CW01667560

THE GOOD SCHOOLS GUIDE 2011

25th Anniversary Edition

www.goodschoolsguide.co.uk

Purchasers of this book qualify for 20% off the price of The Good Schools Guide Online, which offers (in addition to all that's in this book and in our Special Educational Needs Guide) subject-by-subject results analysis for English schools, catchment area maps for English state schools, extensive search facilities, links to school websites and inspection reports, and much much more.

LUCAS
PUBLICATIONS

Sixteenth Edition published 2011

by Galore Park Publishing Ltd

19/21 Sayers Lane, Tenterden, Kent TN30 6BW

www.galorepark.co.uk

ISBN 978 1 905735 47 1

Printed by Lego S.p.A Italy. Layout by Theresa Hare Optima Information Design

A CIP catalogue record for this book is available from the British Library.

Writers:
Nicky Adams
Juliet Austin
John Richard Badham
Carolyn Benaroya
Godfrey Bishop
Janet Breeze
Kalantha Brewis
Susannah Camps Harris
Janita Ronny Clamp
Elizabeth Coatman
Alison Cooper
Charles Cowling
Sarah Drummond
Arabella Dymoke
Suzanne Everest
Richard Field
Sue Fieldman
Sara Freakley
Lisa Freedman
Judith French
Elizabeth Grahamslaw
Paul Grahamslaw
Rosemary Groves
Debra Hamblin
Susan Hamlyn
Bernadette Henniker
Kate Hugh Smith
Martin Husbands
Sandra Hutchinson
Ali Hutchison
Sophie Irwin
Christine Jefferson
Emma Lee-Potter
Elizabeth Moody-Stuart
Grace Moody-Stuart
Patrea More Nisbett
Carolyn Murphy
Beth Noakes
Charlotte Obolensky
Harriet Plyler
Anne Prendergast
Catriona Prest
Deirdre Shields
Mary-Ann Smillie
Jenny Swann
Rosemary Taylor
Carolyn Thomas
Anthony Verity
Janette Wallis
Sally Wheatman
Sue Wood

Jacket design: Annie Finn, James Finn and River Design

Editorial review by Susan Hamlyn and team:
Elizabeth Coatman, Beth Noakes, Anne Prendergast

Research by Annie Finn and Shari Lord

Thanks to telephone team Kathryn Berger, Tania Berlow, Amanda Perkins

Brilliant administrator Shari Lord

Everything organised by Anthea Palmer

Acknowledgements

We should also like to thank the countless friends, pupils, parents, staff (not to mention moles because they would rather we didn't) who have contributed enormously valuable information and to whom we are deeply indebted.

Contents

Hackett Rugby
Little Britons
HACKETT
LONDON

Introduction

Welcome to *The Good Schools Guide* in its 25th year, and to our website (see page 13) where you will find much to interest and delight you.

Less happily, do not miss our section on school closures on page 62. Recessions usually hit independent schools two or three years late. There's no easy way to predict who will be affected – but there are measures you can take to protect yourself.

The Good Schools Guide is written by parents for parents. We choose which schools to review on the basis of what parents say to us – no school can pay to be included (or pay to be excluded if we want them in, for that matter). We are outspoken and independent in our views and there is always a good number of schools in *The Guide* who are cross, sometimes angry, about what we have written. Some of them advertise with us nonetheless.

We visit all the schools ourselves (mostly these days we are welcomed, sometimes we have to go in disguise) and, since we were first published in 1986, have visited most of them many times over, both formally and informally. To put them into context , we can compare the strengths and weaknesses of one school with another. We have a team of local writers who bring us news and views from all over Britain, and help us find the good schools that only their neighbours know about.

Visiting is, of course, only a start. We also spend many happy hours talking to pupils, staff, heads, educationalists of all sorts, matrons – even the school dog. Most importantly, we listen to you. We would like to hear what you think of the schools that you know. All information will be gratefully (and confidentially) received – no detail too slight to mention. Suggestions for schools to be included in the next edition would also be welcome. Send your opinions and experiences to us through the website (there's a comments button on each school's page) if that suits you – it makes life easier for us – but we welcome your views by email, fax, letter or telephone.

This is a GOOD schools guide, but what's good for one child may be useless for another, what is one parent's dream may turn another sick with horror. We try not to impose our own views of what a school should be like but try rather to be guided by what the parents who like a school like about it, and to write our descriptions from their point of view. So read between the lines.

Our write-ups are intended to be portraits of the schools, not inventories of their assets and achievements. The schools' prospectuses are the best sources of the factual background – or would be if the schools' marketing departments had not got at so many of them. If you are a subscriber to *The Guide* online, you can click straight through to the schools' websites – some of them are excellent.

If a school is not included in *The Guide* this does not necessarily mean it is not a good school – our selection is a personal one. In any event, we are in the process of gently expanding our coverage to include more good local schools. If you know of one that we have missed, or have got wrong, please tell us: it's parents like you who have made *The Guide* as good as it is.

You can reach us via the website:
www.goodschoolsguide.co.uk
or by email: editor@goodschoolsguide.co.uk
fax: +44 (0)870 052 4067
telephone: +44 (0)20 7801 0191
and post: 3 Craven Mews, London SW11 5PW

Ralph Lucas, Editor

tedious uninspiring dull tedious uninspiring dull
Expect more from your next trip.
We offer over 85 family adventures and from that expertise comes a variety of exciting school trips.
If you want an exciting journey of discovery you're in the right company.
adventurecompany.co.uk/schools
THE ADVENTURE COMPANY
FIRST FOR ADVENTURE
IATA
ABTA
ABTA No. Y0768

Which route to The Good Schools Guide's expertise?

The Good Schools Guide Advice Service

The Good Schools Guide Advice Service is a tailor-made service for individual families covering every aspect of educating children. Our advisors work to help parents find the right school for their child, whether state, independent, junior, senior, day or boarding – and deal with a wide range of other educational quandaries.

We take no commission from schools and no school can get into *The Good Schools Guide* by paying for it. *The Good Schools Guide* selects its schools on the basis of parental recommendation first and then on our own experience when we research and visit them – nothing else. The advice that we give is completely independent.

The Good Schools Guide advisors are our most experienced writers, editors and consultants. These are hand-picked experts who visit hundreds of schools, talk with heads, with parents and with pupils. *The Guide* itself – even our constantly updated website version – is only a glimpse of this unique bank of inside knowledge and experience. *The Good Schools Guide* is the expert source that other educational consultants rely on. We can put our expertise and our wide network of personal contacts to work for you and your children.

How can we help?

Because The Good Schools Guide Advice Service is a personal service, run on a one-to-one basis, we can help you in whatever way you need us to. You tell us what you need and we tell you how we can help. And then we do!

For example?

Your child is in primary school and doing well, but you're not happy with the senior schools in your area. Should you move house to be in the catchment area for a grammar school? Or should you take the plunge and aim for the independent sector? And what can you do to prepare your child? We can untangle it all for you.

Or...

You are living overseas but you want to send your child to board in the UK. He is dead keen on sailing and will need to keep up his Arabic. Oh, and the school must be near an airport. Can we help? Of course! You will tell your advisor exactly what you need and he will help you find it, guiding you every step of the way.

Or...

We hope it doesn't happen but your daughter has been badly bullied and her school is not dealing with it properly. You need to move her – fast. Call us. We will find you a sympathetic, knowledgeable and effective advisor who will be on the case at once.

Is that it?

It might be. But The Good Schools Guide Advice Service can offer you far more. We have built up relationships with the best experts in fields such as Special Educational Needs, educational psychology, tutoring, English language preparation for school entrance and many others. Just tell us what you need. We will find an expert schools and education advisor to work with you.

And we advise on more than just schools. Our expertise extends to tutor agencies, sixth form colleges and even university applications.

So what should I do?

Phone us on +44(0)207 801 0191 or send us a brief email to advice@goodschoolsguide.co.uk outlining what you need (do include the age of your child and whereabouts in the country you are considering, plus your contact details). We will then get in touch with you – within 48 hours of your initial phone call or email – and make sure that we match you with the right education advisor. Consultations are mainly conducted over the phone, however, our advisors will be happy to meet you, depending on where you are. Urgent enquiries are dealt with urgently. We can find an advisor to speak with you within the hour if necessary.

How much?

We provide one of the most competitively priced tailor-made advice services in the UK. Check our website or call +44(0)207 801 0191 for current fees.

Introductory Service: A 30 minute personal advice session to help with queries and dilemmas of limited scope e.g. deciding between two schools.

Standard Service: No set format – this service provides exactly what individual parents need. An initial consultation to establish exactly what is required, then schools (or educational) research, followed by e.g. a list of schools to meet your requirements, advice on place availability, interviews or entrance exams, weighing up merits of comparable schools, post-visit discussion. Charges for consultations and advisory services involving more than mild SEN will be arranged on an individual basis.

Premier Service: all that is included in the standard service, plus up to two days of accompanied school visits – or visits on behalf of clients – help with all paperwork, all liaison with schools etc.

Call us on +44(0)207 801 0191 to speak to one of our educational experts and to discuss how we can help (or alternatively email advice@goodschoolsguide.co.uk and we will get back to you).

All information is treated in the strictest confidence. We act as agent for our advisors, and they will agree terms directly with you. See our website for current prices and for full terms and conditions.

The Good Schools Guide Promise

We will refund your fee if you are not entirely satisfied with the results.

HOLMEWOOD HOUSE

CONSTANTIA PRAESTA

An independent day & flexi ~ boarding school for boys and girls aged 3 ~ 13 years

Top Prep School

THE GOOD SCHOOLS GUIDE

Come and see for yourself

To arrange a private tour of the school,
please contact our Registrar, Mrs Karen Gwinnett, on

01892 860006

or email her at registrar@holmewood.kent.sch.uk

Registered charity no. 279267

LANGTON GREEN • TUNBRIDGE WELLS • KENT TN3 0EB
TEL: 01892 860006 • E-MAIL: registrar@holmewood.kent.sch.uk
www.holmewood.kent.sch.uk

COUNTRY LIFE®
The weekly magazine for the finest homes on sale
COUNTRY LIFE
SEPTEMBER 15, 2010
EVERY WEEK £3.20
Smaller Country Houses
More than 95 pages of property
'I wish I'd bought that' Top agents confess
Dream House: making eco chic
On sale every Wednesday
Find the best homes on sale through the best estate agents and keep up to date with latest news and opinions from the countryside.
PLUS
Property
News
Arts & Antiques
Gardens
Find new properties daily at countrylife.co.uk the home of premium property

The Good Schools Guide on the Web

www.goodschoolsguide.co.uk

*20 per cent discount for owners of this book

There is so much more to *The Good Schools Guide* than we can fit in this book; we'd need a tome the size of a trunk to fit it all in! Fortunately *The Good Schools Guide* website captures all things educational and makes it personal.

Online you will find all the school reviews that appear in *The Good Schools Guide*; a wealth of advice for your education journey from nursery to university; catchment area maps; in-depth examination of results; a directory of ALL schools in the UK, with data from us, comments from schools and from you; Special Educational Needs; links to inspection reports, schools and others and so much more!

Use www.goodschoolsguide.co.uk to answer your questions.

How do I search for schools?

Whether your criteria are simple or complex, our new 'Find a School' search is unsurpassed.

My child has special educational needs – help!

We have a wealth of expertly written articles, offering advice on all aspects of SEN and we've number-crunched, so you can see how well English state schools serve children with special needs. Plus, thousands of schools have completed our detailed, searchable SEN survey.

My child is gifted/talented – do you cover this?

As well as giving advice, we identify grammar and selective school provision; feature scholarship and specialist schools' information; show (for senior schools) how many pupils go to which top universities, and include gifted/talented feedback in our SEN survey.

Can I find results by subject?

Our online schools pages detail subject results by gender and popularity. Alternatively, choose a subject and level and see which schools made the grade and who should do better!

How do I know if a school is good for my child?

We offer advice on what to consider when choosing a school and our value-added data, for English state schools, show how well a school does for all children – bright, average or struggling.

What about catchment areas?

We've got admissions covered. See where children at a school come from or use our unique, interactive catchment maps to see the schools you are in catchment for.

Where can I study A level Archaeology and Physics?

Use our search to help locate subject combinations and compile a list of schools. You can even compare them to find the best for you; a school may be great for one subject but not so hot for others.

Wow! I can't wait to get started – where do I find you?

www.goodschoolsguide.co.uk

We add to and constantly update our website. Some information is free but ALL this is yours if you subscribe to *The Good Schools Guide* online, for a year – or just for a month.

SPECIAL OFFER

*If you own this book you are (at the time of going to press) entitled to 20 per cent off the usual price of an annual subscription purchased from us; keep this guide close, you'll need it at check-out.

Special Needs and The Good Schools Guide Online

> 'Practical, fearless, frank, sympathetic and lively.'

So said best-selling author, **Nick Hornby,** of our guide to special educational needs and schools. Our aims were clear: to detail schools with great provision for children with special needs and to ensure parents understood what they should be asking of all schools.

In the five years since we first produced *The Good Schools Guide* – Special Educational Needs (edited by Sandra Hutchinson) there has been a notable shift, both in attitudes towards SEN and in the understanding of what is required to help children make progress. All that invaluable information now appears online at www.goodschoolsguide.co.uk. There, in our dedicated SEN section, we detail: different types of special needs, help and support to be found in and outside of school and the classroom; the law, specialist help and school choices. For individual English state schools we examine the value-added to children with registered special needs and, because attitudes are paramount, we have invited all schools to respond to our in-depth, searchable SEN survey. There are still some schools like The Lyceum, an independent prep school in London, that shriek in response to this survey:

> 'We do not take children with special educational needs.'

Fortunately others offer a reply at least akin to that of Eton College:

> 'The school has a well-established Special Needs department, the Learning Centre ... supports boys arriving at Eton with specific learning difficulties, for example dyslexia and dyspraxia ... Boys in the school receive such assistance for as long as they need it. A high degree of success is achieved in ensuring that they can do full justice to their abilities.'

Hurrah! These wake-up calls, echoed by many other schools, shows they understand that special needs plus special attention equals excellent results – and that the teaching habits learned in the process benefit everyone else too.

Read between the lines; the responses (where completed) reveal not only the level of provision within a school but their attitudes towards children with SEN, and their understanding of how all children learn.

See also Special Educational Needs – that's not my child ... is it? (page 37)

The Good Schools Guide International

Whether you're moving abroad, or coming back to the UK ... you need this Guide!

www.gsgi.co.uk

The Good Schools Guide International does for international schools what *The Good Schools Guide* does for the UK ... finds, visits and reviews the best ones for children 3–18, state or independent, wherever they are.

Like *The Good Schools Guide*, the GSGI is completely independent, forthright, and doesn't shy away from judgement calls. All school reviews are unsolicited – selected and paid for by *The Guide*, not the school. That means complete editorial freedom, so we pull no punches. Its crisp, clear advice will give you the inside scoop on schools, headmasters, sports, school runs and local traffic, and life on the ground for expats.

All GSGI editors are expat parents themselves and know which schools in their host cities should make the cut. Schools are in (or out) whether they like it or not.

Aimed at English-speaking expatriates, the GSGI:

- reviews top British, American, IB and international schools in over 55 cities worldwide
- offers brisk, personal expat and educational overviews for each city
- includes real-time updates, red alerts (coups d'état, evacuations, closures etc)

Over 280 articles explain and decode:

- curricula and exams (GCSEs, SATs, IB, AP etc)
- special educational needs
- transitions (between curricula, systems, hemispheres, countries)
- accreditations and inspections (the real vs the bogus)

Purchasers of *The Good Schools Guide* are entitled to a 50 per cent discount. Go to: www.GSGI.co.uk. Enter the reference code GSG412P and answer the question about *The Good Schools Guide.*

There's even a Good Schools Guide International Advisory Service. GSGI advisors can give you (by phone, email or face to face):

- insider info on top (or not) local schools
- pros and cons for your own child
- overviews of local education
- advice for expat survival in their host cities
- a network to other parents and expats
- schooling and entertainment suggestions, even for small children

Want to help spread the word? If you help us successfully contact and secure a new corporate subscriber who then becomes a GSGI customer, we will pay you 10 per cent of our net receipts from them, for a period of five years. To read more about this offer, and for terms and conditions in full, go to www.gsgi.co.uk/articles/want-to-work-for-us/finders-fee-for-new-corporate-subscriptions.

Know someone living in a distant corner of the world who might be qualified to work for us? Go to www.gsgi.co.uk/articles/want-to-work-for-us.

Harriet Plyler, editor, *The Good Schools Guide International*

The Good Schools Guide Tutor Guide

The Good Schools Guide Online now offers advice on finding and using tutors.

There are reviews of the top tutor agencies, tutorial colleges and 'crammers'. Watch out during 2011 for exciting new publishing to help you find the best tutoring, and advice from our experts.

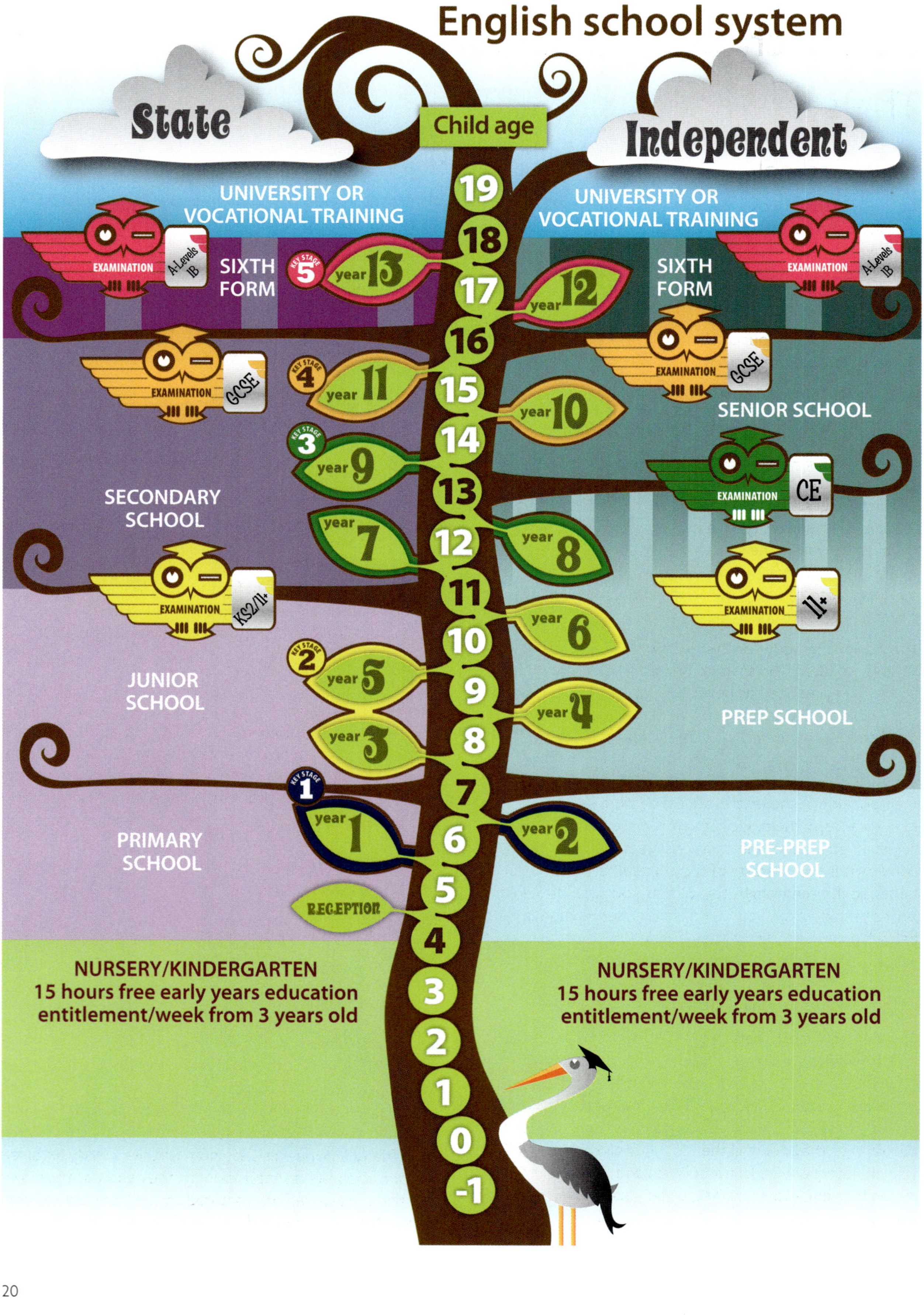
English school system
State
Child age
Independent
UNIVERSITY OR VOCATIONAL TRAINING
UNIVERSITY OR VOCATIONAL TRAINING
EXAMINATION
A-Levels IB
SIXTH FORM
KEY STAGE 5
year 13
19
18
17
16
15
14
13
12
11
10
9
8
7
6
5
4
3
2
1
0
-1
year 12
SIXTH FORM
EXAMINATION
A-Levels IB
EXAMINATION
GCSE
KEY STAGE 4
year 11
EXAMINATION
GCSE
year 10
SENIOR SCHOOL
KEY STAGE 3
year 9
EXAMINATION
CE
SECONDARY SCHOOL
year 7
year 8
EXAMINATION
KS2/11+
EXAMINATION
11+
year 6
KEY STAGE 2
year 5
JUNIOR SCHOOL
year 4
PREP SCHOOL
year 3
KEY STAGE 1
year 1
year 2
PRIMARY SCHOOL
PRE-PREP SCHOOL
RECEPTION
NURSERY/KINDERGARTEN
15 hours free early years education entitlement/week from 3 years old
NURSERY/KINDERGARTEN
15 hours free early years education entitlement/week from 3 years old

Before choosing a school

The system

Starting school

You may need to book a place soon after birth in the private sector; for the best state schools you have three or four years to move into the catchment area. If you are after a religious school, take a careful note of its admissions arrangements, and of the admissions arrangements of the religious secondary school too (you can miss out on some secondaries because you did not baptise your child within 6 months of birth); at the very least you are likely to have to go to church every week.

Education is compulsory for everyone in the UK. Year 1, in the English state system, is the year beginning in the September following the child's fifth birthday. Children born late in the school year are at a disadvantage – on average they will do less well throughout their school careers, and the latest research suggests that they are perhaps 20 per cent less likely to make it to university. The problem appears to be one of social status within the school – younger children ending up at the bottom of the pecking order – rather than an intellectual inability to catch up. So avoid getting pregnant between July and November inclusive!

The obvious remedy for this disadvantage is to allow those younger children who seem to be falling behind to drop back a year. This practice has never been popular in the UK, and was made particularly difficult by the government's former practice (only abolished in 2005) of reporting schools' GCSE and A level results as if children who had been held back had failed all their exams, so that senior schools (conscious of their position in the league tables) became extremely reluctant to accept them. Government policy seems at last to have turned around, and to have accepted that what should come first is the interests of the child rather than the league tables: so if it seems right to you that your child should drop back a year, or take a year out of school (see Home Education below), this is a battle that you ought now to be able to win. Some boarding preps, in particular, will help out by keeping a summer-born child on for an extra year – but it's the attitude of the senior school that's crucial.

The main choice is between state and private education and nowadays you can definitely mix and match. Although, how you do it will very much depend on where you live (are there good local primaries, excellent comprehensives, grammar schools?); the sex of your child (in general pay for boys before girls, they need all the help they can get); the religion you practise (convert to Catholicism and go straight to education heaven); and, of course, upon your child's personality and ability.

State education

The advantages are that it's usually close by and part of the community; a free school bus operates in some country areas (often but by no means always avoiding the need to become full-time driver); a broad social mix; no school fees; a slight edge on the private sector when it comes to Oxbridge entrance (if your child has the determination and confidence to get straight As in a state school); often greater understanding of the wide world at the end of it.

Free schools

These are a new initiative and the first ones are expected to get off the ground in 2011. The idea is that charities, universities, businesses, educational groups, teachers and parents can apply for and be allocated government money in order to start new schools. It's an interesting idea and one seized on with enthusiasm by parents who believe in state education but who feel that their local authority denies them the choice they want for their children. Look at http://www.education.gov.uk/schools/leadership/typesofschools/freeschools for the latest information.

Private education

Advantages of the private system are usually a greater chance of doing well in public exams, especially for an average child (although there are many exceptions); often better academic (as opposed to pastoral) care; a wider range of extras and often at a higher standard; smaller classes; the opportunity to study subjects such as Ancient Greek and start modern languages earlier; the opportunity to board.

Montessori Education

Pioneered by Maria Montessori to educate the poor in Italy, this method is a hot favourite in many middle-class enclaves. The Montessori method concentrates on personal development and progress; homework, testing and exams are seldom found. Mostly confined to early years education in the UK.

To the uninitiated, Montessori methods may seem like a free-for-all. However, the reality is carefully thought out and planned learning aims, objectives and outcomes. What isn't prescriptive is the route a child will take to get there; creativity, exploration and problem-solving are encouraged, children move freely around the classroom and are wholly involved with and absorbed in their learning, they work at their own pace and are assisted or prompted to solutions only as necessary. Older children join forces with younger, they become

instructors and befrienders, revising and reinforcing their own knowledge by working with and helping younger ones. The apparent lack of structure can be a problem for some youngsters; others relish the freedom to explore.

Steiner-Waldorf Education

Designed by Rudolf Steiner, with a strong emphasis on creativity, Steiner education aims to develop the whole child. Steiner believed in fulfilling potential but not in pushing towards adult goals. Like Montessori, underpinning Steiner education is a belief that children should be enthusiastic about and enjoy learning for its own sake, not to pass exams, so enquiry and exploration are encouraged. Play, storytelling, drawing, and nature are fundamentals for younger children, with the three Rs reserved principally for the post-7 brigade, yet foreign languages are taught from an early age. Children are often immersed in a subject over a prolonged period. Steiner schools (several are featured in this Guide), have a 'college of teachers' rather than a headteacher and the usual hierarchy. Often seen as a helpful alternative for children who don't 'fit the box', but not totally alternative: Steiner education still offers a route to GCSEs and A levels.

Summerhill

If you really want an alternative education, where children are free to attend lessons or not, Summerhill may be the ticket. A haven for those who find school challenging, but not for the challenged or problem teenager, it emphasises knowing yourself and friendship, rather than scurrying into the rat-race. Children have the absolute right to attend or not attend classes and they regulate their lives through a democratic meeting where everyone, regardless of age, has an equal vote. As one parent told us: 'You send your children to Summerhill if you believe that learning has as much to do with connaitre, as it does with savoir, and if you believe that academic learning is something that can and should go on throughout your life.' For some, Summerhill is exciting not because it offers the freedom to opt out of education but because it extols the joys of opting in.

The exploding curriculum

The curriculum and examination systems in the UK are in a continuing state of flux. There is now a wide range of curricula on offer, and more on the way – with the fitness of the old stalwarts of A level and GCSE questioned. For parents who can move to take advantage of all these new opportunities, this is an unalloyed good. This section is a rough guide to the alternatives. Use the system diagram on page 20 to see where these exams fit in.

Pre-14 Curricula

6 months to 4+

Nursery/kindergarten, particularly in the private sector. All nurseries are required to follow the Early Years Foundation Stage framework with goals in six areas of learning and development. There's no testing, but observers will write a summary of each child's progress in the final term of the year in which the child reaches the age of 5.

7 and 11 Standard Assessment Tests (SATs), Key Stages 1 and 2

The National Curriculum was originally designed to ensure some consistency across schools. Children are tested at 7 and 11 in state schools – but only for core subjects, and with external assessment at 11 only. Tampered with more times than a test match cricket ball, the most recent developments sensibly give schools a bit more time and flexibility to do their own thing. In general though, the National Curriculum remains over-prescriptive and encourages too much emphasis on 'teaching to the test' at 11. The new government in England will set about further change, including a different emphasis on what shared knowledge and understanding all pupils should have. That at least should be good news.

In England, SATs are designed to show the level a child is working at, or towards, at that moment in his/her career. In Scotland, where there are 5–14 curriculum guidelines, pupils pass or fail levels but should only be tested when they are 'ready to pass'. The brightest child who reaches the dizzy heights of level F of the 5–14 curriculum will have been tested six times in core subjects.

11+ or 13+ Common Entrance (CE)

Independent schools are free to do as they choose. What is surprising is how many – especially at prep school level – choose to be hamstrung by the National Curriculum. Many preps merely provide a glorified version of it, complete with multiple terms devoted to teaching to the intricate requirements of Key Stage tests. Other preps assess or examine on entry but do little else until Common Entrance (CE) at either 11+ or 13+. CE tests youngsters in the core subjects with a range of other subjects, sometimes including Latin and Greek. Papers are offered at different levels to suit the ability of the child. These are marked and graded by a child's proposed senior school. The schools are free to set their own grade boundaries, so a grade C at one school does not necessarily equate to a grade C at another. Children do not fail CE but many schools set minimum CE admission requirements, with those requesting 60 per cent or above usually considered very selective. You can find practice Common Entrance papers on our website and order practice papers and books of past papers from Galore Park, www.galorepark.co.uk.

The CE curriculum generally results in a better spread and depth of knowledge than the National Curriculum – mostly because of the freedoms inherent within it – but preparation for whatever test is to be taken becomes focused and ferocious for the last two years. It could do with a thorough overhaul.

Other 11+ entrance examinations

There are almost 250 state schools in the UK which are selective in whole or in part, and there are many senior independent schools which use their own examinations. Generally these examinations will consist of a combination of verbal and non-verbal reasoning – supposed to be something that you cannot practise for, but experience suggests otherwise – and English and maths. Often the English and maths requirements go beyond that which will have been taught as part of the National Curriculum, and you will need to study specifically for the exam. It is common to use private tutors to assist with this extra education. You can find extensive practice material on our website.

Pre-16 Curricula

GCSE

The principal exam taken at age 16 in England – and a pretty decayed set of uninspiring courses it is too. Assessment methods have suffered the same degradation as A level, and the course content suits neither the bright (who have seen much of the intellectual challenge removed) or the ordinary (who are being asked to study material of little value to them). There are signs of some significant shake-ups: modular exams and coursework, the causes of much controversy, are being phased out in some subjects.

IGCSE

Much used abroad – hence the 'I' for International. It's closer to the old-style O level, and is becoming increasingly used by private schools who despair at the narrowing and lack of academic ambition of the main GCSE courses. A very good course for the naturally academic. State schools were prevented for years from offering IGCSEs: mediocrity for all was the government's cry. This was overturned by the new government, and you can expect to see IGCSEs appearing in state schools. Because the IGCSE did not count for the performance tables (we hope that they will be included for 2010) some top independent schools appeared to be performing ridiculously badly.

IB Middle Years

The IB organisation provides a structure for the years running up to the diploma, which can embrace whatever national curriculum it finds itself surrounding. No exams – moderated teacher assessment. Since it does not provide formal qualifications at the age of 16, you need to be sure that it will be accepted by whatever educational institution or employer your child will face next. Well-understood internationally, but only available in a few schools in the UK.

Standard Grades

The Scottish alternative to GCSE though often with less, if any, coursework. Qualifications can be built up over time, encouraging students to progress to the highest level they can achieve. An incoherent but generally OK system. Headed for major reform – abolishing individual subjects in the years before, replacing the exam with 'General Grades' – if this was England you'd be sure it would be a disaster, and it still smells that way from here.

Vocational qualifications

There's an incredible variety on offer. With such specific qualifications, it is crucial that you quiz each school on (a) what proportion of pupils finish the course, (b) what proportion just pass, and what proportion do really well, and (c) what pupils have gone on to do afterwards. A good school running a good course will keep in touch with as many of its graduates as possible: in a few years time they will have become sufficiently senior to be employing the next generation. If you want to keep your options open, look carefully in this data for evidence that pupils who have set out on a vocational route have been able to come back to more academic study later on.

Exotics

Faced with the widespread dissatisfaction with GCSEs, individual entrepreneurial schools have begun to go their own way. There are a great many qualifications – either offered by individual schools or by other accredited bodies – far too numerous to cover here. You may come across Vedic mathematics (in the St James's group of schools), or Bedales' BACs (GCSE alternatives which aim to offer more room for imagination and exploration for non-core subjects, and which are an innovation that we are totally delighted by). You may, as a result, not find it quite so easy to jump ship at 16; perhaps that thought hasn't even entered the schools' minds? If that is not a worry for you, all you need to be sure of is that it will result in a qualification that your target universities or future employer will welcome. Perhaps it is with this in mind that Haileybury School has enrolled its first students onto 'The Introduction to Investment Award', a qualification accredited by the Securities and Investment Institute and a requirement of many entrants into London's financial services industry. With promises of work experience in leading institutions on offer for the best, it's not surprising this offering is over-subscribed.

All these changes may seem disturbing, and certainly the newspapers are trying (as usual) to get us worried about it. However, we see it as enormously positive. Parents will have a wider choice of schools, schools will be able to choose the curriculum which suits them and their pupils best, and a bit of serious competition should do wonders for the quality of A levels and GCSEs.

University entrance exams

A levels

The main end-of-school examination in England, Wales and Northern Ireland, much revered but suffering from a long trend towards rote learning with standardised questions, and little to generate the joy of learning. Being improved in response to the threat from the IB and Pre-U, they are pretty good exams for someone who has already been bitten by the bug for a subject, and hard work should result in a reliably good grade. Great freedom of choice in subjects (especially when 'applied subjects' are included), and those with a particular bent can focus on it (physics, chemistry and maths is a common combination, for instance) rather than carry on with subjects they hate. All are now unitised rather than based on a final exam. An A level course usually consists of a mix of AS awards taken at the end of the first year of A level study and A2 courses in the second year. Students can choose when to cash in their awards and thus maximise their grades. As a result, well over 20 per cent of students get the top grade. An A* grade was introduced for the first time in 2010, in response to complaints that top universities were finding it hard to choose between students. The A* grade has already become a requirement for some university courses, but it is not yet clear to us that it reflects brilliance rather than a combination of long hours of study and a good memory...

A levels in Applied Subjects

Often considered a Cinderella qualification, VCEs have been given a makeover and renamed GCEs/A levels in Applied Subjects. Intended to provide a broad vocational base, they are frequently identified by the 'studies' tag: art and design, business, leisure and media. Most are available as AS and A level single and double awards but many have reduced currency for entry to top-flight universities (except on specific courses). Cambridge, for instance, will only recognise a six-unit VCE or applied A level as a third A level, or as an additional fourth broadening subject, and then only if the 'essential' and 'highly desirable' subjects required are covered. See www.cam.ac.UK/admissions/undergraduate/requirements/ for details.

The IB Diploma

A very well-regarded qualification in use all over the world – so good currency if you might want to consider university overseas. Astonishingly highly rated by UCAS in relation to A levels, and even if you apply the sort of discounts that Oxbridge or a Russell group University might do (discounting the core subjects, or ones considered a little light), it still feels like a pretty good way to get into a top university. Can be much more fun to do: more scope for exploration, less emphasis on facts and recitation. Suits best those with a broad intelligence, as you have to do a range of subjects – you can't give up maths, or indeed a foreign language. You choose three subjects to study at higher level (rated by UCAS as equivalent to an A level), and three at standard level (rated by UCAS as two-thirds of an A level) – so you can see that pupils have a lot of work to do. Both higher and standard levels are marked out of seven, with the compulsory 'core' of an extended essay, community service etc marked out of three – so the top score is 45, achieved by 1 per cent of pupils each year. Increasing rapidly in popularity, notably among academic state schools, but rejected by some top schools because of the restrictions it places on choice of subjects.

Scottish Highers

A handful of independent schools in Scotland follow the English system; for the rest it's Scottish Highers. As a rough guide Highers, taken after a year of study, are similar to AS and Advanced Highers, a second-year course, similar to A2. In Scotland, some universities will admit students with Highers alone, but only for students doing a foundation year first. Most English universities accept students with Advanced Highers on a similar basis to those with A levels. The Scots claim that Highers are better than A levels, the English that they are easier. They are both right. Scottish exams have their own complexities and there is also a whole raft of intermediate exams as the Scots are not allowed to re-sit Standard grades. Check these out carefully if it's unfamiliar territory to you.

The Cambridge Pre-U

An alternative to A levels developed in Cambridge, aimed at preparing students for good universities. Launched in September 2008, so we don't yet have a clear view of how well things are going, but we believe it to be more challenging than A level, and to require those skills of analysis, understanding, logic and imagination which have gone missing along the A level way. If you are aiming at a top independent school, it's worth asking if they are one of the ones collaborating in this venture. For the latest news see www.cie.org.uk.

Advanced Extension Award (AEA)

AEAs are a kind of starred A grade for A level, with the bonus of additional UCAS points for those checking out with merit or distinction. Take-up is patchy – serious use is mostly confined to independent and grammar schools – and they are now being abandoned.

Diplomas

Just coming into use in English state schools, these were conceived by the thankfully defunct Curriculum and Qualifications Authority and inflated by a series of ministerial egos. They were supposed to provide the definitive vocational pathway, but have turned out to be overweight, unfocused and uninspiring. At the core of the best of them (such as Engineering) is a well-crafted vocational course worth about 4 GCSEs or, at the higher level, a couple of A levels – we hope that they survive in this form. Their academic variants were supposed to take over from A levels in 2013, but have been binned by the new government.

Other Vocational Qualifications

BTECs and other long-lived vocational qualifications are well-respected exams. If you're considering taking one, expect the school or college to be able to demonstrate the excellent careers or courses that they have led to in the past – with vocational qualifications reality is much more important than a paper grade.

Finessing the state and independent sectors

All those scary newspaper statistics about the long-term costs of keeping your child in nappies and birthday presents pale into insignificance when set beside the £100,000+ you'll need to educate a child privately from nursery to university.

But paying for a private education from finger painting to Freshers' Week is no longer the necessity it was once. There may be more people than ever before opting for the independent sector but those without private means or surplus wealth often choose to pay selectively. Obviously the longer you defer paying the longer you'll have to save.

However you choose to play the education game, you should bear in mind – something often neglected by parents transfixed by a system as complex as Grand Master chess – that no decision is final. If something is not working out for you or your child at any point, it's almost always possible to change, and often much easier to do at a stage when not everyone else is making the same decision.

Move at Year 3, age 7/8

State primary school works particularly well if you have an able child who finds little difficulty with the three Rs – particularly since the government is now putting considerable energy into programmes for the 'gifted and talented'. At the other extreme, those with serious learning difficulties, particularly if they are 'statemented' (officially recognised as needing support) will be given one-to-one help at no charge to you.

Those in the middle may be the ones who thrive least well in a busy primary school – as much psychologically as academically. A hard-pressed teacher with a mixed-ability class of 30 children often simply doesn't have the energy to focus on this unexciting middle group, and a parent with an under-confident, just-getting-by child may decide it's worth pinching pennies for the extra attention that a private school can provide at this stage.

If you want to check how a primary school matches up to the private sector, one of the best indicators is the percentage of Year 6 children (10–11-year-olds) who achieve level 5 in their Key Stage 2 SATs – the level that would be expected from the great majority of children in a good prep school. These figures are now included in the performance tables and you will find them on our website.

Some parents choose to use the state system for the early years only, intending to change to a prep school at 7 or 8. However, some over-subscribed London prep schools make little allowance for a child who cannot read and write as fluently as candidates from more results-driven pre-preps so you may want to consider coaching at home. Country preps and less pressured schools, on the other hand, may delight in taking youngsters who need their small-class nurturing to bring them along fast.

Move at Year 7, age 11

State to private

Many independent schools too, ever mindful of those A level league tables, are increasingly keen to attract the brightest and the best, so much of the emphasis of the 11-plus entrance test is now put on raw IQ, which is generally gauged by verbal and non-verbal reasoning tests (English and maths are also on the menu at many schools though fewer every year). The high-flying City of London School for Boys, for example – which has always had a broad intake in terms of means and social class – takes two-thirds of its 11-plus entrants from the state sector and adjusts its marking according to the provenance of the candidates, giving leeway to those from state primary schools. Even academically and socially elite public schools such as Westminster and Eton are now eager to attract the ablest 11-year-olds from the state sector, and are prepared to educate them in the years between 11 and 13 at their own or allied prep schools. Harrow now provides free prep school education to the brightest boys aged 11–13.

IQ alone, however, is not the only factor. Parents keen to make the transition at this point may wish to hire a tutor (or tutor them themselves) from the middle of Year 5 (Year 6 is too late!) to solidify their child's literacy and numeracy and prepare their child for the unfamiliar and idiosyncratic verbal and non-verbal reasoning tests. Keep in mind, however, that virtually all private schools offer their own entrance test as an alternative to CE for state school pupils. Alternatively, many prep schools welcome pupils aged 10 or 11 to train them up for senior school entrance at 13 – although this mostly applies to boys' or co-ed schools.

Private to state

If you live in an area such as Kent or Buckinghamshire, still primarily served by grammar or selective state schools, the approach is often to concentrate expenditure at primary level. However, if you feel your child doesn't have the raw

material to compete in these immensely cut-throat exams be prepared to go private all the way. It is hard for some parents to accept that their child's expensive prep school preparation will not help them through grammar school entrance tests which are increasingly just reasoning papers – and increasingly done online. And the state schools don't, mostly, interview.

The more difficult debate – admittedly only a conflict for a small number – is the choice between, say, a scholarship to City of London, a place at Westminster and a place at one of London's leading grammar schools. Thinking of all the other things you can do with the money solves that for most people but you lose out on the breadth and social cachet that the fees buy.

Move at Year 12, age 16/17

Social issues are, of course, as important for many parents of children at independent schools as the education itself, but some of the benefits conferred by attending a leading public school are now under pressure from the government's attempt to widen access to university.

It may now be slightly more difficult for some public school-educated candidates to study some subjects at some universities, but Oxbridge – despite all its best efforts – still takes 50 per cent of its candidates from the independent sector. Independent school sixth forms often have scholarships for those with talent in music, art, sports or academics.

Transferring to the private sector at this stage can make financial as well as scholastic sense. However, there are reasons for going the other way too. Many move to state sixth forms for a greater range of A level options. Or you may wish to do the IB, though there's an explosion in the number of state schools offering it so check the local state schools' plans. Sometimes a move after GCSE is an opportunity for a pupil to make a fresh start and can revitalise interest in academic work; a move from single sex to co-ed can also be a source of motivation (though sometimes a mixed blessing). Catchment areas become more flexible at this level as do religious schools' requirements of church attendance and so on; older students can travel greater distances without feeling bereft of old friends to walk to and from school with.

Sussing out schools

Ask each school you are interested in to send you the prospectus, a copy of the school magazine, a list of governors, and request the last three years' exam results (for senior schools) and leavers' destinations (for all schools), the latest Ofsted or equivalent inspection report (and the school's reply to it), and any other bumf – and read it. Ask each school you are interested in to send you the prospectus, a copy of the school magazine, a list of governors, and leavers' destinations (for all schools) and any other bumf – and read it. Do not forget to check out the obvious: registration dates, subjects offered, school hours, exeats etc. Some special and specialist schools will require additional information before sending a prospectus or inviting you on a visit. On our website www.goodschoolsguide.co.uk you will find the latest Ofsted or equivalent inspection report and (for English schools) in-depth analysis of each school's examinations. You will even find links to the school's own website. However, increasingly stringent data protection means very little of the school and its pupils may be in evidence on their web - ask if they have a parental-portal or equivalent and what information is stored there – the best have your child's reports, school photos, newsletters and other communiqués.

NB Ofsted reports, good as they are, are written in obscure language by educationalists, can be hard to penetrate, and may entirely fail to see the school from a parental point of view. ISC reports can be too cosy by half, although we have seen some excellent ones recently. And league tables are just one, often unreliable, indicator of how a school performs. None of the above will tell you which is the right school for your child.

Make an appointment to see the head, and book a tour round the school (being shown round by pupils is best). You may find you are fobbed off with an open day or registrars and, for big schools with large numbers of applicants, this is an understandable way to start. It is, however, time-consuming for you: remember you have to meet the head – no number of wonderful buildings make up for a rotten one. Make a note of how the receptionist or secretary who answers your telephone call or greets you on arrival seems to you – they often absorb the underlying character of the school and play it back amplified.

What to wear? Project the right image – not too smart (particularly if you are looking for a cut-price offer), but not dowdy either. No school wants to feel it is attracting dull people, and if you have something to offer, however humble, say so. Have a look at page 47 for some things to look out for during your visit to the school.

ECB CRICKET FACTORY

www.cricketfactory.co.uk

Run

ECB Cricket Factory Core Skills Set

Bowl

Bat

Catch

Throw

For further information email:
enquiries@cricketfactory.co.uk

or phone:
01423 780373

What the league tables don't tell you

League tables have caused a lot of agony and misunderstanding. As raw statistics, they are more or less meaningless. You will observe, for a start, that results swing wildly according to which newspaper you happen to look at. Among other things they don't tell you:

- The pupils' IQs: Two Ds for some pupils is a triumph of wonderful teaching.
- The pupils' backgrounds: How much help/support are they getting at home?
- The school's background: Is it academically selective or mixed ability?
- The school's policy towards A levels: Does it allow pupils to 'have a go' or to take an extra A level (for stretching/breadth), or does it operate a policy of dissuading borderline candidates from taking a subject? We are hearing some disturbing stories these days of schools chucking out pupils who have not done well enough at AS level, to keep them from polluting the school's A level results.
- The school's policy at sixth form: Is it pinching, for example, bright girls from neighbouring girls' schools? Or is it turfing out the less able pupils? Does it insist on very high (A grade) GCSEs in proposed A level subjects for those entering the school at sixth form?
- Good years and bad years: Is this a blip, a one-off? There may be exceptional circumstances, such as the death of a teacher six months before the exam.
- What examinations are taken? The top score in the International Baccalaureate is rated in the tables as worth 5 A grade A levels – a considerable overestimate, so IB schools appear higher up than they perhaps deserve. The International GCSE – taken by many independent schools – is not counted at all, rendering the GCSE tables valueless for assessing the independent sector (this may change for the 2010 tables).
- What subjects are taken? Some, e.g. business studies and classical civilisation, are considered easier than others (and are marked down by Oxbridge as a result). The league tables do not tell you which schools are taking general studies at A level: A level general studies can push league table ratings up no end.
- The spread of subjects at A level: Which are popular? Which neglected? Does that profile fit your child? Does it reflect the relative quality of teaching, or just the spirit of the school?
- Whether a large enough number of children are doing really well, especially in subjects that you are interested in. A cohort of excellence will give leadership and confidence to the rest of the school. Are sufficiently few pupils failing, to avoid the reverse effect?
- The quality of education overall: Depth, breadth, all-round, music, debating... things that help pupils learn to think for themselves. By sheer swotting, exams can be successfully passed – but at the expense of what?
- The reliability of the figures: The more pupils there are, the more statistically significant the results are.
- Watch out for Scottish schools lurking within the newspaper league tables: Many Scottish schools offer two systems – Scottish Highers (usually for the weaker brethren) and A levels. Only the A levels show up in the league tables.
- And while we are on the subject of statistics, treat class size figures with care too. How you teach, what you teach and to whom all govern the size that a class can be before performance deteriorates. The only certain thing about small class sizes is that they mean large bills.

Interpreting results (as best you can)

This is what you need to ask the schools you are interested in:

1. Have they anything to declare – any special circumstances? Understanding the school is the key to understanding its statistics.
2. Next study the extensive analyses of examination results that are available on the schools' pages on our website. They incorporate the most recent 3 years published results, and you can use them to get deep under the skin of the schools' league table positions.
3. Look to see where the weaknesses and strengths are to be found. Which subjects are most popular when compared to similar schools? – This can be an indication of the quality of teaching, or of the spirit of the school ('only girls do art'), or both. In which subjects do pupils do best, relative to the same pupils' performance in other subjects? Mostly this is due to teaching quality. Is one subject pulling the overall results up? Or down? Or is a 100 per cent A grade pass in Norwegian translated as one pupil (with a Norwegian mother)? Is it pure coincidence that the best two subjects at A level are Chinese and mathematics? Look at our analysis of university destinations. This will show you something of the level of ambition that the school has instilled in its students and indications of the directions in life which it has encouraged them to take.
4. How many pupils are taking exams over all? A school with a sixth form of 40 (three children doing each

subject) should find it considerably easier to come high on the league tables than a larger school. The more taking any one subject, the more commendable when the results are strong, and the wider the scope for failure.

5. For state schools, look at the analyses of pupil performance on our website. You can see how selective a school is from the profiles of pupil attainment at Key Stage 1 (for primary schools) and Key Stage 2 (for senior schools). You can see how well they do by bright children, and children with SEN, and how good their value added is overall.
6. For independent schools ask for the ALIS/MIDYIS/YELLIS (systems covering the A level, middle and primary years respectively, managed by the University of Durham) or other value-added data, which should show how good the results really are, allowing for the quality of individual pupils. There are several competing systems – all good in their ways – so a school that has none is (by modern standards) not taking as close an interest in its pupils' performance as it might. This will give you quite a good idea of what is going on, and where the weak teaching might be.
7. Now you are in a position to ask the head to explain those appalling geography results, and to tell you what is being done about the situation. Listen carefully, because all schools have weaknesses, and the important thing is what is being done to remedy them.
8. All schools, even the highest achieving, have some less-than-stellar teachers. Their influence may be masked by stars in the same department. Ask pupils when you go round the school or, less directly, ask what systems are used to monitor pupils' and teachers performance, and how they are linked to remedial action – if the school is well run and up-to-date they should happily tell stories of lost sheep found.

Inspection reports from Ofsted and others

Log onto Ofsted – www.ofsted.gov.uk
ISI – www.isi.net (for independent schools)
HMIe – www.hmie.gov.uk (for Scottish schools)
DENI – www.denidata.nics.gov.uk/applnspRptsSearch/IRMain.aspx (in Northern Ireland)
or Estyn – www.estyn.gov.uk (for the Welsh) for inspection reports online.

As with most reports there's a code to decipher and a few questions to ask. The local school gets a glowing report, yet you know half the population are banned from the shopping centre; mothers with young children dodge the area, avoiding it altogether at dropping off and kicking out times. Oh and then there's the rumours about teachers being attacked, drugs, knives – just rumours, yet last year's local primary Year 6 pupils all opted for a school a tricky bus ride away. Puzzling?

So just what do inspection reports tell us and have they any value? The answers are lots and yes, if you know how to read them. Each section is headed and graded. Grade 1, outstanding (and we've seen several of these), grade 4, inadequate with good and satisfactory in-between. Where a section isn't grade 1, helpful comments will be made about what the school should do to improve.

They grade overall effectiveness, achievements and standards, including how well learners with disabilities or learning difficulties progress, personal development and well-being of pupils including behaviour and healthy lifestyles (so the coke and chocolate machines are a no-no then, drat) and how well learners develop workplace skills (no, not how to have a sneaky fag break). As you'd expect, the quality of provision is reported on. This isn't so much about how pretty the corridors are (though undoubtedly these will make an impression), it's how effective teaching and learning is in meeting the full range of learners' needs (teaching to the middle no longer an option then).

A key part of the leadership and management section refers to how effectively management raise achievement and support learners (but not really about how they support staff in doing so); governors can expect to be grilled (and they don't even get paid for the privilege of doing their job!), plus a comment on what pupils and parents think of the school (though the parent and student questionnaires have gone).

Use your imagination and read reports with care – inspectors have seen too many schools and tend to think everyone knows what's meant by, e.g., 'low-level disruption'. Nothing much then? No! They actually mean the most annoying kind, where the teacher can't nail the kid but would love to actually throttle him. Where lessons are constantly spoiled and marred by a handful who know how to play the system, throw bits of paper when the teacher writes on the board, make silly noises, call out inappropriately. The sort that's much worse for other pupils than the occasional, spectacular blow-out followed by a quick expulsion.

On the whole, despite the obvious improvements, we have our doubts about the current system. Mechanistic (relying on statistical analysis), not getting under the skin of a school, unsupportive, are some of the complaints we've heard.

In England, the most outstanding schools will be named as such, with the consistently great assigned to The Ofsted Hall of Fame – complete with framed certificate. At the other end of the scale, just under one in ten blot their copybooks and are either given a 'significant improvement judgement' (formerly a notice to improve – a kind of could/should do better) or are placed in special measures – a must do better or else! Being placed in special measures prevents a school from applying for, or becoming a specialist school (with an emphasis and specialism in a particular curriculum area) but those given significant improvement judgements can be awarded specialisms, even in areas where they're not making the grade! Confused? So are we!

Don't be fooled into thinking specialist status means the school really is the best in the area for a subject – only one school can have the status. If another school nabbed maths and science first, schools may be left with limited options to grab the extra cash that goes with the status.

Ofsted have also taken over the 'care' inspection of boarding schools, to check they meet national minimum standards. This part of the inspection is taken seriously, and though we have yet to see a disastrous report (boarding schools are much better than they used to be) you may gain some insights from reading it.

Money matters

Schools in this country are mostly state-funded, that is, they're paid for by the government and local authorities from taxes. A small proportion are private, funded mostly from fees paid by parents, but also indirectly by the state, given that most private schools enjoy charitable status. Approximately 7 per cent of children in education are at fee-paying schools. Fees range from under £1,000 per term to £7,000 and above per term for a day pupil, with wide variations depending on the age of the child, the staff/pupil ratio and so on – and up to £9,000+ per term for boarding.

Fee-paying schools: bargain hunting

Scholarships

With the pressure from the Charities Commission mounting, schools are directing more and more of their academic scholarship funds into means-tested bursaries – see below – leaving scholarships as mere shells, with all the honour but none of the cash. Scholarships designed to attract the otherwise talented (art, music, science, sports, all-round and one or two amazing ones – for chess at Millfield, for example) often remain substantial. Getting your child up to grade 5 in music by age 11 can be a profitable investment. Girls' schools, alas, offer fewer and less valuable scholarships. As a rule of thumb, the old famous foundations are the richest: they may well disclaim this, but all is relative. Scholarships awarded by HMC and GSA (the top schools' trade organisations) schools now vary widely. Few are now as much as 50 per cent of the full fees and most are capped at around 10–15% but almost all schools offer to 'top up' your 'scholarship' with a means-tested 'bursary'. If you have a bright, talented child and no money, you could find his or her education is pretty much all found by the school. Some schools (e.g. Eton, Westminster, St Paul's) also have a statutory number of full scholarships to offer – and from them 'full' may include the cost of uniforms and travel to school.

Look out for esoteric scholarships for, for example, sons and daughters of clergy, medics, single mothers. Licensed Victuallers' in Ascot gives discounts to children of parents working in the licensed drinks trade (from bar staff to brewers). If your name is West and you live in the parish of Twickenham there could be a bursary waiting for you (at Christ's Hospital). Scholarships to choir schools are worth thinking about, but they will not cover full fees and the children work incredibly hard for them (and it is worth asking what happens when their voices break). But this could well be the beginning of a music scholarship into public school. If you are after a musical scholarship then this book, Music Awards at Independent Schools from the Music Masters and Mistresses Association, by Jonathan Varcoe, may be just what you need.

Keep your eyes open for internal scholarships which run at various stages, sixth form especially. Of course, there are also increasing numbers of schools luring pupils in at sixth form with generous scholarships: might be worth moving schools for.

Useless scholarships – don't fall for them. It is a false economy to be flattered into going to the wrong school for £200 off the bill. You may be much better off with a school that charges slightly lower fees to start with but no scholarship on offer.

By the way, it is well worth lobbying for 10 per cent off, or even more in this climate, in any case – if you have three children you should be able to negotiate a job lot. Heads are used to this, wary of it – but take courage: this is the way the world now is. Of course, you may get a raspberry.

Bursaries

Assume that any school with charitable status, and many without, will offer bursaries. You will need to prove genuine need – no school should wish to risk falling foul of the Charities Commission.

Charitable trusts

Charitable grant-making trusts can help in cases of genuine need. ISCias (the Independent Schools Council information and advice service) warns parents considering this route: 'Do not apply for an education grant for your child unless the circumstances are exceptional. The grant-giving trust will reject applications unless their requirements are satisfied.' The genuine needs recognised by the grant-making trusts are:

- boarding need, where the home environment is unsuitable because of the disability or illness of the parents or of siblings
- unforeseen family disaster, such as the sudden death of the breadwinner when a child is already at school
- need for continuity when a pupil is in the middle of a GCSE or A level course and a change in parental circumstances threatens withdrawal from school
- need for special education where there is a genuine recognised barrier to learning which cannot be catered for at a state school.

If you want to explore this road, the key books are The Educational Grants Directory (specifically directed at funding for schoolchildren and students in need), The Guide to the Major Trusts (in three volumes), The Directory of Grant Making Trusts and the Charities Digest. Most come out annually with a year suffix to the title, and you should be able to find one or more in your local library.

Other cheapos

Certain schools are relatively cheap. The Livery Companies, such as Haberdashers and Mercers, fund various schools, e.g. Haberdasher's Monmouth, Gresham's. Such schools are usually excellent value – not only cheap(er), but with good facilities.

Also cheap, but with fewer frills, are the Girls' Day Schools Trust (GDST) schools.

It may well be worth considering sending your child as a day pupil to a big strong boarding school. This way you will reap the benefits at a lesser price (although sometimes the day fees are ridiculous).

Fees

Take great care in comparing fees between schools. Some quote an all-in fee, others seem cheaper but have a load of unavoidable 'extras' that can add up to 25 per cent to the bill.

Things that you may have to add in include:

- Lunches. Many day schools charge for these on top.
- Uniform. Many schools have a flourishing secondhand shop – Eton has several.
- Books. An extra in some schools.
- Trips. At some schools almost all included (bar holiday expeditions); at others you will pay even for ones that are part of the curriculum. The greater likelihood, though, is that trips that are nominally optional will be socially compulsory.
- Transport to and from school can be very steep indeed at some day schools.
- Capital levy. Usually a large, one-off impost, supposedly to pay for new buildings.
- Special education (such as one-to-one aid in classroom, dyslexia support or tutoring) or EFL.
- Insurance.
- Unusual subjects e.g. languages, where there are fewer than, say, four in a class.
- Seriously hefty deposit on a firm offer of a place (£2,000 and rising in London, to try to stop well-off parents keeping their options open).
- Keeping up with the Joneses. In a money or status-conscious school, all sorts of possessions or expenditure may be required for a child to remain one of the in-crowd.

Special Educational Needs – that's not my child ... is it?

Special educational needs describes children who may have any of the following difficulties: social, emotional, intellectual, behavioural, physical, sensory or a mixture of some or all. Children with SEN may think or learn differently to others. They are sat in mainstream classrooms nationwide, and always have been, and are the children who:

- have spider hand-writing;
- are disorganised or 'forget' to do homework or revise for tests;
- trip over their own feet;
- avoid eye-contact, are shy and withdrawn;
- make odd noises at inappropriate times;
- refuse to read aloud;
- don't pay attention when the teacher addresses the whole class;
- declare they 'hate maths' when in reality 'they don't get it';
- are articulate but can't or won't put pen to paper;
- engage in disruptive or aggressive behaviour.

These are all characteristics of normal childhood too, which is why some SENs are difficult to spot. Teachers and others working with children are becoming notably more alert to SEN, and supportive of formal assessment.

Many schools now routinely screen for specific learning difficulties and a good classroom teacher will be alert to special needs. However, formal assessment for SEN is not something a classroom teacher can do, they have neither the time nor the training. It is carried out by Educational Psychologists (don't be put off by the title, the good ones are friendly, helpful and accommodating). Many of us at *The Good Schools Guide* have used them, to excellent effect: we keep a list of the ones we like, as do most SEN charities and many schools. If you have any reason to suspect SEN, assess: bright children can be very good at hiding their difficulties or compensating for them, and we have come across cases where bright but undiagnosed severe dyslexics have made it to Oxbridge.

SEN of one form or another affects approximately one in five youngsters. Children do not outgrow SEN but, with help, learn to cope. SEN affects all social classes and intellects. Typically SEN children will need additional or special assistance or consideration to put them on a level playing field with their peers. For some, equality can be achieved by relatively simple measures: having a scribe or being given extra-time in exams; for others, even Specialist equipment and many to one teaching will not make life equable.

Helping the child who is struggling at school

On line we feature schools for children with a range of special needs; in this guide we include a number of Dyslexia Specialist Schools as well as many mainstream schools that offer good provision for children with dyslexia and related specific learning difficulties. On the whole, these schools subscribe to the view that the needs of the learner are paramount. They are likely to: teach a child one thing 20 ways, not 20 things one way; to understand the learning process; use multi-sensory learning styles and understand that when a child's needs are not being met the child may suffer from low-self-esteem and possibly exhibit adverse behaviour as a result of the frustration caused by education appearing to be out of their grasp. Dyslexia Specialist schools will usually expect a formal diagnosis to have been made via an educational psychologist's assessment; equally mainstream schools may well recommend an assessment if you don't already have one.

> The child with specific learning difficulties can be hard to spot. Often intelligent and articulate, it is their own sense of frustration that is frequently the first clue.

Choose your school with care, don't assume any school with a good special needs department will be perfect. Timely (and possibly individual) intervention is great but will only be really effective if set against a backdrop of understanding across all teaching and support staff. A sympathetic Special Needs Coordinator (SENCo) is a great starting point, but the head's attitude to special needs will have a pervasive influence on the school, if they are cautious you should be wary. A child doesn't abandon their difficulties when they leave the learning support department; dyslexia may be mainly associated with reading and writing, but it affects more than just English lessons: the writing and sequencing demands of history can be a problem, and the multi-tasking of many sports can create difficulties if the coaching style is not empathetic.

The type of school and provision that you should look for will depend very much on your child's abilities and on the extent to which their disability affects their learning. A dyslexic child may well have a very high IQ yet struggle to read, scan, write or spell. Look at your child, their innate ability, hobbies and interests: a mainstream school should be doing well by non-SEN children with the same skills. Look at the extent to which your child's disability is affecting their progress: you want a school that happily talks of success with pupils who face similar challenges.

Schools where we particularly rate the provision for children of average to high ability who have a specific learning difficulty

Treat the list below as a prompt. There are many other schools in this guide where their SEN provision may suit your particular child. If a school appears perfect in all other respects, get in touch and find out how they would be prepared to help. The schools below offer a range of provision from fairly minimal intervention to tailor-made curricula; read the reviews with care and check online too www.goodschoolsguide.co.uk to view the school's response to our SEN survey.

Abbots Bromley School for Girls, Nr Rugeley (S)

Aiglon College, Chesières-Villars (S)

Alton College, Alton (S)

Angmering School (The), Littlehampton (S)

Appleford School, Nr Salisbury (J)* Specialist

Barnardiston Hall Preparatory School, Suffolk (J)*

Beeston Hall School, Cromer (J)

Blossom House School, London (S)* Specialist

Bloxham School, Near Banbury (S)*

Box Hill School, Dorking (S)

Bredon School, Tewkesbury (S)*

Brighton College, Brighton (S)

Brighton College Prep School, Brighton (J)

Bruern Abbey School, Bicester (J)* Specialist

Calder House School, Chippenham (J) Specialist

Centre Academy, London (S)* Specialist

Centre Academy East Anglia, Ipswich (J)* Specialist

Clayesmore Preparatory School, Blandford Forum (J)*

Clayesmore School, Blandford Forum (S)*

Clifton College Preparatory School, Bristol (J)*

Cobham Hall, Gravesend (S)*

Cranleigh Prep School, Cranleigh (J)

Danes Hill School, Oxshott (J)*

Dover College, Dover (S)*

Dover College Infant & Junior Department, Dover (J)*

Dominie (The), London (J)* Specialist

Downs School (The), Bristol (J)

Eton College, Windsor (S)

Fairley House School, London (S)* Specialist

Fairley House School Junior Department, London (J)* Specialist

Foremarke Hall, Derby (J)

Forres Sandle Manor School, Fordingbridge (J)

Frewen College, Rye (S)* Specialist

George Watson's College, Edinburgh (S)

Glenalmond College, Perth (S)

Gresham's School, Holt (S)

Gryphon School (The), Sherborne (S)

Hazlegrove School, Yeovil (J)*

Hordle Walhampton School, Lymington (J)*

Howell's School, Llandaff (S)

Impington Village College, Cambridge (S)

James Gillespie's High School, Edinburgh (S)

Kilgraston School, Bridge of Earn (S)*

King's Bruton, Somerset (S)*

King's Rochester, Kent (S)*

Knowl Hill School, Woking (S)* Specialist

Leighton Park School, Reading (S)

Malsis School, Nr Skipton (J)

Malvern St James, Worcestershire (S)*

Mark College, Highbridge (S)* Specialist

Mayville High School, Southsea (S)*

Mayville High School Junior Department, Hampshire (J)*

Millfield Preparatory School, Glastonbury (J)

Millfield School, Street (S)

Milton Abbey School, Dorset (S)*

Moat School (The), London (S)* Specialist

Monkton Preparatory School, Bath (J)

Monkton Senior School, Bath (S)*

Moon Hall School, Dorking (J)*

More House School, Farnham (S)* Specialist

North London International School (The), London (S)

North London International School Kindergarten (The), London (J)*

North London International School Lower School (The), London (J)*

Northease Manor School, Lewes (S)* Specialist

Nunnykirk Centre for Dyslexia, Morpeth (S)* Specialist

Plymstock School and Sports College, Plymouth (S)

Putney Park School, London (S)

Riddlesworth Hall Preparatory School, Norfolk (J)*

Roche School (The), London (J)

Rose Hill Westonbirt School, Tetbury (J)

St Aidan's Church of England High School, Harrogate (S)

St Bede's Prep School, Eastbourne (J)

St Bede's Senior School, Hailsham (S)

St Bees School, Cumbria (S)*

St David's College, Conwy (S)*

St George's School (Edinburgh), Edinburgh (S)

St John's-on-the-Hill School, Chepstow (J)

Seaford College, Petworth (S)

Shapwick Prep School, Bridgewater (J)* Specialist

Shapwick School, Bridgwater (S)* Specialist

Sheen Mount Primary School, London (J)

Sherborne Preparatory School, Sherborne (J)

Sibford School, Banbury (S)*

Sidcot School, Winscombe (S)*

Slindon College, Arundel (S)* Specialist

Stanbridge Earls School, Romsey (S)* Specialist

Stonyhurst College, Clitheroe (S)

Strathallan School, Forgandenny (S)

Sunnydown School, Caterham (S)* Specialist

Unicorn School (The), Abingdon (J)* Specialist

Westonbirt School, Tetbury (S)

Wolverhampton Grammar School, Wolverhampton (S)

Wycliffe College, Stonehouse (S)*

Wycliffe Preparatory School, Gloucestershire (J)*

*Registered with The Council for the Registration of Schools Teaching Dyslexic Pupils (CReSTeD)
S= in the senior section of this guide
J= in the junior section of this guide

Sandra Hutchinson
Special Needs Editor *The Good Schools Guide*

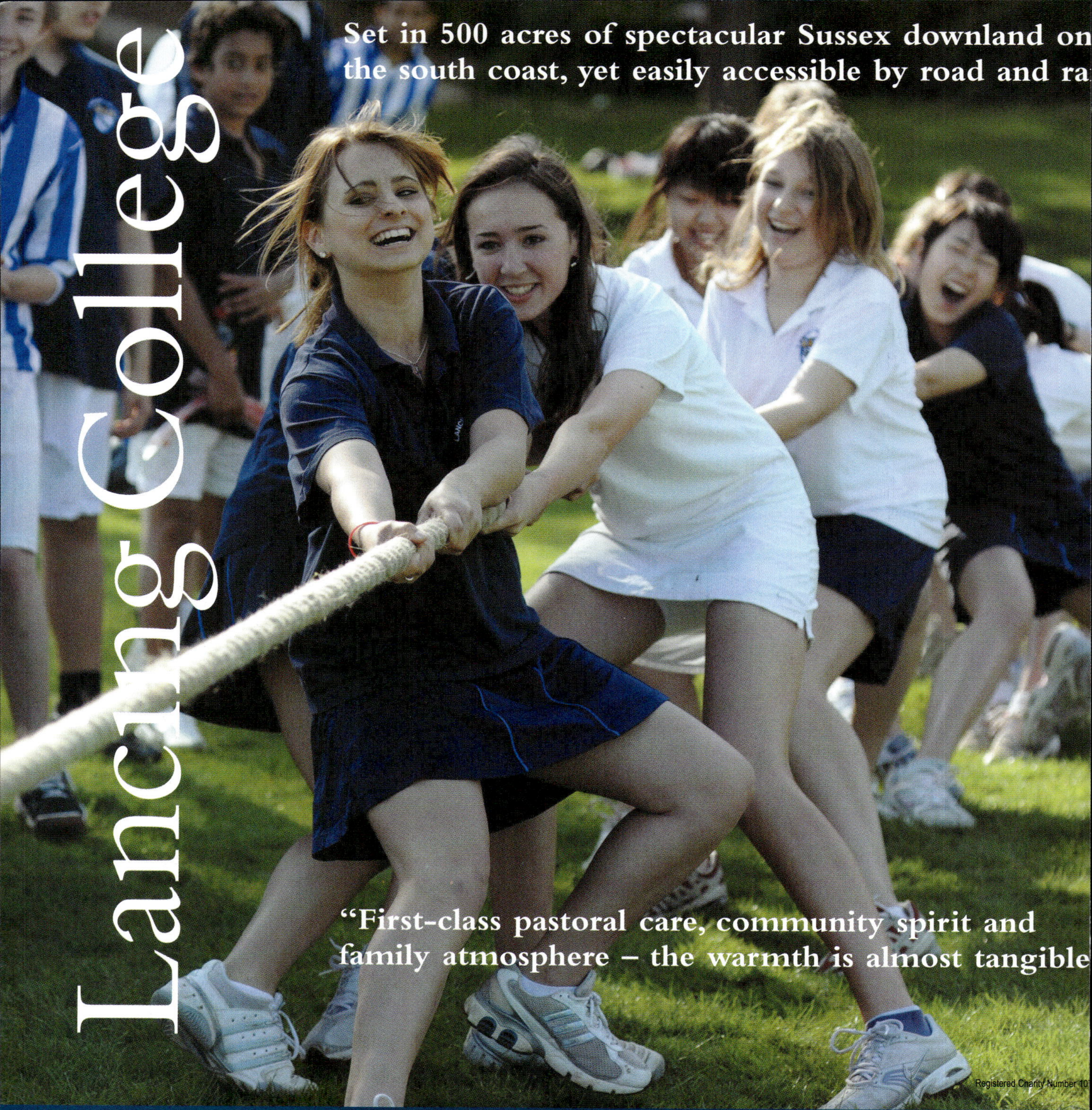
Lancing College
Set in 500 acres of spectacular Sussex downland on
the south coast, yet easily accessible by road and ra
"First-class pastoral care, community spirit and
family atmosphere – the warmth is almost tangible

Boarding schools

Traditionally, heartless British parents sent their little darlings off to school at seven or eight and didn't think about them again until it was time for university. Think Tom Brown's schooldays ... and go to the bottom of the class. Cold showers, initiation ceremonies and enforced runs are more or less a thing of the past – the Care Quality Commission or Ofsted would hastily intervene.

So why board? It depends on where you live. If you happily live near a seriously good state or independent day school, and that is the most rewarding solution either morally or financially, then don't even think about it. If you live in the depths of the country or overseas, or in that educational desert, central London, then boarding may well be your answer.

But beware, boarding schools are not a universal panacea. Putting your child in boarding school implies partnership and trust between school and parent. It is no use sending your utterly revolting child away to school and assuming you will get an angel back at half-term: boarding schools can, and will, expel your child for a variety of reasons (drugs, serious bad behaviour, bullying etc) and – following a recent ruling which involved Marlborough – you will have no recourse. So think carefully before you embark on what is a seriously expensive process. This can often be ameliorated by scholarships, bursaries, kindly grandparents, employment benefits or services bursaries (though at the time of writing these are in jeopardy); in the case of the last you can't just chop and change schools at will but must stick with the one you first thought of.

Do not be taken in by charming heads or their marketing genies entertaining you with PowerPoint presentations and handing out videos (always taken on sunny days and always displaying the best of everything). Again, give some thought to what sort of character you want your child to turn out to be. Boarding schools, because they enfold your child for so much of the year, will make a substantial contribution to their character, and different boarding schools mould character in very different ways. You will never pick this up from the school's marketing material: they all want to appear blandly wonderful.

The Good Schools Guide does its best to capture the character of a school, and you should be able to get a taste of it when you visit. Have a clear view, too, of where you want your child to go on to next. It is easier to get a guide to whether a school is the right place for this ambition: all schools publish lists of where their pupils go on to, and if the education that they provide and the spirit that they inculcate is capable of taking your child where you want them to go, then other children will have gone that way before, probably in some numbers.

Remember that not all boarding schools are in the UK. Most European countries have one or two. Switzerland has some which follow the English academic syllabus (although many 'Swiss boarding schools' no longer live up to their almost mythical reputation for academic excellence), and so do many of the Middle and Far Eastern countries. Some follow the traditional British A level syllabus and some the IB. Ditto Australia and New Zealand (which have several really great boarding schools). There's less boarding in the Americas, though Canada and especially the US have a surprising number of very good ones, and there are a few in South America – particularly in former British colonies. And then there's Africa. There are schools in South Africa that appear to be so British the only real difference is the minuscule fees (but caveat emptor ... as is true anywhere, there are still cultural differences beneath the surface).

NB Some of the above schools have made the cut in our sister publication, *The Good Schools Guide International*, and some have not.

For families from outside the UK, one of the first things that you have to look at is the weekend arrangements ('exeats'). Some schools, prep schools in particular, now work on a formula where the whole school is expected to close down for the weekend every other week. If there are no handy grandparents, godparents or accommodating family friends you must find a guardian. Many schools have a list of wonderful tried and trusted guardians who have taken dozens of tinies under their wing, turn up for speech days and school performances and really provide a second home. But we have heard of a number of distinctly commercial guardians who charge the earth, restrict their input to the barest minimum, and bill for each expense and extra hour. See 'Finding a guardian' (page 45) for more advice.

If you leave boarding until your child has done his/her GCSEs or equivalent they'll have developed a reasonable degree of maturity and independence. Many schools now have expanded sixth forms and happily take children either from the UK (state or other independent schools) or from further afield for a two-year sixth form course leading to A levels or an IB and university entrance globally. Take care to suit the school to the student: the range of styles is particularly broad at this age, from the disciplinarian academic to the 'almost-university'.

Our writers have experienced boarding schools as expats and as locals, as members of families who have used boarding schools for generations and as parents who are tackling boarding for the first time. All of them confirm that, in the words of one editor, 'boarding schools are brilliant, children make friends for life, share the experiences and cultures, and learn tolerance for their fellow man'. That writer remembers finding her eldest son in tears during his first half-term holiday from prep school: 'Mummy, there's no one to play with at home.' That said, there are still many children who end up miserable: you need to take care to match the child to the school, and to watch how things develop thereafter. It should be totally obvious if things are going well.

LEITHS

SCHOOL OF FOOD AND WINE

Leiths School of Food and Wine is a leading London cookery school, teaching cookery for over 35 years. We run a range of courses to suit all abilities and time frames. Whether you are new to cooking, looking for inspiration, or would like a career in the food industry there is a course to suit you.

Enthusiast Classes, for keen home cooks

1 Day Workshops - From chocolate, bread and pastry, to Thai, Japanese and Italian cookery. New classes added throughout the year.

Saturday Morning Classes - Cook a 3 course meal in the space of a morning and sit down and enjoy it for lunch.

Evening Courses - Choose from a range of levels, held one evening a week over 4 or 10 weeks.

Evening Drinks Classes - Match food with wine, Champagne or beer and learn more about this fascinating subject.

One Week Classes - Choose from a range of levels and improve your cookery skills on our intensive hands on cookery weeks.

Certificate Courses, for a cooking career

Career advice is offered through our affiliates **Leiths List** (agency for cooks) and **Leiths Food Solutions** (business consultancy). All courses include food hygiene and health and safety certificates.

4 Week Essential Certificate - For those wanting to learn an essential life skill. Especially suitable for those looking to cook privately for families, B&B's, Chalets or holiday homes.

10 Week Foundation Certificate - Offering a through training in all essential cookery skills, ideal for those looking to work in private catering.

Leiths Diploma - (September - July annually) This Certificate is well recognised in the food industry and leads to exciting and varied careers such as food styling, recipe development or restaurant work.

2 Term Diploma - (January - July annually) For those with previous cooking experience the Leiths Diploma can be taken in 2 terms.

LEARN A SKILL FOR LIFE

CALL NOW FOR YOUR PROSPECTUS +44(0) 20 8749 6400.

FURTHER DETAILS ON ALL OUR CLASSES CAN BE FOUND AT WWW.LEITHS.COM

LEITHS SCHOOL OF FOOD AND WINE, 16-20 WENDELL ROAD, LONDON, W12 9RT

Notes for foreign parents

Most UK schools are now genuinely thrilled to welcome foreign students, and no longer regard a cosmopolitan mix as a matter for shame (that they cannot fill the school with home-grown products). Foreign students are perceived to add breadth, excitement, new horizons, not to mention fantastic exam results in exotic languages (Turkish, Norwegian, Polish, Mandarin, Japanese, Gujerati, Urdu among the most common), high intelligence (often), motivation and – last but not least – cash.

The best schools in this country are outstanding by any standards. Beware, though, of being fobbed off with second-rate places.

Here are a few thoughts from overseas parents who are already in the UK system.

1. Do not assume a school is good simply because it is famous: an obvious point, but you would be surprised how many people believe famous equals good.
2. Consider doing a summer/holiday course before opting for mainstream schooling. There are courses which take place in British public schools, for example, which will give your child a 'feel' for what's in store – and get the English up to scratch. The British Council vets most such courses, and lists the ones that it approves of.
3. Various 'international study centres' have sprung up, most attached to solid private schools. The best of these do a good job in preparing children with little English for entry to British boarding schools. Beware those that are too newly established, and make sure to ask for a full list of the schools that pupils move on to.
4. Educational agencies will give you a list of schools in the UK which have places available when you ask – beware, though, as these are usually no more than lists, and do not differentiate between the good, the bad and the ugly. Such agencies are usually paid fat commissions by the schools they recommend, and may be reluctant to mention those schools that do not pay them a commission (this includes many of the best ones).
5. Look for a school that is popular with the British as well as with foreigners – talk to personal contacts if possible. British Embassies Abroad (www2.tagish.co.uk/Links/embassy1b.nsf) and the British Council (www.britishcouncil.org) are often useful initial points of contact, but don't rely on their advice over particular schools.
6. The majority of schools in this country are not geared to teaching the English language to pupils who don't know it. Beware of schools which have a high proportion of foreigners, but no real way of teaching them English. Schools which have very few foreigners in the school are another matter – being immersed in a language without the option can sometimes be the quickest way to learn, particularly for younger children.
7. If a school says it has got 'provision' for teaching English as a Foreign Language (EFL) ask exactly what that provision consists of, and whether it will cost extra. EFL teachers need to have a proper teaching degree/diploma AND an EFL qualification: the latter alone means very little. However quick at learning your child is, he/she will certainly struggle at public exam level – the pressure of work is just too high.
8. Be prepared to 'sell' yourself a bit to the school. Private schools in this country have a tendency to ask what you can do for them, rather than what they can do for you. This shocks parents from other countries, but it is a fact.
9. You will usually be asked to appoint a UK guardian for your child – someone with whom the school can deal on day-to-day matters, and whom your child can turn to for help, outings and so on. Read 'Finding a guardian' on page 45.
10. Always go and see a school you are interested in yourself – or at least send someone whose judgement you trust (and who knows your child). You will be surprised how much you can learn about a place from even a brief look. Read 'What to look out for during a school visit' on page 47.

SKINS

Finding a guardian

British boarding schools will not admit an overseas pupil under the age of 18 unless he or she has a local guardian. It can seem an unnecessary annoyance, especially for older children, but most schools have had enough grim experiences (such as children left unclaimed on day one of the Christmas holidays) that they have learned to demand it.

Guardians perform several roles. They provide a place for your child to stay during the – sometimes numerous – school holidays (and many schools also have compulsory exeats and half-term breaks when all pupils have to vamoose). Guardians may also need to serve as your representatives, making some decisions for your child, signing forms, attending parents' evenings and being available in an emergency – for instance, if your child falls ill or is temporarily or permanently excluded from school (it happens more often than you think). Guardians may need to assist with transport to and from school or from airports etc. In addition, guardians are sometimes required to act as a sort of bank, doling out pocket money, funds for school trips etc. In general, the younger the pupil, the more comprehensive the service will need to be.

How do you find a guardian? Start by asking friends in your own country who have used one. If they had a good experience with a firm, there is a good chance you will too.

If you don't know anyone who has used a guardian, then ask the school your child will be attending. Most schools will be reluctant to recommend one guardianship firm – they don't want to be responsible if you end up with a duff one – but if you ask them to name a few companies that have supplied guardians for their pupils in the past, schools will often give you good leads. Schools have a lot of experience with guardians and will be likely to know of the smaller, more local (and perhaps less expensive) firms that may be just what you need. Be on guard, however, if a school is tied to one particular firm. There may be a financial relationship between the two that can lead to a conflict of interest – do you really want your guardian in cahoots with the school when Johnny and his housemaster have a conflict that you would like the guardian to help resolve?

Many schools will point you towards one of two accredited associations of guardians. The largest of these is the Association for the Education and Guardianship of International Students (Aegis) (www.aegisuk.net email;secretary@aegisuk.net). Aegis members include such giants in the field as Gabbitas and Sutherland Education. Members of this organisation are vetted and insured and all their host families are carefully checked.

There are, of course, alternatives to using a professional guardianship agency. The first choice for most expat Brits, and for many foreign families, is to house children with British relatives. The benefits are that it is cheap and the guardian is likely to have a genuine interest in the welfare of the child. On the downside, relatives may be working people who will find a long journey to fetch their cousin's wife's niece a bind, not to mention looking after her for a week or more, or even between terms. Financial arrangements with relatives can also become a strain, as they will need to pay out in advance for your child's travel expenses, entertainment, clothes etc. Occasionally, schools will not accept relatives as guardians if they live very far away from the school.

Language schools and tutorial colleges will sometimes have families on their books who can take in older teenagers, thereby sidestepping guardianship firms. You will need to find out how carefully the families have been checked and whether there is any back-up from the school if the family can no longer fulfil its role. You should also ask for references on the families (ideally from pupils who have previously lodged with them) and check them rigorously.

Some parents try to dispense with formal guardians all together, looking to house their child with the local exile community in exchange for some light work. Parents of older teenagers often ask if they can billet their youngsters in a bed and breakfast during school holidays rather than fuss with the expense of guardians. While we admire their ingenuity, these parents are leaving themselves open to trouble if anything goes wrong. And you would be amazed how things can go wrong. Schools sometimes find themselves on the phone to guardianship agencies at the last minute asking for help with a student whose guardian has proved to be non-existent.

Ideally you will want to meet the family your child will be staying with. If that is impossible, you can cover a lot of ground on the telephone or via email.

Questions for guardianship firms

1. What exactly will I be paying for? Go through this with a fine-toothed comb. You do not want to pay for more than you will need, nor do you want to be caught short.
2. Will my child be able to stay with the same family throughout the time they are educated in the UK?

3. Can my child move to a different host family if things don't work out?
4. Do you offer 24-hour cover in case of an emergency?
5. Are you fully insured?
6. Who will be the legal guardian – the host family or the director of the guardianship firm? Who should my child contact if he or she is having a problem? It is key that you establish this because in many firms the appointed guardian is actually the director of the firm, not the host family.
7. How do you choose and inspect your guardians? Are they CRB (Criminal Record Bureau) checked?
8. Will my child's host family have other overseas pupils staying with them? Will the others speak my child's language (there are pros and cons)?

Questions for the host family

1. Do you have children of your own? What ages?
2. Have you been a guardian before?
3. What are your rules on television viewing, homework, going out with friends, use of telephone and computer, drinking (for older teenagers) etc?
4. What will the arrangements be for pocket money and my child's other financial needs?

Emergencies can arise when you least expect them. Quest Guardians in Dorset remembers the SARS outbreak in 2003 when scores of Southeast Asian pupils were stranded after returning from their Easter holidays. Some British schools, including Eton, had made sudden decisions not to readmit them until they had been quarantined for ten days. Host families were also reluctant to harbour the potentially contagious pariahs. It is testing times like that when a guardianship firm (hopefully) proves its commitment and its value.

Whilst choosing a school

What to look out for during a school visit

See several schools – it's a process of elimination and comparisons are vital to make. Does the head impress you? You don't have to like him/her but it helps. Does he/she appear in control of the situation? The head really does make or break a school. Is there a member of staff at the school on the same wavelength as you? There must be someone you can turn to (particularly true of boarding).

We've got a list of things you could look out for and questions you might ask but in the end you know your child – and your family – best. Pay attention to your gut reaction. Did you come out of the school feeling good?

Every single reference book on schools indulges in advice on this. Lists of questions tend to make headteachers bristle but going in as a parent can be daunting. The following is a list of guidelines we drew up as we went around Take note of the Boarding School, Non-UK and Resident Parents and SEN sections if that is your focus.

Atmosphere and attitudes

- What are the pupils like? Do you want your child to be like that?
- Bearing of pupils – politeness, neatness. Bearing of staff, ditto. Do they look clean, bright-eyed and bushy-tailed (or whatever you like)?
- Attitude of pupils to staff and vice versa. Does the head know who they all are (not often practicable in big or house-based schools)? Do pupils flatten themselves against the wall as the head passes? Do they flatten him/her against the wall as they pass? (If so, do they stop and say sorry?)
- Watch the interaction of staff and pupils: it should be easy and unforced, but respectful.
- Is self-confidence universal, or confined to just some kids (and if so, which ones?) Is the atmosphere happy? Fraught? Coerced or co-opted?
- Do you fall over pupils smoking in corners, or did you pass a huddled group on the way in? How many are slumped in front of the television (key question when visiting around 1.30pm especially)?
- What does the school smell like? What is the state of the paintwork – a glance at the ceiling will usually tell (not that it matters per se).

Classes and teaching

- Grab an exercise book or three in passing and look at the standard of work and the standard of marking – this can tell you an enormous amount. Check the size of teaching groups – it's amazing how often numbers do not tally with the official version.
- What is the average age of the staff? All old can mean not enough dynamic new ideas or energy; all young can mean too inexperienced and also, possibly, too transitory.
- Ask if you can pop in to a class, or have a good long look through the peep holes, and see what is really happening. Are the children dozing? Is the teacher dozing? Is there rapport between the teacher and the taught?
- What's on the walls? Look for evidence of creativity and the celebration of pupils' achievements.
- Look at noticeboards for signs of plenty going on, and names you know (for grilling later) – and how up to date the boards are kept.

Where is the head's study: in the thick of things, indicating a finger on the pulse, or still in an ivory tower? (For some heads unbreakable precedent governs where they reign from.)

Resources

- Observe the state of the library: rows of dusty tomes look impressive, but bright, new and dog-eared is healthier. Where is the library – is it in a useful position, do the troops use it? What is the annual book budget?
- What are the computer facilities like? Are there enough for all the kids all the time? According to the school? According to the kids?
- How common are laptops? Laptops are a pain in the fundament to most schools, parents and even pupils who have to worry about losing them and – if their parents are buying them rather than the school supplying them – have to worry about whether their model is sufficiently cool.
- Are keyboarding/typing skills universal (a great plus for later life)? Is good use made of the internet, and is internet access fast? Do all teachers use computers/interactive white boards in class as an integral part of lessons, or just some of them? Is the school proud of its imaginative use of computers?

Finally, do you like the look of the parents, and would you be happy for your children to mix with theirs?

At a boarding school

Be sure to meet your child's houseparents and the matron as well as the head. These three are the ones who really make a difference to the day-to-day happiness of a boarder. And if your child is to have a tutor who stays with them throughout their time at school, meet them too. Get the home phone number of whoever has charge of your child's welfare, and ask if you can call at any time.

Ask how parent and child communicate. Weekly letter? A phone for each 50 pupils? Or nightly emails and a mobile phone? This is definitely something to talk to pupils about when you visit.

Be relentlessly questioning about any requirements which are particular to you. If your child has special educational needs (and there are many boarding schools in the UK which make superb provision for these) you will need to know exactly what is on offer, and how the school proposes to make you part of the decision-making process on such questions as whether to include or exclude your child from particular lessons. How good are the EFL lessons, and how much extra do they cost? What provision do they make for your faith? Don't just take this on trust, talk to a co-religionist who is already at the school and find out what really happens.

Some problems that are easily tackled by local parents become much harder to deal with when a parent is distant. Discover whether matron will replenish (and mend) school (and home) clothes and if she can do it out of the secondhand shop. At the very same time you can be sussing out whether matron, and the under matrons, are cuddly, or moustachioed dragons who grump. Find out if boarders are allowed into town at weekends. How does the school control what they get up to? How can parents ditto? It helps a lot if a child has a bolt hole in town where they can go rather than be dragged into some den of iniquity by their friends because they have no alternative. Do you have a friend or relative who is willing to let them have a key?

The same problem of distance applies to bullying. Being able to recharge courage and self-confidence at home makes a child much more resilient in the face of low-level bullying than a child who has no such resort. Don't be satisfied with the mere absence of stories about bullying; look for stories (particularly from gentler pupils) about how well bullying is dealt with.

As a non-UK resident parent

- What arrangements does the boarding school have for exeats (weekends when the pupils are allowed away from the school premises)? If your child is likely to find itself at school on weekends when many have departed, how many other children will be in the same position? There is an increasing tendency in the UK towards 'weekly' and 'flexi' boarding where pupils can go home any weekend they want. If you live overseas, this is obviously bad news. It is best, if you can, to opt for a 'full' boarding school, which has a proper programme of activities at weekends, and one or two pre-arranged exeats per term.
- What will the school would do if your child were to be found guilty of a serious misdemeanour (drugs etc)? You do not want to find him/her ejected from the school at a moment's notice.
- What arrangements are made at the end of public exam terms? There is an increasing tendency to send pupils home early once they have finished their exams – sometimes weeks early. If this suits you, then that's fine. If not, then you need to know that the school has a proper programme of activities to keep pupils occupied until the last official day of term.
- How many other pupils from your country are there? Will there be arrangements for children from the same country to be in different dormitories (otherwise they form cliques, never learn English, and might as well have stayed at home). And while on the subject of dormitories, will your child have any real privacy at all?
- Research the travelling logistics, particularly if you want to turn up for the school play. Cheapo air fares have done wonders for the UK boarding system. Think Stansted, think East Midlands, think Edinburgh or Glasgow – long- and short-haul flights land at these places regularly, so you are not restricted to Heathrow and the M4 corridor.

SEN needs

If you're choosing a mainstream school for a child with a relatively mild/moderate SEN request a copy of the school's special educational needs policy and ask how much extra you will have to pay for the support that you want.

A good school will:

1. Test /screen all children, for SEN, on entry.
2. Likely have other pupils in the school with special needs supported by qualified specialist teachers.
3. Ensure special needs support is an integral part of the school, with a two-way flow of information between specialists and subject teachers. Schools where SEN support is an 'add on', are really only suitable for very mild cases.
4. Give careful consideration to what a pupil will miss out on to receive extra help.
5. Have a supportive head. If the head is not enthusiastic about helping SEN children staff may not be as supportive or understanding as they should be.
6. Seek to build self-esteem – to find something your child is good at and encourage your child's areas of strength.
7. Use multi-sensory learning and teaching methods with lessons in relatively short sections.

8. Have full regard to the SEN code of Practice and make use of concessions for exams, such as providing a laptop, or an amanuensis and train children in the use of these. For public examination concessions you will need an up-to-date educational psychologist's report.
9. Never ask 'Is this the best you can do?' For some children with SENs pastoral care can be as important as specialist understanding of a particular disability.

When you visit, talk to some pupils with the same diagnosis as your child – are they bubbling with pride and confidence?

Questions to have up your sleeve

Obviously not all are applicable to every school: ask even half of these questions and you will probably never be invited back again, but it does no harm to take them along for prompting. They are divided up into questions for the head, a senior staff member and pupils – however, if you get a sparky sixth former showing you around they will probably be the best source of information, get them chatting.

For the head

Atmosphere and attitudes

1. What are the head's ambitions, for the school and personally?
2. How long as he/she been there? Until when is he/she 'contracted'? Is he/she about to leave?
3. What does he/she regard as most important?
4. What does the head really want for the pupils in the long run?
5. What is his/her history?
6. Is he/she married, with children (hands-on experience)?
7. How old are the children, and where are they at school?
8. How are pupils selected? What is the school looking for in the pupils it takes?
9. Who are the pupils and where do they come from, both geographically and socially? How many Brits and, in particular, how many non-Brits whose first language is not English? Too many of the latter can grind teaching to a halt – very few schools can afford to cater for them separately.
10. What does the school do about bullying? Bullying is universal, so 'we don't have it here' probably means they don't look, and there's lots of it. A good sign is frequent examples of dealing well with it. Who chooses the prefects?
11. What is the head's attitude to discipline? Drugs? Sex? Alcohol? Homosexuality? Stealing? Bad language? Breaking the more petty school rules? What form do punishments take? Are prefects allowed to mete it out? Ask for a copy of the school rules – this can be illuminating – and ask how they have been established (from on high? with pupils?). Be conscious as you ask these questions that the answer you want to hear for your sheltered 10-year-old may not be the answer that you want when she is sinful and 16. How many people have been expelled, asked to leave, suspended in the last two years? (This could pinpoint specific problems.)
12. Who would not be happy at the school?

Classes and teaching

1. What are the results like? Watch the whites of their eyes as they give you the answer – and see 'What the league tables don't tell you'.
2. Which exams do you expect to be doing when my child takes them? All is ferment at the moment – A levels and GCSE, the IB, IGCSE and Pre-U, various specialist university entrance exams, and alternatives to GCSE from e.g. Bedales and Wellington. See 'The exploding curriculum' on page 23.
3. What are the 'value-added' scores like? Most schools now use one system or another for monitoring value added – the improvement in pupils' performance over the years. What's the overall value added compared with the national average? Is this consistent over all subjects, or is the good news all in one or two areas?
4. Is there automatic promotion from the junior school to the senior? If not, in what circumstances are pupils rejected, and how many each year? How much notice should you expect to be given that your child is not among the chosen (look for a minimum of two years).
5. What are the present numbers in the school? What has the trend been like over the last five years, and why? How many are imported into the sixth form from outside? This may well affect the school's results and needs to be looked at with a beady eye – it may be reaping the benefits of another school's hard work. You need to look at the trend within age groups to see which bits of the school are popular, and also factor in any change to co-ed. Any substantial trends will have a reason – e.g. news spreading of the school's quality or lack of it – and may also have consequences, such as closure.
6. Does the school feel responsible for pupils once they are accepted – or will it fire misfits/slow learners if they don't shape up quickly? (May not be confessed to: always ask how many leave post-GCSE and where they go. Girls to co-ed, non-selective to selective or to a good sixth form college are usually pupils jumping rather than being pushed). If pupils are encouraged to leave, how well are they supported in this decision: are they given lots of notice, and experienced help in finding somewhere else?

Scholarship
Complete set with marking guidelines
11+
Core subjects with mark schemes
English
Maths
Science
ISEB
COMMON ENTRANCE EXAMINATION AT 13+
SCIENCE
BIOLOGY

Resources

1. How much does the school spend on staff training, and what does it train them to do? Do any of the staff write school books or work as chief examiners? What is the turnover of staff – do too many stay too long? You are unlikely to get a straight answer to this.
2. Who owns the school? If privately owned – though few are – are there any checks and balances, such as governors or PTA, and to whom do you make out your cheque? Who takes over when the current owner calls it a day?
3. What about cost: fees, plus real cost, i.e., the size of the bill? Some schools quote an 'all-in' fee; others quote tuition fees only and charge massively for extras (such as lunch!). 'Extras' are usually listed on a separate sheet of paper (because they constantly rise) and are tucked into the back of the prospectus. What does music tuition cost? The price of a half-hour piano lesson can vary by 100 per cent from school to school.
4. What scholarships are available and won? What bursaries and funding are available when finances come adrift?

For the head of curriculum, houseparent or senior staff member

Atmosphere and attitudes

1. How much pocket money is suggested?
2. At prep/junior schools: Do staff sit with pupils at meal times and supervise table manners and behaviour or is lunchtime intended to be a break for the teachers?
3. For boys' schools which have gone co-ed in the last 20 years: How many female academic staff are there? How many girls are there? What provision is there for the girls to play games (small numbers mean no hope of making up teams)? What facilities are there for them? What is the school's policy on boy/girl relationships?

Classes and teaching

1. What are the sizes of the classes – biggest and smallest?
2. NB A good teacher teaches any class size competently; bad teachers do not become good teachers by reducing class size.
3. What languages are genuinely on offer? Exam results do not tell you as they may include exams taken by native speakers in languages the school does not teach.
4. What is the ratio of full-time teaching staff to pupils? How many part-timers are there? How part-time are they?
5. How does the school monitor progress (pupils and, indeed, staff)? The best will use regular tests integrated with the value-added system, which allows the school to pick up underperformance quickly (within a term). They are equally as good for teachers as for pupils and, if they are working well, will result in lots of happy stories about pupils rescued and teachers made good.
6. Does the school have special help on tap for learning difficulties? If so, how much help, in what form, and is it going to cost you extra? Mainstream schools that do well by children with SENs are often excellent places for others too.
7. How does the school report to parents? How often are school reports issued? Monthly? Termly? You would be surprised how many fee-paying schools only provide one written report a year.

Options

1. How many pupils learn a musical instrument, and for how long? Are practice sessions timetabled? What proportion of these are taught privately outside the school? This can be quite telling if you are trying to suss out the strength of a school's music department.
2. Every school says it has plenty of extracurricular activities, but don't take its word for it. Ask for a timetable of what happens when and who is eligible. Are the choir and the dance club by audition only? Is your talented flautist unlikely to get into the orchestra for years because there are plenty of flutes already? Does the trampolining club actually happen, or is the teacher off on maternity leave for a year?
3. If your child is keen on sport but unlikely to make the First XI, find out the school's attitude. Are there house teams, fourth and fifth teams, sports clubs open to everyone? Or does the school concentrate all its efforts on the top performers, with no opportunities for those who just like to play for fun? How much choice is there? – many boys' schools insist on rugby. Are there options for the boy who refuses to play rugby or the girl who loathes hockey/lacrosse or wants to avoid team games altogether?
4. If you think school trips are important, find out what actually happens. How many times a term will the average class get a trip? Is the German exchange trip open to everyone, or is it first come, first served? Does the head think that outings broaden the education or disrupt the timetable?

For the pupils

Atmosphere and attitude

1. What's the temperature at the school in the winter? A question for Scottish and seaside schools particularly.
2. What's the food like? Fresh ingredients? Is fruit easily available around the school? Does the tuck shop sell good food or junk? For boarding schools: What time is supper? Is there nutritious food (containing protein) available after supper? Is the food different at

weekends? Is there a designated member of staff with a special responsibility for food at the school?

3. What is the school's policy on attending or missing meals? How aware is the school of the dangers and signs of anorexia? Is there a cafeteria system or a table laid and 'table talk'? Who oversees the tables: the staff at each end? Or prefects? Or is it a free-for-all?
4. Are drinking water fountains placed conveniently around the school? Are pupils allowed to take water into classes?
5. Why did you (or your parents) choose this school?
6. What is the structure? What houses are there, if any? Do you have a brother or sister? If so where do they fit in? What is the school hierarchy? What's it cool to be good at – in order – work, sport (which sports?) social life, drama, art?
7. Do lots of people have boyfriends and girlfriends or don't long-term relationships happen?
8. Is there a shadowing system for new pupils? Any special arrangements in place to welcome a pupil who comes in at an odd moment, such as the middle of term?
9. Who would you go to if you had a problem? Tutor? Houseparent? Favourite subject teacher? This should tell you what the pastoral care is like, who is responsible to whom and whether problems are spotted early.
10. What emphasis is there (if any) on religious teaching? Daily chapel? Daily assembly? Weekly chapel? Are special arrangements made for any other faiths – and what are they? Some schools claiming to cater for Roman Catholics, for example, make it quite hard for them to get to mass. How many of each faith are in the school?
11. What do they call the head? Do they see him/her outside assembly? How does he/she run the school? Does it work?
12. If you had a magic wand, what would you change about the school? What's the best thing about it?

Classes and teaching

1. What special projects are currently on the go?
2. What is the pressure of work? Amount of work? Homework? Setting? Streaming?
3. How involved are parents with the school? Can parents talk to (or email) teachers when they want to? Is there special provision for parents on the school website?
4. Is there a holiday reading list, and is there holiday homework? Ever? Never?
5. How is the school coping with exam pressure? Are pupils taking an interesting spread of courses – or have they relapsed to 3AS, 3A2s and the rest not taken seriously?
6. Where do pupils go on to? How pupils see themselves, their confidence, their ambition – all show through in their choices. What is the careers advice like?

For the local shop/taxi driver/estate agent

What is the school like? This can produce a flood of enlightening comment.

Careers departments and how to judge them

The careers department, too often that neglected airless cubicle occupied by uninspiring books and a sidelined teacher, could (if it is any good) make a big difference to the value your child gets out of his or her years of education (and perhaps a good deal of your money too). No school can now command places for its students at the best universities, so what they teach their pupils ought to be aimed as much at the lives which will follow university as at those dreaded examinations – and the careers department ought to be a strong part of that focus. Undergraduates who started the career decision-making process at school will be likely to make better, more focused, use of their time at university, and do much better at the gladiatorial pre-graduation milk round than their unprepared counterparts.

Some schools seem to bundle the assistance that they give to pupils in choosing university courses in with 'careers advice', and lump the two subjects together as 'careers and further education'. There is some logic in this for those few professions where particular subjects and degree courses are required, but for the vast majority of pupils the choice of degree will have little consequence for what they do afterwards.

A school which has begun to wake up to the benefits of good careers advice will have appointed an impressive (is your child going to follow advice from someone who is not?) 'head of careers', sometimes supported by a small team of helpers. Some will go to the trouble of arranging the school's annual (or, worse, bi-annual) careers fair, rounding up recent alumni and parents to talk to the pupils (not that this guarantees coverage of the best options, or depth of wisdom). If they are doing better than this, then you are in luck.

Here are some questions for the head of careers or headteacher (or a sixth former), just pick a few that appeal to you.

1. How do you make your pupils interesting to future employers? Have those who study sciences read a novel or learnt a language? Are your arts students numerate? How do you advise your pupils to present themselves in all respects ranging from the sartorial to the written word (letters and emails) and body language? Do you provide advice and training on CV writing and successful interview technique – after all, the job interview process normally has a significant subjective element and those candidates who have a polished CV and are skilled at interview technique will normally do better than those candidates who arrive at the interview unprepared.
2. How do you make pupils aware of their various career options? Have they been exposed to people who understand what particular careers are really about? How large is the careers team and what are their roles? Are they employed full-time or part-time? This should help you determine whether the school defines 'filling in university application forms' as 'careers advice'.
3. Does the school actively seek work experience opportunities for its senior pupils? If so, what is the process? How much time is spent with pupils one-to-one helping them to think about their career options? Do they programme sessions or do they sit back and 'provide a service' to which pupils can go to if they are sufficiently interested? Is advice offered to them about leadership qualities and the attractiveness of this trait to future employers?
4. Does the school contact university careers departments to bridge the work that they (the school) have been doing, in order that the university careers department can continue to advise? What advice is given to pupils on the best use of their gap year for adding to their attractiveness to future employers?
5. Now find a sixth former or two. Do their experiences with the careers department bear any resemblance to what you have just been told? What sort of advice have they been offered on choosing a course, perhaps one that they haven't studied at school e.g. anthropology? Have they had good advice on writing their personal statements? Have Oxbridge/medical candidates had practice interviews and entrance exams? Have they been encouraged to aim high or to aim safe? Some of the highest ranking schools offer surprisingly little help.

Compiled by Mark Somers of The Inspirational Careers Company, www.informandinspire.org

A quiet word about child protection

If you are preparing to entrust your precious child to a school – whether day or boarding – you will probably assume without question that your child will be safe and that all members of the school's staff will take the greatest care to ensure that this is always the case. The chances are that your expectations will be fulfilled. However, we have all read news reports of bullying and abuse and may have shuddered at the thought that those very people who smilingly welcome our children into their care may be the last people to whom we would entrust them, did we know all.

It can be hard to keep a sense of proportion faced with the emotional battering from media and pressure groups. Things were much worse in the past; prisons would have been full of staff, and older pupils, had current rules applied 40 years ago. Schools, and society generally, have improved out of all recognition. Successive governments have legislated to protect children and the abuses of the past are now far less likely to happen. Indeed it may seem that the pendulum has swung too far, with the demand that 11 million adults in the UK get CRB checks (common sense may yet prevail here).

We take the view that parents should trust schools, but should nonetheless be on their guard. The effects of abuse can be horrid and life-long. Children tend to keep their miseries to themselves. The film *Chosen* – www.chosen.org.uk – is an uncomfortably well-made documentary of suffering that was once commonplace.

Parents do well to warn their children – gently but seriously – of the dangers, however remote these may be, so they feel that it is easy to speak to you should they meet them. It is worth pointing out that abuse can come from anyone – even a teacher or an adult they know well.

It is also worth thinking about raising your own antennae at any school you may be considering. Most prospective parents feel awkward enough asking head teachers about exam results or careers advice without the almost unbearable discomfort of probing them on how they protect pupils from teachers and other adults. Which is why parents almost never bring it up.

Keep your questions neutral and matter-of-fact. As always, much can be gleaned from the head's attitude – and eyes – when questions about child protection are asked. Is he or she ill at ease? Dismissive? Or are they happy to engage, and proud of the steps their school has taken?

Openness is what you're looking for. Do not rule out a school because a case of abuse has been brought to light there. Tabloid coverage can be the price the school has to pay for handling a case of abuse or bullying honourably and openly.

For those with the courage to ask – and for our editors, who don't have to worry about getting onto the wrong side of the schools – these are the questions :

1. Where can I find the school's child protection policy? Every school is required to have a child protection policy that is made available to staff, volunteers and parents on request. But you may have to dig to find it. When we ask a school for its written policies (which we do when we review them for this Guide) it is rare for a school to volunteer one on child protection. All schools – independent or state – are supposed to publish their child protection policies on their websites. However some schools publish only a small part of the policy or carry it only on their internal site, so you have to be a school parent before you can see it – we wish inspectors would be more rigorous on picking them up for these defaults. We seem to be re-living the long years when schools thought that being open about bullying policies would frighten off parents – the opposite of the truth. Child protection policies should be trumpeted loudly.
2. Where can I and my children find out who the child protection officers are? Ideally, a school should have more than one and they should be named on a public notice board, so that everyone knows who to talk to.
3. There are some more intrusive questions which *The Good Schools Guide* can ask, and which we feel inspectors should cover in their reports so that parents do not have to:
   What training do staff receive in child protection? Training is mandatory every two years for designated officers, and every three years for all staff who work with children.
4. Is it the school's written policy to report child protection allegations to the Local Authority Designated Officer (LADO)? This can be a very uncomfortable issue for schools, who will be aware of the possibility of mistaken or malicious allegations, and will naturally wish to protect staff from these. Nonetheless, where an allegation is received by a school that a staff member or volunteer has behaved in a way that has harmed a child, or that indicates that he or she is unsuitable to work with children, a referral should be made to the LADO, so that an independent, expert view is obtained. A good head will have broken bread with their LADO, so that both can have confidence that incidents will be well managed.
5. How many 'Notifications' have been made to the Department of Education in the past three years? A Notification means a member of staff has left the school in circumstances which indicate they were unfit to work with children. Whether a notification is a good or bad thing depends on the circumstances – spotting a wrong-un early and hoofing him out, or keeping eyes closed until the stench becomes overpowering, both score 1 on this scale.

After you've chosen a school

You've been and looked at your shortlist and made a decision about where you want your child to go. What next? The path is different in the state and independent sectors but get armed with all the information as soon as you can, the process of entrance can be long and convoluted.

If, once your child is in a school, he or she tells you about being miserable/homesick/bullied – believe them. Act at once by telephoning the school and explaining the problem. If the problem persists, consider taking your child out of the school and finding another, more compatible one. Better a temporary disruption to your child's schooling than permanent damage.

Entrance – state sector

State schools in England

Start looking early – you may need to move house. Get the admissions booklets from your Local Authority, and any neighbouring Local Authority whose schools you might consider – they should give you a good idea of what you will have to do to get in. Apply for your chosen schools a good year before the likely date of entry if they are not part of a 'co-ordinated admissions policy' (see below).

Geographical location is one of the key factors in admission criteria. This can be defined many different ways – distance as the crow flies, distance by a safe route, catchment area, previous school attended etc – and liable to change each year as applications vary. Parents have been known to rent houses within the requisite area of the school in order to establish residence there, or 'borrow' an address, or invent one. Heads of schools particularly affected have resorted to peeking through letterboxes to see if there's someone really living there, or asking to see electricity bills – '£10 for the quarter and you say you were living there ...'

Getting into the nursery class at a primary school does not guarantee admission to the main school and, vice versa, you do not usually have a lesser chance of getting into the main school if you choose another nursery school. You may be able to secure a place in the main school by applying for a place in the reception class – but once you've accepted it you can defer entry, but no later than the term after your child's fifth birthday.

For all England, there is a system of co-ordinated admissions arrangements, and applications are all (or almost all) made through the local authority. You will be faced with arrangements that require you to state your preferences in order of priority. You put the schools that you like (up to three, usually, but six in some places) in order of preference; the Local Authority passes these choices on to the schools concerned but does not tell them if they are your 1, 2 or 3. Each school then assesses its applicants against its admissions criteria and tells the Local Authority who it will accept. The Local Authority looks to see what acceptances you have received, and passes on to you the acceptance that you gave the highest priority to – let's say that it is number 2 on your list – and that is where, barring appeals, you go.

Or is it? Because schools will have had some of their acceptances disregarded by the Local Authority (because parents have put another acceptance higher up their list) they will have some unfilled places, for which they will issue acceptances to children who just missed the cut on the first round. If your child gets offered a place by your number 1 choice in this way, then you can choose to go there and rescind your place at number 2. Up to a dozen rounds may be required to sort everyone out. Complicated for the Local Authority? Certainly. Uncertain for schools? Indeed so. But wonderful for parents and something to be grateful to this government for.

Take care, though, that you have a rock-solid case for getting into at least one of the schools you are aiming at or you're liable to land up in a dump if none of your long-shots hit.

If you get what appears to be a 'no' on any count you have the right of appeal, stating to an appeal committee why you think little Edna should go to Grunts and not St Dumps. One of the most successful reasons seems to be health: if you can get a doctor's letter stating that your ewe lamb gets asthma and will only flourish in the pure air of Grunts, you are half-way there. Like any other appeal you need to lobby like mad – the head, the governors, the doctor, the local authority, your MP, the lollipop man – whoever seems good to you. The admissions section of the Department for Education website www.education.gov.uk has hitherto been a good place to bone up on appeals procedures. However, with the change of government in May 2010, policy has been under review and up-to-date guidance from your local authority is the best reliable source of help. Don't get your hopes up too high – 70 per cent of appeals fail. Some small businesses and other organisations offer help with appeals, and claim that they double your chances – we don't endorse any, but you can find names on our website.

You must study the current version of the particular (and often peculiar) admissions criteria of each school that interests you – and do take a look at the catchment area maps on our website. Key factors are usually:

A 'banding' system to ensure that their intake is a fair reflection of the ability spectrum of their applicants or neighbourhood – this inevitably leads to different geographical limits for each ability band – you may need a local tutor to help your child do badly. Some schools set bands according to national averages, others according to applications made to the school (so loads of applications from on-the-ball parents will push up the percentage of their children in the school).

Sibling policies are a real pain if you're trying to get your first-born into a school – geographical boundaries can fluctuate wildly year by year, depending on the percentage of places taken up in this way. Thereafter, of course, they are a real blessing. It is noticeable in our catchment area maps how many families, having secured the first place, move out to nicer – and cheaper – houses.

Ballots are starting to appear in popular city schools. If there's an over-subscription, places will be allocated by random ballot. No known way of working this system to your advantage, and when lots of schools in an area ballot for entry it can lead to parents having no effective influence on where their child goes. Works best when it's only the occasional school in an area, or for out-of-catchment pupils only.

Religion. Some of the best UK schools have a religious foundation, and are more or less devoted to educating children of that religion. You need to start attending church weekly at least a year before conception to have a chance at some schools. Make sure that you have thoroughly studied the admission requirements of the schools that interest you. Do it now. As a result of pressure from all sides, the boundaries are moving on this. The Church of England's policy for its schools is now that they should offer 25 per cent of their places without religious requirements, and the more socially selective entrance policies such as attendance at Sunday school are being whittled away. The good Catholic schools will remain 100 per cent Catholic, however – and they are a vital component of the state school scene in such educational deserts as Central London.

Attainments. There are still almost 200 academically selective schools in England, and others that have special admissions arrangements for particular talents – they may specialise in languages, science or sports, or they may admit a few talented musicians. Understand how the criteria work, and consider some targeted coaching. Ask those whose children succeeded last year and who have no younger children – they have nothing to lose by letting you in on their secrets.

SEN or medical grounds. If this might apply to your child (even cleaner air for an asthmatic), get your case documented – it can be an overriding criterion. See below.

An expressed preference by parents for some special character of the school, e.g. single-sex education or boarding.

State schools in Scotland

The system in Scotland is pretty much catchment-area based, though with a right for a parent to ask for another school. As the government website says: 'If you have a child who is due to start primary school or who will be transferring to secondary school soon, you have a right to express a preference for a particular school. Your Council will probably suggest that you should use the local school designated by them, and of course you may be happy to do so, but the Council must also tell you of your right to choose a different school, and give you an address where you can get help in making up your mind.' Some councils are more helpful than others.

State schools in Wales

You have a right to attend your local school but can apply for another. Your choice will be respected if (as far as we can see) the school and the Local Authority feel so inclined.

Entrance – independent sector

As a rule of thumb this is what you do:

1. Register your child's name at the school(s) you have chosen. Telephone the school and it will send you an application/registration form. If your child is still in the cradle, and the schools you have your eye on are very over-subscribed, you may decide to register before visiting.
2. Filling in the form has to be done at the right moment or the 'list' may be 'full'. Embryos are acceptable at some schools; the lists for many successful schools will close several years before the date of entry — Radley closes shortly after birth. It will usually cost a registration fee (most are non-returnable) ranging from £25 to £200 or more.
3. The school will then contact you and your child's current school about the next stage (it doesn't hurt to telephone and check, though, if you think it may have forgotten you – and don't forget to tell the school if you change your address). They will usually get a report from the head of your child's current school and attention is paid to that.
4. Your child is usually, though not always, put through their paces, which might (at a young age) mean an exam, a test or two, 'meaningful play' or whatever. (NB You might also – openly or surreptitiously – be put through your paces as well: Are you a good parent? Is there discipline in the home? Are you educated? Are you a complainer or a worrier? Have you some wonderful attribute the school might be able to use? For entry to senior schools there may be a scholarship/entrance exam or, in the private sector, 'Common Entrance' – a standard exam, but marked by the school of first choice.
5. All being well, the school will then offer a firm place. You must write and confirm acceptance of this place or it may be offered to someone else. NB You will probably be asked for a large non-returnable deposit at this stage, which can be many hundreds of pounds – many, many hundreds of pounds in London (especially the lower ranked schools, which offer places earlier in a bid to catch the nervous parents of bright pupils) or in schools that offer places years in advance of entry dates (see below).
6. Pay school fees – in advance of the term is normal practice, alas.
7. Read any contract you have to sign carefully: if in any doubt – such as what do they mean by 'a term's notice'? – a little legal advice at this stage can save you a lot of agony later.

There are variations on this theme. For example, some may accept entries up to the last minute, though there will be an official date for closing the 'list', from about three weeks to three terms before the entrance exam.

One exceptionally tiresome and damaging/convenient and helpful (delete according to circumstances and prejudices) current trend is for senior schools to 'pre-test' – putting 10-year-olds through the mill to see if they're likely to pass at 13. Eton has an excuse for this, as it frees up parents to look carefully at other good schools while there's still room, but now all and sundry feel the need for an early test or interview to prove that they too have overflowing waiting lists. Opponents of this development — and that includes most of us at *The Good Schools Guide* — point out that many 10/11-year-old boys will by no means have come into academic flower yet, and face stress and rejection as a result. Advocates say that rejection frees the parents to look at other good schools while there is still time. If you're determined on a pre-testing senior school, choose a prep school that trains children for it. If you are considering senior schools that do not pre-test, you'll have the luxury of choosing a prep that spends its time educating rather than coaching your child.

The pre-test is now virtually uncoachable for, dependent as it largely is on a computerised reasoning test which, the schools who have paid mega-bucks for it claim, is a better determiner of final achievement than the trad English/maths exercises are. Get junior to build up speed on VR and nonVR tests and don't be conned by anyone who tells you they can tutor for the real thing. Not yet they can't.

TIP: All things being equal, always have a go at the school you think is right for your child. Even those schools you have been told are jam-packed may have a place. Don't restrict yourself to trying at the 'normal' entry periods. Dare to try mid-term, and mid-academic year, or even the day before term starts. If you get a no, don't be afraid to try again. NB Some schools simply refuse to consider non-standard entries. Play the rules as far as you can.

Interviews

'I'll always be grateful to Gordon Brown. Not because of his macro-management of the economy, but because his name was the correct answer to my son's 11-plus interview question: 'Who is the Chancellor of the Exchequer?' It was the possession of this crucial piece of information that, in my view, tipped the balance in my son's search for a secondary school place. A year later the right answer would have been Alistair Darling, and all would have been lost.'

The school interview is one which tends to send the applicant's parents rather than the actual applicant into a spin. Parents feel considerably more responsible for their child's social presentation than for his or her ability to do long division or conjugate French verbs. And, while a school may breezily describe the interview as 'just a chance to get to know the child better', this hardly overcomes concerns about sending young Daniel or Daniella into the lion's den.

The London prep or senior day-school interview is perhaps the most straightforward. Over-subscribed at every point, the selective urban independent tends to concentrate on the academic. The majority usually only meet the child after a written exam (generally used as a first edit), and the interview itself will contain a significant component of maths, comprehension or reasoning. The aim here is to probe intellectual strengths and weaknesses in order to select from the central bulk of candidates or to pick scholarship material. Finding out a little about a child's character is only of secondary importance.

Even the most academic schools, however, are not necessarily just looking for those guaranteed to deliver a stream of A*s. Jane Sullivan – for many years the headmistress of one of the country's top selective prep schools – used her 7-plus interview as an opportunity to create as balanced a community as possible:

'I didn't want all extroverts or all eggheads. Most children who sat our exam scored between 40 and 65 per cent in the written paper, so I was looking for an individual spark. At the age of 7, too, the interview is a crucial counter-balance to the exam. Those born between September and December always scored higher marks in the written paper. At interview we would go back to the list and bring in some younger children.'

Concerned parents often do their best to control the outcome of the interview, but professional preparation is seen as a waste of time, both by those who interview and by teachers who send children to be interviewed.

'I always tell parents if they're paying to coach 3-year-olds, they might as well burn £20 notes,' says Jo Newman, headmistress of North London Collegiate Junior School, who has the daunting task of selecting 40 4-year-olds from 200 applicants in a two-tier interview. 'The only useful preparation is to talk to them, play with them and read them stories.'

Further up the system, the advice is equally non-prescriptive. Jenny Aviss, head of Wetherby School in west London, does her best to relax the 7-year-olds she sends to prep school interviews by providing them with as much factual information as she can beforehand. 'I try to prepare them for what they'll find. I usually describe the head – because I'm a smallish woman they might expect all heads to be like me – and I'll tell them what the school looks like. Beyond that I just say, "Look them in the eye, answer carefully and be honest." Children sell themselves.'

Some pre-preps and prep schools provide mock interviews, some will carefully guide children on what books or hobbies that might show to best advantage, but most interviewers say they always know when a child has been coached, and honesty – at least in theory – is the quality they're looking for. 'I tell children,' says one private tutor who prepares children for 11-plus, 'to say what's in their heart, not what their teacher told them to say.'

Those moving from state to private will undoubtedly have to take any preparation into their own hands. Some particularly pro-active parents of our acquaintance have used job manuals and professional coaching techniques to ready their child. One parent videoed his daughter to give her positive feedback on her strengths and weaknesses; another asked a friend unknown to the child to conduct a mock interview.

Personality, of course, will always be the most variable aspect of any interview and all interviewers have a personal bias. They may hate boastful children, or those who say their favourite leisure activity is computer games; they may prefer Arsenal fans to Tottenham supporters, but some schools do make a strenuous attempt to counteract the sense of one adult sitting in judgement on one child. City of London School, for example, sees candidates individually before sending them off to a lesson where they can be observed by another teacher as they work in a group. At Rugby, every child is interviewed by at least two people.

The best interviewers can and do overcome the limitations both of the written examination and of the child. 'Children, even very shy ones, like to talk about themselves, their friends, their families and their pets. I'd get them to describe what they did on Sunday, or I'd turn my back and ask them to describe something in the room,' says Jane Sullivan. 'Sometimes I'd even get a child to sing or dance. I was looking for sparkly eyes and interest. If a child just sat there like a pudding, you usually didn't take them.'

Some schools get over the 'what to talk about' dilemma by asking children to bring along a favourite object. Rugby sensibly provides a questionnaire about hobbies and interests to fill in in advance, which not only provides a talking point, but also allows parents to feel they've done what they can. If, however, the child pitches up with a copy of Proust or boasts a collection of Roman ceramics, parents shouldn't be surprised if the interviewer is somewhat sceptical.

Children themselves tend to be annoyingly honest. The headmaster of one highly selective north London school dealing with 7-year-old entrants always used to ask what the Roman numerals on his clock stood for. One carefully prepared child answered correctly, and then added, 'My parents told me you were going to ask that.'

Although a number of leading boarding schools – Marlborough, for example – still rely solely on the prep-school report and Common Entrance papers, most now feel that the interview can identify serious pastoral concerns. 'We sometimes discover that a child really doesn't want to come to boarding school,' says Hilary Morrish, registrar of Rugby. 'The interview is also very helpful in establishing the academic level the prep-school is working at. We ask children to bring in their exercise books. Some London prep schools are so geared up at that point that all the child is doing is practice papers. Country prep schools tend to be more relaxed.'

Although most heads are honest in their report about a child – after all, their reputation depends on it – the interview can also benefit them. 'Occasionally, a prep-school head knows perfectly well that a child is not suited to our school, but the parents just won't listen,' said Hilary Morrish. 'Coming from us it doesn't sour the relationship with the school.'

Boarding schools, of course, tend to have another layer to their selection process and interview when they match boys and girls to an appropriate house. Here the parent, even more than the child, can be in the spotlight.

Dr Andrew Gailey, now Eton Vice-Provost but formerly housemaster of Manor House, Prince William's house at Eton, always tries to strike a balance of the sporty and industrious, the musical and the generally decent in his annual selection of ten boys but, for him, the parental part of the equation plays an even greater role. 'The boy is going to change, but you have shared management of the child's adolescence with the parents and you have to have some common bond for that to work.'

That's a common theme for those interviews where parents appear – notably in London pre-preps. Most of the time the school is really interviewing you, and it's you who need the preparation while your child can happily be itself. A balance between steady, respectful (schools are ever keen to avoid the parent from hell) and interesting (but nor do they like dull ones) is best.

However anxiety-making interviews are, be wary of a school that doesn't at least wish to meet your child. An interview can fire a prospective candidate's enthusiasm for a school, make teachers more committed to teaching the child and give parents a clearer notion of the school's pastoral style.

Paying the fees

There are any number of wizard wheezes on the market. The schools offer 'composition fees', which means, in a nutshell, you put a sum of money down one year and get a sum of money back later. The 'school fee specialists' offer endowment-backed, mortgage-backed schemes and so on which, in effect, do the same thing. Either way, you are stepping into deep waters. Unless you totally understand what you are doing and all the implications – how the money is being invested, what the returns are, how it compares with any other investment, what the charges are, hidden and otherwise – we think it might be safest to avoid such schemes.

This does not mean you should not save and invest. The earlier you start, the better – obviously enough. We have commissioned a survey of the options: see Finance for Fees on our website.

Scrutinise your bill carefully. We have noticed an increasing tendency to pop in items with a footnote (inertia selling) saying that 'unless you notify the school and deduct the amounts mentioned, it will automatically be charged to you'. For example, the Old Boys/Girls Society; the ISIS membership, your 'contribution' to charities. Do not be shy about deducting these sums from your cheque.

Insurance needs particular care. Often policies are taken out automatically unless you say otherwise – and we know of sickness policies on offer, for example, that only pay up once the child has been ill for at least eight days, but don't pay up for illnesses lasting longer than a term.

Getting in and out of financial difficulties

If you do get into financial difficulties, you will not be alone, and schools are very used to this. Their attitude to bill-paying and money varies hugely. The best schools are wonderful and increasingly flexible over payment, allowing arrangements such as monthly instalments. Bursars are expecting this request – no shame attached. Indeed the bursar has changed from the enemy to being the father confessor (with some notable exceptions – best description received: 'the bursar is a most evil toad').

A lot will depend on how well funded the school is: it is worth investigating this before you go any further. A few well-funded, rich schools will pick up the tab until further notice if you fall on hard times and your child is a good egg. Most of them will do their very best to see you through exam periods, but most poor schools simply cannot afford to do this for long, however much they may wish to.

Don't assume that because they are called 'charities' that they will be charitable to you. Some may send out the debt collectors. They will hold you to the small print – one term's payment or one term's notice to quit really means it. They may well threaten to take you to court – although of course it will be an extremely different matter if your child is especially bright (see 'What the league tables don't tell you').

In these cold times, it is a wise school that reciprocates the loyalty of its parents by allowing them to postpone payment, knowing that they will honour the debt when they can. Of course the school has to have the financial strength to afford this – and the parent has to have shown the loyalty.

Action

1. Speak to the head. Mothers (and sometimes fathers) may burst into tears at this point.
2. The head will immediately direct you to the bursar.
3. Explain your position – as optimistically, positively and realistically as possible.
4. Hope for flexible arrangements: monthly payments or deferred payment.
5. Have all the scholarships gone? Is there a spare bursary?
6. Assess the situation. How vital is it to keep your child in this school? Will the world fall apart if he/she leaves now?
7. If you really feel it is vital the child stays put, try touching a relation for a loan/gift. Grandparents are still the number one source of school fees. Investigate the possibility of an extra mortgage.
8. And if it is not vital, start looking for state alternatives. See 'The System' on page 21.

Obituaries and how to avoid being in them

Girls' schools, prep schools and even the occasional boys' or co-ed school have been closing, at the rate of half-a-dozen a year, for several years now. We expect there to be a higher rate of failure over the next couple of years as the recession bites (independent schools usually feel it a couple of years late). How to avoid being caught in a crash?

In a competitive market, girls' schools find themselves, for the most part, far more recent – and poorer – foundations. They do not have the resources to spend on flash facilities or to fund everyone's choice of subjects. Many girls' schools have suffered a confidence crash over this. In a school with the will to survive, the social and educational benefits of a girls' only sixth form in a school in which you are known should be confidently and unapologetically asserted – by the girls themselves and certainly by the head.

Prep schools face a host of challenges: senior schools looking to the state sector to satisfy the Charity Commission, senior schools transferring to the state sector, grammar schools prevented from expanding, an adverse political climate, reduced funding for diplomatic and military families, improving standards in international schools.

Boys' and co-ed senior schools have dug themselves a grave with a decade of spiralling fee increases. The consequent strain on parents' finances is clear to see.

If the death of a school is sad for us, it can be a disaster for parents. Schools never give much notice of closure – how can they? The moment their state of mind or finance is known, there is a rush for the door. Schools, like marriages, may look harmonious and healthy to the outside world but may be harbouring all kinds of corrosive and ultimately fatal problems under the smiling surface.

Not even we – with all our friends in high – and moles in low – places can be sure we know what goes on, even in 'our' schools.

There are though some runes you can read to give you an idea of what the chances are of your chosen school sinking under you. Look out for:

1. Falling rolls. For English senior schools, look at the performance table data on our website: you can track how each part of the school has been doing over the last five years. For schools in the Guide, we will note where we are aware of consistently falling numbers.
2. Poor finances. Schools that are comfortably off generally feel loved and nurtured when you go round – they are clearly spending money on keeping the place in tiptop order and there are no signs of penny-pinching. Look too for copious bursaries and other signs that the school has funds in hand. Likewise, a school unconfident of its future is unlikely to mount appeals for ambitious projects – a new sports hall or music school. Has your school lost the will to live? Not sacking troublemakers is a sign too, as is cutting corners in the curriculum, the head being away too much drumming up business; cheap labour – gap-year students can be wonderful, but they are inexperienced and they don't last. (It may be you and not the school who hit hard times: rich schools can afford to tide your children over for a year or two.)
3. Loss of self-belief. Many schools have a very particular clientele and image. The whole spirit of the school, and the way that the public and potential parents look at it, is coloured by that. When a school starts to have doubts, to look a little furtive like someone at a cocktail party who is not sure they want to talk to you, they lose their traditional market and often fail to gain a new one. It takes a strong school to proclaim a steady course.
4. In boarding schools, an absence or excess of overseas children. Having no children from overseas at all, particularly in a senior school, can be the sign of a very duff marketing department. More than 20 per cent can make the school an uncomfortable place for the native, unless the school has a segregated facility, as some do.
5. A weak head and an unhappy staff increasingly willing to let their feelings show to parents.

The above applies to all varieties of school. Girls' schools are by no means alone in being in an uncomfortable market position. Boarding is in long-term decline, state schools can provide sharp competition, whatever makes a particular school distinctive may no longer appeal to enough parents.

So who is for the long drop? There are no sure-fire ways to see it coming. The battle between schools is fought out over years and fortunes can ebb and flow. A sudden legacy, a new head, selling out to Cognita, a change in fashions or even the relocation of some large employer – all can pull a failing school back into contention. Senior schools in cities now have the additional option of turning themselves into City Academies, and joining the state system – a catharsis for parents, but at least the school's still operating. It's not over till the chartered accountant sings.

What can concerned parents do about it? If you are really partisan, a talented leader and have a lot of time (and money) on your hands, get involved – school governing bodies can be pretty moribund places, particularly if the bad news has been washing in for a few years. We have seen energetic new brooms make an enormous difference. If you have serious doubts about the stability of your child's school it's as well to prepare an escape route. Check out the alternatives and know who you want to phone should the bad news ever arrive.

Tutorial Colleges

Tutorial colleges – 'crammers' as they are unkindly known – offer intensive teaching in small groups to 'cram' knowledge into your child's head. They may be the answer if your mainstream school has let you down in the results or you think it is going to let you down and a little extra pre-exam tuition might make all the difference.

They may also be the answer if your child can't stand the pressure in her hot-shot school, or if he has been expelled and you are at your wits' end to know what to do next.

Crammers are (or were) mainly aimed at post-GCSE pupils coming in to do A level re-takes, or possibly to do a complete A level course, maybe with a couple of GCSE re-takes at the same time. Some of them have moved beyond this, and are more like schools or sixth form colleges – there for the child who needs that extra measure of independence and responsibility – with much less emphasis on rescue work.

The great plus of a crammer is that it is there, and it takes in the good, the bad and the ugly – though some have a policy of not taking in children expelled for drug-taking. The good ones are also very successful in bumping up exam grades. Minuses are the cost, which is unbelievable (almost as much as boarding school for day students, and considerably more if accommodation is needed too), the lack of 'extras' and the often dodgy pastoral care (crammers are simply not geared to provide a nanny service).

The all-important thing here is the work, and providing this is done, and the (relatively few) classes are attended on time, then pupils are usually left very much to their own devices. This can cause problems if the crammer is in a big city (and most of them are) away from your home. Tales of hanging out in pubs by day, staying out all night and/or not getting up until the afternoon are common.

The crammers, tutorial colleges or just schools with a crammerish aspect which we cover in this guide include: Abbey College, London; Ashbourne Independent Sixth Form College, London; Basil Paterson Tutorial College, Edinburgh; Collingham, London; d'Overbroeck's College, Oxford; Davies, Laing & Dick, London; Hampstead Fine Arts, London; Mander Portman Woodward, London; St Clare's, Oxford; Wallace College, Edinburgh.

Questions for crammers

1. How big is the maximum class size? For A levels, seven is fine, ten is moving into a different ball game.
2. Which subjects do they teach? If it is science, have they an in-house lab? Ask to see it. Ditto art, and the art room. You would be surprised how many practical subjects take place elsewhere.
3. How many taught periods are there a week for each subject?
4. Which exam boards does the place offer? (Don't get stuck with a board that only examines in summer if you want a re-take in winter.)
5. Where do students work in their (bags of) free time?
6. Can I have a copy of your latest value-added data for A levels? This really means something in crammers, as points scored are based on what students are expected to get as a result of their GCSEs, so if students are doing better than expected, then the crammer is doing something right.
7. What proportion of students starting an A level course actually take the exam with the crammer in question?

Useful contacts

The British Accreditation Council
44 Bedford Row, London WC1R 4LL
Tel: 020 7447 2584
Fax: 020 7447 2585
Web: www.the-bac.org
E-mail: info@the-bac.org.

CIFE (Conference for Independent Further Education)
75 Foxbourne Road, London SW17 8EN
Web: www.cife.org.uk
Tel: 020 8767 8666.
E-mail: enquiries@cife.org.uk

The crammers' professional association and your first point of call for information such as: what colleges are in your area, and which, for example, might be persuaded to take little Johnny if he's been sacked from school for drug-taking.

Oxbridge admissions

Judge a tree by its fruit, a man by the company he keeps, and a school by the universities it sends its pupils to? Well, you would miss out on the oak, the saint and many wonderful schools for ordinary children, but the level of Oxbridge acceptances is still a pretty good measure of at least some of a school's qualities. You can find full details of each school's Oxbridge successes (and indeed of the other universities that they send pupils to) on our website.

There used to be a joke about Oxbridge entrance. At some colleges, so they said, when you went for interview, they'd throw a rugby ball at you. If you caught it, you were in. Until recently, as well as training lawyers, clergymen and educators, the ancient universities were partially run as finishing schools for upper-class young men. This is categorically no longer the case.

Much as the two great universities may huff and puff that they always looked for the best, it has taken a great deal of effort by government to push them into using systems that made this likely. Tests have now, say Oxford, 'been designed to look for aptitude rather than acquired knowledge', and they are moving towards a common and understandable admissions system.

The challenge for independent schools has been to respond to the changed times by equipping their students with such confidence and brilliance that they can triumph over a presumption that they are over-educated and inclined to spend their Oxbridge years partying rather than studying. Many of them have done this very successfully, which is why the percentage of independent school pupils at Oxbridge is still barely below the 50 per cent mark.

The challenge for state schools has been to find the time to make their best pupils confident, articulate, sparky, questioning, inventive and learned in the ways of the world while faced with an A level curriculum and marking system that could have been designed to extinguish all these characteristics. A state school that does well in Oxbridge admissions is really something special.

Are these the right universities for you?

For many A Level students, and even more for many parents, Oxbridge is the pinnacle of their academic aspirations, the sine qua non of a university education and a recognised path to fame and fortune. But Oxbridge is certainly not for everyone – even some of the brightest – and it certainly won't guarantee riches, or even a job.

Our main criticisms of Oxbridge are that they are interested in the academic abilities and not in the future greatness of their students, so they draw their entrance criteria narrowly, and that the courses they offer are narrow and (in some subjects) decidedly old-fashioned. All these criticisms might also be cited as virtues – it all depends on the individual student.

There are, of course, many reasons to go to Oxford or Cambridge, not least of which is the beauty of the architecture, but the primary and central benefit of the education offered here is the tightly focused nature of the teaching. All students are taught by tutorial, either one-to-one or in very small groups. To undergo that intensity of education you need to be thoroughly interested in a specific subject and happy to produce a heavyweight volume of work. Many 18-year-olds are still relatively undecided about their intellectual interests (and ought perhaps to be looking to one of the great US universities) and many too would rather dedicate the period between school and work to a more even-handed balance between study and play (in which case they can join the thousands of like-minded students elsewhere in the Russell group of universities).

No matter how great your passion for a subject, however, there's no point applying to Oxbridge unless you are already extremely well qualified academically. It's not obligatory to have straight A*s at GCSE but, particularly since the ongoing tweaking of the entry requirements, the higher your AS grades the more likely you are to get in. You also have had to have chosen the appropriate A levels – Cambridge in particular is getting very sniffy about some A level subjects.

What you can do to prepare

The best academic schools in the country – the ones that send 10–50 successful candidates to Oxbridge each year – often provide specialist preparation both for the application and for the interview.

'We don't do specific training for Oxbridge entrance,' says Helen Turner, head of sixth form at league-table-topping North London Collegiate School, which last year sent 44 girls to Oxbridge. 'But what we do offer in Year 13 is preparation for a university course in a particular subject, whichever university the girl is applying for. We prepare them to be brilliant at their subject. Everyone, too, has a mock interview with someone from outside the school.'

For those without such well-developed sixth forms, the answer can sometimes lie in the specialist businesses set up to help candidates with everything from the choice of course to interview technique.

'I attended a one-day interview seminar,' says Oxford fresher Jo Campbell, whose Hertfordshire comprehensive provided little in the way of application advice. 'I found it very useful in dealing with the kind of question I was later asked.'

The universities, not surprisingly, are unenthusiastic about these businesses and generally tell parents they are wasting their money. But, while it is, of course, essential to choose a reputable supplier, there seems little doubt that some of these outfits are well staffed with knowledgeable experts who may well further your chances of an Oxbridge place. Look on the Web for such as Oxbridge admissions, Oxbridge applications and Oxbridge info.

Uni in the USA

The UK Guide to US Universities

www.UniintheUSA.com

Britain has some magnificent universities, but they are becoming desperately hard to get into. You may be giving Oxbridge or London your best shot, but however well you do you may find yourself among the two-thirds of candidates who have had to accept a lesser institution. Yes, sure, you'll have great fun there. If you find it easy to work hard on your own, and don't get tempted, you will end up with a worthwhile degree. But is a course that only offers you a few hours a week of lectures or tutorials really value for all that money that you are having to invest in it?

Why not look at the USA too? Not only does this give you an extra chance of getting to a top-ranking university, but once you start looking at what is on offer over the Atlantic you will realise how much damage years of financial deprivation have done to UK undergraduate courses. At any of the better US universities you should expect to get 18 hours a week of lectures and tutorials, to have work quickly marked and returned to you, and to find that you are frequently in conversation with the first-rate intellectuals who are teaching you. And if you want to keep your education broad, and are not ready to narrow your range of subjects or to declare yourself set on a firm career path, American liberal arts degree courses may have a particular attraction for you.

Uni in the USA was written by Alice Fishburn, an Englishwoman at Harvard, with the help of fellow exiles at the top two dozen US universities, and has been revised and expanded for its second edition by John Wallis, an Englishman who turned down the USA in favour of Cambridge – so it has a balanced view on all the crucial questions. It describes with great clarity and humour the experiences that you should expect if you venture west, and the qualities of the universities that you might consider. It answers all the questions that you might have about the American university system: who to see, what to ask and when to do it by.

Anthony Nemecek, former director of the educational advisory service of the US–UK Fulbright Commission, contributed to the general advice sections of the book, so you can rely on it for accurate advice about all the hurdles which you need to leap to make it to the USA.

Thousands of us make it to US universities every year and, as Stephen Baldock (formerly High Master of St Paul's) says in his introduction, he has known few, if any, pupils who have regretted it..

Attending an American university is expensive, but don't think that you have to be rich: the excellent financial aid and bursary programs at most American universities ensure that many British students can afford to go, regardless of their educational background or economic status. And with British universities becoming ever more expensive, the additional cost is becoming much less of a factor.

Useful names and addresses

The extensive links section on our website, www.goodschoolsguide.co.uk, is a useful supplement to these pages.

Government

The Department for Education

Sanctuary Buildings, Great Smith Street, London SW1T 3BT
Web: www.education.gov.uk
Tel: 0870 000 2288
Fax: 01928 794 248
E-mail: info@education.gsi.gov.uk

A very helpful site, but use the menus not the inadequate search engine. Has an information division which will give you the names of schools, pressure groups and leaflets, Tel: 0870 001 2345. There is also a publications division on Tel: 0845 6022260.

The Scottish Executive Education Department

St Andrew's House, Regent Road, Edinburgh EH1 3DG
Web: www.scotland.gov.uk
Tel: 08457 741 741
Fax: 01397 795 001
E-mail: ceu@scotland.gsi.gov.uk

Not an easy site to navigate, but if you persevere the information's there.

Department for Children, Education, Lifelong Learning and Skills

Welsh Assembly Government
Cathays Park, Cardiff CF10 3NQ
Web: www.wales.gov.uk

For general education queries: ims@wales.gsi.gov.uk

For statistics and data:school.stats@wales.gsi.gov.uk

Tel: 0300 0603300 or 0845 010 3300

DENI – the Northern Ireland Department of Education

Rathgael House, 43 Balloo Road, Bangor, County Down BT19 7PR
Web: www.deni.gov.uk
Tel: 02891 279 279
Fax: 02891 279 100

Information

The Advisory Centre for Education

Department A, Unit 1C Aberdeen Studios, 22 Highbury Grove, London N5 2DQ
Advice line (10–5pm, Monday to Friday): 0808 800 5793
Web: www.ace-ed.org.uk
Office tel: 020 7704 3370
Fax: 020 7354 9069

A charity founded in 1960. Publishes guides on such subjects as how to approach primary schooling, UK school law and how to deal with the bureaucrats on special educational needs, school choice and appeals, home education, bullying and so on.

Aegis: The Association for the Education and Guardianship of International Students

66 Humphreys Close, Randwick, Stroud GL5 4NY
Web: at www.aegisuk.net
Tel/Fax: 01453 755 160
E-mail: secretary@aegisuk.net

The industry association for guardianship companies; accredits them and offers a complaints service.

CIFE: the Conference for Independent Further Education

75 Foxbourne Road, London SW17 8EN
Web: www.cife.org.uk
Tel 020 8767 8666

The crammers' professional association and your first port of call for advice on which school might, for instance, be persuaded to take on little Johnny when he's been sacked from school for drug-taking. Also covers summer schools and revision courses.

The National Association for Gifted Children

Suite 1.2, Challenge House, Sherwood Drive, Bletchley MK3 6DP
Web: www.nagcbritain.org.uk
Tel: 0845 450 0295
Fax: 0870 770 3219
E-mail: amazingchildren@nagcbritain.org.uk

Independent Schools Council
St Vincent House, 30 Orange Street, London WC2H 7HH
Web: www.isc.co.uk
Tel: 020 7766 7070
Fax: 020 7766 7071

The 'official' site for schools belonging to the Independent Schools Council, about 1,300 of the 2,000-plus independent schools in the UK. ISC members would regard themselves as being the best 1,300. Contact ISCias for information on charities for parents who wish to send their children to fee-paying schools but cannot afford the fees.

For lists of all schools registered in your area (state and private) telephone the county or borough concerned (e.g. Westminster City Council, Suffolk Education Authority). Local authority contact details can be traced though our website, www.goodschoolsguide.co.uk

Lawyers with expertise in educational matters

Woodroffes
7 Beeston Place, London SW1W 0JJ
Tel: 020 7730 0001
Fax: 020 7730 7900
pmw@woodroffes.org.uk
www.woodroffes.org.uk

Peter Woodroffe specialises, among other things, in advising parents about legal matters to do with fee-paying schools.

The Education Law Association
33 College Road, Reading RG6 1QE
Tel/Fax: 0118 966 9866

Network of solicitors who are experts on educational law.

And for home study, Independent Schools Law Custom and Practice by Robert Boyd. Written by a former partner at Veale Wasbrough (a firm with much educational experience, but which acts mostly for schools rather than against them) in magnificently plain English. Intended as a guide for schools and their governors, but so clearly and readably set out that it should prove an invaluable aid to parents brewing up for a dispute with a school, or just wanting to know where they stand.

Books
Most guides to education are, however they are presented, advertising. Beware of books with advertorial entries written by the schools themselves. They will tell you nothing that the prospectus doesn't only they look as if they are 'independent'.

Much comfort may be had from Molesworth by Geoffrey Willans with illustrations by Ronald Searle. A timeless companion for little mites sent off to boarding school, and for their parents.

Glossary and abbreviations

A level General Certificate of Education, second public exam in the UK, taken at age 18

AS level Advanced Supplementary level public exam equivalent to half an A level, formerly taken as a supplement to A levels but now forming the first year of a standard A level course

A2 The examinations at the end of the second year of an A level course

ALIS A system of value-added measurement used by some schools to compare their GCSE and A level results

Amanuensis Someone who sits with a special needs student to help them put their thoughts on paper

ARCM Associate of the Royal College of Music

Assistant A young person from abroad, usually French or German, who helps teach the language (not to mention taking rugby etc)

AVCE Advanced Vocational Certificate of Education. A system of vocational qualifications, formerly GNVQ

BA Bachelor of Arts. University first degree

Bands Different academic levels for students. Some comprehensive schools divide their intake according to bands

BD Bachelor of Divinity

BEcon Bachelor of Economics

BEd Bachelor of Education. A teaching qualification

BHSAI British Horse Society Assistant Instructor – the lowest qualification needed to be a riding instructor

BLit Bachelor of Literature. University qualification

Brill Slang for brilliant

BSc Bachelor of Science

BTEC A vocational qualification – alternative to A level, quite a good one actually – awarded by the Business and Technology Education Council

Bursary Contribution to the school fees, usually given to those who are poor

C of E Church of England

C of S Church of Scotland

CAD Computer-aided design

CAE Computer-aided engineering

Cantab Cambridge (from the Latin)

CAT Cognitive ability test

CCF Combined Cadet Force. Para-military training corps for the young (boys and girls)

CDT Craft, design and technology

CE Common Entrance. Qualifying exam taken usually at 11, 12 or 13 in the private sector for entry to senior schools

CertEd Certificate in Education. A teaching qualification

Combined sciences GCSE exam covering biology, chemistry and physics, counts as one GCSE

Comprehensive school Takes all pupils, regardless of their ability or aptitude. Some are fully comprehensive (no entrance exam whatsoever) and others have some selective measures

Crammers Schools that cram knowledge into the reluctant child, especially those having to re-take A levels because of low grades; not a term the schools use of themselves – 'independent sixth form colleges', 'tutorial colleges' or 'independent further education' is more to their taste

CReSTeD Council for the Registration of Schools Teaching Dyslexic Pupils, a charity that assesses and certifies the quality of teaching for dyslexic pupils

CSYS Certificate of Sixth Year Studies (used occasionally in Scotland)

D of E Duke of Edinburgh Award Scheme. A combination of various different activities, including demanding physical exercise, culminating in a medal

DfE Department for Education

DipEd A teaching qualification

DPhil Doctor of Philosophy

DT Design Technology

Dual Award (Science) GCSE exam covering biology, chemistry and physics – counts as two GCSEs

EAL English as an Additional Language – the latest and PC acronym

EFL English as a Foreign Language

ESL English as a Second Language

Fab Slang for fabulous

Forces The Army, Navy or Air Force, and adjuncts thereto

Foundation school A state school owned by a foundation (generally religious) which appoints some – but not most – of the governing body

FP Former pupil (Scottish expression)

FRS Fellow of the Royal Society (very grand)

FRSA Fellow of the Royal Society of Arts (not grand)

Gap Work experience projects, expeditions etc in year between school and university. Also (when in capitals) name of organisation specialising in this

Gappies Foreign (usually Aus, NZ, SA) students in their gap year working in UK independent schools

GCSE General Certificate of Secondary Education. First public exam in the UK

GDST Girls' Day School Trust (formerly called the Girls' Public Day School Trust). A foundation of private schools

GNVQ General National Vocational Qualification. A system of vocational qualifications, now renamed AVCE

Grammar school A type of school which selects pupils on academic merit and provides a rigorous academic education (and sometimes not much else)

GSA Girls' Schools' Association. Female equivalent of HMC. See below

Highers/Higher Grades Scottish public exam, usually taken one or two years after Standard Grade (qv)

HMC Headmasters' Conference. A sort of headmasters' (and now one or two headmistresses) trade union, mostly for public schools, whose heads belong and are considered 'top' by those in it

HND Higher National Diploma, a well-respected vocational qualification usually taken after A levels or AVCEs

IAPS Independent Association of Preparatory Schools. Organisation of prep schools. Again, generally considered the 'top' ones by those in it

IB International Baccalaureate. A public exam at secondary level, increasingly recognised for entry to university in the UK

IBMYP International Baccalaureate Middle Years Programme

IBPYP International Baccalaureate Primary Years Programme

ICT Information communications technology

IGCSE International GCSE

Inclusion The concept that all children with special educational needs should be educated, if at all possible, in mainstream schools.

Independent Word used by fee-paying schools to describe themselves

Inter-denom Inter-denominational (refers to religious affiliation, supports more than one brand of Christianity)

IQ Intelligence Quotient

ISC Independent Schools Council – inspects independent schools (but not itself independent; owned and run by the schools)

IT Information technology

JMB Joint Matriculation Board

KS (Key Stage) The National Curriculum is divided into four Key Stages according to pupils' ages: KS1 for 5–7-year-olds, KS2 for 7–11, KS3 for 11–14, KS4 for 14–16, KS5 for 16-18

LesL Licencié ès Lettres. French university degree

Lab Laboratory

LAMDA London Academy of Music and the Dramatic Arts

LNat National admissions test for Law

LTA Lawn Tennis Association

MA Master of Arts. University degree

MCSP Member of the Chartered Society of Physiotherapy

MEd Master of Education. Teaching qualification

MIDYIS See ALIS, but this measures value-added up to GCSE

MoD Ministry of Defence

MSc Master of Science. University qualification

NFER National Foundation for Educational Research

NNEB Nursery nurses official qualification

Non-denom Non-denominational (refers to religious affiliation, generally means pretty low-key)

NQT Newly qualified teacher

NVR(Q) Non-verbal reasoning (quotient), a test of ability used by some selective schools

OB Old Boy (former pupil of a school)

OED Oxford English Dictionary

Ofsted Office for Standards in Education. Officially the Office of Her Majesty's Chief Inspector of Schools. Inspects schools and publishes reports on them

OG Old Girl (former pupil of a school)

OSB Order of St Benedict

OTT Over the top, as in unacceptable behaviour

Oxbridge Short for Oxford and/or Cambridge universities

Oxon Oxford

Pastoral care Care of pupil on matters not related to their work, e.g. personal and social ones

PE Physical education

PFI Private finance initiative: off-balance-sheet funding for the government, with private firms providing finance and facilities management

PGCE Postgraduate Certificate of Education. A teaching qualification

PhD Doctor of Philosophy (postgraduate degree)

PPP Public private partnership, see PFI

PSD Personal and Social Development

PS(H)E Personal, social (and health) education (courses)

PTA Parent–teacher association

qv quod vide – which see, i.e., it has its own entry in this book

RC Roman Catholic

RCSLT Royal College of Speech and Language Therapists

QCA Qualifications and Curriculum Authority, a government agency operating in England only

RE Religious education – learn about beliefs

RI Religious instruction – learn to believe

RS Religious studies – learn about beliefs

RSA Royal Society of Arts

RYA Royal Yachting Association

San Sanatorium, sick bay

SATs Tests sat by English state (and some private) school kids at 7, 11 and (until recently) 14

SATS Test sat by American kids to get into US universities

School Action/School Action Plus Extra help/arrangements provided by the school to help children who are not making the progress expected. School Action Plus involves help from outside, perhaps a therapist or educational psychologist

SEN Special educational needs

Services The Army, Navy or Air Force, and adjuncts thereto

Set A group of children of similar ability within a subject and year (children can be in the top set for one subject and the bottom for others, and may move between sets)

Six-inch rule Rule applied at some co-educational schools whereby boys and girls may not come closer to each other than six inches (in case they get over-excited)

SpLD Specific learning difficulties, a portmanteau phrase covering dyslexia, dyspraxia etc.

SSSI Site of special scientific interest – designated as such by the government and, as such, protected

Standard Grades The Scottish equivalent of GCSEs

Stooge A foreign gap-year student employed by a school

Streaming The practice of dividing a year group into streams of similar ability – if you are in the top stream you are in the top stream for all subjects

Suss Slang for find out, get to the bottom of, investigate, sniff out

TLC Tender loving care

Twoccer One who Takes a car Without the Owner's Consent

UK CAT UK clinical aptitude test used by some universities to test a candidate's aptitude to study medicine or dentistry

V very

Vs Versus

Vibes Slang for vibrations

VIP Very important person

VCE Vocational Certificate in Education

VR(Q) Verbal reasoning (quotient), a test of ability used by many selective schools

WASP White Anglo-Saxon Protestant

YE Young Enterprise. A hands-on business studies course

YELLIS See ALIS, but this measures value-added at primary level

YMCA Young Men's Christian Association

SENIOR SCHOOLS

Abbey College, London

22 Grosvenor Gardens, Belgravia, Belgravia, London, SW1W 0DH

• Pupils: 130; mixed • Ages: 14-19 • Non-denom • Fees: £16,900 pa
Two-year A-level • Independent

Tel: 020 7824 7300
Fax: 020 7824 7309
Email: adminlon@abbeylondon.co.uk
Website: www.abbeylondon.co.uk

Principal: Since 2005, Mr Mark Love BEd PGCLME (forties) who, on strength of his performance in HND business studies, was offered a two-year rather than a four-year course in education at Bristol Poly (now University of West of England). Has wide-ranging experience: worked in America, where he established a brewing company, returning to the UK to teach economics in 1990. Previously senior tutor at Barton Peveril College in Eastleigh Hants, then vice-principal of Surrey College. Appointed vice-principal of Abbey in 2004 before grabbing the reins in 2005.

Married with a young family. His wife, a former teacher (they met at college), now runs her own interior design business. Has a keen interest in politics and sport (now very much of the spectator variety). Smart, chatty, informal, he plans to move the college along, to grow organically but not to transform radically. 'We now offer politics, it suits the students we get, but we won't be diluting the curriculum.' With the new premises fully transformed and refurbished, admits he'd like to see a few more bums on seats, but is not interested in all-comers. 'It's not about what the students have already got – we take those with C grade GCSEs; it's about what motivates them, their maturity, drive and energy; students come here for one thing – success.'

Academic matters: Small classes usually capped at 10, but will run courses with upwards of two students. Key subjects are sciences, maths, economics, business studies and accounting. A few additional courses such as art offered in conjunction with nearby DLD College. Lots of contact time; expect to spend 5+ hours in lower sixth and six hours in upper sixth per subject (or 8+ hours per subject if following one-year option). Creditable results: half of all A levels are graded A (70 per cent A or B and 90 per cent A–C) with minimal variation between first time and retake students. Strong showing in biology, chemistry, physics and maths (including further maths). Weaker in economics, business studies and accounting, which in part reflects language barriers and fewer students rather than innate student ability or problems with teaching.

Has a great knack for transforming C grades at AS or A level to A grades via excellent, predominantly traditional teaching and outlook with some modern approaches and styles (IT and smartboards creeping in). Interactive studious lessons, students encouraged to question, problem solve and take charge of their own learning; great preparation for university. A reasonable amount of hand-holding and teaching to the test but not for the fainthearted or work-shy – this is intense stuff for those serious about study. Students we spoke to attributed their success to good teaching and always being able to get individual help whenever it's needed; one student added, 'I didn't know what good teaching was until I came here'.

Games, Options, the Arts: Students don't choose the college for its extra-curricular opportunities. However, those aged under 16 attend PE lessons at the nearby Queen Elizabeth the Queen Mother Sports Centre and the extra-curricular side is in development; occasional curriculum trip open to all – Houses of Parliament a recent offering – plus workshops, e.g. on medical ethics. Students encouraged to maintain outside interests. Planning to offer more during the next two years. Firmly believes, 'Excluding clutter enables the college to focus on ensuring teaching is the best it can be'.

Background and Atmosphere: Established in 1985 as a classic crammer, with students spending a term on retakes in science, by 2000 the college had shifted its focus to cater for overseas and British students requiring two-year courses. The college, now part of the Alpha Plus group, moved from its original base in Notting Hill to the current, leased mansion in 2005. An immaculate Victorian façade minutes' walk from the bustle of Victoria Station hides a thoughtfully transformed interior, complete with fully-equipped science labs and specialist teaching rooms. The crammer element remains, but today accounts for only 10 per cent of all students. Key growth area has been British students underperforming at AS and seeking a fresh start or change in focus. Variety of courses and combinations now offered include: one-term AS retake followed by two-term A level; five-term A level (starting January) and traditional two-year courses. Lots of flexibility, prepared to tailor courses to individual.

Pastoral Care and Discipline: Discipline not an issue; most students come here with one-track minds – success. Pastoral system assists with any issues or anxieties plus usual monitoring and mentoring. Will support and has supported students through tricky times. Lots of help given to those seeking accommodation, be it with a host family or in a local hostel; has good links with Urbanest student accommodation provider. No on-site catering but sandwich man visits at lunchtimes and students have own common-room. Plenty of help given with university applications.

Pupils and Parents: Wide ethnic mix, including British Asians keen to enter the professions. Traditional recruiting grounds of China, south-east Asia and Far East remain fruitful, with sprinkling of white European. Parents tend to be very driven, ambitious and middle class which, for the most part, permeates through to their offspring. Principal interviews all students to ensure college reflects their aspirations rather than simply the wishes of the parents, admitting more than a few micro-manage their children's education.

Entrance: Home candidates, mainly after relative, or complete, failure at AS, often at renowned independent schools. Overseas from a variety of academic backgrounds and stages of education.

Exit: Forty per cent to medicine, dentistry, pharmacy, economics, engineering and business/management at predominantly Russell Group universities. Overseas students focus on ensuring they are accepted at select universities for sought-after courses.

Money Matters: Limited financial assistance via bursaries based on academic potential and need.

Remarks: Does what it says on the tin: few frills or finery. Combination of very good teaching and student endeavour has seen many a sow's ear turned into veritable silk purse; now increasingly a first time choice for the scientific academic. Ideal for the motivated, goal-driven student; ditherers and artful dodgers should look elsewhere.

The Abbey School Reading

Linked to Abbey Junior School (The) in the Junior section

Kendrick Road, Reading, Berkshire, RG1 5DZ

• Pupils: 705 girls, all day • Ages: 11-18 • Size of sixth form: 180 • C of E • Fees: £7,470-£12,060 pa • Independent

Tel: 0118 987 2256
Fax: 0118 987 1478
Email: schooloffice@theabbey.co.uk
Website: www.theabbey.co.uk

Headmistress: Since 2002, Mrs Barbara Stanley BA PGCE FRGS. Educated at Glenlola Collegiate School, County Down, and universities of Belfast and Leicester. A geographer. Headed Bedford High and Alexandra College, Dublin before the Abbey. Direct – 'calls a spade a spade'. Humane, approachable, listens. Knows all the girls by name and levels with them – they like that. 'An educationalist, a thinker – just right for the Abbey in these fast-moving times.' A quietly impressive person who blends strong purpose with open-minded curiosity. Her mission is to urge these exam-clever girls to try their hands at everything. Strong commitment to social responsibility – she is a member back home of the interfaith Corrymeela Community (www.corrymeela.org), which reconciles riven communities post-Troubles.

Academic matters: To have a daughter at the Abbey is to elicit the response 'Oh – ah!' followed by a reverential nod. A premiership school with more about it of Chelsea than West Brom. At A level this year 70 per cent A*/A and 89 per cent A/B, with 54 per cent of girls gaining straight A*/As. Sciences very strong – a benefit of single sex – so we find biology, maths and chemistry as most popular A level options. International Baccalaureate now offered as option in sixth form and in first year of results one candidate got maximum 45 points (top 0.2 per cent in the world!). Students go on to impressive list of universities, and UCAS counselling a real strength. At GCSE it's 99 per cent A*–C, 77 per cent A*–A. Girls know the moment they get their results if they can step up to the sixth form.

An exam factory 'No!' they emphatically say, though a visitor's first impressions are of statistics glistening on noticeboards; everywhere you go you're up against last year's results. Parents – some crossly – assert that more, much more, going on than meets the untutored eye. 'Marvellous teachers', 'They respond to parental queries within 24 hours' – and get pretty good reviews from the girls, too. 'They want to know about problems,' said one mum, 'We wish we'd spoken out earlier'. Teachers' work ethic, the need to pack every day, imposes a focus which, for us as visitors, came over too frequently as blinkered, though warm, well-mannered exceptions. Girls invariably jolly nice. Traditional flavour – not much evidence of rebels or boundary pushers; this is the sort of place where attitude would probably come over as, like, so irrelevant. Tutors urge girls to wander outside the curriculum and follow their own intellectual curiosity – good results are not enough. Progress minutely, scientifically monitored – non-thrivers, 'coasters and sliders' chivvied and egged on by mentors, abetted by parents.

Parents praise the way the school bends over backwards to accommodate unconventional A level choices – 'the timetabler is a genius'. They laud savvy university application advice and the way they back you to the hilt however you opt. They also praise teachers' expert understanding of their daughters, the way they set apt expectations. Marvellous drama and art, inspirationally-led music, terrific sport, all examinable. Sumptuous LRC. Attractively grown-up routines for sixth formers. Own clothes, own classrooms, damn fine commonroom and now choice of IB constitute a counter-lure to local excellent sixth form colleges.

SEN provision not high profile given the requirement to pass the entry exam and cope with the subsequently sprightly pace of life here – notwithstanding an SpLD. Around 50 girls come to the attention of the SENCo, who also runs the gifted and talented programme. Most are mildly dyslexic, some dyspraxic. ADHD is not unknown. Around half of these get just 30 minutes a week one-to-one.

Games, Options, the Arts: Ethos is to coax the reluctant kindly and make it fun – parents agree – and they inspire the very best and catapult them as high as they can go. Hockey, netball and cricket are tops, but it's all top notch – regular county and UK representation. Fine swimming pool and gym and dance. Music very strong – 45+ per cent learn an instrument. Ensembles of all kinds from swing to Stravinsky – thrash metal in your own time, please. Drama is adventurous, art well-resourced in new studios and well done. Considering they're all off the campus by 4pm it's amazing what productivity they get. Good breadth of extracurricular activities – plus D of E (highest participation in Berkshire), Young Enterprise, European Youth Parliament (national winners 2010) – the usual suspects. Many overseas trips and expeditions in the holidays.

Background and Atmosphere: School began in 1887 as Reading High School, then, in 1914, after divorcing the Church Schools Company, took its present name in commemoration of a school which had ceased years before, having had, for two years, Jane Austen on its books. School has now confirmed this link with the new Jane Austen wing, which has transformed the front of the building and added excellent art and ICT facilities. Buildings mixture of Victorian red brick and modern add-ons – new humanities wing and science block being notable ones. Spacious playing fields and netball courts and no sense of the crampedness you get at so many of these off-street city schools.

Pastoral Care and Discipline: Careful attention to best emotional health – a particular preoccupation of the head. Teachers are appraised 60 per cent on their teaching skills, 40 per cent on their pastoral value. Compared with schools with similar pressures to succeed, it's amazing what a sunny lot they are. Sixth formers are buddies to younger girls and talk them through stuff as it happens. No matter how hard we peered, no evidence of anorexia or drugs – parents concurred, praised the PSHE (now Skills for Life) and general caring vigilance. A striking feature, this. Community values and spiritual awareness instilled by hymn and prayers each morning. They look beyond, too: every year group must raise money for charity using their own initiative. Discipline is strict but reasonable. When a girl gets baleful they normally bring her round. Expulsion rare.

Pupils and Parents: Parents are professionals who want a powerhouse. Not all by any means awash with money. New head of sixth form and offer of IB or A level has helped retention rates into sixth form and attracted new joiners from outside. No way snobby – too meritocratic. Not a school for a daffy lass – these are sorted girls, all going for it. Pleasant social atmosphere, sense of pace, but we were charmed to see a little catching game happening in a corridor. They come also from Maidenhead (half an hour) and Windsor (three-quarters). Fleets of buses and close to train station. Busy-bee PTA with pages on school website.

Entrance: Own entry exam in maths, English and reasoning. Interview picks up on any other desirable attributes. Around 50 per cent come up from the juniors, joined by girls from more than 60 other schools including sizeable wodges from Highfield, Caversham Primary, Dolphin and Eton End. New sixth formers need minimum seven GCSEs at A*–C plus glowing reference.

Exit: Sixth formers praise help they are given in university applications. Around 10–20 per cent to Oxbridge. They like London, Birmingham and Bristol especially. Proper subjects at proper places – as you'd expect. Good range, preponderantly scientific. Heard of high-fliers include the late Baroness Brigstocke, Sally Taylor (BBC South Today), Miranda Krestofnikov (BBC Coast), Kate Humble (BBC Springwatch) and Helen Ganly, artist and social reformer. As well as Miss Austen they cherish Elizabeth Taylor, 'one of the great neglected voices of English fiction'. We know how she felt.

Money Matters: Fees decidedly competitive and increased means-tested bursary provision – up to 100 per cent possible. Scholarships to recognise academic achievement available at point of entry to school (primarily Years 7, 9 and sixth form) – 10 per cent. Music awards win free instrumental tuition. Sport, ICT, art and drama awards recognise special talents.

Remarks: It's an anxious business being and staying this good. League table place matters because parents obsess about it (they deny it, of course, and blame politicians). Rivalry with free sixth form colleges post-GCSE has stimulated both a more young adult-friendly sixth form regime and greater efforts in all areas. This is a school which does the biz examwise, no doubt, but also tries with sincerity and enlightenment of purpose, especially under this humane head, to turn out girls who are in touch with everything they can do well and who will go on to be good citizens.

Abbots Bromley School for Girls

Linked to Roch House Preparatory School in the Junior section

Abbots Bromley, Nr Rugeley, Staffordshire, WS15 3BW

• Pupils: 280 girls in senior and junior schools; 80 boarders, also occasional overnight and flexi-boarders • Ages: 3-18 • Size of sixth form: 45 • Anglican • Fees: Boarding £13,560-£22,875; Day £10,590-£13,905 pa • Independent

Tel: 01283 840 232
Fax: 01283 840 988
Email: enquiries@abbotsbromley.net
Website: www.abbotsbromley.staffs.sch.uk

Headmistress: Acting head: Mr Mark Fisher. New head from January 2011, Mrs Julie Dowling, currently director of boarding/resident deputy head Badminton School. MA modern and mediaeval languages, Cambridge, PGCE Bristol.

Academic matters: School describes itself as 'proudly non-selective', so results are commendable, with a spread across the grades but regularly 70 per cent of A*–Bs at GCSE and 70 per cent of A levels A*, A or B, 85 per cent A*–C. The on-site Alkins School of Ballet and the equestrian centre allow girls to pursue vocational courses such as Royal Academy of Dance professional exams and British Horse Society qualifications without sacrificing their academic studies. Each girl's timetable is tailor-made with 'a flexible approach to subjects and number of GCSEs taken to maximise each pupil's potential for success'. A separate sciences option is possible, for example and, whilst encouraged, a foreign language is not absolutely compulsory.

Maximum class size is 20 with maths and English taught in three divisions for ability and flexible movement up and down based on performance. Parents say girls who rub along in the lowest divisions are valued as highly and encouraged as much as the higher flying stars and praise individual teachers. Dyslexia Institute trained SENCo, 'We've some very bright dyslexics here', and all staff have strategies for giving extra help or pushing the boundaries with extension work. Specialist EFL tuition, appropriate for over 10 per cent of girls. Sixth formers help younger girls with maths, gap students help with language and boarding. Charming library with work stations and reading area in gracious bay window and .

Games, Options, the Arts: Here AB really comes into its own, living up to its strap line: 'Much more than a school ... a great deal for girls'. Indeed the school day runs from 8.25am–5.25pm to fit everything in, with vocational dance going on to 6.30pm five days a week. Previous head restructured day to allow longer lunch-break for breathing space. School maintains that boarding is the answer to maximise pupil time and that parental guilt is the greatest hurdle; certainly the 90 or so boarders seem to thrive on it.

At the heart of the senior campus is The Alkins School of Ballet, run by director Russell Alkins, a former examiner with the Royal Academy of Dance and insider in the dance world. The seven-strong staff include his wife, a former international ballerina. Girls audition for vocational course or take dance as part of 'enrichment' (extra-curricular) programme. The three large dance studios are window- and mirror-lined, only pupil grumble is the cold changing-room floor. The stables are found a short, tree-lined walk away, past the jumps – 'I love the pink one,' enthuses one little rider. Ten school ponies and nine belonging to girls, plus the odd Jack Russell greeting visitors, are looked after by a staff of five, three residential. Indoor and outdoor manèges. D of E room in equestrian centre.

For its size, the school holds its own or battles on in competitive sport against much larger local schools, and boasts county-level hockey players and cross-country runners. Fabulous large indoor pool with coach who also teaches life-guarding. All-weather hockey pitch with far-reaching rural views, sports halls and fitness suite. Sports day is a whole school affair. A theatre and the school hall host drama performances and the school orchestras, ensembles, jazz band and choirs. Most girls learn at least one instrument. One wing of school is dedicated to music with computer suite, keyboard studio and 22 practice rooms. Choir sings in chapel, at Lichfield cathedral and on tours; Italy, including the Vatican, in 2006, New York in 2007, Paris 2008, Barcelona 2009, San Francisco 2010. The Cantoria Choir sings for Radio 4's Daily Service twice yearly. AB has both a professional dramatist and artist in residence. David Gleeson's paintings hang in head's study when not on exhibition. Lots of creatively untidy art rooms; every year someone goes on to art foundation course.

Background and Atmosphere: Visiting picturesque, unspoilt Abbots Bromley village is like stepping back in time, and certain aspects of the school are charmingly the same, thanks largely to the strong Anglican influence from its founding Woodard Foundation. Girls meet in mixed-age house groups in the marble floored Talbot Hall to say grace before eating in the dining room, and Friday morning's chapel is known as Eucharist. 'I love it because we get to sing a lot,' say some, others complain the incense 'pongs'. All have to attend but those of other religious groups are expected to develop their own faith too. The prayer noticeboard is peppered with requests, late night vigils aren't unknown and there was standing-room only in the chapel on 9/11. The school is certainly true to its founding principle of 'addressing the needs of the whole child, intellectual, physical and spiritual'.

Formerly there were two schools, St Mary and St Anne, on either side of the village high street; the two were joined in 1921, and more recently the name officially changed to Abbots Bromley School for Girls, affectionately AB. The two sites are linked by a zebra crossing, with the prep department in Roch House, swimming pool, sports halls, Astroturf and medical centre on the St Mary's side. The bulk of the senior activity – teaching, boarding, dance and equestrian centres, chapel, chaplain and head's houses, archives and museum – on the St Anne's side. Commemoration day sees the whole school parading, in costume, through the length of the village. 'Tradition is mindfully guarded here,' says school, 'but we're firmly in the 21st century.' Nevertheless the 1960s academic block does have a yester-year feel though, in 2007, the science labs were refurbished. Other recent refurbishment focused on the boarding quarters which are clean, pretty and homely. IT has been updated with two new 20-station laboratories, and every classroom now has computer access. Overall the facilities are lavish in their provision per girl with acres of available space inside and out. Navy and white uniforms with suits in sixth form and trousers an accepted sixth form privilege. Hair must be tied back, straw boards still used for formal occasions.

Pastoral Care and Discipline: Big on congratulating achievement and praising all merit. AB uses 'restorative justice'. 'The chapel, forgiveness and being able to reconcile are at the heart of what we do,' says school. 'You don't need an iron rod here; we have high expectations and the "I'm very disappointed" line is most effective,' though pupils are wary of head's telling off. Six houses enable all-age interaction socially, for dining, sport and performing arts. Girls can turn to their housemistress/housemaster or form tutor, sixth form mentor, older buddy or the on-site chaplain who leads many of them through confirmation. Some return subsequently to marry in the chapel or have babies christened here.

Some 90 girls board, the younger ones in rooms of three or four, the sixth formers in recently refurbished single rooms on their own floor or on the top floor of St Mary's, which has been competely and extensively refurbished to accommodate the growing number of full boarders; some come down to read bed-time stories. Plenty of common-rooms with pool, football table, sofas, tvs, puzzles, and kitchenettes where girls pile in for toast and squeezy Marmite or chocolate cake. Rooms can be, and are, personalised. Each day girl has three free boarding nights a year, and flexi-boarding is becoming more popular with occasional or regular nights after busy days, to suit home circumstances or just for fun, such as Friday cinema night with an action-packed Saturday to come – 'busy girls don't get homesick'. Performances are videoed for absent parents and the school has some parental accommodation for those visiting from afar. School uses a team of known CRB checked taxi drivers for airport and rail transfers.

Pupils and Parents: School describes typical AB girl as 'herself', and certainly they are gathered from a wide variety of backgrounds. Some from the village and local towns, for some the fees are sacrificial, for others merely incidental. Several overseas boarders from Europe, China, Japan, Hong Kong, the Caribbean, Syria. A few on short stay for a term to boost their English. Most recent (and very positive) ISC inspection said, 'The pupils are articulate; they speak very well and clearly, without any slovenly intonation.' Neither, however, are they remotely hoity toity with undue airs and graces; they're much too busy for that. Rather they are poised (dance and riding?) and friendly. School sends termly glossy colour newsletter home, sometimes with sports news sheet too, cataloguing and celebrating school and individual achievements and happenings. Famous old girls include Sue Nicholls, long-standing character in Coronation Street.

Entrance: No academic selection, although senior applicants may have to take assessments in maths and English, 'just to make sure we're able to meet their educational needs'. Almost all applicants offered a place after interview and reports from current school, 'We're looking for girls who'll unlock their potential', although some years are full, notably sixth form boarding. Plans to increase numbers mainly at the nursery end, but school says they won't go much beyond 350, 'this is a small school'.

Exit: Most to first choice of university or further training. Courses from chemistry to fine art, architecture to sociology, management to equine science all over the country including Durham, Cambridge, Cardiff, Aberdeen, Bath, Oxford, Leeds.

Money Matters: Fees do not cover extras such as £42 a term for swim coaching, but over 33 per cent benefit from scholarships, exhibitions or means-tested bursaries – typically 10 or 20 per cent of tuition and boarding fees for academic promise, dance, drama, music, riding or sport. Ten per cent allowance for first sibling, rising by five per cent for each successive sibling, and reduction for Services, clergy and former pupils' families. Vocational ballet is £800 a term. Stabling seems good value at £85–£95 a week depending on size of pony.

Remarks: Girlie heaven set in idyllic setting for those whose parents can afford it, with fabulous opportunities for excellence in dance, riding, music and performing arts. Turning out poised, grounded and articulate young women and giving a special chance to prospective professional dancers and riders who also want to achieve academically.

Abingdon School

Linked to Abingdon Preparatory School in the Junior section

Park Road, Abingdon, Oxfordshire, OX14 1DE

• Pupils: 860 boys (750 day, 110 boarders) • Ages: 11-18 • Size of sixth form: 290 • C of E • Fees: Boarding: £24,585-£28,515; Day £13,905 pa • Independent

Tel: 01235 849041
Fax: 01235 849 085
Email: admissions@abingdon.org.uk
Website: www.abingdon.org.uk

Head: Since September 2010, Miss Felicity Lusk. A New Zealander, Miss Lusk graduated in music from Victoria University in Wellington, NZ. Her teaching career began in New Zealand where she was director of music at Wellington East Girls' College and then at the co-educational Aotea College.

On moving to England in 1990, Miss Lusk joined the Hasmonean High School in London, initially as director of music, teaching both boys and girls, and latterly as deputy head and also head of the girls' school. She was appointed head of Oxford High School in 1997. During her 12 years at Oxford High, the school earned a reputation not only as one of the leading academic schools in the country but also as a vibrant community, encouraging individuality and self-confidence.

Miss Lusk has also held a number of external appointments, and recently became an independent member of the Standards Committee of the City of London Corporation. She is a past governor of the Guildhall School of Music and Drama and until this year was a member of the Court of Oxford Brookes University.

Academic matters: Very impressive. In 2010, 79 per cent of GCSEs were grades A*/A, with sciences and languages particularly strong. Meanwhile over 91 per cent of A levels were A*/A/B grades. Nineteen boys got three or more A* grades. Maths and science very popular and hugely successful. School doesn't offer what the head calls 'ologies' at A level – sticks to traditional subjects that are more likely to go down well with the top universities. Pupils say teaching is 'very interactive and quite laid-back,' especially in the sixth form. Boys take an average of ten GCSEs (sometimes two or three a year early). Classroom teaching supplemented by specialist speakers, theatre trips, lectures and foreign language exchange visits. Good learning support department helps pupils with mild dyslexia/dyspraxia. Two ICT centres and 400 computers across school. Saturday morning school (not for Year 7 and 8 boys though) and exeats either side of half-term. Three forms per year group for Years 7 and 8, and seven per year group after that.

Games, Options, the Arts: School prides itself on what it calls 'The Other Half' – i.e. the other half of the curriculum. Activities include music, drama, sport, community service, CCF, Young Enterprise, D of E and World Challenge, as well as pursuits like cookery, debating, chess and website design. School philosophy is that all boys should pursue Other Half activities that are 'balanced, physically and mentally absorbing and demanding'. Head defies anyone to 'research what is on offer and find nothing that stimulates their interest or enthusiasm'.

Sportswise, rugby, hockey and cricket are all strong. Abingdon boys (clad in distinctive pink, black and white) compete against some of the top schools in the country – Eton, St Paul's, Millfield etc. Rowing, based at elegant Thameside boathouse opened by Sir Matthew Pinsent in 2003, massively successful. In 2002 Abingdon oarsmen won grand triple – Schools' Head, National Schools' Regatta and Princess Elizabeth Cup at Henley – while in 2008 13 rowers chosen to represent GB teams at regattas. In 2007 two intrepid boys rowed across the English Channel in four hours to raise money for charity. Lots of silverware on display in reception. School hugely proud of its new, state-of-the-art sports centre. It cost £9 million and was officially opened by former sports minister Kate Hoey in 2008. It had only been open for four days when we visited and awestruck boys kept describing it as 'jaw-dropping'. Overlooks 1st XV's rugby pitch and features sports hall, fitness suite, two glass-backed squash courts, climbing wall, rowing ergometer suite, classrooms, physio area and 25-metre, eight-lane pool. Four large playing fields on school site, with 30 acres three-and-a-half miles away at Abingdon Prep too. Games for all but most do far more than the two compulsory periods of sport a week. Boys encouraged to have a go at vast range of competitive and individual sports, including golf, badminton, fencing, athletics, fives, kayaking and wargaming.

Music is excellent – everything from classical to jazz. School won a prized Good Schools Guide award in 2007 for the best results achieved by boys taking AS music at an independent school. Loads of orchestras, bands and choirs to join. Lots of concerts in school's Amey Theatre and further afield in Oxford, Westminster Abbey, even Beijing and Hong Kong. All boys do art and DT up until age of 14. Both popular at GCSE, with 40 taking DT and 45 doing art (either mixed media or graphics). Around 12 a year take A level art and eight or nine do A level DT. Boys clearly keen on product design – everything from heated ice cream scoops to an interactive trophy stand on show in refurbished DT block.

Drama and theatre studies taught throughout school. Enthusiastically supported, with a number of joint productions with girls and staff from nearby School of St Helen and St Katharine. Abingdon even has film unit – documentary made on 2006 trip to Cambodia recently shown at London's prestigious Raindance Film Festival. Boys also play key role in local community – visiting local primary schools, hospitals and old people's homes. One group currently helping to edit an Alzheimer's Society magazine while others are gardening at a local church.

Background and Atmosphere: One of the oldest schools in the country. Moved to its present leafy site in the centre of Abingdon in 1870 but school dates back to the 13th century, if not earlier. Founded by Benedictine monks, it survived the dissolution of the monasteries in 1538 and was re-endowed in 1563 by an old boy, John Roysse, who was also a Mercer. School has retained close links with the Mercers' Company of London ever since. Thirty-five acre site boasts new and old buildings but all merge pleasantly around extensive playing fields and well-maintained grounds and gardens. Beautiful chapel (each year group attends inter-denominational service once a week and RS taught up to the upper sixth). Sixth-form boys based in ultra-smart study centre. Upper sixth get their own individual carrels (wooden desks with high sides) – perfect for concentrating on their studies.

Atmosphere throughout school is focused and busy. 'Most of the boys are the sort who want to engage and it's amazing how much can be fitted into a short space of time,' said last head. Three boarding houses, all run by housemasters with young families. Some full boarders, others weekly. Scope for boys to switch to boarding from 13 if they wish. Boarders' rooms cosy, light and very wholesome. Good range of activities for boarders at weekends – from high ropes to cinema trips. School makes point of listening to boys' views. Spent £1 million on new catering system three years ago in response to pupils' suggestions. School has also made a real effort to go green too. Led by its Waste Force team, it has reduced the waste it sends to landfill sites by nearly 50 per cent.

Pastoral Care and Discipline: House system, with boys belonging to one of nine houses. Two heads of school, along with raft of prefects. Pupils meet their tutors for 90 minutes each week – to discuss academic progress, activities, career choices etc (they change tutors at 13 and on joining the sixth form). Rules on drugs, alcohol, smoking and bullying all clearly laid-out in school's lists book, published annually and given to all pupils. Any boy supplying drugs 'must expect to be expelled immediately', while anyone possessing or using drugs 'must also expect to be expelled.' Smart uniform of navy blazers, school, house or club ties and grey trousers for 11 to 16 year olds. Dark suits for sixth form.

When it comes to the age-old single-sex education versus co-education debate, Abingdon appears to offer the best of both worlds. Boys get to concentrate on their work without the distraction of girls yet school has developed strong links with St Helen's and St Katharine's, both within the formal curriculum (some subjects are taught in conjunction with St Helen's) and in music and drama.

Pupils and Parents: Boys come from wide range of backgrounds. Most day boys live within 20-mile radius of Abingdon, with school buses bringing them in from as far afield as Woodstock to the north and Newbury to the south. Around 45 per cent of the school's 112 boarders from overseas – Hong Kong, China, Germany, Russia, Korea etc. Parents very supportive of and involved in school. One mother told us she liked the way Abingdon offers a traditional, academic, public school education while enabling her son to be a day boy and come home every night. Eclectic list of old boys includes MP Francis Maude, actor Tom Hollander, comedian David Mitchell and all five members of Radiohead.

Entrance: Around 70 boys a year join at age of 11. They arrive from local primaries and schools like Chandlings via the Abingdon School exam, current head's report and interview. At 13 another 80 boys enter the school via pretest (English, maths and reasoning), CE and/or the school's own scholarship exam. At this age most come from prep schools like Abingdon Prep, Moulsford, New College, the Dragon, St Hugh's and Oratory Prep. Increasing competition for places – currently two applicants for every place. Around 15 to 20 new boys join sixth form each year. Three As, two Bs and two Cs at GCSE required (with Bs as minimum in boys' proposed A level subjects) for everyone going into sixth form.

Exit: Virtually all to higher education, with around 20 per cent heading to Oxbridge. Good spread of degree subjects but more opt for science and engineering than anything else. Popular university destinations currently include Imperial, LSE, Bristol, Durham, Nottingham and Warwick. A few boys leave after GCSEs, mainly heading to co-ed schools like the Cherwell and D'Overbroeck's in nearby Oxford.

Money Matters: Good number of scholarships on offer. All means-tested. Up to six awards per year for boys joining at age of 11 – 'to reward outstanding performance in the entrance tests and interviews,' says school. At 13, academic, art and design, music and sports awards offered – plus, in some years, drama too. Handful of sixth form academic scholarships available. Prospective sixth form scholars take exams in at least two of the subjects they want to study at A level, plus a general paper and a reasoning paper. A number of bursaries (up to 100 per cent of fees) offered.

Remarks: A very impressive, high-achieving school which, as it says, combines the lifestyle of a modern boarding school with the energy and buzz of the very best day schools. Purposeful, friendly atmosphere encourages healthy mix of academic success and extracurricular activities. With its increasingly sparkly achievements, Abingdon goes from strength to strength. With Miss Lusk at the helm, watch out for some pretty exciting times.

Acland Burghley School

Linked to La Swap Sixth Form in the Senior section

Burghley Road, London, NW5 1UJ

• Pupils: 790 boys and 465 girls, all day • Ages: 11-19 • Size of sixth form: 355 boys and girls • Non-denom • State

Tel: 020 7485 8515
Fax: 020 7284 3462
Email: genadmin@aclandburghley.camden.sch.uk
Website: www.aclandburghley.camden.sch.uk

Headteacher: Since September 2010, Ms Jo Armitage (fifties), previously deputy head of Kidbrooke School in south

London. Began her career as an apprentice electrical engineer and then worked on intermediate technology projects in developing countries. A technology teacher, she has worked with the Qualifications and Curriculum Development Agency as well as in two deputy head roles.

Academic matters: A genuinely comprehensive school, with no selection by ability or specialist places. Wide ability range, including more than its fair share of students with statements of special education need. A strong cohort of dedicated teachers. Sixty-five per cent 5+ A*–C grades at GCSE, 51 per cent including English and maths, achieved through a broad and varied curriculum that focuses hard on core subjects. Particularly successful GCSE subjects are applied art and design, English literature, history and business studies. The school launched the creative and media diploma last year. Specialist arts college status is evident in the artwork adorning the walls. Students are now set from Year 8 in maths and modern languages and other subjects from Year 9. Students learn French or Spanish, but not both, in Years 7–9.

Teaching and learning, leadership and management, personal development and care, guidance and support were rated good at all key stages in the last Ofsted inspection. Very good learning support department with effective SEN and EAL teaching and enrichment opportunities for gifted and talented students. Sociology is one of the most popular and successful A level choices, with half A or B grades. History, psychology, business studies and media studies are all strong. A good range of vocational courses, including travel and tourism, art and design and business studies. Part of La Swap sixth form consortium that includes other local schools La Sainte Union, William Ellis and Parliament Hill.

Games, Options, the Arts: As previously mentioned, exceptional art teaching, especially in the sixth form. 'It's the best school for art in the world,' said a student. Staff talk of 'visual literacy as a learning style'. All students are offered instrumental lessons. Excellent drama – offers an A level in performing arts, as well as drama GCSE and A level. Has recently opened a multi-million pound performing arts block including recording studio.

PE is good. No grassy acres, but a large sports hall and a gym – refurbished courtesy of a £1.3 million lottery grant. New multi-purpose all-weather pitch. Students also use Tufnell Park playing fields, the Michael Sobell sports centre and Leaside canoeing centre. Everyone does dance and drama in the first three years. Lots of extra-curricular activities, some open to the local community, such as fencing and life drawing.

Background and Atmosphere: A very urban school in the side streets of Tufnell Park. 1960s concrete exterior gives on to bright and cheerful classrooms, including a £900,000 learning resource centre stocked with computers, cd-roms and books, and staffed from 8am-5.30pm. Two-thirds of students are boys, but the school makes sure girls are not overwhelmed. Girls comment, 'It makes us stick together more. And we have boys as friends, which really surprises girls from single-sex schools.' Older students in particular enjoy the equal relationship they have with teachers. 'There's a feeling of co-operation and mutual respect here,' said a sixth former. 'I expect my views to be valued.'

Pastoral Care and Discipline: Renowned for its peer counselling and anti-bullying service, ABC. Students from Year 8 upwards are trained to support others who are having difficulties and to run drama workshops in local primary schools. Students feel that this affects the whole atmosphere of the school. 'You get to know so many people you wouldn't usually meet and there's a real sense of community. It makes the school feel safer and more friendly.'

Commended by Ofsted for good behaviour, but inevitably a few students are less interested than others in arriving on time, sitting down and learning. The school has an innovative 'iBehave' approach to behaviour management; students and staff share the responsibility for meeting behaviour expectations. Skilled at supporting students with emotional and behavioural difficulties, and learning mentors work with students in the lower years. The school's focus on these areas has improved behaviour and academic performance at key stage 3.

Pupils and Parents: A huge social mix, with plenty of children from the tough local estates and from middle class families, who have often chosen Acland Burghley for its friendly co-ed atmosphere over the single sex comprehensives nearby. Around a quarter of students speak English as a second language and 30 per cent are eligible for free school meals – well above the national average. The thriving parents' association runs murder mystery evenings, quiz nights and other social events. Ex- students: Ms Dynamite, Sarah Brown (wife of Gordon Brown), Shazad Latif.

Entrance: Heavily over-subscribed, with a catchment area of three-quarters of a mile. First preference to those with a statement of special educational needs, then siblings, then proximity.

Exit: Ninety-four per cent of Year 11s stay in learning, with about 65 per cent going on to the school's sixth form, part of La Swap consortium. Of these, 90 per cent go on to further or higher education, including many to art college, and about four a year to Oxbridge.

Remarks: Creditable exam results from a very mixed intake, remarkable for its art and for the egalitarian effects of its anti-bullying and peer mentoring programme. 'It's informal, but with clear boundaries,' said a student. 'The staff are good enough at their jobs to enable them to be friendly.' 'There's a real feeling that if you want to do something, you can,' said another.

ACS Cobham International School

Linked to ACS Cobham International School (Junior Section) in the Junior section

Heywood, Portsmouth Road, Cobham, Surrey, KT11 1BL

• Pupils: 1320 boys and girls; 95 boarders • Ages: 2-18 • Non-denom
• Fees: Day £8,480-£18,650; Boarding £29,100-£32,960 pa • Independent

Tel: 01932 867 251
Fax: 01932 869 789
Email: cobhamadmissions@acs-england.co.uk
Website: www.acs-england.co.uk

Head: Head since 1992, Tom Lehman is serious, thoughtful and articulate, and moves with the relaxed ease of a tall, rangy athlete (swimming and baseball). Went to Thiel College and Syracuse Uni (USA), and Uni of London, arrived at ACS in 1987, made head in 1992. He does not mince words, answers questions with care and deliberation – in fact like the philosopher of his undergraduate training – and has a reputation for listening hard and following through. He runs a very busy school with a lot of balls in the air, but families see him as very much out and about on campus. He feels that a large school like Cobham offers a bigger pool for students to find more opportunities – for developing confidence in one's skills, for finding friends with common interests, for developing individually thereby contributing to the whole.

Academic matters: American preparatory honors courses (towards American High School Diploma), with 14 Advanced Placement courses and the International Baccalaureate (IB Diploma) offered in the upper grades, maximum 20 in classes for all grades. Lower school emphasis on personal progress rather than grades, using carefully designed rubrics assessing progress (that can be readily translated into letter grades for transition to other schools). Very concerned that student gets a truly sound foundation and understands where he has been and where he needs to go, not compete against each other at this age. Strong fundamentals in maths; even those arriving not properly prepared are strengthened by the process (in one example going from 40s to 90s in ERB maths scores). Children work well together in teams, share ideas; are mixed well in terms of letting different ones lead, 'even forced into leadership'. Parents report that these are exceptionally empathetic teachers. There is a certain amount of traditional lecturing in the upper grades but the school encourages and looks for 'proficiency in the Socratic method,' teachers who are excited, engaged in inquiry-based, collaborative teaching, and are themselves learners. Frequent professional training in academics and all aspects of dealing with young people.

Exhaustive efforts to make educational experience work and to find (and keep) teachers who feel that education is a vocation and bigger than the sum of its parts. Students are placed according to proficiency in maths and languages, mixed but challenged in other classes. Super language choices; courses in nine languages, classes arranged for other languages not offered or in native tongue. Very good exam results, especially considering there are so many EAL students: 92 per cent IB pass rate with 4 or above (out of possible 7); 133 students took 257 AP exams, 62 per cent made a 3 or above (out of possible 5).

SEN assistance is good and getting better – new specially trained teachers in lower and upper grades are particularly good at helping kids deal with learning difficulties, and teachers deal with kids' disabilities and different learning styles.

Very strong EAL assistance, both in specific EAL classes and mainstream classroom help. Fifteen per cent of students arrive speaking no English, by ninth and tenth grade may still receive assistance but, by high school, must be proficient to handle the workload.

Games, Options, the Arts: One of the strongest sports programmes of all the American schools, no doubt because of endless acres of playing fields (and six hole golf course, baseball diamond, tennis courts etc) but especially now because of the 'healthy schools initiative'. New, very competent staff has been brought on to expand the PE offerings and see to the drop-dead terrific new sports centre. Few gyms, clubs, or schools in the world have such state-of-the-art aquatic facilities (computerised touch pads, movable pool bottom, water temp that can change at will depending on activities, UV-based cleaning all but eliminating heavy, eye-stinging, chlorinated atmosphere), or individual computer-card operated work-out equipment, plus suspended wood floors in the dance studio and gym, in a stunning light-drenched interior that looks like an ocean liner. All hands do sports in middle school, for skill and fun.

By high school, teams are selective (varsity teams compete in ISST competitions around Europe), but so many options (total of about 24 teams in various sports and ages per season) 'any student in this school who wants to do sports, can'. Even by the intensely academic senior year, elective classes are so appealing that most people, including non-athletes, stay in at least one. As everywhere else in the school, teachers come up with an optimum match that fits students' interests while it gives them something they need. Even in their dreams, staff can only come up with one thing more they might desire – maybe an outdoor skills component (to complement D of E programme) with an indoor climbing wall. Not unexpectedly, there are excellent facilities and classes for visual and performing arts, community service like Habitat for Humanity, international academic competitions, clubs, and a million field trips – cultural, historical, or service throughout London and the UK, Europe, Namibia, you name it.

Background and Atmosphere: Started in 1972 in attractive 1820s manor house built by Prince Leopold (later King of the Belgians) for his mistress. Finding herself too far from the bright lights of London, she promptly upped sticks and left, but ACS families who move here love it (poor Leopold would have appreciated today's 30 minute train trip to Waterloo). Apart from said love nest, most of the upper school buildings are contemporary, purpose-built and highly functional (of dark brick and rather in the stepped style of 1970s Florida golf condos), a bit dark in the halls but the rows of glass in classrooms and dorms help. Additional Early Childhood building housing purpose-built classrooms and office space was completed in 2005. The school has the snappy feel of a first rate large public American high school, without the overwhelming numbers.

Pastoral Care and Discipline: In lower school, family buddies are matched with families of same aged children. Boarders are watched over by a sympathetic team of houseparents, the head of which feels the school nurtures teachers and staff as well as it does students. School rules are clearly stated, with a staged process of discipline depending on severity. A peer group buddy system for students, plus parent, teacher and student training for sensitivity to drugs, sexuality, bullying etc (using self-assessing interactive software, weekly group discussions, speakers) all keep awareness high to catch problems as they arise. School feels it's failed if someone must go; the process even for expulsion is compassionate – concerned with what is best for the child as well as the school.

Pupils and Parents: Fifty-one per cent American and 10 per cent from the UK plus students from 55 other countries. Standard louche appearance of non-dress-code-restrained teenagers, but alert and amiable with each other, attentive and focused in classes. Kids love the international diversity, say 'someone closed-minded wouldn't like it'. Capable, involved parents help throughout the school; enormously successful international parents' committee integrates non-English speaking families, initiating and maintaining contact parent to parent in their own languages – quickly creating a high level of confidence and excellent network of communication. Good parent support seminars, welcoming picnics, transition meetings, and close contact throughout with administration. Families move here because of the attractive town and more space for children, yet easy commuting distance from London. Boarders are often children whose diplomatic or corporate parents don't have appropriate schooling in their current posting, or because kids want to finish here once they've started.

Entrance: Roughly 25 per cent turnover of student body from year to year but most of it occurs during summer – average stay is three years, due to vagaries of corporate moves. Selective entrance, looking for children 'willing to take on or grow into the challenge, given the space.' School tries very hard to see how they can address any child's needs, whether in achievement, language, or learning difficulties.

Exit: Colleges attended cut across spectrum of usual suspects, from Harvard to Stanford Uni, Yale, Princeton, with large handfuls going to good British, European and Asian Universities. If students stay in the country but leave after middle school, it is usually for a completely different and perhaps smaller school experience.

Money Matters: Strong financial stability thanks to the private corporate ACS owners; no endowment, fees fund the school and include tuition, loan of books, classroom materials, curriculum-related field trips. Quoted boarding fees do not include tuition, but do include autumn break holiday trip. Some financial assistance available.

Remarks: Outstanding suburban, bustling, something-for-everyone school, with high school IB (93 per cent pass rate 2010) and AP courses; the only one of the three ACS schools with boarding students as well as day.

ACS Egham International School

Linked to ACS Egham International School (Junior Section) in the Junior section

Woodlee, London Road, Egham, Surrey, TW20 0HS

• Pupils: 550 boys and girls, all day • Ages: 3-19 • Size of sixth form: 140
• Non-denom • Fees: £8,480-£18,410 pa • Independent

Tel: 01784 430 611
Fax: 01784 430 626
Email: eghamadmissions@acs-england.co.uk
Website: www.acs-england.co.uk

Head of School: Since September 2010, Mr Jeremy Lewis, who had been head of Istanbul International Community School since 2005. He has also worked at the International School Ho Chi Minh in Vietnam.

Academic matters: They believe here that every child can succeed, and lots of attention is given to helping each student do his/her best. IB programme at all levels – there are ten words that define the system from three to 18, and you see them everywhere: communicators, thinkers, enquirers, risk-takers, knowledgeable, principled, caring, open-minded, balanced and reflective. Great expectations!

The IB primary years programme uses an inquiry based approach, helping the children understand the world they live in, acquire knowledge and apply the knowledge received in an effective way. The IB middle years programme prepares the students for the academic rigours of the Diploma programme in Years 11 and 12. It encourages awareness and strong communication skills. Teachers give the students every opportunity to express themselves and they are very approachable. Although not exactly on the IB syllabus, we witnessed an interesting debate between a student and a history teacher on the merits of the Chelsea Football Club.

Each high school student receives an ipod for educational purposes. The last two years are tough, and the students are expected to put in what it takes to maintain the 100 per cent pass rate the school has had for the last four years. Trust is the key word – the kids trust the teachers and the teachers trust the kids. That is why it works so well.

Small classes of no more than 16 are the norm. French and Spanish are taught from first through twelfth grade. Spanish is offered from the middle school and the native language enrichment programme (NLE) give students the possibility to maintain their own language. ACS will provide the teacher and will finance the class if there are more than three students, otherwise, parents pay for the classes. Examples of languages on offer are Dutch, German, Hebrew, Japanese, Swedish and Urdu.

Reports are sent by email often, and if there are any problems the child study team steps in right away to review all options for help. Each term there are student-led conferences with parents and faculty: the school feels that the student is the main player and should take responsibility for his education. ISA (International Schools' Assessment) tests are given to students from ages 8–15, to assess progress.

The faculty is well qualified, caring and creative. The school makes funds available for career development and there is recognition pay for quality teaching. Appreciated and well liked by students – 'They become almost best friends'.

Some special needs can be accommodated and each case is assessed by the child study team. If specialists are brought in, parents must assume the costs. English as an Additional Language programme supports pupils in regular classes with specially trained EAL teachers, who help each student acquire basic vocabulary and vocabulary relevant to classroom topics. They make the school fit the child.

Games, Options, the Arts: A code of 'students first, winning second' means that everyone takes part in sports. In the middle school, every student can be on a team, regardless of ability. The high school takes on the competitive varsity sports, but once in the final two years, sports take a backdoor to the more academic work – there just isn't enough time. The lower school offers soccer, gymnastics, tennis and track and field during the school day and the Saturday morning sports club offers a variety of sports for all.

Two gyms are well equipped and hi-tech. Each student has an electronic card which has his/her gym programme, assessment and progress registered. Cameras in the gyms help the teachers with their weekly evaluations. Lots of beautiful outside playing fields.

After-school clubs are a big feature with all the old favorites like chess, cooking, language and some unusual ones like Habitat for Humanity. The art studio is bright and airy and obviously well used. Multi-purpose rooms for music, drama and dance. Impressive design tech studio deals with projects from conception through development to the end product – students work with plastics, metal and wood, not just to make an object but to understand why and for what it was made. A musical is put on every year, with a professional choreographer.

Recent community service activities include creating a wildlife garden, recycling paper, building houses in Zambia and raising funds for street children in Kenya.

Background and Atmosphere: Drive through the gates, past the ever-present security post, down a tree-lined road, and you eventually arrive at ACS Egham. The campus is set in rolling hills with a Victorian manor house in the centre, complete with a tower and manicured gardens. Classrooms in the main house are bright and sunny. The rest of the classrooms, labs, and studios are tucked into sturdy low built brick buildings, surprisingly attractive considering they were built as a WWll solders' rehab centre, still connected by sloped paths, gardens and lawns under large trees that also provided excellent camouflage during the war for the secret testing of armoured vehicles. Even though the school was created in 1995, it has a 'been here forever' feel to it.

The lunchroom is noisy but controlled with teachers roaming around. Kids bring their lunch or can buy it with a lunchcard system. No one leaves the campus during the day, but who would want to? There are two libraries with decent budgets, and computers everywhere with a budget 15 times as high. High schoolers can bring their own laptops. No uniform, just good judgement.

Pastoral Care and Discipline: In such a small school, teachers and students know each other. Problems are quickly detected and the child study team steps in to review and resolve problems with the family and the school. The caring atmosphere means that bullying doesn't work here. Health classes, drug and alcohol prevention seminars keep the students informed. Zero tolerance for drugs and drinking (three expulsions in ten years). Students' unwillingness to disappoint parents keeps everyone out of trouble.

Pupils and Parents: Fifteen per cent British, 40 per cent American and 43 other nationalities. Lots of ex-pats, also Brits who are looking to an alternative to A levels. Turnover in the past has been over 20 per cent, but in the past few years families are choosing to stay longer, so it is down to 17 per cent. Kids are eager and confident, relaxed among faculty, and seem very comfortable at this school. It would be perfect, if only 'friends didn't move'.

Parents are active in all areas of the school. They volunteer in classrooms, the library, and on field trips. They sponsor school teams. There is an active PTO which supports the school in many ways. They hold a fall family festival and special interest workshops. The school and the PTO organise parent education classes which include sessions on how maths is taught and student assessments made.

Entrance: Non-selective. The school feels that any child can succeed in the proper environment and that the IB programme can help those who struggle in other systems to thrive. Applications are accepted throughout the year. Send school records, teachers' recommendations and personal statements from students aged ten and over. There are waiting lists at every level, but the school does its best to help.

When the children join the school, the parents join as well. ACS feels that a smooth transition is vital for families and tries to help in many ways. The housing office and PTO help find homes in the neighbouring towns and with settling into the area and offer parent support groups. Lots of experience of helping children adapt and, since the students themselves know what it is like to be the 'new kid', it's an easy process.

Exit: If children leave before graduation, it is most often due to families being transferred. The school offers the course-work needed to fully satisfy the requirements for an American high school diploma. University guidance is started in grades 9 and 10, and grades 11 and 12 are given one-to-one advisors to help with the application process. Most go to their first choice: an equal split between US and UK universities. All the top UK names are on the list including Oxford. Boston University, Purdue, NYU, Georgetown and lots of big state universities in the US are favourites.

Money Matters: ACS Egham is privately owned, fee supported with no endowment. Money has been available to finance growing pains and ever improving facilities. Limited need-based financial aid.

Remarks: The individualised approach to education means that both the child who doesn't blossom in other systems and the curious and intellectually-demanding student can do well.

ACS Hillingdon International School

Linked to ACS Hillingdon International School (Junior Section) in the Junior section

Hillingdon Court, 108 Vine Lane, Hillingdon, Middlesex, UB10 0BE

• Pupils: 580 boys and girls • Ages: 4-18 • Size of sixth form: 240
• Non-denom • Fees: £8,820-£18,560 pa • Independent

Tel: 01895 259 771
Fax: 01895 818 404
Email: hillingdonadmissions@acs-england.co.uk
Website: www.acs-england.co.uk

Head of School: Since 2002, Mrs Ginger G Apple (fifties). Parents tell us she is still observant, gracious and composed, and there is no question she is an asset to the school. As soon as she arrived she quickly absorbed the Hillingdon culture. Has worked her way through meetings with every single student three at a time, and moved with sure but deliberate steps to make her own imprint on a school she thought was already very good. Has taught or run international schools from South America to South Africa, Zambia to Scotland, and has degrees from Miami

University (Oxford, Ohio),Trenton State College (NJ) and an EdD currently underway at Oxford Brookes University (UK) in educational research.

Academic matters: American college prep programme leading to the American high school diploma, with Advanced Placement Courses (12) and/or International Baccalaureate (IB) and very good results – usually about half the graduating seniors are IB diploma candidates, with a 93 per cent pass rate in 2010. In 2010, 25 students took 57 AP tests: 53 per cent passed with 3 or better. School says its results 'place them among the top fifteen independent schools in the UK'. Spanish offered from fourth grade, French from sixth grade through twelfth, EAL available from kindergarten through tenth grade. Hard to tell what impact EAL students have on native English speakers, but clearly students must be fluent to handle strong academics in last two years. Adequate and growing IT (portable pod of laptops available to classes as needed, plus five computer labs), with innovative training offered to teachers.

Small classes of no more than 20 in most grades. Some special needs assistance in lower grades (pull-out programme approximately two hours a week); special needs classes plus specific learning strategies for use in regular classrooms available in middle school.

Games, Options, the Arts: Middle and high school students may do intramural sports (PE compulsory through twelfth grade) or compete in three varsity and JV sports per year, girls' and boys' teams, with tournaments in UK and abroad. Student-run drama and musical productions with multiple departments contributing; major concerts for band and choirs, solo and ensemble performances held in the beautiful rococo Red Room. Great field trips in all grades to London, UK and abroad.

Background and Atmosphere: The heart of the school is the beautifully restored, white, C19th neo-classical Hillingdon Court, surrounded by eleven acres of formal garden and woodlands, and ten acres of playing fields nearby. By contrast, the substantial addition in which the lower school and most of the middle school are located looks dishearteningly like a corporate headquarters. But it's functional and well-maintained and the high school classes, library, music, and meetings take place in the marvellous, light-filled, baroque interior of the original house. New music centre plus digital recording studio, rehearsal rooms, practice studios and computer lab for music tech. Students sharp, interested and like their school. In fact, they actively like the activities both during and after school – writing workshop, sports, art. One, after assuring us that he wouldn't mind missing his bus and staying on at school the rest of the day, pointed out that even the less studious like to learn, because there 'are a lot of activities and not just desk work'. Teachers often go above and beyond, scheduling time to help students on Saturdays and over spring breaks.

Pastoral Care and Discipline: Students say, 'A person who wants to slink into the shadows and disappear might not choose to come here but, once he came, we'd make it work.' They comment that peer helpers and teachers keep in touch with students and parents and are on the look-out for problems, and stress how accepting this fluid, international student body is. International students stay an average of three years, so 'no real time to set up fiefdoms'. Problems are handled quickly; serious offences like drugs could trigger immediate suspension but coupled with counselling. Students allowed to make mistakes and grow past them but protection of other students is key.

Pupils and Parents: About 46 per cent American, 12 per cent Japanese, 7 per cent British, 35 per cent from 51 other nationalities; heavy preponderance of international corporate families, therefore a 25 per cent turnover within the student body during the year; families move to the area just for this school as well as the English suburban village experience, but some 32 buses take students door to door as far as central London as well as in the catchment area. Strong PTA, particularly transitional assistance network (TAN): over 60 volunteer parents, plus students, of every nationality help in family transitions.

Entrance: Non-selective, looking for ways to serve most children who apply, have good character, want to learn and can do the work.

Exit: Graduates go to a range of American first and second tier large universities and small liberal arts colleges, but even more go to good British, European and Canadian universities, with an additional smattering to ones in Japan, South Africa, and Australia. When younger students leave it's because of family transfers, usually going on to another international school or back to the US.

Money Matters: Fees include loan of textbooks, lab fees, classroom materials and day-long field trips (except theatre tickets); one-off debenture payment; some sports, daily bus, travel, tutoring expenses are extra, depending on needs and activities of the student. Also IB mother-tongue languages with fewer than three students are paid for by the parent. Hillingdon is supported by its fees but owned by a private company, so no endowment as such. Some financial aid available.

Remarks: Large enough for lots of extracurricular options but small enough for easy interaction amongst teachers and students. Solid suburban American international school offering strong academics through AP classes and/or high school IB, for families who want to be out of the city but with an acceptable commute and a good school enabling ease of transition anywhere.

Aiglon College

1885 Chesières-Villars Chesières-Villar Switzerland • Pupils: 325 boys and girls, almost all board • Ages: 9-18 • Size of sixth form: 130 • Ecumenical • Fees: SFr 45,800-SFr 64,600 annually for boarding • Independent

Tel: +41 24 496 6161
Fax: +41 24 496 6162
Email: info@aiglon.ch
Website: www.aiglon.ch

Headmaster: Since 2009, Mr Richard McDonald MA (Oxon); obviously a sporty person, strong and wiry, and with his beard could almost be a naval captain. He comes across as a very disciplined man, with a wry smile and twinkle in the eye as soon as you mention his school. Educated at Christ's Hospital and Lincoln College Oxford (studied French and German); taught at Charterhouse; returned to Christ's Hospital to teach modern languages and be a housemaster; became headmaster of Aiglon from 1994 to 2000. Moved on to be director of strategic development at College Beau Soleil in Villars, but returned to Aiglon in July 2009.

After five head teachers in eight years, the leadership of this prestigious mountain school is back in very capable hands. To say that Mr McDonald is passionate about the school and the capabilities of its staff and students would do him a disservice. He literally lives and breathes the school – even eats with the students every meal-time – and has certainly hit the ground running since his return, having obtained IB accreditation in November 2009. He says he is 'vision and inspiration driven', and you can see the results, not only in the move to the IB diploma, but also in his determination for Council of International Schools (CIS) re-accreditation, and the evolving new campus plan which started in May when the building of the sports centre began.

His staff may see him as overly optimistic but they don't think this is a negative. The students are perhaps still a little wary of him: he has a reputation for being a strict disciplinarian, not for small things such as a uniform in disarray, but on breaking school rules and therefore trust. He sees a successful student as one who goes on to the best university to which he or she can aspire.

Academic matters: The school follows the British curriculum in Years 9 to 11 when all students take GCSEs or IGCSEs depending on their chosen subjects. Students are streamed according to ability in maths, English and languages. In September 2010, the sixth form moved to the IB diploma programme. Given the number of different nationalities in the school, around 50, the GCSE results are not bad. Last year they achieved an 85 per cent A*–C pass rate compared with the UK average of 67 per cent. As one would expect, foreign languages are good, but there are notable weaknesses in all three sciences despite excellent facilities.

For a relatively small sixth form, they are able to offer a good range of subjects for the new IB Diploma at both Standard and Higher levels – the three sciences, maths, English, humanities, foreign languages (French, German and Spanish, plus Italian, Russian, Portuguese, Arabic and Japanese on a private tuition basis), art, drama, music, plus philosophy, economics, business and media studies. There are also IT and astronomy on offer at IGCSE, with a hope that the latter may become an IB subject in the future.

Many students have English as a second language, but thanks to the excellent ESL teaching – a mixture of class and individual support from a team of professionals – this is not seen as a barrier to taking any exams. Around 50 per cent of students go on to US universities, so the school is also an accredited SATs centre: amongst those sitting the SATs, scores range from 1240 to 2140 (out of a possible total of 2400, 800 per exam) for critical reading, maths and writing. [NB Remember, these are the US SATs, taken in high school, not to be confused with the UK SATs, taken at a younger age and mentioned later in this review].

Small classes mean that students get individual attention and can develop at their own pace. Purpose-built classrooms for science, a recently-completed modern languages centre in the old post office building, whiteboards and their own computer network system mean students and staff have access to state-of-the-art teaching and learning materials and methods. Students with mild learning difficulties are given extensive support by the learning support department.

Games, Options, the Arts: A light and airy art studio shows off the talent of many students both in 2D and 3D art. Some students also get the opportunity to display and sell their work in a gallery in Geneva. The music and drama departments allow students to develop other artistic talents. The music department takes over the ground floor of the JCB building, the heart of which is the Oudang room which takes up to 60 musicians. Many students learn an instrument from the traditional orchestral to the bagpipes and many take part in the various college bands, ensembles and choirs. Those less musically talented can get involved with the technical side of the recording or radio studio or the keyboard lab with specialist music computers. The drama department uses the purpose built Exeter Hall and puts on a number of productions annually, including a dance show, and is also home to the school's Comedy Club. The two departments worked closely together on the last school theatre production *Woyzeck*, which involved the whole school – students and staff alike.

Stuck on a mountainside, one can forgive the school for not having British style playing fields but they do their best with the limited space available and PE is compulsory for all students. The new sports centre should be completed in January 2012 and will house a 1,080m multi-purpose hall that can be divided into two basketball courts as well as a fitness centre, indoor climbing wall and a cafeteria. The school does well in the SGIS athletics competitions – it must be all that walking up and down a mountainside all day that keeps the students very fit. Football is popular (they do have an Astroturf pitch), as is tennis supported by five courts scattered about the campus, which also double-up as basketball and volleyball courts. Other sports available are swimming, seven-a-side rugby, uni-hockey, golf (the course is just up the road) and of course skiing. Although based in the mountains, the students aren't on skis as much as one would imagine. In winter, students have four hours of skiing a week as part of their PE course, but they are also free to ski on Wednesday and Saturday afternoons. Members of Aiglon's ski race team follow a much more stringent training and competition regime throughout the autumn and winter months and are proud of their successes.

Expeditions are part of the unique Aiglon experience. Two weekend and one three-day expedition are compulsory for all students each term. In the autumn and summer term these usually involve hiking and camping whilst in winter it's ski-touring. These Exes are deliberately physically (and often mentally) rigorous and challenging but are the one thing that all students seem to remember and talk about with affection. They are however, very strictly monitored and the school has four fully qualified mountain guides on staff. One member of staff remarked that it is these expeditions that forge the special relationships between students and staff and gives them all a great opportunity to get out of school and into the open air to fend for themselves. It is also interesting to note that many of the students go on non-compulsory expeditions at weekends too.

Being a boarding school, there is an extensive options programme (including the very popular astronomy in the Kalouti observatory) which varies depending on the time of year and the specializations and interests of teachers. When asked if they played computer games in the evening, a group of students remarked that with all the other things to do, they didn't have the time or the inclination.

Background and Atmosphere: Located in the alpine ski resort of Villars, the school was founded in 1949 by John Corlette, a former teacher at Gordonstoun, and is based on the educational principal of self-reliance developed by Kurt Hahn, Gordonstoun's founder. Originally a boys-only school, it went co-educational in 1968.

Since its founding, the school has grown from a few students and teachers in a single building to an international community of around 320 pupils and 50 different nationalities. In the early years, the school grew by expanding into existing buildings in the village. In the last twenty years, the school has been able to improve the campus with purpose-built Junior School premises, the John Corlette teaching building (JCB) and the new Delaware boys boarding house.

Scattered over the mountainside, some buildings have magnificent views of the Alps. There are six boarding houses in the Senior School, all single sex, three boys/ three girls, with the opposite sex only allowed on the ground floor. One was an old sanitorium, with very 1930's architecture, otherwise think large chalets with lots of wood indoors and out. No British boarding school style dormitories: rooms are usually three or four bedded study rooms, although doubles and singles are more common for the sixth form. Children of different nationalities are encouraged to share a room. Breakfast is still eaten in each house, although there is a cooked breakfast option in the main dining room. Each house has a house captain and inter-house competitions are fiercely fought.

The quality of the food is much improved since it's now outsourced from a proper catering company, with lunch and dinner served in the very chic looking dining room where a lot of the students' art is displayed. There isn't a huge amount of choice, but the food is definitely healthy – salad bar, vegetarian option, invariably pasta and lots of fruit. You'll see fruit bowls scattered around the boarding houses and students are allowed to cook in the house kitchens – home made cakes were seen in all, even the boys', boarding houses. The students certainly don't starve.

School uniform is informal and practical – white polo neck shirt, cream trousers and when we visited, a dark blue sweater with the school emblem – and is compulsory only until the sixth-form. (Although it was noted that most of the prefects wore their special scarves or ties and blazers – or perhaps that was just for our benefit.) All the students were well turned out, uniform or not. As well as typical British style prefects and house captains, there is a head boy and a head girl, but at Aiglon they are known as Guardians.

Meditations are a distinctive feature of the school – don't think New Age, just a different form of daily assembly. Teaching staff and sometimes guests give a short talk on a specific topic which is preceded and followed by a period of silence. In this day and age, it is unusual for a whole school to come together every morning and the students seem to really appreciate this quiet time of reflection.

Aiglon is also a Round Square school which means they devote a lot of time and effort to participation in community service and work projects at home and overseas. These often humbling experiences give students a strong sense of personal development and responsibility.

Junior School: Only 80 pupils so far (age 9 to 13), but numbers will increase in 2010–2011. About half the children are day pupils, but the girls have a true chalet style boarding house, the boys are in the main chalet. It is a small nurturing environment, no high pressure – although a British curriculum, no SATS – with kids from many countries.

Pastoral Care and Discipline: House-parents, personal tutors and most of the staff are on hand to help. The house-parents seem totally devoted to their charges and duties and appear very aware of the difficulties that can arise with different nationalities living close to one another. There is also a well-established PSHE programme in place. Very traditional British boarding school discipline is in place: laps, gating, suspension and even the rare expulsion. Mr McDonald does not hesitate to mete out the appropriate disciplinary action. There is no smoking anywhere on campus, although difficult to enforce over such a widespread area. Wine and beer are allowed for over 17s – a very strict rule given that the legal drinking age for wine and beer is 16 in Switzerland.

There is a zero tolerance of drugs, and regular random testing takes place. A strict pocket-money allowance is in place – refreshing to hear, given that most of the students come from very privileged backgrounds. Public displays of affection are discouraged but let's be realistic, this is a co-ed boarding school.

Pupils and Parents: Over two-thirds of the students are, not surprisingly, European, with the largest group being British – nearly 20 per cent. The next largest group are North American (11 per cent) followed by Far Eastern (seven per cent) and students from every continent. Around 80 per cent enter with English as their mother-tongue or with a high fluency level. A number of more recent pupils are children of alumni. In fact, one student recounted that she and her brother couldn't wait to get to Aiglon, having heard stories about the school from her father and his old school friends. Parents have to have quite a bit of money, whether self-made or inherited, in order to be able to afford the fees, so they form a fairly elite group. However, there are scholarships available for those from more modest backgrounds, including a special scholarship for students from African and Oriental countries.

Entrance: The school has its own series of admission tests, plus an interview with the head and references from the present school are needed. For admission into the sixth form, satisfactory GCSEs or equivalent are required. Mr McDonald states that Aiglon is a 'de-selective' rather than 'selective' school.

Exit: High university fees are not a problem for Aiglon students and around 50 per cent go on to US universities. You will see a smattering of Ivy League, but also other top schools such as MIT, Stanford and Tufts in the US, and McGill in Canada. Entry into UK universities is about equally divided between the Russell and 1994 Groups, plus the occasional Oxbridge entry along with Durham, Bristol, Manchester, Edinburgh and St Andrews as well as the London University colleges of Imperial, Kings and UCL. Some students stay in Switzerland and go on to the prestigious EPFL (Ecole Polytechnique Fédérale de Lausanne) and hotel schools.

Money Matters: In addition to fees there are the usual extras, including school uniform and of course ski passes. These do rather add up. Aiglon is a not-for-profit school and gathers funds from full fee-paying students, donations and registered charitable trusts in different countries. The Aiglon College Alumni Eagle Association is also active in raising funds. There is a serious amount of fund-raising currently going on to try and bring to life the aspirations of Mr McDonald – a new library and media centre and a performing arts centre are just two of the plans on the drawing-board.

Remarks: Not a school for spoilt brats or prima donnas – the expeditions (Exes) and service projects make sure of that. It prides itself on offering a prestigious education in the broadest definition and, on the whole, it delivers. Highly academic it is not, but the kids do get an all-round education. Students leave here with a strong feeling of self-confidence not arrogance, having been humbled by active service (and not by bullying – something that sets them apart from many of their contemporaries).

Akeley Wood School

Linked to Akeley Wood Junior School in the Junior section

Akeley Wood, Buckingham, Buckinghamshire, MK18 5AE

• Pupils: 570 (280 girls, 290 boys); all day • Ages: 11-18 • Size of sixth form: 130 • Non-denom • Fees: £10,095; Tutorial Programme £12,930 pa • Independent

Tel: 01280 814 110
Fax: 01280 822 945
Email: enquiries@akeleywoodschool.co.uk
Website: www.akeleywoodschool.co.uk

Headmaster: Since 2005, Dr Jeremy (Jerry) Grundy MA PhD (forties). Educated at Leeds Grammar, then read PPE at St Anne's, Oxford, followed by doctorate at McGill University in Montreal. He began his teaching career as head of RS and housemaster at St Albans School, before moving to Magdalen College School in Oxford as head of sixth form. He introduced philosophy A level there, a phenomenally successful move. An infectious enthusiast, he is adamant that 'happiness is central to pupils' learning', and that if youngsters 'feel happy and secure in their learning environment' they will realise their potential. Historically, Akeley Wood had a weak sixth form. There were only 40 sixth formers prior to Dr Grundy's arrival but now there are 129. 'I've always felt that the engine behind a good school should be its sixth form, and that is very much the case here now,' he says. Masses of good PR about the school locally. 'When I arrived I drew up a ten-year development plan and my view is that the plan will be achieved in half that time'. Recent additions include dedicated sixth form centre, new science labs and classrooms, more interactive whiteboards and full-size Astroturf.

Dr Grundy is hugely proud of the school and what pupils have achieved in recent years. There's no doubt he has raised standards and, equally important, raised pupils' own aspirations and expectations of what they are capable of. He doesn't teach regular classes but runs the philosophy discussion group, contributes to the sixth form lecture series and frequently pops into classes to observe lessons and contribute to what's going on – 'more on the humanities side,' he says, 'although I have been known to try my hand at scientific experiments!' Dr Grundy is also keen to involve himself on the sporting side – he referees school rugby matches and pitches his hand against pupils on the tennis court. Wife, Ginny, teaches art at Akeley Wood and they have two sons who attend the junior school.

Academic matters: Under the aegis of the Chris Woodhead-led Cognita and with the head's leadership, the school is firmly on the up. In 2010, 33 per cent of GCSE grades were A*/A. Small classes throughout – never more than 20, and much smaller in sixth form. Total of 21 subjects on offer at A level – all the usual, plus business studies, sport studies, psychology, photography, music technology, textiles etc. Setting for maths, science, and French. Languages taught are French, German and Spanish. School is one of only 12 in country to be involved in Autology, e-learning system which gives pupils access to more than 200,000 online resources, including textbooks, audio and video.

When we visited it was history week, with a myriad of lessons and activities focusing on the Battle of Trafalgar. A group of Year 10s were clearly gripped by an account of Nelson's last moments, while even the canteen staff had been inspired to add ship's biscuits and pease pudding to the lunch menu! We weren't sure how modern-day youngsters would cope with such culinary delights but school food gets the firm thumbs-up, especially the homemade bread.

IT provision good. Two IT rooms – pupils get 70 minutes a week from 11 to 14 and many go on to take IT at GCSE and computing at A level. Six science labs and triple and double award science available. Youngsters receive effort and achievement grades every three weeks. New self-assessment system encourages them to look at their own progress and set targets. School also offers impressive Tutorial Programme for children with dyslexia, dyspraxia, dyscalculia and those requiring a greater level of support. The classes run parallel to other classes in the year group, catering for a maximum of ten pupils in each year. System has been widely praised and seems to build youngsters' confidence and self-esteem. One former head boy worked his way from the Tutorial Programme to win a place at Warwick University to study biological sciences. Most recent ISI report (2006) described the achievement of pupils following the Tutorial Programme as 'outstanding'. Some youngsters do study skills instead of talking a second language and can also attend study sessions at lunch-time.

Games, Options, the Arts: Sport good, with lots of matches against local schools; impressive haul of silverware on display in school cabinet. Main sports for boys are rugby, football, cricket and athletics, while girls enjoy netball, hockey, rounders, athletics and tennis. Equestrian team very successful. Pupils can try other sports at after-school clubs – everything from karate to Pilates. Brand new Sports Dome 2009.

Music has grown massively in recent years. Around 60 per cent play instruments. Music is very popular at GCSE and A level. School orchestra, wind bands, brass group, choir and rock bands galore. High point of school calendar is 'Akeley Woodstock', school's annual rock festival. Even the staff band appears onstage, with the head on vocals! Art, textiles and DT all impressive – around eight pupils do art A level each year and 30 currently doing art GCSE. Sixth form has its own art room while younger pupils get to create their masterpieces in prize-winning art department housed in old stable block. Stunning artwork displayed throughout school.

Drama previously weaker link, but new drama space at Tile House Mansion with flexible lighting equipment, combined with a collaborative approach to the performing arts as a whole (drama, music and dance), has seen new inclusive culture of experimentation.

Young Enterprise and D of E widely taken up, with regular expeditions to the Forest of Dean and Peak District. Annual ski trips and recent visits to Paris and the battlefields of Belgium and northern France. Excellent guidance on universities and careers. 'The head of the sixth form is the world's living expert on UCAS,' the head boy told us appreciatively.

Background and Atmosphere: The school as a whole has seen an enormous £8 million investment. New IT suites, food technology and art rooms, Astroturf and Sports Dome – all at the junior school; science lab, IT suite, food tech suite, DT workshop, art room, textiles room, heated Sports Domes, Astroturfs and new teaching block over the two sites of the senior school.

Main school building is a splendid mock-Tudor hunting lodge set in 22 acres and dating back to 1867. The school started out as a traditional boys' boarding school called Hillcrest in 1946 and went co-ed in 1972. Boarding ended in 1980. School expanded in stages. Its junior school and nursery (12 months – 11 years) at Wicken Park was acquired in 1988. The 11–13 year olds are at Tile House Mansion and the 13–18s in Akeley Wood. As we said last time, there's still a faintly boys' prep school feel to the senior school. Lots of wood panelling, no big assembly area and former billiard room stuffed with electric guitars. Place has slightly cramped feel (while lower school seems huge!) Pupils are devoted to the place, though, and say facilities have improved by leaps and bounds since advent of Cognita. 'But I'm really pleased it's still kept its friendly atmosphere,' one pupil told us. Sixth formers very pleased with their smart new sixth form centre, complete with common-room and kitchen.

Pastoral Care and Discipline: School describes itself as 'an unpretentious and civilised environment, where good behaviour, good manners and a smart appearance are paramount'. It prides itself on not being over-regimented or having too many trivial rules and regulations, yet it is crystal-clear in what it expects of pupils. One pupil told us, 'compared to other schools, Akeley Wood really builds your confidence. It has made me who I am and leaving it behind will be very sad'. Good PSHCE programme and 'no trouble' with booze or fags. Pro-active drugs awareness talks and strong anti-bullying programme (although pupils say there isn't any 'nastiness'). Youngsters well supported by heads of year, tutors, school counsellor and prefects.

Bottle-green/grey uniform up to Year 11, own smart jackets/suits for sixth form. Four houses – Hillcrest, Stuart, Pilgrim and Thompson – with house captains, reps from each year and lots of inter-house competitions. House points awarded for academic and sporting achievements as well as effort in the classroom. Head boy and head girl voted into office by staff and pupils. Raft of prefects, with several assigned to help Year 7s settle in – although all sixth formers make a point of being friendly and supportive to their more junior counterparts. Some pupils are strikingly modest about their achievements. We were shown round by a boy who had just won a music scholarship to Cambridge and a girl who is a member of Britain's dressage team and an aspiring Olympian. Neither mentioned these triumphs themselves – but their peers spilled the beans! Whole school assembly at beginning and end of term. House and year assemblies every week.

Pupils and Parents: Fleet of eight school buses bring pupils in from 25-mile radius – from both rural and urban areas, including Buckingham, Aylesbury, Milton Keynes, Towcester etc. Up to ten pupils from countries like China, Taiwan and Thailand enter the sixth form each year, living with guardians, staff and local families.

Entrance: Selective. At 11, pupils either move up from junior school (entry is automatic for them, unless head advises otherwise), while others come from range of local primaries and preps. 'We want to ensure that the pupil and the school are a good match, so that we can support and extend them and help them to thrive,' says the deputy head. He adds that low grades aren't necessarily a barrier for pupils entering the school's Tutorial Programme, but 'it's vital that they are committed to learning'. All prospective pupils spend assessment day at the senior school. Entry into the sixth form requires minimum of five Cs at GCSE (including Bs in the subjects youngsters want to study at A level).

Exit: Some leave after GCSE for local grammar schools or FE colleges. Virtually all sixth form leavers go to university, choosing vast array of destinations. Recent subjects range from architecture and physics to Assyriology and midwifery.

Money Matters: Number of academic, music, art, and sport scholarships available – up to 20 per cent of the fees. Sibling discount across all three Akeley Wood schools.

Remarks: Happy mainstream school that caters for wide range of abilities. Lots of good new-build. Great for boosting pupils' confidence and self-esteem and spotting talents that might have gone undetected elsewhere. Youngsters are happy, engaged and eager to sing the school's praises. As deputy head says, 'it's not the cool thing to be anti-school here'. Akeley Wood is on a roll – and the interesting developments look set to continue.

Albyn School

Linked to Albyn Lower School in the Junior section

17-23 Queens Road, Aberdeen, Aberdeen, AB15 4PB

• Pupils: 385 girls, 165 boys; plus 115 in the nurseries • Ages: 2-18 • Size of sixth form: 60 • Non-denominational • Fees: £5,710-£9,785 pa • Independent

Tel: 01224 322 408
Fax: 01224 209 173
Email: information@albynschool.co.uk
Website: www.albynschool.co.uk

Head: Since 2008, Dr Ian Long BA AKC PhD FRGS FRSA (fiftyish), who was educated at King's College School,

Wimbledon, read geography at King's London and, after a brief spell with Shell (always good to get the outside perspective) worked in a variety of schools – all girls, co-ed, that sort of thing, before becoming head of sixth form at Brentwood, followed by eight years as (academic) deputy head of City of London Freemen's School, during which time he also did his doctorate (in rural council housing). A lapsed rower and a clever clog who came to a school on the cusp; the previous head had worked miracles, but some were a tad expensive. Has tightened up the finance side. No more babies (staffing ratio hideous) and huge increase in both nursery and chaps throughout the school. 'Always wanted to work abroad' but hadn't quite expected to find Scotland, and possibly Aberdeen in particular, quite so different from his previous experience.

Fair amount of movement in the governing body, new head of the governors 'super chap'. Long runs the school with two deputy heads, one pastoral, and one in charge of timetabling et al. Mrs Karen Thomson is in charge of lower school and the nurseries.

An engaging and entertaining head with a sparkling sense of humour, he is also dead efficient and our request for detailed exam results by subject over the previous three years arrived at our computer before we did. His wife, Gwyneth, was deputy head at Channing School in Highgate, having started her teaching career at St Leonard's School down the coast in Fife as a Latin teacher and assistant housemistress. She teaches classics in the school.

Academic matters: Scottish system: broad range of subjects and results 'achieved with girls of varying ability', (boys' results must wait till next year) occasional glitches, biology, English, French and maths do well, ditto chemistry and physics. No apparent weaknesses, info systems obviously not yet up and running, but business management and modern studies good. School did well in the league tables, particularly at Highers (all subjects can be taken at Advanced Higher). German not currently the flavour of the month. Drama the latest addition with higher level PE now on offer. Certain amount of almost individual teaching; the results are impressive (if hardly cost-effective. Some Spanish in upper sixth. Impressive showing in maths challenge and problem-solving.

Maximum class size 20, with low teens for practical subjects (school says 20, but in practice this is much smaller; most classes are 10/15). Comprehensive computer system, class-taught as well as in suites, laptops abound, pupils can bring in their own. All pupils have their own email and can email homework and queries to staff. European computer driving licence available, keyboarding taught early in the school; some interactive whiteboards.

'Sort of set' maths and English in primary, handwriting important. Jolly phonics in nursery, which has been proven to cut the incidence of dyslexia by 75 per cent. All assessed on entry, two learning support teachers cover the whole school, and a pupil's IEP follows throughout their time at school. No problems with dyslexia, dyspraxia and mild Asperger's, and in the past did well for a pupil who was profoundly deaf. No EFL help available as such ('not needed' says the head), but 'lots of support in the classroom', SEN teacher takes individual groups and double teaches a bit – she is very 'willing' – and was off to help out in a German lesson after we talked. She would need to be. Scribing, readers and all the rest; extra time available for exams – this is no longer a blanket 20 per cent per pupil per exam, but different pupils may need different concessions in different subjects. Case must be made for each. No extra charge for SEN help. Digital exams being mooted by SQA, school is investigating voice recognition programmes.

Games, Options, the Arts: Main games field at Milltimber five miles away – pupils are bused, fabulous athletics track. In 2009 the school started to use Aberdeen's state-of-the-art sports village for a number of sports: athletics, hockey, football, netball. Positive netball and hockey with regional representation and masses of individual sports: national representation in several. With boys now in the senior school, serious thought was given to what sport the boys would play in the senior school: 'Both rugby and football have fervent adherents among parents of the boys, but the latter may be more realistic if we are not to be beaten 80–0 for the next five years. Rowing may be the answer.' And so it is. Boys (only at the moment) are already competing successfully in coxed quads, with footie as a minor – albeit successful – sport for both boys and girls. Scottish gold medallist coach.

Stunning art department, with a number of pupils going on to higher things in the art world. Very jolly with papier mâché, acrylic and silk screen work. Hot on costume design and much use made of local museums. Always a joy to come here. Strong art and architectural stream. Fantastic music – 'most girls play a musical instrument' – and loads of participation in either choir or instrumental ensembles. New head of music. Good representation in the National Youth Orchestra plus jazz, ceilidh bands. Blues band. Keen drama and dance (Dancercise important). Couldn't do better. Enthusiastic Young Enterprise and highly competitive D of E with oodles of golds. Strong club culture – quizzes, chess, gardening but alas no more Scottish country dancing. Keen on public speaking and debating. Head has encouraged trips: Borneo, Barbados, and cultural tours to Italy. (Some – mainly local – parents, are not entirely convinced of their necessity).

Background and Atmosphere: Founded in 1867 by Harriet Warrack, who started teaching girls at home, advertising locally for pupils. Albyn Place (just down the road) became the school's home in 1881, hence the name, and Albyn School for Girls moved to Queen's Road in 1925. The son of one of the gardeners at Duff House, Alexander Mackie was an early moving light, writing books on English (he was a university examiner) and made the school an Aberdeen institution, with emancipated Albyn girls on Aberdeen University student council by 1907. The head was pleased to find his original desk in a passage and it now graces his office (the roll-top concealing all manner of educational detritus).

School based in four attached Victorian merchants' houses, with fantastic ceilings, one well-used library and the predictable garden expansion. Harriet House houses the toddlers, aged two to three years, while the juniors have a splendid new-build, with classrooms clustered round a splendid hall (with windows on the first floor) giving both extra light and affording entertainment, tiny people were performing a skipping dance during our visit. Lifts in junior school make disabled access almost available everywhere. Kitchen and dining area dramatically revamped, junior school order in advance, seniors pay-as-you-go. Plans afoot for an amalgamated nursery, and a new science block, with better integrated connections between the various houses; the existing school has a family feel, but logistically it is a complicated complex of corridors and levels between the houses. Fire doors everywhere. The new-build will be part cantilevered over the existing playground which will have the advantage of deflecting some of the granite city weather. Impressive music department above hall/gym (can accommodate the whole school) in the west end of the school, has undergone a significant makeover. School hopes to increase numbers to 650. Boys started in the junior department in 2005 and are working their way up.

Pastoral Care and Discipline: School divided into four quite competitive clans, mainly for games. No tutors; pupils can, and do, relate to form teachers and guidance staff when in difficulty. Wickedness equals a yellow card, followed by a red card, usual punishment is an essay. Sense of community – school aims to boost the confidence of the shyest child. Policy of zero tolerance for drink 'n' drugs 'n' rock 'n' roll, so expect to be out for persistent bullying or drugs. Cigarettes and alcohol on school premises = detention followed by exclusion followed by out. 'Bullying is usually changing friendship groups' seems about right, but actual bullying is regarded as a no-no. If there is real cause for concern, then parents are summonsed for a 'discussion'. Queen's Cross church used for Easter and Christmas (Scotland's first gay minister – which upsets some of the parent base).

Pupils and Parents: Mixture of professionals – a lot of oil and gas, but farmers and marine engineers in the parent body. The former often have to either move or install their young at short notice. Fair number of first-time buyers; parents can drop off early and pick up late (6.15) for pupils in the lower school but there is an extra charge. International bias, but lots of home-grown ones too; strong middle class ethos with girls neat in check dresses or kilts (any tartan, but proper kilts, not skirts – though we didn't see the full eight yards) compulsory for girls from October to April. Some wear them all year round. Boys are allowed to wear kilts but only a few do, mostly on special occasions.

Entrance: Entry assessment for junior school; however, entry from junior to senior is automatic. Pupils can and do join at any time – throughout the year (assuming space available). Not many come post standard grades. The nursery is committed to 2011, waiting lists throughout the junior school and for the first two years of the senior.

Exit: Only about five leave post Highers; most (95 per cent or so) go to university, often after a gap year, a majority to Scottish ones. Aberdeen popular. One recent candidate to Cambridge, the odd maverick to Sheffield, Belfast, film studies in Southern California, international business at London, marine science at Miami; the usual medical and law courses at Edinburgh and Glasgow abound.

Money Matters: Incredibly strict scale of rules for payment but (Aberdeen, remember) parents can get a two per cent discount if they pay the whole annual whack within a fortnight of the beginning of the autumn term. Discounts of five per cent for second child from pre-school nursery up, and 50 per cent rebate for third and subsequent children. School 'will do what it can to help parents in difficult times, as long as they are open and talk to us'. Can, and will do, 100 per cent bursary if need be.

Remarks: The school is now nearly co-ed throughout: numbers increasing along with the facilities. New lower school came on stream in 2007 and more improvements planned. This is a school on a roll, small enough for every child to be known as an individual and big enough to offer the best in modern teaching methods.

Aldenham School

Linked to Aldenham Preparatory School in the Junior section

Elstree, Borehamwood, Hertfordshire, WD6 3AJ

• Pupils: 450 boys, 110 girls; 50 'proper' boarders (from overseas) + 75 flexi-boarders, rest either day or weekly boarders. • Ages: 11-18 • Size of sixth form: 170 • C of E foundation with ecumenical overtones • Fees: Boarding £25,569; Day £17,583 pa • Independent

Tel: 01923 858 122
Fax: 01923 854 410
Email: admissions@aldenham.com
Website: www.aldenham.com

Headmaster: Since 2006, Mr James Fowler MA PGCE (mid-forties). Previously deputy head at Highgate, before that head of sixth at Brentwood. He grew up in the area, having attended Merchant Taylors, Northwood, so came with a useful understanding of the neighbourhood and likely clientele. A former choral scholar at New College, Oxford – musicians often make decidedly civilised heads; married with two sons. Impresses immediately in an ungrand way. At ease, clearly highly competent and in tune with his school's very particular and, in this area, rare ethos, steadily building on his popular predecessor's short, but effective, tenure. Candid and expansive – a solid, astute head to whom you'd have no hesitation in handing your children.

Academic matters: Not for single-minded scholars nor does the head talk about climbing the league tables. When asked whether he is hoping to 'up the academics' he replies, swiftly, 'If you're asking me whether I want to ensure that all pupils here get the very best out of what we provide, of course I do.' Touché. That said, the academics are good and those who want to get to Oxbridge, and have the brains, will do so. But this is not what Aldenham is about. It takes a broad spread of ability – the fact that most enter at an untestably early age and stay the course more or less ensures that. Later arrivals are refugees from more pressured local schools and come not because of any lack of ability, but because they want school to be about more than that. And it is, here.

Classes are small – we saw, in fact, almost nothing but learning in groups – concentrating faces in friendly fives and sixes. Average class size is 20, down to 11 in the sixth. Setting in maths and science. At GCSE, everyone takes a core of two English, three science, maths, a language, RS, PE and IT, plus options from a predictable list. 65 per cent get A*/B, which is wholly respectable. At A level, a good range of subjects: business and economics popular, as are DT (graphics and resistant materials), media studies, PE, music, music technology and art. In 2010, 54 per cent of exams got A*–B. Latin survives, as does German – hooray!

Around 12 per cent on the learning support register, the vast majority for mild dyspraxia and dyslexia. Two statemented pupils – mild Asperger's – and provides for them sensitively. Excellent learning support area with several little rooms for one-to-one, much used by the 40-odd overseas pupils who receive EAL help. Praise for provision though head not keen to be known as a school 'for' special needs – which it isn't. More could be done to stretch the most able, as head admits and has plans to do so. Value-added achievement is high and much praise in inspection report for the promotion of independent learning.

Games, Options, the Arts: The triumph of Aldenham. The pitches, fields, courts, Astroturf and sports facilities here need to be seen. Over 100 acres of glorious green belt land stretch away, much of them part of the school's playing areas – the rest gently wooded, cottaged or be-cowed in a way that belies the school's actual position inside the M25. Football is main boys' game in the autumn term, for girls netball and hockey in autumn and spring terms. Spring brings hockey for the boys and summer cricket for boys and rounders for girls. Shooting range, cavernous sports hall plus fitness suite, climbing wall – you name it, they've got it, except, yet, for a pool of their own. Lots of options – athletics, tennis, sailing, fives, judo etc ad exhaustionem. Lots of success too, and tours to lovely places – in 2007, 1st XI football to Villareal, in 2008 cricketers to Barbados and a football tour to Deportivo la Coruna. Planning afoot to send girl netballers to Spain soon. CCF returned (after 17 year absence) in 2006 and has become speedily popular, largely because of the trips it offers.

Excellent art – we loved the ceramic skydivers, the Impressionistic line drawings and witty black 'n' red linocut self portraits which greeted us; DT work similarly ingenious – metal sculpture, pottery, textiles, graphics; very colourful work everywhere. Photography popular, as is working on the production of sumptuous school magazine. Music thrives and everyone enthuses, especially about 'house music' – clearly an exciting and important annual occasion. Music housed in the school's former chapel, cleverly built around so that odd bits of beamed roof or column find themselves in the middle of practice rooms or the recital hall. Drama housed in theatre opened in 2006 – on a traditional school hall model, i.e. rectangular, with stage area at one end and stackable raked seating for 130 but allowing for flexible productions and much-enjoyed. Refreshing to see a lively list of recent productions with scarcely a musical among them – One Flew Over the Cuckoo's Nest, Speed the Plow, Our Country's Good, The Taming of the Shrew – along with The Beggar's Opera and, yes, Grease. Someone here cares about real theatre and gets on with it, inspiring others along the way. Good programme of trips and outside speakers. All this activity means that the day school day ends at 5.30pm.

Background and Atmosphere: Founded by Richard Platt, a brewer, in 1597. Queen Elizabeth I granted him letters patent to build 'the Free Grammar School and Almshouses' at Aldenham for elementary pupils. The Brewers' Company thereafter had a controlling interest in the school and links remain strong. In the 19th century, the original Tudor building was demolished and replaced by two new schools – one providing an elementary education for the local population, the other a grammar school for fee-paying boarders. What must then have been a remote location and an unpromising one for pupils from all but local farming families is now in prime, protected green belt with the benefit of plenty of well-heeled local villages, prosperous suburbs and satellite towns from which to draw pupils. The school hit a rocky period a decade or two back and some areas of the campus could still do with renovation and upgrading but, for the most part, the school feels comfortable with itself and on an upward curve. The green belt location means that the school is in what the head calls 'a leafy bubble' and cannot grow any bigger, and is all the better for that.

Huge range of architectural styles – everything from the attractive Old School building (Victorian gothic with gables, tower, turret and crenellations), beautiful post-WWI library, splendid panelled dining room, depressing mid-20th century municipal style brick and pipework blocks and some sensitive recent building with light, air and heart-gladdening colour, e.g. languages and media block. Lots of well-kept gardens – each house has one and the head's garden is a gem. A rather extraordinary chapel – crematorium-like on the outside, started pre-WWII and finished just after – sits over the road that bisects the school. Inside it is vast, white and surprisingly welcoming. School uses it well – e.g. 'chill-out chapel' – and no-one in the school's mixed population withdraws from services. Stanley Spencer was commissioned to paint altarpieces for the building in the late 1950s but horrified everyone by producing a Crucifixion in which he depicted the cross wedged across Cookham High Street 'like a crashed airliner'. The pile of earth in the foreground with the figure of the fainting virgin lying on top was inspired by the pipe-laying operations going on in the High Street. Spencer bemused the boys by telling them, 'I have given the men who are nailing Christ on the cross Brewers' caps, because it is your governors and you who are still nailing Christ to the cross.' The altarpiece was sold to provide much-needed funds in the 1990s and was replaced by a large and striking ironwork cross and dove which is somewhat less disturbing.

Girls have been in the sixth form for ages but arrived in the lower forms in 2003. They now make up a fifth of the school but numbers are growing and the aim is that they should be a third of the school by 2013. They have their own house, as have the lower school children – Martineau's – in which Years 7 and 8 make a gentle transition from the prep to the senior school, while using all the senior school facilities. Boarding houses not de luxe – no basins in rooms and some lower school rooms for three or four not huge – but good games/commonrooms, carpeting throughout, the girls have a terrific kitchen, everyone seems comfortable, the sixth form single rooms are good and a programme of renewal and repainting which is brightening things up. Small school in which everyone knows everyone in a supportive, friendly community.

Pastoral Care and Discipline: Strong pastoral care – parents comment that their children feel 'looked after and safe'. 'The staff take immense care – there is always someone my son can go to. The fact that all the children have a place in a boarding house, even if they don't board, makes for a really friendly, family atmosphere.' House tutor and/or matron always on duty. 'The staff are wonderfully protective – especially of the girls,' we were told. Few 'incidents' and school takes a 'sensible' attitude to alcohol, e.g. a little bar in the sixth form 'club' in which they are allowed a couple of beers two nights a week – something they love and wouldn't abuse. Much freedom for boarders to go out at weekends – with permission. Given this freedom, little need to transgress. Boarding is very flexible for those who want it – an excellent resource for families. 'I stay whenever I can,' more than one misty-eyed pupil told us. Food has 'much improved' and looked good to us. Sensible uniform. Lots of democratic consultation – pupils' opinions sought on all manner of subjects and respected. Busy Saturdays and quiet Sundays with extra EAL for overseas boarders who need it. Optional trips and work with a local disadvantaged school at weekends.

Pupils and Parents: Day pupils can sign up to one of eight useful coach routes; most come from north, or north of, London, as far away as Hampstead or within walking distance. Most live within 20 miles. Lots of first-time buyers, lots of busy, professional London parents who like the boarding/day flexibility uniquely on offer here. Around 10 per cent Asian, five per cent Afro-Caribbean British, around 25 per cent Jewish, fewer Muslims; about a third of boarders from Germany, then from China, Japan, Hong Kong, Austria and a scattering from elsewhere. School does well to mix everyone up and integrate them. Parents who send their children here do so for positive reasons and have taken the trouble to find a school which promotes a broad curriculum and a breadth of extracurricular opportunities in a relaxed environment. 'Balanced' is the word we heard most often from staff, pupils and parents. Notable Old Pupils include General Sir Richard Gale, Commander in Chief, British Army of the Rhine, 1952–1956, Jack de Manio, Dale Winton, Professor Sir Martin Sweeting, Karren Brady, three bishops plus a lot of, mostly legal, worthies.

Entrance: Immense care is taken. Head meets all outside applicants – parents and children; a huge job. Forty-five places offered at 11+ for which 130 apply. Those who don't come from the school's onsite prep (see review) try from around 15 local preps, e.g. St Martin's, Edge Grove, Lochinver, Keble etc. A reference from the pupil's present school is sought and all sit school's own tests in English, maths and reasoning. No CE. If interviewees come along after the tests, head sees them 'blind', i.e. not knowing how they did. At 13+, around 85 apply for the 25–30 places – around five of those offered places likely to be girls. Around 15 in at sixth – many from overseas but must be in tune with what the school is about and achieve at least five C+ at GCSE.

Exit: Around 15 leave after GCSEs – some to schools/colleges nearer home, some to the state sector, a few to employment. Most stay on and leave for a range of universities and courses. The occasional Oxbridge entrant, around half to the newer universities to study business and vocational-based courses, the other half to the likes of Nottingham, Manchester – to study subjects mainly with a career-orientation rather than an academic basis. A few historians, chemists, archaeologists etc. Some to employment and around 10 per cent to gap years.

Money Matters: Good clutch of scholarships and bursaries – academic, musical, arty, technological and sports. Check with school for details.

Remarks: Balance is what you get here – an education and a school life in a balanced and stimulating environment, relaxed, secure and civilised. And in an open and rural-seeming setting that is a barely believable half an hour from London.

Alderley Edge School for Girls

Linked to Alderley Edge School for Girls Junior School in the Junior section

Wilmslow Road, Alderley Edge, Cheshire, SK9 7QE

• Pupils: 605 • Ages: 3-18 • Unified Christian • Fees: £8,995 pa • Independent

Tel: 01625 583 028
Fax: 01625 590 271
Email: schoolmail@aesg.co.uk
Website: www.aesg.info

Head: Since 2009, Mrs Sue Goff MA (mid-fifties). Passionate, forthright and fast talking, the sort of thoroughly good egg any girls' school would want on their team. Russian and French degree from Durham where she rowed for the university, PGCE from Oxford where she rowed for St Hilda's College. Came from deputy headship of Woldingham (qv, RC, boarding), and before that head of languages at Sevenoaks School (qv), to what she describes as 'the ideal school for me, all girls with a church foundation'. Catholic herself, 'it's hugely important to me, I don't ram it down people's throats but it's what made me who I am', and talks of developing the good in each girl, thinking of each as 'God's creation'. Parents say 'she exudes a warmth, yet she's quite a toughie'. Has three grown daughters (and a grand-daughter) and, as part of school's 'joint partnership with home', encourages parents to keep in touch, email and drop in. Tissues on the side in her study bear witness to her listening ear but she's also not afraid to nudge parents 'with the greatest respect' towards strong parenting themselves. Anti, for example, girls spending hours on Facebook, 'what they do at home does have a knock-on effect'. Passionate about enabling each girl to 'go for it; whatever their area of expertise we're about helping the girls really believe in themselves and aim high, about them becoming confident but not arrogant, not to bring glory to the school but so they get what they themselves deserve'. Started at the same time as prep head Mr Groves who she describes as a kindred spirit. Still teaches some French and believes in being 'out there, getting to know the girls, after all it's all about them'. Plays piano, loves music, opera, ballet and dog, Meggy.

Academic matters: No longer just embracing arms under those who slip through other nets at 11+. In 2010, six out of 32 girls achieved the equivalent of at least four As at A level, two of them five As including some A*s, regular 70 per cent results A*–B. Cambridge Pre-U taken alongside A levels. At GCSE over 80 per cent of results are A*–B, over half A*s and As. Almost all RS GCSEs are A* or A grades. The ability profile is above average but the ISI inspection in 2009 also described the educational experience here as outstanding and the curriculum as excellent. Three classes to each year with a maximum promise of 25, and when Year 9 classes overfilled they were divided to form additional group. Some sixth form teaching sets are tiny. From

Year 7, girls conduct self-evaluation and review their own progress. No shortage of computers or study areas with four ICT suites, a library and designated sixth form computer and study rooms under an apex roof with girders and skylights. Setting for maths from Year 7, science from Year 9, 'with plenty of chances to change groups if you do well'. Maths clinic every lunchtime, other subjects on various days and girls say 'the teachers here teach because it's their passion and not just their job'. Eight pupils helped with learning difficulties and head has re-launched gifted and talented scheme.

Games, Options, the Arts: Three all-weather pitches, two large gyms, a verdant sports field and a modern drama and dance studio with mirrored wall. On sports corridor walls motivational quotes undergird photos of the girls playing sport and a photo-wall of fame celebrates diverse individual successes, some at national level, from horse riding and ice skating to dance, squash and tae kwon do. Teams play in Cheshire leagues with netball particularly strong, regularly reaching NW finals, and a keen football team includes a Manchester City youth player. Girls say, 'music here is massive' with several bands, orchestra and choirs. Keyboard suite, lots of girls take singing lessons. Music exams, and success in renowned Alderley Edge Music Festival, celebrated at prize giving in Manchester's Bridgewater Hall. Art displayed everywhere with particularly exciting 3d models outside main art rooms. The head of art, here 28 years, clearly loves the place 'and the girls we turn out are so well rounded'. Separate sixth form art room where each girl has own space. Lots of after school clubs, 'best thing about school' say some girls, trips and exchanges, Comenius European links, DofE, Mock Trial, charity fund raising and links with Kenyan school and women's project.

Background and Atmosphere: Founded in 1999 from the merging of Mount Carmel RC convent school on the present site and the Anglican St Hilary's run by the Woodard Corporation from the south end of the village. AESG now describes itself as an ecumenical unified Christian school with the motto line 'aspire not to have more, but to be more'. Prep school on same site and shares some facilities. Compulsory monthly Eucharist is 'boring' in some girls' books, and they're not afraid to say so, but most accept it happily. Four houses named after saints Emilie, Francis, Joan and Hilary, three chaplains, visiting clergy and rallying assemblies; 'we're not turning them all into nuns but it sets a moral framework and builds positive self-image, esteem and worth,' says head.

Fabulous poster-sized professional photos of the girls at work, rest and play lining every corridor do much the same thing and detract from the uninspiring hotch potch of red brick buildings once you pass the modern front facade. Girls seem happy and relaxed, corridor manners more hurly burly than stuffy. Breakfast available free from 8am and the dining room is a sociable place where younger girls dine first and staff cluster chatting too. Bread and pastries at break for a nominal charge. Sixth form privileges include not queuing for lunch, 'handy on Friday chip day', a wider range of muffins and buns from their own all day coffee bar and a new 'chill out' common room in which to enjoy them, and a natter. An annual highlight for pupils and staff is the house entertainment afternoon, organised by the captains, where everyone performs or backstages.

Pastoral Care and Discipline: Much emphasis on rewarding good behaviour and effort with certificates, letters home and even chocolate. Merit system includes personal and house points; in 2010 14 girls with the most were taken to the ballet and meal out in Manchester by the head. Referral cards for work related and behavioural lapses but 'we have high expectations and don't stand any nonsense'. Big sister scheme teams VI formers with Year 7s while they settle in. Girls describe friendship and 'knowing everyone' as the best thing about AESG, as one sixth former said, 'we genuinely don't want to leave; this is a school where everybody knows your name'. They're not quickly forgotten as a leavers' destination board carries large photos of smiling girls, no pouting here, and inspiriting news of where they are now. Parents agree; 'the pastoral care is great, you can ring them at any time', and 'my daughter's extremely happy there, all the girls are so nice'.

Pupils and Parents: Overwhelmingly white and middle class although there are 21 with English as second language. Not all regular church goers, even small minority from other faiths, 'I've not noticed the Christian stuff,' one parent told us. Neat navy uniforms introduced as a new colour when the two schools merged and girls don't seem to push the boundaries. Instead they look unspoilt and innocently young with minimal make up and jewellery. Girls come from as far as central Manchester and Stoke on Trent, a few who didn't pass Trafford Borough's 11+. Most however, hail from rural local areas, so Cheshire set strongly represented, though as one Mum put it 'there are lots of fat cars in the car park but I'm not the only one who sacrifices to send my daughter here'. Good bus network and near train station, traffic congestion at pick up time.

Entrance: Open to any who are sympathetic to school's ecumenical ethos. By maths, English and verbal reasoning exams, interview and reference looking for a broad band of ability, girls who'll fit in. Has catch-all reputation of not setting bar over dauntingly high although head says school regularly turns away girls 'due to their academic profile not being sufficiently high to cope with our academic curriculum'. Entry higher up school includes science and Language papers. Half Year 7 straight from prep, at home here from the off. Some reduction for siblings. Some automatic academic scholarships, others by application for music, sport and art and a few means-tested bursaries and academic 13+ and sixth form scholarships. School runs taster day for prospective year six girls to really see what it's like.

Exit: Some 75 per cent straight to university and art foundation with Leeds, Manchester Metropolitan University and Sheffield closely followed by Durham and Exeter as top choices. Occasional Oxbridge success. Mix of courses from neuroscience, pharmacy, and French to quantity surveying, media studies and politics. The rest leave for gap years which may include a welcome back at school for post A level uni applications.

Remarks: Charming girls' school just beyond the very southernmost outstretched fingertip of Manchester's conurbation. A new vigour of academic purpose mingles with the strong Christian ethos that so celebrates and values each girl here, urging her on to be all that she can be.

Alexandra Park School

Bidwell Gardens, London, N11 2AZ

• Pupils: 1,400 boys and girls; all day • Ages: 11-18
• Size of sixth form: 340 • Non-denom • State

Tel: 02088 264 880
Fax: 02088 882 236
Email: admin@apsch.org.uk
Website: www.alexandrapark.haringey.sch.uk

Head: Since 2008, Mr Michael McKenzie, (early forties), MSc (Nottingham), PGCE (Institute of Education). Educated at a comprehensive in Birmingham, Mr McKenzie read chemistry at Nottingham, then did his teacher training at The Institute of Education. Head of year at William Ellis School in Camden, head of sixth form at La Swap, followed by deputy and associate head at Beal High School in Redbridge. Familiar and comfortable with the APS ethos before he applied as the founding head had been his teaching mentor. Finds his pupils, 'very entertaining, thoroughly enjoyable' and they (and their parents) feel McKenzie is a relaxed and positive addition. 'He's always about and knows a lot of the kids by name. He's very on the ball,' said one mother. Married, no children.

Academic matters: Alexandra Park's motto is 'Success for All' and the school pulls off the very tricky achievement of being a successful London comprehensive welcoming the full range of abilities and full social spectrum. 'Unlike other schools round here, it doesn't pick and choose. It's very inclusive,' says one parent. The intake may be all-encompassing but the academic values remain traditional. 'We don't play any games with the curriculum,' says the head, and the school is notably strong on core subjects. More than decent results at GCSE (83 per cent A*–C, with 82 per cent in English, 76 per cent in maths and 78 per cent in science reaching the target figure). English GCSE results are in the top percentile nationally as are maths results. Most pupils take 10 GCSEs, including all three sciences. Spanish and French standard languages (and you can take either or both to GCSE), but Turkish also an exam option for GCSE and A level. APS has specialist status as a science and maths school and an international school. More than 200 students last year had the opportunity of studying in partner schools in France, Spain, South Africa and China. Mandarin on the curriculum here and is more than token. Students can spend time on an immersion course in Beijing, with 30 studying the language pre-GCSE, a dozen or so in the sixth form. School also offers a certificate of business studies in Chinese and is considering training up a member of staff to enable Mandarin to become a curriculum subject.

A National Training School, indicating the importance the school places on appointing the best practitioners and ensuring they receive the latest training.

Some setting from Year 7, depending on the department head – so maths and science are setted, English is not. Arts and media studies – unsurprisingly in this heartland of the media classes – are notably good so, to counterbalance the trend, APS has opted for specialism in science and maths, with a dramatic upswing in results. Good vocational curriculum, with BTecs in sport, business, art, salon services, construction crafts, performing arts, health care and catering, some taught at the College of North East London. 'It means children who might have been less engaged have something positive and interesting to do, and those taking academic exams have the space to focus,' says one parent.

Strong gifted and talented programme (12 pupils with all A*s at GCSE in 2010) and G and T pupils take early exams in maths, statistics, astronomy and classics. Also notable SEN support under dynamic head of special needs, with additional support in Year 7 for those who've not yet achieved the requisite level in maths and English. Some parents, however, feel the extreme ends attract the bulk of attention: 'I think it was be quite difficult to get support if your kids come in the middle,' said one. 'You have to be very proactive.' Popular sixth form, now in its fourth year. One hundred per cent pass rate past two years, 71 per cent A–C, Over 50 per cent grades A*–B – putting APS results in top 10 per cent nationally. No minimum benchmark to transfer from GCSE to A level, though those without at least grade C may need to resit. Twenty-seven subjects on offer – strongest include English, French, physics and 'a really happening' history department.

Games, Options, the Arts: Busy, busy, busy. Specialist music and drama with a media suite and dance on offer. Last year's huge, all-encompassing drama production of Hairspray attracted a cast of 250 kids and staff. Energetic visual arts with A levels in photography, art and product design, plus a Creative and Media diploma for those wishing to create large-scale projects. Both BTec and A level music. School choir, with an international schedule. Trips a big feature, with 106 different excursions last year, including a three-week exchange to Beijing, science in South Africa, French in the south of France, art in Spanish in Spain, politics to Washington.

Though relatively limited onsite space for sport, games spill over into adjoining Dunsford Park and plenty of variety to suit all tastes. Basketball, football (Newcastle United striker Nile Ranger used to star in the APS team), cricket, netball are main sports, but judo, aerobics, tennis, badminton, wrestling, rugby and golf also part of the offering (aspiring Nick Faldos can daydream their hole-in-ones gazing out from the classroom onto Muswell Hill golf course). Online student newspaper. Eclectic range of after-school clubs, includes knitting, astronomy, fashion, pursuit cycling, and cheerleading. 'Kids come up with the ideas,' says the head. Good careers advice with visits to unis and higher educational conferences. State-of-the-art sixth form centre, with study centre and purpose-built social space.

Background and Atmosphere: Local parents lobbied the local authority to create a new school in the area and APS was eventually founded on the site of a former FE college. A relatively constricted site, which feels more spacious due to the surrounding greenery of Muswell Hill golf course and Durnsford Park. The original mix of pleasant brick buildings, some from the 1950s, some from the 1980s, have now been joined by a sleek modern extension (winner of a 2006 Civic Trust Award) and the recently finished sixth-form centre. Parents unanimous on the remarkably welcoming atmosphere. 'Everyone from the lady on the gate who checks uniform to the school receptionist makes you feel at home.' Even the police officer seeing kids onto after-school buses does it with a smile. Parents also enthuse about the school's multi-culturalism and inclusiveness 'they really try to be for everybody and genuine concern. It's far more nurturing than some of the other local comprehensives.' But concern is not cosseting. 'My children came from quite a sheltered primary school, but I feel they've learnt to cope with life here and cope with London.'

Pastoral Care and Discipline: Traditional values apply. 'Kids need firm boundaries and it's important for the school to set them,' says the head. 'We expect them to be at school, on time, in uniform, ready to work.' Smart red, grey and black kit is strictly enforced. 'There used to be a gang who wore their uniform in a special way and that's now all ended,' said one parent approvingly. Behaviour in general is good and school hopes to keep it that way by instilling a sense of responsibility. 'We're training pupils to choose to do the right thing.' Misdemeanours promptly and firmly dealt with. 'When my son got into a fight, there was absolutely no messing. They threw the rulebook at him.' Drugs not a notable issue. 'It's bizarre,' says the head, 'at a previous school we had an incident every week. Here perhaps they're more savvy – or more mature.' Weapons, too, conspicuously absent.

Year 7 has their own 'transition manager'. Pupils remain in the same tutor groups for five years with a director of studies for each year. Also supported by learning mentors and counsellors. About 40 pupils with a statement of special needs have mainly cognitive rather than behavioural difficulties and the school copes well with autism, Asperger's and Downs. Communication between parents and schools clearly a strong point. 'All my emails, however trivial, get answered promptly.'

Pupils and Parents: Wide social spread from the comfortable middle-class suburbs near the gates to some of the most deprived kids in the country. 'There is a high proportion on the cusp of social needs.' Middle classes tend to dominate the PTA, which runs endless jumbles sales and bazaars and is strongly involved in the day-to-day running of the school, but the kids themselves mix well. Very supportive parents. 'Parents helped set it up and want to make it work.' The school's popularity has reduced the catchment and the launch of another new school to the east is likely to make the intake more socially homogenous.

Entrance: 1340 applications for 216 places. Usual priority to looked-after children, those with statements of special needs and siblings, then distance from the gates, which is now less than a mile. A bulge from adjoining high-achieving primary Rhodes Avenue, as well as from Bounds Green, Our Lady of Muswell, Bowes, Coldfall and Hollickwood. Majority of existing pupils continue into sixth form. 340 in sixth form; 70 per cent come up from Year 11, the rest from other local schools. Open access, provided courses are available and attendance and attitude good enough. External applicants for A levels should have five GCSES minimum A*–C, with Bs in A level subject choice.

Exit: A few encouraged to leave at GCSE. In sixth form majority apply to university, a good showing at Russell Group, three to Oxbridge in 2010.

Money Matters: Specialist science status brings in extra funding for new science labs and small class teaching in science and maths.

Remarks: A notably welcoming place for children (and adults) from a large swathe of the borough. Not an academic pressure cooker but a school with high standards for all.

Alleyn's School

Linked to Alleyns Junior School in the Junior section

Townley Road, Dulwich, London, SE22 8SU

• Pupils: 585 boys, 585 girls; all day • Ages: 4-18 • Size of sixth form: 305 • C of E • Fees: £11,538-£14,013 pa • Independent

Tel: 020 8557 1500
Fax: 020 8557 1462
Email: registrar@alleyns.org.uk
Website: www.alleyns.org.uk

Headmaster : Since September 2010, Dr Gary Savage MA PhD Cantab (fortyish) a historian of 18th century France. Previously under master at Westminster School, before which ten years teaching at Eton, where his roles included community service coordinator, head of history and housemaster of the Scholars' House. State-educated, he grew up in Suffolk, where he developed his enthusiasm for sport, particularly football, and he remains a loyal supporter of his then local team, Ipswich Town. Married to Natalie, a freelance television and film producer. Has a passion for the arts; enjoys film, theatre, dance and literature. Recently, he has taught himself German and enjoys exploring Germany and discovering German culture. A polymath, we think. 'Generally well thought of and a delight to talk to ... knowledgeable and inspiring,' comment parents. Seemingly, also, popular with past pupils at Westminster who lament 'our loss is definitely a gain for Alleyn's.'

Academic matters: 2010 GCSE students achieved 88 per cent A*/A grades. At A level, 93 per cent got A*/A/Bs, including 75 per cent A*/A grades, and 34 per cent A* – the best result ever by some margin. Everyone takes the three separate sciences for the first five years and then can take them as individual GCSEs or as a dual award. Modern languages now being further developed to allow for enthusiasts to take three at GCSE if they so choose, as well as Latin. Greek still holding its own. This level of opportunity is rare.

Previous head introduced philosophy, politics and psychology which, together with business studies, photography, theatre studies, media studies and RS, get respectable numbers of takers at A level as well as the more traditional subjects. English attracts large numbers and does well. History and geography also among the stars. Good IT suite; school recently upgraded resources here and the use of IT throughout curriculum – though not as a religion. SENs are quickly spotted and well supported – 'We have a brilliant SENCo'. Those who need it get an individual learning support profile (ILSP) . Buzz words here are 'choice', 'opportunity', 'warmth and kindness' – parents speak appreciatively of the opportunities available in all areas of the curriculum.

Games, Options, the Arts: Opportunities for everything. Games are big here but less sporty types are encouraged to do less competitive and intimidating things like fives, swimming, fitness, fencing, contemporary and ballroom dancing, trampolining. Very strong representation at county level in many sports – superb cricket and hockey, and football now very strong. Good pool – 'if they can't swim when they arrive here, we make sure they can by the end of their first year', super huge sports hall, vast range of sports available and teams travel far for fixtures. School buildings spread around good fields; more fields plus an athletics track across the road. This is good provision in a grand suburb with a fair bit of local competition for large open spaces.

Opportunities in other areas: an excellent carousel programme for the first senior school years so everyone has a shot at food technology – they design, cook and eat their own meals and love it, and CDT in metalwork, woodwork and graphic design etc. All taught in small groups. Results are weird, wonderful, clever and exciting. The art – taught in five studios – is astonishingly good – among the most impressively assured and proficient painting we have seen. Music thrives in converted brewery, loads of ensembles of all sizes and types. Recording studio, CDs, tours, concerts large and small, both on site and in grander venues like St John's Smith Square and the Queen Elizabeth Hall. A biennial concert with the two other foundation schools. Drama does remarkably well: splendid new RIBA award-winning Edward Alleyn Building including the state of the art, 350-seat Michael Croft Theatre, a new sixth form study centre with IT suite, a lecture theatre, a university and careers centre, housemasters' and pastoral meeting rooms and café bar. The National Youth Theatre started here and the school has developed the link by providing south-of-the-river rehearsal space.

Over 40 clubs and activities, thriving D of E and CCF – the largest voluntary corps in the country, we're told. Volunteering is busy locally. Loads of trips to everywhere, educational and adventurous, and a good range of language exchanges. Posters advertising interesting speakers from outside make you want to book a seat.

Background and Atmosphere: In 1619 Edward Alleyn, actor and theatre manager, who made most of his money from bear-baiting and who, at the age of 57, married the 19-year-old daughter of John Donne, founded his 'College of God's Gift' in Dulwich. This became Dulwich College, but it had always had a lower school. In 1882, this lower school became a separate educational establishment – the present Alleyn's – moving to the present site in 1887, though continuing to share the same board of governors until 1995. The third school in the Dulwich estate is JAGS – the James Allen's Girls' School – which dates from the mid-19th century. (Don't ask about the missing 'y'!) The schools are a unique triumvirate, dominating independent education in this, mostly prosperous, part of south-east London and providing a rich – sometimes difficult – choice for local parents. Alleyn's is the co-ed one, the first independent school in London to go fully co-ed over 30 years ago, and that is its particular distinction and selling point.

The main building, with its broad, unpretentious, four-storey redbrick façade, on quiet Townley Road, faces chic Dulwich village to the south and newly trendy East Dulwich to the north. Behind is the main site with landscaped quads and recently opened £13.5m Edward Alleyn Building with dramatic glass atrium and walkways. The Derek Fenner library (named after pioneering past head) is terrific – well-run, well-stocked and here, almost uniquely, silent study seemed to mean just that. Sciences taught in a separate block and most subjects have their own teaching areas.

The atmosphere is relaxed, with the feeling of any well-run, mixed comprehensive except that, for the most part, it's in good nick, feels very orderly and well-resourced. Pupils are polite, friendly, articulate. Relations with staff seem open and cooperative. You get the feeling everyone is pleased to be here. Plain and sensible uniform. Good food – vegetarian option and salad bar – served efficiently in huge canteen with separate staff area. Sixth form have their own large common-room with snacks available all day and their own servery at lunchtime so they can maintain their separate space – feels like a university student bar. Hot breakfast available for everyone.

Parents speak warmly of the speed with which most pastoral problems are sorted out, especially in the lower school, of the good communications, excellent SEN support and happy children. The 'fantastic' music and brilliant sports are cited and the caring nature of the staff in general. Some feel that girls go there because of the boys, some feel that girls become cliquey in ways that don't happen in single-sex schools but, for the most part, it's happy families all round.

Pastoral Care and Discipline: Junior school starts at four and school hopes for a nursery before too long. Lower school is for the 11–13 year olds, middle school for the 13–16 year olds and upper school is the sixth form. Lower school is comfortably separate from main school so the youngsters have a haven, but they are in the main building for about half their classes. Everyone has a tutor and, on entering the middle school, also joins a house. In Year 9, heads of houses take over as tutors and establish close relationships with tutees. Also academic tutors from Year 10. Full-time school chaplain. School encourages pupils to be self-reliant and sort out their own problems but support is there if needed. Lower school staff highly praised for 'having it sussed'. Drugs policy clear but seldom needed – supply would mean 'out' and random testing used on rare occasions if felt necessary. Bullying is 'nipped in the bud' very quickly, we're told, and most concur. School says, 'Like any school, we do tread a fine line between allegations being made and evidence of bullying actually taking place. We always take it seriously.' One parent insisted, 'Our son came to Alleyn's after finding himself trapped in a vicious cycle of bullying and low self-esteem at his previous school. The transformation in him at Alleyn's has been quite remarkable.'

Relaxed and orderly atmosphere is fed by the space and fields around the school site – less pressure from a harsh external world means less within. A sense that 'the community values everyone,' School says they have taken a stronger line in matters of uniform and dress code and that we should not mistake their 'relaxed, friendly but purposeful atmosphere' for a lack of discipline. 'Suspensions are used and are presented to all involved with the utmost gravity. The pupil has a responsibility to the wider community of staff, parents and pupils, and therefore their personal conduct and actions must be of the highest standard'.

Pupils and Parents: Strictly co-ed – any imbalance due to 11-year-old girls outperforming boys at 11+ is levelled when more boys than girls arrive at 13. Pupils come from a wide range of socio-economic and ethnic backgrounds, inner and outer London boroughs, nearish bits of Kent. Common denominators are brains and attitude and a relish of the all-round nature of what's on offer here. At 11, around a third of new intake comes from state primaries –

much-admired head of lower school now spends a day a fortnight visiting these schools, telling them about the 58 scholarships and bursaries on offer (current total of 171 scholars and 71 on bursaries) to encourage more applicants. Notable former pupils include actors Julian Glover, Sam West, Nancy Carroll and Jude Law; director Felix Barratt; writers CS Forester and VS Pritchett; surgical scientist Professor the Lord Kakkar; defence systems designer Professor RV Jones; musicians Benjamin Wallfisch and Florence Welch; industrialist Sir Ronald Leach; and banker Sir Keith Whitson.

Entrance: Entry is now automatic from the junior school. Exams taken by all in maths, English and reasoning. A report is requested from the head of the applicant's school and, if they reach a satisfactory standard in the examination, boys and girls are invited for interview. Interview given equal weight – not just the numerically top candidates are chosen. Priority to siblings and 'those with a prior connection'. Over-subscribed, of course. 125 places on offer at 11; four times as many apply. 15 places at 13. Up to 20 places post-GCSE.

Exit: Lots of gap years. Otherwise to as wide a range of courses and destinations as anywhere – medicine at Bristol, Sheffield, Newcastle, Southampton; architecture at Edinburgh, Manchester, Nottingham; English at York, KCL, Leeds; History at Durham, Warwick, Nottingham; various kinds of engineering or IT courses everywhere. 2010 saw 22 to Oxbridge (18 in 2009) and one to Harvard. Given the standard of art here, surprisingly few to art schools – but maybe that's where all the gappers end up.

Money Matters: Benefits both from the Dulwich estates' (£1m) and Saddlers' Company (£250,000) support – both of which fund generously. Scholarships at 11+ and 13+, for which all candidates are automatically considered. More scholarships at 16+ are worth up to a third of fees. Means-tested bursaries at 11+ and 16+ worth up to 100 per cent of fees. Art, music and sports scholarships at different stages worth varying percentages. All worth serious investigation.

Remarks: Who would get on well here? Someone prepared to take part and who has their own opinions, someone happy in a relaxed set-up. Perhaps the most academic, shyer girls will still head for JAGS. For boys the choice depends even more on individual personality. The new head needs to assert himself promptly and make his mark in this highly competitive enclave.

Alton College

Old Odiham Road, Alton, Hampshire, GU34 2LX

• Pupils: 2000 • Ages: 16-19 • Size of sixth form: 1,935 full-time
• Non-denom • State

Tel: 01420 592 200
Fax: 01420 592253
Email: marketing@altoncollege.ac.uk
Website: www.altoncollege.ac.uk

Principal: Since 2004, Ms Jane Machell MA BA PGCE. Educated at Wirral Grammar School for Girls, read Spanish and Iberian studies at Southampton University, master's from Queen's University, Canada and PGCE from Leicester. Came from Brockenhurst College, where she was deputy principal. Before that was a teacher and manager at Queen Mary's College. Has experience as an Ofsted inspector and a wide knowledge and understanding of the post in the education sector. She has three vice principals who keep a beady eye on quality and standards, e.g. through lesson observation, staff self-assessments, teacher training.

Academic matters: An active campus with a very friendly atmosphere. The majority of 16–19 year olds are here for A levels, of which there are many – the variety of subjects is a big draw for many pupils. High pass rates way above world averages and past students in the top 1.5 per cent globally. BTEC National Diplomas, Awards and Certificates are offered in selective subjects offering range of vocational options including engineering, sport and fitness, health and social care, media, IT, business and childcare and even a few GCSEs – handy for retakes. Dazzling Ofsted report – judged outstanding (grade 1) in all five areas inspected in the last two inspections in May 2006 and November 2009. Awarded Beacon College status in 2006.

Psychology the most popular A level subject, but very large numbers do sciences, maths, business studies and history. Few opt for modern languages, but pupils say Spanish is excellent and exam results back this up. Over 100 school trips last year. English department takes pupils on an annual battlefield literature trip. Annual geography trek to South Africa. Fantastic library with loads of study facilities for private work. Huge silent IT centre with wall to wall pupils working at computer screens. Principal is keen to expand engineering facilities – DT and CAD – both for vocational engineering students and for the many mathematicians and physicists who leave to do engineering degrees.

Alton College received Beacon Award for its relationship with Treloar College. Around 36 Treloar students with severe physical disabilities study at Alton while boarding at Treloar, which provides their care, therapy and learning support; they are integrated into mainstream A level classes at Alton. Very wheelchair friendly – awarded a disability access award in recognition of this. Strong learning support for pupils with dyslexia and dyscalculia, also helps with time management etc. Gifted and talented pupils go on leadership courses and attend tutoring sessions for applications to Oxbridge in competitive courses, e.g. medical/veterinary study.

Games, Options, the Arts: Lots available – fine sports hall. Football is strong and teams have toured abroad. Team games, especially basketball and netball, holding their own. Music very strong – excellent examination results, huge range of ensembles including a composers' ensemble and a new music ensemble, a specialist jazz course linked to Trinity College of Music and a rock school regional centre. Also runs two area ensembles for local young musicians – Alton string workshop and Alton area wind orchestra, and the Life Force Festival, a professional concert series linked to education workshops. A large number of public concerts – during the last academic year, The Jazz Factory had a monthly residency at a local pub, whilst students also played at The Anvil, Basingstoke, and the Farnham Festival, where they premiered new pieces by students and staff of the College, and to round the year off, its three jazz ensembles played at the Swanage Jazz Festival.

Art exam results are superb and the department runs art trips to destinations including New York, San Francisco and Beijing. Loads of extra-curricular activities, e.g. the school radio station and magazine, mock trial competitions, D of E and debating. A student recently won the national Audi Young Designer of the Year Award for the 'land-board' he built as part of his DT product design course.

Background and Atmosphere: Alton College was the first purpose-built sixth form in the UK and opened in 1978 under Principal Michael Gray. Under his leadership, it grew from 240 students to 1,640 sixth formers and 1,840 adult students when he retired, but has since grown to over 2,000 in the sixth form. The purpose-built buildings are set out like a university campus and they have won awards for their design. Over £20 million has been invested since 2002 with an explosion of development – a new IT/ library/learning resources centre, sports hall and a fabulous science centre. In 2006, the Michael Gray music and arts centre opened, incorporating teaching and performance studios for art and design, textiles, music and music technology. To deal with the influx of students, the refectory has doubled in size and now offers Fairtrade options. The most recent investment has been £10.3m project for the Berkoff performing arts centre, which was opened by Steven Berkoff and houses dance and drama studios and a fully-equipped theatre. The Austen Building was completed in October 2008 and houses English, humanities and modern foreign languages as well as offering professional media facilities with TV and radio recording studios and editing facilities. There are Ofsted-regulated child-care facilities on site which are very important for some of the students; pupils who are parents can apply for a means-tested grant to cover child-care costs. Students are appreciative of the attractive, grown-up environment which forms the perfect bridge between school and higher education.

Pastoral Care and Discipline: Tutorial programme is well thought out with lots of themed weeks – diversity, health awareness, human rights etc – and projects to focus tutor group discussions. Students' Union is active here – office-holders meet with principal once a week and are able to contribute to making things happen for the students; also runs very successful charity and student events. Students say they value being treated like adults – teachers called by first name, mutual respect, can come and go from campus as they wish, lots of independence, could never go back to sixth form at their old schools. Principal (and parents) see the school as a stepping stone where students have independence, but not too much freedom.

Pupils and Parents: Mostly within a 20 mile radius, but the majority come from local partner schools: Amery Hill, Bohunt, Eggar's, Mill Chase, Perins, The Petersfield School, Robert May's, Weydon, and St Nicholas's, while a high number come from local independent schools. Transport (train and bus) is subsidised and double decker busses bring students to college from far and wide in Hampshire and Surrey. Students travelling in by train can get substantially discounted season tickets. Many families move into the area for the college. Parents mainly ecstatic and kept in the loop via parents' evenings, newsletters and electronic reporting system.

Entrance: Oversubscribed. No catchment area – proximity to the school does not affect your chance of admission. Apply between December and March – but the earlier the better. All pupils interviewed twice – once after application and again after GCSE results. Five A*–C GCSEs required with Bs in subjects to be carried on if sciences or maths. Waiting lists for some specialist courses, e.g. music. Over 20 per cent of pupils come from independent schools.

Exit: Like everything else here, a tapestry, and carefully monitored. Alton provides the best analysis of leavers' destinations of any school or college we have ever visited. So we can tell you that up to 82 per cent of A level leavers go on to higher education; 64 per cent of vocational course leavers do so and 100 per cent of art foundation leavers progress to HE courses. Top university courses are (in this order) art/design, business studies, sport sciences, computer sciences, English, media studies, mathematics, physical sciences. The top universities have been (in order) Brighton, Portsmouth/Southampton, Bournemouth, Kingston and University of Plymouth. Nineteen Oxbridge offers in 2010.

Money Matters: Foundation offers scholarships worth up to £1,000 available in many subjects (including music, art, engineering, English, languages and sport) to high-achieving pupils. The bursary scheme, launched in 2009, is targeted at encouraging academic excellence through the provision of funds for a specific activity or item which a student or their family cannot afford. Two art scholarships worth £250 for talented pupils on one-year art foundation course.

Remarks: High calibre sixth form college where everything is possible. An exciting place to be.

Altrincham Grammar School for Boys

Marlborough Road, Bowdon, Altrincham, Cheshire, WA14 2RS

• Pupils: 1,215 boys; all day • Ages: 11-18 • Size of sixth form: 300 • Non-denom • State

Tel: 0161 928 0858
Fax: 0161 924 3888
Email: trichardson@agsb.co.uk
Website: www.agsb.co.uk

Headmaster: Since 2003, Mr T J Gartside MA (Hons) Edinburgh University (history). (Late forties.) A calm and understated authority who has led school through £4m of grants and development. Staff like him, boys like him, parents also. Fact is, he's thoroughly likeable; approachable, grounded, without airs, graces or spin; hard to know if he's picked up the character of the school or if it mirrors his, but both are 'good sorts'. Was educated and then taught at Hulme Grammar School for Boys so this post was a 'coming home' and, with two children still in school locally, he seems settled. 'Where would I find anything better to move on to? And besides, there are always new exciting opportunities and developments, always new challenges.' So stagnation is not on the agenda. Quietly ambitious;

initial aim was to rival Manchester Grammar School and many would agree the gap has shrunk enough to make deciding between the two at 11 a really tough call, especially for local boys.

Academic matters: Consistently very strong. Last Ofsted peppered with 'excellent' and 'outstanding'. Bumper crop of results in 2010 when 80 per cent of A levels gained A*–B, 22 per cent the new A*, 'that's more than any other local school,' head emphasises. Of GCSEs (and most boys take 11) 73 per cent gained A*/A. All take three sciences, taught in the time most schools give to the GCSE dual science award, many take a language early and boys routinely gain two maths GCSEs as school pilots new syllabus. 'Furthermore' head says 'boys tend to rise to where the bar is set,' and while some parents feel 11 subjects is too many, others are grateful subject choices remain wide at GCSE. Head delights in really good staff in their ability to teach the curriculum with care whilst also enjoying freedom to branch out. Maths and science traditionally strong, Science College status since 2009, with Olympiad and National Challenge success reflecting this. Language College status. French, German, Spanish, Latin, Greek and Chinese in the curriculum, 'and it's not just about the language but the culture too,' say boys. Italian, Arabic and Russian as extras, and a strong community programme of evening classes. Only Greater Manchester school to offer Latin and Greek to A level. Sixth formers praise university application help.

SEN provision responds to needs arising, which are relatively few, mainly dyslexia. Physical access now includes ramps and lifts. Library burbling with activity at lunchtime, no stuffy silence here, instead a happy place and even, on Fridays, live music against the racks of periodicals, quality daily papers, the weekly Spanish El Pais. DVDs to rent, 'and if you take them on Friday you get to keep them for the whole weekend'. 'They're educational,' points out the librarian and, indeed, a few in foreign languages nestle amongst the popular titles.

Games, Options, the Arts: Sports facilities to die for since 'The Grammar' halls and fitness suite opened in 2008 with views over new floodlit Astroturf, four new tennis courts and 16 acres of fields beyond. Used by the community until 10pm and at weekends, during the day Year 11 boys get to lunch behind the plate glass and blue steel. Boys from Year 9 up can use the fitness machines and a trainer puts together fitness plans including programmes to support high level sportsmen. Football and rugby enduringly popular with boys proud to use the Sale Sharks training ground. North of England u13 and u14 champions for tennis. Several England hockey players. Ambitious, 'now we've got the facilities, to become big hitters in the school leagues'. Table tennis also popular.

Parents describe music here as 'excellent' and rejoice, 'it's cool to be musical'. The legendary swing band performed at the 2010 LibDem conference in Liverpool, and both it and the concert band have reached national Festival of Music finals; the swing band won in 2008. Manchester's Hallé Choir recruits here. Private lessons for 12 instruments, strings currently particularly encouraged. No bespoke drama studio, or GCSE, but the acclaimed annual production involves girls from local schools, sometimes in the cast, always in the adoring audience.

Lofty two storey art room and impressive works bedeck corridor walls. Too many clubs for lunchtime and after school, some take place before the day begins. At lunchtime, a fallow classroom is rare though the odd quiet space can still be found. By and large, though, this school teems with life with boys engaged over homework, on some of the 433 networked computers (yes, some doing homework) or in a myriad of clubs. Active charity fund raising, community action opportunities. Younger boys marvel as they reel off lists of what they can make in CDT, chess club meets every day and in a dusty cupboard under the stairs in the tech block, radio club tunes into global conversations, sticking pins triumphantly in a map of the world.

Background and Atmosphere: Approaching its centenary in 2012, the original redbrick buildings at the heart of school lend a solidly traditional air. The corridors, therefore, are narrow. You take your life in your hands entering the sixth form centre as they pour out for lessons. But if you are not trampled underfoot (and we weren't) they are welcoming. Nowhere seems out of bounds; all ages including staff, mix genially together and even Year 8 guides with a visitor trot happily into the hallowed ground of the sixth form common room. This, built in 2006, boasts leather sofas, bistro tables and its own 'servery' where chips and muffins sit unashamed alongside fruit. Sixth form council hopes to introduce a tv news feed here and new ties for the centenary year. Across the corridor, younger boys dine with a smartcard, in no particular order, in the airy Stamford Hall. Packed lunch can be eaten at clubs as well and breakfast is available. New food tech department being built for 2011, and much of today's school is either new or newly refurbished. Links with nearby St Mary's Church for concerts and services. Grant maintained since 1996, now actively considering Academy status.

Pastoral Care and Discipline: Parents describe pastoral care as 'really helpful', one new mum praising school for being pro-active at keeping in touch when her new starter took time to settle. At the other end boys who need, for some reason, to apply to UCAS after they've left seem unreservedly welcomed back for help with that. Discipline falls to much respected senior staff, and parents tell us care is taken to fit the punishment to the crime. 'Compared to the girls' head, Mr Gartside doesn't evoke much fear in the students,' say boys, although a Saturday detention isn't relished. 'Boys can make mistakes,' says head 'the most important thing is that they learn from them'; no histrionics here. Head always in school on Saturdays to support sport and known to be readily available to parents.

Pupils and Parents: Unpretentious, middle class. Sixty per cent from up-market Bowdon, Hale and Altrincham swarming home in green blazers with red trim. 40 per cent from classy Cheshire and the less affluent parts of Trafford borough. A fifth of boys from ethnic minority groups, a third with English as second language, mainly professional families. Ofsted said 'diversity is respected and inclusiveness is celebrated by all' and as well as individual faith groups, school has an inter-faith society called Co-exist. Fair smattering of children of Old Boys. OBs include local Tory MP Graham Brady who lent his voice to the refurbishment grant appeal. Cricketer Paul Allott and Ian Livingstone, creator of Tomb Raider, Lara Croft and Dungeons and Dragons, Games Workshop and Eidos. New IT suite bears his name after substantial donation.

Entrance: Hugely competitive with four applying for each place. Standards are kept high, 'consistent' says head, using own maths, verbal and non-verbal reasoning multiple-choice papers, and a short story, one Saturday in September. Places offered based on bald results, 60 per cent to top local boys, 40 per cent using a wider net. Many are tutored or brought up to scratch in small independent prep schools so playing field isn't level. Head maintains hot-housing won't make the difference (hmm) and counsels against pushing to just pass the threshold and then struggle, and we agree with him there. School does however, strongly advise familiarity with exam content and format and makes example papers available.

Exit: A couple of handfuls leave and join at sixth form. Ninety per cent from sixth form to higher education to a wide variety of courses. Ten per cent to Oxbridge. Vast majority to solid unis; Sheffield, Leeds, Manchester, Birmingham, Warwick and Nottingham top the list.

Remarks: Undoubtedly the top boys' state school for miles. Relaxed and happy in its own skin, AGSB exudes friendly enthusiasm while producing, after seven happy years, polite, can-do young men. Legions of very satisfied parents and no wonder.

Altrincham Grammar School for Girls

Cavendish Road, Bowdon, Altrincham, Cheshire, WA14 2NL

• Pupils: 1,265 girls, all day • Ages: 11-18 • Size of sixth form: 295
• Non-denom • State

Tel: 0161 912 5912
Fax: 0161 941 7400
Email: admin@aggs.trafford.sch.uk
Website: www.aggs.trafford.sch.uk

Headmistress: Since 1999, Mrs Dana Ross-Wawrzynski BSc MSc (applied biochemistry) (fifty-ish). Educated in Scotland, studied at Glasgow and Strathclyde Universities. Twin boys, post MGS, at Cambridge. Friendly, but won't compromise on issues she feels strongly about – e.g. sixth form uniform, taking girls out in term time. Rose through the ranks at a wide variety of schools from inner-city comprehensives to grammar schools, holding two deputy headships before Altrincham.

She is a National Leader of Education and influences educational policy locally and nationally. Last year she was executive head at a north Manchester school and, with other colleagues, helped the school to increase the percentage of pupils with five A*–C grades at GCSE (including English and maths) from 16 per cent to 42.5 per cent. This year she will be advising and supporting other Greater Manchester schools.

School has moved forward during her reign – justly proud of improved results, buildings, technology, particularly proud of positive value-added score, but 'always looking to improve – there is always work to be done'. Wants to produce 'young women who are working and influencing, all over the world'. Quite candid that school has high expectations and one or two girls do not keep pace – 'finding that Altrincham is just not for them, especially in sixth form, when deadlines and pressures do begin to tell'.

Respected by pupils, who are also wary of being stopped in the corridor over a uniform issue or other misdemeanour. Parents broadly pleased with results, but some expect more, and sometimes clash with a head who won't compromise. One parent said of her, 'It's her way or no way!' Head listens to parents' views but, in her words, refuses to over-indulge them at the expense of the overall school. 'We are going to give you and your girls the best that we possibly can, but we won't do everything that you want us to. If parents want to be indulged a little more, that is not for us.'

Academic matters: Up with the best – and local competition is from some excellent independent schools. At GCSE, 87 per cent A*/A; 87 per cent A*/A/B at A level. Expectations from parents and school are high so the work ethic is strong. Average class size 26 for pre-16, usually 16 for sixth form. Setting in maths from Year 8 and in first foreign language from Year 9. Language college since 2002 – French, German and Spanish within the curriculum with other languages offered outside it.

Girls take nine GCSEs including three sciences or double award. Head discourages girls from going for more – 'Better not to overload; best to get eight good ones than 11 not so good'. Girls take four subjects to AS level, three to A level, plus general studies.

Uses a eight-day rolling timetable to ensure lesson hours are apportioned fairly, so maths might be first thing on Monday one week but first thing Wednesday the next. Altrincham girls have to learn to be organised, especially the tiny number with some SEN. Progress closely monitored through learning plans, problems addressed and solutions sought. Informal clinics provided (and used) to help girls get extra help. 'We ensure that no girl will fail due to a lack of support from the school.' Results are important, 'We live in a world where results are the key to the next stage in life'. Harnesses the best of IT but values 'passionate teaching' more. Became DfE training school in 2007, which focuses on training the whole workforce to benefit ultimately the girls' education.

Games, Options, the Arts: Builds on language college status to give girls 'a flavour of what is going on in the world'. Has ties with schools all over Europe and in South Africa, China, South America and Japan, which result in trips, exchanges etc. Not seen as holidays but a way of understanding and learning about other cultures. Exchanges knowledge and techniques with other schools worldwide too. Foreign trips allow girls to 'test their own reserves in a controlled environment'. Typical trips go to France, Iceland, Russia, Germany, India, Canada, South Africa and Japan.

Sport is strong and inclusive. Netball, hockey and gym in winter; tennis, rounders and athletics in summer, from Years 7 to 9, plus dance from Years 7 to 8. Years 10 to 11 are timetabled one general PE lesson per week plus the option of GCSE PE and/or dance. Features regularly in National Schools' finals – currently U16 hockey champions – and girls have represented England in hockey, netball and athletics. Great facilities include two full-size, all-weather hockey pitches and six netball courts, converting to tennis courts in summer. 'I love sport and have found the teachers really, really good.'

Breathtaking list of 70-plus extra-curricular activities. 'If a girl has an interest we will try to help her develop it,' says head. Activities range from art to astrophysics, badminton to birds, figure drawing to flute and running to jazz – you get the picture, with Duke of Edinburgh thrown in. Strong links with the Manchester Literary and Philosophical Society.

Background and Atmosphere: Buildings on three separate sites in affluent Bowdon, separated by relatively busy roads. One of very few northern grammar schools not to go independent. Lots of admirable new building; more to come. The differences in style between traditional and new and the layout of school give an open, varied atmosphere, with each building taking on a character of its own.

Non-denominational but with a Christian ethos. Strict on uniform, which becomes smart business attire in sixth form. 'This might not be popular but it is what we, as an institution, would like our girls to be seen in.' All (staff, school support, governors, parents) are expected to play an active part in the school and their contribution is valued.

Its work as a National Support School is a two-way process. Altrincham Girls' staff are stretched and acquire new knowledge and skills which they bring back into their own departments and classes.

Gained coveted Teaching School status in December 2009. Staff deliver high-quality teaching and learning programmes to their own colleagues and those from other Greater Manchester schools. Has direct impact on lesson delivery.

Pastoral Care and Discipline: Works hard to educate girls and parents on drugs, alcohol and self-harm, and takes great care to avoid girls suffering stress due to pressure of work. Signs of anorexia are carefully watched for. Works on positive ethos – rewards good work to try to eradicate poor work or behaviour. A commendation system encourages self-esteem. Works closely with parents when discipline or standard of work becomes an issue.

Pupils and Parents: Majority white middle class, from South Trafford and Cheshire areas. Around 75 feeders but none linked. Creams off best of catchment area via entrance exams.

Entrance: Tricky – the school is so popular it could be filled many times over; has up to 60 appeals a year. Head's worst job is 'turning children away'. Admissions system part academic, part location. Entrance exam includes maths, verbal and non-verbal reasoning. Girls have to reach a required mark to move on to the location stage (measured in a straight line from the school to the residential home address, see school policy).

Much use of independent prep schools to maximise chances in the entrance exam, and many move house to be within range – with the sibling policy resulting in larger than usual year-on-year variations – the closer the better.

Admission into the sixth form requires six GCSEs, four As and two Bs plus a minimum of Grade B in English language – this applies to internal and external candidates.

Exit: Vast majority to university, including Oxford/Cambridge plus Kings College in London, Imperial College, St Andrews, Manchester, Bristol, London, Sheffield, Liverpool, UCL, Birmingham, Warwick, York, Durham, Leeds and Nottingham. High numbers go into medicine.

Remarks: Uncompromising in its pursuit of the best results for its girls. Some parents might balk at a perceived lack of flexibility over some issues but no-one could dispute that the school does what it says on the tin and turns out well-educated girls with a sackful of qualifications, ready for whatever challenges are ahead.

The American School in London

1 Waverley Place, London, NW8 0NP

• Pupils: 1,350 girls and boys • Ages: K to Grade 12 • Size of sixth form: 465 in High School • Non-demon • Fees: £18,600-£21,700 pa • Independent

Tel: 020 7449 1200
Fax: 020 7449 1350
Email: admissions@asl.org
Website: www.asl.org

Head: Since July 2007, Mrs Corner Hester, Stanford University BAA, MA. Most recently head of Hamlin School in San Francisco for 10 years, she was Gal's high school principal from 1995–1997 when her children, Tyler and Molly, attended the school. Early in her career, Mrs Hester taught English at University Light in Grosser Point, Michigan. Later, she spent ten years at the Brannon School as teacher, dean, college counsellor, assistant head and interim head of school. She was also previously director of the Western Region Educational Services.

This energetic Californian inherited a well-oiled machine in a newly renovated campus. Learning about learning and attention to the programmer will be her priorities. Her ambition is to make the already highly qualified teaching staff even better. Well liked by both staff and kids, Mrs Hester seems to be very much at home and approachable.

Academic matters: You don't have to look at the exam results to understand that academics are king at ASL. Parents expect it to be good and students want it to be the best; they're challenged to achieve their full potential. In the lower school the project approach to learning is used. Classes are no larger than 20 and children are encouraged to take risks and view mistakes as natural learning. Positive self image is fundamental to help students feel good about themselves, their work and their ideas. Italian is taught from K to grade 4. It builds appreciation of other cultures and languages and is integrated into other specialist courses, e.g. PEE.

The middle school programme is designed to nurture the development from childhood to adolescence. Independence and organisation are stressed. High school is definitely preparation for higher education. Lots of options in several subject areas (over 15 AP subjects). The kids like to be pushed, appreciate the variety and feel all the departments are strong, albeit languages aren't always a priority. If a subject isn't available, an independent study class can be arranged. Students are encouraged to assume leadership roles, challenge themselves and take advantage of London. Field trips, not just in London but all over Europe and Africa, are organised to broaden perspectives.

In 2009, 211 students sat 464 AP exams, 63 per cent scored grade 4 and grade 5 (out of a possible 5), and 87 per cent scored grade 3 or above. The average SAT I scores are 640 in critical reading, 643 in maths and 644 in writing (out of a possible 800 in each). 32 SAT II were taken in nine subjects and the averages were in the mid-600s.

Two libraries which are always busy. Computer terminals are all over and all students have computer classes. Grades 7 and 8 are given laptops which they are expected to master. High school students can bring their own or use the many on site. Seventy per cent of the faculty have master's degrees or higher and turnover is very small. They are encouraged and subsidised to pursue professional development. The 2003 strategic plan's primary goal was to hire, retain and compensate the best faculty and staff, and its efforts have paid off. When asked what is the best thing about ASL, the students answered, 'the teachers!'

ASL can handle students with mild learning problems. The specific learning difficulties department (SLD) gives individual support to kids with specific problems and who need a programme to help them develop effective compensatory skills. Spaces are limited – there's an additional fee for the programme. The lower school has a full-time reading specialist who catches problems at Grades 1 and 2. Two speech/language therapists work at the lower school; they see all K1 and K2 classes and they help students through grade 8 with specific language problems.

The English as an Additional Language (EAL) programme helps non-English speakers up to grade 4 come up to speed and eventually integrate into mainstream classes. Intermediate and advanced English speakers are integrated up to grade 10. After that, total fluency is required to handle the rigorous academics.

Games, Options, the Arts: Beautifully framed paintings, drawings and photos done by former students line the wall at ASL. They form part of the school's permanent collection. This sets the tone for the arts. Eight practice rooms are available to the musicians. Photo labs and art studios are full at any given moment of the day. The Annenberg Theatre has been renovated to make it bigger and better for a never-ending schedule of plays and concerts. Middle schoolers all take up an instrument and join the choir. These enthusiastic musicians then take up seats in the bands and orchestras at the high school level. Opportunities are available to travel in Europe with the choir and orchestras.

Sports are important at ASL. At least 85 per cent of high school students play on at least one school team. There are two gyms, 21 acres of playing fields a tube ride away, over 40 high school teams and a huge display case filled with trophies, not to mention the fitness centre open after school. Winning is important but any child who wants to play gets on the team. Students try out for teams in grades 7–12. Teams play other international schools both in the UK and abroad. After school clubs are available at the lower and middle school level.

Special interest clubs are far too many to number – all the usual ones and lots of unusual ones. The PTO funds up to £1,000 for a well-thought-out one-time project put forward by faculty, students or staff. The head has a fund to support the unusual project (a robot building project ended with the club flying to the US to enter the finished machine in a competition).

Every September all high school students participate in the Alternatives Program. They can choose from recreational, academic or cultural activities done over four days. There is always a member of the faculty with the students and it encourages cooperation and social interaction.

Background and Atmosphere: Founded in 1951 for American diplomatic and military children, this central London school uses every inch of its space. Compact cement buildings set on one city block encase the 1,300+ student body. Security is tight with fencing around the perimeters and smart security men keeping a watchful eye on all comings and goings. All students, staff and parents have electronic ID cards for access. The plus side to the fencing is that small outside spaces have been created which have been adapted to different age groups.

Everything is bright and shiny, as the school has recently finished a big development project, adding an extra floor, a new gym, new labs and lots of light. The lower school has a pod centre for each level; classrooms radiate from a central information room housing computers and other teaching tools. The middle school students move around between classes more, and the high school is what you would expect: animated kids rushing around halls, definitely happy to be there.

Middle and high school classes run for 80 minutes with an hour for lunch. The dining room is noisy but controlled with teachers roaming among the tables. Lots of kids bring their lunch but there is a paying cafeteria which is very good. It even has sushi!

An open campus policy for grades 9–12. They can leave the school at lunch or when they have a free period, which causes concern with some parents, but after the first few weeks of school, they pretty much stay on campus. No dress code, but jeans seem to be the uniform of choice. You do see the odd shirt and tie, which means some team is off to an away game.

Pastoral Care and Discipline: Mutual respect and understanding are the call words for ASL. The staff keep an eye out for bullying and catch it early. Lots of preventative work for drugs and drinking is done with specialist classes and workshop; it's better to 'show by example how we want to be, instead of rules about what not to do'. When there are problems, they are looked at case by case. They give the students the benefit of the doubt, 'Good kids can do one stupid thing'. As one student explained, 'You have to work pretty hard to get in trouble.'

Parents have access to teachers through email and reports are sent out regularly. Once a week the parents receive an electronic bulletin with all school news and information. Also a website – parents are given an access code. If a child is having problems, the student support team (SST) reacts very quickly, evaluates the problem, contacts the parents and proposes solutions.

Pupils and Parents: The school may be in London but the tone is definitely American. 63 per cent of the 1,350 students hold US passports, 24 per cent are multi-passport holders and they come from over 40 countries. It seems that no matter what the accent, after a few weeks everyone speaks American.

Lots of 'third culture kids' (parents with different nationalities and raising children in a country not their own), and ex-pats from the finance world. These kids are bright, open-minded and used to change. In the past the turnover was about 20 per cent but, in recent years, it is down to 15 per cent. Families are staying in London longer, so getting a space is more difficult – wait pools at every grade, and even though the admissions office tries to accommodate families, they are not always able to take in all the siblings.

Entrance: Wait pools at all grades. Apply directly to the school. Selection is based on school records, teacher recommendations and standardised test results. Interviews and tours of the school are encouraged. The school is looking for students who are self-motivated, hard-working and open-minded. Community at ASL doesn't just mean students and staff but also parents – they even have their own swipe cards. The PTO helps new arrivals by giving guidance and support. They hold seminars, coffees and a huge array of activities to help both the school and families. They have a newsletter and their own page on the school website. The admissions office helps new parents settle in London and the faculty have lots of experience helping new kids adapt. Since the school has a rolling admission policy, there is always a new kid.

Exit: Most students leaving before graduation do so because of family transfers. The guidance department starts the university preparation work in grade 11 for students and parents. Each student is assigned a college counsellor and meetings are set up through grades 11 and 12. The head of the department wants to make the process as 'human' as possible. Graduates go on to all the big and little Ivy League schools, as well as the major state universities.

Money Matters: ASL is a non-profit, independent American school. Fees cover 95 per cent of what is needed with the remainder covered by annual fundraising. Fees include textbooks, lab fees, all required activities, including Alternatives, and laptops for grades 7 and 8. Not included are music tours for band, orchestra and choir members; language trips; and grade 6 overseas social studies trip. Extracurricular activities such as athletics or Model UN are not included. Needs based financial aid is available.

Remarks: Head spoke about 'striving for the best in American education' in her opening letter to the parents. Well, this school isn't far from that. The tools and facilities available are excellent, attitudes are positive and results are good. Bright, curious, hard-working kids do well here, and those who are in the middle of the road end up surprising their parents. As one student said, 'Going to ASL is better than a vacation.'

Ampleforth College

Linked to Saint Martins Ampleforth in the Junior section

Ampleforth, York, North Yorkshire, YO62 4ER

• Pupils: 615, girls and boys • Ages: 13-18 • Size of sixth form: 270 • RC (Benedictine), but not all are • Fees: Boarding £27,375; Day £17,265 pa • Independent

Tel: 01439 766 000
Fax: 01439 788 330
Email: rf@ampleforth.org.uk
Website: www.college.ampleforth.org.uk

Headmaster: Since 2004, Fr Gabriel Everitt MA DPhil (fifty). Educated at Dundee High School, read history at Edinburgh, then Oxford (first in theology, doctorate in medieval history); ordained Anglican curate, converted 1989, joined Ampleforth community 1990, ordained 1994. Successively head of Christian theology, housemaster of two houses, third master 2000. A gentle, thoughtful and candid man, excellent listener, very bright and clear-sighted about how he believes the school should develop. Benedictine values fit him as neatly as his habit, which must partly account for the sense of shared purpose current in the school.

Academic matters: Top of the Catholic league but is proud of non-élitist intake – from A stream scholars to IQs around 100 who get extra help with English and maths. Ninety per cent of the slowest workers get three A levels, which bears out the college's mission statement, in fact an extract from the Rule of St Benedict: 'The strong should have something to strive for and the weak nothing to run from.' 'They never discard,' says a parent. 'The pupils gain self-respect, the staff have an ability to unlock potential.' Fr Gabriel prudently adds that sometimes pupils cannot or will not cope, and 'We try to reach an agreement with parents about them leaving'. Overall aim is everyone to fulfil, and preferably exceed, their academic ability. The most able are challenged by membership of an unashamedly intellectual discussion club.

Core curriculum plus Christian theology throughout, Latin and Greek too. Half GCSE year takes separate sciences, half (of all abilities) double award. Own English literature exam instead of GCSE makes higher academic demands. Humanities traditionally have more takers and the edge at A level but maths and science continue to strengthen (£4.2m science centre opened in 2000). English very strong (most get A or B); history and Christian theology regularly successful. Twenty-five per cent of staff are female, 12 per cent monks.

Dyslexics taught 'for the most part' in main stream; additional specialist one-to-one teaching available. EAL provision for pupils whose first language isn't English.

Games, Options, the Arts: Traditionally powerful games school (games are compulsory). Very strong first XV, feared throughout the north. John Liley (Leicester and England) recently appointed as director of rugby. Recent cricket tour to Barbados, cross-country, hockey (new Astroturf area), netball (recent tour to Malta), lacrosse, athletics (own track), squash, golf (own nine-hole course), fly-fishing, renowned, independently-owned beagle pack, shooting (brace of pheasants recently spotted hanging on coathanger outside boarding cubicle). Phenomenal 20 rugby sides – 'we want wide participation in school teams', ten cricket sides, eight tennis teams, and so on. Sports hall, with plans for £1.5m extension, 25-metre pool. Strong DT and art (centre includes photography and electronics). Excellent drama (three recent Oscar winners are OAs). Voluntary CCF and D of E flourish. Music outstanding – Schola Cantorum choir tours regularly, singing in Catholic and Anglican cathedrals, also impressive girls' Schola Puellarum. Talented chamber music group. Annual pilgrimage for seniors to Lourdes. Own charity, run by students, raised funds to build school in Nepal and to sponsor East European students in school's sixth form. Also several other eye-openingly worthwhile international projects.

Background and Atmosphere: Founded 1802. Magnificent setting in 3,000 acres of lovely Yorkshire valley, very calming to the soul. Though fairly remote it is, 'in fact easy to reach – with some determination – from all parts of the country and world'. Fast trains London-York take about

1 hour 45 minutes. Beautiful Victorian Gothic main wing plus Giles Gilbert Scott's huge abbey church and school buildings (1930s), with late 1980s additions and much recent building, classrooms and boarding houses. 'The Benedictines have joined forces with the Holiday Inn,' commented an architect; the school observes that other views are possible! Huge central hall, 'rather like a liner,' commented one pupil. £20m spent in recent years on improving facilities.

Houses vary considerably in character, with deliberate spread of ability – seven for boys and three for girls, the latter run by married housemistresses. Girls originally in sixth, co-education now growing throughout school; transition seems to have been remarkably smooth, girls claim to be happy with their lot. Three boys' houses run by monks; all lay-run houses have monk chaplains. Some boys' houses still a bit tatty but scheduled for improvement. School keeps in touch with outside world through excellent lecture programme and far-away projects, e.g. Chile and E Europe. No exeats except for one in winter term, otherwise half-terms. Handy list of local hotels, restaurants and B&Bs sent to parents in very comprehensive booklet, *Your Questions Answered.* (Publicity and information generally of a very high standard, giving off an air of thoughtful competence and understanding of parental concerns.) Not unknown for parents to rent a local cottage during their child's time at Ampleforth.

Warmth of hospitality legendary – 'part of the Rule of St Benedict is to welcome guests as Christ welcomed his'. Central feeding now in operation, but pupils sit by houses. The Ampleforth community was part of a 2003 fly-on-the-wall documentary, 'My Teacher's a Monk', which pushed up parental enquiries. 'It looked too much like a holiday camp,' says Fr Gabriel. 'There was much more purposeful activity going on than appeared.'

Pastoral Care and Discipline: Consciences worked on rather than harsh restrictions imposed, all with the aim of turning students into responsible adults. At the same time, says Fr Gabriel, 'this means clear structure and boundaries; St Benedict was not lax'. See the useful booklet on promoting good behaviour. 'They have it absolutely right,' says a parent. 'It's no good succeeding in life if you fail yourself.' Bad language censored – 'They see tennis stars disputing and footballers spitting; we ask for different standards'.

School and monastery handled recent sensational publicity about past abuse cases with deftness and humility; there is a thorough child protection policy now in force. Parents commend the monks for being priests and friends, especially with academic or social strugglers. 'In return, there is a loyalty from pupils, who return to the abbey to be married and have their children christened.' New development is a central chaplaincy, to foster initiatives in keeping with Benedictine character of school. No uniform, but dress code of jacket and black trousers for boys and black skirts or trousers for girls.

Pupils and Parents: From all over the country plus abroad. Scions of top and middle Catholic families (80 per cent); the rest mainly Anglican, but special welcome for orthodox. Old Boys include Rupert Everett, Hugo Young, Lord Tugendhat, Lord Nolan, Sir Anthony Bamford (JCB), Michael Ancram, Sir Anthony Gormley, Lawrence Dallaglio.

Entrance: Common entrance, or school test, and interview. Exceptions 'for faith or family', but no one admitted if he or she won't be able to cope with curriculum – even from St Martin's Ampleforth (rare). Sixth form entry: at least five GCSEs at B or above. Non-Catholics expected to take full part in school's religious life; to be willing to explore their own faith, and to 'delight in virtue'.

Exit: Ninety per cent to university, on average 10 per cent to Oxbridge (which is pretty good, given the school's entry policy).

Money Matters: Generous financial help. Academic, music and all-rounder scholarships. Nearly 13 per cent receive means-tested bursary help. In last two years, 22 pupils have attained scholar status after entry.

Remarks: Unfailingly civilised and understanding top co-educational boarding Catholic school that has suffered from time to time as a result of its long liberal tradition. Things have been tightened up, without losing sight of its essential nature. Advent of girls a good thing for all – development plan aims to reach the standard (for co-ed independent schools) 40 per cent girls. A refreshing openness and honesty about the place these days – though they still go into mourning when the first XV loses. It has been said that people who leave Ampleforth take with them a 'compass for life', a personal direction finder, which allows them to hold on to their moral bearings.

Anglo European School

Willow Green, Ingatestone, Essex, CM4 0DJ

• Pupils: 1,350 boys and girls • Ages: 11-18 • Size of sixth form: 300
• Non-denom • State

Tel: 01277 354 018
Fax: 01277 355 623
Email: enquiries@aesessex.co.uk
Website: www.aesessex.co.uk

Co-headteachers: Since 2005, Mr David Barrs and Mrs Jill Martin. David Barrs MA BEd (Hons) Cert Ed NPQH (fifties) was educated at London and Bristol Universities and St Paul's College, Cheltenham. Has taught in Basildon and Saffron Walden and was joint deputy head here from 1994–2005. Interests include the United Nations and international affairs, cricket and golf. Jill Martin BA NPQH (fifties) was educated at Liverpool University and was joint deputy head here from 1994–2005. Interests include saxophone and piano, reading and gardening.

Academic matters: This is a state comprehensive with about a third of pupils from families with strong overseas links. It was the first British state school to offer the International Baccalaureate (1977) and the first to become a language college (1995). Everyone studies French and German from Year 7 and can add Russian, Spanish, Italian, Mandarin or Japanese in Year 9. Nearly everyone takes two languages other than English at GCSE since this is an expectation. In the thriving Section Bilingue, geography and history are taught in French and German. Extensive study visits: nearly all Year 7s visit Belgium for two weeks, and there are two-week exchanges available for the other year groups. Year 10 pupils can spend four weeks in Reims or eight weeks in Frankfurt.

Good GCSE results in 2010 with 69 per cent obtaining five A*–C grades including mathematics and English; as one would expect language results are very good across the age and ability range. The sixth form was rated outstanding. The school offers the IB and A levels. Many students take a mixture. The IB tends to attract the academically stronger students and results are above the world average. All sixth form students are required to study a language at a variety of levels. In 2010 the average points score was equivalent to ABB at A level.

The school has accommodated children with cerebral palsy and sight and hearing impairments as well as the more usual learning difficulties. 'We have a very positive attitude towards students and staff with disabilities.' The extensive overseas visits can be challenging for children with special needs, 'but we try to make reasonable adjustments. Some people think that if you've got special needs you can't learn languages – we do not accept that. Plenty of our children with learning difficulties are bi- or tri-lingual'.

There are 77 languages spoken in the school. Those for whom English is not their first language are well supported. 'We will try to find someone who speaks the same language: for example, a Russian pupil could communicate with one from Afghanistan who also speaks Russian. We try to foster learning from each other.'

Games, Options, the Arts: All the usual sports, including badminton, trampoline and dance; three inter-house competitions every year, fixtures against other schools and a very successful and inclusive sports day at the local athletics stadium. PE is an option at GCSE and A level but all students must take part in it – if they have any permanent or temporary handicap the curriculum will be adjusted to meet their needs. Excellent indoor facilities and a wide range of sports clubs, plus partnership agreements with local trampolining, tennis and tae kwon do clubs.

Good performing arts, with enthusiastic school musicals and talent shows including an annual Eisteddfod and a large subsidised peripatetic music programme. A wide range of music, drama and sports clubs. Everyone in the sixth form takes part in the IB creativity, action and service programme, which can include helping younger pupils who have special needs, organising a Christmas party for local elderly people and teaching sport in primary schools.

But the raison d'être of the school is the international dimension. 'International awareness is at the very heart of education,' says the school website. It has 19 partner schools in Europe and further afield including three in China; around 600 pupils travel abroad with the school each year; older pupils represent other countries at annual Model United Nations events; citizenship classes lead to the Diplôme du Citoyen award. Sixth formers take part in international conferences; art visits to Paris and Amsterdam, business studies visits to the Czech Republic, World Challenge expeditions to Peru, Argentina, Thailand, Cambodia and Namibia. The school is a corporate member of Amnesty International.

Background and Atmosphere: Opened in 1973 in this small Essex village on the site of a secondary modern, which the local authority had been determined to close. A committee campaigned to keep a school in the village, and as Britain joined the Common Market, and employers such as Marconi brought international families into the area, there was pressure to set up a school with a European outlook. It opened with 180 pupils from the old secondary modern and another 180 new pupils in Year 7, and was founded with the idea that children of different cultures should be able to work harmoniously together. 'We're about respecting other people's cultures including their own. Most importantly, our children learn to become decent human beings.' Ofsted commented: 'The emphasis the school gives to personal development ... has an exceptional impact on its students, who are confident, articulate and aware of their responsibilities to both the school community and the wider community.'

Pastoral Care and Discipline: Relaxed atmosphere with good relationships between staff and students. With such a large school in a small suburban village tensions are inevitable, but the school is proactive and believes it has positive relationships with its immediate community. Bullying can occur but is dealt with firmly and is not a significant problem. High standards are set and reinforced.

Pupils and Parents: Local children rub shoulders with children from virtually all parts of the world. Pupils travel from London by train and elsewhere in Essex by bus or train. They tend to be mature, articulate and pleased to be at the school. Partnership with parents is an important priority.

Entrance: Local children living in the parishes of Ingatestone, Mountnessing and Margaretting get priority, then siblings. All the other categories involve children 'who have been strongly and positively influenced by a different culture and language other than English'. These include having lived abroad for some time and parents who promote language learning. Broadly, a holiday home in Spain or cousins in Australia won't count. 'We're trying to identify parents likely to support the ethos of the school rather than those who are just looking for a school that gets excellent exam results.' Applicants: 651 for 210 Year 7 places in 2009. Children are offered places according to the international criteria on the basis of a points score.

Entry to the sixth form is more straightforward, with varying minimum requirements depending on courses to be studied. However, it is likely that an admissions policy will need to be introduced as the popularity and success of the sixth form grows.

Exit: Around 60 per cent go through to the sixth form. Most of these go on to higher education, with science, engineering and medicine amongst the most popular degree subjects. Other popular subjects include languages, politics, international relations and law. At the end of Year 11 those not in employment, education or training (NEETS) have numbered zero for the past four years, which the school is very proud about.

Remarks: Exciting, successful state comprehensive with an international dimension and unusual commitment to language learning, in an unlikely situation in a small Essex village. Just the place to broaden your child's outlook on life.

The Angmering School

Station Road, Angmering, Littlehampton, West Sussex, BN16 4HH

• Pupils: 1,150 boys and girls, all day • Ages: 11-18 • Size of sixth form: 165 and rising • Non-denom • State

Tel: 01903 772 351
Fax: 01903 850 752
Email: office@angmering.w-sussex.sch.uk
Website: www.angmeringschool.co.uk

Head: Since 2003, Mr David Brixey BSc NPQH (mid-fifties), who was previously deputy head and then acting head. A chemical engineering graduate, taught in two schools in Bolton before returning to his roots in the south. A serious, dedicated and pragmatic head, immensely ably supported by his deputy, Ms Geraldine Tisdall, who has vast experience in SEN and whose responsibility the onsite Lavinia Norfolk Centre (LNC) was. As deputy head it continues to be her responsibility. Both impress by virtue of their commitment, both to each individual child and to the school community as a whole. They answer every question with reference to the need of this or that individual which they have striven to meet. Both believe in total inclusiveness and a sense here, as one parent told us, that 'anything an able-bodied child wants to do they make sure the disabled children can do too. Whatever is going on, they can join in'.

Academic matters: This is a mainstream specialist sports and science comprehensive and its results are pretty mainstream too. A levels – in 20 predictable subjects – included predictably popular options like media studies, IT and sport studies, with most results respectably in the B-D range but increasingly A grades. English literature also popular with a spread of results from A-D, with more at the upper end. Psychology and sociology are options but languages again showing real strengths with groups in both French and German in collaboration with the partner secondary school. At GCSE, PE is also compulsory and everyone, yes everyone, finds four sports they can do. BTecs in e.g. sport and art and design; food technology is popular. Sports Young Apprenticeships enable some to do sport-related topics for more than half their week. College day courses are increasingly popular and enhance the offer.

GCSEs are more interesting. Dance is big here and the takers achieve highly. Results in French and German are a decent spread; most results in maths, English, science (double) and IT are in the B–D range but an impressive number got A*/A in English. Some 48 per cent achieve A*–C in five or more subjects including maths and English. School recently achieved a second specialism in science and is making links with local schools, pioneering ways of developing scientific thought – holds a science fair for parents each term. Library is excellent – well-stocked and well-run and we encountered a reading lesson, silent despite fierce summer heat and mowing noises outside.

For a truly comprehensive intake with a far higher proportion of children with some kind of SEN than in most schools, these results are not unimpressive. Mr Brixey's aim is clearly to up his pupils' academic aspirations and performance. 'I want us to be in the top 25 per cent nationally when value-added is taken into consideration,' he says. Support for the very able includes 'twilight' languages, ICT, sports, dance and science clubs. Languages are well-supported, which makes the relative lack of take up at A level disappointing. The school works with local primaries to develop KS2 language work, it offers both French and German in Year 7 and pupils with learning difficulties or deafness are taught French in helpfully small groups. British Sign Language is offered as an alternative language from Year 8 both as an academic option and as a club.

Under Ms Tisdall's aegis, an occupational therapist assesses individuals' needs and every effort is made to find what will best enable children to learn. Special hard and software with, for example, predictive text; voice-activated software where needed, videos/DVDs with subtitles and laptops for KS4 students. The SEN department is huge – with lots of specialisms, 30 LSAs everywhere work with everyone, as needed, many can sign; physio comes four times weekly, a speech and language therapist and counsellors and school buys in extra skills when needed. Some students spend 3 years or more in Years 12–13, learning life skills, art and sports. No typical SEN student here. Twenty with a hearing impairment, more than forty with severe physical disabilities, some with ADHD and mild to moderate ASD, plenty of dyslexics. Emotional and behavioural problems are understood and supported in a special centre – an attitude of 'no problem if children can't always cope with lessons or with teachers they're not used to'.

We enjoyed a round table 'back-up' session with two cheery LSAs and seven children – some with physical disabilities and some with ASD or behavioural problems – all working on their own assignments and chatting constructively together. Relaxed, safe, collaborative, orderly. Mostly, however, children are included in mainstream classes. As a parent told us, 'they need to learn to help each other. Society has a wide variety of people and it should be in school as well.'

Games, Options, the Arts: Unusually well-provided for with playing fields, monster sports hall, gym, courts etc and fitness suite used by everyone – though no Astro. This is a specialist sports college with a gold Sportsmark. Inclusiveness is in the fabric with the children with disabilities encouraged to be fit and compete along with the rest. So many become expert in, e.g. wheelchair hockey – handbikes for racing and pictures of Dame Tanni pour encourager les autres. Sport for physically disabled pupils is seen as entirely natural here and school is busily developing hopefuls for the Paralympics. 'We are pushing them to try different things so we can identify their talents.' An excellent hydropool, and a dance troupe for the able-bodied and disabled together practises in very good, dedicated studio. The school needs and is now fund-raising for an adapted indoor sports facility for disabled. Lots of activities include visits from the Royal Engineers, who take leadership and construction courses.

Art and DT are strong here – we saw beautiful screen prints, lively ceramics, impressive graphics (airline food packaging) and bold, colourful painting. Product design and systems controls are options and we enjoyed some super models – Brighton and Hove FC's stadium and a cool and delicate sculpture garden. Woodwork and metalwork well-provided for. School won Artsmark Gold in 2006. Music – well, guitar – is popular but also lots of keyboards and music technology facilities, recording studio etc. Orchestral instruments make do without an orchestra and mostly perform solo at concerts. Range of clubs includes 'Eco-gangsters', which endeavours to greenify the school community – litter has now lost the fight.

Background and Atmosphere: School set in quiet, Sussex coast, village of Angmering but takes from quite a large, mixed catchment. Many children walk across the fields to school and most from tight local communities. School buildings are mostly low-rise, 1970s functional and no-one would be inspired to take up architecture by spending their formative years here. A new two-storey block is being built, however, so that huts will finally go. Estates Manager, Steve Jackson, has revolutionised the site, removing litter, re-naming blocks and signposting as well as improving general maintenance. A new sixth form and IT centre opened in September 2010; functional canteen with healthy eating drive and salads/fruit available and burgers and chips are now strictly rationed. Increasing numbers of students eating there.

The Lavinia Norfolk Centre, named for the late Duchess of Norfolk, a much-loved and much respected supporter of, inter alia, riding for the disabled, is central and houses the various support areas and facilities for pupils with SEN. It is a recent addition, with some automatic doors and the fitness suite. It feels a little cramped but is clearly a valued and unique resort and resource. It is situated next to the car park and on the main route into the school and we were disturbed by the number of parents determined, it seemed, to up the numbers of the physically disabled by the speed with which they drove round to drop their own offspring. More and fiercer speed bumps have been added and a very useful large pick-up area for adapted transport, to keep students safer.

Policy of 'looking at each child as an individual' has resulted in adaptations of all kinds, e.g. very high or very low loos, lots of loos for the disabled around, and even, if needed, special beds or chairs in strategic places, and recently some new hoists on tracking to save staff backs. School raising funds when we visited, and continue to do so, to buy wheelchairs actually suited to the pupils' needs – not the standard issue types (cheques welcome!) – 'we want these children to go at least as fast as their peers'. Disability sport is now a real strength of the school. Parents full of praise for the staff – 'I like the fact that they have the same tutor – someone they can bond with – all through'; 'Aall the teachers are fantastic'; 'if you want to speak to someone they're always there'; 'my son had all kinds of problems and we had lots of good support'. General feeling is that the children based in the LNC are entirely integrated into the school, though some niggles among the rest that 'they get away with things we never would' and can be over-privileged. Bless!

Pastoral Care and Discipline: Overall, an orderly, well-run community and problems inherent in the local community which used to find their way into school are dealt with by the Police Support Officer, so less 'leakage' of outside behaviours into school. Mr Brixey will go to the police if drug dealing or theft – on or off-site – is suspected and it's 'something we're continuously working on'. Permanent exclusion almost certain for dealing – no such exclusions for use necessary for several years. Pupils based in the LNC not perceived as targets for bullying, though feuds begun outside school hard to keep under inside. 'Bully-box' system of anonymous reporting helps, as does a new dedicated mobile phone. Electronic tagging system to track the few with behavioural problems who are thought to need it. Atmosphere seemed to us cheerfully collaborative, combative and healthy. You'd not be coddled here but would learn robustness and to take responsibility for yourself and belongings.

Pupils and Parents: A large school with a fairly balanced intake – slightly more boys than girls. Pupils come from tiny local primaries to larger three-form entry juniors. SEN pupils from a far wider catchment. Significant number from 'social housing' but also from leafy lanes with large detached houses. As mixed as you can get except that practically everyone is white. Parents helping raise funds for a variety of extras.

Entrance: Over-subscribed and dealt with by the local authority. Priority given to SEN applicants though numbers necessarily limited. Very little local choice at this level – an explosion in local new-build, and this and the nearest competitors have been bursting at the seams, although numbers are now falling overall. When is West Sussex or Schools for the Future going to, at the least, rebuild this school? A first step is the new specially-designed sixth form centre and six new classrooms replacing outdated hutted accommodation, which opened in September 2010.

Exit: Just over half leave post-GCSE, mostly for further education, the rest leave at 18 – around three-fifths to university/college, the rest to employment. In recent years, all who applied for university achieved a place.

Money Matters: Local authority funded school with additional funding for planned places for students with physical and sensory disabilities and formula – funded SEN for the rest. Hope that's clear. As yet no specific funding for students with ASD but the school has put in place a very good support structure for these students.

Remarks: A sound and solid school trying its best for its mainstream pupils. An exceptional opportunity for those with a range of SENs who want a mainstream school but who might, elsewhere, be offered only special education. 'We fail on some, but it's nice when we succeed,' says Ms Tisdall. If they do fail, it's not for want of trying.

Archbishop Tenison's School

Linked to North Lambeth Sixth Form Centre

55 Kennington Oval, London, SE11 5SR

• Pupils: 515 boys, all day • Ages: 11-18 • Size of sixth form: 200 boys and girls across 3 sites of North Lambeth Sixth Form Centre consortium • C of E • State

Tel: 020 7735 3771
Fax: 020 7793 8519
Email: school@ats.lambeth.sch.uk
Website: www.tenisons.com

Head: Since 2006, Mrs Elizabeth Sims BEd MA, (early fifties) married with two grown-up sons. Prior to her headship at Archbishop Tenison's she was deputy head at St Saviours and St Olave's. Mrs Sims is a committed Christian and promotes a caring Christian ethos throughout the school. Her interests include reading and politics.

Academic matters: Some 78 per cent got 5+ grades A*–C in 2010, 63 per cent of those include English and maths. This may be a medium achievement nationally but it is a steady and impressive improvement for Archbishop Tenison's. Girls admitted to sixth form, which is part of the North Lambeth consortium. The school has been cited as an example of good practice in a Lambeth report on Raising Achievement of Black Caribbean Pupils.

Pupils tested on entry to school for cognitive ability and banded into three streams. Class sizes are 29, and 22 for those who need most support. 20 per cent of pupils have SEN and are either provided with a classroom assistant or LSA in class or withdrawn to a specialist classroom. Those deemed gifted, talented and able (about 25 per cent of each year) learn science as three separate subjects. Everyone starts GCSE courses in Year 9. French is timetabled and Spanish run as a taster course. The extended day gives an extra period of learning for the smartest and plenty are keen to take up to 13 GCSEs – including Latin. Not surprisingly RS and art are very strong here – the school received specialist arts college status in 2004 and has a fantastic new sky-lit art studio. Strong links with galleries such as Tate Modern, Dulwich Picture Gallery, Gasworks and the Saatchi Gallery encourage a practical outlook on the art world.

All classrooms have interactive whiteboards and the pupil to computer ratio is about 4:1. Well-equipped DT rooms are popular and great results emerge from them. The library is open and staff are available for homework support until 4.30pm. Learning is broadened through carefully budgeted school trips.

Games, Options, the Arts: A game of football starts in the playground as soon as the first two children arrive (about 7.30am)! A rooftop fitness suite with sparkling machines is well used and the gym enables on-site PE and basketball practice. Rugby players, athletes and tennis players take the train to the playing fields in Motspur Park, there's swimming at the Shell Centre pool in Waterloo and the connections with the Oval over the road encourage cricket.

Termly drama productions and music performances; the school choir sings at a number of venues round the borough. Soloists often replace recorded music in the daily assemblies. Individual music lessons are greatly subsidised and bursaries awarded to pupils who gain grade two on any instrument. Band and choir practice, guitar ensemble and coursework coaching all take place in after-school clubs.

Public speaking encouraged with in-school debates and practical external successes – a recent presentation of a travel plan to Transport for London and a brief to a parliamentary committee on the needs of street-children in the Democratic Republic of Congo for the charity War Child; the latter resulted in pupil awards for citizenship from John Moores University and four recommendations being carried out by Lord Alton! The school's involvement with War Child began during 2005's Make Poverty History campaign and continues with sixth form help on the development of its website. Locally, an outreach campaign involves pupils with a primary school, special school and a Golden Years group – documented by an impressive student shot and edited DVD.

Background and Atmosphere: Founded in 1685 in St Martin-in-the-Fields by the Archbishop of Canterbury, moved to its site opposite The Oval cricket ground in 1929. Boys pour through the gates up to an hour before school and a member of staff checks their appearance – blue blazer for the juniors, black for the seniors. Plain silk ties for prefects and sixth form wear their own smart clothes. No jewellery, no trainers and no hats allowed in school. You can spot the boys with their badged school bags on trains, buses and bikes heading into the Oval – a different coloured crest signifies a different year. This smart uniform and the school's emphasis on polite behaviour has made a real difference to its local reputation.

The boys are respectful and file silently into well-planned assemblies where class members take turns to light the peace candle – this ritual was initiated 'after 9/11 to remind us to be peaceful in all that we say and all that we do'.

Young staff with a low turnover and emphasis on training (inset days and help from the Southwark Diocese Board of Education) ensure a sense of stability; the size of the school (92 intake each year) encourages a family atmosphere and this is helped by all catering and cleaning staff being on the payroll. The dining room with its healthy food is a gathering point for younger boys; no fizzy drinks, chocolate or crisps allowed and there are no vending machines on site.

Pastoral Care and Discipline: Parents and teachers use homework diaries and one target is set for every subject with three others covering the curriculum, each accompanied by a strategy and a monitoring arrangement. The system is centralised online so that all background information can be pulled up with one click. The school captain, prefects (Years 10 and 11), school council (all years) and peer mentoring are all involved in identifying issues such as bullying and theft. A traditional system of detentions, warnings, letters home, form reports and head's reports is used. After this there are fixed term exclusions, but these rarely result in permanent exclusion.

Pupils and Parents: 50 per cent of boys have English as a second language but very few are not fluent; 25 per cent are Afro-Caribbean, with minority ethnic pupils making up 80 per cent of the entire school, and most are the first in their families to consider higher education. Many parents are looking for a 'mission school' in London, trusting Archbishop Tenison's to continue their children's Christian education while they themselves are doing two or three jobs. Attendance: 95 per cent at bi-annual academic reviews shows parents are keen to work with the teachers.

Entrance: There is no catchment area and intake is split 70 per cent church attendance and 30 per cent open. The school is over-subscribed each year.

Exit: North Lambeth Sixth Form is a collaboration of three schools in the borough – Archbishop Tenison's, Charles Edward Brooke (girls' specialist media school) and London Nautical (boys' specialist sports school) so the sixth form choices are widened over the three sites. All those who stay on in the sixth form move on to some form of higher education, and most artists gain places at Chelsea or Camberwell.

A number of boys from Archbishop Tenison's are awarded bursaries from the Livery Company of the Dyers whilst studying in the sixth form and, over the last three years, a number have been awarded financial assistance from the Livery Company of Chartered Surveyors to help with their university costs.

Remarks: A vital school in a deprived area with rising academic results, enterprising teachers and the boys at the centre of everything. The constant celebration of achievement – wall displays, credits, merits, prizes or even just a comment in a homework diary – makes a massive difference to pupils' confidence. The structure of daily worship and parent/carer school communication has proved essential to the growing success of this school.

Ardingly College

Linked to Ardingly College Prep School in the Junior section

College Road, Ardingly, Haywards Heath, West Sussex, RH17 6SQ

• Pupils: 490 boys and girls, 245 weekly and full boarding (30 per cent in first year, 80 per cent by sixth form) • Ages: 13-18
• Size of sixth form: 210 • C of E • Fees: Day £18,990-£19,470; Boarding £25,320-£25,950 pa • Independent

Tel: 01444 893 000
Fax: 01444 893 001
Email: registrar@ardingly.com
Website: www.ardingly.com

Headmaster: Since 2007, Mr Peter Green MA PGCE CertRE, a geographer (mid-forties). Began at Strathallan School before moving to Uppingham where he served first as head of geography and then as boarding housemaster. From 2002, second master of Ampleforth. A rugby-keen Scot, he talks fast, sensibly and a lot, full of good tales and good ideas, anchored by strong faith. Loves his job – always wanted to be a teacher – pupils find him much more approachable than his predecessor, to be found (by parents, pupils, staff) under the archway at the beginning of every school day. Teenage son at Worth (Worth's head returning the compliment with his daughter at Ardingly) and daughter at Ardingly; married to Brenda who co-hosts the Thursday prefect dinner.

Strong leadership team with prep (external appointment 2007) and pre-prep (external appointment 2010) heads, lots of new blood recently, but it seems for natural reasons rather than character clashes. Predecessor invested money and time in school, leaving a good financial, environmental and academic foundation for what he called 'the best kept secret in Sussex'.

Academic matters: Up to six sets in maths and English for Shell (Year 9), GCSE subjects include Mandarin, PE and drama plus all the usuals, with 22 per cent achieving all As and A* grades. Fantastic new language labs on previously ignored floor, subject rooms much more spread out than in the past. Science labs traditional but effective – all manner of ponds and wildlife to use for practicals.

IB offered since 1996, now around 50/50 IB/A level. Students say IB great for those who thrive with exams, new A levels best for those who are crippled by stress and prefer modular work. Parents say school does not pressurise pupils to get highest grades but encourages those who can reach them. Good choice of A level subjects – theatre studies, business studies (popular) along with more traditional options (biology very popular, RS too), languages – French, German, Spanish and Latin. IB big pulling point for Europeans – Germans especially, with exchange rate and government incentives; this will be a safety net for school numbers even in recessionary times. Lots of overlap encouraged between different subjects, combined trips etc. Apparently 'legendary' teachers in English department encouraging creative writing – we imagine Robin Williamsesque invocation of carpe diem?

ICT seen as a tool, big PC suite, ceiling-mounted data projectors, lots of networked computers both in and out of teaching areas – Wi-Fi available in all the boarding houses and the school library. Light, bright and well-catalogued library – DVDs, books and periodicals; librarian responds with initiative to requests and moans. More staff because of IB, so good pupil:teacher ratio. Long-serving and well-appreciated SENCo who makes sure mild to moderate SEN pupils cope. Success stories include senior dyslexic studying history at Oxford.

Games, Options, the Arts: Stunning environment in good weather, blustery and gloomy in bad. Pupils really appreciate the surrounding green – from being distracted from personal study by the sight of sheep wandering across a hilltop to being able to go for a run through woods and discover something new. School set in 275 acres, a third of which is let as fields. Newly covered Astroturf pitch used for hockey or tennis (12 courts), plus hard courts, plus use of reservoir for sailing (inter-house competition) and rowing five minutes' walk from main buildings.

More than 80 sports offered during the year and school especially successful in cricket, netball, football, girls' hockey, cross-country. Post of director of sports (filled by ex-England rugby cap) seems to be working well – head stirred up tradition by replacing football goals with rugby posts on one pitch ... Sports not compulsory but everyone finds something they like (horse-riding is back). Indoor hall built in 2000 but no weights/fitness rooms or viewing area. 'Hideous old gym' used as back-up, great 25m indoor pool. Duke of Edinburgh Award scheme is popular here, as is CCF – about 25 per cent girls, not just shooting and camping ... .

Music very strong under charismatic director, voluntary choir of 80-odd invited to sing at St Paul's, St George's Windsor, Chichester, Southwark, Westminster, Paris etc. Peripatetic staff give individual lessons and also perform in the London Philharmonic, The Sixteen and at Glyndebourne. The study of production and recording skills are sourced when needed – but most of pupils' energy is channelled into more traditional forms – string quartets, piano trios, house singing and music competitions.

Drama and art more adventurous; a production per year by each year group and a full school show as well – recently a play that the head of drama had seen win a fringe first at Edinburgh. Drama team delighted to use projection and non-theatre space to explore pupils' ideas. Art now housed in fantastic purpose-designed conversion – pupils walk through naturally lit and high-ceiling display gallery to get to studios, daily inspiration. Art library, IT suite (with video editing capability), new teacher for animation and video, kiln room, textile room – particularly popular around Leavers' Ball time ... Fine art displayed all over campus, art trips to Europe and beyond. DT facilities in dire need of upgrade.

Background and Atmosphere: The jewel in the Woodard crown – 23 independent C of E schools in England and Wales (another 22 state school affiliated), founded in the mid-19th century by Canon Nathaniel Woodard. Ardingly moved to this imposing, three storey, H-shaped redbrick building in 1870, high on the Sussex downs and with marvellous views over the landscape in all directions. Grandly solemn vaulted chapel (stained glass windows in restoration programme) used for weekly Eucharist, whole school and other house assemblies. Not a rich foundation and somewhat shackled by buildings' Grade II listings and doubtful privilege of being in an 'area of outstanding natural beauty'; school is continuously improving facilities – and ideally keeping more elderly ones like 'a well-scrubbed monastic corridor'. Good management, prudent changes, summer lets all help to provide major investment (over £11 million in last 10 years). IB fees paid in Euros should help in current financial climate.

Boarding in cluster of three storey houses, moments from main building. All have a house computer (for Skype and facebook, only allowed at weekends), well-equipped games rooms (Wii for the girls, table footie, snooker, karaoke and X-box for the boys), and kitchens or 'brew rooms'. Girls start off in junior house (all named after old heads) and then in lower sixth are thrown in all together – although they still return to make pancakes for and mentor the girls in their old houses. The boys are in the same houses up until the Upper Sixth – when both genders mix in one boarding house, Woodard. There the sexes are separated by the Forum (interconnecting doors locked at 10pm), a space with table tennis, table footie, huge plasma (mostly playing music videos unless football, The Apprentice or Skins is on), two brew rooms (where mostly girls make burgers, pancakes, toast, pizza etc) and a bar (open on Saturday night for beer, wine, alcopops and J20s paid for out of house funds ...). Boarding facilities best in the refurbed younger houses, Woodard's bathrooms are next on the list (phew). More pupils sharing each room (beds, desks, corkboards for posters) in the lower years, age and study load earns you seclusion and a better view – none of the rooms are spacious but all in good condition. Lots of ipod speakers, well-liked matrons, house parents on site to maintain calm.

Lots of tasty and healthy choice in the dining room, monitored by some staff and prefects. Pupils say school is not cliquey (Chinese and Germans groups could form). They seem confident and quick humoured, few exclusive romances – just lots of fun, socialising across years too. Perceived isolation of school is not seen as a negative factor – 'you can get on a train to London and there's so much to do here, you feel exhausted in a good way by the time you get to the weekend'. Very friendly and reasonable both inside and outside school – e.g. turning up to a parent-hosted party with a crate of Carling under one arm, sleeping bag under the other, cheery cleaning up by all in the morning.

Pastoral Care and Discipline: Everyone is assigned tutor on arrival – pupil's confidante, broker and spokesman and school's link with parents. Can switch if tutor's subject speciality is incongruous with pupil's choices. Thereafter, hierarchy of support/discipline ending at the top. Parents say you'll get an email reply from a teacher within a day and probably a follow up phone call.

Sixth form has dress code, lower forms have uniform – trouser option for girls. Iphones not to be used in lessons, laptops only for dyslexics, school email accounts and controls on surfing, some relaxed at the weekend. Head boy and head girl – staff nominate, pupils vote, discussion with housemasters and SMT then head picks – and deputies have weekly meeting with head, prefects' dinner at head's house each Thursday.

Clear drugs and drinking policy – automatic out for class A/B and possible police involvement; second chance over cannabis with testing/counselling/collaboration with parents regimen. Surprising lack of drinking issues for school surrounded by copses/potential shebeens! Flexi-boarding must help – and also responsibility taken early, heads of house in lower sixth and informal mentoring seems almost instinctive.

Pupils and Parents: About 40 per cent of pupils live within 50 minutes drive of the school, 25 per cent come from overseas. IB is prime attraction for Europeans – restricted intake of Germans to 12 per year (but 300 apply). About 20 other nationalities represented, largest group HK Chinese. Parents say great for all-rounders and siblings with different talents. A broad social spectrum – families are doctors, surgeons, lawyers, city commuters, diplomats, landed gentry – just entered the Tatler Schools Guide ... According to a recent questionnaire, a third attracted by the Woodard ethos, in general families are unpretentious. 'It all feels normal – people might go off on their yachts in the holidays but they won't flaunt it!' Good social network of parents, many used to walk their dogs on grounds after dropping children off – recent dog embargo put paid to that (proliferation of signs to that effect irritates some locals). Old Ardinians include racing driver Mike Hawthorn, Ian Hislop, composer Stephen Oliver, actors Terry-Thomas and Alan Howard.

Entrance: Selective via scholarship, CE or other exams depending on point of entry – English, maths, VR tested. half from the prep, half external (St Paul's, Westminster, Westbourne House, Great Walstead, Prebendal, Hurst, state schools). Over-subscribed at present – spaces may appear in current financial climate.

Exit: Around 15 leave after GCSE, mostly to local sixth form colleges. Rest stay and go on to everything from Oxbridge (49 interviews in past couple of years, about eight got in) to aviation studies at Kingston (also Imperial, LSE, Princeton, Stanford, Edinburgh, Lancaster) – 95 per cent to Russell Group universities or equivalent, 40 per cent take 'constructive' gap year (not much loafing around and working in local pub any more).

Money Matters: Academic, music, art, drama, sport and DT awards on offer at 13+ and 16+ various stages – up to 50 per cent tuition remission. Special awards for clergy, Services, Sussex and Old Ardinians' children. Worth scrutinising the literature. Maybe not one to go for if finances are unpredictable – not as strong on tide-you-over bursaries as many.

Remarks: Wide-ranging staff, confident and down-to-earth pupils, beautiful grounds and improving facilities – bit of a mystery as to why more people are not raving about this school. Relatively new head; perhaps he will sing loudly about it to local preps and beyond – otherwise it may well continue to be one of Sussex's best-kept secrets.

Arnold School

Linked to Arnold Junior School in the Junior section

Lytham Road, Blackpool, Lancashire, FY4 1JG

• Pupils: 550; 50/50 girls/boys – all day • Ages: 11-18 • Size of sixth form: 150 • Non-denom but Christian ethics • Fees: £6,831-£8,925 pa • Independent

Tel: 01253 346391
Fax: 01253 336250
Email: admissions@arnoldschool.com
Website: www.arnoldschool.com

Headmaster: Since 2010, Mr Jim Keefe (early forties), educated at University of Newcastle, BA in economics. Previously deputy head at Arnold and before that a housemaster at Bedford School. Wants 'a happy, busy and disciplined environment in which pupils aim for, and regularly achieve, academic excellence'. Very open and honest, admitting that school isn't perfect, 'Which school really is?' But wants no frills, airs or graces. Bluntly admits, 'we are broadly selective so you would expect our results to be good'. Hopes that school can live up to its motto – 'Honor Virtutis Praemium' (honour is the reward of virtue). Teaches economics – 'it's good for parents and staff to see the head teaching – plus there are very few jobs that give you the same job satisfaction as teaching, and I don't want to lose that'. Wife works in marketing and is now president of Arnold's Ladies' Luncheon Club. Two daughters, both at Arnold.

Academic matters: Seventy per cent A*–B at A level in 2010, with 40 per cent at A*/A grade. Puts good results down to good teaching, a good relationship between teachers and pupils and support from parents.'We live by the belief that you only get one crack at life and if you are not careful life will pass you by. We like to produce confident students who will take life by the scruff of the neck.' A parent told us, 'when they say they try to meet the needs of individual pupils they do just that – other schools claim to but don't'. Head positively looking forward to next inspection. 'Inspectors now would find a better blend of the old with the new. We still have assemblies, traditional games and so on but now with better facilities – not least in ICT.'

The whole school enjoys a lunch/activity period from 12.55pm to 2.15pm before lessons resume until 4pm. An 'express' group can take GCSEs a year early. Has introduced International GCSE in maths because traditional GCSE was not stretching. Class sizes kept below 25, usually 20 at KS3 and 16 at GCSE. 11 pupils per one full-time equivalent teacher. One parent told us, 'Arnold creates an atmosphere where working hard and achieving is the norm and within that atmosphere children do work and do achieve'.

Games, Options, the Arts: Vast range of sports – the girls' U14 hockey team were national champions in 2010. Other notable successes in recent years include international fencers, footballers and netball players as well as regional and national success in hockey, swimming and rugby. Sport is inclusive. 'Anyone who wants a game can get a game,' says head.

Puts on at least three major productions a year. Regularly wins awards and former students often go on to RADA, LAMDA and many others. Not surprisingly has seen ex-pupils win roles on television. Music is valued highly and regularly contributes members to the National Youth Brass Band and National Youth Jazz Orchestra. 150 singers and musicians stage a Choral Convert each Spring. Also has thriving swing band and many smaller groups.

Travels far and wide. In 2007 the rugby players went to Chile and Argentina and in 2009 the hockey players went to Australia and Fiji. Last Christmas the choir went to Krakow. Combined Cadet Force (one of biggest in the country) extends pupils' travels throughout UK, Spain and the Red Sea. The school raises funds for the village of Buigiri in Tanzania.

Pupils (many from business stock!) have strong entrepreneurial spirit and jump at chance to set up their own company through Young Enterprise. Duke of Edinburgh is popular with nearly 30 doing gold award each year. Millennium Volunteers help seriously ill, underprivileged children, blind, disabled etc. School raised more than £60,000 for local charities in the last five years.

Background and Atmosphere: Just a stone's throw from the bustling heart of Blackpool, from one entrance you can see the Tower, from the other the Pleasure Beach! Within the school the atmosphere is one of work hard, play hard. It is relaxed rather than frenetic, purposeful rather than hothouse.

Situated in once-affluent part of Blackpool before the money moved out to the sticks. Mixed architecture: school has grown by acquiring former hotels at the front but expanded and added new buildings to the rear. The school joined United Church Schools Trust (UCST) in 2008.

Pastoral Care and Discipline: School divided into lower, middle and sixth form, with four forms in each of Years 7–11 and a tutor for each form responsible for pastoral care along with heads of year. Sixth formers become mentors to help Year 7 pupils to settle. Pupils divided into houses.

'We are not the sort of school where you hear screaming down the corridor, and bad behaviour is rare,' affirms head. 'No head can claim there is never any unpleasantness between pupils, nor that they have never heard of drugs! But we have our rules, rewards and sanctions and we take action where necessary. We do suspend pupils when behaviour requires it.' Merits reward younger pupils and most merits helps secure the house cup. Sanctions include detentions and, ultimately, exclusion.

Pupils and Parents: Around half come from Arnold Junior School, and then some from other feeders including St Pius X and Highfield Priory School in Preston, Hall Park School, Lytham, Roseacre Primary School and others in Blackpool. Covers a geographical area of Blackpool Fylde, Wyre, Preston and the south of Lancashire.

Many are children of local businesspeople, members of entertainment world, hoteliers, arcade owners etc, who want to spend their brass on giving their children the best. Increasing number getting financial support from school. Mainly white Christian but significant minority of other faiths including Jewish and Muslim. A small number have learning difficulties. 'A northern, hard-work ethic prevails and expectation from parents is high. They call a spade a spade and tell us when we don't get it right,' reckons head.

Links with home are strong: has a parent email contact system to keep them up to date with the school plus a parent forum each year to discuss bigger issues and regular parent surveys. A parent who had had three children at the school told us, 'All three were very different, with different personalities, and all have done extremely well at Arnold.'

Lists among famous old boys Blue Peter presenter Peter Purves, Pet Shop Boys singer Chris Lowe and soccer player Jimmy Armfield. Most recent Jonas Armstrong (new TV Robin Hood).

Entrance: School has own junior school and many progress from there. Otherwise exams in English, maths and non-verbal reasoning.

Exit: Regular progressions to Oxbridge and other major universities, especially in medicine, dentistry, science and business-related subjects. Strongly academic school but realistic about achievements. 'We have some extremely clever children who go on to Oxbridge and others of more modest ability who go to other universities and get just as much out of that,' opines head.

Money Matters: Offers some scholarships of varying amounts and chance of a means-tested assisted place.

Remarks: A lovely school, where the hard work ethic doesn't overwhelm the pleasure of learning and growing up. Unashamedly offers opportunity that traditional grammar schools used to and which is rarely available in the state sector.

The Arts Educational School (London)

Cone Ripman House, 14 Bath Road, Chiswick, London, W4 1LY

• Pupils: 205, about a third boys, all day • Ages: 11-18 • Size of sixth form: 70 • Non-denom • Fees: £11,490 pa • Independent

Tel: 020 8987 6600
Fax: 020 8987 6601
Email: pupils@artsed.co.uk
Website: www.artsed.co.uk

Headmaster: Since 2007, Mr Oliver 'Buster' Price BEd. Has taught in a wide variety of schools, starting as English, drama and PE teacher in a Leicester comprehensive. Thence head of PE at Dartford Boys' Grammar School, followed by a ten-year stint as deputy head of the lower school at St Dunstan's College in south-east London, before he was appointed to the post of headmaster of a day and boarding co-educational independent school in East Sussex. Has written a number of plays for schools, played county cricket for Kent and coached the Kent Schools' under 18 rugby squad. Mr Price is married to the registrar at Fairley House (qv), and the ethos of that remarkable institution clearly informs his own commitment to supporting those of his charges with SEN. The school was full of verve and energy when he arrived, but the organisation was also a touch 'artistic'. He has done much to tighten up structure, security, finance and admin and it shows. The academics have also been beefed up since his arrival and the school now has a purposeful feel in all areas. The numbers are up – especially in the sixth. Immensely affable, open and likeable, Mr Price clearly inspires affection and loyalty in the school community. He has exciting plans to develop the school – especially at sixth form level – and clearly understands his pupils. 'They get so used to performing that they grow in confidence – they're happy to talk to adults, to voice their opinions and to listen to others.' Serious, but fun, focused but relaxed, enthusiastic but not artsy, the right man for the job.

Academic matters: 'Arts Educational School is not a stage school. The academic emphasis in the school is equal to the vocational importance and the aim is to produce well-rounded, interesting and interested young people who have the confidence to perform both on stage and in the classroom.' This might come as a surprise to visitors who are surrounded by leotards and leggings, girls' hair scraped into buns, choruses and piano rehearsals booming out of each room. But the complex timetable is firmly balanced and pupils not working on the vocational side are neat in traditional turquoise (known here as 'lagoon') uniforms – which match the classroom doors and look quite demure.

At GCSE, everyone takes biology and chemistry, along with two Englishes, maths – setted from the off – expressive arts, French and three options from a number of blocks – art, dance, drama, geography, history, music and media studies. The most able also do physics. Head of modern langs speaks seven langs himself and would find teachers for any lang a pupil wanted to take. The academic corridors look much as anywhere and good displays on historical topics make a reassuring change from the glitzy pictures of past productions elsewhere. Around 20 have SEN – mostly dyslexia and, as Mr Price says, 'so many dyslexics can communicate through performing when they cannot on paper'. Wise words. School now runs two parallel courses in the sixth form: a trad A level course along with classes in dance/drama/music or two ASs and two As plus a foundation course in musical theatre, which is now an accredited BTec. More pupils are choosing to stay on and a number of new students come in at that stage. 10 AS/A level subjects offered – including philosophy, history, photography, maths, history of art and media studies, plus the musical theatre course. Excellent results.

Games, Options, the Arts: On admission in Year 7 you choose to major in either dance or drama – but both groups have classes in both subjects. Sport is offered twice a week at the nearby sports centre but, as one parent said, 'the school is so full of energy and they do so much physical activity, neither of our children feel locked in or worried about the lack of outside space' – which is just as well as there isn't any and you'd be wise to go elsewhere if you need to get seriously muddy twice a week. Everyone dances their socks off to take exercise and yoga, 'combat fighting' and dances like hip hop also use up surplus energies. A gym/weights room for the sixth form. Vocational courses include spoken voice, audition technique, text in performance, choreography, expressive arts, dance of all kinds and music. Music is impressive – loads of individual lessons, good resources – now with excellent facilities for music tech and no-one now leaves unable to read music. Everyone has music twice a week. Four choirs, various instrumental groups including a jazz group, and many pupils have private music lessons too. Everyone performs all the time and it is most refreshing to go into a studio and see 13-year-olds, of both sexes, improvising without self-consciousness – no blushful hanging back here.

Three major productions a year – aided by professional wardrobe and set-building staff and every corridor has racks of costumes just waiting to be donned. Pupils help on the backstage side and learn about the technical aspects of production, as well as film techniques. Production values are professional and exacting. Unlike at stage schools, however, pupils are not encouraged to have agents and to take off long periods for professional work – school-life and work come first. However, film producers do drop round to choose children for roles – some in major productions, some in ads. The art-rooms are a quiet relief and art is a popular GCSE and A level here. Work is varied, colourful and clever. Sixth form now has eight new laptops for photographic work – very popular. Plenty of trips to concerts and galleries.

Background and Atmosphere: It's a long, three-storey, plain redbrick building, unimpressively occupying about 100 yards of prime Bedford Park along the Bath Road in pricey west London and surrounded by leafy roads housing TV executives in semis which go for £1m++ apiece. Inside it's a different world – once you are past the new turnstile and security system – and security now stops you at each corridor, for which you need an ID card. Plain corridors, plain rehearsal rooms – dozens of them, which all look much the same to visitors, apart from some being black and curtained and others bright and light, but clearly have very different feels to the students, e.g. 'That's where I do tap; I couldn't think of acting in there,' etc. A proscenium arch theatre, lots of storage space for costumes and sets, a good-sized, adaptable studio which mimics 'fringe' conditions – everything is geared to preparation for the outside reality.

Students look bright-eyed and busy – you cannot coast here and drown quickly if you try. Parents rave about 'the positive energy of the place'. Little recreation space – the sixth form has space which acts as a common-room but that's it and no outside. Little time for traditional teenage bickering here – 'It's very friendly and you have to work together,' says sage 12-year-old student. A good canteen and good food, though not cheap. Most pupils eat a hot meal at lunchtime – lots of pasta, always a vegetarian option and all prepared on site by unusually friendly staff. Good salad bar. Breakfast daily from 7.45 – a good idea, considering that some pupils commute from as far as Kent or Reading. It's a long day, especially for dance students – 8.30am-5.30pm.

The school shares a building and facilities with the schools of acting and musical theatre. So the foyer and common areas are full of creatively dressed and coiffed students who mingle indistinguishably from the sixth formers. Lots of hugging and kissing and a real sense of cooperation and mutual support. Local area is moneyed and attractive though we were met by a warning about muggings and the advisability of going around in groups in the evenings. School hires the local fringe theatre, The Tabard, and the excellent Questors Theatre in nearby Ealing for performance space, as well as dance studios at nearby Rambert and other space at Watermans, Brentford. Offers of useful space to the head, please! And a second bathroom for the girls!

Pastoral Care and Discipline: Ambiance is energetic, purposeful and the emphasis is on self-discipline. Few, having got here, would want to jeopardize their place and few drop out though some, obviously, realise after a while that the life of a performing pro is not for them. Carefully-structured tutorial system. Students are remarkably focused and learn quickly that success isn't easily won. Drugs, cigarettes and alcohol are seldom a problem at the school because the students are too busy and committed to their chosen courses to have time for such things. Clear policies on all these sins. Pupils appear to love their teachers – 'they aren't "show-bizzy" – they're here to help us with technique' ... 'my daughter's science teacher is a hero to her – even though she's not at all into science!' ... 'the teachers are all so friendly – I mean, not too, friendly but just, well, lovely and they are brilliantly supportive' ... 'my second daughter isn't into performing but her sister is so happy there, it seemed unfair not to send her too and the academics – more her thing – have been excellent'.

Pupils and Parents: From a huge radius round London and very mixed in all ways: the common denominators are talent, a willingness to work, enthusiasm – and parents who can afford the fees. Some sixth formers from far afield are put up in local digs. Very beautiful and talented young people who may have stars in their eyes but definitely feet on the ground. Many parents are in the business and appreciate the school's values – 'the performances are always professional ... an excellent training for young aspiring actors and it is, most emphatically NOT a Stage School and all that implies,' we were told. 'I wish I'd gone there,' mused one noted actor. Former pupils include Julie Andrews, Sarah Brightman, Darcey Bussell, Martin Clunes, Joan Collins, Leslie Crowther, Janie Dee, Nigel Havers, Cherie Lunghi, Will Young and Glynis Johns and loads and loads of others. Lots of high calibre thesps among current parents – all clearly loving the school.

Entrance: By audition. Pieces prepared for audition depend on which course you are applying for, e.g. dance solos, drama monologues, sung or instrumental pieces. Then participation in unprepared workshops and classes. Tests in English and maths. Don't come along seeing yourself as the next soap star or Billy Elliot: 'We're looking for team-workers'.

Exit: Most to performing arts courses – Urdang is popular. A few stay on and join the degree courses in the same building. Some to other degree courses at e.g. Royal Holloway, Birmingham University.

Money Matters: No govt or local authority help. The school has a bursary fund to help existing pupils and is currently looking at ways of increasing it. Various charitable trusts might help out an existing pupil in case of collapsed finances but the bottom line is, you'll have to find the fees – which are very reasonable given what is provided.

Remarks: For those who are serious about the work involved in performing arts – with the accent on the work. It's huge fun but you need energy, commitment and camaraderie. Now with excellent academic teaching too. If you can cut the mustard at audition, you'll have a ball.

Ashbourne Independent School

17 Old Court Place, Kensington, London, W8 4PL

• Pupils: 200 boys and girls in total (60/40 per cent split) of whom half are in the upper sixth (resits, condensed A levels or special university foundation year), 75 in lower sixth (AS) • Ages: 16-19; plus 25 in the GCSE stream • Size of sixth form: 150 • None • Fees: £18,000-£19,800 pa • Independent

Tel: 020 7937 3858
Fax: 020 7937 2207
Email: admin@ashbournecollege.co.uk
Website: www.ashbournecollege.co.uk

Principal : Since 1981, Michael (Mike) Hatchard-Kirby, BApSc, MSC (fifties), who founded the school. Read aerospace engineering and statistics at the University of Toronto in his native Canada, then a master's in maths at Birkbeck College, London. Fell into teaching in the UK 'more or less by accident'. Tutored at a major London tutorial college as head of physics before setting up Ashbourne in 1981. Member of CIFE (the Conference for Independent Further Education) and the British Council Education Counselling Service. Married with two grown-up children and a young child. A slow-speaking, giant of a man with a crushing handshake and friendly, open manner, has a clear-sighted and down-to-earth approach to the college he's nurtured for nearly 30 years. Runs the college with the director of studies, John Wilson, an Oxford graduate with a degree in biological sciences.

Academic matters: Tucked away from the shopping temptations of Kensington High Street, Ashbourne is a small, independent, sixth form college, which concentrates on A level and university entrance, but also teaches a small number of GCSE pupils. Tutorial-style classes of 6–10 ('As soon as it hits 10 we split it'), offering an extensive array of subjects, from Vietnamese to sociology ('If a student wants a subject we don't provide, we'll take on a teacher to teach it') and any combination, provided you register before the start of September term. As well as traditional academic subjects – maths is a forte – the college is also unusually strong in art and design. Drama, too, is an increasingly popular option (with full drama scholarships available for talented thespians).

Ashbourne prides itself on the quality of its teaching – 'many students here will have the best teaching and the most attention they'll ever get at school or university' – and results seem to justify the boast. Since 2003, over half its A level candidates have been awarded As and Bs, with an average grade of B. University admissions (mainly to Russell Group and Oxbridge) also a key part of the service, with guidance on subject choice, personal statements and interview as well as art school portfolio preparation for creatives. The college also offers specific BMAT training and does particularly well with its aspiring medics – over 60 per cent of candidates have won medical school places in the past three years. (Both Kirby and his deputy might sit as lay members of the admissions panel for medicine at UCL.)

Long-serving staff give their all, with 50 per cent more contact time than generally available in schools and plenty of out-of-lesson support for those who need it. In lessons, exams are very much the message and exam papers (past and specimen) provide the focus, accompanied by regular testing and formal exams every six weeks. Plenty of reports, too – five times a year – keep pupils and parents up to speed with grades, effort, attendance and punctuality – 'we expect them to work very hard' – so little opportunity to slip behind.

Elsewhere, flexibility is the key. Main start dates are January and September but unexpected new arrivals can be slotted in whenever necessary. Course length, too, is adaptable, with A level courses offered over one or two years and – a rare boon – specific tuition for AS resits. GCSEs can either be taken in the standard two years or as an intensive one-year course.

Games, Options, the Arts: As might be expected, extra-curricular is not the college's main attraction, but it does its best to ensure it's not all work and no play with a range of outings (including a visit to a major European city), some sport (a five-a-side football team), an annual revue and fashion show and a reasonable range of clubs (chess, music, drama).

Background and Atmosphere: Ashbourne is definitely a college rather than a school, with the feel of a rather well-furnished modern office and no running-around space. The approach, too, is pretty business-like, with a long, full-on day, stretching from 9am to 6pm and lessons taught in two-hour blocks (six periods a week per subject).

Overseas students live in warden-supervised hostels or with approved families.

Pastoral Care and Discipline: Discipline inside the school is firm – 'What pupils do outside is their own business but they mustn't bring drugs or alcohol onto the premises' – and attendance is strictly monitored with registration taken every two hours.

Pupils and Parents: About half the students come from outside the UK and a chunk more from embassies and international businesses.

Entrance: What would once have been called a 'crammer', Ashbourne still sees its primary role as taking students successfully through exams, but now selects only those who are willing and able to cope with the rigours of A levels. 'A levels are academic exams and, if that's not what they're looking for, they should consider an alternative.' Hatchard-Kirby looks for pupils with above average intelligence who are genuinely keen to study and go on to university. 'We interview to make sure we're getting the right candidates. If someone's just doing it to please their parents, this isn't the right place for them. I love kids with outside interests – but I support the idea of focus.' Behaviour, too, has been nudged up the agenda, and a history of misconduct counts as a black mark – 'in the end, we decided it just wasn't fair on the other students'.

Remarks: You have to be reasonably mature and focused to make the most of Ashbourne, but it could be an excellent solution for those for whom the traditional classroom has never been the perfect fit. Efficient, calm, friendly place that delivers what it promises and does so with a positive attitude.

Ashford School

Linked to Ashford Friars Preparatory School in the Junior section

East Hill, Ashford, Kent, TN24 8PB

- Pupils: 450 (of whom 140 are boarders); fully coed • Ages: 11-18
- Size of sixth form: 160 • Christian but all faiths and none welcome
- Fees: Day £14,286; Boarding £21,810-£25,425 pa • Independent

Tel: 01233 739 030
Fax: 01233 665 215
Email: registrar@ashfordschool.co.uk
Website: www.ashfordschool.co.uk

Head: Since 2005, Mr Michael Buchanan (mid-forties) BSc PGCE NPQH, previously ten years at Highgate School in north London, where he left as principal deputy head. Part of his brief there was to bring in co-education, and he has done a similar job at Ashford with great success. Educated at Downside and King's College, London where he read physics and trained as a teacher. Businesslike and charming, has a passion for physics, sport and choral music – he is a highly experienced, lead ISI inspector. Still teaches and referees sport when he can. Married, two daughters in the school, his wife works for a bank in London – says the whole family felt welcomed from the moment they arrived at Ashford.

Academic matters: Performing very well – takes a range of averagely academic children, with most in the top 25 per cent nationally – and gets very good results and high value added. Many experienced staff and a healthy dose of new, highly qualified teachers since the head's arrival. Three or four forms of 18–24 pupils. Setting in most subjects from Year 7. Huge range of activities on offer – over 80 at last count. Stunning 24 per cent A*s and nearly 80 per cent A*–B grades at A level. Maths is strong at all ability levels, with a good uptake of further maths at A level. Science a strength, students encouraged to take individual sciences at GCSE. Nine labs currently being updated – all excellently staffed. Maths, the sciences, art and design and economics the most popular A levels but there's photography, textiles, sports studies and theatre studies too.

Pupils are taught the essential ICT skills by specialists and apply them generally. They can take the European Computer Driving Licence (ECDL). Fine computer suites and an interactive whiteboard in every classroom, a new language lab in 2007 and design studio in 2008 – and all staff have been trained how to use them. School is now using radio voting handsets in lessons to encourage pupil engagement and improve assessment. The school intranet (virtual learning environment) can be accessed from home. Internet access in every classroom and wireless access in most areas. Fine learning resource centre where pupils can work on their own but with subtle adult supervision and support. New information scientist teaches research skills. Good careers library where students can sign up for an interview and receive individual advice. Newly appointed careers adviser was formerly a senior lecturer and admissions tutor at a leading UK university and is now playing the UCAS system to the benefit of the Ashford School applicants.

Thirty children need some sort of learning support for mild learning difficulties. They are assessed before arrival to see if they can cope and to ascertain if they have the potential to go on to university. Learning support teacher will either teach the students herself or make sure a plan is in place. Classroom assistants support pupils in selected lessons. 80 pupils with varying degrees of EAL need. Full-time EAL specialist. Pupils taught either one-to-one or in small groups. Sixth form prepared for IELTS exam (university entrance requirement) and get outstanding results.

Games, Options, the Arts: Sport for all approach – children are expected to play if they are selected for a team but there is always some flexibility. Team sports growing stronger each year and new director of sport in 2008 having a significant impact. Some outstanding individuals with Olympic potential. The girls play netball, rugby, hockey, rounders and tennis and boys play rugby, hockey and cricket as the main sports. Plenty of grass pitches, tennis courts, all-weather Astroturf, three smallish gymnasiums and an indoor pool. School has recently acquired a further 25 acres of land to develop as sports fields and has taken a lease on a nearby defunct cricket club with stunning views of the Downs. Further facilities planned including a sports centre. Activities programme built into the timetable with a minimum number of compulsory activities for all; at last count over 80 on offer. Food studies up to Year 9 – cooking with healthy eating thrown in. Young Enterprise Scheme, CCF and Duke of Edinburgh Award as well as team-building exercises help develop an enterprising attitude. Highly successful arts festival in the last week of the year. Upper sixth spent a day at the Challenge of Management conference focusing on life beyond A levels and university. Wide range of trips including China, skiing, languages, sports tours and cultural expeditions to Europe and beyond.

Art work all round the school, amongst the best we have encountered – wonderful pottery, textiles and ceramics and papier mache shoes on display in the hall. Lots of students get As at A level and three pupils were among the top ten A level students in the country for art and textiles in 2009. Large numbers study art and design at university. Up to Year 9 the pupils study fine art and, at GCSE, they can choose either fine art or textiles. The sixth form art students are invited to spend a week painting in Minorca. Photography added to the mix in 2006 when specialist studio and darkroom were created.

Head of music is a colourful character who has transformed the musical life of the school; numbers participating have shot up as has the standard. Musical performances every couple of weeks with major concerts in venues such as Canterbury Cathedral; usual array of choirs and orchestras. Musician in residence is a budding professional concert pianist and helps run ensembles, groups and orchestras as well as working with individuals. All pupils are expected to perform and seem to relish this challenge. Annual school musical and house music competitions as well as productions by GCSE and A level students. House music and drama events include everybody. Students also have the chance to have fun e.g. Junk Funk (making music with dustbin lids etc). Students take part in the Canterbury Festival, and sometimes go street busking in local towns and play at the local hospice. An Ashford girl was chosen for a role in the latest Harry Potter film.

Background and Atmosphere: In 2005, Ashford School merged with Friars' Preparatory School, a co-ed prep with a good academic and pastoral reputation based at Great Chart on the outskirts of Ashford. The new school now operates in three sections – the nursery, from the age of three months to three years, at Bridge House in the town centre; the prep school, from three to 11, on the old Friars site in Great Chart two miles away; and the senior school, also in the town centre. A shuttle service runs between the two schools so children can be dropped at either site. Record numbers joined the senior school in 2010 and coeducation is now firmly established. Excellent inspection reports in 2009 and 2010.

Founded in 1898 with the aim that the pupils should play an active role in the life of the town – still prevalent today – and visits to the elderly and community service seen as important. Pupils are expected to engage with life and the head says he does not want passengers in the school either as staff or pupils. Christian values and traditions but welcomes children of all faiths. The school became part of the United Church Schools Trust in 1999 and a huge amount of money is being invested in refurbishment and new facilities. A detailed development plan is reviewed each year.

The senior school is at the foot of the High Street, securely enclosed by high red-brick walls with plenty of lawns and greenery stretching down the hill – a tranquil green haven on a 25 acre site in the middle of Ashford. The main building is ivy clad and charming, with new additions built sympathetically with brick arches and rose-clad pergolas. Pathways lead to quiet benched areas for the students to meet or contemplate.

A very international and friendly community with a busy and purposeful air about it and with an emphasis on the integration of domestic and garden staff into the life of the school. Meals served on a cafeteria style basis with plenty of choice and healthy salad options. Many compliments and very few complaints about the food. A new atrium cafe is also open to parents at drop off and pick up times. No lessons on Saturdays but children are expected to come in for sporting fixtures. Boarders can visit Canterbury, London and elsewhere and have a programme of activities at weekends.

Pastoral Care and Discipline: Support from heads of house, tutors and boarding staff, a chaplain, and the director of the senior school, who joined in 2007 from Caterham and is making her mark by raising expectations of dress, appearance and academic rigour. Pastorally strong. Boarding houses recently refurbished and now with en-suite facilities and all rooms wired for the internet. New junior boarding house opening in 2011 to accommodate demand. Younger boarders do prep in boarding house computer room so that they can be supervised. Inter-house competitions in music and drama and house assemblies encourage interaction between the year groups. There are currently just over 140 full boarders (many from overseas – Hong Kong, China, Nigeria, Europe) and some UK based weekly boarders. The school can accommodate some flexi-boarders when there is space but does not advertise this. The boarders are made to feel an integral part of the school and are not allowed back to their houses during the day as this aids integration. Boarders have a three-day induction at the start of the year. Lots of boarders' events throughout the year – international evenings, celebration of Chinese New Year, Christmas pantomime etc.

Pupils and Parents: An international feel to the school with 24 nationalities represented but school keen not to overdo any one culture. Growing number of Services families and the school is actively seeking more by offering Forces Bursaries. School also looking to boost number of 10+ pupils as full or weekly boarders from London now the high speed commuter train has cut the journey time to/from St Pancras to 37 minutes. Pupils seem a happy, friendly bunch, nothing toffy, and achievement and challenge is predominantly the cool culture. As one pupil put it, 'I like the competitive environment at Ashford. It encourages me to be ambitious.' Ashford is not leafy suburbia and many parents struggle with the school fees but the town is growing fast and folks are moving down from London and taking advantage of the high speed train link. Mainly local families within a 45 minute radius benefit from the good train and bus links and the school's network of pick up points.

Entrance: Seventy per cent from the prep school and others from local independent and primary schools. About 45 per cent of children in the school were unsuccessful in the Kent Test for the grammar schools but still beat their grammar school colleagues at GCSE and A level by a long way. Have own 11+ in English, maths, science and non-verbal reasoning plus a taster day when the school looks for potential. If the head believes they will thrive they are accepted, but if a child would struggle getting six A-Cs at GCSE, he would recommend trying somewhere else; most do much better than the minimum. Small but growing intake at 13 from local prep schools and again at 14 – mainly boarders from abroad. Significant entry for the sixth form, mainly boarders from abroad but some locals as well. Sixth form awards to encourage joiners from state schools. Will always find space for the right type. Foreign students have a telephone interview to assess their level of English and then a written assessment on arrival. A level and GCSE students need to have good English – more relaxed for younger pupils.

Exit: About 90 per cent stay on for A levels; a few leave for other independent schools and some for other further education. Careful guidance given to pupils who might need a less academic environment and there is usually a natural drop out, often because the more vocational A levels are not on offer at Ashford. Of those who stay on, 15 per cent to one of the world's top ten universities in most years, lots to London and other top universities and a good number to art college every year.

Money Matters: A healthy handful of scholarships on offer at age 11, 13, 16 for the able child and bursaries for those who fall into financial difficulty. School runs its own assisted place scheme for 11+ entry to allow a means-blind approach to entry. Special bursaries available to the children of clergy and Services families.

Remarks: Head made his ambitions for the school clear on arrival – to be one of the leading co-educational schools in the UK. With growing demand for places at the school and outstanding results it is clear he is succeeding. Ashford is fast becoming a top-notch co-ed school catering for that neglected breed, ordinary children, as well as for the higher fliers.

Ashmole Academy

Cecil Road, Southgate, London, N14 5RJ

• Pupils: 1,335; 690 boys, 645 girls; all day • Ages: 11-18 • Size of sixth form: 250; 50/50 girls/boys • Non-denom • State

Tel: 020 8361 2703
Fax: 020 8368 0315
Email: office@ashmole.barnet.sch.uk
Website: www.ashmole.barnet.sch.uk

Head Teacher: Since 1997, Mr Derrick Brown MA MBA DipEd, whose degree subjects were psychology and business (mid-fifties). Prior to his headship at Ashmole, Mr Brown was vice principal at Leigh City Technology College in Dartford and then senior deputy at Cranford School – both schools much the size and diversity of Ashmole and in comparable outer London suburbs. Quietly spoken, serious, relaxed and impressively focused on getting things done, he is an outstandingly successful head. Ashmole, as it is now, is substantially his creation, though he pays tribute to the contribution of parents and professionals who have assisted in building both the fabric and ethos of the school. With the site sorted he can now concentrate on the curriculum – 'the beauty now is that we can focus on the rest – music, PE and raising results'. He is supported by a good set of governors who 'want Ashmole to be the first choice over the independents'. Contracted till his retirement, several years away, he has every chance of consolidating Ashmole's reputation as a provider of comprehensive education at its best.

Academic matters: Strong value-added. The school is entirely non-selective so the results are impressive. Way ahead of the other non-selective schools in the area. Ashmole is a specialist science school and recently added a second specialism – music. It is one of the few schools in the country combining these two specialisms and it says a lot about the ethos. Much is made of the need to teach so that neither sex is disadvantaged and, interestingly, boys here do at least as well as girls. 'It requires a firm, highly structured and disciplined approach with boys but allows girls to show flair and creativity.' Classes are setted in main subjects – 'mixed ability doesn't work except in certain areas,' says Mr Brown. Sensibly, the brightest take maths, and in the future, will take languages, early at GCSE – this allows them to get ahead with their ASs and have more time on As. Everyone takes short GCSE course in RE.

2010 GCSEs saw 95 per cent achieving five or more A*–C (78 per cent including English and maths). Results are high at the top end with 34 per cent gaining five or more A*/A grades. A levels saw success with 100 per cent A*–C grades in applied art, art, economics, English, French, history, media, PE, RE and business studies. French is popular at A level, and 83 per cent of entrants gained a grade C or higher at GCSE. The school has a very strong exchange link with the twinned town of La Raincy, a suburb just outside Paris. Spanish and German are also offered at GCSE and A level, but are less popular. No sense here now of a science-orientated school ignoring the languages, thank goodness. Science staff come in for special praise from pupils – 'they are so dedicated and help us so much'.

Just under a quarter of the school has English as an additional language, and support in place to make sure they progress – either through extra help or in-class intervention. Around a fifth have some kind of SEN – about 2.5 per cent with statements. Learning support faculty housed in grim 'temporary' – they never are – building comprises team which supports both in class and via withdrawal. Most support given in class. The weakest 25 per cent drop languages after Year 9, taking business or ICT instead, and the very weakest will have extra support with the basics.

Attractive library in which there are displays of new books and periodicals, but the stock is woefully thin in many areas and needs major investment.

Games, Options, the Arts: Wonderfully off for space and facilities: has a huge floodlit Astroturf court, playing-field, sports hall and separate studio for dance, aerobics and net sports but no pool. Outstandingly successful in both boys' and girls' football and seems to win almost everything in Barnet championships. School now building its orchestra and numbers of pupils taking individual music lessons. Drama is popular – big, well-equipped studio – and successful, and school mounts major musical production each year – standards high and all great fun. Art good and varied – bold colour, lively textiles: we saw some glam evening dresses made by Year 10; popular graphics, clay sculpture, fabric painting and photography. Enrichment groups in the sixth offer a choice of cultural, entrepreneurial and environmental activities. New venture is school's own radio station. Lots of good before- and after-school clubs and classes.

Background and Atmosphere: If you knew Ashmole School in the old days you wouldn't recognise it now. It had survived in pretty dire conditions for years but, on his arrival in 1997, Mr Brown organised the sale of six acres of school land and began a visionary building programme with the proceeds. Design of new buildings the result of collaboration between the school, its very engaged parents and the architect. Re-homing happened in 2004. School now buzzes along in smart, functional and not-hideous buildings. There is plenty of outdoor space and the school is sited on rising ground in quiet, residential Southgate – middle class, respectable and easy both into and out of London proper.

This is a school which is proud of itself and one in which everyone works to maintain its shiny smartness. Remarkably free of the litter and chewing gum which seem to breed in comparable schools, it has wide corridors, banks of sensible-sized lockers, spacious classrooms, labs and studios and an air of getting-on-with the-job. Attractive functional refectory and sensible menu – much emphasis now on healthy eating – and drinking – no fizzy pop. We saw melon being chopped up and bunches of grapes and wanted to stay and chomp. The atmosphere is orderly, collaborative, friendly. Classes we peeked into were, for the most part, disciplined and quiet; there is, overall, an atmosphere which encourages work and discourages messing around. Pupils we spoke too expressed a pride in and gratitude to the school we have rarely met elsewhere. 'I want to be a teacher because of this school,' said one.

Pastoral Care and Discipline: No mobiles allowed except for the sixth form, and they are confiscated if they go off in lessons. Zero tolerance of drugs, weapons and violence – on or off the premises. 'The school is very good about bullying,' we were told by a contented sixth former. Disruptive or abusive pupils are sent to the Individual Learning Room where they are under supervision, have no contact with their friends and hate it. Two or three days there usually does the trick but head will exclude for serious offences – two exclusions in 2009–10 – e.g. threatening behaviour, theft, fighting and disruptiveness. The result of what reads like a strict disciplinary regime is a school in which pupils feel secure and comfortable and everyone knows the score.

For such a large school, there is an unusual amount of interaction across the year groups – encouraged by the cultural and charitable activities. Pupils feel they have friends in all years. Great faith is expressed in the pastoral care given by the school – certain individual members of staff, e.g. the school nurse and deputy head, seen as especially approachable and reliable if something needs sorting. General sense of self-discipline and a fostering of civilised behaviour at work here.

Pupils and Parents: Vast ethnic mix as you'd expect, though more Cypriots – Greek and Turkish – than anything else. Main religion is Christianity of all sorts, second is Islam. Mostly working parents so little involvement in school during the day, but a supportive and hard-working PTA makes big contribution to the school's development and 90 per cent turn up to parents' evenings. Pupils are cheery, focused, ambitious and involved.

Entrance: Admissions unusually simple. All pupils live within less than a mile. Over 1,000 apply for the 224 places – of which siblings will take 50–80. You'll get in if you have a sibling there, you're a looked-after child and if you live near enough. Otherwise, no chance.

Exit: Few leave after GCSEs, and most of those will go to local FE colleges to study vocational courses. The rest stay on, mostly progressing to university with one third going to Russell Group universities and another 40 per cent to other top universities such as Queen Mary, London. Most study science, medicine, law and humanities. There is also a good size group going off to study arts and media and 10 per cent study a language. Notable former pupils include Amy Winehouse, former S Club 7 member Rachel Stevens, musician Stephen Sidwell, goalie Mark Bunn, Oscar winning producer Graham King, lead vocalist from The Feeling, Daniel Sells and Channel 5 tsar Sham Sandhu.

Remarks: Slick, sensible and effective. Check out the housing market.

Ashville College

Linked to Ashville Junior School in the Junior section

Green Lane, Harrogate, North Yorkshire, HG2 9JP

• Pupils: 780 boys and girls; 115 board. • Ages: 4-18 • Size of sixth form: 160 • Methodist • Fees: Day £10,890-£10,980; Boarding £17,070-£21,495 pa • Independent

Tel: 01423 566 358
Fax: 01423 505 142
Email: ashville@ashville.co.uk
Website: www.ashville.co.uk

Head: Since 2010 Mr Mark Lauder MA (Hons) (early forties), educated at Hermitage Academy, Helensburgh, did an MA in English Literature and History at the University of Aberdeen, spending his Junior Honours year at the University of Oregon, Eugene, USA. After graduating he embarked on research at St Edmund Hall, Oxford, where as well as winning a graduate scholarship, he achieved two half Blues in rowing. Previously deputy head of Felsted School, Essex, head of history and then housemaster at St Edward's School, Oxford, and before that head of history and master in charge rowing at Shiplake College, Henley-on-Thames. Married to Caroline, with two sons, both at Ashville College, one in pre-prep, the other in junior school. Older pupils describe the head as confident, open-minded, approachable and dynamic, younger ones as 'cheery and easy to talk to.' Interests include rowing, rugby, politics and restoring a 17th century Yorkshire parsonage, in between long walks in the Dales, and all things Scottish. Believes strong positive relationships between teachers and pupils is key and adds, 'Listening to pupils and understanding their point of view is crucial to engaging them and helping them realise their ambitions and potential'.

Academic matters: Good value-added, especially at GCSE; approximately 55 per cent of all passes are graded A/A* with 94 per cent graded C or above. Approximately 65 per cent of A level passes are graded A* to B, 99 per cent A to E. Science, mathematics, economics, PE and DT all very strong subjects at A-level. At first glance holds a fairly lowly place in the league tables but isn't highly selective in the first place. Taken as a whole, results wouldn't set the world on fire but most pupils exceed predicted potential and very able pupils do this particularly well.

Average class size 18 (Years 7 to 11), dropping to 12 or fewer in the sixth form. Shortish school day – 4pm finish and no Saturday school, but option of after-school activities and clubs. Area winners of the Physics Olympiad in 2009 and frequently sweeps the board in design and technology competitions. All Year 7 pupils (and Year 3 in the junior school) are screened for dyslexia using the Philips and Leonard Screening test with further testing and screening as necessary. No pupil has a statement of special educational need but the school identifies almost 70 pupils, mostly boys, as in need of some special provision. Over half of these require extra English as English isn't their first language, and approximately one-third are dyslexic, for whom specialist help is available. All access full curriculum and are educated in the mainstream classroom by the class teacher with support as required. The norm is for pupils to be withdrawn for one period per week when assessments are carried out and help given on an individual basis. Individual education programmes (IEPs) are included in school reports. Those with dyslexia thrive thanks to the caring environment and carefully planned programmes of study; indeed in recent years only one child didn't get the benchmark five A–Cs at GCSE and most gain at least a B in English.

Games, Options, the Arts: Well resourced music suite is home to a selection of choirs and bands. Talented musicians play in the National Children's and National Youth Orchestras but playing and performing opportunities for those just starting out too. Plenty of productions – latest offerings, Feel the Spirit by John Rutter and Pirates of Penzance, well received. Dedicated art studios and drama facilities always busy. Sports facilities – two gyms, 30m swimming pool, fabulous climbing wall, squash courts, fitness room and ample pitches – show importance of sport.

All usual suspects on offer plus American influenced disc golf – something for everyone.

Background and Atmosphere: Founded in 1877 by the Methodist Church, the pleasant, uncontroversial site sprawls across an otherwise residential area. Evacuated to Windermere during the war as the premises were requisitioned for the war effort and used by Air Ministry. Run as a Christian school in the Methodist tradition. Plenty of well-kept facilities – atmospheric Memorial Hall is home to lectures, meetings and some concerts, with larger gatherings filling the school hall. Recent extensive refurbishment programme with most classrooms and the library being totally modernised. Refurbishment of co-ed junior boarding house recently completed and girls' boarding house refurbishment begun in 2010 and due for completion in 2011. Plans in place for work to start on final classroom refurbishment and planning permission has been granted for an Astroturf pitch.

Pastoral Care and Discipline: All Year 7 are taken to the Lake District for a bonding weekend early in the autumn term; this receives rave reviews not only from the new pupils but also from sixth formers, who work as liaison prefects. Those lucky enough to be assigned to Year 7 go on the trip too. Duke of Edinburgh award scheme available for pupils from Year 10. Trip for older students to Malawi ties in with charity fundraising to support the Open Arms Orphanage which has close links with the school. School viewed as a day school with boarding. Four boarding houses are comfortably furnished with usual facilities: kitchens, commonrooms, games areas and computers. A new co-educational junior boarding house was opened in September 2009 for children from 8–12, already proving very popular with parents and pupils.

Approximately one-third of boarders are from South East Asia – this has reduced in recent years with more emphasis on weekly boarding and more recruitment from the Armed Forces, especially at the junior end. Girls and boys encouraged to socialise, with trips regularly organised at weekends and half-termly theme evenings provide fun for all boarders. Plenty of activities on offer after school but all optional – pupils think everyone should do at least one or two to get the most out of boarding life. Fines if caught smoking, with possibility of exclusion for repeated offences. Drugs: out for intending to or supplying. No issues in recent times.

Pupils and Parents: Hail from local professional and business families, quite a few first time buyers of independent education. A number of Americans from nearby Menwith Hill military base. For about ten per cent of pupils English is not a first language and overall approximately 14 per cent come from a variety of minority ethnic backgrounds. Thriving Friends of Ashville runs regular well-supported activities. Old boys: Ian Dodds (designer of the Moon Buggy), Commander Ian Grieve (head of anti-terrorism Scotland Yard), Ian Coucher (head of Network Rail).

Entrance: Interview, report from previous head and day of tests: academic and practical for Year 7. Sixth form entry is via interview and satisfactory reference, minimum five grade Cs with grade Bs in subjects to be studied. Exams, interview and reference are norm for entry at other times. Majority of pupils come from own junior school and nearby preps: Belmont Grosvenor and Brackenfield in Harrogate, Westville and Ghyll Royd in Ilkley and Richmond House and Moorlands in Leeds, plus local state primary schools.

Exit: Just under ten per cent leave at the end of Year 6 and 25 per cent at the end of Year 11. Almost all sixth formers go on to higher education, a couple to Oxbridge, rest to a wide range of the better universities.

Money Matters: Academic, music, sports, art and drama scholarships are available in the senior school. Scholarships are awarded on entry into Year 7, Year 10 and Sixth Form and are reviewed at key stages. Means-tested bursaries of up to 100 per cent of fees are available either in conjunction with scholarships or on a stand-alone basis. Additional discounts are awarded to the children of Methodist ministers and parents in the Armed Forces.

Remarks: Plenty of happy pupils in a nurturing environment. Popular with locals and overseas pupils alike. Worth a look if one school from nursery to university suits your child.

Atlantic College

St Donat's Castle, Llantwit Major, Vale of Glamorgan, CF61 1WF

• Pupils: 340 girls and boys from 80 countries • Ages: 16-19 • Size of sixth form: 340 • Non-denom • Fees: £21,000-£23,000 pa • Independent

Tel: 01446 799 000
Fax: 01446 799013
Email: jan.bishop@atlanticcollege.org
Website: www.atlanticcollege.org

Principal: Since September 2007, Mr Neil Richards, previously head of Yokohama International school.

Academic matters: Students follow the International Baccalaureate Diploma (IB). On average 95 per cent pass and over a third achieve very high scores (top 30s/40–45 points). English is not the native language of most students but both teachers and fellow students are actively engaged in helping them become fluent. Students have also taken up the suggestion that for one day everyone speaks to each other in their second language – which is being pursued with gusto!

The College prides itself on a challenging, internationally-focused, broad and balanced educational experience, with an emphasis on service and leadership that goes way beyond formal teaching and that prepares students for life beyond the classroom.

Games, Options, the Arts: Academic work in the morning; afternoons are given over to community service and student-led activities. On offer is a broad spectrum of experiences that aim to give the students practical skills, that emphasise the need to work together in tackling a task and which encourage the development of initiative and responsibility. College students and staff crew the local inshore lifeboat service and act as lifeguards, along with the Vale of Glamorgan rescue service. The campus includes an organic farm, complete with sheep; students, unfazed by mud and blood, can help out with the lambing. Indoor and outdoor swimming pools. Music is strong; the school choir tours internationally every year and there is a vibrant arts centre on the college campus. Students have a vital role in helping to organise social and sporting activities – they put up a notice and get on with it.

Background and Atmosphere: Kurt Hahn and others founded Atlantic College in 1962 – the first of the United World Colleges (UWC) aiming to enable young people to become responsible citizens, committed to peace and justice. Set on a Welsh bay with the campus centre in the 12th century St Donats Castle; the college owns and farms the surrounding 150 acre estate. Restored terraced gardens lead down to an extra-mural centre on the seafront which is used for residential courses. Students live in seven co-educational residential houses with boys and girls on separate corridors. Four students of different nationalities share each room – a bit cramped but there's plenty of space elsewhere. New projects include a bio-mass heating system that heats part of the campus and a recently refurbished student residential house, designed and refurbished to environmentally-friendly specifications.

Runs a two term system, with short half term breaks. First years arrive in mid/late August for a year that breaks for about four weeks over Christmas, then runs to late May. Second years return at the beginning of August to spend time on community projects.

Pastoral Care and Discipline: Students are treated as though they were at university rather than at school. A community code and the UWC code of conduct set out clear guidelines as to what behaviour is expected. Students and teachers are on first name terms, but this seems natural given the atmosphere. House parents attached to each student house; there's a system of peer listeners and a part-time student counsellor.

Pupils and Parents: Students come from some 80 countries, about a third from the UK. Selection process is designed to establish if they have the necessary skills to cope with the IB (basically a broad intelligence and an ability to work hard) and the temperament to mix in with a multi-cultural community. Seems to be effective: we saw how well students supported each other, much like the energy generated in the film version of Fame.

Entrance: Apply for selection through your UWC National Committee – see www.UWC.org. Each national committee (around 125 of them) has an allocation for Atlantic College (and indeed other UWC colleges). British students have approximately 20 places at Atlantic and another 16 at overseas UWC colleges. If it is not obvious which Committee is yours (e.g. you are Chinese but have lived in the UK for more than five years, or you have become detached from your country of origin due to war or other social circumstances) ask for a ruling. The deadline for applications is during the January in the year of entry.

Sometimes a few places not allocated as above are filled on a full fee basis, but students must meet the normal entry requirements. Ask the college about this.

Exit: Almost all of the students move on to university, about a third in the UK, a third in the USA/Canada (largely Ivy league colleges) and a third in their native countries.

Money Matters: The UWC is committed to a policy of selecting students on merit and potential, regardless of ability to pay – with financial support provided on a needs basis. Candidates will be means-tested upon selection, which means that some parental contribution, often substantial, may be required.

Remarks: Read carefully the college's full and accurate explanations of the type of education on offer and what students are expected to contribute. If you can sign up to that, then this small island of internationalism in a stupendous and improbable setting on a Welsh bay, with palm trees in the gardens and ever-changing light, should be high on your list.

Aylesbury Grammar School

Walton Road, Aylesbury, Buckinghamshire, HP21 7RP

• Pupils: 1,290 boys, all day • Ages: 11-18 • Size of sixth form: 370
• Non-denominational • State

Tel: 01296 484 545
Fax: 01296 426 502
Email: office@ags.bucks.sch.uk
Website: www.ags.bucks.sch.uk

Headmaster: Since 2008, Mr Stephen Lehec BA (Soton), (late 30s), previously deputy head since 2006. Gained degree in English and history from King Alfred's College, Winchester, then PGCE at St Anne's, Oxford, in history and games, followed by Maidstone Grammar (assistant head of history, ran school football, assistant head). Wife Penelope; two daughters, one at a local primary, the second daughter pre-school. School went from Ofsted good to outstanding in his first year as head. 'I am a strong supporter of openness, transparency and tradition.' Hopes to develop academic excellence 'whilst maintaining a focus on the individual and their needs in and out of the classroom.'

Academic matters: A flagship school and among the top state grammars in the country. It has the sort of feel – and the sort of boys – you might have imagined had gone with Jennings, Derbyshire and Mr Wilkins. But if you think it might be stuck in an academic time warp, think again. It became one of the first specialist technology colleges in 1997 and changed this specialism to science in 2006, when it was designated a specialist language school as well. It added a third specialism, maths and computing, in 2007. Clearly, forward thinking is a feature – the IT block dates from 1985 and now boasts two computer science labs, as well as six computer suite. Results are good across the board and, in some cases, spectacular – e.g. mathematics and statistics at GCSE, history at GCSE and A level and all three sciences, studied individually (no double or single award here) at GCSE and A level. All of these subjects are taken seriously here and by very large numbers. Other popular A level subjects are English, where both literature and language and literature are offered, and economics and business studies, both offered at GCSE and A level. All sixth formers do a complementary studies option, ranging from a full A level in general studies to Italian and Japanese GCSEs, and much in between, which 'gives a structure to the broad, balanced curriculum and makes them more motivated to do well.'

Modern foreign languages hold up very well here – Spanish, French and German all well supported. In this enlightened school, a good linguist can take three languages at GCSE – something we have seldom encountered elsewhere. Classics in the form of both Latin and ancient history is available throughout. All take three sciences at GCSE and the vast majority of students end up with between ten and 13 GCSEs – 'most of them don't want to give up any subjects – the more they can do, the happier they are'. GCSEs generally strong, especially in sciences, maths, history, economics and languages. Sports studies and drama are relatively new options at both levels. 99 per cent achieve five A*–Cs at GCSE but more significantly, over 75 per cent achieve five A*/As. The average grade at GCSE is an A grade. Class sizes average 30 in first three years but fall to the 20s at GCSE and below 20 at A level. The pupil:staff ratio is currently 16:1. An even divide of male and female staff at the school; both deputy heads are female whilst the three assistant heads are all male. The staff age profile is very balanced. A freshness of approach that suggests learning is very much alive here.

SEN very well-supported. Everyone is screened on entry and school takes dyslexia, dyspraxia and Asperger's Syndrome in its stride, most children being helped individually. Full-time and experienced teacher – 'very good at recognising more complex special needs, e.g. autistic spectrum, and referring them on'.

Games, Options, the Arts: Rugby (12 teams) is the main winter sport but Year 9 upwards also plays football on a regular basis. Cricket and athletics dominate the summer. Sport is big here and they have the space and facilities to do it properly. Excellent on-site pool, good pitches on site and two minutes' walk away, courts, a multigym, a small gym and a vast sports hall. Squash (seven times national champs), basketball (county champions three years running) as well as many other sports, including boxing and chess, enjoy success. Was named area school of the year for sport in 2009 and 2010.

Music is outstanding – auditions for the house music competition took place as we toured and we were impressed by the range – solo Bach cello followed by a rock choir cum brass band – and the competence. Most boys seemed to be carrying instrument cases and music was blasting, mostly painlessly, from everywhere. Good recording studio and new additional practice rooms as well as traditional assets. Drama also strong: a new drama studio in 2006 – a splendid addition, invaluable to GCSE and A level cohorts as well as to younger classes. School hall and the Aylesbury Civic Centre, used for larger productions – mostly collaborations with Aylesbury High School for Girls, which is adjacent. Art looked good and we liked the emphasis on basic drawing/painting skills as well as the ceramics and textiles.

Large and excellent library, new sixth form study room and superb lecture theatre which holds entire sixth form. Colossal number of visits abroad and at home, supporting all areas of the curriculum and fun.

Background and Atmosphere: Venerable. It was founded in 1598 as Aylesbury Free School by Sir Henry Lee, who was the Buckinghamshire MP in Queen Elizabeth's parliament. Lee was the originator of the annual Accession Day Tilts on 17th November, the most important Elizabethan court festival, and the first person to hold the office of Queen's Champion, which he resigned in 1590 when the annual tilts were held at Westminster, acknowledging that his 'golden locks Time hath to silver turned'. Originally it was the champion's duty to ride, on a white charger, fully clad in armour, into Westminster Hall during the coronation ceremony. There he threw down his gauntlet and challenged any person who dared to deny the sovereign's right to the throne. Lee was made a Knight of the Garter in 1597, one of very few commoners to have enjoyed that honour. A second substantial endowment was given to the school in 1714 for instructing poor boys of Aylesbury and Walton and neighbouring parishes. The boys were to be instructed in Latin, writing, arithmetic and accounts so they would be fit for apprenticeships to good trades. The school admitted girls in 1903, and in 1907 – with 75 of each sex – it moved to its present site. The girls and boys separated in 1959 to form the present two schools, which maintain close links. The school became voluntary aided in 1952.

School is on a quietish road just off the nightmare of roundabouts and arterial roads which, to the uninitiated, Aylesbury seems to be (if you're a local, you can probably cope fine). It is housed in archetypical twentieth century grammar school buildings – a mix of the soundly robust, one-storey, red-brick-and-tile main building and various later accretions inspired by the municipal architectural mind which seems sadly universal. Resources are carefully garnered and husbanded. The new head has set about removing the luminous, almost fluorescent colours, and much of the school is now in calm hues in the public areas and bright, lively colours in the classrooms. However the site and its buildings are a sight better maintained than many – the buildings include a number of recent, impressive additions and the whole site has a pleasant feel, considerably less depressing than most.

Pastoral Care and Discipline: The six houses are important here. Rivalry is intense and loyalty important. Wellbeing and progress are overseen by heads of house, tutors and heads of year. A trained counsellor is on site two days a week. Prefects have weighty responsibilities and help with supervising and patrolling. Formal and traditional manners – boys stand (and tuck shirts in) at the start of lessons. Staff take uniform seriously and can be heard pulling up boy after boy on infringements 'take that hoodie off', 'tuck your shirt in', 'that's not a school jacket,' etc, but we certainly saw (with some sympathy) at least as many shirt-fronts out as in. Sixth form council consistently votes to keep their uniform, but do wear coloured shirts, jumpers and representative ties that separate them from the rest of the school. They appreciate greater independence in other areas of life, especially having their own kitchen, staffed and run for them by the catering team at the school. Drugs, smoking and alcohol policy clear and enforced – 'Any involvement runs the risk of exclusion'. The head has excluded a number of boys over the years and was backed by the appeals panel in those instances when the exclusion was challenged. School's behaviour policy, however, strikes the right note as far as we could see: 'The vast majority of students ... are a credit to themselves, their families and their school and the reason there is so little need for serious sanctions is the self-discipline and enthusiasm shown by so many of our boys'.

Breakfast served daily, substantial snacks around for break and school lunches are popular, nutritious and good value – and eaten by staff too. Much made in-house.

Pupils and Parents: From a 12 mile radius and most from inside Bucks. More or less reflecting the diverse mix who live both inside Aylesbury and in the villages surrounding – up to Milton Keynes. Bright-faced, articulate and friendly boys with middle-class accents and the 10–12 per cent from ethnic minorities – largely Italian, Chinese and south Asian – seem well integrated. Interestingly, they make no claim to well-known OBs – so, all you prominent Old Aylesburians, show yourselves!

Entrance: Administered centrally by the local authority. Everyone takes the 11+. Don't bother with maths and English coaching – the assessment is purely via a test in verbal reasoning (with a bit of non-verbal thrown in). Thereafter the only thing that will weigh is your distance from the school, though having a sibling there already may help. Entrance into Year 12 requires 356 points from the best eight GCSEs with at least a B (often an A in some, e.g. maths) in your chosen A levels.

Exit: To the whole range of higher education and other pursuits. From Oxford PPE to professional football, from advertising to law at Kent.

Money Matters: School less impoverished than many grammars with a solidly based foundation, generous bequests and parents who like fundraising. The results are palpable, audible and visible.

Remarks: A thumping good state grammar and a very good argument for the cause.

Backwell School

Station Road, Backwell, Bristol, BS48 3BX

• Pupils: 1,700 boys and girls • Ages: 11-18 • Size of sixth form: 355
• Non-denom • State

Tel: 01275 463 371
Fax: 01275 463 077
Email: mailbox@backwellschool.net
Website: www.backwellschool.net

Head: Mr Julian Baldwin MA PGCE (early fifties), educated at Chichester High School before reading French and Spanish at Queen's College, Oxford. Previously deputy and then acting head during predecessor's illness. Taught for 20 years at Parrs Wood High School, Manchester. Staff view head as 'steadfast, caring and with a sense of humour'. Still teaches and likes to be 'out and about' in the school. Head says Backwell is a 'marvellous place in which to work and learn' because of its 'can do' culture. Expects staff to share his commitment to excellence. Married to Gill, who teaches languages at Backwell; they live in village. Eldest son, Max, graduated from York, Matthew works in IT and daughter Kate is studying Philosophy and French at Sheffield. Loves sport, literature and cooking.

Academic matters: Over 55 per cent A and B grades at A level with strong individual performances and a regular Oxbridge places. Boys outshine girls in maths and physics whilst girls perform better overall. In 2010, 66 per cent of candidates obtained five or more A*–C grades at GCSE including English and Maths, with majority of pupils taking 10 subjects, including six options drawn from creative areas, languages and humanities. Strong in core subjects and majority takes at least one modern foreign language. Backwell is a training school with innovative courses for older staff as well as induction and graduate training programmes. Student teachers include some native French speakers.

Wider than usual choice at AS and A2. Critical thinking encouraged as an additional AS option in Year 13. BTec in leisure and tourism offered as a Year 12 course for less academic. Lower down, mixed-ability teaching operates across half the age group with setting in mathematics from the outset, and in modern languages, science and geography from Year 8. Short GCSE courses in PR (philosophy and religion) and ICT for most. Creative and media and business, administrative and finance diplomas are offered in the sixth form. Enrichment programme styled Xtra Bytes runs twilight GCSE lessons in Latin, full ICT and RE courses plus fast-track music and a welcome chance for most to take separate sciences from Year 9. Strong PSHE course with lots of careers guidance. Plenty of computer suites but not OTT, plus Apple Macs for graphic work. Lots of buzz in DT and loads of original designs. Some vocational courses in sixth form but demand is greater for academic A levels.

Has a well-earned reputation for special needs including its gifted and talented programme. 'Having the right attitude towards special needs has helped raise expectations of pupils across the ability range,' says Head. School puts its money where its mouth is by providing priority accommodation for special needs on ground floor of stunning new building; lift provides wheelchair access to maths classrooms above. We saw one boy with cerebral palsy manoeuvring his wheelchair happily around site and one of 14 pupils diagnosed with Asperger's participating fully in a food science lesson with learning support. Thirty-six children currently with statements, some visually and hearing impaired. All children screened on entry for dyslexia with about 160 currently receiving individualised support. SENCo manages specialist staff including 13 LSAs.

Games, Options, the Arts: Range of sports (including swimming in Years 7 and 8) offered as part of core PE provision but not timetabled in sixth form. Plenty of sports available during extended lunchtime and after school; free late bus for those staying for activities. Pupils use adjacent leisure centre as well as school's sports hall and eight new floodlit all-weather tennis courts. No Astroturf but extensive playing fields which provide room to breathe at lunch-time during drier months. House competitions and some inter-school matches with teams practising and playing after school. Steady flow of representative players at county level. Community sports leadership award is a popular addition for some.

1950s theatre needs a revamp; studio theatre for smaller productions. Outreach work in primaries and participation in local festivals. Full orchestra and range of bands, choirs and ensembles. About 20 per cent of pupils have instrumental lessons and chamber choir recently sang in St Mark's, Venice.

Lots of trips within curriculum (art department were at Tate Modern when we visited). Sixth form leavers go on World Challenge expeditions biennially.

Background and Atmosphere: Opened in 1954 as a secondary modern; reorganised in 1969 as a comprehensive, with its own sixth form since 1979. In recent years has expanded rapidly and built reputation over a wide area for good discipline and academic success. Carefully concealed but close to village centre. New canopied entrance leads to a modern reception area and spacious foyer, where displays include plenty of art plus evidence of recent school successes. New buildings for special needs and mathematics (with a multicoloured glass roof) and new visual arts studios with vibrant, student-designed art on external cladding. Library is at heart of school life and includes a separate fiction classroom with 7,000 titles, all supervised by a doubly qualified teacher/librarian; equipped with laptops for online quiet study by sixth formers; identikit fingerprint technology used successfully for checking out loans. A new sixth form and media building is scheduled to open in December 2011.

Pastoral Care and Discipline: Common sense prevails – mobile phones are allowed for emergency use but are confiscated if used otherwise during working day. Pastoral system is strength of the school – parents and pupils emphasise how supportive and helpful they find the teachers. One mother described how she received a 'prompt and effective response' when her daughter was subjected to some 'low level irritation' from another Year 7 pupil. The large numbers are broken down into manageable units – school maintains a separate dining facility for Year 7; Years 8–11 share two kitchens between their four houses. Sixth formers have their own centre, so GCSE pupils are interviewed regularly by head of house to gauge progress, and sixth formers have lots of support too.

House areas double up as social and teaching areas with little evidence of fabric suffering as a consequence. House assemblies in own areas but year assemblies held in theatre. Trained school nurse also monitors attendance and 'uses some discretion' before contacting parents. Nice balance between long-term, experienced staff and younger teachers who move for promotion elsewhere. School council plays part in shaping policies and includes representatives from all age groups with meetings attended by a governor and clerked by school bursar. Part-time adult mentors help with management of behaviour and learning programmes for relatively small number of disaffected.

Pupils and Parents: Predominantly well-behaved, motivated pupils from affluent rural suburbs eight miles south-west of Bristol. Parents expect school to deliver a rounded, orderly, academic education and generally seem pleased with results. Years 7–11 look comfortable and smart in navy sweatshirts over white polo shirts trimmed with house colours. Sixth formers lack 'attitude' and generally wear sensible gear. Presence of a large sixth form helps to 'foster strong work ethic'. 'Some teachers don't believe in homework,' reported younger pupils, but plenty for exam candidates. One girl who was repeatedly 'picked on' at a rival comprehensive said she'd never had a moment's bother here. Active parents' association with fund-raising and donations to school's coffers. Former pupils include film director, Kirk Jones, plus loads of media types, academics and sportspeople.

Entrance: LEA manages admissions to Years 7–11 – those from catchment area will get a place but there is heavy demand from elsewhere. School places siblings in same house and takes care to avoid pupils from one feeder school dominating any tutor group. School handles entries into its sixth form, which attracts some from Bristol independent schools.

Exit: 20 per cent go to FE colleges at 16, much less than from most comprehensives in the LA; a few go directly into employment, but the majority remain in the sixth form. Most Year 13 leavers proceed to higher education across a wide a range of courses and universities.

Money Matters: Local authority funded, with constant belt-tightening constraints. Local management enables some creative balancing acts. Parents contribute to school fund to assist with societies and expeditions. Financial support available in cases of hardship in accordance with school's comprehensive ethos.

Remarks: Much friendlier than you would expect given its size. House system ensures pupils in Years 7 to 11 have a strong sense of identity. Hugely successful sixth form. Lots of younger, enthusiastic and committed teachers. Positive and reassuring buzz through busy working day confirms how well this place justifies parents' description of it as 'a really good all-round school'.

Badminton School

Linked to Badminton Junior School in the Junior section

Westbury Road, Westbury-on-Trym, Bristol, BS9 3BA

• Pupils: 435 girls of whom 60 per cent board and 40 per cent in the senior school are day girls • Ages: 3-18 • Size of sixth form: 120 pupils • Non-denom • Fees: Boarding £27,330; Day £15,360 pa • Independent

Tel: 01179 055 271
Fax: 01179 628 963
Email: admissions@badminton.bristol.sch.uk
Website: www.badminton.bristol.sch.uk

Headmistress: Since 1997, Mrs Jan Scarrow BA PGCE FRSA (early fifties). Educated in the north, read history at Manchester, previously deputy at Stonar. Married to an engineer. 'Borrows' a history set for a fortnight or so and then hands them back, 'it's lovely'. Works on the timetable ('it helps me know what's going on') and has an impressive and detailed knowledge of the school throughout. The rumour that 'Scarrow is scary' does not come from within – the girls like her and parents speak of her as 'approachable, compassionate when necessary, sensible and wholly committed to the school'. No jargon-spouting, arm waving, self-important theorist, she gets on with the business of quietly educating and inspiring. 'Collective mediocrity is not an option,' it says on the website – her phrase, her belief. But don't think Margaret Rutherford and waving hockey sticks – think conviction. Wholly sympathetic to the non-conformist ethos of the school, she is prepared to take risks and is keen for girls and staff to be challenged.

Academic matters: Consistently way up in the league tables and so perceived by some as a cherry picking hothouse – vigorously denied by parents, staff and pupils.

The intake from the junior school and independent prep schools is broad and inclusive. 'The real value-added strength of the school is that it takes average girls and turns them into high performers,' says a mum with three very different daughters in the school. The bright girls are not made to do more than three A levels and breadth of interest is encouraged; girls do not go home for the holidays groaning under the weight of homework. Younger girls are given a rolling annual introduction to Latin, German, Spanish, Italian, Mandarin, thereby 'cutting the primacy of French'. By the time they are thirteen they may choose from three languages.

Subjects are not blocked before the girls have said which ones they wish to do. 'We can't always accommodate all the permutations but we minimise constraints,' says the head. Maths and sciences strong. So how are those excellent results achieved? 'I wish I knew,' said an envious head; 'I can't quite work it out myself,' pondered a parent, 'but I think it's because the school is consistent and thorough. As a result there is no great hiatus when it comes to exams.' 'The teachers are enthusiasts,' says a leading academic. 'Badminton girls don't faint,' says Mrs Scarrow, a reference to girls in the 19th century finally being allowed to sit for public examinations when other girls were 'routinely expected to faint before the arithmetic paper'. 'We enjoy the work,' say the girls, and in the sixth form, 'we're allowed the freedom to work in our own way.' That sense of freedom is central to Badminton – no honours boards, no speech day prize giving, no trumpeting of individual successes.

Games, Options, the Arts: 'A few years ago I might have indulged in a mild bleat about the games,' a parent told us, 'but not now.' The facilities are excellent, the girls are healthily competitive in their approach; county and national players. Everyone is encouraged to find a sport they enjoy. Music thrives from its purpose built headquarters with about 80 per cent learning instruments. Orchestras, ensembles, jazz, choirs, rock groups, quartets. The bright and airy creative arts centre is an exciting place from which are fired inventive and colourful textiles, imaginative jewellery and terrific photography. The overall effect is stunning. Drama too is hugely popular, with up to seven productions a year and opportunities to become involved on and back stage.

Background and Atmosphere: Founded in 1858, it has always been different. The founder's aim was to give girls as good an education as their brothers. Initially its nonconformist origins and belief in a serious, free-thinking intellectual approach, rather than deportment and sewing, shocked the more staid members of Bristol society. Right from the start it was concerned with the global picture (the first boarder was from the West Indies) and girls were encouraged to think for themselves and not be merely decorous and demure. In 1924 the school moved from Clifton to its current site of 20 acres. Centred around the elegant Northcote Manor with its lovely rose garden and unusual topiary, the campus is full but doesn't feel crowded, thanks to the predominantly light brick and cream paint used for recent additions. A new 'green' boarding house has just opened. That will herald the start of a lot of 'exciting relocation' of classrooms, seminar rooms and offices. Girls are cheerful and friendly (rows of them walking along with linked arms and smiling faces) and the atmosphere is calm and happy. Lots of trips abroad, some in the company of boys' schools, as well as D of E expeditions.

Pastoral Care and Discipline: No school chapel but boarders are free to attend church if they wish to. Tutoring is done in year groups. There are few rules – the girls seem to be guided by commonsense and courtesy with much mutual support. Very, very occasional suspensions. 'A culture of disappointment is what reins in any thoughtlessness,' says the head. The sixth form is housed in its own very cleverly designed building: comfortable, homely but not flashy. Sixth formers are trusted and given a lot of freedom. Wearing their own clothes, as opposed to the school uniform, is an outward symbol of this. Head girls are elected by the pupils. 'Discipline really isn't an issue,' we heard over and over again.

Pupils and Parents: Pupils still come from all over Europe and the world (20 per cent of boarders). Those from abroad are fully and comfortably integrated and local girls appreciate the opportunity for making international friends. Some mild anxiety expressed about getting the balance right – not too many from the same country – but 37 countries are involved so no obvious conveyer belt. Parents come from a cross section of professions – Bristol is that sort of city – and are happily included in many activities. Famous alumni include Iris Murdoch, Indira Gandhi, Rosamund Pike, Polly Toynbee and Phyllida Law.

Entrance: At all junior levels and then mostly at 11, 13 and 16. Very few from the junior school are denied entry, though they sit the entrance exam at 11 in English, maths and verbal reasoning, same as other aspirants. 'They are always prepared to be flexible and genuinely seek bright-eyed all-rounders,' says successful prep school head whose school regularly feeds. Eggheads don't necessarily get in: the school is looking for girls who will fit in and appreciate the idiosyncratic atmosphere and ethos. Entrance examinations in November for 16+ and in January for other age groups.

Exit: All to university and on average 15 per cent each year to Oxbridge. Some 25 per cent go on gap years – the experiences gained are reflected in the girls' all-round performances at university, where there are reports of girls rowing, directing plays, broadcasting and generally getting stuck in. No reports of post A level burn up. Thence mostly into professions. Medicine, science, engineering, finance and law seem to be particularly popular, though, as with everything at Badminton, no pigeon-holing.

Money Matters: Means-tested bursaries and the usual range of scholarships (academic, art, music and all-round) on offer at 10+, 11+ and 13+. Foundation Awards of up to 100 per cent off fees available for 2011 entry for Years 5Years 5 and 7.

Remarks: 'Badminton babes', as some boys refer to them with a mixture of awe and admiration, are feisty in argument, independent in mind and spirit, loyal to the ethos of their school, friendly and courteous. Individuality, coupled with commonsense, is genuinely celebrated and girls are given freedom and time to develop within a sensitively constructed framework. Don't take too seriously the carpings of envious schools and ill-informed assumptions about Badminton's academic success. Yes, there are, perhaps, too many pictures of girls celebrating exam results, but that's only part of the experience. For girls who can handle freedom and match up to high expectations, this school is a beacon.

Balcarras School

East End Road, Charlton Kings, Cheltenham, Gloucestershire, GL53 8QF

• Pupils: 1,300 pupils (650 boys; 650 girls), all day • Ages: 11-18
• Size of sixth form: 310 • Non-denom • State

Tel: 01242 515 881
Fax: 01242 250 620
Email: admin@balcarras.gloucs.sch.uk
Website: www.balcarras.gloucs.sch.uk

Headteacher: Since 1996, Mr Chris Healy BA MEd (fifties), educated at Xaverian College, Manchester before reading history and politics at Nottingham. Returned to Manchester for his PGCE and picked up his MEd from Leicester university whilst teaching in Milton Keynes. Worked his way up through five comprehensives (including deputy headship of Tewkesbury School and headship of John Masefield, Ledbury) before appointment at Balcarras. Has raised academic profile here dramatically and is a great supporter of all extracurricular activity. Parents describe him as 'switched on' and attribute much of the school's success to his leadership. 'He knows how to attract the right staff and sorts any problems out quickly,' reported one satisfied parent. An approachable head who knows both pupils and staff well despite the size of the school. Married to estate agent, Penelope, both their daughters went through Balcarras prior to university. 'Little time for leisure,' he says but enjoys relaxing at home with his family when he can. A 'head who makes things happen,' say staff who know he is behind them: last four deputies proceeded to headships. Head regularly undertakes 'pupil pursuits' (shadowing pupils from different houses for a whole day) to gain a pupil's eye view of the school. Keen player in specialist schools' trust and enjoys working with other schools to help raise their standards.

Academic matters: Specialist technology school which outperforms all other Gloucestershire comprehensives with 80 per cent achieving five A*–C including English and maths at GCSE; impressive value-added scores too. A level results place Balcarras up with Cheltenham's big name independents and ahead of some of the county's selective schools – quite extraordinary. Over 30 courses through to A2 level in sixth; about 30 take critical thinking. Now offering AQA baccalaureate which involves 100 hours additional input from students. Results are all the more remarkable given that Pates in Cheltenham creams off a proportion of would-be Balcarras high flyers. We met pupils, though, who had turned down the chance to sit for Pates and were glad they had done so. Emphasis on lively lessons which hold pupils' interest. Number-crunching deputy has put lots of systems in place to evaluate pupil data and maximise pupil potential. Some parents we spoke to rated maths, business and science departments whilst others pointed out modern languages and English. The school's six dedicated ICT suites are well-managed and heavily-used. DIDA (diploma in digital applications) modular course is taught once or twice a week after school for those who can't be fitted into the timetable. Impressive technology areas underpin school's specialism: usual carousel arrangements to end of Year 9 then all pupils pursue at least one technical area to GCSE. We watched an industrious and keen bunch of Year 10 pupils in food technology, admired the products of the jewellery option as well as the high standard of woodworking and manufacturing. Some pupils act as mentors in food rooms for weekly visit by different groups from 'feeder' junior schools. We also watched Year 8 pupils working in textiles area as part of 'mad hatter's project'. Modern languages remarkably strong here with French, Spanish (strong links with Spanish school) and (commendably) Russian holding up well through AS and A2 levels. 80 per cent choose at least one MFL to GCSE level. Maths strong (60 A level candidates in Y12 and 11 taking further maths); 30 taking physics – all groups taught by qualified specialists. School benefits from close link with Gloucestershire university education department: six trainees in school at any time. Lots of checks, it seems, on homework and classwork by HODs and senior staff to keep everyone up to the mark.

Well-developed individual learning department provides additional help for 10 per cent of pupils who need it. Positive attitude throughout school towards learning support. LSAs assigned to different departments; lots of in-house expertise. Nine statemented pupils and several seriously challenged pupils come under the care of this well run department. Sixth formers receive training to help Year 7 pupils through paired reading. All pupils are screened for SpLD using NFER and other tests. 'Pupil passports work better than old style IEPs,' says SENCo who uses them to alert staff to pupils' particular learning needs. Plenty going on to enrich experience for pupils identified as gifted.

Games, Options, the Arts: Students here revel in the arts: acting, music, art and dance all grab their interest: lots go off to festivals and love getting involved in productions. Highly successful art department – 85 GCSE candidates. We saw exhibition of GCSE examination work which highlighted pupils' range of technical skill and creativity. Best AS results in country. As many as 40 take art to A2 level with 20+ going on to foundation course at Cheltenham. Four large art studios with plenty of space for different age groups. Some pupils choose to do photography (includes film making and animation) and many work on their art projects during the lunch break or after school. Purpose-built drama studio with separate lighting studio hosts non-stop productions. Second drama studio has been created from former art room. Dance is also popular and takes place in gym or drama studio. Staff say that head is 'terrific supporter of the arts.' 'Fantastic music department,' say parents: eight different ensembles including hugely popular soul band. Two main music classrooms, recording studio and seven practice rooms: terrific buzz amongst musicians when we visited. House music is very popular with input from sixth formers.

Sport is promoted strongly and nearly all younger pupils participate in team games and extracurricular sporting activities. Full size, floodlit Astroturf and good grounds for rugby, cricket, athletics. Boys' and girls' hockey and plenty of tennis/netball courts. So-called 'pavilion' provides a modern space for dance, conferences and presentations. Super sports hall plus fitness suite used by Year 10 and above. Pupils rate PE teaching and senior staff will come out to cheer on Year 10 rugby players. Lots of activities at all levels: scores participate in D of E up to gold award; biennial World Challenge expeditions as far afield as Mongolia and Costa Rica. Recent county and area winners in Young Enterprise; sixth formers last year were county winners in ESU Debating Mace, national finalists in Bar Mock Trial at Old Bailey. Annual activities week for Years 7–9; camp for Year 9 and work experience for Year 10 all come at end of summer term.

Background and Atmosphere: Positive atmosphere grabs you right away and despite large numbers feels like a smaller school. History on this site stretches back to 1958 when the co-ed Charlton Kings County Secondary School moved here. Balcarras was formed in 1986 as a result of a shake-up in the local education system which scrapped single sex schools. Architecturally a product of its era but with lots of modern infilling and a succession of stylish newer blocks to match the earlier ones. The sixth form centre opened in 1998 and the modern languages block a year later. Lovely playing fields behind and imaginative use of areas between buildings help to give the school a different feel. Whole school has a 'cared for' atmosphere which more than compensates for the utilitarian buildings. We liked the way that the sixth form area interconnects with the main school and the lay-out of the common room where we attended a personal pre-A level assembly given by the head which held students' interest and made good points at a crucial time. Separate computerised study carrels for lower and upper sixth – very impressive and heavily used by students including after school hours. Well-resourced library used by all years though somewhat small for the number of pupils.

Attractive canteen is widely used: lots of healthy eating, good hot meals plus 'grab and go' sandwich bars which are popular. More pupils' cycle to and from school since erection of new cycle sheds and three 'empty car park' days a term when 'even the head cycles to school.'

Pastoral Care and Discipline: Red hot on attendance – best in county. Strong house system (named after four prominent Gloucestershire personalities) through main school with seven or eight classes in each year. 'Houses are cornerstone of school's success,' say some. Discipline is based upon committed house staff; for once we saw teaching staff doing lunch-time duties. Senior staff regularly walk the local area to make sure all is well – this goes down well with the community. Common sense underwrites what goes on; head has to rack his brain to remember last suspension. 'Children don't overstep boundaries,' said one teacher and we felt staff succeed in creating just the right kind of relationships with pupils from the youngest to the sixth form.

Pupils and Parents: Very mixed lot socially but switched on to achieving good results whatever their background. Confident, happy pupils who hurry to lessons and work hard when they get there. Sixth formers less interested in Cheltenham's 'spiky' night life than a few years ago, according to head. Sensible, attractive uniform with polo shirts in summer denoting colour of houses in main school and well-interpreted dress code for sixth formers. Those we met were articulate and well-motivated with a confidence based on a 'can do' attitude. Access for disabled – two currently in wheelchairs and one mum spoke of how greatly one boy had benefited from the 'can do' attitude at Balcarras. Sixth formers organise lots of social and fund-raising events. Former pupils include modern pentathlete, Jamie Cooke. Really supportive parents who count their blessings

Entrance: Admission criteria have changed to serve immediate catchment area of Charlton Kings. Previously, children living only a mile from the school were losing out to those in villages now served by Cotswold School or others. 'Seems to be a much fairer arrangement,' says head, but one which inevitably pushes up local house prices. Two Bs and three Cs (including English and maths) minimum requirement to enter sixth, which attracts large numbers from local state schools and also from independents.

Exit: Most stay on after GCSE. Mainly to university after A level – complete range of courses, colleges and universities. Two or three a year to Oxbridge.

Remarks: Here's a school whose success owes much to the head who moves it onwards and upwards every year. 'Don't ask me to give my son's place up,' joked one father. Great to see a comprehensive raising the bar in a highly competitive local educational market. Must be worth considering a move to Charlton Kings.

Balerno Community High School

5 Bridge Road, Balerno, Balerno, EH14 7AQ

- Pupils: 800 boys and girls, all day • Ages: 11-18
- Size of sixth form: S5 125, S6 90 • Non-denom • State

Tel: 0131 477 7788
Fax: 0131 477 7707
Email: Susan.Donald@balernochs.edin.sch.uk
Website: www.balernochs.edin.sch.uk

Headteacher: Since 1995, Mr Rory Mackenzie BEd MEd (fifties), who is married (his wife is a principal teacher: support for learning) with a daughter still at school, and he does not intend going before she is through with her education, which means he will be 62 when he retires. Educated at Rudolf Steiner in Edinburgh, followed by Telford College, Stevenson College and Edinburgh University. He has worked his way round the Lothians, starting by teaching English at James Gillespie's, followed by assistant principal teacher of guidance at Craigroyston, assistant head teacher at Blackburn and deputy head of Broxburn. A splendid head, who guides this conglomerate with a steady hand and gentle sense of humour, and weathered the glitches of a couple of years ago with aplomb. ('Magnet school as far as disabilities go?' we asked. 'Yeah, yeah, and we co-teach,' was the reply.) Immensely proud, not only of the school, but also of the input of pupils, he dismissed the criticisms of the (Feb 2004) HMI report, 'We are operating well above average,' though he did agree that they needed to provide more vocational courses for the less academic. (HMI's other concerns focused on monitoring of pupil and staff progress.) Balerno is a community high school, a way of life, and the head, whatever he may say, is inextricably involved with the whole community.

Academic matters: An inclusive school with a broad intake. Good support for learning provision, with a dedicated staff of three plus classroom assistants and learning assistants; ICT plus scribing, individual sessions and withdrawal from class all available, comprehensive tutorial support, use of ICT (laptops available) and extra time in exams. Surprisingly, the HMI suggested that more could be done and that guidance and special needs should work more closely together. Extra help from dedicated staff for non-native English speakers, but not a large number of these. Six computer suites, used for proper lessons as well as ICT. For a long time the school led the computer revolution in Edinburgh.

'No particular bias by subject,' said the head. Science results at Higher level seriously impressive. Maths equally strong, English top of comparator schools for Standard grade, Higher and Intermediate 2, whilst German (which the HMI praised as 'being above average') only managed a trickle at A and C; ditto French. Huge improvement in physical education exam performance. The first state school in Edinburgh to teach Mandarin. Accounting and computing in the ribbons, as is economics, and outstanding music, good PE and art. Art-room computer-linked. Good Intermediate 2 in graphic communication, hospitality (practical cookery) and woodworking skills and well below in biology – which doesn't tally with the Higher results. 'Some pupils may be too lazy,' said the head. 'The intermediate courses are really good.'

Games, Options, the Arts: 'The sports facilities look nice but we badly need an Astroturf.' Hockey and rugby 'really strong with internationalists and good representation on the junior East of Scotland football squad (for boys and girls in both cases) plus a rep in the wado kai karate team that competed in the European Championships. Swimming and kickboxing equally popular. Terrific drama – the studio is also connected to the internet. Powerful music, with a variety of orchestras, choirs and bands.

Good international outlook and masses of exchanges including Beijing: twinned with 11 different schools in Europe, plus a two-way project with Romania, with pupils doing a joint project on violence in society in connection with a Fulbright exchange with Bellevue High School in Seattle – an amazing school adjacent to Microsoft HQ. Has won the Lothian finals for Young Enterprise. Work experience for all at S4 and work shadowing in sixth. Parents and school find the positions – a joint effort. Popular clubs post school, at lunchtime and in the evening: Spanish, web development, electronics and publishing as well as extra-curricular dance, snowboarding (Hillend and the real thing), hockey and athletics. D of E. Keen charity input.

Background and Atmosphere: Has historic antecedents – the charming logbook kept by the principal teacher of St Mungo's Episcopal School in Balerno during the nineteenth century is a joy: 'Wet and windy all week. One child was blown into the Water of Leith but was fortunately rescued. One child was bit by a dog ... .' School itself was opened in 1983, on a glorious greenfield site on the banks of the Water of Leith. (Head has a stunning view from his office.) As an 80s build, it was an imaginative concept to include community presence, but oh, the wasted opportunity! The building has all the worst of the 60s' overtones: huge long passages, bare concrete staircases with scaffolding poles as banisters and narrow staircases. Moving around the school during a busy time feels like an endless computer game. There are few ceilings (indeed, 20-odd years on the school is still installing them) and the place feels like a cross between an aircraft hangar and an airport lounge in the developing world.

Built on a grid system. The squares of hitherto neglected grass between interlocking classrooms are being turned into delightful mini-themed areas, with pupils working in their free time: running water for Japan, a chess set – all part of 'an eco-school biology project' (Balerno is striving for Green Flag status). The community affiliation provides the school with all sorts of ancillary activities including a serious 20-metre swimming pool as well as some outstanding public areas. For the stranger it is a bewildering entrance – two reception areas with strategically placed tables and no real feel of school or, oddly enough, sense of purpose and bustle. The pool and the gym, which doubles as a dance studio, are both used by the community when not time-tabled for school use, and the area next to the learning resources centre doubles for school and community groups, including an after-school club, all next door to the school crèche. The Riverside café is used by locals popping in for a coffee and serves as the school refectory – open from 8am for breakfast. School uniform for all, worn with a certain amount of panache in some cases.

Pastoral Care and Discipline: Strong new anti-bullying strategies in conjunction with S6. All pupils join one of four houses called after local areas, siblings in same house; heads of houses are in charge of pastoral care and guidance. Tutorial system for all, same tutor throughout the school, good contact for parents on academic matters. Head Start for 'vulnerable' pupils before they begin at Balerno, when the new S1, sixth form and staff spend a week confidence-building. S1 pupils also spend a bonding week with their guidance and pastoral staff at one of four residential centres during their first term (Monday to Friday). Regular year group and house assemblies.

Pupils and Parents: A tremendous cross-section – local farmers, farm-workers, professionals who drop their children off from four-by-fours. Five per cent from ethnic minorities, mostly the service industries. Excellent and supportive parent council and parent-staff association that does massive amounts of fundraising.

Entrance: From three dedicated primaries: Dean Park, Ratho and Kirknewton, plus huge numbers of requests for placements – there are 29 requests for this year from as far away as Buckstone and Sighthill (which are not next door). Pupils from outwith the area may have problems with the regular school bus but parents' council helps to provide extra buses.

Exit: A few leave to try their hand in the workplace after S4 (low employment rate), some go on to tertiary education elsewhere. Most stay on for Highers in S5 and S6, about 30 or so leave annually after S5. Seventy per cent or so go on to university; strong links with the local high-tariff universities: Edinburgh, Heriot Watt for science, Aberdeen and Glasgow, plus a small trickle, one or two a year, to Oxbridge.

Remarks: School and community thriving.

Balfron High School

Roman Road, Balfron, G63 0PW

• Pupils: 970 boys and girls, all day • Ages: 11-18 • Size of sixth form: 200
• Non-denom • State

Tel: 01360 440 469
Fax: 01360 440 260
Email: balfronhs@stirling.gov.uk
Website: www.balfronhigh.org.uk

Head: Since 2002, Mrs Val Corry BSc (Eng) ARSM PGCE SQH (fifties) who took an unusual course into the heady world of academe. Educated at Morpeth Girls' Grammar School and Imperial College London where she read metallurgy and engineering, her first job was researcher for British Steel which she swapped for teacher training at Moray House followed by Grangemouth High and a post partum dabble in ceramics then back onto the academic ladder where she leapfrogged through Linlithgow Academy (she lives in Linlithgow), and Stirling and Wallace High (depute head). She still teaches (physics, PHSE, maths and chemistry) well worn lab coat on the back of her door, 'does people good to see you teach'; and tries to have 'real contact with at least half the school every year' by interviewing pupils individually and in small groups. Last year she reckoned to speak to a third. Sharp, elegant role model, she has transformed this zinging new school into a 21st century flagship and is totally at ease with the current gov-education-speak (though one or two less savvy locals mutter about 'modern educational mumbo jumbo'...).

Academic matters: School has taken to the curriculum for excellence with a vengeance. The three existing houses act as mother-ship for three school-lets (known as schools, following the American model) with a ninth of each year in each school. The form teacher for each year stays with that class throughout their time in school. Class teachers are responsible for the pastoral care of their children and may well teach their form for some seven hours a week, so all pupils know there is someone out there batting for them. Max class size 20 in the first year, in practical subjects and in maths and English in S3, with extra maths and Eng in S3 if needed. Slightly complicated system of mix-and-match with hist and geog (social subjects course) – 'a standard rota used by schools and not complicated', says head; specialist staff from S2. Fiercely academic – 'Not so', says head, 'we do far more here than concentrate on academic subjects' – and high uptake in all advanced higher subjects. Strong science school with marvellous labs (but marvellous everything, see below); biology lab has a greenhouse incorporated into its roof. Labs are an astonishing, carpeted, 90 metres square.

Good, solid, run-of-the-mill academia. French and German on offer, Spanish and Russian in sixth. Scottish BAC next year in science and langs. Head thrilled that number of pupils getting five subjects at higher level has grown from 19 to 30 per cent since 2007. Flexible learning not a problem and sixth formers and local adults (evenings) can log on to do distance learning courses; sociology the current flavour of the month. Strong links with Forth Valley College and Skillforce for less academic. Computers abound, three pupils per machine, and emails for all. Whiteboards in every classroom. Problems picked up early, and reported immediately, so that any child finding difficulty should be 'sorted out' quickly – via house meeting, which will include deputy head plus support-for-learning teacher and other appropriate staff, and remedial strategies discussed: professional support, psych eds pulled in if needed. Qualified head of support for learning plus three others and four assistants in school. This is an inclusive school, capable of dealing with physical disabilities. Terrific library overlooking the atrium, with views out over the games pitches to The Campsies.

Games, Options, the Arts: School incorporates a fabulous leisure complex with pool, sports-hall and weights much used by the local community and open from 7am to 10pm 365 days a year. (Fantastically fit local community then? – not immediately obvious from mass of adult humanity passing through reception whilst we were waiting!) Excellent swimming (25-metre pool), Astroturf, pitches and athletics track. Masses of games after school, Stirling Council (and the lottery) provide a sports co-ordinator; rugby good – both national and international players in the school, and list of names of all national players of any sport in reception. Art is state of, with every possible medium catered for and finished products creeping onto the walls and a rather chic patio. Computer-linked CDT mass of machines. First year must do home economics, thereafter optional between third and sixth – flash new kitchens with microwaves. Terrific theatre and drama, the theatre available to the community, and masses of music, with local involvement. String, wind and jazz plus Teudan Teth fiddle band, myriad choirs and boy groups plus countless talent shows and clubs at lunch time. Work experience for all at 14. Masses of trips and exchanges, for culture and education (i.e. skiing is out). Strong links with school in Malawi and a huge amount of exchange – staff as well as pupils. School will underwrite those who can't afford it. Huge amount of charity work and much local involvement, including a guide dog puppy called Faith. Huge amount of charity work and much local involvement.

Background and Atmosphere: Opened in May 2002 by Helen Liddle, who celebrated the partnership between Stirling Council and Jarvis by sticking the first leaf on the 'school tree of learning', which climbs up the corner of the atrium adjacent to the dining-room, where pupils either bring their own or use swipecards (which conceals the free school meals problem – about four per cent). Graduands (to continue the American theme) have their name embossed on a leaving leaf, which is firmly fixed to the 30 foot high tree by the intrepid janitor.

A magnet school. State-of-the-art in every dimension – each subject has a pod of rooms off the main core, terrific views, marvellous outside area (the sun does occasionally shine north of the Highland Line). The school was built under a PFI scheme by Jarvis of Railtrack fame – now bust; catering and maintenance provided by same staff but now employed by SGP and, apparently, 'brilliant'. Magical food with mass of choice. All the rooms are networked for sound (as well as inter/intra netted) and at 10.45am loudspeaker announcements about sin on the school bus, praise for work well done and extra music lessons boom over the speakers. Electronic noticeboard advertising week-end jobs at the local pub. School became a community school proper in 2003 but the old boards still reassuringly in place. School uniform for all: trainers out, otherwise just polo shirts, sweatshirts etc atop some of the shortest skirts we have seen this year; smart blue blazers with green trim loaned annually to sixth formers, who must have them cleaned before they are returned.

Pastoral Care and Discipline: State system of pupil support, good PSHE and anti-bullying strategies in place. 'Balfriending' is a buddy system between first and sixth years which really works. Masses of contact, sixth pick up problems early; incidents are logged, the victim supported and the bully sanctioned – sanctions range from verbal warnings through 'the imposition of a written exercise' (restorative exercise' = reflections) to temporary or even permanent exclusions and ed psychs etc. Head maintains that most bullying is really just 'a breakdown in relationships'.

Pupils and Parents: Huge catchment area: 800 children bused in each day. Good middle class ethos prevails – 'we are a comprehensive school', the head reminds us – combo of real country plus incomers, friendly and welcoming children; few from ethnic minority backgrounds. Enthusiastic parents' council which seems to spend time worrying about 'incidents' behind the (unused) bike shed and why special praise seems to be singled out for athletes. Head stresses that they raise money for the school, help with careers advice and interviews, and work with school to manage road traffic problems.

Entrance: From local primaries, capped at 180, usually 30 or so placing requests.

Exit: Few leave after Standard Grades, around 90 per cent stay for Higher of whom 70 per cent will stay till sixth form. Most to Scottish universities – Ed and Glasgow top of the pops with the odd one or two to St Andrews and occasional trickle to Oxbridge.

Remarks: Stunning school, happy staff, good work ethos, some of the best views in Scotland. Worth moving to the Trossachs for.

Bancroft's School

Linked to Bancrofts Preparatory School in the Junior section

611-627 High Road, Woodford Green, Essex, IG8 0RF

• Pupils: 790 boys and girls (equal numbers) • Ages: 11-18 • Size of sixth form: 230 • C of E, but Jews and Muslims properly provided for, all other faiths welcomed • Fees: £12,558 pa • Independent

Tel: 020 8505 4821
Fax: 020 8559 0032
Email: office@bancrofts.org
Website: www.bancrofts.org

Head: Since January 2008, Mrs Mary Ireland BSc DipEd Member Soc of Biologists, Chartered Biologist (early fifties). Mrs Ireland's career began with Proctor and Gamble, but light dawned and she took her teaching qualification and has taught all three sciences and maths in both state and independent schools. Prior to succeeding the very popular Dr Scott at Bancroft's, she was deputy head of Christ's Hospital, before which she had been housemistress at Ardingly and head of science at King's Hall. Mrs Ireland – married, with a grown-up musician son – is brisk, open, energetic, easy to talk to, with an attractive Scots intonation. She is a true, professional head, clear about her modernising agenda – she lost no time in implementing changes – and as clear about the values upon which Bancroft's was founded and which still inform its ethos. She has clearly been won over by the school and its community, 'the buildings have a wow factor – though I tell parents that they are not what the school is about – but the thing that really appealed to me was the children. They are London children who tell it how it is, they are multi-racial, striving children who want to do well – they are incredibly competitive. They do everything here that we did at Christ's Hospital, only they cram it into a school day.'

Mrs Ireland is a safe pair of hands – and not hands that mind getting dirty – she cleared up a lunch that slid off a pupil's plate onto the floor when we visited. She is involved, busy and available. Some of her changes not entirely understood by school community – restructuring of the school council and the popular Stars in their Eyes extravaganza being two. Introduction of new Virtual Learning Environment – internet school-home communications system – hit by predictable teething troubles and much groused about but will be a useful asset when smoothed out. She manages to teach some GCSE biology – we applaud. Bancroft's should continue to thrive under her eager eye and hands-on regime.

Academic matters: Notable results across the board but maths is a star performer by any standards. In 2010, 87 per cent got A*/A at GCSE. English more of a spread despite reports of some brilliantly inspirational teaching. Modern langs getting a boost from a Mrs Ireland innovation of allowing a choice between French, German and Spanish. Greek and Latin have healthy numbers. Remarkable science results – especially in chemistry. Hist and geog also impressive. Few takers for art, music and DT – surprising given the facilities – but this is a school which takes its academics seriously. No trendy subjects though drama has just seduced its way into the timetable and options list. A particular, enlightened feature is that A level subjects can be chosen not, as elsewhere, from 'blocks' but from the whole curriculum. If they can manage it at Bancroft's, why not everywhere? A level results similarly impressive, with 63 per cent A*/A in 2010. Most popular are maths – 76 takers in 2010 from a cohort of 125 pupils. Unique, as far as we know – and the results! – 67 of the 76 got A*/A/B. Chemistry again popular and successful (44 candidates in 2010). Economics and geography good and, at this level, English also impresses. Greek and Latin survive though the numbers taking modern langs are, we would suggest, a cause for concern, though may reflect the immense diversity of backgrounds here.

A place where serious learning happens and in which learning is taken seriously. The library, recently revamped with a stylish new mezzanine floor, beautifully integrated into the whole, is a proper scholarly resource – not something you see everywhere these days when for 'library' you can so often read 'IT suite'. Pupils appreciate the library and its staff – 'they are fantastic – they get in anything you need'. Sixth form will be getting new dedicated library in 2011. New, university-type lecture theatre – used for societies, debates and visiting speakers. IT everywhere – lots of rooms with new PCs, including a brand new tip-top language lab which should give the langs a deserved boost.

Learning support dept screens all at 11+ (the prep also screens at 7+). Mrs Ireland appointed the school's first SENCo and has also ensured that all new staff get some training in SpLD. All on the LS register (mostly mild dyslexics) have an IEP and get some kind of individual support – the younger ones come out of different lessons each term and older ones get one-to-one. A TA in class helps those who are happy to be helped in that way. Lower sixth get help to 'develop individual learning skills'. 'They are wonderfully flexible over special needs,' says a parent.

Games, Options, the Arts: Sports are 'big' and well-resourced. Large playing fields on site plus vast sports hall with 25m pool. Five minutes away is school's own West Grove with pitches, courts, tracks etc. Achievement to match – 2009 saw triumphs in netball, rugby and cricket as well as tours in these and hockey to e.g. New Zealand, Australia South Africa and Sri Lanka. Heart-felt pupil and parental complaints that sport is too elitist – 'if you're not in a squad they don't give a monkey's' – seen by Mrs Ireland as a priority and B and C teams now being developed, along with soccer. 'We are encouraging more staff to help so we can run more teams. It's something we need to work on'. CCF is huge, very popular and enthusiastically pursued by those who surprise themselves by how much they get out of it. 'It's taught me how to get on with people I'd never mix with normally.' 'It's good that the sixth form help with it – you can have a bit of a laugh with them.' Not common in what is still, more-or-less, a London school. Highest number of D of E gold awards of any London day school in 2009. Thriving Sea Scout group with cubs, scouts and explorer sections.

Equally, Mrs Ireland is determined to boost time for arts across the school and has already increased provision. Music and drama enthusiastic and popular – annual concert in Drapers' Hall the big annual event with bands, solo performances and musical mix the main features. Vast range of instruments studied – music maybe more pop and jazz than classical, though we are told there are around eight classical concerts each year. Drama had a recent fillip with conversion of old gym to good, large new studio and subject now on the curriculum at all levels. Not all musicals here, either – The Caucasian Chalk Circle and Macbeth among recent productions. Art, electronics and DT depts produce lively work – we liked the clever clocks, mobiles and the remote control cars and, within the remit of the task, pupils are given their head to be creative with the actual design. Art, exceptionally well-displayed throughout school, originates in one of two studios – light, spacious and full of quiet artists. Nice ceramics. Art could and should be bigger here – perhaps textiles and photography – on the way – as more than a club? New art studios due to open in 2011 should help. Tons of trips and tours – though some parental gripes about not enough places on trips for eager applicants. Extra-curricular stuff is good though some cries for more from the inexhaustible.

Background and Atmosphere: Founded in 1737 by the Drapers' Company on behalf of Francis Bancroft as a school for poor boys; moved to Woodford from Mile End in 1889 into the present large and imposing red-brick Victorian Gothic revival building – clearly designed to impress with serious scholarly credentials by architect, Sir Arthur Blomfield – also responsible for Selwyn College, Cambridge, The RCM, much of Charterhouse, The Bank of England, Wellington, Eton Lower Chapel etc etc as well as an astounding number of parish churches. This, one of his more benign and attractive buildings with towers, crenellations and Oriel windows, a splendid central quad and admirably generous corridors which, though originally intended for 200 boys, still feel spacious for today's quadrupled numbers. It's a truly impressive school with twisty brick staircases and leaded lights which grab eager ten-year-olds immediately – 'I chose it because it was like Hogwarts,' – a unique selling point in Essex, to be sure.

Some typically dismal 1960s add-ons but much better later additions (such as enormous multi-purpose sports hall) and adjoining buildings e.g. vast head's house now used for admin and offices too – with head's garden open to everyone for quiet time and 'well-respected'. Integral chapel one of the best bits (complete with much-loved chaplain who is, 'lovely, a wonderful person for a chat, a laugh and advice – he takes Salsa club') – into which everyone comes once weekly for an ecumenical service. Brass plaques to former heads and a vast stained glass east window set the tone for the services which are inclusive in all ways, given the mix of pupils. Chapel also used for arts events – words and music etc – a classy extra-curricular feature here. Large Great Hall – typical of date and type. Excellent Courtyard Building with colonnaded atrium and sitting area, dining room – in which all eat together – servery and sixth form common room and cafe – large and well-used. Parental tributes to general efficiency of school and its communications. Sense of order, purposeful activity and common sense all-pervasive. Good food though popular vegetarian option can run out too fast for true veggie latecomers, we're told.

Pastoral Care and Discipline: When asked what was good about the school, all the parents and pupils we spoke to – lots – said, as with one voice, 'the pastoral care'. We can't recall such unanimity on any other school feature anywhere. Tributes to the teaching staff, the overall friendliness, the care and attention given to individuals pour from everyone and are a delight to hear. 'My teacher is amazing – he's given me extra lessons every week. He's ordered in around 30 extra books just to help me. They'll help with anyone – not just the Oxbridge candidates.' 'The teacher gave my daughter as much time as she needed when she was struggling.' 'The staff commitment is excellent; pastoral care couldn't be better.' 'My children love it – they look forward to every day.'

Pupils and Parents: From as far away as Potter's Bar, Winchmore Hill and Cheshunt though most from between 10 and 20 minutes drive away. Vast ethnic and social intake – 'very well-handled by school', say parents. Around 30–35 per cent S Asian, 10–15 per cent Jewish, 40 per cent 'white Essex'. Most parents first-time buyers who 'work very hard to pay fees'. OB notables include Dennis Quilley, Sir Frederick Warner, Sir Neil McFarlane, Hari Kunzru, Adam Foulds, Yolanda Browne, Andrew Saul, Anita Anand and Lord Pannick QC.

Entrance: At 11, 50 come up from the school's own prep. Around 400 apply for 60 additional places. Tests in maths and English plus interviews. In practice, around a third of those whose first choice is Bancroft's will get in. Umpteen feeders though several from St Aubyn's and Loyola. Around a quarter from state primaries. Candidates for the sixth need six As at GCSE plus the usual references. Around 20 places at this level – very few leave.

Exit: Virtually all to worthy courses in worthy places – around 11 each year to Oxbridge and many more to e.g. Durham, Nottingham, Leeds and the London University colleges to read everything from architecture to zoology via medicine, management and Japanese.

Money Matters: Fifteen Drapers' scholarships offered annually at 11+ worth a quarter to a half of fees. No means-testing – based solely on performance at entrance exams. Also music schols worth half or quarter fees plus free tuition in one instrument. Several Francis Bancroft schol awards – means-tested but with a generous financial threshold – these are worth up to full fees based on a sliding scale dependent on family income.

Remarks: A splendid school, catering for bright children and those who will seize opportunities. Deservedly oversubscribed. Brings glory to Essex well beyond its immediate catchment.

Basil Paterson Tutorial College

66 Queen Street, Edinburgh, Midlothian, EH2 4NA

• Pupils: 35 boys and girls. EFL College operates separately on same site. • Ages: 16-19 (but currently some in their 20s) • Size of sixth form: 20 • Non-denominational • Independent

Tel: 0131 225 3802
Fax: 0131 226 6701
Email: info@basilpaterson.co.uk
Website: www.basilpaterson.co.uk

Head: Since 2009, Susan Shaw. Previously director of studies at Edinburgh School of English for nine years. Aims to build on college's strong academic reputation and increase numbers. Also looks after students' welfare, guiding them through subject choice and the UCAS application process.

Academic matters: Edinburgh's oldest and most famous tutorial college, founded in 1929. Currently owned by the Oxford Intensive School of English (OISE). Huge number of subjects on offer: Scottish Highers, Advanced Highers, Intermediates and Standard Grades plus all three of the English exam boards GCSE and AS/A levels. A team of part-time tutors to cover the various examination subjects (Edinburgh is rich in tutors). Maximum class size six, plus many individual lessons where necessary. Well-equipped lab and art room on site. Four lessons' tuition per subject for Standard Grade/GCSE per week, five for Highers/AS levels and six for Advanced Highers/full A levels. An accredited exam centre for all four boards. Impressive success rate. Excellent Highers results. Good careers advice, help with UCAS and clearing. The full-time course includes supervised study as well as the social programme.

Popular Easter revision courses run in (almost) everything. In addition, flexible tuition offered in any subject, which is very popular with both parents and pupils.

Background and Atmosphere: In superb premises at 66 Queen Street, it comprises two light, airy Georgian buildings joined together with some original ceilings still visible, and boasts state-of-the-art computers, a student common-room and study centre, a wireless area for students to use their own laptops, 12 excellent classrooms and an outside café area. Classes can flow over into the EFL side during the busy Easter period. New computers with email access for all. Good self-study area. Social programme provides students the opportunity to interact with each other and EFL students. Good camaraderie between students.

Pastoral Care and Discipline: Students on the whole live with families or in flats in and around Edinburgh; accommodation no problem for those from abroad or further afield. Students are expected to take a certain amount of responsibility for their own studies. Each student and parent/guardian must sign a student support agreement to agree to abide by the school rules.

Pupils and Parents: Currently 10 per cent from abroad plus first-time candidates, retakes and those hopeful of upping previous marks.

Entrance: Enrollment form must be completed and deposit paid before starting classes. Students are encouraged to meet with the head before starting to discuss subject choices, suitability etc.

Exit: Most go on to universities across the UK. Past students have gone on to study at (among others) Glasgow, Edinburgh, St Andrew's, Aberdeen, Leeds, Newcastle, Strathclyde, Heriot-Watt, University of Manchester, Edinburgh Napier University and Goldsmith's.

Money Matters: Fees are per subject per year and are invoiced termly or by other arrangement.

Remarks: Up and running and delivering the goods. A great stepping-stone between school and university.

Beaconhurst

Linked to Beaconhurst Junior School in the Junior section

52 Kenilworth Road, Bridge of Allan, Stirling, Stirling, FK9 4RR

• Pupils: mixed; 370 boys and girls plus nursery 40 (partnership status); all day • Ages: 3-18 • Fees: £6,510-£9,456 pa • Independent

Tel: 01786 832146
Fax: 01786 833415
Email: headmaster@beaconhurst.stirling.sch.uk
Website: www.beaconhurst.com

Head: Since 2005, Mr Iain W Kilpatrick BA MEd FRSA (forties), whom we did finally meet. (Our previous attempts had been blocked by his dragon of a receptionist who didn't like the sound of *The Good Schools Guide* – 'we have fulfilled our advertising budget' – and no matter how much we explained that it was our choice whether any school went into The Guide, dismissed our request to visit and so, apparently, did the head.) 'Not so', he said, and was profuse in his apologies. Indeed this year's attempt – as requested – was met with an 'I'll just check his diary before I commit him to something that might be a lot of nonsense.' In the event, the reception team were all sweetness and light when we turned up in person. And Mr Kilpatrick is a delight, sensitive and thoughtful; much concerned about the impact the financial recession may have on his parent base.

Mr Kilpatrick has had an unconventional career path; educated at The High School of Stirling, he spent the first four years of his working life with The Royal Bank of Scotland before going to uni at Stirling to read English and drama followed by a PGCE in Edinburgh. He started his teaching career at Strathallan, down the road, where he rose to become housemaster for five years and still helps out in the classroom when the need arises – 'it's why I came into teaching.' He runs the school with a deputy and a four-strong team responsible for the tutorial base, PSHE, careers and pupil support plus a vast and dedicated army of teachers; mixed age common room. He took over from Mr Clegg, who had been in place for some twenty years and is said to be 'much more relaxed'. Married to a pharmacist, he has two children in the school.

Academic matters: Small classes, max year group is 30; the 40 currently in transition (P7) are split in two certain amount of streaming in core subjects. Dedicated tutors from transition, max 14 per group. Italian from Junior school (P1) with French and German until S2. Lang labs and 'successful' pupil exchanges. Scottish system, combo standard, intermediate II, Higher and advanced Highers, no detailed analysis of results, but a pleasing number of A/Bs amongst them, all must do Eng, maths and courses in IT, core PE, social education, enterprise and young enterprise at S6. Otherwise all the usual suspects with Spanish club at lunchtime. Product design popular. No classics, strong maths (regulars in Scottish maths challenge) and science. Pupils can add to their higher portfolio or do advanced higher in S6. Enthusiastic business admin. Four computer suites, younger pupils use them too, and whizzo multi-coloured computer in the nursery where pupils do jolly phonics and only move up to junior school when 'they are good and ready'. Functional looking labs, where, for some reason, offerings from the art dept appear to proliferate (stuck on the door, hanging from the ceiling – apparently they are made in the science labs – a sort of do it yourself atom – 'science department being creative'). Assorted sized grubby white lab coats hang from a couple of nearby racks – 'help yourselves'. Interactive whiteboards abound (we spotted a couple of staff carting two new ones during our interview – 'cheaper to do it yourself rather than employing a contractor to rig them up') plus data projectors. School heavily into IT, and have adopted the Virtual Learning Environment – where pupils can access course work remotely and email both homework and queries to staff.

All pupils assessed for dyslexia and other learning difficulties at J1, though some may have been picked up in nursery. Terrific support for learning, with three support for learning teachers plus a collection of part-time qualified (SLAS) assistants throughout (the latter are often older, the qualification takes a year, and they are a 'really valuable support'). Withdrawn, co-teaching, school claims they can 'deal with anything'. Keyboarding skills are mainly enforced in the learning support unit, but touch typing from J1 and 'developed all the way through' Scribes, readers, extra time in exams, digital exams – you name it – the systems are in place.

Games, Options, the Arts: Boys' footie team plus hockey teams for both sexes, girls had fun trip to Canada a bit ago. School 'two minutes' walk' from stunning sports complex at Stirling uni and make full use of all facilities – swimming pool athletics, basketball. Sports students help resident PE staff, regular matches on Sat am. Dedicated sports hall below school dining room with cricket nets shrouding the walls when we visited and available to rent for £150 a pop, presumably with footwear restrictions for the former.

Extensive expressive arts: orchestras, singing for all, and really professional drama – compulsory – either to perform or to work backstage – brilliant for talent spotting. Choir performs on occasion at Dunblane Cathedral, acclaimed jazz band, some quite talented young players. Quite small music house away from rest of school for individual lessons. Awards in both. Strong links with Scottish Opera. Charming head of art, who explained she could cover most disciplines, pottery, sculpture, fabric design (but not fabrication), though the offerings on show were a tad mundane, better stuff on the walls around the school.

Geography, theatre et al trippettes to Glasgow, Edinburgh, wherever. Ski trip to proper abroad, plus visits to Fir Park at Tillicoutry, skiing part of standard grade sport, but not really factored into the Scottish scene, the odd weekend perhaps. High emphasis on (compulsory) outdoor week with real rock climbing, bonding time for prefects at local outward bound centre; D of E to silver: compulsory. Young enterprise, work experience. Variety of clubs and splendid charity fund-raising with one girl recently arranging a sponsored hair cut (wow!). Hands on charity in India – Beyond Barriers, one year fund raising, next year visiting. No home economics which seems a missed opportunity.

Background and Atmosphere: The school boasts a slightly larger site than its neighbours (a random collection of B&Bs and rather grand family homes – the one on offer at £835,000 went for over a million) but it is incredibly up and downy, with fairly shallow steep steps in all directions. Windy. For some reason a bus-stop-like shelter has been plonked half way up the steps from the science labs to the main campus. 'The weather is awful here,' said our guide, 'and it is really really useful.' Assorted collection of fairly pedestrian classroom blocks shoe-horned into what is really quite a small area. Jolly hopscotch and dragons painted on strips of tarmac for youngsters to play on and dedicated nursery area – though no obvious buggies or trikes during our visit (apparently there were garaged). The dilapidated Cameron Hall is no more, and an assembly phoenix is arising (on penalty time). The main house (1868 and not that much bigger than its neighbours) which was the original Beacon School for Girls (founded 1919, dreary dame school, long outlived its usefulness) has been much mauled around (historic Scotland?) and boasting a harum scarum collection of classrooms, store rooms and reception. A tiny (and admittedly 'much neglected') library boasts computers and a good collection of fiction but not much for research – ok computers are fine but paper research is sometimes more rewarding (subject matter stuff is apparently in subject depts). Library open over lunch and post school. Head made much of the (two) comfy sofas, but the sixth formers whom we met were busy at the table (sums) or the computer, and an outgoing bunch they were too. Not often are we asked 'where were you at university?' (Paris).

Beacon School amalgamated with Hurst Grange, a boys' prep in Stirling to become Beaconhurst in 1976, dropped the boarding and transmogrified into an all day 3–18 school during the '90s. Chaps, with varying length of hair and girls neat in (Black) Douglas kilted skirts plus rather expensive looking blazers with bound edges do the school proud. School aiming for eco green flag.

Pastoral Care and Discipline: PSHE throughout, with emphasis on healthy living and 'appropriate progression'. Tutor groups, strong prefect programme interlinked with a four house system and 'senior pupils' 'take on responsibilities within school and work with younger pupils'. Our guide said school was small enough to pick up any possible cliques or possible bullying. Pupil council. No religious bias. Only new dining/sports hall complex wheelchair friendly, but inner driveway makes for a certain amount of accessibility.

Pupils and Parents: Large number of first time buyers plus amorphous middle class parents, fair geographic spread, bused, school mini bus meets train at local station. Congestion problems with collection at tiny car parks, no dedicated visitors parking! Apart from local small business, farmers etc, some work in oil refinery in Grangemouth which employs a number of non Brits.

Entrance: Tinies spend session in nursery and are informally assessed otherwise two day taster for all, prospective pupil 'buddied' for first day, joining in all lessons, followed by tests in literacy and numeracy and verbal and non-verbal reasoning with the cognitive ability aspect taken by learning support department. Automatic throughout the school thereafter. Some waiting lists.

Exit: Occasional trad family exit to the wider public school system – and not many of those, some to Dollar et al for wider choice of Highers (or bigger pond to play in), and one or two leave early for vocational or other reasons, most into some form of further education, with the occasional gap year. Business and sports studies and IT popular, but horses for courses, beauty therapists, civil engineers and medics. Most to Scottish unis.

Money Matters: Scholarships available both to those already in school and external candidates. Some form of means-tested bursarial help may be available.

Remarks: Charming little school, grown from a couple of fairly non-performing boarding/day preps (The Beacon School for Girls and Hurst Grange) to a thriving fully fledged grown-up school in the last 24 years. Stunning little two class Junior Start which got a most impressive Care Commission Report recently.

Bearsden Academy

Stockiemuir Road, Bearsden, G61 3SF

• Pupils: 1,183 boys and girls (55/45), capped at 210 first-year intake (seven classes of 30); all day • Ages: 11-18 • Size of sixth form: 350 • Non-denom • State

Tel: 0141 955 2344
Fax: 0141 942 5949
Email: office@bearsdenacademy.e-dunbarton.sch.uk
Website: www.bearsdenacademy.e-dunbarton.sch.uk

Head: Since 2008, Mr George F Cooper (forties), who neither wants to talk to us, nor to 'give any more details': he comes from Ayr Academy, where he was depute head and was previously head of English. He was – to quote our informant – 'at Ayr for many many years' and came to Bearsden Academy in the footsteps of the legendary Mike Doig, who turned the school around, following a period of some unsettlement. Cooper has faced a serious challenge: the school moved in August 2009 to a new site on the perimeter of St Andrews Primary, on the old college site, a term later than planned.

Academic matters: School takes Standard, Intermediate I, Intermediate 2, Highers and Advanced Highers. (Pupils may also be presented for both Intermediate 2 and 1 instead of the Standard; they have different weighting.) German and French but no Spanish, and three separate sciences; maths and English results 'consistently strong'. Pupils are setted in their second year for English, maths, French and sciences. Not a vast choice of subjects but totally adequate with the non-academic well represented. Most pupils take eight subjects at standard grade.

Pupils are allocated a guidance teacher during their last year at primary, who acts as tutor throughout their time in secondary. Smashing library which also includes a careers office and much-used sixth form study centre. Six fully-equipped computing/business rooms – the library has a well-equipped computer room – fabulous dedicated space (books being added to all the time). Work ethos is important here, ditto homework, and homework diary must be signed by parent or guardian but pupils can complain 'to their Guidance teacher if they feel that they are unable to cope with homework'.

Support for learning throughout, with learning support staff visiting the linked primary schools to ensure a smooth transition. Four support for learning assistants, who work with children both on an individual basis and in class, scribing if need be; can deal with normal (mild) Aspergers et al, no currently diagnosed ADHD. New-build wheelchair friendly, no (real) problems with profoundly deaf or visually handicapped pupils. EAL on hand, over 22 different nationalities in the school, many of whom do not speak English as their first language.

Games, Options, the Arts: Stunning games hall and, as a community school, this is much used by locals too. Good spread of games pitches; school does remarkably well at rugby, football, with athletics well-represented. Outstanding success in football and basketball. No tennis courts or swimming pool but skiing, snowboarding are popular options, regular trips abroad – the Alps as well as Aviemore. Superb home economics facility, with pupils learning how to wash and iron, as well as cook and operate electronic sewing machines.

Cultural trips to Paris and Florence and large successful art department, fabric design as well as pure art. Music fantastic, choirs and orchestras of all descriptions, rock band seems to be on the wane. Drama extra-curricular but a popular club – pantomime and Shakespeare in alternating years. Long-standing Young Enterprise. Work experience in fourth year, with loads of private placements. Clubs highly popular, and the board game club specialises in esoteric conundrums that make the mind boggle; enthusiastic web club. Massive charity input from seniors in particular, with five-figure sums raised every year. World Challenge Expeditions to Thailand, Mongolia, Tanzania et al.

Background and Atmosphere: Now on swish new site. Prefectorial duties include keeping a weather eye on behaviour around school premises. Pupils all neat and tidy in school uniform which is mandatory, with a very strict dress code – no advertising, track suit tops, denim, baseball caps or trainers outwith PE and particularly no football colours or any item of clothing which could potentially cause friction.

Pastoral Care and Discipline: Exemplary. School has a very positive attitude to bullying – 'Friends against Bullying', senior pupils volunteer to work with the first year group, visit them first thing each day and wear badges indicating that anyone who feels they are being bullied can come to them to discuss the problem. There are also 'supervised' lunch time clubs that youngsters can come to, as well as study-buddies. Chaplaincy team of five – Church of Scotland, Baptist, all take a year each – Church of Rome declines to allow Catholic priests to join this ecumenical team which is a bit odd considering one of the local primary schools (St Andrews) is Catholic and 90 per cent of their pupils come on. Room set aside during Ramadan for prayer.

Strong discipline code, range of punishments, from Behaviour Card which must be signed by all staff, with the ultimate sanction being exclusion. Pupils who persist in being disruptive or who are late are sent to the Behaviour Support Base for the rest of the lesson which they have disrupted and often for the next lesson in that subject; they also have detention at lunch-time. Previous head would exclude but only temporarily; drugs not previously a problem and they were patted on the back by drugs supremo Maxi Richards, who has an input in the senior PSHE programme.

Pupils and Parents: Four per cent on free school meals; a good middle class bunch from Milngavie, Bearsden, Canniesburn as well as Drumchapel, north west Glasgow. 'Somewhat' over-subscribed, school has a good reputation and is handy for buses and trains. Priority to siblings, followed by East Dunbartonshire location (distance from front door to front door). Large number of ethnic backgrounds, over 100+ youngsters from non-English speaking families – most Asians and Chinese but Africans, Middle Eastern and east Europeans are well represented. Absolutely no problems with the mix, the school is a 'seriously harmonious group'. Good PTA with parents getting quite deeply involved with the school programme of speakers and interview skills as well as the trad charity role.

Entrance: Automatic from local primaries; then by formula. New arrivals can get immediate entry if space available.

Exit: Only 10 per cent leave post-Standard to do further education elsewhere or go into employment. A few leave post-Highers with university entrance qualifications but most stay for sixth form, notably those going to uni down south. Majority of leavers go to central Scottish universities – no particular bias – industry, dentistry and medicine popular. Regular two or three to Oxbridge annually. Some to study music, some to art school. Youngsters tend to go straight to uni, but an increasing gap year take up.

Money Matters: State, with help on hand to supplement low-income families to go on school trips. Two forms of financial help available to those who stay at school after the age of 16. Footwear and clothing grant for those whose family or guardians qualify as low-income; and the other, the Scottish Executive Education Maintenance Allowance Scheme (EMA)), for any pupils living in the area and going to school in East Dunbartonshire.

Remarks: A positive school, firmly setting its sights on the 21st century. Exciting times on new site; we will watch this space with interest.

Bedales School

Linked to Dunhurst (Bedales Junior School) in the Junior section

Church Road, Steep, Petersfield, Hampshire, GU32 2DG

- Pupils: 470; 220 boys and 250 girls. 330 boarders, 140 day.
- Ages: 13-18 • Size of sixth form: 185 • Non-denominational
- Fees: Boarding £28,815; Day £22,650 pa • Independent

Tel: 01730 300 100
Fax: 01730 300 500
Email: admissions@bedales.org.uk
Website: www.bedales.org.uk

Head: Since 2001, Mr Keith Budge MA PGCE (fifties). Read English at Oxford. Rugby blue. Previously a housemaster at Marlborough and head of Loretto 1995–2000. Married with three children. Not yer typical head but then this ain't yer typical school. Not by a long way. In open-necked shirt, discreetly striped jacket and subtly – though differently – striped trousers and unsubtle candy-striped socks, Mr Budge, Keith to everyone, has slowly, quietly and resolutely established his authority in this school and its diverse, vociferous constituency. He is relaxed, though serious, in conversation. While his commitment to the school and its ethos is measured in expression, it is genuine and profound. Parents criticise him both ways – 'the school isn't achieving academically as it should' – 'Bedales has become more ordinary and interested in academic results at the expense of its traditional ethos'. You pays your money.

Mr Budge treads a narrow – but clear – line between maintaining and improving academics and maintaining and enhancing what Bedales is about. And he is doing it effectively. Witness the appointment in 2009 of a new 'managing head' of Bedales to allow Mr Budge to oversee all three Bedales schools with a view to working on the schools' distinctiveness and performance. 'I am in charge of which staff and students come into the school – i.e. appointments and admissions. I also come in when disciplinary matters get to a certain point – whether with a student or member of staff – I have crucial oversight of who comes and who goes and I lead on all areas of policy.' The new 'managing head', since September 2010, is Mr Dominic Oliver who came from Malvern College, where he was head of English. He succeeded Mr Leo Winkley (son of Stephen) who begins a new life as head of St Peter's, York. Mr Budge is guiding Bedales with the necessary firm grip but light touch.

Academic matters: Different. And it gets more different as you go further up the school. In Block 3 (Year 9) you study a pretty trad curriculum plus one of classical civ, German, Latin or Spanish and, crucially, 'outdoor work' – one of the unique Bedalian features. From Year 10, you take GCSE courses in English and a modern lang, plus an IGCSE in maths and dual award science plus up to two more GCSEs in history, ICT, music and three Bedales Assessed Courses (BACs). What? The BACs are confident exercises in real education devised and assessed by the school in, currently, 13 different subjects which include Eng lit, product design or textiles, classical music and philosophy. The approach is cross-curricular and broadening in all respects. 'We had inspirational teachers who were doomed to teach dull and crass curricula,' explains Mr Budge. Yes. And parents concur: 'most teachers are exceptionally dedicated and enthusiastic – they live on site and love engaging with young people.' 'My daughter did the BAC philosophy – she had to produce a massive journal full of her ideas on moral and ethical issues – wonderful.' For those who believe that education should be about education rather than processing and assessment, they can't really send their children anywhere much else. 'And UCAS is hugely supportive,' says Mr Budge. That's all right then!

A levels persist, though, and nothing too revolutionary makes its way onto the timetable, apart from Pre-U music and an option to complete an assessed piece of independent learning – the Extended Project. Eng lit, at this and at lower levels, has long and famously been outstanding and the uptake at A level outstrips all else. Art (see below) is also outstanding and popular. Likewise, history attracts the many and with good results. Smaller numbers for langs and the sciences, though those who take maths and drama do well. In 2010, 66 per cent A*/A/B grades. SENs here mostly consist of mild dyslexia/dyspraxia and affect around 25 per cent. One weekly support lesson – occasionally two – is offered and pupils are not withdrawn from classes. More than that needed and you may want to look elsewhere. Wheelchairs are no problem and school also takes those with hearing/visual impairments and integrates them well. No EAL – reflecting small numbers who come from overseas.

'Outdoor work' is key at all levels. Bedales has its own farm and, over the five years, everyone has a chance to herd sheep, keep bees, learn the skills of fencing, coppicing, gardening, hedging, renovating paths, barns and stone walls, draining and maintaining ponds and all kinds of construction, land management and conservation techniques. We saw home-made coracles, wool being carded and spun, smithing and, unaccountably, a 'trap that was used in *The King and I* being lovingly renovated. Everywhere is green – gardens, orchards, meadows surround and abut the school buildings and we loved the historic timber-frame barns and workshops – turned to all kinds of uses – which one discovers on a ramble around the extensive farm village of the school.

Games, Options, the Arts: Unlike in other schools, here one cannot detach the outdoor life from the rest. Nonetheless, there are extensive playing fields and an Astroturf, yer actual massive sports hall plus super pool, courts, pitches – everything – and sport is no longer a bit of a blush and smirk at Bedales. All have a weekly double PE lesson and all the major sports are offered – even rugby. Art is uniquely well-resourced and, perhaps, uniquely proficient. Studios and gallery space create a mini art school-within-a-school. The quality of work would do credit to a degree show and we hugely admired the imagination, technical skills, mix of media and the confident handling evident in the work we saw. Life drawing, portraiture, photography, metalwork, pottery, stonework and sculpture, colour and texture experimentation – all impress along with an informed and liberating grasp of tradition and classical precedents. This is exceptional provision delivered with exceptional dedication and producing exciting results. Music and drama flourish likewise. Lovely drama studio in adapted workshop. Excellent flexible theatre. Productions attract the masses and most enthuse about the last show they were in. They learn production techniques e.g. sound and light too. Music block unappealing on the outside but truly warm and inspirational inside – baby grands everywhere and deep painted walls and dark wood doors. Most learn at least one instrument and lessons are timetabled. Music tech is well-resourced but seems not here, as in so many other places, to have become what music is all about. School has its own arts programme coordinator and runs an impressive and inspiring programme of events which brings in top professionals to perform and run workshops. The posters around the place for upcoming and recent events made us feel we were attending a permanent arts festival.

Background and Atmosphere: Started by visionary John Haden Badley and his wife in a house called Bedales, near Haywards Heath in 1893. In 1899 – having begun to admit girls to counteract any undesirable masculine boorishness – they acquired a country estate in Steep and constructed a school – including state-of-the-art electric light – which opened in 1900. Dunhurst – a prep to feed Bedales – was started in 1902 on Montessori principles and a pre-prep school, Dunannie, was added in the 1950s. No chapel – Badley's approach was strictly non-denominational – hence its attractiveness in its early days to liberals, intellectuals and non-conformists of all descriptions – both British and European. This was contributed to by the coterie of writers, musicians and artists who settled around Steep from the 1920s onwards. The school grew rapidly in the 1960s – the heyday of its a-la-modishness – and became the school of choice for the children of the super-cool. Lawrence Durrell, Simon Raven, Robert Graves, Cecil Day-Lewis, Peggy Guggenheim, Ted Hughes, Edna O'Brien, John Mortimer, Frederick Raphael, Joseph Losey, Peter Hall, Peter Brook, Laurence Olivier, Susan Hampshire, Mick Jagger, Pete Townshend, Sandie Shaw, Trevor Nunn, A. Gill, Roger Waters, Twiggy, Hayley Mills and Kirsty MacColl have all been Bedales parents. Few eyesores – Bedales boasts two Grade 1 listed Gimson designed arts and crafts buildings – the delicious Lupton Hall (1911) and the Memorial Library (1921), and two, contemporary, award-winning buildings – the Olivier Theatre (1997) and the Orchard Building (2005). Fabuloso library – would grace an ancient Oxbridge college – makes you want to immerse yourself in the cerebral.

The ethos has survived but there have had to be concessions; the school has long since taken day pupils who now make up 30+ per cent of its population; academic results do count – even committed Bedalians want something on paper – and the informality of its core values have needed strengthening with some more recent rigour. Some worried in Mr Budge's early days that he would dispel the relaxed ethos but no-one fusses much now. 'Greening Bedales' involves laudable initiatives on many environmental fronts which other schools would do well to study. Also informs school's policies on trips and exchanges – not just extravagant junkets for the super-spoiled as elsewhere.

Pastoral Care and Discipline: Unique mixed-age dorms. All in first four years have a lower sixth in the dorm and dorms are for one to five students. Rooms and comfortable and friendly – girls' more than boys' – 'twas ever thus. "Boys' flat" (boarding), was designed by a prison architect', one inmate confided but it didn't look bad to us and no bars on the windows for sure. Jolly nice garden, bird tables and bbq. Steephurst, the girls' house, is lovely – the original farmhouse which began the school. Really nice, comfy common rooms – someone here understands about sofas. Bizarre bathrooms in Steephurst – three abutting baths per room – 'you can have a bath with your friends – it gets slightly noisy,' one girl bubbled. 'Pastoral care is really good – they try terribly hard,' a parent said. Good food eaten by everyone together. Upper sixth in own floors in main building – 'Quad' – with kitchens, study rooms, (shared with day pupils) and common-rooms – inviting and very much a separate world.

Most really love and conform to the 'take responsibility for yourself and get on with it' ethos, though 'some people get distracted by all the opportunities and don't work – others don't make enough of the opportunities and doss around,' one wise youngster confided. Very few stay in at weekends and little is laid on – but they have the run of the place and expeditions and outings organised on request. Also 'cosy teas' and 'fireside games'. Own clothes means exactly that – though uniform seems to consist of lots of mini-shorts 'n' tights, track suit bottoms and trainers. Sanctions for e.g. smoking/drinking/lateness/lying usually means gating. 'It's a brilliant school if you're responsible,' a 14-year-old asserted, 'but if you need rules and boundaries it's not the school for you.' Not many find they can't hack it here, so we were saddened to learn that, in June 2010, the school had dispensed with six of its pupils on account of drug abuse. A spokesman said, 'six students admitted to drugs offences involving marijuana at the end of last week and all have subsequently left the school as a result.' Liberal the school may still be but this incident made it very clear that drugs ain't on here.

Pupils and Parents: Money counts now – the school is one of the top 10 most expensive in the UK. But Bedales parents are those who understand what the place is about and choose it in preference to the more conventional routes to wisdom and fulfillment. And that includes many London families. Pupils are open, friendly and articulate. We met many on our visit and all were thoughtful and eager to explain their school to us. They are genuinely appreciative of what they have and the differences between their school and those their friends elsewhere attend. Very few overseas nationals – perhaps the Bedales ethos of no uniform and 'outdoor work' is not what most people abroad associate with a British boarding education! However, always a sprinkling of the well-connected, minor royal and generally savvy and liberal from all over the country.

Entrance: Around 55 come up from Bedales' own on-site junior school, Dunhurst; the rest of the 90-strong year group from outside. Many from Windlesham, Highfield, the Thomases, The Dragon, Amesbury, Newton and West Hill Park. Those who want to are pre-assessed 18 months before entry and most thereafter come for a two-day residential in January before entry plus tests in maths, English and reasoning. Around 75 per cent of these will gain places. As in everything, Bedales is unconventional – 'we back our hunches. We disregard scores when we know someone is right for us.' Many more girls apply for places at sixth form than boys. Assessment via interview – 50 points at GCSE expected (taking A* as 8, A as 7 and so on, based on a nine-subject programme) plus A*/B in A level subjects but, as ever, flexible if they like you.

Exit: Lots of artists to Central St Martin's, Camberwell etc. Rest to every kind of course – relatively few scientists and linguists. Oxbridge numbers in recent years unimpressive and school now addressing this with more enrichment and targeted preparation. Recent Old Bedalian mused, 'I wish the school had been more ambitious for me – they didn't push me'. Another regretted that no-one had told her that her choice of A levels would be seen as 'soft' by universities. Mr Budge now setting 'where they go on to' as one of his missions. Notable OBs include half the unconventional, creative and arty types you've ever heard of, among them: Amanda Craig, Lily Allen, Sophie Dahl, Minnie Driver, Daniel Day Lewis, Ivon Hitchens, Alan Jay Lerner, Sir John Rothenstein and John Wyndham.

Money Matters: 13+ scholarships – all means-tested – for outstanding ability in almost anything, plus a separate category for music. At 16, scholarships for academics, art and music and, occasionally, science. Some awards for drama and design at the end of lower sixth.

Remarks: 'If you want an exam factory go somewhere else,' a parent advised. If you want a relaxed, happy and wholesome school with good teaching, real values and a rich outdoor life look no further. Few Bedalians regret their school days.

Bedford High School for Girls

Linked to Bedford Girls School Junior School in the Junior section

Linked to Dame Alice Harpur School (Senior School) in the Senior section

Bromham Road, Bedford, Bedfordshire, MK40 2BS

• Pupils: 460 • Ages: 11-18 • Size of sixth form: 200 • Christian ethos but respects other faiths • Fees: £10,983 pa • Independent

Tel: 01234 360 221
Fax: 01234 353 552
Email: head@bedfordhigh.co.uk
Website: www.bedfordhigh.co.uk

Headmistress: Since 2007, Mrs Julie Eldridge BSc MBA (fifties). Positive and enthusiastic, clearly understandably delighted with their recent ISI report which, unusually, has no recommendations for improvements. A geography graduate from Bristol, she began her teaching career at Sandy Upper School before taking a break to have her family. While her two, now grown-up, children were young she resumed her interest in swimming, competing in British, European and World Masters' competitions. Returned to the classroom in 1984 as teacher of geography and geology at Bedford High School. Later became head of department, director of studies and deputy head before, slightly reluctantly (which she'd rather we didn't say), taking over the reins. First three years were hard but, after implementing, not always popular, changes, her new management team is now up and running efficiently and the school is moving forward. In 2004 she completed an MBA in educational management at Leicester University. In her spare time she enjoys badminton, swimming, walking and travel.

NB BHS and Dame Alice Harpur Junior Schools merged in September 2010. The new school is called Bedford Girls' School. The senior school will follow in September 2011. No new day pupils into BHS after September 2010. Any girls taking their GCSE/A level/IB exams will be able to stay on until 2011/2012 to complete their courses. Boarders still admitted into Year 12. All the current students will either transfer to BGS or other schools in September 2011, and there will only be two year groups, 11 and 13, on the BHS site after that, finishing their exam courses.

Academic matters: Broad and varied curriculum with a strong emphasis on languages and the sciences. French, German and Spanish all introduced in the junior school. Setting in maths from the beginning and English from Year 9. Dual award and separate sciences, setted in GCSE years. In the sixth form, girls can either follow the A level or the International Baccalaureate diploma programme. They hope that the IB/A level balance will move closer to 50/50 within the next three years as they feel that the IB is possibly more stretching for the brightest girls. They are pleased to have been given the International Schools Award.

Girls expected to work hard and those we talked to did not object. Class sizes in the sixth form rarely exceed 12. Staff to pupil ratio 1:11. About 25 per cent male teachers. They could probably do with a few more. Average age of teaching staff 48. About 20 per cent have been at the school for more than ten years.

In Years 10 and 11 most overseas girls take EAL as an option as support for their GCSE subjects. Some opt to take the full GCSE quota and take EAL as a paid for extra. Younger girls can take EAL instead of a modern foreign language. IELTS preparation classes available in the sixth form.

Girls with SEN offered support sessions by specialised teachers but no classroom assistants and they are not taken out of classes. Young, part-time SENCo feels that girls respond to the very structured approach to teaching in the school and the challenge to really stretch themselves. She runs phonic and thinking skills workshops and is available for girls with problems during break time. The G & T programme is, we were told, the main area of focus for next year, so there should be improvements.

Games, Options, the Arts: Excellent sporting facilities; you name, it they play it. The array of cups is impressive. Several representatives, past and present, at district, county and national levels. First in the Pony Club Mounted Games at the Horse of the Year Show, bronze and gold medals in the British Indoor Rowing Championship, u15 Midlands Lacrosse Champions, National Schools Champions under 14 and under 16 in hockey, Under 13 County Tennis Champions. These are girls to be reckoned with. They even got a gold medal in the National Judo Championships. Lots of eager participants in the Duke of Edinburgh Award Scheme and all three branches of the CCF, organised jointly with their brother school, Bedford School. The sports and performing arts complex, opened in 2005, provides opportunities to try many other activities. The extra-curricular list is extensive. Girls (+ a parent if they like) can swim before school breakfast or visit the fitness centre. Also a multitude of different exercise classes. Sport and fitness play an important part in the school lives of these girls.

Fantastic theatre, the venue for extravagant dance, music and dramatic productions, often in collaboration with Bedford School. Everyone can have a go at something. Our guide was very excited about having recently played the lead in Grease. We looked at the photos. Great props and costume stores in the vaulted basement/crypt.

Exceptional music block with two recording studios and lots of practice rooms. Music lessons for all from the beginning and lots of different instruments to try. Over 50 per cent have individual tuition. We were delighted to spot one girl practising on a harp. An orchestra, several bands and choirs: music really is available for everyone. Music technology is a huge strength with 100 per cent getting A or B grades at A level.

Background and Atmosphere: Typical Victorian school buildings don't give a particularly exciting initial impression but, once inside, everything changes. It is all surprisingly light. The head sits in a small corner of a huge room just inside the main entrance. It is light but imposing and could be quite terrifying for a recalcitrant child. But, she assured us, it isn't usually, only when she needs it to be. Thank goodness for the cosy corner where she can sit and chat to worried parents.

The school is large and rambling yet everything has its place and is bright and welcoming. Children amble along the corridors chattering happily. Subject rooms double up as classrooms with bright blue lockers along the walls, holding a jumble of clothes and books. It all feels very relaxed. Well, until you walk into a classroom that is; then there is air of intense concentration – these girls are here to learn and they seem determined to do their best. It's certainly all there for them. Great labs, fully equipped; a pottery room with interesting GCSE projects at full throttle; colourful geography rooms with illustrations of recent exciting journeys; sewing rooms with individual garments hanging along the walls – 'Ooh, I remember making one of those last year,' said our guide. The art rooms display a huge variety of different creations, and the food technology rooms sported rows of recently-baked cakes when we were there. Mmm. Three computer labs, one specialising in art projects. Interestingly, computers are not in evidence in the classrooms and there are virtually no interactive whiteboards. Apparently it's not until sixth form that every girl works on a computer of her own.

Further along is the amazingly modern sports and performing arts complex, neatly filling the gap between the senior and junior schools. Temporarily, we are in a different world where high tech rules and Victoriana is forgotten. Heaven for all fitness and performing arts addicts. A modern glass building which somehow interlinks with the old Trinity chapel.

Useful school uniform shop on the premises. Up until sixth form all the girls wear smart navy blazers and kilts. After that they wear check skirts instead and are sometimes allowed to wear black skirts or trousers to prepare themselves for office life in the future. Black trousers and veils permitted if religion demands.

They are particularly proud of their main school hall and its magnificent ceiling. Both our guides said that it was this ceiling that first fired their wish to attend the school, when they gazed up at it as visitors to a school concert.

Four boarding houses, about 10 minutes walk away, give the boarders a sense of going home at the end of the day. Fairly unexciting places but they do have a homely feel. There is a good programme of week-end activities – important as so many of these girls live overseas. Most sixth form boarders have their own room, usually en suite.

A good variety of food in the large canteen. An interesting selection of hot and cold, catering for the many different tastes and traditions that abound with such a multi-cultural mix. Teaching staff sit, somewhat unapproachably, at their own table on one side of the room. Breakfast available for day girls and parents alike after, for instance, that early morning swim. Boarders can eat either in their houses or, more substantially, here.

Pastoral Care and Discipline: A good pastoral team with an efficient monitoring system. A happy and well-balanced school with the older girls looking out for the younger ones and the boarders looking out for each other, with a code of conduct to which all girls are expected to adhere. The pastoral team are, according to the SENCo, particularly sensitive to SEN children and will make sure that they are not over-pressurised when they first join the school. Otherwise no real concessions given. The head assured us that they have been working hard on communicating with parents and concerns are dealt with speedily. A significant improvement in the last three years. Now an absolute maximum of 36 hours from contact to response. She is always willing to see parents, no matter how small the problem, although the parents don't always seem to know this.

Mobile phones allowed but they have to be switched off during school hours. They like to promote great cultural awareness. Head feels that the multi-national side of the school aptly reflects the huge multi-cultural community in Bedford. 'I really believe my pupils are colour blind,' she says. 'There is absolutely no discrimination'. The international support department is, apparently, particularly strong, and EAL teachers are available throughout the day to help girls with the English language and to provide pastoral support for those from overseas. Support is available for all these overseas girls to help them in their academic subjects. Important when there are at least 100 of them. Active school council exists for pupil input. Girls put themselves forward for election by their peers.

Pupils and Parents: Wide socio-economic mix with pupils from both prep and state schools. Mostly local families, within a 45 minute drive of the school. Parents have joined forces to offer a comprehensive bus and coach service from early to late. 70 per cent of boarders come from overseas. Since they started offering the IB there has been an increase in those coming from Europe. Otherwise it is Hong Kong, China, Africa, South Korea, Brunei, Thailand and even the USA amongst others.

Entrance: Junior school girls sit the entrance exam for the senior school alongside incomers, although it is unusual not to transfer. At 11+ they are examined in maths, English and verbal reasoning. At 14+ science is added to this. Girls coming from overseas are tested in EAL and maths. If a girl meets the entrance criteria and if the school feels they can deal with any special needs she may have, she has a very good chance of a place. This applies to girls coming in at odd times of the year as well. They will fit her in if they can.

Exit: Some leave after GCSE but most stay and go on to university or further education. Some to Oxbridge, a few to Imperial or University College London, otherwise Bristol, Manchester, York, Hull, Leeds and others of that ilk. More than a few go further afield to Hong Kong and other overseas universities. Their most distinguished old girl is Olympic pentathlete, Dr Stephanie Cook.

Money Matters: The school is one of four whose premises are owned by the Harpur Trust, a Bedford charity which benefits from the generous endowment of 16th century merchant Sir William Harpur and his wife Dame Alice. Bursaries and awards, which are always means-tested, are available for needy pupils. Some are kept for emergencies, and there is a fund maintained for hardship cases with priority for those in examination years. Further development plans for the school in the next few years are, apparently, well catered for.

Remarks: An academic school full of relaxed, confident, hard-working girls bursting with enthusiasm. Not for wilting daisies; but for those who want to go far and are prepared to work and play hard in order to achieve the best they can, there are opportunities here for the taking in a multi-cultural, multi-national environment. Merger with Dame Alice will cause heartache but, we hope, will create a stronger overall presence in this area.

Bedford School

Linked to Bedford Preparatory School in the Junior section

De Parys Avenue, Bedford, Bedfordshire, MK40 2TU

• Pupils: 460 day boys 255 boarders • Ages: 13-18
• Size of sixth form: 285 • C of E • Fees: Day £15,294; Boarding £23,955-£24,771 pa • Independent

Tel: 01234 362 200
Fax: 01234 362283
Email: info@bedfordschool.org.uk
Website: www.bedfordschool.org.uk

Head Master: Since 2008, Mr John Moule MA (late thirties). Young but with a wide range of experience, a head really in tune with his school. Educated at a comprehensive school and sixth form college, he won a history scholarship to Lady Margaret Hall, Oxford and left with a first. Taught history and politics at Dean Close School, Cheltenham, then moved to Stowe as head of history and later became a housemaster, then senior housemaster. He joined Bedford as Vice Master in January 2006 and, in 2008, when the estimable Dr Evans retired at 60 – earlier than some had expected – was delighted to have his application for the headship accepted. Some parents were slightly wary at first but soon got over it. He is seen as a definite change for the good, perhaps more approachable than his highly-academic predecessor, and all love his informative, monthly newsletter. Married with three children, two at Dame Alice Harpur and one at Bedford Prep, he is a committed Christian and passionate about the boarding school ethos, which he feels has a positive impact on any school, improves the ability to nurture and provide good pastoral care and enables them to develop 'the whole child'. Mrs Moule 'is thoroughly involved in terms of entertaining and attending school events – we do an awful lot of this!'. He feels lucky to have taken over such a good educational establishment where dramatic change is not necessary. He is ambitious for his school, which he feels should be up there with the big names. We agree with him.

Academic matters: Top results at GCSE, A level and the IB; here is a school full of bright boys who work hard under excellent teachers and fulfil their potential. Average class size 19 reducing to groups of eight or nine in the sixth form. Average age of staff 44 and teacher/pupil ratio approximately 1:8. The teachers are focused, enthusiastic and full of praise for the school and their pupils. No wonder over half have been around over ten years. Relaxed and friendly relationship between boys and teachers.

Well-structured curriculum. Separate sciences, and all boys learn at least two languages (one of which could be Latin) in Year 9. For overseas children ESOL takes the place of one of these languages, with about 50 per cent of them taking IGCSE ESL instead of English language/literature. ESOL lessons may be a condition of entry and are billed. Twinning with school in China enables exchanges, joint projects etc.

Sixth form boys opt for either the IB or A levels. Around a quarter to a third takes the IB. This is liable to increase as the school increasingly popular with European parents, particularly in Germany. Results for both are excellent: one boy in 2009 achieved what less than two per cent of other students achieve worldwide, maximum IB points.

Academic support department helps SEN boys in the way they feel is best for each individual. Two of these boys were offered places at Oxbridge in 2009 and one boy, who joined in Year 10 and was only diagnosed with dyslexia in Year 13, obtained straight As at A level. Parents certainly feel that 'they have got it right'. Embryonic plan for a centre of excellence in the pipeline. Would also help G & T children.

Games, Options, the Arts: Head is passionate about sport and feels every boy should have a chance to be part of a team. 'It is important for everyone to experience training, winning and losing.' Key sports are rugby, cricket, hockey and rowing but lots of others to try, the majority of which enter teams for competitive events. For those who like bangs there's an on-site rifle range. International honours in rugby, cricket, hockey, rowing, golf and fencing; Daily Mail U15 Rugby Champions in 2006 and the East of England U18 Hockey Champions in 2009. Recent cricket tour to St Lucia and to Australia to play rugby. Boat club has history dating back to 1861 and tradition of winning. Boys represent Great Britain in junior championships and Old Boys have gone on to row for their universities and their country. This is true of most sports played at Bedford. Even the less athletic boys have fun. The head told us of a boy who just couldn't stop talking about the training and the games he was taking part in – no, he wasn't a high flyer, he was playing for a C team. This is what head feels it is all about.

Plenty of individual activities on offer, including swimming (our guide was justifiably proud of the swimming pool), archery, tai kwan do and golf. CCF strong in all three branches as is the Duke of Edinburgh. These in conjuction with sister school, Bedford Girls' School, which adds some attraction for the older boys.

Music particularly strong with a state-of-the-art music centre built in 2005. Several boys read music at university, some Oxbridge choral or organ scholarships, and in 2007 a horn player got a scholarship to the Royal College of Music. You name the instrument – they can learn it. Lots of choirs, orchestras and bands. Impressive music technology suite. Light and airy concert hall. The slightly eccentric, very popular, head of music seems to be able to inspire every boy, no matter how initially reluctant, and they all love it. Parents rave about his ability to open up their children's sensibility and expand them musically. One parent told us that the house singing evening, which the boys take very seriously, is full of extraordinarily good performances and is one of her highlights of the year.

Well-equipped theatre also used by visiting companies. What other school has its own resident astronomer operating from an on-site observatory with a planetarium next door? The resource centres are used by visiting adults as well as lucky Bedford boys. Less displayed art work than at other schools but the facilities are there. Excellent DT labs.

Background and Atmosphere: Interesting mix of modern and old, the school's buildings surround the playing fields, giving a green and open feel. Country life in the middle of town. An historic school which celebrates its own history but does not hesitate to move into the modern age.

Main school building, gutted by fire in the 1970s – arson, says our guide – was rebuilt to retain its character. The magnificent hall is the focal point, around which classrooms are grouped on four levels. Excellent computer labs but so far only a few interactive whiteboards. Focus is on teaching, not gimmicks, and, according to parents, it works. Spankingly up-to-date library in its own very modern building – 'it's a great place to work in,' says our guide.

Boarding houses informal and friendly. Comfy sofas encourage lolling in front of an enormous television screen. Good-sized bedrooms with individual areas for personalisation. Singles for Year 13s. Homely atmosphere and caring house parents. 'Our boys are so happy,' said a parent, 'they don't want to come home at weekends.' Few overseas boarders but no-one complained of cliquiness and parents feel they integrate well.

Whole place has the feel of a country boarding school. In fact, some parents think that better marketing would result in more boarders and that would be a good thing. But that would mean a different development plan: the boarding houses are full.

Innovative and enterprising Bedford School Study Centre. Here, up to 30 international students (boys and girls) spend one to three terms, mostly in intensive EFL, in preparation for entry into a variety of mainstream UK schools. Only two or three a year remain at Bedford, but top guidance and advice is given to all. Full integration at all ages provides an excellent introduction to British schooling.

Pastoral Care and Discipline: Head is keen on policies and there are policies to cover every contingency. 'They are good for helping to think things through,' he says, 'and for producing a framework for action. I had to expel four boys last term, for drug-related reasons outside school; one learns from these sorts of things'. A parent said, 'They are learning that they have to address the drug problem at a younger age group than usual'.

A good pastoral framework. '99 per cent are good at verbalising', says the sensible and sympathetic hockey coaching SENCo who has been at the school for nine years. There are 20–22 boys in each year group who need some sort of help and one-to-one tuition is available when necessary, as an extra of course. 'There's always someone to talk to', she says, and feels they are quick to diffuse a problem if they spot it brewing. 'These are all very bright children and they often see the answer themselves and say "I should have said or done that" when talking it through with us.' The tutor system also helps. It would seem that they all look out for each other. This was underlined by a parent – 'the bigger boys look after the little ones'. Bullying virtually non-existent.

No student council but senior boys can join committees to discuss academics, sports, arts, innovations and, from next year, technology. Those wanting to become monitors – and they do because they can then wear a coloured jumper and brown shoes – have to 'apply' in a written letter.

Pupils and Parents: Currently 16 per cent overseas boys, mainly boarders, from 26 different countries including Hong Kong, Germany and Russia. The rest from a spread around Bedford and surrounding counties. Day boys mainly live up to within 40 miles. Ideally suited for boys who are individuals, but extrovert rebels might find it more difficult. Not particularly selective, so all are welcome to try, but those with exceptional learning difficulties unlikely to make the grade. 'They need to be able to cope.'

Long list of notable OBs includes Alec Dankworth, HH Munro (Saki), Harold Abrahams, Paddy Ashdown, John Fowles, Al Murray, Andy Gormasall, Alastair Cook and the reprehensible Lord Haw-Haw.

Entrance: Mainly from the prep at 13 but also from other local schools. Prospective pupils from other preps sit Bedford's scholarship exam and Access Award Assessment papers. Those from state schools are further tested in the key subject areas. Some extra places at 14, then 25 more at 16, which require six passes at GCSE for those going on to do A levels (B grades in the subjects to be studied) or an academic assessment for those following the IB. They rarely turn away day boys. Boarding places are at more of a premium.

Exit: Mainly to good universities. Nottingham particularly popular. Several to Oxbridge, Bristol and the London colleges. Otherwise all over, nearly always in the UK. A broad range of serious subjects.

Money Matters: Bursaries and scholarships means-tested beyond 10 per cent. Their own Access Awards, decided upon following an innovative assessment process that seeks to measure potential to excel. Again, means-tested. Head will always talk to parents hit by financial troubles.

Part of the Harpur Trust but financially independent – the Trust now puts its money into other projects around Bedford but continues to govern the school. Has been well run for a long time and is strong enough investment-wise, so no problems envisaged.

Remarks: An oasis in the middle of a busy town, a predominantly day school with a boarding school ethos. An unpretentious school which has everything a boy could need.

Beechen Cliff School

Alexandra Park, Bath, BA2 4RE

• Pupils: 1170, mostly boys but 65 girls in the sixth form. All day
• Ages: 11-18 • Size of sixth form: 280 • Non-denom. Assemblies with Christian theme • State

Tel: 01225 480 466
Fax: 01225 314 025
Email: headmaster@beechencliff.org.uk
Website: www.beechencliff.org.uk

Headmaster: Since 2005, Mr Andrew Davies, (mid forties), history graduate of University of Sussex. Married to Anne, an assistant head, with two teenage children, one at his school, one at local girls' independent. Career has followed normal trajectory (teaching, head of dept, head of humanities, deputy head) in five local authorities, plus a spell in the commercial sector as principal of Kings International College in Surrey. Has worked in the most and least desirable bits of SW England, so no airs and graces. Direct, engaging and warm, he is passionate about providing his flock with all manner of opportunity to extend and test themselves. Refreshingly liberated too from some spectres of state education: 'We are not slaves to Ofsted', he says, but with a major success story on his hands, he can afford to. Still teaches – he offers GCSE in humanities to Year 9 boys in their own time: take-up and results are good. Keen shot, cricketer (coaches both) and general outdoor type who involves himself in school endeavours, such as the Centurion Challenge, 100 mile slog in 48 hours as a Roman foot soldier. Proud of his school, and encourages his pupils to be the same. Well liked and respected by parents, who reckon he's 'good at dragging the goods out of the non-academic' as well as the academic.

Academic matters: Completely non-selective on entry but tends to get more able boys by default. From now on, all Year 7s will be assessed with cognitive ability tests on entry to enable better setting than SATs scores provide. Results at GCSE and A level have crept up over last few years and academic aspiration encouraged. In 2010, 70 per cent achieved at least five grades A*–C at GCSE including maths and English, and over 99 per cent passed their A levels, with 10 per cent A* grades: impressive for a non-selective school. Gained Specialist Technology College status in 2004 and founder member of Bath Educational Trust set up in 2009, a collaboration between Hayesfield School (Beechen's sister school), Bath University, City of Bath College and global engineering firm Rotork, headquartered in Bath, which aims to 'to provide a better experience for children'. In fact it provides a lot of good practical stuff too, such as far more options post-16, resources and economies of scale in terms of buying power, as well as a smart minibus to shuttle pupils between sites. BET will evaluate its efforts by tracking pupils' early careers until the age of 25. Thriving and over-subscribed sixth form where IB has been offered since 2009 jointly with Hayesfield: take-up as yet modest (20 in first cohort) but those who teach and those who learn are unequivocal in their praise. A level choices still extensive at 27 subjects, with the possibility of more at Hayesfield or Bath College. 12 or so apply to Oxbridge each year, of which three got places in

2010, across a range of subjects; some extra tuition on offer. The less brainy can choose Route 2, where they spend a year doing more vocational things at Bath College, along with retakes of English and/or maths GCSE.

Enthusiastic and proactive head of sixth form has gone down well with pupils and their parents. The academically precocious are encouraged to push on and take GCSEs early or AS in Year 11; maths and further maths are taught within the same timetable. Most pupils start a second foreign language in Year 8 (German, Spanish, Italian) and there's classics on offer after school. Clearly the message is that pupils will be given extra chances to get ahead, but the onus rests firmly on them. Nonetheless, a few parents worry that a good work ethic is not sufficiently instilled in the boys, and that to be labelled a 'keener' is social death; it is fair to add that the school comes down hard on this. Less able pupils taught in smaller sets and emphasis placed on extra-curricular opportunities and successes for those in the bottom set for everything.

Busy SEN dept caters for most needs one would expect to find in mainstream, the difference perhaps being that, in tune with the school's general ethos, pupils are expected to take responsibility for their own learning – 'I can't be doing with this excuse culture in education', states the head. Lessons seem a good blend of purpose and fun, with lots of participation, and hi tech infrastructure to support them. Significant amounts of homework from Year 7 compensate for short day – school ends at 3.40pm.

Games, Options, the Arts: Simply masses on offer, particularly for a state school, due in part to the all-hours culture where so much happens after the school day and at weekends; indeed it is the only comprehensive in Bath to take on the independents at Saturday fixtures. Impressive array of sporting successes in rugby, football, hockey, cricket and shooting borne out by the honours board in the entrance hall, where Amy Williams (GB's only gold medallist in the 2010 winter Olympics) appears, along with fellow Olympian Jason Gardener – and Roger Bannister. Competitive sport taken pretty seriously and winning is encouraged; some parents feel that the school's rugby and cricket coaches select more top players from city clubs than those outside Bath, but the school strenuously asserts that team selection done strictly on merit. Amazing results emanate from barely adequate facilities, though plans advance for a further all-weather pitch. Tennis and athletics in summer. Super sports barn has exterior climbing wall on one end, funded through parental gift aid. Strong links with top notch facilities and expertise at nearby Bath University too. Enough choice for sixth form girls, including rugby, but they say they are not compelled to do anything in the sporting line.

Art and DT have their own well-equipped if dilapidated block – and a committed following producing high quality work. Provision in photography hugely enhanced by the arrival of an industrial printer, bid for by the head of art, who has other grand plans (e.g. gallery space), if only funds would permit. Music attracts fewer takers, despite avoiding the trap of being a girls' preserve below sixth form, but there's a good range from brass to folk, and they do compete and succeed in the Mid-Somerset Festival, and tour Europe. This year the school held its first internal young musician competition. A new music centre is planned – definitely needed. Some plays done in collaboration with the (all female) Royal High; choices like Tartuffe and *A Midsummer Night's Dream* suggest no lack of ambition.

Beechen Cliff also makes its mark locally at Model UN and debating with other schools. Much 'boys' own' stuff goes on in terms of outdoor activities aside from team games: Ten Tors race, Centurion Challenge, D of E and all the opportunities offered at Tir-y-Cwm, the school's cottage in the Brecons, a gem of an asset. All of Year 7 go for a weekend's bonding near the start of their first term; thence participation in orienteering, climbing and caving is voluntary. Trips on offer compare well with far better resourced schools, and go beyond the confines of Europe, to Africa for charity work and Canada for ski-ing.

Background and Atmosphere: Feels and looks like a boys' grammar, (which of course it was), with a 'perky atmosphere, despite being slightly disgusting,' according to one mother. It became a comprehensive in 1972, after amalgamating with the then boys' secondary modern, and takes its name from the hill on which its 1930's buildings stand. Its future was touch-and-go in 1990, but its head and governors mounted a huge campaign ending in the High Court to get it grant maintained status, and keep it open. Beechen remains prominent on the Bath scene in every way, but close up it is very, very tatty: 'We do what we do here despite our buildings, not because of them,' said a sixth former, who went on to wax lyrical about the 'can-do' culture. We agree: one parent left a recent open evening wondering why he had shelled out so much money on independent education for his children, when he could have had so much of it for free at Beechen. Definitely a sense of tradition about the place (boys are addressed as 'gentlemen', 'gents' or 'chaps'), but it's not oppressive: all seem to absorb the values of discipline, courtesy, academic confidence and pride the school promotes, not least in its first ever year book, The Gryphon. Loyalty and considerable affection from its old boys/girls (Old Sulians) and former members of staff come in to teach extra sessions – for love. This year the head has beefed up the house system, renaming them after illustrious authors, after whom local roads are also named (this part of Bath is known as poets' corner); introducing a house tie and vertical tutor groups within houses to engender a spot of house loyalty. He's hot on uniform too: boys are picked up on untucked shirts and half-mast ties even outside school, no trainers and wild hair either. Some feel, however, that sixth form girls get away with murder as far as dress is concerned. Food is terrific too: Beechen's award-winning chef has broadened gastronomic horizons no end, producing yummy breakfasts, innovative lunches and buffets for functions from the new facilities he designed and implemented as a result of winning a recent trade competition. Take-up for school meals much higher than average and prices are fair. There's a real effort to source food locally – indeed some of the salad and veg are grown on site by the pupils! Popular snack bar for sixth formers is a tangible sign of the more mature treatment they get. Some parents worry that they are given too much leeway by being allowed offsite in free periods – 'they are still at school after all' – and that staff do not crack the whip sufficiently over punctuality or wasting time in free periods.

Pastoral Care and Discipline: Undoubted reward culture for all achievement is balanced by traditional sanctions for those who play fast and loose with expected standards, academic or otherwise. Anyone re-interpreting the uniform can expect to receive 250 lines on the vice of scruffiness, slackers get academic detentions on Saturdays. 'Pupils need to see consequences for their actions', as the head says. Parents report good relationships within school and quick response times from staff; the school takes concerns seriously. Sixth formers provide pastoral input to junior boys within tutor groups, in class on occasion and as directors in music and drama. Expectations of them are laid out in the sixth form code they sign before entry. No-one mentioned smoking, drink or drugs – possibly because they are strictly extra-curricular?

Pupils and Parents: 'Middle class and aspirant, reflecting Bath as a whole', according to the head, who woos newcomers, parents that is, with Pimms and lemonade. Mostly white and very local: the catchment area is strictly drawn. Much emphasis put on the partnership between parents and the school, and it is the sense of shared values rather than class or money, which unites them. The vast majority are totally supportive – 'it really wouldn't suit non-conformists or anyone with authority issues,' said one mother. Strong family connections too. Active PTA runs a gift-aid scheme, whose funds are doled out to successful bidders from amongst the staff or pupils for extras that wealthier schools would take for granted – a climbing wall and better stage lighting, for example. Old Sulians include several sporting greats (see above), as well as Arnold Ridley (Private Godfrey in Dad's Army), Andrew Lincoln (Drop the Dead Donkey, This Life, Love Actually), Curt Smith (Tears for Fears), research scientist, Nobel prize winner and generous benefactor Sir Richard Roberts and the current head of MI6, Sir John Sawers.

Entrance: At age 11, 162 places on offer, 'without reference to ability or aptitude', to boys living within the Greater Bath Consortium. When it's over-subscribed, precedence is given to normal state sector criteria of boys in care, followed by siblings. Applications taken in October for the following September. Admissions policy below sixth form is rigid – worth scrutinising the local authority website, especially as they prefer applications online. In practice, boys come from nearly 20 different primary schools – and the odd prep. Sixth form entry by interview, but conditional on five GCSE passes, ideally with B or above for subjects chosen for A level.

Exit: Between 50 and 60 per cent of upper sixth leavers to universities all over the country to pursue a diversity of courses. Some gap years, but not the norm. Plaudits from work experience placements indicate that those who start work straight from school are well equipped to do so.

Money Matters: Well supported by its parents' fundraising. Less advantaged pupils are able to take part in trips and music lessons by means of a special school fund. Staff keep a sharp eye out for opportunities to bid for or win equipment there is no school budget for; an entrepreneurial culture prevails.

Remarks: A Bath institution and good counterweight to local independents, in that it manages to offer much of what they do – for free, but for boys-only below sixth form. If a fairy godparent were to invest a few million, this would be an outstanding non-selective choice for almost any boy, or sixth form girl.

Belmont House School

Linked to Belmont House Junior School in the Junior section

Sandringham Avenue, Newton Mearns, Glasgow, Glasgow, G77 5DU

• Pupils: 216 boys and 84 girls including nursery 13 boys and 7 girls (partnership status); All day • Ages: 3-18 • Size of sixth form: 23 • Non-denom • Fees: £4,281-£9,711 pa • Independent

Tel: 0141 639 2922
Fax: 0141 639 9860
Email: admin@belmontschool.co.uk
Website: www.belmontschool.co.uk

Principal: Since 2006, Mr Melvyn D Shanks (forties) BSc DipEd MInstP CPhys SQH who was educated at The High School of Glasgow, read physics and maths at Glasgow uni (a 'lapsed physicist', he still teaches maths 'a little bit'.) followed by Strathclyde. Ridiculously overqualified. Spent five years at his alma mater before coming to Belmont as head of physics in 1990, then deputy head in 1997 and says that, 'the most difficult thing was to move from being in the common-room to becoming deputy head'. 'Really, really excited', though it was slightly daunting 'becoming CEO'. Very much on the ball, he has a deprecating sense of humour and showed us round the school with pride. Married, with one son a newly-qualified teacher and another in the junior school (who, apart from not giving his father a hug, followed us round with a variety of comments and suggestions). Has appointed a new internal senior vice principal and a vice principal. Keen on staff development and people management, he runs the school with a senior vice principal, the head of junior school, one vice principal and a general manager. No obvious problems in getting staff.

Academic matters: Tiny classes, results fluctuate. Higher Grade results in 2010 were very strong with one-third of Senior 5 achieving five or six Highers, with many pupils achieving four, five or six A passes. School once managed a surprising 105 per cent, the result of chaps joining post Standard grades. Max class size 20 with core subjects, English and maths in the mid- teens, and most other subjects only nine or ten per class. Setted throughout in English and maths, compulsory to Standard grade along with French (from age three) and computing. Three sciences, history, geography and modern studies also on offer, plus art and PE (plus German, taught from age 12 but 'not popular'). No classics. Spanish, taught as an exam subject only, pupils can do it post Standard grades, ditto admin and business studies. Eight Standard grades the norm, with intermediate II an option in many subjects. Most stay on for advanced Highers and can add the odd free standing modules in sixth. No particular bias – strong on the science front and on languages. White boards, digital, overhead projectors, the lot. Keyboarding for all in transitus. Class room lay-out varies according to whim, with juniors either grouped round their teachers or working in standard classrooms.

Vast array of cups for academic and personal excellence. Good range of computers, throughout school and not just in suites, two trolleys of laptops motor round classes. Learning support; all tested on arrival (cognitive ability), broad intake, and siblings give the school an even broader base. High functioning children with Asperger's, dyslexia, dyspraxia et al are OK, two qualified support for learning staff who follow pupils throughout; either withdrawn from class, or double teaching and strategic advice – free unless ed psych needed. Post-school tutorials in all subjects 'given by all staff, including the principal' from October through May. Free. Computers ok in exams if needed, ditto scribes and readers. Main school (1840 mansion) not that wheelchair friendly (but only six classrooms not accessible). Pupils withdrawn from class, double taught in class if need be and can use the after-school/lunch time tutorial system in all subjects if they feel the need. Stunning recent inspection, school could have written it themselves.

Mixed age common-room, some of the staff looked as though they were on the wrong side of the desk, but all truly dedicated. 'Granny' was coming in to tell a class of seven-year-olds what it was like when she was growing up (we met her, very smart in Burberry she was too).

Games, Options, the Arts: For a small school they do 'not too badly' at rugby; three girls' netball teams, all play volleyball and basketball. School has playing fields some half-a-mile away, but are bused. Jolly art room, variety of different disciplines, fabric strong and fun fashion on display. Kiln. CAD part of the syllabus. New head of music: music important, all learn glockenspiel, guitar or drums in six week chunks, or they sing. Terrific and popular choir, recently won the Xscape challenge, orchestra (and junior orchestra – based on ability not age). Good charity concert output. Extracurricular drama. Variety of clubs, D of E well supported. Strong on public speaking and take part (a little bit) in local competitions, debating club. Keen on tennis and golf, regulars in the British Ski Championships. Lots of inter-house athletics. Not really a school that does brilliantly in team games against other schools. Oodles of clubs, Lego popular; eco-monitors.

Background and Atmosphere: School founded in the heart of Newton Mearns in 1929, moving to this jolly white stucco building on the Broom estate in 1930. The school had magical plans for re-location nearby, which was turned down on planning, so they have now re-grouped, demolished the old wooden hall and acquired a new games hall which is adjacent to the kitchen and doubles for dining (two sittings, takes ten mins to fold up and stow the tables). Junior school pre-orders their lunch for the week and pays with cheque on Mondays, seniors pay as they go. Windows overlook hall on first floor, along with four science labs, and two IT rooms and a music suite, as well as drama and general purpose classrooms. Splendidly light and airy. Lifts and dead posh loos. Bit of the old rabbit-warren still at the back where juniors are ensconced in highly decorated opening-up classrooms. Nursery, in temporary building in the playground, due for demolition and rebuild shortly, and there are plans afoot to rehouse the rabbits. On a personal level this editor thinks that the resulting extension has to be the worst of both worlds with a charming early Victorian villa (gorgeous ceilings, cupola needs help though) carbuncalised (as in Prince Charles speak) by a grotesque modern slab of a façade, neither the roof line nor the windows are in any form of harmony with the original. The planners should be shot. After five years of marking time whilst the planners cogitated, the original building has been somewhat neglected. The stucco needs help at the back (basically a paint job) and some of the floor coverings (1930s lino?) in the classrooms could do with a change.

(NB: nice touch: school colours are purple and those chairs that are upholstered around the building are covered in matching purple). After school club for up to transitus (homework too) 3.20 to 6 pm, £5 per session.

Pastoral Care and Discipline: HMIe reports 'the behaviour of children and young people is outstanding'. Not really a naughty school, standard disciplines apply. Detentions the favoured punishment. Bullying stamped on, graffiti instantly removed. Buddy system for younger pupils. Pupils have tutors (a promoted position) with each tutor having 20 tutees, possible to change tutors if there is a personality clash. Strong discipline, children line up in the playground in twos at the end of break. Charming. Older pupils open doors and stand aside to let us past (only once chap seemed to be confused when we went through the art room door). Twice weekly ecumenical assemblies: all faiths represented and holy days celebrated.

Pupils and Parents: Good middle class collection: 10 per cent from the Glasgow Asian population, most of whom have 'strong traditional family businesses'; core of Jewish pupils, smattering of Chinese etc, broad multi-cultural community. Pupils come from as far away as Ayr, Kilmarnock, East Kilbride, Paisley as well as nearby Pollockshields plus one or two from 'north of the river'. Buses. Good supportive governors.

School has been co-ed since 2000 but has always had a policy of having only one school captain as opposed to having head boy and head girl. First-ever female school captain appointed for session 2010–2011.

Entrance: 'Low-key informal assessment' for nursery, automatic transfer to junior and senior schools, separate test for children from age seven upwards based on CAT school reports and interview if necessary. Can join mid term if space available ('we accelerate the entrance process').

Exit: Almost all stay on for either Highers or advanced Highers. Some may leave post Standard to follow vocational training, others leave to join the family business. Most go to Scottish universities, Glasgow popular, Aberdeen, Dundee, Strathclyde, Edinburgh, St Andrews. Occasional one or two to Oxbridge but none recently. Tranches of medics, lawyers, vets, accountants, engineers and architects. The odd gap year.

Money Matters: Not a rich school, but will do their darndest to hang onto pupils to next public exam if parents who fall on hard times are upfront about it.

Remarks: Super; the perfect local school, works well. Tiny classes, almost a third girls. Dedicated staff. Definitely worth considering.

Benenden School

Cranbrook Road, Benenden, Cranbrook, Kent, TN17 4AA

• Pupils: 525 girls, all board • Ages: 11-18 • Size of sixth form: 182
• C of E • Fees: £29,070 pa • Independent

Tel: 01580 240 592
Fax: 01580 240 280
Email: registry@benenden.kent.sch.uk
Website: www.benenden.kent.sch.uk

Headmistress: Since 2000, Mrs Claire Oulton MA, an Oxford historian, married (mid-forties). One daughter at Benenden, one left July 2009. Previously head of St Catherine's, Bramley for six years – very young for a first headship – prior to which she taught at Charterhouse, having begun her career at Benenden. Mrs Oulton impresses immediately, with an engaging mix of fervently-expressed principles and commonsense based on experience. She has, clearly, a thorough knowledge of her girls and their concerns. 'We put as much emphasis on developing the heart and soul as on the brain,' she asserts, 'helping girls to become confident, compassionate and courageous – I use these words all the time. If they can go out into the world like that, it will be good for them and good for the people they meet.' She is svelte, on the ball and candid. 'I am dedicated to giving my pupils the best possible experience of school. We're not complacent, but if you can concentrate on being a really good school and on making it better all the time, it works. Our best advertisement is the girls and their parents.' Much admired by her fellow heads.

Academic matters: Very impressive. Benenden is pretty much always in the top 50 independent schools nationally and sometimes in the top half of the 50. Small classes, high teacher:pupil ratio of 1:6, a general air of calm and relaxed discipline all contribute. Outstanding Spanish, French and Latin. Good to see healthy numbers for Latin and Greek. At A level, good results across the board – of the most popular subjects, biology, chemistry, economics, English, government and politics and history were the stars, with 31 of the 42 mathematicians gaining A*s or As in 2010. Some feel the school could offer a greater range of A level options but the breadth is there if you look for it. Introduction to psychology course since September 2007. Head committed to developing modern languages and, since 2007, all girls in Years 7–9 – barring real strugglers – take two of French, German, Spanish or Mandarin. Range of minority languages also available. Head's approach is practical and refreshingly sensible – 'we have loads of trips abroad to bolster the languages'. But also, 'I think children get tremendous confidence from learning how a language is constructed.' D'accord!

Good, well-stocked and efficient library. Some feeling among parents of the brightest that academics are celebrated less here than sports and drama but bright girls we quizzed demurred. Brightest and those with SEN all supported by study skills department. Extension programme for gifted and talented throughout school. Everyone screened on arrival and individual plans for anyone deemed in need. Thereafter all girls monitored regularly. Head quickly acknowledges that dyslexics can be among the brightest pupils but feels that 'severe' dyslexics will be better helped elsewhere. 'We need to be sure from the beginning that we're teaching in a way that's going to be helpful to them.' School aiming to be wheelchair-friendly throughout but is a large site with ups and downs and isn't there yet. 'We're keen to be aware of what our pupils may find difficult ... we look after our girls in a sensitive, caring way – we can cope with wheelchairs in most areas.' School takes very positive attitude to girls with individual physical difficulties.

Games, Options, the Arts: Playing fields on the crest of the Kent High Weald spread out gloriously in all directions. Sports hall, fitness suite (open 7am – 10pm and much the most popular facility on site) and 25 metre pool. Everyone plays lacrosse, most play netball and rounders and a choice of 15 or so other sporting activities including ballet, riding, sailing, trampolining and, most recently, rugby. Two U18 7s won the first Kent tournament in 2007. 'Girls love the outward-bound things,' says head, 'windsurfing, abseiling – you name it.' Games popular and successful. Lacrosse always top flight and squads regularly in top few nationally. Several county and regional players. Swimming also impressive.

Dance is strong and combines with drama and music to create imaginative and popular events. All given a huge boost with opening in 2007 of terrific new theatre plus dance studio – one of the best school theatres we have seen in terms of space, flexibility, finish and overall specifications. Full time theatre technician – girls learn the range of sound, lighting, stage management. Built on site of old tennis courts and one of a list of major projects that will continue the updating and development programme that is thoroughly and imaginatively underway. Music wing – music technology is popular now – no-frills and practical, housing teaching and practice rooms. Lively music programme and two-thirds take instrumental/vocal lessons. Special feature is the Hemsted Forest Youth Orchestra, two-thirds of which is Benenden girls, the rest from local preps and seniors – 'it draws talented musicians from the whole area and gives them the chance of playing in an orchestra which is even better than a school orchestra'. Admission 'very much by audition'.

Strong art and design – excellent DT workshops in which 'anything' can be made using 'every possible process' (materials include wood, metal, resin, plastics); computer-controlled gizmos along with traditional techniques. 'We have to hold back visiting fathers,' we were told. Jewellery especially popular. Six art-rooms in which we saw good – some outstanding – painting and witty textiles and particularly liked the sixth form studio with its individual desks and screens for pinning up work in progress – large and successful A level uptake for art and history of art. Lively cultural programme of events and varied lectures – some compulsory, at which there is some chafing, and others not, mostly much enjoyed and recalled with appreciation years later, aimed at nurturing more than the narrowly academic. Weekends packed with activities – girls affirm that this has improved beyond recognition in last few years.

Background and Atmosphere: In the heart of the Kent countryside, this is real traditional girls' boarding – Benenden village is a stroll away but offers nothing in the fleshpots line. The site is vast – 240 glorious acres of field and forest overlooking more rolling miles of hills and woodland. Benenden's trees alone merit a visit – a fabulous lime tree avenue, broadleafs and a 400-year-old wood are some of the delights of the site. Others include the old walled garden likely to be reclaimed from the ground staff and restored, and a set of water gardens, recently excavated and restored to form a valuable and beautiful resource for the ecologically-minded. A new eco-classroom has been built, completely sustainable and carbon neutral. The teaching buildings are close and linked at the heart of the site, and boarding houses spread out hither and yon. No specially distinguished buildings among them, though the main house is a remarkable 1860s re-build of the original Tudor mansion, using brick, fireplaces, panelling etc salvaged from a fire. The overall effect is a kind of Victorian Tudor Gothic. It boasts some reception/meeting rooms and an entrance hall which both impress and gladden the heart with architectural felicities.

Other good things – the wisteriaed 'cloisters', which are a popular meeting place in sunny months, the useful school shop, the large, light dining-room in which food, legendary for the best reasons, is enthusiastically ingested, and the yellow-painted endless corridor, in which excellent – and current – art is displayed. Otherwise, most areas are functional in aspect – this is not a frilly school. Depressing manifestation of this was the small, grim chapel which had no outlook, barring a brick wall, and sank the soul. However, we understand that it has been refurbished to include a big new stained glass window occupying the end wall and specially designed furniture. Boarding rooms are good. School still has up to seven girls to a dorm in younger years and it is cramped, but girls assured us they love it. For older girls, single or double rooms – much more spacious and well done. All are networked. Good kitchens, games rooms, but plain and sensible – nothing smart or showy.

Pastoral Care and Discipline: Happy girls. 'It's more like a community than a school,' we were told. 'Your housemaster might be your English teacher – the teachers really care about your pastoral side as well as your academic work.' Most parents concur though some feel that almost too much latitude is given on occasions – 'They're incredibly indulgent,' felt one. However, 'The house staff are delightful and they are in touch with the real world.' 'My daughter's housemistress knows her so well and is very on the ball,' are more common comments. Some feel the divide between the sixth and the rest is too great, but older girls enjoy their privileges and are less inclined to defect to co-ed as a result. Uniform for all, even the sixth, but they're allowed to dress theirs up with scarves etc and, as there's no-one but each other around to wow, they seem contented.

No serious problems – not one drugs incident since Mrs Oulton's advent nor for many years before that. A palpably traditional air about the place, but it isn't fuddy-duddy, and a sensible, balanced approach to life in general prevails. Also a sense of fun – along with the usual school photos, generations have also had fun photos taken, grotesque versions of the real things in which girls dress down, pull faces and adopt extravagant poses. 'Those are the ones my mum frames,' said one, cheerily.

Pupils and Parents: All are full boarders, though some go home for weekends; two fixed exeats a term. Flexibility about being taken out at weekends for meals etc. About 20 per cent from abroad, half of whom are ex-pats. Of the other 10 per cent, most are from Hong Kong with a sprinkling from other far eastern countries. Girls attest to there being a genuine mixing – no segregated groups as elsewhere. This achieved partly via lots of whole year team activities, e.g. raft building. Solid, traditional clientele – Home Counties and London and from a range of preps – who know what they're paying for and trust their choice. Many daughters of Old Girls; most come here via word-of-mouth recommendation – 'we've not advertised for five years,' says the head. Supportive parents who love the place. School has grandparents' day and lots of family events, also socials in London and surrounding counties. Prominent Old Girls include The Princess Royal, Princess Basma of Jordan, Dame Eliza Manningham-Buller, Rachel Weisz, Fiona Shackleton, Liz Forgan, Sue Ryder, Janny Scott.

Entrance: School over-subscribed and lists now closed two or three years ahead. Head works closely with prep schools. Pre-tests and interviews at 11 and 13 effectively allow for school to be confident about those likely to make it through entrance exam or CE, those who have a good chance but may need some extra help, and those best advised to look elsewhere – head writes along these lines to each individual family. System now pretty streamlined and numbers tend to work out on target. Entry to sixth dependent on exam, interview and current head's report but few places available as very few leave.

Exit: Eight to Oxbridge in 2009. Also popular are Bristol, Edinburgh, Leeds – seemingly a girls' school thing at the moment – London and Nottingham; the subjects taken cover the range.

Money Matters: Awards of up to 10 per cent of fees in academics, sports, music, art and design, DT and drama available at different stages – 11, 13 and sixth form. Generous means-tested bursaries available both for those temporarily in need or for longer term support of those otherwise unable to come to the school. Worth exploring.

Remarks: Everyone's idea of a traditional, upmarket, girls' boarding school, though not remotely hidebound by tradition – cutting-edge and unconventional in multiple ways, in a stunning setting and underpinned with commonsense.

Berkhamsted School

Linked to Berkhamsted Preparatory School in the Junior section

Overton House, 131 High Street, Berkhamsted, Hertfordshire, HP4 2DJ

• Pupils: 1,495, 40 boarders, 835 boys, 660 girls. Single sex teaching from 11-16 and co-ed in prep and sixth form • Ages: 11-18
• Size of sixth form: 325 • Christian • Fees: Day £13,800-£16,200; Boarding + £5,475-£9,600 pa • Independent

Tel: 01442 358 001
Fax: 01442 358 040
Email: admissions@berkhamstedschool.org
Website: www.berkhamstedschool.org.uk

Principal: Since 2008, Mr Mark Steed MA (Cantab) MA (Nottingham) theology, formerly headmaster at Kelly College, housemaster and head of religious studies at Oundle, and before that taught at Radley and The Leys, Cambridge. Mid-forties, married with three children, two at the school. Ten or so years on from the successful merger with the prep, girls' and boys' schools all agree it was time for closure and to move on, and that he's the right man for the job. He has a no-nonsense approach to change. Improvements, for example to the uniform, computer systems, sixth form block and girls' campus, quickly agreed and underway, all without ruffling feathers unduly. He has his own blog and a determination to overhaul school website and make it much more user- and parent-friendly. 'Amazed by how few schools have a vision.' He does, though, along with a strong and diverse management team to take it forward. Approachable, energetic and a keen and accomplished sportsman, generally well liked by both pupils and parents.

Academic matters: The school adheres to a traditional philosophy of education in seeking to provide opportunities for broad development. The wide choice of 26 subjects at A level not to mention the enrichment studies undertaken in Year 12, are consistent with this approach. Quantity does not compromise quality, however. Recently it has enjoyed a 100 per cent pass rate at A level with 87 per cent graded A or B. A level art and photography students have been in the top five nationally for the AQA exam board repeatedly in recent years. Maths, politics, geography and English are other areas of strength. Care is taken to steer particularly able pupils towards the more academic subjects while others are nudged towards less demanding curricula. New headmaster of sixth form appointed to encourage sharp academic focus and pupils to aim high. Staff praised for being readily accessible and other assistance comes in the form of drop-in maths workshops and lectures from leading experts, organised through the local chapter of the Geographical Association to which the school is host.

While some enter the school lower down having been denied grammar school entry, parents feel that the non-academic would probably not be happy here. As with A levels, results at GCSE have seen improvement over the past six to seven years. One in five achieve at least 10 A* or A grades. Again, good performance in most subjects, although some think modern languages could be better. All are required to take GCSE in RS and many go on to A level. More IGCSEs are in the pipeline to ensure they remain challenged, but according to the principal the school is not, and will not become, a 'sweatshop'. The Learning Support Department conducts assessments if requested and supplementary lessons are organised as necessary. There are two ESL teachers.

Games, Options, the Arts: The school receives just recognition for its sporting achievements. It recently won the regional lacrosse championships and former and present pupils regularly represent the country and compete at regional and county level across a range of other sports. Emphasis placed on teaching sport well and ensuring that everyone has fun and is able to benefit. Netball and boys' hockey given new emphasis of late. Rugby, hockey, lacrosse, cricket, football, swimming and tennis compulsory depending on age and gender. The new sports pavilion has opened up wider possibilities both to pupils and the wider community, including squash, aerobics, yoga, badminton and weight-training.

Over 50 per cent opt to study singing or an instrument of some kind. A talent competition to raise money for charity and Young Musician of the Year are relatively recent additions to the school calendar and audiences are overwhelmed by the diversity of talent. The Friends provide Pimms, soft drinks and strawberries for 'Proms in the Quad', and all leave with fond memories of rousing and moving performances from solo vocalists and musicians. The ever-popular swing songs from the mixed pupil and staff Big Band ring in their ears. Drama is a popular option at GCSE and beyond, and there are inter-house competitions to encourage all to take to the stage. Some grumbles from parents that staff compete fiercely for pupil time when schedules conflict, but generally a much-appreciated aspect of the school. 'My son's speech at our wedding anniversary was faultless. They even found time to teach him public speaking.' May well have honed his dance floor skills too, at the Strictly Come Dancing fundraiser, one of many community events at which the girls and boys come together.

A tour of the school may well take in the historic armoury. CCF is well established and attracts large numbers of recruits each year. The choice between this and D of E is often a hard one, but few can keep up with the demands of both. In addition to special visits, cadets are offered at least one training weekend a month and the D of E expeditions take candidates anywhere from the wet and wind-swept Lake District to the altogether more clement foothills of the Dolomites. High level of commitment found. Out of a D of E enrolment of 200, and against a national average of 50 per cent, 74 per cent completed their award.

Background and Atmosphere: Christian foundation school which dates from 1541 and amalgamated with the 1888 girls' school in 1997 and the mixed prep the following year. Boys and girls still have their own campuses but some facilities shared. 'Little school feel, big school infrastructure,' says the principal, and indeed there's a general feel that all parts of the school come together and meld peaceably with the pretty and historic town. The Castle Campus, which mostly houses the boys, but also the mixed sixth form, has some slightly scruffy houses and common-rooms but these are more than compensated for by the neat grass quad, well-preserved exteriors and assembly rooms, including the grade 1 listed Tutor hall and 19th century Venetian-style chapel. Some modern classrooms and labs and an ultra-swish new dining hall. Little wonder parents queue up for those tasty charity breakfasts. Games on the Eton Fives courts provide a popular spectacle and seats under mature trees a traditional girls' meeting place. Perhaps not surprisingly, lots of boys milling about nearby. No-one suggests the girls are hard done-by comparatively – 'our art room is more authentic, a Parisian atelier' – but can't say King's Campus is quite as impressive. To compensate, the new sports centre is right on the girls' doorstep and a more spacious dining hall and classroom block are due for completion in September 2011. Boarding houses are within easy walk of the school and indistinguishable from surrounding privately-owned flats. Recently refurbished, bedrooms are comfortable and tasteful pictures, vases of flowers and modern furnishings give a lovely homely feel to communal areas with quiet and noisier common-rooms to suit your mood.

Smart suit dress and sanctioning of moderate make-up help prepare pupils for life after school. Work experience after AS with targeted placements. Good decision-making support in the form of advice from teachers, careers fairs and lunches with parents and others to open their eyes to the world of work. In fact introduction to career choices starts much lower down the school, with research, profiling and guidance interviews in Years 8, 10 and 11.

Pastoral Care and Discipline: A community school. Many enter the prep early and stay the course. Up until GCSEs, the separation of boys and girls allows them to be themselves and be less inhibited while extra-curricular activities ensure they are not cut off completely from the other sex. Sixth form very much run along the lines of a college, geared towards preparing pupils for the outside world. Many choose the school for all these reasons. A great feeling of pulling together and mutual support pervades throughout. A vertical house system facilitates friendships across and in between year groups. 'This is where we meet to do our prep.' 'We come here to do presentations, sharing our knowledge of specialist subjects.' There's spiritual teaching in the chapel with all faiths welcome.

Pupils wearing smiley badges gather up lost souls and answer questions. On more serious or personal issues, pupils and parents are encouraged to communicate directly with house tutors. Is there bullying? Well, yes, some, but the caring attitude of staff and fellow pupils usually keeps it to a minimum. 'The kids are pretty sensible on the whole.' No real worries about drink or drugs though recently a discussion forum has been established. 'Schools should provide a moral lead beyond the school boundaries,' says the principal. Concentration of overseas students in the boarding house doesn't seem to create a divide between them, flexi-boarders and day pupils. Boarders participate in wider weekend school activities but also organise activities and outings tailored to their interests. ESL lessons held on Saturday mornings and visits to London's China Town and markets to buy African foodstuffs reportedly very successful.

Pupils and Parents: Generally families live within 40 minutes or so of the school. Small number of MOD and expat families. Number of first time buyers along with the more comfortably affluent. The boarding community largely made up of upper school overseas nationals, mostly from Far East and Africa. Overall mix and town location mean that no feeling that they are living in a rarefied environment. Suits those that are willing to try everything out and contribute across the board. Pupils friendly, open and fun. 'Well-mannered and a pleasure to have in your house.' The Friends organise regular social events, including coffee mornings. Good chance to meet other parents and put views across to the principal who attends when he can. Very vibrant OB association with regular sporting fixtures against the school, meetings with fellow professionals, reunion dinners and regular charitable donations to support school activities. Most famous OB Graham Greene, whose father was the school's head. Others include explorer Robin Knox-Johnston, composer Sir Alexander Goehr, Sir Kenneth Cork (former Lord Major of London), Michael Meacher MP, musician Anthony Hopkins and actress Emma Fielding.

Entrance: Seventy or so move up from the prep each year. There is a wide range of feeder schools in Hertfordshire, Buckinghamshire and Bedfordshire. They include Abbot's Hill, Beacon School, Gateways, Lockers Park and Maltman's Green School. Home-grown thought to have an advantage but all have to take an entry exam. This comprises verbal reasoning, English and maths testing at 11+ and additional modern languages tests at 13+. Can enter in Years 8 or 10 when testing also takes place. Push to raise the number of girls and even out numbers. Approximately 40 apply for sixth form from outside. One in two turned away, based largely on GCSE results. Minimum requirement of at least five B and two C grades which may possibly include a short course (usually RS) with A or B in the four subjects chosen for AS level. A grade required if choices include English literature, maths, modern languages or science. Prospective students meet the head of sixth form and are required to provide a reference from their current school.

Exit: Most go on to further education, many after a gap year, with five to six gaining Oxbridge places each year. Other destinations include Durham, Southampton, Birmingham, Nottingham, Bournemouth and Manchester. Art, engineering, history, economics, business and management are popular.

Money Matters: Fees for extras considered reasonable and fair. Limited number of academic, music, drama, art and sports scholarships available awarded on merit. Also bursaries in case of need.

Remarks: Combines the best of a single sex and co-ed school. Study coupled with a strong spiritual basis and community ethos produces confident all-round achievers.

Beverley Grammar School

Linked to Beverley Joint Sixth

Queensgate, Beverley, East Riding of Yorkshire, HU17 8NF

• Pupils: 840 boys, all day • Ages: 11-18 • Size of sixth form: 350, joint with the girls' school • Non-denom • State

Tel: 01482 881 531
Fax: 01482 881 564
Email: info@beverleygrammar.co.uk
Website: www.bgs.eriding.net

Head: Since September 2006, Mr Christopher R Goodwin BSc Hons. Zoology degree from London University. He taught in California and has travelled extensively. An author for Oxford University Press and has a great interest in rock music. He first joined Beverley Grammar School in 1975 as a biology teacher and progressed to be head of science and deputy head before taking charge of the school. Very proud to be the head of the oldest state school in the country and believes passionately in the development of the whole child. He supports the view that education should be enjoyable and, as a parent noted, 'The mutual respect and atmosphere between staff and students is what makes the school so special.'

Academic matters: A high performing specialist school with three outstanding Ofsted ratings. School graded A* at key stages 3 and 4, putting it in top five per cent of schools nationally. In the joint sixth form, almost half of all grades are either A or B. Students can also study for NVQ in engineering and GNVQ in IT. Sixth form blocks at both boys' grammar and nearby girls' high school so students divide their time between the two. 'I argue that it's a good halfway house between the school where they feel comfortable and what it will be like going to university where everything is new,' says head.

Games, Options, the Arts: Strong on music by state standards – about 120 have individual music lessons. Various choirs, orchestras, bands including a Year 7 choir for all new intake. 'If any of the boys are reluctant, we take the view, "what do you mean you don't sing? Everybody sings!" And because it's the norm, they all do.' Drama has included an all-boy production of Macbeth. 'We had a boy as Lady Macbeth. It didn't cause a ripple.'

Also strong on sport ('you name it, we do it') and highlights include annual cross-country race. 'The boys love it. I can't work it out – I used to hate it,' confessed previous head. And extra-curricular is, well, take your pick: 'If a boy wants a club to be started, we find a member of staff to start it'.

Background and Atmosphere: Founded in 700 AD, Beverley Grammar is England's oldest state secondary school. Cherishes its traditions but prides itself on moving with the times. On its present site since 1903 and now mix of the old (museum-piece of a hall) and the new (£750,000 sixth form block). Though a grammar by name, it's a comprehensive by nature. There are no entrance tests, no fees and it takes all-comers from its catchment area.

One of a handful of free-standing voluntary aided schools which means it can bid direct to the DfE for some of its finance. Downside is that the trustees have to find 10 per cent of the cost of major building projects. Recently granted specialist status in engineering bringing investment in technology, maths and science. All prizes at speech day awarded for effort – 'at least as important as achievement,' says head. 'We operate on mutual respect and a friendly environment in which all our students are valued.'

Pastoral Care and Discipline: Uses more carrot, less stick approach to learning. 'We believe in working hard, but having a lot of fun doing it so there's a lot of leg pulling goes on in the classrooms. And because we have a relaxed approach to learning, the boys learn because they want to, not because they're being threatened with what will happen if they don't.' 'We encourage everyone to show respect for everyone else and that's often about the little things – the way staff talk to pupils, the way teachers hold doors open for the kids as well as the kids for the teachers.'

Parents involved at earliest stage over any slips in discipline. School's own social worker may visit child's home to talk over problems. Only one permanent exclusion in three years and exemplary behaviour around school. Creditable reward system of 'green slips' which lead to certificates and ultimate prize of special school tie. And mentoring system with a difference to keep learning on track: as well as teachers, mentors can also be volunteers from the community – industrialists, careers advisers, etc – to drum home the value of learning. Head says, 'we use counselling and praise to modify behaviour. It works better than punishment and threats. We are a happy place where everyone achieves.'

Pupils and Parents: Very supportive parents, encouraged to be involved with school from the off. Parents of new intake invited to sit with their child for half a day of lessons. One mum, fresh from a science lesson, described school as 'absolutely brilliant. There's such an eagerness and keenness here. It's renewed in my son that excitement for learning'.

Entrance: Living in catchment area – Beverley and the surrounding villages of Tickton, Walkington and Bishop Burton – is pretty much a must. Heavily over-subscribed.

Exit: About 70 per cent go on to sixth form and many more into some other form of further education. Ultimately, most go to university.

Remarks: A grown-up school, mature enough to nurture mutual respect and to know when to let its hair down. A school with a sense of humour. No wonder boys love it.

Beverley High School

Linked to Beverley Joint Sixth

Norwood, Beverley, East Riding of Yorkshire, HU17 9EX

• Pupils: 850 girls, all day • Ages: 11-18 • Size of sixth form: 350 in joint sixth form with Beverley Grammar • Non-denom • State

Tel: 01482 881 658
Fax: 01482 870 935
Email: admindept@beverleyhigh.net
Website: www.beverleyhigh.net

Head: Since September 2009, Ms Sharon Japp. Previously deputy head.

Academic matters: Breathtaking 85 per cent of pupils achieve 5 or more A*–C grades in GCSEs. 'We had one of those Kelly Holmes moments when we saw the results,' says head. 'You raise your arms in celebration and then can't quite believe it until you've been back to check.' Also good A level results at joint sixth form with Beverley Grammar (see their entry for details of sixth form).

One of only 18 schools in the country designated an ambassador school by the National Academy for Gifted and Talented Youth. Children with particular skills, whether academic, arts, sporting or even leadership, have their talents nurtured. Gifted A level science students from surrounding schools have joined them for lectures given by experts at top of their field. Key stage 3 pupils get together for weekend study sessions at a local hotel to aim at the highest levels in English and maths. Successful summer schools held for bright students from within the school and also from feeder primary schools. Open University modules are offered to sixth form.

And for the less gifted and talented? 'If you do your best for the gifted and talented pupils, research shows that it benefits everybody in the school. By challenging all in the classroom, it moves everyone on,' says head. Students closely monitored and pace of work is fast but hope is to encourage everyone of all abilities. Aim is that somewhere around the school, every child's name should be highlighted for some kind of achievement. Subjects are taught in mixed-ability groups apart from maths and languages at KS3 and science at KS4.

Games, Options, the Arts: Drama, dance, music and art promoted through the curriculum. Choirs, orchestras, annual carol service in nearby Minster and summer music concert in St Mary's Church. Sport very popular and enhanced by new £1.5m sports hall, shared with community. A new technology block and art block will follow. New developments are not a moment too soon. School, with its small hall, is desperately short of large meeting space.

Twenty-five clubs meet during the week, judo to Japanese. Strong links and student exchanges with a school in Japan helped to win British Council's International School Award. Highlights of school year include more than 60 trips to places at home and abroad. Fund-raising for charities chosen by girls.

Background and Atmosphere: A Tardis of a school with a small frontage onto a main road hiding extensive buildings and wooded grounds. Almost 100 years old but at the forefront of change. Became a technology college in the first flush of schools adopting specialist status in 1998. A school where teachers give of their best. 'We have some wonderful teachers here who work hard to make learning fun and interesting,' says head. But much is expected of students, too. Classroom noticeboards show details of what pupils need to do to strive always for the next level of attainment. A girl expecting a B grade would never be in any doubt about what was needed to lift herself to an A.

An atmosphere of maturity and trust. School has three computer suites where girls can work unsupervised between lessons. Girls value the resources and look after them.

Pastoral Care and Discipline: Each form has a captain and deputy who keep their rôles for a term so that everyone gets a chance at leadership. Merit system in lower school and good behaviour encouraged in upper school by a points system – students can gain or lose points according to behaviour. Rewards on a sliding scale from a 'wear what you like' day to a trip to a theme park; those who earn most points reap biggest rewards.

Pupils and Parents: Very supportive parents encouraged to share school's ambition for their girls. Pupils are drawn from local catchment area and take a real pride in their school.

Entrance: Substantially over-subscribed and draws pupils almost exclusively from catchment area – Beverley and the surrounding villages of Tickton, Walkington and Bishop Burton.

Exit: A hefty 97 per cent of Year 11 stay in education, mainly in school's joint sixth form or the local colleges. Most of Year 13 go on to university.

Remarks: A school that drives students forward, putting in extraordinary effort to help them stand on tiptoe and reach out for the very best they could achieve.

Birkdale School

Linked to Birkdale School Preparatory School in the Junior section

Oakholme Road, Sheffield, South Yorkshire, S10 3DH

• Pupils: 510 boys in the senior school; 150 boys and 50 girls in the sixth form. All day. • Ages: 11-18 • Size of sixth form: 200 • Christian, but all faiths welcome • Fees: £10,317 pa • Independent

Tel: 0114 266 8409
Fax: 0114 267 1947
Email: admissions@birkdaleschool.org.uk
Website: www.birkdaleschool.org.uk

Headmaster: Since September 2010, Dr Paul Owen, previously academic deputy head at Wellington School in Somerset.

Dr Owen has 18 years teaching experience, teaching mostly physics but also some IT, chemistry, maths, astronomy and critical thinking. He has considerable pastoral experience (day housemaster) and this, together with his Christian faith, should support continuing commitment to good pastoral care. He lives on site with his wife, Gail, and their three children.

Academic matters: The sciences, maths, English literature and the humanities appear the most popular and successful A levels. 2010 was best ever for A level results with a pass rate of 100 per cent; 22 per cent A* and 72 per cent of all entries achieved A/B grade. General studies for all at A level. 2010 GCSEs also outstanding with 97 per cent getting A*–C; 28 per cent of pupils gained A*. Spanish now on the curriculum and thriving. Greek on offer at lunchtime and can be taken to exam level. Dual award science at GCSE.

Open-door policy in the common-room – pupils can approach staff for help at any time. Dyslexia provision costs extra, mild dyslexics only. Huge library, many computer rooms, all linked, with email addresses for all; strong DT presence, subdivided into electronics, graphics and resistant materials. Rather jolly ecology pool and masses of trips for geographers and historians.

Games, Options, the Arts: Lively school magazine with quizzes as well as the usual sporting achievements. Rugby important here, with trips to New Zealand and Fiji. Footie very popular and school has joined the independent schools' competition. Girls do team or individual sport, making use of a 30 metre sports hall and designer gym with weights room. Sports field some ten minutes' drive away, with a new £2 million sports pavilion completed 2006.

Fabulous art complex run by husband and wife team, concentrating on perspective when we visited via a rather complicated machine of their own design 'which never fails'. Truly exciting work here. Regular As and A* at A level and GCSE respectively, masses of good 3D stuff and the walls of the art department were positively papered in lively pictures. Nice 3D guitar and some Modigliani lookalikes. Well-equipped drama studio at Johnson House, with recording capabilities and an impressive wardrobe room. Theatre studies at A level. Much use made of the local countryside with trips to the Peak District, D of E. Whole school supports a school in Nepal, with annual visits both from members and friends of the school.

Background and Atmosphere: School founded at the turn of the twentieth century as a boys' private prep school, went up to 16 in 1988, then 18, and added girls in the sixth form only in 1996. Moved into current site in 1998; pleasant bit of Sheffield but hideously complicated campus, embracing Oakholme Road, Ashdell Road, Endcliffe Crescent and Fulwood Road. Masses of to-ing and fro-ing between the various Victorian/new-build houses on an incredibly steep site. Good octagonal concert hall, school hall bursting at the seams that doubles as a dining room and badminton court, as well as stage – extension still planned.

Pupils are encouraged to get involved in a wide variety of lunchtime activities. Separate sixth form block, the Grayson building, which also includes computers. Elegant Johnson House with listed marble fireplaces (£20,000 to replace, said our guide), and RE department on the top floor with a quote from Micah painted on the wall: 'What does the Lord require of you? To act justly and to love mercy and to walk humbly with your God'. Pupils not allowed to go down the main staircase (one-way system). Lockers line the broad passages throughout. As we said before, the atmosphere is lively, scruffy and fun. Steps all over the place and no use for wheelchairs.

Pastoral Care and Discipline: Strong Christian ethos, pastoral care important here. And according to the school's policy statement, 'It is the policy of Birkdale School to promote a Christian lifestyle ... any illegal use of controlled drugs by either staff or pupils will be treated as serious misconduct', the first time we have seen staff mentioned in such context. Dealing in drugs equals out and no questions. If found using on the premises, the matter is 'taken very seriously' and previous conduct is taken into account. Pupil might be allowed to remain under a strict regime of testing. (Hasn't happened yet.) 'Drugs are contrary to all our teaching.' Smoking on site rare in school, would result in detention, increasing in severity if problem persists. Ditto alcohol. Occasional incidents of bullying are dealt with by (usually) confronting the perpetrator – 'might suspend', 'would certainly involve parents'. Head of year groups plus form tutors for all. Tutors first point of call if a pupil has problems but prefects equally used. Prefects spend a training weekend in the Peak District. School uniform throughout the school – blue, grey and white with dashing striped ties for the boys.

Pupils and Parents: Local lads and lasses, many first-time buyers; huge catchment area. Parents operate local buses from as far away as Bawtry, Doncaster, the Peak District and North Derbyshire, over a thirty-mile radius. OBs Michael Palin, a couple of judges, a racing driver and an MP or two.

Entrance: Entrance test for all at 11, including those in the prep school, who don't come up 'if it is not the right school for them' – perhaps a handful each year. CE at 13, but tiny intake then. Girls (and boys) join sixth form from many local schools, around 30 each year. Five passes at GCSE, with four Bs minimum, and at least B at GCSE in any subject to be studied at A level.

Exit: Excellent careers library and on-line for sixth form. Leeds the most popular university, plus ex-polys, which often offer more esoteric courses: De Montfort, Leeds Metropolitan etc. Nine per cent annually to Oxbridge. Business, medicine, engineering, computing and law are popular degree subjects.

Money Matters: Not the rich school it appeared to be, having lost assisted places. Certain number of academic scholarships on offer, which can be topped up in case of need. Will carry a pupil to next stage if in real financial need.

Remarks: School has had a meteoric rise from a boys-only prep school to a full blown senior school with girls in the sixth. No current thoughts about girls throughout, though anything is possible. Happily ensconced in Sheffield's education alley; strong and both academically and socially tough.

Birkenhead School

Linked to Birkenhead Prep School in the Junior section

58 Beresford Road, Oxton, Prenton, Merseyside, CH43 2JD

- Pupils: 11-18: 330 boys, 65 girls; prep school 315 boys and girls
- Ages: 3-18 • Size of sixth form: 95 boys, 10 girls • No affiliation but C of E by tradition • Fees: 1£6,522-£9,426 pa • Independent

Tel: 0151 652 4014
Fax: 0151 651 3091
Email: enquire@birkenheadschool.co.uk
Website: www.birkenheadschool.co.uk

Head: Since 2003, Mr John Clark MA ('just 50'); read modern languages at Exeter College, Oxford, taught at St Paul's School, head of department at Whitgift, deputy head at Birkenhead 1996. A charming, civilised man; apparent diffidence masks a quiet authority; 'Outstanding,' says a happy parent. He knows exactly what goes on in the school, is respected by pupils for this. A good listener; compares favourably with more pushy and gimmicky heads in his concentration on the proper business of education, his excellent communication skills and readiness to take his position seriously, but not always himself. Not to be detected talking or writing about 'learning platforms'. Loves the 'huge family' of his relatively small school in a realistic, grounded way. Ably backed up by energetic deputy, Mr David Edmunds.

Academic matters: Strong pretty well all round, results well ahead of local selective grammars, its main competitors. 2010 A level: 84 per cent A*/A/B, two pupils got four A* grades. Majority opt for maths and science (excellent results); largest humanities entries in history and geography. English looks a little sad by comparison. GCSE produced 28 per cent A*, 54 per cent A* + A. Clearly school's policy of offering (and staffing) wide option range across only three-form entry pays off in terms of small classes and sets, e.g. language choice from Latin, Greek, French, German, Spanish. Separate sciences for most to GCSE. Special needs coordinated by staff member, now helped by learning support teacher with no other teaching commitments. Parents pay for one-to-one tuition.

Not much staff turnover – it's a very nice place to teach and live. A general impression of fervent commitment to setting high classroom standards – and indeed to life outside the classroom.

Games, Options, the Arts: Games record amazing for size of school: cricket first XI ranked second nationally in Wisden list; current captain has played for Lancashire second XI; Under 15 rugby side recently top of national rankings (mind, this does depend up to a point on how strong/weak your fixtures list is). Otherwise, most of the usual sports, including very successful hockey; soccer in sixth form. Since September 2008, senior girls' teams in hockey, netball, lacrosse. School has policy of sport for all, through which individuals find their niche and improve fitness: 'We're not simply interested in natural athletes'. Enormous range of outdoor activities: CCF (all three sections), shared with local RC girls' school; D of E (32 taking gold level); 'biggest scout troop in Birkenhead'. Usual tours and expeditions.

Lively music: choral concerts with Liverpool Sinfonia, most recently Verdi's Requiem; much instrumental tuition; chapel choir, claimed unique among day schools in holding weekly evensong during term, involving pupils from age 10 to 18. Active drama.

Background and Atmosphere: Founded 1860, became direct grant, then independent in 1976. An unusual campus, hinted at in school's suburban address. Walking along the four comfortable, tree-lined roads that define the school, you won't guess at the existence of a lively school of 700 lurking behind the screen of large houses and sundry buildings. In fact, it's an agreeable jumble of old and new, including a handsome Victorian chapel and a fine cricket field. Years 7 and 8 housed in an elegant mansion, with its own playground and Year 8 prefects, helping transition to serious senior school. At present, a handful of girls in the sixth, but they're building up in the prep school and due to fill out ages 11–16. Co-education originally planned with Birkenhead High School, but this has now become an academy, so school is going it alone – to everyone's relief, it seems. Integration of girls in prep has gone smoothly (excellent head), and should continue; campus is a civilised place, and supervision of all ages discreet but effective. Recent ISI inspection noted 'exemplary' pupils' behaviour.

Liverpool proper may be just across the water, but it feels miles away. The Wirral is a pretty conservative place, and the school is happy with its own traditional elements: little boys wear caps, prefects wear gowns, and the head enters assembly to the head of school's cry of 'School!', whereupon all stand up. Trendy potential parents may not like this.

Developments on the way include more prep school classrooms (including science and IT), extensions to sixth form block, improvements to pavilion; a swimming pool is a gleam in the eye. *In Focus*, a superb termly newsletter, full of pictures, is the brainchild of the head's remarkable PA and school lynchpin.

Pastoral Care and Discipline: Traditional day school system; interlocking staff responsibilities mean it's very hard to fall through the pastoral net – commended in ISI report as 'outstanding'. Report also quotes a boy: 'We don't do bullying here.' One expulsion for drug use in last five years; pupils can be temporarily excluded for rudeness and vandalism. Hooray!

Pupils and Parents: Pupils mostly from the Wirral and as far as Chester; some walk, some use public transport, many use school bus system shared with Birkenhead High. Pupils seem articulate, confident, happy with work ethos, and yes, a touch conventional. Their alternative sixth form prospectus is worth a read, though hardly very shocking. Parents mostly professional and business, heavily committed to all aspects of school. Flourishing former pupils society, sharing *In Focus* with school. Most famous old boy was FE Smith, Lord Birkenhead.

Entrance: Increasingly, from own prep; existence of local grammars draws state primary pupils away at 11+. May have been a brief wobble over numbers before the co-education decision, but situation now seems to have steadied, as many parents opt for independent education from the start. Prep pupils not tested at 11+ unless applying for a scholarship – assessed internally, and those not likely to make grade flagged up in good time for parents to find alternative schooling. External candidates tested in English, maths and VR. A few leave at 16+, more than made up for by external entrants. School operates GCSE hurdle for A levels.

Exit: Vast majority to good universities, to read hard subjects; a handful to Oxbridge each year, most to Russell Group, especially Durham. Law, medicine/dentistry, engineering popular.

Money Matters: Was hit by end of assisted places scheme, but now stable. About six academic scholarships a year, a few at sixth form level, some limited-term for music; usually ten per cent of fee. Birkenhead Foundation Trust bursaries support about eight pupils a year; full remission possible.

Remarks: A confident, humane, non-flashy school in the best grammar school tradition, offering an astonishing array of opportunities for personal development in and out of classroom. Not as driven as some famous ex-grammars in urban areas. It feels nearer Chester than Liverpool, more like Bootham than, say, Bolton. Head's claim of an 'open, happy community' rings true, but parents of young thrusters shouldn't be put off.

Bishop Luffa Church of England School, Chichester

Bishop Luffa Close, Chichester, West Sussex, PO19 3LT

• Pupils: 680 boys, 720 girls • Ages: 11-19 • Size of sixth form: 300 • C of E • State

Tel: 01243 787 741
Fax: 01243 531 807
Email: webadmin@bishopluffa.org.uk
Website: www.bishopluffa.org.uk

Head: Since 2000, Mr Nick Taunt MA (early fifties), educated at Exeter College, Oxford. Previously head of creative arts at Harwich School and then deputy head of

Hedingham School. Married to a social worker, they have three children (two youngest came through Bishop Luffa) and one grandchild. Quietly spoken, he is totally committed to ensuring 'everything we do is consistently outstanding'. Feels that citizenship, like faith, is learnt through experience rather than didacticism and that this is a vital part of life at Bishop Luffa. What surprises him most about his school is 'that so many feel so happy for so much of the time!' Still teaches English to the sixth form, plays the violin, sails and likes to walk on the downs – his interests are reflected throughout the school.

Academic matters: Impressive results for a non-selective school. GCSE 80 plus per cent A*–C, A level 55 per cent A and B grades. Encourages children's individual side, whether artistic or scientific. Able pupils take up to 12 subjects at GCSE. Class sizes are 25–30 but teachers hold focus well, interactive whiteboards used in many of them. The compact campus is organised by subject with three main IT rooms and small ones for maths and science. Most of the direct IT teaching is practical, concentrated on databases and building websites, but ICT is also used to facilitate learning in all subjects.

Parents approve school's innovative teaching of mathematics, although some feel science could be more inspiring with a greater continuity of teachers. A modern language is compulsory throughout main school, also an option in Year 8 of a second one or Latin. The latter is popular – 'It is useful for law'; German less so at present – 'A good choice if you want a smaller class!' Pupils help teach languages to primary school pupils as part of the school's Leading Edge work. Pools resources with 10 others and an FE college in its area and acts as the hub for A level German, further maths and Latin.

Everyone learns RE up to Year 11 and all take GCSE but religion is not oppressive here, more the reverse – a Leavers' Eucharist was described as 'great fun'. Christian Union strong and led by the sixth form.

Pre-GCSE the pupils carousel through graphics, product design, home economics and textiles each year. The six rooms devoted to product design with excellent DT equipment meet school's status as a designated technology college. Food tech rooms are good and three art rooms for those taking it through to A level. Textile room is lined with sewing machines and work is up on the walls – we saw an exciting range of recycled clothes (looks better than it sounds). Throughout the school subjects have a practical aspect – in this case regular charity fashion shows. The media workshop teaches pupils to make and edit adverts and short films – enough video cameras to cater for groups of six or seven working together.

The library stages its own Book Award programme that promotes new fiction titles. Visiting authors, poets and storytellers (among them Philip Reeve, Robert Muchamore and James Riordan) keep reading lively.

About 35 pupils with statements but the well-run learning support department does not just deal with these children. A document which is updated every term and a talk from the SENCo (often an informal workshop) ensure that all staff focus on behaviour and inclusion and are aware of differentiated ideas and materials. Five dedicated teachers and 10 LSAs go out into the classrooms and help pupils to access the curriculum as individuals or in little groups. At key stage 3 those needing extra help sometimes come out of lessons, and at key stage 4 supported study is timetabled into the day. The department focuses on ASDAN qualifications. Also lunchtime clubs for those who need to be away from the fray and homework clubs for those who are not getting it done out of school. Toe by Toe programme (delivered by LSAs, little and often) helps improve spelling and reading on an individual basis. At key stage 4 a small numbers of pupils pursue vocational courses for one day a week in college.

Games, Options, the Arts: Extensive playing fields, climbing wall, gym, sports hall and the new MUGA (multi-use games area) all contribute to achievements in sports (Sports Mark awarded for past six years and a number of pupils in county or UK under-18 teams); popular ones include volleyball, hockey, basketball, cricket, athletics; tennis is played at breaktime too. Consideration for neighbours has been given a scientific twist with the construction of a grassy mound to reflect the sound of the school at play away from sensitive ears.

A couple of choirs, a barber shop, an orchestra and a swing group are some of the by-products of individual tuition, and of learning eight bar blues and rhythm and beats on a shared keyboard in a group lesson. Children compose their own music for productions. Much of the drama curriculum is linked with the English department; many productions and pupils work alongside professional actors and are members of the Chichester Festival Youth Theatre.

Duke of Edinburgh is taken up by many from Year 10 upwards, with a young team of leaders – all teachers we saw were enthusiastic with a great rapport with pupils. Lots of trips including skiing, a Year 7 excursion to the Isle of Wight, geography ones to Morocco, Iceland, history ones to Russia and Washington DC – basically if a teacher is interested in a particular place (and a lot of them are) they sort something out. If a child really wants to go and the parents cannot afford it, help is available. The trips normally happen in half terms and if they are residential and take up class time then lessons take place in situ.

Background and Atmosphere: Purpose-built in 1963, in a residential area on the edge of Chichester, as a church school, following requests by a group of parents who wanted a Christian-based education for their children. They have been expanding and adding buildings ever since. A very busy place with a warren of corridors. A quiet area was created as a memorial after the deaths of some pupils – a piece of land between the science block wild garden; not a memorial garden but a place for escape from the bustle of the limited campus.

Lots of pupil participation. Food is healthy and popular, pupils having an input on choices through catering meetings, though many children bring their own lunches or pop to ASDA. Year 7 have their own cafeteria line, ensuring they develop healthy habits (away from the louder bigger kids). The sixth form make sure no one eats outside and keep the queue in order – their perk being the fact that they don't need to line up themselves – and pupils on house detention help the cleaners clear the hall after lunch. The eco group arranged for three new compost bins (yet to be used to their full capacity).

Some cycle to school, 70 per cent come by bus and many sixth formers drive (although on-site parking is at a premium). Wall displays of writing, art and topical issues (holocaust survival, slavery). Compulsory work experience in Year 12 and Year 10 embeds the children further into the local community. Around 50 in each year take part in the Young Enterprise scheme (they've won national prizes), making as much money as they possibly can; a recent project began with a volleyball tournament and a music competition to raise capital for a stock of pen drives which gave the team a £3,500 profit.

The sixth form has an area with slouchy sofas, a pool table and its own kitchen. The three rooms (one with computers, due to be renovated and converted into a library) have been painted and decorated by the kids themselves so feel scruffy but well-used and totally loved.

Pastoral Care and Discipline: House system. The register at the beginning of the day gives each child 25 minutes of tutor time (eight tutorial groups in each year) and it is at this point that worship is conducted, competitions and notices are announced, and you can get airtime for your pet project. Mentoring scheme with training given to help tackle peer problems, organisational and emotional. On-site school nurse dispenses everything from tea and comfort to EpiPens. A member of the clergy team is linked to each year group and comes into lessons and assembly; all this contributes to strong sense of community.

A child would be sent home for rudeness to a member of staff, persistent disobedience, smoking or drinking. Permanent exclusion for drugs.

Pupils and Parents: From a diversity of backgrounds since the school is non-selective. Mainly local, also from Littlehampton, Midhurst, Bognor, Selsey and as far as the border with Hampshire. Five places are offered on compassionate grounds. Past pupils include journalists Jonathan Thompson, Amanda Ursell and Rupert Wingfield-Hayes, theatre director Paul Millar, Catherine Hartley (polar explorer), musicians Jonathan Ansell (of G4) and Zoe Rahman.

Entrance: At 11 from 50 different Sussex primaries, both state and independent. Always over-subscribed. Complicated hierarchy of admissions sets and rules – may change, so look up the latest – but the great majority of places go to the children of C of E churchgoers (weekly for at least two years) resident in the deaneries of Chichester, Arundel and Bognor and Westbourne. Lesser number of places reserved for other Christian denominations and reserve category for less attentive Anglicans (may not be reached). 10 per cent of places allocated to those living close to the school – no religious qualification required.

Exit: A handful leaves at 16 to go to local colleges, most stay for A levels. 90 per cent go to university most years, some take a gap year, some to Oxford and Cambridge; other popular choices are London, Durham, York, Bristol and Cardiff.

Money Matters: Very supportive parents and friends association helps less well-off children pay for school trips, foreign exchanges and in some cases instrumental tuition. Also send four or five children a year abroad to do Christian charity work in Nepal, South America etc.

Remarks: Definitely worth rekindling your faith for this one! Parents say it brings out the best in their children. A really interesting place to visit; the pupils are charming and quick-witted – obviously stimulated and entertained. The cramped site is its one major drawback but the atmosphere more than makes up for this.

Bishop Wordsworth's Grammar School

11 The Close, Salisbury, Wiltshire, SP1 2ED

• Pupils: 890 boys, all day • Ages: 11-18 • Size of sixth form: 300 • C of E • State

Tel: 01722 333 851
Fax: 01722 325 899
Email: admin@bws.wilts.sch.uk
Website: www.bws.wilts.sch.uk

Head: Since 2002, Dr Stuart Smallwood BSc PhD NPQH (forties). Educated at Harvey Grammar School, Folkstone, then a glittering selection of academic qualifications: BSc (Hons) in geology from Leeds University, PhD from Cambridge and PGCE from Bristol. NPQH refers to the National Professional Qualification for Headship, in case you are wondering. First taught at Sir Thomas Rich's School in Gloucester before being appointed deputy head at Bishop's in 1998. Wife Charlotte teaches English at Bishop's sister school, South Wilts. Three children at local state and independent schools. We met Dr Smallwood in his tracksuit and can verify that this is one superfit headmaster. Runs the school's cross-country and broke off our interview to take the lads out for their run. Boys describe him as a 'strong disciplinarian'. Has introduced geology as an AS subject which he teaches jointly with the head of South Wilts, who also happens to be a geologist.

Academic matters: Excels across the board at GCSE. Became a specialist language college in 2004, which has brought innovation. Choice of French, Spanish and German Year 7, all boys pick up a second language in Year 8. Also offers Italian, Russian, Mandarin and Japanese enrichment and will offer Latin to GCSE. Outreach programme in modern foreign languages for local primary schools. Head wants to buck the national trend of boys not learning languages – 'This school swims against the tide!' – and hopes languages will open doors for his boys to work overseas. A level results strong, with economics, chemistry, physics, history and geology consistently outstanding. Art also excels, though few study it at A level. ICT, business studies and theatre studies have had less imposing showings. The boys we talked to singled out history for highest praise and English also got a keen thumbs up. Extensive collaboration in teaching with South Wilts allows the sixth form to offer a wide range of A levels. Class size a constant irritation but school works to keep this under control and boys looked attentive. Mixed ability teaching in Year 7, with setting in maths and languages introduced the following year. IT provision very good after substantial recent investment. Special needs does not unduly trouble the school. Learning Support Department looks after 'very small number with dyslexic tendencies and your garden variety 'chaotic' boys. Virtually no ESL.

Games, Options, the Arts: You can play any game here, as long as it's rugby. OK, just kidding, but it is fair to say that Bishop's takes the game seriously. Not unusual for the school to turn out 10 plus rugger sides for its Saturday morning matches. Fixture card dominated by games against independent schools like (arch-rivals) Bryanston, Dauntsey's, Millfield and Sherborne, though they will play against state schools in the area that can be counted on to give them a good game. Has done well in the Daily Mail Cup and at least one team is county champion most years. Several boys play for SW England or England development teams. Some boys grumbled that to be head boy or deputy you had to be in the first XV.

Athletics and cross-country also strong – over 50 boys represent Bishop's at local cross-country fixtures. Regular representation at national level competitions. Football 'growing' with three sides recently in the county semi-finals, 1st XI very successful in schools' FA Cup. Hockey and basketball going well and biathlon team were national champions in 2010. Brilliant new sports hall inspires shock and awe. Clubs like judo, karate and trampolining on offer. Playing fields a half mile jog away – 'Good exercise!' said one mum, loyally. Despite games emphasis, parents insisted that the slow and ungraceful can prosper here. 'There are plenty of nerdy boys who don't play sport.'

Huge range of well-chosen school trips – can't be cheap. Recent overseas extravaganzas have included art trips to New York and Barcelona, a language exchange to Peru, rugby tour to South Africa, skiing in France and USA. Amazon expedition 2006 (and we mean the one with the rainforest), Peru 2007, Zambia 2009, India Himalaya 2011 – also smaller expeditions to Morocco, Turkey and Croatia for younger travellers. Annual language exchanges to France, Germany and Spain. Outstanding music department housed with maths across main road (take your life in your hands!). Narrow, winding, wooden staircase takes you through a fascinating warren of small rooms containing pianos, computers, instrument cases and other music paraphernalia – a world unto itself. Up to 100 boys sing in the choir, which performs in the Cathedral and annually elsewhere in UK and France. Lots of concerts, both within school and outside, wind bands, string ensembles, jazz groups – over 150 boys learn instruments. Societies include the popular Christian Union, strong chess, drama, debating, public speaking, a sixth form book club, D of E (around 150 boys enrolled annually) and an active community service programme. Lovely drama studio. Annual major play, plus smaller productions.

Background and Atmosphere: Founded in 1890 by Bishop John Wordsworth for the 'purposes of education in connection with the Church of England'. A compact site. Hemmed in on one side by one of Salisbury's most traffic-choked roads, Bishop's other three sides back on to the city's green and pleasant historical centre. Salisbury Cathedral towers above, both literally and figuratively, with the Bishop of Salisbury and one of his Canons amongst the school governors. School bumf warns, 'Please note that Bishop Wordsworth School is a Church of England Voluntary Aided School offering denominational teaching in Religious Education and Collective Worship.' A charming school chapel also serves as a war memorial for Bishop's boys and there is a monthly service in the cathedral. You don't have to be a believer but confirmed atheists or rebels might cringe. Main building, 'Number 11', is old, quaint, dilapidated. But feverish building agenda in recent years has given the school a spectacular new 'E' classroom block – a lovely square of classrooms whose sliding glass doors all open onto a green courtyard; a brilliantly refurbished art block and IT suite; a luxurious sports hall; new art school and DT block; splendid Sixth Form Centre. Some temporary buildings remain – among them the most humble common-room we have ever seen, though further redevelopment scheduled. School day finishes at 4pm but boys can stay for study or activities until 5pm.

Pastoral Care and Discipline: Boys speak solemnly of head's zero tolerance of vice, though reality is a bit less severe. In this cradle of middle class civilisation, bad behaviour is not what it might be elsewhere. House system thriving after many years of slumber – 'a bit Harry Potter', say the boys – while clearly enjoying the rivalry. Canteen serves standard school fare and about half the boys bring lunches; a few go home. Many sixth formers use the small, but welcoming, library for work and quiet chat.

Pupils and Parents: Less of a colourful ethnic rainbow than a homogenous pail of milk. That said, we were much impressed with the boys we met here – easier to talk to and keener to meet your gaze than at a lot of boys' schools we could name. Many Services families. Boys arrive by bus, train and car, from as far away as Warminster, Andover, Ringwood, Southampton, Blandford, Shaftsbury. OBs: actor Ralph Fiennes and rugby internationals Richard Hill (both of them!). William Golding wrote Lord of the Flies while teaching English here from 1945–62. Ex DPP Ken Macdonald.

Entrance: Selected boys take tests in VR, maths and English in November before year of entry. 300 plus candidates going for 120 places. Loads of appeals. Main feeders include local primaries, St Mark's C of E and Harnham C of E, and independent preps, Leehurst Swan and Chafyn Grove. Around 60 new entrants come into sixth form, many from the local secondary modern, Wyvern College; six A*–B GCSEs required with minimum of a B in the subjects you wish to continue; many subjects look for more. Places allotted at other ages as available and always after examination.

Exit: With 11 boys off to Oxbridge in 2009 and another 15 in 2010, the school clearly has a handle on how to play the system. Engineering leads the charge, with medicine, sciences, PPE and history following. Good numbers to Bristol, Warwick, Bath, Cardiff and Exeter. A clutch to art foundation courses at the Bournemouth Institute. Heaps of gap years. Around eight per cent leave after GCSEs, mainly to sixth form colleges.

Money Matters: The school depends heavily on parents coughing up annual voluntary contributions (which altogether come to £80–90,000) to keep class sizes down and to help fund extracurricular activities.

Remarks: Heavy-weight state grammar blooming after extensive face-lift. Rugby, discipline, priceless historical setting – only the Nissen huts remind us that this is a state school and education is available (almost) for free.

Bishop's Stortford College

Linked to Bishops Stortford College Junior School in the Junior section

10 Maze Green Road, Bishop's Stortford, Hertfordshire, CM23 2PJ

• Pupils: 570 boys and girls; 105 full-time and weekly boarders and 80 flexi boarders. • Ages: 13-18 • Size of sixth form: 240 • Non-denominational • Fees: Day £14,445; Boarding £20,355-£20,970 pa • Independent

Tel: 01279 838 575
Fax: 01279 836 570
Email: admissions@bishopsstortfordcollege.org
Website: www.bishops-stortford-college.herts.sch.uk

Head: Since 1997, Mr John Trotman MA (mid fifties), educated at Alleyne's Grammar School, Stevenage, and Oxford, where he studied English; previously deputy head at The Leys, Cambridge. Two sons, both former pupils, one studying for a PhD in English at Cambridge. Writes poetry, interested in an eclectic mix of current affairs, historical events, nature – whatever inspires him. Personable, chatty, quickly puts all at ease. Staff say he's 'interested, aware and has a genuine open-door policy.' Parents full of praise, 'He's fantastic and understands children and what they need'. Held in esteem by youngsters; more than a few mentioned his not-so-funny jokes in assembly, with one diplomatic teenager commenting, 'But we still laugh – it would be rude not to and, anyway, we would rather have an approachable head with a sense of humour than one who's boring and distant'.

He's certainly had an exciting life of late – in 10 years as top man was celebrated with a well-earned sabbatical, touring distant parts of the world, confident school would steam on in the steady hands of his fizzy and enthusiastic team, which of course it did. Loves the outdoors – acknowledges his sabbatical was a great indulgence of his passions for birdwatching, trees and nature, yet, like the English cricket team, he was bowled over by the Aussies and caught by the Kiwi spirit. Loves the double life teaching affords and believes he is blessed, 'I have full-on socialising during term time, where I can gain inspiration and creativity from others, coupled with the freedom and peace of holidays, the luxury of being able to throw a canoe on the car and paddle off ... '

He is retiring in July 2011. His successor will be Mr Jeremy Gladwin, currently head of St Edmund's, Canterbury. A geographer, he is an accomplished athlete, keenly interested in sacred choral and classical music, and is married with two teenage children.

Academic matters: Results improving from modest 68 per cent A/B A level pass rates a couple of years ago to over 80 per cent A*–B in recent times; no mean achievement considering constitution of cohort remains unchanged. Maths, English literature and history are most popular subjects with strongest showing in theatre studies, Chinese and maths. At GCSE, a commendable 65 per cent of passes are A*/A, with all pupils gaining at least a C in virtually all their subjects. French for everyone, German for the top three sets; Latin optional, Japanese offered in sixth form; lack of Spanish may soon be redressed (GCSE Spanish offered in sixth form only). Extensive, generously-resourced library and good teaching facilities including usual range of ICT. Pioneering use of geographical information system technology and fair few accolades give geography a deserved high profile. School has a new, interactive science centre, designed and developed by the dedicated science department – whizzy, experiential, comprehensible. When we visited, a number of children from local schools were animatedly making the most of this exciting 'must see, must do, do touch' facility.

Pupils have a real appetite for hard work and their efforts are rewarded with merits or, for some, the prestigious '10 club'- tie for A/A*grades at GCSE. Streams and sets for most subjects meet needs of all, including the gifted. Team of two sensitively supports 30 students with mild SEN (charged as an extra), including dyslexia and Asperger's. All international students are offered one or two EAL lessons a week and reach IGCSE level (required for university admission).

Games, Options, the Arts: Successful sports: unbeaten seasons in rugby and hockey now the norm – then again, they're lucky enough to have England U16 national squad and England senior A team coach (boys' hockey) and legendary rugby coach in their midst. As well as being county hockey champions, they're district netball and swimming champions. Fabulous, recently-constructed pool has raised profile of swimming from minor to major sport; tennis and waterpolo also on offer.

Music strikes a chord with around 10 per cent of pupils performing to grade eight or beyond. Good facilities – piano in most boarding houses, recording studio, plenty of airy practice rooms. 20 concerts a year including one for pupils, parents and staff, plus a couple of grandioso ventures into the world of opera. Purpose-built theatre seen better days but does the job. Art good but cramped; pupils hopeful new art block (under construction) will give budding Badalocchios room for creativity, composition and exhibition. Trips and tours across the globe including China, Iceland, New Zealand, Africa, St Lucia, Barbados, and a fair few closer to home too. Wide choice of extra-curricular activities including D of E, debating (standing-room only for some hot topics) and community work.

Background and Atmosphere: Founded in 1868 as a nonconformist boarding school, with aspirations of being 'the Rugby of East Anglia', originally sited on the outskirts of Bishop's Stortford. Despite recent new developments and proximity to town, the 135 acre campus still has a rural feel. Buildings are well maintained with thought given to new additions, though smattering of Portakabins and odd corner seem somewhat incongruous. Boys only (apart from sixth form) until 1995 but opening of new girls' house should see ratio (currently 60:40) nudge close to 50–50.

Pastoral Care and Discipline: Offers termly, weekly, flexible or extended day boarding (pupils stay until after prep). Full-on Saturday school for all from 8.30am until 3.30pm has its detractors, but most accept it's necessary if children are to make the most of all that's on offer. Food (central dining) improved of late but still odd grumble. Very strong house system – all pupils go into either a day or boarding house, under the care of highly regarded housestaff, 'They're in control and are aware of what goes on and quick, yet discreet, in response,' said one thankful parent. Masses of competitions for everything, from singing through sports to cooking, generate fierce competition and promote house loyalty.

Pupils encouraged to appreciate diversity and to support and applaud each other. Good accommodation, homely rather than hotel, atmospheric and friendly, ensures boarding a bigger hit than ever. Odd parental moan that not all staff are contactable by email but applause for improved communication with parents. Regular assemblies, hymns et al, in listed Memorial Chapel; one parent suggested the school should do much more to promote Christianity (school is non-denominational), yet the pupils universally praise the Chaplain, citing his thought-provoking assemblies and penchant for 'really smart debates' as a privilege. Excellent careers guidance ensures pupils make appropriate, yet ambitious, choices. Few discipline problems – believes, 'Zero tolerance would result in information embargo; we try where possible to seek to give pupils a chance to get it right'. Admits to odd alcohol issue – 'What school hasn't?' queried head.

Pupils and Parents: Most from within daily travelling distance; boarders mainly from east and SE England but around 10 per cent from Europe and the Far East, 'The blend of nationalities bringing a welcome diversity to the college,' says school. A broadening social mix, though not for those seeking county cachet – majority of parents are middle class professionals: doctors, 'something in the city', or lawyers. Parents' association puts on range of activities, many fund-raising, some for fun.

Long list of distinguished former pupils includes presenter Andy Peebles, rugby player Ben Clarke, writer Dick Clement and educationalist Professor John Ferguson. The world of espionage features prominently via former heads of MI5, Sir Stephen Lander and Sir Dick White, and Peter Wright, author of Spycatcher. Current pupils have a wonderful skillset: a combination of confidence without arrogance, considered intelligence, an appetite for hard-work and play, and a seemingly refreshing openness – truth or bluff, they certainly put us off the scent, for we failed to discover anything untoward lurking in the corridors or under the beds!

Entrance: Pupils are selected via interviews, entrance tests and school references; takes a range of abilities, not just academic high-fliers. At 13 majority come from the junior school but takes some 10–12 external entrants annually; small number joins at 14, in time for GCSEs. Some 30 join in the sixth form – entrance is by interview and written tests; need at least five B grades at GCSE with A*–B in A level subject choices.

Exit: A handful leaves after GCSEs to study A levels elsewhere. All head to university, most to a top 10 for their chosen course, increasing numbers to Russell group, small number to Oxbridge.

Money Matters: Academic, music and art scholarships offered, plus some assistance for those in financial need. 'A considerable proportion of our income goes on scholarships and bursaries,' says the head. 'If a child is talented but his or her parents can't afford us, we will do what we can to help.' Bursar a happy bunny, following recent benevolent bequests.

Remarks: Had a niche as a strong co-ed independent; now, thanks to a great team, improving results, excellent value-added and quietly determined, friendly pupils, it's nudging comfortably past a number of its competitors. A busy, energetic school, going from strength to strength. Difficult to say who it wouldn't suit; highly satisfied parents tell us school not only finds something each child is good at but does so with aplomb.

The Bishop's Stortford High School

London Road, Bishop's Stortford, Hertfordshire, CM23 3LU

• Pupils: 1,040 boys aged 11-16, plus large mixed sixth form; all day
• Ages: 11-18 • Size of sixth form: 370 boys and girls • Non-denom, but strong Christian ethos. • State

Tel: 01279 868 686
Fax: 01279 868 687
Email: office@tbshs.org
Website: www.tbshs.org

Headmaster: Since 1999, Mr Andrew Goulding BSc (late forties). Educated at De-Aston Grammar School, Market Rasen; BSc in mathematics at Hull, followed by PGCE at Cambridge. Previously taught at John Bunyan Upper School, Codsall High and Haybridge High, then deputy headmaster at King Edward IV, Handsworth. Married with two grownup sons and a daughter. Enjoys golf, gardening, theatre and musicals (used to sing quite a bit); spoke animatedly and enthusiastically of school's recent production of Les Mis. Doesn't teach and says it would be impossible to know all pupils by name. When we reported that pupils would like to see more of him and for him to be the one openly celebrating their key achievements, he seemed genuinely touched. Confident, ambitious, receptive to new ideas; says 'nicest things about the school are the harmonious relationships and team spirit,' adding he's 'pleased and proud to be here'.

Academic matters: Results showing year-on-year improvement, with A level A/B passes up from just over 50 per cent a couple of years ago to almost 60 per cent in recent times, girls outperforming boys. Business studies and economics strong; two pupils achieved top A level marks in psychology in recent times. Sixth form limited to those with academic bent – anyone seeking sub level three should look elsewhere. Usual subjects offered plus film, Latin and critical thinking, with option to study courses such as art textiles through the local consortium. General studies course has attracted speakers including Douglas Hurd, Boris Johnson, Linford Christie and Lord Puttnam.

Class sizes, around 30–32 in the early years, fall to 24–26 for GCSE and 13–19 for A level. Over 80 per cent of pupils achieve the benchmark five A*–C passes at GCSE, with approximately 25 per cent of all passes graded A*/A. Setting by ability begins in Year 7 with fast track in maths and French. ICT (received national excellence award) is a fundamental part of the school, and was certainly much in evidence, across all subjects, when we visited. Lots of success in maths, including 10 or so maths challenge gold winners annually. See themselves as a research-based school, encouraging pupils to be creative, discuss learning and develop thinking skills. Benefits from having well below average numbers of pupils with SEN (a mere four with statements); those who get through the gates do well here, particularly those with behavioural issues, who profit from the school's order and discipline. Boys feel staff could be less strict and as quick to praise as they are to condemn, but applaud them for their willingness to help solve problems and the time they put into providing activities outside class.

Games, Options, the Arts: Parents praise the very many extra-curricular opportunities offered, everything from regular, and very successful, rugby football and cricket fixtures (known to field up to 15 teams) through to chess, public speaking, debating, subject-related clubs, D of E and more. Pupils agree, with one perceptive chap saying, 'It's all well and good getting results, but leaving as a rounded person is what really matters, and the extra-curricular activities allow for just that'. Music strong – music technology, recording studio and loads of Yamaha keyboards, thanks to school doubling as a Saturday morning venue for budding musicians. Performing opportunities via swing band, choirs, concerts, plays etc plus annual showcase, run by sixth formers, open to all. Head of drama working on an innovative, international project involving seven Dutch schools which will eventually culminate in a joint production. Art success includes work of one pupil selected for display at the RSBA summer exhibition. Number of trips and tours abroad; sixth formers get opportunity to visit far-flung places and take part in social projects via school's Interact club.

Background and Atmosphere: School has extensive playing fields and an excellent sports ground (35 acres) some three miles away. Built in the 1950s, utility was clearly the driving force behind the school's functional design. Additional accommodation has been provided in recent years but school bursting at the seams, no more so than in the sixth form centre. We were disappointed to see the friendly caretaker clearing litter from corridors after lunch – shame it was there in the first place; however school is generally well kept; odd area lacks atmosphere and would benefit from displays and a lick of paint, but majority have it just right.

Pastoral Care and Discipline: High standards of behaviour and dress (blazers de rigueur) are expected from pupils – not a pair of trainers or 'shirt-dress' in sight: bliss! Disciplinary procedures are clearly laid out and a recently established 'sin-bin' – few spend more than a day or so in isolation. Aims to help and support those who find it difficult to conform.

Boys a polite, likable and articulate bunch but not immune from perennial problems of teenage life (self-harm, family problems, bullying etc); younger pupils felt they were left to get on with the transition from primary to senior school and, although work wasn't a big issue, social elements were. School disagrees, saying 'An awful lot goes into this process and this is not a fair reflection'. Wealth of support is on hand via excellent counsellor, structured pastoral setup and a fantastic community police officer, who, we're told, is simply wonderful with the kids. Boys help themselves too – the active school council addresses key issues of concern; recent successes include the identification, and subsequent elimination, of bullying hotspots around the school; good to see important issues being tackled from the bottom up.

Pupils and Parents: Not a comprehensive intake (minuscule percentage qualify for free school meals) – school is in a prosperous part of town, and the parental mix reflects this. Parents a satisfied bunch; as one said, 'If I had to select again, I would still choose to send my boys here'. Many see the school as a cheap alternative to independent education. PTA organises regular events: quiz evenings, race nights, candlelit suppers etc, and raises impressive amounts of cash. Parents kept informed and involved – imminent move to online reporting set to take parental communication to the next level. Old Boys include Ben Skirving (rugby) and Greg James (Radio1 DJ). The 100 or so girls in the sixth form are a welcome addition, bringing calmness, élan and fresh perspectives.

Entrance: Demand for places far exceeds supply. School has a reputation for suiting the more able, but head insists this is a great school for the academically challenged, saying, 'It's a myth we don't suit the less able – we get good value-added from lower ability pupils'. Places are awarded firstly on the basis of compelling medical reasons, secondly by sibling link. 10 per cent of places are allocated 'to pupils with a proven aptitude in music or sport', who have to be outstanding in their field. The remaining places are allocated according to where pupils live (the school has a traditional catchment area, defined by postcodes) and primary school attended. Obtain a copy of the latest criteria and study carefully. The co-ed sixth form has 60 places open to pupils who have not attended the lower school – good results, with a minimum grade B in subjects chosen for AS/A2, essential.

Exit: Vast majority of sixth formers to a diverse range of courses at recruiting and selecting universities (roughly a 50/50 split), handful take a gap year, 20 or so to employment. 15 per cent leave at 16, majority to college, to pursue vocational courses.

Remarks: With its emphasis on respect, looking smart and working hard, the school's values may appear reminiscent of a 1950s school, but use of technology and up-to-date methodology brings it very much into the 21st century. Suits most, ironically especially the less able or those with difficulties, as they not only benefit from good role models and a house system that allows all to shine, but also the drive to maintain standards means greater help and support for those needing an extra push. Continues to serve locals well.

Blackheath High School GDST

Linked to Blackheath High School (Junior Department) in the Junior section

27 Vanbrugh Park, London, SE3 7AG

• Pupils: 300, girls, all day • Ages: 11-18 • Size of sixth form: 60
• Non-denom • Fees: £12,006 pa • Independent

Tel: 020 8853 2929
Fax: 020 8853 3663
Email: info@bla.gdst.net
Website: www.blackheathhighschool.gdst.net

Headteacher: Since 2000, Mrs Lisa Laws BA PGCE (midfifties). Vibrant, dedicated, a head with a mission. Seemingly very relaxed but determined to make and keep her school at the top, and she is definitely succeeding. She believes in a holistic approach, education of the whole person, and the importance of the international dimension in schooling today. In her multi-ethnic, multi-cultural school girls are encouraged to be individuals, to strive for excellence and to look after each other. Parents like the fact that it is not an academic hothouse yet its results are excellent and right up there alongside all the top South London schools. Mrs Laws is proud that it has been awarded full international school status by the British Council and its partnerships with schools in Europe and the Far East enable exciting and fascinating joint projects. Her vision has brought the school right into the 21st century. It is not a big school but it seems to be able to offer facilities and opportunities way beyond its size. The excellent 2008 ISI report bears this out.

Academic matters: Small classes, a broad curriculum and an exceptionally wide variety of extra-curricular activities enable pupils to get the most out of the excellent teaching available here. Languages and science are strong – our guide is planning to read astrophysics at a top university. She had nothing but praise for her teachers, who she found easy to talk to and dedicated to helping her get the results she wants. Certainly the 77 per cent A/Bs at A level and 68 per cent A*/A at GCSE in 2009 impress. Technology is used to its limits – interactive whiteboards everywhere, computerised laboratories and laptops for every sixth former. Everyone has access to the GDST portal whether working at home or in school.

Confidence building is deemed important including risk-taking and outward bound courses starting in Year 7. European work experience available for all language students. We asked about the IB but they feel they are providing sufficient breadth via early entry ASs and the huge extracurricular programme in which everyone is encouraged to take part.

Lots of structures in place for children with learning difficulties and every girl closely monitored from the day she starts. Quick to identify problems and communication between parents and teachers is good. Children are helped within the system rather than being withdrawn from class although, if needed, additional lessons are available. It is not a school for girls with serious special needs and anyone applying to join will only be accepted if the school feels that she will be able to cope with the work level. No particular language support programme – parents are expected to provide English lessons out of school hours if needed.

Games, Options, the Arts: Own five acre sports field nearby with full size all-weather pitch and lots of tennis courts. Hockey, netball, cross-country – you name it, they can try it. Inter-school matches and competitions here and overseas. Some 95 per cent do the Duke of Edinburgh programme which starts in Year 9. Nearly all take the bronze, some the silver and 13 completed their gold assessment expedition in 2007. They have a national judo champion, a gymnastics silver medallist, a county swimmer and, believe it or not, one girl was in the winning national team in a cheerleading national tour to the USA.

Several different choirs and orchestras which all are encouraged to join. The Year 6 choir won the Beckenham Festival Award in 2006. About 50 per cent learn an instrument; everyone in Year 7 can learn to play an instrument of their choice for free. Lots of drama, including backstage and technical, stage and costume design. New purpose-built theatre on site. Part of the curriculum from Year 7 and available as both GCSE and A level options. Several girls take the LAMDA exam. Inter-house competitions and amazing looking full school productions in their beautiful new theatre. First rate art, ceramics, other 3D work, textiles and photography. Eight art students gained GCSE scores amongst the top 10 in 2008. Great pictures all over the place and inspired dresses hanging in the senior artroom, a relic of a recent fashion show. They were even commissioned to paint the hoardings for the Borough Market development project – what fun!

Plenty of trips and outings. The biennial history trip to Russia ensures history remains popular. Our guide was keen to show pictures from a recent art trip to New York. Skiing in Switzerland, singing in Italy, D of E expeditions all over – these girls have opportunities galore. Even a trip to China on the cards.

Background and Atmosphere: This was the first purpose-built GDST school and opened in 1880. Now in larger premises, it maintains the tradition of a thorough academic education for girls for highly competitive fees. A true 21st century version of a Victorian dream. The somewhat plain exterior hides an exciting inside. We followed our guide along corridors in the old and new parts of the building, upstairs to the sixth form's private area and down and around into good sized, airy classrooms, where relaxed, happy-looking girls seemed to be enjoying their lessons and interacting with their teachers. The younger girls all dressed in typical GDST uniform, the sixth form in 'smart enough to wear to the office clothes. No jeans'.

Each corridor is subject grouped. We admired the well equipped science lab, the biology room with three guinea-pigs, the artrooms, the drama studios, the modern theatre and the huge fully equipped sports hall. We saw the brand new cookery room gleaming with stainless steel where sixth formers can learn to cook before going to university and were amazed by the very grown-up fitness suite. What would the Victorians have thought of the school's digital radio station? We particularly liked the library/resource centre and the language laboratory where a class was working at individual computers electronically linked to their teacher for help and direction. Our guide was very proud of her school.

The students are passionate about green issues and like to keep their teachers on their toes. The school has achieved the healthy schools award and has silver eco-school status. Apparently there was a winter draught problem, so the sixth form set up a knitting club and knitted excluders for the windows. Their potential is limitless. One Year 9 girl was invited onto the National Children's Bureau government advisory panel where she had to do a presentation on sustainability. Phew! She is still one of 25 teenagers advising ministers on young people's issues.

Pastoral Care and Discipline: A general culture of support throughout the school amongst teachers and pupils alike and, according to our guide, a bright, confident lower sixth former, a peer mentoring system that really works. The policy is 'to nurture an enjoyment of learning in an atmosphere of mutual respect and celebration of achievement'. They are sensitive to emotional problems and the excellent school counsellor supports child and parents alike. A real understanding of each girl is important to them. The re-introduction of a house system has proved successful and the school council gives the girls the opportunity to air their views and feel they really are involved in the running of their school. Stress seems minimal, perhaps due to the fact that they are all encouraged to do yoga or pilates during their lunchtime break. Alexander technique is also about to be introduced.

Pupils and Parents: A broad ethnic and social mix with over 25 different languages spoken. 'A real reflection of London's population and a proper preparation for the world they will meet later.' The majority lives locally, Blackheath, Greenwich, Lewisham etc, but others come in from Bexleyheath and Dartford and the school runs two minibuses, one south of the river to Rotherhithe and one north of the river to Canary Wharf and surrounding areas. The common denominator is that all the parents are looking for the best education for their daughters and are willing to make sacrifices to get it. Their involvement and support are manifest.

Entrance: A lot come up from the junior school. Otherwise predominantly at 11+ and 16+ by interview in the autumn term and examination in January. No sibling policy – every girl is assessed on her own merits. If there is a space any child will be welcomed at other times, as long as the school feels that she will be able to cope.

Exit: Mostly to good universities, often in London; KCL and UCL the most popular at the moment. An impressive diversity and level of achievement – these girls can go anywhere. OGs include Mary Quant and Baroness Jay.

Money Matters: An exceptional number of scholarships and bursaries, most, according to GDST policy, for up to 50 per cent of the fees. At least one HSBC academic scholarship per year funding full fees and uniform. Always worth enquiring if your child has a particular talent.

Remarks: 'We are not posh!' they say. Maybe not, but parents are putting the school down as their first choice – girls really want to go here. It is a forward-looking school with traditional values and opportunities for all, providing a well-rounded education thoroughly focused on the future. Here you find the young women of tomorrow being prepared to take their places in an ever changing world. They will be ready.

Blossom House School

8a The Drive, Wimbledon, London, SW20 8TG

• Pupils: 110 boys, 40 girls; all day • Ages: 3-16 • Non-denom
• Fees: £24,258-£29,940 pa • Independent

Tel: 020 8946 7348
Fax: 020 8944 5848
Email: admin@blossomhouseschool.co.uk
Website: www.blossomhouseschool.co.uk

Principal: Since its founding in 1983, Mrs Joanna (Joey) Burgess (fifties) DipCST MRCSLT Dip RSA SpLD PGCE. Educated at St Paul's Girls' School and Oldry Fleming School of Speech and Language Therapy. Married to Patrick, a retired stockbroker, with four grown-up daughters. Wealth of experience gained in part from previous employment as a speech and language therapist, dyslexia therapist and teacher. Has a good business brain coupled with real empathy for parents who've been through the mill – 'If there's a problem she'll help sort it'.

Academic matters: All follow the national curriculum, adapted as necessary. An abundance of highly qualified and experienced teachers and therapists – occupational, speech, art, music and physiotherapy – support the children's educational, emotional and physical needs. Many staff trained in teaching specific learning difficulties (SpLD). The school has been awarded Crested status and also runs an OCR dyslexia course. Each child has an individual learning programme (ILP) with personal learning styles taken into consideration. Classes are multisensory, with much 'over-teaching'. The provision of visual cues such as timetables of the day and of each lesson helps with communication. All (from seven and up) learn to touch-type. Classes are small, 10 or fewer, with children divided into groups of three or four for literacy, numeracy and speech and language therapy (some have individual sessions). Classrooms are spacious, well-organised and calm, but playtimes are as lively and as rowdy as in any school.

The positive ethos continues throughout the secondary school alongside high academic expectations according to the individual pupil's abilities. Senior pupils work towards GCSEs and entry level exams, vocational qualifications and practical courses in a range of subjects including English, maths, science, media studies, astronomy, food technology, ICT, D&T subjects and the arts. They have their own laptops. Pupils work towards Duke of Edinburgh and Sports Leader Awards. An open meeting to settle the perennial homework debate found that many parents wished for more, while others say, 'Homework (a project to do by end of term) is too open-ended – children can't cope with this. I feel like it's the parents who end up doing all the work that teachers should be doing'. Other parents praise 'highly motivated' classes and 'focused teaching' for enabling their children 'to cope so well with all that is required'.

Games, Options, the Arts: Sport and the arts are an important and integral part of the curriculum. A wide range of opportunities encourages pupils to understand the benefits of physical activity. The school has been awarded Activemark by Sport England. Strengths are football and hockey – all get the chance to participate in team games. Fantastic PE teachers who really motivate the children, run lots of activities after school, organise matches, camping trips etc. Two annual drama productions; again, all may be involved. Regular visits by children to art galleries and plays, and sessions in school with artists. Music a strength – lively, run by a professional musician, regular informal concerts and performing opportunities. All have group music lessons, many have individual instrumental tuition and take external exams – a few have even recorded their own CDs. Three music therapists work with pupils to help them acquire a sense of identity, build self-esteem, develop creativity and encourage interaction and communication. Both music and art therapy are available and use a psychotherapeutic approach to help pupils focus on the emotional aspect of their difficulties.

Background and Atmosphere: In a quiet residential road close to Wimbledon Common. Started life as a junior school but now takes pupils up to 16. House system throughout the school. Moved recently to larger modern premises with a large sports hall. A young(ish) staff, mostly in their 20s and 30s (first names used throughout). Head likes staff to be flexible, prepared to adapt and develop – little room for those who've 'always done it this way'. Friendly, but thoroughly professional atmosphere.

Pastoral Care and Discipline: Parents say pastoral care is wonderful and appreciate the good ratio of male staff – 'Incidence of autism is higher among boys so it's lovely to have so many positive male role models'. School rules are simple and clear. Ethos of positive reinforcement means consequences rather than punishments for bad behaviour. Emotional issues are taken very seriously and dealt with sensitively. Some say scope for closer dialogue between home and school: 'We don't know what's happening on a daily basis so it's difficult to reinforce at home.' School says, 'Others praise the open-door policy and feedback meetings; communication between school and home is always encouraged.' Termly curriculum and feedback meetings held for parents and an active FOBH (Friends of Blossom House). Parents invited to talks by professionals during inset days if possible.

Pupils and Parents: From London and Surrey. Fees are high. Over 90 per cent of pupils have statements and are funded by their local authority. However it can be very difficult for parents to get LEA funding. 'Those of us prepared to go to a tribunal are more likely to get here, but it's not easy and some parents just don't have the stamina or know-how.' The school offers advice and support for parents in this situation.

Entrance: School caters mainly for children with speech, language and communication impairments; most also have overlapping conditions such as ASD, dyspraxia, sensory integration difficulties, dyslexia and ADHD. Children with language disorders may have associated difficulties with behaviour but the school is not set up to take children with severe behaviour problems. From 3+ into the nursery; term of their fifth birthday to the junior school; 11+ to the senior school. Admission is possible throughout the year. Entry is by detailed assessment – need to ensure child will benefit from the specialist education available and school best placed to meet child's needs. Many go to tribunal.

Exit: Most now stay at 11+, others to specialist schools: More House (Farnham), Moor House (Oxted), The Moat, St Dominic's Godalming, Sibford, St Catherine's. A few to (supported) mainstream state schools: Wimbledon College, Ursuline Convent etc.

Money Matters: Around 90 per cent are LEA funded. Hopes to offer some bursaries in the future.

Remarks: A very special school for special children; continues to expand. Parents full of praise, describimg staff dedication and patience as 'admirable'.

Bloxham School

Bloxham, Near Banbury, Oxfordshire, OX15 4PE

• Pupils: 273 boys, 163 girls (52 per cent board) • Ages: 11-18 • Size of sixth form: 140 • C of E • Fees: £14,730-£26,980 pa • Independent

Tel: 01295 720222
Fax: 01295 721 897
Email: marketing@bloxhamschool.com
Website: www.bloxhamschool.com

Head: Since 2002, Mr Mark Allbrook (fifties) MA PGCE, educated at Tonbridge and read classics at Trinity Hall, Cambridge where he gained four cricket blues. Previously deputy head of Felsted. Free time spent golfing or at equestrian events with his wife, Mary, who takes the school's popular horsy activities. Says he's at Bloxham for the foreseeable, though he'll have a way to go to match the years put in by some members of staff.

Spearheaded a number of changes, brought in some new blood, had the sense and vision to look at what was needed, rather than what he might like; delivered his five year plan in three! Staff say he's driven, passionate but inclusive, has raised the game and recognises and values the contribution of all, from 'handyman to head of'. Parents say he's approachable, caring and genuinely interested; visible presence at matches and always ready to chat on the touchline. Pupils respectful; one said it was 'quite scary to be taught by him but okay once you got to know him'. A hands-on head, keen to raise standards; still teaches – prefers to spend his time in school rather than chasing markets or selling his soul.

Academic matters: Takes children with a broad range of abilities, but brightest and best can, and do, get to top universities (fine to be clever); lets pupils mature and make academic strides without undue pressure. Regular and increasing number of activities for scholars; intensive Oxbridge help on the cards. School is striving for academic improvement – A/B passes at A level 66 per cent in 2010; penny numbers taking most subjects but business studies and geography top the popularity polls, with English lit and textiles enjoying particular success. Approximately 45 per cent graded A/A* at GCSE. All take IB tech qualification which covers the whole spectrum of ICT skills. Free laptops for all, from 14, with smart internet café on site for fun and games. Attractive, well-resourced library.

School has CReSTeD DU status, so it's a great place for bright dyslexics (IQ 120+, maximum 20 in school at any one time) who not only benefit from the direction, ebullience and experience of SENco but also thrive across the school, thanks to staff awareness, understanding and expertise. Not surprisingly, school attracts a number of children with minor needs, and identifies a fair few more (all screened) on entry. That said, only mild needs – Asperger's, ADD, HI, dyspraxia and some medical difficulties – can be met; those with greater needs or requiring regular individual input should look elsewhere; all must be capable of GCSEs and eventual university entrance. School great at motivating those who might otherwise fall by the wayside. As one boy said, 'I've never been a lover of school but found lessons at Bloxham really engaging, especially biology (do ask about the snakes!) and English.'

Games, Options, the Arts: Wide range of sports on offer: hockey, rugby (regularly fields 11 teams – sports line for matches) and netball, through to fives, squash and very serious clay-shooting. Plenty happening on the equine front: a highly-acclaimed polo team, cross-country, showjumping and dressage all feature (no livery on site). Girls and boys participate successfully at national championships in a range of sports on a regular basis and enjoy a couple of overseas tours annually. All play hard, possibly because just as much credibility in turning out for the thirds as firsts. Head praises all great performances but isn't afraid to issue a 'could do better', if needed. Says, 'I challenge a keen sporting pupil not to be fulfilled at Bloxham.' Good facilities: couple of Astros, modern sports hall, two charming cricket grounds (cricket professional recently appointed). Super indoor swimming-pool, two glass-backed squash courts and climbing wall are much used by pupils and locals. Separate sixth form club-room situated above the cricket pavilion.

The place is singing once again – music facilities and opportunities massively improved and improving; concerts, sung Eucharists, choirs, instrumental lessons and 'Blox-Idol' cater for a range of tastes. Drama is the weak link, (handful of plays a year) but with a musical in the offing, this Cinderella subject may soon be given a welcome boost. Purpose-built Raymond Technology Centre offers good facilities; no cooking/home economics yet but it's on the burner; art strong, ceramics exciting, textiles innovative. Young Enterprise, CCF, D of E, successful debating squad, oenology etc – you get the feeling that if something is desired, wherever possible it's either allowed for or will be provided. One parent told us, 'They try to accommodate passions and will flex schooling/times for something really important.'

Background and Atmosphere: Founded in 1860 and given to the Woodard Foundation (group of schools originally founded by Canon Woodard to promote muscular Christianity) in 1896. Handsome building of Hornton stone, quarried from below the foundations, with stunning chapel on first floor. The well-maintained school proper is contained in a playing field filled 80-acre campus with a number of outhouses, pitches and buildings, none more than an eight minute amble away. Lower school housed in a magnificent transformation of the former White Lion pub overlooking the main street. Uniform for all though sixth formers may wear a suit.

A boarding school at heart – day pupils must stay till 6pm but have the option of pursuing activities and heading for home at 9pm. School buses for day-boarders ferry them from convenient pickup points. The week ends on Friday for the lower school, the rest released from 4pm on Saturday. Boarders are 'expected' to be in for the first weekend of term and the first after half term, frequent mass exodus on non-compulsory weekends. Boarding (weekly only) for Years 7 and 8 provided in Park Close, a former, rather grand manor house with commanding views and very capable house-parents at the helm. One of the best kitted-out junior boarding houses we've seen – looks and feels like a real family home (which it is). Senior girls' houses smarter than boys', though boys confided they quite like the 'lived in look' – less to worry about. Girls graduate early from dorms to individual study bedrooms while boys more likely to progress to shared studies. Good atmosphere, girls and boys readily mix (intra-house, boy/girl visiting in communal areas only).

Pastoral Care and Discipline: Many parents choose Bloxham because of its deserved reputation for nurturing and great pastoral care. A caring school with a family feel – children thrive here because, regardless of skills or abilities, they're given confidence and encouraged to have a go. Faith important – emphasis put on living a Christian life in a Christian community, 'actions, rather than possessions'; a goodly showing in RS at GCSE. Lots of systems in place to ensure no-one falls through the net – strong tutorial system via houses, impressive peer listening, chaplain, counsellor etc. Odd grumble by parents about communication with the school but most felt they could readily contact staff, who would swing into action no matter how small the anxiety. Disciplinary matters usually nipped in the bud; urine testing on demand if drug use suspected, followed by suspension for a week if positive, and random testing thereafter; repeat offences will result in expulsion. Alcohol not a major problem – the villagers complain if they drop litter in the (very pretty) village, and the campus is too busy to find a quiet corner. First class food, healthy selection, friendly staff and excellent surroundings make dining an enjoyable and sociable occasion; nevertheless staff and pupils vigilant for eating disorders.

Pupils and Parents: Most from an hour or so away; lots of first-time buyers. Parents with children in the state sector come because they see it as 'an upmarket alternative', parents from the independent sector because they want a smaller, more local school (as opposed to Stowe, St Edward's, Uppingham etc). Basically north Oxfordshire, farmers, businessmen, the Services; eight per cent from abroad – Germans, Russians, Hong Kong Chinese, French, German, Spanish, Russian plus ex-pats. Produces cheery, confident, polite pupils, interested and interesting.

Entrance: At 11, own test and assessment; CE pass-mark 50 per cent; sixth form entrance via interview, report from previous school and GCSE results. Large tranche from state primaries at 11 plus, Carrdus, St John's Priory and The Croft School; at 13 from a wide range including Ashfold School, Beachborough, Bilton Grange, Swanbourne House and Winchester House.

Exit: Small leakage after GCSE. Majority go on to higher education. Great variety – from Russell Group to former polys and universities; Birmingham and Southampton popular; study a wide range of traditional and exotic courses including PPE, business/marketing, sound production and engineering.

Money Matters: Parents in real need still get helped via the dreaded blue form means test. Woodard Foundation can give help in an emergency for children of Old Bloxhamists. Huge collection of scholarships for everything from music, sport (not at 11+), DT, art and academic, for all ages – take as many as you want, at 11+, 13+ and 16+, but will be withdrawn if child doesn't continue to measure up.

Remarks: Being welcomed into Bloxham is akin to being embraced into the heart of the family. As one pupil said, 'You feel like you're wanted; the teachers always seem pleased to see you.' Academically more challenging than before but content, as ever, to take a broad church. What you see is what you get – a cheerful, family school, with Christian values, all mod-cons and the knack of turning out happy and fulfilled youngsters in a quintessentially English setting.

The Blue School

Kennion Road, Wells, Somerset, BA5 2NR

• Pupils: 1,455 girls and boys; all day • Ages: 11-18
• Size of sixth form: 195 • C of E • State

Tel: 01749 678 799
Fax: 01749 836 215
Email: office@blue.somerset.sch.uk

Head: Since 1999, Mr Steve Jackson (fifties); joined as deputy head in 1989, so has seen it all. Used to teach design technology and PE. Married to a deputy head; three children. Insists on showing new parents and visitors around the school himself. Except us, who were asked not to visit what is already a chronically over-subscribed school. 'A good front man,' said a parent, but 'not engaged in the day-to-day life of the school'. Publicity, website, school profile etc seemingly low on the agenda.

Academic matters: A genuinely comprehensive school. Standards are high at GCSE and consistently good in the core subjects of English, maths and science. Most recent Ofsted report in 2007 is peppered with 'outstanding's, particularly in relation to sixth form. Earlier concerns raised about provision for the less academic at GCSE have been addressed with entry level history and French, and four science pathways to cater for all abilities. Links with Strode College for the more vocationally-minded. At A level there is a broad selection of subjects on offer, though – as ever – take-up for modern languages low. Was awarded specialist school status in science and mathematics in 2003. Outstanding work in design technology and PE. Much use of ICT within the classroom and brilliant ICT provision throughout. The staff seem genuinely keen to embrace the new technology; they feel ahead of the game thanks to local company support.

On arrival in Year 7, boys and girls are taught together and in mixed ability groups, apart from English and maths where they are setted. At GCSE almost all subjects are setted. Generally little staff movement and a considerable proportion has been at the school for longer than 10 years, perhaps why one parent said he thought the school was resting on its laurels and that a few teachers were merely going through the motions. A strong belief that if a child is well-motivated then they can do very well here, less so if not. Some think the school should instil a better work ethic early on so children deal better with GCSE pressures.

SEN provision appears to be good, with close liaison between departments and the SENCo and a flexible approach. Pupils struggling with literacy are helped within class or withdrawn for small group work at behest of subject teachers; SENCo runs assessments on request, esp from parents who suspect difficulties. Maths dept more autonomous, with its own specialist TA who sets up in-class/individual/small group sessions according to need. General assessments done in class, which means first week of new academic year can be 'a bit chaotic', until all five sets are sorted out. Bottom sets might number only eight pupils. Pretty well all behavioural issues are catered for, as befits an inclusive school. SENCo says that the school 'does not hunt out children with emotional or behavioural difficulties but tries to support them in their education. However, [parents of] kids on the autistic spectrum hunt us out, even transferring into the area to attend "The Blue".'

Games, Options, the Arts: Walking into the design technology block feels like entering an art school department – fabulous work and ambitious projects. Regularly wins design awards e.g. Arkwright Scholarships etc and has established close working links with local businesses for funding and work placements. Bench seating in the historic Palace Fields gardens in Wells was designed by A level pupils at the school. The presence of the sports development centre means that there is a huge choice available in addition to the traditional – including caving and rock climbing actively pursued in nearby Mendips – and the school produces a smattering of county players every year. Music is prominent with orchestra, wind band, jazz band, choir and guitar group – so plenty of opportunity to get involved. Drama a strength with regular productions, and not frightened of tackling ambitious works e.g. Peer Gynt. Several trips abroad each year, often exotic – witness two World Challenge expeditions, to Africa and the Himalayas, in two years.

Background and Atmosphere: Dates back to 1641 when it was established as a charitable foundation via the legacy of local churchman Ezekiel Barkham. The name was adopted over time owing to the blue dyed uniforms provided for the original pupils. A big school plonked in a spacious 33 acres. Slightly elevated position means a fantastic view. Three gyms, a school hall and three dining areas. £2m science block opened by the Princess Royal in 2006 incorporating six laboratories, prep rooms and a large state-of-the-art ICT facility for use by own students and those from partner primary schools. The 'Blue' theme is carried throughout the décor – blue carpets, chairs, blinds, lino, walls, though 'it all looks a bit tired', said one parent. Work is in hand to make the school more environmentally sustainable, with the lead coming from the unusual 250-person school council, hailed nationally as an example of best practice. 25 council teams raise awareness and funds for what really matters to them, e.g. Fairtrade, buddying, fitness, cuisine. A great way to demonstrate passion and commitment amongst the young. Dining facilities have won healthy eating awards; in fact 'The Blue' is first school to be awarded FEAST status, by Raymond Blanc no less, which conferred swish catering training facilities for use inside and outside education. Locally-obtained fresh meat and vegetables are used and free chilled water is provided in each of the main buildings. Students also grow some of their own produce.

Pastoral Care and Discipline: Although a church school, no overt signs of Christianity. An assembly every morning with hymn singing and reading from appropriate texts; however the format is guided by 'worthship' rather than worship. Achievement is valued – every opportunity is taken to publicise (bulletins, posters around the school and regular contributions to local press) and praise. A firm but realistic attitude towards all matters of discipline.

Smoking within the building results in a one-day exclusion, as does swearing. The headteacher holds half-termly Saturday morning detentions for students who need redirection.

Pupils and Parents: Serves an area of generally advantaged, white, British, English-speaking households; the strong PTA reflects this and raises considerable sums for major purchases, e.g. a new minibus. Liaison with parents is good, with regular newsletters, meaningful reports and parents' evenings and a recent initiative 'Parent Pay' (how true ...) where payment for school meals, trips etc can be made online.

Entrance: Around 250 a year from local primary schools – mainly from within the city of Wells and surrounding villages. Oversubscribed and estate agents don't help this problem. Worth getting a map of the catchment area from the school.

Exit: Over 50 per cent stay on to do A levels at sixth form (though weaker A level candidates encouraged to bail out if AS results disappoint) and, of those, about 80 per cent move on to higher or further education.

Remarks: Solid state option sailing serenely on within a sea of local independents. The emphasis is on motivation and enthusiasm, amply demonstrated by the range of subjects and activities on offer.

Blundell's School

Linked to Blundells Preparatory School in the Junior section

Blundell's Road, Blundells Road, Tiverton, Devon, EX16 4DN

- Pupils: 575; 335 boys, 240 girls (400 board/weekly board, rest day)
- Ages: 11-18 • Size of sixth form: 185 (boys 110: girls 75) • C of E
- Fees: Day £16,815; Boarding £26,070 pa • Independent

Tel: 01884 252 543
Fax: 01884 243 232
Email: registrars@blundells.org
Website: www.blundells.org

Head Master: Since 2004, Mr Ian Davenport BA (forties). Born in northern Quebec, educated first in Switzerland and then at Bloxham. Read politics at Durham. Taught politics at a community college in North Carolina (USA) before returning to the UK for his 'yuppy' phase – five years in the City in the mid-'80s working for Morgan Stanley and Kleinwort Benson. Returned to teaching first at St George's Weybridge and later at Radley, where he was a busy man – started up the economics and politics departments, was a senior tutor, coached the first XV and fives, and taught economics at Oxford University in spare time. Not a grand, imposing headmasterly type – but quietly does the job well. Married with a son at Blundell's and a girl at the prep. A keen music-lover, one of his first aims was to improve the music department's facilities.

Academic matters: Does well, given the broadly comprehensive intake. Top of the tree recently for RS, history and – perhaps surprisingly for rural Devon – languages. Two pupils were placed in the top five students in the country in German and French GCSE; Spanish and French A level results superb. A level maths and film studies(!) also stand out. 60 special needs pupils 'are not over-looked'. 'Some' special provision for dyslexia – one or two sessions a week. 65 per cent of sixth formers have own laptops (50 per cent of pupils in general). Head eager to raise the school's intellectual tone, so there are now more academic societies, a newish director of studies, new honours award system (full colours for service to school, not just for sport), much IT investment. Newly-opened academic centre comprising classrooms, IT suites, design and technology and seminar rooms – a £1.5m investment.

Games, Options, the Arts: Rugby for boys and hockey for girls are the heavyweights. Registrar's wife was an international hockey player and coaches the first team. Head says Blundell's has strongest sports teams of any school in Devon – perhaps not too bold a claim. All mainstream sports offered, plus strong equestrian team and pupils effuse over the delights of kayaking. 50 acres of playing fields, double sports hall, outdoor swimming pool. Harkens to the great outdoors. Adventure and leadership programme for pupils in lower years involves eight weekend activities over the year (camp-craft, survival skills, vehicle maintenance, fixing plugs and taps etc) leading toward a three-day expedition in the summer. CCF compulsory for two terms in Year 9 (and pupils may carry on to Year 10), Ten Tors hike each May a big event and D of E taken seriously.

Particularly strong arts. Very good music department largely due to long-serving 'brilliant' director of music and possibly some intake from Exeter Cathedral prep. Choir tours central Europe each year (most recently Venice). New building project has doubled the size of the music department and provides an electronic recording studio. An exciting place for drama too, and the Ondaatje Theatre (named after OB Christopher, brother of Booker Prize-winning Michael) is a big asset. New, young head of art has introduced a special art status standing for the school's most talented pupils. Drama and art frequently overlap here (the theatre was being used for a solemn session of A level life drawing on the day we visited). Photography also popular. Good workshops (textiles, silver-smithing, cabinet making, engine repairs).

Background and Atmosphere: Set in 90 acres, bisected by a busy public road. Dignified collegiate main blocks, cloister and chapel; over the road the newer music block, huge and lovely dining hall where staff sit among pupils and the Ondaatje Hall housing theatre, art, photography, pottery. Library refurbished – looks great. Amazing, round Old Boys' pavilion overlooks playing fields – 'The Old Boys paid for it so they could have a perfect view of the rugger'. Long and illustrious history since being founded in 1601 at the bequest of local clothier Peter Blundell, one of the wealthiest merchants of Elizabethan England. The school's timeline includes 'school used as Fairfax's HQ in siege of Tiverton Castle' (1645), 'maths teaching begins' (1823) and 'schoolrooms heated for first time' (1828). School mentioned in Lorna Doone by (Old Blundellian) R D Blackmore. Moved premises within Tiverton in 1882. Fully co-ed from 1993. Tiverton is 'proud to have it on the doorstep' but Years 9–11 must wear school uniform into town. Tawny 'Blundell's tweed' jackets for 13 to 16-year-old boys, bright red blazers and navy skirts for the girls; sixth form boys and girls now wear navy blazers; sweatshirts and ties for the younger pupils. Cars allowed in upper sixth only for going to and from school.

Pastoral Care and Discipline: Seven houses: two girls', three boys', plus School House for 11–13 year olds and – hold on to your seats – a co-ed upper sixth house called Westlake. School House is like a sort of middle school within a senior school. Has its own character, own matrons, changing rooms, play areas and structure, e.g. no Saturday school. School House boarders have own weekend programme; boarding pleasant, four to six to a room, with appealing common-room. Girls' houses pleasant, if a little sleepy. Single rooms for lower sixth. Boys allowed 'just inside the dogrun door' – a quaint reference to past times when Blundell's boys would walk the young hounds for the local hunt. Blundell's describes Westlake as a unique pre-university experience, with individual rooms for boys at one end, girls at the other and both mixing in the central common area. Allows these older students to form new friendships across house divisions and must do wonders for sixth form retention. Association we saw between boys and girls in upper sixth common-room was informal, and in several cases – how do we put it? – very friendly. There is much to be said for this relaxed arrangement, but it may not suit everyone. Head points out that 'the past three years have seen significant academic success and much of this is attributable to the new Westlake project, so it has enhanced the academic focus here'. Separate boys' and girls' common-rooms upstairs for slopping around in dressing gowns etc, very important for the girls – 'so we don't have to worry about hair and make-up'. Full kitchen, widescreen TVs, no set bedtimes, internet access and basin in each room. Almost everyone boards in sixth form.

One or two suspensions for bullying, which shows school is taking it seriously. Drugs not at the top of school's worry list – this is not a school where drugs are cool. Head says anyone caught with them should expect to be out, but a second chance with regular testing is more likely. No more sixth form bar, but occasional dinner-dance with limited alcohol available. Drunken pupils face temporary exclusion.

Pupils and Parents: Wholesome. Not much make-up on girls or hair statements on boys. Farming intake has dropped from 20 to two per cent. Parents working in the professions (probably also looking at King's Taunton); increasingly from the West Country (large contingent of boarders from Cornwall who don't have a lot of choice), many London families relocating to Devon. Some far-flung including Londoners with local connections. Fair number of Services children. 10 per cent are foreign nationals, especially German – Munich agency sends high-class pupils. Others from Eastern bloc, Japan, Canada. Two full-time EFL teachers – pupils needing extra English get three lessons a week in place of French. Strongly loyal and supportive Old Boys (school has a busy development office) include Christopher Ondaatje, Michael Mates MP, Jack Russell (1809–14) of terrier fame.

Entrance: Official entry points 11, 13 (especially boys) and 16, but other years often OK. CE at 11 and 13 from traditional prep schools (e.g. Mount House, The Downs, St Michael's and King's Hall) – pass mark 50. Many from own prep (has own ten acre site on the Blundell's campus; known until 2006 as St Aubyn's, this independent prep was bought by Blundell's, removed and completely rebuilt within it). Good sprinkling from local state schools. Internal and external candidates for sixth form need at least five C grades at GCSE.

Exit: Some 90–95 per cent to university; average of five annually to Oxbridge (two in 2010). Business management, medicine and music are popular career paths; more recently graphic design. Not much migration towards London. Reading and Cardiff popular at the moment. The school has traditional links through Peter Blundell with Sidney Sussex, Cambridge and Balliol, Oxford.

Money Matters: Generous number of scholarships – academic and also for music, art, sport and drama, at different ages. Approximately one-third of entrants hold awards of some sort, up to 50 per cent off basic fees. Foundation awards allow local boys and girls to attend as day pupils. Exquisitely precise fee structure with different prices for boarders, local boarders, weekly boarders, local weekly boarders, flexi-boarders, local flexi-boarders, day pupils and local day pupils (whew!).

Remarks: Distinguished rural school, of ancient lineage, dealing creatively with challenging times.

Bolton School Boys' Division

Linked to Bolton School Boys Division Junior School in the Junior section

Chorley New Road, Bolton, Lancashire, BL1 4PA

• Pupils: 915 boys • Ages: 11-18 • Size of sixth form: 205 • Non-denom
• Fees: £9,099 pa + lunch • Independent

Tel: 01204 840 201
Fax: 01204 849 477
Email: seniorboys@boltonschool.org
Website: www.boltonschool.org/seniorboys

Headmaster: Since September 2008, Mr Philip Britton MBE (fortyish). Unassuming, relaxed and very bright, with a first from Oxford and an MBE for services to physics. Best performance prize from his PGCE at Cambridge, a Masters (with distinction) from Leeds in 1998, a secondment to the Institute of Physics advancing the physics curriculum and writing text books and, in 2009, an international award for his contribution to physics education. Came here from 17 years at The Grammar School at Leeds (qv) where he was head of physics at just 23 and latterly deputy head for five years. Lives near school with his wife and two sons, both in the infant division, and enjoys the extra-efficient service he receives in local shops from 'his boys' on their Saturday jobs. Loves outdoor pursuits and sailing, 'but first and foremost I like learning and an academic life'. Boys say he's 'young, modern, unorthodox in a good way' and like his GSOH: 'he's funny, self-deprecating and he cracks good jokes in assemblies'.

Academic matters: Results reflect solid education of boys from the top 25 per cent of the ability range. Over 70 per cent A levels gain A*, A or B, about 70 per cent of GCSEs A* or A. Long tradition of choosing medicine or engineering so science and maths (the only subject with IGCSE and setting from Year 8) are strong, but humanities and languages also fare well and are popular. Some 20 per cent take two modern foreign language GCSEs, a few take three, helped by native-speaking teaching assistants housed in cottages by the games pitches. 30 took Russian GCSE in 2009 with 74 per cent A* or A results, there's a full-time Russian assistant and a biennial trip to Russia. Greek and Latin on the menu with classics sharing sixth form teaching with the girls' division (qv).

Six forms of 24 in each year but, by GCSE, average teaching group size is just 17 with a maximum of 15 for A level. By A level most choose heavier subjects – sciences, maths, geography and economics, although some A level courses are run for tiny numbers; in 2009 one took RS, two Russian and one theatre studies – all scored As. High flyers encouraged to soar with AQA Bacc extended projects, Olympiads and Nuffield scholarships. Head introduced critical thinking at A level, boys also take general studies. Two libraries, lots of journals, the quality dailies and plenty of computers for working. High-powered staff, lots of PhDs, new ideas and teaching styles from younger teachers. One young pupil told us, 'we've probably got one of the best sets of staff in the country' – certainly boys appreciate teachers' availability and willingness to go the extra mile, and feel that what's expected from them is just that they do their best.

Games, Options, the Arts: Ten per cent of the timetable is given over to games; 'boys need to run around and let off steam'. Soccer, rugby and hockey in winter, cricket reigns supreme in summer. Fabulous 25m pool means swimming and water polo are also strong. Two sports halls, one with a climbing wall, a multigym and pitches descending the hill on 'the levels'. 'Our ground staff are brilliant but we would like an all-weather Astro to practise more to defeat our rivals,' boys say. 'One day,' says head; so it's on the development radar.

Until Year 12 every boy spends half a week a year at school's Patterdale Hall on Ullswater. With outdoor challenges and team-building, 'the Patterdale experience' is designed to build character and give lifelong memories. Sixth formers use it for business enterprise training courses. Many other foreign and residential trips including white water kayaking and coast-to-coast cycling.

Music is strong, about half the boys take instrument lessons, annual gala concert at Manchester's Bridgewater Hall. Strong drama too (Sir Ian McKellen was a pupil here) in both a studio and the theatre in the arts centre. Three huge art rooms, one with a kiln, and exciting paintings on display, 'never a problem finding a cover for the Boltonian magazine'. Special mention for the DT department for building Tenacity of Bolton, a 48 foot sailing ketch just outside the DT department, during ten years from 1998. Over 1,000 boys helped teachers, parents and friends of the school create what's now a mobile outdoor pursuits centre and sailing education resource – 'and MGS (qv) haven't got one of those,' say boys.

Sixth formers take enrichment classes from car maintenance to finance skills, and all give at least 20 hours to community service, some many more. Heaps of extra-curricular clubs and activities and form tutors check that each boy is involved and busy beyond his school work. One parent said, 'look at the end product: they're so well-rounded; they can talk, they can communicate, they're ready to take their place in the world'.

Background and Atmosphere: Imposing, baronial, pink sandstone buildings on 32 acres of well-to-do west Bolton suburb. The girls' and boys' divisions lie either side of a manicured quad with modern arts centre beyond, newly extended junior and brand-new infant divisions are just down the road along with a 'Kidzone' building offering care from 7.30am – 6pm and holiday clubs.

Founded in 1516, but re-endowed and re-built in 1913 by the community minded, first Viscount Leverhulme. It's spacious and splendid with magnificent stained glass, sweeping staircases and oak doors and panelling at every turn. It would be easy to slide straight into Oxbridge architecture from here, the buildings themselves seem to imbue boys with an unstuffy self-assurance. Up a little staircase is a rooftop glass-house so Hogwartian one might imagine germinating mandrakes. Much teaching is traditional with rows of desks; some labs are refurbished, some not; but the refectory tables and benches certainly feel like a step back in time – although the plentiful grub, prepaid with fees, is bang up-to-healthy-eating date. At the sixth form common-room butty bar, Auntie Carol serves bacon sarnies for £1.10 and beans on toast for just 50p against the telly tuned to a music channel.

Pastoral Care and Discipline: Discipline is quietly maintained through form tutors and year heads with a good dose of common sense emphasising owning up, taking consequences and everyone moving on. Few rules, lots of mutual respect, developing 'emotional resilience – stuff happens in life and we want to find the correct place between a traditional stiff upper lip and the arguably modern culture of crying at every opportunity'. Boys encouraged to be 'cheery', as befits leaders of the future. There's a school nurse available to all in the girls' school building and a school counsellor. Boys feel they have a voice on one of three pupil councils. Four houses provide a vertical structure for inter-age mentoring. Boys of 'old boys' and siblings kept in the same house. Four house days a year with sport, quizzes and board game contests. There are 53 prizes on speech day, some for community action and outdoor pursuits. Boys stand for teachers and exercise corridor courtesy. Uniform shop on site and open daily.

Pupils and Parents: These are good lads, down-to-earth, open and articulate. Half from Bolton which head points out 'is not a northern grit town but middle and upper middle class, a town with considerable affection for the school', and plenty of RP here. Many OBs live in the area and the Old Boltonians' Association is strong. Lots walk to school but 46 per cent arrive on one of 22 coach routes from North Manchester, Rochdale, Preston, Warrington and rural areas. The wide geographic catchment and one-in-six boys on bursary assistance gives a broad social mix. Fifteen per cent ethnic minority boys, mainly Asian, reflecting Bolton's make up; some Muslim, some Hindu and a small Jewish presence.

Star in the Old Boys' crown is Sir Ian McKellen CBE, who speaks fondly of the school, but the list includes city bosses, judges, professors and top sportsmen. Sir Harry Kroto FRS won a Nobel prize for chemistry, hence the Kroto Chemistry building at school. Radio presenter Mark Radcliffe, Chess Grandmaster (from the age of 19) Nigel Short MBE, Leslie Halliwell, author of Halliwell's Film Guide, Paul Horrocks, editor of The Manchester Evening News, Martin Milner OBE, leader of the Halle Orchestra, BBC Apprentice finalist Alex Wotherspoon, and Ralf Little who plays Anthony in BBC's The Royle Family to name but a few.

Entrance: Over two applicants per place. NFER VR, NVR and maths tests with school's own creative writing paper in January, interviews and school reports considered, looking for boys who'll get 5s in KS2 SATs. A bit of movement at sixth form, entry depends on reasonable GCSEs.

Exit: Nearly all to university, a yearly ten or so to Oxbridge, medicine and dentistry, engineering, science, maths, humanities and languages all popular in a variety of top destinations but Manchester, Newcastle, Durham, Sheffield, Nottingham, Imperial London and Liverpool particularly favoured.

Money Matters: Impressive BSSL, Bolton School Services Ltd, generates revenue for bursary fund from venue hire, catering, the pre-school nursery and by running 12 buses as a coach company. One in six pupils receives bursary assistance, means tested rather than academic scholarship. Financially all four divisions of Bolton School – girls', boys', junior and infants – function as one unit. Lunches included at £160 a term.

Remarks: No-nonsense, solid, traditional grammar school. If you thought 'they don't make 'em like that any more', think again and be glad. One mum in a family with three generations of Boltonian men said 'you can't better this school, it's "belting",' and we are inclined to agree.

Bolton School Girls' Division

Linked to Bolton School Girls Division Junior School in the Junior section

Chorley New Road, Bolton, Lancashire, BL1 4PB

• Pupils: 1,300; 805 girls, all day in senior school and 200 girls in juniors; 305 mixed in nursery and infants, 0-7 • Ages: 0-18
• Size of sixth form: 220 • Non-denom • Fees: £9,099 pa • Independent

Tel: 01204 840 201
Fax: 01204 434 710
Email: seniorgirls@boltonschool.org
Website: www.boltonschool.org/seniorgirls

Headmistress: Since 2005, Mrs Gill Richards BA MEd (early fifties). Read history at University of Wales, Bangor. Previously deputy head of Belvedere GDST, Liverpool (1996), then head (1997). Taught in comprehensives in Shropshire and Chester, then senior teacher in charge of staff appraisal at Rhyl High School. MEd in pastoral care, SEN, assessment and teacher appraisal. Career in boys', girls' and mixed schools has brought unusually wide experience of the young, and a conviction that girls and boys need different teaching styles to bring the best out of them. She knows about her girls' hopes and anxieties and about boys as well – very useful for everyone. Has an easy, approachable yet direct and confident manner; 'Gill' to all staff, but there's no doubt who is in charge. Has recently appointed a (male) ICT expert as deputy head, to set up tracking and monitoring system for pupils. Married with grown-up children; keen skier, walker and fisher with her family, enjoys cooking.

Academic matters: Predominantly academic school, though not to the exclusion of all else. Head believes in 'working hard and playing hard'. Exam results place school consistently in top one or two per cent in country. Curriculum broad. Four-class intake in Year 7. Class sizes quite big in Years 7 and 8, around 30 for most subjects, though this tapers considerably as girls go up the school. Wide range of optional subjects in sixth form studies, in imaginative curriculum enrichment programme. Girls and boys join up for specialist/small class courses, e.g. RS in girls' division, technology and classics in boys'. Pupils go to shared centre in Patterdale (Lake District) for, e.g., modern languages weekends as well for usual outdoor pursuits. Mrs Richards keen to encourage personalised learning and individual target-setting, also identifying coasters (can be overlooked in big school). Average results over three years – 78 per cent A*/A at GCSE, 53 per cent A grade at A level, 78 per cent A-B. Perhaps not fair to pick out subject results at A level, but history is quite remarkable. Maths also very good; chemistry and biology popular. Specialist staff teach in junior school upper forms, which helps transition at 11.

Games, Options, the Arts: Something for everyone. Sport strong, athletics, lacrosse, netball, badminton, swimming (school has pool shared with Boys' Division). Notable for netball and lacrosse. One pupil voted first ever BBC Young Sports' Personality of the Year. Lunch-time clubs across all areas of activity. Arts centre, drama productions in well-used theatre. Music flourishing – many girls learning instruments in school. 300 instrument lessons given each week with others taking lessons outside, beginners to grade 8+. More merits and distinctions than straight passes in Associated Board exams.

Background and Atmosphere: Founded in 1877 by local Bolton citizens; then in 1913 amalgamated with Bolton Grammar School (for boys) as joint foundation endowed by Viscount Leverhulme, and moved to present shared 32-acre site in 1928. Attractive grade II listed building in monumental sandstone, set in wooded site one mile from centre of Bolton. Wonderful wide corridors, superb main hall – what a school ought to look like. Contact between Boys' (qv) and Girls' Divisions fairly frequent, including shared facilities and opportunity to mix socially at lunch-times, as well as occasionally in class for minority subjects. Twenty per cent ethnic minorities, mainly Asian; Muslim families particularly like single-sex education (16 entered sixth this year from Bolton Muslim GS). Hijabs and short skirts mix easily and without comment; room set aside for Ramadan retreat. All attend all assemblies – 'and they sing hymns,' says head. Parents comment on easy but respectful relations between staff and pupils. Governing body rather dominated by the good and great in the business world but head claims this is a reflection of the north west in general and does not find it necessarily at odds with educational objectives. And they raise a great deal of cash for development. Mrs Richards has her eye on a new infants' and juniors' school, and turning existing buildings into a sixth form centre.

Pastoral Care and Discipline: Yearly form tutors (two per form in Years 7–9) meet with class daily and report to heads of school. Pupils say that 'teachers pick up on problems really quickly'. In addition, sixth form pupils offer confidential service to younger girls, with touching motto 'no problem too small'. In sixth form, girls describe teacher/pupil relationship as 'like friends'. Lower down the school, teachers take a stricter, more formal line. A very friendly and committed staff. Traditional, elected prefect body, strong school council, 'not just a talking shop'.

The absence of any signs of rioting in the long and hungry queue for lunch (hot food, including a vegetarian option, salads and sandwiches all get the thumbs up from their young consumers) suggests that discipline is firmly under control.

Pupils and Parents: Pupils reflect typically northern grammar school attitudes – hard-working, purposeful, frank, unpretentious, drawn from a wide range of primary and secondary schools and from many different social and cultural backgrounds. Unlike its obvious competitors, Bolton has no Cheshire base, though more middle class parents with new-found wealth are moving into the area, and the profile of the parents changing accordingly. Old Girls include Angela Williams, Director UNRWA Affairs (Syrian Arab Republic), Ann Taylor MP, Harriet Steele MP, Monica Ali (nominated for Booker), the Baroness Morris of Bolton and Dame Janet Smith DBE.

Entrance: Own exam at 11, English, maths and VR tests, and interview. Highly competitive, three applicants for every place. Almost half pupils from state schools, the rest from own junior department and handful of other prep schools. All their own junior girls take the exam. If it's thought a girl would struggle at senior level the case is flagged up with parents at least a year before. Nearly all make it. Some entry at sixth form, preferably including A/A* grades in proposed sixth form subjects. Many pupils local, but school also attracts children from wider geographical area served by school buses – Wigan, Worsley, Preston, Rochdale and Oldham.

Exit: Almost all to university, studying a wide array of subjects from Anglo-Saxon to optometry. Very few on academically soft courses; medicine, law and history well represented. Destinations predominantly northern (following national trend to favour places easily reachable from home – or is it partly northern caution?). About ten every year to Oxford and Cambridge (last year's batch included engineering and materials science).

Money Matters: Last cohort of assisted place students has now left. A number of foundation grants maintain, as far as possible, the 'principal objectives of the first Lord Leverhulme – that no boy or girl of potential who qualified on academic grounds but whose family were able to offer limited support would be debarred from entry to the school'. Likewise several Ogden Trust bursaries may also be available. School can and will help in unexpected financial crisis.

Remarks: Big, action-packed school achieving high standards for hard-working and ambitious girls. Its size (according to head, the biggest girls' independent school in the country) dictates need for slightly daunting (at least to new parents) degree of organisation. Systems certainly seem to be well in place, oiled and functioning. Despite this, room for healthy signs of eccentricity and non-conformity – school encourages 'individuality'. Girls very loyal to school, proud to be part of its success.

Bootham School

Linked to Bootham Junior School in the Junior section

51 Bootham, York, North Yorkshire, YO30 7BU

• Pupils: 270 boys, 210 girls and 140 at Bootham Junior School • Ages: 11-18 and 3-11 at the Junior School • Size of sixth form: 160
• Quaker foundation (but other faiths welcome)
• Fees: Day £13,785-£14,820; Boarding £14,985-£24,900 • Independent

Tel: 01904 623 261
Fax: 01904 652 106
Email: admissions@boothamschool.com
Website: www.boothamschool.com

Head: Since 2004, Mr Jonathan Taylor BA (fiftyish), read English at Lincoln College, Oxford, MEd from Sussex. Previously 16 years at Collyer's, Horsham, head of sixth at Ousedale Comp, Newport Pagnell, then deputy head (eight years) and acting head for four terms at Bedales. Not a Quaker but clearly in tune with Friends' ideals; articulate, unstuffy, approachable; clear-sighted about his vision for Bootham, he brings needed energy and experience to the school. He describes Bootham as his 'ideal headship'. Wife, Nicola. Interests include the arts, gardening and the outdoor life.

Academic matters: As far as results go, in recent years school has transformed itself from middle-of-the-road into a Yorkshire leader. Staff not exactly sure how this has happened but point to an infectious work ethic ('It's OK to achieve'), backed up by individual attention (Quaker maxim, 'seek that of God in everyone') and powerful sense of community. School may also have become more academically selective in recent years. About 50 per cent A*/A at GCSE, 70+ per cent A*/A/B at A level. Bootham sees itself as a 'premier science school', and results back this up. English and history popular, excellent art and maths. Class sizes throughout emphatically on the small side. Staff aim to fit A and AS combinations round pupils' choices – quite a feat in a smallish school. 'Give them room and they'll deliver.'

There are specialist science facilities, a music school, art and design studios and an IT centre. Wireless network recently installed to help laptop users. Excellent John Bright library is much used. Teaching lively and interactive; common claim that pupils take responsibility for their own learning and interrogate their teachers carries more weight here than in many schools – an aspect, perhaps, of the Quaker principle of 'speaking truth to authority' (= don't take it lying down). Wide range of special needs catered for, including dyslexia and, in recent past, deafness and physical handicaps. Unsurprisingly, school goes out of its way to help – ground floor biology lab created to enable pupil with a motor disability to learn alongside her peers.

Games, Options, the Arts: Quakers aren't happy with competitiveness ('Testosterone-fuelled heroes don't really fit in here,' said a laid-back senior boy), but sport is played by everyone for enjoyment and, yes, success. Tennis and football traditionally popular; teams in all sports accommodate everyone, not just the talented. Even so, Bootham doesn't produce only happy losers – basketball team has been district champion and individuals have become an international fencer, an Olympic swimmer, county netball, hockey and cricket squad members, and Leeds academy footballers. No rugby. Head has plans for an integrated sport plus well-being programme.

Outstanding design work has received national critical acclaim. Vibrant art department, with wonderfully creative pupils' work. Over 60 per cent learn a musical instrument – mainly for enjoyment – but several get to grade 8 and beyond, as well as scholarships to London music colleges. Well equipped technology suite; regular buffet concerts held in main hall. Drama also strong.

Expeditions to exotic places like Bolivia, Peru and Iceland, regular exchanges with France and Germany. School has its own well-used observatory (lovely polished brass fittings), and boasts oldest natural history society in the country. Hard to be bored here; plenty to do, regular weekend trips and activities for boarders.

Background and Atmosphere: Founded in 1823 on liberal, intellectual, tolerant principles. No need to belong to Society of Friends, or even to be Christian, but non-credal umbrella, underlined by weekly half-hour Meeting, does seem to work a kind of magic, and parents willingly buy into it. Originally for boys only, became co-ed in 1983. From busy main road, within shouting distance of the Minster, only visible part is fine Georgian terrace, which conceals spacious and tranquil campus, towards which a number of new buildings have crept. Head is overseeing ambitious new master-plan, aimed mainly to consolidate boarding provision, rationalise building use, and provide some new facilities. Original buildings are homely or shabby rabbit warrens, depending on your view (some rooms happily colonised by the young with their own brand of organised chaos).

Relationships between pupils and staff clearly very good. It really is a largely non-hierarchical place, where staff are often addressed by first names, yet one doesn't detect any absence of respect. Younger pupils wear a kind of uniform, older ones go about in a variety of inventive outfits, but overall impression isn't sloppy. Very few neckties on male staff or boys; the head wore one – possibly not to put prospective parents off – while his deputy, a Quaker, did not: a considerable man, much respected by pupils for his open door policy ('it's important to find time for what matters to the pupils'). Not a touchy-feely pandering to the young, simply treating them as valuable individuals – and incidentally helping them grow into responsible adults. Self-run school council is more than a talking shop and can subject authority to awkward questions about how the school is run.

Pastoral Care and Discipline: Given the emphasis on a warm, family-type atmosphere, it would be easy to assume a mushy, rule-less school which sold the pupils short on structure and guidelines. Not so – expected standards of behaviour are clear, 'All the usual systems are in place': no alcohol allowed on premises, suspicion of drug-taking renders a pupil liable to random testing, drug peddling leads to expulsion. The difference is that discipline is based on mutual respect, where boys and girls are encouraged to consider the effect of their actions on others.

Good standard of boarding accommodation; good wholesome food, plenty of choice. Day pupils can try boarding in one of many flexible options. Contact with distant homes possible through email and video-conferencing.

Pupils and Parents: Regarded locally as the thinking parents' school; many children of university teachers, doctors, first time buyers; some well-heeled, but not the kind to flash their cash. Quaker reference point clearly appeals; all welcome at weekly Meeting.

Day pupils mainly from York and up to 25-mile radius. 30 per cent of boys and 20 per cent of girls board; from UK and worldwide, all English-speaking or near-fluent if not. Pupils happy, confident, savvy bunch, accepted for what they are. Active parents' association holds regular coffee mornings, walks, lectures etc; has even introduced a grandparents' day. Notable former pupils: AJP Taylor, Brian Rix, Philip Noel Baker (Nobel Prizewinner and Olympic medallist), John Bright (parliamentarian), Stuart Rose (head of Marks and Spencer), Silvanus Thompson (physicist).

Entrance: Main feeder school (since 1997) is Bootham Junior School (formerly Ebor Prep School qv). Entrants at 11 and 13 sit school's own exam. For sixth form entry a minimum of seven Cs or six Bs at GCSE required, which must include maths and English. Head interviews all applicants and asks for report from previous school. Bootham fills up quickly, so don't leave it too late to apply.

Exit: A few leave post-GCSE, mainly to local sixth form college, either for vocational courses or to avoid Saturday school. Many take gap years. Five or six a year to Oxbridge, rest mainly to good universities (Leeds, Sheffield, Newcastle, Warwick) to read proper subjects.

Money Matters: Not a rich school: most income generated through fees and fund-raising. Some academic scholarships (means-tested), music scholarships (not means-tested) and some special provision for Quaker families.

Remarks: On a roll at present, bags of confidence all round. Does well by all, especially the lost sheep and the 'different', but don't expect to find a community of meek souls. End result is a bright, articulate and considerate individual. Parents say Bootham is addictive – it gets under your skin – but it may not suit the highly competitive and the attention-seeker. Take a look at the impressive DVD.

Bournemouth School

East Way, Bournemouth, Dorset, BH8 9PY

• Pupils: 1,060 boys, all day • Ages: 11-18 • Size of sixth form: 320
• Non-denom • State

Tel: 01202 512 609
Fax: 01202 516 095
Email: office@bournemouth-school.org
Website: www.bournemouth-school.bournemouth.sch.uk

Headmaster: Since 2009, Dr Dorian Lewis (mid forties), previously deputy head at mixed comprehensive, Queen Elizabeth, Wimborne, notching up experience managing curriculum, doing the National Qualification for Head Teachers. A chemistry graduate form Southampton (did his PhD there too) originating from Wales, Dr Lewis taught at Thomas Hardye school in Dorchester until his appointed to head of Science at Wimborne. Married with three children in local schools, he relishes his teaching, taking extra chem for exam years and thriving on personal contact with staff pupils and parents. A smiling and reassuringly cuddly demeanour conceals iron determination to get the very best for his boys and a razor sharp awareness of what needs doing. His biggest shock as a new head was the amount of time spent in 'fruitless' meetings, so he immediately set about reorganising the management to produce more 'fruit'.

Feeling the 'good' standards reported in a 2008 inspection left room for improvement, Dr Lewis saw his first year as a 'quiet revolution'. 'Last year a complete development plan for staffing and curriculum, this year the same for buildings.' 'Continuous cohesive management' is his term for galvanising everyone on his 'very talented and capable staff', from the cleaners to the super-efficient business manager, in his own 'velvet revolution'. Busily considering the cost benefits to the school of academy status at time of our visit but will only jump if he is absolutely certain the academic intake can be protected.

Academic matters: Impressive 61 per cent A*/As at GCSE and a steadily improving record of A levels are only to be expected of such a selective school. Dr Lewis agrees with the inspectors that the teaching, though successful, is pretty traditional – lots of chalk, talk and write – all fine but needing a little 'oomph', which he is rapidly providing – interactive whiteboards, classroom technology etc etc. Boys at all levels were clearly engaged with their work and most talked enthusiastically about it. Classes of 24–31 in first 3 years study the basics plus art, music and technology, with Latin (but no Greek) and French plus another language chosen from German, Spanish, Italian, and Mandarin Chinese. All take at least 12 GCSEs with 'fast track' being phased out in favour of the biggest possible bunch of the very best grades. ('It's what the unis want.') Classes average 24. The 22 plus 'mainstream' subjects on offer at A level include a raft of technologies, government and politics, further maths, psychology and sports science. Results appropriately sound, though there was a bit of a glitch in music and, for a Specialist Language School, the take-up of all but French and Spanish is regrettably low. (Dr Lewis has already homed in on this and on this and is 'holding the line' on a compulsory GCSE language for all.) Sixth formers can add General Studies, Mandarin Chinese, the Institute of Financial Services Certificate, or a smattering of other courses with Arabic, Portuguese etc now sprinkling the results list, while drama and sociology are done with the girls at the 'sister' Bournemouth School for Girls, down the road. (Inevitably sibling rivalry flourishes!)

The 'individual learning needs' service is focused mainly on the potential problems of the very bright, coping with a higher than average percentage of Asperger's or similar. Four teaching assistants give in-class and individual support. Lots of personal supervision by 'designated teacher' for children who need 'looking after' and a 'Gifted and Talented Co-ordinator' ensures that exceptional students get enough curriculum enrichment and acceleration to keep them on task.

Games, Options, the Arts: Unashamedly, an academic hothouse (some parents would like to see it a bit 'more rounded'), but there is a vast range of sports, activities and hobbies all pursued with a determination generated by 1000 plus highly intelligent and competitive boys. Dr Lewis protests that there is actually too much rather than too little but is immensely proud of sporting successes, giving a ball-by-ball account of the final matches of the Glanvill and Aegon team tennis cups. (They were runners up in both.)

Music is on a grand (and loud) scale featuring and Big Band and Concert Band with fifty plus players apiece, lots of brass and lots of singing. Most years a distinguished performer or two go on to music college. Choirs and singers abound as is to be expected from the school which produced Gareth Malone! The enormous Javanese Gamelan (takes a whole room) which has highlighted the identity of the music department, is departing for a museum, so perhaps Gareth could come back and identify another area of musical excellence to keep the side up!

Smashing portraiture on show in the music department and a stunning front hall display of one versatile student's work. Art department bristles with artists in residence and has an ongoing links with the Bournemouth Arts University College.

Terrific sports centre, and all-weather pitches. Football teams in every year group scooped up prizes in local and county competitions, as did the first rugby team. Athletics etc and oodles of cricket. Duke of Edinburgh is pretty new with Prince Edward visiting to give it a boost. Mammoth CCF with masses of activities for all three services and (another) band with a new female bandmaster. Sea Scouts take pride of place in a list of other extra curricular bursting with technological activities (a group built and raced a car) and cultural/arty enterprise (links and visits to Japan/China etc).

Loads of chess, films etc etc and a current student won Tesco's junior Masterchef, perhaps spurred on by the brand new shiny cookery kitchens in place for lower school lessons and a pre-uni cooking class.

Background and Atmosphere: Born the day Queen Victoria died in 1901, the school moved to its current hallowed portals as WW2 erupted. Only staff and prefects can use the echoing front hall and staircase where walls groan under notices of awards and achievements. Spectacular for sheer length and solidity and the outsize central clock tower, the buildings are otherwise unremarkable, having been consistently modernized in strict rotation (i.e. a lab one year means an arts classroom the next) with the result that nothing is really out of date but nothing stands out. Functional new maths block, 'managed in house which saved thousands' and all mod cons everywhere: wireless computer networks eat money though don't look spectacular but all technology is bang up to date.

Extensive wooded grounds including the 'copse' much loved by Gareth Malone freely available to roam in since 'Bournemouth boys can be trusted'.

Only the best is good enough here and boys appear to thrive on cut-throat competition. Not for the fainthearted but the feel is friendly and boys respond to Dr Lewis' mantra of 'hard work – discipline – smart appearance – respect' by showing real interest; even junior mathematicians seemed enthralled. Most were reasonably tidy, happy to converse and making responsible use of the facilities left open to them at down times.

Sixth form area buzzes with music/TV/conversation/work all going on at once. A helpful sixth form pastoral assistant is on duty at all times to give support on UCAS etc.

Masses of older boys at work in the library with a quiet academic hum and comfortable feel conducive to intellectual conversation or the odd game of chess. The library is generously staffed and light and airy at the top of a newish building with lecture hall and small classrooms, which make it ripe for development into a self-contained sixth form and adult education area. Sixth formers have freedom to come and go as they please so their bicycles litter the inner courtyard chained to any available railings, unlike lower school bikes which are stowed neatly underneath it. Courses such as sociology and drama are taken in the girls' school and the pin-striped sixth form boys socialise freely with their less formally clad female counterparts. Spaces between buildings are nicely got up for sitting in summer and one courtyard has a horticultural feel though the veg was struggling a bit.

Pastoral Care and Discipline: A competitive house system complete with tutor groups 'helps you to make friends' as well as providing a forum for informal monitoring of progress and social issues. Uniform is pretty neat with quite well-cut grey suits (no one looked baggy-kneed) and own choice suits in sixth form where long hair is a not much used privilege. Prefects on duty in the dining room. Dr Lewis says they virtually run the school. Discipline, when needed, is firm, based mainly on temporary exclusion, though Dr Lewis has not shrunk from permanent exclusion when absolutely necessary and the school is successfully draconian about bullying in any form. Parents can get immediate access to the head if he is there (in a curiously unadorned meeting room since he has opted for a tiny working office). Any whisper of drugs results in parental involvement and appropriate 'severe sanctions'.

Pupils and Parents: A broader academic mix than might be expected especially at sixth form where entry to courses may be less demanding than some less academic schools. Being Bournemouth, Anglo-Saxons predominate, though there is an ethnic mix. Flourishing parents' association and a star spangled list of OBs from the 60s comedian Benny Hill to Sir David English of the Daily Mail, Blur guitarist Alix James, educationalist Mike Tomlinson and news reader Mark Austin.

Entrance: No specific catchment but those outside Bournemouth have to apply via their own LA. Boys admitted by exam process which starts with an application, or 'expression of interest' in October. Testing is Year 7 maths, English and verbal reasoning and the school takes the top 150. Borderliners who may have done less well in one of the papers are considered by a panel. Later years admitted by assessment, if a vacancy comes up, but not open to those who failed at 11. Sixth form has extra 50 places and is by GCSE results: six or more A*–C including maths and English.

Exit: Mainly (91 per cent) post-A level to uni though the very occasional earlier exit to work. Eight out of 147 to Oxbridge, six to vet/medical schools and general scattering of blue chip and others.

Remarks: Solid as the rock of Gibraltar and nearly as traditional though Dr Lewis is bringing in some innovative teaching and ideas. His breath of fresh air approach has already transformed the prospectus, made major organisational changes and set some even more ambitious targets. Definitely for the intellectually tough! A school to be reckoned with!

Bournemouth School for Girls

Castle Gate Close, Castle Lane West, Bournemouth, Dorset, BH8 9UJ

• Pupils: 1,110 girls, all day • Ages: 11-18 • Size of sixth form: 290
• Non denom • State

Tel: 01202 526 289
Fax: 01202 548 923
Email: office@bsg.bournemouth.sch.uk
Website: www.bsg.bournemouth.sch.uk

Head: Since 2004, Mr Alistair Brien (mid-forties) – after being deputy head for five years. Educated at The Royal Grammar School, Guildford, read German and history at Exeter before PGCE at Birmingham. Spent his first three years of married life as housemaster of senior girls' boarding house at Keswick School – so is clearly dedicated and experienced in shepherding teenage girls – then head of sixth form at the Arnewood School, New Milton. Approachable and easy-to-talk-to rather than authoritarian, his affability covers a meticulous attention to detail and a steely determination for the school to serve his girls well. Parents and girls agree that he does. Keen on promoting school ethos and traditional values, with a 'firm but fair' approach to discipline, using carrot (stickers and approbation) rather than stick. Definitely 'prefers seclusion to exclusion' as a sanction by which he means spending a day under his own supervision. Regrets that he is now far too busy to continue writing German textbooks. Three children – the two daughters at the school.

Academic matters: An undeniably academic school, out to produce scholars and scientists – with considerable success. Awarded specialist status for humanities in 2005; more than justified by a comprehensive programme of history (early and modern offered separately at A level), politics, geog, social sciences and psychology plus religious studies for all at GCSE. Not surprising then that part of the spanking new Spreadbury building is for social sciences while RS has had its own building for a long time. More recent designation as a science specialist school attracted funding from the Wolfson trust for spectacular refurbishment of two chemistry labs, now all singing, dancing and resplendent in saxe blue. Current pupil (head girl in lower sixth) was a national finalist in the young scientist of the year competition in 2009 and is up for the European finals. She also pioneered the school's 'big sister' mentoring pairing scheme for pupils – so not just a boffin! Mr Brien agrees with the perception of many parents that the school is 'good' and 'solid' and is working hard to make it 'academically groundbreaking' as well.

All do 11 GCSEs, including triple science and compulsory RS, though outstanding athletes etc are allowed to drop a course to gain training time. Results are spectacular. Two-thirds of GCSE pupils got 5+ A or A*, 54 with 10 or more A/A*, while 50 got two or more A*/A grades at A level. Exam results and consequently UCAS points have improved steadily over the last few years. A bit of tail of D, E and U grades at A level, accounted for by the 'open access policy' which allows pupils coming into the sixth form from local schools to pick subjects in without having A/B grades at GCSE – in the interests of giving maximum opportunity to all.

Smashing A levels in biology, chemistry, maths and Eng lit but less strong in 2009 for psychology which has the highest take-up. A levels in theatre studies, economics and business, plus sociology run with boys from Bournemouth School, while PE and minority languages (Sp and Ger) are done jointly and girls go to the boys' school for business studies. Mandarin Chinese and Arabic taster courses on offer.

Class sizes average 27 in the first few years, shrinking to around 16 by sixth form. No setting in first three years except for maths. Only around 40 special needs pupils, few of these with learning disabilities, but the school does well by them. The 'learning centre' with one full-time staff member currently has a small counselling-style space but is expanding to larger premises. It offers support to any student struggling for personal as well as academic reasons.

Games, Options, the Arts: Definitely not just an academic sausage machine! Parents report a lively sporting programme with some really competitive teams and something on offer for everyone. Team sports not the centre of life but then this is a highly academic 'Gifted and Talented Lead School'. Newly introduced football, basketball, rugby and dance proving popular. House system (Mr Brien's initiative) has hotted up sport generally, encouraging friendly competition. A few super-talented pupils notch up national success at sailing, trampolining, dancing and archery and in 2009 BSG reached national finals in rounders, swimming, sports acrobatics and trampolining. PE staff mentor sports stars and are even hoping for a few Olympic competitors. School hosts national netball competitions but still shares sports hall with boys, though a complete revamp of the gym is on Mr Brien's wish list. Superlative new art studios and pretty solid results at GCSE and A level.

Food technology, textiles and ICT rooms all comprehensively equipped and used by all girls in lower school on a rota basis. (Another area on the list for re-planning and refurbishment.) Music and drama blossoming in the new performing arts centre: 'a cutting edge development'. Regular co-productions with Bournemouth School. Bags of choirs ensembles, orchestras etc. Trips to America, Austria, Belgium etc. The school has a link with St Anne's school in Kenya and staff and pupils visit both ways. Debating and public speaking are also very strong with team reaching national finals in the English Speaking Union's contest and the 'Debating Matters' competition, which they claim to be the 'hardest of all'.

Background and Atmosphere: Younger sister of Bournemouth School up the hill and sharing a pleasant green site. Their playing fields meet, sixth form share courses, pupils from both socialize at lunch break and activities like CCF and D of E are offered jointly. Parents think BSG is more pupil-friendly – not just an academic hothouse – gives a more 'rounded education'. Feels like an ambitious school but not a ruthless one. Outward-looking and community-minded, it is co-sponsor with Bournemouth School of new local Church of England academy and recently became part of South West Academic Trust, a group of grammar schools in south west working with Exeter University. Distinctly utilitarian sixties architecture has been overtaken by pristine new buildings with good in-between spaces which potentially shift the centre of the school away from the unprepossessing front façade – possibly aiming for a new entrance in the foreseeable future. Originally designed to house 700 'young ladies', the current 1100 plus just about fits into the still-evolving complex of new and middle-aged facilities. Once inside, staff are welcoming, while corridors and classrooms bustle with busy girls. Half of a lovely mural showing the pre-1961 school in central Bournemouth brightens up the reception area wall with the other half, cunningly forming a gallery behind a glass wall (sadly obscured by redundant notice boards in a post open day clear-up on the GSG visit). Spacious library is staffed at all times and has a large careers room, also staffed. The new Virtual Learning Environment available via the schools network is the latest addition to technology. State-of-the-art IT is taken for granted here!

Pastoral Care and Discipline: Pupils and parents endorse the 2008 Ofsted judgment: 'tremendous clarity of purpose and superb relationships' and 'girls' personal development and well-being outstanding'. Sixth formers mentor younger girls and organise the six houses, named after (dead) famous women rôle models. All new Year 7 pupils have a 'big sister'.

Pastoral care is delivered in the main by the house system, which has a good reputation for dealing well with problems including bullying 'mainly the fall-out from Facebook', which is always tackled quickly and generally successfully. Social education in drugs/ internet/ personal relationships etc is provided by heads of houses. Mobile phones turned off in class and confiscated if they ring. Drugs seldom a problem though Mr Brien would expel anyone selling them. His main weapons, used extensively by staff as well, are listening, talking and discussing. Parents have 'Open House' access to head without an appointment every morning from 8–8.15, otherwise heads of houses are first port of call.

Pupils and Parents: Mainly from Bournemouth but about a third travel from as far as Brockenhurst (east) and Ringwood (north), though Poole (Parkstone Grammar) mops up the western catchment. Parents arrange several bus routes. The canteen opens at 7:45am for parents dropping girls off early, though not after the 3.35 end of teaching when the school lets girls stay until 5:30pm. Supportive Parent School Association with lots of social activities raises substantial sums to provide equipment such as the recording studio in the new arts block. Old Girls' Association has just been disbanded as pupils rely on Facebook, Friends Reunited etc. Better-known past pupils include Charlotte Moore (800m runner) and Lisa Dillon (actress).

Entrance: Apply on local authority application form in October. No catchment area – girls can come from anywhere. Around 430 hopefuls sit tests in English, maths and verbal reasoning on a Saturday in November, all vying for 162 Year 7 places. Offers sent out in March. Practice papers available to all, and virtually everyone who sits the test will have practised – if you're too lazy to bother, then this isn't the school for you! A few from the independent sector but most come from over 50 state junior schools. Among feeders are Bethany Junior, West Moor's Middle, St Thomas Garnet's Preparatory School and King's Park, Moordown St John's, St Mark's, Queen's Park, the Epiphany and Winton Primaries. Admissions panel takes advice from junior school heads on borderline cases (true for those schools where heads are willing to comment – those opposed to selective schooling can be unwilling to get involved). 40+ pupils enter at Year 12, mainly from local 11–16 schools like Glenmoor and Avonbourne: six A*–C GCSEs the bottom line requirement for entry.

Exit: Vast majority to higher education – Exeter, Warwick, Southampton, Durham, Cardiff popular and a handful to Oxbridge. A sprinkling directly into employment and an increasing number (just over 20 per cent) to gap years. A pretty impressive proportion goes into law, medicine, veterinary, and tougher science courses with a fair share of art, drama etc.

Remarks: A real local grammar with a highly academic but up-to-date curriculum and a surprisingly cosy atmosphere. Certainly not wearing scholastic blinkers.

Box Hill School

Mickleham, Dorking, Surrey, RH5 6EA

• Pupils: 425; approx half day/boarding; 65 per cent boys, 35 per cent girls • Ages: 11-18 • Fees: Day £13,650-£15,600; Boarding £20,700-£26,250; International Study Centre £28,770 pa • Independent

Tel: 01372 373382
Fax: 01372 363942
Email: enquiries@boxhillschool.org.uk
Website: www.boxhillschool.com

Head: Since 2003 Mr Mark Eagers MA (Cantab) MA (Bath) PGCE (forties). Previously deputy head of Ardingly College, was a senior examiner for IB (history) and is an NCA coach (cricket). Married to Jane, who teaches economics, business studies and ESL at the school. They have three children, youngest two at the school. Loves sport especially cricket, enjoys hacking round the golf course and spending time with the family. Pupils say head goes by his name – Eager by name, eager by nature. Personable, chatty, popular, his boundless enthusiasm and energy have lifted the spirit and atmosphere. Had a mandate to kickstart the school in what is a highly competitive market.

Spent first year settling in and prioritising, then started on the very many (and much needed) planned changes and upgrades. Not just facilities (more later) but a school council, greater communication with parents, captains' dinner, more sport etc. No room for complacency on the academic side; most staff swept along with him, a few voting with their feet, some retiring (staff profile older than in many schools). Staff say, 'He has vision, holds onto what's strong and good,' and that, although changes are good, speed of changes has rattled a few cages, 'but he knows where the school is going and where it needs to be.' Head gets universal thumbs-up from pupils who say, 'School is more active, lively; he's younger, plays games with us, knows us all and has children the same age so he's in touch'. Teaches younger years and gets really involved in sport, especially soccer matches (coaches the thirds) where he's often heard cheering on the lads and occasionally questioning the referee. Pupils love the fact he's revamping things and making everything more student friendly; younger ones agree, adding, 'He's funny and nice; even if you're naughty he makes sure you understand what you've done'.

Academic matters: Teaching styles vary but pupils say most staff work hard to make lessons interesting and accessible and use TVs, interactive whiteboards or OHPs to help. School introducing laptops for all from Year 7 (included with fees). Smallish classes average 16. No Saturday school but prep on Saturdays for boarders. Positive value-added with art, English language, French and history scores showing pupils gaining a grade higher than anticipated at GCSE. Lowest (though still positive) value-added found in sciences and maths. Only IB Diploma now offered in sixth form. Awarded Good Schools Guide Award for art and textiles in 2007.

Parents and pupils full of praise for SEN and learning support. Get one-to-one or small group support as necessary. One mildly dyslexic boy with poor organisational skills was thrilled to achieve two As in GCSE English, another told us, 'I was quite severely dyslexic when I came here but I'm not so bad now; teachers help you at every stage. You learn to get on with it. My teachers collaborate with the dyslexic teacher – it makes a difference.' Keen not to flood classes with learning difficulties as they don't have room for classroom support. Work on literacy and English plus strategies to help pupils in the classroom and with organisation, though older pupils may be given subject-specific help. Majority come out of activities on rotation but some drop a subject to fit learning support in. Department produce IEPs and meet, liaise and interact regularly with all teachers. Learning support staff say strength is the staff; all teachers are SEN aware and dedicated. Range of SENs catered for: physical difficulties (though not junior girl boarders), dyslexia, dyspraxia, mild Asperger's, cerebral palsy, moderate hearing impairment, OCD and dyscalculia. Mild to moderate only. A quarter of pupils receive ESL tuition, 30 of whom attend the International Study Centre full time.

Games, Options, the Arts: All usual sports, good range of facilities: gym (doubles as main hall), small outdoor heated swimming-pool, super climbing centre adjacent to a fantastic outdoor high ropes setup, brand new assault/team-working course, a well-used, equipped and supervised multigym.

New music school including recital room, recording studio and percussion room opened in 2009. Plenty of opportunities to perform in concerts, productions, tours (Lake Garda for past three years), cabarets etc. Don't have to be grade 8 and gifted to join in – enthusiasm counts. Practical art, theatre, drama all popular. An hour-and-a-half compulsory activity slot is built into the daily timetable with diverse choice of activities ranging from candle-making to ice-skating. Plenty of outings – Years 7–9 go on camping/outdoor pursuits-orientated expeditions twice a year; a big hit with pupils. Senior years do D of E (10 golds recently) and older children get opportunities to go overseas.

Background and Atmosphere: Founded as a co-ed school in 1959 by Roy McComish, a master at Gordonstoun. Still very much a Round Square school, following Kurt Hahn's principles of allowing children to discover themselves, furthering international cooperation, serving the community and participating in adventurous activities calling for initiative and responsibility. Main school in pleasant village of Mickleham, an important and integral part of the community. Pleasant redbrick building believed to have originally been a wedding present from DH Evans to his daughter. Mix of the old, modern buildings that blend well and incongruous ugly prefabs well past sell-by date. Much refurbishment in progress.

Pastoral Care and Discipline: No plans to turn into an academic hothouse, believes education should be enjoyed, not endured. Stresses importance of finding something child is good at as success in one area enhances confidence, makes child feel better about self, leads to success in other areas. International centre attracts lots of overseas boarders – indeed it accounts for a high proportion of those who board in sixth form, though some stay with guardians.

Boarding facilities vary considerably. Smart new house just built; other houses vary – mansions, cosy but comfortable, modern blocks in need of an upgrade and the externally hideous Ralph House (another brown pre-fab). Grim and impersonal living space in the junior girls' house – the girls loathe it. Much improved new dining hall. Food ranges from healthy salad bar to stodgy puddings; not that anyone should go hungry – there's a school shop and vending machine. Over 18s are allowed a couple of visits a week to the King William pub in the village (landlady checks ID) though we're told, 'Anyone coming back hammered will get punished, but the cost of a pint in Surrey tends to limit quantity consumed anyway!' Sensible drinking allowed for older students at formal dinners. Clear guidelines are issued for those caught smoking, drinking or involved with drugs; random testing may be used.

The tutor group system comes in for universal praise – pupils, parents and staff love it; only disadvantage is that it is house-based so you end up with single-sex tutor groups. Good and staged discipline system of coloured cards works well. Head introduced a student council which sixth formers praise but younger ones want improving – say they'd like to be asked for their opinions, not just rely on a rep who doesn't always do the job properly.

Pupils and Parents: Lots of first-time buyers of independent education. Majority from Surrey or Sussex, a quarter from overseas (30 nationalities). Pupils say it's more sporty, less academic than other schools they looked at and entry assessment procedure is more relaxed. 'I didn't want to be stuck in a classroom all day and knew the school really didn't approve of bullying and would do a lot to stop it.'

Children love the fact it's a small, close-knit community, where everyone knows each other. Need a 'have a go' attitude, good for the sporty. Couch potatoes and the vain may struggle as outward bound expeditions are compulsory. A couple of girls told us how they hadn't fancied caving (water and the dark) but were made to try and found they thoroughly enjoyed it. All agree expeditions are a highlight of the year, a great way to get to know people and make new friends. Pupils struggled to say what they hadn't enjoyed, other than exams. All agree school isn't known for its academic prowess, will never soar up the league tables, but it does well with its intake and those capable of getting to Oxbridge do.

Entrance: Selection is by tests in maths and English and by interview, with previous school reports considered. Majority enter in Year 7 or Year 9 with selection days held in November and February prior to year of entry. Numbers are up and school is meeting challenges to find extra space. A truly comprehensive intake from those who achieve five top grade A levels and take up Oxbridge places to those who struggle academically but may have talents in sports, the arts etc.

Exit: Handful leave after GCSEs for local colleges. Majority of sixth form go to a range of universities, some to study for degrees, others HND. Odd one to Oxbridge, otherwise range from Imperial to Thames Valley. Handful take a gap year, couple into employment.

Money Matters: Range of scholarships and bursaries offered, mainly means-tested and worth up to 50 per cent of fees.

Remarks: We've been in far smarter schools with much better facilities but, as a pupil told us, 'You don't need state of the art sports halls to play football – it's the package: the teachers, the atmosphere, the community; everyone is positive and the school really helps you to develop your talents.'

Bradfield College

Bradfield, Reading, Berkshire, RG7 6AU

• Pupils: 485 boys, 250 girls. 620 boarders, 115 day • Ages: 13-18 • Size of sixth form: 300, of whom 130 are girls • C of E • Fees: Boarding £28,425; Day £22,740 pa • Independent

Tel: 0118 964 4510
Fax: 0118 964 4513
Email: headmaster@bradfieldcollege.org.uk
Website: www.bradfieldcollege.org.uk

Headmaster: Since 2003, Mr Peter Roberts MA PGCE (mid-forties), an Oxford historian. Immediately impresses with his mental database of pupils and a seemingly instant recall of who is who and their minute-by-minute concerns. 'How was the Spanish oral?' he called out to one we passed and 'Was the golf cancelled?' to another – and he brings to mind with microchip accuracy the history of any given Bradfield student. He came from Winchester College where he was in charge of the scholars, but his focus at Bradfield is far from narrowly academic. Value-added is exceptionally strong here. Mr Roberts stresses the family nature of the school, its 30 per cent of siblings and his determination to teach to the children's varying levels of ability. 'We want children who will contribute across the range,' he says, unusually, these days, not making a play only for the academic high-flyers. That Bradfield's results are on the up reflects his conviction that, 'the all-round education we offer informs what goes on in the classroom'.

Tall and rangy, intense and somewhat inscrutable. ('This description sounds like The Demon Headmaster,' he feels.) 'Warmth and inclusiveness are at the heart of what I try to achieve.' We don't doubt his success. Parents are happy – 'he thinks out of the box,' said one; 'the school is going well on his watch,' said another.

Academic matters: On the up. Does well in value-added tables which means, in effect, that pupils of all abilities do better here than they would elsewhere. Maths in particular has improved. Good range of subjects on offer includes at A level: dance, DT, ethics and philosophy, music technology, textiles, but much the most popular are business studies, economics, maths. Languages getting a much-needed boost including Latin and Greek – all had been at lowish ebb despite influx of German native speakers which one year produced a stunning 30 out of 31 takers getting As at A level. Best performers among the major subjects are history, economics, film, art and theatre studies, but overall the percentage of A*/Bs at A level a creditable 73 per cent. At GCSE in 2010, 49 per cent A*/A grades. Accelerated learning groups take some subjects early. Head teaches all Year 9 English sets in rotation to get to know them – which clearly works. A state-of-the-art Science Centre, using the very latest in sustainable design technology, opened its doors to pupils in September 2010. Includes 10 sophisticated laboratories, with a focus on hands-on learning and technology. The school is seeking accreditation to run the IB alongside A-levels.

'Some of our most intelligent and able pupils have SENs,' says Mr Roberts, who, on his arrival, wisely re-sited the study skills department right at the physical centre of the school. He is 'very interested' in SENs and is, in fact, an SEN governor of a number of preps. 'We're very good with bright dyslexics and dyspraxics,' he says and parents agree, though head feels that those on the autism spectrum might not be best suited to board here. School site is very hilly so would not suit wheelchair users or those with difficult mobility, though the houses have good access arrangements internally.

Overall, a sense that school is good at teaching children to their own level and helping them to outperform expectations. A parent told us, 'The facilities are there for the brightest, who want to press on and are Oxbridge-bound, but also for those who need to go more gently'. Library – large and well-stocked, though shelves were perhaps disconcertingly full, considering it was exam time when we visited – reflects this approach. We saw *The Tabloid Shakespeare* alongside Frank Kermode's erudition on his language and DVDs of *The West Wing* as borrowable as the Olivier *Richard III*. Also periodicals from T3 to *Poetry Review*, *Der Spiegel* and *The National Geographic*.

Games, Options, the Arts: The playing fields are gorgeous and the facilities here, in the terminology of a Year 9 neophyte, 'immense'. Tennis courts – all-weather, covered and other – everywhere. On-site glorious nine-hole golf course and space, space, space. Huge sports centre, pool, fitness suite and lots of courts of all kinds. Two all-weather pitches. Most – both sexes – play football and hockey. About a quarter play golf; also on offer are athletics, cricket, sailing, squash, fencing, polo, riding and more. Winners of the Micklem Golf Trophy thrice in the last five years. ISFA National Sixes winners and National Schools' Twenty20 Plate winners in 2009. Competitive and successful across the board. Sport well established for junior as well as senior girls.

Arts similarly strong. Art happens in a Victorian primary school, part of what had been Bradfield Village, on site. Perhaps the most varied and exciting range of media that we have seen, taught in a range of studios and rooms by a highly enthusiastic and creative team – most practising artists themselves. Much good use made of older and contemporary artists as influences and traditional skills taught expertly too so pupils here can paint and draw, sew, print – in various media – photograph, model, carve and sculpt. 'Pupils are encouraged to follow their own ideas in different media while working on the same theme – it's a personalised educational experience,' we were told, and certainly we saw no two pieces that resembled each other.

Music, enhanced by Starship Enterprise-style music school, is very strong and much praised by parents. A third of pupils learn one or more instruments; regular ensemble, choir and orchestral concerts and tours. Good recital room along with 1960s concert hall. Major annual productions on three-year cycle – Greek play for which Bradfield is famous, musicals and major drama, e.g. Shakespeare. So drama is high profile here and standards are high. Vast choice of extra-curricular activities includes African drumming, Amnesty, ballroom dancing, digital animation, D of E, knitting, CCF, cinema, clay pigeon shooting. 'I can't understand,' shrugged a Year 11 boy, 'that anyone could ever be bored here.'

Background and Atmosphere: Bradfield is a village – it has a minor road running through it which pupils need to learn to be sensible about. The original college buildings were built on top and as an extension of the Elizabethan flint and tile manor house, Bradfield Place. The surrounding cottages in the 18th/19th century hamlet abound with cute redbrickery, sloping roofs, chapel, leafy lanes and hillside walks. Founded as a school by the combined local rector and lord of the manor for the education of sons of the clergy in the 1850s, it was very much part of the Oxford Movement. Bit by bit the school took over the village and the village became the school so it includes, in addition to the old school, the old mill – the stream and mill race still rushing away – and, gloriously, a fabulous arts and crafts manor house with stunning quadrangle and quite beautiful gardens, most recently re-designed by Jane Fearnley-Whittingstall. The grounds are among the best-kept we know – immaculate; the National Trust would do well to come and learn. It's a big site and although most teaching happens pretty centrally, a certain amount of fast walking is needed to get from one end to the other. A few privately-owned houses still in the village but most is school-owned – a unique feature in the south of England – and plans are afoot to build more staff houses to increase the palpably family-centred feel and rationale of the place.

Bradfield is five minutes from junction 12 on the M4 and in fact the motorway is visible from the site. It is also minutes from the high speed rail link into London; both factors are important in terms of its clientele which is, to a great extent, from London. So it's a local, national and international school and, in the last five years, has accepted children from an amazing 120 feeder schools. It is now fully co-ed. Bradfield is unusual in never forgetting the schools from which its pupils came. This shows in its literature, which prints the name of the pupil's prep after his or her name throughout the child's career – 'We value very much where they've come from,' says head. He is keen on the idea of continuous education and the unique pastoral arrangements for Year 9 are very much emblematic of this.

Faulkner's is the self-contained village within the village part of the school entirely given over to Year 9 and head sees it as 'continuing the nurturing of the prep schools'. It is an attractive, seamlessly linked group of houses which accommodates the Year 9 day pupils and boarders – the houses having their own staircases and family atmosphere with large communal areas, games rooms and a separate building in which eating and activities happen. Faulkner's is universally praised. It integrates 150 pupils from a huge range of previous schools and backgrounds so that they all become acquainted and know each other when, at the end of the year, they are grouped in houses. A few rooms are four-bedders, the rest are ones and twos, which is true school-wide. Rooms are spacious and well-appointed, with basins, desk and powerpoints.

'We really do think we have invented 20th century boarding,' says head and we can see why. All the houses – four girls' and seven boys' – are small and organised on similar lines and the house staff popular and seen as friends. 'All the tutors are good,' we were told. 'It's informal so you don't feel you're being interrogated – you can just go and chat.' Houses, to which pupils feel great loyalty, are spread over the foresty site and occasion some gripes that informal socialising between residents of houses – not allowed – is a problem after prep. Pupils in Years 9–11 would like the freedom to go between houses but school, understandably, feels this would be awkward to police. Temptations to sin are minimal in general – no shops, no pubs – but no-one seems to mind too much.

Pastoral Care and Discipline: A Year 9 pupil told us, 'It's much stricter than my prep,' and his friend added, 'But the teachers here are really calm and friendly'; a parent confirmed that 'the discipline is sensible and relaxed but it is discipline'. The house staff are central to the pastoral care and maintenance of discipline and we heard little but praise for them all. 'My son's housemaster has been superb,' said one mother, 'and the matron too. My son is not a conventional child but they are malleable and it suits him wonderfully.' Disruptive behaviour isn't tolerated, for the sake of the rest, but 'there are surgeries for those who need help'. Head sees discipline as 'like wallpaper – not in your face the whole time but very much there'. But, 'On the grisly issues you have to be really firm'. Possession of drugs is an expulsion offence but there is a régime for testing which he has put into practice two or three times thus far.

Pupils and Parents: About 70 have EAL help. No vast numbers from any single country. Most who come at 13 have been at UK prep schools and school takes from a vast number of preps. Popular with ex-pats. However majority from the surrounding counties and, now increasingly, from London. School is exceptionally good at being accommodating to busy working families. Who wouldn't fit in? Only someone who refused to involve themselves, thought pupils. But, one added, 'Really there's a niche for everyone.' Notable former pupils include (Lord) David Owen, Richard Adams, Louis de Bernières, Michael Scott-Joynt, Bishop of Winchester, Tony Hancock.

Entrance: School takes 150 pupils into Year 9 – roughly 60:40 boys:girls. Selection, from the 200 or so applicants, by visits, prep school reports and a minimum 55 per cent pass at CE, although the intake covers a wide academic spread. Top three sets are taught as divisions in Year 9. No pre-testing, but borderline CE candidates are screened to help preps and parents with choice of senior school. Sixth form numbers are bigger due to influx of new boarders, some from abroad. The College's on-going waiting list is a true indication that things continue to move in the right direction.

Exit: To the whole range of further education. Exeter, the London University colleges, Bath, Bristol, Durham, Leeds, Manchester, Newcastle and West of England most favoured. An impressive number to art school. Some now to universities in the US, Ireland and Europe.

Money Matters: Scholarships, exhibitions and awards at 13+ and 16+; competitive exams, assessments and interviews.

Remarks: Pastoral, extra-curricular and academic aspects all strong in a very beautiful setting. Unusually family-friendly and with exceptional boarding.

Bradford Girls' Grammar School

Linked to Lady Royd Preparatory School in the Junior section

Squire Lane, Bradford, West Yorkshire, BD9 6RB

• Pupils: 290 • Ages: 11-18 • Size of sixth form: 80 • C of E
• Fees: £10,533 pa • Independent

Tel: 01274 545 395
Fax: 01274 482 595
Email: headsec@bggs.com
Website: www.bggs.com

Headmistress: Since Easter 2009, Mrs Kathryn Matthews BSc (mid-forties), educated at Loreto Grammar School in Manchester, then maths and an MA in education at Leeds University. Taught maths at The Oratory, London; deputy head at Gateways School, Leeds. ISI team inspector and governor at Westbourne Prep in Sheffield. Married with three teenage sons. Enjoys theatre, visiting art galleries, reading and rugby union.

Warm and approachable, astute, honest, humorous, in touch with the wider educational world; enjoys teaching maths (does one quarter of a timetable, up to GCSE). Values individual teachers who can enthuse pupils and is keen to foster staff talent; wants to maintain the school's high academic standards and enable girls from less privileged backgrounds to succeed. Parents say she deals with problems 'promptly and appropriately' and makes herself available in a flexible way.

Academic matters: Strong on value-added. Consistently good results at A level in a surprisingly wide range of subjects (28) for such a relatively small sixth form, including Japanese, Russian, graphics, with subjects run for just one or two girls; bigger numbers for maths and sciences than arts and languages; excellent art. Class sizes up to 10. Good careers advice/university preparation.

GCSEs also strong (24 per cent all A/A* 2010), especially sciences (all three) and several languages (Greek available); usually nine taken. Moved to IGCSE maths this year, science starting next year and English under consideration. New business and communication option very popular and successful. Year 10s do a health and safety qualification. All learn Latin in the first three years. Home economics chosen over food technology because of its focus on practical cooking skills and nutrition knowledge. Several awards in national science competitions. Classes average at 18; 23 maximum. Staff described by girls as 'very supportive'; 'They make lessons fun'. Parents say: 'Very approachable'; 'They know all the pupils individually.'

Exceptional design and technology department with an inspirational, immensely energetic male head who has procured an impressive amount of industrial equipment for the workshop – Knex, Lego and airfix kits also used, girls make go-karts and pedal cars and enter lots of competitions; also a one-year GCSE engineering option – foundations for this year's Cambridge and Durham engineering offers.

Well-led SEN department takes advantage of LEA and national resources and liaises well with parents ('They're good at targeting individual needs') and teachers – confident it could handle any kind of difficulty. Dyslexia Action visits half a day a week for assessments and one-to-one/two support (parents pay it directly); also free outside classroom support for dyslexia and EAL – the school is very aware of a growing need to provide the latter.

Large number of computers, but in need of upgrading. Pleasant, well-stocked and used library, with 72 carvings of mice in the Yorkshire Mouseman furniture tradition to spot.

Games, Options, the Arts: Has Sportsmark Gold. Good facilities include an Astroturf and purpose-built sports hall, but only a half-size swimming pool, with changing-rooms needing refurbishment. 17 sports offered – successful in county, regional and national competitions, notably in synchronised swimming (very popular); table tennis teams also strong.

Keen interest in ecology – aiming for Green Flag status. Extensive D of E; debating throughout the school; lots of success in competitions, e.g. engineering, Young Enterprise, marketing. Sixth formers do Community Sports Leader award, Global Young Leaders, Millennium Volunteers. Wide range of charities. Two – carefully selected – girls visit Auschwitz each year.

High standards in drama, modern dance and art, e.g. some very elaborate textiles work. About half learn instruments – lots of concerts and clubs (steel pans, jazz, soul). Annual large-scale, themed open day for local primary schools, designed to supplement their curriculum with arts, modern languages and ecology activities, organised by Year 10s. Sports and academic trips to Canada, Europe, South Africa, Malawi.

Background and Atmosphere: The main, 1930s building is square, with soothing views from corridors of a grassed quadrangle dominated by a huge cherry blossom tree; all the new developments blend sympathetically with the original Pennine sandstone. Seventeen acres of games areas, lawns and gardens. A very attractive, airy conservatory with wicker furniture and large pot plants serves as a waiting area off the entrance hall. The brightly-coloured modern cafeteria offers a wide choice of food catering for all diets. A spacious atrium for the younger girls to relax in with green walls and café furniture and more pot plants. Some drab classroom and corridor walls due for refurbishment, brightened by colourful displays; an orderly, focused atmosphere within. The separate, very attractive, purpose-built Foster Beaver College feels comfortable.

Girls say the school is welcoming and close-knit, not competitive:'We're encouraged to be independent and set our own goals'; the sixth form is 'like a family.' They are encouraged to take responsibility – elected form prefects, school president with two deputies and sixth form committee, plus school council.

Pastoral Care and Discipline: Excellent pastoral care. Small key stage 4 tutor groups. The school is alert to the usual problems coming from girls putting too much pressure on themselves to succeed, but 'nothing that can't be managed' by working with parents, according to Mrs Matthews. Sensible, enlightened bullying, sanctions and rewards policies.

Pupils and Parents: Mixture of middle-class professionals (several doctors) and self-employed plus some working class; ethnically mixed – a large number of Asians, with very supportive parents. Buses from Ilkley, Leeds, Huddersfield, Halifax. Girls are hard-working, articulate, confident, happy, tolerant, enthusiastic – 'mature and intellectually curious', individual and very proud to be at the school, says Mrs Matthews. Strong links with parents and old girls, who include Barbara Castle, Rebecca Sarker (TV actress), Jill McGivering (BBC foreign correspondent), Isobel Hilton (journalist) and Pippa Wells (CERN astrophysicist).

Entrance: Two-thirds from the prep school, the rest from state primaries – it looks to take from the top 50 per cent nationally. Maths, English and VR tests plus a short, informal interview with the head.

External sixth formers: interview plus five A*–Cs at GCSE, with A/B in prospective AS subjects, but some flexibility here.

Exit: Just under a half leave at the end of Year 11 for local state or independent, co-educational sixth forms, e.g. Greenhead College. A high proportion of Year 13s enter the best universities, including Oxbridge and the top London University colleges.

Money Matters: Means-tested bursaries up to half fees, with one free entry at 11 and one for the sixth form. Will relax bursary rules to help existing parents with unexpected difficulties.

Remarks: A very good girls' grammar blending the traditional and modern. It would be enhanced by greater financial resources but gets the really important things right – high standards, very good relationships and a wide range of opportunities.

Bradford Grammar School

Linked to Bradford Grammar Junior School (Clock House) in the Junior section

Keighley Road, Bradford, West Yorkshire, BD9 4JP

• Pupils: 695 boys and 415 girls, including 120 boys and 65 girls in the junior school (Clock House). All day • Ages: 11-18; junior school 6-10
• Size of sixth form: 250 (100 Girls & 150 Boys) • Non-denom
• Fees: £10,205 pa • Independent

Tel: 01274 553702
Fax: 01274 548 129
Email: hmsec@bradfordgrammar.com
Website: www.bradfordgrammar.com

Head: Since 1996, Mr Stephen Davidson DL BSc PGCE (fifties), educated Tynemouth Grammar School, read metallurgical engineering at Manchester University. Previously head of middle school at Manchester Grammar School. A traditionalist and an engaging, unpretentious and deservedly popular man who loves to talk about his school; thinks he has the best job in England. A hands-on head, he doesn't believe in spending time away from Bradford; claims to know every pupil. Wife Carol much involved in school 'family', one son in Year 11 at BGS. Retiring in December 2011.

Academic matters: A powerful, academic school, emphasized in prospectus and other publicity, with strong traditions across the curriculum range. Very wide spread of A levels, including PE, Greek and Latin. Three full-time teachers of design and technology. 100 per cent pass rate overall in 2010, including 87 per cent at A*, A or B. 71 per cent overall A*/A at GCSE. School will stand by pupils even if they aren't making the BGS grade. AS favoured, 'good for stretching'. Expectations high, and pupils prepared to work hard. Extra time allowed for Oxbridge preparation.

Staff 'amazingly devoted and committed' – and teach sixth formers 'as if they were university students,' said a parent. 2005 ISC inspection notes that 'independent learning has improved to being very good'. Low turnover of staff.

Games, Options, the Arts: Very strong rugby (considerable national success) and netball (in national finals for last three years), cross-country; cricket good too (well, this is Yorkshire, where they take it seriously, like religion), and some outstanding results in tennis, table-tennis and rowing. Keen drama. Music very lively and wide-ranging, both inclusively and at the able top end. Plenty of outdoor opportunities in Lakes and Dales.

Background and Atmosphere: School dates back to the 16th century. Formerly a free grammar, became direct grant, then independent. Pleasant, spacious setting on Bradford outskirts, all games on site. Monumental gritstone buildings 'planned with incredible foresight'. Pleasing feel of space to corridors and quads between buildings, all very spick and span. Subjects grouped together in departmental suites. Large modern library and well-equipped IT rooms. Lots of new buildings opened in 2002 by Duke of Edinburgh, including competition-size swimming pool, music school, auditorium, attractive sixth form centre – academic and social hub. Also junior school extension and superb multi-media language centre.

Bradford has changed in recent years, and the school reflects this: Yorkshire chippiness on the way out, replaced by more tolerant, open community. Pupils seem very much at ease with each other and staff, confident and cheerful – though still competitive and fully stretched. Co-education fully established, not a boys' school with girls in it. Head aims to keep the best of the old, and some will find the school quite hierarchical (no bad thing). Christian assemblies twice a week.

Pastoral Care and Discipline: Lack of self-discipline heavily frowned upon, relatively rare. Theft likely to lead to expulsion. Northern hard-working ethos very much in evidence and plenty of space to let off excess steam. Well-structured 'horizontal' pastoral care system. Good peer support.

Pupils and Parents: Sons and daughters of local professionals and business people; 12–15 per cent Asian origin. Strong parental support – Bradford has always been proud of its grammar school. Large catchment area, efficiently connected by buses and trains, mainly in an arc running NW to SW of city, but also extending into rival Leeds. Old Boys include David Hockney, sympathetic to school and president of recent appeal, Denis Healey, Adrian Moorhouse. Lively Old Bradfordian Association, with more than 5,000 active members.

Entrance: Average school IQ is 120+, so entrance exam pretty selective, but any candidate 'showing sparkle' in any part of exam is interviewed for selection on potential rather than performance. Half of entry (also via exam) comes from junior department (Clock House), which has expanded in recent years and is going strong, tucked away next to main school. Rest of entry mainly from local primaries. Sixth form entrants need 20 GCSE points (A* = 4, C = 1).

Exit: A dozen or so to Oxbridge every year. Nearly all leavers to good universities, majority to read hard/traditional subjects; much medicine and engineering. Popular destinations are Durham, Bristol, Newcastle, Nottingham, Edinburgh, Manchester, Liverpool, Birmingham.

Money Matters: Fees kept amazingly low – an unbreakable Governors' principle and a tremendous bargain for parents. School doesn't believe in borrowing money for capital projects. 130 bursaries available from home-grown scheme, funded by Old Bradfordians, Ogden Trust, HSBC, and other corporate benefactors; this enables school to preserve traditional social diversity.

Remarks: First-class, academic and outward-looking grammar school offering high quality all-round co-educational education.

Bramdean School

Linked to Bramdean Preparatory School, Kindergarten and Pre-Prep in the Junior section

Richmond Lodge, Homefield Road, Heavitree, Exeter, Devon, EX1 2QR

• Pupils: 120; ratio of boys to girls 60:40 • Ages: 12-18 • Size of sixth form: 12 • Inter-denom • Fees: £9,075 pa • Independent

Tel: 01392 273 387
Fax: 01392 439 330
Email: info@bramdeanschool.co.uk
Website: www.bramdeanschool.co.uk

Heads: Since 1978, Miss Diane Stoneman NAHT (timeless), joined 'some ten years later' by Mr Tony Connett. Miss Stoneman is warm-hearted, generous-minded and effortlessly scholarly. To her great regret, she no longer teaches ('swamped by hideous paper work') but in her time has taught virtually every subject. She is also a wonderful artist. Mr Connett, described variously as a 'maverick' and 'idiosyncratic', is dedicated to the shamelessly old-fashioned virtues of education, daily chapel, good manners and the happiness of the pupils. Mr Connett is an independently-minded headmaster of a genuinely independent school. He prefers common sense and directness to regulations and euphemism. He specialises in a desert-dry drollery designed, perhaps, to deflate the pompous, but there is no disguising his underlying shrewdness, experience (he had a fascinating life in industry before seeing the light) and his concern for the welfare of the children in his care. The two complement each other and it is typical of their modesty that there is no mention of them either on the website or in the prospectus. When asked about that Mr Connett said, 'The school is much more important than its heads.' Actually the two are indistinguishable.

Academic matters: Over the last 10 years the school has achieved an average of over 95 per cent of pupils achieving five or more academic GCSEs at A*–C. Candidates sit an average of nine subjects. A level results are equally impressive and classes are small.

The heads have gathered round them an impressive and enthusiastic staff. The head of physics spoke of his great good fortune in teaching maths and physics A level to small sets. 'They're more like tutorials and if we decide to do a practical as a result of a discussion then we can do it straight away.' All subjects have that intimate feel. The headmaster's love of traditional teaching has not blinded him to modern educational tools. He is no Luddite and the classrooms are impressively equipped with white boards and interactive white boards, computers, excellently laid out science laboratories and a large modern home economics suite for teaching cookery and learning about nutrition. All work is closely monitored and recorded in the colourfully helpful prep book with which each pupil is issued. Parents and staff sign and comment.

Games, Options, the Arts: Subjects are not confined merely to the classroom: as well as reports written on the various expeditions, the termly newsletter has lively articles by subject teachers, designed to link the classroom with the world outside. There are challenging expeditions such as the Ten Tors, the Exmoor challenge and Duke of Edinburgh Award. Staff regularly take 20 or so pupils to the South of France for a PGL activity holiday.

Bright, airy music department complete with electric piano and a suite of Yamaha key boards. Involvement is total and judging by the CD of hauntingly lovely Gregorian chant, the choir is superb. They have broadcast on Sky, CNN and the BBC. Listen out for them.

Delightfully intimate recording studio built (recently) to professional standards with CD and analogue video recording, high band TV cameras and editing facilities. Drama is taught in the lower and senior school and there is at least one school production each year involving all the pupils. The drama studio has a sprung floor for various types of dance.

Across the road from the school is the games field. In the Lent term football is presided over by Xavier Martin, former coach at the Barcelona FC Football Academy, with striking results; rugby is played in the Michaelmas term and cricket in the summer. Keith Brown, former vice-captain of Middlesex CCC, is overall in charge of games. Girls play cricket, hockey, netball, rounders and athletics. All learn to swim at the nearby university; tennis is also available there.

Background and Atmosphere: Founded in 1901, it was bought by Miss Stoneman in 1978, since when there has been much building. All stages of the school – the kindergarten, pre-prep, prep and senior school – are housed in the same area of buildings. The original Regency building, which houses the meeting and greeting rooms as well as the well-resourced libraries, is very handsome. The chapel, designed and built by Mr Connett, is an absolute gem of a building: clear, airy and elegant, with two organs and very fine choir stalls. It is an oasis of tranquillity in a bustling world where the air is loud with the sound of music practice and the shrieks of netball players in the covered sports hall, floodlit for evening activities.

A happy atmosphere pervades the school and the children wear their good manners lightly, greeting openly and courteously. Clearly they are used to talking to alleged adults and the breadth of ages assembled in such a space lends for a genuine family feel. No cafeteria but good home-cooked food and three separate sittings, presided over by teaching staff and lovely, motherly kitchen staff.

Pastoral Care and Discipline: The size of the school is a key factor here. Children carry around in their prep books a copy of the all-embracing school rules and expectations and know where they stand. The system of progressing through a series of form heads ensures that staff know their pupils well, 'can spot unusual patterns of behaviour and lend support and love.' A wonderful qualified matron seems to be in attendance non stop. Zero tolerance over drugs.

Pupils and Parents: Parents come from a wide cross-section of society and most live within a radius of 25 miles or so. The end of boarding has inevitably reduced the catchment area, but occasionally people from abroad can be boarded out with designated families.

Entrance: Children admitted to kindergarten and pre-prep at three and five respectively. The majority remain in the prep school, where they progress by ability rather than automatic chronology. Essentially pupils may enter at any stage: the school is not selective but everyone takes common entrance. For entry into the sixth form, pupils need five GCSEs at A and B grades.

Exit: Numbers leaving post-GCSE vary but may lose one-third to sixth form colleges. Of those remaining, the majority go on to university.

Money Matters: Fees are very competitive and the heads are justifiably proud of the financial support they offer in a multiplicity of scholarships and bursaries. Don't be afraid to ask.

Remarks: This is an unusual school and will not suit everyone. For some it would be too small; for others its size would attract. Those who talk to staff and pupils may well feel they have stumbled upon an undiscovered jewel, where the aims are high and education lives on. You certainly won't find many other schools like it.

Bredon School

Linked to Bredon Junior School in the Junior section

Pull Court, Bushley, Tewkesbury, Gloucestershire, GL20 6AH

• Pupils: 230; 20 per cent girls; 60 per cent board • Ages: Lower school 7-14, upper school 14-18 • Size of sixth form: 16-19 • C of E • Fees: Boarding £16,635-£24,165; Day £8,085-£15,405 pa • Independent

Tel: 01684 293 156
Fax: 01684 298 008
Email: enquiries@bredonschool.co.uk
Website: www.bredonschool.org

Head: Since September 2010, John Hewitt. He is 49 years old, married with three children and has a BA (Hons) degree, a PGCE and an MBA. He was formerly a boarding housemaster at Sevenoaks School and deputy head of Churcher's College. A former Irish international rugby player, he now has to content himself with his other passion: for drumming in a rock band.

Mr Hewitt is keen to drive Bredon on as a school which caters for all abilities, although it has a national reputation for developing those with learning difficulties.

Academic matters: Maximum 15 to a class but, in reality, probably seven, often with a teacher and support assistant. School is good at identifying pupil needs and designing programmes to suit. 'They really get to know and understand the individual child, how they learn, what makes them tick, but, most importantly, my child has grown in confidence and he's happy.' Good facilities, interactive whiteboards, lots of visual and kinaesthetic teaching.

Results wouldn't set the league table world on fire but children often achieve beyond expectation and prediction. This isn't a special school – they take a range of abilities – but some 50 per cent of all children have a recognised learning disability, primarily dyslexia or dyspraxia, with others such as Asperger's, ADD and ADHD well catered for. Has a nine-strong learning support team; parents say its head is bringing the department on in leaps and bounds – she's not afraid to try out new ideas and avenues. This has a knock-on effect for those who don't have an SEN – they look at the individual, e.g. if taking GCSE maths a year early is right for a child, that's what they'll do. 'Giving confidence won't cure a child, won't turn an average child into a brilliant scholar, but will help them find themselves and develop learning potential.'

Support is provided in class and at the Access Centre where small group or individual tuition is offered (charged as an extra). Outside support via occupational therapy, speech and language, educational psychologist etc is used as necessary. Help also on hand for the five per cent with EAL requirements. SEN is not viewed as a hindrance. The recent speaker at Founder's Day, Jon Merricks, a multi-millionaire ex-pupil, said Bredon had been his last hope – previous schools saw only an angry, lazy child; Bredon uncovered a dyslexic with ADD and gave him vision and confidence. He says he believes dyslexia and ADD are gifts: 'I came to see that while I may not be any good at detail and concentration, I am gifted with vision and being able to see the bigger picture.' Recognised the ADD traits when he met Bill Gates: 'I was just the same – had to sit on my hands to concentrate.'

As well as all the usual curricula, a wide variety of vocationally-orientated courses including GCSEs in catering, art and design, drama, rural and agricultural science, astronomy, dance and PE. A level options are limited but the core subjects are offered. Also provides a range of alternative sixth form studies including vocational courses (GNVQ, AVCE, BTec etc) in areas such as business, sport, media, countryside and environment, health and social care, engineering, hospitality and catering and ICT.

Has working farm that children use via the curriculum and provides practical, hands-on learning opportunities – hoping to add a teaching area in the near future. Children help with lambing, muck out the pigs, tend sheep or look after some of the thousands of bedding plants grown in the school greenhouses. This year they have added Forest School to their growing curriculum provision, too.

Games, Options, the Arts: All usual sports with a range of others including basketball, trampolining, badminton, tae kwon do. Plays regular competitive fixtures. Older students encouraged to work for awards such as sports leader, basic education leader (BELA), British Canoe Union (BCU), D of E or to become qualified lifeguards – recently had six Gold D of E awards. Music not a strength but guitar and woodwind popular, with opportunities to perform each term. Range of other activities offered including Warhammer, nature studies etc. Good art, into different media: textiles, sculpture, plus woodwork, metal work, plastics. Array of design projects on view – BBQ stands, trailers, go-karts etc.

Background and Atmosphere: Founded in 1962 by Lt-Col Tony Sharp OBE and Hugh Jarrett with just 17 boys, expanded rapidly under the second headmaster – Brian Llewelyn Thomas. Hit a sticky patch in the late 1990s (school very open about this) but has built up reputation steadily since. At the heart of the 84-acre school campus is Pull Court, a super, Victorian mansion, complete with sweeping staircase and surrounded by park and woodland. Many acres are given over to the school farm but plenty left over for the BMX cycle track, adventure play circuit, climbing wall, assault course, zip wire and open-air swimming pool. On-going programme of updating with a major building project just completed. Pupils stand up when adults enter the room, healthy mutual respect. Children recognised for their individuality. Now owned by the Spanish-British education group Colegios Laude.

Pastoral Care and Discipline: Parents impressed with pastoral care, see it as a strength of the school – 'My son was very averse to school before his time at Bredon. But Bredon boosted his confidence and self-esteem'. Pastoral care system recently overhauled and largely separated from the academic – introduced houseparents and additional nursing staff; children seem more comfortable with this régime. Parents assure us any problems are sorted immediately – say staff listen, then act. Bullying not an issue but any that arises immediately stamped on. Mobile phones allowed, child protection issues always taken seriously.

Boarding options are flexible – no Saturday morning school so children can enjoy long weekends at home if they choose. Plenty of activities for those who stay including outings, e.g. to Cotswold Wildlife Park, plus regular shopping trips, as well as free time to relax, chill or simply explore and play in the extensive, safe grounds. A new, purpose-built, sixth form area but much of the boarding accommodation is on the basic side, though clean and tidy with lockers etc. A healthy eating initiative – salads always available – with choice of warm dishes; that said, we're told the food could be better, especially for fussy eaters, and apparently the chips are too greasy!

Entrance: Via interview and assessment. All prospective pupils invited to spend taster days in school. For those with SEN, school will consider both current reports and own assessment to ensure needs can be met by the learning support centre.

Exit: 80 per cent to college or university. Range of courses but typically business studies, agricultural/environmental studies or leisure and tourism.

Remarks: A nurturing school ideal for any child battered and bruised from not ticking the usual boxes. Provides a restorative experience. Parents say they would recommend it to anyone who has a 'sensitive' child with SEN and their other siblings, as they cater well for both.

Brentwood School

Linked to Brentwood Preparatory and Pre-Preparatory School in the Junior section

Ingrave Road, Brentwood, Essex, CM15 8AS

• Pupils: 1,195 boys and girls, roughly 60:40, including some 75 boarders • Ages: 11-18 • Size of sixth form: 215 boys and 140 girls • C of E • Fees: Boarding £24,345; Day £13,560 pa • Independent

Tel: 01277 243 243
Fax: 01277 243 299
Email: headmaster@brentwood.essex.sch.uk
Website: www.brentwoodschool.co.uk

Headmaster: Since 2004, Mr Ian Davies (fifties), formerly head of St Dunstan's College, south London, and previously head of Lower School at Latymer Upper. A graduate of St John's Oxford, he is a theologian, married to a teacher. Likeable, committed, strong on moral values and discipline. An ISI inspector, helps select naval officers for training at Dartmouth for the Admiralty Interview Board and is on the DfE National Advisory Council.

Academic matters: Takes a wider spread of ability than its main competitors – the Chelmsford and Colchester grammar schools – and does pretty well by its pupils across the board. Has been criticised in the past for not stretching the most able but the head points to school surveys showing that the brightest two-thirds get as good or better results as their counterparts at the grammars. 'And the bottom quarter still do well – why would we not want to educate them?' In 2010 60 per cent of GCSE grades were A* or A. 50 pupils got nine or more A*/A grades.

A good spread of A level choices including DT, sport and PE, psychology, theatre studies, ICT. In 2010 32 per cent A*/A grades.

Started offering the IB in September 2007. The head introduced it at St Dunstan's and is 'keen on its philosophical underpinning, holistic approach and vision of a "well educated human being",' plus its ability to stretch the most able. The 2010 results averaged 33 IB points.

Good learning development department, which includes two full-time SENCos and other trained staff. Pupils are withdrawn for support where necessary, and have differentiated tasks in lessons.

The Sir Antony Browne Society (SABS), now open to younger pupils as well as sixth formers, is a forum for the most able pupils to discuss and debate topical issues and is part of a gifted and talented programme which includes other academic clubs and activities.

Games, Options, the Arts: If you are aiming for the Olympic fencing team (or to play premier division football) this is the school for you. Eight pupils represent Great Britain at fencing and an ex-head boy has an international Olympic scholarship to help with his preparations for the 2012 Games. Two coaches are Commonwealth Games silver medallists and Olympic 2012 hopefuls. Has won the Public Schools' Fencing Championships for the last two years. Other pupils represent the country at cricket, sailing, skiing, netball and chess. Large numbers play for the school or their house at the more traditional sports: football, rugby, netball, swimming, cross-country. Acres of playing fields and courts, all-weather floodlit pitch, sports hall with squash courts and excellent swimming pool including learner pool for the pre-prep.

Performing arts block with extensive music teaching, specialist rehearsal and practice rooms and a Sibelius computer suite. One of the largest music departments for a non-specialist school, with large numbers of A grades at GCSE and A level. Some two-thirds of pupils learn at least one instrument; many play in the symphony orchestra, the string orchestra, concert band or Big Band, which has many outside engagements, raising funds for charity. Pupils play in the National Youth Orchestra and National Children's Orchestra. Several choirs and concerts throughout the year.

Plenty of high quality drama, including a production of Les Miserables, praised by John Cameron, orchestrator of the score, as the most exciting he had ever seen. The school is also currently building a 400-seat auditorium to house productions, which will be complete in September 2011. Art, once in the doldrums, now impressive, as is DT, housed in the Hardy Amies Design Centre with some of his original sketches on the walls.

Huge choice of extra-curricular activities, including the largest voluntary CCF corps in the country; popular community service unit. Pupils enthuse about tackling the high ropes course on the CCF summer camp, singing in Siena Cathedral on the music tour to Italy, seeing the Northern Lights during a geography field trip to Iceland, competing in the house pancake race, helping disabled children to learn to ride. School raises some £40,000 a year for charity, mostly via inter-house events organised by pupils.

Background and Atmosphere: Founded in 1557 by Sir Anthony Browne, on the site where William Hunter had been burned to death at the age of 19, for refusing to accept the doctrine of transubstantiation of bread and wine into the body and blood of Christ. Browne had sentenced Hunter when a Justice of the Peace for the area, and founded the school as a penance. A school song commemorates the young martyr. In 1622, statutes were drawn up for the school by Browne, John Donne and George Monteigne, Bishop of London, requiring that all boys should be instructed in Virtue, Learning and Manners.

Was a boys' grammar school, principally boarding, for many years. Admitted girls into the sixth form in the mid 1970s and into the main school in 1988. Now has one boys' and one girls' boarding house, for around 70 pupils. Probably uniquely, the boys all get single rooms (varying in size from cubby hole to spacious), while the girls are never more than four to a room. Pupils and parents seem happy with the system of educating boys and girls separately from 11–16, meeting for extra-curricular activities.

72 acre site bordered by woodland, with different departments housed in separate buildings of varying architectural vintage: the 'Old Big School', which dates back to not long after the school's foundation; the 1867 chapel; the wood-panelled memorial hall with proscenium arch and organ; sixties boarding house; Courage sports centre; red-brick performing arts block. Terraced cottages on the perimeter house up to 50 staff, several of them ANZACs on a three-year stint in the country. A handy journey to school, but with the disadvantage of having one's quiet drink in the garden in full view of any pupils wandering by.

Pastoral Care and Discipline: Hot on manners and tidiness. 'It's about being clear about expectations. They're expected to be ambassadors for the school inside and out.' Indeed, the grounds are pristine and the pupils in general are startlingly well-turned-out, aided by the fact that the Hardy Amies-designed girls' skirt is more-or-less impossible to roll up at the waist – and very elegant it is too. Hot on pastoral care as well, with senior pupils trained to act as mentors for younger ones and bullying, by all accounts, not a significant problem.

The school is a Christian foundation – 'We take it seriously' – and though other faiths are welcome everyone must attend chapel once a week.

The boarding houses are run by husband-and-wife teams, who, said the ISI, 'are so committed to the care of the pupils that they have simply extended their own family life to encompass the boarders, providing them with the next best thing to home'. Boarders have access to all the school facilities at weekends, though there are few formal activities arranged except for Saturday morning matches and some clubs and EFL lessons, and most of the UK boarders go home.

Pupils and Parents: Most come from within a 15-mile radius, which includes the idyllically rural and decidedly urban parts of Essex. 'We are very much a local school, and the local community wants us to be part of it.' Boarders include those from further-flung parts of Essex and overseas, from Europe to Hong Kong. The IB is attracting interest from German families in particular.

OBs – who include several teachers at the school – are a loyal lot, and there is a mailing list of over 7,000. Local ones tend to send their children to the school and many help with careers advice, a mentoring scheme and work experience. The Society of Old Brentwoods runs sports teams, bridge clubs, dinners and outings. Eminent OBs include Sir Robin Day, Douglas Adams, David Irving, Sir Peter Stothard, Griff Rhys-Jones, Noel Edmonds, Jack Straw, Frank Lampard, Jodie Marsh and Sir Hardy Amies.

Entrance: Selective intake at 11, with a small 13+ entry. Around a third comes up from the prep school but must take the same maths, English and verbal reasoning exams as outside applicants. Another third from local state primaries. Applicants who fall down on one of the papers have a supplementary interview to give them a second chance, and those with dyslexia get extra time. Aims to admit those in the top 50 per cent of the ability range. 'We do a good job for high-flyers and for the middle-of-the-road student who might get lost elsewhere.'

Asks for six Bs at GCSE for those who want to move on to the sixth form, 'and nearly everyone gets that. We have a loyal approach to sixth form progression – we will stick with them if they work hard and contribute to the wider life of the school.'

Exit: Around 30 or so move on after GCSEs to e.g. sixth form colleges. Nearly all A level leavers to university – half a dozen to Oxbridge; double figures to art foundation courses; business studies, engineering and economics popular at a range of mostly old-established universities.

Money Matters: Used to be a direct grant school, charging according to income, and offers 10 full-fee bursaries each year as well as up to 25 academic, art, music, sports, drama and boarding scholarships. 'We want a good social mix and are moving towards a means-blind admissions policy. If a child wants to come to Brentwood we want to give them the opportunity.'

Remarks: Extensive grounds and excellent facilities; a handy commute from London. Very strong on all aspects of the extra-curricular, and provides a well-rounded education for a wide ability range in an ordered environment.

Brighton and Hove High School

Linked to Brighton And Hove High Junior School in the Junior section

Montpelier Road, Brighton, East Sussex, BN1 3AT

• Pupils: 425 girls, all day • Ages: 11-18 • Size of sixth form: 70
• Non-denom • Fees: £9,696 pa • Independent

Tel: 01273 734 112
Fax: 01273 737 120
Email: enquiries@bhhs.gdst.net
Website: www.bhhs.gdst.net

Head: Since January 2010, Ms Lorna Duggleby, formerly head of Bromley High School, another GDST school. The school has a reputation for being traditional and academic – a new head is sure to bring fresh ideas. Rumours (as at several Girl's Day School Trust schools) of co-ed sixth form (in the manner of Howell's School in Cardiff) but no plans to change as yet. School assures us that she is already restoring previously low morale.

Academic matters: Academic results excellent, dedicated staff passionate about their subjects. Bright, stimulating, independently minded, confident girls – a description approved by parents, staff and the local general public. Pupils are very conscientious and pile the pressure on themselves but are encouraged to progress as individuals rather than through peer rivalry. English very popular; particularly hot on poetry and awarded first place by the Keats House and The Poetry Society for the school Poetry Landmark of the Year. For Book Week 2005 they lured the Poet Laureate to work with the girls on war poetry.

Also involved with raising funds for the British Library for the specific conservation costs of editions of Pride and Prejudice and Robinson Crusoe. A published author is on staff; the Book Week runs as a cross-curricular activity involving history front page competitions, geography travel brochures and a dress-up day – the old head dressed as Cruella de Vil calling the staff her 'puppies'. History is taught well – we popped into one lesson and witnessed a virtuoso performance in how to elicit facts and develop arguments with a captivated audience of Year 11 girls. Some parents report that a watchful eye had to be kept on the volume of homework. Many girls leave for sixth form colleges because of the limited range of subjects available here; old head was keen to e.g. extend languages beyond Europe and introduce Mandarin.

Excellent exam results in 2010, with 83 per cent A/B grades at A level and just under 70 per cent A*/A grades at GCSE.

Careers programme impressive with close links with the local careers service and employers. Year 9 girls receive individual careers guidance with consultants; all girls have free psychometric testing in Year 10 and prepare their own action plan. There is an intensive programme of visiting speakers and workshops.

Games, Options, the Arts: Facilities much improved by the addition of modern new light sports hall with disabled access (lifts), two outdoor netball courts and an Astroturf court. Winners of the U12/U13 netball County Championship for the last three years, and recent Athletic Sports Champions. Plenty of clubs appear to be on offer, but the general consensus is that sport is not hugely high profile. Girls remark, 'if you are very keen on sport, you wouldn't choose this school or would have to follow up with activities outside the school' – disputed by school which considers that they fully support good athletes in their chosen sport.

Parents laud the singing. Policy of music for all, plenty of experimenting with instruments and sound. Drama well taught, housed in a brand new studio. The Art and Design block has a bright, industrious fizz about it. Excellent photography, sculptures, textiles/costumes.

Background and Atmosphere: The original building (the Temple) became part of the GDST schools in 1880. Still central to the site with pillars said to represent inverted cannons. The school has vastly changed in the past few years – the GDST has carried out extensive improvements, refurbishment and contemporary glass additions so that the past dowdiness has been transformed into a bright cluster of buildings. Food most acceptable – although many pupils bring packed lunches.

Pastoral Care and Discipline: Strong pastoral support system with form teachers and sixth form tutors and year heads – set up for easy communication and accessibility. Sixth forms and Year 10 offer a mentoring service for younger girls – this is made easy by the amount of inter-year, inter-house contact through drama, sport competitions and end-of-year entertainment. Imaginative PSHE – we have encountered this in other Trust schools – the special events and whole days given over to topical issues all help to raise awareness and assist pupils with self-expression on current affairs. Parents agree that the school fosters a disciplined, respectful, industrious environment that suits an ambitious, organised, self-motivated pupil. Some believe that within this there is still room for the individual eccentric, others feel that staff are fazed by combative girls. One past pupil told us, 'They often celebrated feisty pupils – but distinctly rebels with a cause and not those without – there was plenty of room for spirited girls but not for those who did not value what the school offers'. Bullying not a problem – the school would take a serious stance and anti-bullying workshops are held.

Pupils and Parents: Principally Brighton with a good percentage coming from surrounding Pulborough, Eastbourne, Worthing, etc. A real social and ethnic mix and, due to competitive fees, a good economic mix. OGs Karen Pickering MBE, Olympic Swimming Gold Medallist, Heidi Cooper, who won the 2004 Young Director of the year (IoD), Beth Cordingley from The Bill, several recent University Challenge competitors. One girl from the school won the Minerva Prize this year – national GDST award for all round excellence and jolly good egg! The Minerva network puts girls in touch with past pupils who are successful in the career in which they are showing an interest.

Entrance: Not as heavily over-subscribed as in the recent past; girls come from a wide range of local maintained and independent schools and also the junior school. GDST entrance assessment for the main school, at junior level there are a range of tests, see children at play and interview them. Entry at sixth form requires five GCSEs at C grade or above with A or B in subjects to be taken at A level.

Exit: Some 20–30 leave at 16+ to enjoy co-ed at the local sixth form college, or because other institutions offer a wider range of subjects; some leave to go to co-ed private education. New head will need to stem this tide. Those who stay are mainly destined for serious universities studying serious subjects, many into medicine, including medical science and veterinary medicine, sports science, natural sciences, earth systems science, geology, zoology, engineering, etc. 37 per cent have taken science degrees. A handful take a gap year.

Money Matters: A healthy bundle of bursaries. Academic scholarships up to 50 per cent of the fees.

Remarks: At its best, a successful and thriving school where girls grow focused and confident in their abilities. New head busy bringing a fresh start.

Brighton College

Linked to Brighton College Prep School in the Junior section

Eastern Rd, Brighton, East Sussex, BN2 0AL

• Pupils: 780; 435 boys, 345 girls; 535 day, 240 board • Ages: 11-18 • Size of sixth form: 300 • C of E • Fees: Day £12,192-£17,958; Boarding £23,778-£27,477 pa • Independent

Tel: 01273 704 200
Fax: 01273 704 204
Email: registrar@brightoncollege.net
Website: www.brightoncollege.net

Headmaster: Since 2006, Mr Richard Cairns, MA (early forties), left Oxford with a first in history; his path to

Brighton led him through a law firm in Australia, a Palestinian refugee camp, Stewart's Melville in Edinburgh, The Oratory in Reading and the deputy headship of Magdalen College School, Oxford. Now he is looking to buy a house in Bordeaux! Not a man to let the grass grow under his feet, he hit national headlines within a week of his arrival when he announced compulsory Mandarin and English literacy lessons for all pupils. Has overseen development of Brighton College's first new outpost – in Abu Dhabi – and the appointment of its new head in late 2010 – to start in September 2011.

A strategic thinker – 'as a head you have to have ideas; will our leavers in 2015 be ready for the world?' – this head has cut the average number of GCSEs taken to 10 and rationalised the school day, so making more time for the extra-curricular activities now explicitly appreciated by universities.

For new parents, a young head is reassuring since they know their child will have efficient consistency throughout their time at school. Mr Cairns is keen to demonstrate his commitment to being an active, visible head through hand-written letters to pupils congratulating or comforting them on achievements or difficulties respectively. He is a passionate yet measured speaker and best one-to-one. At first meeting, he may underplay his effectiveness: 'I took over a school which Anthony Seldon had already transformed. My role is to take it to new heights.'

Refreshingly honest, 'you can do a lot when people don't know you,' Mr Cairns initially concentrated on getting the intake back to the record levels in his predecessor's heyday (applications up over 80 per cent since his appointment), yet keeps in touch with the pupils by teaching history to all Year 9s. 'I will not allow bad teaching in my school. I want every lesson a child attends to be great, so that they leave enthused by what they hear and see and tell their parents about it in the car on the way home.'

He has breakfast with the prefects and invites sixth formers to dinner in his house every Thursday. The pupils love getting to know the head in this way (one of seven children, he certainly knows how to cope with a large dinner table) and relevant issues, ranging from divorce to cricket, often emerge casually.

Academic matters: Great results and they are getting better: 76 per cent A*/A at GCSE; this is up with the best in London too. One of top value-added schools. Since Richard Cairns replaced Anthony Seldon, results have soared from 77 per cent A/B at A level in 2006 to 95 per cent A*–B in 2010 – the best results of any co-educational school in the UK. The *Financial Times* featured it in their list of the top five UK schools for academic progress over the last two years. 26 subjects offered at A level. There is a 60/40 split arts/science at A level; biology (often combined with PE) and maths are particularly popular (the latter taken by about two-thirds of the pupils). About a quarter do four A levels all the way through, and in 2010, 72 per cent of grades were A*/A and 11 pupils got four straight A*s. Advice given to A level students is integral to their choices: there is a year group assembly on careers and outside speakers (John Major, Boris Johnson, Viv Richards, David Dimbleby, David Starkey, Jeremy Paxman ...) visit in a Wednesday afternoon slot. Each department runs both a subject-specific and a general Oxbridge activity which obviously pays off with a goodly number of pupils heading up to Oxford or Cambridge – it's cool to study hard here.

Languages are popular, not just through the Mandarin innovation – compulsory in the pre-prep since September 2007 and now a GCSE option with graduate students from Chinese universities to assist – but also Latin, French, Spanish and Greek. The burgeoning Mandarin option is now confirmed as a USP, with the school being awarded Confucius Institute status by the Chinese Government as a centre of excellence for the teaching of the language – the first such honour for a UK school. The school-wide recommendation of only nine GCSEs encourages a good balance between academic and extra-curricular.

All new pupils attend a literacy class and the dyslexia unit is nationally famous, specifically helping around seven per cent of pupils. English is taught within the centre (instead of timetabled French) for Years 7–11 in groups no larger than seven, individual help available in sixth form. Taking complete control of English makes a huge difference, removes embarrassment and stress. School actively seeks out and welcomes the bright child with dyslexia. Entry based on recent EP report, CE assessment morning (observed in groups) and interviews by head and excellent head of centre. Approximately 160 taught in centre, from all three schools. Group work means that children become fantastically supportive of one another, concentration on remediation with younger ones and study skills with older. Time to finish tasks is not an issue – a good end product motivates students.

The bright but small library is in the main building and is used to provide quiet working space for the sixth form frees. The dedicated sixth form centre also has computers (Hotmail used more often than school addresses!) but is generally more social and noisy. Saturday morning revision classes on offer in the summer, mostly to boost confidence before exams. Class sizes average 18 up to GCSE; after GCSE, the average is eight.

Games, Options, the Arts: Year groups of 135 mean that someone will always be into the same thing as your child. Everyone has to do dance, PE and drama. House drama, house song and up to 15 different productions a year (including visiting companies, A level and GCSE performances and Commedia dell'Arte). Dance boasts 100 per cent A at A level and A/A* at GCSE in a state-of-the-art performing arts studio (outside classes offered to the community) and the Montague studio is five minutes' walk away.

The new arts building can only improve an impressively productive performing arts department – 142 options including sudoku and street jazz – documented in what looks like a glossy festival programme! Half the pupils have one individual music lesson per week, and there's a choir, orchestra, concert band and various chamber groups, with participation in the National Chamber Music Competition as well as tours to Prague and Moscow.

Sport is enormously important here, with most pupils taking part in games twice a week and, when we visited, 14 girls and boys playing for England in a variety of sports. Cricket, rugby, athletics, soccer and netball (seven out of eight county titles in 2007) are popular, and pupils sail at a local reservoir. Girls' cricket is conspicuously strong and coached by Clare Connor, former captain of the England Women's cricket team and ex-pupil, housemistress, head of PR and English teacher. Sussex captain, Chris Adams, is also on the staff. Squash courts, rounders, cricket, swimming-pool and rugby on campus and four more rugby pitches, three hockey Astroturfs in the extra sports field 15 minutes' walk away.

Community service is a vital part of school life – pupils visit elderly people and help disabled children, raise money for charity; some have visited a Romanian orphanage and there's a new link with a school near Nairobi for gappers.

Background and Atmosphere: Compact campus in Kemp Town, just four blocks from the sea front. Imposing buildings purpose-built in 1840s by Gilbert Scott (designer of St Pancras Station and the Albert Memorial). The entrance halls, visitors' room and headmaster's office all give an impression of being part of a comfortable stately home. The plain and functional atmosphere of some of the boarding houses was transformed in 2008 with a £1 million refurbishment which is drawing in new boarders. Boarding numbers are at their highest for 50 years. The school is now mid-way through an ambitious £23m building programme.

Sited in the heart of the campest area of 'London by the sea', the school succeeds in being fashionable, practical and innovative – the lack of Saturday morning school means that everyone can have a full weekend and the chance to be part of the town instead of just being educated within it. This can put some parents off, since Brighton, like many seaside towns, has its fair share of drug addicts, drunks and loons. Most sensible local parents realise that their children are going to come to Brighton at the weekend anyway, and it is far better that they feel comfortable in their favourite cafés, bars and shops rather than loitering round Churchill Square ...

There is a good social mix here and the pupils are aware that they are privileged. The sixth form wear smart business-like clothes with some restrictions that are flouted when girls fancy tottering on high heels. They can drive themselves into school but must use street parking – new council charges are unpopular. The whole school benefits from a good sense of the outside world, whether it is through exchanges with schools in Russia, Africa, America and Australia, the perspective offered by pupils from an inner-city school, or the opportunity to twist their tongues round a year's worth of Mandarin Chinese. A link with Kingsford Community School in Newham, East London, began with the heads' discovery that they shared a desire to make Mandarin mandatory, and has grown into an HSBC sponsorship of three Newham pupils' education in Brighton for a year.

The chapel, just big enough for the whole school, is used three or four times a week for secular and multi-faith assemblies as well as Christian ones. Tradition still holds firm here (the oldest co-educational public school in Sussex) with the heads of school taking it in turns to sit alone in a pew, yet the chaplain is entertaining and eccentric ('He has to be to keep us interested – he got one of the first XV to rugby-tackle him in front of the altar to illustrate a topic!').

Subsidised teacher accommodation and the attractions of Brighton mean that many of the staff are young, motivated and just as excited as being at this school as the sixth formers.

Pastoral Care and Discipline: As the head comments, this is 'a town school that is part of the real world, not apart from it'. At the beginning of every term he reiterates the ground rules on theft, bullying and beyond: expulsion and no second chances is the line on drugs and the security at the school gates is tight, yet cheery.

Ten pupils to a tutor, 11 houses, two boys' boarding and one girls'; five boys' day and three girls'. Pastoral side has been developed recently with three separate section heads, two new houses and fourth boarding house recently completed. The head of the lower school and the headmaster meet every single registered pupil in their own school before they enter Brighton College. This reduces the fear about attending a new school and gives the pastoral staff a heads-up on what house and friendship group might suit a newbie. There is also a brand new health centre and counselling on-site.

Two options at meals and dishes containing wheat and peanuts are labelled. Food is also available in the Café de Paris – below the drama studio.

Pupils and Parents: A great social mix from the children of butchers to highbrow TV presenters and a smattering of Conservative MPs; 24 per cent boarding, most weekly but seven per cent overseas (five per cent Asian). No Saturday school (weekly boarders can leave Friday 4pm, return Monday am) is popular with parents. School buses from Lindfield, Wivelsfield, Worthing, Angmering, Eastbourne, Horsham, Uckfield and Pulborough. Pupils are generally cheerful, enthusiastic, friendly and polite and have an easy, relaxed relationship with teachers.

Entrance: Around 30 pupils come all the way through from the pre-prep, another 35 or so from the prep. 70 more from other preps including St Christopher's Hove (now run by Brighton College). Now adding extra capacity at 11 in the newly-built lower school to cope with those who lose out in the Brighton state school ballots. Entry at 13, by CE if they come from a prep school; if not, after an assessment. Children who achieve 55 (used to be 50) per cent at CE are accepted, especially if they excel at music, sport or another activity. Around 70 new pupils at sixth form mostly from Burgess Hill, Brighton and Hove High School, Eastbourne, Hurst and Lancing. Placed first nationally in league tables amongst co-educational schools, inclusive not exclusive.

Exit: A handful after GCSEs to local sixth form colleges, almost always for financial reasons. 100 per cent to university – 96 per cent to first or second choice. Around 16 per year to Oxford and Cambridge (15 in 2010). Famous Old Brightonians including Peter Mayle (writer), Lord Alexander of Weedon (lawyer and banker), Lord Skidelsky (historian and politician), David Nash (sculptor), Sir Michael Hordern (actor) and Jonathan Palmer (racing driver) testify to range of successful careers which may ensue.

Money Matters: At a recent open morning, parents were wondering about what extras Brighton College might offer to justify its fees being higher than rival local schools' despite its limited campus space – half an hour later they were totally sold, having been treated to a Commedia dell'Arte take on the drama, a booty wiggling synchronised dance by nine teenage girls and the heads of schools speaking about the high quality lessons. Many parents struggle to pay the fees but bursaries and up to 20 academic awards (5–50 per cent off basic fees), one big music scholarship (up to 50 per cent off), art, drama, dance, sport and all-rounder awards (up to 25 per cent off) and a DT scholarship (up to 15 per cent off) are available at 13+. Extras include £195 per term per musical instrument, £45 per night occasional boarding, £65 for weekly boarders remaining over the weekend and £545 per term for the use of the dyslexia support centre.

Remarks: Happy and forward-looking town school with a wide and healthy spread of pupils and parents. Essentially a day school with boarders but the balance is shifting (boarding numbers are at their highest since 1931, with a new girls' boarding house opened in September 2009). Bright, energetic, robust pupils who like to keep busy will thrive here. The shy and retiring will be coaxed or tempted out of themselves by the energetic staff and/or the staggering range of opportunities. A good bet to become an even more impressive school in the future.

Bristol Grammar School

Linked to BGS Infant And Juniors in the Junior section

University Road, Bristol, BS8 1SR

• Pupils: 920 pupils: 365 girls, 555 boys; all day • Ages: 11-18 • Size of sixth form: 295; (130 girls, 165 boys) • Non-denom • Fees: £10,590 pa • Independent

Tel: 0117 973 6006
Fax: 0117 946 7485
Email: recruitment@bgs.bristol.sch.uk
Website: www.bristolgrammarschool.co.uk

Head: Since 2008, Mr Roderick Mackinnon BSc PGCE (early fifties). Educated at Aylesbury Grammar School before reading engineering at Leicester. From university followed father into army – commissioned into Royal Artillery and promoted to Captain. Returned to Leicester for PGCE, then to teach science at The Minster School, Southwell. Head of physics at Tiffin Girls', then deputy head at Colchester Royal Grammar School for four years before promotion to headship of Bexley Grammar School, where he remained for 13 successful years. Somewhat reserved initially but is actually warm and personable with an infectious passion to educate. Believes that 'a rising tide carries all boats' and that school's role is to enable effective learning. No children from former marriage but 'wonderful father figure' around school, say colleagues. Parents say that he is 'prominent' and 'a breath of fresh air'. Listens to parents' and pupils' views and is now starting to initiate change. 'Will go out of his way to give individual pupils a few words of praise when they do well,' said one admiring mother. Realistic about pressure as a head – limits himself to teaching learning skills and is out of school as little as possible. Hit headlines when he took IGCSE into Bexley GS – adding to debate over standards at key stage four. Needed little persuasion to move to BGS where he has more academic freedom and looks set to up the tempo. A lover of history, country walks and classical music.

Academic matters: Impressive A level results and high value-added with 60 per cent A*/A grades (97 per cent in A*–C range) – impressive given the large numbers involved. At GCSE, 69 per cent of entries at A*/A. Parents choose BGS because it is 'serious about standards,' said one father. Head is moving candidates into IGCSE: first came maths (80 per cent of first cohort in 2008 achieved A*/A with four in top ten nationally). English IGCSE introduced 2010 with sciences and history now following – will stretch students better though head insists that school is 'not an academic hothouse'. School aims at quality rather than quantity in terms of entries and doesn't express groups. 30 further mathematicians and impressive performances in maths Olympiad and UKMT junior maths challenge in 2009. EPQ now introduced for the sixth form. Parental opinions on teaching standards vary: general satisfaction and one parent described her daughter's teachers as 'inspirational'; criticism though of weaknesses amongst some of the 'old guard'. We sat in on an A level English lesson in which inspired teaching steered the discussion to undergraduate standard.

Full curriculum in Years 7 and 8 includes Latin for all; Greek and Russian appear as options in Year 9; 26 subjects currently studied in sixth form to A2 level. Successful DT department now extended to food and textiles; super work in product and graphic design witnessed by impressive displays. Pupils set own (mainly high) targets for themselves in this and other subjects. Year/subject bases fringe open areas; lower school pupils share same site at present – not ideal, we thought, though little ones seemed unfazed and get to use a range of senior school facilities. Expect homework from the outset here – properly monitored and marked; builds up to three subjects per night plus GCSE coursework by Year 10. Internal exams for Years 7–10 in summer term used for assessment purposes. Selective nature of school does not preclude some SpLD needs and school has SENCo to co-ordinate support for SpLD mainly in junior years. Scholars' programme main stimulus for 100+ gifted and talented pupils, but general diet is rich and varied.

Games, Options, the Arts: Excellent sports facilities include Failand complex (a 20-minute minibus ride away): two floodlit Astroturfs, a vast expanse of pitches, low ropes (assault) course in woods plus wow factor £2m sports pavilion which outdoes any other Bristol school and accommodates up to 350 players, with super changing and recreational facilities. Large-scale participation on Saturdays in inter-school competitions as well as on weekly games day. Heavily-used modern facility on site includes super glass-back squash courts, a dauntingly vast climbing wall (professional outside staff lead this activity) and full size sports hall. Graveney (an old boy) Room is the dance studio, also used for judo and other activities. Cricket pros come in for net practice, fitness suite heavily used by older students and effective use made of salle for fencing (school has specialised in this sport for many years). We watched mixed junior PE class – lots of fun with young, energetic staff. Sports studies now an option at A level and GCSE and Dance, DT:Food and Textiles also being added although academic choices predominate. Outstanding girl athlete has reached international level, current independent schools' judo champion, national fencers and plenty of representative team players in variety of sports.

Large numbers doing art (65 GCSE candidates in 2010) so quirky new base on Elton Road bursts at seams (being extended at time of our visit to give same space for AS students as provided for A2 candidates) – high quality work on display here and around school but no separate gallery as yet.Head of art (previously at Dulwich College) places emphasis on 'giving pupils their creative voice'; lots of print-making and timely expansion of digital art.

Next door we found a vibrant music department (apart from 'vanishing violinists') with all you would expect from a large school: main orchestra with lots of offshoots in terms of ensembles, jazz band, woodwind, brass groups and 20 main concerts/competitions during the year. 'My daughter has taken up the sax and loves it,' glowed one mother. In addition to individual lessons, pupils in Years 7–9 have two class-based music lessons per week; option choices for GCSE (much use made of Sibelius software and Macs for composition at this level) and beyond. School rents one of Bristol's premier venues (St George's) for annual concert where works like Schubert's Unfinished get the full BGS treatment.

Drama is high profile with 10 students a year taking A level – Mackay Theatre (opened by no less a person than Sam Wanamaker) provides professional-standard studio space with enough fold-away seating for most productions plus pro-tandard sound and lighting; house plays each year and full scale musical biennially. HoD also manages 'stage crew', which takes all-comers to work behind the scenes. Major sixth form drama at end of winter term (recently Michael Frayn's *Noises Off* was very successful) and lively outside pantomime in summer term performed by Years 7–9 in amphitheatre. Fringe Society performs at Edinburgh Festival. Head keen to put new performing arts centre at top of his wish list.

D of E and Ten Tors get loyal following. Leadership a big thing here with co-ordinated visits; leadership diploma in the offing; recent expeditions include Peru, the Arctic and Morocco: sparked great interest in supporting education for girls there (over £20K raised in four years to build girls' hostel). Activities programme one afternoon per week in Years 7–11; lunchtime and after-school clubs include mentoring, debating, textiles, chess and a whole lot more.

Background and Atmosphere: School founded in 1532 by the Thorne brothers – Bristol merchants made good. School motto: 'ex spinis uvas' ('from thorns to grapes') makes a play on their name. Other benefactors (some of whom linked to Bristol's slavery-based prosperity) have been downgraded – witness re-naming of newly opened Thorne entrance after effective lobbying by school council (meets six times a year and exerts a real influence) against school's now blackballed choice of Tyndall.

BGS is shoe-horned into site it has occupied since mid-nineteenth century. Disparate collection of buildings covers whole gamut of architectural styles (trademark Pennant stone with Bath stone edges much in evidence); unexpectedly peaceful despite central Bristol location. Modernised science wing, new classrooms for art and music, and modernisation of music practice rooms are all recent developments. Impressive (now double-ended) glass entrance doors lead into central Victorian building with stairs sweeping up to what must be one of the grandest school halls ('Great Hall') in the land. Full school assembly a weekly tour de force: former headmasters stare down from gilded frames on panelled walls, whilst current one speaks from rostrum flanked by senior staff and pupils. Unexpectedly intimate style in assemblies given grand setting – a real sense of a family gathering, we felt. School (all wear daffodils) goes en masse annually to cathedral for Charter Day service and singing of school song in Latin. Successful allocation of outdoor spaces for different age groups – includes one sitting out area with skylights over DT department below: a most successfully-designed area opened in 1994. Ownership of six adjacent Victorian villas in Elton Road provides a variety of characterful outposts for modern languages, music and art. Lots of long service medals amongst staff – more than most day schools.

School is ICT savvy: plasma screens keep everyone up-to-date with events and diary; 11 suites of pcs dotted around site and smart boards are used to good effect – we watched enthusiastic Year 9 Russian class learning vocabulary with a difference via the smartboard; Russian word lists constantly changing on the screen prompted enthusiastic pupil participation. Four laboratories per subject in science – all high spec. School library is best we've seen in south west – open until 6.00pm, it clocks nearly 500 pupils a day through its turnstile; hub of BGS literary activity. Recent outside speakers have included Michelle Paver, Jeremy Strong, Michael Wood, Frances Kay and Michael Morpurgo.

Pastoral Care and Discipline: Boys still outnumber girls but the latter thrive here too from what we observed. 'Phlegmatic boys helped my daughter cope better with stresses of exams,' explained one mother, who thought single sex would not have been helpful. Kind introduction to senior school life provided in induction programme. Head of Year 7 visits every feeder school; pupils have taster day in summer term prior to entry.

Well turned out collectively – 'Individualism shines through ideas,' says head, who praises their world awareness and consideration. Pupils 'love their house fleeces enough to go to the local shops in them,' said one teacher. Parents get email contact with all staff – works well, say parents. Pupils placed in one of six colour houses (named after their heads) which operate form-wise for Years 9–11. Well established peer mentoring system which works well and has reduced teasing. Staff use restorative justice to good effect and school is short on petty rules. Pupils are happy and girls especially 'make friends quickly,' said Year 7 mothers. Overlap between heads of houses (still all male, we noticed) and year heads works to pupils' advantage with lots of co-ordination over pastoral concerns and academic needs. 'Misconception is that BGS is too big, but family atmosphere of the house system addresses that,' we were told. No overall house championship.

Sixth form has own centre which successfully combines a social area (café open until 2.00pm daily) with facilities for private study; 30 tutorial groups of 10–12 students; experienced head of careers on hand to guide as necessary. BGS prides itself on its small-scale approach through its house system within context of a big school, and parents like way any problem is sorted out quickly.

Lunch gets rolled out in the university refectory adjacent to the school – works well, given the numbers and choice/standard seemed fine; breakfast club operates daily for pupils and parents before school; pupils generally use topped up smartcards to pay for meals. Great careers suite; world of work day in Year 9 and user-friendly approach to resources backed by full-time head of careers to guide and encourage: 'Follow your passion,' she urges sixth formers.

Pupils and Parents: Broad profile in terms of ethnicity, majority from professional background including high number of academics. Parents' evenings 'reflect how teachers really know pupils' and lots of social events throughout year (head cut an impressive dash with Tanya Perera on dance floor at a recent bash). Strong alumni association and former pupils include Lord Franks, Nobel laureate Sir John Pople and Rabinder Singh QC.

Entrance: Applications accepted at any stage for entry to all years except 11 and 13. January entrance examination principally for main entry (135 pupils) at 11+. Half annual entry comes from BGS lower school and remaining 60 or so places from up to 30 primary schools across city and beyond. Combination of multiple choice verbal and non-verbal reasoning tests plus papers in English. Acceptance on basis of performance on tests, confidential report and predicted grades. Some candidates called for interview with head – either to determine suitability or to assess for scholar's programme. Interview evening for sixth form applicants according to proposed A level choices. Offers conditional on GCSE results.

Exit: A few may slope off to state alternatives after Year 11 (some for financial reasons) but loyal majority proceeds to sixth form. Virtually all to 50+ universities (many to Russell group) and 12 last year to Oxbridge. Economic/business studies, English, philosophy, medicine and engineering amongst favourite areas for higher education.

Money Matters: Not a hugely wealthy school, but has come through the post-assisted places era well and is able to give bursaries to 10 per cent of pupils. More may be on table soon. Also 15 scholarships, each worth 25 per cent of fees, for Year 7 entry from 2011 with 13 awarded on academic merit, one for sports and one for performing and creative arts. In addition, scholarships are awarded for entry into Year 9 in September 2011, each worth 25 per cent of fees. Four will be awarded on academic merit, one for sport and one for performing and creative arts.

Remarks: Proximity to university creates a useful sense of 'an educational continuum', commented some parents. A school where care is 'profound rather than superficial' – something we picked up from all those we consulted – and where 'it's cool to be bright'.

BRIT School for Performing Arts and Technology

60 The Crescent, Croydon, Surrey, CR0 2HN

• Pupils: 900, roughly two-thirds girls; all day • Ages: 14-19
• Size of sixth form: 650 • Non-denom • State

Tel: 020 8665 5242
Fax: 020 8665 8676
Email: admin@brit.croydon.sch.uk
Website: www.brit.croydon.sch.uk

Principal: Since 2002, Mr Nick Williams (fifties), previously head of Thomas Tallis Comprehensive School in Blackheath. A neat, engaging, silver-haired man, he teaches English and has overseen a steady rise in exam results across the board. 'But we haven't sacrificed creative vision for academic standards – one has fed on the other. It's a virtuous circle of confidence.' Although this school is all about nurturing talent, he is passionately inclusive, keen to give a chance to those who have failed to thrive elsewhere.

Academic matters: The only state-funded specialist performing arts college in the country – students here are aiming to tread the boards in the West End or headline at the Reading Festival rather than study classics at Cambridge. Nonetheless, the emphasis on performance goes hand in hand with a strict academic regime. All the Year 10–11s take a BTec first diploma in their chosen arts strand, which could be a performing arts subject, broadcast and digital communication, or visual arts and design, and which counts as four A*–C grades at GCSE. In 2010, an impressive 80 per cent got distinction (including 61 per cent with a starred distinction) and 13 per cent merit.

They also take GCSEs in the core academic subjects and optional subjects that include modern languages, sociology and history plus, as one would expect, art, dance, drama, media studies and music. A commendable showing, with 97 per cent of students getting at least five A*–C grades in 2010, though this does drop to 65 per cent with maths and English included. Maths is undoubtedly the weaker of the two but money and effort are going into improving performance with 68 per cent of pupils getting an A*–C maths grade in 2010. 'Our aim has been to make sure that the academic and the artistic sides work well together – and we've achieved that. But we never accept that it is good enough.'

Sixth formers take a BTec national diploma in their chosen arts strand, equivalent to three A levels. Musical theatre, theatre and dance are particularly popular and extremely successful. The distinction rate overall was 85 per cent per cent in 2010, with virtually all the rest getting merit. Many also take one or two A levels, in subjects such as English literature and media studies, mostly gaining B or C grades, or additional vocational qualifications. One student in 2010 got three distinctions for her national diploma and two A grades at A level, whilst another got three distinctions and an A*.

Quite a few of the staff have come from the performance industry rather than from a teaching background and do a graduate teacher programme on the job. Ofsted commented that the teaching is 'outstanding' and that 'students make impressive progress'.

Lessons make the most of students' interests, with a history class role-playing a debate on the League of Nations while a maths class works on the economics of putting on a show. 'They're really strict about written work,' said a student. 'If you haven't finished it you're not allowed into rehearsals or out to events.' Students from different strands work together on cross-curricular projects, e.g. a dance created round art installations.

Some stay on to do a Year 14 arts management course, which involves projects such as setting up a theatre company or organising the BRIT Idol competition, with a record industry panel choosing the top musicians in the college. This is a useful year for building up skills, making industry contacts and gaining extended work experience.

Students with special needs – varying from dyslexia and dyspraxia to autism and Asperger's and even blindness – are welcomed and well supported. 'We never turn students away on the grounds of special needs as long as they have an aptitude within their chosen arts area. We take people whose salvation is that they can dance or act.' The top floor learning support room with comfy sofas is open to all – 'It's a really good place to go if you get stuck,' said a student.

Careers advice – which can include avoiding dodgy contracts as much as honing one's audition skills – is a vital part of the process. 'We have a great progression team. Because of the way we work with industry, most students will have had plenty of work experience and had talks from industry practitioners. We have the contacts, which helps to be able to point people in the right direction.'

Despite the creative industries' reputation for exclusivity, the head believes that these are some of the most important growth areas. 'Our students know what it takes to succeed and they know how to market themselves. We're not interested in setting people up to fail. One of our jobs is to provide knowledge of other routes if acting, for example, doesn't work out. Students need to be flexible and resilient.'

Games, Options, the Arts: Students here do play football/basketball, use the multigym, go canoing, even take a PE GCSE, but it is fair to say that sports are a peripheral activity – the focus of attention is acting, singing, dancing, art and music-making. The star-studded list of alumni bears witness to an environment that enhances creativity as it hones technical skills. A group of music students sits strumming guitars on the floor in the reception area, which is lined with pictures of the BRIT Awards ceremony. Dancers limber up on the mezzanine gallery. The school day stretches to include extra-curricular dance classes, music lessons and rehearsals.

Large amounts of community work – 'Our programme is the biggest of any school in the country'. This includes taking shows into primary schools, prisons and hospices, as well as the Edinburgh Festival. For the second year running, the head bravely packed his wellies to accompany a group of students to Glastonbury 2008, where music students performed programmes based around HIV and Aids awareness on the Left Field stage, with film and technical theatre students as roadies – 'We like to bite off more than we can chew'.

Background and Atmosphere: The school was founded in 1991, funded by the government and the British Record Industry Trust (BRIT). This enables it to pay for state-of-the-art equipment in its radio and TV studios, music rooms, 350-seat theatre, costume and props departments. The main building, purpose-built in concrete, glass and steel, looks as incongruous amidst the shabby backstreets of Croydon as the streams of exuberant students who make their way from the station every morning. In the next door redbrick, stone-floored, ex-grammar school, 'more academic building', as a student put it, national curriculum subjects are taught alongside musical theatre and theatre. The large theatre space, full of intricate lighting and sound equipment, is the emotional centre of the school – 'Everyone wants to spend their time here'.

A huge sense of engagement, with students immersed in developing dance moves, rehearsing a musical theatre scene, preparing a radio show for the annual BRIT FM summer broadcast. 'It's about giving them a sense of ownership,' said a media teacher. 'I teach them the technical stuff but they generate the content.'

The school foyer can, as one journalist put it, seem like 'a cross between the green room at the London Palladium and a junior fashion show'. But students are grounded as well as exuberant, willing – nay, eager – to spend hours developing their skills.

Pastoral Care and Discipline: Many students who were square pegs in round holes at their previous schools find salvation here, including some from pupil referral units – 'though we would be wary of violent offenders'. Exclusions are almost unheard of, the drop-out rate tiny. Shared interests are more important than racial or social differences. Students are given increasing amounts of responsibility, expected to rehearse without supervision, organise shows, work together as a team. 'It's about professionalism,' said a student. 'You have to get along, or you'd never get anything done.'

Runs five eight-week terms with two week holidays – four in the summer. Older students often expected to stay till 6 or 7pm, but no complaints – 'It's more difficult to get them to go home'.

Pupils and Parents: Virtually all come from state secondary schools. Many travel long distances, rising before dawn to take trains and buses across London. Confident, showy, articulate teenagers with something of a local reputation for cockiness – but that could be envy. Alumni include Amy Winehouse, Kate Nash, Katie Melua, Leona Lewis, Adele, The Kooks, The Feeling, Lynden, David Hall, Wayne Williams and numerous other singers, actors, dancers and DJs.

Entrance: The catchment area is more-or-less all of Greater London plus some of Kent and Surrey. Some sixth formers from further afield lodge in Croydon during the week. Around three applicants for every place. No academic baseline, though in fact most entrants are above average achievers – students are selected for their aptitude and commitment within their chosen specialism. Takes 140 into Year 10 and around 200 new students into Year 12.

Applicants must explain on their application form why they are applying for their chosen strand and what they hope to achieve by attending the BRIT. Those with special needs can submit the application as a tape or use a scribe. Most applicants are invited for audition. 'We're looking for potential and we're trying to favour those who haven't necessarily had the opportunities already. If you're keen, enthusiastic and show aptitude, you'll stand a good chance of getting in.' Everyone invited for audition can have another go if they don't get offered a place the first time – 'We're very inclusive and very keen to give people a chance'.

Exit: Around 90 per cent of Year 11 students go through to the sixth form. Half of the sixth form generally moves on to higher education: Kingston University, Central School of Speech and Drama, London College of Fashion, Rambert Dance School, RADA, Bournemouth University et al. Others go straight to jobs in creative industries or stay on for the Year 14 arts management course, which acts as a bridge to work, further study or training.

Money Matters: Tuition is free but charges for extra dance and music lessons and some school trips. Sixth formers are asked to pay £40 and may have to provide their own specialist equipment, e.g. musical instrument. Some discretionary grants for travel and peripatetic lessons.

Remarks: For a teenager with talent and commitment who is definite about wanting a career in the world of the arts, entertainment or communication, there can be few better foundations. Provides outstanding academic and creative teaching – and the students are obviously having a wonderful time.

Brockwood Park School

Bramdean, Alresford, Hampshire, SO24 0LQ

• Pupils: 65 • Ages: 14-19 • Size of sixth form: 20 • Non denom, enquiry about all aspects of life encouraged. • Fees: £15,700 pa • Independent

Tel: 01962 771 744
Fax: 01962 771 875
Email: enquiry@brockwood.org.uk
Website: www.brockwood.org.uk

Co-principals: Since 1998, Mr Bill Taylor and, since 2006, Mr Adrian Sydenham, both in their fifties. Mr Taylor came to Brockwood in 1983 as a mature student and then member of staff. He returned to his native New Zealand five years later to earn a degree in English literature and language at Waikato University before resettling at Brockwood for the long haul. He is married to a former Brockwood teacher, Leila, and they have one grown daughter. Mr Sydenham has taught psychology at Brockwood for 10 years and holds Masters degrees in modern languages, environmental planning and international criminal justice. Why two principals? 'We'd like to avoid the notion of the Heroic Head,' says Bill. They both, in common with all residential staff, are committed to the teachings of Jiddu Krishnamurti, inspirational writer and speaker on philosophical and spiritual subjects.

Academic matters: Exams 'are not our main thrust', says 'Bill', with understatement, 'but are seen in perspective alongside things like yoga, working in the garden, and care of rooms' (all compulsory). No GCSEs. The school uses Cambridge International Exams for A levels and mixed results are achieved (hard to draw out any trends from such a tiny number of students). Some retakes taken at local sixth form college and many pupils will be returning to their home countries for higher education so British exams not the be all and end all. No fixed academic timetables into which pupils must slot – each programme is created afresh for each child with plenty of scope to concentrate on a single passion. An 18-year-old musician we met had secured two free days a week to spend on intensive piano work. Another had dropped all academic subjects to study only art, yoga and pottery. Others were focused on more traditional subjects.

No pressure; no punishments if homework is not done; lots of one-on-one teaching. SEN support offered on individual basis – one weekly session is covered by the fees, further help is charged for. ESL for newcomers. Computers discouraged but permitted. 'K Class' compulsory once a week to study Krishnamurti, held in soothing white-carpeted room with scatter cushions. Lots of sitting on floors here. 'Inquiry time', when the whole school gets together to discuss a theme – e.g. why are we vegetarians?; why do we value silence? – a core part of education. Staff comprised of renaissance men and women, most teaching two or three subjects at any given time. So, some teaching inspired, while some a bit patchy 'and teachers can suddenly head off on sabbatical or stop offering a subject,' said a parent. Non-residential specialist teachers are brought in to fill gaps.

Games, Options, the Arts: Health and fitness, yes. Games, no. Some sort of exercise is scheduled twice a week (there is a gym with fitness equipment). Not keen on competition. No prizes. Have been known to play football against another school, but never in anger. Music inspiring and given space to flourish, with two concerts a year and a variety of instrumental lessons offered. 'It's not about excelling,' a teacher told us, 'It's about a feeling of enjoyment'. Five pianos, a drum kit and a recording studio on hand – pupils can record their own albums. Art barn, designed by Keith Critchlow in the Arts and Crafts Cottage style, is the fine art centre. Dance, drama , photography, pottery – all the arts – are thriving.

Background and Atmosphere: Founded by Krishnamurti in 1969 with a gift of £40,000. This was meant to be his retirement fund; instead he bought Brockwood Park and 40 acres of inspiring, serene grounds within South Downs National Park. The school still has the same gentle feel he would have liked, with the main building housing admin, classrooms and girls' dorms. Beautiful octagonal assembly hall used for silent meditation before breakfast, whole school meetings (twice a week) and concerts. A huge rambling and impressive library with interesting selection of books e.g. on alternative medicine. Boys' rooms, 'the Cloisters', surrounding small pond – exceptionally nice, like a boutique hotel (though boys speak of noise reverberating through the thin partition walls and single glazing).

Originally set up to be international, fully boarding (no day pupils, and pupils may stay over half terms) and small – and has remained so to this day ... 'but we could get a bit larger,' says Bill. Has softened its early ascetic, socialistic ethos, when staff were discouraged from having children of their own. Yet remains curiously spartan. No TV 'except news and football' on one aged set 'that receives three channels!' No cleaning or kitchen staff. All members of the community, including teachers, do their own laundry and help clean/clear tables/wash up meals. Kitchen fully vegetarian and mainly organic. Smaller 'eco-kitchen' available to the students. Garden and greenhouses lovingly tended by all, produces everything from pumpkins to watermelons – all eaten at the school. Seeds are gathered for the following year. 20 chickens provide eggs. Care for the environment a priority and recycling has been given its own room. Roughly 10 'mature students' (early 20s) an important cog in the Brockwood wheel. They do the cooking and some other work within the community in exchange for room, board and the opportunity to study and bask in Brockwoodian tranquillity.

Pastoral Care and Discipline: No school rules. Instead pupils and parents sign an 'open letter' – a group of agreements including meat-free diet, attending morning meeting, staying in rooms after 10pm and no smoking, booze or drugs. No automatic punishments for anything – everything open for discussion. 'Fear is a destructive force in education. Take away fear and authority and pupils can be creative, willing to try things. It's important to discover what they love to do,' says Bill. Relationships, getting along in a community, solving problems are key. Drinking a big no-no, whatever a pupil's age: this may be the first school we have visited where drinking and smoking are highly uncool. All that said, the school does have to expel the odd pupil, for the usual reasons. And there can be tension between providing structure for younger pupils and freedom for the 18 and 19 year olds. Some 30 members of staff, plus the mature students, live on the campus and students work and live alongside them – the school's greatest strength, or a weakness, depending on how you look at it. Telephone numbers of school's 'independent listener' and of Childline prominently displayed around the school.

Pupils and Parents: International. 12 out of 66 from the UK – none local. Others Spanish French, German, Dutch, Danish, and then from literally everywhere. Everyone looks quite normal – not much inclined to purple hair or facial piercings – and is impressively verbal, eloquent and soft spoken. Most pupils come from families with an interest in Krishnamurti. Others find it on the web (key words vegetarian, holistic or alternative). Some parents consider Brockwood Park alongside other alternative schools e.g. Bedales, Frensham Heights, St Christopher's, the Steiners esp Michael Hall, Summerhill (A S Neill got some of his educational ideas from Krishnamurti). A few come from Inwoods, the 'small school' within Brockwood Park grounds educating 30 children age four – 11 (started as a school for staff children). School estimates that around 1400 men and women have now been educated at Brockwood Park and is keen to involve them more in the school through workshops, fund-raising etc.

Entrance: Same process for prospective pupils and for staff – a trial week followed by a meeting of the school community to share impressions of the visitor. Up to a third of applicants are turned away. Maturity is the essential qualification according to the pupils – 'we won't take someone who ruins the community'. Despite the school's unorthodox ethos, it is most definitely not a magnet for alienated teenagers. 'We're low profile,' says Bill, 'and don't want to be a sink school for problem kids.'

Exit: Students leave equipped for life, though not necessarily for higher education in the UK. However, most students will go to university, either straight away or eventually – frequently overseas, especially the USA.

Money Matters: Fees kept low. All residential staff are paid the same (frugal) salary so are, in effect, subsidising the running of the school. One third of pupils receive some level of bursary. Working on plans and funding to build seven new 'boarding pavilions' and a sports hall/theatre. All will have a self-build element and be 'as green as possible'.

Remarks: Uplifting and unique school with the modest aim of completely transforming consciousness and creating a new human being. 'The bar is set high', said one member of staff. 'Feels a bit like an academic retreat,' said a student trying to sum up the school's ethos. Or a kibbutz. The sort of school that changes lives. Intellectual curiosity will flourish here – but exam results may be elusive.

Bromley High School (GDST)

Linked to Bromley High School (GDST) Junior Department in the Junior section

Blackbrook Lane, Bickley, Bromley, Kent, BR1 2TW

- Pupils: Approx 900 girls, including 310 in junior school • Ages: 4-18
- Size of sixth form: 125 • Christian, non-denom • Fees: £12,018 pa
- Independent

Tel: 020 8781 7000
Fax: 020 8781 7002
Email: admissions@bro.gdst.net
Website: www.bhs@bro.gdst.net

Head: Since January 2010, Mrs Louise Simpson (early forties) BSc, PGCE, married with one daughter, educated in Wales and Ireland. She has had an exciting career in teaching at Ratcliffe College & Gresham's then as head of biology at King's Rochester and deputy head at Brighton College. Having worked with Richard Cairns and Anthony Seldon she should bring some dynamic education management skills to Bromley. Ms Simpson is ambitious and keen to build on everything she has inherited from the previous, head Lorna Duggleby. She hopes to utilise some of the unused spaces around the school and generally make Bromley High more welcoming and user-friendly. She has already established a new community service programme to help the school integrate with the local community.

Academic matters: Academic results consistently high – 94 per cent A*/B at GCSE and 87 per cent A*/B at A level. Science and modern foreign languages remain particularly strong and a number of girls go on to study these at top universities. Modern foreign languages department has links with France, Germany and Spain and arranges much better than average exchanges, visits and work experience placements. All subject areas have dedicated heads of department who ensure high standards and excellent results. Parents say the teaching is solid and fairly traditional, maths teaching is especially impressive and it is a top subject choice in the sixth form. The head and her senior management team work extremely hard to make sure that the curriculum is really flexible so girls can have as much choice possible in all the age groups and fit in extra GCSE subjects if they want. Smart modern classrooms and sparkling labs inspire the girls to work hard and care for their environment. All pupils have a personal tutor who tracks their progress and sets targets with them for their academic and personal development on a regular basis. Well stocked library looking out onto woodland provides an inspiring place to work before and after school. Two part-time SENCos provide additional support on a one-to-one basis for pupils with specific learning differences and run study skills programmes for all pupils. EAL is available as required.

Games, Options, the Arts: Great opportunities for the sportswoman here, acres of space, athletics track, three hockey pitches, including an Astroturf which can be hired by local clubs. Pupils frequently win awards at national, county and borough level across athletics, gymnastics, hockey and netball, tennis and swimming. Ms Simpson was once a national level rower herself. A number of specialist coaches are employed to enhance sporting opportunities via school clubs. Indoor swimming pool and gym which is made available to staff and families out of school hours. Duke of Edinburgh scheme and annual world challenge expeditions both flourishing, along with international cultural exchanges to Asia and China for sixth formers.

Performing arts and dance studios recently updated to create an incredibly clever and versatile performance space. Regular in-house drama and music festivals and pupils achieve distinctions in LAMDA and ABRSM exams including musical theatre. Music department to be enjoyed, producing a lovely range of concerts; everyone is encouraged to learn an instrument or join a choir. International tours for the various choirs and orchestras and there is a yearly middle school music tour to Paris. Art work is of a very high standard, some talented GCSE students do really well, textiles and photography recently introduced as A level choices for budding artists.

Background and Atmosphere: Originally founded in 1883, 2008 saw Bromley celebrating their 125th anniversary with a fantastic concert at the Royal Albert Hall. Junior and senior pupils acted, danced and sang in a memorable performance. In 1982, the school moved to its present 25 acre site complete with woodland and a lake. Cool calm atmosphere pervades the corridors which are lined with notice boards announcing forthcoming events and successes. One area is dedicated to the school's history and a gallery of portraits. General impression is of a busy and active school. Dreary but practical maroon and grey uniform with smart dress for sixth formers.

Pastoral Care and Discipline: All pupils have a personal tutor whom parents can contact at any time to discuss pastoral or academic matters. Democratic elections run for the selection of two head girls and four deputies. Sixth form girls can train as peer counsellors and there is access to a professional counsellor on a drop in basis or by appointment. Older girls are encouraged to mentor younger pupils and gain work and life experiences by helping in the junior school. Ms Simpson has recently updated home-school communications to provide clearer information about school dates and events and set up email contact between parents and tutors.

Pupils and Parents: Predominantly local families, however some travel from all over Kent and south London. Parents mainly hard-working types from the professional classes, small social and ethnic mix. Dedicated parents organise the active PTA running fund raising events and the school bookshop. Ms Simpson has established a parents' forum to discuss school issues and to foster good working relationship between staff and parents. Old girls include Margaret Hodge, Prof Joan Walsh; Richmal Compton was once a member of the teaching staff.

Entrance: Competitive entrance exams at 11+ involving creative writing, non-verbal and verbal reasoning, an interview and reference from junior school. Sixth form entrance requirement is a minimum of six GCSEs A*–B grade.

Exit: Sixth formers all go on to higher education, mainly Russell Group Universities, 6–10 per year to Oxbridge. A few leave at 16+ to attend coed sixth forms or local grammars.

Money Matters: Everyone sitting the 11+ entrance exam is automatically entered for academic scholarships, music and sports scholarships are also available in year seven and year twelve. Sixth form scholarships for art music sport and academics. Means-tested bursaries, Founders Awards, are available for students entering years seven, ten and twelve worth 50–100 per cent Assistance with fees is also available for existing pupils at the head's discretion.

Remarks: A selective school, offering a wonderful range of opportunities to widen horizons and develop new interests. Suits academically able girls with lots of drive.

Bromsgrove School

Linked to Bromsgrove Preparatory School in the Junior section

Worcester Road, Bromsgrove, Worcestershire, B61 7DU

• Pupils: 805: 340 boarders (200 boys, 140 girls); 460 day (245 boys, 220 girls). • Ages: 13-18 (many join the prep school at 11) • Size of sixth form: 380 • Middle of the road Anglican • Fees: Day £12,450; Boarding £24,435; International Boarder £27,345 pa • Independent

Tel: 01527 579 679
Fax: 01527 576 177
Email: admissions@bromsgrove-school.co.uk
Website: www.bromsgrove-school.co.uk

Head: Since 2004, Mr Chris Edwards (forties), a Liverpudlian educated at Merchant Taylors' School and Merton College Oxford (first class honours in English). Married to Karen, no children. Interesting educational career: formerly head of English at St Paul's School, Sao Paulo, Brazil, latterly deputy head and acting head of Stowe. One of the brightest stars in the independent school firmament.

A builder – beautifully refurbished sixth form centre, 18 new and refurbished science laboratories and two new sixth form boarding houses (bought a local hotel which had been the former home of A E Housman, the best-known former pupil). Wants to see Bromsgrove become the leading West Midland independent school, 'offering breadth, quality and scholastic excellence', rather then attempting any further growth in numbers. Concerned to counter what he sees as society's moral black hole by ensuring that Bromsgrovians are firmly rooted in all that the school has to offer – not just the narrowly academic. Enormously proud of the social and academic mix within the school. A very approachable and likeable man.

Academic matters: Bromsgrove is in a difficult market place. It competes with the seriously academic King Edward's Schools as well as a number of well-respected local public schools such as Malvern, King's Worcester and Shrewsbury. Until the 1980s Bromsgrove was generally regarded as the weakest of this group. It was the place where the dimmer sons of industry tended to congregate, those who could not manage the academic rigours of King Edward's or the social aspirations of Malvern and Shrewsbury. All that has now changed, and Bromsgrove inhabits the academic stratosphere with its 200 upper sixth formers achieving 86 per cent A*, A or B grades at A level. The IB Diploma is now also offered and take-up has been high.

All departments strong. Three areas of special excellence are the humanities, which have just acquired a purpose-built teaching block with every possible modern gizmo one could imagine; art and design, where a recently-built centre is full of the most wonderfully expressive and creative work (the workshops have a range of machinery which would not disgrace a small factory and is perhaps one reason why a significant number of pupils go on to read engineering); and mathematics, where the school has the pretty unique distinction of having three further maths sets at A level – around 85 per cent A*/A grades for maths, further maths and physics in 2010.

It is not entirely easy to explain why all this has happened. One suspects it is a combination of outstanding leadership, especially from Tim Taylor, followed through by Chris Edwards, as well as some outstanding teachers. Edwina Curry was a teacher of economics at the school in the '80s and the current director of studies was a member of Gordon Brown's think-tank: the common-room must see some pretty sparkling discussions. It goes without saying that classes are small. Yet perhaps the key elements in all this are the very strong systems for monitoring pupils' progress and for tutorial support.

Games, Options, the Arts: Games at Bromsgrove are outstanding. It benefits from some quite spectacular facilities such as a wonderful swimming pool, weights room, Astroturfs, as well as acres and acres of playing fields. Excellent coaching – recent coaches have included Paul Mullan, the England under-18 rugby coach, and James Fair, international hockey player. Bromsgrovians have been capped at international level in a range of sports but especially rugby and cricket; the most famous current example is Andy Goode, the England rugby international. The school's greatest successes are in team ball games, though clay pigeon shooting figures high amongst the list of available options. The previous head was from Millfield and one can detect something of the Millfield sporting ethos here. It is certainly true that Bromsgrove, like Millfield, does not like or expect to lose.

A wide range of activities on offer. The CCF is especially strong and perhaps reflects the relatively large number of military families here – good discounts on offer. The obvious enthusiasm displayed by the cadet corps is impressive. The Duke of Edinburgh Award scheme is equally strong, as is a lively community service programme.

A unique Saturday morning programme – optional for most pupils (though all staff are in) – offers a titanic range of intellectual, cultural and physical activities, from Oxbridge extension lessons and innovative design work to RADA qualifications and jazz dancing. This programme, combined with flexible finishing times on weekdays (day pupils may now leave at 5pm if they wish), means the school is appealing to a still broader base of pupils and parents.

One of reasons why activities are so strong is the long day all pupils used to spend at the school. Whilst barely 50 per cent board, there used to be Saturday school and day pupils did not return home until 7pm at the earliest. This was clearly a great strength and an important selling point for many parents. However, it was equally, if not perhaps more of, a sticking point for those potential customers who like to see their children in the evenings. The head introduced a more flexible approach to the school day in 2007 – Saturday morning school became optional and pupils could leave as early as 5.00pm on weekdays.

Background and Atmosphere: Founded as a charity school in the 15th century, refounded in the reign of Edward VI and revived again at the time of William III. Some beautiful 17th century buildings survive. The school is virtually invisible from the road but, when one enters the school campus, the vision is a revelation. The main gates are squeezed between suburban villas on one of the main thoroughfares into the town and one is surprised by an attractive cluster of buildings focused on green, well-tended lawns. What is even more remarkable is that spreading out from this are 100 acres of playing fields, woods and fields – one could be in the middle of nowhere. Many new buildings, the fruit of over £20 million investment in the last decade or so, including an amazingly well-equipped library complex which would do credit to a university.

The school tradition is middle-of-the-road Anglican. The chapel (which was built by Gilbert Scott in memory of the Old Boys killed in Great War, who include a number of VCs) is a delight and is right in the centre of the campus. Religion is taken seriously here with regular chapel services and assemblies. The school mission statement focuses on the words: 'Flair, discipline and academic rigour', and these aspirations are very evident in the appearance and demeanour of the students. One has rarely seen smarter uniforms worn with a real sense of pride. Bromsgrove is strict in upholding these traditional values.

Half boarding, half day, so neither a 'proper' boarding school nor a day school. This does not seem to detract from its appeal and boarding, especially in the sixth form, is over-subscribed. Opened (2005) the Bromsgrove International College in Thailand.

Pastoral Care and Discipline: Because Bromsgrove is such a large school it is felt to be especially important that pupils are recognised as individuals and that their needs take primacy. Traditional house structure, with some interesting variations. Each house has its own parents' association which provides a genuinely close family/school partnership in dealing with issues of discipline or pastoral care. Also a system of student listeners and pupil buddies which goes some way to avoid individual isolation which is so often the source of unhappiness and unresolved bullying. In addition to all this, a PHSE programme and an out-of-school counsellor. The pastoral system, with a mix of year and house pastoral support, is clearly designed to reflect the mixed day/boarding population and seems to be particularly successful.

Pupils and Parents: A predominantly local school drawing most of its pupils from the West Midland/Worcestershire areas. School transport provided into Shropshire, Birmingham, Solihull and Worcester. Quite a few students from the Far East (Hong Kong and China especially) but this does not detract from the overwhelmingly 'British' feel, and they have done much to enhance Bromsgrove's academic reputation.

Not a 'posh' school – unpretentious. Its core market is the commercial and professional middle-classes of the West Midlands. Has a wider social catchment than many of its local competitors and the head has extended that still further.

Pupils are bright, articulate and refreshingly lacking in false sophistication, with an endearing straightforwardness and pride in their school which is rather old fashioned, but no less attractive for that.

Entrance: Has its own very large and successful preparatory school. Many pupils enter it at 11 plus after taking a simple English, mathematics and intelligence test. A minority enter the senior school at 13 plus either through common entrance or via the school's own test. Many children come from local primary schools, others from local preparatory schools including Winterfold House and Bluecoats Edgbaston. Entry to the sixth form massively over-subscribed, GCSEs at B or above essential.

Exit: Virtually all to university, usually double figures to Oxbridge, although not as many as are capable of this: 'It does not appear to be the culture here,' says head. Many go to UCL, Durham, Bristol, Nottingham and Birmingham.

Money Matters: The head has set up a foundation so that bursary funds might be commensurate with the spectacular facilities and build programme. Head and governors are passionate about widening access.

Remarks: Now firmly in place as one of the top schools in the West Midlands, with its own particular style. (Head claims they are even better than this, as they are always in the top ten, and sometimes top five, of the national league tables for co-ed day/boarding schools.)

Bruton School for Girls

Linked to Sunny Hill Preparatory School in the Junior section

Sunny Hill, Bruton, Somerset, BA10 0NT

• Pupils: 310; 115 boarders • Ages: Girls 2-18; day places for boys 2-7 • Size of sixth form: 70 • Fees: Day £4,500-£12,510; Boarding £16,335-£22,605 pa • Independent

Tel: 01749 814 400
Fax: 01749 812 537
Email: info@brutonschool.co.uk
Website: www.brutonschool.co.uk

Headmaster: Since March 2006, Mr John Burrough BA PGCE (fifties). Hails from Milborne Port in Somerset. Graduated in mathematics and education from York. Apart from four years teaching maths at Welshpool High School in mid-eighties, whole career has been in Somerset and Dorset. Made sideways move to Bruton from The Gryphon, Sherborne, in 2001 to become head of sixth, then swift internal promotions leading to appointment as school's first male head.

His background suits Bruton well and he feels a deep commitment to the girls' best interests. Parents like the way that he 'gets on with the job in hand' and say that he may be quietly spoken but he is also 'forthright when he needs to be'. Not a showman but understands the need for improved marketing at all levels. Advocate of 'human scale' activity, he supports endeavours that fit this model. 'A good listener' and 'approachable', say both girls and staff, who seem reassured by his style. Has not made huge waves, though appointment caused a few raised eyebrows initially. Private person with grown-up daughter and son; enjoys drama and singing; passionate about the relevance for the students of world events and politics.

Academic matters: Has continued to achieve best public examination results in Somerset even in post assisted places era. Around 80 per cent A*/A/B grade at A level; courses run subject to demand. Sensible balance struck between new and traditional subjects – e.g. classics plus French, German and Spanish all available, as well as psychology, drama and theatre studies. AS critical thinking. Recent dip in sixth form entry but head has fought back with numbers creeping up. Maths and sciences particularly strong but good results across board testify to positive work ethic. We were struck by the variety of schemes, awards and initiatives: not many small schools have two language assistants or a postgraduate researcher in the science department. Top results reached by international pupils in unglamorous but vital IELTS exams, and 65 per cent A*/A at GCSE level with strength in core subjects. Average class 15 girls in Years 7–9; 13 in Years 10–11 and eight in the sixth, though many groups smaller (e.g. three girls taking A2 economics). Modern languages popular; visits start with 40 Year 8 girls spending a week boarding at Maison Claire Fontaine in Burgundy; GCSE Spanish students visit Seville, plus individual exchanges in France, Spain and Germany. Taster sessions in Mandarin. Three-quarters of staff female with fifteen teachers on staff over ten years. Girls rate help given with university applications and careers, with OGs involved in talks and local firms such as Westland giving 'real' experience to sixth form physicists. Home bred courses for gifted and talented in association with NAGTY. Top award for Year 10 student in recent national mathematics contest. Our teachers 'go extra mile,' say senior girls.

New SENCO from state sector: support to wider range of girls, especially in spelling and number work, follows them seamlessly from prep to senior school. Improved sense of inclusivity means school 'would consider' mild Asperger's, says SENCO, but site unsuitable for visually or physically challenged.

Games, Options, the Arts: Parents like 'the broader perspective' offered. Strong PE and games with plenty of fixtures at all ability levels. We watched as Year 7 ergo rowers practised in fitness suite (head's baby) aiming at repeat gold medal performance in national indoor championships. Lots of staff coaching teams after school. High quality floodlit Astroturf and tennis courts; dance studio and large gym provide for most sporting needs. Outside grass area reserved mainly for athletics in summer. Hilly surroundings make for a testing cross-country course. Tag rugby now proving very popular thanks to expert staff coach. County players in netball, hockey, tennis and cross-country. Fifty girls took part in last ski trip to French Alps. Recent hockey tour to Singapore and Malaysia scored a hit.

No shortage of choice when it comes to activities: self-defence, beauty therapy and the much vaunted Leith's cookery course, to name but a few. Public speaking includes even international pupils: English Speaking Board advanced certificate and LAMDA awards.

Music school, built 30 years ago, has proved more than 'fit for purpose': large rehearsal space for choir and/or orchestra plus effective soundproofing between practice rooms. Fourteen peripatetics – instrumental and singing. Healthy sized choir (which we saw practising after school) is one of 17 music groups that meet weekly, plus frequent tours to Europe and around southwest cathedrals. Year 10 student recently had rôle in fully staged Pergolesi opera, La Serva Padrona. Year 11 girl danced lead in English Youth Ballet performance at Yeovil's Octagon Theatre. Successful art department in airy studios – visual evidence of homegrown talent around school, but no gallery, alas! Annual arts week in February includes book character day and 'poetry slam' competitions. The Gleam (echo of Tennyson and also school song), school's lively magazine, largely product of girls' input (hooray!).

Lots of Year 10 girls go for D of E bronze award and some tackle silver and gold in sixth form. Keen group of riders uses local stables but no on-site equestrian facility yet; school now hosts hunter trials; good results obtained in inter-school show jumping and one girl selected to represent GB at three-day event in Ireland. School has in-house driving school ('A major reason for me staying here for the sixth,' said one senior girl, who couldn't say enough good things about the scheme). Budding racing drivers have fun and success with school's electrically powered 'greenpower' car at circuits including Goodwood and Castle Combe.

Background and Atmosphere: Founded in 1900 by Henry Hobhouse and William Knight, head of Sexey's School in Bruton. Sunny Hill might not always live up to its name weatherwise but a warm enough atmosphere. Enjoys great location on edge of small town. Incoherent collection of buildings but it doesn't seem to matter. Science block works well within and new studio theatre even looks good from outside too. Mellow 'old house' building lends an almost collegiate feel from main road. Much is being done to improve look of the place including landscaping an amphitheatre in the heart of school. Carpeted corridors help soften noise; chairs in assembly hall suggest surplus stock from an Indian restaurant but serve a purpose. Small-scale rather than grandiose with refreshing lack of pretension. Regular assemblies, links with local church, annual Cranmer awards, Christian union and confirmation suggest healthy spiritual ethos for those who seek it, but otherwise not overtly religious. Long days with many there after lessons for activities but no Saturday lessons. Lots of Saturday sport and varied programme for boarders (many of whom choose to stay back).

Pastoral Care and Discipline: Well-ordered school with staff quick to troubleshoot if necessary. Parents' view is that 'school is very strict in policies' but only needs to weigh in very occasionally. Seniors good rôle models for juniors: organise impressive range of competitive, social and fundraising events. Triumvirate of senior girls (who run 'open door' policy) seen as a stepping stone for juniors and help to nip potential problems in the bud. We liked the first term tutorial setup for Year 7 when they are 'babied a bit' by senior staff. Everyone seems happy with food arrangements – attractive dining area, sensible range of healthy options.

Deputy head oversees boarding and pastoral arrangements. Realistic attitude to boys, who can visit 'on ground floor only' of senior boarding house. Mumsy housemistresses with assistants to mop fevered brows where necessary. Separate house tutor groups for Years 7–9, 10 and 11, then sixth form. Girls divided into 'halls' for competitions. International girls scoop double bedrooms on grounds of accumulated clobber.

Pupils and Parents: 'Girls come out confident and speaking up for themselves,' said one ex-parent. We met a group of unusually articulate Year 10 girls who were all positive, whilst their seniors were well informed, poised and able to 'think on their feet'. Commendable initiative shown by ex-Cheltenham Ladies' teacher in charge of eight girls who spent summer in Tanzania building houses for Habitat for Humanity charity (funds were raised partly through quiz nights in local pubs). Girls come up with some original ideas for raising money for other charities (e.g. Children in Need and Goodwill Villages in India) and eco projects – Bruton obtained Eco Schools silver award status recently. Overseas pupils requiring EFL teaching capped at ten per cent. Old Girls include Ethel Knight (UK's first female vet) and Clarissa Farr (current head of St Paul's Girls' in London).

Entrance: Own entrance papers in English, mathematics and verbal reasoning plus science for 13+ entry (about 10 girls enter Year 9). Minimum of five Bs at GCSE to get into sixth. Over 90 per cent transfer from prep to senior school at 11+. Growing entry at 13+ welcomed by head. Tradition of some entrants from state primaries. Overseas applicants tested in English and in subjects they want to study.

Exit: Fewer tempted away at 16+ as tales of regret filter back. Regular trickle to Oxbridge and most to first choice universities.

Money Matters: Fee levels what you'd expect without too many extras. Discounts for siblings and Forces. Head keen to fund more bursaries.

Remarks: Success without frills; not trying to prove anything and more inclusive than one might expect given its academic reputation. Has everything you'd look for and more besides. 'Good value for money,' report satisfied parents.

Bryanston School

Bryanston, Blandford Forum, Dorset, DT11 0PX

• Pupils: 380 boys (320 board); 300 girls (255 board) • Ages: 13-18
• Size of sixth form: 270 • C of E • Fees: Boarding £28,560;
Day £23,418 pa • Independent

Tel: 01258 452 411
Fax: 01258 484 661
Email: admissions@bryanston.co.uk
Website: www.bryanston.co.uk

Head: Since 2005, Ms Sarah Thomas BA (forties). Educated at Birkenhead High School, GDST and read lit hum (classics) at Hertford College, Oxford. PGCE from King's, London. Brings experience from helping to run two of Britain's most successful co-ed public schools. Deputy head at Uppingham for six years and before that spent 13 years at Sevenoaks teaching classics, housemistressing and eventually heading the sixth form. Informal, unguarded head, au fait with the pomp and circumstance involved in heading an important school. Has underpinned

Bryanston's tutorial system as the school's 'jewel in the crown' by improving staff training etc. Also created a head of sixth form, and is striving to keep breadth in sixth form education when the outside world is pushing pupils to 'jump through hoops'. Married to Adrian Boote who teaches at a local prep school, has published several children's books and also 'cooks, entertains and is involved in various clubs and activities at school'. Two daughters: one at Bryanston and one now at university.

Academic matters: Revolves around the modified Dalton Plan – a scheduling system that allows for assignment periods – non-lesson time throughout each week to be used for study, prep, catchup or extra-curricular obligations (e.g. music lessons). In their first three years, pupils spend assignment periods in subject rooms/libraries supervised by a teacher from that department. Older pupils usually work in their houses. These assignment periods, along with two sessions of prep each night, help pupils stay on top of their work. Prep set a week ahead so pupils learn to organise their time in preparation for sixth form and university. Teachers see pupils in subject rooms, in class, and individually in weekly tutorials where pupils receive assessments from every single one of their teachers via the 'eChart', an online markbook. So, no shortage of opportunity for teacher/pupil rapport to blossom then.

Exam results good given broad intake; excellent VA scores. Setting in maths, sciences and languages. Economics, history, maths and biology most popular A level subjects in 2010. Sciences stand up well, with some inspired teaching, and the impressive new Sanger science and maths centre, named after OB Frederick Sanger (double Nobel Laureate biochemist), should further buttress the subject. All three sciences compulsory – either dual award or as separate subjects. Classics outstanding. Latin compulsory for all in first year; it and Greek both dazzle at GCSE with many A*s (13 pupils took GCSE Greek last year and 9 the year before). Good Latin A level results as well. Range of A level courses surprisingly narrow for a progressive school. No psychology, no music technology, no philosophy (although these are included in the non-examined humanities programme). Mac-based IT rather than PCs reflects (dare we say it?) arts leaning.

For non-native speakers good English a must, although a handful receives ESL help. Not a school one would seek out for SEN but 'the potential of each pupil is achieved'. A fifth of pupils require special provision for learning disabilities. Pupils not taken out of lessons but receive up to one hour a week of help. 2007 inspection report noted 'a rather too casual atmosphere still exists in some lessons and a clearer insistence on pupils' attention and engagement would aid their learning'. School says it's addressing this with 'a programme of lesson observations within and across departments to enable the dissemination of effective teaching and learning methodologies across the school'. Some old-time Bryanston parents grumble the school is becoming too exacting in terms of academics, saying for instance that pupils who muff their GCSEs were being encouraged to look elsewhere for sixth form.

Games, Options, the Arts: Much emphasis on rugby – surprising at this progressive school, and too much, according to some parents. Top rugby talent much sought after and nurtured and many boys have gone on to glory. Hockey (for both sexes) also strong. Lots of sports options a godsend for many. Fives, fencing and kayaking some of the more exotic choices. Rowing important and an annual rowing training trip to Switzerland (why Switzerland?). Two artificial pitches for hockey and tennis (one floodlit). Indoor pool; swimming club, the Bryanston Barracudas, competes in galas. Riding uneven – some years going great guns (two girls in U18 GB training squad), other years deathly quiet. All depends on how many pupils bring horses, school says, but we wonder if they are missing a trick (riding does form part of compulsory, second year adventure training programme). Soccer a nonentity. Sailing at Poole Harbour. Those who really, really hate sport can get away with doing a bare minimum, parents say.

Brilliant art – lovely creative arts building, partly funded by the Conran Foundation (another OB) which houses cooking and textiles. The art department's teaching is second to none, the range of projects undertaken enormous, the results a joy to behold. Head of art full of enthusiasm and humour and not shy of the occasional tussle with pupils over which background music to play. Ceramics bask in massive, industrial kiln (it was on special offer). DT department also buzzy and impressive. Very hot on producing electric guitars at the moment (chap from Fender comes to adjust them so they play gorgeously). Kids put together a Caterham car each year and then sell it back to the company. DT GCSE results brilliant lately; A level 90 per cent A*–B in 2010. We receive mixed reviews of the drama department but there is certainly loads going on. School says, 'Drama is now flourishing, culminating last autumn in what was arguably the best musical the school has ever staged – a highly-polished and emotionally-charged production of West Side Story'. Drama/theatre studies examined at A level only (not GCSE). Professional theatre, the 600-seat Coade Hall, hosts touring companies – hard to believe it is 40 years old. School's own TV network shows recordings of school performances, videos and information. Music active with range of ensembles, several choirs, London concerts. All pupils must try a musical instrument in their first year. Some talented scholars wash up here from Salisbury Cathedral School – one sixth form violinist gained scholarships to all three of the main London music conservatoires. Good facilities for rock bands: six guitar teachers, 150 guitarists, 70 drummers, a recording studio. Music building has seen better days but school currently working with Hopkins Architects, designers of the Sanger Centre, on plans for new music school. Lots of community service (known here as 'pioneering'). Fabulous list of extra-curricular activities with everything from welding for beginners to salsa classes. No CCF.

Background and Atmosphere: Very long drive from the front gates, through untamed woods, past riding centre and across 57 acres of playing fields to distant conglomeration of school buildings, sets tone for this unusual school – 'uninstitutional' and 'unschooly' are how pupils describe it. Ostentatious Norman Shaw House for Viscount Portman is 'more like a town hall than a private house', to quote John Betjeman, but makes an aesthetically inspiring heart of the school (wood panelling and parquet flooring throughout). Majority of modern additions are architecturally outstanding – can't be cheap. Set in 400 acres. Founded 1928, went fully co-ed in 1975. Religion low key but most Sundays pupils must attend either assembly or church. First year pupils have compulsory weekly chapel in basement of main building. Pupils may go home at weekends from the end of classes/sport on Saturday until bedtime on Sunday but many stay in. Day pupils can't be picked up until 9pm, after prep – some local parents wish it were earlier (they do the late night school run in their pyjamas). Famously good, creative nosh served in a newly-refurbished dining hall designed by Conran Architects. Fab new healthy eating café (smoothies, flapjacks, pizza) has replaced tuckshop.

Pastoral Care and Discipline: School has reputation for giving pupils a loose rein but is little different from other co-ed, liberal schools. In fact, pupils are more closely monitored here than at most places. 'The great thing about the school,' said a parent, 'is that it has an atmosphere of great liberation while in reality keeping more control over pupils than any school I know.' Obsessive, almost excessive, pastoral care makes it close to impossible for misery/despair/going off rails to go undetected. Member of staff has recently been made responsible for co-ordinating pupils' extra-curricular involvement, making sure no one is hideously over-extended – a brilliant innovation. No uniform, but dress code has been tightened up. Ages 13 to 16 wear polo shirts (of any colour) and black or navy trousers or skirts ('avoiding extremes of length'). Sixth form must just look reasonably together.

We continue to get reports of student misbehaviour – the full range – but equally hear from students who were at the school for five years and seldom caught a glimpse of anything untoward. Upper sixth bar open Friday and Saturday nights. Boys and girls may visit each other's houses until 9.30pm. Security guards monitor woods etc. 'I'm not an expeller,' the head told us, 'though certainly wouldn't rule it out, and pupils have been asked to leave in the past.' Those busted for drugs given second chance but must submit to testing. Alcohol misdemeanours dealt with personally by head, not housemasters, to send a clear message that the school takes it seriously.

Boys enter one of two first-year houses (40 boys in each). The idea is to protect them from the rough and tumble, eradicate opportunities for bullying and allow new boys to make solid friendships. Thereafter they move into mixed age houses. Not much rivalry among houses or between year groups – much promotion of older pupils looking out for younger pupils etc. Girls go straight into mixed-age houses. Sky TV in every house.

Pupils and Parents: Has become more local than last time we were here. Half from not much more than an hour's drive away. Most of these have chosen the school for its ethos, but there is also a contingent of pupils who didn't quite make the Canford and Marlborough academic cut (school disputes this). Many pupils from preps: Dumpton, Castle Court, Knighton House (which is sited on the same estate), Hanford, Port Regis and Sandroyd. Some 15 per cent from London. There are 22 ex-pat families; very few foreign nationals – a half dozen Germans come for a year or less.

Many of these middle class pupils tend to see themselves as non-conformist semi-rebels and Bryanston as a centre of cool, while actually sporting polyester blend polo shirts and playing hockey and rugby. Most are very fashion-conscious and, unlike other no-uniform schools where grunge rules, pupils here care how they look. 'Face Odyssey', a beauty club, is popular. OBs Lucian Freud, Terence, Sebastian and Jasper Conran, John Eliot Gardiner and Mark Elder (conductors), Quinlan Terry (architect), Phil de Glanville (rugby) and pop star Amy Studt, though we don't think she quite stayed the course ... also Howard Hodgkin, Emilia Fox, Ben Fogle and Nigel Barker.

Entrance: No need to organise years in advance – 18 months before September of entry will do nicely. At 13+, CE (50 per cent pass required) or school's own tests in English, maths and French, plus school report. Always strives to accommodate siblings. Entry to sixth form requires interview with head, test in maths or English and a general aptitude test in November before year of entry.

Exit: Some 98 per cent to higher education, up to 70 per cent first taking a gap year. Up to a dozen to art colleges. University destinations change enormously year on year. Five to Oxbridge in 2010 and one most years to an American university.

Money Matters: Up to 27 scholarships: academic, music, art, ICT, DT, sport and all-rounder awards (all in February). For the last of these, leadership potential is an important criterion. Academic, music and sport scholarships available at sixth form. School is not wealthy, despite appearances. Bursaries available.

Remarks: Friendly, relaxed, non-traditional school where management has miraculously succeeded in making pupils feel they are treated like adults. Supportive relationships among pupils, and between pupils and staff, keep most everyone whistling while they work. Distinctive feel – most people know if it's right for them before they've even turned off the engine in the car park.

Brymore School

Cannington, Bridgwater, Somerset, TA5 2NB

• Pupils: 130 boarders, 40 day; all boys • Ages: 13-17 • Inter-denom
• Fees: £7,950 pa • State

Tel: 01278 652 369
Fax: 01278 653 244
Email: office@brymore.somerset.sch.uk
Website: www.brymoreschool.co.uk

Acting headteacher: Mr Mark Thomas is acting headteacher until Easter 2011.

Academic matters: Brymore's three Rs are 'resilience, responsibility and resourcefulness'. Doesn't mean that traditional three Rs are neglected – quite the opposite. We spoke to parents of able boys who have not suffered academically by moving to Brymore: 'He studies better because of the practical work,' commented one happy dad. Slower learners do particularly well here. Over last four years around 40 per cent of pupils have achieved five A*–C grades at GCSE, though figure drops to around 30 per cent if English and maths are included. Lower ability boys 'clamour for extra help,' say staff: many boys see Brymore as a 'second chance'. Engineering, agricultural and horticultural subjects occupy one-third of timetable and lead to an NVQ qualification alongside GCSEs. We were mesmerised watching self-confident Year 10 boys pouring molten metal into moulds and then knocking out their castings – awesome! Drawing office and computer lab (mainly for CAD work) enhance DT facilities. Year 12 students opt for either a BTEC first award in an agricultural subject or level two NVQ in engineering. Art, dual science and geography sit alongside core GCSE subjects. RE and PE provide half a GCSE each. No MFL after Year 9.

Outstanding special needs provision lies at heart of school's recent academic improvement. 'Financial support needs to be maintained,' pleads SENCo. Staff are given specific guidance by SENCo for each of the lower ability groups (where staff: pupil ratio is 1:7). Fast-track phonic revision for these boys in Year 9 using a multi-sensory approach. SENCo always on look-out for suitable non-fiction to interest boys. Dedicated specialist staff (three f/t and five p/t teaching assistants, each of whom specialises in a subject area, plus three LSAs to 'plug the gaps'). 'It's all about relationships at Brymore,' explains the exuberant SENCo, who has to take on some entrants with reading ages as low as seven on entry. SEN expertise ranges from SpLD to ADHD and Asperger's. About 30 boys are on SEN register plus loads more with difficulties of various kinds. Learning support in every prep session and reading offered before school and at lunch-times. Learning mentor helps to 'retrack' individuals and also works with small groups. Staff encouraged to use target-setting and self-assessment. Boys are generally 'up for it,' says SENCo, who promotes literacy as 'relevant to life'. 'Message gradually sinks in,' she says with a smile. Six-day timetable of 54 lessons: each of 35 minutes; doubles and triples for practical subjects. No options beyond year nine so parents must be sure that what is on offer is going to suit. School puts maximum 24 boys in top (B) set of each year, 20 in middle (R) and 16 in lower (Y) one. An 'average ability' boy leaves with five or six GCSEs and an NVQ qualification. Post-16 provision poised for possible expansion.

Games, Options, the Arts: Sport is important at Brymore with emphasis (in keeping with school's ethos) upon team rather than individual effort. Most boys play rugby: 'We give Millfield B teams a good run for their money,' says head, and fixture list looks impressive. Hockey attracts about 20 boys, and cross-country is particularly strong with boys doing school's three-and-a-half mile ('Chads') course at least once a week. Failure to do this or missing fitness sessions results in team deselection. Super athletics: Brymore has been Somerset champions for 19 consecutive years and dominates under-17 age group. Hefty representation at county level; hammer, pole-vaulting, cross-country, road running and walking make nationals – two boys currently representing England. Multi-purpose hall used for volleyball, table tennis etc. Enthusiastic golf, fishing and mountain biking. Caving and karate current favourites. One mum runs chess activity; staff take boys deer and badger watching on nearby Quantocks; also popular for hill walking and D of E (bronze and silver) expeditions. Annual ski trip still draws great support. Young farmers' club. Business incentive scheme linked with Barnardo's offers Year 12 chance to gain experience whilst raising money for charity. Little music or drama outside the curriculum, though some boys have peripatetic drum or guitar lessons.

Background and Atmosphere: The Brymore School of Rural Technology was established in 1952 for sons of Somerset farmers on an impressive 60-acre site on the edge of Cannington, between the Quantocks and Bristol Channel. A half-mile tree lined drive affords first sight of extensive farm buildings and impressive new accommodation. Head has been given mandate to 'change the culture but retain the ethos'. Brymore has won lion's share (over £3m) of national lottery money going to state boarding. Two new (50-place) boarding houses opened in January 2009, followed by refurbishment of existing Dickensian provision in main house. Mini dormitories for four boys apiece plus common-rooms and staff quarters. Long overdue, though many boys still hanker after larger dorms. Should sell boarding concept more easily to nervous mums, though. New classroom block will have 'rural look' similar to boarding houses. Funded by LEA, it will be a massive step forward. Boys 'won't know what's hit them,' say staff. Head of art 'can't wait' to move in after years as a hut dweller. Some mobile classrooms will remain on site but these are modern and quite acceptable. Main building will remain the 17th century mansion originally owned by a notorious Civil War figure, John Pym, Oliver Cromwell's right hand man. The original stable yard complete with clock tower has been converted to sizeable metal and wood workshops, plus two blacksmiths' forges and foundry to industrial standard. No wonder the ghost of John Pym still roams this part of the school (sound of restless horse hooves on cobbles at night)! Motto: 'diligentia et labore'. Together with a spur motif it forms school crest, visible on blazers (worn for formal occasions and for assembly every morning).

Boys bid for plots to grow vegetables in impeccably-kept one-acre walled garden dating from 1753. Pupils are responsible for upkeep of entire estate: tree-pruning, grass-cutting, weeding, planting flower beds all lead to an NVQ. A self-financing farm is at the heart of this unique set-up – lambing a flock of 50 ewes, rearing free-range chickens, beef cattle and pigs ('more of which should end up on boys' plates,' complained one mum) and milking cows at 6am on a crisp winter morning are essential parts of the learning. 'Backing a tractor through a gateway and getting 10 out of 10 in a spelling test are of equal value here,' says the head. Prince Charles visited in school's golden jubilee year (2002) – no doubt a 'home from home' for HRH.

Pastoral Care and Discipline: No written rules. Staff talk 'with' rather than 'at' boys; no raised voices when we visited. Loads of patience which boys appreciate. Common sense and co-operation paramount – we watched a new boy being offered spontaneous, genuine help in a DT lesson from an older hand. Great! Teenage boys without that sullen, 'back off' expression and no backchat. Lots of friendly conversations overheard in and out of classrooms. Yes, really! Sloppiness not appreciated here – especially by boys appointed (after interview) as heads of department on the farm. 'Boys thrive on the level of responsibility they're offered at Brymore – you don't get it elsewhere,' emphasised one father. Tidy appearance underpinned by common-sense dress code – once assembly is over boys don black sweatshirt or working rig. Hooray! Inter-denominational; assemblies usually include a hymn, but we watched a clever video presentation by head on the power of advertising which got boys laughing first thing. Older staff than in most schools but younger blood may fill current vacancies. In addition to kindly matrons (who provide 24 hour health cover) boys have access to two counsellors who visit regularly. Tasty grub and plenty of it, with only one caveat mentioned above. Two deputies and head all residential; new boarding staff will raise number on site to ten. Some teachers described as 'quirky' by parents; boys rate them highly. Staff give loads of time outside the classroom.

Pupils and Parents: Head takes boys who haven't thrived in mainstream. Not everyone a wurzel – present head boy from London (he's a national champion 5km road walker now); two overseas at present (Anglo Saxon escapees from France, we think) and around 50 per cent from Somerset. We met boys from the Isle of Rhum and Northumberland, which suggests that 'word has got around'. Mixed bunch socially but mostly boys used to 'doing what they're told'. Head marched 12 of them down to barber's at beginning of term – 'Uniform includes head and feet as far as I'm concerned,' he asserts. Assembly has retro look – shirts tucked in and ties properly knotted. Boys learn independence – 'After a few weeks at Brymore my son told me to stop fussing over him at home,' said one mum, whose enthusiasm for the school has resulted in friends sending their sons to Brymore too. 'If your son is a day boy, you have to be prepared to pick him up at odd times,' said another mum, whose sons like to stay late for activities.

School takes exhibition trailer to county shows but mostly admits through word of mouth. Boys here don't have to be farmers in the making, but a love of the open air and practical work are essential. What kept impressing us was the level of concentration and co-operation on practical tasks around the whole school. Former pupil teaches blacksmithing: great role model for boys who can see how the practical Brymore education can be basis for a successful business in later life. Other OBs include MEP Neil Parish, Mark Irish – England U21 rugby player, Julian Anderson – world windsurfing champion.

Entrance: Approximately 60 boys admitted at 13 plus the odd one at any stage: when we visited, two boys had joined Year 10 after spring half-term. Day boys (head now refers to them as 'out boarders') will need to board when on farm duties. All boys quizzed on their 'suitability for boarding' – the school's only selection criterion. Current one year post-GCSE course open to applicants from outside. All must accept six day week.

Exit: Over 70 per cent to further education colleges such as Lackham, Sparsholt, Kingston Manward, Duchy College, Cornwall or closer to home – Canninton College and Bridgwater. 'Brymore boys often get fast tracked at college,' said one farmer dad. Some boys progress to degree level. Some into apprenticeships, others to work-based learning or employment. Many former students now run their own businesses.

Money Matters: Boarding fees being increased slightly (quantum improvement in boarding facilities seen as justification for this). Some pupils obtain educational grants from home LEAs.

Remarks: Deserves wider recognition and should be heavily over-subscribed. A unique boarding school with a sense of purpose and a special atmosphere. By no means a boot camp – boys treated with respect. When pupils leave, staff 'see no resemblance to the boy they were sent'. Look no further if your son isn't afraid to get stuck in and is currently feeling swamped by worksheets and undervalued in a 'rubbish' school. Bit of a fracas in September 2010, resulted in change at the top – though character of previous head widely appreciated in the school community and unbesmirched. Perhaps some understandable tension between what Brymore offers and the 'pupil protection at all costs' policy of the Local Authority?

Burford School and Community College

Cheltenham Road, Burford, Oxfordshire, OX18 4PL

• Pupils: 1,145 boys and girls (90 board, the rest day) • Ages: 11-18
• Size of sixth form: 185 • Inter-denom • Fees: Boarding £9,300 pa Tuition free • State

Tel: 01993 823 303
Fax: 01993 823 101
Email: head.4040@burford.oxon.sch.uk
Website: www.burford.oxon.sch.uk

Headteacher: Since January 2008, Mrs Kathy Haig BA MEd (forties). Educated at Burford School (her family lived at nearby Shipton-under-Wychwood), followed by Leeds University, where she studied food science and nutrition. Taught at schools in Hull, Keighley and Preston before moving to Ellesmere Port Catholic High School in Cheshire. Spent 12 years there, rising to become deputy head. 'I consider myself fortunate that very early on in my career I realised I wanted to teach,' she says. Still teaches GCSE health and social care to Years 10 and 11 (four periods a week) – 'I like teaching,' she says. 'It's what a school is about.' Chatty, full of ideas and keen to stress the pride pupils take in their school. Married to management consultant and has two children, one of whom is a pupil at Burford.

Academic matters: Rural comprehensive with rare boarding element (one of only 30 or so state boarding schools in the UK). Offers wide range of subjects to wide ability intake. Setted on ability for maths, science and languages. Overall GCSE grades well above national average – 69 per cent 5+ A*–C grades in 2010 (61 per cent including English and maths). At A level, 49 per cent A*/A/B grades. Total of 23 subjects on offer at A level, including business studies, economics, PE and sports, psychology. Most youngsters take at least nine GCSEs. Homework plays integral part, with parents asked to sign children's student record books once a week up to GCSE. Learning support unit, housed in own block, was judged 'outstanding' in 2006 Ofsted report. Deals with wide range of special needs (dyslexia, dyspraxia, Asperger's, Year 7s who arrive with lower than average reading ages) and helps pupils achieve. School is now a specialist science and technology college – good for status and cash. All Year 7s do French, with German and Spanish on offer from Year 8. Group of key stage 3 youngsters (11 to 14 year olds) recently linked up with Oxford University students to learn Latin. Two computer suites and all do ICT. They're also ahead of the game when it comes to cookery lessons, which the government is making compulsory for 11 to 14 year olds from 2011 – Burford already teaches food technology. One vocational course – applied business studies for Year 12s (business and communication studies, word processing etc). Average class sizes around 25 up to GCSE, 15 in sixth form.

Games, Options, the Arts: Lots of wonderful green space and very committed sports staff. All pupils get one PE lesson and one games lesson a week – hockey, football, rugby, netball, tennis, athletics, keep fit and dance. Gym in main school, separate sports hall (only building large enough to house the whole school), rugby and hockey pitches, tennis and netball courts etc. Loads of matches with local state and independent schools.

Light, airy art block with different areas for art, design and technology, textiles. Stunning work on show in foyer, from wall-mounted magazine racks to stylish jewellery and ceramics. One pupil even made a ferret house! Drama is popular. Around 20 took part in the 2008 national Shakespeare Schools' Festival, performing a 21st century version of *The Taming of the Shrew.* Around 25 per cent of pupils learn a musical instrument – everything from classical to jazz and rock.

Impressive library, with more than 23,500 resources and own website. Pupils encouraged to read for pleasure as well as work, with authors Jacqueline Wilson, Anthony Horowitz and Charlie Higson getting the thumbs-up. Book of the week on display at front desk. After-school homework club held in library three times a week.

Voluntary extra-curricular clubs held every lunchtime, and most youngsters keen to participate. 'We do everything from sailing and skiing to dance and computer clubs,' says head. Good takeup for D of E – around 75 Year 9s doing bronze award. Lots of Year 12s do Young Enterprise and Year 10 engineering pupils regularly involved in Formula Schools, where they get the chance to design, build and race model cars at Silverstone. Many trips to foreign climes and school rightfully proud of its 14-year link with a school in Uganda. The scheme is the longest-running reciprocal exchange link with a school in Eastern Africa.

Background and Atmosphere: School was founded by charter in 1571 and still celebrates Charter Day in November every year. Has been on present 36-acre site (also owns 40 acres of farmland) since 1949, when Burford Grammar School was enlarged to form Oxfordshire's first comprehensive school. Maintains many old grammar school traditions, including house system, prefects and uniform for all but sixth form. Head girl and boy voted for by staff and sixth formers. Main school situated on the busy A40 on edge of beautiful Cotswold town of Burford (just over an hour from London on a good traffic day). Original building has been vastly added to and site is a maze of interconnecting buildings, although a chirpy Year 8 assured us, 'You soon get the hang of it'. Around 80 boarders live in Lenthall House, a listed building in the town itself. Behind the honeystone walls, it's a bit of a Tardis, with modern facilities and warm, cosy rooms. Boarders come from all over – from Oxfordshire to Hong Kong. Boarding places highly sought after. 'I could fill the boarding house three times over,' admits head. 'It's a safe environment and a kind of halfway house between school and university.' Weekly and full boarding available.

All pupils (and staff) belong to one of four houses named after school founders – Falkland, Heylin, Warwick and Wysdom. Fiercely competitive, with contests ranging from creative writing and fashion to Monopoly and ultimate frisbee. House points given for homework, effort, presentation etc. Pupils attend assembly twice a week. School council with two representatives from each form. Sixth form housed in their own block, with common-room and study area. Pupils reckon food is 'very nice', with daily choice of hot meals, pasta, salad, sandwiches and vegetarian options. Cashless system, where they use swipe card to pay for school dinners.

Excellent induction programme for new pupils. Year 13s get special training to act as peer mentors to Year 7s. Teaching assistants on hand to guide the youngest to classes in early weeks. Year 7s also get a three-day residential trip to the Isle of Wight during their first week as part of their settling-in process. Year groups divided into eight forms, each with own tutor.

Smart uniform (black blazer with school crest, black trousers/skirts, house tie and white shirt) for younger years. No uniform for sixth form – but expected to dress 'appropriately', i.e. no flip flops, T-shirts with offensive logos, ripped trousers etc.

Pastoral Care and Discipline: Well-defined rules set out in excellent student record book – smart navy hardback given to each pupil at start of each year. Contains everything from equipment needed for school, spelling lists and tips on how to present classwork to home-school partnership agreement and what to do if the school bus is late. School's central tenet is that 'everyone will act with care and consideration to others at all times' and it seems to work. Head runs a tight, stable ship, with pupils comfortable and secure within a firm list of dos and don'ts – dos include using 'polite and courteous language' while don'ts include not distracting others. 'It's not an overly strict school, though,' a sixth former told us. 'We get treated like grown-ups.' Youngsters wanting to talk about problems can go to their tutor, head of year or any other member of staff – plus school counsellor who's on site three days a week. Firm policies on drugs, drink and smoking and school anti-bullying policy crystal-clear.

Pupils and Parents: Youngsters come from wide variety of backgrounds, from quite posh to disadvantaged. Buses (some local authority, others organised by parents) bring children in from 10-mile radius, including Lyneham, Kingham, Carterton, and Witney. Pupils very polite – they open doors for visitors and behave well; 'This is a school where staff can teach,' says head. 'It's not about crowd control.' Old pupils include Gilbert Jessop (cricketer), Simon West (film director) and Alice Freeman (who won a bronze medal at the 2007 World Rowing Championships).

Entrance: School is over-subscribed but children living in catchment area and attending one of Burford's nine partner primary schools virtually guaranteed a place. Around 35 per cent come from outside catchment area though, with priority given to those with siblings already at the school. Head says it's always worth prospective parents talking to her and explaining why they want their children to come to Burford. Number of Year 7 places has been upped from 200 to 210 this year. Some new pupils also join higher up the school, particularly in sixth form.

Exit: Around 40 per cent leave after GCSEs, for local FE colleges, apprenticeships or to join family businesses. Most of sixth form go to university – to read everything from astrophysics to naval architecture. Exeter, Southampton, Bristol and West of England currently very popular.

Remarks: A happy comprehensive school that offers a good, all-round education and some boarding places too. Pupils are keen to do well, know what is expected of them and rise to the challenge admirably.

Burgess Hill School for Girls

Linked to Burgess Hill School For Girls Junior School in the Junior section

Keymer Road, Burgess Hill, West Sussex, RH15 0EG

• Pupils: 700 girls, boarding and day • Ages: 2½–18 years • Size of sixth form: 94 • Non-denom • Fees: Boarding £22,875; Day £12,975 pa • Independent

Tel: 01444 241 050
Fax: 01444 870 314
Email: reception@burgesshill-school.com
Website: www.burgesshill-school.com

Head: Since 2006, Mrs Ann Aughwane (fifties), graduated from Loughborough, joint honours maths and education, previously deputy head of the school and prior to this head of mathematics at Guildford High. Interrupted her career to be a maths research associate at Edinburgh University. A bubbly, warm personality, keen on smiling faces in school. Had no plans to make sweeping changes but her motto, 'extending opportunities – extending horizons', led to the introduction of Mandarin and other less commonly taught languages. Concerned that there is still a tendency to self-doubt within the female psyche and wants to engender a philosophy of confidence and even risk-taking. She is excited about and animatedly overseeing the new extensions to facilities.

Academic matters: Not for the work-shy. Very good results all round. At A level, the A/B percentage rose from 66 per cent in 1999 to 84 per cent in 2003 and has remained consistently above 80 per cent since – 87 per cent in 2010. There is no stereotyping in terms of subject choices with large numbers attracted to psychology, maths, English lit, chemistry and biology amongst 24 subjects offered. GCSE results steady, 76.5 per cent A*/A in 2010. Girls talk of inspirational teachers. Quite a handful of male staff although predominantly women. There are two very well-equipped laboratories for each science discipline where the girls can unselfconsciously enjoy the sciences unencumbered by gender expectations. New chemistry laboratories opened in March 2010. Science is split between the dual award and the individual sciences. Head of sciences denies that the dual is lightweight – 'many girls still go on to study medicine and sciences at university but it allows them more flexibility with other subject combinations.'

Uses MidYIS data for academic tracking, showing very high value-added. Only junior school participates in SATs at key stage 1 and 2. Streaming in maths and French begins in Year 7 and for science in Year 9. Some grumbles from the girls who would relish more subjects on offer – school says, 'a diverse and balanced sixth form programme' is on offer. Parents happy, although they have to keep a vigilant eye on girls' stress levels as homework can be over-demanding. SENCo appointed to interpret psychological jargon and nip problems in the bud. General ethos is academic, however, and the school does not boast any kind of specialism in special needs.

Games, Options, the Arts: Sports facilities are not extensive, one manicured hockey/athletics field and one other rather sloping pitch. One floodlit and four other courts. Very good-sized gym and main hall for indoor sports. Good modern sports/drama block. Efficient, popular staff and plenty of sporting success in hockey, netball with coaches employed for aerobics, squash and trampoline. The girls are bussed to the nearby Triangle sports centre for the use of the pool and other facilities.

Exciting music and drama departments. A truly bustling music block, all practice rooms lively with orchestra, practising flute ensemble; 60 per cent learn one or more instruments, plenty of choirs. Sixth form produces a performing arts festival each year, with fashion, art, drama, dance and music. Good range of children's artwork colourfully prominent around the school and a quality display – good thoughtful compositions making one want to linger. Both junior and senior school very up-to-date with IT equipment and girls use computers in all subjects. Smartboards in all classrooms, including the infant/ junior house. Well-stocked and modern library with full range of daily papers and flat computer desks with recessed computers (under smoked glass/wood desks, no Margins here).

Ambitious building programme. Netball/tennis courts and a practice astro turf completed in 2006, now has planning permission for new sports hall.

Background and Atmosphere: School founded in 1906 as a PNEU (Parents' National Education Union) school by Miss Beatrice Goode, steadily grew and moved to present site in the 1930s. Now an independent charitable trust with 'an industrious, supportive bunch of governors,' says the head. Set in residential suburbia, a good mix of modern redbrick buildings and old turn of the (19th) century houses are linked by some elegant glass corridors. All buildings, including the nursery, junior school, senior school (Webb House) and the sixth form (Cedar House), sprawl across a 14-acre site interspersed with large pockets of lawns, ancient trees, attractive paved quad, fenced pond – a colourful, happy atmosphere.

Takes care to accommodate special requirements e.g. prayer routines and festivals, religious diets, and even bathroom fittings. The three boarding houses, on the surrounds of the school fields, are comfortable and spacious with room to take more. Only the senior school boards; upper sixth have single rooms, Year 9 three to a room. Excellent kitchens, new common-room, sick bay, bathrooms adequate. Full programme of activities for boarders: ballet, fencing, drama workshops and theatre. Sunday is their day off, although they spend most of the day working. The majority of boarders are international.

Food more than worth a mention – anything but traditional stodge, a dining room and food any good restaurant would be proud of. Good hot food choices, excellent display of 12 different salad options, vegetarian option, halal meat for Muslims, and quality fruit. Queues too lengthy, grumbled some girls, but 'well worth the wait.'

Extension to the sixth form centre opened in 2006; new nursery and infants school opened in 2008.

Pastoral Care and Discipline: Heads of lower school, upper school and sixth form strengthen the pastoral ethos of the school.

Pupils and Parents: Catchment wide and mixed – semi-rural and urban. Majority from professional/business backgrounds. Typically both parents work, often first timers to independent education. International contingent of Chinese (HK and China proper), Russian, Malaysian, Korean and UK make up most of the boarding populace. Teachers and pupils have ready beaming smiles – most charming and confident. Some pupils sweetly sidelined us to hymn their teachers' praises. Notable Old Girls include Haydn Gwynne (actress), Holly Willoughby (TV presenter) Caroline Atkins (cricketer) and Dr Francesca Happe (world authority on autism).

Entrance: Almost automatic from junior school so long as pupils can cope and are comfortable with the work ethos. External entry for Years 7, 8 and 9 (the school will accept entrants at any year) – maths, English, verbal reasoning. Entering Year 10 – maths and English paper plus formal interview. Head likes to interview in threes to see how pupils interact with each other, plus helps them to know familiar faces when starting school. Some minor dyslexics will be accepted – although no open policy on special needs.

Exit: A wide spread to universities, drama school etc, and 95 to 100 per cent of pupils go to their first college of choice.

Money Matters: Numbers have always stayed steady, so there are no financial blips or disasters and the governors' current policy is to remain debt-free. Scholarships and bursaries are awarded for talented individuals and those who will thrive in the school environment.

Remarks: Good results, steadily improved reputation, emerging as one of the most popular choices for girls' education in the area.

Caedmon School

Airy Hill, Whitby, North Yorkshire, YO21 1QA

• Pupils: 460 boys and girls • Ages: 11-14 • Non-denom • State

Tel: 01947 602 570
Fax: 01947 820 315
Email: admin@caedmon.n-yorks.sch.uk
Website: www.caedmon.n-yorks.sch.uk

Head: Since 2001, Tony Hewitt BEd MA NPQH (fifties). Attended Gateshead Grammar School, then Leeds and Huddersfield Universities. Taught in four state secondary schools. Still a principal examiner in history – sets GCSE papers for AQA examining board – and is a secondary consultant headteacher. Has written nine GCSE history textbooks and teachers' guides. Married to Jenn, a special needs teacher. Two adult children. Enthusiastic, committed, with unstuffy sense of humour.

Academic matters: Key Stage 3 results are king. And, boy, does it show – Caedmon's results are regularly in top five per cent nationally. Across ability range, pupils judged to leave Caedmon a full academic year ahead of the progress they were expected to make on intake, which means a flying start on GCSEs at their next school.

Also working on 'demystifying' exams by offering volunteers a chance to take information technology and food technology GCSEs at 14. Impressive results from pupils – and even some teachers who were brave enough to sit the exam alongside them. A Wednesday afternoon option programme allows pupils to study GCSEs in food technology, ICT, statistics and general studies, alongside opportunities in music,drama,construction and outdoor education. School prides itself on doing well by less-able pupils, including special needs. Intense monitoring means that any slip in standards is noticed and acted on. The school was awarded the Dyslexia Quality Mark in 2007.

Ofsted in 2005 reported 'no weaknesses' and head got an invitation to St James's Palace 'as head of an outstanding school'. 2006 saw the school selected to represent the youth of Great Britain at the G8 conference in St Petersburg – along with students from seven other countries, they advised the world's leaders, resulting in accolades from across the world. The visit concluded with meeting all eight world leaders and morning coffee with the prime minister at number 10. In 2007 the school was selected for a visit to Pakistan and works closely with schools in the Middle East. In 2008 and 2009 the school sent representatives to speak at the UN in Geneva.

Games, Options, the Arts: Huge grounds including own wood for cross-country. £500,000 new floodlit Astroturf, the first in the town, completed 2004. New classrooms and changing facilities finished in 2007. A new music and drama centre built in 2010 and new science facilties planned for 2011. Some pupils opt for junior sports leadership awards and pass on their skills in primary schools. Others return to coach Caedmon's athletes in their lunch hours after they leave. Wealth of after-school activities, including clog dancing and boxercise.

Good music and drama, including two productions a year – though expect the unexpected. The sublime – performing a home-grown play on board the replica of Captain Cook's ship, *Endeavour* – was soon followed by the ridiculous, Caedmon's own *Stars In Their Eyes*, with staff and parents doing their routines. These events regularly raise over £1,000 for school charities, including the sponsorship of a classroom destroyed in the tsunami five years ago.

Background and Atmosphere: Get up early, very early, to see what puts Caedmon in a class of its own. Its open school policy means that pupils welcome from 7.45am onwards to use the library, computer rooms, do their homework or just socialise. The last pupils drift home around 6.00pm. And still the 1960s building, above Whitby Harbour, is as tidy as your grandma's front room on Easter Sunday. So how do they do it? Largely through a very structured system of rewards and merits and efficient prefects given a heady level of responsibility, which includes running the school council and helping to suss out job candidates – hard to believe they're still only 14. They even have their own common-room.

And if you thought the days when house points meant anything in state comprehensives were long gone, Caedmon has found a way of making them doubly precious – the more points your house gets, the more balls it's awarded in the school's weekly lottery. And the prize? First place for your year in the school dinner queue. Priceless.

Pastoral Care and Discipline: Part of its success is down to knowing its pupils well, and while most would claim the same, it's small enough to mean it. Teachers pool knowledge of individual pupils at staff meetings – as much chance of disappearing in this school as of scooping a double rollover. Those who work hard are rewarded, those who don't are under the microscope. The head, who tours school several times a day, also does spot-checks on pupils' books. Bad behaviour means formal warnings and sometimes a phone call home to Mum. And the ultimate deterrent? Saturday morning detention in full uniform. 'You see this forlorn figure in white shirt and tie trudging into school? They don't do it again,' says head.

Pupils and Parents: Very supportive parents who appreciate that Caedmon goes that extra mile. Accessibility to head verging on saintly – gives parents his personal email address and mobile phone number: 'I know if they use that number, they're desperate to speak to me'. And a newsletter goes home every Friday. That's more contact than most adults have with their mums.

Entrance: Mainly, but not exclusively, down to catchment area. About 20 per cent come from outside in one of those rare instances where parental choice means you can actually get into a very good school without having to move into the grounds.

Exit: Most go to Whitby Community College, the local 14 to 19 state school. Some come out of private sector for their three years at Caedmon.

Remarks: A peach of a school which combines respect and responsibility and still finds room for some classroom banter. You don't just send your child there – you wish you'd gone yourself.

Caistor Grammar School

Church Street, Caistor, Caistor, Lincolnshire, LN7 6QJ

• Pupils: 295 boys, 335 girls; all day • Ages: 11-18 • Size of sixth form: 170 • Non-denom • State

Tel: 01472 851 250
Fax: 01472 852 248
Email: administrator@caistorgrammar.com
Website: www.cgs.lincs.sch.uk

Head: Since 1996, Mr Roger Hale MA MA(Ed) (forties), a driving force. Educated Huddersfield New College and Cambridge (law and history), he is a modern headmaster with a top-flight MA in education management and administration, and his finger on the pulse of what's happening in the world of education. Was deputy head here for three years. Previous schools include Tewkesbury School (a Beacon School) and Haberdashers' Aske's, Elstree. Married with two children. Subtle, capable and switched-on, ensuring that his school gets the most of what is on offer. Respected by staff and pupils alike for his commitment to the school – 2008 Ofsted report, once again, refers to his 'outstanding leadership'. Proud to head the county's best grammar school and one of the country's top ten mixed state schools but certainly doesn't gloat about it; always on the look-out to make improvements where possible. Other half of the impressive double act is hugely popular and energetic deputy head, Eddie Cook (also Cambridge). School in Ofsted 'Hall of Fame' three times and received, yet again, an 'outstanding' judgement from latest Ofsted inspectors.

Academic matters: Results at GCSE and A level consistently break school records. Nearly 100 per cent get A*–C at GCSE and most of those are taking 10 or 11. The average point score for A level candidates has been over 30 for five years. Results especially strong in English, history and geography but also in sciences. Smallish range of subjects on offer reflects size of school. Latin and/or classical civilisation is on the curriculum. All sixth formers do three A levels complemented by general studies, 'to broaden horizons,' say students, cheerfully. Good support is provided for those with learning difficulties. There is a mentor scheme for students in Year 11 and a paired support scheme where sixth formers provide support for younger students as well as extra teaching. The school has recently become a Humanities Second Specialism School bringing new opportunities for personal development, along with extra funding.

Games, Options, the Arts: Since 2005, the school has been a Specialist Sports College allowing them to set new goals, develop facilities for students and serve the wider community, with fitness suite, multi-use games area and new pavilion. The school works alongside other schools promoting sport, sending out students as ambassadors. Pitches are a five-minute jog from the main school buildings, as well as floodlit all-weather area and tennis courts on separate field. A good range of sport is available – football, hockey, rugby, netball, dance, gymnastics, volleyball, badminton, cricket, tennis etc, with a number of students playing at county level. Music quite strong and all students are encouraged to play an instrument (tuition is subsidised by the school). Diversity of skills amongst students – one is eighth in world Irish dancing. The art block is small but subject keenly-supported. Interesting work hangs on the walls around the school.

A mass of extra-curricular activity – house plays, exchange visits to France and Germany, public speaking teams (often successful up to county level), a school newspaper (highly commended in the TES competition), theatre trips to Stratford, ski trips, many Leadership Awards in sports, drama, music and modern foreign languages, chess club, Young Enterprise Scheme, the Duke of Edinburgh Award scheme and a host of designated days, e.g. Disabilities Awareness Day, RE Day, World Issues Day, Safety Day, Enterprise Days etc. There's also a partnership scheme with a school in Senegal. Lots of careers advice on hand and help for students to get the most out of their gap year.

Background and Atmosphere: Caistor Grammar lies along a narrow lane in the somewhat crumbling and faded Georgian magnificence of Caistor. Founded in 1631, the school is an attractively higgledy-piggledy collection of buildings, one of which dates from the original foundation. New building provides much-needed extra space but it is a marvel that the school manages to fit so many students into a comparably small area. Maximum benefit seems to be extracted from every inch. The buildings are generally in good shape and kept tidy, which is a necessity. Lots of computers available around the school. Sixth formers have their own house for private study.

Pastoral Care and Discipline: The school feels happy and with a strong sense of purpose in the air – smiling students and staff. Teachers are strikingly popular and much mention is made of friendliness and supportiveness. Considerable quiet pride in being at the school. 'Pupils feel they've been given a great opportunity,' says the head. 'They've seen the publicity and they're very conscious they're the next generation, carrying the baton, and they don't want to let the school down.'

All the sixth form are prefects and the head boy and girl plus senior prefect team are elected. There is a school council with representatives for each year to discuss various issues. Lunch – good healthy choice on offer, with majority opting for this rather than packed from home.

Pastoral care is outstanding, says Ofsted. The school is small enough that every person is known and valued as an individual. Form tutors to keep an eye on things. The head is keen that non-teaching staff support school in other ways so that everyone contributes to school life. Academic problems are quickly identified and appropriate action swiftly taken. The pupils look after each other – a weekly mentoring system operates whereby older students help younger ones with study problems. Given the size of the school, most of the outside areas are overlooked by class rooms, staff and various offices, something that parents must welcome.

Pupils and Parents: A fairly middle class school (parents are doctors, lawyers, businessmen, farmers) but far from exclusively so. Quite a lot from Grimsby but many also from villages. Pupils are well-mannered and open, keen to talk about the school, its achievements and the opportunities on offer. Most notable Old Girl is Dawn French, 'but I'm sure there'll be many more quite soon,' says Roger Hale.

Entrance: Children are required to sit two verbal reasoning tests, assessing natural ability rather than subject knowledge. If the applicant lives within 6.5 miles of the school, they will need 220 marks out of a maximum 280 (i.e. they will be in the top 25 per cent of ability range). Then they are guaranteed a place. For those out of catchment, it's a case of competing for whatever places are left over, typically about 40. There are 90 places in total per year and about 300 applicants. There are usually a few places each year subsequently. Applicants to the sixth form are particularly welcome.

Exit: All sixth formers leave for higher education. A good proportion go off to study science in some form or other. Universities include Cambridge, Imperial College – London, Leeds, Newcastle, Nottingham, Sheffield, Warwick, York.

Remarks: The school continues to reach new heights, seeking to 'use lively minds, to work hard, to develop all talents; to grow through sharing'. They make more than most of what are, admittedly, not lavish facilities and could teach a number of well-endowed schools a thing or two. 'We seek to build on the distinguished past,' says Roger Hale, 'to create our even better future.'

The Camden School for Girls

Sandall Road, London, NW5 2DB

• Pupils: 970; all day • Ages: 11-19 • Size of sixth form: 420 sixth form of whom 125 are boys • Non-denom • State

Tel: 020 7485 3414
Fax: 020 7284 3361
Email: csg@camdengirls.camden.sch.uk
Website: www.camdengirls.camden.sch.uk

Head: Since April 2010, Ms Elizabeth Kitcatt, who has been at the school for 15 years and was previously head of English at Parliament Hill School in Highgate Road.

Academic matters: Banded entry taking a quarter from each of four ability groups, ensuring sufficient high fliers to keep up the Camden classics tradition: everyone studies classical civilisation in Year 8 and chooses between it and Latin in Year 9. Ancient Greek lessons available before school (and as a mainstream sixth form subject). Everyone tries out French and Spanish in Year 7, choosing one of these at the end of the first term. Strong encouragement to keep studying a modern language to GCSE – hooray! – and about 80 per cent of pupils do, though studying two is not an option. The less academically inclined can opt for beauty therapy, business studies or child health and social care alongside the core GCSE subjects. The school is 'signed up to support developments' by the local authority to offer the new diplomas, but unlikely to run them in house.

By general consensus a gentle start to secondary school life. 'We weren't sure that anything was happening to begin with. But in Year 10 she realized that she had to start working hard. The ethos encourages self-motivation. They aren't nagged or nannied. They're encouraged to be independent of mind.' Teaching a 'mixed bag' of the inspiring and the less impressive, say pupils and parents. But school is strong on tracking students. 'They know how everyone is doing,' said a parent. 'We were never concerned that she was going to under-perform.'

Setting for maths and science from Year 8 with five ability groups; two groups each for French and Spanish. One nurture group in English in Year 10 for those needing targeted support. In 2010, 90 per cent of pupils got 5+ A*–C GCSEs, 74 per cent including maths and English.

The year groups more-or-less double in size in the sixth form, with a large part of the first term spent bonding as a group, including an adventure activities week. The sixth form is unashamedly academic, with a baseline for entry of five grade Bs at GCSE, including maths and English. GCSE retakes are not on the timetable, though maths retake does sneak into the enrichment slot. The subject range widens to include drama, economics, media studies, photography, philosophy and more, plus vocational business and ICT. The bias is definitely towards the arts, with English much the most popular subject, history a close second, physics low down the list. At A levels 79 per cent A*/A/B grades in 2010.

Gifted and talented programme from Year 7 onwards sees pupils working with eminent architects, photographers, poets, dancers et al. 'We are not afraid of identifying talented pupils and moving them forward.' Sixth form masterclasses challenge students outside their chosen subjects. 'They are open to anyone, in true Camden style, but we would expect those with particular talents to take part.'

Good, very nurturing SEN support inside and outside the classroom. Mentors aim to raise aspirations of those who would not otherwise have considered higher education. 'There is lots of casual employment in Camden and they need an understanding of the benefits of further study.' Investment bankers from JP Morgan link up with sixth formers to give them help with CV writing, interview techniques, researching higher education. 'Everyone can benefit from someone showing a special interest in them.'

Games, Options, the Arts: Has a music specialism and the music is, indeed, 'very inspiring'. Strong links with the London Symphony Orchestra – pupils might find themselves playing alongside LSO musicians at the Barbican, hearing their composition played by an LSO group, or taking part in a project on Mahler. 'It brings an amazing breadth to our students' experience.' Ambitious choral and orchestral performances; popular parent/staff choir.

Art excellent and popular with inspiring work on display round the school and good results at GCSE and A level. DT also strong, particularly textiles. Drama is an A level but not a GCSE option – plenty of opportunities to get involved in exciting school productions, including sixth form musicals.

Limited sports facilities on site – gym, basketball court and dance studio – but the school uses the next-door Cantelowes sports pitch and the newly-refurbished Kentish Town baths, plus other facilities in Market Road and Finsbury Park. Football, netball, rounders and athletics matches against other schools, and dance, trampoline, gym and basketball clubs.

Enrichment classes for sixth formers range from rock-climbing to stage management. Plenty going on throughout the school from talent shows to ski trips, from sponsored cycle rides to language exchanges. Pupils talk of fantastic dance projects, fascinating after-school philosophy courses, inspiring jazz workshops.

Background and Atmosphere: Founded in 1871 by Francis Mary Buss in her mother's home in Camden Street. Moved to the Sandall Road site, previously occupied by Ms Buss' other school, North London Collegiate, in 1956. Originally a grammar school, it turned comprehensive in 1977. Cramped site off the busy Camden Road, but extensive rebuilding and refurbishment over the past 20 years has seen most of the school modernised, with plush new DT rooms, music house, sixth form centre etc.

A strong sense of tradition engenders self-confidence and ambition. 'My daughter has really found herself here,' commented a father. Relaxed, informal atmosphere with a very strong ethos of social engagement and a sense of loyalty and belonging. 'Even the boys are proud to be "Camden girls",' said a parent.

Pastoral Care and Discipline: A small minority have 'challenging behaviour'. Some of these have severe emotional or mental heath problems. 'I will fight tooth and nail to get them into a more suitable therapeutic environment.' Most of the others come round and there are few permanent exclusions. Excellent pastoral care, very inclusive and nurturing. Influential school council responsible for running anti-bullying support group, choosing drama productions, organising charity events. Pupils encouraged to take on responsibilities, speak in public, express their views.

Pupils and Parents: Hugely diverse ethnically and socially, including many middle class families who did a tactical move to the area in the late primary school years, plus large numbers who may speak Bengali, Greek or Somali at home. Undoubtedly adds a premium to local house prices. OGs include Emma Thompson, Arabella Weir, Geri Halliwell, Lily Donaldson and Julia Hobsbawm.

Entrance: Massively over-subscribed, so will only accept applications for its 112 Year 7 places from up to 220 girls who live less than 1.2 miles from the school. These all take a banding assessment and are divided into four ability groups, with equal numbers from each group offered a place. Priority to girls with an SEN statement naming Camden as the most appropriate school; then looked after children; then siblings; then by distance. This varies according to band but is nearly always less than half a mile.

Also up to eight music places, selected by audition, for which distance is not a criterion. Applicants must have passed grade 3 or be playing at that level, but in practice successful musicians tend to have reached at least grade 5.

Takes up to 150 new students – generally around half of them boys – into the sixth form, many from independent schools. They must have a minimum of five grade Bs at GCSE, including maths and English, and higher requirements for some A level subjects, e.g. further maths. The number of appeals has been rising at sixth form level and the school may no longer interview candidates, nor can it continue to select 'on a touchy-feely criterion of supporting the school ethos'. So priority to looked-after children; then those already in the school; then siblings; then 15 music places; then exceptional medical or social need; then those 'selected on the basis of their school reference regarding their suitability for A level study and their predicted GCSE grades', with proximity as a tie-break. The school expects to offer places to students living within about three miles but this depends on spaces being available in their chosen courses. Those wanting to study ancient Greek or further maths are more likely to be accommodated than, for example, budding philosophers.

Applicants for the 15 sixth form music places are expected to be playing at grade 5 or above – probably rather higher – on an orchestral instrument and taking part in an orchestra. They are chosen 'to support the distinctive orchestral tradition of the school' and must provide a copy of their latest music exam comment sheet and contact details for two referees – usually their music teacher and orchestral conductor.

Exit: The five grade B baseline for sixth form entry trips up a few, and generally around 30–40 girls leave after GCSEs, mostly for more vocational options elsewhere. Sixth form leavers virtually all go on to higher education, including around 15 a year to Oxbridge, a similar number to art colleges and some to read music. Courses such as international relations, anthropology and classics more common than science/medicine.

Money Matters: Voluntary aided, so must find 10 per cent of funds for refurbishments etc. Luckily parents are supportive, committed and skilled at raising money.

Remarks: Extremely popular and successful comprehensive, consistently rated 'outstanding' by Ofsted, with a liberal ethos of social concern and hugely loyal pupils, strongly committed to their school. New head – a rare internal appointment – should maintain happy, productive and stable atmosphere.

Canbury School

Kingston Hill, Kingston Upon Thames, Surrey, KT2 7LN

• Pupils: 65; mixed • Ages: 11-16 • Non-denom • Fees: £12,855 pa • Independent

Tel: 020 8549 8622
Fax: 02089 746 018
Email: head@canburyschool.co.uk
Website: www.canburyschool.co.uk

Head: Since 2002, Mr Robin Metters BEd (late fifties). Mr Metters' teaching career spans thirty years. He was principal of Woodside Park International School in North London for sixteen years before taking over at Canbury. Married with two grown-up children, Mr Metters enjoys sports, particularly sailing and golf. Time permitting, he is keen to join in sporting activities with pupils and is an enthusiastic spectator at all school events.

Academic matters: Small, inclusive school catering for children who would not necessarily thrive in large comprehensives. Good range of subjects on offer, the majority of pupils take around nine GCSEs. Considering the school is non-selective, results are impressive, especially for maths and English. Options at 14+ now wider with additional GCSEs subjects. Small class sizes enable teachers to provide that ever important individual attention, staff pupil is ratio 1:7. Sensible amount of homework with clear guidelines for each year and an optional homework club. A number of children with SEN, mostly dyspraxia, dyslexia and mild Aspergers/ASD One-to-one support with specialist teachers in-house to ensure individual needs are meet. Local speech therapists and occupational therapist work with the school as required. English as a foreign language tuition is also provided on a one-to-one basis or small group depending on the needs of pupils.

Games, Options, the Arts: Excellent range of sporting activities for a smaller establishment, so something to suit everyone's tastes. The school takes advantage of the numerous local sporting facilities in Richmond Park, Kingston and on the Thames for sailing, canoeing and rowing. Cross country running is a major sport in which pupils compete successfully and everybody gets the opportunity to learn to swim. Visual arts are strength, colourful expressive art displays and many different media are used; parents say three-dimensional design, ceramics and collage are particularly popular. Class music is taught for the first three years and some children have individual instrumental tuition and enjoy performing in informal concerts. Drama taught mainly through small group work with an emphasis on developing communication skills and building confidence. Younger pupils tend to be the actors, with older ones taking on technical roles and directing the productions. A variety of clubs run at lunchtimes and after school, table tennis, karate and arts being popular. Good variety of excursions and field trips arranged each term for all to help pupils develop new interests. The school prides itself on taking the children out and about.

Background and Atmosphere: Founded in 1982 by John Wyatt, Canbury is accommodated in a large Edwardian house on Kingston Hill. Whilst the site is compact it has the advantage of backing onto Richmond Park where many of their sporting activities take place. Recent renovations include a new science lab changing facilities and complete redecoration, the IT suite and art room recently made over too. The school is fully accessible and is able to consider applications from children with physical disabilities. Canbury is an educational charity administered by a board of governors whose aim is create a genuine community where individuals can be happy and motivated to achieve their maximum potential. Despite pupils being hard at work there is a calm and less formal atmosphere in comparison with many other schools.

Pastoral Care and Discipline: Pastoral care is high on the agenda to ensure wellbeing and self-esteem. This is a caring school, where everyone is treated as an individual and taught to feel good about themselves and their abilities. Form tutors are always available to deal with any day-to-day problems, home work diaries are used to convey messages between home and school. Two members of staff are trained counsellors and pupils have a school council. Clear set of school rules are presented in a booklet, The Canbury Code.

Pupils and Parents: Mostly professional parents come from all walks of life and a range of backgrounds, both international and UK based. Families tend to be fairly local from a 5 mile radius from Richmond to Weybridge, handful come from central London. A school council is run by staff and parents to raise funds for the chosen charity of the year.

Entrance: At 11+ pupils spend an assessment morning at the school. Places are offered following a meeting with the headmaster and satisfactory reports from previous schools.

Exit: At 16+ most choose to go to further education colleges, Epsom, Esher and Guildford. A few opt for sixth forms at local schools Coombe Girls.

Money Matters: Both current and prospective pupils can apply for means-tested bursaries.

Remarks: A good choice for children who require a sympathetic approach to their education. The school definitely fills a gap in the education market, comment parents. A positive and warm atmosphere, where everyone is made to feel welcome.

Canford School

Canford Magna, Wimborne, Dorset, BH21 3AD

• Pupils: 365 boys, 270 girls (245 boys board, 120 day boys; 180 girls board, 90 day girls) • Ages: 13-18 • Size of sixth form: 268 • C of E • Fees: Boarding £26,970; Day £21,000 pa • Independent

Tel: 01202 847 207
Fax: 01202 881 723
Email: admissions@canford.com
Website: www.canford.com

Head: Shortly after Mr John Lever MA PGCE (fifties) settled himself at the helm in 1992, the Church of England voted to accept women priests and the Queen referred to her Annus Horribilis; earlier Betty Boothroyd had been elected the first woman Speaker of the House of Commons. That's how long ago it was and at least two of those events must have sent tremors down to the idyllic acres of Canford. Budding Boothroyds and women priests began to fill the school shortly after his arrival. A product of Westminster and Trinity Cambridge, where he read geography and won a rowing blue, he arrived at Canford after a brief spell at St Edward's, Oxford ('I don't think I did any teaching there') followed by 16 years at Winchester, where he did teach and was a housemaster. Married to Alisoun, with three children.

The prospectus, one of the very few we have read which can be enjoyed for its literary and thought-tugging merit, is largely scripted by the headmaster. Nor does he disappoint when meeting him. Articulate and witty, he does not belong to the turkey-cock school of heads firing off sound-bites and trumpeting successes, while exuding self-importance and power. He talks of the old virtues with originality and sensitivity, is totally lacking in pomposity, enjoys the fact that, when it comes to change, Canford, as a young school, has the 'manoeuvrability of a speed boat' and enjoys the company of the pupils – 'rebels included'. Sitting in his extraordinarily decorated study with exquisite views over the manicured grounds, he can watch with interest boys and girls drifting by. Many of them look in as they pass; some smile, a few wave. This is not an ogre in his den. 'He's got a great sense of humour but he's no pushover,' said a boy who looked as if he might have experienced both characteristics. Most parents think he is terrific; one or two thought he might be running out of ideas, a suggestion which was howled down by the majority. 'I never cease to be amazed by his capacity for thinking up new ways of encouraging individual growth within a sense of community,' says a neighbouring head.

Academic matters: Do not be fooled by the relaxed and informal atmosphere that pervades, even when A levels and GCSEs loom. This is a school where there is some cracking good teaching going on and the staff we met were fizzy, fun and focused. What's more, pupils seemed to acknowledge and value that, frequently volunteering respect and affection for their teachers – even when out of ear shot. The excellent relations between staff and pupils which really do seem to exist at Canford are founded on trust and willingness, as much in the classroom as out. Indeed divisions between inside and out are frequently invisible: whether it's the school lobster sloughing his shell, wounded seahorses finding solace with the biology faculty, brown trout being launched into the river, setting out for Lyonesse in search of Thomas Hardy and Tennyson, down to St Ives for painting and artists, much of what is taught and disseminated involves wholeness. This is not gimmicky stuff: it's education in the round. Education for life.

Statistically-minded league table bibbers ought to be impressed by the results published in the prospectus pack and on the internet: they make good reading. Canford's GCSE and A level results are right up with co-education schools with more illustrious names. Considering the breadth of intake, that speaks volumes.

New boys and girls try every subject available in a kind of academic circus including Connections, a non-examined course in every year group involving PSE, citizenship and general knowledge. Everyone takes a language at GCSE; very, very few people drop below a B. The system precludes cutting out subjects too early and gives a far more realistic foundation from which to choose A levels. Breadth, breadth, breadth. Facilities are good: glorious library, innovative new IT room, lively DT space (more girls than boys taking A level this year – so one in the eye for critics who say that co-education polarises subject choices), good science laboratories (55 per cent in the lower sixth doing sciences. 'The quality of teaching for the sciences is one of the best-kept secrets in Dorset,' says a delighted parent.) Languages are 'fun' and imaginatively taught but numerically not as popular; music and art results excellent (the latter taught by the man who runs the first XV). All this is supported, encouraged, broadened by visiting authors and scientists, poets and politicians: fresh air from without as well as expeditions and trips abroad, trips to the theatre and other places of interest. No boundaries. Good provision for those with learning difficulties. Learning skills can replace a GCSE and help with dyslexia is in-house and available on a one-to-one basis.

Games, Options, the Arts: Notable successes on the games field at every level. Rugby, hockey and cricket for boys; hockey and netball for girls are the main team games, though a sizeable number of boys and girls take to the river and propel themselves backwards as fast as they can. Some recent successes at Henley and more local regattas, and a magnificent feat on the part of a boy who last year sculled over the channel only 10 minutes outside the world record. There is a Royal/real tennis court (not many of those around), a delightful golf course as well as numerous Astroturf pitches and a huge sports hall with room for indoor cricket nets, indoor hockey, weight-lifting, dance practice rooms. Everything. The old swimming pool is leaking water and money; a new and snazzy indoor one, haemorrhaging school funds but reckoned to be essential, is due to open shortly. The CCF is popular but not compulsory, with an exciting assault course and the opportunity for challenging expeditions; alternatively, younger pupils take part in conservation project work, while the majority of sixth formers are involved in a local partnership project such as working with disabled young people or helping teach science and languages in local primary schools.

The Canford Northam project is a more ambitious community project with an inner-city youth club in Southampton. Always the outside world beckons. Nowhere is this more obvious than with the Canford Partnership which, founded with money raised from the sale of the

Assyrian bas-relief, annually sends parties of young Canfordians to orphanages in India, Argentina and a village school in Kenya. Pupils raise money over the year and then visit with practicalities and spirit, helping to build tangibly and, as importantly, build bridges of understanding and friendship. Staff and pupils are 'humbled by the experience' and feel they have a 'clearer and wider window on the world'. Again, this is not a gimmick; rather a life-enhancing experience.

Music is terrific and has been for some time. Concerts for all and by many abound; a great number play instruments and are encouraged to perform at any standard. Drama – in the hugely attractive Layard theatre – built specifically for teaching purposes but home to travelling thespians and countless home grown productions – is lively, innovative and popular. 'Anyone can get involved, from actors to lighting and sound boffins', and they do. Art flourishes in a minimalist building designed by a previous art master, offering a wide range of media from oil paintings and ceramics to glass work and objects from abandoned cars. Creativity, the courage to experiment and challenge boundaries, individuality and skilled draughtsmanship are all in evidence. The building is open at weekends.

Background and Atmosphere: Dull would he (or she) be who failed to respond to the beauties of Canford and its Capability Brown landscape. Here, where a building of some sort has stood since the Domesday book, is a monument to the ambitions of the Guest family of GKN fame and Sir Charles Barry, architect of the Houses of Parliament inter alia. The Norman origins remain in the evocative John of Gaunt's kitchen, no longer used for the purpose, and the delicious church in the grounds, too small to take the whole school but used for smaller gatherings. The main building is 19th century at its most baronial. Eating is enjoyed within a magnificent Arthurian hall where in 1888 Edward, Prince of Wales, danced after a ritual slaughter of birds at a shooting party. Nowadays cafeteria meals offer a wider choice of good food with breakfasts allegedly 'amazing'. Founded in 1923, great names from the past are given to key buildings but sit lightly on the superb modern buildings dotted around 250 acres complete with wonderful arboretum, a constant source of delight and research. That and the river with its suspension bridge and mill pond offer a whiff of Eden – as well as teaching aids. The beautiful surroundings play an integral part in this purposeful paradise and it's all only two hours by train from London.

The three day houses are mixed and a day pupil told us that they feel integrated, though many go home at 6pm. The most interesting accommodation is within the main buildings – School House, for instance, has a state bedroom, wonderful old rooms and a maze of corridors. More recent house accommodation is well-designed, with good chilling out areas and kitchens, computer rooms and study bedrooms for older pupils. Girls have bright and airy accommodation comprised of single and double bedrooms with wash-basins, sewing machines and areas for socialising with the boys. A recent group of inspectors described the accommodation as 'outstanding', not a word that is selected lightly from their bland vocabulary.

Prefects are chosen less for their role as bloods, more for their ability to identify minorities and to care. All this supports the feeling that the aim of the school is to promote well-rounded citizens rather than slaves to league tables. The head of school is chosen after a series of interviews and prefects act as conduits between staff and pupils. No swaggering. Pleasant tuck shop known as 'the grubber', much to the delight of the press when the Assyrian bas relief was recognised as genuine, complete with holes from darts. Excellent Health Centre makes up for not having house matrons living in, and there is an impressive new sixth form centre, though the school is still wrestling with how best to use it. The overall feeling we got was of space and friendliness, with pupils ready to talk and laugh. All very happy. Special mention for the sixth former whom we discovered lolling on a sofa reading Dante on his ipod – at least that's what he claimed.

Pastoral Care and Discipline: The matter of child protection once more drew that rare word 'outstanding' from the inspectors, something which did not surprise our guides. 'There are so many people you can talk to if you're worried or unhappy.' Each house has a married house-parent, three tutors (one resident in each boarding house) and a matron. Bullying is very rare though, not unusually, there can be some jostling to establish pecking order among the first year. The point is, no one need feel isolated. There is an official counsellor and a listening service for those who feel some objectivity is required. Sixth formers choose their own tutors – not necessarily from a subject teacher – and meet regularly. There is a zero tolerance policy on drugs (though our guides couldn't remember the last incident); illegal drinking, though dealt with firmly, is more of a challenge. Smoking, it is said, is no longer a problem. Senior pupils may, with permission, visit the fleshpots of Wimborne for dinner on Saturdays and are required to show restaurant receipts. Reins are lightly held but never dropped.

Pupils and Parents: This is not an international school nor, surprisingly, a national school. The head is 'content to remain below the radar' and is pleased that the majority come from less than two hours away. 'It makes it easier to get to know the parents if they are regular visitors.' A smattering come from London and six per cent of boarders come from the Channel Isles. There are some foreign nationals – a few from the far east, from Africa and Europe – but by no means the shopping trolley loads imported by some schools. Day pupils can come and go by bus, and for them occasional overnight accommodation may be offered; senior pupils may use their own cars. The school does not empty at weekends – indeed for 10 weekends of the year pupils are required to stay at school; otherwise arrangements for home leave are sensitively handled. The majority of parents come from local professions with a high preponderance of medics. Those to whom we spoke appreciated the contact they have with the school.

Entrance: The benchmark is 55 per cent at CE, though the school will exercise its discretion in favour of potential flagged up by prep school heads. Relations with prep schools are good and this year's batch of scholars came from 20 different schools. There are over 40 on their books. About 30 join annually post-GCSE.

Exit: Some 97 per cent to universities. Bright pupils are encouraged to set their sights at Oxbridge – 'it's a healthy challenge' – and around 30 do. Over the last four years the school has averaged 16 Oxbridge places per year. This is a school which is not overly fussed about league tables, so isn't in the business of weeding out pupils who may bring them down a little – providing they are really striving for their potential. Occasionally the head will suggest some would 'do better in a different environment' but that's usually enough to do the trick. Traditionally strong on engineering and medicine but an increasingly wide variety of subjects are read at over 30 different universities.

Money Matters: A range of scholarships is available at 13+ and into the sixth form.

Remarks: This is a very special school. Superb facilities in an almost matchlessly lovely environment; first-rate teaching with pupils who really do seem to find joy through achievement. A school of opportunities with windows open to the world outside. Unpretentious and sensitive, at ease with itself but without a trace of smugness. A school which can hold its own with the most popular in the country but one which has, perhaps, benefited from not being fashionable. The question is, for how long will that bonus remain with them?

Canon Slade CofE School

Bradshaw Brow, Bolton, Lancashire, BL2 3BP

• Pupils: 1,680 • Ages: 11-18 • C of E • State

Tel: 01204 333 343
Fax: 01204 333 340
Email: contact@canon-slade.bolton.sch.uk
Website: www.canon-slade.bolton.sch.uk

Head: Since 2006, Mr P Williamson BSc PGCE CPhys MInstP (late forties). Taught physics. Was assistant head here from 1994, moving to headship of Holy Trinity Senior School, Halifax in Jan 1998, returning as head in 2006. Describes himself as a practising Christian and parents say, 'He brings a real Christian influence'. Pupils remark that he always attends drama performances, 'He's so encouraging; he treats us like adults; he doesn't shout at you but tries to work with you'. That he loves the job is evident – 'To be the head of Canon Slade is the best job in the world; I'm here until I retire, I love the place'.

Academic matters: Intake from the whole ability range yet results consistently well above average with over 80 per cent achieving A*–C at GCSE including English and maths, 56 per cent of GCSEs A*–B and 27 per cent A* and A. At A level 75 per cent results are A–C and at key stage 3 most scores level 6 or above, 94 per cent at least level 5. Performing arts particularly strong reflecting specialist college status; top school nationally for the AVCE vocational performing arts for boys and pupils regularly hit the top five per cent of results nationally at all levels in drama and dance, as well as in modern languages. One exception is ICT where results have been notably disappointing in comparison but head promises, 'We are working on this.' Ambassador school for NAGTY with ambitious gifted and talented programme of its own. Target setting through all years – 'You've got to be prepared to work hard here,' say pupils, 'but they don't leave anyone behind; everyone's encouraged to do their best.' Pupils praise teaching staff who're 'always on hand at lunchtime and after school to give extra help and who run extra revision classes before public exams'.

Annual 'walking on water' competition with physics department giving teams £50 from gifted and talented budget to design and make shoes that'll race across the surface of the swimming pool. History trips to European battlefields and language exchanges with France, Germany and Spain as well as with twin schools in Germany, Spain and Japan. Classics and Latin available at both GCSE and A level, even for just one student: 'We'd be loath to give it up,' says head who, along with senior staff, dons his gown every morning for assemblies. Newly refurbished library; computers here and elsewhere round school for students' own work. Sixth formers grumble there aren't enough in their block but admit they could make the effort to walk to one in main school.

Games, Options, the Arts: Specialist college status for performing arts with extensive opportunities. Drama and dance studios with full length mirrored walls, brand new state of the art sound recording studio with full time technician and school hall with traditional stage for renowned high standard productions. Over 20 per cent of pupils play an instrument and contribute to more than a dozen varied ensembles and 'Young Musician of the Year' competition as part of school arts festival. 'We're sympathetic to those offered contracts with theatre companies or orchestras,' says head, 'as long as their academic life doesn't suffer.' Extensive art rooms are ripe with fruit of pupils' labours – 'You have to knuckle down in here,' they say, 'and we've got our own kiln'. Range of design and tech rooms full of beavering students and from the food tech room a view of the out-of-bounds pond that's protected habitat for an endangered gold crested newt population. PE offered at GCSE and A level: 'We've got fantastic sports facilities and loads of opportunities,' say pupils. Half yearly sports assembly for handing out stripes; some blazers groan with these. Bright, clean refurbished 17m indoor swimming pool also used by staff three times a week. Pool, floodlit Astroturf, gym and studios all used by local community. Footballer pupils enjoy workshops with Bolton Wanderers FC. National level cross-country success due in part to school's 57 acres which include 'agony hill'; national schools' finals hosted here. Ambitious basketball led by former England U18 coach; school's U16 and U17s have been recent national champions. National stars include golf and U18 fly fishing champions and last year's winner of two events at the Great Britain Open Disability Swimming Championships is a sixth former here. Dozens of extracurricular clubs, 'The car park in early evening is full of parents collecting children from after school drama, music, sport and other clubs,' says head. Pupils also busy with D of E, Young Enterprise, community service and substantial charity fundraising. Lots of awards including Artsmark Gold, Sportsmark, Investors in People, Leading Edge Status, Excellence in Mentoring among others.

Background and Atmosphere: Founded in 1855 by Canon James Slade for 'classical and moral instruction in conformity with the principles of the Church of England'. A lifesize oil still oversees the hall and the annual Founder's Day service commemorating his death is much loved by all. A girls' school opened in 1879 and the two joined in 1902. The current buildings grew up decade by decade from the 1950s as a direct grant grammar school and then a C of E voluntary aided comprehensive, with selective entry ending in 1978. The modern, airy chapel was added in 2004. Pupils say they'd like to 'change the aesthetics – you've got the lovely chapel at the front and then the grotty bit', although they themselves could help this by taking better care of the dejected lockers that stand broken in the corridors. Pupils are, however, proud of their otherwise good reputation in the wider community.

Pastoral Care and Discipline: Distinctive Christian ethos. Full time chaplain and team described as being 'at the heart of this community of 2000, which is his congregation'. Each day a different form group has communion service in the side chapel and all have daily Christian assembly, form prayers or service in main chapel. School motto, 'Ora et Labora', the imperative forms of the Latin literally translated as 'You must pray and you must work', sets the ethos. 'It's no mistake that the prayer comes before the work,' declares the head and pupils say, 'Oh, yes, most people are real Christians here but the Christian stuff isn't pressurised'. Ofsted said, 'Pupils' spiritual, moral and cultural development is excellent.' Pupils describe the school as caring with very little bullying. 'We have a low threshold of tolerance for poor behaviour, 'says head. 'If we deal with low level problems like undone top buttons, the rest takes care of itself. We don't tolerate a child being cheeky to a teacher and if they were to swear at a teacher they'd be excluded.' Detentions and contacting parents are first steps, followed by isolation in school and eventually exclusion. Pupils say, 'Isolation doesn't teach anything – it just causes aggravation,' but parents like the firm hand saying, 'The children have a healthy respect for the discipline system and the teachers and we welcome the new head's gentler touch'.

Sixth formers describe their common room as relaxed and friendly but some of them feel that 'the sixth form rules are petty, especially over uniform', and their parents wonder if the identity of sixth form is confused, the promised freedoms scuppered by unchanged strong discipline. Overall, however, pupils do feel they have a voice through form captains, school council and several committees – anti-bullying, catering, worship and environment.

All carry ID badges which double as pre-paid cashless catering cards for breakfast, break and lunch, which pupils describe as 'very healthy – whoever heard of a tuck shop that only sells fruit?' before admitting they can buy fairtrade chocolate as well. Long outdoor queues for the canteen mean that some flout rules by eating packed lunches in playground to delight of scavenging seagulls who rake through a surprising amount of litter. 'We are lazy about rubbish,' pupils confess. First four years wear green blazers, Year 11 graduates to black sweatshirts as transition to smart casual, 'but no denim', of sixth form. New intake, 270 in ten forms, has outward bound bonding, lower sixth an induction day of Pennine pursuits.

Pupils and Parents: Pupils come from far and wide from seven LEAs – Bolton, Manchester, Salford, Bury, Blackburn with Darwen, and as far afield as Lancashire and Yorkshire. Over 1,000 travel on fleets of public and school buses and public trains, some 700 under their own or parental steam. The low percentage of ethnic minorities does not reflect the catchment areas but may, head admits, 'reflect the church-going population. Our pupils have a head start because most of them come from stable homes where their parents want them to do well'. Lower than average percentage eligible for free school meals.

Entrance: Not for those ambivalent about the Christian faith. Children from committed Christian families with a lengthy proven track record of regular church attendance stand the best chance of bagging one of the heavily oversubscribed places. Points given for church attendance as verified by an ordained minister and places offered to the 270 applicants with highest scores through LEA co-ordinated system which matches offers with children's given choices. Entrance to sixth form is based on GCSE performance and not on faith criteria. Over 50 per cent of pupils stay on to sixth form taking 90 per cent of places. The rest are also over-subscribed and attract a broader ethnic mix as other faith groups are drawn to overall ethos of school.

Exit: Some 90 per cent to university with plenty of success for medicine and dentistry and one or two to Oxbridge.

Remarks: Fantastic opportunities for performing arts and deserved success from hard work across the board in a caring and unstuffy but distinctly Christian atmosphere.

The Cardinal Vaughan Memorial RC School

89 Addison Road, London, W14 8BZ

• Pupils: 920 boys, plus 130 girls in sixth form; all day • Ages: 11-18
• Size of sixth form: 310 • RC • State

Tel: 020 7603 8478
Fax: 020 7602 3124
Email: mail@cvms.co.uk
Website: www.cvms.co.uk

Acting headmaster: Mr C Eynaud is acting headmaster since the early retirement of much-loved head, Mr Michael Gormally, due to ill-health. Mr Gormally saw his unique school as something of a bastion against the 'moral chaos raging outside', and there is undoubtedly chaos raging at the time of writing. A row over admissions criteria between the school governors and the Westminster diocese – the diocese objected to the parental involvement criteria as discriminatory against poorer parents (see Entrance)- has resulted in a purging of the governing body, injunctions and a stalemate which has, so far, prevented the governors from meeting to select a new head.

Academic matters: Consistently impressive results and school makes no bones about aiming for academic excellence in its comprehensive intake. School has specialist status in mathematics and IT and computing is BIG here – though some would like to see computer science on the curriculum in addition to IT. A level results 79 per cent A*/A/B grades in 2010. Range of subjects offered not immense but includes economics, music tech, philosophy and sociology. It has to be said that the 'newer' subjects do not attract vast numbers. School also offers applied A levels in business and travel & tourism – Bs and Cs for most. Most popular – and successful – A level subjects are maths and Eng lit – both astonishing good. GCSEs – again not a huge range of options – French and Spanish now the only modern langs though Latin thrives and Greek is up-and-coming. Most popular subjects are engineering – a double qualification – French and ICT. Everyone takes RS. 57 per cent A*/A grades overall in 2010 – and remember this is a comprehensive school.

This degree of success is not achieved by having independent school sized classes. In the lower school class sizes are 28–30 though music, DT, art and IT groups have 20 pupils. At KS4, class sizes vary but core subjects are taught in groups of 25–30. Most sixth form classes are under 20. Girls and boys seem to achieve similarly though there are some mutterings about AS candidates being 'encouraged' to drop subjects rather than continuing to A2 if it is felt they are unlikely to do well. Accolades abound – the Vaughan is in the top 20 of just about every league table – often near the top. It is regularly named 'top Catholic comp in the country' by those who have such plaudits to give away. Parents and pupils, for the most part, add to the encomia. No-one could eulogise the school's shiny new facilities – apart from all the IT stuff – or accommodation. The level of achievement here is down to the quality of the teaching and the staff and pupils' pride in the place. We heard of 'lovely teachers', the good monitoring of progress and much high praise, especially, of the music dept. Bright pupils speak warmly of their 'inspiring' teachers, 'they are amazing – best in the business', and they mean it.

All applicants are tested – to ensure that school takes across the ability range and to better enable banding once they arrive. School takes 'more than our fair share of statemented children' and it is a beacon of hope for those parents of children with significant difficulties, seeming, as it does, to offer real education in a compassionate community. Majority with SEN, though, are mild dyslexics and dyspraxics. Who goes where is decided, of course, by the LA but school is concerned about the sheer additional physical space taken by extra LSAs who accompany some of the children with more severe SEN. And this is understandable. Many rooms are small and rather poky and corridors are not spacious. Busy SENCo and others give in-class support but parents give mixed reports. One parent felt that her dyspraxic son's problems were picked up very late and that the support he was subsequently offered was barely adequate. Similar reports from others. School, however, tells us that such comments are 'vastly outweighed by parents delighted with our SEN arrangements'. School unashamed of its high octane essence. 'Here we have traditional, hothouse academic teaching. It can be a bit of a shock for those who come in from outside.' G and T pupils offered Greek – where else in the state system is this a growth area?

Games, Options, the Arts: Very little space on school premises. This is hardly uncommon in London, but it cannot help the potential for the school's sporting excellence to parallel its academic prowess that, for the most part, games depend on a coach trip 30 minutes away to Twickenham – a major part of any school day, however inspiring the location when they get there. Games, nonetheless, played with immense energy and enthusiasm and, especially on the rugby pitch, done well. Cross-country also popular and successful – especially for the girls; rock climbing and indoor rowing equally so – four rowers being offered schols to train for 2012. Football and basketball also played with vigour and rigour. Complaints of too little sport in the recent past now being remedied.

Over 30 per cent of pupils receive individual music tuition and music is a glory of the school – now enhanced by superb new space and facilities on the top floor – big rehearsal/recital rooms, lots of practice rooms and music tech facilities which must induce composing even in the tone deaf. All under a busy and smiley head of dept. Lots of ensembles include the popular Big Band. Schola Cantorum – the celebrated choir – tours and gives concerts all over the place. In London, this includes Westminster Cathedral, Westminster Abbey, St John's Smith Square, The Royal Opera House – they recently provided the boys in Turandot – The Barbican and the Queen Elizabeth Hall. Outside the UK, this includes Italy – all the grandest places in Rome – plus Spain, Greece, Holland, Germany, the USA and France. In 2007, they sang High Mass at Notre Dame. The Schola now has its own Songschool – just like in a regular cathedral choir school – in which the choir rehearses – a real boon. Drama, never a strength here and not an academic subject is, however, enthusiastically pursued and results in popular productions of, mostly, musicals. School's original main building began life as a theatre and we wondered why so little use is made of it in this way – the stage and gallery are intact, if a little dog-eared. Good art – we liked what we saw of the ceramics, sculpture, mobiles, printing et al – lively creative stuff – and equally good DT – wood, metal and plastic work. Lots of imaginative and rewarding extra-curricular trips and visits – especially for the musicians – parents glow.

Background and Atmosphere: The Vaughan is located in posh Holland Park – wide, quiet streets lined by well-appointed Victorian villas and mansion blocks. Shepherd's Bush, on the other side of the monster roundabout round the corner, is a world away, whereas Kensington High Street – about 15 minutes walk the other way – seems a natural neighbour. Founded in 1914, the school is a memorial to the third Archbishop of Westminster, Herbert, Cardinal Vaughan. It began life as an independent school with 29 pupils but became a grammar school in 1944 and a comprehensive in 1977. Girls were first admitted to the sixth form in 1980 and their presence – 'an adornment to the school', according to Mr Gormally – is established. No chance of going co-ed throughout – simply no room. The original building – Addison Hall – was a musical theatre, but its exterior – possibly what attracted its purchasers – is more reminiscent of a Rinascimento palazzo in pink stone. It now boasts an entrance with highly-wrought grillwork in which the school's motto, Amare et Servire, and crest are displayed. 'The Old Building' as it is known, houses Years 11–13. The 'New Building' was built in the 1960s and much added to since then. It has an attractive exterior with a pretty little garden and an impressive reception area which abuts the main hall – full of pupils on supervised private study when we visited – no 'free' periods here. DT and IT are housed in the Pellegrini Building, named after Mr Gormally's predecessor. Some roomy places inside but the overall impression is of a rather cramped school with little space – especially outside – and many rather bleak areas. Most rooms have air-conditioning but we almost passed out in the heat of some of them. Few rooms or corridors have displays or much colour and the ambiance is not so much monastic as a little neglected.

Situated in these leafy, pricey avenues, you'd expect an upmarket local school population. But it isn't so. School takes from all over and the only common denominator is a commitment to the Roman Catholic faith. Mr Gormally was wearily, but pugnaciously, defensive of the charge of being socially or academically elitist. In his 2008 report he wrote, 'people ask why our pupils' performance goes so far beyond national averages. After all, our top results at A level and at GCSE, over the last five years, have improved six times more than national results. Is it because, as some would like to believe, we "cherry pick" pupils from privileged backgrounds? I don't think so. More than 18 per cent – almost a fifth – of those boys who achieved such staggering results at GCSE last year were on free school meals. The national average of pupils on free school meals is 14 per cent. So much for the slander that the Vaughan is socially selective.' Maybe the slander persists because the staff wear academic gowns – must be anathema to Dave Spart, head of St Jargon's, and those who pump out new brainless 'initiatives' every morning.

The life of the school is imbued with its Roman Catholic inspiration. Everywhere are photographs of pontiffs, cathedrals and the school's own choir singing in various glorious cathedrals. Year groups go on retreats at Tyburn Convent and at Farm Street and the school day and week are punctuated by regular Mass, confession, Benedictus, angelus and so on – all lessons begin and end with the Sign of the Cross and some teachers have prayers in each of their lessons – to a degree rare even in RC schools. But there is also a spirit of enquiry. Vaughan pupils address seriously 'the Dawkins Delusion', 'the problem of Free Will' and 'the Just War theory'. Philosophy pupils attend Heythrop College for talks on philosophy of religion, epistemology and ethics and theology pupils explore the history of Israel. The ethos is embraced and warmly defended by pupils when appropriate. They are aware of the privilege of being here and of the secular – and other – pressures that might have it otherwise. While most parents express great satisfaction with the school in general, we heard a few murmurs from those who are less than ecstatic. 'It's fine as long as all goes well' ... 'they're not brilliant at dealing with problems' ... 'they're not great at getting back to you' – (school says, 'we pride ourselves on excellent communications with parents and prompt responses to their queries') – and 'it's best for the really bright'. School warmly disputes this too. And most are truly grateful for what they receive.

Pastoral Care and Discipline: Discipline is tight but, by now, so well-established that it works and few transgress. Sixth formers have more latitude though their commonroom is open only at breaktimes. Occasional bullying is 'firmly and speedily dealt with'. Zero tolerance of drink or drugs is seldom tested. The occasional idiot caught smoking in the streets – sixth form pupils are allowed out of school in breaks – is punished. We saw lots of Vaughan pupils out and about and they definitely do not frighten the horses. 'Old-fashioned good manners' expected and, in general, displayed. The atmosphere is orderly and we saw only quiet classes. Catholic ethos underpins everything and is palpable. Sex ed taught 'by the RS dept for the moral side and the science dept for the biological details'. Four houses – Campion, Fisher, Mayne and More. Real sense of camaraderie between pupils.

Pupils and Parents: Pupils come from a wide area covering most of London, some from as far away as Hertfordshire and Surrey. 51 per cent are from ethnic minority groups. 30 per cent speak English as an additional language. Here the offspring of a few of well-heeled 'old' RC families from Kensington learn alongside those of their Filipino, Portuguese or Spanish live-in domestic staff and the children of Irish immigrants from Wembley, in a context hard to find elsewhere. Parents very appreciative of parents' evenings when teachers come to find them rather than the usual ghastly queuing for a two minute slot with a glazed-eyed teacher. Notable former pupils include actors Richard Greene – Robin Hood in earlier days – and Roger Delgado, footballers Bernard Joy of Arsenal and Fulham and the last amateur to represent the England national football team, Paul Parker and Eddie Newton, novelist Helen Oyeyemi and comedian Dominic Holland. Also WWII flying aces Donald Garland VC and Paddy Finucane DSO and recent Olympic rowing gold medallists Martin Pross and Gary Herbert. Many seem, however, to have worthy careers in the City.

Entrance: Pupils come from over 50 schools. Around 725 apply for the 120 places at 11+. At sixth form, around four apply for every place. Most of the sixth form entrants will be girls – lots from Sacred Heart – and the entrance requirements at that stage are academic, rather than devotional – As and Bs in the subjects they will study in the sixth. Simple. Alas, not so simple the requirements at 11+ and, at the time of writing, even more fraught than hitherto. School is beset not just by requirements made of admissions criteria by the secular authorities but, lamentably, since early 2009, by muddling (and meddling?) directives from the Archdiocese of Westminster. School has long been (in)famous for the rigour of its admissions' criteria and stories abound of devoted little church-goers being rejected on account of imperfect catechism or knowledge of parables. 'Nonsense!' bellows school. Early baptism, weekly attendance at Mass, first confession and communion – all are taken for granted in applicants but now the crux seems to be the criterion of family 'involvement' in the church. It is sad – and confusing – to see a schism in this community over such an issue and we hope to report a resolution soon. It may well be that the new Archbishop – just appointed at the time of writing – will sort it out.

Exit: A regular mighty handful to Oxbridge – 12 in 2010 – all doing solid subjects at real colleges. Most of the rest to heavyweight universities to do heavyweight subjects – law at King's, maths at Imperial etc and a sensible fistful to e.g. sports psychology at Bournemouth. A notable number to architecture and engineering. Around 20 per cent leave after GCSEs – most to join other schools, a few to employment, another few to other RC colleges.

Money Matters: Voluntary aided. School asks for a voluntary contribution of £300 pa for The Governors' Fund and the vast majority stumps up – some more, some less but no-one comes after you if you don't. A few instrumental bursaries for sixth form entrants who must have reached at least grade VI on an orchestral instrument.

Remarks: A unique opportunity, not to be missed if you can meet the requirements and stay the course. The kind of school parents everywhere cry out for and few, very few, ever find.

Casterton School

Linked to Casterton Preparatory School in the Junior section

Kirkby Lonsdale, Carnforth, Cumbria, LA6 2SG

• Pupils: 295 girls (60 per cent board) • Ages: 11-18 • Size of sixth form: 90 • Christian foundation • Fees: Day: Seniors £12,252-£14,673, Prep £6,570-£12,252; Boarding £17,949-£24,600 pa • Independent

Tel: 01524 279 200
Fax: 01524 279 208
Email: admissions@castertonschool.co.uk
Website: www.castertonschool.co.uk

Headmistress: Since January 2010, Mrs Maxine Lucas, a graduate of Lancaster University, where she read French and Italian, master's degree in French at Bristol University. Brings a wealth of experience from her former school, Tudor Hall in Oxfordshire, where she worked as assistant head.

Academic matters: Punching well above its weight academically and pushing grades higher each year – ranked number 25 in the Financial Times top 1,000 schools list (2009). Broad range of ability on intake and, to its credit, topping the tables for value-added in the independent sector. No obvious weak areas – both arts and sciences excellent; new multi-media lab 2006. Learning support offered as necessary at extra charge; strong work ethic is evident – it is 'cool to succeed'. Useful curriculum course guides provided for all ages giving detailed information of subjects covered and both types and timings of assessment. Average class size 12, maximum 18. Average age of staff 35+.

Games, Options, the Arts: Raising the profile of sport with England cap players coming in to coach. Hockey, lacrosse and tennis have parity of esteem in representing the school at county level. Also swimming, cross-country, dancing, sailing and D of E. Riding is ever-popular – you can bring your own horse, aficionados compete in the Horse of the Year show. All-weather pitch and attractive sports pavilion doubling up for social functions. Wonderfully inspirational creative arts centre displaying very high quality work. Music and drama also particularly strong – majority have individual music tuition; choirs and ensembles perform demanding works, all available on CD.

Background and Atmosphere: Founded in 1823 as Clergy Daughters' school; Charlotte Brontë's portrait hangs in the entrance hall. An eclectic mix of buildings with neat, attractive grounds and surrounded by glorious countryside, with stunning views from every window. Various buildings denote faculty areas, some more attractive than others, and you might get wet when it rains dashing from one to another. The school has 'grown like Topsy', but future plans should ensure a sympathetic and cohesive approach to new building development.

Boarding remains popular – increased numbers in lower school and over 70 per cent boarding in the sixth form, boosted by the launch of a full programme of weekend activities, and new boys' schools adding to the mix for socials. New junior boarding house has been built and a sixth form house is on the way.

Secure traditional feel without being dowdy – the place looks and feels cared for and girls and staff are on good terms. Not just 'academic cannon fodder' – the commitment to an all-round education means what it says here: majority involved in extra-curricular activities. Girls are 'decent' – confident without being arrogant. Peer pressure is supportive – girls say: 'There are no cliques,' and that here, 'You can work, be beautiful and have a boyfriend' without compromise.

Pastoral Care and Discipline: Horizontal house system 12–17 plus prefects. A 'moral compass' is offered – an emphatic 'Yes!' to both discipline and fun. Teachers adopt a fairly relaxed style, small classes making this manageable without threat to academic rigour. Strength of character is much admired, a good range of intellectual, spiritual and physical challenges are on offer, and a highly supportive atmosphere amongst the girls themselves and between staff and girls means that most are prepared to get involved and give it their best shot.

Pupils and Parents: Girls come from all over the north, including Scotland, and as far south as the Midlands, with a few venturing from the south, if they can find it on their radar. Also popular with daughters of Old Girls, Services and ex-pats; brothers attend Sedbergh, Merchiston, Shrewsbury, Giggleswick, Fettes and Lancaster Boys' Grammar. Small influx from Europe, Japan and Hong Kong. Parents are a mix of farming families, old and new money – staunch girls' school supporters who know the value of a good set of academic qualifications and appreciate girls who are bright, lively and curious but not overly sophisticated.

Entrance: Not especially rigorous – which of course highlights results at the other end. Own exam (maths/English/VR) at 11, or common entrance. Mix of girls from primary schools and prep schools, including Casterton Prep. Entrance at 11+ by school exam, CE for 13+. Sizeable intake also at 16+.

Exit: Huge majority stays on for sixth form, a few depart for co-ed, their places filled by new girls, some from overseas. Most go on to HE, vast majority to Russell Group universities and, for those who can, Oxbridge. Notable old girls: Brontë sisters.

Money Matters: Scholarships at 11+, 13+ and 16+. Bursaries are means-tested.

Remarks: The school development office has a real challenge in an area where sheep outnumber people by at least 40:1 and where a Barbour is a necessity rather than a fashion statement. However despite the geographical and demographic challenges, it continues to attract those who prefer a small school feel, strong academic rigour and a lack of social pretensions. A real buzz about the place these days, a go-getting attitude with encouragement for girls to show the world what they can do and to 'get their lip-gloss on and get out there'. Charlotte Brontë would have approved.

Caterham School

Linked to Caterham Preparatory School in the Junior section

Harestone Valley Road, Caterham, Surrey, CR3 6YA

• Pupils: 830 boys and girls, roughly 3:2 • Ages: 11-18
• Size of sixth form: 275 • Christian • Fees: Day £13,275-£13,896; Boarding £24,594-£25,926 pa • Independent

Tel: 01883 343 028
Fax: 01883 347 795
Email: admissions@caterhamschool.co.uk
Website: www.caterhamschool.co.uk

Headmaster: Since 2007, Mr Julian Thomas BSc MBA PGCE, following the immensely successful, innovative and likeable Rob Davey, who retired after 12 years. Previously second master at Hampton School, Mr Thomas is a computer science graduate who gained experience in the business world at Lloyds Bank and BP before he went into teaching. Previously taught maths and was director of studies at Portsmouth Grammar. Six maths textbooks under his belt. Qualified rugby, cricket, hockey and netball coach – and an experienced player himself. Other interests include drama, environmental issues – he had a leading role in making Hampton the world's first carbon neutral school. He is married to Julia and they have two small children.

Academic matters: Caterham can now hold its head high in any company, especially in maths, the sciences and religious studies. 2010 results included 70 per cent A*/A grades at GCSE and, at A level, 93 per cent A/B grades. All students go on to university and consistently over 80 per cent go to one in the 'top tier'. Something is going right here. A good set of subject options (international students can take their own languages) includes business studies, economics, government and politics, textiles, psychology, photography and theatre studies, in addition to the usual staples. Modern languages, though encouraged by many foreign trips of all kinds, need beefing up to encourage more takers – Mr Davey made great strides here. Excellent language lab helping. Greek survives here – hooray! Years 7 and 8 take a course in citizenship and all sixth formers take general studies. A good combination of the traditional and the trendy but all in a sensible, purposeful manner. SENs are efficiently diagnosed and well-supported here, though those with physical disabilities would find parts of this valley/hills site difficult to negotiate. Parents pay tribute to the caring and dedicated staff who 'really enthuse the pupils' but don't have unrealistic expectations of them.

Games, Options, the Arts: On-site playing fields, pitches, all-weather surfaces abound. Superb sports hall, plus pool, giant fitness room with 25 plus exotic-looking machines plus plus plus, opened in 1996 by Sebastian Coe and open to members, i.e. school families, former pupils etc. Superbly maintained home field for athletics etc. Boarding football enthusiasts coached by a trainer from Crystal Palace FC and school achieves highly in sports which include swimming, rugby, hockey, lacrosse, netball, cricket and cross-country. Riding and fencing too. CCF, Young Enterprise and D of E all popular.

Lots of drama though no designated studio; *Les Miserables* a recent success. Drama an A level option. Workmanlike, well stocked workshops for IT. Art is well catered for (the art building has just been refurbished) and popular, especially with girls. Printmaking, graphic design, pottery and photography among many options. Interesting interdisciplinary enterprises like a recent, beautifully-produced pamphlet of art and writings – a truly imaginative exercise done just for the pleasure of it and wonderfully encouraging for those whose work appears. Flourishing music with many in school lessons on around 20 different instruments and every kind of band and ensemble – a range of small recitals to major choral concerts in the Humphreys Hall. Arcane and eclectic choice of other extra-curriculars includes Amnesty, circus skills, chemistry, Christian Union, debating, various languages and minority sports and the splendid Melting Pot – a chance to exchange multicultural experiences with over 20 countries represented. Visits here, there and everywhere – Tanzania, Ukraine, Iceland, USA, skiing, France, Germany and Spain.

Background and Atmosphere: In 1995 boys' school, Caterham, founded in 1811, merged with nearby girls' school, Eothen, founded in 1892. Both Christian foundations. Caterham had been set up to educate the sons of Congregationalist ministers – even 30 years ago around a third of pupils were Welsh and the relationship with the United Reformed Church is still close. Christian background informs the ethos and is neither exclusive nor punitive. In fact, this is about as inclusive as a school can get.

School moved to its present 100 acre site in 1884. One arrives at the school down a quiet lane out of Caterham centre with substantial, well-spaced detached houses on one side, and the school appears on rising ground to one's left. A three-storey, immensely long, red-brick building, it is imposing though built in a plain and solid style – free from the excesses of later in that century. It faces banks of glorious, tree-festooned hills and its own sports grounds. Battalions of white minibuses wait on hard standing. Further down is the prep and pre-prep, wonderfully secluded, be-treed and traffic-free. Later building has added necessary facilities and some views can seem a little cramped but, in general, there is a sense of space and light.

Inside the main building, redbrick and tile corridors which could be prison-like but aren't, thanks to sensitive lighting and general decoration. Boarding for girls and boys recently expensively upgraded. Years 7–9 in good sized rooms for 6, Year 10 for 4, Year 11 for 2 and Year 13 students all have good rooms with ensuite loo and shower – better than most recently built undergraduate rooms. Good kitchens, lots of staff living in and school well up on parents' need for flexi-boarding and very keen to help. New science block and dining-hall completed in 2006. New sixth form centre opened in 2008. Uniform a sensible black/white/grey mix though 'smart business suits' for sixth form girls interpreted somewhat surprisingly by some.

Pastoral Care and Discipline: Commitment to excellent pastoral care evidenced by huge and touchingly accessible booklet, strong PSHE curriculum and general air of happy purposefulness everywhere. Clear but flexible structure. House system. Around 70 per cent stay in over weekends – good programme. Many staff live on site, either in purpose-built houses or in boarding houses. Boarding staff seen as parents rather than staff.

Pupils and Parents: Most boarders from abroad, currently from 23 countries. Largest numbers from Hong Kong, China and Eastern Europe. Day pupils from Surrey and a few from Kent or Sussex borders. Good bus services bring from all over. Large proportion of city and professional families, many first-timers – this is easy, prosperous, commuter country. Perennial problems of getting some hard-working foreign students to join extra-curricular activities and to mix generally being keenly tackled, but remain an issue. Former pupils include Angus Deayton, Jon Finch, Michael Jecks and cricketers Alastair Brown, James Benning and David Sales.

Entrance: Getting harder for those outside school's own prep, especially as more folk grasp the fact that boys and girls from 3–18 get a pretty unbeatable start in life here. Usual tests at 11 and 13, via interview, and six good GCSEs expected at 16.

Exit: In 2010, ten pupils went to Oxbridge, six to Imperial College and seven to UCL; 82 per cent chose top tier universities.

Money Matters: Good number of scholarships awarded at 11, 13 and 16. Extra science scholarships at sixth form. Also art, music and sports awards. Bursaries available for children of clergy, OCs, Services and foreign service personnel. Bursaries also available for the able but less well off.

Remarks: A top school – surprisingly little known. Well appointed in virtually every area and performing outstandingly in maths, science and RS, it is set to build on the achievements of the last decade. The site is leafy, spacious and comfortable. Hard to beat if a co-ed school in the Home Counties with a boarding option is your thing. It is exceptionally well placed for commuters and those for whom Gatwick/Heathrow are significant – connections couldn't be better. 2010 inspection commented: 'Pupils throughout the ability range are highly successful in their learning and personal development ... The pupils' personal qualities are outstanding and are promoted by the friendly and supportive atmosphere.'

Central Newcastle High School

Linked to Central Newcastle High School Junior Department in the Junior section

Eskdale Terrace, Newcastle upon Tyne, Tyne and Wear, NE2 4DS

• Pupils: 620 girls, all day • Ages: 11-18 • Size of sixth form: 180 • Non-denom • Fees: £5,760-£9,627 pa • Independent

Tel: 0191 281 1768
Fax: 0191 281 6192
Email: cnhs@cnw.gdst.net
Website: www.newcastlehigh.gdst.net

Head: Mrs Hilary French MA Oxon MEd PGCE NPQH (fifties). A historian. Four years as deputy head at Teesside Prep and HS, followed by five years as head. Married to Durham University lecturer with one daughter. Welcoming and approachable, she is determined to shrug off any hint of the 'little bit aloof, closed door' image she feared the school had gained. Has adopted more open approach, welcomes closer links with parents. 'I think people thought we closed the doors and got on with it – don't question us. We are very different now.' Masterminded a £5m-plus revamp which also physically opened up the school, particularly the entrance. Knows every girl by name and aims to produce confident girls able to achieve their potential. On the board of Centre for Evaluation and Monitoring which 'helps me keep a finger on the pulse of education'.

Appreciates that the girls may well have a 'portfolio' career, but believes that a good, sound education built on moral values, respect, courtesy and hard work will stand them in good stead. Attitude is to build self-confidence, celebrate successes and the rest will follow. Loves the buzz of coming to school and meeting the girls and working with them and their parents. Girls and parents like her. 'She is very warm and approachable and that now sets the tone for the school,' says a parent.

Academic matters: Keeping an eye on the demands of universities to see if the International Baccalaureate qualification becomes the next 'must have'; in the meantime working within the A level system. Reviews curriculum every year to meet needs of new intake.

Four class intake and all the way through from Year 7, roughly 20–25 per class, 28 maximum. Smaller groups for sets and options. Setted in January Year 7 for maths and Year 8 in English, speedy set for languages who then take the relevant GCSE early. Beyond that no further streaming. 'We are already selective so they start out at a certain level and we don't want to move them around too much. We don't want any of the "not in the top set" attitude that can make you feel a failure.' SENCo, whose knowledge is 'encyclopaedic', carries out individual assessments and girls with learning difficulties are supported. Formal extra support comes at extra cost, less formal support not charged for.

Huge variety of subjects on offer at A level; best school in the area for GCSE/A levels. 76 per cent A*/A grades at GCSE. Philosophy for all. Strong classics; outstanding results in the sciences, which explains why many go off to be doctors and vets – more than half take three separate sciences at GCSE. Good library, computers all over. Exchanges to France, Germany and Spain and languages equally strong; digital language lab in a separate building. New library, art school, ICT resource centre, sixth form common-room, English school (strong success in debating) and an additional state-of-the-art science lab. Brand new sixth form work area. Sixth form split into lower/upper. Improvements to outside grounds have improved the girls' leisure facilities. 'We are not a hothouse that crams girls – you can see that by walking around. We give them 100 per cent commitment, build their confidence. Success comes from that. We are an academic school but you can almost take the academic side for granted. It is the rest that makes the school. We want the girls to be part of something that is exciting, vibrant and lively,' says head. Parents agree, 'The school provides a good, rounded education'. Students appreciate their opportunities and the help they get, 'The teachers are fantastic – you feel like you want to go round and thank them one by one'.

Happy with single sex success, 'Egos are fragile and the girls need the space to have a go, make mistakes without living up to any sterotypes. When they go on to university they are streets ahead of their co-educational sisters in confidence and ability to tackle the outside world, not timid, shy girls.'

Games, Options, the Arts: Very strong in sport; ethos of everyone gets a turn, but success on a national stage is celebrated. Examples include hockey and netball tour in Fiji and New Zealand; national schools' tennis finalists and the LTA Tennis School of the Year not so long ago.

Dance now offered throughout the school including at A level and plans for a new dance studio. New development completed to link the music school to the super sports hall and creating new drama studio. 'Music is stunning,' says the head. Subject has own building with keyboards, a fine wigwam-shaped recital hall and recording studios. Drama includes regular full school productions. Dazzling arts curriculum: ceramics, jewellery-making, photography, fine art etc and a lot of fabric work. Girls run their own fashion shows. D of E very popular, one of the largest participating schools in the area; navy and army CCF with field days and camps. World Challenge trips to Tanzania, Chile and India; sports tours to New Zealand and Australia; ski trips to Europe and the US.

Background and Atmosphere: Founded in 1895 and set in a selection of new-builds and converted Victorian villas. Big investment in opening up the school has paid dividends, now less stuffy. 'I think environment is important because you spend a lot of time here and it needs to be fresh, tidy and modern.' Away from main building, a former synagogue with fabulous stained window gives stunning light for art department – filled with art and models. Close to metro station/main roads for ease of access. Stage used to take up half the hall and has been removed to allow a whole school assembly at least once a year. It is also a multi-use space to include dining at lunchtime.

Pastoral Care and Discipline: Excellent PSHE with full new programme; year heads in charge of pastoral care and monitoring progress, keeping an eye on individual ups and downs and safeguarding the 'quality of life', plus form teacher/tutor, plus qualified counsellor. Anti-bullying policy – but it 'isn't a problem' as girls have respect drummed into them from the off. Merits and de-merits promote the good and punish the bad. Girls educated about the risk of drugs.

Pupils and Parents: Solid middle class intake from throughout region as far as Alnwick, Co Durham; loads of professionals and very wealthy parents, but no snobbery in the playground. Rich mixture of regional accents and healthy mix of different cultures. Working hard to engage parents more. 'You want to be invited in to see what your daughters are doing at times when you can get there' – head. Using pastoral system to underpin better communication – heads of year and form teachers take the lead. Email is a favoured communication tool for 'hard-pressed, working parents'.

Transition from junior to secondary is sensitively handled with little ones offered an 'experience day' and then 'big sister' sixth formers help them settle in. 'They very soon blossom from the opportunities that they get and are soon coming in via the metro like all the others' – head. We picked up that it isn't quite as easy to settle in if you are joining the school from a different junior school and not from CNHS's own.

Articulate and friendly girls. School uniform, flat-soled shoes, all very smart. Sixth form in their own clothes, though some students would like uniform there too. 'I would prefer to be in uniform; I think it's nice when everyone looks the same,' a sixth former told us. Interesting.

Entrance: Natural progression from own junior school and competition for other places is fierce. Entrance exam and interview to get in at Year 7. If 10 leave post-GCSE, then 10 more come in.

Exit: Handful leave after GCSE. After A level, medicine a popular career choice, also other sciences, regular stream to art colleges, normally 10 or so a year to Oxbridge. Other choices include Leeds, Nottingham, Edinburgh, Glasgow, St Andrews and Manchester.

Money Matters: GDST funds bursaries and scholarships. All bursaries are means-tested annually.

Remarks: Having lost the 'aloof' accusation that apparently affected the school, pretty much doing everything right. Produces confident, bright and articulate girls without the 'like' and 'whatever' attitude of others of their age-group. Marvellous.

Centre Academy

92 St John's Hill, Battersea, London, SW11 1SH

• Pupils: 45 boys, 15 girls; all day. • Ages: 9-18 • Non-denom
• Fees: £25,500-£26,400 pa • Independent

Tel: 020 7738 2344
Fax: 020 7738 9862
Email: info@centreacademy.net
Website: www.centreacademy.net

Principal: Since 2007, Dr Duncan Rollo BA MA PHD (sixties), born in Scotland, raised in the USA. A professor of English in the States, he returned to the UK some 21 years ago. Awarded postdoctoral fellowship LSE; has penned numerous articles on various aspects of education and written three books on effective communication.

Popular with parents, personable and empathic with a can-do approach that, say parents, has made a real difference. Knowledgeable and charming, an expert on SEN matters, he is also refreshingly honest – if mistakes are made or something needs improving he takes it on board. Enjoys working with younger ones but now mainly mentors older students ('Possibly my age,' he confessed).

Academic matters: Small classes averaging five or six pupils enable group work as well as individual teaching. Every effort is made to adapt the curriculum to the needs of the individual with timetables monitored daily by tutors. Broadly follows the national curriculum to Year 9 (age 13), thereafter GCSE, USA high school diploma or vocational courses – whatever suits; the continuously-assessed American system works particularly well. A well-regarded work experience programme runs with additional guidance provided by Connexions and university applications are wholly successful. School has its own in-house language and occupational therapists and all staff attend regular specialist training sessions. Pupils are confident about their learning – in recent years almost all have achieved A–C in GCSE English. The quality of teaching is on the up – that's not just our observation; a recent Ofsted inspection highlighted some outstanding elements.

Games, Options, the Arts: Annual trips to adventure camps, places of interest and, for older students, overseas. No on-site sports facilities so pupils make full use of the local sports centre and nearby playing fields. Drama important, not just for fun but for supporting language and communication skills too, with the neighbouring church hall providing much-needed space for the expressive arts. Art studio is a hive of activity – traditional drawing, painting and sculpture is offered alongside weaving and embroidery; plenty of opportunities to develop fine motor skills and concentration. Regular clubs include arts, sports and community service offerings.

Background and Atmosphere: Founded in 1974 and housed in an attractive Edwardian, but small, building with limited outdoor space close to a busy road. A well-equipped ICT room, small science lab, art room and a new library are evidence of a continuing programme to improve facilities. Welcome plans are afoot to replace part of the property with theatre facilities and a gym. Had some bumpy times, probably not helped by the size of the building and its location, but the arrival of Dr Rollo calmed the waters. An active school council is helping to revitalise the community spirit and a smart new uniform promotes pride and identity.

The school has recently opened a new school, Centre Academy East Anglia (qv), near Bury St Edmunds. Similar ethos and programmes, but also has a boarding facility for 8- to 16-year-olds.

Pastoral Care and Discipline: At the heart of the pastoral care system is a preventative approach to every-day problems – everyone has a mentor whom they meet with three times a day. Many of the pupils have not fared well in other schools and so clearly appreciate the friendly staff; one boy confided, 'This is the first school where I have felt confident enough to ask the staff questions without fear of getting into trouble'.

Life skills are an integral part of the curriculum, with pupils encouraged to use their initiative and get involved, hence the recently-opened pupil-run tuck shop for break times. A highly experienced counsellor runs an impressive support team. Home-school links considered essential; masses of help given with organisational skills, and homework can be completed at school during the daily prep period.

Pupils and Parents: Complete mix from all over London and home counties, but with an international flavour – mostly British with a few from USA, Europe and the Middle East. Around 50 per cent are funded by LAs.

Entrance: Admission from 9+ years, then as places become available; caters for a range of needs including milder autistic spectrum disorders, dyslexia/ADD/dyspraxia and complex processing difficulties. Eccentricities can be managed but not aggressive or violent behaviour. We've heard mutterings from a few parents that the school isn't always receptive when making initial contact and can be 'funny' about sending out information. We raised this with Dr Rollo, who promised to investigate – his concern clearly about the distressed parent who is seeking a school like this, rather than any over-riding marketing concerns. He did note that the prospectus is not sent to parents until he has had a brief phone chat to ascertain the appropriateness of the school for the child. Officially, first step is to have a conversation with Dr Rollo to check the school is what you are looking for. If all agree it may be suitable, the next stage is to send in the relevant documentation e.g. medical and psychological reports. The family will then meet with Dr Rollo, and the child will be invited to spend two or three assessment days. Assessment is two-way, to see how the child copes and to ensure the school will be able to meet particular needs. If the trial period does not work out, Dr Rollo will try to assist with finding an alternative placement for the child.

Exit: A few return to mainstream schooling before the end of KS3. 18+ mostly to university, odd one to FE college; UK universities have been happy to accept the four-year USA high school diploma as an equivalent to GCSE and A level.

Remarks: Special strength is its wholly individual approach and dedication to preparing pupils for their future and beyond. A unique school that recognises one size definitely does not fit all.

Channing School

Linked to Channing Junior School in the Junior section

Highgate, London, N6 5HF

• Pupils: 360 girls, all day • Ages: 11-18 • Size of sixth form: 95
• Non-denom (Unitarian) • Fees: £13,395 pa • Independent

Tel: 020 8340 2328
Fax: 020 8341 5698
Email: info@channing.co.uk
Website: www.channing.co.uk

Head: Since 2005, Mrs Barbara Elliott MA (late forties). Educated at Lancaster Girls' Grammar School and New Hall, Cambridge, where she read Spanish and French. PGCE at King's, London. Taught at Haberdashers' Aske's School for Girls, lectured at the College of Further Education in Aberdeen ('But I prefer chewing gum and socks,') before returning to England and St Columba's College, St Alban's, where she was headhunted on an open day. Head of languages at St Alban's High School for Girls, then deputy head, then acting head. 'I realised, I can do this.' Husband in the City, four sons. No-nonsense with charm, she clearly loves the job – 'I was born to be in a school and haven't been off for a day since 1983'. She has evidently made her mark. 'The girls love her,' notes one pair of parents.

Academic matters: In the past few years Channing has risen rapidly up the league tables and is now right up there near the top, the result of a bespoke education applied to brighter and brighter girls. 'It's an upward spiral,' says the head. Classes are small, 20 max and sharply down from there, average in the sixth form just seven. 'It's more tutorial work than classroom teaching.'

Very strong teaching throughout – 'They make it interesting and everything's taught in a sensible and logical manner,' says one admiring parent. 89 per cent A* and A at GCSE, 87 per cent grade A*/A/B level in 2010. Generally nine subjects at GCSE, though business and communication can be taken as a tenth. Double award science. Four ASs (plus critical thinking and financial services as additional options) and generally three A2s. Sixth form options built round what a girl wants to study. Modern languages already a strength – French from Year 5, German, Spanish, Latin and ancient Greek from Year 9 and head also thinking of adding Russian and Italian.

Games, Options, the Arts: The pretty grounds are ornamented with six netball-cum-tennis courts, a junior performing arts centre, a specialist music suite and some good modern arts studios, but facilities don't compete with some London independent senior schools (no pool, for example). 'If you want an 800-seat theatre you won't find it here – yet,' says the head. 'But you won't find better drama teaching.'

Not unduly competitive approach to sport – 'Channing girls love the opportunity to play tennis, especially when the sun is shining,' reads the school magazine – and health and well-being take precedence over cups won. Nonetheless, wide range of sports on offer – the usual netball, hockey, rounders and athletics, but also aerobics, badminton, basketball, gymnastics, table-tennis, trampolining, yoga and polo.

Art, music and drama undoubtedly strong. Inspiring art studio with panoramic views of London and a full range of techniques from computer design to etching, photography and ceramics. Two-thirds of the girls learn an instrument, many two. Two orchestras, three choirs, wind and jazz bands and various string groups. Joins with neighbouring Highgate to perform a major choral work each spring and orchestral concert in May. Drama, too, a strength. Timetabled drama for Years 7–9, theatre studies at A level. Whole school production every autumn, plus the occasional musical.

Lovely, light, well-equipped library staffed by a full-time librarian. Plenty of trips. Duke of Edinburgh, Young Enterprise. Fully equipped careers library, with careers advice from Year 9 and an organised convention for Years 10 and 12. Visits, lectures and workshops to prepare girls applying for university.

Background and Atmosphere: Founded in 1885, Channing sits in an idyllic seven-acre site on Highgate Hill, with its junior school just across the road. Delightfully housed in a selection of rambling Victorian buildings with high ceilings, beautiful views and oodles of light. Plus a range of purpose-built contemporary buildings to reflect the expanding demands of a modern education. Has the charm of a well-run private home with the same sense of relaxed control. 'A hidden treasure,' says the head. A relatively small school, with a real sense of community, kindness and mutual support. 'It's very warm and encouraging,' says one happy mother. 'Like an extra pair of hands going round my daughter.' Because of its scale, many girls get the opportunity to run projects – the Spanish club, the Mandarin club, the recyling programme are all girl-driven initiatives. Also feels very much part of the local community with brown-clad girls (and their fashionably-dressed mothers) dominating the high street at various times of day.

Pastoral Care and Discipline: An unusually decorous environment. 'Behaviour is exemplary,' gushes the schools' inspectorate and the head confirms, 'Discipline is just not an issue here'. Rare cases of bullying are stamped on immediately and general order is 'strict but fair,' says one parent. The relatively small size of the school means every student is carefully monitored – 'If a girl wobbles, she won't wobble for long' – and clearly the head developed a pretty firm grasp of who's who very quickly. Established by the Unitarians, the school is now non-denominational, though every girl is still encouraged 'to be strong in her own religious faith'.

Pupils and Parents: Largely local, though a few from Totteridge and Islington, because well-served by public transport. Professional parents, with less of a racial and religious mix than elsewhere in north London. Old girls include Baroness Cox, Peggy Vance and Princess Sarvath of Jordan.

Entrance: Main intake into the junior school at 4+. Girls from the junior school normally proceed seamlessly to the senior, without sitting the entrance exams, unless applying for a scholarship, so only 40 places available for external candidates. At 11 part of the North London Independent Girls' Schools' Consortium, with exams in English and maths. Significantly over-subscribed at all points. Siblings given 'careful consideration', but no guarantees. Sixth form entry requires six GCSEs at C or above with Bs in chosen subject (except maths, where you need an A).

Exit: A few leave after GCSE, some to state schools, some to co-ed sixth forms. Thereafter, almost all to Russell Group universities and leading art colleges. About 10 per cent annually to Oxbridge.

Money Matters: Scholarships, exhibitions and means-tested bursaries at 11 and 16. Music scholarships (50 per cent of the fees) and exhibitions (25 per cent) on the results of an audition after the applicant has passed the academic entrance exam.

Remarks: A sheltered, friendly school in a beautiful setting, less pressured than many London girls' schools but still getting excellent results and producing self-assured young women.

The Charter School

Red Post Hill, London, SE24 9JH

• Pupils: 1100, 610 boys, 490 girls • Ages: 11-18 • Size of sixth form: 240 • Non-denom • State

Tel: 02073 466 600
Fax: 02073 466 601
Email: info@charter.southwark.sch.uk
Website: www.charter.southwark.sch.uk

Head: Since September 2007, Mr David Sheppard MA NQPH PGCE (early fifties), promoted from acting head to the real thing, having been part of the foundation team that led up to the opening of The Charter in 2000. His predecessor, Chris Bowler, was tempted away to lead a city academy in Slough at short notice. Mr Sheppard has plenty of experience with aspirational inner-city kids and parents. His former responsibilities as deputy head included a focus on the links The Charter has with local businesses and larger corporates.

Academic matters: Over 90 per cent A*–C at GCSE, which is excellent given the range of children. A focus on learning and achievement at all levels – many children have feelings of minimal self-worth, though the most able pupils do as well at GCSE as in many selective schools. It's not enough to be a good teacher here – you must have an amazing range of skills to motivate children. Many of the staff are outstanding and choose to be here despite more lucrative offers elsewhere – job satisfaction must be very high. Most are in their 20s and 30s (the older ones are those in management positions) and many have only ever worked at The Charter School. The Charter School has been declared outstanding twice in a row by Ofsted.

Class size is around 27 at KS3, drops to 24 at KS4 and, in the sixth form, ranges from six to 20+. Up until Year 9 all classes are a mixture of all-ability and setted groups; after this everyone is setted in English, maths and science. Subject study always has a practical aspect: in English, when looking at poetry from different cultures, you might kick off with a two-minute interview of your neighbour to find out where they come from – with the reassuring discovery that very few children or members of staff, whether black or white, have a parent of wholly English descent.

School zones dedicated to different subjects, e.g. humanities, citizenship, science, maths, communications. Around 10 pupils study Latin each year and Mandarin and Italian are possible options for the future. Citizenship classes strong.

Level 2 and Level 1 sixth formers who don't take A levels spend two days per week at The Charter and two at Southwark College – this makes the transfer to college much easier with connections already in place. These pupils take particular advantage of the impressive sixth form learning resource which has around 40 computers hidden in slick desks. SEN kids and their LSAs use this too.

The Charter School is designated a specialist business enterprise college and practical links with local businesses encourage realistic choices after school. The school has won every business and enterprise competition that it has entered in the past two years – flyers for The Charter's own Dragon's Den were pasted everywhere when we visited. Being part of HSBC's cluster of excellence means that The Charter and 12 other London schools share good practice. Science is a second specialism and triple science results are consistently at A*/A.

Experiencing teaching from the other side of the desk through peer to peer mentoring is very popular here. Pupils see the effort that goes into preparing and evaluating a lesson and the value of clear target-setting – encourages empathy and concentration. At present this takes place with four Year 7 and Year 6 (local primary) classes in English, business, maths, science and art and is being rolled out in modern languages and across all year groups.

Parents of children with SEN see the school as a place where their kids will be supported whatever their needs – the school has full wheelchair access. The Charter takes about five per year group though successful SENDIST appeals may push this number up. There is nonetheless great tolerance among the pupils of their peers' complex needs – if it is explained to them that a boy might cry out without warning, they just take it in their stride. The library is light and well-equipped with different areas for KS3, KS4 and sixth form – SEN students and their LSAs can also work in this space. There are lots of books on CD and tape and listening posts with beanbags (memorably, an ADHD student became so relaxed listening to a story that he curled up on one and nearly fell asleep).

Games, Options, the Arts: England's hockey goalie inspires players and sports facilities have been transformed from the worst to among the best across Southwark state schools – a £4 million sports hall opened in 2008; school has a 20 year lease on neighbouring playing fields and new changing rooms. Football is very strong here (links with Millwall, Fulham and others) and rugby and cricket getting stronger – beating Dulwich College being the goal (a tall order, given the regular practice on gleaming pitches that the private school provides). Well-connected parents provide opportunities such as swimming club at JAGS.

When we visited, the GCSE art show was being hung in the entrance atrium, and all manner of people – from facilities manager (painting a stand) to the head (had his eye on a new painting for his office) – were involved. A fashion show was planned on a catwalk around the paintings to showcase the textiles. Impressive progression of work and peer-to-peer mentoring in art classes. Music department has plenty of keyboards and hundreds of children have private lessons; percussion is particularly popular. Whole school (including staff) takes part in a yearly production (e.g. *West Side Story*). Hall, a smaller, dedicated theatre and drama studio used for productions.

Bronze Duke of Edinburgh Award offered in Year 10 and the gold in Year 12 – the only state school in Southwark to offer the latter. In 2009, 33 pupils got bronze, 23 gold.

Background and Atmosphere: One hundred metre drive (no smoking on this either) off Red Post Hill up to security gates of school (everyone has a swipe card for ID which also enables them to pay for or get free school meals) which is shared with JAGS's sports ground. A school has been on this site (right by North Dulwich train station) for years but, after being closed due to poor behaviour in two previous incarnations, this one came about in 2000 after an 18-month campaign by local parents. They wanted a local community school that would give an education to rival independent neighbours James Allen's Girls' School (JAGS), Dulwich College and Alleyn's.

The building has been revamped (rather than rebuilt), meaning that the hot pink walls of the entrance cohabit with the impressive dedicated reception area. The canteen was refurbished this summer and is bright and airy. Pupils pay for meals using the latest payment recognition technology. The courtyard has also been revamped. Classrooms are light and clean, the corridor floors have been re-linoed in bright colours and very little graffiti to be seen, but still some points which suggest the school was designed more as a middle-class planner's fantasy rather than through detailed analysis of its pupils' needs. The site is compact (the playing fields were sold off in the 1980s, so now girls from JAGS play lacrosse just over the fence ...) but the available space is being re-assigned with particular input from the school council, including the installation in 2009 of an outdoor gym.

Involvement of the pupils in the running of the school is obviously vital to its atmosphere: this ranges from children conducting interviews of prospective teachers, through their re-design of the school uniform and building use to their evident ease of communication with the current teaching body. It's a south London hub school for student leadership, with year councils and a vigorous and positive school council – no political apathy here; everyone votes. It's also a hip place for teachers to work, so a lot of young staff who have their own social life (based around Dulwich Village and East Dulwich). You hardly hear a member of staff shouting – you have to like children to work here and if you don't, you won't last long.

A transparent-walled cyber café is shared by sixth formers and staff and is in use at all times of the day. The main dining room seats 180 and the queues and sittings are self-organised. 25 per cent eat packed lunches outside in the adjacent courtyard under the 1970s mosaic or in the main assembly hall, which has specially-designed tables for the purpose. Each year has a 20 minute assembly weekly and a key stage one twice a term – no full school gathering.

This school aims (according to Ofsted and locals, successfully) to create a haven of peace/calm/civilisation for children whose journey home may often involve interactions with those from less disciplined schools and those who may have been excluded. For some children there are few rôle models for manners or educative application in their home environment.

Pastoral Care and Discipline: Hoodies and caps are banned, taking away a layer of anonymity and disguise from teenagers. One stud per ear, no mobiles or mp3s and all staff addressed as Sir or Miss. Inflexible line on drugs, violence and smoking: after being caught smoking, a pupil must report to a meeting room on entry and exit to the school, and if they continue after that they will be excluded. Staff barred from smoking on site too. School police officer shared with Alleyn's (every Southwark secondary school – state or independent – has one assigned) present for part of every school day and carries out searches of children if any inkling of drugs. Multi-agency contact (with YoT, CAMHS, social services etc), an educational welfare officer and preventive activities like circle time and an anti-bullying project.

Complex behaviour management system here (featured in the recent BBC documentary Class Act – directed by a parent) with non-teaching behaviour officers as well as an inclusion manager who help pupils reassess their attitudes to learning and behaviour. Three learning mentors are linked closely to the behaviour manager and two separate pupils' support units for KS3 and 4. Children are given four warnings in class before being sent out – at this point both teacher and pupil have to go through a process of restorative conferencing. The hierarchy of discipline goes through year leaders to directors of learning (one each for KS3, 4 and sixth form) and the head only deals with exclusions. Basically, pupils can't just be thrown out from this school if their attitude does not fit the ideal work ethic; skilled tactics must be employed instead – they are, and they are working.

An isolated parental criticism is that this drive to deal with disruptive behaviour leaves minimal resources for the pastoral care of those with less noisy problems – a teenager's depression was dealt with by his tutor but the issue received no attention from more senior staff and no counselling was offered. The school assures us that this was a one-off occurrence and that links with council services are excellent and well used.

Pupils and Parents: 70 per cent from Dulwich Village and East Dulwich (privileged) and the rest from the neighbouring estates; 50 per cent white with majority of the non-white Afro-Caribbean or African – few Asians. With a near 50 percent gender split, boys and girls happily mix and share successes and feel very prepared for adult life when they leave. Complete range of ability in the children, over three per cent with statements. Participation in the Black Pupils' Achievement Programme brought up the question of how to groom people to stand for election to the board of governors – the confidence issue is not just restricted to pupils.

Entrance: Biggest group from Dulwich Hamlet Junior School (The Charter takes more of their Year 6 – about 75 – than any other school), and four other main primaries. Totally over-subscribed (900 applications for 180 places) with the head's secretary very experienced in dealing tactfully with desperately keen parents. Transition methods are held up as a model example locally.

Exit: Some 97 per cent stay on for sixth form or go to Southwark College for more vocational options or a change of environment. Sixth form has reached full home-grown capacity and everyone who applied for university got a place –school trips are run to popular choices, e.g. Edinburgh. Pupils consistently achieve placements in the top Russell Group of universities as well as Royal Academy of Music, Royal Veterinary College and medical schools.

Remarks: One ex-head who went on to advise the government, another head-hunted for a fresh city academy, a local MP who is now minister for the Olympics and London, a BBC documentary about discipline in the classroom – this school is held up as an example in many worlds. It is a truly comprehensive school and parents praise the commitment of teachers to getting the best out of individual brains. The pupils look you in the eye, are sparky, involved and really grow during their time here. A small number enter with some pretty big problems, but when they leave they are all good citizens.

Charterhouse

Admissions Office, Godalming, Surrey, GU7 2DX

• Pupils: 655 boys; 125 girls in sixth form. All board except 15 day boarders and 27 day pupils in the new Sixth Form Day House • Ages: 13-18 • Size of sixth form: 395 • C of E • Fees: Day boarding £24,330; Boarding £29,430 pa • Independent

Tel: 01483 291 501
Fax: 01483 291 507
Email: admissions@charterhouse.org.uk
Website: www.charterhouse.org.uk

Head Master: Since 1996, the Revd John Witheridge MA (fifties). Educated at St Albans School, University of Kent and Christ's College Cambridge. Also Ridley Hall Theological College, Cambridge. Who says headmasters must follow a conventional ascent incorporating housemastership and deputy headship? The Revd Witheridge started life as assistant chaplain at Marlborough College before being personal chaplain to the Archbishop of Canterbury, Robert Runcie, from 1983–7. He returned to school life as

Conduct of Eton. After Charterhouse's low period in the late '80s and '90s culminated in the abrupt departure of the head (don't ask), John Witheridge was catapulted to headship. Twelve years later, the school is humming like a well-oiled machine, entry lists are jam-packed and exam results have sailed up the league tables. The 'head man', as he is called by the pupils, is universally respected and seen as competent, competent, competent. Careful with his time, succinct, formal, but always straight-talking – when business allows, he is an extremely interesting chap to chat with. A gifted public speaker, 'his sermons are outstanding,' said a parent. Spends free moments writing biographies and has a particular interest in 19th century church history. Married to Sarah, who is much involved in the place, e.g. running cooking class for new boys, coffee mornings for the girls and generally stoking the engine of the Charterhouse train. Four children, now all in their 20s.

Academic matters: Brainier and brainier. 2010 saw 71 per cent of GCSE grades A*/A. Has bravely embraced IGCSEs – thought by many educationalists to be superior to GCSEs – in English, all sciences, maths and history; where will it end? Maths, history and economics vie for most popular choice among A level students, followed by all three sciences and English. The school's dissatisfaction with A levels (not rigorous enough, inconsistent marking, not convinced by the AS/A2) has caused it to look about for alternatives. Now many departments teach the Cambridge Pre-U and all public exams are taken terminally, freeing up the summer term of the lower sixth for teaching. From 2011, the IB will be offered as an alternative, and it is expected that about 30 per cent of pupils will opt for it.

Frank about being academic first and foremost. Two hours' prep per evening in the first years and builds from there. In 2007, Charterhouse teams came first and fourth in the Surrey Schools' Mathematical Challenge and the deputy head boy appeared as a panellist on BBC 'Question Time'. We are told that the average class size in the lower school is 16.85 (not to be confused with 16.84 or 16.86) though they can go as high as 24. Sixth form more intimate. 52 teachers have been at the school over ten years – amazing what subsidised housing will do for staff retention – but lots of important new appointments, including multi-talented head of English who used to teach modern languages at Winchester. Around 60 pupils have mild SEN; one pupil statemented. An English teacher is in charge of SEN – mainly mild dyslexia, which head notes is common among the scholars. So SEN not a bar to achievement here, but certainly not a school one would seek out for a child with learning difficulties.

Games, Options, the Arts: A football school – Charterhouse is credited with inventing the art of dribbling, which emerged because boys were confined to playing their ball game within the cloisters. 'It's such a relief not to have rugby-worship ruining everyone's life,' said a mother with a second son elsewhere. For a traditional school, enlightened when it comes to games choices. 'Yearlings' must trudge through the major sports but even they take part in a minor sport each term. From then on choice is paramount – 'I gave up hockey in my second year,' our guide told us – unless you are required to play for a school team. Variety of sports on offer really is unbeatable and includes riding, rackets, rowing and even a little rugby for sixth formers (one school rugby team). Plenty of inter-house activity and A–F school teams means that not only the superstars get to take part. Girls' main sports are hockey, lacrosse and netball. Sports hall that was state of the art when built over a decade ago now looks – well, state of the art.

Eager to celebrate culture as much as sport; you can now win house colours for art, music, drama and every Under School pupil must attend three cultural events per term. Newish head of music has raised the standard of choral music enormously and is well-liked. One of the few public schools that can cope with a genuinely talented musician but, if your child wins a music scholarship, be aware that the time commitment will be immense – for some 'unmanageable'. Everyone happy with the art department at the moment, though pupils described it as free and innovative while management stressed its focus on good old drawing and painting. The director of art won the BP Portrait Award in 2009. Photography also very good. Ben Travers theatre no longer as impressive as it once was, now that so many schools have built similar versions, but still an asset. Much competition each year to be chosen as part of the school's delegation to the Model United Nations in the Hague. D of E and CCF, of course. The Royal Marines Section won the prestigious (and very tough) Pringle Trophy in 2007 and 2008.

Background and Atmosphere: Founded, together with an almshouse, in 1611 by wealthy businessman Thomas Sutton on site of an ancient Carthusian monastery, hence Carthusians. Moved to the current site atop a hill just outside Godalming in 1872. Public schools are always torn between the competing necessities of saving money (this is a school) and appearing elegant (this is a lifestyle) but Charterhouse manages to exude good taste at almost every turn, barring the odd plastic chair. Gothic spires, turrets and mellow stonework; cricket pitches flat as a mirror. A great favourite with the Daily Mail etc (teacher's sex change operation several years ago was memorable – the master returned briefly as a mistress). Girls admitted into sixth form since 1971, as was the vogue, but one of the few such schools not to then extend co-education down to age 13 (and emphatically will not be doing so).

Loaded with historical touches, e.g. cloisters built as memorial to former pupils who died in the Boer War, main school chapel built in 1920s to commemorate 700 Carthusians who died in the Great War. We note, however, that the Charterhouse Museum no longer features on the school tour – most of the treasures from antiquity that it housed were sold in 2003 to fund the rebuilding of the library (completed 2004 – beautiful). Social sciences centre opened 2006 and modern languages block opened by Pérez de Cuéllar – the head girl's grandfather – in autumn 2007. School tells us new website is now 'fabulous and easy to navigate ... with secure Parent Portal'. School's 400th anniversary in 2011 to be the focus for development activities (school-talk for fundraising). Hoping to create an endowment to ensure it can not only prosper but also admit able pupils of modest means. Hopes to offer places to 25 'public benefit boys'. Also considering slight increase in the number of sixth form girls.

Pastoral Care and Discipline: List of school rules informs us that a 'sack attack' and 'debagging' are both unacceptable. Rules regarding prep: 'Should a beak not arrive at a hash you should remain and work quietly for the remainder of the hash. At the next strike of the school clock, it is the duty of the member of the division highest in alphabetical order to inform both the beak in the nearest hashroom and the headmaster's secretary of the beak's absence.' Quite. School also publishes exceptionally clear statement of principles and practice that lays out every detail about how the school works in less than three pages (much less entertaining to read). Twelve houses – new day house, Fletcherites, opened in September 2010. Saunderites, Verites, Gownboys and Girdlestoneites are in the heart of things in the original school buildings. The New Houses, a collection of modernistic multi-storey '70s blunders, have stoically weathered the decades – and have been rewarded by coming back into style, or nearly. Boys fiercely loyal to their houses and all think theirs best, though Weekites is current flavour of the month. Girls do prep and socialise in their ('boys') house (one upper sixth girl is currently head of her house) but leave around 10pm to go home to their boarding accommodation. Upper sixth girls all board in Chetwynd: extremely nice; all individual bedrooms. Lower sixth girls in one of four homely houses – rotate each term. Boys not allowed anywhere near.

Girls wear attractive black skirt suits and the occasional black trouser suit. Many come from all-girls' schools and appreciate being able to start fresh with other girls, rather than entering a co-ed school where girls have already forged friendships. Also like the more university-style existence here. And the boys. Presence of girls helps to tone down teenage boys' tendency to macho excess and dilutes bullying. Pupils may go into Godalming – not London or Guildford – two afternoons a week. 'Pub leave' only for over-18s with permission; school has own sixth form bar open to over-18s from Christmas onward. Lots of social events, bands playing, toga party etc. Can be a robust environment, and school is strict if perhaps unimaginative on bullying. Comes down hard on vice, especially drinking. If a boy is suspended for bad behaviour, it is treated as a final warning – 'I never suspend twice,' says the head. Recent appeal by family of expelled boy upheld school's decision. Pupils are tested if a suspicion of drugs. If drugs found in system the pupil may be expelled. If the pupil is suspended, he or she will have to submit to random testing for the rest of their time at school and will be expelled if a second test is positive. Currently around a dozen 'second chance' boys (drugs or alcohol). The handful of day boarders must stay at school each night until at least 9pm (can be much later). Parents warn that the 24/7 demands of the school make it virtually impossible to be a day pupil unless you live less than a mile away. Boarders may pop home most Saturday nights but must be in on Sunday if needed.

Pupils and Parents: Girls here do not HAVE to be attractive, confident and from a well-heeled family – but it certainly helps. Ditto for boys, though they are more of a mixed bunch. We watched boys earnestly trudge round the school clutching ring binders – something that would have been considered impossibly uncool a decade ago. Little in the way of trendy hair, no piercings etc. Mostly from south London, Surrey, Sussex and Hampshire; 20–30 from ex-pat families, 10 per cent foreigners in the under school with more joining in the sixth form. Long and distinguished list of Old Boys: Joseph Addison, John Wesley, William Thackeray, Ralph Vaughan Williams, Robert Baden Powell, Robert Graves, Jonathan and David Dimbleby, Rachel Portman, who was the first female composer to win an Academy Award (for the 1996 film Emma) and had a premiere of her work at the 2007 BBC Proms. And who could forget Peter Gabriel and the rest of the lads in '70s art-rock band Genesis?

Entrance: Around 125 chaps enter Year 9, most take CE or scholarship exams, but school has own test for boys coming from an alternative universe (state schools or abroad). Register at least three years before entry. Guaranteed places offered two-and-a-half years before entry based on satisfactory report from prep school (conditional on 60 per cent CE pass). Parents then asked to fork out deposit. In November of year before entry, parents pay a second deposit and commit themselves to Charterhouse as their first choice school. Around 15 boys (mainly from abroad) and 50 girls enter at sixth form, most with a tidy stack of mainly A* and A GCSEs. Much over-subscribed for girls' places. Some prospective parents of girls put off by school's coolness of manner – 'You get the distinct impression when you apply for a girls' sixth form place that they are doing you a favour rather than vice versa'. Selective examination and interview for sixth form places conducted in the November of the year prior to admission.

Exit: Almost all to higher education – 60 per cent taking gap years. Edinburgh was the most popular university destination in 2010, followed by Leeds, Newcastle, Durham and Manchester (25 to Oxbridge). Carthusians were admitted to over 100 different courses. One boy a year might be asked to leave at the end of his first year if attainment and effort are not up to scratch, two or three ditto after GCSE mocks, after much consultation with parents.

Money Matters: Fees (slightly) lower than Eton – so no joke. Intelligently aware of the danger that public schools could eventually price themselves out of the market. Hopes that fundraising may provide a future source of support for the school so that fee increases can be kept under control. Scholarship exams sensibly late in the year (May). Ten Foundation scholarships worth 10 per cent of the fees, plus five exhibitions worth five per cent. Probably the only school in England to offer a closed award available only to – wait for it – sons of lawyers. Peter Attenborough awards for all-rounders, plus music, art and sports scholarships also available. At sixth form, several academic awards, plus music (generally, and also particularly for organ) and art. School offers bursary programme for bright but genuinely needy boys 'in keeping with the intentions of the founder Thomas Sutton'.

Remarks: Traditional public school with all the trimmings. A class act from top to bottom. 'An academic school,' said a boy, 'that would be wasted on someone who was merely academic.'

Cheadle Hulme School

Linked to Cheadle Hulme School Junior School in the Junior section

Claremont Road, Cheadle Hulme, Cheadle, Cheshire, SK8 6EF

• Pupils: 1,380 boys and girls, all day • Ages: 4-18 • Size of sixth form: 265 • Non-denominational • Fees: £9,156 pa • Independent

Tel: 0161 488 3330
Fax: 01614 883 345
Email: Registrar@chschool.co.uk
Website: www.cheadlehulmeschool.co.uk

Head: Since September 2010, Ms Lucy Pearson (late thirties), the first female head in the school's 154 year history.

Oakham School, Keble College, Oxford, for a BA in English literature and language, and an Open University teaching degree. She coached cricket and hockey and sang in the choir while head of the sixth form at Solihull School (qv), until moving to deputy head post at Wellington College in 2006 where she was also vice principal of the newly-formed Wellington Academy. Statuesque at 6'1", she is perhaps best known for being one of England Women's cricket stars; player of the year in 2000 and 2003, and consistently a lead wicket-taking fast bowler. She's notched up 62 women's one day internationals and 12 women's test matches, and is only the second woman in over 79 years to take 11 wickets in a test match. . Also a musician, she was once in the National Youth Choir. She describes herself as passionate about co-education and making sure school education includes skills beyond the curriculum to prepare young people for 21st century working life.

Academic matters: Selective from top 25 per cent of ability range, a wider band than some competing schools, with consistently impressive results. Almost a third gain nine A* and A at GCSE and at least three As at A level. Pupils say they like the wide range of teaching styles and most are confident that while overall grades are of interest to the school, they as individuals are more important: 'We're pushed to achieve our academic potential but without undue pressure'. Parents praise most areas of teaching, 'The head of maths is inspirational; whatever she's got needs bottling', and thank the head for dealing firmly with teachers who don't deliver. Head says experienced teachers 'age well', retaining enthusiasm, but also likes newly-qualified teachers for the life and ICT savvy they bring. Maths and French IGCSE, extended project and Pre-U on offer.

Games, Options, the Arts: Pupils proud of competitive and successful sports teams, which spawn county and even international players. However, one quietly told us, 'there is sport in lessons but I wish there were B teams and more social sport if you don't make the high level teams'. There's certainly plenty of sport space with Astro pitches, playing fields, year-round indoor pool and large gym and plans for a larger pavilion.

Last inspection described extra-curricular activities as 'outstanding' and pupils appreciate the big-name speakers the school can attract to its wide range of clubs and societies – the newly-refurbished food and nutrition department recently opened with a Ready, Steady, Cook night starring Paul Rankin, Clare Short gave the Dubs Lecture last year. 'There's so much going on outside the classroom, there's always somewhere for you to fit in'. School has initiated The Cheadle Challenge in place of D of E, 'more challenging without some of the constraints'. Lots of trips with plenty of warning for time to save up.

Pupils keen to show off creative, life-filled art rooms, interactive whiteboards, banks of computers, the stationery shop and the librarian, who won't tolerate any noise, 'and she knows where every book is'. They like both their traditional biology benches and the space age chemistry labs; 'there's no lack of equipment here'. Drama is nurtured in two atmospheric studios with black drapes and lighting, while performances of every kind take place in the old-fashioned, undersized Holden Hall. One parent described the music department as 'outstanding, there's something for everyone from classical to rock, big band and jazz to samba, plus they combine with drama for fabulous musicals'. Brass and woodwind have had great success in competitions, at the expense of strings say some parents, but we're told this is now being addressed and a new singing teacher is transforming choral life at the school.

Background and Atmosphere: Established in 1855 for 'orphans and necessitous children', modern teaching blocks sit comfortably alongside Victorian buildings on this leafy campus site that's clearly visible from the Manchester to London train. Newly cleaned and re-roofed, the Victorian splendour of the main building gives way to unexpectedly 'grand designs' modernity with bright rooms and glass corridors and, near reception, an in-depth history exhibition from the 150 years celebration. Purposefully busy but relaxed, no 'keep off the grass' signs here. Separate common-rooms for upper and lower VI and lots of yummy choices from their own butty bar where Brenda knows everyone's names. Year 7 has its own block, 'but how have they managed to timetable all my lessons as far apart as possible?' laughed one, 'at least I am getting to know my way around'. Green uniform until sixth form when it's blue, but still only skirts for girls, although female teachers wear trousers. Pupils we met in school defended this but a few we know outside school think it's 'pants'.

Pastoral Care and Discipline: Most pupils are motivated and compliant and their parents can't praise pastoral care highly enough: 'The relationship with form tutors is great and the children are all known very well'. However, one recent parent, who admits their son was difficult, told us he couldn't wait to leave for a sixth form college, where 'his teachers really liked him and gave him back some self-esteem'. In general, though, pupils say problems are picked up quickly and that there's always somewhere to turn from peer mentors to staff, where 'the relationship with teachers gets more human the older you get'. The atmosphere seems very civilised and grown-up, perhaps because zero tolerance for disruptive behaviour in class means tricky non-conformists have been asked to leave. School council of 14 sixth formers who represent views of all pupils; younger ones would like more of a voice of their own.

Pupils and Parents: Mainly from South Manchester suburbs, but also further afield, arriving by bus, train and bike with school pick-up from local station and a drop and ride scheme from Styal to reduce parental traffic on local suburban streets where neighbours also object to sixth form parking – 'school council and staff working on it'. Extensive bus routes with subsidised and private services; the Hulme Hall School buses are recommended as better value if the route's right. A few parents haven't liked the increasingly egalitarian meritocracy from the bursary scheme but most welcome it. Varied ethnic backgrounds. 'We're Christian with a small c', says head, 'but tolerant with a capital T', although *Jerusalem* is still the school song. Good share of celeb offspring, mainly footballers and actors. Significant alumni include Lord Alf Dubs, ITN's Katie Derham, BBC's Nick Robinson and The Guardian's political writer Lucy Ward.

Entrance: By examination at 11, interview of child and optional parental 'chat', so wear something decent. Oversubscribed, six applicants per place. Applicants for one of 20 places in sixth form need GCSE As in intended subjects and at least passes in English and maths.

Exit: Fantastic help with choosing university and subject, the application process and mock interviews; 'they really help with the spadework,' say pupils. Diversity applauded with applications to shipbuilding and paramedic science courses in 2009. School aims to submit all UCAS forms, except for ditherers, by October half term putting its students firmly ahead of the field. Almost all to solid universities and more than a handful to Oxbridge each year.

Money Matters: Competition with other Manchester schools keep fees reasonable. Lunch swipe card, £2.27 a day. Increasing numbers of bursaries based on financial eligibility, and academic and music (particularly strings now) scholarships. Excellent web site has all the info you could need.

Remarks: Vibrant, action-packed, friendly school where motivated students are well supported to achieve their full potential. But forget the school's previous '11+ safety net' reputation; it's probably no longer the right place for those who just don't quite get in elsewhere.

Chelmsford County High School for Girls

Broomfield Road, Chelmsford, Essex, CM1 1RW

• Pupils: 870 girls; all day • Ages: 11-18 • Size of sixth form: 270
• Non-denom • State

Tel: 01245 352 592
Fax: 01245 345 746
Email: office@cchs.essex.sch.uk
Website: www.cchs.co.uk

Headteacher: Since 2007, Mrs Nicole Chapman (fiftyish). Born in Burgundy, France, but says she feels 'like a local girl' having relocated to Essex soon after gaining her Licence ès Lettres (BA Honours equivalent) in English with Spanish and French at university in Tours. She has a son and two step-children and joined CCHS after six years as head of a girls' grammar school in Gravesend, Kent – 'they're slightly less super-selective there', she says – and before that a mixture of challenging and high-achieving grant-maintained and foundation schools. Perspicacious and single-minded, she is certainly a safe pair of hands for Chelmsford's stellar girls' grammar and is revered for her tough stance on standards ('girls here are delightful but they will take advantage if you let them'), for inspiring them to greatness ('being the leaders of tomorrow is something of a mantra here') and for her tireless scouring of the state's coffers to make sure that her super-bright girls have access to the best possible facilities and resources ('they deserve them,' she says, simply). Some new pupils – and their parents – admit to being slightly startled by Mrs Chapman's determined approach, but she has impressed with her willingness to re-visit the issue of uniform just a few years after the introduction of an unpopular design and her efforts on the funding front are much appreciated.

Academic matters: A real star of the league tables, twinkling brightly among the UK's top 10 states and outshining all but the most hefty-fee-ed of the public schools, CCHS is one of just a rarefied handful of secondaries in the country to have triple specialist status – modern languages, technology and music. Academic achievement is famously sky high, with eleven A*s at GCSE common and regular achievers of four As at A level. No wonder then that parents, from the London boroughs to the coast, get themselves in a twist when it comes to priming their daughters for Essex's notorious 11+ entrance exam, leading to a frenzy of tutoring that, for some academically-promising girls – or those with clued-up parents – can begin as early as year four. There are rumours of occasional drop-outs, but the vast majority of girls are genuinely of the intellectually-gifted variety and relish the challenge. 'There are girls here who have been coached through the exam and then struggle, but we do our best for them,' says the head. 'It's sad because it does dent their confidence.'

Unsurprisingly, given its specialist status, sciences and languages are particularly strong at CCHS, and this despite the decidedly outmoded facilities – 'a triumph of good teaching and bright pupils over an increasingly unsuitable complex,' says the head, who is working hard to rectify the situation with a new £2.5m modern foreign languages block and a plan to add more labs.

Girls cite the single-sex environment as a factor in their willingness to throw themselves into the more traditionally male technological pursuits, without fear of opprobrium. All learn French, German and Latin and a growing trend towards internationalism at the school has seen the introduction in 2009 of a fledgling IB course including ab initio courses in Italian, Russian, Spanish and Mandarin, to which AS students are also welcome. 'IB as a package is ideal for bright, hard-working girls who want to stand out from the crowd,' says the head. She is at pains to point out, though, that she has no intention of going over to the IB completely – specialism at A level suits many at CCHS, particularly those who have a clear idea of a future career in a narrow field. CCHS already has a long and commendable tradition of community service, with almost all sixth formers involved and girls forming strong bonds with local special schools and retirement homes, often giving up their free time to continue beyond the prescribed sessions. That said, the head is anticipating a three or four-year settling in period as the IB becomes established. 'Understandably, parents here can be slightly reticent towards change and we'll need to convince them.'

Games, Options, the Arts: Despite the academically-biased two-week timetable, which means that the necessary enrichment subjects can be confined to one hour-long lesson a fortnight, less bookish pursuits are also encouraged at CCHS. Every half-term a cross-curricular Enrichment Day sees all students off timetable working on an extended project or activity, often offsite. PE is compulsory all the way to the top and Years 7–11 have two one-hour lessons a week. At least one sporty club every lunchtime and every day after school including gymnastics, fencing and trampolining alongside team games. Tennis, netball, hockey and athletics are particular strengths and the school collects trophies from national and district competitions.

About a fifth of the school learns a musical instrument and the orchestras and choirs are of a frighteningly high standard. Art is also pursued with enthusiasm and amazing talent. The list of lunchtime and after-school clubs reads like a novel and every department makes a contribution. French film club, football, netball, musical theatre, hockey, cross-country, netball, junior choir, History Society and debating are just a fraction. Also student-led professional societies for future doctors, lawyers and the like are evident. Lunchtime is an hour so there is plenty of time for a 30–40 minute activity and then food, though girls often combine to save time. Chinese has been introduced as an after-school club and there are plans to shoehorn it into the curriculum – there is a link to China through the British Council immersion initiative, and as Essex is twinned with the Jiangsu province, CCHS has a partner school in Nanjing. Unusually for a girls' school there is CCF – shared with the boys at King Edward VI Grammar School down the road.

Background and Atmosphere: A traditional red-brick Edwardian grammar school on one of the main roads into the county town of Essex, CCHS will bring back memories for any grammar school girl of the last century. Opened in 1906, it has remained largely unchanged since, save for some tacked-on additions and the impressive music centre, which opened in 2008, complete with a recording studio, which as the head says, 'shows up the rest of the school'. Plans are underway, though, for a new languages centre to be built right at the front, freeing up space at the rear for an extension to the science block and for a new sports hall, which the school is severely lacking. The swimming pool was recently refurbished and there is an all-weather hockey pitch and playing fields. The performing arts block is a real asset with a large drama space, and sixth formers have their own house for relaxation and study. A café has recently been set up to encourage girls to eat food cooked on-site rather than frequenting the local take-aways.

Pastoral Care and Discipline: In a close-knit community of fewer than 900 girls, discipline is hardly an issue. Stress, however, is and pastoral care is evident across the board. Parents thrilled by their daughter's 11+ success are often reluctant to airlift her out of such a rarefied social milieu in favour of the local state secondary, so Mrs Chapman focuses her efforts on helping flounderers to rise to the intellectual challenge of CCHS through close monitoring, confidence-building and occasionally making adjustments to individual curricula, lightening the GCSE burden. A specialist mentor spends lunchtimes supporting girls who are not performing as expected, because says the head 'we have to make sure that the girls enjoy being here and do well. They need to keep up with the pace and cope with being among very bright girls, so we often have to work hard to build self-esteem – there is a self-fulfilling prophecy about the bottom end of grammar schools.' Despite parental grumbles about teachers who warn that a B is nowhere near good enough, Mrs Chapman asserts that the pressure often comes from the girls themselves and that those who also have friends outside school are better at keeping perspective.

As might be expected, CCHS has an ordered atmosphere – students take responsibility for their property and their actions, work confidently and are extremely self-motivated. The school's behaviour policy is sent to all students on entry and parents are asked to sign an agreement outlining the expectations that the school, the parents and the student all have of each other. A logbook is used to record homework and as a regular channel of communication between form tutor and parents, who monitor progress and commitments and comment as necessary. A mature staff with an average age of nearly 45 is on hand to address concerns. Canteen lunches are promoted, as much for the social opportunity as the nutritional value.

Pupils and Parents: Hard working and very able girls from supportive homes travel up to three hours a day to CCHS – no specific catchment area here. Consequently the ethnic mix does not reflect that of the immediate locality and almost a tenth of students have English as an additional language. When we visited, 44 students were noted on the Special and Additional Needs Register – the vast majority with identified medical or pastoral needs. The Register is reviewed termly with student progress managers and staff are made aware of changes and additions and are encouraged to report worries about any students not mentioned.

Entrance: Applications are on the up but, despite rumours in the press, the extra numbers are coming principally from the state sector, which pleases Mrs Chapman. 'We don't want to give the impression that we are a free alternative to independent education – grammar schools exist to provide an education for the very brightest, whatever their background.' Girls have come from more than 200 feeder schools over the past three years, and although a few years ago almost half were from preps, that proportion is now down to about a quarter.

Admission is determined solely on performance in the Consortium of Selective Schools in Essex 11+ exam, held in November. Places are offered by the Local Authority on National Offer Day in March to the 120 girls who have performed best in the selection tests and have not been offered a place at a higher preference. A waiting list stays open until the end of the autumn term. Occasional vacancies further up the school are filled by inviting all girls on the waiting list to sit a test. Vacancies in the sixth form – often created by girls being tempted away by the mixed sixth form at the local boys' grammar – are readily filled and a further 30 places are made available, bringing the sixth form year group totals to around 150.

Exit: Only a smattering opt out of higher education while more than 85 per cent win places at their first choice of university. Around 15 a year go to Oxbridge. Old girls worthy of particular note include the United Nations' first woman Under-Secretary General, Dame Margaret Anstee, Dragons' Den dragon Rachel Elnaugh, sculptor Catharni Stern and BBC correspondent Emma-Jane Kirby.

Remarks: An intellectually stimulating environment that gives a flying start to the brightest of girls.

Cheltenham College

Linked to Cheltenham College Junior School in the Junior section

Bath Road, Cheltenham, Gloucestershire, GL53 7LD

• Pupils: 360 boys, 240 girls; two-thirds full boarders. • Ages: 13-18
• Size of sixth form: 250 • C of E • Fees: Boarding £28,515-£29,415; Day £21,360-£22,260 pa • Independent

Tel: 01242 265 600
Fax: 01242 265 630
Email: registrar@cheltenhamcollege.org
Website: www.cheltenhamcollege.org

Head: Since September 2010, Dr Alex Peterken BA MA DEd (mid-thirties), previously deputy head. Dr Peterken was educated at The Prebendal School (he was head chorister and head boy!), thence as a music exhibitioner and academic prize winner in history and theology at Eton. His first teaching post was at Charterhouse, where he spent 11 years. He held several senior posts at Charterhouse, and joined Cheltenham College as deputy headmaster in 2008. He currently also teaches RE. Passionate about classical music, he sings semi-professionally with various choirs and plays the piano. A keen theologian, he has a deep interest in church architecture and the history of science and theology. Also a keen sportsman. He is married to Clare, an SEN teacher and ex-deputy head. They have three children – the elder two are both at Cheltenham College Junior School. He says, 'Educating boys and girls together is the most natural, productive and enriching experience there is in education and I am honoured to be the next headmaster of such a prestigious and successful school'.

Academic matters: Distinct focus on the education of the whole person, as well as upgrading of academic rigour, with deliberate emphasis on learning and responsibility. 'We are determined to help pupils understand the way in which they learn and foster a work ethic that stands them in good stead for the modern world,' says new head. Record breaking 2010 GCSE results (the IGCSE is a prominent exam). Higher selection targets – at least 50 per cent in all subjects at Common Entrance and five Bs at GCSEs (formerly five Cs) for admission to the sixth form. New deputy head team, one male, one female – a first in the college's history – and new female director of learning (moving over the road from the Ladies' College) due to start in January. Strong, traditional timetable which has been tightened up to make sure that core subject teaching and individual tutorials, a big strength of the college, do not suffer through the proliferation of sports and their related fixtures, a key part of school life. Maths has long been a star subject here and continues to be so, with more than 50 per cent gaining A* and A at IGCSE and more than 75 per cent As and Bs at A level. History and geography also up in performance and popularity. English a strong performer, with record IGCSE results in 2010 and the bulk scoring As and Bs at A level. Design and technology is well established and popular with boys and girls, as are the sciences. Art has high numbers and results are good, with the endearingly messy artroom testament to its popularity. Languages on the up (French, German and Spanish A levels) and great improvement in higher grades awarded at GCSE and A levels. Nine pupils have featured in the top 10 UK places at A level over the last couple of years.

Definite feeling that it's a new era for the college, with an ambitious new head already making his mark. Two new national firsts this September: an accredited leadership and life skills course in the sixth form, based on Sean Covey's *Seven Habits of Highly Effective Teens,* and an accredited Apple Mac digital media course in the third form. 'We have beautiful traditional buildings; our aim is to be a dynamic, cutting-edge learning community within them,' says head. Good mix of younger and more mature staff, including the noted eccentrics of the science department, reflecting both the need to look forward and retaining Cheltenham's sense of its own history. Information Technology is playing an ever-increasing part in all aspects of school life, with a college wide intranet, laptop-enabled teaching facilities throughout (all pupils are issued with a laptop on arrival at school), homework posted on the school's intranet, Powerpoint science projects, airports and internet connection. Apple Macs are everywhere and much more is planned, all maintained by a dedicated IT department. A mix of modern and traditional classrooms, with some in need of a lick of paint, although excellent work, including some outstanding art and DT projects, is proudly presented all over the school.

Games, Options, the Arts: Sport is an important aspect of the character of the school and very popular. The core games through the year for boys are rugby, hockey, cricket, tennis and rowing, while the girls do hockey, cricket, netball, tennis and swimming. Many other sports flourish, including rowing (the college has its own boat house), polo (pupils are consistently National Schools' Champions), golf, shooting (clays and targets) squash, rackets (the college is consistently in the top two schools in the country), swimming and badminton. Support from a number of distinguished professionals in various team and individual sports. New scholarship and talented athlete programmes launched last year and many links fostered with both local and regional clubs.

Vast array of activities including eco club, photography, film making, pottery, CCF, community service, third form programme of outdoor skills, plus orchestra, wind and jazz bands. Very popular Duke of Edinburgh Award; large numbers for bronze and gold; annual Nepal trekking expedition and far-flung trips. Facilities are extensive and relatively recent, with an excellent and well-used pool and a large sports hall. Pupils have resultant reassuringly healthy glow. There is a strong tradition of community service, with visits to local nursing homes and primary schools and two long-term humanitarian aid projects by staff and pupils to maintain and support Romanian orphanages, with reciprocal visits between the two groups, and the renovation of a school in Kenya. Drama very popular, with school and house plays. Lots of music options and outstanding choirs (many ex-cathedral choristers and organ scholars) – and the gusto with which the daily hymns are sung in the chapel is legendary.

Background and Atmosphere: Traditional, and traditional-looking, Victorian public school, opened in 1841 to cater for the sons of gentlemen and now fully co-educational. Longstanding Services connections, but balance has shifted so that, although boarding is still thriving, many pupils come from within an hour and a half radius of the school. An impressively Gothic array of buildings of Cotswold stone, set off by the expanse of the cricket pitch and its elegant pavilion, makes a statement to the visitor, although some of the interior, awaiting its refit, does not yet match it. The most notable exceptions are the grand 'new' chapel (completed 1896) and the only slightly less grand original chapel, now pressed into service as a well-used dining room after its position, light and acoustics proved to be all wrong. The library is also lovely, an oasis of calm and quiet (kitted out with wireless technology as well as newpapers, magazines and ranks of books) – and is due to be lovelier still after a planned overhaul. Pupils are chatty, polite and neat, particularly impressive given that the uniform brief seems fairly wide, with lots of different ties in evidence.

Pastoral Care and Discipline: House system is at the heart of the school, with girls' and boys' houses divided into boarding and day. Ports of call for support include housemaster or housemistress, tutors, chaplain, matron, teaching staff and other pupils. A college wide peer-mentoring network has been introduced new this year and is a big hit with pupils. Each house also has its own 'vertical family', linking up pupils from each year group to support and mentor each other. Bedrooms are initially large and shared, graduating to single rooms in senior years. These are fresh and, by teenage standards, reasonably neat, with the older buildings having been newly upgraded to a high standard. Communal areas are thoughtfully equipped, with sofa-sized beanbags and snooker tables. Houses are spread along both sides of the road (the A40, busy elsewhere along its route but quiet here) and pupils are able to come and go from main school to house as they need to. The on-site medical centre has the added bonus of having Cheltenham Hospital, complete with A & E, directly opposite. Discipline continues to be quietly tightened – drug taking, bullying and general slackness absolutely not tolerated. Some recent less-than-happy reports reaching us about bullying not well-handled and children in difficulties not picked up and dealt with as one would expect. 'Bullying is never acceptable. Poor behaviour must not get in the way of other pupils' happiness or fulfilment; hence an expulsion and two final warnings last term,' responds new head. Pupils are made responsible for these issues also; indeed a cohort have set up their own cyber-bullying support and education programme across the college.

Pupils and Parents: The older boys are smart but express themselves with hair styled in all directions, while the girls are stylish rather than overtly fashionable. All wear uniform from first to last year. Well-integrated as a co-ed school, with girls first admitted to the sixth form in 1969 and from 13 in 1998. Ratio is around 60:40 boys to girls, nearing parity in the sixth form. It feels like a good, comfortable balance, producing confident, affable students. Popular with local families, who often find their children ask to board like their friends, even if they live just around the corner. Ex-pat quotient varies from year to year – strong links with Kenya. Lots of well-known Old Cheltonians: Scott of the Antarctic's companion Edward Wilson, General Sir Michael Rose, actor Nigel Davenport and his son, Pirates of the Caribbean actor Jack Davenport and journalist, Rageh Omaar.

Entrance: Most take Common Entrance – and will need good percentages in all parts to get in. About forty per cent are drawn from its own junior school, with others from a variety of preps. Those entering from the state sector take an entrance exam. So do those wishing to enter at 16, who must also get at least five B grades at GCSE; there is stiff competition for places.

Exit: A handful leaves at 16, either to attend other schools or because pupils are not sufficiently committed to working to keep up – 'Taking responsibility for independent learning is important, not just to succeed at A level but in life in general,' says head. Dedicated support to those applying to Oxbridge or US universities. Current favourites include Manchester, Nottingham, Leeds, Exeter, Bristol and Durham, with art, medicine and music colleges also popular. One in five takes a gap year.

Money Matters: Big range of 13+ and 16+ scholarships, including art, sport, DT, drama music and all-round potential as well as academic, geared towards prep school entrants, although non-independent school pupils welcomed. Bursaries and generous Forces discounts also offered.

Remarks: Strong all-round traditional public school, where league tables matter less than a complete educational experience – but matter more than they used to. We hope they are not losing touch with their softer side; exciting times expected under the new head.

The Cheltenham Ladies' College

Bayshill Road, Cheltenham, Gloucestershire, GL50 3EP

• Pupils: 870 girls; 645 board, 225 day • Ages: 11-18 • Size of sixth form: 300 • Christian but welcomes and respects all faiths • Fees: Day £18,621-£21,174; Boarding £27,735-£31,242 pa • Independent

Tel: 01242 520 691
Fax: 01242 227 882
Email: enquiries@cheltladiescollege.org
Website: www.cheltladiescollege.org

Principal: Since 1996, Mrs Vicky Tuck MA BA PGCE (fifty-ish). Came from City of London School for Girls where she was deputy head, formerly at Bromley High, previously modern languages teacher. Married with two sons, cool and collected, keeps in touch with what is happening in the classroom by shadowing a girl twice a year for the day. Large school so pupil/head contact fairly limited (unusual in a girls' school).

Leaving in July 2011 to become director general of The International School of Geneva.

Academic matters: Continues to be seriously strong – in 2010, 94.6 per cent A*–B at A level. GCSE consistently impressive – 94.9 per cent of girls achieved five or more A/A* passes in 2010. Maths, English, chemistry, physics, biology, economics and government and politics the most popular A level subjects; a few do Greek (one classical and one modern in 2010). Girls can now opt either for the International Baccalaureate Diploma or choose from the existing wide range of A levels offered by the school. Spanish, German, Mandarin on offer, Japanese classes available. Prides itself on allowing almost 'any combination of subjects at every level'.

IT strong: all leave with an ICT qualification, masses of computers, internet and email for all using wireless technology and laptops. Contemporary art, design and technology block complete with artist and photographer in residence. Huge staff – low turnover. Two well-equipped libraries both with full-time librarians. Strong support offered for mild learning difficulties (approximately 40 in college). New professional guidance centre encompasses support for higher education and careers advice and work shadowing.

Games, Options, the Arts: Excellent 'big' school facilities – huge gym in main building, games hall, two fitness rooms, up to 24 tennis courts, competition-sized indoor swimming pool which generates great enthusiasm and spectacular results. Two all-weather pitches, one floodlit, proving immensely popular. Teams for everything at various levels – a good number of girls play at county and national level. Increasingly popular alternatives to the traditional lacrosse, hockey and netball are fencing, rowing and judo. Off-site riding facilities – girls are allowed to bring ponies (popular among younger children especially) and polo is an option.

Immensely strong music as always – over 900 music lessons weekly, all packed in round subject lessons, five choirs, three orchestras, dozens of chamber groups and lots of girls compose. Drama and dance strong. Clubs for all ages and a plethora of productions including the annual Edinburgh Festival offering. Debating strengthening with societies dedicated to debating and public speaking – a team of sixth formers successfully defended the title of ESU UK Public Speaking Champions this year. Several College teams enter Young Enterprise each year, with one team winning best overall company in the 2007 Gloucestershire Young Enterprise Awards.

Active D of E programme. Two staff members dedicated to outdoor education programme – much growth here. Some 40 to 50 extracurricular activities on offer ranging from animation to business modelling. Adventure club invites girls to 'live life' by trying orienteering, canoeing, skiing, kayaking, scuba diving and the like. Something for the less adventurous (or active) too – like card making, needle skills, German cookery and magazine club. Strong on charity work through Community Links – helping in primary schools, animal shelters etc; 'Mrs Tuck's big thing,' said a pupil.

Background and Atmosphere: Founded in 1853, granted Royal Charter in 1935, main school revolves round huge purpose-built Victorian campus, with magnificent stained glass, marble corridor, Princess Hall, vast library, in the middle of Cheltenham. Boarders 'go home' to their house for lunch, tea and at night – friendly homely atmosphere; it really works. All houses are about 3–10 minutes' walk away. Junior boarders live either in rooms converted into 'cubs' (cubicles) or in open-plan dormitories.

New tutor arrangements strengthen the links between academic and pastoral care; housemistresses' job to ensure contact as frequent as possible. Most junior housemistresses and all sixth form housemistresses have academic responsibility. Sixth formers have dedicated houses (one day, four boarding), boarders sleep and work in charming individual rooms, but retain strong links with their junior house. Sixth formers can 'have dinner in town' (taxi there and back) and invite their boyfriends back – 'The boys often become house friends'.

Called 'greenflies' by townsfolk, new uniform, designed in consultation with the girls, recently introduced – trousers an option for sixth formers. Food has undergone a recent review. Few anorexics. Girls carry their books in 'sacks', send internal messages via 'slab' and have names for almost everything: Slodge (Sidney Lodge), St Mag's (St Margaret's), the bunny run. No bells, just clocks. Very highly structured, feels big (it is).

Pastoral Care and Discipline: Head feels that this is good and lots of safety nets have been put in place. Bullying is 'taken very seriously'. All girls have tutors. The three junior day houses are based at the newly refurbished day girl house, each with their own housemistresses. Confidential counselling service available to all girls run by professionally trained counsellors – 'No shame attached,' said a girl. Also 'Daisy', a pupil-led advisory service for younger girls. Very comprehensive and tough drugs policy – nothing mealy-mouthed about it. Occasional misdemeanours involving drink but rare. Older girls encouraged to take responsibility in school affairs – prefects elected by staff and senior girls, with each one given a portfolio of responsibilities.

Pupils and Parents: Ambitious parents of academic offspring – school has to manage the parents' expectations as much as the girls'. Broadish social mix, majority professional, not the 'posh' place the tabloid press think it is (accents are well-spoken but not smart). Lots of ex-pats. Around 20 per cent are international, mainly from Hong Kong and Singapore. Girls are good natured, bright and sensible, robust, astute and articulate, perhaps a touch 'solid'. Girls' priorities are work, sport, art, drama and shopping. Old girls: Rosie Boycott, Mary Archer, Cheryl Gillan, Rachel Lomax (first woman deputy governor of the Bank of England), Katharine Hamnett, Fiona Mactaggart MP, actress Kristen Scott Thomas, journalist Sue Lloyd-Roberts, Amanda Wakeley.

Entrance: Selective at 11, 12, 13: CE or own exam but able, enthusiastic learners encouraged to apply – stiff competition. Those from overseas need to have 'fluent and accurate English' before entering. Own competitive exam into the sixth form (lots join then and love it).

Exit: 25 offered Oxbridge places in 2009. Others to traditional universities – Durham and LSE most popular in 2009 – and art colleges. 'All girls are destined to have careers.'

Money Matters: Expensive but definitely provides value for money. At last count, 4.8 per cent of fee income available for bursaries. Large number of scholarships (by girls' school standards) available.

Remarks: Famous and strong traditional girls' boarding school, with large numbers of day girls. Impressive results as always. Full and busy timetable. Described by Ofsted as an 'exceptional school' where emphasis on personal development – even for the timid girl – is encouraged.

The Cherwell School

Marston Ferry Road, Oxford, Oxfordshire, OX2 7EE

• Pupils: 1,785 boys and girls, all day • Ages: 11-18 • Size of sixth form: 430
• Non-denom • State

Tel: 01865 558 719
Fax: 01865 311 165
Email: head@cherwell.oxon.sch.uk
Website: www.cherwell.oxon.sch.uk

Head: Since October 2010, Mr Paul James, previously deputy head, and acting head since the precipitous departure of Mr Neal McGowan, who left after only a year. This kind of instability does no school any favours and we wish Mr James well.

Academic matters: One of the best state secondary schools in Oxfordshire. Wide and interesting range of subjects at GCSE, including health and social care, product design and astronomy. German, French and Spanish on offer, with other languages subject to needs and backgrounds of pupils. Traditional academic route supplemented by a mixed bag of college courses – construction, hairdressing, engineering etc, plus ASDAN awards, Cope and skillforce, whatever is best for the pupil. Strong showing in history, English (mixed ability teaching), modern languages and science at GCSE – no real weaknesses. A/B pass rate at A level has varied, from just under 50 per cent to almost 70 per cent in recent years; few fail altogether. Strong too in the sciences, economics, history and maths.

Very inclusive school: well-staffed learning support department led by SENCo, offers a continuum of provision for more than 300 pupils who are currently on the SEN register. Transition programme for those with statements begins as early as Year 5. Two specialist units on site (separate admissions policies), one for autism, and the hearing impairment centre for Oxfordshire, complete with outreach staff. All those in the oral, hearing-impaired unit attend mainstream classes with appropriate support to ensure curriculum can be fully accessed. Works to ensure suitable acoustics, staff training etc. Those in the autism unit spend majority of their time in the unit but will attend mainstream classes if deemed beneficial to the pupil and not detrimental to the learning of others. School believes units are real assets – 'They teach our youngsters tolerance, understanding and acceptance of people who have differences'. Has behaviour base, for vulnerable students, not necessarily those with SEN. Not a sin-bin, though it is used for transgressions, the base also acts as a refuge and support centre – anger management, assertiveness training, social skills, counselling etc on offer.

Accelerated classes (NACE Challenge Award too) for the very able means new groups of students rise to top, to be best of the rest. School currently focussing on student voice and personalised learning, so pupils know where they are and what they need to do to move on – still a work in progress. Already target gifted and talented (currently 23 per cent on register, no gender bias), SEN and those on C/D grade boundaries; now focusing on getting to all pupils.

Games, Options, the Arts: School has three gyms and good all-weather tennis courts, basketball area plus lots of green space for a range of sports, including hockey, basketball, rugby and football, played by boys and girls. Site borders Ferry sports centre, which houses pools, larger sports hall and squash courts. Art, drama, music ever-popular, with regular trips, visits and productions plus Artsmark award. Music taken seriously and to a high standard – around a quarter take individual music lessons. A recent Young Musician of the Year was a Cherwell pianist; a current Year 7 boy has written his own symphony. Regular concerts from school orchestras and wind band; hoping for a resurgence of choral music. Thanks to goodwill of the staff, a host of lunchtime and after-school clubs and activities are on offer; has a massive knock-on effect with positive pupil relations. Sixth form art students study abroad for a week each year. Linked to schools in France and Germany.

Background and Atmosphere: Opened in 1963, as a small secondary modern, for ages 11–16, surrounded by allotments and fields near Oxford's upmarket Summertown area. Two 1970s events shattered its peace: first, the building of the inner Oxford ring road; secondly, the shakeup of Oxford's schools. School became an ever-growing comprehensive upper school (ages 13–18), separated from its main feeder middle schools (9–13) by fast-flowing traffic. Its original box-shaped buildings were supplemented by a library and sixth form block and then, when the money ran out in the 1980s, rows of ugly temporary classrooms. When building restarted in 1991, a music and drama block and new permanent classrooms were added. The site was also landscaped with help from the parents' association. Now a revamped 11–18 comprehensive following a major reorganisation of Oxford City's schools in 2003, the school is on two sites, linked by a subway. Key stage 3 students are on the south site and key stages 4 and 5 are on the north site. This helps to preserve identity and pupil individuality, in what could otherwise be a large anonymous school.

Pastoral Care and Discipline: Form tutors are first port of call for general matters, well-supported by heads of years and non-teaching assistants. Works hard to prevent gang/laddish culture from surfacing; common-sense, 'firm but fair' rules and formal detentions coupled with a positive approach result in, for the most part, decent behaviour and polite young people, though handful disrupt lessons on occasions. Temporary exclusions used sparingly, usually for bullying or fighting, and permanent exclusions very rare. Trained staff from local businesses act as e-mentors to pupils in danger of being disaffected by school. Mentors are invited into school to lunch with their mentee – 'it's a great motivator, especially where children are invited into the workplace'.

New healthy eating options victim of own success with complaints of frequent scrums in the dining hall. Uniform viewed as irrelevant but the lack of such leaves some looking decidedly like 'Kevin'. Little wonder some of the younger ones would like to return to the security of a sweatshirt or similar.

Pupils and Parents: Pupils are generally all a school could wish for – bright, encouraged at home, used to academic endeavour, imaginative and ambitious to realise their dreams. Parents are often academics or work in the mass of white-collar, highbrow and highly-paid jobs on offer in Oxford. There are, however, pockets of poverty and disaffection in the heart of Oxford and Cherwell has its share of troubled and troublesome children; it also has delightful children from poorer backgrounds, grateful for their places at this sought-after school and a real credit to the place. Famous ex-pupils include Rachel Seiffert (novelist) and Yasmin le Bon (model).

Entrance: Only distance from school matters – unfortunately, this varies from year to year according to numbers applying. Oversubscribed – distraught parents falling just outside the boundary make up ever-increasing number appealing; handful succeed. Most come from within a small radius (cycling to school popular), a few arrive from private prep schools in Oxford. Admission to the autism unit or hearing impairment centre is via the local authority – all will have statements of SEN.

Exit: Around 80 per cent go on to sixth form, 70 per cent staying at Cherwell and the remainder usually joining Oxford's FE college. Almost all A level students go on to higher education, while others take vocational qualifications and a small number start work. 15 or so a year to Oxbridge.

Money Matters: Usual issues facing state schools but in pretty good shape, all things considered.

Remarks: A true comprehensive, offering something for everyone. Stars rise from across the academic and social spectrum. Changes at the top clearly destabilising but the school is, we feel, strong enough to weather them.

Chetham's School of Music

Linked to Chethams School of Music Junior Department in the Junior section

Long Millgate, Manchester, Lancashire, M3 1SB

• Pupils: 295, mostly boarding (65 day pupils) • Ages: 8-18 • Size of sixth form: 125; 55 boys, 65 girls • Non-denom • Fees: Day £23,988; Boarding £30,987 pa • Independent

Tel: 0161 834 9644
Fax: 0161 839 3609
Email: chets@chethams.com
Website: www.chethams.com

Head: Since 1999, Mrs Claire J Hickman MA (late forties). Read modern languages at Oxford. Previously housemistress and deputy head at Rugby School. Before that, taught languages at Croydon High School and Sevenoaks. Professional but warm, informal, humorous. Married to Richard Hickman, music examiner and consultant – previously in charge of the Federation of Music Services. Teenage son at Abbotsholme School. Interests are music, literature, theatre, travel and walking. Plays classical guitar in private. Appears to be holding down two full-time jobs with no sign of madness or hysteria. The first is running Chetham's. The other is, in her words, 'building a whole new school'. For Chetham's – Manchester's refined haven of classical music – is in the throes of constructing an 'iconic' new building as part of a £35 million development project in concert with Manchester City Council's urban regeneration. The new building is rising on land previously owned by Network Rail (between the school and Victoria Station). As well as classrooms, the block will house a sumptuous 400-seat concert hall for both school and public use. A huge and exciting undertaking – Mrs Hickman stands in the eye of the hurricane, coordinating between Manchester City Council, English Heritage, funders, the Victorian Society (who object to pulling down one of the school's current buildings) – and we watch progress with interest.

Academic matters: About one-third of timetable devoted to music. In view of this, and the fact that the school is academically non-selective, exam results are exceptional. Director of studies points out that although the intake is comprehensive in theory, in practice most pupils are academically high calibre. Most pupils ambitious across the board, not just as musicians. School careful to ensure that 'a decent Plan B' is in place, for those pupils who don't make it in a musical career or don't wish to pursue one. Fewer GCSEs and A levels taken than in most schools to make time for all that music – though not many fewer: generally eight GCSEs and three AS levels; a few take less – music colleges only require two A levels so some pupils drop a subject after AS; many take more.

Range of subjects slim but adequate. German the main foreign language, with French also offered (and occasionally Italian). Pupils from overseas may prepare for exams in their mother tongue (out of school). Setting in maths. Science facilities very good. Classes small – average size 15, maximum 22. Ratio of staff to pupils 1:7. Junior school pupils are entered for KS2 exams. 50 pupils have some form of SEN tuition provided by three members of staff: typically 20–30 pupils get help for dyslexia or dyspraxia; 16 currently require ESL support; two statemented pupils (autistic spectrum and hearing and visual impairment). Mostly disability-friendly, barring the library.

Musically, the school is acclaimed nationally and internationally. Pupils say no single department shines brighter than the others, although brass is particularly good, perhaps owing to the Northern brass band tradition. A few parents pointed out that although jazz and electronic music are growing (superb music tech and recording suite opened 2006), the vast majority of pupils remain firmly within the classical tradition and virtually all the music played in school concerts is classical (though not necessarily 'classical'). The underlying premise is that 'music comes first', but NB the tension between academic and musical commitments still exists – the academic work doesn't just disappear. It is done, and generally to a high standard. Fantastic array of ensemble opportunities from chamber music, big bands, choirs and full symphony orchestras.

Games, Options, the Arts: No team games but tailor-made fitness programmes for each pupil. Friendly matches, e.g. between staff and pupils, do take place. Basketball and football in the yard, underground gym and small swimming pool, plus weekend walking trips, sailing activities etc, to get out of the city. 'Some kids do miss team games,' said a parent, 'but you simply cannot have them breaking their fingers or spraining their wrists.' 'Loads of stairs everywhere keep us fit,' say pupils wryly; the school lifts are for teacher use only. Drama popular.

Background and Atmosphere: The largest of Britain's five specialist music schools. Small site, 15th-century listed buildings at its core, and located in the heart of Manchester city centre – the word 'oasis' is not out of place. Was once a grammar school; became a school of music in 1969. The main building is something of a town landmark – took us no time at all to find it, but half an hour to work out how to get in. Hint: don't try the front door! Dripping in history – Chet's roots as an educational establishment go back to 1653, while the beautiful Baronial Hall which is used for school concerts was built in 1421. Foundations within the school form part of Manchester's original city walls. Chetham's houses the oldest public library in England – it began acquiring material in 1655 and Karl Marx leafed its collection.

The only specialist music school based in a city centre, there is a palpable buzz from its mega-urban setting. Easy access to Bridgewater Hall, opera house, conservatoire (Royal Northern College of Music) and other cultural opportunities. Atmosphere of school is tangibly charged with the excitement and enthusiasm of the pupils and has all the pros and cons of any tight-knit community. School has fairly close relationship with Manchester Cathedral (it educates the choristers) but has multi-ethnic and international intake and looks for common spiritual ground between people and religions rather than following any particular doctrine. The diversity of backgrounds of pupils is viewed as a plus. Loads of outreach, workshops, classes and special projects for the community. The northern branch of the Nordoff-Robbins Music Therapy charity is based in the school and there is a new pre-school music initiative.

Pastoral Care and Discipline: Things have certainly changed since the 1970s when pupils had to parade in the yard and have their shoes inspected before breakfast! Pupil handbook, setting out anti-bullying policy, general information and school rules, is a model document ('Busking is strictly against the rules' – hard luck on the more entrepreneurially inclined pupils). Various people to whom pupils can and do turn in difficulties. Relationship with instrument teacher generally very close. Houseparents, tutors, are available, also house assistants who are often a popular choice of confidant/e. Older pupils look after the younger members of the school and are touchingly fond of their 'little ones'. Head says she is tough on vice – 'If kids are being subsidised by British tax payers, then they need to commit themselves fully'. Out for dealing drugs. If caught experimenting, then will have to submit to testing. If persistently busted, then out.

Boarders must stay in school until Saturday lunch. The majority remain in all weekend – they live too far away to get home easily. Homesickness an issue as students tend to come from further away than at most boarding schools. A mother we spoke to was full of praise for the way the school handled her daughter's homesickness (although eventually the girl decided to leave). Quite a lot of controlled access to the city, particularly for the sixth form.

Bedrooms not big but not too many sharing. Sixth form boys get a lovely view of the cathedral, as well as internet connection, and there are quite a few en suite single rooms. Roomy middle school dorms we visited slept four chaps. Common-room with huge windows looking out on skyscrapers in every direction. Girls' boarding also good, with kitchens and hands-on laundry room; sixth form girls mainly in individual en suite rooms. Victoria House junior boarding in separate boy/girl corridors. Each Victoria House pupil is assigned a sixth form mentor available for chat, outings etc.

Pupils and Parents: Most are encouraged to apply by their music teachers or existing students. However we came across a range of other avenues including 'my mother happened to be walking by the school and thought it sounded interesting', 'the government funding made it affordable – we could never have paid for a normal private school' and – our favourite – 'well, a film crew was making a documentary about the school when I visited and they wanted to film me so I thought I'd better continue to the next stage and audition'.

Vast majority of pupils desperate to come here. Occasionally parents push their children into auditioning with a predictably unhappy result once the child is here. Increasing numbers from EU students for whom there are reciprocal funding arrangements for sixth form places. Parents from many countries and all walks of life. Many are active in the musical world themselves, others are the opposite and are astonished to find themselves with a musical prodigy on their hands. Students view 'modesty' and 'having your feet firmly on the ground' as essential prerequisites to happiness at the school. Mutually supportive atmosphere, in which students 'live or die' by remembering to read the noticeboards (there is a long corridor of them) and checking school's intranet several times a day – the more absentminded students being suitably organised by the switched-on ones. Student population heavily weighted toward the oldest age group, with nearly half of the students in the sixth form. Famous old boys/girls include organist Wayne Marshall, pianist Peter Donohoe, pop musician and actor Max Beesley, choral conductor and organist David Hill, conductor Daniel Harding, three BBC Young Musicians of the Year (most recently Jennifer Pike who won the competition at the age of 12) and many others: an impressive list ... yeeessss, but possibly less impressive than one would expect given the calibre of the students who come here.

Entrance: The only criterion for entry is exceptional musical ability, which is assessed by two auditions. No academic criteria. Instrumental students from age eight. Voice students come for sixth form only. The largest intake is in the lower sixth. If interested, you can first ask for an optional advice audition, to see if you're up to the mark. If you get a thumbs up, then register and attend an assessment audition (30 minutes). If that goes well, you pass to the main audition in front of the director of music and a panel of other school bigwigs. Here 'You'll be asked to develop specific musical elements based on what we heard at the assessment audition'. Not sure what this means but it sounds scary. DVD or video performances can be accepted from overseas applicants who, incidentally, need fluent English. You can apply and audition at any time of year, but the school encourages students to apply before Christmas for a place for the following September. Head says the standard for entry has risen during her time here, partly owing to students of genuinely world class ability from abroad raising the bar. However the DfE places will always go to UK/European applicants. Choristers for Manchester Cathedral can apply between the ages of seven and ten.

Exit: Majority (about three-quarters) to music conservatoires and colleges; most of the rest to university either to study music or – surprisingly often – other subjects. A good proportion to Oxbridge. Strong links with the Royal Northern College of Music, virtually next door, to which many Chetham's students proceed.

Money Matters: Over 90 per cent of students receive some level of government support via the DfE music and dance scheme. The government's contribution is means-tested and ranges from full fees for the poorest families to a drop in the bucket for families with incomes at the top of the range (£160,000). Students not receiving DfE funding are either choristers (who are funded through alternative schemes), very wealthy or from outside the EU.

Remarks: Fabulous, muscular, urban music school literally vibrating with musicality and flair. Very special students but not remotely 'precious'. Whereas a lot of schools like to pass themselves off as one big, happy family, Chetham's actually feels like one.

Chew Valley School

Chew Lane, Chew Magna, Bristol, BS40 8QB

• Pupils: 600 girls; 560 boys, all day • Ages: 11-18 • Size of sixth form: 195 • Non-denom • State

Tel: 01275 332 272
Fax: 01275 333 625
Email: chewvalley_sec@bathnes.gov.uk
Website: www.chewvalleyschool.co.uk

Head: Since 2003, Mr Mark Mallett LLB MA PGCE (early fifties). Read law at University College, London, then completed his PGCE and MA at the London Institute. Son of a Methodist minister, sent first to Kingswood, Bath, then Reading School and finally Maltby Grammar School, Rotherham. Discovered passion for teaching whilst a graduate gapper in Algeria and later taught in Borneo with VSO. Early career in Greater London, then HOD at rival Backwell School, North Somerset (qv) before six years as deputy at QEH, Hexham. Committed to comprehensive ideal. Still teaches English enthusiastically. Rushed off at lunchtime when we visited to learn Italian with students. Leads regular choir practices and 'always pushing the performing arts,' say colleagues. Keen musician who 'loves East European composers'. Plays flute and piano, sings with City of Bristol choir. Now into gear in first headship and keen to raise cultural standards; admits he 'much prefers ballet to cheerleading'. Married with a daughter at Oxford and son at another comprehensive.

Academic matters: Rated 'very good' by Ofsted; consistently good examination results from a very wide intake. Around 50 per cent A and B grades at A level with 76 per cent gaining five A*–C at GCSE (69 per cent including English and maths) puts it in top drawer of Somerset comprehensives. Some local uncertainty about breadth of sixth form choice but majority are happy with what Chew offers its A level candidates. Thirty subjects and the AQA Baccalaureate offered in sixth form, with small class sizes. History rated particularly highly by pupils, who had been to Washington DC as part of AS course. English, maths, sciences and geography all impressive in volume and level of results.

Most GCSE pupils follow a traditional route but about 25 per cent have more vocational and skills-based work. More modern languages here than at most schools, with top set doing German in Years 8 and 9. Year 7 parents need to state first language preference (French or Spanish); maths setted from first term. All ages seem to cope well with 50 minute lessons. Triple science offered at GCSE to most able but most do double. Enterprise option in Year 9 gets pupils planning an event.

Science area was extended in 2003 and provides modern laboratories. A brand new sixth form centre opened in September 09. Plenty of ICT with interactive whiteboards but not a software driven school – fizzy lessons are considered most important. Special needs team seen as 'absolutely fantastic' by parents – deals sensitively with 30 statemented pupils including Tourette's and Asperger's. Site is largely wheelchair-friendly with three lifts installed. Sixth formers volunteer to help with reading etc. SENCo's base is seen as 'safe haven' and behaviour management includes time out where necessary. Excellent screening and testing for special needs and close liaison with feeder primaries. Happiness of pupils seen as top priority. Mentoring and inclusion initiatives to support least academic partly based in former caretaker's house on site. Lots of extra-curricular stuff for gifted and talented with financial support from LEA where necessary. Critical thinking at AS level for about 15 sixth formers.

Games, Options, the Arts: Energetic head of PE faculty sets pace for sport plus diverse outdoor pursuits, games and activities programmes; parents really appreciate the effort put in by staff. Teams compete annually in 35, 45 and 55 mile Ten Tors challenge on Dartmoor. Outward-bound team spent some of previous summer in India's Himalayan mountains and refurbishing village schools. This year a similar project with a partner school in the copper belt, Zambia. Next year a sports exchange to South Africa. Close links with Bristol football academies. County representation in all major sports. International performances include swimming, riding, fishing, squash and dragster racing. Top sports people supported through new 'performance centre' initiative aimed at serious athletes. Acres of playing fields, floodlit Astroturf, excellent lottery funded leisure complex includes massive gymnasium with sprung floor ideal for dance and tae kwon-do. Large sports hall, squash courts and fitness suite all in heavy school and community use – 'not much else to do here,' quipped one parent. Rugby, netball and football teams particularly successful, as is sailing on nearby Chew Valley lake.

Music is flagship performance area with superb facilities including state of art recording studio; school puts out own Chew Valley radio programmes 106.6 FM. About 25 per cent of pupils have individual music lessons up to grade 8. Ensembles, choirs, orchestras and bands (including keen swing band) are a feature of life here. Pupils enthuse about music in a way which is unusual in comprehensives. Drama and dance are also lively with a heavily-subscribed annual dance festival and lots of dance year round. Current drama productions vary from a full production of Midsummer Night's Dream to Little Shop of Horrors, and generally take place on the main stage, but also a small studio for lessons and intimate performances.

Good facilities for art and DT. Lots of linked visits and activities including curating exhibitions at galleries in Bath. Sixth form artists were at St Ives when we visited and Chew Valley dragsters have scooped prizes at annual competition run by Bath University. However we would have welcomed more visual displays around the school to enhance the environment.

Background and Atmosphere: Began life in 1958 as a rural secondary modern and had a successful sixth form by early seventies. Reputation has attracted growing numbers from south Bristol in addition to own catchment. Not many state schools enjoy a setting like this – low impact buildings spread across pleasantly landscaped site with outlying playing fields. Too many bare breeze blocks in corridors but head aims to improve décor with pupils' input. Mezzanine area in library provides excellent ICT area for sixth formers. Purposeful and orderly atmosphere throughout. Good arrangements for midday hot meals with new bistro alternative; hardly a crisp packet or sweet paper in sight.

Pastoral Care and Discipline: Senior staff get out and about to jolly things along. Lots of effort goes into ensuring a smooth transfer from feeder primaries with buddy system operating once they've got here so 'not at all daunting,' say parents. Heads of faculty intervene quickly and insist on seating plans for all lessons at key stage three. Heads of year, SENCo and tutors are main players in maintaining good discipline. Exclusion room used internally; suspensions for more serious breaches. New student council initiative to involve 120 pupils in action teams targeting healthy eating, fundraising, toilets, buildings, energy, recycling and environment. Plenty of charity giving in recent times including a Peruvian project, Children of the Andes, co-ordinated by a former teacher. Hooray for the simple uniform – school polo shirt and sweatshirt over it leave little scope for subversion. Elasticated 'daps' supplied for any who 'try it on' (probably not more than once?) by turning up in trainers.

Pupils and Parents: Looking at this lot it's hard to believe you're not in a selective school, though socially it's pretty mixed, which parents like. Lots of parents relocate to be within the catchment area and house prices reflect this. Ready volunteers for projects such as memorial garden made for a former, much-loved science teacher. Lots of enthusiasm – over-subscription of school and student councils speak volumes for morale. Very active school society runs successful fundraising and social events. Former pupils include John Garden (keyboards in The Scissor Sisters); recording flautist Nicola Woodward and professional percussionist Justin Woodward.

Entrance: School is full in lower years and draws about a fifth of intake from outside its catchment area. Apply direct to LEA in October of year before entry. Outside entry into sixth form requires five A*–C GCSEs but motivation and behaviour are key factors.

Exit: 65 per cent remain for sixth form and head would like to retain more. FE and sixth form colleges in Bristol and Norton Radstock now provide serious competition post-16. Some modern apprenticeships and a few straight into employment. Majority of Year 13 leavers go into higher education including a few to Oxbridge. Some seek vocational training.

Remarks: School measures success by 'happiness of children'. Performing arts permeate life here and make a huge difference to pupils' experience. Staff love teaching at Chew Valley and their enthusiasm makes it easier for pupils to contribute above and beyond norm.

Chigwell School

Linked to Chigwell Junior School in the Junior section

High Road, Chigwell, Essex, IG7 6QF

• Pupils: 510; 275 girls; 230 boys. 30 full boarders, to rest day • Ages: 13-18 • Size of sixth form: 170; boys and girls nearly 50/50 • C of E but welcomes all • Fees: Day £9,696-£14,532; Boarding £22,335 pa • Independent

Tel: 020 8501 5700
Fax: 020 8500 6232
Email: hm@chigwell-school.org
Website: www.chigwell-school.org

Headmaster: Since September 2007, Mr Michael Punt MA MSc PGCE (thirties), a physicist who lives on site with his wife Gill and their three sons, one of whom has just started at the school. His calm and positive influence is palpable throughout the school, although he modestly describes his many successful initiatives as 'just tinkering'. Parents know better, saying he's 'approachable, liked and respected'. One even tells the tale of a parent who was torn between three schools for her child but plumped for Chigwell on the basis of meeting Mr Punt.

Academic matters: Results of 79 per cent A*/A at GCSE, and 80 per cent A/B at A level; ISI inspectors to describe attainment in public examinations at Chigwell as 'excellent' in their recent report. They put this down to the 'pupils' positive and conscientious attitude to learning and their excellent relationship with the teachers'. Experienced, dedicated staff and a free choice of options outside of the core subjects are major factors, says the head, and he is keen to offer a wide range at A level, including those required for a wide choice of university courses to pique the interest of his academically inquisitive students. History and geography are the long-established favourites here and good results can be credited to an experienced department, says the head. Economics, maths and sciences are also strong at A level but drama and DT are on the rise too, enforcing Chigwell's reputation as a place for the all-rounder.

Maths IGCSE is taken and pupils are setted 'loosely' in Year 7 in preparation. Three-quarters take separate sciences at GCSE and sets for these start in Year 9. New heads of languages and English have recently been appointed to try to boost take-up and results, which have lagged behind the other subjects in the past. English is set in Year 10 and languages are now more popular choices for GCSE and A level thanks to the early introduction of Spanish and German in the junior school.

One of Mr Punt's most successful recent innovations has been the change of lesson length from 35 to 50 minutes, which has increased teaching time for sixth formers and given teachers the scope to introduce more pupil-centred activities. It seems to be working – the ISI concluded that pupils are 'well educated' and that the school 'fully meets its aims to provide a high quality rounded education where pupils reach high standards of achievement and develop of a love of learning'.

For those who need help, a dedicated SENCo is on hand. Junior school pupils are screened for SEN on entry and then undergo further testing in the senior school. Learning support is used mostly in the junior school rather than the senior, but high ability students are developed beyond the classroom with extension activities.

Games, Options, the Arts: Parents are pleased with the balance of academic work and life experiences – 'valuable pursuits such as art, drama, music and sport enhance the atmosphere of positive competition,' says one.

Playing fields surround this small school (75 acres) but indoor facilities are relatively modest in comparison to many of Chigwell's peers, with an unfancy sports centre and a small outdoor swimming pool. Hockey is strong for both boys and girls and this is set to build now the school has its new Astro pitch. Chigwell competes well on the football pitch too and the school numbers several county players in netball and cricket – the school has its own all-weather nets. PE pursuits are rotated half-termly, with basketball and badminton on the menu. Golf is played at the nearby club and sixth formers can visit the local gym or use the on-site fitness equipment.

The Drama Centre is a real pride and joy – an eye-catching red-brick building with impressively professional facilities. There's a foyer big enough for pre-theatre drinks receptions, plus rehearsal and teaching rooms, and the auditorium has 200 moveable seats. The two productions a year and the sixth form play are highlights of the school calendar. A dozen students each year take drama A level with great success. Music at Chigwell is very inclusive. Every other pupil learns an instrument and the annual Prom concert is open to all. The annual house music competition, the Chigwell Young Musician of the Year event and performances by the many musical ensembles add to the cultural richness of the school. Chigwellians have a huge choice of extra-curricular activities, from D of E and Scouts to art exhibitions and the inspiring and thought-provoking talks run as part of the Williams Project, named after philosopher and Chigwell alumnus, Bernard Williams.

Background and Atmosphere: Set on the approach road to the historic high street, Chigwell was founded in 1629 by the Reverend Samuel Harsnett, the local vicar who became Archbishop of York and Chancellor of Cambridge University. Today the original red-brick schoolhouse forms the centrepiece to this pretty village of neat buildings, punctuated by gardens and quads planted with blooms and trees. The surrounding playing fields stretch as far as Epping Forest and give a rural aspect to the school and some lovely views from the windows of the attractive, low-rise teaching blocks. None of the facilities are more than an easy and pleasant stroll apart. The music block is positioned centrally so that the odd note and phrase float across the greenery, and the drama centre is a well-designed modern addition. When we visited, the new dining hall and kitchens were under construction and the pupils were excited to be taking their meals in the Harry Potteresque main hall. The new food facilities were later decared open by Michel Roux. There's also a new Astro and plans are afoot for a pre-prep and a sixth form study centre.

The 1920s chapel was built in tribute to fallen alumni and is a mainstay of life at Chigwell. Twice weekly services embrace all the beliefs represented at this multicultural school and speech day includes a passage from each of the six major world faiths. Indeed respect and a sense of community are integral to life at Chigwell. 'This is a happy school', says the head and there does seem to be a sense of harmony at work. There is no need for intrusive bells to mark the change of lessons – pupils make their way around the school in an ordered fashion and newbies of any age wear a plain tie so they can be spotted and helped when in need, in typical caring Chigwellian fashion.

Chigwell has its own nomenclature for year groups, from removes (Year 9), through lower fifth, upper fifth and lower sixth to middle sixth (Year 13).The school's intranet – Chigwell's Gateway – is heavily relied on for submission of homework and essential admin, such as notices and timetables. An electronic noticeboard system is also well used and life at Chigwell seems to flow in a stress-free fashion.

Pastoral Care and Discipline: 'Excellent' was the verdict of ISI inspectors on pastoral care at Chigwell and it's easy to see why. A strong four-house system – and staff who 'really know their pupils' according to the head, mean students are comfortable in the knowledge that they are being 'looked out for'. Pupils' personal development was described by inspectors as 'outstanding', and they put this down to the school's promotion of a society in which everyone takes responsibility for each other and the wider environment.

Sixth form students from abroad add to the mix and are valued for the insights they provide into other cultures and ways of life. Mostly from Central and Eastern Europe, and China, they are encouraged to give talks on the issues affecting their homelands. These students are the only ones to board in four homely houses on-site, and their constant presence gives the school a lived-in feel. Boarders are also attached to a day house and take a full part in activities there.

Food is said to be plentiful and good, with healthy options and popular themed days. Children spoke enthusiastically of tasting lobster on seafood day, and sausages were dished up all round to celebrate St George's Day. The uniform is smart and sober – kilts or plain trousers with a navy blazer, though the sixth formers wear office attire.

Pupils and Parents: This leafy, middle-class suburb is spoilt for choice education-wise, with several good fee-paying schools on the doorstep and some of the best grammars in the country a short hop on the train away. Even Old Chigwellians admit to investigating the competition before signing up their offspring, but one was pleased to note that 'the school has retained one of its key attributes – to ensure that pupils attain their potential'. Equally though, the school appeals to first-time buyers, notably British Asian families who are attracted by the excellence in maths and sciences, and those who see Chigwell's strength in 'creating confident, well-rounded people'. Although this is undoubtedly an affluent area, and children are drawn mainly from a four or five-mile radius, the head is aware that families often make sacrifices to send them.

There are slightly more boys than girls in the seniors, but as the juniors are now 50–50 that is set to change in the future. The pupils we met fell over themselves with helpfulness and had a relaxed, confident air. Parents have many opportunities to speak informally with staff about their children's progress and well-being at breakfast get-togethers and afternoon teas, and the Friends of Chigwell put on a programme of social events.

The list of distinguished alumni includes William Penn, Sir Arthur Grimble, Austin Bradford Hill, Edward Vulliamy and Sir Bernard Williams. Sir Alan Sugar lives virtually next door and his grandsons are pupils here, as were their fathers.

Entrance: Most come across from the junior department and there are very few vacancies at 13. At 16 there are no advertised places and those moving up to the sixth form are expected to have achieved at least Bs or above in six GCSE subjects and As or A*s in their A level choices.

Exit: 'Students here have high aspirations,' says the head. The Oxbridge dreams of 10 per cent are realised currently but he fully expects that proportion to rise as attainment improves throughout the school. The majority go on to their first choice of university, though few Chigwellians venture north. Four or five choose medicine, and marketing and economics are other favourites. However as many as 10 Chigwellians a year go on to study art.

Money Matters: Academic scholarships are available at 11 and 13 and schols for art, drama and music are offered at 13 and 16. Means-tested bursaries are available.

Remarks: A relaxed and happy school with a real family feel, this is a very civilised place to nurture confident, caring all-rounders.

Christ College

Brecon, Powys, LD3 8AF

• Pupils: 190 boys, 150 girls. 210 boarders; 130 day pupils • Ages: 11-18 • Size of sixth form: 130 • Christian • Fees: Boarding £16,800-£21,465; Day £12,210-£13,890 pa • Independent

Tel: 01874 615 440
Fax: 01874 615 475
Email: enquiries@christcollegebrecon.com
Website: www.christcollegebrecon.com

The Head: Since September 2007, Mrs Emma L Taylor MA (early forties). Educated at St Antony's Leweston, Sherborne and Canford, won an exhibition to New College Oxford, where she read PPE. Taught philosophy, religious studies and economics at Stowe; then housemistress at Canford and deputy head at Dean Close. Her husband is a modern linguist, now a househusband. Two daughters, one at the school.

Academic matters: Wide ability range – results are extraordinarily good: 26 per cent of A level grades at the challenging new A* level, 78 per cent of all grades achieved A*, A or Bs. Maths and the sciences particularly strong as well as photography and art. Nearly 60 per cent of all GCSE grades achieve A* or A with 100 per cent of pupils achieving A*–C in the core subjects of English, maths and science.

The range of subjects offered in such a small institution amazes one. Enormous choice offered for GCSE and even more at A level. Sixth form teaching groups often very small with individual progress being very closely monitored – a particular strength. Indeed the school prides itself on the high degree of individual mentoring and support it provides for all of its pupils. Not a school that has compromised its scholastic ideals in the pursuit of transitory success in league tables. The vast majority of sixth form pupils are undertaking real and demanding subjects even if this depresses the school's league table showing. Strong learning support provided (unusually) as part of the basic fee. The 17 per cent foreign student contingent is offered considerable assistance with English, again as part of the basic fee.

Games, Options, the Arts: Brecon is fundamentally a boarding school but its day pupil numbers are growing too. This means that, even nominally, day pupils will spend at least 10 hours a day in school and sometimes as much as 14. The school is a hive of activities with the glorious Brecon Beacons being well used as a resource for adventure training and CCF activities. Christ College is perhaps most famous for its prowess on the rugby field. The annual match (perhaps better described as a battle!) between Brecon and Llandovery is a highlight of the Welsh school rugby scene. However, all sports are taken very seriously but with the emphasis on participation and enjoyment. Now the college is co-educational this is particularly true of hockey, netball and equestrian pursuits. If proof were needed of the sporting focus of the college, the 30-plus pupils who have represented their country in 10 different sports over the last three years or so surely speaks volumes.

Art one of the particular strengths, and some extraordinary work in photography. The way the pupils' success in this area is acknowledged and even celebrated shows that Brecon has shrugged off the bone-headed rugby image it once had. Also shown in the fine dramatic tradition the school has developed. Major dramatic productions take place in most terms and involve as many pupils as possible. *A Midsummer Night's Dream* and *The Music Man* are recent examples that do precisely this, as well as exploiting and developing Brecon's strong choral tradition. A new director of music appointment has seen an upsurge in activity, and the new post of head of choral music gives a clue as to the direction the school is taking, with closer links being forged with the neighbouring Brecon Cathedral and its musical director.

Background and Atmosphere: Founded in 1541 by Henry VIII, together with Eton one of the two independent school royal foundations. Nestles on the edge of the small, safe Welsh market town of Brecon – views are truly spectacular and whole assemblage is reminiscent of an idealised Dylan Thomas film set. Campus nicely compact with boarding houses, chapel, games fields and classrooms all jumbled together in a rather eclectic mixture of architectural styles. In truth one would not celebrate the majority of the post-war developments, yet on the whole the campus is of a human scale that enhances the very modest and unpretentious atmosphere. The Hubert Jones Science Centre opened in 2009, however, is a superb addition to the campus. The key to Brecon's success is the friendliness and warmth that pervades relationships here. The head's determination to be accessible to all is a key factor. Her office right in the centre of the campus ensures that pupils and staff can pop in if need be.

Pastoral Care and Discipline: Very strong house system with excellent back-up from tutors. Head focused on the need to deliver top quality pastoral care. A huge amount of money spent in recent years on upgrading the boarding accommodation with some superb enhancements for boarders in the Junior (Year 7/8) house. The two girls' boarding houses are very attractive with charismatic and effective housemothers. Whilst the school expects high standards of behaviour from its pupils (and usually achieves them) discipline is enforced with a light touch. The emphasis is on the quality of personal relationships and community relations. Escapes some of the more extreme drugs and drink difficulties that plague schools closer to the fleshpots of the south-east.

Pupils and Parents: Most of the pupils hail from within 50 miles, though its catchment area is expanding, pretty evenly divided between those from Wales and from the English marches. Small numbers from a total of 19 different countries as well as significant and, unusually, not declining, numbers of military and ex-pat families. Not a smart school and has never attempted to be so. Significant numbers come from an agricultural background. The growth in the number of refugees fleeing London to the good life in Powys suggests that the English proportion will grow.

Entrance: About 40 per cent of the intake at sixth form – a very popular choice to do A levels – and 40 per cent at 11, who spend two years in the delightfully prep school atmosphere of the Junior house, mostly from relatively local Powys and Herefordshire primary schools. A significant and growing intake from prep schools at 13 plus: St John's on the Hill, Llandaff and Moor Park. Entrance is by a mathematics, English and verbal reasoning test and not usually Common Entrance. The popularity of the school has made it more selective than it was but it remains relatively relaxed in its selection criteria.

Exit: Some 97 per cent go on to university, between two and four a year to Oxbridge. A larger than expected number go on to read science degrees, a reflection of the College's particular strength here.

Money Matters: Grown its numbers again this year and has its largest school roll since 1998. Provides extraordinarily good value. Very generous scholarships and bursaries for the able and deserving. A rare and very attractive feature is that despite a competitive fee level there are no compulsory extras. The Financial Times recently put school in the top three of all independent boarding schools in terms of value for money.

Remarks: No one is going to choose Brecon as an elitist haven but it's a school that is very much on the up and achieves much more than one would expect, given its size and location. Offers at least as much as many more prestigious and expensive alternatives. Check it out.

Christ's Hospital

Horsham, West Sussex, RH13 0YP

• Pupils: 415 boys, 400 girls (most board but a few day places)
• Ages: 11-18 • Size of sixth form: 255 • C of E • Fees: Boarding £0-£24,500; Day £13,500-£17,000 pa • Independent

Tel: 01403 211 293
Fax: 01403 211 580
Email: enquiries@christs-hospital.org.uk
Website: www.christs-hospital.org.uk

Head: Since 2007, Mr John Franklin BA Dip teaching MEd admin (mid-fifties), came from nine years of headship at Ardingly. Born in Australia and quietly-spoken yet firm, his experience is spread across both hemispheres – six years as a deputy at St Peter's Adelaide, the oldest school in mainland Australia, prior to that an English teacher and acting housemaster at Marlborough for three years. Kim, his wife, teaches English part-time and he hopes to return to that as well. In the meantime he mixes with the pupils by walking the school and sports pitches (with or without his dalmatian and golden retriever) and eating lunch at high table every day.

Lots of fresh blood in his senior management team: a new bursar, a couple of new deputies, a new chair of the school body, a new treasurer – a chance for governance structures to be brought into the 21st century? After 456 years, CH finally has its own governing body, legally separating the school from the foundation. Behind the scenes, the head is integrating his five-year development plan with the foundation organisation and also planning on increasing the number of teaching staff. On the pupils – 'To say emotional baggage holds some pupils back explains the problem but does not excuse it. Every child must be happy, achieve their academic potential and have a rounded education'.

'I am a great improver': he's implementing much of what proved so successful at Ardingly – a more organised and supportive tutorial system; he's already tightened up discipline. He aims to introduce into the school a limited number of Direct Entry full-fee paying day pupils and boarders, some of whom may be from abroad – 'The international element – Europe, America, even Australia – will flesh out the social spectrum and boost our income'.

The school will be marketed during his headship (a first), resulting in increased numbers of worthy applicants, more donations and more teaching staff aware of what CH is up to.

Academic matters: Junior class sizes are around 25; this shrinks to about 11 at A level. GCSE subjects are chosen in Year 8. Pupils must choose history or geography and French, German or Spanish. Tutorial groups and HoDs give advice before the Year 8 parents' meeting. Everyone is setted. Four subjects at AS and most continue all of them through to A2 (20 doing Latin, Greek GCSE about to be re-instated). IB arrived in September 2010. A double period of careers with a range of external speakers in the lower sixth; the final year get a weekly lecture on topics ranging from Picasso's Guernica to John Glenn's experience as an astronaut. All Senior Grecians (upper sixth) get laptops provided by the school with a link to the internet, hotmail filtered out.

The campus is arranged by subject blocks, all with high ceilings and plenty of space and equipment – science and language labs. The ugly sister is the IT department – the 15 classrooms above it are next in line for refurbishment or a move and fresh build. A small SEN unit with one full-time SENCo; plans to expand this by a part-time assistant and PHSE teacher. Any problems are picked up by MidYIS in Year 7.

Libraries – one main one, with a 16th century painting (cut to size in the move from Newgate a century ago; unfortunately the signature was a casualty of this trim) and a mezzanine level with extra computers. Practically every department has its own subject library, saving searching time and keeping the crowds down.

Games, Options, the Arts: Huge choice of extra-curricular activities. The pupils have to decide what they can fit in, with more personalisation as they move up the school, a preparation for university life. The main sports are hockey, netball, football, rugby, cricket and tennis – the sports centre is dual use with the public, 25m pool, double-sized sports hall, six squash courts, spin bikes, split-level fitness suite, vending machines and a café. A scout hut, CCF and D of E on offer too.

500-seat theatre, modelled on Shakespeare's Globe, with padded red benches instead of the standing yard. Used by travelling drama companies as well as the school (contemporary dance as well as curriculum-relevant plays). Music has a respected and talented director who's very good at encouraging even the coolest Grecians to sing their hearts out in chapel. Learning is certainly not all grade-focused – four organs, we saw a couple of harps, 140-strong chapel choir, orchestra, jazz ensembles and marching band that performs at the Lord Mayor's Show (and plays everyone into lunch daily).

Energetic art department, successful and focused on working on pupils' own ideas, which produces an enormous range of work. Three floors of bright and naturally-lit space, an artist in residence, art historian, three full-time staff, print-making, kilns, a sewing room (which is so popular it may expand and textiles re-enter the curriculum), a computer suite (although the primary source of each project is drawing, digital images are always involved) and a library full of glossy books – all open from 7.15am to 10.00pm. Art has always been good here but department now co-operates much more freely with others – joint trips with philosophy, business studies, DT to New York, Rome etc. DT department occupies almost as large a space and is just as well-equipped with a laser cutter, a graphics area etc.

Background and Atmosphere: Moved to the current 1,200 acre campus in 1902, into a building designed by Sir Aston Webb (who also did the façade of Buckingham Palace and King's College, Cambridge) to house 1,000 pupils and Ingress Bell. Fascinating school history – a museum on site dedicated to it, under-visited at present but rumours that this will change. Since most of the main buildings were constructed over a century ago, an ongoing conservation programme.

The covered cloisters that enclose the quad are studded with commemorative marble plaques alternating with padded felt noticeboards detailing sports teams. The chapel and dining hall face each other across the quad. Lunch served in two sittings, food is good, choice of hot and cold, apparently a chef's theatre to show off the back kitchen skills – and over £8 million earmarked to update the facilities.

The uniform has hardly changed since Edward VI founded the school in 1552 in Newgate – the britches are a bit less itchy, senior girls can wear tights – yet pride in the mustard coloured socks and figure-disguising Tudor coats is obvious – current pupils reckon that 95 per cent of them would vote to keep it. A bit more individuality in hairstyles and jewellery, and after lessons are over you can change into contemporary clothes.

CH runs in three-week blocks before a leave weekend – some children don't want to or can't go home; they can stay in or get matched with a friend and spend the weekend with their family – 'There's no one way to be a CH pupil'. This diversity is the school's strength – whatever obstacles or advantages your home life might present, everyone is equal as soon as they tie on the bands of their uniform. The new 'deps' (deputy Grecians, lower sixth) probably find the acclimatisation most difficult. Pupils learn within the first year to live with a huge range of personalities, which stands them in good stead in later life. Well-adjusted, confident and accepting children.

Pastoral Care and Discipline: Chapel services are important – not least because it is a space big enough for up to 840 pupils to gather on Tuesdays and Sundays. The school was founded partly in response to a sermon preached by the Bishop of London – and sermons are still powerful today; even if every pupil is not touched, they definitely pay attention. Lots of children here whose parents or carers are ill or struggling, so faith can be a real touchstone.

Sixteen single-sex boarding houses along The Avenue and then two co-ed built in 2000. Each is looked after by a married couple (practically all of the 90 staff live on site), often with their own families, so that every child gets a taste of parental and sibling relationships that may well be lacking in their own home. A recent revamp has left these boarding facilities sparkling – no junior shares a room with more than three others, big common-rooms with ping-pong and snooker, bright kitchens, a phone room (for the first two years everyone hands in their mobile at night). Every new arrival gets a nursemaid in the year above, and this relationship produces a family tree stretching across year groups.

The two Senior Grecian houses (the nomenclature comes from the sixth form historically having to study classics) would be the envy of any university student. Often more space than the children might have to themselves at home – big windows, a sink in each (senior's) room, double-height communal spaces, bowls of fruit, kitchens shared between eight, a BBQ on the deck, a little library area with a piano and students' art displayed. A third of the Grecians might be in long-term (more than a year) relationships with each other – no peer pressure to do this. The proximity of co-ed living space means that sex could be problem, but the co-ed nature of the full school normalises boy/girl relationships.

Minor misdemeanours mean getting up for 7.15am and a dress parade. Mini-detentions on Sunday am, the big one is on Saturday night, and a card system which restricts free time by having to sign in – for smoking, bullying, drinking alcohol. Apparently the new senior management team is particularly strict on smoking and 'night walking' (previously popular with the boys). 'Swearing at the staff is unacceptable' (suspension) and continued difficulties will result in a behaviour contract between the pupil, parents and school – a line drawn in the sand. Drugs – class A or supplying – mean immediate expulsion with the involvement of the police; for cannabis there will be one chance, after which the ongoing drug testing policy is implemented. Family circumstances are always taken into account – parents really appreciate consistent and accessible staff.

Pupils and Parents: The pupils know they're lucky to be here – for everyone who gets in, four or five are turned away. Accepts pupils from all over the UK, in reality about 30 per cent from London, 30 per cent from Sussex, 30 per cent SW and home counties, rest from Scotland, Wales, north of England (most from further afield enter at sixth form, but only if they have some extended family in the SE). Historical links with Richmond, Newbury, Reading and Twickenham – the towns on the route of John and Francis West (17th-century scriveners) to Christ's Hospital.

Many children have a parent or sibling who is ill or has behavioural problems or an addiction. Only 42 per cent of pupils have both parents resident at home, and lots of aspiring middle class and freelancers. Some of these would appreciate more potential for communication with each other outside school. Parents, even those of children who have left, will spread the word via posters and leaflets in doctors' surgeries etc.

A limited number of pupils pay the full fees (their parents want their child to come to a school that's a good social mix and reflective of society); everyone else plays a fraction according to their means. If CH does its job, then former pupils will be ineligible to send their children to their alma mater, unless they pay the full fees.

Entrance: Most at 11, 25–30 after GCSE. No feeder schools but a very good relationship with south of England state primaries – 85 per cent come from these, the equivalent of each school sending one child every other year. A primary school workshop programme is held twice a year in a variety of subjects so that children and the staff can experience the learning environment, find out what type of child will thrive at CH, and then talk to interested parents in their areas. The initial application form elicits lots of information about family circumstances and finances – from the previous school, the local church, social services; the staff in the foundation are at the end of the phone to answer questions, and baffled or swamped parents really value this.

The child also completes a form and comes to the school for a residential initial assessment – with a maximum of 299 other hopefuls. They stay in one of the boarding houses and spend two days experiencing chapel, English, maths, verbal and non-verbal reasoning, an interview, sports and a chance to demonstrate special skills such as music or art. Mild dyslexia and dyspraxia accepted but competition is fierce – only one in five applicants gets a place. The foundation advises on the best method of entry: presentation (by individual governors or corporate bodies, RAF, Guy's Hospital, the Church), special categories (specific areas of residence, parental occupation) or competition (most pupils). No preferential entrance requirements for siblings. Now a limited number of academically-able students can join through Direct Entry – day and boarding places at 11, 13 and 16 for pupils whose parents can afford to pay an all-inclusive fee without the normal means-testing. These places are non-competitive, offered on a first come, first served basis, subject to candidates meeting the required academic standard. Scholarships have been introduced – up to 20 per cent remission for both Direct Entry (full-fee) and Foundationer (means-tested) entrants.

Exit: Around 10 leave after GCSE for vocational courses, and then over 90 per cent to their first choice university – the Upper Grecian houses are a real stepping-stone to life there. To Edinburgh, Oxbridge, Durham, Manchester, Sheffield, Leeds, London, for medicine, archaeology, sport, classics, law, music, maths. Artists seem to take it in turns to go in posses to Wimbledon, London College of Fashion, Central St Martin's. Famous Old Blues (the dead ones have boarding houses named after them) include Coleridge, Middleton, Peele, Barnes Wallis, the cricketer John Snow, comedian Mark Thomas, the academic Alan Ryan, the MP Martin Linton.

Money Matters: A ready-reckoner has been introduced on the website as a guide to fee contributions. Currently 16 per cent pay nothing, 23 per cent pay an average of £1,323 per year. Parental contributions are assessed on the total family income of the home in which the child resides, interest and dividend payments plus a percentage of any financial and other assets above £25,000. Most DSS benefits are included but not housing benefit, disability allowance and carer's allowance. Reviewed each year, discounts for siblings within school. Tudor-style uniform is free. Extras include £20 pocket money per term, music contributions (means-tested again), a dictionary and a bible. CH has a big endowment but, like every other school, lives beyond its means. Curriculum-based trips are partially funded by the foundation, means testing applies. Old Blues provide travel grants for gap years etc.

Remarks: In the words of the head, 'This is the most noble school in the country' – it is the only independent school that escapes the state school prejudice when attracting principled teachers. The Old Blues are incredibly loyal and you can see why – with 75 per cent of them in the top quartile of income in their later life, CH turns many lives around in an unpretentious and joyful manner; admirable work.

Churston Ferrers Grammar School

Greenway Road, Churston Ferrers, Brixham, Devon, TQ5 0LN

• Pupils: 900 boys and girls; all day • Ages: 11-18 • Size of sixth form: 275 • Non-denom • State

Tel: 01803 842 289
Fax: 01803 846 007
Email: secretary@churston.torbay.sch.uk
Website: www.churstongrammar.com

Headteacher: Since 2007, Mr Robert Owers BA PGCE CFES NPQH (forties), educated at Gaynes School, Upminster before reading history at Warwick. Taught at two large co-ed comprehensive schools in Essex before promotion to deputy headship at top performing Chelmsford County High School for Girls. Limits his teaching here to general studies and 'learning to learn'; appointment raising school's academic profile in Torbay area. Parents feel that he is making positive changes to make pupils more independent in their learning. 'Approachable and relaxed style,' commented one mother. Lives locally with wife, Justine (who teaches drama part-time at CFGS) and their two children – still at village primary school. Strong background in sport: represented his university and Essex schoolboys at football; plays cricket locally. Able, energetic and communicative head who is intent on moving this school into the top five per cent of co-ed grammars.

Academic matters: 74 per cent A and B grades at A level with honours fairly evenly spread between departments rather than relying on a few 'big guns'. 99 per cent five A*–C grades at GCSE (64 per cent at A*/A). Good 'value-added' education – pupils leave with better results than parents often anticipate. Head is keen to provide 'more than the exam treadmill' but knows good grades matter. School has foundation and specialist humanities status. We were particularly impressed by the geography department – video conferencing with an adopted school in Peru was not something we had expected nor partnership over climate change with schools in Spain, Finland and Estonia involving foreign visits and hosting a final conference at Churston. MFL department also makes good use of this facility as well as own computer lab. D & T includes food technology to GCSE and textiles (annual 'catwalk' fashion show has become a popular event). 'My daughter has really been encouraged in her art from year seven upwards,' said one mother. Usual carousel arrangement for practical subjects in Years 7 and 8; product design a popular A level subject. Recent gold medallist in British Biology Olympiad and top student in the country for chemistry. Similar successes in national maths contests too. Academic needs of every pupil are taken seriously and include re-jigging the timetable if necessary: 'they really care and do what's best for the individual,' commented a parent. Twenty-three subjects on offer at A level including good numbers in psychology, sociology and business studies. Six computer suites and plenty of smart boards but not overburdened with ICT. Learning support is taken seriously: two pupils are currently statemented with access to a designated LSA according to need and a number receive individual or small group help for SpLD outside the main timetable. Initial screening occurs when literacy issues are raised by the English department but further diagnostic tests are paid for out of learning support funds using an outside agency. Ofsted gave CFGS an 'outstanding' for all 36 categories in 2009.

Games, Options, the Arts: Sport is a big deal at Churston – good facilities and some successful teams. Top sporting strength is basketball: winning two national championships thanks to two England coaches on its staff. Football, netball, hockey and athletics also produce county and some national players. Enterprising individuals also achieve sporting success outside school – recently in national Tae Kwon Do, octopush (underwater hockey) in Portugal and south coast coastal rowing.

High quality productions are always a sell-out. Eye-catching artwork; dedicated computer suite in art room. Recent Year 11 involvement in community art project with primary school pupils at nearby Greenway House culminating in impressive exhibition. 'Music is improving,' say parents: orchestra and choir perform at festivals as well as at in-house concerts; wide range of lunch-time and after school musical activities. Sixth formers encouraged in public speaking. Serious about environmental issues and has a thriving 'Force for Change' movement. Dedicated Combined Cadet Force for Year 9 upwards, managed by armed forces sergeant. Organised trips through CCF; BTec award in public service part of scheme; D of E (to gold standard) and Ten Tors (35 and 45 mile teams) only available through CCF. Other recent school visits include exchanges with French and German schools, a dozen sixth formers going to Russia, rugby tour of South Africa and expedition to Kenya.

Background and Atmosphere: New learning resources centre (named 'The Cube') catches the eye before one steps into the attractive, modern entrance foyer. Very relaxed atmosphere is immediately obvious, a non-invasive 'beep' indicates each lesson change and pupils move more calmly than in most schools. Churston Ferrers, set on the edge of a picture postcard Devonshire village, is the only co-ed grammar for the Torbay area. Surrounding tranquillity interspersed with idyllic 'Railway Children' style steam train running alongside school – originally a popular mode of transport to it and still used by some.

School extensively developed since opening in 1957 – lots of new classrooms (including new modern languages suite), well-equipped science labs plus sports hall with fitness suite, drama studio and assembly hall. Sixth formers have own study and social area (extended by them during a recent summer holiday). There is a pleasant café ('the greenhouse') for civilised sandwich eaters and the like which also serves up pasta in a variety of forms. Smallish outdoor heated pool and lovely playing fields plus hard courts for netball and tennis. No Astroturf as yet. Strong links with Lucre in Peru – fair trade calendar with proceeds going to the Peruvian primary schools that produced the art work; active in local community and lots of national charity giving: Childline (from sale of blue ribbons during national anti-bullying week); Leonard Cheshire Foundation, shoe boxes for Children in Need and others. Commitment to sustainability includes termly newsletter going digital and six recycling zones around school.

Pastoral Care and Discipline: Ask parents why they choose Churston and they'll reply 'pastoral care' which they rate as 'much better than at neighbouring grammars or comprehensives'. Five groups of 26 pupils placed in houses at beginning of Year 7. Experienced pastoral team provide guidance and support; Year 11 prefects trained in listening and restorative justice. Problems are 'dealt with promptly and effectively'. Active school parliament. Smoking and drugs policies adhered to with some good educational input too in these areas. Minor bullying problems resolved by bringing together those involved. Parents, teachers and staff alike view atmosphere as 'friendly but purposeful' and relationships as 'easy going and relaxed'.

Pupils and Parents: Modern grammar school pupils – no longer in blazers. White shirt, tie and school crested sweatshirts for Years 7 to 11 (flexible dress code in sixth form). Size means everyone gets to know each other – 'very friendly,' say pupils. 25 feeder primaries including Brixham, Dartmouth and Paignton. Year 5 primary pupils are introduced to Churston via a one day induction and incoming Year 7 have an induction week at the end of Year 6. Parents can e-mail school; termly reports and well organised parents' evenings. Parents say that the school 'knows its pupils and encourages them to excel without undue pressure'.

Entrance: Foundation status allows school to set part of tests itself. Around 250 first choice applicants for 130 places in Year 7. Apply through LEA, with supplementary application form direct to school. English, maths and verbal reasoning tests; those only passing two of the three will be ranked in a border-zone that takes account of additional academic information from the primary school. Between 30 and 35 students from Brixham and Dartmouth Community Colleges join sixth form (six B grades at GCSE the minimum requirement) annually.

Exit: A few drop out after Year 11 but sixth form takes in more than it loses. Some 95 per cent to university with especially strong links with Exeter, Plymouth, Cardiff, Bristol, University of West of England and Bath. Falmouth Art College also popular. Two or three annually into the Services. Ninety per cent continue into sixth form, others migrate to nearby community colleges and South Devon FE college.

Money Matters: Online 'parentpay' system means trips and activities can be paid for with credit and debit cards from home.

Remarks: Caring and close-knit; feels more like a rural comprehensive than a grammar but delivers the goods academically. Strong pastoral system, increasingly effective teaching. A lovely example of 11–18 co-education working well.

Cirencester Deer Park School

Stroud Road, Cirencester, Gloucestershire, GL7 1XB

• Pupils: 1,070, boys and girls, all day • Ages: 11-16 • Non-denom • State

Tel: 01285 653 447
Fax: 01285 640 669
Email: enquiries@deerparkschool.net
Website: www.deerparkschool.net

Head: Since 2003, Mrs Chiquita Henson BA(Hons) NPQH (forties). Read English at Sheffield University followed by PGCE at Bristol; subsequent professional training in leadership and headship. Educated at a comprehensive school herself, Chiquita Henson has been at Deer Park since 1989, becoming head of English when the school still had a sixth form and then deputy head from 1994 to 2003. Knows the patch inside out and has been at forefront of school's development as a High Performing Specialist School. Outwardly reserved but combines steely professionalism with a passion to drive Deer Park forwards. Makes full use of ex-accountant director of support to do the number crunching she finds a chore. 'Incredibly hard-working,' said one parent; 'Children find her a bit scary,' said another. A modern, no-nonsense head who is good at getting recognition and money for the school. Partner, Tim, is a science teacher with children at primary school in Stroud where they live. Still teaches some English. General parental agreement that she is good news.

Academic matters: Currently has five specialisms under High Performing Specialist Schools, including technology, arts and applied learning. A truly comprehensive school with results fluctuating from year to year – 84 per cent 5+ GCSEs at grades A*–C in 2010, 61 per cent including maths and English. Has averaged 70 per cent plus over past four years; consistently impressive KS3 levels and improving results in value-added tables with boys and girls doing equally well. Around 20 per cent gain five or more A* and A grades at GCSE.

Curriculum structure is divided into modules across a 50 (hour-long) lesson fortnight, run by faculties and overseen by mentors – brings the nearest thing to a personal timetable by GCSE level. Interesting links with industry. Mix of traditional and newer courses at GCSE where the normal subject load for pupils is 11.5 to 10.5 subjects. Non-examinable PE (five hours per fortnight) and global citizenship. Dual award science was quite a challenge for those who went to academic science sixth forms – opportunities now for triple science. 'Fabulous maths teaching,' said a parent; we saw a class tackling probability with plenty of intelligent participation. Innovative maths and drama scheme for Year 7 pupils. 'Faculty in Focus' puts pupils and staff from a given area into the spotlight for a short period – visits to 'Starlab' and 'Maths Magic' have resulted. Parents like homework which they described as 'challenging without being too difficult'.

Well-sited learning support unit adjacent to art area. SENCo carries out audit in Year 7; 16 statemented pupils; about 20 per cent of pupils receive help in some form: extraction, spelling and literacy groups; alternative curriculum pathway with support from teaching assistants based in different faculties; value-added results highlight successes, with one pupil achieving five GCSEs at grades A*–C from a baseline VRQ of 70. Enrichment activities for gifted and able have included finding alternatives to fossil fuels with postgraduates at the University of Manchester and Bath and exhibiting at the Royal Society.

Games, Options, the Arts: Recent head of expressive arts determined to build on predecessor's success. Orchestra, choir and jazz band with music tours abroad. Major drama production every two years with plenty of shorter works in between. We saw a drama class which was totally absorbed and never noticed us watching. NCFE award in music technology, rarely found in 11–16 sector. Good sports hall plus larger Astroturf for football, hockey and lacrosse, and smaller one for netball. Plenty of teams and extra-curricular sports activity. Art is well taught (parents amazed at what their offspring have achieved); adequate accommodation with some impressive pieces on display. Stand-still days give each year group a chance to do something outside the curriculum and the annual enrichment week approaches citizenship from a different angle, e.g. 'European Awareness' for Year 8 and 'Personal Challenge' for Year 9. Hosts South Cotswold Science Fair – a fun event to bring science into every-day experience.

Background and Atmosphere: Celebrated 40th anniversary as a comprehensive school in 2006. Origins stretch back to middle ages but 1960s legacy evident in featureless external appearance. School shares attractively wooded site on western edge of town with Cirencester College next door and the Royal Agricultural College opposite. Youngish staff with the average age below 40 but over one-third have taught here over ten years. Specialist technology status translates into computers everywhere plus digital projectors and interactive whiteboards in every classroom; Powell's Learning Centre a hive of activity and remains open after school. Some aesthetically pleasing internal features such as the drama studio, atrium social area and art exhibition corridor. We liked the simple polo shirt uniform and the positive buzz in lessons and corridors.

Pastoral Care and Discipline: Strong pupil services team with non-teaching learning co-ordinators for each year supported by tutors and mentors. We felt that pupils here have a positive attitude to work and an understanding of a good range of global issues. Pastoral database is bought by other schools. Emphasis on restorative justice. Good attendance levels point to policies working.

Pupils and Parents: Mainly middle class catchment but with some from surprisingly deprived areas in Cirencester. Friendly, polite bunch who get stuck into the challenging work environment. Year 11 pupils seem more mature for age than in average 11–18 school. Some pupils were involved in an unusual exchange with Inuit children from Canadian Arctic, though more recently it has been the usual European exchanges. Most of school's governors are parents. Friends of Deer Park is active in supporting school events and raising funds. Website allows parents access and publishes weekly newsletter.

Entrance: Over-subscribed – comprehensive intake with geography and siblings most important criteria. Majority from Cirencester primaries and outlying villages but quite a few come from Stroud direction, where it is seen as an attractive alternative to secondary moderns for some.

Exit: About 90 per cent go into further education with majority going to Cirencester College next door. Significant number go further afield to sixth forms such as Pate's in Cheltenham where Deer Park pupils have done extremely well.

Remarks: 'Can do' philosophy rubs off on everyone: 'Everything is an opportunity,' said one teacher. Plenty of human endeavour and creativity behind the high-tech world on offer here which 'doesn't take over'. Quite a place, with pupils liking the modern approach and responding well across the board.

City and Islington College

The Angel, 283-309 Goswell Road, Islington, London, EC1V 7LA

• Pupils: 1,350 students, roughly 60 per cent girls, 40 per cent boys
• Ages: 16-19 • Non-denom • State

Tel: 020 7700 9333
Fax: 020 7520 0602
Email: courseinfo@candi.ac.uk
Website: www.candi.ac.uk

Director: Since 1999, Ms Keren Abse (fifties). Has a BA in English, an MA in history and a PGCE in English, all from the University of Sussex. Taught at Reynolds High School in Ealing and Quintin Kynaston School in Westminster before joining what was then Islington Sixth Form Centre in 1984, as English teacher and then deputy director. Praised by Ofsted for 'exemplary' leadership.

Academic matters: An inner London sixth form college, nicknamed Candi, that takes in a very mixed student body, often with modest GCSE grades, and sends most of them to university. 'The staffing makes our institute special. We have high expectations of the staff and they are very enthusiastic.'

English has extensive enrichment activities such as theatre trips and creative writing workshops. Science, with a heavy emphasis on practical work, is growing in popularity year by year, in contrast to national trends. Candi offers Italian, German, Spanish and French – an unusual breadth of languages for the state sector – taught in state-of-the-art language labs. It will never be amongst the top league table performers but adds huge academic value. Most popular subjects tend to be English, psychology, sociology and media studies. A parent commented approvingly that the college was willing to run advanced extension English classes for just two students. The A level choice is huge: 37 subjects ranging from electronics to Turkish. Has offered the IB since September 2010.

Nearly all the teaching is mixed ability though there are weaker science and maths groups that can have extra sessions. Gifted and talented students are identified and encouraged to take part in a range of extension activities.

A few students, mostly from linked Islington schools, retake GCSEs at Candi. Many of these have arrived from abroad fairly recently, and most stay on to take A levels. Was one of the first colleges to introduce the new Diplomas, now offering five – environment, business, creative and media, IT and society, health and development.

Candi has links with several universities. Queen Mary, for example, runs a mock interview programme, Sussex organises a media residential school and City contributes to the Law Support Group. In 2000, Candi formed a 'Partnership for Excellence' with University College, London, committing both to work closely together. Staff have developed strong links and Candi students have lectures and masterclasses in subjects ranging from electrical engineering to geography. Candi students can have UCL library cards; there is a weekly 'medics link' programme of lectures and meetings; UCL students run an astronomy club. 'One of our key strengths is the effort we put into encouraging students to apply for higher education. Many come from families with no culture of going to university. UCL doesn't drop grades for us but increased numbers of our students are applying there.'

Around 10 per cent of students speak English as an additional language; many of these are refugees. These get excellent support; some who arrived in their teens with little or no English gain top A level grades. In 2008, a student who had come from the Congo three years before got a place at Oxford to study maths. There is a drop-in writing facility open all week: students who need help with academic writing can pop in for advice.

Games, Options, the Arts: Sport is not high on the agenda here, though there is a five-a-side football/basketball pitch round the back. But there is a varied enrichment programme on Wednesday afternoons, which includes a range of scientific and political speakers, student magazine, robot club and street dance. Art students visit Rome, politics students go to Brussels, and there are many local outings to theatres, ballets and galleries. 'We put a lot of effort into enrichment, as many of our students would never visit the theatre or ballet otherwise.'

Spacious top floor art, photography and design studios, with lavish facilities and plenty of imaginative 3D, textile and artwork on display. Dance, music, drama and theatre studies and performance studies are all A level options. The college has its own well-equipped performing arts centre, with two studios that open into a theatre space, and produces a whole college musical each year. Students have also worked with companies ranging from the Welsh National Opera to Rambert Dance Company and Comedie Francaise.

Background and Atmosphere: The Sixth Form College is part of City and Islington College, which also includes the Centre for Business, Arts and Technology, the Centre for Lifelong Learning, the Centre for Health, Social and Child Care and the Centre for Applied Sciences. The other four centres, on sites around Islington, concentrate on vocational courses for adults as well as teenagers.

Candi moved in 2003 from two Victorian buildings close to Holloway Road to a £9.2m landmark building somewhat akin to a cruise liner moored alongside Goswell Road near the Angel. The Kalwall finish appears white, translucent and calming during the day, and glows at night. There is abundant glass, giving views across the City from the sixth floor.

'If you wonder what's happened to all the money spent on education over the past few years – well, it all seems to be here,' commented a parent. All rooms are linked to the internet, all the classrooms have projectors linked to computer, video player and whiteboard. It is accessible throughout for people with disabilities and has a good range of specialist equipment.

Pastoral Care and Discipline: This is a sixth-form college, with an atmosphere to match and a lighter touch than most schools. 'You need to be self-motivated,' said a parent, 'because they won't stand over you.' However, Candi is particularly praised for its academic support, with students' progress carefully monitored and regular reports to parents. The discipline is strict, with no quarter for bad behaviour, but very strong pastoral care from tutors and from the student counselling and advice service. Highly rated for its equal opportunities and support for disabled students.

Pupils and Parents: From over 100 schools right across London, particularly Islington, Hackney, Haringey and Tower Hamlets, with a huge cultural and ethnic mix. Around three-quarters of students are from ethnic minority backgrounds ranging from Bangladeshi to Turkish.

Entrance: Candi acts as the sixth form for six Islington secondary schools that do not have their own. These students get first priority, providing they apply by the end of the spring term and gain the requisite GCSE grades. All courses require at least five grade Cs – applications usually close early in February. Applicants must include a reference from their school, and must attend a course guidance interview. Final enrolments take place once students have received their GCSE results, in the date order in which they applied.

Exit: Around 80 per cent generally go on to higher education, including several to Oxbridge. The others go on to a range of jobs, some applying to university later on as mature students. Many Candi students stay at home while studying for financial or cultural reasons, and the most popular universities are London ones, including Westminster, Middlesex and City. Sussex is the highest ranking outside the capital. Business and related studies top the list of degree subjects, followed closely by English and media studies. Art foundation courses are also popular.

Remarks: A beacon in an area with historically poor educational achievement. Its student body mirrors its inner-city location and many arrive with lower than average GCSE results. But excellent teaching, wonderful premises and strong support means that most leave for university with creditable A levels (or, in future, IB results) under their belt.

City of London Freemen's School

Linked to City of London Freemen's Junior School in the Junior section

Ashtead Park, Ashtead, Surrey, KT21 1ET

• Pupils: 850; 430 boys; 420 girls; 50 boarders • Ages: 7-18
• Size of sixth form: 210 • Inter-denom • Fees: Boarding £22,887; Day £10,710-£14,382 pa • Independent

Tel: 01372 277 933
Fax: 01372 822 416
Email: admissions@clfs.surrey.sch.uk
Website: www.clfs.surrey.sch.uk

Head: Since September 2007, Mr Philip MacDonald MA. An Oxford classicist (in his fifties) with a long career in education: experience in single sex and co-ed schools, day and boarding. Married with four teenage children, all pupils at CLFS. His previous post was nine years as head of Mount St Mary's College, Derbyshire. In his palatial office, Mr MacDonald exudes self confidence and experience. He is 'very interested in the idea of educating the whole person' and explains this as 'including sport, drama, debating, music, providing wider opportunities for children to find fulfilment and thus happiness.' Parents find him 'quite aloof and reserved,' they feel they don't know him, one saying, 'I wouldn't know him if I passed him in the street.'

Academic matters: Very good solid results year on year at both GCSE and A level. Not a pressured academic hot-house. Parents are universally complimentary about the teaching, singling out physics, English, politics and business studies. 'Teachers fabulous with lots of them there a long time.' 'Teaching is excellent and without high pressure.' Superb teaching facilities housed in the Haywood Centre (named after the previous, long serving and very popular head). This hub of the senior school, opened in 2000, is an airy and attractive, well equipped block of classrooms, IT and multimedia rooms plus a large library open until 6 pm for individual study.

Not a first choice school for a pupil with significant SEN and ask lots of questions for a child with mild SEN just to make sure the school can help. SEN support is limited; head tells us there are very few pupils with SEN statements. He would ask parents to consider whether this is the right academic environment for their child, he feels it 'may not be suitable for pupils with formal SEN statements'. A parent of a mildly dyslexic pupil reinforces this view saying 'there is little specialist help but teachers are kind and supportive and do the necessary such as extra time in exams, maybe it wouldn't be suitable for a child who is quite dyslexic.' A head of learning support provides help within the curriculum for mild needs, such as a slow reader, and support classes are available for children who are struggling in English. A parent of a pupil accessing this help praised it saying 'the kids call it the remedial class but they have a very positive attitude towards it'. Mr MacDonald tells us they have had hearing impaired children and wheelchair users and says the issue is 'can we enable a youngster with special needs to access the curriculum?'

Games, Options, the Arts: The stunning facilities at CLFS are not aged and beautiful but they very much contribute to an environment which cannot fail to impress a pupil (or perhaps even more their parents). Sports facilities are outstanding and would compete easily with the best of the public school fraternity. Glorious and extensive grass pitches, huge Astro pitch for tennis, football and hockey, a vast sports hall, an enviable 25 metre indoor swimming pool, two squash courts and a multi activity room for table tennis and aerobics. Sport is well and truly part of life here, parents report there's a 'massively active programme but it's not forced' and sport is 'made fun not a chore'. It is very much a 'come and try' atmosphere, rather than a 'team place or else' school. For the seriously sporty, A and B teams are fielded in the more popular sports. Most fixtures are scheduled on Saturday mornings and squad members are required to attend.

Drama occupies as central a position as sport, both within the curriculum and in extra-curricular clubs. A hugely enthusiastic head of drama (who maintains a dedicated drama website for the school), plus more terrific facilities including a professionally equipped theatre, mean plenty of productions. Good GCSE and A level results and some impressive acting alumni. Music is encouraged, with plenty of choirs, ensembles and an orchestra putting on about 30 performances and concerts. Musical theatre productions performed to sell-out audiences in a nearby 800-seater public venue are described as 'great,' and 'the highlight of the musical year'. Students' artwork of a high standard is displayed around the school and the art and design technology facilities, like all of the facilities at the school, really are top class.

A huge range of lunchtime and after school clubs cater for all tastes and interests. Senior pupils run some of these clubs and can even start them on their own initiative. Trips out of school include an annual whole school visit to the City of London to celebrate the school's close ties with the City, plus many regular field trips both locally, within the UK and abroad – the list of destinations is long.

Background and Atmosphere: Founded to educate orphaned children of the Freemen of the City of London, the school is owned by the Corporation of London. Support staff are employed by the City of London and governors are largely from the Court of Common Council (i.e. City officialdom). The Corporation provides financial support for capital projects which helps to keep fees to a minimum. HR, planning and management all operated by the City, which leaves the head and school free to run and manage the education, 'a burden lifted!' says Mr MacDonald who describes the Corporation as 'forward looking with a long term view, also traditional and a little bureaucratic'. A little bureaucratic may be something of an understatement. All our interaction with the school was slow and slightly difficult. The admin side worked like an old fashioned office, hierarchical and by the book, one gets the impression the whole school probably works like that as everyone ultimately refers to a more senior authority.

Ashtead Park's 57 acres are owned by the City of London Corporation and the grounds are subject to open spaces regulations. Expansive, formal and well kept, with zebra crossings and double yellow lines, the City of London coat of arms on railings and bins really do make it feel like a London park. The feel is of a campus with pupils moving between various buildings. Parents particularly appreciate the 'beautiful setting' and 'great atmosphere to work in.' The 'mansion house' in grand country house style, houses music practice rooms and the dining room (which are rather small and old fashioned) and reception rooms, offices and girls' boarding. The girls' accommodation in the main house is by no means trendy and high tech, in fact, quite the opposite – rather old fashioned and fusty. Boys' boarding house is a rather uninspiring building due to be completely renewed.

Boarding is part of the school's statute and must be provided. (There are to this day a small number of 'foundationer' places – they have their fees, be it boarding or day, met in full). However, boarding at CLFS is not like other boarding schools – it is used almost exclusively by pupils from abroad (vast majority of boarders are sixth form entrants). The boy boarders are from Hong Kong and Russia apart from seven English pupils. All the girl boarders are from Hong Kong or the Far East. The girls' housemistress said she had to make them 'stop working sometimes and go out for a walk' – they are under immense personal and family pressure to succeed. With their very strong work ethic and extremely high standards, the boarders are often culturally different from the local day students.

All pupils and staff are in one of the three houses – good opportunities for positive relationships between age groups. Each house holds a weekly assembly and accumulates merits through music, sporting and other achievements and good work to win the annual house competition. The sixth form has its own centre and is run 'almost like a separate school'.

Pastoral Care and Discipline: Parents are positive describing pastoral care as 'excellent' and 'second to none'. Pupils have a daily tutor group and parents are encouraged to get in touch if they have any issues, they feel 'it's made clear who is responsible' and they 'always have somewhere to go, staff have an open door policy'. The spirit of the school is respectful and listening and pupils are encouraged to be kind and helpful. Parents and staff describe it as 'a family school with lots of siblings across the school,' the environment is 'caring and very friendly,' 'boys and girls mix well' and 'they grow up to be rounded on gender issues'. Pupils report that 'staff treat them with respect,' which sets a good example and gives them self confidence. Senior pupils mentor juniors and volunteer as class prefects and to run extracurricular clubs.

Discipline is laid down in clear policy and stuck to firmly; bullying is not tolerated. Incoming pupils sometimes find the regime initially rigorous as they learn the rules, but it is seen as fair. Parents say there's 'no bolt out of the blue, problems are flagged up early' and it's the 'right balance'.

Pupils and Parents: Pupils neither scruffy nor especially tidy – just nicely ordinary. Despite our request to be shown round by a pupil, we were, unlike at most schools, put firmly in the hands of the marketing manager. Both boys and girls we met en passant were communicative and pleasant when asked questions. Pupils predominantly from surrounding Surrey towns of Ashtead, Epsom, Banstead, Leatherhead, Esher and Cobham, but some travel down from south-west London and even a couple from north London. School transport from most of these local areas plus a shuttle bus to Ashtead station help parents avoid the school run. Families come from a wide range of backgrounds and plenty of families with both parents working. Parents say this 'adds to the rounded normal feel of the school'. Many find the variety comfortable with lots of ordinary families. Definitely not posh, does not even try to compete with its neighbour Epsom College (qv). Some CLFS parents we spoke to were positively anti 'the four wheel drives and mothers dressed for tennis one upmanship' of some other local schools.'Everyone is friendly,' parents can get involved if they want and there are regular parent and family socials.

Entrance: Entry to the Junior School is via entrance exam, school report and interview, with 60 places at Year 3, increasing to 80 at Year 7. Majority enter the senior school directly from junior school with no entry tests. Parents love the fact their children can go straight through from the junior school and see this as a major advantage to dispense with 11+ and CE worries. A further 25–30 are added from local preps including Downsend, Danes Hill, Cranmore and Lanesborough. Entry is competitive with screening tests at 11 and 12 confirmed by entrance exam or common entrance at 13. Head is pleased to add a little variety from other schools to 'leaven the mix'. Sixth form entry on predicted GCSE grades, school report and interview. About 20 join, including overseas boarders.

Exit: About 10 per cent leave after GCSE to taste life in a sixth form college or another school. Those who stay expect to go to university and do, mostly to Russell group. About one in ten to Oxbridge, other current favourites are Birmingham, Durham, and Edinburgh.

Money Matters: Generally perceived by parents to be excellent value for money and cheaper than other 'comparable' schools in the area. Academic and music awards at 11, 13 and sixth form available to current pupils and incomers. Means-tested bursary awards available, sponsored by the City Livery Companies and often tied to certain professions. A very small number of children of Freemen who have lost one 'family breadwinner' parent attend completely free as Foundationers.

Remarks: A good, solid school, not quirky or elitist, in fact quite the opposite. It does what it says on the tin: genuinely providing pupils with wide opportunities and an all-round education including consistently good academic results, without a hothouse atmosphere.

City of London School

Queen Victoria Street, London, EC4V 3AL

• Pupils: 910 boys; all day • Ages: 10-18 • Size of sixth form: 260
• Non-affiliated • Fees: £13,050 pa • Independent

Tel: 020 7489 0291
Fax: 020 7329 6887
Email: admissions@clsb.org.uk
Website: www.clsb.org.uk

Headmaster: Since 1999, Mr David Levin BEcon MA FRSA (fifties). Educated in South Africa, read economics at the University of Natal, then did a research degree at Sussex. Originally a solicitor, he was second master at Cheltenham College, then head of the Royal Grammar School, High Wycombe, before joining City. Keen on sport, he swims for an hour after school in the school pool; we hear that late visits are, on occasion, enlivened by encountering him striding around in Speedos. During the cold, wet summer of 2007 he swam across two chilly Cumbrian lakes in horizontal rain to raise £12,000 for charity. Tall, dark and 'divine', said a parent. By common consent a strong, solid and popular head. Very much the outward face of the school – his role involves networking and fundraising in the City as much as the day-to-day academic minutiae. His wife, Jenny, is a management consultant.

Academic matters: This is an academic school of high expectations rather than high pressure. 'You work as hard as you need to work,' said a sixth former. 'You know who is good at what – and you accept that.' 'They welcome your strengths, whatever they are,' said a parent. Talented linguists can take French or Latin GCSE in Year 10, whilst also studying Russian or Greek. Musicians, too, can take their subject a year early and some boys do additional maths alongside maths GCSE.

Generally, 75 per cent of A level grades are As and there are few GCSEs lower than B. 'Most departments have at least one amazing teacher,' said a sixth former. A good mix of long-serving and newer staff. Strong emphasis on science in the sixth form – several boys coming in from linked state schools with science scholarships; history also extremely popular, with numbers taking it to A level second only to maths.

Excellent support for those with mild dyslexia/dyspraxia – 'It needs to be mild or they wouldn't cope' – with 100 or so boys receiving extra help in small groups. 'It's wonderful and very low key,' said a parent. The building is accessible for wheelchairs, but so far only boys with a broken leg have made use of this.

Games, Options, the Arts: In Tardis-like fashion, the compact-looking school building encompasses a sports hall, gym and swimming pool as well as squash courts and fencing salle. 17 acres of playing fields a half-hour coach ride away and a couple of concrete playgrounds on site. 'When I looked out before school this morning there were four cricket matches, a football game and some basketball going on,' said a sixth former.

Teams have reached London cup finals at cricket, football and water polo, and the school fields teams in 12 competitive sports, including golf and sailing – 'Sailing suits our boys because you need a mixture of intellectual and physical aggression and you don't have to train too hard'. Pupils have represented their country in fencing and table-tennis in recent years, with recent successes in football and athletics. The head is keen to up the school's sporting profile, with more teams in the lower years playing matches against feeder prep schools.

But it is fair to say that the average City boy is not a fanatical sportsman. He is likely to be equally interested in debating, singing in the choir, playing Warhammer. 'We push debating and public speaking because it makes the boys more thoughtful and considered. It counters any yob culture.' Zillions of clubs before, during and after school: Model UN (with annual conference); railway society (with its own model railway room); Jewish society (generally involving food); Square Mile club (with eminent speakers such as Jeremy Paxman, John Bercow and Nick Robinson) et al. 'I'm very keen on being an outlooking school. The boys will have to make their way in a global setting.'

Pupils in Year 9 get to know their city well on eight visits to, e.g., the Museum of Surgery and the Globe. Over 140 other school trips ranging from a Chinese exchange to geography field trips to Namibia, Iceland and Peru. European work experience in Year 12. Extremely popular CCF, with hundreds of pupils learning to fly, going camping at home and abroad, skiing, canoeing, driving powerboats – 'It was one of the best things I've done at school,' said an ex-pupil. Community service is an alternative and charity fundraising is high profile – over £58,000 raised for READ International.

The school theatre was revamped and drama is strong, with frequent theatre visits and many productions in conjunction with City of London Girls' School. Joint orchestras and choirs, too, bolstered by the choristers who join at the age of 10. The music is 'fantastic', said a parent, and a sixth former agreed, 'If you're good you become sucked into the music department and your life revolves around it'. Two terms' free instrumental tuition for everyone in the younger classes.

Background and Atmosphere: Has its origins in a 1442 bequest of land to support the education of poor men's sons. This endowment became so valuable by 1834 that it enabled the Corporation of London to found City of London School in Milk Street, near Cheapside. Unusually for the time, it was a day school that did not discriminate against non-Anglicans and offered a practical and progressive education which included science and English (as opposed to classical) literature. It moved to Blackfriars in 1879 and to its present red-brick purpose-built facilities in 1986.

Wonderful site with many balconies and windows looking out across the Thames to Tate Modern, adjacent to the (alas no longer) Wobbly Bridge, with St Paul's right behind. Very urban, very buzzy. Keen on outreach – staff seconded to help East London state schools with maths, sports, drama etc. Boys not cosseted, expected to be independent, used to getting about London on their own from the age of 10 upwards. A teacher recounts approvingly how she overheard a group of 11 year olds, who had finished exams early, organising their own trip to a pizza restaurant across the river to celebrate. 'The boys are immensely proud of being part of the City of London,' said a parent.

Some boys who joined at 13 found it took time to integrate; they also mention an atmosphere far less pressured than their prep schools, with time to coast for a while.

Pastoral Care and Discipline: Strong anti-bullying culture. Pupils report some scapegoating in the younger classes, but no physical abuse, 'And people soon grow out of it'. 'They work very hard to deal with it,' said a parent. 'It's a very welcoming place. There's space for all sorts of diversity – black and white, rich and poor.' By general consent a complete lack of racial tension. Clear expectations, rules strictly enforced. 'It's relaxed but firm,' said a pupil.

Pupils and Parents: Extremely cosmopolitan. Few local families so nearly all travel in by tube, train or bus, from all points but particularly north and west. The huge catchment area and generous bursaries encourage a rich ethnic and social mix emanating from St Albans to Mile End. 'It makes teaching RE very interesting. In a class of 20 there will be a hundred different opinions, and they educate one another about their own religions.' OBs include Daniel Radcliffe, Julian Barnes, Lord Levine, Kingsley Amis and Herbert Asquith.

Entrance: Takes 24–40 boys at 10, some of these Temple Church or Chapel Royal choristers on scholarships. The main intake of 60–70 boys is at 11. Around 60 per cent of these come from state primaries. Another 40 come in at 13, almost entirely from prep schools. Around 15–20 join the sixth form, often with science scholarships, and mostly from state schools, including linked schools Stepney Green and St Thomas the Apostle.

Exit: Around 12–15 leave after GCSEs, almost invariably for state sixth forms. Always gets 20+ Oxbridge places (28 in 2010), with the vast majority of the rest going to Russell Group universities, many to read science or engineering.

Money Matters: A good place to try for a scholarship or bursary. Has a total of 106 full fee means-tested bursaries throughout the school, plus 30 academic and music scholarships a year.

Remarks: Very urban, very happening, very cosmopolitan school that achieves high standards without undue pressure and produces independent, outward-looking boys. 'We're happy as Larry,' said a father. 'We'd recommend it to anyone.'

City of London School for Girls

Linked to City Of London School For Girls (Prep School) in the Junior section

St Giles' Terrace, Barbican, London, EC2Y 8BB

• Pupils: 700 girls; all day • Ages: 7-18 • Size of sixth form: 140
• Non-denom • Fees: £13,131 pa • Independent

Tel: 020 7847 5500
Fax: 020 7638 3212
Email: admissons@clsg.org.uk
Website: www.clsg.org.uk

Head: Since 2007, Miss Diana Vernon BA PGCE (forties), who comes from a headship in the rolling green acres of Woldingham School in Surrey, and was previously a housemistress and biology/business studies teacher at Downe House. However, the City is familiar territory, as she once worked nearby in PR and she comes across as very much a PR professional: smart, dynamic, ambitious, keen to extol the merits of her school. 'She's fantastic ... really wonderful ... down-to-earth,' say parents. 'She's made huge efforts to get to know all the girls and they really like her.' Girls concur, 'Even in the first week she knew people's names. She's something very good that's happened to our school.'

An excellent manager. 'I really feel she takes things on board and will follow them up,' said a parent. She has instigated popular breakfast meetings for parents from different year groups. 'Because the girls all make their own way here, you don't see parents much. It's useful to put faces to names and I want them to feel that they can come in and see us when they need to. And it helps them to know what's going on here. We haven't been singing loudly enough about what we do.'

Although she has taught entirely in independent, selective, girls-only schools, mostly country boarding schools, she was inspired to become a teacher whilst a governor of a south London comprehensive. She feels that City's location is one of its great advantages – 'right in the heart of a vibrant, cosmopolitan city. You can visit the Tate Modern during an art class and it's very easy to attract interesting speakers.'

Academic matters: Up there with the top selective schools. Nearly 98 per cent A*/A/B grades at A level in 2010, with maths, history and English the most popular subjects. Praised for imaginative teaching methods. Everyone does two modern languages from Year 7, choosing between French, Spanish, German and Mandarin, and studies at least one to GCSE. Some take Spanish a year early; most get A*s and then start the AS course. Fifty per cent of girls achieved 10 A*s or more at GCSE in 2010. Top set mathematicians do additional maths alongside GCSE maths, and everyone studies three single sciences. The school now teaches thinking skills to Year 10 and 11 pupils, who can take the AS exam alongside GCSEs; 80 per cent got an A grade in 2010. 'It's good for university assessment tests and interviews and I like to give them the opportunity to be stretched.'

Is part of the East London Schools' Consortium, exchanging good practice with other girls' independent and state schools, and hosting the Urban Scholars Intervention Programme Saturday school. Some 60 gifted and talented state school girls from surrounding boroughs follow a varied programme encouraging them raise their aspirations and attainments.

Games, Options, the Arts: Music particularly vibrant, with numerous orchestras, ensembles, groups and choirs, many run jointly with City Boys. 'It's very inclusive,' said a parent. 'Anyone can go along to the orchestra and they all get a good experience of performing.' Most peripatetic teachers come from the nearby Guildhall School of Music. High quality art and DT – the innovative coffee tables in the reception hall were designed and built by a student. Often produces Arkwright engineering scholars. Plenty of drama – 'lively and good,' said a parent – again, often in conjunction with the boys' school.

'It's not the place for someone who wants to chase a ball around playing fields,' said a pupil, 'but they do pack things in.' It particularly suits those who shine in the compact arenas of swimming pool, netball court and gym, with successful swimming, fencing, gymnastics and netball teams. Diving, canoeing, climbing, running and water polo are other sporting options, alongside cricket, hockey and football on the new five-a-side Astroturf pitch. City girls always make up a large proportion of the City of London team for the London Youth Games and pupils have represented England at karate and fencing.

Makes good use of its central London location, with numerous outings to museums, art galleries, concerts and theatres, as well as strong connections with City banks and businesses. Sixth formers set up and run lunch-time clubs ranging from Asian society to cheerleading, with plenty to choose from. Residential trip destinations range from Bideford to Beijing.

Background and Atmosphere: It was founded in 1894 with a bequest from coal merchant William Ward as a school for girls that 'would correspond, as near as may be, to the City of London School ... making all proper allowance for the difference of the sexes'. It moved to its purpose-built five-storey Barbican home in 1969. Uncompromisingly urban, surrounded by multi-tiered flats and office blocks, it shoe-horns in everything from a food technology room to a multi-gym to a new sixth form centre with pool table, bean-bags and computer suite, looking out over a khaki-coloured lake. Corridors are lined with notice boards crammed with information.

Buzzy, busy atmosphere. Girls are encouraged to be independent; nearly everyone arrives by public transport. 'Our girls are pretty savvy. We give them support and advice on dealing with potential problems and they're streetwise in the nicest possible way.' Plenty of emphasis on ambition and women in leadership, with City mentors, visits to City institutions and talks by scientists and journalists, bankers and army officers.

Joint activities with City Boys include concerts and plays, lectures, careers conventions and mock Oxbridge interviews, plus social events organised by parents for the junior classes. 'By Year 9 they prefer to organise their own social life.'

Pastoral Care and Discipline: No easy ride academically. But the pressure to succeed comes from students as much as staff. 'There's a focus on academic success,' said a pupil, 'but everyone wants to do well. And staff are aware of other things going on in your life apart from work, so you feel supported.'

Four houses give a strong sense of identity and belonging, as well as opportunities to get involved in drama and sports competitions. Strong pastoral support. 'They do look out for them,' said a parent. Parents can even log on to keep tabs on what their daughter ate for lunch and what she has to do for homework.

Pupils and Parents: Girls travel from Chelmsford and Croydon, Bromley and Buckinghamshire, though the majority are the children of 'North London intellectuals and City bankers,' said a parent. A fair social and ethnic mix. 'It's a melting pot of girls,' says the head. 'They learn to respect each other and value other people's opinions.' Girls tend to be independent, opinionated and ambitious, inspired by the location of their school.

Entrance: Part of the North London Consortium, which sets joint maths and English exams each January. Applicants to City also sit GETINTU – a computer-based congitive test – in November. From some 500 applicants, 280 are interviewed to choose an intake of around 70, who join the 20 or so coming up from the prep school. Has now abolished its Year 10 intake in favour of four, rather than three, Year 7 classes. A few girls join the sixth form. 'We have a strong means-tested programme, so we have the flexibility to give bursaries to those who need it.'

Exit: A fair outward trickle after GCSEs, mostly to co-ed state or private sixth forms. All sixth form leavers go on to university, art or music school, with around 20 per cent to Oxbridge and the rest to a variety of the top universities. History, politics, philosophy and languages are amongst the most popular degree subjects.

Money Matters: Scholarships and bursaries help support 23 per cent of pupils. Academic, drama, art and music scholarships, generally worth £1,500 a year, available at 11 and 16, plus means-tested bursaries.

Remarks: Vibrant, ambitious, high-achieving school in the centre of London, producing confident and articulate girls.

Clayesmore School

Linked to Clayesmore Preparatory School in the Junior section

Iwerne Minster, Blandford Forum, Dorset, DT11 8LL

• Pupils: 265 boys, 160 girls; 240 board, the rest day. • Ages: 13-18 (but Clayesmore Prep offers 2-13 on the same site) • Size of sixth form: 140 • C of E • Fees: Boarding £27,597; Day £20,190 pa • Independent

Tel: 01747 812122
Fax: 01747 813187
Email: hmsec@clayesmore.com
Website: www.clayesmore.com

Headmaster: Since 2000, Mr Martin Cooke BEd (Hons) FCollP (mid-fifties), an ex-St Paul's chorister and organ scholar who was educated at Monkton Combe and did his

BEd in music at Sussex. Describes his hobbies as music in general, playing the organ and information technology. A human dynamo, he originally came to the school in 1994 as head of Clayesmore Prep. We met and lunched with him and his wife, Eleanor, who plays an active part in both schools. Previously head of music at Bembridge School and, whilst he no longer teaches, plays the organ for chapel on occasion and 'interferes' (his word) with the musical output 'occasionally'. He reckons that running a music department is excellent training for a headship as 'you do a lot of handling of people, dealing with the whole "congo"' (as in congregational choir practice).

Trenchantly hands-on, keeps himself well-informed on all pupil issues including bullying. Lots of new appointments since he took over; has focused his attention on making the sixth form an exciting environment and spruced up the school's image. 'We are now a small school of 420 rather than of 300,' but no intention of changing the central ethos of a small, caring school dedicated to bringing out the potential in each individual child. Wish list included a new prep school building and classrooms (which are now opened), improved boarding facilities plus new upper sixth house and an extension to the chapel.

Academic matters: Year groups of 90, five sets in most subjects except maths for which there may be six. Pupils setted in French, science and maths. French, Spanish and German all available to A level. 98 per cent average A level pass rate in the last three years. Tiny class sizes equal more attention from committed staff. Tutors responsible for a small group of pupils and monitor assessments every three weeks. Fantastic new extensive builds all over the shop including the award-winning Jubilee Building housing an entire new science department, two large computer suites and the new learning support centre with small lecture hall. Plus the Spinney Centre, which opened in 2004 with new classrooms for geography, history, business studies and careers, all bristling with the latest computer technology. Impressive.

A school on a roll. All the dys-strata catered for. Outstanding learning support for children with moderate to medium learning difficulties from one full- and 12 part-time staff (all fully qualified) in the superb new learning support centre (LSC) atop the new Jubilee Building, 'and anyone can get there,' though, sadly, the senior school SENCo was on a school trip in Rhodes during our visit. All children are assessed, by an educational psychologist if needed, extra help in maths, English and science (but not modern languages). More than 35 per cent of all pupils have some form of support, and a 'tiny number' have serious needs. Progressively more group lessons, particularly in study skills. 'We need children to laugh and feel successful.' Pupils generally come out of language classes, and extra sessions can be timetabled if necessary, plus evenings, but can pop in whenever – early morning sessions, exam and coursework, 'Try anything'. Good communication between LSC staff and subject teachers means that each pupil will have the individual attention they need, detailed pupil profiles for each. Help for the most able too. CReSTeD category B – CreSTeD listing essential for 'forces stock', who will be deprived of 'unlimited help indefinitely' if the school is not part of the system. Strong EFL too, with up to six hours a week, either individual or in pairs. Extra charge for both, from £26.43 for individual lessons to £6.73 for lessons shared by up to five.

Games, Options, the Arts: All pupils do sport three times a week. You name it, they play it: swimming, rugby, squash, badminton, hockey, football, netball, athletics, cross-country, rounders, sailing and tennis. Lots of matches and some notable successes against bigger schools. A good sprinkling of county players. School is 'potty on orienteering' and regularly in the ribbons. Locals use the leisure complex on site with pool, gym, squash courts and modern fitness suite, including weights (from 16 and under supervision) and a mirrored salle, but pupils say, 'The public are not that much of a hassle'. Presumably a planning requirement. Sports science strong. CCF opportunity for pupils in Years 10, 11 and sixth form, and enthusiastic D of E participants – tranches of golds et al. Sailing at Ringwood popular.

Thriving music school in purpose-built building run by enthusiastic head of music. Vibrant, terrific impromptu piano recital during our visit ('Actually my main instrument is the flute'), in a classroom filled with primitive instruments collected from all over the world – and some of them sound amazing. Sophisticated electronic keyboards too, recording studio and good participation in national choirs and yoof orchestras. Composition master class in Salisbury, loads of internal concerts, plus masses of travel; pupils can play almost anything, plus woodwind ensemble, brass group, flute choir and string ensemble.

Strong thespian tradition, with a terrific head of drama, whom we met in the (tiny) black theatre, but he is keen that actors should give several performances and not just be a one-off. Tremendously strong, with masses of tripettes: Bristol, the Old Vic, London. Pupil technicians (approximately 60 in the school at the moment) as important as actors themselves; fantastic costume department, with sewing machines and London type input. 'Reading plays' give access to more pupils, who need not learn the part but can perform, on stage, in costume, with script in hand. 'Theatre studies A level and drama work closely together.' Mystery plays for all, including the prep, at Christmas. Outstanding art department housed in lovely old primary school past the pub in the village – pottery, photography, textiles, drawing, painting and ceramics, really bustling and fun, sixth formers have a dedicated work space.

Trips to galleries in London and Paris. Huge range of extra activities four afternoons a week and all staff expected to run at least one. Pupils can do anything from fencing and yoga to textiles and pottery.

Background and Atmosphere: Idyllic setting: large country house set in sixty two acres of well-maintained grounds with lake, in the pretty village of Iwerne Minster in rural Dorset, five miles north of Blandford Forum, which boasts a post office and butcher's (and an awfully large collection of those blue/grey morris minors). Some slightly surprising room divisions in the main house but fireplaces to die for (and glorious computer room on ground floor). Well-used social centre, lots of inter-house competitions. Superb grub with salads and vegetarian option. Good cross-cultural influences – staff helped the small group of Chinese pupils cook a celebration meal for Chinese New Year and school meals are occasionally themed around different international celebrations.

Pastoral Care and Discipline: Head keeps a well-practised eye: 'No overt and terrible sin'; the odd cigarette equals letter home and it can get more severe. A tiered system of punishments ranging from academic 'satis' for prep missed/inappropriate clothing etc to gating and suspension for more serious behaviour problems. Tight eye kept on discipline by the deputy head. Pupils air complaints and suggestions at pupil forum with the head, who is well on top of the situation and not as relaxed as you might think. Has a 'very bad memory' for sin, which means that the next time a pupil sins 'he is down upon him like a ton of bricks', but otherwise the offence is deleted.

'Fantastic collection of houseparents' currently; five boarding houses (three boys' and two girls' houses) – all on site except one boys' house in the village. Traditional smell of toast, pupils graduate from dorms to study bedrooms. Houses run by married staff often with small children and dogs, with full support staff of matrons and house tutors (choose own in sixth form) – 'a good school for the expatriate child who might otherwise have been lost with parents far away'. Campus living in a small school is a double-edged sword: on the one hand this big family feel with lots of people to turn to; on the other, there can be pervasive claustrophobia; great efforts made to have buzzy weekends for boarders, including discos, talent contests and popular sixth form parties, houses take turns to organise.

Shopping buses organised to local towns such as Blandford, Shaftesbury and Sherborne (none of which will set the world alight). The Southampton shopping mall streaks ahead of the rest, staff go too. Duty staff organise excursions to local places of interest such as Bath (ditto) after Sunday chapel. Children of any denomination welcome.

Pupils and Parents: Number of day children, local buses: Salisbury, Poole, Bournemouth, Dorchester and the A30; can't flexi-board, but can stay over if late night activities, weekly boarding OK (casual boarding, for parents' or pupils' convenience, £20, post school function £10). Senior pupils can bring their own cars. Progressively more London refugees (this is getting to be the norm), home counties and a good sprinkling of ex-pat children (Services, diplomatic etc) plus a small number of foreign students – Dubai, Russia and Germany. Fair number of first time buyers. No great green wellie influence. Two-night exeats.

Entrance: By common entrance at 13 (50 per cent) and interview with the head, who looks for potential and the all-roundedness of prospective boys and girls. Just under half come through from the prep with the rest from a variety of local (and some further afield) prep schools: Forres Sandle Manor, Hordle Walhampton, Highfield, Durlston Court, Port Regis, Dumpton, Sherborne Prep and Castle Court plus local maintained schools. Rash of academic, music and art scholarships, several species of all-rounder awards made each year. Sixth form entrants need five A/C passes at GCSE.

Exit: Mainly universities, certain number of Oxbridge candidates, some Services, some vocational courses. School turns out vets, medics, all the usual suspects plus strong art, drama and music stream.

Money Matters: Oodles of scholarships – sixth form up to eight, with a minimum of four reserved for those not presently in the school, plus for local candidates (means tested) plus internal, plus music (string players preferred). Trillions too (though not quite so many) of scholarships, exhibitions and bursarial help for academics, music and art for entry into senior school, plus continuity awards from 11 to A level via the prep school (bursarial help available here too) and more closed awards at 13 – means-tested again. Plus closed bursaries for serving members of the Services. Impressive collection.

Remarks: A well-structured school, ideal for a child needing a supportive environment, with a bubbling far-sighted head in charge. Not a snooty school – perfect for the child who needs extra care.

Clifton College

Linked to Clifton College Preparatory School (The Pre) + Butcombe Pre-Prep in the Junior section

32 College Road, Clifton, Bristol, BS8 3JH

• Pupils: 715 boys and girls (60 per cent board) • Ages: 13-18 • Size of sixth form: 340 • C of E but many faiths welcomed • Fees: Boarding £27,300-£27,750; Day £18,750-£19,350 pa • Independent

Tel: 0117 375 7000
Fax: 0117 315 7101
Email: hwilliams@clifton-college.avon.sch.uk
Website: www.cliftoncollegeuk.com

Headmaster: Since 2005, Mr Mark Moore MA (late forties). Educated at Wolverhampton Grammar School and Downing College, Cambridge, where he read English, captained the university Eton Fives team and was world champion. A wonderful all-round games player who converses intelligently and interestingly about sport – 'he really understands games players,' said a hero-worshipping hockey player – but absolutely not a hearty. In fact he's a mighty talker on a range of subjects and is refreshingly iconoclastic about a number of educational issues, including league tables and some individual A levels. Teaches A level English – 'I love it'. One bright boy described him as a 'brilliant' teacher.

Engaging, witty, a strong advocate of co-education (girls have broken the breathless hush of the Close for 20 years and he has taught at Marlborough), he is committed to a 'broad church' in terms of entry into the school. Passionate about Clifton and its traditions, though with a clear eye to 21st century needs: he has a shrewd eye on the global scene – 'we have boys and girls from over 20 countries' – and is keen to inculcate an understanding between different faiths and nationalities. 'He may appear a little aloof,' said one senior boy, 'but he doesn't miss much.' He listens to pupils' initiatives and they feel encouraged. Above all he expresses a real affection for, and interest in, the pupils and a sympathetic understanding of rogues. Has instituted a school council. He and his wife, Jo, a fabulous cook with a wicked sense of humour, entertain a lot: staff, praeposters (prefects), pupils of all ages, prep school heads and visiting lecturers.

Amidst all this they have four children, two boys and two girls, all within the various stages of the school. After Marlborough he had seven years at Eton followed by 11 years at Radley, where he was head of English. This is his first appointment as head, though he's no greenhorn in terms of schoolmastering and has worked under some illustrious heads.

Academic matters: Good teaching (and preparation at prep schools) has resulted in good value-added at GCSE. A broad range of subjects with non-examined courses designed to feed the all-round pupil and a balance of art and sciences, the latter mostly taken separately. A thoughtfully flexible timetable allows for great diversity of subject choice. Over the last six years an average pass rate of 95 per cent A*–C.

A levels offer a broad spectrum of subjects from psychology to Chinese and from ancient Greek to sport and physical education. In total 31 subjects. No sense of narrowing down to A levels and breadth is encouraged. Most pupils choose four As, some more. Last year over 50 per cent of candidates scored A grades and 43 pupils scored AAA or better – you can play the statistics game till you swallow your abacus. The crucial point is that bright pupils are served well and less bright pupils are encouraged to reach their potential and made to feel good by doing so. As one grateful mum said, 'Pupils are never discouraged from pursuing a subject because they might not do very well and so lower the school's position in the league tables. Help and advice is given but it's individual rather than political.' 'The school offers exemplary help and advice with university entrance,' said a senior university don who is also a parent, 'and the co-curriculum stands them in very good stead when it comes to balancing the different aspects of university life.'

For dyslexics and others with learning difficulties excellent one-to-one teaching where the emphasis is on support and building self-esteem. Evidence of the success of this programme lies in boys and girls who have had learning support and then won Oxbridge places.

Games, Options, the Arts: Beyond the classroom it offers an extraordinary range of activities with amazing facilities. In the pursuit of manly chivalry, it was one of the first schools in the country to make sport compulsory; now the damsels have joined in for different reasons – such a range on offer that 'everyone can find something they are good at,' said a satisfied parent. Rackets, fives, squash and tennis courts abound. A sports hall with indoor cricket nets, an indoor swimming pool, a huge gymnasium bursting with instruments of torture and one of the most beautiful cricket grounds in England. There, year after year, WG Grace piled on the runs, and in the summer of 1899 schoolboy prodigy Arthur Collins made the highest individual score in the history of the game: 628 not out. The crowded score book is on view in the prep. In the winter term, rugby is played including the oldest rugby fixture between schools in England, Clifton v Marlborough, the Governor's Cup, first competed for in 1864.

That's just on the Clifton side of the river. Cross over by the thrilling suspension bridge – even Cliftonians don't swim across – and you come to Beggar Bush (safely referred to as BB). There, under the expert eye of the head groundsman, an old Cliftonian, stretch acres of playing fields with new international-standard Astroturf hockey pitches, a new covered pitch allowing year-round tennis and netball, 24 tennis courts, a Real Tennis court, a new fitness centre with pavilion for entertaining, all open to the public at set times. When we visited, huge earth-moving machines like prehistoric monsters were filling in dips and valleys with building rubble for, inter alia, a full-sized all-weather rugby pitch. Girls' and boys' hockey thrives and produces its generous crop of internationals and county players who regularly go on tours as far away as South Africa and Australia. Rowing on the Avon and further afield in Plymouth adventurous mariners can experience The Moosk, a 55ft gaff-rigged yawl built in 1906 and fully restored.

So much for burning up physical energy. What of the creative juices? Music and drama thrive. The new Joseph Cooper Music School is proving a huge success. The building is stuffed with pianos and practice rooms as well as modern technology in the shape of synthesisers and computerised composition suites, and recording studio. Choirs, ensembles, orchestras, bands abound and perform regularly; the chapel choir sings nationally and internationally. Named after old Cliftonian Sir Michael, the Redgrave Theatre, a surprisingly spacious building which offers little hint of its opportunities from the road, hosts over 40 productions a year including visits from travelling thespians. Pupils are in the National Youth Orchestra and the National Youth Theatre. The House Drama week, a festival of pupil-produced plays, is hugely popular with everyone, including parents, and offers opportunities for anyone keen to participate. Upper school production for 2010 was *Les Misérables* and the preparatory school production was *The Pinafore Pirates.*

Art and ceramics are stunning (look at the prep school art to see the talent being fed through). Evidence of further improvement is everywhere: a scrappy old dump has become a new all-weather play area, tatty old tennis courts have been made playable. The science school has been totally refurbished offering the latest new facilities. A room in one of the houses has been converted into a ballet and dance studio where even the 1st XV have practised for a musical. Pshaw!

The Close with its statue of Earl Haig and its striking war memorial to those killed in the Boer war, to say nothing of the haunting arch commemorating the dead of the two world wars, are constant reminders of Clifton's connection with the Services. The CCF is large and girls participate as enthusiastically as boys. D of E is very popular and the school has its own property in Wales as a base for orienteering and walking weekends. Mountaineers cling on to rock and heather all over the world. Everyone is involved in some sort of community service. Overseas expeditions have included Artic Circle 2009, Borneo 2010 and Ecuador 2011.

Background and Atmosphere: The Victorian buildings, conveying as they do the impression that Clifton College has been around for much longer than its foundation in 1862, are very handsome – especially where the stone has been cleaned and the brick repointed. The jewel in the crown is the Percival Library, modelled on Duke Humfrey's mediaeval library in the Bodleian. It has been tactfully refurbished combining traditional scholarship with information crunching: elegant bookcases in the body of the building; functional banks of computers in the foyer.

After its foundation and the early building, the school set about building or buying houses. Thus Houses are houses, for the most part. Recent refurbishment has resulted in bright and airy rooms equipped with modern accessories – running water and power points, for instance – plus comfortable lolling space with plenty of sofas and armchairs. 'Home from home,' said one happy girl. Day pupils have their own houses and enjoy all the amenities of boarders, minus the bed and breakfast, with facilities for sleeping over if parents are out gallivanting. The head has introduced matrons for each day house, which has not only improved the medical backup but also added further depth to the counselling and befriending in houses. New houses for the girls reflect the increase in numbers. Traffic (if that's the right word) between houses for boys and girls is civilised and, of necessity, restricted. CCTV cameras are thicker than on the M1 but that, we were assured, is to catch or deter Burglar Bill. Overall a bustling, friendly atmosphere and pupils smile and greet. We heard of a boy currently at a big, powerful London school itching to join Clifton at sixth form – 'the kids are so normal there'. Big School is a big dining room but with small tables and attractively presented food – consumption does not disappoint. A newly created cafe in the chapel crypt complements the school shop, called, inevitably, Grubber.

Pastoral Care and Discipline: Clifton is a town school, unless you're at BB. Not far from the leafy suburbs and impressive houses, Bristol offers its attractions and its temptations. The newly appointed Marshal, a man who used to work in counter-espionage, is responsible for overall discipline, rule keeping and self-restraint. 18-year-olds are allowed to visit certain pubs with strict provisos – 'they guard that privilege jealously'. Staff say that, by and large, the pupils are pretty sensible about visiting pubs and clubs. One pupil we asked shrugged his shoulders with a grin – no animosity there. Sanctions are in place, so is trust. The chapel is a monument to 'muscular Christianity', complete with stained glass window depicting a cricket match, the game of life. A popular and charismatic figure, the chaplain ensures that the chapel remains a focus of spirituality and a forum for discussion and discovery, e.g. when we attended a service, a group of boys were talking about the many facets of love – they were sensitive and unflinching in their treatment of the topic.

An effective tutoring system based on the houses – pupils spoke with appreciation of the friendly atmosphere and good relations they enjoy with the staff. Above all they appreciate the way they are allowed to develop as individuals. Interestingly, pupils spoke warmly of the support team: the porter, the ground staff and the secretarial branch.

Pupils and Parents: Parents, mostly professional, come from a cross-section of society working in media, law, engineering, academia and lots from the Services. Day pupils are on the increase. Boarders make the most of the flexi, weekly and full boarding options and the proximity of Bristol Airport has brought cohorts of Europeans from further afield. The strong, historical Jewish connection brings pupils from Lithuania and neighbouring countries, even from Siberia – a cosmopolitan school and celebrating it. Famous old boys include three Nobel Prize winners, seven winners of the VC, two Field Marshals and scores of gentler participants including LP Hartley, Sir David Willcocks, Trevor Howard, Simon Russell Beale, John Cleese, John Madden and Richard Foster – the list is impressive.

Entrance: 70 per cent enter from the prep school – communication between the schools is effective so the entrance exam is for setting purposes. Common entrance is pitched at 50 per cent and potential. The school has its own exams for pupils applying from the state system or abroad. Few leave after GCSE and the sixth form is massively over-subscribed.

Exit: Despite lowly entrance requirements most go on to first choice universities over a wide geographical area – good universities, too. Oxford consistently among the most popular – average of nine Oxbridge places a year.

Money Matters: Scholarships, awards and bursaries are awarded for the usual things, and discounts available for children of armed forces and the clergy.

Remarks: In many ways Clifton can be summed up by its excellent magazine, one of the few which can be read with interest even by strangers, containing a scholarly interest in the past and a celebration of the present. With such a variety of good schools in the area, it has got to work hard to justify its expense and its less tangible position in the market. For many it's the dinner party school, watched closely and much discussed. Inevitably gossip throws out unattractive stories hinting at a certain arrogance, even a degree of philistinism – extraordinary when you see the standard of art, music and drama. After a brief period dedicated to climbing the league tables, Clifton has returned to teaching for potential.

These are exciting times for Clifton. It is not yet riding the crest of the wave but a huge wave is building up. There could be some good surfing.

Clifton Hall School

Linked to Clifton Hall Junior School in the Junior section

Clifton Road, Newbridge, Edinburgh, EH28 8LQ

• Pupils: 70 boys and girls, all day • Ages: 11-18 • Size of sixth form: 4
• Non-denom • Fees: £9,255 pa • Independent

Tel: 0131 333 1359
Fax: 0131 333 4609
Email: headmaster@cliftonhall.org.uk
Website: www.cliftonhall.org.uk

Headmaster: Since 2005 (and here, he promises, until 2015 at least), Mr Rod Grant BA PGCE (early forties). Came from Hutcheson's – having been principal teacher of English and responsible for literacy; his brief stretched through primary to S1. From Prestwick in Ayrshire (where he has a second career as a 'property developer' – he lets out flats that he owns), and educated at Merchiston, followed by Edinburgh where he read English, but abandoned this to join his brother in a wine bar venture. Returning to academia, he completed his degree at the Open University (having, in the interim, been housemaster at Drumley House School – deceased – in Ayrshire), doing his PGCE at Paisley and cutting his teeth in Broxburn at a state primary.

Less than three months into his headship, Grant was approached by the governors of the tiny St Serf's school (94 pupils aged 5–18, lousy prep inspectors' report, mediocre senior report) suggesting a merger – and, after much gubernatorial activity, the schools amalgamated in September 2008.

Grant is putting his previous business experience to good use (it sometimes feels as if you're talking to an accountant rather than a headmaster, what with .6 and .4 of teachers) and has obviously got the building bug – new kitchen adjacent to games hall and new sports pavilion under construction plus refurbishing '57 parts of the school'. Rumours rife about the £1.5 million the merger realised – Grant is not so upfront, 'we spent what we got'.

Certain amount of tinkering with previous head's innovations: coffee mornings weekly, rather than daily – 'they were becoming cliquey'. Chatty and open on his own, but gave us a somewhat whistle-stop watch-consulting tour of the school, with little chance to talk to either the staff or the children. Very positive, his common-sense view on bullying and some of the wilder health and safety regulations ought to be circulated round the heads' grapevine. His wife, Helen, is a supply teacher and on the school books, though with a toddler she might be a bit preoccupied (Grant also has three step-children, some of whom are in the school). They live on site.

Academic matters: Difficult to judge as yet. Three pupils in upper sixth, two of whom are hoping for Oxbridge. Head says that all subjects are covered with 24 part-timers 'and timetabling OK', though we found two Intermediate English classes with three pupils in each running simultaneously (with one of the dishiest masters we have seen in a long time). Proper French, German and Spanish in P5 (aged 10), option of Italian and Russian in the pipeline. Two pristine computer suites (one Apple, one PC) used by all for timetabled lessons as well as IT – networked, intranetted, wireless. Stunning new lab designed by science staff, complete with prep room and adjacent scientific classroom. School follows Scottish system.

Two SENCos (an unusual arrangement). Pupils either withdrawn from class individually, in groups or offered dual teaching. Can cope with minor physical handicap – senior classrooms are upstairs – and Asperger's (mild).

Games, Options, the Arts: Apparently enthusiastic music and drama (fab photograph of young bridal couple in hall) though neglected during our interview with the head; peripatetic staff. Exciting art, some very intricate dress design going on. Eco committee, school currently bronze and going for silver. Charity involvement via houses, children choose their own projects.

Games hall (with bars and benches) doubles as dining room – two-and-a-half hours out of the day and charming swimming pool with timetabled lessons for all. Senior school a bit dodgy on team games, though lots of clubs (judo, ballet, fencing, swimming) – no tennis courts seen, but smashing-looking sports pavilion under construction. Gym, swimming pool and sports facilities can be hired out by locals. Nine hole par three golf-course on horizon but no all-weather pitch as yet.

Background and Atmosphere: School based in a magical Bryce house, complete with impressive paintings and the odd bit of antique furniture, in 54 acres of child-inspiring grounds just off the Newbridge roundabout – the junction of A8, M8 and M9. A boon for parents to the west of Edinburgh, who can either take advantage of the school buses which leave Bathgate, Livingstone and the West End of Edinburgh (primarily to accommodate the fallout from St Serf's) daily at 8am (and departs at 5pm each evening) or drop off their poppets on the way into work (school open 8am to 6pm).

Senior, junior and nursery all have their own dedicated playspace, where the head can watch from his study and has been known to invite concerned parents to watch their darlings at play. Weekly menus handed out to all, so that parents don't cook the 'same for their tea'. Lots of parent participation. Previously painted in rather jolly prime colours, particularly in the basement, school has opted for airforce blue – light-absorbing, and besides which, this editor would never employ those painters again: hasps left on doors (and painted over), woodwork not prepared properly. Outdoor classroom under pupil construction (in Scotland?). This is brave stuff. The gorgeous doo'cot is about to have serious input from Historic Scotland.

Amalgamation appears to have gone well. Expensive (90 quid) blazer worn by all, though seniors don't have the natty trim. I think it is the first time this editor has seen amalgamation completed so uniformly: normally the young wear their existing kit until they grow out of it – impressive.

Pastoral Care and Discipline: Head has common-sense attitude. Small enough school to care – tinies walk down school paths hand in hand. Matron sign still visible on first floor door. Children devised own set of 'Golden Rules' (representatives from each class on pupil council) – each pupil must have both a request and a thank you.

Pupils and Parents: The main catchment area is West Lothian: Livingston, Linlithgow, Bathgate – Silicon Glen. Parents 85 per cent or more first-time buyers, ditto both working. A complete mix. More popular now with traditional parents, many of whom will be sending their young off either at eight or 13 to traditional schools, often down south. FPs include Rory Bremner and Jim Clark.

Entrance: Mainly through the (non-selective entry) nursery – a proper nursery school (member of the Edinburgh City Partnership Scheme) with many of the children wearing a uniform. Otherwise by assessment and interview. Overbooked for nursery and first few years of primary. Space available aplenty in the senior school, suck it and see at other ages. Will accept pupils at any time; head, reckons to have a good 'conversion' rate of potential parents, emailing them within three days of interest being shown, and keen on first names.

Exit: Too soon to call.

Money Matters: Fees include almost all extras; trust fund on hand to pick up financial hiccups 'for a year or two' – 'safety net' rather than 'safety blanket'.

Remarks: 'School is going places and it is growing.' Governors very bullish – and so they should be. New head has maintained and even increased momentum.

Clifton High School

Linked to Clifton High Lower School in the Junior section

College Road, Clifton, Bristol, BS8 3JD

• Pupils: 510; 235 lower school; 275 in upper school; 3 family boarders, rest day. Co-ed in the lower school and sixth form, and throughout from 2009 • Ages: 3-18 • Size of sixth form: 75, including 11 boys.
• Non-denominational with a christian ethos • Fees: £10,905 pa
• Independent

Tel: 0117 973 0201
Fax: 0117 923 8962
Email: kboltonjones@cliftonhigh.bristol.sch.uk
Website: www.cliftonhigh.bristol.sch.uk

Head of School and Clifton High Sixth: Since 2008, Dr Alison Neill (early fifties), a former research scientist with long service at Clifton High, she started as a biology teacher, and worked her way up via head of sixth form to head of school and Clifton High sixth. Parents describe her as fair, kind and taking a personal interest in the children. 'And amazingly elegant at the same time,' said one parent. Dr Neill works with her executive team, Mr Tony Richards, head of lower school, and Mr Guy Cowper, the director of operations in charge of business matters.

Long years at the school haven't made Dr Neill narrow-minded: some radical rethinking has gone on since she took on the headship, from the move to co-education at all ages to the links between different parts of the school. Even the head's office was not sacred: down came the curtains to let the light in – possibly a symbolic gesture as much as an interior design choice. The head says the decision to admit boys to the secondary school was triggered at least in part by her disappointment at having to send her own son elsewhere at 11, but that personal feeling was backed up with intensive research into current educational thinking and visits to other schools practising different models of co-education.

Academic matters: Not an academic pressure cooker, but results are good for the intake – 98 per cent A level pass rate, 68 per cent at grades A*, A and B – and small classes mean plenty of support is available. There are a few bright stars in each year, but staff stress they are even prouder of those who struggle to hard-won Cs and Ds at A level and go on to higher things. GCSE and A level options are as flexible as possible, with no option block system. In 2009 all four students who applied and interviewed for Oxford were offered a place.

Parents talk about a 'sense of fun' underlying the serious academic work, and this could be seen on our visit with a Year 8 class firing rubber bands at a ball during a physics lesson in a practical demonstration of forces.

Boys and girls are taught together in the junior school and sixth form (and will be taught together for the two pre-GCSE years when boys reach that level) but in Years 7 to 9 they are taught separately for English, maths, sciences, IT, French and games in a system known as the 'diamond model' (also used in a handful of other schools in the UK). Early days, but parents and teachers seem happy that system is working so far, and it is seen as a good compromise for parents wanting the best of both single-sex and co-ed models of education.

Languages are a strong point. A new 'carousel' system for trying out the three modern languages offered (French, German, Spanish) in Years 7 and 8 started in September 2010. Wide range of overseas trips offered, and full-time native-speaker assistants for each language. Latin is strong and popular (helped by an innovative head of department); Greek is no longer officially on the menu, but has been offered on demand if a group within a year is desperately keen. Classical civilisation an option at A level. Science provision is good. Large numbers taking biology A levels, possibly helped by a popular and young new head of biology, but take-up of other sciences at A level is increasing. Business studies, psychology and IT are relatively new additions to the A level option list.

The special needs coordinator makes sure that everyone is screened periodically so dyslexia and other issues can be picked up at any stage, and individual or small-group help offered, but school does turn away some needing more support than it can cope with. Physical disabilities adjusted for as far as possible, but the age and layout of buildings make accessibility an issue.

Games, Options, the Arts: Drama is popular and inclusive – regular productions for all school levels are 'very creative'. There is an option of extra speech and drama lessons during school hours (leading to external exams) for the keen, and lots take drama at A level. Lively musical scene, with most instruments offered, and lots of chamber groups plus school choir and orchestra.

Two tennis/netball courts, gym and pool are on the main site, but playing fields are off-site on a large development shared with the university at Coombe Dingle, with good modern and spacious facilities including indoor sports courts and more outdoor tennis courts. The full-size swimming pool is a perk not available to most of the other independents in central Bristol. Small numbers of boys as yet mean that the school cannot realistically field full rugby or cricket teams for inter-school sports, but it does have arrangements with sports clubs sharing the Coombe Dingle pitches. Tennis players have the example of old girl, Jo Durie, to look up to. The recent appointment of a head of boys' sport is already making his mark upon sport throughout the school.

Historically stronger on food and textiles than the more masculine variants of design technology, but that is changing. The lower years curriculum for textiles has been rejigged for gender neutrality with the advent of boys – less fashion, more kites and other items – and some new options are being introduced, such as graphic design.

Background and Atmosphere: Clifton High still feels, for the moment, like a girls' school – upper school boys are a conspicuous minority, but that should change quite rapidly. Indeed the school as a whole is already one-third boys. Bigger batches of Year 7 boys expected after the initial guinea pigs, and there will be boys in every year group by 2012. The teaching staff is also still female-dominated (roughly two-to-one ratio), but the school is making an effort to recruit more men; alongside the new male head of boys' sport there is a new male head of food technology.

Pupil numbers took a dive a few years ago, with rumours for about the school's future in the over-supplied Bristol independent school sector. Dr Neill's bold measures seem to be having the right effect: numbers are now steady or rising. Teachers and parents rave about the school's warmth and friendliness, partly due to its size but also deeply rooted in its attitudes and culture.

The school has expanded from its original cluster of impressive 19th century houses with various less-attractive 20th century additions around a central lawn. Cramped in parts, but the use of space is efficient, and the heart of Clifton location helps keep the image upmarket. Classrooms and corridors look a little shabby in places, but all the equipment you would expect is there, from interactive whiteboards to computerised language-labs, and it is clean and well-lit.

Everyone from junior and senior schools (staff included, though on separate tables) has lunch in the cheerful hubbub of main school canteen – a good choice of hot and cold meals, plus salad bar (more limited choice for the little ones). There's also a cafe opening on to a courtyard for breaktime and after-school snacks. Sixth formers have their own eyrie in the main building: study and common-rooms with Wi-Fi (all are issued with laptops) and a more grown-up feel.

Pastoral Care and Discipline: Pupils generally agree that staff are approachable and relations are friendly, and parents are full of praise for the firm but caring attitude of the staff. 'No one gets lost in the crowd,' said one. Pupils encouraged to talk to any member of staff they choose about a problem – they don't have to stick to their own tutor if they find another teacher more sympathetic. The school nurse (shared with the lower school) has a suite of rooms and is there for anyone who feels unwell or needs a chat.

Sixth formers assigned as peer mentors for Years 6 to 8, seen as the peak danger years for bullying. Bullying is taken 'very seriously'; school uses strategies to build resilience, and tries to work through issues openly with dialogue.

Discipline system of merits and demerits in place, most often used for handing in work late or not at all – three demerits lead to a detention – but apparently most staff rarely use them.

Boarding has shrunk from whole-school to now only being offered in the sixth form, with a handful of boarders living with local families rather than on-site, but school says it is keen to promote the boarding option (new boarding coordinator recently appointed).

Pupils and Parents: Family backgrounds are varied, but on the whole not as wealthy as those driving past the school to Clifton College up the road, or as high-pressured as the ones at some of the single-sex Bristol girls' schools. Lots of sibling groups, and some second or even third generation pupils. A large proportion of the staff send or have sent their own children to the school, including the head, which can be seen as a vote of self-confidence. The big shift to co-ed doesn't seem to have fazed the parents – only one apparently upped and left in protest, and most are supportive of the thinking behind the diamond model.

Old Girls include Jo Durie, Sarah Keays, Mary Renault, Stephanie Cole, Elizabeth Filkin and Bernice McCabe (current head of North London Collegiate).

Entrance: Intake is from a wide range of local primaries throughout the junior years and at 11, with some movement from other Bristol and regional independents. Boys joining the upper school under the new system include some first-timers, but also some sixth-formers who spent their primary years at CHS. Entry at 11 via tests in NVR, maths and English, plus a chat with the head – informal for most, more formal for scholarship or bursary applicants.

Progression from the junior school is automatic, with only those hoping for scholarships taking the entrance tests. Potential scholars are identified from entrance examinationn and interview by the head. Any juniors seen as unlikely to make the grade are given plenty of warning, usually at least a year or so before they would need to make a move. Sixth form applicants taken on the basis of GCSE results or predictions, previous school reports and interview; some may be asked to sit in-house tests in relevant subjects.

Exit: Most stay on after GCSE, though a few have always opted to leave for co-ed sixth forms – too early to see if this will change with the arrival of sixth form boys – or to take up subjects not offered. A handful dispatched to Oxbridge most years, with a high hit-rate for those who apply, and nearly everyone else goes on to some form of higher education – destinations cover the whole range of universities and art colleges – except for those taking a gap year or two.

Money Matters: Not a rich school, but there is enough in the pot to help 30 or so pupils a year, with support ranging from token academic scholarships to full assisted places or bursaries for three or four. Fees are in line with the other Bristol day schools.

Remarks: Bouncing back from a rocky patch. Now with a dynamic new head, closer integration with the lower school, and boys joining the upper school and sixth form – though taught separately in some subjects for the lower years. Still not an obvious choice for seriously sporty boys, although this is changing, but sporty girls have plenty of scope here, and the relaxed, friendly atmosphere and small class sizes have plenty to offer for more academic or arty types of both sexes. 'It's very calm and grown-up feeling,' said one girl.

Cobham Hall

Cobham, Gravesend, Kent, DA12 3BL

• Pupils: 185 girls; 90 board • Ages: 11-18 • Size of sixth form: 70
• Multi-faith • Fees: Boarding £20,700-£26,100; Day £13,800-£17,400 pa
• Independent

Tel: 01474 823 371
Fax: 01474 825 906
Email: ferrerss@cobhamhall.com
Website: www.cobhamhall.com

Principal: Since 2008, Mr Paul Mitchell (late forties), unmarried. BSc in maths and PGCE from University of Newcastle. Previously deputy head at St Mary's School Cambridge, and before that taught at Royal High Bath, Godolphin in Salisbury, Radley College and in the state sector. A keen interest in sport a factor in his career choice, granting him the flexibility to keep at the top of his field as an international pentathlete; he represented Britain for 10 years. Out of hours now more often to be found at the stables with his two horses than on the track, but brought his enthusiasm for sport to the school. Not someone to put too much emphasis on this or that standard, far more on the individual and how each can find their niche and come to life at the school. Keeps tabs on them all. He speaks with disarming candour and while evidently fiercely loyal to the school and conscious of economic realities (he has appointed a marketing manager and plans to boost the boarding community), you feel his genuine openness in his appreciation of openness ibn others. 'I'd approach him about anything, but he'd probably know and have done something about it already,' we were told.

Academic matters: Recent introduction of the IB to replace AS and A levels seems almost tardy, given the traditional internationalism and Round Square ethos of the school. Certainly likely to be a draw for overseas parents, as is the pre-IB course. UK parents also value the broad, values-based education, consistent with the IB but, in a school not known for its academic rigour, will their girls be able to cope? GCSE results have improved, with good performances in modern languages and IGCSEs in sciences, but A*–C pass rates in, for example, English, history, geography and ICT disappointing in the past. Parents don't seem overly concerned and are quick to mention cases of teachers generating interest and unexpectedly good results in particular subjects. The school's mantra and Round Square motto is 'there's more in you than you think' and with small class sizes (12–15 in the lower school, middle 10–12 and a small sixth form) enabling a high degree of individual attention, parents are confident that staff bring out the best in them, in and outside the classroom.

The Susan Hampshire Centre was established in 1990 to cater for pupils requiring learning support. Predominantly, pupils using the centre have dyslexic/dyspraxic tendencies or Irlen Syndrome. For each, an IEP drawn up covering literacy, maths and study skills, according to their needs. Two full-time specialist EAL teachers.

Games, Options, the Arts: Head says that the school was somewhat at the 'egg and spoon race' stage a few years back but this is changing. The girls enjoy their sport and relish a more competitive approach, the introduction of lacrosse and the greater focus on field and track. Notable recent successes in the biathlon, high jump and 1500m. Some new specialist sports coaches; enthusiasts enabled to go to county netball and local hockey club training. Rounders also popular, and if that doesn't tickle their fancy there's always badminton, dance, aerobics and swimming.

Just under half the pupils study a musical instrument or sing and have the opportunity to join instrumental groups and one of four choirs. Regular lunchtime concerts and a major performance each term in the fabulous Gilt Hall. Drama is evidently innovative and fun and there are inter-house drama and music festivals every other year in which all have to participate. Being an extra during the filming of *Wild Child* at the school must also have been a real thrill for some.

Good sporting and other facilities include an indoor heated pool, indoor and outdoor tennis courts, dance studio and fitness suite. Bikes encourage the girls to be more active. Well-equipped theatre and, judging by the art and sculptures on display, artistic talents well catered for. Programme of lunchtime and after-school clubs and, at the weekend, film, culture and shopping trips keep boarders occupied.

In truth, the activities and the D of E are not out of the ordinary. What excites most is the school's membership of the Round Square and the opportunities for adventure that creates. It's obviously a subject of much discussion and anticipation amongst the girls who come up with varied fund-raising ideas – fashion shows, bake sales and sponsored cycle rides – to enable them to travel to and support community projects in far-flung places. School exchanges and international conferences also a regular feature. Parents love all this character-building and eye-opening stuff plus the sense of security which comes with the school's 40-year Round Square association and vast international network.

Background and Atmosphere: Cobham Hall is only a stone's throw from major motorway links, but passing through the gates is like entering a time warp away from the noise and bustle of modern life. A Grade II listed Elizabethan building comes into view, all more modern classrooms and boarding houses discreetly tucked away out of sight so as not to detract from the 150 acres of beautiful parkland. The buildings are made accessible for various events during the year and, in the spring, grounds opened up to the public who can gaze in awe at the carpet of flowers. Inside, many rooms are beautifully preserved with the help of English Heritage, and scattered about with wonderful nonchalance are portraits of past owners, framed historical documents, and even a horse-drawn carriage resting idly at the end of the main library.

Since its establishment in the early 1960s, the school has had internationalism at its core, and cultural integration and enrichment are still very much a part of life here. On Friday nights pupils tell stories from around the world, and assemblies feature explanations of different religious beliefs and traditions. Nonetheless, as one pupil put it, it does feel a bit of a 'bubble community', a small world of its own. No bad thing, say parents of, in particular, younger pupils, as it allows, indeed encourages, them to develop a strong values-base on which to build their future lives. Pupils are proud of the community and individuals' achievements and, through the various student committees and leadership structures, play an ongoing and important role in promoting them. If they didn't like the head – and most do – arguably they would have themselves to blame: after all, they interviewed him before he got the job.

Pastoral Care and Discipline: 'We're a close community. We all know each other and everyone has the freedom to be who they want to be.' Quiet, outgoing, musical, academic, sporty, the school accommodates all bar perhaps those who want to break away and form their own group. It has a gentle and friendly atmosphere with real thought and care taken to ensure that, whatever your background, you settle in well. In this nurturing atmosphere even the shyest gain confidence.

Sixth form boarders housed in dedicated blocks, with cooking and other facilities to reflect their greater independence. Younger full-time and flexi-boarders are in the main old buildings which are comfy and spacious. Little touches like putting a teddy in a flexi-boarder's bed, the big sister system to look after newcomers and peer mentoring are examples of how the girls look out and care for each other. Day pupils are encouraged to try out boarding as part of the induction and get five 'free' nights per term – part, perhaps, of the school's current strategy to tip the balance more in favour of boarding. This, and the fact that many day pupils stay late, means there is no great day/boarder divide. Some parents comment that it would be good if boarders were invited out more regularly but, with

80 per cent or so staying in at the weekends, it is rare for anyone to be at a loose end.

Discipline is 'tough but fair'. Incidents of a serious nature are rare, as is bullying, problems mostly limited to minor fall-outs, perceived as inevitable amongst teenage girls. Where parents have had concerns of this nature or in relation to academics, they find staff accessible and responsive.

Pupils and Parents: 'Outside, they think we're all posh but we're not,' says one girl. This is backed up by a parent's observation: 'There's anything from old bangers to Rollses come up the drive each morning'. Most boarders are international. Living in a small community while acquiring a good level of English is clearly a strong draw amongst the 31 nationalities represented.

Parents say pupils are polite and chat quite happily with them in a relaxed and mature way. They are supportive of each other in work and play and tend to just get on with whatever they are tasked to do. In the all-girl environment, parents celebrate that there is little pressure to grow up too fast. Sixth formers allowed to wear own clothes; few uniform infringements lower down school.

The Unicorn (parents) Association is very active and welcoming – 'you almost have to beat them off'. Regular teas before exeat weekends, coffee mornings, school events, salsa and jazz evenings provide ample opportunities to meet other parents. The wide catchment area can otherwise make this and sharing transport difficult. Former pupils include BBC newsreader/journalist Mishal Husain, Susie Forbes, editor of Easy Living, and Kate French, who hopes to represent Britain in the 2012 Olympics pentathlon.

Entrance: At 11+ and 13+ applicants sit a maths and English test, provide a report of recommendation from their current school, attend an interview and take part in a group activity. Those wishing to enter the sixth form sit English and maths exams, must achieve five GCSEs at grade C or above and A or B grades in the subjects they wish to study as part of the IB. Day pupils mostly come from local state primaries or prep schools.

Exit: Approx 45 per cent move on after GCSEs, mostly to larger mixed schools or sixth form colleges. The introduction of the IB has had little impact on sixth form numbers. Of those staying on until 18, a small minority take a gap year. Most pursue further studies in their countries of origin or in the UK at a variety of universities and colleges.

Money Matters: Discounts are available for daughters/granddaughters of old girls. Reductions for those staying on in the sixth form and bursaries for British Services families, diplomats and families working for UK charitable trusts overseas. Few scholarships. Fees for extras are considered reasonable and there is no extra charge for day pupils on boarder taster weeks or for breakfast and supper when they are involved in clubs.

Remarks: A friendly and caring environment with strong international links and the premise that everyone achieves, given belief and support.

Cokethorpe School

Linked to Cokethorpe Junior School in the Junior section

Witney, Oxon, Oxfordshire, OX29 7PU

- Pupils: 660 boys and girls; all day. • Ages: 4-18 • Size of sixth form: 120
- Joint C of E and RC foundation • Fees: £9,885-£14,385 pa
- Independent

Tel: 01993 703 921
Fax: 01993 773 499
Email: admissions@cokethorpe.org
Website: www.cokethorpe.org.uk

Headmaster: Since 2002, Mr Damian Ettinger BA MA PGCE, (early forties). Educated St Joseph's College (Beulah Hill), Universities of Manchester and Surrey. Previously head of theology and housemaster, Prior Park College, Bath, 1989–96; head of St Oliver's and head of theology, Downside 1996–2002. Married with four sons and one daughter. Brisk, relaxed, confident, personable, impatient: 'It drives me bonkers that things need to happen quickly but don't'. He's ambitious, and adamant the school should be the school of choice, not playing second fiddle to some of the many other (very good) schools in the area. A keen sportsman, ex-Bath flanker (seconds, he adds).

This isn't a man seeking to massage his ego; this is a man on a mission, who cares, who genuinely wants the best because he believes that's what the kids deserve. He's far from a soft touch but the children, staff and parents all seem to love him: 'He's so funny, hilarious,' said one pupil, and a host of others grinned and nodded. 'He makes me laugh every day; he's a joy to work for.' That so many staff have embraced his vision is testament to his enthusiasm, his passion, his personality. That more than a handful have fallen by the wayside demonstrates his dislike of 7/10. 'If someone is graded 7/10 what does that mean? What's it saying? I so dislike 7/10. Five, that says something; nine? Yes, but not seven.' A tough, modernizing head who wants his own high standards reflected in all areas.

So mediocrity isn't in his vocabulary, but consolidation? He set out a five-year plan in 2002, so what now? A new challenge, more of the same elsewhere, head-hunted? No. He insists he wants to enjoy a period of stability, that he's here for the long haul; he likes the fact he can meddle in the finances, tinker with the maintenance, ride a tractor ... His family are settled (three at the school) and family matters: 'I go home; I'm soon grounded; I have to help out, get stuck in, do as I'm told'. And for relaxation? Jazz, or the MGB roadster, a pair of overalls and a spanner or two.

Academic matters: Results have improved dramatically, with 94 per cent of GCSE passes graded A* to C and 59 per cent of A levels A* to B. Not extraordinary, but the school has a high proportion of children with learning difficulties, and this represents a considerable improvement and, no doubt, for many, a huge achievement. Small group sizes make it difficult to select star subjects with results fairly evenly spread. Also notable is that more good candidates are now staying on here post-GCSE, and school keen to build on this. Sixth form has doubled in size over last three years, with retention at 86 per cent. New sixth form centre opened in September 2009. A range of new A level subjects – philosophy, politics and law – sit alongside the traditional. £80,000 spent on upgrading ICT.

All do French in Year 7 and Spanish on offer from Year 8. An assortment of trips and visits, home and abroad, support both the curricular and extra-curricular programmes. Head has introduced discrete subject setting – you are setted separately for each core subject, not, as before, put in the same set for everything irrespective of your varying aptitudes. He has also moved to a two-week timetable of one-hour lessons – more flexible and better for consistent work.

Used to be known as a bit of a special needs school but has very much shaken off this image now, so what's the current attitude to SEN? 'Definitely a bit wary; we'd love to be fearless, sing from the hills about our provision, but we're not quite in a position to be. When I arrived I was worried by the emphasis on special needs; I'm more relaxed about it now. We're certainly not a special school but we are very good at mild/moderate special needs, across the whole ability range. Parents of children with special needs choose schools like ours precisely because they're not full of special needs kids.' Currently 15 per cent of students have some kind of help, mostly for dyslexia or dyspraxia, but other SEN will be considered. Readers, writers, laptops, extra time in exams, dedicated provision, help in and out of class demonstrate continued commitment to children with difficulties who will get a lot out of a Cokethorpe education.

Very much a school where a tradition of learning support benefits all. Teaching is often (though not universally) sparky, practical, hands on, teacher:pupil ratio is good – most classes 5–15 pupils and never more than 20, and pupils stress teachers are willing to give extra help whenever it's needed. Head wants good 'middle order batsmen' with a starry top and a slower bottom and aims 'to get the best out of every child'. 'I'm interested in maintaining the 20-60-20 balance of the school, 20 per cent very able, 20 less able and 60 from the middle. We assess children but we're not academically selective – we want children with a spark, a personality. If a child has a sense of humour, of adventure, I'd far rather that than a mousy egghead who will contribute little to the place.' So what of those who say special needs kids can't get a look in? Priority places go to those from the junior school and invariably there are far more applicants competing for the 20 per cent of places offered to the less able than for the most able, for whom there are a handful of schols. The ablest are stretched and extended through activities and events, including extra classes in the things they're good at. 'We want to challenge and extend the children, see what they're capable of. What's more, some kids have special needs and are gifted and talented – it's good they get extra time to do what they are successful at, as well as where they have problems.'

Games, Options, the Arts: School has 150 acres of parkland and a vast sports hall. Clay-pigeon shooting is a passion here – available four times weekly and very popular. Lots of pitches, tennis courts and brand new Astroturf, climbing wall, multigym. Head has reintroduced house system, importantly, for competitive sports, and believes in excellence – 'We're élitist about our sports'. Flexible curriculum possible for those whose sporting standard requires more intense training. Rugby, netball, tennis, hockey, football, golf, fencing, riding (very successful equestrian team), canoeing, aerobics and judo a sample of sporty offerings.

Music department revitalised over recent years. All Year 7 encouraged to take up an instrument. Good DT workshops. Art dept expanded 2009 and packed with striking examples of student work in an array of different media. Graphics, textiles and photography all on offer. Drama very popular so converting old huge maintenance hut to make new performing arts space seating 200+ a good move. Hundreds of clubs – chess, sketching, cookery, design, film, even neuro-linguistic programming and worldwide wines (for 16+); something for everyone and if not, you can start your own!

Background and Atmosphere: An attractive, solid-looking Queen Anne house – The Mansion – greets the visitor. It's set in acres of flattish but undeniably rural parkland with grazing sheep, and even has its own Norman church – St Mary the Virgin – a hundred yards or so from the house and used for services and assemblies. The mansion fronts four courtyards, around which teaching takes place, mostly in subject blocks. Some new buildings have been added to complete the quadrangular arrangements – all sensitive and in the appropriate Cotswold stone. New 'magnificent' dining hall, 2009, seats 250. Lovely features like a centrally placed little round building – formerly a dovecote, now the school shop – and a rather grand arch to one side of the estate.

Site is well maintained and orderly. It still feels something like the boarding school it was until 2003 but also something like a fee-paying, mixed comprehensive which, essentially, it now is. When we visited, the entire school gathered in the quadrangle for a mid-morning recital by the Madrigal choir. For a moment, you almost expected Morse to appear! The sweet notes pleasured the ear, but, alas, the eye discerned an array of legs, some with tights, some socks, some bare, a few shirts out, the odd tie askew, though all (except nattily suited sixth-formers) in smart blazers and pinstripes – a successful move by the head in his drive to create a more trad public school ethos.

Entrance is lovely and were it a country house hotel, you'd be impressed. What it lacks is the sense that you are entering a school – feels more like a hotel reception. More celebration of pupils' work and achievements would not go amiss.

Pastoral Care and Discipline: Joint RC and C of E foundation underpins ethos. The school has long had local reputation for good pastoral care and Ettinger Effect – 'I want pupils to stand up when I come into the room and feel proud of their uniform; I can't stand children eating and walking; I can't stand mobile phones' – hasn't detracted from that; if anything it's focused the pupils. Refreshing that despite the ever-increasing numbers, older and younger pupils agree the overwhelming plus of the place is its friendliness – 'It's not cliquey here. I belong to different groups for different things. We know everyone. Pick out someone and we can tell you something good about them – we have younger ones in the houses, we see them getting certificates in assembly or know them because they're someone's kid sister'. Younger ones wholeheartedly agree: 'There's a family atmosphere – you don't get left out. I was petrified at first but I soon settled'. School lunches look appetising and mainly healthy.

Pupils and Parents: From wide catchment area; school busses in 400+ children – a real plus for working parents. Children come from as far as Oxford, Swindon, Wantage,

Witney and all villages round about. Some complain of the long school day – it can be tough if you have an hour's journey each way on top of a school day that ends at 5.00pm. Wide range of families – old school to sizeable proportion of first-timers. Parents increasingly involved – head sees this as essential.

Entrance: Getting tougher – days of taking anyone are long gone (waiting list operates). Entrance exams in maths, English and VR assessed along with applicant's social and sporting skills, so other aptitudes taken into account. 'If he's a fantastic fly-half I'd be interested even if he's not academically strong – the question is, what can he offer the school?' says head. Criteria for sixth form entry also upped – must have 5+ GCSEs at A*–C including maths, English and a science plus good grades in your A level subjects. Seniors from outside come at 11 via Chandlings, The Manor, Ferndale, Our Lady's Abingdon, or, at age 13, from Abingdon Prep, The Dragon, New College School, Christ Church Cathedral School and St Hugh's.

Exit: Some to redbricks, e.g. Manchester, occasional one to Oxbridge, most to newer universities, e.g. Sheffield Hallam, Oxford Brookes. Handful embark on a gap year or pursue vocationally orientated courses. Care taken at application stage ensures almost all get university of choice.

Money Matters: Lots of means-tested schols/bursaries of all kinds – academic, art, music, sports, drama, classics, modern langs, and all-rounder. Minor schols for two years from 11. All gauged on exam performance and interview with head.

Remarks: That this is such a changed school is no mystery: teamwork, hard work and, importantly, a head who knows what needs to be done – who won't rest until the job is complete (actually who'll probably never rest, regardless). If Morse were in town he'd discover one of Oxford's gems; that it glistens but isn't pristinely polished adds to its appeal.

Colchester County High School for Girls

Norman Way, Colchester, Essex, CO3 3US

• Pupils: 785 girls, all day • Ages: 11-18 • Size of sixth form: 230
• Non-denom • State

Tel: 01206 576 973
Fax: 01206 769 302
Email: office@colchestergirls.essex.sch.uk
Website: www.colchestergirls.essex.sch.uk

Headteacher: Since 2010, Mrs Gillian Marshall, previously deputy head at the mixed comprehensive Notley High School, Braintree. Took over from the long-serving Mrs Ward.

Academic matters: The buzzy, bright girls here have fought their way through the rigorous Consortium of Selective Schools in Essex 11+ exam, the cream of the crop. No need for setting then – apart from the addition of an accelerated maths class – and girls are taught in their form groups until the end of Year 9. French and German are begun in Year 7 and Latin kicks in in Year 9. Sciences are taught separately and are popular A level options – reflecting CCHS' status as a specialist college for both science and languages.

Taking 11 GCSEs in the norm and most get A*–C in every one with 81 per cent scoring As and A*s in all. A level results are impressive across the board – 90 per cent of those taking it regularly achieve an A in maths, for example, but so do nearly all of those entered for A level PE. 84 per cent of sixth formers take A level critical thinking as part of the school's ambition to promote independence of mind.

Such stellar achievement in all areas can cause anxieties, but bringing perspective is something the school does well, according to parents. 'Girls here are in a relatively small ability range but it's easy for them to forget that,' said the previous head. 'We have to remind them that they would be top anywhere else and it doesn't matter where you are here.' Only 20 girls are on the school's SEN register and a variety of needs are represented. An assistant headteacher takes on the additional role of SENCo and support is generally offered on an individual basis – there is no in-class assistance as the school does not have teaching assistants. However staff themselves are constantly updated on individual students' needs and the school works closely with students, parents and the Student Advisor and external agencies if need be.

A recent Ofsted report was largely flawless – with a barb about a requirement for more publicity about charity work, smacking of desperation to find a hole to pick. Nevertheless, it ruffled the feathers of the school, who retorted, 'Initiatives here are for educational purposes, not to tick a box.' Indeed there is plenty of community cohesion, with CCHS sixth formers teaching philosophy classes in local primary schools and running courses to boost the educational aspirations of secondary school girls in CCHS's capacity as a Leading Edge school. As well as having close local ties, there are international links, most notably with Japan, where girls undertake science projects with Japanese students under the guidance of professors from Kyoto University. 'There's a huge amount going on and they're the links we think it is important to make.'

Games, Options, the Arts: Numerous musical groups, ensembles and choirs, many instigated by the girls themselves. The regular music exchange with a school in Giessen, Germany is a popular trip. Drama also strong – when we visited an external drama coach was taking a class in the hall for a lively session. The lack of facilities does not hamper the girls' sporting performance – they like to win on the hockey pitch, netball court and athletics track. While the elite are picked and trained in squads, those with more enthusiasm than talent have many active clubs to choose from, including dance and fencing. Most clubs take place at lunchtimes due to travelling home arrangements and there is a huge range, from the academic and the vocational to the fun, some run by senior pupils, and staff are generous with their time and encouragement. D of E is thriving with many golds.

Background and Atmosphere: CCHS was founded at the turn of the century but relocated to its current site, a campus setting on a quiet road a mile from the centre of Colchester, in 1957. A collection of rather characterless buildings typical of that era, which have to be made the best of. The main teaching block is chilly in winter and boiling in the summer, despite an attempt to insulate the vast windows. There is the superb new m-School, which encompasses the so-called 'music, mathematics and mind' departments. The 'mind' is the critical thinking department, which has a showcase high-tech i-Lab where students scrawl their thoughts on the wall and then recall them at a later date for further study. The music department has two large teaching rooms, a recording studio and a computer suite fitted out with Apple Macs, keyboards and composition technology. Maths has – well, what do mathematicians need anyway?

Sixth formers have their own common room and private study area. Gym is pleasant and high-ceilinged. There are playing fields on-site, though rather bleak, and the outdoor pool was distinctly verdant when we visited, but is set to be spruced-up with a glass enclosure to allow year-round use. Picnic benches are arranged on the scant greenery in between blocks for girls to gather on at breaks.

The girls rave about the food and a one-man band buys fresh every day and even tries out recipes suggested by the girls. A bright dining space serves hot and cold food, paid for in the old-fashioned way, and girls who have lunchtime clubs can request cold food to be speedily collected and eaten wherever is most convenient.

This is an ordered environment, but without the stuffiness that extremely academic schools sometimes find it hard to avoid. Cloakrooms are reassuringly untidy although each year group has PE bags in a specific colour and there are lockers for books. Girls are credited with the self-discipline to get themselves to and from lessons promptly and to keep on top of their belongings without the need for endless rules and recriminations – a real plus point say parents.

Pastoral Care and Discipline: With so much talent in a relatively small space, CCHS could be something of a pressure cooker environment; however, locally this is known as one of the more laid-back of the local grammars. The strategy is to use PE and PSHE lessons to teach coping skills, approaches to revision and even breathing exercises at crucial times. School is in any case fairly relaxed, with teachers preferring to 'check up on pupils' effort rather than their attainment', which has prompted some interesting discussions with Ofsted inspectors.

The girls themselves say they feel well supported by the staff, who are generally long-serving and who move up through the years with their charges as far as the sixth form. Girls appear to get along happily together. Self-discipline is exemplary, and although a system of detentions was introduced in 2002 it is rarely called into play, and there have been no exclusions for more than 15 years.

Pupils and Parents: Girls here come from around 65 different primary schools across central and north Essex and south Suffolk and from varying backgrounds. A handful have English as a second language, although their fluency has enabled them to get through the entrance exam. Statemented pupils tend to have hearing or sight impairments.

Many girls are extraordinarily bright and that can bring its own challenges, although the school emphasises that 'we enjoy the eccentrics, the quiet girls and those who don't approach things in the normal way – we think that's refreshing and a great gift so we encourage them and allow them to develop.'

Keeping in touch with parents is not easy given the geography, but there is a monthly enewsletter and parents are largely supportive of school events and also raising money for badly needed new buildings – the fund for which is presided over by old girl, gardener and writer Beth Chatto OBE, who hosts an annual concert in her gardens.

Entrance: One of the top-performing schools in the UK, it's no surprise that places are highly sought-after, though seemingly less of a scrum than at the grammars closer to the capital. Entrance is granted to those 112 girls who choose the school and perform the best in the notorious Consortium of Selective Schools in Essex 11+ exam, one half verbal reasoning, the other maths and English in equal part. The minimum entry requirement is AAAABB for the 15 students coming in for the sixth form, including English language and mathematics and grade A/A* in the subjects to be taken at A level, and many travel from far and wide, some lodging in Colchester for convenience.

Exit: Only one or two choose not to go on to university, and around 20 – only slightly less than a fifth of the cohort – win Oxbridge places. Law, medicine and academia are established career paths.

Remarks: A relaxed and purposeful academic school, where self-motivated high-achievers are gently steered towards success.

Colchester Royal Grammar School

Lexden Road, Colchester, Essex, CO3 3ND

• Pupils: 780 boys and girls (girls in sixth form only), all day, apart from 30 sixth form boarders (boys only) • Ages: 11-18 • Size of sixth form: 300 • Christian • Fees: Boarding £6,900-£9,000 pa • State

Tel: 01206 509 100
Fax: 01206 509 101
Email: info@crgs.co.uk
Website: www.crgs.co.uk

Headmaster: Since 2000, Mr Ken Jenkinson (fiftyish). Educated at Danum Grammar School, Doncaster. BA in French and German from University of Leeds and MA in French from University of Sheffield. Started his teaching career in a Doncaster comprehensive, then moved on to Blundell's where he was head of modern languages. Five years as deputy head at Colchester Royal Grammar before becoming head. Enjoys sport (football, rugby and cricket), travel and spending time with his family. Authoritative but pleasant and friendly manner with pupils. Married to Jackie, a librarian currently working as a school secretary. Two daughters.

Academic matters: Extremely high academic standards. No setting in Years 7 or 8. French and maths setted from Year 9. 'But this is only a question of pace,' says the head. 'Set four pupils will still be expected to achieve A* at GCSE.' French and Latin in Year 7, choice of German or Greek in Year 8. One of the very few state schools to offer Greek – the Greek government funds a teacher. For a state school, an above average number go on to study classics at university. Fantastic results at GCSE and A level; regularly among the top five state schools in the country for A level results. Occasional SEN pupil with physical disabilities; any EAL pupil will have had a high enough standard of English to pass the selection tests. Top school for A level results in official rankings for the last three years.

Games, Options, the Arts: Cricket and rugby particularly strong. Regular fixtures against state and independent schools. Hockey and netball for the sixth form girls. Many other sports available as extra-curricular activities including athletics, sailing and weight-training. Also plenty of non-sporting activities. Great music department with loads of opportunities for any pupil with any musical ambitions.

Background and Atmosphere: The school is directly descended from a Colchester town school that existed in 1206 and was granted royal charters by Henry VIII in 1539 and Elizabeth I in 1584. Set in an affluent residential area of Colchester, the main buildings date back to the late 19th century. Latest additions, which include a new history and classics block, a new art block and renovated music and drama facilities, fit well with the attractive old school buildings. Lovely, well-tended gardens of a standard unusual in a state school and featuring quiet and private sitting areas for pupils. Extensive playing fields five minutes' walk from the main school and a heated outdoor swimming pool. Two boarding houses with a mixture of single and double bedrooms; family-style facilities, with five resident staff members for the 30 boarders. The uniform includes a vivid purple blazer not very popular with the boys (school begs to differ!) no uniform for sixth formers but smart dress is required.

Pastoral Care and Discipline: Generally very high standard of conduct and not many discipline problems. Punishments include loss of privileges and lunchtime and after school detentions. There have been few expulsions in the head's time at the school. Zero tolerance of drugs – possession leads to expulsion.

Pupils and Parents: Years 7–11 mainly from Colchester and surrounding area but pupils travel up to an hour each way each day. Sixth formers come from further afield. The boarding house caters mainly for those who would have too far to travel to school each day and pupils from abroad; the school is very popular in Hong Kong and a member of staff visits the country each year to interview potential sixth formers. Very active parents' association raising funds for the school. Old Boys include Telegraph columnist Giles Smith, economic commentator Tim Congdon, costume designer and double Oscar winner Jim Acheson, founder of Freeserve, John Pluthero and BBC education correspondent Mike Baker.

Entrance: Highly competitive 11+ exam – 50 per cent verbal reasoning, 25 per cent English and 25 per cent maths. 'Places will be awarded in rank order to the top 96 boys in the order of merit who have named Colchester Royal Grammar School as a preference.' The exam is set by the consortium of selective schools in Essex, which has 12 members, and is held in November at the school. Candidates do not have to live in Essex. Four places available for entry to the school in Year 9, but the competition is stiff – report, plus tests in maths, English, science and a modern language. Minimum of three A and two B grade GCSEs for entry into sixth form for internal and external candidates. The 60 or so external entrants (half of them girls) also require a school report and must satisfy the school's academic requirements. Candidates for sixth form boarding places must meet the academic requirements. Overseas boarders must be British or EU passport holders.

Exit: Virtually all pupils go on to higher education; 25–35 to Oxbridge each year.

Remarks: One of the country's top selective boys' state schools, rivals many independents. Any academically able and hard-working boy (and sixth form girl) should thrive here.

Colfe's School

Linked to Colfes Preparatory School + Pre Prep And Nursery in the Junior section

Horn Park Lane, Lee, London, SE12 8AW

• Pupils: 500 boys and 250 girls, all day • Ages: 11-18
• Size of sixth form: 180 • C of E • Fees: £12,483 pa • Independent

Tel: 020 8852 2283
Fax: 020 8297 1216
Email: head@colfes.com
Website: www.colfes.com

Head: Since 2005, Mr Richard Russell (forties). Attended Methodist College in Belfast and went on to read classics at Cambridge. Teaches Latin; lives in nearby Blackheath with his wife, who is in energy markets in the City. Spent his first year surveying his new demesne before appointing new head for the prep and taking on an academic deputy head (previously head of classics at St Paul's). Frankly admits that he became a teacher because of the long summer holidays which were used to indulge his passion for archaeology, 'looking for bits of pots' in central Greece. Was at Sevenoaks for 15 years. Co-ordinator of the IB there which 'was a fantastic challenge'. Needed to sell it to parents and universities, which he did with such success A levels were dropped and numbers doubled. Not planning IB at Colfe's as it 'only makes sense in a multi-national school'. He is, in fact, a fan of A levels – 'very British. They suit British kids and are a tremendous preparation for university'. Diversity/alternative pursuits can be created in a school in other ways, he avers. Mr Russell is quietly ambitious and clearly intends to raise the profile of his school by the example of his own high standards, undoubted courtesy and clear vision for the future.

Academic matters: Good variety of subjects offered and all pupils study for a total of nine or ten subjects at GCSE. At least one option must be a modern language (French, German or Spanish) and another has to be history or geography. English, maths and science also compulsory. All pupils study Latin for their first two years. Good results and improving.

The sixth form aims to offer a competitive but social environment with a wide range of subjects including psychology, medieval history, economics, further mathematics, Latin. Media studies has a strong department and is a popular choice. Most pupils take four subjects to AS and then three or four to A level. The two years of sixth form are designed to act as a bridge between school and the more independent style of learning expected at university. 70 per cent A*/A/B grades in 2010 and the head has assumed personal responsibility for raising Oxbridge offers above single figures.

Games, Options, the Arts: Sport is big here – all pupils have an afternoon of games every week. At the heart of the school lies an enormous games pitch, and a huge indoor facility has recently opened with a 25-metre swimming pool, fully-equipped gym, cricket nets, goal posts, basketball and netball courts. The junior school, parents and local community make good use of it too. New Astroturf busy with tennis or football. Minutes away by minibus is the Leathersellers' – a dedicated sports field with five rugby pitches, athletics track and cross-country course. Inter-house matches throughout the year and matches in all sports organised against other schools. Netball very strong at present.

A wide range of inter-house competitions – quizzes, chess, drama, concerts. Fantastic new centre for musical and dramatic productions with state-of-the-art equipment, a computerised music room and individual sound-proofed practice studios. Swing bands, orchestras, choirs. For the visual arts a dark room for photographers, an amazing art room displaying students' work, a kiln for ceramics. On top of this there are expeditions, cultural visits, sporting tours and clubs after school or during lunch. Something to suit everyone.

Background and Atmosphere: Abraham Colfe, Vicar of Lewisham, founded the school in 1652, 'To educate the poor boys of Blackheath'. The school was then left in trust to the Leathersellers' Company whose livery members make up the governing board. Colfe's will runs to several volumes and is extremely detailed, even to the point of dictating the length of the Colfe sermon to be delivered on the second Sunday in June! When the Lewisham site was bombed the school was evacuated to Tunbridge Wells and then Somerset. It came to its present site in the 1970s as a state grammar school. Opted to go independent rather than comprehensive in the late 1970s. The rather dull brick buildings give a false impression – inside it is much less sprawling suburbia and rather more 'rus in urbe'. There's an abundance of greenery with trees and shrubs and plants dotted amongst the classrooms. Atmosphere is one of calm and order and quiet purpose.

Pastoral Care and Discipline: Pupils are relaxed and self-disciplined. Pastoral care is excellent. Head views it as important that all staff are prepared to go the extra mile. Has been fully co-ed since 1999 and is the better for it. No bullying – 'It's just not what we do here,' says a pupil. School counsellor is very active and is the first port of call if pupils have a problem. Excellent links between home and school: email addresses of each head of year available to parents and regular correspondence takes place via homework diaries. School rules are strict – dress and appearance regulations are upheld. Pupils remain on site throughout the day except for sixth formers who may leave during the lunch hour only. Chewing gum, mobile phones and ipods are banned.

Pupils and Parents: Mostly middle class professionals from Blackheath and Lewisham, which are both a mile either side of Lee. Lee itself is a leafy suburb 20 minutes by train from Charing Cross. Social variety is lacking since the abolition of the assisted places scheme, but the head is keen to address this and is actively recruiting pupils from local state primaries – he doesn't want to operate in a middle class monoculture, and sees it as a significant part of his job to raise awareness of the school in places like Kidbrooke and Peckham; he is currently setting up a working relationship with the Damilola Taylor Trust. Emphasises that bursaries are not handed out just for being poor – you also have to be very good indeed.

Majority of the families have two working parents so school opens at 7.00am and the library is supervised till 6pm. The library is also available to pupils during study leave – not an option offered by every school.

Entrance: 11+ entry by interview and school reference followed by January entrance exam in maths and English. Moderately over-subscribed. Places in the sixth form are offered on the basis of interview and reference and predicted results at GCSE.

Exit: Incredibly varied, from film studies at Canterbury to English at Oxford.

Money Matters: Very good value. The less-than-attractive buildings have a hidden advantage for parents – they are cheap to maintain so overheads are kept low. Scholarships and bursaries: academic, sport and music.

Remarks: A school that is going somewhere. A happy, uncomplicated atmosphere where the needs of the pupils come first.

The Collegiate Foundation

Linked to Chapter House Preparatory School in the Junior section
Linked to Queen Ethelburgas College in the Senior section

Thorpe Underwood Estate, York, YO26 9SS

• Independent

Tel: 0870 742 3300
Fax: 01423 333 912
Email: info@queenethelburgas.edu
Website: www.queenethelburgas.edu/private-school.htm

Remarks: See Queen Ethelburga's.

Collingham Independent GCSE and Sixth Form College

23 Collingham Gardens, London, SW5 0HL

• Pupils: 220 in total: 30 in GCSE dept, 190 over two years in senior dept; roughly 50/50 boys and girls • Ages: 14-20 • Size of sixth form: 190 • Fees: £16,650 pa • Independent

Tel: 020 7244 7414
Fax: 020 7370 7312
Email: london@collingham.co.uk
Website: www.collingham.co.uk

Head: Still under the thriving leadership of Gerald Hattee, who has been in the position since 1989. Educated at St Peter's, York and read history at Keble. Teaches history and politics. Very amiable man who clearly has a good rapport with the students, whose welfare is paramount.

James Allder, BA, is in charge of the GCSE department in Queen's Gate Place. A keen skier and snowboarder.

Academic matters: Offers an impressive range of subjects and in any combination. Popular ones are English, history, maths and economics. The modern languages department is consistently successful. Sciences strong with a number of students going on to read medicine. Overall, 97 per cent pass rate at A2.

Students can join a course half-way through and the college will pick up the threads, preparing the student for examination. Class sizes on average five at AS and A2 with a maximum of nine at GCSE. It's a long day, starting at 9.30am and finishing at 6pm with lessons taught in two-hour slots, with a short break in the middle. Students can expect six hours' tuition per subject a week at A2, with individual lessons if deemed necessary. For January retakes, this goes up to eight hours.

The college runs Easter revision courses for A, AS and GCSEs, fitting in a staggering amount of tuition, enabling a keen student to thoroughly revise three AS/A2s or six GCSEs. Not surprisingly, these are very popular.

Games, Options, the Arts: The college makes use of its location in central London, with gallery and theatre visits. Weekly football match in Wandsworth – voluntary but very popular. Students can keep fit using the facilities at Imperial College where there is a pool, gym, squash and tennis. Sport compulsory in the GCSE department. Chess has taken hold of the college; also a thriving debating group.

Background and Atmosphere: Founded 30 years ago. Housed in a seven-storey building in a leafy residential square and in good condition. Space obviously a limitation but the house has been cunningly divided up, making 27 classrooms, with three well-equipped laboratories, a digital arts studio, plus art and dark rooms. You couldn't expect the facilities to be state-of-the-art but they are surprisingly good, and combined with teaching excellence, it all adds up to the provision of a sound education. The library, with a bank of computers, overlooks the square, providing a tranquil place to study, and always monitored by a tutor. The coffee room in the basement allows students to meet and sandwiches are made to order. For a tutorial college, there is a strong sense of community that seems to go beyond the boundaries of the classroom. There is an air of inspiration about the place.

Pastoral Care and Discipline: The college prides itself on its pastoral care and is clearly good at it, cleverly bridging the gap between the care that you would expect to find at school and the degree of freedom that the students enjoy here. The support of staff is subtle but highly effective. The over-riding mood is decidedly upbeat on both the student and staff fronts. The head's door is always open and he is happy to talk. He is keen that students develop and succeed in their own interests outside school hours.

Registers taken at the beginning of each class and should a student fail to show, this is followed up immediately. Students have personal tutors for their two years, who are adept at picking up on problems and praising triumphs.

No boundaries within the building, so tutors and students are free to go wherever they like, which promotes openness. The smokers can usually be found on the pavement opposite the school at break and are not fussed when a member of staff pops out for a word. Mr Hattee prefers to have them in sight rather than round the corner.

Pupils and Parents: You might expect a London tutorial to be full of misfits. This is certainly not the case here. Many come from the larger public schools where for one reason or another it hasn't worked out. They may have found the set up just too large or the rules too confining. The friendly environment provided here is often the catalyst needed to fire the imagination and the will to succeed.

It is often the first time that the students themselves have been in part responsible for making a decision about their future education. This means that they are unlikely to fight the system and consequently put more effort into their work.

Students are largely local, travelling in by public transport. Generally there is parental support, with a parent or guardian at the end of a telephone, should the need arise.

Entrance: Students are interviewed and need five GCSE passes to get a place in the sixth form. The student also has to assure the head that he really wants to come.

Exit: Students are taken through the UCAS process with a number of presentations and given guidance with personal statements. The majority go on to the major universities and art schools. A number to Oxbridge.

Remarks: Appeals to children who haven't quite fitted into the public school system. The level of support given to students is exceptional, reflected in a growth of confidence and the desire to succeed.

Coloma Convent Girls' School

Upper Shirley Road, Croydon, Surrey, CR9 5AS

• Pupils: 1050 • Ages: 11-18 • Size of sixth form: 283 • RC • State

Tel: 020 8654 6228
Fax: 020 8656 6485
Email: sellis@coloma.croydon.sch.uk
Website: www.coloma.croydon.sch.uk

Head: Since September 1995 Maureen Martin (fifties), BA economics and history then additional RE and education management qualifications. Whilst on the foreign postings with her family, Mrs Martin has had a varied teaching career in international schools including deputy headships at Alice Smith International School, Kuala Lumpur and El Collegio Britannico, Mexico. Mrs Martin grew up locally and attended Coloma as a child. Bounding with energy and ideas, deeply committed to educating all young people to the highest possible level. She is equally committed to ensuring the staff access additional qualifications and attend continuous training programmes. Much-admired by the local and school community, she will make time for you, but she can be hard to catch as she is so very busy! Alongside all her sterling work at Coloma, she is executive principal at The Quest Academy – Coloma Trust, a non-denominational, mixed secondary school in Croydon. Last year she was involved in transforming the lives and education of primary school pupils by taking their school out of special measures.

Academic matters: Outstanding results, constantly in the top 30 comprehensive schools, specialist status for music and science. Every pupil is tracked and monitored throughout their school career to ensure that they are taught and learn properly and achieve their potential. Subject teaching across the curriculum is considered to be very strong; where weaknesses are identified they are dealt with swiftly. Years 7 to 9 are mixed ability, with setting from Year 8 for maths and sciences. Staff continually research and develop ways to assist pupils' learning and much time is given to researching work-related courses and activities. Head of economics has recently introduced the personal finance GCSE to ensure the girls understand how to manage money as well as the consequences of redundancy, unemployment and recessions. Language choices are French, German, Spanish, Latin club and Italian in sixth form; annual European trips and home-stays are arranged. Further developments include establishing a modern foreign languages network so good practice can be shared. Dual award or three separate sciences as well as food and nutrition can be studied in well-resourced labs.

Full-time learning support coordinator oversees additional support in maths, English and study skills, including organisational and life skills. Specialist staff visit the school to provide one-to-one tuition as required. Reading ages of new entrants are assessed as part of tracking and monitoring scheme for each individual pupil. Those identified as struggling to make progress regardless of ability are offered support. Inclusive sixth form centre aims to suit many, offering 28 A level choices, IB diploma and Cambridge Pre-Us; development plans include introducing some further BTec/diploma courses. Sixth formers gain experiences and skills from an extensive range of extracurricular and enrichment opportunities on-site and in partnership with other schools. Well-established tradition of public speaking, debating, musicianship and business enterprise; the girls scoop countless prizes at competitions and national events.

Whole school benefits from a managed learning environment; web tools are used to enrich learning, access homework and help home-school communications. Good mixture of male and female staff, a number of whom have dual roles. Scholarly and generous types who are willing to share their skills and talents throughout the school.

Games, Options, the Arts: Exceptional and active music department: about 400 pupils learn an instrument, two orchestras, several choirs, including gospel choirs, and large instrumental ensembles. Regular winners of awards at the National Festival of Music; around half the pupils belong to one of the choirs, which tour and perform all over the world. As a specialist music college the school has developed additional recording, composing, and performance facilities and provides courses in music technology and performing arts. Over 40 musical and dramatic events are organised every year in-house, at the Fairfield Halls and beyond. A new building for the performing arts will be completed this year and the whole school play will be reinstated, aiming to include all ages and talents, staff welcome too. Range of sporting options; standards are high, netball, lacrosse and tennis are admired and a number of girls go on to play for local and national teams. Indoor and outdoor facilities for all weathers, girls' football and cricket clubs increasingly popular, a new 3G floodlit pitch has just been installed. Dancers were recently invited to perform at Sadler's Wells. Duke of Edinburgh Award scheme runs and CCF is available as a joint venture with neighbouring Royal Russell school. Year 9s go on very popular annual trip to a trust house in Austria, where pupils can ski and spend time in an Austrian School.

Background and Atmosphere: Founded in West Croydon in 1869 by a Belgian order the Congregation of the Daughters of Mary and Joseph, led by Reverend Canon Van Crombrugghe. The school opened with three nuns and one pupil; after a couple of years they moved to a larger house. 1965 saw the move to the present large, leafy site on the edge of Shirley Hills, and in 1978 the convent became an RC comprehensive. Ever developing and striving for excellence by keeping in step with modern educational demands, Coloma was awarded music college status in 2005, high performing specialist status in 2008, and in 2009 science specialist school. A bright, clean, hard-working environment, highly structured but also welcoming and inclusive. Coloma celebrated its 140th birthday with a huge party in the Royal Festival Hall, with music specially composed by Howard Goodall. The celebrations were widely attended by members of the convent, school, friends and old girls who are also active in helping to fund-raise for school enterprises. As a Roman Catholic foundation, the school has a special ethos: 'Every member of the school community is motivated to see that they can make a positive difference through love, commitment and service. Prayer, respect for one another, integrity, kindness and compassion are greatly valued.'

Pastoral Care and Discipline: Some girls feel the school rules are a bit strict, but most parents and pupils feel pastoral care is thoughtfully planned and helps to ensure everyone feels equally valued. Home-school contact is thought to be very good, with most documentation provided in 'read friendly' format, but alas not on the website as yet. Full-time pastoral manager supports staff, ensuring the daily well-being, behaviour and progress of each pupil. Hand-picked counsellors visit the school and referrals can be made to other agencies. The PSHE programme is boosted by outside organisations and special issue days. Girls learn to be considerate, reflect on others' feelings and on the possible consequences of thoughtless actions. Staff and pupils join disabled children on the annual Easter pilgrimage to Lourdes

Pupils and Parents: No particular catchment area or feeder primary schools. Girls come from all over south London, Kent and Surrey. Hard-working, motivated and committed Catholic families who wish to support their daughter's education along with all the charitable projects Coloma is involved in. Champions of fund-raising, staff, pupils and parents organise a magnificent number of events for school buildings, equipment and numerous charitable projects. Events manager assists the charity committee coordinating events from concerts, fetes, readathons and quizzes to the annual rag week, which alone can raise as much as £28,000. Coloma helps to fund a school in Uganda, in addition to supporting other charities at home and abroad. Pupils become very pro-active in creating new ideas and opportunities to fund-raise. Christmas fete has included an ice rink. Unsurprisingly, many girls choose to work in education, social and caring professions.

Entrance: At 11+ non-selective; statemented and looked-after children and then a points system to assess practising Catholic credentials. Entry into the sixth form includes students of other denominations and faiths, who are in sympathy with the ethos of school

Exit: Majority stay for the sixth form; leavers head for local colleges or co-ed schools. At 18+: almost everyone to university; approximately 35 per cent to Oxbridge and Russell group.

Money Matters: Most parents make a voluntary contribution to enhance the quality of their daughter's education.

Remarks: Truly remarkable school for its vision, academic achievements, charitable activities and contribution to society. Considering it operates on a budget less than 40 per cent of an independent school, must also be commended for economic genius. Produces well-rounded, articulate and innovative young women.

Colyton Grammar School

Whitwell Lane, Colyford, Colyton, Devon, EX24 6HN

• Pupils: 800 boys and girls • Ages: 11-18 • Size of sixth form: 205
• Non-denom • State

Tel: 01297 552 327
Fax: 01297 553 853
Email: admin@colytongrammar.devon.sch.uk
Website: www.colytongrammar.devon.sch.uk

Head Teacher: Since 2008 Paul Evans BEd, having served 11 years at the school as deputy head, which he described as a 'long apprenticeship'. As the school's 2007 Ofsted report enthused, 'Leadership and management at all levels are outstanding', and Mr Evans is set to continue to build upon the strengths of the school. He trained at the College of St Mark and St John before teaching in comprehensive schools in Newbury and Reading. Head of biology, then science and finally senior teacher before moving to Colyton in 1997. Married to an assistant head teacher with one daughter who is considering following in her parents' footsteps.

Academic matters: Revolutionary. In 2005, the school struck out on an exceptional path by introducing a three-year sixth form. GCSE work begins in Year 9 and exams are taken a year early at the end of Year 10. All pupils then spend three years studying for the English Baccalaureate, which is similar to the IB but incorporates A level study. All students follow a programme leading to three or four A levels plus A level general studies and AS critical thinking. The idea is to give pupils more breadth, depth and time for community service and extra-curricular activities. Students will all complete an independent extended study as part of the over-arching baccalaureate diploma. We applaud the school's courage in overhauling its exam schedule. Only drawback is that pupils can be boxed in – no one can enter the sixth form from outside because they will be a year too old; Colyton pupils can't leave after GCSE because they will be a year too young for courses elsewhere. Students could transfer to other institutions but virtually none choose to; the school is not seeking to take in extra students to the sixth form.

Test results all levels all subjects, are eye-poppingly brilliant. As the school's Ofsted gushed, 'The performance of this outstanding school continues to improve and accelerate away from that of similar schools.' Every year pupils win examination board top performing students awards, often in a range of subjects. Science and maths results particularly good in this science specialist school. Annual successes in National Mathematics Challenge, British Biology Olympiad, Physics Olympiad and Chemistry Top of the Bench (national finalists). Colyton students have represented Britain in the International Physics Olympiad. Exchange links fostered with France and Germany extend to work experience to encourage linguists. Huge emphasis on helping pupils to become good learners, which means allowing pupils to take intellectual risks. All pupils study critical thinking. Breadth is valued – at this bastion of full-on academia not a single pupil did three sciences at A level last year. Staff superb – despite off-beaten-track location, teachers queue up for positions in this intellectually rewarding state school environment. Setting for maths, sciences, English and French. Class sizes pushing upper limits – GCSE up to 30, A level up to 25 but average 17.

Provides assistance to two statemented profoundly deaf children – something of a mini-specialisation here. Beyond this, few customers for the SEN department. An Ambassador School of the National Academy for Gifted and Talented Youth.

It is a trust school working in partnership with the University of Exeter and four other south-west selective schools. Has just been recognised by the DfE as a highly performing specialist school. Already works in partnership with local selective and comprehensive schools as the lead partner in a Leading Edge partnership programme and has recently taken the role of Leadership Partner School as a third specialism.

Games, Options, the Arts: Pupils carry their high-achieving spirit onto the games field: girls' netball and hockey very strong; ditto boys' football, cross-country and cricket. Good sporting facilities with dedicated playing fields, newish sports hall and floodlit all-weather Astroturf for tennis and hockey. Recent acquisition of a neighbouring field has doubled the area for sport allowing more scope for future athletes and cricket and soccer fixtures. Definitely not what one could call a thrusting rugby school, but the game is played and Years 9 and 10 had a recent rugby development tour to Dublin and Barcelona. Students gain county honours in many sports and some participate at national level in hockey, golf, sailing and fencing.

Music said to be good; 40 per cent have peripatetic tuition with some excellent results. GCSE/A level results were flagging a bit but GCSE over 80 per cent A*/A this year, A level nearly 70 per cent A*/A grades, so catching up fast. Choir is popular and enjoys a national reputation, performing at the Barbican, Westminster Abbey, the Edinburgh Festival and overseas, e.g. Dublin, Venice, Prague, Santiago de Compostela. Orchestra, wind, brass, jazz bands etc with lots of concerts. Visits from performers of international standing. Drama studio lives in what, in another age, was the dainty main school hall. Huge Cottrill Hall (once the school sports hall) now used for exams, theatrical productions and assemblies. Bright new art centre opened in spring 2006, with lots of teaching and display space plus a darkroom and kiln. Additional science laboratories and extended sixth form accommodation opened September 2008. Also new study areas for sixth form, two new labs and totally refurbished technology centre with CADCAM facilities opened. Loads of extra-curricular activities – a pleasant surprise to some parents who expected the school to have a narrower focus. Young Enterprise regional winners and national champions of both the National Magistrates' and the Crown Courts' mock trial competitions. Regularly enters at least two teams in Ten Tors and Exmoor Challenge. D of E popular too with, for example, 80 per cent of Year 9 following the Bronze programme. Healthy Schools Status 2006, Silver EcoSchools Award 2008 and has recently been awarded the International Schools Award.

Background and Atmosphere: Founded 1546 in a room over the porch of Colyton parish church, CGS is one of the oldest state schools in the country. Current school was built in the 1920s, originally to educate 100 pupils. Main building now has dozens of additions, but school remains surprisingly small – everyone knows everyone – and absolutely no plans to expand. Attractive low-level redbrick school with views of the sea from playing fields. Constant renovation and upgrading, e.g. chemistry block refurbished to cutting edge, 2005. Happy atmosphere which comes from the top, with teachers made to feel integral part of team. Every pupil we spoke to emphasised the superb relationships between themselves and their teachers. Trust is also highly valued with e.g. pupils being allowed into ICT rooms without supervision. School lunches have benefited from healthy eating push, but head would love a bigger canteen.

Pastoral Care and Discipline: In this Devon backwater (build in an extra half hour to unearth the school if you plan to visit – and remember, it isn't in Colyton!) social problems are not what one might call entrenched. There have been exclusions but so rarely that the head cannot remember the last one. Backpacks are strewn thither and yon with no fear of them being pilfered (the last case of theft was three years ago). Pupils, by and large, aware of their good fortune in being here – they value the school and work hard. Uniform worn neatly: shirts tucked in; hair plain; hardly any make-up or jewellery. Either we have entered a time warp or pupils are less fashion-conscious and streetwise than at most schools. Oddballs and individuals well-accepted. Super sixth form centre and lots of sixth form responsibilities, e.g. organising assembly, extra-curricular activities, teaching in primary schools.

Pupils and Parents: A mix, but largely rural families living in stable communities, away from the glare of big city life. Families apply from over 100 primaries; many will move to the area if their child wins a place. Others travel from as far as Dorchester, Taunton and Exeter. About 50 per cent of students live in Axe Valley and the parents' association organises buses. OBs include Sir Rex Richards, President of the Royal Society of Chemists and former Vice Chancellor of Oxford University; Ben Way, a Young Entrepreneur of the Year who, despite being dyslexic, made his first million in his first year of work.

Entrance: The school maintains it is not highly selective: 35–40 per cent of those who take the test will qualify for a place. Still, a pupil must come in the top 25 per cent of the ability range nationally (NFER maths, English, VR) to be considered (a few get in on other evidence, even if they don't quite make this hurdle). If more qualify than the 120 available places allow for, preference is given to those with siblings at Colyton. Biggest feeders are the half-dozen nearest state primaries, but pupils come from a 30-mile radius, including a few from prep schools.

Exit: At least 95 per cent of the sixth form enter university, with 10–15 to Oxbridge. A wide range of degree courses but more than average head for science, medicine and engineering. A few leave after GCSEs, mainly because of families relocating.

Remarks: Unique rural grammar with astonishingly fine exam results. Ground-breaking three-year sixth form. Worth moving house for.

Comberton Village College

West Street, Comberton, Cambridge, Cambridgeshire, CB23 7DU

• Pupils: 1,412 • Ages: 11-16 • Non denominational • State

Tel: 01223 262 503
Fax: 01223 264 116
Email: thecollege@comberton.cambs.sch.uk
Website: www.combertonvc.org

Headmaster: Since 2001, Mr Stephen Munday MA PGCE (mid-forties). Read economics. Previously director of sixth form and deputy head County High Saffron Walden. Young-looking and refreshingly unaffected – reference to the recent outstanding Ofsted provokes a boyish glow. Well liked by all, his tendency to deliver morning assemblies with a fair amount of movement is affectionately referred to as 'the Munday dance'. Attends all those conferences that successful heads seem to frequent and now also works for the DfE on several projects. However, he still manages to teach AS economics after school – his spacious, egalitarian office is home to a rather menacing portrait of hero Keynes, a gift from a past pupil. Married with three children and a regular church-goer. Enjoys playing sport and supports Everton 'even though they never win'.

Academic matters: Mantra of achievement backed with an array of targeted interventions – 'They do jump in if kids are underachieving'. Cracking GCSE results for a comprehensive: 45 per cent 5+ A*/A and around 80 per cent 5+ A*–C, rising to about 90 per cent if English and maths aren't included. Pupils value contributions from their peers and lessons are predominantly interactive – teacher-led questioning and comments from the floor the norm. Impressive commitment to languages with Spanish taken by all and productive links with schools around the globe. Top sets have to take a second language but, according to a mole, this can be 'a bit of a disincentive' if interests lie elsewhere. Gifted and talented are stretched with extension work plus after-school options – AS economics, history and critical thinking as well as an additional maths qualification. Hard workers who aren't necessarily academic can follow vocational pathways.

Self-contained suite of rooms, within the main body of the school, is home to the calm, well-resourced SEN department – a welcoming refuge for those with educational or emotional needs. Intelligent, flexible approach with pupils attending mainstream lessons as much as possible. 'Our philosophy is neutral,' and they really do 'look at what's best for the individual'. Extensive list of supportive strategies range from in-class teaching assistants to music or Lego therapy.

Up to nine pupils with Asperger's syndrome, not necessarily from within catchment, are based in two diminutive mobiles with cheery pots of flowers softening the entrance. Work here is centred on the development of social skills while as many lessons as possible are taken in the mainstream. Good understanding that little things can upset and staff readily adapt to remove potential barriers – 'We might need to find a room where there isn't a sciency smell'.

Games, Options, the Arts: 'Sport is the best,' enthused our tour guides. Not overly competitive according to parents, but varying degrees of sportiness are well served. All the usuals plus PE and dance at GCSE and/or BTec – an individual timetable can be seriously weighted in the direction of sport. Inclusive and popular approach for the older ones. Choices include off-site golf, skiing or rowing and 'leadership' – pupils take part in sport or dance and deliver sessions to children in feeder primaries. Good facilities: several large gyms (with one for trampolines), Astro, outdoor swimming pool and dance studio where a hip hop dancer recently ran two classes – 'so much fun'. Sporting pictures done by pupils add a touch of colour to the corridors. Sports clubs are 'never cancelled because of a lack of numbers. There's usually a waiting list so we have to get our names down quickly'.

Music is enjoyed – 'We can relax but still get the work done'. Gospel, blues and reggae feature and end of term concerts, in the new performance hall decked with tiered seats, showcase musicians who're 'worth a watch'. If BTec and GCSE art are taken in tandem, timetables can be heavily biased for the arty – 'Our son is thrilled by the quantity and quality of it all'. Pleasing to see GCSE after school for those who can't fit it in on their main timetable.

Voluntary activities and clubs run from 3–4pm every day with 75 per cent of the school attending something sporty. Mandarin and Latin plus D of E, which goes from strength to strength – by the time they leave around half will have taken bronze, and if any pupils have started gold the enthusiastic teacher in charge has made arrangements for completion at Comberton.

Background and Atmosphere: Founded in the 1960s as a village college, it's continuously grown to meet the needs of several hugely popular rural villages close to Cambridge. The wider community is a gentle presence and is seen using sporting facilities or visiting a branch of the local building society based in the reception area. Functional, unassuming buildings are in good repair and amazingly we didn't spot a gob of gum anywhere – 'We just don't,' according to a pupil. Fresh, well-ordered feel to the place but, as it's now on the verge of becoming uncomfortably large, governors have set a ceiling of no more than 1,500 11–16 year olds. To cope with the demand for additional places, a federated school at Cambourne is on the cards. Excellent induction programme makes sure that 'new children aren't totally at sea' whilst the team of Year 10 and 11 mentors and system of keeping the same form tutor all the way up reinforce a perception 'that there's always someone there for you'. Pupils encouraged to be independent and responsible – all have opportunities to succeed, and when they do there's ample recognition. College has yet to develop the distinctive character which prompts leavers to say more than 'We'll miss our friends,' but this should come when the new sixth form for 350 students (major £7 million state-of-the-art building under construction) is opened in September 2011.

Pastoral Care and Discipline: 'We don't feel intimidated here' – a big school which manages to make pupils feel at ease. No herding in the corridors and staff a visible presence during break and lunch time. Each year group tends to congregate in their own designated, clearly-delineated outside area where large sweeping canopies give shelter from the elements. Pupils have a say via the school council and they've promoted recycling – there's no litter anywhere – and helped devise a school uniform which solves the problem of dangling shirts and low slung ties: neat, pale grey polo shirts and sweatshirts with yellow trim and school logo top black trousers, but Year 11s are allowed black sweatshirts – a popular but depressingly sombre ensemble.

Children are actively involved in drafting behaviour policies and the sorting of issues tends to be pupil-led. Parameters are clear and detentions known as MODs or SODs, an interesting acronym for 'serious offence detention', deal with most transgressions. Permanent exclusions, usually relating to illegal substances, very rare. Parents fully back the non-negotiable policy of zero tolerance.

Healthy eating promoted – 'we only get chips one day a week' – but parents say there's a lack of choice for the end of the queue and 40 minutes isn't long enough for a lunch break. Given the numbers involved and diminutive serving stations, they have a point. Head won't make major changes but has instigated ways to use time efficiently, e.g. cashless payment with debit cards which are topped up away from the dining area, quality vending machines and additional outlets serving hot soup and baked potatoes.

Pupils and Parents: Confident, cheerful children who know the value of education. Predominantly middle class with relatively few from ethnic minorities. Parents move to the area because of the school and pay a premium to be in catchment – stories of sealed bids or camping in rented accommodation until a property comes on the market aren't unusual.

Entrance: Admission criteria in order of importance: resident in catchment, sibling, from a feeder primary. Popularity of the school and new builds in catchment have made entrance a potential nightmare. Lots of appeals and on the odd occasion bussing of Comberton children to a different secondary. Preferred solution to the problem seems to be a new comprehensive in Cambourne which would remove the village from Comberton's catchment – not an idea that goes down well with those who bought a house in Cambourne on the basis that it was within Comberton's catchment area. As yet nothing's been decided but double check with LA about timing of possible changes.

Exit: Vast majority to one of the sixth form colleges in Cambridge, but this is likely to change with the opening of the new sixth form.

Remarks: The popularity of this well-organised comprehensive is justified. High standards and enthusiastic staff. A sixth form should give the finishing touch.

Concord College

Acton Burnell Hall, Shrewsbury, Shropshire, SY5 7PF

• Pupils: 215 boys, 205 girls; 380 board • Ages: 13-18 • Size of sixth form: 303 • Inter-denom • Fees: £24,900 pa • Independent

Tel: 01694 731 631
Fax: 01694 731 389
Email: theprincipal@concordcollege.uk.com
Website: www.concordcollegeuk.com

Principal: Since 2005, Mr Neil Hawkins MA (forties), previously director of studies at The Leys School, Cambridge. His wife, Vanessa, continues the tradition of principal's wife looking after the girls' welfare. Oversees the relaxed yet focused atmosphere that has helped Concord develop from a lesser-known international college to perhaps one of the most respected and successful in the entire country.

Academic matters: In recent years Concord's A level league table position has rocketed to the very top – currently the top co-educational independent school in The Times league. Remarkably, Concord has now left very prestigious local public schools such as Shrewsbury and Malvern in its wake, despite the fact that most of its students speak English as a second language and selection criteria are very broad indeed. The reasons for this success are many, but first amongst them is the atmosphere of focused endeavour that pervades the institution. In some sense it is refreshing that there is little attempt here to lay claim to a liberal educational agenda. The public school tradition of chapel and games field simply does not exist here and student status is a consequence of academic effort and success. This celebration of avowedly meritocratic values underlies everything the college stands for. One student secured eight A grades at A levels and she, together with other successful scholars, has her photograph and achievements prominently displayed and celebrated. Academic work is the first priority and every other aspect of college life plays second fiddle to this. To emphasise this point, all students sit internal examinations every Saturday morning. This, according to the principal, ensures a very close monitoring of progress and gets students used to the experience of examination nerves.

80 per cent of all A level teaching is science-based – no attempt to massage league table position by offering soft subject options. Science teaching facilities, already extraordinarily good, have just become even better with the building of yet four more laboratories. Up to 25 per cent of all students go on to read medicine at British universities. The balance of the curriculum in the sixth form is somewhat skewed by the emphasis on science. History and geography are now now offered at both AS and A level, to give those opting to pursue a non-scientific track more options alongside economics, law or business studies, all of which are extremely strong.

In 1995 the College expanded from its strictly sixth form identity to develop a lower school of pupils aged 13 to 16. The lower school is now over 100 strong. A significant local day element as well as Concord's international mix of students and, in atmosphere and ethos, it is very similar to the core sixth form. GCSE results have been improving with 81 per cent at A*/A and 98 per cent A–C grades in 2010 but, in truth, these results do not yet compare with the exceptional achievement of the A level scholars.

Games, Options, the Arts: A wide range of games and activities – remarkable freedom of choice. The policy is to offer what the student wants rather than demanding that the student accepts what the college can provide. Rugby was reintroduced two years ago and the college now runs a junior and a senior team. There is also a demand for kickboxing, so facilities and coaching are provided.

Some lovely art facilities are to be found in a separate house in the local village. Art is popular, not only for its own sake but also because quite a few students aspire to architecture as a future career. Despite some wonderful music facilities, only 70 pupils take individual tuition – a consequence of the primacy of academic matters. It would be wrong, though, to suggest that Concord is merely a glorified crammer and it is clear that it possesses a lively and creative cultural life. The musical standards are high and informal concerts are a regular feature of college life. A brand-new theatre/concert hall which must rate as one of the most opulent anywhere, and especially in so small an institution. Drama, too, is a regular feature of life here but, like music, the emphasis is on informality and personal choice.

This consumer-led approach to games and other activities is one of the great strengths of Concord. Students really feel that their views and concerns are central to college policy. They seem to feel that their wishes are taken seriously by the college management. However, the essentially voluntary nature of these activities means that it is difficult for the college to compete effectively with local rivals and is one reason for its relatively low profile within the local community.

Background and Atmosphere: The campus is centred on Acton Burnell Hall, which was once the family home of the Smythes, who were a leading Catholic gentry family. The building has a fascinating history and, during the Napoleonic wars, housed what later became the Benedictine schools of Ampleforth and Downside. The building is maintained to an extraordinarily high standard, and the feel is one of a particularly prestigious country house hotel. Furniture and decoration are all of the highest quality and do much to enhance the civilised feel of the college. The library is especially attractive, housed in the Strawberry Hill early 19th century Gothic chapel. The many new buildings (approximately one a year over the last 20 years or so) are sympathetically styled to fit into this quintessentially English landscape. The position of the college in the stunningly beautiful Shropshire countryside, hard by the market town of Shrewsbury and close to Birmingham, makes it a popular venue for summer schools which are offered every year to students from overseas, but not yet from the UK.

The college recruits its students from all over the globe. Around 85 per cent are overseas pupils and, of these, the largest component are from south east Asia; however, growing numbers from Eastern Europe. It is very careful to avoid developing national cliques – the various national and religious groups mix freely with a real sense of mutual respect and tolerance.

It is keen to stress its lack of any religious affiliation. However, great efforts are made to accommodate various faiths with transport provided to church and mosque if required.

Pastoral Care and Discipline: Concord has avoided the English educational obsession with uniform and traditional ethos and rules. The atmosphere is very relaxed, with students free to wear more-or-less what they want. However, this is not a free and easy institution – the students are expected to be polite and considerate of others. And they do seem to be – very much the result of old-fashioned, high-profile staff involvement. Teaching staff are all expected to be fully involved in all aspects of pastoral care, with particular responsibility given to the 12 house-parents. The principal considers evidence of such a committed attitude to be an essential component of staff selection. Rules only exist when they are deemed essential and this seems to avoid the often mindless rule bashing one sees often in some English schools. Essentially, the students are trusted but, if that trust is abused, the consequences can be dire. Smoking and drinking are not tolerated and can quickly lead to expulsion; any drug-taking will ensure the immediate departure of the offending student.

One unique feature of the college is that overseas pupils can and do stay during part of the Christmas and all of the Easter holidays, as well as half-term holidays, at no extra cost. Sometimes as many as 250 are to be found resident during these times – a remarkable service that does much to enhance the college's popularity with overseas parents.

Pupils and Parents: Generations of the same family have often attended the college. Pupils tend to hail from the richer and more socially mobile groups of south east Asia, central Asia, Africa and Eastern Europe. However, the opening of the lower school has made Concord attractive to some local families. Local prep school heads are taking the college increasingly seriously.

Entrance: An informal online test of mathematical and English ability is the only real requirement. Beware – you only get one chance!

Exit: Ten to Oxbridge in 2010, 20 going on to do medicine, veterinary science or dentistry. The vast majority go on to British universities, although a growing minority now aspire to American, Australian and European higher education.

Money Matters: The fees are very competitive – especially so when one considers that pupils may stay for most of the academic year. The college is very generous in providing bursaries and scholarships, setting aside as large a proportion of its fees as many grander and richer public schools.

Remarks: Offers a fascinating and creative alternative option to overseas pupils aspiring to a British education. Combines strong pastoral care, fabulous facilities and an extraordinarily focus on academic achievement and the sciences.

The Coopers' Company and Coborn School

St Mary's Lane, Upminster, Essex, RM14 3HS

• Pupils: 1,320 boys and girls, all day • Ages: 11-18 • Size of sixth form: 440 • Christian • State

Tel: 01708 250 500
Fax: 01708 226 109
Email: jjn@cooperscoborn.co.uk
Website: www.cooperscoborn.org.uk

Head: Since 2007, Mr David Mansfield. Previously headteacher at Southend High School for Girls and before that deputy at KEGS in Chelmsford.

Academic matters: 'This is an exceptional school of real excellence that provides a high quality of education all round,' said the 2003 Ofsted report. The school has been at, or near, the top of the league tables since its inception. Though most of the intake is of above average ability, eight local grammar schools cream off many of the 'gifted and talented', so its outstanding GCSE results are all the more impressive. 95 per cent gained five or more A*–C passes including English and maths in 2010, with 41 per cent at A or A*. A levels are equally impressive, with more than 61 per cent with A*, A and Bs in 2010. Lower attainers seem caught up in the heady atmosphere and achieve remarkably well, too.

The kids are undoubtedly keen, the staff equally so. 'The best thing about this school is the lessons,' said one randomly chosen sixth former. 'They're almost never boring.' Ofsted, too, eulogises the long-serving staff (an unusual number of whom have doctorates) and teaching in virtually every subject – 'often inspirational' – with particular praise for geography, design and technology, PE and biology.

Class sizes are large because so many parents go to appeal, and can reach 33. Roughly 25 at GCSE, 20 in the sixth form. The curriculum is traditional and academic, with a compulsory GCSE core of Eng lang and lit, maths, double science, a modern foreign language, PE and RE. Some setting in maths. One modern language (from French, German and Spanish) in Year 7, with another in Year 8, and the option to continue both to GCSE. Very large sixth form, with approximately equal numbers of boys and girls. Most stay on – despite the demanding requirements of eight GCSE A*–Cs – with As or Bs in A level subjects. As well as three A levels and one AS, all take a general studies A level. Strict homework policy with two or three subjects a night.

Few with special needs – only four with a statement – though there's a SENCo and three teaching assistants as well as a special needs assistant.

Games, Options, the Arts: Recently been awarded humanities and training school specialism status, enabling it to build an impressive new £350,000 pavilion. PE is compulsory to GCSE and all students must do some form of sport throughout their time at the school. Vast range on offer, from the trad (rugby, football, hockey and cricket), to the more rarefied (scuba diving, fencing, trampolining and skiing – taught on a dry slope nearby). 25 acres of green-belt playing fields include an indoor pool, tennis and basketball courts, a recently refurbished all-weather pitch, a sports hall and a gym. The school fields national finalists in 14 different sports.

Music a major strength, led by a passionate head of department who oversees 26 orchestras and bands. Half of the students play musical instruments. Dynamic art and drama, with a wide range of productions, from Shakespeare to *Guys and Dolls*. Careers education – 'a model of good practice,' says Ofsted – includes some enviable Year 10 placements, at Channel 4 News and shadowing an MP. Loads of trips, curriculum-related (business studies to New York, French to France etc), general (boat trips, walking weekends, skiing trips) and as part of the school's annual involvement with an international charity (e.g. to Bolivia to help build a school kitchen, to Fiji to build a dormitory, to Zambia to build a school).

Background and Atmosphere: Dating back to the 16th century, the Coopers' Company and Coborn (which is still involved with the Worshipful Company of Coopers) is the product of a merger between two East End schools which moved jointly to their current site in Upminster in 1971. The buildings – which, for conservation reasons, are crammed into one corner of the site – are low-built, seventies brick, with some glamorous modern additions – science block, music block, pavilion and art extension. Internally, not the sanitised perfection of some – with significant stretches of undiluted primrose paint – but the new-built pockets definitely give it a lift.

Teacher-pupil relations unusually friendly and relaxed. No locked classrooms, no clocks and no bells – except for the fire alarm. 'The teacher decides when the end of the lesson should be,' says the head. 'It's more peaceful that way.' Not a clock-watching school in any sense. Both pupils and staff are heavily and passionately engaged in a wide range of after-school activities. Everyone is part of the team. The school is run on a 'success culture' and the noticeboard is crammed with newspaper stories, both local and national, which attest to the wide range of pupils' achievements.

Pastoral Care and Discipline: Disciplinary problems virtually non-existent. Zero tolerance of drugs, graffiti and smoking – exclusions, too, for anybody caught smoking off school premises but still in school uniform. There's little doubt that these self-assured and motivated pupils want to please. 'You learn quickly to behave,' said one Year 12 with a smile. 'They're very strict in Year 7, more relaxed as you go up the school.' Detentions given for poor or unsubmitted work, mobile phone use and for chewing gum, but only doled out in the smallest numbers.

Assembly held every day, in the senior school twice a week. Pastoral care – both for work and personal problems – revolves round the form tutor, with pastoral time twice a day. Extensive PSHE – delivered by the form teacher – includes careers guidance and advice about university applications as well as sex and drugs and citizenship. Inelegantly named 'pastoral support manager' since September 2007 to ensure good communication between heads of year and parents.

Pupils and Parents: Very much a local school but 'local' includes the less affluent districts of Mile End, Stratford, Barking, Dagenham and Ilford as well as the residents of comfortable Hornchurch and Upminster. About one in ten from numerous ethnic minorities. The entrance procedure ensures that both children and parents are highly motivated – and seem to stay that way, with parents unwaveringly rapturous about the teaching, the head, the extra-curricular programme and the school's capacity to bring out the best in their child. The dedicated parents' association raises an average of £50,000 a year to fund such things as a new music block and interactive whiteboards.

Entrance: Massively over-subscribed. Extra-curricular activities no longer a criterion for admission; priority to looked after children, then siblings, 10 per cent talented sportspeople, those with 'exceptional need', Christians and members of other world faiths. Of the last category, 70 per cent by proximity to the school and 30 per cent who live nearest to the historic school site in Bow. About 30 join the sixth form.

Exit: A few leave at GCSE but the overwhelming majority continue to A levels and higher education, the bulk to Russell Group universities. An average of five a year to Oxbridge.

Remarks: A happy and friendly school with outstanding results and enthusiastic, confident, mature pupils who come out very well-equipped for further education and for life. Most impressively, the school manages to takes the solid middle ground and turn them into stars.

Copthall School

Pursley Road, Mill Hill, London, NW7 2EP

• Pupils: 1,100 girls, all day • Ages: 11-18 • Size of sixth form: 190 • Non-denom • State

Tel: 020 8959 1937
Fax: 020 8959 8736
Email: enquiries@copthall.barnet.sch.uk
Website: www.copthallschool.org.uk/

Head: Since 2005, Ms Jane Beaumont, who started her career here as an NQT in the early 1990s and has not strayed very far since. A geographer, who also teaches ICT, she has been assistant head/director of sixth form head at Acland Burghley school and deputy head at both The Compton and Fortismere schools. 'I live locally and that's very important. I know and understand the local community.' Straightforward, down to earth, has her school well under control. Her husband is head of a Redbridge comprehensive school.

Academic matters: Good solid results – 85 per cent five plus A*–C grades in 2010 (76 per cent including English and maths where value-added is very good). A good range of traditional and non-traditional options, including food tech, ICT and leisure and tourism. Refreshingly, everyone does a modern language to GCSE – 'We're educating young women for a global economy' – and the school got specialist language college status in 2006 to add to its business and enterprise specialism.

Plenty of opportunities to develop business acumen – 'All our enrichment activities are designed to develop entrepreneurial skills'. These may include raising money for a World Challenge expedition, baking and selling biscuits, or organising a north London-wide fashion event. PHSE includes modules in personal finance.

Wide range of A levels with maths, biology and chemistry all popular (as elsewhere, few opt for physics); 51 per cent A*/A/B grades in 2010. Psychology and sociology also get large numbers of takers. Has advanced skills teachers for science, dance and business education.

The school organises some learning by ability rather than age – able linguists can take language GCSEs in Year 9 then start on ASs; Year 10s and 12s taking BTecs in retail or child care may study together. 'It is more like a workplace, with people of different ages working together. We can offer a greater range of courses because combined age ranges make them more viable.'

Everyone is tested in Year 7 and those in need get extra help in class or in small groups. Five teaching assistants manage Year 7 and 8 pupils with complex needs who require full-time support. Learning co-ordinators keep an eye on pupils' progression and those who are struggling with work and behaviour may embark on an intensive six-week programme in the inclusion centre, which puts most back on track. The school welcomes pupils with physical disabilities, including one wheelchair-user and two with severe visual impairments. The site is not yet fully accessible, 'but we are doing our level best'. There are stairlifts and wheelchair-lifts, height-adjustable furniture and teaching assistants to lend a hand.

Games, Options, the Arts: Strong on a range of practical subjects including art, DT and performing arts, with small classes for practical subjects, state-of-the-art facilities and inventive creations on display.

Dance and drama popular and successful, with good GCSE results. Nice dance studio with sprung floor and more facilities are also planned on site. School runs summer performing arts school for gifted and talented pupils from feeder primaries. Lots of performance opportunities in school and trips to, e.g., Royal Opera House, National Theatre, Sadler's Wells.

GCSE PE is now an option, with plans to offer it at AS and A2 in future. The school has its own sports hall, netball courts and hockey pitches, with Barnet Copthall Stadium more-or-less next door and the Power League Football Centre down the road. Offers basketball, trampolining, aerobics, table-tennis alongside more mainstream sports. Inter-form and inter-school matches, lunch-time clubs, and keen sportswomen join Barnet sports clubs.

Background and Atmosphere: Leafy suburban site amidst woods, playing fields and upmarket housing. Named for Copt Hall, the local 17th century manor house, Copthall opened as a grammar school in 1936, and merged with Woodcroft School in 1971. It became a girls' comprehensive in 1973 and operated as a single school on two separate sites, until extensive rebuilding enabled its amalgamation on one site in 1996.

Some of the original buildings show their age, with narrow corridors, high windows and an assembly hall that reminded this editor of her own school days. Eight demountables in the grounds are well past their sell-by date, and with luck, and a wodge of cash, will soon be history. But the newer buildings are bright and facilities mostly good, with plenty of computers and whiteboards, refurbished science labs, well-equipped DT and art rooms, purple business suite.

Pastoral Care and Discipline: These are mostly nice, well-behaved girls. Fixed-term exclusions are relatively high, though falling; as a result, says the head, the permanent exclusion rate is very low, averaging one a year. 'Most bad behaviour is outside lessons. We draw a clear line in the sand about what is and is not acceptable behaviour. We have a very close partnership with families; we insist that parents come in after a fixed term exclusion, and they do.'

Peer mediation, buddying and anti-bullying council help to protect more vulnerable pupils. The school council is strongly involved in planning for the future: it researched healthy eating, worked on changing the structure of the school day and runs governors' meetings for parents. Has lobbied successfully for student representative as associate governor.

Pupils and Parents: A great ethnic and social mix, with lots of middle class girls and those from tough estates. 'We don't have large numbers from any particular ethnic minority or social class, which gives us a nice breadth of views.' Parents mostly very supportive, and the school runs plenty of out-of-school activities for parents as well as pupils. 'Parents hold the school in high esteem. We have a strong sense of partnership with them.' Many of the teachers have daughters at the school. 'It shows a trust in what happens here.'

Entrance: Organised by the LEA, with looked-after girls and those with particular medical or social needs first on the list, followed by siblings and then those living closest – generally less than a mile-and-a-half away. Around 30 or 40 come into the sixth form each year, many from local 11–16 schools.

Exit: Around half the year leaves after GCSEs, mostly for local colleges, many to follow vocational courses. A level leavers go on to a range of universities, old and new, including quite a few in London, e.g. Imperial, LSE, City, Westminster. Five or six a year try for Oxbridge. Popular subjects include medicine/biomedical, psychology, art/fashion, economics and business. Good work experience and careers advice.

Money Matters: Barnet is officially viewed as leafy suburbia and thus not in need of urgent government cash for, e.g., replacing portable classrooms. Stable staff but turnover not helped by the fact that they can get inner-London weighting just a few miles south. However, its specialisms bring extra funding, and supportive parents help with raising cash.

Remarks: Good, solid, popular local school with a strong sense of community that does a good job looking after its diverse pupils. Plenty of scope for developing a bent for science, languages or making a million at business, while picking up performing arts or food technology skills along the way.

Craigholme School for Girls

Linked to Craigholme Junior School in the Junior section

72 St Andrews Drive, Pollokshields, Glasgow, G41 4HS

• Pupils: 450 girls, all day • Ages: 3-18 • Size of sixth form: 030
• Non-denom but Church of Scotland roots • Fees: £3,615-£9,405 pa
• Independent

Tel: 0141 427 0375
Fax: 0141 427 6396
Email: admissions@craigholme.co.uk
Website: www.craigholme.co.uk

Principal: Since 2004, Mrs Gillian C K Stobo MSc BSc (mid fifties). Moved from High School of Glasgow, where she was educated herself. Glasgow through and through, she read chemistry at Glasgow Uni and did her Dip Ed at Jordanhill. After 'a bit of teaching' followed by about ten years raising a family, she joined the High School as part-time chemistry teacher in 1993, progressing to head of chemistry, then Assistant Rector but finding time to complete her MSc thesis on learning support for able pupils. Now she's working on her doctorate – quite a role model.

Severely smartly suited, her impressiveness is lightened by her warmth and genuine passion for girls' education. She runs the school with the senior management team of junior and nursery heads plus the newly appointed business manager, seeing the school as a 3–18 unit, friendly, purposeful with success rooted in 'knowing what girls need and providing it right through from the nursery'. Well versed in 'education-speak', she focuses on 'the real and different needs of girls' widely varied modes of learning', concerned for the 'mismatch between technology in school and how the young actually use it'. Backed by 'a strong board', she has moved the school forward, managing the inspirational £2m sports development in Pollok Park (home of the Burrell collection) and hopes that, if it becomes a training venue for the 2012 Olympics and 2014 Commonwealth Games, it will put Craigholme even more firmly on the map.

Academic matters: Still a determinedly academic and very Scottish school using Scottish Standard Grade, Intermediate 1 and 2 (subject heads taking decisions on which best prepares for Highers), Highers and Advanced Highers. Despite small numbers the school will put on Ad Highers for individuals, though contact time may be reduced and pupils use Heriot Watt's internet-based 'Scholar' for support. Impressive results and small classes (12–16). French at four for all with German from S2 and Spanish from S1, though classics have gone the way of all flesh. Specialist science and art using senior facilities for J7. Strong emphasis on science, taken as three separate subjects all through, perhaps at the expense of history etc which is studied in rotation in S1 and 2. Chemistry offers an S6 forensic chemistry module, human biology at Higher and Advanced Higher is 'particularly well suited to pupils interested in the biomedical sciences and professions allied to medicine'. Physics runs a supporting engineering club.

Smashing light-filled study library with permanent staff to hand, tucked attractively under the eaves with every conceivable study aid. It goes without saying that computers and high tech equipment, interactive whiteboards et al support every aspect of teaching as well as a discrete computing course. Classrooms well planned into subject specific areas and light, pastel painted and modern for all their pretty moulded ceilings, elegant Edwardian windows and tasteful white blinds.

Dyslexia screening with trained help and Ed Psych support. Sizeable Asian intake seldom in need of help with English. Pupils are given individual or in-class help as appropriate and the school 'prefers looking for pupil's alternative strengths to flagging weakness'.

Games, Options, the Arts: Teams, choirs, orchestras, clubs in all disciplines travel to every corner of the globe. Florida last year – choirs winning at a Disney festival – Vietnam next with geography, not to mention regular Paris, Aberfeldy, Lake District, London and more local trips for both the usual round of D of E etc and for curriculum enhancement. Strong music has forged links with Africa and Australia, hosting visits when there are no trips happening. Both the school and indeed sport for women have become higher profile in the surrounding area with the appointment of a school-based Community Sports Coach, with Craigholme spear-heading holiday sport camps, sport for Asian women and training for the 2014 Commonwealth games. Hockey, tennis and athletics have dominated with bags of success, and recently new facilities have allowed pupil initiative to pilot other areas such as netball. Drama including Shakespeare much in evidence in both junior and senior school, thanks to the Mitchell theatre's festival. Home Ec has smashing new facilities which have tempted back Year 6 to do a cake-icing module (supposedly great training in manual dexterity for dentists!)

Background and Atmosphere: Three affluent Victorian residences have been cunningly joined by purpose-built stone and glass halls to form a nearly harmonious whole. Large reception rooms and linking social spaces including a multipurpose assembly hall intersperse airy classrooms and useful gathering points. The three houses are linked by the 'Dungeon', a subterranean passage, rightly named despite cream paint and gaudy lockers. This provides wet weather access to all the buildings, gives a cafe, common-room and acres of cloakrooms cheerfully crowded with girls in unusually tidy scarlet blazers and `Craigholme tartan' kilts. Plans afoot but currently on hold 'for recession', to make the redundant gym hall into a canteen and to create much-needed play space and an extra classroom, which would create a real asset from a depressing though valuable space. Girls like the food. Up to S4 cafe attendance is compulsory though packed lunches are allowed. Sixth formers more forthcoming than younger girls and clearly enjoy their roof top common-room. Unanimously enthusiastic about the school, they insist that being all-girls is no curtailment to social life in a city environment. Seeming very much at home, they take responsibility for granted, not really surprising since some had been at Craigholme for 14/15 years! Almost every inch of wall space crammed with evidence of activity with a strong sense of the relevance of education to the local and wider community. And vice versa! News reporting a recurrent theme with the seniors – BBC Newsday contribution echoed in the J7s complete newspaper, a cross-curricular medium for some really exciting learning.

Pastoral Care and Discipline: Houses – Scottish Castles – run vertically from start of junior school and evidently evoke competitive identity, though form teachers are first point of contact for parents. Bullying prevented by careful placing and management of vulnerable pupils rather than by sanction. Teachers' care for and knowledge of individual pupils and their needs is evident. A minimum of major problems thanks to monitoring, small tutorials and good PSE.

Pupils and Parents: Largely affluent middle-class catchment spread over south side of Glasgow with three school buses and a good train service, bringing girls from as far as Cumbernauld to Ayrshire, including some areas north of the Clyde. Numbers of first-time buyers and ethnic minorities. School open from 8am to 6pm (for an extra charge up to J6). Supportive parents raise funds for the Foundation and give their time and expertise to extend the pupils' life skills. Amongst past pupils are scientist Rosalynne Watt (won the Siemens prize at Cambridge while doing PhD and the Institute of Physics Young Researcher in Combustion runner-up prize in 2007), Paediatric Emergency Physician Joanne Stirling, artist Sally Carlaw, crime novelist Louse Hughes, ex editor *Scottish Field*, Claire Grant and TV journalists, Victoria Lee and Carla Romana.

Entrance: Assessment for all, even the nursery. Main entry points J1, J7/6 and S1 though a few join S5/6. Despite the exam Craigholme will take girls 'who have abilities in other areas'. Sample exam papers not available, as 'potential rather than achievement' is the key. Numbers steady during recession though the entry pattern has changed with parents nervous of committing from the start of J1.

Exit: Almost exclusively to Scottish, predominantly west coast unis with a few to Edinburgh or Aberdeen. Lots of tough options in science, medicine, engineering, dentistry and a tranche to law, international relations or architecture. Few fall out along the way and the majority of girls from juniors form a core of about half of S1.

Money Matters: Not a rich school but will support parents in financial crisis. Approachable attitude encourages early consultation about potential problems. All assistance is means-tested rigorously (including capital/investment income). Bursaries mainly for S1 entrants and for those whose circumstances change

Remarks: Still a nice school with nice girls in a nice part of Glasgow. Impressive staff and up-to-date, open-to-change teaching and leadership.

Cranbrook School

Waterloo Road, Cranbrook, Kent, TN17 3JD

• Pupils: 450 boys, 325 girls; 245 board • Ages: 13-18 • Size of sixth form: 330 • Non-denom • Fees: Boarding £9,765; Sixth form £11,715 pa • State

Tel: 01580 711 800
Fax: 01580 711 828
Email: registrar@cranbrook.kent.sch.uk
Website: www.cranbrookschool.co.uk

Head: Since 1999, Mrs Angela Daly (sixtyish), married with two children, one of whom attended Cranbrook. Feisty, down-to-earth and approachable. She was head of Tunbridge Wells Girls Grammar School for six years and prior to that deputy head at St Bede's, Redhill. Read English at Bangor, teaches GCSE Religious Studies. Very ably supported by her two deputies.

Academic matters: At GCSE, 64 per cent A/A*; 87 per cent A–C at A level – a high quality intake and good value added, but a spread of lower grades too. A wide (but notably academic) range of A levels include Latin and music technology. Computer studies and psychology available to AS level. Students can also take vocational A levels in leisure and recreation and travel and tourism through Cranbrook's link with Angley School up the road.

Has been a specialist science school for a number of years – popular, separate sciences for all at GCSE, and good labs. Results good but not spectacular. Increasing uptake of all three sciences at A level with chemistry being particularly popular with the girls. A community science and astronomy society uses the school's new observatory, which is equipped with several telescopes. Has recently also become a specialist language school; French, Latin, German and Spanish on offer, only 20 per cent take a language A level: better than average but room for improvement. Does notably well in French. Overseas students including Chinese given the opportunity to take GCSE and A level in their native language, but any teaching is done outside the curriculum. Strong humanities: history particularly so at all levels, plus politics and geography. Setting for maths and French – some children can take these GCSEs early. Large well-equipped kitchens for pupils to learn food technology. Lower sixth are all required either to take a critical thinking AS level or do an extended project which encourages independent learning.

One part-time SEN teacher and a part-time assistant – will accept those with academic or physical special needs so long as they would 'benefit from a grammar school education' i.e. generally mild dyslexia. Irregular sessions mainly to give pupils strategies for coping. They do have one statemented child and another joining, but remarkably few pupils overall are recorded as having any level of SEN.

Lots of extra-curricular activities, sixth form lectures and visits plus a number join Young Enterprise Scheme, setting up and running their own business. All children required to do two weeks work experience after GCSEs.

Games, Options, the Arts: Philosophy of 'Sport for all' and they do it well. Lots of opportunities for everyone, compulsory games once a week plus various sports clubs.

All the usual sports. Lots of teams and lots of matches. First XV rugby team won all but one match in 2009–10 season. Recent rugby and hockey tours to New Zealand and Fiji. Outdoor heated swimming pool, squash courts, Astroturf for hockey and tennis plus sports hall with dance studio, climbing wall and multi-gym.

Active music department with a director of music and 16 peripatetic music teachers. About 180 children learn an instrument. Orchestra, big band, two choirs as well as various chamber music ensembles and rock bands. The Performing Arts Centre has music teaching/practice rooms, a chamber music room, music library, recording studio and concert rooms and a drama studio. The Queens Hall is the home of the drama department and is a fully-equipped and recently refurbished theatre, largely run by the pupils but also used by outside touring companies. Annual house play festival as well as junior, senior and whole school productions.

Background and Atmosphere: Founded in 1518 by John Blubery, and in 1574 Queen Elizabeth I granted the school its Royal Charter, still displayed in the library, and the school began its life as the 'Free Grammar school of Queen Elizabeth in Cranbrook' The school is centred on School House, a fine Georgian mansion, and has 70 acres of buildings, gardens and playing fields close to the centre of Cranbrook. Co-ed since 1972.

Went through a period of complacency and was seen to be resting on its laurels, but things seem to have tightened up recently and pupils' academic progress now monitored more closely, although one parent said that it still needs a bit more 'oomph'. It is now becoming cool to be clever again. Particularly suits proactive self-starters who do not need to be spoon-fed – if children want to do something, they need to make it happen. Struggling children are spotted early and high achievers well managed. Good food – very pleased that they have recently managed to recruit the chef from Benenden School down the road.

Pupils seem have a lot of fun here and a thriving social life. Lots of opportunities for foreign adventures – link with a community in Tanzania and every other year a group of pupils go out to work alongside local people – places much sought after and pupils have to earn money to pay their way – lots of money-making projects set up in the local area in run up to the trip. The Tanzanian teachers are then invited to come to Cranbrook to work alongside class teachers. Exchange partnership with a school in Kerala, South India plus trips to battlefield sites, Paris, Vienna and many more. British Council's International School Award for bringing the wider world into the classroom through a range of international projects. Active CCF, both an Army and RAF section with an annual camp, regular field days and adventurous training camp.

Pastoral Care and Discipline: Strong house system for day pupils and boarders. Each child is allocated a tutor on arrival who will monitor academic and activities programme as well as social progress and work closely with the head of house. Effective mentoring system in place and some senior pupils opt to become 'listeners' and are trained by the school and a local counsellor to hear and help those with personal difficulties. Students in the Lower School are expected to take part in two extra-curricular activities whilst sixth formers are encouraged but not compelled to get involved. Although non-denominational, the school has close links with the parish church and the vicar of Cranbrook is an ex-officio governor of the school. The chaplain is a member of the teaching staff and is always available for consultation and advice. Religious education studies continue into the sixth form. Bright, airy, well-decorated houses for boarders, some in small dormitories but most in study bedrooms. Activities are laid on for them at the weekends and many go to stay with the day children.

Pupils and Parents: Parents tend to be middle class professionals – some London commuters, some local. Generally interested in their children's education and hugely supportive of the school. School has strong links with parents – frequent parents' evenings and assessment reports sent home regularly. Parents encouraged to contact the tutor whenever the need arises. Very few families on benefits and very few super-rich either. Confident, natural children without arrogance. Well-spoken, chatty and polite. Children are expected to get on with it and those who are highly motivated and well-organised get the most out of their time at Cranbrook. Independence is strongly encouraged. Boarders tend to be either those just outside the catchment area who cannot get a day place plus a number from London and about a third of boarders come from overseas – anyone with a British passport or right to residency can get a free education, and this includes Hong Kong Chinese, Nigerians and anyone from the EU. EAL tuition is offered free of charge to anyone who needs it. Sixth formers given lots of responsibility – running clubs, committees, technical support in computer rooms, specialist help with lighting in the Queen's Hall etc. Old boys include: astronaut Dr Piers Sellers, Harry Hill, Tim Smit of Eden Project fame, Sir Charles Wheeler and sports commentators Peter West, Brian Moore and Barry Davies.

Entrance: Competitive entrance at 13+ (unusual for a state school). Objective NFER test (verbal and non-verbal reasoning) plus school's own papers in maths and English. Set against top 25 per cent of national ability range. Always over-subscribed but even more so in the current economic climate. Very rare for places to become available in Years 10 and 11. There may be some extra places available for sixth form entry but there is no guarantee of this, especially for boarding. Entry to sixth form is a minimum requirement of six Bs (but in reality pupils are likely to achieve far higher grades than this) plus a letter from the student's current head and a meeting in the spring term before GCSEs. Anyone who does not achieve six Bs at GCSE is asked to leave.

Day pupils MUST live within 6.2 miles from the school on normal roads – i.e. no cutting through forests in 4x4s as has been tried in the past – and houses reputedly cost £20,000 more within the Cranbrook School catchment area. This policy is very strictly adhered to and if a child has already joined the school and the governors discover a fraudulent or deliberately misleading application, the child may be asked to leave. Transfer between boarding and day and vice-versa depends on places and the 6.2 mile catchment area still applies. There is a slightly different admissions procedure for boarding places and there is often marginally less competition, but the pass mark remains the same. Owing to the 13+ start many children have been to private prep schools – lots from Dulwich College Prep School (Cranbrook). About 30 per cent come from Angley School in Cranbrook – these children will have come from the local state primaries and spend two years in the fast track at Angley before taking the entrance exam at 13+. Angley understandably does not want to lose their brightest and best at this stage and do not prepare them for the exam. Parents tend to get outside coaching. Contrary to popular belief, there is not a quota system from Angley and it is first past the post wherever the child comes from.

Exit: Some 95 per cent go on to a good range of universities and colleges. Up to seven per year to Oxbridge – lots of help with personal statements and interview practice etc. A few move into the independent sector after GCSEs.

Remarks: Feels like a public school and indeed many local parents choose it over public schools even if they can afford fees. Does not have the hothousey atmosphere of the other grammars in the area and pupils appear relaxed and even 'laid back', but there must be lots of paddling under the water to get the results they do.

Cranleigh School

Linked to Cranleigh Preparatory School in the Junior section

Horseshoe Lane, Cranleigh, Surrey, GU6 8QQ

• Pupils: 405 boys, 200 girls; about 70 per cent board • Ages: 13-18 • Size of sixth form: 235 • C of E • Fees: Boarding £27,795; Day £22,650 pa • Independent

Tel: 01483 273 666
Fax: 01483 267 398
Email: enquiry@cranleigh.org
Website: www.cranleigh.org

Headmaster: Since 1997, Mr Guy de W Waller, MA MSc PGCE FRSA (fifties), educated at Hurstpierpoint, read chemistry at Worcester College and educational psychology at Wolfson College. Cricket and hockey blue. Former headmaster of Lord Wandsworth College. Obvious enthusiasm, energy and self-confidence. Clearly doesn't feel he has to impress anybody – PR machine definitely switched off the day we looked round; also a tendency to be rather glib and flippant (he doesn't have much time for this guide!). Describes himself as a 'frustrated housemaster – definitely not a career headmaster'. Feels that co-ed schools 'reflect the world we live in'. Has no doubts that school is doing it right – right balance of boys and girls, right approach to education. Describes the school fondly as 'this crazy place with heart'. Still teaches chemistry and philosophy – believes being in the classroom 'focuses you'. Likes to be kept informed and involved with pupils and says 'the key is to have a good team in place'. Cuts something of a controversial figure amongst parents – variously described as 'charming, dynamic, running a tight ship' as well as 'distant, arrogant, autocratic, doesn't listen to parents', and all range of comments in between. Has in the past been criticised for rather resting on his laurels, but the last year alone has seen the opening of a huge new academic centre for science, modern languages and maths; the opening of a four-storey art and design building; the addition of a (fourth) all-weather sports pitch and a complete refurbishment/extension of the cricket pavilion. For others, he can do no wrong.

Academic matters: Although academia is not wholly what Cranleigh is about, results have improved greatly of late, not least because of the introduction of girls throughout the school. At GCSE 64 per cent A/A* with particular success in English, history and drama. At A/AS level, individual strengths vary from year to year but drama, economics, English, history, languages, maths and the sciences usually up there with good grades. At A level 80+ per cent A/B grades. Head says that pupils 'don't have to be superstars,' but one parent commented that the academic side is definitely hotting up and 'B and C students may struggle'. School employs a SENCo who screens all entrants, support offered for those who need it – one-to-one sessions which cost extra.

Games, Options, the Arts: 'Sport is a very important part of just about every Cranleighan's life,' says head. The sheer range of sports available is staggering – there really is something for everyone. Facilities extremely impressive – 100 of the 200 acres of the school land given over to playing fields – and include the Trevor Abbott sports centre, four all-weather pitches, one of which converts to 12 tennis courts in summer to add to the other 12 courts (all packed with Wimbledon wannabees when we visited), indoor and outdoor swimming pools, cricket and rugby pitches stretching as far as the eye can see, championship standard squash courts, six Eton fives courts, nine hole golf course, stables with own horses (pupils can bring their own horse(s) if desired), and so on. Key sports include rugby, cricket, hockey, lacrosse, netball, tennis and athletics. Football nowhere near the same emphasis as rugby – might put off a soccer-mad boy. Opportunities for all levels of talent – parents with non-sporty but enthusiastic children say that they really enjoy what they do. But certainly don't bother applying if your child absolutely loathes sport.

Art generally praised but one informed parental critic 'wasn't that impressed'. Drama particularly strong with fantastic theatre facilities (very professional tiered auditorium) and a new technical studio, and lots of chances to perform throughout the year in a variety of different shows. Musically, opportunities vast, with choirs, orchestras, individual instrument tuition, concerts throughout the year. Interestingly, though, music not hugely popular at either GCSE or A level.

Head does not feel the description 'after-school activities' is apt for Cranleigh: 'It's not an expression that fits with our ethos as here, after-school activities equal going to sleep – you have to be careful not to say "going to bed" in a co-ed school'. Quite! However, call it what you will, other than sport, the options are wide-ranging and children have lots of opportunities to fill their day – 'too many,' says head.

Background and Atmosphere: Founded in 1865 for farmers' sons, going through something of a renaissance and currently wildly fashionable – 'The school has become very popular since Guy Waller became head,' was how one prospective parent put it. Another described how it was her daughter's 'dream come true' to get in. Set in stunning grounds, it certainly fulfils every expectation of an English boarding school. Beautiful, impressive façade – breathtaking architecture which continues inside to the chapel, library, quad.

Six houses: four boys', two girls'. Boarding houses seem well designed – the newer ones obviously more swish with bright and airy feel; dorms (generally sleep four) for younger pupils (individual rooms for older ones) on the whole seem like the typical teenage bedroom – posters on wall, clothes strewn everywhere, but a homely atmosphere. Dining hall atmospheric, pupils help themselves from a choice of food – 'Rather like motorway services,' says head.

Boarding actively encouraged – majority do board, not out of necessity but desire to engage in all the school has to offer. If you are looking for a school where the kids are home at 4pm lounging around and chatting to parents, forget it – this is not the school for you. Absolutely key at Cranleigh are the sporting/extra-curricular opportunities and a long school day – whether boarding or not. A parent of a day pupil commented, 'She loves the social whirl and doesn't want to come straight home.'

Pupils encouraged to eat, sleep and breathe Cranleigh and are busy from dawn till dusk – school day is from 7.30am until potentially 9pm at night. 'If they really want to go home after that, they can,' says head. Everyone expected to participate in the school fully and the head very pro boarding and quite disparaging of what he calls 'five day' schools.

Everyone has Saturday school virtually every Saturday, and over a third of boarders stay at the weekend – although one boarding pupil said, 'We all go home at the weekend,' so it depends what a particular peer group does. A number of parents we talked to felt that there should be more weekend exeats. 'My children aren't usually home till 6.30pm on a Saturday, which makes going away for the weekend or seeing friends very difficult,' said one parent of day pupils. Boarders need to be back by 7pm on a Sunday, so an even shorter weekend for them.

Pastoral Care and Discipline: Christian values underpin school society. Huge crackdown in recent years on sloppy discipline – drugs definitely not tolerated in any way; two boys expelled recently for drugs' possession, although 'those expulsions surprised nobody,' says a not-particularly-shocked parent. Personal possession of alcohol and smoking also big no-nos leading to a variety of sanctions including gating and detentions. Persistent offenders suspended. Sex education, not surprisingly, quite high up the agenda here and romantic attachments between pupils definitely discouraged. 'Inappropriate' sexual behaviour leads to suspension or expulsion.

Head says whole feel of school is 'more like a university' and that pupils will need self-reliance. Pupils' daily pastoral care managed within each of the six houses and weekly meeting between head and tutors allows specific problems to be discussed. Bullying tackled via the tutorial/house system where pupils can talk in confidence. Individual housemasters and housemistresses have their own views on mobile phones, going out etc – it's the luck of the draw. ('Nonsense!' says the head. 'The only variation is whether the house actually collects phones overnight/during prep.') Surprisingly, considering tough line on transgression, school not a pageant of well-turned-out pupils – lots of customised uniform in evidence and funky hairstyles. Sixth formers wear suits – but for some the word 'suit' is ambiguous, and Mr Waller is trying to tidy them up. All this trendy dishevelment and urban cool seem a bit incongruous in such glorious surroundings.

Pupils and Parents: Interestingly, for a predominantly boarding school, parents tend to be from quite a small, local radius (certainly no more than 30 miles the norm) – and it's not unusual for parents to actually live in Cranleigh. Parents are 'a mix of backgrounds,' says head – although as the school is hardly cheap, presumably most are well-heeled (though Mr Waller keen to stress that a significant number have bursarial assistance). One parent said that school is 'like a movie set – full of beautiful people', and certainly pupils are particularly cool souls who come across as mature, self-possessed individuals.

Entrance: Entrance list opens in May, two-and-a-half years before September entry. Candidates and parents interviewed for interests/values/aspirations – conditional offers based on these and prep school reports, pending CE results. Very over-subscribed so can afford to be choosy about who gets in. Head looking for pupils who 'enjoy being at school and have the capability to be interested in a wide range of things'. For entrance to the sixth form (about 15–20 come in at this stage) the expectation is to have gained six points at GCSE, with two points for an A* or A grade and one for a B grade. Also at least a C grade at GCSE for maths and English language. Candidates will also be interviewed and reports sought from previous head.

Exit: Around 15 or 20 a year leave at 16 for 'places offering more diverse AS/A2 courses than us', but the vast majority stay and go on to a wide range of universities – most popular recently include Nottingham, Exeter, Bristol. Leeds, Oxford Brookes, with 10–12 a year to Oxbridge.

Money Matters: Fees by no means cheap, but most parents seem to feel that 'you get what you pay for' with the huge amount on offer. Scholarships available – academic, music, art and the Eric Abbott for candidates of 'strong academic ability and at least one other area of excellence', e.g. sport/drama – up to a maximum of 25 per cent of fees for the top awards. Other than that you'll need to remortgage.

Remarks: Hugely popular school with lots on offer, strong academia and mega street cred. Ideal for the sporty, energetic, sociable and independent child.

Croydon High School

Linked to Croydon High Junior School in the Junior section

Old Farleigh Road, Selsdon, South Croydon, Surrey, CR2 8YB

• Pupils: 420 girls, all day • Ages: 11-18 • Size of sixth form: 100
• Non-denom • Fees: £12,006 pa • Independent

Tel: 020 8260 7500
Fax: 020 8657 5413
Email: info2@cry.gdst.net
Website: www.gdst.net/croydonhigh

Head: Since May 2010, Mrs Deborah Leonard MEd, BEd Hons (forties). Deputy head of Nottingham GHS, Mrs Leonard arrived towards the end of the academic year as acting head for the following year after only brief tenure of predecessor. Previously deputy head of Thetford Grammar and head of PE and school development at King Edward's Birmingham. Her Masters is in management and learning and she is passionate about girls' education. A very keen sportswoman, she has been a national league hockey coach and plays golf. She grew up in the Lake District and enjoys climbing and walking.

Academic matters: GCSE results excellent, more than 77 per cent A/A*, after that mainly Bs. Good all-round education with a strong performance from the science, maths, English and modern foreign languages depts. French, German, Spanish and Latin offered; talented linguists can take up to three options at GCSE putting linguists on a par with the scientists. Newly-decorated, bright, clean science and language labs, with recently updated resources. Parents report very solid teaching in maths, virtually no one fails to achieve the GCSE and quite a few go on to take maths and further maths at A level. A new tracking and monitoring system recently introduced to help move towards more individualised learning, the aim being to ensure everyone meets their potential.

Year 9 girls encouraged to try out subjects and choose a balanced mixture of GCSEs before making A level choices – always guided towards their strengths. Subject choices at A level now expanded, around 80 per cent A and B grades. Sixth formers link with Whitgift and benefit from a good range of sporting, artistic and practical enrichment activities. Accessible Careers Centre which maintains links with outside agencies; girls also encouraged to get involved in voluntary work and help run school clubs and undertake some supervisory roles with younger children.

ICT centre and library stay open until 5 pm, library is run by a much-appreciated and knowledgeable librarian, who facilitates book groups and a number of other literary related activities. Pupils volunteer to assist in the library designing information posters and leaflets. Girls say library comfortable to work in, with desks overlooking attractive grounds, a popular place to be, good stock of books, audios, periodicals and DVDs. A few wobbles recently on the staff front but we hope now settled down. Reasonable mix of long-serving and new, younger staff. Part-time SENCo organises some additional support provision which includes screening and study skills for all age groups.

Games, Options, the Arts: Something for everyone, energetic sporting calendar, hockey, netball, tennis, cross-country, rounders and gymnastics. School has won the netball national finals 14 times in the last three decades, and is successful in many other national events. Large sports centre which doubles as a private club, houses gym, sports hall, dance studios and pool, where the highly successful swimming teams train. Recreational sports include badminton, self-defence, table tennis, aerobics and salsa. D of E award scheme thrives, also regular field trips as well as adventure holidays, music tours and skiing. Year 7 go to an activity centre in Devon for a week of outdoor activities. Traditionally strong music, say parents, instrumental tuition available on most instruments including tuba and harpsichord. Wonderful choirs, orchestras and bands in-house and Fairfield Hall concerts are always a sell out, musicians are involved at local and national levels. Own annual chamber music composition competition judged by an external adjudicator. Music and drama departments work together to produce spectacular musicals each year. Surprisingly few choose to take music GCSE or A level, a shame for such an innovative group of musicians. Art teachers continue the open-door policy so pupils can use facilities – which include pottery studio and dark room – outside timetable classes. Girls also get out and about and take part in national and local competitions; enthusiastic debating groups and Year 7 made it into the finals of a recent national spelling bee.

Background and Atmosphere: Founded in 1874, the school moved in 1966 to its present purpose-built site which accommodates the junior and senior schools. The buildings, which are rather utilitarian from the outside, provide excellent well-proportioned rooms. Spacious landscaped grounds provided superb sporting and recreational space for both juniors and seniors. A few well-loved school pets enjoy the grounds too. Comfortable atmosphere pervades, possibly influenced by the many links encouraged between older and younger girls. All appears to be quiet and purposeful.

Pastoral Care and Discipline: School code of conduct is included in pupils' yearly planners; school rules are mostly common sense or based on health and safety requirements. Sixth formers train as peer listeners to befriend younger pupils. No outside counsellor, however referrals can be made through the school nurse. All girls are encouraged to look out for each other and respect each other as individuals. Teachers are available to pupils on a drop-in basis first thing in the morning.

Pupils and Parents: From around 70 feeder independent and state primaries. Catchment area stretches from south London to rural Surrey although the majority lives within a five-mile radius of the school. Pupils come from a range of backgrounds, mostly professional; proportionate racial mix with around a dozen different nationalities attending. The school has a link with Shenzhen in China so a small number of Chinese students are able to live locally to attend the sixth form. PTA runs fund-raising events and sixth form fashion show often raises around £4000 for charity. Alumnae: Jacqueline du Pré, Helen Chadwick, Elizabeth Laird, Jean Ure, Jane Warr, Marilyn Cutts, Rabbi Helen Freeman etc etc.

Entrance: At 11+ annual entrance test in November and informal interview with the head or deputy. All those offered places attend a special induction day during the summer term before entry. At 16+, interview, report from the previous school and seven GCSEs, B grade for subjects to be studied at A level, A grade for mathematics, chemistry, physics and modern languages.

Exit: Mostly all to university, a handful a year to Oxbridge, otherwise anywhere from London to Edinburgh. Combined degrees becoming particularly popular, e.g. engineering or law with a modern language. Around 25 per cent leave at 16+, mostly to co-ed schools or state sixth form centres and colleges.

Money Matters: Standard GDST scholarships and bursaries are available. Music, art, drama and sports scholarships for Year 7 entrants. Jacqueline du Pré music scholarship and sixth form scholarships.

Remarks: Consistently good results across the board, and with a new headmistress this school should flourish. Pupils present as highly-motivated and accomplished, but maybe too rigorous a place for a more sensitive soul.

Culford School

Linked to Culford Preparatory School And Pre-Prep in the Junior section

Culford, Bury St Edmunds, Suffolk, IP28 6TX

• Pupils: 650 girls and boys; 190 board in senior school • Ages: 13-18 in senior school; 7-13 in prep, 3-7 in pre-prep • Size of sixth form: 145 boys and girls • Methodist foundation • Fees: Day £15,240; Boarding £22,740-£24,660 pa • Independent

Tel: 01284 385 308
Fax: 01284 729 146
Email: admissions@culford.co.uk
Website: www.culford.co.uk

Headmaster: Since 2004, Mr Julian Johnson-Munday, (early forties), educated Norwich School, Leicester (Eng lit) and Durham (MBA). Previously housemaster at Cranleigh and deputy head at Mill Hill. Married with one son. Highly approachable, unstuffy and energetic, he refers to himself as a 'shameless hustler' when it comes to furthering the interests of the school. Busy giving the school a higher profile, has invested heavily in the boarding side (the senior school aims to maintain 50 per cent boarding) and has already done a lot to improve the provision of weekend activities. School, he says, should be 'challenging, enriching and fun'.

Academic matters: Results are very sound, considering the wide ability range, with 97 per cent achieving 5+ A–C grades at GCSE and 84 per cent A*–C at A level. The 2002 inspection was concerned that provision was not as good as it could be at the top and bottom of the spectrum. Now, an excellent SEN teacher liaises with subject staff to support pupils with difficulties (individual help is an extra), and scholarship pupils (and anyone else who wants to) attend an extra-curricular course of challenging lectures, organised by a newly-appointed head of scholars.

Many classrooms are now very high-tech – there are computers, laptops and interactive whiteboards everywhere – and ICT is thoroughly integrated into lessons. The classics are alive and well, with extra-curricular Greek attracting good numbers. A choice of French or Spanish is largely compulsory at GCSE, with German as the other modern language. Science is very strong and has its own state-of-the-art centre. Roughly half do separate sciences at GCSE. Choice of subjects at GCSE and A level is, at least for the moment, fairly strictly mainline academic. Psychology now offered at A level, the only other -ology being biology. ICT also available.

Classes are small (average 16, maximum 24 across the school, average 10 in sixth form). The school day is quite packed, with a very short 40-minute lunch break, to accommodate eight periods (four on Saturday), plus every day after-school activities. Day pupils don't leave until 5.30pm. A well-established system of rewards for good work (which add up to bronze, silver and gold medals), and closely monitored sanctions for unsatisfactory work.

Games, Options, the Arts: Provision for sport is nothing short of spectacular – a 25m indoor pool, squash courts, fitness suite, huge sports hall, floodlit Astroturf and games pitches as far as the eye can see. Competition within the school and with other schools very much encouraged. The head has introduced CCF and clay pigeon shooting to add to an already impressive list of outdoor activities, as well as an indoor climbing wall. A new indoor tennis centre offering development for all abilities and a high performance programme for the élite.

A new studio theatre provides wonderful facilities for drama and music; also a very good dance studio. Wide range of choirs, bands and orchestras, plenty of concerts and two major dramatic productions annually. Phase one of the redevelopment of the music school completed at the end of 2008. Art is imaginatively taught in pleasant, lively studios but it would be nice to see more of the pupils' efforts around the place.

Background and Atmosphere: The main building is a fine, late-18th century mansion (with much older bits), originally belonging to the Cornwallis who lost the American War of Independence, and it is gloriously set in 480 acres of beautiful well-kept parkland, with a fine grade one listed bridge and a garden designed by Humphry Repton. The interior of the main building, now changed by the studio theatre, is ravishing. The head's study was Lord Cadogan's morning-room, the very fine library served as Queen Alexandra's dining room, and giggling new pupils may be taken to see the loo where Edward VII once sat enthroned. Dotted about are various pleasant purpose-built subject blocks (some the result of handsome bequests) and boarding houses. The latter are currently undergoing a major overhaul. Comfort in the two already finished is definitely five star.

Everywhere is amazingly tidy, well-equipped and well cared for. Uniform is worn throughout the school, with girls in long pleated skirts looking rather quaint and elegant. Pupils and parents alike rate the school highly, and one has the feeling of a quietly self-confident, happy establishment.

Pastoral Care and Discipline: A thoroughly efficient hierarchy, responsible for care and discipline, in which everyone seems to know where they are and who to turn to. Discipline problems are very rare – it helps, of course, that the school is well away even from the very minor fleshpots of Bury St Edmunds.

The ethos is decidedly Christian, with two religious assemblies a week, but not overtly denominational. The parish church in the grounds is used by the school.

Pupils and Parents: 25 per cent of boarding pupils are Services children, 11 per cent from overseas (about 10 German girls and boys doing a year or two at the school, and a fair number of Hong Kong and mainland Chinese). Otherwise pupils are very much East Anglian, coming from within a radius of 50 miles, and from middle class professional and business backgrounds. A sizeable number of families have attended the school for generations. Old Culfordians are generous in their support, e.g. one funded the building of the splendid science block.

Entrance: Not highly selective – entry is by exam and interview at 13, and seven A–C passes are required for the sixth form, with B grades or better in the subjects to be taken at A level. Pupils come from local prep (including Culford Prep) and state schools.

Exit: Almost all go on to further education, with a good smattering making it to Oxford and Cambridge.

Money Matters: Various academic, sport, tennis and arts scholarships (25 per cent of tuition fees) and exhibitions (10 per cent), renewable annually. Up to four boarding scholarships (25 per cent of boarding fees), various bursaries and Services allowances. NB School charges overseas boarders £555 more than UK boarders.

Remarks: A well-rounded, thoroughly reliable school, in a wonderful setting, which deserves to be better known.

Dame Alice Harpur School (Senior School and Sixth Form)

Linked to Bedford Girls School Junior School in the Junior section
Linked to Bedford High School For Girls in the Senior section

Cardington Road, Bedford, Bedfordshire, MK42 0BX

• Pupils: 600 girls, all day • Ages: 11-18 • Size of sixth form: 175
• Fees: £10,398 pa • Independent

Tel: 01234 340 871
Fax: 01234 344 125
Email: enquiries@dahs.co.uk
Website: www.dahs.co.uk

Head: Since September 2010, Miss Jo Mackenzie, previously deputy head of Ipswich High School. She has the complex, challenging but exciting task of overseeing the merger of DAHS with Bedford High School into a new school to be called Bedford Girls' School. The merger began in September 2010 with the junior schools. Bedford Girls' School Junior School is in Cardington Road, on the Dame Alice Harpur site. The senior school will follow in September 2011.

Academic matters: Not too highly selective but excellent results nonetheless. In 2010, 61 per cent A*/A at GCSE; 77 per cent A*/A/B at A level, with history and business studies the most popular. Setting in maths from Year 3; girls in Year 7 choose two out of three languages (French, German and Spanish) and add Latin. Every girl takes nine GCSEs and is expected to achieve at least eight passes to go into the sixth form, with at least B grades in the chosen A level subjects. Traditional subjects offered at A level, also Spanish and English language and now psychology. In the sixth form a range of examined and non-examined supplementary courses, including fitness training, preparation for driving, self-defence and study skills. Class sizes in Years 7 and 8 can be 24 or 25, but this reduces in subjects with setting, and girls are taught in groups of, at most, 24 in science and in half form groups for all practical activities. Class sizes further reduce as GCSEs approach.

Games, Options, the Arts: Excellent facilities on site include a floodlit, all-weather area which provides one full hockey pitch, two seven-a-side hockey pitches, 12 tennis courts and six netball courts. There is also a gym, excellent indoor pool, fitness suite and versatile sports hall which stages indoor hockey events. Hockey is the main sport but, because of the school's closeness to the Great Ouse, rowing has grown in popularity over the last decade and girls have enjoyed increasing success in local and national events – some internationals.

Excellent music and drama, with 400 individual music lessons and 45 speech and drama lessons taking place each week. The girls often join forces with pupils from other schools to put on productions – from small informal gatherings to major concerts where the other three Harpur Trust Schools (Bedford High, Bedford Modern and Bedford School) combine to fill the Birmingham Symphony Hall. Girls can also join the CCF along with boys from Bedford School, where they can learn to scuba dive and fly, among other things. Thriving clubs including debating, polo and a popular Saturday youth theatre group.

Background and Atmosphere: The school was opened in 1882 to receive 58 girls, who were among the earliest in the country to enjoy an education previously reserved for boys. One of four schools of the Bedford Charity, the Harpur Trust, which benefit equally from the generous endowment of Sir William Harpur (a Bedford merchant who became Lord Mayor of London in 1566) and his wife, Dame Alice. Moved to its present site, a short walk from the town centre and by the banks of the Great Ouse, in 1938. Makes education available to as many girls as possible through the Harpur bursary scheme. Modern buildings surrounded by attractive gardens and playing fields. Two listed Georgian houses provide a sixth form centre and music facilities. A purpose-built drama studio and separate drama room have been sympathetically added. The most recent building projects have included enhancements to the art and textiles facilities and an extensive redevelopment programme of Dame Alice House – a 'fabulous' building used as the school's sixth form centre.

Pastoral Care and Discipline: Discipline does not seem an issue. No 'rule book' – girls know what is expected of them.

Pupils and Parents: A wide mix from a large catchment area attracting pupils from many corners of Bedfordshire. Some parents make considerable sacrifices to send their girls here. A mix from state primaries and prep schools. Some girls come by train; others make use of the coach service which has been set up jointly by local coach companies and parents. Old Girls include Jean Muir, designer – who famously designed Diana Rigg's wardrobe for the 1965 series of The Avengers, including her famous PVC catsuit – and Gail Emms, Olympic silver medallist in badminton 2004 and winner of the world championships in September 2006.

Entrance: At 11, 12 and 13 girls have a group interview, then take a test in English, maths and non-verbal reasoning. The head insists on writing to each girl individually to say whether they have been successful or to explain why they have not met the required standard – 'I believe it's important to explain why I don't feel a girl will benefit from a Dame Alice education rather than just telling them they haven't got in'. No waiting list but parents can contact the school at any time to see if places become available.

Exit: Some girls leave post-GCSE, for financial reasons or to pursue courses not available here. Most go on to university or further education. A handful to Oxbridge.

Money Matters: No scholarships. The head and governors feel strongly that a Dame Alice education should be available to as many girls as possible and are able to offer a number of bursaries through the Harpur bursary scheme.

Remarks: The merger with Bedford High is a bold move and one we will watch with interest and optimism. Will be a very large school, cornering the market in the area.

Dame Alice Owen's School

Dugdale Hill Lane, Potters Bar, Hertfordshire, EN6 2DU

• Pupils: 1,400 boys and girls • Ages: 11-18 • Size of sixth form: 430
• Non-denom • State

Tel: 01707 643 441
Fax: 01707 645 011
Email: www.damealiceowens.herts.sch.uk
Website: www.damealiceowens.herts.sch.uk

Headteacher: Since 2005, Dr Alan Davison (early fifties). Read theology at Durham, gained his master's and doctorate in education leadership from Leicester University. Two previous headships: the first at Notley High School in Braintree, then Mill Hill County High, Barnet. Spent two years with London Challenge developing leadership across schools in London under the directorship of John Coles – 'It was a privilege to work with John and I learnt a great deal from the experience, but I missed working with the pupils and the very hands-on experience of running a school'. Married with four children, enjoys skiing, travel, theatre and cinema, has eclectic tastes. Hails from Whitley Bay though the accent, like Spanish City, has all but disappeared.

Interesting and interested, he's described by staff as a head who is prepared to get his hands dirty and who takes a task-orientated approach to leadership – pushes things forward, won't fix things that aren't broken but might improve them. Rattled a few cages on arrival but, in a recent well-being survey of staff, they were described as the 'happiest in Hertfordshire'. Odd parental moan, when he took up the reins, that his focus on driving up academic standards, discipline and expectation that parents should fully support the school may be misplaced and unnecessary, but notable improvements since and he seems to have won the majority over. 'He listens and acts and has made a good school even better,' commented one.

Academic matters: Almost 40 per cent of pupils are selected either by academic ability or musical talent; a strong sibling policy further skews the largely middle-class intake; not all are bright as buttons but the majority performs exceptionally well. Results and facilities, though possibly not class sizes, are a match for independent schools in the area. Approximately 95 per cent of pupils achieve five GCSEs at grade A* to C. Good A level results too: average 73 per cent graded A/B. Particularly strong showings in chemistry, mathematics, French, economics, English literature, geography and Spanish. Wide range of academic A levels, plus maths AEA, applied business studies and ICT but no other vocational offerings.

At 11, pupils are placed in an upper or middle band until 14 with some setting introduced. Class sizes around 30, reduce to 20 or fewer in some GCSE subjects. Science (specialist status recently granted) is taught on an integrated basis for two years, then separately in Year 9, all do additional science as a second subject. Huge take up at A level with 80 students studying chemistry and healthy numbers in other sciences and maths. Good facilities backed up, say students, by 'fantastic, well-prepared staff who make lessons entertaining and fun'. One added, 'We did a study to discover what kind of learners we were and found most teachers were already catering for our different styles.'

The school was awarded language college status in 1996 and offers Spanish, Italian, Mandarin, Portuguese, applied linguistics and Japanese as well as French and German plus Latin. At 11, pupils take French, Spanish or German, then, in Year 8 all, bar a few with SEN, study an extra language. Regular exchanges including work experience overseas in Year 10 ensure maximum exposure. The vast majority of pupils stay on for A levels. Handful leave to pursue GNVQs elsewhere as only ASs and A2s offered here. Parents say children are pushed academically and given lots of homework, but generally sufficient help and support in place too.

Approximately 100 pupils are on the SEN register, of whom 23 are statemented for a wide range of needs (including ASD, BESD and SpLD). School has had pupils with sensory impairments too. A team of learning support assistants are assigned to departments rather than pupils. Individual education plans are made available to teachers with general and specific strategies suggested. 'It's a calm school which suits many SEN children.' Much improved since arrival of current SENCo but still battling in some corners to ensure staff fully understand and are conversant with pupil needs. Two gifted and talented coordinators look after the demands of the brightest and ensure they are given appropriate challenges and opportunities including visits, visiting speakers, master classes, NAGTY membership etc.

Games, Options, the Arts: Extra-curricular opportunities, in and out of school, provide something for everyone, regardless of talents or bent. Odd minor grumble about coaching for teams rather than all but equally acceptance that staff already give more than enough of their time. Sports facilities are impressive for a state school – large sports hall, floodlit Astroturf pitch and games field. Boys enjoy soccer, rugby, hockey, cricket, athletics, cross-country, gym, badminton and basketball. Girls play football, netball, hockey, badminton, cross-country, athletics, tennis, rounders and crickets. 2012 hopefuls plus county and national representatives in many sports. Judo, dance, gym and cheerleading some of the alternatives.

Music is exceptionally strong, with some 10 pupils a year selected solely on musical prowess. Approximately 400 learn a musical instrument; two symphony orchestras, five chamber groups, three bands and four choirs. Students perform to a very high standard: a few play in the National Youth Orchestra, two finalists in the BBC Young Musician of the Year and the two orchestras recently gained first and second in the National Festival of Music for Youth at the Royal Festival Hall. The regular music tours abroad provide performing opportunities and fun. Increasingly popular drama (regular productions) now vies for space in the fabulous Edward Guinness performance arts centre and concert hall.

Background and Atmosphere: Alice Wilkes, thrice widowed by a brewer, a mercer and lastly by Judge Thomas Owen, established a school for 30 boys from Islington in 1613. She entrusted the running of the school to the Worshipful Company of Brewers who, for the best of the past four centuries, have supported and encouraged the school. A girls' school was added in 1886 and, in the late 60s, a search was made for a new location. The new school opened on its present site – 35 acres on the southern borders of Potters Bar in Hertfordshire – in 1973. Today, all Year 7s receive one crown each at a ceremony at Brewers Hall in the City of London, with annual 'beer money' until they leave.

Buildings are modern and purpose-built. Sixth form has own block, dining facilities etc. In 1989 the trustees provided the Edinburgh Centre to house computer suites, labs and a high-tech library. On-going building work limits outdoor space, better in summer when grassed areas, pond and paddock are in-bounds. Smart school uniform graduates to business dress for sixth form.

Pastoral Care and Discipline: Overwhelming belief that the sense of community, care and staff-student relations make the school special. 'Teachers make you feel secure and most of us have good parental support too,' said one youngster, adding, 'Sometimes people mess about in lessons but if anyone is naughty they're dealt with quickly; there aren't any horrible kids here or gangs.' Sixth formers would like more integration between year groups, but even they were hard pushed to suggest areas where the school should improve, one adding, 'It gets better all the time because of its good reputation. At 11 I didn't realise how lucky I was but I do now'.

Pupils and Parents: A wide mix from a large catchment area attracting pupils from the northern reaches of Hertfordshire through parts of Essex and down to north London, majority described as 'ambitious middle class'. 'The pupils here are amazing,' said one teacher, adding, 'They are in a different league to other schools I've worked in; pupils' willingness to learn and the support for, and value placed on, education from families is extraordinary.' Undoubtedly, the pupils are an articulate, competitive bunch; said one member of staff, 'They feel very strongly if they are deprived of an opportunity'. Opportunities for parents to get involved too – not just PTA but library duties etc. Notable former pupils include Gary and Martin Kemp of Spandau Ballet, Sir Alan Parker, Dame Beryl Grey and Joss Ackland.

Entrance: Unusual admission rules. Well over-subscribed – some 1,200 children compete for 200 places. Siblings take priority, then 65 places awarded on academic ability. Tests in English, maths and verbal reasoning. Ten places for musical aptitude, 20 places to children living or at school in Islington. Then places offered to applicants from specific parts of Hertfordshire, Barnet and Enfield: 300 compete for approximately 25 additional places at A level. More than a match for local competition: QE Boys', Haberdashers' Aske's, St Albans, Latymer etc.

Exit: About five per cent leave post-GCSE to pursue courses elsewhere. Five GCSEs at grade C and above (including English and maths) plus minimum Bs in subjects to be studied very much an absolute minimum requirement for sixth form – vast majority have A grades. Most to higher education after A levels to a wide-range of mainly selecting universities, e.g. Nottingham, Sheffield, Bristol, Manchester. Oxbridge places average 17 a year – lots of help and support for those who wish to apply including in-house guide to getting in.

Remarks: A star, shining bright, for the lucky few who claw their way in. A state school where teachers can teach, pupils value the joy of learning and parental support really makes a difference.

Dame Allan's Boys' School

Linked to Dame Allan's Schools Centre Linked to Dame Allans Juniors Fenham in the Junior section

Linked to Dame Allans Juniors Forest Hall in the Junior section

Linked to Dame Allans Girls School in the Senior section

Fowberry Crescent, Fenham, Newcastle upon Tyne, Tyne and Wear, NE4 9YJ

• Pupils: senior: 305 boys, 230 girls; juniors 65 boys, 45 girls. Plus Linden Prep (separate entity with 100+ boys and girls). All day • Ages: Seniors 11-18, juniors 8-11; Linden Prep 3-11 • Size of sixth form: 215 • Christian foundation • Fees: Junior £7,467; Senior £9,501 pa • Independent

Tel: 0191 275 0608
Fax: 0191 2751502
Email: enquiries@dameallans.co.uk
Website: www.dameallans.co.uk

Principal: Since 2004, Dr John Hind, (late forties), MA (history) from Downing College, Cambridge, MEd (Newcastle), PhD (history) Durham. Previously deputy head of Kingston Grammar and before that at Durham and Exeter. Affable, enthusiastic exponent of 'our school is a community, not a hothouse' philosophy. Approaches each pupil with 'let's work together and see where we can get to' attitude.

Walks tightrope of preserving 300-year traditions and modernising, 'honouring the past and welcoming the future'. Married to Ginny, a dentist, with two young daughters. Outside school, campanology rings a bell.

Has two vice-principals: Bill Lomas, head of boys' school; Janet Middlebrook, head of girls' school.

Academic matters: Seventy-six per cent A levels at A*, A and B in 2010. At GCSE, 36 pupils got all A*/A grades. Diamond structure sees juniors mixed, ages eight to 11, then split into single sex schools from age 11 to 16 (co-ed for music and drama) before returning to co-ed sixth form. Split allows for more focused approach – boys and girls to learn in their own ways: boys fidget, compete to answer questions; girls are neater, less competitive, have greater emotional intelligence. However subjects are zoned in different parts of the building (science, maths etc) so integration is inevitable and allowed. IT is good and planned to get better. Each pupil has own space on system.

One girl who joined in Year 9 from a mixed school, told us, 'It didn't seem strange at all and I certainly didn't miss the boys in class with their noise, disruption and stupid questions. I would have missed not having boys around school at all, though.'

Games, Options, the Arts: Fantastic opportunities abound. Excels in music, drama and especially dance (including rugger-playing lads). Took honours in National Musical Theatre Competition and boasts jaw-dropping dance studio straight out of *Fame the Movie*. Pupils perform with National Youth Choir and National Youth Music Theatre.

Sport is valued as much for its inclusivity (everyone gets chance to represent school) as its excellence. For half a century boys have represented their country at rugby, but range of sports on offer is dazzling. Weightlifting, archery, tennis, running, taekwondo and netball have all produced internationals. Sport transports away from muddy fields of Tyneside to tours in, for example, South Africa and Italy (rugby), Barbados (cricket), Canada (hockey and netball).

More travel offered by World Challenge participation. Has seen pupils go to Uganda, Kenya, Bolivia, Mongolia, China and the Indian Himalayas. Exchanges flourish to France, Germany etc and school is in Relais De La Memoire – joint initiative with French, German and Polish schools to nurture continued learning and respect for victims of war and holocaust.

Background and Atmosphere: Founded in 1705, marked tercentenary in 2005 with a visit by the Queen. Girls' school believed to be one of the oldest independent girls' schools in the country. Founded by Dame Eleanor Allan, daughter of a city goldsmith and widow of a wealthy tobacco merchant, to provide a 'proper' education for 40 poor boys and 20 poor girls. Keeps that ethic but has shaken off the pre-1980s girls at one side, boys at the other and never the twain etc.

Hemmed in on all sides by mid-war semis, rescued from claustrophobia by square green lung of a playing-field. Strong sense of community and family. Cherishes church links – historically the cathedral school and retains links with St Nicholas' Cathedral and Church of SS James and Basil. Places community, charity/fund-raising work on a par with academic and sporting achievement.

Lower down school space is at a premium and one girl told us, 'The dream would be a common-room for each year'. Youngsters are at ease in a friendly atmosphere. One girl told us, 'There is so much to do and it is such a nice, friendly family atmosphere. Everyone knows everyone else and the relationship between staff and pupils is really good. I'm in the orchestra, a ceilidh band, in drama productions, concerts and choir and, though I'm not very good at sport, I have enjoyed hockey here too.'

Brilliant new sixth form centre, well received and well used by students. Old boys/girls include Sir David Lumsden, Ian La Frenais, Elizabeth Fallaize (pro-vice-chancellor of Oxford University).

Work has just begun on a new building to house Junior School, anticipated to be ready in 2012.

Pastoral Care and Discipline: Form teachers/tutors perform pastoral role. Has a trained counsellor to listen to any particular problems and effective pupil counselling system called 'Link' where sixth formers provide a listening ear and guiding hand. Flexible merit system keeps pupils on course. Typically a demerit is a warning sign, two prompts letter home and three invokes detention. Pupils report zero-tolerance of bullying and drugs.

Pupils and Parents: Catchment is Newcastle and hinterland (Tyne Valley, coast, Durham area, plus wider north east). Pupils mainly from LEA first and middle schools, Newcastle Preparatory School and Linden School (linked). Socially mixed background with several on bursary. Most have English as first language though several have other languages spoken at home.

Entrance: Entry is predominantly at eight, nine and 10 plus respectively for juniors and 11 and 13 plus for seniors. Junior and main schools have entrance examinations (in January/February) with papers in English, maths and verbal reasoning, followed by an interview.

Exit: Higher education beckons, with solid numbers heading for Oxbridge, but closer to home Newcastle, Northumbria and Durham also popular.

Money Matters: Not a rich school.

Remarks: A diamond in many senses. Hemmed in and short of space but the split structure works well. Pupils take full advantage of many opportunities to learn, travel and grow. Stiff local competition – Dame Allan's tries harder.

Dame Allan's Girls' School

Linked to Dame Allan's Schools Centre Linked to Dame Allans Juniors Fenham in the Junior section

Linked to Dame Allans Juniors Forest Hall in the Junior section

Linked to Dame Allans Boys School in the Senior section

Fowberry Crescent, Fenham, Newcastle upon Tyne, Tyne and Wear, NE4 9YJ

• Fees: Juniors £7,467; Senior £9,501 pa • Independent

Tel: 0191 275 0708
Fax: 0191 275 1502
Email: enquiries@dameallans.co.uk
Website: www.dameallans.co.uk

Remarks: For Good Schools Guide entry see Dame Allan's Boys' School.

Dane Court Grammar School

Broadstairs Road, Broadstairs, Kent, CT10 2RT

• Pupils: 1,150 boys and girls, all day • Ages: 11-18 • Size of sixth form: 320 • Non-denom • State

Tel: 01843 864 941
Fax: 01843 608 811
Email: admin@danecourt.kent.sch.uk
Website: www.danecourt.kent.sch.uk

Executive head: Since 2004, Mr Paul Luxmoore (forties). He is executive head of the two federated schools, Dane Court Grammar and nearby King Ethelbert. Read history at University College London and trained to be a teacher at the Institute of Education, London. Taught at Chelmsford County High School and says this has had a very strong influence on him. Came here from being acting head at Bourne Grammar School. Dapper. A personable and articulate man with lots of energy and commitment. Ofsted inspection in 2007 found school to be 'outstanding' in every category and he was found to be an outstanding headteacher.

Believes in state education and has always taught in it. Has introduced a house system, which has gone down well, and is working on involving the sixth form more in the life of the school. Realistic about the school but clear in his aim to take it up a level; believes, for instance, that all in the sixth form should aim to go to university (not the norm in this economically-stretched part of Britain). Wants the school to do better by exceptionally able students.

Head of school is Mr Simon Pullen, previously deputy head of Dover Grammar School.

Academic matters: Superb results, both actual and value-added, by the uninspiring standards of the Thanet area, and not at all bad by national standards – in the top 25 per cent. Almost all get the requisite 5+ A*–C grades at GCSE; around 50 per cent A/B grades at A level – 'an indication of the very hard work done by both staff and students,' says Mr Luxmoore.

The school is a specialist language college – though this is not obvious from the A level results – it shows more in a determination to develop an international approach to the curriculum and in students' attitudes – the International Baccalaureate Diploma Programme was introduced in September 2008.

French, German and Spanish are taught to GCSE. French and German at A level, with Spanish to be introduced in 2010. Students are particularly enthusiastic about media studies and English. Physics popular – always a surprise – and Ofsted found that teaching and learning in general is 'outstanding'. Boys keep up with the girls – another welcome rarity. Facilities reasonable, much new spending on ICT. A £20 million rebuild project is now underway.

Splendid SEN provision. For the past few years, Dane Court has been a designated grammar school for visually impaired students. A handful scattered throughout the school; one student is profoundly deaf, one is completely blind. A significant number of students have dyslexia, dyspraxia or Asperger's. Staff training for SEN is a high priority: five are qualified in braille. Each department has its SEN coordinator to ensure continuity of provision and staff work closely with families. SEN children are featured in an album, ensuring all staff are aware of their needs. Other students are accepting of SEN pupils and rather proud of them being there and being involved in the life of the school. Genuinely inclusive.

Games, Options, the Arts: A strong PE department, with successful teams at all levels, some students competing at county level. Successful climbing team. Art very good, with vivid and skilful displays around the school. Music strong, with a large number of orchestras and bands.

Background and Atmosphere: Shabby. Years of neglect and tight budgets. Faint but pervasive smell of school dinners. When head arrived he was dismayed by the premises but soon found that, compared to other local schools, facilities are good. School, though, feels full of pupils who like being there and are busy. The Building Schools for the Future initiative, started in 2008, is radically changing facilities. 50 per cent of the school is being rebuilt under the new plan and the other 50 per cent significantly refurbished.

The spirit of the school shines through. Forward-looking, enthusiastic, aiming at widening the often narrow parameters of pupils' and parents' aspirations.

Pastoral Care and Discipline: Sixth form 'buddies' (also a club run at lunchtimes where Years 7–11 can meet others, play games and talk to the staff) and 'form friends'; senior students very much involved in helping younger ones. Much appreciated. Sixth form generally given responsibility and a strong involvement with the house system. The sixth form centre belongs entirely to them – they have a telly, do their own decoration. Sixth form newspaper and year book. Firm policy on drugs – the few incidents rapidly dealt with; apparently not much of a problem with alcohol. Bullying not tolerated, 'I can't stand it,' says the head, and he sees to it that any infringements are dealt with appropriately and the right message gets across.

Pupils and Parents: Varied socio-economic backgrounds, with much deprivation. School spirit gets through to parents as well as kids – many parents involved in e.g. language evening classes, PTA activities and fund-raising. Free Spanish evening classes for parents and pupils attracted 240 people, so another tutor has been recruited. The highly-presentable sixth formers who showed us round were chosen at random and told us, 'we don't know anyone who doesn't want to be here'.

Entrance: From local primary schools by the Kent Test – the county's version of the 11+. Sixth form entry not tough – five A* to C grades with B grades in the subjects studied at A level.

Exit: To university or other FE if the head has anything to do with it, and not just to the local branch of Canterbury Christ Church University down the road, either. Although that's perfectly good, he is keen to encourage wider horizons, and two went off to Cambridge in 2009.

Remarks: A good school in less-than-easy circumstances, showing the way on inclusion and aspiration. Clearly heading for greater things.

Dauntsey's School

West Lavington, Devizes, Wiltshire, SN10 4HE

- Pupils: 790: 430 boys, 360 girls. 40 per cent boarding overall: less in first two years, but approaching 50 per cent at the top of the school
- Ages: 11-18 • Size of sixth form: 270 • Inter-denom
- Fees: Boarding £25,380; Day £15,060 pa • Independent

Tel: 01380 814 500
Fax: 01380 814 501
Email: info@dauntseys.org
Website: www.dauntseys.org

Head: Since 1997, Mr Stewart Roberts MA (fifties). Educated at Birkenhead School and St Peter's, Oxford, where he read physics. Previously housemaster at Shrewsbury School and the founding head of Chand Bagh School, Lahore, Pakistan. Briefly second master before being offered headship. A very funny, witty man ('though he can be very serious,' say parents) and a super, high-power head. Despite having been boss for over ten years, remarkably open to new ideas. Married to Anna, who teaches piano at the school, with a son and daughter, both at Dauntsey's.

Academic matters: Without anyone quite knowing what or where the school is, has shinnied up the league tables from mid-ranking, co-ed, mystery school to first division heavy-weight contender. Its handsome exam results barcharts show an unrelenting curve onward and upward as the school seems to ratchet up what little room for improvement remains. A level results especially outstanding in English and maths, less so in the sciences. Art and theatre studies results a sea of As and deserve special mention. Music technology, a niche subject, also super dooper. GCSEs very good across the board; dual and single sciences offered.

Class size around 16 in GCSE years. Three full-time staff provide thoughtful SEN help. Greatest call is for help with mild dyslexia and as a safety net for the organisationally challenged but, 'If pupils pass the entrance exam,' says the head, 'it is rare for us to say we can't cope with their special needs'. Fully wheelchair accessible. 30 foreign pupils receive EFL tuition. Computers and interactive whiteboards everywhere – has virtually reached IT saturation point.

Games, Options, the Arts: Sport three times a week. Boys' hockey and rugby faring well with some delicious victories against arch-rivals, Marlborough and Bishop Wordsworth. Girls' hockey and netball also thriving. Vigorous cricket – the first XI cricket team recently toured Grenada – although purists may disapprove of the school's active involvement on the Twenty20 front. Football played as a mainstream game alongside hockey. Some notable individual successes in fencing, rifle shooting, athletics. Facilities include indoor swimming pool, two handsome Astros, sports hall. Athletics track a hike away, a source of grumbles for a few. Gym a bit macho with scary weights and levers crammed into too small a space.

Music department buzzy – you can tell that attention is paid to it. Healthy numbers of pupils on instrumental teachers' lists; plenty of ensembles and concerts. Glorious music room, once the main school hall in some bygone day, with what can only be described as a 'cute' pipe organ. Practice sessions timetabled for junior boarders. Art housed in spacious building with teaching, pottery and computer rooms, plus display area. Head of art keen on observational drawing. Sixth form course allows lots of room for trial and error. Pupils very proud of drama and upper sixth pupils took a play to the Edinburgh Fringe. Gloomy Memorial Hall serves as theatre (plus assembly hall, plus concert hall, plus chapel) but is made up for by 'Annabel's', a truly fabulous, newly-refurbished drama studio. School made a big effort to expand number of clubs and activities on offer. It certainly seems to stop the boarders, rather marooned in a quiet Wiltshire backwater with only a Costcutters mini-market to pass for excitement, from becoming bored.

Distinctly outdoorsy flavour to the place. Outward-bound charging about – known here as 'strenuous pursuits' – is a big part of proceedings. The Year 9 Moonrakers programme offers camp-craft, map reading, rock-climbing and shooting. D of E, Ten Tors, Brecons Challenge and the Devizes to Westminster canoe race are all popular. A group of sixth formers recently spent a month in Kenya and Tanzania doing volunteer work and climbing Mount Kilimanjaro. Curiously, given that Wiltshire is a landlocked county, the school owns and maintains its own tall ship, The Jolie Brise, a gaff cutter that won the Millennium Tall Ships race and three Fastnets – if you understand any of that, this may be the school for you. All pupils have a chance to sail in her and some become seriously involved, taking part in overseas voyages. Plenty of school trips – modern languages to Spain and France, geography to Iceland, classics to Athens, rugby to New Zealand, skiing in Italy.

Background and Atmosphere: Dauntsey's was founded in West Lavington in 1542 on the deathbed largesse of William Dauntsey, master of the Worshipful Company of Mercers. Present school opened in 1895. Mercers' Company still provides six governors, occasional financial help and annual knees-up for its associated schools. (Mercers' are involved in an unlikely spread of schools, from St Paul's School in London – both boys' and girls' versions – to Peter Symonds College – state sixth form in Winchester – two new city academies and The Royal Ballet School – who'd have thought?) Dauntsey's was once described to us as a sort of public school 'lite' – meant in the best possible way. If you take a very grand public school and peel away its National Trust property style buildings, over-the-top acreage (much of which pupils never use), hugely expensive facilities and atmosphere of self-importance, what you are left with is Dauntsey's – nice pupils, good teachers, beautiful (enough) surroundings, fresh air, good facilities, good results. As one parent said, 'A five star hotel it is not.' Perhaps a bit countrified for some hardened Londoners – until 1930 the school was known as Dauntsey's Agricultural School. Buildings mainly piled up in a heap in one corner of the grounds, which helps give the campus a stimulating feel, and you never have to worry about being late for the next lesson.

Super, bright and airy new library; the exposed desks/computers down the centre of the building may not be everyone's cup of tea (where do they hide the sweet packet?) but more sheltered study space is available upstairs and fooling around can be done in the cybercafé or in the tuck shop. Lessons finish at 4pm and it is technically possible for day pupils to creep off then, but most stay on for prep or take part in clubs or sports until the mass bus exodus at 5:20. Boarders have two hours of prep in the evenings, one just before and one after supper.

Pastoral Care and Discipline: '17 Club' is the hub of sixth form social life. We never cease to be amazed by the ingenuity boarding schools have shown in the face of the new licensing laws. Dauntsey's solution is to give sixth formers two free drinks each week so the whole question of purchase is neatly sidestepped. These need not be alcoholic, of course. Surprisingly uncompromising on drug use – immediately out. Listening service (trained sixth formers) plus a school counsellor, and parents have commented that pupils always seem to have a staff member they can go to if they have a problem. Girls' uniform an attractive check skirt with blue blouse and pullover. Boys in blue shirt and grey-blue jacket. No uniform in sixth form but smart dress required (suits or chinos, tie and jacket for boys and at least a nod towards suitishness for girls, though there is room for quibbling here). Boarding houses all better than good, with new girls' house, Evans, particularly elegant (all rooms en suite). Sixth form girls all have own rooms. Upper sixth boys also have own spaces, though share in lower sixth. World-class san. Lovely lower school boarding house, The Manor, for 11–14 year olds in separate 100 acre site.

Pupils and Parents: Key to the school – not obsessed about social status or they would not have chosen it. 'Pupils come into the school unsnobby and uncliquey and that is the way they are when they leave,' says the head. Boys and girls mostly wholesome-looking but not smart – very little makeup. From Wiltshire and seven surrounding counties. Has particularly stepped in to fill the gap for boys' independent education in Salisbury. Big clumps also from Swindon (especially), and Marlborough, Calne, Westbury. A wide range of activities on offer for boarders on Sundays – over half now stay for weekends. Some 20 pupils from British ex-pat families, mainly Services, and 50 overseas, mostly from Hong Kong, also Germany, Switzerland, Russia, Spain and US. Old Dauntseians include Thomas the Tank Engine creator Reverend Awdry, anthropologist Desmond Morris, TV theme writer Simon May (Eastenders) and Sydney Olympic rowing silver medallists Miriam and Guin Batten.

Entrance: Main feeders Chafyn Grove, Norman Court, The Mill, St Francis's (Pewsey) and St Margaret's (Calne), plus many local state primaries. Largest entry is at 11+ (mainly, but not entirely, from state schools) via school's own exam (maths, English, VR and optional music and art interviews). Places offered ten days later. Choosier than you would expect – head says school's selectivity is similar to the Salisbury grammars', which is not a walk in the park. Everyone who sits the exam is automatically considered for a scholarship and around 15 pupils out of 80 admitted will receive an award. At 13+ school is looking to take around 30 boarders (mainly) via CE or scholarship exams; day places at 13+ are limited and do not qualify for scholarships. Does not take pupils into Year 10. Some 30 pupils join the school for sixth form, many from abroad – a minimum of six Bs at GCSE is required from UK pupils, plus interview.

Exit: Almost everyone to university, with Nottingham, Cardiff, Durham, Exeter popular. Few to London. A few to Oxbridge each year – sometimes more than a few. About 10 pupils leave after GCSEs.

Money Matters: Much more aware than many schools that parents' resources are not infinite. The vibe from parents is that day fees here particularly good value for money. A few nice touches: music lessons cost the full whack for first instrument but less for second and subsequent ones; a 10 per cent reduction for siblings who are boarding at the same time (this is a very sibling-friendly school). Mercers' connection a help when it comes to funding building projects but not bottomless pit. Currently fund-raising for new mega-project – a performing arts centre.

Remarks: Excellent academic results and steadily improving facilities. Now on the map big-time and worrying the heebie-jeebies out of bigger name schools in the area. Friendly, down-to-earth, independent education with absolutely no snobbishness or arrogance.

Davies Laing and Dick College

100 Marylebone Lane, London, W1U 2QB

• Pupils: 325 boys and girls • Ages: 15–24 • Size of sixth form: 280
• Non-denom • Fees: £16,400 pa • Independent

Tel: 020 7935 8411
Fax: 020 7935 0755
Email: dld@dld.org
Website: www.dldcollege.co.uk

Principal: Since January 2008, Mr David Lowe, who read English at Gonville and Caius College, Cambridge, where he was a choral exhibitioner. He also studied solo singing at the Mozarteum Music Academy in Salzburg, Austria. Previously principal of Cambridge Tutors College, since 1997. Married with five children. A team inspector for the Independent Schools Inspectorate, a trustee of UK Council for International Student Affairs, and board member of the British Council's Education UK Partnership.

Academic matters: A small minority of pupils are there to do one-year GCSE courses, the rest one- or two-year A level courses. Also retake courses of varying length. Maximum class size 10. Commendable results from a mixed-ability intake. Most GCSE students take eight subjects, from a limited list that includes the basics plus French, Spanish, business studies, ICT, art and drama. Latin, Greek and German are available via individual tuition. Generally over 85 per cent get 5+ A*–C grades.

A level students get a choice of 35 subjects, including music technology, photography, film and media studies, in more-or-less any combination. Art, economics, religious studies and philosophy are consistently popular, alongside English and maths; nearly 27 per cent A*/A grades in 2010.

Some students are disaffected when they arrive – 'But it is unusual for them to be anti-education after a few weeks. It's important to fit the right course to the right student. Because of the small class sizes they get lots of individual feedback and huge amounts of encouragement, and most start making progress very quickly'.

The college can cope with a wide range of special needs, generally picking up several previously-undiagnosed cases each year. Most need group support with study and essay-writing skills; individual help is also available at extra cost. 'Our SEN students get more-or-less the same level of results as the others – due to getting the subjects right, and to plenty of support.'

No quarter is given academically – 'We will not accept scrappy work. We believe in raising standards and in making students believe they can move up to the next level'. Many staff are from Oxbridge and come from non-teaching backgrounds – the theatre, the City, the BBC. 'They work unbelievably hard,' said an insider. 'They put in a lot of effort for the students.' 'DLD stands for determination, learning and distinction,' says the head.

Games, Options, the Arts: A surprisingly arty college – A level art and photography are two of the most popular and successful subjects and several students are refugees from high-powered academic institutions where the creative side is less valued.

The main aim of most students is to pass their exams, and extra-curricular activities are not high on the agenda except for those in plays and sports teams. A level students, in particular, often work long days. However, all GCSE students play sport at local centres on Friday afternoons, including football, basketball, tennis, netball and aerobics – sports clubs and matches after school. The DLD youth theatre puts on two performances a year; the house band – organised by the drummer of Van der Graaf Generator, who is also the music technology teacher – plays well-attended gigs; film, debating and art clubs.

Background and Atmosphere: Now one of a group owned by Alpha Plus, the college was founded in 1931 to provide tutoring for Oxbridge and Colonial Service entrance exams. After World War II it began to specialise in A and O level teaching. In 2004 it moved from Notting Hill to light, airy, refurbished premises in Marylebone, with an 80-seater theatre, recording studio, three art studios, science labs and photography studio.

Informal atmosphere, closer to a college than a school, with staff and students on a first name basis. 'They're unfussy about clothes and about students in clinches on the stairs,' said an insider. 'But academically they're pretty tough. Students don't get away with things.'

Pastoral Care and Discipline: Strong pastoral system. 'Many students have had a shifting lifestyle and it's a real haven for them,' said an insider. 'There is a lot of respect because students know we care about them.' A register is taken in every lesson and parents are texted or emailed. Each student has a weekly meeting with their personal tutor to talk about progress and future plans and the College has five directors of studies working closely with the personal tutors. Tough sanctions for misusing drink and drugs; those under suspicion are sent for drugs tests, to general parental approval. 'There are a few troubled and troublesome students,' said a parent, 'but most buckle down eventually.'

'Occasionally there are students we don't manage to turn round,' says the head. 'Then I'll often suggest to parents a gap year in the middle of the sixth form, preferably working in Waitrose. It concentrates their minds on the consequences of failing to work and the difference in maturity when they come back is often amazing.'

Sanctions include supervised study; also a system of verbal and written warnings based on employment law. Bullying is taken very seriously.

'They don't care about superficial things,' said an insider, 'but on work, drink, drugs and bullying they clamp down very quickly.'

Pupils and Parents: Most students have come from private schools. Some have had enough of boarding; some have been ill; some have found their previous school too rigid or too stressful. Others come from peripatetic diplomatic families. Some lack confidence and need to learn good working habits. Most thrive in the informal but structured atmosphere.

Entrance: Those going into the sixth form need a minimum of six grade Cs at GCSE; if they haven't passed maths or English they will need to retake these. Everyone is interviewed and previous schools are asked for references. The college will not consider students who have been disruptive elsewhere.

Exit: A few GCSE students move on elsewhere – perhaps to state sixth form colleges – but most go through to the sixth form. Those aiming at Oxbridge are given an intensive course including lectures, seminars, mock interviews and individual tuition; around half a dozen a year generally get places. Extra help also for potential vets, doctors and dentists, via a bespoke medical programme. Arts foundation courses are popular; other students move on to a huge range of courses varying from mechanical engineering at Edinburgh to sports and exercise science at Brighton.

Money Matters: Several scholarships available, worth 10–100 per cent of fees, plus bursaries.

Remarks: Good at stimulating the very bright as well as re-motivating the disaffected. Informal atmosphere with strong staff/student relationships underlies a structured regime where everyone is kept up to scratch.

Dean Close School

Linked to Dean Close Preparatory School in the Junior section

Shelburne Road, Cheltenham, Gloucestershire, GL51 6HE

• Pupils: 270 boys and 240 girls: 220 day; 290 board • Ages: 13-18
• Size of sixth form: 220 • C of E (Anglican Foundation) although all denominations welcome • Fees: Day £19,680; Boarding £27,870 pa
• Independent

Tel: 01242 258 000
Fax: 01242 258 003
Email: office@deanclose.org.uk
Website: www.deanclose.org.uk

Headmaster: Since late 2008, Mr Jonathan Lancashire FCA. Read maths at Cambridge. Taught maths and house-tutored for seven years at Radley after graduating but then qualified as an accountant. Then became bursar at Rishworth School before moving to Dean Close in 2000. His wife is head of history and politics at Cheltenham Ladies' College; two children at university. A keen sailor, outdoor pursuits man and keeps pigs and chickens.

Academic matters: Some clever clogs here get six As at A level, which tweaks league table performances nicely to show Dean Close well ahead of local rival Cheltenham College and even nudging out Pate's Grammar School in terms of points per pupil. The fact is that school has been rising steadily over recent years: 14 per cent grades at new A* and 74 per cent A/B grades at A level with stunning successes in English, maths, physics and art. 'Astonishingly good' head of maths described as a 'one in a million teacher' by one parent with a Cambridge maths degree. Ironically, mathematics is taught in 'temporary' classrooms tucked away from the main (and better) buildings. Government please take note. Good to see other barometer subjects like geography and religious studies riding high too. Classics thrives: three classicists made Cambridge in current year. RS compulsory to GCSE but appears as philosophy and ethics thereafter with a faithful following (as you would expect). Surprisingly few taking DT. Proliferation of exotic languages reflects the international boarding element more than the proximity to GCHQ. Good range of choices for GCSE with 62 per cent achieving A*/A grades, with English, maths and physics achieving a plethora of A*s. Home economics a popular and successful choice. We watched an English lesson which kept pupils mentally alert and inquisitive. Classrooms and laboratories we saw were modern and well-resourced. Teachers strike as energetic and well on top of their subjects. Two librarians manage well-resourced facility which includes much vaunted careers section. Lots of help with UCAS, work experience, gap years etc. Tutorial system (linked to house system) underpins academic organisation and sixth formers get to choose their own. ICT networked throughout school with 'virtual learning platform' under development to allow pupils access to learning resources from home as well as in school. Weekly monitoring of progress by tutors with self-assessment an important feature in sixth form.

Literacy or numeracy support provided on one-to-one basis for usual reasons, but school draws line at ADHD or anything more than the mildest Asperger's. School prides itself on doing well with sows' ears.

Games, Options, the Arts: National reputation for hockey, which recently celebrated its centenary. Boys' 1st XI won national title in '09 and finalists in '10. Sport generally given a tremendous boost by opening of hugely impressive sports hall with its deluxe gallery, fitness suite and sporty buzz. Phew! Rugby strong enough to more than hold its own in rabidly oval ball area; recent girls' and boys' hockey tour to South Africa was huge success. In summer, cricket for boys, rounders for girls; tennis and athletics for both. Two Astroturfs host high-quality hockey matches and county trials and bring total of outside tennis courts to 20. Separate indoor 25 metre swimming pool and squash courts, climbing wall and indoor rifle range. Growing choice of sports (especially for sixth formers) includes horse riding, polo and eventing. Equestrian team won div 2 of national girls' SUPA polo tournament – could the green wellies be making inroads?

Exceptionally well-conceived two-storey art and design centre incorporates inspiring studios, BonBernard gallery and individual carrels which enable sixth formers to leave their work out ready for the next flash of creative genius to strike. It's all here, including digital art and mixed media. Great to see loads of art around a school and such obvious fun producing it. Frequent trips to Paris, Barcelona etc. Busy drama department stages up to eight productions a year. Individual lessons for 150 pupils who are entered for RADA, LAMDA and Victoria College exams. Small studio used for class work at GCSE and A level and some presentations. We watched a lively GCSE class composed (untypically) mainly of boys. Major performances staged in professional-standard Bacon Theatre. Annual auditions for those wanting to join sixth form Close Up company, awarded sell-out status at Edinburgh Fringe for seven consecutive years. We also watched rehearsal of a house play (three of these a year) but were assured that school productions are in a different league. 'Lavish' musical staged biennially – Christmas 2010, *Cabaret.* Some go on to drama schools and recently to American Academy of Dramatic Art in Los Angeles. A 400-seat outdoor theatre is used for some summer productions.

Purpose-built music school features elegant Prince Michael Hall, specialist classrooms, recording studio, library and individual practice rooms. 25 full time and visiting teachers and over 50 concerts a year of all kinds. Strong choral tradition – we watched 60-strong chapel choir practising Bernstein's Chichester Psalms in Hebrew with choral director (shared with Tewkesbury Abbey) impressively in charge. Chamber choir tours abroad. Orchestra tackles major works and will be at Westminster Abbey for HMC evensong there. Jazz band performs at local festivals. Number of pupils selected for national youth orchestras and tradition of choral and organ scholarships at Oxbridge and admissions to top conservatoires. 'My daughter is a scientist but Dean Close has given her a love of singing devotional music which she wants to continue at university,' said one appreciative father.

Five term Leith's cookery course heavily over-subscribed by sixth formers. Strong CCF tradition, compulsory in first two years and many continue beyond. Most Year 9 pupils achieve D of E bronze award, first aid certificate and RLSS lifesaving award. Close on a hundred clubs and societies range from debating through film making and robotics to outdoor pursuits. Decanian magazine (format slightly resembles in-flight glossies) published annually, reflects life across school community but could be enlivened with more student input, we felt.

Background and Atmosphere: 'Offers everything a bigger school does,' claims head and we would concur – not that the school could be described as small. Buildings date from Victorian era with additions over the years of varying merit – mostly hidden until inner confines of school are penetrated. Imaginative use of glass and light in many areas, especially in hugely impressive refurbishment of boarding houses. Confusing system for numbering years has fourth form followed by Remove, then fifth form – puzzled? We were. Victorian chapel squeezes whole school into facing oak pews with school motto: 'God's word. A guiding light' emblazoned on vertical banners the extent of sacerdotal embellishment. Only occasional Sunday chapels these days but whole school comes together for evensong on Fridays.

Ski lodge appearance to modern dining hall – high table for staff, efficient service counters and good variety on offer. Sixth form societies and special occasions provide for more refined tastes whilst snacking in boarding houses is ever popular. Big on charity giving. All sixth formers involved in community action programme which includes establishing a link school in Uganda and visiting each year to take out raised funds and muck in with building programme.

Pastoral Care and Discipline: Committed Christian ministry within school with dynamic female chaplain punching well above her weight. Huge following for CU with anticipated range of bible studies, Christian summer camps etc. Nothing imposed – 'whether you buy it or not doesn't really matter,' we were told and investigation bore this out. Four boarding houses and three day ones with 'day boarding' options allowing a couple of sleepovers a week. Boys' houses the best we've seen for a while and girls' houses also great. Lovely staff in charge with just the right balance between supervision and friendliness. Not massive amounts of 'hanging out': pupils kept too busy for that. Many have been together for as long as they remember, which helps keep relationships on an even keel. Sixth formers not given undue authority and head will come down hard on any sign of drugs (testing on suspicion) or drunkenness. Parents feel school has got balance right.

Pupils and Parents: Not a place for loafers – pupils get stuck into what school offers. Parents amazed at how school turns out such 'confident, willing young people'. Trust between pupils and staff seen as important.

Entrance: Close liaison with feeder preps (mainly own prep and local ones) reduces number of disappointments. 50 per cent required at CE or minimum four Bs and two Cs at GCSE though much depends on examination and interview. Growing popularity with London families for boarding; lots of ex-pats including strong links with HSBC and forces. International pupils from far and wide.

Exit: Handful leave at 16+ for state sixth forms. Sixteen into Oxbridge last year and even a smattering to LSE (perhaps harder). Vast majority to first choice universities.

Money Matters: Strong finances enable huge numbers (about 40 per cent) to benefit from some sort of award. Scholarships galore: academic, art, music, all-rounder, drama, music, art and sports. Bursarial help automatic for clergy children and popular with the Services. Tough on non-payers but helpful at times of genuine crisis.

Remarks: Sees itself as more 'local' and 'down to earth' in its origins than rival Cheltenham College. Has moved upmarket in recent years, though, with county folk and Londoners swelling the ranks plus loads from abroad. Academically mixed entry but tremendously successful at getting pupils to succeed beyond parents' wildest dreams. Not one to be discounted as too churchy – open minded, challenging and unpretentious, ticking the right boxes for many.

Devonport High School for Boys

Paradise Road, Stoke, Plymouth, Devon, PL1 5QP

• Pupils: 1,150 boys • Ages: 11-18 • Size of sixth form: 240 • Non-denom • State

Tel: 01752 208 787
Fax: 01752 208 788
Email: headteacher@dhsb.org
Website: www.dhsb.org

Headmaster: Since 2008, Mr Kieran Earley BA MA NPQH (late thirties) educated at John of Gaunt School, Trowbridge, before reading English and drama at Bangor and PGCE at Bath. Has studied part-time for multi-disciplinary MA and further educational qualifications. Family roots lie in the Navy and in Plymouth – had to pay back Navy university scholarship when he decided that his future lay in the classroom rather than at sea. Began teaching English and drama at Bishop Heber High School, Cheshire then took a year out to run 'Sound and Fury' – Shakespeare and music educational workshops; next came a year at King's College, Madrid, then three appointments in Cheshire over eight years, culminating in assistant headship back at Bishop Heber. Deputy head at Torpoint Community College for just two years prior to current appointment.

Ideas man with vision; pupils and parents welcome his energy and involvement. 'Has settled in very well,' they say. Compared first year at DHSB to 'drinking from a firehose' but seems to be surviving. Boys 'like him' and add that he is 'out and about' talking to them and to staff. Married to maths teacher, Alex, with three sons currently at their village primary school in Cornwall. Looks young for a head: he's on a mission to see DHSB achieve 'outstanding' levels in all areas. Aside from time with the family, he enjoys playing football and cricket for local teams.

Academic matters: Consistently good results at GCSE and A level. New head is raising the academic bar and has appointed deputy from Torquay Boys' Grammar to help achieve this. After a massive brainstorming exercise involving staff, parents, governors and pupils, head is condensing KS3 curriculum to Years 7 and 8. This exercise has involved a lot of cross-curricular dialogue and some radical thinking. Setting from Year 9 where Latin (compulsory still in Years 7 and 8) becomes part of a mini option scheme. Mandarin recently introduced from Year 8. Curriculum shake-up at junior end will allow more time for boys to get into their KS4 workload (all boys study 10 subjects to GCSE plus RE and PE). Astronomy now a GCSE option.

Parents say that maths and science teachers are good at getting pupils to 'think out of the box'. Boys generally take four or five AS subjects in Year 12 and three or four A levels in Year 13. Head has plumped for AQA baccalaureate to extend sixth form curriculum – projects in the pilot group included producing and performing in a Pinter play and sustainable building. As a G and T opportunity, DHSB offers Level 2/3 diploma courses and Young Apprenticeship schemes in engineering and art (DCFS granted school specialist engineering status and judged it as 'high performing'). School has also obtained a second specialist status in view of its European studies centre in France and its new engineering-based relationships in Germany and other countries. Numbers opting for languages in sixth is on the increase and all take at least one MFL to GCSE. Hooray! Lots of languages initiatives with fifty boys participating in an on-site Chinese enrichment day and some boys selected for Euroscola Day at European parliament in Strasbourg. Third specialism granted to DHSB in field of applied learning: this is developing a more independent and innovative learning community and giving boys the opportunity to develop workplace skills in proper industrial contexts.

Sixth formers can study alongside girls at other schools in the consortium which includes DHSG, Notre Dame, St Boniface and Eggbuckland. Teachers' rôle increasingly that of facilitator: we watched sixth form English class directed into research and composition using individual laptops. Psychology growing in popularity; science and maths seen as strengths alongside engineering. New virtual learning platform (FROG) allows pupils to access work from home and includes a facility for uploading work and having it marked electronically.

Boys are screened for SpLD and SENCo operates from a cottage on site which also provides a useful sanctuary for any needing it. School ('lynchpin of the citywide campus,' says head) provides lead for Gifted and Talented programmes in science, maths and engineering across the city.

Games, Options, the Arts: Strong sports tradition – enviable record at county, regional and national levels. Consistent local success in a dozen sports. Nearby civic pool is used for swimming. Hockey off campus for 50 boys involved – Astroturf is high on head's wish list. Cross-country and orienteering take place either on Dartmoor or at picturesque Mount Edgcumbe Country Park.

Lots of engineering activities – e.g. a team of Year 8 boys recently won 'best use of electronics' award in a national competition for remote controlled 4x4 vehicles in schools. Art, taught in refurbished studios, popular at GCSE and A level and also operates as a club activity. Music is based in a separate house on site which includes a classroom, recording studio and individual practice rooms. After school activities include school orchestra, swing band, choir and rock club. Recent production was *Joseph and the Amazing Technicolour Dreamcoat.* Drama gaining popularity: good numbers taking GCSE and A level courses and making advantage of splendid new theatre with pull-out seating for 300. Separate ATC building on school grounds with participation from both within and outside DHSB. Wide range of before and after school clubs from robotics to rock climbing; involvement in Plymouth youth parliament and local success in ESU competition. D of E and both 35 and 45 mile teams for Ten Tors (on doorstep) perennial favourites. SW regional champions in Schools Challenge. Up to 400 (including Year 7) benefit annually from school's own French centre at Uzel in Brittany where, for under £250 for five days, pupils get to practise French and participate in orienteering, canoeing and riding. Other recent trips abroad include art to Paris, skiing on Jungfrau and, classicists visiting Rome and the bay of Naples. Sino-DHSB co-operation includes a link with Xiuzhou Modern Experimental School.

Background and Atmosphere: Founded in 1896 by first headteacher, Alonzo Rider, to give educational opportunity to able boys from less well off backgrounds. Aims reflected in school motto: 'Prorsum Semper Honeste' ('Forward Always with Integrity'). New mantra is 'helping families raise their sons' as school adjusts to 21st century changes in technology and the learning environment. School moved to its present site in 1945 to occupy a huge Grade 2* listed building which had formerly served as a prison during the Napoleonic wars and as a hospital during WWII. Some of the interior remains rather barrack-like and battered but recent additions and improvements include the new Edgcumbe theatre, library and sixth form centre plus an attractive refectory. Sports hall and fitness suite are heavily used; five engineering workshops – all boys take at least one D&T subject. New food technology base currently under construction. ICT used throughout school (universal access to digital teaching resources) with departmental laptops and four IT suites. Extensive playing fields for a city centre school provide some room to breathe; tight packed buildings however mean boys can move relatively quickly between lessons.

Pastoral Care and Discipline: Strong pastoral care team includes heads of year; six houses into which boys are placed on entry with one form per house. Separate head of sixth form. Purposeful atmosphere and a real effort by staff to sort out any problems quickly – 'come down heavily on wrong-doers,' say parents. One mother praised how the school had helped her son overcome insensitivity from his peers. Still a bit scruffy at the edges but boys gain confidence as they progress. Devonport Voice is the school's initiative for incorporating pupil opinion and is gaining momentum with its vision of 'words into actions.' Head recognises achievement in fortnightly full school assembly: recently noted successes range from six D of E gold awards and grade 8 piano to a national indoor rowing champion and year seven boys raising over £1K for Lepra charity.

Pupils and Parents: New initiative has been to appoint a parent support adviser – a welcome move given the very mixed social catchment including Chinese and other ethnic groups. Supportive parents with an active PTFA – initiatives include fund-raising discos and a link with a local charity shop to recycle school uniforms to help reduce excessive growth spurt costs. Pupils travel from within 750 square-mile catchment area. Parents from the three Plymouth grammars have organised contracts with local bus company for eight double-deckers to bring children from the city's neighbouring districts. Boys from 160 feeder primary schools desperately want to come here and often pressurise their less committed parents. DHSB takes up to 12 per cent of Plymouth's boys. Old Boys include Sir Austin Pearce, chairman of British Aerospace, a smattering of admirals, professors, current Bishop of Truro and Anne Widdecombe's dad.

Entrance: Written English paper (comprehension and composition), two multiple choice papers on maths and verbal reasoning. PTFA organises a 'mock paper' at £30 a shot – real thing is held on two successive Saturdays. Oversubscribed: candidates selected on basis of their score which is standardised. Transfer into all other years (except 11 and 13) is possible dependent upon availability of a place and satisfaction of entry criteria.

Exit: Eighty per cent to sixth form (others to college, apprenticeships or local employment). Ninety per cent of sixth form to higher education. Good smattering to Russell group universities and Oxbridge (five to ten annually). Some into medicine; generous sponsorship from Engineers' Employers' Federation and BAE Systems results in large number heading into engineering and science courses.

Remarks: Moving from the traditional into a more modern concept of selective education with a head who is likely to make the place come alive. Good local reputation for turning out worthy citizens.

Devonport High School for Girls

Lyndhurst Road, Peverell, Plymouth, Devon, PL2 3DL

• Pupils: 830 girls • Ages: 11-18 • Size of sixth form: 230 • Non-denom • State

Tel: 01752 705 024
Fax: 01752 791 873
Email: dhsg@devonportgirls.plymouth.sch.uk
Website: www.devonportgirls.plymouth.sch.uk

Head: Since March 2009, Mrs Anita Hemsi, previously acting head.

Academic matters: High standards. 100 per cent of all GCSEs A* to C, 60 per cent A/B at A level. Choice of 20 A level subjects, further options including politics, psychology, sports studies and media studies – part of a consortium, the Link Partnership, which allows more timetable flexibility. English, the sciences and maths are particularly popular A level choices and students often sit additional Institute of Biology British Olympiad exam. French, Italian, Latin, Spanish and German available at GCSE and A level and new language block opened in 2010 to support this. Budding engineers invented collapsible mobile platform to lift equipment on and off ships, which has been adopted by the Royal Navy. Weaker achievers or students with SEN receive ample support.

Games, Options, the Arts: Thriving basketball squad. Dance taught in main school hall. Sporting stars have made national squads in hockey, netball, basketball, swimming and athletics, and improved sporting facilities are likely to further boost success. Music is a strength with more than a third of girls playing an instrument and achieving grade seven or eight by Year 10. Flourishing orchestra and choir perform a carol concert in the city church each year. Drama group teams up with St Boniface College for Boys and Devonport High School for Boys for annual production. Active Christian Union. Duke of Edinburgh available elsewhere through local YWCA; windsurfing and sailing offered through school.

Background and Atmosphere: Founded in 1911, moved to its present purpose-built site in 1937. The redbrick building is off a busy road opposite parkland. No great views and access by car is somewhat puzzling. Originally built for three forms of entry but since expanded to four – still waiting to dispose of ten temporary classrooms. Low turnover of staff – teachers almost seem relieved to be here, 'Pupils listen and like to learn'. Sixth form has own centre with kitchen and study. Every girl has access to internet and own email.

Pastoral Care and Discipline: Good level of care and support; discipline is a 'quiet word in their ear'. School nurse and youth counsellor from Youth Enquiry Service run weekly drop-in sessions. School council instead of prefect system – each form elects a member. Girls have been sent home for minor incidents but no exclusions in previous head's 15 year history; letter sent home to parents if caught smoking. Sixth formers expected to dress as if at work; body-piercing items must stay home. Everyone in school is 'expected' to contribute to school's chosen annual charity. Good attendance record and extremely positive attitudes.

Pupils and Parents: Attracts girls from some 50 feeder schools in Plymouth, west Devon and south-east Cornwall. Many professional parents from doctors and nurses to lawyers and scientists.

Entrance: Plymouth exam: multiple choice and written English – two successive Saturdays in January. Pupils admitted in the order of their exam score until the maximum intake of 120 is reached. Sixth form entry is open on interview to students who have achieved at least five GCSEs at grades A*–C with B grades in subjects (or equivalent) they wish to pursue at AS and A2 level. Average point score of 46.

Exit: Some 85 to 90 per cent migrate into sixth form, others move away or choose vocational courses. A few go into modern apprenticeships. Most continue to further education, although gap years popular. About four Oxbridge candidates annually. Cardiff, Exeter, Bristol, Southampton and London universities are favourites.

Remarks: Currently preferred choice for parents wanting single-sex selective education for girls. Students seem well prepared not just for academic success but also for life after school.

Dollar Academy

Linked to Dollar Academy Prep And Junior School in the Junior section

Dollar, Clackmannanshire, Dollar, Clackmannanshire, FK14 7DU

• Pupils: 1,240 boys and girls, 50:50; 80 board, rest day • Ages: 5-18 • Size of sixth form: 285 • Non-denom • Fees: Boarding £21,177-£22,383; Day £9,810 pa • Independent

Tel: 01259 742 511
Fax: 01259 742 867
Email: rector@dollaracademy.org.uk
Website: www.dollaracademy.org.uk

Rector: Since September 2010, Mr David Knapman BA (maths) DPhil, (forties), who came from Hampton School where he was deputy head and 'established a non-nonsense reputation but was also notable for his work with charities and the local community'. Educated at Morrisons, 'doon the road', followed by Sheffield and Exeter. Married to Brigitte with two sons, (younger one is in the school) he enjoys tennis and 'playing the piano badly'. Already seems well-settled at Dollar. Has a dry sense of humour: when asked how his son felt about moving to Scotland he explained that the bribe of a new puppy had been more than sufficient. Hugely enthusiastic and 'very popular – going down well' and 'doing just fine' say our spies.

Academic matters: 'Science in Dollar is outstanding,' and the results certainly show an impressive collection of As. The Scottish school centre for biotechnology, with funding from the Wellcome Foundation, which underwrites 'half a member of staff' annually. English and langs not too bad either, German and French more popular than Spanish or classical studies (heroes for zeros). All three langs on offer from junior school. Good take up in Japanese (regular rugby tours and exchange visits to Japan), plus Russian, Italian, as well as philosophy, car mechanics and other jolly options. Pupils choose the subjects they want to study and classes are worked round them, rather than the trad system of block choice. Broad streaming for English (with EFL if needed), tight setting maths, and mixed ability in most subjects, plus a compressed science option on offer for 15, 16-year-old high flyers aiming for medical school. Equally popular compressed business option which combines economics, business management, finance and accountancy. There is a distinct emphasis on the academic rather than the vocational.

Classes of 18–26 in junior school and 5–22 in senior school. Efficient support for learning in place, with rector getting progress reports. One to one, small groups and support learning in class all on offer. School has a positive approach to those with ADHD: pupils can drop into the dyslexia centre at any time. Serious homework, carefully spelt out in a smart little green book full of info for parents which interestingly persists in referring to the school as the Academy. 'Whatever else, we expect that all pupils in the Academy should have enough work to occupy their evenings and any child who indicates otherwise misunderstands.' Not quite all singing and dancing new computer system, touch-typing for all as well as the Scottish word-processing Higher course for all, thus cutting out the need for short courses in keyboarding at university. Specialist ICT course to Higher grade.

Games, Options, the Arts: No sport is compulsory. That said, boasts a first XV rugby team unbeaten for the first seven years of this century. Regular tours to Europe and further afield: regular and successful trips abroad, Canada, Japan, Italy et al. Shooting 'phenomenal' (Dollar was half of the UK U18 team), and always a strong showing at Bisley. Hockey hot stuff – Midlands Champions 2010. Individual pupils regularly get through to county level in major and minor sports – golf, skiing and badminton particularly successful, as well as the more esoteric activities such as shotput, curling, table tennis, equestrian vaulting (gymnastics on horseback) and triathlon. Large collection of games fields, sixty-three acres of school grounds, as well as much used hall and swimming pool (the word BATHS, neatly carved in stone above the doorway. Fantastic Maguire Building opened in December 2005 – sports, arts, drama, million pound bequest from FP Brian Maguire; second bequest from the Price family resulted in a new 5.3 metre inflatable for the navy section. All weather surface has now been officially opened by Linda Clement, Scottish Ladies' hockey captain.

Strong volunteer CCF – good following, not just because of the trips to Canada; amazing pipeband, all of whom wear the McNabb tartan, which has been Scottish Schools' champions for the last eight years and this year were world champions. Fabulous art, now in the splendid Maguire Building – we saw a jolly fifth form exhibition in the sugarpink-painted library when we visited ('Don't call it "sugarpink" – call it "regency coral".') Strong drama club and masses of productions – the head of drama specialises in doing sound commentaries for the blind on films. Clubs for everything, oodles of choirs, orchestras, jazz bands, a raft of choice. Munro bashing (Munros = mountains over 3000 feet), fabric technology and D of E, work experience at home and abroad, plus ballroom dancing on Fridays. Participants learn Latin American and rock 'n' roll – medals (bronze, silver, gold or Scottish Awards) which they wear proudly on their blazers thereafter; Scottish country dancing too – but no medals. Seventy-six options in total; terrific facilities; powerful charities committee.

Background and Atmosphere: Captain John McNabb, a former herdboy who rose to become a ship's captain and, latterly, a ship husband – literally looking after ships in port – died in 1802, leaving half his fortune, £55,000, to found a school to educate children of 'the parish wheir I was born'. Rumours abound whether the monies came from slavery or piracy but they were certainly augmented by bribes from ship owners eager to be first past the post, and the Rev Andrew Mylne opened Dollar Academy in the elegant Playfair building in 1818. McNabb's ashes are entombed in the wall above the main Bronze Doors; this is the only school in the land where pupils pass under the founder every day. By 1830, the grounds at Dollar had become an Oeconomical and Botanical garden, boasting some of the rarest trees in the country – certainly the most northerly tulip tree, as well as a Corsican pine. The interior of Playfair's original building was gutted by fire in 1961 and a certain amount of rearrangement dates from then, with a zinging concert hall (the Gibson Building) and much improved science block. Current wish-list includes a new technology, engineering science and earth science building – to be built out of 'funds'. The grounds are open to the public daily.

Formerly a direct grant school, Dollar became independent in 1974 – a day school with an international boarding element. Easily accessible from most of Scotland and just a short hop from the Forth Road Bridge and Edinburgh Airport. The boarding houses are small, no more than 25 in each; Heyworth house has had recent half million pound facelift and many of those who do board have rellies round the corner. Wet weather a feature of the place and masses of matches are rained (or snowed) off. NB The school uniform includes beanies (first time ever for us on a clothes' list) and macs with fleecy linings.

Pastoral Care and Discipline: Automatic out for drugs. Lousy work equals detentions post school or early morning – dead unpopular with parents, plus out if 'The pupil is not deriving benefit from being at the school or indicates by his/her conduct that he/she does not accept the rules of the Academy'. Pupils not particularly streetwise – 'Pupils have a reasonable amount of self-knowledge but on the whole they are not young people obsessively interested in the major interests of the day; it is no bad thing for them to remain children for a little longer'. Victorian values, with clear rules; many of the petty restrictions have been done away with, and the kilt may be worn by chaps at almost any time, though most prefer to be 'breeched', except for dances or reels.

Pupils and Parents: The vast majority comes from within a 30 mile radius – impressive number of buses, plus Services' children and a contingent from the Scottish diaspora worldwide. Dollar itself has the reputation of having the 'highest percentage of graduates of any town in the country'. School has a long tradition of looking after the children of tea-planters, missionaries and engineers – still. Perhaps a tad parochial and 'mercifully' free of Sloanes. Very strong and active FP network, including Sir Frank Swettenham, the first

Governor of Malaysia, Sir James Dewar, the inventor of the vacuum flask, and the sculptor, George Paulin. The governing body is mostly FPs, which ensures that the place has freedom to develop but an awareness of its history shapes the thinking – no bad thing.

Entrance: At 5, 10 or 11. The latter two by examination, which is very selective. Well over-subscribed for entry at fifth and sixth forms; each case individually considered; good GCSE or Standard grades required plus good refs and an ability to put something into the school. No open days as such – 'School is open every day'.

Exit: A handful to Oxbridge each year. Otherwise most students head for the Scottish universities: Edinburgh, Glasgow, Aberdeen, with barely a quarter going south or abroad. Not much gap year take up: either a reflection of the recession or the "get on with it" mentality. The chairman of governors and his wife have just set up a trust with more than £1 million to encourage the youngsters to take up challenges overseas. If that doesn't persuade entrepreneurs overseas ...

Money Matters: Collection of means tested-academic bursaries at 11 and 12, plus ESU, Service and boarding bursaries (means-tested, with tuition not covered). Very reasonable; governors tough on non-payers. Travelling scholarships for Dollar's seniors to study abroad – pour encourager le gap, peut-être?

Remarks: Very sound – this large, solid, co-ed school provides education in the best old Scottish 'get on with it' manner, facing the twenty-first century with the traditions and values of an earlier age, mercifully free of most of the excesses of the sixties. 'Robust teaching and meritocracy' are important here. March 2005 brought an outstanding Inspectors' report. Up there with the best of the merchant schools, though possibly 'not quite so trendy'.

Douglas Academy

Craigton Road, Milngavie, Milngavie, G62 7HL

• Pupils: 1,015 boys and girls • Ages: 11-18 • Size of sixth form: Fifth form: 190; sixth form 135 • Non-denom • State

Tel: 0141 955 2365
Fax: 0141 956 3231
Email: office@douglas.e-dunbarton.sch.uk
Website: www.douglas.e-dunbarton.sch.uk

Head: Since September 2008, Mr Seamus Black MA (Hons) (fifties) who was educated at St Xavier School, Coatbridge (a local-ish lad then) he read Italian and French at Glasgow uni, and came to the old Douglas Academy for a year – 'to get to know the traditions', having been previously deputy head of Shawlands Academy. He still teaches when he can, and is often 'out and about' – a wandering head, he keeps a beady eye and is incredibly proud both of the new school and of the 'high quality' of his staff and 'pupil attainments'. Keen on parent involvement, he runs the school with a management team of seven, including the head of music. He also talks incredibly quickly and is very on the ball. Married, his family lives in Dunbarton.

Academic matters: A strong school, results consistently high; and the HMI report is peppered with 'very good's. Three sciences on offer, many take two, pupils do well in science and maths challenges. French and Italian, Spanish option at sixth form, plus Mandarin. Fair amount of autonomy in employing staff, 'but if there are teachers free within the authority, then we have to take them' (an iniquitous system that caused much grief to England, high time it was abandoned here too); otherwise school advertises and can make their own appointments. Regular success across the board at Standard Grades, music specialists take both Standard and Higher music without fuss and, 'effortless'. Specialists take 'specially tailored courses', but see below. Most pupils get a 'variety pack' of eight subjects at Standard Grade, including core subjects; most stay on for Highers and Intermediate courses, and a 'goodly proportion' stay for Advanced Higher – school responds to 'the needs of the pupil': a certain amount of mix and match with Intermediate grades. Asterisked (i.e. outstanding) performance noted in history, modern languages, art and English.

Staff visit local primaries and meet new pupils the term before they hit big school. Children are setted for maths in October of their first term, and for some other subjects in their second year. Classrooms equipped with IT, interactive white boards and learning wall, as you might expect with a top notch new build: teachers happy and au fait with the most modern of facilities and the results speak for themselves.

Extensive support for learning, with a strong team which offers both guidance and support in class, offering help for the brightest as well as for those with learning difficulties, and with an acknowledged expertise in Asperger's.

Games, Options, the Arts: The school does well at rugby, hockey and athletics. 'Strong competitive edge'. This is not a school for layabouts, this is a doing school. State of the art all-weather rugby, football and hockey pitches, huge games hall plus two gyms, fitness suite, much used by the community, who also do evening and keep-fit classes here. Tennis, cross country course. Mass of charity involvement. (beat the High School of Glasgow!) and national award winners.

School became a Centre of Excellence for Music in 1979 and boasts a first orchestra of 'almost professional standard' plus 'an outstanding chamber orchestra, senior wind band, second orchestra – very full (60+) which often has first year pupils playing, as well as non-music specialists. Chamber choir, junior choir, senior choir, who swept the board at the most recent Glasgow Music Festival with the former beating the adult section to boot. On a par with St Mary's Music School in Edinburgh. Music lessons carry a nominal charge for non-music specialists, and local concerts are always a sell-out, particularly the annual Christmas concert at St Paul's in Milngavie. Almost equal numbers of boy and girl choristers: serious senior choir, the junior one is merely 'good' but, by any other school's standards, it would be outstanding. Most of the music staff have top jobs in Scotland's orchestras and choirs. Adjectives tend to fail when dealing with Centres of Excellence but take it as read that any superlative would be inadequate. Pupils follow the normal curriculum, but 20 per cent of their time is spent on music. Music specialists come from all over Scotland, Ullapool to Newton Stewart, and their chosen instrument can be in any discipline from fiddle to piano. There are no quotas for entry, around about eight or ten annually, currently 49 dedicated music scholars, places at the school are free and open to all (help given with transport), with pupils from further away boarding at Dalrymple House, (about 75 per cent) opposite the Botanic Gardens in Glasgow's west end (they share with pupils from the Centre of Excellence for Dance at nearby Knightswood). Two homework tutors.

Background and Atmosphere: Superlative new build in old school grounds with magical views of the Campsies to the North. Transition was more or less 'seamless'. School dress equals blazer (S6 pupils), white shirt/blouse, school ties, trousers or skirts and NO trainers. 'Parents and pupils have high expectations.'

Pastoral Care and Discipline: Team of ministers from local churches welcome involvement with the school. 'Drugs not an issue' in the school and good (state) guidance system in place ('highly effective'), plus link tutors who have informal relationships with the pupils offering both emotional and social support. Clearly defined rules about bullying and loads of staff back-up. 'Good extended team'.

Pupils and Parents: No 'significant number' from ethnic minorities and no problems with religious festivals – 'praying (as in five times a day) never an issue'. Parents 'feel welcome', and good fund-raising and pastoral parents' association in place.

Entrance: Parents 'feel welcome', and good fund-raising and pastoral parents' association in place.

Exit: Four associated primary schools; one of which is tiny and rural. Pupils from (the Catholic) St Joseph's may come here, and almost all do, or they may prefer to be bused the 30 minutes or so there and back to the local secondary Catholic school in Kirkintilloch. Excellent child-orientated joining handbook.

Remarks: Stunning state school for musicians, which moved to a split new – and fantastic state of the art campus in 2009 – worth moving house for if you are not in the catchment area, even if you ain't a musician. Exam results impressive and getting even more so. Outstanding recent HMI report. Strength through knowledge, the school motto, very much a byword.

Dover College

Linked to Dover College Infant And Junior Department in the Junior section

Effingham Crescent, Dover, Kent, CT17 9RH

• Pupils: 355; 50:50 boys/girls; 2/3 day pupils to 1/3 boarders - ratio reversed in the sixth form • Ages: 3-18 (boarding from 11) • Size of sixth form: 100 • All faiths welcome • Fees: Day £5,940-£12,585; Boarding £17,304-£25,437 pa • Independent

Tel: 01304 205 969
Fax: 01304 242 208
Email: admin@dovercollege.org.uk
Website: www.dovercollege.org.uk

Headmaster: Since 2004, Mr Stephen Jones MSc MLitt (mid forties), previously social tutor (housemaster) at Radley for eight years, where he taught maths and coached rugby, sailing and fives. Before that he taught at Berkhamsted, Cheltenham and The Dragon. Educated at Hurstpierpoint, Lord Wandsworth College and Durham University. Married to Katie, a priest, who occasionally conducts services in the school. Three children, one of whom is in the sixth form here. Very enthusiastic about the school, warm and approachable, knows all the children.

At first meeting we felt it was rather surprising that someone of this pedigree and quality should have ended up somewhere so un-smart as Dover, but he appeared totally happy here and committed to the place and its ethos. However, we were not amazed to learn that he will be off in July 2011 to take up the prestigious job of Warden at St Edward's, Oxford. A real loss to Dover but he will leave them much to be grateful for.

Academic matters: A refuge from the Kent grammar school system and smart, selective independents, there is a strong international flavour. Grades of 54 per cent A/B at A level are pretty respectable, given the intake, and pupils speak warmly of good teaching, small classes and lots of support. Few get three A grades but then almost nobody fails, either. BTech in sports, business studies, drama, ICT, DT, textiles, photography; music offered at A level as well as core subjects.

Foreign students start off in the International Study Centre and gradually move into more mainstream lessons. Do IGCSE in English, PET English test and International Language Testing System (IELTS) needed for university. Staff draw up individual study plans for English as a second language leading to university accredited qualifications. About 60 children have some form of EAL requirement.

Dyslexics, dyspraxics well supported here (CReSTeD category WS), but probably would not suit a child with very severe problems as no LSA or teaching assistants. Some children with hearing impairments. Children withdrawn from lessons (but not from maths, science or English) – rotate through the other subjects and then given time to catch up on what has been missed; some extra help available. Would not, for example, take a very artistic child out of art lessons. Computers networked, with special software packages to support literacy and numeracy. Three well-qualified SEN teachers; specialist maths support too. Year 7s screened for reading and spelling; NFER and CAT testing for all. Some problems still emerge later but close eye is kept on all children by subject teachers and through the house system. Difficult to slip through the net here, even if not picked up by previous schools. Exercise programmes and INPP (Institute for Neuro Physiological Psychology) developmental course – a respectable outfit despite the weird-sounding name, and we know children who have benefited considerably from their programmes.

Saturday school every other Saturday with lessons until lunchtime and sport and activities until 4pm; works well as non-lesson Saturdays used for whole school events – play and music rehearsals and sponsored walks etc, so as not to waste lesson time.

Games, Options, the Arts: Not a notably sporty school – it's just too small to make for competitive teams, but sport is much enjoyed and taken seriously; some examples of excellence in individual sports. Boys play football, rugby, hockey, cricket/tennis and basketball. Girls play hockey, netball and rounders/tennis. Major sport is compulsory up to fifth form. Sixth form have to do some form of exercise but it doesn't have to be team games – fitness classes a popular option, particularly for the girls. Can do art instead of team sport. Sailing with Dover Sailing Club. Some notable sportsmen, including Oleksiy Udovenko (Kent Cross-country League Champion) and Ashley Burton (captain of England independent schools' soccer XI).

Music, drama and art are what the pupils like to put their surplus energies into. Burgeoning music, strong choral tradition. New music building opening in early 2011 to provide music classrooms and sound-proofed pods. Art good but headmaster keen to develop it further – would like to make an art gallery to exhibit pupils' work and that of local artists. As head says, drama is good but could be better – recent investment in new technical equipment, lights etc. Lots of plays throughout the year – major school and individual house productions. 11–13 year olds do outdoor play in King Stephen's Garden in the summer – wonderful walled garden where King Stephen is apparently buried.

Background and Atmosphere: Founded in 1871 by a group of local businessmen to educate local children and housed in the grounds of St Martin's Priory, an oasis of green in the middle of Dover with wonderful views of the castle and nestling behind the famous white cliffs. Went co-ed in 1974 – one of the first boys' schools to do this; now 50:50. Although much of the original Priory has been destroyed, still a feeling of history here and the overall impression is uplifting, despite the hotchpotch of buildings added as the school has grown over the years, from late Victorian houses through the 1930s and 1950s and uninspiring modern.

Although not part of the Round Square group of schools (Gordonstoun et al) it follows many of Kurt Hahn's principles of service to the community; the headmaster is keen to strengthen this element. Children are expected to be involved in some form of service which could be through Duke of Edinburgh (good haul of golds) or helping with sport and music in local primary schools. Leadership training trips to the Italian Alps and Wales. A school council, and the children are encouraged to be concerned with environmental issues. Despite the strong military traditions of the school no CCF – a previous headmaster abolished it and knocked down the armoury!

Pastoral Care and Discipline: A broadly Christian school. The headmaster does not believe in multi-culturalism but in the celebration of all cultures. Everyone required to attend chapel three times a week, very much a spiritual whole-school event. A comfortable, caring place, high on TLC; headmaster says they try to be proactive through the house systems; low self-esteem and lack of confidence picked up pretty quickly. The children we met seemed thoroughly happy and at ease with themselves.

Usually about 100 children in at weekends and pupils tend to want to 'chill', but shopping trips to Canterbury etc organised with, perhaps, a celebration of different cultures – e.g. each member of house might cook their national dish. All children, both day and boarding, belong to a house – Priory and five others; three boys' houses, two girls'. Younger children (11–13) start off in the Priory House (mainly day with about 10 boarders) – 'wonderful pastoral care and lots of feedback,' according to one parent. 'Housemaster really seems to know the children and what they are up to.' Ethos of tolerance throughout the school; people look after each other.

Pupils and Parents: Around 30 per cent from abroad; over 30 nationalities in the school. Lots from mainland Europe – Germany, Russia, Belarus, Ukraine, some from Nigeria. Everyone gets on well with each other and with the English – all the hoped-for benefits of international diversity are here. The mainland Chinese find integration a little more difficult than everyone else (as always). A number of Services children – headmaster wants to encourage families from all ranks to send their children here. Some refugees from the state system cannot believe their luck in having an average of 15 per class for GCSE and an average of five in the sixth form. Popular with those who have not made it in the Kent Test for entrance to the grammar schools.

Children are well dressed, thoroughly natural, altogether comfortable. Lots of mixing between ages and interests: a delightfully hierarchy-free school. Old Boys include Sir Frederick Ashton of Royal Ballet fame, film producer Guy East, Simon Cowell of Pop Idol and The X Factor and Nick Cowell of Big Brother and The Block.

Entrance: Almost non-selective. Most come in at 11, 13 and sixth form but pupils can be admitted at any time if there are spaces. 11+ by entrance exam and interview, 13+ by common entrance and at any other time by interview and a report from previous school.

Exit: Some movement after GCSEs – some to local sixth form colleges but more come in. Most on to further education – some to major universities, e.g. Leeds, Edinburgh, plus others to newer universities and to performing arts, film and media and fashion courses.

Money Matters: Fees widely regarded as good value and then a number of useful academic, music, arts and sports scholarships, means-tested to ensure that the most deserving families get the biggest discounts. Also special armed forces bursary for those entitled to the educational continuation allowance, where a 10 per cent parental contribution is required.

Remarks: One of those crucial and hard-to-find schools which sets out to do well for the ordinary child and succeeds. A happy, relaxed place. Jeffrey Archer taught here as a young man and apparently proved to be an excellent teacher! Now needs an A1 replacement for Mr Jones.

d'Overbroeck's College

The Swan Building, 111 Banbury Road, Oxford, Oxfordshire, OX2 6JX

• Pupils: Sixth form – 245, mixed; 55 per cent girls; half day, half board. Leckford Place – 150 mixed, all day • Ages: 16-19; Leckford Place 11-16 • Size of sixth form: 245 • Non-denom • Fees: £12,255-£17,955 + accommodation £4,860-£9.195 pa • Independent

Tel: 01865 310 000
Fax: 01865 552 296
Email: mail@doverbroecks.com
Website: www.doverbroecks.com

Principal: Since 1996, Mr Sami Cohen BSc (early fifties). First educated in Baghdad, then A levels in London, before reading chemistry and French at Leeds (an admittedly odd combo but others have since followed his example). Came to d'Overbroeck's to teach French in 1979, two years after sixth form founded. In 1992 left for Paris, but four years later invited to return to run the whole show. Always wanted d'Overbroecks to be full 11–18 setup – achieved ambition with launch of Leckford Place. Leckford Place (on separate site in north Oxford) has now built a fine local reputation under head Mark Olejnik. Cohen oversees both halves of school. Married (wife Emily, an EFL specialist) with three daughters. Cohen still clearly loves what he does and has no intention of moving on. Charismatic and exhaustingly enthusiastic. Adores (and has enormous respect for) staff and students alike. Immensely proud to be in charge of a college that deliberately sets out to be different and offers a real alternative to traditional independent education. Felt establishing Leckford Place 'was one of the biggest contributions I could make to this place'.

Leckford Place head: Since Sept 2005, Mark Olejnik (fifties). First class history degree from University of Wales. Later head of Bury Lawn School, Milton Keynes, where taught for 18 years and where his popularity among pupils and parents made headline news. Wife Susan is primary school teacher, three children. Infectiously keen and active Roman historian, both in and out of school hours.

Academic matters: Sixth form – almost 40 subjects at A and AS level to choose from ranging from accounting to Japanese, ancient Greek to music technology, further maths to film studies. The norm for three subjects in second year sixth. Currently celebrating record year – 27 per cent A* and 59 per cent A* and A. 'Academic excellence is not just a measure of results but the quality of teaching and learning manifested in results,' says Cohen. Small classes – none bigger than 10, average is seven. Means lessons are lively and interactive. Students report, 'The relationship with teachers is very different here. They treat us like adults, listen to what we have to say. We're encouraged to speak our minds.' Teachers agree. One senior staff member comments, 'There's lots of inter-action. No-one's treading on egg shells. We work in an environment of mutual respect.' Self-motivation essential although staff make sure students don't slack. Cohen describes it as 'independence with a safety net'. Top subject choices are sciences, maths, English, economics and business studies, closely followed by politics and communication studies. Offers the AQA Baccalaureate for high fliers: A levels plus critical thinking plus independent research project plus enrichment activity. Oxbridge and medical programmes.

Leckford Place – boys and girls arrive mostly at 11 and 13, but entry considered at other times. Again, small classes – 10–15 pupils – with discussion and participation much encouraged. Over 40 per cent A*/A GCSE grades in 2010. Clever design, resembles ship's upper deck with shelves and study areas situated around large well. Surprisingly quiet as well: looks directly down onto student common-room. Superb use of space. Classrooms and science labs modern and extremely well-equipped. Teachers make good use of state-of-the-art facilities, and vibrant teaching methods certainly appear to keep pupils' full attention. Full range of sciences (all three elements), humanities, languages etc. offered as after-school extras. Considerable emphasis on music, arts, debating and drama. All pupils enjoy a wide variety of sport and are able to compete at a high level; exciting extra-curricular programme. Great community spirit and sense of everyone working together.

Learning support available for mild difficulties like dyslexia and dyspraxia. Every case looked at individually and decision made on whether it's felt Leckford Place is right place. Olejnik says, 'We have always had provision to support a small number of children of average or above ability who, while expecting to do well in their GCSEs, nevertheless require some help in the form of specialist tuition to guarantee their success. There is a limit both in terms of numbers and nature of the need.'

Games, Options, the Arts: Sixth form and Leckford Place have made concerted effort to increase and broaden sports and extra-curricular activities. Annual freshers-style fair at start of year to gauge interest in everything – from rugby, rowing and netball to x-box, jazz and the college magazine. Between 25 and 30 clubs in all each week. 'If there's enough demand for something, and it's not on offer yet, then we'll do our best to provide it.' Games and clubs mostly happen twice a week. School doesn't have own playing fields but has use of fantastic facilities at nearby Oxford Brookes University and other pitches in north Oxford. Variety of extra-curricular activities. Exceptional drama on both school sites – sixth formers choreograph as well as perform regularly in own productions. Musicals, concerts, dance, debating, enterprise club, speaker programme (chief executives, sports people, leading journalists etc) all contribute to very full programme of events and activities. Younger students at Leckford Place also show great promise. Some very talented artists on both sites – work on show was imaginative and impressive. Music and music technology popular exam choices. About a third of Leckford Place pupils learn an instrument; school also has orchestra and both sites join forces for annual musical.

Background and Atmosphere: Sixth form founded in 1977 and now in two buildings a short distance apart in north Oxford. Science labs, computer room, art and photography in one; pretty much everything else, including student common-room and library, in the other. Students travel to performing arts department at Leckford Place less than five minutes away for music and drama studies. The short walk between buildings was the only moan students could dredge up when invited to find fault with d'Overbroeck's. But a 15-minute break between lessons should give them bags of time to make the trek. Real college feel to the place – not like school at all. Everyone on first name terms. No uniform. Informal and energetic atmosphere. Students instilled with sense of personal responsibility. No dining room but filled rolls available in the common-room at midday, lots of local sandwich shops or cafes, and water coolers everywhere in the college. 'It's important we keep the sixth form separate from the younger pupils so we can run it in a more collegiate way,' says Cohen. 'The fact it's more grown up and not schooly is what draws a lot of students to d'Overbroecks.' Lots of staff are lifers, but not the tired dried-up old sticks you might expect. In fact, just the opposite – they're lively, buzzy, still excited to be sharing a wealth of knowledge.

In the late '80s d'Overbroecks decided to extend downwards into GCSEs. Not long afterwards, intake lowered to 13 and, since 2005, children able to join at 11. Leckford Place was opened in the former Phil and Jim's (state primary school) site on corner of Leckford Place, an ingeniously-designed new building that not only transformed the residential area but also the school's ambitions.

Original school hall is central to school activities. Healthy lunches served here (sweets and sugary drinks confiscated) before space morphs into theatrical venue. Max pupil numbers will be 220 – now at 150. Aiming to be 50/50 boys and girls but currently slightly higher percentage of boys at the top of the school. Increasingly parents' first choice. Staff and students seemed equally keen to be there. First name rule applies here too, also little or no uniform. Cohen insists, 'It's a well-disciplined school. By using first names, pupils see that teachers are real people too.' Questionnaire circulated among parents 'touchingly positive'.

Pastoral Care and Discipline: Sixth form – very regular contact with parents through meetings and reports. Good feedback. Around 50 per cent of students board in college boarding houses or with host families. Live-in warden, supervised study periods and curfews. No drugs tolerated with total exclusion for offenders. Bullying 'not part of this environment,' says Cohen. All students assigned own director of studies who's there for pastoral and academic purposes. Can also talk to trained college counsellor in confidence if preferred. Academic progress, attendance, punctuality, work rate and general well-being monitored very closely. Pastoral care outstanding.

Leckford Place – no boarding at this age. Form tutors head pastoral care team. Open door policy means parents welcomed any time and pupils encouraged to turn to tutors with any concerns. Usual anti-bullying policy.

Pupils and Parents: Majority have already been in independent sector for a while. Quite a mixed bag of grafters and high-achievers. Most have one thing in common – they're opting for an environment where students are treated as individuals. All students (whether at Leckford Place or in sixth form) treated thus – high fliers and strugglers handled with sensitivity and success in equal measure. Value-added features in spades at both sites (sixth form is one of the top in England). Have yet to meet a dissatisfied parent. In sixth form, 40 per cent of students from overseas. Wide spread – some government-sponsored Thai scholars, others from Germany, eastern Europe and USA.

Entrance: Sixth form – intake from Leckford Place, but majority from other schools. GCSE requirements at least eight A* to Cs,including four Bs, though most have higher than this and the college looks for higher grades for certain A level subjects. Looking especially for students who will 'contribute'. 'They should throw themselves into the life of the college as much as they can as then they get more out of it,' says Cohen.

Scholarships available (academic, science, art, performing arts). Recent additions have been the Environmental Awareness Award for a student interested in this and able to raise awareness within the college, and this year the Enterprise Award for future entrepreneurs.

Leckford Place – not just one entrance exam day for 11+ and 13+ students. A good number of pupils now enter through the scholarship examinations. Scholarships are offered for academic excellence and in art and performing arts at 11+ and 13+. Prospective pupils assessed both academically and for individual strengths, such as sport or music. Head says school not overly academically selective, but still wants children who can do well at GCSE and progress to sixth form. Assessment involves test and interview. Pupils must also supply school report and latest key stage results. Some cynics suggest all-comers welcome to bump numbers up quickly, but slow increase of roll tells different story.

Exit: Sixth form – approximately 10 per cent to Oxbridge. Other top choices include Imperial College, London, Oxford Brookes, Leeds, Bristol, King's College, London and Newcastle. Fairly high proportion of medics, also social sciences and arts feature prominently. All get in to first choice unis. Plenty opt for gap year.

Leckford Place – most move up to d'Overbroeck's sixth form, a few leave for well-thought-of local state Cherwell (just along the road).

Money Matters: Academic, science, art and performing art scholarships all available up to maximum of 25 per cent tuition fees. Value is at discretion of college. College also offer means-tested bursaries.

Remarks: Leckford Place is now an important part of the local community and is Oxford's only coeducational independent day school for this age group. Aims to give children the chance to discover and develop talents which may have been overlooked in 'larger more impersonal environments'. Sixth form already well-established in parents' minds as quite possibly the leading independent sixth form in the UK. It's a place of energy and laughter, of single-minded determination among students to do the best they can, and d'Overbroecks doesn't let them down.

Downe House School

Cold Ash, Thatcham, Berkshire, RG18 9JJ

• Pupils: 575 girls, 550 boarders • Ages: 11-18 • Size of sixth form: 165
• C of E • Fees: Boarding £28,875; Day £20,895 pa • Independent

Tel: 01635 200 286
Fax: 01635 202 026
Email: correspondence@downehouse.net
Website: www.downehouse.net

Head: Since 1997, Mrs Emma McKendrick BA (forties), quietly-spoken, thorough, thoughtful and firm, has two little boys and a banker husband. Previously head of the Royal School, Bath for three years but chose Downe House over the headship of the merged Royal School Bath/Bath High because of the boarding – 'Having that extra time is glorious'. Read German and Dutch at Liverpool but does not teach any more, instead concentrates on finding different ways to get to know the girls. She meets with each of them (grade reading) one-to-one, nominally to look at their academic progress but with no set agenda. As a result she greets girls by name on the way into chapel or lunch and asks after siblings or extra-curricular projects – pupils are really impressed by her knowledge and feel valued (handwritten birthday cards for each). This individual attention is at the heart of the school – 'We're not aiming to produce a Downe House girl, but a common value system'.

Academic matters: Sparkling results. Not as academically focused as Wycombe Abbey, more so than St Swithun's. 100 per cent grade A to C at GCSE – you only need to do eight but 99 per cent do 10 or 11 – with 84 per cent grade A or B at A level (English, maths, biology and French most popular), 45 per cent three grade As. Girls are encouraged to excel in their chosen subjects – you go as fast as you can but are pressured if it seems necessary. Downe has recently taken up the Pre-U in a big way too. Parents comment that both arty and academic girls succeed and judge that the quality of teaching rises further up the school, with a strong pitch for girls to remain in the sixth form – this is not seen as a given.

A term in the Dordogne for 12 year olds improves everyone's French and is a highpoint of school life for those entering the school before CE; it provides a real chance to build friendships and focus on projects independent of the national curriculum. Many other languages on offer: Italian, German, Latin, Greek, Chinese and Spanish (now massively beefed up by recruitment of new member of staff – rare specimen in that he is a highly successful Cambridge Pre-U expert). Separate science (double award and distinct, top sets can sit AS at same time as GCSEs) and IT blocks fully-equipped, although most girls have their own laptops.

Geography extended through trips (Iceland), English classes emerge from the cloisters they are taught in and head to the theatre in Reading. Work in a disabled school in Newbury provides first-hand experience for those interested in medicine. Similar use of external examples throughout teaching, e.g. speakers talk on politics, Einstein's theory of relativity and superstring theory. Prep is not supervised in the sixth form, so girls learn to organise their own study during free periods, which stands them in good stead for university. Older girls comment that staff are hot on spotting difficulties and offering help. Learning skills department (staff of four includes one EFL/speech therapist) operates an evolving list for extension and encouragement, whether ad hoc or ongoing.

Games, Options, the Arts: The art department looks very impressive – or certainly as May Music Weekend approaches and visitors are expected! Experienced teaching (head of department 15 years in tenure so far) backs up this parade with examples of work used as best practice in their latest publication for teachers. A yearly mural project brightens the corridors leading to other subjects. Ceramics less popular with older girls.

Preparations for the school's centenary in 2007 included the composition of an opera about Downe House during the war. Music practice in nuns' former cells (cells are now offices) contributes to a strong chamber orchestra and choir, and a hugely enthusiastic head of department who arranges tours to places like Venice and St Petersburg – 'ideally somewhere without too much night life!'. Impressive performing arts centre buzzes during house drama, concerts and fashion shows – girls involved in every aspect of performance and Radley boys often pulled in too.

Rows of tennis courts, fantastic pool, hockey begun recently, strong on netball and lacrosse; if you are in a team you really practise sport – if not you sort out your own exercise outside PE: options are there and staff open to arranging new ones – yoga, dance, gym (plug your iPod in and get on a machine), judo, sailing. Off-campus riding on a Wednesday evening works very well for girls with their own or riding school horses.

A successful jewellery business created as a previous year's Young Enterprise encourages new ventures. World Challenge is also very popular – trips with Radley boys to Borneo, China etc. New plan for each house to link with a school or an orphanage in the developing world should ensure girls' privileged life is anchored in a global reality. Many keen to explore this contact further during gap years. Places on the Leith's cookery course are coveted – great for stints as a chalet girl – so allotted by ballot.

Background and Atmosphere: Established in 1907 by Roedean- and Oxford-educated Olive Willis; moved from Kent to Cold Ash in 1922. Main building purpose-built for a silent order during World War I; today the chapel and cloisters remain the physical centre of the extended campus, with Greek Steps overlooked by the staff common-room, so not many girls hang out there – at the tuckshop instead.

Real effort to mark transitions for girls who attend the full seven years – the youngest ones are in separate houses, one a bus ride away from the campus, with firm rules to get girls used to communal living and long days. These are relaxed slightly by the house-mistresses of the five mixed-age houses where girls from 13 to 16 learn to co-habit and watch Home and Away together! The first opportunity to mix with your entire year is in the sixth form house, which generates independence and enormous excitement – new friends, cooking and washing facilities, and a resident maths teacher on tap for prep help. Separate refectory here with reputedly better food than in the main dining room. At present, half the upper sixth is in solitary splendour and the other shares a roof with the lower sixth. Future plans include consolidating this final year in an upgrade of the boarding houses. (Now Willis House houses the L6 and York House the U6.)

No litter in the grounds, but atmosphere is relaxed enough to have book piles on the floor outside the art block and some girls getting away with Converse under their uniform. Sixth form have more elegant dress code and can wear jewellery. Fads spread across the school but they range from a recognisable Downe House hairstyle (loose pony tail, in line with fashion) to gobbling books during a Readathon – none centred on exclusive cliques. The owner of the PO in Cold Ash obeys headmistress's request not to sell cigarettes to the girls and has no complaints about them, sees them mostly at weekends and judges them an international lot. A neighbour reports that the girls who come to collect tennis balls mis-hit into her garden are very polite.

Seems to be a huge amount on offer and not enough hours in the day/week to try everything. Scheduled 'chill out' time for the youngest ones after which you learn your limits by experience. Weekend activities stretch from shopping trips to Bluewater to the ballet in High Wycombe, with Greek dinners and reeling with boys' schools in between. Staff are delighted to be involved in these and also invited around to houses by girls for tea parties – this friendliness is obvious.

Pastoral Care and Discipline: House-mistress is the first port of call for teenage angst and graver matters; daily meetings with tutor for academic and administrative issues. A foundation of trust often develops between certain pupils and particular teachers – can be a subject teacher, the chaplain or a housemistress. Staff walking dogs are a deterrent to smoking in the woods, suspension if it happens inside. Rare drinking episodes, even rarer drugs ones – suspension and expulsion respectively.

Pupils and Parents: Lots of affluent country parents (local, Scotland, Norfolk) and a big London contingent, with 70 per cent rich professionals – bankers, businessmen, doctors, accountants – and the rest are diplomats or from the military. Five per cent non-UK nationals. All shapes and sizes of girls here, open, charming and talkative – according to a Downe House alumna visiting recently, the latter is the one characteristic common to all generations! Old girls include actress Geraldine James, comic Laura Solon (winner of 2005 Perrier Award at Edinburgh Festival), Fru Hazlitt, CEO Virgin Radio, the late Dame Rosemary Murray, first woman vice chancellor of Cambridge, TV and radio presenter Clare Balding and explorer Jennifer Murray. Oh – and Kate Middleton – until she went to co-ed Marlborough for her sixth form.

Entrance: Three applicants for every place, around 65 per cent enter through CE at 11+ and school exam at 12+, the rest at 13. A few enter thereafter. Minimum of seven GCSEs at A or B grade for entry at sixth form, and entrance exam and interview for the few that enter from outside.

Exit: Eight per cent leave after GCSE, usually to boys' schools taking girls in sixth form, e.g. Uppingham, Marlborough. Almost all to university and gap years popular (Bristol, Edinburgh, Leeds, Newcastle, Durham); Oxbridge and US Ivy League take about 10 each year.

Money Matters: Scholarships and exhibitions (art, music and academic) with a nominal remission of £1,000 and £600 per annum thereafter. Additional funding and bursaries available via means testing and bursaries. Sport scholarships for internal candidates at 14+ and 16+ only last two years.

Remarks: A green and spacious school which leads its pupils into independence as they move round the campus, and makes sure they experience life outside it. Grounded and confident girls in great facilities (plans to improve these include a new music school and Astroturf) achieve results that match their individual focuses.

Downside School

Linked to Downside Junior School in the Junior section

Stratton-on-the-Fosse, Radstock, Somerset, BA3 4RJ

• Pupils: 425 pupils: 250 boys, 175 girls; 85 per cent board • Ages: 11-18 • Size of sixth form: 140 • RC and Christian • Fees: Boarding £20,037-£25,227; Day £12,285-£13,668 pa • Independent

Tel: 01761 235 103
Fax: 01761 235 105
Email: registrar@downside.co.uk
Website: www.downside.co.uk

Head: Since 2003, Dom Leo Maidlow Davies MA BD STL (mid-fifties), a Benedictine monk who has been at Downside man and boy, departing only to read archaeology and anthropology at Cambridge in the '70s, and theology at London and Rome in the '80s. Since then, he has taught classics as a novice master, been a housemaster and still teaches RS to the sixth form. His steepled fingers, intense spirituality and learned air thinly veil a delightful sense of humour and turn of phrase: Downside is undoubtedly a Catholic school 'but I don't need a beauty parade to see just how Catholic pupils are'. Working out of a charmingly messy book-lined study overlooking the quad, he appears to enjoy the right degree of respect and warmth with his flock. His faith is at the centre of everything he does: 'The glorification of God is important and this school does not tuck a little bit of religion away on the side', yet he is much in tune with the transient preoccupations of the young and addresses them with apparent sensitivity. Commercial necessities and front of house are well handled by his management team, an effective foil to this most cerebral of men, yet some parents feel that he should exhibit more honest-to-goodness leadership, particularly in dealing with less than effective teaching.

Initiatives introduced five years ago now bearing fruit in terms of much better results, and integration of the girls, currently a 40/60 split. 'The centre of gravity has changed – there's a stronger sense of inner ambition,' claims the head, and it's become cool to be clever and to work. The girls' houses have lost some of their sparkling newness and are thought by some to lack soul compared with the homely antiquity of the boys' accommodation – apart from bathrooms which take antiquity too far. Any lingering male resentment has mostly gone.

Academic matters: Greatly beefed up in recent years, especially at A level with 71 per cent A*/A/B grades in 2010; creditable GCSEs too, at 47 per cent A/A*, some of which attributable to determined new director of studies, and insisting on a 50 per cent average at Common Entrance since 2006. Value-added particularly strong here. Subjects offered at GCSE and A level are 'properly academic and recognised by leading universities'; this causes some pupils wanting more choice and/or creativity to bail out for sixth form. Most take 11 GCSEs, including at least one modern language; RS compulsory for all but the most alienated foreigner. Some parents critical of academic snobbery, e.g. a society for Oxbridge pupils (only).

A tutor is assigned to each pupil and they're around the houses during prep to offer sticks/carrots as appropriate. Grades every three weeks mean progress can be closely tracked and problems dealt with; lots of academic clinics on offer. Academic societies in every year group exist to 'ignite an appetite for higher achievement' (a very Benedictine aspiration) and there are essay prizes for all subjects and year groups. Refurbished library is enough to provoke intellectual endeavour in anyone. Latest IT sits comfortably in some historic classrooms but not all and some parents worry that ICT is an add-on, insufficiently integrated into lessons; 'they're asleep on IT' said one dissatisfied dad. The labs also let the side down but funds for a facelift on the way, not before time; pupils reckon that 'humanities far outstrip sciences', and that one or two teachers should be given the heave-ho.

The school claims 'long experience of supporting pupils with mild special needs, especially dyselxia (sic) and dyspraxia', though points out that pupils must be able to cope with a mainstream academic curriculum, albeit with one-to-one support where needed. There is a dedicated unit which also caters for moderate learning difficulties and some behavioural issues, though there is no provision for autistic spectrum disorders. Its low profile assures discretion to its users. EAL provision supports foreign pupils. All special tuition is chargeable.

Games, Options, the Arts: Around 500 verdant acres mean pitches almost as far as the eye can see, plus tennis/netball courts, a running track and an Astro in need of resurfacing. As well as traditional rugby, hockey, football, cricket, tennis for the boys and hockey, netball, tennis and rounders for the girls, more exotic activities are on offer. Some, e.g. sailing, promise more than they deliver. Super sports hall and beautifully-refurbished swimming pool accommodate those less keen on the great outdoors. Philosophy tends to be team participation for all, rather than winning at all costs, (though 1st XV 'repeatedly victorious' at the time of writing), and there's an upscale fixtures list. Some parents feel that the approach and organisation could be considerably sharpened up. Top players can join local clubs and county/regional squads. Thriving CCF, compulsory for part Year 9, can morph into D of E or Ten Tors for the less pugnacious, but Downside maintains a proud and distinguished military tradition.

Pupils' art adorns the walls of the main building's wide corridors, with their quaintly wonky parquet floors. Innovative work in all media and remarkable photography, some of which appears in the school's own publications, oeuvres of extraordinary glossiness – and paucity of content.

Drama very strong and they're fortunate to have a theatre seating 600, with a stage built wide enough to perform Gilbert and Sullivan, in the days when it was fashionable. Plays put on for all age groups and in each house once a year, and everyone gets involved, on or off the stage. Fantastic music and art provision mean enough competent players, singers and set designers to ensure productions are almost always pupil-led.

Music outstanding – and so it should be, with the prospect of singing mass every Sunday in the sublime setting of the abbey church. The Schola Cantorum performs major choral works throughout the year and has several CDs under its belt. No less than four chamber choirs of only 16 voices each (boys, girls, mixed, junior) invite only the especially talented to audition. Players shine too, either in the orchestra, chamber groups or pipe band, and the jazz band, Slaughterhouse 7, has played in every continent. Organists lucky enough to have two quality instruments to play on site. More contemporary fare trumpeted at the battle of the bands and charity showcase, held at nearby Writhlington School, but considerable feeling that modern and/or alternative music (e.g. folk) should get more airtime than it does. Oddly enough, music tech pretty good after recent investment.

Background and Atmosphere: Rearing up from the surrounding countryside, the abbey is visible for miles around and dominates the sleepy, slightly run-down village of Stratton-on-the-Fosse. The present, somewhat austere, buildings date mostly from 1814, when it had become safe for Catholics once more to provide education in England, but the school is over 400 years old. The spiritual life of the monastic community permeates the very fabric of the school; this veteran of many schools had never experienced anything quite like its atmosphere. As the head remarked, 'It would be hard to leave Downside without a sense of what a spiritual life was'. The monks are vital to the life of the school; some teach and their presence in the chaplaincy is particularly valued, but their role is one of influence rather than power. 80 per cent of the pupils are Catholic; those that aren't are asked to 'recognise the distinctively Catholic nature', but a few feel somewhat sidelined, including parents, who chose the school for its pastoral care and spiritual grounding, yet resent being referred to as 'protos'. Nonetheless, these aspects do not disappoint, and the way in which the schools lays down the foundations of faith – whatever the pupils then go on to make of it – is widely praised; 'an anchor for life', as one father put it.

Atmosphere and setting remain distinctly traditional, helped by wonderfully anachronistic uniform of black jackets and pinstripes for the boys, and classic mid-length kilts and tweeds for girls (even in sixth form, astonishingly), designed by a committee of mothers. Sports kit cooler, if lurid. Magnificent though slightly gloomy refectory (nb) serving unspectacular food; some complain there isn't always enough of it for hungry boys at supper time, but the theatre café opens in the evenings, filling any gaps, and there are kitchens in all the boarding houses. Gripes about food or any other matter raised at school council. Strong house allegiance to each of the six senior houses for boarders and day pupils; after Plunkett House, the school's junior section, the boys spend their first year in Powell, before moving on, girls straight in. In common with most boys' schools, no change at sixth form.

The girls' arrival in 2005 has breathed new life into the place, 'the making of it', according to one mother of three sons, though a few dissent! 'We are no longer preparing boys and girls for different roles,' says the head, then adds 'but our primary purpose is not to produce chaps who will be useful to the economy'. Oh dear, not too many sons and daughters of Old Gregorians in the pipeline then ... however, a palpable family feeling about the place. Parents also like the notion of service the school promotes. It does all feel rather insular though and remote from modern life: there isn't even a shop in the village, so unless pupils take advantage of a weekend minibus trip into Bath 12 miles away, they have to walk a mile to the nearest (tiny) co-op in the next village. Certainly wouldn't suit more urban types, which is perhaps why some parents choose it! Others feel strongly that a small school so rurally located definitely needs socials with other schools. Downside has determinedly kept its ethos as a full boarding school, with 85 per cent boarders and a full weekend activity programme. Some day pupils elect to spend much of the weekend at school; when we visited, everyone was preparing for a Roman banquet on the Saturday night – no stuffed dormice, we hope.

Pastoral Care and Discipline: Excellent pastoral care and tolerance for the individual produces happy kids, some of whom have found Downside a refuge after the rough and tumble of other schools: 'My daughter is respected for who she is and her confidence restored', said one relieved mother who moved her from the local state offering. Each pupil has a tutor to oversee academic matters but they liaise closely with house staff, so that the overview is seamless. Policies strive for consistency; there is a dedicated head of pastoral care. Problems of smoking and drinking are 'manageable' – the school aims to educate the pupils though the pitfalls. Parents are kept informed of all but the most minor misdemeanours and sanctions tend towards privations at weekends, such as detention, gating or the wearing of uniform. Pupils report some inconsistencies in the awarding of punishments, but they agreed that owning up was likely to be in their best interests, both in this world and the next. No reports of inappropriate relations with the opposite sex; perhaps all that moral guidance pays off.

Achievements of all kinds are celebrated at house or school level; certificates in 'seemly Latin' are handed out at headmaster's assembly six times a year, along with sporting colours and caps. He marks lesser successes with a hand-written postcard, a nice touch.

Pupils and Parents: Lots of different backgrounds and educational experiences united by 'common values and aspirations to a spiritual life' – plus Catholicism in majority of cases. Strong family ties. A certain amount of Catholic snobbery but not so much social – this is not a flashy school. Most enjoy a good and mutually supportive relationship with the school, though some report that 'feedback is not always welcomed, let alone acted upon'. The pupils struck us as articulate, thoughtful, focused (though not alarmingly so) yet somewhat unworldly, seemingly immune from the teenage temptations of sex, drugs and rock 'n' roll. (Perhaps not in the holidays.) Mostly local families, but increasing numbers from London, fleeing the intense competition for places at decent schools, or metropolitan distractions. A sprinkling of foreigners, 10 per cent or so.

Entrance: Entry below sixth form has had a shake-up. The junior section has recently been reorganised and renamed Plunkett House, where entry is now only into Years 7 or 8 (curiously Year 6 too in the past), via the Downside Assessment Test, a computerised aptitude test with no possible preparation, with assessments in maths, English and general reasoning, plus interview and reports from the previous school. The expectation is that once a child has got into Plunkett House, he/she will be fit for the senior school. Nonetheless, all pupils still sit common entrance or common scholarship in Year 8 – results determine sets in the senior school. Conditional places sometimes offered to less confident performers, who then have to 'pass the CE exam threshold', currently set at 50 per cent across all subjects. Normal whirligig of open/taster/induction days. Sixth form entry depends on interview, previous school's reports and references and tests in subjects intended for A level. B grades at GCSE, but As for sciences, are required to pursue any subject to A level.

Exit: Almost all to higher education; mostly university but one or two to art college. Success at Oxbridge shows a 'pleasing upward trajectory' over the last few years: eight in 2009, with an even stronger current upper sixth. Approx a third take gap years and apply post A level, something the school encourages; we hope that the school offers the same degree of support over UCAS forms as it does to those still in the school. Director of studies intends to track leavers' destinations more closely in future; more information would be useful. A little fall-out after GCSE, mostly pupils seeking a wider or more vocational choice at A level.

Money Matters: Fees in line with, if not cheaper than, comparable schools. A 'substantial number' of scholarships and exhibitions available, the size and distribution of which are at the head's discretion. Usual offer of music, sport and all-rounder, plus choral awards of anything up to 50 per cent of fees. Discounts of up to 15 per cent for scions of Old Gregorians and 10 per cent for siblings, also means-tested bursaries.

Remarks: A culture of aspiration, whether spiritual or academic, pervades this rather rarefied school. Sheltered by the abbey and guided by its faith, pupils are cocooned from less welcome bits of modern life and allowed to concentrate on acquiring a thorough intellectual and spiritual toolkit, and to grow up in their own time, with idiosyncrasies intact. Very special, and not for everyone we suspect, but a great choice for practising Catholics and those seeking strong spiritual direction in a school.

Dr Challoner's Grammar School

Chesham Road, Amersham, Buckinghamshire, HP6 5HA

• Pupils: 1,300 boys; all day • Ages: 11-18 • Size of sixth form: 380 • Non-denom • State

Tel: 01494 787 500
Fax: 01494 721 862
Email: admin@challoners.com
Website: www.challoners.com

Headmaster: Since 2001, Dr Mark Fenton MA MSc PGCE PhD. Now in his early forties, became head in his early thirties and remains an ebullient and boyish figure, with a nice sense of irony, passionate about his school and about delivering an education that isn't all about exam statistics (one of the few heads we've met who genuinely doesn't have the figures at his finger tips). Educated at Brentwood School, Essex, followed by Peterhouse, Cambridge, where he read history, graduating with a first. PGCE at the Institute of Education, then squeezed in his PhD (on how parents choose schools) while already working. Started out at Chelmsford, at a mixed comprehensive, then taught history and politics at King Edward V1 Grammar School for six years, rising to assistant head. Then deputy head, Sir Joseph Williamson's Mathematical School, a grammar school in Rochester, before proceeding to Dr Challoner's as one of the country's youngest heads.

Feels the school he took over was not only run down but a bit insular and old-fashioned. He has spruced it up physically, socially and academically, transforming its traditionally élitist (some would have said arrogant) approach to one where 'intelligent awareness' is the norm. 'Now it's a softer place,' he says. Wants the education he provides to be 'broad-ranging and rounded', to teach about perseverance, responsibility and risk – 'I want boys to be able to reflect on what they've done; I want them to understand collaboration'.

Parents feel he has come tightly to grips with the organisation; most find him very approachable – 'When it snowed and half the boys couldn't get in, he just said, "Right, let's go out and have a snowball fight," and the teachers all joined him'. Continues to teach (citizenship to Year 8, politics A level) and, according to one father, knows 'endless boys' by name. Recently appointed a national leader of education by the National College for School Leadership, one of about 100 heads in the country.

Academic matters: Now Buckinghamshire's top-performing grammar and consistently in the top 20 nationwide, though not a school where undue pressure seems the norm. Breadth considered a desirable commodity – Dr Fenton believes that the more pupils learn the better they become at learning. Most take 11 GCSEs, with a compulsory language and humanity plus four options. Two-thirds take four A levels – 'research shows that if you take four subjects you do better in all four'. About 85 per cent of boys get five or more As and A*s at GCSE, nearly 80 per cent A*, As and Bs at A level.

Specialist status in science and maths since 2002 – 'the science teaching is incredibly strong,' said one parent – and carts away loads of awards from the Royal Society of Chemistry. Recently took on a second specialism in languages. 'We asked: where is there most scope for improvement? Boys and languages can be a bit of an uphill struggle; we wanted to put it front and centre in an innovative way.' As well as French, Spanish and German, Mandarin and Russian now offered as sixth form options and language teaching approached in a creative fashion using music to help aid speech rhythms, plus cultural enrichment days and work experience exchanges abroad.

The head is an enthusiast for more adventurous teaching and learning methods all round – 'The point is for them to work things out and then explain how they've done it'. Staff are trained to understand boys' strengths as learners and boys do specialised induction days in Years 7, 10 and 12 devoted to reflection on learning. Teaching (and indeed everything else) praised as excellent in recent Ofsted inspection (though one parents felt the school was still stronger on the science side than on the arts). 25 A level options. Standard classes of 30 in the early years, 20–30 at GCSE, 15–20 higher up. All teachers are involved in SEN and, if necessary, individual education plan will be drawn up, with some individual tuition where required.

Games, Options, the Arts: Sport played at top competitive level – 'We knew the school was academically strong,' said one parent, 'but our son wouldn't have survived if it hadn't had good sport as well and he absolutely loves it'. Headmaster very keen on cricket, which is reflectively buoyant. Regular sports tours abroad – football to Holland, cricket to the Caribbean. Very successful soccer team, hockey up-and-coming. National finals of the under 19s squash. National junior cross-country champions. Annual activity week lets boys try out the more unusual sports, like climbing and golf. Sport for all with house competitions and lunch-time clubs. Two sports halls and the Centenary sports pitch, opened in 2004, which includes a floodlit all-weather pitch, a new cricket square and pavilion.

Music also hugely strong with a good boys' choir, professional standard jazz band and swing band operated jointly with the matching girls' grammar school down the road. Lots of other co-ed activities, including lively drama – annual drama, musical and senior play, plus showing at the Edinburgh Festival. Debating enthusiastic and strong. Wide range of stimulating education visits (geographers to Iceland, historians to Russia). Six houses with plenty of inter-house competition in sports, music and science.

Background and Atmosphere: Founded 1624 under the will of Dr Robert Chaloner (sic), former rector of Amersham and Canon of Windsor. Moved to present site in 1905, when it became co-ed. Due to expanding numbers, girls got their own premises in 1962. The boys' school is still focused round the 1905 core but has expanded higgledy-piggledy with a motley mix of buildings from creaky '50s to state of the art 21st century. Definition added with a new entrance in 2007. Still not the most coherent or beautiful site, but now well equipped with the requisite facilities to house and stretch its 1300 or so bright and well-behaved young men.

'Excellence with integrity' is the school's motto – it prides itself on the responsibility it gives to pupils. 'This school respects students, gives them responsibility and trusts them,' said one. Very active student council – 'It teaches negotiation and leadership,' says the head. 'We regularly consult students and student groups undertake research, then present their findings to the senior leadership team. It work across the ages and helps them understand both research and presentation.' Sixth formers given considerable degree of freedom – attendance compulsory till lunch, then free to go if no lessons. Large number of boys given official responsibility in the sixth form, with 60–80 elected prefects, head boys, house captains etc. Boys supervise lunch with walkie-talkies and mentor new boys. Healthy hot lunch for younger pupils, sixth formers have their own café with slightly less PC snacks or leave the premises to make their own eating decisions. Blazer and standard tie pre-GCSE, own suit and tie of authority thereafter.

Pastoral Care and Discipline: In general, a sensible, well-behaved lot ('I'm sure there must be drugs but I've never seen any evidence of them,' says one long-term mother). School confronts traditional problem areas head on. 'We bring in search dogs unannounced and have a drugs counsellor,' says the head. 'Since we introduced this policy five years ago, we've not had a single drugs-related incident.' One or two challenging students and usual tiresome teenage misconduct, treated firmly but with understanding. 'One boy couldn't fit a pornographic film on his memory stick so he tried to upload it onto the school computer,' says the head wryly. 'He got a one-day exclusion. I don't mind the odd misdemeanour but I get fed up when they can't learn from their mistakes.' Pupils themselves have drawn up the bullying charter, displayed in every classroom. Student development team and support staff with a counselling qualification.

Pupils and Parents: Solid middle-class parents from the surrounding solid middle-class landscape. Ethnic minorities (about 15 per cent) and free school meals very much less in evidence than elsewhere; nonetheless parents and pupils range from the very poor to the significantly well off. Coaches deliver boys from more remote spots but the school also nicely near the tube.

Entrance: All applicants take the Buckinghamshire Test (the best score of two tests in verbal reasoning) and anyone who gets 121 (with 141 the top mark) is entitled to a grammar school place. Technically, this means the top 34 per cent will be eligible, though occasionally successful candidates will fall below the benchmark, including some boys who qualify through the appeals process. Catchment area is defined by the council. Ever-more-heavily over-subscribed, it used to take boys from more than seven miles away, now rarely more than six miles – don't even think of applying if you live out of county. 20 places for external applicants at A level – candidates must have 386 points from their best eight GSCEs, plus at least a grade C in English and maths. Some subjects have additional specifications.

Exit: Three or four leave post GCSE, some to private schools. 'When we offered our sons the choice of any independent school they wanted, day or boarding, they all decided they'd prefer to stay at Challoner's,' says one mother. 27 Oxbridge offers – more 'Ox' than 'Bridge' this year – with the most popular subjects, now as always, maths, physics, engineering and PPE. The rest to other leading universities.

Money Matters: Strong PTA fundraising but parental financial support is optional rather than press-ganged.

Remarks: An outstanding boys' grammar school, particularly strong in science, which produces well-qualified, level-headed, responsible adults, able to fit in anywhere. A friendly, purposeful, down-to-earth place, where boys enjoy a good social life with their peers and with the neighbouring girls' grammar school.

Dr Challoner's High School

Cokes Lane, Little Chalfont, Buckinghamshire, HP7 9QB

• Pupils: 1,055 girls, all day • Ages: 11-18 • Size of sixth form: 280
• Non-denom • State

Tel: 01494 763 296
Fax: 01494 766 023
Email: office@challonershigh.com
Website: www.challonershigh.com

Head: Since 2006, Miss Peg Hulse BA (mid-fifties), previously head of Portsmouth High since 1999 where she was nominated for, and gained, the South East Award for Leadership in a Secondary School, in 2002. Taught English and drama for 13 years at Newcastle-under-Lyme School, then deputy head at Northampton High. Cheerful, tall, slim, but steely; a culture-vulture – especially loves anything innovative, avant-garde and well-performed; packs in theatre, galleries and exhibitions on trips at home and abroad. Reads a lot and is a keen walker.

Approving noises from staff for this head, the third in recent times. They say, 'she's very approachable, has got to grips with things and fits in well.' Popular with parents – 'she consults and listens, is open to ideas and is keen to build a community, ensure growth and cohesion'. Girls comment, 'she takes a real interest in us and is very enthusiastic, impassioned and omnipresent.' She admits to being passionate about girls' education, particularly for the relatively able, and insists it's important to stay at the forefront of education. Keen to 'turn out young women who have the skills and personality to be responsible for the world and themselves', and 'We must develop and use their talents to the best, while ensuring they remain happy and balanced'. A Quaker, so responsibility, valuing others and making a difference not only sit well with her beliefs but she also recognises that at her desks may sit the next Jocelyn Bell Burnell or Elizabeth Fry. Retiring July 2011 after a long and admirable career.

Academic matters: Max class size 30, unstreamed except in maths, though plenty of differentiation to ensure all needs met. Staff think as a collegiate body, look to challenge rather than give answers. At GCSE in 2010, 81 per cent A*/A. At A level 88 per cent A*/A/B. Believes in quality not quantity, so enrichment very much a part not only of the whole curriculum but also of personalised learning. Early language diversification with French and Spanish or German on offer plus Latin at KS4 and Mandarin at sixth form; girls can choose two languages for GCSE.

Double or triple sciences, large take-up in English literature, biology, chemistry and maths at A level. Economics and history strong, politics popular – girls enjoy the intellectual challenge. Significantly fewer opt for physics at A level than the other sciences but results creditable. Tough to find any weak areas but unanimous that maths is the strongest – 'Staff are enthusiastic and organised and the teaching is very good,' commented one further maths A level student, who had been given additional support to get to grips with the subject when in Year 7.

Some support for those experiencing learning difficulties – monitoring and assessment as required. Raft of activities both within and beyond the classroom, including pioneering pilot language leader programme, stretch and challenge the most able.

Games, Options, the Arts: Superb arts and technology faculty; quality art festoons the building – not all displays tip-top but at least they're refreshed on a regular basis. Masses of drama, mostly via English department, plus A level theatre studies in conjunction with Dr Challoner's Grammar School (qv). Plenty of opportunities for all to sing, dance, act and play via annual musical production and concerts; string, wind and brass ensembles and instrumental lessons (300 learn an instrument in school). Swing band tours Europe bi-annually.

Sport extremely popular and well supported via enthusiastic staff; fully developed sports leadership programme for sixth form and junior athlete education programme for those at county, national and international level. High standards across athletics, hockey, netball (third in national finals), fencing (U16 public schools winners – had to get dispensation to compete), basketball (national finalists), cricket, football, rugby, world-ranked sailor and swimming (but no pool). Plenty of extra-curricular opportunities though it would be good to have more for younger girls, perhaps with a compulsory feel, to encourage them to try new (and old) things out and join in. Work experience, D of E, and many clubs for everything; debating popular and fiercely contested, with regular trips to Oxford Union. Economics Society invites key people from the government and the world of finance to give lectures. Currently launching a new society for those who want to explore things culturally and intellectually with the intention of stretching minds, perhaps via writing of an academic/research-type paper. Lots of foreign visits; strong charity involvement – especially with link school in Mvumi in Tanzania, working on dream teams' project. Enthusiastic contributors to a county initiative for rights-respecting schools which uses the United Nations Convention of the Rights of the Child as a basis and looks at the rights and responsibilities of all pupils and adults in own school.

Background and Atmosphere: Founded in 1624 by Dr Robert Chaloner (sic), becoming co-ed in 1906. Girls hived off to Little Chalfont in 1962, concentrating, in the words of the then headmistress, 'not on looking backwards, but upon a forward vision'. The splendid suburban site, a short walk from the Metropolitan line tube station, incorporates mature trees and acres of playing fields. The school is a combination of typically featureless, flat-roofed 1960s buildings, paradoxically placed alongside marvellous '90s curving, brick-built extension encompassing an outdoor amphitheatre. Latest additions include a large, modern, versatile sports hall and new reception. Head keen to continue to smarten the school – 'It's what the girls deserve'.

Pastoral Care and Discipline: Girls have the same form tutor from arrival to sixth form. Not many behavioural issues so pastoral care concentrates on support and ironing out the usual friendship problems. Relatively few grumbles from girls – 'It would be good to see coursework spread out; there are times when we're inundated,' and another added, 'This is a very teach-yourself school, and for those who aren't so clever, class sizes can be problematic'. They did agree, though, that they were encouraged both to take responsibility and have fun. Discos back on the agenda – 'It's important the girls let their hair down but in a safe and controlled environment'. Sixth form support about to be restructured.

Pupils and Parents: From south-east Buckinghamshire and Chiltern district; sixth formers may enter from further afield; predominantly middle class, with fair share of ethnic minority backgrounds. Parents can visit the school at any time, with head's 'clinic', once a month, for queries. Girls are a busy, confident, dynamic bunch and, in the main, happy to be pushed, though some merely bright girls feel they live in the shadow of the highly able.

Entrance: Selective. 150 pupils each year at 11; administered by LA. School has no say in intake (it's done by Buckinghamshire selection procedure) though preference given to siblings and girls within the catchment area (grammar schools in Bucks take approximately top 30 per cent of ability range, though Ofsted says this represents top 5–10 per cent nationally). Sixth form entrants apply direct to school, need minimum five GCSEs at B or above, B minimum in the subjects they want to do at A level.

Exit: Very few leave after GCSE (usually to do different A levels elsewhere), otherwise 95 per cent to university and 10–12 annually to Oxbridge.

Money Matters: State funded. Very supportive parents' association involved in fund-raising events including marvellous mums' and daughters' indulgence days with manicures, makeovers, mini-massage and more ...

Remarks: A powerhouse of a school where girls are smart and proud to be so, but a difficult environment for those on the margins, especially those who needed pushing through the 11 plus.

Driffield School

Manorfield Road, East Riding of Yorkshire, Driffield, YO25 5HR

• Pupils: 2,000 boys and girls • Ages: 11-18 • Size of sixth form: 300
• Non-denom • State

Tel: 01377 253 631
Fax: 01377 256 922
Email: office@driffield.e-riding.sch.uk
Website: www.driffieldschool.net

Acting headteacher: During 2010–11, Mr Simon Jones is acting headteacher, with Mr Martin Green as co-headteacher. Mr Green, who started his career as chemistry teacher in Hull area, later deputy head of Winifred Holtby School, Hull, and head of Withernsea High School and Technology College, is on half-time secondment for the year to the National College for Leadership of Schools and Children's Services.

Academic matters: Exam results on oxygen-sapping uphill gradient as children benefiting from changes in recent years reach exam age. Some 63 per cent of pupils achieved five or more GCSEs at A*–C including English and maths in 2010. A level results currently among the best in the East Riding – half of all grades A*/A/B. How do they do it? By tracking every single child in every subject all the time. Teachers log progress of pupils every four weeks on an electronic registration system. Computer flags up any student who fails to make hoped-for progress and hapless pupil is brought up to speed in whatever way the school decrees, be it extra homework or late study. Child is attached to a mentor – a teacher designated to get them instantly back on track. Parents love it, school loves it, even students accept it's for their greater good. Apparently. And it's not all bad news for pupils. The mentor can negotiate deadline extensions etc for a student genuinely snowed under.

SEN dept, now called Student Services (i.e. inclusive), can cope with (almost) any learning difficulty from moderate to severe – the entire dys-strata, ADHD, plus severely (rather than profoundly) deaf (the school operates a sound field system). 200 children on the register with IEPs for all including 49 with statements. One-to-one, one-to-two, small groups, anything from one hour to three hours a week, alpha smart (computers) – in and out of school, and all networked. 18 teaching assistants, all highly trained; most remedial help is provided in class, but occasional one-to-one, max one and a half hours a week, but 'can buy in more'. Very accommodating, 'can adapt to different needs'; special co-ordinator for their able, gifted and talented programme too.

Games, Options, the Arts: International recognition for performing arts. Winners many times of international Rock Challenge competition for dance, drama and music. Represented UK in Australia in 2003. Strong on sport, particularly cricket, rugby, hockey. Thriving Duke of Edinburgh scheme. Range of activities outside lessons excellent. Extra-curricular activities given priority because of rural catchment area where, for many children, school is core element of their social life.

Background and Atmosphere: A whopper of a school, among the biggest in the country, set in a vast 40-acre site and with most of the students' home villages in the Yorkshire Wolds. Feels less like a school, more like a campus, not least in sixth form which boasts own internet café. School only 50 years old but has just spent millions on new design and technology, specialist performing arts and ICT blocks with imminent building of new sports hall and swimming pool.

Biggest asset? Its own residential studies centre in the North York Moors National Park for everything from geography field trips to intensive study seminars. Pupils encouraged to use school with its 600 plus internet-linked computers out of hours. Doors open at 7am and library is open until at least 7pm, sometimes later. Children can go home for a meal, then catch special late bus back to school for more study or activities before school bus takes them home again.

Pastoral Care and Discipline: Potential for feeling swamped enormous as intake mostly from small rural primaries. Problems prevented by putting students into six houses and having registration forms comprising six students from each year group. New pupils instantly taken under wing of older ones – one of many ways school encourages responsibility. The 16-year-old student governor says views of pupils are taken seriously: 'They really listen to us.'

Discipline tight. School prides itself on standing no nonsense. Will not tolerate pupils disturbing lessons and disrupting education of the majority.

Pupils and Parents: Parents from wide range of backgrounds but many have caught school's ambitious bug and work hard to support it. Pupils' progress reports to parents three times a year and full report annually. Newsletters to parents via email so no chance to 'lose' that letter about extra homework. Parents' briefing evenings about, for instance, study leave.

Entrance: Seriously over-full and only takes pupils from 130-square-mile catchment area.

Exit: Most stay on to sixth form and then to universities including Oxbridge.

Remarks: A beacon state school combining innovation and risk-taking to fire up the ambitions of a whole community. Outstanding. Recently designated a specialist maths and computing school.

Dulwich College

Linked to DUCKS (Dulwich College Kindergarten and Infants School) in the Junior section

Linked to Dulwich College: The Junior School in the Junior section

Dulwich Common, London, SE21 7LD

• Pupils: 1,285 boys. 130 boarders • Ages: 11-18 • Size of sixth form: 400 • C of E • Fees: Day £14,184; Boarding + £13,257-£14,787 pa • Independent

Tel: 020 8693 3601
Fax: 020 8693 6319
Email: info@dulwich.org.uk
Website: www.dulwich.org.uk

Master: Since 2009, Dr Joseph Spence BA PhD (fiftyish), previously headmaster of Oakham. Was Master in College at Eton from 1992–2002, so had charge of the scholars, one of the top academic jobs in independent education. A history and politics graduate, he is disconcertingly multi-talented: he writes and directs plays, has written several books on Anglo-Irish history and culture, and plays sport 'quite well'. A personable, enthusiastic and charming man, he is married to a lawyer, with two sons and daughter. 'Great news for the college,' say parents.

His predecessor spent much time and energy on developing Dulwich College franchises overseas. His appointment represents a rebalancing of priorities in the eyes of the governors. He is clear that 'my job is here. I value our commitment to the Dulwich College schools abroad, for they are impressive and can enhance our reputation, and I want to develop real educational links with them, but my focus is SE21.' He is keen for the three foundation schools (the others being JAGS and Alleyn's) to work more closely together, and has already formed closer links with JAGS.

Back in a boys-only environment after seven years, he says: 'It's only when you leave the co-education setting that you realise how much social engineering you have had to do to avoid gender stereotypes. Here, you don't have the issue of having to persuade boys to be in the orchestra, the choir, the play.'

He is 'determined to harness the history of this place. I want to give everyone a sense of pride in where they find themselves and an understanding of the status of our extraordinary College. I want to make it as good as it's ever been by the 400th anniversary in 2019.'

Academic matters: Dr Spence feels that Dulwich has been punching slightly below its weight academically. 'I don't want us to be a pale imitation of St Paul's or Westminster. We take the top 20 per cent of boys, in terms of academic ability, they take the top five per cent – but you can do as well here as if you are in the top five per cent. I am committed to the cause of learning beyond the classroom (and away from the test), but we must never lose sight of the academic basis of our work.'

The academic basis isn't bad – 85 per cent A*/A grades at GCSE in 2010 (up from 80 per cent in 2009), with sciences and languages still looking particularly strong and English, previously thought to be a weaker link, having delivered 40 per cent A*s (and over 85 per cent A*/A) from a cohort of 200. Maths is the most popular A level, sciences and economics close behind, undoubtedly influenced by the scientifically-minded boarders from China and Eastern Europe. Ninety per cent A/B grades at A level in 2009 and 2010, and 68 per cent A*/A in 2010 across a remarkably wide range of challenging subjects.

Screening for dyslexia in Years 7 and 9, with some boys referred for an ed psych assessment. Learning Support dept helps those diagnosed with a learning difficulty, who may use a laptop at school and in exams.

Dr Spence's first job has been to look at the 13–16 curriculum and iron out any kinks in the system, e.g. over-rigid setting which has resulted in an aptitude for science being a pre-requisite for the fast-track French course. No plans to introduce the IB but is setting up the 'Dulwich Diploma', which is similar in its outlook: four A levels, an extended essay and a real commitment to service, plus attending the Master's series of five lectures a year. 'I will write to every admissions tutor about the Dulwich Diploma to make sure they know what we are doing.'

Games, Options, the Arts: 'Extraordinary work going on beyond the curriculum.' Sport has always been a big deal here and the greater academic emphasis won't change this. Seventy acres of playing fields include two full size all-weather pitches and an athletics track plus numerous courts and pitches, a swimming pool and a vast sports hall. Rugby is a major sport – 40 teams play regular matches – and has spawned quite a few international players; boys also compete at football, hockey, cricket, badminton, golf et al. They fence, they row (boathouse on the Thames at Putney), they play water polo. Most recently there's been an evident encouragement of another sport at which Britain has begun to excel: cycling. There are plans for the College to support the redevelopment of the Herne Hill Velodrome. As in most large and sporty schools, boys need major talent to make the top teams.

Edward Alleyn theatre hosts numerous performances by all age groups, including one big upper school production each year in conjunction with JAGS, and inter-house drama competitions. Theatre studies an A level option and, in 2009, all Year 13 thespians got 100 per cent for their devised physical theatre piece. All art staff are practising artists and everyone who took art A level in 2009 got an A. Plenty of artistic options from ceramics to animation. Music also strong with lots of orchestras, bands, ensembles and choirs – including the college Chapel Choir – playing and singing in regular concerts, in such as St John's, Smith Square and the Queen Elizabeth Hall.

All Year 7s visit the school field centre in the Brecon Beacons for hiking, rock-climbing, canoeing etc. D of E, scouts and CCF popular; huge variety of clubs and societies. Lots of language exchanges, sports, music and drama tours, field trips, trekking, sailing and skiing expeditions.

Background and Atmosphere: Founded in 1619 by the wealthy, flamboyant actor and businessman, Edward Alleyn. He set up the foundation Alleyn's College of God's Gift and endowed it with the ancient manor of Dulwich, including considerable land. Part of the foundation funded the education of 12 poor scholars by resident Fellows. Its successor charity, the Dulwich Estate, owns what land remains, and distributes its surplus income to the schools within the foundation, which include Dulwich College, JAGS, Alleyn's and several state schools.

The college moved to its present site in the mid 19th century; the main buildings are grand, confident Victorian redbrick, embellished with stucco worthies in cream niches. They include such treasures as the panelled great hall, the masters' library and the Wodehouse library (PG is an Old Alleynian), with archives including 'the largest and most important collection of material on the professional theatre and dramatic performance in the age of Shakespeare to be found anywhere'. Ernest Shackleton is another OA, and the James Caird – the terrifyingly small boat in which he sailed the stormy southern ocean from Elephant Island to South Georgia – is berthed in the North Cloisters.

Not a school you could walk past without noticing. The manicured pitches surrounding the (mostly) gracious buildings give the impression of a country public school or traditional university campus. But the boys – 30 per cent of whom receive some sort of help with fees – cheeringly reflect their multi-ethnic south London environs.

It is part of the Southwark Schools Learning Partnership, which includes five state and three independent schools working together on a huge range of projects. Also sponsors the new Isle of Sheppey Academy – a mutual learning relationship which is likely to include the College helping with aspects such as modern languages and Oxbridge preparation whilst learning from the Academy about innovative teaching methods.

A multi-national arm franchises three schools in China and one in Korea, and an Events and Enterprise element runs the school bus network and rents out the college facilities for e.g. wedding receptions. This helps to bring in funds for improving facilities and increasing bursaries, and should provide opportunities for international exchanges.

Pastoral Care and Discipline: Boarders in a small minority here – 130 out of around 1,300, mostly sixth formers and many from the Far East. They inhabit swish boarding houses – sixth formers have their own rooms with en suite bathrooms – and can take advantage of all London has to offer at weekends. Dr Spence has plans to develop boarding further, increasing weekly boarding and integrating boarders better with the day boys. 'We have the feel and the facilities of a boarding school, and we need to make more use of them. I'd like to widen our appeal beyond the Far East and Europe.' House-parents work hard to create a home-like atmosphere. All the boys are members of day houses, which provide opportunities for making friends and mixing with boys in other year groups, to say nothing of competing against one's peers at anything from sport to chess to debating and recitation.

General praise for the pastoral care, with carrots more evident than sticks. 'They're pretty good at motivating boys who don't want to work,' said a parent. Those found with drugs are out, say college rules, but the school is not heavy-handed on this. Will give a second chance to boys excluded from elsewhere who are keen to join in the wide range of activities.

Pupils and Parents: Mostly local, though many take the buses run in conjunction with three other local schools – providing excellent opportunities for socialising, say boys. Good ethnic and social mix, including, of course, the international boarders, though it is fair to say that the core clientele is the solidly middle-class families of the Dulwich/Blackheath/Greenwich/Clapham surrounds. This is a very large school, and particularly suits confident boys who don't need encouragement to take advantage of all the off-piste opportunities. OAs include PG Wodehouse, Sir Ernest Shackleton, plus Raymond Chandler, Lord George of St Tudy, Bob Monkhouse, Lionel Barber, CS Forester, Karol Sikora, Graham Swift and Michael Ondaatje. The school has produced more than its fair share of international sportsmen, including England Test cricketer Trevor Bailey and the present-day England and British Lions rugby player, Nick Easter.

Entrance: Takes 70 boys into Year 7, plus around 60 coming up from the junior school. All applicants take maths, English and verbal and non-verbal reasoning tests; junior school boys must pass the tests but are not competing for places with outsiders. Another 60 join Year 9, again after English, maths and reasoning tests. Those trying for an academic scholarship must also take French, science, history and geography papers. Up to 40 places, mostly boarding, for outsiders joining the sixth form. These largely go to international students, many from Hong Kong, assessed by entrance exams. UK candidates – like boys already in the college middle school – must get A*/A GCSE grades in their four A level subjects and at least two more grades B or above, including maths and English.

Exit: A few – probably around half a dozen each year – likely to trip over the sixth form entrance requirements and leave after GCSEs. Nearly all sixth form leavers to university, including around 10 per cent to Oxbridge and one or two to American and Hong Kong universities. Also many to Bristol, Leeds, Manchester, Nottingham and Imperial. Medicine, economics and engineering particularly popular.

Money Matters: Academic scholarships of between 10 per cent and a third of fees available to boys joining in Year 7 and Year 9. Music scholarships, of up to a third of fees plus free tuition on two instruments, also available at Year 7 and Year 9. Art scholarships of up to 10 per cent of fees and sports scholarships of up to a third available at Year 9 and Year 12. Means-tested bursaries also available, all but a handful from Year 7 and above; about a third of boys have some sort of help with fees.

The 1940s–60s was the era of the Dulwich Experiment, when the school offered free places, funded by the local authority, to boys who could pass the entrance exam. 'I've met hundreds of 60 to 80 year olds who benefited from those and wax lyrical about the school and what they got from it,' says Dr Spence. 'We need a new Dulwich Experiment, with a move towards needs-blind admissions.'

Remarks: Huge operation that manages to encompass sixth-month-old babies and 18-year-old school leavers, to say nothing of franchises in the Far East. Exudes a traditional public school ambience of stalwart Victoriana amidst enviable manicured acres, but houses a cheerfully diverse mixture of south London and international boys. The new Master is intent on upping the academic ante whilst encouraging the vast range of activities outside the classroom, and drawing on the sense of history that enriches the Dulwich College experience.

Dunraven School

94-98 Leigham Court Road, London, SW16 2QB

• Pupils: 1200 day boys/girls 50/50 • Ages: 11-18 • Size of sixth form: 250 • Non denom • State

Tel: 02086 772 431
Fax: 02086 647 242
Email: info@dunraven-school.org.uk
Website: www.dunraven.org.uk

Principal: Since September 2003, David Boyle (forties) BA, NPQH, FRSA, married with a young daughter. Has worked in various London secondary schools, including a deputy headship at Burntwood, and is committed to creating excellent schools. A terrific manager who is able to relate to all his client groups, say parents – a great compliment as not all heads have this skill. Lots of energy and a good communicator. Ofsted described him and his team as 'outstanding' in their most recent report (May 2009).

Academic matters: One of Lambeth's top performing schools, GCSE and A level results moving ever upward and already beyond national averages. A strong emphasis on core subjects with a good balance of languages, geography, history, arts, drama, music and PE. Has specialist status for maths, technology and computing. Languages on offer are French, Spanish, Latin and Mandarin; native speakers are encouraged to take GCSE in their first language. Pupils can take dual or triple award science GCSEs.

Sixth form opened in 2004 – housed in its own brand new block, it offers a broad range of academic and vocational courses. Each student is given individual guidance on selecting higher educational courses and careers advice. Residential, day trips, theatre and opera visits are part of school life, enriching all areas of the curriculum.

SEN pupils are catered for on an individual or group basis. Funding is limited but this school understands that one size does not fit all. Accelerated learning groups for more able pupils who may take GCSE exams early. Annual activity week is a non-uniform week – staff and pupils participate in numerous activities both on and off site, anything from circus skills to foreign travel. Well-stocked library is open all day and after school for homework or personal reading.

Games, Options, the Arts: Range of sports – basketball, volleyball, cricket, tennis, gymnastics and football – popular with both girls and boys; even the head joins in some games. School has Sports Mark and members of their fencing club in the Lambeth team. Sports provision has been boosted by a state-of-the-art new sports hall. Strong musical tradition continues – large team of music teachers visit offering tuition on over 20 instruments. Individual and group lessons with some tuition subsidised by the school. Choirs, jazz group, quartets and other ensembles perform regularly. School also has a link with the Royal Opera House and the Young Musicians' Centre. Drama also significant – school works with outside organisations including the National Theatre. Charming wood-panelled octagonal theatre for school performances. Gold Arts Mark; the school has an artist in residence, runs a number of creative projects and a life drawing class. Extensive range of extra-curricular activities including electronics, martial arts, debating, film studies, sports and arts.

Background and Atmosphere: The upper school and sixth form occupy the former Phillipa Fawcett College with extensive grounds including tennis courts, games area and attractive gardens, a luxury for an inner city site. Younger pupils accommodated across the road in a former 1960s adult education building, rather a stark place.

The school has done its best to enhance the premises with small garden areas and brightly colour-coded corridors. Children wear smart blue and grey uniform; an orderly and focused air about the place. Building and grounds look well maintained and clean. School patron is the Earl of Dunraven – the school is named after his great grandfather.

Pastoral Care and Discipline: Clear code of conduct for the children to follow. The emphasis is on treating all with courtesy and consideration and encouraging pupils to feel and want their school to be a really pleasant place. A school counsellor and a learning mentor. Anyone behaving recklessly or causing damage will be sent home. All pupils have homework organisers which must be signed by parents. The website, 'Parent mail' email system and a termly magazine help keep parents in touch with school events and achievements.

Pupils and Parents: Representative of a large London comprehensive school – a diverse mix of pupils from many different nationalities.

Entrance: At 11+ admission tests for five ability bands, 20 per cent from each band are allocated places. Needless to say, heavily over-subscribed as any high achieving state secondary school, but don't let it put you off. Class sizes are large.

Exit: At 16+ one-third to college and vocational courses, a handful to work. Two-thirds remain in sixth form for A level, 98 per cent to university of first choice and around five a year to Oxbridge.

Money Matters: State funded foundation school – receives many awards and grants due to its success and, probably, dynamic staff. At present they have a grant for running a science and engineering club.

Remarks: Has become one of the most popular south-west London secondary schools. Relationships between staff, parents and pupils are part of its key ingredients, also the knack of finding an individual's strengths and developing them.

Durham High School for Girls

Linked to Durham High School For Girls Junior School in the Junior section

Farewell Hall, South Road, Durham, County Durham, DH1 3TB

• Pupils: 600 girls, all day • Ages: 3-18 • Size of sixth form: 100 • C of E, accepts all faiths and none • Fees: £6,090-£9,660 pa • Independent

Tel: 0191 384 3226
Fax: 0191 386 7381
Email: headmistress@dhsfg.org.uk
Website: www.dhsfg.org.uk

Head: Since 1998, Mrs A Templeman MA DipT (mid-fifties), previously deputy at Haberdasher's Askes, Elstree. Married with three children; calm, reflective, gentle style; teaches classics. Educated at Watford Grammar School for Girls and at St Hugh's, Oxford (lit hum). Anglican minister. Wants girls who are 'excited about life and learning', encourages hard work and dedication alongside a social conscience.

Academic matters: 2010 saw 68 per cent of entries A*/A and 92 per cent A*/B at GCSE. 47 per cent of A level grades were A*/A and over a quarter of the year group obtained at least three grade As. Stronger than average take-up in maths and science; geography and religious studies also strong. French, German and Latin taught from 11, though not the widest range of languages for keen linguists; a safe but not expansive range of A level options includes politics and sociology. Average class sizes; a number of age groups surprisingly not yet at capacity. Some girls with mild to moderate dyslexia, the occasional one with other special needs; teaching assistance offered at extra charge.

Games, Options, the Arts: DHSfG is a sports academy for girls. A great deal of sport going on, hockey, netball and tennis being favourites; represented at county level in hockey, national level in tennis and gymnastics. A multi-skills coach on staff. The school is closely associated with the work of the Durham Lesotho Link. Each year sixth form pupils visit Lesotho to work with orphans in a scheme that greatly enriches the life of the school. Duke of Edinburgh awards also popular; community service and charity work encouraged. Music workshops, outdoor activity trips and overseas visits invite the wider world in and encourage the girls out; music, art and drama popular with larger productions held in Durham's Gala Theatre – the girls not afraid to tackle the occasional all-male play with an all-female cast.

Background and Atmosphere: Founded in 1884 by the Church of England, now accepts all faiths and none. Relatively new site with mostly modern buildings and programme of refurbishment throughout. Attractive open location in good residential area, convenient for city centre. Juniors in attractive new buildings, including delightful Rainbow Hill Nursery ('the promise of a good beginning') which now includes superb outdoor learning environment. Early years funding is also available for up to 15 free hours. Upgraded library, ICT and science labs. A translation of the school motto causes some consternation: 'the fear of the Lord is the beginning of wisdom' (which, for avoidance of misunderstanding, rarely surfaces these days). Yet reminders everywhere that this is a church school: the affirmation of faith and 'spiritual growth' are mentioned throughout. The recent appointment of a lay chaplain proved a great success, inspiring girls with her desire to learn salsa dancing as well as her teaching. Staff are 'wonderful and slightly whacky'; average age 44; a number of 'characters' generating real fondness between staff and pupils.

Pastoral Care and Discipline: House system has been developed; all houses have choir competitions on founder's day, St Cuthbert's Day, then raise money for charity. Form tutor for each class. Staff and girls vote for head girls and deputy. Buddy system; nurturing approach to discipline.

Pupils and Parents: Very diverse social spread: significant number from educational action zones in East Durham, others from business and professional families. 10 pupils on free places; 20 per cent of senior house on bursaries. Intake chiefly from County Durham and Sunderland; fairly narrow cultural spread, reflective of the local community. Supportive Old Girls' association. Girls are bright, vivacious and enthusiastic with that refreshing naivety that they can take on the world – and win. Free (but not too free) thinking, challenging but not ground-breaking; girls are glad to be here and feel 'safe'.

Dress-code for sixth form now evidently less relaxed: they wear 'smart suits'.

Entrance: Assessed by observation for nursery and reception, appropriate testing in subsequent years for junior house. English and maths tests at 11 based on key stage 2 SATs with references from junior heads and interview – style of testing reflects intake from local feeder state primary schools. For entry at 16, five GCSE passes A* to C, references and interview with head.

Exit: Some leave post-GCSE for local state schools, most stay for sixth form, then go on to traditional, predominantly northern, universities, plus a good number of Oxbridge candidates. Notable old girls include Wendy Craig (actress), Joanna Burton (opera), Wendy Gibson (BBC journalist), Sarah Blair (sister of ex-PM).

Money Matters: Generous number of scholarships and bursaries 'to attract bright, enthusiastic and gifted pupils who can make a real impact on the life of the school'.

Remarks: A refreshing change – a school that doesn't oversell itself. A combination of all that is new in education with core traditional values.

Ealing Independent College

83 New Broadway, Ealing, London, W5 5AL

• Pupils: 125 boys and girls • Non-denom • Fees: From £1,490 per subject pa • Independent

Tel: 020 8579 6668
Fax: 020 8567 8688
Email: ealingcollege@btconnect.com
Website: www.ealingindependentcollege.com

Principal: Since 2001, Dr Ian Moores BSc PhD, a chemist with impeccable independent education credentials, in his late forties but looking a decade younger and definitely 'cool'. Previously taught at Wellington College, then head of chemistry and science at Bedales and latterly head of science and IT at Cheadle Hulme, Cheshire. Something of a polymath – a sportsman and musician – his main commitment is to 'the individual' – the currently small scale nature of his college allows for all-comers to be given close individual attention. 'I'm an innovator,' he says, 'very flexible and adaptable.' Certainly easy to talk to and very open about the challenges of the job – those he has already confronted and others to come. Relaxed but focused, with an intensity and quiet purposefulness which makes this college an interesting prospect for the future.

Academic matters: Its raison d'être. No-one would come here for the ambiance or the architecture but it is a place in which work is palpably central. Not much else to do anyway, and the importance of consistent work – often neglected in comparable establishments – is stressed here. Results are quite hard to evaluate – partly because, for example, the GCSE cohort consists of early and late takers, resits and of candidates of varying ages. 2010 saw 75 per cent A*–C grades. At A level, students achieved 55 per cent A/B grades.

Not a great range of subjects offered – college disagrees – but they will get in tuition for minority subjects and 2010 saw papers taken in Greek, accounting and psychology. Permanent part-time staff in accounting and law. Business studies very popular, supported by Dr Moores' new back-up programme of visits to companies, talks from outside speakers, work experience and IT, in tandem with new medical sciences programme to support aspirational medics with visits to hospitals, speakers etc. Music now a GCSE option, as are geography, history and Spanish. PSHE compulsory at GCSE level. Economics, psychology and sociology among available A level options. No qualified SEN support though an English teacher is available for extra help. This is not the place if you have SpLD but EFL help is available, though 'We won't take a child whose English is very poor'.

The strength of the place is in the tiny classes, the teaching – 'crucial,' says principal – and in the close monitoring of all students. GCSE students work in a supervised study room when they don't have classes. Every lesson/study period begins with registration and parents are telephoned in cases of no-show. A level students have supervised study programmes worked out with their personal tutors. Everyone has an individual learning plan and parents get written feedback every five to six weeks. One-to-one tuition also on offer as an extra and, unusually for a college of this size and type, a large proportion of the staff is full-time. League tables – in as much as they are an indication of anything – suggest that, at A level, the college performs as well as the smarter, up-town competition and better than some.

Games, Options, the Arts: Nothing on-site. Sport is compulsory for GCSE students, who are bused to a local sports centre. A 'circus' of games is offered around the year: football, badminton, tennis, handball, rock climbing and swimming. No formal games programme in the sixth form but football team meets weekly, voluntarily. Music newly available and college will arrange private lessons if required. No art, music ensembles, drama – no space and, as yet, no demand, though locality abounds with classes, clubs and courses of all kinds for those who want out of school arts.

Background and Atmosphere: College began life as Ealing Tutorial College in 1992 in even smaller premises. Moved in 2001 to present three-storey building – ex-social security offices – just off the Broadway in the centre of Ealing. The building itself is entirely undistinguished – a glass and steel cube with a bumpy tarmac car park, all in need of renovation. The rooms are smallish but the right size for the small group teaching they accommodate. Good IT suite, two neat labs for chemistry and physics but no library and principal keen to develop that area, though Ealing Central Library – an excellent resource – is minutes away. College has good computer facilities with links between home and staff.

Low ceilings, strip lighting, carpeting awaiting replacing when we visited – it isn't cosy. Much could be done to refresh the inside with displays/posters on the walls, which would not be at odds with the austere purposefulness of the ambiance. Ealing Broadway is a lively shopping area with plenty of cafés and bars and students get their lunches from these or bring their own – eaten in the sizeable common-room, which has vending machines for coffee and chocolate bars (and is out of bounds during lesson times). Bus and tube connections are excellent – students come from quite a wide area: Hammersmith to Uxbridge, Harrow to Richmond.

Pastoral Care and Discipline: Everyone is in a tutor group – 10–12 students to a tutor and the tutors are responsible for academic and pastoral matters. Close supervision picks up problems and links with home are crucial to progress and welfare. Principal holds a compulsory weekly assembly followed by meetings with tutors – an unusual and healthy feature for a college of this kind. A cheery atmosphere prevails and a sense that individuals who were unhappy or uncomfortable elsewhere could find a niche here. 'We're good at individuals who need to be pinned down more,' says principal. 'They're not lost in the crowd here. We get several who have been bullied. That doesn't happen here.' Lateness, late appearance of work and erratic attendance are now minor problems due to reporting system, letters home and sanctions. 'We put them on probation if necessary', says principal. For the majority, the approach works well and results are showing it.

Pupils and Parents: A few come as young as 13 and they do, indeed, get a privileged education – taught alone or in tiny groups. Great for tuition and they get used to co-existing with older students but – otherwise socially and in terms of extra-curricular opportunities – this must be an outside option for most at this age. The largest cohort in this small college – only 90 students, with a capacity of 130 – is at A level; these overwhelmingly are there to study the sciences – though this may broaden according to demand. 65 per cent of students are Asian, 20 per cent white; the rest a mixture reflecting local population. Some from overseas – local accommodation is found in hostels or with host families. Special link with school in Singapore. Common denominator is a willingness to pay for top tuition to achieve results.

Entrance: On exam results, reports from schools and interview. Principal likes to give those who have failed elsewhere or been expelled – once, no more – a second chance. Place could be a lifesaver for those who have seen the light.

Exit: Some stars – several leavers with straight As off to read medicine or dentistry at top universities. Sizeable number to Brunel and other more local universities – engineering, sciences and business subjects, obviously, dominate. Some with no places after results, often due to unrealistic parental aspirations which push offspring into applying for unrealistic courses. The majority does end up in the newer universities.

Money Matters: Fees according to subjects taken and number of lessons. Seven or eight subjects at GCSE works out at £9,790 pa. Three or four A2s works out at £10,495 pa. More lessons are given for retakes and one-year courses, which are proportionally more expensive. A few scholarships available, up to 50 per cent of fees.

Remarks: College keen not to be seen as second option or refuge for those who have failed elsewhere, but this may well be a mistake. It meets a real need in unglitzy west London for a haven for those with support – financial and moral – from home who need a second chance or for real individuals, oddballs or bullied who will find a haven here and be taught expertly, monitored closely and given every chance to succeed. Not the place for those for whom the extra-curricular side is what schooldays are all about. Some will opt out wherever they go and whatever support they are given, but this college offers an unusual opportunity for those with the wit and maturity to seize it.

Easingwold School

York Road, Easingwold, York, North Yorkshire, YO61 3EF

• Pupils: 1,365 boys and girls, all day • Ages: 11-18 • Size of sixth form: 265 • State

Tel: 01347 821 451
Fax: 01347 823 301
Email: admin@easingwold.n-yorks.sch.uk
Website: www.easingwoldschool.n-yorks.sch.uk

Head: Since 2001, Mrs Carey Chidwick, BA Hons Diplomée (fiftyish). Friendly and outgoing. Popular with pupils and staff. Qualified King's College, London. Previously head at Berwick-upon-Tweed Community High School. Began as a modern languages teacher in Kent. Became head of department and joined Kent education department's teacher training team. Then went to Northumberland as adviser/inspector for modern languages. Qualified as an Ofsted inspector in 1992 and continued to participate in inspections after returning to mainstream schools. Knows most of the children's names and chats to them in the corridors.

Academic matters: Around 70 per cent five A* to C grades at GCSE. As proud of the less academic student who achieves D at A level or E at GCSE as of those who record straight As. Expectation is high but not too driven by league tables. This philosophy embraces children with special needs, championed by an achievement manager whose job title says it all. School caters for children with a range of special needs such as Asperger's, autism, hyperactivity, ADD, learning difficulties, and speech, vision and hearing difficulties. Not bound by the SEN register – help is targeted at children who need it, regardless of whether they are on register or not. Aim is to get children off the register, not perpetuate their place. Parent of a special needs student told us, 'the school values every pupil individually and the staff are amazing. We have been absolutely thrilled, and for our son it has been marvellous, he has come on in leaps and bounds.' School works with primary schools to get a picture of the pupils before they come to Easingwold, and an idea of any special needs they may have. Does not prejudge, but those needing extra help will get an individual plan, including specific targets, regularly reviewed. Recently introduced, at Year 10, a computerised tracking system monitors individual children's progress and alerts school where they are in danger of under-achieving. A model of inclusive education with reams of enthusiastic parents.

Traditional subjects studied at GCSE, with all pupils taking core subjects – English, maths, science etc – and selecting two options from art, business studies, child development, music etc. In sixth form students take intermediate (GNVQ) courses or AS/A levels. A variety of vocational studies on offer throughout. Life after Easingwold is important. School includes careers education as part of the curriculum. Quality of work placements recognised with national award and work-related learning is strong thread in the curriculum. Always looking for ways to do better, using both national and international research to identify best practice. Staff encouraged to develop their own learning while they teach: teaching assistants go on to qualify as teachers, teachers get Masters degrees, and so on.

Games, Options, the Arts: Fabulous sporting pedigree. Regularly excels in competitions on a Yorkshire-wide/ regional basis in cricket, football, basketball, rugby, netball and hockey. Many other sports are offered and there is a pool and multi-gym. Music (choirs and orchestra that tour home and abroad) and drama (strong tradition with frequent productions and theatre visits) with good facilities. Lots of extra-curriculars, and plenty of opportunity for language exchange visits and many other trips, community work, IT access and Duke of Edinburgh Awards.

Background and Atmosphere: Opened as a bilateral school in 1954 but roots can be traced to the foundation of Easingwold Grammar School in 1784. Has outgrown its buildings. Uninspiring corridors hide pleasant and vibrant classrooms, decked in the children's own impressive work, filled with attentive children working, enjoying.

School is proud of its achievements – sporting and academic – and the noticeboards are testament. One pupil told us, 'Easingwold is a very friendly school and very nice, there is always someone there to help when you need it'. Most pupils feel very positive about their school and its sense of community.

Pastoral Care and Discipline: Well structured; form tutors and house system. Praise and punishments graded, gradual. Mentoring system to pick up children who develop any difficulties – academic, emotional, behavioural – and address them.

Pupils and Parents: 10 miles north of York, on outskirts of market town of Easingwold; pupils also come from York, Thirsk, Helperby and surrounding rural villages. An outward-looking school. Almost all pupils are English and white – but school is aware that this inhibits pupils' learning about cultural diversity and addresses this. Designated a Specialist Language College with International School status in 2006 and hopes to expand experience of different cultures and offer broader employment prospects to pupils. Strong cultural links with French and German schools with regular exchange visits. Very much part of the community – Friends of Easingwold as much social as educational.

Entrance: Popular. Preference for SEN, then for locals. Panic-stricken appeals succeed more often than usual (the alternative school may be many miles away).

Exit: About two-thirds go on to school's own sixth form after Year 11, with many others going on to further education elsewhere. Post A level, 75 per cent to university and other higher education.

Remarks: A happy comprehensive school where it is a pleasure to teach and be taught. Pupils and staff are at ease, know what is expected of them and strive to achieve their best.

Eastbourne College

Headmaster's House, Old Wish Road, Eastbourne, East Sussex, BN21 4JX

• Pupils: 370 boys and 260 girls; 50 per cent board • Ages: 13-18
• Size of sixth form: 275 • C of E • Fees: Day £17,295; Boarding £26,130 pa • Independent

Tel: 01323 452 323
Fax: 01323 452 327
Email: admissions@eastbourne-college.co.uk
Website: www.eastbourne-college.co.uk

Head: Since 2005, Mr Simon Davies (mid-forties). Previously vice master at Bedford school, prior to which he was head of biology and senior housemaster at Abingdon School. Married with children; wife runs a literary charity, is involved with school publications, and hosts dinner parties for new staff. Two of their three children attend the school. Mr Davies is affable, approachable, intelligent, warm, unpretentious, you get the feeling you can trust him (even though he was previously a derivatives broker in the city, 'but not something he ever intended making his career'). Described by some as an inspirational biology teacher.

He enthuses about what education should and should not be. It emphatically should not be about league tables and measurement. It should be about 'how well a child does in relation to his or her ability and aiding them make their choices'. He asserts that his school is 'selective but not highly selective' and the school measures success more in value-added terms than in absolutes. He has hundreds of conversations with pupils, parents, staff to ensure this message is communicated and he listens to what others have to say. He likes the school to be relaxed, never casual and always purposeful. He makes a point of getting to know the pupils and parents and can very impressively recount details of pupils past and present.

He quotes de Bono – 'there's no point being brilliant if you're brilliant at the wrong thing' – and believes too many schools proclaim their brilliance at just the wrong thing. 'We are not the Chelsea Flower Show', but more in tune with Capability Brown, i.e. not an exhibition of bloom on show for a short burst but developing saplings that will continue to grow and fruit for years to come.

Academic matters: A wide sweep of subjects at GCSE (can take French, German, Portuguese, Spanish, Latin and Greek). This freedom of choice is evident through the curriculum e.g. a pupil can study many creative subjects such as architecture, textiles, music tech, and not be bogged down with subjects that he/she is not interested in. A real strength of the school is the value-added – from the academically gifted to those for whom academic success is tough. Time and again pupils entering with Bs and Cs emerge with As.

School aims to include all SEN pupils where possible but there is specific provision for mild dyslexia, G&T and TEFL. One full-time and one busy part-time teacher. All children are screened on entry. Individual SEN lessons are charged for – £43.80 ph for one and £24.20ph for two pupils reducing to £12.90ph for group of four. There is no separate cost for the G&T provision however, which is department specific e.g. BioSoc for biology. DT entered a

RIBA parliamentary design (finalists). A G&T coordinator monitors the challenge to these pupils. Academic whole school societies for G&T i.e. Hayman society, the New Academy and Casson society etc (details on website).

Not a huge breadth of subjects at A level e.g. no psychology, sociology, politics. May consider politics if they found the right candidate but few requests from parents or pupils for 'pop' subjects such as psychology. So, a traditional curriculum is what traditional parents want? 'Not so,' say a few parents, more on offer at A level would be interesting e.g. Italian was taught inspirationally to GCSE but the plug was pulled for A level, much to the disappointment of some fired-up pupils. IB programme not on the horizon here. Good enrichment programme for gifted/talented pupils, as well as those less academic. Every dept has a gifted coordinator so that staff engage pupils according to their ability. Since the introduction of A* for A level they have a '100 per cent club' for the elite achievers.

School feels they are ahead of the game in the way they use and integrate ICT through the curriculum. Reports are produced online every three weeks showing pupils' grades for effort and achievement. Science block is new, sporting 12 laboratories and some of the most spacious we've seen – results accordingly exceptional. Worth a mention is the level and scope of the DT work. Housed in a large new block, staff have commercial and industrial backgrounds. Winner of the GSG DT and Textiles award in 2007; after a trip around the many rooms, it is easy to see why. Many pupils leave to study project design, textile engineering, architecture etc. School works closely with renowned local architects, professional designers who offer constructive criticism. Excellent architectural models on display, pupils currently designing a local House of Parliament soon to be followed with a design for Westminster to be displayed on site. Fantastic range of high tech equipment that industry would die for, 50 per cent take-up for GCSE. At present building cars with sustainable themes, green power and a lot of awards for resistant materials use, graphics etc.

Games, Options, the Arts: Strong at the top level, plenty achieve national status and some international and offer excellent competition on the local circuit. Two good recent appointments. A level 5 rugby coach and a head of netball raising standards. Fives, shooting, swimming, recent addition of fencing, golf are taken up by more senior pupils if team sports are not for them. Most are engaged on a daily basis and the school fields many teams for some fixtures; some consternation that the less conscientious and the D of E team can slip detection and be seen munching pizzas in town! 'There's a certain glamour for the first XV and those that excel in sport but 'if the child doesn't jump at the school, then the school doesn't jump at the child'. The manicured rugby pitch dominates the front of the school but the main sports fields are a five min drive away.

Some interesting art work on display. Graphics not offered. Plenty of drama productions and musical events, bands, choirs, rock and swing bands, soirees in the houses etc but again it would be prudent to enquire what is done for the pupil who is reluctant to raise his head above the parapet. Plenty is open to the community, clubs, societies etc, e.g. silver surfers' club whereby the pupils act as agents to help ageing locals with ICT skills. CCF and D of E flourishing. Fertile links with local sports clubs so that facilities are shared, and they host regional prep school rugby and hockey tournaments – good outreach for prospective pupils and talent.

Background and Atmosphere: The seventh Duke of Devonshire founded the school in 1867. The current Duke is President of the Eastbourne College Council along with other influential Eastbourne residents. The school is not socially exclusive but rooted in the Meads community. Main school is an imposing red-brick building, amid an aesthetically pleasing mix of others, old and sympathetically new and ensconced in the heart of Eastbourne. No ivory tower feel, though it is fronted by a large pitch and bordered by five-storey Victorian houses and retirement homes. There is constant traffic of hearty pupils hotfooting around the perimeter hurrying to lessons. It is close to the railway and next to Devonshire Park, home to the pre-Wimbledon Men's and Ladies' Tennis tournament. Themed dinner parties for the sixth form, catered for by the college. The standard of food is very good, excellent range of choices, although pupils impressed with lunch but were critical of teas. Plenty of inter-house competitions, concerts, soirees etc.

Pastoral Care and Discipline: Very, very strong indeed, very nurturing, excellent loops of communication with pupils, parents and staff, definitely the throbbing pulse of the school, and possibly why it is so successful at reaching all abilities. Head of boarding came from Sevenoaks and thus brings plenty of experience. He believes the boarding works so well because they focus on 'character and relationships which are fundamental to the way the school is run'. Parents and pupils concur that pastoral philosophy is backed with action and not self-promotion. Good system of buddies and sages for the new boarders. The school is run as a full boarding school, 50/50 full boarders to day boarders with the day finishing for day pupils at 8pm. No weekly boarding. School revolves around the house: all pupils are registered in the common-room of their house, assemblies, announcements are all made in house. The boarding houses all are spacious, light; all have good facilities with their own garden. They each have a tuck shop run on a profit basis; one house bought two goats for an Indian community. Junior boarders share three to five to a room, reducing up to the sixth form, where they have large single rooms. House parents or matrons are the first port of call for any confidences.

A generally wholesome and happy bunch, they give the thumbs up to the quality of boarding staff and to the blend of home and school it achieves. 'Good manners go with the turf and discipline has been tightened up,' says one parent. 'One strike and out' policy for drugs brought into the school and socializing between sexes is kept strictly to the common-room (perhaps more vigilant these days since the embarrassing incident reminiscent of *Notes on a Scandal* captured on a pupil's mobile phone!). It was testament to the head that the incident was dealt with deftly and didn't become a major media event. The head remarks here that this happened a few years ago and is not representative of life at Eastbourne.

Pupils and Parents: Varied social mix. On one side you have the Sussex Downs and the rolling Sussex countryside. It attracts families wanting a boarding-style education. The international contingent makes up only eight per cent of the school – Chinese, Nigerians, Germans. These students integrate properly and don't stay in packs. Flourishing parents' and friends' society that organizes social functions.

Entrance: Overseas pupils are accepted provided their level of English is proficient. Candidates for Year 9 entry sit CE or the college's own entrance exams or scholarship papers. The hurdle for sixth form is B grades or better at GCSE. About 30 pupils enter for sixth form from surrounding state or private schools.

Exit: Mr Davies talks candidly; clearly his less academic pupils aren't also-rans to be sold down the river and replaced by clever-clogs from other schools at sixth form. At 18, mainly to further education to a mix of redbrick, Russell group and vocational colleges; up to 10 per cent go on to Oxbridge, about a third take a gap year. Rather a high proportion of girls leave to study public relations, business, media related studies, leisure management.

Money Matters: The school is full although could accept a few more at a push. Scholarships available for most subject areas and a foundation director oversees the fundraising and bursary fund. He is aiming to build a pot by contributions from parents and staff to allow financial help to the struggling. The headmaster introduced the idea of all staff contributing the price of a pint per week to the fund. This equates to approx £250 a week and thus £15,000 a year. This philanthropic pint fund consequently translates to a) a full bursary for a fortunate and worthy pupil and b) a thirsty staffroom! The fees remain highly competitive by comparison to other full boarding schools. Music scholars receive free tuition, international students pay EFL fees as a lump sum arrangement or an hourly rate e.g. one-to-one is £43.80 per hr or group of four is £12.90 per hr.

Remarks: Good for all abilities and school is snug in its own skin. More about developing integrity in the pupil than about clawing its way up the league table, but equally relishes seeing top notch scores from those capable of such.

Edgbaston High School for Girls

Linked to Edgbaston High School For Girls Preparatory Dept in the Junior section

Westbourne Road, Edgbaston, Birmingham, West Midlands, B15 3TS

- Pupils: 490 girls; all day • Ages: 11-18 • Size of sixth form: 105
- Underlying Christian ethos and respect for all traditions
- Fees: £9,117 pa • Independent

Tel: 0121 454 5831
Fax: 0121 454 2363
Email: admissions@edgbastonhigh.co.uk
Website: www.edgbastonhigh.co.uk

Head: Since 2006, Dr Ruth Weeks BSc PhD (mid-fifties). Formerly head of Redland High in Bristol, a city with possibly an even more ferociously competitive educational environment than Brum, and which has clearly schooled her in what needs to be done to up the admiration factor for this arguably under-appreciated school. She's not a PR hot-airhead by any stretch, but she's got a good story to tell – she's improved communications with her market admirably, started an excellent weekly e-newsletter, and holds informal coffee mornings where parents can drop in and sound off. A wholly unterrifying sort of head, nothing of the dragon about her at all. Easy, charming, sincere, principled and, phew, bright. She's a chemist and finds time to teach Years 7 and 13. A Brummie by birth and breeding, she has come home. Married, two daughters.

Academic matters: Everyone knows that it's the King Eds that do best, so does that make Edgbaston a plucky but undeniable second best? A good many unsentimental parents clearly think so and migrate at 11+ if their child can get in. They nevertheless leave behind lots of good brains and, increasingly, best brains, because this school does things the way more and more parents loyally like. Raw scores demonstrate good teaching all round. Superb value-added scores more than merely attest to this. Real breadth here, with girls going on to do the whole range of subjects at university from medicine to fashion. Science and maths are strong, art simply stunning. They still do Latin and Greek, resist silly subjects but listen to their girls, so soon home economics and perhaps digital photography will add to the (excellently taught) PE and psychology. IT excellent and everywhere. Mild SENs only.

Games, Options, the Arts: Passionate about enrichment – who's not? – but a lot goes on here outside the classroom. They're a sporty lot and, though a city centre school, the four-acre site enables them to play a good range of games including football. Sparkling new pool, sports hall, all-weather pitch. Dance and drama are strong in their seriously fabulous new performing arts centre. Masses of lunchtime clubs. Music is pervasive and everybody studies it all the way through.

Background and Atmosphere: Non-denominational but with Quaker and Unitarian roots and a Cadbury connection, where elements of no-nonsense nonconformity linger. Utterly unpretentious. Friday assemblies are spent silently listening to music. Strong emphasis on charitable work. School population almost matches the city's racial mix and the girls we spoke to were totally colour-blind. Single sex education has always been very much a Birmingham thing, a good thing for those whose culture and religion require it. The school is unable to lay on halal lunches but provides a salad alternative. Assemblies offer up praise to God, but no specific God – each to their own. In this affectionate environment it works.

Comely 60s buildings erected when the school moved from the city centre, with a charming recreation of the old reception room inside and some very fine portraits of former heads. The prep school is separate, integral and shares the same ethos. This is the cleanest, shiniest, unschool-smellingest school you'll ever see – it really is remarkable. Splendidly resourced classrooms, very civilised meeting areas. Really nothing else they need, but plans for a sixth form centre are gestating. The setting in this leafy suburb, bang next door to the Botanical Gardens and among university buildings, is highly agreeable.

With an investment of £3.5 million, the school has significantly improving facilities with a new extension which includes a new state-of-the-art sixth form centre, library, classrooms and a fitness suite.

Pastoral Care and Discipline: Pastoral care here is a major strength. In addition to tutorial support, senior girls mentor younger ones. Girls praise teachers for the individual attention they give. It's an un-cliquey place, they assert – impossible, you would have thought, in a girls' school, but the influx of new girls at 11+ brings about a healthy remix. This really is a notably inclusive, supportive environment and, of course, small size is a factor. The girls wholeheartedly buy into the ethos.

Pupils and Parents: Pupils come from all over Birmingham and an outer ring which takes in Redditch, Kidderminster, Tamworth and Stourbridge, so some long journeys here – that tells you something. Increasingly popular with university lecturers. Thriving parents' association, Edgbaston High School Parents' Association (EHSPA), who organise everything from second-hand uniform sales to social jollies. Current high achievers include Molly Dineen, filmmaker; Lydia Hislop, racing correspondent for *The Times*; Professor Sally Davies, director of research and development at the Department of Health; Robyn Jones, Credit Suisse Outstanding Woman in Business 2006; Philippa Lett, top model; and Kate Williams, author and TV historian. Quite a spread.

Entrance: Starts at two-and-a-half. Entry tests at five, 11, 13 or when places are available. Entry to sixth form non-automatic, but departures hardly ever happen. This is a selective school, it's no pushover and it's nudging its bar upwards.

Exit: Good Russell Group universities. Nottingham especially popular. Usually a few Oxbridge.

Money Matters: Not a rich foundation, but very keen to reach out and help where it can. Bursaries available – ask about them – and some scholarships. Fees more-or-less on a par with rivals.

Remarks: Anything but a sink-or-swim sort of place – lots of rigour as well as kindness. An easy school to be very fond of, waking up at last to the need to proclaim the good news about itself, a matter of urgency as straitened times return.

The Edinburgh Academy

Linked to Edinburgh Academy Junior School (The) in the Junior section

42 Henderson Row, Edinburgh, Edinburgh, EH3 5BL

• Pupils: Pupils 1025, 705 boys, 320 girls • Ages: 2-18
• Size of sixth form: 180 • Non-denom • Fees: Senior £8,850-£10,980; Junior £5,850-£7,980 pa • Independent

Tel: 0131 556 4603
Fax: 0131 624 4994
Email: enquiries@edinburghacademy.org.uk
Website: www.edinburghacademy.org.uk

Rector: Since 2008, Mr Marco Longmore BA, Edinburgh historian (early forties). Previously senior deputy head of Alleyn's School (qv) prior to which he taught history and modern studies at George Heriot's School, and then moved to George Watson's College as head of history and modern studies.

Elegant, relaxed and exuding confidence, Mr L reports a 'management restructuring' with two 'senior deputes' to cover senior (senior depute rector) and junior school (headteacher) and further depute rectors in both. The senior school is re-divided into 'transition' (11/13), middle years (14/16) and sixth form (17/18). New heads of these areas, plus assistants, manage academic and personal supervision, 'supporting families and allowing information giving and gathering'. This provides a 'sense of progression' and more effective 'delivery of the school's as well as the parents' expectations'. Edinburgh gossip indicates that this may be a necessary move.

An enthusiastic sportsman with a keen interest in theatre and public debates, Mr Longmore believes so strongly in the values of the 'co-curriculum' (stressing the 'co-rather than extra-curriculum') that he has started a rector's book of outstanding achievement so he can personally acknowledge this. He and his wife, Karen, have two children, both in the school.

Academic matters: Hybrid public exam structure with GCSEs for all across the board, followed by either Higher or AS and then A levels (A2); children showing an interest in a Scottish university are encouraged to take Higher English. Those with a target of A levels and/or university in England might go for the AS route, depending on the subject.

Overall, results pretty strong, English, maths and mod langs particularly, and most subjects good at A level with new A* above the national average. Science department invigorated by new science building and numbers going on to science-based subjects at university high. Business and finance courses also growing in popularity as new head of dept hits his stride and now popular at university. History and modern studies hit a wobble last year but dynamic new head of dept will look to boost.

Sport and PE are popular and getting good results. Latin and music have small uptake but terrific results and school keen to keep such subjects in exam years to retain breadth. French, German and Spanish all doing well in big department and this session Chinese Mandarin is introduced on trial basis. Good range of subjects at Higher, though some parents find it frustrating that specialist subjects not available (such as Russian, law or psychology). Depute rector says that no-one has expressed an interest in these for some years.

Staffing levels good. New appointments made and turnover has been steady with lots in internal and external appointees. Some changes made very late last year as a result of recruitment from another Edinburgh Independent school that closed late last session. Feedback from parents very positive: the academy was very dynamic and supportive in assisting, and built special one-off curriculum for S4 group.

Expect a broad academic range of pupils. Junior years largely mixed ability with the exception of maths and English. Further up school, teaching groups defined largely by blocking scheme, though set by ability where possible. Maximum class size is 24 in younger years though generally lower. Support for learning department is strong and growing. Support spread between extraction and collaborative teaching in classes and pupils with learning difficulties are treated positively. Results commendable given the mixed intake , 'But,' says the rector 'remember that a C or

D grade may represent a great triumph for an individual and the others things they achieve in sport or music, for example, are also hugely important'. The top end of the exam list will indicate the school's expectations of academic children. The tradition of 'dux', the brightest boy or girl in the school (Magnus Magnusson was dux in his day) is extended to include wider group of high achievers, the Dux Club.

Games, Options, the Arts: The school tradition for providing a mini squad for the Scottish rugby side continues and this year is no exception, with usual rash of caps, would-be caps and waiters in the wings. Merchiston and The Academy celebrated the 150th anniversary of their annual match – the longest-running fixture in world rugby – with a slap-up dinner at Murrayfield, which raised £34K for Hearts and Balls (sic) which fund-raises for rugby injuries. (Merchiston won – but only just!). In 2010 the School won the Brewin Dolphin National Schools U18 Cup.

Main games field down beside the junior school with its fantastic (community) sports hall shared with lucky local residents. No pool (Mr Longmore says the wish list is still under debate) but specialist weights and gym and two new all-weather hockey pitches. Girls now have their own competitive teams in sports such as hockey, netball and athletics. Emphasis is on mixed sex sport for the girls, though the boys retain their, admittedly distinguished, team identity.

Outstanding art department with notable achievements in every discipline, brilliant ceramics; life class in the evenings a popular option. Dashing but philosophical young head of art said that this year's theme is Substance and Appearance. The department, complete with tools, books and other comforts, occupies a central space. Music outstanding, all-singing and dancing. Superlatives from our informants reach awesome proportions. Lucky singers and orchestra just back from a tour of Sorrento. Any pupil learning an instrument can play in concerts 'even if it is only three notes and child has been learning the trombone for three weeks'. Concerts outstandingly professional (the odd radio concert).

Drama immensely enhanced by the sympathetic conversion of the lovely old physics building to a state-of-the-art performing arts centre, the Magnusson Centre for Performing Arts (£2.5m): theatre and dance studio with girls' and boys' showers and changing for every imaginable activity below. Inside is breathtaking, though original features have not been vandalised: outside some additional curious tiled 'ears' provide ventilation for the new activities.

CCF hugely popular (everyone has to join, including the girls) – great flurry of battledress and airforce blue evident on Remembrance Day; piping particularly strong, with successes in both quartet and trios. Keen D of E; lots of hobbies – jewellery-making the most recent, attracting boys as well as girls – and good charity input – the charity committee does a massive amount of fund-raising (£16.5k for four local and national charities) and even the last rector was known to take part in a charity sleep-out. Well, Mr Longmore?

Background and Atmosphere: Lord Cockburn and Sir Walter Scott founded school in 1824 amongst others. Built in traditional Edinburgh-inspired sandstone (Greek mode), the Greek motto on the main portico reads, 'Education is the mother of both wisdom and virtue'. Buildings in main school a mixed bunch, some obviously designer-inspired additions including a fabulous oval assembly hall, plus a mass of add-ons as well as classrooms and impressive new labs around huge bleak tarmac courtyards, although new seating and planting across the school helps to soften the traditional yards. Pleasant gardens surround the administrative areas. Stunning music department. Look for generous Edinburghoisie-sponsored libraries etc; successful FPs remember their font of learning with pride. Boarding houses, now sold, have made a good nest-egg for further developments (still to be prioritised). School owns a field centre in Angus.

Boys wear bright blue blazers; girls, when visible, look neat in a tailored version. All-through co-ed at the academy is cold news now. Girls now 29 per cent in both senior and junior, and 50 per cent in nursery; entry applications indicate an increase. Girls are now in occupation, scattered unevenly over all year groups with more at top and bottom, but it still looks and feel like a boys' school. Feedback from parents indicates that this is changing, however.

School sold five (disused and needing money spent on them) tennis courts several years ago (little boxes built on them) which caused a press furore, and built the James Clerk Maxwell science building, which is now fully functioning. Outstanding interior with exciting scientific photographs forming whole walls, tiptop labs, colour-coded to match the textbook coding of red for chemistry, blue for physics and green (of course!) for biology, which also boasts nature garden complete with pond and a magically beautiful fishtank embedded in the entrance hall wall.

£2 million upgrade of nursery school, also housing juniors up to second year, recently completed. 'Very well received,' says rector. Numbers of pupils at the junior school had fallen and girls have taken up the slack. The new-build also houses after-school care for juniors available up to 6pm.

Pastoral Care and Discipline: Pupils divided into four 'divisions' (houses), pastoral care via depute rector (pastoral and personnel), heads of year plus form takers (class teachers); good PSHE. Head ephor (prefect) is a key link with rector and school. School 'not complacent that drugs are confined to an area south of Princes Street', or 'stop at the railings – incidents do occur'. No automatic exclusion unless dealing is involved. 'If at all possible we give the pupils a second chance'; parents are involved. 'Pupil may forfeit the right to remain in the school (for a varying length of time).' City temptations are close. One or two teeny reports of bullying still around, but really just aggravated teasing and no more than any nit-picker might expect.

Pupils and Parents: All sorts, with a large traditional intake of the Edinbourgeoisie. Small tranche from abroad, mainly Europe. Rector and head of junior school keen on playing down traditional middle-class image of the school – hence extended and very popular nursery hours and 8am breakfast for seniors. On the whole, pupils are pleasantly self-confident and polite – occasional lout but not more than teenage adolescence. Robert Louis Stevenson and Archbishop Tait of Canterbury are FPs, as are partners in many of Edinburgh's institutions today. Girls still outnumbered by boys and parents still a little hesitant to send the less confident.

Entrance: Traditionally patronised by the great and the good of Edinburgh (the Edinbourgeoisie) and does well by them, plus an increasing number of first-time buyers (around 40 per cent). Entry handbook makes ages and stages for entry very clear, despite the contortions of language and ingenuity required to make the Scottish and English education systems fit into a coherent whole. Girls' advent has, as expected, increased the application rate (for both sexes we understand) but not changed the system.

Exit: 'Around 90 per cent' to various universities, roughly 60 per cent to Scottish, the rest elsewhere, with fewer recently taking a gap year first. Steady trickle (five last year) to Oxbridge – as ever, sciences and engineering feature strongly, with creative and social subjects on the increase. Art something of a speciality. Enlightened careers department (rector again: 'Very very good'). Quantities of embryo lawyers, doctors and merchant bankers, plus, it has to be said, a plethora of pupils going off to university to read engineering, physics, technology, English, modern languages, sports studies, history, international relations. 'What they do thereafter may be different – but they are not cloned down the three routes which you mention. Some into the professions, but progressively more into art, drama, interior design and administration.' School can manage SATS (for American universities). Unconditional offers from Scottish universities based on Scottish Highers taken in (lower) sixth year do not always make for academic concentration in seventh (upper sixth) year.

Money Matters: Good crop of scholarships for musicians and academics plus means-tested bursaries; school may support pupils in financial difficulties in a number of ways depending on the circumstance, until the next practical exit point. 'No endowments per se – majority scholarships and other bursaries come out of fee income.' Familial discounts for third child (and more). The Edinburgh Academy Foundation's primary goal for next year is to support the annual giving programme. Bursaries are means tested up to 100 per cent fees in line with OSCR expectation.

Remarks: Now the dust has settled a bit, the academy emerges as a popular school with huge potential and rapidly improving facilities. Girls are now 29 per cent of both junior and senior – not perhaps for the shrinking violet, but well worth watching.

Edinburgh Rudolf Steiner School

Linked to Edinburgh Rudolf Steiner Lower School in the Junior section

60 Spylaw Road, Edinburgh, Edinburgh, EH10 5BR

• Pupils: 250 boys and girls • Ages: 3-18 • Non-denom • Fees: Upper school £6,990 pa • Independent

Tel: 0131 337 3410
Fax: 0131 538 6066
Email: erss.admissions@steinerweb.org.uk
Website: www.steinerweb.org.uk

Chair of the College of Teachers: No head as such – role of chair is rotated: current chair, Philip Shinton, has been in position for a year. Major educational decisions are taken by the college of teachers and executed by the school's management team in conjunction with teachers. The bursar, board of trustees and college of teachers are responsible for finance, admin and building development. Forget trad hierarchy – teachers in the Steiner Waldorf world 'share responsibility and authority for the daily running of the school and the educational programme'. Forget too, uni backgrounds and PGCEs (though school adds 'most of our upper school teachers have PGCEs and most of the teachers do have a degree'); Steiner teachers are trained in-house, and the Ed SS is one of four training centres. Prospective disciples come from all walks of life, some are former pupils, some former parents and some come from trad teaching backgrounds (sometimes they stay with Steiner and sometimes go back to mainstream). The part-time course is spread over three years and includes an introduction to Rudolf Steiner and Anthroposophy, the Esoteric Science, Goethean Science and artistic practice (and this is in the first year), plus Parsifal: Biographical Questions with Reference to the Grail Legend, eurythmy, creative speech, painting drawing etc. During the second and third year all must do teaching practice. Senior members of the college are part of the interview team for new staff, with each school deciding its own pay scale. Some schools have a definite scale, other schools pay according to teachers' needs and circumstances. The Edinburgh School comes under the first category (but, staff confess, they are hardly overpaid).

Steiner schools do not follow the (now largely historical) orthodox attitude to education, but treat each child as a blank canvas to be filled with interlinking academic, artistic and practical information delivered in such a way as to incite curiosity, encourage creativity and an awareness of others. The Edinburgh Steiner School has long been regarded as a 'school offering alternative education to somewhat scruffy children in hippy clothes, who took no exams and pretty well ran riot'. However, since the Scottish government introduced their much vaunted curriculum for excellence the Edinburgh Steiner School has become an educational flagship, albeit an holistic one. To quote The Scotsman: 'All schools strive for innovation but one that does more than strive is Edinburgh's Rudolf Steiner. It lives and breathes innovation'. The educational philosophy that Rudolf Steiner put into practice in 1919 for the children of the employees of the Waldorf-Astoria fag factory has finally come home to roost.

School holds an open day one Friday each month and visitors (usually prospective parents) are welcome and allowed into classrooms while lessons are in progress, which wasn't quite what happened to this editor: we overshot our briefing session and only managed the art class.

Academic matters: Pupils start each day with a 'wake-up call': rhythmic time/or morning verse followed by the main lesson, a two-hour slot when 'topic blocks' are covered in four-week chunks: astronomy, philosophy, history of architecture, whatever. These are not necessarily exam fodder, but the Open College Network (OCN) recommended that the 'narratives' main lesson be 'accepted without amendment and accredited,' OCN levels 1 and 2 are equivalent to A or B/C at GCSE. We saw few books during our tour; we had previously said that no reference was made to a school library, school disputed this ('but the school does have three libraries in house!') and we were shown the lower school library at the top of the house – a random collection of what looked like paperbacks – though most of the room seemed to be shrouded in blue polythene. Apparently a remedial lesson was in progress, the pupil was bare-foot, and books were thought to be distracting. However, hot news is that they have allocated £80,000 for a new build which will include £10,000 for a library – quite). School also says 'pupils are encouraged to read widely and to make full use of the extensive range of academic resources available to them in the libraries, galleries and museums of this wonderful city'. 'Pupils make a day book for each subject': the one we saw was beautifully illustrated and the pupil concerned could hardly fail to understand angles after many diagrams and pages of colouring.

Spanking new computer room though computers still thinner on the ground here than in many schools; most classrooms equipped with computer-generated projectors (they 'ripped out the whiteboards' we were told) and computers not encouraged (nor telly) till age 14. Either at home or at school. Computer lessons include deconstructing and reconstructing old PCs as well as designing websites (school one impressive). As in Europe, formal education starts at six, with pupils reading first from what they themselves have written (having been 'familiarised' with the letters), and learning both French and German. (Those who join the school later may have to take extra lessons, and pay extra to catch up). Five-week trips to proper French and German Steiner schools – funded by pupils themselves via jumble sales/pizza cook-ins and the like. No 'real' homework until aged nine. Classes of about 20, brighter pupils can leapfrog, and vice versa; EAL for older foreign nationals (charged), the younger ones pick it up as they go along. 'Huge learning support'. Regular testing for all for dyslexia et al in lower school and again on entry to senior school at 14, some pupils with statement of needs. School follows a multi-sensory approach with the emphasis on co-ordination and 'curative' specialists. Qualified staff in both lower and upper school, plus one 'floater'. General dyslexic (dyspraxic etc) help is covered within the fee structure, but if parents request extra, it costs. Scribes. School has reputation for a caring environment (NB not to be confused with Camphill School in Aberdeen), and a number of children with quite hefty special needs have personal assistants whose expenses are covered either by the local authority or their parents.

School offers GCSEs, Standard grades, intermediate I and II, Higher and AS levels (though may be moving to OCN, or possibly the 'Waldorf certificate' – think IB 15 years ago). The normal two-year GCSE syllabus is studied over one year, with maths, English, German and French GCSE taken aged 16, followed by humanities, the sciences and art at 17, and either Highers or AS levels at 18. No academic selection, results are good: some seriously good, top marks in GCSE chemistry last year, and joint highest mark in physics. But difficult to judge overall: our request for exam result breakdown by subject and grade not forthcoming. Lots of practical science with hands-on lessons taught in rather antiquated labs – everything taught 'experientially and children learn by doing'. 'By teaching science, art and religion in this integrated way, we hope to implant in our young people a holistic view of life, so that they may regard the world with understanding and serve it with respect.' Loads of exchanges globally with other Rudolf Steiner schools.

Games, Options, the Arts: Small basketball court, cricket and hockey; seven-a-side rugby at Meggetland 'dead popular'. Timetabled PE and gym, acrobatics a recent addition; pupils wear Steiner tee shirts and track suit bottoms. Hall used for gym, theatre etc. Options and the arts integrated into syllabus – art exam results consistently very good (with an astounding two pupils getting 100 per cent in 2009 at GCSE). Fabric design, weaving, knitting from age six. Music and drama ditto and inclusive, *Oliver* in 2009. Cooking lessons for all, baking in kindergarten during our visit. School lunches, 90 per cent organic (following the principles of Steiner's bio-dynamic organic movement), locally sourced, menus provided and prepared daily by older pupils. Lunch price quite reasonable; the seniors, with a nod towards encouraging enterprise, make a modest profit on the lunches, which they use to pay for their end of term trip.

Background and Atmosphere: Three trad Edinburgh Victorian villas, in a residential area, set betwixt George Watson's extensive campus and various parts of Napier University – this is conversion land in Edinburgh (school thought we meant conservation: we mean large villas flatted). Various modern additions, exciting Swiss chalet for tinies. Mother and toddler group. Parking 'borrowed' from a church opposite, though masses of parking meters on road outside. Three acres of tidily shoe-horned campus, children playing anywhere and everywhere neatly segregated by age. Proper pupil gardens. Every bit of space is used, some tatty areas, nothing precious – the whole place smacks of a lack of funds, though the paths are better maintained than previously. Skool protests as 'work is ongoing to renovate classrooms'. Pupils' work on display adds interest to otherwise lack-lustre classrooms, with a huge and amazing felt hanging in the main reception area. Christian school, everyone enjoyed a Michaelmas feast the week before our visit, other faiths' holy days celebrated.

Pastoral Care and Discipline: Small school, variety pack: some pupils come up via kindergarten, others join for logistic or other reasons further up the school. Staff are caring bunch. One child asked to leave in 'living memory'; otherwise school does its best to bring out the best in each and every one 'instilling life-long learning'. We were surprised to see one pupil eating a banana in class.

Pupils and Parents: In addition to Steiner aficionados, parents are a disparate collection of mainly middle class enthusiasts who are fed up with, or whose children do not get along with, other local schools. Plus some 'out-boarders', pupils from further afield, who stay with local families, plus some exchange students from Rudolf Steiner schools elsewhere, as well as those from non-Steiner schools. This is a hands-on school and parents are expected to contribute during the term, as well as 'helping with redecorating etc' during the work week at the end of the summer term. Relaxed dress code – no uniform; a (very) general policy states that pupils should be clean and tidy – no logos, football strips, ripped jeans, hair colour or excessive jewellery; fairly impressive standard of make-up on some of the older girls; no hajibs (by choice). Pupils are comfortable in the company of visitors, happy to chat and share their work, interests and aspirations – no obvious teenage angst or reticence here – and quite honest about how they were bullied at their last school.

Entrance: Suck it and see: visit school, take child to interview, with a second and longer visit if need be. Pupils come throughout the year: any time. Either through kindergarten or, often age 12, when they have either discovered problems with their current school or need to have their self-confidence boosted.

Exit: Some 95 per cent of pupils leaving at the upper end of the school go on to some sort of further education – eventually. Gap years popular, furthering the Steiner philosophy wherein journeying is an important part of life. Oxbridge 'not out of the frame', but doesn't figure recently; wide selection of universities, drama, music, art schools.

Money Matters: Some £20,000 available for those in financial need. England has a state funded Steiner school as do most of the European countries and Steiner aficionados are currently – somewhat unsuccessfully – campaigning the Scottish parliament to secure state funding North of the Border.

Remarks: Founded 70 years ago, the Edinburgh Rudolf Steiner offers cradle-to-grave still slightly alternative education, with some brilliant teaching and perfect for the child who finds the trad schooling system difficult.

The Ellen Wilkinson School for Girls

Queen's Drive, Acton, London, W3 0HW

• Pupils: 1,400 girls; all day • Ages: 11-18 • Size of sixth form: 350 • Non-denom • State

Tel: 020 8752 1525
Fax: 020 8993 6632
Email: office@ellenwilkinson.ealing.sch.uk
Website: www.ellen-wilkinson-school.co.uk

Head: Since 2004, Ms Chris Sydenham BSc MEd (early fifties), previously deputy head at the school from 2000. Had a 'very mobile' education in areas ranging from Yorkshire to Cornwall, studied maths at Royal Holloway College and did a maths PGCE at Kings College London, pausing in between to work in technical information research. Then taught at several west London comprehensives, becoming head of maths, then assistant head at Greenford High, and then joined Langleywood Secondary Modern in Slough, leaving as it emerged from special measures. Energetic and enthusiastic, she is a passionate advocate of comprehensive schooling and has the school firmly under her thumb.

Academic matters: Steadily improving results, with 77 per cent of students getting 5+ A*–C grades at GCSE in 2009 (29 per cent of exams with A* and A grades) and in the top 15 per cent of schools for value added at advanced level. English, sciences, languages (including Arabic and Latin) all strong. A specialist maths and science college – a healthy proportion take maths, biology and chemistry A level (increasing numbers opting for physics with plenty of A grades). Arabic, further maths, psychology and philosophy are recent additions to the A level choices. Several vocational options at level 2 and 3 too, including business studies, travel & tourism, health and social care and ICT. A 2-year KS3 programme introduced in 2008 with a wide range of options planned at GCSE and beyond from Year 9. Runs maths and science taster sessions and masterclasses for feeder primary schools, with excited pupils trying out practical experiments in real science labs.

Some 50 per cent of students speak English as a second language – EAL support is excellent. 'Most speak English enough to be understood. The difficulties arise with subtleties of language – maths terminology, for example.' So both English and EAL lessons focus on the specifics of language and learning foreign languages can help with sentence structure. Drama is particular helpful for some girls who get little conversation practice outside school because their close female relatives do not speak English. Good SEN support, in and out of the classroom. Extra-curricular gifted and talented enrichment activities. Scores very well on value-added basis, and is probably the best-performing Ealing school that does not select on academic or religious grounds.

Games, Options, the Arts: Limited indoor PE facilities have been transformed by new sports and performing arts building, completed early 2009. Plenty of outdoor space, with grass and all-weather hockey pitches and netball/tennis courts. Sport is popular and high on the agenda – 'Because we're an all-girls school it's cool to be sporty'. Successful basketball and netball teams, lots of clubs, e.g. dance, trampoline, badminton, ultimate frisbee, inter-form matches. 'We do competition here. We celebrate people taking part but we reward winners too. Students need to be resilient.'

Art studios ablaze with papier mâché, silk screen printing, life model drawings. The (smallish) canteen is decorated with exotic designs created during the Year 7 arts and crafts day. Everyone does drama in Years 7–9 and a fair number carry on to GCSE and A level. Plenty of performance opportunities: Christmas musical extravaganza, school musicals, Year 12 pantomime, orchestra, rock band and choirs.

Gardening is a popular club – paths are lined with daffodils and crocuses, flowers bloom in brightly painted pots, herb gardens and vegetable gardens. Other clubs include Amnesty, debating, chess, film. Students go on geography field trips, D of E, language exchanges; they take part in mock bar trials, science, technology and maths challenges, debating competitions, classes with visiting artists, musicians and actors.

Background and Atmosphere: Named for Mancunian Ellen Wilkinson, who was a Labour MP during the '20s, '30s and '40s, one of the leaders of the Jarrow March in 1936, and became the first female Minister for Education in 1945. The school sits amidst comfortable, leafy, mock-Tudor suburbia, though few pupils live in the immediate vicinity. Brick buildings, mostly one or two storeys high, flanked by grass and flower beds planted by the gardening club, with a tube line running behind a high wall round the edge of the playing fields. New sixth form centre and music rooms; a new library and resource area planned for 2010/11 and refurbishment and remodelling on the horizon through the government Building Schools for the Future programme.

The only all-girls state school in Ealing. 'This makes them unselfconscious: they're happy to sit and make daisy chains in the summer, they're keen on sport, they're very appreciative of each other. They don't grow up quite so quickly.'

Pastoral Care and Discipline: Well-ordered. Girls are put in one of four divisions – similar to houses – and stay in these throughout their time at the school. 'It's like having a smaller school within a bigger school, with a family feel.' For some girls from difficult backgrounds, school is the most stable aspect of their lives, and discipline is based round 'catching them being good'. Learners of the Month are celebrated, awards for perseverance and commitment. Most are well-behaved girls, who give the school a good name. A member of the audience during a recent class trip to the National Theatre wrote to the school to praise the exemplary behaviour of its students.

Pupils and Parents: Great ethnic mix, with around 20 per cent white, 20 per cent black, 20 per cent Asian and 20 per cent Arabic. The rest come from a variety of backgrounds, e.g. Polish, Chinese. Most of the well-heeled residents in the immediate vicinity patronise independent schools, though some Japanese girls from the local enclave join the sixth form. So the catchment area tends to spread along the local tube lines and bus routes.

Entrance: Increasingly over-subscribed, with over 600 applicants for 216 places in 2009. Priority to siblings, looked-after children and those with specific medical or social needs. Then 10 per cent from linked Ealing primary schools. Other Ealing primaries get next preference, with the remaining places filled by those living nearest. In practice, this probably means less than two miles away.

About 30 girls from other schools join the sixth form each year, with a baseline of 5+ A*–C GCSE grades for A level courses, including Bs in their A level subjects. Those who don't make the grade can take level 2 courses.

Exit: The 30 per cent or so who leave after GCSEs tend to go to mixed sixth forms or colleges, or follow vocational courses elsewhere. A few high-fliers are lured by scholarships to local independent schools.

Sixth form leavers mostly go on to university, with a trickle to Oxbridge, but some potential students find it socially alien and the majority stays in London. Imperial is particularly popular. Biomedical sciences, business and law figure highly, with English close behind.

Remarks: An increasingly successful and popular school. Huge social and ethnic mix, egalitarian traditions. Strong head, stable staff, nice girls, few discipline problems. For many pupils it is a haven and a springboard to academic success.

Elmhurst School for Dance

249 Bristol Road, Edgbaston, Birmingham, B5 7UH

• Pupils: 190 total – 110 girls, 80 boys – majority boards • Ages: 11-19 • Size of sixth form: 90 • Non-denom • Fees: Boarding £22,419-£24,168; Day £17,490-£18,126 pa • Independent

Tel: 0121 472 6655
Fax: 0121 472 6654
Email: enquiries@elmhurstdance.co.uk
Website: www.elmhurstdance.co.uk

Principal: Since September 2010, Ms Jessica Ward BA Hons Dance Theatre, Post-Graduate Diploma in Dance Performance, QTS, NPQH (early thirties). She started dancing at the age of two, and continued to study ballet and other dance throughout her school years. Degree from the Laban Centre (now Trinity Laban); joined the resident company, Transitions, where she taught as well as performed, and gained her post-grad diploma. Set up dance department at Islington Green School (whilst also head of year) – dance now a high-profile GCSE and BTec subject in the school, which has a 40-strong boys' dance company. Then worked for EdisonLearning (sic), an educational services provider, as part of its senior management team at Turin Grove secondary school in Enfield. Described by Ofsted as a 'highly effective leader'. Has also run workshops for trainee head teachers and created programmes for Teachers TV. Phew – all this by her early thirties.

Keen for Elmhurst students to leave with high academic achievements as well as outstanding dance skills, and comments: ' I look forward to strengthening our relationship with Birmingham Royal Ballet even further, to place Elmhurst firmly as a centre of dance excellence in Birmingham, the UK and beyond.'

Academic matters: First and foremost a ballet school but academic studies do still matter. Regularly found midway down the schools' top 500 league table, also winner of three Good Schools Guide awards in 2004 (for dance and performing arts, inevitably). But still very good results for a school with no academic selection and a timetable spotlighting vocational training. In GCSEs, latest figures show 100 per cent passes A*–C, with 51 per cent of all grades A* or A. Usual curriculum subjects as you'd expect but with science only as a double award and French the only language choice. As principal explained, 'French is the language of the school – it's the language of ballet.' Most students take six core GCSEs, another two from a list of options plus RE short course. English taught as additional language to lots of overseas students.

Some learning support for mild to moderate dyslexics. Subject choices at A level very restricted due to nature of Elmhurst's three-year sixth form, which is heavily vocational. All graduate with qualified dance teacher status (the national diploma in professional dance is degree level), plus A levels in, say, art, music, French, English literature or GCSE office skills. No science. Previous principal insisted the curriculum is 'broad and balanced'. As the prospectus points out, 'In the event of a career cut short by injury or a change of aspiration, they (non-vocational qualifications) constitute a reliable insurance policy'. Lots of non-ballet careers followed by former pupils would seem to support this. State-of-the-art ICT room, also interactive whiteboards in bright airy classrooms, well-stocked library as well as plenty of books in departments and boarding houses. Class size 30 max, with English and maths streaming in GCSE years. Six-day week starts at 8.20am, finishing at 8pm after prep; there are five meal or snack breaks during that time.

Games, Options, the Arts: Exclusively classical ballet since move to Birmingham. Tap, contemporary and jazz only taught as appendages to ballet rather than disciplines in their own right. Superb dance studios with slightly sprung floors rarely out of use. Surrounded by both external and internal windows so young dancers can get used to being on show. World-class dance teachers under the artistic directorship of Desmond Kelly OBE. Each class has own piano accompanist. The school is closely associated with Birmingham Royal Ballet and students perform with the company on a regular basis: 'It's the kind of experience dance students would normally only be able to dream about'. BRB director David Bintley CBE also school's artistic advisor.

Fabulous 250-seat theatre at hub of school which is hired out for summer school/ conferences. Great evidence of artistic ability on show, with students' own work adorning the walls. Sports necessarily limited. No team sports like rugby or hockey but students put through Sthenos body conditioning (exercise) programme and allowed to use neighbouring school's swimming pool. Can also kick a football around school grounds. Music, not surprisingly, extremely popular. There are around 200 individual music lessons (both instrumental and vocal) a week as well as class music for all for the first three years, then music as GCSE, AS or A2 option.

Background and Atmosphere: Relocated to Edgbaston area of Birmingham in summer 2004 from its former home in Camberley, Surrey, the culmination of five years' planning and building. 'We believe it's the first purpose-built ballet school in Europe for this age range,' says school. Originally set up in 1922 by Helen Mortimer as the Mortimer School of Dancing, re-named Elmhurst Ballet School in 1947. Uncertain future in Surrey forced total rethink and its now purpose-built, edge-of-city campus is the glorious result and 2005 winner of Birmingham Civic Society's new building prize. Previous principal John McNamara was first to admit that, despite present day delight, the move was traumatic. Only 11 staff could relocate (including him and wife), mostly on the academic and pastoral side. 'At least that meant there was a sense of continuity for students and their parents,' he said. Vocational (dance) faculty built up from scratch. Move had total support of parents, pupils and governors though. Two other bits of Camberley relocated – an old painting of the former Elmhurst, and a bronze 'Girl with Otter' standing outside a boarding block. School designed so dance studios and classrooms form ring around theatre, while medical centre and boarding houses do same around small outdoor amphitheatre.

Two nurses, two medical care assistants and two physiotherapists on the payroll, so help always on hand. Treatment room always busy as the least twinge is quickly repaired. Never a dull day on site. Constantly buzzing with visitors (Friends of Elmhurst were sitting in on dance classes the day of our visit and you could hardly move without bumping into a governor or two) but students plough on regardless. The overall impression was of complete contentment – the smiles never stopped coming. And even though the aroma emanating from the school bistro smelt like school dinners, the food looked very different. Choices ranged from salads to curries to jacket potatoes and pupils sat at tables with plates piled high. 'We have our own catering team so we have total control over diet and nutrition,' says the school. 'We take eating disorders very seriously and our menus are regularly reviewed by a leading dietician.' Each boarding house has live-in house parent and resident tutor who are responsible for the daily health and welfare issues the young people might have. The students have a comfortable common-room, kitchen and communal areas within each house. Year 7 and 8 boys live next to the Medical Centre, Year 9, 10 and 11 boys next door and Year 7,8 and 9 girls in the adjacent house, all sharing double rooms while Year 11 students have spacious single study bedrooms with en-suite shower-rooms. There is an off-campus house five bus stops away for the first year sixth formers (with resident members of staff). Students in 6:2 and 6:3 live in rented flats and houses: 'It gives them the independence they need at that age'.

Pastoral Care and Discipline: Pastoral care primarily the responsibility of tutors and house-parents. But it's a responsibility taken on by everyone where older pupils also help and support younger ones. Bullying quickly stamped on through mediation rather than sanctions. Both sides (including parents) brought together to sort it out. Would have zero tolerance of drugs if they became an issue but school stresses, 'There are no drugs.' In such event, the course pursued would be 'negotiated withdrawal'. Discipline generally not an issue either. The discipline students show in the dance studios spills over into their daily lives. (Certainly true if the state of classrooms and study bedrooms is anything to go by.) Head of pastoral care told us, 'the difference is that all our students want to be here. They know how lucky they are to have a place here and they're happy'.

Pupils and Parents: Numbers up significantly since move to Midlands – especially among the boys, put down to the Billy Elliot effect. Both boys and girls are bright, cheerful and totally focused. 'They have an emotional maturity you don't normally find in youngsters of that age.' Come from far and wide. Now 13 nationalities represented. Full range of backgrounds dictated by sliding scale of fees support. 'The children blend together seamlessly because they have one thing in common – the common concern with excellence.' OBs and OGs (known as Old Elms) include actresses Helen Baxendale, Hayley Mills, Juliet Mills, Jenny Agutter and Joanna David, singer Sarah Brightman, and ballet dancers Dame Merle Park, Diana Fox and Isobel McMeekan.

Entrance: By audition only. No formal academic test. Selection made on 'perceived potential' and 'commitment' rather than technical brilliance. 'That can be taught, but this isn't a place for recreational dancers.' Auditions held between October and March (fee non-refundable). At least 12 applications for each place, so youngsters really need to be something special. Big sixth form intake to replace those weeded out.

Exit: Around 20 per cent lost before sixth form to dance careers or other vocational schools more suited to them. Regular assessments throughout school career will have identified weaker members who will be directed elsewhere. Ruthless, maybe, but school explains, 'We're all about producing classical ballet dancers. It's a very demanding art form and there's no point in giving youngsters false hope.' Of those who stay the course, most each year secure contracts with international ballet companies before leaving and 95 per cent are in professional employment within six months of leaving.

Money Matters: One of eight specialist schools that get government support through music and dance-aided places scheme. School receives funding for 102 aided places across lower school, and sixth formers helped through national dance and drama awards. Means-tested support given to most gifted and eligible 11 year olds, with funding continuing until end of Year 11 if youngsters get through artistic appraisal in Year 9. When visited, school had 145 students on state scholarships. Fees not extortionate compared with similar specialist schools. Few extras include text books, exam and audition costs, and any medical expenses not covered by compulsory medical insurance.

Remarks: A very special place for very special students. It was easy to forget at times that Elmhurst was, in fact, a school as pupils looked happier than they had any right to be! Certainly not a school that would suit all, though, but then that's the whole idea. Only the best need apply – it's as simple as that.

Eltham College

Linked to Eltham College Junior School in the Junior section

Grove Park Road, Mottingham, London, SE9 4QF

• Pupils: 570 boys plus 60 girls in the sixth form. All day. • Ages: 11-18 • Size of sixth form: 210 • Christian Free Church • Fees: £12,525 pa • Independent

Tel: 020 8857 1455
Fax: 020 8857 1913
Email: mail@eltham-college.org.uk
Website: www.eltham-college.org.uk

Headmaster: Since 2000, Mr Paul Henderson BA FRSA (mid fifties). Educated the Leys School, Cambridge, Nottingham University and postgraduate in education at Cambridge. Captained first X1 cricket at school, at university and played in first XV rugby too. Taught at Norwich School for 15 years, where he was director of studies, head of classics and, for a brief while, acting deputy head; then, second master at St Albans for six years before taking over headship of Eltham College. Keen sportsman and loves singing. Says that perhaps the most important things that he does are 'employing staff and getting children through the door'. Teaches everyone in Year 7, so that he can get to know them. Comfortable with what is being done at the school and feels that it is an exciting place to be. Believes there is now 'a good balance of stable staff and young newcomers'. Feels strongly that the school has an important role to play in the community and has built up good relationships with local state schools. Introduced a community scholarship, targeting over 20 primary schools that are within a mile and a half's radius. Extremely excited about the links they are forming with schools in China and elsewhere. Parents find him approachable and like the general open door policy of the school. Married with two grown-up children.

Academic matters: As their results show, (excellent A level results in 2010 with 67 per cent A*/A grades and 88 per cent A or B), a highly academic school where pupils are stretched to the limits of their abilities. Yet, parents tell us, this academia is nurtured into them and they are taught to be well-organised and to want to succeed. The teaching is, on the whole, parents say, about 90 per cent excellent and teachers are always prepared to give extra help and support if a pupil asks for it. Teacher/pupil relationships appear relaxed and respectful.

Broad curriculum and the school works hard to identify the particular strength(s) of each child and build on them. Languages very strong, many taking two or three at GCSE level. French and Mandarin compulsory in Year 7, German in Year 8 and Spanish can be taken up in Year 9. Latin also compulsory in Years 7 and 8 and all do short course in GCSE RS. The three sciences studied separately unless circumstances exceptional. 'Science is fun,' we were told by a boy, 'all theory is backed up by experiments!' Maths and science are taken as IGCSEs. Three streams in each subject, according to parents 'top, middle and could-be-better', no-one here is 'bad' at anything.

Full-time learning support teacher. All new pupils screened on entry for possible difficulties and, if anything arises, parents immediately involved and a programme devised. Support and encouragement is part of the school ethos and, according to parents, communication is easy and as frequent as necessary. When we asked about G and T, we were told that really every child in the school is gifted or talented and that, because of the huge range of activities in the school, everyone should be properly stretched. Also that teaching is always done to the top level, on the assumption that all are perfectly able. We're not sure that parents of middle-of-the-road, less motivated boys agree or are happy with this.

Games, Options, the Arts: Sport is considered an essential part of school life and everyone is encouraged to participate. With 42 acres of playing fields and an all-singing-all-dancing sports centre, there is something for everyone. In the sixth form it could be just table tennis but before that rugby, hockey and cricket are tops and are played competitively at all levels internally, against other schools and nationally. Also regular overseas tours. Plenty of other options as well, the girls have a couple of strong netball teams, foil and epee fencers recently qualified for the British Championships and there was even a golf team in 2009. Swimming also popular. Duke of Edinburgh Award Scheme followed to gold level though parents said the expedition costs seemed rather high. The less sporty can still find their niches and are encouraged to excel in their individual talents.

Plenty for budding thespians. Drama is on the curriculum for all in Years 7–9 and can be taken at GCSE and A levels. Productions range from Shakespeare to blockbuster musicals, so something for everyone and a great theatre in which to perform. Pupils thrilled with the experience of taking *Oliver!* to the Edinburgh Festival. Music very impressive. Chances for everyone to join in and the head thinks good for teamwork. Lots of choirs, orchestras and jazz bands. About 65 per cent learn an instrument. A parent said she makes a point of going to every musical occasion and is in total awe of their capabilities. Apparently choral singing an exceptional strength, several pupils also members of local and national youth choirs. A lucky group will be picked to perform with Simon Rattle and the Berlin Philharmonic in 2011. The Last Night of the Proms, when there is music and picnicking in the grounds, is a popular end of year event.

Great art on display in the main entrance hall and elsewhere. Lots of talent here. On average a dozen take art A level, all getting A or B, mostly the former. Sculpture displayed outside along route to Junior school. A multitude of trips or, as they call them, journeys every year. Art galleries and museums home and abroad, adventure courses for younger pupils and advanced D of E, languages in their countries of origin, geography, biology, history, theatre, music, any excuse for adventure. This school really does believe in breadth, encouraging research and getting out and about and exploring the world. Some of the sixth form even went cycling in China and younger pupils are scheduled to take part in exchanges with schools in Beijing. Parents praised this cultural aspect and exceptionally happy with the organisation of language exchanges.

Background and Atmosphere: Originally started as a small boarding school for the sons of missionaries, still a strong Christian foundation with the importance of caring for the community and travelling far and wide as part of its ethos. Since moving, in 1912, to this elegant 18th century mansion surrounded by green fields, it has grown in size, stopped taking boarders, introduced girls into the sixth form and become thoroughly part of the 21st century, opening up great opportunities for today's youth. Yet its aims are still very much the same: to produce polite, caring, focused young people ready to go out into the world knowing what they want and where they are going.

Buildings very much the usual mixture of old and new. The central hall and the chapel, where pupils attend a service every morning, could not be more traditional, but the surrounding classrooms and buildings are bright, up to date and contain every modern technological element. Good resource centre for languages, excellent science labs, computers everywhere. Several exciting projects, particularly perhaps the 'green car challenge', voluntary at any age, where, every other year, students design and build an electric car to run at Goodwood. Wow!

Hard-working atmosphere prevails. Reasonably turned out, well-mannered pupils smiled at us wherever we went and looked thoroughly involved in their lessons, whether mechanical or creative. Excellent library, the use of which is built into the curriculum, with quiet areas for study and where prep can be done before going home. A green oasis in the middle of busy, bustling SE London that still has a bit of a boarding school feel about it. A warm welcome greets anyone walking across the threshold, and the enormous statues in the central courtyard, representing power and speed (they came from the old Tricity Building in the Aldwych and were donated by, amongst others, old boy Dr Gerald Moore), illustrate the sense of purpose that exists equally amongst pupils and staff.

Pastoral Care and Discipline: Comprehensive anti-bullying policy and zero drug tolerance. Parents sign contract outlining, amongst other things, acceptable behaviour in school. Fairly strict, disciplined environment. Tutors expected to know everything about the children in their care. Pastoral team meets weekly to discuss potential or ongoing problems. Popular school nurse always available for chat. Head of girls for those in sixth form. Communication lines between school and parents excellent, problems answered promptly. House system also enables peer mentoring.

Pupils and Parents: Solid SE London, mainly from within five-mile radius. Good social mix with a wide range of backgrounds, all keen to ensure good education for their children. Lots of working mums. Pupils can be dropped off at 8am if necessary. Several school busses ferrying backwards and forwards. Lots of social occasions for parents to meet and mingle. Ex-pupils include early sons of missionaries Eric Liddell, Olympic runner, after whom the sports hall is named, and Mervyn Peake, author of fantastic Gormenghast trilogy. More recently, Major Phil Packer, military hero, and Jim Knight, ex-minister of state for schools.

Entrance: Some 75 places at 11+ of which about 50 per cent come from the junior school, the rest from about 60 local primary and private schools. Occasional spaces at 13+. Girls included in 16+ entry which increases the sixth form by about a third. School insists no specific quota. Head interviews all candidates, looking for those that 'want to have a go'. Says 'sponges' would not do well here, pupils need to have drive and really want to do well. Regards interview as most important part of entry process.

Exit: Pretty well all to top universities. About a dozen to Oxbridge each year and ten or more each to London and Bristol. The rest spread around the UK, Nottingham and Warwick being particularly popular in the last few years.

Money Matters: Up to 20 academic scholarships available at 11+ and 15 more at sixth form level for art and drama. Also several for music and sports. Bursaries available for the needy. Apparently fund-raising in last three years been very effective, so the money is there. Five to six percent currently benefiting from bursaries. The school would like this to continue and grow.

Remarks: An academic arena for those who know what they want and are willing to give anything a go. For children with enquiring minds, there are adventures to be had, the world to understand, chances to learn, to give to others and to grow. Those who are kind, considerate and passionate about something will flourish here, but the insecure, and those who need more than a gentle nudge, may not get as much out of it. Fantastic opportunities here for grabbing; boys and girls emerge with a well-rounded, worldly education, ready to take whatever chances life may give them.

Emanuel School

Battersea Rise, London, SW11 1HS

• Pupils: 460 boys, 240 girls, all day • Ages: 10-18 • Size of sixth form: 130 • Christian Foundation • Fees: £14,139 pa • Independent

Tel: 02088 704 171
Fax: 02088 771 424
Email: enquiries@emanuel.org.uk
Website: www.emanuel.org.uk

Headmaster: Since 2004 Mr Mark Hanley-Browne MA (late forties). Educated St George's College, Weybridge, BA in natural sciences at Oxford then PGCE at Cambridge. Previously, taught at Sevenoaks for five years, assistant master at Charterhouse for nine years and deputy head (pastoral) at Highgate for seven years. Enthusiastic and ambitious, has led the school forward and academically upward, making some 'dramatic changes' along the way. Particularly proud of two new computer suites named after old boy, Sir Tim Berners-Lee, creator of the World Wide Web.

Is 100 per cent pro the A level system and has no intention of introducing the IB. 'Specialising at 17/18, is the right timing, four subjects is enough. After all, they will have to specialise even more at university. And we do quite a lot of the extras the IB offers, more self-motivated research and involvement in charities and community support.' Believes that all children should be doers and really want to participate; 'the child who is quite good at everything but not excellent at something' would not really fit. All prospective pupils interviewed which he believes is the most important part of the entry procedure; woe betide anyone lacking a focal interest, no matter how bright he/she may be. Parental views seem to vary. Some say he is 'a bit aloof' ', others say 'affable', 'approachable' and 'often seen about the place'. Married to Rachael, who works for an American business school. They live locally.

Academic matters: Seems to be steadily pulling its socks back up again. Results now higher at A level than they were five years ago, with 92 per cent A*–C grades; 43 per cent A*/ A grades at GCSE. Head 'not in the least interested in league tables' and has withdrawn from them. He feels that he is giving his pupils a far broader, all-round education than exam results alone can possibly show.

Parents certainly happy with the experience their children are getting, 'the teaching quality is good' and the staff 'dedicated and supportive', particularly the heads of year. Although they also spoke about some finding it difficult to keep control over classes. The head says 'getting good staff has been my top priority'. Pupils feel that, on the whole, teachers are 'brilliant and inspiring' and that there have been several new ones in the last few years, who are 'great'. The majority of children in the first year (6) come from local primary schools and parents feel are probably disadvantaged where maths and French are concerned. But they seem to catch up quickly enough.

Certainly the facilities are all here. Science labs, language labs, design technology labs, computer rooms, they are all spankingly up-to-date. We saw children working with wood and metal, experimenting with science, heads down solving mathematical problems; they all looked happy, positive and intent, with relaxed-looking teachers keeping them absorbed. Classrooms are well equipped with the latest technological aids.

An active, imaginative learning support department has its own room with computers and other important aids, alongside a team of specialists who also have their own area of teaching, so are also fully involved in school life. Open door policy when possible but chaplain always around to act as counsellor as well. Pupils are assessed and continuously monitored with constant parental consultation. As far as practical, try to keep one-to-one sessions out of lesson time. Head doesn't really like children being withdrawn from classes. Also run a homework club after school for those who need help. Between 12 and 15 per cent have mild learning difficulties.

Games, Options, the Arts: Fantastic sport, music, art and drama. This is where the school really wins hands down. Rugby, netball, rowing and cricket their major sports. Compete at all levels both at home and abroad. Girls' first netball team unbeaten in 2009 and in cricket the first X1 won 60 per cent of their matches. Overall, rugby teams won 55 per cent and both girls' and boys' rowing squads provided stiff competition in annual regattas. On-site games fields, access via a private gate to the facilities on Wandsworth Common plus 14 further acres of sports ground at Blagdons, near Raynes Park; own fantastic sports hall which includes a climbing wall, exercise rooms, ergometers, as well as a PE classroom; large swimming pool which pupils say is 'great' but changing facilities 'pretty scruffy'. Believe this is one of the head's next update plans. Huge boat house at Barnes housing 45 boats. No wonder so many Emanuel pupils win sporting awards at all levels, from local to international, and some even go on to represent the country in their chosen field. Girls as well as boys. All do pretty well in, what they deem, minor sports as well, athletics, swimming, fives, rounders, dance and tennis.

Music and drama very strong. Several orchestras, bands and choirs. Something for everyone. Pupils we talked to particularly keen on number and variety of bands. Children sing in the National Youth Choir and play in the National Youth Orchestra. Plenty of chances to learn individual instruments, we were told 250 music lessons given weekly. Eight grade 8 passes in 2009. Concerts and recitations regular events, even put on Bach's St John's Passion in 2010. Very excited, when we were there, about current production of Oliver. Plenty of parts for everyone. Pupils said drama department 'very brave', presumably for putting on ambitious productions. Certainly they have the facilities. We would probably say that to put on Tom Stoppard's *Arcadia* was pretty brave. But they did and it was a great success. Another of the head's projects is to widen the theatre.

Art studios amazing. Recent project on 'passions and obsessions' produced fascinating results. Enthusiastic teacher with equally eager pupils. Head is a great art fan and views the school as a showcase. Certainly everywhere we went pictures hung on walls. Apparently, lots more also stacked in storage rooms. Some really wild and wonderful. Says he commissions pictures from students every year. Lots of trips, home and abroad, to expand their horizons. Singing in Venice a recent highlight.

Background and Atmosphere: Originally richly endowed by the Dacre legacy in 1594, there's a courtyard in the middle of the main building dedicated to three Queen Elizabeths. The first on the throne at their foundation; the second who planted the central tree, Queen Elizabeth, later the Queen Mother, in 1951; the third, her daughter who made a royal visit in 1994. Surrounded by glass, this is typical of the traditional/modern mix in this school. Old buildings house modern facilities and new buildings grow up out of old ground. The library, which could be said to be the hub of the school, is a good illustration. With silent areas behind glass and a circular staircase leading up to an archive room full of school history, it is a great place for pupils to gather for meetings, research or quiet study. A good learning resource centre. Librarian relaxed and welcoming, pupils often stay to do homework there; which would explain why one parent said her daughter never seems to bring much home. Its renovation one of the head's decided successes.

Main building originally a Crimean War orphanage, taken over by Emanuel in 1883. Although, internally, it has been through many changes, the Chapel, on the first floor, remains and assemblies held there daily. This is still a Christian school bearing Christian values and commitment to the community outside as well as within. Pupils are polite, open and, according to those we talked to, have good relationships with their teachers. Also spoke positively about their headmaster. Year 9s talked about team-building, peer mentoring and the way older years interact well with the younger ones. School council seems to help this, as does the house system. They say school seems to recognize what each child is good at, really promote it and thus create confidence. Out of the mouths of babes. Must be good. Whole place feels happy, friendly and welcoming. Parents say school good at making sure course-work is done on time otherwise 'big trouble'. Girl/boy ratio now about 40/60 per cent which, given the large number of single sex girls schools in the area, is how it is likely to stay.

Split of school day seems to work well with two classes before a short break, then two more before half an hour's assembly and two more before lunch at 1.15. Excellent food, say pupils, good choice, but queuing system not good if you are late. Lovely to have tables outside in summer. Sixth form thrilled with their new common-room and café (only open at certain times and not for lunch), very grown-up. Whole sixth form area with all its own facilities is brill. Parents say very friendly and lots of activities and involvement for them as well.

Pastoral Care and Discipline: Tutor system combined with house system and easy access to head of year ensures that any problems that arise should be spotted and dealt with quickly. We asked pupils where they would go if they needed to talk to someone sympathetic and they agreed that that it would probably be the head of year first and then the chaplain. Chaplain also has sixth form team to help him when necessary. Christian ethos is important and responsibility for others would seem to be endemic. Big emphasis on being part of community and charitability. Natural interaction and mutual respect between teachers, pupils and year groups does appear to be working.

All pupils carry conduct cards recording homework timetables, commendations and misconduct records – five commendations and you get a chocolate, but get a misconduct signature and you have to start again. Beware of getting five misconduct records: Saturday morning detention looms.

Separate, comprehensive policies on bullying addressed to parents, teachers and pupils. This is something almost bound to occur, in some form or other, in a school full of alpha boys and girls. The majority of parents we talked to were not worried and felt that school handled problems well. However, some think there should be zero tolerance and, at the moment, don't feel this is happening. Most praise the pastoral care whole-heartedly but a few doubts remain over the handling of difficult or sensitive cases.

Pupils and Parents: Mainly local, 85 per cent from within three mile radius. Typical South London mix. Many working to make sure their children get a good education. Ex-pupils include Michael Aspel, Andi Peters, Michel Roux, Issey Cannon (recent member of under 21 England women's cricket team) and Peter Hain.

Entrance: Competitive at 10+, 11+, 13+ and 16+. Must get 55 per cent in entrance test and show special aptitude somewhere. Good command of English, both written and spoken, essential. Priority for siblings as long as performance report from previous school OK. Popularity has surged, recently 500 applicants for 85 places at 11+ and 700 overall. Interview mandatory. Must have special interest but need not be academic. They are looking beyond pure academia.

Exit: A few at 16, if they don't make the grade or would rather go elsewhere, but most stay for A levels. One or two a year to Oxbridge and about 78 per cent going to Russell Group and other good unis. Nottingham, the various London colleges and Bristol most popular recent choices.

Money Matters: Lots of bursaries, not only academic but also music, sport, art and drama. Varying degrees of financial support. Strong bursary fund, constantly growing aiming for self-perpetuation. Big fund-raising drive with ex-parents. Old boy, James Wates, created special fund; six children benefit from his bursaries at the moment.

Remarks: An amazing campus to find in an urban area close to Clapham Junction. For parents who can scrape the fees together, in a borough sadly lacking in good secondary schools, it is ideal. For sporty, arty, musical children, the opportunities to expand their talents and their horizons are all here.

Epsom College

College Road, Epsom, Surrey, KT17 4JQ

• Pupils: 730: 460 boys of whom 220 board full/weekly; 270 girls of whom 125 are full/weekly boarders • Ages: 13-18 • Size of sixth form: 315 • C of E • Fees: Day £19,263; Boarding £25,731-£28,200 pa • Independent

Tel: 01372 821 234
Fax: 01372 821 237
Email: admissions@epsomcollege.org.uk
Website: www.epsomcollege.org.uk

Head: Since 2000, Mr Stephen Borthwick BSc Cphys FRSA (fifties). Married to Glynis, a modern linguist, they met while both at University of Wales in Bangor. Previously head at Aldenham; before that was deputy head at Bishop's Stortford and head of physics at Marlborough. Has overseen eight years of change for the school, primarily completion of the move to co-ed and a multi-million pound buildings and improvement programme. A businesslike chap, he works from a traditional, well-appointed office under a clock tower in a beautiful administration building. Views his job as 'fantastic – it's an absolute privilege to be involved in so many lives and to bring on an institution such as this'.

Rather a remote figure: one first year boy we spoke to did not know where head's office was. Not one of the super-smooth parental charmer brigade – we had a strong sense that parent contact is not usually with him. But some who have spoken to him one-on-one rate him highly. 'Brilliant,' said one mother. 'I don't really have a handle on him, but he's obviously doing something right,' says another, and a third thought perhaps he is 'not so good with large groups.' However, all credit him with assembling a first rate team: deputy and expert bunch of housemasters and mistresses much praised. He, meanwhile, is not resting on his laurels. 'I want to enjoy the fact this school is in the best shape it's been for years – and I've got more plans,' he says. Epsom has just launched a partnership link with Lambeth Academy in Clapham, designed to provide particular help to Lambeth's new sixth form by an exchange of ideas, skills and experience.

Academic matters: First division: strong overall performance and consistently among top schools in the south east – but it's no St Paul's. 'The academic side is good, but I don't think it's why people come here – it's a good all-round option,' said one mother. 'We chose Epsom for its sport and music as much as because we liked its science bias.' At GCSE 84 per cent A*/A. Popular optional subjects include history, geography and drama. At A level it is just outside the top 100 schools nationally, but still very much up there with 84 per cent A/B grades at A level. Most popular subjects are maths and science (especially physics – a pat on the back on this score with the subject so much out of favour elsewhere), history, economics, French and English (now following the exciting new Cambridge Pre-U syllabus). Critical thinking available at Year 11 and lower sixth form, leading to Perspectives: extended 4,000 word essay project in sixth form. High value added.

Academic programme spread over six days, most of the teaching in the morning. Average class size 20, decreasing to an average of 10–15 at sixth form. Most subjects have their own dedicated teaching block with library, but also a smart main library (fantastic space as converted from the old gym) with full-time librarian and link to careers department. Nice place to spend time and makes the most of its function as a community area with broad selection of newspapers, magazines and CDs. Economics, business studies, history and geography are housed in impressive Mackinder Building.

Good special needs provision. Long school day means all SEN tuition takes place outside timetabled lessons so pupils do not miss an academic class. Happily caters for dyslexia, dyspraxia, ADHD and other emotional, social and behavioural needs (about eight per cent have one-to-one help). Parental experience bears out that support is good – one mother was delighted that the school diagnosed and 'sorted' her daughter's borderline dyslexia. A handful of EAL students in each year group – a dozen in sixth form. Timetabled lessons only if they don't do FML and private individual tuition available.

Games, Options, the Arts: Strong sporting tradition where enthusiasts thrive and facilities are fab – it's all here from first class pitches and huge sports halls (one with cricket nets) to a high-tech fitness centre that posh private clubs would admire. Plenty of national and county players – 'It drives the youngsters to know there are older boys here playing for England,' says head. Particular success in rugby, judo, athletics, golf and rifle shooting (school has its own .22 range and has been national champions for three out of last five years). More than 25 sports available and large number of teams means almost everyone gets to represent the school at some point during the year. Not the school for wimps and couch potatoes as CCF compulsory in the second and third year – splendid CCF assault course.

Music and drama good and the school is strong in performance – lots of chances to sing, including in the splendid chapel choir. Annual musical theatre/opera production – Monteverdi's The Coronation of Poppea, Sonheim's Sweeney Todd, Mozart's Marriage of Figaro. Tons of ensemble music. Superduper shiny new concert hall opened 2007. Modern music block with own recording studio. All-singing, all-dancing performing arts centre recently completed – including theatre, dance studio and dressing-rooms – with state-of-the-art sound and lighting facilities. Some 350 instrumental lessons in school each week, again not during academic time. Timetable is organised so that these lessons, along with voluntary activities, clubs, rehearsals etc take place in the afternoon – pupils can also use this time to continue art, IT or DT projects or use the library. New creative arts compulsory programme for younger pupils (craft, art, dance, Mandarin, electronics etc).

Background and Atmosphere: 'Girls have civilised the place – it's more positive, co-operative and relaxed,' says head. 'And also a lot noisier.' School was founded in 1853 by Dr John Propert as The Royal Medical Benevolent College, as part of his foundation to help the orphans and widows of the medical profession. The good doctor aimed to provide a 'liberal education' for 100 sons of 'duly qualified medical men' for £25 a year. Opened by Prince Albert and granted (still existing) royal patronage by Queen Victoria in 1855. Strong links with the medical profession remain (although school is now providing a far broader education) – has helped to produce more doctors than any other school, and the Royal Medical Foundation, which promotes the founder's aims, is still on the school site. Superb setting and many of the handsome red-brick Victorian buildings remain, but are now joined by impressive new 21st century facilities, well blended, creating collegiate atmosphere. Majority of the 80 staff live alongside pupils on site.

Girls began arriving in numbers in 1997, and the school has now reached what seems to be the standard ratio for former boys' schools of 60:40 boys:girls. 'Epsom is fine for girls,' said one mother, 'albeit the ones that get the best out of the school would be the ones with an inner strength.' Girls are very visible around the place, head talks about them a lot and the school has just closed down a boys' house (ironically, in the face of demand from boy applicants) to further tip the balance towards co-ed. But still, we feel, not the ideal place for a real girly girl.

Fifty per cent of the pupils board for some of the time and there are (four) boys' and (three) girls' single-sex, self-contained, boarding houses – homely enough, quite cosy (strong smell of toast when we visited mid-morning), dreary in places though school protests, 'Many of our houses have been refurbished recently'. Each house has own small library, common-room and IT facilities. No more than four to a room, numbers reducing gradually to single rooms by upper sixth.

Day pupils stay until 6pm (3pm on Saturdays). Be warned – the first term can be very tiring (which can make for very grumpy children) for those used to short prep school days. 'It can take a while to get used to a long and differently structured day,' says one mother. 'The children need to learn about managing their time.'

Weekly boarders leave after games on a Saturday until Sunday evening. Day pupils can stay over on occasions. All meals compulsory – great comfort to parents of potential anorexics. Plenty going on for full boarders – and trips galore round Christmas time. Despite growing day population, school still ticks over nicely as a boarding school with all the consequent opportunities, commitment and support. Typical public school type atmosphere. 'It's a wonderful environment for kids,' says one mother who has found it the right place for all three of her very different children. 'They have a very good time. We were looking for an adult version of their very vibrant prep school and feel we found it here.' Very social – buzzy.

Pastoral Care and Discipline: Healthy house system runs well and forms the framework around which care and discipline is based. Parents rate pastoral side as 'fantastic'. Good support from medical centre staff, school counsellor and two chaplains. Also house prefects. Some feeling that parents should pay close attention when choosing a house, as 'there are differences, particularly in flexibility'; school says parents are asked for a preference rather than to make a choice of house and that the options for a day pupil or a boarding pupil are the same, regardless of the house they join.

Fairly strict as you would expect – it's a traditional place with good old-fashioned values, plus the added in loco parentis responsibilities of a boarding school set-up. Fine chapel at the heart of things. Fair number of rules and regulations – sanctions begin with a verbal reprimand and after that scale up as necessary. On drugs use, parents sign agreement giving head flexibility of punishing according to seriousness of offence – head spent first four years in fact showing no flexibility at all, requiring all offenders to leave. Now generally understood it is a line not to cross – no problems for the past five years. Incidences of drinking or smoking (naturally also no-nos) treated more leniently, but only to a point. A first offence would be punished but tolerated, get to a third – and wave bye bye. Such flagrant disobeying of the school rules is simply not on. And absolutely zero tolerance of sexual activity – even hugs: 'While the person doing the hugging might just mean "Well done!", the person being hugged doesn't necessarily know the motive, or enjoy the experience,' says head. 'But while you have to have a line on sex, drugs and rock and roll, none are actually issues here.' Sanctions are all balanced with an equally well-administered rewards system to recognise achievement, effort and behaviour.

A few rumblings of parental discontent in the past about aspects of home-school communication – but most parents seem happy and enjoy web-based access to information separate from pupils. As well as the annual full report, pupils are graded for effort and achievement twice a term.

Pupils and Parents: Come mainly from Surrey and fringes – typically a 30-mile radius of the school. Pupils are an orderly bunch – well turned out (traditional uniform with a few permitted variations denoting house and seniority) and well-to-do. Normal middle class teenagers. Lots of siblings. Sixth formers we met were a credit to the place.

Epsom is one of the richest areas in the UK (and the EU), hence lots of moneyed (a mix of old and new money) parents with high percentage of professionals and company directors; also doctors and a sprinkling of celebrities. OB network strong. Former pupils include artists John Piper and Graham Sutherland and, for no obvious reason, a number of TV reporters including Nicholas Witchell, Mark Mardell, Jonathan Maitland and Jeremy Vine, together with his brother, Tim Vine, the comedian. Lots of medical luminaries and some politicians and other notables, including Lord Alex Carlile and Sir John Scarlett.

Entrance: Currently reducing the entry number of boys to get the co-ed balance right – 'Further expansion would be an easy route – but not the right route,' says head. Entrance is selective – but not ruthlessly so. At 13+ 130 places – via CE for prep school pupils (account for approximately 70 per cent of places); non-prep or overseas candidates sit school's own entrance exam. For CE, 60 per cent average is a comfortable pass, under 55 at a key subject is a fail. (Also an optional 11+ in English, maths and verbal reasoning.) Places can be reserved three years prior to entry (£1,000 deposit). Offers made subject to satisfactory reference and reports from previous school and pass in relevant entry exam. School says it looks for 'able all-rounders who are hard-working, talented and want a challenge'. List generally full 12 to 18 months prior to entry. 'Anyone can apply at any time, and as early as they wish,' says the school. 'Whilst the headmaster likes to keep families together where possible, every child would have to pass our entry requirements – there are no special concessions for siblings other than sympathy!' Huge list of feeder schools.

Sixth form intake of about 50: 35 girls, mainly from independent, single-sex day schools, and 10/15 boys, mainly from overseas. Entry subject to exam, interview and GSCE results. For existing pupils, sixth form entry depends on GCSE results (not usually the problem) and attitude. School quite fierce in denying a chance to stay if a pupil's report card over the years has been full of poor effort grades and comments. Head will ring warning bells, usually during Year 10.

Exit: Less than five per cent leave at 16 – usually headed for alternative independent schools or sixth form colleges. At 18, an average of 20 plus (out of 165 leavers) set off for medical school – 'That leaves 145 who are quite normal,' jokes head. Business, economics and law attract a large chunk. 75 per cent of pupils gain a first choice university place. Lots to Leeds, Exeter, Cardiff and Nottingham. A dozen or so to Oxbridge.

Money Matters: Consensus is that the school is value for money – even non-boarders are in school from 7.50am to 6.30pm, returning home with homework done; 'What price on that?' muses one happy mother. Scholarships 13+ and 16+ for academic, all rounder, art, DT, music dram and sport – but most money devoted to bursaries; head is very keen to extend his Widen our Access scheme aimed to help attract less traditional public school entrants rather than prop up investment bankers who have fallen on hard times. But most families here have rather a lot of money and a pupil scraping in from the state system (or the ranks of the impoverished middle class) may feel rather a poor relation – some rather fancy trips and extras to fork out for.

Remarks: A generally slicker outfit these days. Excellent on-site facilities, well resourced, good academia and you don't need to live in to gain the benefits of the boarding atmosphere. Especially suits self-contained, robust and sporty types – social drive too brisk for shy and solitary souls.

Ermysted's Grammar School

Gargrave Road, Skipton, North Yorkshire, BD23 1PL

• Pupils: 805 boys • Ages: 11-18 • Size of sixth form: 245 • none • State

Tel: 01756 792 186
Fax: 01756 793 714
Email: admin@ermysteds.n-yorks.sch.uk
Website: www.ermysteds.n-yorks.sch.uk

Head: Since 2008, Mr Graham Hamilton BA PGCE, previously deputy head. Unassuming but quietly determined to move school forward. Adds 'aiming for excellence' to school motto of 'follow the truth' – 'Excellence in whatever they are able to achieve – academic, sporting or cultural. I have to ensure that this one chance is the best it can be for any boy'. Seeking change, particularly curricular, but favouring evolution over revolution. 'Last year we got our best results for 10 years – why make wholesale change?'

Parents seem pleased with the continuity, 'It is early to tell whether anything will change, but they have an excellent teaching team at the school and I think that is key'.

Academic matters: Selective – boys work hard and achieve 77 per cent A/B at A level. Average class sizes 29 at KS3, 30 at KS4 and 20 at KS5. French and German taught from Year 7; Latin in Years 8 and 9. Gained specialist science status 2006. Maths and science among best in country. One parent spoke of 'excellent, inspirational teaching' of economics but was less impressed with the French teaching, though results are good. Food Technology being offered from September 2011, new building in progress.

High-achieving school – looks to ensure boys fulfil potential and are well rounded, able to cope with life. Curriculum review imminent – which ought to lead to greater personalisation, e.g. a wider choice of GCSE courses and early entry for some examinations. 'We don't want the boys to tread water,' opines the head. Review will focus on transferable skills, preparing boys for 'jobs that don't exist yet'. Aware that entrance to best universities gets ever tougher and wants to help boys keep up. 'A good, old-fashioned state grammar that gets as good, if not better, results than the fee-paying options in this area,' said a parent.

Plans for astronomy GCSE and PSHCE as separate subjects. Links with Girls' High School for some sixth form subjects – PE, Latin, theatre studies, politics – but jealously protects benefits of single-sex education.

Expectation is high. 'I have never felt pressurised, but I do like to be stretched,' one student told us. Gifted and talented benefit from personalisation in lessons plus strong enrichment programme. Caters for SEN and currently has nine on SEN register and one statemented; 43 have English as an additional language.

Games, Options, the Arts: Football rapidly catching up rugby, cricket and athletics – strong in cross-country and school is represented at both county and national levels. National fell-running champions 2008. In 2006 the junior team were runners-up in the English Schools' Cross-country Championships; in rugby, the first XV (under 18) reached the quarter-finals of the national Daily Mail Vase Competition. International honours at orienteering. Great sports hall for team games and school functions. Parents' Association funded a challenging climbing wall. Proud of its music and drama; school visits valued by parents, notably geography trips to Iceland, annual exchange with Tassilo-Gymnasium, Simbach, Bavaria, and partnership with Zahira College, Sri Lanka.

Background and Atmosphere: Founded circa 1492; unfair to say it hasn't seen a paintbrush since but some parts are a little worn. Mishmash of new and old buildings showing signs of age. Head accepts 'accommodation is an issue for us'. Listed building status restricts wholesale change but gradual investment is improving things. 'What would we prefer – a new set of text books or beautifully painted corridors? I know what I prefer and any money we do get is spent on learning and teaching,' asserts head. Reasonably new refectory and two ICT suites. Purposeful in its atmosphere. Summer 2009 saw complete refit of library and creation of sixth form learning resource area – a sixth form library.

Pastoral Care and Discipline: Induction is carefully managed – with 50 feeders it has to be. Staff visit boys in their primary schools and among other things there is a pizza party for upcoming year sixers. House structure and merit system work well. Rewards all endeavour through assembly recognition, personal praise and letters to parents. Traffic light system monitors progress. Parents like lack of any issues with drugs or bullying and exclusions are rare.

Pupils and Parents: Main intake from Craven, Ilkley and Barnoldswick. Head boy had a 40-mile round trip but catchment area priority now reducing huge geographical spread. The diverse population is a strength. Parents like the grammar ethos without the fees. Placing increasing importance on its communication with parents. Students like the opportunities. 'There is a lot to do here, a chance to make of school what you want or what you can, academically or in sport, drama or music,' said one student.

Parents fund-raise for the school. Old Boys include Iain Macleod (politician) and Simon Beaufoy (scriptwriter of *The Full Monty*).

Entrance: For entry at 11, LA oversees testing procedure – verbal and non-verbal reasoning tests with admissions following the set criteria. Strong priority now given to boys living in catchment area because demand for a place from parents over a wide geographical area was great. Entry to Years 8 to 11 if places available. Tests in mathematics, English, science. Entry to sixth form needs six GCSEs at grade C+ including at least B in subjects to be studied at AS (some exceptions – e.g. grade A in GCSE mathematics required).

Exit: Majority stay on to sixth form; of these by far the majority go on to good universities (Newcastle, Leeds, Durham, Oxbridge). Small number into industry and the Services.

Remarks: Don't let the shabby entrance and occasional corridor put you off. Does pretty much everything right and great prospects for the future. Change is coming and it's in good hands.

Eton College

Eton, Windsor, Berkshire, SL4 6DW

- Pupils: 1,300 boys (all boarding) • Ages: 13-18 • Size of sixth form: 520
- C of E (other faiths 'excused' chapel, but many attend anyway)
- Fees: £29,862 pa • Independent

Tel: 01753 671 249
Fax: 01753 671 248
Email: admissions@etoncollege.org.uk
Website: www.etoncollege.com

Head Master: Since 2002, Mr Anthony (Tony) Little MA PGCE (early fifties) who was educated at Eton, read English at Corpus Christi (where he was a choral exhibitioner) and did his PGCE at Homerton. Previously head of Oakham, having taught English at Tonbridge and Brentwood, and was head of Chigwell ('a steep learning curve') before Oakham. Keen on music, the theatre, film and rowing (nostalgically the latter). A lovely man; he speaks immaculate English, in paragraphs, with 'whoms'.

Though the appointment was greeted with some shock – 'He hadn't even been head of a first division school and now he is head of the heap' – he has proved to be an excellent and innovative head man (as all Eton heads are known). He instituted a parent/teacher evening in E and F block, before long leave in the first half (Eton speak: read before half term in the first term) – a dramatic turnaround by Eton standards. Good at working the public and the parents, 'super directed, makes a terrific impression'. 'Keen on raising the public perception of the school.' 'Not a stuffed shirt and always open to new ideas.'

This is a head who reckons that, 'There must be a regular appraisal of teachers and housemasters'. Health and safety are also much involved, and there has been a proactive appointment. The head's wife, Jenny, is very involved in school activities ('Too involved,' said one beak – i.e. teacher); 'Not at all hands-off,' said the head man; she regularly acts as school guide. The Littles have a grown up daughter.

Academic matters: First class all round, though not necessarily first class in all the league tables (the school takes some IGCSEs, which don't count). Outstandingly good teaching, Eton can pick and choose (and cash has quite a lot to do with it – heads of departments elsewhere join the also-rans for extra pay). Prospective staff have a series of interviews, spending time in the department, taking a class (head man is 'keen that everyone should be in a class with boys') and culminating with lunch (knives and forks test). Boys setted by ability from the first year. All boys take a mixture of GCSEs and IGCSEs, then A levels or pre-U in the sixth form. Plenty of va et vient among sets, boys are constantly changing beaks and peer groups.

Tutors allotted for junior boys, who may then request their specialist tutor post-GCSE. Highly structured, lots of sticks and carrots. Monthly order cards and show-ups. Certain amount of irritation from older beaks about 'having to fill in the class register by computer'. Fabulous languages, one of the most successful departments in the country in terms of results – packs in talk and chalk. Japanese, Chinese, Arabic are options (NB if Eton offers a subject it really happens – unlike many other schools which often have an element of window dressing); the results here are (mostly) not native speakers clocking up an easy A – regular colony of OEs have 'gone east, young man' to seek their fortunes in China. Proper language exchanges throughout the school (e.g. two weeks in Japan). Indeed exchanges in every discipline – France, Spain, Russia ... Plus Casa Guidi in Florence for history of art and Italian.

Vast choice of A levels, results outstanding. Humanities, art and languages much more popular than in similar schools, maths too, but sciences a poor relation in both popularity and results. English results are phenomenal. Twice yearly internal exams ('trials' – the top boys' results are read out). Boys are treated much as university students and need considerable stamina and self-discipline to cope with the workload, though help is usually given to those who fall by the wayside through illness or computer-games addiction or whatever.

School reports sent to parents have an unusual formula: beaks report to tutors, who in turn report to housemasters, who in turn write to parents, enclosing relevant reports as well as their personal assessment of the situation.

Whereas in some schools, staff training in SEN means the odd one-day course, Eton has invested heavily in it. An educational psychologist spent a year setting up and coordinating the SEN unit at Eton and training staff. A good dyslexia unit, with one-to-one and group therapy on tap. Parents extol the curricular discretion/freedom that Eton has for dyslexics and others. School has good links with the Dyslexia Association and has had for many years. It's not the easiest place for them, though – 'Too much working on your own,' said one former (mildly dyslexic) Etonian of our acquaintance, and it's still quite a socially tough environment. That said, the learning support system is strong and the school takes in 'a significant number of dyslexic and indeed dyspraxic boys corresponding to the proportion in the general population ... and does so consciously at the point of selection where their potential is recognised, and it then provides them with extensive support'. Though pupils and beaks alike agree that 'It is not really the best place for pupils who are seriously challenged,' the school can cope with those with Asperger's or ADHD, on the 'mild to moderate' spectrum as well as the 'dys' strata.

Most of Little's previous headships have leant in the direction of co-education and/or the IB. When we asked him about the possibilities of such radical change his reaction was to say, 'I first learnt that we were going down the IB route on the radio when I was filling the car with petrol in Norfolk'. He doesn't reckon it is 'good for enthusiasts, nor for scientists', but is 'much better for girls'. 'The best part of the IB is the extended essay or theory of knowledge – complete with footnotes – but now that all lower sixth do divinity' (which he teaches) 'this acts as an embryonic ToK, and we find nuggets of outstanding excellence, exposing as many boys as possible.' Now that Eton has taken on the Cambridge Pre-U (a superior alternative to A levels) a move to the IB seems very unlikely. On the question of girls, we got an enigmatic 'who knows?' (the boys wondered about their uniform).

Games, Options, the Arts: Excellent all round – every conceivable extra-curricular activity is on offer to amazing standards in some cases. IT now in the vanguard, with the local expert maintaining that he had rarely come across such infrastructure. (Head man complains about 'the tyranny of the email culture'.) Each room in every house now with infra-red and net connections; all boys have mobiles and discount-available laptops. Brilliant music, generally acknowledged to be one of the best departments in the country, and attracts the brightest and best in music scholarships. Regular and very polished concerts; wonderful chapel choir.

Superb and inspirational art department, oodles of dosh spent here in the last few years – marvellous open aspect over playing fields to the northwest. Remarkable and challenging work; masses of prizes and scholarships here too – the art department that all other schools envy. Drama important – school and house plays, both housemaster and boy-inspired, plus more traditional stuff.

Main games are soccer, rugby, fives, hockey, cricket – very good – plus Eton's own Wall Game and the Field Game; good fencing, swimming (squad recently trained to swim the Channel), water polo, sailing etc, also judo, polo, beagling. Over 40 teams in action most Saturdays. Sport, perhaps, no longer worshipped the way it once was. Housemasters not pushing hard enough, say some. Head encourages boys to continue with sports through exam terms – brownie points for this.

Huge number of outings, visits and field trips etc, and good provision for amusing pupils post-exams. CCF very popular – pace Harry Windsor – and full-time officer seconded. Excellent and popular post-school camp offers fantastic range of experiences – helicoptering, parachuting, speedboat driving licence (popular this and essential for hiring boats in the holidays). Vast number of clubs and societies, with topnotch speakers, often run by boys themselves, almost all of which boast a variety of club socks, by which Etonians can be easily identified – they usually wear a non-matching pair (warning here: the school bill may well be augmented by several hundred quids' worth of extra 'essential' club kit – socks and scarves only).

Background and Atmosphere: Founded in 1440 by Henry VI (sister college of King's College, Cambridge, which was founded a year later), and 70 King's Scholars still live in the original buildings (most elegant dining hall and really ancient classroom still with original benches and graffiti). Buildings of mellow old red brick, grounds run down to the Thames. Magnificent chapel built by Henry VI and a second chapel for Lower Boys; war memorials all over the shop, deep nostalgia. School has appointed an imam – RC chaplain, Jewish and Hindu tutors on staff too.

Twenty-four boarding houses, including separate one for King's Scholars; single study bedsits for all, from day one. Huge variety in specification – housemasters employ different strategies as to which boy chooses first. Décor differs – one mother described one as 'like a working brothel'; another has carpet up the walls. Boarding houses scattered down the High Street and beyond; houses are known not by name but by the initials of the housemaster in charge – housemasters in the job for 13 years, so of course the name of the house changes, irritating for Eton buffs who like to pretend they know the place. Boys no longer wear bum freezers but tail coats for all, with stiff collars except for office bearers, who wear proper wing collars and white ties. Brilliant for posture, as boys stuff pockets in their tails with all sorts of essential school kit, pulling even the most round-shouldered creature straight. (Must be the cheapest school uniform out, with good second-hand trade both boy-inspired and via the school tailors in the High Street.) Head describes the uniform as 'anally retentive'. Fancy waistcoats worn by members of the Eton Society ('Pop'), most memorable one was entirely made of condoms. However, pupils no longer wear tails across the bridge to Windsor, or even now (much) in the High Street, and much changing and half-changing throughout the day.

Atmosphere very much alive, not easy, and every day is structured and active. Everyone – boys and beaks (often flying round Eton on their bikes, in white tie, with their black gowns flying and trousers tucked into their socks) – on the go. All beaks must wear gowns, which come into their own during their three line whip coffee break – Chambers – when one beak will attract the attention of another by tugging at his gown; this can become addictive, with long lines of tugging beaks forming, 'Like a line of elephants,' says the head man.

Eton has its own traditional but ever evolving school language: halves (terms), long leave (half term) etc; currently the buzz is to add 'age': as in 'pubage', 'birdage', 'tabage' (tobacco), lebage (as in plebs) etc. Excellent school mags (*The Chronicle, The Junior Chronicle*) which are sold on high days and holidays for commission (usually by younger boys). A school rule discourages boys from speaking to the press, which may be the reason why beaks often hear the latest gossip via their houses and not from their peers – this can lead to not so funny situations, when a quick email to all housemasters concerned could calm the matter down. All boys now allowed mobile phones.

Pastoral Care and Discipline: Broad-minded and liberal in principle. Boys who get into trouble seem to be given lots of support, especially from their housemasters. Drugs, alcohol and cigarettes a perennial issue. If a suspicion that a pupil may be dabbling with drugs, then a 'more flexible' view is taken, to 'motivate' the pupil. Parents are informed and the boy signs a contract and is offered counselling and subjected to lectures and random drugs testing. The idea, according to the head man, is to 'turn around the drug culture'; this is not necessarily how it is perceived by housemasters and dames who may be involved. Drugs policy generally pretty mainstream. Very few excluded – more put on probation.

'Not so much boozing' now, but 'smoking is still fairly prevalent'. Expect dismissal for repeat performances. Drunken boys are usually sobered up in house – with much love and care from housemaster and dame; other boys equally supportive. The alternative is an overnight stay in the local (extremely expensive) private hospital with stomach pumps et al. Immediate rustication thereafter, and not a lot of sympathy either. The most normal punishment is 'to go on the bill' – this involves a quick trip to the head man with a praeposter (aka sixth former) within and without the head man's office. The former acts as watchman and the latter as marshal. The only time a praeposter is not used is in the case of bullying, when the head man deals with suspected culprits on his own.

The most popular form of punishment – and here the range is from missing chapel to going AWOL – is early rising. Some pupils are never 'off the bill' and some are never on it. Boys have limited (but increasing with age) rights to escape into Windsor and further afield – but only with their parents' permission. Some parents seem to be quite happy to say that their boys are coming home when in fact they are not. For those left at school, though, masses of extra-curricular activities, choral, dramatic, what have you. The art and music schools are open, as well as the swimming pool, plus organised cross-country runs (strong house competition here), rowing, cricket, football, whatever. This is a school well provided with opportunities as well as the staff to run them, and house noticeboards bulge with information on rehearsals, debates, groups, matches (both inter-house, and friendlies), clubs and activities.

Pupils and Parents: Still the traditional school it always was, with numbers of Old Etonian families in the ascendant again. The Fourth of June (aka school speech day) is still as buzzy as ever, with minibuses decanting lovelies from local girls' schools to join the baying throng of picnickers but (fortunately for the school) the mass of royal watchers have gone, and the hype has subsided (though the school is still described on Google as 'Famous public school popular with the royal family' – much to the school's own annoyance, apparently!). A huge mix of families – scholarship boys from the remote Welsh valleys via a percentage of first time buyers to foreign princelings and the deeply grand.

Numerous notable Old Etonians: Hubert Parry, 19 Prime Ministers, Captain Oates, the poets Gray and Shelley, Keynes, Fielding. Surprisingly few real stars among the living: politicians (William Waldegrave, Nicholas Soames, Douglas Hurd, Boris Johnson), a clutch of journalists

(Charles Moore, Nicholas Coleridge, Craig Brown), also Martin Taylor, Humphrey Lyttleton, Nicholas Charles Tyrwhitt Wheeler, Matthew Pinsent and Michael Chance; plus gaolbirds: Jonathan Aitken and Darius Guppy amongst others. A reunion for a group of leavers from a single year in the mid 1980s consisted of two TV executives, a soft drinks company founder-director, a civil engineer, two architects, a composer, an opera singer, an actor, an obesity specialist, a urologist, a radiologist, a headhunter, a hedgefund manager, a stockbroker, an estate management director, a film production company founder-director, a publisher of children's books, a university lecturer, a politician, two barristers, a country solicitor, an insurance executive, a fund manager, two bankers, an accountant, a homeopathic clinic director, a nightclub manager, a pub chain director, a gambling syndicate manager, two journalists, an army officer, a motorcycle retailer and one managing his own stately home.

Successful old boys tend not to describe themselves as Old Etonians, preferring to describe themselves as 'having been at school', as in 'There is no truth in the rumour that Jeffrey Archer was at school'. Still imparts a very recognisable character to its pupils – school objected to our use of 'solipsistic': 'Utterly baffling. What on earth leads you to that conclusion?' and we agree that was perhaps a bit strong. Coming back into public fashion (after many years where OE ties were only worn in private) in the wake of the entirely un-solipsistic David Cameron.

Entrance: 850 candidates for 250 places; currently from 91 different schools. 'A record,' says the tutor for admissions. New (as in not the traditional 'put down at birth and forget about it' régime) entry procedures appear to be working well. The head man has taken the new exam himself – 'I did pass, but did rather better in the oral part'. Boys do a combination of an interview and a multiple-choice computer-driven exercise and results are marked by five independent assessors who then spend two days discussing their findings. Prep school reports are important, and family background is taken into account when reaching the 'global mark'. It is important that a boy 'will thrive in a boarding environment', and be able to cope 'working under his own steam'.

Successful candidates then make their choice from a possible four houses – as each housemaster has a potential 13 year tenure, the odds of actually getting the particular housemaster you opt for is higher than if you chose him when little Johnnie was two or three months old, so that's a bonus. Housemasters find the extra strain of these late interviews a bit of a bind and sometimes reflect nostalgically on the days of the general list. School makes regular visits to likely prep schools to reassure them that Eton is still the place for their darlings. Prep schools to whom we have spoken report that yes, after the first year's blip, when school seemed to 'be choosing clever creatures without much oomph', procedure does seem to be working well, and the chaps who get in would mostly have been the chaps who got in under the old procedure.

Entries for King's Scholarships (14 per annum) accepted until the beginning of March for exam in May at 12/13+ (these scholarships may be up to 100 per cent, with school paying for uniform, and occasionally travelling expenses). Scholars still chosen by the examiners sitting as an electoral college, looking for imagination and enterprise as much as competence – hopeless Latin forgiven if maths superb, or vice versa. Past papers freely available from the school.

Has abandoned junior scholarships (which placed 10 year olds in prep school for three years) in favour of encouraging state school candidates to take the standard ten and three quarters exam and then steering the best pair towards prep schools who may offer them scholarships – which, as you can imagine, they do with alacrity. They get extra support when they join the school too. Eight scholarships for state school pupils at sixth form – for the whole two years – and four scholarships for state school pupils for entry at 13.

Exit: Average of 70+ boys to Oxbridge, (though not all who might be Oxbridge material apply). School takes great care with applications, matching boys to colleges and avoiding an Etonian overload in any one of them. Successful in organ scholarships to Oxbridge. Most go on to university, to Bristol, Exeter and Edinburgh in droves, plus over 70 different institutions in the UK, 10–15 annually abroad. The army is popular in some quarters (pace Prince Harry), and one or two fall through every net. Tranches of gap year. Thereafter the City, estate agencies, auction houses, journalism, family estates, politics and just about every other curriculum vitae you could imagine.

Money Matters: Pots and pots of money and assets: it is said that Eton is funded not by fees but by rental income; popular sideline from films (*The Madness of King George* etc). Eton can afford to, and does, have everything of the best, and pays its staff very well indeed. Good value. Large number of bursaries etc for parents on hard times, plus eight music scholarships year, plus countless exhibitions. The posh thing is to win a King's Scholarship and turn it down in favour of someone who needs it financially. Regular subsidised summer schools – rowing a popular option for prep school wannabes. Masses of public activity – the rowing lake is used nationally for training international rowers, and the new athletics hall and track are much in demand by locals. Eton is one of the few schools confident in its charitable status and, if it goes, they assume that parents will be able to pay the VAT on fees which is what the government is after. However, currently – reportedly – on mega fund-raising splurge. Seeking £50 million to fund further bursaries; they have raised £31 million so far, allowing for help for one in five pupils, but are aiming for one in three, we gather. Autres temps autres moeurs.

Remarks: Still the number one boys' public school. The teaching and facilities are second to none. School was cross about our saying that it was 'a hard place to be for a boy who is neither one of the lads nor a gifted sportsman', but a quick survey of recent starry leavers thought 'it must have been ghastly' for those whom they regarded as nonentities or nerds; the nonentities disagreed, saying 'they had great fun' and 'wouldn't have been anywhere else for the world'.

Exeter School

Linked to Exeter Junior School in the Junior section

Victoria Park Road, Exeter, Devon, EX2 4NS

• Pupils: 435 boys; 260 girls • Ages: 11-18 • Size of sixth form: 130 boys; 80 girls • C of E • Fees: Senior £9,900; Junior £8,940 pa • Independent

Tel: 01392 273 679
Fax: 01392 498 144
Email: admissions@exeterschool.org.uk
Website: www.exeterschool.org.uk

Headmaster: Since 2003, Mr Bob Griffin (late-forties). First in modern languages (French and Spanish) from Oxford. Taught overseas in Peru before being head of modern languages at Haileybury. Came to Exeter from The Royal Grammar School, Guildford, where he was second master for five years. Teaches English, French and Spanish. Attends everything possible so he knows pupils personally – it is important to him to know something about every child as well as their name. Married with two children, both at Exeter.

Academic matters: Over 80 per cent average A/B grades at A level over the last five years, similarly impressive at GCSE. Top sets in maths and French up to 24 pupils to allow bottom sets to be 10–14. Average GCSE class size 16–18, other year classes average 20. Broad subject choice – 18 GCSEs including Spanish; 25 A level subjects, with strong uptake of all major academic subjects. High numbers in economics and politics. 'There is a good balance of everything at Exeter,' said a parent. Special educational needs have improved since last school inspection, with the appointment of a learning coordinator.

Games, Options, the Arts: Strong rugby and hockey teams regularly win county cups and make regional and national appearances. Dance now also popular, among boys and girls, following development of a professional new dance studio and vibrant house dance competition. Plenty of fixtures in various other sports – cricket, netball, golf, soccer, shooting, cross-country, athletics and swimming. Annual trips abroad include language trips to Nice and Hildesheim and politics study visits to the USA. Trips with British Schools' Exploration Society and Adventurous Training Expeditions popular. CCF, D of E and Ten Tors well supported. Music exceptionally strong: many and varied ensembles; regular recitals in Exeter Cathedral. Artistic talent abounds. Lots of exceptional 3D work produced in various media.

Background and Atmosphere: Founded in 1633, originally for sons of freemen of Exeter. Reverted to independent status in 1976, stopped boarding in 2000. Girls into the sixth form in 1980 and fully co-ed since 1997. Female integration evidently pleasing to both sexes, and most parents – transition 'as smooth as one could expect'. Separate and mixed common-rooms. Head boy and girl and prefects take a prominent role in running the daily life of the school. On 25-acre site with views of countryside and backdrop of Haldon Hills, less than a mile from city centre. Original buildings designed by famous Victorian architect William Butterfield – designer of Keble College, Oxford. School not as lavishly endowed as one might think.

The modern IT suite has 88 computers for pupil use located in three rooms, and 74 classrooms have digital projectors linked to the school's intranet and the world beyond. A grand two-storey library and study centre opened in 2006, improving resource accessibility and affording sixth form pupils in particular a light and tranquil area for private study. Pupils' pride in their school has grown and many come in at the weekends to work. Active and social parents' association – 'great at making parents feel included in the school'. Rivals boarding schools with its active weekend programme.

Pastoral Care and Discipline: Persistent or serious troublemakers not tolerated and would have to leave. Senior staff and heads of house quick to act on minor indiscretions. Pupils failing to produce homework more than once might expect detention. Saturday detention for cigarette smokers. 'Extremely caring staff,' say parents. Parents say, 'My son was being bullied at another independent so we moved him to Exeter. The pupils are the advert for Exeter'; 'They are polite and friendly'. Teachers usually stay for years.

Pupils and Parents: Community of pupils, staff and parents who share great pride in their school. Happy pupils, seem glad to be here, especially appreciative of extra-curricular activities. Past pupils include Chairman of Yell, Bob Wigley, Olympic yachtsmen Ben Rhodes and Stevie Morrison, actor Matthew Goode, high court judge Sir Charles Collingwood, politicians David Bellotti and Tony Speller, Nick Barnes of Radio 1, General Sir Anthony Farrar-Hockley, historian and TV expert on military issues, commanders, generals, actors and a former Bishop of Hull. Middle class parents – doctors and lawyers, farmers and leisure industry professionals; 44 per cent live within five miles of school, the rest up to 30 miles away.

Entrance: Entrance to junior school by informal assessment and school report. Examination and school report for senior school candidates at 11 and 13. No entrance exam to the senior school for junior school pupils starting in Years 3 and 4. Sixth form entry by interview. Pupils come from 60–70 different schools, including six per cent from other counties.

Exit: Oxbridge 10–15 per cent. 90 per cent stay on for sixth form. London, Durham, Bristol, Cardiff, Southampton, Reading, Bath and Nottingham universities popular, with 10 per cent studying medicine, some dentistry and veterinary science.

Money Matters: Strong numbers in recent years have enabled a range of academic and music awards at 11–13 and 16, also a sixth form art award. Governors' means tested awards of up to half fees may be offered to applicants whose parents are unable to afford the full school fees. Special awards from generous local benefactors. Support from Ogden Trust for one sixth form entrant.

Remarks: Unexpectedly unpretentious and relaxed. Produces high-achievers.

Fairley House School

Linked to Fairley House School Junior Department in the Junior section

30 Causton Street, London, SW1P 4AU

• Pupils: 155 boys/girls 4:1, all day • Ages: 5-14 • Inter-denom • Fees: £26,250 pa • Independent

Tel: 020 7976 5456
Fax: 02079 765 905
Email: office@fairleyhouse.org.uk
Website: www.fairleyhouse.org.uk

Principal: Since 1997, Ms Jackie Murray BA MEd Dip Pysch RSA SPLD, (late fifties) educated at Rickmansworth Grammar and Sussex University, teacher training and special needs qualifications in the UK and US. Qualified as an educational psychologist in 2000, Ms Murray has worked as a teacher, run the Watford Dyslexia Unit and trained teachers at London University to work with pupils with specific learning differences. Fairley House has a teacher training facility and runs evening classes for teachers offering the OCR certificate plus bags of expertise which they are eager to share with other professionals. With three grown-up sons, one of whom attended Fairley House before her headship, Ms Murray has the advantage of both a personal and professional understanding of her clientele and what they might have been through.

Academic matters: Regularly inspected and accredited by CReSTeD, the register for specialist schools with provision for dyslexia and SpLDs. Pupils are split into a junior department – five to nine years – and a senior department – 10 to 14 years, class size usually 8–12 pupils. The main emphasis being on numeracy and literacy, everyone is put into a small group to match their ability and skills for maths and English and rejoin their class for other subjects. Children are taught to understand their own learning styles and shown strategies to overcome barriers to learning to achieve their targets. The aim is to return children to mainstream schools as soon as they are able, which FHS has great success in doing. Test results such as SATs are very respectable, especially from children who can have quite pronounced difficulties.

Every child has an IEP which is regularly reviewed by the trans-disciplinary team to monitor progress and ensure that individual needs are being catered for. Mornings start with exercises; depending on the individual, this could be physical, orthoptic or attention focused. All the classrooms, including the science lab, are buzzing with activities, visual reminders and clues, anything that is memorable: models made by the children, word banks for a current history topic or colour coded parts of speech. Every teacher has specialist qualifications which ensure that all classes are fully accessible and multisensory. 'Having teachers who are nice to you and understand has changed my life,' said a 10-year-old. The learning support is an integral part of the whole school approach to teaching. The transdisciplinary approach is used across the curriculum, helpfully allowing therapy delivery to be linked to specific subjects and development. Homework is colour-coded to help with the organisation, and deadlines must be met to prepare the children for returning to mainstream school. Help and advice is on hand for those who get stuck.

Depending on the individual needs of the pupil, speech therapy and occupational therapy are incorporated into classroom learning, art, drama and sports. Younger children will be making 'ch' out of chocolate buttons whilst older ones are baking round pies to help understand and remember the mathematical sign pi. Children are taught to touch-type once they have achieved a reading age of approximately eight years. In-house speech and occupational therapists run their own sensory integration programmes and motor coordination classes. The therapy staff organising the motor coordination classes have been specially trained in America, and continue to attend training in the USA to keep up-to-date.

Games, Options, the Arts: Wonderfully imaginative art displays line the corridors and even the ceilings are decorated in many areas of the building. Pupils make their own ceramic tiles depicting various scenes from history and also design and execute murals. The most recent addition to the school is the newly-built art studio and kiln room. The children enjoy a great variety of artistic activities including textiles, fashion, design and technology, sewing and puppet-making. A range of sports, all the traditional ones alongside canoeing, fencing and yoga. Although the school doesn't have its own playing fields they make good use of local facilities at Battersea Park and the Queen Mother Sports Centre. Music and drama are taught as separate subjects and integrated into other curriculum areas to help children develop good communication skills. Everyone is encouraged to learn a musical instrument and the school runs its own acting awards and music medals scheme. Parents pack into the termly dramatic and musical productions. Extra-curricular activities include museum and theatre trips along with a wide choice of lunchtime and after-school clubs. Club options change regularly depending on the clientele and demand.

Background and Atmosphere: Fairley House was founded in 1975 by a speech therapist, Daphne Hamilton Fairley, as a charitable trust in memory of her oncologist husband, killed by an IRA bomb. The upper school site, originally a church, has been cleverly converted into a four-storey building. The junior school pupils are housed in a Victorian infants' school in the shadows of Lambeth Palace backing on to Archbishops Park, complete with sports facilities and an adventure playground for the children's use. Both buildings are well decorated, with a lot of space dedicated to the children's achievements, visual timetables and fantastic works of art. The atmosphere is purposeful, peaceful and well organised, encouraging pupils to be themselves. Lots of smiling and cheerful faces, nobody should feel the odd one out here.

Pastoral Care and Discipline: There is a structured mentoring system involving 18 members of staff to whom children can refer themselves. The school's aim is to work in a strong partnership with parents to help ensure things do not go wrong for pupils due to simple misunderstandings. Seems to be working as parents feel pastoral care has improved over the last few years.

Pupils and Parents: From all over London, and a few from the edges of the home counties. Everybody and anybody affected by neuro-diversity. By all accounts, lots of very supportive and enthusiastic parents who are keen to get involved with school activities. Most recently the parent group has fund-raised to update and restock the school library. Weekly newsletters, back-up information on the website and parents can use a communication book or e-mail teachers. Comprehensive well-designed website but not 'read friendly' as yet.

Entrance: Children are invited to spend two days at the school where they will have a transdisciplinary all-round assessment to ensure that the school will be able to meet their needs. After the assessment parents are provided with reports from an educational psychologist, speech therapist and occupational therapist and then invited for a conference to discuss how the school can help and support their child. Assessments cost £250 – £850. In the event of the school not being able to offer a place they will suggest other options to parents.

Most pupils have a diagnosis of specific learning differences, usually dyslexia and/or dyspraxia and the related conditions ADD, ADHD and Aspergers. The school is also able to accommodate some pupils who have non-conventional learning styles and find mainstream schools inaccessible.

Exit: The average stay for pupils at Fairley House is approximately two/three years. Some return to junior schools e.g. Newton Prep, Eaton Square, The Hall, Northcote Lodge, older day pupils to Portland Place, Davies Laing and Dick, Royal Russell, Thames Christian College. Boarding choices include St Christopher's, Millfield, Sibford, St Bede's, Bloxham and Bedales.

Money Matters: A few bursaries are available for trainee teachers. As yet, the school is unable to offer bursaries to pupils but will assist parents with tribunals and the statementing procedure. Approximately 26 per cent of pupils have a statement of special educational needs and are funded by their local authorities.

Remarks: Fairley House is certainly good value for money but the fees are terrifying and beyond the reach of many without local authority funding. A remarkable school for its holistic, multi-sensory and transdisciplinary approach. A beacon for children with learning and processing differences and parents who have been tearing their hair out trying to cope in other situations.

Farmor's School

The Park, Fairford, Gloucestershire, GL7 4JQ

• Pupils: 1,200 boys and girls, all day • Ages: 11-18 • Size of sixth form: 230 • None • State

Tel: 01285 712 302
Fax: 01285 713 504
Email: a.stokes@farmors.gloucs.sch.uk
Website: www.farmors.gloucs.sch.uk

Head: Since 2000, Mrs Anne Stokes MEd (forties). Taught English in a comprehensive in Somerset before moving to Gloucestershire and taking up posts in a secondary modern, Linden Secondary School, then at the Catholic St Peter's High School in Gloucester. Joined the teaching staff at Farmor's in 1988, becoming deputy head before taking over the headship. Approachable, friendly and organized.

Academic matters: Very much a school serving its local community, with a broad ability intake, although has in recent years taken busloads of children from over the border in Wiltshire, including a sizeable number from Swindon who opt against lower-performing local schools. Has always been a school where high-flyers shine, with many A grades. Results have risen since Mrs Stokes took the reins. Excellent results in business studies at both GCSE and A level, became a specialist school in business and enterprise in 2004. Real star subject is English, both language and literature, at GCSE and A level – awash with As every year, despite no setting, although maths, sciences and languages are streamed. French GSCE results very good, although few take it through to A level. Sports studies is popular with strong results, psychology and music technology popular too. Consistently good science results, with the most able taking triple science. Vocational choices are limited, but it either supports students through courses elsewhere, such as Swindon College, or suggests alternative colleges. Engineering is newly-introduced, aimed at the most able. Large network of PCs throughout the school, well used by students. Good mix of much-loved long-serving staff and fresh enthusiastic new ones.

Games, Options, the Arts: Lots of space for sport but no large all-weather surfaces. Sports centre on site but school limited by its public usage. Despite that, pupils excel in the main competitive sports of rugby, football, hockey, netball, basketball, tennis, cricket and athletics, with many representatives in county teams and regular wins in district and county sports. Appealing bright spaces for art and design and technology. A quarter of students take individual music lessons – singing a current favourite. Numerous orchestras, groups, ensembles and a choir; regular concerts, musicals and dramatic productions. Lots of foreign trips, mostly sports and language related. Interest in healthy eating initiated by staff and pupils in the form of their Ecobytz meal options project, now continued by the school kitchen. Lots of quiet space for reading and research.

Background and Atmosphere: Modern school with long history in a largely rural area. Founded in 1738 with money left by Elizabeth Farmor and Mary Barker to educate 50 boys in Fairford. Girls were admitted in 1815, became fully co-educational in 1922. Originally in the centre of town, in a building that is now the community centre, but in 1961 it moved to its present site in 18 acres of parkland a short walk away, becoming an 11–18 comprehensive in 1966. Although showing its age in places, the site is very well kept, with older buildings having had a recent facelift and the new business and science rooms being large and airy.

Pastoral Care and Discipline: Clear, open rules pinned up in every classroom regarding bullying, insolence and disobedience – well adhered to: permanent exclusion, the ultimate sanction, not seen now for several years. An air of studious calm.

Pupils and Parents: Intake from Fairford and villages around make it a broadly, though by no means entirely, middle class intake. Parents very supportive of school events and fund-raising. Widely regarded as a decent bunch (the local driving instructor says they are the nicest learner drivers in the area). Neat, polite, enthusiastic and eager to learn. Reasonably well turned out – uniform until sixth form and then 'decent' attire, which translates as jeans and plain tops in the main. Eminent former pupils include vulcanologist Dr Philip Gravestock.

Entrance: Oversubscribed (despite doubling in size in the last ten years) at both 11 and 16. School takes siblings, feeder school pupils, locals, Swindon applicants, independent school pupils and, if room, a few from further afield. Five A*-Cs at GCSE needed for sixth form, with Bs preferred for A level choices, although some leeway allowed.

Exit: Two-thirds stay on for the sixth form; some go to nearby Cirencester to college, although some come the other way. Almost all A level students continue their studies. Favourite destinations include Cardiff, Nottingham, Bristol, Exeter, Swansea and Manchester. A few to Oxbridge.

Remarks: A happy, forward-looking school with excellent academic results where everyone can fulfil their potential.

Felsted School

Linked to Felsted Preparatory School in the Junior section

Felsted, Great Dunmow, Essex, CM6 3LL

• Pupils: 525 boys and girls; (44 per cent girls) 90 day, 195 full boarders, 240 occasional boarders • Ages: 13-18 • Size of sixth form: 235 pupils • C of E • Fees: Boarding £22,485 - £24,705; Day £18,480 pa • Independent

Tel: 01371 822 605
Fax: 01371 822 607
Email: ado@felsted.org
Website: www.felsted.org

Headmaster: Since 2008, Dr Michael Walker MA PhD PGCE (early fifties) previously head of King Edward's in Chelmsford, where he spent 18 years, rapidly rising up the ranks. Before that head of history at Gresham's School. Sought-after to share his expertise at regional and national level. Despite having massively impressive credentials, he places great value on tapping into others' ideas and experiencing for himself all aspects of the school. Pupils and members of the newly formed parents' forum cite numerous examples of proposals implemented. He's made a point of staying overnight at each house in turn, has risen to the challenge of singing and dancing on stage – 'I was utterly petrified' – and will compete cross-country against a sixth former to raise money for charity. All combines to make a strong leader who has injected new thinking and set out a clear path while reportedly remaining approachable, open, kind and low-key.

Academic matters: Not overly selective but each year a solid cohort achieves top grades across the board in both A levels and GCSEs. In 2010, average UCAS score 324, 77 per cent GCSEs A*–B with 97 per cent of grades C or better. Known for its success in psychology, but pupils do well in other subjects – Latin and modern languages, history, maths, science and art to name but a few. More generally it has the reputation of bringing out the best in all. IB now taking off amongst quite conservative local families – currently about a third of the sixth form opts for it – with results improving year on year.

Parents recoil at the thought of it becoming an academic hothouse and support increased focus on individual educational plans with the aim of ensuring maximum academic success but not at the expense of other activities. Recent increase in number of classroom assistants to support the process. SEN pupils, of whom there are about 45, often take one fewer GCSE to allow time for more personalised support. EAL teachers also on hand. Streaming in the lower years and class sizes are kept small – between 15–20 up to GCSE – and often considerably smaller in the sixth form. Staff development encouraged. Recently, staff and pupils were asked to suggest what constituted a good or outstanding lesson and the findings have been discussed openly with all. Can but add to the pressure to deliver!

Games, Options, the Arts: Traditionally sporty. It has produced some outstanding cricketers and Olympic athletes. Games fields and facilities stretch as far as the eye can see. Currently has a tennis player in the top ten nationally. Hockey, cricket, rugby and netball all strong with regular success at regional and national championships. If you don't make the teams, no shame with lots else on offer to keep you fit and occupied. Emphasis very much on participation, be it in sports, regular music events featuring individual talent, the many choirs and orchestras (30 per cent are involved in music of some kind), drama or in the wealth of extra-curricular options which make for very full days and busy weekends. Not perhaps for the retiring, ill-organised or easily-wearied type. Huge take up of D of E – at the last count no fewer than 26 gold awards in the upper sixth – and 220 enrolled in CCF.

Very much accords with the head's ambition of becoming a Round Square school promoting IDEALS – internationalism, democracy, care for the environment, adventurous pursuits, leadership and service. In addition to much appreciated local community activities and links to disadvantaged communities in East London where pupils have been busy promoting cheerleading, the school is reinforcing developing world links. Students queue up for opportunities to break the 'Felsted bubble'. They include visits to the partner school in Ethiopia and jumping aboard a former pupil's Magic Bus which supports children in the slums of Mumbai.

Background and Atmosphere: Traditional, yet progressive, it feeds off its history but is not hidebound by it. Founded in 1564 by Richard, Lord Riche, Lord Chancellor of England, the school's original Guild Hall is still in use with other, later, attractive Grade I and II listed buildings scattered throughout the village, interspersed with well tended lawns and sports fields and cut through by the quiet Dunmow to Braintree road. Most recent additions include the music school opened in early 2009 and the sixth form centre – a great space to access the net and meet informally or at regular social events where the odd glass of wine is permitted. Overall impression of being a happy, happening place with parents content to be swept along for the ride.

Pastoral Care and Discipline: Recent tightening up on uniform and behaviour welcomed by parents and local businesses alike. Swift and decisive action when bullying and other misdemeanours uncovered, although, in truth, such incidents are relatively rare. Good relations between parents, pupils and staff enhanced by the introduction of clearer reporting systems and a new atmosphere of openness and purpose. Standardising flexi-boarding arrangements has overcome some earlier problems concerning integration of full and part-time boarders and there are robust measures in place to help new and international students settle in. Although many local boarders disappear at the weekends, the stayers-in are rarely short of invitations to stay with local families, outings or on-site activities to fill their time.

Two day and seven boarding houses, four for boys and three for girls with plans to expand and provide 28 more boarding places overall. Separate upper sixth form boarding houses. Year nine board in pleasant shared accommodation – all other years have single rooms though some choice of double rooms if pupils prefer it. Homely common room areas and studies.

Pupils and Parents: We hear that Essex is proud of producing self-starting, entrepreneurial and independent spirits. Parents value the fact that 'they're not sausage making' and champion these qualities at the school. Pupils range from the highly-driven and academically-orientated to the more fun-loving and easy-going, but all pretty down to earth. Characteristics of the typical Felstedian recently assessed, based on feedback from various parties, include being ambitious, motivated, accepting challenge and being self-aware.

Long list of notable OFs includes English test cricketer John Stephenson and General Sir Richard Dannatt, until recently Chief of the General Staff. Huge diversity of talent is reflected in the senior positions and success OFs have achieved in science and medicine, the military, politics and public service, academia, business, sports and the media.

While most live within a couple of hours of the school, it is increasingly attracting London-based families. Taking advantage of its proximity to Stansted Airport, international students make up some 20 per cent of pupils – getting towards the high end amongst schools in this guide. Lots of Germans do IB and a similar number of students from China, Hong Kong and all round the world.

Entrance: Many come up from the prep. Other popular feeder schools are Holmwood House, Heathmount, Orwell Park and Edge Grove. Those taking CE are required to obtain 50 per cent in each paper. Others take a verbal reasoning test, interview and submit a confidential report from their current school. They may take tests in maths, French and English for setting purposes. The same is true at 14+ entry. At 16+ there is a similar entry procedure and pupils are required to obtain six GCSEs at grade B or better including B grades in the subjects being pursued. Pupils who do not have English as their first language will be assessed by the head of ESL.

Exit: All but a few go on to good universities with five plus to Oxbridge each year. The most popular subjects in recent years have been business-related, medicine, humanities and the sciences.

Money Matters: Academic, music, sport, art, design and technology or drama and all-rounder scholarships offering up to 20 per cent or £1,000 off the fees are available at 13+ and 16+. There are some assisted places up to 100 per cent on a means tested basis.

Remarks: Real sense of excitement as the new head avidly goes about canvassing views and implementing change to fulfil his vision of making Felsted 'a leading independent boarding and day school, regionally, nationally and internationally'. Well on his way, from what we hear, with parents welcoming a renewed focus on academic performance but not at the expense of individualism and quirkiness. All agree – it's one to watch.

Fernhill School

Fernbrae Avenue, Burnside, Glasgow, Glasgow, G73 4SG

• Pupils: 250 - primary 80 girls, 50 boys; secondary 160 girls • Ages: 3-18 • Size of sixth form: 40 • RC (but all faiths welcome) • Fees: Primary £7,470-£8,190; Secondary £8,532-£8,976 pa • Independent

Tel: 0141 634 2674
Fax: 0141 631 4343
Email: info@fernhillschool.co.uk
Website: www.fernhillschool.co.uk

Head Teacher: Since 2007, Mrs Jacqueline Sexton BSc. Mrs Sexton taught maths and physics in the state sector until 1997, when she became head of physics at Craigholme School in Glasgow. In 2003, she was appointed deputy head of Craigholme, responsibilities including all aspects of the whole school curriculum, SQA examinations and health and safety. She lives in Glasgow with her husband and three children.

Incredibly young-looking, Mrs Sexton fizzes with enthusiasm for Fernhill and her role there. 'A fantastic school. I love my job.' She is energized by her contact with pupils and staff. Since sixth year numbers have doubled since her arrival and IT has been eagerly embraced by staff, it would appear that the energizing is reciprocal! She believes the 'family atmosphere' of the school provides the positive and moral learning environment pupils need, in which to experience a wide the range of activities to prepare them for life beyond.

Her first task has been IT: making sure the school is 'wired to be future-proof.' This has meant linking all buildings with a hard-wired intranet, some reconstruction of the original house to provide central services and a rationalisation of teaching areas with spin-off providing a new feel to the school. P7 (top juniors) now work more closely with senior school and primary has a new general-purpose area which can be used as two rooms or, undivided, as a really large unit. The key has been flexibility of resources and forethought to accommodate future development rather than cosmetic.

Teaching staff, galvanized by Mrs Sexton's personal training and support, have embraced the computer age and 'excellent teamwork' means they share facilities, both dedicated computer rooms and mobile equipment (smart boards/laptops/audio-visuals/LCD projectors etc) effectively and are ready for anything!

In her first year Mrs Sexton has also restructured staffing. Under the leadership of the depute heads of primary and secondary departments, three principal teachers form a pupil support team. Two work in secondary and one in primary with overall responsibility for pastoral, social and health/SEN development.

Academic matters: 'Does very, very well', firmly rooted in the Scottish exam system doing S grade, Highers and, increasingly, Advanced Higher; though some subjects (English, mod langs and Latin) use Intermediate 2 instead of S grade. This is an academic school, which offers a full curriculum, all results are pretty impressive. 'A wonderful spirit of team work' pervades and pupils 'work well together'. Teachers can give real personal attention to pupils of all abilities. Five Highers the norm, with no formal examinations in drama or home economics but music now up to Ad Higher.

Huge investment in IT over the past five years, keyboarding for all, flat screens, local area network, and 40 stand-alone machines. Computing is offered as an exam subject up to Ad Higher level. Staff all dual qualified and can book computer suites for lessons. Two interactive whiteboards to date and around the place. Humanities well taught and good SEN provision. Pupil support taken very seriously and – from evidence of results gained from a mixed ability intake – very effective.

Games, Options, the Arts: Amazing range of sports on offer, rugby for primaries of both sexes, plus all the usual girl-affiliated activities: netball, volleyball, hockey; house matches as well as inter-schools friendlies. The school's size means team sport tends to be participative as well as competitive; for primary athletics Fernhill had a clean sweep at the South Lanarkshire track events. Parents are enthusiastically involved in annual sports days, keen swimming at a local swimming pool nearby (absolutely stunning after another refurbishment) and successful cross-country team. Saturday sports for teams. 'Staff are brilliant at encouraging star quality athletes,' though high fliers tend to go to local clubs for high-level training etc.

Some clubs post-school and a wide variety during lunch. Chess popular, debating important, poetry a recent successful addition. Masses of woodwind and violins, the occasional trumpeter and pianist and, at last, an orchestra, formed just as Mrs Sexton arrived and going from strength to strength. Lots of group playing and house competitions; music is fun here. Regular trips to the Royal Concert Hall in Glasgow and last year a singing trip to Salzburg. No drama – as yet: 'basically this is an academic school'. Airy all-purpose art department including fabric and fashion design, 'band-box smart into the bargain'; pupils design the fabric and follow all the way through to the finished item. Impressive.

Background and Atmosphere: Perched beside a golf course close to the Cathkin Braes, the central Victorian family home, overlooking the city of Glasgow nestles in nine 'nook and cranny' acres. The school is private and very secure with locked gates. It was founded in 1972 as a primary school and pushed the leaving age up – demand and supply. Classrooms added when necessary, though the main quad is splendidly uniform. Two more recent teaching blocks are smart and practical while the collection of cabins and smaller classrooms was brightened with boxes and baskets of flowers on a summer visit. School runs on Catholic ethos and pupils deliciously polite, tons of praise for all, and oodles of cups awards and prizes for a various activities. Immaculate. Strap shoes, caps for boys and round felt hats for girls, even with their summer dresses and long white socks. Strong links formed between senior girls and primary pupils, with buddies at break time. Packed lunches for all, no vending machines, most pupils eat lunch in the hall but senior girls have a bit more privacy in their own common-room.

Pastoral Care and Discipline: Founded on respect for other people and 'treat them properly' ethos reinforced by anti-bullying assemblies and workshops in first and second year secondary. Of course girls sometimes fall out but there is no real bullying. Strong PSE and MRE (social and religious education in old speak) programmes, four houses and tutor system in place. Drugs, smoking and alcohol awareness days. Drugs simply don't happen! This school has a very particular ethos and catchment which means that on the whole children stay children and enjoy their childhood.

Own chaplain and strong links with the local community. All practising RC pupils are prepared for the sacraments of first communion and confirmation within the school. Primary school staff are all practising Catholics, but it is not essential for teachers in the senior school; non-Catholics may be excused services. The school welcomes all: Hindu, Muslim etc. There is no religious or sectarian bigotry. The Asian pupils celebrate their feast days and the school acknowledges other faiths with understanding and respect.

Pupils and Parents: From all over, some travel quite a long distance: North Lanarkshire, Ayrshire, buses. An oasis of middle-class respectability. Can leave pupils from 8.30 am, which is handy for commuting parents but no after-school care (the buses again).

Entrance: Entrance assessment and interview for all pupils – looking above all for potential.

Exit: On average boys leave at age 10, for a number of schools in the independent sector – Glasgow is well served. Girls leave after sixth form with some leaving directly after Highers in S5. Gap years for some post-Higher; 95 per cent go on to university, usually in Scotland. More now staying on for S6 and Advanced Highers. Selection of degree courses including law, medicine, dentistry plus some traditional academics and business – impressive for a small school! Most (12 out of 15 in 2009) go to Glasgow unis. The odd leaver takes a vocational course.

Money Matters: Financial assistance is available and is always means tested. Chair and deputy chair of the board of governors review bursary provision.

Remarks: Still a school serving a very specific Catholic heartland population, but will accept pupils of all faiths looking for girls' only (senior school) and strong moral values. Ideal, of course, for a wide range of children needing small, loving and caring environment with the benefit of a strong religious backbone, but this is an academic and, under Mrs Sexton, an adventurous school with 'some pretty lively pupils and a fantastically committed staff'. Difficult to find – one of Glasgow's well-kept secrets!

Fettes College

Linked to Fettes College Preparatory School in the Junior section

Carrington Road, Edinburgh, Edinburgh, EH4 1QX

• Pupils: 285 boys, 215 girls; 220 boys and 155 girls board, the rest day. • Ages: 13-18 • Size of sixth form: 245 • Non-denom • Fees: Day £19,050; Boarding £25,860 pa • Independent

Tel: 0131 311 6744
Fax: 0131 311 6714
Email: admissions@fettes.com
Website: www.fettes.com

Headmaster: Since 1998, Mr Michael C B Spens MA (sixty), educated at Marlborough and Selwyn College Cambridge, where he read natural sciences. Came to Fettes after five years as head of Caldicott, having previously spent 20 years at Radley where he was housemaster and taught geology, after a short spell in business. The transition between junior and senior schools is always an interesting one but Mr Spens has weathered his double change with charm and élan – one might say nonchalance but that would be harsh, and misleading; quarter is not easily found here: there is a tightly-wound spring beneath the cultivated appearance of charm and relaxation. Expect zero tolerance on the drugs front, 'The students don't want it around', and the Fettesian druggy alcy image no longer makes headlines in the Scottish press. Fettes is challenging all-comers as Scotland's school of choice, surprisingly, even on the day front, 'And we're more expensive than the others,' says the head – but then we are talking Edinburgh (think mink and nae knickers). Married to Debbie, they have three young children (all at Fettes) and a much-loved labrador ('Kiwi, because she's all black'). Charismatic, vibrant, fun. Fettes and Mr Spens are zinging. Currently forefront of the campaign to keep Scottish independent schools' charitable status and all over the Sunday papers.

Academic matters: Almost all heads of departments have changed during the past few years, 'new young staff', 'very good', 'strong', 'Edinburgh is a strong draw'; and, having played the Scottish versus the English system along with all the other big players, Fettes added the IB to its exam choice in 2006. Pupils can choose whether they want to specialise – in which case they will be encouraged to do A levels, or decide whether the broader IB syllabus, with its extended theory of knowledge, will suit them better. Highers are still on offer over one year 'to broaden' those on A level courses. This is a brave decision, but Mr Spens appears to think that it is possible to mix the three disciplines. Pupils will be offered positive advice and encouragement on which route to take, 'but parents' wishes at the end of the day are followed'.

Three sciences on offer throughout, plus trad French, German and Spanish, as well as Mandarin (available for beginners as well as for native speakers). No particular bias, physics, chemistry, history and geography outstanding at GCSE level, maths and English almost equally strong, results in all disciplines equally impressive at A level (84 per cent A*/A/B grades). Art results outstanding throughout the school (three out of the top five A level candidates nationally two years running). Tranche of outstanding French GCSEs taken early. Strong tradition of classics; government and politics and history of art available at A level. Broad range of subjects available but not the biggest take up at A level in langs, classics or further maths.

Foreign pupils with minimal English are no longer accepted willy-nilly unless they happen to be particularly bright, or have siblings in the school. EFL is on hand, but pupils who don't have 'a pretty good working knowledge of English' are encouraged to do an English lang course before they arrive (Edinburgh School of English is popular). Good staff:pupil ratio. 'Computers zooming ahead.' School wireless networked throughout, with all senior school students having their own laptop, school can provide at 1,500 quid a pop including software and insurance, or pupils can opt for their own. A very high proportion of leavers (95+ per cent) go on to university; on average 12 Oxbridge places each year.

Fettes is creaming off the academic élite of Edinburgh, be they boarder or day.

Games, Options, the Arts: Wide range of opportunity for games. 'Rugby is strong, though no longer a religion' (73 blues to date). Needle matches with Glenalmond and Merchiston on the rugby field and Strathallan in hockey. Lacrosse impressive, girls play hockey and netball as well; sixth form not forced to play team games at all – swimming or aerobics also available. Big new sports centre and swimming pool providing a wide range of other sports, old pool (a delicious antediluvian gem) used for sub-aqua, canoeing and the like.

Music 'a huge strength' with loads of bands, orchestras, three choirs and a string quartet etc etc, two popular concerts in spring and autumn plus carol service all in aid of charity. Keen drama with imaginative productions, pupils often perform at the Edinburgh Festival (and win awards). *Frankenstein* the most recent production with over 100 pupils involved. New art centre in pipeline (still) and 'very inspirational head of art' (another one, if you follow) recently appointed. Pipe band popular. CCF, community service, D of E etc. Masses of trips, everywhere, for everything.

Background and Atmosphere: Vast Grimms' fairy-tale of a building, turreted and with acres of wood panelling and shiny black floors (are they granite or stone flags underneath the tarry surface?) purpose-built in 1870 by Bryce. Part of the main building still has the original steam-driven heating which starts up twice a day with alarming groans and wheezes – ripe for the engineering museum methinks.

Various Victorian edifices scattered about the school's wonderful 90-acre grounds plonk in the middle of Edinburgh. 'School uses Edinburgh much more now,' says the head. Spectacular development after school sold 'redundant' acres to build Fettes Village, a collection of neat little boxes which splits the games field and provided the cash for much-needed expansion. The collection of new and converted buildings that house the new prep department are much bigger than they look from the outside, an example of space well used, and about to be extended. New posho boarding house – Craigleith, dead modern – to accommodate the expanded sixth form which is due to increase by 25 per cent. The new-build, which will include a sixth form centre but not a bar (illegal in Scotland – but of course they can leave the grounds and go out for their two units of alcohol) will house 125 upper sixth pupils in two identical wings (surely this should be 126 or 124?) each with their own individual room and will provide a transition between the disciplines of school and uni with pupils being able to cook their own meals if they want to. Planners have accepted a 15-year development plan (well done those architects – difficult with conservation and all that) and whilst funding is in place for the new upper sixth form house, some serious fund-raising looms for the future.

The school has gradually metamorphosed from famous trad boys' school to genuinely co-ed. Girls have been head of school twice in recent years and the flavour has changed from home-grown Scots to more exotic, with an influx from the Far East.

Pastoral Care and Discipline: Despite colourful stories in the Edinburgh press in past years – drugs, booze, etc, grossly overstated, says the head – there is a clear framework of discipline that is well understood by all. This is a school with a zero tolerance policy on drugs. Edinburgh is the drugs capital of the north and running a school in the middle of it is no joke. Under-age drinking is an acknowledged problem. Three tier system on the discipline side: housemaster/deputy head/head = rustication/formal warning and suspension or expulsion. Ditto smoking. Very clear house-visiting rules – no overt demonstrations of affection; bonking equals out. And yes, they do lose the occasional pupil for all these misdemeanours, ditto bullying. Strong anti-bullying ethos. Prefects very responsible – imaginative anti-bullying code involves culprits writing down what they must or must not do and signing it. Expulsion is always an option.

Pupils and Parents: School topped up with many non-Brits in the bad old days, now the mix is veering more towards the British norm but still collections of exotic foreigners – Russians, Chinese, Japanese, Americans, Ukrainians, but fewer Bulgarians than previously. Increasing numbers of locals and Scots from all over. 'Pupils from 40 different countries, East European connection sadly dropping off.' Very strong old Fettesian stream, plus loads of first-time buyers, intellectuals etc etc. Good vibrant mix. Old Fettesians include John de Chastelaine, Ian McLeod, James Bond, Tilda Swinton, Lord Woolf and Tony Blair – remembered fondly for 'his acting ability'!

Entrance: CE or school's own exam for those not coming from UK preps. Approx 40 students a year join the sixth form after GCSE elsewhere, currently much sought after as pupils pile in from other, mainly Scottish, schools.

Exit: University or further education the norm with seven Oxbridge places in 2010 and about one-third taking a gap year; favoured universities are – as ever – Newcastle, St Andrews, Durham, London, Bristol, Leeds, Warwick, Nottingham, Edinburgh, Glasgow and Aberdeen.

Money Matters: Well-endowed with academic scholarships which can be supplemented with bursaries when the chips are down – if necessary up to 100 per cent: 'The level of these awards depend upon parents' financial means and can cover up to the full value of the fees'. Special (Todd) bursaries for Old Fettesians, 12.5 per cent discount for Services (not so many of these around).

Remarks: Undoubtedly the strongest school in Edinburgh – possibly riding too high? To quote one governor, 'It is better to have a challenge, otherwise we become complacent'. Head adds, 'No danger of becoming complacent; the most dangerous thing in a school is to stand still.' Exciting cosmopolitan mix in an exciting city.

Filey School

Muston Road, Filey, North Yorkshire, YO14 0HG

• Pupils: 805 • Ages: 11-16 • Non-denom • State

Tel: 01723 512 354
Fax: 01723 512 165
Email: admin@filey.n-yorks.sch.uk
Website: www.fileyschool.com

Head: Since November 2010, Mr Andy Dickinson, previously acting head.

Academic matters: Awesome improvement in exam results. From 67 per cent 5+ A*–C in 2006 to 74 per cent in 2010 – 46 per cent including maths and English. Now has technology college status, which has helped with funding and to attract best staff, particularly in maths. Winner of government's School Achievement Awards' bonus scheme for three consecutive years and dubbed 'Ofsted-on-Sea' by one national paper. Awarded Highly Effective School status in 2007. Ofsted deemed it 'a good and improving school' in the same year, though the 2010 report described it as only 'satisfactory'. Has International School status, Leading Aspect Award and is a centre of excellence in North Yorkshire for ICT. A true comprehensive – the only one serving the Filey area – with often a below-average ability intake. Does well by SEN students and just as well by the gifted. Now the centre for enhanced mainstream provision for high-functioning autistic children, owing to the SENCo's reputation and the school's track record of success.

A growing school not just in numbers but in breadth of courses offered. Has widened choice from solely GCSE to now offering vocational courses – business studies, ICT, leisure and tourism, applied engineering, health and social care, NVQ childcare. Gained 100 per cent A* to C in business studies and in ICT in 2010. 'Widening course choice has made a huge motivational improvement,' says school. Some students who have the aptitude do all GCSEs, including two modern foreign languages and three sciences; some do the core subjects plus vocational subjects. 'We personalise our courses. We had a young lady who wanted to learn hairdressing – she also did business studies and ended up opening her own salon!' Growth has also seen management team strengthened. School now has one deputy and six assistant head teachers. Additional non-teaching staff have also been added.

Under-achievement is spotted and dealt with. Computerised management system tracks students' progress against agreed targets. Teachers are monitored too with a rigorous programme of performance management.

Games, Options, the Arts: Good sporting achievements but thank the staff, not the facilities. Thriving sports ethos based on the house system and extensive team sports. It's not just the school which lacks a sports centre – it's the town. Head and community now working together on bid for sports centre funding. School also has the only community swimming pool, 30 years old and still open to the public. Shirley Cooper Performing Arts Centre opened 2008 and drama now part of the curriculum. New music suite but as yet no adequate drama space. Usual hobby clubs. Accessible community education with facilities open 50 weeks of the year.

Background and Atmosphere: Built in the sixties, school's growing reputation and thriving population have seen numbers virtually double in 14 years. Recent £1.4m investment saw improved reception, offices, arts station, modern language suite and six-classroom state of the art maths block. Now interactive whiteboards in just about every room. Fully networked for ICT and four, excellent ICT rooms.

Also improvements to design and technology area, with a much improved CAD-CAM room, two well-equipped food rooms (aided by links with local McCain factory). School uses technology to enhance e.g. drama and music, and every subject area is benefiting. The school now has a local studies area used by students and the local community and the library has been transformed into a learning resource centre.

Students treated in a grown-up, respectful way and they give that respect back. Youngsters who once sat on the floor in assemblies now sit on chairs; the canteen, built for 400 and hopelessly too small, has the Ikea look; toilets are graffiti-free. A school buzzing with good pupil/teacher rapport – no wonder they learn.

Pastoral Care and Discipline: School rules mercifully brief and standards of behaviour high. Isolated study, possibly with head, as ultimate deterrent for bad behaviour. A learning support centre to modify poor behaviour was opened in 2006. The school has three learning mentors, to work with youngsters and their parents. Also has extended school co-ordinators.

Pupils and Parents: Parents, desperate to secure children's future in an area hard-hit by fishing and farming decline, treasure school as a focal point in community. Pupils come roughly half from Filey, half bussed in from surrounding villages. Good school/home links. 'Nothing is too much trouble,' says one parent.

Entrance: Same old story: unless you live in catchment area, appealing for a place in this chock-full school is your only hope.

Exit: Two-thirds go to sixth form or further education colleges in nearby Scarborough or further afield. Most ultimately to university. Modern apprenticeships take much of the remainder.

Remarks: New technology college status has helped with recruitment. But if it's gloss you're looking for, not the school nor the town for you. What you see is what you get – good behaviour, good teaching, good results.

Forest School

Linked to Forest Preparatory School in the Junior section

College Place, Snaresbrook, London, E17 3PY

• Pupils: 1,240; 50:50 boys:girls • Ages: 11-18 • Size of sixth form: 270 • C of E foundation with a sizeable proportion of pupils from other faith groups • Fees: Prep £8,901-£10,521; Senior £13,410 pa • Independent

Tel: 020 8520 1744
Fax: 020 8520 3656
Email: warden@forest.org.uk
Website: www.forest.org.uk

Warden: Since 2009, Mrs Sarah Kerr-Dineen MA (forties), read English at Cambridge, postgraduate studies at Oxford. Taught for Open University, at Kelly College, Tavistock, Oxford High School and St Edward's Oxford, where she was a housemistress for six years and director of studies for five. Husband also in education; four children, 14–22, the youngest at Forest School.

Passionate about teaching and pupils' achievements outside the classroom as well as within. Sees Forest as an exciting and important school with happy children achieving well beyond what might be expected, in all areas.

Academic matters: Boys and girls are taught separately from Year 3 to Year 11, so it is tempting to compare and contrast GCSE results. Tempting, but tricky to tease out any substantial differences. Most of the results are, as one would expect, impressive. 2010 results at GCSE were 33 per cent A* and 73 per cent A*/A. At A level in 2010, 19 per cent A*, 55 per cent A* and A, and 83 per cent A*–B – both sets consistently this good and on the increase.

The vast majority of both sexes take three sciences and most do very well. Maths tends to be much the most popular (and successful) A level choice, with English, history and the sciences next in line. Less mainstream possibilities are philosophy and government and politics, the latter another popular choice.

Full-time LDD support. Everyone is screened on the back of the MIDYIS test in the autumn of Year 7 – some 50 pupils get individual education plans as a result and extra help. 'Parents can be worried, but dyslexia is not a reason for us not to offer a place, unless it is severe. However, we do need to know about it, so we can organise help.'

Games, Options, the Arts: Plenty of drama, music and sport. A new sports hall which includes two swimming pools, a gym, fitness rooms and cricket gallery was opened by HRH The Duke of York in 2007. There are 15 acres of sports pitches and tennis courts on site, plus more pitches a short walk through the forest. Strong reputation for boys' football and cricket with plenty of county and national players. The only school that has played in the FA Cup (in 1887). Girls' games increasingly strong – netball and hockey but also athletics and rounders; girls' rounders team includes an England International.

Inter-house music, drama, art and sports competitions are an important part of school life; six girls' and eight boys' houses. The new performing arts centre also hosts major co-ed drama performances. 'We can choose plays which suit boys (such as *Journey's End*) or girls (such as *The Crucible*), but there are also joint productions, like our big musicals.' Four orchestras, five bands and ten choirs, co-ed and single sex. 'You name me a mixed school where it is cool for boys to sing'. D of E and CCF popular; lots of money raised for charities.

Background and Atmosphere: Opened in 1834 with 22 pupils in a row of Walthamstow cottages. Now ten minutes' walk from Snaresbrook tube station, but still surrounded by Epping Forest. Buildings include a Victorian chapel, elegant Georgiana, seventies girls' school and a Hogwart-sesque panelled dining hall, with a glitter ball still hanging from the rafters after the parents' disco. The Warden describes it as 'one school on two bases' (three including the prep school), with each base the centre of gravity for each school. But to avoid duplicating facilities, classes take place wherever works – which may well be in what is technically the other gender's school. Similarly, although staff are appointed to one school or another, most teach in both. C of E foundation school – chapel services compulsory for all pupils, including the 25ish per cent of other faiths. 'Our chaplain is very skilled at being inclusive and invites many speakers from other faith groups. This is a school where you don't cherrypick what you want; we expect everyone to take part in everything.' Early-rising parents can breakfast here with their children from 7.30am.

Pastoral Care and Discipline: Plenty of carrots as well as sticks. Inevitable wobbles, but generally well-behaved children kept fairly firmly under control. Drugs are low on the radar scan; alcohol is higher. 'We have our problems but they are not, on the whole, the problems of affluence.'

Pupils and Parents: The catchment area ranges from Islington to Beckton to Woodford Green and out into Essex, so a good ethnic mix and plenty of street-wise East London pupils alongside those from gentler environs. Hugely supportive parents' association runs quizzes, fairs and balls, raising large sums for improving the infrastructure of the school. Ex-pupils include cricketers Nasser Hussain and James Foster, footballer Quintin Fortune, writer and actor Sharat Sardana, author George Dangerfield, murderer Eric Brown, and first woman Chinook pilot Jackie Smiles MBE.

Entrance: By maths and English, plus interview, at 11+. Those with LDD get extra time. 'The scripts of pupils with LDD are scrutinised specifically and sympathetically as part of the selection procedure,' says the school website. A few ad hoc places at 13. Those coming into the sixth form need at least six good GCSEs, four of them at grade B or above. Quite a few from the state sector at this stage.

Exit: On average 45 per cent of those applying to Oxbridge receive offers. 2009/10 saw 10 Oxbridge offers, all met; and 13 medics. More or less all leavers go to university with strong showings in medicine, law, economics, history and other proper subjects.

Money Matters: Offers the equivalent of 14 full scholarships and bursaries at 11 and eight half scholarships/bursaries at 16. Also four music scholarships (grade 5+), sixth form half-fee art and drama awards and four Ogden Trust sixth form scholarships for pupils coming in from state schools to study science.

Remarks: Highly successful East London independent school situated amidst leafy Epping Forest with unusual mix of single-sex and co-education, which excels at the extracurricular as well as the academic.

Fortismere School

Linked to Blanche Nevile School

South Wing, Tetherdown, Muswell Hill, London, N10 1NE

• Pupils: 1,660 boys and girls; all day • Ages: 11-19 • Size of sixth form: 440 • Non denom • State

Tel: 020 8365 4400
Fax: 020 8444 7822
Email: southwing@fortismere.haringey.sch.uk
Website: www.fortismere.haringey.sch.uk

Head: Since September 2010, Ms Helen Anthony ('the right side of 50'), previously head of Central Technology College in Robinswood, Gloucestershire. This all-boys school was transformed from 'notice to improve' to 'good' in four years under her headship. Has worked in variety of urban and rural schools, in affluent and deprived areas. Mother of two daughters. Her plans: 'Fortismere will have an active mind, a finger on the pulse and a big heart.'

Academic matters: By no means a bog-standard comprehensive. The ability on intake – as well as the income – is significantly above average, and the results reflect this. In 2010, 66 per cent of all A level grades were at A*, A or B. It is a similarly strong story at GCSE with 75 per cent of students gaining 5+ A*–C grades including English and maths. Large and buoyant sixth form – one of the largest in north London – which focuses on traditional academic A levels. Nearly 30 choices, plus a small number of vocational courses including music technology, ICT, business and sports studies. Strong teaching in most areas, with a good balance of experienced staff and those new to the profession.

Has multiple specialisms in maths/computing with music, and foreign languages. All do French or Spanish in Year 7 and more able linguists are invited to add a second language in Year 8, from either German or Mandarin. Setting from Year 7 in almost all subjects. Three sciences offered to top 60 per cent of students. Homework not overwhelming in the early years but work hiked up a notch by GCSE, with study skills days for pupils and evenings for parents. Most pupils take nine GCSEs – though top-set students may take 10 or more. Four ASs, three or four A2s. Exploring the IB for post-16.

Games, Options, the Arts: Strong sport, particularly basketball, football, athletics and netball (two netball teams have been county champions, one soccer team is Middlesex Champion and made the last 16 in the Nationals). New sports hall, plus an assortment of pitches, including Astroturf. High level of involvement with music – over 600 students take specialist music lessons with peripatetic staff. Symphony orchestra, big band, several choirs. Recent tour to Salzburg and performance of Mozart's Requiem in St John's, Smith Square. Enthusiastic drama with 2009 production at Edinburgh Festival. Excellent, well-run library.

Well-developed ICT – interactive whiteboards now in all classrooms. Good range of trips – dance to Spain, art to Berlin, media studies to New York, annual exchanges to France, German and Spain, plus annual ski trips. Duke of Edinburgh, Young Enterprise and industrial link. Two well-used canteens, with increasingly healthy food.

Background and Atmosphere: A bit like a high school in an American TV programme – the pupils are cool, but not threateningly so, articulate, confident and neatly groomed. The school itself is rather less glamorous. Sprinkled out over a large site, it involves a haphazard arrangement of all the usual buildings, with a new(ish) science block, decent-enough provision for art, dance, drama and a brand new music block. The accommodation is functional rather than beautiful (and often rather untidy). The general mood, however, is upbeat. 'I always like coming to school,' said one enthusiastic newcomer and parents feel the same applies to older pupils. A school, however, which works best for the diligent and focused – some do get distracted by rather too cool a peer group. School shares the site with the secondary division of Blanche Neville School for the Deaf.

Pastoral Care and Discipline: This, by and large, is a well-behaved middle-class school, with attentive classrooms and orderly corridors. With over 1,600 pupils, however, there's bound to be an unruly element and discipline is strict. The previous head introduced a tariff system of escalating punishments and rewards. Zero tolerance of drink and offensive weapons, both punished with exclusion. Strong induction programme for Year 7s, with visits to partner primaries in Year 6 and a specialist team of Year 7 tutors, who oversee groups of about 27 every afternoon. The school attempts to put at least one familiar face in each child's classroom when they arrive.

Pupils and Parents: Very much a local comprehensive but, in this instance, 'local' means affluent middle class – quite a few parents here who've contemplated – and rejected – private education for their children. Pupils are mature and confident and parents are the sort who monitor homework, bedtime and exam results. 'My mother made sure I revised for my setting test in maths,' said one conscientious Year 7. 'She was very cross that I hadn't done my revision till the night before.'

Entrance: Haringey is a borough not particularly well served by secondary education and Fortismere is way out in front academically, which means competition to get in is particularly cut-throat for its 243 places. Admissions are administered by the governors under the pan-London scheme and priority is currently given to those in council care and siblings, then 10 per cent musical aptitude, then distance from the gates as the crow flies. In practice, this generally means you have to live within about half a mile and housing round here is correspondingly expensive. Determined parents have been known to rent to guarantee the appropriate proximity. The school gained Foundation status in 2007, and one of the reasons is the opportunity it gives for a transparent admissions process. About 600 apply annually for 230 places in the sixth form – applicants must meet the criteria for the subjects they wish to study (five A* to B grades for academic subjects). Anyone who does should get a place.

Exit: The majority to higher education, over 65 per cent to Russell Group universities. Ten Oxbridge and medical successes this year.

Money Matters: Very active parents' association which underwrote the refurbishment of the sixth form centre.

Remarks: One of the best comprehensives in north London, building on its academic excellence under a new head.

Framlingham College

Linked to Brandeston Hall Preparatory School in the Junior section

Framlingham, Woodbridge, Suffolk, IP13 9EY

• Pupils: 255 boys, 180 girls; 260 board, 180 day. • Ages: 13-18 • Size of sixth form: 200 • C of E - inter-denom • Fees: Boarding £23,706; Day £15,237 pa • Independent

Tel: 01728 723 789
Fax: 01728 724 546
Email: admissions@framcollege.co.uk
Website: www.framlinghamcollege.co.uk

Head: Since September 2009, Mr Paul Taylor BA, formerly lower master (deputy head) at King's School, Canterbury; before that he was director of sport at Tonbridge School. He read history and politics at university; 18 years' teaching experience; also played professional cricket with Surrey CCC.

Academic matters: A well-performing school at both GCSE and A level, with a 2010 A level A*/A/B rate at 67 per cent and GCSE A* and A rate at nearly 50 per cent. Head says, 'Some schools achieve success by carefully selecting students, accepting only those of exceptional academic potential. Our cloth is cut more broadly and we look at the whole person, not just grades on a report sheet.' The College welcomes students from many backgrounds, and its focus is on serving students' individual needs. Provision for ESL and learning support is excellent, with a separate suite of rooms and a lovely atmosphere. Facilities in general, for such a large place, are very sensibly thought out, businesslike and well equipped. This is very much due to the previous head's excellent eye for maximisation of space, of which the superb split-level library is a prime example. Class sizes are small, with rooms deliberately designed to hold no more than 22. Maths very strong through to A level; design and technology department is stunning and produces quite exceptional work.

Games, Options, the Arts: Sport clearly of major importance – a fine new indoor pool and sport and fitness complex – and highly successful. Head makes a point of musical and academic achievement also featuring strongly in inter-house competition. Drama immensely popular – quite a few pupils go on to RADA and the like – with frequent first-rate performances. A state-of-the-art new drama and music building, the Headmaster Porter Theatre. Lots of concerts. Endless interesting leisure activities. Radio enthusiasts have their own room bursting with equipment.

Background and Atmosphere: College founded in 1864 with rather austere (school prefers 'a stunning mock-Gothic', so chacun à son goût) Victorian main building. Beautiful setting, perched on a hillside with a gorgeous view across the valley to Framlingham Castle. Everything beautifully kept, including 50 acres of playing fields. A woman's hand at the helm has helped to give a greater sense of light and cohesion to what was a bit of a hotch-potch. Boarding facilities are pleasant enough and have certainly come a long way since the best boast of a (very) early prospectus that 'each boy has a separate bed'! A comprehensive extension and refurbishment programme now underway. The school is enviably tidy and well-organised. Relaxed politeness the order of the day for relationships between staff and pupils and the atmosphere is tangibly unpressured but businesslike. Some very nice touches, like the airy central meeting hall, where pupils can gather and chat, currently being extended into a charming outside piazza. Ultra-modern design and technology centre and a well-equipped library.

Pastoral Care and Discipline: A major change has been the abolition of day houses and the absorption of day pupils into boarding houses, where they have desks and can sleep over in boarders' rooms – clearly a good move, as now the tutor system looks after day pupils and boarders with complete even-handedness. Prefects are carefully trained (the top ones do a week's residential leadership course) and given plenty of responsibility. Open discussion of problems such as bullying is encouraged and prevalent. The school has a strict policy on drugs and substance abuse. Discipline in general is good – a calm atmosphere prevails.

Pupils and Parents: Pupils are drawn largely from middle class East Anglian families, although a largish contingent of students from abroad, including numbers of German students who come for one year in the sixth form and frequently stay for two. Most integrate seamlessly into the school. The college is highly thought of locally. No problems recruiting on any front.

Entrance: Most applicants and linked junior school Brandeston Hall pupils accepted, but only if the head considers they will cope. Common entrance and interview form the normal means of entry at 13+, but special provision made for students for whom this is not appropriate. Entrance at 16+ normally on the basis of GCSE results and interview or testing, but special arrangements made for overseas students who are not following the British curriculum. Big influx into the sixth form, where virtually all subject combinations are accepted.

Exit: Most to university, with a fair smattering to Oxbridge and other Russell Group universities.

Money Matters: A wide range of scholarships awarded every year for academic excellence, exceptional ability in art or music or outstanding talent in another field, such as sport, available at 11+, 13+ or 16+. Successful candidates can be offered further assistance through bursaries in cases of proven financial need. Siblings' and forces' discounts.

Remarks: Very pleasant, well-ordered school which bears the stamp of the previous lively, charismatic head.

Francis Holland School, Regent's Park

Clarence Gate, Ivor Place, London, NW1 6XR

• Pupils: 465 girls, all day • Ages: 11-18 • Size of sixth form: 90 • C of E
• Fees: £13,890 pa • Independent

Tel: 02077 230 176
Fax: 02077 061 522
Email: admin@fhs-nw1.org.uk
Website: www.francisholland.org/nw1/showpage.asp

Headmistress: Since 2004, Mrs Vivienne Durham MA. Read English at St Hilda's, Oxford. Has always taught in girls' day schools. Was previously very popular deputy head of South Hampstead High. Husband is headmaster of UCS.

Academic matters: Mrs Durham is an academic and her vision of the school reflects this. The target set for all the staff is quite simply to get the best results for the girls. Prefers to appoint specialist, enthusiastic and talented staff to achieve her aims; leans heavily towards Oxbridge or older university graduates as she feels the intensity of study required by their tutorial systems requires the keenest minds. The percentage of A and A* grades at GCSE is consistently high – over 72 per cent in 2010 – with nearly 19 per cent A* at A level and over 98 per cent A–C grades. Offers Spanish, Latin, Greek, French, German and Italian; 'satellite centre' where A level language students can access foreign TV channels.

Games, Options, the Arts: Enthusiastic sport. A fitness area above the modern gym has state-of-the-art running and step machines which are always full during break and lunchtimes. Yoga is hugely popular. Netball, hockey, rounders, tennis, gymnastics, dance, pilates, aerobics, ju-jitsu, kickboxing are all available. Field sports in Regent's Park, water polo and swimming in the newly-refurbished, amazing basement pool which doubles as a meeting room, if you are brave enough to trust the floating floor. Every October the whole school enjoys a sponsored walk round Regent's Park, raising large sums for their chosen charity; dogs are very welcome – in fact, one might say dogs are de rigeur.

Music is very strong with every type of instrument on offer as well as choirs, orchestras, chamber groups and jazz ensembles, including the very talented 'Pink Ladies'. All levels are catered for, but the musical highlight is the annual concert held jointly with Harrow in their speech room accompanied by a professional orchestra. This traditional link with Harrow means that sixth formers enjoy balls and concerts together. Sixth formers also enjoy weekly lectures from visiting luminaries such as Boris Johnson, Anne Widdecombe, Michael Portillo and Joely Richardson.

Background and Atmosphere: The Reverend Canon Francis Holland founded the school (and the one of the same name off Sloane Square) in 1878, but the influence of his wife Mary should not be disregarded. She was rather taken with the educational system current in France, which was somewhat less blue stocking, and emphasised the importance of extra-curricular activities – there are now over 70 to choose from. Her vision remains one of the special elements of the school today. The new Gloucester Wing (formerly a pub!) provides additional classrooms, art studios and performance space in the old bar. Another element is the corridor travelled daily twixt tube and school where pupils and staff fall into step and chat en route. Parents comment on the easy relationship apparent between those who teach and those who are taught. Older pupils look after the younger ones. There is a family feel to the place and it's small enough to be noticed. The best school food in London, say pupils.

Despite its central London location, the proximity of Regent's Park, St Cyprian's church next door and the wood-panelled hall where full school assemblies take place combine to make the quirky, friendly, intimate and welcoming atmosphere peculiar to this school. Mary's vision lives on.

Pastoral Care and Discipline: Voicemail is available for all tutors so parents can raise issues instantly and know they have an immediate point of contact. The head encourages 'a bespoke quality' to the school, which she feels is a 'hidden secret'. The girls are not 'crushed with pressure'. Invites girls to her study on their birthdays to congratulate them – helps keep her in touch and makes her more accessible to the pupils. She knows them all. Head girl cannot recall any problems with drugs or alcohol in her seven years at the school. All girls fiercely loyal to the school and each other.

Pupils and Parents: Many from Hampstead, Highgate and the St John's Wood area but also from Mayfair, Islington, Kensington, Notting Hill. Tube links dictate the distribution, as the school is only five minutes from Baker Street. Parents choose it as an academic school which offers results without the attendant stress and pressure so often found in other high-achieving schools. Girls seeking a place at Francis Holland are mainly from the surrounding prep schools such as Glendower, Pembridge Hall, Sarum Hall, Bute House, St Christopher's, St Christina's, Trevor Roberts, Falkner House, Kensington Prep. The intake from local state schools tends to be from John Betts, St Michael's in Highgate and Fox's in Kensington. The resultant pupils are sensible, down to earth, ambitious, unaffected individuals.

Entrance: In the autumn term at age 11 and also at 16+ (sixth form), though some are accepted for occasional vacancies, especially at Year 9. Registration should be completed by the end of the previous November. Entrance tests and interviews take place in January or February before term starts in September. The school is in group 1 of the North London Independent Girls' Schools' Consortium where the girls sit the same paper on the same day using the same mark scheme. The results are made available to all the schools in the group and offers are sent out to parents early March.

Exit: Bristol, Leeds, Manchester, Nottingham, Durham and Edinburgh are the current favourites, but always some to Oxbridge and LSE. Also a number to American universities. Just under a quarter (but rising) take a gap year. History, English, maths and geography are popular subjects.

Money Matters: Three or more bursaries per year at 11 worth up to 100 per cent of the current school fee. Scholarships for music and for academic ability at 11 and 16. Remission of fees available for daughters of C of E clergy.

Remarks: The school motto is taken from Psalm 144 and asks, 'That our daughters may be as the polished corners of the temple' – a phrase which is quoted happily and with pleasure by former pupils and parents. Mention of a 'polished corner' anywhere in the world always raises a smile and reflects more than anything the special camaraderie which exists in this very idiosyncratic school. Francis Holland is a corner of London which, for some, will be forever polished.

Francis Holland School, Sloane Square

Linked to Francis Holland Junior School, Sloane Square in the Junior section

39 Graham Terrace, Belgravia, London, SW1W 8JF

• Pupils: 290 girls, all day • Ages: 11-18 • Size of sixth form: 65 • C of E
• Fees: £14,205 pa • Independent

Tel: 020 7730 2971
Fax: 020 7823 4066
Email: registrar@fhs-swl.org.uk
Website: www.francisholland.org.uk

Headmistress: Since 1997, Miss Stephanie Pattenden BSc PGCE (fifties). Educated at St Anne's Sanderstead (now defunct), Durham (maths) and King's College London (PGCE). Keen on bell-ringing and hill walking. With an entire career spent in independent London girls' day schools (St Paul's, Lady Eleanor Holles and South Hampstead High, where she was deputy head) she understands the London market well. Efficient, practical and modest, she ensures a balanced perspective, in spite of the King's Road-style sophistication of some of the girls in her care. Parents like her very grounded approach.

Although traditional in her approach, she can be found most days at the door shaking the girls' hands, aims to always make herself available to them regardless of what else is going on and is deeply respected by them. Teaches maths to Year 7 and enjoys her hands-on approach, 'The school is small enough so I can afford to be'. Proud that she has preserved the personal atmosphere of the school while improving academic standards, 'Now we are a serious player in the London market'.

Academic matters: At A level 86 per cent A*/B. Traditional teaching approach 'not for the unmotivated'. Many teachers on staff over 10 years but not fossilised – plenty of young too. Sympathetic to mild special educational needs but no specialist provision, although there are links with the Kensington dyslexia centre – 'We couldn't take anyone who was academically challenged'. Staff track individual pupils where help may be needed and parents are kept informed.

Head wouldn't be drawn on singling out any particularly strong subjects – 'It's a small school and therefore dependent on the girls in each year' – but looking at the last three years together, it's clear that French, Spanish and German are all strong and popular, English and maths are popular; five or so a year take sciences to A level. Latin and Greek offered to A level, with students keen to read classics at university. Will facilitate exams in languages for those who speak them (a number have e.g. Russian and Spanish as their mother tongue) but doesn't offer it as part of the timetable. Small class sizes – typical sixth form class is six to eight; further down school 15 the norm.

Games, Options, the Arts: Passionately committed ballet teacher who has been there forever; Princess Margaret competition held internally each year; lots of links with the Royal Ballet School. Music and drama also strong – regular concerts in St John's, Smith Square and choir trips to e.g. Barcelona and Paris. Strong emphasis on community work – girls recently raised over £10,000 auctioning, among other things, a Tracy Emin mug, to fund schools in Malawi and India. Closer to home they work with the elderly in a charitable settlement in Battersea.

In October 2010, The Duke of Westminster unveiled Carmel Hall, the school's new performing arts centre. Carmel Hall was formerly home to The Grosvenor Club, a working men's club. The new development provides the school with top notch music and drama facilities (including 10 music practice rooms) and also a stunning double-height performance space. This is a really major boost for the school.

Sport – netball, rounders, hockey, athletics – takes place mainly in Battersea Park (also the home of the annual sports day) but the school has the luxury of one netball court on site that doubles up as a playground for the juniors and a well-equipped gym on site. Inter-house competitions in both sport and music.

Lovely bright, airy library where the younger girls can be found curled up on beanbags reading. Lots of help and encouragement with career choices – old girls come back to talk about their work and no hesitation in taking advantage of the range of expertise among parents. London walks; theatre trips; visits to galleries as well as a well-patronised D of E, bronze or silver level.

Background and Atmosphere: Impressively spacious, light-filled school on residential road behind Sloane Square. Wide staircases where considerate girls walk sensibly. An intimate school with lots of space. Relaxed and comfortable sixth form common-rooms with the obligatory magazine pictures plastered over the walls. Bright, functional and well-equipped classrooms. Netball court in the centre of the school separates senior from junior school. Late 20th century blends well with – recently decorated – 1881 portion (including recently extended school hall with stained-glass windows). Affiliation with St Mary's Church; no special emphasis on religion.

Pastoral Care and Discipline: 'Excellent,' enthuses the 2007 ISI report, commenting on the 'strong rapport between pupils and teachers'. Effective systems managed by the deputy head and form tutors ensure that 'nobody escapes attention'. Head declared she would not shirk from suspending, but only in extremis, 'for, say, vandalism or deliberately lying or cheating – not that there have been any cases of these'. For lesser offences detentions (married with a rewards system). Not a huge number in detention each week – 'A sign that they work'. Clear and defined boundaries minimise any escalation of problems. Girls stand up when a teacher enters the room.

Clear communication channels for parents too. Open-door sessions timetabled twice a week for those who want them.

Pupils and Parents: Confident, articulate, self-aware girls who sparkle and appear to have fun while getting their work done. Daughters of doctors, captains of industry and TV presenters, as well as Russian magnates and Saudi royalty. Pretty (though often scruffily worn) uniform – (some very small) grey skirts with blue and white check blouse. King's Road-style own clothes for sixth formers. Old girls include Vanessa Mae, Jemima Khan and Jane Fearnley-Whittingstall.

Entrance: 'We are not the most selective school in London,' says the head, though there are more people chasing fewer places each year (currently eight applicants for each place not taken by the 50 per cent coming from the junior school). Many sisters but no sibling preference. Part of the North London Consortium Group One. Written exam in English and maths at 11, plus interview and attendance at two lessons for assessment. Places do occasionally arise further up the school, especially in Years 8 and 9 when the odd girl might choose to go off to boarding school.

The brightest from the junior school may divert to the more pressured competition, but this is not universal.

Exit: Almost all to university; 10 per cent to Oxbridge. Some choose the London College of Fashion and the Royal Ballet School. Also American universities. Emphasis on matching the pupil to the right course with a wide range of destinations. Courses from law, medicine and maths, marketing and advertising to journalism, psychology and history of art.

Money Matters: Three bursaries up to full fees at 11+, 14+ and sixth form. Academic and music scholarships also available and help for clergy daughters.

Remarks: A traditional school that is relaxed in its approach, but not at the expense of academic excellence. No longer the option 'for your less bright daughter,' says head, but brings out the best in girls who might flounder in a larger, less personal, establishment. If your daughter is fiercely competitive, then probably not the school for you. Here standards are encouraged to come from within.

Frensham Heights School

Linked to Frensham Heights Lower School in the Junior section

Rowledge, Farnham, Surrey, GU10 4EA

• Pupils: 500; 270 boys, 230 girls; 100 boarding, 400 day (boarding from Year 7) • Ages: 13-18, juniors 3-13 • Size of sixth form: 100 • Non-denom • Fees: Boarding £19,965-£23,250; Day £15,690-£19,965 pa • Independent

Tel: 01252 792561
Fax: 01252 794 335
Email: admissions@frensham-heights.org.uk
Website: www.frensham-heights.org.uk

Headmaster: Since 2004, Mr Andrew Fisher BA MA (forties), educated at Geelong Grammar in Australia (where his father was headmaster) followed by the University of New South Wales (history and Eng literature) and a master's in education management at Sheffield. Comes from Wrekin College in Shropshire, where he rose through the ranks to become deputy head. Married to Catherine, with two young children who are not in the school – 'As the son of a head, grandson of a head and nephew of a head, I realise that they must have a bit of a life outside school'. Teaches 14-year-olds, loves teaching. 'Children only get one chance', 'School should be the best experience they ever have', 'Students should get the chance to make mistakes'.

Recently appointed a deputy head academic whose job it is to 'ensure that all pupils fulfil their potential – not with the eye to any league table but with an eye to them not wasting their own time, other pupils' time or their parents' money'. 'Several got quite a bump when head kept his word by not allowing them up into the next year as they had not worked hard enough. It has had a remarkably salutary effect.' Head is, nonetheless, delighted to be fronting this seriously artistic school, but keen on sport too, so watch out for a slight change in emphasis. He is personable and fun; some pupils are still slightly wary of Andrew (this is a first name school) but those who have regular contact were reassuring: 'He's OK,' (highest form of praise), 'You can hear him whistling in the morning' – but not apparently later in the day. Suspect that he is probably a people's person rather than a builder.

Academic matters: Average class size 17. Not the best collection of A levels we have ever seen; 33 per cent A*/A grades in 2010. However, that's not really what this school is about. Science and maths strongest, history OK. Drama, dance, music, art, 3D design, DT and sport options at GCSE. Most take at least two, some take three. A few only take one. AS level sociology recently introduced. Vast range of different and busy A levels, e.g. photography, PE also new addition. Setting in maths and science but not other subjects to avoid labelling perennial slow-streamers. 100+ pupils receive support for mild specific learning difficulties and virtually all get extra tuition. Parents interested in personal development, not league tables. No classics. No RE after age 14 (pupils thought they might like it). Some good, unconventional teaching, using drama etc to get the message across.

Lower school classrooms are dotted along the ground floor of the converted and much-expanded stables, IT in the hayloft (powerpoint presentations the norm), ditto (but not the same hayloft) busy multi-media library, well-used with audiobooks, videos and appealing paperbacks, and classical music buzzing gently in the background. Ceramics everywhere. Library is open till 6.30pm, points for laptops; teaching sessions on how to run a library and use a catalogue, along with quizzes and games for 13+, make this one of the more imaginative libraries we have visited.

Games, Options, the Arts: Head keen on sport; his employment of the ex-director of performance at Southampton football club has already revolutionised the fortunes of the school football teams: first XI has just beaten Charterhouse, 'and are walking about 50 foot tall'. Sport is 'improving' – enormously, 'both in the quality of the schools against whom they play (for instance boys' matches v Eton, Winchester and Charterhouse) and in the results they are achieving – several sides are unbeaten'. Games compulsory twice a week, whole class play the same games up to sixth form, when they can choose. All the usual games are played but probably not the place to send a prep school rugby champion (no rugby). Boys play soccer, hockey and cricket, girls hockey, netball and rounders, plus minority sports, led by tennis, basketball etc. One or two already involved in colt county cricket, new all-weather nets; Astroturf completed September 2009. Sport's profile seems to be achanging – apparently the original cricket ground was laid down by the Charringtons in 1900 so that Daddy could play and Mummy could entertain the Prince of Wales.

The most terrifying high frame ('It looks even higher from the top,' said Andrew) which combines every conceivable movement plus some that even stuntmen would be amazed at. Woods filled with serious and popular climbing frames: Jacob's Ladder impressive. School was the first to be licensed as a centre for outdoor education, and 'The ropes course is partly about personal challenge, but it is actually far more about respecting and supporting others, and taking responsibility for one's own actions, which is why it is a timetabled lesson'. Forges strong staff/pupil links and is much used in summer by business workshops. Forget convention: this is the most imaginative playground we have ever seen. Traditional gym looks Neanderthal by comparison. Certain amount of D of E, but not the religion you find in many schools. Expeditions important, huge range – staff 'give up weeks of holiday time to take pupils to the Red Sea and the Sahara'. Trekking, camping, mountain climbing, survival skills, first aid. Lots of weekend trips away for boarders which day pupils can join – most sound rather scary.

Intimidatingly good performing arts; the building itself has won oodles of awards, with several pupils in current TV programmes and films. Award-winning dance in stunning dance studio: shiny black floor, wall of mirrors and no shoes allowed. New, rebuilt, slightly surprising music centre (fires are in fashion at Frensham: this time it was a squirrel which apparently ate the wires; horrifying photographs of the detritus left by the blaze). Music centre has a glass roof in the main auditorium which means that it is almost useless sound-wise when it rains, and like an oven when the sun shines. Fortunately the house itself boasts a glorious ballroom which can be co-opted for concerts. Music strong, with loads of opportunities to play and sing, including an annual concert tour abroad; 22 peripatetic music staff, some of them international performers, two orchestras, three choirs, string quartets, masses of concerts and a soirée in June – for some reason they also teach the bagpipes. More ceramics dotted all round the place, with children's art on every wall, everywhere – the main hall, the passages. 'We like having our work on show – it is very encouraging,' said our 11 year old guide. Not quite big enough art department (extension probably on next wish-list), but some superb results. Glorious pupil-designed panther in foyer of the performing arts centre.

Background and Atmosphere: Founded in 1925, this was a school ahead of its time: co-ed school capable of taking children virtually from cradle to university with no uniforms, no bullying, no competition, no housepoints, no prizegivings. Creative learning, creative thinking important, plus the arts. Think Bloomsbury in the country. Teachers and students all on first-name basis. No uniform, vague dress-code -'We do insist on more formal dress when the occasion demands,' but no overt fashion dictates.

Magnificent Edwardian pile, built by a brewery magnate, set in beautiful 100+ acre grounds with stupendous views – over fifty miles on a clear day; Frensham Ponds just over the hill. Massive outside use of performing arts centre, which was set ablaze by an electrician's halogen light just days before it was due to open. Fair amount of new build lately and lots of titivating going on. Sixth form centre opened 2006.

No Saturday school, day pupils may leave at 4.10 on weekdays; behaves much more like a day school than boarding school except in the sixth form. Boys' houses across the road, girls live in the main building in recently renovated rooms.

Pastoral Care and Discipline: Very nurturing pupil/teacher relationships with teachers widely available out of school hours. 'If you get a bad mark it's easy to discuss it with your teacher,' said a pupil. Mentors counsel younger students – 'nice and easy to talk to'. Strict about getting prep in, discipline is taken seriously. No smoking; bar twice a week, school gets cross if drink overdone. Drugs the same perennial problem – though Andrew will always give everyone a second chance, even to taking on pupils dismissed by other schools, though immediate expulsion if caught indulging on school premises. Pupils with a drug history coming from other schools must agree to a contract, and will be subject to regular – periodic – drugs testing. One out last year. No chapel or assembly, but morning (sic) talks on Monday afternoons, varying from the 'enlightened to the mundane'. Annual parent-teachers' meeting, which doesn't seem quite enough, plus parents' committee 'which meets each term to discuss matters of common interest'. (Fly on the wall stuff that.)

Pupils and Parents: Pupils come from state and independent schools in Surrey, East Hampshire, West Sussex and the A3/M3 corridor into south west London. About seven per cent ex-pat and no more than 10 per cent from overseas. Unusual international dimension, echoing the founders' international conscience, with the head keen on bringing overseas children into a 'parochial part of Surrey'. Large numbers of those whom we met lived 'within two minutes' of the school, and neighbouring villages are rapidly becoming school annexes. Lord Moser is an Old Boy (he came as a refugee from Nazi Germany). Many from the arts, publishing, film, entertainment, design etc. Also academics, professionals and IT people.

Entrance: Mainly at 3+, 11+, 13+ or 16+. Assessment, interview and school report at age 10 (or below). Entrance exam required for the older children. Considerably 'over-subscribed for our January entrance exam. There will therefore be those who are not offered places. BUT, and it is a big but, the selection will never be just about academics – the reason why we have our own entrance exam, the reason why we offer all pupils the chance to show us skills/interests they have, irrespective of whether these skills are of themselves scholarship standard'. Success in sixth form entrance exam, and subsequent offer of a place, subject to obtaining six Cs or better at GCSE. A or occasionally B required in subjects to be studied at A Level. Hates to turn anyone away – 'The worst thing you can say to anyone is: you failed. So we encourage families to disclose all problems before getting as far as the entrance process'. Some children come here from schools where they were not happy.

Exit: Some to music conservatories, drama schools and art colleges in the UK and abroad. Most to a wide range of universities, studying everything from marine biology and coastal ecology to Arabic with politics, dance and fashion. The odd one or two to Oxbridge. Some gap years.

Money Matters: Scholarships have, for many years, been restricted to £750 (£450 exhibitions). Means-tested bursaries available for those whose parents would not otherwise be able to afford a Frensham Heights' education. Enterprise Company that helps the school to make a bob or two letting out facilities like the outdoor education centre to visiting schools. Also does a brisk trade in weddings, and competitive music festival and summer schools contribute to funds.

Remarks: Schools with a liberal outlook are thin on the ground so, if this alternative education appeals to you, then Frensham, with its emphasis on freedom and friendliness, is worth considering – particularly for the transfer of an unhappy child or those who do not fit neatly into the traditional system.

Frewen College

Northiam, Rye, East Sussex, TN31 6NL

• Pupils: 100 boys and girls; about one-third board • Ages: 7-17 • Size of sixth form: No sixth form • Non-denom • Fees: Junior School: day £16,200, boarding £23,376; Senior: boarding £29,382, day £21,165 pa • Independent

Tel: 01797 252 494
Fax: 01797 252 567
Email: office@frewencollege.co.uk
Website: www.frewencollege.co.uk

Principal: Since 2006, Mrs Linda Smith BA, PGCE (sixty-ish). Has a background in English and religious education and has held a number of senior management posts in both the maintained and independent sectors, in both senior and junior schools. Most recently deputy head of a mid-sized independent school in Leicestershire covering infants up to GCSE. Main focus is on further enhancing teaching and learning strategies within the school. The experienced business manager and bursar, Mr Jeremy Field, remains in situ and has embarked on some ambitious plans for further development of the facilities.

Academic matters: Individual education plan is one of the two guiding principles here. Targets is the other. Every child knows his own plan. The targets of junior pupils in all key areas are kept on little cards in cups, ready to be referred to at any point in the day. Most classes have no more than six children and all are carefully monitored. The school specialises in supporting dyslexics and dyspraxics with the associated speech and language difficulties such children can have, as well as a small number of children with Asperger's. They do not take those whose primary problem is ADHD or MLD, nor those with profound speech and language problems. The nature of the building and its unalterability (planning regs) do not allow for wheelchair users to come as boarders.

The separate junior school for Years 4–6, in a house opposite the main one, is spacious and incorporates classrooms and a small hall in which a play written for the children and tailored to them as individuals was being rehearsed with everyone contentedly partaking when we visited. There is an IT room, a therapy room for small groups or one-to-one which is used for 'time out' space, especially for Asperger's children for whom class activities can be stressful. There is also a speech and language therapy room, also used for occupational therapy. Here children are helped with social skills and 'good listening' and 'good looking'. Lots of outdoor play – in all weathers – in wellies and overalls. All is overseen by the juniors' own teacher in charge, who is very experienced, enthusiastic and very clued-up.

But the two schools are decidedly one. At Year 7 most move into the main site, and there are very comprehensive transition arrangements in place. A few each year have so successfully caught up they are able to rejoin mainstream education elsewhere, some passing entrance exams to local independents.

In the main school, the small class sizes persist and all the classes we visited were relaxed, with everyone seemingly absorbed and involved. A sense of each child's individual needs is pervasive. We visited an English class where everyone was writing on a PC and we learned how, in public exams, many will use an amanuensis to read the questions and/or transcribe the pupils' dictated answers – all according to the individual needs. Touch-typing, predictive text and voice-recognition technologies have all been introduced, together with brand new e-library.

School follows national curriculum, and most students take and pass seven GCSEs. In latest exams 45 per cent of grades were A*–C. Given careful targeting and recently beefed-up staff, these results look set to continue to improve. Recent successful innovation is the introduction of a daily whole-school literacy session, with all staff and pupils involved in intensive sessions in very small groups. Many pupils have shown significant progress in just a few weeks.

Pupils in Years 10/11 given weekly careers lessons and benefit from an extremely experienced professional careers guidance counsellor who also arranges work experience placements.

Most teachers and TAs have SEN qualifications and school supports several others through distance learning courses at the Dyslexia Institute. Also a full-time speech therapist with audio therapy training, and a full-time occupational and sensory integration therapist.

Games, Options, the Arts: A good outdoor pool in the exquisite gardens at the back of the house – a rarely privileged setting; no sports hall, though good use is made of a new community sports hall just across the road. A cricket field, football and rugby pitches, tennis/basketball/netball courts, an all-weather floodlit five-a-side football and hockey pitch, a good fitness suite in its own house in the old stables. Alternatives to PE for dyspraxics. A recently-appointed Australian head of outdoor activities proving a tremendous boon; the newly-introduced GCSE in PE and Duke of Edinburgh Award Scheme both popular.

We saw enthusiastic DT classes, MDF chairs in mid-construction and an array of imaginative and colourful gardening boxes. Art is excellent: varied in both inspiration and media – super ceramics decorate window sills. The inspirational art teacher is a former senior lecturer from Camberwell College of Art and a recent Tate Modern exhibitionist – a coup for such a small school. Music is popular – many learn individually, principally keyboard, guitar and drums. There is one band (surely scope for more ensemble work here?) but former pupils have gone on to read music at university.

Background and Atmosphere: The main house, formerly called Brickwall, is quite stunning and a bursar's nightmare. The 1617 black and white Jacobean façade, original leaded lights 'n' all, fronts some quite splendid plasterwork ceilings, C17th painted oriental leather wall-coverings, concealed staircases and who knows what behind plus a ghost called Martha – the poor darling ran out with her nightie on fire and expired on the onion patch c1752 (Bursar assures us fire precautions have been improved!). The house came with numerous family portraits, other paintings and furniture and artefacts, the curatorship of which is an abiding feature of the school's management. Fierce English Heritage regulations constrain what can/must be done to alter or preserve and it is easy to forget that this is a school. This is especially true in the glorious Sissinghurst/Knole-style gardens which are a knock-out mix of beautifully planted borders and formal yeweries – maintained by gardener with RHS silver gilt medals. Converted stables house a number of departments. And there are some 'temporary' classrooms – which never are, of course – plus good, newish teaching block with central atrium housing library and display area.

The school is named after the family who owned the place for 300+ years, having made their money in furs and spices. It became, first, a girls' school, then a billet for Canadian forces in WWII, then a boys' boarding school after the war. The last resident Frewen, Admiral Sir John, set up an educational trust in 1972 and decided the existing involvement with dyslexia should become an all-embracing specialism. Frewen believes it was the first specialist dyslexic school. The atmosphere is relaxed, civilized and measured – helped hugely by the spaciousness and peace of this quiet nook where East Sussex peeps into the Garden of England next door. The junior school is housed in an old brick building with sensitive add-ons. Gardens with an adventure playground – gardening club is popular. No good-sized towns for miles – a good place for anyone to de-stress. We heard no raised voices on our visit. Boarding being refurbished but looks pretty good as it is. Year 6s are four to a dorm with en-suites – amps and guitars in rooms. Seniors are two to a pretty spacious en suite room or have a room to themselves. Full boarding offered at no extra cost. Good, wholesome food including salad bar and home grown vegetables, and school works with special diets where necessary. System of three different tablecloths for different types of food – everyone takes something from each to ensure a balanced diet and the school was one of the first to implement fully the last government's nutritional guidelines.

Pastoral Care and Discipline: An established pastoral system but, clearly, 'Anyone can talk to anyone if they want to'. Deputy head deals with most behavioural problems. System of good and bad order marks, leading to yellow and red cards for misdemeanours. Few problems severe enough to reach the head. Excellent 'incentive scheme' devised to tackle problems of litter and minor vandalism highly successful and popular, and school looked very orderly and beautifully-kept throughout – despite massive upkeep challenges. Since Mrs Smith's arrival, one permanent exclusion for theft, none for drugs or bullying. A sense of a whole-school approach here to general welfare – 'Everyone understands the difficulties,' said a teacher and pupils work with maintenance and kitchen staff on work experience – terrific for self-esteem.

Pupils and Parents: Most are local though, in effect, that means a few from south London boroughs, from well into Kent and into Sussex. About 60 per cent supported by LAs and 10 per cent services so a good, homogenous social mix. Girls admitted since 2004 and boarding for girls was a popular introduction in 2009 and already requires an extension. Girls' numbers have doubled in 12 months. Currently about half the senior boys board. Parents mixed in all ways, largely realistic about their children's aspirations, and school works hard to foster links.

Entrance: Infinitely painstaking. All prospective pupils invited for evaluation days and they may stay for as long as a week, participating in classes with all appropriate teachers who then report back. Specialised assessments also made of individual needs and problems – all goes to create fullest possible picture and school will advise if they feel they are not the best place. Ed psych's and current school's reports also important, of course. Now takes children from seven.

Exit: Most to some sort of further education – usually a practical, vocational or art course at a local college. Some straight into work. Given the educational difficulties of some of these young people, an encouraging record: for at least the last six years all have gone on to further education, job training, or employment.

Money Matters: No schols but means-tested bursaries may be made available in cases of need. Bursaries for Service families.

Remarks: Still more to do here in terms of the school's growth and development but the essentials are in place – the main one being a confident, dedicated and enthusiastic staff. With outstanding recent Ofsted and good CReSTed and LA inspections, Frewen provides a privileged setting for its clear-sighted, gentle and encouraging approach. If the school feels you're 'a Frewen child' and takes you, they'll give you of their best.

Friends' School

Linked to Friends Junior School in the Junior section

Mount Pleasant Road, Saffron Walden, Essex, CB11 3EB

• Pupils: 260 boys and girls; 50 boarders • Ages: 11-18 • Size of sixth form: 60 • Quaker • Fees: £13,830-£22,335 pa • Independent

Tel: 01799 525 351
Fax: 01799 523 808
Email: admin@friends.org.uk
Website: www.friends.org.uk

Head: Since 2006, Mr Graham Wigley MA NPQH (late forties). He and wife, Maeve, a teaching assistant, have two sons 'who've just flown the nest'. Read economics at Nottingham, PGCE at Hughes Hall, Cambridge, and an Open University MA in education. Previously academic deputy at Wakefield Girls' High after posts as housemaster and assistant director of studies at Framlingham.

Tremendously smiley and bouncy, but more than a suspicion that Graham, as he's called by the older pupils, is 'steel in kid gloves'. In line with Quaker ethos, he's understanding about the needs of the individual, but has given some areas a timely shake and raised the bar in relation to pupils' work ethic – 'It's not un-Quakerly to set challenges and have high expectations'. Teaches GCSE English ('It's a great way to see youngsters in the middle of the school and helps me appreciate the needs of the staff') and is known to be someone who 'likes to be involved and not just oversee things'. Determined that Friends' 'shouldn't be a well kept secret' and eager to move the school forward, he optimistically proclaims that major development plans, which stalled under the previous regime, will go ahead. Reading, theatre and the odd spot of running fill his spare time.

Academic matters: For a school whose policy is to select as wide a range of pupils as will benefit from its curriculum, it does well. Doesn't worship at the altar of league tables and no policy of withdrawing borderline candidates in order to improve statistics. 'The ethos of the place is to bring out the best and encourage the child,' said a parent. Small classes and three sets in maths and science. Value-added is above average with 88 per cent achieving five or more GCSE A*–C grades and 70 per cent eight or more. Cosy sixth form (most tutor groups only six) attracts those who can't face 'factory farm' sixth form colleges nearby. Tiny groups for A levels (67 per cent A/B grades) and, since Graham Wigley's arrival, several new subjects to broaden provision.

Member of the National Association for Gifted Children; caters for the more able as well as special needs. Three specialists – 'Hugely supportive from day one,' said a mum – in a separate study centre with six assistants for class-based work. Dyslexics predominate but mild Asperger's, impaired hearing and occasionally a statemented pupil can be accommodated – school bumph suggests now a cap on the number with needs in each year group.

Established ESOL department. International students, mainly from Asia and the Pacific Rim, are fully integrated into school life.

Games, Options, the Arts: Given the number of pupils, parents are impressed with how well games fare: 'Really positive teachers realistically boost the children's confidence'. Plenty of team and individual options plus acres of playing fields, hard tennis courts and a 25m swimming pool. D of E for those who're interested.

Inclusive approach in music – 'The subject is brought to life and the kids are encouraged to join in'. Around 70 per cent learn an instrument but practice sessions aren't timetabled. LAMDA exams and flamboyant musicals with casts of all ages. Art department run by an 'approachable lot' appears quite haphazard but work is strong and expressive. The Octopus Art Gallery (in large, interlinking rooms below a disused watertower) provides ample exhibition space for local artists, pupils and the enthusiastic artist in residence.

Background and Atmosphere: Founded in 1702, this well-travelled school began life attached to a workhouse in Clerkenwell. Lifted off to Croydon and, when typhoid threatened, settled on the present site donated by two Friends. Wide barren drive curves up to an imposing Victorian edifice supplemented by several utilitarian additions of various vintages. Eye-catching work by ex-pupils and artists-in-residence cheer the large wood-panelled dining room; otherwise not a penny wasted on vanities. Head acknowledges that some TLC is needed in places and boarding facilities are being upgraded. Sixth formers congregate in a civilized double height space and appreciate the annual dollop of money to spend at Ikea – helps build a sense of shared responsibility. Generally the atmosphere of an unpretentious grammar combined with a small county school with tight community ties. With its well worn, old-fashioned feel it's a place where individuality is cherished, catered for and celebrated.

Pastoral Care and Discipline: Where the Quaker element comes up trumps. Pupils value the feel of the school and the way they treat each other. 'Everyone knows everyone and it's like one big family,' enthused a parent. The emotional and personal well-being of the children is paramount and encouragement abounds. School phobics or those bullied elsewhere thrive here. Recently introduced mentoring scheme for Year 11s (they select a teacher who'll be there for them if things get a bit much in the run-up to exams) and flexi-boarding for day scholars much appreciated by parents and pupils. No uniform for sixth nor, in line with Quaker principles, any prefects – a quartet of senior scholars represent their peers. Banned substances aren't 'condoned'. Where illegal drugs are concerned, students can expect to have their case considered individually, but expulsion or suspension plus future random testing are likely outcomes.

Pupils and Parents: Candidly chatty youngsters who recognise strengths in themselves (and others) and don't see areas of difficulty as weakness. Only a sprinkle of teachers and pupils from a Quaker background, though the governing body is still essentially Quaker. Day pupils come from a 30 mile radius – Cambridge is 20 minutes away – and boarders from London and the Eastern counties. Parents mainly professional and entrepreneurial. Old scholars: BBC Blue Planet producer Martha Holmes, rock star Tom Robinson, Lord Newton of Braintree, educator extraordinaire Naomi Sargant and quite a few of the Rowntree clan.

Entrance: Interview and assessment at 11 – not desperately difficult but needs to be evidence of intellectual potential to achieve C or above at GCSE. 60 per cent from the junior school. Most outside entries to sixth form are currently via EFL.

Exit: Post-16 exodus to sixth form colleges beginning to slow as A level curriculum broadens. Majority who stay for sixth go on to universities ranging from Imperial to Anglia Ruskin.

Money Matters: Scholarships for academic excellence and for art, drama, music and sport in Years 7 and 9. Sixth form scholarships are awarded at the head's discretion (maximum £2000) for those who contribute substantially to school life. Quaker bursaries for Quaker families. Means-tested bursaries are also available throughout the school.

Remarks: Enthusiastic head with the bit between his teeth and tremendously caring staff. Ideal place for the individual or child who would shrink in a high- pressured hothouse.

Gateways School

Linked to Gateways Preparatory School in the Junior section

Harewood, Leeds, West Yorkshire, LS17 9LE

• Pupils: 500 • Ages: 2-18; boys aged 2-7 • Size of sixth form: 60
• Non-denom • Fees: £5,395-£10,335 pa • Independent

Tel: 0113 288 6345
Fax: 0113 288 6148
Email: gateways@gatewayschool.co.uk
Website: www.gatewayschool.co.uk

Headmistress: Since September 2009, Mrs Yvonne Wilkinson BA PGCE NPQH. Started teaching in a comprehensive, then became senior mistress and head of geography at the Algarve International School, Portugal, followed by seven years at Portsmouth Grammar as head of house and girls' PE and games. In 1997, became deputy and then acting head at King Edward VI Five Ways School, followed by headship at Holy Trinity School from 2003. Came to Gateways as a member of the 2006 ISI team and was greatly impressed. Interests are walking, hockey, tennis, squash, narrow-boats and house renovation.

Academic matters: Results getting better year on year (value-added index too) – A*/ A at GCSE: 57 per cent; 42 per cent A* or A at A level; brightest 'identified and pushed' by staff – offered STELLA programme. 100 per cent pass rate in 2010. Girls at opposite ends of the ability range seem to coexist contentedly. English, maths and science outstanding at both levels; art, geography and RS show very well. Some girls entered ahead of or behind their chronological group, thus 'highlighting our policy of treating each pupil as an individual'. Average class size 17, and student:staff ratio 8.7:1. Serious SEN provision: currently three statemented pupils (one-to-one attention), while another 17 get extra support.

Games, Options, the Arts: Games flourish under male director of sports. The usual netball, hockey and swimming, plus some football, and an emphasis on general health; fitness suite. Enthusiastic involvement in drama, art and music (director is an expert on music and liturgy). D of E and outdoor expeditions cater for the adventurous. Green Gateways, LEAP, debating groups and community outreach all well subscribed.

Background and Atmosphere: Founded in 1941, occupies the handsome former dower house of the nearby Harewood estate, midway between Leeds and Harrogate. Plenty of additions since then, much of it good to look at and work in, especially recent science/languages building, sports hall and performing arts centre. An attractive site, if a touch bleak in winter – but these are (mostly) Yorkshire lasses who can cope with a bit of wind and rain. Mrs Wilkinson is a strong advocate of single-sex education, for all the familiar reasons but with a gritty extra dimension – self-esteem in adolescence depends to an extent on experience in risk-taking, public speaking and conflict handling.

Much is made of providing opportunities for these – and preparing girls for a changing world where teamwork and communication skills count for more than old hierarchies – in the school's admirably terse and guff-free prospectus. Fine if it all works in practice; the intention is certainly there. Equally, you find evidence of thought for others, something a good small school can do very well – from 'wraparound care' for the 2–11s (i.e. before and after school provision, charged as an extra) to involvement in the locality (ask about the community outreach programme). A senior girl observed how satisfactory it was that younger pupils weren't altogether separated on the site and that prefects could keep a motherly eye on the little ones as they played. Neat, trad uniform – cherry red blazers and black skirts, with sixth formers in smart business suits. Altogether an impression of quiet, unpushy confidence and girls ready to converse unaffectedly but respectfully with adults.

Pastoral Care and Discipline: As you might expect, a well-conceived pastoral system in which every teacher is involved and just about everyone knows everyone else. Very little problem with the common school sins.

Pupils and Parents: This used to be a faintly posh establishment for girls perceived to be nice but dim and who couldn't make it to boarding school or the grammar schools of Leeds and Bradford. No more – Gateways increasingly figures on the local prep school circuit for parents who choose what it offers in preference to other places. Local primary schools are also taking an interest. Girls come from Leeds' more comfortable suburbs and the affluent arc of villages from its NW to NE; also Harrogate, and further afield from Skipton and York. Parents are typically doctors, lawyers and financiers, also transient foreigners (Danes, Australians, French) drawn to Leeds' booming economy. Plenty of large shiny cars and smart mums in the car park at picking-up time. Prominent OGs: Henrietta Hill, human rights barrister; Frances Segelman, sculptor.

Entrance: Applicants for nursery places spend some time in the school on a carousel of activities; 4–11s assessed. 11+ tested in English, maths and VR and have a 30-minute slot with Mrs Wilkinson, then asked to say what they thought of the process (and each other) – selection 'not on academic criteria alone'. Transfer from prep to main school is automatic; parents warned in good time if this is unrealistic. Relocation at any age considered if the school has room; post-16 candidates need a minimum of five GCSEs at A*–C.

Exit: Majority of girls win places at their first choice university. UK wide – St Andrews to Goldsmiths, London.

Money Matters: New scholarships available for 2010 include academic, music, sport, performing arts, exhibition and Foundation, offering up to 30 per cent fee discount. Means-tested bursaries available and reductions for siblings.

Remarks: An impressive small school on the way up, with strong visionary leadership and a real concern for the all-round development of the individual, but by no means comfy and girly. Increasingly making its mark and respected by big-hitter neighbouring schools. It has suffered little from the amalgamation of Leeds Boys' and Girls' and has the confidence to continue carving out its own niche. Definitely worth a trip into the Yorkshire countryside.

Gems Bolitho School

Linked to Bolitho Junior School (The) in the Junior section

Polwithen Road, Penzance, Cornwall, TR18 4JR

• Pupils: 365 boys and girls; 85 board, 215 day • Ages: infants 4-6, juniors 7-10, middle 11-13, senior 14-16, sixth form 17-18 • Size of sixth form: 35 • C of E • Fees: £5,850-£21,960 pa • Independent

Tel: 01736 363 271
Fax: 01736 330 960
Email: enquiries@bolithoschool.co.uk
Website: www.bolithoschool.co.uk/

Joint heads: Since 2010, Mr Will Ansell (previously deputy head) and Ms Ann Miles. School went into administration at the end of 2009 and was bought by the GEMS group (a well-established schools business with a dozen or so in the UK, including The GEMS Hampshire School qv).

Academic matters: This is the place if you fancy your child learning fluent French. The unique bi-lingual department was introduced in 1997 – starts in Year 4 with eight lessons a week of intensive French, and continues with history and geography – and later RE – taught in French from Year 5 to Year 8. At that point lessons resume in English in preparation for GCSEs. Parents choose whether or not to opt for the bi-lingual department. Some pupils find it too taxing but around half the year generally makes it through to Year 8, taking French GCSE a year early and nearly always getting A* or A. Everyone learns French from reception and can take up German and Spanish in Year 7. Chinese nationals – several pupils from Hong Kong and China – can also take Chinese GCSE, and Latin is available as an extra.

A small, mixed-ability school, with fewer than 35 GCSE candidates a year so far, so results vary according to intake. Generally, however, between 80 and 100 per cent get 5+ A*–C grades. Most pupils take 10 GCSEs, including three sciences and IT; PE and RE are also options. Small class sizes – none are bigger than 15 and most are in single figures – enable pupils to get probably a couple of grades higher than they would have elsewhere, says school. Pupils are grouped by ability for maths, English and science.

Sixth formers study the International Baccalaureate, which involves three subjects at higher and three at standard level, including humanities, maths, science and a language, plus an extended essay, theory of knowledge, and creative, sporting and community activities – particularly appropriate for an international school, as students can study their native language as well as English. All the lower sixth have work experience in Denmark, sponsored by a Danish company. Sixth formers are also working with those from eight other European countries on a three-year project funded by the British Council, producing books and a website for primary schools on life in the nine countries in 1900 and today.

Has a learning support unit, including a dyslexia specialist, but not equipped to deal with severe special needs. International students with little English can join the intensive English section (at an extra £1,100 a term), studying the humanities and languages individually or in very small groups, and other subjects with the rest of the class.

Games, Options, the Arts: Music is a particular strength – around half the pupils learn an instrument. Five rock groups, as well as an orchestra, choirs and other ensembles. Art is growing in popularity; has opened a new art and DT centre. Regular plays and musicals.

Team sports include rugby, football, basketball and rounders. Everyone has a weekly swimming lesson at the nearby public pool and can also go sailing and surfing – the sixth form was, indeed, returning from the beach when we visited. The council has constructed a public sports hall adjacent to the school. Plenty of camping and field trips; many take part in the Duke of Edinburgh Award Scheme and in the Ten Tors expeditions. A school tradition is a whole-school trip to the beach for three days in September, with activities such as writing about the sea, looking for wildlife in rock pools and sketching St Michael's Mount.

Background and Atmosphere: Founded in 1889 by the Woodard Corporation as the Church of England High School for Girls, moved to its present site – a former Bolitho family home with views to the sea – in 1918. It became the School of St Clare in 1928, and was renamed The Bolitho School in 1995, when it was re-launched as a registered charity by a group of parents who saved it from closure and turned it co-educational. Latest incarnation since 2010, and again from the brink of closure, is GEMS Bolitho.

A classic Cornish house with integral chapel surrounded by lawns, shrubbery, trees and playing fields, with separate science labs, music centre, art rooms and boarding houses of varying constructions. Boarders live in comfortable bedrooms of two to four, with house-parents and gap year students to take care of them. Sixth form centre, Clarence House, is a few minutes' walk away.

Pastoral Care and Discipline: In such a small school, disciplinary problems are rare. Students know that drug or alcohol abuse is liable to result in expulsion. School comments that students from Europe are often used to a liberal, laidback environment. 'We try to give them some independence – it's a bridge between school and university. But it's not run like an FE college – there's a clear code of conduct and they know what they can and can't do.'

Pupils and Parents: Local parents range from hoteliers to artists to estate agents. The school runs minibuses from Truro, Falmouth, Helston, St Ives and the Lizard. Many of the boarders are international students – the school takes up to three of each gender from any one country in each year group, mostly from Hong Kong and China, but increasing numbers of German students in the sixth form. An OG is Rosamunde Pilcher, whose novel Coming Home depicts life at the school between the wars.

Entrance: More-or-less first come first served, assuming no great learning problems. 15 join in reception, and one or two more each year throughout the junior school, mostly from local state schools or families moving into the area. Another intake into Year 7, including several international children, who must produce a good report from their previous school; more come into the sixth form. Those coming into the sixth form without good English can take a foundation year before moving on to the full IB diploma.

Exit: Some who do not wish to take the IB move on after GCSEs to local FE colleges or other independent schools. Those leaving the sixth form take courses ranging from medicine, maths, disaster management to librarianship at a range of universities.

Money Matters: 10 per cent sibling and Services bursaries; 50 per cent clergy bursary. Elizabeth Bolitho scholarships of up to 75 per cent attract local state school children into the sixth form.

Remarks: Small, friendly international school in a glorious situation on the Cornish coast, whose bi-lingual section enables pupils to become fluent in French by their teens. The most westerly independent school in the country and the only school in Cornwall to offer the IB.

George Abbot School

Woodruff Avenue, Guildford, Surrey, GU1 1XX

• Pupils: 1,945 boys and girls • Ages: 11-19 • Size of sixth form: 440
• Non-denom • State

Tel: 01483 888 000
Fax: 01483 888 001
Email: office@georgeabbot.surrey.sch.uk
Website: www.georgeabbot.surrey.sch.uk

Head: Since 1999, Mr Daniel C Moloney BEd MA FRSA (fifties), married with two children. Very experienced head – was top man at Feltham Community College before the headship at George Abbot. He is full on, not pretentious nor posh but enthusiastic and proud of his school. In his businesslike office, the school's coat of arms (Latin motto) and a painting of Archbishop George Abbot juxtaposed between an array of students' spectacular artwork and photography, encapsulate the school and the man as the best of both tradition and modernity. Parents recognise his impact on the school, reporting he is 'very dynamic and controls the school well,' and 'he has business management drive, the school has developed hugely in his time'. Parents and children respect his 'personal presence and confidence'. He is all praise for his 'fantastic management team' and feels 'a school this size would take a long time to change'.

Academic matters: A strong academic performer in the state sector. A specialist school for the visual arts since 2001 and took on a second specialism in modern foreign languages in 2008. Ability-setting starts at 11 and is used increasingly in core subjects. The academic focus of the school, reported by parents, pupils and staff alike, encourages hard work and good practice – work must be handed in on time and no lessons missed, tardiness is quickly followed up with a 'pink slip' requiring an explanation from the pupil, a second will trigger a letter home. Pupils feel 'they keep an eye on you'. Progress monitoring is strictly applied with pupils and parents involved in review and target-setting. Action is taken to bring on pupils who are not performing well, everyone matters equally.

Plenty of options, 33 GCSE subjects and 34 at A level. 39 per cent A*/A at GCSE in 2010. Not surprisingly, a huge variety of art and design subjects and photography (very popular at both GCSE and A level), but English, maths and science by far the most popular. Good to see that science and maths are booming, 40 doing further maths A level and over 100 biologists. Average A level attainment is AAB with 65 per cent A*/A/B IN 2010. NVQ options in the sixth form for less academically-able.

Head says, 'SEN children have the highest value-added of any group in the school,' and credits this to a 'dedicated team, including the Director of SEN and a SENCo who came to GA from a specialist school'. Reading, spelling and learning styles are tested on arrival. About 10 per cent of pupils receive help. Withdrawal support in small groups, provision including 'units of sound' programme for dyslexic students and a strong centre for up to 15 visually impaired students. Gifted and talented pupils are catered for with specific summer schools and an 'extensive enrichment programme' overseen by two specialist staff. The 78 children with EAL requirements have provision in liaison with the local authority.

Games, Options, the Arts: As you would expect, arts of all sorts are top notch. Fantastic displays of mature work abound and pupils, not just the artists, really enjoy these surroundings. Past pupils who progress to art foundation courses are all too aware of the advantages GA provided and put their success down to 'plenty of funding, plenty of space and good teaching'. Music also very popular, 'playing an instrument is a very Guildford thing,' a performing arts teacher told us. More than 200 pupils learn an instrument up to grade 8 and perform in school and outside, everything from chamber music to Guilfest (Guildford's answer to Glastonbury).

Sport is the only area of repeated disappointment for parents, though the school says 'a recent independent parent questionnaire indicated a fairly high level of satisfaction with the sport in the school'. Facilities look good, plenty of fields (for a state school), a huge indoor sports hall (doubles up as the Surrey County Cricket Centre, a result of partnership with Surrey County Cricket Club), plus smaller halls and a fully-equipped gym. The school turns out teams for football, rugby, netball, cricket and athletics, pupils display colours on their lapels and honours ties won for sports. Yet many parents feel sport is lacking: 'there's not enough time in the national curriculum,' 'lack of sport is just part of the state system'. Sports are seen as mainly an after-school activity relying on pupils' own commitment.

An enormous list of lunchtime and after-school activities covers curriculum subject catch-ups plus extra arts and sports, some run by sixth formers earning a Sports Leadership award. These are all optional and pupils can get away with doing none. One parent suggested, 'it might be better if they were encouraged to do more'.

Background and Atmosphere: Buildings are institutional blocks but well-maintained and equipped, positively dripping with gleaming new Apple Macs and the like. The huge size of the school is managed by splitting it effectively into four sections; Year 7, 8 and 9, Years 10 and 11 and the sixth form. Each has its own dedicated building and each year group has its own playground. The Year 7s are particularly cosseted: with their form rooms in a dedicated building, they have their own loos and garden as well as playground and they eat lunch separately from the rest.

Sixth form is housed in a brand new building, shared with performing arts. Relationships between teachers and students are more adult at this stage, but it still feels like school and some move to colleges for 'more independence'. Leavers 'graduate' at a student-organised ceremony at local University of Surrey celebrating A levels plus community work, D of E and other awards.

Atmosphere is calm, controlled and ordered. Pupils are expected to work hard and parents are expected to support the ethos. Head's view is 'if you don't like or value uniforms, discipline and manners then don't come here'. The spirit is can-do and friendly, with very little negativity. Pupils and teachers respect each other and 'understand that people are good at different things'. It's egalitarian, provided pupils work hard and to the best of their abilities: 'they are all concerned with how well they are doing and they don't stress the teachers by messing about'.

Our guides on the day frequently mentioned making appointments to see tutors or advisors and booking work sessions in libraries or on computer stations. The whole place is buzzing with a managed, grown-up way of working; pupils need to operate within the systems and take responsibility. It's not particularly parent-friendly but parents put that down to the size of school and increased pupil independence at secondary school. Some parents criticise lack of ready access to teachers. Just one day a year when you get a 5–10 minute slot with each one, otherwise the form tutor is the single point of reference. The school, however, says that parents are advised that they can contact the school and make an appointment at any time throughout the year to meet with a member of teaching staff. 'There is also a clinic held on the first Monday of each month, where parents can attend without an appointment to meet with a member of the senior leadership team.'

Pastoral Care and Discipline: Parents say GA doesn't seem to suffer from discipline problems, 'they deal with the one or two difficult children and don't seem to have the critical mass that makes classes uncontrolled'. Pupils have the same year head through Years 8/9 then 10/11 ensuring they know each other well. Clear, confidential processes to deal with bullying; no-one we spoke to had any experience of bullying though they felt it would be dealt with very quickly. A resident youth worker is available 'to talk to you about anything – home, school, whatever'. One parent, describing how his child had been suspended for involvement with drugs, told us, 'the head was very supportive and helpful through this traumatic time. The school process kicked-in, involving counselling for parent and child.'

Pupils and Parents: GA is located in a middle class area of a largely middle class town. Families here reflect that – the vast majority is motivated and aspirational. The head regards his competition as the independent sector and parents feel they are very similar to families at local independent schools. Even pupils see themselves as more 'like independents' and 'definitely the best state school around'. Sixth formers describe themselves as 'all quite intellectual,' 'motivated and hardworking, few slackers or chavs,' 'pupils all rub along and respect each other'. The head says that '50 per cent of the local secondary heads' children are pupils at GA'.

Entrance: As a county community school, admissions are dealt with by the LA. Like all Guildford maintained schools it is heavily over-subscribed, almost 800 applicants for 300 places. In practice about 50 per cent of places are taken by siblings, statemented and looked after children, who all automatically get in. Highly complex state system called 'equal preference' whereby parents nominate three schools of their choice in order of preference; if they don't fulfil criteria for first choice, it goes on to second and so on. Parents are confused and anxious about the whole system and appeals are a law unto themselves. Mr Moloney says 'if you live in the immediate area you're likely to get in,' and he optimistically tells parents wherever they live that if they feel GA is the school for them then apply. Main feeders Boxgrove, Bushy Hill, Burpham, and Holy Trinity are all linked and are partners in community arts and the local extended school federation.

Selective sixth form entry, stated requirements five A–C GCSE minimum but, in practice, much more – five A*s plus other subject specific requirements depending on A level choices. 25/30 join sixth form from outside – popular with private school pupils (looking for a piece of real life before university?), but it operates very much as a school rather than a sixth form or FE college.

Exit: One third leave at 16 – most for local FE or sixth form colleges, some to work. After sixth form, vast majority go on to university, huge range of courses and locations. Handful to Oxbridge.

Money Matters: Attracts funding as a successful school and applies for whatever is available, running on a budget of over £10 million. Outstanding fund-raising by PTA e.g. towards new buildings. International links mean many opportunities for trips abroad which parents pay for, though there are funds to ensure no-one is excluded.

Remarks: Large, successful comprehensive in affluent area providing a modern, ICT-led curriculum which works for all sorts – the bright and the less so. Particularly suitable for arty, media interested children and those who sit comfortably with the school procedures and systems. Very real option for the sixth form for cash-strapped parents of private school children.

George Heriot's School

Linked to George Heriots Junior School in the Junior section

Lauriston Place, Edinburgh, Edinburgh, EH3 9EQ

• Pupils: 1,565 boys and girls, plus 30 in nursery • Ages: 11-18 • Size of sixth form: 320 • Non-denom • Fees: £6,288-£9,434 pa • Independent

Tel: 0131 229 7263
Fax: 0131 229 6363
Email: admissions@george-heriots.com
Website: www.george-heriots.com

Head: Since 1998, Mr Alistair Hector MA (fiftyish), who was educated at Edinburgh Academy, read modern languages at St Andrews and came to Heriot's from Warwick School, where he was deputy head. Before that he taught at King Edward's School. Started his career at Merchiston, after a spell in Germany teaching EFL. Married, one of his children currently attends the school. Pleased to be back in Scotland and quite liked taking over mid-way through the session – 'You don't have to worry about the timetable and you've got a couple of terms to settle in'. He is head of the whole school. No longer has a timetabled class to teach but pops in and does the 'odd bit of supply teaching for PSHE'; rather misses the daily contact – 'Pupils are the core of what the school does'.

Academic matters: Not easy to extract detailed examination results (by subject by grade) – so keep asking. Solid results at all levels. Maximum class size 26, 'but usually much less'. Classes streamed early, setted for maths at nine; also for English from 11. Steeped in 'Euro-awareness', a sort of Euro-starter course at eight, with either French, German or Spanish at 10. A second language can be taken at 13. Strong sciences across the board but actually no particular bias. Eight Standard Grades the norm; Latin available to Standard and classical civilisation to Higher level is surprisingly popular.

Finely-tuned support for learning but limited in the amount of help they can give, will not take children with a formal statement of needs except in 'exceptional circumstances', but any child with a suspected problem is seen by the support for learning department, which then swings into action. Both withdrawn and team teaching on hand, either individual or in small groups. School will bear the cost of extra lessons and may, in certain circumstances, cover the cost of an outside educational psychologist – they have their own, who is free. Can cope with ADD/ADHD up to a certain degree, Ritalin is not an issue – 'We would consult with parents to see how their children might be best served'. EFL lessons are charged for. Computers all over the shop, loads of new suites.

Games, Options, the Arts: This is a games school. Outstanding rugby and cricket and girls' hockey very powerful; games played at Goldenacre, along with all the other Edinburgh schools mafia; FPs use the pitches too. Pupils bused across Edinburgh, cross-country running and rowing are favourite alternative sports – the school has a boat house on the canal. Badminton and extracurricular football are all in the frame, plus fencing and very good swimming – a small training pool on the (very cramped) site, but basically they use the baths at Warrender. Drama now timetabled and taken at both Standard and Higher levels. New head of music recently appointed, which has done wonders for this department – choirs as well as a variety of chamber and other orchestras. Art streaking ahead, and photography on offer but not to exam level. Sixth year does voluntary service, working in the nursery, helping with lower primary pupils and outside placements, e.g. the outpatients at the Astley Ainslie.

Background and Atmosphere: George Heriot, jeweller to King James the VI (and I), who had started business life in a booth by St Giles, left the princely sum of £23,625 'for the building of a hospital' (i.e. a charity school) on a 'site at the foot of Gray's Close', for boys whose fathers had died. Fabulous ogee curved-roofed towers, the place was first inhabited by Cromwell in 1650 and, whilst principally designed by William Wallace, the magical inner-city school can boast of almost every important 17th century Scottish architect – finishing with the court favourite, Robert Mylne. Claims to be the longest-inhabited school in Scotland. Magnificent Pugin chapel revamped by James Gillespie Graham in 1837; pupils still sit on backless benches. A rather snazzy library in the lower half of a hall has been disastrously (school rejects this epithet – not surprisingly) split in two to provide a concert hall above.

While all schools are perennially short on space, this is the most blatant piece of architectural sacrilege we have ever come across.

Founders day celebrated with 'buskins' (garlands) round the founder's statue on June Day. The foundation was feudal superior of great tracts of Edinburgh, and has close links with Donaldson's hospital for the deaf (the school's after-school club is held there daily). The hospital became a school in 1886, changed its name and the 180 foundationers were joined by paying pupils, but the 180 registration marks are still visible in the quadrangle. Boarding was phased out in 1902 and girls admitted in 1979; became fully independent in 1985. FPs are known as Herioters. Fantastic views of Edinburgh Castle but the site is cramped; hence has recently purchased a site from the Edinburgh College of Art and planning permission has just been granted for a new sports centre. A new sixth year common room and café – plans for the site include expansion of the music facilities. Uniform for all, different ties for prefects and sixth. Trips all over the shop in every discipline.

Pastoral Care and Discipline: Code of conduct equals school's rules, which parents and pupils have to sign, based on 'personal safety, safety for others and respect for others, property and the environment'. Ladder of sanctions. Good PSHE team who are proactive in reducing tension, both sides must face up to an issue. Persistent misbehaviour and not responding = out; detentions and discussions with parents more normal. Occasional suspensions, no real problems with drugs, alcohol and cigarettes but head is on the ball – 'Can honestly say there have been no expulsions because of drugs in my time here'. Concern if school work suffers, no random drugs tests. Church of Scotland chaplain; school uses Grey Friars Kirk (of Bobby fame) for services.

Pupils and Parents: Sturdy middle class lot, Edinburgh-average ethic. Thriving parents' association.

Entrance: Tests (English, maths, VRQ) at primary and senior level, including from own junior school; predicted grades for pupils joining post-Standard Grades.

Exit: Regularly four or five to Oxbridge – runs induction weekends down to Oxbridge along with St Mary's Music School to familiarise pupils with the collegiate system, otherwise mostly to Scottish universities. Some leave after Standard Grades either to employment or further education elsewhere.

Money Matters: Felt the loss of assisted places keenly but is pretty well back up to speed. Foundation still provides 100 per cent bursary for 'children of primary or secondary school age, who are resident in Edinburgh or the Lothians, whose father has died and whose mother might not otherwise afford the cost of private education'. Raft of other bursaries and scholarships, will keep children in place during financial crisis – but rather depends on child for how long.

Remarks: Thunderingly good inner-city school in a spectacular position, doing what it does do well.

George Watson's College

Linked to George Watson's College Junior School in the Junior section

67-71 Colinton Road, Edinburgh, EH10 5EG

• Pupils: 2,335 (boy:girl ratio 53:47) • Ages: 12-18 • Size of sixth form: 450 • Non-denom • Fees: Nursery £3,654-£6,390; Junior £6,078-£7,326; Senior £9,426 pa • Independent

Tel: 0131 446 6000
Fax: 0131 446 6090
Email: admissions@gwc.org.uk
Website: www.gwc.org.uk

Principal: Since 2001, Mr Gareth Edwards MA, (fifties), a Welshman, he claims a 'keen affinity with the Celts'. Educated at Tudor Grange Grammar, Solihull; read classics at Exeter, Oxford, taught at King Edward VIth Edgbaston, before becoming head of department at Bolton Boys, and vice principal of Newcastle-under-Lyme School. He was previously rector at Morrison's Academy in Crieff. Married, with one daughter, he refuses to meet with this editor, having taken a scunner to our previous comments; so alas we are still unable to report on the twinkle in his eye or his taste in ties. A slow-speaking, deep-thinking head, he has all the Welsh charm and a quiet charisma. He is also very giggly, though he was considerably offended by this comment saying that 'a reputable publication such as ours would not pass such personal comments'. Little does he know. Highly respected in the Edinburgh education world, we hear of nothing but 'how sound he is' (and how lovely and giggly). He runs this huge triumvirate with Mrs Heather Wilson, head of senior school and Mrs Linda Fleming, head of junior school.

Academic matters: One of Scotland's most successful schools; currently follows both the Scottish and English system post Standard grades, but is moving towards incorporating IB into the educational mix. Pupils will have that option from August 2011, and whilst Scotland is embracing the IB all over in dribs and drabs, Watson's will be (currently) the only school to offer the SQA/IB combo. We await the requested individual results by grade and subject with interest. The web site has the usual gobbledegook about 'the average number of Highers sat by S5 candidates was 4.51, a pleasing increase on last year's figure of 4.32': which is fine if you like pie charts, but not that helpful if you want to find out how strong the maths dept is. Max class size 25 but 20 (as ever) for practical subjects.

School spear-headed the dyslexia (et al) rescue movement in Scotland with the redoubtable Cabin: problems often picked up in junior school 'by test on observation, as early as pos' and pupils monitored throughout their time at school. Heads of special needs in both junior and senior schools, plus assistants in class (usually in junior school) and either one-to-one or group sessions. Drop-in centre, caters for the brightest as well as those who need oodles of help, or just a short sharp explanation with some bothersome subject. No charge. One of a few schools to teach study skills throughout the school; 'literacy skills' on offer for those who need it, though pupils may have 'to drop perhaps one subject to allow a literacy skills programme and supported study, while reducing the overall curricular load'. Sixth formers (with 'good higher passes') help out, they also scribe. Help too, from scores of parent volunteers who – amongst other activities – record text onto tapes. Surprising that there is no automatic assessment for all at the start of their time in the school. Help available ESOL for non native English speakers.

Careers advice starts from 15 upwards beginning with Morrisby testing so that pupils can make informed choices when deciding on five or six subjects from the choice of 26. (This editor's personal experience of Morrisby is that it is a waste of dosh – but horses for courses). Extension modules and additional subjects available for the last year. Trad langs French, German, Spanish and Italian plus huge Mandarin following: Russian if required (but no automatic 'catering' for ethnic langs). Mass of native speakers and exchanges. Classics and classical civilisation, media studies a sixth form option. Networked ICT dept and impressive-looking labs, school hot on sciences but not human biology. Frequent 'inset' and personal development training for all staff throughout the school.

Games, Options, the Arts: Renowned for their successes on the rugby field. Two sports halls now fully operational with The Galleon sports club open to the general public. Strong rowing team. Both senior and junior World Pipe and Drum Champions. Clubs and societies galore, plethora of choice: at the last count close to 80, including 20 sports clubs, four orchestras, three bands, musical ensembles and several choirs, plus organised games, and strong drama. Something for everyone. Many school trips, at home and abroad. Popular third year 12-day excursion backpacking which tests staff as well as pupils. Amazing art (students sit English board for this).

Background and Atmosphere: George Watson, merchant and financier, left a legacy of 12 grand in 1723 to provide 'post-primary boarding education' to the 'children and grandchildren of decayed Merchants of Edinburgh and of the Ministers of the Old Church thereof' with a preference for those with the surname Davidson or Watson. School finally opened in 1741, operating under the aegis of the Merchant Company until the mid 1980s, having moved to current site in 1932 (after a period in the wilderness) and amalgamating with George Watson's Ladies College in 1974. Splendid and impressive façade: listed building with amazing amount of oak inside, broad corridors, a sweeping driveway and immaculate lawn (aka games pitch). Vast 50-acre campus includes variety of pitches, plus art, junior and nursery schools in a somewhat random selection of architecture. Huge dining hall, school operates a swipe card system for pupils from P4 up, parents can top these up on-line via their credit cards; school provides packed lunches or hot/cold menu which is published on their website, though we couldn't find it. Indeed the web site needs a radical overhaul, we never did manage to download the prospectus: we are told Watson's has two zinging games sheds – aka sports halls – but you would never guess it from the on-line blurb.

Pastoral Care and Discipline: Ethos of respect for others. Well-tried system in place to manage such a large school, with two year heads following pupils all the way through the school. First year pupils keep the same form teacher for the first two years; the next three years follow suit and pupils then choose their tutor.

Sixth formers are actively involved throughout the school. Strong anti-bullying policy, parents immediately informed and consulted if child is involved and, apparently, impressed by the help given in difficult situations. Seven point school charter devised by pupils. Detentions plentiful but expulsion rare. Regular training for specialist guidance staff who help with listening and advising.

Pupils and Parents: Popular (in the trad sense of the word) Edinbourgeoisie, wannabes and incomers. The pupils whom we meet are bright and bubbly, claim never to be bored. Very much a local school but some travel quite a distance. Organised buses from East, Mid and West Lothian. Some boarders housed off campus.

OBs and OGs include Sir David Steel (The Right Hon Lord Steel of Aikwood), Sir Malcolm Rifkind, Chris Hoy, Gavin and Scott Hastings, former Scottish rugby internationals, Sheena McDonald and Martha Kearney, plus Sir Basil Spence, Rebecca West, Martin Bell and Sir Eric Anderson, previously provost of Eton.

Organised buses from East, Mid and West Lothian.

Entrance: At 12 and upwards where vacancies arise by selection taking maths, English and VR papers along with interview. Waiting lists at some stages. Fresh blood post Standard grades (more come than leave).

Exit: 90 per cent plus stay on after Highers for further studies. 90 per cent plus go on to higher education. 80 per cent to Scottish universities, regular five per cent to Oxbridge.

Money Matters: George Watson's Family Foundation: primarily for 10/11 year olds, though awards available in junior school and current pupils 'may apply for short-term help at any stage'. Means-tested. Will keep a pupil to the next public exam in extenuating circs, plus extra help for those with a 'recognised learning disability' A range of up to 11 academic and two music scholarships each year: 25 per cent. Sports bursaries, Enablement Fund and part of Ogden Trust Science Scholarship Scheme. Numerous short-term or long-term bursaries for those in need; with assistance for more than 120 pupils. In 1997 the school's own foundation was established to further the original Watson credo and has recently funded the new music school extension, the GWC Centre for Sport and a lift for disabled students. Fees can be paid monthly by direct debit.

Remarks: Deconstructed former Merchant school: distinguished and deserved reputation. Mega campus, communication with parents and pupils said to be strong. Every pupil treated as an individual.

Giggleswick School

Linked to Giggleswick Junior School in the Junior section

Giggleswick, Settle, North Yorkshire, BD24 0DE

• Pupils: 390 boys and girls (235 board, 155 day) • Ages: 11-18
• Size of sixth form: 155 • C of E • Fees: Boarding £15,615-£25,950; Day £6,105-£17,760 pa • Independent

Tel: 01729 893 000
Fax: 01729 893 150
Email: enquiries@giggleswick.org.uk
Website: www.giggleswick.org.uk

Head: Since 2001, Mr Geoffrey Boult BA. Read geography at Durham University. Previously a housemaster at St Edward's, Oxford. Married to Katie, four daughters. A friendly, good-humoured, youthful figure, well-liked and respected by pupils. Has developed a love of life in the north; appreciates the straightforwardness of northerners who 'tell it like it is'. A committed Christian and keen sportsman, once a county hockey player, now enjoys coaching games and indulging his passion for golf. Has improved academic results through emphasis on individual target setting, blends academic performance with the breadth of opportunities that Giggleswick offers.

Academic matters: Hard working pupils, confident but not arrogant; good solid staff, blend of age and experience. School selective, but not greatly so, good value added. Separate and combined sciences offered, 94 per cent A* to C pass rate at GCSE (100 per cent in single sciences) and new generation of enthusiastic science teachers. Sets for English, French, maths, science. A good selection of A level courses offered – results have improved significantly over the last few years, due to an increased emphasis on target setting and value added. Those wanting to pursue vocational courses are directed elsewhere at 16. 100 per cent pass rate at A level in 2009. No massaging of results here – if you study for a subject you sit the exam. 'Failure not necessarily a bad thing,' says the head. 'Sometimes it can provide a much needed wake-up call.'

Full time special educational needs co-ordinator and successful buddy system where older children with experience of a learning difficulty mentor younger ones. EFL provided (two to four lessons a week), one to one, in study periods, but anyone arriving from abroad must have a basic level of English. Class sizes 22 maximum, 4–12 for A level. Lots of computers, including some in each boarding house; every pupil has email and a computer link in their study bedroom.

Games, Options, the Arts: Keen drama started by Russell Harty – several OGs and some pupils active in the profession, but luvvies and their tantrums not tolerated. The Richard Whiteley Theatre, named after the late TV presenter, who was an old boy and governor, was opened in 2010. Art and design taken seriously – impressively ambitious design work in particular. Public speaking encouraged. A third of pupils learn an instrument (some play professionally), glorious chapel choir and lots of bands regularly tour home and abroad.

Sport keen – traditionally cross-country and rugby; international level coaching over the past few years has led to success in hockey, rugby, cricket and athletics. Seven hard and three grass courts, together with the opportunity to train in Portugal, ensure continued popularity of tennis.

Oozing with outward-bound opportunities including Duke of Edinburgh and CCF (compulsory in Year 10) but plenty of other activities: conservation projects and all the usual opportunities. Exchanges with schools in France and Spain, tours, e.g. sports to Kenya, New Zealand, Grenada, South Africa, cultural trips to Russia and Italy and historians to the WW1 battlefields. Holiday trips charged as extras but those identified as curriculum trips included in the fees.

Background and Atmosphere: Set in the western margins of the magnificent Yorkshire dales beneath an imposing limestone escarpment, 60 minutes' drive north of Manchester. Founded in 1512, moved to present site in 1869. Attractive buildings overlook Giggleswick Village beneath the fabulously restored chapel, complete with landmark copper dome well worth the walk up the steep hill (bring your crampons). Large development plan continues and has included wonderful new library with IT suite and internet café (a popular venue for nightly prep). Other recent additions include floodlit all-weather pitch, two new sports halls and a dining hall (cafeteria system, separate sittings, lots of choice). Girls' quarters in better decorative order than boys', where a lick of paint and the odd new carpet wouldn't go amiss (school assures us that renovation has occurred since our visit). Pupils welcome to decorate their own study bedrooms – most do but some communal areas impersonal. A full boarding school, exeats only one weekend out of three. Happy, relaxed but purposeful atmosphere: James Herriot meets Wainwright. Splendid sixth form centre with bar – alcohol allowed at weekends but consumption strictly monitored.

Pastoral Care and Discipline: Seven houses – four boys', two girls', one junior (Years 7 and 8) mix of boarding and day. Small dorms for Years 7 and 8, study bedrooms for Years 9 and up, shared until Year 11 (boys) or sixth form (girls). Senior house staff tutor Years 7–10, with pupils choosing their tutors in Year 11. Pastoral care is supported by the medical centre, school doctor, professional counsellors and chaplain. Sniffer dogs brought in termly for drugs checks and compulsory drugs testing is used on known and suspected offenders. Anyone caught supplying faces immediate expulsion. Smokers required to attend cessation clinics. Boys and girls are allowed to visit each others' houses but permission must be sought to move away from public areas. Behaviour between sexes 'should not cause embarrassment to anyone'. Staff vigilant for anorexia and similar – system in place to check on pupils suspected of skipping meals, including height/weight monitoring and meal attendance cards. Chapel an integral and important part of the school but faith more important than denomination.

Pupils and Parents: 65 per cent board, the rest are local children from a large catchment area; more boys (62 per cent) than girls, mid-range academically. School fully co-ed since 1983. Fifteen per cent foreign, 15 per cent expats and Services – popular with all these. Suits those who are team players, keen on the outdoors and enjoy the varieties of life. Not for city types, loners or those who mind getting wet. Parents in business and the professions. OGs: James

Agate, Richard Whiteley, William Gaunt, Sarah Fox. OG society well established on the internet.

Entrance: Not a great problem – no formal entrance tests in the Junior School. At 11 Giggleswick entrance exam, at 13 normally CE together with interview and previous school's report. Entrance into sixth form is by a minimum of five GCSEs at B grade – around 35 new sixth form entrants per year. Giggleswick Junior School, the main feeder for Giggleswick, is situated in the same grounds in a newly refurbished teaching building.

Exit: Five or so to Oxbridge, others principally to a wide spread of universities or art foundation courses. 20 per cent do a gap year.

Money Matters: 30ish scholarships a year, including all-rounder, art, music, and locals, ranging in value from 10 per cent for an exhibition to 50 per cent for a top scholarship award; bursaries including Services available. School in good shape financially owing to large gifts from OG Norman Sharpe and more recently Graham Watson (late governor).

Remarks: Friendly, character-building co-ed boarding school serving the locals and the English community abroad. Extremely strong links with business reflected in curriculum and attitudes through the school. Doing a good job for a broad intake in this relatively isolated area. A useful school for the less academic pupil, those who don't know what to do next or the multi-talented who want to pursue a diverse range of interests.

The Glasgow Academy

Linked to Glasgow Academy Atholl (The) in the Junior section

Linked to Glasgow Academy Preparatory School (The) in the Junior section

Linked to Glasgow Academy Dairsie (The) in the Junior section

Colebrooke Street, Glasgow, Glasgow, G12 8HE

- Pupils: 680 boys, 600 girls; (including prep schools, see below)
- Ages: 3-18 • Size of sixth form: 200 • Non-denom
- Fees: £6,690-£9,645 pa • Independent

Tel: 0141 334 8558
Fax: 0141 337 3473
Email: exrel@tga.org.uk
Website: www.theglasgowacademy.org.uk

Rector: Since 2005, Mr Peter Brodie MA, PGCE (early fifties) who was educated at Abingdon and did his master's in English at St John's, Oxford, followed by a PGCE at Oxford and a (later) master's in education management (part time) at Canterbury Christ Church University College ('a good intellectual training exercise'). Chalk is in the blood – his father was a headmaster and his mother taught PE. Having started his teaching career in a split-site comprehensive school, he came to Glasgow Academy from King's, Canterbury, where he was press officer, having risen via the ranks from head of English and housemaster, and more recently 'held public relations responsibilities and was arts festival manager'. Unmarried, he also 'produced numerous plays' and organised a wide range of activities and events, from debating to Duke of Edinburgh Award training.

Bubbly, enthusiastic, fun; keen on teaching with the 'wow' factor and incredibly efficient – he is the only head who, when faced with a barrage of questions to which he did not instantly know the answer, left detailed answers for us to collect with the rest of the bumf from his office. Impressive. He is passionate about 'encouraging children to make the most of the opportunities school can provide,' and believes strongly that 'a culture of high expectations combined with good pastoral care helps children grow in confidence and achievement'.

The rector has done much to reinforce the house system, appointing 12 new members of staff plus eight new heads of houses – 'good mix in staff room'. Potty about postcards, he had 2000-odd printed from some of the best of the art work and delights in sending pupils cards to congratulate them on any success, e.g. a good bit of art, an interesting essay, debating victories, or, when we visited, congratulating the whole of the girls' hockey team on being Scottish champions for the third year running. Keen on bonding – he took the whole of the sixth form off to the Lake District for a weekend camp before he arrived at the school and is (said our moles as well as our guides), 'a good egg'. Sees every pupil each year with 'three bits of work, selected by themselves'. Seriously successful appointment, which is all the more laudable as Mr Brodie was appointed in the midst of the recent spat of educational sectarianism in the south side of Glasgow.

Academic matters: School follows Scottish system, all singing and dancing, with fabulous computer labs, science labs and lots of ancillary add-ons (as you might expect with the amount of cash they got from selling the grounds of Westbourne for upmarket housing). Maximum class size 24, 20 and down for practical subjects: average 19 with five parallel. Sciences, computing studies, geography and maths strong at Standard Grade, Highers and Advanced Highers, as is English; Latin on offer – with a commendable take-up (and impressive results in 2009 with four As out of five at Advanced Higher level), Greek up to Higher level. French and Spanish in modern language labs. Occasional glitch but strong results overall. Links with both Glasgow and Strathclyde Universities: psychology at the former and Mandarin the latter, and a vast and complex sixth form guide details both academic and ancillary courses available, including SCOTCAT credits. Fabulous new computer suites all over; school is wireless and pupils can email queries and prep to staff.

New childcare qualification for sixth formers who can take the early education and childcare SQA Intermediate 2, which includes the REHIS certificate in food hygiene; home economics also on offer (and very popular at sixth form level as part of the life skills course) – this editor and the Rector were offered an amazing selection of sausage rolls, including one with caramelized topping (interesting combination).

Good SEN pickup. Psychological and spatial memory and reasoning for all from P1 plus other year groups assessed on a rolling basis. Remedial help on hand for the lesser and brighter child, laptops in evidence and extra help in exams. No problems with children with ADHD, support for learning much in evidence, learning support based in purpose-designed refurbished accommodation with trained support staff in both senior and prep; support is mainly lesson based with teaching assistants, though child will be withdrawn either for one-to-one or small groups if necessary. Drop-in clinics manned by different people each day, no shame in popping in for a quick explanation; good buddy system with senior pupils helping out where necessary (slightly more girl monitors as far as the three Rs are concerned). Good dissemination of information: all staff are aware of individual teaching strategies for those on the help register. No extra charge for remedial lessons. No problems for the visually challenged – extra large print et al and British Sign Language on the syllabus from next year. Currently one deaf pupil in the (junior) school; masses of BSL hype in the media lately – whether this academic exercise has much real use is open to debate.

Games, Options, the Arts: Serious rugby school (more than 90 FPs have won their Scotland caps). Four playing field areas with Astroturf, floodlight, some hundreds of metres apart from each other at Anniesland (the home of all Glasgow Academy playing fields) plus an all-weather pitch on site in the middle of the campus. Hockey, cricket, footie, athletics, rowing as well as tennis. Recently acquired extra ground from Jordanhill – bought a bit and share a bit. Games are important here – zillions of inter-house competitions as well as inter-school matches.

Masses of inter-house activities at lunchtime. Outstanding pipeband, with lots of exposure – duty band at Murrayfield for a Scotland England match, Kelvinhall etc. CCF non-compulsory but still popular. D of E – trillions of golds. Trips almost everywhere, in every dimension, art as well as skiing: Greenland last summer – to collect live samples of the Greenlandic seed bug (aka Nysius groenlandicus since you ask) with practice of living in snowholes in Glencoe and lessons on how to handle a polar bear featuring largely in the build-up. Skiing at Heavenly in California at Easter, music in Belgium, Italy and New York, rugby and hockey in South Africa, hockey in The Netherlands and geography in Iceland. Language trips to all over. The rector feels a real need to get the Glasgow young out of their cosy environment and see the big bad world outside.

Music is good and strong with choirs for all, as well as orchestra, string, windband and various ensembles, lunchtime concerts back on form and dynamic head of music spearheading musical resurgence – over 500 individual music lessons a week, from harp to clarsach. Twenty-three visiting music staff. Recorder for all aged eight and nine plus keyboard at 10 and 11 (as well as drums, guitar and base guitar). Tranches of exam successes and oodles of productions, often, as in the week before our visit, entirely pupil-led – *The Odd Couple* ('the vice captain of rugby also directs plays'). Pre-empted Andrew Lloyd Webber with a pupil-led (again) production of *The Sound of Music.*

Spectacular art and stunning artroom at the top of the recently converted terrace house in Colebrooke Terrace (now known as Kelvinbridge), dark room, fabric and almost every conceivable discipline. Strong follow-through to art schools all over. Some of the most imaginative school art we have seen, with a fantabulous iron man (mini iron man in window too) and some particularly impressive portraits (artist already operates her own – successful – website). Popular design technology, with a huge number of girls participating, though, as our guide pointed out, this may have something to do with the dishy member of staff in charge (still)!

Background and Atmosphere: School founded as a limited company in 1845 and re-constituted as a memorial to the 327 staff and pupils killed, post the First World War; merged with the girls' school, Westbourne School for Girls, in 1991. Based on the banks of the River Kelvin, with the Glasgow underground system but a hundred yards away, and the western end of the M8 a busy quarter of a mile distant, the handsome Glasgow sandstone main building is surrounded by ancillary music, humanities and science blocks with the random play areas scattered about (and ancillary parking for staff and visiting editors). The hub of school is The Well, or library (full time librarian, naturally), where children can come and study in their free periods, computer linked, it hummed during our visit. Any pupil can ask for any book or any DVD and it is ordered.

School now owns the whole of the lovely Victorian Colebrooke Terrace, which is shut off from the general public with fancy iron gates. The most northerly of these houses have recently been demolished (historic Scotland apparently no problem) and a fantastic six million pound phoenix of a prep school curves round the banks of the River Kelvin. In 2008 the rest of the school expanded into the void left by the prep. Total gain 19 new classrooms. New buildings are planned for site bought opposite the school.

Fifty minute lunch break is filled with inter-house and club activities and only S6 pupils permitted to leave school grounds. Good assembly (Cargill Hall), dining hall complex – looking a trifle tired, even taking into account the detritus of the previous week's production. The Cargill Hall and its ancillary dining area are let out for functions – vending machines (carefully controlled) and good buffet catering, which pupils say is much improved. Pupils have healthy eating card which clocks up goody grub. When pupils get enough points they can claim an ipod; meantime parents can check up on exactly what their little darlings have been eating. All pupils wear uniform and an excellent sixth form chill-out area on two floors in an area which used to be the old 'writing room'. Serious debating – the Gavel Club; FPs come back for the smack. Terrific booklet of information for parents and smashing Glasgow Academy planner with wizard cheats' guide to maths and literacy in the back.

Pastoral Care and Discipline: All pupils join one of four houses and much of the extra-curricular activity is organised through these. Each house has a male and female head, plus PSE and anti-bullying procedure in progress, popular points system, including debating and music. Pupils have their own tutors, two per house per annum, each has 11 or 12 tutees, also heads of year. Good pastoral structure in place and it works. The occasional theft – 'Yes, we're into sin,' said the Rector, no recent problems. Suggestion box – mainly used by first two years senior school, and dealt with by the deputy rector. Positive behaviour committee. School council. Form tutors for all – each has 10 to 12 pupils who stay with them throughout school; the aim is for each tutor to see each tutee for 10 minutes at the start of every day. Sixth form get a wide range of lectures from a variety of speakers, including police and fire brigade. No recent drugs scares. God equals total exposure from a raft of ministerial faiths – pupils actively encouraged to contribute to themes for the week.

Pupils and Parents: The usual Glasgow mafia; excellent links with the west and M8 conurbations, good PTA, basically sound middle class, plus ancillary huge scholarships for the less financially able. Loads of FPs' children, plus first time buyers. Buses from further afield. Previous FPs: Sir Angus Grossart, Niall Ferguson, Sir Jeremy Isaacs, Lord Vallance, Darius, Sir James Barrie, Donald Dewar.

Entrance: Largely automatic from junior schools, school's own test. Some incomers at sixth form level, usual requirement of Grade 1 at Standard for courses to be studied at Higher level. But pupils can arrive at any time assuming space available, though waiting lists at some stages.

Exit: Trickle post Higher, i.e. at S5, otherwise most stay till S6, usually taking Advanced Highers or adding to their existing portfolio. 96 per cent plus to universities, most to Scottish ones, with a steady stream south of the border; oodles of medics, three or four regularly to Oxbridge. Law a popular subject, ditto business and engineering.

Money Matters: The school has worked hard to get comprehensive bursary scheme in place – the hope that is that 'financial need should never prevent anyone'. Priority given to all-rounders rather than nerds. Help often available for the financially challenged to go on trips. Will certainly keep pupils to next available exam stage.

Remarks: A good solid school, with an exciting and dynamic head moving seamlessly into the 21st century. Should not be overlooked under any circumstances.

Glenalmond College

Glenalmond, Perth, Perth, PH1 3RY

• Pupils: 400 pupils, of whom 86 per cent board; co-ed 60/40 boys/girls (230 boys, 165 girls); all board except 60. • Ages: 12-18 • Size of sixth form: 180 • Ecumenical within an Episcopalian foundation • Fees: Boarding: Senior £26,244, Junior £19,674; Day: Senior £17,898, Junior £13,422 pa • Independent

Tel: 01738 842 056
Fax: 01738 842063
Email: registrar@glenalmondcollege.co.uk
Website: www.glenalmondcollege.co.uk

Warden: Since 2003, Mr Gordon Woods MA (Oxon) PGCE, (fifties), educated at Durham where he was head boy. Previously taught at Shrewsbury, where he was housemaster, head of geography and ultimately second master. A keen stroke (with the winning Oxford lightweight crew in 1976 and 1977), he has mellowed in true Glenalmond tradition and, with his wife, Emma, has settled into Perthshire. Mrs Woods, who previously worked in the wine trade, runs 'survival cookery' classes for 17 and 18 year olds, plus formal wine tasting for the upper sixth. Their children are at Edinburgh and Leeds universities (son a medic, daughter studying history of art); the Warden anticipates fronting Glenalmond for 'at least the next six years', by which time both offspring should have graduated and retirement will loom.

A human geographer, he is 'passionate about geography and the part that the subject can play on the way the other half lives ... You must always look outwards.' No longer teaches but has a girl tutor group. Breakfast with new pupils still on the agenda plus lunches with the lower sixth. Charming and articulate, he is pleased with the school roll, to the extent that he was quite relaxed about the recent lamentable turnout at the Isis marketing show in Edinburgh and no, he 'didn't think they needed to go to the big one in London'. Believes 'Glenalmond needs to be outward-looking and not just outward-bound, to retain a strong sense of its own past but to be modern in its approach to pupils and parents. Seeing boys and girls through the teenage years has to be a three way partnership – pupils, parents and the school.' Wishlist would include a medical and well-being centre, another girls' house, better sports facilities and a revamped theatre.

Academic matters: School follows the English system only. An astonishing 24 subjects on offer at A level, including ancient history (four candidates last year), D&T (six) and PE (nine). Two candidates also in Greek and nine in Spanish, tiny presentations of pupils in Latin (two) and music technology (one – 'one of the relatively few schools to offer this as an examined subject'); seven presentations in French. Pleasing number of candidates in the usual suspects – maths, English, history, and geography the strongest both in candidates and success, though the odd D creeps in. Economics popular, government and politics available. Science strong – science and maths block is awkwardly placed on the slope to the north of the main complex and connected at various levels, the traditional build-it-by-numbers confection we see so often, with tubular rails and bog standard three-level classrooms. Some excellent science results but school still leans towards the arts; no philosophy or psychology. Suspect the syllabus may be in a state of change – it can't make sense to present so few candidates in so many subjects in not a very large school. Setting in the third year – core subjects still setted individually, four sets. Good GCSE results with quantities of As and A*s across the board. Loads of class related trips. 2010 saw radical changes with the length of lessons almost doubling and a fortnightly rotating timetable.

Eleven new staff have joined in recent months including new heads of art, chemistry, English, languages and maths; some buzzy young staff around though still one or two who reckon that teaching at Glenalmond is 'a way of life'. Part of the problem is that staff must live on site (though now they are allowed to live off site for three years before retiring), which makes it more difficult to get part-time staff.

Huge investment in computers – couple of suites; internet access in houses (nannynet, intranet, wireless), ten-fold increase in broadband speed. Fibre optics in place, two networks throughout school, apple and PCs, computers in most classrooms. Software used to detect fraud with pupils downloading coursework from elsewhere (does it work, we wonder?).

Dyslexia support now represented at meetings of heads of departments and 'salaried professional' (so we should hope) in charge of learning supports – 'loads of one-to-one lessons'. All screened on entry and certified with educational psychologist's report for extra time in exams. One SENCo and three fully trained dyslexia staff, plus classroom assistant – 'strategies for life as well as time management'. Can deal with most moderate disabilities. Prep club, which more or less acts as a drop-in centre for instant help. Support for the brightest seven or eight per cent of each year group, who have a tightly organised series of compulsory seminars – the Bright Group (called after William Bright), complete with ambitious programme of outside speakers and discussion topics (poet in residence occasionally). But programme of outside speakers for all as well.

Most of the male chauvinists are now a thing of the past – 'Hope so,' said Warden Woods, (who prides himself on being 'somewhat understated').

Games, Options, the Arts: Still a school which majors in outward-bound activities and uses its fantastic site to good advantage – all sorts of activities (and active is the word) – conservation projects, Munro Club, full-bore shooting as well as clays, indoor and outdoor .22 range, Scottish Islands Peaks Race, skiing (own artificial ski slope now out of commission, thanks to health and safety regulations) with regular trips to freezing Glenshee (school boasts a number of past and current members of Scottish ski teams), curling a surprising newcomer, own nine hole golf course at Cairnies (golf scholarship), sailing. Several gold D of E assessors on the staff – hugely popular option, with trips to Norway and the more rugged parts of the USA. Fishing (on the River Almond). Terrific CCF (remember college has strong army links) – fifth form CCF (both sexes) now an option but compulsory in the fourth form, regular camps throughout the term very popular. Strong emphasis on leadership training with college sending more cadets for officer training than any other school in Scotland. Sixth form can visit the elderly or work in special schools instead.

Rugby is a religion but good, rather than sweeping all before it. Boys' hockey coming up fast, girls' hockey and lacrosse strong. Girls now muster full strength sports teams who keep hockey/tennis/netball teams flying the Glenalmond flag. Sports hall; swimming pool used privately in exchange for coaching by former Olympic swimmer. Particularly successful gold scholarship with recipient turning professional and gaining good A levels. Sports are a key part of life here and daily participation is compulsory (the constitutionally disinclined can get by with a spot of umpiring, however) though regular interruption by vile weather. Rich in all-weather spectacularly floodlit pitches.

First XV matches timetabled to ensure that players can participate in music and art – which they do with enthusiasm. Head praised new art department head's 'intensity and passion about her art'. Art department no longer boasting hats on every corner (previous artist-in-residence) but offers a wide range of disciplines and some pretty decent takeup and A level results. Hotshot head of drama (he is also a housemaster and we suggested that the time had come for him to go and seek a headship of his own) runs some of the most exciting drama lessons we have seen in a long time; he also uses it as a medium to reinforce PHSE. Brilliant. The theatre itself is well past its sell by date, however. Strong music assisted by new chapel organ and evidenced by touring chapel choir. Two pipe bands, which hotshot on the charity front: they had a terrific time playing at Lords for an England/Australia International.

Background and Atmosphere: Known to the pupils as Coll. Founded in 1847 by Prime Minister Gladstone, this is Scotland's oldest, most elegant school. Spectacular self-contained quadrangle of cloisters, centred on the chapel and set in its own mini 300 acre estate, beautifully tended parkland and surrounded by some of the smartest grouse shooting in Scotland. Several modern additions stuck round the back, including Basil Spence music block, also the aforementioned science and maths block. Gorgeous library occupies a beautiful chapel-like building in the centre of the front quadrangle, well stocked (real old collection as well as lots of modern stuff) and inviting armchairs; media area downstairs. Uninhabited when we passed through at lunchtime, but our guide, the head girl (who could have sold ice cream to Eskimos) said it was packed at exam time. Stunning bronze statue of Gladstone by acclaimed artist Jemma Pearson unveiled summer 2010.

The mixed sixth form common-room was crowded, noisy and very relaxed. This is a proper boys' boarding school which admitted girls at sixth form in 1990 and went 'all the way' in 1995; admissions now running 50/50. School currently sports five boys' boarding houses and three for girls. New boys' boarding house (old one has been converted into staff quarters) one of the smartest houses we have seen in a long time – 'the largest single investment in the school's history' – providing bedroom and communal accommodation that the school claims is 'comparable with the best in Britain'. Decent-sized single rooms and huge four bedrooms for the youngest with good wide corridors. However the architect obviously took his eye off the ball – the housemaster's garage completely obscures the glorious view from his dining room, and the showers – nasty plastic sort of triangular things – are rapidly showing signs of wear (well, boys will swing from the shower rails). Ditto the silly islands in the Brewrooms (the house is a year old) – the lighting in these is sensor controlled, which makes television viewing and film nights a health and safety hazard. (Ladders required to baffle the sensors – geddit? Ladder climbing not allowed.) The Warden says the architect also designed the accommodation at Stirling University. 'Nuff said.

Fifth form girls (i.e. GCSE year) have been moved to a previous boys' house, Cairnies (now upgraded), quite distant from the main campus, adjacent to the golf course. Same architect. The aforementioned showers, whilst in better heart, are too small for girls to wash their hair (think about it) and they much prefer to use the old fashioned (which the school thought had been abandoned) five bath, power shower room in the basement instead. The double bedrooms are no better than cabins in steerage on a not very good shipping line – not enough space for a rabbit to work, far less girls studying for their GCSEs, though, in mitigation, it has one of the best common-rooms we have ever seen. Cairnies adjoins the housemistress's house and the surrounding garden would benefit from a serious dose of paraquat. Like the tennis courts to the right of the main drive, it is a disgrace, and the image when you drive up is one of total neglect (tennis courts now completely refurbished, says school). This has to be the worst million pounds spent anywhere. (However the Warden maintains that 'This is an unreasonable remark, as the overwhelming reaction from girls and their parents to the accommodation in Cairnies has been wholly positive.')

Boys and girls mix socially during the day and after prep in school, but not in each others' houses, although moves are afoot for each house to have a co-ed common-room for limited access (there is a sixth form common-room). A sixth form bar on Saturdays, though this is currently under review (alcohol may only now be sold in schools with a 'substantial meal'). Rather set apart from the world and protective – you can't just wander round at will. Shopping bus to Perth twice a week. Fixed exeats on either side of half term – 'Parents have free and welcome access to their children at any time and can take them out on Saturdays and Sundays (after chapel).' New trenchant school prospectus and jolly handy prospectus supplement which goes into enormous detail. Weekends said to be more organised. Boy and girl joint heads of college, which scares the pants of OGs.

Other info to be added in: A gorgeous library occupies a beautiful chapel-like building in the centre of the front quadrangle. The tennis courts have been completely refurbished and the upgrading of Cairnies House has been completed

Pastoral Care and Discipline: Previous high jinks some time ago have resulted in a massively impressive tightly worded code of behaviour which covers everything from cycling without a helmet to public displays of affection between pupils, as well as a massive drugs etc document. 'Smoking is a major social gateway to the smoking of illegal drugs. The College may regard persistent tobacco smoking as a reason for asking parents and pupils to agree to future drug testing.' These documents are unique in our experience and we are slightly concerned that sometimes alleged offences may be judged in black and white – and the HMI boarding report was rather fazed by it. Basically, random drugs testing on suspicion, out if positive; smoking equals house gating, Warden's gating and letters home, followed by suspension. Smoking in a building equals suspension even for the first time. Drinking to excess in permitted zones equals Warden's gating, followed by bans and possible suspension, no spirits allowed in the (local) recognized pubs and watering holes. No bringing alcohol back to school under any circumstances. 'Not completely clean,' admits the head – local keepers still complain about empties and other detritus on the neighbouring grouse moor. (We like a tad of spirit!) No reported bullying – senior mistress both neutral and approachable. Anorexia said to be less of a problem – couple of girls under watchful eye, but nothing serious.

Pupils and Parents: Scotland's school for toffs – 'Jolly nice parents'. Traditionally Scottish upper middle and middle class, army, Highland families. About 20 per cent locals and 18 per cent foreigners from all over, plus seven per cent ex-pats. All real foreigners must have guardians, either via parents or contacts or school will fix them up with guardianship agencies 'with whom we have worked successfully in the past'. Large number of first time buyers. Pupils look very smart in their tweed jackets, particularly the girls who have the most stylish, short tweed jackets (often with velvet collars for everyday wear and, what is more, they wear them in the holidays). More ecumenical than an Episcopalian foundation might imply – 20 per cent Catholic, who are prepared for confirmation, plus Church of Scotland confirmation et al. Increase in day pupils (all of whom have either a bed or a station in one of the houses) means regular buses: one third from Crieff (minibus) and two thirds from Perth (coach) – no charge. FPs (known as OGs) a generous bunch and include Sandy Gall, Robbie Coltrane, Miles Kington, Allan Massie, David Sole and Andrew MacDonald (Train Spotting fame), Charlie (Lord) Falconer, erstwhile flatmate of Tony Blair – who was, of course, at arch-rival school, Fettes.

Entrance: Own entrance exam at 12, most at 13+ via CE, oodles from Ardvreck, Craigclowan, Lathallan (who now sport a senior school and currently take pupils up to age 16), St Mary's Melrose and Belhaven, with a clutch from Cargilfield, Mowden etc, as well as state primaries or overseas. Some at sixth form – 20 in 2009, with a number from Germany; six passes at standard grade or GCSE or entrance test and previous school's recommendation. Entrance not a difficult hurdle at the moment ('academic threshold 50 per cent').

Exit: 96 per cent plus to university or some form of higher education, half a dozen to Oxbridge. Some to the Services. Trickle elsewhere post GCSE.

Money Matters: Discounts for siblings of 25 per cent, a whopping 50 per cent for fourth child. A range of bursaries means-tested (from 5% to 100%) according to financial circumstances, including 10 per cent for children whose parents are in the Services, and Fil Cler bursaries for offspring of the clergy. Music (including piping), art, sport and all round scholarships too. Currently offering reduced fee for 'junior entry' for conversion courses from candidates from the state sector. Latest wheeze is for individuals to sponsor deserving but needy pupils by direct giving (anonymously).

Remarks: School popular and highly thought of, saved by the 'belles' after a period of falling numbers – pretty well co-ed now. Not for delicate blossoms, rebels or non-joiners in. We gave the school the soubriquet, 'the Eton of the north', in our first edition; despite its best endeavours, we still don't think it's fully back on form (school says: 'In HMIe inspection last summer (2009) we were rated as excellent for improvements in performance) but getting there.

Godalming College

Tuesley Lane, Godalming, Surrey, GU7 1RS

• Pupils: 1,700, mixed • Ages: 16-18+ • State

Tel: 01483 423 526
Fax: 01483 417 079
Email: college@godalming.ac.uk
Website: www.godalming.ac.uk

The Principal: Mr David Adelman (forty-something at a guess), likes to be known as the Principal. The college was mysteriously negative and unwilling to let us visit, despite our best endeavours to get a foot in the door. The PR person told us that they didn't want us to review the college as 'there aren't any other sixth form colleges in the guide,' which is not true, but hey ho. So we haven't been shown round the place, nor met the elusive Mr A, and some parents told us that they hadn't met him either, although those who have had the pleasure of his acquaintance say he is 'switched on', 'very nice guy'. One parent told us her daughter hadn't said anything about him, which was 'a good thing as she would only say if she didn't think much of him.' Judging by the improvement in student numbers and ambitious building programme (of which more later) he is certainly not letting the grass grow.

Academic matters: A tip-top sixth form college, which competes and hold its head high with the independent schools in the area – hence we are even more mystified why they didn't want us to grace their shining academic portals. Almost 50 A level subjects on offer, so the choice is huge. The college is always in the top 20 FE and sixth form colleges in the country (sometimes the top 10). 2010 results were above the national average with 62 per cent A*/A/B grades. All subjects are well represented and the college has produced top ten national results in subjects such as history, graphic design, performing arts and biology. Art, in particular, is excellent and is a favoured subject of many. Natural sciences and mathematics are also popular and strong.

For the less academically inclined, the college is a very sound choice for those who want to study a vocational subject such as media studies, business studies, travel and tourism, sport or childcare. Progress reports are sent home plus parents' newsletters and an annual report, and there are new parents' induction evenings, parents' evenings and a careers evening. However, one parent commented that the college was 'rarely in touch'. Larger class sizes than at most school sixth forms – typically 17 or 18. Very solid support network available for dyslexia in the form of assessment and one-to-one support plus provision of specialist equipment such as laptops. Students with physical disabilities are actively welcomed and supported. There is also specialist teaching available for EAL students. Those students who struggle with organisational skills and time management (i.e. most teenagers) also get extra support if required.

Games, Options, the Arts: Pupils are encouraged to go above and beyond their A level choices by choosing an enrichment subject in addition to their main studies which should help with character building – all the emphasis on the value-added these days. These range from sport, drama and music to Duke of Edinburgh and citizenship. Some muttering about not enough sport generally, especially for those used to compulsory sport at their former private schools. Plenty of clubs and societies – debating club is particularly popular and successful, winning several competitions; others include lacrosse, martial arts, circus skills and dance – and if there isn't anything to your liking, you can start your own. A fully-equipped gym featuring a programme of workout classes plus individual training sessions is available to all students.

Background and Atmosphere: Formerly the local county school built in 1930, Godalming became a sixth form college in 1978. Original building remains, with rather lovely old façade with not so lovely car park in front. Various other purpose-built buildings have been added over the years and we're told by the school that significant investment during the last five years has resulted in state-of-the-art facilities that rival those found in higher education and in industry. New buildings recently completed include the independent learning centre (what we used to call the library) containing 18,000 books, plus digital and online resources; there is also a large area for private study, plus careers library and a student study centre. A sports hall centre contains a fitness centre and indoor courts and a dance studio is also on site. Parents have praised the facilities as 'fantastic for a state school.' All of this set in some 20 acres. A performing arts centre provides a drama studio, music performance space, recording studio, practice rooms and classrooms, addressing the previously-reported lack of suitable accommodation. A central piazza provides students with an atractive area in which to socialise as well as an outside performance space for arts festivals etc.

It is a huge place in terms of vast pupil numbers and is daunting for some – one prospective pupil was totally put off by the sheer size and the number of students, feeling that she would not have the individual attention she needed. A parent commented that it felt 'impersonal'. For others, it allows an opportunity for a degree of freedom and independence – 'they're allowed to rebel with their clothes and their hairstyles,' said one parent. Big welcome evening for new parents and pupils once a year with talk by the head. For some that's the one and only time they will see him (at least they are one up on us!)

Provides a really good halfway house between school and university but this is definitely not the place for a shrinking violet as, aside from the pupil numbers and relatively large classes, you need to have your wits about you and be prepared to ask for what you need. Socially, it is great for a teenager – 'lots of parties – it's the first taste of university life,' said one mum; there's also the freshers' ball and the delights of rag week to contend with. This party scene can be a bit of shock to the system especially for the rather cloistered ex-private school contingent (see below). There is a many a private school mum who throws up her hands in horror as her hitherto nerdy teenager becomes a party animal when they hit the social scene at Godalming. For some pupils it can be a challenge, to say the least, to get the work/social life balance sorted out.

Pastoral Care and Discipline: Each student is assigned a personal tutor who takes care of them throughout their time at college – a twice a week session to offer support and guidance. Subject tutors are also available. Additionally, an on-site counsellor five days a week and a careers and life skills department which can help with everything from gap year advice, work placements and university subject choices. But this is not a cosy sixth form where everybody knows your name – pupils have to be very self-motivated and independent; it is a college community which thrives on self-reliance. College says, 'Students here are expected to be self motivated, willing to accept responsibility for their own learning programme and to behave as young adults.' One parent commented, 'It's hard to cope when you have come from a private school where you get feedback and motivation all the time.' Interestingly, the college is pretty tough on attendance and has a very strict registration policy – tutors complete electronic registration at every lesson. Three no-shows at lessons results in a letter home for parents – this tough line was 'a bit of a shock as she thought she had left school and was free,' said one mum about her daughter. One parent commented, 'They have a lovely knack of telling parents to back off, that they will handle the discipline and the academia, so parents can be parents again rather than a surrogate teacher.' Another said that it was great to know that their unruly teen would be managed 'through this difficult stage'.

Pupils and Parents: Wide variety of backgrounds as you would imagine for a state sixth form college, but this is posh rural Surrey so in reality it has a very middle class feel. Lots of pupils from the state sector, but well over a third from independent schools (and some of them from the more upmarket ones) who either want a taste of more collegiate life with all the extra freedom or whose parents are fed up with handing out wads of cash for education. The college has a reputation far and wide, so whilst the main intake is local, a significant number live much farther away – the further reaches of Surrey as well as West Sussex, Hampshire, Greater London and Kent. No uniform so every parent's worst fears on dressing/hairdos will no doubt be realised.

Entrance: Dependent on how many subjects you wish to study but generally five GCSEs grades A–C in the subjects to be studied, plus reference from current school. The college is relatively flexible and should the prospective student not achieve the required grades, they will advise on the next step. Applications are accepted from an advertised date during the autumn term followed by an admissions interview.

Exit: A dedicated tutor to support applicants to Oxbridge. Around 80 per cent to more than 80 universities spread far and wide. Approximately 10 per cent choose to go on foundation art courses.

Remarks: A top sixth form college (though shame about the powers that be and their cloak and dagger secrecy about the place). A great choice for teenagers who want a more collegiate lifestyle or who are simply just too cool for a traditional school sixth form. A no-brainer for the confident, motivated and self-reliant type. Not for anyone who needs lots of hand-holding, nurturing, hands-on guidance or indeed the demophobic.

The Godolphin and Latymer School

Iffley Road, Hammersmith, London, W6 0PG

• Pupils: 730 girls; all day • Ages: 11-18 • Size of sixth form: 200
• Non-denom • Fees: £15,525 pa • Independent

Tel: 020 8741 1936
Fax: 020 8735 9520
Email: registrar@godolphinandlatymer.com
Website: www.godolphinandlatymer.com

Head Mistress: Since January 2009, Mrs Ruth Mercer BA (late forties), read history at London University and is passionate about the subject – 'one of the reasons I chose to teach', she says, 'is so that I could continue to learn history'. Previously head of Northwood College, where, after a bumpy beginning, she was a considerable success. She grew up in Preston, but her northern accent is only just discernible after years of teaching in independent London girls' day schools – head of history and politics and Notting Hill and Ealing for twelve years, deputy head here at Godolphin from 1998 until 2002 and thence to Northwood College which she ran for seven years.

Married to the deputy head of Greenford High Comprehensive in Ealing; they have two teenage children, both at single sex schools. 'I practise what I preach,' she says. Wholeheartedly committed to single sex education: 'We fail both boys and girls if we educate them together because we can't meet their very different needs,' she says. Succeeds the highly respected Margaret Rudland after 23 years, but since Mrs Mercer was her deputy until 2002, staff here knew what they were getting and, as one said, 'We were thrilled with her appointment – she is so hands on'.

Thoughtful, honest (prefers careful accuracy to hard sell) and tactful, Mrs Mercer is serious but clearly enjoys humour and is not afraid to join in and make a fool of herself, whether it be in the chorus of Mamma Mia directed by the girls or in a fitness contest, organised by the students, clad in blue wig and hood. Teaches history to Year 7 – 'I need to know what the girls are like as learners as well as individuals'. This is a head who rolls up her sleeves and gets on with it at the coal face. During her first two terms she shadowed several classes, sitting with the girls, doing all the set tasks – 'quite a challenge when you are in a GCSE chemistry lesson and you haven't done chemistry for aeons'. It was an invaluable exercise, one of the results of which was the appointment of a thinking and learning coordinator (a refreshing departure from the usual 'teaching and learning'). She identified that teaching here needs to move away from the didactic – 'predictable hoop-jumping isn't training them for the real world'.

Popular with the girls, who appreciate her warmth and friendliness. None of the parents we spoke to had much, or indeed any, contact with her. They don't seem concerned. As one parent put it, 'She may tweak a few things but she isn't going to screw it up'.

Academic matters: Examination results are impressive – over 90 per cent of A level results at A or B and those doing the IB achieve well too, about half winning 40 points or more out of a possible 45. Average grade per subject is just over six out of seven. English literature, history, maths and biology particularly popular, with chemistry and history of art close behind. A level choices include philosophy, government and politics, music technology, Russian, classical civilisation.

IB take-up varies (about a quarter in 2009) but Mrs Mercer is a great fan because it makes girls think ('exam technique has dumbed down A levels') and is right up the street of your typical self-reliant and busy Dolphin (that's what girls here are known as – past and present). All A level students can now do an extended project so they can be as stretched (nearly) as much as the IB candidates. In 2010, 90 per cent of GCSE grades were A or A*.

Over 50 per cent of staff have been here for over 10 years, 25 per cent of staff are men (not bad for a girls' school). Some parents comment on how results driven the school is – As are expected the whole time and 77 per cent is a poor mark. One mentioned her horror when parents were told in the November of their daughter's first year – two months in – whether their daughter was meeting her expected targets.

Positive noises from the girls. Teachers are supportive and always available to help, they say. No tutor system, however, and, as one parent pointed out, there is no one person who knows your child really well academically and has done all the way through so you can have a productive discussion with them about, say, their choice of A levels.

Full-time individual learning needs coordinator (Mrs Mercer doesn't like using the pejorative sounding 'special needs'). Needs mainly on the mild to moderate dys-strata and organisational skills, though have had statemented children in the past. Each case will be judged individually but girls here need to be able to stand the pace. 'All our girls are Gifted and Talented,' says head and the aim is to constantly stretch and stimulate them with the quality of the lessons. No extra charge for extra help.

Games, Options, the Arts: If your daughter is passionate about sport but gawky on the pitch probably not the school for her. Although the teams – hockey and netball in particular – are strong, if your daughter isn't picked she is likely to get sidelined – a common complaint among parents. Astroturf (floodlit) hockey pitch, courts for netball and tennis – all on site and girls here are competitive and keen. Involvement rapidly declines for the not so sporty and as they move further up the school – one girl told us there is very little sport beyond Year 10. Fencing, yoga and pilates as well as rowing (they share a boat house with Kings, Wimbledon). Not much swimming though they do have use of Latymer's pool.

Drama and music are a different story – very inclusive, ambitious and hugely popular. Girls take responsibility for a number of shows throughout the year – producing, directing and acting in them. Splendid new facilities housed in the Bishop Centre (nothing ecclesiastical meant by the nomenclature – it is in fact named after Dame Joyce Bishop, headmistress until 1963, but building is made up of St John's Church together with the vicarage, which school acquired in 2008). Concerts and theatrical performances take place here with state-of-the-art lighting and seating facilities (though one parent controversially complained that the acoustics were terrible and you couldn't see a thing – 'that's now been fixed,' school assures us). The Rudland Music School is connected to the Bishop Centre by a bright glass corridor. First class facilities for music playing and music making – you can burn discs in high tech studios, store your instrument in a discreet but secure locker and practise in comfortable soundproofed music rooms. A joint orchestra with Latymer Upper School as well as various choirs, ensembles and bands including a jazz band. 'You can get involved even if you have no musical talent whatsoever,' said one pupil, approvingly.

Art is strong. One girl commented that it was best thing about the school. Pottery a little disappointing. They still have a kiln but no longer have any wheels.

Huge range and number of trips – domestic and global – whether it be classics trips to the British Museum, Bath or Athens, skiing in the US or trekking in the Sinai desert. Swimming is not the only contact girls have with Latymer Upper. They go on French and German exchanges together and sixth formers do joint work experience in Versailles and Berlin.

Impressive amount of work in local community, especially with the elderly. One old Dolphin fondly remembers that her first experience of the indignities of old age was while she was at school here helping old ladies onto the loo. A 'social services' team led by about seven girls in the sixth form coordinates whole school charitable efforts – every week they choose a different charity. They raise money by any means possible – cake sales or charging fellow pupils to watch all the staff perform *Mamma Mia* during lunch break.

Background and Atmosphere: Built as a boarding school for boys in 1861, became an independent day school for girls in 1905 and evolved, through different state-aided statuses, before turning independent again in 1977 rather than becoming a comprehensive school or being closed down altogether. Situated at the end of Iffley Road in W6, it's encased by hectic Hammersmith on one side and leafy Brackenbury on the other. There is a definite churchy feel to the architecture.

What was formerly St John's Church is now the Bishop Centre. The original buildings are yellow brick Victorian, with some distinctly church-like windows and a formal panelled assembly hall. Recent yellow-brick additions blend in fairly harmoniously and have provided science labs and art studios, a pottery room, computer studies rooms and language labs. 'I like the way different buildings have different feels,' said a pupil. The ecology garden is used in biology lessons, there's a quad with pond (plus dolphin statue) and a courtyard where girls can eat lunch in warm weather. The spacious top floor sixth form centre resembles an airport lounge with roof terrace and tuck shop. 'We feel privileged to come up our own staircase to our own room,' said a sixth former.

Although almost every girl we spoke to said they loved the friendly and supportive atmosphere, a number of parents complained of poor communication and an 'us and them' attitude from the senior staff – 'they prefer to support the teachers rather than sympathise with the concerns of parents,' said one. That said, it is universally acknowledged that school responds swiftly when something can be done.

This is a close knit community where there is mutual trust between staff and pupils. Girls here are real joiner-inners – for many of them the school day runs from seven in the morning until eight at night. They are given a lot of responsibility and there is healthy contact between younger and older girls. One parent described the atmosphere as buzzing. We would have to agree.

Pastoral Care and Discipline: Head says behaviour is good, and better than when she was here as deputy seven years ago. No instances of drugs found in school: if they were, each case would be dealt with individually, but likely to result in expulsion. Regular surveys about bullying – school council (chaired by head girl – with one member of staff – the rest are girls) produced its own anti-bullying strategy, recently revised to incorporate facebook cyber-style bullying.

Sixth form can go out to Hammersmith at lunchtime – a privilege that can be withdrawn for bad behaviour.

Mutterings among parents about poor communication – 'it's hard to get hold of teachers' – and one said that her daughter's form-mistress hardly knew her: 'They only have ten minutes with the girls in the morning'. A parent of a younger girl said she was still working with the reputation of the school as being a good one rather than what she has experienced – 'I wish I knew what she was doing in the day,' she said.

Pupils and Parents: Parents are professional – city types and lawyers, a few in media and publishing. Ambitious with high expectations. Not as much diversity as there used to be in the days of Assisted Places, though school tries hard with a bursary fund to maintain some socio-economic spread. Lots of Gucci and Fendi handbags at the school gates as well as the odd chauffeur dropping off a daughter of a Russian magnate. Quite a high number of children from the States and France who live in SWs 1 and 3. A few from Ealing, Kew and Richmond and a small number from north London, otherwise it's largely local.

Girls are feisty, confident, independent and grounded. Not afraid to stand up for what they believe in and their teachers let them – its part of the mutual respect that is so valued here. It's cool to be clever and to be responsible. Timid girls tend to blossom, and enjoy – as one parent put it – the slightly Victorian approach to structure and boundaries. Not many of the hair flickers in Starbucks in Hammersmith will be from Godolphin, and one old Dolphin – also a current parent – pointed out that it's fine for girls here to have chunky thighs and to use the wrong hand cream. Old Dolphins include Nigella Lawson, Davina McCall, actresses

Kate Beckinsale, Jemima Rooper and Samantha Bond, writer Sarah Dunant, Professor Dame Susan Greenfield, architect Julia Barfield and singer Sophie Ellis-Bextor.

Entrance: Competitive – about 500 each year apply for a 104 places. About a quarter from state primaries, large number from central London preps – Pembridge Hall, Bute House, Thomas's – over a hundred schools. Member of group 2 of the North London Consortium of girls's schools that set common maths and English exams. All girls are interviewed twice. 'We place a lot of emphasis on school report and interview,' says head. 'We are trying to get at potential, do they have the ability and willingness to think for themselves – are they teachable?' adding how depressing it is when they ask what they do in their free time and are told that most of it is taken up with tutoring. A pretty high standard of raw ability is required if they are to keep up with the fast pace of lessons. Siblings will be turned away if not they're not up to it.

Exit: A small number – about 10 per cent – will leave after GCSE to go to e.g. Westminster, or boarding schools – Marlborough, Wycombe Abbey, Cheltenham Ladies ('but we bring in at least that number,' says head).

After A level or the IB almost all go on to the most selective Russell Group Universities, 15ish per cent to Oxbridge each year, and a high number (12 per cent) to Ivy League universities in the US – Harvard, Stanford, Brown.

Money Matters: A development director raises funds, particularly for bursaries. School will make every effort to ensure that no-one has to leave because their family has fallen on hard times. One or more music scholarships at 11 and music and art scholarships in the sixth form.

Remarks: A stimulating school that does its job well. Produces independent, confident (rather than arrogant) girls that are looked after but appear to be looking after themselves. An excellent choice for your busy daughter who loves to join in.

The Godolphin School

Linked to Godolphin Preparatory School in the Junior section

Milford Hill, Salisbury, Wiltshire, SP1 2RA

• Pupils: 440 girls; one third boards • Ages: 11-18 • Size of sixth form: 140 • Christian foundation • Fees: Boarding £23,661; Day £16,458 pa • Independent

Tel: 01722 430 511
Fax: 01722 430 501
Email: admissions@godolphin.wilts.sch.uk
Website: www.godolphin.org

Head: Since 2010, Mrs Samantha Price MA art history. Started career at Tate Gallery before switching to teaching – trained at Reading Blue Coat School where she was head of Year 8 and ran both the CCF and RAF section, then girls' housemistress at King's Canterbury, followed by deputy headship at Hereford Cathedral School. Keen sportswoman, married to a vicar, two young children – girl (5) at Godolphin Prep and son (2).

Academic matters: Very good GCSE (69 per cent A*/A) and A level results (78 per cent A*/B). A level subject range not huge but includes a few less usual subjects, e.g. history of art and food technology (one girl recently went to study with Gary Rhodes). Strength in most subjects but modern languages (mainly French, Spanish, German) stand out – annual exchange with schools in Berlin and Alicante. Sciences, maths, English and the arts also strong. English language A level offered in addition to literature – English teacher published her first novel *Raffy's Shapes* last year. A few pupils opt for Latin at GCSE and one every few years at A level. Has introduced IGCSEs for sciences, maths and modern languages. No A level or GCSE option blocks – girls choose the subjects they want and the timetable is created around them.

Some twelve girls receive between half an hour and an hour of help per week from qualified SEN teacher. Girls who are falling behind are picked up and given extra support after school on an informal basis by staff. Probably not the place to aim for if your child is used to getting more support than this.

Games, Options, the Arts: Wonderful art rooms with very high quality work on display. Art department is open at weekends and pupils make full use of it. In 2008 one girl came in the top five marks nationally for A level art and design. Photography, ceramics and metal work on offer. Splendid round theatre building, The Blackledge, used for several drama productions a year as well as concerts, debates and talks by visiting speakers. Girls full of enthusiasm for the annual music and drama competitions in which all boarders are involved. A pupil was chosen for a part in the latest *Harry Potter* film, another appeared in the film of Ian McEwan's *Atonement* and a fifth former is a member of the National Youth Theatre.

Instrumental music building a bit scruffy but doesn't seem to hold the girls back (extra space for music in The Blackledge) – 329 music lessons are provided each week, 34 per cent at grade 5 standard or above. Every year students take performing diplomas; the choirs sing services in Salisbury Cathedral at least once a term; occasional music tours. Music lessons are timetabled outside lessons in the sixth form and where possible in GCSE years, otherwise lessons are missed on a rotating basis (some complaints from parents here).

Compulsory sports until year four, when options also kick in. Lacrosse is number one, with hockey, netball, tennis, athletics, rounders, swimming, gym and dance also available. List of options a bit limited: badminton, fitness, basketball, rebounders and volleyball. Fabulous 25m indoor swimming pool. An Astro surface is in the planning stage. Sports tours in recent years to Barbados and Australia; expeditions to Namibia and India. CCF contingent formed in 2000 (a first in a girls' school so lots of publicity). Masses of after-school activities to choose from, ranging from 'glass slumping' to martial arts and special exam revision classes. Debating in conjunction with boys from Winchester and Bishop Wordsworth's.

Background and Atmosphere: Rare to find such an outstanding boarding school – with such good academic results, a rich past and an impressive list of old girls – which is so little known outside its immediate area. 'Friendly, relaxed, happy, nurturing, the opposite of stressed-out,' enthused a parent. 'Girl-centred,' said another, the most obvious example being the school uniform. We must confess to our jaws dropping in disbelief when first confronted by sight of teenage girls unblushingly going about their business bedecked in bright blue pinnies. Girls swear blind that they love them and we believe they do, in a sort of burqa-esque/covers a multitude of sins/Hermione Granger robes way. The pinnies are worn over full school uniform, in case you are wondering. A great leveller because they make everyone look peculiar, friendly, feminine and industrious. A school with no anorexia, little make-up – 'There's no point: we all look like blue marquees' (untrue – they look lovely). Sixth form wear mufti.

Housed in handsome cluster of buildings in a 16-acre campus atop a hill, 10 minutes' walk from the centre of Salisbury. Has close links with the Cathedral. Facilities and classrooms generally very good. Fabulous language lab with IT galore and interactive white board. Library fine but would benefit from a more welcoming area for the younger end of the school. Three very pleasant mixed age boarding houses for girls below sixth form (Douglas is newest) with shared dining hall adjoining them (great for wearing pjs to breakfast). University-style sixth form house (great kitchen) and sixth form centre incorporating study, boarding, careers and leisure facilities recently opened.

Pastoral Care and Discipline: Parents comment on the friendly atmosphere and girls call it 'cosy and not intimidating'. Mixed age dorms mean much mixing between the age groups – 'It's more like a normal family,' said a mum. Being in a town makes a huge difference, say sixth formers, and prevents feelings of isolation that can be a problem in girls' boarding schools. All ages allowed into Salisbury starting with an hour a week for the first years, in groups of five, and gradually extending through the school. Sixth formers may go down freely after afternoon school although, in practice, they rarely have the time (or money) to do so; they may also spend Saturday evenings in town. Weekends are packed with activities after Saturday prep (no Saturday lessons) and many 'Sarums' (day girls) come back to join in. Only thing missing, say sixth form girls, is a brother school with which to share activities, socials etc (school says it is increasing social activities with Winchester College and Bishop Wordsworth School).

Pupils and Parents: Boarding flexible – full, weekly and midweek options. Becoming more and more local, though a few girls come from outside the region. A surprising number of children of old girls. A small handful of foreigners (eight per cent) and quite a few Services/FCO kids. Boarders must spend five full weekends a year in school but may otherwise spend weekends in or out of school, as they and their parents choose. 'Sarums' may spend the odd weekday night in school if they are staying late for activities. Boarding very popular in the sixth form and a press on places, with some coming in from outside. Old Girls include lots of writers: Dorothy L Sayers, Jilly Cooper, Amanda Brookfield, Minette Walters, Elizabeth Lemarchand and Josephine Bell. Also up and coming actress Antonia Bernath and 'Dragons' Den' 'millionaire investor' Deborah Meaden.

Entrance: At 11, 12, 13, 14 and sixth form. Registered pupils invited for a preview day and night in the autumn before CE. Girls come from school's own prep plus Leaden Hall, Salisbury Cathedral School, Stroud, Forres Sandle Manor, Farleigh, Norman Court, Princes Mead, St Swithun's Junior School and Hordle Walhampton. 27 girls from overseas, the majority from Hong Kong (10 require extra English tuition). A dozen girls from British expat families.

Exit: Seven per cent go elsewhere after GCSEs (often to good state options like Peter Symonds or South Wilts). Of those who stay, nearly all to higher education, mostly to universities to do anything from medicine to Japanese. Others to art foundation courses (mainly Bournemouth), music conservatoires and sometimes drama school. About half take a gap year.

Money Matters: Scholarships at 11, 12, 13 and sixth form, up to 50 per cent of boarding fees for outstanding merit and promise in academic work, sport, music or art (13 and sixth form only). In cases of financial hardship additional bursaries may be awarded to scholars. Also six Foundation Bursaries (worth 70 per cent) for girls with financial need who are orphans or from divided families.

Remarks: A good place for bright girls seeking a supportive environment, not a pressure cooker. Buzzes with confident, gregarious girls. Deserves to be much, much better known – but perhaps its modesty is part of its charm.

Gordon's School

West End, Woking, Surrey, GU24 9PT

• Pupils: 680 boys and girls (approx 55 per cent boys); about one third boards • Ages: 11-18 • Size of sixth form: 130 • Inter-denom
• Fees: Boarding £11,427-£12,501 pa • State

Tel: 01276 858 084
Fax: 01276 855 335
Email: registrar@gordons.surrey.sch.uk
Website: www.gordons.surrey.sch.uk

Headteacher: Since September 2010, Mr Andrew Moss, BA Med NPQH. Started teaching in 1992 – has worked in a variety of boarding and day schools, including most recently a headship in a Cognita independent school. Father of two and keen skier.

Committed vision that every child should achieve the best academic result possible but also develop all round character, confidence and compassion; intelligence comes in many forms and the aim is for students to leave believing they are all equally smart and the best they can be.

Academic matters: An academic star in the state system, particularly as it is non-selective. No plans to go selective, despite huge over-subscription. Outstanding Ofsted report in January 2007. It may be mixed ability but the push from the beginning of Year 7 is to work hard – setting from the outset. Not a hothouse high pressure school but, make no mistake, students know where they stand and what is expected of them, i.e. to do their best. Excellent rewards system not just for A grades but also for good effort – even the pupils give the system the thumbs up and concede that it makes them work harder.

Traditional teaching produces excellent results – a school which has fought its way from the depths of educational despair to the top of the tables by sheer hard work and determination. Year on year the school scores consistently

90 per cent or above 5+ A*–C grades. Intensely proud of its exam successes – lots of practice papers, coursework and timed tests, to make sure all the children are as prepared as possible when it comes to GCSE. One-to-one extra tuition available at exam time particularly. Most popular GCSE options are geography, design and PE. Sixth form of approximately 140 pupils and growing. Two thirds of grades generally A or B.

Amount of homework is 'quite fair' – homework diaries are an important part of keeping on top of everything. About 500 computers in the school, all linked to computers in the houses so work done in class can be finished off during prep. Also computers in the well-stocked library. Interactive whiteboard in every classroom, lessons quite formal, with quiet, calm atmosphere, but the students actively participate and are fully engaged.

Fifteen per cent of pupils have special needs of some kind; four per cent have statements. Learning support department headed by a full time SENCo; the department works with needs across the board, including dyslexia and dyspraxia, in small groups and individually.

Games, Options, the Arts: Tip top sport which is hugely popular with the pupils. More than forty acres of playing fields, with cricket nets, rugby pitches, shooting range and athletics track etc. Indoor swimming pool and very well equipped gym. A couple of parents, however, felt the sporting facilities don't actually quite match up to the emphasis the school places on sport and that, compared (perhaps unfairly) to the private sector, they are a bit outdated. Pupils have to do three physical activities each week – the usual, including rugby, football, tennis, badminton, gymnastics, but non-sporty types are not left out. Camera club, ice skating in Guildford, art, drama, tap dancing and pottery etc. Everyone gets a chance to try whatever they want for a term at least. Lots of emphasis on D of E – about 90 pupils achieve awards every year.

Music and drama are a big part of life – a purpose-built music centre, flourishing orchestra, choir and concert band. The pipe and drum band is a major focus of the school – a tradition of parades which the pupils, perhaps surprisingly, love. Marching practice every Friday, and every year pupils go to London and literally stop the traffic when they march down Whitehall to the Cenotaph, ending up at the bronze statue of General Gordon on the Embankment. Each year the school stages two full-scale drama productions.

Background and Atmosphere: Steeped in history, but not living in the past – dates back to 1885, started life as a home for poor boys, 'the necessitas lads'. Established by the Gordon Foundation (the trustees today) at the request of Queen Victoria – she wanted a memorial to her favourite general, who had died at Khartoum. After discussion, it was decided that Gordon would have preferred something more practical and so the home was opened. Since then, the reigning monarch has been the patron.

Built round a large quadrangle, quite bare and military in feel, with the odd bench here and there, where the students hang out during break and lunch if they are not in their houses. The newer buildings, around the quad, have been designed sympathetically and fit in well with the original Victorian buildings. Tucked away from the quad are '60s buildings, not in the least pretty and fairly shabby inside – the school says these will be replaced when money is available. Classrooms are large, light and spacious, in both the older and newer buildings, and well equipped. Lots of displays of recent work everywhere in classrooms, corridors and stairways. Over the last two years two new buildings have been opened – a centre for music and drama and a new science block. Both are, we're told, fitted with the latest state of the art technology. Stunning chapel, built in 1894, which houses numerous school treasures, including a book which lists the names of all the Gordon's boys killed in the two world wars. At assemblies, names are read out to the pupils, to give them a sense of belonging to something with a real history.

Smallish – will not increase in size despite the demand for places. Four boarding houses and five day-boarding houses, but much mixing in between day pupils and boarders. House system is fiercely competitive – everything from table football to rugby. Boarding houses are all quite homely and comfy but well used. Plenty of space in the dormitories – four or five to a room in Year 7 and 8, reducing to double rooms for sixth formers, who have separate houses. The boys' houses are typical male enclaves dominated by snooker tables, table football and satellite TV. Girls' houses much more touchy feely – the ubiquitous table football but many more homely touches with cushions and pot plants galore. One parent said she found the state of the decoration of the boys' houses disappointing – a bit too shabby for her liking, and the girls' houses disproportionately cosy by comparison.

All the houses boast lots of trophies and certificates and are bedecked with photos and collages of pupils' happy smiling faces. We only spotted one play station: a pupil explained that they mostly preferred to be outside playing sport – both refreshing and remarkable. An extended school day to 8pm for all who want it; most of the day pupils stay on for the activities, supervised prep and an evening meal.

Uniform is smart and and adhered to – no skirts 'up to here'; not seen as a problem, although a couple of girls said they would really like a summer uniform to replace the shirt and tie. In sixth form, students dress as if for a day at the office, and as you would expect, are smartly turned out.

Food is generally praised – 'not all pizza and chips like other schools' – but some complaints that it is 'a bit boring', with the same dishes repeated too often. Pupils can voice their opinions on the food and everything else at the school food committee.

Pastoral Care and Discipline: A strict code of discipline backed up by those nine school rules – parents say pupils are very aware of the lines that cannot be crossed. Not an ideal school for the free spirits of the world and one pupil dissenter did complain that some of the punishments, such as long essays, were too severe for minor offences. Zero tolerance of bullying – a culture of 'telling' to houseparents and tutors is encouraged from Year 7 through assemblies; pupils say the odd bullying incident has been dealt with effectively and stopped immediately.

Alcohol and cigarettes are strictly forbidden on school grounds and on the journey to and from school for day pupils. Imaginative punishment for those caught puffing – to write a four-page essay entitled, 'The correlation between smoking and lung cancer', due on the head's desk the morning after the incident or the length is doubled. Drinkers face at least two weeks' exclusion, although this has happened only twice since 1995. Absolutely zero tolerance for drugs. Staff work hard from Year 7 to steer children away from them and anyone caught with them at school is expelled immediately – twice since 1995.

Boys and girls are allowed to mix freely in each other's houses but no boy is allowed upstairs in the girls' boarding houses and vice versa. Houseparents are popular and informal – both boys and girls agreed they wouldn't hesitate to talk to their houseparents or house tutors about any issue. Sixth formers are also assigned houses to help out – an idea much liked by the younger pupils.

Pupils and Parents: Parents are a huge mix of professional, locals and diplomatic and Services living abroad full time. Pupils are polite, confident, happy to talk about their school and proud of their own and its achievements. The disciplined air about the place certainly does not turn out repressed youngsters. They are a bubbly and even quite cheeky lot – in a nice way – with a good sense of humour. They come from very mixed backgrounds including a few straight from the private sector, others having moved from school to school in the state sector with their military and diplomatic parents.

Entrance: In a word, difficult – around 500 applicants for 100 places. Non-selective, so no entry exams. Residential boarding (full and weekly) by 'need to board' (priority to children of families in armed forces) usually means that parents are in the Services, live overseas, or have very complicated dual careers which necessitate boarding – boarders come from all over the UK and abroad.

Day boarding: a small number of places is allocated each year to children with statements of special educational needs, approximately four per cent; otherwise, first priority goes to siblings – usually 50 to 60 per cent sibling entrants to Year 7 annually.

On the home front, a very, very small catchment area – if you live within 600 yards of the school, you should get a place. It's worked out by radial distance from a yellow spot painted on the driveway at the main entrance to the school. Local estate agents are fully clued up about its popularity and catchment area and prospective parents go to great lengths to get in.

The growing reputation of the sixth form means an increasing number of students from neighbouring schools come in at 16. Entry requirement (for both existing and new pupils) is five GCSEs A–C with Bs for subjects to be taken at A level.

Exit: Only about two per cent leave at 16 – one parent said that her child decided to stay in situ for the sixth form particularly because of the sport on offer, unmatched anywhere else they looked. Majority of sixth formers go to university, two to Oxford in 2010.

Money Matters: Bursaries are available.

Remarks: A super state school, ideal for 'head down and work, toe the line' souls, who will benefit from splendid academics and sport and a disciplined atmosphere. Definitely not for the rebel nor the rule-breaker nor those looking for luxury boarding – they would hate the place.

Gordonstoun School

Linked to Aberlour House the Junior School at Gordonstoun in the Junior section

Elgin, Moray, Elgin, Moray, IV30 5RF

• Pupils: 425 boarders, 65 day; boys and girls 60/40. • Ages: 13-18 (juniors from 8-13 in Aberlour House) • Size of sixth form: 250 • Inter-denom • Fees: Day £11,040-£19,860; Boarding £16,497-£26,607 pa • Independent

Tel: 01343 837837
Fax: 01343 837 808
Email: admissions@gordonstoun.org.uk
Website: www.gordonstoun.org.uk

Head: Since 1990, Mr Mark Pyper BA (fifties). Educated at Winchester, dropped out of Oxford and finished his degree externally at London. Father, grandfather and great grandfather were all prep headmasters. Started his teaching career in the prep school world. Came to Gordonstoun from Sevenoaks, where he was deputy head. 'Rather like it here. Suits me.' His wife likes it too, 'She jogs, plays the guitar,' and runs a crèche for staff children. In a world where headmasters are progressively a scruffy bunch, he is unique (in our experience) in wearing a natty tweed suit come summer come winter. Study (drawing room, more like) of lairdly splendour full of Mr Pyper's ancestors in stately frames. 'Likes to give the impression of being laid-back', but would like the world to know that he 'is quite switched on and can be quite tough as well'. HRH The Princess Royal is no longer a governor but is now Warden ('She wanted to keep in touch') and fronts the fundraising campaign 'and is very supportive'. Retiring April 2011.

The new head will be Simon Reid, at present deputy head of Worksop College in Nottinghamshire. Educated in South Africa, he has taught there and at Brentwood School, Stowe and Christ's Hospital.

Academic matters: Academia is not what Gordonstoun is about – 'Students are here for the whole broad experience'; 'The balance is important'. Huge range of ability from children 'at the lower end of the academic scale for whom two Ds at A level are a real achievement' to the really bright who get to Oxbridge. A level exam results in 2009 saw 95 per cent of students gain entry to university of their choice. Maths consistently good, with French, Spanish and German throughout, the latter remarkably successful (but then school has a large number of German students). Classes setted for maths and English from 13. Excellent new networked computer setup on stream, including wireless connection in all boarding houses, New international citizenship course in place, not PSE or RS but examining real problems against a global background. Good remedial support – all pupils are now screened on arrival. Will scribe for exams. EAL available at all levels.

Games, Options, the Arts: Community service is important at Gordonstoun and many chose the school for just this reason. All children must take part and do service training in Year 11 before opting for the fire brigade (the most popular), mountain rescue (MR), offshore and in-shore rescue, ski patrol, visiting the elderly. Lots of exchanges with other Round Square schools – Canada, Germany, Australia. Joint international expeditions to India, Sinai, Thailand, Kenya, Honduras to work on conservation/ecological projects (expensive but students encouraged to fundraise to meet own costs), popular and full of teenage japes. School has its own 80 foot yacht and timetabled sailing weeks (when the weather can be 'pretty wild', according to the skippers), as well as outward bound expeditions. Tall ships' race now a regular feature – has acquired a new 28 foot training cutter.

Mainstream games on course but long distances to other schools for matches cause problems. Good sports facilities – new sports hall opened in 2009 with plans to completely refurbish the existing sports facilities underway – and trips all over – Europe, Australasia, points west. The arts very popular – 200-seater theatre opened in 2005 and new music recording studio and recital room in 2007. Dance offered to A level. Magnificent art, lots of disciplines, graphic design impressive. Particularly strong DT with pupils learning not only to make lights but also to cost them effectively.

Background and Atmosphere: Founded in 1934 by the German educationalist, Kurt Hahn, founder of Salem School in Baden-Württemberg and believer in educating and developing all aspects of children, not just the academic. Grounds and setting lovely – half a mile from the Moray Firth with cliffs and beaches nearby, and not as cold as one might think (the Gulf Stream is useful). Gordonstoun House is a former residence of Gordon-Cumming of card-cheating fame. Beautiful circular stable block (hence the Round Square tag) houses the library and boys' house. Cunning music rooms round exotic chapel (shaped like an open book – magnificent, but repairs to the pews are incredibly botched). New library conversion in round square, sixth form study area in attic area – lots of nooks and crannies; very busy.

Houses spread all over, some quite a hike from the main school. Minimal exeats – distances are huge, but pupils often do not want to go home. Prospectus lists nearby hotels, B&Bs (with prices) and ways of getting to school (a good four hours from Edinburgh but less than that flying from London). Non-stop social life which swings right through the holidays – caveat for Southerners. Excellent prospectus information booklet.

Pastoral Care and Discipline: The Betts parents (father and stepmother of Leah who died after taking one ecstasy pill) give harrowing anti-drugs lectures. Occasional problems with smoking and alcohol – 'not totally whiter than white'. Head tough on perpetual offenders, particularly bullies – 'Children have eventually had to leave the school as a result'. Commendably clear rules. Girls and boys can visit each others' houses with a certain amount of freedom. Each pupil has an academic tutor; house parents and assistant house parents in each house. Shopping bus to Elgin on Tuesday, but only the upper sixth can visit on Saturdays and can 'have meals out in the evening' – Elgin can be pretty rough.

Pupils and Parents: A third English, a third Scottish and a third from the rest of the world – wide diversity of students, some deeply rich, some less so, with the less so benefiting from serious scholarships. Quite a number of first time buyers. FPs include royals, William Boyd, Eddie Shah, the composer of 'The Flower of Scotland' – Roy Williamson, Martin Shea, Alan Shiach, Lara Croft.

Entrance: Pupils come up through the school from the junior school, Aberlour House (usually automatically, at 11), Ardvreck in Perthshire and prep schools south of the border. Assessment for those joining at Year 10 (about ten each year) and influx to sixth form. Pupils are assessed both academically and for personality. Odd places sometimes available for pupils 'at any level of the school for short periods – although not normally less than one term'. Keen to keep up its intake from outside Scotland – may pay travel/hotel bills for prospective parents.

Exit: Some leave after GCSE 'because they believe they might get higher grades elsewhere', some to crammers, otherwise standard 80/90 per cent to universities all over. Newcastle, Leeds, Bristol and Edinburgh currently popular. A few Oxbridge entrants.

Money Matters: Set fee; parents can 'opt above'. Scholarships and bursaries awarded after means-testing. Hardship fund. Success of flourishing international summer school helps with dosh. Despite offering scholarships with a proactive hardship fund, has launched a £4 million appeal for revamping the 1960s sports hall (£2 million), plus extra scholarship fund – to date raised over £3 million. Building of phase one of the new sports complex is now complete and plans are underway for phase 2.

Picked up the tab when Aberlour School was closed earlier in 2004 (it was losing money) – the buildings were sold and the funds realised more or less paid for the stunning new build, Aberlour House, in the grounds.

Remarks: Children and parents appear happy. Fashionable, co-ed, outward-boundish boarding school with vast range of pupil backgrounds. Recent HMI/Care Commission inspection awarded 'excellent' for two out of the five categories and 'very good' in the remaining three. Increasingly popular, particularly with the new younger boarding house. Availability of budget airline flights to nearest airports has proved popular with southern-based families.

The Grammar School at Leeds

Alwoodley Gates, Harrogate Road, Leeds, West Yorkshire, LS17 8GS

• Pupils: 2,300 (1,200 boys and 1,100 girls) • Ages: 3-18 • Size of sixth form: 445 • Non denominational • Fees: £7,092-£10,359 pa • Independent

Tel: 0113 229 1552
Fax: 0113 228 5111
Email: admissions@gsal.org.uk
Website: www.gsal.org.uk

Principal and Chief Executive: Mr Michael Gibbons was appointed principal in April 2010. In his fifties, he has been head of Queen Elizabeth Grammar School, Wakefield. He read history and completed a PGCE at Kings College London.

Academic matters: Academically selective and well up in league tables – 78 per cent obtained A/B at A level in 2010.

Generally a longer male than female tail but very good showing in value-added terms. Good girls' entry in science and maths at A level and GCSE; size enables school to lay on many language options (German, French, Latin, Greek, Spanish. A choice of almost 30 A level subjects. Most pupils relish the academic challenge and appreciate support of well-qualified and dedicated staff (teacher:pupil ratio across whole school is 1:10). A real sense of intellectual purpose about the place. Up-to-date library and IT facilities support teaching. All pupils screened for dyslexia on entry; some help given thereafter. Many new teachers appointed in recent years, committed to coeducational school.

Games, Options, the Arts: Boys had strong reputation in traditional team games (frequent representation at county level and beyond in rugby, and, this being Yorkshire, the 1st XI tend to moonlight in the tough world of league cricket). Football now an official game, taking advantage of both social trends and vast playing fields on new site. Girls' standards have risen (equal users of two huge Astroturf pitches), reached national finals in U14 and U18 netball. Lacrosse taster, mixed hockey, football too, and plenty of other sports, including strong cross-country. Visits to outdoor centre in splendidly wild upper Teesdale centre part of everyone's curriculum. Voluntary CCF, scouts and D of E also on offer.

Girls' school had outstanding art tradition, which continues; boys no sluggards either. Strong food technology department – boys much in evidence in cookery club. Exceptional music: classical, folk, jazz, and 60 per cent learn an instrument. Lively magazine – ambitious and satirical writing, plenty of humour. Good drama, no more need for one school to 'lend' pupils to the other for productions. Very good debating (national successes).

Background and Atmosphere: Girls' school (LGHS) founded in 1876 by Yorkshire Ladies Council for Education, while the boys' (LGS) when Sir William Sheafield left £14.13s.4d. to found a school 'for all such young scholars, youthes and children as shall come to be taught, instructed and informed'. New premises were found in 1624 and in 1857 increasing numbers prompted a further move to a site a mile from the city centre, with confidently gothic ecclesiastical buildings – now part of Leeds University – designed by EM Barry, brother of the then headmaster and member of the famous architectural family. In 1997 lack of space and pressure of curriculum brought the governors' courageous decision to build a completely new school, under Dr Bailey's predecessor, on the north edge of Leeds.

Result is a very handsome set of buildings, 'a blend of function and quality', designed by an architect who did imaginative work at the previous LGS site, incorporating (according to one senior pupil) 'the longest school corridor in Europe'. Vital historical bits from the old buildings are incorporated – few if any major schools start with an advantage like this (visitors are wafted by lift from reception to the elegant administrative area and invited to admire the campanile, piazza and porte-cochère). Though purpose-building didn't come cheap, fee increases over the last four years have been 'comfortably below sector average'.

Recent building in preparation for merger includes new science, maths and music provision, departmental suites, dining hall and sixth form common room; a second sports hall and extension to theatre are planned. Each year group has its own common room and now more intimate sheltered areas for association – something probably more appreciated by girls, who miss the cosier atmosphere of the old LGHS, which gave rise to a strong sense of community. Most (younger) boys have simpler needs, connected with space to kick a football around.

Impression is that all pupils are determined to make the new school work and, in fact, don't always recognise problems that may exercise staff and parents. A buzz of confidence in the air as pupils move about the generous and well-lit circulation space; parents comment on the civilised consideration pupils show for each other. Strong house system throws girls and boys of different ages together for communal activities – not only sports competitions but also maths, masterchef and music.

Girls and boys aged 11 to 16 are taught separately (the so-called 'diamond' system), but pastoral and social activities are in a mixed environment. Sixth form is completely coeducational.

Pastoral Care and Discipline: Both schools had excellent systems and much thought went into new structures, firmly established from day one, and more generously staffed than formerly. Head keen to point out that a big school doesn't mean big units, just a lot more small ones; heads and deputies of each year located in offices next to their groups, to keep a benign eye on things.

Pupils and Parents: From Leeds and a wide arc to the north, well served by public and school-run bus routes. Significant proportion from ethnic minorities, notably Asian, and a strong traditional Jewish element, all reflecting area's cultural diversity. Doesn't serve only the wealthy – bursary fund on its way to second million. Parents generally supportive, many typically outspoken Yorkshire. Former pupils include Dame Pauline Neville Jones, journalist Jill Parkin, comedian Barry Cryer, poet and playwright Tony Harrison, singer Robin Blaze, Gerald Kaufman MP, Ricky Wilson of the Kaiser Chiefs, and golfer Colin Montgomerie (who has given a sports-weighted bursary).

Entrance: Mostly from own junior school (tinies still in Rose Court on original LGHS site, 7–11 located with senior school) and local primaries, some from independent preps. Selection by usual in-house exam, interview and report. Some places available at 16+, heavily oversubscribed since merger; minimum five grade Bs at GCSE demanded including, where appropriate, subjects applicant wants to study in sixth form.

Exit: Nearly all (predictably) to higher education in well-established universities: two dozen a year to Oxbridge. Very few leave after GCSE. Gap years popular.

Money Matters: A number of means tested bursaries available at age 11, a few at 16; a few academic/music scholarships 'for exceptional potential'.

Remarks: Created in 2008 as merger of two excellent single-sex schools, Leeds Grammar and Leeds Girls' High. Despite careful four-year preparation bound to be differences of approach in first year (more among staff and parents than pupils?) to be reconciled. Girls and boys react differently to discipline and surroundings; one parent of girls found rules 'boy-centred', another's daughter welcomed the wide extra-curricular range. But signs that a fresh identity is being forged with both constituencies being taken seriously and suspicions of a male takeover diminishing; much responsibility here on the senior management team and breaking down a 1,500+ school into manageable and pupil-friendly units (see above). All in all, a remarkable school, drawing fully on excellence of both former parts. For many families, it makes sense to have children educated in the same place.

The Grange School

Linked to Grange Junior School (The) in the Junior section

Bradburns Lane, Hartford, Northwich, Cheshire, CW8 1LU

• Pupils: 975 boys and girls, all day • Ages: 11-18 • Size of sixth form: 195
• Christian • Fees: £6,525-£8,730 pa • Independent

Tel: 01606 74007
Fax: 01606 784 581
Email: office@grange.org.uk
Website: www.grange.org.uk

Head: Since 2005, Mr Christopher Jeffery BA Hons (history) York, (mid-forties). Came from deputy headship at The Perse School and history post at Bristol Grammar. Hugely enthusiastic, 'I wake up every morning thanking my lucky stars I've ended up here; it's a joy'. Lives a short walk away and is committed to the local church and community. A people person, liked by all and praised for his ability to remember everyone's names without hesitation. 'He commands respect rather than fear,' say pupils, while staff describe him as 'really supportive and encouraging', 'a good communicator, very friendly, very open', and appreciate his full consultation with them.

Academic matters: Stunning results tables with tiny tails below B in almost all subjects. Many exceed expectations. 'Results day was brilliant,' say pupils. Over 91 per cent A level grades A or B, over 66 per cent As in 2009. At GCSE, consistently over 46 per cent grades are A*s, over 85 per cent over A*s and As, and over 96 per cent A*–Bs. 'We're the top school academically in Cheshire regularly now and produce some of the best results in the country,' says head, 'but I prefer to be judged on the value we add and what our kids are like when they leave us.' Success is attributed to playing to pupils' strengths, so four real choices for GCSEs and pupils can opt to take just one science, for example.

New intake studies French, Spanish and German for a term each so subsequent language choices are informed. IGCSE maths. Spacious, state of the art science labs where first years flock to feeding time for kimono dragons, corn snakes, aquarium and terrapins. Sixth formers take activities that include magic, politics, morality, managing finances and cooking on a budget. 'There's a momentum here, a desire to look forward, to connect with the world and where it's going,' says head. Great emphasis on teaching learning methods and helping each child discover what works for them – sixth can sign up for one to ones for this.

Passionate, on the ball SENCo keeps in touch with some 50 sets of parents, who praise the extension work built into lesson plans as well as the extra help available for SEN pupils. Links with Wilmslow Dyslexia Institute – a specialist assessor visits school (at extra cost). Children with SEN have handbooks, to liaise with parents and other teaching staff.

Games, Options, the Arts: Four house system – Bollin, Dane, Gowy and Weaver (local rivers) – mingles age groups for drama, music and sport. Pupils not chosen for school teams play plenty of competitive house sports in their blue, red, green or yellow kits. Specialist rowing coach, boat-house on the Weaver – the national champion Ford twins are much celebrated by pupils, 'They're machines'. Pupils also very proud of drama department and superb, £3.6 million, galleried theatre – and no wonder. Full range of instrument tuition with over 20 peripatetic music teachers in new music block.

Dozens of clubs – every teacher is encouraged to share a further skill. Strong outdoor education tradition gives rise to some of the spectacular array of possible trips. Some exciting far-flung excursions come in at mega-buck level (California, Ecuador, Thailand, diving in British Honduras), but pupils are philosophical about not being able to do everything and saving earnings, or fundraising to go on a trip that really inspires them. Impressive sums raised for charities chosen by children – £16,500 in 2009 (£7,000 by juniors). 'Our children enjoy a huge privilege coming here and with that comes responsibility,' says head. Annual visit to support sister school of 10 years in the Gambia.

Background and Atmosphere: Founded in 1978 in two demountables in response to prep school parental demand. The first head, Scott Marshall, instilled tradition, and even today academic gowns wait for assembly or high days. Mrs Jenny Stephen, head from 1997–2005 (now South Hampstead HS qv) masterminded impressive forward looking building project. A core of long serving teachers gives stability; newcomers, many bright NQTs, bring bags of energy. Mr Jeffery's arrival began new chapter for investing in people and infrastructure and he is universally thought to be just the man for the job. One overtly Christian assembly a week – 'I hope to increase hymn singing,' says head, 'as a background for the children's lives, for armoury as they get older'. Pay as you go lunches are optional but popular with pupils and staff, especially the pasta and salad bars, as they're delicious.

Pastoral Care and Discipline: Relaxed atmosphere – no formal standing for visitors, but respect and good manners are expected and achieved. Relationships between staff and pupils described as 'exceptional' and 'outstanding' by 2006 ISC inspectors; 'Its quality is something I've never seen anywhere before,' says head, and each group praises the other for being 'brilliant to work with' and 'going the extra mile'. Staff available all hours except for sacrosanct thirty minutes at noon. Pastoral care through peer support in designated room with Childline training for prefects, who also marshal lunch queue and have power to hand out bus misconduct slips. Detentions mostly at lunchtime – 'You'd have to assassinate someone to get an after-school detention,' say pupils. Strong emphasis on encouragement with letters home – one from head is ultimate pat – and badges for achievement, progress and effort. That it's cool right to upper VI for one's lapels to groan under ranks of badges is refreshingly unsophisticated, but perhaps the somewhat less utopian real world will be a bit of a shock?

Uniform recently modernised (though still formal), introduced in both schools in September 2009 and ordered online. Ties follow house colours.

Pupils and Parents: Largely local from rural mid-Cheshire, so mostly white and middle class, and above average numbers of pony owners, though head is keen to point out that for some the fees are sacrificial. Head and other staff have children here. Growing reputation leaves would-be parents from leafy but urban NW suburbs frustrated – no rapid bus for the 20 mile journey. 'We do have pupils from the Cheshire set,' says head, 'but some reject us because we're not prestigious enough.' Some sixth formers' cars have personalised plates. Strong parents' association raises funds, most recently for climbing wall in sports hall. Parents join choral society and help with D of E, rowing, at a careers day and by offering work experience. A parents' Christian group regularly prays for school.

Entrance: Four form entry in senior school with most of two forms coming up from prep school, after same tests on same day as outside entrants – English, maths and verbal reasoning, plus personal questionnaire to unearth interests and personality. Entry to later years when places arise based on similar age adjusted exams. External sixth formers need eight GCSE passes with A or more in proposed A level subjects. Reference from previous school is key in all applications.

Exit: Almost all to university, a few to Oxbridge and specialist art or drama schools, some ten per cent after gap year. Pupils are grateful they're encouraged to aim high. The school hosted a gap year fair in October 2009 and is now offering a number of gap year bursaries to its own pupils and pupils in local schools.

Money Matters: Fees in line with other north west independent schools though, unusually, GCSE and A level exam fees aren't included. Bursary assistance available (up to 100 per cent plus other 'start-up' benefits) and a fund for pupils who fall on hard times, but no background trust fund or alumni support – the oldest leavers are only just hitting their forties. Until now spare cash has gone into bricks and mortar, but developing this area is now firmly on the agenda.

Remarks: Forward looking and determined to enable pupils to achieve their very best. Everyone (head, staff, pupils, parents) seems so happy it's almost too good to be true – even the kimono dragons have 35 eggs! Unpretentious certainly, but what's been described as 'independent education's best kept secret', because of its youth and diffidence, is establishing itself as a top player.

Graveney School

Welham Road, Tooting, London, SW17 9BU

• Pupils: 1,950 boys and girls • Ages: 11-18 • Size of sixth form: 635 • Non-denom • State

Tel: 0208 682 7000
Fax: 020 8767 5883
Email: info@graveney.wandsworth.sch.uk
Website: www.graveney.org

Principal: Since 1989, Mr Graham Stapleton MA (early sixties). Read history at Cambridge and joined Graveney's predecessor, Furzedown Secondary, as a history teacher in 1970, progressing as head of sixth form and deputy head to the top job. Described as 'exceptional' by Ofsted. Energetic, dedicated, a very visible presence and very much the guiding force of the school. 'It's a sense of duty to do something well,' he says. Married with two grown-up children.

Academic matters: 'It successfully challenges even the highest performing individuals and supports those with difficulties effectively and with great care,' said Ofsted, rating the school 'outstanding'. 59 per cent A*/A/B grades at A level in 2010, with 38 students getting A* or A in all the A levels they took. English literature tends to be much the most popular A level subject, with maths, biology and chemistry also high on the list. Business studies and law have been the weakest links and the school is dropping these, while adding archaeology and film studies.

85 per cent of pupils got five or more A*–C passes at GCSE in 2010 – and 81 per cent included maths and English in their five. This is not a school that ups its rating by encouraging the more woolly subjects – everyone studies a foreign language to GCSE and around 95 per cent each year takes three single sciences, all taught by experts. The head is a strong advocate of the 'pure' sciences rather than the softer 'environmental' approach. A technology college, it was the first school in London to become a specialist – 'We specialise in technology in the broadest sense, which includes science and maths as well as IT'. RE and DT are also compulsory GCSE subjects, and music, Latin, Mandarin and statistics are available as 'twilight' subjects before or after school. Understandably, a good proportion of students ends up with GCSE passes in double figures.

Pupils are divided into ability bands as they enter the school in Year 7. Staff have visited all Year 6 children with Graveney places at their primary schools, talking to their teachers and checking their school records. This is no mean feat, as in an average year there will be 70 feeder primary schools. The children are banded largely by English scores and setted for maths from Year 8 onwards, but divisions are fluid and reassessed each year. An extension programme for those nominated by teachers, which includes PE, music and art as well as English, maths and science. Also a lecture programme with visiting speakers open to everyone in the upper school.

Pupils with special needs get 'an immense amount of individual attention', with detailed individual education plans. The school has an above average percentage of statemented pupils, since these can name their chosen school; the trick, says the head, is to identify those just below this threshold and ensure that teachers act on that identification. 'We concentrate on learning styles so everyone is taught in an appropriate way.' In Years 10 and 11, the lowest band follows a narrower choice of options to allow more time for maths and English. It seems to work, as virtually every pupil passes at least one GCSE. However, like most state schools, it has far more pupils with SEN than it has funding to cope with adequately, and some parents feel it deals better with highly motivated pupils.

Graveney seems to have cracked the under-achieving boys conundrum – never much of a gap in achievement between boys and girls. The head attributes this to his 'fantastic upper school team', dubbed the 'three amigos', who know all the pupils and give the boys, in particular, constant, humorous reminders of looming homework and coursework deadlines. 'The students know the three amigos won't let them get away with it.' No-one is allowed to graduate from Year 10 into Year 11 until they have finished their coursework and the school is open over the holidays for those who need to catch up.

Very strong senior management team that is interested and involved in the day-to-day life of the school and always on the lookout for ways to improve. Plenty of support for new and experienced staff, so few recruitment problems. 'The school treasures its teachers as well as its pupils,' said Ofsted.

Games, Options, the Arts: Sports excellent with high quality teaching. PE and dance options at GCSE and A level; softball, climbing and martial arts available alongside more traditional sports. The school has a sports hall, multigym, Astroturf pitch, tennis courts and climbing wall. Close links with the Wandsworth sports development team; many pupils compete at regional and national level.

Music is very important: the school subsidises instrumental lessons and runs many bands and choirs, including those conducted by students. Extensive programme of concerts and shows, at school and in the local community. Many study at the Centre for Young Musicians. Talented musicians are identified in Year 7 and many take exams early.

Plenty of high quality art displays all round the school. A very high proportion of top grades, particularly at A level, and many go on to art college. Drama also strong, with good results at GCSE and A level. Annual school productions have ranged from *Romeo and Juliet* to *Jungle Book*. Also plenty of smaller productions, trips to theatres and workshops run by visiting companies. Sixth formers have recently begun to finance, direct and produce their own musical theatre performances, and have so far staged *West Side Story*, *Grease*, *Moulin Rouge* and *Hairspray*, with *Little Shop of Horrors* in the pipeline. D of E, ski trip, French exchanges, field trips etc.

Background and Atmosphere: The school can trace its origins to Battersea Grammar School, founded in 1669, which went through several incarnations before amalgamating with Rosa Bassett Grammar School in 1977 to form a comprehensive named Furzedown Secondary. In 1986, Furzedown amalgamated with Ensham School to become Graveney. Its nine buildings – Furzedown House is Georgian, most of the rest built around the First World War – straddle quiet, suburban Welham Road in Tooting. Green, leafy campus – a bonus whilst making one's way between classrooms. The large numbers can seem intimidating at break times but the atmosphere is ordered and behaviour good-humoured.

Pastoral Care and Discipline: Quite a few temporary exclusions, mostly in the lower years, but these are combined with a reintegration programme. The social inclusion unit helps pupils to catch up and to develop strategies to avoid unacceptable behaviour. As a result, the school has permanently excluded only three pupils in the last 15 years, and those all very recently. 'It is very labour-intensive to deal with badly behaved pupils and I'm very sympathetic to schools that won't put up with it. But most young people are worth the effort. All our heads of year put enormous amounts of work into avoiding exclusions, and generally it pays off. But in the end justice must be seen to be done.'

The school is careful to ensure that those who behave well are not overlooked. Achievements are celebrated at presentation evenings, with colours for excellence in music, sport and community service, and certificates and special credits for academic success. Sixth former prefects run the school council, organise their own budget and work with younger pupils – 'They play a great part in the running of the school'.

Pupils and Parents: Fairly representative of the area, with around 65 per cent from various ethnic minorities. Supportive parent body – the PTA goes well beyond cake sales and organises workshops on topics such as homework and study skills.

Entrance: All applicants (generally around 2,000) take the Wandsworth Year 6 test. Many will also be applying to the Sutton grammar schools and various independents. The 63 with highest scores in the non-verbal and verbal reasoning papers are offered places. Next in line are siblings, though not – since 2008 – siblings of pupils who got a place on ability. Those with particular medical or social needs, and looked after children, come next; the rest of the 250 places are awarded to children who live nearest – in practice, within about half a mile.

Takes around 150 into the sixth form – at 650 pupils it is one of the biggest in the country. Many of these come from independent schools. Graveney pupils must get at least five grade Cs at GCSE to move up, and nearly all do. Incomers average eight or nine good GCSEs.

Exit: Some 15 per cent leave after GCSEs, mostly for vocational courses elsewhere. The Swan Partnership with other local schools coaches prospective university candidates in public speaking, problem solving and team working skills. Nearly all sixth form leavers go to university, usually between five and ten a year to Oxbridge (11 in 2009).

Remarks: Immensely caring and successful school that, despite its size, manages to treat everyone as individuals. Very few fall by the wayside, with boys achieving as well as girls, and the most and least able nurtured equally.

Greenhead College

Greenhead Road, Huddersfield, West Yorkshire, HD1 4ES

• Pupils: 1,910; 1,110 girls, 800 boys • Ages: 16-19 • Non-denom • State

Tel: 01484 422 032
Fax: 01484 518 025
Email: college@greenhead.ac.uk
Website: www.greenhead.ac.uk

Principal: Since 2002, Mr Martin Rostron BA PGCE (late fifties) who was educated at Chadderton Grammar School in Oldham and read English at Liverpool. Recently made FRSA. He came to Greenhead in 1991 and was previously vice principal. Career entirely in the maintained sector and has taught all ages from 11–18. Has had two sons and a daughter at Greenhead. Has presided over successive outstanding Ofsteds and relishes challenge of living up to that accolade. Driven by desire to treat young people 'as we would want our children to be treated'. Enjoying his time here, 'Life has got to be fun ... People here work extraordinarily hard ... The staff are quite phenomenal and love teaching 16, 17 and 18 year olds' – good intra-staff support. Concentrates on 'developing the positives' in students and passes the college's ethos on to others. Has built on foundations laid by revered predecessor, Kevin Conway.

Academic matters: College is one of three in Kirklees with a concordat whereby, between them, they provide basic AS and A level subjects but each will specialise in a different sphere. Hence Greenhead offers business studies at applied level, as well as A and AS levels in law, government and politics, IT, maths ad infinitum, humanities, sciences, psychology, philosophy and sociology. An astonishing 246 students took maths last year, with 55 per cent getting A*/A. French, German, Spanish and Italian on offer but no classics or esoteric languages – yet. Overall, 99 per cent A level pass rate, with 66 per cent at A*/A or B. 11 per cent of passes at A*. Applied business and applied science up with best results in the country.

Good take-up for OCR (RSA) qualifications. Average class size 20 for A levels and 21 at AS. Most students opt for four AS and three or more As. College will also 'investigate the possibility' of grafting on extra subjects if 'sufficient demand' and if sufficient space. A level general studies for 'almost all'. Also offers extended project and AQA Baccalaureate to give further evidence of academic excellence for demanding universities. Head employs staff who are 'experts in their field', and it shows.

No real break between some lessons – the distances can be quite far – but no bell and a business-like but sensibly relaxed atmosphere prevails. Students have ample room to study and socialise – the library is peaceful and well banked with computers; they can chat and study in the reading room and use a main hall area as a common room.

Seems to have twin pillars of success. Firstly, the open door policy, where students always have access to staff and rarely find a staffroom door closed to them. Friendly staff cluster in subject rooms during their free time and any pupil can walk in and ask for help: 'These are young adults – we don't shut ourselves away in adult rooms and leave them in the corridor'. Secondly, the college's own value-added system developed by Kevin Conway and now built upon and widely followed. It picks up students who are falling behind or deserve particular praise very early and, most particularly and without rancour, helps bring teachers who are performing below par up to scratch.

They have visually impaired students and provide good support for learning – this is, after all, state-funded. Prospective students are advised to contact the college's learning support coordinator for advice prior to admission, so any specialist support or facilities can be put in place (strives to meet all reasonable requests).

Games, Options, the Arts: Recent fitness room, all-weather sports field and changing room block. No large sports hall of their own but has use of one. Major playing fields are five minutes' walk across the park – 93 took PE last year – 70 per cent grades A*/A and B. Strongest football side in the county, cups all over the place, squash, netball, basketball good (boys and girls); two national representatives in hockey – popular; spectacular success in tennis. Olympic skier Fiona Hughes is a former student.

Enormous art rooms in £2 million building, shared with law and business – walls drip with creative work. Music is very strong with the orchestra, plus jazz, string quartets and choir the subject of much pride. Helped by impressive music department with full recording gear and Apple Macs. Vibrant drama, often with play rehearsals at 7.30am as well as pm and at weekends.

Serious enrichment programme. College has 121 teachers and all offer an enrichment subject from a bewildering choice, from creative writing and first aid to power yoga, critical thinking, swing music, poetry, boxercise, archaeology, Scrabble, climbing, golf, skiing, Freudian psychology, D of E – in fact if a teacher can teach it, you can do it – plus hints on how to handle Oxbridge. Every student MUST attend one course, but if you don't fancy any of them, then start your own. Excellent work placement programme – 570 placements last year, home and abroad. Happy to bring in experts to college if the right placement doesn't present itself – 385 on work-based projects.

Background and Atmosphere: A very busy college; tight on space, which makes lesson changeover a little bit London Underground, but the students love it and enjoy being right in the centre of Huddersfield, close to train and bus stations and shops. A former girls' school, it has grown physically and in reputation. A 10-year plan embraces hopes of further new building work. Thanks to five lifts, most areas are now fully accessible. Student Union, self-elected prefects.

Pastoral Care and Discipline: Pastoral system is another secret of success; 22 staff have tutor duties and plenty of time is set aside for students to take up tutor guidance. PSHE for all. College will exclude for violent or abusive behaviour, smoking 'not tolerated'. Students with problems can make an appointment to see a counsellor, and they do. No racial tension. Students report that the college is not cliquey – no sense of all the sports 'jocks' sticking together, for example. Regular 'whole block' assemblies – unusual in most sixth form colleges.

Pupils and Parents: Lots of middle class, but a good cross-section and a better than usual success rate in turning round fortunes of youngsters who did not fare especially well at GCSE. Strong work ethos. Huge catchment area, about two thirds of the students come from partner schools. Students enjoy not calling the staff 'Sir' or 'Mr' and like coming to college. One told us, 'My friends at other colleges don't want to go but I want to come, otherwise I would miss out.' Their only gripe is a lack of space.

Entrance: Regularly 40 per cent over-subscribed so apply well before mid-Feb of the year you want to go to. Fed by 12 local partner schools in the same catchment area and around 55 other schools nearby on a placement basis. Places allocated on the basis of interview, plus results of mock GCSEs and school reports. Six per cent from the independent sector. Open days for Year 11 students and their families.

Exit: Aspirations are high here. About 90 per cent go directly to higher education, including 30 or so to Oxbridge; very strong medical bias – at one point the college was responsible for one per cent of the new medical intake in the country. Five per cent take a gap year (and then go presumably to higher education) and rest to work. Musicians may choose the Northern College of Music or the Conservatoire but, equally, may decide to go to university first and then study music full time.

Money Matters: Some students are entitled to an allowance (EMA – means tested), to enable them to access sixth form education.

Remarks: Up there with the very best state and independents. Superb student/staff relationships foster an excellent, enjoyable learning environment. Turns out successful students again and again, whatever qualifications they first arrive with.

Gresham's School

Linked to Greshams Preparatory School in the Junior section

Cromer Road, Holt, Norfolk, NR25 6EA

• Pupils: 475 boys and girls; (almost 60 per cent board) • Ages: 13-18
• Size of sixth form: 195 • C of E • Fees: Boarding £25,395; Day £19,500 pa • Independent

Tel: 01263 714500
Fax: 01263 712 028
Email: registrar@greshams.com
Website: www.greshams.com

Headmaster: Since 2008, Mr Philip John BA (fifties). Read management and engineering science at Bradford. Previously head at King William's College Isle of Man for eight years. Before that a housemaster and maths teacher at Malvern College. Married to Kathryn – she teaches French in the school and has broadened parents' social forum by introducing Friends of Gresham's and a popular Saturday morning bacon butty club. They have four children and in the hols relax in their house in France. He's not in the least bit stuffy despite a reputation for being business-like – says one of the most important things achieved since arriving is the development of a rigorous administrative structure which includes a marketing and HR department.

Promotion of the IB also a big thing – absolutely clear that it's the way forward and even year niners know that 'Mr John is pretty keen on the IB'. He'd like to see it taken by most pupils (all took it in his last school) and thinks the perception that only the brightest can cope is misguided – 'It's more to do with managing the work load – if you want to do well you have to work hard'. No current plans to scrap A levels, but the head said everyone 'should, like IB students, follow the theory of knowledge' – something which benefits all. Interests include rugby (used to play and coach but now prefers to watch matches on the TV) and music – he plays the cello and guitar at home.

Academic matters: Setting in various subjects and on the whole small classes where children 'don't get lost in a crowd'. Parents speak of a generally unpressured approach where pupils are allowed to go at their own pace – 'The focused kid who wants to learn is thrust forward'. The days of 'the lazy happily meandering' seem to be numbered – comments made by Mr John when we visited led us to believe he'd want to make that a thing of the past. Ten to eleven GCSEs for the majority; 63 per cent A /A*. Strong performances in maths (which offers fast tracking) and the sciences.

For the sixth, A levels or the IB – latter is gaining in popularity amongst the home grown cohort (when introduced nearly half the entrants were from abroad) even though, as one sixther mused, 'You have to be pretty bright to hack it'. IB subject list is expanding – some parents wonder if enough teachers to deliver the IB and A levels (to date A level Latin no longer available, those wishing to study it follow the IB course: an accreditation which gains UCAS points). Good results in most areas – A level: 74 per cent A/B with big boosts from art and maths; IB: average point score of 34. Relatively low interest in languages – improvement may follow recent investment in language lab equipment. Standard facilities spacious and perfectly okay. Useful chemistry lecture theatre and nannied school intranet.

Good noises re learning support, which is given instead of language lessons (three languages compulsory until Year 10 – some in the centre do one, two or none). Parents feel the school doesn't want to advertise just how good they are – that's our impression too. Cap on numbers imposed by the number who can be accommodated in the cosy unit. Sympathetic, well qualified staff (two full time, four part time, plus one who delivers ESL) provide a 'sounding board for all sorts of needs' – dyslexia, dyscalcula, dyspraxia, mild Asperger's and ADD. 'It's a pyramid, there's a big drop in numbers after Years 9 and 11 and pupils only need an occasional visit once they are in the sixth.' Strong links with the junior school, screening for new entrants, IEPs for each child, offer of scribes, readers and voice activated computers. Charges according to the number of sessions in the unit with a cap of £500 at term. Also applies to ESL.

Games, Options, the Arts: Outdoorsy lot who appreciate the inclusive ethos and huge number of teams. Hockey (girls and boys) and cricket particularly strong – rugby still to find consistent form. Ample number of pitches and tennis courts, well used Astroturfs and swimming pool, four refurbished squash courts and a rifle range (justifiably trumpets awards gained by members of the rifle club and the achievements of two pupils who, between them, have been British Junior Ladies champion four years running).

Weights room, gym and rowing machines for extra exercise and sailing for those who feel the call of the water.

Flourishing D of E with healthy number of gold and silver awards. Other options include BASC course (British Association for shooting and conversation) and the CCF. Drama is big here – 'Outstanding – it blows me away,' gushed a parent. The Auden theatre (the real thing with dressing rooms, professional lighting and sound systems) hosts a tremendous variety of performances given by touring companies – well attended by locals and free to pupils. Also a venue for numerous school productions – we enjoyed an impressive offering produced and played with great brio. Music also valued. Wide choice of instrumental tuition (approx 40 per cent have lessons) plus various orchestral, band and choral activities. Rather crusty music facilities due to be upgraded in time for the 2013 Britten centenary.

Grown-up art block with decent studio space. Oil paints from the start and life drawing on a regular basis. Large canvases all over the place – strong, confidently realised representational images. Some 3D work and a new kiln recently installed. Regular artists in residence and exhibitions in the foyer – all very positive.

Background and Atmosphere: Although founded in 1555 as a free grammar school, it wasn't until the 1890s that it became something more. Somewhat random development of the 170 acre site (including 90 acres of woodland) makes for a fair amount of walking – all but the upper sixth have to use a bridge which straddles a road into town. Structures vary from listed to unattractive. Solid Edwardian classroom blocks, a sizeable chapel and 'The big School', a rather fine hall with polished wood floors, rub shoulders with the thoroughly modern Auden theatre and now listed 'temporary' twenties thatched huts (scruff shacks). Everywhere spotlessly clean. Comfortable atmosphere. Friendly, relaxed relationships between pupils and staff despite some predictably unpopular tightening up since new stewardship (sixth have to wear suits and girls are meant to tie their hair back – one or two still manage the tousled look).

Inter-house competition important but doesn't hinder cheerful social interaction (most have known each other since they were tinies in the junior school) – sixth whizz off to congregate at the BOP (bar on premises) with the rest flocking to Dave's Diner for a burger and fizzy drink. All allowed into Holt three times a week – charmingly sedate country town. Boarding houses on a rolling revamp pogramme – some more homely and cared for than others. Full and weekly boarding with over 40 per cent day pupils – working hard to promote full boarding and parents say weekend activities have improved. Some houses can empty if nothing going on, so worth checking which have a higher proportion of full boarders.

Day and boarding pupils are integrated with the former having a base and or bed in boarders' rooms – flexi boarding isn't encouraged ('We're not a baby sitting service,' according to the head) but when activities are full on, pupils can stay the night. Large dining hall where pupils eat at house tables – staff have a table of their own. Adequate buffet fare with vegetarian option – for hungry moments packets of squadgy white bread can be toasted and buttered in the house kitchens.

Pastoral Care and Discipline: A small school where everyone knows everyone. Positive interaction between year groups and approachable staff (tutors, house parents, school counsellor and multi denominational school chaplain) – parents say issues are dealt with promptly. Some pupils find going from junior to senior a big leap, but others relish greater independence and a chance to take responsibility for what they do – new bods are 'buddied'. Polite (lovely to find door holding is de rigueur), biddable lot. Sixth formers have sessions on stress and a clear anti bullying policy. Zero tolerance re illegal drugs. Pretty tough on boozers (although over 18s are allowed to visit The Feathers with permission) and pupils found in their company can expect to be punished. Same applies to smoking.

Pupils and Parents: Fresh faced, friendly girls and boys – their 'confidence comfortably worn' – more upturned collar and bleached rugby shirt than Vivienne Westwood. Most come from East Anglia, Lincolnshire etc – getting that all important driving licence makes getting home for the odd night or two a breeze. Twenty per cent foreign nationals in the sixth (strong German contingent). In the main parents involved in farming, law, accountancy etc. Old Boys include Sir Stephen Spender, W H Auden, Benjamin Britten, Ben Nicholson, Sir Christopher Cockerell (inventor of the hovercraft), James Dyson, Lord Reith, Prof Alan Hodgkin and Stephen Frears.

Entrance: 50 per cent CE plus interview. Keen on siblings but only if 'up to standard'. Eighty per cent come in from own prep school (parents wonder if its popularity means that cherry picking will make the school more 'academic' – potential candidates for the IB?). Rest from local preps or maintained sector.

For the sixth 6 GCSE A*–C with B grades in subjects to be taken in the sixth. IELTS minimum score of 6, or equivalent level of ability.

Exit: Trickle to Oxbridge otherwise all over the place with heavyweights well represented. Number 'reapplying' decreasing. Huge variety of courses with practical subjects like engineering, economics, accounting and business predominant – law, veterinary, medicine yet to show on the radar.

Money Matters: Worshipful Company of Fishmongers, with whom has close links, give generous scholarships – recent launch of Gresham's Foundation will help fund new builds and bursaries. Twelve academic awards (up to 100 per cent 'upon demonstration of financial need'), in addition to art, drama, music, sports and all rounder awards. Sixth form scholarships (academic, art, music etc) for those who've done fantastically well at GCSE and haven't already received an award. Annual award of £1,500 for maths genius and £750 for pupils who 'undertake voluntary work through Student Partnership Worldwide'. For pupils whose parents have fallen on hard times does its best to help them through until next public exam.

Remarks: Has been known as an unsophisticated public school where parents have valued a broad education without an over pressured, hot house atmosphere. Introduction of the IB is already making its mark (an academic deputy has recently been appointed) and Mr John is determined to make it a success. He says it will broaden outlooks – we say the school's attractiveness to a wider, out of county audience. An interesting time ahead.

The Grey Coat Hospital

Greycoat Place, Westminster, London, SW1P 2DY

• Pupils: 1,010 day girls, 40 boys in the sixth form • Ages: 11-18
• Size of sixth form: 235 girls and 40 boys • C of E • State

Tel: 02079 691 998
Fax: 02078 282 697
Email: info@gch.org.uk
Website: www.gch.org.uk

Headteacher: Since 1999, Mrs Rachel Allard BA (fifties). Married with two grown-up children. Previously deputy head of St Saviour's and St Olave's and advisory English teacher for Hackney. Tall, eloquent lady with a special interest in African and Asian literature. Consciously raising the academic profile. Strong management team and governors.

Academic matters: Rated 'outstanding' by Ofsted in March 2009 and at previous inspection in 2005. Best ever exam results in 2009 with benchmark 91 per cent of students achieving 5+ A*–C grades including maths and English, 97 per cent overall. GCSE and A level results are impressive for a comprehensive intake – very few failures in any subject. Specialist language college and training school. Vibrant and well thought of school, strong, teaching staff who are open to new ideas and methodology. 'An enthusiastic and committed bunch,' claim parents. 'Evening Standard' Award for academic excellence is proudly displayed in the head's office. Particularly dynamic languages department offering a good range of choices; girls do particularly well in French. Pupils selected for their aptitude for languages can study three languages by year eight, one of which is Mandarin. European and Asian exchange programmes are run with other schools along with 'culture of the month'. The school also works with local primaries who teach foreign languages. Pupils are encouraged to do well with incentives such as 'mathematician of the month' and debates are welcomed. Single and dual award sciences on offer; girls now benefit from lovely new modern science labs at St Michael's.

Excellent ICT facilities integrated across all curriculum areas. The sixth form open evening is run as a road show, attracting prospective pupils from all over London from both the state and independent sectors. A small number of boys join at sixth form. 'We come for the friendly atmosphere and better facilities,' say boys. Active careers department with business mentors and careers road shows. Head has arranged a link with Westminster School so pupils can study subjects, such as Latin A level, not available at Grey Coat. A head of special needs, a number of learning support assistants and a programme for gifted pupils.

Games, Options, the Arts: Sports Mark – amazingly successful sports, considering the limited facilities, run by a dedicated head of sports. They make the best of the small on-site space; pupils use the outdoor facilities at Battersea Park and local pool. Recently national champions of cricket, they have produced national football and cricket players. Hoards of trophies for almost everything. Year nine have the option of doing junior or community sports leader qualifications or a BTec in sixth form. Strong music and drama, four large choirs that have performed at the Albert Hall, wind band and strings group. Instrumental tuition is subsidized by the school's Foundation. Theatre studies A level and drama GCSE are becoming very popular, several plays are produced annually. Successful competitors in the Mock Magistrates and Bar competitions. Huge list of lunchtime and after school clubs to choose from, D of E awards and community service programmes also run. Brand new arts building to be ready for autumn 2010 housing state of the art facilities for drama, music, art as well as improved facilities across the curriculum overall.

Background and Atmosphere: Founded by concerned parishioners to reduce crime and get urchins off the streets in the days when the parish of Westminster was considered a den of iniquity. In 1701 the governors purchased an old workhouse to set up a school to provide education, board and lodgings and care (hence hospital in the name) for 40 boys and 40 girls. Benefactors' portraits still hang in the Great Hall. There was a murder in 1773 and a rebellion against the dreadful conditions in the school in 1801. In 1874 The Grey Coat Hospital became a day school for girls led for some years by one of the great pioneers of education, Elsie Day. The lower school continues today on the same site, St Andrew's. An additional site, St Michael's, houses the upper school. Both premises have gyms and libraries.

Pastoral Care and Discipline: Girls are expected to be responsible for themselves and considerate to others. Good community feel with plenty of opportunities for spiritual and moral development. Long tradition of caring and solid Christian values; other faiths are also welcome. Older girls have the opportunity to take on serious responsibilities and serve the school. 'Everyone gets a chance to be involved here and staff are approachable,' say pupils. Sensible set of school rules aimed at producing conscientious young people. Many past pupils return for the annual school celebration service in Westminster Abbey. Strict uniform code.

Pupils and Parents: Big inner city mix, few locals, pupils come from all over as catchment is anyone living in the dioceses of London and Southwark. Popular choice for the children of education professionals. Streetwise, polite and (mostly) sensible hard working girls, plus a handful of boys in sixth form.

Entrance: At 11+, 15 selective places by exam for girls showing an aptitude for languages, then standard LEA criteria – 25 per cent band one, 50 per cent band two, 25 per cent band three with priority given to practising C of E families and siblings.

Exit: At 16+ one third leaves to follow vocational courses or A levels elsewhere, mostly because the school does not offer the A level courses they want; a few to work. At 18+ most go to university – London, Durham, Bristol, three or four to Oxbridge.

Money Matters: The Parents' Guild raises money for the school and charity, keeping up the long tradition of serving the community. Parents are asked to contribute a small amount of money on a monthly or annual basis.

Remarks: Ever popular, the pioneering spirit lives on, as does the tradition of care. Regularly on Ofsted annual list of 'outstanding providers' of education and care.

The Gryphon School

Bristol Road, Sherborne, Dorset, DT9 4EQ

• Pupils: 1,500 boys and girls • Ages: 11-18 • Size of sixth form: 330
• Church of England • State

Tel: 01935 813 122
Fax: 01935 816 992
Email: office@gryphon.dorset.sch.uk
Website: www.gryphon.dorset.sch.uk

Headteacher: Since 2007, Mr Steve Hillier MA PGCE, a King's College Cambridge geographer. Variety of teaching experiences before becoming assistant head at the Minster School, Southwell and, prior to taking up his post at The Gryphon, vice principal at Frome Community College 2003–06. Soft-spoken, intelligent and inspires trust rather than operating on the livewire end of the spectrum. Highly regarded by other school heads in the area, and parents we spoke to uniformly described his arrival as good news. Married to Sharon, with three children, two at Gillingham School and one at primary.

Academic matters: Results were the highest ever in 2010, commendable given the non-selective intake. At GCSE, 66 per cent of students gained 5+ A* to C including maths and English – steady improvement here. 48 per cent A/B at A level (big growth of sixth form recently). Very good results in business and economics, as befitting its business and enterprise specialist status (recent Ofsted praised the school's 'exceptional' links with local businesses). The arts, ICT and languages also stand out. GCSE Latin taught by a teacher from Sherborne School – scope for much more interaction with the independent schools in the area and we expect to see that growing.

Sixth form has breadth and variety – 27 subjects including ancient history, law, philosophy and ethics, further mathematics, theatre studies, sports studies and economics. Also offers an increasing range of vocational subjects from equine studies (pupils whizz off on buses at dawn) to motor vehicle maintenance. National winners of the UK Formula One Technology Challenge in 2007 (creating a car of the future).

SEN provision has a strong reputation, attracting students from some distance away. Lots of good inclusive practice, so that SEN students are made to feel an integral part of the school and are given the support they need to do their best.

Games, Options, the Arts: Music a definite strength – Ofsted inspection in 2009 judged provision to be outstanding. Two school bands, three choirs, four ensembles, annual music tours. In 2009 the senior choir finished second in the national BBC 'Songs of Praise' Choir of the Year competition. We were sorry to note, however, that the practice of Gryphon pupils joining the Sherborne Schools Sinfonia, alongside pupils from the local independents, has died out – pupils we spoke to had never heard of it. Recording studio and main music rooms have composing software on fifteen computers. Bright, spacious rooms for art and lots of art trips. Art exhibitions raise local critical acclaim. Ambitious dramatic productions, though less frequent than some students would like. Artsmark Gold awarded 2009 in recognition of results in drama, music, art, design, media and literature.

Leisure centre on site provides fitness suite, squash courts, cricket nets, dance studio, outdoor pool. Pupils and parents miffed that the town's new indoor pool has been built at Sherborne School for Girls rather than The Gryphon, but the school intends to make use of the new facility. Rugby strong with some county players – The Gryphon beat Sherborne in the 'Daily Mail' Cup in 2006 – but team sports further down the school don't often get the attention or the manpower needed to keep them going. The girls we spoke to said they did no sport at all, though two periods of some sort of physical activity is compulsory through Year 11. Lunchtime sports clubs include fitness, squash and ultimate frisbee. Some sort of extra-curricular involvement (usually on a Wednesday afternoon) is a requirement to progress from Year 12 to 13.

Background and Atmosphere: The result of an amalgamation of three schools in 1992 is a bustling, well-marketed, consumer-orientated institution with snappy newsletters. For a purpose-bred school it lacks some essentials (lockers for pupils) but youngsters are cheerful as they hover round architecturally monotonous quadrangles and foyers. Recent poll of parents came back with 96 per cent agreeing that 'My child likes this school'. Ambitiously-named 'conference centre' (2007) provides a valuable second school hall. Engaging and well-used library another asset. Little Gryphons nursery on site, taking little ones from three months old, helps to recruit staff.

Pastoral Care and Discipline: Well thought out. Hugely popular chaplain here three days a week – described by C of E inspection as 'a holy hanger-around' – makes a big difference. Pupil guidance centre so youngsters with problems integrating, e.g. school phobics, can have specialist attention from senior staff in much smaller groups and move back into classrooms as confidence grows. All buildings wheelchair-accessible. Pupils remain in same tutor groups for five years. Sixth form assembly we observed was swift, respectful and information-full. Hot on parent-rapport and student voice – two students have been chosen to be associate governors, attending governors' meetings etc. Pupils from Year 11 up are allowed into town during the lunch break – a few parents worry about this, but school says the privilege is withdrawn for any pupil that transgresses. A bit of rancour between Gryphon boys and those at the 'Boys' School' (Sherborne) – but less than before. One parent singled out the school's effective handling of bullying as its finest quality.

Pupils and Parents: From near (the town) and far (well into Somerset). Many teachers from independent Sherborne schools – and state schools – choose Gryphon for their own children. Nearby Yeovilton airbase instills a drop or two of foreign blood (pilots on three-year stints) into an otherwise white community. Uniform strictly adhered to; sixth form wears mufti.

Entrance: Non-selective but slightly over-subscribed. At least 220 enter at 11 from 80 square mile catchment, 25 or so from local independent schools. Lots enter at sixth form: requires five A-Cs but will make exceptions for students with special needs.

Exit: Post-16, 40 per cent leave, many to Yeovil Sixth Form College, a few owing to a family move from the area, some moving to other schools, a few into employment. Post-A level, 60 per cent to university, 15 or so gap years, 15 to employment/apprenticeships, small handfuls to art foundation courses and FE courses. When we were there, the university adviser from Sherborne School was visiting to offer his advice on university admissions to Gryphon sixth formers, as a topup to the school's own very good guidance.

Remarks: Annual review by the LA judged school outstanding; increasingly popular.

Guildford High School

Linked to Guildford High School Junior School in the Junior section

London Road, Guildford, Surrey, GU1 1SJ

• Pupils: 630 girls (plus 285 girls in junior school) • Ages: 11-18, junior school 4-11 • Size of sixth form: 150 • Christian • Fees: £7,560-£12,744 pa • Independent

Tel: 01483 543 853
Fax: 01483 306 516
Email: Guildford-Admissions@church-schools.com
Website: www.guildfordhigh.surrey.sch.uk

Headmistress: Since 2002, Mrs Fiona Boulton BSc MA (mid-forties). Previously deputy head, prior to that a teacher and housemistress at Marlborough and Stowe. Energetic and enthusiastic, a non-stop soul who somehow manages to run a first rate school and have three young children – 'I throw myself into everything'. Supremely confident in her school and the approach it takes – and makes no apologies for the ambitious academic goals: 'I'm absolutely confident we are the best school in the area, one of the best schools in the country, and it is a privilege to be a part of this community'. Believes that the school is 'very strong' in all areas of school life – academic, sporting, music, pastoral care – and wants it to be perceived as 'at the forefront of everything'.

Roundly commended for her leadership skills and for being 'motivated' and 'very focused', with a universally-praised team of 'fantastic' teaching staff. 'Wonderful on a one-to-one basis,' said a very pleased parent. Her own suite of rooms is a relaxing space with comfy sofas and chairs opening on to a meeting room – conducive to the air of relaxation but also to industry.

Academic matters: Superb academics in a school which constantly pushes the boundaries of achievement. As you would expect from this rigorous approach, results are hugely impressive. 44 per cent of all the A levels sat in 2010 were awarded the new A* grade (placing the school second nationally in *The Times* league table), with 89 per cent A*/A. At GCSE, over 90 per cent of grades were A/A* with 60 per cent A*. Huge mixture of subjects on offer at A level, with languages, sciences and maths very popular, also psychology is much in demand. In the dreaded league tables, the school is 8th nationally at GCSE and 9th at A level – what more could a parent want? The results speak for themselves, but it is the approach to education which is so exciting and ground breaking – the intention is to teach girls 'how to learn, not what to learn'.

Follows the national curriculum, broadened and enriched with a wide variety of subjects. Offers French, German, Spanish, Latin and classical Greek. As well as history, geography and RE, philosophy is taught from Year 7 onwards, encouraging the development of sound argument and the confidence to debate issues publicly. Critical thinking in the sixth form and Year 11. Impressive to see how, in a history lesson, Year 9 girls were split into teams to research a historical figure and analyse and debate their relative merits against another – e.g. Florence Nightingale versus Mother Teresa. This total culture of learning makes for less pressure – 'It's how my school work has always been, so it doesn't feel pressured to me,' says a senior pupil.

A parent commented that the work was 'stimulating but not overwhelming'. Innovative information booklets give a complete insight for parents and pupils as to expectations and curriculum in each school year, including guidelines for parents on how to help at home. SEN support either one to one or within the classroom, but a low key affair. Gifted and talented programme.

Games, Options, the Arts: Strong sporting tradition with four games lessons a week. New state-of-the-art £5 million sports centre – 25m swimming pool with touch pad timing and a sports hall. Girls have done exceptionally well nationally in swimming and schools' athletics; netball and lacrosse tours to Japan and Australia and lacrosse tours to the US. Gymnastics strong, as are tennis and rounders. No miserable little souls hating every minute of sport here – girls are encouraged to have a go, whatever their ability, much encouraged by the 'fantastic' (according to Mrs Boulton) director of sport.

Very strong musical tradition with myriad opportunities to shine – symphony orchestra, chamber orchestra and a number of choirs and instrument groups. 550 individual music lessons a week. Involved with the Light! Project – a musical exchange programme involving schools in Turkey, Austria and Slovakia. Drama very important – a number of productions each year for all age groups, which also provide a welcome opportunity to mix with boys from the nearby Royal Grammar School. Sixth formers write and produce the annual pantomime, performed by Year 7, and girls from Year 11 up can be involved in the senior school play. Art is increasingly important and impressive. A vast number of clubs and extra-curricular activities including debating (very popular), maths, creative writing, chess, art and books. Dazzling array of expeditions abroad – trips to China, Bangalore, France, Germany. These academic girls obviously like to challenge themselves in all areas of school life with 85 per cent participating in D of E.

Background and Atmosphere: Founded in 1888 by a consortium of 'worthy locals'. Member of the United Church Schools Trust consisting of ten schools which share a common governing council. Pleasant leafy surroundings for a city centre school. The main buildings are a mixture of old and the new, sympathetically put together in what can only be described, in polite terms, as a compact and bijou space – i.e. cramped. It is all incredibly well maintained – much effort has been put into upgrading all areas; since she has been head, Mrs Boulton has refurbished a section of the school each year: 'We never stand still'.

Pressurised though space may be, it has all been thoroughly thought out so no corner is allowed to go unused. Dripping with fantastic ICT rooms, well equipped science labs, impressive food technology rooms, pleasing and airy art rooms, very well equipped library (would beat many local libraries into a cocked hat for sheer volume of items available) – the atmosphere as a whole is inspiring and enhancing of creative thought. Main school hall is a vast, multi-purpose space which can house the entire school for assemblies and stage drama productions with professional lighting rigs and sound box. The raked seating at one end can be pushed back to one side for an entirely clear floor space which allows for, amongst other things, the annual parents' bash. The sixth form centre has seen some recent updating: the common room looks a bit like the 'Big Brother' house – very funky.

Mrs Boulton recently pushed for the £1.5 million purchase of the house next door in Nightingale Road – whipped away from the hands of developers, much to the delight of the old lady who had lived there. This provides extra classroom space for sixth formers, plus staff accommodation. It also offers much needed extra green space available for both senior and junior pupils – currently full of lovely garden furniture, perfect for al fresco breaktimes.

She couldn't wait to show us the brand spanking new sports centre just up the road overlooking Stoke Park, which is a triumph of modern architecture. It houses a stunning 25m swimming pool, indoor courts and café area with outdoor balcony, which should add a comfort factor to otherwise potentially miserable winter fixture viewing for parents.

Not an obvious girly atmosphere – different from other girls' school in this regard. 'It's quite sophisticated with its city setting but doesn't come across as élitist,' said one mum. Mrs Boulton has an excellent relationship with pupils and teachers, feels it is all a team effort and has a relaxed informality with senior pupils, whom she treats as adults and equals, imbuing them with responsibility. She has a weekly meeting with senior prefects to touch base on any issues but 'usually we talk about what we're doing at the weekend!' Head feels that the 'cohesive community' is much to do with the happy atmosphere of the school.

Pastoral Care and Discipline: Christian foundation is important to the school, particularly service to and awareness of the community. A formal system of pastoral care, through form tutors, heads of year and the deputy head, which should ensure that girls' problems do not go undiscovered. Bullying, apparently, is infrequent and nipped in the bud. Older girls have a rôle to play in ensuring the younger ones feel secure and happy and Mrs Boulton has encouraged a culture of self-regulation – 'I can't remember the last time I looked at the school rules'. Girls are introduced to the (very small) set of school rules on arrival; sanctions are in place for rule breaking, ultimate sanctions being temporary or permanent exclusion – incredibly rare. A school which inspires self-confidence and independence – 'We have them on a very long leash and it works,' says the head.

Pupils and Parents: Parents are mainly professionals/academics who expect the best of private education, both from their daughters and the school. Parental background is irrelevant – 'We do not ask; it does not matter,' says Mrs Boulton. Pupils are very bright sparks, well spoken, interesting. A more obviously confident lot than at other schools – not a place where you would want your daughter to be bumping along at the bottom of the heap either academically or socially. One pupil said she thought girls were 'mature and realistic', and a parent commented, 'They're the sort of girls who go hiking with the boys, not flirting with them'.

The train journey to school is the much vaunted socialising time – with the girls competing with neighbouring Tormead girls for the attentions of the boys at the Royal Grammar in Guildford. Much friendly rivalry between the two girls' schools in all aspects of school and social life. Not the most gorgeous school uniform we have ever seen but practical nonetheless, and everyone relatively neat and tidy. Old girls include Julia Ormond, Celia Imrie, playwright Lucy Prebble, the chef Sally Clarke and writer/director Ella Hickson.

Entrance: Automatic from the junior school, comprising 45 per cent of entry. Otherwise an hour long exam in maths and English based on the national curriculum, plus an interview, 'so it is accessible to all pupils,' says the head, though in reality fierce competition and only the very top of the pile make it. Private tutoring is a waste of money if your daughter is not up to it naturally. Big range of feeders in striking distance of Guildford including Danes Hill, Downsend, Halstead, Hoebridge, Lady Eleanor Holles, Notre Dame, Rowan, Rydes Hill, St Hilary's and St Ives, and the state star, South Farnham. Girls entering at 16+ need to have A/A* at GCSE in the subjects they wish to study at A level.

Exit: Five per cent leave at 16, usually to experience a taste of life outside at sixth form colleges. Of those who stay on, 95 per cent to university, with typically 25 per cent a year to Oxbridge. Huge range of subjects studied at an equally wide range of universities, but medicine is particularly popular, along with sciences, languages, psychology, geography, history, English. Some to Wimbledon College of Art.

Money Matters: Fees are paid by direct debit, either monthly or termly (slightly cheaper) and include textbooks and stationery. Academic and music scholarships are available at 11 and 16, worth up to a quarter of the fees at 11 and a third of the fees at 16. All candidates are automatically considered and no separate exam. Don't hold your breath for a scholarship unless your daughter really is a super star amongst other shining stars. Bursaries are available to entrants to the sixth form and all scholarship winners at any level, awarded on the basis of financial need. Clergy daughters are also eligible for bursaries. A reduction of five per cent for second child and 10 per cent for the third and subsequent child in one family. Assisted places are available to all candidates at 11, again awarded on the basis of financial need.

Remarks: Aiming for excellence in all things – a top class act from start to finish. A superb school for very bright, confident girls and with room for all personality types – off the wall or quirky, non-conformists included (positively encouraged, actually). Possibly intimidating for some but, for those it suits, a wonderful opportunity to experience an exciting and challenging education which should set them up for all that life has to throw at them.

Gumley House RC Convent School, FCJ

St John's Road, Isleworth, Middlesex, TW7 6XF

• Pupils: 1,180 girls; all day • Ages: 11-18 • Size of sixth form: 250 • RC • State

Tel: 020 8568 8692
Fax: 0208 758 2674
Email: general@gumley.hounslow.sch.uk
Website: www.gumley.hounslow.sch.uk

Headteacher: Since 1988, Sister Brenda (Miss B Wallace BA PhD) (mid fifties). Previously taught French and Italian and loved it. Now a non-teaching head – felt she was not giving enough time to lesson preparation and this was unfair to girls. Read modern languages at Liverpool and a PhD in Italian poetry at London. Diminutive and approachable, whereas her study is large, airy and reassuringly cluttered; 'you'll just have to take us as you find us,' she declared in a soft Lancashire accent. An outstandingly successful inspection by Ofsted in 2006 showed that they liked what they found very much indeed.

Academic matters: For a non-selective state school, very good results. Compares extremely favourably with local and national averages. Comes top in local league tables. 89 per cent gained five or more GCSE grades A*–C in 2009. A and A/S levels well ahead of local and national averages. On vexed subject of A/S levels, head feels weaker pupils benefit from leaving school with some qualification but regrets loss of free study periods, 'so essential for independent learning'. Designated as a high performing Specialist School since September 2007 and asked to take on a second specialism April 2008 – languages.

Very committed to special needs provision. Two fully qualified teachers and fourteen learning support assistants. SENs catered for include physical difficulties, learning difficulties, ASD, dyslexia, Downs Syndrome. To make sure that they miss nobody, policy is to screen for literacy at the start of Year 7 and to organise support as appropriate e.g. literacy tuition, in-class support, reading clubs or monitoring as appropriate. Preferred method of support is in the classroom. Where possible, tries to avoid withdrawing girls from subject lessons. Classroom support now widely accepted by staff and students alike. No stigma associated, in fact the girls often ask for it. Wheelchair access throughout the school seen as part of ethos – 'we encourage concern for the disabled, the marginalised and the needy'. Sixth formers involved in helping younger pupils.

Games, Options, the Arts: Netball, hockey and athletics all very strong. School regularly wins all local tournaments. Eight tennis courts, a new all-weather surface hockey/football pitch set in spacious 10 acres. New dance and fitness studio (very popular), new drama studio. Thriving orchestra and plethora of private instrument lessons on offer.

Background and Atmosphere: Founded in 1841 as a school and convent by the Faithful Companions of Jesus. The Queen Anne house surrounded by lovely grounds creates a peaceful oasis in west London. Strong support from parents, 'we couldn't run it without them'. Superbly equipped library in former chapel (just the place for inspired contemplation), sensational octagonal assembly hall for whole school events. Despite rigorous religious requirements at entry level the atmosphere is cheerful and tolerant with no hint of religious oppression.

Pastoral Care and Discipline: Prides itself on discipline. Truancy very rare. Emphasis on strong school/home links. Distinctive uniform worn with pride. Strong emphasis on religious, spiritual and moral formation of pupils. Very supportive staff.

Pupils and Parents: The catchment area covers a wide area of west London from Southall to Twickenham so a broad mix of intake. Most parents make a voluntary contribution to the school's development fund each month.

Entrance: Non-selective academically at age 11. However (and here's the rub), girls and their parents must be practising Roman Catholics (written proof required from parish priest) and that means attending Mass every Sunday. Other entrance criterion is distance from school. School is heavily over-subscribed; head has no plans for further expansion – 'we'd rather like to keep our grounds as they are'.

Exit: Around 80 per cent and rising each year go on to higher education. The remainder either take a gap year (increasingly popular) or go directly into employment.

Money Matters: Voluntary aided so run by head and board of governors. Funded through the local council but parents' contributions (voluntary) keep it running as a Catholic school, provide extra facilities and offset maintenance costs.

Remarks: For a budding Mr Bennet who is also a fully paid-up member of the Catholic Church, now would be a good time to visit an estate agent in Isleworth. This is an excellent school in lovely surroundings, which will give all your daughters a good education. Well worth a visit.

Haberdashers' Aske's Hatcham College

Pepys Road, New Cross, London, SE14 5SF

• Pupils: 1,900 boys and girls • Ages: 3-18 • Size of sixth form: 495 • Non-denom • State

Tel: 020 7652 9500
Fax: 020 7652 9520
Email: reception@hahc.org.uk
Website: www.hahc.org.uk

Principal: Mr Declan Jones LLB PGCE NPQH of the all-through 3–18 academy. Has had 14 years of senior leadership experience and is an executive member of the Haberdashers' Aske's Federation 'Three Schools One Vision' leadership team. Has extensive experience in developing initiatives to deliver school improvement and a special brief for assessment and ICT across the Aske's Federation. Lots of contact with pupils and parents and is the visible face of the College's leadership team. Teaching and learning of the highest quality are his priorities. He is married with two young daughters, one in primary and one in secondary.

Chief executive of Haberdashers' Federation, led by Dr Liz Sidwell CBE; began her career in the independent sector (previous post was at Forest School) before moving to Hatcham when it became a city technology college in 1991. She led its transformation to the current federation of three academies – the former CTC, now a 3–18 academy, the newly founded Haberdashers' Aske's Knights Academy and, in 2009, Haberdashers' Aske's Crayford Academy. Among other bits of pioneering, she initiated the first independent/state school consortium for training new teachers and the annual Aske's education lecture series, now in its fifteenth year. An associate member of HMC, an Ofsted inspector, a governor at Wellington College, a trustee of the Specialist Schools and Academies and a board member of the National Challenge Trust, in her few spare moments she enjoys visits to the theatre, gardening and walking holidays. A Liveryman of the City of London, was awarded the CBE in 2009 for services to national and local education. Two grown-up sons.

Dr Sidwell oversees this considerable empire, aided by a heavyweight senior management team. Each school and each site has its own principal and senior leadership team. Dr Sidwell's portfolio includes strategy, finance and monitoring standards and leadership on consultancy. A conversation with her is a bit like trying to keep up with a racehorse – energy, fervour and ideas drive the agenda at immense speed. 'We look back with pride and forward with excitement,' she says, clearly undaunted by the recent expansion of her rôle in the acquisition of the former Malory, Monson and Barns Cray primary schools. 'It's made us re-look at everything. The Habs brand of ethos, excellence and responsibility is important to us – it's what people respect and know. We will maintain that and recreate it in our new schools.' Newest project is a primary school for Knights. Her vision is three 3–18 academies.

Academic matters: Entrance selection criteria assure a spread of ability and, given that, the results are startlingly good. Boys and girls taught separately until the sixth form and little to choose between the sexes' achievement at GCSE level. Neither do there seem to be the usual differences in subject choices, which is refreshing. In 2009, 98 per cent achieved five or more GCSE grades A*–C (90 per cent including in English and maths) with many subjects, e.g. biology, chemistry, physics and food technology, mostly getting A*-Bs. Maths not far behind. For a specialist music school, perhaps relatively few takers for the subject at GCSE – only an eighth of the year in 2008, but virtually all got A*-Bs, so that should encourage the others. Good range of mainstream subjects. Mandarin since September 2006. A selection of students does a foundation course in Latin in Year 9 and it's an option thereafter.

A levels similarly impressive – popular subjects include psychology, English literature, maths, history and, in 2009, 100 per cent pass rate with 68 per cent of all grades awarded at A or B. Of the major subjects, English was startlingly good, as were maths and media studies. Of the less popular subjects, sociology and the languages stand out in the results. Music is growing and the music technology facilities are excitingly better than any we have seen elsewhere – studios for making videos and for music production alongside the solid, traditional stuff. A whole technology building has ample facilities: 'You can always get access to a computer,' said a techie sixth former. Innovative idea is to take PCs apart and rebuild – to see how they are made: brave! One computer suite with 27 working machines and a class was the most over-heated classroom we have ever been suffocated in.

DT good – intoxicating scent of wood surrounded us as we enjoyed the collaboratively workful atmosphere in the workshop. Food technology resources also good and pastry-making classes we observed were noisy but focused. Art is lively – we admired pâpier maché animal heads and solid painting techniques in two good-sized studios.

Around one in seven pupils on the SEN register, about half supported in class and around a quarter has additional support with specialist teachers or learning mentors. About 25 pupils with statements for a range of physical or other needs, including ASD, in which the school has a minor specialism; they are supported by the inclusion team, which works alongside the SEN staff. SENs taken and dealt with seriously. Three new lifts to assist wheelchair users. Gifted and talented team supports the very able.

Games, Options, the Arts: Five minibus minutes away are the College's 12 acres of playing fields: two rugby pitches, two football pitches, seven tennis courts and a sports hall – a rare asset for an inner city school of any denomination, comparing well with facilities offered by many fee-paying schools. Range of outdoor games includes rugby, cricket and football – equally popular with both sexes. Indoor activities on offer include volleyball, badminton, weight training, basketball and trampolining. Huge multi-purpose sports hall plus gym with all the machines you'd expect, complemented by swimming at Crystal Palace. Results are impressive, especially in rugby, athletics and cross-country.

Arts and crafts, including textiles, lively and intelligently taught with good results. Good black and white portraiture, lino cuts, paper lampshades and other imaginative work. Music is strong and has had much investment. Suite opened in 1993 by Judith Weir has practice rooms, though no designated recital/performance space, but school uses neighbouring church for performances. However musical life zings – 40 plus public musical events annually, 400 pupils sing in choirs, chamber groups (including two string quartets and a piano trio), orchestras and ensembles, along with bands of all descriptions. Composer in residence. Eleven pupils are members of the London Schools' Symphony Orchestra, more than 60 attend special Saturday classes at the colleges; one got an Oxford choral scholarship in 2005. All students are given the opportunity to receive free instrumental tuition at Aske's, on condition they attend one of the choirs or ensembles.

Drama is strong and popular – an annual college opera and a musical. Designated room with blackout etc, though no studio – yet – but the lecture theatre on the Pepys site, remodelled as a multi-use space, has lighting and blackout and is a dedicated performance space. Trips in and out of the country abound and D of E is a new, thriving enterprise. An enthusiastic sixth former told us, 'I've got everything I've wanted and more from this school.'

Background and Atmosphere: Complicated. Hatcham is one of the Haberdashers' 'family' of ten schools, fee-paying and state, plus one grammar in Shropshire, now federated with an academy. The governing body is made up of committed, knowledgeable and serious educationalists and a determination – hence the acquisition of Malory, reputedly 'the worst school in the country', and its transformation into Knights Academy, and in 2009, Monson (which had notice to improve from Ofsted in 2008) – to grow and develop more schools on the successful model that is Hatcham. College became an academy on the understanding that federation with Knights, six miles away, was agreed – the impact on the area is substantial and promises most interestingly.

Hatcham itself is divided between three sites – Jerningham Road, which houses the lower school, in a huge Victorian redbrick edifice, typical of its time; Pepys Road – 15 minutes' walk up Telegraph Hill to a similar building, only in quieter, leafier surroundings, where the older pupils are, and the primary. All buildings have the air of the great old-fashioned grammars they once were – honours boards in the great hall etc – but innovation thrives – swipe card system in the canteen. The two sites are linked by a constant minibus shuttle, though older pupils can walk. The streets are lined by solid and attractive Victorian houses, the area looks affluent and well-established – but an alarming incidence of muggings, around one a week on pupils, mostly for their mobiles, we were told.

All sites are well-kept and every opportunity to cultivate and maintain a little garden area for sitting outside or small class lesson has been seized. However outside space actually on-site is very limited. Good lecture theatre a real boon and well-used. Classrooms are, in general, not silent, but the buzz is collaborative and amiable. Work gets done here and in relaxed and co-operative style.

Pastoral Care and Discipline: A house system here – and it plays a rôle in every aspect of college life. Pupils like it and feel a real sense of belonging. Strong PSHCE establishes ethos and works preventatively. Anti-bullying website, mentoring by senior pupils, peer counselling and mentoring. Small tutor groups and individual transgressors dealt with individually – no inflexible policy. No exclusions for drugs in two years prior to our visit, no random testing – seemingly no need. Staff/pupil relations respectful and appreciative.

Food in canteen eaten by most and looked excellent – stuffed peppers, hot puddings, salads, sandwiches – dead cheap too.

Pupils and Parents: Pretty reflective of this cosmopolitan and socially mixed area – sixty per cent of pupils are white, around 25 per cent black; a high proportion are Turkish, Chinese or Yoruba speakers – a total of 36 first languages spoken at home by pupils. It all seems to make a relaxed and homogenous whole. Parents wildly supportive. Famous former pupils include Lord Soper, artist Rowland Hilder, dambuster Sir Barnes Wallace, actor Rafe Spall, newsreader Fiona Bruce, footballer Shaun Wright Phillips, fashion designer Georgina Knight and numerous other sportsmen and women.

Entrance: Applicants apply for a place in Year 7 by naming the College on the Local Authority Common Application Form and completing an additional information form for the College. The College is a 3–18 academy and therefore, children in Year 6 of the primary phase have automatic entry into the senior phase. The College received 2136 applications for the places that were available for September 2009 and 105 appeals.

All applicants take a non-verbal reasoning test and the score achieved places them into one of nine ability bands. No point in coaching your child in the non-verbal reasoning test as the college takes children from all abilities.

Exit: To a vast range of courses – some vocational, most academic at universities and colleges everywhere.

Remarks: The most over-subscribed non-selective state school in Great Britain.

Haberdashers' Aske's Boys' School

Linked to Haberdashers Askes Boys Preparatory School (The) in the Junior section

Linked to Haberdashers Askes Boys Pre-Preparatory School (The) in the Junior section

Butterfly Lane, Elstree, Elstree, Hertfordshire, WD6 3AF

• Pupils: 1,200 boys (plus prep and pre-prep school, with 200 boys); all day • Ages: 11-18, prep/pre-prep school 5-11 • Size of sixth form: 300 • C of E • Fees: £14,103 pa • Independent

Tel: 020 8266 1700
Fax: 020 8266 1800
Email: office@habsboys.org.uk
Website: www.habsboys.org.uk

Headmaster: Since 2002, Mr Peter B Hamilton MA (forties). Educated at King Edward VI Grammar School, Southampton, and read modern languages at Christ Church, Oxford. Previously head of King Edward VI School, Southampton. Taught French and German at Radley College, later became head of modern languages and Wren's housemaster at Westminster School. French wife Sylvie, two daughters (one at Habs' Girls'). Big outdoorsy type – into hill walking, riding and sailing. Also likes a bit of karate, classical music and comparative literature when time allows. Sincere, ambitious – wants school to be known as the best boys' day school in the UK. Stresses importance of pastoral care – believes boys need to be happy to truly succeed.

Academic matters: Consistently outstanding exam results: 93 per cent A/B at A level, virtually all pass GCSE at A*–B – failure not an option. Setting in Year 8 for maths. Aims to broaden and extend rather than fast track – recognises exams as essential but not an exam factory; spoon-feeding not needed. Realises that brightest can easily be bored and need challenging so has enhancement and enrichment classes for the most able – Olympiads (always has gold medallists) etc. Lots of national academic successes. All take either aesthetic or design GCSE in Year 10. Classes of around 20/25 at the youngest age, then 10/12 for A level. Learning support on hand for mild dyslexia/dyspraxia with usual laptops, extra time in exams etc.

Science popular – all study three separate sciences at GCSE, even produces own glossy science and technical journal: *Scope.* Computers everywhere, more to come, interactive whiteboards well used. Staff predominantly white, male, especially in senior positions, a good number at school for a great many years – 'terrifically keen teaching,' report many parents. According to one master (of a superior subject?), economics, theatre studies, geography and history are popular with the less able (i.e. those likely not to get straight A grade A levels); head disagrees, saying, 'Some of the very best in the school do these subjects – indeed both economics and history had the highest number of Oxbridge places recently'. Lots of careers advice including help given to choose the right university. Failure hard to take and relative – not only can those who don't secure a place at Oxbridge deem themselves unsuccessful but even a place at St Edmund's Hall rather than Christ Church can prove a bit of a downer.

Games, Options, the Arts: Work hard, play hard – stacks to do and detailed monitoring by housemasters ensures all participate in something. Games, arts and extra-curricular viewed as essential part of all-round education, so activities timetabled into day. Strong on the games field: rugby and hockey both good (regular tours abroad), also a number of budding athletes and swimmers. Badminton very strong, water polo successful. Good games pitches, two Astroturf pitches, sports hall, fitness centre, pool in need of refurbishment.

Super pottery and art department; fantastic design technology, heuristic approach – new laser cutter worth every penny. Drama exceptionally popular – opportunities for all to participate (some joint ventures with neighbouring Habs' girls). Active debating society attracts regular external speakers (Theresa May when we visited). Masses of music, plenty of performing opportunities: choirs, bands, orchestras, ensembles, quartets, quintets ... Biennial gala concert, Barbican in 2006 saw over 450 students on stage. Abundance of clubs and activities, thriving community service, CCF currently popular. See *The Skylark* magazine for an 'insight into a wealth of extra-curricular activities'.

Background and Atmosphere: Founded in 1690 in Hoxton by the Worshipful Company of Haberdashers, who continue to play a powerful rôle in the governing body. Moved to the present site in 1961. Ten year building plan successfully drawing to a close – recent additions include new well equipped science block and gym, which cluster round Lord Aldenham's pretty redbrick former home now housing the admin offices and accommodation upstairs for young teachers. Delightful, fragrant, well maintained grounds (originally designed to rival Kew) with rustic bridge leading towards the girls' school – a pleasure to see a sixth former pick up a discarded wrapper and place in the bin without a second thought. Purposeful, grammar school atmosphere pervades, tolerant of most from the diligent swot or eccentric to the camp or not quite über cool. Buildings have masculine, clinical, feel; pupils not smart or chic.

Pastoral Care and Discipline: Pastoral care prioritised in recent years. ISI report praises enhanced house system, which has improved monitoring and level of care. Most religions represented in the school – Thursday multi-faith assemblies; serene school chapel a popular option. Good food, excellent choice, including kosher and halal, nice to see smoothies, sushi and sweets. School busily fosters links with the home, involving parents in school life and discipline if necessary. Saturday detention for serious miscreants. No recent expulsions but handful 'invited' to leave – help always given in finding suitable alternative.

Pupils and Parents: Polyglot. Parents mainly ambitious, successful professionals but range from wealthy to those who struggle to pay fees. Appeals to first-time buyers keen to get on. Boys colour-blind to ethnic mix. Pupils come from large catchment area – boys and girls are bused in together (parking permits for the lucky few). Old Boys include Sir Leon Brittan, Sir Nicholas Serota, Dennis Marks (English National Opera), Michael Green (Carlton TV), David Baddiel, Sacha Baron Cohen (aka Ali G/ Borat), Matt Lucas, racing driver Damon Hill, Martin Sorrell and Brian Sewell.

Entrance: Tough – over-subscribed and highly selective. Exam and interview at 11, one third comes from Haberdashers' own prep school; about 25 at 13. Some at sixth form – top GCSE grades expected, absolute minimum of four As and two Bs.

Exit: Very small post-GCSE leakage (mainly to sixth form colleges) – pupils expect and are expected to last the course. To university – with rare exceptions. Between 35 and 45 to Oxbridge annually, most of rest to other Russell Group universities.

Money Matters: Keen to ensure bursaries given to those in financial need.

Remarks: Rock solid academic day school for serious minded high-fliers. Work hard, play hard, success-driven atmosphere. Delivers the goods, but expects a great deal from its pupils.

Haberdashers' Aske's School for Girls

Linked to Haberdashers Askes School For Girls, Junior School in the Junior section

Aldenham Road, Elstree, Borehamwood, Hertfordshire, WD6 3BT

• Pupils: 1,140 girls (including 300 in junior school), all day • Ages: 11-18 • Size of sixth form: 250 • Inter-denominational • Fees: £9,468-£11,490 pa • Independent

Tel: 020 8266 2300
Fax: 020 8266 2303
Email: admissions@habsgirls.org.uk
Website: www.habsgirls.org.uk

Headmistress: Since 2005, Mrs Elizabeth Radice MA PGCE (fifties). Previously head of Channing School, prior to which she was head of English at St Helen's and St Katharine's, Abingdon and director of studies at the Royal Grammar, Newcastle. Mrs Radice's appointment followed the lengthy tenure of the loved and respected Mrs Penelope Penney and 'hard act to follow' was the inevitable mantra she encountered, along with a highly successful and well-run school. She is no mere warmer of the magisterial seat, however, and clearly loves the job. She has a powerful agenda – 'I would like to think that the school will continue to foster a genuine love of and thirst for learning which isn't the same as passing exams – that's what a school like this should be about.' She pays warm tribute to her staff and to the girls – 'they have astonishing drive' – and relishes the way opportunities offered by the school are seized upon and made use of. 'Their ideas come tumbling out – teenagers can do so much more than you think.' She is striking, smart, articulate, efficient and warm. The immensity of Mrs Radice's chief executive style office might, briefly, intimidate and she regrets that the demands of the job allow her virtually no teaching but this is management with a human face and heart. We anticipate that whoever eventually succeeds her will be warned about the hard act they have to follow. And Mrs Radice will be leaving in July 2011.

Academic matters: Results are stunning and place the school firmly in the top tranche of every league table. 2009 saw 425 entries at A level with only 21 being graded lower than B. The last three years' A level results average 95 per cent A/B grades. Popular subjects are history, maths, biology, Eng lit, chemistry – with results to relocate for, especially in the first two. At GCSE in 2009, 94 per cent of subjects were graded at A*/A and an amazing 99 per cent at A*/B with lots of girls getting into the top few nationally. No surprises in the curriculum though relatively few of those who take a language in the sixth form continue after AS level. Languages well-supported and resourced and girls who meet lang teachers in the corridors are expected to address them in the appropriate demotic. IT also well-resourced. Few take art A level which must be disappointing given the quality of what is produced here and the top results for those who do. Sizeable contingent, however, take technology and get top results – justifiably from what we admired in the workshop.

Everyone assessed on entry and mostly what is picked up is mild dyslexia. Later the occasional girl with organisational or processing problems is identified and given support by individual learning dept. Screening in Years 7 and 9, and an annual week of subtle observation in all year groups to pick up on any other problems. SENs not big time here. One-to-one support is given and all those with an identified need have an agreed Individual Learning Plan to help them and their teachers address that need. The ILP is reviewed regularly.

Games, Options, the Arts: The school is alive with the sound of music: 90 per cent learn at least one instrument and grade eight is nothing unusual here. The symphony orchestra – fifty strong – is made up of mostly grade eight students; the chamber choir won Youth Choir of the Year in 2005; there are music tours abroad and occasional musical productions with the boys next door, such as a joint Concert at the Barbican in 2009. Bands of all kinds – plenty for those who are not at grade eight but just love doing it – and top notch facilities including for music tech. Superb recital room though we wondered at the choice of black and white tiles – the only unharmonious thing. Music and art share a block with an excellent atrium used for displays – we saw some terrific sculptures and models – evidence of an uninhibited freedom of imagination and a thrilling creativity. No textiles but there is pottery and it was good to see that actual drawing is alive and well here. Evidence of all the basic skills in good heart and joyous to find that girls attend life classes just for the love of it. Superb DT, taken to A level by academic girls who produce knock-out designs and have fun doing it.

Drama very strong – the middle school play the week before our visit had a huge cast – something found for all who wanted to be involved and the pictures suggested an exuberant performance, costumed with flair and ingenuity. Productions large and small, conventional and alternative, dot the calendar. Vast sports hall though no gym with machines as yet or fitness suite or dance studio. Lots of outside space. New pool and fitness suite a great asset. Lots of sporting prowess – teams excel in gymnastics and synchronised swimming and individuals at badminton, lacrosse and athletics. Lacrosse is main winter sport, with netball and swimming; summer is tennis, athletics and plenty of opportunities in everything from football (popular), cricket and dance. Popular D of E. Trips everywhere and of all kinds. Opportunities galore and parents like the way, 'you can dip in and out of things just to give them a try'. Delicious things like 'The Thinker' society.

Background and Atmosphere: Take your satnav. Probably easy to find when you know how, the two Habs schools occupy a vast site moments from the M1 but down a country road where you'd least expect to find them. It's a bit like an industrial park when you arrive – security barrier, car park etc with the splendour of the main Victorian building that is now the boys' school admin hub to your left – and the heart sinks gently at the sight of the girls' school's main building – a featureless, rectangular block on which the only decoration is a plaster shield with the motto 'Serve and Obey'. Inside, however, it is light, spacious and comfortable and one wonders why an architect who could get so much right made so little effort to produce something with a more inviting exterior.

In 1689 Robert Aske (Master of the Worshipful Company of Haberdashers) left £20,000 to found a school and almshouses in East London. After several moves and expansions, the girls' school moved here from west London in the early '70s , following the boys who took over Lord Aldenham's estate, big house 'n' all, a few years previously. So – excellent hall into which whole school can fit. Good sixth form provision though the girls feel their – vast-seeming to us – common room is too small. It has its own canteen though – a boon in a day school. The privilege of this amount of space – 55 acres – for London-based children is unique, as is the happy co-existence of two single sex schools which combine when appropriate and provide, for many, the best of both worlds. Parents like the fact that the sexes can meet in such a civilised way – and they do, at lunchtimes, at the gates – and join up for shows etc – but live and learn separately.

The atmosphere is cheerful, collaborative and civilised with a genuine relish of what can be done here. We have yet to see more smartly turned-out staff and this somehow adds to the sense of politeness and self-respect which permeates the place.

Pastoral Care and Discipline: Parents are happy – one with children at both schools felt 'the girls have more freedom, the boys are more regimented. The teachers are very approachable and put themselves out to deal with an individual's problems.' Girls agree and, for the most part, staff and girls relate easily – though high standards of behaviour are insisted on and some may chafe a bit. We witnessed one girl being met with a very stony-faced mistress at the staff room door when she asked for a teacher, calling her 'Miss' rather than 'Mrs'. Clear policies on narcotics and bullying. Zero tolerance for drugs in theory – head has not had to put it into practice. Bullying 'is not acceptable full stop', says head, 'if the parents or the girl tells us, we will do something very fast'. Little evidence of any such problems here and girls look happy. One told us approvingly of the lack of petty rules in the school. As one parent said, 'the school allows you to be what you are'.

Pupils and Parents: Maze of coach routes brings everyone from everywhere – around 100 pick-up points from St John's Wood to Winchmore Hill to Welwyn, Harpenden, Watford and Ruislip. Result is a highly diverse ethnic, social and cultural mix which, head says, 'we really value'. Weekly split assemblies – Christian, Jewish, Hindu/Jain/Sikh, Muslim and Humanist and, wonderfully, you can choose which you want to go to on any given Thursday. Girls quizzed about friendships between people from different cultures look bemused. Said a parent: 'What really sells Habs are the girls – confident but not cocky, willing to give anything a go and masses of positive energy.' Old Girls include BBC's Charlotte Green, Vanessa Feltz and shoe designer LK Bennet.

Entrance: Fifty come up from junior school. The rest from local preps and state juniors. A four or five form entry annually – around 450 apply for around 115 places. Exams in English, maths and VR – those who perform best invited to interview. A few admitted at sixth form level if they've got what it takes.

Exit: Very few leave after GCSE. The subjects taken and universities chosen cover the range. Around a quarter make it to Oxbridge annually. Medical subjects, English and philosophy especially in favour but law, chemistry, economics and classics in there too.

Money Matters: Means-tested financial assistance (average is £6,000+) annually including free places. Also academic scholarships for up to half fees including music awards. No discounts for siblings.

Remarks: This is what girls' education in the modern world, at its best, is all about.

Haberdashers' Monmouth School For Girls

Linked to Inglefield House in the Junior section

Linked to Haberdashers Agincourt School in the Junior section

Hereford Road, Monmouth, Monmouthshire, NP25 5XT

• Pupils: 630 girls, 130 board (full and weekly), the rest day • Ages: 11-18 • Size of sixth form: 170 • Christian foundation, non-denom • Fees: Day £9,150-£11,445; Boarding £19,203-£21,498 pa • Independent

Tel: 01600 711100
Fax: 01600 711 233
Email: admissions@hmsg.co.uk
Website: www.habs-monmouth.org

Headmistress: From 2008, Mrs Helen Davy (forties), was head of Cobham Hall (qv) where laid foundations for move to IB 2008. Read modern history at Oxford, followed by postgraduate study at King's College, London. Then worked as a radiographer at The Royal Free Hospital for four years before beginning teaching. Has taught history, history of art and politics at Roedean and The Towers Convent School. Before Cobham she was head of the faculty of cultural studies and acting senior mistress at Roedean. During a career break she ran a small fine wine business and still retains an interest. A warm and enthusiastic person who seems to be very much in touch with the outside world. Married, no children; her husband, a biodiversity enthusiast, works in the City and spends much of his time travelling abroad.

Academic matters: Examination results excellent at both GCSE and A levels, sustained over the last five years. Over 99 per cent grades A*/B at GCSE and an average of 79 per cent A/B grades at A level over the past five years. Art, modern languages, maths and sciences popular choices. At sixth form offers over 30 options in conjunction with Monmouth School – co-ordinated timetable and many shared classes. Sensible use made of new technology to support traditional teaching. Learning support available on an individual/shared basis from suitably qualified staff. Scheme to identify and mentor gifted and talented pupils. In the sixth form, study skills taught to equip students for independent learning.

Games, Options, the Arts: Head is keen on a rounded education and has nurtured a diverse extra-curricular programme. Drama and dance popular with first-rate facilities also used by the local community. Wide range of sporting options includes lacrosse, hockey, rounders, rowing, swimming and tennis; several PE staff are international players. Well equipped sports hall, pool with magnificent views, floodlit all-weather pitch and well kept playing fields encourage girls to become involved with sport – we watched some of the younger girls respond with St Trinian's-like enthusiasm during a sports lesson. Girls represent Wales in various sports on a regular basis.

Duke of Edinburgh Award popular as well as local community service. Fund raising has enabled the school to undertake projects in Africa to help local schools improve their facilities. Girls join the CCF at Monmouth School. Strong art department evidenced by work shown throughout the school – on entering one of the artrooms we were confronted by the surreal image of a host of small ceramic Adams and Eves. Annual interhouse Eisteddfod embraces a wide range of skills and activities. Music flourishes – fifty per cent take lessons on an instrument or voice, choirs and orchestras give girls a chance to shine, some current pupils in the Welsh National Youth Opera.

Background and Atmosphere: School founded in 1892 to complement Monmouth School, whose foundation dates from 1614. It was funded by the original bequest of local man, William Jones, a member of the Haberdashers' Company who made his fortune in Russia. The livery company is responsible for the school and provides financial support. The original late Victorian buildings are set on a hill overlooking the market town of Monmouth. Over the last ten years facilities have been improved with sympathetic modern additions, including a glassed atrium linking some of the buildings together.

Flexi-boarding available. Younger girls board in the main school in three or four bedded rooms. Older ones are based in a purpose-built boarding house with sixth formers having study bedrooms. Accommodation is spacious, bright and includes plenty of space for both study and relaxation. Well-developed programme of after school and weekend activities. Food is good and served in a comfortable dining room. Uniform worn by all pupils – badges on jackets worn with pride. Good mix of female and male staff. The girls sometimes gently tease the latter – of course.

Pastoral Care and Discipline: The aim is for it to be a happy place. Pastoral support available from a number of sources: effective peer monitoring from trained sixth formers to younger pupils; heads of year or house, tutors and school chaplain available to talk. Bullying is rare – the girls have good and supportive relationships between themselves. Reserves the right to search for drugs but this has never been a problem.

Pupils and Parents: Wide range of parents including first time buyers of independent education. Catchment area south-west England and south-east Wales. Becoming more popular with overseas parents; fewer pupils from Monmouth itself than in the past. Former pupils include Lisa Rogers, Sandra Huggett and Jackie Ballard MP.

Entrance: A third from their own prep department, a third from other preps and a third from state schools. Entry at 11 by entrance exam, an interview and school reports. At 13 by Common Entrance or own exam. Sixth form entrants must have five GCSE passes at grade B or above and be interviewed.

Exit: A few leave after GCSE. Majority to a wide range of universities – Bristol, Exeter, Cardiff and Durham among the more popular choices. In most years ten to Oxbridge.

Money Matters: Has replaced about a third of the government assisted places scheme and offers a number of scholarships. Fifteen per cent of pupils receive some help with fees. While day fees are now in line with similar schools, boarding fees are very competitive.

Remarks: Friendly school that produces feisty young women.

Haileybury

Hertford, Hertfordshire, SG13 7NU

• Pupils: 765 (including 485 boarders); 460 boys, 305 girls. • Ages: 11-18 • Size of sixth form: 305 • Christian foundation • Fees: Boarding £26,394; Day £19,821 pa • Independent

Tel: 01992 706 353
Fax: 01992 470 663
Email: registrar@haileybury.com
Website: www.haileybury.com

Master: Since 2009, Mr Joe Davies (early fifties), former head of Sutton Valence. Educated St John's College, Cambridge – MA in history. Previously a housemaster at Tonbridge, then six years as deputy head of St John's School Leatherhead. Married with four children; his wife is also a teacher. Parents comment, 'he is going about his job enthusiastically and has a genuine desire to be inclusive'.

Academic matters: A classic example of the wisdom of not trusting the league tables. Around 40 per cent of Haileybury's sixth form take the IB and this results in anomalous showings. You will find them anywhere from 28th (*The Times*) in 2006 to 154th (*Telegraph*) in the 2007 tables to 174th in the Times in 2008. The truth lies between. The IB takers tend to be those who want the breadth it offers, like lots of hard work and a challenge. These make the most of their opportunities and, generally, achieve highly. IB has been here for a decade and it's hard to miss the obvious gleam in some staff's eyes when they extol the IB curriculum over the A level. Nonetheless, the majority still takes A levels and results are strong, if not stratospheric, across the board. No obvious stars, likewise no glaring weaklings. Results have improved conspicuously in recent years and teaching is perceived as all-round good.

GCSEs again overall good though the average is more A/B than A*. Everyone takes combined science rather than the three separate subjects – 'it's a better way of teaching the subject' – thus leaving room for other options and not forcing everyone pointlessly into the same mould. We applaud and would love to see similar enlightenment in other academic schools. School works to a ten (Years 7 and 8) or twelve (Years 9, 10, 11) day fortnight to enable longer single lessons – we like this too. Saturday is a full school day with classes in the mornings and games afterwards.

SEN register of over 100 but vast majority mild dyslexics/dyspraxics. Wheelchair friendly but possibly not the place for ASD spectrum pupils or those with other less common difficulties. Certainly wise to make careful enquiries before setting your heart on a place. School has – head says, 'uniquely' – its own GP i.e. employed by the school – 'this is Rolls Royce provision' – and clearly he is much relied on to attend to individual needs of diverse kinds.

Library not the most impressive of the school's assets – though has imposing bust of Kipling – and stock could use some updating. We were impressed by a range of periodicals which included Pony, Modern Painters, Private Eye, Shoot, The Big Issue and Top Gear. The 'library' in one of the boarding houses boasted 13 uninviting paperbacks.

Games, Options, the Arts: Playing fields you could build a small city on. They made this physically moribund editor want to wriggle into running shoes. Courts, massive sports hall, fitness suite, Astroturf, pool – for those who like to run and play games it's a dream. Sport is big and full of opportunities but also sane. You don't need to be a rugby god to be valued. Nonetheless, recently neither the boys' hockey nor soccer teams were beaten and the school's reputation in some sports is formidable. Dance is popular but has no designated studio – yet. Drama also popular and bold – Sarah Kane performed in 2007 – and there is a nice little studio theatre – the Ayckbourn – flexible and well-used. Drama-freaks would like a bigger one and it is clear that recent expenditure has been more on sports than arts. No performing arts block here – yet. But music thrives and is well resourced – in particular, music tech has benefited from a recently opened wallet or two. Also a musician in residence. Art now zinging under lively and disciplined new director – and we admired much that was clever and imaginative in both art and DT. Some good trad painting skills evident. Unusually challenging and intelligent periodical – the *Haileyburian*.

Befitting its history, Haileybury has one of the oldest and best-established CCFs in the country – all three services are well-staffed and popular. Likewise, D of E. Stacks of other clubs and activities through the week and at weekends. Lots of tours too. Though many do go home at weekends, it must be a wrench as, unlike so many schools where the minority remain on Sundays, this one puts on trips and balls and cabarets and, sorry mummy but I have to be there. People have fun here. Pupils' only criticism was that some of their peers don't make enough of their opportunities.

Background and Atmosphere: Impressive approach – feels rather like one of the more venerable smaller US universities. Spacious and well-ordered. It was built in 1809 as the training college for the vastly influential East India Company, equipping their bright young public school leavers for life in the colonial sub-continent. The vast quad – the largest, it is thought, in Europe – dates from the college's inception and is still partly bordered by the oldest boarding houses and the head's reception room which is Regency gorgeous. Assorted bits of the school's history are to be spotted included a splendid naval dinner gong in the vast and remarkable dining hall. Above the main entrance billows a vast silk flag bearing the motto: 'Fear God Honour the King'.

The site was sold in the mid-nineteenth century, bought, added to and re-opened as a trad public school in 1862, from when the splendid, marbled and rather moving chapel – with its many memorials to the mass of public servants spawned by the place – dates. Big School – the huge hall – is early twentieth century mock Georgian and is home to assemblies, dances and major productions. Various other interesting buildings of different eras – notably Bradby, housing music – the lower school building – modern and separate, giving the younger children space to themselves – and the technology building which is impressive and full of creative energy.

Lower school – for the 11–13-year-olds – has three forms of 18 in each year. Pupils use main school art, PE, tech and science facilities. We watched some classes in which pupils were attentive and engaged. The ambiance is more senior school functional rather than prep school jolly and a sense of orderliness and purpose prevails.

Boarding is good and even the remaining large dorms are carefully divided allowing for private – and reasonably spacious – space. Oldest houses fringe the quad, others all close by, some modern and well-designed. Relaxed feel to rooms, pupils have the freedom to decorate to their own taste and standard of tidiness. Single and double rooms for older pupils feel cosy and homely. Good range of table games and everywhere has wireless internet.

Largely a boarding school and becoming yet more so – around 70 per cent board and around 30 per cent remain in school over any given weekend – remember that only 15 per cent of boarders are from overseas so a vote of confidence for the extra-curricular stuff. Boarders allowed home at 4.00pm on Saturdays and must be back for chapel at 8.45pm on Sunday. Two non-exeat weekends termly. Boarding numbers vastly up since 1999 – from 370 to 485.

Pastoral Care and Discipline: Strong house and tutor system and pupils express confidence in both the care and in matters of discipline. Sixth form offices seen as responsibilities rather than privileges. Clear policies, rigorously applied. 'Anyone about whom we have suspicions (drug use) is liable to be tested at our discretion. Anyone caught is put on a testing regime. Anyone caught twice is out.' Around one a year is foolish enough to come a cropper in this regard. Drink or tobacco infringers incur a four-hour detention and are liable to be breathalysed. Bullying is rare but it happens – as everywhere. One out in last few years on this count. Pupils look secure, relaxed and happy. Trusted trained counsellor visits one day a week.

Pupils and Parents: Over half come from the local area, many choosing to board either from the off or later. Overseas boarders around 15 per cent of total from no dominant continent – currently from 32 countries! Around five per cent from Germany and a good mix overall. Lots of worthies among the Old Boys and Girls – Clement Attlee, Kipling, Stirling Moss, John McCarthy, Alan Ayckbourn, Quentin Letts, Sir Jonathon Band, Dom Joly, Christopher Nolan and Luisa Baldini.

Entrance: 48 places at 11 for which an average of 120 apply – assessed by exam, informal interview and head's report. Up to 40 boarding places. Equal split between boys and girls aimed for. Lower school pupils automatically move into the senior school. At 13, a further 72 places, most of which are boarding. Average of 65 per cent in Common Entrance for day places is expected; for boarders a minimum of 55 per cent. Maths, English and Reasoning papers set for those not prepared for CE. Clearly more boys than girls enter at this stage – worth trying for a place for your bright, enthusiastic 13-year-old daughter. Dozens of feeders, most prominent are Heath Mount, Edge Grove, Aldwickbury, Beechwood Park, Lochinver House, Duncombe, St Joseph's in the Park, Stormont. Places are sometimes available at 14 and places are competed for using tests in maths, English and reasoning. At 16, applicants sit papers in maths, English and reasoning and offers of 6+ grade B+ GCSEs given. Very over-subscribed, especially for girls, at this stage.

Exit: To the widest range of courses and universities imaginable. Ten or so to Oxbridge and then mostly to the redbricks and plate glasses. Lots of practical courses – notably business – estate management, marketing, aeronautics and pharmacy mixed in with the law and medicine.

Money Matters: Lots of schols but most up to only 10 per cent fee remission. Impressive bursarial help for those who merit and need it – from 10–100 per cent fee remission. Well worth investigating if you are deserving.

Remarks: The inspection report of 2006 made good reading and was testament to twelve years of stability, imagination, growth and consolidation under the former Master, Mr Westley's, care. With Mr Davies now at the helm, Haileybury should continue to be hard to beat in the coming years.

Hall School Wimbledon (The)

Linked to Hall School Wimbledon, Junior School in the Junior section

School 17 The Downs, Wimbledon, Putney Vale, London, SW20 8HF

• Pupils: 270 boys and girls • Ages: 11-16 • Non-denom • Fees: up to £12,000 pa • Independent

Tel: 020 8879 9200
Fax: 020 8946 0864
Email: enquiries@hsw.co.uk
Website: www.hsw.co.uk

Head: Since 1990, Mr Timothy J Hobbs MA (fifties) educated at Eastbourne College and St Andrews where he read medieval and modern history. Abandoned accountancy training in favour of a teaching post at Hill House International Junior School which he left six years later, encouraged by parents, to set up his own school – the original Hall Junior School (qv). (In 1999 his brother Jonathan joined as principal of the junior school.)

Unmarried – except to the school, which TJH (as he likes to be known) hates us saying, but there's no better way to describe his passion and dedication to the place. An avuncular figure with quite old-fashioned (in the nicest possible way) sensibilities. He's a stickler for good manners, a strong advocate of books over computers and likes the children to be outdoors in the fresh air as often as possible. Alongside such Blyton-esque objectives, he espouses a rigorous and thorough approach to teaching, tested weekly in his personally-devised homework system (qv).

Works tirelessly at the sharp end and consequently gets to know every child very well. Does some teaching but, more pertinently, personally leads the many school expeditions – basically count him out for the summer term; he's 'on tour'. Traditionally has baked every pupil a cake for their birthday – 'a great way to focus on that child for half an hour and think about their needs in the coming year,' he says. But less keen on thinking about their parents – he's not interested really, he's all about the children. 'I've never met him,' said one mother who has been at the school a couple of years. 'He's very nice,' thought another, rather vaguely. 'But you'll never see him glad-handing at the gates'. TJH happily defends his position; 'I can't know and run the school properly if I'm seeing parents all the time – I have some excellent staff who do that. I am keen that parents speak to the right person to deal with their questions/concerns. If that person is me, then I will meet with them.' Opinionated on occasion, one gets the impression that it is his way or the highway. You either buy into his ethos of the school or go elsewhere. Admits he dislikes detail and dealing with the minutiae of running a school – 'he does tend to wander off,' agrees the school secretary – but he's absolutely your man for some blue-sky thinking, pushing the envelope, outside the box type of approach. Cutting something of a maverick figure, he and his school have a local reputation as being quirky; although actually he and the whole set-up is much more traditional than reputation would have it. Outside school, TJH is interested in culture, particularly art, which he collects and hangs at the school.

Academic matters: For a largely non-selective, mixed-ability school, HSW does extremely well. The ethos is that learning should be a pleasure, not a chore, and that exams are not the be-all-and-end-all – as the prospectus says 'thought is the most important activity taking place at our school'. So no 'teaching to the test' other than obviously complying with the requirements of the GCSE and Common Entrance syllabuses. There's a nod to the 'spirit and content' of the National Curriculum, all combined in school's own 'Work Programmes'. Pre-GCSE the core curriculum includes English, maths, French, German and science, history, geography, religious studies (including a chunk of philosophy), art DT, music and drama. At GCSE the timetable will be written around that year's cohort No ICT GCSE (see below) or PSHE- which is covered 'more naturally' during conversations on school trips, lunchtime and as part of the RS syllabus.

Children are encouraged to believe that all subjects are equal – poetry as valuable as science – with no more praise given to a mathematician than to a pianist than to an athlete. 'It sounds ridiculously clichéd but we do faithfully honour the individual,' says TJH. Forget the league tables and think about the value-added. 'Some of our children will leave with a full set of A*s, while for others a collection of B and C grades will be a personal triumph and just as worthy of celebration.'

IGCSE is preferred in science and maths – largely because they are, 'more child-friendly – we are an international school after all'. Certainly the language used in IGCSE is simpler, making them more boy-friendly perhaps. A 100 per cent pass rate for CE. Results for 2010 exams at 16, 89 per cent A*–C, 39 per cent A*s and As.

Homework is relevant, contained and limited to 45 minutes a night, all designed to reinforce what has been taught in the classroom. It's a system of the school's own device called 'Flints'. Based on a 'little and often' philosophy, the pupils get bite-sized exercises in four or five different subjects every night and are then tested at school on Friday morning in what is called ' a flint wall'. Some parental feeling that CE children pushed a little harder than the rest – which would be unsurprising. Hard to over-emphasise the importance of flints which are an enormous part of the school. 'My child is quite obsessed with them,' says one mother. Certainly parents can see exactly what is going on (particularly valued by those overseas). 'It gives trust and comfort that their children are being prepared at the highest level,' says TJH.

One area where HSW children may not be so highly skilled is in ICT – TJH is not a fan but, bowing to the modern world, such technology is tolerated and available, with laptops permitted where it helps a dyslexic child. School dropped the ICT GCSE because it felt the syllabus did not deliver and was genuinely not useful. Computers are available in classrooms, and there are two dedicated ICT suites. TJH prefers that children are trained to use books as a resource. But it is worth noting, flints is a highly sophisticated computer-based system, so although anti-ICT for its own sake, the school isn't exactly advocating chalk and slate, it's more of a philosophical position. DT is also not strong. There are really only facilities for woodwork and the subject falls off the curriculum after year eight.

The schools says it has average numbers of special needs children for a private school. Lots of dyslexia. So surprising to hear from one parent that her child's dyslexia was neither picked up, nor sympathetically handled – don't assume school has it covered. TJH says 'HSW is diligent about not labelling children, hence possible explanation for this comment. Every child is assessed annually'. There is a SENCO (praised by a parent) who tries to meet most needs within the classroom –inclusivity is everything here. Nearby Kingston upon Thames and New Malden have large Korean and Japanese communities and a third Hobbs brother has links in the Far East – this is reflected in school numbers and the school even has a Japanese-speaking teacher. Good EAL facilities. Predominantly female staff with several long-standing members steeped in Hobbsism.

System of deputies and senior tutors aims to devolve power down from the head. For the future, a sixth form is on the cards – parents would welcome it and school is similarly keen to get stuck into A levels, but space limitations make it no-go at the moment.

Games, Options, the Arts: Lazybones and other such slackers need not apply. Get your children used to the great outdoors – they will be thoroughly aired here with lots of sport and all sorts of clubs. Every day begins with a wake-up call of 30-mins circuit training from 8.30am and loads of sport is timetabled throughout the week – there's some every day and bad weather rarely stops play. Rugby, hockey and netball feature large – no swimming facilities though and no playing fields on site but extensive playing fields and sports facilities nearby. More chances for girls to play in the teams as there are fewer of them in the school. Fantastic place for netball; school is borough champion and long established tour to New Zealand is extremely popular. Boys' rugby tour to NZ recently added. TJH admits to feeling; 'rather galled that Epsom, Cranleigh and Millfield get credit for having international players, who are actually former HSW pupils who got their first touch of a ball with us.' Drama in its many different forms runs through the timetable for all years. Every child has a role to play in his or her year group's annual performances and learn that production, lighting, costume and makeup are just as important as starring roles and comic cameos. Also dance laid on for girls. Well equipped music studios and peripatetic teachers offer vocal, guitar, piano, woodwind, percussion, music theory and music technology lessons. Is orchestra and a choir. A long day school day helps the children fit it all in. Children can arrive as early as 6.30 and can also stay after the official 5pm finish.

Hard to overstate the importance of field trips at this school – usually in the summer term and always led by TJH. They are educational – picking up on the history and geography of whatever location e.g. Northern France and D-Day landings – but also provide an opportunity to talk through PSHE-type issues, undertake physical challenges and bond as a group.

Background and Atmosphere: All very civilised. Original Victorian building has nice features including a 'country house-style' library filled with giant bean bags, although as one parent pointed out, the bean bags are more in evidence than the books. And there's no librarian – all a bit strange for a school that claims to value books so much. Not a glamorous place, and some of the newer parts (from 1980s and 90s) are a bit dismal (the school tells us that they have been recently redecorated), although all floors are carpeted and windows curtained to minimise nasty ambient noises. Walls are decorated with original artwork including TJH's own collection. Not much of the children's work around the place – although we did visit early in a new term. Classrooms are of different sizes, but space is well used and there's no feeling of crush and cramp. Unusually for a secondary school years seven, eight and nine 'stay-put' and the teachers come to them, from Year 10 there's the more traditional set up of children moving around.

The place is boy-heavy; school says 60/40, but perception is more 70/30 as you walk around, it varies throughout the school – current Year 11 has just a handful of girls, whereas year seven has one third girls. Although school says it desires equal numbers, lots of very good girls' schools in the area make for strong competition. TJH says he is very mindful – and keen to change the fact – that some girls might not come to the school because of male feel to the environment. But there is no nasty gender stereotyping– children will see TJH gardening, cleaning and even hanging curtains!

An active place – 'outward bound' style uniforms say it all. Nice to see children (admittedly Year 7s) actually playing at break time rather than skulking around trying to looking cool. Balls allowed – or rather encouraged – and we can't believe this place would have any truck with conker-bans and the like. 'They really celebrate childhood here,' says a parent. 'When it snows they are told to get sledging.' Similarly where many schools would have a ban on running, here running outside is good.

45 minute break mid-morning and a similarly decent break in the afternoon and on both occasions your child will be encouraged to get fresh air. Freshly-cooked food for lunch. As well as birthday cake large enough to share with their class and take a piece home, every child is given a Christmas present by TJH. 'They are simple acts of kindness to show each child that they matter to us.'

TJH conscious that some wariness exists over family-owned schools and is keen to stress that the place is not a 'Tim Hobbs' production. 'There's a proper structure here, with Jonathan (TJH's brother and head of junior school) and I each supported by a very able deputy and a system of senior tutors.' We feel it would be some deputy that made much headway against a Hobbs brother – though TJH disagrees!

Pastoral Care and Discipline: TJH extremely strict on all interaction at the school, proud of the fact it is 'a very safe place,' and of course its small size makes it reasonably easy to monitor. 'I've found that the school watches the children very closely, particularly as they get older,' said one mother. Few rules, mainly commonsense. The fact that TJH displays his own art collection around the place speaks volumes – obviously no vandalism. 'We spend a lot of money on making the school nice and comfortable; they wouldn't write on their parents walls and we don't expect it here either,' he says. Little call for punishments as children quickly understand what's expected of them. 'We try not to create pointless barriers and rules.' But action will be taken if necessary. A child was expelled three years ago for bullying, which the school 'loathes' and is the ultimate no-no here. Widely defined to include even ignoring somebody – this place is very inclusive. Parents all mentioned how their children grew in confidence at the school. If somebody does do wrong, staff are 'shocked and upset' rather than angry. No detentions – school would not want to send a message that break-time activities were not important and could be dispensed with at will. Ever evolving, the school is currently considering providing make-up lessons for the girls. 'We know they're at an age when they are going to want to experiment and better to provide some guidance so that any application is discreet,' says the head. In reality, there's probably no better way to put girls off the whole idea!

Pupils and Parents: About 60 per cent from the rather prosperous local area – which is roughly mid-way between Raynes Park and rather grander Wimbledon. Others from Kingston, New Malden, Dulwich and Clapham with a couple from Kensington, Knightsbridge, Barnes and the like, so a fairly up-market clientele including the odd famous name. Children of all shapes, sizes, nationalities and abilities – parents similarly mixed bunch. No PTA or sports days (by design) so not the easiest place to get to know other parents, particular if you haven't been at the junior school – though the school doesn't accept this comment.

Entrance: By assessment at 11+ – applicants spend a day at the school: interview with deputy and another member of staff, English and maths assessment and they take part in drama, music and games activities. 'We're watching for behaviour too, it's quite an elaborate process,' says TJH. Prides itself on seeing the good and potential in children that other schools might turn down. Consequently this can involve two or three meetings with parents – all handled by long-serving deputy. 'While there is no such thing as a HSW child, we are looking for a good match.' No open-days, 'too fake and laid-on,' says TJH in typical TJH fashion. School says it is full.

Exit: About 10 per cent fall out at 13 after the Common Entrance group leave. HSW pupils go all over the place – locally to King's Wimbledon, Lady Eleanor Holles and Westminster, alongside further afield Winchester, Cranleigh and Millfield and St John's Leatherhead. All out at 16, lots to Epsom College in 2010.

Remarks: A happy school, brave enough to take on children that other London schools might well turn down. Children who are a bit eccentric will be comfortable and accepted here. A humane place that concentrates on all-round development (not just academia – so not for league table obsessed parents) and turns out confident, personable, polite and physically fit teenagers.

Halliford School

Russell Road, Shepperton, Middlesex, TW17 9HX

• Pupils: 415 boys, with girls in sixth form; all day • Ages: 11-18 • Size of sixth form: 80 • Non-denom • Fees: £11,034 pa • Independent

Tel: 01932 223 593
Fax: 01932 229 781
Email: registrar@hallifordschool.co.uk
Website: www.hallifordschool.co.uk

Headmaster: Since 2002, Philip Cottam MA (fifties), previously a senior master at Stowe, housemaster at Sedbergh and an officer in the army. He has two grown-up children from his first marriage and a 17-year-old stepson from his re-marriage – 'I'm sorry I left it so long,' he laughs. Bristling with energy and enthusiasm, his interests include history (which he still teaches 'as an indulgence'), the theatre, concerts and wine tasting. Also a keen skier and climber ('though I do less of that now'). Describes his approach as 'traditional with a soft centre', which also serves as a good description of him personally. The boys like him; long-serving staff are still in post ('He has a very strong team,' stresses one mother) and parents describe him as 'super' and 'very approachable'. More of a disciplinarian than his predecessor and has brought in plenty of new ideas, while apparently retaining the best of the old. 'He has tightened things up all round,' says one delighted mother. Very hands-on, he makes a point of attending most of the school's weekend home matches.

Academic matters: Deserves a pat on the back for genuine willingness to take in the less academic and late developers. Not an academic hothouse – which is part of its appeal for parents – but that's not to say it doesn't get very reasonable results from the mixed ability intake. Almost all get five or more A*–C grades at GCSE. Latin compulsory until Year 9 and mentioned as a highlight by several parents – a fair few boys go on to GCSE (80 per cent A–C passes) and even A level. 45 per cent A/B at A level. Busily recruiting girls to make the sixth form fully co-ed instead of just 'the few girls we have at present'. Everyone takes critical thinking AS.

The first two years are taught in three sets with 22 boys in each. After this, four sets for all academic subjects. Staff are generally very willing to help in lunch hours and after school. Good value-added: head cites example of a boy in the lower sixth whose predicted attainment in Year 7 was two GCSEs; he went on to pass nine and studied for three A levels. ICT has improved – this was one of the few weaknesses. A few pupils have EAL; a dedicated teacher. No provision for SEN – boys with mild dyslexia and/or mild dyspraxia 'are dealt with by virtue of small class groups,' says the school.

Games, Options, the Arts: Certainly a sporty school with bags of opportunity for those so inclined. But don't be put off if you have a not so keen son – it's not rammed down their throats (much of the action is outside the timetable), though several mothers of non-sporty sons said their boys really enjoyed the four timetabled periods of sports per week. Main sports are rugby, football and cricket. Rowing is also popular (Old Boy Steve Trapmore of the Sydney Olympics gold eight is a shining example to today's eager crews) and golf is on offer to the older boys. A new building includes a sports hall the size of four badminton courts, with a climbing wall – all topped off with a viewing gallery.

State of the art theatre – masses of drama, also used for extra-curricular lectures (plentiful and popular), as a cinema and assembly hall, and home to the house unison singing competition and debating society meetings – both Cottam initiatives from Stowe. Art is a strength, music too – drums and guitar popular with teenage boys, of course (too much electric guitar, head grumbles, good-naturedly). Evidence of a rich after-school life, including a wide selection of clubs, all free – some born out of adversity (when building works restricted playground space). The cinema club proved so popular it has been retained for rainy days – though it can take several days to see a whole film, said one pupil, patiently.

Background and Atmosphere: Established 1921, on six acres beside the Thames. Georgian house, behind which, separated by a courtyard, are modern buildings housing light and airy classrooms. Hard surfaced play area is bijou – one mother moans that boys are not encouraged to get out in the fresh air at lunchtime (Mr Cottam disagrees). Sports pitches are plentiful and well used. The school is small (for a secondary), very friendly and nurturing – 'a real boy's school,' enthuses one parent. Good manners seem second nature to the boys: doors routinely held open for others, teachers greeted with respect – and they, in their turn, know all the boys by name. A healthy sprinkling of female teachers (called 'Ma'am' by the boys). 'The staff have a great rapport with the boys,' says one parent. 'They are approachable and not at all stuffy and really seem to get the balance right, so that things are not regimented, more relaxed but respectful.' Several parents mentioned that their son's confidence had been really boosted after just a few months at the school.

Most pupils must have the school dinner – 'They learn to eat what is put in front of them – no bad thing,' says one mother, describing the food as 'slightly better than typical'. Another said the food was 'rather heavy on carbs' – but this is probably necessary for all the rugby players and rowers around. Staff eat it too, with the boys. Uniform is not ruinously expensive – M&S trousers and shirts allowed – but standards are strictly applied: no silly business with ties or untucked shirts is tolerated, also fairly strict rules about hair – no gel and must be kept above collar-length. All this results in smart boys.

Pastoral Care and Discipline: Great efforts to help the boys feel at home from the start, with a honed programme of induction including taster days and a sports day during the term before entry, Q&As sheet – aimed at the boys rather than their parents – answering common concerns, generally plenty of opportunities to make contact with soon-to-be classmates. Healthy house system in operation, which provides the foundations of a discreet, but highly effective, discipline system based on merits and censures. Anti-bullying policy seems equally effective – head claims zero-tolerance. The mother of a (briefly) bullied son has nothing but praise for the way things were handled. Head is keen to stress the importance of distinguishing between a bad dose of adolescence and genuine bad behaviour. Four boys have been asked to leave in recent years for incidents involving stealing, drugs and rudeness – this sort of behaviour is very much the exception.

Pupils and Parents: Not snobbish or full of rich kids. A largely local intake from Middlesex, Surrey and SW London, using good transport links and a school bus service. Fairly equal numbers arrive from state primaries and private preps.

Entrance: Mostly at age 11 – armed with a suitable reference from their previous school, applicants must pass an entrance exam and an interview. 'It's getting harder to get in,' says head – in 2009, over 140 applications for 66 places. Word among parents is that the school will look kindly on applications from siblings (even overlooking a bad test result). 'I definitely believe the interview counts more than the test,' says one parent. Some pupils join at 13, based either on Common Entrance or a separate Halliford exam. For entry to the sixth form, a minimum of five GCSEs (A–C) including English and maths and an interview with the head. School does take boys at odd times – always worth a try.

Exit: Currently approximately 60 per cent of boys move on to the sixth form (school is aiming to increase to 70 per cent). Most leavers at 16 go to sixth form colleges (a glut of them in the surrounding areas) – some to do courses the school does not offer and, for others, head says, 'There is a feeling the grass is greener on the other side with more freedom etc, but we do keep the majority of the most academic'. From the sixth form, it's university in the main, including a 'steady trickle' to Oxbridge (one or two a year).

Money Matters: 'It's one of the cheapest,' admits one honest mother, amid her list of reasons for choosing the school. Offers up to six scholarships to the value of 10 per cent of fees for entry in Year 7. Also scholarships available for entry into the sixth form – academic, artistic, musical, dramatic and sporting. Bursaries available as well.

Remarks: Does well by all; although clearly not first choice for those after a hothouse academic environment, the bright boys who get here are well looked after. Going from strength to strength.

Hampstead Fine Arts College

24 Lambolle Place, Belsize Park, London, NW3 4PG

• Pupils: 120 boys and girls • Ages: 14-19 • Size of sixth form: 100
• Non-denom • Fees: GCSE £14,850; A level £6,000-£15,600 pa
• Independent

Tel: 020 7586 0312
Fax: 020 7483 0355
Email: mail@hampsteadfinearts.com
Website: www.hampsteadfinearts.com

Joint principals: Nicholas Cochrane and Candida Cave founded the college in 1978. Both trained at the Ruskin School of Drawing and Fine Art, Oxford. He worked for several years in the Old Masters' Department at Christie's. He is head of the art department, with a wide experience of teaching drawing and painting at A level and foundation course level. He is a practising artist, registered with the Royal Society of Portrait Painters, and exhibits regularly in London. He appeared as Leonardo the draughtsman in a Channel 4 documentary.

She teaches history of art, and is also an established playwright, with recent plays performed at the Royal Academy, the British Museum, Tate Britain, the National Portrait Gallery, London theatres and in Florence, Bologna and Rome for the British Council.

Both relaxed, chatty, passionate about art and about their college. 'They are very kind and have a very good relationship with the students,' said a parent. Ofsted talked approvingly of the 'vision, conviction and leadership provided by the joint principals'.

Academic matters: Despite its name, does offer a range of subjects at GCSE, but it is fair to say that the emphasis is firmly on the arts side. GCSE students – about 20 in Years 10 and 11 – generally take the two Englishes and maths plus a variety of history, biology, classical civilisation, French, drama, textiles, fine art. A few study, e.g. physics, but this is not the place for an aspiring medic or scientist, with no labs – any practical work is done at a prep school up the road – 'We're big on studios and small on labs'. Results are as variable as one would expect from students who have mostly either come recently from abroad or been unhappy elsewhere, with a fair number of As for fine art in particular, but Bs and Cs more prevalent generally and a sprinkling of Ds and Es.

The college's raison d'être is its sixth form. Here it concentrates unashamedly on what it does best – with plenty of A grades for fine art, history of art and photography in particular (it won the 'GSG' award for the Best Independent School for Girls for art, design and photography in 2004). One student got 100 per cent for fine art A level in 2007. Also offers business studies, drama, classical civilisation, English, film studies, graphic design, Italian, media studies, music technology, philosophy, psychology and textiles. Will run courses for one student. Few grades below C. Also runs a one-year foundation course, with intensive formal training in drawing, painting, printmaking and photography, which prepares students for university or art school. 'We are renowned for thorough teaching. We are one of the last bastions of drawing – we have a good reputation for it.'

Enthusiastic staff who have realistic expectations of their students. 'I reduce it to the fundamentals and build up from there,' said the media studies teacher, who encourages all his students to make short films to submit to festivals. The photography teacher commented, 'I don't impose my own ideas – I work with their interests and develop those, then apply my technical knowledge.'

EAL support available. Quite a few students have dyslexia or other special needs and the individual attention – 'almost one-to-one,' said a parent – enables them to thrive. 'One boy considered "educationally sub-normal" at his previous school got six good GCSEs here – and will get three good A levels. In a conventional system he wouldn't have got one.' 'My son had failed his GCSEs abysmally at boarding school and was seriously behind,' said another parent. 'They turned him around here and he achieved good A levels and a university place in a year.'

Games, Options, the Arts: Sports are not high on the agenda, though the GCSE students do have one afternoon a week doing, e.g., football, tennis, basketball, and a sixth former's timetable was being altered when we visited to accommodate football practices.

The arts, however, are the agenda – 'People come here because they want to specialise in one of the arts in real depth, beyond the A level syllabus, with lots of external visits and talks'. Art students go to, e.g., Rome, Florence or Vienna, classics students to Greece; also theatre, film and book clubs, music recitals, charity fundraising events. Musicians few but talented; drama and theatre studies popular with plenty of theatre trips and devised pieces performed at Hampstead Theatre.

Background and Atmosphere: 'Lovely people, friendly atmosphere,' said a parent. Set up in 1978 to teach fine art and history of art, in 1982 it expanded into a college specialising in the arts and humanities – 'somewhere we would have wanted to go ourselves'. The GCSE programme started in 1993. The main site, round a quiet courtyard in Belsize Park with coral-painted buildings, has a pleasantly continental feel, students on breaks sitting round in groups. Originally a Victorian dairy, these light and airy buildings include specialist art, graphics, music and drama studios as well as lecture and tutorial rooms.

A few minutes' walk away is the photography department with state-of-the-art equipment and other teaching rooms. Extensive libraries in each department: the history of art department has over 10,000 slides and 3,000 books. Atmosphere relaxed, more akin to an art college than a school. Not a slick operation – 'Don't expect great organisation,' said a parent, 'but it all comes together in the end – and they do love it'.

Pastoral Care and Discipline: A minimum of what the principals call 'petty, intrusive regulations' – 'We treat them as we expect to be treated in return. And most react in a spirit of delighted cooperation, because they are so pleased to be treated fairly'. Each student has a personal tutor – they meet weekly to discuss subject reports, study skills and pastoral matters. 'It's good for students who respond to being given responsibility,' said a parent. 'They seem to be able to get the best out of them.'

Fewer than 10 expulsions in 25 years – 'Usually the situation has got to a point where there is no going back. But it's not taken lightly. They have to sign a contract of behaviour setting out what we and they are supposed to do, and we give them every chance'. Hard line on drugs, with expulsion for possession – 'We explain that we don't consider it goes with studying, and the students do respond'.

Some students have been bullied at previous schools, others have a degree of autism or Asperger's, one is profoundly deaf – 'They don't have to conform here. We give them the space and confidence to be themselves. And the other students really look after them'. A parent commented, 'My son was bullied and traumatised at his previous school. This has been marvellous for him. It motivated him to want to do well. They had faith in him and respected him, and he responded to that.'

Pupils and Parents: A mix of mostly local professional/artistic families, who tend to be profoundly relieved that their children have found such a civilised and creative niche. Some of those who come in to do GCSEs have previously been educated abroad. Others have had enough of boarding school, or failed to fit into more conventional schools. Alumni include Orlando Bloom and Helena Bonham-Carter.

Entrance: By interview and references from the previous school – 'It's pretty apparent then if they are going to be too difficult. It is attitude rather than academic history that is important. You can sense if we're not going to be the right place for them'. Some are taken on a half term trial – 'That is an opportunity, and most go for it'. Seldom takes students who have been expelled from other schools.

Those coming into the sixth form should have five or more grade Cs at GCSE – 'We insist on English language, and try to insist on maths, because otherwise they will bump into glass ceilings later on. If they don't have them, we put together a package that includes retakes'.

Exit: Unusually for a college of this sort, virtually all the GCSE students stay on to the sixth form. Nearly all sixth form leavers go on to university or art school, as one would expect, with a good many doing history of art, English, drama, photography and media courses. But also a mix of surveying, estate management, accounting, politics, journalism and other courses at old and new universities.

Money Matters: Means tested bursaries of up to 50 per cent – hard work expected in return. The Laurence Bowkett scholarship, which covers full fees, is awarded each year in memory of the archaeologist who taught at the college for 13 years until his death in 2002. It is given to a GCSE student going on to take A levels who shows great potential as a musician, artist or academic.

Remarks: Peaceful and creative haven for artists and others, many of whom have struggled to cope at more conventional schools – high quality teaching with much individual attention often remotivates the disaffected. 'It was everything we hoped for,' said a parent.

Hampstead School

Westbere Road, Hampstead, London, NW2 3RT

• Pupils: 1,310 pupils; 55/45 per cent boys/girls • Ages: 11-19 • Size of sixth form: 270 • Non-denom • State

Tel: 020 7794 8133
Fax: 020 7435 8260
Email: enquiries@hampsteadschool.org.uk
Website: www.hampsteadschool.org.uk

Head: Since September 2006, Mr Jacques Szemalikowski MA BSc PGCE NPQH CPhys MinstP (late forties), a human generator. Studied astrophysics and taught in and around London for 25 years, before his first headship at The Warwick School, Redhill. Has four young children of his own. Heads don't come more voluble than this – he talks the talk, is on top of all the latest terms, acronyms and initiatives and, through it all, convinces one that he has the soundest – noblest – educational principles and works his socks off to implement them. He could sell sand to a Bedouin. Hampstead is no pushover school – the site and its pupils present immense challenges – but this is an undauntable head whose tenure has already had a powerful impact. His mantra – 'Every child can achieve, every child will achieve, whatever it takes' – is a challenge to his staff, his community and the children themselves. His convictions and attack are unimpeachable and impressive. His governors are behind him. If he is to achieve as highly as he is determined to do, he will need the staff to match his fervour. The signs are good – numbers of applicants for posts are rising and he can increasingly pick and choose. If he stays the course and continues to build his school, Hampstead's future looks shiny bright.

Academic matters: The raw results may look poor in comparison with those of most of the schools reviewed here, but when one takes into account the fact that half the pupils are bi-lingual, five per cent statemented and forty per cent on free schools meals, the value-added data is rather more impressive. Whereas 2008 saw a drop in results, with 5+ A*–C rate including maths and English in the 30s per cent area, in 2009 achieved its best ever academic results, the number of students achieving 5+ A*–C rising to 70 per cent+. Equally impressive is the independent ALPS A level assessment ranking its A level results as two out of a nine point scale ('outstanding ... top ten per cent'). In the top 20 UK state schools for progression into science A levels after GCSE. 78 per cent achieved A*–C in French, 67 per cent did so in Spanish – good numbers of candidates in each case. On offer in the sixth form are six BTecs and 21 A levels. English is the most popular subject and 70 per cent got A–C in 2007. Media also popular. Maths, with 15 takers, achieved 87 per cent A–C. Very few takers of languages at this level.

Large library, though not over-stocked with actual books. Maths alone setted from year eight. Strong curriculum support and SEN help, notably to those who arrive with little English, and catch up is rapid. Somali students make up one-tenth of school's population and have designated home-link worker. Everyone has individually set and closely monitored academic targets. G and T co-coordinator supervises programme, which includes early GCSEs, maths challenges etc and triple rather than double GCSE science. Masses of support is given to enriching the curriculum, and what goes on outside the syllabus perhaps better reflects the academic ethos than a narrow table of results. Parents acknowledge general tightening up undertaken by head – 'He has made his expectations of staff and students very clear,' said one. School now collects and monitors masses of data – head likes data – on every child, and motivated children appreciate this close surveillance.

Games, Options, the Arts: Fizzes with activity – plenty to do. A technology college – well equipped on the IT and DT sides. It was awarded an Artsmark Gold in 2008. The art, DT and textiles are impressive – we saw good, concentrating classes and enjoyed much of what they produced. The art is varied and well displayed in the art corridor, though the school as a whole would benefit from it being spread around rather more. Lively music includes 100 strong showing at the Royal Albert Hall in the Camden Music Festival in 2008. Super and wildly enthusiastic drama – partnerships with The Hampstead Theatre Club, Royal Court and Tricycle all help to inspire. Innovative project on 'maths and drama' exemplifies imaginative approach. 2008 saw school's first ever arts festival. Lots of involvement in multi-discipline regional and national competitions and events – often achieving highly.

Spectacular success in Model United Nations – the only state school entrant – beating all-comers in 2008 for the fourth year running. Strong programme of top class outside speakers – Camila Batmanghelidjh and Shami Chakrabarti recent visitors. Lots of after-school clubs, attended by most, include organic gardening. Has a Sportsmark and sport is big here, despite relatively limited facilities. New Astroturf (September 2008) a good asset. Onsite pool. Many successes, especially in football and cricket.

Background and Atmosphere: The name misleads. The school is not in posh Hampstead but on the fringes of Cricklewood, Kilburn and West Hampstead. The main building also confuses – it was the old Haberdashers' Boys' school and still bears the name and crest on the façade. It was built in 1908 to impress and, despite decay and neglect, still does, being a large and solid redbrick edifice, though now with a ramped approach and plate glass entrance. Through the entrance one sees a vast concrete, central, open air atrium faced by a modern teaching block and broken only by a dark and reedy pond. The school is due for a substantial rebuild and, apart from the outside of the main building, will look very different by 2012. Refurbishment already under way – £125,000 spent recently on new loos: 'The test of any state school is its loos,' says the head – 'it's a touchstone,' and pretty spruce they are, too. Little sign of vandalism or even litter throughout the campus. Good sixth form centre with huge common room overlooking central atrium. A new £2.2m state-of-the-art ICT and catering teaching block opened in October 2009.

It's a daunting site for new pupils from little primaries, but they are carefully absorbed and those we met clearly feel at ease, despite the austere campus. 'It's easy to make friends here,' we were told. Lots of outreach and community work including classes for parents. Commendable efforts to involve the outside world and lots of whole school charity work. School culture involves loads of celebration and reward of achievement and improvement – all testament to head's indomitably positive approach to everything. Pupils are as mixed a bunch as anywhere and the atmosphere is, for the most part, cheery and collaborative, though clearly some members of staff inspire rather more respect than others and we witnessed a couple of pretty breathtaking incidents of insubordination.

Pastoral Care and Discipline: Much to be done when Mr Szemalikowski arrived. Punctuality and attendance have been major issues but are now coming under control – the entire senior management team greets pupils in the mornings until 8.40am, after which sluggards have to report in individually. In the 2008–9 year, attendance improved to 92 per cent from 87 per cent when Mr Szemalikowski arrived. Head re-introduced uniform as part of his self-esteem-raising mission – raised middle class eyebrows and hackles here and there but largely successful, though liberally interpreted in older age groups. Head walks around each day to keep in touch. Automatic exclusion for fighting. Head claims few problems with drugs, alcohol etc, though lighting up as you leave – the sixth can come and go in free lessons – is routine.

Buddying, mentoring and restorative justice schemes all bolster pupils' sense of security. Rewards for positive behaviour – both for those who have improved and those who are 'routinely good'. 'The House' is a cuboid block on the perimeter where you go if you are troubled – or troubling – and is well-staffed with welfare workers, counsellors and other supportive types. Altogether well staffed on the non-teaching side to smooth admin and support the academics.

However, we were disturbed, on our tour, to see – and hear – a number of classes which could most charitably be described as chatty and in which little work was evident, and a few more which could only be described as disorderly. Head's policy of 'non-shouting' not implemented by all and school's dependence on supply teachers may explain some of what we witnessed. Pupils, too, while fervently loyal, admit to a level of classroom disruption which would make all but the most forbearing of potential parents have qualms. Existing parents acknowledge Mr Szemalikowski's tightening up but, clearly, much remains to be done if a relaxed but disciplined learning environment is to be consistently maintained here. A new robust behaviour framework was introduced in September 2008.

Pupils and Parents: From liberal, moneyed Hampstead to recent refugees in temporary housing – perhaps as wide a range in a school's population as anywhere in the world and one admires how it is done. Inclusion inclusion inclusion. Former pupils include Zadie Smith, Rachel Yankey, Julia Drown MP, Alex Bogdanovic, Jake Lensen, Tobias Hill, Jude Law.

Entrance: From up to 40 local and less local primaries – Gospel Oak to Gladstone Park. Admissions managed by Camden. School now full in each year group but not hugely over subscribed – except in the sixth, which takes in 20 per cent of its total at this stage.

Exit: Most stay on for the sixth form, around 60 per cent for A levels and the rest for BTecs. At 18, most leave for an impressive range of higher education – from medical school to Oxbridge ('They get much better Oxbridge preparation than my daughter's independent school provides,' said a local parent), anthropology at Goldsmith's and maths at Manchester to zoology in Wales. Also a spread of vocational and practical courses – advertising at Coventry, event management in Winchester and international business in Roehampton. Some directly into employment.

Money Matters: The school has achieved the Government's financial management in schools (FMSIS) kitemark.

Remarks: The head's energy, drive and unassailable faith in his students should work wonders here. Hampstead has the potential to be an outstanding school and, in its extracurricular opportunities, seemingly already is, but in other respects it ain't there yet. However, its latest Ofsted report cited it as an 'improving school with many good and some outstanding features' – the word 'improvement' being mentioned no fewer than 11 times.

Hampton Court House (Senior School)

Linked to Hampton Court House (Junior School) in the Junior section

The Green, Hampton Court Road, East Molesey, Surrey, KT8 9BS

• Pupils: 190 boys and girls • Ages: 13-16 • Strictly non-denominational
• Fees: £12,825 pa • Independent

Tel: 020 8614 0857
Fax: 020 8977 5357
Email: sarah@hamptoncourthouse.co.uk
Website: www.hamptoncourthouse.co.uk

Head: Since September 2010 Mr Joe Francis BA, latterly head of English at Eton, before that a teacher at Tonbridge and, clearly, a catch. He has been brought in by Lady Eliana (see below) and Mr Tristram Jones-Parry (likewise) to strengthen and tighten up the academic provision and to boost the school's profile to a wider potential clientele. This initiative sees HCH moving more into the mainstream as far as senior education is concerned and promises well.

The founder since its inception in 2001, and now the principal overseeing both schools, is Lady Eliana Houstoun-Boswall ISIT (Paris) ('mid-sixties', she says, though she looks more fabulous at that age than anyone who runs a school has a right to.) Educated at the Lycée Français, New York (clearly a formative experience – good and bad – and one she vividly describes), then Georgetown University, Washington DC. Thence to a postgrad course at L'École d'Interpretes, Paris. A linguist herself, she has a precision and elegance of diction one seldom hears. In addition, her convictions and educational principles –

wildly idealistic though some may think them – are articulated with an intensity that is hard to resist. They are expressed with characteristic fervour on the school's website – pour yourself a glass of something expensive and settle down for a treat.

Eliana (as everyone calls her), has two children of her own – both involved in the school – her daughter teaches English to the tots and her son is Finance Director and Chairman. She co-founded and ran The Harrodian School (qv) – achievement enough, you might think – starting schools was never a push-over. Having gone into property with her husband and made a bit of a pile, after the divorce she bought Hampton Court House – an extraordinary estate with a fascinating history (see below) and took three years and more than £1m to bring it up to the standard required for educating the young. One cannot but admire the courage, drive and vision which did this solo. However, some parental feeling that a board of governors/trustees might lend a guiding hand to the benefit of the school community in general.

The school began as a pre-prep and prep but, as the first pupils got to leaving age, it seemed natural to continue into the complex realms of senior education. (Nonetheless, the schools – housed as they are in one building and with pupils of all ages very much part of one community, it is in some ways inappropriate to separate them into two as, for the purposes of our review, we have done. Hence the duplication of much of what we say in our reviews of each school.) The oldest pupils are now in Year 11 so the school is about to grow a sixth form and hope to introduce A levels in 2011.

'Satisfactory' was the term favoured by Ofsted in its inspection report of early 2010, in relation to almost every aspect of the provision, also recording 'inconsistency' in the teaching styles and approach. Hence the arrival in 2009 of Mr Tristram Jones-Parry as 'advisor' charged with upping the academics, improving 'systems' and generally beefing up all-round discipline. T J-P, as he was known at Westminster School, of which he was, for seven years, the head, is a formidable figure – dedicated to top-class education but not a man, you would think, to stand much nonsense. Clearly Eliana knows a good thing when she sees it (her son is an OW and was taught by T J-P) and grabs it with both exquisite hands. The combination of Eliana's idealistic vision and T J-P's rigour could, possibly, produce an extraordinary school, we said after our last visit. The appointment of Mr Francis is a clear indication of intention and is a bold move. The school isn't yet where it wants to be and we will watch attentively to see how it develops.

Academic matters: Languages, the arts, civilised values and culture reign here. DT is now much better resourced than hitherto but if you are a parent for whom computer expertise and a solid career in the City are the ultimate goals via a rowing blue and an MBA this is probably not your school. If you want your child to be a linguist, to study academic subjects with values attached, to learn about art, music and to develop individual interests in a liberal, relaxed atmosphere, you'll probably love it. And that is what you will get if your offspring is bright, motivated and responsive to opportunities. At GCSE, an admirable range of options for so small a cohort includes 5 langs – old and new – and business studies. We watched an attentive and large class of Year 11, seemingly all girls, doing psychology.

However, results thus far are highly variable. In 2009, 23 per cent of GCSE subjects were awarded A*/A and only 61 per cent A*–C. This can be accounted for, in part, by the number of children with mild dyslexia supported by the school. It is also explicable to some extent by the emphasis on arts – drama especially – and the expenditure of some pupils' effort and time in these rather than academic areas. Also, with an emphasis on self-motivation, if you don't want to work no-one exerts much pressure – and this may also be true of some pupils' families. In addition, there is a lot of coming and going – both staff and pupils have had an unusually high turnover, though we are assured that more staff are now here to stay. T J-P will have an influence here as elsewhere in stabilising and developing the senior academics. Additionally, the school has, until now, positively encouraged – well, at least, enabled – its brightest and best to leave at CE so it is hardly surprising that the results – even given the heady atmosphere – do not impress.

Things will change, especially with T J-P's input but possibly not that much. 'I want more discipline and rigour,' Eliana admits and acknowledges there is work to be done. 'I can put in all the love and Tristram will put in the rigour – eventually,' she asserts. She accepts, reluctantly, the need to become more 'establishment – "while keeping the ethos of happiness"' and clearly the intellectual and cultural values will not be sacrificed to a galumph up league tables – and grace à Dieu for that. But Latin and Greek and the languages, art, music – all acknowledged to be superb – flourish here and year sizes are so small that virtually individual timetables can be made for those who need them – for now. IT now well-provided for with a designated room full of Macs with big screens. Teachers – many from abroad – provide intellectual clout though some parents feel that, while they may be clever and knowledgeable, some are not 'teachers' either by qualification or by inclination. School very accepting and inclusive of SENs. SEN dept consists of a SENCo who comes in 3 days and as needed plus 2 others, one trained and the other very experienced. They work in small groups or one-to-one as best suits the child. 19 per cent of pupils on SEN register – mostly mild to moderate dyslexia but school will support ADHD and dyspraxia. Ofsted praised good use of IEPs. Invitingly crowded and well-stocked, smallish library with views over the park but so cold that the teacher giving an individual lesson in there did so in coat and scarf.

Games, Options, the Arts: Arts are strong, strong, strong and part of the feel of the place. Art seen as anything but a discrete subject but very much part of the philosophy that underpins the educational approach. Delicious things like the band kit set up in the old ice house in the garden, music everywhere – around half the pupils take individual classes and everyone throws themselves into drama and art. Music dept comprises professional, practising performers – an impressive list – and children here are clearly exposed to the best. Several of the children we spoke to had performing ambitions and clearly no shyness about such things prevails here. This confidence also evident in the manner of the children as they move around the school and address each other and the staff. Sports rather more haphazard – coaches and courses seemingly come and go but a considerable range of games and challenges are undertaken – from kayaking on the Thames – what an asset a river is! – to fencing, fitness and a newly launched Do f E initiative. Some older pupils with especial gifts teach the younger ones – guitar and dance were mentioned. Chess is a big thing here – a specialist teacher on the staff.

Background and Atmosphere: Built in 1757 by the gloriously named George Montague Dunk, 2nd Earl of Halifax, the house is stunning. Its entrance hall – as pictured on the prospectus – has to be seen, columns, gallery, ceiling fireplace 'n' all. To say nothing of the view over Bushy Park, the proximity to Hampton Court itself and the fabulous neighbouring houses on the little lane one drives down to reach the gate. The lake, grotto and ice house in the garden were added in 1771 and, when his lordship died, the house was left to his mistress, Mrs Donaldson, and, on her death, to their daughter. Nice work if you can get it. The house then passed through a succession of tenants and in, 1871, was sold to Marmaduke Blake Sampson, city correspondent of *The Times* and Argentine Consul in London. He built the picture gallery, later a ballroom and subsequently concert room. Then a further century of lettings and sales – among them to the tea-planting Twinings – until, in the 1980s, it became a Save the Children home for refugee Vietnamese boat children. You couldn't make it up. Eliana bought it in 1998, spent years and a million doing it up and, voilà!

Children of all ages mix and mingle – lots of hugging in break time which we liked. No uniform though 'you have to look presentable' – and they do – rather more here than in many uniformed schools where the rules are stretched to the scruffy limits. The teachers too – some in suits, other very casual but no-one pushing at the boundaries. Happy parents love the 'warmth and liberality of the ethos – it's just what we wanted. Not perfect but so much better than a hothouse'. Mixed parental reports on school admin and general efficiency – but we had a sense of this, as other areas, being tightened up.

Pastoral Care and Discipline: Discipline is expected to come from within rather than to be imposed. School's philosophy is a belief that all – pupils and staff – should be treated equally and with respect. Politeness and good manners are insisted upon and bullying, we are told, is not countenanced though some parental feeling that, on occasions when it occurs, the bully is accorded rather more TLC than the bullee. School aghast at this allegation but reports of bullying not adequately dealt with reached us more than once. On the other hand, we learned of other such incidents which were swiftly and sensitively sorted.

'It's a wonderful place for children thought elsewhere to be unteachable,' we were told and, assuredly, children who need space and air can breathe here and find that perhaps they do want to learn after all. But some don't last here either and the school's open door policy occasions, perhaps, a less stable – though very accepting – community than has been good for it. Staff a mix of the 'very laid back and the over severe,' parents told us. 'Some are wonderful with the children and really make the relaxed, first-name thing work. Others can't hack it and leave. I've heard teachers swearing at children loads of times.' We witnessed a cheerful confrontation between a teacher and a genial but recalcitrant fifth former on our visit – amicable and polite but clearly a conflict between equals rather than one in which authority was firmly exercised. Children with a more mature understanding of personal relationships will think they've come to heaven.

Pupils and Parents: Popular with French families for obvious reasons though some grouse that the French is not truly bi-lingual which, with the breadth and transience of the school population it could hardly be by senior stage. Pupils from a 30 mile radius – school bus collects and deposits. Attracts the unconventional, the liberal, the arty. Lively Friends of HCH have outings, balls and shopping events to support both school and a Sri Lankan orphanage. Annual Blood Lust Ball occasions a wide range of parental reactions.

Entrance: Via interview with candidate and parents, plus maths and English tests. Eliana must be satisfied that the pupil and family are in sympathy with the school's ethos and approach. From Cameron House, Hill House, Wetherby and local juniors

Exit: As diverse as you could imagine. 2008–9 leavers to University of the Creative Arts, The Brit School, Hampton, DLD, Bryanston, Halliford, Westminster, Richmond or Esher Colleges, Wellington, City of London and a catering college. Some few unaccounted for.

Money Matters: Up to three scholarships – academic, music, arts – annually worth upto 10 per cent of fees and all 11+ candidates are automatically entered. New sixth form also offers three such scholarships.

Remarks: Ideal place to grow and learn for those who will thrive on the relaxed and civilised values of the place. Hitherto seen as a refuge for those who couldn't get on elsewhere – sometimes the obstructive or wayward – but this is likely to change now, though the head will continue to take on those with something to offer that may not be conventionally academic. And so she should.

Hampton School

Linked to Denmead School

Hanworth Road, Hampton, Middlesex, TW12 3HD

• Pupils: 1,200 boys; all day • Ages: 11-18 • Size of sixth form: 330 • Inter-denom • Fees: £14,010 pa • Independent

Tel: 020 8979 5526
Fax: 020 8783 4035
Email: admissions@hamptonschool.org.uk
Website: www.hamptonschool.org.uk

Head: Since 1997, Mr Barry Martin MA MBA FCMI FRSA PGCE (fifties). Educated locally (Kingston Grammar School), with bags of experience of teaching in independent schools and a career in the Bank of England before teaching. A plethora of educational posts to his name – he has been an independent schools inspector and A level chief examiner and has co-authored leading textbooks, now serves on the Education and Academic Policy Committee of HMC/GSA and is honourable treasurer of HMC. One of the heads who established FIDS (Forum for Independent Day Schools) to promote the strengths of such schools. Friendly (but not to an extent that could prejudice his professionalism), generally a traditional head. Respected by boys and parents alike, he has a dry sense of humour, great confidence in the merits of his school, pride in the boys and a very caring attitude to others. Often referred to as 'the BFG', he is described by parents as 'ambitious, yet visible and approachable' or 'a light but firm hand on the tiller'.

Academic matters: A consistently tip top performer locally with already good results moving onwards and upwards. At GCSE, number of A*/A grades has been rising markedly – 86 per cent in 2010 – putting the school in the top independent schools in the country. At A level in 2010, 90 per cent As and Bs keeps the school in the top 100 – without anyone being asked to leave after GCSE (and very few choose to), so no large intake of high-flyers into the sixth form. The extended project qualification now forms an important part of the newly introduced and broad sixth form enrichment programme. Many parents see the absence of a hothouse atmosphere as a strength (and one of the reasons why they choose the school). Wide range of subjects on offer with plenty of take-up in languages and science subjects.

IGCSE science and maths are taught – no coursework and are more testing. Some boys take one or two GCSEs early. Setting is organised to ensure that no boy is in the bottom set for all subjects – 'No Hamptonian should, nor does, see himself as a bottom set boy,' explains Mr Martin. Year 7 boys choose between French, German and Spanish. Latin is compulsory until Year 8. The launch of Mandarin is a proven success with 75% A* grades in the first GCSE entry.

Average class size on entry is 23/24, though the size of teaching groups is often much less. Sixth form sets are in single figures to low teens. A modern extension houses English, technology and art and the myriad of machinery and art equipment gives the impression of being very well used, as are the various IT suites. All boys can now access their computer-based work files from home. A new state of the art teaching block, the Atrium, opened in September 2010, housing 10 fully-equipped new classrooms and an additional biology lab.

The library is welcoming, open even in the holidays, and extremely well-stocked. Careers advice has a high priority and is impressive (although one parent bemoaned lack of advice for A level choices) with efforts being made to think more globally. Plenty of females on the staff. Average age of staff 37 and they are top drawer – six Oxbridge graduates joined in 2010. Several old boys also to be found in the staffroom. Turnover never out of single figures.

Special needs are catered for through a head of learning support, but the school is cagey about how many boys or how much work this entails – delve deep if you want to send an SEN boy here. Provision for children with English as an additional language is negligible.

Games, Options, the Arts: Sport is very strong: 16 current boys have won international honours for England or GB at nine different sports. All the necessary facilities are on site, apart from the spanking new boathouse shared with neighbouring girls' school, Lady Eleanor Holles (LEH) a mile or so away. Each boy chooses the sport he wants to play – a key success factor, according to the school – 'The boys taking part are there because they want to be and there are none who don't, which makes for higher quality sessions'. All sports spawn international players.

The ideal school for a budding Beckham: unlike most private schools, football is a major sport here and Hampton twice won the Independent Schools Football Association Cup and reached the final on two other occasions. Also won the inaugural ISFA Fair Play trophy in 2010 in recognition of on field conduct and respect for officials. Rugby has taken off in similar leagues recently with the 1st XV being *Daily Mail* finalists at Twickenham in 2009 and the U15 team semi-finalists in 2010. Rowing is also big, big news – Hampton is one of the leading UK schools (check the provenance of the Oxbridge Blues next Boat Race day). Also notably strong in cricket. But it is not all brawn and no brain in the place – currently three chess internationals in situ.

Music takes many forms and can be at a very high level. Has just had its first BBC Young Musician of the Year Finalist, now at the Royal College of Music on a full scholarship, and four organ scholars in residence at Oxbridge, as well as several choral scholars. But plenty of light-hearted groups and joint performances with LEH take place each term. Drama productions are also sometimes shared with the girls but often all-male affairs as well. The new '450 Hall' (it actually seats 400 – built to celebrate the school's 450th anniversary) was designed as a centre of excellence for the performing arts and is likely to be an exceptional facility both for the school and for use by the outside community.

The list of extra-curricular activities is so long that you wonder how they can all be fitted in, especially since most boys, reliant on the school coach service, go home promptly at 4pm. The answer is the extended lunch hour – where plentiful and reportedly high quality food is served over a long enough period to fit around all the clubs. In addition to all the extra-curricular activities, a very popular lunchtime programme of eminent speakers – politicians, businessmen, academics, media figures and famous old boys: Dr David Starkey is on the list of speakers as well as Jeremy Paxman, Dr Mary Archer, Iain Duncan-Smith and John le Carré, and don't forget Tara Palmer-Tomkinson. The boys who are busy at their sports clubs don't know what they're missing!

Similarly, so many trips and activities in the holidays you wonder if the boys ever see their families. Beware – all these jolly jaunts are not included in the fees. For those desirous of helping their fellow man plenty of opportunities for helping in the local community, as well as links with African communities in Uganda and Malawi. Jointly with LEH, won first place in the Barnardo's People Recognition awards for their Saturday activity club for children with disabilities – all the result of a huge commitment from the staff to the wider curriculum.

Background and Atmosphere: In the heart of suburbia surrounded by houses and other schools. Parents can breathe a small sigh of relief – girls may be nearby but not a shop or pub in sight. Superbly spacious grounds; buildings not an architectural gem though well-maintained and constantly being updated. Loads of outdoor space – quads, gardens and playing fields which many boarding schools would envy. Interiors are light and airy and remarkably tidy – even the corridor outside the rowing ergo rooms presents kitbags in a long, neatish row. The sixth formers are proud of their common room with its own café selling vital sustenance at break time and a flatscreen TV tuned to Sky Sports.

Claims to be the first school in the country to go 'climate neutral' through off-setting emissions caused by its daily running. Climate Care, the link company, offsets through projects including renewable energy and energy efficiency schemes in Southern Africa and India and forest restoration in Uganda. Has its own bore-hole for irrigation of its playing fields, solar panels and a wind turbine. Continues to raise pupils' awareness of climate issues – the boys conduct regular audits of the school's energy consumption.

Formerly a state grammar school (went independent in 1975); about 50 per cent of the pupils come from state primary schools and is fully committed to a large 13+ entry from prep schools. Many of the parents were not independently educated and this is definitely not a school for Hooray Henrys, although within school the boys look the part in blazers and ties (even in the sixth form). However, the minute they leave the school gates the shirts become magically untucked and the ties unknotted – these guys know the meaning of 'grunge'. A marriage here of public school ethos and London lads.

Pastoral Care and Discipline: Proximity to LEH is supposed to provide 'the best of both worlds' – single sex teaching means that monosyllabic 14 year olds are not intimidated by garrulous girls, but, 'The boys certainly know what girls are,' says the head. The two schools have just audited their joint acitivities with a view to expansion. Hampton has also established sixth form management courses with Surbition High and a junior musical with Waldegrave School.

New boys at 11 are given as much help as possible to settle in with their peers – an overnight team-building exercise is very popular, with boys returning 'raring to go.' Similar jaunt for 13+ entrants. Mentors from the upper school are allocated to newcomers. New boys are closely monitored and any who are found to be struggling with work or organisation given special support and help with study skills. Stringent illegal substance policy – expulsion is a serious threat.

Assemblies celebrate a range of achievements – concentration on success is more important than telling the boys what they have done wrong and exceptional work is presented to the head. Counselling is readily available; a parent whose son had an extended illness felt that staff went the extra mile to ensure an efficient return to school – 'He was even met at the door by the head of year'.

Pupils and Parents: No obvious Hampton boy but, if you want your son to be kept busy, here is an environment to suit all sorts. 'Like most things in life, it's what you put in that counts,' says one parent, 'and most people in the Hampton community both give and consequently receive a lot – it might not be the right school for a boy if he's not the type to roll up his sleeves and join in.' Delightfully suburban – no smart cars, champers and party frocks here on prize-giving day – but a nice mix of keen mums and dads from a wide range of backgrounds. All faiths represented and celebrated, according to the head. Huge west London and Surrey catchment area bolstered by the extensive school coach network shared with LEH (a new service recently introduced from Ealing). Socially, neither the boys (nor LEH girls!) complain about busing, but parents take note – it's not cheap, and be prepared to spend hours in the car at weekends to pick up and deliver from far flung friends' houses. Once a Hampton boy, always a Hampton boy – contacts with ex-Hamptonians are strong.

Entrance: Two thirds come at 11 (mostly from state primaries) and one third at 13, from more than 200 schools. (Denmead School is part of the same foundation but is no more 'tied' than any other.) Majority of 13+ candidates are pre-selected at 11, then they need 65 per cent at Common Entrance. Four applicants for every place at both 11+ and 13+ entry.

Advance place exam available for 10 year olds to avoid the scramble at 11, but boys who don't make it early are encouraged to re-sit with no prejudice. Both the 11+ and 13+ pre-test consist of three papers: maths, words and reasoning, English response and composition. Locally, the tests are perceived as demanding – according to the school, 'The entrance exam is designed to identify innate ability rather than to test what has been taught or coached'. The local private tutors, who make a tidy sum coaching for this and other school exams, would no doubt disagree. Acceptance is based on school's own exam, interview and school report combined with an age allowance. What is clear – it is not enough just to be academic: the school also assesses 'a pupil's likely positive contribution through good behaviour to the aims, ethos and co-curricular life of the school'. Acceptance at sixth form is based on at least six GCSEs at A or A*, interview, school report and personal statement.

Exit: Almost all to Russell Group or equivalent universities. In last ten years 15–29 have gone annually to Oxbridge, though not all the brightest choose to apply – school is relaxed about this. London is proving increasingly popular.

Money Matters: Academic, all-rounder, art, music and choral scholarships. Means-tested bursaries.

Remarks: A super outward-looking school keen to preserve its strengths (not about to go co-ed), but ready to embrace change if it will further educational achievement. Ideal for high calibre all rounders, but don't think of sending toffs, tremblies or tearaways.

Harris Academy

Perth Road, Dundee, DD2 1NL

• Pupils: 1440 boys and girls, all day • Ages: 11-18 • Size of sixth form: 290 • Non-denom • State

Tel: 01382 435 700
Fax: 01382 435701
Email: harris@dundeecity.gov.uk
Website: www.harris-academy.com

Headteacher: Since 1997, Mr James Thewliss BSc PGCE (fifties) who was educated at Broadhurst High in Motherwell, read geography at Glasgow University and did his PGCE at Hamilton College. Previously depute head at Dalziel High in Motherwell and before that depute head at Wallace High. Very experienced, a chap who knows the area, married, with two children, both now up and flying. Charming, articulate and fun, 'Love this job – I cannot believe how lucky I am to have it. Everyone thinks I am nuts'. It's not so easy to get good staff, fairly high turnover, and this problem is reflected in the 2004 HMI report – 'Overall, the quality of learning and teaching was variable'. No change here.

Academic matters: Well above average: no particular bias, but with around fifty per cent of all pupils leaving after standard grades (most go to Dundee College) it is a little difficult to give an accurate picture. Smashing results for those who do stay on to sixth form – way above national average (though with 38 per cent with three highers – or better – it's not that hard a target to beat). Masses of computers etc, all heavily used, with waiting systems in place if need be. Impressive library with yet more machines, class teaching on computers as well as IT. Pupils do keyboarding and basic ICT skills and use the skills in presentations: power point, sound, film-making, animated flow charts. Max class size (legal limit) 33, but down to 20 for practical subjects.

First couple of years all study English, maths, science, history, geography, modern studies, home economics (magic), technology (great) plus one modern language: French, German or Spanish. Latin on hand, but no Greek. Streaming after first year when a fast track for English, maths and modern languages comes into force. Teaching disciplines are a combination of individual, small group, whole class teaching and discussion. Strong learning support.

School attracts a number of ethnic minorities whose parents are billeted to the local university, hospital or area, 14 currently in the school. Russian, Bengali, Urdu and Cantonese the most frequently spoken at home – native speakers can take these at standard grade. EAL is taught by the special educational needs team, and the HMI thought they were a bit stretched. Pupil support staff co-teach where necessary in class, but 'Such support may result in a revised elaborated or alternative curriculum and include individual or small group tuition'. Supported study includes homework clubs, and a teacher is available early on Tuesday mornings or Thursday evenings to help pupils with problems. Good encouragement, too, for the more gifted. Terrific use of external facilities. HMI also a bit dissy about homework – the amount, the marking et al, but that was some time ago, and the results of the recommendations are not yet available. The HMI other comment which concerns us is that brighter pupils 'do not appear to be sufficiently stretched'.

Eight Standard grades for all as far as possible. Languages, humanities and modern studies above average and good showing in the Scottish and UK Maths Challenges; ditto the Dundee Enterprising Maths competition. Wish list includes re-vamped labs on the top floor. Inspiring programme of lectures from outside speakers. Serious advice for all pupils on which road to take. Good choice post Standard with the option of intermediates 1 and 2 as well as Highers and Advanced Highers in a raft of subjects, plus tourism and hospitality at standard grades. Regular assessments and good parental feedback.

School is an important cog in the education of children in the autistic spectrum and, since 2000, takes ten pupils (never fewer) by request and allocation from the west of Dundee and the city itself (Morgan Academy takes those who live East of Dundee). These pupils are scattered across the age range, and school only accepts the next pupil when space becomes available. 'Lovely laddies' (mainly boys, but that's the nature of autism) all have individual educational programmes which are regularly monitored and amended. Some are totally supported individually and educated in the base (only one currently); others attend mainstream lessons but may be entirely supported in class, or allowed to attend certain classes for a short period – e.g. physics: in mainstream for six weeks, and then back to the unit. Most take Standard grade maths and all have speech and oral communication. School OK for physical handicaps – 'Only one lift, but there are ways of moving round the school'. The base is popular with 'normal kids' who choose to join those in the autistic spectrum at lunchtime – a reverse integration. Many of these pupils will go on to Elmwood College in Fife, where the school has close links.

Games, Options, the Arts: Games fields half a mile away, gyms on site plus swimming pool. Large sports complex off-site. PE timetabled and impressive lineup of games (extra-curricular) including the very popular rugby, hockey, football for boys and girls, athletics, basketball (enthusiastic coach) water polo etc.

Art, as you might imagine, deeply computer-linked: ceramics, painting, ICT, no CAD as such but the facility to use computer based design. Computer suite in art room, home economics, metalwork area, all computer based and hands on. Mass of instrumentalists, music strong and popular with ceilidhs and rock concerts (including FPs) – huge charitable input, 'everything and anything'. Choirs, bands, orchestras. Popular theatre club, though not available as an exam subject, despite pupils' requests. Outstanding debating, thrashing all comers; vibrant YE and truly popular D of E, with a whacking list of gold, silver and bronze successes. Not the longest list of clubs we have ever seen, but thoroughly active, mass of trips abroad: humanities with proper exchanges popular.

Background and Atmosphere: Founded in 1885 and 'the oldest public school in Dundee', moved to the handsome granite building in 1931, school then added on a hotchpotch of flat-roofed excrescences in the '60s. Thirties classrooms elegant and airy, with corridors wide enough for children and their bags to pass; '60s nasties – apart from the inevitable flat roof drip – boast beastly narrow passages, scarred by teenage bookbags. Stunning views to the south, with really quite a lot of playground. Tiny dining hall in basement, next to library, students wait their turn in a surprisingly orderly queue at the 'red line'. Work experience at 14; some – less academic – pupils can study vocational subjects; access courses in communication and maths or apprentice-shops locally.

Pastoral Care and Discipline: Sixth formers buddy first formers – 'very protective and good anti-bullying strategy'. Strong PSE reinforced by RME. Pupils are divided into four houses, and the pupil support strategy is handled by house representatives, each house having two guidance and two support-for-learning teachers. Terrific inter-house competition, both in the academic and the sporting field, with marks being allocated for each and house championship fiercely fought over.

Defined sanction system: if pupils disobey one of five clearly defined rules, then they 'may be excluded for up to three days' for continuous disobedience, and head will meet with the parents. He 'is not prepared for disruptive children or anti-social behaviour' to permeate the school and would much rather produce 'decent sensible sensitive citizens' who are a lot 'more use than an anti-social chemist'. To this end (and this is a first for us) he has installed a splendid reward system (Pavlov eat your heart out). Each pupil (who has the school code drilled into them during their first week, 'so they can't say they don't know what is expected of them') is given a personal plan which must be stamped at the end of each lesson. Pupils earning 250 marks are awarded a certificate, can skip an afternoon's school and see a film of their choice – and get a Mars bar. 500 stamps qualify for a silver certificate and a free ticket for Megabowl; gold equals a trip to Alton Towers, with a certain amount of parent input, and platinum a three day trip to London. Platinum winners have to have their cards stamped after almost every lesson to qualify – head just loves these trips. Links with top year of feeder primaries – guidance staff and teacher visit regularly (HMI reckoned the school 'could try harder') and first year pupils all decamp with their teachers to Falkland Youth Centre for bonding and team-building stuff.

Pupils and Parents: A mixed bunch: some here briefly – charming and well-mannered. Good parental support and school booklet encourages this. Farmers, business people, as well as the university and hospitals. FPs include Donald Findlay QC, Bruce Milan, James Crabb (accordion player), the footballer Christian Daily and the much beloved George Galloway – who does not even receive a mention in the FP online site under 'government'. (Should we have checked 'media/television personalities'?)

Entrance: Always full. Pupils come from five main feeders with a couple of dozen placement requests annually. Certain amount of logistical movement. Standard rules about addresses and siblings.

Exit: Either post Standard Grade, or (usually) post sixth form. Some 70 odd per cent to universities, mostly to Scotland but the occasional trickle to Oxbridge. Inspired careers advice.

Money Matters: Free school meals (but the cafeteria is cashless). Help with school uniform (school provides the basics ex-stock) and trips. Grants available. If pupils stay for fifth year the odds are they will stay on to sixth: five Highers the norm; school qualifies for £40 educational maintenance allowance for those staying on after 16, which is a carrot.

Remarks: Inspirational. An outstanding head – pity he can't inspire the building with as much enthusiasm as the children.

The Harrodian School

Linked to Harrodian Preparatory And Pre-preparatory Schools in the Junior section

Lonsdale Road, London, SW13 9QN

• Pupils: 945; mixed • Ages: 4-18 • Size of sixth form: 120: 60/60 boys/girls • Non-denom • Fees: £14,502-£16,350 pa • Independent

Tel: 020 8748 6117
Fax: 020 8563 7327
Email: admin@harrodian.com
Website: www.harrodian.com

Headmaster: Since 1999, Mr James Hooke BSc Hons PGCE (late 40s – yet could still be mistaken for a sixth former here, only smarter and slightly more conventional). Educated up the road at Hampton, read geography at Leeds and then straight to the City as a banker. Soon became bored and took off to Latin America, where he taught at St John's School in Buenos Aires. Impressed the former head, when he arrived here in 1995, with his knowledge of languages and very soon became deputy head. His youthful appearance belies a steady, practical, and considered approach. He loves the job and is totally committed to the pioneering ethos that is being achieved here. His daughter and son are both at the senior school. One parent commented that he seems to float around the place – no one is very sure what he is doing to steer the ship. His subtle touch seems to be effective, though – as soon as the slightest problem is brought to him, it's swiftly and decisively resolved.

While he, as headmaster, runs the school, the principal, Mr Peter Thomson, is central to its public face. A former head of history and surmaster of St Paul's, yards up the road, he ran the school for a short period until he 'retired' in 1999 but is still very much involved. Apart from knowing, and knowing about, everyone, children and parents alike, he imparts avuncular wisdom and experience and turns his hand to any job that needs doing, whether creating an allotment or delivering documents during a postal strike. His quirky sense of fun and enthusiasm for the spirit of what is being achieved here are key to the originality of the school.

Academic matters: High standards without undue pressure is the consistent message. 'Children can learn at their own pace and grow in confidence,' was the observation of more than one parent. Streaming in English, maths and languages. As it becomes more academically selective at every entrance point, and the image that this is a school for the clotted cream of society starts to fade, the results continue to make dramatic improvements. 2010 A level results included 100 per cent passes with 66 per cent A/B. At GCSE 100 per cent five A*–C, 50 per cent of all grades A*/A and 18 pupils scored nine or more A*/As – impressive stuff.

Those with SEN, so long as they are mild to moderate needs, are well looked after. A team of ten support staff run by the experienced and highly praised SENco work closely with mainstream staff. Pupils are taken out of sport or Latin to the appealing suite of rooms tucked away at the top of the main building for mostly one to one attention. No formal programme for the gifted and talented – this is not pegged onto learning support. 'We don't like the implications of branding a child as gifted and talented – it sends the wrong message to others.'

Maverick and colourful members of staff from all walks of life who, unsurprisingly, thrive in such a civilised environment. Muttering among some parents about the high turnover of antipodeans, but Mr Hooke is keen to point out the cultural diversity and energy young Australians bring. Average age of staff is young – 35 to 40 – and 20 have been there for more than 10 years.

The curriculum is mainstream with a heavy emphasis on modern languages – key to a civilised life; how refreshing. All learn French to a more or less bilingual level, taught wholly by native speakers. They can also do Italian, Spanish and German; Japanese, Chinese etc are available by arrangement. Latin and religious studies survive – can offer Greek for those who want to do it. Media and business studies are popular. Graphic design recently introduced as an A level option.

ICT is well provided for – gleaming Apple Macs in three spacious rooms dedicated to ICT as well as in various key rooms around the school. Everyone has a lesson a week plus being encouraged to use it in other academic areas. Interactive whiteboards making slow progress – some but not many. We speculated that the founder's penchant for York stone took precedence but were told firmly that his resistance to state of the art teaching technology is based on educational principles – children get enough screens at it is; he wants to avoid any interference in the teacher/pupil oral interaction.

Overall good, and promising to become better and better -'Academic bar is being raised each year,' says head.

Games, Options, the Arts: One pupil remarked that she contemplated going to boarding school but realised she didn't need to – she could go to the Harrodian. The sense of space (25 acres of pitches, courts, play areas and gardens) and the emphasis on getting plenty of exercise and fresh air (they carry on even in torrential rain) are central to the Harrodian experience. Winning isn't, however: lots of fixtures in traditional sports, as you would expect, but competition isn't the main focus – 'It would be wrong to thump a team 12–0,' says head, and one parent remarked that sports day was a bit of a joke: plenty of races but no one with really any idea of what's going on. 'It's more about happy kids enjoying themselves.' Mr Hooke is keen to counter that while they have an inclusive approach – A, B, C and D teams – the A team is competitive. Plus a highly qualified team of sports coaches, high tech equipment that can record a match so you can replay it MOTD style to comment on technique, as well as the best sports equipment.

Building work is soon to commence on a swanky sports hall which will provide a gym as well as fencing salle and dance studios. In true Harrodian style it's not just the conventional that is on offer either – a smattering of glamorous options, e.g. a racing ski team will compete in France and attend a three day training camp; golf is being developed at Dukes Meadows; yoga, karate and self-defence as well as boxercise and volleyball. Small but heated outdoor pool in attractive colonnaded courtyard – only open in the summer.

Lots of dynamic and bubbly music – from opera (*The Magic Flute* recently performed by the prep school) and musicals to the hugely popular Battle of the Bands judged by a celeb from the music industry. Bands allowed to record CDs on site and make their own photographed cover. Intimate recital/theatre studio with fixed raked seating and individual practice rooms housed in the music school, which bursts with activity of all kinds – three senior choirs, orchestra and smaller groups. A less than confident guitarist may be called upon to accompany a singer in assembly – while excellence is recognised and valued, it's not over-lauded.

Drama is dynamic and innovative. Pupils here are confident about getting up on stage and often take the initiative themselves to write and perform, e.g. comedy sketches. One boy in the prep school took a few terms out to perform in the film of 'Peter Pan'. Artistic endeavour is encouraged, opportunities valued. Art happens in three different rooms around the site – all equally pleasantly cluttered; twenty per cent take art at GCSE, impressive photography and graphics studio – we saw haunting models of WW1 soldiers recreating the carnage of the trenches. Very little cookery, textiles club popular with girls in the prep school but not much evidence of it in the senior school. DT markedly absent – surprising in such a creative school.

Background and Atmosphere: As eccentric as you would expect. In a previous incarnation it was the country club for Harrods employees. Sir Alford and Lady Houstoun-Boswall – a couple with a vision – bought it in 1993 (pipping The Lycée and St Paul's Boys' at the post), he the eighth baronet, she an American multi-lingual teacher, headmistress and restorer of historical buildings (see Hampton Court House), and proceeded to create a dream – a co-ed school run according to civilised values in a civilised environment to produce relaxed, happy children. The original intention was to create a prep school but two way expansion occurred and now it runs from 4 to 18. Strong sense of family ownership and involvement – Sir Alford's sister, Mrs Moore, lives in a flat in the school and has a pastoral role, he has an office and comes into the school most days and his elderly mother can be spotted eating lunch in the dining room with the children (she has a flat over the coffee shop).

The dream appears to have been realised – this is one of the least institutional schools we have visited: no sign of industrial carpets and concrete here. York Stone courtyards embellished tastefully with inessential but elegant and stylish jeux d'esprit – little fountains and stone vases, olive trees, loggias and parterres. Spacious reception areas with sweeping staircases, three piece suites nestled on landings and in comfortable corners. No signs, no bells, no uniform, and no common rooms for staff or pupils ('Reduces the chance of any whispering behind doors,' says principal). Real three course lunches eaten on tablecloths in a dining room that could seamlessly become a ballroom. A coffee shop, complete with open fire, latte and floor to ceiling plush curtains (no crisps, no coke). And yes, the children are relaxed and are happy and seem surprisingly unspoilt by the privileges they enjoy here. We heard tales of some children returning, having left, and others ecstatic when they didn't get into another school.

Pastoral Care and Discipline: We were fully prepared to witness a level of chaos; not a bit of it. One parent described the discipline here as 'contained liberalism but certainly not lax'. Boundaries are clearly defined and pupils respect that, while enjoying an unusually equal and positive relationship with staff. If you miss homework you will be given a detention; these can take place on a Saturday morning (when no school) but the number of detainees is small – a reflection, we were told, of how well the system works. Zero tolerance on drugs – 'I have expelled children for drugs and wouldn't hesitate to do so again,' says head. Pupils have a mature self regulating approach but it's not the place for someone who persists in pushing the boundaries – 'They wouldn't fit in,' says head. Ofsted 2008 opined, 'The spiritual, moral, social and cultural development of pupils is outstanding.'

Pupils and Parents: Increasingly trendy media and fashion types from central London, with a fair helping of celebrities, but the core group of middle class professionals from affluent Barnes are still here too. A few first time buyers who are coming to grips with what is meant by a Russell Group university. Plenty of money, though – not many families here are scraping to find the fees and this is reflected in the lavish activities and trips that your child will want to attend. Children less bothered than their parents by this – thank goodness – and are confident, relaxed but polite, and relishing the space and the stimulation of the place.

Entrance: Huge waiting lists for the pre-prep – 'It's getting to the stage that you may wish to plan your Caesarean at the beginning of the month,' we were told, with only a slight hint of irony. Non-selective. Strong sibling policy. Competitive at 8+ and 11+ and for occasionals. 11+ applications from a huge range – local state primaries as well as local preps; 'Girls' schools are less sniffy now,' head said. Becoming increasingly competitive – 250 applicants for 20 places. Two thirds of candidates are interviewed, in some cases on the strength of an excellent school report notwithstanding a poor exam result. Despite evident delight at the quality and calibre of applicants in recent years, head keen to preserve the ethos of not creaming and cramming.

Takes a few more at CE. Entry to the sixth requires 6 or more Bs with As in the subjects chosen for A level. Standards less stringent for internal applicants.

Exit: A decreasing few at CE to trad boarding schools (Eton, Harrow, Charterhouse, Marlborough, etc) and the odd one or two to single sex London day schools (St Paul's Girls', King's College School etc). Will lose a few in the sixth form to, e.g. tutorial colleges and boarding. Most leave for good universities after A levels to read a well balanced mix of arts and sciences, creative and practical courses.

Money Matters: Fees pretty average for location and what's on offer, but very little help available to pay them – limited bursaries (the funds are kept for a crisis emergency) and no entrance scholarships. Academic awards are offered at 13+ and 16+.

Remarks: The secret of this unique place is undoubtedly out, as the gap continues to narrow between its local reputation as a country club for kids and the experience of those on the inside that it's possible to achieve high standards without being tense and worried about doing so. The challenge will be how the school manages to maintain that ethos, as competition to experience such a delightful way to learn and grow becomes ever more fierce.

Harrogate Ladies' College

Linked to HLC Highfield Prep School in the Junior section

Clarence Drive, Harrogate, North Yorkshire, HG1 2QG

• Pupils: 320 girls; 120 board, 180 day • Ages: 11-18 • Size of sixth form: 120 • Christian Foundation • Fees: Boarding £22,626 (International £26,907); Day £12,966 pa • Independent

Tel: 01423 504 543
Fax: 01423 568 893
Email: enquire@hlc.org.uk
Website: www.hlc.org.uk

Headmistress: Since September 2009, Mrs Rhiannon Wilkinson MA (Oxon), PGCE (Bath), MEd (Manchester), a historian (forties). Married, she and her husband have four children between them. Two are grown-up and two are school-aged. A breadth of experience, having taught in the maintained independent (day and boarding) and international sectors. Previously director of pastoral system at Cheadle Hulme School, deputy principal at Jerudong International School, Brunei and latterly director of studies, then senior mistress at Haileybury. The product of an excellent girls' grammar school and St Hugh's College, Oxford, she has returned to her belief in the success of single-sex education for 11+ girls. She is a great believer in the importance of pastoral care and in a culture of high expectations and ambition. Her early intentions are to revitalize boarding (she has already instituted vertical houses for girls 10–17) and to create one-schoolness across the Harrogate Ladies' College group of schools.

Academic matters: Improving – regularly registers individual subject results in top five nationally. 96 per cent A* to C pass rate at GCSE. 84 per cent A*/A and B grades in 2009. Strength is with sciences, a particular bias in the sixth form, but modern languages are fine – normally only the odd D at GCSE, otherwise all A*–C. Only a handful (three or four per language) opt for modern languages at A level but achieve good results. Teaching is generally very good – friendly good-humoured staff and girls feel both known and supported. Practical subjects good too – impressive art throughout the school and girls using a wide range of complex design and technology equipment, with an after school group delighting in dismembering an old moped for spare parts for their go-cart. Super new food technology room. Overseas students encouraged to sit exams in their native language, additional English language tuition available (and certainly encouraged), prior to start, at no extra charge. EAL students take IELTS rather than GCSE English. 82 per cent of A levels graded A*, A or B. Computer facilities excellent. A brand new business school provides outstanding teaching facilities for those students who wish to take economics, business studies, accountancy and psychology courses in the sixth form. Over the past four years, 32 per cent of girls have pursued a business-related degree course. Young Enterprise a regular and successful feature.

Good and stimulating facilities, displays everywhere – a striking balance of pupil work and thought provoking material, alongside posters from house captains rallying the troops. Good provision for a range of special needs and specific learning difficulties. Class size averages 18 in lower school. Reports always discussed with head or tutor prior to being sent home.

Games, Options, the Arts: Sport, the life-blood of the school, is keenly pursued by all. Lacrosse ('lackie') is king (at expense of other sports?), current holders of northern schools' lacrosse title. Super much-used sports facilities include plenty of tennis and badminton courts, multi-gym, 25-metre pool and an enormous indoor general-purpose sports hall which doubles up as a venue for social events, speech day etc. The extra-curricular menu embraces sub-aqua, golf, sailing and ski trips as well as keen D of E and masses of charity and community work. School also boasts a flourishing ham radio station (call sign GX0HCA) – historic triumph was a hook-up with the Mir space station and the International space station.

Dedicated music house accommodates ensembles galore. Music is a real strength and majority of girls learn an instrument or two. Choir regularly features on BBC Radio, at cathedral services across the land and on tours, Eastern

Europe being a favoured destination. AS and A level theatre studies on offer with plays and productions acted out in the suitably equipped drama studio. Curriculum supported by regular trips to concerts, theatre and cinema. Many girls take LAMDA lessons (honours and distinctions the norm). Careers education taken seriously – two weeks' work experience for all followed by presentation and lunch.

Background and Atmosphere: School founded in 1893 on a nearby site and is one of the Allied Schools. Within walking distance of the busy town centre, in the heart of Harrogate's leafy prime real estate, originally part of the Duchy of Lancaster. The pleasant Victorian mock-Tudor buildings with sympathetic additions blend gently with the locality. C of E (own chapel, resounding hymns et al) in small doses for all without exception. Separate sixth form centre in main school complete with common rooms, study centre, kitchens, AV room etc. The six well-presented boarding houses each have generously sized attractive study bedrooms, a common room centred round the TV, kitchen and games room.

Up to four share a room in lower school but most sixth formers have their own room with internet access for all in studies and bedrooms. Friendly comfortable feel, not snobbish or overtly feminine, girls mix well with the sense of a supportive sisterhood. Girls are encouraged to mix across the ages with a buddy system operating for new pupils. Upper sixth housed in Tower – a half way house between school and university where pupils prepare and eat breakfast and a couple of evening meals in house and have greater freedom than lower down the school (team building exercises at start of upper sixth aid the bonding process). Flexi and weekly boarding as well as day and full boarding, weekends brimming with trips and activities. Food is now provided by an external catering company, which has seen a marked improvement in the choice and quality of meals available; a magnificently refurbished dining room. Residential staff and girls dine together in main house, self-service at lunch, grace and formal sit-down at other times. School council meets regularly, though girls would like it to be less of a talking shop and to exert more power. A new uniform (predominantly navy) has been introduced throughout the school whilst keeping the traditional green cloak. The sixth form wear a smart, practical navy business suit.

Pastoral Care and Discipline: Manners strictly monitored. At 16+ girls are allowed out one night a week. Occasional links with other schools but not into creating artificial exposure to boys. Drugs and similar problems uncommon and treated with firmness, head retains discretion, expulsions rare. Health centre, specialist counsellor, tutors and staff all on hand to help if things go wrong.

Pupils and Parents: Mostly from Harrogate and the environs. Number of boarders from overseas, especially high number in the sixth form, including Hong Kong, USA, China, Thailand, Spain, Brunei, Germany, France and Baltic Republic currently being marketed. All faiths and none in the school. Parents predominantly from the usual professions, many Harrogate glitterati, also self-employed and some farming families, popular with the Services. Turns out informed, assured, polite and articulate girls, cooperative rather than competitive. Strong OG network, including Anne McIntosh MP, Jenny Savill (author), Juliet Bremner, Claire King and Henrietta Butler, and working hard to encourage more recent leavers to stay in touch.

Entrance: Own entrance test (maths, English, verbal reasoning) taken on assessment day together with reports from previous school. Main entry points are 11, 13 and 16 but school flexible. Highfield Prep is the linked feeder school. Minimum seven GCSEs at grade C or above required for entry to sixth form.

Exit: Several Oxbridge girls in 2010, otherwise to a widespread selection of universities including Durham, Imperial and Leeds. Lack of boys cited as main reason for handful of pupils leaving at 16.

Money Matters: Academic and bursary scholarships of up to 25 per cent of fees. Regular armed services scholarships of up to 15 per cent. Music, art, sport and drama scholarships also awarded.

Remarks: Could do with a few more local girls to balance the top end in particular, but playing the balancing act and gaining strength both academically and financially from its overseas intake. Frequently described as 'a genteel school in a genteel town', but that description does neither any favours. Dig a little deeper and you find that both the school and the town have a great deal to offer the academic, the sporty, the musical and the keenly ambitious, whilst being small enough to provide a safe and welcoming haven for those who require a little more TLC.

Harrow School

1 High Street, Harrow on the Hill, Middlesex, HA1 3HT

• Pupils: 800 boys (all board) • Ages: 13-18 • Size of sixth form: 350
• C of E (but 135 RCs) • Fees: £29,670 pa • Independent

Tel: 020 8872 8007
Fax: 0208 8872 8012
Email: admissions@harrowschool.org.uk
Website: www.harrowschool.org.uk

Headmaster: Since 1999, Mr Barnaby Lenon BA PGCE (mid-fifties), previously head of Trinity, Croydon, having been deputy head at Highgate and head of geography at Eton before that. 'One of the most remarkable men in education,' we were told by a colleague. Pin-striped with scarlet braces, rimless specs and black brogues, he is a true and unswerving educator without a trace of jargon. Firm of view, incisive of expression, with a controlled, energetic wit, he is also faintly and disarmingly theatrical – a pretty winning and successful combination. He has put his own stamp on Harrow – not a pushover with 400 years of tradition thundering at you from all sides.

We applaud his educational principles and convictions, 'We are great believers in late developers ... I'm not going to fail (at CE) someone who is only very good at some things and not others' (not a view we hear at all comparable schools at present). 'Most boys are not motivated to work – we've got to motivate them to do subjects they're interested in' – and enjoyed his take on many matters – see below for the Lenon view on IB, SEN and bullying. He teaches – yes, really – three subjects to A levels and a fourth to GCSE – we doff our hats to him. Married with two daughters, locally educated. His was an inspired appointment and one which, had he stayed his full term, would have seen him preserving and powering on this ancient-modern school into the third decade of the millennium. Sadly not to be, though: he's retiring in July 2011.

His successor will be Mr Jim Hawkins MA (mid forties), currently head of Norwich School. Read maths at Brasenose. Taught at Radley College before becoming head of maths at Forest School, then deputy head at Chigwell School. Upright and courteous, he enjoys rowing (coaches some of the boys) and music (turns up to concerts, large or small, and is a member of the school choral society). An interesting match and we wish both halves well.

Academic matters: Much improved during Mr Lenon's tenure and the boys see themselves as at an 'academic' school. Not that Harrow hasn't always had some splendid minds (on both sides of the desk, of course) – it numbers many writers of scholarly books on its staff, past and present. Masters – the 15 women teachers are also 'masters' – tend to stay. Results are impressive across the board. Popular GCSE subjects are maths, the sciences and history. At A level, a good spread of options includes government and politics, photography, ancient history and DT, alongside all the traditional subjects. Languages – old and modern – are in goodish health, though here, as elsewhere, German teeters on the edge of extinction in the sixth.

Overall, in 2010, 85 per cent of GCSE papers taken achieved A*/A – remarkable, and testament to the nature of full boarding and the flexibility it facilitates. At A level, overall, 74 per cent of papers gained A*/A. Allows boys to take exams when they are ready to do so , which can result in 15 year olds already having clutches of GCSEs and leavers having managed to amass 4, 5, 6 or even 7 A levels – sometimes all with A*/A grades. No plans to adopt the Pre-U – 'Completely untried – don't tell me the average Oxbridge admissions tutor knows anything about it' – or the IB – 'No way – we force boys here to do far more than the IB does ... Most boys here do critical thinking' – and professes himself 'satisfied' with A levels, especially in view of the recent reforms (A*s etc).

Not so GCSEs – moving to the IGCSE in six key subjects – some already up and running – for greater rigour. 'Set Zero' consists of fast-tracked mathematicians who venture well beyond and outside any standard curricular maths and generally end up as Oxbridge latter-day Pascals. An inexhaustible range of academic opportunities here. Many take the option of the extended project, which equates to an AS level – has an engineering scheme with local companies, e.g. Kodak and BMW, taken by many of the high-flying scientists. 'Off-timetable' options include Japanese, astronomy; Mandarin is timetabled throughout.

Around five per cent of boys on the SEN register – all are screened on entry by the learning support department. Most are mild dyslexics and all have individually-based support as needed, though 'Every teacher has instruction on how to help them'. No special G and T provision – 'I'm assuming that every boy here has some gifts and some talents,' says head – and boys are encouraged individually to stretch themselves and take on more challenges (some feel almost too challenged in terms of Oxbridge application). Not conducive to wheelchairs, being scattered between umpteen, mostly elderly, buildings and on an undulating hill. 'If,' asserts Mr Lenon, 'a good, disabled boy applies, I'll take him like a shot.'

Games, Options, the Arts: Not easy to see what you couldn't do here. Cricket the main game, though rugby and football run them close, hockey and athletics also popular. Games of course happy and glorious, though rugby recently less victorious than hitherto – swimmers and athletes currently much bemedalled. First XI cricket team has lost only two matches in the recent years – therefore one of the strongest in the UK, beating Eton at Lord's four years in a row. Football team wins 90 per cent of matches (one player also trains with QPR). Much expected of new director of sport. Several county and some national players at all levels. Has own nine-hole golf course. Many other sports such as shooting, fencing, badminton, polo – both the wet and the less wet – plus 'Harrow football', all played on fabulous pitches, tracks, courts and fields. Harrow football is played with a pork-pie shaped ball which absorbs the wet and can be propelled by any part of the body, and is integral to the great Harrow song tradition – see below.

Art, music and drama all very strong. Art is everywhere – space here for masses of painted, sculpted, crafted and welded pieces. Displays it all over, and thoroughly deserving it is, too – we saw things that would do credit to many an art school and rejoiced to see evidence of the traditional skills of drawing and figurative work being practised. Work is witty and beautifully made across the whole spectrum of art and DT. Photography thrives. Outstanding music – ensembles, concerts and tours all enabled by superb teaching and facilities. Seventy five per cent of the boys who learn an instrument – around half – gain grade 8 while at school. Excellent Ryan Theatre seating nearly 400, of professional quality and adored by aficionados, with recent productions of, e.g. *Donkey's Years* and *Les Miserables*, but the annual Shakespeare productions take place in the stunning arts and crafts Speech Room – a huge, wood-panelled, half-moon with authentic Globe-style staging and seating the entire school. Made us want to pull on our breeches and buskins.

Perhaps unique range of other opportunities – no lounging about with nothing to do on Sunday afternoons. Eighty eight activities listed in the school's 'Some extra-curricular activities'. Corps now not compulsory but one of a wide choice of worthwhile options, e.g. community service, life saving, first aid. Has own farm, conservation area and museum – this last housing an extraordinary rich collection of artefacts, pictures and books, most connected with the school, its former pupils and benefactors, and open to the public. Its curator, an art historian, introduces all pupils to the collection and takes regular trips to London galleries. An immensely privileged provision, and so good to see a school not hiding away its treasures in vaults. Huge programme of top notch speakers, trips and visits. Rather nice tradition of the Harrow Prize –'awarded to boys in the upper sixth who have shown particular commitment to an all-round education'.

Background and Atmosphere: Believe it or not, only two other all-boys, full-boarding schools now left in the UK: Radley and Eton (Winchester has a fistful of day boys). Which would make Harrow something of an endangered species except that it, plainly, isn't. And, despite some OH huffing that it has 'lost its distinctiveness', this is not evident either to its current population nor to the visitor – tradition and history are everywhere, celebrated with pride by most boys. Sits atop a high hill overlooking the spread of London – of it, yet remote from it, physically superior to it, yet indivisible from it in all practical ways. Boys have been educated here since the thirteenth century, though it was officially founded by John Lyon under a Royal

Charter of Elizabeth I in 1572. (The new house, due in 2011, will be, belatedly, called "Lyon's".)

Emphatically populates the little suburb of Harrow-on-the-Hill, housed in a range of buildings covering a sizeable acreage – everything from the original 17th century 'Old School' to subject-specific, well-sited, sensitively designed brand new blocks. Old School contains the original schoolroom, which needs to be seen. Every inch of deep panelling has a name carved into it – history (and vandalism) enshrined in wood, redolent of four centuries of boydom. The deceptively commodious Vaughan Library designed by Gilbert Scott has chess sets on tables, is open late during exam periods and is well-supplied, as you'd expect, with books and PCs. The War Memorial Building commemorates shockingly large numbers of fallen OHs. We relished the vigorous bagpiping coming from a downstairs room as we walked round. We were profoundly moved by the Alec Fitch Room – a joy in wood panelling and stained glass with a fabulous Cromwellian refectory table, given in honour of her son, dead at 19 in WWI, by a grieving mother, for the purpose of boys meeting their mothers.

The church atop the hill overlooks London – you could touch the Wembley Arch, it seems – across to Canary Wharf and beyond. Harrovian Byron sat here and contemplated. Everywhere are plaques and memorials commemorating quirky events: Charles I rested here while preparing to surrender, the very first fatal traffic accident is dubiously recorded on a wall, and little inclines have names like 'Obadiah Slope' – wittily adopted by OH Trollope for his unctuous character. Most of the other buildings are very solid nineteenth century redbrick – the sense of the whole place is of solidity, confidence, permanence. Worth noting are The Copse, a secluded, smallish, flint building, perfect for English and bookishness, the massive, highly flexible DT building of 1986, in which miracles happen, and the MFL block of 2006 with a superb view and facilities to match.

Meals eaten centrally – won the Tatler Schools' Food Award in 2008 (boys concur). But in general houses are all-important. The housemasters do most of the admissions assessments (see below) and give the house its character and reputation; the houses themselves generate fierce loyalty. Care is taken to spread overseas nationals and sports and music stars between houses for 'balance'. House rivalry is fostered though innumerable competitions –'friendly,' we are assured. The importance of your housemaster and his staff and family cannot be over-emphasised and houses are chosen primarily on the strength of this.

Boarding here is not state of the art. Two boys sharing is the norm in the first year – rooms have cabin beds (not always long enough), cupboard, shelves and PC point, but no basin and not spacious. By the sixth form you have your own, much larger room (some boys have fridges), well-furnished with desk and shelving, but no basin. All boys share communal bathrooms. Common rooms and games rooms with plasma TV, pool and tabletennis tables – comfortable but not luxurious.

Has its own argot, of course, e.g. 'skew' = a punishment, 'tolley up' = permission to work late, 'torpids' = house sports teams etc. Harrow songs are legendary: no Harrovian – Old or current – will fail to mention the strength of feeling these engender and the tear in the throat and lump in the eye they provoke – for ever.

Pastoral Care and Discipline: Meticulous pastoral care. Highly structured system of housemasters, matrons, 'mentors and shepherds', plus a health educator/counsellor, picks up all but the most subterranean distress. Two school chaplains play an important rôle for many. Bullying an occasional problem here as everywhere, but 'mostly in the first year and we do a bullying survey every winter' – an eight-sided anonymous paper which picks up anything undesirable: 'All staff fully understand that any bullying is totally unacceptable'. In a full boarding school you have to get along and everyone seems to, as we were repeatedly told by boys, staff and parents.

Rare cases of unauthorised nipping out punished by automatic suspension and final warning; drinkers/smokers 'a permanent minor irritant' – anyone found with spirits also suspended and warned. Possession of drugs of any kind anywhere means out – consequently, these days, a rarity. Discipline is clear and firm but the place feels pretty relaxed. A parent told us, 'There's a very good balance between giving boys the boundaries they need while allowing them freedom to develop,' though for some, the lack of independence, especially by the sixth form, becomes a trial. However, 'We're a full boarding school and demand is growing. We don't feel we need to change,' says head.

Uniform is attractive with unpretentious dark blue jackets ('bluers'), grey flannels ('greyers') and white shirts and ties; boys wear – or carry – boaters and either love them – 'We love them!' – or hate them – 'They're such a bore to carry around'. Shirts are reassuringly out in many cases, though officially in. Sunday wear is black tailcoat and the whole kit and caboodle. Two exeats a term, one each half plus half term holidays.

Pupils and Parents: The head stresses that Harrow is a 'national school' and one in which a Yorkshire farmer's son will be sharing a room with the offspring of a City banker. Seventeen per cent are scions of OHs, 16 per cent from overseas, the largest number from Hong Kong, who come in for the sixth form, often on music scholarships. Rest mostly from the Middle East (King Hussein was an OH), Malaysia (a former king was an OH) and Thailand (ditto). Vast majority are, nominally at least, C of E, with the second largest contingent being RC. Small numbers of all other main faiths or no faith.

Honourable tradition of housemasters' daughters being accepted as pupils – currently one, whom we met, who seemed entirely at ease: we boggled with admiration. We spoke to a large number of her colleagues and, though some were a little wary, we were impressed by their friendliness and pride in the school – no-one wished to be anywhere else. Parents highly complimentary – 'The reports are good and detailed' – but some feel school-home communications should be better and not all queries are dealt with as swiftly and comprehensively as they should be. Parental feel that communication with some housemasters is better than with others.

OHs include numerous foreign royalty, seven British Prime Ministers, amongst them Sir Winston Churchill, umpteen local and foreign politicians, e.g. Jawaharlal Nehru, John Profumo, Bill Deedes, Sir Jeremy Greenstock, Lord Shaftesbury and Sir Keith Joseph; the Lord Cardigan who led the Charge of the Light Brigade and General Sir Peter de la Billière, plus countless other military men of high renown, including 19 VCs; a dazzling list of achievers in both arts and sciences, e.g. Sheridan, Byron, Galsworthy, LP Hartley, Rattigan, Trevelyan and Trollope, Francis Wheen, Alain de Botton and Richard Curtis, Sir Joseph Banks and William Fox Talbot, Lord (photographer) Lichfield, Victor Pasmore, Michael Denison, all four Fox brothers, James Blunt, Julian Metcalfe (founder of Pret à Manger), Benedict Cumberbatch (see Wikipedia), Crispin Odey (one of the world's top hedgefunders – hmm!) and Tim Bentinck (David Archer to you) amongst them.

Entrance: See the prospectus – they do what it says. Around 600 apply for the 160 places at 13, ideally by the time the boy is 11. They meet a housemaster and 'if they like each other', a boy is 'pencilled in' for that house. A reference from the boy's prep school is sought and then he will take a pre-selection IQ test. 160 places will be offered at this stage but those – the majority – who are rejected are invited to try again later since, as the head acknowledges, many will make fast progress in the next year or two, and some of the 160 will go elsewhere. Many apply after this process and are tested the following year. Sixty per cent expected at CE. 'Some weight' is allowed for the sons of OHs and to the brothers of boys already in the school – but this is not a given. 'It has got harder to get into Harrow over the last ten years,' admits Mr Lenon, 'and the brother of an existing pupil of similar ability will find it harder now to get a place.' Some 200 apply for the ten or so places in the sixth form, around half will come in on bursaries. All sit tests on their proposed AS subjects.

Exit: Largest single number usually to Oxford, with Bristol, Edinburgh, Leeds, Newcastle and Durham also popular. Around ten annually to US colleges. They study across the academic range, though Harrow mathematicians are a class apart.

Money Matters: School has given franchises to 'Harrow Beijing' and 'Harrow Bangkok' – successful enterprises carefully monitored by the mother school but unashamedly for the purpose of funding generous bursarial schemes at home. Prominent and most admirable of these are the Peter Beckwith scholarships for talented boys of 10 or 11 without the funds to pay for a Harrow education. The scheme pays for the boy to attend a good prep to bridge the 11–13 gap which so often confounds the hopes of parents of state school educated boys of their winning places at schools which begin at 13. A range of other scholarships and bursaries at 13 or 16 which can cover up 100 per cent of fees – some for talent in a specific area, one for the sons of OHs, some for local boys. Well worth investigating if gifts are plentiful but your pocket is empty.

Remarks: If you want blue chip, full boarding, all-boys' education, is there anywhere else to go? Well, is there?

Haydon School

Wiltshire Lane, Eastcote, Pinner, Middlesex, HA5 2LX

• Pupils: 1,800; 50/50 boys/girls; all day • Ages: 11-18 • Size of sixth form: 295 girls; 255 boys • Non-denom • State

Tel: 020 8429 0005
Fax: 020 8868 8213
Email: haydonschool@hillingdongrid.org
Website: www.haydonschool.com

Headteacher: Since 2007, Mr Steve Robson MA PGCE NPQH (fiftyish), first joined school in 1986 as a geographer. Married with two children, both of whom have now left home. Son graduated from Kingston University and daughter graduated from UMIST and now works in the City. Read geography at Swansea University and received his MA from UCL. His interests are travel, ornithology, photography and reading. Building on the on the excellent work of the previous head, with results in 2009 the best ever at both GCSE and A level. The school has upped the overall performance by a clamp-down on discipline – grudgingly accepted by the pupils who acknowledge its positive effects. More to do – the school is far from being a showcase – but the atmosphere is positive, the faces are smiley and the results speak for themselves.

Academic matters: A specialist language college and, since 2007, an applied learning centre. The aim is to increase the range of vocational subjects to ensure that the curriculum provides progression and opportunities for success for all students. The language opportunities here lift the heart. It is particularly impressive that a student survey rated Italian and French as the two most popular subjects. Everyone in year seven takes either French and Italian or German and Spanish and the ablest are selected by the end of the first term to add either Latin, Manadarin or Japanese. They can continue with all three to GCSE and flexibility so that German can be added to French or vice versa if desired. This kind of thing allows the school to recruit and retain good language teachers – not so elsewhere. Science results, previously unimpressive, have soared with appointment of bright new head of science.

GCSE results in 2010 were a record for the school with 76% of students reaching the benchmark figure of 5 A*–C including English and maths. Italian the most popular and successful of the languages with 51% getting A*–A; French mostly Bs and Cs. Maths more of a spread with the bulk getting A/B. Popular options include business studies, geography, history, PE, media and sociology.

Excellent A level choice includes every language you could imagine. Popular subjects are psychology, media, IT and law, which all do well, and many subjects getting mostly A–C. No fewer than 20 A level subjects were rated as 'outstanding' in 2009 by an independent organisation (ALPs) that rates the performance of schools and colleges. Good extras, like a BTec in health and social care supported by experience at nursery school which adjoins site. Everyone takes general studies. Average A level point score in 2009 was 838 and the percentage of A grades was 30 per cent and 24 per cent B. In 2008 14 students achieved top 10 placings in the country for GCSE, including in Italian, Japanese, Russian, geography, business & economics, Spanish (four students!) and an astonishing five of the national top 10 in art. At AS there were one each of the top 10 performers in physics and general studies. A fifty minute citizenship slot on Mondays. Decent library, well-used, but stock badly needing updating in several areas.

SENs are well-supported and the school is now accessible to everyone, with lifts, stair-lifts and positive attitudes helping. 21 statemented pupils and 355 on the SEN register with a teaching staff of five – one full-time – supported by two HLTAs, 15 LSAs and nine special needs assistants who work with individuals according to their needs – right up to sixth form. Everyone tested on entry for reading, spelling and cognitive ability and then assigned individual support if needed. Very sensibly, emphasis is put on literacy, so that weaker Year 7 pupils are withdrawn from mainstream English to bolster their basic English skills. These children might well do only one language and have extra English up to Year 9. SEN supported by specific computer programmes for reading, spelling and maths and dept led by able and compassionate head. 190 children have EAL and a vast range of languages is spoken at home. A real sense of support and integration.

Games, Options, the Arts: Lots of space. Oddly, the main (mostly at the extreme end of unlovely) buildings are all cramped up at one end of the extensive site and much land that could – and probably will, eventually – be used to extend the built facilities. So lots of green, though nothing flat, a good sports hall, though no gym or weights or fitness suite or anything comparable, and several hard courts for ball games. Main sports are football, rugby, athletics and cricket and some golf, cross country, swimming, badminton etc. Success especially in gymnastics. Lots of outward bound and Duke of Edinburgh type opportunities.

Two drama rooms and a real 1950s school hall with small backstage area, helped by workshops with professional companies from outside, somehow contrive to produce a lively mix of work and major productions, and the occasional leaver studies drama thereafter. Good range of musical activities well-supported by instruments and electronic wherewithal – wondrously left in unlocked rooms quite safely. The school has just opened a £5.5 million art and design building funded by the expansion of successful and popular schools scheme. We saw some expert painting, drawing and collage work along with some witty 'funky' hats made in a Year 8 textiles class. Carousel system of trying out the DT and art options – all enjoyed. Food tech also specially popular, it seems. Good range of trips, mostly for older pupils.

Background and Atmosphere: A 1950s school, and it shows – most buildings are frankly tragic. Much has been done to improve and the plans are impressive, but the interiors speak for themselves in terms of the numbers they accommodate and the neglect of successive local authorities. We saw broken blinds and lockers, lights with dead bulbs and several areas that made the heart sink. Barn-like sixth form work area/common room. The school fights the ubiquitous battle against litter and sanctions against it, but accumulations of jettisoned bottles and crisp packets here and there suggesting this is a battle not yet won. A general air of dinginess rather than decrepitude.

School occupies an elevated position on the Northwood Hills side of Pinner and is surrounded by uninspiring 1950s and 1960s developments. It's quiet and orderly and parents of 11-year-olds don't fear to send their children through these streets. The atmosphere isn't sedate – nor especially polite: on our hour-length tour, no-one held a door or allowed us to go through one first. But everyone smiled and our guide had gentle, disrespectful joshing from his peers as he steered us through the hubbub. Classes were, for the most part, clearly purposeful, silent and good-humoured. Teachers seemed relaxed, confident and in control, though we wondered at the sight of one munching a biscuit bar as he directed his class from behind his desk. If the pupils take less of a pride in their environment than they might, the environment doesn't inspire them to do so. However they clearly do take a pride in their abilities and their achievements and that seems the right way round.

Pastoral Care and Discipline: Discipline much tightened up in recent years and pupils, while grumbling, acknowledge the knock-ons in terms of the overall ethos and level of achievement. Well-understood system of sanctions, though some pupils feel the punishments to be not best suited to the crimes. But it seems to work. One recent exclusion for disruptiveness but otherwise nothing much, though the head acknowledges the need for sanctions against smoking, drink and or drugs on site. Dealing would mean out. Parents of 'challenging' pupil feel the school is 'very helpful and patient and keeps us very well-informed ... very good at working with us'. Others 'can't praise the school enough'. Head picks up pupils on uniform infringements, which are manifold, and says, 'We need a purge,' on occasions. Overall feeling that discipline is important but not obsessive.

Pastoral care good. Children feel occasional bullying but school gets onto it and sorts it pronto. Lots of anti-bullying literature and it's a pretty high-profile issue here. House system for all the usual competitive activities and taken for granted. One of the best student handbooks we have seen. Head has CCTV on in his room, flicking from loos to lockers to playground etc – but no sense of Big Brother's eye on them seems to worry his charges. Food – good range and lots of it – especially break snacks, very varied and popular. Chips only on Fridays.

Pupils and Parents: Increasingly diverse ethnically and socially – 'Welcome' is printed in 22 languages in reception. Intake truly represents neighbourhood though catchment has narrowed with school's more visible successes. Parents are encouraged to involve themselves and many do. Pupils are open, articulate, sparky, cheeky and on the ball.

Entrance: Previously reported as impenetrable, we're told the criteria are standard pan-London rules. However the school is over-subscribed 3:1. If you don't manage to be a sibling and/or have a statement, all you can do is apply and wait. School accepts students into the sixth form with six Cs, but higher grades are needed for some subjects.

Exit: The school is underselling itself – as the head acknowledges. Lots of university entrants but not enough apply to the top universities – to which they would surely have a good chance of entry. Head has appointed member of staff to up the aspirations of the sixth form. As it is, multiple places at City University and universities of Kingston, Westminster and Herts; good numbers also to Brunel, Nottingham, Royal Holloway and Queen Mary (London) and Sheffield. One to Cambridge and three to Oxford in 2008. Subjects studied cover the entire range. Some to vocational courses or employment.

Money Matters: Parents expected to pay for trips etc but no-one excluded on account of low funds.

Remarks: A school which lifts the spirits, despite the uninspiring ambiance.

Headington School

Linked to Headington Preparatory School in the Junior section

Headington Road, Oxford, Oxfordshire, OX3 7TD

• Pupils: 720 girls; day, weekly and full boarders • Ages: 11-18 • Size of sixth form: 225 • C of E • Fees: Day £12,639-£12,885; Boarding £21,357-£24,945 pa • Independent

Tel: 01865 759 113
Fax: 01865 760 268
Email: admissions@headington.org
Website: www.headington.org

Head: Since 2003, Mrs Anne Coutts BSc MEd. Educated at King's High School, Warwick, and Apsley Grammar, followed by Warwick University, where she read microbiology and virology. Research posts at Oxford Institute of Virology and Nuffield Institute, then taught at Trent College and Edgbaston C of E College. This is her third headship, following Sutton High School and Eothen School, Caterham.

Married to a C of E clergyman, with two grown-up daughters. She lives in a house in the grounds, lunches alongside the girls and teaches chemistry and RS. Popular with parents, who describe her as 'very approachable', 'vastly experienced', 'really in tune with the girls'. Leaving in December 2010 to become head of Canberra Girls' Grammar School. New head has been announced, Mrs Caroline Jordan, currently head of St George's, Ascot (qv).

Academic matters: Parents say happily that they can take a back seat and rely on the school to keep the girls on track. 'It's fair to say that my daughter is of average ability and the school has pushed, focused and nurtured her to get top grade GCSEs.' 'They get good results without serious pressure.' The percentage of A*/A grades is generally in the high 70s, with most taking separate sciences. A levels average around 90 per cent A/B grades, with a very good take up for biology, maths and chemistry – 'I'm a chemist, so I know it's important'. Geography is another popular subject. Twenty top ten candidate awards in 2008 at GCSE and A level, including four for ICT GCSE and five for Spanish GCSE. Started teaching the IB in September 2009, with some 20 students signed up for the first year.

The school is 'not aggressively selective' and can accommodate those with mild dyslexia and dyspraxia. It has on occasion welcomed pupils with sight or hearing problems and one with cerebral palsy. Extra help is usually included in the fees, unless it is 'very specialist and very frequent', in which case it costs £30 an hour. Foreign students can get help with cultural English from the EAL department. Everyone is given achievement and effort grades six times a year and decides in consultation with their teachers what to aim for in the next half term. 'In the younger years we are much more interested in the grades for effort.'

Games, Options, the Arts: Rowing is 'sensational,' said a parent – 'the total sporting strength of the school. They all row at national level.' The newly-opened floodlit Astroturf pitch (six years in the planning) has revolutionised ball sports, which have been known to take second place to rowing. Enthusiastic teams compete at netball, hockey, rounders, fencing, cross country etc and seven are county champions. Sports hall, fitness suite, swimming pool and assault course in the woods that fringe the site.

Light, airy, galleried art and design building with a dark room, kiln and history of art room. Plenty of impressive artwork on display including ceramics, photographs and textiles. A good takeup for art and history of art at AS and A level, and several students each year go on to art foundation courses.

The impressive Headington Theatre is used by outside companies as well as school thespians, with concerts, dance displays, musicals and plays alternating with school fashion shows, comedies and lectures. School drama is 'excellent', say parents, often in conjunction with the boys of Magdalen College School.

A new music school opened its doors in 2009 and boasts state-of-the-art equipment including electronics studio and recording studios. With airy teaching rooms for individuals, ensembles and full classes, and performance spaces both indoors and out, the facility will take music at Headington to a new level. Speaking at the opening of the new Music School, parent Brian Eno said, 'It is fitting that a progressive school such as Headington should choose to add to its music department this kind of facility for new music.'

The house system encourages everyone to take part in inter-house sport, music and drama competitions. 'It's one of the best things about the school,' said a pupil. 'You get to know people from all the different years and it's all organised by the students.'

Pupils agree that the emphasis on so many different activities makes Headington special. 'You join because you've heard the music or the drama's good, then you find that so many other things are too.'

Background and Atmosphere: Founded in 1915 by a group of evangelical Christians to provide 'a sound education for girls to fit them for the demands and opportunities likely to arise after the war'. It occupied various large houses in Headington before moving to its present site, the main school built in neo-Georgian style in 1930 amidst 26 acres of grounds including four boarding houses. It is still run by a Christian foundation and boarders attend Sunday church services run by a lay chaplain. 'But it is very open – a service may be on a theme such as thinking about others and all the girls are happy to attend.'

Around a third of the school boards, half of the boarders from abroad. Full, weekly and flexi-boarding with different age groups in different houses. The younger girls, some from the prep school, share bright, cheerful dormitories with posters and teddies abounding. Nationalities are mixed and girls move room each term to prevent cliques forming. 'They can ask to share with particular friends but don't always get it.' Older girls get twin or single rooms and increasing freedom, with permission to go out for a meal or off to the pub.

Instead of gap year students, beginning to employ graduate assistants in the boarding houses, mostly en route to PGCE courses – 'I want people who are really interested in the girls'. Plenty of activities to keep homesickness at bay – from table tennis tournaments to chocolate fondue evenings to London theatre visits. Some older girls who live nearby choose to board for the last year or two to prepare for going off to university.

'My daughters have both been incredibly happy there,' said a parent. 'I haven't got a bad word to say about it,' said another. 'We get on really well with most of the staff,' say sixth formers. 'They look for good things in everyone.'

Pastoral Care and Discipline: Drugs, alcohol and smoking all banned on school premises; the head feels that alcohol is the greatest threat to teenagers generally. Strong pastoral support system includes mentoring by part-time staff, who see those in need of extra care once a week for perhaps six weeks at a time. 'It can make a real difference to have that injection of extra attention and it seems to get them sorted fairly quickly.' Anyone can book an appointment with the school counsellor. 'She's really great,' say students.

The school keeps in close touch with parents. 'A student is a jig-saw puzzle – different people see different parts – and we may ask how things are going at home if she doesn't seem to be performing as we would have expected. And sometimes parents need reassurance, especially if she is their eldest child.' One parent praised the school's reaction to a family crisis: 'They were excellent, very calm and supportive, and arranged for her to board for a week until things blew over'. Another, whose daughter was off sick for some time, commented, 'They were amazing and very understanding when she came back.'

Plenty of effort is put into encouraging foreign students and other boarders to integrate with day girls, with everyone joining in international evenings and events such as the rock challenge dance competition. 'We find out what the shy girls are interested in. The Brunei girls, for example, performed their national dance.'

Pupils and Parents: From some 30 countries, including Brunei, Hong Kong (20 sixth form places), Italy, Russia and Australia. Day girls come from a 30 mile radius, with quite a few weekly boarders from London catching a coach which drops them right outside. A mixture of different backgrounds including wealthy country people, professional parents and academics. 'They're a nice bunch of normal girls,' said a parent. OGs include Baroness Young, Julia Somerville, Lady Longford, Christina Onassis and Emma Watson.

Entrance: Ninety-six pupils join the school at 11, of whom about 40 have come up from the junior school. Another 15 or 20 come in at 13. These have all sat the Common Entrance. About half the new entrants at 11 are from state primaries – some 58 different feeder schools. Not ferociously selective – about two applicants for every place. Sixth form applicants sit exams in their chosen A level subjects and are expected to get at least six A/B grades at GCSE. Overseas applicants all sit exams, including an EFL paper if English is not their first language. Twenty girls from Hong Kong join the sixth form, chosen by the head from a field of 100 – 'They integrate much better now we interview them all personally'.

Exit: Most GCSE students go through to the sixth form. Around 10–15 move on to co-ed sixth forms or sixth form colleges. All sixth form leavers to university, about 10 per cent a year to Oxbridge, with a good proportion going for science/medical degrees, and a few to art foundation courses.

Money Matters: Academic, art, drama and sports scholarships all worth £300 a year; music scholarships for tuition on one instrument and a Loft Simson music scholarship for tuition on two instruments for an exceptional candidate.

Means tested bursaries of up to 100 per cent of fees are available to applicants for entry at 11, 13 or 16, and Services/C of E clergy bursaries also available.

Remarks: A nice, happy school that manages to turn out girls with admirable exam results without undue pressure and with rich extra-curricular experiences along the way. 'The staff make sure that life's not all about work,' say students happily. 'You leave school with so much more.'

Heathfield School

London Road, Ascot, Berkshire, SL5 8BQ

• Pupils: 220 girls; all full boarders • Ages: 11-18 • Size of sixth form: 80
• C of E • Fees: £26,397-£27,897 pa • Independent

Tel: 01344 898 343
Fax: 01344 890 689
Email: registrar@heathfieldschool.net
Website: www.heathfieldschool.net

Headmistress: Since 2009, Mrs Jo Heywood BSc PGCE (late thirties); a chemist. Mrs Heywood began her teaching career in a large comprehensive in Surrey, thence to St Mary's, Ascot – a shuttlecock's flight away. She stayed there for eight happy years as teacher of chemistry and head of house. Concerned that she should not become 'complacent', she moved down the road to Heathfield in 2005 to become deputy head (pastoral). When her predecessor, the late Mrs McSwiggan, became ill, Mrs Heywood became acting head and, after Mrs McSwiggan's death, the decision of the school's governors to appoint her to the headship was a popular one with, it seems, the entire school community. 'She's so Heathfield,' one girl enthused – 'she understands the homeliness and the traditions and also what we need to get rid of.'

And it is not hard to see why they wanted her. She is the fifth head in ten years. The school has been dogged by change and misfortune of all kinds – the death of Mrs McSwiggan being the latest and most shocking. As deputy head with pastoral responsibility, Mrs Heywood 'knew everyone' and was ideally placed to bring stability and personal commitment to a school she already loved. She provided, however, more than much-needed continuity. She is a warm, commonsensical head with youthful enthusiasm, generosity of spirit and a firm belief in what Heathfield is all about, which are just what's needed here. 'She's lovely,' said a parent. And she has taste – her newly refurbished room is peachy and beautiful – hits exactly the right note. Heathfield survived the previous difficult decade in remarkably good shape. A good long spell of steady renewal and growth under an excellent head should restore this unique school to robust health and stability.

Academic matters: Warm and friendly atmosphere. In 2010, 24 per cent A* pass rate at A level and an increase of 5 per cent across the board A–B. Now offers accounting, further mathematics, classical civilisation and Latin. Maths popular and successful. At GCSE the A*–C passes a little down on last year but good valued added for this cohort. Single sciences, drama, music and geography stand out; also strong English and maths. Small class sizes.

Games, Options, the Arts: Everything done with energy, enthusiasm and friendly collaboration. Core sports are netball, lax, tennis and athletics but loads else on offer and, in particular, equestrianism gathering strength. 'We punch above our weight,' says Mrs Heywood – 'around 15–20 now play polo, we have some fantastic eventers and around twenty per cent now ride.' Team successes in several sports and notable individual stars include an international skier, national skating and lax players. 'We will always help if they need to go away to play their sport,' says the head, as if it were quite the most normal thing in the world. Occasional trips and tours to exotic places. New cookery room invites the rolling up of sleeves. Everyone learns in the first three years, no-one does in Years 10 and 11 (except as a leisure sport) but Leith's available in the sixth and very popular. Room also used imaginatively – we observed a biology class learning about micro-organisms in food. Yum! New theatre building (opened 2009 by Mother Winsome late of St Mary's Wantage and diplomatically named 'St Mary's') seats 300 and includes drama room, music rooms (including music technology) and attractive conference room, complete with founder's splendid polished table as centrepiece. Drama is adventurous and strong, considering the small forces available. Theatre balcony cleverly overlooks sports field, rather like the grand stand at Lord's! Textiles and photography are exceptional and art in general is varied, imaginative and surely outstanding, again, for so small a school. Masses to do at weekends, though, according to parents, 'This is when good friendships become great'.

Background and Atmosphere: Founded in 1899 by Eleanor Beatrice Wyatt, who began by starting small schools for girls in London but, on deciding that out of London would provide a healthier environment, acquired this eighteenth century house, built in the style of a restrained Italian villa for the Paravicini family. Off the main road out of Ascot – very discreet sign: you need to know. The white-painted, modest exterior belies the pleasures of the interior – most notably the splendid drawing room now given over to the lower sixth as its privileged common room. Elsewhere, the interior of the main house provides unremarkable but pleasant accommodation with some distinctive attributes – the classrooms are huge for these small numbers and most now boast areas with comfortable chairs and sofas as well as the usual desks and tables. The common rooms are exceptionally well-appointed – every year has one – though girls would always like more, of course! The upper sixth kitchen looks more like a real family kitchen than any school kitchen we can remember.

Beautiful and rather special chapel of which the girls are clearly proud and in which they spend ten minutes each morning. Dining room now less formal – no more top table, thank goodness. Food definitely good. The grounds are charming – lots of huge trees and plenty of space everywhere. Virginia creeper and other sensitive planting around its buildings old and new (newer ones are low and attractive) make these real gardens. In a unique and privileged location just outside Ascot (which has a station), six miles from Windsor and Eton (Windsor bus stops at school gate), ten from Heathrow, twenty from London, this school has a relaxed and country house feel and everything is on an inviting human scale.

'Merged with' – well, devoured St Mary's Wantage of affectionate memory in 2005. Lots of gain in terms of dosh from sale of Wantage plus a few migrants and some excellent staff, but also pain as many St Mary's devotees deeply saddened by their considerable loss. Mrs Heywood is keen to lessen the grief and issues invites to St Mary's OGs in hopes they may come to feel at home in their land of adoption, but much gnashing of teeth still audible to the west.

Heathfield now the only small boarding school for girls in the UK. Rightly proud of this unique status and all that it offers to the right family. Numbers inevitably fell over the last difficult decade but look healthier now and set to rise – though not too much. Boarding is good – everyone who wants to has a single room from Year 10 upwards and a choice of single, double or dorm for those below. In the fourth form, you get a trial week in the upper sixth bungalows – such fun and sense of independence engendered by this canny move that no-one now leaves after GCSEs: they can't wait to experience the freedom and fun the top year enjoys. They are allowed to cook their own breakfast and do their own washing – quelle joie!

Pastoral Care and Discipline: New four-house system – Austen, de Valois, Seacole, Somerville – felt by girls to have improved inter-year relationships in general. All but the upper sixth wear uniform – trad navy with blue tie; upper sixth wear their own clothes. Lower sixth swear this is their choice. Quaint system of 'bows and bearings' – badges for conduct and manners, kindness, deportment etc apparently much prized; girls wear these and other honours in long chains down the front of their jerseys. Very few disciplinary concerns. Focus always on the individual. 'The school could not have been more helpful when my daughter joined at an odd time,' a parent told us. 'Instead of punishing people,' said a sixth former, 'Mrs Heywood tries to help them.' 'The head of boarding has been here for ever,' said another. 'She knows every trick in the book. She can read your mind.' Excellent pastoral support within the full boarding system but no rigidity – 'If the dog or the horse has died, we're not so Dickensian that we won't let them out for pastoral reasons'. Girls enthuse – 'Our house mothers are so lovely!' Friendships lauded – 'we all get on – you have to in such a small community'; 'It's so nice knowing everyone'; 'You can't afford to be cliquey here'. 'The teachers are on the side of the girls and get the best out of them.' Proper support for boarding families includes transport help and luggage storage.

Pupils and Parents: Lots of daughters, nieces and granddaughters of Old Girls. But newcomers too – all drawn by the palpable sense of tradition and, now, a sense of a school firmly in the 21st century, in many ways, while weird, anachronistic things like writing real letters still encouraged. Not falling into elephant traps into which so many others have been lured –'We've been through a bit of a time and we could fill the school with overseas pupils, but we're not going down that road,' says wise Mrs Heywood. Fifty per cent from London, 20 per cent from Home Counties, 13 per cent from overseas – everywhere: no dominant nationality. Up-market clientele – this school has lost none of its cachet, though parents claim, 'It's not for snobby show-offs – the girls are lovely and natural: they have no "London edge"'. Lots of social stuff with Eton, Wellington, Radley and Harrow.

Entrance: Around two applicants for each of the 18 places. The usual tests but much emphasis put on report from current school. Better chance at 13. At 16, hitherto some have left for boys or wider options; however 2010 the first year for many in which no-one goes – therefore no places (but worth a phone call to check).

Exit: A lively list of destinations and courses includes mechanical engineering at Bristol and at UCL, Northumbria University for photography, event management at Solent, history at Exeter, chemistry at Sheffield and one to RADA. No stereotypes here.

Money Matters: Generous bursaries available to means-tested applicants; the Old Girls' Association also offers financial assistance to deserving cases. Academic scholarships awarded, though these dish out prestige rather than dosh.

Remarks: Unique now in offering traditional, full boarding for lucky girls in a close, happy, small community with all mod cons and opportunities. Sensible, sound and super.

Heathside School (Weybridge)

Brooklands Lane, Weybridge, Surrey, KT13 8UZ

• Pupils: 1280 pupils; girls and boys • Ages: 11-18 • Size of sixth form: 210
• Non-denom – but affiliated to the diocese of Guildford • State

Tel: 01932 846 162
Fax: 01932 828 142
Email: mail@heathside.surrey.sch.uk
Website: www.heathside.surrey.sch.uk

Principal: Since January 2009, Mrs Anne Cullum.

Academic matters: Has grown dramatically in size and stature since 1988 when it had only 487 pupils. It is now a well established foundation community technology college (in affiliation with the Diocese of Guildford) with modern foreign languages as its second specialism. Gets very good academic results and GCSE and A level results put them up with the top performing comprehensive schools nationwide. Although it is a specialist college, offers a broad and balanced academic curriculum. For the first three years, all students follow a general foundation course (including French and German or Spanish) with a fair amount of extra ICT work being included in all subject areas. Students work in mixed ability groups and are also setted for others. However, by Year 9, setting is more extensive. A wide choice of subjects on offer for GCSE including a number of vocational qualifications. The sixth form offers AS and A levels. Class sizes are larger than in many fee-paying schools but, at an average of 29, perfectly acceptable (drops to 8–15 in sixth).

Design and technology and IT are particular strengths; also wonderful art. Works closely within the community and has links with many outside agencies, both in education and business. It is part of the Elmbridge Consortium. A well-equipped learning resource centre is at the heart of all student-directed learning.

A separate sixth form centre, where most lessons and relaxation take place. The commonroom with kitchenette provides students with the autonomy they feel they need. No uniform requirements in the sixth form, only an understanding that dress be 'acceptable'. Careers area located in this centre is open all day for student use. Strong links also being formed with the traditional universities (particularly Oxbridge) to widen the options available to the students. A number of additional opportunities also exists for sixth formers, such as acting as senior councillors on school council, working with industry mentors (meet on a regular basis with a mentor from a local business) or directing and managing large drama productions, producing the annual year book and mentoring younger students.

Games, Options, the Arts: Many students come because of its strong sporting profile – sports hall, gym, tennis courts and hard play area. All encouraged to participate. A number of district, county and international players in several sports. Teams for netball, football, rugby, cricket, basketball and rounders are strong within the district.

Drama and music important with plenty of activities. Large concert band (70 players), jazz group, choir, and a number of ensembles. Students regularly perform in local venues and choir has appeared at the Albert Hall and Docklands Arena. Over three hundred students have individual music lessons. Annual school production and weekly drama club. Duke of Edinburgh, book, science and art clubs and many others.

Background and Atmosphere: Tucked away down a side street in Weybridge, Surrey, surrounded by trees and looking onto playing fields. A great deal of refurbishment has taken place in the last two years to improve the learning environment, foyer and canteens – healthy options: fresh fruit salad, salads, panini and stir fry vegetables as well as trad meals. No fizzy drinks sold on site. Recently awarded healthy school status.

Pastoral Care and Discipline: Good pastoral care system with an advanced mentoring scheme whereby all new pupils in Year 7 are linked with trained student mentors from the upper school, responsible for them throughout their first year. Tutors and student welfare/key stage co-ordinators form the additional rungs of support through close monitoring of students and constant feedback with parents. Ofsted in March 2008 stated, 'Relationships between adults and students are excellent. The staff know the students very well and care for them superbly.'

Strong culture of discipline within the school, which works very closely with parents and the community to ensure it is upheld. Zero tolerance of substance abuse. Close co-operation with Surrey police and involvement with Youth Against Crime scheme. School does not stop at the gates and it takes complaints from members of the public very seriously – every complaint is followed up. Firm anti-bullying guidelines.

Pupils and Parents: The students are reflective of the Weybridge, Walton, Hersham area and a good international mix. Most social classes and faiths are represented; up to 21 feeder schools – St James School, Cleves School, Sayes Court School and Ashley School the main contributors.

Entrance: The closing date for applications is in October the year before entrance. Siblings at the school and proximity of home to the school can affect admission. Will also consider applicants who live outside the catchment area who show exceptional musical, sporting, science or design and technology skill and are successful in the challenges in these skills.

Exit: Many students opt to remain for the sixth form and numbers have steadily increased – now 216. A few seek employment. Many traditional university choices. In 2008, the vast majority of students gained their university or college place of choice. In March 2008, the sixth form was graded as 'outstanding' in all areas.

Remarks: A thoroughly all-round school that will prepare your child well for the demands of the 21st century.

The Henrietta Barnett School

Central Square, Hampstead Garden Suburb, London, NW11 7BN

• Pupils: 690 girls; all day • Ages: 11-18 • Size of sixth form: 230
• Non-denom • State

Tel: 020 8458 8999
Fax: 020 8455 8900
Email: admissions@hbschool.org.uk
Website: www.hbschool.org.uk

Headteacher: Since 2006, Mr Oliver Blond (early forties). Educated at Calday Grange Grammar School in West Kirby, then at Essex University, where he read English, European literature and philosophy. PGCE at Homerton, Cambridge, followed by teaching posts at a variety of selective girls' schools. Former head of English and drama at Wimbledon High School, deputy head at North London Collegiate School. Laid back and friendly, he still teaches drama and philosophy. His primary objectives since coming to the school have been to stabilise it, improve the opportunities on offer to girls and to bring it up to date with the help of a large government grant. He seems to be managing these with the maximum efficiency and minimum fuss. Married to a teacher, with two young children, he has a keen interest in theatre, literature and the arts.

Academic matters: Consistently top or very near the top of the A level league tables, Henrietta Barnett seems to achieve that position without any of the obvious pressure found elsewhere. 'It's very uncompetitive,' said one parent. 'I's much more about collaboration and co-operation.' 92 per cent A and A* at GCSE, 98 per cent As and Bs at A level in 2010. Dedicated band of long-serving teachers teach clever and motivated girls. Most do nine or ten GCSEs, four or five AS, three or four A2s. Results strong across all subjects. A good range of languages. French and German for all in Year 7, Latin for all in Years 8 and 9. Plus Ancient Greek and the recently added Spanish. The head has updated the curriculum in a number of other ways, bringing in drama in the early years and enrichment courses at A level. The bias at A level is currently towards maths and the sciences, though French and English have a healthy representation. The head wants to improve the balance. Goodly amount of homework – 'But they're not driven hard. It's the engagement with other people that makes them think. They should be excited in the classroom.' Three-form entry. Class size 24–31 in early years – with no setting except in maths – falling to 10–13 in the sixth form.

Games, Options, the Arts: Possibly not the most sporty school and certainly somewhat hampered by its restricted grounds. Four tennis courts, two polished but petite gyms, a new fitness suite with a range of exercise equipment and a variety of pitches available on the nearby Hampstead Heath extension. Two double periods of games a week, with a wide variety of exercise alternatives, including golf, swimming, rock climbing, orienteering, fencing, box exercise, yoga, Pilates and dance.

Awarded music college status (with English as a subsidiary) in 2007. 'This is a very clear area of excellence and part of the majority of children's experience, which goes beyond subject teaching,' says the head. Already very active music department. Specialist music house for peripatetic lessons, with its own music library. 11 or 12 music groups meet each week, with teachers and pupils playing together. Music status has brought new performance space, a music technology suite, a band room and a rehearsal space for rock music.

The head, with his wide experience of the independent sector, is making a determined effort to broaden the extra-curricular offering, with more drama, inter-school debating with local independent schools – 'The girls can be a bit shy and it helps to build up their confidence' – plus an artist-in-residence working on site all year. 'You need to work at building up confidence, self-esteem and achievement beyond the academic,' says the head. 'They will all leave with good qualifications but we have to teach them how to make a success out of life.'

The library, with its stunning views, could benefit from more space, and the basement canteen is currently a bit dingy, but both are in line for a revamp.

School trips, through each subject department, take every year group out once a year. French and German exchanges. Lots of day trips. Founder's week, held in the summer, provides an entire week of outings. Own field study centre in Dorset, which every pupil visits for one week during their early years at the school.

Background and Atmosphere: Founded in 1911 by formidable social reformer Dame Henrietta Barnett, who wished to establish a school to educate bright girls regardless of their means. Housed in architecturally stunning Grade II* listed buildings by Sir Edwin Lutyens, the school sits, like a minor stately home, in a calm and soothing sea of green. The floors are polished parquet, the windows as high flying as the pupils, and the overall effect is of light and airy rooms straight out of an Angela Brazil novel. Nonetheless, parts of the building are fairly down at heel – the result of a long shared ownership with the local adult education institute. The head is gradually reclaiming the territory and buffing it up. 'The building is beautiful and the girls are very proud of it but it's not entirely fit for modern purpose.' A £7.5m government grant paid for the complete refurbishment of the science wing over the summer of 2009, and a new music and drama school and art and DT centre are due by the end of 2010. The school will be even more desirable.

Pastoral Care and Discipline: 'They're very well behaved and always do their best. Discipline is hardly needed here,' says the head. Polite and friendly girls are treated as adults from the word go, rules are explained and pupils tend to live up to the high expectations. Elected student council – which helps choose the head. Tutors in sixth form for groups of 10, seen individually to ensure problems, both academic and pastoral, are dealt with promptly. Junior and senior school have their own assembly halls for non-denominational assemblies, plus twice termly whole school assemblies.

Pupils and Parents: Girls bright, curious, well supported and very keen to learn. When the school was founded the intake was largely local but, since the arrival of league tables, the catchment has broadened considerably (now a parent-run bus service to cater for those who can't easily get here by the restricted public transport). Wide ethnic mix – about a fifth Indian and a fifth white, the rest from serendipitous backgrounds. Well below average number on free school meals. Girls work unusually well together. 'There really are no cliques here,' said one parent with a daughter in the sixth form, but after-school social life is not necessarily as vibrant as elsewhere.

Entrance: One of the most competitive entrance tests in the country with 1000+ girls applying for 93 places. First round is two separate tests in NFER verbal and non-verbal reasoning, which takes it down to 500. Then testing in English and maths – 'It's fairly straightforward, but we do try to challenge the most able'. Pupils come from 50–60 primaries. A further 40–45 places (with approximately 100 applicants) in the sixth form with six A grade GCSEs minimum requirement plus As in intended A level subjects. Girls coming up through the school must also meet this requirement.

Exit: One or two leave after GCSE to go on to larger (co-ed or independent) sixth forms. 23 this year to Oxbridge. Lots to medicine, economics and law at other leading universities. The head has introduced a specialist UCAS adviser to help girls through their university applications and help raise expectations of what can be achieved – 'We want to keep the blinkers off'.

Money Matters: The school has been awarded a grant of £7.5m towards a partial new build to provide a music and drama school, an art and design & technology school and refurbishment of the science block. An active PTA and a parental support scheme to which many parents regularly donate.

Remarks: One of the top academic state schools in the country, providing a gentle, inspiring education in a wonderful setting for very clever girls.

Hermitage Academy

Cardross Road, Helensburgh, Helensburgh, G84 7LA

• Pupils: 1,400; mixed • Ages: 12-18. • Non-denominational • State

Tel: 01436 672145
Fax: 01436 671338
Email: enquiries@hermitageacademy.argyll-bute.sch.uk
Website: www.hermitageacademy.argyll-bute.sch.uk

Head: Since 2007, Mr Geoff T Urie (forties), who was educated at Paisley Grammar and read geography at Glasgow University. He first came to the school as depute head before spending a couple of years at Ardrossan Academy – 'I had to come back to move to the new campus'. He runs this conglomerate with a depute and staff of over 100: no apparent difficulty with getting new teachers. He is proud and welcoming and was pleased to spend some time with this editor, who dropped in out of the blue.

Academic matters: Scottish system. All do Standard grade English and maths (for which they are setted) plus personal and social development, PE and RE. Three sciences throughout. Courses on offer vary between foundation, general and credit levels – huge choice from graphic communication, hairdressing, home economics, motor vehicle engineering (City and Guilds), woodworking, as well as uniformed and emergency services (popular), terrific fashion and textile, design, health and food, plus product design, baby sitting and accounting, and all the usual subjects. Maximum class size 30, but in reality much lower – with half below 20. French, German and Spanish offered to exam level, Spanish and Italian lunch time clubs as well. Exam results show a pleasing number getting good grades.

IT everywhere, whiteboards and overhead projectors. Student planner and fairly strict homework expectations, can email queries to staff, much use is made of GLOW and HABIT revision programmes. Help on hand for weaker students – two dedicated teacher plus the support team (this is an inclusive school, with some pupils getting a mega amount of help) led by 'a DHT pupils' support and eleven principal teachers, as well as ten principal teachers of guidance and a principal teacher of support for learning'. Learning support either short sharp bursts out of class ('the kick-up' room), or assistance during lesson time. IEPs where necessary and good links with 'Get It Right For Every Child', the local partnership agency which oversees what happens next.

Games, Options, the Arts: Splendid sports hall with electronic scoring, two proper gyms with ropes and strong gymnastic following; terrific dance studio, weights room – 'busy all the time'. No pool (uses local one, but currently under refurbishment), two football pitches plus Astroturf, tennis courts. A couple of football players spent some time training with AC Milan – which has to be a senior mega moment. Sports activities are, in the main, extra-curricular – massive amount nonetheless (funded through the Active Schools programme), with senior pupils helping official coaches and enthusiastic (and successful) involvement in football, swimming, athletics and golf. Three Peaks race, Young Enterprise (rather jolly tartan recently accepted and registered with the Scottish Tartan Authority, scarf currently on sale, but watch this space). Activity days and rash of clubs.

Big school, big bands: symphony, wind, brass, swing with samba on the cards. Choirs, and hefty trad Scottish in/output with fiddlers, Gaelic choir and pipe band. The best fabric ever, ditto fashion design. Drama – latest offering *Casualty Jane*. Amazing record of charitable activity. Has strong links with Comenius and different European schools – Germany, the Czech Republic, with loads of trips in every discipline.

Background and Atmosphere: Drop dead gorgeous modern building in stark black and white opened in 2008 – built to hold 1700 and not currently full. Overlooks the Clyde – all singing and dancing. Long wide passages, two huge spaces (architects of new school builds always seemed to economise here) with a splendid ground floor dining hall: holds a thousand and, when we visited just as lunch was finishing, it was quiet, orderly and remarkably tidy – the cleaners had perhaps one small waste paper basket full of detritus; stage at one end with ancillary green rooms and storage, professional lighting and rather posh red plush curtains. Pupils operate a swipe card system which disguises any free school meal stigma. Glorious assembly hall above (seats 1300, sound-proofed and used for exams as well), stunning views with amazing decorative mega pipes at roof level – probably nothing more mundane than the central heating system but it looks 22nd century stuff.

Terrific library with cunning circular window roof lights (head always coming in and turning lights off in the interests of economy, forgetting that those furthest from the windows are then studying in the dark). Library pupil led – everything state of the art, can't fault it. Vast car parking area, see-through bike sheds hold 80 bikes (but you can't smoke behind them). Head had rather hoped that the local fuzz would turn up to 'keep an eye' at admission time, and is not quite sure whether he is pleased or disappointed that they refused: not enough naughtiness apparently. Traditionalists are happy that the old HS (Hermitage School) shield has made the transition, as has the wheel of the Lucy Ashton, which for so many years greeted pupils at the previous academy.

Pastoral Care and Discipline: Managed by group of depute head teacher and heads of every year, plus dedicated guidance teachers. Strong PSE; pro-active anti-bullying strategy in place with all newbies being given an anti-bullying card, 'It's OK to talk'. Sixth year pupils active in Friends Against Bullying – their photographs are displayed on notice boards, and oodles of anti-bullying programmes in place. The odd exclusion. School uniform for all – prefects wear red ties.

Pupils and Parents: Everything from farmers to local business folk, to Service personnel based at nearby Faslane – inclusive in every possible way. Strong parent-teacher body.

Entrance: Some placement requests, otherwise school has ten linked primaries from as far as Arrochar, Cardross and Kilgreggan; also has 'close links' with Parklands School in Helensburgh, which is Catholic – pupils might well be expected to attend an RC secondary RC, but 'find it more convenient' to come here. Operates a 'hooked on Hermitage' programme – masses of to-ing and fro-ing by learning support and subject teachers; all P6/7 pupils spend two days at Hermitage in June to meet their guidance teacher and S6 buddy, plus two pupil/parent evenings throughout the year. Serious input into changeover – works well.

Exit: Impressive careers advice which extends beyond a pupil's time at school. Currently 172 pupils in sixth year – about 85/90 per cent stay on after standard grades, of whom a further 90 per cent stay on thereafter. Latest statistics show that some 60 per cent either went into further or higher education.

Money Matters: Funding available for essential (or non essential, come to that) trips for those who couldn't otherwise afford it.

Remarks: Impressive new build, inclusive school – appears to work exceeding well.

The Hertfordshire & Essex High School and Science College

Warwick Road, Bishop's Stortford, Hertfordshire, CM23 5NJ

• Pupils: 1,035, mostly girls; boys in the sixth form • Ages: 11-18
• Size of sixth form: 242 • Non-denom • State

Tel: 01279 654 127
Fax: 01279 508 810
Email: admin@hertsandessex.herts.sch.uk
Website: www.hertsandessex.herts.sch.uk

Headteacher: Since September 2009, Mrs Cathy Tooze, previously head of Hadleigh High School in Suffolk. Positive and authoritative, her manner is relaxed, though you feel she can be firm when the situation demands. Her husband works in telecoms and they have two teenage sons and a young daughter, which helps her to see things 'from the parental perspective,' she says. She spends her leisure time with the family, who particularly enjoy watersports and skiing holidays together.

Academic matters: A very successful school, a particular feat given the fact that it is totally non-selective. Eleven GCSEs the norm and 95 per cent score A*–Cs. 'Quality rather than quantity,' says the head, who puts the exceptional grades down to 'exceptional standards of teaching and learning' and the very positive work ethic. But, she adds, 'This is a caring school, not an exam factory.'

The traditional curriculum certainly works well for the students, many of whom are of an academic bent, but modern aspects too and new technology is embraced where appropriate. Teaching is very hands-on. Pupils are set targets with progress tracked three times a year and each has a mentor to get them back on course if they should stray. 'This is how we notch up the outcomes,' reveals the head. 'We can raise expectations just that little bit higher every time.'

Generously staffed, and good admin support allows teachers to spend more time in the classroom and less on pen-pushing. All teach their degree subject, which, the head says, means they are focused, committed and keen to broaden the students' experiences through a huge variety of trips and extra-curricular activities. As a science specialist college, it's maybe no surprise that science success is high – many take triple science, which stands them in good stead for A levels. Languages are growing in popularity. French is setted from Year 7 and compulsory until Year 9, and Mandarin has recently been introduced. Working closely with the local Polish community to enrich the curriculum further. Media studies and sociology are attracting students' attention and, for many, the technologies are a good contrast to the more academic classes. Top sets can number as many as 28, but the lower classes are often much smaller.

Very wide choice of subjects at A level, particularly as part of the local consortium, which pools its resources to host minority interest subjects. Herts & Essex offers dance, further maths and German. Although undoubtedly a timetabling nightmare, this scheme allows for great breadth. Psychology is another popular A level option. Sixth formers have a half-day of enrichment on Wednesday, which includes D of E, pilates, extra languages and sport, and also listen to struggling readers in Year 7.

Assesses the needs of all students on entry and monitors their progress closely throughout their time. A whole school approach to learning support – able, gifted and talented students are identified, in addition to those who will benefit from individual learning plans, plus differentiated learning materials to provide educational challenge for all students. Where a student has a particular need (for example, a visual impairment) learning materials are adapted and staff training put in place, so that all teachers are fully aware of the adaptations they can make to their planning and preparation to ensure access to the curriculum. Four teaching assistants timetabled to offer both in-class support and some small group literacy sessions. Ground floor access is good throughout the site. Where some of the school buildings are inaccessible to wheelchairs above ground level, rooming considerations are taken into account when timetabling.

Games, Options, the Arts: Sporting facilities are good and the students take full advantage of them. Netball is a strength – girls recently represented the east of England, coming third in the under-16 national championships. Tag rugby, pilates, yoga and judo are popular and indoor rowing is an unusual forte. Sixth formers continue with their interest in sport and the boys compete well on the football and rugby fields. Hard courts for tennis, netball and basketball, four rounders pitches plus a football pitch onsite, as well as a 25m indoor pool and dance studio. Has its own large playing fields with hockey pitches and a grass running track five minutes' walk away.

Art taken seriously – makes use of the Rhodes Centre in the town for exhibitions, raising the school's local profile. Work displayed in public places throughout the school too. Large numbers attend art clubs and workshops. Good use made of proximity to London and Cambridge, with their wealth of art galleries – visits by students independently, or with their families, also encouraged. Students are inspired to produce work that is original, personal and skilful; A level options in art, art and design and fine art printmaking.

A separate music school across the road is a hive of activity. One of four local schools to give entry to eight pupils who show exceptional musical aptitude at age 11 – 'It's about an innate aptitude for music, not experience,' says the head. Plenty of other students with musical ability entering through usual channels, though – ten per cent learn an instrument. The head describes the concerts as 'breathtaking', several choirs, an orchestra (the only one in a state school in the town) and ensembles for regular playing practice.

An International school – a genuine focus on global citizenship. Close links with a school in Uganda – teacher exchanges and an annual trip for Year 13s. New similar arrangement with a school in India, thanks to student fundraising. Leadership partnership status, which involves staff, students and the community in sharing good practice. Benefits include staff mentoring, coaching programmes and many student leadership opportunities.

Background and Atmosphere: Dating back to 1909, the original buildings, in a leafy residential road just a mile or so from the town centre, have the feel of a grammar, though in fact The Bishop's Stortford Secondary School for Girls was opened to prepare girls for a career in teaching for a fee of £3 a term. In 1944 fees were waived and the school was granted self-governing status by King George V, who presented a portrait of himself that hangs in the impressively panelled school hall to this day. New teaching blocks have been added in the intervening years and a house over the road was acquired to make a very suitable music school.

Sixth form study rooms, English classrooms and an exhibition space added recently, but no more expansion on this site, as planning permission is being sought for brand new buildings, in conjunction with the boys' Bishop's Stortford High School, on green belt land in the town. Local residents unkeen. With a burgeoning local population, a need for a new location, points out the head, and the planned huge swimming pool and eight-court sports hall will also be available for community use. The intention is for the girls' and boys' schools to remain discrete entities in separate buildings, and although a whisper of sixth forms being merged, this is yet to be decided. But crossovers and joint provision to the benefit of all concerned, says the head.

Pupils are often canvassed on their opinions – recently asked if they wanted to change their distinctive uniform of brown kilt and beige jumper: the response was a big 'no', although the hemline was raised slightly. Sixth formers are expected to turn up in suitable business dress.

Pastoral Care and Discipline: Pupils known individually and closely mentored. Leadership is strong, with a head boy and girl as well as a swathe of prefects and a school council. Sixth formers are trained as peer mentors who support pupils lower down the school by acting as 'buddies'. A form per year for each of the five houses – a tradition – with competitions in sport and music, but no need for rewards for good behaviour, says the head – 'It's just expected'. She reports no real discipline problems, although an immediate one-day exclusion rule for use of bad language. A recent annual pupil survey showed they felt safe and were confident any bullying would be properly dealt with.

Pupils and Parents: Parents realise that their children are spoilt for choice in Bishop's Stortford, with several very good state secondaries right on their doorstep. Herts and Essex is often picked ahead of the local fee-paying institutions, with the traditional approach to education and the largely single-sex environment a vote-winner. 'Students here want to learn,' says the head, and girls and sixth form boys strike one immediately as being focused and sensible, with a very savvy attitude to their studying and related future prospects. Very supportive friends' association, a pro-active governing body and a parental forum, which has real input into changes of direction and provides feedback. Parents are kept in touch with newsletters four times a term, and any requests to see the head are usually granted the next day.

Entrance: Except for musical and sporting stars, non-selective – regularly three times as many applicants as Year 7 places. Medical and social grounds for entry are prioritised, then looked-after children, then siblings. Ten per cent of places are reserved for students with an aptitude for music and sport and their development is monitored throughout their school career.

Not many pupils leave, so very few spots open up in other year groups. New sixth formers occasionally bring a younger sibling with them. Any gaps that do materialise are filled from the 'continuing interest' list , in accordance with the admissions arrangements, with those with siblings already in the school jumping to the top.

Sixth form entry is by four pathways, depending on the number and quality of GCSEs amassed. Pathway one requires seven As or A*s for those who are on course for an Oxbridge or Russell Group exit. These usually number about 50 students, who sit five ASs and are mentored for the top universities. Pathway two is for the 60 students who have Bs and above – they have the choice of most of the A level subjects on offer. Pathway three, where Herts & Essex's own students are prioritised above external applicants, requires Cs and above at GCSE – they're offered about a dozen, less academic A level options, including health and social care, applied science and sociology. Pathway four is the diploma course, offered at local consortium schools. 'It's about setting children up to be successful,' says the head.

Applications from boys for Year 12 are on the up, but the head is keen to cap the number admitted at a third of the sixth form population. The offer of philosophy and ethics, Latin, media studies and film studies combined and the science specialism draws them in, and many transfer from the local Anglo-European school, which only offers IB.

Exit: Up to 40 per cent leave after GCSE. 'There's always a number of students for whom we don't have a provision at sixth form, but there are great courses elsewhere that suit better,' says the head. 'The focus is on getting to the university of choice and that isn't going to be accessible to everybody.' Straight A* students at GCSE are expected to go all the way to the top universities and all-round skills prepare some for Oxbridge entry – a handful every year, more than other schools in the town. Durham, Bristol and the US are favoured otherwise.

Remarks: A positive learning environment for hard-working girls and sixth form of both sexes, striking a balance between traditional values and a modern approach to individual attainment.

High School of Dundee

Linked to High School Of Dundee Junior School in the Junior section

Euclid Crescent, Dundee, Dundee, DD1 1HU

• Pupils: 680 (50/50 boys/girls) • Ages: 11-18 • Size of sixth form: 200
• Non-denom • Fees: £6,930-£9,840 pa • Independent

Tel: 01382 202 921
Fax: 01382 229 822
Email: admissions@highschoolofdundee.org.uk
Website: www.highschoolofdundee.org.uk

Rector: Since 2008, Dr John Halliday (early fifties) previously head of Albyn School (qv). Educated Abingdon School, followed by BA in Germany, linguistics at Exeter and PhD at Cambridge on German and Austrian satire in WW1. Married with three children, two now at university and one at school in Edinburgh, he misses the buzz of teaching but compensates in other ways. In a large school this takes positive effort – interviewing achievers in any field, helping with sport, playing in the orchestra (as an accomplished viola player) and attending all school occasions. After a baptism of fire at Rannoch, (now defunct) which he, none the less, remembers as 'inspirational', he initiated coeducation at Albyn School in Aberdeen with a resulting huge increase in numbers. Easy on the eye and quietly confident about his role in Dundee, despite plunging in with an almost completely new senior team (he had a hand in the appointments) and facing a triple anniversary for the school. 'Like Dundee,' he says, 'the school is modest about its achievements, which are considerable.' The same is true of Dr Halliday. His first task has been to build a strong close management team, which includes his much valued bursar, and to improve internal communications through more regular meetings. Keen to develop an 'integrated curriculum' making the 'co-curriculum' more co-ordinated and giving a range of opportunities to take account of multiple types of intelligence, and to build teamwork, leadership and self reliance. 'Not just ticking boxes but trying to systemise' it all while maintaining Dundee's high academic tradition. This should improve prospects, especially for middle ability students. A new performing arts centre is a high priority for him and space is available, though plans not yet formulated.

Academic matters: A Scottish school through and through, with high expectations, using Standard Grades and Intermediate 1 and 11 followed by Highers and Advanced Highers. A solid range of subjects with French from year P6. Results pretty good generally, and spectacular in modern langs, chemistry, history. Most teaching in mixed form groups but English, maths and languages are set. English dept was delighted to have two finalists in the Pushkin Prize for short stories. The take up in French, Spanish and German has improved and outstanding in history, which, understandably, gets its fair whack of the S1/2 curriculum, not being reduced to a share of rota system as in many schools. English and maths Higher taken by the most with good grades. Not much take up for Latin and minimal for Greek (on offer, plus Russian in S6) but a good range of marginal subjects – sociology, technical studies, PE, managing environmental resources etc – together with some academic toughies – philosophy, economics – and respectable numbers taking all sorts of maths specialisms: stats, mechanics etc. Class sizes from three or four to mid-twenties. Masses of techno equipment – PCs, internet link via Abertay University etc and trolleyed laptops for class use in the Junior School. S6 can do enhancement courses at Dundee University.

Learning skills centre with three dedicated staff provides support and specialist teaching in junior and senior schools for 'mild to moderate specific learning difficulties' (dyspraxia, dyslexia, ADHD, mild Asperger's). Early intervention encouraged. Support also for the super bright. Few need ESOL which tends to be given in class at primary and rarely needed at secondary. Much used library with areas for different ages and activities and full time librarians on hand and arranging multifarious library talks and activities.

Very good exam results 2010 – 91% of Standard Grade at Credit; for the second successive year three quarters of all exams at the top grade, 40 pupils with eight straight As and 64% at least seven top grades. Higher pass rate of 92% – 50% A grade and a fifth with five straight As. Very high standard for Advanced Highers – 48% at A grade and 74% A or B.

Games, Options, the Arts: Pupils mostly bused to games in the multi million Mayfield sports centre, though swimming is in the Dundee University pool. Strong rugby, girls' hockey, netball and athletics, tennis, cricket etc etc. D of E has really flourished with 16 achieving Gold. CCF, a pipe-band – with girls as well as boys – riding and skiing teams (the latter swept the board at the 2010 schools championships) are the tip of an iceberg of physical activities from line skating to golf.

Art department, chilly with a garret view of intriguing Dundee roof-scape, serves curriculum and co-curriculum using, for instance, the skill of the textile classes to teach the scarf making club, while the jewellery class – with boys as well as girls – gets help from the enthusiastic chemistry department in decorative fusing of metals. Music very strong with concerts in the town and a musical production biennially – *Dido and Aeneas* as a bit of a contrast to *Tin Pan Alley*! Numerous orchestras, groups and choirs.

Drama strong with productions at all levels. Art, music and drama all available as exam subjects up to Advanced Higher with some very good results, so we wait with baited breath for what they can do if the new creative arts centre materialises. Formidable debating in true Scottish school tradition helped by the fact that the debating coach also manages the Scottish schools debating team.

Background and Atmosphere: This is school in the grand tradition of Scottish education, founded in 1239, making it over 770, and eventually receiving its charter from Queen Victoria in 1859. Princess Anne followed her great grandmother's example by visiting to mark the double celebrations 175 years on. The High School is a City 'treasure' and has a governing body drawn partly from the City's great and good, the 'Guildry' and 'Nine Trades', partly elected from among parents, past pupils etc and some co-opted for their skills.

The neo-classic, portico-ed façade, beloved of Scottish school architects (a little grubby) sports the celebratory banners designed by a sixth year pupil. Completely surrounded by some of Dundee's better buildings (including the newly opened McManus Gallery much used by the art department) it faces a huge half-moon of tarmac, elegantly railed, and fiercely patrolled by janitors to provide a safe recreation area during school-time but open to parents who would have no hope of parking in Dundee at the end of the school day.

The impressive Doric front is flanked on one side by the 1880s Margaret Harris Building, once the girls' school, which now houses the juniors, and the on the other the (ex) Trinity Church, which provides a hall, not big enough for the whole school, the ground floor library and attic drama space.

Departments are cunningly grouped in a collection of buildings, some quite grand, gradually accumulated along Bell Street and curiously interspersed with courtyards, one of which sports tall, thin climbing wall. Roomy and light teaching rooms, plenty of space, though not much greenery. Pupils mill about, open, friendly, and happy to talk about their work. Some corners/staircases a bit dark and 'schooly' but most bright and clean, though neither corridors nor pupils are unnaturally tidy! Boys wear navy blue, while girls wear 'softer' grey blazers with a grey Dundee High tartan skirt. The tartan looks best as pinnies for the tinies. Blazers up to £90 in larger sizes but there is a parents' thrift shop.

Pastoral Care and Discipline: Four vertical houses, with continuity from juniors to seniors, run by guidance staff, have two forms each in each year group, the guidance teacher being the first point of contact for pupils and parents. Despite freedom to go into town at lunch breaks, the rector reports far more phone calls from citizens complimenting the helpfulness of pupils than complaints. No spectacular problems but guidelines are clear – suspension for first offence for smoking and the like, while a pupil with drugs can expect to be expelled.

Pupils and Parents: Fifty per cent from Dundee, 50 per cent from Fife, Angus and Perthshire, up as far as Forfar and Blairgowrie etc, with 5 different bus routes. A mix of farmers, professionals and people working for universities and hospitals. Pupils can bring own cars but not drive others. Former pupils include William Wallace, AL Kennedy. Lord Cullen and Lord Ross, and more recently Andy Nichol, Mark Beaumont, Frank Hadden and KT Tunstall. BBC's Andrew Marr had a short spell in the juniors.

Entrance: By assessment at all stages, with two thirds coming into seniors from juniors. Demand and waiting list not much hit by recession, though bursary applications are up.

Exit: Few leave post S4 and S5. Almost all to university, generally Scottish with a smattering of Oxbridge and other English ones.

Money Matters: The very first school inspected and passed by OSCR (Scottish charity regulator), the school gives about £700,000 in bursaries every year (approximately 13/14 per cent of its annual turnover). Bursaries, all means-tested, are normally awarded to form 1 but applications from current parents in financial trouble will be considered. Stringent means-testing for all. Number of independent trusts which also give financial support to individuals in the school. No specialist scholarships for academic, art, music sport etc.

Remarks: Still a warhorse of a school, doing an impressive job for Dundee and its surroundings. The fine tradition of Scottish education is alive, well and living (independently and at a price) in Dundee. New developments eagerly awaited.

The High School of Glasgow

Linked to High School Of Glasgow Junior School in the Junior section

637 Crow Road, Glasgow, Glasgow, G13 1PL

- Pupils: 685 boys and girls in the senior school; all day • Ages: 10-18
- Size of sixth form: 195 • Non-denom • Fees: £3,141-£9,696 pa
- Independent

Tel: 01419 549 628
Fax: 01414 355 708
Email: rector@hsog.co.uk
Website: www.glasgowhigh.com

Rector: Since 2004, Mr Colin D R Mair MA Cert Ed (fifties), who was previously depute rector here. Originally a classicist, educated at Kelvinside Academy, St Andrews, honours arts from Glasgow and Cert Ed at Jordanhill, thence to The High School in 1976. He became deputy rector in 1996, having previously been head of classics and housemaster. Charming, affable and well-versed in the ways of the school, he reluctantly relinquished his teaching rôle (classics) when he became rector but 'would be keen to cover whenever the chance arises'. He would also be keen 'to help out on either the cricket ground or rugby pitch' and hopes that being rector won't 'make him too remote' from the school itself' (not a chance, says this editor, who has met him on earlier visits to the school).

Academic matters: Scottish system exclusively. A thunderingly good school on all fronts. 80 per cent 1/A, 96 per cent Credit /A–C for 811 exams at Standard Grade/Intermediate 2; 60 per cent A, 83 per cent A/B for 522 exams at Higher; and 42 per cent A, 70 per cent A/B for 158 exams at Advanced Higher level in 2010. Previous years' exams have shown strong results across the board, with perhaps less take-up in home economics. A pleasing 30 out of 30 got grade A in Intermediate art. English, history and modern studies, modern languages and music particularly strong, but impressive results across the board in all disciplines. Classical studies on offer as well as Latin (good results).

Latin for all first two years, French and German throughout, Spanish offered at third year and as a crash course in the sixth year. Business management popular. Serious and successful representations as ever in last year's Olympiads and 58 awards in the intermediate maths challenge, including 17 gold, and 38 with 15 gold in the junior challenge. Fewer girls than boys doing Higher physics, though still a few. Greenhouse attached to new biology lab on first floor; school offers human biology as well as the 'normal' option, and pupils can take this as a crash subject in their final year at school – useful for those entering the medical profession (Glasgow University is popular for medics). One of the best sixth form handbooks we have ever come across, complete with university entrance requirements and advice – other schools would do well to copy.

Huge variety of subjects and options, home economics and sewing for all – fluffy toys and embroidered lined denim bags being sewn in the lunch hour. Max class size 26, with 20 for practical subjects. Excellent and organised learning support throughout, with masses of liaison from junior school, and good follow-on in all disciplines. Dyslexic pupils from junior school teamed up with senior pupils for the first three years, to encourage and help them with any organisational difficulties and with homework etc. Impressive library, computers everywhere; dedicated for the fifth and sixth form only, during their study time, but all pupils can and do use them during their lunch break. New IT suite opened 2003, science extension opened 2008.

Games, Options, the Arts: School surrounded by 23 acres of games fields and car parks; masses of district, county, country players (Alison Sheppard FP, Olympic swimmer), lots of representatives on West of Scotland teams in almost every discipline. Huge range of activities, including sailing, skiing (trips to Canada popular) as well as D of E. Cultural trip to China in 2009 and visit to Cuba in 2010. Visits to elderly and strong links with local group of autistic children. Lots of charity projects, often house-based. Masses of popular clubs, lunchtime and post school.

Impressive debating skills – silver mementos of previous glory all over the shop: 'The Observer' Mace, the Cambridge Union, the Oxford Union and ESU. Finalists in 2006 and 2010 ESU debating competitions and 2007 Law Society of Scotland Donald Dewar Debating Competition.

Massive and exciting drama and music, trip to Prague 2005. The former in super new purpose-built studio – always interesting to have the theatre on the first floor – but much use too of sponsoring – the Fraser of Allander lecture room, Wolfson Foundation in Science and suchlike. Regular spectacular productions. 'Really exciting music department', which has won chamber music awards in recent years. Smart new music practice rooms with mirrored walls. Choirs and orchestras abound, trips abroad, travelling for competitions and the like. Fauré 'Requiem' in Paisley Abbey and orchestral/choral concerts in Glasgow University Chapel highly acclaimed. Sparky art department with a gallery, but not much take up at higher levels – work is a serious matter in the west. Rector challenges this, saying 'an encouraging take up at Higher levels with pupils regularly going on to art colleges'.

Background and Atmosphere: Founded as The Choir School of Glasgow Cathedral in 1124, gained grammar school status during the 15th century and became a high school in 1834. Despite (because of?) its high academic standing, was closed by Glasgow Corporation in 1976. An appeal launched by the High School Former Pupils' Club funded the new purpose-built senior school on the sports ground at Anniesland Cross, already owned by the FPs, and the new school opened the day after the old school closed – a triumph. The High School merged with the former PNEU dame school, Drewsteignton, in Bearsden, three miles away, now the junior school. New history, *The Town School*, just published.

The flat roofed building at Anniesland has expanded considerably; with new additions sprouting all over the place (usually on the roof), though fortunately without any obvious loss of playing fields. Square split level assembly hall, artificial floodlit pitch, new stand complex. Sixth form area houses coffee shop and loud music as well as dedicated computers and work areas. School uniform for all, with girls in tartan skirts. The old house system remains, with each house having its own particular area in the school.

Pastoral Care and Discipline: Highly defined house system with colours but not names carrying on from junior school, siblings follow siblings into the same house. PSHE largely house-based with house staff playing a major rôle in extra-curricular and social activities. 'Transitus' (11/12 year olds) pupils are lovingly tended with lots of back-up from junior school, particularly with learning support.

The Rector has enormous parental support and says that he 'is not complacent, but no problems'; no recent drugs cases, though a couple have been asked to leave in the past for going OTT, but certainly would expel if drugs were brought into the school. Suspensions for 'major offences'. Otherwise punishments range through sanctions, lunchtime detentions, clearing up litter (black bags) – how about scraping the gum off the tarmac? – to school detention after school on Fridays.

Excellent blue booklet on promoting positive relationships – good PSE step guide, practised from the junior school.

Pupils and Parents: Ambitious, strong work ethos, almost half come from the affluent Bearsden/Milngavie complex and the remainder from different parts of Glasgow and outlying towns and villages. Bus system, some pupils from Ayrshire, the Trossachs (aka the edges of Argyll). Popular amongst the middle classes. Pupils can and do drive to school, large pupil car park. The geographic jump from the centre of Glasgow to the West End has changed the bias of the school, which now has fewer Asian and Jewish pupils (no synagogue in the West End), though a significant number from the South Side. Still large element of first time buyers plus one or two recently arrived Europeans – Russians and the like. Previous pupils include Bonar Law, Sir John Moore of Corunna, Campbell Bannerman, Lord Macfarlane of Bearsden, Sir Teddy Taylor, Lady Cosgrove and Lesley Riddoch.

Entrance: At 10 and 11. Automatic from junior school (qv), otherwise three times over-subscribed – 50–60 applicants for approximately 32 places at Transitus and 30–40 for first year. Odd vacancies in most years, own entrance exam, small number after Standard Grades, 'not many, really'. Fifth year candidates should have grade 1 passes in virtually all their Standard grade exams, or As at GCSE if they have come from England. Sixth year entrance based on exam results and school reports.

Exit: 98 per cent to degree courses all over, with a fairly high percentage to Scottish universities, a regular few to Oxbridge and about 15 per cent going elsewhere. About 10 taking a gap year this year (out of 94), but numbers rising. Work experience popular and all sixth year encouraged to undertake community service.

No particular bias in career – medics, engineers, accountants, IT course, lawyers, possibly less enthusiasm for the humanities.

Money Matters: School sympathetic to genuine problems, no academic scholarships but 40–50 bursaries awarded on a financial need basis (and Rector is pleased when he can help pupils of a suitably high calibre in financial need). On-going bursary fund.

Remarks: School on a roll, going from strength to strength. A remarkable success story – and, as we said before, a high school truly worthy of its name.

Highgate School

Linked to Highgate Junior School in the Junior section
Linked to Highgate Pre-Preparatory School in the Junior section

North Road, London, N6 4AY

• Pupils: 950 pupils in the senior school; boys and girls in Years 7, 8, 9, 10, 12 and 13. • Ages: 11-18 • Size of sixth form: 270 • C of E • Fees: £15,120 pa • Independent

Tel: 020 8347 3564
Fax: 020 8340 7674
Email: hmoffice@highgateschool.org.uk
Website: www.highgateschool.org.uk

Head Master: Since 2006, Mr Adam Pettitt MA (forties). Educated in state schools in East Sussex and read French and German at Oxford; taught at Eton, Oundle and Abingdon and was second master at Norwich School. Married – his wife is a French teacher, though at present caring for their youngest child. The two older ones are at Highgate pre-prep. Very confident, good public speaker, say parents, excellent manager, a stickler for good manners and appearance – as we toured the school he frequently ordered a tucking in of shirts and doing up of buttons. A marathon runner, he helps with the cross-country club and leaps up numerous flights of stairs with aplomb. Teaches linguistics to Year 9, 'which keeps my hand in', and 'lunches my way' through Years 11 and 12. 'I feel terribly proprietorial,' he told the school magazine. 'This is my school, these are my pupils; I care about them.' He added, 'I think the most important thing you can learn at school is to serve others, rather than be self-serving.'

Academic matters: Historically, this was a school slightly outside the frenzy of the most highly academic north London selective schools. However, with its decision to turn co-ed came an upping of the academic ante and its entrances are now ferociously competitive from the age of three upwards, with little quarter given at transfers between the three sections. Academic levels are rising consistently. 'I hope that the results are getting better because we're putting scholarship at the heart of what we do and because I and my predecessor have recruited some excellent and exciting teachers,' says the head.

Around 75–80 per cent of GCSE grades tend to be A* or A with sciences and languages particularly successful. These include Russian and Spanish and Mandarin from since 2009. Also offers Latin, Greek and classical civilisation. Sciences taught as three separate subjects.

Around 90 per cent A/B at A level. Maths and economics very popular, followed by sciences and English. Very much an academic curriculum, though the head has introduced RS, philosophy and theatre studies (but not drama GCSE). 'We unapologetically stick to the canon of academic subjects. But we don't want exams to determine what we teach. I've asked staff to look at what students will need to know to study any particular subject at a good university, and teach from that.'

Has replaced sixth form general studies with a programme of academic forums (compulsory for scholars and encouraged for everyone else) which function on a seminar basis and are designed to make connections between subjects and stretch students' knowledge beyond the curriculum.

Parents praise good teaching in the core subjects but comment that some is unimaginative. The ISI commended teaching as 'effective and in some lessons outstanding'. With thirty-one new members of staff appointed last year, many are yet to make their mark.

Setting from Year 7 for maths and French, and from Year 9 for science. 'We try to do it so they're not too aware of it. But it is not set in stone. We're ludicrously flexible.'

A full-time educational psychologist runs the SEN department, helping with organisational skills as well as difficulties such as dyslexia. 'We know we can cope with a degree of dyslexia as long as, for example, their maths is strong. We like to talk to them before they sit the entrance test to find out what reasonable adjustments have been made by their previous school and work out if we can do it too. But some are so well adjusted that I only find out about their special needs when I read their referee's statement on their UCAS form.' One or two pupils with long term illnesses. 'We look at how we can make life easier in terms of start times and what we can take out of the educational package without the whole thing collapsing.'

Has links with St Michael's Primary School over the road, which provides a safe passage through to the sports fields and art department. Maths staff teach enrichment classes there before school and joint science sessions. Has lots of links with other schools through its programme of summer schools in Haringey and Camden to help gifted and talented pupils.

Games, Options, the Arts: Wonderful new art and DT building, the Mills Centre, was opened in 2005. It is a refurbishment of the School House, built in 1880, which used to be a boarding house and housemaster's residence. Its basement, extended underground with turf roofs and Japanese-style basement gardens, has DT workshops and electronics room. DT here tends towards the engineering side. Upstairs are art, graphics, photography and pottery studios, with kiln, darkroom and history of art library. Art GCSE results, in particular, have not been outstanding, given the sumptuous surroundings, but pupils comment that the new head of art is 'absolutely brilliant', and great improvements are expected.

Strong music includes orchestra, choirs, chamber ensembles, jazz and swing bands. Joint orchestral and choral concerts with nearby Channing Girls' School. 'They have really encouraged my son's talent for singing,' said a parent. The music here is of an unashamedly classical bent but it seems that most north London teenagers nowadays have formed rock bands and several OCs (Old Chomeleians) are now members of groups such as Razorlight.

Glorious 20 acres of playing fields, all the better for being so close to central London. Facilities also include the Mallinson Centre with sports hall, swimming pool, weights room, squash courts and Eton fives courts, and the new Caen Wood Hall for dance and fencing. Alongside the more usual sports (fields D football teams and 4th XIs, so plenty of scope to play for the school as well as one's house), offers golf, sailing, fencing and water polo. Pupils compete nationally at clay pigeon shooting, handball, polo and fencing.

Despite the lack of curricular drama, plenty of opportunities for getting involved in plays of all kinds ranging from *Les Misérables* to *Blood Wedding* to new plays written by staff and students.

Oodles of clubs, e.g. bee-keeping, puzzle, reptile and vinyl. Trips to theatres, galleries and museums; also Sahara Desert, Isle of Purbeck, Maastricht, Essen etc. The school has an outdoor centre in Wales. Visiting speakers have included politicians, adventurers, surgeons and stage directors; a philosopher-in-residence gives talks on aesthetics.

Background and Atmosphere: Founded as the Free Grammar School of Sir Roger Chomeley, Knight at Highgate, in 1565. By the 1870s it was no longer free and changed its name to Sir Roger Chomeley's School at Highgate, becoming Highgate School in the late 19th century. The chapel and main buildings date from the mid-19th century, a period of great expansion. By 1965, the school occupied a large site in Highgate Village, with extensive sports fields and several boarding houses (now refurbished for other use) nearby. Owning so much valuable land and property has enabled the school to spend large sums on its facilities, as well as to offer staff accommodation in a very expensive part of London.

This is a Christian foundation but an inclusive one, with Muslim and Jewish assemblies and speakers from different religions on a weekly basis.

The whole school is in the process of becoming co-educational. Girls joined the sixth form in 2004 and Year 7 in 2006. Years 7 and 8, once the top two forms of the junior school, have now moved to the senior school. Girls still much in the minority – 'A girl needs to be able to hang in there with the boys,' said a parent. 'But they have tried very hard to integrate the girls. They're willing to make it work – and that's a good spirit.'

While Years 7 and 8 have class teachers, Year 9 pupils upwards are based in houses, with their housemaster acting as tutor. The houses are allocated geographically, to encourage local friendships, and housemasters visit pupils at home before they join the school.

Pastoral Care and Discipline: This is not a laid-back school – strict rules on uniform and discipline. 'I'm insistent on good behaviour, good manners and punctuality.' But it is generally acknowledged to be a kind one, particularly to those with no huge rebellious streak. 'My son is not easy,' said a parent, 'but they've been very good with him.' Huge praise (from all faiths) for the full-time padre – 'He's very much there for pastoral care and they adore him. His door is always open.'

Few expulsions – 'Behaviour and academia are often closely linked, so we will try to sort that out. But once they are running up against the buffers we may have to agree a departure with child and family'.

Pupils and Parents: Mostly wealthy families from the surrounding area, which gives the school a nicely local feel. Parents of girls in particular often come from mixed nationality backgrounds. 'It's our pioneering spirit,' said one. OCs include: Rt Hon Charles Clarke, Rt Hon Anthony Crosland, Michael Mansfield QC, Johnny Borrell of Razorlight, Zak Starkey of Oasis and The Who (son of Ringo Starr), Sir John Tavener, Barry Norman, Gerard Manley Hopkins and Sir John Betjeman.

Entrance: Takes about 40 girls and boys at 11 to join those coming up from the junior school. Tests in maths and English with interviews in pairs for a large proportion of applicants. At 13+, takes girls as well as boys but only 20–25 in total, as the balance has shifted towards the two form entry at 11+. Tests in maths, English, science, French, verbal and non-verbal reasoning, with interviews for most.

Around 40 pupils, mostly girls, join the sixth form. Assessment includes subject-based and general interviews, and the school is keen to encourage state school pupils to apply.

Exit: Transition between different levels of the school 'is not automatic but is expected', but apparently getting harder as competition for places increases. A few leave after GCSE for sixth form colleges or state school sixth forms, e.g. Camden School for Girls. Virtually all sixth form leavers to university, over half to the élite ones and around 10 per cent to Oxbridge (20 per cent in 2008).

Money Matters: Academic and music scholarships at 11, 13 and 16. Also internal awards at various different points. 'Around 20 Year 9 students have an award of some sort, for example. We like to recognise and acknowledge our pupils' endeavours and to encourage a culture where it is cool to work hard.' Means-tested bursaries, funded from the school's non-fee income and from the Friends of Highgate School, support those who could not otherwise afford the fees and pupils already at the school whose families get into financial difficulties.

Remarks: A London school with acres of playing fields and enviable facilities, which provides particularly rich extra-curricular opportunities. Its decision to go co-ed has helped to put its popularity and academic standards on upward trajectories. 'They have brought out the best they could in my son,' said a parent. 'Big tick – well done, Highgate.'

Hills Road Sixth Form College

Hills Road, Cambridge, Cambridgeshire, CB2 8PE

• Pupils: 1,820 girls and boys • Ages: 16-19 • Non-denom • State

Tel: 01223 247 251
Fax: 01223 416 979
Email: aclarke@hillsroad.ac.uk
Website: www.hillsroad.ac.uk

Principal: Since 2008, Mrs Linda Sinclair BA (early fifties). Languages and linguistics at Essex, followed by three years in banking. Retrained as a teacher with most of her career at Hills Road teaching economics and business studies. Became deputy principal in 2003. Definitely not a big 'I am'. Instead a democratic, likable manager – someone who's able to field questions with a beguiling smile and placatory answer. Some new initiatives – nothing radical – coupled with a resolve to maintain high standards and keep this huge, fluid place running like clockwork. She says, 'The College caters for ambitious students,' and her intention is to ensure they're 'provided with the right tools for the next stage'. Teaching is out of the question, but she tries to keep in touch by visiting lessons, meeting groups of students and attending extra-curricular events. However, this is a place where student – and parental – focus is clearly directed towards the tutor or subject teachers, so the response, 'Who?', in relation to the principal, isn't surprising. Spare time is filled with family – she's married with two teenage children, making gardening or reading a rare luxury.

Academic matters: Nothing but praise for this side of college life – whatever they tell you, Hills Road is chosen first and foremost for its academic credentials. High expectations all round – a remark that 'A grade C really isn't good enough' sums up the thinly disguised view of many. Bright, focused, super keen young adults who relish a challenge. 'Firm but fair', well qualified staff. Lunch time surgeries in all subjects for extra help. Top notch facilities in every department plus trillions of computers. All in all perfect ingredients for impressive results – 74 per cent A/B, 89 per cent A–C. Outstanding status awarded by Ofsted and often tops the league tables as the highest achieving sixth form college.

Over 40 A level subjects on offer. Every student takes at least four AS subjects in their first year – seems to be very little give here. History is popular, but the crowd pullers are biology, chemistry and maths, which gets praise from everyone – 'They're always finding new material and addressing individual needs', 'There's always someone there waiting to offer help' and 'If I went into teaching I'd like to be like Mr ******'. In their second year many still take four subjects – AS critical thinking, world development, science in society or the extended project are possible topups.

Alongside examined subjects, first year students have to produce a compulsory 3,000 word research project which needs to demonstrate quantitative and qualitative research methods – a sort of extension programme linked with study skills. Good idea, but in a place where huge emphasis is put on student choice, this is the only area of compulsion which is greeted with a universal groan.

At some stage during their time at Hills Road about a quarter of the students will seek help from the excellent study skills centre, which deals with everything from time management, handwriting and essay writing skills to ESL, dyslexia and Asperger's syndrome. It also provides assistive technology, in-class support and timetabled sessions.

Games, Options, the Arts: Year 12 students must attend at least one enrichment session once a week – something for everyone and real appreciation for the level of choice. For the physically active, 30 different options – all the usuals plus the possibility, if enough interest, of rustling up provision for something new. Regular representation in national teams and, in 2008, two Olympians in hockey and the triathlon. Sizable cricket hall bedecked with droopy nets, five professional indoor tennis courts, sports hall, squash court, fitness suite bulging with muscles and, just a hop away, ten acres of sports fields. Alternatively drama (it flourishes in the small but perfectly formed Robinson Theatre funded by a millionaire old boy), music (range of ensembles and good facilities) or art, which regularly hosts an artist in residence.

Huge number of student-led clubs and societies funded by the student council – we fancied ultimate frisbee or global citizenship. Young Enterprise and community service going strong. D of E as well but, as students have until they are 26 to complete all the elements, it isn't clear how many actually go on and get gold.

Work placements in Germany for linguists coupled with worldwide visits and exchanges, including links with partner schools in Mthatha, South Africa and Shanghai, explain recent International Schools award, which acknowledges the effectiveness and diversity of links.

Background and Atmosphere: One glance at the sophisticated, no expense spared prospectus and the message comes over loud and clear – this is 'niversity': nine tenths university or, as one mum put it, 'university with someone still doing the washing'. These are students, the central area is the quad and the place to meet is the buzzy student café, which could sit quite happily in a shopping mall. Continual coming and going of the multitudes – students love the freedom of only having to be on site for timetabled lessons – makes a sense of cohesion or belonging difficult to achieve. Students say the first two weeks can be daunting, but guidance from day one ensures almost all come to flourish in this heady mix of independent learners. Many find it's the first time they can get something from 'school', whilst others have found friendship with like-minded souls – spods, boffs and swots don't have to keep their heads below the parapet: they can fly.

'We're not interested in the past – only the students' future,' said a big honcho, so we'll do the history bit. College started life in 1903 as a selective grammar – nearby

Perse complained to the government and tried to get it closed down. Relaunched in 1974 as a co-ed college for 600 sixth formers. Subsequent ballooning to 1,820 now makes the place a giant, bright pond – the original buildings have been neatly linked to tasteful, well designed modern blocks (depressing 'social area' in the basement is the only real blot, but this is now being refurbished and should be completed by August 2010).

De luxe pluses are contacts with the university and a stream of celebrated speakers – Stephen Hawking, John Major, Lord Dearing, Zandra Rhodes, Sir Martin Rees, the Astronomer Royal, and Tony Juniper.

Pastoral Care and Discipline: So much is 'up to the student' and, although they 'won't let you drown', students have to take responsibility for their learning and post A level plans. Self discipline is a prerequisite; subtle reinforcement comes from the super efficient pastoral system based on daily email contact and 19 'specialist' tutors, who have offices in the new student guidance centre. 'Luck of the draw which tutor you get' – the best are 'fantastically helpful' or 'always there for you while you cry'. No hope of swaps if things aren't quite so positive – one or two seem to 'only think about academic individuality' – but, as one pragmatist said, 'You only have to see them once a week, so you sit there and put up with it'.

Adult behaviour is expected and most meet expectations – strict rules re attendance for lessons and meeting of deadlines are made clear from the start and regular 'goofers' (non attenders, to you and me) who don't change their ways are 'helped to find alternative routes'. Concerns can be voiced through the student council, who've been consulted on most college rules – two members are on the board of governors. 'As there's not much missing', focus is on fundraising for charity and social functions – freshers' disco and two annual balls are highlights of the year.

Pupils and Parents: Mature, generally biddable bunch, who have academic aspirations. Some commute a considerable distance – buses stop outside and it's a ten minute walk to the train station. Cyclists living over three miles away can apply for a termly £30 incentive to be green – a sprawling knot of bikes clings to the railings outside the college.

87 per cent of students from maintained sector in and around Cambridge. The rest lured (finance and freedom oft quoted reasons) from independents (especially the Perses, Leys and Kings Ely). Parents (they're likely to sniff at Classic FM and laud Radios 3 and 4) are involved, committed and tremendously ambitious for their offspring. Former students include prominent government officials, Anil Gupta (director of the TV programme, *Goodness Gracious Me*) and Tom Heap (journalist and BBC presenter).

Entrance: Becoming increasingly selective – B or better in subjects or related subjects for proposed A levels ('better' is more realistic, given level of over subscription and academic credentials of most). Priority for those from the Cambridge 14–19 partnership area. Feeder schools are contacted to gauge applicant's suitability. Reference also required, with predicted grades, behaviour, level of commitment and ability to make the most of opportunities being key. Interviews for all qualified in-area candidates (parents are included and are under no illusions as to how hard students will have to work) – a phenomenal feat, given the numbers. However not all entrants from outside the area (most come from within a 30 mile radius of the college) are interviewed.

Exit: Effective programme for budding medics, vets and dentists, plus full time careers advisor and several tutors with relevant expertise. Almost all to degree courses at a wide spread of institutions – Leeds seems to be the new Nottingham. About 75 a year to Oxbridge – admission tutors come in to talk to students. College will help with gap year arrangements and about a third take up the option. Small proportion don't last at Hills Road, but retention rates are well above sixth form college norms.

Money Matters: The college has 'outstanding' financial status and has also been very successful in recent years in bidding for a number of QIA grants to support innovative projects and share good practice. A £5m building project was recently completed and plans for a new £3m project are under way.

Remarks: Powerful, top of the range sixth form college. An exciting place, especially for bright, questioning go-getters who are ready for some independence. Not quite as fizzy for the faint-hearted or less than determined.

Hockerill Anglo-European College

Dunmow Road, Bishop's Stortford, Hertfordshire, CM23 5HX

• Pupils: 710 boys and girls; 225 boarders • Ages: 11-19 • Size of sixth form: 140 • Non-denom • Fees: Boarding £9,450-£12,783; Day boarding £5,031 pa • State

Tel: 01279 658 451
Fax: 01279 755 918
Email: admin@hockerill.herts.sch.uk
Website: www.hockerill.herts.sch.uk

Principal: Since 2008, Mr Simon Dennis, previously head of South Wolds school in Nottingham for seven years, where he introduced the International Baccalaureate, the bilingual section, achieved language college status and was judged to be 'outstanding' in his leadership by Ofsted. He has six children and is a keen sailor.

Academic matters: Recognised (and therefore awarded additional funding) as a language college, music school, a leading edge school and a training school by the DCSF. Pupils are setted from Year 7 and those with an aptitude for languages are not only fast-tracked in a modern European language (either French or German) but also learn history and geography in their chosen language in Years 9, 10 and 11 up to GCSE. All pupils also take their first foreign language GCSE one or two years early and nearly all achieve an A or A*. Across all subjects, GCSE grades are now well above the national average and improving. Hockerill's GCSE results last year were amongst the top 20 comprehensives in the country. In *The Independents*' league tables of post-16 schools it has been top for four successive years. The 2007 Ofsted report judged Hockerill to be outstanding in all areas.

No provision for A levels – all pupils study for the International Baccalaureate Diploma. In 2009, 100 per cent were successful, with many gaining a bilingual Diploma and displaying equal competence in two languages. Lessons are held on approximately two out of every three Saturday mornings but school holidays are longer than those of state day schools (an extra three weeks in the summer, for example).

Games, Options, the Arts: Floodlit Astroturf pitch; plenty of sporting fixtures, including soccer, rugby, hockey, netball, basketball, tennis and athletics, against both state and independent schools.

Wide range of extra-curricular activities, including D of E, CCF (both army and RAF), community service and golf, to keep the boarders occupied, but day pupils are strongly encouraged to join in too. Numerous exchange trips and foreign visits – Year 10 pupils are offered two weeks of work experience in France, where the college has a rural base.

Background and Atmosphere: Set well back from the road and close to Bishop's Stortford town centre. Dates back to 1852, originally an Anglican teacher training college, and only set on its present course since 1994. Traditional Victorian buildings with the addition of standard modern blocks, overall appearance and atmosphere of the 20-acre site is very pleasant. Uniform is blue blazers, pinstripe trousers and striped tie for boys, blue jackets, distinctive blouses and pinstripe trousers or skirts for girls. Sixth formers wear plain dark suits. Uniform rules strict.

Pastoral Care and Discipline: 'Our approach to behaviour and discipline is generally old-fashioned,' says the principal. Pastoral care for boarders is highly rated, with a recent (November 2009) judgement of outstanding from Ofsted, although pupils think that they are treated rather strictly. Good behaviour by the boarders rewarded with a system of privileges.

Pupils and Parents: Boarders come from around the world and seem to mix well. On the day we visited a history class studying the causes of the second world war included a group of Germans. 'We have plenty of lively and stimulating discussions,' said the very enthusiastic history teacher. Hockerill has found favour with the local middle classes over recent years, so day pupils are increasingly from relatively affluent backgrounds.

Entrance: It's getting more difficult to get a place here every year – seven or eight applicants for every day and every boarding place. Top priority goes to applicants with a brother or sister on the roll at the time of admission, then those with a compelling medical and/or social reason for admission. Then ten per cent to those who attain the highest scores in the college's language and/or music aptitude test. After that those who can demonstrate that they may need to take advantage of the college's boarding facilities at some point in the future. All other places are allocated according to the primary school the applicant has attended.

Out of 107 Year 7 places, 35 are allocated to boarders. Boarding places are heavily over-subscribed. Entrance is by suitability, interview and then demonstration of a boarding need. Entrance to the sixth form is dependent on GCSE (or equivalent) results and interview.

Exit: All of 2009's sixth form went on to higher education, including a few to Oxbridge and other top European universities. A high proportion studied law or medicine.

Remarks: In little more than eight years has changed from a relatively unknown school with places to spare to a very highly regarded and massively over-subscribed academic institution. Even for those who don't regard language as a priority, this school has plenty to offer.

Holland Park School

Airlie Gardens, Campden Hill Road, London, W8 7AF

• Pupils: 1,570 boys and girls, all day • Ages: 11-18 • Size of sixth form: 170 • Non-denom • State

Tel: 020 7908 1000
Fax: 0207 908 1098
Email: info@hollandpark.rbkc.sch.uk
Website: www.hollandparkschool.co.uk

Head: Since 2001, Mr Colin Hall BA PGCE (late forties). What he inherited was a disenchanted fiefdom, with low attendance, low academic performance and more than its fair share of inner-city problems. 'Standards are not high enough,' lectured Ofsted crisply and 'behaviour is unruly'. Since his arrival, Mr Hall, an energetic terrier of a man, has worked 14-hour days and six-day weeks to transform the school into one of Britain's 'most improved'. The 2007 Ofsted described Hall's leadership as 'charismatic, inspirational and transformational' and few would disagree.

Mr Hall attended Durham Wearside Grammar School, read history at Sheffield, followed by a PGCE at Cambridge. Started out as a history teacher, before transferring to English at Thurston Community School (now College) in Suffolk, then at Harrogate High School in north Yorkshire. Rose rapidly through the management ranks, firstly as director of sixth form at King Edward VI Morpeth, in Northumberland, then deputy head at Cheney School in Oxford. First headship was Longford Community School in Feltham, Hounslow, a tough inner-city school, where he quickly drove up GCSE results from 16 per cent A*–C to 40 per cent before being headhunted for Holland Park. The school he joined was on the verge of special measures and it soon became apparent that Mr Hall and existing staff were not on the same wavelength. 'My job involved assisting people's passage to places where they might flourish,' is his velvet-glove description of these 'ugly' times. His own views are clear and consistent – 'Adults run the school. That's what makes it a safe and agreeable place to be'. Mr Hall describes his job as an obsession: 'I'm not good at the work-life balance. This is a passion, the best thing I could have ever done with my life'. His long-time partner, Ann, is another head teacher.

Academic matters: The school has seen a steep and continuing rise in results. In 2010, 95 per cent of pupils got 5 A*–C at GCSE, 67 per cent including English and maths. 'We're aiming for 100 per cent, 75 with English and maths,' says Mr Hall. The school has a banded intake, with four bands selected on the basis of verbal and non-verbal reasoning before entry. All are then re-assessed in the middle of their first term and setted for each subject. It's clearly a method that works, but some students find it creates a 'them-and-us' mentality. The quality of the teaching is strong and the dedication of staff unquestioned. 'I'm looking for robust teachers, open minded, passionate about what they do, with an energy beyond their subject,' says Mr Hall. 'If children love a subject, it's because of the person who's teaching it.'

Pupils have nothing but praise for the staff. 'The teachers are really, really dedicated,' said one sixth former. 'They'll stay in school till 8 or 9. Even on their birthday. They never take a day off.' Teacher development is very much part of the programme. Younger staff observe their more experienced colleagues and can take specialist courses on the weekend for aspiring leaders. 'Once you've found them you want to hook them,' says Mr Hall. Preparation and monitoring are meticulous. Classrooms are laid out in advance of lessons. 'It's about rigour and order' – and that applies to students, who all have chic student planners for parents to sign weekly.

The school has a humanities specialism and English is clearly strong, with graphic displays of themed work on every wall. Other departments that come in for special praise are history, art, dance and PE. The approach to the curriculum is relentlessly innovative. Latin now on offer for GCSE and compulsory BTecs in media studies, sport and art. Dance, music and drama taught as separate subjects in Years 7 and 8. Modern languages are French and Spanish ('We tried Italian and German, but they didn't root'). About to launch a three-year GCSE programme, in which most students will already have acquired their 5 A*–C grades by Year 10 ('They can see the end point more quickly'), leaving Year 11 to focus on English and maths. Sixth form is now, as always, primarily academic, with some very small classes. ('It's like a free private school,' said one pupil.) Results here, too, are on the up, from 15 per cent A and Bs in 2003 to a pass rate of 100 per cent in 2010 (85 per cent A–C, 27 per cent A*-A). English and maths most popular A levels. SEN has had a recent boost with the advent of a 'brilliant' new head of dept – parents cannot praise highly enough. 220 pupils on the register of emotional and learning needs overseen by the SENCo and 15 teaching assistants in specialist accommodation.

Games, Options, the Arts: Hall wants Holland Park to be a 'life-transforming institution' and has worked as vigorously to develop the extra-curricular as the academic. Art rooms are large, light and lively. The school has a highly praised director of dance and collaborates with several dance companies including English National Ballet. Poet Simon Armitage is a friend of the school. Music, with new teachers and increased funding, is an ever more popular choice at GCSE and pupils have performed at the Royal Albert Hall.

Currently, sports facilities, particularly out of doors, are reasonably restricted (though a pool and large, well-tended gymnasium), but this will change when/if the school gets the final go-ahead for its costly rebuild. Sport is important (and recognised by a Sportsmark award). 'Sport can build up or destroy confidence,' says the head, who's recruited a specialist to up the ante in rugby and introduced rowing at Barn Elms rowing club. The cricket team has played at Lords and Ampleforth. Amongst the wide range of clubs available, sports fans can do football, rugby, cricket, judo, baseball, gym and swimming. An annual garden party celebrates outstanding sportsmanship. School trips, too, are seen as a foundation pillar of the education and are underwritten by a £1m trust, enabling every child in Year 7 to visit Stratford (for *Romeo and Juliet* and dinner in a restaurant), Year 8 Rome, GCSE historians Auschwitz, and the entire sixth form Florence and Rome. 'The trust enables us to benefit the children of families who don't have those kind of resources.'

Background and Atmosphere: Designed by the architect of the Royal Festival Hall, Sir Leslie Martin, and built at the then astonishing cost of £1m, Holland Park opened in 1958 as one of London's first purpose-built comprehensives. The school, set in eight leafy acres of London's most costly square footage, has always been controversial and Kensington locals weren't entirely happy with its arrival. Naturalist Peter Scott (who claimed the children would frighten away nightingales), John Betjeman (who worried about the trees), and the High Commissioner of South Africa (who feared for his garden parties at nearby 'High-end') were only a few of those who inundated *The Kensington Post* with their concerns. At the time, the feeling was that the school would 'reduce Campden Hill to Earl's Court'. Early fears, however, were soon confounded. The school quickly attracted high-profile, left-leaning pioneers convinced that state education was the answer for a more egalitarian age.

Celebrated former peer and socialist minister Tony Benn transferred his two oldest sons from Westminster and Charles Jenkins, son of Labour cabinet minister Roy, joined the sixth form from Winchester. Hardly surprising then it was soon dubbed, 'The Eton of comprehensives'. In the '60s and '70s, the school became increasingly progressive and undoubtedly cool (Anjelica Huston was a pupil, as were the children of the Marquess of Queensbury), but the '80s and '90s were not so kind, and cool turned to chaos.

Today, its pristine, light-filled classrooms are once more an oasis of well-ordered calm. The corridors are polished, the reception ornamented with fresh-cut flowers and the pupils themselves, in smart grey suits, would do credit to any independent school brochure. 'The environment,' says Mr Hall, 'is part of an attitude, a landscape for learning. It transmits that we care about young people and, as a result, students want to work hard and feel they belong.' Certainly students are proud of their school. 'It's a shining hall of hope,' said one, 'a fantastic place to be,' commented another. A controversial £80+m new building is under way, which will add outside space, an Olympic-sized pool and a more compact and SEN-friendly interior. The head sees the rebuild as his next main goal. 'I want to come out into the new school before I hand it over to someone else.'

Pastoral Care and Discipline: Where once mayhem, now tranquillity, and pupils higher up the school notice it most. 'When I came here it was completely chaotic – now it's an incredible school,' said one Year 12 boy. 'There is a very special thing about the school, an openness and willingness,' says the head. 'Pupils behave with good grace and enthusiasm.' They definitely feel comfortable here. 'It's very close knit, like a family. It looks after the kids and cares about how you are,' says one. The head aims to create a safe and secular, humanist community and instil a sense of spirituality. 'We live in such a ready culture – we don't want to replicate what happens out of school.' Pupils meet twice a week with their House Leaders, once with the head and deputies, listen to choral music and poetry –

'Not because it's of use in exams, but because it takes them beyond the everyday passions'.

Praise is very much part of the mix and an annual awards dinner, Perfect Tense, recognises outstanding achievements, attitude and contributions during the year. Award winners portraits ornament the corridor walls. Vertical tutor groups about to be introduced, for a better understanding across the years ('and less bullying,' said one pupil). Behaviour is generally good, 'though not without its challenging moments'. Permanent exclusions for offensive behaviour, trafficking, physical assault or any 'significant intent'. On average, four to six exclusions annually, though none in the past five years for drugs. For lesser misdemeanours, a range of sanctions, from detention to an extended school day. There is a behaviour support centre for students with challenging behaviour and a student needs team co-ordinates the identification, tracking and support of the vulnerable.

Pupils and Parents: From a vast range of ethnic backgrounds (90 languages spoken): 50 per cent speak English as a second language, about 10 per cent are refugees, mainly from Somalia and Eastern Europe. Fewer than 20 per cent are actually English by origin and language but, as was the original intention, investment bankers ('we felt the head was a great leader, a visionary person; we took a gamble, but we're delighted with it') and intellectuals (Will Self) are once more happy with their local state provision.

Entrance: Over 1000 apply for 240 places. Banding tests held in November/December. The school operates a sibling policy, then distance from the gates. Makes every attempt to ensure parents understand that if you live more than a mile away your chances of entry are slim. (Last year 60 appeals produced only one extra place.)

All sixth form applicants, internal and external, are interviewed by an assistant headteacher, who leads the sixth form. Places offered on the basis of a school report and predicted grades. A*/A required at GCSE: 'It's not absolutely rigid – some students are bored at GCSE'. Year 11 students the school wants to retain are wooed with 'an extra bit of love and a series of suppers'.

Exit: A number leaves post-GCSE to sixth form colleges, with different curricular offerings. Last year every Year 13 leaver to university, one to Cambridge to read medicine. Usually two or three to medical school. All have one-to-one guidance on university choice and a programme of visits, with time and effort put into personal statements and developing 'cultural capital'. Most to London universities and others in the south east – 'It's a rare student who goes to Lancashire'.

Money Matters: Now, as always, Kensington and Chelsea's flagship comprehensive, very well funded by the borough.

Remarks: A school which has gone rapidly from 'could try much harder' to 'outstanding in most departments', under a dynamic and inspiring head. Now, once more, a model cosmopolitan, inner-city comprehensive. Suits those, according to one student, who are 'hard-working and opinionated, who strive to do their best. It's not for someone with a blasé attitude'.

The Holy Cross School

25 Sandal Road, New Malden, Surrey, KT3 5AR

• Pupils: 750 day girls • Ages: 11-18 • Size of sixth form: 200 of 410 (federated with Richard Challoner) • RC • State

Tel: 02083 954 225
Fax: 02083 954 234
Email: hxs@rbksch.org
Website: www.holycross.kingston.sch.uk

Head: Since 2001, Mr Tom Gibson MEd NPQH BSc DipEd,(forties). Educated Wimbledon College, read physical education and sports science at Loughborough University. Previously taught at St Joseph's, Beulah Hill, Glyn ADT and St Gregory's, Kenton. Married to a fellow teacher, four children. Well experienced in different areas of education, a pleasant, unassuming gentleman who looks set to brighten all horizons.

Academic matters: A mostly long-serving, committed staff of all age groups delivers an 'innovative curriculum' (Ofsted 2004) in an outstanding school (Ofsted 2007). Class sizes are around 30. A level results improving and with a high level of value-added; GCSE results have been consistently over 90 per cent A*–C. Awarded Specialist Science College status from September 2003 which enabled the school to develop its provision in science, maths and ICT over four years. Independent working habits are encouraged. A £5.4 million building project has provided excellent facilities for drama, music, science and IT. New sports hall and dance studio opened in September 2007. Staff and students developing a video conferencing project with NASA and China. School tells us that due to the high level of academic achievement, the school has been designated a high performing specialist school. The sixth form is in partnership with a local boys' school, Richard Challoner, enabling them to offer a wider choice of subjects – much appreciated by pupils and parents. SEN and EFL are catered for by specialist teachers throughout the school.

Games, Options, the Arts: Two garret-style studios provide an inspiring setting for art and DT. A hard-working music teacher is making new waves with the orchestra in a state of the art music suite and individual instrumental tuition on most instruments can be arranged. The school trains year ten as Wimbledon ballgirls. Creative drama department in purpose-built drama facilities is growing – many do GCSE. Duke of Edinburgh Award Scheme along with an extensive selection of after school clubs, including astronomy and young engineers.

Background and Atmosphere: The Sisters of the Holy Cross founded the school in 1931. It became grant maintained in 1993 and in 1999 became a voluntary aided school within the diocese of Southwark. The original buildings have been much added to, updating and redecoration is currently underway. Caring and moral values help deliver a smooth, organised atmosphere. Whilst Roman Catholicism predominates, all other faiths are welcomed. Pupils are encouraged to be involved in the community through voluntary work.

Pastoral Care and Discipline: Sensible school rules – girls are expected to be mature and aware of others' needs; all have form tutors. Strict uniform code – girls ticked off if not properly dressed. Sixth form pupils expected to be self-disciplined and present themselves well.

Pupils and Parents: Good ethnic mix; 90 per cent are Catholics. 'We are from all walks of life here, professionals to refugees; most are somewhere in the middle.' The common interest is a well-balanced and Christian education. Serious PFA.

Entrance: Pupils come from a wide catchment area. First preference to practising Catholics. 143 places available in Year 7.

Exit: Currently 80 per cent of students return into the federated sixth form, with 15 per cent moving to local colleges and a small number to the world of work.

Remarks: With a young and dedicated head, a school for parents to watch develop. October 2007 Ofsted stated that Holy Cross 'is an outstanding school. Christian values and concern for others are at the heart of its work.'

Howard of Effingham School

Lower Road, Effingham, Leatherhead, Surrey, KT24 5JR

• Pupils: 1,575 pupils; girls and boys • Ages: 11-18 • Size of sixth form: 350 • Non-denom • State

Tel: 01372 453 694
Fax: 01372 456 952
Email: Howard@thehoward.org
Website: www.howard-of-effingham.surrey.sch.uk

Executive head: Since 1999, Mrs Rhona Barnfield MA BSc (fifties). She is executive head of the Howard Partnership, a federation of Howard of Effingham School and Thomas Knyvett College. 'She comes over as very committed and probably quite determined,' says a parent. Mrs Barnfield declined to be interviewed. The actual head of Howard is Mrs Sarah Kieran.

Academic matters: 'The Howard' – as it is known locally – enjoys an excellent reputation and many families move into the catchment area to enable their children to attend. It is a mixed comprehensive school that achieves very good results. 90 per cent plus get five A*–C grades at GCSE; average point score at A level in 2009 was 344 with 54 per cent A/B grades. Has larger classes, lesser facilities and fewer resources than most of its Surrey fee-paying counterparts yet its results are as good, if not on occasions better, than some of its private competitors, particularly when you consider its mixed intake. Modern languages, art and design and technology are particularly strong with great examples seen all over the school. Latin, too, is offered as an additional subject option from Year 9. Light and airy new science labs (sponsored by Brown & Root).

The Howard was among the first 24 schools in the country to become a science college. With support from businessman, Peter Harrison, it has built a brand new lab and ICT suite; older labs have been refurbished. A cyber café was opened, plus new courses in applied sciences at KS4 and A level and science-based events for the wide community.

In the core subjects, maximum class sizes likely to be 30, but numbers do get smaller higher up the school. Very few foreign students so no current EFL requirements. Some special needs support – sixth form students also get involved, giving up one free period a week to help. It works out to about two hours per fortnight and sixth formers seem to enjoy the challenge. Also a reading scheme that helps Year 7 students achieve required levels (operated on a voluntary level by sixth formers).

A large sixth form resulting in a wide range of options. Vocational A levels on offer and praise for the sixth form teaching – 'The teachers are very helpful and friendly – we get a lot of support, yet a lot of opportunity to work on our own,' said one (ex-private school) sixth former, whose only fear was of turning into a couch potato in the state system. 'I'm not particularly sporty – there should be proper timetabled PE lessons, but at least now we have voluntary sports lessons.' Adequate sixth form block has relaxation area and study classrooms.

Games, Options, the Arts: For a comprehensive school, a lot of sport on offer. Facilities could be larger for the number of pupils but uses additional fields from a nearby sports club as well as the facilities of the Effingham Community Sports Centre. Hockey, netball, football, cricket and rugby are major sports, with tennis, badminton, athletics, basketball, rounders, cross-country, squash, volleyball, softball, orienteering, dance and gymnastics also available.

Drama and music play an important rôle in the life of the school with regular musical activities each week – numerous choirs, a jazz band, orchestra and ensembles. The orchestra provides the music for many of the drama productions and both orchestra and choir have performed at the Albert Hall. The drama productions are popular, with the sixth form being very involved in the lighting, sound and staging. Any other extra curricular activities take place before and after school and at lunchtime. The Duke of Edinburgh Award Scheme is available from Year 10 onwards and enjoys popular support.

Background and Atmosphere: Named after the second Lord Howard of Effingham (admiral who commanded the fleet which defeated Spanish Armada in 1588), built in 1940. Although it has since been extensively enlarged and expanded, feels as if it is bursting at the seams – so many pupils it operates a one-way system during lesson changes to avoid congestion in the narrow pale green corridors. Yes, it needs a coat of paint in places and it would be nice if green lawns where black tarmac, but instead of window dressing, it seems to be spending its funds on great teachers and educational resources. 'The staff seem extremely committed and very hands-on,' says one impressed parent. Food is adequate, say pupils – hot and cold options, plus snacks. Many pupils bring their own packed lunches.

Pastoral Care and Discipline: Conscious of the need for strong pastoral care in such a large community. House system in place to encourage co-operation, community spirit and competition. Older pupils are encouraged to be rôle models for younger ones. All new pupils are invited for an induction day in July before they join. School has a code of conduct which pupils are expected to adhere to. 'If there are any difficulties, the staff are in there pronto,' says a parent.

The size is undoubtedly an issue – but it bothers some more than others. One pupil did say that if she could change one thing at the school it would be the class sizes, because 'you sometimes feel as if you could disappear'. A parent shared this view and said, when discussing her child with a teacher, she was not sure whether the teacher really knew who she was talking about. However, another parent had the opposite view and felt, despite the school's size, the staff had a good insight into her daughter. Lots of consultation with parents re any changes.

Common complaint from outsiders is the scruffiness of the pupils – the usual parade of micro skirts skimming their backsides, school socks disappearing into clompy shoes and shirts and ties for both boys and girls worn at ever more rakish angles – although head and staff are trying very hard to encourage pupils to take more pride in their appearance. Not a particularly authoritarian school but encourages children to behave responsibly with respect and consideration. Policy on drugs and smoking is firm, according to pupils, as is anti-bullying one.

Sixth form is relatively autonomous. Fewer pupils in each class and, as the students feel closer to and more relaxed with their teachers, they really seem to enjoy themselves – 'My daughter found her feet very quickly, and there was no prejudice whatsoever that she had come from a private school. She is very happy,' said one impressed mum. Sixth formers don't wear uniform but have to conform to a standard of acceptable dress, which was certainly adhered to when we visited. Biggest gripe of the older students seems to be that not enough parking for their cars.

Pupils and Parents: Main catchment areas are very middle class – Horsley, Effingham, Bookham and Fetcham, although a few pupils come from the equally upmarket Cobham and Oxshott areas. Most pupils are bused in, as parking facilities are limited – parents are discouraged from dropping their children off. The school is popular and usually over-subscribed. Pupils seem well-mannered and happy. A smattering of real scruffs and others the school would not be proud of, including the odd smoker or two, spotted on their way to or from school – a fact of life unfortunately common to many schools and something they can do little about.

Entrance: At 11. The closing date for applications is usually around mid-November of the year before a pupil is due to attend (for example, Nov 2009 for entry Sept 2010). Siblings at the school and proximity of home to the school seem to be the main factors affecting admission. Places are then offered during the spring term and, if unsuccessful, one can apply to be put on a waiting list. Also an appeals procedure.

Impressive A level results mean that the school is popular with outsiders, including ex-private school pupils, for sixth form studies.

Exit: Approximately 65 per cent stay on into the sixth form; the students who leave tend to enrol at a local college to pursue more vocational courses, and a small number take up employment or join training schemes. Sixth form leavers to many traditional university choices, about 20 per cent via a gap year, a good few straight into employment. A good half dozen to Oxbridge each year.

Remarks: A very large, but very successful, state school that offers a good alternative to the ubiquitous Surrey private schools. It doesn't have the manicured grounds and gracious old buildings of the private environment, but it does boast many pupils whose parents are teachers in both the private and state sectors.

Good academic results mean that the school is an option for cash-strapped parents of private school pupils at age 11. However, 11 year old timid girls and shy, awkward boys – particularly those from cloistered private schools – may feel overawed by the sheer sink-or-swim size of the place. At A level, the school comes into its own and can hold its head up high with the private schools academically and with the big plus of an atmosphere and social mix more in tune with university life.

Howell's School, Llandaff, GDST

Linked to Howells School Junior School, Llandaff in the Junior section

Cardiff Road, Llandaff, Cardiff, South Glamorgan, CF5 2YD

• Pupils: 800; girls from nursery to Year 11, all day; co-ed in the sixth form • Ages: 11-18 • Size of sixth form: 200 co-ed • Non-denom • Fees: £9,630-£9,818 pa • Independent

Tel: 02920 562 019
Fax: 02920 578 879
Email: admissions@how.gdst.net
Website: www.howells-cardiff.gdst.net

Principal: Since March 2007, Mrs Sally Davis BSc PGCE (late forties). Educated at Bassaleg Comprehensive School, Newport and Bedford College, University of London, where she studied geology. Taught at a number of inner London comprehensives before joining Howell's as deputy head in 1992. Bubbly personality who consults with her management team but appreciates the buck stops with her. Married to a teacher and has two children. A theatre is top of her wish list for the school.

Academic matters: Results remain strong – 84 per cent A/Bs at A level, with 31 per cent A* and 32 per cent A, and 72 per cent A*/A (42 per cent A*) at GCSE in 2010. Science is very popular. The range of subjects available has expanded in recent years. The average class size is 22. Staff a mix of young and older teachers. We sat in on a practice for a debating competition and it was clear that pupils are encouraged to ask questions.

A clearly defined SEN policy and Dyslexia Action Cymru has an on-site satellite on the campus. Parents are expected to pay for any SEN referrals. The needs of moderate dyslexic/dyspraxia pupils can be met. Also procedures in place to identify gifted and talented pupils and ensure they are academically stretched.

Games, Options, the Arts: Examples of pupils' art are shown all round the school. Drama is popular and we sat in on a very lively improvisation session. Over half the school play an instrument, many at county or national level. Concert hall and practice rooms are well used by the many choirs, orchestras and groups. An annual Eisteddfod is held which encompasses a wide variety of activities designed to give as many pupils as possible a chance to take part. The spirit and history of Wales is alive here and well supported by both parents and staff.

Sport taken seriously. Apart from lacrosse, hockey, netball, tennis, athletics and swimming, rugby has been introduced for the sixth form boys. Fencing, badminton, cross-country running and dry skiing among other sports available.

After school activities are well supported and range from ballet to Mandarin. Duke of Edinburgh award a firm favourite. Award winning careers advice programme with a dedicated careers coordinator supported by outside speakers and the GDST Minerva network, which offers a supportive scheme for sixth formers including on-line information and practical training courses.

Background and Atmosphere: Merchant Thomas Howell on his death in 1537 left a large sum to the Drapers' Company for the benefit of orphans. Howells, founded in 1860, benefited from this legacy. Joined the Girls' Day School Trust in 1980. A short distance from the centre of Cardiff off a busy road, the campus is more extensive than first appears. The main buildings have a Hogwarts look about them with a Grand Hall complete with fresco, turrets and impressive staircases. Improvements and extensions have been added over the years as required. Younger pupils wear simple but smart uniform. Sixth form have no uniform but a dress code. Good food with plenty of choice. Multi-cultural entry with over 30 different languages spoken. Communication with both pupils and parents is given a high priority – examples of this include a revision guide for parents and handbook for new pupils. A buzzing feel to the school – pupils seem keen to learn and enjoy what is on offer. The sixth form college is based in two Victorian houses, over the road from the main campus. Sixth formers are treated more like university students and have space both to study and chill out.

Pastoral Care and Discipline: It is made clear to pupils that the school expects them to take responsibility for themselves and to respect others. Strong anti-bullying policy is part of a proactive pastoral system. Drugs, alcohol and smoking not an issue but will be dealt with severity if found.

Pupils and Parents: Catchment area from Cardiff to Newport, Bridgend and the Valleys. Wide range of backgrounds, which makes the school socially inclusive. Many first time buyers of independent education. Notable former pupils include Baroness McFarlane of Llandaff, Professor Rosalie David, Emily Barr, Jane Crowley QC, Lucy Cohen, Linda Mitchell, Jemma Griffiths the singer, known as JEM, and Charlotte Church.

Entrance: Entrance test at Year 7 in maths and English. The principal then interviews all candidates being considered for a place. Entrants to the sixth form are expected to have a minimum of six grade C GCSEs and above, including grade B or above in their chosen A level subjects, and are also interviewed.

Exit: A few leave after GCSE. Majority go onto a wide range of universities – Bristol, Exeter, Swansea, Cardiff, London and Durham being popular choices. In most years several to Oxbridge (nine in 2010). Medicine, dentistry, veterinary sciences, law and engineering are among the more popular degree subjects.

Money Matters: The GDST Minerva Trust and the Thomas Howell Trust support bursaries – means tested and currently about 20 per cent of the senior school receive them. Also a small number of scholarships.

Remarks: A school that nurtures the pursuit of learning and the arts while celebrating Welsh culture.

Huish Episcopi Academy

Wincanton Road, Huish Episcopi, Langport, Somerset, TA10 9SS

• Pupils: 625 boys, 615 girls; all day • Ages: 11-18 • Size of sixth form: New sixth form opened September 2010 • Non-denom • Independent

Tel: 01458 250 501
Fax: 01458 250 262
Email: office@huishepiscopi.somerset.sch.uk
Website: www.huishepiscopi.net

Principal: Since 1996, Mr Graham Roff BEd MEd AdDipEdMgt (mid fifties). Educated in Stockport, then Madeley College, before reading geography and education at Keele and adding further qualifications along the way. Has moved around the country and was deputy head at Cheadle Hulme High School for six years before coming to Huish Episcopi. Lives locally and wife Pam teaches infants in Ilminster; both their sons have gone through the school. Takes a keen interest in sport, particularly basketball which he used to play. Enjoys hill walking and foreign travel but says he has little time for these. Slightly reserved but shrewd, with a pragmatic approach to educational issues. Likes to engage with parents and staff; chats to pupils informally in corridors and says that they are 'comfortable' about seeking his help when needed. Proud of what has already been achieved and would love to see school develop a sixth form. Ofsted graded leadership in the school as being 'outstanding'.

Academic matters: Head believes in setting children from the outset. School operates two distinct 'populations' (or bands) in each year group. Two 'top ability' groups identified within each band for English and a number of other subjects, but 'tight' setting in maths and science. Choice of second foreign language from Year 8 (for all except those with 'extreme' special needs) allows pupils to see whether to continue with one or two languages from Year 9. GCSE results have improved consistently over recent years. More than 70 per cent have gained 5+ A*–C grades at GCSE for the past six years. In 2010 74 per cent of students achieved 5+ A* to C grades including English and mathematics (best results and significantly above county average). Noticeable effort being put into making teaching livelier and more flexible. Strong emphasis on ICT with more than 420 computers in the school; specialist science, languages and 'applied education' status has provided funding for additional laboratories. Majority takes dual award science. BTec science 3 also offered.

Most able pupils can take AS levels in maths and history and achieve good results. Particularly impressive GCSE results in English, art and geography. Science, history and French also good. The majority of the highest achievers are girls, but in 2009 boys out-performed them for the 5+ A*-Cs measure. All take short GCSE courses in

RE and citizenship. Some pupils follow an optional extra subject after school. Large laboratories accommodate up to 32 pupils in top sets, allowing lower ability groups of 16–19. Less flexibility in other core subjects. Links with Yeovil College and South Somerset 14–19 consortium now provide a wide variety of additional (mainly vocational) courses in Years 10 and 11.

All Year 7 children are screened on entry using computer based (CATS) testing, despite close liaison providing plenty of information beforehand from feeder primary schools. SENco works with staff to support pupils with SpLD and other special needs largely within normal timetable and the 16 learning support assistants work alongside mainstream teachers. Small numbers of statemented children. Few with Asperger's traits get help with socialisation and use of free time in school.

Games, Options, the Arts: Long-standing reputation, especially in boys' football, girls' hockey and cross-country, with huge numbers involved. Successes include county championships in football, cricket and hockey; also individual representation at district and county level. Has produced national champions in athletics and high national placings in cross country. PE is a popular option (now BTEC qualification) and pupils have benefit of purpose-built leisure centre on site, which is shared with the community and includes fitness centre, dance studio and superb squash courts; floodlit multi-use outside courts, heated 25 metre open air pool and extensive playing fields.

Music and drama join forces for many productions with good results. Dance is popular but not a GCSE option yet. Lower school hall doubles up as a drama studio. Well-resourced music area where pupils get hands-on experience in lessons. 100 learning music instruments plus choirs and ensembles with regular concerts. Art is well displayed despite the limitations of the buildings; innovative and enthusiastic department which gets good number of students into specialist art and design courses at local colleges. Purpose built art spaces within the new sixth from centre allow students progression to level 3 qualifications.

Background and Atmosphere: Motto: 'Conemur' ('Let us strive') which head feels is as appropriate now as ever. The unassuming, single storey, red-brick buildings at the front of the school date from 1939 with seven subsequent additions behind them. From outside and on entering it still feels like a small, rural school. No nine day wonder, it has built up a reputation locally as a school which 'gets the best out of children' who go there.

School opens up inside like a Tardis, but despite its multiplicity of specialist accommodation, the original appeal has not been lost. The assembly hall, which doubles up as a dining (snacking is probably nearer the truth) area, can only accommodate a year group at a time. We witnessed an unusual Year 10 assembly which used overhead projection of a Liverpool FC footballer as a positive rôle model and succeeded in carrying pupils along in a way which had relevance for them. Five lessons per day of one hour duration – four before lunch break (which doesn't start until 1.20pm) – a pattern which brings good trade for mid-morning snacks (breakfast for some). Old style classrooms can be viewed from corridors, which are now too narrow during lesson changeovers (fortunately not too frequent). Many groups seen knuckling down to real academic work.

Pièce de résistance is the vanguard pupils' loo – all gleaming hardware and surfing murals – which has provoked local media interest. CCTV 'not infringing pupils' privacy' has stopped vandalism. Languages and science suites particularly impressive with results to match the facilities provided. Study centre is perhaps the greatest success of all, offering multi-media facilities including well stocked library – a real oasis of civilisation where pupils are allowed to bring food into a hugely popular weekly storytime. Workshops with visiting authors for both the gifted and those with low literacy levels.

Sixth form opened in September 2010, offering 22 AS level qualifications within purpose built learning spaces. The new build boasts teaching rooms, laboratories, cafe, multi use drama and performance space as well as socialising areas. Learning is supported by dedicated study areas and ICT spaces, including a suite of 32 Apple Mac computers. Has aspirations to increase its offer of vocational BTec courses at level 2 and 3, providing coherent progression routes for all learners within the academy.

Pastoral Care and Discipline: Pastoral care in hands of experienced senior staff and year heads, who make themselves accessible to parents. Year 7 head is especially active around feeder primary schools to make sure children look forward to joining senior school. Attendance is carefully monitored with dedicated staff member to ensure first day notification of absence. Small but adequate learning support area in the heart of the school and separate student guidance and learning centre introduced recently to tackle the educational and social needs of the disruptive and disaffected few.

Pupils and Parents: From within and outside a 200 square mile catchment area. Slightly undersubscribed at present, which is good news for those parents willing to ferry their offspring. Martock parents have clubbed together to run their own coach. Informal parental car sharing gets pupils back home if they stay for sports, rehearsals etc.

Parental views are sought and involvement is maintained through regular newsletters; turnout at parents' evenings is usually about 90 per cent. We heard no parental gripes about discipline or teaching standards but some criticism of homework policy as being both too little and too much. School tries to strike the right balance but may have to work harder with parents on this one. Parents' strong support for sixth form was revealed in a recent survey.

A certain amount of scruffiness, but staff chip away at keeping pupils' appearance up to the mark. Children we met definitely enjoy the school and thought the teachers were good – 'No evil teachers,' said one – and were keen to show us the best bits. Interesting array of former pupils include fashion designer Alice Temperley, winner of the Walpole Award for British Excellence, as well as Sarah Ball, creator of 'Bob the Builder'.

Entrance: Children come from about thirty villages across mid-Somerset, including 18 per cent from outside the catchment area.

Exit: At the end of Year 11 students have the opportunity of staying on at Huish sixth or securing places at other local tertiary providers.

Remarks: Friendly, close-knit and not daunting for the younger ones. Not many 11–18 comprehensive schools do as well as this. Academy status and the new sixth form promise well.

Hurst Lodge School

Linked to Hurst Lodge Junior School

Bagshot Road, Ascot, Berkshire, SL5 9JU

• Pupils: 160 girls, 20 boys (aged 3-18); 20 boarding (weekly and flexi), 160 day • Ages: 3-18 • Size of sixth form: 6 • Non-denom • Fees: Boarding £21,045; Day £12,930 pa • Independent

Tel: 01344 622 154
Fax: 01344 627 049
Email: admissions@hurstlodgesch.co.uk
Website: www.hurstlodge.co.uk

Principal: Miss Victoria Smit (fifty) is a former Hurst Lodge girl. Unusually for a head, she doesn't have a teaching background. Spent early part of her career in industry and reckons it helps to have worked 'in the real world'. A dynamic, hands-on, open-minded head with great sense of humour, she is a 'chronic dyslexic' who tells pupils she's never let it stop her doing anything. 'If a child ever says, "I can't do that – I'm dyslexic," I tell them that I am too,' she says, matter-of-factly. Miss Smit knows all pupils by name and encourages girls to pop into her study to chat about successes and/or disappointments. Spends spare time learning Chinese and going to theatre.

Academic matters: In 2010, 95 per cent of students gained 5 GCSE grades A*–C with 38 per cent at A*/A. A level candidates achieved 89 per cent A–C grades. School firmly believes in tailoring approach to student' needs and abilities. Small classes – rarely more than 16. Pupils are setted for English, maths and science. Strong learning support department.

Games, Options, the Arts: Sport definitely on the up. Small numbers used to mean that teams regularly got walloped but no longer the case. Children enjoy swimming (open-air pool) and also holds annual biathlon and cross-country championship for local schools. Performing arts form a key part of school – past pupils have gone on to work at the RSC and the National. All pupils have timetabled dance classes every week up till Year 10 and ballet, tap, modern dance, jazz and musical theatre offered as extras too. Three performing arts studios for ballet shows, drama productions, concerts etc. Student creativity encouraged as much as possible – must be one of the only schools in the country to allow two and a half tons of sand to be deposited in its performing arts studio for a drama production. Around 85 per cent of students take music lessons, with singing far and away the most popular choice. Junior and senior choir as well as ensemble groups and a mini recording studio where students can compose their own music. Art and photography very popular at GCSE and A2 and loads of extra activities on offer, from flower arranging and cookery to football and judo.

Background and Atmosphere: Founded as ballet school in London in 1942 by Doris Stainer, sister of Oscar-winning actor Leslie Howard (*Gone with the Wind*) – 'A very formidable woman with a cane,' recalls present head, who was one of her pupils. School later moved next door to Agatha Christie in Sunningdale and then to leafy 22-acre site on outskirts of Ascot in 1997. Main school building a rambling Victorian country house. Poignant rolls of honour from First and Second World Wars take pride of place in tiny chapel, now used for choir rehearsals. Despite small numbers, the school fizzes with activity from dawn till dusk. The few boarders live at far end of house – traditional dorms for younger girls, with older ones getting singles or doubles.

Strong family atmosphere abounds. Despite its posh reputation not in the least bit snooty. Smart frocks, suits and a marquee for prize-giving are 'as posh as we get,' says principal, who hands out gongs for all sorts – from the kindergarten child with smiliest face to the Spirit of Hurst Lodge award, given to the pupil who embodies 'all the things we think are important, like enthusiasm, politeness and hard work'. A smart new uniform recently introduced. Sixth form wear suits, though they look more like trendy art students than city-slickers.

Pastoral Care and Discipline: Emphasis placed on good manners, respect for others and integrity. Clear list of school rules – students getting fresh air at break times and making sure they eat properly at lunch – but discipline not a problem here. Principal says can count on fingers of one hand the number of times she's ever had to raise her voice. Very helpful welcome book for new pupils lists everything they need to know, from what to call the teachers to the stationery they need in their pencil cases. Head student and prefect system, as well as three competitive houses – one named after Miss Stainer and the others after ballet legends Margot Fonteyn and Ninette De Valois. Students also run buddy system to look after new pupils and offer friendly ear to anyone who needs it. Head prides herself on regular contact with parents and produces weekly newsletter to update them on forthcoming events. Each form has parent rep who attends a termly school management meeting.

Pupils and Parents: Day pupils from up to 50 miles away, boarders from as far away as Hong Kong. Weekly boarding and flexi-boarding only – guardians occasionally used. Friendly, personable students who are very proud of their school and stand up when teachers or visitors enter the room. Notable old pupils include Duchess of York, actresses Juliet Stevenson and Claudie Blakeley and TV presenter Emma Forbes.

Entrance: Entrance exam at 11. Girls entering at other stages spend day at school and have interview with principal. Girls starting Year 7 often come from own junior school, others from local primaries and preps. School looks at educational psychologists' reports but always keeps an open mind. 'Reports sometimes bear no relation to the child we see,' says principal. Girls entering sixth form must have a C or more in chosen A level subjects and 'a commitment to work hard'.

Exit: Sixth form leavers head in loads of different directions, to university (LSE, Exeter etc) studying everything from languages to law, art college and performing arts careers.

Money Matters: Academic, dance, drama, music and art scholarships on offer, as well as the school's annual Racov award – three terms of basic fees given in memory of eminent neuroscientist, Achi Racov.

Remarks: Mainstream school that caters for all. Great for raising self-esteem and getting the best out of pupils in nurturing, friendly, purposeful environment. Splendid performing arts and more academic than sometimes given credit for. School caters for a wide variety of ability but is particularly good at helping pupils who have the ability to succeed academically but may need individual help.

Hurstpierpoint College

Linked to Hurstpierpoint College Preparatory School in the Junior section

College Lane, Hurstpierpoint, Hassocks, West Sussex, BN6 9JS

• Pupils: 595; 345 boys, 250 girls; 325 board: full, weekly or flexi • Ages: 13-18 • Size of sixth form: 245 • C of E • Fees: Boarding £23,535-£27,750; Day £18,495 pa • Independent

Tel: 01273 833 636
Fax: 01273 835 257
Email: admissions@hppc.co.uk
Website: www.hppc.co.uk

Headmaster: Since 2005, Mr Tim Manly BA MSc (mid forties), an Oxford classicist. Took an MSc at the LSE, went into consultancy and then, having seen the light, did a PGCE and jumped into teaching. His first job was at Sevenoaks, where he became head of classics and housemaster of School House. Thence to Oakham as deputy head. Both his previous schools, then, gave him plenty of experience of the fully co-ed, boarding and day mix he found here, as well as of the International Baccalaureate – pioneered at his first school and now firmly established at the second. Married with four young children, the eldest in the senior school with the younger three currently in Hurst Prep.

Dashing, enthusiastic, confident and engaging and seems to have most of the tight Hurst community batting for him. He has a mission – 'to make sure that every child knows what they can achieve and how to get there' – and practical plans to make it happen. Pupils are appreciative, 'He's so approachable ... His door is open ... You can walk in and talk to him about anything you want'. Since his arrival, the numbers of pupils throughout the College have increased dramatically from 630 to 920 in all three schools. The 2007 ISI report commented that Mr Manly, with the support of staff and governors, has achieved a great deal in a remarkably short period of time.

Academic matters: 'We're never going to be a league table chaser, but we're ambitious for our pupils rather than for our school,' says head – but we have yet to meet a head who did admit to craving statistical success. Results now showing more consistency and overall class with approximately one third of the 2009 GCSE cohort obtaining eight or more GCSE grades at A* and A and a pass rate A*–C grades of 97 per cent. Overall, entirely respectable, with data averaged over the last four years indicating that the college's performance at A level places it in the top 17 per cent of schools nationwide for adding value and the top quartile of independent schools for value-added at GCSE.

Previously reported weaknesses in some areas of the curriculum, but since our visit, head has 'significantly strengthened the academic life of the school, introducing monthly challenge grades, the results of which are immediately emailed directly to parents and, in September 2006, introduced a two-weekly timetable that increases the focus on academic studies whilst still accommodating the school's extensive cultural, sporting and extra-curricular activities'. Re-introduction of Latin and inclusion of new subjects such as psychology and dance. With his impeccable IB credentials, it seems likely that a consideration of moving, at least in part, à la Oakham, to the IB will be on the cards.

Good new learning resources centre, i.e. upgraded library, with lots of internet-linked PCs and three full-time librarians, now open 12 hours a day and a well-used, serious place of work, though the bookshelves were so full we did wonder whether any books were taken out! Pupils pay tribute to 'very good careers advice'.

Head says, 'We can't put our hands on our hearts and say we could deal with special needs as well as other schools could. We've probably taken more of these children in the past but I want to get away from the idea that "Hurst will look after them". We will take mild dyslexics and have one or two with mild Asperger's or ADHD, but can't really offer more than one or two periods a week – withdrawals on rotation.' A sixth former told us, 'I'm dyslexic. The SEN department is very strong. I got a good grade at English AS level due to the help they gave me and my teacher in the English department gave me loads of extra time. And they are like counsellors too – if you are low and fed up with being a dyslexic, they chat, pat you on the back and cheer you up.'

Games, Options, the Arts: More than a third of school's lavish magazine is devoted to sport, which is big, successful and popular. Facilities are good, though pupils would like more Astro pitches – a second Astro is now being planned. All boys in the first years play rugby, hockey and cricket and girls play hockey, netball and rounders. Both do athletics. Lots of teams and fixtures. Loads of other activities including polo, swimming and scuba diving in school's pool, volleyball, squash, climbing, kayaking, weights, sailing and golf. School achieves impressively given its size – at the 2009 Sussex AAAs the squad brought home 28 medals; U15 netball Sussex Knock-out cup, champions and U16 netball SISNA runners up; the girls' 1st XI hockey runners up in the Sussex Schools championship; the girls' football XI runners up in the Independent Schools National six-a-side tournament; Hurst golf team won the West Sussex Golf Club Independent Schools trophy; lots of representation in county teams and even occasionally in national squads. Vast, Swedish built, pine-clad sports hall – less chilly and off-putting than most, good fitness suite with a personal fitness trainer to oversee fitness programmes and rehabilitation from sports injuries and, overall, a feeling of room to move.

Drama is good and well-established; 2004 saw the opening by Simon Russell Beale of super studio theatre and smallish dance studio. Studio theatre seats 120 and is used for debates, meetings and theatre studies lessons – one of the nicest, best-equipped little modern theatres we have seen. The technical side of production is popular here. Good main theatre, seating 250, with pronounced raked seating, well-used. Many chances to take part in drama with productions throughout the year, from the Shakespeare Society's annual play in the Michaelmas Term to musicals and plays with auditions open to all pupils in the whole of the senior school. Performances for local arts festivals and productions taken on foreign tours. In 2008/9, 18 separate drama productions. The school's dance company takes productions into the community – for example children's homes.

Music school has good practice rooms adjacent to the inviting, light and spacious performance hall also seating 120, which was fully renovated in 2006. Music tech recent innovation and immediately popular, with a purpose-built studio opened in 2006. Busy choir now numbering some 125 members. Music led by dynamic husband and wife team, with choirs and musical ensembles performing not only at school events but also at venues ranging from Chichester Cathedral to the local residential homes. One third of pupils learn an instrument.

Art is in suite of studios – maybe more space to be creative in here than anywhere else we've seen. Dark room, pottery, sculpture studio and varied, imaginative work in all areas. A sense of pupils being encouraged to do their own thing – now with more staff on hand to help. Long and strong tradition of overseas sporting tours and trips. Recent biology expedition to South America and the Galapagos; mixed hockey tour of South Africa, a cricket tour to Dubai, Shakespeare Society performances of 'King Lear' in China, a classics trip to Italy, a netball tour to Spain, white water kayaking and rafting expedition to Nepal and India, ski and adventure sports trips to the Alps and language trips to France, Germany and Spain. Phew!

Background and Atmosphere: The first impression on approaching the site, set among fields a mile down the road from Hurstpierpoint Village, is of a monasterial community, self-contained and orderly, going about its monastic business. The sight of trendy young things in blazers and short skirts comes as something of an anachronistic shock. The hyperactive Oxonian, Nathaniel Woodard, who founded it in 1849 – along with nine others before and after – believed in the value of a Christian based, holistic education and this is made tangible in the modest, knapped flint buildings with college-type quads and cloisters, clearly intended to inspire a seriousness and unpretentiousness in a childhood given to learning and community. It is one of the most venerable in the Woodard Foundation, which now comprises over forty schools – independent and maintained. These days the cloisters are softened by pastel wall colours and grassy places to sit and the atmosphere is very different, with young of both sexes, most of whom live at home, from what Rev Woodard witnessed at its inception.

Set in 150 acres of Sussex downs close to Brighton and the sea, it's a pretty idyllic location. The Oxford college influence is felt most profoundly in the imposing chapel – large enough for the whole school. The Friday evening service held there brings to an end the working week. The old school theatre, with a splendid beamed ceiling, is now a grand dining hall. The school has expanded westward since Woodard's day – into newer and frankly undistinguished teaching blocks and boarding houses which do no credit to whoever planned and built them. Not so the newest block – St John's House – housing the upper sixth, very easy on the eye and far more in keeping with the school's architectural tradition. Ambitious plans for campus development began in July 2008 with the building of an extension to the classroom block to provide 18 new classrooms, with further updating of teaching space and facilities to follow.

Pastoral Care and Discipline: Clear pastoral system includes system of 'guardians' in each house/year group. These are chosen for their approachability. Head has strengthened the house team and 'adults are around modelling good behaviour'. All underpinned by 'a strong sense of Christian principles'. Head has been blitzing bullying – 'There's a feeling that I'm taking it too seriously, but when you want to send a clear message, you have to push the pendulum harder than you might like.' Moreover, 'I've taken a pretty strong line and have suspended a few. We've still got things to do but they're generally pretty giving and forgiving'. An unusual approach to drugs – 'I'm very keen on sniffer dogs – use them a lot; they come at least once a term. Prevention is absolutely key. I can be pretty confident that I can make this a drug-free campus, but I need to have parents on side'. Alcohol seldom a concern and smoking not really an issue.

Food is good – we saw a pasta bar with an inviting menu, plus hot dishes including lamb in red wine and plums, Mediterranean vegetables and quorn, a salad bar and a good choice of desserts and fruit. Lower sixth have chic coffee bar known as 'Costa' with polished wood floor, leather-look sofas, coffee tables, soft lighting and the papers. All pupils – day and boarding – have a study. Boarding rooms unusually large and unusually individual for the upper years – all upper sixth formers have single rooms (though no ensuites yet). First years share up to five in a room – rooms again decorated with care and flair we've not seen elsewhere. New annexe to girls' boarding house in 2008 and brand new girls' day house opened in 2009.

Pupils and Parents: Diverse – or as diverse as southish London, Surrey and Sussex can muster. Increasingly, takers are busy working families who like to see their offspring at weekends, so the mix of weekly/flexi boarding and day places offered here is just the ticket. The vast majority live within short driving distance. Good bus service from as far as Hove, Worthing, Horsham Copthorne, Forest Row, Crowborough, Lewes and Seaford. Parents get close and rapid communication from school via school/home internet links, particularly by e-mail. Under five per cent are full boarders and these only in the sixth form, with a few from overseas – China and Germany biggest contributors.

Famous former pupils include Admiral Sir Michael Boyce, Chief of Defence Staff in the Gulf War, former German Minister of Defence, Volker Ruhe, various MPs and ambassadors, former General Secretary of The National Association of Head Teachers, Sir David Hart, actor Michael York and film director Ronald Neame.

Entrance: At 13+ mostly via CE from external prep schools – 'comfortably over 50 per cent' expected, though 'I will always listen to the prep school head,' says Mr Manly. Entry from Hurst Prep is by assessment. Get in while you can, as entry threshold likely to rise to 55 per cent in the next year or so as school becomes seriously over-subscribed. At 16, you need Bs in your A level choices and a minimum of six passes at GCSE.

Exit: Most to university and around 80 per cent get to their first choice. To universities old and new – a handful to Oxbridge, a large number to London (Imperial, King's, LSE and UCL) with Durham, Edinburgh and Exeter also popular. Subjects over the whole range – a good varied mix of everything.

Money Matters: Lots of awards. Scholarships: academic, musical, artistic, dramatic, sporting and in D&T, IT and for all-rounders. Varying amounts but all worthwhile. Supplementary means-tested bursaries available for scholarship entrants. More of the same in the sixth.

Remarks: It's been a good, happy, smallish school for ages. We predicted that under Mr Manly it would become better and bigger in all respects, and the significantly increased numbers, combined with local reports, suggest we weren't far wrong.

Hurtwood House School

Holmbury St Mary, Dorking, Surrey, RH5 6NU

• Pupils: 325 girls and boys. Mainly boarders. • Ages: 15-18
• Non-denom • Fees: £32,100 pa • Independent

Tel: 01483 279 000
Fax: 01483 267 586
Email: info@hurtwood.net
Website: www.hurtwoodhouse.com

Joint heads: Mr Richard Jackson MA (late sixties). Began working in marketing, then became a prep school master before founding Hurtwood in 1970 in a National Trust rented house with 17 pupils and a dream. He wanted to re-create what he views as the idyllic prep school atmosphere of security and discovery for A level students. He feels that at 16 it is time for a change and seeks to bridge the gap between school and university. His drive, enthusiasm and inspiration have got the school to where it is today and he admits he will never totally relinquish his day to day involvement in its organisation, not, that is, 'until I am taken out in a box'. His wife, Linda, is school bursar and currently responsible for catering and domestic arrangements.

Cosmo Jackson BEd (fortyish), his son, came straight from Bristol University to work for his father. No attempt at any other career for him – he knew exactly what he wanted to do and his enthusiasm and flair are equal to it. It is difficult to discover the division of labour – both talk about their school projects and achievements with excitement and well-deserved pride. Perhaps Cosmo says 'my' a bit more often – he is probably more involved with the day to day administration, but they still seem to be a team and it is very much a family concern. His wife, Tina, teaches history and assists with careers. They have two children, currently at local prep schools. Will his son want to carry on the family tradition? That is a question yet to be answered.

Academic matters: Excellent results all round. Small classes and top level teaching have proved a recipe for success. Their results 2006–2010 put them into the top fifty independent schools and the top three co-educational boarding schools in the UK – an achievement to be proud of.

Large range of available subjects that can be combined any way desired – for instance biology and chemistry could go with theatre and music, if that is where a student's talents lie. Theatre and media studies are the most popular, with maths, business studies, art and English literature coming close behind. Good languages and sciences as well.

Although the general appearance would seem rather liberal, the structure is certainly not. All students are graded weekly and their progress carefully monitored by tutors and teachers, a system designed to keep everyone on their toes. Parents appear to really like this – they can review their child's performance at any stage and know he/she is not lagging behind.

No specific special needs help, but a co-ordinator for dyslexia, and extra lessons can be provided where necessary. Extra ESOL lessons available plus a one year foundation course with GCSE options for overseas pupils needing a more intensive introduction to English, and an introductory summer course for foreign students.

To encourage breadth of experience, each student has to spend specific times each week on subjects in which they are not taking exams, a programme imaginatively called 'Enigma'. This is compulsory and they are not allowed to miss sessions. The Enigma range is enormous – life skills, fitness, media, arts: a student's creativity is challenged and channelled.

Games, Options, the Arts: Games are an option, not compulsory, but a variety of sports/activities is available every afternoon and they do manage to produce enough teams to play external matches and go on overseas tours. Playing fields and all-weather courts. Termly outward bound expeditions.

Perhaps the greatest strengths of this school are its media and theatrical facilities, which are to die for – a theatre with a revolving stage, roll up seating, totally professional lighting and sound equipment; as Richard Jackson says, 'Could be the Donmar'. These students learn all aspects of film making, theatrical productions, music and dance – someone really keen could do up to 12 hours' dance, on top of his/her academic studies. A television studio opened September 2008. Performing, shooting, recording, cutting, mixing – studios for everything, and they do the lot with spectacular results, often up to professional standards. A utopia for creative minds – no wonder they have such high pass rates in theatre studies, media studies and music technology.

Great art, textiles, design – modern and traditional: here are some talented students being well taught. 30+ take art A level, of whom 100 per cent have achieved A/B passes over the last three years – or perhaps more impressively, over the last five years, 202 out of 209 students have got A grades. Look at their website and you will understand why.

Background and Atmosphere: As you drive along narrow leafy Surrey roads, following outward bound style directions, finally turning into a drive marked inconspicuously, 'Hurtwood House', you begin to slightly wonder whether you have made a mistake and this is someone's private residence – it does not feel like a school. Cars parked outside the house and a fleet of buses presumably fresh from ferrying students from their not too distant boarding houses to the place where they will spend the rest of their day – no-one is allowed back to their house during school hours – but absolutely no institutional feel and no sense of nearby easily reachable towns with irresistible attractions beckoning vulnerable teenagers. No transport – this school is a big protected place (from the parents' point of view) where you can learn and be yourself (from the students').

The main house, a huge country mansion perched high in the Surrey hills with fantastic views across to the south coast, has an old fashioned feel about it. Walk in and ahead you'll see an elegant staircase leading to students' comfortable informal accommodation – at least two to each bedroom; turn left and you'll be let in through a secure plate glass screen into the central hall. At the far end leather sofas and a gigantic television set, perfect for showing examples of school productions etc.

The classrooms, laboratories and studios are all very cleverly built into the grounds, below the eye-line, some underground. A feeling of wonder grabs as you walk round the performing arts complex and meet students animatedly editing film, mixing sound, working creatively in a setup bound to enthuse 17 and 18 year olds – their idea of heaven. Walk into the classrooms, all at ground level, and you find small informal groups with their teachers, some interactive whiteboards (only where they will be used properly), some pupils using laptops – technology is there, where it is needed, and bang up to date.

At break time students sit casually on steps and walls chatting, no uniform, most of them in jeans but looking tidy. All students join together so no one is coming into an alien environment – they make friends quickly. As a stepping stone between school and university this seems a good place to be.

Pastoral Care and Discipline: Housemasters, in-house tutors, personal tutors – students have plenty of people to talk to and are being constantly monitored. The atmosphere is grownup and informal – staff are called by their first names. No prefects which, the Jacksons say, together with the fact that all the students are new at the same time, eliminates serious bullying. Zero tolerance of and random testing for drugs. Three things that are totally unacceptable, says Richard Jackson: bullying, drugs and stealing.

No organised activities at weekends – theoretically they can all go home, but often drama rehearsals for the next production, so the houses are never totally empty. Permission always needed for exits. Staff purport to know where anyone is at any time.

Pupils and Parents: Young people who have got fed up with school, want a change, are artistic with ambitions in the world of television, cinema and theatre, whose parents can afford to send them here, a lot boarding for the first time. Twenty five per cent from a broad overseas spread – currently about 25 different nationalities.

Entrance: Non-selective. 'We interview each candidate,' say the headmasters. 'They must want to come to the school.' No expelled or suspended children.

Exit: Some to drama school or art college, others to trad universities, Leeds, Bournemouth, Sussex, for instance, to read media related subjects, or UCL, Manchester, Imperial etc for economics, languages and the occasional biochemistry or engineering degree.

Money Matters: Fees pretty high, but what else would you expect with all these facilities? Worth checking on available scholarships, some for performing arts and some for maths/science. A possible scheme in the air, with support from parents, to include less privileged children.

Remarks: More for the seriously creative than the seriously academic, though 60 per cent go to Russell Group universities having achieved academic A levels. But the creative part dominates and some might find it all too much. For those looking for change, needing smaller classes and lots of nurturing or wanting somewhere to expand their creativity, it could be just the right place. A different and exciting environment, somewhere that develops confidence and encourages disciplined methods of learning – young people discover that hard work creates happiness and fulfilment. A place where 'students can make things happen and school can make things happen for them'.

Hutchesons' Grammar School

Linked to Hutchesons Grammar Primary School in the Junior section

21 Beaton Road, Glasgow, Glasgow, G41 4NW

• Pupils: 860 boys and 725 girls. • Ages: 11-18 • Size of sixth form: 160
• Non-denominational • Fees: £9,228-£9,473 pa • Independent

Tel: 0141 423 2933
Fax: 0141 424 0251
Email: admissions@hutchesons.org
Website: www.hutchesons.org

Rector: Since 2005, Dr Ken Greig MA (Oxon) PhD (forties), a geologist by inclination and teacher by trade. Educated at George Heriots in Edinburgh, where he was Dux, thence to a first at Oxford (maths) followed by a PhD in practical geology and a stint with BP as an exploration geologist. He was previously head of Pangbourne, where, amongst other things, he was part of HMI team. He started his teaching career at Christ's Hospital School in 1987, thence to Dollar as head of maths and housemaster. A man o' pairts then, he is young to be on his second headship and, as one of his staff said, 'Our Dr Greig is absolutely super; everything we wanted, and good looking and charming into the bargain'. (He is all of that.) Married, with two children in the school, he and his wife are settled in south Lanarkshire. Greig arrived post interregnum, the previous head having been hounded from office in a witch hunt which would have done Salem proud, and has spent time 'binding the community together', improving the ethos to 'make the school more at ease with itself'.

Runs the school with a senior depute rector plus four deputes, one of whom is known as director of curriculum (overseeing academic and ancillary activities including the arts) and one 'director of ethos'. Three further deputes in the primary school. Sits in on one lesson each day and has a follow-up meeting with both children and staff, which is, he says, 'a way of getting to know them all as people'. Coffee in the common room on Fridays is now a popular sounding ground, not only for mixing up the departments – 'There's just the danger that the separate departments will become isolated because of the size of the school and the geography of the building' – but also to thrash out future plans. The rector has a 'three to five year' plan, but nothing too radical – at least nothing that he would share, though his eyes did light up when we mentioned possible building expansion (all those lovely flat roofs). 'Anything,' he agreed, 'might be possible, but now is not the time'. A keen golfer, he goes for geological yomps when he can.

Academic matters: Fantastic results – strings of As in Highers with pupils regularly getting six or more in S5 (i.e. fifth year) and eighty per cent or so staying on to top up with extra Highers, advanced Highers or A levels in sixth year, despite the fact that they will already have university entrance qualifications in the bag. Heads of departments chose whether A level or Scottish syllabus and teach accordingly – in all cases two years' study is truncated into one. Results in 2010 were excellent – lots of A grades at Higher (58 per cent of all results) and 51 pupils (almost one third of year group) achieved five or more A grades.

Results per pupil make other schools quake with envy and broad enough pupil base to offer a moving feast of ancillary subjects. Classical Greek comes and goes, as do classical studies and Greek itself – new head of classics may just make Greek a serious higher contender. This is very senior stuff. School is open early and late, staff will hold individual drop in sessions if needed. Biology no longer top of the pops (pupils do human biology too) – maths, English and chemistry head of the pack; pupils encouraged to take as wide a spread as possible – and they do. Only French, German and Spanish on the language front – new head of languages appointed recently, so this may change. Native speakers can and do take highers in their own tongue. Language labs, satellite TV. Vast classics department – Latin compulsory till third year.

Double-decker library at the forefront of technology uses finger print recognition and is stacked with as many DVDs (Shakespeare on film) as books, and computers everywhere intranetted and internetted. EFL on offer for the handful of non-English speaking foreigners – we are, after all, on the edge of Silicon Glen.

No setting for first year – 'Got to find their feet first – this is a big step' – though setted for everything thereafter. All pupils screened at 11 – any problems with reading and writing picked up by SENco, who will 'work within the context of the class', no withdrawn lessons, but fierce academia means that those seriously dyslexic may be either screened out earlier or given the tools to succeed – Hutcheson's primary department particularly hot on this. Class sizes of 20/25 at bottom end of the senior school, reducing in number as specialist subjects kick in.

Games, Options, the Arts: Brand new sports stadium opened November 2009 on old playing fields at secondary school. Incorporates Astroturf hockey pitch and international training standard Tartan athletics track. Astroturf hockey pitches at Clydesdale ground adjacent to the school, which also has international cricket ground. Pupils are bused to Auldhouse for rugby. No swimming pool on site (problems with old coal minings underneath); huge sports hall with fitness centre and gym (open to the general public). All the usual games – rugby almost a religion, like so many schools in Scotland, but it has to be said that last year's results showed more Ls than Ws in the top XVs (better results lower down). Hockey (couple of staff in the UK Olympic team) etc, plus rowing (Rector was a rower) and '25 sporting options'. Curling growing in popularity – Olympic win did wonders for the sport. Trophies in every discipline.

Good and busy drama – consistent finalists in the Scottish drama and music festivals. Three big productions each year – last year 'Oliver!', 'Hot Mikado' and 'Annie'. Terrific music – several orchestras, newish pipe band, Rector is 'potty about the pipes', and quite often plays too – is 'delighted to wear the school trews' but, as a Lowlander, is 'not at all keen on the kilt'. No CCF; granny bashing and masses of charity work popular; recent links with local state schools – the Mark Scott Leadership for Life Award was set up 'after the tragic sectarian murder of Mark Scott' in 1995. Art fantastic, with kiln, fabric design plus home economics – though less of a takeup of this than previously. Huge raft of other options: pupils can do advanced driving (fairly strict rules in place about driving other pupils), archaeology, first aid, Italian and Portuguese. Lots of trips abroad and pupil exchanges. D of E et al.

Background and Atmosphere: Both Hutcheson's hospital and school were founded in Ingram Street in 1641 by the brothers Thomas and George Hutcheson. In 1841 the school moved to the 'quietness of the situation, good air, roomy and open site' of Crown Street in Glasgow's Gorbals, before moving to leafy Pollokshields in 1960, five minutes from the M8 and easily accessible from both sides of the river. Good local buses, plus a fantastic train service. Amalgamated with the girls' school in 1976 (the primary school then moved into the girls' school) and went independent in 1985; the board of governors is full of the great and the good of Glasgow: the Merchants House, Hutchesons' Hospital, the Trades House plus the Church of Scotland Presbytery, some ex-officio, some co-opted.

Large, flat roof, wide open corridors, huge blocks of classrooms. Super chunks of new-build on what is basically a sixties flat roof horror; masses of photographs, good pupil-inspired art. Subjects are grouped either horizontally or vertically, superb – if dated in places – facilities, though a certain amount of moaning about more labs being needed NOW – they only have fifteen, five for each science subject. Dining area extended, still pretty busy at all times.

The latest development is the Fotheringay Centre, which incorporates the existing Congregational church, complete with internal stained glass window and red Glasgow sandstone walls (one of them new) and comfy red purple and grey chairs for the congregation. The former church hall has been converted into a whizzy auditorium with collapsible seating – school not sure now how they ever managed without it. Auditorium is home to weekly sixth year lectures, Talking Points, held on Friday mornings and ranging from Mind power: Fact, Fiction and Fakery via The Genetics of Engineering to Eating Disorders. The series is open to all by ticket – mega wows. This is architecture at its best, incorporating the entire music centre, with practice rooms in the crypt and all manner of exciting performance space, plus the computing centre – for computing lessons rather than for use as an alternative teaching area. Would that all schools could be so imaginative.

Weekly assemblies are divided by year group – the Rector delivers four assemblies a week, two to each group. Individual year groups hold separate assemblies on alternate days elsewhere. 'The trouble with such a large school,' said Greig, is 'there is nowhere large enough to take the whole school at the same time.' Apart from the library, operates on swipe cards – the original cashless economy: pupils top up their cards and use them to buy lunch (very good, lots of veggies and salads), breakfast or whatever. Pioneered no fizzy drinks from vending machines. School uniform in regulation black and white, no obvious anomalies that we saw.

Pastoral Care and Discipline: Divided into four houses for games, competitions and the like. Seniors 'buddy' littles when they join senior school. Strong emphasis on PSE, with fatigues or detention in place for minor wickedness, though individual teachers may set their own punishments – the ultimate deterrent is expulsion. Tutors for all over a two-year period. Rector admits to 'a bit of bullying', but strictures in place to combat it, and his own children, who moved here from the south of England, 'found it a friendly place'.

Pupils and Parents: A mixed bag – 'social, ethnic and economic A-Z'. Cosmopolitan collection of parents, about a third bus their children daily – over 20 miles – from Paisley, Renfrewshire, Lanarkshire, north of the river. Pupils from as far afield as Ayr and Falkirk, made possible by improved road links and school bus service. The odd 'real' foreigner, who may be staying with relations nearby in order to benefit from the Hutchie magic, but fewer Koreans than before. Long tradition of having a significant number of Jews – separate assemblies for them; perhaps 10 per cent from Asian backgrounds. Muslims may go to the mosque at lunchtime on Friday, have separate lessons for gym and no problem with scarves. Number of FPs' children. FPs include John Brown of the shipyard, plus John Buchan, Russell Hillhouse, Carol Smillie, James Maxton, Richard Emanuel, Lord McColl, Ken Bruce, Lord Irvine, Olivia Giles.

Entrance: Either from local prep or (usually) state, the odd refugee from other independents. A hundred a year more or less automatic up from the primary school, plus a 100 extra (all pupils then get mixed up), otherwise by written test. Admission for all usually in August but, if space available, can join at any term.

Exit: 95+ per cent to universities: 15–18 a year regularly to Oxbridge, and many leave with firsts; an impressive list of firsts (and double firsts) from all graduates. More gap years taken than previously – lots do work experience and then travel; most to Scottish universities, but a fair trickle down south. This year 29 hope to become medics, and most 'get to universities of choice'.

Money Matters: Currently discounts for siblings, around 40 full-fee bursaries and some prizes for sixth formers. More funds being actively sought. All bursaries are means tested. But 'there should be no bar to a really able pupil profiting from a Hutchie's education' – full bursaries are not unusual.

Remarks: Awesome. Fiercely academic but pupils achieve their impressive grades from a fairly unselective background. Traditional teaching with enormous breadth, at its very best and using the most up to date tools available. As a previous rector said, 'It's cool to succeed here' – no change in that. It is good to see Hutchesons' back under firm direction again – Thomas and George would be proud.

Hymers College

Linked to Hymers College Junior School in the Junior section

Hymers Avenue, Hull, East Riding of Yorkshire, HU3 1LW

• Pupils: 980 boys and girls • Ages: 8-18 • Size of sixth form: 200
• Non-denom • Fees: £8,694 pa • Independent

Tel: 01482 343 555
Fax: 01482 472 854
Email: enquiries@hymers.org
Website: www.hymerscollege.co.uk

Head: Since 2006, Mr David Elstone (forties), read history and geography at University College, Cardiff, and has taught at a variety of independent schools, most recently as depute rector at Hutchesons' Grammar School in Glasgow. A former cricket and hockey master.

Academic matters: Average class sizes 27 in lower school to 12 post-16. Academically selective on intake, 'though not as selective as most grammar schools'; standards and expectations are high and exam results very commendable. This school has a high credibility rating in the academic stakes, little, if anything, to match it locally. Traditional teaching styles prevail – classrooms are formal with a nod to modern technology, desks in straight rows very much the order of the day, even in the all-new junior school. Science is popular – widespread aspirations (both pupils and parents) towards medicine. French, German, Spanish and Latin on offer, though linguists in the school would appreciate even more choice. Several pupils in top ten nationally in A levels in recent years. No specialist SEN staff – parents advised to seek professional (external) help; about thirty dyslexic pupils in school.

Games, Options, the Arts: Where talent is recognised, be it in sport, music or the arts generally, then pupils are expected to demonstrate commitment and be prepared to give extra time and effort after school and on Saturdays – opting out isn't an option. Games compulsory – rugby and cricket for boys, hockey and netball for girls, tennis (notably successful) and athletics for both; boys and girls well represented in national competitions. Successful and nationally recognised music department, eight pupils in National Youth Choir. Army Cadet Force (voluntary and after school) popular with some, though my pupil guide seemed a little unsure, 'They go in those sheds over there and do whatever they do ... ' A hugely successful Duke of Edinburgh scheme is run by some enthusiastic staff and regularly attracts over 100 senior pupils.

Background and Atmosphere: Opened in 1893 as a school for boys, its founder, The Reverend John Hymers, Cambridge fellow and Rector of Brandesburton, leaving money in his will for a school, 'for the training of intelligence in whatever social rank of life it may be found among the vast and varied population of the town and port of Hull'.

'It's hard to get excited about Hull,' as its most famous adoptive son, Philip Larkin, wrote – 'I wish I could think of just one nice thing to tell you about Hull ... Oh yes, it's very nice and flat for cycling'. Harsh perhaps, but it does capture something of the character of a town that reaches few heights, physical or otherwise. But despite such unpromising geography, Hymers is to be commended for scaling the heights of academe. A curious mix of tatty classrooms, a fine old assembly hall and attractive new buildings – labs, theatre, sports hall, sixth form centre, junior school and swimming pool – clearly extensive recent investment in new facilities, perhaps at the cost of refurbishing the older ones. Appealing site, well-maintained playing fields, all-weather pitches and even a lake for those keen ornithologists on balmy summer post-exam days. Hard core of long-established experienced teachers, average age forty-five, majority ten+ years at the school. The boy/girl ratio is 60/40.

Pastoral Care and Discipline: Apparently the children are expected to 'jolly well behave themselves'. Good, that's that sorted then. Pupils can expect to be expelled for serious misdemeanours, such as bringing drugs into school, but no expulsions for ten years. Head rarely gets involved with disciplinary matters – this is picked up through the robust pastoral care system, where pupils feel 'genuinely supported' but understand the rules and know they will be pulled up quickly, probably by 'a furious but fair' deputy head, if they get it wrong. Good pupil/staff and pupil/pupil relationships, all fairly relaxed for much of the time.

Pupils and Parents: Large catchment area – Hull, East Yorkshire, North Lincs, buses in all directions. The school reflects the lack of ethnic diversity in the area. Wider social spread than most independents, due mainly to generous bursaries and lower than average fees, remaining true to its founder's intentions. About fifteen fee remission places per year, mostly full fees. Parents mostly first-time buyers, ranging from professionals (preponderance of medics) to owners of local takeaways. Pupils bright, cheerful and enthusiastic, and most apologetic when our car was hit by a football for the third time; uniform, like some classrooms, scruffy around the edges.

Entrance: For entry at 11+ competitive entrance exams in maths, English and verbal reasoning, plus interview. Four-form entry, 108 places in all, about 30 for external pupils, remainder transferring from own junior school. For sixth form, five GCSE grade B or above passes, usually about 12 enter at 16.

Exit: 90 per cent stay post-GCSE, favoured universities mainly in the north/Midlands – Leeds, Newcastle, Durham, Nottingham, also a good number annually (around ten) to Oxbridge.

Remarks: Hull is a conventional, unpretentious place and the school mirrors this. 'Perform and conform' could be the school motto, though isn't, but that's the message coming over loud and clear. Do this and the school will support and deliver quality traditional learning at its best.

Ibstock Place School

Linked to Ibstock Place School, Preparatory And Kindergarten in the Junior section

Clarence Lane, Roehampton, London, SW15 5PY

• Pupils: 460 boys, 420 girls, all day • Ages: 3-18 • Size of sixth form: 100 • Inter-denom • Fees: £11,520-£14,985 pa • Independent

Tel: 020 8876 9991
Fax: 020 8876 9915
Email: registrar@ibstockplaceschool.co.uk
Website: www.ibstockplaceschool.co.uk

Headmistress: Since 2000, Mrs Anna Sylvester-Johnson BA PGCE (fifties) – 'Mrs SJ' to the pupils. Previously head of English at the Green School for Girls in Isleworth for nine years and, thereafter, at The Lycée. Then head of The Arts Educational School, London. Prides herself on knowing all faces and sends personal notes of congratulation home when half-termly pupil reviews merit it; sees the friendly community of the school as vital. Has the final decision as the head but relies heavily on discussion with her staff.

Academic matters: Results now over 70 per cent A or A* at GCSE – was rated seventh nationally for value-added. Head of sixth form (at cutting edge of IT) is second master and also teaches English literature. Mathematics, modern languages, science and psychology very popular at A level, reportedly because of teachers. At least two languages from age 11; Mandarin since 2006. These, maths and sciences are setted. Critical thinking is mandatory from age 11 and staff have been trained to encourage this questioning throughout all subjects. ICT is integrated into teaching everywhere – computers in every form, access to intranet from home and headsets in the business/language lab. About 24 pupils in the senior school need SEN help, mostly for dyslexia or dyspraxia.

Dedicated and responsive teachers who report on each pupil every six weeks (every three weeks in sixth form), which means no surprises. What everyone is reading is important – during World Books Day teachers read aloud over lunch. School trips support teaching. Science labs and DT in both senior and junior schools mean facilities are now commensurate throughout.

Games, Options, the Arts: Definitely a sporty school, with swimming pool on site and eight acres of playing fields and new sports hall over the bridge next to Roehampton Club (reciprocal relationship with their facilities, golf, squash etc – and The Bank of England Sports Club). Has rugby connections with Rosslyn Park and a full fixture list for that, hockey and swimming. Ping pong tables (new Mandarin teacher a champion player) on the terrace by the orchard in fine weather, rolled into the conservatory dining room when inclement.

However, plenty of chances for non-sporty group activities – dance, debating, jazz concerts in the hall or, more informally, in the atmospheric but cosy library, a fantastic new cookery room which everyone is keen to use – including the head! Fine art, pottery and drama are on the other side of Clarence Lane, with some really effective teachers and exciting ideas. The music room is equipped with keyboards and headsets, staff and pupils play in orchestras and ensembles and a fair few head off for more tuition to the Royal College of Music every Saturday.

Many opportunities for children to realise how lucky they are without becoming patronising – local MLD state school kids come in and use the pool; Ibstock Place staff and pupils help them through EFL and Duke of Edinburgh Award Scheme. Worldwide sports tours, World Challenge and also trips to Cambodia and Thailand linked with charity work for children from troubled families.

Background and Atmosphere: Founded in 1894 on the principles established by Friedrich Froebel, and started life in a small house in West Kensington with only four pupils. Moved to former private residence designed by GK Chesterton just outside Richmond Park after World War II. New senior school building under construction which, when completed in October 2010, will provide 16 new classrooms, 6 laboratories, a double storey library and resources area.

Tricky to get to – school shuttle buses from Barnes Station at each end of the school day – with main road bisecting campus, but a bridge over it provides extra step training! Security code at entrance, surrounded by Roehampton University and Roehampton estate nearby – the latter apparently less notorious and more studenty now. Sixth form move to the top of the school metaphorically and literally – they register with fingerprint recognition, as do the rest of the senior school; the sixth form common room has more computers, sofas and a pool table. Careers library is very well resourced.

Stately entrance to hall with mirrors and walls hung with pupil art, a quiet area named after a former pupil below the grand stairs, which lead to a piano and sofa where sixth form wait for classes. A new building for library, English, maths, modern languages, science and a sports hall accommodates the expanding school. Campus atmosphere; separate buildings housing nursery, junior and senior school with the beautiful orchard in the middle. Kids race in and chuck their bags into hutches on the terrace; an enterprising teacher videoed them doing this and held an assembly on how it could be tidier/more efficient. Bustling with pupils waving at each other and staff as they go from lesson to lesson. Entire school, including nursery, eats in sittings in the conservatory.

Pastoral Care and Discipline: Courtesy is a cornerstone of the school – autonomy and self-discipline also encouraged – with traditional methods such as dismissing a form row by row to avoid a crush still used. Mobile phones are confiscated if they are seen or heard, although sixth form may use them in their common room. House masters, house tutors, head of pastoral care and school nurse are part of the formal side of pastoral care; school council (meets fortnightly), prefect team, sports' captains and all of the sixth form are involved in planning and running the school. Four houses compete in debating, sport and music. Anything against school rules is disciplined. On the whole, the frequency and detail of pupil reviews picks up issues before they turn into problems. Trust between parents and school is key, founded on comprehensive and responsive reporting; the energetic and well cared for staff and supportive PTA make this possible. School is open at the weekends and in the holidays, with a summer camp in July – all excellent for working parents.

Pupils and Parents: Intake drawn from around Richmond Park, Barnes, Sheen, Richmond, Putney – four by fours dropping off those who do not get buses from Barnes; breakfast provided for early birds. About 60 – mostly European – pupils speak English as a second language. Sporty children from parents with a wide outlook on life, looking for a gracious school with a family atmosphere – a weekly newsletter keeps them up to date. Neat and straight backed pupils who look visitors in the eye and listen to what they say. Iris Murdoch was an alumna.

Entrance: At three, four, 11 and 16; call to see if places appear due to parents being posted abroad. Register at birth (long waiting lists) – siblings given priority for entry into nursery class of 24. One more class introduced at age four and then two all the way up to age 11, when year size doubles. At 11 all applicants interviewed and tested in maths, English and reasoning, and potential assessed in one modern language and one practical subject (science/DT/ICT); 300 applicants for 48 places in 2010. At 16, exam and interview day.

Exit: 25 per cent leave before A levels for local sixth form colleges – Kingston, Richmond – or St Paul's, Westminster, KCS Wimbledon, Latymer; others to board at schools such as Bradfield. School introduced sixth form in 2005. Many A level students take gap years, inspired by World Challenge and school trips.

Money Matters: Exhibitions, academic, art, drama, dance, music and sports scholarships at 11 and more at 16. Auditions and interviews every January.

Remarks: An ambitious co-ed school which turns out well-rounded adults.

Ilford County High School

Fremantle Road, Barkingside, Ilford, Essex, IG6 2JB

• Pupils: 865 boys, all day • Ages: 11-18 • Size of sixth form: 250
• Non-denom • State

Tel: 020 8551 6496
Fax: 020 8503 9960
Email: enquiries@ichs.org.uk
Website: www.ichs.org.uk

Headteacher: From April 2010, Mr Michael Capon, who comes from a deputy headship at St Martin's School, Brentwood.

Academic matters: A strong, academic, highly selective grammar school, which in 2004 became a specialist science college and, having been awarded high performing specialist school status as a result of an 'outstanding' Ofsted report in November 2007, is also now a language college. The admission test is by verbal and non-verbal reasoning alone. Tests all new boys again in October and uses the data as a baseline for monitoring progress and target-setting. Loads of extra help given to those who need reading support, with professionally trained older boys mentoring younger ones, 'You'll find pockets of sixth formers all over the schools reading with Year 7s'.

All do 10 GCSEs (99 per cent A*–C): English lang and lit, maths, chemistry, physics, biology, a modern foreign language (French, German, Spanish), ICT – plus two options. Setting in GCSE maths only and class sizes kept down to 20 in English, maths and science. Twenty five A level options. All Year 12s take four academic A2s, plus an AS in critical thinking – 'It's more useful than general studies for those thinking of medicine or law'. 'Our boys are nothing if not pragmatists,' says the head. 'Their view is, "What does my career or university ask? I'll do that to the best of my ability".' Clearly a successful strategy since the average point score is 330–360. Very strong biology, economics, English, history, mathematics and physics.

Homework from five to seven hours a week in Year 7, up to 20 hours a week at A level. 'Though not all the parents agree, there's enough homework,' says the head. 'Boys need time to watch television.' All pupils given twice yearly assessments of progress and an annual full school report known as a record of progress. Also one-on-one pupil interviews once a year to discuss progress. Reports sent out at times when most useful to parent and child – in Year 7, before parents' evening; in Year 9 before GCSE option choices; in Year 12 before mock GCSEs; otherwise at the end of year.

Six well-equipped, air-conditioned computer rooms, plus interactive white boards in many classrooms. Two trolleys of laptops also accessible to every department. Ten labs, including one period piece from 1935 and another recently refurbished. New learning resource centre opened in 2007, replacing the old library. Built in the old gymnasium, as well as housing an extensive book collection, the centre has 75 computers and elearning resources. Designed for flexibility, it can be converted into a venue for concerts, assemblies etc.

Games, Options, the Arts: State-of-the-art sports hall was opened by Sir Trevor Brooking (an Old Boy of the school) in 2006. Main sports: football, rugby, cricket and swimming, with two football pitches, a rugby pitch, a swimming pool, tennis courts and indoor and outdoor cricket nets. Also access to excellent facilities at the Old Boys' Association grounds less than ten minutes away. Strong sporting tradition outside the curriculum and boys are fanatical about cricket ('winter, summer, rain or snow,' says the head).

Music is good – jazz a strength, full range of classical orchestras and ensembles, as well as the usual medley of rock bands. Also caters to its ethnic population with a sitar teacher and traditional eastern instruments on offer. Concerts and plays are multi-cultural. While probably not the place for aspiring fine artists, pleasant art rooms with some strong work and excellent teaching, but these boys favour traditional academics and few do art at A level. Drama, too, not a major component of the curriculum – taught only as an academic subject in Year 7 – but now housed in a new drama studio in the new sports centre, with a lot of fun clearly had at the annual talent competition.

Wide range of educational trips – World War 2 battlefields for history, the UN for economics. Definitely not, however, all work and no play – end-of-year activities week includes outings to Alton Towers and paint-balling. Popular after-school clubs – often organised by the boys – include table tennis, maths, Warhammer, sailing and Sudoku. Sixth formers also recently won The Schools 'Question Time' Challenge and presented with a Helping Unite Generations Award by HM Queen for over 20 years' work with the residents of a neighbouring old people's sheltered housing complex.

Background and Atmosphere: Moved to its current site in 1935 – the main core of the building is still two gracious floors of art deco-influenced brick built round internal courtyard gardens but elsewhere the fabric is somewhat patchy. Strong family feel, relaxed but respectful: ties must be tied, shirts tucked in, but the odd sweet wrapper is tolerated. Older boys in particular given a fair bit of autonomy. Most of Year 12 made prefects from midway through the year plus three head prefects and six senior prefects, selected by formal interview. Very little communal non-academic space. Only a small playground, for example, but boys are allowed into the building and their form rooms during breaks and lunch-times with very little supervision. The canteen, a walk away from the main building, has recently been re-equipped and now provides healthy options – awarded healthy school status in 2007.

Pastoral Care and Discipline: All religions welcomed and celebrated. Weekly whole school and year group assemblies, given by boys and topped and tailed by staff. Separate assemblies on Tuesday and Thursday for Sikhs, Hindus, Muslims, Christian and Jews. Also recently introduced a non-faith assembly. Behaviour admirable – courtesy and consideration in evidence without prompting. Very much operates an open-doors policy – discipline firm but reasonable. Fixed-term exclusions can, very occasionally, be followed with permanent exclusion. Truancy virtually unheard of.

Pupils and Parents: Supportive parents with high expectations. Primarily from Redbridge, but also from most of the neighbouring boroughs. Extremely ethnically diverse, with a high percentage of pupils whose main language may be English but who speak something else at home. About 30 per cent white British, then largely Asian (Indian, Pakistani, Sri Lankan, Bangladeshi), with increasing numbers of Afro-Caribbean and Chinese. Few free school meals.

Entrance: At 11, by age-adjusted verbal and non-verbal reasoning tests set by the local education authority, Redbridge. Top 120 given places. Level of ability very high; over-subscribed by about nine to one. Fifty feeder primaries and independent prep schools. Gaps occasionally appear higher up the school. About 30 new boys admitted to sixth from with a requirement of six A*- B, with A*/A in A level subjects.

Exit: A handful at 16, to co-ed sixth forms or schools with a different choice of A levels and facilities. Thereafter, the majority to Russell Group universities to read practical, career-orientated subjects including law, medicine, dentistry, business, economics and mathematics. A consistent number to Oxbridge (nine in 2008). Old boys include Lord Shepherd, former chairman of Grand Met, England footballer Trevor Brooking, West Ham manager John Lyall, and conductor Bramwell Tovey, musical director of the Vancouver Symphony.

Remarks: A friendly, orderly school, which takes able, focused boys to exam and career success without undue pressure and with considerable enjoyment.

Immanuel College

87-91 Elstree Road, Bushey Heath, Bushey, Hertfordshire, WD23 4EB

• Pupils: 260 boys, 235 girls • Ages: 11-18 • Size of sixth form: 125
• Jewish • Fees: £12,945 pa • Independent

Tel: 020 8950 0604
Fax: 020 8950 8687
Email: admissions@immanuel.herts.sch.uk
Website: www.immanuelcollege.co.uk

Headmaster: Since 2000, Mr Philip Skelker, MA (Oxon) PGCE (early sixties). Attended Colfe's School in south London, before reading English at St Catherine's College, Oxford. PGCE at Cambridge, then taught English at Watford Boys' Grammar before becoming head of English at Hasmonean High School and Watford Girl's Grammar. First headship, King David's School, Liverpool, then Carmel College in Wallingford, Oxfordshire. When Carmel closed, he taught for a year at Eton, before becoming head at Immanuel. Still teaches English at A level and to all of Year 7 (which means he knows every child by name). A firm believer in Jewish schools and in the education offered by Immanuel, which 'equips pupils to lead a Jewish life in a modern world'. A gentle, erudite man, with a lively sense of humour, greatly liked by pupils and parents. 'The head is a delight,' said one. 'Loving and warm.' Married to a teacher with six, mainly grown, children, two of whom attended the school. A voracious reader, he also enjoys bird watching and walking.

Academic matters: The focus of the school is the provision of a nurturing education centred on a core of Jewish studies. Very small classes (18 pre GCSE, as little as three or four at A level) mean all pupils are well known. 'The small classes meant my daughter reached the top end of her ability,' said one mother. Though selective at 11, the academic range is reasonably broad, albeit skewed to the more able. 2010 GCSE results – 84 per cent A*–B; A level – 80 per cent A*–B. Probably works best academically for the child who needs close care and attention, rather than the one who needs academic extension. 'I had two children in the school,' said one parent. 'My daughter got a very, very good set of GCSEs; the school really added something she would not have got elsewhere. My son is very able and I'm not sure it stretched him.' Some concerns, too, about curriculum monitoring at A level. Considering the Pre-U and 'revisiting' a discussion on the IB – 'Though we don't really feel it suits our learning profile. It's not good for those whose maths is wobbly'.

Boys and girls are taught separately Years 7–9 – 'Girls need a respite from male competitiveness and being scrutinised,' says the head.

Independent learning project in Year 8 to develop research and study skills. Years 10 and 11 now setted and co-ed. IGCSE in maths, history, music and science. Top set takes triple science IGCSE.

Jewish studies a fundamental part of the curriculum. Modern Hebrew taught in Years 7, 8 and 9 and students have the option to study biblical Hebrew as well as textual Jewish learning. Three religious study options for sixth formers: A level RE with Judaism and ethics; preparation for Jewish life and an intensive textual course (some pupils go on to study at yeshiva and seminary). Secular A level options include sociology, theatre studies, PE, maths and psychology.

Lively, relaxed engaged teaching and excellent teacher-pupil relationship. Head interviews again and again if applicants don't meet his (high) standards. Once appointed, teachers (half of whom are not Jewish) tend to stay. 'There are some very, very good teachers,' said one parent. Good and caring special needs provision (with two teaching assistants) for both physical and learning difficulties. Despite the upstairs-downstairs site, a specially adapted lift makes all things possible. Outstanding specialised support and individual learning plans.

Games, Options, the Arts: Art particularly vibrant, with good numbers going on to places at leading art schools and art rooms packed in lunch hours with pupils polishing their portfolios. Music part of the core curriculum but only a handful take it at GCSE. Head, aiming to up the numbers, firing up potential young talent with an American band and subsided music lessons. Three concerts a year, two drama productions.

Not a school where parents prioritise sport – 'We had our biggest attendance at sports day ever – ' says the head wryly, 'it rose to double figures,' and high-level competition certainly not part of the creed. Head, however, wants pupils to reach a decent level in all their hobbies 'to improve their quality of recreation'. The sport on offer has improved in recent years with a keen young staff who, in 2008, arranged 250 fixtures. Football played with enthusiasm and success, good showing in basketball. Boys offered football, basketball, tennis, athletics, cricket, badminton and trampolining, girls football, netball, rounders, tennis and dance (very strong). Adequate rather than inspiring facilities: prettily positioned running track, well-used tennis courts.

A strong and enthusiastic following for debating. Teachers contractually bound to help out with the extra-curricular and school trips definitely a strength. The whole of Year 9 to Israel, the entire Year 12 to Poland. 'The four-week trip to Israel is a real bonding experience. It creates friendships for life,' says one parent.

Background and Atmosphere: Founded in 1991 by the then Chief Rabbi, Immanuel Jacobovits, who wanted to establish a religious school to rival some of north London's most famous academic names. The core of the building is a magnificent turreted Victorian pile (formerly a convent school) described by Pevsner as sitting atop its 11 acres of Hertfordshire green belt like a 'Harrogate Hotel'. The original high-ceilinged rooms with their elaborate plasterwork are still in use for art classes and classrooms. Plenty of later additions. This, however, is not some pristine show home, rather a comfortably shambolic family house.

Unlike some of its Orthodox state school competitors, it has a more modern approach to the faith – 'We study contemporary literature and a range of religions'. Not as academically competitive as the private schools it was set up to rival, it provides a more intimate and nurturing atmosphere. No bar and bat mitzvah programme at the moment but under consideration. Programme of social action in Jewish and wider community a high priority. 'We could do much better,' says the head modestly, but the list of charities funded seems long and all-encompassing. Friendly and encouraging community in a protected and protective environment. 'Because of the size, it has a real family feel,' said one parent. Head aims to turn out 'young people who are kind and confident, know themselves and help others. They understand where they are going, have a loyalty to being Jewish and a relationship with their faith that is going to continue'. Food is kosher, healthy, appetising. Staff share pupils' dining room, which offers a calm and orderly place for all to sit, eat and enjoy civilised conversation.

Pastoral Care and Discipline: Pastoral care very fine tuned. Head of year plus four tutors in Year 7, designated pastoral leaders in Years 8 and 9. Deputy heads constantly available to pupils and parents (as, indeed, is the head). Prefects are self-selected – those who are keen to take on responsibility apply for the post and are interviewed. Once appointed, they play a large part in the life of the school, helping younger pupils to read Hebrew, organising social events and charity fairs. Prayer is a fundamental part of the ethos. Years 7–11 have compulsory prayers every morning before class. For sixth formers, prayer is primarily voluntary, though compulsory before the major festivals.

Not a school where discipline is a significant issue – 'The worst problem here is that pupils talk too much,' jokes the head. Certainly no serious concerns about drugs: 'We have a programme of education – we'd be mad not to – but it's a day school and it's common sense for pupils not to put themselves in a position of vulnerability'. Some after-school detention but it's not prominent – 'Teachers are very good at classroom management'. Inconsiderate car parking by sixth formers tends to irritate the locals.

Pupils and Parents: Applicants must be Chalachic Jews, as defined by the Chief Rabbi's office, but after that the school takes in the full spectrum, from the seriously observant to those who don't attend synagogue but have an attachment to the Jewish way of life. Particularly popular with Sephardic Jews. Pupils tend to be articulate and creative – 'They're nice, decent kids, not too cool or street smart,' said one observer; parents affluent professionals from a broad sweep of north London and Hertfordshire. Coaches bring them in from near (Bushey and Pinner) and far (Hampstead Garden Suburb, St John's Wood.) Coaches at 4.15 and 5.45pm – pupil groupings at school often divide into coach-journey buddies.

Entrance: Selective entry but not overly so. Head aims to take those 'who can pass GCSE at grade C or above. We're looking for someone eager to learn, excited by being on the planet. We want someone curious, rather than just academic'. Small intake into the sixth form.

Exit: Good preparation for universities – series of seminars after AS, plus tailored individual advice. On our visit a sixth former was searching through university courses with the deputy head and being warned about how courses might suddenly disappear – 'No stone is left unturned. We find courses that suit pupils' strengths'. Also prepares students for any additional tests required for degrees such as medicine or law. Generally a handful to Oxbridge, otherwise to Nottingham, Birmingham, Leeds, Manchester, universities with a large Jewish centre. Many do their gap year in Israel.

Money Matters: Not a rich or well-endowed school. Some symbolic scholarships, but most extra money used to help those who have hit rocky times. Entrance exhibitions in art and music of up to £2000 a year. Some scholarships of up to half the fees.

Remarks: Produces confident and well-qualified young people with a deep understanding of their faith.

Impington Village College

New Road, Impington, Cambridge, Cambridgeshire, CB24 9LX

• Pupils: 1,370 boys and girls, all day but provision made for far-travelled pupils to be put up locally • Ages: 11-19 • Size of sixth form: 280 • Non-denom • State

Tel: 01223 200 400
Fax: 01223 200 419
Email: office@impington.cambs.sch.uk
Website: www.impington.cambs.sch.uk

Principal: Since 2007, Mr Robert Campbell BA PGCE MPhil (early forties). Married with three school age children (two at the College themselves). This English graduate, who has quickly climbed the educational ladder and already has a previous headship under his belt, is seriously conscientious and totally wedded to the job. Proactive, direct and thoughtful, he's a great believer in inclusivity and is good at promoting IVC (Impington Village College). Acronym speak occasionally pops up, but as his vocation is to be active within the school, he doesn't sit on committees or live behind a desk – currently teaching GCSE English. Interests include fiction, history and music – he plays the guitar and clarinet. Also an international orienteer who has represented England and hopes to do so again. On top of all of this he often runs to school from Cambridge Station and joins staff in the weekly 'circuits' – at 7.20 am. As someone who has 'endeavoured to be everywhere for everybody', he must be, as one parent commented, 'Superman'. We rather agree.

Academic matters: A school with a split personality. Pre-sixth a happy, sound community comp where the ordered teaching environment lauds the bright and gives sensitive help to the less able. Comments from parents that some have learnt to be middle of the roaders are countered by the head. He assures us this is a thing of the past now there are two tutors per form. The learning tutor and assistant learning tutor stay with their charges all the way through, making under-achievement less likely.

At GCSE, a solid performance given the mixed intake – 64 per cent with five A*-Cs including English and maths in 2010. Students start key stage 4 in Year 9. Applied learning schemes for those in this year and above. Courses in catering, construction, life skills, hair and beauty – a salon on site. Has specialist language status – it provides a French teacher for local primaries and has a clutch of European teachers on the staff. All in Year 7 learn French and Spanish. Option of Spanish and Japanese at GCSE and Russian in the sixth. Greek, Italian, Latin and Chinese also on offer and some fast tracking for super linguists. At the other end of the scale, the sensible alternative of an international award which increases awareness of other cultures.

Now to the extraordinary sixth form where 75 per cent take the IB – introduced in 1991 – with most of the rest taking A levels in the arts. A bona fide international college with a well regarded head and students from 33 nations. 'The way international students raise expectations and level of competition is an eye opener for the home cohort,' commented one parent. Results at the top end are impressive – typically, over 90 per cent IB pass (international average is 79 per cent) and average points of 32, equivalent to three A grades.

'Hugely inclusive' place – a quarter have special needs. The spacious, purpose-built Pavilion provides a perfect base for SEN and treatment centre for those with physical difficulties. Where appropriate, designated lessons and/or in-class support. In addition, the school boasts an IDEAL unit which provides 25 places for young adults with moderate to severe learning needs, including those with Down's syndrome. Some of the 25 are from out of catchment – the rest LA referral. All join mainstream pastoral activities and, where appropriate, mainstream lessons. We were impressed with the positive interaction between some of the IB students and members of the unit.

Games, Options, the Arts: Verdict from the punters is that 'sport is brilliant' and appreciation for staff who not only put in extra time but are scrupulously fair when selecting teams is unanimous. College has a Sportsmark award and there's a fine choice of team and individual games at all levels. Pupils are encouraged to try everything and boys genuinely enjoy dance lessons in the sprung floor studio – an enthusiastic ex-pupil has returned to teach in the school which inspired him to dance. Games aren't compulsory in the sixth and enthusiasm for team sports found lower down the school seems to fizzle out.

Performing arts are particularly strong and a composer, fine artist and professional dancer are in residence. Impressive drama. Excellent and often challenging performances – not many places where you'd find a production of Spring Awakening (of the German expressionist genre) put on by Year 11 GCSE students playing to a full house. Workshops run by external talent, ballet classes before school and a post 16 School of Performance.

Introduction of two-weekly timetable has given more time for extra-curricular activities. Lots of clubs including an active Amnesty International group. D of E is popular (several gold awards each year) with the IB requirement of 150 hours of community service readily accommodated. Many trips overseas and international exchanges – a Year 11 student recently gained a scholarship to spend five months in Japan.

Background and Atmosphere: On the outskirts of Cambridge, the college was founded in 1939 under a scheme (devised by Cambridgeshire's education secretary Henry Morris) where rural England was to be provided with educational and social centres serving all ages – college continues to offer adult education and maintains a sports centre open 364 days a year from 6am to 10pm. Walter Gropius, of Bauhaus fame, designed the main building which, although jaded on the outside, still makes an interesting architectural statement, particularly in the curved wing where the head has his office. Large entrance hall serves as the 'prom' where younger children congregate and happily chatter. Newer buildings radiate across the ample site.

Good facilities including indoor pool, new and impressive sports centre with first-rate gym and sauna, library with a sound proofed sixth form area, a history department set around clusters of computers and an editing suite with top notch equipment. Children are well behaved and appear pleasantly relaxed in this straight forward, well tended environment. Jolly touches give a lift to otherwise bland spaces – cronky metallic structures donated by a local sculptor and bright graphic images in the Year 7 eating area. Improved, healthier food and cheery canteen. A shame children have to buy water and relatively little space for eating at tables – but giant leap into the 21st century with 'Vericool' (note the creepy name): a finger print recognition system which has effectively cut queues at tills and signing in points. Orwell and '1984' come to mind, but pupils predictably think it's 'cool'.

Sixth, who don't wear a uniform, have their own building with a buzzy, welcoming common room. New mezzanine floor hasn't done much to alleviate crowding and the head hopes for a new centre to accommodate ever increasing numbers. Community spirit is strong and charitable events abound – a project to raise money for children in Ghana has already given some the opportunity to go to school. Students have also been to Bangalore to help the street children.

Pastoral Care and Discipline: Caring, friendly atmosphere predominates, and true to its egalitarian principles, no prefects – very Impington. All have access to a male or female counsellor – a great help with stress and all sorts of problems. Bullying isn't swept under the carpet but dealt with straight away – as one pupil commented, 'This is a big school and we are children'. Students and a teacher recently refined the behaviour policy and volunteers are involved with a mentoring scheme. Highly rated community support officer, employed by the school, is based in the college – 'He's an excellent rôle model, up to mischief in and out of school, and works with the child, their family and the college, and every school should have one,' enthused the head. 'Absolutely brilliant,' commented one mum.

Pupils really feel they have a voice. Large, unelected and active student council, co-ordinated by a member of staff, is open to all. Head believes in being firm but fair and developing pupils' sense of responsibility towards the college. Occasional permanent exclusions. All cases are looked at individually and support is given to students and families, but the policy re banned substances is clear – permanent exclusion for dealing or exclusion for possession including alcohol.

Pupils and Parents: Parents of 11–16 year olds range from Cambridge academics to the seriously underprivileged. In the sixth form, pupils come from all over. Some are local whilst others are from a range of countries – mostly in the EU. International students and those from outside Cambridgeshire are housed (carefully) with local host families. Sixth formers we met (of several nationalities) were delightfully open, mature and self motivated. 'The work is extremely challenging and we have to work hard, but the atmosphere in this school is so good that I really regret having holidays. It is just a wonderful school.' Praise indeed from someone who's come from abroad.

Entrance: At 11 from local primaries in catchment. Oversubscribed but appeals often succeed, boosting class sizes above the target level of 28 (20 in the sixth).

Four distinct courses in the sixth. For the selective IB, pupils need to be well motivated and have an average B grade profile at GCSE; according to a sixth former, if students don't work that's their problem – they'll sink. For A levels – mostly arts based – normally five Cs or better. For the School of Performance, which provides a vocational training for those planning a career in dance, theatre or music, academic qualifications aren't an issue, but students are informally auditioned and are likely to take one or two A/AS levels. Special post-16 one-to-one course for those with severe learning difficulties.

Exit: At 16 about two thirds to local colleges (Hills Road, Long Road etc) for wider range of A levels and vocational qualifications. 87 per cent of sixth formers to university; destinations are a wonderfully eclectic mix – last year included University of Rome (medicine), LMO Munich (pure economics), University of Plymouth (sports management), Sussex (psychology), University of Tu, Delft (aeronautical engineering), Northern Contemporary Dance (dance degree), Bristol (architecture and planning). Quite a few gap years and deferred entries.

Money Matters: No fees unless non EU families re locate to the area. Entitlement to free education – or assistance – is determined by the visa status of parents.

Remarks: An exciting, forward looking place which has much to offer all sorts. Energetic head looks set to make pre sixth equal to the sixth form, where the international cohort makes IVC exceptional within the state system.

International College, Sherborne School

Newell Grange, Sherborne, Dorset, DT9 4EZ

• Pupils: 135 pupils: 50 girls, 85 boys. All board. • Ages: 11-17
• Non-denom • Fees: £31,500 pa • Independent

Tel: 01935 814 743
Fax: 01935 816 863
Email: reception@sherborne-ic.net
Website: www.sherborne-ic.net

Principal: Since 1997, Dr Christopher Greenfield MA MEd EdD (late-fifties). Previously worked for the Quakers in the Middle East for four years, then became head of Sidcot (Quaker) School for 11 years. Currently chair of the Joseph Rowntree Reform Trust, which is funded from the legacies of the Quaker chocolate entrepreneurs and social reformers. The ideal man for the job, he describes his work as 'doing my small part for increasing global peace and understanding'. Dr Greenfield is away from the school a fair bit, taking less part in the day-to-day running of the school than most heads. An active politician, he has stood as a Liberal Democrat candidate four times. Slightly less starry-eyed than when we last met him, but still proud that the school is providing a sound education to many countries' future leaders. Married to Gill, their two children attended Sidcot School. The college is owned by Sherborne School.

Entrance: At ages 11 through 16. First come first served. No entry test but (translated) school reports checked to screen out bad apples. Pupils' academic abilities and knowledge of the English language vary widely. Students entering the one-year intensive GCSE programme need to have at least Lower Intermediate Level English (equivalent to IELTS score of 4+). It may well be that those coming with minimal English are better suited to the programmes here than those whose English is fairly sophisticated. School also runs a highly successful and flexible summer (and Easter) course that caters for some 300 pupils.

Exit: To wide range of mostly well-known independent schools – an impressive list, given the broad intake. The 'future schooling adviser' is devoted to slotting pupils into good schools when they leave International College – each pupil visits up to three schools, which some feel is too few, and is groomed for interviews. A chunk end up going to the main Sherborne School, the odd Einstein to Eton or Winchester, several to top schools like Sevenoaks, Harrow and Charterhouse, but quite a few to Hurtwood House, hardly a traditional British boarding school, and even – gasp – Bellerbys.

Remarks: The original and the best. Founded in 1977, the college was the brainchild of Robert Macnaghten, then head of Sherborne School, who was frustrated with having to turn down applications from non-English-speaking boys. National origins of the student body have always reflected international economic and political trends. Started off with three Iranian boys – a sign of the times in the late '70s. Later became dominated by pupils from the Far East. Now numbers from the former Soviet Union have rocketed: pupils not only from Russia, but also from Ukraine, Azerbaijan, Georgia, Uzbekistan, Kazakhstan ... The school could host its own Eurovision Song Contest. Indeed, the biggest change in the school since we last visited is the increased number of nationalities represented. The college keeps a low profile in the UK, but is promoted by 250 agents overseas, plus plenty of personal recommendations.

Very close academic supervision with mini-reports on each pupil every three weeks, though some feel the supervision is rather programmatic and inflexible and not too tailored to the individual. Excellent teachers all trained in EFL as well as their subject of instruction. Most pupils stay for one year, preparing for CE or GCSEs, but the college offers a two-year GCSE course (along with a more demanding 'express' course – essentially a one-year crammer for older children, some of whom may have covered much of the material already and just need to nail down some exams and spruce up their English). Unsurprisingly, the subjects studied lean towards maths and sciences, where language ability is less crucial. Class sizes tiny: up to eight for the main academic subjects and for options like art or IT. Last year, 85 per cent of the pupils on the GCSE courses earned 5 A–C grades (results in English were particularly impressive) – a super achievement considering the linguistic hurdles.

A mixture of handsome stone farm dwellings and sympathetically designed purpose-built school blocks close to the centre of town and Sherborne School. Strong feeling of industry and purpose – parents are not coughing up this kind of money for their children to have a holiday. 25 small classrooms, a small library, computer room, eight science labs, playing fields and basketball courts. Much of the school could benefit from improved ventilation – a bit of fresh air would do wonders. Plenty of sport available using Sherborne's superb facilities (but no rugby) and a surprising number of matches are organised against other schools. Music particularly well-provided-for with concerts and good tuition. The most talented can join the main Sherborne School orchestra. Lovely canteen with piles of fresh fruit, plus evening snacks available in the boarding houses.

Friendly atmosphere with boys playing basketball in the sun and girls chatting in small groups when we arrived at break time. Technically, pupils allowed to speak in their home language only after prep in the evenings and at the weekends, but this is impossible to enforce. Boarding facilities much better than at most boarding schools. Older boys live on site in single or double rooms. Girls, and younger boys, board a three-minute minibus journey away in the very lovely Westcott House, a converted Georgian residence (they are bussed to and from school). 11–13 year old boys live in their own wing of the house. A few pupils are sometimes housed with local families in sets of two. Pupils age 13 and over are allowed to wander freely in town (must sign out and wear school uniform) and can be found hovering in newsagents and over the sushi display in Sainsburys. An education in itself, and lovely Sherborne is an ideal town in which to wander. Much emphasis on instilling British manners, culture etc alongside learning the language. Little in the way of SEN provision – these kids have enough on their plate without adding learning disabilities to the mix – though currently one pupil with mild dyslexia.

Not cheap: £30,000+ for one year – costs more than a year at Harvard. But you get what you pay for. Just don't expect the college to turn your disaffected son into a scholar. Schools that have accepted International College pupils tell us that they find their levels of English and general academic ability do vary widely. The college follows the pupils' fortunes after leaving and while many go on to earn three As at A level or stellar IB scores, others are earning mostly Cs and Ds. And do be clear what exactly you are signing up for and just what your obligations are if you take your child away early. Former pupils: King Mswati III of Swaziland, Crown Prince Tamin of Qatar, Princess Marie-Gabrielle of Luxembourg.

International School of Aberdeen

Linked to International School of Aberdeen, Preschool and Elementary in the Junior section

Pitfodels House, North Deeside Road, Pitfodels, Cults, Aberdeen, AB15 9PN

• Pupils: High school (15-18) 110; middle school (12-14) 95; elementary (5-11) 170; 40 in pre-school (3-4). Variable ratio boy/girl • Ages: 3-18
• Fees: £16,205-£18,145 + £2000 capital fee pa • Independent

Tel: 01224 730 300
Fax: 01224 865 558
Email: admin@isa.aberdeen.sch.uk
Website: www.isa.aberdeen.sch.uk

Head: Since 2002, Dr Daniel Hovde PhD (forties), who came to the granite city from the jungles of Sumatra, where he was head of an International Services contract school, contracted to Chevron. Before that he taught in the Canadian Academy in Japan, which was founded as a missionary school in 1913 and was home to some 35 different nationalities. Dr Hovde, who is married to Karol, a counsellor with the school (they adopted their daughter in China whilst in the far east), was educated in Seattle, studying history, social studies and majoring in education from Washington State University, followed by a master's in education and a doctorate in educational leadership – 'It seemed to take forever'. He taught in between his lengthy education and was pleased to come to Aberdeen, as it was 'the right size and make-up for himself and his wife and good for the daughter'. They could 'all work in the same place'. Delightful, outgoing and friendly, he runs the school with a pair of principals and positively bounced this editor round the school.

Academic matters: School nominally follows the IB, but they also cover High School Diplomas. Those pupils who only do the IB diploma average 33 credits (24 is pass). Pupils get advanced credit for having taken the IB, but it is by no means suitable or even needed by all. Some standard grades taken 'for curiosity benchmark'. Fair mish-mash. Massive amount of to-ing and fro-ing, over 35 nationalities are represented in the student population, 32 different languages spoken, most pupils come for two or three years, some only for one, and 'odd much beyond five'. Pupils go on the roll of honour (spelled, of course, 'honor') society if they have done well in the realms of academe, leadership and service. All very American and fairly in your face.

Sixty per cent of all staff are British 'local' hire, with husbands in oil, or 'just living here', and 40 per cent have a mixture of backgrounds, from English-speaking countries in the main, though native speakers employed for Spanish and French (the two languages offered for IB) and Dutch. School appears to run as a commune with 'no heads of departments', and two counsellors – whilst senior pupils seek advice from staff, younger pupils are ambivalent about whether they go to a teacher or an older pupil ('natural helpers') for help.

EAL where necessary, and three dedicated teachers. Roughly 30 pupils in each year group, 13/20 per class. Choices accelerated, and learning support available – two dedicated members of staff. School is brutally honest – if pupils need more than 20 per cent support per week, then they will have to go elsewhere, i.e. local mainstream. Three dedicated computer labs, and flat-screened computers in the class rooms, a fully networked library/media centre, science labs, language lab equipment in language classrooms, home economics also in a classroom ('A cooker and a sink in the corner' – sorry, chaps – we missed it).

Games, Options, the Arts: Stunning sports hall housing a double gymnasium, fitness centre and multi-purpose spaces; trad games football and golf (which they also play internationally and in the Scottish league) plus basketball and volleyball. Teams visit London, Stavanger, Spain and Portugal, as well as running their own internal league. Cabinets of shining silver.

No orchestras, but number of instruments taught, ditto choirs – pupils make music outside school. Rather clever computer programme which goes red when you hit the wrong note – deeply popular. Fine new arts centre offering a 300-seat theatre, drama, vocal and instrumental music areas. History of lavish drama. School has a high charity presence – sleepovers for the homeless, shoe-box appeal and the eight year olds visit local 'rest' homes and read and perform to them. American boy scouts, cub scouts, girl guides and brownies but no D of E.

Background and Atmosphere: School founded in 1972 by Mr McCormick, and bought by the oil companies in 1980. They own the buildings (and undertake all the improvements – wish lists et al), leasing them to the school for a peppercorn. The school is run by a charitable trust, with the members of the board being appointed in proportion to the number of employees' children in the school at one particular moment. A local solicitor sees fair play.

School owns six, fairly cramped, acres on the north of the Dee, with an almost-impossible-to-see sign tucked away up the drive at a rotten angle – perhaps it might be more visible were one to drive on the right? (Prospectus details 9.5 acres of land, school secretariat appears to plump for five, including an acre bought last year – looks more like nine or so.) Huge spaces, huge magically filled classrooms, wide passages. Pupil pictures abound, so not that soulless.

Pupils eat by year group in the dining room – choice of healthy option, main meal, veggie meal (pretty pathetic – mini waffles and spaghetti hoops; come in, Jamie Oliver) or panini and pud. Menu for whole week, and really pretty expensive. Not quite the overflowing library one might expect, but humming with more computers and boasting a book hospital. All pupils have lockers, decorated in rather uninspired wrapping paper on their birthdays. Lots of singing of 'Happy Birthday' at lunch. Much talk of how super Scotland is, and a certain amount of Celtic indulgence. Trips all over the shop. Tinies have dedicated play area outside with squidgy tar.

Pastoral Care and Discipline: Head anxious to dispel the myth of spoilt little rich boy – keen PSE and strong RME. Guidance by clans or houses. Staff are trained in different cultures and dealing with people in a different fashion. No overt bullying – more 'teasing because of personality traits'. Drug presentation evenings, and head has 'on occasion' disciplined and suspended (never expelled) miscreants for a day or two – details of all suspendable offences in handbooks complete with list of drug test cut-off levels. Head keen on independent study and motivation and no gum may be chewed in school.

Pupils and Parents: No school uniform, but of course everyone conforms. Most students arrive via school bus. Good contact via weekly newsletters.

Entrance: Whenever.

Exit: Universities in America and Britain the most popular.

Money Matters: Fees paid by oil companies, otherwise one or two non-oil American expats. Bursaries and financial aid available so that school more reflects the cost of a 'normal' British school. IB academic scholarships available for final two years.

Remarks: Smashing school – an eye-opener, and totally logical, of course, to follow an international programme but, with such an influx of non-native teachers, it might be possible for a family to be billeted in Scotland for a year or so and experience no native culture at all.

International School of London

Linked to International School Of London in the Junior section

139 Gunnersbury Avenue, London, W3 8LG

• Pupils: 345 boys and girls • Ages: 3-18 ECP and primary 145, secondary 150, sixth form 50 • Size of sixth form: 30 boys, 25 girls • Non-denom • Fees: £17,500-£19,750 pa • Independent

Tel: 020 8992 5823
Fax: 020 8993 7012
Email: mail@ISLondon.com
Website: www.ISLondon.com

Director: Since 2009, Mr Huw Davies MA PGCE. He has extensive experience as a former deputy head, IB Diploma coordinator and higher education advisor, as well as being involved in governorship of a number of schools in London. He has worked as a member of IB authorisation teams visiting prospective Diploma schools in the UK. He has also been on the board of directors of two London theatres – the Lyric, Hammersmith and the Riverside Studios. His key priorities for pupils at the school are learning, achievement, wellbeing and the promotion of international understanding.

Academic matters: School has followed the IB programme since 1976. It has been offering the PYP and the MYP since 2002. Accredited by Council of Schools (CIS) and International Baccalaureate Organisation (IBO). Member of European Council of School (ECIS) and London International Schools Association.

The IB is well and truly up and running with 90 per cent getting the diploma in 2010 (100 per cent 2002, 94 per cent 2005 and 80 per cent 2006). Students can take almost any foreign language in their IB syllabus. Homework important with diaries for parents to monitor. Diploma students get up to 15 hours a week. Parent/teacher interviews in the autumn and spring terms, but assessment is continuous and is well defined in the fully comprehensive parents' and students' handbook. Communication with home is supposedly good, but one comment was, 'I wish they were as transparent as schools are in my country – they don't keep us properly informed'. That having been said, the communications tools are worthy of note – a good admissions booklet, a comprehensive guide to the IB diploma and an excellent website.

Approximately 75 teachers, of whom 39 are full-time. The majority of the part-timers are, not surprisingly, language teachers. Very low turnover in recent years. One computer room with 100+ laptops. Smartboards in all classrooms. Small classes, never larger than 20.

Two learning support teachers for children with special needs. The school is not keen on taking children with an already identified problem; however, if the problem becomes apparent as the child progresses through the school, they will provide the necessary support. No statemented children. Mother tongue lessons available for all pupils if wanted, and only at extra cost (£600 a term) if fewer than five children studying a particular language. EFL and EAL always available, in fact essentially so, as only about 15 per cent pupils are purely English-speaking, though several do have one English-speaking parent.

English is the language of the classroom and the playground, so 'depending on their age, students are placed in an appropriate group to acquire fluency as quickly as possible'. By the last two years, the Diploma work is too rigorous for anything but complete fluency, so no question of sketchy English slowing down the rest of the class.

Games, Options, the Arts: PE part of the curriculum. Football and basketball played competitively against other international schools and in tournaments home and abroad. Several cups proudly displayed in the school corridor. Swimming at Brentford Leisure Centre weekly for Years 1–6. Other sports such as yoga, karate, fencing available. Tennis and athletics in Gunnersbury Park as well as football, volleyball and basketball. Lucky it's so close by, as the school's concrete playground is not quite so encouraging. Sports day fun for all once a year.

Music timetabled to Year 10. Probably about 45 per cent of school learn an instrument but no school band. Drama presented on school stage. Last year a Year 11 group called themselves 'Rough and Ready Theatre Productions' and entertained with their own version of *Macbeth.* Lots of trips here, there and everywhere – educational, sporting, historical, bonding, foreign or local, you name it. Participation in the Model United Nations conference (last year in St Petersburg) a fantastic opportunity for the IB diploma students. As seems to happen in all aspects of this school, students see interest and opportunities in each other's cultures: the presence of four Icelandic students inspired the idea of possibly taking the annual ski trip to Iceland.

Background and Atmosphere: The school was founded in Camden in 1972. In the late 1980s it merged with the Catholic school which stood on the present site. It is a not particularly attractive redbrick building, situated on the busy North Circular road with cars and lorries zooming noisily past the front entrance. However pupils can be bused door to door (£800 per term) and, once behind the iron barriers, they can't escape.

The atmosphere is informal and friendly. Loads of bright colour in the infant section, where each classroom belongs to one year group. These younger pupils are in a separate building, called the Annexe, apart from Years 5 and 6, who have their own section in the main school, which gives them a foretaste of hustle and bustle and makes the transition from PY to MY easier.

A warren of corridors in the rest of the school with specific subject classrooms on either side. Lockers in several different locations and loo-paper-strewn cloakrooms. The top floor dedicated to lots of language rooms with the relevant name on each door. Good science labs and a great two tiered artroom full of original creations and extraordinary remains of past projects. Some recent expansion and re-organisation of buildings with more planned. Small dining room which, according to our guide, a bright Swiss IB Diploma student planning to study medicine in London, provides delicious home cooked meals representing several different nationalities. A very happy feel to the school – polite 'hellos' wherever we went, even when we put our heads into the senior commonroom. Lessons looked as if they were serious but fun, and the only seemingly inattentive child suddenly came to life and responded to a teacher's question quickly and accurately.

Pastoral Care and Discipline: Parents' and students' handbook lists strict rules (full of commonsense) which must be adhered to. Mobile phones allowed but must not be used without permission. No serious bullying problems but counselling available if needed. Seems to be an openly discussed subject and pupils appear to be supportive of each other. Zero drug tolerance. No uniform, except for sportswear, but a reasonable dress policy. Sensible 'code of expectations' for both parents and students.

Easy transition at all stages is part of the school strategy and it seems to work. As the majority of pupils move on after two to three years, the school tries to make the process easy. The fact that few barriers to newcomers here seems to speed up the settling in process.

Pupils and Parents: An amazing mixture with 51 different nationalities represented and 90 per cent expats. Mainly corporate families used to moving around. At the time of our visit 13 per cent Italian, ten per cent French, six per cent Japanese and six per cent Dutch, but that can change according to the economic climate. Of the rest, about ten per cent are American or English, with smatterings from Spain, Kazakhstan and Saudi Arabia, to mention but a few. Children and parents may come from all over the world, but that does not stop them from mixing together and getting to know each other's cultures. In fact that and small classes seem to create cohesiveness rather than cliquiness.

Friendship is big in the school's ethos. Even parents are catered for by a zippy PTA, which provides them with lots of getting-to-know-each other activities, including expeditions and multi-national cookery demonstrations. New parents are contacted by someone who speaks the same language who will give them all the help they need to ensure an easy move. The monthly newsletter, taken home by everyone, tells of past and future events concerning pupils and parents and acts as a voice for the school and the PTA.

Entrance: From all over. Need previous school records and interview. Because of the fluid nature of the school normally 'always room for one more'. Ability to speak English not necessary up to the age of 15. After that, unless circumstances are particularly unusual, a non-English speaking child probably won't be accepted. All those already there will be fluent enough. Main intake in September and January but can join at other times of the year if necessary.

Exit: Mostly to university anywhere in the world. Some stay in England after their parents have left. Others take SATs here (recognised testing centre) and head for America. Aside from European universities, destinations include Oxbridge, Manchester and Imperial in the UK and Boston, Chicago, Michigan and Vassar in the US. Strong science bias.

Money Matters: No scholarships as such as most pupils have corporate allowances, but school will keep a child in extremis if a disaster occurs – 'We don't want a child to leave because of money'.

Remarks: The most cosmopolitan group of children and teachers we know – very good training for the United Nations. Global issues do not seem to affect them at all. Yet despite all that, and its modern soulless shell, this feels reassuringly like a typical, small, English independent school. The solid IB programme allows easy transition from anywhere to anywhere.

Ipswich High School

Linked to Ipswich High Junior School in the Junior section

Woolverstone, Ipswich, Suffolk, IP9 1AZ

• Pupils: 415 girls • Ages: 11-18 • Size of sixth form: 75 • Non-denom
• Fees: £9,627 pa • Independent

Tel: 01473 780 201
Fax: 01473 780 985
Email: admissions@ihs.gdst.net
Website: www.ipswichhighschool.co.uk

Head: Since 2006, Ms Elaine Purves BA PGCE (early forties). Read English and German at Hull. Previously deputy head at Royal High School Bath. Married with two young children. Delightfully breezy and determined on issues of gender and marketing – not a feminist but an egalitarian who is proud of her maiden name and wants to demonstrate that identities can be maintained within an established order. Clearly a devotee of the GDST – absolutely no hint that boys in the sixth are an option. Instead she's overseen improvements in sixth form facilities and introduced new blood into the staff room. All her time outside school is for the family.

Academic matters: Continues to maintain its position as top academic school in the county – and value added is well above average. 80 per cent A/A* at GCSE. Combined science at GCSE plus the popular, recently introduced sports science. Relatively narrow selection of mainly academic subjects at A level but what they do they do well – 88 per cent A*–B.

Keen learners and high expectations – parents are impressed that best practice starts from day one. Generally traditional, not unduly pressured approach. Problems are spotted quickly and plenty of support, especially in maths, where groups are small. In the sixth form help is there if needed, but 'We're encouraged to be responsible. It's good preparation for uni – if you don't get on with your work it's your loss'.

SEN provision isn't a feature but 'children with learning impairments aren't disbarred – they need to show potential or be of above average intelligence'. A 'lady' (that speaks volumes) comes in one day a week to provide support in English and develop study skills, whilst maths support is given at lunchtime by a member of the maths department.

Games, Options, the Arts: Usual three for girls, with county champions at several levels. Some sixth formers say they would like more than the single lesson of PE a week but, 'If a kid is good at sport and is selected for a team they have a good time'. Fine facilities including a top notch sports hall and swimming pool which is open to the public. Lunchtime clubs for team players with fencing on offer plus the popular football club – a link with Ipswich Town FC, who provide a spot of training.

Over one third of the school have singing or instrumental tuition and annual concerts at Snape Maltings are 'fantastic'. Drama is strong and popular – the department has a generous theatre. Parents enthuse over recent appointments and innovative approaches which have 'pushed standards to the highest levels'. Self contained, spacious art department with a dedicated sixth form area. Students can take A level critical and contextual studies or squeeze in an additional GCSE. Predominantly two dimensional work that's expressive and well informed.

Range of extra-curricular activities mainly at lunchtime. Bronze D of E has a good takeup but only a few take silver. Food studies was welcomed back onto the curriculum in 2009 with purpose built cookery rooms – taught to Years 7 and 8 as part of their core curriculum and available as an extra lunchtime or after-school club for all other year groups, and the sixth form as part of their co-curricular enrichment programme. Interesting development and one we will follow with interest to see if it is emulated elsewhere.

Background and Atmosphere: Founded in 1878, this GDST flag flier 'nurtures alpha females in a lovely way'. A fair ethos where manners and respect foster good relations between staff and pupils – a civilised and harmonious place. The idyllic out of town site, home to the school since 1992, provides something of an oasis away from the pressures of everyday life. Girls genuinely appreciate their surroundings and, despite those cutting easterlies, relish the freedom to roam over most of the 80 acres of parkland, with its grazing sheep and slopes on the edge of the Orwell. All the buildings, including the central hub, a Grade One, pedimented, be-urned Georgian pile, are well loved, and not a spot of litter to be seen. The same is true of the sixth form area at the top of the main house where students have their own work-station and laptop. They also have a comfortable common room with pool table and bistro kitchen kitted out with café style furniture, dishwasher, fridge and microwave – all very grown-up.

Lunch in the old orangery is a chatty affair, food is plentiful and healthy. Sixth use a separate dining area (rather dingy) which overlooks the grounds and River Orwell beyond, but each half term are invited to a meal in the smaller of the two libraries and are introduced to guests who share knowledge of the world of work. 'We're encouraged to meet new people and speak confidently,' said student. No uniform for the sixth – love it or loathe it cerise and grey for those lower down.

Pastoral Care and Discipline: No houses – inter-form competition instead and a tutorial system which is at the heart of effective pastoral care. Mentoring for Year 7s, who are befriended by a senior girl, plus societies and clubs where a healthy mix of year groups. Girls know who to seek out if the need arises whilst 'shrewd teachers see beyond the veneer'. Unobtrusive discipline with few serious problems. Theoretical zero tolerance of illegal substances has yet to be tested.

New initiatives are run past the girls and the head listens to their thoughts and ideas. Eco issues, driven by the pupils and a deputy, are high on the agenda – a 'blitz week' with the school monitoring its energy use and making an effort to keep consumption to a minimum alerted all and brought amazingly positive results. An organic vegetable plot, tended by the girls, is being developed and it's planned to provide cut flowers and produce for the canteen.

Pupils and Parents: Mostly local girls from a wide catchment with 60+ pick up points for coaches – the journey, lengthy for some, is seen as part of the school's social life. Families very mixed – strong professional contingent and quite a few in farming. Charmingly unaffected girls.

Entrance: At 11. Majority from the junior department. 35 or so from state or independent juniors. Entrance tests in English, maths and verbal reasoning – plus school report.

For the sixth – five GCSEs with B or above for AS subjects, except for maths where the requirement is A/A*.

Exit: After Year 11 some of the brainiest to the free alternative over the county divide. Post A level a few to Oxbridge with most of the rest to heavyweights – healthy spread of courses. No starry OGs but a good proportion are successful in many professions.

Money Matters: As one of the 26 schools of the Girls' Day School Trust, the fees represent excellent value. At 11 and 16 a few scholarships awarded on merit. Academic, art, music, drama and sports scholarships at 11 and 16 for up to a quarter of the fees. Means-tested bursaries, awarded on need and academic merit, up to full fees. Short term assistance available if needed.

Remarks: Definitely not a girly place but echoes of an august girls' boarding school, especially in its setting. Highly desirable for the down to earth academic.

Ipswich School

Linked to Ipswich Preparatory School in the Junior section

Henley Road, Ipswich, Suffolk, IP1 3SG

• Pupils: 810; 515 boys, 295 girls; includes 40 boarders. • Ages: 11-18
• Size of sixth form: 240 • C of E • Fees: Boarding £16,623-£20,262; Day £10,254-£11,241 pa • Independent

Tel: 01473 408 300
Fax: 01473 400 058
Email: registrar@ipswich.suffolk.sch.uk
Website: www.ipswich.suffolk.sch.uk

Headmaster: Since September 2010, Mr Nicholas Weaver BA (late thirties), previously deputy head (academic) of The Portsmouth Grammar School. He read engineering at Cambridge and is married with three young children.

Academic matters: Children are encouraged – and, according to parents, pushed – as far as they can go. Fast tracking for the super brainy and in some cases additional lessons before school. Around 67 per cent A/A* at GCSE. IGCSE maths for all, with a fair range of options including Russian and dual or separate sciences. They're after results in the sixth and students know what's at stake if they don't do their stuff. 'No' to the Bac because 'we do the Ipswich Bac – there's a similar balance with four ASs plus our compulsory enrichment programme'. And 'they really pile it on,' said one mum. Lure of the Essex grammars has been countered with a broader A level curriculum which now includes Russian, Spanish and some 'softer' subjects – results have recently leapt to 80 per cent A/B.

All Year 7 entrants are tested for SEN – two part-time learning support teachers; only mild needs accommodated. Support in the form of one lesson a week focuses on either organisational skills, learning difficulties or English for overseas students.

Games, Options, the Arts: Sport with a big 'S' – they're on a mission to compete and win. Being part of a team is important and members are expected to put in huge amounts of time and effort – a general understanding that commitments have to be balanced, although one parent commented that the less than robust can get steam rollered. Major three sports for boys with hockey – with top coaches to hone skills even further – being the one parents justifiably crow about. Girls' sport is beginning to get its act together and catching up fast. Cross-country, sailing in the summer and fives also on offer. Modern sports hall, immaculate cricket pitch at the heart of the school, indoor nets and 35 acres of sports fields near by – dreams of a new, all-in-one sports centre.

They say music – a third take individual lessons – and drama, now offered at GCSE, are on a par with sport. Two theatres, one seating up to 400, and resident wardrobe mistress. Thoroughly impressive 1999 design technology centre with multimedia workshops and burstingly keen head of department. Observational skills are developed early on and art work, both 2D and 3D, is well executed – it's worth having a peek at the school calendar crammed with lively examples.

Older ones have activities on a Thursday afternoon – options include the high profile CCF and community service. D of E also features with about 10 taking gold every year. Long list of clubs and societies – journalism, photography, robotics ...

Background and Atmosphere: Although an ancient foundation (possibly 14th century), has only been on its present site in a leafy residential area of Ipswich since the 1850s. The main building, a mock Jacobean extravaganza, adjoins newer blocks which work well together. Neatly designed heated 'loggia' with picnic tables for middle school relaxation. Sixth, in their converted house, socialise in a rather cramped area but have a general factotum on hand to keep the place in a civilised state. Charming chapel and stunning library – an unusually inviting space where students enjoy the calm working atmosphere – with four John Piper stained glass windows depicting the seasons. All is carefully tended. Manicured flower beds plus imaginative architectural adornments lift the place way beyond the merely functional – altogether a very pleasant environment.

Conventional, somewhat subdued atmosphere. Parents speak of the way the the ethos is set without heavy-handed policing – it just seems to run like clockwork. Plenty of tie tightening and shirt tucking before crossing the threshold in the morning. What a shame that the only pupils we were allowed to engage with (fleetingly) were the chaperoned head boy and girl – charmingly polite but clearly constrained.

Pastoral Care and Discipline: House and year group tutorial system with the chaplain and school matron seen as important pastoral cogs; pupils are encouraged to think about others and their feelings. Children are expected to be well organised – more swim or sink than hand holding – but all know who to approach for help, which can be very good. Definite expectation that rules will be followed – 'Rebels aren't tolerated' – and, to balance varying degrees of detention, a merit system for good behaviour. Good eggs are rewarded with a book token – reading is encouraged, e.g. the school produces an excellent booklet with reading lists for all tastes. Occasional serious transgressors are dealt with on an individual basis – 'We wave a big stick'.

Pupils and Parents: A mix of rural and urban, Essex and Suffolk, preps and primaries. Many farming families but also those who commute to London. Booklet with useful information and comprehensive coach service to help with transportation. 25+ overseas nationals, from Europe and the Pacific Rim, live with weekly and flexi boarders. Girls in the minority and are likely to remain so – ratio of less than 1:2 up to Year 11 but 1:1.5 in the sixth. Pupils appear relaxed and quietly purposeful.

Entrance: At 11 exam, report and 'chat' with the head. Large number from the prep – 'no surprise' policy ensures problems are flagged up in plenty of time. At 13 Common Entrance or the school's entrance exam. Outside entrants need to be of above average ability to cope – a fair amount of cherry picking; entrance is becoming increasingly competitive. (Occasionally parents have used the school – obviously not something it encourages – to get their children up to speed before sixth at the Essex grammars.) For the sixth, six GCSEs at C or above with Bs in the subjects to be taken at AS.

Exit: Wide range of courses and institutions. Respectable showing from the heavyweights with Oxbridge growing in prominence – a push in that direction with a special programme which includes a member of Cambridge University, who's also a governor, helping with the application process. Old Boys include Rider Haggard, Nobel laureate Sir Charles Sherrington and physicist, Sir Charles Frank. Also Edward Ardizzone and composer David Sawer.

Money Matters: Maximum and Queen's scholarships equivalent to half the fees. Some smaller awards made each year. On entry at 11 and 13, academic, music and art scholarships with sport at 11 and all rounder at 13. On entry at 16, academic, music, sport and all-rounder scholarships. Limited number of means-tested bursaries at 11,13 and 16.

Remarks: A tightly run, substantial school that's full to the brim – perfect for those who are prepared to have go but aren't looking to rock the boat.

Italia Conti Academy of Theatre Arts

23 Goswell Road, London, EC1M 7AJ

• Pupils: 20 boys and 80 girls; all day • Ages: 11-16 • Interdenominational • Fees: £10,635-£14,190 pa • Independent

Tel: 020 7608 0047
Fax: 02072 531 430
Email: admin@italiaconti.co.uk
Website: www.italia-conti.com

Head: Since 1975, Mr Clifford Vote. Educated at universities of New South Wales and London (economics, psychology and education). Previously taught in secondary schools in Australia. Affable Aussie with a more or less lifelong dedication to the school. Regular team member for Independent Schools Inspectorate and board member of the Council for Dance, Education and Training.

Academic matters: Theatre schools are not judged primarily by their academic results, but with generally upwards of 80 per cent of pupils getting 5+ A*–C grades at GCSE, the school performs creditably. Learning and behaviour, said the ISI, are 'overwhelmingly good or very good'. The school recognises that for its pupils the vocational parts of the day are the most important. 'They get academia more or less by default without realising. The fact that most of them get through eight GCSEs at an average of grade B is a huge achievement.'

Everyone takes English language and literature, maths, single science, drama, dance, history, French and art GCSE courses. Those 'who demonstrate a profound incompetence in a subject' may be allowed to drop it, and several from each class give up French, a few history or art. Maths is strong, science greatly improved, French rather weaker. 'Modern foreign languages depend on cumulative learning: because they spend so much time on vocational subjects, our children are more inclined to flit from topic to topic.'

Most teaching is mixed ability, though maths is mostly taught in ability groups from Year 8 upwards. 'Mixed ability in small classes harnesses the ability of children to learn from each other as well as from the teacher, which is a huge advantage for children who have problems with didactic forms of teaching.'

The academic entrance test is largely diagnostic: 'They cover the curriculum in half the time available to normal schools, so they must be reasonably bright'. They must also be willing to learn: 'In our small mixed ability classes a few children who weren't interested would have an appalling effect. They're training for a career that will offer them an extraordinary range of experiences: they don't have the right to circumvent their academic obligations.'

Limited SEN support, so can take few dyslexic children. 'We just don't have the space to accommodate more staff. And there is a huge amount of help available elsewhere; I would advise parents to spend their money on that rather than our fees.'

Games, Options, the Arts: Art is very successful, especially in view of its cramped space. The ISI praised its 'creativity, vitality and sense of industry', and nearly everyone who takes the GCSE gets a good grade. No sport – performance is the raison d'être here, and half of each school day is spent dancing, singing and acting. While some classes, clad in traditional blue school uniform, get down to maths coursework or studying the Second World War, others in leotards are rehearsing for a modern dance exam or putting together a performance. The skills, teamwork and dedication are outstanding. No theatre on site – in July the whole school decamps to Wimbledon for a week to mount 'a humdinger of a production' of variety performances, demonstrating a phenomenal range of musical theatre skills.

All the pupils are represented by the Italia Conti agency and are not permitted to attend auditions except through it. But although many of the pupils have appeared in *Harry Potter* films and the like, outside professional work is not a major part of the school experience. 'Whilst you're out working you can't be in class learning technique, and those who are out too much won't be up to the standard of training we offer at 16 plus.'

Background and Atmosphere: If you climb the steps of an office block opposite the Barbican to find dance students practising moves in the reception hall, you are probably at Italia Conti. This is the oldest theatre arts training school in Britain, founded in 1911. It grew out of the first production of the children's play, *Where the Rainbow Ends.* Italia Conti, an established actress with a reputation for working with young people, was asked to take over their training. The play was a triumph, and the school was born in basement studios in Great Portland Street. Now it shares nine floors of an ex-office block in the City, traffic roaring by outside, with over-16s doing full-time performing arts courses. Classrooms are cheek-by-jowl with practice studios; students training at the barre have views over the City skyline.

Pastoral Care and Discipline: Self-discipline and teamwork are an integral part of performing arts training, and the pupils are in the main so delighted to be at the school that discipline and relationship problems are few. Many of the vocational classes are mixed in age groups, with older pupils acting as mentors and rôle models. A full-time matron deals with medical and emotional upsets. 'They learn to live the lifestyle of a performer, which is partly about having the skills but also about being able to cope with success and rejection.'

Pupils and Parents: About half the pupils have already attended the associate weekend schools in places like Chislehurst, Guildford, Wokingham and Tunbridge Wells, so a strong southern home counties contingent. Pupils are confident and friendly. 'Socially, they are amazing. I expect them to be able to get their own way nicely. If people want to be with you, there are few obstacles to a successful career.' Ex-pupils include (amongst many) Noel Coward, Gertrude Lawrence, Patsy Kensit, Tracey Ullman and Leslie Phillips. More recent graduates include Danny Bayne, Newton Faulkner, Claire Goose and Kelly Brooke.

Entrance: The twelve associate schools act as feeder prep schools, though pupils audition successfully from a wide range of backgrounds. Around 12 or 13 pupils come into Year 7, with more joining over the next few years, to a maximum of 20 in a class. 'Very few live within five miles, so it tends to take persistence for them to persuade their parents that they're old enough to make the journey.' The academic test is largely diagnostic; students also prepare a song, two speeches and up to three types of dance. 'We're looking for exceptional ability in one and trainability in all three.' All those who are considered right for the school are offered a place. 'We try hard to select children who will thrive. The school would be purgatory for children without the physical abilities.'

Exit: A few transfer to state or independent sixth forms to do A levels, but the vast majority move on to the one- or three-year intensive performing arts courses in the same building run by the Italia Conti Academy of Theatre Arts. One of these, the three year performing arts course, produces 'audition ready' graduates with a degree equivalent national diploma in professional musical theatre from Trinity College, London. Government dance and drama award scholarships are available for this course.

Money Matters: A number of full and part scholarships for children from the associate schools. No open scholarship auditions. Some charities help to fund places.

Remarks: Children with a talent and passion for performance will thrive here. 'It's a wonderful place to grow up,' says the head. 'There's so much to see and do and so many talented people to emulate.'

James Allen's Girls' School (JAGS)

Linked to James Allens Preparatory School (JAPS) in the Junior section

East Dulwich Grove, London, SE22 8TE

• Pupils: 1,070 girls; all day • Ages: 11-18 • Size of sixth form: 210 • C of E Foundation but all are welcome • Fees: £12,975 pa • Independent

Tel: 020 8693 1181
Fax: 020 8693 7842
Email: julie.ellis@jags.org.uk
Website: www.jags.org.uk

Headmistress: Since 1994, Mrs Marion Gibbs BA MLitt FRSA (fifties). Read classics at Bristol, where she also did her PGCE and part-time research. Was an HMI and has also inspected for Ofsted and the ISI. She has taught in state and private schools including Burgess Hill and Haberdashers' Aske's School for Girls. A passionate classicist, she has been an examiner and written books on the subject, and teaches citizenship, Greek, Latin, Greek mythology and classical civilisation to different age groups. 'How can you manage your school if you don't know all your pupils and where they are coming from?'

A highly efficient operator, particularly good one-to-one. 'She's dynamic, she's sensible, she knows what she wants and achieves it,' say parents. 'If there's a problem, she's on the phone, you're straight in there, and it's dealt with very quickly.' Girls say: 'She's a brilliant head. She knows everyone's name and what you're doing. She's in tune with the students – we are her focus.'

Academic matters: Has so far avoided following the byways of IGCSEs, Pre-Us or the IB. 'We've looked at the new exams but decided against taking them up at the moment. Ideally, I want the girls to take the same exams as everyone else, rather than helping to form a two-tier system where independent schools take separate exams.' A very strong showing, with 36% A* at A level in 2010 and 95% A*/A/B and 67% A* at GCSE and 94% A*/A. A wide range of languages offered to GCSE and A level, including Italian, Russian, Spanish, German and Japanese, with a good take-up at A level. Maths, biology and chemistry are other popular A level subjects, alongside English and history. 'Our daughter has learned to work hard without pressure from us,' said a parent. 'She's had some fantastic, enthusiastic teachers who have really inspired her.'

A few girls have mild dyslexia/dyspraxia and the school has also accommodated children with sight/hearing problems. It does not provide one-to-one help, except for those with a statement of education need, but the SENCo liaises with staff and parents to ensure that girls are coping within normal classes, that they are provided with e.g. laptops where necessary and get extra time in exams if they are entitled to it.

Part of the Southwark Schools Learning Partnership, which includes five state and three independent schools working together on a huge range of projects. 'A real partnership is organic. It develops out of shared interests. We all have something to learn from one another. If we're having a theatre company or a speaker in, or a training session, we'll invite other schools over, or we may go to them.'

Games, Options, the Arts: Several pupils said they had chosen the school for its music – indeed, a huge variety of orchestras, choirs, ensembles and groups to choose from, playing in over 30 concerts each year. 'There's something for everyone, whatever you play,' said a pupil. Ralph Vaughan Williams and then Gustav Holst were the school's first two music teachers. At the planning stage is a community music centre, to be open to the community after school and at weekends as well as for school use during the day. Art also very strong, including fabric and textiles, with six art rooms and several students most years going on to art foundation courses. 'The art department really pushes you,' said a pupil. 'You learn such a lot.' Drama is 'exceptional,' said a parent, including joint productions with Dulwich College and trips to perform at the Edinburgh Festival.

A very sporty school; plays an extensive and generally successful programme of inter-school matches, with house competitions giving the less physically-talented a chance to shine. One pupil commented, 'You have to be really good to play for the school'. PE GCSE and A level options. Facilities include a sports hall with squash courts and multigym, a dance studio –'We do everything from flamenco to Bollywood to street dance' – and an elegant swimming pool with a large spectator area, plus extensive playing fields, artificial turf and courts. A wide range of sporting opportunities in the upper school, including ice skating and dry slope ski-ing. 'But there's so much to do you have to choose. You may not be able to be in the school team and the orchestra,' commented a student.

Background and Atmosphere: Part of a foundation established by talented Elizabethan actor Edward Alleyn, which includes Dulwich College and Alleyn's School. The school was founded in 1741 by James Allen, a Master of Dulwich College, as a free reading school for local poor children. He died five years later, leaving a bequest to secure his school's future. It has been girls only since 1845 and moved to its present site in 1886.

Much development since, culminating (so far) in rather swish dining room and Deep End café in what used to be the swimming pool. Grammar-schoolish dark wood stairways and window frames in the older parts contrast with light and airy glass, white paint and pale wood in the newer areas. Fabulous library, dance and drama studios, 200 seat theatre, labs and DT rooms, walls lined with notice boards crammed with photos, lists, cuttings and posters.

But best of all are the 22 acre grounds, where girls are free to wander at will during break times, which alongside sports pitches and courts include botanical gardens (originally planted over 100 years ago by pioneer ecologist and head of science Dr Lilian Clarke), engagingly shaggy woodland and wetland areas, and even a tree-lined country walk. Also a bridge over the railway line which runs through the grounds, with views down the line to North Dulwich station. The school has its own environmental manager who runs a biology club, welcomes children from nearby state primary and special schools for nature trails and pond-dipping and spreads the ecological word to other schools in the area.

The head is keen for the girls to share their privileges with the wider community – 'You need to get in the habit of giving something back. We're training them to roll up their sleeves and do something'. So, as well as sharing their sports and other facilities with other schools and local people, girls are encouraged to visit the nearby Cheshire Home, work with Romanian children with special needs, help with the Saturday literacy scheme for local children, join Kids Company children in their art activities.

Pastoral Care and Discipline: Unashamedly old-fashioned over behaviour: no bad language, no graffiti, no chewing gum. Best suited to girls with no great inclination to rock the boat. Has excluded permanently for bringing drugs to school and temporarily for physical violence and being caught smoking more than once. 'If there's any chance of pupils misbehaving outside school, they'll be down like a ton of bricks,' commented a parent. However, the head says that sanctions are rare, 'We're tough but we don't have a lot of discipline issues'.

A many-tiered pastoral system which includes form tutors, heads of year and the two school nurses, who are also trained counsellors. Girls say they like having a range of people they can go to for help but report most people rub along well together. However, some felt that occasionally, stressed students are not noticed and that the pastoral net does have the odd hole. The school says it has worked very hard to improve pastoral care over the last few years and keeps a look out for stress and anorexia, 'But they do mostly enjoy their food. When we banned sweets and cakes from the tuck shop they came up with charity cake sales'.

In the main school girls are usually allocated forms according to their houses, with staff and students getting together in fund-raising events such as sponsored space hopper race, teacher karaoke, film-and-cake club. Sixth formers have vertical tutor groups, including Year 12s and Year 13s, so the younger girls can learn from the older ones' experiences of going through the UCAS process.

Pupils and Parents: Diverse ethnically and socially, with plenty of girls on bursaries and some 50 home languages. Girls bright, buzzy, focused. 'They come out very confident, streetwise kids,' said a parent. 'They're used to standing up for themselves and arguing their point.' They travel in from a wide area by train or bus, mostly from south of the river but increasing numbers from the north (12 minutes by train from London Bridge). OGs include Anita Brookner, Lisa St Aubin de Terain, Dharshini David and Sally Hawkins.

Entrance: Hot competition. Everyone is interviewed in the autumn term. Maths, English and verbal reasoning exams in the spring term. Around a third comes up from the junior school, and some 40 per cent of new entrants are from state primaries. Sixth form entry for outsiders depends on entrance exam, GCSE results, school reference and interview. Generally 10 or so join at this stage.

Exit: Around 10 girls a year leave after GCSEs, mostly for co-ed sixth forms. A level leavers virtually all go to university: usually 20+ to Oxbridge, a few to art college, the rest largely to top universities to study anything from drama to dentistry.

Money Matters: The last part of James Allen's bequest was used to establish a Scholars' Fund to replace the abolished government assisted places in 1997. Seventeen James Allen's Bursary Places, which can pay for up to full fees plus help with uniform, lunches and school trips, awarded each year. School also gets an annual grant from the Dulwich Estate, which pays for more scholarships and bursaries. More than a third of pupils are on some sort of financial assistance. Up to 20 scholarships at 11+, including music, art and sports awards. Major scholarships of £1000 pa and minor scholarships of £500 pa can be means tested up to full fees. A few 16+ scholarships of £1000 awarded on the basis of GCSE results.

Remarks: High-achieving school at work and play, with a strong social conscience. Suits bright, well-ordered girls who are keen to get involved. 'You feel really proud that your daughter's at JAGS,' said a parent. 'You know she's set up for life.'

James Gillespie's High School

Lauderdale Street, Edinburgh, EH9 1DD

• Pupils: 595 boys, 540 girls • Ages: 11-18 • Size of sixth form: 310 • Non-denom • State

Tel: 0131 447 1900
Fax: 0313-466-7035
Email: admin@jamesgillespies.edin.sch.uk
Website: www.jghs.edin.sch.uk

Head: Since 2005, Alex Wallace BSc, MA (fifties), who first came to the school in 1991 as assistant head of learning and teaching, rising to senior depute head teacher, acting head and thence head. An expert on methodology, he wrote the seminal book on Higher Still and is the expert on 'methodology and emotional intelligence' in the country. Educated at St Andrew's High School in Kirkaldy, followed by geography and race relations at Edinburgh University, did his PGCE at Moray House; his previous post was at Craigroyston (which we agreed would have been interesting). A sympathetic head with a dry sense of humour, who describes Gillespie's ethos as being particularly good, especially on the bullying front – 'a listening school'. Married with three children, two of whom are up and flying, with a younger daughter still at Gillespie's.

Academic matters: Class size 30 (20/25 for practical subjects), setted early for maths in the September of their first year, second year setted for English. Three separate sciences for all from the third year onwards. No classics, but French, German, Spanish and Urdu, a tiny number also learn Gaelic (a feeder school where pupils do all subjects in Gaelic). All languages are taught up to Higher level. School does complicated mix of Standard, Higher, Advanced Highers and A levels for physics, art (in order to form a portfolio), Urdu and geography – an interesting diversification for a state school. Good support for learning, dyslexia, dyspraxia, and help with exams, both withdrawn from class and team teaching in class. ADHD is OK – 'Most reasonably well-behaved'. 250 of the pupils come from 40 different countries – 'the most diverse population in Scotland': EFL available (free) for all who need it. CDT is 50/50 craft and design and all computer-based – 350 computers in the school. Recent BECTA award for best website.

Games, Options, the Arts: PE and swimming on site; huge games hall plus Astroturf, much used by local community. Football, rugby, hockey pitches about 1.5 miles away at Kirkbrae, pupils are bused. Games are basically extra-curricular, girls' football and netball are popular. Short lunchbreak, 45 mins, so no lunch clubs – pupils either go home or to the local carry-outs, rather jolly dining room. Massive music uptake, with carol service normally held in the Usher Hall, over 350 regularly on the stage. Senior orchestra, junior orchestra, lessons free, but music department needs drastic revamping. Ditto labs, DT, libraries and PE area. Strong, spectacular art, photography, 'the lot', impressive fabric design. Huge dance area, media popular with lights and editing studios, three drama studios. Wizard home economics department – better than most homes we know. Trips all over the place, in many disciplines – skiing, Paris for art, historians to the trenches, geographers to do glacial research in the French Alps.

Background and Atmosphere: Founded in 1803 as a result of a legacy from James Gillespie, 'a wealthy Edinburgh manufacturer of snuff and tobacco', who was born in Roslin. Started with 65 students and one master and led a peripatetic existence. At one point the prep school for the Merchant Company's secondary schools. By 1908 had a roll of over a thousand, including girls, and offered secondary education under the aegis of the Edinburgh school board, moving to Bruntsfield House, just off The Meadows, in 1966 and going fully co-ed in 1978. The earliest building on this site dates from 1300, and the current building, Bruntsfield House, was built in 1605, with later additions and improvements. Sir George Warrender, whose family was to be awarded the title Bruntsfield, bought the house from the original owners and was intrigued to find that if you hung a sheet from every window you could access from the inside, still sheetless windows outside. A secret room was discovered, with bloodstained floor, ashes in the grate and a skeleton under the wainscot. The Green Lady haunts the top storeys to this day.

The head has a grand office in the main building, with a spectacular ceiling and an impressive fireplace, almost exactly replicated by the music room not quite next door. Now surrounded by predominantly sixties-type classroom blocks, relieved by swards of green and mature trees with a singular clock in the middle of the campus which, despite thousands spent on renovation, will never work properly as the hands were found to be too long. It remains as a memorial to the follies of the architects of the day, though interestingly, Colin MacWilliam has nothing but praise for the design. The campus is hidden amongst decent Victorian tenements – more grass and trees than you would expect. Woefully short of space – a certain frisson when the local electricity board sold an adjoining substation without first offering it to the school, which desperately needs room to expand.

Pastoral Care and Discipline: Follows the state guidelines – good PSHE, good anti-bullying strategy in place: 'We get the youngsters to talk it through ... We bring them together and get the bully to accept their behaviour is wrong'. 'No current problems' with cigarettes, alcohol or drugs, but head will exclude on either a temporary or permanent basis if necessary. Last head only ever made two drugs-related temporary exclusions, but it would be permanent if any hint of dealing. Also out permanently for a violent attack, though merely temporary exclusion for 'physical violence'. Homework books which must be signed by parent or guardian. No uniform, which is going slightly against the current Edinburgh trend – 'If it ain't broke, don't fix it'.

Pupils and Parents: Free intake, so diverse: 35 languages spoken. Large number of professional families (Marchmont is a popular area for the university) plus 'a significant group of working class, with relatively poor backgrounds'. Huge ethnic mix, with some girls wearing the chador – they may well do PE and swim wearing full leggings and long-sleeved T-shirts (though parents can ask to withdraw their daughters from these lessons, few do). Lifts being installed next year for wheelchair-bound pupil, minor physical handicaps OK. Strong parent/teacher involvement.

Entrance: First year capped at 200; catchment area recently re-drawn but some places still available by request – very popular, with pupils from as far away as Penicuik and Musselburgh. Obliged to take children on a first come first served basis, waiting lists. Certain number of pupils who have obtained university entrance elsewhere in the independent sector join in sixth form for Higher Still (and a better chance at Oxbridge).

Exit: Number leaves after Standard Grades, either to further education or work; good proportion to universities, mainly Scots, studying medicine, science, art college, followed by social subject and music in that order. Annual trickle to Oxbridge.

Remarks: Can't fault it.

JFS

The Mall, Kenton, Harrow, Middlesex, HA3 9TE

• Pupils: 1,030 girls; 1,045 boys • Ages: 11-18 • Size of sixth form: 575 • Jewish • State

Tel: 020 8206 3100
Fax: 020 8206 3101
Email: admin@jfs.brent.sch.uk
Website: www.jfs.brent.sch.uk

Head: Since January 2008, Mr Jonathan Miller BSc MA NPQH (late forties). Educated at Carmel College and Imperial College London, he has been at JFS for many years. A former head of chemistry and head of science, he was responsible for planning the school's timetable and IT strategy when it relocated to Kenton, also deputy head. Articulate and highly respected, considered even handed, even tempered and level headed, well able to cope with the current dilemmas facing the school concerning admissions, as well as to preserve the happy balance which exists between pupils of a wide range of religious observance within the school.

Academic matters: A very large comprehensive that compares favourably with many grammar schools in terms of results. Last year 86 per cent of A level grades A/B, while 93 per cent of students gained 5+ A*–C (90 per cent including English and maths) at GCSE. School graded 'outstanding' by Ofsted in 2009 in every one of the 39 judgements made.

New pupils are admitted in four ability bands, and all subjects are set by ability in Year 8. Both upper and lower ends are given unusually strong support. The gifted and talented have accelerated classes from Year 7, while the large special needs department – with over 80 statemented children – has its own suite, six special needs teachers and six permanent teaching assistants. Those struggling at the bottom of the middle band are perhaps the least well served. French for all in Year 7, Spanish from Year 9. IT bang up to the minute, with interactive whiteboards in every classroom. Science, too, unusually well equipped with 15 laboratories.

First-rate, highly sought after, academic sixth form with 574 pupils, housed in its own discrete space (though with some lessons taught in the main school). Large expansion of the curriculum at this point, with applied art (including photography and graphics), economics, business studies, psychology, sociology, childhood studies, theatre studies, media studies, politics and critical thinking added to the GCSE basics. Masterclasses, too, for the 25 or so Oxbridge candidates, including some pupils from neighbouring boroughs.

A core of long-serving staff provides some outstanding teaching in all subjects. 'A child who wants to work could not receive a better education anywhere in the country,' said one mother, whose son recently left for a top-flight university. Teaching is carefully monitored, with videoing of lessons – prides itself on its continuing professional development and places the training of teachers from a number of teacher training institutions high on its agenda: about a third of its trainees stay on as teachers, so few problems with recruitment.

Games, Options, the Arts: Outstanding range of facilities, which include 14 acres of playing fields, two sports halls, a dance studio and a multi-gym for students and staff. Games lessons focus on athletics, ball games, gymnastics and dance.

Strong music department – all students take music in Years 7, 8 and 9 and about 15 per cent also take instrumental lessons with visiting staff. Ten practice rooms, keyboard laboratory, recording studio, two specialist classrooms, plus music master classes. Large auditorium which seats 900, plus a concert hall for 450. Amphitheatre for outdoor concerts and performances. Five interconnecting art rooms, plus a sculpture terrace. Media studio with professional standard film and television equipment and an editing suite. Well-equipped library.

Annual reading festival and poetry competition. Excellent range of school trips, including Poland (for 6th form Holocaust studies), Israel (Year 9 residential scheme), Prague, Strasbourg, Flanders and Paris. Duke of Edinburgh, Young Enterprise. Kosher kitchen with a healthy and balanced diet – no other food can be brought into school.

Background and Atmosphere: The largest Jewish comprehensive in Europe, has a particularly distinguished history and tradition. Founded originally in the East End in 1732, it had, by the 19th century, become the largest school in the world, with 4000 students, mainly poor Jewish immigrants. Bombed in WW2, it was re-built in Camden Town in 1958, but by the time it transferred to Kenton in 2002 the accommodation had, in the words of its previous head, become a 'cesspit'. Perhaps previous head Dame Ruth Robins's most significant achievement was guiding the complex negotiations which secured the large and leafy site in north-west London and overseeing the design and building of the new school, with its light, modern buildings, wide curved corridors, and state of the art technology. Has a strong family feel – often parents, grandparents and even great-grandparents are former pupils – with an outstanding sense of continuity, community, warmth and commitment. The social side of school life is particularly prized by parents and most students enjoy coming to school and make life-long friends.

Pastoral Care and Discipline: Blue and white uniform, which meets the demands of the most Orthodox – so girls in skirts with arms covered, respectful necklines and 'no ironmongery', boys with heads covered with skull caps (albeit some only when they see the head approaching).

In such a large school, the organisation of the pastoral side is of vital significance. On entry, the intake of 300 is subdivided into ten groups of 30. Each student joins a tutor group and is assigned a tutor – who stays with them throughout – a year manager and director of studies, so three adults looking after every child. Also buddy and peer mentoring systems. The ethos is strict, determined but kind – discipline is certainly not a major issue, with quiet and orderly classrooms. Famous detention room – Room 17 – for any persistent offenders and a designated behaviour team to deal with transgressors. 'One or two per cent take up all the time, but I don't know of a single child we haven't turned around,' said the previous head.

Outlook and practice is Orthodox and one of the key aims is to further Jewish values. Very strong Jewish studies programme – 'outstanding,' says Ofsted – and all take GCSE in religious studies. Modern Hebrew and Israel studies are included as part of the Hebrew education programme. Accelerated GCSE in modern Hebrew. Daily services, led by students. Wonderful light, purpose-built synagogue with delicate stained glass windows, where volunteers teach additional Jewish education to the most Orthodox. All pupils can choose to have a bar or bat mitzvah at the school.

Pupils and Parents: A very broad spectrum of religious belief, from 'those considering rabbinical studies to those who've never seen a candle lit on Friday night'. Nonetheless, you would probably not feel comfortable here if you didn't want your child to be involved with the Jewish experience. Indeed, for some non-practising parents, it offers a religious opportunity they feel they can't provide at home. 'We're not observant,' said one mother, 'and one of the nicest things about the school was that it enabled my son to have a bar mitzvah.'

Entrance: Six hundred applicants for 300 places. In 2009, following a much-publicised court case, the applications process altered and it was forced to abandon the principle of giving priority to those children who are Jewish according to the religious principles stated by the Chief Rabbi. Instead, last year it gave priority to those who met a test of religious practice. Parents for Year 7 places had to provide a certificate to testify to synagogue attendance, evidence of a formal Jewish education and/or of family activity in the Jewish community. Places were awarded on a points system, which also applied to siblings and external applicants for the sixth form. Following a further case in the Supreme Court in late 2009, the 2010 admissions process may change again. Those applying for admissions in 2011 should study the criteria carefully.

Exit: About 6–12 to Oxbridge, half the rest to Russell Group universities.

Remarks: An outstandingly well-run comprehensive, with a warm and well-ordered atmosphere, in bright and spacious modern buildings. Ideal for those looking for a strong education within a secure environment and Jewish cultural tradition.

The John Lyon School

Middle Road, Harrow, Middlesex, HA2 0HN

- Pupils: 580 boys, all day • Ages: 11-18 • Size of sixth form: 150
- Non-denominational foundation, welcoming pupils of all religions
- Fees: £13,560 pa • Independent

Tel: 020 8872 8400
Fax: 020 8872 8455
Email: enquiries@johnlyon.org
Website: www.johnlyon.org

Head: Since September 2009, Miss Katherine Haynes BA MEd NPQH, a mathematician (fortyish). Miss Haynes was the first woman to be appointed head of an HMC, boys only, school – a notable milestone. Previously head of maths at Warwick School (qv), prior to which she held the same post at Edgbaston High (qv). This is a look-you-straight-in-the-eye-plus-firm-handshake head, one whose palpable intensity of purpose masks, you feel, warmth and a sense of fun. She is articulate, forthright, focused. 'What a school provides needs to match its location… I want teaching that is dynamic and energetic, that enables boys to learn in the way that is best for them.' She is realistic about the physical limits of the school site – 'It's a question of going with what we can do rather than "what if?"' Perhaps less visible about the school than her popular and relaxed predecessor, Miss Haynes initiated a crackdown on 'standards' and discipline from day one – clearly a bit of a bombshell for some but appreciated by most. All recognize that 'she is keen to do good things with the school'…'she is going to up its game' …'she's obviously keen to do her best'. Whatever uncertainty and scepticism might have rippled through the school on her appointment, it sure as anything isn't there now and parents, staff and boys look puzzled at the idea that a woman in the job is unusual. She has taken on an interesting school at an interesting time – boys' only day schools are thin on the ground these days. In her hands, John Lyon is a school of which north west London is going to sit up and take notice.

Academic matters: Mainstream trad curriculum. Maths much the most popular A level subject and 31 out of 45 candidates in 2010 got A*/As. Chemistry and economics also with good uptake and results mostly in the A/B band. Biology and history more of an A–C spread. Few modern linguists – nothing unusual there in a boys' school – though Spanish now an ab initio option with French which may strengthen both. School also offers psychology, drama and music tech at this level. At GCSE, likewise, no curricular quirks. In 2010, 65 per cent of subjects taken gained A*/A. Maths IGCSE taken and results are exceptional – all but 4 of the 93-strong cohort achieved A*–B. All three sciences also strong, the Englishes get mostly A/B. Three boys sat Latin in 2010. German now, sadly, dead. No obvious weak areas. Able to take advantage of big brother school up the hill, i.e. Harrow, for individual language specialisms among other perks. IT hitherto seen as integral to learning in general and not as 'a subject' but this is changing – all take it in the first two years – no shortage of computers about the place – and an A level in the subject is 'probably on its way'. No DT though – simply not possible given the constraints of the site and, seemingly, no pupil or parental pressure to bring it into what otherwise might be seen as a natural home.

Learning support dept works in classroom and via withdrawal. Around 60 on the register at the time of our visit. Mainly assists dyslexics and dyspraxics – of a mild to moderate kind – and has boys on the ASD spectrum too. Site is a bit up and down but most is accessible and wheelchairs are 'not impossible'. We grilled many parents and boys and no subject seen as weak – most staff, in fact, praised for the support they give. Library full of PCs and much fiction. Somewhat eclectic stock otherwise and what appeared to us an unusual cataloguing system.

Games, Options, the Arts: Drama clearly lively and popular – possibly not unrelated to the fact that girls from several chic local schools e.g. St Helen's, Northwood College and North London Collegiate compete at auditions to play opposite the boys in big, well-appointed, productions. We witnessed some younger boys improvising with none of the coyness and self-consciousness common elsewhere at this age group. Provision is good – two studios and the big hall though no performing arts centre here – no space. Parents enthuse about productions. Music also exceptional despite unglamorous accommodation – school musters all manner of ensembles and boys play a great range of instruments. Good to see, alongside the bands and R and B, a motet choir and string ensembles. Music tech growing. 'The standard of music and drama is amazing,' a parent told us, 'the last concert was so moving I came out in tears.' Art in a series of studios and some good displays of pupil work here and there in otherwise rather uninspiring corridors. Good to see art done by staff on display – and not just by art staff. Sports hall – though not of the cavernous size found elsewhere – and provision otherwise is good – impressive fitness centre, excellent pool, playing fields up and down the hill and much borrowing of Harrow's fields and pitches also enhances opportunities. Cricket an exceptional strength. Lots of popular expeditions – sporting, educational and charitable – classroom building in Uganda, India and Vietnam occasioned particularly zesty response – along with mountaineering in the alps.

Background and Atmosphere: It's tucked into a winding road on the Harrow hill, still reminiscent of the quiet leafy village this must have been. Harrow School dominates the hill and its fields and structures abut John Lyon's but this is a happy brotherly co-existence and the cadet school benefits in many ways from the senior. School sits on the edge of two conservation areas which concentrates creative thinking as far as development is concerned. The main school building is Victorian gothic. One planned small new-build will – under the 'estate strategy' – enable it to change its designation from housing economics and dining to become a new sixth form centre and teaching area. Pretty arts and crafts villa, now housing the sixth form centre, shortly to become admin hub – hence dismal internal state at time of our visit. Most corridors, painted white under fluorescent lighting and with municipal carpet, are pretty stark. Good-sized school hall, with picture windows and views on two sides. The site is not spacious and few buildings delight the eye but it doesn't feel crowded – partly because of the surrounding pitches and fields. Limited space means that the population has to stay at more or less its present size – the relative smallness of the school seen by all as a great attraction. Parents are united – 'everyone knows everyone – they all mix, older and younger, especially on the school bus and all are very accepting of each other'... 'sport and drama means they make good friends across the age groups'... 'because it's small they get a lot of individual attention and that develops and strengthens their confidence'. Three quarters eat school food which, reportedly, 'could be better' and assuredly needs a more comfortable home. Atmosphere is healthily but not aggressively male – good number of women teachers probably helps. Parents pay tribute – 'the school is very good at bringing on their confidence'... 'it's academic but not pushy'... 'it's an academic school but people aren't separated into geeks and jocks'.. 'not cliquey...everyone is treated equally'... 'good at parent-teacher contact'. 'My son is very happy there.'

Pastoral Care and Discipline: All lessons start and end with boys standing for the teacher – we approve. Year 13 boys are peer mentors for the younger boys – trained and monitored by professional school counsellor. Clear disciplinary structure – detentions and brief suspensions sort most problems and these are mostly related to late work or behaviour. Two exclusions since Miss Haynes's advent – both for unacceptable behaviour. Drugs/smoking/drink infringements seemingly unknown. Bullying managed by prevention so very little goes on. Self-discipline is the ethos and it seems to work. Pupils clearly proud to be here.

Pupils and Parents: Huge ethnic and social mix reflecting the local area. Thirty-odd home languages. Around two thirds a mix of Asians – mostly Indian. All seemingly mix and co-exist with the school needing to do very little to help it along. An overall ethos of work and collaboration does all that's needed. Most live within two miles of the school but they do come from further afield into e.g. Ealing, Hounslow, Watford and Bucks. Five bus routes. Noted Old Boys include actors Julian Rhind-Tutt and Timothy West, writers Geoff Atkinson and Liam Halligan.

Entrance: Main feeders at 11+ are Alpha Prep, Reddiford; at 13+ St Martin's, St John's, Quainton Hall, Clifton Lodge. At 11, c60 places and c40 at 13. Heavily over-subscribed at both levels. Selection via exam – an online test and an essay at 11. Then an interview with some mental maths. At 13, exams in maths, English and science plus optional papers in e.g. history, geog or RE. Plus interview. At 16 there are additional places and well worth applying. A grades needed in A level subjects and a decent spread of good grades overall.

Exit: A range of subjects and universities – economics, IT, business and dentistry loom large. Mostly to Russell group or plate glass – several to London colleges. Lots, seemingly, reapply post A level results – better matching their results to their choice of course, perhaps, and school offers good support.

Money Matters: Good number of bursaries – all means-tested and worth up to 85 per cent of fees. Scholarships worth up to 20 per cent in academics, sports, art, music, drama and all-rounder. If you have a gifted son and no money you could get a fabulous deal here.

Remarks: Solid, sound and sensible. Deserves to be far better known.

Jordanhill School

Linked to Jordanhill School Primary in the Junior section

45 Chamberlain Road, Jordanhill, Glasgow, Glasgow, G13 1SP

• Pupils: 590 boys and girls, all day • Ages: 11-18 • Size of sixth form: 180 • Non-denom • State

Tel: 0141 576 2500
Fax: 0141 576 2555
Email: info@jordanhill.glasgow.sch.uk
Website: www.jordanhill.glasgow.sch.uk

Rector: Since 1997, Dr Paul Thomson BSc PhD Dip Ed (fiftyish), educated at Dollar Academy and took combined honours in maths and physics at Glasgow University, where he also did his PhD, and then did his teacher training at Jordanhill College next door. Started his teaching career at Boclair in Bearsden, followed by Chryston High School, where he was principal teacher of physics, then assistant head at the Vale of Leven and depute head at Hermitage Academy: a speedy career path. Dr Thomson, whose wife is depute head of St Margaret's High School in Airdrie, has two children; he is also exceedingly keen on cooking. That apart, he has a fearsome intellect and spouted facts and figures faster than most heads we have met, adding all the while 'that it is available on the web page'.

Jordanhill is the only direct grant-aided non-special school in Scotland, runs its own budget and indeed so does each department. A block grant comes from the Scottish Executive Education Department to whom the school is answerable. Dr Thomson regards himself quite rightly as a CEO, working 'with the staff' and running the place with a budget of £5,000 per child per annum. Was one of the youngest heads – state or independent – in Scotland; he says he has no intention of moving, though he obviously misses teaching, and his entire demeanour changed during our tour round the school: whenever we found a child to be talked to – about anything – gone was the efficiency question-answering model and in its place appeared an interested smiley friend. (He also does all the 'early' UCAS references.) But youngsters apart, we suspect he does not tolerate fools with ease (he thinks he has 'mellowed a little' recently). The school has just constructed a new all-weather pitch and extended the refectory. A major new teaching block was completed in May 2008. Unlike many heads, Dr Thomson regards this as a pupil necessity and therefore worth spending time and thought on, rather than as an end in itself to glorify Jordanhill and his own cleverness in getting the funding.

Academic matters: The school is inclusive, but is still the most successful state school (albeit grant-aided) in Scotland. Four classes of 25 (rather than the trad legal limit of 33) with practical classes of 15 (max 20). Some setting in maths and French. French from primary, Spanish taster at 13 and enormous success with credits all over the shop at intermediate II; German is available in S5 and S6. The school plies both standard and intermediate II (and results have become sharper in the last eight years). English, French/Spanish and maths results are impressive, as are art, biology, physics and chemistry. Masses of external activity in the science department with pupils doing project work with the University of Lyons, taking part in the Royal Society of Chemistry quiz and challenges run by Paisley University.

Outstanding music results. The recent HMI report praises the economics results. Higher psychology in conjunction with Anniesland College and a good partnership developing. Terrific art. Excellent use of computers – everywhere, in the art rooms as well as the classrooms, three hundred of them, interactive whiteboards all over the place too. Smart new media studies room which doubles for English having interesting star-shaped six seater tables and two overhead projectors with an interactive whiteboard. Pupils won a prize with their first film. One of the best equipped schools we have visited – ever. Clusters of lap tops motor round classrooms.

Homework clubs and some homework on line. Ditto supported study. Several groups of pupils doing research projects have direct links with staff. Power point demos by all, from P7; P6 are observers and rector then discusses the P7 presentation with them (face lit up like a beacon when he described this). Loads of interaction. Evening support classes for exam years, labs are open at lunchtime and post school. Good modern library, more computers and even more in the careers department. Special needs well catered for, 'If they can cope then we will take them, unless their needs are such that the school cannot accommodate them', some pupils have a record of needs. Two dedicated staff who work across both primary and secondary schools, plus a host of pupil support assistants, scribing where necessary. Lifts and ramps all over the shop. With one or two exceptions, the staffroom looks incredibly young and vibrant.

Games, Options, the Arts: Fantastic games and oodles of caps – capped pupils wear green ties. Rugby, hockey, football, volleyball, basketball and athletics. Two gyms and a recently acquired sports hall nearby. Stunning if cramped art complex – new and expanded department being created in the new building. Excellent art on display all over the place. None of it too big, but impressive. Kiln and new silk screen machine in place. Sculpture and good CDT. Drama strong, though not the biggest studio we have seen. Inspiring music, with specialist staff from P6 up. 'The best music department in the country,' says Dr Thomson – 300 plus pupils play an instrument, 26 different ensembles, serious orchestras. All swinging, and particularly keen on composing.

Clubs for everything, chess particularly popular – a current pupil is in the international squad. Hot on debating, and citizenship. Home economics a serious contender now, but rather more post standard grades, when students also study international cuisine (head's face lit up again). Ambitious outdoor education programme with pupils spending afternoons or weeks away depending on year group: Raasay, Castle Toward, senior pupils have a bi-annual trip to the developing world, part project part tourism (forty in Thailand when we visited). World Challenge in Malawi in 2007. Oodles of trips abroad: Euroscola at the European Parliament in Strasbourg, Paris, Spain et al. Massive charity involvement – both fundraising and community work in the locality. Jolly pupil-produced school mag, clearly laid out with brilliant editing – nice one, easy to read, with none of the trendy undershadowing that doting grannies find so irritating (not to mention GSG editors).

Background and Atmosphere: Founded in 1920 as a demo school for Jordanhill College of Education and became direct grant aided in 1987. Handsome classical grade B listed building. Rector has stunning panelled offices (think Eltham Palace); super huge classrooms with wide pupil-proof corridors. School surrounded by (some) games pitches but a high fence now divides them from the university. Strong links with local Jordanhill Parish church. Strong links too with Glasgow state schools – joint improvement meetings for staff and pupils, whilst the latter have a joint pre-vocational programme plus Your Turn project involving pupils across the city. Pupils from other schools can come to Jordanhill to pick up the odd higher or advanced higher not catered for in their own schools.

Pupils are neat in brown uniforms – except for the primary when we visited, who were in mufti, as were their staff, the head of primary particularly dashing in a black T-shirt. Efficient and fairly unforgiving uniform guide-lines in the prospectus supplement. Sixth year have a dedicated common room and two separate ones for boys and girls in S5 – the new build will give them better social areas. JOSS operates an after-school club for tinies in the nearby church hall.

Pastoral Care and Discipline: Four houses, the heads of houses are guidance staff with a combined office and interview rooms. Pupils have tutors who are responsible for PSE and the school policy is to clamp down hard on any form of bullying. Neither Dr Thomson nor his predecessor have ever permanently excluded; a clearly defined code of sanctions, including letters home, litter duty (brill) and detention. Regular links between sixth form and littles – combined reading and the BFG club. Minister from Jordanhill Parish church takes assemblies, but this is an ecumenical school, with all religions' festivals observed – rector is keener that pupils learn 'to conduct themselves properly in church' and understand other faiths (by, e.g., visiting local synagogues, mosques and temples) rather than pay lip service to any particular religion.

Pupils and Parents: Serves a predominantly owner-occupier area – professionals, who form an enthusiastic parent- teachers association, with parent volunteers in primary department and loads of fundraising. Seven per cent ethnic minority.

Entrance: Inclusive, by address, over-subscribed, waiting lists. Siblings get priority. Some places (never advertised) available post standard grades. First come, first served.

Exit: Some 75 per cent to university. Trickle to Oxbridge, certain number to universities down south – Imperial for engineering, Liverpool, Manchester, the odd musician to the Royal Academy of Music, and tranches to art school, with or without a foundation course. But most stay in the west of Scotland. Dentistry, medicine and veterinary school all popular.

Remarks: Outstanding, with an inspirational, slightly left of centre rector. Better resourced than many schools in the independent sector – and it's free. A beacon. Glasgow independent sector eat your heart out.

The Judd School

Brook Street, Tonbridge, Kent, TN9 2PN

• Pupils: 960 • Ages: 11-18 • Size of sixth form: 305 (includes 60 girls)
• Non denom • State

Tel: 01732 770 880
Fax: 01732 771 661
Email: enquiries@judd.kent.sch.uk
Website: www.judd.kent.sch.uk

Headmaster: Since 2004, Mr Robert Masters. Educated at The Harvey Grammar School, Folkestone, Reading University (BSc maths) and Bristol University (PGCE). Previously taught at Gravesend Grammar School for Boys and Torquay Boys' Grammar. Married with three children. Believes strongly in 'the old traditions of grammar schools', i.e. academic strength, leadership, social concern, wide programme of extra-curricular activities.

Academic matters: A high achieving school – the result of creaming off the top 15–20 per cent at 11 and excellent teaching staff. Judged 'outstanding' three times in a row by Ofsted.

Maths popular and strong – the top maths set can take GCSE from Year 10 and go on to study statistics or pure maths or give more time to other studies; the maths staff generally need to be pretty sharp to keep on top of the crucifying questions being fired at them. 10 science labs, four very modern, the rest museum pieces. Good IT and effective IT-based parents/pupils/staff communications. Sixth form economics/politics/business studies described as 'exceptionally good with A1 teachers', and the sixth form generally is highly valued, because the school tailors the curriculum to each individual based on a lengthy personal interview – attracts many pupils from surrounding schools. Not a huge variety of subjects on offer, e.g. lacks psychology, sociology, media studies but, as the headmaster commented, 'These are not subjects accepted by some universities and thus resources are better utilised elsewhere'.

Maths is the only subject which is streamed (from Year 8) but otherwise the head is keen to keep four equal groups with a range of ability in each. These are regrouped in Year 9 – often for social reasons. Every boy is given a full dyslexic test on entry (the 11+ in Kent is pretty writing-free). 'This highlighted a weakness in my son, who was immediately given extra tuition,' says one parent. Parents affirm, 'This is as much a school for the plodder as the boffin.' Homework surprisingly undemanding and the culture full of encouragement; the boys become organised very quickly.

Games, Options, the Arts: Very, very strong games – does exceptionally well at all levels on a competitive circuit. Loads of rugby and cricket teams, basketball reached final of Kent Cup, virtually no soccer. Cross-country team second nationally and produces regular national finalists in athletics. Good swimming and tennis teams.

Music built into the very fabric of the school, described as inspirationally good with many excellent musicians, some first class, yet all abilities catered for. Director oversees an impressive roll call of orchestras (professional and training), choirs, wind and swing bands, chamber music and countless rock groups. 'One of the perks from a stressful profession is to have the spirits uplifted when attending concerts performed by the pupils,' says the head. Designated a specialist music college – one of very few in the country. Vast expansion into music technology planned. Colourful art department. Drama good – timetabled once a week, one main production plus Year 12 charity revue annually, plus plenty of mini productions. The usual excursions and adventures on offer including Borneo jungle complete with leeches. CCF (army and RAF) occupies a shack on the periphery of the playing fields – very well attended. Vast Duke of Edinburgh Award participation.

Background and Atmosphere: Opened in 1888, after the local burghers, unable to afford the fees for Tonbridge School, asked the Skinners' Company to provide an affordable academic education for their sons. A traditional, outwardly attractive, late Victorian red-brick building complemented by handsome red-brick/Cotswold stone buildings and annexes. The rear sports three pitches (including an all-weather) but school also uses some approximately five minutes away. The corridors and classrooms of the main building are still undistinguished and Dickensian, however a traditional, snug feel to the place – sixth form common room has been given a major makeover, including a servery and study facilities.

Pastoral Care and Discipline: A happy relaxed atmosphere, although a traditional grammar school – nothing staid or finger-waggingly strict. Small school feel enhanced by house system for pastoral care and competition. The care of pupils high on the agenda for the head – 'You can be any sort of person here (e.g. quirky, dyspraxic) but still feel accepted, valued and thrive'. Very experienced staff who are used to dealing with individuals. Pupils with any concerns have access to a mentoring system supported by the staff and sixth form.

Pupils and Parents: Pupils are unpretentious, alert, unstifled and look you confidently in the eye. A complete mix from high-flying parents to those who qualify for financial help with outings etc (all done discreetly). Famous past pupils include Admiral Sir Terry Lewin – Chief of the Defence Staff, Neville Duke – WW2 test pilot, Royal portrait painter Bernard Hailstone and Cecil Powell – Nobel prize winner (physics).

Entrance: Selection at 11 with an exam set by Kent CC. Always over-subscribed, the top 125 are chosen in order of merit. Distance from the school is a very minor factor.

Parents and staff alike speak of misapprehensions and the 'fear factor' of the school's academic reputation and some refrain from applying, but head of lower school feels the 'overall standard is more within reach than people assume'. Care is taken to put pupils in with friends, as 60+ feeder schools. Waiting lists still for Years 8 and 9. The sixth form admits 150 students, including around 30 girls from surrounding schools – external applicants likely to need 4 GCSE A*s.

Exit: Almost 100 per cent to university.

Remarks: Not uncommon for parents to hop county borders to ensure they are in the catchment area of a first class education. Very normal, honest, able pupils amongst similar staff, bristling with confidence and intelligence.

Kelly College

Parkwood Road, Tavistock, Devon, PL19 0HZ

- Pupils: 350: 200 boys, 150 girls; 50-50 day/boarding • Ages: 11-18
- Anglican foundation but all faiths and denominations welcome
- Fees: Boarding £20,700-£24,600; Day £11,400-£14,100 pa • Independent

Tel: 01822 813 100
Fax: 01822 612 050
Email: admissions@kellycollege.com
Website: www.kellycollege.com

Headmaster and principal of the Kelly College Foundation: Since 2008, Dr Graham Hawley BSc, PhD, PGCE (early forties). Educated at Mill Hill School, followed by Durham and Exeter. Not a pin stripe suited, hands on lapels, sound bite delivering headmaster of the bullfrog sort, a modest and gently amusing conversationalist who listens sensitively ('He really understands us,' said one of the girls) and has sane and realistic ideas about Kelly College and its constituents. After a spell at Ardingly as housemaster, he moved on to Warwick School as deputy head – a job 'I was surprised to be offered'.

He was even more surprised to be offered the job at Kelly, but 'if there is an opportunity....' Was attracted to the school for its most obvious qualities: its size, the location with its natural beauty and the opportunities it gives the young for enjoying childhood. 'For the most part the young here are gloriously unsophisticated.' Those initial attractions are what continue to sustain him.

'Before I discovered plankton' is an unusual paragraph opener from the headmaster of an independent school. Dr Hawley's 1st class hons in natural sciences and his doctorate have taken him to solitary places: the west coast of Scotland, Devon, Cornwall, India, Bangladesh and Sumatra. Do not think Gussie Fink-Nottle. Think someone who is highly intelligent and articulate, with a close eye for detail and the willing ability to notice and pay attention to everyone. Everyone we spoke to, from ground staff and cooks (those vital people) to pupils, staff and parents, spoke of the head's interest in and concern for individuals – 'He stands outside every morning and greets us by name'. Married to Rachel, they have two delightful children who attend the Kelly Prep School.

Academic matters: If you are interested in those ghastly league tables you may be disappointed. 'Education is not about league tables' – a point of view expressed by an increasing number of heads who no longer enter their schools. Kelly is one of those. However if you are a results junkie and need a fix before considering Kelly, the results are published on the website : in 2009 31per cent gained A grades and 78 per cent gained A to C grades. This is not a selective school when it comes to academics. 'We will ensure that pupils do as well as they can but we are not an exam factory,' says the head. Class sizes are small – sometimes very small at A level – and without exception pupils we spoke to were full of praise for the extra help offered by their teachers when necessary. A good range of subjects on offer – proper academic subjects, not raffia dolly making and flower arranging – with excellent language and IT areas. Parents spoke of the expert and sensitive advice they had had from staff when trying to help their children choose the most suitable subjects for them. There remains a school of thought that says, 'Better to go further afield if you want a real academic education,' but that lobby is 'less vociferous these days,' a very satisfied parent told us. Parents and pupils speak very highly of the help given to those with special needs.

Games, Options, the Arts: For those in the know, has an awesome reputation for sport – particularly swimming. The list of champions and Olympians is impressive (over thirty Olympians in the last thirty years) and endless county and national champions. But it does not feel a hearty place: it is old fashioned enough to insist on old-style school blazers with ribbons and badges festooned all over athletic gods and goddesses, but musicians, artists, thespians and prefects can be equally decorated – the school is just good at celebrating and acknowledging. The groundsmen look after the pitches marvellously, but we felt it was significant, or at any rate interesting, that all these successes came without a sports hall. Stories were told of opposing teams begging to be allowed to leave the Astroturf over the road and play inside, only to be told, 'We don't let the weather interfere'.

On the other hand, a splendid and most interestingly designed performing arts centre with superb facilities for music, drama and debate – to say nothing of interval entertainment. Close by is the art building with evidence of creative painting and pottery. Outdoor activities are legion. We were left gasping in admiration at the number of boys and girls who had completed the 125 mile canoe marathon from Devizes to Westminster; completed the Ten Tors race; trained as divers, rifle shots and mountaineers. So much to do and so much enthusiastic willingness to have a go.

Background and Atmosphere: Very close to the attractive town of Tavistock, with its historical connections with the Duke of Bedford, who donated the land, founded in 1877 by an Admiral Kelly. Sculptured into the side of the hill overlooking Dartmoor, the main building is a wonderful example of what Victorians felt a public school should look like. The result is long corridors with gothic archways, stone floors, wide staircases, mullioned windows: all very Hogwarty but generously softened with skilfully chosen colours, pictures, honours and, when we visited, wonderful heraldic banners as part of that year's theme, created by the younger children with enthusiastic support and encouragement from the seniors – a tribute to the universal friendliness pervading throughout. That really is one of the impressive aspects of the school, which must account for such keen willingness in so many activities. Handsome library presided over by enthusiastic librarian; slightly forbidding but impressive chapel, used four times a week. Boarders spoke enthusiastically of the sixth form centre and the activities arranged at weekends. Flexi boarding is very flexi.

Attractive new buildings higher up the hill behind the Victoriana, one of them the delightful Conway House where the eleven and twelve year old boys and girls live in comfortable harmony before joining the senior houses. 'It's a good way of settling in,' one of them told us, 'and the staff are very friendly.' As for the co-ed question, has been doing this for nearly forty years and it all feels very relaxed and natural.

Pastoral Care and Discipline: Lunch in the dining room (excellent Yorkshire pud) was a good insight into the relationships between staff and pupils. Clearly mutual respect and genuine affection, with enough of both to allow friendly banter on occasions. The pupils themselves were forthcoming, friendly and honest in their conversation with us. While accepting that bullying was always a possibility, they felt that the tutorial system in place was a good safety net and protection – always someone to talk to; Ofsted categorised the standard of pastoral care as outstanding. Pretty sensible school rules based on common sense – 'We don't have much trouble,' said one senior member of staff.

Pupils and Parents: Parents come from a broad spectrum of professions and choose it for a variety of reasons. One said to us, 'Kelly is famous for its swimming. My son can swim but hates it. But he gets stuck into lots of other things and that's the point. I take the view that excellence breeds excellence. It's good to have it around.' The pupils we met and observed were open, friendly and trusting and we noticed how much interaction there was between the different age groups. It really did feel like a family – even the bunch of genial rogues we spoke to were very friendly, funny and loyal.

Entrance: About 50 per cent of entries into the first form come from Kelly Prep, just down the road. Academically the emphasis is on literacy and numeracy, with as much attention paid to potential as to knowledge. Entrance at sixth form is based on GCSE results (or equivalent) – normally about twenty new sixth formers joining each year. The important thing is to be alert, bright-eyed and willing to be taught. That applies as much to rugby players as potential Nobel Prize winners.

Exit: Around 98 per cent go on to universities with an average of two Oxbridge places a year. Popular universities include London, Bristol, Bath, Southampton, Manchester.

Money Matters: Scholarships and bursaries are available. Naval and Services families may receive ten per cent discount. Don't be afraid to ask.

Remarks: A delightful, small and happy school which offers wonderful opportunities to anyone who is prepared to get stuck in, where effort is rewarded and friendships flourish, unhampered by bogus sophistication and false glitter.

Kelvinside Academy

Linked to Kelvinside Academy Junior School in the Junior section

33 Kirklee Road, Glasgow, Glasgow, G12 0SW

• Pupils: 610 • Ages: 3-18 • Size of sixth form: 90 • Inter-denom
• Fees: £9,360-£9,897 pa • Independent

Tel: 01413 573 376
Fax: 01413 575 401
Email: registrar@kelvinsideacademy.org.uk
Website: www.kelvinsideacademy.org.uk

Rector: Since August 2009, Mrs Lesley Douglas BEd CMath MIMA SQH, formerly deputy head of The Mary Erskine School and Assistant Rector at High School of Glasgow. Mrs Douglas is married with two children.

Academic matters: Follows the Scottish system, with Standard Grade, Intermediate 2, Highers and Advanced Highers. School traditionally strong on maths and sciences, 'science within the class' but strong across the board. Max class size 20, parallel classes, upper school setted for English, maths and modern languages. Good work-shadowing arrangements. Strong learning support with trained teachers in each faculty.

Games, Options, the Arts: Lots of music – masses of tinies carrying instruments bigger than themselves were struggling off to junior orchestra when we visited, a lovely sight. Drama timetabled and impressive. Masses of extras. Liberal studies includes a wide range of classes – e.g. philosophy, psychology, cooking.

Rugby and cricket powerful, girls play hockey. PE is mixed and can be taken by staff of either sex. Two serious gyms, CCF compulsory for all for one year, thereafter voluntary. DofE and camping at Rannoch (costed into fees).

Background and Atmosphere: Technically The Kelvinside Academy War Memorial Trust, in a purpose-built building in Kelvinside. Has expanded down to nursery level, with parents dropping off early and collecting late (late waiting till 6.00pm). Super computer complex which includes a multimedia lab 'that anyone can use', and a small lab for the website, with conference and digital enhancing facilities. Rather a fine double-decker library. Stunning new Gilchrist Theatre opened in Kennedy Mall (Nigel Kennedy was major donor). Certain amount of spreading across the road – the two houses here are destined to become a sixth form house – and plans are afoot to roof over part of the frankly disorganised area at the back of the school proper to form a social area.

Pastoral Care and Discipline: House system, strong PSE. 'A certain amount of smoking' – 'We flush the smokers out'. Only one recent drugs incident; will use random testing if suspect evidence of involvement; counselling on hand but miscreants are probably out anyway. School boasts 'a strong partnership with parents'. Holiday club to help with baby sitting problems.

Pupils and Parents: Middle class, professional, a significant number of first-time buyers, lots of travelling. From Gairlochead, the Trossachs, to Dunlop in Ayrshire. Bus from Newton Mearns/Southside.

Entrance: Through the nursery, or wherever; traditionally at 5, 11, 12 or sixth form level. Not academically selective – by interview and assessment.

Exit: Over 80 per cent to universities – usually Scotland; Glasgow and Strathclyde Business School popular – 'We're a parochial lot' – but trickle elsewhere and the very occasional Oxbridge candidate. Lots of engineers.

Money Matters: Usual discounts for siblings, bursarial fund in place. Will help 'wherever possible' if financial difficulties occur.

Remarks: Strong traditional school. The girls look as though they have always been there.

Kent College

Old Church Road, Pembury, Tunbridge Wells, Kent, TN2 4AX

• Pupils: 410 girls (90 board). • Ages: 11-18 • Size of sixth form: 100
• Methodist but other faiths welcome • Fees: Day £15,474; Boarding £24,945 pa • Independent

Tel: 01892 822 006
Fax: 01892 820 221
Email: seniorschool@kentcollege.kent.sch.uk
Website: www.kent-college.co.uk

Head: Since 2008, Mrs Sally-Anne Huang MA, PGCE (late thirties). Educated at Bolton School for Girls and Lady Margaret Hall, Oxford where she read classics and English. She took her PGCE at King's College, London. Married to Alexis, a management consultant whom she met at Oxford. They have two young sons. Spent six years at Sevenoaks School where she taught English and classics and was latterly a housemistress. Moved to Roedean as sixth form housemistress, then senior housemistress and spent four years as deputy head before moving to Kent College. Has raised the academic standards and increased numbers and would like to raise standards still further but is determined to keep a wide ability range. Has a very good relationship with the girls and operates a genuine open door policy so girls feel comfortable to go and see her at any time.

Academic matters: Apart from the usual subjects, film studies, product design (textiles), food technology, drama and theatre studies, psychology and PE are offered at A level. 80 per cent A*- B grades and 45 per cent A*/A grades. GCSEs 96 per cent A*–C. 82 per cent A*–B . The usual subjects offered, plus textiles, food technology, Latin, Spanish, German, French, drama, and PE. Option to take all three sciences separately or as a dual award. Inspirational textiles teacher has taken the subject to new heights. Science is strong and a pupil recently won bronze in the International Chemistry Olympiad.

RE taught to all up to the sixth form and all younger girls take food technology. Healthy eating is covered in PSHE. The careers department is proactive and helpful and sixth form attend a higher education preparation programme with weekly sessions on interview technique, gap year planning, money management etc. Due to the recent increase in pupil numbers, several new teachers have joined so there is a healthy mix of new younger teachers and others who have been in the school for many years. Plenty of male teachers – one a housemaster. Good support for minor learning difficulties and good communication between learning support and mainstream teachers.

Games, Options, the Arts: All the usual sports – girls have competed at national level at swimming, hockey and gymnastics and are U13 south east area cross country champions. A Gymnast Academy was set up in summer 2009 and is run by ex Olympian Natalie Davies – also open to outsiders on Saturdays. Outdoor activities seen as important and the school has appointed a head of outdoor education who oversees the Duke of Edinburgh programme and various adventure trips at home and abroad. A 'Confidence Course' has been built in the grounds which includes a scramble net, a 12 ft wall and a 30ft abseil tree – school officers in sixth form have a team building weekend using the course. Sixth formers are required to take part in sport for one double period a week but this could be trampolining, aerobics, aquarobics, Salsa or more mainstream team sports. Everyone encouraged to get involved.

Lots of clubs before and after school and at lunchtime, from Tae kwon-do to public speaking lessons and clay pigeon shooting and girls are encouraged to initiate activities and start clubs e.g. a street dance club and gospel choir. Astonishing that they can fit so much into a day. They are even good at bee keeping and the school's honey was commended at the National Honey Show.

Top two years have enrichment programme where they work in a small team on a project of their choice to gain a Record of Achievement by the Open College of the North West. This could be producing the school magazine or a cooking course leading to Leith's certificate in food and wine, an extended essay and community service. Young Enterprise scheme where they can run their own business for six months , working in mixed groups with other local schools. Charity Committee organises fund raising events. Plenty of opportunities to hone public speaking skills and look at the bigger picture in World AIMS (Action in Methodist Schools) Weekend where such issues as the arms trade, climate change and development are debated and at the Global Students Forum and model United Nations events in Tunbridge Wells and Bath. Girls Schools Association recently held an annual conference at Kent College where the girls debated 'Are women taking over the world?' – lots of thought provoking and challenging stuff. Sandi Toksvig was a recent visitor and she signed copies of her book 'Girls are Best'. Drama impressive with productions in the purpose-built Judi Dench theatre – 'the school has very high expectations of the girls and they always seem to step up to the plate'. Music on the up with a modern music centre and Apple Mac computer suite where girls can compose. LAMDA and English Speaking Board exams and every girl will speak in at least one assembly a year.

Background and Atmosphere: Founded in 1886 in Folkestone and moved to its present site in Pembury, just outside Tunbridge Wells during World War II. The school is one of nine belonging to the Methodist Independent Education Trust and managed by the Trust's board of management – but they do this with a very light touch. The school also has its own governing body half of whom are members of the Methodist Church or members of a Christian Church. Methodists state that their schools aim to be 'caring, family communities committed to the development and full potential of each individual, having regard for their personal attributes as well as their academic aspirations'. Kent College certainly does this and caring for the individual is central to the ethos of the school – each girl's wellbeing is paramount.

Modern and well designed boarding houses and classrooms cluster around the original baronial style Victorian house and everywhere has a light and airy feel. Since the new headmistress arrived, there has been a huge amount of refurbishment and building projects with new science labs and IT suites already completed and more specialist classrooms planned.

Pastoral Care and Discipline: The school has a warm and welcoming atmosphere and girls are happy and relaxed while leading incredibly busy lives. A strong Christian ethos is a subtle part of the school routine; girls are expected to take part in assemblies but the celebration of other religious festivals is an integral part of school life. A spirit of tolerance and respect is part of the ethos. Relaxed and comfortable girl/staff relationships. The tutor system ensures any problems are picked up early – mentors are allocated to girls who struggle and there is a school counsellor. Girls are supportive of each other across the year groups and the house system means that different year groups pull together in sporting competitions and charity work. Day girls are allowed in the social areas of boarding houses and are encouraged to try flexi-boarding and older girls help supervise younger ones at bed time. New girls are integrated quickly and attend an induction programme which includes an overnight camp in the school's orchard. Discos and socials with local boys' schools are popular.

Pupils and Parents: The school seems to breed great enthusiasm and loyalty. Twenty per cent of boarders from overseas from e.g. Nigeria, China, Russia, Thailand and mainland Europe but nationalities carefully balanced and the school takes trouble to prevent cliques forming. About 25 children need extra help with their English. About 20 per cent of boarders come from Services families. School sees itself as a small global community. There does not seem to be a typical Kent College girl but they do have a great zest for life and want to try everything. The school produces extraordinarily confident girls with a 'can do' attitude who are encouraged to surpass their expectations and believe that they can be anything they want to be – and yet there is no hint of arrogance. They come from as far as Bromley and Tenterden – good network of school buses. Great variety of parents from all walks of life – great tolerance of difference but mostly from business and professional families. Famous old girls include the Countess of Wessex and Sarah Sands, the first female editor of the Sunday Telegraph. Good links with parents who feel involved at every step. Active parents' association who organise social events throughout the year – a ball, coffee mornings, new parents' social evenings and a pamper evening. There is also a thriving old girls' association and active Friends of Kent College Association which includes ex staff, parents and governors.

Entrance: Not overly competitive – broad intake and can cope with a wide range of abilities as there is lots of individualised care. Most enter the school at 11+ and attend the entrance day in the November before entry when they are interviewed and sit the school's own exams in English, maths and verbal reasoning. The school also requires a letter from the girl's current head. Entry at 12+ and 13+ with exams in the January before when they are also tested in science and French. A taster day and overnight stay are strongly encouraged. Those who come up from the Prep School also have to take the test. Sixth form entrants need 6 GCSEs at C or above and A or B grades in the subjects they wish to study at A level. Children come from a wide range of local prep schools and primaries including Holmewood House, Rose Hill, Sevenoaks and St Michael's Otford.

Exit: About 5–7 leave after GCSEs usually for the co-eds e.g. Sevenoaks or boys' grammars. Sometimes girls come back and have been known to repeat the lower sixth year rather than stay somewhere else. Most go on to some form of further education to a huge range of destinations from pharmacology at Edinburgh, chemical engineering at Cambridge, land management at Royal Agricultural College, Cirencester, retail marketing at Loughborough, Spanish at Oxford, criminology at Cardiff. Lots of help with UCAS forms and personal statements and Oxbridge preparation lessons including interview practice with a local boys' school.

Money Matters: Academic, music, drama, music, art and sport scholarships offered at up to 10 per cent of fees. Means-tested bursaries also available.

Remarks: The school has improved hugely since the arrival of the new headmistress. The numbers are up and a major refurbishment programme has been implemented – recent glowing report from the Independent Inspectorate. Girls leave with great self confidence and strong sense of purpose.

Keswick School

Vicarage Hill, Keswick, Cumbria, CA12 5QB

• Pupils: 1,075; 545 boys, 530 girls; all day except 45 boarders
• Ages: 11-18 • Size of sixth form: 240 • Non-denom • Fees: Boarding £7,500 pa; Tuition free • State

Tel: 017687 72605
Fax: 017687 74813
Email: admin@keswick.cumbria.sch.uk
Website: www.keswick.cumbria.sch.uk

Headmaster: Since 1996, Mr Mike Chapman MA (late-fifties). Cambridge natural scientist, taught biology at City of London School, then from 1980 at Sexey's School, Somerset, where he ran boarding and sixth form, became deputy and briefly head. Fast-talking, buzzy non-northerner, up-front leader, has made quite an impact in Cumbria. Full of ideas, ambitious for the school, with its growing reputation for good practice; loves it here and so he should, with the finest study window view in England. Believes in 'sheep-dogging' – claims chivvying pupils to observe minor rules helps to set right conditions for getting big things right.

Academic matters: Results at GCSE and A level remarkable across the board in view of non-selective comprehensive entry. GCSE A*–C passes around 80 per cent; English regularly does well and science too (unusually, separate sciences taught by specialists to almost all pupils – school has been awarded science specialist status). Setting in most subjects from Year 8. A level taken by about three quarters of original year group; vocational courses laid on for Year 12 leavers, including popular applied business. A/C passes at A level 75 per cent in 2010. Few take modern languages but do well. Art regularly gets many As and Bs. Some provision in small department for SEN; other local schools specialise more in this area.

Teaching styles lean towards the traditional. Facilities are excellent (see below). Staff tend to stay in Keswick (who wouldn't?); about half have been there more than 10 years, average age is about 40. Pupils appreciate staff commitment and teaching quality. School has Leading Edge and Training School status and Ofsted 'outstanding' status for boarding and sixth form (good overall).

Games, Options, the Arts: All the usual team games, with regular successes at county level; extensive playing fields, dry ski slope, lottery-funded sports hall shared with local community. Particular emphasis on outdoor education (strong staff team, Lake District on doorstep). Music thrives – much instrumental and singing tuition, very successful choir. Serious efforts made to overcome geographical isolation through visits abroad and, e.g. to theatres.

Background and Atmosphere: Re-founded in 1898, briefly grant maintained, now voluntary-aided again – one of that rare and under-vaunted breed, a state boarding school. A lot of civic pride about, strong sense of identity. Moved in 1996 to one half of original split site, on town outskirts. New buildings are airy and good to work in, blend with refurbished older ones, all surrounded by stunning vistas of lakeland fells. Up to date ICT network throughout means internet access from anywhere, video conferencing etc; all can email. Circulation areas generally tidy and litter-free. Striking bottle-green and maroon uniform; only sixth form are allowed into nearby tripper/tourist town.

Pupils are cheerful, busy and positive. Not much sign of small-town doziness (pupils don't see rural setting as a disadvantage), though inevitably life moves in a more uncomplicated way than in a big city. Boarders (boys and girls together, in purpose-built house) add variety and breadth to the school atmosphere – a particular enthusiasm of Mr Chapman. Originally intended to accommodate children from remote settlements, the boarding list is now made up of UK and EU passport holders from all over the world, including Scots escapers; applicants are carefully weeded on academic and personality grounds, i.e. they have to fit in.

Pastoral Care and Discipline: Efficient and unfussy pastoral system, plus the now common formal home/school contract. 'Conduct and discipline' is an important area. Keswick attracts the usual holiday town bad behaviour but drugs and alcohol are not a real problem. Governors may permanently exclude persistent offenders.

Pupils and Parents: Most of the school's catchment area beyond Keswick is occupied by sheep, hence it draws substantial numbers from the decaying industrial belt of west Cumbria. Aspirational parents, e.g. from Sellafield, run a large fleet of buses from as far away as Egremont, which broadens the social intake and parental support helps to push up attainment. Some have moved into Keswick, which has allegedly inflated house prices.

Entrance: No entry tests, though headmaster asks for recent report from current school, for information but not selection (feeders are overwhelmingly state primary). Preference given to siblings, prospective boarders. Out of catchment applicants considered on strict basis of distance from school. Small intake into Year 12.

Exit: About 15 per cent leave after GCSE and a further 15–20 after Year 12. Ninety per cent of Year 13 leavers go on to university, mainly in the north; a handful each year to Oxbridge.

Remarks: In some ways, more like a traditional country independent school (but without the pretentiousness) than a rural comprehensive. Headmaster – 'Not "headteacher", please' – happy with this aspect, as with his unashamed advocacy of middle class values, but he and the staff are proud of the school's history of service to its all-ability, wide social range.

Kilgraston School

Linked to Kilgraston Preparatory School in the Junior section

Bridge Of Earn, Perthshire, Bridge Of Earn, Perthshire, PH2 9BQ

• Pupils: 325 girls (+14 day boys in the nursery); 160 boarders, the rest day • Ages: 2-18 • Size of sixth form: 90 girls; (60 boarders). • RC, but plenty of non-Catholic pupils (including Muslims) • Fees: Day £7,875-£13,590; Boarding £19,050-£23,175 pa • Independent

Tel: 01738 812 257
Fax: 01738 813 410
Email: headoffice@kilgraston.com
Website: www.kilgraston.com

Principal: Since 2004, Mr Michael Farmer BA PGCE (forties), who was educated in the state system in Leicestershire, did economics at Portsmouth and then became a yacht skipper. He did his PGCE at Bristol and comes from Headington School in Oxford, where he was deputy head and head of sixth form (having moved there from Godolphin with the erstwhile headmistress Mrs Hilary Fender). A Roman Catholic. Heads a school very different to that to which he first applied – it absorbed the 8–13 section of the much loved girls-only prep school, Butterstone, at the end of the summer term 2003. The girls from Butterstone have now all gone (most went down south) and Kilgraston has grown by over 30 per cent.

An open door head, his wife Mary Ann 'is deeply supportive' and runs the sixth form creative cuisine course. Comments that 'Mr Farmer has done loads for the school but is not necessarily child-friendly' and that 'his eyes tend to glaze over'. However, school says that recent parental survey 'very positive'.

Academic matters: Not the sleepy place it used to be – now has a good academic record. Academic success has helped the population grow by an impressive 50 per cent in the past five years with the school roll now full, boarding by even more and now over-subscribed.

Runs primarily on the Scottish system, with Standard grades followed by Highers and Advanced Highers to university in sixth form. Certain number of fast track standard grades in French and English. Science on the up, with new head of physics, excellent science labs. Good remedial unit (CReSTeD WS status – wow), with specialist teachers for dyslexia and dyspraxia – one to one teaching and EFL on offer. Language labs popular. Many exchanges, French, German and Spanish (both pupils and staff) via Sacred Heart network.

Games, Options, the Arts: Superb indoor 25 swimming pool complex opened in 2008, magnificent sports hall (also incorporating a fitness suite and climbing wall) faced in sandstone, with niches echoing those in the stable building (well converted into prep school with attached nursery) – Historic Scotland at its best. Wide choice of sports. Eight newly resurfaced floodlit tennis courts, a new international sized all-weather floodlit hockey pitch. The only school in Scotland with equestrian facilities on campus – centre with 60m x 40m floodlit arena and livery. Sport is a big focus with newly appointed director Pauline Stott (GB Olympic hockey captain, Sydney 2000) and head of curriculum PE Louise Baxter (Scotland and GB hockey).

Strong drama, and inspired art – 'going from strength to strength'; the art department overlooks the Rotunda and currently boasts an enormous computer-linked loom. Tremendous ceramics and regular master classes. D of E, debating, leadership courses. Music centre in the attics, with keyboards and 14 individual sound-proofed study rooms; guitars and stringed instruments everywhere and a sound recording studio. Writers' group. Cooking and brilliant needlework, the girls make their own ball gowns for the annual ball with Merchiston. Dedicated director of weekend and outdoor activities encourages all sorts of co-curricular options such as whitewater rafting, canoeing, sailing.

Background and Atmosphere: Founded in 1920 – one of 200 networked schools and colleges of the Society of the Sacred Heart. Moved to the handsome red Adamesque sandstone house in 1930, masses of extensions including spectacular Barat wing, light and airy with huge wide passages. Mr Farmer has removed many of the statues of saints from the Central Hall, feeling this would be an excellent place 'to show off some of our superb artwork'. Indeed pupils' work does look smashing, but school looks a bit bleak. Bedsits from third year, tinies' dorms now divided into attractive cabins for each. Much investment going on in the dorms area with newly refurbished rooms, moderated WiFi access and single rooms with washing facilities for girls from age 12.

School stops at 4.10 on Fridays for day and weekly boarders, but masses of alternative activities for those who stay back. Computers, games hall/courts, art, music and sewing rooms open throughout the weekend. God still important here – most attend assembly and mass on Sundays, Feast days still special.

Pastoral Care and Discipline: Sacred Heart ethos prevails – staff enormously caring, 'will go the extra mile'. Pastoral conferences every week, independent counsellor on tap. Disciplinary committee, gatings, suspensions, fatigues round school for smoking. Drinkers are suspended and a not so recent problem was 'nipped in the bud'. Will test areas, not girls, if drugs suspected – the girls here are not the dozy lot they used to be. Counsellor on hand, and bullying handled by BFG (Big Friendly Group). Charming little handbook for new pupils full of helpful advice.

Pupils and Parents: Day children from Fife, Dundee and Perthshire and even as far afield as Stirling. Boarders from all over Scotland and beyond (including this year several from London). Currently 37 from overseas ('The internet is handy,' says the head).

Entrance: Not that difficult, although boarding places are currently at a premium. Scholarship exams in February. Junior school entrants also do CE. Otherwise 11+ from primary schools and 12+ from prep schools. Pupils can come whenever, half term if space available. Sixth form entry – 'good Standard grades/GCSEs to follow A level course'; pupils come from overseas or local state schools and are steered to 'appropriate' levels of study.

Exit: About 98 per cent to higher education including leading universities – recently Aberdeen, Bath, Cambridge, Edinburgh, Glasgow, Oxford and St Andrews.

Money Matters: OK financially – the nuns left rich pickings – as evidenced in the current capital investment programme (swimming pool, new theatre, bistro style dining room, international-sized all weather hockey pitch etc).

Up to ten academic, art and music scholarships. Also riding, tennis and sporting scholarships. Almost one third receive assistance of some sort. School is 'good at finding Trust funding' for those who have fallen on hard times.

Remarks: The only all-girls' boarding school left in Scotland and popular. Small, gentle, not overtly Catholic, with terrific facilities. Useful prep facilities; Scots parents see it as a viable alternative to St Leonards.

King Alfred School

Linked to King Alfred Lower School in the Junior section

Manor Wood, 149 North End Road, Golders Green, London, NW11 7HY

• Pupils: 615 all day, 50:50 boys:girls • Ages: 4-18 • Size of sixth form: 75 • Non-denom • Fees: £13,635 pa • Independent

Tel: 020 8457 5200
Fax: 020 8457 5249
Email: pressoffice@kingalfred.org.uk
Website: www.kingalfred.org.uk

Head: Since 2003, Mrs Dawn Moore (mid-forties), BSc, MA (London), PGCE. Grew up in Nuneaton (daughter of a teacher), where she attended Higham Lane School, before proceeding to UCL to study genetics. PGCE at the Institute of Education, MA in education management at Kings College, London. Started at King Alfred as a science teacher in 1986, recognising at once that this was somewhere she felt at home: 'On my first visit, pupils came up to me and said, "Hello. Who are you? Can we help?" They weren't afraid to talk to adults. It was so different from my teaching practice'. After having her two daughters (now in the senior school), she took a couple of years off. Returned as a part-time science teacher, then deputy head – 'There was no favouritism. I had to apply for every job'.

A warm, unpretentious enthusiast, completely committed to the school's ethos, 'Dawn' operates an open-door policy and knows most children, from the tinies to the sixth form, by name. Parents see her as an intelligent, anchoring presence: 'Dawn is wise and good at putting your mind at ease,' said one. 'The head is lovely,' said another. A trained and practising schools inspector, in her limited spare time she loves reading and cooking.

Academic matters: A school where exams are famously not the priority (pupils sit no exams whatsoever until Year 10, and even then only because 'it's necessary to assess what they can and cannot cope with prior to GCSE'). That said, prides itself on being able to teach to the highest standards – 'If a child can get four or five As, we'll get them there,' says the head. Pleasing results at GCSE (most pupils take nine), with about 50 per cent getting A* or A; equally solid at A level, with 42 per cent getting As. Exams may not be the focus, but 'personalised learning' definitely is, and parents feel happy that every child is treated as an individual. 'We have no idea who the clever children are,' said one. 'All are special – they're not compared to one another.'

Not a vast range of subject choice at GCSE (only curriculum languages French and Spanish); good variety at A level, with 20 options, and every attempt is made to accommodate any combination. The classroom approach, as with the whole-school approach, is relaxed – 'Teachers are not that strict,' said one senior school pupil. 'It can sometimes take quite a long time for lessons to begin, but you're still motivated to work.' Homework and marking, however, can be a bit too relaxed for some – 'The school believes that children should be children,' said one mother. 'I like the fact that it doesn't force them to do two hours a night, but sometimes I think they could push a little more.'

Sixth form particularly strong in the expressive arts (photography amongst the best in the country) and arts subjects (English, history); scientists generally find themselves in a minority. A few vocational options post GCSE (business studies and music technology) – 'Some children are not ready to leave school at 16,' says the head. Special needs well catered for with a qualified SENCo in the lower school and generously staffed curriculum support in the senior school. Mild dyslexia and dyspraxia, ADHD, mild autism and Asperger's and physical disabilities (has a lift) not a problem. Those with behavioural difficulties, however, would struggle, since 'self-regulation' is a central theme.

Games, Options, the Arts: Known for its creativity and the strength of its visual arts teaching, all lower school classrooms have ovens for baking; has its own forge. Thriving drama, with theatre, 'black box' studio and master classes often given by parents, who are themselves leading lights in the profession. Music, too, is popular, with orchestras, band and ensembles of all kinds. Two well-stocked libraries, one for seniors, one for juniors.

Sport played enthusiastically, but 'go, fight, win' is not what this school is about. 'We don't have a first eleven in each year – often we just have a mixed-ability team,' says the head. The spirit, however, is strong, and an eager crowd turns out to support the home team. As well as the usual ball sports, sails three (school-built) boats on Welsh Harp. Games aside, for a London school an outdoorsy place. The large central playing field is at the heart of the campus and even on the rainiest day is filled with fresh air enthusiasts. Considerable emphasis on self-sufficiency. Den building very much part of the experience and whole-year camping trips take place from Year 4.

'Extra-curricular', too, is core to the curriculum. In the senior school, Years 7–11 required to make their choice from a wide range of activities, from pottery to golf; sixth form options include screenwriting for films, emotional intelligence and Mandarin. Strong commitment to volunteering throughout, with pupils helping out at the local special school and raising significant sums for international causes (including building a school after the tsunami in Sri Lanka). Good careers advice (which kicks off in Year 7) helps with GCSE and A level options and UCAS applications pre and post A level. As one might expect, green is high on the agenda – one of the first schools to introduce solar panels and recycling bins. Delicious, exclusively healthy lunch with plenty of fresh salads, yoghurt and water.

Background and Atmosphere: Founded by parents in Hampstead in 1898, original aim was to provide an education based on what was best for the child and encourage learning for its own sake. Part of the progressive movement, sees its kindred schools as Bedales in Hampshire and St Christopher in Letchworth. Moved to its current site, a leafy patch of north London opposite Golders Hill Park, in 1921, and has recently expanded, with a new school building for the infants across the road from the main site at Ivy Wood, once the home of Anna Pavlova. Attractive, if compact, grounds, with a mixture of periods and styles (new fitness studio, music and drama block, lovely arts and crafts dining hall) grouped around a central village-like common. Star attractions include a wooded amphitheatre, an arbour (Squirrel Hall), formed from the sheltering branches of two ancient chestnuts, and a diminutive farm, complete with chickens, ducks and bees.

The original ethos – liberal, progressive, egalitarian, child-centred – remains core to the school's values today. Parents and pupils agree that the needs of each child are foremost – 'They try to act very holistically. They look at the individual and find out what makes them shine'. In many respects, too, operates as a large extended family, without the rigid age divide found elsewhere. 'It's a really friendly school,' said one Year 9. 'Older kids look out for younger ones and you'll see sixth formers play with Year 7s.' Most children seem to enjoy their time here – 'They skip into school every day,' said one long-time parent. 'Even after the holidays, they can't wait to get back.'

Pastoral Care and Discipline: Has always believed in minimal rules and flat hierarchy. Teachers are called by their first name, pupils are expected to be self disciplined, co-operative and self-motivated. Head sees the mutual respect between teachers and pupils as one of the key strengths of the school, 'We trust them to be sensible'. The expectation, too, is that wrongdoing is likely to be an accident – 'We enable children to learn from their mistakes. There are no quick sanctions. It has to be worked through. Equally there are few re-offenders'. Those who cross the line between liberty and licence – 'being irresponsible in the science labs' or 'putting others in danger' – are given a 'blue form' and sent to the head. Children can be devastated – 'I've seen 16-year-old boys cry,' said a member of staff. Offences too serious to talk through – inappropriate behaviour towards their peers, bullying – can result in suspension. Expulsion for drugs on the premises, but head can't remember the last incident and the school has a 'huge' drugs education programme. 'The kids are pretty mature about sex and drugs,' said one parent. No uniform or dress code, but pupils tend not to push the boundaries, preferring standard-issue jeans and jumpers.

Four counsellors – 'We know what's out there and make it our business to be pro-active'. Help too from other pupils – peer mentoring, school 'Cits', pupils' council. The end result is a happy bunch of kids. 'I've seen other parents go through miserable teens,' said one mother with two teenage children at the school. 'King Alfred teaches them a lot of confidence.' Non-denominational – pupils of every faith and none.

Pupils and Parents: An arts and media favourite, parents often choose it for its informality and creativity. 'They come from both ends of the spectrum,' says Dawn Moore. 'There are those who are so liberal they think we're conservative and those who are conservative with a small "c".' Popular, too, with former pupils. New converts are often those who disliked their own, more traditional, schooldays: 'I'd have killed to go to a school like this,' said one. 'They make it such fun.' Pupils, mainly from the wealthier suburbs of north London (Hampstead, Golders Green, Highgate, Muswell Hill), are confident and articulate and expect to be given equal weight as adults. Quite a large international contingent – Americans, South Africans, Israelis, Swedish, Germans, Spanish, Italians.

Entrance: For entry at four, names down at birth, then first come first served (100–200 apply for 40 places): 'We go down the list'. New entrants come for a half-day assessment, are interviewed by the head of the lower school and observed by teachers – 'We soon pick up on how they function'. Seventy or so apply for a handful of places at 11 – 'A lot of thought goes into the mix of classes'. Not highly selective at A level – four GCSEs minimum for those already in the school, five for 12 or so newcomers, with A*–B in chosen subjects. All candidates, however, interviewed to ensure they'll fit into the school culture.

Exit: One or two leave in Year 6, another handful post GCSE – 'Some children have been here since they were four and it's quite a long time to spend at one school,' says the head. About 90 per cent to further education, a good chunk (8–12 each year) to art foundation, then to the full spectrum of universities, from PPE at Oxford and maths at Cambridge to Manchester, Sussex, UCL and Bristol. Carefully guided, the vast majority get into their first or second choice.

Money Matters: Though not particularly well endowed, attempts to keep fees as stable as possible while keeping facilities up to date. No scholarships, a small number (about four) of means-tested bursaries in Year 7 and sixth form. Also hoping to start a bursary from reception.

Remarks: A kind, liberal, creative school that suits the self starter, the sophisticated and the artistic (pupils and parents). Will get the best out of most children, but possibly not ideal for those who require competition in the classroom or on the games field. Good, too, for the square peg and those who might find a more traditional environment oppressive. Not a school for parents obsessed with league-table position or those looking for children who jump to attention when an adult enters the room.

King Edward VI Five Ways School

Scotland Lane, Bartley Green, Birmingham, West Midlands, B32 4BT

• Pupils: 1,175 girls and boys, all day • Ages: 11-18 • Size of sixth form: 390 • Non-denominational - broadly Christian • State

Tel: 0121 475 3535
Fax: 0121 477 8555
Email: office@kefw.bham.sch.uk
Website: www.ke5ways.bham.sch.uk

Head: Since 2003, Mr David J Wheeldon BA BEd MSc FRSA (mid fifties). Educated at Alleynes Grammar School, Uttoxeter. Read history at Birmingham, later studied politics. Returned to King Edward (was deputy for eight years), having spent six years as head of Altrincham Grammar School for boys. Married with two grown-up sons, he spends much of his free time travelling, dabbling in antiques and gardening. A Rotarian for many years, says he still flies the flag (but badly, he adds).

Friendly, exuberant, enthusiastic, with seemingly boundless energy, pupils say he's very pro getting involved and is really pushing things along. Despite the confident, sociable façade, you sense this is a man who not only likes but is used to getting his own way. We wonder what happens to the jolly persona on the odd occasion when he doesn't ('I go home and metaphorically kick the cat,' he jests). Insists he must defend and maintain the school's ethos but acknowledges it's equally important it moves with the times – 'We mustn't be set in aspic – we have to produce 21st century citizens who know how to learn, be wise, be good neighbours and be well qualified'. He wants and expects the best. When he says he wants to be the top co-ed school, he means it. Not that being co-ed in an area surrounded by quality girls' schools is easy – 'Parents of boys want co-ed schools, parents of girls often prefer single sex, but the girls themselves can and do win out and get the co-ed they prefer. That said, it's a difficult circle to square'.

Academic matters: Very good indeed. 66 per cent of GCSE passes at A*/A in 2010. 82 per cent of pupils gained 5+ A*/A grade. 87 per cent of A level entries are graded A or B. No weaknesses but particularly strong in English and economics. All usual subjects on offer plus sixth form additions of psychology, philosophy, government and politics, classical civilisation and media studies. Pupils take three single sciences. All study two languages from French, Latin, German and Spanish from Year 7. All take GCSE IT in Year 9 and GCSE RE or citizenship in Year 11. All sixth formers take AS and A2 together with A2 general studies and functional skills, brightest can take advanced extension awards (AEA). Accelerated KS3 curriculum and GCSEs begun in Year 9. IB to be introduced (with A level) from September 2011.

Classes average 25 in the main school, reducing to 20 at A level. Extra help on hand in most subjects. Maths workshops/clinics held four days a week, not just for standard help but for fun and to develop skills too. Only a handful are identified as having special needs, two with statements. Support given as needed.

Games, Options, the Arts: Good sports facilities including gym, sports hall, sports pavilion (doubles as additional lunch area), immaculate, county standard cricket pitch and own pool (recently refurbished to include sound and light system for aquarobics). A brand new, large, state of the art fitness suite. Climbing very popular – superb indoor climbing wall built when one in locality closed. All usual sports. All belong to a house; range of competitions held weekly – lots of sports, spelling bees, Call my Bluff etc. Art shows recent signs of improvement (including a new conservatory studio). Food tech offered to younger years. DT ordinary, nothing spectacular. About a tenth learn an instrument in school, with a handful playing to grade 8 standard. Good drama – seven productions a year.

Lots of trips to everywhere, for everything, emphasises 'Five Ways, five continents' – growing number of international links in Africa, India, China, New Zealand and Chicago. Plenty of extra-curricular on offer including D of E, chess, and debating – something for everyone, whatever their level of talent or expertise.

Background and Atmosphere: An aided, co-educational selective school, one of the seven King Edward Foundation schools (all bursarial work carried out jointly), founded in 1883. Funded by the state with additional help and funding from the Foundation. Moved from Five Ways to current 30-acre site on the southwest tip of the city in 1958. Formerly a grant maintained school, became co-ed in 1998. Has been designated a high performing specialist school, recent award of specialist status for humanities and a second specialism in science helping boost the coffers and drive the curriculum; school is a centre for The Royal Geographical Society and the Ordnance Survey.

Immediate area deprived but bordering open countryside – views of the reservoir and fields mingle with small terraces and high-rise. School steadily being smartened, still has feel of a 1950s grammar, the odd scuffed edge but more building, renovation and development in the pipeline – a new £2.2m sixth form study centre opened 2007. Super, well-kept grounds (full-time groundsmen work particularly hard). Pupils enjoy being at the school, say there's a good atmosphere and it's possible to have fun with their teachers.

Pastoral Care and Discipline: Firm discipline – anti-social behaviour not tolerated. Pupils say they get lots of support but also do a lot off their own backs. Have designated counsellor but are encouraged to talk to whoever they feel comfortable with. Peer tutoring being introduced. Assembly hall complete with fabulous church organ can, and does, accommodate the whole school, all seated since the opening of a 200 seat balcony in 2009. Three whole school assemblies a week including a traditional Christian assembly complete with hymn (nice touch).

Pupils and Parents: Pupils travel from all over Birmingham with some forty per cent from outside, primarily Worcestershire and the Black Country. Expected social and ethnic mix

– super origin chart on display shows many pupils' families originally from Ireland and India, handful from Africa, smattering from America and the Caribbean. Getting smarter (will push as far as they dare) but frequent uniform purges keep most looking reasonable ('We will smarten them up,' insists the head). Active Five Ways Old Edwardians Association. Notable OEs include: Kate Ashfield (actress), Ben McCarthy and Ben Wright (BBC journalists), David Cannadine (historian), Michael Checkland (Director General of the BBC) and Tom Butler (Bishop of Southwark).

Entrance: Competitive – 1,800 pupils vie for 150 places at 11. Pupils accepted by strict rank order of scores, no interviews, no concessions for siblings or proximity to school, though parents do appeal. No fixing to get 50 per cent girls (more boys than girls apply, school roughly 40 per cent girls, thanks to popularity of girls in sixth form). All applicants need to complete a grammar schools of King Edward VI application form and the LEA preference form supplied by their resident LEA. Each of the King Edward VI schools counts as a separate choice. Occasional places at other times.

Approximately 70 places per year for sixth form. Applicants tend to have straight As; some will have missed the boat first time around but worked extremely hard to earn a coveted place. Head enthused by additions, says they tend to be hard working and diligent, give a bit of a kick to some pupils who may have rested on their laurels.

Exit: Majority at 18, around ninety per cent to traditional universities, rest take a gap year. Around 12 a year to Oxbridge (growing numbers, says head).

Remarks: A top-flight, state, co-ed grammar school that competes well, but not quite on an even footing, with independent rivals. Very much about the education, not the school, a bargain for the middle classes, gives wings to the able but less well off.

King Edward VI Grammar School, Chelmsford

Broomfield Road, Chelmsford, Essex, CM1 3SX

• Pupils: 870: 805 boys, 65 girls in the sixth form. All day • Ages: 11-18
• Size of sixth form: 310 • Non-denominational • State

Tel: 01245 353 510
Fax: 01245 344 741
Email: office@kegs.org.uk
Website: www.kegs.org.uk

Headteacher: Since 2008, Mr Tom Sherrington BSc (Hons) MSc NPQH (forties). Previously head of secondary section at the British International School, Jakarta (a high performing school, we're told). Also deputy headteacher at Alexandra Park School, Haringey, and assistant headteacher at Holland Park School, Kensington. His interests include writing and performing music, playing guitar and piano.

Academic matters: In terms of academic achievement one of the top ten state grammars. In 2010, 79 per cent A/A* at GCSE, with 86 per cent A/B at A level (not including general studies, which is taken as a compulsory subject). Outstanding commitment from staff who, according to a parent, 'go a thousand miles beyond the call of duty and don't just stick to the curriculum. They give a proper education'. 'Teaching isn't obsessively focused towards exams,' and a love of learning is engendered right from the word go. Younger boys enjoy 'creative lesson plans' ('Blackadder' to illustrate a point and volcanoes made from bicarb of soda) whilst older pupils, according to a sixth former, are 'challenged and taken to another level'.

Extensive use of computers in all subject areas, each of which has its own website with lesson resumés and question sheets – big boon for team players who miss a lesson. Awards for those who tot up the most effort marks. 'The school values you if you try your best. We had a letter from the maths department praising our son for the work and effort he'd put in this year,' said a mum. Some feeling that the odd coaster slips through the net but head is adamant: 'Every child gets the provision they need – we try to find out what's causing a block'.

Full-time counsellor on hand if help is needed. General perception that boys are nurtured – 'Any difficulties are identified early on and strategies are given to help,' said a parent. Very few have special educational needs but a SENco for one-to-one assistance and ILPs. Visual impairment, dyslexia, dyspraxia and Asperger's syndrome are accommodated. Understanding, inclusive approach – 'circle of friends' sometimes recruited to look out for particular individuals.

Games, Options, the Arts: Not known as a particularly sporty place but rugby's faring well and full range of fixtures in all major sports. Sixth get the chance to play squash or swim at the local sports centre. Multigym, for all comers, recently opened after representations from the unteamy, who wanted somewhere to let off steam.

Welcoming art department – veritable Aladdin's cave crammed with lively work, especially by the younger ones. New music block – parents are impressed with the standard of concerts and way their children enjoy this side of school life. D of E, CCF, trips and good selection of clubs enrich beyond the curriculum. Best for those who live nearby – a long journey home can thwart involvement.

Background and Atmosphere: Founded in 1551, nearly three hundred and fifty years before it settled on the present site close to the town centre. Last hundred years have seen numbers increase eight-fold and buildings, permanent and 'temporary', added behind the original low-key redbrick frontage. Absolutely no frills, though. Library housed in the school's first hall – beanbags for the younger ones and friendly librarian who, according to a pupil, 'has an encyclopedic knowledge of every book'. The Darwin Centre – new sixth form centre – opened in September 2009. This three storey state-of-the-art building contains a spacious study area, high-tech careers library, new classroom and spectacular sixth form social area on the top floor. The project was funded by a legion of extremely generous donors and is the largest and most rapidly off-the-drawing-board-onto-the-foundations building project of any state school in the country.

Strong sense of community where the acquisition and sharing of knowledge exude from every pore. Contented, well behaved kids are absorbed in the learning process. Typical boyish inattention to sartorial matters (although a recent uniform drive has smartened them up significantly) but no deviation from the standard white shirts and black blazers – customised with a bright red stripe round collar and reveals. Plain blazers for boys and girls in the sixth with a free choice of shirt colours.

Big drive to improve school lunch has seen fizzy drinks banished and an emphasis on locally sourced meat and veg. Accessible web site gives menus for the term and clear indication of the odd dish that hasn't been prepared in house.

Pastoral Care and Discipline: Transition to the school can be difficult but parents find staff approachable and understanding. Slightest sniff of bullying is instantly investigated – support from staff mentors, who are available at any time. Active school council encourages a high level of civilized co-existence and lack of confrontation – 'My son's hair was slightly off the wall after the summer holidays. I was impressed with the way they managed to agree on a compromise,' commented a parent. But no exception to clear rules regarding banned substances – Mr Sherrington is determined 'to preserve social order within the school'.

Pupils and Parents: Pupils from as far afield as some London boroughs. Diverse parent body – range of occupations and backgrounds. Old Boys include Lord Fowler, Simon Heffer, Grayson Perry.

Entrance: Hugely competitive. In recent years, over 800 of the brightest examined for the 112 places. Parents say at least a couple of years of coaching are a must. Wide catchment area with over 60 feeder schools – prep and primary.

Almost all on to the sixth. Minimum four As, four Bs – plenty of warning that this is non-negotiable.

Exit: Virtually all to university – on average 16 per cent to Oxbridge. Spread of locations and courses – the traditionally demanding dominate.

Remarks: Inspired approach towards teaching. Staff are passionate about their subjects and students thrive in an atmosphere where it's cool to study.

King Edward VI High School for Girls

Edgbaston Park Road, Birmingham, West Midlands, B15 2UB

• Pupils: 550 girls; all day • Ages: 11-18 • Size of sixth form: 160
• Non-denom • Fees: £9,735 pa • Independent

Tel: 0121 472 1834
Fax: 01214 713 808
Email: ct@kehs.co.uk
Website: www.kehs.org.uk

Head: Since 1996, Miss Sarah H Evans BA MA (fifties); educated at King James' Grammar School, Knaresborough and Sussex, Leicester and Leeds Universities. Previously head of the Friends' School, Saffron Walden, and before that taught at Leeds Girls' High School, also Fulneck Girls' School. A delightful, calm Quaker; graceful, poised, knowledgeable (a look of Helen Mirren, we thought), exudes warmth, has a wonderful genuine smile. Teaches young ones library skills, older ones presentation skills and runs weekly current affairs, breakfast club. Is passionate about the girls and their education. Adored by girls, respected by staff, who say she is a wonderful head. Focused on community – working with other schools, Birmingham University – and on breadth – building characters for life. Wants to give her pupils 'wings to fly somewhere unexpected'.

Academic matters: Outstanding academically for decades, one of the country's top academic schools (placed at the pinnacle of league tables, A grades the norm). Superb, innovative, vibrant, creative teaching and an ethos of hard work. Biology, chemistry, maths and English are currently the most popular subjects – Latin not far behind. RS well liked, 'We get to debate politics and religion – it's really very exciting'. Practical and problem solving activities aplenty including 'paper clip physics' and participation in the education engineering scheme. 'Good Schools Guide' award for the best independent girls' school for A level business and economics, and also for classics, proudly on display. Many staff of long standing – excellent, lovers of teaching, passionate about their subjects, want girls to delight in the joys of learning, not be suffocated by the confines of exams and assessments. Lots of individual attention – help is available from all and any staff at all times.

Wide academic syllabus. Maximum class size 26. Over 60 per cent of pupils take A level sciences (and must follow a non-A level English course); one third takes arts (and must follow a non-A level maths course) and one third mixed. General studies taken as fifth A level – and girls get mostly As in this too. Russian, Italian, German and Spanish on offer. Classics department flourishing and innovative. School moved to IGCSE maths in 2005 – 'Much more fun and challenging', we're told.

Nine science labs, two computer rooms – equipment recently upgraded, super library (with high numbers of girls opting to study in school during exam period). Classrooms double as subject rooms, with old-fashioned desks in some, but filled with pupils' work on display – we particularly liked the facial symmetry and golden ratio in maths. Some classes taken with King Edward's School (qv). 'Outsiders sometimes think teaching here must be a soft option,' commented one member of staff, 'because all the girls are bright, but the fact is that a little doesn't go a long way – they lap it up and want more.' Girls are adept arguers and class discussion and debate are encouraged from the earliest forms.

Games, Options, the Arts: One of the few schools where enrichment is genuinely as important as the academic. Plenty of trips, masses of fundraising and community service, including Bolivia as part of World Challenge. Swimming outstanding, formidable hockey teams. Netball, tennis, athletics, fencing, basketball, good, strong dance group, aerobics popular. Girls picked for county squads in several sports, 'They get madly keen'. Good facilities: sports hall, Astroturf, squash court, fitness centre, pool. No sports day, GCSE PE on girls' wish list. 1983 Centenary art and design block filled with textiles plus traditional painting and superb ceramics (we liked the busts produced for A level). Girls combine A level art with science and arts subjects.

Many concerts, plays and dance productions – most shared with the boys from over the drive; school symphony orchestra outstanding but lots of performance opportunities for all levels. Drama/theatre studies shared – popular, challenging and deservedly famous under 'very professional ... inspirational' (according to latest Ofsted) and extraordinary teacher. Productions big and small to top standards. Music also outstanding – combined again. Fabulous video technology room with TV cameras, full editing suite, mixing etc. Younger pupils do compulsory creative living, a carousel of ceramics, still photography, electronics, food. Older students are encouraged to do non-exam courses such as sports leadership, video or food technology. Careers advice and work experience all on offer (records kept of university interview experiences and past UCAS personal statements to help current applicants). Stacks of extra-curricular: debating, creative writing, living history and film-making a mere flavour.

Background and Atmosphere: Part of the King Edward Foundation group of schools (all bursarial work carried out jointly), founded in 1883 and followed King Edward's School to present site in 1940. Shares same architect – campus is a pleasing blend of redbrick plus usual later additions; feeling of space and calm inside. Direct grant school until 1976. Girls wear uniform until sixth form, when free rein is given to fashion. Perhaps the happiest and most cohesive staff we've come across – that they are valued (collegiate approach, equal professionals doing different jobs) and encouraged to pursue their interests, not tied down with policies, paperwork and the latest government initiatives, must surely be significant. Part of graduate teacher scheme: 'This is a good place to learn to teach,' says head.

Pastoral Care and Discipline: Liberal outlook – girls of all ages trusted and encouraged to take and share responsibility. Staff hold a short weekly meeting to discuss concerns, but have 'been very lucky'. Girls follow a pastoral care and personal decision-making programme and can discuss problems with any member of staff. No prefect system, no head girl, no houses (many girls say they would like houses, especially for sports competitions). No school drugs offence policy – 'Any cases would be dealt with on an individual basis'. No exclusions or 'asked to leave' during current head's tenure. Recognises they also have to help high fliers deal with failure. Staff send girls cards wishing them luck in their exams – a nice touch. Good parental contact. In principle, parents can contact senior staff, head or her deputy 'certainly within the hour', if it is clearly an urgent matter (other schools please note).

Pupils and Parents: Seriously bright children of professional families, middle to lower middle class. Not the tidiest bunch we've seen, not particularly girlie girls, but they are confident, savvy, happy to get stuck in and share responsibility. They take learning seriously (absolutely fine to be clever), live life to the full but enjoy it and have fun along the way. Shares transport system with boys at King Edward's; girls come from as far away as Lichfield, Bromsgrove, Wolverhampton, Solihull. 'Not a school in this league for miles and precious few anywhere,' say parents. Approximately 35 per cent ethnic minorities, as you might expect – no problems here. Ecumenical outlook. Active school council – black jumpers and recycling among recent initiatives. Established OG society; currently working to draw more Old Girls into today's school community.

Entrance: School's own very selective test 'designed to test the children, not their teachers' (nice one). School spends two weeks searching the completed tests 'for potential, not raw marks'. About half come from state primaries. Tough entry post-GCSE (and girls are 'warmly welcomed' at this stage) – school's own exam in relevant subjects, plus interview and previous school's report. By their statutes girls have to be resident in the area of the West Midlands with their parent(s).

Exit: Very few after GCSE (having the boys next door removes the urge to fly off to a co-ed), and does not throw girls out for doing badly at GCSE but stands by its commitment to them. 10–20 to Oxbridge and the rest to the top range of universities – Bristol, Leeds, Nottingham, London etc, almost always to their first choice. After university to the professions, arts, media, industry, business; school records 'noticeably more and more high achievers – no glass ceiling'.

Money Matters: Assisted places have been replaced by an 'equivalent governors' means-related' scheme – up to 14 places a year. Academic scholarships up to the value of two full-fees at 11 (not more than 50 per cent per pupil).

Remarks: One of the country's top academic girls' city day schools, turning out a long line of academic high-flyers, and an example to the grammar school tradition of how this can be combined with breadth, civilisation and fun. Only for the seriously able and talented.

King Edward VI School (Southampton)

Wilton Road, Southampton, Hampshire, SO15 5UQ

• Pupils: 595 boys, 375 girls; all day • Ages: 11-18 • Size of sixth form: 250 • Non-denom, with C of E ancestry • Fees: £11,235 pa • Independent

Tel: 023 8070 4561
Fax: 023 8070 5937
Email: registrar@kes.hants.sch.uk
Website: www.kes.hants.sch.uk

Headmaster: Since 2002, Mr Julian Thould MA – Pembroke College, Oxford. He's a historian and therefore, arguably, leavens the atmosphere of this notably scientifical school. Worked in industry before beginning teaching at Westminster School and arrived at King Edward's via Cranleigh and King's Worcester. A man whose brains can be read in his eyes and demeanour – alert, astute, assiduous. Decidedly likeable. An educationalist and a humanitarian, capable of radical action, probably always with his feet on the ground. He did remove the school from the league tables but is now back in (well above the snow line) and is determined that, in addition to superb exam results – 'Parents take those as read' – the school will turn out pupils with 'well-tuned minds'. He wants his school to be 'happy and safe', busy in and out of the classroom. His big things are outward bound, charitable work, sport, new technology and creative arts. Has developed strong links with local state schools, especially in the teaching of science, and you can see he'd like his school to be accessible to children from deprived backgrounds. Still a strong whiff of direct grant about this place, a very agreeable aroma of old-fashioned grammar, and Mr Thould asserts, 'We are only doing here what a state school should do'. He's proud that over 200 children receive financial support. The school is making a big bow wave under his headship and he's getting rave reviews. Parents like him, say he's a good communicator. Pupils 'love him – he's always having new ideas, he lets them in on the plans and asks them what they think'. Well up, too, to having an apple shot off his head at a medieval banquet. Very much a family man – two children at the school, the eldest two having passed through its ranks.

Academic matters: 'We are the leading school in the area, and known to be,' says the head without vanity or vainglory. Exam results speak for themselves – superb in all respects. For all the pupils' penchant for sciences, the arts are just as well done, history and English in particular. Why are the sciences so popular? Partly because a lot of medical parents, partly because this is what the school is known for – to which we may add, perhaps, the reflections of a sixth former, 'I did history AS. Writing those essays took forever. I can do my chemistry homework in half the time'. They're all-rounders. The range is broad – three modern languages at A level, theatre studies, philosophy. In 2002 the school inspectors worried there was too much focus on exam teaching. By now, the head's breadth-making policy has dissolved that criticism. The sort of work ethic here you would expect wherever a thousand or so very bright people are gathered together and, yes, they know they are expected to butter the parsnips. In the classes we saw the atmosphere was purposeful, civilised and, in the sixth form, urbane. We shan't quickly forget a GCSE design technology class where boys and girls were designing board games. Independent thinking and high intellect were generating seriously clever projects. An attractive school to good teachers, you can't help but reflect.

A fair amount of decamping, post-GCSE, to sixth form colleges in recent years. The flow is being stemmed both by a more young adult-friendly régime, plus uniform to match, and also by a growing perception that, when you see how the émigrés get on, staying here offers the stronger certainty of best grades. Parents praise university selection and preparation which, for Oxbridge interviews, leaves the syllabus far, far behind. Lots of recent refurbishment in the science zone part funded by the Abraham Trust. No shortage of space anywhere, everything bright and kempt. Marvellous concourse, a great meeting area with highly readable notice boards. Mild SENs addressed – literacy and numeracy support from SENCo, but you've got to be able to keep up: SEN has been a blind spot for years.

Games, Options, the Arts: Sport a serious matter for the sportiest and well resourced – acres of playing fields, sports hall, Astros. Compulsory for all – sixth formers do minimum one afternoon; unsporty types do merrymaking lollopy things. Very inclusive; top coaching – 'We probably win more than we lose'. Website has multimap links for all competitor schools. Sailing especially strong – double Olympic gold medallist Iain Percy was here. Also Keith Wiseman (past chairman of the Football Association), John and Simon Francis (county cricketers), Dudley Kemp (England rugby cap and past president of the RFU) and Rob Moore (hockey Olympian). Parents like the Saturday fixtures – they keep 'em out of town.

Lots of good art going on, especially the drop-in session at lunchtime when you do just as you please, radical as you like. Purpose-built, in-the-round theatre doing good stuff. Plays well supported by fellow pupils. Lively music, Henry Mancini to Henry Purcell, lots of public performance, often with a charitable fundraising focus. Christmas carols in Romsey Abbey. Fifty-plus clubs, many of them formidably intellectual – sure, cooking and wargaming, but also chess, Conversationalists (they debate someone's essay), classicists and creative writing (popular, we note, with all academic persuasions).

Raising money for good causes is a big thing, thinking up events – £18,000 raised last year: summer camp for deprived children, links with an orphanage in Romania. D of E is big, too – lots of gold awards – the school has a recently refurbished rural studies centre on Dartmoor. Young Enterprise does very well. They're a busy lot and egged on to be so. The school is, say parents, very good at picking out wallflowers and discreetly nudging them into things. Last Easter hols 50 per cent of the teaching staff took groups away on residential trips.

Background and Atmosphere: Founded by William Capon in 1553 to elevate the customary impoverished wretches. Though non-denom now, the school maintains its historic relationship with St Mary's Church. Has been at its present site since 1938, the period feel of the buildings imparting, you can't help thinking, their bit to the ethos.

Pastoral Care and Discipline: Notably relaxed, adult relationships between pupils and teachers, a collaborativeness about them that's very good to see. No better insight into this than the superb school magazine, entirely produced by sixth formers. They even have to get print quotes and oversee every aspect of production – a truly adult expectation. The writing is sprightly, irreverent, funny, intelligent, unmediated by teachers and a huge tribute to the confidence of the school – read it and you will know the place. An annual revue, too, another excellent window. Rules try not to be petty, uniform is worn mostly as intended, attitude met with intelligent, unpatronising debate, though the school is impatient of recalcitrance. No earrings for boys, no nose studs for anyone. You pass the beadle-like deputy head's office on your way in, and she picks up on the slightest. Lots of drugs education. Is this a worry? Say parents, 'Not an issue.' Food has been Jamie Olivered, now a source of pride. Boys and girls observably natural in each other's company. Tutorial system works. One mum reported a teasing thing at breakfast and was phoned back before she got to work – sorted.

Pupils and Parents: Unstuffy, unsnobby. That's how parents want it and that's how they intend to keep it. They want a traditional, co-ed grammar school and they inhabit a 25-mile radius. No local competitor. Around a third come from Winchester. School has its own buses but, a tradition, certainly a green touch, this, around a hundred flood in by bike or on foot. So does the head, and so do quite a few teachers. The school is rooted in its community and, hard though it is to get in, it doesn't do exclusivity nor does it breathe rarefied air. Typical of its values, it has never borrowed a penny to build anything. Ethnic mix evident, testimony to its meritocratic nature. Buzzing PTA, KES Soc – secondhand uniforms, social events.

Entrance: Hard, of course: around two up for every place (reputation depletes aspirants). Entry exam: maths, English and reasoning plus interview plus previous school's report. Around half from state primaries, then from around 25 local independents, with big lumps from Stroud and Sherborne House. For sixth formers (own brochure) you'll need six GCSEs at grade B including English and maths.

Exit: Almost all to Russell Group universities – the cream. Around 10 per cent to Oxbridge. Recent OEs range from Hugh Whitemore (playwright and dramatist) and Michel Vickers (pop group Manfred Mann) to Michael Langrish (Bishop of Exeter), Ian Bruce (president of the RNIB) and Sir Edward Abraham FRS (Oxford academic – groundbreaking work on penicillin and synthetic antibiotics). Also His Honour Judge David McCarraher, Sir Michael Bichard and Her Majesty's Ambassador Richard Kinchen MVO.

Money Matters: Bursaries, means tested, 100 per cent remission for the most deserving. Scholarships, academic (up to 10 per cent) and creative arts (up to five per cent) of the fee. Entry at 11, 13 and sixth form.

Remarks: We arrived through the tight-squeeze entry at the back of the school in the middle of break, air thick with balls, shoals of flushed boys, gaggles of chatty girls – not much enchantment to the eye here. Yet from the moment the bell dissipated, those first impressions fell away to reveal not only top-notch teaching but also great charm. This is a downright and a decent place, an independent school socially comfortable in its surroundings.

King Edward VI School (Stratford-upon-Avon)

Church Street, Stratford-upon-Avon, Warwickshire, CV37 6HB

• Pupils: 545, all boys • Ages: 11-18 • Size of sixth form: 165, all boys • State

Tel: 01789 293 351
Fax: 01789 293 564
Email: admin4601@we-learn.com
Website: www.kes-stratford.org.uk

Head: Since 2010, Mr Bennet Carr BA FRGS (fortyish). Undergraduate studies in geography at Queen Mary's College, London, then PGCE at Institute of Education, followed by The Bishop's Stortford High School (head of geography and sixth form, assistant head). Influential deputy headmaster of St Olave's Grammar School, London ('Sunday Times' State School of the Year 2009) for eight years.

Married to Beverley; two young daughters, one at a local primary, the second pre-school. Chose KES because it's a small school where he can get to know boys and their families. A driven, "hands-on" head. Unashamed of traditional values and proud of the school's Shakespeare connection and its rôle in the town of Stratford-upon-Avon. Forward-looking and business-like yet sceptical of educational initiatives, genuinely committed to education in the widest sense. He has a lifelong interest in sport, especially rugby union, and has become a keen runner since ending his playing days.

Academic matters: Economics and science strong, maths very strong. But results, especially at A level, impressive in most areas, including the far less popular humanities. French seemingly the only casualty – very few continue after the compulsory GCSE whereas German and Spanish, in their small way, flourish. In 2010, 46 per cent A*/A results across the board at A level, 72 per cent A*–B; 66 per cent A/A* at GCSE.

Teaching mostly good across the curriculum and boys enthuse about some individual teachers. Not a big school so the range of subjects isn't dazzling but, as one boy said, 'Most people here are academic and we're pretty well provided for'. And the list is growing – D&T now means electronics and resistant materials, RS has given way to philosophy and plans to reintroduce Greek as a timetabled GCSE – alongside the Latin that everyone takes for the first three years. Theatre studies a new A level in 2006. All sixth formers take A level general studies, some do an AS in critical thinking and around a third take four academic A levels. Options extended by collaboration with other local schools/colleges and some commuting of pupils now for, e.g., sports science, French etc – equally, some come in from outside.

IT dramatically upgraded under remit given to deputy head and the new science block includes a special IT suite. The block is not only a boon for science but releases much-needed space elsewhere, including for better sixth form facilities. Library not huge but well-stocked in unbeatably inspirational accommodation and all Year 7s have a weekly period therein for reading.

SEN not huge here but statemented boys not unknown and IEPs drawn up and implemented where necessary. SENCo works with parents and outside agencies and everyone carefully monitored. Currently school has boys with dyslexia, dyspraxia, ADHD, Asperger's and eyesight problems. Gifted and talented coordinator well supported by the tutor system.

Much tinkering with timetable has resulted in standard single lessons being only 35 minutes long. Older boys have more doubles, of course, which are generally preferred, but younger boys dislike the shortness of singles, 'You can't get anything done'.

Games, Options, the Arts: Drama is central to life here but then if one of your schoolrooms is the one in which William Shakespeare learned his little Latin and less Greek, it is understandable, nay most natural, forsooth! School is less than a minute from The Shakespeare Memorial Theatre and the town breathes and lives off its Tudor dramatic heritage. So no sense of a stifling tradition here. School has close links with The Royal Shakespeare Company – borrows its costumes, goes to its workshops, sees the productions and, uniquely, boys parade annually with other local bodies on the anniversary of The Bard's birth. And they're good at getting the stuff on themselves – lots of plays (Sophocles the night we visited) and a buzz around the subject almost audible throughout. Debating likewise popular and accomplished.

Lots of music too – how enlightened to offer each boy in Year 7 a year's free tuition on an instrument of their choice. Lots of ensembles, bands, choirs and concerts and, in this as in other areas, collaboration with the girls of the girls' grammar down the road. Good music technology room under the eaves with Sibelius 2 and other essentials of life.

Lively work in art and DT – the art studio hung with golf bags, musical instruments, cat-cages, windows, chains, miners' lamps, drums, helmets and bikes, among other unaccountable and evocative ephemera. Good painting and we enjoyed purposeful work in quiet, uncrowded workshops.

Games fields are a mile away – younger boys are bused, the rest walk – and facilities there are good. Range of games and activities, including sculling on the Avon, basketball, athletics and cricket but, if you worship the round ball, look elsewhere. School provides district and county players in rugby and cricket and has a distinguished record in fencing and rowing. Lamentably, decent-sized school pool now in disrepair and looks ghostly in its bluey half-light. Too expensive to renovate, too good to demolish, too sad for the boys who'd love to use it – any suggestions (+ cheque!) on a postcard welcome. Large tarmac playground surrounded by the school buildings the only space available in breaks – not much for 500-odd chaps. However, smart Levi Fox Hall – huge and multi-purpose with flexi-seating and gallery – used for productions, sport, meetings. Gym area plus machines and 'old gym' also useful for boosting or expending energies. D of E strong. Lots of expeditions – no teachers fighting shy of form-filling here. 2006 saw two teams off to Ecuador. Pupils speak warmly of the 'Third Reich Tour' – not everyone's cuppa but clearly effective in both friendship-building and grim but necessary educating (some even go twice).

Background and Atmosphere: Tourists ambling round Stratford are spoiled for choice of half-timbered marvels and relics – authentic and recreated. This is the real thing. You wouldn't imagine that the low, brownish half-timbered building along the south side of Church Street is a school and has been one for nearly seven centuries. The Bardlet probably arrived here in 1571, aged about seven, when the school was already about 150 years old. The main building – the old Guildhall – still houses the library and, in the old muniments room, the librarian. Above is Big School – a splendid long room with an extraordinary beamed and cantilevered ceiling, ancient, notched and graffitied desks at least 200 years old – all still in use – and this was where young Will first sharpened a pen.

Opposite is The Pedagogue's House, once the home of the schoolmaster and now a hotchpotch of small offices plus the head's domain. Adjacent is The Old Vicarage, a fine house of a later period in which live the current head and his family – a rare thing in a state grammar. Attached is the Guild Chapel shared by the town and the school in which admirably brief but significant daily services are held.

The rest, around the other three sides of the tarmac area, is wholly undistinguished, mid to late twentieth century, low-rise municipal-build and a testament to how unimaginative architecture can be even when in, one would have hoped, inspiring surroundings. For the most part it's in goodish nick. However, some parts are unforgivably dingy – especially around the maths area – though it appears to have minimal effect on the standard of work. We witnessed a morning-full of lessons and saw nothing that wasn't quiet, purposeful and interesting.

School is central in Stratford – both geographically and in its consciousness. Everyone knows KES and the boys feel conspicuous and have a sense that they are seen almost to belong to the town and its people. This has its privileges but also its strains – 'You feel proud of the school's history,' we were told, 'but sometimes people have unfair expectations.'

Pastoral Care and Discipline: School operates vertical tutor system – i.e. 18–20 boys within a house, three to four from each year group, under care of one tutor for their entire career through Years 8–13, a popular system which ensures continuity and a real relationship. Head is a tutor – feels system has improved behaviour, defuses tensions and has done much to eradicate bullying. Backed up by two weekly tutors' meetings. No drugs, alcohol or significant smoking incidents despite S Warwickshire's acknowledged problems. 'I believe we don't have it because of the ethos of the school,' says head. Younger boys pretty firmly kept in line but we heard no complaints. Older boys warmly appreciative of their teachers – 'I'd be happy to socialise and talk to them about my life,' said one. 'They're very relaxed but they won't let anyone slip up.' 'Our teachers are much more prepared to put themselves out for us than at other schools ... They go that little bit further for us,' said another.

School dining room does full English breakfast, popular on cold mornings. Good range of hot and cold snacks at break – muffins, bacon sandwiches, apple Danishes and pains au chocolat. Good, varied and sensible lunch menu, competitively priced – all paid for on a smartcard system.

Pupils and Parents: Majority from S Warwickshire primaries or preps, though some come from as far as Banbury. Vast majority white middle class. Currently no pupils need EAL. The ones we met were articulate, polite and relaxed. Parents very supportive – three separate parents' committees: the Friends, one for tours and one for the performing arts. These raise large sums enabling boys to take up opportunities they otherwise couldn't. Notable old boys include biblical scholar Arthur Peake, Rex Warneford VC, Croix de Guerre, Tim Piggott-Smith – and that other thespian mentioned above.

Entrance: Two verbal reasoning tests administered by local authority for this and the other four Warwickshire grammars. Distance from home/siblings not taken into account. However borderline children get looked at again and their recent schoolwork considered, along with reports from their present schools. Not surprisingly, the local comprehensives want to lose as few as possible of the brightest so fight to keep the borderline children, but an appeal is worthwhile – KES has places to fill and appeals are often successful.

Exit: To a range of good university courses including a clutch to Oxbridge annually. Despite the heavy science/maths bias, fewer than you'd think to engineering/science courses but to everything from history at Aberystwyth to economics at York and most else besides, though linguists not in abundance.

Money Matters: Voluntary contribution to school fund of £140 pa per family – used to subsidise extra-curricular life. Plentiful leaving scholarships awarded to A level stars, which contribute to their first university term. Additional leaving scholarships available for specific subjects, e.g. veterinary science, medicine, plus numerous other awards.

Remarks: Now with new head for whom all the world could be a stage, if he continues the good work done by his predecessor. If all state schools were like this, the independent system would be struggling. If you have a bright lad and fancy the Bardshire idyll, it could all be as you like it!

King Edward's School (Bath)

Linked to King Edwards Pre-Prep And Nursery Linked to King Edwards Junior School (Bath) in the Junior section

North Road, Bath, BA2 6HU

• Pupils: 675; 245 girls, 430 boys, all day • Ages: 11-18 • Size of sixth form: 205 (65 girls, 145 boys) • Non-denom • Fees: £10,965-£11,091 pa • Independent

Tel: 01225 464 313
Fax: 01225 481 363
Email: headmaster@kesbath.com
Website: www.kesbath.com

Headmaster: Since 2008, Mr Martin Boden MA (late thirties). Educated at Bolton School (where he was asked back to teach after his PGCE) and Jesus College, Cambridge, where he read French and German. Spells at Cheadle Hulme School and Bradford Grammar as head of modern languages preceded his arrival at King Edward's as director of studies, whence he was appointed head, after a turbulent period with three heads in six years. A boy wonder. Married to head of geography, Jane, with an infant son.

Proud of grammar school career and academically very ambitious for his school. It shows: as director of studies he redesigned the school day to lengthen lessons to 60 minutes, necessitating a move to a two week timetable to 'underline philosophical aim of depth in education'. Something's clearly working – KES is up there in the top 50 independents, having recently achieved 91 per cent A/B grades at A level and 74 per cent A/A* at GCSE. Anxious to dispel local reputation as hothouse however, by taking every opportunity to flag up everything else the school does: he claims its stunning results are attributable to 'the quality of the teaching', not merely the innate ability or industry of its students.

Although relentlessly on-message when we visited, we did uncover a keen footballer – 'Though I have learnt to love rugby since coming to Bath' – and the drummer in the staff band. Parents reckon he is straightforward (what you see is what you get) and professional and respect him, not least for his intellect and ability to think strategically – though some feel he has yet to perfect the art of delegation.

Academic matters: Exceptionally strong across the board. Prominent Oxbridge entrants boards (eight or so per year) draw the eye on the way in, setting the tone and expectations. 'The school takes great pleasure in its rude academic health,' states the head, who also claims intake is not off-puttingly selective. That myth will take some dispelling locally, where it still prevails. Nonetheless, pupils are not pushed into taking absurd numbers of public exams: the norm is nine or 10 GCSEs, four subjects at AS, dropping to three at A2 in most cases. A small group of enthusiastic Year 9 classicists is now able to pursue Greek as well. A level options have been enlivened by trendier non-trad additions like photography, but intellectual rigour is applied and delivered here too.

SEN provision has been massively developed since we last reported – the head says, 'It has been embraced by pupils, parents and staff'. Learning support now has its own department, one of whose staff has close links with the junior school. 100 per cent screening for Year 7 has just come in. Individual support lessons in school time as a chargeable extra (after assessment), but the head concedes that the school would find it hard to accommodate severe cases of dyslexia, dyspraxia or dyscalculia.

Games, Options, the Arts: Sport is king here and woven into the fabric of the school. Keenly competitive rugby, hockey, football and netball: fearsome local reputation extends to cricket, tennis and athletics in summer. Much participation at county level, some at national, and individual quirks accommodated, such as pole-vaulting and the Devizes to Westminster canoe race. Indoor sports complex, Astroturf and an athletics track on site, grass pitches a mile away at Bathampton. No swimming pool, but close enough to the university's superior set-up. Head conscious of managing the tension between winning at all costs v sport for all. Sixth form options include walking the inhabitants of the local dogs' home, as part of community service.

Drama an increasing strength: one recent Old Edwardian, Tom Payne, has become a star of stage and screen, and at least one production has been to the Fringe. Music facilities small, uninviting but high tech. Staff mad keen, though, and try their best to enthuse: recent appearances of the highly selective chamber choir, 16 in number, and the non-auditioned one have been very well received and instrumental groups gain plaudits at the Mid Somerset Festival. Notable individual successes too (e.g. National Children's/Youth Orchestra, fast track GCSE group getting all A/A*), yet music still seems to have an undeserved image problem for non-participants.

Visual arts emanate from a well-used department with an enthusiastic following and a fantastic annual exhibition. Graphic design and photography well catered for with their own designated space, and DT has its own bang up to date CAD/CAM workshop. Loads of trips every year, mostly Europe but recently Kenya as part of Global Schools Partnership, and Antigua for the cricketers. Very active CCF, Duke of Edinburgh awards and Ten Tors Challenge teams, plus an annual activities week remove pupils regularly from the confines of Bath. Charitable initiatives undertaken with typical seriousness of purpose.

Background and Atmosphere: Ancient grammar school founded in sixteenth century but wears its history lightly if at all, having abandoned its historical but unsuitable buildings right in the city in the 1960s in favour of the southern slopes. Buildings scattered over a steepish site: largely functional but not beautiful, exceptions being Nethersole House, a Georgian mansion housing the parts the head's visitors will see first, plus history, politics and classics, and B block, a sensational new high tech teaching space opened in 2008. Some parts could do with smartening up, such as the dining hall and locker spaces – cheerless in winter, we suspect; short on commonroom space below sixth form. Food gets thumbs up, though – all done in-house with plenty of hot and cold choices. Impression is busy busy busy, but not frenetic. Lessons have a real buzz: no-one's snoozing at the back. Actually they wouldn't be allowed to – academic commitment and performance are what count here, though, as the head is so keen to point out, that's not all that counts.

The shortish day – lessons end at 4.00pm and even the keenest are shooed out of the library by 5.30 – means most clubs – over 60, from the cerebral Aeolian (the hot air club?) to the practical Young Life Savers – are fitted into lunchtimes. Takeup is reasonable and pupils say everything they want, but some parents worry that that 'there is too much time to hang about and obsess'. Earlier reputation for being two dimensional (i.e. kids who weren't bright and/or sporty didn't count) gradually fading, though some pupils reckon this is not a school for nonentities, passengers or those without particular skills or gifts. It is certainly cool to be clever here, and an air of academic seriousness is quite discernible. The head conceded, when pressed, that children who don't throw themselves into their work and at least some of what is on offer at KES might not thrive.

Personal independence and eco-conscience encouraged too: large numbers of pupils make their way to school by bus, train (school runs a shuttle service from the station), bike and on foot; space for sixth formers to park. Lively social scene after hours with other Bath schools, but partying which invades the groves of academe, literally or otherwise, strongly discouraged.

Pastoral Care and Discipline: Strenuous attempts to rid itself of persistent reputation for being tough seem to have met with some success – current pupils and parents praise support given to them, particularly when the going gets rough, academically or otherwise. The post of pastoral deputy head was created in 2008 and a p/t chaplain from the Bath Abbey is now on board. We witnessed one teacher truly going the extra mile with an evident straggler in her lunch break; apparently discussions about pupil welfare predominate over crosswords and gossip in the staffroom too. Inordinate trouble taken not only by tutors but also by subject teachers over personal statements. Academic expectations are high, but pupils are helped, not bullied, into meeting them by effective tutors, who enjoy just the right kind of rapport with their charges.

Senior management occasionally exercised over pupil behaviour in town on Saturday nights and not afraid to expel those who supply drugs. Sixth formers are expected to be rôle models and mentors to the lower school: in lower sixth they can try out the rôle of deputy prefect for three weeks before standing for election. Forty per cent of upper sixth then become prefects, with ten or so senior prefects, from whom a head girl and boy are appointed.

Pupils and Parents: Wide social and economic cross-section coming from a 25 mile radius, with a refreshing lack of snobbery for an independent school. Pupils are articulate, open and direct but without brashness, and they are proud of their school. The head likes to remind them that having all those opportunities does not make them better people. Parents are academically ambitious for their children ('But not at the expense of all the extras,' he says) and support the school in all it does, including active fundraising for extras; interestingly, one said it was hard to 'give the school money', so determined is it to be financially independent. Amazingly few gripes of any description. Most famous Old Edwardian is comedian Bill Bailey. Older notables have reached prominence in industry, academia, finance and the military.

Entrance: At 11, 90-or-so places up for grabs by passing an entrance exam in maths, English and verbal reasoning. 50 per cent of the intake comes from its own junior school, tucked away at the top corner of the site, nearly all the rest from a range of local-ish primaries.

25–30 places offered at sixth form, conditional on good GCSE passes (A/A* desirable for A level subjects), interview and references from previous school. Sixth form entry tends to attract more girls, who even up the numbers and give the sixth form a genuinely co-ed feel.

Exit: Vast majority to university of first choice with few gap years, including approximately eight per cent to Oxbridge. Scottish and northern universities popular, with London and Wales attracting their share. Wide diversity of degree courses but medicine and geography particularly strong. Sports and art-related degree choices also feature. Hardly anyone leaves after GCSE.

Money Matters: Widely acknowledged by parents to be a 'complete bargain', for the calibre of teachers and range of opportunities it provides. Approximately 15 per cent of pupils receive means-tested bursaries, total fees in exceptional cases. Bursary forms routinely given to prospective parents; the head very keen to encourage able but impoverished candidates to apply.

Remarks: Bath's most academic school, where bright, confident, motivated achievers will thrive on the constant intellectual stimulus it provides in and out of the classroom. Totally unpretentious in site and clientele, with the feel of a grammar school, but edgy – for Bath. Specialises in producing independent thinkers.

King Edward's School, Birmingham

Edgbaston Park Road, Birmingham, West Midlands, B15 2UA

• Pupils: 840 boys; all day • Ages: 11-18 • Size of sixth form: 250
• C of E/multi-faith • Fees: £9,900 pa • Independent

Tel: 0121 472 1672
Fax: 0121 415 4327
Email: admissions@kes.org.uk
Website: www.kes.org.uk

Chief Master: Since 2006, Mr John Claughton, MA Hons (an Oxford classicist) (fiftyish). Educated at King Edward's, he was previously housemaster at Eton and then headmaster at Solihull School 2001–2005. Married with three young sons. Loves cricket, having gained his blue at Oxford and subsequently played county cricket for Warwickshire.

Academic matters: School gets outstanding results by means of first-rate teaching, a well-organised curriculum and an emphasis on educating the whole person, not merely turning out impressive exam statistics. Roughly 12:1 boys to full-time teachers, no class bigger than 26, sixth form 16. Results among the best in the country, especially so in maths, chemistry and geography. In 2010, 57 out of 67 candidates got A* or A in maths, out of 45 chemistry candidates 37 got A*s or As and 26 out of the 32 boys who took geography got an A* or A. French compulsory to GCSE, other languages having to be taken as options.

Virtually 100 per cent passes at GCSE, the overwhelming number of grades in all subjects being A*s or As (85 per cent). The recent full inspection regarded the school as 'outstanding' in many respects. Sixth form moving to the International Baccalaureate Diploma (IB) in 2010.

Games, Options, the Arts: Main sports rugby, hockey, basketball, cricket, athletics. Boys can also take archery, badminton, cross-country, Eton fives, fencing, golf, orienteering, sailing, squash, swimming, table tennis, tennis and water polo. Boys participate in many regional teams in various sports, also in national sides in basketball and water polo (under 18 national champions 2010). Extensive playing fields, extraordinary in a school one mile from centre of city. Also huge Astroturf pitch shared with King Edward's VI High School for Girls (qv) which shares the school's vast campus and many activities, facilities and some staff. Extra-curricular options include conservation and environmental studies, leadership, CCF. Arts are famously good. Drama to professional standards under inspirational, unequalled teaching and production values. Music similarly outstanding – school justifiably proud of both. Art also impressive.

Background and Atmosphere: School founded in 1552 by King Edward VI, now flagship of King Edward Foundation group of seven Birmingham schools, including King Edward VI Camp Hill, an excellent grammar and school's main academic local rival. The Chief Master is head of the Foundation though each school is autonomous. School moved to a famous Charles Barry building in 1838, but in true Birmingham spirit of renewal and regeneration, this was demolished and the school moved to its current impressive 32-acre site in 1936.

Buildings are 1930s redbrick and solid-looking, and manage to be both elegant and functional, though the length of the corridors might daunt newcomers. Newer buildings have been sensitively incorporated, including latest addition, an imaginative 'tea pavilion' for the entertainment of parents during matches and so on. Much recent refurbishment, especially flooring and lighting, greatly improves ambiance. Major building project has started – performing arts centre in collaboration with the girls' school and also an integrated sports centre for the boys' school.

The adjacent King Edward VI Girls' High School, founded 1883, is a real boon to the school, especially in matters dramatic, musical, social. Good friendly working relations between the two schools, assisted by some shared staff. Most pervasive feeling in school is a genuine warmth and unaffected enthusiasm among both staff and pupils and a sense of privilege – of the best kind – and good fortune in being there. The school has a sense of being geared to the realities of working life. A cooked breakfast is served every day and school uniform buying arrangements are geared to a working parent's schedule.

Pastoral Care and Discipline: School publishes an impressive-looking pastoral handbook with a carefully constructed code of conduct and policies on sex education, PSE, drugs, bullying etc, as well as advice on whom to speak to in the event of 'matters of pastoral concern'. System, however, is not restrictive and boys are encouraged to talk to person who is right for them, rather than to specific tutor or master. School has trained student counsellor. Also very approachable masters, including deputy chief master. Prefect system. Head would assess individual infringements of rules individually but hypothetical serious issues, e.g. drug selling, would mean instant expulsion.

Pupils and Parents: Intake reflects greatly diverse local ethnic and social mix. About 50 per cent of boys from ethnic minorities, only 35 per cent from the city of Birmingham, many commute from as far as Coventry, Wolverhampton, Lichfield and consider it 'worth it'. 45 per cent from primary schools and 55 per cent from prep schools. Uniform throughout the school but sixth formers don't seem to mind. Liberal attitude to self-expression in hair etc and on 'own clothes' days. A place at this school clearly regarded as a prize by parents and pupils alike.

Entrance: Highly competitive (600 candidates for 120 places) at 11+. Entrance tests in English, maths, verbal reasoning, interview for many, report from current head. Five or so places available at 13+. Sixth form entry dependent on entrance examination, Headteacher's report and interview. Academic scholarships decided on performance in entrance tests. Music scholarships (up to one-half fees) also offered.

Exit: Vast majority take up places at good universities. Unsurprisingly for a school which is so strong in maths and science, recently maths, science and medicine accounted for 37 leavers; engineering and economics made up a further 17. But the traditional bias towards science has changed over recent years; leavers are now fairly evenly divided between science and the humanities. Old Edwardians include Tolkien, Enoch Powell, Nobel medical Laureate Sir John Vane, Kenneth Tynan, Bill Oddie.

Money Matters: School – and pupils – hugely fortunate to have Foundation able to compensate to great extent for loss of government assisted places. Up to 25 places a year still funded out of school resources (King Edward VI Foundation, Old Edwardians, etc). Means-tested remission of up to full fees; 30 per cent of pupils have financial help of some kind and of those 10 per cent have free places. Additional help in subsidising educationally useful school trips for those who need it. Altogether generous help for the genuinely worthy. Fees compare very favourably to comparable schools elsewhere.

Remarks: On all counts this is a very impressive school, combining academic excellence, a real commitment to wider values of education, genuine exuberance and enthusiasm and turning out unpretentious, independent-minded, well-behaved and confident young men. Worth moving for.

King's Bruton

Linked to Hazlegrove School in the Junior section

Plox, Bruton, Somerset, BA10 0ED

• Pupils: 220 boys, 95 girls; 225 board, 95 day • Ages: 13-18 • Size of sixth form: 145 • Christian • Fees: Boarding £25,455; Day £18,486 pa • Independent

Tel: 01749 814 200
Fax: 01749 813 426
Email: office@kingsbruton.com
Website: www.kingsbruton.org.uk

Head: Since 2009, Mr Ian Wilmshurst MA PGCE (mid-forties) educated at The Edinburgh Academy, where he was head boy, then Pembroke, Cambridge, where he read geography. Started career at Highgate as geography master, house tutor and games coach, then back over the border to Merchiston Castle, where he was a housemaster for five years, as well as teaching geography and coaching 1st XV rugby, before promotion to deputy headship at Royal Hospital School, Suffolk. Wants to breathe more commercial realism into a school which has perhaps sometimes suffered the financial consequences of misplaced priorities. Married to Helen, formerly in marketing within pharmaceutical industry: she plays an active part in school life (is a house tutor in a boys' boarding house inter alia). Their two daughters, Anna and Natalie, are currently at Hazlegrove.

Head's strong sense of justice has already rattled a few cages, but most parents are behind his disciplinary stand and feel that he 'will raise profile of the school'. Wants to improve academic standards (which new head doesn't?) whilst keeping the school's traditional warmth. Time will tell, but putting a brake on spiralling costs seems like a good starting point. 'Not afraid to change things,' reported pupils (who 'really respect him') whilst parents thought he would 'pull up on any sloppiness'. Claims not to be ambitious personally. Parents are getting to know him and say that 'he is a very nice man' and 'much more personable than first impressions might suggest'. He is excited about King's and is already more relaxed about his rôle. Enjoys hill walking, the odd round of golf and time out with his young family.

Academic matters: Consistent if not superlative – school admits a wide spectrum of ability. 2010 A levels: 15 per cent A*, 74 per cent A*–B and 89 per cent A*–C, with a 100% pass rate. 40 per cent A* and A at GCSE. IGCSE is offered to all pupils in maths and to most able as separate sciences; two out of three languages on offer can be chosen in Year 10 – teachers choose courses to play to pupils' strengths with brightest sitting ten subjects. May not match high flyers in Bath or Bristol but delivers more than King's parents often expect.

Head of teaching and learning – a new post created to focus on stretching the more able and to improve independent learning. Pupils are fast tracked (e.g. scholars in Latin, which is still offered within timetable for year nine and at A level but is taught as an activity at GCSE) where appropriate, flexible timetabling to meet individual needs and expanding provision for gifted and talented. 13 AS pupils currently involved in extended project qualification.

Huge range of subjects (17 or 18) in year nine; small class sizes a great plus point; setting in core subjects. ICT is not taught as a separate subject; lots of computers and smartboards but some subjects have been ICT shy, it seems; good use is made of intranet in some GCSE (e.g. sports studies) and A level (e.g. geography) work. Surprising location of food technology (very popular with boys – ten pupils currently taking AS) in science building rather than with D&T. School benefits from involvement in Mid-Somerset consortium to bring new blood into teaching from other backgrounds – two trainee teachers currently on this GTP programme.

Valued learning support department (it has a long tradition here) with its inviting base conveniently located alongside the library. Head of learning support is keen that pupils receiving help are 'not seen as different'. She helps organise the annual ISC conference on SEN and is very experienced at managing provision: 20–25 per cent of pupils currently receive some measure of support. All entrants are screened for reading comprehension, spelling and processing speed. Numeracy is covered from within maths department and two teachers are employed to work with EAL pupils (currently over 20 of 80+ overseas pupils receive support with English). Insists that Bruton's learning support is not about 'old ladies in cupboards' but aims to enable pupils to 'make the most of their talents'.

Games, Options, the Arts: Sport (compulsory three times a week including Saturday) counts for a lot – 10 per cent of pupils have performed at representative level. Tennis players reached girls' and mixed finals nationally; other recent national finalists include biathlon and gymnastics plus top equestrian events. Sports teachers are ex-internationals; loads of teams in major sports; increasingly attracting girl athletes; universal participation in some events (e.g. annual cross-country). Opportunity to shine in a team at King's as opposed to being one out of two hundred overlooked players elsewhere. Large sports hall with gallery and fitness suite; two squash courts, fives court, acres of playing fields and Astroturf. Swimming at nearby Sexey's or Hazlegrove. Range of sporting activities (from archery to trampolining) offered throughout the week. Strong art department (14 currently in A2 group) with good studio spaces (including photographic studio) for exciting range of work and new school and community gallery about to happen, thanks partly to success of recent art auction. Sixth form curriculum includes life drawing and history of art also on offer.

Music (includes music technology to A2 level) is very popular under new director: formal choir and full orchestra through to jazz and rock. Battle of the bands and open mic evenings for the extrovert. About 150 pupils currently play an instrument and opportunities to perform include big band, chapel choir, string orchestra and military band (which recently took part in Lord Mayor's Show in London). Big band goes down a storm at annual black tie dinner dance, 'Swing into Spring', for parents and friends. We listened to lovely chamber choir, which presents range of modern and traditional music with high level of competence. Lots of concerts each term. Drama offered to A level with productions put on by pupils at all levels in impressive Fitzjames Theatre.

CCF very well established: gliding, sailing and camps all feature regularly, with some opting for D of E programme instead. Varied and extensive activities programme covers everything from girls' cricket or rugby to Arabic and Scottish reels. Recent visits include year nine to the World War One battlefields, language students in Barcelona, lower sixth to Paris, biologists at Nettlecombe Court near Exmoor and historians experiencing Nuremberg and Leipzig.

Pupils raise money for charity and annual sponsored endurance challenge in Morocco (organised by the chaplain) funds gap year students (to the tune of £1k+ each last year) who go out to Salem in India to work at a Christian orphanage. School's rural location makes work experience difficult to organise and all but a few miss out; successful careers convention for Year 12 involves former pupils in giving advice and information. Strong local links exist mainly through weekly community service which involves 65 pupils working with groups ranging from primary pupils to senior citizens. Innovative international committee organises events such as European Languages Day and Chinese New Year.

Background and Atmosphere: Mellow yellow stone wonder located at centre of this unusually scholastic country town, in shadow of landmark Dovecote. Founded in 1519 during reign of Henry VIII, the school shut its doors after only twenty years and was then re-opened in 1550 under Edward VI – difficult for pupils here not to have a sense of history. Straddles busy road to Castle Cary – no zebra crossing yet to make crossing it safer – and sits conveniently alongside main railway line to south west. Has added buildings (e.g. impressive Hobhouse science centre and 'badly needed' reception area) without destroying the harmony of older ones. Old House (complete with turret added by a former housemaster) is oldest part of school whilst smallest boarding house of seven is Arion – a girls' house. Neighbouring parish church doubles as school chapel twice a week; assemblies are held in beamed Memorial Hall: refurbished in 2010, thanks to +£90K raised within King's community in memory of Ben Ross (see below). Adjacent John Davie room (used for small functions, concerts and meetings) could be next on the list. Purpose built, inviting music 'hub' provides for individual and group lessons.

IT is wireless networked throughout school; separate computer rooms available for classes or study periods. School intranet includes useful lesson notes and reviews for pupils. Excellent, active library works closely with English department (e.g. accelerated reader scheme) to get even the most reluctant reader involved and lots of literary happenings (e.g. on national poetry day, world book day etc). Dreary staff room, we thought, and ubiquitous 'Tardis' litter bins suggest past bursarial priorities. Boarding houses vary in quality (some very good but others have been cause for parental concern) with a programme of upgrading apparently now well under way.

Dynamic and popular chaplain (doubles as a rugby coach) insists he's not tried 'to do anything clever' but has upped the Christian vibes here with 'TGI' – a weekly get together – plus drop-ins at lunch-time. Nothing forced – which goes down well with the neutral majority. Definitely a major element in building a positive ethos at King's (chaplaincy programme described as 'vigorous and popular' by inspectors). Teachers tend to stay here (14 have been at King's over ten years) and at forty-five, the average staff age is on older side.

Large, airy dining area provides wide range of menus (usual thumbs down for supper but other meals considered 'good' by pupils). Pupils can cook up own grub in houses after prep and are provided with basic rations. Take-aways (referred to by pupils as a 'Sun Inn') are limited by houseparents to one at weekend and one during week (apparently the local pub has cornered this lucrative market and delivers to houses). New head has a keen eye so a general tightening up is taking place.

Pastoral Care and Discipline: 'Family atmosphere' is what attracts parents and pupils – 'friendly children and good mixing between year groups' praised by one father. 'Fantastic' pastoral care, said one mum, whose son is now in fourth year of boarding. Some pupils trained to act as mediators where cases of harassment arise. Well established PSHEE programme includes sessions on stress management to help pupils cope with exam pressures. Medical centre provides for day pupils and boarders; free physio sessions on offer for all those sports injuries and visiting counsellor to provide additional support.

Smoking less of a problem these days (we didn't have time to check behind the bushes) but rigorous sanctions for those discovered. Sixth form club serves alcohol on Wednesday, Friday and Saturday evenings for an hour or so; junior common room a great success: we were told that 'friends just click with each other here'. Head 'takes all circumstances into account' before applying sanctions in areas such as drugs or illicit sex.

Pupils and Parents: All-round trad education sought by King's parents is steadily moving towards a more focused academic one. Sophisticated incomers appreciate it as much as locals, who prefer its 'slight scruffiness' to more lah-di-dah alternatives. Pupils appear confident and purposeful – apparently they get ('unfairly,' they say) occasional anti-toff flak at inter-school events (e.g. annual 'Bruton's Got Talent'). Boarders are in vast majority and though girls are well established here (first admitted in 1969) they remain outnumbered by boys 2:1. Internet savvy parents can enjoy seeing sports and other activities on school's 'gallery' (thanks to input from a local parent employed to provide all the visual media) even if they can't attend functions in person, regular newsletters and 'plus one card' sent to parents via house staff whenever an achievement has been recognised.

Long list of worthies going back to Hugh Sexey – auditor to Queen Bess and James I and founder of still extant Sexey's Hospital in Bruton. Lots of military top brass (including more recently Air Chief Marshal Sir Peter Squire) plus less worthy William Dampier – a seventeenth century explorer and buccaneer – and author of 'Lorna Doone', RD Blackmore. Also 'The Sunday Telegraph's' Mandrake, comedian Marcus Brigstocke and Sergeant Ben Ross – killed by a suicide bomber in Helmand, Afghanistan, who became the first Brutonian to be killed in action since the Korean War.

Entrance: About half of Hazlegrove's leavers move to King's. Remainder from Chafyn Grove, Perrot Hill, All Hallows, Port Regis and a host of others. Wide ability range as parents tend to choose King's for its own sake rather than its league table position.

Exit: Nearly everyone to higher education – half to Russell Group universities and remainder to every which course anywhere.

Money Matters: 20 per cent discount for Services' families. Fewer scholarships (still available for academic, sixth form and music) than previously but increased number of means-tested bursaries.

Remarks: 'Fairly useful,' said one dad clearly not given to hyperbole, whilst another parent stressed how King's 'does very well at catering for a wide range of ability'. Parents like the family feel of King's – its safe setting and sense of traditional values make it a popular choice. Moving forwards in curriculum terms but should guard against losing its warmth in a drive to be more ambitious.

King's College (Taunton)

Linked to Kings Hall School in the Junior section

South Road, Taunton, Somerset, TA1 3LA

• Pupils: 165 girls, 265 boys; 100 girls board; 175 boys board – the rest day • Ages: 13-18 • Size of sixth form: 170 • C of E • Fees: Boarding £25,170 pa; Day £17,040 pa • Independent

Tel: 01823 328 204
Fax: 01823 328 202
Email: admissions@kings-taunton.co.uk
Website: www.kings-taunton.co.uk

Head: Since 2007, Mr Richard Biggs (mid forties). Much admired at his previous school, Lancing, where he was deputy head and, for a time, acting head. Prior to that he was director of studies and a house tutor at Magdalen College School, Oxford. Degrees from the Universities of Cape Town (BA in physics) and Oxford (MA in maths and philosophy), where he was a Rhodes Scholar. Very bright, but not intimidatingly so; he has a wonderful sense of humour and has made a tremendous impact on the school. 'Inspirational and on the ball,' says one delighted parent; ' he's brilliant,' says a pupil, 'he knows everyone's names and leads from the middle.' An interesting concept but as we toured around, it became clear what was meant. He pops up every where: joining campers over night and staying, watching on the touchline, attending plays and concerts, teaching top maths sets and generally wandering about, observing and encouraging. Prep school heads and teaching staff at the college, alike, talk of his energy and interest in what they are doing.

Shrewd, open to ideas and clear about implementing the best, he has a refreshing vision for the school and is on the way to implementing it. He is ably supported by his charming wife, Sarah, and their two young children, who attend King's Hall.

Academic matters: 'There are far too many exams and too much attention paid to league tables,' says the headmaster. 'I'm less interested in the grades than the process of learning away from exams. I want teachers to be passionate about their subjects.' A new third form curriculum has been devised to make it stimulating and not merely early steps towards GCSEs. The head of English tutors the young scholars, inspiring and challenging; prep is not sacrosanct and can be used for rehearsals and discussion groups: pupils are encouraged to plan and use their time effectively. The dismissal of league tables is not a defensive game founded on sour grapes: separate sciences for most at GCSE and value added is very impressive, a clear sign of good teaching and hard work. An average of 63 per cent A/B grades across the board is further evidence of good practice. The school enjoys strong links with Exeter University and beyond, performing well, academically, but not for the sake of league tables.

Games, Options, the Arts: Flourishing. Games are taken seriously ('but there's no embarrassment if you're not all that good, you can always find something you can do'). Still holders of the Rosslyn Park 7s cup (this year was washed out), designated a centre of excellence by the English Cricket board (the legendary Dennis Breakwell still reigns supreme), successes at fencing, cross-country, netball, hockey; Senior School Choir of the Year in the BBC Songs of Praise of 2007; wonderful jazz CD with other musical delights sent out to prospective parents; new art building, clever adaptation of an old house, with stunning work being produced under inspirational head of art and artists in residence; new theatre and drama studio, an outstanding new swimming pool and absolutely amazing DT. Superb building for it – and how well it is used: cars stripped down and repaired, inventions mushrooming, skilfully drawn up plans converted with real craftsmanship. No wonder they have won the Good Schools Guide Award for Design and Technology three times. And it could happen again: this year's GCSE results saw 92 per cent of candidates gain A*/A grades.

Background and Atmosphere: Founded in 1880 to mark the 1,000th anniversary of the death of King Alfred, with pleasing ecclesiastical Gothic complete with obligatory tower. 100 acres of good playing fields and, by and large, interesting new buildings. A member of the Woodard Corporation, there are regular services in the large, plain but impressive chapel with its popular chaplain. Services are varied and with scope for open discussion as well as more formal worship. Very fine gothic dining hall and the Woodard room is an excellent facility for concerts, functions and conferences. When we were there, it was bursting with a very lively careers seminar. Thanks to the generosity of an OB, funding has been made available for a brand new, IT-rich modern library. Popular sixth form centre with attractive alpine-looking bar. The overall feeling of the school is warmly friendly and it was not unusual to see pupils of different ages chatting away convivially – that is when they were not tearing about.

Pastoral Care and Discipline: Seven houses, two recently built, mix day and boarders. Day pupils are welcome to stay over night, by prior arrangement, and we were told of several instances of that which resulted in permanent boarding. Boarding is very popular: week-end activities are arranged by houses and boarders are expected to be in residence for most week-ends. Those we spoke to were delighted to be so. 'Week-ends are the best time of the week,' said a young boarder and then grinned sheepishly. This is a school which takes boarding seriously and where the boarders are absolutely not day pupils who live too far away to go home. As far as discipline is concerned, common sense and courtesy really do seem to prevail, though the authorities are not stupid!

Pupils and Parents: This is not an overwhelmingly grand school: there is more aspiration than pretension and this is reflected in the clientele. A number come from the Services, others are from business, farming etc. 10 per cent come from abroad. The parents' association is active; indeed one of the things we noticed when talking to parents was their loyalty. OBs include Geoffrey Rippon, cricketer Roger Twose, rugby internationals Tom Voyce and Matthew Robinson, historian John Keegan, singer and broadcaster Alexandra Edenborough and children's broadcaster Dominic Wood.

Entrance: Via Common Entrance or VRQ at 13. 50 per cent or so come from King's Hall, the excellent partner prep school just out in the country; the rest from a wide geographical area: Exeter and Salisbury Cathedral schools, Jersey, Port Regis and around. A number enter at sixth form.

Exit: 98 per cent go on to universities; five or six a year to Oxbridge.

Money Matters: Academic and sports awards of a third fees at 13. Several music scholarships, plus art, drama, DT awards. At sixth form sports, music and academic scholarships held in November each year. Special scholarships for those from state schools.

Remarks: A sound, well balanced school, setting out into new exciting waters with a very able skipper at the helm.

King's College School (Wimbledon)

Linked to Kings College Junior School (Wimbledon) in the Junior section

Southside, Wimbledon Common, London, SW19 4TT

- Pupils: 760 boys; all day • Ages: 13-18 • Size of sixth form: 310
- Anglican foundation with own chaplain • Fees: Senior £16,680 pa
- Independent

Tel: 020 8255 5300
Fax: 020 8255 5309
Email: admissions@kcs.org.uk
Website: www.kcs.org.uk

Head Master: Since 2008, Mr Andrew Halls MA (late forties), previously head of Magdalen College School, Oxford. A double first in English from Gonville and Caius. Was head of English at Bristol Grammar School and deputy head of Trinity Croydon before becoming headmaster of Magdalen College School, a school stuck in a time warp, and made a stunning success of it. A good listener. Not scared of upsetting people if convinced he's right or has silent majority support. French wife Veronique teaches French at Godolphin and Latymer School. Two daughters. Firm advocate of single-sex education up to 16 but believes that in the sixth form, boys and girls benefit from being taught together – the school has taken girls into the sixth since September 2010. Mr Halls has consolidated the school's academic success, strengthen links with its partnership schools and introduced girls into the sixth form in order to make 'King's one of the most distinctive and sought after schools in the world'.

Academic matters: Excellent exam results in the top league, outstanding at International Baccalaureate, average score of over 39 points per pupil, amongst the top scores in the world. IB completely replaced A levels in 2008 – in 2010 11 boys gained the full marks score of 45 points. Good variety of subjects on offer plus international GCSEs widen the range of exams – pupils take between 10 and 13 subjects. Setting in most subjects, sets are arranged individually for each year to meet the requirements of each particular year group, extending very able pupils and identifying those who may need a different pace. English and mathematics brilliantly taught, fantastic standard of teaching throughout the departments, comment parents. Some innovative teaching in the sciences. Very strong results in modern languages where 98 per cent of grades at GCSE were A or A*.

Pupils write and edit their own newspaper. Community service is particularly strong, a compulsory part of the IB – amongst the many activities, every Friday sixth form boys host tea parties for the elderly. Pupils are encouraged to share their good fortune with others as much as possible – school works hard to widen the boys' outlook on life. KCS runs the partnership programme with local schools, offering many children access to sport, music and other classes not often available in the state sector.

Games, Options, the Arts: Just about every sport imaginable on offer from table tennis to water polo. Hugely successful rugby, tennis, golf and cricket teams. In addition to on-site facilities, school has a further 24 acres of playing fields. Sports tours all over the world, rugby team to South Africa in 2010, cricket team to Caribbean in 2009. Previously ranked at number one in the UK for fencing and for tennis. Rowing is also popular – school has its own boathouse at Putney. D of E gains a high number of gold awards. Thriving drama department – heart throb Ben Barnes – Prince Caspian – a recent old boy, as is 'Kite Runner' star, Khalid Abdalla. Boys often win the schools' category at Edinburgh Festival.. Very strong music – superb concerts of a professional standard, say parents. Art and design centre produces spectacular work that can be seen all over the school, ceramics and sculpture also of a high standard. Numerous clubs and societies run at lunchtimes, before and after school. No chance of being bored here.

Background and Atmosphere: Founded in 1829 by Royal Charter, KCS was originally based in the Strand. The school was an immediate success and moved to Wimbledon in 1897, enabling it to expand and also establish a junior school several years later. Original buildings are 18th century, then various additions to accommodate modern demands. Seventeen acres of playing fields and laid-out gardens including an international sculpture garden, a traditional flower garden and a spectacular Millennium Archway, partly of fish made by the pupils. All very well kept – an inspiring place to be.

Pastoral Care and Discipline: Head master, Andrew Halls, tells us, 'I have found parents waxing lyrical about KCS pastoral care.' KCS has adopted the holistic approach – boys have a personal tutor to guide them in all aspects of school life. The school is an Anglican Foundation, the chaplaincy provides worship and pastoral care. The chaplain, a female these days, is available at regular times to see pupils. The school's counselling service is off-site, ensuring confidentiality and anonymity. Two full-time staff man the learning enrichment centre, providing a range of supportive techniques for any pupil, of whatever ability, who may need some differentiation in their learning. Genuinely good relationships between staff and pupils throughout the school. Regular newsletters and a parents' handbook keep all well informed. Bullying is not tolerated. Co-educational sixth form has been widely welcomed.

Pupils and Parents: Once predominantly south west London and Surrey, the catchment area has expanded over the years, reflecting the school's popularity. In particular the IB has increased numbers, partly of a more international nature, coming from central London. Mainly professional middle class parents. Active Friends' group organises social events and is famous for fabulous firework displays. Many fundraising activities run for the benefit of the local community and links abroad. 'Make a Difference' days raise money for charity, provide services for the less fortunate and raise awareness of those who have made positive contributions to society.

Entrance: Two-thirds from school's own prestigious junior school; all candidates are pre-tested at 11. CE pass mark 65 per cent upwards, musical and sporting ability also a plus. Very competitive.

Exit: Virtually all to university – Bristol, Durham, Exeter and Edinburgh, plus around 30–40 to Oxbridge annually. Law, medicine, engineering and architecture are likely careers. Some to USA Ivy League universities.

Money Matters: Funded entirely by fee income. KCS Enterprises helps swell the coffers. A number of generous scholarships and bursaries awarded every year, academic, art, music and sport. Sixth form awards include an organ scholarship. School committed to increase bursaries significantly, at 11, 13 and 16. Money for scholarships is being devoted to this purpose.

Remarks: Only for the academically able. Boys work and play very hard in this wonderful school community. 'The great thing about schools like KCS is, on the whole, whatever they do, they do it so well,' say enthusiastic customers.

King's Rochester

Linked to Kings Preparatory School in the Junior section

Satis House, Boley Hill, Rochester, Kent, ME1 1TE

• Pupils: 275; mostly day, 20 per cent board • Ages: 13-18 • Size of sixth form: 130 • C of E • Fees: Senior Boarding £25,000; Day £15,420 pa • Independent

Tel: 01634 888 555
Fax: 01634 888 505
Email: admissions@kings-rochester.co.uk
Website: www.kings-rochester.co.uk

Head Master: Since 1986, Dr I R Walker KCG St G, BA, PhD, LTh, ThG, ABIA, F CollP, FRSA etc etc (mid-fifties), a philosopher, classicist, linguist, artist and general phenomenon. Dr Walker arrived at King's over twenty-four years ago (from Dulwich College, where he'd been head of RS) – a super-young, dynamic Australian, seen by some in the HMC as a maverick. Since then, he has built King's into a centre of all kinds of excellence and perhaps the most intelligently structured school we know. He is now the longest-serving HMC head and, legendary for his dedication to his pupils, he has acquired a unique eminence among his peers, several of whom see him as a mentor. Simultaneously suave and irreverent, he has a profound respect for tradition, along with a principled and rollicking capacity to debunk the pretentious and hypocritical. Dr Walker is his pupils' best advocate – 'I'm very proud of them and very, very rarely ashamed of them' – and they are his – 'He's, well, just brilliant'. Married to Kerrie, a solicitor, who has also given over twenty-four selfless years to the school, they have two children.

Academic matters: Value-added is good here – in an area known for the quantity and quality of its grammar schools, King's does remarkably well by its academically broad mix of pupils. Unique feature is German – taught to everyone from reception upwards and taken at GCSE level at 13 and at A level, by those who choose to, at 16. Other languages include French, Russian, Latin and classical Greek – Dr Walker himself will teach Egyptian hieroglyphics if asked. Languages well supported by lots of trips and exchanges, including the D of E gold award in France – results correspondingly impressive. Strong showings also in DT, art, biology and Eng lit and several smaller subjects. Refreshing to see no mandatory three sciences here, though one is compulsory and many take more. However, since Sept 2006, pupils take the IGCSE in sciences and maths – seen as a return to the rigour lost in the persistent dilution of the current curriculum. Everyone takes RS at GCSE. The diploma in digital applications is taken at GCSE level – this chosen in preference to standard ICT courses as it allows pupils to develop projects actually using their IT skills, e.g. designing websites etc.

At A level, subjects include Latin, Greek, economics and PE. 100 per cent pass rate and 60 per cent A*–B. RS, English, biology and chemistry the most popular with a spread of results. General studies for all. Small classes at this level and a collegiate feel mean that most pupils exceed expectations.

Team of qualified SEN teachers supports the quarter of pupils who have some kind of special educational need – mostly mild dyslexia, though school happily accommodates and makes provision for those with educational needs and physical disabilities where possible. An attitude of inclusiveness, can-do and helpfulness, and pupils are assisted in class, through withdrawals and with IEPs. Head takes small group who write a novel together and the super-bright are 'stretched by really good teaching. I encourage the staff not to stick to the syllabus,' says Dr Walker. The seriously good teachers will, of course, need no such encouragement.

Games, Options, the Arts: Main sports are rugby, hockey, badminton, netball, rowing, cross country, fencing, swimming (in school's super pool) and cricket. Netball shines in the honours lists and individuals achieve highly in rugby, otherwise a mix of results, but all played with huge enthusiasm on the beautiful, centrally sited pitches. Skiing is excellent; shooting also on offer with D of E and CCF. Pupils would love an Astroturf on-site – but it's hard to see where they'd put one. Music is exceptional – this is a cathedral school and the chapel is the Rochester Cathedral, which dominates the site. Every morning begins there and glorious music is a given for the lucky congregants. Lots of ensembles, concerts and musical occasions of all kinds. Art is good and DT inspired – both achieve highly, though a smaller range of applied arts available here than elsewhere, perhaps. Performing arts very strong – lots of high quality productions despite lack of actual designated studio/ theatre. Loads of clubs – around five choices each evening. Young Enterprise and debating.

Background and Atmosphere: Remarkable and something of a surprise, even to Kent locals who never penetrate the venerable and picture-book centre of Rochester. The second oldest school in the country, founded in 604, at the heart of ancient Rochester, the cathedral and the castle all part of the mix of buildings – Norman, Tudor, Georgian, Victorian, twentieth century and very recent indeed – which make up the school and its environs. Sixth formers housed in The College, a 17th century gem/Victorian gents' club – panelled and painted rooms, beautifully furnished, immaculately kept and self-policed, an education in civilised behaviour in itself. Pop in to the cathedral while you visit and find the mural painted in honour of the school's 1,400th birthday – and see if you can spot Dr Walker peeping out of a window. Round about is the less glamorous but also less recognised Medway region, which includes both deprived and highly privileged areas. This breadth and diversity is appropriately reflected in the school community.

Dr Walker's twenty-five years have had a dramatic and permanent impact on the school's fabric. Venerable buildings are now equipped and furnished to top standards and several new buildings set standards for elsewhere. Most recent is the conference centre 2006 – elegant, with a super-duper IT spec and imaginative decorative features – which provides a versatile space for gatherings big, small, formal or relaxed. Purpose-built pre-prep 2000 is a model of what a pre-prep should be. New girls' boarding house (see below) similarly classy. Brand new nursery with superb facilities for the youngest children, in the school opened within the pre-prep building, Chadlington House, in 2010.

The whole place is beautifully maintained. It looked its best on the day we visited – all gorgeous colourful borders against old brick walls on a sunny July day; it's immaculately kept and standards of appearance – for flower-beds and pupils alike – are high. Standards high altogether – behaviour, manners, respect, courtesy, consideration and order are the core values inculcated. A feeling of space, at odds with the reality in some respects – no-one looks crowded here. Pupils value the school's history and tradition as well as Dr Walker's determination to make the 21st century facilities second to none. 'The atmosphere's really friendly,' said one sixth former. 'You couldn't get better.'

Pastoral Care and Discipline: Unashamed Christian ethos and equally unashamed valuing of and respect for the faiths of others. Everyone takes RS to GCSE, but it is taught from an ecumenical point of view and Buddhists, atheists and everyone contribute to chapel services and the spiritual life of the school. Each day begins in the cathedral where the service is 'always challenging and provocative, as it's crucial to understand religion and its impact on society'. Two chaplains available and the prospectus says, 'The pastoral, sympathetic care of each child is the responsibility of every member of the school staff'. House system – everyone has a house tutor who monitors all aspects of tutees' lives. Zero tolerance of drug selling on or off-site – two expelled in 2006 for this. No random testing – 'It's a gross intrusion into people's lives and is immoral,' says Dr Walker – but suspected transgressors are 'vigorously investigated and judiciously dealt with'. Alcohol, smoking and drug use on site virtually unheard of in Dr Walker's time. Bullying? 'I dive in with my size nine hobnails and stop it.'

Boarding is small but offers as much as many full boarding schools, along with a close family feel. The boarding houses – central on the site and surrounded by gardens, with nice touches like a barbecue and picnic tables – are exceptionally well-furnished – all carpets and fresh paint, and the rooms, especially the new ones, are large, have four data points each and excellent en suite bathrooms. Nicer than average common rooms with vast plasma TVs, games etc, plus PC suite – we met several happy boarders. Half remain in school at weekends and exeats are allowed every weekend. Lots of activities and trips. Good food all freshly prepared and a very varied menu. We were especially impressed with the boarders' supper menu – not just soup and a roll, as so often elsewhere, but the works in three courses, and very munchable.

Dr Walker has had time to establish his own brand of friendly formality and cordial mutual respect in this community. Discipline is tight but the manner is relaxed, and pupils and parents pay tribute to a rare degree of tolerance and community spirit in which oddballs flourish alongside the sports captains and Oxbridge hopefuls. A parent volunteered, 'I like the healthy eccentricity which is also one of the most important aspects of any education. For example, Dr Walker teaches two subjects – divinity and manners. That is fantastic!'

Pupils and Parents: From up to 30 miles away and increasingly from the smarter Kent towns, e.g. Tonbridge and Sevenoaks. Also from the less manicured Chatham and Maidstone and towards east London. Everyone from old Kent families with centuries-old school connections to first-time buyers of private schooling, often second generation immigrant families who value the all-round start in life the school offers. Boys outnumber girls 2:1 in many years, though a better balance is gradually being achieved. Parents deeply involved and organise events with passion and fervour. Pupils a mix of the very bright, for whom public school was always the only option, to numbers of 11+ near-misses whose families scrape up the necessary and, seemingly, never look back.

School publishes 'Eminent Roffensians', a fascinating social history – said ORs are a sterling mix of the military, divine, artistic, athletic and bizarre. Among them are Richard Dadd, artist and parricide, composer Percy Whitlock, actor David King, John Selwyn Gummer and his brother, Peter, now Lord Deben and Lord Chadlington respectively (the first time in history two brothers have served in the House of Lords) and lots of brigadiers.

Entrance: Via interview and test, though school sees itself as essentially non-selective academically. Most come from the prep school on-site and certainly this is the best way in. We met happy 18 year olds who'd been there since they were four – the sense of cohesiveness derived from a shared childhood was palpable. Intake at all ages, although mostly at 11, and smaller one at 13, though no rigid pass mark at CE. Some arrive for the sixth form – often refugees from the grammars. School takes great care to look at the individual child and his/her circumstances and every candidate is seen by one of the school heads.

Exit: Virtually all to university to study the full range of academic and vocational subjects. A decent number to Oxbridge and more to the University of London colleges.

Money Matters: Good range of valuable scholarships – up to 30 per cent minimum remission, means-tested up to 75 per cent, for King's Scholars. Also means-tested awards and awards specifically for those from the state sector. Scholarships for specific aptitudes, e.g. music and organ playing. Remission also for clergy, service families and for siblings.

Remarks: Rigour and compassion blend in a classy school which, were it in Wiltshire or Berkshire, would be turning them away in coachloads.

The King's School (Macclesfield)

Cumberland Street, Macclesfield, Cheshire, SK10 1DA

• Pupils: 500 boys, 370 girls; all day • Ages: 11-18 • Size of sixth form: 270 • C of E • Fees: £9,225 pa • Independent

Tel: 01625 260 000
Fax: 01625 260 022
Email: mail@kingsmac.co.uk
Website: www.kingsmac.co.uk

Head: Since 2000, Dr Stephen Coyne BSc PhD MEd (chemistry/polymer science) (fiftyish). Grammar school educated before studying at Liverpool and Manchester Universities. Taught at Merchant Taylors', Crosby and The Manchester Grammar School, becoming head of science at Arnold School, Blackpool, and deputy head at Whitgift School, Croydon. Married to a teacher, no children, and is very happy here; softly spoken, quietly confident with clear ideas and ambitions for the school. Quite understated but appears to provide good leadership for the King's foundation. Makes his presence felt at both sites, regularly making the mile journey between the two.

King's has had the reputation of being a sports school and, whilst anxious not to diminish this, the head has brought improved academic results, putting it on a level with other academic schools in the area. Since his appointment he has tightened up on 'housekeeping' issues, e.g. uniform, presentation of the school and monitoring of standards ('Many more assessments of academic performance,' comments one pupil). He enjoys teaching chemistry to the sixth form – 'the only way to keep in touch at ground level'. A believer in breadth of education, not academic pressure cookery.

To retire 2011. His successor will be Dr Simon Hyde, MA and doctorate from Oxford in modern history. Currently deputy head of Haberdashers Askes Elstree, he is an old boy of the school.

Academic matters: Now a leading school in Cheshire. Maximum class size is 25 with average sizes around 20. Sixty two per cent A*/A grades at GCSE, 76 per cent A/B grades at A level. A wide range of subjects on offer, including psychology, classical civilisation and geology. A gifted and talented register offers opportunities for exceptional pupils and learning support is available for pupils with dyslexia (for which a fee).

Games, Options, the Arts: Excellent facilities include 40 acres of playing fields, all-weather pitches, gym and squash court. The girls' division has a sports hall and Macclesfield leisure centre provides a swimming pool. High pupil participation in all sports, with teams of all abilities playing on Saturday mornings. Hundreds of sporting fixtures occur throughout the year and many pupils achieve county and national success; regular tours abroad to places such as Kenya, Singapore and Australia. Outward bound activities are particularly well catered for, including a compulsory programme of activities in Years 7 to 9, making use of a variety of centres in the Peak District: rock climbing, pot holing, sailing, mountaineering, orienteering – the list goes on.

Music is important – timetabled lessons in Years 7 and 8 provide a broad exposure to the subject and include hands-on learning in the keyboard lab. Thirty peripatetic teachers provide individual lessons. A full programme of recitals by the choirs (BBC choir of the year in 2003), barbershop, and chamber groups as well as orchestras, wind bands, percussion and string groups; the more talented musicians, boys and girls, combine to form the Foundation choir, orchestra and big band. Results at GCSE and A level are excellent. Art and design are well catered for with dedicated art rooms at both sites and an impressive technology rooms at both sites. Pupils enjoy residential weekends and workshops and hold biannual art exhibitions.

Background and Atmosphere: Founded in 1502. Originally a grammar school, its status has evolved over the years and it became an independent fee-paying school in 1946. C of E foundation but an ecumenical ethos. The King's School Foundation is organised in four divisions – the boys' and co-ed sixth form divisions at the Cumberland Street site that the school has occupied since 1855, whilst the girls' and co-ed junior divisions occupy the site formerly known as Macclesfield High School for Girls. Boys and girls are therefore taught separately between the ages of 11 and 16 but mix for some extracurricular activities – promotes the advantages of single sex and co-ed education at the different stages of development.

Boys and the sixth form occupy an impressive site with lawns sweeping up to the imposing main building. A new purpose-built sixth form centre was opened in September 2007. The girls' and junior site is less grand but situated on the edge of the Peak District with glorious views over open countryside. We reported that the girls' division had a bit of a poor relation feel compared to the dynamic boys' division, but the girls extol the virtues of their division and the head, disagreeing with us, points out that the girls represent much of the academic success of King's. A house system works at both sites, encouraging achievement, academic or otherwise.

Pastoral Care and Discipline: Head likes to deal with antisocial behaviour before it reaches the point of bullying. The few cases that occur are dealt with quickly and in close liaison with parents. A peer support network enables younger pupils to turn to a known older pupil with problems they may be unwilling to take to a member of staff. Drug offences would invite expulsion, but head comments he would look 'at circumstances of each individual case'. Warnings and detentions for other troublesome behaviour. School councils (pupil run) operate at many levels. The sixth form council has its own boardroom and seems to have real clout.

Pupils and Parents: Majority professional, some farming families and a sizeable minority of blue-collar workers.

Traditionally rather WASPish but now popular with families relocating to the area, so has an international element. Good parent support. Head 'rarely buttonholed at events with concerns or complaints'. Pupils are relaxed, chatty and warm, clearly enjoy school. The head girl was outstanding – very confident, articulate, with oodles of charisma, clearly going places. The rest are a sociable bunch with their feet on the ground, polite and fiercely loyal to their school. They defy any pupil not to find a niche here.

Entrance: The school draws from a large geographical area within Cheshire, Derbyshire and Staffordshire. Non-selective entrance into the infants. Assessment for entry into juniors plus report from feeder school. Entrance is not automatic from own infants. At senior level, entrance is by examination, report and interview; again no automatic right of transfer, though vast majority does. At sixth form, two As and four Bs or equivalent are required by internal candidates, higher for externals. The majority at senior level come from the junior school, the local state schools and local prep schools.

Exit: A small number leaves post GCSE to go to sixth form colleges. The vast majority of sixth form leavers go on to higher education – a mix of universities, including the new universities and art foundation colleges. Around 10 each year go to Oxbridge (support and preparation for candidates). Pupils praise the careers advice.

Money Matters: Bursaries (means tested) for bright children with limited resources are available. Some minor scholarships. To mark the quincentenary year, a fund to provide for sixth form bursaries was launched and many students have gone through on this scheme.

Remarks: A relaxed, friendly school offering oodles of opportunities for its pupils. Academic results have steadily improved under the current head. He comments that bright pupils are challenged and stretched here, but pupils who may not have achieved in a pressured environment also do well because they enjoy school, find that they can excel in an area and hence their overall performance improves.

The King's School (Worcester)

Linked to King's Saint Alban's School in the Junior section

Linked to Kings Hawford School in the Junior section

5 College Green, Worcester, Worcestershire, WR1 2LL

• Pupils: 515 boys, 425 girls; all day • Ages: 11-18 • Size of sixth form: 270 • C of E • Fees: £11,874 pa • Independent

Tel: 01905 721 700
Fax: 01905 721 710
Email: info@ksw.org.uk
Website: www.ksw.org.uk

Head: Since 1998, Mr Timothy H Keyes MA (fiftyish). Educated at Christ's Hospital, read classics at Wadham College, Oxford, then PGCE at Exeter. First headship. Came from Royal Grammar School, Guildford, where he was second master, having previously held classical teaching posts at the Perse, Whitgift and Tiffin. A committed and active Christian. Says, 'I think that's important because the school is run on Christian principles.' But keen to stress all faiths 'welcomed and valued'. Sings with Worcester Festival Choral Society, also a keen campanologist. Sits on the board of UCAS so able to give solid advice on higher education. Outgoing, friendly and infectiously enthusiastic - he's a man on a mission. Knows all pupils by name and what's going on. 'I'm interested in every one of them,' he says. 'I hope they know that.' The friendly face of authority, but not a soft touch. Wife Mary Anne teaches maths and science to juniors (King's St Alban's) and takes Christian Union club. Two sons – both in higher education. Lurcher, Tess, rounds off family unit.

Academic matters: Usually to be found in league tables' top 150. Selective though flexible intake with generous approach to lower entry exam marks if child excels in other areas. Much emphasis placed on 'unlocking potential' and pupils 'doing the best they possibly can'. Class size maximum 24 with setting introduced pre-GCSE in maths and English. May be more setting in future but not much as head believes it can be 'demoralising'. GCSEs 98 per cent A*–C grades. A levels in 2009, 100 per cent pass rate with 78 per cent at A or B grade. Maths and sciences (separately or as dual award) consistently good at both GCSE and A levels. Modern languages equally impressive – 100 per cent A*–C in German (Bravo!) with French and Spanish coming up fast. Geography shines in sixth, English lang and lit good to average. Interesting observation by head. 'GCSEs and A levels are very important but their shelf life is very short,' he says, their main use being to secure university places. 'It's our responsibility to produce people who can work in teams, manage themselves, take responsibility, who can lead and who are well-balanced.'

Options includes drama, music, theatre studies and textiles. Classrooms bright, freshly painted and well organised with mixture of eyes-front and huddle teaching according to year group. Changeover from boarding to day school freed up loads more rooms giving lessons new lease of life and increasing year (but not class) sizes. Science labs in typical 1960s block but labs themselves have all been recently re-fitted with great effect. New award-winning £2m library 2006 – central to academic life and fully integrated with a very active careers department – it is well-stocked and e-friendly putting bytes on more equal footing with books. Elsewhere computers much in evidence. Dedicated IT rooms as well as classroom provision. New art school opened in 2007. New D&T department finished in 2008 along with a new Lecture Theatre. Specialist help for mild learning difficulties only.

Games, Options, the Arts: Awarded Sportsmark Gold in new millennium. Sport an important part of school life – but not an obsession, says head – with fine facilities like sports hall, fitness suite and 25-metre pool, also used by outside bodies. Games played once a week. Very competitive and successful – in particular the girls' rowing eights (recent national champions), an impressive rugby XV, strong cricket, hockey and netball. In 2008, one recent leaver played rugby for England and one won an Olympic gold in rowing. Dance a popular activity among both boys and girls. Outstanding art – and lots of it. Might have been the unsung hero a few years ago but deservedly celebrated from the rooftops now. More A grades than any other at A level. In the 2008 GCSE exams, 17 students from King's were among the best in the country. Art school in separate building secreted behind red brick wall but visitors discover a paint-splattered Aladdin's cave inside. Extremely high-quality work. Work shown off well in dining room, around school and in specially designed and lit gallery.

Much music, as you might expect at a choir school. 18 boy choristers boost ranks of cathedral choir (until voices break so most come from junior school). Over 100 musicians, three school orchestras (two pupils recently in National Youth Orchestra), two school choirs, a wind band and brass group. Two school organs for pupils' use. Oxbridge organ and choral scholarships not unheard of. Flourishing drama department with Actor in Residence. Newish 310-seater theatre in frequent use for plays, concerts and big screen presentations. A full-time theatre manager adds an extra dimension to the activity. Plenty of opportunities for travel, home and abroad. King's accepted onto EU-funded Comenius Scheme which involves joint projects with schools in France and Germany. School's own outdoor pursuits centre in the Black Mountains hugely popular; art and language students, historians and geographers also venture far and wide. National finalists in Young Enterprise Scheme. Very involved in local community (sixth formers help young readers at local primaries and host events for the elderly and for a local special school) and further afield (young Nepalese student sponsored through university). Extra-curricular can mean anything from chess club to climbing the Himalayas. Innovative relationship with a local comprehensive based on shared extra-curricular activity and common ethos. The school day might not be long (8.30am to 3.50pm) but it's certainly packed. School remains busy until 5.30pm each day.

Background and Atmosphere: Superb green setting under the watchful gaze of Worcester cathedral, founded in 1541 by Henry VIII after the suppression of the priory. Described by head as 'an oasis of calm' at heart of busy modern city. Head sees this location as of great benefit to pupils, enabling them to build relationships with leading city institutions and businesses. Oldest part is 14th century former monks' refectory now serving as vast and imposing assembly hall. Despite school's great age, no school motto (dismissed as fatuous by head). Closest it comes to one is Greek inscription (translated for us by classicist) on heavy oak assembly table: 'I learn what may be taught; I seek what may be found, and I pray for what heaven may grant.' (Well, that just about covers all eventualities.)

Despite hundreds of years of history and tradition, it feels refreshingly unpretentious. School completely co-ed since 1998. From early age, pupils encouraged to look beyond school gates, to try new things and help those less fortunate. Keen communicators internally and externally. Slightly stodgy but worthy annual school mag The Vigornian, regularly supplemented by a more upbeat four-page bulletin, various newsletters, tabloid newspaper, The King's Herald (free) and countless activity leaflets. King's underpinned by two junior schools – one right next door (King's St Alban's) shares senior school facilities; the other more recently acquired (King's Hawford) lies to north of city in country setting. Have own individual heads but Mr Keyes is supreme head.

Pastoral Care and Discipline: Pastoral care still run, unusually but very successfully, along boarding school lines, based on old house system. Newcomers at 11 put into groups of 20–22 for first two years to make friendships and settling in easier. For remaining five years pupils assigned to one of eight houses (around 80 per house) with six tutors per house responsible for pastoral issues (staff paid extra to take on this rôle). Sixth formers act as mentors for youngest pupils. Active school council and pupils also have voice through elected monitors and sitting on food and uniform committees. Imaginative team-building events early in the year for new pupils. Pretty hot on rules – suspension for smoking and drinking (even in Worcester city centre). Drugs more complicated: automatic expulsion for dealing, final warning for using. 'We are very tough when we have to be,' admits head. Best summed up as firm yet fair. Parents always contacted and consulted, particularly in rare cases of bullying. Daily matters of appearance, behaviour, punctuality and so on dealt with through system of coloured papers issued by staff which collectively give overview of pupils' activities.

Pupils and Parents: A fairly mixed bag. Reputation for old money but far more professionals and new money these days plus a number of strugglers. Many give generously towards bursaries for current pupils and are supported by a professional and effective Foundation Office which coordinates alumni activity. Large numbers of former pupils return each year to share expertise and the benefit of experience, some as part of 'barnabas group' (leaders in their fields who address full school assemblies). Annual fête or charity walk regularly raises tens of thousands. Parents prepared to travel some distance too since King's went day (Stratford, Birmingham and Evesham, to name but a few).

Pupils smart, interested but above all confident – from the youngest up. Well-mannered, not afraid to speak up, enthusiastic. 'We are not seen as having a mould,' says head. 'We turn out interestingly different characters. The example set by sixth formers to younger pupils is superb.' OVs (Old Vigornians – they take their title from the Roman name for Worcester) include TV presenter Chris Tarrant and comedian Rik Mayall.

Entrance: Selective entry exam at 11 (qualifying for those coming up from the two junior schools, competitive for external candidates). 130 new places at 11. Own entry exam at 13 – vacancies vary in number each year but usually between 5 and and 10 places. School looking for 40–50 per cent minimum pass but considers all-round performance and potential. About 25 places fall free each year in sixth – at least five Bs and two Cs needed at GCSE. Entry to junior schools also selective. Chorister voice trials held throughout the year. A good voice is not enough in itself to win school place.

Exit: At least 95 per cent to higher education with a few heading for Oxford and Cambridge. Medical studies perennially popular, as are languages, art, drama and mechanical engineering. Few losses post-GCSEs. No weeding-out policy to improve overall A level results.

Money Matters: Good crop of scholarships (worth up to a third tuition fees) up for grabs in the junior schools and at 11, 13 and 16. Includes academic, music and all-rounder awards. Boy choristers awarded 50 per cent scholarships by cathedral to cover their time in the choir. Head says, 'the school will do its very best to make sure no chorister has to leave after that scholarship ends.' Growing number of bursaries available. Big appeal under way to make more funds available (growing at 15 per cent per year, with 12 pupils on free places this year), recently boosted by single gift of £1 million. Small discount for third and fourth siblings.

Remarks: Big enough to offer much, small enough to keep it personal. Individual choice and achievement count for a lot here, with boys and girls given the right mix of guidance and freedom to discover their own strengths. A real feeling of relaxed respect among students and staff with co-operation seen as the key to reaching goals. 'It's quite simply a lovely school,' says one parent. Very well thought of locally (even by those who haven't got childen here) and much sought after. Book early.

The King's School Canterbury

25 The Precincts, Canterbury, Kent, CT1 2ES

• Pupils: 785 pupils: 425 boys, 360 girls (610 board, 175 day). • Ages: 13-18 • Size of sixth form: 320 • C of E • Fees: Boarding £29,175; Day £21,555 pa • Independent

Tel: 01227 595 501
Fax: 01227 595 595
Email: admissions@kings-school.co.uk
Website: www.kings-school.co.uk

Headmaster: Mark Lascelles, Lower Master, is interim head, but Mr Peter Roberts, head of Bradfield College, appointed from September 2011 – appears to have been met with universal approval: prep heads and parents most enthusiastic. One prospective parent stated this was a perfect match.

Academic matters: Very successful, producing excellent results – academic achievement highly rated here. Over 80 per cent A/A* at GCSE and 99 per cent A*–C. 92 per cent A*–B at A level with 92 candidates gaining at least one A*. All-round academic strengths – no single area dominates, though modern languages always excellent and in 2009 a number of national awards in physics and chemistry. Top sets can take French GCSE early; 28 to Oxbridge in 2008. The tutor system provides strong support for the pupils and ensures that any problems are picked up early. Impressive library on the St Augustine site across the road – very pro-active librarian ensures library is at the centre of academic life – open until 10pm every night of the week. Somerset Maugham and Sir Hugh Walpole both left their personal libraries to King's.

Great strength is intellectual growth – constantly encouraging children to find out more and aim high. Languages department staffed by mainly native speakers, all housed in The Old Palace. Specialist laboratories for chemistry, biology, biochemistry and physics; 'Young Scientists' online science journal designed and managed by a team of pupils. Specialist IT laboratories plus networked workstations with printers all over the place, plus sockets in every pupil's room in the houses; school intranet. Purpose built CDT building. SEN support available, although only minor difficulties can be coped with – laptops available.

Games, Options, the Arts: Thriving sports department – sport held in high regard by pupils; trophies all over the school. Girls' sport particularly strong, especially hockey – Kent champions at various age levels, regional finals at three levels. Rugby on an upward curve – new master in charge this year, two England internationals in last season's team; football being expanded. Acres of playing fields about 15 minutes' walk away, with modern sports centre incorporating pool, indoor courts, climbing wall, café and gym. Has produced international players in various sports, particularly fencing and rowing (boys and girls). Talented sailing squad. Mark Ealham is the cricket professional.

Long tradition of excellent drama and music – annual house plays, short GCSE and A level productions, drama competitions at different age levels: 'Wherever there is a quiet corner, you will find a rehearsal going on'. Fabulous new music school. Crypt choir tours annually – most recently to South Africa and Swaziland, 'Carmina Burana' with international soloists; jazz very strong, lots of house concerts, choral awards to Oxbridge. Art department in a sympathetically converted twelfth century priory, different artist in residence each year. Countless clubs and activities including D of E, international science journal and archaeology – staff always keen to add new options. CCF totally reinvigorated; something going on all the time.

The famous King's Week at the end of the summer term is the highlight of the school year and is a festival of music, drama, and dance with events being staged in all corners of the school every day for a week – parents and friends come bearing picnics and it is a major social event culminating in Commem Day and the leavers' ball – so the leavers get a great send off.

Background and Atmosphere: Set in the shadow of Canterbury Cathedral, it has to have one of the most inspiring settings for a school. Stunning ancient buildings and cloisters and beautifully kept gardens – with the busy city life going on outside the gates. Pupils enjoy the contrast and the fact that the City with its shops and cafés is on the doorstep – 'Makes us feel part of the real world,' as one girl put it. The origins of the school date back to 597 AD when Saint Augustine arrived in Canterbury. In 1541 it became part of the Cathedral Foundation of King Henry VIII with a core of 50 King's Scholars and soon became known as the King's School. It went co-ed in 1990.

A forward looking school with a great sense of history and an ancient feel to it. Children can wander round the cloisters and into the Cathedral. Six main boys' houses and five girls' plus three day houses and a smaller sixth form girls' house – rich variety of architectural styles. Half the houses clustered round the cathedral and the other half across the road at the St Augustine site, where they have their own dining hall – pupils equally happy to be in houses in either location. Very easy and comfortable relationships between boys and girls.

School is a sponsor of Folkestone Academy and pupils can attend activities not available at King's, like cookery in a full teaching kitchen. Atmosphere of ancient customs and traditions in fact totally at odds with the truth – that a small school on the site was turned by Canon Shirley (head of King's 1935–62 and one of the great pioneering entrepreneurial heads) almost overnight into a place with smart uniforms and quaint customs, in a marketing exercise of which any captain of industry would be proud.

Pastoral Care and Discipline: Smart uniform – pinstripes and jacket with wing collars, like little barristers; monitors wear purple gowns. Big effort to address everyone's needs and happiness – several staff/pupil committees to ensure all have their say. Boarding houses friendly and welcoming with areas where pupils can make their own snacks and relax. Younger children housed in small dormitories, sixth form have their own study bedrooms. Large and popular social centre open to the whole school during the day and sixth formers in the evening. Current head very keen that pupils should know where he (and they) stand re partying and other jollies. Excellent food, consistently praised by all – 'restaurant standard', according to one parent.

Pupils and Parents: Good mix socially and culturally – popular with locals, London and county sets, expats and foreigners (France, Germany, Nigeria, Hong Kong, Russia and others – a wide spread with very few from any one country). Very popular with Foreign Office families. Scholarship pupils are encouraged from all backgrounds and nationalities.

The King's Society, a cultural, social and educational society for parents and friends of the school, going from strength to strength and now has over 300 families. Members organise lectures, dinners, trips etc. Thriving Old King's Scholars Association. Old boys and girls include David Gower, Michael Morpurgo, astronaut Michael Foale, supermodel Jacquetta Wheeler, Patrick Leigh Fermor, Olympic silver medallist and world champion rower Frances Houghton, William Somerset Maugham, Christopher Marlowe, Anthony Worrall-Thompson, Lord (Charles) Powell, conductor Harry Christophers.

Entrance: Very popular at the moment – need to book at least two years in advance. At 13+, by Common Entrance, or special exam for those coming from abroad who have not been prepared for CE. Pass mark around 60 per cent but school has good relationships with prep school heads and takes their reports very seriously. They do not overbook so will only fail those who they feel would struggle. 25–30 places available for sixth form entry by exam held in November (80–100 usually apply). Children come from a wide range of Kent and Sussex prep schools and London day schools plus 30 per cent from Junior King's, although no special dispensation for children coming from here.

Exit: Virtually all to a wide range of universities: Cambridge, Durham, Leeds, Bristol and Oxford being top five in 2008, with an increasing number going to American universities and Trinity College, Dublin. Languages, English, history, religious studies and economics still hugely popular, but physics, with a young dynamic woman at the helm, has gained the top spot this year (65 studying the subject in the lower sixth). Bio-chemistry the most popular of the sciences, followed closely by medicine. Five or six a year leave after GCSEs, usually to go to London day schools or local schools.

Money Matters: Up to 20 King's scholarships and exhibitions of up to 10 per cent of fees. Up to 12 music scholarships for up to 10 per cent of fees and free tuition in two instruments, plus art and sports scholarships (the Gower sports scholarship) all with a rigorous selection process. Three or four sixth form scholarships awarded for outstanding performance in the sixth form entrance exam. Greater emphasis on bursaries – the King's Foundation has been set up to fund both scholarships and bursaries: lots of fund raising activities – a recent ball in London raised £60,000.

Remarks: Thriving school with highly motivated pupils who work hard and never seem to stop but still have a huge amount of fun. Not a heavily religious school but the Benedictine tradition of care for body, mind and spirit is very much in evidence. Religion a light touch and other faiths welcomed. Not a school that wants to mould people and produce a type – tolerant of quirkiness. A fast flowing river 'but open to a wide range of abilities and personalities' – humane ethos. Now with a rocky patch to overcome.

The King's School (Chester)

Linked to Kings Junior School in the Junior section

Wrexham Road, Chester, Cheshire, CH4 7QL

• Pupils: 995 girls and boys • Ages: 7-18 • Size of sixth form: 150 boys and 70 girls • C of E, cathedral foundation • Fees: Juniors £7,797; Seniors £10,173 pa • Independent

Tel: 01244 689 500
Fax: 01244 689 501
Email: admissions@kingschester.co.uk
Website: www.kingschester.co.uk

Headmaster: Since 2007, Mr Chris Ramsey MA (mid-forties). Previously head of King's College, Taunton, deputy head at Cranleigh, head of languages at Wellington College. Educated Brighton College and Corpus Christi, Cambridge. Quick thinking, fast talking, fizzing with enthusiasm, this new head has bounded into King's determined to make it 'the great co-ed day school of the North'.

Sitting (not still) in pinstripe suit with braces and silk tie, on the aubergine sofas on the teal carpet in the newly colourful head's study, he brings not a breath but a gale force gust of fresh air to the place. He admits that not everyone has enjoyed him challenging the status quo. 'He has ruffled feathers,' confess older staff, while pupils say, 'he rules with an iron fist,' recalling a mass detention for tardy compliance with new locker rules.

Publishes weekly blog musings on school website. Says his three children here 'are very happy, but I'm forbidden to talk to them', 'I'd like to see her through the school'. Intriguingly, his dapper dressing (check out his blog picture) seems to contrast with the endearingly small R reg Rover in the Head's parking bay.

Academic matters: Extremely ambitious – 'We're quite keen on league tables' – and no wonder. In 2009, King's rose a hundred places with a bumper crop of 66 per cent As at A level, 82 per cent of GCSEs an A or A*; add the B grades and you've got 96 per cent of the GCSEs – 'making us not just very good but now a leading school,' says head.

Pupils are quick to give 'fulfilling my potential' as a top reason for coming here, 'We work in a productive environment, with teachers available in classes before and after school and approachable at lunch times for extra help'. Teachers must expect head to pop in to lessons, 'to take an interest, be visible, be encouraging', in a spirit of respectful, constructive criticism. IGCSE maths and accelerated maths A level to fit in another subject. Taking three sciences at GCSE is compulsory – 'Universities are hungry for science' – and contentious with pupils for limiting other choices, partly because provision for music, art, DT, ICT etc is so temptingly good. Three Arkwright scholars in 2009 reflect progressive approach in DT; plenty of prizes in other national Olympiad challenges. A biology department greenhouse overflows with verdant 'herbology'.

Newly refurbished library, open from 8.15am–5pm, attracts 800 visits a day to its 16,000 resources, which include 85 journal subscriptions. ECDL instead of GCSE ICT, plenty of computers everywhere, whiteboards and netbooks in some classes. UVI trialling extended projects in 2009 and in life skills learning how to manage money, cook and drink sensibly as a student and change a plug.

Games, Options, the Arts: Strong rowing tradition since 1877 from boathouse on the Dee. King's is a top rowing school which grows a steady supply of national rowers: Tom James, 2008 Olympic medal, Olivia Whitlam, world U23 champion in 2007, 2008 Olympic finalist. Girls now making their mark in competitions; most importantly, King's had the edge over arch-rival Shrewsbury on the water last year. Fiercely competitive in all sport including girls, with 'Kings are Queens' headline from paper proudly displayed outside the galleried gym. Acres of pitches, courts, floodlit Astro, indoor pool and tradition of inter-house sport so all can take part.

New music school (2005) boasts bright recital hall with floor to ceiling apex windows, recording studio, classroom full of computers and six individual practice rooms. About half take individual instrument lessons in school and 20 orchestras, ensembles and choirs, including Schola Cantorum, which leads services in the Cathedral. The music head, described as 'fantastic' by parents, has direct phone and email on school website. Art is celebrated in an exhibition space near entrance foyer with the superb DT creations too. Thriving CCF and DofE, Model United Nations, varied list of extra-curricular activities from Scrabble club to meteorological society. 'This is a school for people with aspirations and a wide range of interests; the school does such a variety to a good level,' say pupils. Huge range of trips and charity partnership with school in Madagascar.

Background and Atmosphere: Founded by King Henry VIII in 1541, the school left its city centre cathedral site in 1960, moving to acres of greenness leased from the Duke of Westminster, who takes an interest in the CCF. The campus has a newly spruced feel in line with head's crack down on pupil and indoor untidiness, 'We've pulled our socks up'. Pupils complain they don't have time to visit lockers between activities, especially during break and lunch, but unattended bags are confiscated and detentions issued as they're reclaimed – 'a matter of responsibility,' says school against background of pupil grumbling, but the corridors are clear. Most classrooms are hugely spacious too, which contrasts with the cramped dining hall, where lunch is compulsory, although a new theatre and dining hall are on the cards. A sense things are still settling since change of head, although one unruffled duck and drake have carried on with two years' duckling production in the school quad.

Pastoral Care and Discipline: Pupils describe this as 'a very friendly school' and parents praise the effort made to help children settle in here at all levels. Prefect and sixth form mentoring and form tutors form backbone of pastoral care. Whole school devised and subscribes to core values of 'ambition, benevolence and co-operation'. Last ISC inspection mentions 'the excellent relationships between pupils and staff ... engendering an atmosphere of trust and security'. Strong Cathedral links endure, although Mr Ramsey perhaps gives Christian traditions less emphasis than former head. One of two weekly assemblies now includes 90 second 'Quite Interesting' public speaking slot for pupils to share their interests – 'We want them to discover that knowledge is delicious'.

Achievement is recognised across the board and head is quick to point out, 'There's something for everyone with glory, not just for the goal scorers and A*s'. Pupils stand for teachers and visitors and in the main wait their turn at doorways. Choosing not to fulfil responsibilities, such as not storing bags correctly, brings the consequence of sanctions such as detentions, simple as that, but, apart from teething problems with the new locker system, discipline doesn't generally need to be heavy handed; this seems to be a pretty civilised community. A full time nursing sister mans the sick bay.

Pupils and Parents: Proportion of girls has grown to 33 per cent since their arrival in 2003 and the school now feels properly co-ed with girls of all sorts, not just robust pioneers. Despite school becoming more image conscious, pupils remain disarmingly normal and charming – apart from the odd characterful hairstyle we saw no hint of a cool in-crowd, and all ages politely but naturally hold their own in adult conversation; they're a very nice bunch.

From Chester and Cheshire, the Wirral and North Wales, in their distinctive navy, green and white striped blazers and ties. Sixth formers move on to crested navy blazers with ties denoting activities and status and senior prefects get to wear academic gowns for special occasions. Largely middle class and white, professional or farming backgrounds.

Entrance: By 11+ examination in January, with English, maths, non-verbal reasoning and group discussion to assess thinking skills. Selecting from the top 25 per cent, about two applicants for every place. Sixth form requires A* or A in intended subjects and seven GCSE Bs or above. Assessments for the Junior School at 7+.

Exit: The opening line on school website states, 'From your child's first day at The King's School at seven years of age, we are preparing them for graduation and beyond'. University is unapologetically assumed from the off. Most to a university from 'Times' Top 30 list, handful to Oxbridge (some to keep rowing), over ten to medicine and dentistry in 2009 and recently one a year to St Martin's Art College. Sixth form support for course and university choice very strong, with all UCAS applications submitted by end of October. Notable old boys include TV's Martin Lewis, talkSPORT's Mike Parry, Ronald Pickup (actor), Tom James MBE (rower), Nicolas Grace (actor), Sir John Vanbrugh (architect), Steve Leonard (TV vet), Freddie Owen (cricketer) and Admiral Sir Peter Dennis who, after leaving in 1730, reportedly invented mayonnaise.

Money Matters: About 80 senior pupils receive some kind of means tested bursary; 10 have free places, with plans to increase bursary provision to help more pupils over next decade, returning somewhat towards school's founding principles of helping 'poor, friendless boys'. Top achievers in the first term at 11 bag a one off £500 scholarship and keep the term King's Scholar for their school career.

Remarks: Confident school with top notch facilities and all round education, that's becoming ever more academically ambitious under dynamo new head. Thankfully pupils remain consummately friendly and unassuming.

The King's School Ely

Linked to Kings School Ely, Junior School in the Junior section

Barton Road, Ely, Cambridgeshire, CB7 4DB

• Pupils: 460; 185 day boys, 115 day girls; 95 boy boarders, 65 girl boarders • Ages: 13-18 • Size of sixth form: 165 • C of E • Fees: Day £16,395; Boarding £23,730 pa • Independent

Tel: 01353 660 700
Fax: 01353 667 485
Email: admissions@kings-ely.cambs.sch.uk
Website: www.kingsschoolely.co.uk

Head: Since 2004, Mrs Sue Freestone GRSM MEd LRAM ARCM (early fifties), married with grown-up son and daughter. Trained at the Royal Academy of Music and Bristol University. Previously head of Sibford (a Quaker school) and prior to this appointment was a conductor and director of music at Colston Girls' School.

An approachable head with bags of energy and enthusiasm. Morality and a religious conviction are important to her, and she wants to show that it is possible to have these traits without being stuffy. Behind her bubbly exterior a razor sharp mind and a determination to get things done. Has already engineered some big changes – senior girl choristers to complement the boys and the genesis of a gifted and talented partnership scheme with a local comprehensive.

Academic matters: Pupils aren't spoon fed but are encouraged to make the most of opportunities. No undue pressure, but feedback is honest and dedicated staff give plenty of support – value added is well above average. Five sets for all academic subjects lead to small groups that benefit the individual student. The school works hard to ensure that the less academically able feel valued – 'I didn't feel that I had learning difficulties – everyone is valued'; 'We're helped to understand ourselves'. Some mumbles that, once in a set, particularly in the middle bands, children might become complacent or stuck. The head said that she 'didn't believe in coasting' and 'there is some mobility between sets.' 24 subjects at GCSE (97 per cent A–C) including single sciences, geographie (geography in French leading to a dual award – often taken by the more able) and religious & moral philosophy, which is compulsory. Wide spread of subjects at A level (100 per cent pass rate and 40 per cent A). Biology, business studies, maths, psychology are popular and top grades in textiles and art, although not many entrants after AS.

Dyslexics and dyspraxics are thoughtfully accommodated with an emphasis on flexibility – the setting system is geared towards particular needs; a designated area (with sofas) where pupils can drop in if they want additional support. At GCSE it's possible to substitute a subject with learning support – 'The director of studies was very flexible and understanding'. The Kings International Study Centre equips approximately 50 foreign students a year with the language and study skills needed for transition to UK independent boarding schools – classrooms and accommodation are separate, but some fraternising with the main school in sports and dining areas. A wide spread of nationalities and good success rate at GCSE.

Games, Options, the Arts: Emphasis is not purely on the academic – plenty of areas where children can develop, especially in music. 'It's woven into the fabric of the school and it's hard not to become involved,' remarked one parent. Over 50 per cent learn an instrument and 'intriguing stuff at all levels' – musicals, choirs, orchestra, jazz bands, groups, electric guitar etc. Excellent facilities, including practice rooms that are open until 10.30pm. The scheme for girl choristers (own boarding house) aims to attract high achieving girls and tighten the bond with the cathedral – which, the head commented, 'helps underpin Christian values'.

Not a big drawback if pupils aren't particularly turned on by music or have interests elsewhere. The unusually tidy art department produces carefully controlled work. Sensitive textile pieces and some expressive ceramics – all tastefully displayed. Sport is enjoyed and plenty on offer – but after the re-instatement of rugby no competitive hockey for boys. Otherwise the usual majors for both sexes and a good range of alternative activities. Rowing, according to one girl, is 'taken verrrry seriously'. Own boat house, specialist coaches and a potential member of the GB rowing team in Year 11.

The Ely Scheme (outdoor pursuits programme) is compulsory in Year 9. Pupils can opt (and do) to continue in year 10 and then apply to become a scheme instructor – good opportunities to take responsibility and develop leadership skills. Very positive feedback from older pupils – 'It's taught me how to work in a team and break a problem down into steps'.

Background and Atmosphere: Idyllic setting in the centre of Ely with glimpses of the Fens and the ever present cathedral. Access to the town is relatively free – 'It gives a taste of real life – albeit of a small town. A gentle feel'. The school is housed in an assortment of buildings – modern (classrooms) to medieval – which are spread around public spaces to the north of the cathedral. Although several minor roads cross the campus, pupils move around sensibly. The monks' barn is now a lovely dining hall – food, particularly the breakfast, really is as good as they say. The library, reached by a well-worn stone spiral staircase, is in an ancient building that has been modernised to make a top notch facility – eager librarian on hand to help and order books needed for research. A terraced cottage is used for the sixth form centre – although it's a bit of a warren and on the small side, just enough room for a pool table and a giant plasma screen, which has pride of place. Boarding accommodation isn't plush but everywhere is well tended and clean – no litter anywhere.

Friendly staff communicate with parents increasingly by email. Consultation and dialogue are actively encouraged between the staff, parents (regular heads forum) and pupils. The school council isn't just a token – things happen and the head is open to new ideas; one pupil said, 'She really listens if you have evidence to support your argument'.

Pastoral Care and Discipline: An on-site counsellor and parents report that pastoral care is very good – 'Staff have their fingers on the pulse all the time – not just when there's a problem'. Pupils are given a fair degree of freedom but rules, particularly in relation to boarding, are strict. Pupils know that they must comply – 'Feels like they trust us unless we break that trust'. The Christian ethos and sense of community have a big impact on school life.

Pupils and Parents: Farming, clerical and service but increasingly entrepreneurial and professional. Predominantly from the Eastern counties plus a good smattering from Europe and the Pacific Rim. Pupils are polite, well behaved and quietly confident. Uniform until the sixth, when boys wear suits and the girls something tailored – all very sensible and tidy. Past pupils include Lord Browne of Madingley (chief executive BP), Alan Yentob (BBC), Ms Jo Marks (multi-million mobile phone business), Matthew Amroliwala (broadcasting), Olympian Goldie Sayers.

Entrance: Own exam at 11; Common Entrance type exam for entry into Year 9, though Common Entrance may be sat (75 per cent from King's own junior school). Entry to the sixth form – minimum of six A–C grades at GCSE but at least B grades expected in the subjects to be taken at AS. School says it is 'becoming increasingly difficult' to get in, but the overall picture of the student is taken into consideration.

Exit: Some students leave after GCSE, usually to the sixth form colleges in Cambridge. Post A level all go on eventually to further education (anything from Oxbridge to art school) with a sizable number of gap years before students take up their university places.

Money Matters: A wide selection of bursaries/scholarships – discounts for the clergy and Services. Boys who were junior choristers and remain in the choir receive a 33 per cent bursary. Girls in the senior girls' choir receive a 33 per cent bursary on boarding fees.

Remarks: Connections with the cathedral are important – the Christian ethos is at the heart of everyday life. Not an academic hothouse but plenty of opportunities for all-comers to shine. A worthy school run by an ambitious and dynamic head. One to watch.

Kings' School

Romsey Road, Winchester, Hampshire, SO22 5PN

- Pupils: Total: 1675 boys and girls, roughly 50:50. Boarding (boys only) 32
- Ages: 11-16 • State

Tel: 01962 861 161
Fax: 01962 849 224
Email: kings.school@kings-winchester.hants.sch.uk
Website: www.kings-winchester.hants.sch.uk/

Head: Since 2005, Mrs Sue Lawrence (50s). Previously at other Hampshire schools as head of year, English teacher in an 11–18 school and deputy at King's. Before she took over, the school's physical environment was, by all accounts, rather dull and lifeless. Neither of those qualities would suit this glowing ball of Celtic fire. Modest and generous in her acknowledgement of staff and pupils, she is justifiably proud of what she has achieved. In more ways than one she has brought light and colour into the school – burgundy and cream are everywhere, helping to give it a sense of identity; even Mrs Lawrence's lipstick was colour coordinated with her surroundings on the day we visited. 'That's just a coincidence,' she said, but the fact is, as one teacher told us, 'She lives and breaths the school'.

The school rules and expectations, with their insistence on smartly worn uniform, punctuality and consideration for others, have a splendidly old fashioned ring about them, what the head in her introduction to the prospectus refers to as 'traditional values' – 'Children are happiest when they know where they stand,' she says. 'I want the pupils to accept ownership and be encouraged to grow from within without any autocratic interference.' Happiness and fulfilment – it works.

Nothing autocratic about her, and certainly nothing pompous, but a powerful sense of determination, good sense and warmth. Also much strength of will and loyalty to her charges: woe betide anyone who uses too much jargon or mistakes quantity for quality. The targets she believes in meeting are individual, nor governmental – in a school of over 1650, individuality is not swamped by bureaucracy. Glowing recent Ofsted report on 'inspirational' leadership and 'exceptional' management. Now just takes a number of 'Head's lessons' – ' We discuss anything that crops up. There's no opportunity for interaction during assemblies but there is in these lessons. The pupils can be very frank. I learn a lot'.

Academic matters: Impressive results considering not an academically selected hothouse, e.g. 2010 GCSE: over 50 per cent Latin A*, 100 per cent Chinese A*, 91 per cent five+ A*–C. Lessons bridge the academic with the practical – good preparation for the outside world. Purposeful atmosphere.

Games, Options, the Arts: Excellent facilities for every sort of activity. Thanks to careful budgeting and a well conceived application to the National Lottery, a fully flood-lit Astroturf pitch and large multi-surface flood-lit playing area with six tennis courts and space for basketball and netball. Recent large sports centre which links the new swimming pool and sports hall; beautiful cricket pitches.

In 2008 took over the management of the nearby Tower Arts Centre, a very attractive Victorian water tower, considerably refurbished with a new stage, up to date lighting and sound system, a printing press and art studios. We saw some extraordinarily beautiful creations in the art department, where pictures were being assembled for GCSE; impressive work in the excellently equipped science and technology department and a thoughtfully designed business centre for sustainable businesses – companies set up and run by the pupils with help and interaction from business partners. Everywhere you look the work of pupils is celebrated and held up for inspiration and admiration.

Background and Atmosphere: An amalgamation of two underperforming single sex schools, linked into one twenty five years ago, in a leafy and spacious area of suburban Winchester with views over the downs. The older parts – the original girls' school – have long, narrow corridors, once dark and forbidding, now enlivened and enlightened with pictures, posters, photographs, many reproduced and blown up to giant size, thanks to the school's printing press, one of its sustainable enterprises; also more modern buildings with wider corridors.

Pastoral Care and Discipline: 'About 97 per cent of the pupils want to be taught,' said one teacher. It shows, but without any dampening of youthful noise and energy. Moving about the school the decibel count is healthy; once lessons begin it is appropriate.

A designated school for pupils with physical disabilities – to stand in the middle of the school when pupils are moving to different classrooms between lessons is to witness very movingly how well this aspect of Kings' concern works: compassion and understanding are manifest in this intelligently run school.

Pupils and Parents: Lots of grateful local families and mostly happy pupils – one eleven year old boy gasped out, 'I just love this school!' Another older boy announced he was 'pleased to be leaving,' but added with a grin, 'It's been quite good, though' – high praise from an adolescent. Pupils greet and smile and in conversation reveal themselves articulate and relaxed – it was difficult on occasions to remember we were talking to sixteen year olds and not sixth formers. On the whole town and gown work well together – one local described the school to us as a 'lovely lot'.

Entrance: The prospectus gives information about entry, administered by the Hampshire County Council, so no control over who comes to them. Parents express preferences – consistently the most over-subscribed school in the area – but the council ultimately assigns pupils to one of the three secondary schools in the area. Thanks to shifts in local demographics, parents may now apply from outside the official catchment area. Always appeals and waiting lists. Children or families who have a serious medical, physical or psychological condition receive preferential treatment for admission. A boarding house for around 30 pupils, some of whom come from abroad.

Exit: 96 per cent go on to Peter Symonds Sixth Form College, a few to other sixth form colleges and the remainder to vocational courses. Interestingly, some stay on in the boarding house because they like it so much.

Remarks: By any standards an outstanding school – if all state schools were as good as this, the HMC would be a much slimmer body.

Kingston Grammar School

London Road, Kingston Upon Thames, Surrey, KT2 6PY

• Pupils: 460 boys, 365 girls; all day • Ages: 11-18 • Size of sixth form: 120 boys, 100 girls • Non-denom • Fees: £13,908-£14,283 pa • Independent

Tel: 020 8546 5875
Fax: 020 8547 1499
Email: registrar@kgs.org.uk
Website: www.kgs.org.uk

Head: Since September 2009, Mrs Sarah Fletcher MA PGCE, an Oxford historian (late forties) and, according to parents, a breath of fresh air. She came from a deputy headship at Rugby where she had been for twelve years. Previously taught at Wycombe Abbey, St George's Montreux, Habs Girls' in Elstree and Lawrence Sheriff Grammar in Rugby – an admirably varied career with child protection, housemistressing and Pre-U experience along the way. Mrs Fletcher is pretty, softly spoken, sparkly, diplomatic and clever. One of the new breed of heads we are meeting more frequently, now that governors have learned that women can do the job superbly without being remote administrators and while being warm, human and effective. A 'can do' head, she has plans to 'green' the school i.e. to landscape it and plant it so as to soften its somewhat austere aspect. We approve. She's also smartened up the pupils. Parents say, 'She is wonderful. She has lots of new ideas and is only holding back so as not to overwhelm people. She's good at consulting – she really wants our views'. And pupils agree. 'Her door is always open. She wants us to come in'. Under Mrs Fletcher, the school is opening up in all ways. 'I believe in creativity, independent learning, helping people think for themselves and stretch themselves. I want opportunities for everyone.' An inspired and confident appointment for an inspiring and confident school.

Academic matters: Now does IGCSEs in maths, English, sciences and langs. No Pre-U yet though under consideration as an alternative to A levels. Maths is popular at both levels and results are outstanding – pupils praise the brilliant teaching and even those who say they aren't mathematical find it hard to resist. Eng lit, physics, biology and history also star. Smaller take-up in langs despite good teaching. However, this will pick up under enthusiastic support from head who wants her pupils to encounter as many langs as possible, maybe taking to the 'virtual classroom' to link with schools over the globe. Current dept currently musters 14 langs between them. Greek taught in collaboration with Tiffin Boys. In 2010, 88 per cent achieved A*/B at A level across the subjects. No great surprises in the curriculum though sports studies and theatre studies offered at A level. A few pupils yearn for cookery. IT a tool not an end in itself and all sixth formers take the European Driving Licence in IT. Learning Support dept helps those on the dys strata, mostly mild, a few moderate. Learner profile compiled for all children seen by Ed Psych or specialist teacher and head a great believer in constant monitoring and tracking to ensure progress. Site pretty accessible and school will put itself out to support mobility if needed. Lots of laptop users and open to those with aural/visual impairment – 'so long as they can cope with the site'.

Impressively stocked library, actually called 'the library', not 'the resources centre'. And books actually used. Most reassuring. Pupils praise their teachers and librarian unreservedly – 'they will always run extension classes if you ask'...'they'll order anything in for us'. Parents praise the academic ethos – 'It's not pushy but they do get the results'. 'They really encourage them to think for themselves.' 'They're quick to pick up on people's talents and nurture them – even talents the children didn't know they had.'

Games, Options, the Arts: In an area full of good schools – and some of them are free – this is what gives Kingston the edge and makes it the first choice even for those whose children are super-bright and might well gain a place at a local grammar. The extra-curricular opportunities here are seemingly limitless or, at any rate, fill a 40 page booklet. Half a dozen activities pre-school, a dozen or more in the lunch break and a further dozen after-school make for a busy, busy life. Pupils we spoke to said they stay after school every day – though this, of course, not true of everyone. Loads of trips – local, national and international, an excellent programme of outside speakers – and an expanding sports programme – ('one of our new teachers, an ex-army officer, thinks anything is possible', says Mrs Fletcher) – which includes girls' football, now countering erstwhile grumbles of sport being only for the best. Netball no longer a poor relation but zooming. Boathouse on the Thames provides rowing option – 'it's huge!' we were told. CCF very popular with the first year's cohort, tails off thereafter though masses of opportunities for RAF flying, summer camps (very popular) and some get schols to Sandhurst at the end. 'The Cage' – two onsite courts with soft surfaces – due for upgrade but most sport takes place on the Fairfield – a field behind the main site or off-site at Ditton Fields – a bus ride away. New stress on community service. Older pupils admit that 'it's a bit of an eye-opener' for those who had, hitherto, looked inwards rather than outwards to those, locally and beyond, less fortunate than themselves.

Music acknowledged to be outstanding and, again, strengthened by the Fletcher approach. Music tech new and burgeoning – already growing out of space – but trad music also supported, though small academic uptake. Head says, 'I want music that will appeal to everyone but which has a high class end'. Drama, well-housed in excellent, flexible and well-equipped performing arts centre, produces classy shows, including annual Shakespeare festival and real plays – good to see something other than High School Musical and Grease, for once. House drama, Ad Lib and annual dance fest much enthused over, even by boys. Art and DT are exceptional; masses of workshop/studio space and we drooled over brilliantly conceived and executed mini-dresses made from e.g. sweetpapers or exquisitely embroidered canvas. Professional quality furniture made by GCSE class, perspex clocks and clever ceramics make you want to get your hands gummy. Previously blank walls now acting as showcases for pupil work – a welcome and humanising change. The list of national awards, prizes and achievements across the extra-curricular spectrum fills several pages.

Background and Atmosphere: In the midst of Kingston's tarmac tangle, it's fine if you know your way but, if you don't, leave an hour or so to locate it and then park – no parking on site and even the staff have an efficient system of sharing lifts and spaces. The school itself looks like a real old-fashioned grammar on the outside – solid, brick-built and purposeful – though, once you get inside, the modernisation and bright, light spaces change one's initial impression. The trad grammar style persists in the school hall from your parents' childhood, with honours' boards, memorial tablets to those who fell in the two wars and faint echoes of Praise My Soul the King of Heaven lurking in the curtains. Give Mrs Fletcher a couple of years and the place will look different – she plans trees, umbrellas, picnic tables – 'you can create an illusion of space,' she thinks, 'we've all got to muck in and make do'. And space is certainly not lavish here though the school is less cramped than some of its central London peers.

Pupils wear white shirts and black or grey uniforms. They look sensible and tidy. 'Mrs Fletcher has really cracked down on very short skirts – she wants everyone to look smart. It's made a huge difference,' we were told by one rather elegant sixth former. About half the school eat school lunches, acknowledged to be much improved and gaining support. It looked good to us and lots of choice. The place feels relaxed and welcoming. Pupils like the House system which enables friendships between the years. 'We feel far more like a real community now.' Good café for sixth form – into which staff also pop (it's OK – they don't come in in large numbers') – with TV, stereo system, drinks and snacks. Good home/school IT links – email used all the time now, we were told. The most appallingly ear-lacerating school bell we have ever heard.

Pastoral Care and Discipline: Good system of heads of year and form tutors – 'they get to know you really well' – but discipline scarcely an issue here. 'They're really hot on bullying'...'they've always got time to talk to you if you've got something you need to sort out'. Misconduct marks, summons to head of year, rare Saturday detentions generally all that's needed. No smoking, drink or drugs problems that anyone can recall. 'The pastoral care is extremely good,' a parent told us, 'they're quick to pick up problems and to keep parents in touch. It's in the culture of the place.'

Pupils and Parents: From only around a 3 mile radius, so they probably know how to navigate Kingston's surreal road system. From over 150 primaries, 65 per cent came from state schools in 2010.

Notable former pupils include Edward Gibbon (The Roman Empire one), Michael Frayn, Jonathan Kenworthy, James Cracknell, Neil Fox and Andy Sturgeon (imaginatively roped in to help with the reshaping of the school's landscape).

Entrance: Changing. School so popular and over-subscribed now scrapping the 10+ entry – no longer needs to snaffle those unsure of getting in somewhere good at 11. More or less equal number of boys and girls arrived at through merit not engineering. Interview seen as important, 'We are not academically exclusive in our selection – we look for potential'. Mrs Fletcher works closely with the feeder schools – especially at 13+ so as to not to encourage unrealistic applications. 'I don't believe in disappointing people.'

Exit: They spread over the country – from Edinburgh to Exeter. Of 109 leavers in 2010, 94 went to university and 4 to art school. Annual sprinkling to Oxbridge, lots to London, Manchester and the biggest range of courses you could imagine.

Money Matters: Scholarships worth 10 or 20 per cent of fees available at all entry points and awarded on results of tests. Bursaries worth up to 100 per cent of fees also at all entry points and means-tested. Worth a serious look if you are, local, clever and strapped.

Remarks: Great school, great new head, great future.

Kingswood School

Lansdown Road, Bath, Bath and North East Somerset, BA1 5RG

• Pupils: 650 boys and girls, 480 day, 170 boarding • Ages: 11-18 • Size of sixth form: 200 • Methodist • Fees: Day £11,220; Boarding £17,634-£24,183 pa • Independent

Tel: 01225 734 200
Fax: 01225 734 305
Email: enquiries@kingswood.bath.sch.uk
Website: www.kingswood.bath.sch.uk

Head: Since 2008, Mr Simon Morris MA (Cantab) modern and medieval languages, especially German (late forties). Educated at Ipswich School, then a spell in the City after Cambridge, 'But in my heart of hearts, I always knew I'd be a teacher'. Despite exclusively independent school career, has taken pains to cut the mustard by doing his PGCE and NPQH, the latter quite unusual amongst independent school heads. Previously deputy at St John's, Leatherhead, via housemaster and head of modern languages at The Leys and head of German at Warwick School.

First ever non-Methodist head of this Methodist school – openly C of E but embraces Wesleyan philosophy of service. Might seem unassuming but isn't: passionate about instilling high but attainable standards in every individual – in everything they do. Married to Caroline, who teaches modern languages in the school and has lots of state school experience. Three children, all pupils here. Supported by triumvirate of deputies, all good foils to the others. Takes junior PHSE programmes as a chance to stay in touch/get to know the newly arrived. Visible, approachable, welcome and frequent spectator; keen cricketer. Appears to have 'gone down brilliantly' with parents and sixth form, in particular. Firm of handshake and of purpose, a round peg in a round hole.

Academic matters: Strong performance across the board – super results. Well over 60 per cent A/A* at GCSE and 85 per cent A/B grades at A level. Vies for second place in Bath league tables with Prior Park (Kingswood edged ahead last year), behind local academic hot-house, King Edward's. Must do really well on value-added, then, for a school which claims not to be 'narrowly selective'. Masses of choice, with 23 subjects to choose from at GCSE and 26 at A level. Languages lag behind in terms of takeup, despite German being compulsory alongside French in Year 7. Two languages too much pressure, some parents think. Main teaching block (The Ferens) utilitarian and colour coded inside according to subject. OK labs and lots of IT throughout. Unlovely but much loved sixth form block (The Dixon) houses some teaching, the HE and careers department, studies and chill-out space, including a kitchen. Magnificent Gothic splendour of a library enough to make anyone work; sixth form has Perspex platform of privilege at far end. Cosy seminar room at entrance.

Not a huge number of diagnosed SENs but 1:1 help on offer (paid as extra) for those who need it. Head keen to take 'any child who can access the Kingswood curriculum', including those with dyslexia and on the autistic spectrum. Inclusive, non-stigmatised provision. Head's personal experience informs his attitude.

Games, Options, the Arts: Plenty of pitches/courts/Astroturf, flattened out on three levels of alarmingly sloping grounds, imaginatively named lower, middle and upper, the latter a short minibus ride up the hill. Usual rugby/hockey/tennis terms for boys, hockey/netball/tennis for girls, but tempting options too for the less sportingly inclined, e.g. the slow running club(!). Not queuing up to show us the swimming pool.

Strong links with Team Bath at the University – makes good use of its facilities and expertise. Sport taken seriously but no discernible 'jock' culture – in fact current captain of rugby also a musician of note. Head's plans include splendid new multi-sport pavilion/bar/social space on the Upper, which also hosts Bath Rugby Club in this rugby-obsessed city. A 2012 swimmer's timetable has been pared down to fit training in; a promising young golfer is also in the slips.

The arts generally acknowledged as outstanding and have their own awards ceremony. Charming arts and crafts style studio produces works of exhibition standard in all media; a local gallery has chosen more Kingswood work than from any other Bath school. Sixth formers and staff wear enviable monogrammed smocks.

Music school a super light space boasting a top-notch recording studio and an 'inspirational' head of music who embraces everything from Bach to the Beatles, and whose students recently recorded for Children in Need at Abbey Road. Something for all performers of all styles and standards. Drama right up there too, with proper theatre as well as a studio. Productions for all ages, which neighbouring schools attend, plus a massively popular comedy club for (brave) aspiring stand-ups. Shows are collaborative, with pupils involved with writing, producing, publicising as well as performing. Theatre also twice a venue for BBC 'Question Time'.

Background and Atmosphere: The only school founded by John Wesley (who believed that education should engage the heart as well as the head) and first ever Methodist one, spawning over 700 across the world since. Moved from Bristol in the early 1850s because of unreliable water supplies and has occupied an imposing pile of purpose-built Victorian Gothic on steep northern slopes above Bath ('Satan's throne', according to Wesley) ever since, almost opposite the Royal High School. Other buildings of varying degrees of age and beauty are dotted around its 140 acres of manicured grounds, including the chapel, too small these days to house the whole school, which gathers for religious and secular assemblies in the theatre. Not at all horribly worthy, as its history might indicate.

Has managed to hang on to the feel of a co-ed boarding school with day pupils. A long day for everyone (5.30pm finish after activities or, rarely, prep) and mixed day/boarding houses from Year 9 right up to upper sixth. No Saturday school but good activity programme for boarders, plus usual sporting fixtures on Sat pms. Littlies spend their first two years in Westwood, a gentler introduction to the big school. Boy and girl boarders occupy separate floors of immaculate dormitories for six to eight, out of bounds to day pupils, who share the slightly dark living space downstairs. Room sizes go down while mess goes up in the six single sex senior houses, where the feel is cosier and autonomous. Space for occasional over-nighters.

A spirit of service (to the school/local/global communities) expounded by the head and lived out in the school, e.g. by close involvement of sixth form with junior pupils, lots of unglamorous charitable stuff in Bath as well as abroad, e.g. bricklaying in Malawi – Uruguay at planning stage. Green credentials measure up too: holder of Eco-Schools Green Flag, fluttering proudly from flag pole; in-house (and excellent) catering sources as much food as possible locally or from Fair Trade; sustainable development committee currently looking at ground source heating, reducing food waste and an improved travel plan. Head talks convincingly of 'our responsibilities to the planet'. Right mix of respect and banter between pupils and staff, and pupils at the top and bottom of the school – 'They really look after each other,' said one mother, echoing several others. Central dining in splendid Gothic setting helps all 600 pupils get to know each other.

Sees itself as an innovator amongst Bath schools, e.g. Model UN, and quite keen to show them how it's done. International flavour: pupils come from 15 countries, but an eye is kept to see that no one nationality dominates and all get an esentially British boarding experience. Pupils love it – 'I've got friends all over the world,' declared a sixth former, with an eye to his gap year.

Pastoral Care and Discipline: 'Outstanding,' according to parents – 'They're just so nice to each other – and that goes for kids and staff,' said one, whose son fled bullying at another school (it gets zero tolerance here). Touchy-feely stuff not at the expense of academic rigour or general endeavour, however: expectations are laid down early and slacking discouraged. A clear system of sanctions looks good on paper, but we didn't find anyone who would admit to being on the receiving end of it! Emphasis definitely on support and redirection, rather than on chastisement, and all felt help for any problem was very much on hand.

Pupils and Parents: Moderately to exceedingly affluent but not especially posh. Wide range of professions amongst parent body, offspring of (more successful) actors, musicians and sportsmen/women amongst pupils. 'Incredibly supportive – and reasonably demanding,' says the head. Pupils are engaging and confident without arrogance, and startlingly uncritical of their school. Most come from north side of Bath – crossing the city at peak-time is hideous and plenty of provision south of the river.

Entrance: 50 per cent from own prep school, some from other prep schools mostly north of Bath, good few from local (excellent) primary school, St Stephen's, where they have strong links and collaboration. Maths, English and non-verbal reasoning tested at 11+ to try to ensure fairness; coaching not expected and discouraged. Head sees all entrance papers.

Exit: 90 per cent plus to university of first choice, preceded by gap year by 40 per cent or so of leavers. Handful to Oxbridge and to art and music colleges, others to diverse degree choices all over Britain.

Money Matters: Good value for what's on offer: third cheapest in Bath with lots of extras thrown in. Some parents resent those long holidays, which can be a problem for those working so hard to fund it all. Academic and special talent scholarships offered at Years 7, 9 and lower sixth. Head keen to increase bursary provision throughout.

Remarks: Super school which has finally gained its place in the competitive galaxy of Bath secondaries. Setting and atmosphere suggest privilege without pretension; particularly good for budding performing or visual artists who require results too. Takes the best of Methodist philanthropy and adapts it for a secular multi-cultural world. Truly global in feel and outlook for an English school.

Knowl Hill School

School Lane, Pirbright, Woking, Surrey, GU24 0JN

• Pupils: 60; 15 girls and 45 boys • Ages: 7-16 • Predominantly Christian • Fees: £15,789 pa + therapy • Independent

Tel: 01483 797 032
Fax: 01483 797 641
Email: info@knowlhill.org.uk
Website: www.knowlhill.org.uk

Principal: Since 2005, Mr James Dow Grant MA Ed PGCE IE Dip Dip DS Cert SpLD Cert Prof Std AdvDip (Behaviour), member of NASEN and PATOSS, has spent 15 years at the school, four as deputy head. Pupils say, 'He's very nice, charismatic and clever; knows his stuff and what he's doing but he can be strict.' Hopes to continue to work on specialised therapy programmes and keep school moving forward and progressing, including internet-based learning. Various therapy programmes now available in auditory processing issues.

Succeeded founder Mrs Angela Bareford AGSM Teachers Dip Ed AMBDA (Dys Inst Dip) IE Dip, who started school in 1984 when she was unable to get help for her own dyslexic son (now in his 30s).

Academic matters: Maximum class size 8 but smaller groups and one-to-one as required. Good range of compact specialist facilities, science lab, small library, photography studio, art and textiles room, fully equipped OT room, large room for assemblies and lunch (packed lunches only, healthy eating actively encouraged). All follow national curriculum (modified as appropriate) and take key stage tests. No foreign languages, though older pupils participate in conversational French. Senior pupils study for GCSEs or, for those unable to cope with GCSE, literacy and numeracy tests. Great emphasis on the multi-sensory, holistic programme for literacy skills (either Dyslexia Action's multi-sensory literacy or their units of sound programmes). A similar approach is used in maths for those with dyscalculia. Integration of speech and language and occupational therapy is central to learning programme. The therapists go into and run some lessons – the SaLT runs social skills session and assists with English Speaking Board (ESB) preparation – helping pupils focus on voice production, breathing as well as organisation of language, vocab social skills. Some pupils can take AS/A level art, textiles and photography, following the upgrading of the art department facilities. Some links with outside agencies allow for practical ASDAN programmes as part of the school's curriculum, for example metalwork, plumbing, perhaps car mechanics, animal welfare.

Additional therapy, tailored to the needs of each child, is available to small groups or individually (extra charge). LEAs prefer blocks of therapy, but school feels strongly (and is prepared to argue the case) that regular integrated support is more beneficial. All learn to touch type (but active handwriting policy encourages good pencil grip and cursive writing) and each pupil has use of a laptop (wireless networked). ICT playing an increasingly important role in teaching and learning – enhanced by use of interactive whiteboards. All have an IEP, regular reports and bi-annual testing, supplemented by statutory annual review for those with statements or annual appraisal run along broadly similar lines for rest, with regularly monitored and updated targets for all.

Games, Options, the Arts: Good facilities in new creative arts block for art, pottery, 3D, CDT, photography and drama. Art a strength – 'Some pupils have spatial difficulties but we show them tricks and teach techniques'. Drama important and used to give guidance, social training and act out day-to-day problems. Limited sports on offer within school, principally football and basketball, but good use made of local facilities. Compulsory educational trips including annual overseas visit (Iceland this year, Barcelona next) seen as integral and important to building confidence, encouraging independence, reinforcing sense of community and developing social skills. A variety of clubs including choir, sports, archaeology, IT, art, origami, prep and electronics keeps pupils gainfully occupied at lunchtimes and after school. Rare sports fixtures and little instrumental tuition at present (school hoping to address latter) but pupils have instrumental enrichment and the listening programme uses specific music to channel ideas and concentration. Good links with community and local army base provides outward-bound opportunities and PSHE support.

Background and Atmosphere: The charming, redbrick, former Victorian schoolhouse occupies a small but well-maintained site in a pleasant village location. Sympathetically extended over the years – especially the two-storey art block; the compact but modern, pristine facilities adequately support the curriculum. Much thought has gone into all aspects of the school's development – even the playground is carefully divided: a yard for those needing to let off steam or simply enjoy a game of footie or basketball, a quiet area complete with fountain for those wanting to de-stress, a work/picnic area and a well-equipped adventure playground.

Pastoral Care and Discipline: 'Some children have spent a considerable amount of time out of school; it's important that we provide an empathetic atmosphere and environment so we work hard to develop confidence and foster enthusiasm for school.' That doesn't mean misdemeanours go unchecked – a sliding scale of sanctions and detentions exists and the occasional pupil is excluded if behaviour merits it – 'We have to consider safety and the wellbeing of all our pupils and balance that with the needs of the individual'. Merits and rewards aplenty, including collective rewards for the best class. Pupils very positive – 'If you need help you get it'; 'It's like a family'; 'Knowl Hill is the best thing that happened to me'. Pupils appreciate smallness of the school – 'You get more friends here because everyone knows each other'. Careers advice via Connexions. Regular counselling available (charged as an extra) or open door drop-in sessions (free). A school council set up to enable pupils to express their views and suggestions, in response to their request.

Pupils and Parents: Children of varying backgrounds all rub along nicely. From a large catchment area – Richmond, Cobham, Weybridge, Kingstone, Hampshire, Windsor and Maidenhead and various London boroughs. Majority are English plus a few Americans referred from the two local American schools. Most epitomise the severe dyslexic – they are appealing, they like talking, are creative but have significant problems with organising, sequencing etc. A significant minority have had very negative experiences of school life and some are so traumatised by past experience that a graduated programme is used to integrate the child into school – 'We might start with the child attending for a couple of days a week or maybe just mornings – whatever it takes'. Parents very positive – 'It's made a tremendous difference, we just wish we'd sought out help sooner'.

Entrance: All pupils have to be dyslexic and may be dyspraxic. Additionally, pupils may have hearing impairments, elective mutism, epilepsy or mild emotional difficulties requiring either a modified or mainstream (plus support) curriculum. Won't take those with behaviour problems and all accepted on a half-term's trial basis. Referrals may be made privately, by educational psychologists (EP) or by local education authorities (currently eight different LEAs refer pupils). Expected that prospective pupils will already have an EP report.

Initially parents come to look round the school and have an interview with the head. 'Parents are often worried, upset and don't know where to go for help and advice – even if we can't help, we can usually point them in the right direction.' If school thinks they can help, they'll invite the child for a two-day visit to see how they integrate in class and in the school. If appropriate, a place will be offered. Mainstream education often has a devastating impact on these children – 'They're bright and know a lot, but they can't get it down on paper – that's where we come in'.

School won't usually go to tribunals with parents – feels it's better to have an independent eye. Pupils come at almost any time, though rarely in Years 10 and 11. Hope is that after a few years, where appropriate, some can return to mainstream, either to an independent or state school.

Exit: Majority to mainstream education or sixth form college.

Money Matters: Several means-tested bursaries worth up to 50 per cent of fees.

Remarks: A caring school with a happy community feel; refreshes the parts other schools failed to reach.

Knox Academy

Pencaitland Road, Haddington, East Lothian EH41 4DT

• Pupils: 415 boys, 425 girls, all day • Ages: 11-18 • Size of sixth form: S5 132, S6 90 • Non-denom • State

Tel: 01620 823 387
Fax: 01620 823 186
Email: knoxacademy@knox.elcschool.org.uk
Website: www.ka-net.org.uk

Head Teacher: Since 1997, Mrs Janis Craig MA (Hons) MA (education) (fifties), educated at Dorking County Grammar School and studied history at Edinburgh (the 'best history course in the UK'). She took her PGCE at Moray House in Edinburgh and promptly went into non-academia: cinema usherette, Marks and Spencers, archivist at Falkirk Museum and working in the complaints department of Scottish Gas, followed by teaching. She came to Knox from Currie, where she was depute head, and before that Preston Lodge, where she was assistant head, and before that Craigshill, where she was head of department. Well versed in local education, she is a feisty lady and truly hands-on – she was juggling next year's timetable, waiting for a phone call to reassure the parents of a child who had got appendicitis during a school trip and trying to locate the whereabouts of an SEN pupil who had mislaid his class during our visit. Her wish for the school – to make 'a comfortable and welcoming place where people achieve'. Definitely one of the regiment of women – John Knox would be proud of her.

Academic matters: Does well. No particular bias, though, interestingly, they offer Italian, rather than the more commonplace Spanish at 13, along with French and Latin (trips to Rome) in the language department. Most do English, maths, science and five other subjects at Standard grade. Classical civilisation, but no Greek, and a host of science labs, neatly ensconced in the new build. Good choice of subjects, with craft and design available at Standard grade; hospitality at Intermediate II, plus a variety of subjects at Intermediate I.

Impressive list of Highers, including administration, business management, music and religious, moral and philosophical studies. Also available at Advanced Higher level, along with a host of other options – a school which caters well for the academic and the ordinary mortal. Raft of computers – 40 in the computer department and a further 60 in the business education department; more in the very jolly library, which has rather noisy air conditioning and also houses the careers department. The careers officer comes once a week and pupils can either just pop in or make an appointment for one to one consultation.

Pupils with mild(ish) SEN are catered for. SEN and guidance staff work together and share a bright passage of individual rooms; pupils with special needs 'do not necessarily attend all classes', special computers with huge type available for the visually challenged and laptops to help the dyslexic. Mixture of 'learnings' on hand with support either on an individual basis or in class.

Games, Options, the Arts: PE timetabled and on offer to Higher level. Games fields on site, all the usual suspects: rugby popular, volleyball, basketball, hockey, netball, girls' and boys' footie teams and golf. Badminton courts on site; school currently swims in the local Aubigny centre and does remarkably well in competitions; good support from the East Lothian sports development officers, and a physical activities co-ordinator based in the school who also manages the huge (and we mean huge) outdoor education department. Sixth form have a team-building weekend early in the year, and pupils who were not on exam leave were doing an activities week during our visit: from extreme sports to visits to Paris, the Alps, Italy and London, day trips to Edinburgh, the Dynamic Earth, spooky Mary King's Close or the Science Museum in Glasgow. Alternatively, a variety of home-based options: hospitality, fishing and making digital films – impressive. Myriads of trips abroad; young explorers' trust et al.

Superb music in the old building. Musicians give two concerts annually, oodles of orchestras, choirs, and bands. Stunning art department – good selection of paintings in view. Magical and truly inspirational fabric and hatting department, buzzing when we visited, plus ceramics and all the rest. Home economics equally buzzing – the smell of newly baked bread was mouth watering. School seriously into Europe – representatives went to the first Youth Eco-Parliament in Berlin. The Alice Burnett twinning scholarship is popular and school encourages languages via a language week when all the school goes French, Italian or Latin for the week; good links with France, Italy, Finland, Sweden and now Rwanda. School recently gained its second British Council International School Award (2008–2011) – the first Scottish school to do so.

Buzzing citizenship course, 'part and parcel of the curriculum'; the school council has a training day for all with proper speakers and a grown up agenda. All do work experience at S4 (the school has a core list of placements if pupils can't find their own). Pupils have to write letters of application and go through the whole gamut – excellent practice. In 2006, the school won the BBC 'Schools' Question Time' and pupils were involved in producing a televised programme. Strong CCF, 'badged' to The Royal Regiment of Scotland, but no pipe band. Good YE which extends as far as 13 year olds, who are currently decorating flowerpots to sell. Profits go to charity – school is keen on 'the big traditional charities' like UNICEF.

Background and Atmosphere: The most recent in a line of education establishments in Haddington dating back to 1379 – was dedicated to John Knox at the end of the nineteenth century. The building, which still has a statue of John Knox in a place of prominence, is now sheltered housing for old folks. The school moved to its present site in the 1930s – loads of additions since. The new-build looks spectacular, cleverly organised so that the gym and sports hall will be available to locals with access to the dining hall. Food here is good, healthy eating a priority (eat your heart out, Jamie Oliver) though, to be honest, the cooked menu was a little drear; sandwiches on offer though no salad bar. Dress code for the whole school with white shirts, school ties and black trousers or skirts. School blazers mandatory for post Standard Grade pupils, and gold braiding for prefects. Second-hand shop.

Pastoral Care and Discipline: Strong discipline, with letters home to parents and detention as the ultimate deterrent. Pupil points system where pupils can gain or lose points and receive certificates once a certain level has been reached. Pro-active anti bullying strategy, sixth formers doing a buddying routine with first year pupils.

Pupils and Parents: Eclectic, though predominantly white middle class, like its catchment – a mixture of East Lothian farmers (usually well founded) and locals. Supportive parent-school partnership and KASG (Knox Academy Support Group) – an excellent and effective fundraising initiative.

Entrance: Automatic from King's Meadow Primary, St Mary's Roman Catholic Primary in Haddington, ditto Yester Primary in Gifford. The rest by placement requests.

Exit: Good follow through to S5 and university entrance – most choose Scotland, though regularly Oxbridge candidates. Of those who leave after Standard grades, some go on to FE elsewhere, others into industry.

Remarks: Excellent. No adverse comments from any of our contacts – so go for it, but make sure you are in the catchment area first.

La Sainte Union Catholic Secondary School

Linked to La Swap Sixth Form in the Senior section

Highgate Road, London, NW5 1RP

• Pupils: 1,200 girls, all day • Ages: 11-18 • Size of sixth form: 335 (including 45 boys) • RC • State

Tel: 020 7428 4600
Fax: 020 7267 7647
Email: general@lsu.camden.sch.uk
Website: www.lsu.camden.sch.uk

Head: Since 2008, Mrs Maureen Williams (forties). Educated at a convent school in Hampshire, read English and medieval literature at Exeter University before taking her PGCE at Digby Stuart College, Roehampton. Taught English at St Joseph's College, Croydon and La Retraite Roman Catholic Girls' School in Lambeth, before taking over from long-serving head Sister Teresa and becoming the school's first lay principal, charged with a mission to gently modernise while maintaining the traditions of La Sainte Union. A calm and competent presence, no doubt the school's illustrious tradition remains in safe hands. Married to a senior probation officer, she enjoys running, walking and good food in her spare time.

Academic matters: One of Camden's top-performing schools. In 2009, 81 per cent of those who sat GCSE gained A*–C (over 75 per cent including English and maths) – a significant achievement for a school with no academic selection, and not reached by any fudging of the exam system. Pupils here take a demanding curriculum, with nine and half subjects kept going until GCSE, including a compulsory modern language, ICT and RE. Has specialist status in science and maths and 25 girls a year take all three sciences. Everyone, however, benefits from the science enrichment programme with a multitude of speakers from UCL and Imperial College (both of which offer work placements). 'Many of the girls come from backgrounds where there is limited experience of higher education,' says the head. 'The programme raises their aspirations.' Science results have improved significantly, though A level physicists are still a relative rarity. Setting in maths from Year 7, broad banding in science, English and languages (French and Spanish) from Year 8. The gifted and talented are led along at a brisk pace, taking some subjects early and adding to the basic diet with astronomy, geography, Italian and statistics. 'The school has some really clever girls,' said one mother, 'and they really nurture them.'

All abilities and interests, however, are well catered for, with young apprenticeships and diplomas increasingly popular. 'Not everyone has to be brilliant, but everyone has to achieve what they can,' commented a parent. 'They say, this is your goal, go for it – but not everyone's goal is the same.' About 70 per cent proceed to the sixth form, which forms part of the popular local consortium of four comprehensives, La Swap. A commendable 97–98 per cent pass rate at A level, though results post-16 are not quite as starry as at GCSE. 'We could raise the entry requirements,' says the head, 'and attract a higher ability cohort, but we know we can achieve these results without doing so.' Strongest subjects include RE, sociology, English, maths and art (most pupils got As in 2009). Twenty pupils have statements of special needs, including one with Down's; has wheelchair access by means of lifts. 'They try to help everyone,' commented one parent.

Games, Options, the Arts: Music is a particular strength ('Super,' says Ofsted) and is based here for the entire consortium sixth form. The standard of singing is unusually high with a 'talented' voice coach in residence. Whole school enthusiasm manifested in a 130-strong gospel choir (a Tour Choice, which performed recently in Barcelona Cathedral), a Year 11 jazz band and a strong chamber choir. About one third of pupils take individual instrumental or voice tuition.

Definitely not a 9am-4pm place – 50 clubs operating, before, during and after lessons, everything from rowing and trampolining to keep fit and cookery. For hard-pressed working parents, the homework club, with supervised study before and after school, is a real boon – as it often is for girls. Thriving art department. The spacious walled grounds include a decent range of pitches, made full use of for two hours' compulsory weekly sports, including rounders, netball, athletics, basketball, trampolining, football and aerobics. 'There's no sitting on the side here,' says the head.

Background and Atmosphere: One of a number of schools founded by the Sisters of La Sainte Union de Sacre Coeur, a teaching order founded in the early nineteenth century. The Camden school has now been in the borough for the past 150 years. Housed in a gracious Victorian building (with later additions), maintains the stately and soothing presence of the former convent boarding school it once was. The classrooms in the main block are light and high-ceilinged, the floors polished to a mirror sheen, the gardens to the rear are elegantly laid out with a small orchard and an ample stock of summer roses (sensibly, girls are required to keep to the path and admire from a distance).

Though now very much a modern comprehensive, with a broad intake of practising Catholics from across the capital, still has the purposeful air of calm you might expect from its history. The last teaching sister departed in summer 2010, but the tradition of the founding order and those of the Catholic faith are well maintained. 'We see our mission as promoting the values of the gospel and spirituality, preparing children for a life centred on Christ, celebrating the sacrament and providing links with other parishes and the international LSU community,' says the head. Has its own pretty chapel and pupils attend mass once a weekly rota. Founder's Day is marked with mass – and ice cream.

Pupils wear the distinctive uniform of tartan kilts and white stockings with pride – and recently voted to retain this particular tradition. Strong sense of community, both local and international, including its sister school in Tanzania. Vocal school council (with elections for president and vice president) has its say on bullying and school food as well as uniform.

Pastoral Care and Discipline: Despite its affluent north London location on the lower slopes of Highgate, intake is anything but indulged – 65 per cent of pupils are on educational maintenance, twenty per cent on free school meals. The student population reflects the Catholic population of London – a third speak English as an additional language; a sizeable percentage are first and second generation immigrants from Nigeria, Ghana, the Congo, Poland, South America and southern Europe. Parents are active in their own churches and in the school. 'There is a real sense of community,' said one. No linked parish but many families attend nearby St Joseph's, Highgate and St Dominic's in Kentish Town.

Pupils and Parents: 'This is an inner-city comp,' insists the head, though anyone dropping in from outside might be excused for thinking the term doesn't match the orderly space within. Behaviour is generally exemplary but, for those who stray, bad marks and detentions, as well as fixed-term exclusions. Girls with difficulties are certainly not left to fend for themselves. 'Some girls are from families with real problems and they would rather be at school on weekends and holidays than at home,' says one mother. 'This is a safe place to be.' Offers both parental support and additional help with behaviour management and conflict resolution. Teaches about the temptations of drugs and alcohol but drugs are not a significant issue, at least on site. Problems mainly concern friendship disputes that change social boundaries. Good induction day in Year 7 brings pupils from disparate locations and homes together. 'My daughter has really blossomed here,' says one happy parent.

Entrance: Around 180 girls admitted to the heavily oversubscribed Year 7, mainly from Catholic primary schools. No selection on ability but must be practising Catholics baptised in the first year, then able to demonstrate regular church attendance for at least three years. Pupils arrive from seven boroughs – from Walthamstow to Barnet – as distance is measured by public transport rather than metres from the gates. Eighteen places offered on musical aptitude, with an objective tests and a small audition. Entry to La Swap sixth form requires a minimum 2Bs and 3Cs for A level. All girls who enter between 11–16 base themselves at the school for the sixth form.

Exit: About a fifth to Russell Group universities, with UCL a favourite option. Popular subjects include English, history, business studies and art foundation. Medics get specialist coaching for BMAT tests. One or two to Oxbridge each year, including medicine.

Money Matters: Despite the fact that two-thirds of parents here are on a joint family income of £30,000 or less, most manage the £100 a year voluntary contribution. 'Parents are very generous' and very active, constantly raising funds with second-hand uniform sales etc. 'This is not a rich school,' said one, 'but the school and parents make every effort to give the girls the opportunities that others might take as a given.'

Remarks: A calm and orderly universe, demanding (and getting) high standards of achievement from girls who might not always be expected to reach this high.

La Swap Sixth Form

Linked to La Sainte Union Catholic Secondary School in the Senior section

Linked to William Ellis School in the Senior section

Linked to Acland Burghley School in the Senior section

Linked to Parliament Hill School in the Senior section

William Ellis School, Highgate Road, London, NW5 1RN

• Pupils: 1300 • Ages: 16-19 • Non-denom • State

Tel: 0207 692 4157
Fax: 0207 284 1021
Email: laswap@williamellis.camden.sch.uk
Website: www.laswap.camden.sch.uk

Head: La Swap is a sixth-form consortium composed of four neighbouring comprehensives – Parliament Hill, La Sainte Union, Acland Burghley and William Ellis, and the heads of the four schools (Ms Sue Higgins of Parliament Hill, Ms Maureen Williams of La Sainte Union, the acting head of Acland Burghley and the acting head of William Ellis) share the headship. They meet monthly to plan a strategic overview.

Academic matters: These four comprehensives, geographically within a few hundred yards of each other, created an amalgamated sixth form to provide the widest possible subject variety and range of qualifications. Lucky sixth formers here can study a remarkable 39 A levels, as well as BTECS, NVQs, a Certificate in Childcare and GCSEs (for those who need further preparation before going on to A levels). About 80 per cent of students follow a purely academic course, the rest sit vocational exams, but those who want to can mix and match. Results are above national average with a 97 per cent pass rate in 2009; 74 per achieved A–C. The consortium's strengths lie in vocational subjects, the visual arts (with consistently outstanding results) and arts subjects, like RE, media studies and English. Still possibly not the ideal location for scientists.

Teaching (with over 300 teachers) is enthusiastic, knowledgeable and well prepared. 'We've generally found the teaching to be very good,' said one parent, 'though, as always, you'll get the odd dud.' Some criticism for not always taking into account the wide range of ability in this relatively unselective sixth form, but not all would agree. 'In my classes, some people have 10 A*s and others mainly Cs, but I haven't found that a problem,' said one boy. All students are allocated a base school but most study on a number of sites. Some subjects are taught on all the sites, the more rarefied – philosophy, textiles and dance, for example – on only one.

Each pupil is given target grades on entry based on GCSE results and is carefully tracked thereafter, with good exam preparation and help with study skills, as well as twice yearly reports. 'The communication with home is excellent,' says one parent. 'If my son has done something well they email me. Equally, if he's not doing his homework, they'll let me know.' The academic side is clearly complex, but well organised. 'I wanted to change one of my subjects early on,' said a pupil. 'I went to see the head of year and it was sorted by the end of lunch hour.'

Games, Options, the Arts: The extra-curricular here is a significant part of what La Swap has to offer, being as varied and extensive as the academic range. The generous enrichment programme – which largely takes place on Wednesday and Thursday afternoons – provides 35 options, from ballet and debating to theatrical make-up, D-jaying and maths master classes. Off-site sports include sailing and climbing. The programme is not compulsory, but everyone is encouraged to have a go, regardless of previous knowledge or expertise.

Background and Atmosphere: The four schools (La Sainte Union, an all-girls' Catholic school, William Ellis, an all-boys' former grammar school, Acland Burghley, a co-ed comprehensive, and Parliament Hill, an all-girls' comprehensive) decided to unite their sixth form offering 25 years ago. Each school retains its distinctive ethos and pupils generally enjoy the change of pace. 'I really like the different atmosphere in each school,' said one. All four schools retain the pupils they take in at 11 and each has its own director of sixth form and heads of year.

One great plus of the model is the half-way house it offers between school and sixth-form college. 'My daughter originally wanted to leave and go to college,' said one mother, 'but once she'd started at La Swap, she found the teachers treated her with more respect and she was given much more responsibility for her assignments.' The advantage for students who opt for continuity is that they remain in familiar surroundings while meeting new people and conquering new horizons. 'In the earlier years, my daughter's friends were all local,' said one parent. 'In the sixth form, she suddenly had a whole new set of friends from all over London.' New students, however, don't feel excluded. 'I felt everybody was in the same position as I was,' said one. 'People had friends from their original school, but they didn't know anyone from the other schools.'

La Swap is careful about taking both existing students and recent arrivals to a more independent level of study, with a well-planned induction programme, including a thorough briefing on the outline of each course and relevant dates and department procedures. Students like the friendly, laid-back but organised approach and strong sense of community.

Pastoral Care and Discipline: All students register at their base school, where they take most of their lessons. Here they have a head of year and a tutor who monitors their work and wellbeing, with regular interviews to discuss problems and set appropriate targets. Also a confidential professional counselling service, a Connexions personal adviser and regular PSHE, with outside speakers, group work and discussions.

Pupils and Parents: Students, from a huge range of ethnic and social backgrounds, apply from a vast swathe of north London. Despite the consortium's leafy surroundings on the eastern edge of Hampstead Heath, all four schools are inner-city comprehensives with a socio-economic intake reflective of the term. Generally, pupils are confident and mature and get on well.

Entrance: LA Swap has about 1300 places on offer. 800 of these generally go to existing students, a further 300, however, are up for grabs. The entrance procedure is intricate and careful attention must be paid to every step and date. First step is to register interest online by the end of the autumn term. Then, armed with a ticket and a parent, prospective candidates attend the open evening in January. Applications must be submitted by post or by hand in early February – those who miss the deadline are immediately put on the waiting list. All applicants who meet the deadline are offered an interview at the school in February or March to discuss subject choice and given conditional offers based on GCSE grades. Those with offers must attend the one-day induction course held before the start of the summer holidays, when summer assignments are set. Post GCSE results, further interviews and places are confirmed.

Exit: About 400 students go on to 60 universities to study 50 different subjects, from medicine and accountancy to drama and international relations. About 20 per cent to Russell Group universities. A large contingent to leading art colleges, mostly to the University of the Arts, London (Central St Martin's, Chelsea, Camberwell and London College of Fashion etc). A handful to Oxbridge.

Remarks: A good compromise between school and a sixth form college, with an extraordinary range of subjects on offer. Tends to suit the motivated and the self starter but not ideal for those who will be distracted by studying on a number of sites or who require the disciplined parameters of a school sixth form to function at their peak.

The Lady Eleanor Holles School

Linked to Lady Eleanor Holles School, Junior Department (The) in the Junior section

Hanworth Road, Hampton, Middlesex, TW12 3HF

• Pupils: 880 girls; all day (690 in the senior department; 190 in the junior department) • Ages: 7-18 • Size of sixth form: 180 • C of E
• Fees: Senior £13,800; Junior £10,560 pa • Independent

Tel: 020 8979 1601
Fax: 020 8941 8291
Email: office@lehs.org.uk
Website: www.lehs.org.uk

Headmistress: Since 2004, Mrs Gillian Low MA Oxon PGCE Cantab (early fifties). Immaculate pedigree: previously head of Francis Holland School for six years, before that deputy head of Godolphin and Latymer School. Began her teaching career in state sector at various comprehensive schools. Educated at North London Collegiate School, then read English at Oxford. After university she had a brief spell in industry as a management trainee with Courtaulds. 'But I missed my subject and took a positive decision to move into teaching,' she says. 'I've been very lucky in always having worked in good schools, but this job in particular is a real joy.'

Lives in central London with her three children – her parental credentials ensure she is absolutely in tune with 'the teenage girl world': 'I know what it is like on both sides of the fence,' she says. 'Coping with friendship issues, boyfriends, how you are getting back from wherever – it's all going on in my house too; along with exams and university applications.' Time and time again parents mention her empathy and the most popular adjective used to describe her is 'approachable'. The door to her (newly-decorated, cream, very smart but homely) office is open as often as possible.

She is everything you would expect of the head of a top girls' school – immaculately dressed and groomed, with a definite air of authority and completely on top of her brief. In her spare time, she enjoys travel, art, e.g. working on her own mosaic pieces, theatre, cinema and reading. President of GSA 2010.

Academic matters: Generally over 90 per cent A* and A grades at GCSE – 98 per cent in 2010 – and most girls take 10 subjects – separate sciences taken in preference to the dual award. Popular GCSE options are geography, history, Latin, biology and chemistry. Similar success at A level – in 2010, 93 per cent A and B grade passes (excluding general studies) with 76 per cent of grades at A* and A. English literature and geography are most popular, followed by psychology, history, maths, chemistry and biology. Girls mostly take four subjects (or three plus an AS) together with general studies and additional options such as PE or word processing. . Alongside the usual, the school offers theatre studies, classical Greek and music technology. Slightest smidgen of interest in the classics will be seized upon and encouraged – good takeup of Latin (taught in Years 8 and 9), cleverest also take Greek. French and German taught from Year 7. Formerly some parental grumbling about language teaching, but new head of modern languages department and new head of French have raised the game.

A school of great expectations: a B grade is B for 'bad', particularly at GCSE – from day one the girls are working towards A* and A grades. But parents don't feel their daughters are overly pressured. 'Anyone bright enough to get here in the first place will be able to cope once they are in,' says one mother. 'There is a lot of self-motivation and peer pressure to do well.' Lots of homework from the off and a longish (9–4) school day – can be a big shock for an 11 year old. Typically two to three hours of homework a night by GCSE stage, plus one day at the weekend. Parents say their daughters are 'pushed', but again, 'not unduly pressured'.

Girls are mixed for some lessons such as science and ICT, but only setted for maths. Average class size is 20. Stable staff, average age mid-forties (lots of male teachers) and almost 50 per cent have been with the school for over 10 years. Most have a good relationship with their pupils and parents are happy that teaching is generally very good. 'Nowhere's perfect and we have a few past their best-before date, but overall they are a good bunch,' says one mother. 'They always seem to know the girls really well – parents' evenings are really worthwhile, useful events.' Well-resourced library and careers room (very impressive careers resources).

Won't take every SEN but very good provision in place for girls it does take, largely for dyslexia and dyspraxia, where one-to-one study skills lessons with specialist teachers are available for an extra charge. Similarly, support can be arranged for pupils with EAL requirements. Fairly flat site is good for wheelchair users, and a lift.

Games, Options, the Arts: Bags of things to do and fantastic facilities. Famed locally for its very strong sport – 'although it's not actually quite as good as you expect once you get here,' says one mother, who grumbles that only the best get a chance of regular matches. Another mum of a B team player moans that her daughter was mainly practice fodder for the A team girls, who went off for all the fun matches. Other parents, however, are quite happy that the system of squads as well as teams means everyone gets a go. Lacrosse and netball in the winter, tennis and athletics in summer. Among the current cohort are three under 18 internationals and five girls aiming for the Olympics. Swimmers revel in the indoor heated pool. Rowing an optional extra with great facilities – has a shared boathouse on the Thames.

Music very strong both in performance and as an academic study. Around 300 girls learn an instrument – from a choice of 20 on offer – to an average grade 6, some to grade 8. Loads of choirs, orchestras and groups, an annual music competition and an annual choral and orchestral concert with boys from neighbouring Hampton School tackles some major works. Similarly lots of drama within the curriculum and as extra-curricular. Sixth formers mount annual drama festival, drawing their casts from the entire school. Wide range of clubs and societies – many during the long lunch break, others after school – including Scrabble, chess, debating, and Christian Union. CCF available via Hampton boys next door and Young Enterprise groups much in evidence in the sixth form. D of E now back on the agenda following a break. Notice boards (well used and up to date) burst with information on everything from fixture lists to ideas for things to do in the holidays.

Background and Atmosphere: One of the oldest girls' schools in the country. Established in 1711 in Cripplegate, City of London. Current premises were purpose built in mid 1930s – architecturally unremarkable but set in wonderful 30 acres of space, including playing fields, gardens and many, mostly modern, additions to the original building. In the entrance and main hall splendid honours boards are engraved with the names of past pupils and school captains, and gleaming cabinets house memorabilia and countless trophies – a nice nod to the school's heritage. But be in no doubt that this is now a thoroughly modern operation, with fantastic boarding school type facilities and space. Splendid sixth form centre – separate common rooms with kitchens and cafeterias for upper and lower sixth – very comfortable and clean, and a world away from the untidy mélanges we've encountered elsewhere. Old girls report that their university facilities are not as good as the ones they left behind.

Overall the place has a very calm, organised and ordered air about it – but nothing ordered about the girls' appearance. A surprisingly scruffy bunch: very un-stuffy uniform – grey sweatshirts are preferred to more formal ties and blazers; the addition of clumpy scuffed black shoes and black laddered tights was one fetching combo on view. Mrs Low has introduced a new-style pleated skirt from Year 7 in an effort to stop the girls rolling up their waistbands to shorten their skirts. No uniform for sixth formers, nor are they steered towards the 'business-dress' style beloved of similar establishments.

Good security – all the girls have biometric or swipe card access to buildings and services. The girls can invite Hampton boys into their common room (and vice versa) and spend time together on social and cultural events ('best of both worlds,' says a pupil). To help the pupils overcome what would otherwise be tricky and time-consuming travel arrangements, LEH and Hampton share a school bus system covering 22 routes to all points north, south, east and west. On the surface a most satisfactory arrangement – though a persistent drizzle of complaints from parents about the cost (approaching £250 per term). The school recently trialled a late after-school coach service for girls involved in after-school activities, but lack of takeup means it has not continued.

Pastoral Care and Discipline: General parental approval for pastoral care – usual system. Full time school nurse in situ. Several parents cite instances where they were delighted by the personal touch of a letter or phone call over and above what they expected, but overall this is not a cuddly school – 'Little to no allowance made for the girls being new or tired,' says one mother. School prefers, 'Self-sufficiency encouraged'.

No formal punishments or detentions system. Staff rule by consent – parents will be contacted if homework fails to appear. Smoking and worse obviously all forbidden. Head said all cases would be handled according to individual circumstances: she seems realistic about teenager experimentation, but not condoning. Short suspensions an option for more major misdemeanours. Mrs Low has suspended (for one day) a girl caught smoking in a car in school car park. Every school has bullying (never believe a head who says there is none) but parents we spoke to had not come across any specific examples, and head and parents give examples of girls being supportive of each other and also of drama/music/sport activities involving all year groups helping to foster friendship between different year groups.

Pupils and Parents: Not as much a snob school as people may think. Smart Mercedes owners jostle for car park space with the beaten up Volvo owners who can just about afford to do their best for a bright child. No mega-merchant banking types. 'Nice straightforward bunch,' says one seasoned parent. Pupils generally very confident and self-motivated – obviously cases of little quiet ones blossoming, but generally a school for go-getters: go for it girls from go for it families. Mix of nationalities – plenty of white middle class but also lots of Asian girls and a few from African community. Strong links with Hampton next door – some 90 families have children at both schools. Don't be too free and easy offering lifts to your daughter's friends – intake is from such a wide geographical area that they may live miles away.

Entrance: Tough and over-subscribed by three to one. Girls are examined in maths and English and general knowledge – hard to cram for, no sample papers available. Then interview (girls only – no parents) for those who have made the grade academically. Interviews described as 'general – we are looking for doers,' says head. 'What can they bring to us? They must have time to do things outside pure academic study – success in one area will spin off to others.' School is not interested in heavily coached girls who will then struggle to keep up.

Up to one third of the places go to girls joining from the junior school, who follow the school's own transfer arrangements (see separate entry). Other main feeders are private preps including Newland House, Rowan, The Study and Bute House. About 20 per cent from state primaries. For the sixth form entrance exams in maths, English (essay, comprehension and analytical thought) and a subject of candidate's choice, followed by interviews for those who pass exams. Average of eight to ten places available to replace leavers. Coffee-table worthy prospectus includes DVD.

Exit: At 16+ most go on to sixth form. 'There's a general feel that it's not a good idea to leave,' says one parent. Of the 10 or so who do go elsewhere each year, some are looking for a mixed sixth form college, or boarding school, and a few want to head into London. Mass exodus in search of male companionship is forestalled by strong links with Hampton Boys' School next door. Head says very few leave at school's suggestion. 'My main goal is the girls' happiness and self-esteem. There would be lots of early warnings and consultation with parents if we really felt that their daughter would do better elsewhere.' At 18+ a very definite expectation of university – almost all go to Russell Group and other traditional establishments. Always a notable chunk to Oxbridge.

Money Matters: Some scholarships (for academic work and music) for 10 per cent of tuition fees (dependent upon parental income); means tested bursaries. Apply as part of the enrolment process.

Remarks: Deservedly one of the top girls' schools in the country: it is exactly right for naturally confident, very bright young things who thrive on lots of work. Highly sought after for its academic delivery, celebration of female success, top of the range facilities and cream of the crop intake. Set to remain a 'destination' school.

Lady Lumley's School

Swainsea Lane, Pickering, North Yorkshire, YO18 8NG

• Pupils: 1,005 boys and girls • Ages: 11-19 • Size of sixth form: 245
• Non-denom • State

Tel: 01751 472 846
Fax: 01751 477 259
Email: post.master@ladylumleys.net
Website: www.ladylumleys.n-yorks.sch.uk

Headteacher: Since 2007, Mr Richard Bramley. Former deputy head at Chelmsford County High School and recently advisory teacher in Islington, North London. Wife also teaches. Daughter and son in sixth forms in Chelmsford. Loves the school and enjoys every minute of his headship. Believes that everyone in the school community can be inspired with a love of learning and, by being so, maximise his or her life chances. Pupils say, 'He's lovely!'

Academic matters: Good GCSE and A level performances. No prima donna departments here – school claims its strength is quality of teaching across the whole curriculum, especially at key stage 4, and Ofsted largely backs that up. Strongest performances consistently in the basics – English, maths and science. Able linguists given the option of taking GCSE French a year early, with German to follow in year two. Early results impressive.

School also does well by less academic pupils – 15 and 16 year olds can take a double GCSE in engineering, studying partly off-site with engineering firms. Others opt for GCSE health and social care, drawing on links with GPs and hospitals – would-be paramedics, chiropodists etc please note. Vocational path can continue into sixth form with packages including modern apprenticeships. Students encouraged to pick and mix, customising education to boost chances of achieving career goals. Strong, award-winning careers education and guidance, and work experience programmes.

Games, Options, the Arts: A specialist sports college with extensive sports facilities in a glorious rural setting. New fitness suite and floodlit all-weather pitch used by pupils and local sports clubs with benefits to both. Sports hall, gym, good athletics facilities, all helping to encourage all-round sporting achievements. Drama taught in every year group and those with a musical interest can join the orchestras and choirs. All the usual extra-curricular clubs and societies too, but pupils have to risk indigestion to join. One downside of a sprawling catchment area is that buses whisk pupils away at the final bell – makes for busy lunchtimes, with sports practices, science clubs, revision workshops and even dreaded detentions all competing with the butties.

Background and Atmosphere: Set on the edge of the market town of Pickering, Lady Lumley's is a mix of every architectural style over five decades. The older buildings are offset by a new £1m+ administration block, sixth form and community learning centre, with a conference centre for use by school and community. Besides, who couldn't live with a bit of dodgy fifties architecture, when the view is of sweeping school grounds framed by countryside, with even the puff of an old steam railway in the distance? Good disabled access, including lifts.

Biggest surprise? Classroom doors are left open during lessons and all you can hear in the corridors is the teacher's voice. Cloakrooms have been replaced with lockers with a key for pupils, which have been very successful. Even the morning rush into school is orderly. No school-run congestion because of the buses and an uncanny absence of the teenage sillies.

Pastoral Care and Discipline: A no-nonsense school which sets high standards and expects pupils to meet them. 'It irons out problems before they escalate,' said one parent, which seems, to use a third metaphor, to hit the nail on the head. Unacceptable behaviour is dealt with quickly and efficiently. Students are given 'cool off' time, which can include that most excruciating of all punishments – writing a letter of apology.

School policy to keep children busy, in and out of lessons, and 'treat them like human beings', giving them the courtesy of decent catering, clean toilets and graffiti-free walls. Strong on caring and community, and rolls up its sleeves to practise what it preaches. School still collects food to make into harvest festival parcels and gets pupils to deliver them to nominated neighbours over many miles. One of a dying breed, we suspect.

Pastoral care boosted considerably by Lady Lumley's Education Foundation, named after its founder, an Elizabethan landowner. Her bequests to the school mean that it can still spend upwards of £20,000 a year on pupil support, from subsidising trips to encouraging pupils' projects. A very nice carrot indeed.

Pupils and Parents: A true comprehensive, drawing from an area of affluent professionals and farming communities – lots of the Range Rover set, but also its fair share of children from disadvantaged homes. Good rapport with parents, who receive a report in every term of every year. Pupils' progress tightly monitored with regular tutorials – no hiding place here. Parents talk of a happy school and are pleased with children's achievements.

Entrance: Living in the catchment area is the only way to be sure of a place. A whopping 22 per cent of pupils come from further afield after winning appeals, but if your heart's set on Lady Lumley's, you might have to move house to get in – people do.

Exit: Almost 60 per cent of pupils stay on into the sixth form, expected to increase as vocational courses expand. Around 85 per cent of sixth formers go to university.

Remarks: A solid school which feels part of the community it serves. Recent letter from newly qualified graduate thanks school for giving out-of-class tuition to him and others who needed that extra push. 'It has made all the difference to my future. You made me feel I was somebody and I could achieve my goals,' he writes. Says it all.

Lady Margaret School

Parson's Green, London, SW6 4UN

• Pupils: 670 girls; all day • Ages: 11-18 • Size of sixth form: 205 • C of E • State

Tel: 020 7736 7138
Fax: 020 7384 2553
Email: admin@ladymargaret.lbhf.sch.uk
Website: www.ladymargaret.lbhf.sch.uk

Headteacher: Since 2006, Mrs Sally Whyte BA (Hons) French and Russian, PGCE NPQH . Formerly deputy head at Dr Challoner's High School in Buckinghamshire and assistant principal at Exmouth Community College in Devon. A charming, cheery lady who undoubtedly has the school firmly under control and clear plans for the future – Ofsted praised the 'exceptional capacity of the recently formed senior leadership team'. 'This is a lovely school to be head of,' she says.

Academic matters: Traditional, rigorous teaching produces invariably good results (English was rated outstanding by an Ofsted subject inspection in 2009) – 'We're now fully staffed with excellent teachers'. Everyone – except the few girls with statements of special educational needs – takes a foreign language to GCSE and RE is also compulsory. English literature, history, mathematics, biology, chemistry are the most popular A level subjects. Art and design subjects also have a very strong showing – over half of the grades in art were A* in 2010. The sixth form is expanding with a new state of the art building which has allowed the introduction of new subjects at A level, including economics, psychology and music technology.

The school missed an 'outstanding' rating in the latest Ofsted inspection because of variable progress between subjects and year groups – the most and least able have tended to make the best progress. The head, however, is beefing up the systematic monitoring of each girl's academic progress so no-one should be overlooked in future.

'They add tremendous value in a lot of cases,' said a parent, 'as long as the girl is not resistant to having value added.'

The girls with SEN – mainly dyslexia – are well looked after, with excellent targeted support. Very few with behavioural difficulties – they would be likely to struggle in the traditional, closely-regulated environment. 'Parents tend to realise that if their daughter's not going to be able to cope here, it's not right for her to come.'

Games, Options, the Arts: Art and textile design are popular and successful A level subjects, with a high proportion of A grades, and quite a few pupils go on to art college. Plenty of impressive art on display. Music 'permeates the whole of the school', and large numbers learn instruments. Plenty of ensembles and choirs – a musical production such as 'Annie' or 'Oliver!' every other year. Inter-house music, debating and drama competitions. But performance space is limited – no drama studio or theatre and no drama GCSE or A level.

Not ideal for the sports-mad child – facilities on-site are limited to some tennis/netball courts and a gym (yoga, basketball and dance amongst activities on offer), though older girls use the local sports facilities. Netball, rounders and football matches – 'We play and achieve well'. Amazingly, 28 girls are currently studying GCSE PE and the school offers A level PE.

Background and Atmosphere: Has its origins in Whitelands College School, founded in 1842. In 1917, when Whitelands was threatened with closure, the Second Mistress, Miss Enid Moberly Bell, and other school staff 'rescued' a large number of pupils, who joined the new Lady Margaret School, named after Lady Margaret Beaufort, mother of Henry VII, founder of St John's and Christ's Colleges, Cambridge. The school is in three listed Georgian houses facing leafy Parsons Green, with a gym, hall, impressive technology block, classrooms and landscaped garden beyond.

Very strong sense of community, happy atmosphere, tightly regulated; parents comment that it has the feel of an old-fashioned girls' grammar school.

Pastoral Care and Discipline: A traditional school with a strong Christian ethos and pastoral imperative that includes taking on girls with health and social problems. A parent commented, 'They have an impressive record of nurturing.' Strict about uniform, homework and manners, and everyone takes part in collective worship in the mornings, 'Though the Muslim and Jewish girls I know feel extremely valued,' said a parent. A very few short term exclusions, virtually none permanent. 'The vast majority come here wanting to work, get exam results and have fun.' The PHSE programme covers careers, study skils, citizenship, sex, drugs, alcohol etc.

Pupils and Parents: The intake reflects the surroundings of this very leafy part of south west London. The new entrance system is changing the makeup of the school. 'But there's still a critical mass of well-supported, compliant girls,' said a parent. Incredibly committed parent body, plenty of whom could have afforded to go private. Some impressive fundraising goes on – the latest summer fair day raised some £20,000. Pupils strongly supportive of each other, confident, lively. OGs: Janet Street Porter, Jill Saward, rape law reform campaigner.

Entrance: Fifty places (called foundation places) are reserved for girls who have been to a C of E church at least fortnightly for the past three years. The other forty are open places. The main criterion is walking distance to the school. Everyone takes a maths and English banding test and is placed in band 1 (top 25 per cent), band 2 (middle 50 per cent) or band 3 (lowest 25 per cent), with places allocated in those proportions. A few places go to those with an SEN statement and looked after children. Very over-subscribed – over 500 applicants each year for the 90 places. NB You must complete and return both the local authority common application form and the school additional information form.

Those hoping to go through to the sixth form must have at least six A*–C grades at GCSE, including B grades in the chosen A level subjects; mathematics, languages and sciences need A grades. An increasing number of girls join the sixth form from other schools.

Exit: A few don't make the grade to go through to the sixth form and some go off for a wider range of courses – 'We offer quality but not quantity'. Nearly all sixth form leavers go on to university, over 40 per cent to the élite establishments over the past five years (fourth comprehensive in the country on this basis), including five to ten a year to Oxbridge.

Remarks: Small, traditional, friendly church school with high standards and family atmosphere in a quiet green setting. The social mix is changing but, in this part of London, it will always attract a high proportion of bright, hardworking girls, and the head is not letting the school rest on its laurels.

Lancaster Girls' Grammar School

Regent Street, Lancaster, Lancashire, LA1 1SF

• Pupils: 890 girls, all day • Ages: 11-18 • Size of sixth form: 335
• Non-denom • State

Tel: 01524 320 10
Fax: 01524 846 220
Email: lggs@lggs.lancs.sch.uk
Website: www.lggs.org.uk

Headteacher: Since September 2007, Mrs Jackie Cahalin BA (forties), a historian, three previous years as deputy head at LGGS, only the ninth head in the school's 100+ year history. Married, with two children, and living some distance from the school, she commutes daily by train, often with pupils for company. A friendly, calm yet authoritative presence, she clearly enjoys the company of the girls and this appears to be reciprocated.

Academic matters: Very sound, one of the top 20 schools nationally, aspirations to be in the top ten. Tremendous results at GCSE, marginal dip at A level as the intake is broadened, though still very impressive. Strong languages (French, German, Spanish), language college status awarded in 2006 and more recently international school status awarded by the British Council. Extracurricular Mandarin Chinese growing in popularity and Latin before school – 'dawn Latin' – is over-subscribed.

Large numbers of girls opt for sciences in the sixth form, skill and interest level being strengthened by studying three separate sciences at GCSE. Maths is the most popular A level subject. Marked technology emphasis (specialist status since 1995); sponsorship and collaborative projects including Leading Edge work with partnership schools; enviable technology and IT teaching provision. High computer count, interactive whiteboards everywhere ('Lots more than the boys' school,' say the girls). Able staff (about one third men), age profile creeping upwards – they don't want to leave, and you can see why.

Games, Options, the Arts: By their own admission, not the best sporting facilities, essentially due to lack of space. Sports fields 5–10 minutes away from school. Astroturf pitch and would like a sports hall – but where to put it? A dance/drama studio is on the cards, though. Dance flourishing with many clubs run by the girls themselves and after school GCSE dance classes. Sport is important and keenly played, especially hockey and running (representative successes). Much variety beyond these, including rugby, fencing and swimming. Old-fashioned gym brought up to date by the addition of an immensely popular Wiifit screen. Music strong and multi-form, house music competitions one of the girls' favourite annual events; has its own musician in residence. Joint ventures in music with boys' school; also drama and public speaking. Largest centre in the area for D of E. Strong international links include a link school in India and World Challenge to Madagascar. Plenty of European overseas trips and exchanges and representation at science fairs in South East Asia.

Background and Atmosphere: Founded 100 years ago on central site, with more modern additions and surrounded by private houses. Very limited parking and limited outdoor space for play or socialising. However site restrictions have brought about some inspired and resourceful use of space as buildings are updated and transformed according to the changing needs of the school. Newer additions include impressive technology, cooking and IT areas.

Girls appear very academically focused – they have earned their place here and tell us they are 'eager to learn and like the fact that they don't have to wait for others to catch up'. Busy girls, hardly a moment when they are not occupied, thriving on the many challenges and opportunities. Hint of academic snobbery from a few – a little dismissive of 'less academic' subjects at A level; however 'You can be yourself here,' they say, and appear happy in that. The head concurs – 'Girls are braver in lessons in an all girls' school and it's OK to do your homework and to take on leadership rôles.' Girls genuinely feel they have a voice on the school council and have been actively involved in uniform updates. Has a healthy eating award and food is 'pretty good', with plenty of choice for all. Was grant maintained, now has Foundation status, which allows a degree of control over its destiny, including (vitally) academic selection.

Pastoral Care and Discipline: Usual form tutor system, backed up by heads of key stages, works well. Relaxed but far from lax – great emphasis on trust, self discipline and good old-fashioned standards of behaviour; make-up, nail varnish, piercings and hair colour all forbidden – the girls know and, for the most part, respect it.

Pupils and Parents: Straightforward girls who are proud to be here and keen to get on and to do their bit for society. They want to do well and make their mark on the world and it's not hard to believe that they will. Wide range of parental backgrounds, not surprising in middle-size county town. Parents rightly assume high academic standards but also value the 'what else?' factor – Year 7 parent says her daughter settled easily and well, despite friends going elsewhere, thanks to good pastoral care on transition from primary school. Another parent, with three daughters through the school, places huge value on the 'real-life perspective' of the place provided by numerous opportunities to interact with students both from the local boys' school and overseas, via inter-cultural exchanges.

Entrance: Four-form entry and heavily over-subscribed at 11+. Admission is 'according to ability and aptitude' – tests in maths, English and VR. Entrance exam in September and results come fairly speedily to aid the admin selection process. First chance goes to inhabitants of Lancaster and District (map available from school), then residual places to families living outside these. If at first you don't succeed, try again later – up to one third of post-GCSE year group has entered from other schools with only a minimum qualification of five or more GCSEs at C and above, including three at grade B; this is a huge attraction and draws from local maintained schools and the independent sector.

Exit: A very few leave after GCSE; almost all go on to higher education, six to ten annually to Oxbridge.

Remarks: Awarded 'outstanding' in four consecutive inspection reports, a confident, sought after and successful state grammar school. A place where, despite (because of?) the smallish county town background, girls are encouraged to look outwards as well as inwards, resulting in refreshingly open-minded, ambitious and worldly-wise young women.

Lancaster Royal Grammar School

East Road, Lancaster, Lancashire, LA1 3EF

• Pupils: 1,050 boys, including 200 boarders • Ages: 11-18 • Size of sixth form: 350 • Christian foundation • Fees: Boarding £8,100-£8,700 pa; Day – free • State

Tel: 01524 580 605
Fax: 01524 847 947
Email: sknight@lrgs.org.uk
Website: www.lrgs.org.uk

Headmaster: Since 2001, Mr Andrew Jarman MA (early fifties). Read maths at Oxford, taught at Aylesbury Grammar, Portsmouth Grammar, Haberdashers', Cheltenham College (director of studies). Energetic, enthusiastic, bags of unaffected charm, voluble, strides around the place with evident pride and pleasure. Still teaches, though 'not enough'; a grammar school boy in head and heart, sets and maintains high standards. Aided by capable and experienced senior management team, most appointed by him. Keen golfer, lists 'family' among his interests.

Academic matters: Superb tradition – regularly near top of table for state grammars, strong value-added results. Aiming high taken for granted, as is the graft to support it. Very much the traditional grammar school ethos, challenging boys to 'fulfil their potential in a competitive environment'. Narrow ability range, so no setting (except maths and French) up to GCSE; class size averages 28. Maths outstanding, stronger classics than in most independents. All do technology up to GCSE; school has had Technology College status since 1995, with languages, mathematics and computing specialisms added since. Sciences taught separately up to GCSE and all three are popular sixth form options. Modern languages not quite up to exalted standards of the rest at GCSE, but climbing and better at A level. Most pupils do four A levels, a third manage five, general studies taken as read, literally, as it's not taught, but the school teaches an enriching life course, developed internally but partly lifted from the IB, which can include anything from leadership to conversational Italian to the lyrics of Bob Dylan. Special needs (e.g. dyslexia, Asperger's) looked after in-house. The especially gifted are stretched by further enhancement schemes and wide-ranging extra-curricular provision.

Games, Options, the Arts: Team games rather than individual sports dominate here. Strong rugby and cricket, taken seriously – they beat most independents. Frequent tours – Hong Kong, Australia, Japan, Barbados and sometimes High Wycombe. An impressive list of other sports, plenty of outdoor pursuits in nearby Lake District and rowing on the Lune leading to some successful pairs at Henley. Much encouragement to join in; couch potatoes don't seem to figure. Music popular, regular drama productions (often with sister school in Lancaster). Very good art and design results.

Background and Atmosphere: An ancient foundation, in existence by 1235 and endowed in 1472. Now has voluntary aided status. Queen Victoria donated £100, hence its 'Royal' tag – and the school still receives the same amount (sadly not index-linked) annually from the Duchy. Buildings gather around a crossroads on hilly East Road, 'possibly the most academic crossroads in the northern hemisphere'; PE to biology means crossing two roads but doesn't worry the boys and 20mph speed limits are enforced. Mixture of Victorian houses and purpose-built blocks, leading to impressive newer additions (science and business/design centres, new boarding houses). Parking is tricky but most walk or use public transport. Though the school in most ways resembles its independent competitors, it differs in that there isn't much money to do the things that the private sector usually takes for granted. It doesn't matter, of course, since the school concentrates on the important transaction of the classroom, but it does mean the place can look a touch untidy at the edges. Real sense of history and tradition about the place: 'Juniors love wearing blazer and tie,' says Mr Jarman. Boys scuttle purposefully between classrooms that range from slightly tired-looking to smartly refurbished. Older parents will be reminded of the grammar school of their youth; 'no-nonsense, no-frills,' says one successful and grateful old boy. An ambitious and exciting 50-year master plan is attracting support from old boys – a real drive here that leaves you in no doubt that it will happen.

Boarding gives the school an edge and identity and attractive new facilities have understandably brought a resurgence of interest. Younger boys have a splendid boarding house with views to die for and a back garden of immaculate cricket pitches. Dorms are cheery, comfortable and well-furnished, with sitting rooms and homely kitchens for tea and toast after school. Seniors are housed in a very attractive and well-designed conference centre-style building adjoining a Victorian villa, with comfortable ensuite single studies alongside relaxed sitting rooms and a modern kitchen, allowing the boys both privacy and companionship as and when required.

Pastoral Care and Discipline: Boys respond to the no-nonsense direct approach of staff in a school that thoroughly understands them. The school looks to recruit 'schoolmasters' (of either sex) rather than 'teachers'. Heard the saying, 'They don't make them like that any more'? Well, they do here, apparently. Thorough care systems for both boarding and day work well; pastoral staff heavily committed to pupils' welfare and relations between boys and teachers admired by parents and inspectors. High personal standards expected. Not much evidence of real wickedness; Mr Jarman suspends for possession and would expel for dealing – and the boys know it.

Pupils and Parents: Lancaster is a city with a small town feel and boys come from every walk of life and are a very genuine mix. Still 'the school on the hill' to some, yet no wish for this to become a middle class enclave – rather it is open to any boy, from any street, who can cope with living and working alongside a future Oxbridge don. Local day boys given preference; about 50 places go to those further afield. Boarders come from all over but must be a UK subject or have an EU passport and a UK guardian. Boys and parents very proud of school and its regional standing. One parent – 'No child of mine would ever go to a boarding school' – absolutely delighted to see her son thriving both academically and relishing life as a boarder also. Parents are easily persuaded to contribute regularly to the development programme – not a burden, given free day education and bargain boarding fees. Old boys include Prof T Hugh Pennington, microbiologist; Kevin Roberts, CEO Worldwide Saatchi & Saatchi; Sir James Crosby FSA, Government advisor; Jason Queally, Olympic cycling champion; Brigadier Alex Birtwistle, foot and mouth star; Tom Sutcliffe, journalist and Sir Richard Owen (dinosaur man).

Entrance: By over-subscribed competitive exam at 11 (English/maths/reasoning). Three strands of entry: local day, regional day, boarding. Boarders have separate test but all 'must be of an aptitude and ability suited to an academic curriculum'. All leave at 16 and then reapply for sixth form places: 'Tell us why we should give you a place here' – great practice for university UCAS or even the real world. Regularly increasing intake at 16 and growing interest from independents for sixth form places; grab a boarding place whilst you still can.

Exit: A few leave after GCSE; vast majority to good universities, mainly in the Midlands and North, though some dipping a toe into southern universities such as Bristol and London. At least 10–15 annually to Oxbridge.

Remarks: Buoyant selective grammar school with big reputation in the region; chiefly a day school but also offers excellent boarding provision. Has managed to retain marked degree of independence within maintained system, offering a curriculum above and beyond the norm, including classics – 'If we don't offer it, which state school will?' says the head. A wide range of extra-curricular activities which, according to a parent, 'suit a boy's needs extremely well'. Unashamedly academic but takes all-round education seriously and delivers.

Lancing College

Linked to Lancing College Preparatory School at Mowden

Lancing, West Sussex, BN15 0RW

• Pupils: 525: 350 boys, 210 board; 175 girls, 120 board • Ages: 13-18
• Size of sixth form: 240 • C of E • Fees: Day £19,395; Boarding £27,750 pa
• Independent

Tel: 01273 452 213
Fax: 01273 464 720
Email: admissions@lancing.org.uk
Website: www.lancingcollege.co.uk

Headmaster: Since 2006, Mr Jonathan Gillespie (early forties), formerly a housemaster and head of modern languages at Fettes. Married to Caroline (an ex-civil servant and part-time church secretary) with two sons, he and his wife operate a headmaster's table at lunch a couple of times a week to get to know more pupils. Kept the boat steady in his first year; his most high profile (and very popular) change was the introduction of two exeat weekends per term. Plays the bagpipes, wears tartan trews on special occasions and is stretching into his first post as headmaster.

Academic matters: Impressive results, given the low hurdle on entrance, with more than 63 per cent A* and A grades at GCSE. In recent years A level A and B percentage consistently above 80. In 2009, 40 per cent of A level candidates got at least three A grades; 59 per cent of entries were A, 85 per cent A or B. In the lower school, setting according to ability and performance in entrance exam. Average class size 15, with maximum of 23. Choice of separate science subjects or dual award at GCSE and sleek modern labs (converted from Victorian style lecture theatres), but science A level results nothing special. Lots of languages on offer – French, German (strong department), Spanish, Italian, Chinese, Latin and Greek; a pilot scheme in Italian offered to 13 year olds for those who have not done French or don't take to it. Maths (with the usual boost from Chinese students), economics and history are popular and successful choices.

Religious studies compulsory (to end of year 10) and includes personal, health and social education, together with comparative religion. Great new library building with good, up to date stock, mezzanine level with 25 networked computers. Very impressive new DT building crammed with brilliant work – loungers, rowing machines, even an aeroplane simulator.

Clinics held once or twice a week by subject teachers for pupils to catch up or seek clarification. Around 50 pupils here with SEN and a learning skills coordinator but no unit, so pupils will be advised to try elsewhere if the school does not have the facilities to cater for them – 'Ultimately the pupil needs to be happy'.

Games, Options, the Arts: Excellent music provision with two directors – one responsible for instrumental and academic and the other for chapel music. Highlights include a choir that periodically tours Europe, annual concert by candlelight with the chapel full to capacity (a sight to behold), Christmas carols broadcast on TV and Mozart's 'Requiem' at St Bart's as part of the Brighton Fringe. The choir has recently released a CD – 'Surrexit' – celebrating 500 years of choral music. At any one time about 200 pupils learning at least one instrument and playing in orchestras, bands and ensembles.

Art very strong with a committed and popular head of department – popular and successful at A level; spanking new zinc, steel and glass studio. The area of outstanding natural beauty in which the school is sited encourages plein air work. A level photography well provided for.

A soccer school (players in the Public Schools' squad), but rugby is an option and hockey grew larger with the arrival of the head, who umpires in the national league. Squash traditionally strong here with some nationally ranked players. Netball, rounders, fives, 22 tennis courts (including six grass), cricket pitches and a team of groundsmen who do a fantastic job. 25 metre swimming pool that the prep school tiddlers swim in too; the use of it has led to competition at a national level – the girls beat Oxford University recently. Recent sports tours to Hong Kong, Thailand, Holland and USA and traditional links with Kamazu Academy in Malawi – trips there every other year, with much charity fundraising done in preparation.

Great drama – nearly everyone gets a chance to sing or dance, or work above or backstage in one of more than 12 productions annually ('West Side Story', 'Romeo and Juliet' set in Brighton, house plays) both in the indoor (seats 200) and open-air theatre (400).

Saturday morning school means that Tuesday and Thursday afternoons are devoted to sport and extra-curricular activities. CCF is popular with both girls and boys; the alternative is the school's Outreach (community service) scheme, but the chance to learn to shoot wins more recruits. Debates in the library, sailing on River Adur, Duke of Edinburgh awards, clay pigeon shooting and conservation projects also available. The school farm offers the children the chance to pet (or clean out) alpacas, lambs, pigs, sheep and rabbits.

Background and Atmosphere: School founded by Reverend Nathaniel Woodard in 1848; The Woodard Corporation (commemorated in the chapel's Rose Window) is now the largest group of independent schools in England and Wales, with Lancing as its senior school. Tradition is strong and for most, very comforting; Eucharist weekly in the chapel, where all staff don gowns and sit in pews along the edge, looking a bit like icons in niches. The senior girls wear sweeping cloaks in their house colours to keep out the wind (can be a lot up on this hill) in the winter. Most of the school is ushered up the aisle by prefects (also in gowns) to the altar for communion or a blessing, but this is relaxed enough to allow for some chat while everyone streams down the side aisles to return to their seats. Largest school chapel in the world, of the upturned pig school of architecture. Stunning – in either sense of the word. The Chaplain is well-liked – he knows how to communicate, at the right level and holding attention.

Boys and girls have good, modern accommodation. The dining hall is lofty (sixth form bar with no alcohol but table football, pool and beanbags instead) and a good range of food, including salad and vegetarian choices. The sixth form can order pizza and Chinese takeaways (even mid-week). A café is planned as the final stage of the art centre shift around.

Everything is available on one huge site (550 acres) looking out over the River Adur estuary (50 per cent of the staff live onsite). Somewhat isolated, although pupils can visit Shoreham and the sixth form (co-ed for 30 years) can go to Brighton. Although Lancing only went fully co-ed ten years ago, the school is not laddish and girls fit in well.

Pastoral Care and Discipline: The houses have strong identities and compete healthily. Each has its own commonroom, often with a pool-table and plasma screen, although in the summer everyone mixes up in the quads. A year group forum, but pupils assure us everyone ends up knowing everyone else. Peers really support each other here and the house matron normally has a stratagem (like a dog to hug) to deal with young ones' homesickness. An official counsellor as well. Thirteen year olds are given a fair bit of freedom in their use of time during the day and so have the chance to make their own decisions, since 'mistakes are a key part of the learning process'.

School rules clearly defined in the pupils' charter, given to all new pupils. Compulsory attendance at chapel and a voluntary Eucharist on offer every morning in the crypt below the chapel, but faiths other than C of E welcomed. Bullying, alcohol and drugs dealt with severely and generally not a problem. Noticeably relaxed and warm atmosphere.

Pupils and Parents: Mainly from south east, 22 per cent from overseas (at present 13 per cent from Hong Kong and China, seven per cent Europe). School transport services from Horsham, Brighton, Hove and Lewes have widened the day catchment area. Parents mainly local business people, professional, financiers and academics, with some commuters but, as one parent says, 'well away from the pushy, yuppie London types'. Pupils from many prep schools in the area and, now, Lancing Prep in Hove. Former pupils include playwrights Sir David Hare, Christopher Hampton and Giles Cooper, lyricist Sir Tim Rice, novelists Tom Sharpe and Evelyn Waugh, Shakespeare scholar and writer John Dover Wilson, singer Sir Peter Pears, Archbishop Trevor Huddleston and TV presenter Jamie Theakston. Not a snobby school.

Entrance: Not very selective at CE with a 50 per cent pass rate; pupils from state sector separately assessed. For entry into the sixth form, outsiders need a satisfactory reference from present school and good GCSE results; they undergo interviews and a verbal reasoning test and have to produce an essay on their interests and aspirations.

Exit: Oxbridge popular as well as Nottingham, Bristol, London and other redbrick universities. A couple every year to art or agricultural college.

Money Matters: Around 45 awards annually up to 50 per cent of annual fees. All awards can be augmented up to a maximum of two-thirds of the full fees, depending on family circumstances. Special awards for music and art, drama, sport and all-rounders. A number of awards (academic, art, music, organ) available annually for sixth form entrance; again, these can be augmented.

Remarks: First class pastoral care, community spirit and family atmosphere – the warmth is almost tangible. Very good results from a mixed intake. Distinguishes itself as a boarding school with day pupils; local parents enjoy Friday night/Saturday morning to themselves with dedicated family time with their kids for the rest of the weekend.

Langley Grammar School

Reddington Drive, Langley, Slough, Berkshire, SL3 7QS

• Pupils: 1025; girls and boys • Ages: 11-18 • Size of sixth form: 300
• Non-denom • State

Tel: 01753 598 300
Fax: 01753 810 858
Email: school@langley-grammar.slough.sch.uk
Website: www.langley-grammar.slough.sch.uk

Head: Since January 2010, Mr John Constable BSc (forties), was deputy head of Wycombe High School and before that posts at Sir William Borlase (Marlow), Watford and Aylesbury Grammars. If his cv seems to show a trend then no surprise to learn that Mr Constable is a 'classic grammar school boy', the product of a town grammar in Suffolk (but no, he isn't related). Not quite a seamless move from learning to teaching, he took his degree in Engineering Science and Management at Durham and worked for Unilever for a couple of years before evolving into that highly prized creature, a physics teacher. Acknowledging polarised opinions on the subject of grammar schools, he believes that, when it works, the model, certainly as represented by Langley, still has the potential to transform lives. Married with two young children, he sails, is a qualified dinghy instructor and cub scout leader, enjoying the chance the latter gives him to work with younger children. Other interests are hill walking and photography. 'It's hugely important to do other things,' he says.

This is Mr Constable's first headship, a school where there are ten applications for every place and which was declared 'outstanding' by Ofsted; so, where does he intend to go from here? 'Outstanding doesn't mean perfect,' he says, there is scope to 'review the curriculum' and boost students' independence. So far, so virtual; if he has more specific plans (beyond building works) he's not letting on. Immensely likeable, quietly charming, he is also understandably guarded – these are early days and one feels that he is keeping his powder dry.

Academic matters: Among the top state grammars in the country and highly valued locally, this is a school where expectations are high. A specialist maths and computing school since 2004. GCSE A*–C grades are over 96 per cent with more than half of these A* or A; at A level, grades are equally impressive. Such results are particularly admirable given that, on entry to the school, 40 per cent of students have a first language other than English. Booster classes in English, particularly essay writing skills, and by the end of key stage 3 the majority of pupils exceed expectation. The library plays a key role in this, its indefatigable staff organise all kinds of initiatives to get everyone reading widely; its SOAR (switch off and read) Fridays for Years 7–9 are a great idea: all electronic distractions are disabled and

10,000 books regain their rightful place as the library's main attraction.

Very strong in all academic areas and formidable in maths. There is an 'expectation' that the majority will take three separate sciences at GCSE and most do so along with choices from the wide range of arts, technologies and languages (French or German). No Latin or Greek here but classical civilisation is an option for GCSE and there are plans to offer it at AS level. Psychology, sociology, philosophy & ethics and law all offered at AS and A level. Head is considering IGCSEs but 'has yet to be convinced'.

Classes are broadly similar in size to those in other grammars – 30 at Key Stage, mid twenties for GCSE subjects – but the prevailing air of studious quiet is enough to indicate that at Langley this is not a barrier to learning. As the head comments, 'part of that is us, part of that is because the majority of our students come to us well-motivated and with a respect for learning'. On our visit the view in every classroom is of heads bowed or hands up, 'You've got to like your book work,' commented one of our guides. Small number on SEN register, mainly for dyslexia or other SPLD and students' individual needs catered for by SENCo, a gifted and talented coordinator and school counsellor.

Games, Options, the Arts: Music and drama facilities are spacious – the main sports hall can accommodate the whole school – and professional looking; foundation status means it can make its own choices about how to spend money and, notwithstanding the science and maths bent here, sport and the arts are impressively resourced. One of our guides said of the sports facilities, 'it's only when you go to away matches that you realise how lucky you are'. Whole school drama productions, house and school concerts are a key part of school life; instrumentalists are served by the borough's peripatetic music teachers and a recent 'push' to encourage take up of brass instruments has apparently been successful. Not surprisingly, chess is particularly strong as the silverware in the trophy cabinet in reception goes to show but Langley is equally successful in the less cerebral sports. 'This is not a rugby school or a hockey school,' the aim being to offer the widest possible range to appeal to the maximum number of students. Two hours of timetabled sport a week is augmented by plenty of lunchtime and after school activities and matches; the girls' basketball team has been county champion for two years in a row. Sixth formers can also earn money working in the huge sports centre – facilities are open to the local community out of school hours.

Background and Atmosphere: Sitting comfortably among quiet residential roads, the grounds and immediate vicinity are immaculate, not a crisp packet or drinks can anywhere to be seen. The school presents a smart, purposeful face to the world both outside and in. This isn't an ancient foundation; built in 1956, the style is post-war municipal Brutalist, softened with age and summer bedding. Inside the original core buildings are beautifully maintained with gleaming linoleum and polished wood. The school is fortunate to be surrounded by plenty of green space and playable surfaces are extended by a floodlit all-weather pitch.

A 'redundant' strip at the edge of the site was sold for housing in order to finance a significant building programme. Classrooms have the requisite whiteboards, computers etc, and even in the older parts everything is scrupulously clean and well maintained. In the corridors, subject notice boards are up-to-date and colourful but pupils' work is not prominently displayed in public areas. A much needed refurbishment and extension of the dining room was under way when we visited, the student council was involved at all stages of its design ('including the colour scheme,' remarked the head) and attended all presentations. This cashless café style area with small tables and squashy sofas will provide a continuous service, including breakfast, with the emphasis on healthy eating. Sixth formers can eat in the common room or outside at picnic tables. The food is, apparently, much, much better than it used to be.

Slough's education system is rather mix and match – of the twelve secondary schools in the borough, four are grammars. According to Mr Constable there are 'interesting philosophical differences regarding selection but heads are working together very effectively' to raise standards for all. Not much in the way of philosophical difference if you talk to parents or locals though: residents are fiercely proud of these schools and the opportunities they offer young people. Even parents we spoke to whose offspring did not get into Langley are refreshingly unchippy. Local primaries don't teach to the 11 plus but Langley is involved in a great deal of outreach work with younger children, especially in the area of IT, to share the school's equipment and expertise. It also actively supports three non-selective schools with senior staff involved in training NQTs and peer mentoring schemes and contributes to another partnership (readers are being spared an alphabet soup of acronyms here) aimed at raising achievement in a group of local schools.

One is struck by how calm everything is. Bells have just been abolished and pupils walk quickly to their next lesson chatting quietly in groups, no crowd control needed here. Green blazers with the school insignia for boys, green jumpers for girls, traditional enamel badges for positions of responsibility worn proudly. Sixth form uniform smart variations on a theme of monochrome.

Yes, this is a focused and academic school but it is not inward looking; it has been awarded International School status for its 'outstanding development of the international dimension in the curriculum' and sixth formers in particular are very enthusiastic in their fundraising for charitable causes abroad.

Pastoral Care and Discipline: The head describes his school as a 'good mix' and the student population as 'harmonious' and pupils we spoke to confirm this. Understandably the ethos of the institution is broadly secular, there are no religious clubs but plenty of discussion supported by an assembly programme of visiting speakers. The response to bullying is 'prompt and effective' action by tutors and heads of year. In addition, there is a peer mentoring scheme for which pupils are trained and a website that allows students to report incidents or request support anonymously. Staff are energetic and experienced, just the right combination of new ideas and old wisdom, and pupils receive a high level of pastoral support particularly in the first couple of years when boys and girls arrive from unusually diverse geographic (the school has no catchment area) and cultural backgrounds. Our Year 13 guides had fond and grateful memories of the buddy system which pairs small groups of new pupils with a sixth form mentor.

There is what the head describes as a 'fairly traditional house system,' with lively inter-house sporting fixtures and music competitions with external judges. No school bus – public transport network here pretty good – but a car share scheme operates too. School day ends at 3.15 and a full extra-curricular programme of sport and other activities takes place after this and in lunch hours. Some funding is available to support the purchase of uniform or pay for trips in cases of hardship.

'Code of conduct' and the 'usual range of sanctions' for those who break this. Major transgressions are rare – a commendable zero racist incidents, for example. The head believes in tackling any potential problems head-on and claims that he and his senior staff spend as much time as necessary face to face or on the phone to parents.

Pupils and Parents: Pupils enter from a wide geographical area and over 80 primary schools. About 40 per cent come from Slough borough but, because the school is close to the boundaries of other authorities, 'out of borough' entrants can also live relatively nearby. Two thirds of the school's intake is from what are officially described as 'minority ethnic groups,' just over half coming from Asian/British-Indian backgrounds. Pupils are charming, polite and very proud of their school.

Entrance: Verbal and non-verbal reasoning papers taken in November. Slough is not a selective authority so parents must opt in for their children to take the test set by a consortium of Langley and two other grammars. Places are allocated according to rank order of performance, thereafter distance from school is only possible advantage. Coaching? 'Of course there is,' says the head. There are roughly 20 sixth form places for external candidates and admission is on the basis of GCSE performance and specific grades stipulated for A level subjects chosen.

Exit: Mainly Russell Group universities, King's College London and Imperial particularly favoured. Overwhelmingly science, medicine, engineering and computing but some choose other traditional academic subjects such as history or English – nothing remotely fluffy. Not as many as one might expect applying to Oxbridge and the head believes there is work to be done here. Gap years are not the norm and the school continues to provide support for pupils after they leave, especially those who delay university entrance.

Remarks: Huge local pride in Langley and the other Slough grammar schools; it seems that the noblest ideals of the old fashioned grammar survive here untarnished. Perhaps because of its location, the school is relatively untroubled by sharp-elbowed incomers looking for a private education on the state. Hard working, serious minded school, indeed one feels that pupils sometimes might need to be encouraged to look up from their books and spend a few minutes day dreaming. Langley is at the heart of its community, providing invaluable opportunities and changing lives; as a charming sixth former remarked, 'if you're willing to give everything a go, it's all there for you and the teachers help you to achieve'.

Langley Park School for Boys

South Eden Park Road, Beckenham, Kent BR3 3BP

• Pupils: 1,510 boys; 185 girls in the sixth form; all day • Ages: 11-18 • Size of sixth form: 540 boys and girls • Non-denom • State

Tel: 020 8650 9253
Fax: 020 8650 5823
Email: office@lpbs.org.uk
Website: www.lpbs.org.uk

Headteacher: Since 2000, Robert Northcott MA (fifties), an energetic man with a bone-crushing handshake. In his third headship. Married to a psychology teacher, with four successful grown-up children. Astonishing energy and charisma, passionate about his school and about education, whilst being a complete maverick. Hugely popular with parents, pupils and colleagues. 'He IS the school – it wouldn't be the same without him,' as one parent put it. 'He's amazing!' said at least three pupils we spoke to. 'And funny,' added another.

Academic matters: Intake is non-selective. Boys join in mixed ability tutor groups, then 'tightly setted' for subjects – seven entry forms divided into 10 ability-based learning groups. Head very enthusiastic about this, and the school's results explain why: English language GCSE is consistently in the top five per cent nationally, and success in maths and science is impressive. Specialist status in maths and computing, with links to other schools to offer master classes. School re-introduced engineering at GCSE and A level five years ago, and now has its first Oxbridge success with the subject. Also won the Spirit of the Event Team Award in the Shell Ecotec Challenge (designing a fuel efficient car) three years running.

Head actively recruits teachers from the top universities, training them at Langley. The result is a good mix of experienced longer-serving staff and dynamic newcomers. Students rave about them: 'The teachers are really helpful', 'They always help you out if you ask them', 'Languages here are fun, really in-depth', 'Science lessons are great', 'The staff are fantastic – I've never met one I didn't like', are just a few of the comments we received. Culture of going the extra mile, combined with imagination and innovation: Bobby George, the darts champion, was booked to give a masterclass in mental maths. Thriving co-ed sixth form, which girls leave the independent sector to join.

Excellent SEN provision, with statemented pupils completely integrated into school life. Gifted and talented programme for more able pupils, results compare favourably with those from grammar school. 'All three of our sons have blossomed here,' said one parent. 'We couldn't be happier.' 'My daughter loves it,' added the mother of a sixth former. 'She's so much more confident now.'

Games, Options, the Arts: 'We're the only state school who's played Eton at Fives!' enthused head, adding, 'We got slaughtered.' Notwithstanding, sport here is very strong, rugby and hockey particularly so – a boy described the recent rugby tour of South Africa as 'unbelievable – I'd recommend it to everyone'. Links with professional sportsmen keep the profile high; gold Sports and Artsmarks. Art is truly amazing – OB Henry Mee's mural is still there from

1973, and has been joined since by hundreds of remarkable and thought-provoking artworks, all by students and all proudly on display. Drama and music both flourish, with regular productions, choral tours and concerts – Catfish Blue, the school's jazz group, did well at the National Festival of Music for Youth in 2009 and went on to play the Royal Albert Hall in the Schools' Prom. 'The performing arts are huge drivers of motivation and confidence,' head believes. All boys learn to ride a horse at the end of Year 9. Lots of trips abroad and dozens of refreshingly different extra-curricular opportunities, including comedy club and fly-fishing.

Background and Atmosphere: Previously the Beckenham and Penge County Grammar, it became comprehensive in 1976 and moved out of Penge to its present green field site. Buildings are now showing their age and head clearly loathes them, but brand new school is in the process of being built. Meanwhile, as one pupil said, 'We just get on with it.' Co-ed sixth form since 2001 started with seven girls, now has 181, and has, head says, 'Transformed the feel of the school, hugely benefiting both our learning and our extra-curricular' – adding, endearingly, 'Girls are brave, you see'. Staff/pupil relationships extremely good, and head really does know every child in the school by name. Uniform is smart and smartly worn, formal dress for sixth formers.

Pastoral Care and Discipline: Described by one student as 'excellent', and parents endorse this. 'The head doesn't just sit in his office – he's out there setting the tone,' said one father, and everyone we spoke to praised the staff and the example they give. Students are expected to be courteous, cooperative and sensible. Sixth formers given responsibilities such as library and lunchtime duty and helping younger pupils settle in.

Pupils and Parents: Drawn from the immediate locality, mostly Beckenham and West Wickham. 'A nice area – we are privileged,' admits head. Majority of parents are aspirational, expecting their children to work hard and do well. Students likeable and down to earth. One turned down a place at a local independent school, because 'Langley was friendlier'.

Entrance: School is massively over-subscribed at 11 – only siblings and those living less than 1.07 of a mile away can hope to get in. Predictably, local house prices reflect this. Priority also given to children in care.

Exit: 'Vast majority' of boys stay on at 16. At 18, most go on to university and usually get their first choice. Between two and four Oxbridge successes most years.

Remarks: A wonderful success story of a school. Comprehensive education at its very best.

Langley Park School for Girls

Hawksbrook Lane, South Eden Park Road, Beckenham, Kent, BR3 3BE

• Pupils: 1,635 day girls • Ages: 11-18 • Size of sixth form: 480
• Non-denom • State

Tel: 020 8663 4199
Fax: 02086 636 578
Email: info@lpgs.bromley.sch.uk
Website: www.lpgs.bromley.sch.uk

Head: Since 1994, Ms Jan Sage MA (fifties), considered an excellent manager and tireless fundraiser for her school. She encourages the staff to work closely with parents to form effective home school partnerships. A rather glamorous lady who runs a tight ship, with a commitment to helping all pupils. Moving on to other things in December 2010.

Dr Anne Hudson takes over as headteacher from January 2011.

Academic matters: A successful single sex comprehensive offering strong competition to some of the selective schools in the area. GCSE and A level results moving ever upwards. Languages strong: French, Spanish or German in year seven; pupils can add second language following year. An after-school distance learning course runs for those wishing to study Latin, and the modern languages department arranges interesting trips and foreign exchanges. Design & technology very strong; individual science subjects on offer. Setting in maths, the girls do very well in external competitions. Good monitoring of progress and support; gifted and talented programme, and additional support is available to those identified as having SEN. Staff provide an excellent guide for parents on study skills and supporting your child in school. Has accumulated four specialisms: technology since 1996, leading edge status since 2002, languages since 2006, sports since 2007.

Games, Options, the Arts: Lots of competition between the girls to get into the various sports teams – after-school sports tends to be only for those selected for the teams. Well used floodlit all-weather pitches and courts. Music department has come on in leaps and bounds over the last few years – dynamic head of music runs many different musical groups, also music tours, everyone can join in. Huge jazz band, string groups and two choirs regularly provide much appreciated entertainment. Concerts are wonderful, say parents, staff and girls. Through the student council pupils are encouraged to have a say in what extra-curricular activities they want. Many take part in the D of E awards and World Challenge expeditions. Has been awarded a Charter Mark for excellence in public services a number of times.

Background and Atmosphere: Originally Beckenham Grammar School and moved to its present site in 1959. Further extensions added throughout the 1990s – now boasts sports halls, sixth form centre, drama studios, art and food workshops. Welcoming entrance hall with a most impressive display of the school's awards and achievements. Shares a huge green site with Langley Boys' School.

Maintains its good local reputation with many community links and works.

Pastoral Care and Discipline: Outstanding reputation for well-behaved pupils, clean and tidy in their smart navy and tartan uniform. Staff-parent communication is effectively managed and all queries are responded to within 24 hours – most parents feel the school responds very well to parental and pupil concerns. Gordon Brown recently visited to gain an insight into 'Beat Bullying' incentive. Monthly parent bulletins and termly newsletters.

Pupils and Parents: Very local Beckenham and West Wickham types, small ethnic mix – mostly hard working parents who wish to see their children achieve their potential. Active parents' group helps raise funds for various local charities. Past pupils are encouraged to stay in touch through the Adremian Association.

Entrance: At 11 always over-subscribed; priority is given to siblings and those living closest to the school.

Exit: At 16 plus around a third leave for coed sixth forms or vocational colleges. Quite a few join the sixth form from neighbouring Croydon. At 18 mostly to their first choice university.

Remarks: A school committed to developing the whole person, a serious consideration if you're lucky enough to be allocated a place.

Lathallan Senior School

Linked to Lathallan School in the Junior section

Brotherton Castle, Johnshaven, By Montrose, DD10 0HN

• Pupils: 185 boys and girls throughout the school; some weekly and flexi boarders • Ages: 6 weeks-18. • Non denominational
• Fees: Day £14,658; Boarding +£3,510 pa • Independent

Tel: 01561 362 220
Fax: 01561 361 695
Email: admissions@lathallan.org.uk
Website: www.lathallan.org.uk

Headmaster: Mr Richard Toley joined Lathallan in 2006 as director of studies from nearby High School of Dundee. In 2007, Mr Toley was promoted to head of the new senior school and his rise to the top means he is, now at 37, we think, the youngest head of any comparable school in Scotland. A historian, he is the eighth head of Lathallan since it was founded in 1930.

Academic matters: Scottish curriculum – 17+ subject options for Standard Grades. French and Spanish, plus the usual suspects – maths, English, three sciences, history, geography, business and classical studies, art, PE and drama, plus managing environmental resources, which is a new boy on the block. Pupils streamed for maths and English and taught in newly refurbished classrooms (one with interactive whiteboard) in the castle. Maximum class size 16; interactive whiteboards introduced in the resource centre. Good strong dyslexia help, plus help for the brightest, withdrawn from class once or twice a week. Loads of new staff, including part timers. Specialist staff also for junior school. IT impressive – Dell computers all over the shop with Apple Macs in senior school.

Games, Options, the Arts: Music everywhere – bagpipe boxes all over the porch and hall when we visited, both girls and boys in pipe bands much in demand for charities and have entertained Princess Anne of late. Scottish country dancing and strong drama. Has re-introduced a new formal schoolwide traditional PE programme, which 'through age-appropriate indoor exercises aims to improve co-ordination and mental agility both in and outside the academic classroom'. We say not quite enough pupils for strong senior school team games (school says, 'Strong senior school team games, given small numbers'). Keen games in junior school, but OK rather than thrashing all comers – school prefers 'competing well against all comers in junior school' – but size will out. All seven plus year olds play sport daily, tennis courts double up for netball (Astroturf), ten acres of playing field overlooking the North Sea and own beach (bracing), plus refurbished gym. Lots of jolly rugby trips and girls' netball tours.

Background and Atmosphere: Lathallan school was founded in the imposing Victorian Brotherton Castle almost eighty years ago. Originally a traditional boys' boarding prep school, set in 62 acres of woodland and catering, in the main, for 'the folk over the hill', it is now a thriving nursery through standard grade co-ed school offering weekly or flexi-boarding only. All dormitories in castle, with boys in quite large, east facing ones now benefiting from trendy (free) eco-friendly woodchip boiler; girls cosily ensconced in former servants' quarters. Library and resource centre in main building with classrooms and nursery in bright converted stable block with massive additions. Some lessons in temporary classrooms. Masses of eco-input. Pupils have newly refurbished commonroom for senior school pupils only. School uniform provided in house, with rather jolly fleecy waterproof jackets which the staff wear too; they also all have to take the minibus test.

Pastoral Care and Discipline: School small enough for every child to be known, strong anti bullying policy. Civilianship a popular subject.

Pupils and Parents: Increasing number of first time buyers, very supportive, strong parental input, will drive many miles out of their way to drop off their tinies in the nursery. Return buses for older children from Stonehaven and Aberdeen with coaches from Brechin and Montrose. Aberdeen business community plus local farmers, commuters and the like, from within one and a half hour radius (which would actually take you to Dundee). Rob Wainwright an old boy.

Entrance: At any time to any year group if places available, but recommends joining in form 5 (P7) ready to start two year Common Entrance course. Taster day recommended. Informal tests in English, maths and verbal reasoning.

Exit: Senior school pupils an unknown quantity. In the junior school, some pupils are still opting for traditional secondary schools, as in Glenalmond, Strathallan, Fettes, Merchiston etc, plus tiny dribble down south, St Margaret's

Eskrick, but their number is diminishing. Magnificent record of scholarships.

Remarks: Senior school seems to be settling in remarkably well. Brave new venture – bated breath ain't in it.

The Latymer School

Haselbury Road, London, N9 9TN

• Pupils: 1,360, 710 boys, 650 girls; all day • Ages: 11-18 • Size of sixth form: 470 • Non-denom • State

Tel: 020 8807 4037
Fax: 020 8887 8111
Email: office@latymer.co.uk
Website: www.latymer.co.uk

Headteacher: Since 2005, Mr Mark E Garbett (fiftyish) MA MEd NPQH. Formerly head of Stretford Grammar School, Trafford, Manchester; for five years before that at Skegness Grammar School and Royal Belfast Academical Institution. Also taught in the private sector as head of maths at Framlingham College and as a maths teacher at Dean Close. Two daughters. Plays the piano, sails, run for pleasure.

Academic matters: One of the country's most over-subscribed grammar schools with outstanding exams results – at A level 'comfortably' within the top five per cent of schools nationally. In 2009, over 90 per cent of grades at A level were A or B and over 90 per cent were A or A* at GCSE. Pupils are highly motivated and conscientious, teaching challenging and often inspiring. School teaches learning skills and critical thinking to enhance the basic exam fodder. Strong in everything – maths the most popular A level – but outstandingly strong in music, modern languages, history, design technology and art.

Nine GCSEs only to reduce the pressure. 'We believe in the liberal tradition of developing the whole person and allow plenty of time for that,' says the head. Setted in maths from Year 9 and language at GCSE, but in nothing else: 'There's no need – the academic spread is minimal'. French or German in Year 7, with the option to add a second language in Year 8, including Russian or Latin. All do one language at GCSE and combined science.

Established, experienced staff monitor progress carefully. 'I don't think they let people slip through the net – they notice everything,' says one positive parent. 'There's a high level of expectation but it's done gradually, so there's not the endless pressure and competition you find elsewhere.'

Teacher-pupil relationship unusually strong, with respect and affection on both sides – 'My son, who's in the sixth form, couldn't imagine not inviting his teachers to his leaving party'.

Games, Options, the Arts: Full range of sports but most highly rated are soccer, rugby and cricket for boys, cricket, hockey and netball for girls. Lavish new sports complex, which doubles as a dining hall, has expanded the range to include badminton, volleyball and a fitness centre.

Residential centre in Wales, where Years 7 and 9 spend a week and older pupils attempt the 14 Peaks hill-walking challenge. Regular exchange programme with France, Germany and Russia. Drama tours and other subject tours: classicists to Italy, artists to New York, athletes to Barbados, musicians all over Europe, plus ski trips. Well-stocked careers room.

Music outstandingly strong – virtually professional standard – with five orchestras, a concert band, various choirs and a plethora of instrumental ensembles. Regular performers at the National Festival for Music and Youth, the Schools' Prom and carols in Trafalgar Square. Recent pupil led the National Youth Orchestra. Main school play is either a large musical or a heavyweight drama, plus house drama festivals and junior drama evening.

Vast extra-curricular offering: Duke of Edinburgh, Basic Expedition Leadership Award and Young Enterprise (where pupils frequently reach the London final). Students, organise a multitude of lunch-hour clubs including politics, debating, psychology, philosophy, animal rights and juggling. Very active, too, in charity work. Strong relationship with Amnesty International and Fair Trade.

Background and Atmosphere: Founded originally in the 17th century, Latymer moved to its current site in 1910. Not particularly picturesque inside or out but well-equipped and well-maintained. Surrounded by 12 acres of playing fields, the oldest building is Edwardian but continual additions and revisions since then, including a performing arts complex with air-conditioned practice rooms, opened in 2000, and the new sports hall cum dining hall, opened in 2006 by Princess Anne. The library, which holds 20,000 volumes, is attractive and well run by a professional librarian.

Pastoral Care and Discipline: Each year group split into six classes – one for each of the school houses – and remains together till end of Year 11, meeting for registration and form periods daily. This develops a strong sense of coherence and team work. Each class has a class tutor who takes responsibility for pupils' welfare while at school and, in the lower school, teaches PSHE. Also a head of year, who stays with the year group from Years 7 to 11. In the sixth form, students retain their house links but join mixed form groups. Expects self-discipline and a sense of community – and they get it. Homework nightly, from one hour in Year 7 to two and a quarter in Years 10 and 11. Discipline generally not a problem.

Pupils and Parents: Anyone and everyone who is 'very clever', though the school wisely lists acceptable postcodes in its admission criteria. This includes half from Enfield, then from a wide surrounding area which takes in Hackney, Islington, Tottenham and Essex. Old boys include footballer Johnny Haynes and 'Strictly Come Dancing' host Bruce Forsyth.

Entrance: Around 1,800 compete for 180 places at 11. Cut to 600 on the basis of non-verbal reasoning, then internally set exams in maths and English. 20 places for music – 'though you still have to be able to cope with the academic pace'. 390 applicants for sixth form – they have to do a test, then about 80 offered places on six GCSE grade As or better.

Exit: About five per cent at 16 years for education elsewhere. Then 95 per cent to degree courses, mainly Russell Group and specialist music and art colleges. In 2009/2010 27 to Oxbridge.

Money Matters: The Latymer Foundation, as well as funding the Snowdonia Field Centre, funds selected capital projects and helps those who cannot afford uniform or school trips. The financial side is looked after by the bursar, who is on the senior leadership team.

Remarks: A top-notch academic grammar school which produces mature, confident pupils. 'I've been absolutely bowled over by every pupil I've met who's recently left this school,' says a parent. 'They're dynamic and articulate, with their feet on the ground, and have none of that snottiness you can sometimes find in academic schools elsewhere.'

Latymer Upper School

Linked to Latymer Prep School in the Junior section

237 King Street, Hammersmith, London, W6 9LR

• Pupils: 1,045, co-ed started in 2004 from Year 7, now fully co-ed with 25 per cent girls. All day • Ages: 11-18 • Size of sixth form: Mixed • Non-denom • Fees: £14,460 pa • Independent

Tel: 0845 638 5800
Fax: 020 8748 5212
Email: registrar@latymer-upper.org
Website: www.latymer-upper.org

Head: Since 2002, Mr Peter J Winter MA (Oxon) (late fifties), formerly head of King Edward's School (Bath), educated at Trinity School, Croydon and Wadham College, Oxford, where he read French and German. Taught at Latymer Upper and Magdalen College School (Oxford) before going to Sevenoaks School, where he was head of modern languages, then ran the International Centre, the sixth form boarding house for boys with his Ghanaian-born wife, Adwoa. Two children. A keen all-round sportsman and Francophile, he is a strong advocate of co-education and is happily overseeing Latymer's transition. 'I have never been more fulfilled in my work.' 'He clearly has his hands on the reins,' said a parent, 'and he seems to have the support of a good staff team. I value his recognition of all the pupils – including those who don't win the prizes.'

Academic matters: Results have improved year on year for the past six years – 86 per cent A*/A at GCSE in 2009, 91 per cent A/B at A level, 29 going to Oxbridge in 2010. Impact of clever girls is clear. English and maths followed closely by history and RE, and then sciences, as most popular A levels, from a total of 35, including government and politics and photography. Very big staff changes here; the head has done some weeding out and now says confidently, 'We don't have any weak staff any more'.

A learning support department which backs up classroom teachers with diagnoses, advice and support.

Games, Options, the Arts: Rowing is a particular strength. Plenty of opportunities too for more conventionally sporty types, including cross-country, badminton, netball as well as football (girls as well as boys) and rugby. Sports ground at Wood Lane, a 20 minute bus ride away, completely refurbished in 2004 at a cost of £4.2 million, with a new pavilion and changing rooms, grass and Astroturf pitches. 'We want to give the girls the same quality and range of sport as the boys.' Large sports hall with swimming pool and fitness suite on site.

Very strong art. Arts Centre includes three-store gallery and two floors of art studios. Well-equipped Edward Latymer Theatre with galleried seating; drama is another strength – timetabled throughout the school. A brand new performing arts centre was opened in 2008 housing a dedidated dance/drama studio and a recital hall. Strong musical tradition – joint orchestra with Godolphin and Latymer and exchanges with The Johanneum in Hamburg, plus bands and choirs. Saturday music school for local children.

A new building, with a library and resources centre on the ground floor, and three floors dedicated to science above, opened in September 2010 and is used by all pupils.

Each summer, all the pupils who are not doing public exams go off for an activities week – which might include caving on Dartmoor, rafting in the Alps, surfing in Newquay or visiting the Futuroscope in France. Other school trips include language exchanges, classics tour to Sicily, geography field trip to Switzerland and art trip to New York. Lots of pupils get silver and gold Duke of Edinburgh Awards. Plenty of extra-curricular activities, e.g. bridge, karate, French, drama, debating, dance, chess.

Background and Atmosphere: Founded in 1624, the school moved to its present site in 1895. It was once a direct grant grammar school and still has a somewhat hybrid feel: jammed and very urban from the front entrance, straight off a busy Hammersmith road, but with a vaulted great hall lined with Oxbridge scholarship boards and a boathouse emerging onto the banks of the Thames at the back. An elevated section of the A4 was actually built through the playground after WW2. But an underpass emerges by a tarmac sports pitch which leads to a lawned garden, swimming pool, sports hall, boathouse and the elegant town house with river views occupied by the prep school. Italianate piazza with plants, seats and tables has been created in the centre of the site, giving a spacious and airy feel and room for outdoor recreation away from ball games. The cars have been exiled – hooray!

Pastoral Care and Discipline: Historically, not a place for shy, sensitive souls – quite a few stories of bullying. 'We do not tolerate bullying,' we are told, though we used regularly to hear otherwise (school says no longer true). A very good structure of year heads and division heads to ensure that children do not fall through the net either socially or academically. 'We've sent out some strong signals. I now have a first class pastoral team and we are serious about our pupils' welfare.' School tells us that in its 2007 Inspection, the pastoral care was described as 'outstanding' – we're keeping our ear to the ground. But we might not send a sensitive, artistic or eccentric soul here.

Lamentable incident in June 2010 at sixth form leavers' ball when three pupils were caught with cocaine and others turned up to the event drunk, with one girl having to be taken to hospital. Expulsions and a suspension ensued, alongside much gnashing of teeth. Mr Winter was quoted as saying, 'Latymer Upper has a clear and unequivocal policy on drugs. Most Latymer parents welcome this strong line, although by no means all. Statistics would suggest that there will be some parents who take drugs themselves, and there are certainly others who seem to have little idea what their son or daughter gets up to at weekends'.

Pupils and Parents: This is an inner-city school that still has a grammar school feel and parents value the social mix that comes from taking in plenty of state school children at 11. Its clientele is mostly local – middle class professional families, including plenty of media and acting folk, many races and creeds. Turns out 'hard-working, solidly unpretentious chaps'. OBs include Sir James Spicer, George Walden, Mel Smith, Hugh Grant, Alan Rickman, Professor Lord Stern, Adam Balon, Dave Hendy and lots of MPs.

Entrance: Going co-ed has naturally upped the ante on the entrance front. About 40 boys and girls come up from the prep. The rest are chosen at 11 (and a few at 13) from a variety of state and private schools – at 11, around 50 per cent come from state primaries. Lots of competition – this being the only independent co-ed in the area – means it's pretty much a seller's market and potential parents report a less than welcoming response if they want to visit outside normal open days. The school will be over-subscribed whatever. 2004 was the first mixed gender entry and the whole school is now co-ed. Around 40 to 50 places in the sixth form. Extra time is allowed in entrance exams for those with formally recognised SEN – receipt of report from educational psychologist needed.

Exit: To a wide variety of universities, including 25+ a year to Oxbridge, to do a wide variety of courses ranging from sports science to theoretical physics. University of London is particularly popular.

Money Matters: A rich enough school, which offers a range of scholarships, bursaries and awards including academic, music, sports, art and drama. The school's aim is to raise sufficient funds for many more bursaries, 'so that academic ability is the only entry criterion'.

Remarks: Popular with local parents who know their sons and daughters will emerge with creditable results. Image softening under this head, needs to soften further. Aims to set new standards for co-education in west London.

Lavant House

Linked to Junior Lavant House in the Junior section

West Lavant, Chichester, West Sussex, PO18 9AB

- Pupils: 160 girls; 20 board, 140 day. Considerable flexi-boarding
- Ages: 11-18 • Size of sixth form: 16 girls • C of E • Fees: Day: Junior £6,210-£10,770, Senior £13,020; Boarding: Junior £17,085, Senior £20,490 pa
- Independent

Tel: 01243 527 211
Fax: 01243 530 490
Email: office@lavanthouse.org.uk
Website: www.lavanthouse.org.uk

Headmistress: Since 2009, Mrs Kate Bartholomew (late forties) BA MA PGCE, educated Universities of East Anglia, London, Cambridge, specialist subject history. Previous posts in the maintained sector in London, Suffolk and Berkshire. Internally appointed after ten years as senior mistress and then head of sixth form. Keen to develop the latter, academically and pastorally – obviously successfully, as ten years ago three pupils in it and now twenty. Attentive, charming and composed and radiates pride in her school.

Aims to 'build success upon success' with a clear vision of what she wants for the girls' education: 'The key to our success and how we manage the school is in its size. We are a small school with small numbers and have no aspirations to grow much larger. We make sure they have a childhood and, being a girls only school, they can develop without self-consciousness and feel comfortable with being themselves'. Developing music, e.g. by increasing the scholarships, now at 11 as well as 13+, and introducing academic mentoring for girls taking their GCSEs. She lives with her farmer husband approximately seven miles from the school and has two teenage children, one boy, one girl.

Academic matters: Small and traditional school with a broad range of abilities. Head says that more academic mentoring as well as pushing each girl's grade boundaries is achieving academic success. However, this school is about much more than the sum of its results. Because of its small numbers it can accommodate individual needs and thus the value-added is high. When working on their GCSE options the girls are required to rank their subjects on a scale of 1 to 10 and a flexible timetable is constructed to include their choices. This flexibility extends to A level, e.g. classes of just one for Spanish and economics. Science rated as very good by the pupils and staffed by enthusiastic teachers. Because of the small numbers in the labs (now being updated), 'A high proportion of time can be spent on experiments and a lot of practical work; the pupils really engage and get involved'. Art and media popular and results good. French is taught from Year 1, Latin from Year 7 and Spanish from Year 9. All staff have 'SEN awareness training' and are kept up to speed with any emerging problems, which are 'nipped in the bud,' we're told. Learning support dept, specialist SEN teacher and TEFL teaching for foreign students – but very few international students.

Games, Options, the Arts: Facilities are good for a small school – an outdoor pool, 3 netball courts (soon to be resurfaced), a good old fashioned gymnasium plus hockey pitches. Head of sport popular with the girls and a wheelchair user – chosen for 5 different disciplines in the 2012 Olympics. Main sport is netball – they do well on the local circuit and 50 girls are taken each week to the West Sussex netball club to train. Separate stables on the periphery of the school – many girls own horses and love to ride at weekends. Active Duke of Edinburgh Award scheme, with the school being perfectly placed for such ventures amongst the Downs.

Music is crucial for the head as she develops more ensembles, string groups, orchestra, a harpist, an emerging flute group and, bearing in mind the size of the school, this is some achievement. Art is a big strength – pupils' work adorns every available nook and cranny and is housed in a long light studio with some exciting textiles on display. Offers the unendorsed GCSE course that includes digital photography, printing, some sculpting. Fine art and textiles but no food technology nor DT. They make good use of the neighbouring Pallant House gallery for visits and workshops and are introducing an integrated arts evening in the summer terms – a production of varying scenes performed around the lovely grounds, particularly the orchard, to include the music, art and drama department. Many girls take GCSE drama – not many performances, however, as teacher feels drama should be more about process than performance. Abundant trips to, e.g., nearby Goodwood House, Fishbourne and Bignor Roman villas, Chichester Theatre, plus trips to Auschwitz, Flanders battlefields. Year 9 spends a week off timetable exploring the tunnels, cellars, roof spaces and ice house of Lavant House and plenty of camp outs at school.

Background and Atmosphere: A former large country house – Dora Green founded the school in 1952 originally for her own children, one of whom is still on the board of governors. The main building is a mix of flint and 18th century red brick with spacious rooms and well-tended grounds. Additions of studios, a cottage, the Scott Building, named after the last headmistress, and multi-purpose large hall merge well with surroundings. The school is approached on a long path surrounded and cushioned by the Sussex Downs and fields of horses and stables. A long terrace to the rear provides a safe and pleasant place for afternoon teas and evening barbeques. Teachers love teaching here, and why wouldn't you? The deputy head was internally appointed six years ago and has been at the school since 1980.

Presently twenty boarders housed in the eaves of the main house; rooms are cosy, fastidiously tidy, with some unattractive wall colours, although apparently chosen by the girls themselves. Flexi-boarding is very popular – plenty of beds to cope. Accommodation ranges from single rooms to dormitories of seven for those that like company. Four sixth form boarders who have their own small cottage in the grounds – individual rooms with a small sitting room and kitchen. Plenty of activities and outings for the boarders; the head of boarding is also, very usefully, PE trained and thus sets up stool ball, swimming, croquet, rounders etc. A safe path that the girls can ride their bikes down to West Wittering beach – the stuff childhood memories are made of. Food is good with a daily large salad bar, vegetarian and dish of the day. Warm family feel throughout the school.

This is an established school, grounded in Christian values – a traditional grace said before lunch. To some this may be non-PC but the head is unapologetic, 'as this is what our school represents'.

Pastoral Care and Discipline: Head of pastoral care is also the head of art and says the care is about constant communication with the nurse, counsellor, matron, staff and parents – 'The most important thing is that the staff are approachable, so that any girl can talk through a problem'. Discipline is not a problem – 'No teacher needs to raise their voice here: a raised eyebrow is enough,' said one parent.

Pupils and Parents: A broad social mix described by one as 'ranging from the country wellies to the Gucci brigade'. One parent chose the school after bumping into a group in the Chichester Theatre car park – 'The school minibus arrived, the girls disembarked and we found ourselves walking into the theatre with them. We noticed how well they conducted themselves and how very appropriately dressed they were, not very made-up but an assured and classy set of girls – an encounter of more value than all the marketing'. Another parent chose the school because of the amount of back-up literature and details of events etc sent to them after their visit, keeping them totally in the loop: 'They were too attentive to be resisted'. The girls mix well and feel they are very supported and not inhibited from being themselves. 'It's cool to be clever or not,' say some girls. Day girls come from a radius of twenty miles, boarders further afield, some Services children and small handful of overseas boarders, mainly from France and Spain and presently two Chinese.

Entrance: Pupils can and do join at various stages, mainly 11 and 13. Formal assessments in maths, English, NVR (11+) and science (13+). Entry to the sixth form is dependent on GCSE results (the fact that the school does not stipulate specifics here indicates flexibility).

Exit: More now stay on to the sixth form and then to diverse destinations: a few Russell Group universities, English and classics at Leeds, medicine at Peninsular, a few study art and design, law at Middlesex, nutrition, business in Hong Kong and some take a gap year. Links with an Australian independent girls' school, Abbotsleigh – exchanges after sixth form (the girls' rooms overlook Sydney Harbour).

Money Matters: Music and academic scholarships at 11 and 13. One fully funded place for year 10 and Year 11 based on academic merit and parents' financial situation.

Remarks: Small size of this school its huge strength – very flexible in accommodating individual pupils' needs. It can cope with the academically able, although that is not its raison d'être. You can rely on good manners, integrity and the well roundedness of these girls.

Leighton Park School

Shinfield Road, Reading, Berkshire, RG2 7EE

• Pupils: 505 girls and boys; 140 board • Ages: 11-18 • Size of sixth form: 140 • Quaker (all faiths welcomed) • Fees: Boarding £23,220-£26,430; Day £17,328 pa • Independent

Tel: 0118 987 9600
Fax: 01189 879 625
Email: admissions@leightonpark.com
Website: www.leightonpark.com

Head: Since 1996, Mr John Dunston MA AICL FRSA (fifties), grew up within earshot of Wembley stadium, then to Selwyn College, Cambridge where he read modern languages, followed by PGCE at York. Early career at Pate's GS, Cheltenham, then Bancroft's, Essex before becoming first Jewish head of a Quaker school (Sibford in 1990 – where parents 'rated him highly'). Firm supporter of Quaker education – 'They offer spirituality without the dogma,' he asserts and feels 'that their time has come again'. Has overseen period of considerable diversification and expansion at LP. Parents describe him as 'approachable and receptive'. Takes a genuine interest in every pupil. Wife teaches at a local prep, two children (both at LP). Called 'John' by pupils – reflects Quaker belief in equal worth of all. Has been a JP, chairman of SHMIS (Leighton Park was first HMC school to join) and was awarded a Winston Churchill travelling scholarship to work with choirs and conservatoires in China. A Liveryman of the

Musicians' Company – has accompanied school choir and orchestra on USA, Prague and Italy tours (sings baritone and even appeared on 'Top of the Pops' in early seventies). A fervent supporter of Reading FC but otherwise every inch a headmaster.

Academic matters: In 2010, 70 per cent A*/B grades at A level. Twenty-three subjects on offer. Almost half A level students take maths, about a third physics or chemistry – extensive labs with separate wet and dry areas. Head of science spent years in industry and encourages pupils to use science as a route to any career. Sciences taught separately as three subjects. History and politics both popular. New multi-media languages centre opened in 2005, followed by well appointed but architecturally incongruous maths building in 2007. Great workshop space for DT – popular at GCSE; some continue to A level. No food studies (shame) or textiles (some included in art syllabus). Fortnightly timetable and fifty-five minute lessons. Class sizes across school average 15 (often smaller in sixth form). Boys perform as well as girls despite national trends. 99 per cent achieved five or more A*- C grades at GCSE, with 53 per cent at A*/A. Pupils averaged nine passes each. School launched IB as an alternative sixth form syllabus in September 2009. Religious studies (called 'beliefs and values') includes philosophy of Quakerism.

Pupils love individual learning centre (mainly for dyslexia) with highly skilled and friendly staff (two f/t and four p/t). 'Not a soft option,' says SENCo, who looks after ninety or so pupils. 'Most of them wouldn't hit radar in other schools,' she confides to us. Range of needs includes Asperger's, dyspraxia, dyscalculia and (currently) two visually impaired.

Games, Options, the Arts: An impressive list of county athletes, runners, hockey, netball and rugby players – 'We punch above our weight,' says head of PE. A rugby and hockey South Africa tour in 2007 made time for bush excursions and ocean safaris, as well as visiting a township school. Floodlit Astroturf and beautiful games pitches – space for 400 metre athletics track in summer. HOD adds, 'When we play we want to win,' but is adamant that 'how you deal with winning is more important'. Recent individual successes include rowing, cycling, ice dancing, swimming and world-class sailing. Parents are pleased with way that sport has come of age at LP in recent years. Walled area provides sheltered netball or tennis courts. Super 25 metre indoor pool 'boosts confidence' of many tentative swimmers; more than adequate gym but sports hall is on the wish list. Wide choice of hobbies: ceramics, debating, good causes, Duke of Edinburgh (some take gold), photography, textiles, plus wide choice of sports and musical groups. Young Enterprise is an ambitious throng.

Music area (linked to main hall) is currently being expanded. Over half school learn a musical instrument – from beginners to grade 8 and occasionally diploma level. Huge range of ensembles and groups with loads of opportunity to perform at regular concerts. Choir and orchestra tour Europe regularly, recently to Sweden and Denmark. Talented jazz musicians have made impressive 'Liquid Silk' CD. We watched Year 7 music class sharing own compositions and opinions; we liked the way the music teacher prefaced his own observations by, 'Shall I tell you ... ?' – authority is not taken for granted here. Pupils practise hard before school/in lunch hour/evenings. New music technology studio and mobile 'Music Mac' trolley very popular – 25 Applemacs armed with software such as 'Garageband' for composition. Annual house music competition an annual highlight of gladatorial proportions.

Great stress laid on aesthetics at LP – ranch-like art studios provide more creative space than in most schools this size. Separate gallery to exhibit home grown talent; artist in residence works closely with pupils. Drama uses studio in adapted (former) squash court and theatre style concert hall. We watched thirty Year 11 pupils preparing nine GCSE drama presentations on the day we visited. Two major productions a year with bi-annual musical (recently 'Grease' and 'Under Milk Wood'). Pupils ooze talent (some already acting professionally).

Masses of cultural exchanges – recently with a lycée in Nantes; Barcelona, Hamburg, and joint ventures with other Quaker schools. Trips galore – when we visited some pupils had just returned from a joint English and geography expedition to 1st World War battlefields and others were going skiing in the USA. Adventure training trips recently include Ecuador (senior students) and Pembrokeshire (Year 8) plus Ladakh in 2008, skiing in Canada and Pembrokeshire (Year 8). Sixth form bi-annual cultural trip (Russia 2008, China 2006). 'Sixth Special' on Friday afternoons welcomes a range of speakers. 'Litebytes' enhancement programme for sixth includes critical thinking, Mandarin and dance. Amnesty group; sixth formers get to attend Quaker events hosted by school, e.g. peace conferences organised by Forgiveness Project (Martin Bell and Jill Hicks were recent participants). Close link with Penn Charter (Quaker) school in America and Friends' School, Hobart, Tasmania.

Background and Atmosphere: Quaker ideals permeate LP – first name terms throughout emphasise equal worth of all; unexpected moments of stillness during day – we experienced this at 'Collect' (the morning assembly) and, remarkably, twice during lunch. At weekly 'meeting for worship' silence is longer. Worship is not 'led' but anyone can 'witness' (or speak out their inner feelings) – this sometimes leads to poignant and emotional moments, felt individually and collectively. Younger pupils 'find silences difficult at first' but soon latch on. Older pupils speak movingly of how the Quaker ethos has made a deep and lasting impression. Sixty acres of parkland (as school name suggests) – a welcome oasis of greenery; calm and (mainly) gracious buildings provide a welcome change from Reading's maze of tarmac, cheek by jowl with the University of Reading, close to M4 corridor and Heathrow. Some areas of meadowland and a lovely natural pond help create a rural feel on hot summer days. Keen eco school (bronze award) and in partnership with local state schools; 'Save the Planet' group active and inspired by one year 'ecologist in residence' (appropriately clad in green when we met her).

Not as old as some other Quaker schools, LP began as a public school in 1890 with the specific intention of educating scholars for Oxbridge. Nicknamed 'the Quaker Eton' at the time, it still has style but in a modern, forward thinking kind of way. Current improvements are enabling planned expansion to a maximum of 510 pupils. The 'old school' is a fine Georgian building with a gracious reception area; outside, a small lawn and ha ha date from its origins.

All boarding houses now adapted for co-education and former dining areas converted into enviable recreation spaces. Some areas of school have a 'collegiate' feel whilst others are futuristic. Fryer House (where 11–13 year olds live) has retained in-house eating for breakfast and supper. A lively, warm environment with lots of space for recreation/prep/outdoor activities housed in a self-contained building. New (2006) sixth form centre – The Caradon Centre – with areas for IT, study and relaxation as well as kitchen and meeting rooms plus own garden. Careers also based here – school uses ISCO's all-in package with pupils going on university taster days, conferences etc.Circular dining facility – very trendy 'Oakview', offering wide and healthy choice of meals for the whole school community (breakfast, lunch and tea) plus sixth form café. 'Soups are finest in the land,' claimed one teacher. Library to die for on top floor of old school with themed, artful displays prepared by a librarian who lives to make people want to go in there and read.

School regularly hosts visits by authors, some being Berkshire Library book events. Head proud of Radio 4 broadcast in BBC 'Sunday Worship' to 1.75 million people worldwide – BBC and listeners (judging from postbag afterwards) greatly impressed but Auntie 'found managing the silences a challenge,' chuckled head.

Pastoral Care and Discipline: 'Anyone can fit in,' say pupils. Hasn't abolished corporal punishment – it was never introduced in the first place. 'Pupils here learn about self-discipline,' says head and a mum praised how school manages to create a 'sense of responsibility between the pupils'. All belong to either Fryer (junior) or one of four senior houses. Lovely environment for juniors (Fryer started life as a children's sanatorium) and has 'home from home' feel despite smell of floor polish. Kitchenettes in all houses where pupils 'learn to provide for themselves' from an early age. Pupils raise loads of money for charity, led by active 'Good Causes' committee – e.g. 'Ray of Sunshine' for seriously ill children or currently a community in Malawi. Flexi-boarding ('cheaper than a babysitter') available on request – many pupils sleep over once or twice a week. Facilities for day pupils and boarders in each house – improve as pupils move up school. Not much division between day pupils and the rest – many stay for evening meal and supervised prep if required. All pupils participate in residential week of team building/adventure training.

Anyone bringing drugs onto premises permanently excluded. Alcohol is banned. Head boy and girl chair monthly school council meetings. Pupils like the way staff don't impose beliefs but 'accept pupils for who we are'. Sick bays in each house plus 24 hour medical cover at health centre; separate room where school counsellor visits two half days per week. Well established and highly rated pupil mentoring scheme.

Pupils and Parents: Parents often from IT plus lawyers, business and university types. Head says, 'Parents are articulating need for something more from a school than good exam results.' All major faiths represented here. 20 per cent from overseas and a sprinkle of expats but mainly from Berkshire, Oxfordshire, north Hampshire and Bucks. Only five per cent of pupils Quaker. Youngest pupils have uniform (with symbolic oak leaf emblem on jumper); 'collect dress' for middle years and 'business dress' for sixth form 'allows pupils to express some individuality,' claimed head, but we weren't totally convinced.

Parents love the fact that 'pupils make friends across the age groups, unlike at many other schools'. Lots of day pupils choose to have breakfast and supper (no extra charge) at school. 'My friends can't work out why I choose to spend so much of my spare time at LP ... but I just love it here,' beamed one Year 11 girl. No Saturday lessons – so many of the boarders are weekly – hence exodus on Friday nights, though much to do for those remaining. Long standing link with German school provides trickle of Teutonic one-termers.

Old Leightonians: Sir David Lean, Sir Richard Rodney Bennett, Jim Broadbent, Michael Foot, Lord Caradon, Lord Frederick Seebohm (who reformed social services) and a fair clutch of MPs, Rowntrees, Cadburys, Clarks, Reckitts, Morlands and Frys.

Entrance: Tests January following entrance for Years 7–10 (though alternative dates can be set if needed); tests in maths, English, non-verbal reasoning. Pupils chosen on previous report, interview and reference from current head. Mostly Common Entrance for Year 9. At sixth form about 35 enter from outside with at least six A-Cs with A*–B grades in chosen subjects (A/A* for maths). Large number of feeder preps and primaries in Reading and wider area. Overseas pupils from about twenty countries, including USA, China, Australia, Europe.

Exit: Most to universities (often getting firsts). About twenty per cent take a gap year. A few leave at 16 for sixth form colleges. One or two annually to Oxbridge; wide range of other universities and specialist colleges, conservatoires etc.

Money Matters: Several major and minor awards for art, music and sport. Means tested bursaries. Friends' schools' bursaries given to those with Quaker parents. David Lean Foundation awards one annual scholarship for 100 per cent of day fees, for academic excellence.

Remarks: Many schools vaunt their 'special atmosphere' but at LP it's tangible. No room for hypocrites (staff or pupils) here. One of the most distinctive schools we've visited – it gave us a renewed sense of hope for the future. More schools would do well to adopt the LP model – it has 'integrity and honesty at heart'.

Lenzie Academy

Myrtle Avenue, Kirkintilloch, Lenzie, East Dunbartonshire, G66 4HR

• Pupils: 1,350 boys and girls (50/50 split); all day • Ages: 11-18 • Size of sixth form: 415 • Non-denom • State

Tel: 0141 955 2379
Fax: 0141 777 8121
Email: office@lenzieacademy.e-dunbarton.sch.uk
Website: www.lenzieacademy.e-dunbarton.sch.uk

Rector: Since 1997, Mr Roderick (Roddy) McLelland BSc PGCE (fifties), who first came to the school as head of maths in 1985 and was previously assistant rector. He started his teaching career at Paisley Grammar, followed by five years at Williamwood High. Educated at John Neilson Institution in Paisley, studied maths at University of Strathclyde and did his PGCE at Jordanhill College of Education. Married with three children, two of whom have now graduated; his daughter is at university in Glasgow and his wife is a principal teacher of pupil support.

A pro-active, open door head, friendly and helpful, but very much an iron fist in a velvet glove – were the charming, articulate pupils who had recently won the YE local final, and were due to appear in Edinburgh shortly, who came to borrow the trophies, primed? We think not – the encounter was too relaxed and natural. He runs the school with a management team of six whom we met for coffee – much talk of chocolate biscuits, each contribution examined with obvious delight, and much use of walkie talkies to keep in contact throughout the day. Head keen for pupils to enter as many competitions and extra-curricular activities as possible, lots of celebrations of achievements of citizenship. A rector who believes in carrots rather than sticks – impressive. This is a school moving as one.

Academic matters: Max class size currently 30 in S1/S2, with 20 for practical classes, English and maths. A number of new heads of departments appointed recently – no problems with getting top class staff. Huge range of Standard Grades on offer; three sciences. Good take up of French and German, impressive variety of foreign exchanges at junior level and two week European work experience placements for older pupils in 5th and 6th years. Standard Grades the norm, but Intermediates available too, 18 Advanced Highers on offer, 23 Highers: subjects include tourism, food technology (looked and smelled delicious), photography and dance – all the usual suspects found in some, but by no means all, of the top end of the independent sector.

A magnet school – pupils from other (state) schools come to Lenzie to study Highers not available in their own schools. Stunning computer studies results at all levels, geography is also particularly strong ('progressive,' says the rector), interactive whiteboards much used. Good use, too, of the eight computer suites, for teaching as well as IT. Psychology is taught by distance learning – the SCHOLAR programme, provided by Heriot Watt University. Maths results strong across the board, school makes much use of the Glasgow Maths Association lectures and joins with Strathclyde both for maths and using their biology lab for DNA work. 'Welcome Host' customer service course.

Dedicated special needs team, (this is an inclusive school) with half a dozen profoundly deaf children happily integrated, some of them with special interpreters who sit in class with them. (The East Dunbartonshire Council Sensory Service was relocated here some six years ago.) Over 100 pupils do not have English as their first language and extra help is available. Homework club at lunch time and supported study classes post school – 200 pupils regularly stay on – when pupils can access the ICT suites. Smashing library, with roll of shame for sixth formers who have overstayed their allotted book time; computers, too, and pupils have a say in what books are stocked. Altogether a superb set up.

Games, Options, the Arts: Sports hall built eight years ago, not quite as big as anticipated – a top floor was on the original plan – but financial constraints meant that this stunning building is perhaps not as versatile as anticipated. Sports facilities are 'slightly limited' but good links with local sports clubs; rugby, football, volleyball, plus hockey, athletics, cross-country, and regular trips abroad, with a fund to help those who couldn't otherwise afford it. Basketball, golf, dance, sailing – they win races even though the school has no boat.

Jolly art rooms but no great airy windowed space to paint in, though good and interesting work. 'Strong art and design,' says the rector, with pupils entering local competitions; ceramics as well as flat art. Good computer interaction, CAD available and nice line in CDT. Drama extra-curricular and post school; the school competes successfully in national competitions, but music highly integrated with huge department on top of the new wing, good representation in the West of Scotland youth orchestra, lots of little bands and excellent and exciting concerts, the Christmas concert particularly popular. Good jazz, keen public speaking, superb YE – since pre Jamie Oliver they have had a healthy food tuck shop (bottled water and nutrigrain bars). Clubs post school and at lunchtime for everything, chess popular plus maths, debating and sport, fashion shows. Staff stay on unpaid. Tremendous charity input – £10,000 a year for Children in Need (wow!) plus Comic Relief and other appeals. Keen on World Challenge: Australia, Ecuador, Costa Rica, loads of fund raising and good for self-sufficiency.

Background and Atmosphere: Founded in 1886 as Lenzie Academy, originally a private school started by Donald McQuarrie, based in what is now the primary school on the main street, and moved to the current site nearby in 1960s. Surrounded by mixed housing, Victorian villas around a large housing estate and games pitches. Good, wide corridors in all but the latest wing, where a one-way system has been installed. Uniform de rigueur, but some slightly surprising hair styles amongst the male of the species. Effective school council – year groups meet with staff and raise matters of concern (hence the padlocked lockers for each student), vibrant interactive house competitions, regular school assemblies. New build includes provision for the disabled, fabulous social areas – including dedicated area for S6 and new dining facilities.

Pastoral Care and Discipline: Strong and effective PSE, a school with zero tolerance for bullying and abusive behaviour. A number of exclusions but pupils know where they stand. Permanent exclusions are rare, though the occasional parent prefers to remove their offspring rather than have them excluded – perhaps one every two or three years. Sixth year pupils act as mentors for younger ones, helping with reading and dealing with minor bullying issues – they receive training from Childline.

Pupils and Parents: Loads of professionals. Decent middle class ethos prevails, mass from Glasgow, universities and local hospitals, with a fair number of ethnic minorities. In 'Mirror'-speak this is leafy Lenzie; school has four dedicated primary schools but currently takes pupils from over 30 primaries and regularly has over 500 placement requests. Pupils come from nearby Glasgow, Bishopbriggs, East Dunbartonshire, North Lanarkshire (the train station is handy). Very supportive parent council.

Entrance: Either automatic from dedicated primaries or by placement requests. School has strong links with local primaries; SEN staff and guidance staff spend time at the primaries during the summer terms. Every pupil coming to the school receives a letter of introduction from a current first year pupil telling them what it is like. Incoming pupils spend a three day induction period in the school following a specimen timetable.

Exit: Some leave post Standard Grades, some, but not a lot, arrive. Sixth form visit the Glasgow careers forum, 65 per cent or so to universities, more to FE colleges, and a regular trickle of three or four to Oxbridge – a local seminar for senior students.

Remarks: Smashing school, academically and socially strong, but some areas could do with a makeover.

The Leventhorpe School

Cambridge Road, Sawbridgeworth, Hertfordshire, CM21 9BY

• Pupils: 1,150; boys and girls; all day • Ages: 11-19 • Size of sixth form: 355 • Non-denom • State

Tel: 01279 836633
Fax: 01279 600339
Email: education@leventhorpe.net
Website: www.leventhorpe.net

Head: Since 2008, Mr Jonathan Locke (forties), degree in maths from the University of Wales and PGCE from Cambridge. A keen rugby player forced to retire through injury, he now spends his free time running and cycling but also enjoys relaxing trips to France with his language teacher wife Celine and their two young children. A natural communicator, he believes that, 'Whenever you make a decision it's impossible to see it from every perspective – someone's opinion always hits you from left field, so that's why it's important to speak to as many people as possible to make sure all opinions are taken into account'. To that end he's 'freely available and very approachable to parents and children,' says one parent, and hosts a listening lunch every month to sound out the staff on new developments, gripes and suggestions. Another parent comments, 'He holds discipline and achievement high on his agenda but encourages all aspects of a young person's development.' His positive approach to education is certainly infectious, and his efforts to ease the curriculum into a more pupil-centric way of thinking have been very well received.

Academic matters: SATs results determine setting for new Year 7s in English, maths and languages, and these are checked up on throughout the first two years – 'It's fluid,' says head. Year 9 is an 'enrichment year' with pupils offered a broad choice of subjects: additional literature in English, experiments in sciences plus a vocational option, PE theory, philosophy, sociology – refined when the time comes for GCSE option decisions. A very wide selection of subject options at GCSE – some clever timetabling software ensures that 95 per cent are able to study their chosen combination.

Enthusiasm high and reflected in results – around 92 per cent get five A* to Cs at GCSE and A levels hover around the 56 per cent A*/B mark (90 per cent A*/B in English language and psychology also successful). Open University modules can be studied alongside A levels and this – and the fact that the place is buried in computers – typifies the ethos of independent learning. In fact it provides one of the largest school OU cohorts in the country. 'Our aim here is to encourage pupils to take ownership of their education and to develop a sense of responsibility that will transfer to further and higher education and into the workplace,' says the head.

Games, Options, the Arts: Land sales financed the striking and badly needed new building – to be completed in spring 2011 – which will house a sports hall with a dance studio and fitness suite. In spite of its previous lack of good facilities, does well on the sports field and makes the most of close ties with the local cricket and rugby clubs.

Music facilities are 'reasonable,' says the head rather generously, but even so music is thriving: 300 students have lessons, a school orchestra and a choir that goes on tour every few years – the staff choir shows the way. Musical aptitude places are available to a handful of year sevens from out of the area, and free lessons encourage them to develop their talent. A few go on to music college each year.

The art rooms are hives of colourful activity and the annual fashion show gives young designers the chance to strut the catwalk in their own creations. The expanded sixth form provides a pool of leaders for activities: they have revived the Student Council themselves and take it very seriously, recently having the casting vote on the restructuring of the school day.

Background and Atmosphere: A collection of rather plain 1960s buildings – has the advantage, though, of being nearly all single-storey with wide sunlit corridors and classrooms off. This makes for an easily navigable, light and airy school with few bottlenecks and plenty of space for displays. Being set back from the main road just on the edge of this small town and backing onto playing fields and farmland, it has a tranquil, rural aspect.

Well resourced by state standards – impressive ICT suite with pop-up monitors and a face-recognition registration system in the sixth form block, for instance. Food technology on the way back with the completion of kitchens.

Although this is a sizeable secondary and pupils come from a scattering of villages on both sides of the Herts-Essex border, it has a small-town community spirit. Pupils seem proud of their school and coming here is generally a given – 'Why go anywhere else?' asked one pupil in bafflement. Uniform is fairly traditional – blazers and white shirts with a kilt for girls and plain trousers for boys, sixth formers smart in business wear with suits for both and ties for the guys. The overriding impression is one of purposeful industry – and smiling faces all round.

Pastoral Care and Discipline: House system is all-pervading and trumpeted through distinctive ties for boys, the house name embroidered on gtirls' shirts and coloured blazer badges. Pastoral care is funnelled through the tutor and head of house, and sixth form mentors look out for Year 7–11 students. As well as inter-house competitions, achievement in the classroom is rewarded with points for the house and the totals are eyed with enthusiasm. Celebration of success is key – the new Headteacher's Commendations are listed every fortnight in the school newsletter and achievements of both pupils and staff are highlighted. 'It's through rewards that behaviour can be modified, not through sanctions,' says the head, but is quick to point out that the school has very few problems with discipline and pupils on the whole are purposeful and law-abiding.

Except in the case of major misdemeanours, exclusion is eschewed in favour of 'inclusion' – a day spent working under adult supervision in isolation on school premises: 'A day at home can be seen as a reward,' says Mr Locke. Minor transgressions are dealt with by tutors. Although mobile phones may be brought to school, using one in lesson time leads to confiscation and a call to a parent to collect the offending item from Mr Locke himself. Bullying is dealt with effectively – the heads of school run a listening panel of senior prefects and trained student counsellors to support any pupil who feels they might be affected. No exclusions this year and the Thursday after school detention session is the only one – generally fewer than a dozen children in it.

Pupils and Parents: Since the arrival of Mr Locke, parents have appreciated being kept in the loop with increased school-home communication and a constant dialogue. Pupils are dispatched with PDAs to canvas opinions at parents' evenings. Feedback informs school policy: 'If a parent posts a message via the school website saying that they think standards of appearance are going downhill, we post a teacher on the gate to check uniform the following Monday morning'. Parents generally appreciative – an interactive revision night, when parents and pupils were instructed by three key subject teachers on revision techniques and useful websites, was singled out for praise.

Entrance: Children from eight feeder primary schools in Sawbridgeworth and the surrounding villages – usually a place for every child in the catchment who wants one. 16 places for children with musical aptitude from outside the catchment, who sit a standardised test in common with other good state schools in the local area, and are then encouraged and often financially supported in their musical endeavours.

Scraps over good sixth form students with sixth forms in Bishop's Stortford and Harlow: two Bs and three Cs, including at least a C in maths and English at GCSE, needed to get in.

Exit: After Year 11 nearly all move on to own sixth form, which has ballooned of late from 200 to 350 due, says the head, to 'good marketing and fantastic results'. All who want to go to university do, although not always to their first choice. Three to Oxbridge for the past few years and medicine and dentistry successes are picking up. 'They don't just want students with a string of A*s,' points out the head. 'It's their ability to conduct themselves and communicate, and that's what our curriculum develops for everyone.' A strong link with the head's alma mater, Cambridge, with good preparation and support for those anticipated to make the cut.

Remarks: A very businesslike establishment with a forward-thinking head who seems likely to take it to greater heights. An innate sense of community – pupils take pride in themselves and their school.

Leweston School

Sherborne, Dorset, DT9 6EN

• Pupils: 240 girls; 110 boarders (full and weekly) plus up to 20 flexi • Ages: 11-18; plus co-ed prep on site for ages 2.5-11 (girls may board from Year 3 • Size of sixth form: 70 • RC - but the majority are other denominations • Fees: Boarding £17,385-£23,625; Day £14,655-£15,270 pa • Independent

Tel: 01963 211 010
Fax: 01963 211 080
Email: admissions@leweston.dorset.sch.uk
Website: www.leweston.co.uk

Headmaster: Since 2006, Mr Adrian Aylward (forties), former headmaster of Stonyhurst. Educated at Worth and Oxford, where he read classics. Spent ten years in the City and industry, becoming MD of a plc before entering education – parents see evidence of this practical business background in his running of the school. Likes to spend rare moments of free time fishing. Wife Caroline participates in the artistic and musical life of the school and has started a prayer group. Three children – two girls at Leweston and a son at Downside.

Academic matters: Hotting up as the school sharpens its focus on exam results. Geography, music and the sciences popular and outstanding most years. 2009 saw the best ever set of GCSE results with 62 per cent of all grades an A or A* (32 per cent A*). A level results have been consistently good for the last few years and 100 per cent of the recent applications to medical and veterinary schools have been accepted. Language results also good, bolstered by native speakers. All year 10s spend eight days in an 18th century French manor house near Caen studying their normal curriculum plus French language and culture. Girls can also take Spanish, German, Italian, plus Latin and Greek. Range of A level subjects wider than you might expect for a small school, including art history, health and social care, psychology, politics. Since September 2008 has offered the new Cambridge Pre-U qualification in music, history, history of art, English lit and 'global perspectives'.

Takes pride in offering almost total flexibility in subject choices ('We create the timetable to work around girls'). GCSE maths and French may be taken early. Many enthusiastic and devoted teachers, beloved by the girls and their parents. Good support for EFL, dyslexia and, the school adds, the gifted and talented. Small classes; lots of 'value added'.

Games, Options, the Arts: Excellent and active music department – over half learning at least one instrument and gets some very good exam and festival results. Stellar A levels too. Top musicians join pupils from other independents in Sherborne for joint Schools' Sinfonia Orchestra. Lots of LAMDA acting and speech exams and racks up much glory at the Mid Somerset Festival of Speech and Drama. Theatre from a bygone era but in very good nick. Sports popular and successful. Cross country going strong: U15 girls are currently the English Schools' Cross Country Cup champions. Much success in horsey pursuits – showjumping and one-day eventing. A girl we spoke to singled out the equestrian team as her favourite thing about the school. Hockey and athletics also triumphant. Fencing club every Wednesday. A good clutch of D of E silvers, bronzes plus one gold last year. Lots of inter-house competitions (theatre, sports). New debating club.

Background and Atmosphere: Well, the name change – dropping the 'St Antony's' – was a surprise, especially to Old Girls, but everyone seems used to it now. Remains a caring, relaxed school founded by the Sisters of Christian Instruction in 1891. Weekly boarding a new and welcome option. 46 acres on a lovely, open site, a three mile drive south of Sherborne through apple orchards and country air tinged with the scent of manure. The grounds offer a warren of wild paths through splendid nature. An ethereal calm pervades with, sometimes, a feeling of a few girls knocking around a huge site. Peaceful – perhaps not the place for a girl who suffers from agoraphobia. Never famed for its architectural coherence, today an astounding jumble of discordant styles. But once the shock has worn off, it is possible to appreciate the floodlit all-weather pitch, lovely DT, art, jewellery, cookery and ceramics rooms, science labs, sports hall, outdoor pool, terrific health centre and new cavernous library. Attractive, bright new dining room with loads of fruit and hypnotising conveyor belt for trays. Cosy common rooms for different year groups – a nice touch. Three prefab classroom blocks are an eyesore (cold in the morning and hot in the afternoon, say girls) but school has launched £2m appeal to replace them and in the first year has raised a very healthy £600,000.

The era of Sherborne School partnering both Sherborne School for Girls and Leweston in merry bigamy seems to be coming to a close, as the two Sherborne schools snuggle up together (joint marketing, bursaries, sixth forms, IB – 'as if Leweston doesn't exist!'). Accordingly, Leweston is working to raise its profile and runs joint school trips with other boys' schools, including Winchester and Milton Abbey.

New director of boarding has 'transformed' the boarding with new structure and staffing in the boarding house, plus much improvement of the facilities. He also introduced weekly boarding – boarding numbers up 10 per cent year on year since he has arrived. Dormitories outstandingly tidy and pleasant – maximum six to a room to start with, gradually working up to singles by sixth form. Money has been spent on sixth form accommodation: now a kitchen and laundry and internet provision in every study bedroom. Mr Aylward says the school has strengthened its commitment to academics, boarding and spirituality.

Pastoral Care and Discipline: More noticeable emphasis on RC foundation than previously. Head, who is chairman of the Catholic Independent Schools' Conference, says the student body is 40 per cent RC (30 per cent was quoted last time we visited). Has established chaplaincy team and a lecture series open to the outside community with subjects like 'Was Shakespeare a Catholic?' The girls are well cared for, feminine, outdoorsy, well-mannered. School says the sixth form now has more responsibility for school administration and discipline. Pupils may go into Sherborne town in the afternoons (minibus takes them once a week, taxis available other days). Upper sixth may visit the Sherborne School bar.

Pupils and Parents: Mostly local (school says, 'or regional' – they come from up to 80 miles away); a few from London. Virtually all the girls from the school's own prep come up to the main school where they are joined by pupils from All Hallows, Sunninghill, Knighton House, Perrot Hill, Hazlegrove, Farleigh, Kensington Prep. 15 per cent from overseas, many from Spain, Mexico, China. Parents like the mixed ability range – 'Nice', said a mum, 'and very Christian'. Numbers slightly down: a question mark hovers over whether enough young ladies exist to fill the surfeit of girls' boarding schools in the vicinity. School points out that registrations for future years, open mornings, taster days etc are all up, so things are heading in the right direction. Old girls: actress Kristin Scott Thomas, novelist and radical anti-feminist Erin Pizzey, Serena De La Hey, artist and creator of the West Country's 'Wicker Man', BBC producer Anuschka de Rohan.

Entrance: Mainly at 11, 13 and 16 but girls can enter intervening years as well. Entrance is via CE, scholarship exam or school's own entrance test.

Exit: Majority to university – London, Bristol, Warwick, Cardiff, Exeter, Durham. Business, administration, hotel management etc popular, but the spread of subjects is wide. Some to art foundation courses.

Money Matters: Scholarships offered at 11, 12 and 13 for art, drama, music, PE, sport and academics. Sixth form scholarships offered in the same.

Remarks: Caring school, quietly bringing out the best in its pupils. 'We chose it because the girls can climb trees and run around barefoot after school,' said a parent. 'They are allowed to be children.'

The Leys School

Linked to Saint Faith's School in the Junior section

Trumpington Road, Cambridge, Cambridgeshire, CB2 7AD

• Pupils: 560; 335 boys, 225 girls (370 boarders, 190 day) • Ages: 11-18, plus associated prep St Faith's 4-13 • Size of sixth form: 180 • Methodist/ inter-denom • Fees: Boarding £18,495-£25,410; Day £12,060-£16,905 pa • Independent

Tel: 01223 508 904
Fax: 01223 505 303
Email: admissions@theleys.net
Website: www.theleys.net

Head: Since 2004, Mr Mark Slater MA (early fifties), two daughters and faithful dog. Read modern languages at St Edmund Hall Oxford. Taught at Lord Wandsworth School and Wellington before headship at St Lawrence Ramsgate.

Polished and urbane, has tightened things up since taking over. 'Lots of minor changes and tiny tweaks that have made a difference,' commented one parent – 'especially the work ethic and uniform.' Likes to keep contact with the children in the classroom particularly the younger ones – he teaches French to Year 9s. Hot on pastoral care – the happiness and security of the pupils are top of his agenda. All lower sixth, Years 11 and 9 get to have lunch with him in groups of five or six at least twice a year – he says it gives a barometer on issues within the school.

Seen at most events and, when time, likes walking, skiing and playing tennis.

Academic matters: Traditionally middling but in recent years results have steadily improved. 65-ish per cent A/A* at GCSE – vast majority take separate sciences, physical ed (pupils see it as a big plus that it can be taken regardless of other options) and religious studies (compulsory) taken in year 10. 80 per cent A/B at A level – strong results from maths, physics, economics, geography and history. Sets for maths, languages and sciences.

According to parents, a good selection of teachers (mixed bag from the mature to young sporty South Africans and Australians who come for a couple of years). They 'keep an eye on what's going on and make sure that the children achieve as much as possible'.

School doesn't flaunt its SEN credentials (dedicated department with three staff, one full-time) but garden variety learning disabilities well supported in a low tech way (do own up to known problems well in advance – the school's literature is a bit threatening on this point). As the head said, 'Extreme cases wouldn't survive here.'

Games, Options, the Arts: Games (compulsory three afternoons a week, also offered after lessons) are important and popular – a common response from the kids is that they're 'the best thing' about school. Caters for all sorts – 'Those who aren't sporty aren't sidelined'. Plenty of flexibility, flourishing minor sports and the not so brilliant put into a less competitive sets. 'Lots of teachers on the sidelines at matches joining in and doing their bit,' commented one parent. Results for the major sports aren't always in the top drawer but girls' hockey lower down the school is doing well. School participates in the Cambridge University Leagues for some sports and gifted athletes are assured of top level competition. Swimming and rowing are strong. Top notch facilities are an attraction – first class sports hall (shared with local sports clubs), floodlit Astroturf hockey pitch (converts into twelve tennis courts in the summer), rowing from own boatyard on the Cam.

The bright and inviting Rugg Centre houses DT, art, photography and ceramics. Music department, now in the smart, well equipped music school, runs a large orchestra, string groups, choir and parents' singing group. LAMDA exams are taken with plenty of success – three pupils recently gained national communication and performance awards: justified crowing here as only ten are given each year. Masses of school trips and all sorts of events during the year including a specialist literature group which brings in authors to talk to the kids and get them fired up about reading – 'Above and beyond what would be expected,' enthused one parent.

Background and Atmosphere: Opened in central Cambridge in 1875 with 16 Methodist boys. Red-brick Gothic buildings, modern additions, sporting facilities and a dotty miniature railway (with several halts) ring central playing fields. With additional games fields nearby the school has an ample 50 acres. Went co-ed in 1994 and maintains a roughly 60:40 boy/girl split. Pupils can be boarders (the majority), home boarders (at school for all but breakfast and sleep – the best of both worlds according to several) or day pupils (home by 6pm).

Still a relatively small school with a friendly atmosphere and strong sense of community. Open, approachable house staff (some with babes and buggies) underline the family feel. NB Home boarding carries the distinct advantage of being able to return home after Cambridge rush hour, but only available from age 13. Girls' boarding rooms (much nicer than boys' – as usual) housed in a modern block with balconies for sunbathing and plants.

Kids are trusted to go off into town from an early age and are good about getting back in time. Bikes are allowed (some houses have house bikes which can be borrowed) – 'We can get into town more quickly'. Sixth form club open every evening after 9pm for an hour or so – limit of two pints a night or two glasses of wine: 'Not so good,' according to one sixth form connoisseur (no surprise, at 50p a glass). The head has listened to suggestions from the pupils – town time has been marginally increased and snacks have been provided for later in the evening.

Standard uniform pre sixth. Mackenzie tartan kilts for the girls hark back to the war when the school was evacuated to Pitlochry. Sensible summer Fred Perry shirts get over the flashing shirt tail but dress code isn't absolutely rigid especially in the sixth. 'Depends who sees you,' said one fifth former.

Pastoral Care and Discipline: Parents and pupils are impressed by the pastoral care – the key to its success is the tutorial system. Each child is treated as an individual and staff 'go out of their way to sort things out'. Small tutor groups and regular emailing between staff, the pupil and their parents ensure all are well informed. The school produces a brilliant information booklet with, amongst other things, details of dozens of Leys parents who are willing to be contacted and grilled mercilessly about the school. Chapel can be up to three times a week – 'The Christian ethos is essential to the ethos of the school,' says the head. The chaplain is 'amazingly supportive in times of need,' reported one parent, but day pupils and home boarders not desperately enthusiastic about having to occasionally attend on a Sunday.

The school maintains an admirable balance between tradition and discipline on the one hand and progressiveness and brotherhood on the other – 'Traditional but not formal,' according to a teacher. Easy going rapport between teachers and pupils. Bullying well handled. Sensible, pragmatic approach to banned substances (not punitive but supportive). The odd expulsion and one or two 'asked to leave' each year.

Pupils and Parents: Hefty 15 per cent international component – mostly in the sixth, a good mix from all over (ESL support available). Ten per cent expat, otherwise UK residents, mainly within a two hour drive of Cambridge. 'A mixed lot – senior professionals, surgeons, people from IT and the City,' said a member of the active PTA. A real push to get parents involved – a parent rep for each house liaises with the housemaster and reports back to the parent body.

Leysians range from the earnest to Cambridge preppy. Self assured and relaxed. 'Seems to produce nice individuals,' said one parent. Known locally as the 'rounded' option (with obvious reference to the highly academic Perse schools up the road). Old boys: Martin Bell, Sir Alastair Burnet, Richard Heffer, mathematician Sir Andrew Wiles, J G Ballard and England cricket captain Freddie Brown.

Entrance: At 11 and 13. High proportion from St Faiths (same foundation), Dame J Bradbury and local preps. Own entrance exam – tightening up here: need to be at least moderately bright with a view to going on to university. For the sixth – usually no fewer than six Bs at GCSE.

Exit: Most day pupils and a few home boarders to excellent, local sixth form colleges at the end of the fifth. Majority of those who remain, or join the sixth, to university, with a fair number taking gap years. London remains the most popular destination, then an even spread across the field. Courses biased towards business and humanities.

Money Matters: Scholarships of up to 15 per cent of fees to great brains at 11, 13 and sixth form entry. Host of other talents considered at 13 and sixth form entry. Some special bursaries to children of Old Leysians and Methodists.

Remarks: Comfortable school with dedicated staff and head who's steering a tighter course. Well rounded kids who flourish as individuals.

Lincoln Minster School

Linked to Lincoln Minster Preparatory School in the Junior section

The Prior Building, Upper Lindum Street, Lincoln, Lincolnshire, LN2 5RW

- Pupils: 770 girls and boys • Ages: 2-18 • Size of sixth form: 145
- Inter-denominational • Fees: Day £10,728+; Boarding £20,760+ pa
- Independent

Tel: 01522 551 300
Fax: 01522 551 310
Email: enquiries.lincoln@church-schools.com
Website: www.lincolnminsterschool.co.uk

Principal: Since 1999, Mr Clive Rickart BA PGCE, previously head of the prep school from 1996, when the United Church Schools Trust merged the Cathedral School for Boys, St Joseph's School for Girls and Stonefield House School. Prior to this was boarding housemaster at Stamford School and head of Oswestry Junior School. His tenure has seen the school grow steadily in terms of pupil numbers and development, with a new £10m music school and a magnificent sports hall opened in June 2010.

Academic matters: A perfect environment for learning. Interactive whiteboards and Activexpression handsets in each classroom, to help students get the very best out of every lesson. Pupils who miss a lesson are able to print off material or access it on the school's network. Science, IT and art facilities are fabulous, some with far reaching views across the Trent Plain. Given that the school is mixed ability, the results are an indication that the school is clearly adding value. At GCSE, an impressive 93 per cent A* to C.

Subjects spread well across the board, with sciences and history popular at A level. 2010 saw record results with 100 per cent pass rate at A level and 50 per cent grades A* to B.

Games, Options, the Arts: Music plays a very large part in the school's curriculum with its close relationship to the Cathedral. The director of music's role is divided between the Cathedral and school, which provides 40 choristers, so the standards are incredibly high, with a number of orchestras, bands and groups making for a busy concert programme. A GCSE express music course for Year 9 pupils which allows them to complete the full course two years early. Drama thriving and taught to A level. All year groups encouraged to take part.

Sports field is a short walk away in Lincoln's conservation area and the new sports hall will no doubt fuel the school's already high standard of team and individual performance. Will go to great lengths to look after an individual talent, e.g. a young swimmer who represented Great Britain at the Beijing Olympics – to fit in with absences for training, he was able to keep up with schoolwork over the internet. Also has riding teams who compete regularly at events across the country. Sailing is offered as an extra-curricular activity; a high level of involvement in the Duke of Edinburgh Award Scheme and a very full outdoor and adventurous programme being augmented this year.

Background and Atmosphere: In the shadows of the Cathedral – magnificent setting. Successful new build – old bits there, but the feel is modern. A new sixth form centre and resource area opened in 2007 and the new £10m music school, recital hall and sports hall are bringing in many more musicians and sporting enthisiasts form the county and nationally. Food exceptionally good and the atmosphere in the dining hall one of enjoyment.

The new boarding house adjacent to the school has been a real hit with the boys, who enjoy the spacious grounds and airy rooms. The other houses do look a bit tired when compared to the modernity of the new facilities; however the houses are cosy and spotlessly clean and run by kind and sympathetic staff. The plan is very much to develop the boarding and the new house sets the standard for the future.

Pastoral Care and Discipline: A strong sense of Christian values. Issues spotted early and dealt with immediately. Tutors are always on hand to help pupils and answer parents' concerns. Prefects, too, are approachable, even by the younger members of the school.

Pupils and Parents: A county school attracting children from Lincolnshire's further reaches, with buses ferrying them in, as well as a number of Services children.

Enthusiastic, happy kids, tidy, look you in the eye and chat easily.

Entrance: The majority of children from the Minster's prep school move up to the senior school. Others attend a personal assessment day in January, which largely indicates the breadth of ability, although entrance is not based purely on ability.

Exit: Durham, Newcastle, Leeds, Reading, Nottingham. A few to Oxbridge. The award-winning Virtual Careers Library, which can be accessed from computers outside the school, is a tremendous resource for leavers.

Money Matters: Well endowed under the auspices of the United Church Schools Trust. Scholarships for academic, art, music and sport. Means tested UCST assisted places.

Remarks: State of the art facilities. Turns out well-rounded and thoughtful children, who want to succeed.

Lomond School

Linked to Lomond School Junior Department in the Junior section

10 Stafford Street, Helensburgh, Argyll and Bute, G84 9JX

• Pupils: 510 boys and girls; all day except for 55 boarders • Ages: 3-18 • Size of sixth form: 90 • Non-denom • Fees: Senior Day £9,120; Boarding £10,380 pa • Independent

Tel: 01436 672476
Fax: 01436 678320
Email: admin@lomond-school.org
Website: www.lomond-school.org

Headmaster: Since August 2009, Mr Simon Mills (forty-ish), formerly senior deputy head at The Portsmouth Grammar School, where he greatly enjoyed working with Service families and developing a high value co-educational school. Cambridge geography graduate, worked with BP Oil. Boarding housemaster at Stamford School (also head of department) and Blundell's School. Grew up in St Andrews and educated in Perthshire. Married to Ruth, a primary teacher, three children, all at Lomond School.

A great believer in developing young people to their fullest potential and a strong supporter of the extra-curricular life of the school. Passions include skiing, windsurfing, sailing, golf and all things outdoor. Academic extension, strong pastoral care, pupil leadership and developing a wide co-curricular programme are of greatest importance to him.

Academic matters: Tranches of As across the board. Setted in English, French and maths at the age of 12, French taught from 8, German from 11. Huge range of subjects on offer, including such esoteric ones as graphic communication, modern studies and business management, as well as French, German and Spanish and French, German and Spanish writing. Three sciences. Latin GCSE taught by video conference link and distance learning. School takes Standard Grades, Intermediate 2s, Highers and Advanced Highers – notably in the sciences, maths, statistics etc and the humanities.

Maximum class size 20. Sixth form were working supervised (which is unheard of at that age) in the library when we visited. Homework very important – children keep a diary and expect to do at least two and a half hours each night in their Standard Grade year. Has strong links with a private school in China and in Germany. Computers everywhere, networked, and all have access to the internet; keyboarding skills for all, electronic interactive whiteboard presentations for all by all. Tutors for all. Good support for learning, with scribes and readers (and now provision for those with ADD or ADHD), both withdrawn and team teaching on offer. English as a second language on hand.

Games, Options, the Arts: Huge playing field just along the (tree-lined) road. Recently opened floodlit Astroturf hockey pitch. Also new rugby pitch and changing rooms. Rugby and hockey the two main winter games, with tennis, cricket and athletics in the summer and oodles of add-ons. Swimming in the local pool, option of squash, riding and badminton. Inter-house matches popular. Mass of lunch time clubs, D of E popular and, of course, sailing, The Scottish Islands Peaks Race, Lomond Challenge (a beastly tough triathlon) – not a school for sissies. New games hall, adjacent to the Astroturf, includes badminton courts, climbing wall, dance studio, fitness suite and indoor cricket lanes. Further development to include another smaller Astroturf.

Traditional Scottish music important – clarsach players, fiddlers, pipers and singers are in regular demand. Strong music, based in the old stables – one wall entirely covered with guitars, not just for decoration, judging by the enthusiasm the guitar teacher generated. Recording facilities in place but tape only. Big bands and chamber orchestras, over 20 instruments on curriculum with some 150 individual lessons. Sparkling art department, with old school desks press-ganged into use. Huge variety of disciplines – photography with spit-new kit, magical screen printing, jewellery making as well as the more prosaic (which it wasn't) sculpture, painting and etching. Tremendous enthusiasm here; enchanting flower costume, complete with design, basque and wings, made for last summer's play, on show. Strong drama.

Background and Atmosphere: Based on the northern edge of the posh, sleepy, seaside town of Helensburgh, originally housed in a series of Victorian villas. Present school is an amalgam of Larchfield, founded in 1845, and the girls' school, St Bride's, founded in 1895. The schools combined in 1977; later a stunning re-build. The resulting school is a curious combination of old and new, with three floors replacing the original two and subject rooms being grouped in series. Most impressive – massive amount of glass, super new dining hall, good gym and terrific entrance hall with glorious views out over the Clyde. Burnbrae now the most modern boarding house in Scotland – boys and girls share the same building but are separated by a state of the art security system using biometric readers. All pupils wear uniform (kilts for females) – neat and tidy with ties and a thoroughly purposeful air.

Pastoral Care and Discipline: Strong anti-bullying procedure in place – the 'no blame' circle appears to be the most effective. Confidential suggestion boxes all over the school are really part of the anti-bullying programme. Good PSD programme. CCTV cameras throughout. Children not 'given a lot of rope' – taking a puff of the odd joint equals letters to parents and discussion, dealing equals straight out. Smoking is apparently 'not happening just now', but smoking in uniform is 'not on'. Tries to educate 'through' booze, but expulsion would, in any case, be the last resort.

Pupils and Parents: An upmarket lot – solid middle class, from the surrounding area (they organise the buses), some from as far away as Glasgow; picked up quite a few with the closure of Keil School in Dumbarton. Number of Services families, Faslane next door, and some from further 'round the bay' send their children here. (The local state school thought to be too state.) A few mainland Chinese usually come for most of their secondary schooling, plus connection with Germany, whence the occasional pupil comes for a year or a term – not much take-up of Scots going to Germany in exchange.

Bonar Law was educated at Larchfield, as well as John Logie Baird – his school report, displayed in the dining room, apart from showing that he was fourteenth out of fourteen in maths, expresses the hope that he will eventually 'go on and do something with his life'.

Entrance: Either up via nursery or from local state primaries.

Exit: Usual dribble away after Standard Grades and could fill up the resulting places several times over, trickle leaves after Highers; some, e.g. those going south to university, tend to stay and do their Advanced Highers. Most will end up at university, usually two or three to Oxbridge. Gap year popular, particularly the Chinese option, where girls and boys have their fares paid, receive two thirds the normal salary and teach in China for a year, complete with lessons in Chinese.

Money Matters: Not a rich school. Will support pupils in financial difficulties; an increasing number of means-tested bursaries (up to 100 per cent) available at the age of 10 and 11 and post-Standard Grades.

Remarks: A jolly, busy school, perfect for those who want to keep their children at home without the hassle of going daily to Glasgow, with one of the most outstanding heads we have come across. Will watch new head's activities with interest.

The London Oratory School

Linked to London Oratory School Junior House (The) in the Junior section

Seagrave Road, London, SW6 1RX

• Pupils: 1,330; all boys except for 80 girls in the sixth form; all day
• Ages: 7-18 • Size of sixth form: 360 • RC • State

Tel: 020 7385 0102
Fax: 020 7381 7676
Email: registrar@los.ac
Website: www.london-oratory.org

Headmaster: Since 2007, Mr David McFadden BSc MA (fiftyish), a round peg in a circular hole. An Old Boy, began his career here, thence to Australia, where he spent twenty years teaching and, ultimately, headmastering. His previous two schools were Aquinas College and the Christian Brothers' College in Fremantle.

Mr McFadden retains an Aussie twang with a characteristic Aussie candour and relaxed confidence which we found engaging and reassuring. He has a clear sense of his school and what he wants to do there and, while paying tribute to his long-serving and much-admired predecessor, made pretty radical – and generally approved of – changes in his first, fast-moving year. It was not a honeymoon. He has been extraordinarily busy, engaged, among much else, in a huge consultation process to find out what the school community sees as priorities for change. This led to an impressive and far-reaching strategic plan – a massive agenda of 'things to do'. And he's already doing them.

Boys, parents and staff enthuse: 'He's very involved'; 'He's exceptional ... dynamic ... very approachable'; 'He seems to know what you're thinking ... and (most importantly) the lunches are heaps better'. We can't think of many heads we know who better fit their posts and we look forward to a further flourishing of this unique institution.

Academic matters: Selective only on the grounds of Roman Catholic practice – the level of academic achievement is therefore remarkable. Parents and boys attribute the results to good teaching, high expectations and the discipline which, though too strict for some, clearly pays dividends. At GCSE in 2007, outperformed the two, highly academically selective, local girls' schools and gives the independents a run for their money. 2008 GCSE results show 88 per cent A*–C grades with 37 per cent A*/A. In 2009, 97 per cent A*–C grades. Languages do exceptionally well here – refreshing in a boys' school; especially heartening to see German thrive. A level results similar – A–C in most subjects with 72 per cent A/B in 2008; 2009, average points score per pupil was 363. Popular and high-achieving are languages, maths and English, with excellent showings also in art, physics and chemistry.

Parents and pupils pay tribute to the 'challenging' curriculum, which makes a virtue of teaching beyond the syllabus, and to the efforts of the staff, who see strugglers individually and dollop out support and encouragement. The less academically able are offered a sixth form course in advanced business – a hybrid of two A levels and an AS, leading to qualifications in business and computing, a practical alternative to a sixth form college course for those who can't bear to leave. Classes felt by some to be too big, especially at sixth form level. However overall standards are high, high, high, to the extent that, in the recent Sutton Trust report, it was ranked top amongst all non-selective state schools, second amongst all selective state schools and thirtieth against all schools, including the independent schools.

SENs catered for – attracts standard numbers of the usual spread of needs: a few with Asperger's but no other ASDs at time of our visit. In-class help along with withdrawal where appropriate. Wheelchair friendly and SENs seen, in general, as just part of life.

Games, Options, the Arts: Outdoor space is in short supply and boys are bused to Barn Elms – a round trip of not much less than an hour. Rugby is big here, with six teams in the first form alone and more than twenty in total – becoming more available to all. Mr McFadden speaks of 'heart and hand' – seeing the development and nourishment of all parts of a pupil as central to his education. Rugby played mostly against the independents and at weekends, so a big commitment for the privileged few. Weights, water polo, rowing and basketball are other main activities at present; also a good, well-used, on-site, 17m pool. World Challenge, a popular activity since 2002, has more participants than any other school in the country – state and independent – and sends boys on exciting, self-financed trips of a lifetime. Also popular D of E. CCF perhaps the biggest in any state school, both army and RAF – tours, camps and expeditions of all kinds. Lots of sixth involved in community work – helping at local schools, at soup kitchen on Saturdays, at the offices of a local charity etc.

Music is very big, fuelled by those who come up from the Junior House, all of whom have exceptional aptitude. Six hundred plus pupils learn at least one instrument. Bands, choirs and orchestras thrive and are well-housed in the arts centre. The Schola is a choir of professional standard and considerable significance in the world of RC – and secular – music: three visits to Rome in as many months in

2007, including representing the Vatican in Al Gore's LiveEarth initiative. They record for films and TV and are regarded with deserved respect.

School's on-site arts centre is an impressive asset and includes stunning 300-seat galleried theatre in which full scale shows are mounted – 'Pirates of Penzance' in production when we visited. Good display spaces – a stimulating photo show by member of staff was good to see, along with a vast Paolozzi Brutalist sculpture. In 2006, eighteen pupils went on to study art/art history or architecture at prestigious institutions. But pupils' art/ceramics/DT etc not much in evidence – more of their efforts around the school would help the ambience and encourage les autres. No photography or textiles on offer.

Background and Atmosphere: Founded by the Oratorian Fathers, 145 years old. It moved to its present site and buildings – in the lee of Chelsea FC's massive stadium – in the 1970s and has worn surprisingly well. Some rooms and corridors, notably in the sixth form areas, are dilapidated but, in general, the place was imaginatively designed and feels looked after. We liked the brick courtyard with its lead flashing. New block built 2008 provides English department classrooms, learning support rooms and a function room to aid parental involvement. Has the look of a less than well resourced independent school, but the faces of the boys and staff belie that – an air of engagement and pride, a sense of collaborative energy and achievement which transcend the physical shortcomings and lack of space in some areas.

Some clearly unsatisfactory aspects – lunch (now good and with vegetables, though no sandwich option) is eaten in house rooms, which are also used for teaching after the metal grilles are rolled down and the servery disappears. Some year groups have no social space to speak of and are cramped and crowded. The large sixth form common room doubles as a fencing salle. Much of the school has a rather austere feel, which you couldn't describe as 'monastic' and, therefore, perhaps, good for the soul. We felt it to be bleak when we visited but, since then, the paintbrushes have been out and more displays put up, which must lift the spirits.

The Chapel, opened in 1992 by Basil Hume and dedicated to St Philip Neri and St Edward the Confessor, is simple in design and has a warm and gentle feel. Major ceremonies held in the famous, huge, Italianate Oratory Church in South Kensington. The Catholic ethos underlies all aspects of the school but not obtrusively or obsessively – it is simply a given and central also to Mr McFadden's plans to develop the community involvement of the school. Long standing commitment to local primary schools and charities – such as SURF and the SVP soup kitchen – with sixth formers carrying out voluntary work and the music department involved in outreach programmes.

Pastoral Care and Discipline: Discipline is acknowledged to be tight – rules are strict and enforced strictly. Any mobile phones spotted on the premises will be confiscated and have to be collected by parents. Eight boys were expelled or left in Mr McFadden's first year after two cannabis smoking incidents. 'You need a clear-cut policy, but you have to have a listening ear and heart.' The approach is 'compassionate', but zero tolerance for physical violence – automatic suspension for anyone who tries to sort a problem by 'raising a hand against someone else'. House system encourages friendships between the year groups and boys in the sixth can mentor those younger who need support over a subject or a problem. Parents of older boys still to feel the benign and hospitable effects of the new régime, but parents of newer pupils warmly praise the staff for their pastoral care, especially the deputy heads – both of whom have been in the school for twenty years since the start of their careers. Head keen to grow the 'heart and hand' of each boy – to integrate his learning into what his life is about, both individually and in terms of his service to the community.

Pupils and Parents: From a vast geographical area, most London boroughs, inner and outer – some leave home at 7.00am to come here. Over fifty languages spoken at home; serious Roman Catholicism the only – but unifying – common denominator. Parents are warming to head's drive to involve them in all ways – social, educational and practical. Parents' groups for sports, music and food and more to follow. Reports are now termly and home-school contact far more a normal thing, though some complaints persist of parents not being kept in touch. Children appreciate the knock-ons of greater parental involvement and find it supportive and helpful. The boys themselves are relaxed, friendly, ambitious and hard-working. Classes are head down and concentrating. We heard no raised voices, saw few inattentive faces. Pupils have a sense of pride in themselves and in the school which one would wish to see replicated everywhere. The only boy who wouldn't like it there, we were told, was someone who didn't want to involve himself.

Sixth form girls are no mere modern import designed to boost results. They date back to a link with a girls' school in the nineteenth century and were incorporated into the sixth in the 1950s after a merger. Their numbers are small but, says head, 'They add so much to the school'. It was good to see girls and boys out and about in the lunch hour clearly in relaxed friendship and at ease – no cattle market or points system here. Notable former pupils include Simon Callow and Haley Atwell. Oh – and David McFadden.

Entrance: Simpler than hitherto, but heart-sinking for anyone other than an assiduously practising Roman Catholic family with lots of community involvement. In fact, don't bother to apply unless you are a pillar of your local church and known to your priest, who will have to vouch for your bona fides – both pupil's and family's. No facility now even to rank your preferred schools in choice order. Eight hundred plus apply for the hundred and sixty places. Junior House boys transfer automatically and parents praise the seamless transition. Sixth form also oversubscribed. Forty places for girls attract two hundred applicants and, again, the RC credentials are what counts. Girls join from Sacred Heart (qv), – virtually the whole year applies – Gumley (qv), the Ursuline Convent and a few from Lady Margaret's (qv).

Exit: Most stay on after GCSE; almost 400 in sixth form. Regularly wins Oxbridge places with a dozen plus each year covering the range of disciplines. Otherwise to good universities everywhere to read everything. Refreshingly few silly subjects pursued – these pupils have been properly taught and sensibly advised.

Remarks: Much that is excellent, but also much potential for building this school – in bricks and mortar terms as well as educationally and spiritually. Destined for stardom.

Lord Williams's School

Oxford Road, Thame, Oxfordshire, OX9 2AQ

• Pupils: 2,150 boys and girls; all day • Ages: 11-18 • Size of sixth form: 450
• Non-denom • State

Tel: 01844 210 510
Fax: 01844 261 382
Email: Headteacher.4580@lordwilliams.oxon.sch.uk
Website: www.lordwilliams.oxon.sch.uk

Headteacher: Since 2005 (at first as acting head), Mr David Wybron MA (fiftyish)). Previously head of lower school and deputy head of Lord Williams's overall, he joined school in 1991 as head of humanities faculty. History graduate from Swansea University who taught in Cambridgeshire and Great Missenden, Bucks, before settling in Thame. A softly-spoken Welshman whose drive and determination should not be under-estimated. 'I am passionate about this place,' he assures us. Wife a secondary school teacher.

Academic matters: Still one of top state schools in Oxfordshire. A level results seen as major success in 2010 with 97 per cent pass rate, 46 per cent A*–B grades and 73% A*–C grades. GCSE results far exceed national and county averages – 80 per cent gained five or more A*–C grades in 2010 (69 per cent 5 or more A*–C grades including English and maths). Focus now on intervention strategies to support underachieving students. As children of all abilities entered for exams, results are sound and school commended by Ofsted for adding value. Huge curriculum choice at every level.

Special needs very well catered for. Resource unit for 20 children with autism on site, also plenty of classroom and extra help for others with dyslexia and other learning problems. Well-stocked libraries in both lower and upper schools, regularly updated. ICT taught as subject in its own right to all from Year 7, also as learning support for later studies. 10 purpose-built computer networked suites boast latest technology and are in constant demand. Good enrichment programme for gifted and talented students.

Games, Options, the Arts: Sports College status, also awarded an Artsmark silver award for its creative arts provision. Both areas of school impressive, highly productive and successful. But head keen to point out, 'We are not just a sports school – we haven't slanted things so that it's just about sport'. Happy with the health, leadership, fitness and community agendas. Shared use of Thame leisure centre (right next door to school), acres of playing fields and a new all-weather pitch. Regularly produces county (sometimes national) players and winning teams. Art studios well used and well resourced. Good displays at lower school. Good music uptake – individual lessons as well as compulsory class music for all early on. Traditional orchestras now complemented by assortment of bands. Drama, dance and theatre studies all popular time-table and exam options. Impressive results too.

Background and Atmosphere: A true comprehensive. Known affectionately as Lord Bill's, it's a big school – much bigger than average secondary with 2,100+ pupils – but split over two sites about two miles apart. School founded by Lord Williams of Thame in 1559. Current set-up dates from 1971 when Lord Williams's Grammar and Wenman Secondary merged. Both sites on leafy edge of market town, well spread out, and despite high numbers on school register, room to breathe. Buildings mixed in age and mostly functional, parts much in need of TLC, but well laid out and absolutely buzzing. 'It's an ideas place. There's a sparkiness here about teaching and learning.' Students allowed voice in decision making process. 'Sometimes people are afraid of the student voice,' says head. 'But we harness it.' School sites very open but security measures are good – CCTV installed at cost of £38,000 at lower school. Maintains close ties with local primaries through well-established system of networking. Much effort made to ease the transition to 'big' school through team-building activities.

Pastoral Care and Discipline: Pastoral care is solid throughout the school. Nurture groups set up for students who are particularly vulnerable. In Year 7, children shown how to deal with own problems as well as being encouraged to seek help. Few serious misdemeanours but guilty parties swiftly dealt with – sliding scale of exclusion periods for offenders. No instant dismissal for drugs, but police will automatically be involved. Head readily admits bullying exists, but is not tolerated. All unacceptable behaviour dealt with initially in the same way, with a range of sanctions used – systems of warnings, detentions, internal isolations and fixed term external exclusions.

Pupils and Parents: Confident, sometimes out-spoken, but articulate and secure. Hard workers will achieve and the less academically able are being increasingly supported. Students seen on our visit appeared focused and involved in their lessons. Their relationship with staff seemed generally relaxed and informal. A socially mixed catchment area obviously results in a wide social mix at school. Some from professional backgrounds, plenty of rural and an increasing number who qualify for free school meals. Parents range from the supportive to the demanding, rather than the apathetic.

Entrance: From Oxfordshire state primaries in Thame and surrounding villages like Chinnor and Tetsworth, but also a number of Buckinghamshire schools (like Brill and Long Crendon) due to school's proximity to county border. Head describes Lord Williams's as 'truly inclusive'.

Exit: Up to 70 per cent stay on to sixth form; most of those leaving after Year 11 go on to college courses or into employment. Majority go to university or college after A levels, annually two or three to Oxbridge. No single area of expertise evident – courses and jobs right across the board.

Remarks: A perennially popular school which maintains a good local reputation through its ability to do well by its students. Seen by some as a safety net for Bucks grammar school failures but hard-grafters won't be disappointed. In many respects worthy of first choice status, certainly not second best.

Loretto School

Linked to Loretto Junior School Aka The Nippers in the Junior section

1-7 Linkfield Road, Musselburgh, East Lothian, EH21 7RE

• Pupils: 350 pupils, 230 boarders, 120 day • Ages: 12-18 • Size of sixth form: 130 • Non-denom • Fees: Senior: Boarding £17,085-£26,130; Day £12,810-£17,760; Junior: Boarding £15,465-£17,085; Day £6,975-£12,255 pa • Independent

Tel: 0131 6534455/4444
Fax: 0131 653 4445
Email: admissions@loretto.com
Website: www.loretto.com

Headmaster: Since 2008, Mr Peter Hogan B Com PGCE MA FCollT FRSA. Married with two teenage children. Formerly warden (headmaster) of Llandovery College, Wales, where he opened a new prep school and technology centre, doubling the size of the school. Prior to that he has been a deputy head, head of business education and marketing and has taught economics and history, coached numerous sports and directed a number of school plays. He is author of two musicals and two radio plays broadcast on BBC for younger children. Also wrote numerous business studies texts and is a governor of the University of Wales.

Loretto prides itself on being 'a family school' – the headmaster talks to the whole school, on his own, two or three times a week (known as doubles). This is unique in our experience.

Academic matters: Monthly tutorial assessments, which are 'minuted and followed through' with pupils and parents. School exclusively follows the English system – GCSEs for all, plus AS and A2s. 43 per cent of 2010 A level papers A*/A and 91 per cent of GCSE passes A*–C. Normally pupils take four ASs, followed by three A2s, though, increasingly, top end pupils go for five ASs and four A2s. Yet another AS can be added in the upper sixth. Other recent introductions include a new classics programme, a new IT programme across the school and the AQA extension project scheme, which contributes UCAS points.

Maths, biology, physics, art, government and politics, history, geography and business studies the most popular subjects. Traditionally strong on science and engineering, A level physics course now has encouraging numbers of girls. AS results have pleasing numbers of As across the board. New AS level in music technology. French, history, geography strong at GCSE, Spanish increasing in popularity. Russian and Mandarin additions at all levels.Three sciences standard at GCSE, though one can be dropped for art.

Setted in English, maths and languages, according to ability – from third form, most subjects setted. The girls apparently set the academic standard and boys try to match them. The staff we met were all bright, bubbly and enthusiastic. ESL (extra cost) and learning support available throughout. Smartboards in class rooms and networked computers everywhere, even in study-bedrooms if requested. An impressive visiting lecturer programme averages one per week, plus members of upper sixth regularly give lectures; interview practice for all.

Games, Options, the Arts: Singing as ever good and keen – the whole school sings in the war memorial chapel choir, also performers at the Schools Proms at the Royal Albert Hall. A burgeoning orchestra, most of the second (i.e. 12 year olds) study one or more instruments and, as always, an acclaimed pipe band which performed with Sir Paul McCartney on his world tour this year. Drama on the up – theatre studies now available at AS and A2 levels, as is PE. Art scholars take life classes as well as screen printing and textiles. Campus and online Loretto radio station as well as all mod cons music recording studio.

Sport is strong – girls' athletics and lacrosse do well; the appointment of a head of girls' games has given real impetus to it. Additional sports stars appointed as coaches, Michael Powell (formerly Warwickshire CCC and England 'B') director of cricket and South African Danny Rossouw, director of rugby. Impressive string of wins on the rugby pitch over the last two years has put the Loretto 1st XV firmly back in the top league. Impressive all-weather court now surrounded by a security fence – as much to keep out the local ungodly (what happened to the "honest toun"?) as to pre-empt the Right to Roam Act.

The golf academy, which opened in 2002, is flourishing (school has a long tradition of senior golfing FPs), and golf is professionally coached throughout the school, with all pupils using top class practice facilities on campus, including a nine-hole Huxley all-weather putting green. Rounds are played at the local Craigielaw golf club and three other challenging golf courses. Older pupils can have their lessons re-jigged to accommodate coaching. Recent accolades include HMC foursomes champions 2009 and 2006, (runner up in 2007), winner Welsh Amateur 2010 and winner Intercollegiate Individual Final 2010; three golf scholarships to leading American universities and wins in many of the county championships. Summer residential golf campas are run to encourage new golfers to apply.

Background and Atmosphere: Founded in 1827, and bought by Hely Hutchison Almond in 1862 (a distinguished scholar of unconventional convictions – Scotland's answer to Dr Arnold), went fully co-ed in 1995. The traditional East Lothian ochre-coloured buildings straddle the main road. Swimming pool off-campus. Libraries full of books, learning support and EFL, and head of ICT has 'ambitious plans'. Plexi-glass now covers all but the memorial window in the chapel.

Various outbuildings, including The Nippers, across the River Esk. Holm House (with lift for disabled access) and Balcarres, the two girls' houses, are adjacent to the (small) sports centre. Junior girls' house and girls' sixth form house. Study bedrooms in sixth form house. Senior common rooms for sixth form with a certain amount of male access, Linkfield, the sixth form bar, open at weekends, barbecues are popular at the girls' houses and attended by all. All six houses completely refurbished 2007 and additional boarding accommodation created in 2010. The famous haunted Pinkie House, with its important painted ceiling in the gallery under the roof, is home to some of the sixth form boys – though we understand the ghost is not much in evidence. It also houses the new exam centre and function room for lectures.

Kilts on Sundays – some remnants of the traditional uniform remain. Red jackets the norm for all, with navy collars distinguishing sixth form. Still no ties for daily dress. An absolute ban on any form of platform heels – no more 'tottering on the asphalt'.

The CRC (Communication and Resource Centre), now houses a sixth form centre – designated areas for independent academic study, university admissions, individual tutoring and socializing. The aim is to create an ambience more like a university's and provide good opportunities to develop leadership skills.

Full boarding, weekly boarding and flexi-boarding on offer as well as day pupils. Buses from all over – mainly East Lothian – and more in the pipeline. Operates a six morning, three afternoon schedule, and day pupils can and do go home during the week at 4.30pm if they have no further activities (otherwise it is 6.30/8.30pm).

Sixth form boarders can get permission to go into Edinburgh on any night of the week 'providing that their work is in order'. They can go to a film, to the theatre, to concerts (rock or otherwise), and the upper sixth can go to the races in Musselburgh. The young told this editor that they take taxis, though apparently buses are gaining in popularity. Younger boarders take the school bus of a weekend to Kinaird Park, which houses a collection of utterly desirable shops – a great improvement on Musselburgh. This is a chilly corner of East Lothian and the east wind whistling across the race course from the North Sea is an almost permanent feature (headmaster is not so sure!).

Pastoral Care and Discipline: Small school, so great family feel, much emphasised by the head. Zero tolerance for drugs no longer the norm – automatically out for being caught actively using any drug or for dealing, 'But the alternative policy, which can be adopted if the facts are not clear, involves the whole truth from everybody, and no disciplinary consequences if drugs have been involved'. Instead parents are told, counselling may follow and the pupils concerned go on random urine testing for the remainder of their school career. A positive test would then mean expulsion. School is tough on persistent bullying ('We spend hours on it – please don't use the word "tough"'). Recognised ladder for punishments, no longer entirely in the houseparents' domain: breathalyser, gatings, rustications and out for alcohol; gatings and letters home for smoking.

Pupils and Parents: Usual Scottish collection – not a lot of foreigners here; large number of OLs' sons, daughters and grandchildren, some of whom join for the sixth form only. Fair number of first time buyers. Not really a Sloane/Charlotte Ranger school. OLs include the current headmaster, plus a gang of MPs, Lord Lamont, Lord (Hector) Laing, Andrew Marr, Alastair Darling, and the current chairman of the governors Roy Martin QC.

Entrance: Own entrance exam or CE from Scottish and northern prep schools; pupils come up from The Nippers en masse. Special exam and interview for those from the state sector, or from overseas. Six GCSEs at C and above for entry into sixth form. Scholarships and bursaries are available.

Exit: 99 per cent or so to tertiary education with a regular four to six to Oxbridge – 90 per cent getting into their first choice of university.

Money Matters: Scholarships for academics, musicians, drama, art, sport, golf, plus scholarships for those from the state sector, and for those coming up from The Nippers etc etc; also sixth form scholarships and bursaries awarded to those 'who have deserved well of Loretto'.

Remarks: A famous Scottish public school, now co-ed, for gentle middling souls in need of nurturing – back in the frame.

Loughborough Grammar School

Linked to Fairfield Preparatory School in the Junior section

Linked to Loughborough High School in the Senior section

Burton Walks, Loughborough, Leicestershire, LE11 2DU

• Pupils: 1,005 boys; 55 boarders, 950 day • Ages: 10-18 • Christian - non denominational • Fees: Day £9,960; Boarding £15,834-£17,994 pa • Independent

Tel: 01509 233 233
Fax: 01509 218 436
Email: registrar@lesgrammar.org
Website: www.lesgrammar.org

Headmaster: Since 1998, Mr Paul Fisher MA (mid fifties). Taught at Prior Park College in Bath and Marlborough College. Teaches RE to half of year 10. A very likeable person who clearly has huge support from his staff, pupils and their parents. Plenty of humour, which is reflected in the extremely happy atmosphere of the school. Married to Helen, who teaches Spanish and French here; two boys.

Academic matters: Not an academic sausage machine and all boys given full opportunity to shine in any way they choose. Having said that, A level results are very good indeed. Both maths and English have exceptional results – though not exceptionally popular. Popular subjects are biology, chemistry and physics. Maths and a modern foreign language are compulsory subjects to GCSE level and Latin to the end of Year 8. The first three years are used to emphasise the fun in learning and boys go confidently into their GCSE years. Average class size 19, maximum 26. Average age of the staff early to mid forties, with about 50 per cent having 10 or more years' service.

Superb language lab with state-of-the-art facilities proving very popular and encouraging. Phase I of an ambitious building programme for the sciences just completed – new chemistry building opened September 2009. Computers evident all around the school and much used. Although selective on academic grounds, every pupil is screened and, if necessary, assessed for SEN. The school is highly supportive with about 60 boys currently receiving extra help – individual targets, very confidence-boosting.

Games, Options, the Arts: Sport in good variety and much enjoyed; compulsory in some form twice a week with matches on Saturday afternoons. Rugby remains very popular, as do hockey, basketball, swimming (own heated indoor pool) and cross-country, with cricket, athletics and tennis in the summer. Popular extra-curricular activities include D of E, CCF, music and drama. A hugely popular lunchtime and weekend bridge club boasts national and international players and a karting club where boys have built their own go-karts and then raced them with much success at national level.

Drama studio allows for some marvellous productions, once a term in conjunction with the girls' High School, and as an integral part of the school. New music school for all three schools on the same campus provides excellent facilities available to pupils of all ages and standards. Approximately 40 per cent of the boys play at least one musical instrument. Music staff are very enthusiastic and numerous bands, concert bands, orchestras, ensembles, choirs etc. One of the big bands was selected for the National Festival of Music for Youth at the Queen Elizabeth Hall in London, and bi-annual tours abroad, e.g. Prague, Italy, Austria, Spain and Malta, often on sea-front bandstands as well as at concert halls.

Background and Atmosphere: Founded in 1495, now part of the Loughborough Endowed Schools and shares the same extensive campus as Loughborough High School for Girls and Fairfield School, the co-educational junior school. Although independent of each other, the three schools share a common board of governors and the links joining the three are very tangible. Some joint sixth form teaching but not a co-educational senior school.

All boys from all backgrounds are fully integrated and made to feel welcome and part of the community. Although generally Christian, with 20 per cent of pupils from other religious denominations, all faiths are celebrated and included in the curriculum. Lovely mixture of old and new buildings surrounding an attractive cherry tree-lined grassed quadrangle – boys behave better because of the way the place looks and feels, for instance a distinct lack of litter and general dumping of schoolbags and blazers.

Pastoral Care and Discipline: Small tutor groups, with a great deal of support at all levels; staff always have time to talk and help where necessary, said one pupil, a view echoed by others and parents. Boys are made to feel that they contribute in some way. Anyone who is prepared to join in and have a go, in whatever capacity, will fit into this school. In a sixth form with a broad ability range, those boys who come out with lower grades at A level are made to feel that they have really achieved something and are encouraged to apply to university.

Pupils tell us that bullying is really not a problem. If it does occur, it is dealt with quickly at the root. Boys seem to be able to separate what is acceptable at home and at school. The two small boarding houses offer a homely atmosphere with comfortable dorms and sitting rooms both within easy reach of the campus, so sports facilities can be used outside school hours. Staff always willing to find the time to talk to parents.

Pupils and Parents: Some middle class, others not; about 25 per cent from ethnic minority backgrounds as well as approximately a dozen boys from mainland China and Hong Kong and a few from other parts of the world. Buses from all over Leicester, Derbyshire and Nottinghamshire, as well as the immediate local area. Old Boys include the late Johnnie Johnson, Felix Buxton of Basement Jaxx, Stephen Mitchell (head of BBC Radio News), Giles Kristian (author of 'The Raven' series), Ben Murphy (current leader of the Red Arrows) and David Collier, Chief Executive of England and Wales Cricket Board.

Entrance: By own examination, at 10, 11 and 13, or CE at 13, with about 40 boys coming in at 11 from Fairfield School. Sixth form entry based on GCSE grades – overseas pupils may sit an entrance exam in the subjects to be studied in the sixth form.

Exit: About 10 per cent leave after GCSE, usually to go to a sixth form college or other school that offers a specific course that Loughborough Grammar does not. University places are varied, from Oxbridge (15–20 each year), reading law, theology, natural sciences or maths, to other universities, reading medicine, dentistry, engineering or computer sciences etc. Generally a good range of subjects being read at a good variety of universities.

Money Matters: Financially secure and not pressured into taking students who would not fit into the school. A number of scholarships at 10, 11 and 13, awarded on academic merit, regardless of parents' means. Some music awards each spring for boys entering the following September. Foundation bursaries are available upon request.

Remarks: Any boy willing to have a go and join in would be welcome here. A very happy, productive school, excellent facilities and support from staff and pupils. Very well respected in the area and beyond, the current head is continuing to attract a wide range of boys who really contribute to the success of the school.

Loughborough High School

Linked to Fairfield Preparatory School in the Junior section

Linked to Loughborough Grammar School in the Senior section

Burton Walks, Loughborough, Leicestershire, LE11 2DU

- Pupils: 605 girls, all day • Ages: 11-18 • Size of sixth form: 160
- Non-denom • Fees: £9,279 pa • Independent

Tel: 01509 212 348
Fax: 01509 215 720
Email: admin@leshigh.org
Website: www.leshigh.org

Headmistress: Since 2002, Mrs Bridget O'Connor MA (early fifties). Read literae humaniores at St Hugh's College, Oxford. Taught classics at Francis Holland and became head of classics and year head at Old Palace School, Croydon. Moved to Haberdashers' Aske's School for Girls as head of classics and head of sixth form, then deputy head, before moving here. Married with one daughter. Very keen to make improvements, particularly extending the IT department and further developing the science departments. A very fair head, with a good sense of humour, liked by her staff and pupils.

Academic matters: Very academic school with excellent results. Impressive GCSE results, particularly in double science, English literature and maths, leading on to equally impressive A level results – 89 per cent plus A/B. Huge support from teachers who, according to a number of pupils, 'really care how well you do and therefore put themselves out for us'. The most popular subjects at A level are biology, chemistry and maths, closely followed by history. Classics in Year 7 (taught by the head), Latin compulsory in Years 8 and 9 – those who continue this through to GCSE level generally get A* or A. German or Spanish as additional modern foreign language in Year 9. Five computer suites. All classrooms have a computer and many have interactive whiteboards too. Some specialist rooms with banks of laptops.

Does not cater for statemented children, but pupils with diagnosed specific learning difficulties are put on the school's own Individual Education Plan. Excellent library, with computerised fingerprinting instead of library card very popular – 'I kept losing my library card before this was introduced,' said one girl. Lots of computers in the library and a separate resource room with internet access. Appears to be very well used.

Games, Options, the Arts: Traditional sports – hockey, netball and cross-country in the winter, tennis, athletics and rounders in the summer and additional recreational sports such as soccer and tag rugby. Great use made of the recently refurbished Astroturf. Some excellent achievements in all sports at county level and many national team representatives too.

Music very popular with about 85 per cent learning at least one instrument; some very talented musicians amongst the pupils including several who play at national level. Very well equipped music school opened in 2006 facilitating joint ventures with the boys' Grammar School. Excellent art department with some really superb work displayed throughout the school; a great variety of media and small group taking art at A level. Lively drama department with a brand new, fully equipped drama studio – a good mix of productions from traditional plays to musicals, often in conjunction with the Grammar School. Popular lunchtime drama clubs.

Plenty of extra-curricular activities, including a very popular mind games club at lunchtime in conjunction with the Grammar School, chess, Chinese chess, bridge, Scrabble and Go, as well as other games that many people may not have heard of. On the day of our visit, pupils were playing a Japanese game called Pini.

Background and Atmosphere: Founded in 1850 and one of the oldest girls' grammar schools in the country. Academic work and excellence are central to the philosophy of the school, though personal and social development receive much attention. Pupils commented that the school offers such tremendous support and friendship that it is just like one big happy family. Popular school council chaired by the headgirl and her two deputies discusses changes in the school, the introduction of new curriculum subjects, a change in the school uniform. Staff sit on the periphery, listening and allowing the pupils the chance to debate. A separate food committee discusses the dining accommodation and school menus.

Pastoral Care and Discipline: Staff and pupils are really attentive to each other's needs and each girl treated as important. Staff always available and willing to chat, go out of their way to iron out problems.

Pupils and Parents: From a 40 mile radius covering Leicestershire, Derbyshire and Nottinghamshire. Huge variety of backgrounds including Asian and European – a recent survey showed 21 languages spoken by families and extended families. Parents and pupils very enthusiastic about the school; the happy atmosphere really shines thorough as you are shown round.

Entrance: Exams at 11, also 12, 13 and 14, when a foreign language is tested, usually French, but an alternative if French has not been studied. Entry at 16 is on the basis of an interview. Approximately 35 per cent come up from Fairfield Preparatory School (part of the Loughborough Endowed Schools), others from prep and primary schools (and state secondaries at 12,13 and 14).

Exit: A few girls take a gap year but almost all go on to university, about half a dozen to Oxbridge, the rest to universities around the UK, reading a diverse range of subjects. Many choose the sciences, others subjects such as anthropology, economics, a variety of languages, architecture, law, medicine and classical civilisation. Not many leaving after GCSE, only those wanting either to board, go on to a sixth form college or, more usually, to study a subject not offered at Loughborough.

Money Matters: A number of scholarships for academic and musical ability are offered on entrance at 11, 12, 13 and 14. Separate applications need to be made for the musical awards. All are eligible for the academic awards, which are given on performance in the entrance exam. Means-tested Foundation bursaries are assessed on an individual basis.

Remarks: An excellent and very friendly school for the academic girl who has lots of energy and commitment together with a love of learning, and who can keep up with the rigorous pace.

LVS Ascot (Licensed Victuallers' School)

Linked to LVS Ascot (The Licensed Victuallers Junior School) in the Junior section

London Road, Ascot, Berkshire, SL5 8DR

• Pupils: 890 (370 girls, 520 boys). 170 boarders from age 7 • Ages: 4-18 • Size of sixth form: 160 • Non-denom • Fees: Day £13,200-£13,410; Boarding £23,550 pa • Independent

Tel: 01344 882 770
Fax: 01344 890 648
Email: registrar@lvs.ascot.sch.uk
Website: www.lvs.ascot.sch.uk

Headmistress : Since September 2010, Mrs Christine Cunniffe BA MMus, previously director of music and assistant head. Three children currently at LVS.

Academic matters: Results unbelievably good, given the school's non-selective admissions policy. Parents say all praise goes to the teachers, who are left to teach and not expected to be managers. Most subjects setted according to ability. Some less academic A level subjects on offer, e.g. photography and media studies. Vocational A levels in sport and leisure, business and finance. Careers advice very good and parents very pleased with school's rôle in securing some plum work experience placements – 'It made all the difference for my son', said one. 80 special needs children, mainly mild dyslexia and dyspraxia.

Games, Options, the Arts: Sport for all, rather than for the élite. All the usual games – football, hockey, netball and rugby. Competes mainly against minor independents and the strongest state schools. One hour of games and one hour of PE per week – a few parents grumbled this isn't enough, but lots of co-curricular sports available after school and in lunch hour. Very good indoor swimming pool. Music recital room and chapel area for boarders to use on Sunday mornings. Fab music tech room and recording studio. Standard assortment of musical ensembles available. Every year the choir performs in Disneyland Paris – a good gig. Fine drama studio seats 100 – used for lessons and small performances. Larger impressive, state of the art theatre with steeply sloping seating – lots of shows and concerts.

Background and Atmosphere: When it comes to governing bodies, we thought we'd seen everything, but how wrong we were. LVS is owned by the Licensed Trade Charity, which represents anyone 'whose main job is, or has been, to serve, produce or deliver alcohol'. Founded by the Society of Licensed Victuallers in Lambeth in 1803, the school was intended to provide 'a wholesome and airy environment' for the children of those working in the drinks trade. When Lambeth became un-airy, LVS moved to Slough. In the late 1980s the Slough site was bought by Tesco; the governors bought another school in Ascot and re-built it in an architectural style strangely evocative of that great retail colossus.

Set in 26 acres of good playing fields, woodland and lake, looks more like an upmarket American high school than a British boarding school. Classrooms are clustered on two levels around 'The Street' – a central hub fitted with American-style lockers. In keeping with the light and airy aim, all walkways and stairs are on the outside of buildings, but under cover. Architecture and atmosphere provide no hint whatsoever that this is a boarding school, and it certainly does not feel like one. School day ends at 4pm, with activities until 5.15pm. Boarders then have prep until supper (and sometimes after) and evening activities. Fine sixth form commonroom.

Pastoral Care and Discipline: Contrary to what you might expect, no sixth form bar and no alcohol is allowed on site. No sixth form uniform, just business wear. Boarding numbers very healthy; facilities jolly. Boarding houses named – wait for it – Carlsberg, Gilbey, Guinness and Bass, after sponsors. Experienced boarding house staff: 'Outstanding,' said a parent. Up to three quarters of boarders go home on weekends, but a solid quorum remains in school most Sundays. 11–16 year old boarders allowed off-site on week-ends. Older pupils can sign out when they wish. Year 7 boarders live in the junior school boarding house. Lunch provided for all within fees.

Pupils and Parents: A microcosm of 'normal' society – not your run of the mill public school, this. Parents attracted by school's wide scope – can take all ages, both sexes, all abilities, boarding and day, all the way through their schooling – and attractive price tag. Particularly suits big families with children of differing abilities. Parents also like the un-grand tone, the unpretentious campus. As a parent said, 'Their approach is to target the average 80 per cent – after all, there are more of us to target.' Quite a few pupils come who failed to get a place in the state school of their choice, plus a smattering of kids who muffed the Reading or Bucks grammar school tests. About ten per cent of pupils are children of publicans etc, some here with full bursaries; others come from much more affluent families.

Affordable boarding from age seven a big draw for overseas Brits, especially Services families – currently 80 expat children. Around 40 overseas students from Far East, Nigeria, Russia, Switzerland, South Africa, some of them getting extra help with their English. Day pupils from Windsor, Gerrards Cross, Slough, Maidenhead, Camberley, Woking, Feltham, Staines, Ascot, Bracknell, Virginia Water.

OBs: flashy circus impresario Billy Smart; frozen food brothers, William, Frank and Peter Brake (sponsors of the current dining hall); Burn Gorman, who stars in 'Dr Who' spin-off, 'Torchwood'.

Entrance: Mainly at 4+, 7, 11, 13 and 16+. Not academically selective: one of the increasingly rare breed of schools that requires no entrance exam, though reports and interviews are used. At age 11, 40 per cent of the intake is from own junior school. For sixth form entry pupils need five GCSEs at least grade C. School becoming increasingly popular, so do not leave things until the last minute.

Exit: 95 per cent of sixth form leavers go on to a degree course or higher education. 2007: 14 per cent took courses in science, ten in engineering and technology, 16 in humanities and social sciences, 40 vocational subjects, 20 arts.

Money Matters: Good value for money. Financially well-managed, with a focus on cost control. And the alcohol link has got to be a plus – as one parent said, 'With their connection to the drinks industry, they're never going to be short of money'. Children of parents working in the licensed drinks trade (from bar staff to brewers) get a 20 per cent discount and may apply for bursaries of up to 100 per cent. 15–25 per cent fee reductions for Services children. Ten per cent reduction for third children. Usual variety of scholarships available for up to half fees, but mainly much less.

Remarks: In well-heeled Ascot, cheek by jowl with some of the most upper-crust educational establishments in the land, LVS has created an alternative universe of independent schooling. This is classless, no-nonsense, independent boarding education for all.

Lycee Français Charles de Gaulle

Linked to Ecole André Malraux in the Junior section

Linked to Ecole Charles de Gaulle - Wix in the Junior section

Linked to Ecole Marie d'Orliac

Linked to Ecole de South Kensington (Primary School of the Lycee Français) in the Junior section

Linked to Lycee Français Charles de Gaulle (British Section)

35 Cromwell Road, London, SW7 2DG

• Pupils: 3,900 (including primary and nursery school); all day (but see below) • Ages: 3-18 • Size of sixth form: 400 (100 in the English section; 300 in the French) • No religious affiliation • Fees: Primary £3,531; Bilingual class Wix £4,308-£6,597; Secondary £4,311; British Section £8,472 pa • Independent

Tel: 02075 846 322
Fax: 02078 237 684
Email: proviseur@lyceefrancais.org.uk
Website: www.lyceefrancais.org.uk

Proviseur: Since 2007, M Bernard Vasseur, previously head of French schools in various European and Eastern European countries. 2003–2007 deputy head of the French Schools Abroad in Paris.

Head of English stream: Mrs R E Nichol.

Academic matters: Prepares students to follow the official French curriculum from nursery to the Baccalauréat. The results put the school at the top of French league tables and in the top 50s on the UK charts. Classes start at 8.30am and last for 55 minutes. Up till 13 years old, all follow pretty much the same programme. After 4ème, the children choose between the British Section (GCSE and A levels) and the Baccalauréat. At 15 they move from Collège to Lycée, where they spend three years preparing the French Baccalauréat. They choose between the literary, economic or scientific streams. Students are evaluated each term by all their teachers, a member of the administration and student and parent representatives. A written report is sent to the parents and any problems are highlighted.

All students take philosophy in the final year, which cumulates in the very demanding Baccalauréat exams, spread over ten days. Once the written sections are over, the orals begin. The results are excellent with a pass rate of 99 per cent, of which 80 per cent receive honours.

Following staff/parent meetings and consideration of end of term reports, children from the age of 14 have the option of moving to the British section, which prepares them for GCSE and A level examinations. Pupils entering this are bilingual but usually more at ease in English. It allows pupils to maintain their contacts with the French language and culture and follow the British curriculum (French GCSE and A level are mandatory for all here). Results are excellent. The scope of subjects offered is not as broad as a British school but what they lack in quantity, they make up for in quality.

The teachers are dedicated and hard working, and the atmosphere is caring, almost family-like. 210 students in this section and, since most of the students came from the French section, the two groups all mix well. One of the strengths of the French system is training the young to become good at analysing and expressing themselves.

Very long days in the secondary school and heavy homework loads are normal. No school on Wednesday afternoon in the primary school, but over recent years Wednesday afternoon clubs and activities for these students have flourished, to the delight of the children and parents. Class sizes at all levels are around 30, including at primary level.

Language support: Priority is given to the French language. English is taught as a second language from the primary school through to Terminal. English is the teaching language in the English section for all classes, except, of course, French classes.

Games, Options, the Arts: Considering the time limits and the distance of the playing fields (Raynes Park, near Wimbledon), the sports department does its best. Basketball and volleyball are keenly played, but it is up to the parents to make sure the children can let off steam on the weekends.

Art is everywhere on the walls, from posters done by the students about human rights and child slavery to projects done in the fine arts classes. An orchestra and thriving choir, not to mention the photototography, chess and graphics clubs.

Background and Atmosphere: London disappears when you walk into the main building on Cromwell Road – you feel you are in France. The halls are noisy and busy. The pupils are urban, stylish and cosmopolitan. The campus takes up the entire city block, sharing a corner with the French Institute. The first Lycée opened in 1915 in Victoria with 120 French and Belgian refugee children. The present set of buildings ranges from Victorian stucco buildings to the main 1950s building and a more modern primary complex on Harrington Road with playgrounds, gardens and auditoriums. Has recently undertaken a considerable programme of adaptation and renewal of the buildings in order to have more space. A new primary school was opened in Fulham in September 2008 which, like the Ealing and Clapham annexes, feeds into the secondary school.

Although the French language is dominant, you hear Italian, Spanish, English, Russian and Arabic. The whole place feels French, down to the chic staff and even the attitudes. The neighbourhood is frenchified with boutiques, butchers, patisseries and bookshops. The cafeteria is big and buzzy. As might be expected, the food is good: even the Michelin 'Guide' gave them the thumbs up – boeuf bourguignon, filet d'haddock sauce fines herbes or cuisse de poulet au confit de citrons are just a few of the choices. Contrary to popular belief, pommes frites are not the favourite – a recent poll showed the students prefer lasagne. The nursery children have a small dining room, where everything is just to their size.

Pastoral Care and Discipline: A no tolerance policy for drugs is applied. Bullying isn't much of a problem with such a diverse mix of students – in fact, they are proud to be open-minded and in general are polite and courteous. Surveillants (college students) monitor the halls and cafeteria so teachers can teach. Spiritual matters are left to the parents.

Pupils and Parents: Confident, self assured and eclectic, about 80 per cent French, but over 40 nationalities represented. No dress code but everyone has style. Parents come from all walks of life – from ambassadors to bankers, civil servants to dress makers, expats to actors. The parents' association (APL) fundraises, helps new families settle in and brainstorms with the administration. APL also organizes a careers day attended by 120 participants from the professions as well as from universities in the UK and France.

All Lycées are the same the world over, so arriving mid-term isn't a problem and these cosmopolitan students just get on with it.

Entrance: Fluent French is mandatory. The few places available each year are given to the French families with children already in the French system. Anything left over is allocated following strict rules. Applications should be made online – information on the school's website.

Beware: unless someone in the family is French, chances of admittance are very low.

Exit: The British section offers half-day course for UCAS preparation – helps with personal statements and demystifies the online application process. They also help those who want to sit the Oxbridge entrance exams (2008 saw ten offers). The French section's main aim is to send as many students as possible to France – about half do get into the Prepas and top universities. The other half choose the British system and some go to the States. Counsellors arrive from France for a few days each term to advise parents and students, and applications are processed, but it is up to the families to research the available options. Imperial College, King's, Bath, Edinburgh, LSE, Cambridge and Oxford are very popular. Duke, Yale and Princeton and McGill are favourites as well.

Money Matters: 11 scholarships – recipients selected by the French Education Department. Fees are more than reasonable because the school is maintained and subsidised by the French government

Remarks: The school is huge, with few extra-curricular activities, as is usual in the French system, yet it produces outstanding results and confident and open-minded students.

Lymm High Voluntary Controlled School

Oughtrington Lane, Lymm, Cheshire, WA13 0RB

• Pupils: 1,990 boys and girls, all day • Ages: 11-19 • Size of sixth form: 440 • Non-denom • State

Tel: 01925 755 458
Fax: 01925 758 439
Email: sch_lymm_head@warrington.gov.uk
Website: www.lymmhigh.co.uk

Head Teacher: Since 2008, Miss Angela Walsh – head of Ridgeway High School on the Wirral for the last 13 years.

Academic matters: Lymm High School ranks in top 30 non-selective state schools for results. 97 per cent plus 5+ A*-Cs at GCSE. Specialist language college since 1996 – five language assistants, in separate block of eight classrooms with state of the art technology, offering German, Spanish, French, Italian, Japanese and Mandarin – 80 language on-line learning packages available. Staff from LHS teach and support language learning in partner primary schools – regarded as exemplary practice by CILT. Languages are taught in all of the vocational subjects in key stages 4 and 5. Many students take intermediate and advanced vocational BTecs each year, most passing at the highest level. International cuisine course, with the opportunity for study/work experience in France, and sports vocational course with work experience in Spain. The health science course in key stage 5 completes its work experience in Germany. Established courses in art/design, fashion, public services, travel and tourism, construction. As a result of being judged outstanding in the 2008 Ofsted inspection and being awarded 'high performance school' status, has now secured two additional specialisms, in sport and training.

Good provision for dyslexia and dyspraxia in designated block – currently 200 pupils identified as having special educational needs. School works closely with parents of SEN children from Years 5 and 6 before transition to secondary school. Huge developments in SEN provision over past decade from single SENCo to learning development team of 25 staff, working to evaluate and improve support. Extra literary sessions at 8.15am before school, lunchtime typing/homework club popular for those who need extra help and those escaping hurlyburly of playground. Wheelchair-friendly sixth form, lift and automated doors. Timetabling for ground floor access if necessary lower down school.

Has links with schools in South Africa and is supporting developments at Quashana High School in a black township near East London, which is also supported by one of Lymm's partners, Glen High in Pretoria.

In recent years has developed a strong personalised learning programme which encourages students to take responsibility for their own learning both at school and in other environments. A transparent home learning policy, supported by an active VLE programme, available to parents and students at all times. Students have the opportunity to develop their skills and competencies through residential learning at the school's outdoor centre on Anglesey

Games, Options, the Arts: Sport is a key strength – employs teachers who are county coaches for hockey, has appointed an England U16 squad coach for soccer and strong club-school links for rugby. Vastly improved fixture lists against some of the best independent schools in the north west have resulted in winning the U18 'Daily Mail' Vase in 2006 and the U15 'Daily Mail' Cup in 2007 at Twickenham. A number of county players in hockey, netball, rugby, cricket, football, tennis, athletics, cross-country – including two female county players – and under 18 male and female water polo nationals. Pupils frequently selected for England U18 Rugby Union.

Rowing established at junior and senior levels – won the gold medal at U15 in the National Schools' Championship and two silver medals in the National Championships. The 22 metre pool, gym and sport hall double as local community leisure centre. Water sports a strong feature, with students representing Great Britain in rowing, water polo and sailing. Full size all-weather pitch, and recent land purchases mean the sports fields stretch out in several directions with additional pitches. Now leads a school sports development partnership involving 50 schools in Warrington and Cheshire. Climbing is latest sport – very popular with staff and students of all ages and ability.

Half a dozen dinghies are over-wintering in one of the quads – the school has 14 GPs, Mirrors, Lasers and Toppers and sails every weekend from April to October at local Budworth Reservoir and Tatton Mere. Summer sailing courses held at Roscolyn on Anglesey, where the school has an outdoor residential centre in 38 acres – Ty'n-y-Felin is a 1600s farmhouse with new dormitory wing where all first years bond in form groups and which is busy all summer with camps. Long list of clubs and societies, several bands (one has cut CD), mainly meeting in lunch hour. D of E, Young Enterprise, Whole School Enterprise Challenge. Lots of trips to exotic locations and international sports tours (Australia 2004, South Africa 2007). Music is also a strong element of the school. All students in Year 7 have musical tuition in strings, oboe, bassoon and brass free of charge. Music is also taught by LHS staff in partner primary schools.

Background and Atmosphere: School (Lymm Grammar until 20+ years ago) serves a wide area of rural England. Set on a hillside with far reaching views over the Cheshire plain, all the outlooks are green. Easy access to the motorway network makes Lymm an ultra-leafy suburb – recently acclaimed the most expensive place to live in the north west, with average house price over £200,000+. The school grounds are well presented and cared for, with work, projects, trips and very impressive ceramics on display everywhere. Prefects on entrance doors at breaks and lunch – a nice touch and welcoming. Staff and pupils friendly and communicative. A busy place with leisure and language centres and on-site uniform shop open every day. Healthy eating policy – recently a large sum of money spent on refurbishment to improve lunch time provision.

Notable past pupils include Ruth Lea, director and economic adviser at the Arbuthnot Banking Group and governor of the London School of Economics; Maurice Flanagan CBE, group managing director of Emirate Airlines; Catherine Bruton, author; Neil Fairbrother, cricketer; Richard Eggington, rower, and David Strettle, current England rugby international.

Pastoral Care and Discipline: Parental concerns that size of school is daunting for first years – addressed by established Five Halls system, so each child belongs to smaller unit. Two forms from each year in each of five halls – Arley, Dunham, Moreton, Tatton and Walton, each with own tie. The Halls are the backbone of the school and afford many more students the chance to succeed. In 2006 school achieved the Healthy Schools award and in 2007 was the first school in the authority to be awarded the national standard. In 2009 year system was introduced to complement the Hall system and to support tracking of pupil progress.

Pupils and Parents: Mainly white, rural Cheshire, fully reflective of society. Ethnic minority faces and faiths almost non-existent. Christian with a small 'c' – no church connections. Parents say they're 'bowled over' by the school and describe it as 'the cream of secondary schools for miles'.

Entrance: Non-selective. Place virtually certain for children from one of nine feeder partnership primaries. Heavily over-subscribed locally, so entrance difficult from out of area – for 11+ rejects from neighbouring Trafford, for example – but some with grammar school places choose it in preference.

Exit: A good handful to Oxbridge. About 90 per cent go on to higher education, most to university.

Remarks: A forward looking, happening place – full of life and more opportunities than you would expect even from a large secondary school. Good results with a lot of fun to be had along the way.

Magdalen College School

Linked to Magdalen College Junior School in the Junior section

Cowley Place, Oxford, Oxfordshire, OX4 1DZ

• Pupils: 700 boys; all day (including 100 in junior school); 30 girls a year into the sixth form from 2010 • Ages: 7-18 • Size of sixth form: 155 • C of E • Fees: £13,068 pa • Independent

Tel: 01865 242 191
Fax: 01865 240 379
Email: admissions@mcsoxford.org
Website: www.mcsoxford.org

Master: Since 2008, Dr Tim Hands BA AKC (theological diploma) DPhil (fifties), previously head of Portsmouth Grammar, where he carried through many ambitious and imaginative ideas. A state school pupil turned down by Cambridge ('I was told by the careers adviser at my grammar school that I wouldn't get to university at all'), he read English at King's College, London then on to St Catherine's, Oxford, followed by Oriel, where he ended up as a lecturer. He became housemaster at King's Canterbury then second master at Whitgift School. He comes from a long line of teachers, including both parents and an ancestor who was schoolmaster on HMS Victory. Likes sport and music – he was co-leader of the London Schools Symphony Orchestra and conductor of the Oxford University Chamber Choir, the Schola Cantorum. He is the author of several books about Victorian literature and teaches English A level.

'He's very approachable. Boys and staff all like him,' said a parent. Another commented, 'he comes across as very human and down to earth, not at all in an ivory tower. It must be very hard to be a head in Oxford where lots of your parents are masters of colleges and they all have very high expectations'.

He is married to Jane, a solicitor, and has two sons.

Academic matters: 'This is a school full of A*s,' says the head, and its results are undoubtedly up there in the firmament – nearly 75 per cent A*s at GCSE and over 97 per cent A/B grades at A level in 2009. Tim Hands is a fervent supporter of the new A* A level grade and feels that universities that fail to make it part of their offers for the next few years are 'craven and pusillanimous'. This can, commented a parent, make a child feel that getting an A is an abject failure. However, another recounted how kind and helpful the school had been when her son achieved (relatively) duff GCSE results. 'They were very positive and he felt they were on his side.'

A strongly traditional school in many ways. It was founded as 'a school of the university and within the university' and is focused accordingly. Everyone does three sciences (though one parent commented that 'actually my son would have preferred to have been able to do another humanity instead') and classics is a given – 'they take it for granted as a way of training the mind'. A narrow range of subjects – philosophy, politics and further maths are the only extra A level options. Media studies did creep in briefly and was swiftly banished; economics and theatre studies are under consideration.

However, says the head, 'our curriculum is on the other hand quite liberal'. One afternoon a week in the lower sixth is spent on Waynflete studies (the school was founded by William of Waynflete), which involves a series of talks by experts in their fields on anything from world economics to swine flu. Boys then choose their research topic (generally, but not always, closely linked to their likely university subject) and are taught initially by lectures and seminars at school then in individual or paired tutorials by teachers from Oxford University.

By common consent very high teaching standards. 'My son finds virtually all the teaching exciting and the staff are very interesting and helpful.' 'You have a real sense that they are on the boys' side. My son says, "the masters are really cool – you feel that they love their subjects".' Hard work is expected – 'it's not for the academically idle' – and certainly the previous head hauled the school up through the league tables. 'Lots of the boys have sisters at Oxford High, and their parents felt that they should be achieving the same high grades,' said a parent. Most parents agree that their boys are not hot-housed – 'they don't feel that their noses are to the grindstone' – but they are expected to buckle down and work long hours at home. However, the mother of a talented sportsman was impressed by how flexible the school was prepared to be over his training schedule. 'There was a good symbiotic relationship and he didn't let them down.'

Games, Options, the Arts: Compact site, which includes a sports hall with a multi-gym and squash court and floodlit tennis courts. The 13 acre School Field is just over the Cherwell – rowers can launch straight from the school – and the school also has access to a range of college and university sports grounds, athletics tracks and swimming pools. The main team sports are rugby, hockey, cricket and tennis – girls will play hockey, netball and tennis when they join the sixth form in 2010 – with sailing, rowing and badminton also popular. Pupils have competed in national teams at shooting, rowing and sailing, and many school teams are county champions. The school sounds slightly bemused to find itself very successful at sailing – twice British Schools National Champions.

The junior school recruits the 16 Magdalen College choristers and music is an integral part of life in the senior school too. Singing is particularly strong, as one would expect, with several choral societies and choirs. Choristers sing from the top of Magdalen Tower on May Day morning, Madrigals Society sings from punts on the river, the Oxford Sixth choir – including sixth formers from several Oxford schools – sings in Magdalen College Chapel. There are also orchestras, bands and ensembles. 'The standards are fantastic. A lot of boys are incredibly talented,' said a parent.

Drama is not a GCSE or A level option (yet) – 'we don't have the facilities. But we will have'. The school hall doubles as a chapel and theatre, with an altar and stained glass windows at one end and a stage at the other. The school joins with Oxford High to perform large scale musicals – Grease and Anything Goes are recent successes – but the head has greater plans. 'By 2016 – the quartercentenary of Shakespeare's death – we want to have established ourselves as a performing centre for early modern drama – Shakespeare and his contemporaries. We have already put on a fantastic performance of The Tempest on the School Field, and we are planning a quasi-courtyard theatre.'

The inaugural Arts Festival in June 2009 included a concert in the Sheldonian Theatre, incorporating a celebration of Haydn and Handel. 'I found it simply uncanny to think that Haydn had stood on that spot to get an honorary degree.' It also included An Evening with Tony Benn, a performance of Dracula, art workshops, a Battle of the Bands and many more. 'We want to liberate all the creative forces around us.'

Background and Atmosphere: Founded in 1480 by William Waynflete to educate choristers and prepare other boys for Magdalen College. Former masters include Cardinal Wolsey, former pupils St Thomas More and William Tyndale. It moved in 1890 from its original location in Magdalen College to its present site just the other side of the bridge, opposite St Hilda's. Buildings of a variety of pedigrees, from the School House, built in 1893 and now housing the junior school, to the 2008 New Building which includes the swish new canteen (serving rather tasty lunches) and fabulous top floor art and design rooms with views to die for. Like other former direct grant schools, it has the feeling of a city grammar rather than a public school, with a relaxed approached to uniform and heaps of school bags in random corners. 'We're a little Byzantium, situated where east meets west, where Cowley meets Oxford, very multi-faceted and multi-ethnic.' An overtly Christian school, with non-denominational services in chapel every morning. Boys can opt out, but very few do. 'I like going to chapel,' said a sixth former. 'The whole school gets together, and people enjoy singing.' Boys are relaxed and friendly. 'They don't have that public school arrogance,' said a parent. 'A typical Magdalen boy is high achieving but modest.' 'Most boys can find a niche here,' said another. 'There's such a mix – bookish, geeky ones, sporty extroverts – they're not clones. It's fine to be eccentric.'

Pastoral Care and Discipline: Pastoral care is 'a speciality,' says Tim Hands. 'It is fantastic, and I sense it has been fantastic for a long time. We have a light touch; we're disciplined and liberal simultaneously. Lessons can go from quite chatty to silent concentration when necessary.' The pastoral system is based round the six houses, which are organised by home location and compete at sports, singing, debating etc for the house cup. Expulsion (rare) for theft, systematic anti-social behaviour or involvement with drugs. A parent commented: 'When we've raised any issues they've been prompt and sympathetic. They're worldly-wise about what teenage boys get up to.' 'They run a tight ship,' said another, 'but boys do need boundaries.'

Pupils and Parents: Mostly academic and professional families, including some who are scarily high-powered on the academic front and quite a few who struggle to afford the fees. 'You're not up against much "big money",' said a parent. Many Oxford boys, but private buses serve far-flung areas such as Abingdon. OBs include (amongst many) Ivor Novello, Sam Mendes, Misha Glenny and Ben Goldacre.

Entrance: At 11 by maths, English and verbal reasoning tests and an interview. At 13 by common entrance for prep school boys, after pre-test in Year 7. By school exam for state school boys – maths, English, verbal reasoning and a modern foreign language or Latin. For the sixth form, by verbal reasoning test and interviews with the Master and a subject specialist. Boys (and girls from September 2010) are expected to get A* GCSE grades in their chosen A level subjects.

Exit: A few leave after GCSEs, mostly for local state sixth forms. About a third of A level leavers to Oxbridge (Oxbridge preparation apparently 'super-delux'); the rest nearly all to other top universities e.g. Bristol, Durham, UCL. Sciences probably more popular than humanities, anything from aeronautical engineering to cognitive neuroscience.

Money Matters: Scholarships and exhibitions for academic and extra-curricular excellence – modest amounts, but can be topped up by means-tested bursaries. Choristers get a 66 per cent fee remission. Will generally try to help families who fall on hard times.

Remarks: Up there with the top of the academic high-fliers. Uses its Oxford connections – intellectual, sporting and creative – to the best advantage, creating a niche where sports stars and geeky bookworms are equally at home. 'I feel the school is in safe hands,' said a parent. 'It's a very impressive place.'

Malvern College

Linked to Downs (The), Malvern College Preparatory School in the Junior section

College Road, Malvern, Worcestershire, WR14 3DF

• Pupils: 380 boys and 280 girls; 520 board, 135 day. Plus own prep and pre-prep schools - 310 boys and girls. Ages : 13-18; prep 7-13 and pre-prep 3-7 • Ages: 13-18; prep 7-13 and pre-prep 3-7 • Size of sixth form: 340 • C of E but ecumenical • Fees: Day £19,392; Boarding £29,256-£30,279 pa. • Independent

Tel: 01684 581 500
Fax: 01684 581 615
Email: enquiries@malcol.org
Website: www.malcol.org

Headmaster: Since 2008, Mr Antony Clark MA HDE (early fifties), previously head of Gresham's School for six years – 'When I hit 50 I thought it was time to move on or stay for ever'. Educated in South Africa and at Downing College, Cambridge, where he read history and narrowly missed a cricket blue, he was head of two demanding multi-racial schools in South Africa before he took over Gresham's. Friendly, open, intelligent and modest ('My predecessor did much of the strategic planning from which we are now benefiting'), he has brought 'stability and leadership' to a school which has been through choppy waters and is relieved to have him at the helm. 'We know where we're going now,' says one member of staff; 'Just what we needed,' says a grateful parent. 'What we like about him,' said a sixth form girl, 'is that he has instituted more rewards for success. It isn't just sporting activities which are acknowledged now – he notices a lot and it feels good.'

His wife, Brigitte, has built up the family law section at the law faculty at the University of East Anglia and teaches there three days a week. 'Pretty good for a recycled South African,' says the head, adding with a twinkle, 'I'm very proud of her'. A good rôle model for the girls, she is much more than a mere consort adept at pouring tea and making small talk – boys and girls who know her enjoy her company. The Clarks share the view that education should include 'fun and laughter' as well as appreciating the capacity of the individual within a group. 'Malvern has suffered from over-governance,' says one local prep school head; 'But not any more,' says another. 'This excellent new head has already made his mark.' He has had to exhibit a degree of firmness since his arrival and a small body of parents 'hope he's not going to spoil the fun' – wait and see. Either way, he is not a grey anorak sort of head and examples of his integrity are widely admired.

Academic matters: Malvern was the second school in the country to adopt the IB and runs it alongside A levels – 50 per cent study each. Statistically minded parents reading through the welcome pack (new prospectus and DVD this year) will love all the facts and figures. Up front about its academic results and deserves to be – the good results are right across the board: English and maths, business studies and languages all do well, as do the sciences – separate and dual. Little Latin at A level; Greek at A level and IB. Recent introduction of a three year build up to IB and A levels, largely aimed at bringing non-native speakers up to scratch to prepare them for the English system – lays firm foundations for the subjects taken at the highest level.

Very good facilities – orchards of Apple Macs stretch over the campus and obvious efforts to fully incorporate the use of computers in a creative and positive way, encouraging intellectual curiosity rather than relying on them to give quick answers. This is evident, for instance, in the art school and very impressive library, as well as the whiteboards and reactive whiteboards in all the classrooms. As befits a school which pioneered the Nuffield Science course, good laboratories (a Nobel prize for Chemistry was won by an old boy early in the last century). The teaching areas are bright and purposeful and the teaching 'lively and encouraging,' says one satisfied dad. 'Pretty good,' agreed an A level student, who probably meant much the same. As far as learning difficulties are concerned, one pupil we spoke to was full of praise for the help he had received with his dyslexia. The overall impression we received was that help with more serious difficulties was less apparent, though bags of sensitive advice and support.

We detected that running the IB as well as traditional A levels was not all plain sailing – not difficult to identify a touch of tribal rivalry between the two camps: pupils we met indulged in healthy discussion/arguments over the comparative merits of each. One argument says that the IB stultifies extra-curricular activities and produces breadth at the expense of depth; the other side appreciates the breadth of IB and that their last term ends at half term. Everyone commented on the nigh impossibility of playing for a senior cricket team while working for the IB. Perhaps most important is the thoughtful and expert guidance from heads of department, housemasters and teachers in general, acknowledged by pupils and parents alike. Only one pupil commented wistfully, 'I wish we were all in the same boat together,' and added, 'for social reasons.' One interested observer with a professional interest in Malvern spoke of 'boringly studious Europeans dampening the atmosphere'. In reply, the school talks of celebrating its global links and actively seeks to promote understanding of the world beyond, not merely through the IB community service.

In an attempt at tackling what the headmaster refers to as 'the boredom many bright pupils feel', he has appointed a school-friendly academic development co-ordinator with special responsibility for challenging and extending the more able pupils. The aim is to identify particularly gifted and talented pupils and encourage a lively sense of intellectual curiosity. Numerically Malvern is top-heavy – a hundred more pupils in the sixth form than in the first year – and the wish is to inculcate a 'mini university feel' – in the academic sense, of course. A burgeoning partnership with Hereford Academy, including an annual scholarship into the sixth form.

Games, Options, the Arts: In the history of Malvern, the decision to play rugby in the winter term and football in the spring – implying, as it does, a greater importance attached to rugby – is comparatively recent. That has not yet proved an unqualified success, though younger teams are performing excellently and plans afoot to improve the standard of games. 'The College has not been performing to the standards we would hope for,' says a rheumy eyed Old Malvernian. Last year the College opened a large sports complex complete with indoor cricket school used by Worcester CCC, which contains a double sports hall, 25m swimming pool, climbing wall, squash courts, fitness suite and shooting range. The two rackets courts have been recently refurbished and now offer tournament quality standards for play. Recognising that facilities alone are not enough, the school has appointed an Olympic athlete to run the sports development, with the aim of creating a centre of excellence. Wonderful cricket pro strives to maintain Malvern's reputation as a cricket school. Already an abundance of sporting and outdoor opportunities, and in the midst of the hockey and lacrosse a very successful girls' football team.

Much opportunity for music making – the music school is housed in a wonderful Victorian monastery with the cells providing atmospheric practice rooms approached via an impressive staircase. Lots of concerts – orchestral and smaller groups as well as choral. Close by, a handsome church now serves as a concert hall as well as a venue for lectures and meetings; the crypt has recently been converted into a hugely appreciated sixth form chilling out centre with an attractive bar, supervised by staff.

The art school is pretty dreary from outside but inside positively fizzes with creativity and energy under its dynamic director. Genuinely exciting examples of work, all over the campus and constantly rotated, are testament to the high standards achieved and a feature of the school. Fine art most popular, though the variety of media pursued is wonderful. The DT building, linked to the art school with an amazing bright, glassy staircase with bags of display areas, is heart-lifting. Functional and inspirational building within which cars are constructed and developed and budding designers are encouraged to stretch the boundaries of possibilities. Both buildings are open at the weekends and used. One boy told us, 'I virtually live here.' Popular at GCSE.

Strong CCF and D of E with plenty of opportunities for adventure, not least at the school's cottage in the Brecon Beacons, which everyone attends during their time at the school. Much community service.

Background and Atmosphere: Founded in 1865, quickly expanded – now eleven houses scattered around the 200 or so acres, terraced out of the Malvern Hills. Justifiably famous for its setting, it is not just a country school, as it is so often labelled. True, the town of Malvern doesn't give the impression of bright lights and the lure of sin, but the school does not feel out in the sticks. No whiff of fertilizer drifting over when the wind is in the wrong direction; no distant sound of cattle winding slowly o'er the lea – in fact, the approach past handsome Victorian villas feels a little cramped, as you thread through the parked cars. Once through the tower of the main entrance, however, the scene below is breathtaking and there it does feel like a country school. So although it isn't a city school, by any means, it does benefit from the proximity of the town and can play both cards. Pupils appreciate the town's change of atmosphere and one girl told us how excited she was to be sitting in a café with her boy friend when Simon Callow walked in. (The town's theatre, only yards from the school, stages a wide range of productions before going on to London and is much appreciated by staff and pupils.)

Has been fully coeducational for 18 years and feels happy with it. Pupils still eat in houses – a recent move to go for central feeding was met with fierce and triumphant resistance. The advantages of this – especially with a good catering company in overall charge, so none of the old business of starting the month with caviar and ending with baked beans and last week's bread – include the homely feel of guzzling with chums, the opportunity for house parents to observe behaviour and feel the atmosphere, and for girls to be girls/boys to be boys. Socialising areas downstairs for boys and girls, otherwise it's strolling in the grounds or tea in the town. 'The staff treat us with great maturity and sense,' said an apparently serious pupil. We were lucky enough to have lunch twice and to appreciate not only the very good food but also the excellent company of the pupils, clearly used to talking to alleged adults.

About to embark on an ambitious upgrading programme for boarding houses: two new ones have been most sensitively designed with 21st century pupils in mind within a 19th century ambience. Thereafter one house will be used as a 'decanting house' while another is being refurbished and on goes the merry-go-round. Younger pupils sleep in small dorms with separate studies before graduating to bed sitters. Day pupils are attached to boarding houses and flexi-boarding is available when room.

Pastoral Care and Discipline: As with so many boarding schools, revolves around its house system. Parents almost unanimous in praising the quality of the house parents. A few little gripes, as expected, but an overall appreciation. Each house has a resident house tutor and house assistant; one of the spin offs of house feeding is that members of staff lunch in different houses on different days of the week, which means they get to know a wide circle of pupils outside the classroom and vice versa.

Junior pupils are assigned a tutor up to GCSE; thereafter they may choose their tutor – and not necessarily one who teaches their subject. The attitude to bullying is clearly laid out, as is the complaints procedure. The safeguarding officer regularly visits the houses, is known to all and freely available for consultation and support. Pupils who wish to become involved with peer mentoring and how to listen. A good safety net is in place and no one need ever feel isolated. Time after time we heard that from pupils.

The school's policy on drugs is clearly displayed and well known to pupils. Personal sympathy and offers of help will be shown and counselling offered, but basically, if you're dealing or caught in possession, you can expect to be expelled. Testing is an option if reasonable suspicions are aroused. Drinking is dealt with on a graded system from sin bin to red card; smoking is also dealt with on a graded scale leading to rustication. Above all common sense and the law of the land are the guidelines.

Pupils and Parents: A good cross-section of parents, mostly from the professional classes. 40 per cent of pupils come from abroad and from 27 countries – lots from Europe and an increasing proportion from Africa; an annual clutch comes every year from Germany, mostly for two years (now a German Old Malvernian on the Council). The international feel lies easily – pupils talked openly about the pleasures of getting to know children from far flung corners of the world. A smiling and greeting school, from the excellent porter to the pupils who showed thoughtful courtesy when directing us.

Entrance: Initial dealings are with the legendary registrar. Once registered, entrance is via CE (50 per cent pass), scholarship or, in the case of children from state schools, a paper set by Malvern in English, maths and science. 30 per cent from The Downs, the school's associated and updated prep school, the rest from some 25 other prep schools. About 70 sixth formers join every year either via entrance papers in the subjects they wish to read at A level or IB or the scholarship.

Exit: 100 per cent to university: 16 to Oxbridge in the last three years, five to the States. Some to European universities.

Money Matters: Scholarships are available for a wide variety of talents both at 13 years old and sixth form. Bursarial help is available after means testing – don't be afraid to ask.

Remarks: A school of thought says Malvern has had to be innovative in reaction: the demise of assisted places, for instance, and falling numbers in 1992 (Lloyds etc). Whatever the explanation, it has shown a degree of flair and imagination, reaching high standards without ever reaching the peaks – perhaps it has been slightly off the boil over the last few years. The prospectus speaks of entering 'an exciting phase of development' – certainly the current mood is buoyant. It needs to be, with so much financial investment, in these tricky times. Recent interest has grown dramatically. Perhaps, as someone has suggested, 'The giant is awakening' – watch for Brobdingnags in Worcestershire.

Malvern St James

Avenue Road, Great Malvern, Worcestershire, WR14 3BA

• Pupils: 395 girls; 180 full boarders, 15 weekly boarders, 200 day • Ages: 4-18 • Size of sixth form: 145 • C of E • Fees: Day £12,330-£14,085; Boarding £15,345-£27,825 pa • Independent

Tel: 01684 584 624
Fax: 01684 566 204
Email: registrar@malvernstjames.co.uk
Website: www.malvernstjames.co.uk

Headmistress: Since 2010, Mrs Patricia Woodhouse BMus (Hons), educated at former Stafford Girls' High School, then music at London University, early career divided between working in the City and as a freelance musician. Has been involved in educating girls for over twenty years in a variety of schools – director of music at Wimbledon High School, sixth form housemistress at Queenswood, deputy headmistress at St Mary's Wantage and formerly headmistress at Abbots Bromley School for Girls. A governor of Bloxham School, on the Advisory Board of The Old Vicarage Preparatory School and an ISI Inspector.

Academic matters: The former Malvern Girls' College and St James's both had fine academic reputations and consistently high exam results and the new school looks to be following suit. In 2010, Malvern St James scored 98 per cent passes at A level with 82 per cent A*-Bs and 58 per cent A*-A. At GCSE, it got 94 per cent A*–C grades, 60 per cent A*-A. Maths particularly popular – nearly 70 per cent of current Year 12s doing A level maths.

Malvern St James says it offers 'first-class teaching adapted to the needs of individual pupils,' combined with top-notch facilities like science centre, multimedia language centre and impressive drama studio. Whiteboards, digital projectors and computers galore, plus four ICT suites. School has recently introduced electronic registration – staff mark attendances and absences on their laptops and at the press of a button numbers whiz through to reception.

French, Spanish, German and Latin taught, with Mandarin available for sixth formers. Well-stocked library with 26,000 books and resources (Harry Potter, Ian McEwan and the Brontes perennial favourites) plus a bookshop next door. When it comes to SEN, one-to-one support available for dyslexia, dyspraxia, EAL. School also offers critical thinking ('a really good way of expanding your mind,' says head) to Years 7 to 13. Around 35 girls currently taking AS critical thinking too.

Games, Options, the Arts: Lots of opportunities for boarders and day girls alike. Full range of sports on offer – netball, hockey, lacrosse, tennis, rounders etc. Facilities excellent – all-weather surface, 25-metre swimming pool and indoor sports centre. New state of the art £4.5 million sports hall opened in 2008, complete with six-court hall and dance studio. Competitive house system, with lots of inter-house sports competitions.

Masses of music groups to join, including orchestras, jazz and big band, and drama and dancing too. Stunning choir, much in demand to sing at charity events locally, and two-thirds of pupils take instrumental or singing lessons. Receptionist sitting outside hall where chamber choir practice being held beamed appreciatively and told us, 'this is the best place in the school to have your desk!' Arts strong and school has been given Artsmark award for its programme of drama, music, design, literature and dance. Stunning artwork on show throughout school, from vividly patterned textiles to fine art.

Background and Atmosphere: New school formed when Malvern Girls' College amalgamated with smaller St James's. School based on a 40-acre site in imposing former Imperial Hotel in the heart of picturesque 19th Century spa town. Main building is in leafy road opposite Great Malvern railway station, so very handy for boarders! Officially opened in autumn 2006 by the Duke of Gloucester – plaque unveiled and hundreds of blue and gold balloons released into the sky to celebrate. School is very much part of local community. It opened its doors for recent English Heritage open day and was amazed to get 200 visitors arriving for tea, croquet and a guided tour of landmark Victorian building.

Main school building houses stylish new entrance hall (complete with trendy curved glass reception desk and plasma screen showing details of school menus, activities and pictures from key school events) classrooms and the York Hall, a stunning art deco assembly hall opened by the late Queen Mother (then Duchess of York) in the 1930s.

Girls can board from the age of seven upwards, with full-boarding, weekly and flexi-boarding on offer. Boarders live in four houses, organised in age groups. Two houses are a few minutes' walk away, while the rest are on main school site. All houses offer a full weekend programme. Youngest girls sleep four to a dorm, while sixth formers get their own rooms. Girls wear smart navy uniform (tartan skirts and neat navy jackets) up till 16. No uniform for sixth form – but girls discouraged from jeans, flip-flops, heavy make-up etc.

Day girls and boarders very well integrated. Day pupils stay till 6pm every night and often come in at weekends to take part in activities. No Saturday school – typical weekend includes house parties, netball, hockey and lacrosse sessions run by international coaches, theatre trips and a photography competition. School food served in two dining rooms. Lots of choice (hot, cold, vegetarian, salad bar) and staff always eat with girls.

Pastoral Care and Discipline: Few rules but school prides itself on very strong code of conduct. Head believes in listening and being fair but says that where there are rules it's important to enforce them. In fact, discipline problems are virtually unheard of. Zero tolerance on drugs, alcohol and smoking. Head is a realist though and says that if a sixth former is suspected to have been drinking she would be referred to the sixth form council. 'My feeling about alcohol is that we should help them learn to be sensible.'

Bullying rare – staff know pupils well and if they spot any girl being left out they swiftly pick up on it. Peer support group made up of year 10s and up, all of whom receive training. All girls allocated to tutor group of 12, with tutors reporting to assistant heads. Girls of all ages mix well – head says it helps to create a 'happy environment'. Head girl and deputy head girl in place, with raft of 15 prefects – each attached to a form and actively involved in areas like games, PR and communications, showing prospective parents round etc. School has full-time chaplain and girls can pop into chapel for a few minutes' reflection in their spare time. Head regularly holds suppers in elegant yellow drawing room for tutor groups from Years 11 to 13 and teas for Years 3 to 10 so she gets to know pupils outside classroom as well as in.

Pupils and Parents: From all over. Day girls live up to an hour away (minibuses from as far afield as Hereford and Ross-on-Wye) while boarders mostly from the Midlands and London. Large international contingent – a quarter of pupils from abroad – Hong Kong, Thailand, Brunei, Russia, Eastern Europe, Russia, Spain, Germany, Canada etc. Head is proud of the fact that girls are 'confident without being arrogant' and girls we met seemed helpful, smiley and enthusiastic. Clara Furse, the first woman chief executive of the London Stock Exchange, the late HRH Princess Alice, Duchess of Gloucester and the childcare expert Penelope Leach are former pupils of St James's School while Malvern Girls' alumnae include the late Dame Elizabeth Lane, the first woman High Court Judge, and writer Aminatta Forna. More recent former pupils include BBC correspondent Hannah Hennessy, journalist Elizabeth Day, surgeon Abbie Franklin and city high flyers Helen Freer and Elizabeth Sharpe.

Around 50 girls aged four to 11 in junior school but numbers growing steadily. Juniors housed in own section of main building, with separate playground, but get to use main school facilities like swimming pool and drama centre.

Entrance: All prospective pupils are interviewed by head. Own junior school provided ten pupils into Year 7 this year, with rest coming from local primaries and prep schools like The Downs, The Elms, Kitebrook House, The Croft, Stratford Prep, Godstowe and The Carrdus. At 11, girls sit cognitive ability and comprehension tests while others do CE at 13. Main entry points are Years 7, 9 and sixth form. Girls looking to enter sixth form must take a written paper in one of the subjects they wish to study at A level and a general essay paper (or EAL paper for girls from outside UK).

Exit: After GCSE, the majority stays on. Virtually all sixth form leavers to university. Popular destinations Oxbridge (six in 2007), Imperial College, LSE and University College London while courses in vogue range from medicine and veterinary science to law and economic management.

Money Matters: The school offers a number of academic, music, sport, art and drama scholarships, which are worth between 20 and 40 per cent of fees.

Remarks: This newly-merged school has got off to a flying start. A lively, creative place with impressive academic results and lots on offer to occupy pupils outside the classroom too.

The Manchester Grammar School

Linked to Manchester Grammar School Junior Section (The) in the Junior section

Old Hall Lane, Rusholme, Manchester, Lancashire, M13 0XT

• Pupils: 1,420 boys; all day • Ages: 7-18 • Size of sixth form: 400 • C of E links, but basically non-denom • Fees: £9,660 pa • Independent

Tel: 0161 224 7201
Fax: 0161 257 2446
Email: general@mgs.org
Website: www.mgs.org

High Master: Since 2004, Dr Christopher Ray BA PhD FRSA (youthful late fifties). Educated at UCL, Churchill College, Cambridge, and Balliol College Oxford. Taught at Marlborough, then a spell teaching in universities before returning to schools when he was 40. Came here from three years as head of The John Lyon School, Harrow. He has written two books on the philosophy of space and time and is currently chairman of the HMC academic policy sub-committee and a member of the ISC education committee.

We find him enigmatic, but parents talk of his discreet and calm authority, without arrogance or any swaggering about. Some may interpret this as a lack of charisma but his seems to be a background presence, an under-girding strength, and they praise him for allowing others to take the credit for the school's success and 'incredible pastoral care', saying, 'He must be very good at his job because the school runs like clockwork'. Many also welcome his changes to the curriculum, especially introducing iGCSEs. Those who have little direct contact with him say it's because 'the initial structures for dealing with problems are so efficient and robust' – he is known for being 'approachable and not intimidating, viewed by the boys with respect and awe rather than fear'. We've also heard that, as far as he is able in such a big school, he takes an interest in every pupil, occasionally involving himself 'directly on a personal level with pastoral care or motivation of a single boy'.

Academic matters: Consistently formidable, with over 85 per cent of GCSEs at A or A*, 95 per cent of A levels A/B; over half of the boys get three or more As. Introduction of IGCSE spreading from maths and the three sciences to almost all subjects: 'Able children need serious challenges if you are to get the very best out of them,' is HM's opinion. Most parents seem to agree, and so do we. School offers A levels almost exclusively in 'hard' subjects, with strong results across the board. The first batch of IB students (about 20 per cent of the sixth form) took their exams in 2010. Since 2008, some 30 a year have taken IB.

Love of learning is a given for many of the boys and, in most subject areas, the education goes way beyond the official curriculum – attentive boys absorb a vast store of general knowledge. Staff are a mix of long timers with much experience and newer bloods with masses of enthusiasm, many of them textbook authors and leaders in their fields; some offer talks to other schools as part of a new visiting speaker programme. A good proportion of women teachers. A level classes rarely exceed 12 pupils, 25 the norm lower down the school, and the homework expectations of an hour a night for 11 year olds up to 16 self-directed hours a week for sixth formers seems to parents to be 'about right'.

Two fabulous, well used libraries – lower and upper school – open from 8am–6pm. New archive library being developed in lead-up to 500 year anniversary in 2015. Great success in national and international Olympiads and challenges. Links with nearby Withington and Manchester High girls – the Hugh Oldham lecture day invites over 200 boys and girls from some 20 schools to preparatory workshops and to hear a visiting speaker of note, Douglas Hurd in 2009. MGS teachers also help with Oxbridge preparation at other local sixth forms. SEN, within the usual limits for highly academic schools, carefully attended to; 80 per cent of buildings are wheelchair accessible.

Games, Options, the Arts: Fantastic sport both in variety and the level played. Lots of local and national players and a rich programme of competitions and tours, particularly for those who are keen or in top teams. Some parents would like school to instigate a more robust system for 'boys who don't put their hands up' to get involved as a matter of course.

Water polo deserves a paragraph on its own. School points out that this rests on a foundation of exceptionally strong swimming.

Art continues to wow. New 200 seat, plus two wheelchairs, theatre, funded by donations, due to open in 2010 – even without it drama excels, ditto music. Unique full-length play-writing award, the Robert Bolt Memorial Prize, open to any pupil and judged by Royal Exchange Theatre (£500 for winner). An extra-curricular something for everyone and lots of top achievers prove that 'the more you do, the more you can do'. D of E; every imaginable academic and arts society and club – no excuse to be bored or inactive. Impressive charitable fundraising – long standing friendship with Mwiri School in Uganda, and more recently with Nawaikoke School also. Many trips at varying costs to Europe and beyond, outdoor centres in Derbyshire and the North Pennines and much loved camps. A team of four MGS boys represented Great Britain at the Linguistics Olympiad in Poland. Older boys bent on altruistic travels can apply to school travel fund.

Background and Atmosphere: Founded in 1515 by Hugh Oldham, Bishop of Exeter, a year before he founded Corpus Christi College, Oxford (with which links still exist), to 'educate able boys regardless of their parents' means'. Now the largest independent boys' school in the country on an airy green site just south of Manchester city centre.

A tree-, bus- and car-lined drive, flanked by pitches and courts, leads to an arch into the quad with science blocks and the junior section off to the left behind the cricket pavilion. Inside former high masters look down on long lists of MGS's war dead in the traditional hall where one often finds a pupil practising the organ or another instrument, giving a timeless feel, a solid sense of the weight of generations. Lunch is by termly ticket with packed option for those organised enough to request it when on activities. Uniform is flexible and economical with blue blazer and grey trousers, blue or white shirt from any outlet and the badge and tie available from school office. The parents' association struggles manfully to organise lost property.

Pastoral Care and Discipline: Pastoral care is generally outstanding, especially if parents are forthcoming, and usually it's easy to reach the appropriate person. Commendations for excellence, notes home and detentions as sanctions; rigorously implemented drugs policy including random testing for previous offenders. MGS says, 'One of the important features of the policy is that we consider MGS to be a community of people, not just a collection of buildings and playing fields. Thus the policy is implemented beyond the physical confines of the school estate and the random testing component is used principally for those whom we know have used drugs out of school. This is both to give us and their parents confidence they are no longer involved and to give the boys a credible way of saying no if/when they are offered drugs in the future.' Gold prefects chosen by peer and staff vote, with school captain, who'll be forever recorded in gold paint on an entrance hall board, selected by interview with senior staff. Shirts are meant to be tucked in and ties tied, but boys round school look reassuringly teenagerly and a feeling that, in the main, school doesn't 'sweat the small stuff' – everyone's too busy with far more fascinating things.

Pupils and Parents: Extremely diverse in every way and from a huge geographical area. Long journeys therefore for many. The city centre, Cheadle and Altrincham supervised school shuttle buses (which run both after school and after later activities) have proved very popular. (Bus journeys can be stressful for younger boys who don't yet appreciate the networking opportunity with girls.) Parents praise the fact that MGS is a place where quirky, eccentric or anoraky academic boys can exist happily beside trendy boys who ooze street-cred kudos. Many ethnic and faith backgrounds; separate assemblies on Fridays including a secular option.

Dozens of distinguished Old Boys, including rows of FRSs, not least Sir Michael Atiyah. Also Mike Atherton, Michael Wood, the Crawley brothers, actors Ben Kingsley and Robert Powell, Robert Bolt, Steven Pimlott, and National Theatre head Nicolas Hytner, writer Alan Garner, John Ogdon, LSE boss Sir Howard Davies, Thomas de Quincey, plus several members of the Sieff family and Simon Marks (partner of Spencer).

Entrance: Looking for the very most academically able boys, to the extent that the 2009 intake is a form smaller than normal because MGS is committed 'never to lower the bar on quality'. Sixty places taken by graduates of MGS's own, new, junior section, reducing the intake of new boys at 11+ to just 122, from some 450 applicants. All outside applicants invited to an exam day with four papers in January and to a further assessment day in school, with the hope of diminishing hothouse tutoring for 11+ hoop jumping. Each boy's previous school report also carefully considered. Average of A at GCSE needed for sixth form entry, when a bit of movement in and out for a variety of reasons.

Exit: Great record of bagging top courses at top institutions – 38 to Oxbridge in 2009. London, Birmingham, Nottingham, Durham and Leeds popular, more than a few stay in Manchester. Excellent guidance through the UCAS process with bags of experience and inside advice. Five applied to Harvard in 2009 – four gained offers and two accepted places there.

Money Matters: Good value for money at senior level, especially given the calibre of education. Discount for siblings and (in 2009, perhaps to be repeated) an option for parents to pay last year's fee if they pay in advance for the whole year. Uniform and lunch relatively inexpensive. Impressive bursary foundation, over 240 receiving assistance and over a hundred families receiving full support. MGS was the only one of five independent schools to pass every section of the Charity Commission public benefit test without qualification – in our view MGS community contribution is fulsome and impressive. Furthermore, school tells us that it has quadrupled its hardship funding – 'Considerable assistance has been given in the present climate; no parent has been required to remove their child precipitately – we take the view that MGS is a community and that if we can help we will'.

Remarks: Still the tip-top senior school choice for boys in the Manchester area, offering superb and well-rounded education and the best chance of stunning results, as befits pupils drawn from the very top of the academic bands. New junior division since September 2008 (qv).

Manchester High School for Girls

Linked to Manchester High School For Girls Preparatory Department in the Junior section

Grangethorpe Road, Manchester, Lancashire, M14 6HS

• Pupils: 950 girls, all day • Ages: 11-18; preparatory department 4-11
• Size of sixth form: 195 • Non-denom • Fees: £9,270 pa • Independent

Tel: 0161 224 0447
Fax: 0161 224 6192
Email: administration@mhsg.manchester.sch.uk
Website: www.manchesterhigh.co.uk

Headmistress: Since January 2009, Mrs Claire Hewitt BSc. Educated at Wakefield Girls' High School, chemistry degree plus PGCE from Sheffield University. Taught science at Harrogate Ladies' College, then head of chemistry at Fulneck School, West Yorkshire. Head of chemistry at Sheffield High School, followed by director of studies, then deputy head teacher until 2005. Came from a headship at King Edward VI Grammar School, Louth.

Academic matters: Outstanding A level results in 2010– 100 per cent pass rate and 94 per cent A*–B; GCSE: 87 per cent A*/A. Awarded International Baccalaureate (IB) World School status in 2010 and now offers IB Diploma alongside A levels.

Form groups average 28, with smaller teaching groups. Great facilities – plenty of ICT provision, two state of the art language labs, refurbished science labs and stunning sports complex. Broad curriculum includes graphics, textiles and food technology, GCSE PE and, more recently, A level too. GCSE in dance an option and all year 10s take the RS short course. Well used extra clinics in maths and science – 'The teachers here are amazing, giving up their frees to really help you'.

Games, Options, the Arts: Fabulous, up-market new sports complex, opened by Dame Kelly Holmes. Huge hall has climbing wall and five star viewing gallery complete with leather sofas. Bright air conditioned multi-use dance studio, extensive fitness suite for older girls and staff, indoor pool. Wales' hockey coach on staff, tennis also strong, county players in various sports. Super music house with 12 sound proof practice rooms. Two orchestras, two choirs, wind band, quartets and over 400 girls take individual instrumental or singing lessons. Speech and drama lessons also a popular option; drama studio has floor to ceiling views of gardens and black out drapes. Main hall fits all seniors on stacking tiered chairs which are rolled away for exams or events. All girls have to take three extra-curricular activities a year – some hardly pause for breath.

Background and Atmosphere: Founded in 1874, 'to provide for Manchester's daughters what has been provided without stint for Manchester's sons'. Plenty of siblings at nearby Manchester Grammar and joins with boys there for societies, drama, music events and, of course, on the bus. Current school rebuilt after WW2 bomb damage. High quality, modern architecture gives spacious, bright and purposeful feel and all is softened by immaculate, very pretty gardens with manicured lawns and internal quad with clipped box parterre. Just two miles from city centre yet a verdant oasis bordered by public parkland.

Spick and span classrooms – the newly refurbished areas positively sparkle. Even the extensive locker areas are neat and tidy; respectful girls in cream and black open doors and stand for the head. A friendly, culturally diverse community where girls say, 'Individuality and difference aren't just accepted – they're celebrated'.

Pastoral Care and Discipline: Usual peer and staff hierarchy for pastoral care, but first port of call is often the much loved, long term, full time-school nurse, whose four bed sick bay doubles as a listening room and general refuge for wide ranging problems, minor and major. Extra classes are timetabled at exam times to talk about coping with stress and pressure, but staff and girls say overall most problems come from friendship issues in the younger years. Minor discipline matters are addressed firmly and fast (detentions for chewing gum) and the full age range on site engenders thoughtfulness. A parent praised school for working hard with her 'wayward adolescent daughter'.

All doors security protected with CCTV and caretakers keep an eye on things, including main road crossings to bus stops. Girls say that despite proximity to the city, they always feel safe and secure and praise head for listening to their ideas via student council – 'What's the point unless they've got a real voice?' says head. Water dispensers are a result of this process. Staff enjoy excellent work preparation room as well as daily cakes (at cost to the individual, school points out) and common room – 'I believe in looking after the staff,' says head. 'They're our most important resource.'

Pupils and Parents: Gathered from all points of the compass, far and near, served by well established buses, some of them supervised, designated MHSG and favoured by the prep girls. Lots of professional families and all cultures and creeds represented – Friday's optional assemblies include Christian, Jewish, Muslim, Hindu, Sikh, humanist and secular gatherings. No specific prayer room but a classroom is set aside for special religious festivals. Old girls include, famously, a clutch of Pankhursts; assorted businesswomen such as Clara Freeman OBE, Marks and Spencer's first female executive director; Merlyn Lowther, the Bank of England's first female chief cashier, whose signature's on every bank note; leading lawyers such as Ann Alexander, who acted for the families in the Shipman case; and, doing her bit for the cult of TV celebrity, Judy Finnigan, of 'Richard and Judy' fame. Plenty of less daunting rôle models too in entrance foyer hall of fame, where distinctly non-celeb girls doing great things for charity are also featured. Pupils say the old girls' network is strong – 'It's easy to contact them via email for real opinions on universities or careers,' they say.

Entrance: Academically selective at 11, initially by exams in maths, essay writing, comprehension, verbal and non verbal reasoning. Then by interview and primary school report, whittling down four applicants for every place. About fifty per cent come from state primaries. Cleverly produced promotional DVD with prospectus will have parents clamouring for a place.

Exit: Impressive leavers' destination lists – all to higher education, some via a gap year, most to solid courses at established top notch universities or art schools. About 7 per cent to Oxbridge, with success for about two thirds of those who apply. Pupils praise careers provision, which is integrated into school life from Year 8 and includes careers aptitude testing.

Money Matters: A few academic/music/sports/dance scholarships for age 11, plus means-tested bursaries and two free places (conditions apply). One of the nation's top value schools based on A level points per pound in a survey by The Halifax Building Society. Twenty per cent discount for a third child in the school.

Remarks: Lovely surroundings; excellent all round education turning out irrepressibly articulate girls. One parent said, 'By the time they reach sixth form they're pretty impressive young women.' Subtle but discernible Pankhurst legacy underlined by the prospectus strap line, 'Today's students, tomorrow's successful women'.

Mander Portman Woodward (MPW)

90-92 Queen's Gate, South Kensington, London, SW7 5AB

• Pupils: 525 boys and girls • Ages: 14-19 • Non-denom • Fees: £16,821-£20,955 pa • Independent

Tel: 020 7835 1355
Fax: 020 7259 2705
Email: london@mpw.co.uk
Website: www.mpw.co.uk

Principal: Since 2010, Steven Boyes BA, MSc, PGCE (mid-forties). First became principal in 1997 and now back at the helm after four years, during which he was worked on a number of development projects for the MPW Group. Read geography and English at Lancaster University before going on to do a master's degree in management sciences. He has subsequently published articles on aspects of physical geography and is a textbook reviewer for two publishers. He was a senior A level examiner for over a decade and is a serving inspector for the Independent Schools Inspectorate. Was appointed chairman of the Council of Independent Further Education (CIFE) in 2010. Married to a lawyer, Melanie, with two children aged 10 and 12. A former county level squash player, he still plays a variety of racket sports and golf. Other hobbies include collecting crime novels and political biographies and crosswords.

Academic matters: You can take or retake GCSEs and A levels here, in one or two years or even a over a term. You can also come in for after-school private tuition, for a week's revision course at Easter or for extra Oxbridge preparation. Never more than eight in a class and those retaking in a year are taught in a different group from those in the second year of a course. Will run courses for single students but with half the normal teaching hours – 'if you're being taught one-to-one you whizz through the syllabus'.

A staggering range of 43 subjects in any combination at A level – from ceramics to geology to statistics. The 'reassuringly expensive' fees fund a high enough ratio of staff to students to provide a genuinely personalised curriculum, with staff willing to set extra practice work when necessary or go over tricky subjects with individuals after lessons. 'And because the classes are so small, they can stop and explain anything you don't understand,' said a student.

The latest ISI report commented on an over-reliance on worksheets and model answers at the expense of independent learning, though most classes we saw involved staff and student discussion. 'I felt the comment was a bit unfair,' says the principal. 'If you are providing someone with a one year A level, you have to do it in ways reminiscent of the old crammers. But pedagogy needs to be increasingly diverse. I was amazed when I arrived by the quality of the teaching staff here.' MPW stands or falls by its exam results and university places and a high proportion of staff are also public examiners – 'This can be a double-edged sword: great expertise but sometimes too great a focus on exams'.

Students get plenty of timed tests and exam practice. Parents are kept up to date with twice-termly reports and can also log in to see test results, what homework has been set and whether or not it has been done – 'particularly useful for those who are overseas'. They are also encouraged to pick up the phone to personal tutors whenever they have a query. 'They put themselves out to be helpful,' said a parent.

Helping students get into Oxbridge was MPW's original raison d'être, and it has added medical, veterinary, dental and law school applications to its expertise. Indeed, it publishes books on these and several other related subjects. It provides interview practice, seminars and specialist preparation for university entrance tests, plus detailed guidance on completing UCAS forms. 'The director of studies was very helpful over my son's personal statement,' said a parent. 'I didn't get involved at all, which was such a relief.'

Historically, SEN help was not high on the agenda. But the principal has appointed a head of academic support – 'I didn't want to ghettoise particular learning difficulties' – who is a qualified educational psychologist. Staff are being trained to use academic support plans and set appropriate targets for students, such as always writing down verbal instructions. 'We're not an SEN school but I think everyone is getting something out of having a SENCo. It is a growing area of need.'

Games, Options, the Arts: Offers fine art, ceramics, photography, textiles and graphics, separately or combined into a single A or AS. It has art and ceramics studios, two darkrooms and a well-equipped history of art library. It organises two exhibitions each year, with work by ex-students at art college or university on display alongside pieces by current students and staff, and helps those aiming at art college to put a portfolio together. Art historians visit Florence or Paris as well as local galleries.

A donation from a grateful ex-student now at Cambridge has re-equipped the theatre studies studio, used for extra-curricular activities such as yoga as well as examination practicals. The new drama club has staged its first performance, *The Real Inspector Hound.*

Sport is not a major part of college life, particularly in the sixth form, where it is voluntary – GCSE students have one compulsory and one voluntary session a week. However free membership to the nearby gym is extremely popular and enthusiastic football and rugby teams. Netball is, by popular request, another option.

Background and Atmosphere: Founded in 1973 by three eponymous Cambridge graduates to offer small group A level retake and Oxbridge entrance tuition. Now greatly expanded, with sister colleges in Birmingham and Cambridge, it occupies three listed stucco buildings in smart South Kensington, where enviably large sums have evidently been invested in facilities and decoration.

Buzzy but relaxed atmosphere, with staff and students on first name terms, no dress restrictions and a lack of petty rules – 'You're not going to be told to do your tie up or tuck your shirt in here'. Some students find it hard to make friends, since communal activities and space are limited and fellow-students may be there for only a short period of time. 'But everyone's very friendly,' said a parent, 'and my son really likes all his teachers – they treat him like an adult.'

Pastoral Care and Discipline: 'I feel they're actually concerned about you,' said a student, 'which I never felt at my last school.' Personal tutors, who have a light teaching load, are responsible for students' work and welfare – 'Too often schools divide up the pastoral and the academic. Our tutors are a one-stop shop for parents – the buck stops with them'. Parents are full of praise – 'They are very open to any kind of discussion. And unlike his previous school, we get lots of communication'.

Despite the relaxed atmosphere, strict about turning up on time and getting work done. Registers are taken at the beginning of each lesson and the registrar is liable to phone absconders' parents, even if it is 3am where they are. 'It is very difficult not to work here. We are a very disciplined place. We give masses of homework and you get a lot of feedback. The students always say that MPW stands for "makes people work".'

Will expel for 'any involvement with drugs on or off the premises', violent behaviour or even persistent smoking in the vicinity (fair to say that groups of illicit cigarette smokers were conspicuous by their absence). 'If you're clear about boundaries most will push it as far as the limit, then stop. Parents never say we didn't warn them.'

Pupils and Parents: Virtually all from independent schools. GCSE students tend to be recent arrivals from abroad – 'Lots of foreign students come in by chauffeur,' commented a parent – or those who have had differences of opinion with their previous school. A level students may have outgrown boarding school, lost confidence in their previous school or had medical problems. An increasing number transfer into the upper sixth after disappointing AS results elsewhere. Plenty of diplomatic and business families.

Entrance: By interview. Will never take anyone who has been expelled for drug-taking, but will consider perpetrators of long-term low-level misdemeanours or one-off mistakes. GCSE applicants take English and maths tests: those applying to join Year 11 may be advised to go into year 10 to build up their skills or English fluency. A level applicants generally need at least six grade Cs at GCSE, with Bs in their A level choices, but can retake English or maths if necessary alongside AS levels. Those whose English is not fluent can study EFL alongside other subjects until they catch up.

Exit: Around five per cent a year to Oxbridge and up to ten per cent to medical/dentistry/veterinary schools. 'As a non-selective school we do very well across all subjects. We have good connections with medical and dental schools, and they know we know what we are talking about when we recommend a student.'

Money Matters: Scholarships and bursaries of up to 100 per cent at all levels by competitive exam.

Remarks: Relaxed, collegiate atmosphere combined with a strict attitude to attendance and work. Small classes, great flexibility, plenty of communication with parents and a strong emphasis on what it takes to pass exams and get into university.

Manor House School

Linked to Manor House School Junior School in the Junior section

Manor House Lane, Little Bookham, Leatherhead, Surrey, KT23 4EN

• Pupils: 190; all day • Ages: 11-16 • Christian non-denom
• Fees: £12,510 pa • Independent

Tel: 01372 458 538
Fax: 01372 450 514
Email: admin@manorhouseschool.org
Website: www.manorhouseschool.org

Head: Since 2008, Miss Zara Axton BSc PGCE (forties). A varied teaching background – starting with maths in a Catholic comprehensive and progressing through to four years at Kent College as pastoral deputy and head of sixth form.

Miss Axton tells us she has an open door to parents, is informal and likes to meet people 'by being around'. She describes her input so far as having 'slightly rebalanced towards the academic, reviewed processes and sharpened up,' whilst also maintaining the nurturing and fun ethos. We found Miss Axton very comfortable when she talked about her thoughts on the school – she is proud of the girls' only status of Manor House and 'would worry about girls' self confidence in an environment dominated by boys'. However, she was decidedly not relaxed nor keen to talk about herself. Her 'more reserved approach' (than the previous head) has meant that she cuts something of a controversial figure among parents. Some we spoke to have yet to warm to her or were reserved about her – largely because they all felt that they did not know her and that she has yet to make her personal presence felt. On the other hand, one parent told us, 'I like her and she had brought in good ideas and changes. Anyone new will upset a few people, often the vocal ones'. 'I really like her,' said another. 'I find her approachable and my daughters go in for a chat with her.' All parents we spoke to felt she was generally running the school well.

Academic matters: The range of abilities is genuinely broad, from high flyers who want to work without pressure, to those who struggle with academia. GCSE results are excellent from such a spectrum, pitching the school well against the local competition, just over 50 per cent GCSEs are A or A*. Most popular GCSE subjects are art, Spanish, French and geography, less so the sciences. High flyers in English can take GCSE a year early. Nice to see plenty of vocational options at GCSE – food & nutrition, child development, art, music, PE and drama.

The head feels all abilities are catered for 'because we teach in small groups and have stable staff who know the girls well.' About 27 per cent of the senior school teachers have been there more than 10 years, a few taught current pupils' mothers and clearly have great affection for both the school and the pupils. There has been some staff movement with the arrival of Miss Axton – commonplace as all new heads make their mark. As the school only has pupils to 16, young ambitious teachers would have to move on if they want to teach A level. Class sizes average 20 – parents all agree good academic results are gained by small class sizes and the small scale of the school, telling us 'the girls are a bit spoon-fed,' but the work ethic is positive and 'being clever is OK not geeky.'

The full time head of learning support provides help to girls throughout the school (junior and senior), individually or in small groups. No SEN assessment on entry but about 10 per cent are referred by their teachers for additional help; anything more than a couple of sessions are charged extra. Girls have a positive view of the help they are given at all levels.

Games, Options, the Arts: Sports are a big part of life here; all the usuals and matches most afternoons for A through to D teams whenever possible, so most gain match experience, much appreciated by parents and girls. Games teaching widely praised, 'the PE staff work incredibly hard'. Some girls very involved and with excellent results. On-site outdoor facilities (including pool) and sports hall good; changing rooms for each year dotted around school, but no showers – which can be a problem for the older girls.

Music, art and drama all enjoyed as part of the fun, have-a-go ethos. Busy, inspirational art room buzzing with girls and their pretty and impressive artworks. Drama is praised by parents as very strong with a 'wonderful teaching team'. Girls of all ages take part in productions both on stage and backstage. New director of music is 'young and full of enthusiasm'. Individual music lessons taught by a variety of peripatetic teachers, standards range from beginner to Grade 5, the majority at Grade 2 or 3, with plenty of opportunities for performance in school.

Background and Atmosphere: Housed in a classically beautiful Queen Anne house set in formal gardens and parkland, tucked away in a surprisingly quiet and leafy Surrey lane close to the busy A3 and M25. The house can be hired as a wedding venue via a completely separate events company. The lovely gardens, sweeping lawns, as well as the 'safe feeling' location, are much appreciated by parents and many of the girls. Inside the house feels as much like a rather grand home as a school, with a central staircase leading up to classrooms on the upper floors. Behind the main house are a number of newer blocks housing the art room, school hall (doubling as a theatre and gym) and classrooms for the oldest girls and, separately, the nursery and preparatory sections. Unusually, there is a well equipped home economics department, girls are taught nutrition and diet as well as child development and textiles – and good old fashioned sewing.

Truly a through 2–16 school, there is little, if any, separation between early years, juniors and seniors; it is one community. This is a major 'USP' the school uses to differentiate itself from the competition. Although the juniors and seniors do have some separate playing areas they are involved in each other's school lives on a daily basis, with most of the senior girls having a role – prep and subject prefects, house and sports captains – with responsibilities across the whole school. They are greeted with excitement, hugs and kisses by the juniors who love the seniors to bits. Miss Axton describes it as 'a small, friendly, nurturing school where everyone is known'. Parents generally like the small size, especially at the younger end, feeling 'it's a good choice for a quiet child,' but sometimes find that 'in such a small environment one girl can upset the applecart.' Delightful website, (in fact one of the best school websites we have seen) with loads of pictures of happy smiling girls, gives a real flavour of the place.

Pastoral Care and Discipline: 'To love is to live' is the school motto and generally fits well; girls all know each other and are friendly across age groups. The girls we met on our visit were charming, polite and confident without a hint of precociousness. Huge praise from every parent we spoke to for the pastoral care -'second to none'. Parents describe the caring environment as 'cosseted' and 'like being wrapped in cotton-wool,' acknowledging that a few find it too much so in their latter years – although Miss Axton says 'no parent or girl has ever raised this with me'.

A counsellor visits for one day each week, providing confidential advice and support for both girls and staff. Issues of potential teen angst – alcohol, drugs, eating disorders, cyber-bullying, self esteem – are covered in class. The head reports very few problems, explaining they work 'with clear policies and consistent boundaries' and discuss bad behaviour and its effect. Parents tell us 'girls who have been particularly unpleasant are taken for a chat' – Miss Axton says, 'I can assure you these are not cosy chats! I do, however, give them the right of reply and the opportunity to put the situation right.'

Pupils and Parents: Parents choose Manor House to avoid the academic pressure and competition of the 'Surrey schools mafia,' they are a varied and non-judgmental lot who mix comfortably. They feel Manor House suits 'girly girls', 'quiet girls' and families who are 'not too pushy'. There are plenty with family ties, mothers who are old girls, as well as lots of sisters. Girls look fresh faced and tidy, with swinging pony-tails and sensible skirt lengths. Manor House is not for the wild child – the rebel or rule breaker – she would stick out like a sore thumb.

Pupils come from around a 10 mile radius from Epsom to Guildford, school minibuses pick up in the morning. No homebound school transport is laid on, but a minibus runs to Effingham station before and after school.

Entrance: Most girls move seamlessly through from the junior to senior school here; the largest external intake is at 11, with pupils coming from a scattering of local state and independent schools. An entry testing day is held in January prior to entry in September – verbal reasoning, English and maths and an informal interview with Miss Axton. She also chats to parents; she's looking for girls 'who want to be here' and the school accepts a wide range of abilities from the very academic to those whose interests are in other areas of school life.

Exit: All girls leave after GCSE, mostly to study for A levels. Around 50 per cent go on to local independents – St John's Leatherhead and Reeds sixth form are popular choices. The rest largely to the very good state sixth form provision in Godalming College and Howard of Effingham School. A few head in different directions such as child care, hairdressing or the arts. A few jump ship at age 13 – particularly girls who have been at Manor House all through nursery and juniors (4 out of a year size of 40 in 2010). Current fave destination is the newly offered girls' places at St John's Leatherhead.

Money Matters: A few scholarships of limited value at 11, including one for the top state school joiner. Annual means-tested bursaries are available, in line with the school's charitable status, for new and existing pupils. Theoretically covering up to 100 per cent of fees, though the head is keen to manage expectations, applications for bursaries need to be made by February for the following September and involve a home visit as well as consideration of the pupil's contribution to school life.

Remarks: A charming, small, friendly school, ideal for girls who need a caring environment to reach their full potential, be they very academic or otherwise. Wholesome unpretentious girls mix with other 'nice' girls (no fears they would lead each other astray). Pupils work hard, play hard and form friendships for life – a school, which though fully embracing the new, harks back to a wonderful bygone era. Think Enid Blyton's Malory Towers (without the boarding) – in the nicest possible way. (Think, but do not say: the head takes huge exception to the comparison.)

Mark College

Blackford Road, Mark, Highbridge, Somerset, TA9 4NP

• Pupils: 80 boys, 5 girls • Ages: 10-18 • Non-denom • Fees: £5,884-£16,261 pa • Independent

Tel: 01278 641 632
Fax: 01278 641 426
Email: markcollege@priorygroup.com
Website: www.priorygroup.com/markcollege

Principal: Since September 2010, Michelle Whitham Jones, BSc PGCE MEd NPQH. Married with an adult son. Has taught children, for over 15 years, from ages 2–19, in both mainstream comprehensive and SEN – SBED,

PMLD, SLD, MLD, ASD, specialising in physical disability and language disorder.

Academic matters: Takes boys and girls of 'average and above average ability' with severe dyslexia. CreSTeD 'specialist provision' status and chosen by DfES as a beacon school for dyslexics. Some real experts amongst staff with all the right training and experience; school geared up for students getting information from sources other than books. Some extra input from psychologists and therapists when needed. Students follow national curriculum with core subjects including media studies (rather than English literature) and ICT. Assessed at beginning of year 10 to determine level of help required (e.g. reader and/or scribe) in public examinations. In most cases students choose three more subjects from DT, PE, geography, history, drama and art.

ICT support makes sense for dyslexics with voice activated software (highlight a word and you hear it) from Year 9 upwards to help get good ideas down on paper. Academic input 'second to none', according to one father who fought an expensive two year battle with his LEA to get his son funded. Students say teachers 'try different ways' to explain things and recognise their difficulties in reading, self-organisation etc. Meets challenge more often than you'd expect to get students GCSE grade C in English (most enter school with reading age of seven) and pupils attain well above national average in maths and humanities; most come out with pleasing results overall. Sixth form offers seven A levels on site, plus a full range of subjects which can be chosen from Strode College, with full support given for pupils' dyslexic needs through Mark College.

Foreign nationals can take a GCSE in their mother tongue, but otherwise languages are not taught here. Saturday morning lessons for all enables longer holidays, which families prefer. Good ICT suite in basement of Mark House, with boys and girls able to use own laptops in classrooms and in internet lounge for Years 10 and 11 in their boarding house.

Games, Options, the Arts: Main rivals nearby Shapwick (slightly larger school for dyslexics); other Wednesday fixtures either with local comprehensivess or schools on Independent Schools' Association circuit. Students see selves as sporty (school has won Sportsmark award with distinction) and even dyspraxics achieve here. Good-sized sports hall on main site with much used multi-gym; games pitches visible on other side of main road, plus a new addition of nine hole golf. Pupils compete nationally in cross-country and some county representation in athletics, rugby (sevens particularly strong) and cricket. Twenty per cent of pupils learn a musical instrument: piano or keyboard, electric guitar or drums, but no choir or orchestra. Close liaison with Connexions on careers front. Cosy library is supervised by matrons during breaks.

Art department looking to expand from present garret; much artwork on display (including in principal's study). Drama and DT would also benefit from more space. Laboratories and classrooms aren't large but work well here – we were impressed by the quality of lessons seen and especially by positive vibes between staff and pupils. Parents say plenty of sport and practical activities like car club are just right.

Background and Atmosphere: Founder, Steve Chinn, taught dyslexics in USA before opening Mark College as a leap of faith in 1986. School has grown like Topsy but remains unpretentious and relatively small scale. Recent acquisition by Priory Group to become their flagship dyslexic school is allowing school to 'upgrade and expand', according to Julie Kay. Administrative offices, staff room plus some teaching and boarding facilities centred in listed, red-bricked Mark House. Cluster of newish and converted buildings all close by on peaceful 24 acre site lined by splendid trees and backing onto farmland, which is strictly 'out of bounds'. Easy access to junction 22 on nearby M5 enables frequent visits (now in MPVs more than in minibuses) to coast and nearby towns for shopping at weekends etc. Dining hall accommodates whole school and is used for assemblies. Pupils say food OK – best at weekends when numbers are smaller. Exchange with sister school in Boston, USA, is a highlight for students and staff.

Pastoral Care and Discipline: Mainly long-serving, experienced staff, but some young matrons and teachers. Parents comment on 'good pastoral support'. We saw boarding arrangements with privacy for older boys and girls plus good commonrooms with recreational and some self-catering facilities. Small dorms in Mark House for younger pupils help them to get to know one another. Head of care is a qualified nurse; married houseparents with babies, dogs etc make for a homely atmosphere. Most Year 11 students become prefects with extra privileges in return for duties; withdrawal of extra tuck or early bedtimes used as sanctions but heavy discipline uncommon.

Pupils and Parents: Unpolished but engaging boys and girls who get along well with each other; school raises self-esteem and it shows. Complete social mix here; many have chequered earlier school history; a few from overseas. Lessons designed to cope with short attention spans: ADD 'goes with the territory', according to principal; she won't accept emotionally disturbed pupils or severe Asperger's. A few day pupils stay for prep before going home and can arrange to sleep over.

Entrance: Parents send educational psychologist's report before initial visit is arranged. Prospective pupils spend a day at school for informal assessment. Normally one class entry (maximum eight pupils) in Years 7 and 8, with two classes or more in Years 9–11. But this varies – when we visited over one third of boys were in year 10. Some each year from specialist dyslexic schools, e.g. Appleford in Wiltshire and Belgrave in Bristol.

Exit: Most stay on or go to schools on CreSTeD register that offer continued support, though some leave already able to cope with mainstream 16+ education.

Money Matters: About 40 per cent of pupils receive post-tribunal LEA funding; remainder fee-paying, but many parents can't afford full five years. We hope that fees will be maintained at their current 'reasonable' levels and feel that current principal really wants this – time will tell.

Remarks: Now with girls. Focused and specialist teaching; size and setting allow a committed and interestingly diverse staff to 'achieve what they set out to do'. No frills approach with emphasis on meaningful delivery rather than show – 'value for money' is paramount, so don't expect loads of flashy gizmos. Lucky ones who get here (after what has often been an impossible situation in mainstream education) often 'enjoy school for the first time'.

Marlborough College

Marlborough, Wiltshire, SN8 1PA

• Pupils: 550 boys, 330 girls. A very few day, rest board. • Ages: 13-18
• Size of sixth form: 390 • C of E • Fees: Boarding £29,310; Day £22,245 pa
• Independent

Tel: 01672 892 300
Fax: 01672 892 307
Email: admissions@marlboroughcollege.org
Website: www.marlboroughcollege.org

Master: Since 2004, Mr Nicholas Sampson MA PGCE (mid-fifties), a highly experienced head. State educated himself, he read English at Selwyn College, Cambridge and did his PGCE in Oxford. He spent ten years at Wells Cathedral School and six as head of Sutton Valence. Thence to the celebrated Geelong Grammar in Australia for four years. Mr Sampson is affable and likeable but perhaps not the easiest man to read – hence mixed parental reports. Some find him remote and disengaged and others feel that the school has become complacent in recent years but the reality is a quiet, thoughtful and assiduous educator, working hard behind – rather than in front of – the scenes – building up the academic excellence of his Common Room, developing an exciting new school in Malaysia, strengthening the College's internationalism and its engagement with social responsibility. An example of this is the College's active involvement with the Swindon Academy and the turnaround this has effected.

The Master is mistrustful of the PR industry on which much independent education depends, stands and falls these days. He is temperamentally averse to the showmanship that characterises headship elsewhere – 'the first person pronoun in school management is a real pain…I don't think school leadership is all about The Great Me… This job is about empowering teachers.' We applaud but this is a difficult balance to maintain in such a high profile school and one with a demanding traditional constituency – some of whom clearly want to see him more in evidence and more prominent in the school's public image. Such parents are likely to remain dissatisfied but, under Mr Sampson, the College is steadily being modernised. His legacy will be a stronger – if, perhaps, less glamorous – Marlborough.

Academic matters: Now offering A levels, the IB and the Pre-U – something for everyone. That is really the keynote here in general – a wealth of opportunities of all kinds. Results vary from outstanding – geog, drama, Latin at GCSE and English, maths, history of art, history and Latin and Greek at A level – to surprisingly low English at GCSE and A level biology – all in 2009. Overall, around 70 per cent of subjects taken at GCSE got A*/A. Options include astronomy – school has the Blackett Observatory which houses the best telescope in any UK school and everyone gets a chance to use it in Year 9. Outreach also brings in users from local primaries and preps and various other groups – a real gift. 24 A level options include 4 mainstream langs, business, class civ, DT and, very popular, politics. Surprisingly few – compared to elsewhere – for music tech. Massive numbers for English lit, biology, history and maths. Modern langs getting much-needed beefing up from new head of dept coming Sept 2010.

Excellent innovation is 'Form'. Children in the first year – 'Shell' – follow a course which integrates English, history and RE – all taught by one teacher. Sounds like real education – is anyone in government listening? The IB – 'we won the Common Room over' – now getting under way. The Master was keen because of its international perspective, because it 'offers a safety route in case A levels get further devalued', because of its 'philosophical attraction' and the 'remarkable intellectual challenge' it offers the Common Room. The first year has a small but keen cohort and will build. Good new staff intake – many from the top London day schools. Exceptionally high teacher:pupil ratio. Excellent library – a delight for the mind and eye.

Around 1 in 9 pupils have some kind of learning support – 3 full-time SEN staff see them either one-to-one, in-class or withdrawn; some is free, some charged for e.g. lots of individual support. Very extensive site but can and will accommodate wheelchairs; ramps and general access being upgraded as we write.

Games, Options, the Arts: Terrific games – aided by good staff (including former capt of Leicestershire cricket) – recent addition an Olympic gold medallist – and fabulous facilities which include a swimming pool, 25 metres long, with an adjustable floor – either sloping or deep for diving – everyone we spoke told us about this! Individual and team successes in, particularly, fives, lacrosse, rugby, netball, hockey and football. College has produced 38 rugby internationals and four England captains. Football coached by pros from Swindon FC. Lacrosse by former England international. Lots more including shooting, polo and everything else you can think of. DT excellent and we saw wonderfully creative artefacts derived from field trips – e.g. litter bins, benches and butterfly feeders. Casting in all kinds of materials here. Around 30 per cent of DT A level candidates are girls. Art is everywhere – art school (2005) a big, bright, airy place full of eager beavering. Art a serious matter here – great tradition of history of art (see Old Marlburians below) – seen as culturally and intellectually central to the ethos. Film editing suite, photography, varied and imaginative ceramics.

Superb music under outstanding, internationally renowned, head of dept, with wonderful facilities. Everyone involved in some kind of music and around half learn one or more instrument. 'They've encouraged my wholly unmusical boys to play instruments – inspirational teaching'. Concerts in and out of College, and a good range of music here – not just guitars and drums but the real thing – along with guitars and drums. Recent concert of opera scenes impressive. Drama – the College has lots of quality performance space – also outstanding – recent productions from a York Mystery play to *The Seagull* and *A Winter's Tale*. School moving towards a surer sense of its place in the outside world. One knock-on will be a greater emphasis on socially responsible trips – 'rather than super-charged tourism' – a loss for some but addressing the gripes from some parents who feel that the very expensive trips the school has offered are, of necessity, exclusive. Plenty to do at weekends – though some feel there could be more for the less academic and non-sporty. Loads of trips and tours – art to NY, geog to Tenerife, Russian scholars to St Petersburg, netball to Barbados and 'Wilderness trip' to S Africa. Oh to be a child again!

Background and Atmosphere: Founded in 1843 for the sons of the clergy for the south of England. Imposing red-brick quadrangle, with elegant Queen Anne building at the head of the court, contrasting with Memorial Hall built after World War I, and archaeologically important earthwork known as The Mound in the middle of it all. Mix of interesting buildings from all eras since includes vast and glorious chapel in late Victorian Gothic – perhaps the most impressive we know – pupils clearly proud of it. Also the War Memorial Assembly Hall – 'the best piece of American campus architecture this side of the Atlantic' – with a stunning theatre rather like the Harrow 'Speecher'. Extraordinary features here and there e.g. a real Egyptian mummy, found by some pupils in a store cupboard, now glass-cased in the foyer of the languages and classics dept. Grounds and gardens are beautiful and include the Master's garden with a quite wonderful vast beech tree under which we saw a glorious pool of mauve crocuses.

School has its own argot – the year groups for instance are: Shell = Year 9, followed by Remove, then Hundreds, then, prosaically, sixth form. Wide range of views from parents, 'in some ways it's very progressive,' we were told, 'in others it's incredibly dyed-in-the-wool and needs to move into the 21st century'. Most agree that the end result is a well-mannered, sensible young adult. New head of Upper School will up the notion of service in the school's extra-curricular activities – going some way, perhaps to meet the complaints of some parents who feel the school is too inward-looking and insufficiently socially responsible. This is a case Mr Sampson is decidedly on. Witness latest new-build which has solar panels and a ground source heat pump – 'this is the way society ought to be moving,' says the Master. School is building a branch in Malaysia – not a franchise but a real partner and much exchanging is planned. Also a new International Study Centre planned for 2012.

Pastoral Care and Discipline: Fourteen houses – five each for boys and girls and four mixed – though the sexes are segregated on different floors, wings etc. This is, in all ways, a full boarding school though a very few local day pupils also attend. No plans – or pressure – to offer weekly/flexi boarding. Provision varies – pupils move rooms each term with no choice of room-mates but a feeling that this works well and prevents exclusiveness. Good kitchens 'brew areas' and lots of excellent single rooms for the older pupils. Some houses have decision-making democratic 'year group councils'. Good common rooms – TVs, sofas, PCs and everywhere is intranetted. 'Outhouses' i.e. those houses which are more than five minutes away, have their own dining rooms and breakfasts and dinners are taken there. Lunches and all meals for everyone else in vast dining room – 'can feed 1500 in 1 ½ hours'. Food good. Excellent onsite medical team – surgery held daily. Good support for travel arrangements at starts and ends of terms.

All parents we spoke to emphasised the importance of getting into the 'right' house. In other words, visit, ask questions, be sure it feels right. Girls' boarding – for which we have previously reported that you needed to be 'robust' – now seemingly 'fantastic' and we heard only ecstatic reports. Not so, in all cases, boys' boarding. Much of it also 'fantastic' and house staff reported 'lovely' though too many reports of the, 'the housemaster is so lovely but he's not strong enough' kind. Also, however, reports of bullying not properly dealt with, far too much cavalier nicking of other people's possessions and a careless attitude among staff over such things in some houses. We even heard reports of 'initiation rites' still current in one or two houses – not quite the roasting over an open fire but still not on. College assures is that these matters are being dealt with. Some parental feeling that the dame system for younger boys could be more caring. In other houses, not enough care taken to ensure boys get to bed early enough. New Proctor has a responsibility for fair discipline across the whole College community.

Plans to up the number of girls but not by much – 'it wouldn't work – the girls would steam-roller the boys'. And the girls who come in for the sixth do balance the numbers and seriously impress. They generally go into a mixed house 'so as not to disrupt friendship groups' – for example on an upper floor over the junior boys. Lots of rules in school almanac – dress code largely adhered to but rules on mobiles only in houses in the evening clearly now 'relaxed'. Ongoing boyfriend/girlfriend relationships manifest in the way some pairs had their arms around each other – very sweet, we thought, and nice that they don't feel it has to be hidden. Out for dealing drugs, a one-chance testing policy otherwise. 'We make plentiful use of breathalysers and we've a drive on smoking at the moment – there's too much of it,' says the Master. Only good reports of sixth form boarding but clearly work still to do lower down.

Pupils and Parents: All the girls we saw had uniformly long hair and were very pretty. A generally relaxed feel though a certain prevailing sense that you still need to be 'tough' if you're boy and young. Families largely traditional boarding types, though much new money and some few from overseas. Notable OMs include William Morris, Anthony Blunt, John Betjeman, Nicholas Goodison, Wilfrid Hyde White, James Robertson Justice, Lord Hunt (of Everest fame) Francis Chichester, Peter Medawar, Louis MacNeice, Siegfried Sassoon, James Mason, Bruce Chatwin and Frank Gardner. Along with synods of bishops and messes of generals, brigadiers etc. Oh – and Sam Cam and Kate Middleton came along for the sixth form.

Entrance: Visit any time after birth. Three years prior to entry go to an Open Day, visit houses, chat to housemasters/mistresses; then come back in the September two years before entry to see more houses and have more chat; then apply by November 5th in Year 7 at which point the College will write to your prep for an assessment which will count for 50 per cent of your assessment. Individual arrangements are made for overseas pupils or those at primaries but all candidates are assessed at the College. 10 per cent of assessment via the 'Durham test' – an ingenious online reasoning/number skills exercise – 'very expensive' – and very subtle and 'much more accurate than CE'! It even takes into account dyslexia and dyspraxia. Remaining 40 per cent from interviews. Official CE pass is 60 per cent but this is flexible. 'We don't want to be an academic hothouse'. Don't hear that too often. Around half the applicants get places. For sixth form entry, a minimum of 6 GCSEs at B, including English and maths.

Pupils from everywhere but many from Cheam, The Dragon, Farleigh, Highfield, Port Regis and Windlesham.

Exit: Not all parents impressed with careers and university guidance. 'We had to do it all on our own,' we heard.

However, careers now being given a shake-up by being moved to the centre of the College. Around three quarters take gap years. Manchester, Bristol and Leeds the most popular destinations for several years now and much the most popular courses are in history, art history, modern langs. Annually between 15–20 to Oxbridge. Very few to the London colleges and no sign yet of an exodus across the pond as elsewhere.

Money Matters: Lots of awards at 13 and 16; unusually generous provision for a) Services children b) clergy children. Worth getting ordained for but also worth getting the booklet – far too much up for grabs to describe here.

Remarks: The quintessential English boarding school, now moving towards a more international, more modern future.

The Mary Erskine School

Linked to Stewart's Melville College in the Senior section

Linked to Mary Erskine and Stewart's Melville Junior School (The) in the Junior section

Ravelston, Edinburgh, EH4 3NT

- Pupils: (SMC) 725 boys (almost all day), (MES) 745 girls (almost all day)
- Ages: 11-18. (Separate entry for junior school) • Non-denom
- Fees: Day £8,916; Boarding £17,790 pa • Independent

Tel: 0131 347 5700
Fax: 0131 347 5799
Email: principal@esmgc.com
Website: www.esms.edin.sch.uk

Principal: Since 2000, Mr David Gray BA PGCE (fifties), who was educated at Fettes, read English at Bristol, where he did his PGCE. Taught English in a Bristol comprehensive, before moving to a language school in Greece, then taught English and modern Greek at Dulwich College and was head of English at Leeds Grammar, before heading Pocklington School in East Yorkshire, for eight years. Since the Stewart's Melville vast conglomerate forms the largest independent school in Europe, it is not surprising he feels he is in a position here 'to give something back to Scotland, having been away for almost a quarter of a century'. Brought up in Inverness, he is proud of his Scottish roots and sees himself and Stewart's Melville/Mary Erskine as at the 'most exciting cutting edge of Scottish education', and stresses that he's the first overall principal who is actually Scottish. Mr Gray spends part of the week in each school. We visited him at his base in Mary Erskine, where he was busily involved in compiling a history of the school for his teaching contact with the girls.

Very much a hands-on head, the principal reckons to keep sane (and fit) by swimming and jogging at 7am each morning, and is a familiar sight as he cycles between the two campuses. He also 'works the room' quite beautifully – 'We all think we know him well and that he knows our children almost as well as we do,' said one father (a gift no doubt inherited from his politician father?). Keen on promoting self-confidence in his pupils, he sees himself as an 'educator' and is teaching English and coaching cricket at Stewart's Melville. After eight years he feels pleased that the school has 'become a gentler place' and that the 'children are wedded to our ethos of reasonable, sensible behaviour'. No need for draconian action on the discipline side recently – when silliness occurs, 'the student body can be very conservative on behaviour,' while parents 'don't want to be ashamed of the school'.

Mr Gray runs the twin senior schools with two deputy heads and the head of the co-ed junior school, Bryan Lewis, who is also vice principal. Mrs Linda Moule took over as deputy head of The Mary Erskine School in August 2009; she was previously vice principal of New Hall School, Chelmsford. Mr Neal Clark, depute head of Stewart's Melville for the last ten years, describes himself as a 'grammar school boy, in tune with Scottish social culture'. All school facilities have been upgraded in the last ten years, 'so future plans are for maintenance rather than development'.

Academic matters: The principal and three heads have agonised together over the pros and cons of single-sex v co-ed. All four speak with the same passion – and often the same phrasing – of their 'best of both worlds' system. Boys and girls educated together at junior school, separately from age 12–17 – gains for girls (being able to get on with learning) and boys (feeling free to talk about poetry etc); then the social etc gains of co-education for the sixth year and all activities. 'Not a highly selective school' – however described by an educationalist as a 'grade one academic machine'. Classes of up to 25 (20 for practical classes) setted, with groups subdivided to extend the most able.

School has embraced the new Advanced Higher in depth – greater analysis, independent study, projects and dissertation. Mr Clark – though pleased that this year's SMC sixth year averaged two AH passes – would like three to be the norm. Recent results show a pleasing number of As and Bs across the board in both schools, with some outstanding successes in history, sciences and maths. Higher results impressive, particularly at MES 'on the languages front' and for SMC in history and geography. French, German, Spanish and Latin on offer to Advanced Higher Grade.

Since 2002, Standard Grades phased out (except drama) in favour of Intermediate 2 (which is based on the same assessment pattern as Highers). Results pretty impressive here too.

Very good links (still) with the Merchant Company, which provides masses of business breakfasts and connections with professional firms around Edinburgh. Single IT network across all three schools with 'massive schools' intranet', interactive whiteboards galore and close on 1000 computers. Biology department links with the horticultural department of the world famous Edinburgh Botanic Gardens. Impressive careers structure across both schools and excellent library facilities. Pupils sign in for private study.

Schools combine for sixth form, most extras and pastoral structure. In the interests of integration, sixth formers have to take academic courses from both schools – a feat resulting in limitless (almost) variety of course permutations, miraculous timetabling and quite a few bus journeys. Outstanding back up for those with learning difficulties – school has its own educational psychologist; 'some on Ritalin'; 'will never abandon anyone'.

Games, Options, the Arts: Big is beautiful, providing a list of over 75 different clubs for all, from goldsmithing to Greek, costume design to curling and cross country, lunch time and post school – popular. Major sports have separate clubs for ages/stages and 27 rugby teams. Good at football too. Girls prefer hockey and basketball, still better at shooting than boys, and both sexes join the voluntary CCF (trillions of girls, over 400 members in all). A second super new floodlit Astroturf at MES, 'so everyone gets a chance'; dramatic wavy roofed swimming pool (at Stewart's Melville) with co-ed sixth form slump-out room adjacent, new gym (at MES), cricket pavilion (MES again). FPs and current pupils share sporting facilities at MES; extra games pitches at Inverleith. Needle matches in almost all disciplines, with FPs representing both county and country across the board.

Incredibly strong drama – regular performances at the Edinburgh Festival and throughout the year at the Playhouse etc. Masses of every sort of orchestra. New £2.5m performing arts centre's opening splash was 'Snowman' composer, Howard Blake, and Scottish Chamber Orchestra. Centre took 12 years in the planning – seats 800 with a 'retractable' stage and dividing walls, replacing the old assembly hall, which was huge and impressive, and jolly nice in its way. Pupils can learn to fly and ski (Hillend and the real thing: the Alps, Canada). Brilliant debating team – regularly the Scottish Debating Champions and European Youth Parliament finalists; SMC has represented Great Britain abroad all over the shop. Good home economics. Art spectacular – dramatic artroom atop MES (with adjoining pottery and greenhouse).

Background and Atmosphere: Stewart's Melville campus is based round the magnificent David Rhind-designed Daniel Stewart's Hospital, which opened in 1885 and merged with Melville College in 1972. Fairy-tale Victorian Gothic with a cluster of necessary modern additions, surrounded by ever-decreasing games pitches and car parks. The old chapel is now a library, complete with organ and stained-glass windows. Stewart's Melville is also home to the senior department of the junior school – see separate entry.

Mary Erskine was founded in 1694, as the Merchant Maiden Hospital, moved to Ravelston in 1966, changing its name to The Mary Erskine School, and amalgamated with the boys' school in 1978 (girls wear charming Mary Erskine tartan kilts). MES clusters in decidedly 1960s architecture – with now quite a lot of more modern extensions, round the pretty but sadly overwhelmed Ravelston House (1791): swimming pool, tennis courts, games pitches, Astroturfs etc, the last much used by FPs. The nursery department and the youngest classes of the junior school are also based here – see separate entry.

Smart dining room complex serves all juniors and 80 per cent of seniors opt in. Sixth form coffee bars with stunning overview of school and pitches.

Two boarding houses, Dean Park House and Erskine House, furnished like large (and very well equipped) family houses and based on the edge of the Stewart's Melville campus. Tremendous family feel – boarders are encouraged to invite friends home, caring house parents, only 60 boarding places.

Regular buses from East and West Lothian and Fife service both schools, which operate as one, under the auspices of Erskine Stewart's Melville Governing Council. Each school, though, is fiercely proud of its individual heritage.

Pastoral Care and Discipline: Both schools have a tutorial system for the first year, followed by house system in upper schools. Houses are common to both schools and house competitions have mixed sex teams. Good links with parents. Brief is that 'all children have a right to be happy here'. Code of conduct established by consulting pupils so 'they know exactly where they stand'. Excellent anti-bullying policy: wary pastoral staff and peer-support group 'with professional training' stop 'children slipping through the net'. Sophisticated PSE programme right up the school, including study skills. Buddy system for those coming up from junior schools.

Automatic expulsion – 'zero-tolerance' – for those bringing in illicit substances – 'Those on the periphery of the same incident will not necessarily be excluded, but can come back in as long as they agree to random testing'. Smoking 'unacceptable and pupils suspended'. Alcohol 'not an issue in school'.

Pupils and Parents: Edinburgh hotch-potch of New Town and suburbs, with many first-time buyers and lots up from England. Siblings and FPs' children. Taking over a third of Edinburgh's independent secondary pupils, it's less élitist and perhaps less dusty than some city schools. Children living far out can spend the night when doing evening activities. Parent-teacher group ('the red socks brigade') slightly better organised into a Friends of the School group – fundraising, ceilidhs, 'good cash cow'.

Entrance: At 11,12, 13 or sixth form – otherwise 'by default'. Automatic from junior school. Entrance assessments held in January but can be arranged at any time. Waiting lists for some stages but just go on trying. Entrance to upper school is by interview, plus school report plus GCSEs/Standard grades (five credit passes for S5 entry.) Numbers up overall.

Exit: Minimal leakage pre Highers; most sixth year (96 per cent) go on to university (gap years growing in popularity, especially for girls), most opt for Scottish universities but a few Oxbridge, London, Bristol etc. SATS (for American colleges) not a problem. Art college, music/drama are popular alternatives.

Money Matters: Scholarships/bursaries available, some linked to the Merchant Company, others sibling directed. 'No child will be left wanting in a (financial) crisis.'

Remarks: A glance at the school mags, *Merchant Maiden* and *The Collegian*, sums it up: bags of boys' poetry, multiple hockey, rugby and cricket teams, nine Oxbridge places, fabulous art, photos and writing, plus fascinating glimpses from boys and girls reporting on the same activities with subtly different views.

An outstanding school: happy pupils, happy staff – focused on self-development with impressive results.

The Maynard School

Linked to Maynard Junior School (The) in the Junior section

Denmark Road, Exeter, Devon, EX1 1SJ

• Pupils: 440 girls, approx 100 of whom are in the junior school. All day pupils • Ages: 7-18 • Size of sixth form: 100 • Non-denom • Fees: £9,891 pa • Independent

Tel: 01392 273 417
Fax: 01392 355 999
Email: admissions@maynard.co.uk
Website: www.maynard.co.uk

Headmistress: Since January 2009, Ms Bee Hughes, after seven years as deputy head of Hitchin Girls' School and a wide-ranging career including fifteen years in Hong Kong at Island School and West Island School (where she captained and coached national hockey team). Strong academic background: has an MBA and was heavily involved with University of Cambridge initial teacher training programme. Teaches in senior school, and philosophy in the extended studies programme in the sixth form.

Academic matters: Consistently excellent results: 71 per cent at grade A* and A at A2 level with 92 per cent A/B grades and 83 per cent A* and A at GCSE in 2009. No SATs. No early entries – 'Girls should enjoy GCSEs,' says head. Outstanding mathematics department (two thirds take it beyond GCSE). Further maths plus good number continue subject at university. Sciences strong too – modern labs and dedicated staff. We watched a year 10 biology group conducting chromatography experiments to test for food additives. Outstanding English department also bags top grades. 23 subjects taken to A2 level – lots of small sets. Geography will benefit from new classrooms. Food science (super refurbished facility) and textiles have regular takers but DT as a separate subject disappeared some years ago – accommodation apparently unsuitable; a pity, we thought.

Commitment to learning support has helped make school more inclusive. SENCo (an OG) fell into post by default but has made it her own. Only one girl statemented (with hearing impairment) but 35 girls currently have 'profiles'. Full assessment for SpLD and look-out for difficulties in maths. Free learning support generally offered when first required. ESL teaching as required. School counsellor comes in to see girls on regular basis. Head believes shape of day is important – six lessons in morning, long lunch break for activities, then assembly and two further lessons. We liked the idea of lower 3 (Year 6) girls having lessons in senior school prior to transfer at 11+. Parents confirm younger Maynardians 'aren't overburdened with homework'; head has wanted girls to get as much as possible done in lessons. Fair enough – especially given distances many of them travel daily.

Games, Options, the Arts: Art and music housed in separate building, provides creative hub at centre of school. Separate sixth form art studio allows girls to spread work out as they like. Dark rooms for girls specialising in photography (not a separate A level, however). Two other spacious art studios for younger girls, plenty of strong and imaginative work on display. Music strong at all levels, 'charismatic teaching,' say parents. Some win music scholarships to specialist colleges and universities. Three orchestras, three choirs, plus a chamber orchestra and choir, jazz and wind bands, then various ensembles. Summer and autumn concerts and lots of less formal recitals. Six practice rooms and pianos everywhere.

Mostly in-house drama productions (handy little drama studio tacked behind main hall where major productions take place). Drama studied for GCSE and A level. LAMDA exams; girls participate in Exeter Competitive Festival each spring. When we visited girls were recovering from four successive nights of *Sweeney Todd* production. Girls and parents excited about new appointment in drama: professional actor who has appeared regularly on TV and on stage. Sounds promising.

Surprisingly sporty for an academic school. Three on-site netball and tennis courts. Super-sized sports hall and magnificently refurbished gym, where we watched thirty or so sixth formers going through kick boxing paces led by a Rambo-like male instructor. Phew. Other activities include fencing, golf and aerobics. Girls walk to external swimming pool but are bused to nearby university Astroturf for hockey. National reputation for netball and basketball.

Overseas visits have included Russia and, more recently, Iceland. Annual ski trip to Austria (travel by coach to save parents money and use British instructors who 'understand what is required'). World Challenge – twenty girls spent a month in Ladakh in summer hols. Work experience abroad is popular and gap years taken in far flung places. Young Enterprise well established and Maynardians participate in European Youth Parliament each year as well as public speaking competitions. Ten Tors and D of E hugely popular. Loads of voluntary and charity effort, especially in sixth (e.g. 'Singing for the Brain' – Alzheimer's charity; helping at hospices or schools for deaf or partially sighted). Popular weekly ESP (extended studies) programme for sixth form provides a wide choice from animation or ethics to self defence and sign language. Girls see it as a welcome change from formal studies. Sixth formers claim they 'can concentrate better in all girls' school' and that they 'motivate one another'.

Background and Atmosphere: Founded in 1658 so school celebrated 350th anniversary in 2008. Moved in 1882 to its present 'island' site close to main competitors and a stone's throw from city centre. Former incarnations included boarding and direct grant status. Blue Boy statue commemorates historic link with St John's Hospital Trust, which still provides money for bursaries. Non-denominational and proud of it. 'Might seem a bit chaotic sometimes, but girls have a whale of a time and produce wonderful results,' declared one parent. Assemblies (sixth formers attend and take one assembly a week) generally have a Christian theme, though we watched Year 9 girls performing classical Greek *Lysistrata* (somewhat censored). Lovely piece about women's power over men, though a shame one of the Greek 'women' dropped her 'baby' on stage – laughter all round. Girls and staff clearly on side with performers.

Attractive mosaic floor tiles create a sense of continuity with past generations. Honours boards around newly refurbished main hall also echo past glories. Some fine new buildings – Pring, Ryan and new classroom block, the

Murdin Link (named after Dr West's predecessor) – infill every available space; garden of reflection (created in memory of a girl killed in a train crash) and rose garden provide welcome intrusions of nature into an otherwise congested site.

Not overrun by computers, though good IT facilities in main and Pring buildings as well as in attractive sixth form centre. Laptops available for girls where needed. New building provides five extra classrooms and includes a lift for disabled access. State of art learning areas with 'nice clean lines'. Girls love reading and well stocked libraries are popular. Celebrating world book day with a competition – turn your classroom door into a book jacket, a novel idea, we thought. Low staff turn-over (many have twenty plus years' service). About a third male – 'I appoint whoever is best,' says head. 'The Maynard is a teaching paradise,' said one new arrival. 'It's bliss to teach in a place where pupils are enthusiastic,' commented another. Parents talk up school's friendly staff and atmosphere and confidence it inspires.

Pastoral Care and Discipline: Girls encouraged to behave responsibly. Rare misdemeanours dealt with sensitively by staff. Zero tolerance of bullying. Persistent bullies will be suspended, counselling provided. Smoking not tolerated ('by girls,' we were told) on or near site, let alone worse substances. Tutorial system overseen by heads of year responsible for academic progress and general welfare, girls see tutors twice daily. Carefully structured and monitored PSHE programme in all years. Plenty of careers teaching and hand holding through UCAS minefield. Two weeks' work experience for all girls at end of Year 11. Innovative careers fair held in October – 'Jobs for the Girls' for girls across the city. One head girl and three or four deputies elected by peers and staff attend annual GSA leadership conference. Year 11 girls and below held to high standards of appearance, though uniform is practical rather than fussy – no tie, blouse designed to wear over kilt.

Year 10 girls trained to act as one-to-one peer supporters for Year 7. School council run by head girl team comprises two reps from each form. Recent victories include return to 'proper' cutlery in dining-hall and better provision for storing kit on site. Small dining hall provides good choices including daily vegetarian and salad options – 'Girls love the meals,' said one mum. Some bring sandwiches – especially if they're busy at lunch-time. Sixth formers can make own snacks or go into city centre (few do). Lunch-time clubs run by sixth formers for younger pupils (see entry in Junior section). 'Sixth form atmosphere more like university,' say girls, who clearly enjoy comparative freedom and being taught by staff they know well. Parents praise way staff motivate their daughters and 'give extraordinary amounts of time'. Girls are 'encouraged to do lots of things and are recognised for their achievements'.

Pupils and Parents: A really mixed bunch. One third from city, remainder from as much as fifty miles away: Plymouth, also Taunton, Barnstaple, South Hams and Lyme Regis. Parents operate successful bus schemes to serve main Exeter independents.

Most parents are professionals, business people and university types. Very few overseas. Lack of pretentiousness. We liked fact that girls give feedback to head when prospective staff are interviewed. Parents help with careers advice etc and say, 'There is never a feeling of not being wanted'. Parents' association does plenty of fund-raising and socialising. Old girls include Professor Dame Margaret Turner-Warwick – first woman president of British Medical Council; Claire Morall, author, short-listed for Man Booker Prize 2003; Diana Brightmore-Armour, MD Lloyds TSB corporate banking division.

Entrance: Admission from seven to 15 is by entrance assessment and interview. Selection not just on academic results: girl with artistic potential was offered a place on basis of her portfolio though she had some weaknesses. 'Now her schoolwork has improved too,' said head. GCSE grades and interview for sixth form. Seamless entry from Junior school with no further qualifying hurdles to clear between Lower 3 (junior) and upper 3 Year 7 (senior). Feeder schools include local state primaries plus Maria Montessori, Exeter Cathedral Prep, St Peter's, Lympstone and The New School, Exminster. Head likes school being used by outside groups (e.g. sports clubs, Stagecoach and local churches) at weekends.

Exit: Virtually all sixth form proceed to higher education. Remarkably few drop out after Year 11 and any who leave (for financial or other reasons) are replaced by new arrivals. High proportion read sciences, medicine or maths at university.

Money Matters: Governor assisted bursaries pay up to forty-five per cent of fees for those in need. Two scholarships and two exhibitions awarded annually for music for Years 7, 8 or 9. Sixth form scholarships are available for academic, music, sport and art. Sibling discounts offered. Governors deal sympathetically with extreme hardship. Sourcing trust funds has been very successful to support students. No major endowments.

Remarks: Leaves you with a good feeling. Academically successful but not at expense of friendly atmosphere. 'We chose the school because we liked the finished article,' said one mother. Girls have loads of support from one another as well as staff. Girls are 'kindly and thoughtful'. Parents seem relaxed and trust school to do a good job.

Mayville High School

Linked to Mayville High School Junior Department in the Junior section

35-37 St Simon's Road, Southsea, Hampshire, PO5 2PE

• Pupils: 500; 255 boys, 250 girls, all day; nursery 35 girls and 45 boys; pre-prep 40 girls and 40 boys; junior school 65 boys, 70 girls; senior school 100 boys, 105 girls • Ages: nursery 6 months-4; pre-prep 4-7; junior school 7-11; senior school 11-16: • C of E • Fees: Senior £7,965-£8,040 pa • Independent

Tel: 023 9273 4847
Fax: 023 9229 3649
Email: Enquiries@MayvilleHighSchool.com
Website: www.mayvillehighschool.com

Headteacher: Since January 2009, Mr Martin Castle BA PGCE, previously deputy head, taught here since 2000. A historian who still makes time to teach – we like that. He joins children on trips, e.g. accompanies them to the

Portsmouth Guildhall while they perfomed in Rock Challenge, an event that Mayville always shines in. Took a group to Spain to the Dali Museum for an art trip. Very unsnobbish, demands people respect each other and is strict about appearance and manners.

Academic matters: The spectrum is broad. They do particularly well by dyslexics and those who need the nurturing of a small, caring school. It's all about focus on individual needs, of course, and it's this that's made them locally famous – 'Others say they do it – we have to'. Class teaching is trad, structured, careful with we saw it happen the clever being stretched while the rest work at their own level, and no sense of anyone looking down – or up. These children rate each other according to personal attributes, not marks, and that's instilled by the teachers. Parents say, 'They lay down the building blocks of learning one by one and don't move on until everything is consolidated, no matter how much reiteration is necessary. It's very systematic.'

It's also segregated. Boys, they reckon, develop differently from girls, so they teach them maths, science and English separately, the boys for shorter periods according to male attention span, and bring them together for modern languages, history, geography, art, drama and sport. This is increasingly popular with members of ethnic minorities, the separate sex education in particular. One father praised the way his daughter can wear the hijab with pride, attend festivals and is encouraged to tell the other pupils at assemblies all about her faith – 'They accommodate individuality at no cost to the community'.

A number of children here are victims of the coercive, target obsessed national curriculum – they fell behind, gave up on themselves and became the prey of all manner of emotional fallout. Refugees from other independents here, too. Mayville turns them around by, first, 'understanding the problem,' say parents, then making them feel secure, reacquainting them with success and giving them 'an amazing sense of belonging'. Discipline is strict in terms of expectations, never heavy-handed. Teachers here understand learning styles – they're up to date, not a bit faddish and unusually well qualified. Relationships are warm, often giggly. Say parents, 'They know them and they like them.' But it's 'not cushy' – believes that 'hitting barriers gives them the strength to overcome and learn. It sets them up for life. Our job is to keep them going though this period'.

The dyslexia unit (CReSTeD DU) is justly lauded by inspectors, who know what's what, and by parents, who see the difference. Highly qualified teachers do all the right polysyllabic things – multi-sensory, kinaesthetic – and they do it expertly, but this isn't the half of it. Remediation has to be much more than a mechanical process because every dyslexic is different. Kindness matters most, and it is the emotional intelligence of those who work here that generates their best work. It's all about how children feel about themselves, and one thing they certainly don't feel is sorry – this is a victim-free zone. Lots of one-to-one – 'expensive but worth it'. In addition to GCSEs, some pupils are entered for dyslexic-friendly BTecs. Some parents say they'd like to see more vocational subjects – and wish the school wouldn't worry so much about league tables. Well, it wouldn't if they didn't.

Not a school for the marginalised – conventionally bright children here, too, who benefit in all the ways the rest do; they resist the urge to go off to Portsmouth Grammar at 11 and pick up fine GCSE results. Currently developing a programme to stretch them even further.

Games, Options, the Arts: Sport four times a week, fixtures with schools of similar size and they play in local leagues. Drama is big because 'it's a whole life skill'. Public speaking big, too – they win Rotary Youth Speaks competitions. Art good. Music doesn't stretch to orchestras but super choirs, a jazz group and rock bands. All learn recorder, then a brass instrument and violin for a term each. Fab after school clubs and supervised prep: they are open (would you believe it?) from 8am till 6pm, 50 weeks a year.

Background and Atmosphere: Now has a brand new purpose built hall and classroom block. All 5–11 year olds now in purpose built classrooms. Excellent facilities for drama and dance – a studio theatre for drama is a huge boost for creative arts. Also a new library for the junior department, a design technology area and a third science lab for the senior school.

Pastoral Care and Discipline: Strict uniform – smart blazer – and strict behaviour codes underscore the sense of security the school instills. Justly famed for its standards of care. One mum says, 'I wish I could be a fly on the wall to find out exactly how they do it.' Teachers 'very approachable. Any problems, they pick up the phone or write a note'. Expectations of parents are rigorous, 'They let you know early, and they expect your backing'. Children notably pleasing in their manners and demeanour and shiningly proud of their school.

Pupils and Parents: Local. Some move to be near the school, some make quite long daily journeys. Down to earth, unsnobby. Active PTA.

Entrance: No academic hurdle. Interview. They recruit for balance, so where SENs are concerned they do turn away 'the one too many'. Dyslexia's the big thing, but they also consider dyspraxia, ADHD and mild ASD. No emotional and behavioural disorders – 'There's only so much we can do'.

Exit: Havant College very popular. Local sixth form colleges and independent sixth forms.

Money Matters: Fees decidedly competitive and after-school care a real bargain. Academic and creative arts scholarships worth 50 per cent of fees. Some means-tested bursaries up to 80 per cent.

Remarks: Very much its own place. Very inclusive. The point is this: a raging little success story.

McLaren High School

Mollands Road, Callander, Callander, FK17 8JH

• Pupils: 665 boys and girls • Ages: 11-18 • Size of sixth form: 110 in the fifth, 80 in the sixth • Non-denom • State

Tel: 01877 330 156
Email: mclarenhs@stirling.gov.uk
Website: www.mclarenhigh.co.uk

Rector: Since 2004, Mr Peter Martin MA, who was deputy head for seven years prior to that. A geographer who knows the school and the catchment area well. Strong commitment to quality improvement. Keen on using outdoor education as a vehicle for delivering other educational objectives – leads annual ski course to the Alps.

Academic matters: Follows Scottish system. All mainstream subjects. Good results all over. Careful setting, max class size 30, with no more than 20 for practical subjects. Pupils work in flexible ability groups – 'individual timetables' and varying amounts of work experience where necessary. They are encouraged 'to aim for the best', 'take as many (exams) as you can'. A strong emphasis on support, both academic and pastoral, for everyone, the gifted as well as pupils with additional needs. IT is good and the physics website is second to none, with pupils logging on to do their homework – they can ask for and get help online. Attainment in SQA exams well above national average.

Games, Options, the Arts: Given the time restrictions, manages to pack in a lot – lots of clubs and activities in the lunch hour and after school. Choirs, jazz, swing, guitar ensembles plus violin groups (i.e. fiddle – pupils do well at the Mod). In-school music festival with outside adjudicators – over a hundred pupils took part last year. Lots of excursions, skiing popular with regular course to France and Austria. Has reinstated the role of dux ludorum, i.e. the head of games, a title which dates back to 1904 and is now awarded (by medal) to the top boy and girl in the games field. Uses the on-site McLaren leisure centre for PE and fitness sessions. New residential experience at outdoor centre for all first year pupils during activities week.

Background and Atmosphere: Donald McLaren, a banker from the Strathearn area, originally endowed the Free Church School in Callander in 1849 with a view to providing a 'salary of sufficient amount to induce men of superior talents and acquirements to become and continue to be teachers in the said school'. McLaren High was established in 1892. After Donald McLaren's death in 1894, 'His daughter Mary McLaren ensured that the McLaren educational trust endowments were used for the benefit of the children throughout West Perthshire, including Balqhuidder, without distinction of income or class' and the school handbook is still supported by the Clan McLaren.

Stunning site on the edge of the river just south of Callander. Only secondary within the Loch Lomond and Trossachs National Park. Has recently undergone a comprehensive refurbishment to provide a school fit for the 21st century.

Masses of student involvement, student forum includes the top team – i.e. the head boy and girl, plus deputies. Pupil representatives are involved on local civic panels. Active pupil council of all ages meets regularly to discuss specific concerns. First year pupils have a 'buddying system' (the McMentor system) to ease their transition into the senior school. Community service volunteers. Very strong PTA. This is true community spirit at its best. All pupils wear uniform (parents who don't support the uniform code must give their reasons in writing). Prefects wear rather smart gold edged blazers.

Pastoral Care and Discipline: 'ORCA' values important here (order, respect, care, achievement). Time-keeping is emphasised, good community policing. Very high profile prefects. Letters to parents and 'withdrawal of privileges'. The head of each year group is tutor to that year group throughout. Hosts visits from the local Presbyterian Church of Scotland, the Roman Catholic church and the Episcopalian Church in Scotland.

Pupils and Parents: All sorts, from a 600 square mile catchment area – tourism, farming, home-workers, Stirling University.

Entrance: By registration; automatic, places for all.

Exit: Some 27 per cent go to higher education – Glasgow, Edinburgh, Aberdeen Universities all popular; large numbers to further education locally and some straight into work.

Money Matters: Tiny foundation (not a lot of income); well supported by local businesses, which can and will provide extra funds for excursions etc.

Remarks: Sound, much admired school on the edge of the Highlands with lively friendly pupils. 2007 HMI report identified 'the very positive ethos of the school based on its core values and high quality relationships between staff and pupils'.

Merchant Taylors' School

Sandy Lodge, Northwood, Middlesex, HA6 2HT

• Pupils: 860 boys, all day • Ages: 11-18 • Size of sixth form: 285
• A multi-faith school rooted in Anglican values and traditions
• Fees: £15,250 pa • Independent

Tel: 01923 820 644
Fax: 01923 835 110
Email: admissions@mtsn.org.uk
Website: www.mtsn.org.uk

Head Master: Since 2004, Mr Stephen Wright MA. Educated at King's School, Macclesfield and Queen's College, Cambridge. Formerly head of Borden Grammar School in Kent for six years and deputy head of The Judd School, Tonbridge. Also taught at Framlingham College in Suffolk. Married to Penny, who is MTS admissions secretary. Three children – one son went on to Cambridge from Merchant Taylors', one daughter at sister school, St Helen's, Northwood. He has a passion for teaching and learning and maintaining the school's traditions of offering an all-round education, rather than a narrowly academic one. Very keen on sport – volleyball half blue at Cambridge – and continues to teach history and general studies. 'It's essential to keep in touch. I have lunch with the boys every day.' Enthusiastic gardener and opera buff. Jolly, down to earth, diplomat, who is continuing the school's evolution to excellence. 'I see my job to develop and refine, not break with the past.'

Academic matters: An area where parents keep a keen eye on league table performance. 2010 outstanding results – nearly 33 per cent of A levels awarded an A*; 79 per cent A*/A and 96 per cent A*/A/B. 92 per cent A* or A at GCSE – very high up the league tables indeed. But the head is prouder of the school's value-added in every subject and says: 'The examination success of the boys is very pleasing, but education is lighting of a fire, not the filling of a pail – and the current obsession with league tables represents a frightening impoverishment of the moral imagination and educational values espoused by the school for 450 years'.

Glowing 2008 inspection commended the "stress on love of learning for its own sake, the ... activities which enrich pupils and the community both socially and intellectually ... (and) the learning environment of considerable beauty". Teaching clearly a major strength, with teachers going the extra mile both for those who are struggling and those who need stretching. Predominantly male staff oversee classes of 20 up to GCSE, 10–15 at AS and A level. All boys take nine or 10 GCSEs – up to 50 per cent do maths and/or French a year early. Four ASs; most take three A2s.

Wide range of subjects on offer – over 20 in the sixth form. Traditional academic curriculum (plus theatre, ICT and psychology) – no business or media studies. Science taught as three subjects from 11. Maths, English and science offer more stretching IGCSEs. Science taught as three subjects.

Very strong modern languages department in superbly equipped, purpose-built, centre with three state-of-the-art labs. Two thirds take two modern languages to GCSE, 50 per cent at least one at AS. All boys study French and Latin in Years 7 and 8 and begin either German, Italian, Spanish or ancient Greek in Year 9. French, German, Spanish offered at AS and A, plus Russian, Japanese and Mandarin as part of the general studies programme. English offered as three different A levels (lang, lit and lang & lit).

All boys screened on entry to the school and those with additional educational needs looked after by learning support co-ordinator and supported by a dedicated learning support specialist.

Extensive, written reports two or three times a year. Grades and comments sent to parents each half term, plus a full parents' evening once a year with teachers, tutors and headmaster. Study skills built into the curriculum. Once a year, each boy writes his own report in considerable detail and discusses it privately with his tutor. Bright, modern library – 'a jewel,' waxes the Independent Schools Inspectorate – with over 18,000 books, periodicals, tapes and CDs. Homework six hours a week in Years 7 and 8, nine in Year 9, 20 at A level.

Games, Options, the Arts: Games taken seriously in this outstandingly well-equipped school. Fabulous on-site pitches, large sports hall, cricket nets, heated indoor pool, two floodlit all-weather hockey pitches, lakes for sailing and windsurfing, grass and hard tennis courts, squash and fives court, fencing piste, huge, level playing field for athletics etc. School teams in rugby, hockey, cricket – as many as four a year – and PE includes basketball, athletics, swimming and tennis. Soccer, badminton, croquet, cross country, golf and shooting also on offer. 'We would rather have an F team and give everyone the chance to participate rather than an elitist A team,' says the head, and the boys undoubtedly love it. 'You couldn't possibly not find a sport you liked here,' said one. Facilities now being strengthened with the new pavilion, running track and pitches.

Art, too, is outstanding – 'The art department is what you'd like every department to be,' says the head. 'The teachers are total and utter enthusiasts. They tell boys that they can create wonderful art, and they do.' Light, spacious and well-equipped art block with well-used display space. Gallery trips and lectures, exhibitions in school and beyond, residential courses include a week painting at St Ives. Excellent design & technology department. Self-contained music school arranged around an octagonal 150-seat recital hall seating. Annual concert at the Merchant Taylors' Hall in the City, plus a medley of orchestras, band and choirs. Active drama department, with numerous large and small-scale productions. Links up with St Helen's for drama, music, CCF, Phab (work with disabled children) and other activities.

Impressive range of extra-curricular options. Over 50 clubs – everything from Scrabble to outward bound – including a Young Enterprise business company to form rival businesses and a school bank run by senior boys as a branch of Barclay's. Large cadet force – army, navy and air force – with purpose-built HG, assault course and shooting range.

Community service important part of the school with a Physically Handicapped and Able-Bodied Residential Care Week held annually and funds raised throughout the year. Amnesty International, Aid for Tibet, Protect our Planet, plus a pupil-run Charity Drive. Strong links with the local community – boys help in local primary schools and inner-city scheme as well as with residential holidays for the disadvantaged.

Enviable reputation for quality of food – which head has made increasingly healthy. Popular tuck shop – 'The Lun' (short for lunch) – for mid morning and after lunch.

Background and Atmosphere: 2011 is the 450th anniversary of the school's foundation. Founded in the City of London in 1561 by the Worshipful Company of Merchant Taylors and Linen Armourers, it was then the largest school in the country. In 1933 moved to current impressive 250-acre green-belt site, which remains one of the outstanding features of the school. Core of (listed) buildings still date from that period, with a dominant Deco angularity complemented by beautiful formal gardens and lakes in the grounds. Playing fields surrounding the school are an impressive sea of green. Funding clearly not an issue, with recent additions including a new library and information centre, computer centre, politics and economics centre, entrance hall and sixth form common room. No lack of direction here – administration and management evidently clear and precise.

Has the feel of an Oxbridge college, with the same sense of unhurried calm and timeless beauty. The boys, too, seem remarkably unstressed. 'I think the beauty of the surroundings contributes to their good behaviour,' said one member of staff. The school's philosophy, too, is about achievement without pressure – 'It's a place to breathe and experience a childhood'.

Pastoral Care and Discipline: Eight houses and a very strong tutor system for individual guidance. Each boy is allocated a tutor on his arrival, whom he sees at least twice a week throughout his time at the school and who monitors his progress – academic, sporting and extra-curricular – and reports regularly to parents by email. Relationships are conspicuously civilised and the school has always treated the boys as gentlemen in embryo, with whom it is best to discuss intelligently and reasonably, rather than wave a rule book under their noses. 'We don't call it discipline,' says the head. 'There's not much need for it. The tutor keeps an eye on everything and snuffs out problems at an early stage.' All the boys under the supervision of one tutor meet as a group once a week, so older boys and younger boys can work together to resolve problems.

Two whole-school assemblies a week, plus one house assembly. Religious leaders from different faiths invited to address the whole school. Christian services held in the Chapel, plus a Muslim prayer room, Jewish society and Christian discussion group. All faiths work happily together with tolerance and consideration. A good percentage of Jewish boys, although the school is probably not suitable for the strictly observant since a significant number of activities take place on Friday evenings and weekends. The whole-school assembly is something the school insists on, so that all boys have knowledge of and respect for each other's faith traditions and are prepared to meet the challenges of a spiritually pluralistic society.

School rules kept as simple as possible. Boys encouraged to show kindness, common sense and respect in their day-to-day behaviour – and good manners here are clearly not restricted to high days and holy days, with evident courtesy displayed in boys' dealings with each other. Around 40 members of the Junior Common Room (prefects) and boys take considerable responsibility at registration, lunch times and assembly. Also run the Duke of Edinburgh's Award, the Asian Culture Club and house-based teams and activities.

Series of lessons and courses on health and diet, sexual behaviour and risks of alcohol and substance abuse. Qualified school counsellor, with whom boys may book appointments and talk in confidence.

Pupils and Parents: Pupils reflect the affluent, suburban, middle-class area in which the school sits – the traditional parental clientele supplemented by Asian, Jewish, and commuter-belt Wasps. Well-balanced global village – many first time buyers – working and living together in peace and harmony. Intake embraces an area from Harpenden down to Marylebone and across to Ealing and points along the Metropolitan Line – Moor Park Station, a five minute walk. Coaches from Beaconsfield, Ealing, Harrow, Mill Hill, Radlett, Stanmore and Harpenden.

Old boys include Sir Edmund Spenser, Clive of India, Titus Oates, the artist Samuel Palmer and the founding editor of 'The Times'; and, more recently, Reginald Maudling, Lord Coggan, Archbishop of Canterbury, Sir John Sulston, Nobel prize-winning medic, the sculptor Lynn Chadwick (whose work graces one of the many manicured lawns), Conn Iggulden, whose *Dangerous Book for Boys* was a 2006 best seller, Michael McIntyre, the comedian and Riz Ahmed, the film star and musician.

Entrance: 11 plus entrance (about 50 per cent from the state sector) by January exam in English, maths and verbal reasoning. Boys who do well are asked to return for interview. Some 300 apply with 150 offers made. Main entrance at 13 plus – need to be registered a year in advance, with interviews in autumn preceding entry. School's own exam in all CE subjects with the scholarship exam running at the same time. Scholarship candidates invited back for further interviews.

Sixth form places by examination in March – candidates must register by January 31 and will be tested in the subjects they wish to study, followed by interviews. School is looking for all-rounders and prizes quirkiness and scholarly potential rather than cramming. It offers sports, music and 'all-rounder' as well as academic scholarships. 'You don't have to be a genius to get in but we do want enthusiasts. There needs to be something about a boy – flair, if you want to call it that.' Good sportsmen as welcome as the academic élite and scholarships available. The 450th anniversary is the occasion for an ambitious development campaign for bursaries ("Forward to our Roots") to realise the dream of the school's founders in 1561 that up to 200 boys in the school would receive some sort of financial assistance.

Exit: Two or three leave each year after GCSE, occasionally because they don't make the sixth form entry requirement of three As and three Bs. 'Though ultimately each individual case is considered on its merits,' says the head. About 20 to Oxbridge and another 10 to medical schools, most of the rest to a broad range of academic subjects at Russell League universities – Nottingham, Warwick and Birmingham have strong contingents.

University and careers advice clearly a strength. Each sixth former is assigned to a senior head of department who acts as his university adviser. Careers guidance from Year 7, with a careers test and a careers conference offered later. Work experience – some of which can be done abroad – is highly developed, including a Companies Links Scheme with helps boys find work in major companies in varying sector of business and industry. 'You're set up really well for university and for UCAS,' says one positive sixth former.

Money Matters: Bursaries: school welcomes applications from parents from all walks of life whose son's life would be enriched by attending it. Means-tested bursarial support is available up to 100 per cent of the fees, at whatever point a boy enters.

Scholarships: no separate exam – honorary academic scholarships (20 at 13 and 10 at 11); scholars receive glory plus an enriched programme. A clutch of sports and all-rounder scholarships at 11, 13 and 16. For sport, high performance in rugby, hockey or cricket required, plus other strengths. Music scholarships at 11, 13 and 16 include one up to 25 per cent of fees, one at 15 per cent and two at 10 per cent. Cost of tuition of up to two instruments is also available.

Remarks: A tightly-run but relaxed, high-achieving academic school in stunning surroundings preparing well-rounded and courteous boys for good universities and good jobs.

Merchant Taylors' Boys' School

Linked to Merchant Taylors' Stanfield – Mixed Infants and Junior Girls' School Linked to Merchant Taylors' Girls' School in the Senior section

Liverpool Road, Crosby, Liverpool, Merseyside, L23 0QP

• Pupils: 795 boys including Junior School • Ages: Junior School 7-11 and Senior School 11-18 • Size of sixth form: 160 • Non denom
• Fees: Juniors £6,606; Seniors £8,928 pa • Independent

Tel: 0151 949 9333
Fax: 0151 949 9300
Email: info@merchanttaylors.com
Website: www.merchanttaylors.com

Head: Since 2005, Mr David Cook (early forties); read history at Birkbeck College, London, taught at Caterham, housemaster and head of history at Giggleswick, deputy head at QEH, Bristol. Held short service commission in Cheshires. Sharp, decisive and energetic, mind clearly spilling over with ideas for school. Good listener, not without gravitas. Ready to build on solid achievement of predecessor, Simon Dawkins, head for nineteen years. Son in school and daughter in sister establishment.

Academic matters: Traditional curriculum, including German, Spanish, Latin, Greek; separate sciences. GCSE results 75 per cent A/A* in 2010. Relatively few go on to arts subjects at A level, where science and maths rule. Things may change after current radical curriculum review (head has some interesting ideas about early GCSEs) but few stronger science departments in the north. A level overall 86 per cent at A/B in 2010 – the best ever results for the second year on the run, and no soft subjects. Recent innovation is system of one-to-one back-up clinics for pupils having academic or organizational difficulties. SEN overseen by head of learning support. Teaching staff experienced and effective. Big staff turnover, due to retirement, over past few years. Big opportunity then.

Games, Options, the Arts: Only room for a few pitches on site, but main fields within walking distance. All the usual sports, taken seriously, plus strong rowing on Southport Marina. Plenty of representation at regional and national levels. Enormous and vigorous CCF (all three services), shared with sister school (250 in all). Plenty of expeditions and trips. Good art and lively drama: several shared productions with girls' school, plus usual in-house plays. About 25 per cent learn an instrument; annual family carol service in Philharmonic Hall raises money for Merseyside charities. Joint debating society with girls is over 100 years old.

Background and Atmosphere: Founded in 1620 by London Merchant Taylor John Harrison, moved to present agreeable site in 1878, in respectable suburb; handsome Victorian main building. As in most schools, facilities for different subject areas; sports hall on shopping list – a new sports complex has been started and is due to open in May 2011. Special emphasis on ICT: latest software as teaching tool, and though a day school, every boy has email address and access to many campus computer sites. New school council seems to be more than a talking shop, if pupils' recent victory in matter of toilets is anything to go by.

Atmosphere decidedly northern ex-direct grant grammar school. Academic work a serious priority, more important perhaps than glitzy facilities – some classrooms are on the shabby side but serious refurbishments and new builds are in progress. Merchant Taylors' Schools have recently undergone a re-brand – now a new joint schools' prospectus and website.

Pastoral Care and Discipline: A small school, so it's claimed every boy is known. Usual day school network of form teacher/ year head/pastoral deputy head means no-one is overlooked. Chaplain also available to talk through problems and independent counsellor drops in once a week for chats in total confidence. Personal health taken seriously. As in all good schools, aim is to develop self-discipline. Drug dealers face the sack.

Pupils and Parents: Families from all over Merseyside area. Professional, business, etc, only two to three per cent ethnic minorities, but broad range of social background – 'We are academically, not socially, selective'. Fourteen buses operate daily from as far away as Wigan, South Liverpool, Southport and Warrington; convenient suburban rail link as well. Boys cheery, frank, polite, academically ambitious, a mixture not always understood by southern incomers. Probably a greater community of interest between school and parents than in similar conurbations. Old Boys include Nigel Rees and ex-England rugby international Ben Kay.

Entrance: Academically selective and over-subscribed at 11+. Best chance is via infant and junior boys' school, which makes up 40 per cent of entry; any boy not likely to make it to seniors is flagged up well before exam time and discussed with parents. Ten to fifteen lost every year to sixth form colleges (some then want to come back), numbers made up by sixth form entry (six Bs required at GCSE).

Exit: 18+ leavers nearly all to Russell Group universities, to read traditional subjects (engineering, science, economics, medicine); about six a year to Oxbridge.

Money Matters: Probably the cheapest HMC day school in the country – a huge selling point. 'Considerable numbers' on sliding scale in own assisted places scheme. Some merit scholarships.

Remarks: Good, solid, dedicated former grammar school in northern mould, where nearly all work hard in and out of classroom. Now in the process of a twenty-first century update, but not likely to lose its traditional ethos of commitment and emphasis on the daily transaction of the classroom.

Merchant Taylors' Girls' School

Linked to Merchant Taylors' Stanfield – Mixed Infants and Junior Girls' School Linked to Merchant Taylors' Boys' School in the Senior section

Liverpool Road, Crosby, Liverpool, Merseyside, L23 5SP

• Pupils: 565 • Ages: 11-18 • Size of sixth form: 135 • Non-denominational Christian • Fees: £8,928 pa • Independent

Tel: 0151 924 3140
Fax: 0151 932 1461
Email: admissionsmtgs@merchanttaylors.com
Website: www.merchanttaylors.com

Head: Since 2006, Mrs L Robinson MEd BA NPQH (forties), previously headmistress at Howell's School, Denbigh. Avid fan of girls' schools – ex-Bolton School and Manchester Girls High – keenly committed to the values of single sex education. Married, with a son at university; she is a mathematician and computer scientist, teaches mathematics to first years. Unassuming yet warm and welcoming with a shrewd and pragmatic approach; now into her second academic year here, she is keen to make her mark and with a strong and clearly capable team around her, is committed to leading the school forward – no resting on laurels here. Academic rigour is important, and whilst pastoral care is well managed, the head makes it clear that this is not a soft touch school and strives to ensure that her girls 'are fully aware of the possibilities that life holds for them'.

Academic matters: Academically selective on intake, girls are competitive and hardworking, GCSE and A level results consistently good; maximum class size 23. All subjects appear to be strong – no obvious weaknesses; classics a real powerhouse; French, German and Spanish taught as standard, Mandarin available as extra-curricular. No language labs but recently purchased i-pods provide individual listening facilities and girls download the curriculum to practise at home. No streaming but setting in French, maths and science. Post-16 collaboration with nearby boys' school has increased opportunity for widening A level options in minority subjects, but still only dipping a toe in here and girls (and some staff) remain wary.

Some provision for special needs – small percentage of dyslexic pupils, pupils supported and monitored at no extra charge. Dedicated ICT rooms for main school, sixth form and staff; whiteboards dotted throughout classrooms and one in the library too. Large group of gifted and talented identified at sixth form and given additional opportunities to excel and grow, 'widening intellectual horizons'. English and classics department both this year awarded a 'Good Schools Guide' award. Unusual level of competitiveness for a girls' school, with pupils achieving very high levels in maths, history, Shakespeare competitions and a science Olympiad, to name but a few.

Games, Options, the Arts: Tennis and netball courts on site; girls are bused to playing fields a short distance away and share the use of a pool on the boys' school site. Hockey, netball and athletics are main sports on offer, broadening post-16 to badminton, volleyball, trampoline, pilates; rowing (with the boys) has obvious appeal. Slightly dated but functional sports hall/gym on site. Notable achievements at national level in a variety of sports. Enrichment fairs at the start of the year (a kind of freshers' week) lure girls into a myriad of extra-curricular activities and ensure they are kept busy all day and every day. Plenty of music with recent addition of brass, and choirs, D of E, CCF and drama (joint productions with the boys' school) and lectures from visiting speakers. Classics trips are the star turns. Work experience offered home and abroad.

Background and Atmosphere: Little kerb appeal hitherto, but always worth stepping inside to see the eclectic mix of very old buildings complete with stained glass, parquet floors and stone mullioned windows; more recent buildings added sporadically, some rather more attractive than others. New glass front on the main building has given the school more of a presence on the road and addressed some health and safety issues. Spacious sixth form area with individual study space and microwaves for lunch on the run. Outside space limited but attractive and popular for summer picnic lunches.

Classrooms dotted around the site, upstairs and down, the whole larger than it appears. Feels reassuringly traditional and secure, yet somehow not old-fashioned. The buildings are lifted throughout by vibrant art work. Sited on a busy road, parking and access very restricted and therefore troublesome; girls are encouraged to travel by school bus to avoid the chaos. Busy street with a few shops, sixth formers out and about getting a shopping fix at lunchtime, though nothing really to buy here.

Hard core of long-established, experienced teachers, average age 46, proud of the girls' achievements and ambitious for them. Whilst the girls are clearly capable, results also suggest good solid teaching throughout. Staff and girls are comfortable rather than cosy with each other and both are happy with that.

Pastoral Care and Discipline: Limited but effective handholding in the early days; beyond that, there as necessary. Exclusion for anyone posing a danger either to self or others; 'inappropriate behaviour' excludes approximately one per year. Neat navy uniform for most, dress code for sixth form with rules upheld. Dining room not especially inviting – given a choice, girls and staff would eat elsewhere (though we're told it has been recently renovated and is more attractive), food wholesome but basic and limited choice proving a challenge for one vegan pupil. Two written reports per year, plus consultation and information evenings. Thriving school council, run by pupils.

Pupils and Parents: Wide catchment area, including Southport to the north, Wigan to the east and down to south Liverpool and Warrington – new bus route from Warrington added 2009. The wider than average social mix means that girls here have that city edginess about them – confident but not arrogant, articulate, feet firmly on the ground but take nothing for granted and don't appear to feel that the world owes them a living. They're here to work and do so because it's expected. Relatively small percentage with English as a second language. The fact that staff are friendly ('They can afford to be – we don't cause them too many problems') is appreciated and valued by the youngest and the oldest. A wide-eyed new girl, the only one from her primary school, said it 'felt strange' on the first day but by day two was 'just great', and she hasn't looked back since. Parents are generally a new-money mix of professionals, semi-professionals and 'property' who enjoy getting to know one another via various speed-dating socials early in the year. The girls choose a new charity to support each year and work with enthusiasm in fundraising for the less fortunate.

Notable old girls: Professor Janet Finch, Vice-Chancellor, Keele University; Romily Menzies, BBC producer; Winifred Lambert – lost both legs to a bomb, became social worker of great distinction, working in housing for families and disabled, was a lifelong faithful member of the Communist party; Jane Greenwood, Tony award-winning fashion designer; Joy Swift MBE, creator of the original murder mystery weekends; Jane Garvey, Radio 4 presenter.

Entrance: For entry at 11– English, mathematics and verbal reasoning tests, approximately 70 per cent of entrants gain a place, though 50 per cent of entry is from own junior school.

Exit: Around 85–90 per cent stay post-GCSE with only a handful migrating to sixth form elsewhere. Favoured universities Russell Group and some Oxbridge, though most stay in the north.

Money Matters: 22 per cent receiving some form of financial support.

Remarks: Describes itself as a member of the Merchant Taylors' 'family' of schools, working closely with the boys' school and junior departments. As with all families, just a hint of sibling rivalry – impossible to mask the satisfaction of nudging slightly ahead of the boys' school in most subjects. It's not a pretty or a fussy school and yet somehow all the more likeable for that. Nothing flamboyant here and lacking frills, but it's a workhorse and does the job extremely effectively.

Merchiston Castle School

Linked to Merchiston Juniors (aka Pringle) in the Junior section

294 Colinton Road, Edinburgh, EH13 0PU

• Pupils: 480 boys; (70 per cent board, 30 per cent day) • Ages: 8-18 • Size of sixth form: 170 • Non-denom • Fees: Day £11,385-£17,940; Boarding £16,140-£24,780 pa • Independent

Tel: 0131 312 2200
Fax: 0131 441 6060
Email: Admissions@merchiston.co.uk
Website: www.merchiston.co.uk

Headmaster: Since 1998, Mr Andrew Hunter BA PGCE, educated at Aldenham and Manchester University where he read combined studies: English, theology and biblical studies. Came to Merchiston after eight years at Bradfield, where he ended as housemaster of Army House and, before that, eight years at Worksop, housemaster of Pelham House. Trails of glory on games fields: ex-county hockey, squash and tennis player, now enjoys running – Tennis Academy, launched in partnership with Tennis Scotland, allows him to keep his hand in with racquet sports. An expat, he was brought up on a Kenyan coffee farm and started school at Kenton College, Nairobi. Married to the glamorous Barbara, who teaches art and design. The Hunters have three children, one son a Merchistonian now at university, one son at college and a daughter also now at university. Keen on the arts, theatre, wine tasting etc. He goes from strength to strength – spot of tinkering with the syllabus, trawling all over the UK, Europe, and the world on behalf of school, plus a dabble into building. Latest great project is the sixth form house, opened in 2009, after an eight million quid fund raiser. Excellent Hunter-inspired forty-five page information booklet that is undoubtedly the best guide to any school we have ever seen, plus a really comprehensive leaflet on exam results including a rather complicated value-added section – other schools please note.

Academic matters: School continues to ply the mainly English system, though a few sit a combination of AS and Scottish Highers over two years. All boys must do two separate sciences at GCSE and goodly whack go on to study science at A level. Maths, English and science results very good; humanities good, too, and increasingly popular. A level critical thinking and classical civilisation and junior school Mandarin launched in 2006, with economics added in 2007. The labs have all been refurbished – interesting design, repeated throughout the school, a mixture of trad tables and octagonal plinths, projectors in many classrooms, interactive white boards in a few. Increasing use of computers as teaching tools (staff and pupils take their European Computer Driving Licence), some pupils have their own laptops and a good IT suite plus more computers in the magical, double-decker Spawforth Library, but prep is not necessarily done online. Good showing in out-of-school activities, maths, physics and chemistry Olympiads and the like.

Snazzy new Pringle Centre provides a teaching block for eight to ten year olds – we enjoyed a treatise on tropical fish from the youngest year group; computers in every classroom but no dedicated IT area for the youngest. Pupils must score 100 in IQ assessments to follow main curriculum and do the standard eight or nine GCSEs.

Learning Support teacher dedicated to the juniors. School has CReSTeD B status, though head of support for learning was fairly noncommittal about this. No pupil taken who can't 'access mainstream education'. She heads a team of one full-timer (dedicated to junior school) and roughly three part-timers. All pupils are assessed on entry on a whole year group basis for their reading, writing and maths. Support is specially geared for each pupil – all have individually tailored profiles. Timetabled support varies from year to year, with small groups for foreign languages and Latin, as much to get boys up to speed as for actual diagnosable problems. In-class support too, plus 'concentrated units' for spelling, reading and individual subjects. Maths on the whole catered for by the maths department, whilst the SEN specialists provide support lower down the school – sometimes via withdrawal, sometimes in class. Complex problems need more info and background than she feels the SEN department can give. Support for the gifted too. Mrs Watson appears to be a one woman, 24 hour, referral unit – boys can and do come at all times. All the dys-stream catered for, plus two or three currently with 'mild Asperger's' diagnosed in-school; ADHD not a problem, physical disability not 'a real problem': classes are relocated if access complicated; profoundly deaf boy recently went through the school with a (free) monitor paid for by West Lothian authority – wow! Can scribe in exams and pupils get extra time both in school and public exams. Really quite a large number of boys 'in the system'. Laptops not provided by the school, but masses in the special needs department, all on the school network, and parents often buy their own.

Games, Options, the Arts: Rugby popular, cricket, athletics, curling back in favour, hockey growing, skiing, sailing. Well-used sports hall, very well used swimming pool, weights room replaced by fitness centre. New tennis academy jointly with St George's and Tennis Scotland – serious ambitions. Golf encouraged. Wide variety of activities and successes in many areas. Popular CCF, community service and work in special schools a viable alternative, rifle range built into school wall. The head and the dean of sixth form extremely keen on outreach so the latest initiative is a group of lower sixth formers mentoring in several Edinburgh primary schools. Masses of trips all over the place in every discipline. Fantastic pipe band, sounding good during our visit, with some of the smallest pipers looking like embryo masons lugging their oblong bagpipe cases with grave determination. Strong choral tradition, including close harmony group, and a number of orchestras and bands. Super art department, with terrific paintings both in the department and displayed all over the school; apparently not much takeup post school. DT uses Cad Cam – good juxtaposition with computer suite and music hall, open till late.

Background and Atmosphere: Founded in 1833 by scientist Charles Chalmers, school moved from Merchiston Castle (now owned by Napier University) to the rather gaunt, purpose-built Colinton House in 1930 (ruins of Colinton Castle in grounds). Set in 100 acres of park-like playing fields, with stunning views to the north.

Pringle House, for junior boarders (aged eight to 12 or 13) recently much extended and a bit rabbit warreny, enclosed in its own private (secret) garden, own houseparents. Boys can climb the tree as far as the white mark, and generally allowed to be their own age without being pressurised 'to join the grown-ups'. Book inspired dayroom, plus obligatory television and rather complicated game of Diplomacy up on the wall. School in good heart, well used, nothing flash here but no signs of real distress either – just some minor blemishes in the chipboard desks and cabinbeds. Huge amount of cash recently spent on revamping loos and individual showers.

Boys work in their dorm areas and day boys have desks in the same area. Wicked posters. Sixth formers are billeted to each house for the year to act as monitors and have pretty snazzy kitchens to make their tasks less onerous. Cooking the flavour of the month, both in Pringle and, certainly, in Chalmers West – stunning pupil inspired kitchens. Pringle boys are running a self-financing cook-in. Older boys are encouraged to deviate from pizza and Pepsi. 'Steaks would be good,' said our guide and housemaster. Impressive new sixth form boarding house, Laidlaw House, opened in January 2009–126 ensuite bedrooms, modern kitchens, a café area, multi-gym and open plan social spaces with stunning views of Edinburgh.

Sick bay with visiting sports physiotherapists, own ultrasound machine and a delightful bubblegum pink isolation room (which would put any self-respecting boy off thoughts of malingering). Dining hall surprisingly small, with new servery and buffet service. Food good – soup, meat and veg, acres of white bread and rice pudding when we visited, impressive salad bar for a boys' school too. Boys praise the new arrangement: 'The food is still good at the end of term' – when the budget is low.

First floor Memorial Hall doubles as a chapel (service inter-denominational) and dance hall and boasts Cameron tartan cushions on removable pews, with an impressive tartan stair carpet up to the entrance. Girls are regularly corralled in from (primarily) St George's but also Kilgraston and St Margaret's for reel parties, with lots of practice before the real thing. Merchiston boys are regularly voted the best dancing partners in Scotland. Visiting girls 'not a problem' – they come and go at weekends and can join the boys in the sixth form club. Various departments already plotting what they will do with the redundant areas which have been freed up with the opening of Laidlaw; we heard three possible uses within the same number of hours. Vast number of trips and options for boarders, day pupils can join if space available.

Pastoral Care and Discipline: Good rapport between pupils and staff. The horizontal house system is said to have made bullying practically 'non-existent', and 'Anyway, physical bullying has been superseded by text bullying from mobile phones'. Head will and has asked pupils to leave. Believes in tough love, though a couple of prefects to whom we spoke obviously hadn't heard the phrase before. Mr Hunter is keen on parent/pupil/school partnership; will take in boys who have been excluded elsewhere – both boy and parent will sign a contract and the boy will be subject to very stringent and regular drugs testing routine. Expect to be drugs tested if either caught or suspected of dealing, or dabbling, followed by (but nothing in black and white) temporary or permanent exclusion. Ordinary misdemeanours (alcohol, smoking etc) are treated on their own demerits. No longer cool to smoke. Discipline seminars. Jolly school policies booklet, re-printed every year, of which head is justifiably proud, lists all the dos and don'ts of the place. Purchase of cigarettes or alcohol on or off the campus and dealings with betting shops are no-go areas. Betting is a new one to the GSG, but perhaps other schools aren't as clear-cut in their expectations.

Pupils and Parents: 'A down to earth school, rooted in values,' says the head. The only all-boys boarding school in Scotland. Strong middle class ethos, good values – no change here. Record number of pupils in the school. Sixteen per cent from abroad, of whom about five per cent are expats. Real foreigners come from all over, Japan, Hong Kong and Mainland China as well as the States, Mexico, plus a number from Europe, usually for the sixth form. Germany popular at present. No quick short stay fix – pupils must stay the full year. Head keen not to lose the boarding ethos and littlies at Pringle are encouraged to flexi-board. Day officially ends at 4.10pm, but pupils can stay till after tea (and presumably supper) if they want to – must be the cheapest babysitting service in the country. Senior boys can flexi-board too, often without charge if they are about official business – 'debates, plays and the like' – but £30 a night if for 'parental convenience'. Housemasters spend their ill-gotten gains on boy treats: microwaves, new cookers. Boys open, friendly and well-mannered.

Entrance: At eight, 10, 11, 12, 13 and 16, always via exams; 55 per cent pass mark at CE; boys come from prep schools all over Scotland and the north of England. Entry to sixth form automatic from inside school, others need a satisfactory report from previous school.

Exit: Refer again to the useful little booklet for details of the favoured universities – almost 80 per cent to England (Durham, Bristol, London, Newcastle etc, ten per cent to Oxbridge), the rest stay in Scotland (Edinburgh, Glasgow, St Andrew's, Aberdeen). Science, engineering, economics, management/business and languages/classics/English the favoured subjects. Pupils go on to be fully paid up members of the Edinburgh mafia – law lords etc.

Money Matters: Myriads of scholarships and bursaries for almost everything but all are now means-tested – scholarships are awarded for the honour alone. Sibling discounts with Kilgraston, Casterton and Queen Margaret's York. New Laidlaw scholarships donated by Merchistonian to pay full fees for several boys each year – targeting 'talented individuals whose financial circumstances would not otherwise allow them to attend Merchiston'.

Remarks: No change. Still the top boys' school in Scotland (indeed, the only boys-only boarding school north of the Home Counties) which extraordinary position has been achieved by defection to co-education by the rest – and it is on the way up anyway, as it was named Scottish Independent Secondary School of the Year 2009 by *The Sunday Times*. Charismatic head, boys are encouraged to 'try their hardest, make the most of their talents and look after each other'. 'No thoughts of going co-ed,' say head, staff and boys – the latter positively shuddered at the idea.

Michael Hall School

Linked to Michael Hall Lower School in the Junior section

Kidbrooke Park, Forest Row, East Sussex, RH18 5JA

• Pupils: 540; 280 girls, 260 boys; (up to 20 can board with local families) • Ages: 0-19 • Size of sixth form: 40 • Non-denom: Member of Steiner Waldorf Schools Fellowship • Fees: Upper School £10,300 pa • Independent

Tel: 01342 822 275
Fax: 01342 826 593
Email: info@michaelhall.co.uk
Website: www.michaelhall.co.uk

Chairperson of the College of Teachers: No head – instead a chairperson of the College of Teachers appointed annually, along with chairs of faculties (early years, lower and upper school). The school is a charity, with its only trustee a company called Michael Hall School Ltd. The trustees and directors of this company (council of management) are evenly split between parents, teachers and independents – all elected by members of The Michael Hall Association. The system is designed to avoid hierarchy and promote the transfer of skilful teachers into managerial positions.

Some parents find the lack of direct accountability disturbing, especially when faced with the substitution of specialist staff and/or the management of high-spirited children. Ideally the 45 members of the College of Teachers will together know all the children and the school will develop organically through their growing knowledge and experience, rather than there being sudden changes of direction when a new head takes over.

Academic matters: Kindergarten feels like a farmhouse kitchen, homey and calm. Earthy rather than bright colours are used in the decoration, pictures are wiped clean or taken home rather than being put up on the walls – children are left to find their own level of creative play and imitate the adults with plenty of repetition and ritual. Each of the four classes (age range three to six and a half) has access to its own garden, where apples are peeled, crushed and juiced in the autumn – a strong seasonal rhythm.

In the lower and middle school ideally one class teacher from seven until 14, some specialist teachers for maths, English and languages from 12. The classroom layout is traditional, with a rolling blackboard, games and music used in lessons. Children are taught to write before they read (seven or eight – usual in mainland Europe, startling in the UK); they learn manually and are encouraged to do before they understand.

Range of ability is huge – one parent complains that the classes (of 25) are all taught at the pace of the slowest pupil, resulting in bored bright ones, while another delights that her bi-lingual children get to expand their language skills creatively while less fluent children are coached. This variety of experience must stem from the skill of the teacher, which used to be a bit of a lottery, less so nowadays with tighter appraisals and continuous training. The mnemonic power of free ranging discussions and holistic links cannot be underestimated – caesarean sections while talking about Rome. The purpose-built library is well stocked with old Steiner favourites and eight computers available for project work, the ICT department has 20, the labs and learning support department three each (and alpha smarts).

Kindergarten and the lower school teachers keep records as well as planning their lessons – but no external targets or tests until mock GCSEs. The classes are regularly screened by the learning support department (two full-time and two part-time staff). End of year reports are ramped up to come out twice a year in the upper school. This organic schooling relies on a three-way partnership between the child, the teacher and the parent – communication between these is vital for success. Some parents have been frustrated during parents' meetings (once a term) by the lack of focus on individual children – a separate meeting must be set up for that type of discussion. Lower school teachers frequently do home visits to enable a good dialogue to take place between parents and teacher about the child.

A level choices in upper school (14–19) mean more select groups, even though the main lessons can be in a community of around 30. These operate concurrently with A level choices – each one lasts a shorter time than they did in the lower school, but the curriculum still covers a huge range of topics (e.g. ecology, meteorology, economics, gym, drama). Subject cross-pollination is ubiquitous. In a maths main lesson golden geometry leads to an exhibition at a London gallery and pupils compose a haiku. In a science main lesson, children cling to each other in threes mimicking atoms combined together to make a molecule of water. A recent student initiative resulted in a hand-bound book of work in the upper school, a beautiful record of an individual education. This breadth of education is really appreciated by the upper school – they feel it is one of Michael Hall's USPs. A relatively traditional range of A level choices on offer and some courses are validated by the Open College Network (OCN).

Games, Options, the Arts: Balance between practical and academic disciplines is the aim: each class of 11–12 year olds has a chance to cultivate a bed in the two and a half acre walled garden. The seasons run through the timetable too: whole school assemblies mark natural festivals as well as the end of term – Michaelmas, Advent. Poems learnt by rote and recited, costumes, lighting and sets designed for productions in the theatre. Learning games involve singing and later the playing of wooden flutes. Other instruments and the reading of music are introduced from eight.

And there's Eurhythmy – described by Rudolf Steiner as 'visible speech and music'. At first glance it looks like a bunch of kids clanking metal pipes to the accompaniment of a piano, kept in check by a softly spoken lady in a kaftan. However, no denying that it aids the development of rhythm, teamwork and coordination – and it's fun; an upper schooler admitted he had spent a while wishing they could learn dance instead, but now he was right back into it.

Everyone learns woodwork as well as to knit and sew, moving from a case for their flute to their own shirt. In art, colour is the essence of the work until the age of 15, when a period when only black and white is used – to link in with the 'I love this, I hate this' period of development. Drawing is also integrated into all topics – e.g., while studying the Renaissance, everyone will draw a room with perspective.

The multi-purpose gym is used by children in the lower school and above, with lots of imaginary narratives to link different disciplines together – balancing, climbing, skipping, trampolining, trapezing. No organised games until middle school and then only ones that use the hands, e.g. basketball, netball, tennis – but no football (Waldorf Steiner development philosophy encourages upright throwing of a ball rather than kicking and heading). Some parents miss the kick-around in break as a traditional way of burning off their sons' energy. The year after they enter the lower school, everyone takes part in the Olympic Games (this coincides with the study of ancient civilisations in the curriculum). Steiner schools from all over the UK come and camp and compete – but with enough categories to ensure everyone receives a medal.

Background and Atmosphere: In 1919 the Austrian philosopher and scientist, Rudolf Steiner, began a school in Stuttgart for children of the workers at the Waldorf-Astoria cigarette factory, using a curriculum based on nurturing emotional and cognitive intelligence. Today 958 schools and 1,600 early years centres in over 60 countries now use this holistic approach, making it the fastest growing independent education system in the world. Their curriculum is unique and, in the lower school, all teaching is done 'through the teacher and not via text books'. Michael Hall, founded in 1925, is the longest established of the 34 English Steiner schools to offer national curriculum exams.

Many families move to Forest Row so their children can attend, as local estate agents well know. This makes for a community feel – 'You can drop your homework round to a teacher if it's late'. Some school buses to Tunbridge Wells, Lewes and Brighton – you can walk down the hill (the estate consists of 60 acres of park land) from the A22, along the Cow Path, to the main building (Georgian listed). An ongoing plan for site development. However, many of the buildings are modern and distinctive, e.g. the Kindergarten (Hobbitshire-like – the Waldorf Steiner font on all signage begs more Elvish references), the gym, the theatre. Pupils built climbing frames, edged a path (both class building projects in summer before GCSEs start) and help to maintain the bio dynamic garden – this produces food for the kitchens, sells to the community and feeds a compost dragon each year.

The site and school do feel magical and slightly removed from reality – a huge spider's web woven onto a tree is a legacy of a middle school project – but reassuringly, still some sulky-looking teenagers milling around. The school council is very strong – they recently managed to get student cards issued to enable discounts: children are clear thinking and effective. This school is a beacon of professionalism among the Steiners in the UK – inter-school appraisals and assessments are vital to the self-regulation of this strand of education.

Pastoral Care and Discipline: The class teacher is the first point of contact in the concerns procedure, followed by the chair of faculty. Each upper school child also has a tutor – he or she can request a particular teacher for this rôle, choosing one to suit a particular subject choice or emotional support. Ideally the one class teacher for eight years in the lower school should be a constant, could well see you through your parents' divorce, puberty, your gran's death. Obviously character clashes – children go through love and hatred of parents and class teachers – and this system teaches you to confront the things you don't like, instead of turning away from them. If open and honest conversation fails, the child may move into the parallel class (in the lower school) or leave. Some parents hold back from complaining for fear of jeopardising their child's relationship with the teacher and instead resort to out of school tutors.

Pedagogical stories are used a lot in the younger years – remarkably effective (obviously this does not work so well in mid-teens). A points system in upper school for behavioural, alcohol or drug incidents – resulting in anything from detention through a behavioural contract and finally to exclusion.

Pupils and Parents: Practically all local families – some as far as Lewes, Tunbridge Wells, Nutley and London. Twenty-five per cent non-UK born. Lots of small to medium sized business owners – natural risk takers, musicians, architects, lawyers, teachers. Can be roughly divided into three groups – the New Age-ers (instinctively want their children to have as much of a childhood as possible before being forced into tests), the anthropops (done a lot of reading on the Waldorf Steiner philosophy) and the cosmopolitans (moved from Holland, Germany or a Scandinavian country where their children attended a state-funded Steiner school). Lots of Steiner pupils send their children to a Steiner school and many return to teach or volunteer.

Coffee and tea are served in the canteen each morning (a cheerful yellow hut) by parents and staff for parents and staff. Those parents who are frustrated with the unconventional way the school is run are those who are least involved. The community surrounding this school looks after its own – but the outside world can be a bit of a shock for some pupils. A girl who left to go to Lewes Sixth Form College wanted to return after three weeks – no exercise, she missed mixing with a wide peer age-group and she didn't like the regimented way subjects were taught.

Past pupils: Oliver Tobias, Sean Yates (cyclist), Bella Freud, Esther Freud, Marty Boysens (mountaineer),

Prof John Pearce (author and professor of child psychiatry at Nottingham University), Stuart Korth (osteopathy centre for children).

Entrance: At no specific age – 'the younger the better' and natural breaks in the Steiner curriculum occur at six and 14 years old. Non-selective in academic sense, although much effort to ensure class communities mesh. Mild dyslexia and dyspraxia fine (often diagnosed and always supported by learning support department) – more severe conditions sometimes OK as long as children are in system from kindergarten and their needs do not detract from quality of whole class education. Class teacher will interview potential parents/pupils – previous experience of French or German and music an advantage. Brighton Steiner and Steiner School of south west London are main feeders at age 14. Sixth form entry by interview.

Exit: Up to15 per cent leave at age of 12/13 to enter public schools. Fifty percent after GCSE for sixth form college in order to take more vocational A levels. Sixty per cent of upper schoolers go on to degree courses. Some UK universities (e.g. Plymouth and Roehampton) accept OCNs and many European ones take Steiner pupils without external qualification.

Money Matters: No scholarships, means-tested bursaries, discounts on fees for siblings. Government's early years funding operated for three and four year olds. No big trust fund – plans in place to set up a charitable foundation at present run on legacies and current account.

Remarks: A gentle school which aims to keep children from rushing into adulthood before they're ready. Will not work for every child, nor every parent – both must be tremendously involved in the educative process. Very difficult to explain a Steiner school without direct experience – hippy stereotypes abound – yet the children who emerge are confident, articulate, international, open-minded and grounded. Lucky them.

Mill Hill County High School

Worcester Crescent, Mill Hill, London, NW7 4LL

- Pupils: 1,700; 55 per cent boys and 45 per cent girls; all day
- Ages: 11-19 • Size of sixth form: 455 • Non-denom • State

Tel: 0844 477 2424
Fax: 02089 596 514
Email: admin@mhchs.org.uk
Website: www.mhchs.org.uk

Head: Since 2004, Geoffrey Thompson MA MBA(Ed) FCMI (mid-fifties). Formerly head of Duchess's Community High School in Alnwick, Northumberland. Educated at Campbell College, Belfast, then read music at St Catharine's College, Cambridge. Married with two sons and a daughter, he still practises the piano daily and has given a recent recital at the school. A dapper soul with a dry sense of humour and a certain cynicism when it comes to government jargon. Formerly a keen mountaineer – once led an expedition to the Himalayas – and skier; still a keen mountain walker, with a philosophy that derives from the sport: 'The straw never broke the camel's back – if I can take the last step I can take the next'. Has what he describes as 'boringly predictable interests' like travelling, the opera and Shakespeare.

Academic matters: In 2009, 75 per cent got five or more A*–C grades at GCSE including maths and English, 76 per cent A and B at A level, with 43 sixth formers getting three A grades or more. Some of the best results in north London. 'The percentage of GCSE and A level candidates who originally came in by selection has gone down from 45 per cent to 25 over the past three years, but the statistics haven't changed,' says the head.

Most subjects setted according to ability. Core, applied and additional science at GCSE. All students take French in Year 7, with the option to add German or Latin in Year 8. A technology college since 1994, the school recently acquired languages college status as its second specialism and more languages are planned. OCR National in leisure and tourism, and ICT offered both as a OCR National and as a half GCSE. Also GCSEs in economics, business studies, dance, drama and music.

A very big comprehensive (eight form entry) with large classes – average 27, but plenty with 30 and top sets can have 31 or 32. The school also has the largest sixth form in Barnet, which enables it to offer a wide range of subjects – including psychology, economics, media and film studies, music technology, as well as music, dance and drama – and an unusually wide range of subject combinations, but does mean can be 20ish in a class. 'It can be fantastically fertile,' says the head. Four ASs, generally three A2s. 'Otherwise, when do they get time just to be?' Sixth form curriculum includes PSCHE, ICT, careers guidance, preparation for university application and a variety of enrichment activities.

Games, Options, the Arts: Main school sports are football, rugby and netball in the winter, cricket and athletics in the summer, but huge range of other sports from trampolining to Tae Guk. Wide array of pitches and courts, including a gym, sports hall and all-weather cricket pitch. All students taught football, netball, hockey, rugby, basketball, badminton, cricket, rounders, swimming, trampolining, gymnastics, table tennis, tennis, pop lacrosse and volleyball.

Music unusually strong. Over 25 per cent have instrumental lessons. A school orchestra, three wind bands, four choirs, a jazz band, a chamber orchestra ('We have loads of string players, which is unusual in a comprehensive'), brass group, wind group and guitar group, plus award-winning rock bands. Major concerts every half term and annual musical. Dance and drama also strong with drama and dance clubs, autumn drama festival (plays written by head of drama) and an annual dance medley. Art came in for criticism in the last Ofsted but 'Staffing changes have been made and we have moved forward a long way,' says the head.

Exceptional extra-curricular programme with wide range of trips – to the Atlas mountains in Morocco, Honduras, Mongolia, Madagascar and India, plus skiing and regular field trips. Head's Challenge, Duke of Edinburgh, World Challenge Third World expeditions (100 students enrolled in past year). Consistent enthusiasm for charity fundraising – 'There could be something going on every day but we have to be selective'.

Background and Atmosphere: This very large school was formed by a gradual process of amalgamation. Its roots lie in Orange Hill Boys' Grammar School (founded 1931) which joined with Orange Hill Girls' Grammar School in 1971 and then, in 1983, merged with Moat Mount School to form the current school.

Attractive 21-acre hilltop site in a salubrious suburb with views over the surrounding greenery. Complex layout because of unplanned expansion over many years – 'I've been here a year,' said one member of staff, 'and I still get lost' – but very good facilities nonetheless. The atmosphere is purposeful and directed with confident, well-behaved children. 'An overwhelming majority of our pupils want to get on,' says the head. 'They're pupils who value learning and we have teachers who want to help them learn.'

The school also runs Oak Hill, a successful facility for 32 emotionally and behaviourally disturbed children in Barnet, four and a half miles away.

Pastoral Care and Discipline: Happily considers itself 'very traditional' in terms of school discipline. Maroon and navy blazers worn by all. 'They mostly wear their uniform with pride,' says the head. 'They don't wear it to look like Britney Spears. Last time I stood at the gates and watched nearly 1,700 children go through, only two had their top button undone.' High expectations, too, of student behaviour – 'There's an explicit expectation that students will respect their elders and try to be a pleasure to teach'. Zero tolerance for drugs.

Pastoral care excellent – each student placed in a tutor group on arrival, remaining with the same tutor and head of year throughout Years 7–11. Sixth formers provide peer mentoring and also help with literacy in Year 7. System of merit awards for service to the school and academic achievement. Good careers guidance, with school's own work experience organiser and higher education consultant.

Pupils and Parents: The school is quite difficult to get to by public transport (no tube nearby) and the majority come from affluent Mill Hill and surrounding leafy suburbs – parents buy carefully to be in catchment. Selective places enlarge ethnic mix and size of catchment but still predominantly middle class. Old Boys include Sir Ronald Cohen (venture capitalist), David Dein, Angus Fraser, Middlesex cricketer, and style journalist and broadcaster Robert Elms.

Entrance: Heavily over-subscribed at 11–1,822 applicants for 240 places; queues round the block plus security at the gate on open days. To meet local demand, the number of places allocated by distance from the head's office has been increased to a minimum of 90. Siblings get next preference (about 28 per cent of places in 2007), then ten per cent on technological aptitude (abstract reasoning), ten per cent for music by aural test and performance audition (generally at least good grade 4, though aptitude, not attainment, assessed and exams play no part) and five per cent for dance, by audition. Any places left added to the 90 allocated by proximity to the head's office. Waiting list places, too, on geographical proximity. About 450 apply for 40 or 50 Year 12 places – five GCSE Bs minimum requirement. Five Cs for vocational courses.

Exit: Virtually all existing pupils proceed to sixth form. 'Once they are on the roll, we never throw anyone out, unless they have no realistic chance of an E grade or better' – though those looking to do maths or sciences A level must have A grades at GCSE in those subjects. 'We have severe accommodation problems, so we have to be selective.' Most pupils to higher education and an astonishing range of universities and courses, from child care to medicine. Some 36 to Oxbridge in the last five years. 'We help our students to do what's right for them.'

Money Matters: High performing specialist school status, economies of scale and enthusiastic parents mean school is not short of funds.

Remarks: A purposeful, well-run school, with excellent teaching and results, which provides an all-round education for a wide range of motivated and well-behaved children.

Mill Hill School

Linked to Grimsdell Mill Hill Pre Preparatory School in the Junior section

Linked to Belmont Mill Hill Preparatory School in the Junior section

The Ridgeway, Mill Hill, London, NW7 1QS

• Pupils: 420 boys, 190 girls (about half of boarders are from abroad)
• Ages: 13-18 • Size of sixth form: 240 • Non-denom • Fees: Boarding £25,479; Day £16,125 pa • Independent

Tel: 020 8959 1176
Fax: 020 8201 0663
Email: registrations@millhill.org.uk
Website: www.millhill.org.uk

Head: Since 2007, Dr Dominic Luckett BA DPhil FRSA (forties). Educated at the University of Leicester and Magdalen College, Oxford, where he did his doctorate in Tudor history. Taught at Harrow, where he became both head of history and an assistant housemaster, then at Worth, where he was deputy head. A tall, serious, quietly spoken man, he continues to teach history to the fourth form – 'You can't talk to other teachers about teaching unless you do it yourself'. Attracted to Mill Hill because it mixes day with boarding and because of its location in north London – 'It's a bit more edgy'. Has come in with no desire to change the fundamentals – 'It's a really nice place, with a chatty atmosphere' – but has already tightened up appearance and manners and aims to raise the general academic standards by carefully monitored teaching. He is a serving inspector with the ISI. Married to Cara, a barrister, his hobbies include paragliding, skiing and hill walking.

Academic matters: Takes in a reasonably broad spread of academic ability and aims to get the best out of each child by helping them to learn effectively. 'We're not a hot house,' says the head. 'We're never going to be the top academic school in the country, but we want to make teaching accessible and enjoyable and give children high expectations. That said, we have some very bright children. It's a question of identifying what each child is capable of and providing what each child needs.' The head feels that when he arrived the school was suffering from a 'slight lack of ambition' – 'I think expectations could have been higher, particularly with the good middle of the roaders'.

Head aims to achieve each child's full potential while working in a way that makes them feel comfortable – 'For some, three Bs at A level is a real achievement, but others here get three, four or five As. Some children, too, require a lot of pressure to achieve and others buckle under pressure'. Currently, 70 per cent get As and Bs at A level, with particularly strong results in maths, drama, art and history. 24 subjects on offer at A level, including Chinese, business studies and government and politics. Pupils setted in ability in subject groups from Year 9. Good spread of languages: French, Spanish, German, Greek and Latin, plus Portugese and Chinese as extras. Wonderful new teaching block, the Favell Building, provides a light and airy contemporary home for the social sciences, modern languages and RE, plus a splendid venue to display student artwork. Science labs, on the other hand, where Nobel-winning scientist Francis Crick once studied, still have a quaint old-fashioned feel, though these too are in line for an update. They certainly don't seem to hold pupils back, however, since Imperial College was the most popular university destination last year.

Good teaching, though it has been criticised by the ISI for being a bit 'limited in range'. The head is focusing on developing learning plans appropriate to pupils' abilities. Learning support provision also being built up – the special needs co-ordinator and two full-time learning support assistants will be joined by another part-time LS teacher.

Games, Options, the Arts: Has always had a reputation for outstanding sport – 'Though it's not a religion,' said one boy – and that continues unabated, with masses of opportunities and county players in many sports. Rugby particularly successful – in 2009 the 1st XI had an unbeaten season. Cricket also very strong and golf big and growing, with a 'super' golf professional and a golf scholarship (no golf course, however – pupils play at nearby Hendon). Tennis also very strong, with competition results proving it to be one of the strongest schools in the south east.

Music, drama and art also strong. Enthusiastic director of music encourages all comers and rock given as much encouragement as classical (Alicia Chilli in 'The X Factor' is an Old Girl). 250-seat theatre is the venue for the popular house drama festival (about a third do drama at GCSE). Lots of other opportunities to shine, too: annual fashion show a highlight of the year; CCF, which is compulsory in the first year, also gives many an opportunity to take on responsibility and show their mettle. 'You can do anything here. What's wonderful is that if you have an interest, the school will take that seriously and facilitate it,' said one pupil. Thriving charitable work with partnership programmes in Nicaragua, Ethiopia, Tamil Nadu, in which pupils stay with local families and involve themselves in fundraising.

Background and Atmosphere: Founded in 1807 by a group of non-conformist Christian ministers and city merchants, who placed their school outside London because of the 'dangers, both physical and moral, awaiting youth while passing through the streets of a large, crowded city'. Many parents still see this pleasant isolation as a key advantage – 'I like the fact that my daughter is busy six days a week with her friends in a nice environment, not hanging round Brent Cross,' said one. The original, handsome neo-classical building, with its pillared entrance and sweeping views across parkland, is still an undoubted selling point and it very much has the feel of a country boarding school, with the same sense of rural isolation and expansive parkland (120 acres of Green belt).

In fact, only about a quarter board, but Saturday morning lessons for all and a busy afternoon games schedule, so you really only choose Mill Hill if you're happy with a long day and a one-day weekend. 'A lot of parents like Saturday school,' says the head. 'It gives a bit more space in the week, a bit more breadth, with slightly less pressure and a broader range.' Boarders are now allowed home Friday nights for the night, but the head is not interested in flexi-boarding. Very much a campus school, too, with little access to urban reality some distance from the gates. Day pupils stay on site during the academic day, boarders are allowed out post lessons to the local (limited) high street. Boarding houses slightly tired. Head has tidied up the walls (personal memorabilia now restricted to neat little notice boards) and redecoration is high on the agenda. Still compulsory chapel once a week, but the school is non-denominational.

Pastoral Care and Discipline: Considered to be a kind and gentle school, consistently praised by parents and officials for its outstanding pastoral care. Head a little firmer on dress and courtesy than his predecessor (but 'not Stalinist,' said one pupil) – 'I want to make sure pupils are making the most of their opportunities'. Realistic but not lax on drugs – 'Drugs in London are a fact of life. If someone is selling them, I don't want them in my school. If I find someone taking them, they're allowed one mistake and no more'. Uniform pre-GCSE, lower sixth dark suit with one of a myriad of ties, upper sixth can wear their own suit. Dress code and other regulations now strictly adhered to – 'My son got a detention for having his shirt out of his trousers when he was at the local tube station,' said one mother. 'Another for forgetting his swimming kit on a Saturday.'

Pupils and Parents: No typical Mill Hill pupil. Quite a lot live locally, even boarders, though in the sixth form, a significant influx from China, former Soviet Republic, Germany, Albania and Russia. Strong entrepreneurial element and urban professionals among the parents, quite a number of first-time buyers. Former pupils include Richard Dimbleby, Francis Crick, Simon Jenkins, Timothy Mo, Denis Thatcher, Katherine Whitehorn and Norman Hartnell.

Entrance: Some 140 places in Year 9, with about 70 or 80 going to pupils from the junior school, Belmont – 'There is the expectation that if they want to come here they can, though there's no absolute guarantee. We have to feel that they are going to flourish'. 20 to 25 places reserved for boarders. Sets its own exams in January before entrance in English, maths, French and science and uses the Common Entrance pass mark for setting. In 2008, the school was three times over-subscribed, so 'we want to know what a child will bring. It's partly personality, and partly other factors like sport, music or drama'.

Entry to the sixth form is two As and three Bs, a requirement that applies both externally and internally. These requirements have not always been strictly adhered to, but one of the head's first acts was to enforce it, involving about 15 pupils leaving – 'We've always had a minimum grade requirement, now we're insisting it's met. If pupils are getting Fs and Us, this is not the right place for them. We are just encouraging them to work harder'.

Exit: Majority to university, with a sprinkling to Oxbridge.

Money Matters: A selection of scholarships in academic subjects, the arts and sports. Fully-funded bursaries and a range of other bursaries up to 90 per cent of the fees, on a carefully graded system of finance – 'The bursar goes to see parents. The bursaries are not here to help the impoverished middle classes, but to broaden access'.

Remarks: Suits a busy, engaged child happy to try out a wide range of activities and use all the facilities and range of a boarding school, while still being able to go home at night (unless, of course, they board). A well-balanced school, with a head determined to put the academic underpinning firmly in place.

Millfield School

Linked to Millfield Preparatory School in the Junior section

Butleigh Road, Street, Somerset, BA16 0YD

• Pupils: 1,220 boys and girls (80 per cent board, the rest day). 365 girls board/105 day; 590 boys board/160 day. • Ages: 13-18 • Size of sixth form: 550 • Inter-denominational • Fees: Boarding £28,020; Day £18,855 pa • Independent

Tel: 01458 442 291
Fax: 01458 447 276
Email: admissions@millfieldschool.com
Website: www.millfieldschool.com

Head: Since 2008, Mr Craig Considine (fiftyish), former headmaster of Wanganui Collegiate School, New Zealand. An Australian, married with four children, twin 12 year olds at Millfield Preparatory. Wife, Penny, a social worker with experience of working in boarding schools in Australia and New Zealand, is very supportive of husband's move to Millfield. Mr Considine played professional Australian Rules football and was in the Australian Commonwealth Games team for decathlon. Has a passion for the outdoors and was involved in outdoor education, especially at Timbertop at Geelong Grammar. Set up year 10 experiential education programmes in New Zealand.

Academic matters: You name it, they do it, or very nearly. Huge range at GCSE, from dance to design by way of classical Greek and, of course, physical education. More than 40 A levels as well as vocational A levels in leisure & recreation and BTEC in art & design and sport. Languages a movable feast depending on the origins of the intake, more popular here than in many schools, with French particularly strong, although with 50 nationalities represented it is not surprising. Academic Society for the brightest and the best.

Staff constantly irritated by some outsiders' perception that Millfield's truly comprehensive, all-ability intake makes it a school solely for the nice but dim. Individual results attest that brilliance is enhanced as much as struggle is aided, and overall grades and points tallies have steadily increased over the last six years. School results highlight 100 top scores rather than dwell on the huge spread that reflects the ability range.

Well-stocked library open from 8.30am Monday to Saturday. A full 10 per cent of pupils are non-native English speakers who receive EAL teaching from specialist staff. Millfield is dauntingly large, yet classes are pocket-sized (maximum 15, usually much smaller) and the pupil:staff ratio a long-standing constant 1:7.5. Boys do just as well as girls, bucking the national trend. Staff usually stay for the long haul and, with 200 academic and coaching staff, Millfield boasts the largest common room of any school in the UK.

Millfield's expertise in specific learning difficulties goes back a long way: Jack Meyer was summoned to London in 1941 to discuss the possibility of Attlee's 'word blind' son entering Millfield. He passed his exams to enter the School of Navigation at Southampton eighteen months later and Millfield's reputation for helping dyslexics was made. We get the feeling from parents, though, that a slight dip in emphasis and the school becoming reluctant to take more complex cases. Un-PC language flared up when we were told that the pupils with SEN benefit from very small numbers in the 'lower sets'. Currently some 240 children get SEN support – down from a few years back.

For those with lesser difficulties help may be only once a week when they are taught in groups, but an entire English class in each year (of a greater or smaller size – can depend) who are taught English in the SEN department, with proper classrooms as well as individual teaching units. Strong emphasis on spelling as well as on personal attention spans; each challenged pupil has an individual pupil profile which is constantly updated. Unit is open before school, during break and at lunchtime with a drop-in centre (well used during our visit) plus some mainstream guidance for those in the main school. No shame in visiting the unit. Sixth formers meet with the unit at the start of the year, can do preps here (some concentrate better in an organised environment). Dyslexics, dyspraxics, mild Asperger's, autism, ADHD all assisted – some come with statements of needs and educational psychologists' reports, others are identified during their school career. 'Jolly nearly' wheelchair friendly but can certainly cope – enough classrooms on the ground floor; one child at the school is deaf, hearing aid rather than monitor. Five full-time staff and two part-timers, all qualified teachers and either dyslexia qualified or with loads of experience. No extra fee for SEN support.

Games, Options, the Arts: 'Outstanding' barely covers the range, quality and availability of the fantastic sporting facilities for which Millfield is justly famous – 25/30 pupils compete internationally each year. Olympic-sized swimming pool, freshly upgraded sports halls, equestrian centre with indoor and outdoor arenas with fabulous accommodation for the pupils' own horses, recently increased in size: a waiting list for horses, polo very popular and played at Millfield Prep. Pupils can take their BHSPIC, as well as competing against the outside world. Purpose-built fencing salle, nine-hole golf course with indoor tuition centre (and golf clubs everywhere), indoor tennis centre (plus lots of all-weather courts), plus running track, three water-based Astro hockey pitches (you scoosh it with water at half time and it remains super smooth), acres of playing fields, fabulous cricket pavilion and a growing reputation for clay pigeon shooting and skiing. To further aid the quest for physical excellence, a well-staffed physiotherapy department and weights rooms. Predictably, Millfield teams trounce all comers as a matter of course – two pupils have been selected for the English Schools' athletics team, one representing Great Britain at the European Youth Olympics. As head says, 'I could cover my walls just with pictures of famous Millfield sportsmen and women;' (the admissions stairway is covered, anyway, with winners from all walks of life). Highly competitive, losing not really an option – some disquiet from those who have suffered cold shoulder when on a losing Millfield side. Sadness in some quarters that sport seen as so very important, 'It can take away the enjoyment'. Two PE lessons a week the norm, including dance or orienteering for the less overtly muscled. Trips to everywhere in most disciplines.

Fantastic fine arts centre teaches everything from photography to painting, with regular artists in residence, but closed on Sundays so budding painters will have to do it elsewhere. Regular exhibitions – fab new space – showing visiting artists as well as staff and pupils. Outsiders invited in. Impressive new food technology department under Leith's aegis popular, and massively increased design technology department, positively humming (BTEC as well as GCSEs on offer).

In 2006, a 320 seat concert hall and music school was completed and have increased musical awareness in the school and huge numbers have individual music lessons and tripettes all over the place. One pupil currently in the National Youth Orchestra. Interest in academic music tends to tail off at A level. Drama well-supported, with pupils having the 500 seat Meyer Theatre at their disposal, as well as a professional-standard TV and recording studio. Eight pupils in the National Youth Theatre last year.

Background and Atmosphere: Always a pleasure to come here – the immaculate campus is dotted with sculpture, some by artists in residence (and pupils watch them grow) and some specially commissioned, courtesy of the Millfield Sculpture Commission. Founded in 1935 by Jack Meyer with seven Indian pupils, of whom six were princes, and swiftly adopted the Robin Hood principle – squeezing money from the exceedingly rich to subsidise the needy, talented poor. From day one, in a large, rented Somerset house, he set about promoting individual ability, in whatever sphere. Enormous sixth form rather dominates, according to some parents, making the whole feel less like a school than an old-style university campus, with buildings in all directions in a mishmash of styles. The new on-site boarding houses are particularly impressive, smashing kitchens with Sky and huge commonrooms, almost all upper and lower sixth have individual cabins. The old boarding houses, mainly ageing manors around Street and Glastonbury, have almost all been sold off, three only remain, pupils are bused in and out. Over three hundred acres of ground and school is still adding to its portfolio.

Millfield is proud of having been built up from nothing and owing nothing. Used to paying its way – school hosts range of Easter revision courses and summer English language courses as well as conferences. A large dining hall, notable for its finer than average fare, sits at the heart of the campus and is given a universal thumbs up by pupils, even the vegetarians. One wall consists entirely of pics of Olympic contenders. Fantastic glass fronted sixth form bar, which serves real food. An incredible new cricket pavilion, the glass walls etched in cricket balls (this editor thought they were coffee beans until put right). Clubs for almost everything.

Pastoral Care and Discipline: Seems to have eased off the throttle of 'one strike and you're out' methods of old, no doubt helped by now having a larger number of boarding pupils on campus and in clear sight. Head judges any case of bullying, drug-taking or drinking on its individual demerits, although on-site drug dealing would inevitably earn a one-way ticket home; 'one sniff' and off with his head, 'unless there is a good reason why not'. Posh parents no reason to keep the blighters, and we hear of pupils disappearing virtually overnight. Random drug testing for individual pupils by agreement with the parents.

Head acknowledges bullying cases, particularly at boarding school, can be complex – needs of the victim a priority, though. All pupils are in houses. Not for wilting wall-flowers; for rest, houseparents are usually the first port of call with problems – caring, family-orientated people making boarders feel at home. School keeps going throughout the term with activities for those who live abroad (though guardians etc pick up during half term). Long-standing, and successful 'no private assignations' rule – couples would need houseparents' permission to meet. Definite sense of separation from more worldly atmosphere of nearby Glastonbury – a relief. Chaplaincy centre a haven for exam-stressed pupils, plus other counsellors in the place, dedicated prayer room for Muslims. Strong community service locally.

Pupils and Parents: Pupils from a wide range of backgrounds, from the dyslexic sent by a local authority in north Wales to a Middle Eastern prince wallowing in cash – makes for some challenges. Ties for every achievement and the headgirl has a swish gold brooch, senior prefects the same but in silver. Expected to work hard and play hard – not for those lacking confidence or who duck out of being part of a team. Day pupils mostly local, boarders from anywhere and everywhere, with 18 per cent from overseas. Increasing numbers (24 per cent) from London and the Home Counties, 'We seem to have been discovered by the trad parents and not just the first time buyers'. Some parents of girls felt that they were too much in the minority, but school points out a lot more girls here than at most girls only schools. The list of alumni, famous and notorious, is endless, with Duncan Goodhew, John Sergeant, Tony Blackburn, James Hewitt, Ben Hollioake and Sophie Dahl just the tip of a very eclectic iceberg.

Entrance: Interview and previous head's report the usual route in, with CE used to determine set for core subjects – 'We have 23 maths sets in Year 9!' For overseas pupils, no written test is required – a huge selling point for many. Millfield has anything up to 80 feeder schools but by far the largest day number come from its own prep school (see separate entry). Quite a lot of pupils begin at Millfield – and leave – at odd times.

Exit: Most go to universities here and all over the world (America a big favourite), seven last year to Oxbridge, one to Harvard, quite a number to sports courses at university, Bristol is popular, also accounts, business management and law. Around 60 leave after GCSE, but twice as many enter, and 36 left after lower sixth last year.

Money Matters: Loads of scholarships (£4.2 million per year's worth, to be precise) at all levels for all-rounders, sportspeople (was the first school to offer these), academics, musicians (instrumental and choral) artists and even chess players. Sixth form scholarships said to be more plentiful than 13+ (fewer years for the school to shell out). All are individually assessed (vestiges of the Robin Hood principle linger), nearly 50 per cent get some form of award, with higher special bursaries for local hardship cases. Reassuringly expensive for the affluent – in top 20 for big-budget full fees. School setting up a foundation to be able to offer more help to more.

Remarks: Impressive, good-looking school great for those who value independence and street-cred. Strong in every area and a great confidence builder for sporty kids and those who have struggled elsewhere. Not for those content to hide in a corner or needing lots of TLC.

Milton Abbey School

Milton Abbas, Blandford Forum, Dorset, DT11 0BZ

• Pupils: 220 boys, 15 girls in the sixth form • Ages: 13-18 • Size of sixth form: 105 • C of E • Fees: Boarding £28,350; Day £21,300 pa • Independent

Tel: 01258 880 484
Fax: 01258 881 194 or 01258 881 250
Email: admissions@miltonabbey.co.uk
Website: www.miltonabbey.co.uk

Headmaster: Since 2010, Mr Gareth Doodes, who has been the deputy headmaster of Milton Abbey since September 2009. Educated at Eastbourne College and St Andrew's University, where he read history. He started his career at Taunton School before moving to Oakham, where he was first master of scholars, overseeing the appointment, development and appraisal of the school's scholars, and then, for five years, a housemaster.

He says, 'I want Milton Abbey to have big ambitions, big achievements and a big heart.'

Academic matters: Huge range of ability – IQs between 80 and 156; very frustrated bright boys (and girls) and the rest. A key school for helping pupils with learning difficulties, dyslexics are integrated with the rest (lots of remedial help where needed and instant tutorials on anything at any time). School is anxious not to be known as a 'specialist school' and all pupils must be able to access mainstream education. That being said, thirty per cent of the pupils come with an educational psychologist's report, a summary of which stays in the staffroom, so tutors and staff have instant access. Four dedicated SEN teachers plus three classroom assistants and more to come – 'dual teaching is the way forward'. Some pupils withdrawn – usually from French – have five lessons a week, either one-to-one or in small groups but it varies according to need.

Extra time in exams, scribing, amanuenses, laptops – 'Exams are a really exciting time', with invigilators for every pupil with an amanuensis or a scribe, each in separate rooms. School now CREsTeD (i.e. indefinite learning support paid for by Services et al). No DORE or trendy exercise gismos – 'scaffolding rather than tricks'. GCSEs taken ad nauseam, no shame in failure here. AS levels often taken over two years and, though the A level results are perhaps not as convincing as they might be, many get A*s in their practicals, which subsequently lead to job offers after school. Grade D or E at A level is often way beyond anything that might have been predicted. Modules as far as possible in everything. Smallish classes, (16 the norm, much smaller in sixth form).

'No problem' in getting staff, 'though sometimes the choice is restricted', much emphasis on staff training. Academic tutors do study skills and monitor progress; teaching staff set aside two periods each week for official tutorials or help with problems. IT popular and computers everywhere – most boys and girls have them for private study, and laptops both in class and exams. Business studies linked to economics department; excellent take up in BTecs (equivalent of two A levels, a 'fantastic good qualification'): countryside management popular – two boys recently organized the delivery of 140 pheasants, with 40 boys up at crack of dawn to welcome them to their release pen. The game farm was so impressed that they delivered 40 partridges for free the following day and boys organized a shoot the Saturday before our visit, with nearby fathers bringing guns in on the day (no, they did not shoot 180 birds). BTecs also in equine studies – school recently bought adjoining land and stable yard – sports and exercise management and hospitality management, with the school currently offering a popular chalet cooking course in Shaftesbury and planning its own cooking course in the kitchens, which are about to undergo a serious facelift, ditto the food (wood-burning ovens, making own bread and cutting down on the Es – which 'lengthens the attention span').

Games, Options, the Arts: Compulsory activities on Tuesday and Thursday afternoons, huge choice: art, very active theatre, boat maintenance, clay-pigeon shooting (popular), fencing, model making etc. Art and design re-vamped with the addition of good, practising (commercial-eyed) artists and 'excellent' photography. Natural history still strong with moth traps shining through the summer months. Boys do regular head counts of birds. Ferrets (captain of etc). CDT popular, as well as CCF. School has strong links with Royal Armoured Corps at Bovington as well as the Royal Navy and masses of D of E (oodles of golds). Indoor heated swimming pool popular, games hall has sexy under floor heating – a bonus in winter; new Astroturf. Peter Allis inspired golf course (his son was here) and very enthusiastic sailing (lots of prizes) plus success in off-shore yacht masters' certificates and day skipper courses. County participants in athletics.

Background and Atmosphere: Friendly, caring, prefects are called pilots and a 'big brother' atmosphere is encouraged, particularly where new and vulnerable pupils are concerned. Weirdos are not picked on and almost all recent Old Boys report that they 'loved it' at the school, though – as ever – the occasional chap slips through the net. Approving noises from prep school heads.

Magical listed grade one building, with fabulous plasterwork (begun by Sir William Chambers and taken over by James Wyatt), set in fold of valleys and Dorset hills. Abbot's Hall and King's Room breathtaking. School does weddings in the holidays and is used for the occasional film and telly set; the Sallie Army has a couple of summer schools a year. Rather jolly prospectus with masses of brightly coloured inserts. School owns the fabric and grounds, diocese of Salisbury owns the Abbey, which is gorgeous – a peculiar arrangement: the diocese bought it when the place was up for sale in the thirties, to prevent it falling into 'the hands of a faith-healing group'. Locals occasionally worship here too and school uses it daily. Each year group takes chapel and even the most dyslexic reads a lesson or say a prayer. School founded in mid 1950s. Modern blocks cleverly hidden, stable block converted into light classrooms plus art, music etc. Stunning theatre, with efficient CDT below (very cunning), all classrooms/sports hall/theatre quite close to hand. Houses, now with carpets, being revamped, all in main building, each with its own territory.

All housemasters (one of whom is a woman) are married, family atmosphere pervades – boys know each other well, graduating from dormitory/common rooms (i.e. with working spaces round the beds – and much less cramped than previously) to single study bedrooms, still untidy and refreshingly scruffy. Lots of new paint everywhere, some surprisingly bright (and some currently looking a trifle worn), head aiming to bring the school 'somewhere towards the 20th century', and is going for 'the faded country house look', 'buildings and the whole environment are so important'. School not as bulging as when we first visited and could hold one or two more, but no wish to grow.

Boys are kept busy in this isolated school. Lovat trousers and jerseys, suits on Sundays, ditto for girls. Certain amount of to-ing and fro-ing still with local girls' schools – St Mary's, Godolphin, St Anthony's – and stunning new basement sixth form centre ('the best night club in Dorset'). Two fixed exeats, plus half term, but enormously flexible. Saturdays off for hunting (still), polo, 'They would lose the same time if they had to go to an away match'. NB This is the only school where reception has 'Hurlingham and Country Life' to read and a glossy on sporting achievements as well as other recent school mags and prospectuses.

Pastoral Care and Discipline: Housemasters, who are normally also academic tutors, plus assistant house tutors. School is small enough to pick up any worrying vibes via the bush telegraph and head usually knows within hours if drugs have been brought back: 'Boys don't like drugs because it forms cliques, which are unpopular in a small school'. Rehabilitation and random drugs testing on suspicion (boys apparently like to be able to say, when offered drugs during the exeats, 'No thanks – I am tested at school' – even if they aren't). Not automatically out for drugs but out for dealing or going OTT. Booze a permanent problem, with parents tending to slip a chap the odd six pack in the hopes that a beer here or there will keep them off drugs, and the introduction of girls will compound the problem, ditto the recent government diktat that schools can only have a bar if food is served, hence the introduction of school feasts – a massive Saturday night blow-out followed by gassing to staff 'over a beer or two'.

Pupils and Parents: Gents, plus a handful of first-time buyers, more so than previously, and from further away. A handful of real foreigners, slightly more expats, and an increasing number of Services children. Pupils are courteous, relaxed and friendly and 'really miss it when they leave'. 'Boys here have three great loves in their lives – their ma, their pa and the head'. Geographically widespread. Monthly rendezvous for old boys at the 'Duke of Wellington' pub, Eaton Terrace. Presumably girls will turn up there too.

Entrance: Via CE – very flexible, though; 'It's not really the school for children who need the bright lights and the Kings Road'. (Staff too, have to come for a twenty-four hour interview rather than a short sharp committee quizzing.) Boys come from all over, over 100 feeders, including all the top preps, plus state system. Girls currently from Cranleigh, Westonbirt, St Mary's Shaftesbury and the maintained sector. Entry post-GCSE if they have the right qualifications – currently five Cs or even Ds at GCSE is 'good enough'. 'But we have to be very frank and honest and say if a child is not up to it.'

Exit: Around 90 per cent to some form of further education, with 50 per cent to degree courses. (The chap who went to Peterhouse, Cambridge, at 14, graduated in 2001.) An 'increasing number choose not to go to university, preferring instead to get a positive life experience', e.g. two years before the mast, a year in an African game park, coaching sport in a shanty town in India and then hitting the jobs market. But still Cirencester, Newcastle, Bristol WE, Bournemouth, Oxford Brookes, Manchester Metropolitan all popular, as are colleges of higher education like Cheltenham and Gloucester. Boys given career briefing from the moment they arrive, and tend to opt for careers where 'they have to sell themselves' – very entrepreneurial. Practical subjects such as business studies, the record industry and hotel and catering are popular. Some leakage (to sixth form colleges everywhere) this year post-GCSE, 'Chaps tend to get restless,' said our guide.

Money Matters: Some scholarships, including academic, music, art, drama, sailing. Will carry pupils through exam year in cases of hardship.

Remarks: Boarding school which resolutely continues to give good, experienced, professional help to those with learning difficulties, now with an increasing number of girls in the sixth form (a third of whom have learning difficulties). A great confidence-building place which runs on kindness and encouragement. Don't take our word for it – read Dr Rae's 'Letters to Parents' (Harper Collins). 'What is more, the self-confidence gained by the school's pupils is the self-belief that comes from fighting back and proving the pessimists wrong.' We await the impact of Mr Doodes on this special place with much interest.

The Moat School

Bishops Avenue, Fulham, London, SW6 6ED

• Pupils: 70 boys, 20 girls • Ages: 11-16 • Fees: £23,850 pa • Independent

Tel: 020 7610 9018
Fax: 020 7610 9098
Email: office@moatschool.org.uk
Website: www.moatschool.org.uk

Head: Since September 2001, Ms Abigail Gray BA PGCE Cert SpLD, graduate of School of Oriental and African Studies, teaching assistant in a busy special needs unit in central London, teacher and subsequently SENCo in a city technology college before deputy head here. Completed her specialist teaching qualification in her first year at The Moat – has since made specialist teacher training a priority for all subject specialists here. Lives in Mortlake with her partner and nine year old daughter.

Academic matters: Max 10 to a class, three or four typical for GCSE – 'We teach as they learn, so we learn and adapt'. Average value-added is a commendable two grades to GCSE – a quick scan of GCSE results shows exponential dividends in the past three years: A* to C pass rate has risen from 29 per cent to a very commendable 65 per cent, with over half the pupils gaining the benchmark five or more A*–C passes (though no A* grades yet). Art, design technology, science and business studies popular and successful – English and maths have poorest showing. No modern foreign languages or classics, otherwise all usual subjects on offer. Extra time and laptops in exams the norm.

Occupational therapist visits once a week but input extends beyond that – working with staff, parents and child to ensure delivery of a full and integrated programme. Onsite speech and language therapists work with pupils one-to-one or in small groups. Weakest have two periods of speech and language to support GCSE. Aware that their pupils have to work much harder to succeed and that moving from their comfort zone can cause stress – 'We have to ensure pupils cope – there'll be few concessions in the world of work; we have to ensure they're at ease with dyslexia and dyspraxia and will put their hands on the controls of their life. If you're in a car and hit a hill you slow down, but you don't stop ... '.

You'd be hard pushed to find a staff more in tune with specific learning difficulties – all are offered continuous training and development: 'The head accepts that once we're highly trained we'll probably move on, but we're all encouraged and supported – teaching and non teaching staff. We get on very well, have a lot of fun and mix socially too'. Creates lots of in-house, tailor-made resources, shares good practice. Definitely a happening place for staff – 12 are currently studying for the Dyslexia Institute postgraduate certificate in dyslexia and literacy accredited by York University. Keen to provide outreach support, be inclusive and share expertise with others – about to launch first conference on how to get SpLD learners to write narrative (requires sequencing – not easy for the SpLD learner). Won the KS3 stage of the *Times Educational Supplement* 'newspaper in a day' competition (national, open to all schools) in 2004 and has been highly commended on various occasions.

Games, Options, the Arts: Lots of music and performing arts. Careers advice provided by Connexions. Art aplenty, supported by trips to London galleries and exhibitions (art teacher is author of books specifically for SpLD learners). Plenty of extra-curricular clubs including rowing (on boat race route), filmmaking, wargaming and yoga. All play sport; new head of PE inspired and enthusiastic – 'He's ex-army, so we really benefit from his skills and experiences – he's even managing to get us more fixtures,' said pupils.

Prejudice abounds – not here but in the locality: 'We're a special school, so some local mainstream schools are reluctant to organise fixtures against us' – outrageous! Maybe it's the fear of losing to a small special school that's hard to stomach? Bright, intelligent, articulate and often gifted youngsters – you'd be hard pushed to notice anything different about them if you met them in the street, except perhaps a confidence about who they are.

Background and Atmosphere: Part of the Constable Educational Trust, a charity. The first five pupils and seven staff crossed the threshold in 1998. Has grown and is at capacity in most years. 'We're out of step with fashion – a specialist school in the age of inclusion, but we see inclusion as an entitlement to mainstream education, not a compulsion.' In a residential part of Fulham but overlooking parkland, externally a 1930s carbuncle – metal windows, dreary redbrick, one half given over to a state primary, the other The Moat. Step inside and the tired exterior is belied by the deceptively spacious, all mod-cons interior – 'We even had a colour specialist assigned to ensure colour matched purpose' – it works. The full national curriculum is offered with facilities to match – well-resourced science labs, food technology, DT, art studio, music technology room, IT suite, all pupils use laptops, wireless technology throughout; super gathering room used for assemblies, lunches (packed lunch only), drama, some games. No separate gym but a playground and football/basketball/netball pitch, plus tennis courts across the road and access to local sports facilities, so deficiencies well catered for. 'Our driving force is the knowledge that failure isn't an option. The outside world has kicked these children – there's a great financial sacrifice and emotional cost involved; we're morally obliged to succeed.'

Pastoral Care and Discipline: Breaking school rules not tolerated – two pupils expelled in the lifetime of the school. 'If they really can't follow our code we won't accommodate ... It's disappointing when they're not as responsible as they might be. Pupils want to come here – the school has high aspirations for them and shame hurts; we try to addict child to success.' A small school with high staffing ratio, so pupils get a lot of teacher time and – the flip side – get away with very little. A member of staff has developed a comprehensive reporting and recording system – at the touch of a button, 'Teacher's Pet' churns out the good and bad on any pupil: learning, test scores, targets, homework, merits, absence, so it's difficult to conjure up excuses. All staff and pupils have access to school intranet and email support so no excuse for not doing homework. Usual merits, detentions, report card system for misdemeanours. Pupils are divided into two competitive houses – Bishop and Palace. Seniors nominated and trained as prefects and alerted to responsibilities under Child Protection. Daily gathering taken by pupils on Fridays seen as an opportunity to present ideas and to celebrate.

Pupils and Parents: A mixed bag in part because those statemented (40 per cent) receive funding from LEA; the rest are partly or wholly privately funded – sometimes involving great financial sacrifice, even hardship. Professional parents tend to be from arts and media – several dyslexics among parents. All share a strong sense of relief, even those making huge sacrifices. It's fine to be smart here; no one personality typifies a Moat pupil. We met quiet ones, the forthright, funny, sporty, academic, creative, dramatic – 'Think "Moatenders",' said more than a couple – but they rub along well together, sharing a tremendous team spirit and great respect for the individual. Lots of famous patrons – no famous old boys/girls yet, but one of the original pupils has gained a place at Cambridge, so we're guessing it won't be too long ...

Entrance: School caters for high performing child with dyslexia, dyspraxia and a few with language issues, such as expressive language difficulties or problems with auditory processing – maximum 20 a year. Entry via detailed assessment including reports from previous school, educational psychologist, SaLT, OT reports and copy of current statement where applicable. Procedure praised – 'It was really thorough – they picked up on our child's strengths and interests and were happy to accept him, but the LEA wouldn't support a place for our son, said insufficient OT provision; we were really disappointed'. No sixth form but extended age range allows for entry outside of chronological year group. All interviewed and tested, then spend an 'acquaint day' at the school. From a variety of schools including Fairleigh House, the Dominie, Blossom House.

Exit: Majority of leavers to date move on to mainstream sixth forms, a few to employment.

Money Matters: Not a rich school – all capital funding raised charitably; currently fundraising to improve school playground and outdoor facilities. 'We'd love to have a sixth form but we need £200,000 just to underwrite the costs, so it's probably not going to happen yet. It's a shame – there is a clear demand but we just don't have the cash.'

Remarks: Something special. Not for wilting wallflowers wanting to be cosseted and comforted, but a hard-working haven for bright, determined dyslexics and dyspraxics who know what they want from life and will achieve when given a chance.

Moira House Girls School, Eastbourne

Linked to Moira House Junior School in the Junior section

Upper Carlisle Road, Eastbourne, East Sussex, BN20 7TE

• Pupils: 360 girls day and boarding (from 10 years) • Ages: 2-18 • Size of sixth form: 90 • C of E • Fees: Boarding £17,805-£24,555; Day £6,000-£13,950 pa • Independent

Tel: 01323 644 144
Fax: 01323 649 720
Email: info@moirahouse.co.uk
Website: www.moirahouse.co.uk

Principal: Mrs Lesley Watson MA(Ed) has been the principal since September 2006.

Academic matters: In 2010, the overall pass rate at A and AS level 97 per cent, with 67 per cent achieving A*–B grades at A level and 84 per cent A*–C grades. At GCSE, the overall pass rate was 86 per cent, with nearly half of all grades being A*/A and 79 per cent passing five or more subjects. Good careers counsellor. Intensive language courses offered by the EFL department to help integrate foreign language speakers.

Games, Options, the Arts: Very strong music and drama – girls perform at local theatres plus tours abroad, recently Hong Kong and the USA. Horse-riding, watersports, first girls' school to play cricket, successful swimming teams. Girls selected as the ball girls for the international ladies' tennis tournament in Eastbourne.

Background and Atmosphere: Founded in 1875 and established on its present site in 1887 by Mr and Mrs Charles Ingham, pioneers of female education. Set in 15 acres on the outskirts of the historic town of Eastbourne, very traditional feel to the site – several Victorian buildings, headgirls and prefects known as Knights and Standard Bearers.

Study areas, commonrooms and kitchens for the boarders, full programme of activities at the weekends – day girls can join in. Far-reaching minibus service

Pastoral Care and Discipline: Close links with parents. Grades for academic achievements, effort and attitude given regularly – girls encouraged to discuss their reports with the principal, seen as an 'invaluable system'.

Pupils and Parents: Wide cultural mix, particularly in the sixth form – local girls and from all over the world. Parents and Old Girls very involved, e.g. Prunella Scales, Susannah Corbett (actor Harry's daughter), author Rumer Godden, explorer Virginia Fiennes, whistleblower Katherine Gunn, who founded the Truth-Telling Coalition – talk about their career choices to pupils.

Entrance: Mainly from other junior schools. Non-selective.

Exit: The majority to university in the UK, a few to USA, Hong Kong and Japan. A strong bias towards science subjects, business, and finance.

Money Matters: A certain number of scholarships and bursaries available annually.

Remarks: Friendly, family-orientated school with a good academic record. Given the example of other girls' achievements throughout the school, even the most retiring female would come out of her shell – very non-threatening and supportive. 'Moira House Girls are confident and articulate and go on to a wide variety of careers' – *The Independent.*

Monkton Senior School

Church Lane, Monkton Combe, Bath, Bath & North East Somerset, BA2 7HG

• Pupils: 385; 250 boys (150 boarding, 100 day); 135 girls (80 boarding, 55 day) • Ages: 11-18. • Size of sixth form: 135 • Church of England, Evangelical • Fees: Day £13,794-£16,656; Boarding £19,464-£26,274 pa • Independent

Tel: 01225 721 102
Fax: 01225 721 181
Email: admissions@monkton.org.uk
Website: www.monktoncombeschool.com

Principal: Since 2005, Mr Richard Backhouse. Probably late thirties but could pass for half that owing to well-preservedness and an engagingly boyish side to his disposition. Former pupils rib him about this. Educated at Marlborough and Selwyn, Cantab (economics) where he was vice captain of boats – a sound qualification for heading up Monkton. He ran the College Christian Union, too – an even sounder pedigree. Arrived here via Oundle and Bradfield, where he was a housemaster. Clearly very bright and at ease with his capableness. Open minded, inquiring, with an excellent sense of humour. Has good egg written all over him. Some say he's visionary. What's undoubted is that he will move the school forward – and, despite the headway made by his much-liked predecessor, really quite a lot to be done. Has already naffed off pupils by tightening up on appearance – jewellery out, shirt-tails in. A spot of dietary dissent, too – the tuckshop sells sweets no more; instead, meals have been overhauled and improving snacks made available in place of E-junk. Parents all for it. Mr Backhouse calls in pupils and parents, lets them say how they feel about it, then does what he reckons to be right – 'He's gone to a lot of trouble to find out what people want'. Not afraid to lob cats among pigeons in a good cause. Married to Debbie. Two children, one of each, aged twelve and ten. Has been a force in his local church, enjoys a spot of golf and gnashes his teeth weekly in support of Southampton FC.

Academic matters: Four years of best-ever results. Everyone claims this, of course, as devaluation of standards dishes out laurel wreaths to all comers and also rans. But recently a drive on, led by excellent director of studies, and the force is decidedly with him, assisted by some natural wastage of poor teachers. Given the pupils' brain-range – 'We are broadly non-selective' – academic accomplishment is impressive. In the dry view of an indifferent expert, 'For a state school the GCSE results would be excellent and the A level pretty damn good'. Parents give across-the-board thumbs up – 'The brightest are definitely stretched'. Class sizes 18–20 up to GCSE, smaller thereafter. Predictable curriculum. Mandarin now available at KS 3. Post-16 courses lack a leavening of vocational options but a softie AS in critical thinking and an AS/A2 in DT. Theatre studies strong, one of the teachers a recovering actor. RS scores highest, surprise, surprise. New £4m maths and science centre opened in September 2008 – also has a very smart learning resource centre. Art room too small and no kiln, but they are scheduled to be things of the future soon. Mr Backhouse is very keen to banish tattiness. Good-oh.

The Monkton emotional climate, of which more anon, clearly helps the less able and the boyishly disinclined. One former pupil entirely lacking sedentary proclivities praises the school for its affectionate insistence – 'It's just what I needed'. Relationships between teachers and pupils shine with mutual esteem, mostly. Up to 10 Oxbridge applications per year – usually three or four get in. A goodly wodge go to Russell Group universities. For a year group of 65, that's something not to be in the least bit bashful about.

International tradition strong and long established. 20-plus nationalities, with an overseas cap of 15 per cent. Many need masses of ESL when they arrive, some throughout, for whom there's a dedicated department and an induction programme which addresses cultural acclimatisation, too. Good.

The learning support unit is similarly well rooted, and the school is registered CreSTed category D. SpLDs catered for are mostly dyslexia and dyspraxia. Students get 45 mins a week one-to-one, some more, some a bespoke less intensive programme. All teachers are tuned into special needs and work with the LSU. Some study skills offered to all, and all to some.

Games, Options, the Arts: Sport as strong as you'd expect in a school where most board. The customary big three for boys: rugby, hockey, cricket. For girls, hockey, netball and tennis. Rowing also very big – Rowley Douglas and Steve Williams, Olympian golds, first dipped oars here. Given the small size of the school, Spartan valour as exemplified at Thermopylae is often called for, but the quality is high. Half a dozen tennis students funded by the LTA board here. You don't have to be sporty – but it helps. After Year 11 a keep fit programme for lollopers – students assure us it's quite okay to be one of those. Good Astro surfaces, good sports hall, gorgeous thatched cricket pavilion.

Music suffers a bit from small school syndrome, so the orchestra's a touch squawky, the ensembles far sweeter. Jewel in the crown is the jolly good jazzy big band, replete with snazzy red bow ties – tours a lot locally and even internationally. Rock bands abound. Parents of musical children happy. A new director of music just appointed and new music centre planned for 2011. Drama rated highly – ambitious productions, professional approach. Art very strong though under-resourced at present. Ex-prep school pupils build on the inspired work of the excellent Mr Baker. Photography good. Visiting artists and workshops, links with local galleries and Bath University. Art trips abroad every other year – Berlin next.

The cadet force (CCF) is an attractive if compulsory option – girls like it, too; a community service option for sixth formers. Duke of Edinburgh Award Scheme – small numbers but increasing. Range of out-of-school activities limited by school's small size – one parent notes lack of Croatian basket weaving – but pupils complain the school day isn't long enough.

Background and Atmosphere: A clerical foundation. Established in 1868 by the evangelical Revd Francis Pocock, the local vicar. His original five pupils have increased and multiplied. From the start the school was popular with clergymen and missionaries – still is. In 1992 they merged with a girls' school next door and went fully co-ed, also a prep and a pre-prep. The setting at the bottom of a deep-cleft valley is ravishing; proximity to Bath makes it convenient; the cordon of countryside around it keeps the troops of Midian and the tawdry allure of secularism at bay. Good, informative website and DVD.

A strong Christian tradition here – it's what the school is all about. It's distinctive and it's humane, neither doctrinaire nor gimlet-eyed, and anything but joyless. This is what parents buy into, and they don't get it anywhere else. What parents want is one thing; what children want is often another – not here. The vibrant Christian Union is run entirely by the students and around a third attend every week. Of around 200 boarders in school on a Sunday, between 160–180 go and worship. A big accent on service, and many gap-year students go off to Africa in particular to work, say, with children orphaned by AIDS. Lots of charity work in school, too. What are the pressures to conform? Unstinting investigation reveals none – it's quite all right to be an atheist and no one hassles you. The values of this species of Christianity express themselves altruistically – even if you were to fall out of faith, it would be impossible to fall out with your friends. The result is a social atmosphere which is notably tolerant and unselfish, where people put themselves out for each other and where they make deep and enduring friendships. One mum, who married a former pupil, says you can always tell who went to Monkton – 'They're much more genuinely interested in you than anyone else'.

Pastoral Care and Discipline: 'Pastorally brilliant,' say parents, for many of whom this was their reason for going with Monkton. For boarders the customary house system, pupils looked after by a husband and wife team. Much praise for the time they give and way they let their charges over run their own homes. We stayed for a weekly after-prep soirée and observed a respectful informality in relationships between staff and pupils, delightful to see, highly characteristic of the place and with frequent gales of laughter. Day pupils belong to boarding houses, so they don't feel much different. They can sleep over if they need and most go home so late it hardly seems worth it. All houses have academic tutors who also do their pastoral bit. Boarders say plenty to do at weekends, borne out by the frankly astonishing number of day pupils who come back to school for their social life – a touching tribute. A prefect system, and induction for prefects which teaches them to be kind, not martinets. We watched them in action, supervising the little ones in prep. As in all boarding schools the social atmosphere is robust and joshy, but it is definitely kind and engagingly unsophisticated. No big school strutting arrogance here. When the Government social care inspectors questionnaired the pupils and asked them if they were being bullied, every single one said no. This most unusual statistical return inspired fulsome praise, justly so. Friendships across the age range, unusually. One parent says, 'They really look after each other.' Discipline is neither overt nor heavy handed. The school has plumped up some tricky rejects from other schools – they say that rebels tend to end up as priests, anarchists as missionaries.

Pupils and Parents: Popular, of course, with evangelical Christians and those who want the values – still lots of sons and daughters of clergy and missionaries. Lay folk with faith move to Bath to be close by – not all by any means are Christians. Services parents like the seven-day boarding week. Wide geographical range enriched by the many from abroad – 10 to 15 per cent. Popular with M4 corridor-dwellers. Nothing a bit snooty about this school – children natural, unaffected, jolly nice; those brought up in the fast lane of fashion might reckon themselves B-roaded. Pupils from abroad carefully looked after by international officer, a club for them, too, and an annual evening of song, food and fun. Former pupils promoted to glory on earth include former spymaster Sir Richard Dearlove, songwriter and humorist Richard Stilgoe, blockbuster novelist Bernard Cornwell and the late Bishop of Peterborough, Ian Cundy.

Entrance: They look for 50 per cent plus at CE. Standard rising. Special needs evaluated to make sure a pupil will cope comfortably. One of few schools which does not occupy an academic ability niche. Pupils come from Monkton Prep, St Andrew's Turi, Castle Court, Mount House, Rose Hill, All Hallows, Summer Fields.

Exit: Most to universities, the full range.

Money Matters: Bursaries on offer to children of missionaries and clergy – means-tested. A clutch of academic, art, drama, music and sport schols on entry to Years 7, 9 and 12. Has just secured a £2 million donation for the school and is embarking on a £35 million development programme – seriously confident in straitened times.

Remarks: Character comes first here – that's how parents would have it, and it doesn't push academic performance into second place. It's scruffy but tidying itself up. Religion is pervasive but not monolithic, and parents love the way their sons and daughters take the faith they were given and make it their own. Does faith translate into works in the real world? It seems so. These boys and girls go on to do well and do good. Monkton is a genuine and beguiling one-off.

Monmouth School

Linked to Haberdashers Agincourt School in the Junior section

Linked to Grange, Monmouth Preparatory School (The) in the Junior section

Almshouse Street, Monmouth, Monmouthshire, NP25 3XP

• Pupils: 585 boys; 145 boarders • Ages: 11-18 • Size of sixth form: 185 • Anglican • Fees: Day £12,345; Boarding £21,498 pa • Independent

Tel: 01600 713143
Fax: 01600 772 701
Email: enquiries@monmouthschool.org
Website: www.habs-monmouth.org

Headmaster: Since 2005, Dr Steven Connors (late forties). Came from Christ's Hospital where he had been deputy head from 2000. Read English at Swansea University – PhD was on the poetry of William Wordsworth. Started teaching at Denstone College, followed by head of English posts at Queen's College Taunton and Sevenoaks, where he was also head of boarding and housemaster of the sixth form international centre. His wife is a specialist in the education of high functioning autistic children. They have two sons, one at university and one studying drama.

Open manner and a dry sense of humour. In his first term led from the front when he abseiled down from the church tower to raise funds for a local charity. Interests include sport, music, theatre and hill walking.

Academic matters: Good performance at both GCSE and A level, sustained over the last five years. Approximately 90 per cent A* to B at GCSE; consistently around 80 per cent A/B at A level. Modern languages, maths, sciences and history remain popular choices. Lots of A level choice – around 30 options in conjunction with Haberdashers' Monmouth School for Girls.

Learning support is available on an individual/shared basis from suitably qualified staff, although additional charges for both numeracy and literacy support. Boys are given lessons in study skills and encouraged in the sixth form to plan their studies towards what they wish to do later on. Class sizes vary from ten in the sixth form to 22 at the lower end of the school.

Games, Options, the Arts: The school buzzes with a wide range of activities ranging from chess to rock climbing, most of them run by staff who want to share their interests with the boys. Sport has always been an important part of the school. Rugby is coached by former Wales and Lions player John Bevan: as well as coaching the 1st XV he takes the younger boys on tours to Blackpool, Ireland and Italy. Cricket, soccer, rowing, tennis, cross-country, squash, golf, water-polo and sailing all flourish. Several teams in each year group – gives more boys a chance to represent the school and helps identify potential. Good new sports pavilion opened 2008.

Around 40 per cent take instrumental lessons and a varied collection of groups, choirs, bands and orchestras. Drama studio and a new 500 seat theatre which, as well as being used by the school, is the venue for an extensive programme of public performance art including ballet and world cinema. Quality art – we saw the well-equipped art block filled with boys working in a wide range of media. We also observed the popular (co-ed) CCF at work. Numerous foreign trips for groups from choir to scuba divers.

Background and Atmosphere: Founded in 1614 by William Jones, a member of the Haberdashers' Company (one of the oldest Livery Companies in London). A direct grant school until 1975. Rebuilt in the 1880s, sensitive restoration and new buildings in recent years. Fairly compact site but some green areas. Playing fields reached by a pedestrian underpass below the busy A40. Now predominantly a day school with flexi-boarding, but still has Saturday morning school for all but the sixth form – not universally popular with parents but is an important factor in giving the school the time to run outside activities. Five boarding houses. Mid-range accommodation for boarders with an extensive programme of weekend activities. Uniform is plain blue blazer and grey trousers, replaced in the sixth form by a smart dress code.

Pastoral Care and Discipline: Tutor is the focal point for monitoring academic performance, the housemaster looking after pastoral wellbeing. School rules are sensible and concentrate on the standard of behaviour expected rather than a prescriptive list of dos and don'ts. Relations between staff and boys appear relaxed but formal enough to engender respect. Clear policies on drinking, smoking and drugs – not considered a problem, but boys are made aware of the damage they could do to themselves.

Pupils and Parents: Attracts boys from south west England and south Wales. Popular with first time buyers as well as families who have long term links with the school. A few overseas boarders mainly from Hong Kong. A diverse school community who seem to get on well with each other – unstuffy and produces confident but not arrogant young men who are open and independent. Notable Old Boys include Christopher Herbert, Bishop of St Albans, David Broome, Eddie Butler, Major Dick Hern, Lord Moynihan, Lord Ezra, Steve James, Keith Jarrett, Tony Jordan, Victor Spinetti and recent silver medal Olympic rower, Tom Lucy.

Entrance: Three form entry at 11, from its own prep department and from primary schools. Both groups sit the school's own entrance exam. A further one-form entry at 13 from a growing list of prep schools – based on Common Entrance, a foundation scholarship exam or an entrance exam for those at state schools.

Exit: Small number after GCSE. Majority to a wide range of universities – Bristol, Cardiff, Exeter and Swansea among the more popular choices. In most years ten to Oxbridge.

Money Matters: Has replaced about a third of the government assisted places with its own scheme and offers a number of scholarships. Fifteen per cent of pupils receive some help with fees. While day fees are now in line with similar schools, boarding fees are very competitive.

Remarks: A rounded education. Boys work hard but also develop other skills and interests.

More House School (Farnham)

Moons Hill, Frensham, Farnham, Surrey, GU10 3AP

- Pupils: 380 boys, of which 100 are boarders, 35 in sixth form
- Ages: 8-18 • Size of sixth form: 35 • RC foundation but all welcome
- Fees: Day £11,310-£15,855; Boarding £17,805-£24,660 pa • Independent

Tel: 01252 792 303
Fax: 01252 797 601
Email: schooloffice@morehouseschool.co.uk
Website: www.morehouseschool.co.uk

Headmaster: Since 1993, Mr Barry Huggett, worked in the City and scientific research before moving into education. Pleasant, polite and formal, married to Geraldine, the school's admissions tutor, two grown-up children (a doctor and a headmistress). Lives on site, runs a tight ship and is not only incredibly hard working but also always readily available to pupils, parents and staff.

Academic matters: An exceptional, specialist school; the caring and supportive ethos shines brightly. Every boy has an ILP monitored regularly to check progress, with detailed annual reviews for all. Classes are small and carefully structured to take into account everybody's different learning needs. Literacy and numeracy embedded into all subject areas across the curriculum. Most boys receive some individual or small group teaching by specialist literacy teachers and/or speech therapist. Very wide curriculum, all boys take 8–9 GCSEs.

Impressive science teaching and achievement; three sciences are offered at GCSE and A level. Winners for the second year running of the Surrey Scientific Problem-Solving Challenge – no mean feat, especially considering stiff competition from neighbouring, highly selective grammar and public schools. Good choice of GCSEs, BTecs and A levels. Results continue to move upwards and remain considerably above national averages.

Boys are encouraged to, and do, engage with their learning, developing awareness of their own styles and preferences. 'Understanding how you learn best and succeeding is a great motivator and confidence booster,' said a parent, 'particularly as a number of boys arriving here have not always been successful or comfortable in previous schools.' Teachers, speech therapists, occupational therapists and a small army of literary support specialists ensure academic and creative success. Compulsory training every four months keeps staff on their toes – those wishing to do further qualifications for SEN are funded by the school. Recently invested £1,6m in a training school, as many courses are run for visiting professionals.

Games, Options, the Arts: Boys enjoy and excel in many creative areas – performing arts, stagecraft, design. Good facilities including theatre, dedicated music building with a concert hall, heated outdoor pool and specialist rooms. Art continues to flourish – broad range of media: painting, sculpture, ceramics, DT, photography and computer animation. Drama for all to Year 9 and ever popular at GCSE – boys are regulars on stage, whether their own or further afield at the Chichester Festival or National Theatre. Instrumental tuition can be arranged and boys are encouraged to join the various jazz bands, steel band and choirs. Music is offered at A level.

Fabulous opportunities for outwardbound enthusiasts: mountain biking, orienteering, rock climbing, high ropes tree walk, together with the more traditional rugby, football, cricket, athletics and D of E. Actively twinned with a school in Tanzania – has a number of joint projects and some staff exchange positions. Sixth formers visit Africa and is currently sponsoring a student from Tanzania through medical school.

Background and Atmosphere: Founded in 1939 by a forward thinking, somewhat eccentric monk, Joseph Gardner, for boys who were not thriving in mainstream schools. The original curriculum included circus skills, with the school successfully running its own travelling circus throughout the 1940s.

Delightful wooded site, some of the modern additions are built into the hillside creating unique spaces to observe plants and wildlife. Sixth formers have study cabins in the woods. Boarding accommodation recently refurbished; younger boys share dorms, older boys double, with oldest graduating to single study bedrooms. Rooms are adequate and immaculate.

Parents are genuinely pleased with the school – often they and their children have received appalling treatment elsewhere and are delighted that their children can finally make friends in a friendly and safe environment. Atmosphere is genuinely calm and cool, with both pupils and staff palpably proud of the positive ethos, something that didn't go unnoticed when Ofsted inspected.

Pastoral Care and Discipline: Parents appreciative that boys are taught to understand why good behaviour for learning is essential and that poor behaviour can lead to negative consequences, both for themselves and for others. Good staff-pupil relationships are a high priority. Speech therapists double as class tutors for daily support and each boy has a weekly meeting with his mentor; plenty of anticipatory tactics in place to help with planning and organisational skills.

Pupils and Parents: Specialist provision and excellent reputation mean boys come from all over the UK, with a few expats and service families. Always a waiting list for boarding places and day parents organise car pools. School bus meets morning and evening trains from the local station. Parents are encouraged to communicate with each other and some parents have formed Friends of More House, who raise funds by organising events such as the Christmas Fair.

Entrance: Some children are severely dyslexic, often with dyspraxia/ADD, others have autistic/Asperger's traits. Those with base IQ of less than 100 and/or with behavioural difficulties are unlikely to be offered a place. As a first step, parents talk to the admissions tutor and send in any medical and psychological reports for consideration. If it appears that the school can support the student, the parents are invited to meet the headmaster and view the school. Following this, the student will spend an assessment day and an overnight stay, if applying for a boarding place. The main purpose is to see how the child fits into the school environment and to ensure all his needs can be met by the school.

Exit: At 16+ some go to further education colleges, predominantly to study vocational and art foundation courses. The sixth form, now in its seventh year, is increasingly popular, with a number of boys moving on to university. Runs an advice and guidance hotline for ex-pupils in further and higher education.

Money Matters: Different pupils have different needs, so three bands of fees, as some individual specialist help has to be charged for at an extra cost. Fees are kept as competitive as possible – will try to help in cases of financial crisis. Fees for the sixth form are discounted between 10 and 50 per cent, depending on how long a boy has been in the school.

Remarks: 'An answer to our prayers,' said a parent. A truly good place for boys with learning differences.

More House School (London)

22-24 Pont Street, Knightsbridge, London, SW1X 0AA

• Pupils: around 230 girls, all day • Ages: 11-18 • Size of sixth form: 55
• RC, but others welcome • Fees: £13,710 pa • Independent

Tel: 02072 352 855
Fax: 02072 596 782
Email: office@morehouse.org.uk
Website: www.morehouse.org.uk

Headmaster: Since 2007, Mr Robert Carlysle BA MBA AKC PGCE Cert Dysl & Lit MCoIP (fifties). He was founding head of the Moat School in Fulham, a specialist school for children with dyslexia, and has also taught at two independent girls' schools and a co-ed state grammar school. A historian, he is also a keen girls' hockey coach and a qualified leader for the D of E award – both are activities which have developed greatly at More House since his arrival. He teaches IT, English, history, philosophy and ethics.

A comfortable and compassionate man, wearing Bart Simpson socks with his suit, and a committed Catholic, who sees this as vital to the school's ethos. 'It is built on the Catholic notion of worth – that everybody matters. It is part of our ethos to care. It is the head's job to believe in the girls – they need to know that they matter to me.' Parents comment, 'He is very thorough, very kind, very concerned to do the best for the girls. You feel he knows exactly who your child is and how she is doing.' Particularly effective one-to-one, he makes a good team with the deputies, who tend to present the more public face of the school.

Academic matters: A broad spectrum of ability here, including many girls who would sink without trace in larger, more ruthless environments. 'I'd never passed a maths exam before I came here,' said a dyslexic sixth former, who now has a clutch of top GCSEs and the offer of a good university place. GCSE results tend to be around 70 per cent A*–B grades, with history, RS and languages showing consistently good results – but with such a small year group (usually fewer than 30) generalisations are tricky.

Everyone learns French, German and Latin in Year 7, and can take up Spanish in Year 8 or 9. 'We choose German because it's good to have a language that most come to fresh. They often find it easier than French and the Year 7 activities week in Germany gives them a substantial immersion in German language and culture.' Everyone studies RS to GCSE but no obligation to adopt a Catholic viewpoint – 'My daughter's an atheist and really enjoys RS. She doesn't have to pretend to have particular beliefs'. Three ability groups for maths, English and languages from Year 7.

A level subject groups are often tiny, always fewer than ten and sometimes one-to-one. 'We have a moral obligation to run a subject if a girl wants to do it. We're about encouraging them to find out what they want to do with the rest of their lives, so we won't tell them they can't study geography, for example, because they're the only one signed up.' The subject range is necessarily narrower than in larger establishments but encompasses five languages, including Latin and Arabic, RS (very popular), drama and textiles. Generally around 70 per cent of grades are A/B.

Well set up to help those with special needs – 'We're successful because they're not regarded as the mad relative to lock away – staff are well aware of their needs. A school like ours resolves these issues easily because once we have taken them on, we see it as our job to educate all our pupils to the highest level irrespective of their needs – it's our ethos to care for all of them'.

As well as individual help for those with learning difficulties and ESOL lessons for girls whose English is not colloquially fluent, the school now offers weekly lessons with a visiting speech and language specialist.

Games, Options, the Arts: 'We've always had a massively strong tradition in the creative and performing arts.' Art is conspicuously successful, with six GCSE candidates in the top ten nationally in 2008 – a rather staggering statistic in a school of this size. All three art teachers are also professional artists. Artwork of great quality, from life drawings to an intricate ballgown, lines the corridors. The sixth form has its own art and textile room on the top floor, complete with skeleton, and quite a few go on top art and design schools, e.g. St Martin's, London College of Fashion.

Music is also very strong. The school is too small to field a full orchestra, but girls from Year 7 learn composition from a visiting specialist teacher. They play in ensembles and perform in the many school concerts each year, such as the 2009 'fabulous' performance of Mozart's *Requiem* at the Cadogan Hall. The school is known particularly for its choirs, with an annual international singing tour. 'They rehearse really hard. It is clearly a professional music tour rather than a school trip with a bit of singing.' A sixth former described her tours as 'the best memories I'll take away from More House'.

Drama is increasing in profile, with a whole school play each year alternating between straight play and musical, e.g. *Twelfth Night* and *Pirates of Penzance*. 'We have so much fun,' said a pupil. School hall used as theatre, dining room, assembly hall and space for house competitions, and also a dance/drama studio.

Pupils are unlikely to choose the school for its sport, but the head has introduced PE GCSE and A level, 'as well as the concept of exercise being a part of healthy living'. School fields a hockey squad for the London Youth Games, running is popular, girls visit Hyde Park and Cadogan Gardens for lessons and play in inter-school competitions. 'We don't work on an élite squad approach to anything – we encourage everyone to take part.' Fencing and dance are optional extras.

Activities week every year, which can be D of E, and school trips to, e.g., Russia – 'We went on the Trans-Siberia overnight. It was eye-opening'. Sixth formers enthuse about the 'great fun' they have at the Berkeley Dress Show, traditionally the inaugural event of the London Season.

House system is now a central part of school life, with all the staff below deputy head level attached to houses, which field teams in competitions – sport, drama, art, music and even English and maths. 'It gives you a sense of identity in the school,' said a pupil.

The only outside space is a small courtyard but activities abound at lunchtimes, e.g. cooking, keep fit, arts and crafts and movie club, as well as sports clubs. 'You're always so busy,' say students.

Background and Atmosphere: Named for the Tudor sage and saint, Sir Thomas More, the school opened in 1953 at the request of a group of Catholic parents. It moved to its present site in two adjoining redbrick panelled houses a few streets south of Harrods in 1971. Around 50 per cent of the girls are Catholics and mass is held in the school chapel and in the church of Our Lady of Victories down the road. 'But our Catholicism is about service – about how we treat people. We don't see ourselves as an evangelical outpost of the Vatican.'

Small, cosy and friendly, the school suits girls who value its nurturing atmosphere rather than those seeking the bracing winds of competition. 'London girls' day schools can have a reputation for ruthlessness and I came here expecting it to be like a scene from 'Mean Girls'. But I found a family atmosphere – the girls have time for one another and so do the staff.'

Pastoral Care and Discipline: Described by parents as 'a very caring school'. 'The girls really are treated as individuals, with things tailored to their own needs,' said a parent. Minor skirmishes about skirt lengths, with girls being told to wear trousers if their skirt is too short – 'the war of the skirt,' as one parent described it – irritate some, who feel that discipline on such subjects has got stricter. But most girls, says the head, want staff approval. 'Catholics do guilt well. We always distinguish between the behaviour and the person.' He is on door duty every day as the girls arrive. 'It is easy to drop into the conversation that I've heard something good about them. By investing in their self-esteem, you get girls who like themselves.'

Active leadership programme for the lower sixth, who act as mentors for Year 7s and run the lunchtime activities programme alongside staff members. They also have their own private penthouse area with two cosy commonrooms, kitchen with coffee machine ('our favourite toy – it was a present from Mr Carlysle'), IT suite, textile studio and other specialist teaching rooms.

Pupils and Parents: A diverse lot, more international than Sloane. Many European and diplomatic families, with

Catholicism as the draw, alongside London girls travelling in from Hammersmith and Hampstead.

Entrance: Part of the North London Consortium, with common maths and English exams. Interviews everyone in groups before the exams, including a series of lessons to give them a feel for the small school environment. 'I'm interested in what they find interesting, what they find difficult. We begin to build up a picture of their strengths and weaknesses before the exam, and we're very interested in potential as well as performance.' A large number of feeder prep and primary schools, including Hill House, Thomas's, Finton House, Our Lady of Victories and the Oratory primary. Worth trying for places higher up, as international families come and go.

Sixth form entrants are interviewed and expected to have at least five A*–C grades at GCSE, with B or above in their AS subjects.

Exit: About 20 per cent leave after GCSE, to co-ed schools or abroad. After A levels, to a broad range of universities to do a broad range of courses. 'We don't see any one destination as better than another. We try to encourage girls to recognise that it is their life and think deeply about where will suit them best.'

Money Matters: Various academic scholarships, some aimed specifically at Catholic girls, and exhibitions for prowess at art, drama, music or PE, which can be topped up by means-tested bursaries.

Remarks: Small and nurturing school with strong Catholic caring ethos, that does well by girls of a wide ability range. Ideal for those of a creative bent who do not feel the need to compete in the more ruthless worlds of many larger London day schools. 'It is a lovely school,' said a parent. 'My daughter is so happy there.'

Moreton Hall School

Linked to Moreton First in the Junior section

Weston Rhyn, Oswestry, Shropshire, SY11 3EW

• Pupils: 380 girls (and boys in junior school) • Ages: girls aged 3-18 and boys aged 3-11 • Size of sixth form: 100 • Non denom • Fees: Boarding £17,070-£26,380; Senior Day £19,740-£21,390 pa • Independent

Tel: 01691 773 671
Fax: 01691 778 552
Email: registrar@moretonhall.com
Website: www.moretonhall.org

Principal: Since 1992, Mr Jonathan Forster, BA, PGCE (mid-fifties). Educated Shrewsbury School and Leeds University. Girls' housemaster at Strathallan before coming to Moreton in firefighter role: rescued the school from outrageous misfortune. Says he has no plans to move on – they all say that, but we believe him. His achievement is massive financially and educationally, though he won't tell you this, and he wants to be around for exciting developments coming up next – 'I enjoy being part of a success story'. Exudes capability and good humour. None of the exquisite oratorical strokeplay of so many heads, no boasting, no reposing on self-congratulatory laurels for Mr Forster, he's only ever forward looking – 'You've got to push on'. That's what he's all about. Alert to shifting winds in education and his market, he trims this little school constantly to get optimal performance – 'We never forget we are competing, so league tables are important and we've got to win our matches and we've got to hit our targets'. Married to Paula, who helps in the superbly resourced library and teaches English. Two daughters, both ex-Moreton.

Academic matters: Results matter like mad here, but they are wholly averse to flogging girls to death in pursuit of them, so how do they do it? Inspiring teachers, thirty of whom live on the campus, almost half of whom are male; masses of support and a far from joyless work ethic – it's a great team, no doubt about it. They describe their entry policy as 'not frightfully selective' and do a very good job with those who come, with a clutch every year to Oxbridge. Value added scores place them in the top 10 of UK independent schools. Proper curriculum – no silly soft subjects, invidious to name the best. Seriously strong maths and science, excellent English, business studies and geography very fondly spoken of by the girls. Most important of all, no weak links. Plenty of IT, internet connections everywhere.

Good specialist supplementary support for gifted and talented, dyslexia, dyscalculia and EFL (roughly 70–80 girls with special needs) – holistic, all-staff approach and – you don't often see this – no extra charge for it. Meticulous university preparation and sound careers advice.

Games, Options, the Arts: In all things, Moreton punches above its weight. Lacrosse is the sport of sports here and they travel far and wide in search of worthy foes. Splendid sports hall plus fitness suite, all-weather surface, brand new indoor pool – something for everybody.

Much, much music: masses of ensembles – instrumental and choral – and a heartening number of brass players. 18 visiting teachers from conservatoires, successful auditioners for National Youth Choir and National Youth Orchestra, a musical a year and biennial tours abroad. Brilliant art – real art taught by real artists, can do it as a subject or for art's sake. Plucky, plentiful drama, always difficult in a single-sex school.

And then their extraordinary entrepreneurial initiative, Moreton Enterprises. All first year sixth girls take on executive rôles in running businesses – shops mostly and a branch of Barclays. They do the lot – the degree of independence is astonishing. Enterprise girls have just raised funds to build a new shopping mall. Yes, really! The aim is to give girls a taste of real life but, of course, it's a proving ground for those with a taste for it, as former pupils testify. Good range of out of school activities plus D of E. Strong social links with Shrewsbury School.

Background and Atmosphere: Founded in 1913 by Mrs Lloyd-Williams for her own daughters and those of local friends. A homely place – 'We never lose sight of that,' says Mr Forster. Seventeenth century hall fronted by a comely ha ha and the customary hotch-potch of buildings behind it, including an extraordinary sixties creation, all roof, dubbed The Toblerone, which now houses Moreton First. All new building is high spec and all parents praise the excellent facilities. They've spent an unleveraged £3 and a half million in the last five years, all of it raised from income – a separate study centre for overseas students, multi-activity holidays and conferences. 'We never close' – so they never stop earning. Older girls live in hotel-style accommodation, which may just make going to university a bit of a comedown. Fine, spreading grounds across which girls scoot to the petrol station just outside, where they can stock up on comestibles. A rural location but quickly reached by fast roads from every direction.

Pastoral Care and Discipline: Rigour and seriousness underpin all things here, but they don't manifest as furrow-browed Puritanism. Quite the contrary – it's the rigour and seriousness that make the liberal ethos work. This is a notably unstuffy, completely unsnobby place, relaxed and friendly, an easy place to be whoever you are. About 90 per cent board at 11+, but it's not bang-up boarding – it's responsive-to-the-individual boarding ('We go home when we need but there's so much going on'), and that's why most day girls spend between one and four nights at school and why the school is 80–90 per cent full at weekends. Much stress is laid on being nice to one another, living together among friends – 'We're not a school, more of a family'. This is a corny thing to say perhaps but it's the literal truth, so not corny. The girls are unspoilt, unaffected. 'You don't feel under pressure to be anyone or do anything,' they say, but they're all jolly nice, and don't they do a lot? Close monitoring, academic and pastoral, but it's not smothering – it's kind. Girls are genuinely appreciative of the way they are looked after. Induction programme for new pupils praised by parents.

Pupils and Parents: Most live within an hour and a half's distance. From Cheshire, the West Midlands, Wales and, since the Malverns merged, a greater flow from the south. Single sex is a major choice factor – those few single sex schools that have survived have done so because they are the fittest (stats show still an academic advantage). Parents can drop in whenever they want, unannounced. They like to muck in and join trips to the theatre, skiing holidays, even meals, and also like the way they can see the principal whenever required, and that he never seems to need briefing first. Good communications, frequent updates. Informative, vibrant website. Very supportive former pupils; stalwart, canny governors.

Entrance: At three to Moreton First, at 11 from primaries and at 13 from preps. Test, interview and head's report to make sure she can cope. Entry into sixth form, too. Taster visits popular. Superb retention after GCSE – a hallmark of quality. Once in, you're safe: 'If we take them on, we have a responsibility to make a proper job of them'. Lists pretty full, over-subscribed at sixth form. Five per cent from overseas, capped.

Exit: All but one or two to university.

Money Matters: Some scholarships and bursaries. The astute use of the school in holiday time makes the most of your fees.

Remarks: A school attuned to its market, highly responsive to the needs and aspirations of its parents, constantly evolving. Well worth the hike for parents turned off by perceived la-di-da pretentiousness in rival schools. Moreton girls take their place in life beyond school without adjustment.

Morrison's Academy

Linked to Morrisons Academy Junior School in the Junior section

Ferntower Road, Crieff, Perthshire, Crieff, Perthshire, PH7 3AN

• Pupils: 170 girls and 175 boys • Ages: 3-18 • Size of sixth form: 40
• Inter-demon • Fees: £9,675 pa • Independent

Tel: 01764 653 885
Fax: 01764 655 411
Email: principal@morrisonsacademy.org
Website: www.morrisonsacademy.org

Rector and Principal: Since 2004, Mr Simon Pengelley BA PGCE (fifties), historian, educated at Repton, followed by Bristol University and PGCE in London. He has taught up and down the country: Abingdon, Strathallan (head of history), Rossall and now Morrisons, where he has overseen a huge sea change. Boarding numbers had been dwindling for some time and the final boarding house closed in 2007. Former boarding houses are about to go on the market ('silly them – they missed the moment' critique) and 'all sorts of plans are in the pipeline' – though we couldn't find them on the web.

Our visit came just after an exhausting Ofsted inspection: everyone appeared quietly confident (from the nursery up). The Rector's vision (his word) is to make Morrisons the top academic school in the 'locality'. Independent rivals include Glenalmond, Strathallan, Dollar Academy and – the one they really have to beat – The High School of Dundee. This editor was surprised not to be shown ambitious plans for future building, and, with the Rector having stabilised the school (it was in dire straits – both numerically and emotionally when he arrived), by closing the remaining boarding houses while greatly increasing pupil numbers (no mean achievement) wondered whether the M6 wasn't beckoning again. Their three sons are now all at university, but he and his wife, Louise, 'love Scotland and have loads of friends in the area', so that's all right then.

Academic matters: School follows Scottish curriculum: good take up for Advanced Highers and remarkably good results all round. Outstanding results in Highers across the board, slight glitches in business management and English, ditto German. The traditional bias towards science is slightly fading in favour of arts-based courses. Intermediate 2 more or less across the board: 17 Highers, with photography for media at sixth form only on offer. Sciences perform consistently well, also maths; English Highers impressive last year, ditto accountancy, goodish art and design, not really much language take up, humanities OK. No obvious terminal cases; human biology popular at Higher level and results indicate that it is obviously either better taught or more interesting than its bog standard twin. Inspirational English department produces plays 'every other year' as part of the syllabus (alternate years = musicals).

Fantastic flat screen computers all over the place – pupils can take their European Computer Driving Licence, though no-one was quite sure whether the head of the computer department still built his own. Can cope with special needs and programmes much used. Dyslexia, dyspraxia and mild Asperger's not a problem – no extra charge. (Junior school has 1.6 remedial teachers and this continues all the way up.)

Games, Options, the Arts: Masses of pitches at Dallerie, a ten-minute walk from the main buildings, and school plays all the standard games. Good rugby. Swimming pool on site, still labelled Baths (bless). Stronger pipe band than ever, with Scots reclaiming it as their own; parents seem to think that this eruption of interest in piping and drumming is a direct consequence of closing the boarding houses, as the pipe band was previously once almost run as a private fiefdom with Chinese (who made up the majority of boarders) students playing a mega part – made for interesting photographs. Band plays at Murrayfield rugby internationals as part of massed bands. Huge CCF, D of E strong (straight to silver if part of the CCF) – almost all get bronze, lots of silver and gold. 45 extra-curricular activities in total.

Enthusiastic art department in inspired converted attics – terrific fabrics, which were exhibited at The Scottish Parliament, but still no CAD. Music and drama strong (and based in what was once the girls' loos – check out the plumbing in the store cupboard); not totally soundproof practice rooms: 'We can hear what they are working at,' said the head of music. Stunning girls' chamber choir which plays regularly to local acclaim.

Background and Atmosphere: Built in 1859, this Scottish baronial-styled building with its crow stepped gables was described thus at the time: 'Its healthful locality and commanding view of extensive and beautifully romantic scenery cannot be surpassed, if at all equalled, by any such public building in Scotland'. The gift of Thomas Mor(r)ison, who lived in the neighbouring village of Muthill and made his fortune as a master builder in Edinburgh (he was implemental in constructing Edinburgh's new town). He instructed his trustees to erect an institution carrying his name 'to promote the interests of mankind, having a particular regard to the education of youth and the diffusion of useful knowledge'.

Always independent, at one stage the school did have grant-aided pupils, but this finished in the late 1970s. Fabulous buildings revamped following the sale of underused outlying houses. The impressive original school building, with its large open corridors, works well in the noughties, though some of the more recent constructions are less inspiring. The glorious first floor hall, much used for theatricals and the like, doubles for daily assemblies and socials, boasts a new organ and a 'recently restored' floor. Recording studios on the wish list. Re-development of the library, the installation of an artificial hockey pitch and increased ICT in classrooms are all planned for the coming year. A magnificent newer build for maths and jolly attic transformation into a vast art complex. Dining refectory off campus – rector lunches with heads of houses on Tuesdays, food said to be 'OK', though our guide and most of her peers preferred to eat at The Tuckie across the (not very busy) road.

Pastoral Care and Discipline: Excellent pastoral care. Head quite tough on sin, though pupils on the whole 'quite docile' – 'Tobacco could get you suspended', regular boozing could ultimately result in expulsion and use of drugs means that 'you should expect to be expelled'. Not really a street-wise school.

Pupils and Parents: Pupils from all over the middle belt – Falkirk, Stirling, Dunblane, Comrie, Perth (masses), Auchterarder – are bused to school (no trains since Beeching). Catchment area extends to south of Stirling and north: past the House of Bruar and Crianlarich. Not really a toffs' school.

Entrance: Children can and do arrive at any time – during the term and at the start of any term. Interview and testing for nursery and junior school and more or less automatic entrance into senior school from the junior school. Some join the senior school at 11 from the state sector or from local prep schools such as Ardvreck or Craigclowan. Interview and examination. Sixth form entrants are assessed on their potential, taking into account their grades at Standard Grade or GCSE.

Exit: Three or four off to (usually) Scottish independent schools at either 11 or 13. Otherwise a dribble occasionally to Oxbridge, one to Cambridge last year, plus four to London – Imperial and King's. Regular mini stream usually to engineering or allied science at Imperial or Manchester, Newcastle, Leeds. Most stay in Scotland with law, computing, business and sciences prevailing, though sports science and sports medicine in the ribbons.

Money Matters: Discounts for siblings, one or two means tested bursaries, scholarships for the final year.

Remarks: A good proud school which does well by its pupils.

Mossbourne Community Academy

100 Downs Park Road, Hackney, London, E5 8JY

• Pupils: 1300 • Ages: 11-18 • Non-denominational • State

Tel: 0208 525 5200
Fax: 0208 528 5222
Email: enquiries@mossbourne.hackney.sch.uk
Website: www.mossbourne.hackney.sch.uk/

Head: From 2010, when school was opened. Sir Michael Wilshaw (mid sixties), started out in Docklands in 1968, when the area was full of dockers rather than bankers, and his ability to engage with pupils was not immediately obvious. One asked: 'Sir, have you thought of doing something else in your life?' Fortunately, he stuck with his original career path and has now become one of the country's undoubted super heads, recognised by both political parties for his outstanding ability to turbo charge the attainment of those who could easily not attain at all. After Bermondsey, he did a stint in the leafy suburbs as deputy head of a comprehensive in Woodford Green, but his heart lies in the inner city and in 1985, he took on his first headship at St Bonaventure's, an RC all-boys' comprehensive in Newham, one of the country's poorest boroughs, where only five per cent of pupils were then getting five GCSEs at A*–C. During his 18 years there, he transformed that figure into a formidable 80 per cent and in 2000 was knighted for the achievement.

Though he had every intention of remaining at St Bonaventure's until retirement, he was approached by Sir

Colin Bourne, a wealthy Hackney-born businessman, to launch the country's first City academy. Mossbourne, which opened in 2004, was designed to Wilshaw's specifications. A calm and forceful presence, he looks rather like a City businessman, but no doubting his hands-on commitment as a working head. 'The head is always around, always there to talk to,' said one parent. 'He wants to know how the kids are getting on and really listens to what you have to say.' Also director of education at ARK, a charitable education trust developing a number of academies, and, now, one day a week, executive head of Haggerston, another Hackney comprehensive going through a troubled patch. Clearly, a man who knows how to get things done – equally clearly, he prefers to get them done in his own way: with justification. Married, two children.

Academic matters: In 2009, the first intake took their GCSES and the results were truly outstanding, with 85 per cent of pupils getting A*–C, including English and maths. Not only are these some of the best state-school results in the capital, they are all the more extraordinary given the fact that a significant proportion of the pupils arrive in Year 7 hardly able to read.

The country's highest ranking school for 'value added' – how is it done? Well, there is a formula and it bears no relationship to wishy-washy liberalism – a tough-love approach with a strict uniform policy, ferocious discipline, meticulous monitoring with weekly target setting and a 'can-do' culture. Young and enthusiastic teaching staff (who receive performance-related bonuses) have no official office hours and parents universally praise their dedication. 'My kids never complain about their teachers,' said one mother. 'They seem to be in school at 7 every morning. They recognise that not everyone is going to be a rocket scientist, but still manage to make every child feel relevant, included and loved.'

The banded intake is set on entry in all the main curriculum subjects (English, maths, science, humanities, ICT and modern languages), though considerable movement between sets. Music, drama, dance, PE, art and design technology are not set. Three languages on offer at GCSE – French, German, Spanish – as part of the core curriculum, but students also have the opportunity to take public exams in Turkish, Latin, Bengali, Swedish and Italian. Both vocational and academic exams on offer post GCSE (though considerably more academic than vocational), with a BTEC in business studies and level 3 ICT. Homework is set in abundance. Two specialities, ICT and RATL (raising achievement, transforming learning). ICT facilities are therefore state of the art with interactive whiteboards in all classrooms and all students offered access to the internet and laptops. What really makes the school excel academically, however, is the minutely monitored assessment – the 'personalised learning agenda' is certainly not just government jargon at this school.

The SEN provision is particularly remarkable, with its own well-resourced teaching centre and well-qualified specialists who cope with the full range of difficulties from autistic spectrum to dyslexia. All pupils with academic, social, emotional or behavioural difficulties have a learning mentor and those who require learning support work with a teaching assistant (in class or outside), receive specialist teaching and the support of external specialists if required. Handwriting club and homework club. Additional English classes, too, for non-native speakers on Saturday mornings. Strategies to suit all, including the brightest. The head quickly followed up on one parent's suggestion that Latin might be a desirable addition and equally quickly found himself with 30 students, who went on to take GCSE.

Games, Options, the Arts: Extra-curricular here is part of the curriculum, with an additional, compulsory, off-piste period every afternoon from 3.10 to 4.10pm. This time is used to help strugglers, but also to broaden horizons, with more than 70 activities on offer. All pupils required to take a minimum of two extension classes, which include everything from journalism to marathon running. Saturday morning school provides a safe place to have fun and weekend activities include the City Explorers club, to discover the joys of London. Sports include football, netball, basketball and cricket and 'best in Hackney' for athletics. Wonderful head of sport, reports one mother – 'My son had no problem getting up at 6 three mornings a week to be at cricket practice at 7'. Clearly buzzing on all fronts – annual junior concert, dance and drama production; trips to Edinburgh, Belgium, the Isle of Wight, language trips to Spain and German; Spanish play, poetry competition, debating, links with London College of Fashion.

Background and Atmosphere: Founded on the site of Hackney Downs School, once a successful local grammar school, whose alumnae include Sir Michael Caine and Harold Pinter. By the 1990s, however, it had become notorious as 'the worst in Britain' and was eventually demolished. Mossbourne was rebuilt on the same site, a tricky triangle bounded on two sides by railway lines. Sir Michael worked alongside architects, Richard Rogers and Partners, to design a school (costing £325 million) which met his requirements. Now one of the largest wooden structures in England, it was created in a V shape, which holds in its arms a triangular social area. Wilshaw believes that pupils need to be kept under constant observation, so his office and the classrooms all overlook the grounds. No corridors – hotspots for bullying – and no staff room, since Wilshaw feels teachers need to be involved at break times and after school, when most trouble occurs. Indoors, the triple-height space is light and airy and learning takes place in 'learning areas'. Sparkling new sixth-form centre added in 2009.

Pupils' aspirations always focused upwards. Rather than the Lord's Prayer, students recite the Mossbourne reflection: 'Throughout this lesson I aspire to maintain an inquiring mind, a calm disposition and an attentive ear, so that in this class and in all classes I can fulfil my true potential'. Parents without hesitation describe the school as 'absolutely amazing' – 'The kids are plainly very well cared for, polite, helpful and considerate. You feel that they are looked after and they are looking out for each other'. An incredible loyalty between kids from completely different ethnic and social backgrounds. Perhaps the greatest compliment any parent can pay is: 'You walk into the school during the day and there is an air of studiousness and control. I don't think about it anymore – I know the teachers are in charge'.

Pastoral Care and Discipline: As celebrated for its discipline as for its academic success and little opportunity to slip up here. Particularly in the early years, pupils are drilled in army-like expectations. Detentions commonplace – for lost homework, left-at-home games kit, being more than ten seconds late when the morning whistle goes at 8.40am – and students stand when a teacher enters the room. Wherever the potential for rule breaking, staff are on hand – stairwells manned between lessons and students monitored after school. Pre-GCSE pupils wear smart grey and red school blazers and neatly knotted ties, sixth formers graduate to business-like suits and skirts (at or below the knee). No piercings allowed, except for ears, hair must be kept to an acceptable norm (those indulging in the shaven look work in isolation until locks re-grow). Mobiles banned and students not allowed to enter shops on their way home or loiter outside the gates in groups. 'Structure sets a child free,' says the head. And it certainly seems to – a 96 per cent attendance rate.

Pastoral care is as strong as the discipline – few personal problems go unnoticed, whether bullying or self-harm. At the first sign, parents are invited to come and speak to the staff. One grateful mother has nothing but praise for their intervention – 'They made it very easy for my children speak to a counsellor. Mossbourne is a place where you can talk and get support when you can't always get that at home'. Food healthy and delicious.

Pupils and Parents: A large percentage of the intake comes from the adjacent Pembury estate, an urban sprawl which tends to hit the headlines for its shootings and drugs rather than its high educational aspirations. Four-fifths of pupils are from minority ethnic groups (many Turkish Kurds), two- fifths speak English as a second language, fifty per cent are on free school meals. But also a fair number of clued-up, middle-class parents – the kind who used to go private or bus their children out of the borough – who fight from a great distance to get their children the superb education the school offers.

Entrance: 180 places. Now one of the country's most over-subscribed schools with six applicants for every place in 2008. The head is looking for a balanced intake: 'We want a comprehensive – we don't want a secondary modern'. Applicants sit reasoning tests to divide into four equal ability bands. In each band, 60 per cent of places are given to whose who live within the inner zone (1000 metres from the gates); 40 per cent of places go to those outside the zone. For those inside the zone, priority is given to those in public care and statemented children, then siblings, then distance from the gates. For those outside the zone, the order is the same, though the final criteria is not distance from the gates but distance from the home address to a co-ed, non-selective comprehensive. Those who live furthest from that type of school are given priority at Mossbourne.

The lower sixth form has only 125 places and priority is given to those who have come up through the school. Most places are filled automatically, though pupils looking for academic courses need to meet the demanding criteria of 7A*-C GCSEs, including English and maths; those wanting vocational courses need four A*–C. A few candidates come in at this stage from other Hackney comprehensives.

Exit: Most proceed to the sixth form. No higher education destinations as yet, but this year's pupils who took away 15 A* GCSEs shouldn't have too many problems.

Money Matters: Money is not a problem at this well-resourced school. Everything from the buildings to the technology is of the highest standard and whatever the head wants to get done he has the means to achieve.

Remarks: Proof that with sufficient resources and the right direction, the kids who life intended to fail can succeed. Parents rightly fight to get into its safe, inspiring and eco-friendly classrooms.

The Mount School

Linked to Tregelles in the Junior section

Dalton Terrace, York, North Yorkshire, YO24 4DD

• Pupils: 235 girls; 60 boarders, 175 day • Ages: 11-18 • Size of sixth form: 75 • Quaker • Fees: Boarding £20,520-£21,780; Day £13,995 pa • Independent

Tel: 01904 667 500
Fax: 01904 667 524
Email: registrar@mountschoolyork.co.uk
Website: www.mountschoolyork.co.uk

Principal: Since September 2009, Ms Julie Lodrick BA music and related arts (University College, Chichester) PGCE (Kingston University) MA education, leadership and management (OU) professional practice certificate in boarding (BSA) national professional qualification for headship (NCSL) (late thirties). Wide experience in educational management; deputy head of Farlington School, West Sussex for four years. Also a tutor and lecturer for the Boarding Schools Association. Previously housemistress at Queenswood School, Hatfield, Hertfordshire, for five years; head of music at St Margaret's Senior School, West Sussex, for five years.

Academic matters: Strong AS/A level results – about 86 per cent A/B. 58 per cent or more A*/A at GCSE. Maths setted in Year 7 onwards, English in Year 9 onwards. A strong set of traditional A levels on offer with PE, theatre studies, psychology and business studies added due to demand. EPQ and AQA Baccalaureate offered with strong takeup. Good IT provision – interactive whiteboards in most classrooms and two state of the art computer suites; qualifications including OCR National taken in middle school and sixth form. Attractive and well designed new sixth form study centre has revitalised the top end of the school, giving private study areas as well as allowing extra activities such as cookery and social gatherings. York used for local cross-curricular and thinking skills work via 'Investigating York' in Year 7; archaeology is part of history lower down the school; links with university. Does well with all abilities including EAL – support available; also specialist learning support teaching. Girls enjoy lessons and have good relationships with friendly, cheerful and enthusiastic staff. Very good careers education with work experience.

Games, Options, the Arts: Beautifully kept grounds with numerous tennis courts, sports fields for hockey and athletics, an indoor pool and sports hall including a fitness suite. Successful at traditional team games as well as fencing and orienteering. Very strong and varied musical life, from classical to rock; all abilities participate in Christmas concert; regular concerts with other Quaker schools. About one third learn instruments at school; regular speech and drama successes. Huge range of after-school activities, e.g. jewellery making, photography – all take part. Very impressive artwork throughout the school, especially 3D work. Creative writing competition successes. Duke of Edinburgh popular – strong tradition of community involvement. An understanding of the wider world is important – currently enjoying involvement with Peace Jam and electronic links to Quaker schools in Palestine and Lebanon.

Background and Atmosphere: Origins go back to 18th century; present building, close to the centre of York, has a very fine 1857 façade with modern additions. Classrooms are a mix of old and new, very traditional library, which the girls enjoy, and a delightfully modern dining room. Set in 16 acres of gardens and green fields – girls make the most of the outdoor space, practising their tennis strokes, others deep in conversation and even twelve year olds are not too cool to race to the garden swing at break times. Though only a small percentage of staff and girls are Quakers, the ethos is central, manifest in respect for everyone in the community, a high degree of tolerance of differences, caring for others and democratic practices like the school council, which discusses internal affairs and, unlike most, really does have a voice. Morning Meetings include a period of silent reflection. Widespread involvement rather than bald achievement is regarded highly and girls view additional activities, such as lectures from visiting speakers, as 'opportunities not to be missed'.

Pastoral Care and Discipline: Considered very important – girls feel they receive a lot of individual attention. Four sixth form girls to a tutor group. Non-confrontational approach to discipline; exclusion only for persistent offences or major breach of rules (e.g. alcohol abuse) – huge amount of trust around the place, which girls appreciate with a typical commonsense approach – 'If you mess up, you mess it up for everyone'. Plenty of contact with parents – school website, weekly newsletter.

Pupils and Parents: Not just those with Quaker connection (it's the only all-girls Quaker school in England) – large number of local parents, often without an independent school background; not a county set school. Wide range of religions or none. Several boarders from Pacific Rim, South America, USA and Europe and others from a variety of other countries, though 'not too many from any one language group', plus overseas British. Girls wear white shirt, tartan skirt and blue jumper; no uniform for sixth form – 'relaxed' dress code. Famous Old Girls include Dame Judi Dench, Margaret Drabble, Antonia Byatt, Mary Ure, Kate Bellingham, Laura Sayers.

Entrance: Assessments for Years 7–10 entry in English, mathematics and verbal reasoning plus interview with head, who looks for 'spark – interesting girls with wide interests'. School report also important. Average and above average abilities catered for. Six GCSEs A*–C and interview for sixth form.

Exit: A very small number leave post-GCSE, most for local sixth form college. Otherwise to a variety of universities, old and new, several to Oxbridge, most to their first choice; a wide range of subjects studied; some take a gap year.

Money Matters: Year 7 academic and music scholarships; Year 9 academic, art and design, sport, music and drama; lower sixth (College) academic, art, sport, drama and music – all give five per cent remission of fees, to which a means-tested bursary of up to 100 per cent can be added. Music and drama scholars get free lessons. Separate bursary fund for Quaker children.

Remarks: Well-established Quaker girls' school – multi-faith and with an international student body. Lively, creative, warm atmosphere in a framework of orderly calm – mature, articulate and magnanimous sixth formers setting high standards for younger girls. Girls are highly motivated self-starters – collaborative rather than competitive, as you would expect in a Quaker school, nevertheless driven by a determination to do well.

Newport Free Grammar School

Bury Water Lane, Newport, Saffron Walden, Essex, CB11 3TR

• Pupils: 1,030; boys and girls • Ages: 11-18 • Size of sixth form: 185
• Non-denom • State

Tel: 01799 540 237
Fax: 01799 542 189
Email: admin@nfgs.essex.sch.uk
Website: www.nfgs.essex.sch.uk

Head: Since 2006, Mr Sean O'Hagan MA Leeds MEd London (late forties), married with young children. Quietly spoken and, unlike his long-serving predecessor, keeps a fairly low profile at the school. A realist and a pair of safe hands, with a keen understanding of pupil and parent worries and expectations and of the importance of having the right leadership team and dedicated staff. Quiet diplomat perhaps, taking the trouble to write personally to thank a parent for donating a book. Proud of the school's internationalism and the diverse opportunities for involvement offered in terms of travel, music (himself a saxophonist and guitarist), community contributions and sport, his aspiration being that everyone has the means to fulfil their potential.

Academic matters: 'Pretty average,' say some, but more say that its flexible and personal touch brings out the best in academic and non-academic alike, at least up to GCSEs, when overall results are well above average, as they are at AS and A level. Some grumbles that those looking to enter the workforce direct slightly neglected but, 'That's government policy'. Classes up to Year 11 average 23 and are considerably smaller in the sixth form. Some parents concerned about changes in staff over the year and as longer-serving staff take retirement.

Specialist status as a language and science school reflects key strengths, with a good number of GCSE candidates in these subjects and solid results, especially in Italian, chemistry and physics. Art and design also feature strongly. Parents attribute success to the passion and commitment of key staff which fosters widespread respect and motivation amongst the students. Setting lower down the school in French, maths and science and booster lessons over the Easter holidays for Year 11. Robust student tracking systems, previously implemented in the sixth form and commented on favourably by Ofsted, have now been introduced throughout to help identify those falling behind.

With two new deputy heads appointed, further fresh initiatives are likely to be on the cards. Construction of a learning support block is about to begin, reinforcing provisions for, amongst others, SEN pupils, who by all accounts thrive and are made to feel very much part of and contributors to the school community.

Games, Options, the Arts: An independent school manqué is how the head teacher termed it. The wealth of extra-curricular activities is certainly impressive, valued highly and participation very much the norm. As one parent put it, 'They go out of their way to make them citizens of the world.' Visits to inner city mosques and huge takeup of overseas trips and exchanges, strengthened by teachers' enthusiasm and Euro School Net2000, of which a founder member. One of a small élite group of UK state schools whose sixth formers are invited to participate in the Model United Nations General Assembly at the Palais des Nations in Geneva. The D of E award also well established and very popular. After-school sports clubs are well attended and fixtures (some international) regular – rugby, hockey and netball all strong. Frequent drama productions involving pupils across the school; big band members and many others learning an instrument and encouraged to perform. If none of that interests you, then after school offerings include bridge, African drumming and tap, in addition to more standard homework and spelling clubs.

Background and Atmosphere: An intimate and traditional community feel. Set in beautiful countryside a stone's throw from a picturesque local village, houses and shops, where students in blazers and ties wander in pairs and can be seen chattering in groups, it moved to its present 34-acre site in 1878 but keenly asserts its 400 year plus history. It celebrates Foundress Day, and in its library august past masters look down on heavy wooden tables which will have seen thousands come and go. Its newer classrooms and buildings do not always sit well with the cloistered courtyards and red-brick elegance of the past, but adequately house updated arts, IT and science facilities. A welcome and more recent addition is the all-weather hockey pitch.

Pastoral Care and Discipline: Friendly is the term most used to describe the school. Pupils generally fit in and are allowed to be themselves. They look you and staff in the eye and are generally waggy-tailed as they gather together in breaks or go about their business. Few shirts hanging out – an easy way to get your card marked, but little real resentment there. Few reported cases of bullying or disruptiveness – more often what the head teacher terms 'friendship issues'. When they do arise, most parents confident that they are dealt with in a reasoned manner and school congratulated for not attempting to shift the problem elsewhere. Aspiring prefects must be keen with a formal application process and, for senior posts, a presentation in front of the senior school council.

Pupils and Parents: Most families advantaged, affluent and able with high aspirations – as a result pupils are generally confident and precocious communicators. TV chef Jamie Oliver, pig farmer Jimmy Doherty and Irish international footballer Matt Holland are all former pupils. Parents wanting to get involved can usually find an avenue for their energies, and in response to past criticism, a pupil community committee has recently been set up to ensure concerns and ideas are channelled and acted upon more effectively.

Entrance: Non-selective but heavily over-subscribed, particularly at age 11, where in 2008, 605 applications for 168 places. Parents must submit an application form to their local LEA. Those living in the parish of Newport get priority, followed by residents of thirteen other designated parishes and then siblings of pupils at the school. The majority stay on for sixth form, allowing a maximum of 30 students to join from outside, on gaining a minimum of 5 GCSEs at grades A–C and completion of a standard application form.

Exit: Approximately 70 per cent go on to university or further studies, including some to Oxford and Cambridge. Some attracted by larger local schools at 16.

Remarks: Traditional school that remains true to its original aim of providing education for local pupils, regardless of ability. Motivated 'doers' should do particularly well, but scope for all to thrive in its friendly atmosphere.

Newstead Wood School for Girls

Avebury Road, Orpington, Kent, BR6 9SA

• Pupils: 1020 students; Y7-11 all girls; Y12-13 mixed. All day • Ages: 11-18
• Size of sixth form: 335 • Non-denom • State

Tel: 01689 853 626
Fax: 01689 853 315
Email: office@newsteadwood.bromley.sch.uk
Website: www.newsteadwood.bromley.sch.uk

Headteacher: Since 2001, Mrs Elizabeth Allen BA MA FRSA (early sixties) married with two grown-up daughters. Previously head of Altwood (mixed) Comprehensive in Maidenhead. Currently teaches critical thinking to the sixth form but previously taught RS, English and drama to advanced level. She impresses with her understanding of what works best for bright girls and of the educational scene and is immensely proud of what the pupils and staff achieve. Credited for being business-like with clear vision and having the school's best interests at heart. While parents lower down the school have limited contact and pupils tend to be somewhat in awe of her, sixth formers call her inspirational and parents say she is very focused on the job at hand.

Academic matters: Not so much an academic hothouse as the sort of place where, if you don't work reasonably hard, you're the odd one out. The head places great emphasis on staff and pupils 'co-constructing' the learning experience and on staff leadership and development. They should be critical questioners and facilitate, rather than direct, learning. An active school parliament and regular re-writes and performance assessments of the school's mission statement. In addition to termly reports and annual parent teacher meetings, an academic tutoring day each term which includes individual interviews to discuss achievements and set targets for improving learning.

Building learning and thinking skills starts early. Year 7's 'Journeys of a Lifetime' programme encourages pupils to articulate how they learn and where they need to focus and is allied to lots of opportunities to expand and get beneath curriculum subjects. Further up the school, the engineering diploma (Years 10–13) and IB and extended project in the sixth form are designed to promote independent study and breadth of learning. All have been introduced recently and takeup is growing, though parents detect some residual nervousness on the part of staff in relation to the IB. The impressive exam results might also explain why pupils and parents tend to play safe by sticking to A levels, with popular subjects biology, chemistry, maths, English lit and psychology. Advanced extension awards and music grades contribute to an average UCAS points score of over 440, equivalent to almost four A grades. GCSE results are no less creditable – lots of girls with 10 A*s and over 80 per cent of all grades at the school A* or A.

Strong enrichment programme – the usual timetable is effectively suspended for three weeks each year. Specialist engineering and languages status provides opportunities to extend the scope of study (e.g. engineering diploma and Mandarin Chinese and Japanese from Years 8 and 9 respectively). Also a designated G&T lead school. G&T pupils aren't noticeably singled out for special treatment but staff ensure lots to stimulate and push them. Dyspraxic and dyslexic pupils' coping strategies often uncovered during GCSEs. Individual education plans then agreed between pupils, parents and staff to overcome any difficulties.

Games, Options, the Arts: 'Whatever they do, they do well,' says one parent and the evidence seems to support this. Good performances in hockey, netball and gymnastics and, though the school has no pool, it tops the results tables in national and county swimming events. Older girls help the youngsters.

The Year 7 and 8 vocal ensemble was conceived and is run by sixth formers, one of several choirs and orchestras which perform regularly. Music is a real strength and taken seriously and at tempo here (better make sure you rehearse!). Vox CC, its senior choir, has performed at the Royal Albert Hall and in Prague. Drama is popular; twenty plus student societies in anything from debating, politics, history, the environment, medicine to law, all run by Year 12 pupils. Leadership and participation is very much what this school is all about and it's rare to find a sixth former who doesn't voluntarily take on extra responsibilities. For others too, judging by the somewhat overwhelming stream of calendar reminders on the electronic board in reception, little excuse to be idle. Lots of after school and lunchtime activities, as well as positions as sports ambassadors, Arkwright scholars to promote engineering in schools, language teaching in local primary schools, maths and debating competitions, *Dragon's Pen* workshops and charity events – plenty going on.

Background and Atmosphere: Set in a quiet residential area, has wonderful views across the playing fields towards the Downs, but the school buildings, though quite spacious, are unremarkable and jumbled – the 1950s, when it was established, not perhaps the best architectural era. Inside, the walls are brightened with artwork and a lick of paint from the girls over the holidays in the sixth form area. This is to be re-housed, thanks to a successful 2008 bid for £2.5m, which will also largely fund an engineering/design technology block, additional classrooms, staff areas and lab refurbishment. Already has wonderful indoor tennis courts open to the public.

Pastoral Care and Discipline: Ongoing and slightly half-hearted battles regarding sixth form dress code but, in the head's view, it's churlish to make too big a fuss when most girls behave and perform well. In an all-female environment they are generally not interested in acting beyond their years and the school encourages them to assess for themselves what's appropriate in different circumstances. More commonly issues arise through poor organisation or conflicting priorities, typical, the head says, amongst brighter enthusiastic pupils.

As long as you are willing to work with the school, issues are normally swiftly resolved in liaison with staff, the emphasis being very much on motivation rather than chastisement. Parents cite examples of a generally good response to concerns voiced, whether individual (friendship) or more general (chain emails). The school is also alert to mixed expectations relating to academic and home life. In such cases, a counsellor and family worker are available to provide guidance and support. A strong PSHE programme, which, e.g., incorporates financial literacy, in which pupils can gain accreditation. Careers support very good with lots of 1:1 advice, a calendar of related events, a well-stocked library and lots of exposure to different areas of work through placements and contact with professionals.

In general, bullying is stamped on, the girls themselves tending to side with the victim. Informal vertical contact encouraged through extra-curricular clubs and older pupils acting as mentors. The travel buddy scheme is a nice example, combining as it does environmental targets to reduce car use with accompanying Year 7 pupils on public transport their first few weeks. Occasionally girls are to be seen eating and smoking outside the school grounds, but few complaints from local businesses and residents, who seem grateful to have such a well-thought of school in their midst – 'We'd all like our kids to go there'.

Pupils and Parents: Says one parent, 'If they're really not up to and up for it, they won't enjoy it' – i.e. you need to be self-motivated rather than coached to get here. From a range of socio-economic and ethnic backgrounds. 'They stand out for being bright, self-confident and just getting on with it,' says one business regularly offering work experience to pupils from local schools. PA is active and effective, holding a variety of social and fundraising events over the year, as well as organising regular fairs through its careers sub-committee. Notable former pupils include Christine Hancock, Barbara Harriss-White, Emma Johnson (clarinettist who came back to hold a masterclass at the school), Susan Tebby, Josie Long and Kim Medcalf.

Entrance: Most from local state primary schools. For Year 7, entrance tests in verbal and non-verbal reasoning in November. Standards high but the test experience 'more friendly' than for other local schools. Around 650–700 applications for 130 places. When, very occasionally, places come available further up the school, those on the waiting list are invited to take an age-appropriate test and the highest scorers offered a place. From 2010 the 15 places available for outside applicants to the sixth form will be likely go to those wishing to sit IB. A minimum of six GCSE grades A*–C with A* or A in the subjects for further study needed.

Exit: The head makes it clear that those entering at 11 are expected to stay the course and only a few leave at 16, mostly to pursue specialist studies, e.g. performing arts or media studies. Around 15–20 per annum to Oxbridge. Other popular destinations London, Leeds, Bristol, Birmingham, Exeter, York and Durham as well as London art and medical colleges.

Money Matters: Dedicated and enthusiastic PTA raises £30,000–50,000 annually, which funds the artists in residence each year and extra teaching resources. A covenant scheme and continuous fundraising events and activities to support the ongoing developments. Girls raise money for charities during house charity week.

Remarks: Capable and committed girls do really well here, most setting out on their future studies and careers well-qualified and equipped for the challenges ahead.

Nonsuch High School for Girls

Ewell Road, Cheam, Sutton, Surrey, SM3 8AB

• Pupils: 1,245 girls, all day • Ages: 11-18 • Size of sixth form: 350
• Non-denom • State

Tel: 020 8394 1308
Fax: 020 8393 2307
Email: admissions@nonsuch.sutton.sch.uk
Website: www.nonsuchhigh.co.uk

Head: Since 2009, Mrs Karin Rowsell BSc (biochemistry) from University of Bath, MA (management in education) from Open University, NPQH, a Dutch national, educated (Atheneum – Baccalaureate) in The Netherlands. Married with four daughters aged 21 to 26; interests include music, piano, theatre, sailing, skiing. Committed to the education of the whole child and the development of a breadth and depth of skills.

Academic matters: Impressive, as you would expect from one of the top selective schools in the country. Science facilities are excellent – recent new build and all 11 labs now newly refurbished – and results, hitherto not so sparkling, now improved. Several girls take up Nuffield scholarships each year and many progress to careers in science and medicine. Nice to see astronomy available as a GCSE option (school has its own observatory). At A level, English, psychology, sciences, geography and maths are among the favourite options. 'It's almost as if they don't want to be labelled as a girls' school – they are always emphasising the more traditionally masculine subjects,' said one parent. Lots of homework, but parents say it is 'manageable'. 'My daughter works very hard and is definitely stretched here. In Year 8 she was looking at GCSE papers,' says a mother. Definitely not a school for slackers. 'We actually chose this school because we thought it would be less pressured than Tiffin Girls, but we were wrong – it is quite pushy,' says another mother. Little call for special needs support here, but SENCo assists those dyslexic pupils who are able to pass the entry test and some physical disabilities are catered for. Approximately 70 EAL students but no beginners.

Games, Options, the Arts: Sports facilities are excellent and well used, thanks in large part to an innovative deal with a David Lloyd sports club. Nonsuch was the first state school to go into such a partnership – it leases land to the club and in return can use its facilities, including exclusive use of the swimming pool in the mornings and the tennis courts in the afternoon. Additionally, as part of the deal, David Lloyd provided the school with a dedicated sports hall, floodlit all-weather hockey pitch and new music centre. All the usual main sports on offer and pupils compete at national and county level in several, including netball, football, cycling and hockey. Tennis is popular and the school provides the ball girls for the Aegon tennis tournament at Queen's.

Very good reputation for music (old girls include 'cool' singer Katie Melua and harpist Lucy Wakeford) with many choirs, orchestras, and ensembles. Some 250 girls take extra-curricular music lessons and aim for grade 8 by the time they leave. Budding dancers and actresses have traditionally struggled to express themselves and some parents have feel these subjects were the poor relations. However drama now stronger and very popular – a discrete subject throughout KS3 and an option at GCSE and A level, drama suite now situated in a permanent building. Enthusiastic annual drama festival and dance show; a theatre school operates on the site on Saturdays. Clubs and societies from cheerleading to philosophy, salsa and ballroom, CCF and D of E.

Background and Atmosphere: Lovely setting on the edge of the 22 acre Nonsuch Park. Plenty of outdoor space, mix of buildings: admin and some classrooms are in the charmless original building, which has been extended in different directions with newer, fresher facilities and a few separate blocks – workman-like rather than flashy. Girls are lively – even noisy. Strong house system.

Pastoral Care and Discipline: Usual system of tutors and heads of year in place and working well. Issues dealt with rapidly – nothing festers. Discipline is strict. No major discipline problems – 'I tolerate absolutely no nonsense and treat everyone exactly the same,' says the head. Parents feel their daughters clearly know and understand the boundaries. No tolerance of smoking anywhere while in school uniform – including travel time; prefects patrol the huge school site.

Pupils and Parents: A refreshingly multicultural bunch (30 languages). Pupils proud to be here, and generally smart – school uniform kilts are difficult to shorten. Parents are mainly professional, ambitious for their daughters, and supportive of the school. Communications with parents are good – lots of up to date information on the website, 93 per cent of parents opt to receive and send all communication by email.

Entrance: Hugely over-subscribed – in 2009 1300 applications (from some 50 primary schools) for 180 places. Applicants must list Nonsuch as a preferred school on the application form. Two parts to the test (verbal and non-verbal reasoning), no interview. Places are allocated to those who pass, according to proximity criteria (NB admissions criteria have changed in line with the Admissions Code 2007) – families move into the area to be as near to the school doorstep as possible. However the top 80 highest scores get a place regardless of where they live. In practice, maintains a local intake, with 95 per cent of the pupils living within 5 km. 15–25 external students join the school in the sixth form.

Exit: Over 80 per cent of the girls stay on for the sixth form – of the rest, some join colleges (probably in search of a mixed environment) and a few go to the private sector. At 18 most go on to university – 15 or so to Oxbridge, lots to the redbricks and a dozen or so each year to leading medical and dental schools.

Remarks: A super school for the disciplined and hardworking, not for the rebel or slacker.

North Berwick High School

Grange Road, North Berwick, East Lothian, EH39 4QS

• Pupils: 935 boys and girls, all day • Ages: 12-18 • Size of sixth form: 150 • Non-denom • State

Tel: 01620 894 661
Fax: 01620 895 495
Email: northberwick.hs@northberwickhigh.elcschool.org.uk
Website: www.northberwickhigh.net

Head Teacher: Since 1999 Mr Colin Sutherland BSc (early fifties), who comes from the west (as they say in Scotland). He started his teaching career at Garnock Academy, Kilbirnie, in Ayrshire, before spending 11 years at Castlehead School in Paisley. Previously depute at Port Glasgow High School, before that assistant head at Greenock. Educated at Paisley Grammar, 'when it was still selective'. He read maths and geology at Glasgow University plus PGCE and 'masses of courses'. He would love to teach more but still does 'the odd bit, supply teaching mainly', but no set classes as such. Runs the school with four deputy heads responsible for the four houses, plus a whole host of add-ons, in addition to a recently-appointed business manager.

A charming man, thoughtful and very aware of children's needs, he has a lovely sense of humour and 'just loves it here'. An enthusiastic cyclist and walker, he has not yet taken up the North Berwick vice of golf, though is otherwise much involved in the community (he lives at nearby Port Seton, safely out of the catchment area).

Academic matters: School follows Scottish system: Standard Grades/Intermediates followed by Highers and Advanced Highers the following year. Six parallel classes at S1 and S2, with pupils being setted for maths in S1 and S2. Thereafter, the school runs six parallel classes, taking into account option choice, when specialist subject teaching kicks in – 'deliberately made broad to ensure that pupils' needs and interests are met within the national framework'. Maximum class size 25 (head says, 'Could be up to 30, but the school strives to ensure that classes contain no more than 25/26'). 18/20 for practical matters. Since August 2007, the maximum class size in S1/2 English and mathematics is 20.

Consistently turns in best results in East Lothian – recently ranked 37th overall in Scotland for Standard Grades and 17th for Highers. In Standard Grades biology, chemistry, English, French, geography, history, modern studies, music and, to a lesser degree, physics, were outstanding. French writing and German less so, maths had a bad year. Pupils can take Spanish up to Intermediate level in S5/6 – usually the latter.

At Intermediate 2 (which many schools are using instead of Standard Grades) chemistry, English and maths are very strong and this trend continues at Higher level, with excellent showings across the board in English and the sciences, as well as geography, history and modern studies. Pupils take an amalgam of exams, often topping up with another batch of Highers rather than opting for Advanced Highers. Little problem with getting staff – well, it's North Berwick, isn't it? Head is autonomous in being able to choose his own staff.

Good remedial back-up – children with records of needs not a problem, nor those with ADHD. Double teaching in class, laptop computers where required, plus extra time in exams and for those with learning needs 'which cannot be tackled in the classroom', workshops on basic processes, individual educational programmes and individual tutorials. Reading Recovery programme, plus educational psychologists, outreach teachers et al. Support for learning for the most able as well as for those with learning difficulties. Has a number of profoundly deaf pupils, for whom an excellent programme. Blind and partially sighted pupils and wheelchairs all easily absorbed – laudable.

Integrated pupil support faculty includes a pupil support base in which the most vulnerable pupils have a 'sanctuary' with a base for pupils with additional support needs, met in various ways: in class by teachers, auxiliaries and S6 pupils, some extracted to work on particular areas in support base, programme of paired reading well established, Alphasmart and laptop computers in use where required. Individual education programmes in place.

All classrooms have TVs and Promethean multimedia systems, allowing interactive learning and teaching in all areas, plus dozens of wireless laptop computers.

Games, Options, the Arts: Has an enviable collection of games pitches with the local sports centre and swimming pool next door – they have priority over local users. New Astroturf. Two gyms in school, plus dance studio plus mirrors, of course. Strong rugby and hockey – 68 players recently toured Australia and Fiji with great success. Also basketball, hockey (huge fixture list for girls), badminton, netball club, sailing, swimming; local authority development officers on hand for coaching. D of E popular – head would like us to add 'very' – with half a dozen pupils every year going to Holyrood for their gold award. Trillions of clubs for everything.

Music outstanding, though no pipe band of their own – pupils (of both sexes) play with the town band. Bands, orchestras and choirs in every discipline: wind, jazz, brass, piano. Senior and junior choirs – sings carols outside the church for charity at Christmas, plays at The Lodge and provided the brass band for the opening of the local Seabird Centre. Musicians have been known to come back to school and join in the school orchestra – often with no warning at all. Scottish country dancing popular, as are the regular ceilidhs, much to the amazement of the bunch of Kosovan refugees who were billeted in the town a few years ago – 'They loved it' (and came with extra resources).

Recording studio; huge assembly hall used for school drama (very good) and by the locals – for partying as well as plays. Deaf loop in operation. Keyboards, guitars, large number of practice rooms. Whizzy art department, absolutely fabulous, with excellent ceramics and tranches of young going on to art schools all over the country – amazing cutglass, fabulous screen printing (though the sewing-up was less impressive); artwork all over the school. Huge art library and darkroom, CAD and computer links to art department. Impressive DT, though mainly in wood. Home economics but not much take up. Impressive computer suites (one hundred new computers in 2004) set out like an office.

School is twinned, as is the town, with Kerteminde in Denmark – children do exchanges and four-weekly study visits are a regular feature (a growth activity).

Background and Atmosphere: Founded in 1893 with thirteen pupils. Originally North Berwick boasted two schools: the Parish School (which started in 1661) and the Burgh School; these amalgamated in 1868 and joined forces with the High School in 1931. The current buildings date back to 1940, and very impressive they are too. The temporary classrooms which had provided schooling for the extra post-war pupils were replaced during the 1990s and a further extension under the PPP initiative is now complete. Light and airy, must have some of the best views in Britain, with the Law to the south and views over the North Berwick coastline and the Bass Rock to the north. Has strong links with the recently opened Seabird Centre, used for regular study, as well as providing summer and weekend jobs for impoverished pupils – a grade one bonus.

A community school at its best: loads of town participation, a squad recently cleaned up the East Beach and local countryside a haven for hands-on teaching. Masses of interschool/town involvement – the Community Council has recently donated a prize for community service. Huge library, divided into little seminar areas, as well as crannies for private study. The tidiest school we have ever visited – only two bags in evidence, the rest neatly tucked into lockers. However quite a lot of detritus and candybar wrappers lying around, despite the enormous (labelled) litter bins everywhere. Four house system a focus for pastoral care as well as discipline and games – sibling led. Each of the four depute and heads fronts one of them; houseboards vie for imaginative notices.

Pupils wear their school uniform with pride – move currently afoot to introduce fleece jackets, all wear white shirts with black and red ties and sweatshirts. Pupils not encouraged to leave the school at lunchtime but no dining rooms as such – cafeteria-style food available, and can bring packed lunch or eat in the sports centre. Headboy or girl chosen via ballot of staff and sixth form – 'Not a beauty contest,' said the head; the top four are then interviewed before selection. A pretty onerous task – they have to do the Burns Night supper at the local Marine Hotel, which brushes up their public speaking skills. Two prizegivings – the headboy and girl are principal speakers at the prizegiving for S1/2/3 at the traditional time in June, and then return for the senior prizegiving in mid September, which is followed by soft drinks, wine for the adults and nibbles in the library; very popular.

Closes at lunchtime on Fridays for staff training, which may not be over-convenient for working parents. Schoolbus for all outlying districts. Masses of trips, for everything, all over.

Pastoral Care and Discipline: Good PSE and strong anti-bullying programmes in place: 'Secrecy is the worst enemy'. No obvious problems with alcohol, cigarettes or drugs in school, but North Berwick itself had some horrendous publicity a few years ago with children being found paralytic on the beaches during the weekend, and underage drinking is certainly a problem locally. The local community health boys take this seriously and are very 'proactive'. School is much involved in this and 'ever vigilant in educating youth'. Regular smoking patrol.

School uses four chaplains, three Church of Scotland and one Episcopalian, who tackle moral issues. 'An honest school' – no history of theft and most classrooms are left unlocked.

Pupils and Parents: Parents mostly a middle class bunch but a diverse intake, everyone from baby bankers to impoverished shepherds. Incredibly supportive – usually over 95 per cent turn up for parents' evenings and a very strong PTA good at fundraising. Minuscule number of ethnic minorities. Parent-led parent council – parents, staff and a couple of members of the local community.

Entrance: Automatic from local primaries and if children of school age move into the area, at any time. Children from five associated primaries: the huge (over 700) Law Primary, which is adjacent and shares many of the school facilities, including the fabulous local sports centre, and the much smaller local primaries of Aberlady, Athelstaneford, Dirleton and Gullane. Pupils in primary 7 visit the school before their actual arrival here and follow part of the big school timetable.

Exit: Two departure dates a year, one at Christmas, the other at the conventional end of school year. Around 80 per cent stay on for sixth year; some leave to go into further education, some work, 50 per cent to university – quite a mix: medics, law, business administration, economics, English, maths, education. Primarily to Scottish universities but a regular and quite impressive trickle to Oxbridge annually.

Money Matters: No child disadvantaged – good backup from the local LEA, as well as parent-inspired foundation.

Remarks: A stunning and successful local school. Couldn't do better anywhere.

North Bridge House Senior School

Linked to North Bridge House Preparatory School Linked to North Bridge House Junior School in the Junior section

1 Gloucester Avenue, London, NW1 7AB

• Pupils: 195 boys and girls • Ages: 11-16 • Non-denom • Fees: £12,810 pa
• Independent

Tel: 020 7267 6266
Fax: 020 7284 2508
Email: seniorschool@northbridgehouse.com
Website: www.nbhseniorschool.co.uk/

Head: Since 2003, Miss Alexandra Ayre BA PGCE (thirties), an English specialist who still finds time to teach – hooray! Previously taught in the state sector. Pretty, elegant and with a faint American tinge to her voice, she is clearly enjoying the challenge of her small, niche school with its complex history and labyrinthine accommodation.

Academic matters: The senior school is a small school and most of the intake is made up of those children who would not aim for the academic powerhouses of north London. No sixth form, with the sense of impending adulthood and university that tends to lend a school; nonetheless, in the three years of Miss Ayre's tenure, all leavers have gone on to sixth forms elsewhere and thence to university. The academics are gently flourishing here and 2009 saw good GCSE results – 91 per cent five or more A*-Cs (including maths and English). In fact, 55 per cent of subjects taken were graded A*/A. In the Englishes and maths, few pupils got lower than B. Double science – taken by most – achieved an A/B average. French is weaker but Spanish, taken by the abler linguists, scored highly. Everyone learns French in year seven and then Spanish in years eight and nine. Surprisingly wide range of GCSE options for so small a school includes photography and media.

Year 7 taught English, maths and history by class teacher to homogenise all-comers and weld disparate intake into cohesive group. Everyone assessed on entry and SEN specialist supports those deemed to need it – sometimes with up to three withdrawals per week. Some places conditional on parents agreeing to such support. Help given mostly to those with mild dyslexia and dyspraxia.

Games, Options, the Arts: A seriously arty school, partly because of the backgrounds of the children but also through some inspired teaching. Art and photography impress in particular – both in terms of the work and in the excellent results. Art is taught in a real studio with good light and large windows – evidence of sound teaching of basic skills and results to boast about. Attractive collage work and good textiles along with the exemplary photography. Lively drama in basement room and several productions annually. Lots of visits and outside speakers – including cast of actors and artists among parents, who give generously of time and support. Sports in Regent's Park, the Talacre and Swiss Cottage centres. Despite the lack of on-site facilities and small numbers, performs remarkably well in competitive sports, with wins in all usual team games. Main sports are football, netball, rounders, athletics and tennis. Lots of clubs include dance, drama, football, table tennis, cricket at Lords, cookery, choir, touch typing, Amnesty International, science and French culture.

Background and Atmosphere: The convent history is still palpable in the high panelled walls, high ceilings, chapel and maze of rooms on all levels, which have a modest plainness, despite the work on display. The chapel, which doubles as dining room and main hall, is colonnaded, coffered and gilded. A splendid new mosaic depicting the school's multi-national intake adorns the main corridor. The houses are irreproachably called Mandela, Churchill and Pankhurst and all rooms are given their designations in French and Spanish. Along with pupils' work, worthy posters flank the passageways on subjects such as the state of the death penalty worldwide. Quiet prevails and classes are full of concentrating pupils.

Schools now owned by Cognita – chaired by former Chief Inspector of Schools, Chris Woodhead. This has resulted in much investment, sharing of training and resources and a radically different probable future, especially in terms of accommodation.

Pastoral Care and Discipline: Pupils are open, enthusiastic and quite palpably happy. They pay tribute to their teachers who 'are always there to help us and treat us as individuals. They want us to be happy'. One refugee from a less congenial school said, 'I always wanted to look forward to coming to school and I do here.'

Pupils and Parents: Very mixed north London intake ensures no typical pupil. School so small that everyone knows everyone.

Entrance: Around 70 per cent from state sector – frequently parents who had found decent junior schools but are less gruntled by what the state offers at secondary level. Some from preps that end at 11 and the rest from the North Bridge House Prep School. 'We fill a niche – we're not an academic hothouse,' says head. Pupils invited to admissions day and tested in maths, English, vocabulary, comprehension, verbal reasoning and non-verbal reasoning. A reference from the current school is also necessary.

Exit: Many to Camden Girls' (qv) (state comprehensive) sixth form or, occasionally, to Fortismere – a mixed comprehensive (qv). Many to Highgate. Some to sixth form colleges, some to independent day schools, e.g. Channing and UCS, and some to independent boarding schools, e.g. Rugby, Bedales or even Westminster.

Money Matters: Some academic and music scholarships.

Remarks: A gentle school. Could be the answer for your shyer or less robust son or daughter, who will flourish given the opportunities and security available in this close-knit, nurturing nook.

North Cestrian Grammar School

Dunham Road, Altrincham, Cheshire, WA14 4AJ

• Pupils: 290 boys and 30 girls - co-educational since 2008 • Ages: 11-18 • Size of sixth form: 70 in sixth form; co-ed since 2005 • Non-denominational • Fees: £7,980 pa • Independent

Tel: 0161 928 1856
Fax: 0161 929 8657
Email: office@ncgs.co.uk
Website: www.ncgs.co.uk

Head: Since 1996, Mr David Vanstone MA history, Cambridge, then PCGE and sabbatical union post from Goldsmiths' College, London. Youthful mid fifties. Came from six years as deputy head at Stafford Grammar. Former Chair of ISA, director ISC. Passionate about what small schools can offer pupils in developing individual potential, speaking of 'the ethos behind the mission'. Jocular with pupils but commands friendly respect. Pupils like him but say, 'He does like making speeches and the sound of his own voice'. Parents appreciate his pastoral care – 'Once your child is under his wing he looks after them like his own children'.

Academic matters: Founded in 1951 as a grammar school for boys who hadn't passed the 11+ and who might therefore be disadvantaged – fully co-educational since 2008. 'People see us as a non-academic school,' says head, 'but many who have passed the 11+ actively chose our small, personal environment where they're known individually and looked after.' Justly proud of reputation for 'value-added', nurturing unfulfilled potential and enabling dyslexic children to thrive. Two classes of 25, streamed from Year 8. 14 GCSEs and 16 A level courses on offer. 87 per cent GCSEs A–C. Most pupils exceed expectations, delighting parents and themselves, and many go on to university. All encouraged to develop in extra-curricular ways too.

25 per cent LDD with special help for those with SEN, mostly dyslexia. Parents describe extra dyslexia tuition as 'very available, timetabled, sympathetic, open-minded, an extra cost but marvellous'. Some children have restricted curriculum to succeed in six GCSEs rather than struggling in nine, 'so they learn they can cope, to boost their confidence and self-esteem'. Boys and girls seem willing to give up breaks to finish work. Trafford Connexions careers service and parents praise school's help in decision-making during upper years. Sixth form classes average seven pupils. Also new A levels in business studies and music and additional GCSEs in PE and drama.

Games, Options, the Arts: Large sports hall, gym and four tennis courts on site with new music suite, recording workshop and dance studio. A new three storey science block opened in July 2010 paving the way for the creation of a sixth form common room, drama studio and learning support centre. 20-acre playing fields rented from National Trust with modern pavilion and changing rooms, five minutes' walk through leafy suburbs, downhill there, uphill back – 'miserable in the rain after two hours' football,' say boys. Very strong tradition of D of E, accounting for over half local borough's gold and silver awards. The only local school with in-house training to gold. 'Though we're a small school we try and provide everything you'd find in a bigger school,' says head. Strong emphasis on outdoor pursuits during weekends, evenings and holidays, including rock climbing, snowboarding, golf, white water rafting. Well-equipped music and art rooms, private tuition on seven instruments, impressive ceramics on display round school. Recent trips include skiing in Colorado and tracking in India, plus less expensive outward bound nearer home.

Background and Atmosphere: Stately home aura with portico entrance, pink front door to grand carpeted entrance hall with wallpaper. Large front room of 1850s mansion was home to original 1951 intake of 39 boys, now head's study. New hall seats all, by former stable block housing technology. Former hall now home to library with work stations. Outdoor area at break seems cramped. Unstuffy, bustling but relaxed atmosphere prevails. 'The best thing about the school is the co-operation and understanding between pupils and staff,' says head. 'They get the best out of each other.' Parents say a lot of fun here – teachers join drama productions, one even flick-flacks across the stage. Lunches pre-paid, compulsory. Head firmly believes, 'Children need to be fed,' and, while there are healthy options, defends provision of stodge – 'better than them being hungry all afternoon and I abhor Ruth Kelly's abominable attacks on vending machines. This school is full of thin children and we educate them to make choices'. Inevitably, most choose stodge, but do seem to stay thin.

Pastoral Care and Discipline: On very busy A56 but pupils keep to footbridge and nearby pelican crossing. Otherwise very secure with gated grounds sandwiched between Loreto Prep and Girls' senior schools. Pupils stand for staff and the word 'sir' is on the tip of every tongue, though pupil-staff relationships friendly. Head says, 'I know every child, not just their names but their family and whether they need me to shout at them or not.' Four houses – Grenfell, Hillary, Livingstone and Scott. Strong pastoral care, going to great lengths through year heads and form tutors, older prefects mentor lower forms. Parental contact is good, termly reports and homework diary have scope for communicating home. Parents describe school as 'very approachable' with lots of awards for effort as well as achievement, but say that the influx of those who're not thriving elsewhere before GCSE courses begin can be disrupting for existing settled boys and class groups. Head says, 'We rarely fail a pupil and, if we do, they generally end up outside mainstream education.'

Pupils and Parents: Largely white middle class. 10 per cent Jewish, 10 per cent Muslim with strong link to local faith communities. Two thirds from nearby, others travel out from Manchester or in from far flung parts of Cheshire. Diverse but harmonious community embracing those needing extra tuition or nurturing as well as the eccentric and recalcitrant. Co-ed since September 2008 when thirty girls joined in response to local demand from parents, who say, 'There is nothing similar in the whole area where girls can get the opportunities offered to the boys'. 'They'll flood in once word spreads,' says head. Notable OBs include ice skater Nicky Slater, floating weatherman Fred Talbot, Kevin Godley, 10cc rock star, James Goulding, chief executive of Deutsche Asset Management Europe, Justin Pidcock, Olympic hockey medallist, Gary Davies, Radio One DJ and Nabeel Chowdery, millionaire property developer.

Entrance: Relatively undaunting exam looking for GCSE A–C potential, so not all pass. Papers in English, maths and reasoning in autumn term. Entry to co-ed sixth form based on anticipated GCSEs and interview with head. Some exchange of pupils at sixth form, some leaving for a bigger school for better transition to university, others coming here for more individual attention.

Exit: Many to university, some to high flying courses.

Money Matters: Means-tested bursaries available – 'We would like to issue more,' says head, who also offers some academic scholarships based on entrance exam merit.

Remarks: Justly deserved reputation for realising potential, especially in children who, for whatever reason, have not passed 11+ and for dyslexics who can pass entrance exam. Many local children sit exam as safety net, some 11+ passers also choose NCGS for its size and ethos of individual attention. Parents say, 'It's a brilliant school for the right child. I can't speak highly enough of it for our son.'

North London Collegiate School

Linked to North London Collegiate School Junior School in the Junior section

Canons, Canons Drive, Edgware, Middlesex, HA8 7RJ

• Pupils: 760 girls; all day • Ages: 11-18 • Size of sixth form: 240 • Christian foundation, but all faiths welcomed • Fees: £11,472-£13,572 pa • Independent

Tel: 020 8952 0912
Fax: 020 8951 1391
Email: office@nlcs.org.uk
Website: www.nlcs.org.uk

Head: Since 1997, Mrs Bernice McCabe BA MBA PGCE, (a glamorous mid-fifties). Mrs McCabe had exemplary, if not wholly predictable, credentials for this top job in girls' independent education. An English graduate, she spent 23 years teaching in the state sector and was appointed to her first deputy headship in 1986 at Heathlands School, Hounslow. Her various responsibilities there helped her gain the expertise needed for the effective running of a modern school and she took her MBA during her first headship at Chelmsford County High (qv). Chelmsford, under Mrs McCabe's seven year tenure, became one of the country's leading state schools.

She teaches all Year 7 – an excellent principle and one that all heads should practise, in our view. She is not interested in drilling or ranking girls, 'We have no class positions, no prize-giving except when they leave ... I want the staff to find out what the girls are good at and develop their potential, not just teach them to jump through hoops'. She lunches with her Big Six – the committee of sixth form girls who act as a conduit between her and the school community. She fosters a democratic community which is generally appreciated and comfortably taken for granted now.

Mrs McCabe is clever, charismatic and good company. She is also stunningly pretty and elegant – clearly a rôle model in all ways for her girls, who appear to adore her. Her deep dark red nail varnish is imitated by half her sixth form. She is relaxed, dedicated to education in its truest sense and committed to sharing what she and her school has with the wider world, notably with those who teach or learn in the state sector. Hence her directorship of The Prince's Teaching Institute, a high calibre residential project to reinvigorate subject teaching in schools and reinspire the teachers. At NLCS, she is, clearly, very much in charge and the régime is benign, respected and popular. It is also now a long-standing one. 'She is simply wonderful', say parents in unison.

Academic matters: Second to none and, as with all truly top schools, it is achieved through a preparedness to teach beyond the curriculum and celebrate the pleasures of learning for its own sake. NLCS offers the IB in tandem with A levels and IB is now taken by around a third of the year. The IB points score is 'phenomenally high' – an average of 42 points per pupil, something achieved by only three per cent of students worldwide, and three NLCS students in 2010 achieved the maximum 45 points. Top IB school in the UK for last five years. A level results are as good – around 92 per cent of subject grades are A and 99 per cent are A/B. The curriculum has no surprises, though it is good to see a healthy Greek contingent at A level and five modern langs too – French, German, Russian, Spanish and Italian. Mandarin now an option for the sixth. RS is popular, as are biology and chemistry, but maths and English are way ahead of the rest in terms of take-up. GCSE results equally impressive – 96 per cent getting A*/A.

Long-serving, sensible, deputy head is i/c SEN. No current statements and a very few with special needs. Of those, most are mild dyspraxics and some use laptops and have extra time in exams. No withdrawal from classes or in-class support. SEN here mostly means even more gifted and talented than the rest, and the latest inspection report paid tribute to the individual help given to these, as well as to dyspraxics and the use of IEPs where appropriate. School's philosophy was articulated by past head – 'Everyone matters' – and now, in Mrs McCabe's words, 'I try to do everything I can to put them in charge of their own destiny'.

Games, Options, the Arts: The endless playing fields and superb facilities – with which no other London girls' school can compete – inspire sporting enthusiasm and prowess. Options abound – even, now, riding, scuba and golf along with the trad games. Lacrosse especially successful (school has players in national squads) but cross country thrives too. Art practised joyfully by many – as the super paintings and other exhibits round and about demonstrate – witty, fluid in style and imaginative. Music is celebrated and many play to top standards. Good music tech. Very good music hall with gallery – light and inviting. Grand pianos seem to breed here. Numerous ensembles, choirs, tours and concerts and much success in major musical competitions, festivals etc – as you'd expect from girls with this amount of creativity, energy, opportunity and encouragement.

The new Performing Arts Centre (PAC) is a superb facility. Its auditorium seats 350, with a removable floor over an orchestra pit and, helpfully, it is connected by corridor to the music school. Drama, always good here, has now a tremendous buzz – everyone can take part on or backstage and productions are numerous and exciting. Good drama studio in use for smaller productions, exam work, lessons etc. The PAC has a cafe/bar which the girls talk about almost more than anything else – a smart meeting place with coffee and snacks and which is patronised by sixth form and staff – all very cool and chic – 'it's like going out of school with a friend'. The roof terrace, with benches and view over the whole estate, is another great place for coffee and chat and the sixth form love it.

Vast programme of complementary activities. Parents pay tribute to the imaginative and high-calibre opportunities and the girls look almost bewildered by the range on offer – 'You have to prioritise – there's too much to do; you just can't do everything'. Debating especially popular – we enjoyed ads for forthcoming meetings, e.g. 'This house would die young', 'This house would be a boy', 'This house would ban violence in entertainment' etc – many of them pinned onto noticeboards which line the rather stark staircases, reminiscent of a students' union in which everyone has opinions. Charity work a priority, though we aren't sure when they find time to do it and so much of it.

Background and Atmosphere: Venerable and unique. No other school in the history of girls' education in the UK has such significance. It was founded by Frances Mary Buss in 1850 in Camden and set the standard for ambitious, forward looking education for girls on a par with the best of that offered to boys. In 1939 – remarkable foresight or luck? – the school moved to Edgware. It acquired the former estate of the Dukes of Chandos – of Handelian fame – then comprising a splendid, late eighteenth century house, now the school's central building – and 30 acres overlooking formal gardens and down to Canons Park. The original ducal palace – Canons – was demolished in the 1740s after the financial collapse of the first Duke. Perhaps, in his distress, he would have been glad to know what an excellent site for a girls' school his domain would become.

The main building – housing the offices, sixth form accommodation and some teaching – is elegant outside and impressive inside – wood panelling, grand portraits of former heads – some of them the prime movers in girls' education in their day – archival photographs, stucco and cornicing. Later built additions range from functional and boring – e.g. the main teaching block – to inspired and enlightened. This last is especially so of the library – a fine building full of light and cleverly constructed on four storeys. It is also as well-stocked and managed as you'd expect here.

You reach the school either via a walk from the tube across the park or by a meander down Canon's Drive – all large detached houses, much mock Tudor and with more than a whiff of Wisteria Lane. The road goes only to the school or the park so there is a sense of entering a wonderfully secluded world. And secluded, safe and stimulating it is though what is provided here hardly excludes the outside world. There are true partnerships with schools elsewhere – notably in Zambia and in Dagenham – reciprocal visits, educational collaboration, mutually informative and enlightening both ways. And Mrs McCabe's Prince's Teaching Institute also informs the school's ethos and daily life. Outsiders, though, must goggle at the lime tree avenue, the grand aged cedar tree, the sizable reedy pond, formal gardens and sheer glorious green space, overlooked by the very pretty main house.

Food served in huge lunch room is clearly terrifically good – girls don't usually worry about ODing on school food but it's clearly a temptation here: masses of choice and high, high quality. The atmosphere overall is collaborative, enthusiastic and relaxed. Lots of male staff – many of them young – and the average age of staff here is only 32. Old Girls will raise several eyebrows at all this! We can't recall visiting another all-girls school and finding quite this kind of relaxed self-confidence – normal in the best boys' and co-ed schools. 'My fundamental belief,' says head, 'is that anything is possible for the girls – it's about stretching, enrichment, passion.'

Pastoral Care and Discipline: Classes are uniformly orderly, relaxed and full of concentrating faces. Relations between staff and girls are clearly warm, especially so in the sixth form, and girls pay tribute to the time and individual care their teachers give them. A noticeable cachet to sixth form life here – the girls move into the upper rooms of the charming old main house, they don't wear uniform and they chat on easy terms with staff. They are also given responsibilities for younger girls, often running clubs for them – this fosters a healthy bonding between the years and probably contributes to the tiny number of leavers post-GCSE. Strong tutor system throughout. No drugs or other major problems within last five years: 'They're very sensible,' says head. Lots of collaboration with boys' schools – Harrow, Merchant Taylor's, Habs Boys, Winchester and Whitgift – socially and in extra-curricular activities. Occasional bullying dealt with firmly and parents are 'pleased with the approach'. 'The girls know where they stand,' says Mrs McCabe.

Pupils and Parents: Multi-ethnic, multi-faith, multi-brains. We spoke to no two pupils from the same ethnic or geographic origins. In common is a desire to learn and share the fun of doing it here – along with a fair bit of cash, though bursaries help (see below). Notable Old Girls' list is uniquely long and impressive – see Wikipedia – but, for starters: Barbara Amiel, Alice Beer, Eleanor Bron, Tanya Byron, Gillian Cross, Fenella Fielding, Margaret Fingerhut, Helen Gardner, Stella Gibbons, Susie Orbach (expelled), Myfanwy Piper, Stevie Smith, Marie Stopes, Judith Weir, Rachel Weisz and Anna Wintour, along with a great many useful types – doctors, civil servants, scientists, artists and academics.

Entrance: At 11+ by exam in maths and English and interview. 44 come up from the junior school and school has a further 60 places for the 550 who apply. Don't despair – someone has to get them. Junior school children are not in competition for their places – they take the exam like everyone else and, if there is a chance of them not thriving in the senior school, they will have been warned and helped well in advance. At 16+ by exam in their A level subjects and by interview. Around 80 applicants for 25 places.

Exit: Most go through to the sixth form and Mrs McCabe stresses, 'No-one is ever prevented from going into the sixth form. Once the girls are here we never write anyone off'. Later, Oxbridge is the norm – along with London, Bristol, LSE and the best of the rest, including quite a few at Ivy Leagues, notably Harvard. They do solid subjects – lots of medics – at the top places and, unsurprisingly, do well.

Money Matters: Lowish, we feel, for what is offered here and a generous number of valuable bursaries available. Means-tested but offering between 10 and 100 per cent of fees. Scholarships up to 50 per cent and can be held along with a bursary. Music schols too.

Remarks: Possibly the best advertisement for girls-only education in the country.

The North London International School

Linked to North London International School Kindergarten (The) in the Junior section

Linked to North London International School Lower School (The) in the Junior section

Main Office, 6 Friern Barnet Lane, London, N11 3LX

• Pupils: 395 boys and girls • Ages: 2-6 kindergarten and junior (4-6); 6-11 junior; 11-16 senior; 16-19 IB Diploma Centre • Size of sixth form: 30 • Non-denom • Fees: Upper School £13,320-£15,480 pa • Independent

Tel: 020 8920 0600
Fax: 020 8211 4605
Email: admissions@nlis.org
Website: www.nlis.org

Head of School: Since 2005, Mr David Rose (fifties) CertEd BA MAEd LPSH. Married with two grown-up daughters. Softly spoken, clean shaven, well dressed, relaxed, very approachable and much travelled. The majority of his teaching experience has been overseas, including headships in Cyprus, Germany and Houston. Extremely enthusiastic about the school, which he took over as, apparently, the fourth head in four years. Immediately set out to remove disruptive elements from the upper school, modify the school buildings and facilities and move the whole school into true international status. Really enjoys working in the two to 18 through-school situation.

Academic matters: Runs the IB programme at all levels. Average class size in upper school not normally more than 15. Although they would rather a child moved up through the school, they will prepare children for Common Entrance etc if required. Years 7–11 follow the MYP. Years 12 and 13 follow the IB programme according to ability, some pupils opting to follow individual courses which produce certificates (acceptable for university entrance) rather than following the full diploma programme.

Languages are well catered for, French is introduced in the nursery section, Spanish in Year 7 and Italian is an option at Diploma stage. Computers all over the place. Interactive whiteboards in every classroom with linked Macs. Wireless technology enabling laptop use anywhere. No RE, though they say this is covered in global studies and most religious festivals are celebrated, which was evident in photos round the school. Homework regarded as important and students are expected to fill in their diaries and keep to deadlines; can be done in school out of hours.

Computer database covers every pupil, profiling, recording progress, enabling and tracking accurate parental contact. Parents also receive a chatty newsletter from the head at the end of each week, not only containing news but also updates on extra-curricular activities available both to their children and themselves. Excellent website.

Most learning difficulties, or learning differences, as they prefer to call them, catered for; good specialist teachers. Would accept a statemented child but not one with disruptive behavioural difficulties. The QUEST Programme (fees as above) aims to 'teach children with different learning styles to function successfully and independently in an academically challenging mainstream setting'. Sessions are mainly one to one but some class based time if relevant.

English as an additional language (EAL) regarded as essential for children with two non-English speaking parents – two to five lessons a week, one to one or in a small group depending on needs. Native language sessions also provided; special teacher brought in if necessary – Greek, Japanese etc. Would be reluctant to take a non-English speaker after Year 8. Language Heritage Day once a year when everyone speaks their own language. Not only over 35 different nationalities represented by the pupils but also 15 amongst the full-time teachers.

Games, Options, the Arts: Games obligatory once a week per year group – sports field five minutes away by minibus, and has use of Trent Park sports hall. Tournaments not only with local schools and nationally but also overseas – recently cricket in Barbados and football and netball in Antigua. Lots of clubs from chess to martial arts – kendo very popular at the moment – to cater for compulsory activity sessions. Emphasis put on 'healthy exercise' – shirkers beware!

Good music – about 25 per cent learn an individual instrument, orchestra, chamber group and lots of different bands. Very excited about setting up a link with the Barnet Symphony Orchestra; loads of different instruments in the music room, classical and modern – no excuses not to try. Several soundproofed rooms for individual tuition.

Lots of outings to concerts, theatres and galleries as well as trips home and abroad. The Model United Nations Conference of course features and an annual exchange with the Dwight School in New York, but perhaps the most exciting thing the older children have done is help build a village in Cambodia: not only did they organise events to raise funds but some of them also went out to lend a hand.

Background and Atmosphere: School originally founded in 1972 by Dr Stephen Spahn, director of the Dwight School in New York, and Sir Maurice Bowra, Warden of Wadham College, Oxford. Is now fully owned by the Spahn family.

On four sites in two locations. The upper school (nearest tube Arnos Grove) consists of Dwight and Jubilee Hall, both of which are purpose built. Dwight was, once upon a time, Friern Barnet Grammar School, and a few traces of this still remain in scruffy corners and inter-connecting classrooms. Five minutes' walk away, Jubilee Hall is a bright, modern building originally created solely as the IB Centre, but recent modifications now enable both buildings to be run in sync. Classes are timetabled to minimise movement between the sites, which has improved the general timekeeping and removed excuses for tardiness. All children below year 10 are escorted between sites. Good playground outside Dwight and lovely common room for the Diploma students in Jubilee Hall.

Apart from the laboratories and studios, all classrooms non-specific and spacious. When we were there, the library was being used for an English class discussion concerning the amount of television watched – soaps, of course, but not too much, as far as we could gather. Other pupils working quietly at computers in a different area only looked slightly distracted. Enthusiastic teachers and pupils wherever we went, all happy to explain what they were doing. Although a lot of the classrooms seem to be at sub pavement level, no lack of light.

The dining area has been completely modernised since our last visit – now with a coffee shop style cash cafeteria. Food all brought from the kitchens in the lower school ten minutes' drive away. A huge plasma screen on one wall broadcasts the news or other teacher selected items. Year 10 upwards are allowed to make use of the local cafés if they prefer to, with parental permission, of course.

Fantastic art studio overseen by a huge golden eye. All sorts of different creations, paintings, sculptures, models – lots of inspiration from an enthusiastic teacher. Both disciplines of sight and sound expanded in a galleried computer studio overlooking art and music rooms, where Macs are used for creating music, animation and design.

The whole school seems to buzz with exciting projects – children in the physics lab enjoying experimenting; lovely creations in the DT studio, including great clocks made by the younger students; a drama studio in a dark and mysterious room entirely surrounded by black curtains: 'Double, double, toil and trouble'.

Pastoral Care and Discipline: Strict conduct code – IB philosophy of intercultural awareness and respect for the individual thoroughly in place. Very few rules otherwise needed. Mobile phones allowed (upper school only) but have to be left in the school office. A system in place should problems occur, and a counsellor who is apparently popular and fully occupied. Communication links between teacher and parent encouraged and always available.

As each new entrant is individually assessed, transition is normally easy. A child will be placed in the class relevant to stage of learning, even if this occasionally means (temporarily) out of year (for example when arriving from a different hemisphere country). With such a mixture of nationalities and backgrounds and the ethos of respect for all, settling in is not usually a problem.

Pupils and Parents: About two-thirds local north London and just beyond. The rest expats working in industry, embassies or high commissions and the occasional university lecturer. No-one normally more than 30 minutes away. School bus service provided at extra cost. Most families have an international background, usually one English speaking parent. Nationalities include Japanese, American, Chinese, Australian, Swedish, Indian and Greek. Parental involvement encouraged, whatever their experience and talents can provide. Large range of presentation and social events arranged each year.

Entrance: Mainly in September but can also join at other times of the year if required. Interview and report from previous school only real requisites. Many come up from the lower school but others from other local schools or overseas.

Exit: Mainly to university, a lot London based but some overseas. A careers guidance service and they all take the Morrisby test. The link with The Dwight School is extremely useful for those wishing to attend American universities – the head also has an extensive knowledge of US schools. Business and languages are probably the most popular subjects, but science is also an option and they are beginning to make greater inroads into the arts. Last year all IB Diploma students got into their first choice of university.

Money Matters: A variety of scholarships for talented students: academic, music, sports and citizenship. Bursaries for needy students, £500 to £1000 a term, but they will keep a child at 100 per cent if a crisis arises. At the moment two boys from West Ham football academy on sports scholarships and at least one talented musician – flexibility seems to be the name of the game; finances ultimately dependent on the owners' wishes.

Remarks: Ambition to be the number one international school in London. Good management structure and an enthusiastic team of teachers operating the IB programme with imagination and zest. Students enthusiastic, controlled and happy.

Northease Manor School

Rodmell, Lewes, East Sussex, BN7 3EY

• Pupils: 85 pupils, 15 girls, 40 weekly boarders (5 girls), rest day • Ages: 10 to 17 • Inter-denom • Fees: Day £19,416; Boarding £26,550 pa • Independent

Tel: 01273 472 915
Fax: 01273 472 202
Email: pa2headteacher@northease.co.uk
Website: www.northease.co.uk

Headteacher: Since 2008, Mrs Carmen Harvey-Browne BA (mid-fifties) (English lang and lit) PGCE (English and special needs) NPQH. Married to Graham, a chartered quantity surveyor by profession, but also involved with Cabrini Children's Society. They have three grown-up children and used to foster children ranging in ages from five to 16.

Has been in teaching for nearly 30 years and taught all key stages, from little ones to FE. SEN children always gravitated to her – her youngest child had no SEN but never fitted the typical school mould, so she had personal insights – but she resisted being pigeonholed, exploring adult education and teacher training, with teaching English being a constant throughout. 'The longer you are in education, the more you realise there are 3,000 different ways to skin a cat!' Came from a six-year stint as deputy head of More House in Farnham.

New deputy head came from the National Autistic Society and this means parents' and governors' concerns about too big a ratio of autism are unfortunately inflamed – traditionally Northease is a school for dyslexics, but nowadays it caters for a lot more besides. Head is aware of challenge, relishes it ('As soon as I walked in the door of Northease I felt there was a lot I could do') – after a year assessing the situation, a new website, logo and brochure. Appears both pragmatic and bold, yet will revise new initiatives if shown evidence to the contrary.

Academic matters: Average of eight in each class (41 teaching and support staff) means that each pupil gets plenty of adult attention even during their free time. Small groups allow expansion – especially useful in Year 9 and 10, where children may come from a miserable phase in secondary school and have the opportunity to start year 10 again. Core curriculum is taught at the same time in each year group, so cross-year teaching accommodates pupils' differing strengths – gives them an opportunity to shine. Lessons are chunked into small components and laptops are used, as well as the extensive ICT suites. Touch-typing lessons are begun for the little ones in the first term and skill is developed as they grow older. To give pupils full access to the national curriculum a six session day, beginning with assembly at 8.45am and ending at 4pm. After school activities and supervised evening homework sessions for boarders and day pupils who wish to stay.

Everyone has an individual education plan, boarders have a care plan and all of this feeds into Northease's holistic approach, which produces remarkable results at GCSE. Many staff come from mainstream education and welcome the opportunity to pursue their interest in SEN at Northease – most, especially the English teachers, go on to get further SEN qualifications. At present, eight literacy teachers have specialist dyslexia teaching qualifications and the focus on literacy skills has obviously paid dividends – 77 per cent of all Year 11 students achieved a reading age of over ten years. Even in their final year, pupils make significant gains in their reading comprehension (27 to 51 months' gain in ten months). 100 per cent of Year 11 achieved a maths age of over 13 years, 69 per cent of over 14, and 44 per cent of Year 11 had recorded a maths age of over 15 years 5 months by the end of year 10. Year 11 demonstrated accelerated learning by achieving well above the nationally expected half a level per year in maths, science, history, geography and technology.

The teaching, particularly maths, benefits from communication with other schools and visiting international academics. The literacy products of these pupils are astounding – two novels, one illustrated ('The Dyspraxic Ghost'!) and many other storybooks. The technology teaching is especially impressively documented and computers are used not just for CAD but also to help develop pupils' literacy through the spelling of titles etc. Specialist speech and language and occupational therapists (spinning on a trolley attached to a bungy cord is particularly popular) as well as counsellors on staff.

Pupils can remain until 17 if they need to retake a year and, although the academic focus is impressive, Northease's main aim is to provide security and support its students as independent learners, through personal and social development (and marking done in green ink).

Games, Options, the Arts: An outdoor swimming pool, a paved area for wet play, trips to riding stables and a huge field for athletics and football. However, as one pupil commented, no other football pitch like Northease's – you have to score uphill no matter which end you play at! Fixtures with mainstream schools, and Northease created and hosted the Dyslexic Schools Football Festival for three years, before handing the mantle on to More House School.

Strong connections with the local Rotary Club and a seniors' project on the homeless with Lorica St Patrick's in Brighton offer the children perspective. Residential trips to centres such as Hindleap Warren offer more opportunities for learning and socialising.

Art (some amazing creative work involving deer bones illustrates the extra mile staff will go to develop a pupil's interest and talent) and technology are flagship departments – art block divided into a room dedicated to fine art and one to ceramics (two wheels, a kiln); projects can also be carried out using metal in the technology rooms. Drama (keen to develop to enable whole school productions) and PE also popular, newly introduced music and media up to GCSE.

Recent shuffling of timetable to allow solid block of time for seniors' practical activities for key stage four or GCSE school trips etc on Fridays. A whole school initiative twice a term – Olympics day or Young Enterprise, to make things to sell at Christmas carol concert: the students get a lot out of working together across year groups.

Background and Atmosphere: Began life as a privately owned independent school in 1963, which attracted boarders who did not make the grades necessary for more prestigious schools. Roger Dennien turned this into a USP during his 30 year stint as head and it took on charitable trust status in the 1970s. The Grade II listed buildings are in the countryside, just outside Lewes and 12 miles from Brighton. Supervised train travel is provided from London Victoria to Lewes and vice versa, shared taxis and parents bring day pupils onsite. A thatched Tudor Hall houses the dining room (with a pub sign in it advertising 'The Pen and Ink' and some padded beams to protect the heads of the tallest boys) and an auditorium with tiered seating for assemblies and meetings.

The site is stunning; the youngest buildings, where the middle school learns, are pre-fab, otherwise everything is sympathetic to the green backdrop of the Downs. Both formal and wild gardens (out of bounds to pupils without adult supervision) as well as acres of grass, on which the kids lounge and play. A big indoor play area offers pool, air hockey, table tennis and healthy tuck. The school is small, so a real family atmosphere and affection between pupils and staff.

The two boarding houses are sections of the main school and day pupils can negotiate stays when they have late activities. A graded system of independence begins when they enter school, encouraging self-sufficiency as they move up it. Art work and photographs of activities are displayed on most walls, celebrating everyone's achievements. The pupils are cheery, engaging and curious – a lesson about drugs contained real and valuable debate. The uniform is tidy but not restrictive, and teachers are never called by their first names.

Pastoral Care and Discipline: The high ratio of staff to pupils means that issues are picked up rapidly. A sensible home school agreement is part of the registration process and any inappropriate behaviour means being withdrawn from lessons to allow others to work. A personal tutor for each pupil, a houseparent and the head of pastoral care form the basis of the pastoral system. Pupils are taught to laugh with and not at others, and everyone is aware that a lot to be learnt from wrong answers – this is especially important when pupils are improving their meta cognition, whether they be an 'inchworm' or a 'grasshopper' (Dr Steve Chinn's terms).

Authorised absence stands at 11 per cent and no recorded unauthorised. Suspension and expulsion are reserved for serious misdemeanours. The phone numbers of two independent persons are available to all pupils and these two visit the school regularly, sometimes taking an assembly, sometimes having lunch.

Pupils and Parents: Pupils come from varied backgrounds all over the country (these range from wealthy farming families to a child in care). The common factors on their arrival are their previous failure, sometimes avoidance strategies, often difficulties with expressive language and their experience of education as a means of being embarrassed and laughed at. They are used to being asked to try harder when often they are already trying harder than anyone else. They have often been picked on, which means they are more likely to try bullying themselves – this is a well-worn issue that is dealt with effectively by teachers and house parents.

Some parents are also dyslexic but did not have the benefit of a specialist education. Quite often they run their own businesses in a determined manner that they were forced to develop to succeed in a society that did not recognise specific learning difficulties. The style of the pupils' reports takes parents' dyslexia into consideration – not wordy, lots of visuals, plenty of face-to-face meetings; every pupil has an annual review even if they don't have a statement. A parents' association, Friends of Northease Manor School, has been recently developed and the school provides regular workshops on topics such as occupational therapy, IEPs and behaviour management.

Entrance: Approximately 50 per cent from state and 50 per cent from independent sector, 66 per cent funded by LEAs and 33 per cent private. Approximately 60 pupils on waiting list for funding. Most come via word of mouth or CreSTeD. LEAs rarely refer pupils and often they are unsuitable, since Northease is not equipped to deal with severe emotional and behavioural difficulties. Entrance by interview and assessment – sometimes this involves a whole day or even part of a week spent here.

Exit: More than 90 per cent go on to mainstream education: sixth from college, FE college, combination of AS levels and retakes. Some of them go on to university, notably one boy who was at a local maintained school and almost stopped attending, while at Northease got an A* in art when stuck at a reading age of eight, fought to be accepted on the higher course at Eastbourne College and became their star pupil, before going on to Loughborough University. Another gained funding after his mother wrote weekly letters to the LEA and is now a structural engineer with an MA and has competed for Great Britain in judo. Leavers return to talk to 16 year olds very effectively, emphasising to students that skills learnt at Northease will stand them in good stead (recording lectures, purchasing reference books since library loan periods are too short) but that you have to want success really badly to get it.

Money Matters: Bursaries for 20 per cent of fees available; main criterion is that parents have done all they can to secure other funding. Used extensively and invariably makes the difference between a child attending or not – at present nine out of 87 pupils have bursaries.

Remarks: Parents constantly say that they feel they have their child back after a year at Northease. This is a direct result of their regaining their self-esteem and self-confidence, both of which take a huge battering in children with dyslexia, dyspraxia, dyscalculia, pragmatic and semantic language difficulties and social and communication difficulties and who are in the mainstream education system. The school provides a wonderfully safe and supportive environment and achieves its aim: to turn failure into success and produce independent citizens. This is one of the first schools to be DfES approved, so that if the LEA is planning to send a child here, you don't need to ring the Secretary of State to get permission.

The new head reinforces the belief that although children like routine and a strong structure, they have to be taught to deal with change and be given life skills to equip them when they leave the school. Children's needs have become more complex over recent years and the intake has to be balanced so that all the pupils can thrive. Future plans include better use of current facilities and the next big project is to replace the temporary middle school. An innovative school which is not afraid to try new ideas and shares its expertise.

Northwood College

Linked to Northwood College Junior School in the Junior section

Maxwell Road, Northwood, Middlesex, HA6 2YE

• Pupils: 780 girls; all day • Ages: 3-18 • Size of sixth form: 100
• Non-denom • Fees: Seniors £12,600 pa • Independent

Tel: 01923 825 446
Fax: 01923 836 526
Email: admissions@northwoodcollege.co.uk
Website: www.northwoodcollege.co.uk

Head: Since January 2009, Miss Jacqualyn Pain MA MA MBA PGCE NPQH (fiftyish), a theology and philosophy graduate and a most experienced head. Two previous headships, both impressive – Henrietta Barnet 2000–2005, St Albans High 2005–2008 – prior to which she'd been deputy head at Northwood. She'd had no intention of leaving St Albans until Mrs Ruth Mercer, her predecessor at Northwood College, was appointed to the headship of Godolphin and Latymer (qv). Miss Pain, who believed 'so strongly in the ethos of the school – that it does so well by every kind of girl' – couldn't resist coming back and is a round peg in a spherical hole, if ever we saw one. 'The school has changed, of course,' she admits cheerfully, 'because schools must move on, but the underlying principles are the same and I passionately believe in them.' Highly competent, understated, relaxed, elegant and popular, she is quietly but enthusiastically building on the energetic modernisation initiated by Mrs Mercer. She likes cats and chocolate. Northwood College, too long the unsung school in this well provided for part of the world, is lucky to have her back.

Academic matters: Takes a spread of ability – but well above the national average. Value-added very strong here so you should achieve your potential, whatever it is, and not feel pressured while you do it. Your 10 A*s pupil happily coexists with your artsy, mathematical struggler and both feel good about themselves. This is very much the Northwood ethos and the one Miss Pain was keen to come back to and strengthen. At GCSE, all take 2 Englishes, maths, a language, three sciences; options include art, classical civilisation, drama, Latin and Greek, home economics, RE and textiles. RE is the star subject – taken by most with exemplary results; maths (IGCSE) and English pretty good too. 2009 results saw 89 per cent of subjects taken achieve A*/B. At A level, maths, economics and RE impress. Maths, the sciences and psychology are popular. Tiny numbers for history and English (though good results), reflecting the science orientation and aspirations of the school's current core constituency. The same is true for languages, but scope for new HoD from Sept 2010 (a French and Mandarin specialist) to boost numbers and broaden curriculum. Much to be done here, especially in increasing the uptake at A level of a broader range of subjects – parents as well as girls will need to be convinced – and the school, in fact, offers an admirable range.

Most mild SENs managed in lessons with occasional extra temporary support and withdrawals. Can cope with mild ADHD and Asperger's along with dyses. Older parts of site not really set up to accommodate serious motor difficulties, though will adapt where possible.

School is pioneering 'thinking skills' and they approach this seriously from nursery to sixth form via 'cognitive development programme' plus f/t director to coordinate it. We were seriously impressed – junior school pupils feel empowered and the results are tangible. School held a recent 'Dragons' Den' event – with high profile 'dragons' – and even juniors' projects were taken seriously – to the extent of possible commissions from the commercial world outside. Clever stuff, integral to the overall ethos of the place and a real selling point.

Games, Options, the Arts: It's got the lot – in miniature, in some cases. Yer actual sports hall, of course, plus 25m pool – and everyone swims all year. Pitches and courts abut the main campus and most girls are keen. Some parental feeling that more effort is needed and girls should be pushed harder. Brand new performing arts centre, cleverly shoehorned in, and now providing good drama studio, range of music teaching/practice rooms and much-used recital room. No room here for grand theatre or concert hall, but assembly hall does as well and, though hardly glitzy, has all a good school needs. Art is enthusiastic – painting, modelling, textiles, principally. Music likewise, enthusiastic – 50 strong orchestra, jazz bands and lots of fun had in staging productions – more *Oliver!* than *Othello.* A 49 page booklet details all the extra-curricular activities from the physical (trampolining, badminton etc) to the cerebral (Think club, puzzle club, chess) to the fun (book club, bridge, life drawing etc etc) – good stuff. 'Fabulous' trips –'We went to Brazil for a month on World Challenge' – and closer to home, e.g. Regent's Park theatre, and good in-school events, e.g. African drumming evening.

Background and Atmosphere: Founded in 1878 in Endsleigh Gardens, Bloomsbury, with around 25 boarders and a few day girls. Headmistress, Miss Buchan-Smith, who had modern ideas about the importance of the extra-curricular as well as the curricular, and was concerned about the unsavoury influence of the Euston area on her girls, moved the school to Northwood in 1893. Interestingly, this area – now leafy, prosperous and safe as £1m+ houses can be – was, in 1871, described as 'a destitute district near Moor Park'. But the coming of the tube, a few years later, changed all that and made Northwood a jolly useful commutable suburb, which it remains. In 1893, the present, late arts 'n' crafts redbrick with leaded lights building was opened for 20 boarders and two day girls; the next door Briary accommodated little boys. Boys long since gone, but touching tribute paid to their presence – especially to those who went on to fight and fall in the two wars: school still lays an annual wreath at Ypres.

More land has been acquired, more buildings built and the school is now a nest of attractive, disparate edifices, centred on a couple of tennis courts which make a kind of quad. To the side of the school are the pitches and playing fields – the overall feeling is one of a slightly crowded campus made up of pleasant, purpose-built or acquired blocks forming a cosy community. Despite the somewhat cramped feeling, it is a surprise, in a quiet residential street, to find it there at all. The latest additions – the Early Years centre and the performing arts block – are notable assets, in terms both of their additional provision and imaginative design – which cannot, here as elsewhere, be said for the few, lesser, 1960s architectural indiscretions.

Cosy, civilised library in old, converted, vaulted gym. Excellent string of sixth form studies – each shared by five/six girls – for private work in free periods (boarding ended in 1990). Exemplary displays everywhere. Good dining room, cafeteria system, food exceptional – home-made soups and yoghurts, lots of fresh everything; everyone above nursery eats school lunch, which is included in the fee. From 2006, a formal partnership with the nearby John Lyon Boys' School (qv) enabled collaboration on curricular and extra-curricular matters, to the considerable benefit of both communities – a sensible and enlightened move begun by Mrs Mercer and Kevin Riley, former head of John Lyon, and continued by its new head, Katherine Haynes.

Junior school in three buildings on site. The Early Years centre (2009), home to 80 nursery and reception children, is a super building, sensitively conceived and completed. Sensory garden, excellent playground, and lots of lovely touches and thoughtful additions – wellies for rainy days, masses of well-integrated IT, colourful toys, space, cookery, a beautiful library. We loved the collage on the life cycle of a hen and the display about the Philosophy Bear who 'likes to look at things carefully and ask questions'. Years 1 and 2 in Vincent House, 3 and 4 in junior school – both attractive, small scale houses. All safe, well-maintained, full of impeccable and attractive displays. Parents are thrilled – 'My daughter was so shy – they've really brought her out ... They're so caring and nurturing'; 'They take the child and encourage her to be the best she can, but according to their own character – they don't have to fit a mould'.

Pastoral Care and Discipline: Year heads and form tutors handle most pastoral matters. Tutor changes annually. Discipline seldom a problem here – one minor recent drugs incident. Girls feel involved in decisions – 'Miss Pain really wants to hear from us – our ideas about what can be improved,' we heard. 'The girls do as well as they do here because of the way we nurture them,' says Miss Pain, and parents concur. Overall sense of a relaxed, orderly community in which little disturbs and everything encourages.

Pupils and Parents: As you'd expect in this cosmopolitan, well-heeled suburb: majority are British Asians – mostly Hindus – and Christians and sprinklings of everyone else. Little need for EAL. Contingent from local NATO base makes for movement in and out and enriches the mix. Five extensive coach routes bring in girls from Ealing, Edgware, Kenton, Gerrards Cross and Radlett. Proximity to the Metropolitan line makes tubing it easy. Sense of community, and devoted parents from all backgrounds pitching in to support. Former notable pupils include Dame Margaret Booth – a judge – and actress Sue Holderness.

Entrance: At 3+ into the nursery via observation and little tasks, ditto at 4+ into reception. 48 places at this stage. At 7, via maths, English, reasoning and interview – up to ten new places at this stage. At 11, via the exams set by the North London Consortium, to which the school belongs, plus online test and group interview – 30 places. One out of three girls who apply usually gain a place, many off the waiting list. At 16, conditional on GCSE results, plus online test and interview – 20 places. Occasional places do occur in other years – particularly on account of NATO personnel coming and going – so always worth a call. 'We're looking for girls who will fit into the school,' says Miss Pain. 'We're academically selective but not narrowly exclusive – we want people who will benefit from an all-round, holistic education.'

Exit: Lots of gap years. Then majority to a range of Russell Group and newer universities; an extraordinary number of pharmacists and a good number of dentists; otherwise anything from art to retail, English to – well, pharmacy.

Money Matters: A few means-tested bursaries – up to full fees. Also scholarships for academics, art, music and sport.

Remarks: The parents have it: 'My daughter has been given opportunities and she's flourishing'; 'Northwood has given my daughters so many opportunities'; 'It was the best decision we ever made'.

Norwich High School for Girls

Linked to Norwich High School For Girls Junior Department in the Junior section

Eaton Grove, 95 Newmarket Road, Norwich, Norfolk, NR2 2HU

• Pupils: 625 girls, all day • Ages: 11-18 • Size of sixth form: 150
• Non-denom • Fees: £9,579 pa + lunch • Independent

Tel: 01603 453 265
Fax: 01603 259 891
Email: admissions@nor.gdst.net
Website: www.norwichhigh.gdst.net

Headmaster: Since September 2010, Mr Jason Murrow, previously deputy head of curriculum at North London Collegiate – seemingly going down a storm with parents, girls and staff.

Academic matters: 'Concentrated education', according to a parent, and nothing seen as a boys' subject, although some regret that food technology is available only in the junior school. A place where it's clearly 'cool to get an A' – 68 per cent A/A* and 89 per cent A*–B at GCSE. Four main IT suites. Outstanding ICT results (exam taken two years early in Year 9), strong showing in the three sciences and maths – all take IGCSE as 'it's a better preparation for A level'. Bias towards the heavyweights, but a good choice of A levels and willingness to run subjects with only one or two candidates. True to form, results shine, with 83 per cent A/B. Settled staff with two thirds over 40, many in place for at least a dozen years.

Garden variety support for those who are found to have learning difficulties – withdrawal from lessons for 'quality time' with the designated learning support teacher.

Games, Options, the Arts: Competitive and encouraging approach to sport – 'sport catch-up' for those who miss more than two sessions. Pitches and tennis courts just a hop away from classrooms. Good lacrosse (seen as a useful ticket when girls get to university, so still on board, despite teams having to travel miles for suitable competition), hockey, netball, tennis. Rowing on the Wensum and synchronized swimming in the enticing 25 metre pool.

Strong music department – 'It's an international language,' enthuses the head – where all are expected to join in. School's choirs, under inspirational head of department, are especially successful – regularly winning national competitions etc. Barnardo's Choir of the Year 2010 resulted in concerts in all the major London venues. The experience of making music together is a must and younger ones have to take part in class bands. A third of the school has individual music lessons. Usual selection of bands/ orchestras plus occasional performances in the magnificent cathedral under inspirational staff. Voluminous drama hall for budding thespians, useful careers department in lofty garret and visiting speakers to inspire the older girls.

D of E is popular – 'Kids learn stickability, which is valued in this school'; proportionally the highest takeup in an East Anglian school: 104 awards achieved in 2009, including 32 golds – a school record.

Background and Atmosphere: Founded in 1875 (the first GDST outside London). Ordered collection of understated, solid buildings to the rear of an attractive, bow-fronted Regency house. Generous sports hall, studious library, labs and double height art room contrast with tightish classrooms. Pleasantly comfortable sixth form commonroom where the newly installed dishwasher is a welcome addition. As for litter, it doesn't exist.

Navy and green tartan kilts for the lower seniors. Upper seniors love the change to straight skirts, 'even though it's more difficult to race up the stairs'. Supposedly managerial dress code for the sixth, who are happy not to have to wear the 'delicious' uniform, comes in a relaxed form. Food has improved – 'It wasn't nice before' – and lower seniors have to have school lunch. Canteen open from 7.45am for breakfast and from 3.50–5.15pm, so late stayers can get a snack tea.

Pastoral Care and Discipline: Firm but fair parameters and, according to a sixth former, 'Anyone who goes astray is usually licked into shape and encouraged to make the most of what's on offer'. Morality is high on the agenda and the head talks of 'global citizens who fit into a big jigsaw'. Teachers are always willing to help at lunchtime and can be emailed through the Minerva network, which also puts GDST pupils past and present in touch with each other.

Distinctly competitive edge to the various companies (houses) where year groups mingle and offer support. Daily tutor groups and mentoring across the years. The Moot (with representatives from Years 7–11) is listened to, as long as it comes up with suggestions rather than moans – replacement of baggy gym knickers with svelte cycling shorts is seen as quite a coup.

Pupils and Parents: Hard-working, well adjusted girls who want to go places. Predominantly middle class with many parents connected with nearby University of East Anglia, lots of second and third generation girls. Very few from ethnic minorities, but four times more than Norfolk demographics. Wide catchment, but most from a 15 mile radius. Daily shuttle bus from the station (limited places) and range of coach transport organised by parents. School can usually organise buddies to look after new pupils. Notable OGs include authors Pat Barr, Anne Weale, Stella Tillyard, Raffaella Barker and Jane Hissey; sopranos Jane Manning and Elizabeth Watts; dress designer Ann Tyrell and composer Diana Burrell.

Entrance: Exam at 11 – one and a half applicants per place. Most from the junior school (they make up half the intake) carry on into the senior school – plenty of warning if they're not going to make it. (Word on the street – if a girl's on the reserve list, the going could be tough.) Entrants for the sixth need at least seven Bs at GCSE.

Exit: Nearly all to university – loads of help with UCAS. Enormous spread of locations with academic courses predominating. Quite a few join co-ed sixth forms or go elsewhere to be closer to home.

Money Matters: Approximately 15 means-tested bursaries and a few academic or music scholarships at head's discretion.

Remarks: Happy, ordered school where the desire to do one's best is de rigueur. Bright, pleasantly confident girls. New head set to harness the place's talent and make it soar.

Norwich School

Linked to Norwich School Lower School in the Junior section

70 The Close, Norwich, Norfolk, NR1 4DD

• Pupils: 820 boys and girls; co-ed since 2008; girls in all years by 2010 • Ages: 11-18 • Size of sixth form: 280 pupils • Christian • Fees: £11,595 pa • Independent

Tel: 01603 728 449
Fax: 01603 728 491
Email: vagaskin@norwich-school.org.uk
Website: www.norwich-school.org.uk

Headmaster: Since 2002, Mr Jim Hawkins MA (mid forties). Lives with his wife, an artist, and their young child in the cathedral close. Read maths at Brasenose. Taught at Radley College before becoming head of maths at Forest School, then deputy head at Chigwell School. Upright and courteous, dreams that one day the school will be 'means blind'. Really comes alive when talking about scholarship and, though the school doesn't have any direct competition, he isn't complacent. He's ambitious – 'We need to think how we can be even better' – and has recently appointed a second deputy who will monitor the quality of teaching and learning. With a 'burgeoning interest in fine art', he also enjoys rowing (coaches some of the boys) and music (turns up to concerts large or small and is a member of the Norwich school choral society).

Academic matters: Plenty of lively and rigorous teaching across the board – 'superb teachers,' commented one parent. Children are encouraged to (and do) take an active part in lessons – 'In English we learnt without realising it'. A healthy rapport between staff and pupils: 'They're good at knowing what's needed – they're so willing to help,' said a sixth former. The head wants to see pupils stretched 'above and beyond A grade boundaries' and results have steadily risen to the 72 per cent A*/A at GCSE. Relatively limited range of trad subjects on offer – including dual award IGCSE science and IGCSE maths – increases to 25 at AS. Critical thinking is compulsory – 'Carries clout with the unis,' said a sixth former. Most subjects do well at A level (89 per cent A/B). History is particularly popular – director of studies 'is fantastic and writes loads of books on the civil war'.

Help with university applications is given by heads of departments, but some gripes that the sixth form is becoming increasingly geared towards Oxbridge – an Oxbridge co-ordinator and concentrated preparation for candidates; also sense that they get more than their fair share of praise. Head's response that, 'We do talk about successes and every success is valued,' is tempered by an acknowledgement that PR, on higher education offers, could be re assessed.

If bright, those with special educational needs aren't barred. Dyslexia screening for all entering Years 7 and 8, extra time in exams and help given after school, either by subject teachers or external specialists (costs are means related) – all overseen by the SENco.

Games, Options, the Arts: Parents feel a good breadth of music, activities and clubs – 'The school expects the kids to be proactive – they're not spoon fed'. Over 60 per cent involved in music making of one sort or another – instrumental, choral, 'wonderful jazz band'. The department uses a motley assortment of spaces from slightly tired, cramped rooms to high ceilinged halls, but overall the atmosphere is homely and welcoming – friendly, helpful staff and bunches of flowers on window sills. Art work is strong – personal and well informed. Check out the small sixth form printing room and purpose built DT studio where some interesting glass and metal pieces.

Two afternoons a week for games – the usual majors and a good selection of minors for both sexes. Rugby fares well and following representations to the head, girls' hockey is being taken far more seriously – 'We're really pleased that pre season training has been introduced,' said one sixth former.

Debates are well attended and take place in a small lecture theatre twice a week. A recent motion, 'This house will not apply for Oxbridge', was roundly beaten by a floor vote.

Background and Atmosphere: The Close – a traffic free area with open spaces, winding paths and a collection of architectural gems – is home to the school, which nestles around the base of the cathedral. Easy to forget that the city centre is a stone's throw away. Classrooms come in all shapes and sizes – some in old houses, others in purpose built Victorian or 20th century structures. Morning assemblies in the cathedral – an uplifting place to be – whilst small services and organ lessons in the chapel where Nelson was taught. The head readily admits that some facilities are due for a make over, especially the '70s dining block, which works hard to look temporary, and the rather dusty library. Tucked away in locked cabinets is an interesting collection of books on local history given to the school by Augustus Jessop – sixth formers doing related specialist studies are allowed access and can browse through sixteenth century first editions.

Two common rooms for the sixth. The larger, which has a noisy bistro atmosphere, is a recently refurbished vaulted and pillared space – new sofas, tables, TV and trendy lighting. A self regulating area where all sorts rub along happily – 'It's so much better than before'; 'We realise how nice it is and really respect it'.

Introduction of cooked breakfasts has been a popular move and, although the head has further improvements in mind, the drive to raise the standard of food at lunchtime has really worked – one pupil said, 'It was dire before – at least they're using fresh ingredients now'.

Straightforward uniform with bright blue blazer toned down to navy in the sixth – not a shirt tail or low slung tie in sight. Girls also wear a uniform – 'one less thing to worry about' – and are relieved that the Rosa Klebb boxy blazers and high waisted skirts are being updated.

Pastoral Care and Discipline: Energetic conversation at meal times and good behaviour around the school. Strong sense of community – children stay in the same tutor group throughout: 'There are people in my group I'd not normally socialise with but I've got really close to them'. 'Any issues and the school is very responsive – either an email or phone call.'

Girls coming into the sixth in 1994 caused only a momentary flutter – 'At first the boys were really macho. Then after a couple of weeks everything was back to normal'. One girl said she was 'surprised that all the boys open doors for you'. Long may it last.

Pupils and Parents: Children come from a wide catchment area and variety of backgrounds – professional, entrepreneurial and some farming. A general sense of cheerful, purposeful activity. Pupils aren't afraid to question or comment and are an unpretentious lot.

Entrance: Entry for both boys and girls mainly at eleven and thirteen, with approximately 50 per cent from the lower school at eleven. Only external candidates (state and prep) sit an exam, plus interview with the head – also one for parents. Between 50–60, mostly girls, join the sixth form, although that will change as co-education moves up the school: interview plus a minimum of six Bs at GCSE – can be higher, depending on demand.

Exit: Aspirations tend towards the professions and a high proportion go on to well established universities with nearly all to first choice. Wide variety of courses – including veterinary science, history of art, biomedical engineering, medicine, town planning. Oxbridge entrants have steadily risen – on average more than 15 per year.

Money Matters: Fifty per cent off for choristers. Ten per cent off for scholars: academic and music scholarships at 11 and 13; academic, music, sport and art/design/drama scholarships at 16. Bursaries up to 100 per cent fees from 11+ depending on parental means. Scholarships for students of outstanding scientific ability who have been educated entirely in the state sector and wish to join the sixth form.

Remarks: Friendly school with a strong academic bent. Best suited to the bright and enthusiastic – as the head said, 'Not a finishing school for the wealthy'. Big changes now with the advent of girls.

Notre Dame Senior School

Linked to Notre Dame Preparatory School in the Junior section

Burwood House, Convent Lane, Cobham, Surrey, KT11 1HA

• Pupils: 380 pupils • Ages: 11-18 • Size of sixth form: 55 • RC
• Fees: £12,000 pa • Independent

Tel: 01932 869 990
Fax: 01932 589 481
Email: headmistress@notredame.co.uk
Website: www.notredame.co.uk

Headmistress: Since 2003, Mrs Bridget Williams MA. Previous headship at St Mary's Convent, Worcester. Moved back to Surrey for family reasons. Married with son and daughter. A softly spoken, honest and open lady who is smart, efficient and friendly. Her faith and the spiritual ethos of the school are important to her. She quickly gets to know pupils and their parents and still teaches quite a lot because she 'enjoys exchange and interchange with young people'. Has worked hard to increase academic standards.

Academic matters: A wide range of abilities catered for and lots of emphasis on getting the best from each girl. Mrs Williams keen to emphasise that 'the school has the highest value-added in Surrey'. Not a huge amount of academic pressure but academic standards are high and continue to rise, helped by new initiatives such as accelerated learning and learning to learn programmes. 100 per cent pass rate at A level with 74 per cent A/B grades: bright sparks here – girls in the top ten in the country for languages, PE and sport. Sixth form, previously rather small, now is growing and A level options consequently expanding. GCSE: 100 per cent pass rate with 58 per cent A*/A grades. Seventeen girls achieved A* or A in all examinations taken.

Deserves a pat on the back for bucking the trend for sciences in girls' schools – three girls in top five in the country for science GCSE. Twelve per cent of this year's A level students studying medicine at top universities. Fabulous new science facilities already in use. Mrs Williams says, 'The school is at the forefront of science teaching – we teach and train the teachers of other schools in the area'. Already biotechnology workshops – head sees science as growth area and will back this up with future investment.

Everyone does theology and all take GCSE in religious studies. French, German and Spanish from Year 7, Latin from Year 8, Italian as an optional extra at lower sixth. Exchange trips with sister schools overseas reinforce language provision. Good design & technology facilities (food and textiles) with large, well resourced rooms. Average class size 14, split into tutorial groups and set by end of Year 7 in English, maths, languages, sciences, history and geography.

SEN provision is limited – entrance tests used to reveal learning difficulties; mild dyslexia and dyspraxia catered for. Two part-time specialist teachers, but a small number of girls receive extra help.

Games, Options, the Arts: Everyone involved in Sport for All – swimming, tennis, athletics, rounders, netball, fitness, dance, cross country, all compulsory. Netball very strong with tours to Tobago and Grenada. Full-sized heated indoor swimming pool, complemented by newly refurbished changing rooms, showers, locker area and state of the art fitness studio recently completed with financial support from the parent body. Super sports hall. Better use could be made of outdoor space – three tennis courts, running track and area for playing lacrosse, but no Astroturf pitch or hockey pitch, although plenty of room for them.

Art is exceptionally strong and is held as a model of good practice by examining boards (OCR and Edexcel both use photos of pupils' work as examples in their booklets). The pupils' beautiful artwork decorates the school walls and is updated yearly. Two art rooms; facilities recently upgraded with new art suite which consists of large bright conservatory area with patio doors onto gardens, wet area for screen printing and dying, new kiln room, dark room and extended storage facilities. Drama is well resourced – productions each term: Shakespeare festival, Christmas show and productions taken to Edinburgh Fringe Festival.

Investment in music is evident, including music technology equipment and loads of different instruments. Everyone gets the opportunity to learn a musical instrument from a vast range taught by peripatetic teachers. Successful string orchestra and choir, concert band, flute group, jazz ensemble, various choirs (be prepared for religious element to singing groups). Mrs Williams says, 'Parents choose to pay for their daughters to use a coach to travel to and from school – thus after school clubs are limited.' So Wednesday afternoon activities are provided instead.

Background and Atmosphere: First and foremost a Catholic community with a strong family value: parents agree that the head is 'bringing faith and spiritualism to the forefront again'. Opened on its present site in Cobham in 1937 and is part of a worldwide educational order, The Company of Mary Our Lady. Celebrations for the order's 400th anniversary year included sensational choir trip to Rome, pilgrimage to Bordeaux for governors, Sisters and staff during half term as well as magnificent ball and alumnae reunion occasions.

The core is the rather beautiful Burwood House, where four elderly nuns remain in the convent and from which the junior school is run. However a maze of large modern blocks attached to the house has overshadowed it. Stunning library resourced to a very high standard and employs two librarians. A mezzanine floor houses the new sixth form study area that any university would be proud of – real wow factor here. Classrooms are tidy, well maintained and spacious. Girls move about the school in a polite, quiet and orderly fashion and the atmosphere is calm.

The prep school and senior school are inextricably linked (prep school girls regularly use senior facilities and vice versa) – girls move easily between the two schools through a large adjoining corridor. Communal chapel sits between the two. Security around the school is tight. Not near any public transport – seven coach routes laid on from the surrounding areas (for very local families these can be pricey). Alternative is the school run – cars nose to tail down a very narrow road to the school. Children of working parents can use the breakfast club open at 8am. Study centre stays open until 5.45pm for homework at no additional cost.

Pastoral Care and Discipline: Strong pastoral care and a routine of regular contact, including personal, social and health education, forms part of every day. School chaplain lives on site and is available for chats. Supportive mentoring system. A nice touch is the blue post boxes discreetly scattered about the school where girls can post slips asking mentors for help of any kind. Parents say new girls settle in well – particularly important for the 30 or so who are not from the prep school – helped by 'big sister' scheme where each lower sixth girl is given responsibility for four Year 7 girls. This scheme also operates if your daughter joins later up the school.

Pupils and Parents: Although strongly Roman Catholic (with attendance at mass and assemblies compulsory), welcomes pupils from other denominations. In fact, no more than 50 per cent of the pupils are RC. The girls are beautifully turned out and uniform guidelines are strict – hair tied back and no jewellery except a cross if wanted. Any holes in tights are fixed at reception.

Many families dual income professional in and around Cobham, Walton, Weybridge and Esher areas. Majority are British, but strong multicultural feel, which parents regard as a plus (constant turnover of expats from around the world) and some celebs (Chelsea football training grounds are just down the road). Has a long history of charitable involvement in the community and all girls are encouraged to take part.

Entrance: Entrance exam at 11: English, maths, verbal or non-verbal reasoning (non-verbal for girls with learning difficulties). Past papers not available. Of the 72 places available, approx 40 per cent from own prep school. General feeling among the prep school parents is that head 'wants to make the senior school stand out academically', with no longer the guarantee that prep school girls automatically have a place in the senior. Competition for the remaining places comes from up to 20 different schools including Danesfield Manor, The Ursuline Prep, The Study Wimbledon and Holy Cross Prep Kingston. Spaces become available in all years – quite a transient parent population – so always worth a try. Entrants into sixth form need a minimum of five or six subjects at B/C grade or above (A grades for the subjects to be taken at AS level).

Exit: After GCSEs, a number of leavers (majority remain) move to pastures new to experience co-ed sixth forms or to increase their A level options. Big financial input into sixth form resources have encouraged more to stay. Post A level all opt for higher education; universities include Oxford, Cambridge, Durham, Bristol, Birmingham, Surrey, Imperial College London, Exeter and Leeds.

Money Matters: A number of short-term bursaries which are based on personal hardship. In this anniversary year, the number of scholarships, exhibitions and bursaries has been increased – and can be up to 50 per cent of the fees. Also some special awards into the sixth form linked to a particular talent or expertise such as music, drama or sport.

Remarks: A solid, all-round, school with an orderly, nurturing atmosphere and a head who is pushing to drive up academic standards (not least to boost the numbers in the sixth form).

Notting Hill and Ealing High School

Linked to Notting Hill And Ealing High School Junior School in the Junior section

2 Cleveland Road, London, W13 8AX

• Pupils: 580 girls, all day • Ages: 11-18 • Size of sixth form: 150
• Non-denom • Fees: £12,063 pa • Independent

Tel: 020 8799 8400
Fax: 0208 810 6891
Email: enquiries@nhehs.gdst.net
Website: www.nhehs.gdst.net

Head: Since 2008, Ms Lucinda Hunt BSc ARCS PGCE (Oxon) (late forties). Formerly deputy head at St Paul's

Girls, read physics at Imperial. Striking, clear sighted and determined, Ms Hunt is enjoying a meteoric career in education with a year's secondment at Goldman Sachs to boot. Working in a bank reinforced her appetite for teaching – 'when profit is the motivator the bottom line is that it's dull'. In the early years of her career she taught science, maths and geology in Australia and France. Well versed in the ethos of GDST (and very happy with it) – a period at Putney High and eight years at Wimbledon High where she rose to head of sixth form. Here she follows the legendary Mrs Whitfield, who after 17 years has a loyal following. 'I'm not afraid to rock the boat if it needs rocking,' declares Ms Hunt but adds that she is no Hazel Blears, and will only make changes that are needed. Quick as a flash, she has fearlessly cut swathes through the existing management structure. At the same time she is well tuned to the relatively gentle spirit of the place – 'that indefinable quality that makes a school different from the others despite the fact that we all say the same sort of things,' she explains. One of her aims is to open up the windows and doors – 'at the moment not enough people know what we're about'. Parents agree and some comment on poor communication about the day to day. She starts with her own door which, unlike that of her predecessor, is always open to staff and pupils alike. The best thing about the job is the 'wry, intelligent' girls she says and has lost no time in getting to know them despite the fact that she doesn't teach any of them. The energy that she brings to the place is tangible. Here's someone whose influence may restore the school to its former status as one of the best girls' schools in west London.

Academic matters: 2010 results were the best in the school's history: 88 per cent A*/A at GCSE and 98 per cent A*/A/B at A Level . Subjects taught are wide ranging, including philosophy of religion and ethics, and psychology. Maths and geography strong. Chemistry and biology also popular as well as drama, history and English. Year 12s choose a general studies option, can range from jewellery making or music technology to Russian, Mandarin or Ancient Greek. Mandarin compulsory in Year 7, which they learn alongside a European language. Class sizes large for an independent school – maximum 30 in Years 7–9, average 22 in Years 10–11. A lot of young teaching blood. Ms Hunt asserts that there is the usual turnover you would expect in every London school. 20 per cent have been at the school for more than 10 years. One third are men. Pupils speak of the commitment of the staff and generally feel well supported.

Ms Hunt reluctant to be drawn into specific learning difficulties – wary of labelling she explains – but 5–10 per cent of children are eligible to have extra time in exams and school is becoming more adept at identifying who should be screened. The SEN teacher will go into lessons to work with individuals. No extra charge for any extra support. School proud of its success with one girl with serious visual impairment who went on to read English at Durham University. 'The term "gifted and talented" could describe almost every girl in the school,' says Ms Hunt. These are catered for with the various activities that take place during the school week including whole school assemblies. Parents praise an inclusive approach to academics – girls in lower sets are not ignored as 'dunces'.

Games, Options, the Arts: The benefit of being a suburban school is there's a little more space to squash in some facilities. Interwoven into the network of classrooms there is a large indoor pool (girls can go for a swim at lunchtime supervised by sixth formers trained as life guards), music studios, a recital hall (with excellent acoustics) a gym and the largish school hall. Tennis and netball courts on site. For hockey, rounders and athletics they can run or be bused to nearby sports grounds. Not known for its sporting achievements 'but girls get plenty of physical activity,' says one parent. Mutterings among some that if their daughter is not in the tennis team they are left to play among themselves. Ms Hunt keen to introduce some less conventional individual sports – for which you 'don't have to get undressed – so many girls just prefer not to' – fencing currently riding a wave of enthusiasm – other innovations may follow.

Drama jolly good fun. Music well provided for, orchestras, choirs and ensemble groups with about half the school playing a musical instrument – school will accommodate the few who want to do it at A level. Musicians tour to Venice and Paris. Plenty of trips abroad for the non musical too. Artists go to New York, linguists to Paris and Barcelona. 2009 saw a trip to China, in 2008 it was Borneo. Lots of enthusiasm for debating – whether it be competing against other schools in debating competitions, Model United Nations events or mock trial competions. Duke of Edinburgh awards – most girls take bronze, over a third take silver.

Background and Atmosphere: Founded in 1873 – NHEHS is the oldest of the Girls' Day School Trust schools. The school moved from Notting Hill to its present site in a large house (grand entrance with columns) in a broad Ealing residential avenue in 1931 and a number of features of the original building moved with it. The West Wing is the most recent modern extension – a bright and above all functional building with its white washed breeze block walls and hardwearing carpet. People we spoke to commented, rather blandly, on the warmth and friendliness of the school – Ms Hunt attributes this partly to the intimacy created by the leafy central quadrangle that connects the old with the new – lots of meeting and greeting as girls pass each other on stairs. Library ostensibly equally uninspiring – steel stacks of books with computers interspersed – but lots of girls quietly making the best of it. A refurbished and much extended dining room with a bright, airy feel, and plenty of space opened in November 2010.

In March 2010, the school opened a new sixth form centre in a separate building on the south west corner of the main school site. It is in a listed modernist building that had been a children's home and had been lying empty since 2006. It has been gutted and converted to a bright, modern, airy building with seminar rooms, common room (with the obligatory leather sofas!) multigym, café, and outside terrace.

Pastoral Care and Discipline: Girls are noticeably well behaved around the school – some of the quietest entrances in and out of assembly that we have seen anywhere. Head acknowledges that there are instances of bullying (a good sign – it's the ones who deny there is any at all that one has to look out for). New area of concern – not just here – is the opportunity for students to use cyber space to make each others lives difficult. Ms Hunt well aware of this and ready to take on the challenge. With her modern, forward thinking approach if anyone born in the early '60s can meet that challenge she is your woman. A few worrying reports from parents about having nobody to go to talk to about pastoral issues ('don't want to be nuisance and worry the head – she's got enough on her plate'); encouraging signs that school is onto this and attempts are being made to plug the gap.

Pupils and Parents: Families more modest than you would find at most London independent schools – typical GDST parents. Professional, ambitious, looking for value for money but not prepared to compromise on their daughters' education. It's a local school – but some come from as far as Richmond, Perivale, Harrow and Greenford to the west and Notting Hill to the east. Cosmopolitan (particularly Asian), community – reflective of the local area. Lots of doctors and dentists, chartered surveyors, but creative types too – record producers, fashion journalists, business consultants. A wide range – ethnically, culturally and economically. Girls here are focused but enjoying life. Not so pressured as their contemporaries in more central schools – they can work hard without being cowed by expectation and league tables. We saw lots of initiative – girls writing scores for musicals, scripts for witty renditions of the Theseus and Ariadne myth and choreographing amusing Michael Jackson dance routines for mythical monsters. They emerge articulate and confident, full of west London sophistication, but without the trendy, street-wise demeanour characteristic of their peers in more high profile schools in west London. OGs include Angela Rumbold, writer and TV presenter, Bettany Hughes, BBC children's presenter Angellica Bell and Blue Peter's Konnie Huq.

Entrance: Competitive consortium examination in maths and English plus interview. About half come up from the junior school, the rest from west London state and independent schools. Sixth form applicants sit entrance exams in their potential A level subjects plus a general paper; they're expected to get at least seven B grades, with As in their A level subjects. Most go on to the sixth form. For the occasional place in the senior school girls will be tested according to their age and stage.

Exit: Still losing a fair number each year after GCSE – some girls, (misguidedly) still insist on sampling boys at co-ed establishments – even the less academic ones, others opt for the maintained sector. Those who stay continue to do very well. Each year a number of girls go to Oxbridge, some win scholarships. A lot read sciences – and not just medicine. History, politics and English are also popular. Leeds, Manchester and Nottingham favourites at the moment. A few go on to foundation courses.

Remarks: A well run, efficient GDST school that does exactly what it says on the tin. Your daughter will get a very good, balanced education here. Over subscribed but currently in the shade of other schools of its kind. The dynamic Ms Hunt has now settled in and is busily making the school her own – without altering the relatively relaxed, down to earth friendliness of the place.

Nottingham Girls' High School

Linked to Nottingham Girls High School Junior School in the Junior section

9 Arboretum Street, Nottingham, Nottinghamshire, NG1 4JB

• Pupils: 810 in senior school of whom 215 are in sixth form • Ages: 11-18 • Size of sixth form: 215 • Non-denom • Fees: Senior £9,627; Junior £6,978 pa • Independent

Tel: 0115 941 7663
Fax: 0115 924 0757
Email: enquiries@not.gdst.net
Website: www.gdst.net/nottinghamgirlshigh

Head: Since 2006, Mrs Sue Gorham BA MA (mid-fifties). Educated Manchester University (French) and Open University (Education Management). Widowed, three adult children. Hers was a wind of change appointment; Mrs Gorham came from Burgess Hill (qv) with a reputation as a tightener, a tweaker, a freshener-up. Not that NGHS had become the dowdy Duchess of Arboretum Street, far from it, but the time was right just the same. With cheerful courage and steady nerve she ruffled feathers at the outset but in short order won over the glum, the cross and the doubtful. She's here not to build a reputation but to lead from the front and get it right. A moderniser for sure, up to speed with latest thinking and practice, but does not rate processes higher than people. Inspires affection and approval in all constituencies. Girls really like her. She is approachable, she wants to know. One parent says, 'You don't just get the party line, she listens to you, really listens'. An admirable, and likeable head with a notable achievement so far. A gentle revolutionary.

Academic matters: Exam results place the school in the top tier. Traditionally strong in maths and the sciences and once arguably over-focused on them, it has enjoyed an academic culture change and now attaches equal value to all subjects – girls are encouraged to go for what they do best. There has been a culture change in the delivery thing, too. Teachers as a breed don't do change with anything approaching alacrity, they get terribly upset by it, so we can only conjecture what their response must have been when Mrs Gorham, on arrival, had windows put in all classroom doors, opening them to the gaze of those outside, then threw them open to a new way of doing things. Modern teaching methods, best practice sharing and inter-disciplinary team working are how they go about it now.

Lots of brand new IT in sparklingly refurbed classrooms. Watching them at it is to observe lit-up students and animated teachers. We wondered if some weren't perhaps having too much fun. The proof of the pudding is in the exam results; they march from strength to strength with value-added scores to match. There has been some resultant staff turnover and some bright young things brought in. Most girls here like most of their teachers a lot; one mum added, 'Do they ever go home?' The work ethic is shared.

Nottinghamians generally do not, you'll notice this if you're moving here, buy into the intense pressure ethic evident in other big city top schools. They work jolly hard, though. Parents and girls talk of workloads that keep them up o' nights and of teachers who insist it is done on time.

This is a school for achievers all right, one of those that cannot accommodate daffiness and unfulfilled promise – simply can't afford to. Actually they did indulge a bit of that recently and it skewed the results. They've bounced back with attitude since. If your daughter has problems with deadlines, think again. If she doesn't, she may occasionally utter words like 'unremitting' but never 'crushing'. Yes, exam stats matter, that's the way of things, but they really do educate the whole girl here, they care about their well-being and about character and life outside the classroom and life after school. SENs, mild to moderate at most, are supported in the classroom, not one-to-one.

Subjects studied are all gold standard, no sillies, and the full range, of course. Sciences remain especially strong, maths and economics mind-blowingly good, and no weaknesses though art is notably undersubscribed. All Year 9s do a classy three modern languages. Sixth formers can learn Mandarin. Partnerships with local universities have added inspiration and grown-up perspectives with PhD students coming in to talk about their research. Green chemistry is big in this eco-aware school.

Games, Options, the Arts: An impressive range of enrichment activities available but, here's the striking thing, they're not there as ornamental window dressing, they make time for them, they actually really matter. This is a school with a joy ethic, for sure, underlying which is a deadly serious belief that personal qualities and social values count as highly working hard and keeping up, so character-building pursuits are central. D of E and Young Enterprise buoyant. Plenty of music, resurgent under its new choir director. Boys imported from over the road as and when, particularly for drama. Sport is cramped by the school's location and lack of space but they do well with the facilities they've got. Compulsory up to Year 12. Everyone has a go at a wide range from netball, hockey, etc, to kick-boxing and self-defence. There's swimming in the boys' pool. In spite of the lack of rolling acres of freshly-mown greensward the school boasts a pretty impressive roll of sporting success.

Background and Atmosphere: A Girls' Day School Trust school. Sound a bit corporate? Collaborative would be a better word; localism is favoured. Check it out at gdst.net. NGHS was founded in 1875, situated just north of the city centre in an area which has been described as insalubrious – as indeed it until recently was. Nearby Victorian town-houses which had seen better tenants are now being bought by Nottingham Trent University. The area is perfectly safe – charming, actually, with the Arboretum next door. The school is bisected by Arboretum Street and occupies a small site where new buildings jostle old. There are competitor schools which offer more elbow room and more eyecatching facilities. How does the school answer them? By focusing instead on the human scale and the quality of relationships. Among teachers and students there is a strong feeling of shared purpose. This is a warm, kind and purposeful place, neither snazzy nor haughty – and perhaps all the more impressive for that. Much recent refurbing has brightened and improved what there is. Splendid new sixth form centre with its own garden – an essential recruiting tool for itchy Year 11s on the lookout for greener grass. What the school now needs more than merely urgently is a decent performing arts centre.

Pastoral Care and Discipline: This being a school where teachers and students look out for each other as a matter of course, pastoral care really is as good as it gets. We were as much impressed by the shining dedication of those charged with it as we were by the endorsement of students and parents. Problems are addressed speedily. For wide-eyed and apprehensive new girls there's a fun bonding weekend when they arrive.

Food, another important quality of life issue, is very good. Snacks and meals throughout the day and breakfast for students and parents.

Pupils and Parents: Socially mixed they say – and true up to a point – pupils come from up to 30 miles away. Active parent-teacher association. The head welcomes parent involvement – all part of the team working. You find the sort of relaxed social atmosphere you expect in a single-sex school, decidedly affectionate. Males are never too far away: good relations and joint enterprises with the boys' school over the road. Eminent alumni include Stella Rimmington, spy; Helen Creswell and Julie Myerson, authors; Parosha Chandran, human rights lawyer; Jane Smit, England cricketer; Clare Hammond, fiery pianist.

Entrance: At 11 by test (English, maths and verbal reasoning) plus interview. On the lookout more for potential than what a girl actually knows. At any age, 'if we think they'll benefit' – in other words if they think your girl is bright enough. At sixth form, average B in best 8 GCSEs. Any who leave after GCSE and undergo second thoughts, as they do, admitted to sixth form if poss.

Exit: A declining number leave after GCSE despite some superb free competitors, notably Bilborough. Sixth formers go on to good universities, a decent wodge to Oxbridge.

Money Matters: Scholarships and means-tested bursaries available – the bursaries very much targeted on those who would not otherwise be able to afford the fees. The full fee offers good value for money.

Remarks: A school not without strong competitors, especially to the south. Though lacking glitzy, soaring bricks-and-mortar, NGHS more than makes up for it with a most engaging and carefully wrought quality of humanity. Hardware's all well and good, but it's software that matters most, and this is a school with an impressive operating system.

Nottingham High School

Linked to Lovell House School in the Junior section

Linked to Nottingham High Junior School in the Junior section

Waverley Mount, Nottingham, Nottinghamshire, NG7 4ED

• Pupils: 840 boys, all day • Ages: 11-18 • Size of sixth form: 210 • Fees: Senior £10,872 pa • Independent

Tel: 0115 978 6056
Fax: 0115 924 9716
Email: enquiries@nottinghamhigh.co.uk
Website: www.nottinghamhigh.co.uk

Head: Since 2007, Mr Kevin Fear BA PGCE, (early forties) educated at Douai, a historian. His first job, from 1986, was at the King's School, Chester. Then appointed by the High

School in September 2000 as a senior teacher, in 2004 became deputy head with academic and marketing responsibilities. Married to Denise, two children.

Academic matters: This is not a swot-house – boys don't need to be force-fed facts and figures; they are capable of independent thought and enquiry, encouraged to challenge accepted doctrine and discover the joys of serious thought and intellectual discussion. Boys say, 'The school has a reputation for taxing, challenging work, but you find you can do it and teachers will help if you have difficulties.' All pass – 82 per cent of GCSE entries A/A* and commendable around 80 per cent of A levels A/B. Enters lots of academic competitions – maths challenge, maths Olympiad (highest scorers), Engineer for Britain (winner most innovative award), physics and biology Olympiads (gold medal winners), to name but a few. Super, well-kept facilities (save the odd bag strewn on the floor) – school has many generous benefactors and it shows. Wireless networked throughout, interactive technology; excellent library with own laptops, DVDs, periodicals; new arts centre; well equipped labs, DT centre etc.

Class size varies from 16 to 26, reducing to fewer than 10 in the sixth form. Lots of fizzy teaching – uses technology and skills to make lessons come alive; practical demonstrations and the concrete even extend to A level mechanics – believes it's important to appreciate practical applications. Older pupils expected to research, plan and take model lessons – it enhances understanding, makes them think. Pupils clearly appreciate dedication of staff, who willingly give up free time to help boys both academically and with extra-curricular activities (45 staff assist with games alone).

Enthusiastic and very capable head of learning support who has done much rapidly to transform attitudes – lots of inset and training on learning styles, kinaesthetic learning etc. Not only have old-school staff embraced provision but children are also gaining confidence to self-refer. School identifies 70 children as being in need of additional help or support – majority are dyslexics but a handful of dyspraxics and smattering of Asperger's, ADD, ADHD. Staff keen to offer extra help and support. No additional charge for those requiring one-to-one, though outside help such as occupational therapy will incur a fee. They stress that the main thing is pupils requiring additional support are able to achieve. Say to pupils, 'This is you, this is your profile – you can give up, or go for it.' They go for it – SEN input reaping rewards.

Games, Options, the Arts: School motto: 'Together everyone achieves more' (TEAM) summarises the spirit of the school. All are encouraged to do far more than pursue academic interests and virtually all do. Games and music are the mainstay but not the only offerings. Chess plays a large part in school life – national champions and international representation across several age groups. Very good facilities – large sports hall, climbing wall, full size swimming pool and excellent multi-gym – put many leisure centres to shame (even a TV to take your mind off going the extra mile). First-rate sports pitches located a short bus-ride away and used for school matches as well as area and national trials and training; Astroturf and additional tennis courts on the wish list. Sport is an important part of the boys' education – don't gloat over victories, be happy to accept defeat. Rugby (couple of international players) and swimming particularly successful (lots of cups) but sports such as orienteering (national champions) get a look-in too. Trying to encourage and develop sport for all, especially for those where enthusiasm exceeds talent or who have difficulties such as dyspraxia.

Music is active, alive and practical – numbers opting for GCSE shooting up, lots of bands (big band medal winners in Boosey and Hawkes competition), choirs, performing opportunities, and now latest computer equipment adding a new dimension to music technology. Trips and tours aplenty.

Background and Atmosphere: Founded in 1513 by Dame Agnes Mellers (with help of Sir Thomas Lovell) after the death of her husband, Richard, partly in his memory, but also as an act of atonement for his several wrongdoings against the people of Nottingham, with the foundation deed sealed by King Henry VIII. Moved to its present pleasant site in 1868. A long programme of building and development results in today's facilities. Immediate area not the most salubrious – a police raid was taking place opposite the school on the day of our visit and ladies of the night are known to pound the nearby streets (school say police efforts reducing the problem) but, apart from odd incident of graffiti, appears to escape the downfall of its near neighbours.

Pastoral Care and Discipline: Plenty of graduated awards for good work, helping out etc. Celebrates, enjoys and respects success at any level – not just rugger buggers; mutual respect, family feel. Head or deputy sees those with 10 or more distinctions. All belong to a form and a tutor group. Forms have a horizontal structure but crux is the carefully thought out, vertically operated tutor-system – tutor even phones parents to invite them to the introductory parents' evening, they get to know families as well as boys. No detentions for Year 7 but one boy reported that 'detention runs from Years 8 to 11', which we thought a bit excessive. Tutor often the one batting for a boy when chips are down. Students encouraged to seek help, support or advice from any of the school nurse, tutor, form teacher, head of year, form prefect, school counsellor or other person they trust – school medical service open daily. Compulsory testing for suspected drug misuse. Bullying of all kinds dealt with promptly – boys encouraged to report all, however trivial, and certainly the many children we spoke to agreed bullying wasn't a problem, saying they felt the tutor system, where they got to know boys from all years, really helped.

Sixth formers are expected to act as rôle models for those younger than themselves. Usual opportunities for leadership and personal and social development offered through CCF, Duke of Edinburgh, young enterprise, business leadership scheme or as prefects. In addition, the organisation of house teams and events relies solely on the initiative of sixth formers and this is serious stuff – everything from four-part choirs to producing, directing and coordinating up to 50 youngsters at a time in the uniquely inventive and dramatic verse-speaking competitions. Dire threats issued to those who might think about skiving a rehearsal or two. Plenty of joint activities with Nottingham Girls' High School: politics society, arts society, drama club and explorer scout unit, as well as a couple of balls and an annual major dramatic production.

Pupils and Parents: A genuinely mixed bag – offspring of millionaires to those in care. From a wide geographical area: Nottingham, Bakewell, Loughborough, Leicestershire. Half from own junior school, 15 per cent from other independent schools, rest from state primaries. Twenty per cent identify their ethnic mix as other than white but fewer than four per cent have English as an additional language. Boys smartly dressed in blazers distinguished by house ties, suits in the sixth form (tufty tie for those who gain a minimum 10 grade A GCSEs), say they feel privileged to have a first-rate education and fantastic opportunities. These are genuinely grounded, rounded individuals with bags of personality and myriads of interests, not a swot in sight – we doubt arrogance, even a mild dose, would be tolerated by anyone. Many have a string of successes to their bow – grade 8 instrumentalists, national representation in the sporting, academic, and musical world, but they don't let on; they present as great lads, able to hold their own in conversation and debate but with a wicked sense of humour and lovely ability to poke fun at themselves – what more could you ask? A sample of famous old Nottinghamians includes Ed Balls, Jesse Boot, Kenneth Clarke, Geoff Hoon, Robert MacFarlane (author) and Andrew Turner (Olympic hurdler).

Entrance: Majority at 11, a few at 16. Occasional places available at other ages. Tests for all in English, maths and verbal reasoning, plus short interview for non-junior boys. Details about the exam are sent out in January prior to September entry. Advises all to visit school on open day in November. Entry to sixth form is by interview and achievement at GCSE, sixth form open evening held early October. Doesn't admit boys they feel wouldn't be happy.

Exit: Small number (between five and 10) leave after GCSEs. Large numbers to Oxbridge, most of rest to wide range of Russell Group of universities studying for traditional gold standard degrees. Birmingham, Leeds, Manchester, Newcastle popular.

Money Matters: Generous means-tested bursaries (up to 100 per cent of fees) available at head's discretion. Believes any boy who is able should be given all the assistance necessary to attend the school. Part-scholarships also awarded to top performers in entrance exam at 11+.

Remarks: A very good school, hard to fault. Media studies types should look elsewhere, though media types would do very well. Only for the seriously bright with personality and plethora of pursuits and passions. Challenge for the new head to up the game and stay ahead of it.

Nunnykirk Centre for Dyslexia

Netherwitton, Morpeth, Northumberland, NE61 4PB

• Pupils: 40 of whom 15 are weekly boarders. 35 boys, 5 girls • Ages: 9-18 • Non-denom • Fees: Please apply to school • Independent

Tel: 01670 772 685
Fax: 01670 772 434
Email: secretary@nunnykirk.co.uk
Website: www.nunnykirk.co.uk

Head Teacher: Since 2008, Mrs Carol Hodgson BA PGCE NPQH ACFPS(SpLD/Dyslexia) BDA-Approved-Teacher. Appointed on the retirement of Mr Dalby Ball. Has worked at the school for 22 years and for the last seven as SENCo and deputy head teacher.

Academic matters: This is a CreSTeD SP school specialising in dyslexia and all the associated info-processing quirks which huddle under that umbrella term. Ofsted were uncharacteristically charmed by what they saw but couldn't put their finger on how they did it. Cast aside all objective criteria, stop ticking boxes and switch to subjective mode – a good school is an affair of the heart. It's the individual focus, the being known and liked, that enables these children to achieve so far beyond expectation, above and beyond the application of any modish methodology. Teachers go to great lengths to find what works for each child and they keep them at it. One mum says, 'They don't make it easy just because they have difficulties.' Plenty of brilliant rapport, so good to see, heaps of praise and richly deserved mutual admiration. Tiny classes, most 4–5, max eight. Brain gym. One-to-one as necessary. Results put this school in the top five per cent of the value added tables – says it all. Sixth form operational since Sept 2005.

National curriculum, all go for GCSEs, most tackle 5–8, and entry levels for those who need longer. English and maths, good IT, and options spanning history and geography through photography to rural science. No modern languages – 'They can do them later if they want'. More vocational subjects coming soon. Big hands-on element in all things. Science lab completely brilliant – far from brilliantly resourced, you think, then the head points to the French window at the end of the room and says, 'It's all out there, you see ... ' And in your mind's eye you see them clutching nets and jars, heading for the river, theory and practice happily married.

Studies of pigs show that, though they like toys and nice buildings, they'd much rather have a good relationship with humans – children are no different. You don't at any stage feel urgently impelled to write home about the glittering equipment in this school, nor its plushness, but the teachers are just what you'd want for a child dismayed and dented by early experiences and, dare we say it, over-demanding parents. The head picks teachers for their personal and professional attributes, then trains them on the job. It's a tiny staff – they all do lots, are encouraged to develop their own approaches and all run hobbies: 'This is no place for anyone wanting to work 9–4'. Informal and shirt-sleeves-y. They are never substituted by supply teachers – continuity is all. Stability and routine are the foundations of this notably calm, notably busy school.

Games, Options, the Arts: The extra-curricular programme is an essential element of the rescue remedy, not only because achievements in other areas cross-fertilise performance in the classroom, but also because parts of the academic curriculum are embedded in, especially, the rural studies programme.

Much of what they do is vigorous. Sport, given the numbers, is not competitive at school level, but they play the customary ball games and athletics. Swimming and the use of the sports hall in Alnwick, and sailing (RYA quals) at Amble. Playing fields, all-weather surface. Annual endurance race for all, summer sports day with barbie.

Plenty of art, well done. Music brave, if not symphonic. Lots of plays. D of E, of course, and scouts, karting, mountain biking, canoeing, bird watching, cross-stitching, egg painting – all tastes catered for. Rural studies is the big thing – looking after the pigs, hens, ducks, geese and turkeys.

They do it for real – while we were there, Maggie the sow was waiting sadly to be sent on, the arrival of six ewes and a tup eagerly expected. Fruit and veg home grown in the walled garden – 'We eat what we produce'. Fencing, rotavating, shed making – brilliant therapy for the children, all this, developing a sense of responsibility, following instructions (English), measuring out the right amounts (maths). The older ones teach the younger and exert stern expectations punctuality-wise.

Background and Atmosphere: Nunnykirk was founded in 1977 for children not at home in the hurly-burly of bigger schools. Everything presently happens in the Greek revival, John Dobson manor house surrounded by uncounted miles of Northumbrian loveliness.

Pastoral Care and Discipline: Well looked after children greet visitors with unfussed naturalness – these do; no reservations, not even of any kind, on that score. Standards are high, important for those rougher diamonds when they first arrive. Manners are excellent, discipline not an issue, and they all know exactly where the line is. Smoking? Not a blind eye in the house. It's a big deal – parents instantly informed. Drugs? Out.

Weekly boarders come from as far south as Birmingham and as far north as Edinburgh. No more than two to a room in the warren upstairs. It may look well worn, but they don't mind this a bit – it's fun. Supervision levels are high, older ones guide the younger, and a warm welcome – 'It's a big event when someone new comes'. So much goes on in the evening, no time for telly, and it's not missed. Day pupils who can stay on for these activities.

Food is good, the children reckon – high praise. They're not mad, all of them, including parents, about the gluten-free diet, and some pounce on the toaster when they get home. Additives are out, sugar rare, fish oils in, fruit abounds. The head is certain this makes a difference, keeps them calmer and more focused. A written record is kept of what each child eats. Healthy living tuck shop.

A student council. Efforts are made to mix with the local community despite location – excellent work experience for Years 10 and 11 with local businesses. Trips to the cinema and theatre.

Pupils and Parents: Pupils a mixed bunch, socio-economically, spanning the 50 per cent funded by their LEA to the scions of stately homes. More girls needed. Because this is the only school of its type between Oxford and John O'Groats, a big geographic mix, why they offer weekly boarding. For many parents this is not at all what they wanted, so the school goes to great lengths to allay fears and, thereafter, keep in touch – parents united in grateful applause. Day children from 45-min radius. Big expectations made of parents: 'If work is sent home we expect it to be done – and we expect parents to help'. It's all about partnership, which means 'parents have got to make an effort, too'. A training day for parents where you can find out what they do, how they do it, how you can help. If your child thrives remarkably, they won't hang on – but many opt to stay nevertheless; they reckon they'll do even better. Informative website.

Entrance: Careful selection process. All the usual reports, but the (long) interview's the thing. Boys and girls here are refugees from mainstream schools with, most of them, anything from an antipathy to a horror of being educated plus a history of being teased or bullied. Repairs to damaged self esteem are all part of the package, but no entrenched EBDs of any sort – they're outside their specialism: 'If we feel we can't help, there's no point'. IQs reckoned from 95 up. Formal acceptance after a trial half term when, if a child has settled, an IEP is drawn up.

Exit: Careful advice precedes post-16 decision making, finding the right course at the right college. It's a huge leap, obviously, reliant on the self belief they've acquired. They go on to the full rainbow – degree courses to clock making. Decided bias in favour of hands on, fresh air careers.

Money Matters: Some bursaries for private feepayers. For parents seeking to persuade their LEA to apply the statement, the news is that it's getting harder.

Remarks: Delightful and deserving. Restores children to a full sense of themselves and allows them to blossom at their own pace. Do they feel hived off? No – it's great to be where you're not the only one, where you can sometimes get top marks. This is a school you can easily fall in love with.

Oakham School

Chapel Close, Oakham, Rutland, LE15 6DT

• Pupils: 560 boys, 520 girls; 55 per cent board. • Ages: 10-18 • Size of sixth form: 400 • C of E • Fees: Day £13,965-£15,645; Boarding £15,540-£26,190 pa • Independent

Tel: 01572 758758
Fax: 01572 758595
Email: admissions@oakham.rutland.sch.uk
Website: www.oakham.rutland.sch.uk

Headmaster: Since 2009, Mr Nigel Lashbrook BA (late forties). Educated at King's Heath Boys' Technical School (he was one of the last grammar school intake) and Hertford College, Oxford, where he read chemistry, played in the university's 2nd cricket XI and captained his college rugby side. Stayed on at Oxford to train as a teacher and began teaching career at Manchester Grammar School, where he taught science and coached rugby and cricket teams. After eight years moved south to Tonbridge School as head of science and chemistry. Later became a housemaster and, at the age of 40, second master. Jumped at the opportunity to become acting head for a term while head was on sabbatical – he did so well that returning head predicted, 'I don't think you'll be here for long'. Sure enough, he was appointed head of King's Bruton soon after and spent five years at the helm there before moving to Oakham.

Approachable, affable and ambitious, he's taken to Oakham like a duck to water. The previous head, the very popular Dr Joe Spence (now in charge at Dulwich College), left Oakham in very good shape and the new head is, by all accounts, just the man to take it forward. Married to Jill, a geography teacher. They live on site and have three children – a son at university and a son and daughter who are pupils at Oakham.

A firm believer in education not just being about what happens in the classroom, he is proud of the fact that

Oakham manages to be a 'happy and successful' school 'without being a hothouse in any shape or form'. He's determined, too, to open Oakham's doors to pupils who would thrive at the school but whose parents can't afford to send them and is busy developing stronger links with local state schools. Proud of Oakham's sense of community – the school is helping the local comprehensive to introduce Latin, runs Rutland's primary French programme and the school's musicians give free (and very well attended) concerts for the town at All Saints' Church every Wednesday.

Academic matters: Results get better and better. In 2010, a third of A level pupils achieved a clean sweep of A* and A grades, whilst just over 80 per cent of all grades were A*–B. 26 subjects on offer at AS/A2 – all the usual ones, plus business studies, classical civilisation, economics, PE, sports studies and politics. Prides itself on being an innovative school and has offered the IB since 2000. Of the 2010 cohort taking the IB (55 in all – more than a quarter of the year), 100 per cent gained their Diploma. One student achieved the maximum 45 points and 36 per cent scored 40 or more points (worldwide just over five per cent achieved 40+ points). School helps pupils decide between IB and A levels. Deputy head reckons it's a myth that the IB is only for the brightest – 'It depends on the breadth of pupils' academic interest,' he says, 'but it's quite transformative in developing a much broader approach to their work'.

At GCSE, nearly 70 per cent of grades were A*/As, with a third of pupils scooping all A*/As. IGCSEs in maths and the three sciences, with IGCSE English being offered from 2012. Unlike some comparable schools, Oakham still submits its results for listing in the league tables. 'But,' says the head, 'it's just a snapshot. There is far more to what we offer than the league tables show.'

Impressive computerised language labs where pupils learn French from Year 7. German and Spanish on offer from Year 8. Everyone takes at least one language at GCSE, but most take two. Setting for all in maths, French and science from Year 9. Up until GCSE, maximum class size is 24, though often much smaller, whilst A level and IB classes tend to have ten pupils or fewer. SEN supported by team of four learning support teachers. School prefers to give in-class support rather than take pupils out of class – no charge made for this.

Games, Options, the Arts: School talks a lot about the 'total curriculum' and the importance of pupils achieving their full potential in every sense. With this in mind, opportunities galore in sport and the arts. By any measure, a very sporty school – independent school of the year in the 'Daily Telegraph' Sport Matters Awards in 2009, 1st XV rugby side won the 'Daily Mail' U19 national schools' rugby cup in 2002 and 2003. Loads of top sportsmen and women started at Oakham – cricketer Stuart Broad and rugby internationals, Lewis Moody and Tom Croft, to name a few. School has more than 40 acres of games pitches (some so good they're used by county cricket teams), sports centre, 25m indoor pool, two all-weather pitches, squash courts and a fitness centre. Around 30 sports on offer, including cycling, golf and sailing (on nearby Rutland Water), but main sports are rugby, hockey, cricket and athletics for boys and hockey, netball, tennis and athletics for girls. 700 pupils take part in competitive sport, from 1st XV rugby to polo. Some weekends the school fields six rugby or hockey teams per year group. 62 staff involved in sports coaching – 12 full-timers, 20 visiting coaches and 30 teachers from the common room.

Drama is an integral part of the school. 250-seat Queen Elizabeth Theatre hosts four main school productions a year (rehearsals for 'Little Shop of Horrors' in full swing when we visited), along with shows by touring companies. Each house competes for the MacFadyen Shield, given to the school by 'Pride and Prejudice' actor Matthew MacFadyen, a former pupil. Music is just as popular, with 600 instrumental lessons a week (some of the instrumental teachers travel from as far afield as London and Manchester). Around 80 concerts a year. A quarter of pupils sing in a choir and in 2010 a Year 9 girl won a competition to compose a fanfare for the Royal Opera House. Growing numbers taking music at GCSE and A level and go-ahead music department is the first in the school to offer the subject as a Cambridge Pre-U qualification (alternative to A level.)

Art is amazing – everything from life drawing, abstracts and sculpture to textiles and jewellery. Has been offering critical and contextual studies (a modern form of art history) at A level for three years and has won 'The Good Schools Guide's' award for the best results by independent school girls in the subject two years running. DT department rightfully proud of the brand new Jerwoods School of Design, which cost £2m and is equipped with state of the art technology. Third formers (Year 8s) get off to a productive start by making their own USB sticks, whilst an enterprising former pupil recently set up his own business selling the gun box he designed for his DT A level.

On two afternoons a week everyone does activities, trying their hand at everything from aerobics and film production to stone carving and yoga. From year 10 onwards pupils can opt for Duke of Edinburgh Award scheme (in 2001 school was first to achieve 1,000 D of E golds), CCF or community service.

Background and Atmosphere: Founded in 1584, sits in the centre of the prosperous market town of Oakham, surrounded by the rolling Rutland countryside. The main parts have the feel of a Cambridge college – quiet quads, old stone buildings overlooking immaculate lawns and flower beds. Much is owed to pioneering former head, John Buchanan, whose tenure from 1958 to 1977 oversaw the school's move to full independence and co-education, as well as the landscaped garden feel of the whole site.

No weekly boarding – very much a full boarding school, with so much going on at weekends that day pupils often pitch up to join in activities on Sundays. Day boarding, i.e. boarding three or four nights during the week, is a popular option. More flexible boarding is available in the lower school (Jerwoods), where 10–13 year olds can opt for full or transitional boarding. The latter is a great way for youngsters to try boarding life (signing up for one to four nights a week) and see if they like it. As well as half-term, two 'leave-out' weekends every term when boarders can go home.

Lessons take place in two to four-storey purpose-built blocks. Superb Smallbone Library is a match for public library standards – spacious, well-stocked, computerised, it boasts a careers room, first floor for silent individual study and is open every day. Chapel twice a week and all meals eaten in school's light, airy dining hall.

Pastoral Care and Discipline: 16 houses, scattered across the large campus: four junior houses (two day and two boarding), ten houses for 13–17 year olds (five for boys and five for girls) and two upper sixth houses (one for boys, one for girls). Comfortable, well-kept houses are run by staff who have teaching responsibilities too. Useful 'settling in' guide for new pupils, with wise advice from prefects, like 'Don't be shy or afraid to get involved' and 'Give everything a go'. Houses all have common rooms, quiet rooms and games rooms. One housemaster, aware that it would be all too easy for boarders to live in 'this little Oakham bubble', gets his GCSE boys to lead a debate every week – everything discussed, from politics to the Pope's visit to ideas for house trips. Sixth formers get rooms of their own, with younger years usually two, three or four to a room. Parents can express preferences for boarding houses but school has final say.

Rules clearly spelled out in Oakham's 'red book'. Anyone who tests positive for drugs or admits to drug misuse faces suspension or expulsion. Any pupil who supplies or brings drugs into the school is out straight away. One youngster expelled for drugs in last five years. Rules on alcohol and smoking crystal clear too. Head boy and head girl appointed every year, along with 22 school prefects (known as The Decem, because there used to be ten of them).

Plenty of sympathetic ears for pupils in need of advice and help – housemasters/housemistresses, tutors, matrons, chaplains, medical centre and school counsellor. New pupils given mentors to guide them through their early weeks. Uniform is compulsory and pupils look well turned out as they hurry between lessons. Business suits for sixth formers, while boys wear blazers and ties and girls are clad in black and white tartan skirts and blazers. 'We want them to look smart,' says head. 'They are ambassadors for the school.'

Pupils and Parents: Outgoing, enthusiastic bunch, determined to make the most of every second at Oakham. 'It's hard to stereotype an Oakhamian,' the head boy told us. 'There is so much on offer here for everyone and it's given me the chance to have a go at so many new things.' Most come from one to three hours' drive away. Around ten per cent from overseas. Past pupils (known as OOs) are an eclectic lot – they include actors Matthew MacFadyen and Greg Hicks, director Katie Mitchell and international sports stars Lewis Moody, Stuart Broad, Lucy Pearson and Crista Cullen. Parents are a supportive crew – director of sport reckons 60 per cent regularly turn out to cheer teams on.

Entrance: More and more competitive to get in, with 2011 list almost full and filling up for subsequent years. Pupils come from all over the shop – 40+ different preps. At 11, intake is mostly youngsters from local primary schools and preps while 13+ entrants tend to be mostly boarders. Entrance exams at 11+ in maths, English and verbal reasoning. At 13+ CE mark of 55 per cent needed or, for those coming from schools which don't do CE, school's own exams in English, maths, French and science. Lower school pupils don't need to take exam to progress into middle school. Around 40 to 50 new pupils enter the sixth form each year – they need seven Bs at GCSE, with a minimum of Bs in the subjects to be studied in the sixth form.

Exit: A handful leave after GCSEs, mainly to take vocational courses or subjects Oakham doesn't offer (like law, psychology or the dreaded media studies). At 18 virtually all progress to higher education – around 11 or 12 to Oxbridge each year and large swathes to Newcastle, Nottingham, Leeds, Birmingham, UCL and Durham, with the most popular courses including business management, economics, the sciences, engineering, maths, medicine, art and history.

Money Matters: Variety of scholarships on offer – academic and music at 11, academic, music, art, DT, sport and all-rounder at 13. More available at 16, including the recent introduction of two science and engineering scholarships for pupils to join the sixth form from a state school. Oakham scholarships offer five to ten per cent off the fees but the school says greater financial assistance may be available (in cases of proven need, this can be up to 100 per cent).

Remarks: A friendly, unpretentious and forward-thinking school that achieves impressive academic results. Far from being an academic hothouse, has high expectations and achievements across the board. For all-rounders who like rolling their sleeves up and throwing themselves into a staggering range of activities it's a very exciting place to be.

Oban High School

Soroba Road, Oban, Argyll, PA34 4JB

• Pupils: 1,170 boys and girls (capacity 1,300); 80 boarders • Ages: 11-18
• Size of sixth form: 100 • Non-denom • State

Tel: 01631 564 231
Fax: 01631 565916
Email: enquiries@obanhigh.argyll-bute.sch.uk
Website: www.obanhigh.argyll-bute.sch.uk

Head Teacher: Since August 2008, Mr Peter Bain MA MSc PGCE (fortyish) who was educated at Musselburgh Grammar, read history at Edinburgh University, where he did his masters in the science of historical research followed by PGCE at Jordanhill plus courses on headship and leadership. Started life in the civil service, which gives him the strategies to deal with the vagaries of Argyll and Bute Council education service. Six schools under his belt, from the depths of Fife to quite grand Trinity in Edinburgh: he comes from Eyemouth High School, Berwickshire, where he was depute head, and runs Oban High with five deputes.

Bouncy, caring and fun, he is married with two children currently in the next door primary and is potty about surfing and snowboarding (neither of which spring to mind as usual Oban activities), and waxes lyrical about drama. Runs a complex and complicated ship with children ranging from bright middle class, some with a fairly lively hippy ancestry, to off-spring of local farmers and fisherfolk, and, following the closure of Drumore Special Unit, has a dedicated unit for autistic children with severe and complex needs (some of whom need two carers). We high-fived one young man several times during our tour. A fulfilling and challenging job, and one he relishes. 'My vision for the future of Oban High School is to work in partnership with pupils, parents and the local community to ensure that every single pupil becomes a successful learner by developing their knowledge and their talents to the best of their ability. We will endeavour to provide an enriched and broad experience beyond the academic thus ensuring that they become confident individuals and effective contributors within society.' This is what he said, and he seems to be getting there (and how). Last year he commissioned a professional assessment from Investors in People which came out with flying colours.

Academic matters: Full range of subjects offered at Standard grade, Highers and advanced Higher, including Gaelic (both for native Gaelic speakers and for learners – amongst whom the head counts himself, as do many of his staff) plus politics and sociology. Business studies popular and good success here. Results significantly above average for Scottish state schools in most subjects. Good emphasis on the academic. Advanced Higher mathematicians have mind-blowing residential weekends, maths challenge popular. Scientists work alongside the Scottish Association for Marine Science. Exciting new laser cutter (£10k) in design and tech dept. ICT is taught in five well-equipped rooms but other departments have good access to the school's many computer facilities.

Effective learning support operates for those with specific learning difficulties. Class sizes generally smaller than in most state schools, average 23 for academic and 20 for practical subjects. SQA certificate an option. Home economics superb, master classes from chef of the Isle of Eriska Hotel (5 star, two rosette restaurant – that sort of thing) and prize winners in national competitions. Subject choices (choose one subject from each column) include the Prince's Trust and skills for work plus uniformed emergency services (fire brigade), land management, make up, hairdressing and hospitality. Pathways – a structured 24 week timetabled semi-secondment – allows pupils in S4 to try out various (more or less) service activities: the fire brigade were recruiting during our visit, but the police are expected to come on board shortly. Work experience too with the Northern Lighthouse Board – 12 would-be engineers learn how to make buoys. About 8 per cent stay on post Standard grades and a further 70 per cent for advanced Highers.

No real problem getting staff – head has strategies to uncover Argyllshire wannabes, and is contemptuous of applicants who haven't done their homework before interview.

Games, Options, the Arts: Large games/assembly hall, well-equipped dance/fitness studio, two gyms, wide range of sports available including sailing, climbing, basketball, rugby (uses Oban Rugby club as well as their own) grass pitch with flood-lighting. Footie (girls very strong) and badminton plus shinty, basketball, sailing, boxing, dance and cheer-leading. Cross-country running, athletics, hill-walking, climbing, canoeing and gorge-walking are timetabled in PE curriculum from S3 upwards, as is D of E. Number of golds. Serious and successful swimming (off campus). Impressive wind-band, strings section, plus 75 strong prize-winning pipe band, samba band, choir and Gaelic choir (which competes successfully in the Royal National Mod). Music and drama have merged and all S1 and S2 learn keyboards. Dance, in conjunction with Taynult based Balletwest (who also use the hall for their outreach classes), is amazing – we could have been watching any professional troupe, anywhere. Scottish country dancing (hall – splendidly sprung – also used by locals). Fantastic art and really inspiring fabric and design, school took part in Homecoming '09. Air-training corps, Scout troop, sea cadets Plenty of extra-curricular activities on offer, difficulties because of long distances and buses are generally overcome. Variety of trips in most disciplines, free for those on free school meals; no one is excluded.

Background and Atmosphere: Smart looking façade conceals a mass of serious re-build but the old school is still there. War memorials and jolly photographs. Dining hall is cashless and parents' handbook publishes list of food available with prices. S1 not allowed to leave school grounds during their first half term. Certain amount of grubby buildings at the back, due for replacement soon, but the cost of not being able to use private contractors makes it a fairly slow process (though excellent breeding ground for smokers). Previous head seemed to forget about cleaning windows and this is exercising the current staff. Loads of displays throughout the school including an imaginative art gallery exhibiting students' creations.

Uniform is largely adhered to (sixth years wear blazers) with individual styling by some, and a constant battle with girls and ties. When asked by a parent how short the girls' skirts could be, the head replied that if he could see their bottoms when they bent over, then they were too short. Obviously immune to Oban weather, then. Hostel for islanders and those who live afar, recently beset with problems but with a new manager at the helm it is up to scratch. Spare space available for the new S1s to stay and spend a couple of days in the school before their arrival in August.

Pastoral Care and Discipline: All year groups are divided into tutor groups of 20 pupils or fewer. Each has its own tutor and sixth year prefect buddies. Year groups are managed by a head of year and school depute. School boasts an attendance officer, health worker and social worker. 'Good discipline prevails with effective sanctions for those who don't conform' – often involving local social workers. Head reckons to exclude 'about one a week'; five so far this term (one girl four times but each time counts anew). All staff trained in assertive discipline. Successful Truancy Watch scheme operates in conjunction with the local community. Lots of certificates and awards, including trip to Strathclyde Park for winners of 'annual class of the year'. Local ministries (all ten of them) support a chaplaincy centre H20, which in turn supports an array of local services via The Well and two and a half workers who – along with pupils – organise activities for pensioners and the disadvantaged. Huge charity input.

Pupils and Parents: The lot, including incomers, but not many ethnic minorities. Majority Scottish, many travelling long distances from North Argyll and the Islands. Famous Old Boys/Girls: Iain Crichton-Smith (writer), Kirsten Campbell (BBC political correspondent) and Maureen Scanlon (MSP), Shona and Mairi Crawford (British Ladies' ski team) and Lorne McIntyre (author and journalist).

Entrance: Catchment area plus placing requests. Twenty plus feeder primary schools, some are tiny, with perhaps eight or nine pupils in total. Six are on the islands – this involves 'hopping on a plane or a ferry to visit those in J6 who will transfer to Oban that year; takes a whole day, rather than popping round the corner for a couple of hours'. Enormous care taken to ensure S1s are not swamped on arrival – after all, if home is a croft and a few sheep, the bustle of Oban itself is overwhelming: some of the islands are still without mains electricity (televisions don't run that well on generators). Head visits all primary schools, as do the support for learning staff (if necessary) plus new form teachers; J6 pupils and their parents visit the school.

Exit: Automatic jobs for all at the end of the summer term: Oban is a popular tourist destination. Come September/October, some may have gone off to university (mostly Scottish, very occasional Oxbridge), some to further education, training schemes or family firms (fishing, farming) and some may sneak back to school for a bash at further qualifications.

Remarks: Wow. Has to be one of the most challenging and inclusive schools in the United Kingdom. Brilliant – really holds the community together.

Old Palace of John Whitgift School

Linked to Old Palace of John Whitgift School Junior Department in the Junior section

Old Palace Road, Croydon, Surrey, CR0 1AX

• Pupils: 840 day girls • Ages: 4-18 • Size of sixth form: 140 • C of E
• Fees: £10,212 pa • Independent

Tel: 020 8688 2027
Fax: 02086 805 877
Email: info@oldpalace.croydon.sch.uk
Website: www.oldpalace.croydon.sch.uk

Head: Since the merger in 2008, Dr Judy Harris (forties). Head of Old Palace School before the merger and, before that, deputy head at the Abbey School in Reading, where she taught French and PE. Grew up in Purley and went to Croydon High School for Girls. 'My personal background should have no relevance,' she told us, so no further details are forthcoming. But then she appeared to be recovering from a humourectomy at the time and it was kind of her to see us at all. Runs a tight ship, wholly committed to the girls in her care, passionate about education, clearly a terrific head. Modernising the school at a marvellous pace, reminiscent of that notable Russian innovator, Peter the Great.

Old Palace School merged in July 2008 with Croham Hurst School – a neighbour, and a nice enough school, but not at the same academic level. Dr Harris is head of the new school, known as Old Palace of John Whitgift School. The senior school will educate up to 800 girls on the Old Palace site, the junior will serve 500 girls from the Croham Hurst site. This is about 100 more pupils than the two schools educated between them. A nursery section, The Limes, opened in 2008 and is expanding rapidly.

Historically such mergers have not been easy. Either the pupils from the less academic school stay, and the character of the school changes, or they leave and the finances suffer. The Whitgift Foundation has the resources to make sure no ships sink – and they seem to be the authors of this deal. However, undoubted unease amongst parents, who complain of a lack of consultation.

Academic matters: Consistently excellent results, with 66 per cent per cent A*/A grades at GCSE in 2009 and over 73 per cent A/B grades at A level. Several girls in top 10 in the country for their subjects. Science has been strong, with chemistry the most popular subject at A level, and astronomy GCSE offered after school, where staff themselves are amongst those studying it. Modern languages department 'amazing, fun and really cool', according to the girls, with many tongues offered alongside French, and trips abroad 'tripled, even quadrupled' over the past three years. The new language lab is superb and girls can use it whenever they wish. IB was apparently up for discussion at a forthcoming curricular review – no news from the school. Pupils are worked hard and respond enthusiastically – even cover lessons are 'actually a pleasure', according to staff, 'because the girls just get on with it'. The girls in turn describe the staff as having 'passion, thought and consideration'. Watch this space for updates on what is now a much broader academic range.

Newly appointed learning support advisory teacher and the school has staff trained in dyslexia and dyspraxia. 'We aim to support the needs of our intake.' These are now, of course, more complicated, and we await developments. Some 'rationalisation' of staffing levels in process.

Games, Options, the Arts: Sports used to be the Achilles' heel of Old Palace, but a dynamic new head of PE plus dedicated staff have changed all that and things are buzzing. Gym, dance, swimming, rounders, athletics, netball, hockey and tennis are all successful, and football divas have gone on to join Tooting & Mitcham Ladies FC. The school has its own swimming pool, gym and netball courts, and the girls are bused to the Croham site whenever playing fields are needed, proving that you don't need acres of greenery to be a contender.

Art is outstanding, with fabulously creative work on display everywhere you look. Drama, debating, chess and house activities are all lively, with ballroom dancing and the gospel choir particularly effervescent, and Indian dance blossoming. Music continues splendid, with the annual Music Fest playing host to luminaries like the Maggini string quartet. All kinds of instrumental tuition are offered, and the school has staged a number of operas, including *The Magic Flute* and *Dido and Aeneas*. Polyphonic, the school's awesomely good chamber choir, regularly sings in Croydon's lovely parish church and services are 'inspirational'.

Background and Atmosphere: A beautiful, tranquil oasis nestling rosily in the centre of Croydon. Grade I listed English Heritage site, with parts going back a thousand years to 1070, when King William granted the Manor of Croydon to Archbishop Lanfranc. Medieval Banqueting Hall, a fifteenth century jewel, is used for assemblies, and the chapel, still used for prayers, is arrestingly lovely. Library housed in the Guard Room, where the young James I of Scotland was held prisoner. History really breathes in this wonderful old building and girls and staff are deeply proud of it. New buildings are also impressive – the Whitgift Foundation has served its sister well.

A magnificently refurbished preparatory school on the Croham site has transformed life in the junior department and the former Pickford's warehouse over the road now houses a thoroughly modern sixth form centre and a state-of-the-art canteen serving hot lunches that Jamie Oliver would be pleased with. Bad news for the McDonald's round the corner – but you can't have everything.

The community seems remarkably happy and tender, with many girls choosing to spend their entire school career here. The senior girls take particular pleasure in their close links with the junior department and opportunities to work with the little ones are highly prized. 'It's a kind school,' a sixth former told me – 'the girls are just nicer to each other here'. Her mother added, 'The school has always looked after her. It's not just been about results.'

There will undoubtedly be teething problems with the new, much larger venture. Parents fear the school is spreading itself too widely to compete for pupils and may lose its concern for individuals. Certainly they complain of a slow response to questions and lack of concern for their views.

Pastoral Care and Discipline: Discipline is tight, behaviour and manners excellent. Issues with drugs, drink or smoking are non-existent. Staff are caring and approachable: the aim is that all girls should have at least one teacher they can talk to about anything, preferably more than one. Parents report that any problems with studies or with other pupils have been spotted quickly and dealt with successfully – they hope this will continue under the new regime. The school rests secure and serene in its Christian foundation and all girls attend the end-of-term Church services, regardless of their individual faith. Interestingly, the result is an outstandingly sensitive and friendly community, with no racial tension whatsoever between its ethnically diverse members.

Pupils and Parents: As just mentioned, this is a multi-cultural society, with all minorities represented. Catchment is wide, from Bromley to Wimbledon one way, from Southwark to Coulsdon and Oxted the other. Parents are committed, involved and from all backgrounds – good social mix. Many girls have brothers at the foundation's other schools, Whitgift and Trinity, and links between the three are close.

Entrance: Was over-subscribed but not massively so. Entrance tests were tough but not impossible – will now need to accommodate a much broader ability range. Tests for entry at four and 11 given in early January – 11+ tests only in English, maths and verbal reasoning, plus 'very informal' interview, to ease entry from state school. 13+ candidates tested in February. Virtually automatic entry to senior school for all girls in the junior department. Entrance at sixth form by interview and dependent on GCSE grades.

Exit: Overwhelming majority go on to university in London. Numbers to Oxbridge vary widely – eleven in a good year, four in more typical years. Medicine, dentistry and optometry popular. A handful leave at 16 for other schools or sixth form colleges.

Money Matters: The school aims to keep the fees as low as possible and is considered excellent value for money by parents. Whitgift Foundation offers a number of bursaries, plus scholarships for academic ability, music or sport, and many pupils at Old Palace are on financial assistance of some sort, some of it extremely generous.

Remarks: Old Palace was a lively yet caring school where almost all personalities could flourish, though possibly not for subversives. Now it has merged with the academically gentler Croham Hurst, all hope that teething problems will be swiftly overcome to ensure that girls of all abilities can thrive here.

The Oratory School

Linked to Oratory Preparatory School in the Junior section

Woodcote, Nr Reading, South Oxfordshire, RG8 0PJ

• Pupils: 430 boys – 240 board, 190 day • Ages: 11-18 • Size of sixth form: 125 • RC foundation but all faiths welcome • Fees: Day £18,795; Boarding £26,025 pa • Independent

Tel: 01491 683 500
Fax: 01491 680 020
Email: enquiries@oratory.co.uk
Website: www.oratory.co.uk

Headmaster: Since 2000, Mr Clive Dytor MC MA (Cantab) MA (Oxon), (early fifties). Born and bred in Wales, where he attended Christ College, Brecon. Read oriental studies at Trinity, Cambridge. Joined Royal Marines, serving in Belfast and Falklands (where he earned that MC for a night attack on hilltops above Stanley – well worth a Google if you can stand the awe that this inspires). In 1986 read theology at Oxford, followed by Anglican church work and first teaching post at Tonbridge. Conversion to RC influenced strongly by Cardinal Newman's writings. 'A man of integrity and vision,' said one parent, who also placed him 'towards the top' of the strictness scale. Housemaster at St Edward's, Oxford, before Oratory appointment.

Ringmaster minus top hat – cracks whip when required, talks up school's star acts and exudes boundless energy. Ambitious for The Oratory but not interested in hiking up numbers. Likens school to 'a Morgan alongside the Rolls which is Eton or the Bentley which is Harrow'. Hobbyhorse is building a new chapel and converting present one into a performing arts centre. Military attention to detail but sense of fun and has time for everyone. Took Spanish GCSE recently alongside boys (A* result but admitted to finding listening paper challenging) and now embarking on part-time doctorate in Spanish history. Had to remove some dead wood early into headship; has right team now and appears to be advancing steadily on all fronts. Great rôle model for boys – manly devotion mixed with exemplary commitment to high standards. Wife, Sarah, teaches violin and plays professionally; son has gone through school successfully and has place to read medicine at Birmingham; daughter a music scholar at St Mary's, Ascot.

Academic matters: Results have improved steadily since head took over – 75 per cent A*/B at A level in 2010. Art and design department enjoys 'inspirational' leadership, has achieved *Good Schools Guide* overall best in England award for top A level results by boys three years running and is consistently at the top of the tree. Runs own foundation art diploma course whereby most talented can gain direct entry to degree level art courses. Twenty-five subjects on sixth form choice list makes curriculum broader than most schools this size.

GCSE results have bettered national levels of improvement and pulled away from some obvious competitors. Boys have made top five nationally in AQA English lit exam. Lessons delivered with enthusiasm to relatively small groups (overall pupil staff ratio of 8:1 very generous). Good number of 'ledge' (aka legendary) teachers according to boys. Recent construction of new history, art, English, maths, DT and theology departments. No computers in rather dated library, though main ICT teaching area up to the mark and all boarding houses have IT suites. English, maths and sciences all strong. We watched a lively physics lesson on electricity – excellent rapport between teacher and boys. RI compulsory throughout school with some taking RS as exam course. Good choice of languages includes Italian and Mandarin with Latin still offered as GCSE option. Plenty of exchanges and foreign visits. School leans over backwards to accommodate subject choices wherever possible.

Special needs low key but rated by parents whose sons need learning support; new SENCo from Kingham Hill.

Games, Options, the Arts: If you want your son to be spoilt for sporting choice, receive top coaching and be better placed for team selection than in larger schools, then look no further. Games timetabled every working day except Thursday, when CCF takes over. Swathe of manicured grass hosts magnificent cricket pitch on which several international schoolboy players have played for the school first Xl; acres of adjacent football and rugby pitches; magnificent sports complex with (undersize) indoor pool, good squash courts and a superb real tennis court used to host world championships. Current sports tours to India, South America and New Zealand (rugby), Barbados and South Africa (cricket) and Malta (football). Strong racquet tradition overall with 12 courts, six grass (set in exquisite walled garden), six hard. Wet bobs warm up running down to nearby Thames where school has own boathouse. Voluntary fundraising efforts by boys help keep boats up to scratch. In 2006 the 1st VIII won at the national schools' regatta. GB oarsmen have been selected from the school over the last few years. Very strong at shooting (enviable record at Bisley and Cadet Skill At Arms Meeting). Four Oratorians currently in GB teams, one to Canada, one to Jersey and South Africa. Wide participation in D of E scheme with twenty-five per cent of second year sixth achieving gold. School won the *Telegraph* and Norwich Union national sports awards in the Independent Schools' category.

Turbo-charged head of art is 'on a mission': some of the work we saw was far beyond usual school level – huge canvases, exciting sculptures, ceramics and print work showing stunning individuality and flair at all levels. Stress on skill building from junior years – 'We cannot offer freedom without structure' is the approach. New gallery and drawing studios allow the school to showcase quality in depth here and also attract top artists. Boys 'enjoy physicality of art' and 'seem to perform better without girls around,' we were told. DT now brought into fold with innovative product and textile design courses on offer.

Music enjoying a renaissance with a particularly strong choral tradition (new entrants include ex-Westminster Cathedral choristers). Just under half the boys participate in instrumental or singing lessons. Good range of ensemble, orchestral, choral and band activities. Schola Cantorum (school choir) numbers over seventy. Recent successes include selection for national youth choir. Drama gathering momentum under new HOD with termly productions ensuring all age groups get to perform regularly; girls from Reading and Abingdon drafted in where needed. Belloc Society provides keen forum for school debating and cultural activities.

Background and Atmosphere: Started in Edgbaston in 1859 by Cardinal John Henry Newman as an 'Eton minus its wickedness' for the sons of well-to-do Catholics. In September 2010 Pope Benedict XVI conducted a Beatification Mass for the school's founder, John Henry Cardinal Newman, at Cofton Park in Birmingham. Has done well to reinvent itself as a mainstream faith school and to hold its own as a slightly quirky place in a notoriously 'brand conscious' area. Moved to present Queen Anne style manor location at Woodcote in 1942 with just 30 boys. Sympathetic conversion of original building with more recent (less sympathetic) additions but first impressions still make impact. Impressive foyer and portrait adorned 'black room' now used for Saturday teas and a variety of black tie occasions for seniors, informal concerts etc. About £5 million spent recently on providing two new state of art boarding houses, though many boys still prefer older, refurbished one. Physical separation of living and working areas makes sense.

Set on a hill, surrounded by 400 acres of playing fields, greenery and woodlands, the school commands breathtaking views across both Berkshire and Oxfordshire. Hard to imagine Reading a few miles down the road, let alone the M4 corridor or Heathrow to which it is conveniently close. Back lane allows boys limited shopping in Woodcote Village, but otherwise boys are relatively isolated and self-contained, which helps to strengthen the community life here. Over half boys are boarders and bulk of staff live on site or in school-owned accommodation in village.

Pastoral Care and Discipline: Head's mantra ('A busy boy is a happy boy') seems to hold water. Boys really get stuck in here and the strong Catholic tradition maintains a healthy balance between mind, body and heart. Boys like chaplain who presents them with a 'vision of happiness based on something other than money,' insisted an admiring mother. We met a Muslim day boy from a state primary background who said that he had been 'stunned' when he first visited with his parents and was now having 'the time of his life'. All religions fit in here. Daily prayers in houses and weekly assembly for all. Sunday morning Mass a must for all boarders and an option for day boys. Questionably appropriate modern chapel (hence head's pet project) for main school; juniors attend atmospheric old chapel converted from a former tithe barn.

Houses all run by married couples with extra live-in tutors. Tradition of gap year students from Australia and New Zealand to help with juniors at St Philip House (the two we met were certainly good value). Particularly good atmosphere here: discrete playing, social and teaching areas for 11–13s ensure that boys get a lot of attention; presence of five resident staff for junior boarders with no shortage of hands-on experience – current houseparents and deputies have eight children of their own between them.

'Food is awesome.' Head insists on high standards of appearance. Sensible approach to alcohol and smoking.

Pupils and Parents: Majority come from professional and business families in Thames Valley. Oratory parents like fact that, 'boys are not treated as robots or exam fodder' plus 'school doesn't force us to separate siblings just because one may not make same academic grade as the others'.

About half RC (including some from Europe and Africa). Overall, 15 per cent from overseas including Hong Kong and Korea. Boys look you in the eye and are ready to give you their take on the school or life in general. Unashamedly traditional structures with all kinds of tribal differentiations in uniform – customised in the case of prefects (to the disapproval of some, we learned) but arts given same cred as sport. Strong links with old boys; good smattering of professional sportsmen amongst them. Best known Old Oratorian is probably writer and poet, Hilaire Belloc.

Entrance: More choosy now than in doldrums of nineties. Most come from own prep school nearby (co-ed to 13) or on-site junior house, a few from good primaries. Entry test. CE at 13 requiring 50 per cent pass (though more flexibility granted to siblings and OB's sons plus others who make out a good case). Also head's report from last school and interview. Five Cs at GCSE a minimum to get into sixth form.

Exit: Very few leave at 16+ to go elsewhere – a good sign. All sixth form to HE though some take a gap year. High hopes of increasing Oxbridge but finding it more difficult of late to penetrate heavier social engineering barrage. Plenty to Russell Group universities; some to top art and music colleges. A few to military careers.

Money Matters: Scholarships and exhibitions up to half fees available – academic, music, art, sport and good all-rounders. Fees middle of the range. Extra charges for books, cultural and sports trips, laundry and haircuts. Generous bursaries.

Remarks: Refreshingly quirky staff and unpretentious boys. A great place to develop self-confidence and a faith in the nobler things of life.

Oundle School

Linked to Laxton Junior School in the Junior section

Great Hall, New Street, Oundle, Peterborough, Northamptonshire, PE8 4GH

• Pupils: 650 boys, 460 girls; 860 full board, 250 day • Ages: 11-19 • Size of sixth form: 415 • C of E • Fees: Day £13,500-£17,775; Boarding £20,760-£27,300 pa • Independent

Tel: 01832 277 125
Fax: 01832 277128
Email: admissions@oundleschool.org.uk
Website: www.oundleschool.org.uk

Headmaster: Since 2005, Mr Charles (Charlie) Bush MA (mid fifties). Previously head of maths and housemaster at Marlborough before headship at Eastbourne College. Married, with children, he's an energetic pragmatist who's wedded to the school. Wants it to be a 'market leader' and lauds its 'middle Englishness'. Often seen wandering in the cloisters, he makes it his business to see and be seen – a penetrating gaze, verging on a glare, appears intimidating, but his genuine friendliness quickly comes to the fore once he starts chatting. Parents speak of his all-round encouragement and the way he 'turns up to everything, even charity and fundraising events'. Clearly happiest when busy, he fills spare time watching matches, getting to know pupils over a meal at Cobthorne (gem of a townhouse originally built for one of Cromwell's generals) or absorbing absolutely everything there is to know about the school.

Academic matters: Expectations are high and pupils are stretched. According to a sixth former, 'If you're not exhausted by the end of term something's wrong.' Parents comment that a fair amount of pressure and absolutely no mollycoddling. Strong showing at GCSE – 84 per cent A/A*. History shines and is tremendously popular – the department is 'filled with unforgettable characters' – whilst science is a 'major, major thing in the school'. Fast track French for strong linguists is followed by Chinese, Arabic or Italian in the fifth form – several language teachers are foreign nationals. The more demanding IGCSE English, maths and science taken by all. IGCSEs have now been extended to geography, history and religious studies. Triple award science offered for the most able, dual award for everyone else. Impressive 91 per cent A/B at A level – everyone takes at least four subjects. A non-examined extension course is compulsory in the lower sixth and, in response to recent history, Arabic has been added to the list of options. No let up in the upper sixth – most narrow down to three A levels (30 per cent take four) and pupils attend weekly lectures or discussions which make up the stimulating general studies programme. The Pre-U is offered in physics, chemistry, economics, German, mathematics, history of art and government and politics.

Only those who have the mildest SEN will cope here. The learning support department provides one to one help outside lesson times but rarely more than once a week. Additional help is available from individual departments, but clashes with sporting or musical commitments can be a problem. Limited help for EAL students – 'Their English needs to be pretty good'.

Games, Options, the Arts: Has a balanced view of sport – not the raison d'être of life but an important factor. After the fourth form, pupils opt for team or individual activities – 'If the right choice is made it's very good,' said a parent. All the majors including football – plus squash, fives, water polo, rowing, athletics, aerobics, cross country, golf. Tip-top facilities. Apart from a third Astroturf pitch they've got it all – modern multisports complex with its own goodie-filled sports shop, an outdoor synthetic athletics track, a rifle range etc etc. First teams are viewed seriously and plenty of competitive fixtures for those on lower rungs. Under 15 team recently won Lord's Taverners cricket competition and Under 15 rugby team reached the semi-final of the 'Daily Mail' Cup. A small number of sports scholarships will be awarded for 13+ entry for the first time in 2011.

Busy music department with almost three-quarters of the pupils learning an instrument plus a full programme of concerts at home and away. When we visited, lusty singing in chapel was accompanied by an impressively competent fifth form organ scholar. Organ scholarships recently won to Trinity and Jesus College, Cambridge.

Proud that it pioneered the idea of learning through doing and has developed the tradition by neatly positioning, on the northern side of the town, a sizeable sci-tec block. Intended to marry the arts with sciences, it trumpets lofty ideals and has plenty of green credentials. Phase one, filled with 16 laboratories, has opened, whilst the rest will take several years to complete – an exciting development. Meanwhile DT continues to thrive. Atmosphere in the department is more akin to industry than school, with casting, lasers, wind tunnels, micro-electronics and computer aided design. Work from the art department is highly accomplished and pupils appreciate the open door policy at weekends when 'they can get on with their work, listen to some music, relax and chat'. They also get to use the small Yarrow Gallery, which regularly hosts visiting exhibitions. To mark the millennium, pupils' design ideas were used as a starting point for the vibrantly coloured stained-glass windows made for the school chapel – a lively foil to John Piper's sedately beautiful east windows.

Extra-curricular activities are more than encouraged – for some the best thing about the place: 'It's like one big activity camp'. For the first two years 'voluntaries' are compulsory and the extraordinarily varied list of activities caters for all tastes. CCF is compulsory in the fourth form. Up to 50 per cent of the school is involved with the D of E scheme at any one time and fifth and sixth formers help in the wider community through the school's community action programme – a long running connection with Mencap. No idle time and activities run into the hols – 'They don't seem to have time to take breath,' commented a mum – field trips, exchanges, sporting tours and expeditions to the exotic and remote.

For the stage struck the charming Stahl Theatre – funded by an OO (old Oundelian) legacy – provides a professional venue for touring companies and the good and popular pupil productions.

Background and Atmosphere: Founded in 1556 as the local grammar, the school split in 1876 into Laxton for the sons of tradesmen and local farmers and Oundle for the sons of gentlemen. Full co-education, with a 60:40 ratio in favour of boys, came in the early 1990s. Laxton was brought back into the fold as a day house in 2000. Today it's hard to distinguish the extensive school campus from the picturesque market town of Oundle, the two are so closely meshed. Pupils move about as if at university and if time, drop into a coffee shop or join the snaking break queue outside the popular High Street bakery.

Spacious boarding houses – well maintained and of varying degrees of architectural interest – are liberally spread, with the furthest a brisk ten minute walk away from the central Cloisters. A first year pupil plus pedometer managed to clock up seven miles in a day – 'Good exercise,' humphed the registrar. The house system is strong and none of the thirteen houses elicit a groan, but boys still think the girls get a better deal and parents have their favourites – a four year waiting list for one or two. The crucial rôle of housemasters and mistresses – 'Ours is 101 per cent supportive' – and policy of eating every meal in house give an intimate feel in what could be an overwhelmingly large school. Compulsory chapel on Sunday plus two other slots during the week.

The 20,000 volume library offers a book-ordering service and stays open till late most days. Also home to a display case full of fine Attic vases – part of a collection of antiquities left to the school by yet another grateful OO. A major redevelopment of the library will take place in the summer of 2011.

Pastoral Care and Discipline: Pastoral care is based on the house tutorial system. 'No time for hand holding' and pupils heed the emphasis on self reliance – but when the chips are down, personal tutors or housemaster are there to help and keep parents informed via email; a dim view is taken of bullying and it's promptly sorted. Interhouse competitions strengthen the strong bonds within houses and parents speak highly of the support pupils give each other. Demarcations between girls' and boys' houses are strict and fraternising is closely monitored.

Rules are fair and the head, perceived to be 'very, very strict', upholds the policy re drugs and sex – instant exclusion – but allows upper sixth formers the freedom to visit just one pub, which happens to be next door to his house. Exeats are a rarity – officially after the first year only one per annum – but if a pressing need the housemaster will flex.

Pupils and Parents: Oundelians hail from all corners of England and Scotland but vast majority are from the eastern side of the country. Currently over 130 prep schools represented. 10 per cent of pupils come from continental Europe or the Pacific Rim and 12 per cent are children of OOs – the family network is strong. Parents range from the professional to farming folk – open minded but ambitious. Pupils are fresh-faced and courteous, the girls with swishing culottes and the boys with just enough hair gel to conform. High levels of motivation are a must – all work hard and enjoy the social side of school life.

OOs include Arthur Marshall, Peter Scott (ornithologist), Cecil Lewis (aviator), A Alvarez, Anthony Holden (royal biographer), Richard Dawkins, Professor Sir Alan Budd, Charles Crichton (film director), Bruce Dickinson (lead singer of Iron Maiden).

Entrance: Tough. At 11+, 13+ or 16+. Waiting list with sibling preference – 36 per cent have a brother or sister in the school. Feeder schools are well primed and start preparation early, whilst the registrar makes it his business to ensure only those who'll succeed are entered. The majority do much better than the minimum CE requirement of 55 per cent in English, maths, French and science. Pupils must achieve a minimum of three As and three Bs in their GCSEs to proceed automatically into the sixth form.

Exit: From the sixth form virtually all to university. Traditional courses with history especially popular. Healthy proportion to Oxbridge (about 25 places each year). Most of the rest to the heavyweights or, increasingly, across the pond.

Money Matters: Range of scholarships awarded at 11+, 13+ and 16+. Bursaries, which may be as high as 100 per cent, available in cases of proven need – parents need to discuss the matter with the school at least two to three years before entry. Old Oundlean bursaries for the sons and daughters of OOs.

Remarks: Popular, well-oiled, well-heeled, co-educational boarding school which is riding high. Life is full on and pupils and parents relish the opportunities which abound. Idyllic setting provides an oasis of gentility where the bright all-rounder who's prepared to have a go will flourish.

Our Lady's Abingdon

Linked to Our Ladys Junior School Abingdon in the Junior section

Radley Road, Abingdon, Oxfordshire, OX14 3PS

• Pupils: 390 • Ages: 11-18 • Size of sixth form: 85 • Roman Catholic
• Fees: £10,980 pa • Independent

Tel: 01235 524 658
Fax: 01235 535 829
Email: office@olab.org.uk
Website: www.olab.org.uk

Head: Since 2004, Mrs Lynne Renwick (forties), NPQH BEd from Leeds. Previously assistant head at All Saints' Catholic School, York; head of humanities at Dixons City Technology College, Bradford, and head of history at Colegio San Silvestre, Lima, Peru – her first post in the independent sector. Petite and sparkly but also extremely determined, she has a clear-eyed vision for the school's co-educational future, accentuating the positive at all times. Has taught and travelled in South America and is very proud of the school's recent DCSF award of 'International' school (for 'bringing the wider world into the classroom' and vice versa), one of only a handful in the country.

She is not timetabled to teach regularly, preferring instead to 'dot around' and cover lessons when staff are absent, in order to see what's going on in all classes. She maintains 'an open door' for staff, pupils and parents, seeing them as all working together in partnership. Member of the Catholic Independent Schools Conference, a governor of Cranford House School, Oxfordshire (qv) and an ISI inspector. Her husband works in advertising as an illustrator and they live nearby in Bampton. Interests include Spanish culture and literature, travel, walking and ice skating.

Academic matters: Perhaps unfairly, the school's reputation has been somewhat overshadowed by the stellar achievements of the girls from nearby School of St Helen and St Katharine (qv) but results here are still extremely good, with average of 10 GCSEs taken with an A* to C pass rate of 98 per cent. No IGCSEs as yet but these are 'under consideration'. Separate sciences taught by subject specialist teachers throughout but dual award science GCSE only. Apparently the subjects are taken 'beyond' the GCSE curriculum and over 50 per cent go on to study science at AS/A level, where all three subjects are taught. Fairly traditional range of GCSE subjects with business studies and psychology on offer too. Creditable results at A level, results table percentages affected by some small class sizes. The benefit of those small classes is that all pupils get individual attention – lots of active questioning and free discussion in the lessons we observed. Latin offered up to A level, Greek too, although this is an extra (lessons in the lunch hour and after school). Technology has now been added to the list of subjects, prompted by change to co-ed. Good mix of male and female staff, many have been with the school for more than ten years. Learning support described by one parent with dyslexic daughter as 'excellent', one-to-one and paired extra lessons offered, and pupils also benefit from the small classes in lower sets.

Games, Options, the Arts: Head stresses the importance of extra-curricular interests – she is a keen ice skater and to be found on the rink at 6.30am every Saturday. Buses leave at 5pm three days a week to allow time for participation in a varied timetable of after school clubs including astronomy, synchronised swimming and 'Uganda Team', where pupils take part in regular email and webcam communication with their partner school. The indoor swimming pool, right at the heart of the school, means that kayaking, scuba diving and snorkelling are all on offer too. Recent expedition destinations include Everest Base Camp and trekking in South America. A junior and senior choir trip to France, including a performance at Disneyland Paris, is planned to celebrate the school's 150th anniversary. Proud of its strong links with Maryhill High School in Uganda (see above) and regular visits and energetic fundraising activities to support this.

The library is modern and well stocked with separate sixth form study area; helpful librarian who organizes reading challenges and inter-school literary activities. The dedicated computer suite next door does much to maintain bookish quiet. The standard of work in the art department is particularly impressive, much of it is also beautifully displayed throughout the school. Usual range of instrumental tuition offered in what was described by one parent as a rather 'traditional' music department. Two choirs, a wind band, chamber groups and an orchestra perform at two concerts a year and a whole school drama production in the winter term and frequent smaller productions (usually for GCSE and A level drama).

Background and Atmosphere: The school was founded in 1860 by Sister Clare Moore, a nun from the order of the Sisters of Mercy who worked closely with Florence Nightingale in the Crimean War. It was originally co-ed, but then became girls only until 2009, when the governors decided to accept boys once again. Now boys in two of the four Year 7 classes – the school decided to concentrate them in two classes rather than spread them thinly over four – and a handful in the sixth form. According to the head, numbers are set to increase from 2010.

Our Lady's is tucked away in a residential area of Abingdon in a mixture of old and modern buildings. The older parts were once the convent – the junior school (qv) has a marvellous door with sliding grill through which the nuns would speak to strangers. Newer buildings include a spacious entrance hall with versatile open plan space (on the other side of a glass divide is the swimming pool – an unusual centrepiece), an assembly hall which doubles as a theatre space and light and modern sixth form centre, all pale wood and big windows. The newer parts of the school are distinguished by extremely effective use of natural light; by contrast, the older classrooms and corridors seem dingy, although these, like the rest of the school, are much enlivened by displays of the pupils' work. The let down is the dining room, where the low ceiling and awkward layout give a subterranean feel, but plans to improve this and to build a dedicated DT block. Science rooms are well-equipped (new laboratories built in 2008), dedicated art, textiles and home economics spaces are light and spacious and music practice rooms and a keyboard room.

Sizeable outside space for an urban site, large playing field just across the road and the school uses nearby Astroturf facilities (as do other Abingdon schools). The atmosphere is calm, efficient and relaxed and genuine rapport between staff and pupils was notable in the lessons we observed.

Pastoral Care and Discipline: The motto is 'Age quod agis' (Whatever you do, do well) and its influence is palpable throughout the school, undoubtedly helped by an average class size of 14 (max 22), much smaller in lower ability sets. Pupils have half an hour of tutor time/assemblies at the start of each day per day, split between the start and the end of lessons. Although only around a third of the intake is Roman Catholic and no longer any teaching nuns, the school's religious ethos is strongly in evidence – crucifixes in every room, frequent masses and a clear emphasis on service both local and international: on Wednesday afternoons sixth form pupils do voluntary work with the elderly, the local hospital and other community projects.

The head is proud of the enrichment programme (Year 12) that she says is intended to 'prepare pupils for life after school', offering tuition in a range of skills such as financial management, car maintenance and cookery, as well as courses exploring ethics and morality. Standard house system headed by sixth formers with emphasis on sharing responsibilities and tasks throughout age groups. Sensible uniform of blue jumper and kilt will appeal to parents; possibly unpopular (nearby girls' school abandons uniform after GCSEs) sixth form dress code allows pupils to choose, as long as it is smart and monochrome.

Catholic and non-Catholic parents are attracted by school's strong moral and pastoral reputation and parents we spoke to were fulsome in their praise of staff/pupil relations and the ways in which each child's individual abilities are developed. When questioned about bullying (in relation both to school policy and specific incidents), the head pronounced confidently that her school is a 'telling school' where pupils are encouraged, for example in PSHE and whole school assemblies, to report incidents. Any problems are dealt with sensitively and all concerned followed up for some time afterwards.

Pupils and Parents: Predominantly white, from a wide catchment area extending to Berkshire and Gloucestershire, the school's religious character appeals to those who want an unashamedly Christian education for their children. Apparently it was pressure from those with boys in the junior section of school that was partly instrumental in the decision to become co-ed. Unusually for a secondary school, the head actively encourages parental involvement (CRB checked, of course), helping with trips etc. Most recent Christmas Fair raised an impressive £7,000 for charity. Parents we spoke to were fiercely loyal, 'a gem' said one; others praise the school's 'family' atmosphere and the way in which their children are treated as individuals rather than league table fodder. All parents commented on how pleased they were with home-school communication. It's still early days for co-ed integration; sixth formers say that boys have 'not changed the school as much as they thought they would'. We saw Year 7 boys absolutely engrossed in cutting patterns for Mondrian-inspired cushion covers in the textile department. It's cookery for them next term, and that can only be a good thing.

Entrance: Interview and assessment for junior school. Examination in Years 6 and 8 for entry to Years 7 and 9. Sixth form: interview and minimum of 5 GCSE passes at B or above, grade A or B for subjects to be studied at A level.

Exit: Approximately two thirds stay on for the sixth form and are joined by students from maintained and non-maintained sector. Careers teacher is sixth form tutor and has an office near the common room and study areas; these are at the top of the school, spacious and well-designed – usual commonroom mess but an air of serious study too. The size of the school means that A level students benefit from very small classes with plenty of individual attention and advice. Majority of leavers go on to first choice, mainly Russell Group universities (one or two to Oxbridge).

Money Matters: Fees are on a par with the other local independents. Lunches are extra. Bursaries and academic awards that account for up to seven per cent of the annual fee turnover; a number of these give up to 100 per cent remission on fees. Several bursaries funded by The Sisters of Mercy are available for Catholic children.

Remarks: A happy, well resourced school with a secure moral and pastoral ethos and the feel of a thriving community. Great plans afoot for expansion, both architecturally and in pupil numbers. If your child thrills to the competitive pressure of an academic powerhouse, two of these nearby whose reputations have, in the past, partly eclipsed Our Lady's. But perhaps you want something slightly different. If so, take a closer look: this school is strong in all areas with exam results and facilities to match and prides itself on 'revealing the special talent of each individual child'. The brave new world of co-ed status means it is now a much more clearly distinguished part of the Abingdon triumvirate.

Oxford High School GDST

Linked to Oxford High School GDST Junior School in the Junior section

Belbroughton Road, Oxford, Oxfordshire, OX2 6XA

• Pupils: 590 girls, all day • Ages: 11-18 • Size of sixth form: 145
• Non-denom • Fees: Junior £6,774; Senior £9,345 pa • Independent

Tel: 01865 559 888
Fax: 01865 552 343
Email: oxfordhigh@oxf.gdst.net
Website: www.oxfordhigh.gdst.net

Head: For the autumn term 2010, Mrs Olwen Curry MSc MA(Oxon) PGCE, a former pupil, read biochemistry at Somerville, has been head of biology and of sixth form at OHS and has now stepped up from her deputy head rôle to lead the school during the transition before the arrival of Mrs Judith Carlisle – 'It's a privilege and a pleasure to be in charge of the school, if only for a term, at a time of great development and progress which coincides with the opening of the new buildings that have been constructed over the last year'.

From January 2011, Mrs Judith Carlisle, who comes from Dover Grammar School for Girls. She read English and drama at Bristol and worked in the theatre for a few years before doing a PGCE at Goldsmith's – 'As soon as I came to visit Oxford High School I knew it was the school I wanted to lead. The energy, enthusiasm and sheer quality of the pupils and staff make it a very special place'.

Academic matters: Consistently successful in all exams and regularly in the upper reaches of league tables. 2010 A level results were excellent with 36 per cent A*, 81 per cent A*/A and 96 per cent A*/B. Half the sixth form take maths, with sciences extremely popular, supporting successful university applications to medical schools and top universities. English, history, geography and languages (classical and modern) are also popular and strongly taught. GCSE results are equally strong with 91 percent A*/A grades. Mandarin is compulsory in Year 7 and offered at GCSE and AS/A level. Twenty six subject choices in the sixth form, with a curriculum built around the student subject choices, not the other way round. No early GCSEs taken because, as a teacher puts it, 'We want the journey to be as comfortable as possible. We want to engage their curiosity and, by leaving exams until the proper time, the girls' level of understanding is that much greater. We want them to love learning'.

Students work hard – lots of homework set to develop independent working. A girl told us, 'You grow up with the ethos that you work hard, because you're motivated and it's fun.' The school is a regular top performer in science and maths Olympiads and wins national and local essay and poetry writing and classics competitions. Proud to have feet in both camps: ancient and modern, traditional reading and research materials with excellent computer facilities, intranet and satellite links. Special needs help is available – all girls screened, dyslexia or other needs identified and given support with full parental involvement. Participation and exchange of ideas is encouraged in lessons at all ages – learning is a two-way process and definitely not just chalk and talk.

Games, Options, the Arts: Maths and music clearly do go hand in hand, if OHS is anything to go by – at least 300 individual instrumental or singing lessons each week, with the vast majority of girls learning one instrument, many two; five auditioned only choirs or choral groups, African drumming, concert band, four orchestras. The quality of performance is truly outstanding, with pupils regularly members of the National Youth Orchestra. Art, pottery and textiles are also in a league of their own. The work on show in the studios is breathtakingly professional and innovative. Fine examples on permanent display, including a clock and outdoor seating area. Excellent DT, e.g. a superb chaise longue. Drama is dynamic – student directed productions and senior musicals such as *Fame.*

Keen sport – county, national and international representation, including fencing and shooting. Well kept playing fields, a sports hall, tennis and netball courts and magnificent indoor pool. D of E very popular, very successful participation in the Young Enterprise scheme – two or three companies a year gaining local and regional awards and one of last year's companies reached the national finals. Also chess, gardening, sailing, politics, knitting and People and Planet – total of 90 clubs. Fantastic number of expeditions and trips abroad – Nepal, Moscow, Iceland, USA, Italy and Spain. Good careers advice – a coherent programme of activities from Years 8 to 13 and expert support and guidance during the tense period of UCAS.

Background and Atmosphere: The buildings previously described as 'ungainly concrete and glass sprawl ' at the end of leafy residential area of North Oxford are now accompanied by a soaring frontage of the new build in wood and stone, with a proud sunflower illuminated at night.

Over 900 girls attend, including 350 in the two sites of the Junior School nearby (with the boys currently aged between 5 and 7 to be phased out). Despite these numbers, girls insist it is a student centred and student led school and feel it is 'good at being inclusive' and they are encouraged to be themselves. Many parents agree – 'I just don't understand it when people label OHS as a purely academic school,' said one. 'It's far more rounded than that.' Others feel the emphasis on self-motivation can be too great. 'I'm just so glad my daughter found herself a really good group of friends,' a mother told us. 'I have no quibble with the results they get, but it's a very competitive place and you need a network of friends to lean on at times.' Different ages mix for some activities and older girls look out for younger ones when they arrive at the senior school, which is within easy walking distance of the junior school sites. Also city centre theatres, museums attractions etc can be reached on foot.

Pastoral Care and Discipline: On the whole, excellent staff/student relations with free yet respectful exchange of views. Strong tutorial system underpins academic and personal needs of individuals. Daily staff briefing crucial, 'So everyone is aware of what's going on and that maybe you need to go easy on some girl for whatever reason', 'Our pastoral awareness is second to none'. Nurse also involved in PSHCE, plus lessons in self-esteem and self-awareness. Strong influential school council. Self-discipline promoted among girls with rewards for good behaviour rather than punishments for bad. Pupils encouraged to speak out to keep bullying to a minimum. Girls caught with drugs face instant exclusion. Cigarettes or alcohol might warrant short-term exclusion.

Pupils and Parents: A broad mix from a wide geographical area. Intake generally from a 30-mile radius. Traditionally a third has come from dons' families and that's still the case. The rest is socially diverse, but with intelligence and intellectual curiosity in common – staff say, 'You get some absolute gems from the most unlikely places'. Girls agree it's not a 'snobby school' and they're constantly aware of other people's circumstances and backgrounds – 'There's no particular type of girl. You can't put them into a box'.

Very supportive parent group. Activities include fundraising and giving careers talks. OGs include actresses Dame Maggie Smith and Miriam Margoyles; Cressida Dick, commander in the Metropolitan police; journalists Eleanor Oldroyd and Ursula Buchan; Dame Josephine Barnes, the first woman president of the BMA; lastminute.com entrepreneur Martha Lane Fox; Nina Raine, playwright; Mel Giedroyc, TV presenter.

Entrance: Although over-subscribed at all entry levels, it is worth having a go. Selective after nursery and reception – tests in maths, English, reading and spelling at later entry to junior school. Entry to senior school at 11 relies on similar test plus girls invited to bring something with them to discuss during interview. Transfer from junior to senior school generally automatic. External candidates can apply at any age.

At 16, at least five Bs at GCSE (including maths, English and a science) and As in the A level subjects they plan to study. It's a big thing for people to apply to a school like this. People might think they haven't a hope, but they shouldn't write themselves off.

Exit: On average 25–30 per cent to Oxbridge (placed 11th in recent Oxbridge admissions league table), others to other top drawer universities in a wide variety of subjects. Medicine and natural sciences feature highly, languages and politics also perennially popular.

Money Matters: Fees include all exam entries, careers advice, exercise and textbooks. Additional sum for compulsory school lunch until end of Year 11. Academic scholarships (for nominal amount) and music scholarships available at 11 and 16. Also art, sports, drama and all-rounder scholarships at 16, as well as music and academic. Means tested bursaries in cases of short or long term need which can be applied for.

Remarks: As the long list of alumnae clearly goes to show, churns out success after success after success. 'An unbeatable start in life for able pupils, who will be inspired to put in as much as they will get out of it,' we reported after our last visit, and nothing we saw or heard this time has changed our minds. The mix of talented enthusiastic staff and stimulating, challenging students is indeed a heady combination and one which appears to produce the most amazing results.

Palmers Green High School

Linked to Palmers Green Lower School in the Junior section

104 Hoppers Road, London, N21 3LJ

• Pupils: 320 girls, all day • Ages: 3-16 • Size of sixth form: n/a
• Non-denom • Fees: Y7-Y11 £11,355 pa • Independent

Tel: 020 8886 1135
Fax: 020 8882 9473
Email: office@palmersgreen.enfield.sch.uk
Website: www.pghs.co.uk

Headmistress: Since 2002, Mrs Christine Edmundson, BMus PGCE MBA LRAM ARCM. Educated at London (Royal Holloway), Cambridge (Emmanuel) and Exeter. Further music qualifications from The Royal College and Royal Academy of Music. Previously deputy head at the Royal High School, Bath. Believes strongly in maintaining a presence in the classroom and so teaches ICT to Year 6 and RE to Years 10 and 11 and runs the senior string ensemble. Interests include music and travel and, for the last twenty years, many members of her former sixth form have met annually for a summer cathedral singing week under her direction.

Academic matters: All prospective pupils are assessed and interviewed prior to being offered a place. High academic achievement is a declared goal. As a relatively small school with a new purpose-built nursery two miles from the main school, and with the majority going through from age three to 16, pupils receive so much individual attention that it is very hard for anyone to slip through the net.

Although year group sizes can go up to 32, the maximum number being taught at any time is 16 – most subjects, especially at GCSE, taught in much smaller groups. Excellent results – 74 per cent A*/A in 2010. Good range of subjects both at GCSE and IGCSE, with some students accessing AS level course material. All do science and additional science; Spanish available; maximum of 10 GCSEs.

Language and culture courses in Russian, German and French are popular along with the after-school Greek and Japanese courses. Other languages such as Persian, modern Greek, Turkish and Gujarati have been taken as GCSEs.

Games, Options, the Arts: Other than the well-equipped gym, no games facilities on site. Coaches for travel to Southgate swimming pool, Southbury leisure centre and the outdoor sports facilities at the Walker Ground, allowing a wide range of activities. PE (short course) a GCSE option. Many inter-house competitions in main sports. Ski trips to Europe and North America, Mediterranean watersports weeks.

Head very keen on music – several girls reach excellent standards and some follow specialist music courses at Trinity College of Music Junior School or via the Enfield Youth Orchestra. Wide choice of instrumental lessons, choirs, ensembles, chamber groups, orchestras, flute choirs. Light, airy music room with plenty of computers and key boards for composition.

Also art, drama, debating, yoga and the very popular knitting club, 'The Knit-Wits'. D of E from Year 9, annual residential trips for all at the beginning of Year 7 (team building/outdoor activity/ice-breaker course), for Year 8 geography fieldwork and art and modern languages GCSE students.

Background and Atmosphere: Opened in 1905, founded by a Quaker, Alice N Hum, in a building in Green Lanes, Palmers Green. It moved to its present site in 1918, formerly a meeting hall – the utilitarian walls and stairwells, though bravely decorated with art work and collages, recall institutions in an earlier life. Happily, the smells of lunch coming from the dining room do not – homemade, wholesome and appetising food. Purpose built Alice Nursery opened in 2008, 10 minutes' drive from the main school, intended as an academic day nursery.

Atmosphere of hard work, take pride in it, aim to succeed, do your best. Miss Hum chose the motto, 'By love serve one another', to reflect her Christian convictions. Although school is now non-denominational, the sentiment expressed in that motto still obtains. Head wants academic achievement and to see girls develop into capable, confident and compassionate young women willing to make their own contribution to their community.

Pastoral Care and Discipline: As a relatively small school contained in one building, it would be hard for any child's problem or unhappiness to go unnoticed – 'It is quite common for a member of staff to take a girl aside if she seems troubled in any way'. Very good staff-parent relations as all share the ethos of: work hard and your reward will be a good career.

Careers advice is taken extremely seriously. With pupils leaving here at 16, they need clear guidance before taking the next step. Many old pupils return to give talks about their chosen path and pupils practise their interview techniques, e.g. by tracking down school staff, 'to find out what the head's PA really does and what goes on in there'.

Discipline is not a problem. Mobile phones are allowed in Years 10 and 11 but must be switched off. For Years 7–9 all mobiles brought into school must be handed into the school office and can be collected at home going time.

Truancy is just not an issue. All girls sign an anti-bullying statement when they start at the school and staff are vigilant, acting immediately if they see any evidence of bullying.

Pupils and Parents: The mix of ethnicity accurately reflects this area of north London. Parents are mostly professionals who have an enormous regard for the value of education and are prepared to make any sacrifices necessary to send their daughters to this highly respected local independent school. They are viewed as an important part of the school family and kept up to date with relevant matters. The pupils are bright and busy, full of purpose and energy. The building may be dull, but its contents are anything but.

Entrance: Entry normally at 3 into the nursery, 4 into the prep, 7 into the junior and 11 into the senior sections. Most start at 3 and continue to 16. 11+ pupils are selected on the grounds of ability and aptitude. Assessments for the prep and junior schools take place in the spring. Senior 7 (Year 7) school applicants sit their entrance exam at the end of January and those shortlisted are called for interview in February. Assessments for nursery take place throughout the year.

Exit: Several to Haberdashers' Aske's School for Girls, City of London School for Girls or North London Collegiate in the independent sector or The Latymer School, Dame Alice Owen's and Henrietta Barnett in the maintained sector. Sixth form college at Woodhouse College is also popular.

Money Matters: Bursaries and academic awards up to 100 per cent of fees for 11+. Music awards giving free instrumental tuition are also available at 11+.

Remarks: Few frills, as befits its Quaker origins, but delivers the goods. High standards in behaviour, appearance and learning produce smiling, polite, courteous, interesting students.

Parkstone Grammar School

Sopers Lane, Poole, Dorset, BH17 7EP

• Pupils: 1100 girls, all day • Ages: 12-18 • Size of sixth form: 375
• Non-denom • State

Tel: 01202 605 605
Fax: 01202 605 606
Email: enquiries@parkstone.poole.sch.uk
Website: www.parkstone.poole.sch.uk

Headteacher: Since 2001, Ms Anne Shinwell MA (early fifties). Read history and politics at Glasgow. First teaching job was at John Kelly Girls' School in London where she rose to be assistant director of the sixth form and head of careers and economics. Went on to spend eight years striding the hallowed halls of Tiffin Girls', one of the most revered and over-subscribed girls' state schools in the land – most of her time there as deputy head. Leaving no stone unturned, she became head of Queen Elizabeth's Girl's School, Barnet, an academically successful comprehensive. In short, this lady knows a thing or two about educating clever girls. Exudes authority, confidence and joie de vivre. Married to a solicitor who has two children.

Academic matters: GCSEs and A levels almost uniformly excellent. Given science specialist status in 2002 and the subject is popular, successful and well-resourced. In 2008, in recognition of its status as high performing specialist school, awarded a second specialism in modern foreign languages. The school has loosened its compulsory GCSE requirements – the vast majority of students take three separate sciences (more fun to teach, say teachers); AS level science in society, AS food technology and AS citizenship are available at key stage 4. Girls learn French and German in Years 8 and 9 and, since 2008, Spanish is also taught at key stage 3. Since 2004, modern foreign languages have been optional at GCSE but the vast majority of girls still continue with at least one. Pupils may add Spanish or Italian and be examined in three languages – or none at all. Very few GCSEs taken early. Computing and graphics A levels and geology AS courses around the corner at Poole Grammar (the boys came to Parkstone for economics, food technology, theatre studies and politics). Since 2009 many more joint courses available through working in collaboration with Poole Grammar School. Psychology all the rage and media studies has become very popular since its introduction in 2004.

Tries to give girls every opportunity – 'Da Vinci' enrichment classes for Years 9 and 10 pupils with Poole Grammar in subjects like photography, philosophy and Japanese. Overseas trips take girls to unusual destinations, e.g. Russia, USA, Australia, Costa Rica, Uganda and Iceland. A Year 11 homework club and mentoring help to keep motivation high. Class sizes large throughout. A small percentage with SENs including physical/medical and emotional difficulties and school can support those with mobility problems.

Games, Options, the Arts: Sport good and heartily played – up to a point. All girls do PE of some kind through to the end of Year 13, and girls' rugby, cricket and football are popular (Parkstone hosted Dorset's first tournament for girls' rugby). Netball strong, being runners-up in the national U14 championships in 2010; hockey less so. Girls who came here from the independent sector comment wryly how they were suddenly promoted from the D hockey team at their prep to prime position on the school team at Parkstone. School is now enjoying its wonderful new sports hall. Playing fields are ample, with loads of tennis courts. At sixth form, girls can go off-site to local sports clubs etc. Music well-housed and said to be very good, with some very talented girls. A big drama production every second year in conjunction with Poole Grammar and junior musical theatre production held every summer. Theatre studies A level. High quality art and textiles. School was awarded the silver Artsmark in 2009. Unusually good range of extra-curricular activities – some in the sixth form combined with Poole Grammar. Ms Shinwell eager to continue to develop the links between the two schools.

Background and Atmosphere: Founded 100 years ago in nearby Parkstone, hence the name. Moved to 20 acre site, near to the sewage works, in 1961: the smell takes some getting used to – 'only very occasionally,' says head. The main building not a thing of beauty but serves, and several new buildings, especially the sixth form/music block, are downright pleasant. Received funding to build a new art, maths and technology block with state-of-the-art facilities and to refurbish the science and ICT areas. Classrooms bulge with brainy girls who are proud of their school and know they are privileged to be here. Despite their dedicated (and very attractive) common room, sixth form girls say that the school is a bit short of space for their study and computer use. Impressive new lecture theatre. Little canteen opens at 8am for early birds and serves as a social area/study throughout the day. Extended canteen facilities currently under construction. Cheap, very good food.

Pastoral Care and Discipline: Girls usually stay with same tutor group for first four years. Mentoring and big sister schemes help new girls fit in. Uniform quite attractive, though our heart goes out to girls who can't wear yellow. Trousers an option. Sixth form students allowed to wear what they like within reason and seem relaxed with it. Some parents dismayed that the school has permitted nose rings and exposed tummies in sixth form, but this is not a school that wages war over minutiae. A very few girls have received fixed-term exclusions for 'friendship group problems' – head-speak for bitchiness.

Pupils and Parents: Some quite affluent, some poorer – families from across all the socio-economic groups, but few from ethnic minorities (reflecting Poole's residents) and virtually nil who do not speak fluent English. Parkstone Grammar has a reasonable social cachet and families which can well afford to pay for education can be found earnestly coaxing their daughters to swot for the entrance exam. Head laments that still areas in Poole where families say, 'We don't send girls to the Grammar'. Some 65 per cent come from Poole, the rest from up to an hour away. Around 40 per cent of girls come to school by bus – local bus company, city bus or via private arrangements made by parents. Sixth form girls distinctly mature and focused.

Entrance: Poole's current three tier system (junior, middle and senior schools) makes the entry age of 12 out of sync with many schools (the borough has reviewed this system and Parkstone will move to a Year 7 start in 2013). Over 400 girls sit entrance test in late November/early December each year, competing for 168 places. Girls who pass and who live in Poole will automatically get places. Girls living outside Poole are allotted places in exam rank order – distance away from school only counts if two applicants receive the same score on the exam. Further places can be awarded via the Independent Admissions Appeals Panel: 35 extra in 2004 and over 40 extra in 2010!! Appeals on the rise, especially if parents can give a good reason why only Parkstone will meet their daughter's needs.

Girls come from all over but usual suspects include Broadstone Middle School, Baden Powell and St Peter's School, Canford Heath Middle School, Oakdale Middle School and independent preps like Buckholme Towers, Uplands, The Yarrells and Castle Court in Corfe Mullen. Can take up to 50 girls at sixth form – currently, the school requires a bare minimum of six GCSEs at A*–C, with at least a B in subjects to be studied at A level; specific entry requirements for each subject can be found in the sixth form prospectus.

Exit: About twenty leave after Year 11, often to schools nearer home (some competition from good comprehensive sixth forms like Thomas Hardy's and Brockenhurst). Occasionally girls 'return' to the independent sector. However, as some girls go, over thirty students join the sixth form from other schools. At 18, 'practically all' go on to university – loads locally to Southampton, Bournemouth, and Portsmouth. Also Exeter, Cardiff, Bath, Reading, King's College London. Some to Oxbridge.

Remarks: Very together, very confident, very forceful place. We don't know how they manage it but even fragile or disorganised girls seem to blossom here.

Parliament Hill School

Linked to La Swap Sixth Form in the Senior section

Highgate Road, London, NW5 1RL

• Pupils: 900 girls, all day plus 300 in sixth form • Ages: 11-19 • Size of sixth form: 550 in joint sixth form with William Ellis, part of La Swap consortium of 1,250 sixth form students in four schools • Non-denom • State

Tel: 020 7485 7077
Fax: 020 7485 9524
Email: headteacher@parliamenthill.camden.sch.uk
Website: www.parliamenthill.camden.sch.uk

Head: Since 2005, Ms Susan Higgins MA (Cantab) MA (Ed) (fifties), previously head of Brentford School for Girls for five years. She studied English at New Hall (now Murray Edwards) College, Cambridge, after a peripatetic school career as her family moved around the country. The first Oxbridge student from her Bradford comprehensive (Fairfax School, since 'shamed and renamed a few times'), she was enthused by 'an inspirational English teacher'. She was head of English at Walthamstow School for Girls for much of her career, taking time out to become deputy head at Skinners' Company's School for Girls in Hackney and spending time as a school-based PGCE tutor for the Institute of Education before returning to Walthamstow as deputy head. She has two children.

A strong and capable leader with a good back-up team. Parents say: 'I'm very impressed by her.... She's personable and engaging, with great people skills. She has a firm grasp of what needs to be done....The girls love hearing about her experience of going to Cambridge as a working class girl...She's a great role model for them.'

Academic matters: A huge ability range here, with lots of bright girls and also plenty in need of extra support, whether educational or emotional. Accordingly, offers a range of options. Everyone studies for a core of GCSE subjects which includes maths, English, core science, RE, DT and short courses in PE and citizenship. They can add on more GCSE subjects, or choose a vocational BTec from a range that includes business, art and design, ICT and health and social care, or study for one of ten diplomas, or go for a Young Apprenticeship. Most of the latter two options are taught elsewhere in Camden. Everyone is allocated to either French or Spanish classes for the first three years, and can start the other language in Year 9; about a third take a modern language GCSE. Other options at KS4 include additional AS maths and triple science; ICT AS and photography GCSE are taught after school as twilight classes.

English is very strong, maths and science rather weaker. The disappointing 2009 GCSE results – only 47 per cent of girls got 5+ A*–C grades including English and maths – were largely down to poor maths grades. From September 2010, maths taught in ability sets from the second term in Year 7 rather than from Year 9, and the curriculum has been redesigned substantially – 'We're confident that results will be far better in future'. Girls arrive with, on average, much higher verbal than non-verbal aptitude scores. 'But as a technology college we focus on building up their confidence and aptitude in maths and science.' The science department has appointed some very highly qualified teachers over the last few years. 'They're very good at assessing strengths and weaknesses,' said a parent, 'and throwing lots of energy at weaknesses.'

The head is reviewing all the schemes of work in KS3, including building in greater differentiation for ranges of ability – 'In a comprehensive you have to keep revisiting this and doing it better'. Homework and marking – aspects raised by parents as sometimes inconsistent – are other key priorities – 'Every department is producing its own guidelines with clear expectations. Parents need to know these'.

SEN provision has been 'transformed', with a new assistant head leading the way on SEN and inclusion. Consultants brought in recently to review the provision were 'very positive'. Few state schools feel that they have sufficient funds to provide all the help every child needs, but 'we feel we've made substantial progress'. The Extra Mile project targets under-achieving year 10 girls, who are mostly from white low-income families.

Gifted and talented provision focuses on what goes on in lessons – 'In a comprehensive you've got to make sure you're providing stretch in the classroom. We get professionals in to make sure we're getting it right'. Also masterclasses and mentoring, and Year 7 girls recently visited Murray Edwards College, Cambridge, to meet undergraduates and visit the zoology department. 'Many of our girls wouldn't naturally consider applying to a university like this. It's essential they have their aspirations raised.'

Has a joint sixth form with next-door William Ellis School, with co-ed tutor groups. It is also part of La Swap, which includes La Sainte Union and Acland Burghley schools. Each school teaches the core sixth form subjects, but students visit other schools in the group for more minority subjects, e.g. film studies and further maths. The ability range encompasses those aspiring to read medicine at Cambridge and those working for an introductory BTec diploma in health and social care, with appropriate entry requirements. A new scheme in conjunction with La Sainte Union targets very able scientists, who will study together and take part in organised work experience and masterclasses. English is the most popular A level subject at Parliament Hill, with psychology second. Generally around 48 per cent of A level grades are A or B.

Games, Options, the Arts: Everyone takes DT GCSE, with a choice of four options – Year 7s were busy cooking muffins during our visit. The single storey DT block was built in 2005 to an environmentally-friendly design with a green roof, and forms the fourth side of a grassy courtyard, twisting up to meet the original Edwardian building. On another corner of the building is the performing arts block, built in 2006 and clad in green glass, which provides music rooms and dance and drama studios. The top floor corridors are lined with expressive GCSE and A level photography and artwork, and textile designs hang in the stairwells.

Music probably not the highest profile subject here, but many girls have instrumental lessons and play in the orchestra or in the jazz, string or brass ensembles, or sing in the choir. Those on free school meals get free music lessons. Two hours' timetabled PE a week for everyone. Two tennis/netball courts at the front of the school and a grassy area at the back where the football teams practise, plus a rather ageing hall for gym and badminton with a fitness suite. On the wish-list is a new sports hall. All Year 7s learn to swim at Swiss Cottage baths and the head hopes in future to make more use of the Lido, which is more or less next door. Sports teams play successful matches against other Camden schools.

A breakfast club every morning at 8am and plenty more activities ranging from Italian and chess clubs to basketball and rounders. Girls perform in musicals such as the 'excellent and ambitious' production of *The Wiz*, run round Parliament Hill in fancy dress to raise funds for Sports Relief, visit China and go on physics trips to Switzerland.

Background and Atmosphere: Opened in 1906, has an idyllic site on the edge of Hampstead Heath. Plenty of grassy space, including a sculpture park and kick-around area. Buildings range from solid Edwardiana to the 21st century award-winning DT and performing arts blocks. Despite the countrywide school building projects cancelled by the new coalition Government, is crossing its fingers that the promised funds for replacing the well-past-its-sell-by-date Heath Building will after all be forthcoming – 'If they're not, we're all going to lean against it until it falls over'.

Harmonious atmosphere. Despite the huge range of pupils, both ethnically and socially, girls tend to get on well together, with few reports of bullying. Recently one of 11 in the country to win a gold quality mark for cultural diversity. 'They manage the mix very well,' said a parent.

Pastoral Care and Discipline: Many vulnerable pupils here, including refugees and those with learning difficulties, who get 'excellent' support, says Ofsted. Liaises with its feeder primary school to identify girls likely to be in need of extra help with making the transition to senior school. It works with outside agencies that provide therapy or counselling to those in need. It also runs many programmes to motivate disaffected pupils, stretch the aspirations of bright girls and ensure everyone gets a chance to broaden their horizons. Assertive classroom management keeps most lessons running without disruptions.

Older girls are allowed to go out onto Hampstead Heath at lunchtimes, together with pupils from nearby schools, William Ellis and La Sainte Union, and locals have complained about litter problems – 'We're very concerned. The girls regard the Heath as very special to them, and we're doing work on social responsibility to educate them that it's for everyone in the community'.

Pastoral care is very good, report parents. 'I've always felt they know my daughter very well,' said one. 'They've contacted me whenever they've had concerns, and they've dealt with any problems quickly and well.'

Pupils and Parents: 'Amazingly diverse' student population speaks some 50 different languages at home, though few are at early stages of learning English. Over 200 refugees. Nearly half of the girls are on free school meals, but also good support from some local middle-class families. OGs include actress Katrin Cartlidge, BBC journalist Laura Trevelyan and Lola Young, Baroness Young of Hornsey.

Entrance: Takes 180 girls into Year 7, with admissions organised by the LEA. Priority for particular SEN, siblings, children in care and those with exceptional social needs. Then by distance – generally within a mile and a half. Those joining La Swap sixth form to do A levels must have at least eight GCSE passes including three C and two B grades; various vocational courses available for those with lower grades.

Exit: Between half and two-thirds of pupils join La Swap sixth form. Some move on to other sixth forms, e.g. Camden School for Girls or Woodhouse College, others to colleges such as City and Islington or Westminster Kingsway to do vocational courses. Most Year 13 leavers to high education, one or two a year to Oxbridge. Several to art foundation courses, the rest to a wide variety of old and new universities, with many choosing London colleges.

Remarks: Popular girls' comprehensive in idyllic situation on the borders of Hampstead Heath, with a diverse but harmonious student population. Strong, popular head who is a driving force in building on strengths and tackling weaknesses. 'My daughter has been so happy there that she has become an ambassador for her school,' said a parent.

Parmiter's School

High Elms Lane, Garston, Watford, Hertfordshire, WD25 0UU

• Pupils: 1,250 boys and girls, all day • Ages: 11-18 • Size of sixth form: 300+ • None • State

Tel: 01923 671 424
Fax: 01923 894 195
Email: admin@parmiters.herts.sch.uk
Website: www.parmiters.herts.sch.uk

Headmaster: Since September 2010, Mr Nicholas Daymond MA Cantab PGCE NPQH. Started his career in 1985 at Goffs School, Cheshunt, where he became head of languages, head of sixth form and senior teacher. Was appointed deputy head at Beaumont School in St Albans in 1998. Joined Roundwood Park in Harpenden as head five years later.

Proud of the school's past and traditions, enthusiastic about the school's future, always available to parents.

Academic matters: Banded by ability in most subjects in Years 7–9. Setting in maths, sciences and languages from Year 8. Class sizes very good for a state school – around 25 and going down as GCSEs approach. 95 per cent got five or more GCSE A*–C grades including maths and English in 2010, over 50 per cent of grades at A*/A, with maths and English being particularly strong. A levels well above the national average too – 72 per cent A/B grades in 2010. English and maths were the most popular choices. Latin has re-emerged, having previously been squeezed out of the timetable.

A new, modern foreign languages block was built in 2005, a new music centre in 2007, a new sixth form centre in 2008 and drama studio in 2009. Separate sciences as well as the dual award. All children undergo diagnostic testing on joining the school to identify strengths and weaknesses and those with special needs. Holiday courses in maths and other subjects, as well as a week's summer school for gifted and talented students. Three specialisms: technology (i.e. maths, science, ICT, D&T), music and languages. Designated as a high performing specialist school.

Games, Options, the Arts: Proud of its sporting tradition and success, awarded a Sportsmark Gold for its facilities (extensive playing fields, floodlit tennis and netball courts and an impressive new sports centre – new floodlit Astroturf and another new sports pavilion opened in 2004, plus floodlit synthetic pitch for football and hockey) and extracurricular activities. The main sports for boys are football, basketball, rugby, cricket, tennis and athletics. Girls choose from netball, hockey, football, athletics, tennis, dance and rounders. Reaches national level in many sports – national finalists for football and netball in 2006 and notable county successes in nine sports in 2010. Very good reputation for music with some 250 pupils learning an instrument in school; two symphonic wind bands, four choirs, an orchestra, a big band and a recorder group, as well as smaller woodwind, brass and string chamber music groups. European concert tours are arranged biennially.

A host of extra-curricular clubs including dance, drama, trampolining, debating, science, chess, computer programming, languages and technology. D of E strongly supported to Gold Award level, the public speaking team has been national champions and thriving house system. Regular foreign exchanges and visits to France, Germany and Spain, and sixth form exchanges with Eton and Sherborne Girls'. Owns its own field centre in Wales.

Background and Atmosphere: Founded in 1681 in Bethnal Green, moved to its present 60 acre rural site in 1977. As well as public funding from the government, the school receives additional financial support from Parmiter's Foundation, which owns the school and its site. From the outside, modern, seventies style and purpose-built but, on the inside, it has a traditional feel. Portraits of former head teachers look down on you as you enter the welcoming reception area, honours boards give you the feeling you are in a school where achievement is highly valued and recognised. But traditional doesn't mean stuffy. 'It's a traditional school which is progressive and forward looking,' says the head. It's very much a family school. Siblings, regardless of academic ability, take priority in the admissions process. 'We believe every child has a talent and we celebrate it.'

Pastoral Care and Discipline: Minimal set of rules. Pupils are expected to be punctual, tidy, hard working and courteous. Pupils are publicly rewarded for good effort and excellent work. In eight years no pupils have been expelled. Last Ofsted report stated, 'Standards of behaviour are excellent and sanctions rarely have to be applied.'

Pupils and Parents: Vast majority come from Hertfordshire post codes, although some travel from as far away as the Wembley/Harrow/Stanmore areas in north London. Most come from state primary schools, a few from prep schools. Pupils are well behaved and polite and feel they are given every opportunity to reach their full potential. Former pupils include Geoffrey Woolley OBE VC; Tommy Walsh from TV's 'Ground Force'; Steven Finn, Middlesex CCC; Jordan Parkes, Watford FC; Keith Medlycott, international cricketer; Alper Mehmet, British Ambassador to Iceland; senior diplomats, Emrys Davies and Sir Terence Clarke.

Entrance: Partially selective and rather complex criteria for places at 11 plus. 10 per cent allocated to those living closest to the school. Current siblings have high priority, followed by those for whom compelling medical grounds. 25 per cent of places are awarded on academic ability (test in maths and verbal reasoning) and 10 per cent on the basis of music aptitude (test and audition); remaining places are allocated on distance. Entry into sixth form is based generally on B grades upwards at GCSE.

Exit: Around 20 per cent leave post-GCSE to go to further education colleges and occasionally to other schools. More than 95 per cent of sixth formers progress to higher education with around 15 per cent taking a gap year. Six to Oxbridge in 2010.

Remarks: Private-school-standard facilities in a state school. Excellent results at key stage 3, GCSE and A level and excellent value-added.

Pate's Grammar School

Princess Elizabeth Way, Cheltenham, Gloucestershire, GL51 0HG

• Pupils: 950 pupils, 50:50 boys:girls. All day • Ages: 11-18 • Size of sixth form: 360 • Non-denom • State

Tel: 01242 523 169
Fax: 01242 232 775
Email: office@pates.gloucs.sch.uk
Website: www.pates.gloucs.sch.uk

Headmaster: Since 2006, Mr Shaun Fenton MA. Educated at Haberdashers Askes' School and Keble College, Oxford, where he read PPE. Married with two young children. A brief flirtation with accountancy preceded his career in education. Worked for Hertfordshire Education Authority as part of a team supporting schools in challenging circumstances and as head of Sir John Lawes School in Harpenden. Implausibly young, and slightly managerial in appearance, but not to be regarded as a lightweight. An initial sense that one is on the receiving end of a Pate's sales pitch is dissipated by his evident passion for the school, pride in its pupils and determination to develop its ethos and its social as well as academic impact.

An enthusiast for excellence, seeking to build a community focused on 'relationships and individual growth'. A committed Christian whose faith informs his passion for producing young adults who will 'do the right thing' and lead their communities in whatever role they find themselves. Pupils evidently warm to him. What does he believe to be the school's greatest strength? 'The students are fantastic: sensible, grounded, breathtakingly good – they are the best of their generation.' And who wouldn't fit in? 'We'll make the changes we need to, to make it a place where every child feels comfortable and able to succeed'.

Academic matters: Extremely impressive results – strong across the board. 100 per cent have achieved their five A*–C GCSEs with 86 per cent A*/A grades. At A level, 90 per cent A and B grades. The pass rate for all public exams is 100 per cent (except for general studies – taken as a compulsory subject by all). Wide range of subjects – the school is a language college: French, German, Italian, Spanish, Mandarin and Latin are all taught. Also a science specialist college and sciences are also strong – around 85–90 per cent of A level candidates pass with an A or a B in biology, chemistry and physics. Computer science and psychology are also taught at A level. Well organised use of a good library, a good supply of laptops and networked computers and very good technical support. Strong IT is part of the drive towards more 'personalised' learning – pupils remark on the helpful guidance given by staff and the sense of collaboration in learning, especially in the sixth form. An enthusiasm for learning, exploring and developing academically.

Also a beacon school – offers support and curriculum enrichment to twelve local schools. For those on the SEN spectrum, a student focused approach rather than a formal system. For those who have specific needs, TAs under the management of a SENCo. The overarching principle is 'do the right thing for the individual' – personalised care is organised for each child.

Games, Options, the Arts: Where to start? A huge CCF, an active Duke of Edinburgh programme, outdoor pursuits most weekends, rugby, football, basketball, cricket, athletics, swimming, gym, dance etc. A large sports hall with a fitness suite, a climbing wall – if you're a sporty sort, you will find yourself well catered for. Pupils say that the house system ensures that those who are keen but less than brilliant still get their chance to play in teams and participate in the things they enjoy.

Music is very strong with charity concerts, junior concerts and recitals all part of the mix. Orchestras as well as composition classes, a good range of school instruments available to those wishing to learn and good practice rooms. Drama is also a strength with some demanding pieces being taken on (*Return to the Forbidden Planet, Jesus Christ Superstar, A Midsummer Night's Dream,* for example). An active charity committee, formed from the lower sixth, charged with raising 'as much as possible' for a variety of good causes. It's clear that 'good works' are high on the agenda in all spheres of school life.

Background and Atmosphere: Founded over 400 years ago by a local – the eponymous Richard Pate. It was a free grammar school for boys until 1904, when a girls' school was added, the two merging about 20 years ago. It has recently been substantially rebuilt. Pate's is not exactly set in rolling parkland – it's at the less glamorous end of Cheltenham, and perimeter fences make the initial impression somewhat forbidding. However, the school buildings are uniformly well designed, and sited round a large quad, which gives a sense of openness. Good sized playing fields to the back and generally well maintained and well equipped. Food, according to the pupils, is good, varied and healthy. The atmosphere is one of confidence, aspiration and exploration – the pupils seem comfortable without being cocky, and the staff are friendly. Even during exam season the place retains serenity and friendliness.

Pastoral Care and Discipline: Care for the individual child is a priority. The conviction in 2006 of a member of staff for a sexual offence involving a pupil has, understandably, caused a great deal of dismay and soul searching. The head (who joined the school after the matter had come to light) insists that 'nothing but the best is good enough' and that child protection is taken 'extremely seriously'. All policies have been reviewed and the commitment to the highest possible standards 'reinforced'. Additional training for all staff and governors. One new staff member says the pastoral system is 'watertight'.

On a day to day basis, each pupil has a tutor, as well as a head of year, to whom they can refer. A school counsellor, and older pupils from the middle and senior schools act as mentors to the younger pupils. The house system is very strong – both pupils and staff say that it works to strengthen community and opportunity. Pupils say very little bullying and that it is taken seriously and dealt with immediately when it arises. No system of detentions, slips or similar, because it isn't needed. The pupils say they are respected and trusted by the staff and that respect is reciprocated. Staff say the pupils are 'great', with a 'remarkable sense of mutual support among staff and students and between staff and students'.

Pupils and Parents: Pupils are mostly from around Cheltenham but they also come from further corners of Gloucestershire and even Worcestershire and west Oxfordshire. Most parents are middle class and aspirational but the school is also keen to encourage entrance for those from less comfortable backgrounds. An active PTA and communications between parents and school are generally very good, with good turnouts to parents' evenings and positive responses to reports. The pupils themselves are friendly, confident and articulate. They say the school is 'great', 'Coming to school isn't a chore' and 'You're allowed to be eccentric – you can be an individual and still fit in'.

Entrance: Two opportunities for entrance: at Year 7 and again in the sixth form, where an extra 50–60 places available. At Year 7, selection is via the LEA but based on the school's own entrance test (you have to register with both the school and the LEA) and places are offered strictly to the 120 top scorers – usually around 700 apply. These will already have self-selected to some extent, as the school is known for its very high academic standards. Practice papers are are available on the school's website. The competition is quite tough – not for the easily frightened.

Entrance exams (NFER verbal reasoning papers) are in November, with places offered (or not) by the beginning of March. For the sixth form, high GCSE scores plus glowing reports from the pupil's current school are needed. Places for the sixth form are offered by the end of April (apply by February). See the school website for more detail.

Exit: Very few leavers after GCSE. All of sixth formers get places at university. Last year around 27 went to Oxbridge (from a cohort of about 180). All sorts of subjects are pursued, 'not just the old professions'. Those who want to take gap years or explore first leave the school 'ready for university', with the grades to go if they choose to. A dedicated careers room, and pupils say they can talk freely to the careers staff about their interests, strengths and weaknesses.

Money Matters: Although a state school, with no fees payable, the wealth of extra-curricular bits and pieces, trips to China, skiing expeditions and so on could seriously embarrass those of genuinely restricted means, although many less expensive trips. Financial assistance is available to ensure that no-one need be excluded from these activities. The school has its own foundation (The Pate's Foundation) and is also assisted by the Sutton Trust to fund some specific projects.

Remarks: A really outstanding state school. Offers a great combination of academic excellence, extra-curricular enrichment and an inspiring ethos of respect, responsibility, and community. Committed to the individual. For those who seriously aspire to excel intellectually and personally, this is a fantastic place to be. Those looking to join a particular 'set' might feel happier elsewhere.

The Perse Upper School

Linked to Perse Pelican Nursery And Pre-Preparatory School (The) in the Junior section

Linked to Perse Preparatory School (The) in the Junior section

Hills Road, Cambridge, Cambridgeshire, CB2 8QF

• Pupils: 760 pupils, all day. • Ages: 11-18 • Size of sixth form: Co-educational; 2/3 boys • Non-denom • Fees: £13,263 pa • Independent

Tel: 01223 403 800
Fax: 01223 403 810
Email: admissions@perse.co.uk
Website: www.perse.co.uk

Head: Since 2008, Mr Edward Elliott (late thirties), who has been at the school since 1997. Educated at The Royal Grammar School, Worcester, then St Anne's College, Oxford, where he got a first in geography. Tried commerce (a graduate trainee at De La Rue) but quickly moved to teaching at the Whitgift School in Surrey. Married to Sue, a paediatrician; two daughters and a son.

Academic matters: The academic school in Cambridge – where, needless to say, brainpower is not thin on the ground; it aims high academically and has the pupils and staff to achieve the highest standards. Results good across the board, 94 per cent of candidates getting As or Bs at A levels and A*/A at GCSE. Japanese and Russian, sports science and philosophy are among sixth form options. An unashamedly 'seriously maths and science school' and results are especially good in these areas. English, history and geography numbers and results also holding up well. School teaches a technology syllabus that is unusually weighted to engineering and practical skills – its previous emphasis on and reputation for egg-headed intellectualism is now outdated. All labs recently refitted to highest standard.

SEN provision much improved in recent years – all pupils screened on entry, on-site SEN teacher plus liaison with educational psychologists. 50 pupils with some kind of SEN support.

Games, Options, the Arts: Surprisingly for a day school, manages to keep two/three afternoons a week for games and other extra-curricular activities throughout the school. This is, in the main, a very popular policy and pupils relish the opportunities to develop sporting, musical or dramatic skills, along with the various other options on offer – among them CCF, a, perhaps surprisingly, popular choice for many girls. Scout and Explorer scout troops. Excellent sports hall block includes two squash courts and a large and well-appointed fitness suite which – an enlightened and appreciated policy – the sixth are allowed to use in free unsupervised time.

Art is rich and colourful, evidence of inspirational teaching, and includes ceramics and printing. Local artists exhibit in The Pelican Gallery within the teaching space. Good lecture theatre doubles as drama studio seating 180 – big expansion in drama productions in recent years. New music building – an extension to existing block – provides new teaching/practice rooms, space for larger ensembles and exciting new rehearsal hall to accommodate full-scale symphony orchestra with chorus; doubles as concert hall, available to local community. About half learn at least one instrument and musical activities of all types flourish here – baroque string ensembles, jazz, brass, wind and chamber groups, choirs and music technology. The school's musical excellence now seen by parents as a principal reason to apply and attracting correspondingly good budding musicians. Good careers room and resources in sixth form centre, which also has well-used common room area recently expanded to provide a separate work area for growing number of sixth formers.

Background and Atmosphere: The school's history – nearly 400 years of it – is chequered and includes embezzlement in the 18th century, an assault on the head in the 19th and an incendiary bomb hitting it in 1941. Since 1960 it has occupied award-winning, purpose-built accommodation on a 28-acre site. Buildings are low – few higher than two storeys, as is customary in this part of the world – but although not imposing, they are inviting and well integrated into the site. Hall doubles up as dining room, necessitating daily quick setting out and packing away of tables. Meals taken by staff and pupils together perhaps explaining the unusually orderly atmosphere. Two Astroturf pitches, very attractive, tree-lined playing fields, good feeling of space. While being efficient and well-organised, school has room for eccentricities and individuals.

Pastoral Care and Discipline: Three deputy heads in management structure, including one with specific responsibility for pastoral matters. All pay tribute to new system – previous head saw pastoral care as central to his régime. No house system but various vertically grouped activities compensate and pupils mix comfortably across the year groups and sexes. 'Code of conduct' – highly reasonable rights and responsibilities. New, more pastoral role for prefects who are – a novel approach – required to apply for the job. Strong drugs policy seldom needed.

Pupils and Parents: Fees prohibit mass takeover by bright children of poorly paid Cambridge academics, though many still manage it. School ceased taking boarders in 1993, two years before girls arrived in the sixth form – most blossom here, with opportunities and resources few girls' schools can offer. Pupils are relaxed, unpretentious and natural, indicating that, altogether, this school gives them a very good start in life.

Many come for science but also relish new sporting/artistic possibilities. Lots of local competition for pupils at sixth form level (not least from the state sixth form colleges) and about 10 per cent of fifth formers do leave – more than compensated for by those who come in from outside. Majority live close by, though many come from as far as Ely, Saffron Walden, Newmarket, Royston and elsewhere. Annually, a very few from abroad, under special guardianship scheme, seen as bringing new and refreshing dimension to school life. Distinguished list of Old Boys includes Sir Peter Hall, Rev Dr John Polkinghorne, David Tang, Dave Gilmour, Pete Atkin, Sir Mark Potter.

Entrance: At 11, about 50 from Perse Prep, but also 50+ from other local juniors and preps. About 48 more at 13+. Competitive entrance at 11+ and 13+ via own exam and interview. Very good GCSE grades required for entrance at 16+. School stresses that competition for places at 11+ – at about two to one – is tough, but not that tough.

Exit: Many to Oxbridge and top medical schools with a good spread of other universities. Engineering, medical and natural sciences preferred subjects, engineering single largest degree subject.

Money Matters: Scholarships 10 per cent at most. Determined to maintain its direct grant tradition and increase the amount of means-tested financial support available to bursary applicants.

Remarks: Much expanded in recent years and now set to expand again, as it takes girls at 11 and 13 from September 2010. An academic school which has, in recent years, put much effort – and cash – into raising the standard and profile of the other areas of excellence it offers. Justifiably, but not forbiddingly, sought after, will get the best out of its pupils and do the best by them.

Perth Grammar School

Gowans Terrace, Perth, Perth, PH1 5AZ

• Pupils: 1,100; co-ed • Ages: 12-18 • Size of sixth form: S5 160, S6 100
• Non denom • State

Tel: 01738 620 071
Fax: 01738 620073
Email: headteacher@perthgrammar.pkc.sch.uk
Website: www.perthgrammar.pkc.sch.uk

Headteacher: Since 2007, John Low BEd (50s), brought in at a week's notice from the highly sought after Breadalbane Academy as a temporary secondment to sort out the school. After the 2008 inspection showed considerable improvement, he was enjoying the challenge so much that he accepted the headship as a permanent post. 'The school, like a super-tanker, took several miles to turn', but in twelve months he had changed it from a school with 'weak academics, poor behaviour, staff and pupils with low morale', losing lots of its rural catchment pupils to Breadalbane, into one which won £80K in *The People's Millions* TV show, is attracting pupils back and has had to cap its annual intake at 220, having previously averaged about 170. (Mr Low would like eventually to see 1400–1500, but that would need some more building.) Above all, pupils and staff have gained confidence, which he sees as the key factor.

Confidence has been created by bringing in international coaches, Eilidh Child European 400 metre silver medallist, Scottish basketball coach Russell Kesson, creating a sports trust to give them charitable status for fundraising, making the letters of Perth Grammar larger than the signage of any other Perth school, winning the £80K and using it to revamp the theatre, upgrade all pupil toilets and improve the grounds. He looked for 'plus factors', such as first whole school photo, courses for mums and child minders, state of art playground complete with wendy house and little wicker dens for nursery, linking in with childcare course, forging links with China, France and Germany, taking ski trips, winning the Scottish education award for ambition. More recent developments are sports and health, with the school now shortlisted for the Scottish Education award for 'Getting Scotland Active', plus very high profile expressive arts, with a musical productions in the pipe line.

Academic matters: Since the catchment area covers both inner city areas of Perth and part of county Perthshire, courses provide for academic high fliers and direct entry to employment. Initially all classes are mixed ability, but some subjects are set for ability during the course of S1 and S2: maths and French from S1, English, Spanish and German from S3. All do S grades (or Int I /II) or vocational courses – hairdressing, construction. horticulture (new poly-tunnel), engineering, childcare, sport and recreation (all joint with Perth College etc) – and technical – technical studies, graphic communications, home ec, admin, craft/design etc, as well as a solid set of academic possibilities.

S5/6 offers fullish range of Academic Highers and Ad Highers, kept under review according to the needs of each year group. Results and takeup both improving steadily, with 24 As and 3 Bs out of 27 maths Highers last year. Courses in hairdressing (a non-examined level 6 Higher equivalent) and beauty (with Perth College, which has massage beds etc), Professional Development Award in General Insurance (now Aviva is a major Perth employer) etc are tailored by Mr L to fit up-and-coming employment opportunities.

Learning support department of 22 (teachers and support staff) led by Bill Colley, who used to be head of New Butterstone. Children who came in as non-copers are now making out in mainstream. Lots of initiatives: C 20 group with a pre level A life-skills programme – 'Super soups' enterprise group making profits for charity, equalities programme. School now a 'Magnet' school for special needs. New 'assertive tutoring' guidance programme gives one to one support to keep up motivation and work output when necessary.

Games, Options, the Arts: One of the few assets Mr Low inherited is a sports stadium with a proper grandstand and a good running track. This is used by Perth clubs for evening training and Mr Low's team of Scottish national level coaches (G McIntosh – hockey, S Cameron – football, K Munro – netball et al) can make after school practices join up with evening club times. This facility will be shared by the new St John's RC School, just opened on other side of the site. Perth Grammar is a step ahead, already offering sports training to its feeder primaries. Usual range of soccer, netball, hockey athletics etc. 45 per cent of Year 1 took up sports clubs last year, 75 per cent this year. The 'Sustrans' sport health initiative has provided oodles of bike lockers, which are dotted colourfully all over the grounds, and a flash of inspiration provided girls arriving dishevelled from their bike helmets with free access to the hairdressing department for half an hour before school.

Lots of outdoor activities, climbing wall at planning stage and plentiful trips, sporting and other, abroad: ski trip, Rome, Boston and New York last year, China this year and Barcelona next year. Music and drama now getting a turn with a summer musical production in the newly equipped hall. A few competitive activities are adding to the feel-good factor: a girls' team won the under 15 Girls' Final of the SSFA; gardening (Perth in Bloom trophy); science (Perth and Kinross Schools science quiz); architecture (a team designing school leisure space won the Dundee College "Creative Space" competition). Lots of effective fundraising: over £22,000 for Rachel House children's hospice and other projects, such as a very active link with a school in Bangladesh and more planned with Poland and Spain. All these are beginning to open the doors to the world beyond both downtown Perth and rural Perthshire

Background and Atmosphere: Perhaps the most unpromising school buildings ever devised. Gaining admission via an unanswered buzzer, and finding the school office, curiously located on the upper floor some way from the entrance, were only possible because both staff and pupils were so friendly and helpful. Narrow corridors, pretty clean considering, though all still in garish colours, inevitably noisy and battered with the regular passage of 1100 children. Mr Low has prioritised his maintenance budget on classrooms and equipment, often stretching it by buying second hand, with impressive results such as the home ec room, enthusiastically in use by both boys and girls alike.

The extensive suite of art rooms is filled with masses of creative squalor and pupils working with enthusiasm. Sad to see the old tennis courts now used as car parks. The school suffers from its setting, sandwiched between two council housing estates in a semi industrial part of Perth, though this may improve with the extensive, though not universally attractive, new-build round about. The school hall, once the library, is far too small, but has been opened up and given a large screen wall for wet day amusement etc, while Mr Low rents empty industrial space locally as exam halls away from school noise, thus freeing the school from a month of break times spent whispering in corridors. A school canteen serving sensible fare using 'cashless catering', the card system Scottish schools use to avoid having cash in school, but it also supplies a perky kiosk, 'The House of Munch', by the hairdressing Portacabin, with baguettes, hot drinks etc, in an effort to tempt pupil custom from the rather too local McDonalds.

However the shortcomings of buildings and general ambiance are more than made up more by the friendly, welcoming and extremely smart staff, which to a certain extent seems to have brushed off on the pupils, who look on the whole happy and purposeful. No mean achievement in that part of Perth!

Pastoral Care and Discipline: Mr Low's two-pronged approach has been, first, his code of 'pride, respect and ambition', implemented by the second, a team of deputes, three heading the new houses, Almond, Earn and Lomond, and the fourth dedicated to support for staff and pupils, with the aim of further raising standards. Another full time member of staff heads the attendance project. Parents are involved at every stage communicated through 'Group Call', which texts parents both with general school information and, if necessary, about problems, parents' evenings reminders, homework, absence etc. Formal reports covering progress and social issues are only once a year, but the school stresses that parents can make contact at any time, not just at parents' meetings. Social education is managed by the guidance department and includes programmes on bullying etc. Any instance of bullying is dealt with quickly and rules (on website) are simple and practical, including those on mobile phones and Mp3 players. Sanctions are mainly detention and withdrawal from class (into supervised alternative), though exclusion is the last resort. Tutor system based on houses is well enough staffed to allow individual monitoring/support where needed.

Pupils and Parents: The catchment includes the least salubrious parts of Perth and a chunk of 'county' Perthshire, spreading north to Dunkeld and east almost to Crieff. Previously this meant that Breadalbane Academy 'creamed off' the rural bits, but this trend has now reversed, which must make for a dynamic mixture. The Perth sector features alarmingly in Scotland's deprivation stats. 'Dress code' (more PC than uniform) is black blazers, skirts/trousers, school tie, white shirt, and the usual means tested uniform allowance is available. Mr Low is looking for sponsorship for some smart sportswear and casual coats to enhance general attitude to dress. Perth LA does not give breakdowns on ethnic mix – but then Perth is pretty Scottish, anyway.

Entrance: To Year 1 from designated primaries, with a few moving into the area.

Exit: Two thirds stay on for S5 and about half to S6. Approximately 30 per cent to university and a good chunk to all sorts of vocational course, with an increasing swing to apprenticeship type employment. Very few unplaced.

Remarks: Certainly not the Eton of the north, but a school in which every single statistic that should be climbing is doing so, some slowly (academic averages) but all surely, and some exponentially – minor successes, teams and competitions. A long way to go, but everyone and everything seem to be growing on the journey. Nice to see the leafy glens knowing a good bit of Scottish education when they see it.

Peter Symonds College

Owens Road, Winchester, Hampshire, SO22 6RX

• Pupils: 3140 boys and girls; most day, 80 board • Ages: 16-18 • Non-denom but with strong links to C of E • Fees: £9,822-£10,536 pa • State

Tel: 01962 852 764
Fax: 01962 857 501
Email: psc@psc.ac.uk
Website: www.psc.ac.uk

Principal: Since 1993, Mr Neil Hopkins BSc MEd (mid fifties), read maths at University of East Anglia. Something of a sixth form college niche specialist. After teaching maths in a comprehensive he moved to Eccles Sixth Form College and was acting principal at Rutland Sixth Form College before arriving here. Married (wife lectures in further education) with three children, all of whom have been through Symonds.

Expected to come for four or five years and he's still here, watching over a school that has more than doubled in size since he came – now the biggest A level centre in the country. His rôle is essentially general manager – five faculty heads are more in touch with the pupils themselves and he 'only knows the very good and very bad by name'. Relishes the independence of being outside LEA control. Makes its own decisions about staffing and can borrow money, while vaguely watched by the LEA with 'friendly disinterestedness'.

Southampton FC fanatic and bird watcher in his (limited) free time, with a streak of competitiveness – takes a schoolboy's delight in beating neighbouring toff school, Winchester College.

A strong defender of A levels; no plans to do the IB: 'It's still too small and too few people are doing it – I don't experiment with other people's children'. Don't even mention the Pre-U – 'It's an abomination on the face of the earth'. So that's a no then. Also sceptical about university entrance exams like the BMAT – 'They're tough on students and give an advantage to small independent schools that can provide coaching'.

Academic matters: Everything is here, both in terms of subject matter and the full range of human ability, from the star student who became head of the Cambridge Union last year to those who bump along at the bottom with a string of Ds and Es. A level performance on a mega-roll, improving year after year. Exam results outshone Winchester College's in 2009 – 'and we send more students to Oxbridge!' The usual wide array of courses one finds at sixth form colleges, includes, e.g., photography, film studies and environmental science. Everyone takes general studies ('It strengthens university applications') and quite a few go for other non-subjects like critical thinking (very good results) and citizenship. A few subjects beam particularly brightly: maths, art, textiles, music, media studies. Some courses are 'victims of their own success' and students have reported that they could not study their first choices. Candidates may have to audition for dance or performing arts.

Numbers are huge – 21 sets for biology. No streaming. Largish class sizes with 15–19 average – sounds overwhelming in theory but seems to work in practice. Fewer academic students (about 100 of the total) can pursue vocational courses – Level 2 BTecs or OCR Nationals in, e.g., health & social care or business & finance – 'much more useful than re-sitting GCSEs and struggling with A levels'. A few GCSEs on offer for retakes, and good linguists may pick up Italian or Spanish from scratch taking GCSE on the way to A level in just two years. Those aiming for Oxbridge or competitive courses such as medicine or vet science get additional guidance (with governors roped in to provide interview practice).

15 per cent benefit from some form of learning support including essay planning and self-organisation. Wheelchair access to much of the site ('We don't do badly for a sloping site'). Corridor to learning support centre lined with pictures of successful and famous dyslexics. Lunchtime workshops for those needing extra tuition – at both the top and the bottom ends of the achievement spectrum. Students report all the help they need if they ask for it – but they have to ask for it. Organisational ability is important here. 'It's like going to uni,' said a girl.

2008 Ofsted report gushingly rated Symonds 'outstanding' across the board.

Games, Options, the Arts: Strong teams because of its size. Sports hall funded by 'Mercers' money' (loosely part of the Mercers 'cluster' alongside, e.g., St Paul's and Abingdon). Lots of grass about the place but the principal dreams of an Astro. Drama strong and an A level in performing arts is offered. A performing arts centre also on the principal's wish list. Brilliant results in art – course said to be very broad – 'almost like a foundation course'. Former fives court enjoying a second life as a photo studio. DT wedged into one large workshop. Students take part in an extra-curricular programme (two hours a week) with activities chosen from long list (50+) ranging from Amnesty International to creating the high quality American-style yearbook; knitting particularly hot at the mo. Some of these are accredited, such as the Community Sports Leader Award and the Duke of Edinburgh award. Lots of fundraising and local community work.

Fabulous, unique Hampshire Specialist Music Course curiously low profile. Around twelve students a year are selected and study two instruments (free of charge) to a high standard alongside academic music and two or three further A levels. 'Costs a fortune – we spend three times as much on the music specialists as we do on the other students,' says Mr Hopkins. The course gives the college a solid core of talent but music spills out over its edges:140 students are studying music and/or music technology A level. Other music students receive free tuition on their main instrument and can play in a variety of bands, orchestras and choirs.

Background and Atmosphere: Peter Symonds founded Christes Hospital (no relation to the Horsham school – it was a 'trendy name' at the time) in the seventeenth century to look after aged brethren, assist two divinity students and educate four poor boys. Sale of land during the expansion of the railways enabled a boys' grammar school to be built on the current site in 1897, operating first as a boys' independent, then a grammar and finally becoming a co-ed sixth form college in the early seventies. Heads arrive and proceed to make the place their life's work: only six since 1897.

An intense conurbation perched on a hilly spot overlooking the suburbs of Winchester. Original late Victorian building now completely surrounded by dedicated buildings purpose-built in the last ten years, including newish cavernous learning and resources centre (library plus). Everything being used to full capacity – jam-packed with strapping youths. Students socialise in giant departure lounge style commonroom and sunbathe like seals on Hopkin's Hump, a little knoll named after the head. Large canteen plus satellites provide cheap and plentiful food. No uniform (style leans to grungy rather than trendy), teachers called by their first names, 55 minute lessons, no bells: really a halfway house between school and university.

Pastoral Care and Discipline: Sanctions minimal, although a zero tolerance policy on drugs and alcohol on site and smoking is not permitted except in one small fenced off area outdoors. 'Six or seven' students expelled most years – more common for them to leave 'by mutual consent'. Most common reason is 'laziness'; the occasional drugs bust. Full time counsellors available for personal matters. Two boarding houses (girls one floor, boys the other, electric door between). School House is a handsome Victorian building in which students share two-four bedded rooms. Falkland Lodge was opened in 1998: single or twin rooms, all en suite, but it costs more. Feel almost, but not quite, like university halls of residence, with an air of independence, e.g. boarders do their own laundry, aside from bedding. Boarding inspection reports rated it 'outstanding'.

Pupils and Parents: Fifty per cent from the three Winchester 11–16 schools – Kings, Westgate, Henry Beaufort. Perins in Alresford tops the long list of other feeder schools. A further 15–20 per cent from independent schools and the rest from far and wide – Reading, Salisbury and the Isle of Wight included. Student social profile directly reflects Winchester skew towards ambitious middle classes – one teacher remarked, 'Nothing as formidable as a Winchester mother protecting her young'. Former pupils include comedian Jack Dee, Olympic gold medallists Ben Ainsley and Iain Percy, Coldplay drummer William Champion, 'Page 3 girl' Lucy Pinder.

Entrance: 1600 pupils pile into the school at 16. Deadline for application is December. Non-selective, but requirement for A level courses is at least five grade Cs at GCSE level, 'ideally' including maths and English. Maths and science are exceptions – you need a B. Every applicant is interviewed. Vastly over-subscribed – local pupils automatically get in; beyond that pupils are accepted geographically in concentric circles radiating out from Winchester. Exceptions made for musicians, boarders and students from a windswept corner of the South Atlantic (has the honour of being the official sixth form of the Falkland Islands – construction of Falkland Lodge boarding house was partly funded by the Falklands government). Candidates for the Hampshire Specialist Music Course audition in February/March on two instruments, one of which should be at grade 7/8 standard.

Exit: 83 per cent to universities of all descriptions, with a steady 40–50 (sometimes more) to Oxbridge. Students on the music course frequently move on to the top music colleges.

Money Matters: Sixth form colleges receive less money per pupil than normal schools so the management employs meticulous budgeting, plus a dash of sorcery, to keep the whole shebang on the road. Hardship fund available. Students compete for several bursaries each year for gap year projects.

Remarks: A huge, friendly metropolis which falls neatly between school and university in approach. Most people would be happy here, but not those who need spoon-feeding.

Plymouth College

Linked to Plymouth College Preparatory School in the Junior section

Ford Park, Plymouth, Devon, PL4 6RN

• Pupils: 210 girls, 330 boys. 130 boarders, the rest day • Ages: 11-18
• Size of sixth form: 185 • C of E • Fees: £10,740-£22,050 pa
• Independent

Tel: 01752 203 300
Fax: 01752 203 246
Email: mail@plymouthcollege.com
Website: www.plymouthcollege.com

Headmaster: Since September 2006, Dr Simon Wormleighton BA PhD. Formerly head of Grenville College, Bideford. Married with two children, a keen sportsman – hockey and cricket in particular.

Academic matters: Strong academically. Typically, 94 per cent A to C pass rate at GCSE and 98 per cent pass rate at A level. International Baccalaureate available. Very strong economics, physics and engineering students, winning top competitions. Upper sixth students provided two of the four teams in the 2005 national final of the business CIMA Management Challenge Competition – school was runner-up in 2004 and won it in both 2007 and 2008. Won National Young Enterprise in 2009 and Student Investor in 2010. Strong sciences and business studies generally. French compulsory from Year 7. Students can choose Latin, German, Spanish or classical civilisation in Year 8. Pushes strong linguists towards Latin – also useful for medics, lawyers and English experts. Small classes – 5–10 common at AS and A levels; the average of 16 in younger years.

Hot learning support system with some 80 students, including some very bright who have SEN, including three Asperger's. Will take dyslexics with reasonable IQs (i.e. those who are capable of achieving a minimum of eight GCSEs) but not so geared up for ADHD or general learning problems. Any strugglers will be advised to drop a subject and will receive extra help to concentrate on the main ones – 'It really helps your child be the best they can be'.

Games, Options, the Arts: Ample on-site sporting facilities. Excellent sporting reputation. Outstanding rugby teams with Devon Cup champions in each year group – senior player currently in U18 England rugby team. Élite swimming programme with Plymouth Leander club – swimming scholarship pupils compete in international events such as World Championships and Commonwealth Games. Old Girl Cassie Patten won the bronze medal in the Beijing Olympics 10km open water event. Specialist house for swimmers on prep school site. Modern pentathlon and fencing academy with national athletes. County successes in netball, hockey, athletics, cricket and tennis.

Plenty of practice, specialist teaching and performance rooms for music, including a recording studio and performance hall with professional audio and lighting equipment. Discussion groups of a director, producer, editor, DJ announcer and publicity officer develop varied performing skills. Separate art house displays fantastic artwork with very varied styles. Drama is not as strong here, although 'up and coming'. Visiting lecturers from poets to sportsmen.

Background and Atmosphere: Acquired girls' preparatory school in 1995 and the nearby St Dunstan's Abbey in 2004. Founded in 1877, a maze of large buildings with a myriad of corridors and doors making for a quiet and peaceful atmosphere, though must be somewhat daunting for newcomers. The students seem to have masses of space – a table or even a row each. Not an élite or tough city school – adopts a more gentle, seemingly laid-back air, perhaps quietly confident. However, in class, students are attentive and studious – a dream for any committed teacher.

Pastoral Care and Discipline: No behaviour problems in evidence here. 'Very helpful' resident married housemaster and housemistress and a member of the sixth form team support boarders on a one-to-one basis or in small groups. Boys are accommodated in three houses on one side of the housemaster's home, with girls in the three houses on the other side. Two new houses with single rooms for sixth formers opened in 2009 and 2010. Lots to do for weekenders, from surfing to skating.

Pupils and Parents: Overall well-presented and polite individuals. Sixth form senior prefects adorned with graduate-style gowns when accompanying visitors or on special days. Varied social and professional backgrounds. Many from the local area whose parents work at Plymouth's Derriford Hospital. Some 10 per cent foreign nationals – German, Russian, Hong Kong and mainland Chinese, South Korean and African.

Entrance: Only mildly selective, so enormous range of ability on entry, following satisfactory performance in entrance exam. Typically lower ability than neighbouring grammars on entry but GCSE and A level results compete. Six GCSE passes including maths and English with a minimum of three B grades to enter the sixth form. Some 70 per cent enter from prep. Intake likely to be reduced, particularly fewer foreign nationals.

Exit: Over half leave for traditional universities – the trend is to aim for south west universities but a good mix going all over the country. Steady stream to either Oxford or Cambridge as well as other top universities.

Money Matters: Academic, art, music, rugby, golf and swimming scholarships plus other sports awards; also a limited bursary fund. New modern pentathlon programme with scholarships on offer for this discipline.

Remarks: A school with ample space, excellent teaching and many opportunities to excel. Should produce 2012 Olympic swimming hopefuls with this amount of support.

Plymstock School and Sports College

Church Road, Plymstock, Plymouth, Devon, PL9 9AZ

• Pupils: 1,575 boys and girls, all day • Ages: 11-18 • Size of sixth form: 260 • State

Tel: 01752 402 679
Fax: 01752 484 018
Email: info@plymstockschool.org.uk
Website: www.plymstockschool.org.uk

Headteacher: Since 2007, Mr David Farmer, former head of Torpoint Community College. We hope that calmer times lie ahead after a period of disturbances at the top.

Academic matters: Top Plymouth school with 79 per cent 5+ A*–C grades at GCSE (66 per cent including English and mathematics). 25+ A level courses, besides good GNVQ, NVQ, RSA opportunities via a training consortium. Lots of awards. Enhanced specialist provision – centre for communication difficulties and intensive numeracy and literacy programme for SEN in Years 7 and 8. Good extension studies for gifted/talented students through faster moving classes, earlier entry into subjects; supportive services include reading and homework club.

Games, Options, the Arts: Excellent reputation for county, national and international sporting achievements – hence has specialist sports college status. Enviably large, outdoor floodlit sporting area with flat grass track and netball/tennis courts. Newly completed third generation artificial football pitch and very large sports hall. Parents believe separating boys' and girls' groups for PE works. The less academic will not fade here and budding actors still have a chance with drama and performing arts A level. Growing percentage of students do PE, dance and sport studies. The art adorning the corridors shouts high quality. Parents impressed with varied range of musical and dramatic performances from Shakespeare to rock and roll. Work experience in Germany popular for A level German students – a big confidence booster.

Background and Atmosphere: Very attractive school with garden courtyards. Teachers, students and parents work well together. Quiet and hard-working atmosphere of which it is proud. Recent investment of £5m has replaced temporary classrooms with well-resourced dance and drama, modern languages, mathematics, pottery and sport areas. Science, technology and humanities refurbished. Plymstock keeps up with leading edge ICT development – electronic whiteboards in every department, digital music recording. Wheelchair friendly.

Pastoral Care and Discipline: Bullying or behavioural problems are dealt with quickly. It's 'cool to be clever at Plymstock' so ridiculing high achievers – 'boffs' – is out. 'Unreserved support' for any necessary punishment is expected from parents.

Pupils and Parents: Mixed social backgrounds, although Plymstock is more affluent than many parts of Plymouth. Parents are 'proud' to send their children to Plymstock. 'It really encourages individuals to celebrate their talents.' Students believe they achieve because the teaching is good. Olympic swimmer and gold medalist Sharron Davies came here before winning a scholarship to Kelly College.

Entrance: Pupils from eight feeder schools: Oreston, Elburton, Hooe, Dunstone, Pomphlett, Goosewell, Downham, Wembury – belonging to the Plymstock (Plymouth) area Academic Council. This family of schools communicates well. One per cent choose Plymouth grammar schools instead.

Exit: Approximately 75 per cent of Year 11 students progress to Plymstock's sixth form, others head for the local college of further education, the College of Art and Design, employment based training and other schools. Plymstock regularly sends students to top universities, including Oxford and Cambridge.

Remarks: Highly successful and good all-round comprehensive in a pleasant suburb of Plymouth. Now needs period of stability to build on its notable successes.

Polam Hall School

Linked to Polam Hall Junior School in the Junior section

Grange Road, Darlington, County Durham, DL1 5PA

• Pupils: 340 boys and girls age 2 to 18 ; 45 board • Ages: 2-18 • Size of sixth form: 70 (including boys) • Quaker origins • Fees: Day £6,150-£11,160; Boarding £17,355-£21,405 pa • Independent

Tel: 01325 463 383
Fax: 01325 383 539
Email: information@polamhall.com
Website: www.polamhall.com

Head: Since 2004, Miss M Green BA PGCE (early fifties), previously head of English at Withington Girls' School, Manchester. Extremely cheery and welcoming, Bolton Wanderers supporter with one of the warmest handshakes ever encountered; studied English and French at Lancaster, exudes a love of literature. Hugely enthusiastic and genuinely sincere in her affection for the school and for pupils of all ages and stages.

Academic matters: Moderately selective intake, pupils expected to work hard and results impressive with non-high flyers achieving beyond expectations in all areas; maths very strong, bucking the trend with the largest A level group; French, German, Spanish and Chinese all available; art, music and drama vibrant and popular; physics and chemistry labs fully refurbished 2006; ICT much in evidence; comprehensive range of A level subjects for size of school. Very buzzy nursery and junior departments, colourful and enthusiastic displays abound.

Very modest about their SEN provision saying, 'We do strive to support effectively our pupils with special needs, but we do not wish to present ourselves as experts in the field'. However they do have experience of dealing with Asperger's syndrome, dyslexia, dyspraxia and moderate learning disabilities. Their entry in the Public Autism Resource & Information Service (PARIS) includes, 'ASD pupils are usually educated in mainstream classes, with some time designated for support in the learning support unit ... We have a good history of success with ASD pupils at this mainstream boarding school, where the majority of pupils leave us to go to university. Pupils are placed here by our local authority who value the education we provide for this type of pupil. Please contact the school SENCo for more detailed information'.

Games, Options, the Arts: Hockey, lacrosse, netball, cross country, tennis, athletics all popular, cricket, rugby, football; attractive playing fields, courts and sports hall on school premises; school represented on England lacrosse squad; national golfer, two potential Olympian swimmers and a member of the England equestrian team. Major sports tours to Canada, Australia. Purpose-built theatre; termly music concerts; intimate 'coffee' concerts held in the conservatory to showcase developing talent. Orienteering – pre-drive schemes for sixth formers. Duke of Edinburgh Award operating with sustained success at all levels. Extended view of the world encouraged with inspirational speakers, annual overseas visits, World Challenge to Malawi.

Background and Atmosphere: Founded in 1848 by Quakers, with the descendants of founding families still represented on governing body. Tight, cohesive site including main school, junior school and boarding houses, with a number of newer additions to original school house. Residential on three sides, attractive open parkland adjoining school grounds to one side lends a feeling of open space. Major upgrades to the boarding facilities completed 2006.

Hard core of long-established, experienced teachers – fairly stable but with an appropriate injection of new blood; average age 37. Mutually supportive, spirit of goodwill – 'working together for the good of the whole' encouraged by collaborative leadership style.

Pastoral Care and Discipline: Regular assemblies ('Reading') reflecting Quaker foundations; awareness of the wider world and strong spirit of generosity. Successful and enthusiastic fundraising. Before and after school care, and homework clubs. Few formal rules; high standards of courtesy and behaviour expected based on respect for self and others. Strong anti-bullying policy; serious misconduct extremely rare.

Pupils and Parents: A broad cross-section of abilities, backgrounds and cultures here in a community that welcomes diversity. A changing profile with a large influx of overseas pupils mainly into upper school – including proud International Boarder of the Year finalists.

Pupils are friendly, remarkably modest about their achievements and down to earth, reflecting the honest, unpretentious character of this northern school. School council produces manifestos and submits thought-provoking proposals, with even four year olds effectively negotiating the right to wear watches to school. Parents a mixture of urban and rural, first-time buyers and second and third generation Polamites. Strong Parents' Association organising free events for parent body. Parents' focus group presents views/perspectives to head.

Entrance: For entry at 11, diagnostic tests in English, logic and reasoning, interview with head. Scholarships, means-tested bursaries and music awards available. At 16, candidates for the sixth form scholarships sit examinations involving general studies and critical thinking, complete an application pack, and will have an interview with the head. Occasional placement by local authority of pupil on autistic spectrum (Asperger's).

Exit: Varying numbers depart post-GCSE, most remain but small proportion move to local sixth form college or co-ed boarding schools. Students go on to a wide range of universities and courses, including a small number of Oxbridge candidates. Notable old girls Nadine Bell, NASA scientist, Ruth Gemmell, actress.

Remarks: Impressive work adorns the walls and cheery pupils meet and greet. Enthusiasm abounds, busy pupils at work and play with the well-organised, self-reliant manner that children, with support and encouragement, do so well.

Poole Grammar School

Gravel Hill, Poole, Dorset, BH17 9JU

• Pupils: 1000 boys; all day • Ages: 12-18 • Size of sixth form: Around 300 • Non-denom • State

Tel: 01202 692 132
Fax: 01202 606 500
Email: office@poolegrammar.com
Website: www.poolegrammar.com

Headmaster: Since 2004, Mr Ian Carter BSc, PGCE, NPQH, FRSA (forties), member of the Institute of Biology, chartered biologist. One of a very small group of state school heads who are HMC additional members. Educated at Worthing Sixth Form College, then read zoology at Durham and earned PGCE from Pembroke College, Cambridge. Blue chip teaching career includes stints at University College School in London, Cranbrook Grammar School, Monkton Combe and Woodbridge School in Suffolk. Came to Poole from The Perse in Cambridge, where he was senior deputy head. Wife, Suzy, is head of German at Talbot Heath Girls' school, their son is at arch-rival Bournemouth Grammar. Informally arranged hair conceals a stickler for detail. Keen that the school should focus on serving the local population, rather than drawing in the brightest berries on the bush from anywhere. Keen sportsman – played cricket and hockey at university and still surrenders to the call of leather on willow in the springtime. Sings in the local choral society. Lifelong interest in Borneo and spent time in Sarawak 'studying headhunters' in his twenties. Visiting fellow of Harris Manchester College, Oxford University 2010.

Academic matters: A mathematics and computing specialist school and, not surprisingly, maths is the most popular A level subject here. Sciences also big – separate sciences for virtually all at GCSE now – with some stellar individual performances. Surprisingly, the subjects where the results really shine out are the more verbal ones – English, history, French, politics – and also art (though very few candidates for this last).

Enthusiastic and innovative IT. All pupils are entered for short course IT GCSE at end of Year 9 and computing is a popular A level. The school has Cisco and Microsoft Academy status and students can earn the CCNA networking qualification in sixth form. Modern languages expanding with the introduction of Spanish in 2006 to complement French and German. Currently no setting in languages but head appreciates the mind boggling boredom some French whizzes experience when they arrive here and may introduce it (some setting in maths at present). Media studies robust – not the vacuous piece of fluff it can be at some schools. Joint sixth form teaching in many subjects with Parkstone Grammar School (girls). Very good careers programme and all pupils do two weeks' work experience in Year 11. All take A level general studies, with mixed results, with options for the extended project and OU modules available. A few do an AS in critical thinking. Class sizes under control, especially in sixth form.

As grammar schools go, has made thoughtful provision for learning support via a part-time specialist teacher and three full-time learning support assistants. 'We're not afraid of special needs,' says the head. 'We want to celebrate differences.' A teacher at the school agreed, saying, 'We are working harder now to look after boys who are not achieving.' Currently one profoundly deaf boy and several with statements for a range of needs on the Asperger's spectrum. The school has adopted a second specialism in SEN cognition and learning which focusses on gifted and talented individuals and supporting bright boys with a range of needs.

Games, Options, the Arts: Considered a sporty school. Some activity compulsory all the way to the end of sixth form and a significant minority of boys involved in teams. Football the most popular sport but rugby, cricket and athletics are probably more successful. Teams from Poole Grammar have recently been U13, U14 and U15 county cricket champions and South West Schools Athletics champions. Tennis played in the summer on new courts. Two old-fashioned gyms, one with diminutive climbing wall. Sailing (at Hamworthy) plus swimming and squash off the premises. After school participation in games and activities constrained by the bus schedule but much happens at lunch time. In September 2010 a new music school, studio theatre and library (learning resource centre) have been built and provide excellent state of the art facilities. In addition a multimedia suite, music and TV production studios will be available. Music department enthusiastic and accomplished. Unconventional ex-actor has added a certain je ne sais quoi to the drama department. Big theatrical production alternate years with smaller studio play in between. Some boys also take part in Parkstone Grammar's big musicals. Art a little less central here, with a slightly fringe following. Large, multi-faceted DT area, with a different room for each aspect of the subject, including food tech. Keen Young Enterprise.

Background and Atmosphere: A 'late' grammar school, founded in central Poole in 1904. Strangely, the school admitted boys and girls until 1937, when it became boys only. Moved in 1966 to Gravel Hill, a nondescript wooded artery into Poole famed for its speed traps. Large grounds, well cared for, with 'the best cricket square in Poole!' enthused the head. Much recent building, though the contractors seem to have mastered the retro sixties look, as the whole place looks of a piece. New sixth form facilities created out of the conversion of former library. Science labs all upgraded since 2006 – and we saw an unfathomable range of ultra-high-tech equipment. Boys expected to work hard and they do. New food technology, sports science, sixth form art and graphics facilities built in 2010, coupled with new entrance to the school and landscaping. Over 150 academic and non-academic prizes given annually. Although this is a place of work for over a 1,000 manly adolescents, it feels surprisingly civilised and less macho than Bournemouth Grammar, only fifteen minutes away – not sure why.

Pastoral Care and Discipline: Heads of year take responsibility for all boys in the year. Head of Year 8 makes sure the little lambs settle. Their Year 8 tutor takes them into Year 9 and a remixing of forms in year 10. Uniform requirement relaxes over the years – from blazer and tie for Years 8 and 9 to jumper and tie for Years 10 and 11, to ties only in sixth form. Out (either temporary or permanent) for bringing drugs on site – the policy was recently put to the test. Bullying will land you in school's exclusion room for a day. Parents praise the discipline here and the rapt and concentrating faces we saw in lessons certainly bore this out. School holds some social events with Parkstone Grammar.

Pupils and Parents: We dug long and hard but did not find parents who found fault with any major aspect of the school (the demon headmaster?). Families from a range of social backgrounds, mainly united by good work ethic. Not a rich tapestry of ethnic diversity, but this is Poole. Ability range broader than you would expect, perhaps owing to proximity of similar grammar in Bournemouth, plus very good local comprehensives, plus entrance policy that favours local pupils above potentially brighter but more distant applicants (see below).

Entrance: Complex and intensely controversial. In 2009, due to a new admissions code, the school was able to reinstate its desired aim of admitting pupils who live in Poole once again irrespective of where they go to school. Meanwhile, Poole Grammar will continue to take some pupils from outside the borough (not enough Poole boys to fill it). Entries by late October; test (in maths, English and non-verbal reasoning) in early December for 168 places at 12+. Loads of appeals – 33 last year, of which nine were successful. Main feeders: Broadstone, Oakdale and Canford Heath Middle Schools and Dumpton Prep. NB – The borough consulted over moving the entry age to 11+ and decided in favour, which will take place from 2013.

Sixth form entry much less competitive – surprising that more people haven't caught on: 344 points with an A*, A or B in the subjects chosen or in a related discipline. The points used are the DCSF points: 58 A*, 52 A, 46 B, 40 C, 34 D, 28 E. (Maximum = 8A* = 464 points.)

Exit: One or two boys scram after Year 8, often in search of small class sizes and hand-holding at a local independent school. 10 or 20 leave after GCSE to vocational courses or sixth form college. Later, to universities mainly in the south west – Southampton, Bristol, Bath, Bournemouth (for media programmes); also to Durham; few to London. A dozen or so to Oxbridge. Staff includes seven Old Boys.

Remarks: A treasure serving the people of Poole.

Portland Place School

56-58 Portland Place, London, W1B 1NJ

• Pupils: 375 (285 boys, 90 girls); all day • Ages: 10-18 • Size of sixth form: Size of sixth form: 80 (60 boys and 20 girls) • Non denom • Fees: £14,250-£14,985 pa • Independent

Tel: 020 7307 8700
Fax: 020 7436 2676
Email: admin@portland-place.co.uk
Website: www.portland-place.co.uk

Headmaster: Since 1996, when school opened, Mr Richard Walker BSc PGCE CChem FRSA (mid-fifties). Previously head of chemistry at St Paul's Girls' School, then principal of Abbey College (also owned by Alpha Plus group, formerly DLD Group, which owns Portland Place and around fifteen other schools, PP being the only secondary school in its portfolio). Bluff, breezy, voluble and genial, after thirteen popular years in post has lost none of his enthusiasm, bonhomie and zest for the future. He is grateful to leave the financial and legal sides of running a school to the Alpha Plus head office and concentrates on the education – in its broadest sense – he provides for his charges. Parents enthuse: 'He's extremely accessible'; 'There's nothing he won't do'; 'He knows all their names'; 'He really seems to enjoy the kids' – an appreciation of his open-minded and relaxed approach. As a parent told us, he's 'a compassionate man but not of the awful PC ilk' – witness the clear pastoral system ('on which we stand or fall') and the truly collaborative feel around the place.

1996 was a different era – even a Richard Walker might find starting a school in the second decade of this millennium a tall order. But that was then – his was clearly an inspired appointment and this most unlikely of schools – given its location and premises – is thriving. Reputedly a Wagner buff, not much of the Alberich about him but he assuredly is guardian to a bit of a goldmine.

Academic matters: Avowedly and proudly mixed ability and piles on the value added – 'We're top of the MidYIS GCSE tables,' boasts Mr Walker. Small classes – an average of 18 in Years 7–9, and we saw several smaller ones – and of 15 in Years 10 and 11, smaller still in the sixth. GCSE options include business, computing, sport studies and media, along with the trad subjects – but no Latin or Greek and modern languages uptake is less than enthusiastic, though all take at least one. Reasons for this include, probably, the sizeable number of mild dyslexics and the high proportion of those for whom a natural second language would not be the French, Italian and Spanish on offer – 'We have 50-odd languages spoken at home'. Mr Walker determined to persevere with the languages but it's clearly a bit of a crusade. Likewise with RE – very low uptake. At GCSE, 75 per cent get A*–C, 44 per cent A*/B. Some subjects achieve 100 per cent A*–C – these include the sciences, music, art and media. The value added shows at A level, where the results are more impressive, most being in the B-D bracket with a decent sprinkling of As. And this after a fair number departed after GCSEs – a trend now on the wane.

Library manned by full-time librarian and a nice place to sit and read. Lots of fiction, used for competitions, book club and being quiet. As an academic resource it is risible (school prefers 'needs developing' and reminds us that the individual heads of departments keep library resources in their offices). Good IT suites and resources for the popular media and film options. Most teachers spoken of warmly, but a few clearly less than adept at dealing with livelier pupils – 'My son finds it hard to concentrate in classes where the teacher isn't good at controlling the more wayward elements,' we heard. However, most pupils laud their friendliness and helpfulness.

Everyone setted for everything, though the exigencies of the three sites and timetabling can lead to anomalies, e.g. a geography whizz might find himself in the lowest set because his English needs extra support. However, parents approve – 'A child can work his way up, or be dropped down – they are very flexible,' we were told. Takes a lot of children with mild dyslexia but, apart from general support from the class teacher, no other help is available and a staunch policy of no withdrawals from classes (except once weekly for children who have EAL). No screening on admission. However SENCo oversees general provision and monitoring– 80–90 children perceived as having some kind of LDD (learning disability or difficulty), some have IEPs. Most with more than the mildest difficulties seek support outside school. Inside school, the attitude is healthy – 'I'm not treated as if dyslexia is a crime – unlike at my last school,' we were told. Two of the three buildings have lifts but will be helpful if someone breaks a leg and move lessons to the ground floor.

Games, Options, the Arts: Everyone told us, 'Sport is huge,' and we were taken round by a 17-year-old semi-professional footballer! Virtually no facilities on site – a tiny gym and small hall. They are bused or walk everywhere – mostly to Regent's Park, with pitches and courts of all kinds – and the results and achievements, given the conditions, are impressive. Football and netball tour of Barbados in 2009, swimming teams win competitions, masses of medals in cross country and local honours in athletics and team sports. Pervasive pride in school sports – helped, no doubt, by classy Olympians on staff. However most really keen sportsmen and women do their serious sport outside school – no real alternative. Sport now compulsory to Year 12 – one afternoon a week minimum of netball or football.

Music and drama similarly 'massive'. Music means, mostly, pop and jazz – a few violinists and woodwinders amongst the jazz pianists, guitarists, drummers and bassists who predominate, but music taken seriously in general. Wholehearted, whole school major productions annually – *Grease, My Fair Lady, Oliver!* and *Bugsy* are recent offerings; not onsite as no suitable space, though a good drama studio – in local theatres, e.g. The Cockpit. Also lots of year group plays in which most get involved – and not all are musicals.

Art in the lower school is lively and inventive – we enjoyed aboriginal-style models made of wood and paint along with African puppets and a wonderful mobile fashioned from a clapped-out brolly. Art uptake in senior school is small – facilities limited, though a textiles room and it excels in photography. DT similarly energetic – resistant materials, pewter casting, CAD and CAM, though all in rather small and poky rooms in basement. Lots of imaginative extra-curricular stuff, especially for the sixth – we liked the daylong compulsory cookery and two-day self-defence courses. Trips galore – we have seldom seen such a full programme. Much use made of London's galleries, museums and exhibitions, plus the nearby wider world and the opportunities it offers for field, sporting and other educational exercises – here and abroad.

Background and Atmosphere: Robert Adam – did he but know it – designed two schools in the UK: Stowe and this one. Portland Place – the road – is a broad, straight thoroughfare in the heart of Regency London – two minutes from Oxford Circus to the south, two minutes to Regent's Park to the north. It is lined by august embassies – China, Kenya, Poland, Portugal – and the HQs of royal and learned institutions – architects, physicists, radiologists, anaesthetists. The main school building – Portland Place – identifies itself with a modest brass plate and is elegantly splendid. It is rare for us to compliment a school on its décor but a pleasure to do so in this case. Super real blue carpet up and down the stairs – not just on the ground floor for show as elsewhere – magnificent ceilings, cornices, columns, capitals and fireplaces – nowhere more so than in the old ballroom, rescued by Mr Walker from its carapace of false ceiling and fluorescent tubes and very much in use. All in tip-top nick. This building houses the lower years, the hall used for gym and dance, and the top floors – formerly the servants' quarters – accommodate music and languages.

A second building in Great Portland Street, five minutes away, houses the upper years and has a breathtaking eyeball-to-eyeball view of the Post Office Tower – seemingly within grabbing distance. Harford House – also in Great Portland Street and with a façade resembling that of a corporate HQ – is home to art, drama and science. It's a logistical nightmare – five or seven storeys to be up and down all day, three buildings – and the whole has to be timetabled, supervised and navigated. We suppose everyone to be very fit! Head yearns openly – 'My aim is to have a two-site school. PP would be a prep school from Year 4 and we'd have a second building for everything and everyone else – including one room which would house the entire school. It's got to happen.' Apparently it's high on the agenda for the management. Look out – PP already punches above its weight and we predict its becoming bigger and more prominent within five years maximum.

No school kitchen – pupils import packed lunches or order in from local café which delivers dozens of panini etc in little brown carriers. Years 10, 11 and the sixth hang out in the many cafés in or around Gt Portland Street and just love the privilege of this kind of freedom.

Pastoral Care and Discipline: Good use of sixth form mentors for Years 7 and 8 – really fosters inter-age group understanding and friendships, especially helpful in so small a school. Solidly structured pastoral care hierarchy picks up and deals with problems but a pervasive sense of everyone looking out for everyone else. People seem to know each other's little brothers and sisters here. Parents praise the home-school communications and especially the termly parents' evenings. 'The teachers are mostly young and energetic,' enthused a parent, 'and you really get to know them.'

Pupils and Parents: Far more boys than girls – simply because so many more girls' and co-ed schools in London than boys'. Mixed, as befits its location – trad, moneyed independent education veterans, alongside newbies and newcomers from here, there and everywhere, blended with those who couldn't get into the 'academic' schools and for whom PP has been a jolly lucky find. From, now, the whole urban sprawl – no longer just the north and west but around 30 per cent from east and south too. Mostly UK born and based but also from pretty much the rest of the globe, solar system and beyond, in a great undivided family. Brains? Yes, though common denominator more palpably pleasure, pride and enthusiasm for the place.

Entrance: Now an intake into Year 6 – partly to steal a march on the competition and partly to meet the needs of those who dread the 11+ circus and will do anything to avoid it (wise move). 'Informal tests' in English and maths and a chat with the head and deputy. Twelve into Year 6 in 2009. Year 7 has 50 places for whom 120+ apply (a 25 per cent increase 2008/9) – tests in English and maths and a chat with the head. Some places higher up – same format plus additional test in science. Fifteen come in at Year 9. A few join at Year 12, on flexible terms. They come, at 11, from a large number of schools – state and independent. Mostly from north, north-west.

Exit: 30 per cent have left after GCSE hitherto, but the last two years have seen more stayers. Interesting range of post-A level destinations – music at The RA, interior design, fashion and animal management at the newer universities, but also physics at Bristol, politics at Nottingham and a couple to good US colleges. Certainly no typical end product.

Money Matters: Five scholarships for 11+ entry – academic, music, drama, sports, art. All worth 50 per cent of fees. Pretty good for so new a school.

Remarks: It's smart, relaxed, modern and very London. Not a hothouse, but not a dossing place for slouches either. A place for engaged, lively, normal kids – privileged, yes, but Sloanes, no. Find it before your friends do.

The Portsmouth Grammar School

Linked to Portsmouth Grammar Junior School (The) in the Junior section

High Street, Old Portsmouth, Portsmouth, Hampshire, PO1 2LN

• Pupils: 1130 • Ages: 11-18 • Size of sixth form: 300 • Christian non-denom • Fees: Seniors £12,132 pa • Independent

Tel: 023 9236 0036
Fax: 023 9236 3256
Email: admissions@pgs.org.uk
Website: www.pgs.org.uk

Head: Since 2008, Mr James Priory MA (late thirties), previously the school's assistant head and head of sixth. An Oxford graduate (got a 1st) in English, Mr Priory was educated at King Edward's School, Birmingham, and Taunton School, where he became head boy and a hotshot debater, winning the World Public Speaking and Debating Championships. His first teaching post was at Bradford Grammar School where he became head of Year 7, introducing the first girls into the school. Arrived at PGS as head of English in 2000, later assistant head in charge of sixth form.

Became PGS's first internally appointed head in 200 years when he took over the reins from Tim Hands (now at Magdalen College). After the promotion, was permitted an enlightening sabbatical term shadowing heads and scrutinising IB schools all over the UK, USA and Canada – as a precursor to PGS gearing up for the IB programme. Interested in Portsmouth history and culture and teaches a course about Arthur Conan Doyle (who had his first medical practice in Portsmouth) and his links with PGS (one of Conan Doyle's brothers is an OB; a PGS maths teacher, Alfred Wood, was the model for Dr Watson). Has replaced Hands as chairman of the Portsmouth Festivities, a city wide celebration of young people and the arts held each June. Teaches songwriting as a sixth form general studies option and is known for 'getting the guitar out, David Brent style'. Writes and performs songs for leavers' occasions and the like. A stickler for detail, he sent us back our draft of this write-up covered in red ink. Married to another English teacher and they have three young children, all at PGS.

Academic matters: Takes its academics seriously – A level results rock solid, with little movement up or down, year after year. Unique approach: all pupils do four A levels;

exam-free lower sixth – AS modules not taken till January of upper sixth, 'So pupils are taking the exams at their most mature,' explains the head. Last year 28 pupils achieved four straight A grades. Similar strategy for GCSEs – none taken early except maths in the top two sets, and then only by a few months, still firmly within Year 11. A levels lean towards the geeky – maths the most popular A level by a long chalk; sciences also up there with almost as many pupils taking physics as biology or chemistry. English also successful, along with most other subjects really, modern languages excepted perhaps. IB introduced in 2009 with 35 sixth formers – 25 from PGS and ten joining from other schools; expects half the sixth form to opt for the programme eventually. GCSEs impressive across the board. Two modern languages plus Latin compulsory in Years 7 and 8.

Setting in maths and science. Average class size 24 in Years 7–11; down to eight (and often fewer) in the sixth form. Head recollects that he was in charge of SEN when he was head of English years ago; things have moved on – now a learning support department with three dedicated staff for the senior school alone, plus other members of staff with SEN training. Extra support delivered through individual lessons before school, at lunch or in small timetabled groups – pupils not taken out of lessons. Year 8 pupils may have extra help instead of a second foreign language, 'But they still do Latin and one modern language'. Not a school to seek out specially for SEN – Mayfield School down the road has cornered that particular market. Brilliant list of sixth form general studies options includes songwriting (with the headmaster), car maintenance, introduction to medicine and philosophy through film.

Games, Options, the Arts: Extra-curricular activities now have their own deputy head, whose job is to make sure all pupils are squeezing in as much as possible outside the classroom – but not too much. Strong, competitive sport, with many county successes. Placed in the top three Independent Schools for Sport for the last three years running in 'The Daily Telegraph'. The usual games are played one afternoon a week. Has been keen to improve girls' sport, which some felt was the unfortunate stepsister of the boys' programme – netball, athletics and hockey particularly stand out. Cricket is the most popular and successful boys' sport. Sports hall on site, with three squash courts, fitness suite and aerobics/dance studio. No playing fields on site but owns 18 acres at Hilsea, a couple of miles away, complete with all-weather hockey pitch – pupils are bused there for games and matches. Sailing on the doorstep, though mainly pursued outside school. Swimming not a particular strength, but junior school has small covered pool; the senior school uses nearby naval facilities.

Uniquely, a non-denominational cathedral school and member of the Choir Schools' Association. Parents rave about the music, taught in its own building with loads of practice rooms, recording studio and lovely rotunda for concerts. Partnership with the London Mozart Players and promotes new classical music through annual commissions from leading composers for Remembrance Sunday. 'It's very inspiring for young people to be involved with a leading international composer and it brings prestige and a sense of history,' notes the head. Numerous ensembles including a swing band and African drumming group.

School drama energetic and popular – LAMDA exams taken and loads of performances, including a major musical production every year in a Portsmouth theatre and an annual open air Shakespeare production. A school production taken to the Edinburgh Fringe was singled out by 'The Guardian' as the best show produced by children. Art still lower profile than music and drama, but exam results very good. Masses of overseas trips and exchanges, e.g. a trip to Argentina to work on several charitable projects aimed at helping children. D of E now involves over half of year 10. CCF attracts 200 pupils. Debating has risen from ground zero and now has a weekly Model United Nations club – its own conference each March is now a firm fixture on the MUN circuit. Big on fundraising for charities: its 56at45 campaign to raise funds to build a school in northern Cambodia won PGS the Best School award in the community awards run by *The Portsmouth News*.

Background and Atmosphere: Founded 1732 as the dying wish of Dr William Smith, Mayor of Portsmouth and physician to its garrison (mayor of Portsmouth remains a governor). Went independent in 1976 and fully co-ed in 1995. Faint lingering scent of regimented past in the air, mostly owing to the stern, brick, listed architecture, remorseless view of tarmac, brisk sea air and urban setting. Re-development in 2005 produced a new dining and theatre complex, a new library and state-of-the-art science laboratories. Mega science centre open September 2010 set to be a wonder of the Hampshire world and will connect with the already swish 2005 labs. Straightforwardly academic feel (a strong 'culture of aspiration', prefers the head). Cheery Year 6–11 library; another grander one for the sixth form. Sixth form centre with little café a nice touch, as are the house 'bases', with table football, lockers and study areas. Head says Portsmouth has become increasingly international and outward looking, reflected in the ethos of the school (perhaps more inspirationally than actually, thus far). Numbers have steadily increased to almost 1200 in the senior school – presents a challenge for inclusion in school plays and sports teams.

Pastoral Care and Discipline: Four houses, each divided into mixed-age tutor groups, meet three times a week. Tutor stays with same group for two or three years and is the pastoral care lynchpin. Buddying system for Year 7 and 8 pupils to guard against bullying. Sixth formers may go home for the day at 12:50pm if they have no afternoon lessons, but no others allowed off campus. Piles of offputting marketing bumf heavy on fashion-shoot style photos of pupils – not sure why such a fine school has invested so heavily in such froth. An exception is the sixth form handbook – a model student-friendly publication with useful email addresses, times when staff are available to students (including the head, who has a ten minute slot every morning when pupils can drop in) and revision advice. Very occasionally a pupil is asked to leave, usually owing to laziness or 'behaviour'. Head vigilant on cyber bullying and has embraced new technology as a means of combating it. After much consultation decided to allow Facebook on school computers: 'You need to get behind the digital bikeshed'. Staff encouraged to join Facebook; pupils are taught the importance of protecting their identity.

Pupils and Parents: Some travel from as far as Southampton, Winchester, Petersfield and Isle of Wight (and beyond). Six parent-organised coaches bring in the hordes and others take public transport. Pupils not polished but generally diligent and polite. Parents work for IBM, the Navy, professions. Not posh; informal – boys' shirts cheerfully hang out of trousers. Feels a bit like a boys' state grammar or a London day school – 'Feels just like Latymer,' said a teacher. Girls look much more at home than when we visited before; un-tarty. Old Portsmuthians include lots of rear admirals and other military leaders, but also some colourful surprises, e.g. Paul Jones (lead singer of Manfred Mann on their hits 'Do Wah Diddy Diddy' and 'Pretty Flamingo'), James Clavell (best-selling author of *Shôgun* and director of *To Sir With Love*), and Ian Osterloh (inventor of viagra).

Entrance: January entrance tests for 11+ (160 places, but half filled by junior school children) in maths (no calculators), English and verbal reasoning, plus interview. For pupils coming from prep school, CE usually replaces school's own test at 11 and 13. Families frequently transfer in and out of Portsmouth, so places open up in most years at odd times – always worth inquiring. Entry to sixth form requires seven GCSE passes at B or above, with A or A* grades recommended in four subjects to be studied at A level or IB. School's own pupils who fall significantly short may be encouraged to look elsewhere. Minimum requirement to join IB programme at sixth form: four As in GCSE subjects to be continued to IB, Bs in other subjects.

Exit: Almost all to universities far and wide, with sciences the most popular degrees. Bucked the national trend of increased competition for medicine by producing 13 vets and medics in 2009. Good clutch to Oxbridge. Some 15–20 pupils leave after GCSEs, some for a wider curriculum, others because their GCSEs are not up to scratch.

Money Matters: Fees kept low; no lunches included; no sibling discounts. Range of academic scholarships at range of ages bring more status than cash. Bursaries also mostly small, but can run to full fees. Only academic and all rounder awards at 11+, same plus music at 13+. At sixth form also awards for sport, leadership potential and the Peter Ogden sixth form science bursaries for pupils from state schools.

Remarks: Ambitious, frankly academic grammar providing a top quality, seamless education for robust children, from toddler to adult.

Portsmouth High School

Linked to Portsmouth High Junior School in the Junior section

25 Kent Road, Southsea, Hampshire, PO5 3EQ

• Pupils: 500 girls, all day • Ages: 3-18 • Size of sixth form: 70
• Non-denom • Fees: Seniors £9,720; Juniors £7,044; Nursery £5,820 pa
• Independent

Tel: 023 9282 6714
Fax: 023 9281 4814
Email: headsec@por.gdst.net
Website: www.portsmouthhigh.co.uk

Head: Since 2006, Mrs Jenny Clough MA (Cantab) PGCE Institute of Education, a glamorous biologist in her late forties. Varied teaching and management experience in state and independent schools: girls, boys, co-ed, privilege and deprivation – she's done the lot. Portsmouth High via Sherborne School for Girls (deputy head), Priory School in East Sussex (assistant head) and, before that, assistant head of faculty at Riddlesdown High School. Convincing advocate of single sex education (twin sons at boys' boarding school) and great rôle model for her pupils. Open, approachable, knows (almost) every girl by name – she makes it her business, say parents. Her office at the centre of the school belies any hint of an ivory tower. Scientific background now makes her passionate about the arts and modern languages, realising what she's been missing, perhaps. Full of ideas to get the school and girls to break out of their comfort zone by bringing a more investigative mindset into their work and by creating expectations of leadership from a tender age (at least Year 9).

Academic matters: The appealing colour prospectus sets just the right the tone for this school, which offers a remarkable amount from its small urban site. Consistently very good results year in, year out. Outstanding sciences emanate from science block situated off-site, just across the road, where some recently (and splendidly) refurbished laboratories show up the others. Good maths: all sit – and pass – IGCSE papers, some in year 10. Emphasis on languages – French or Spanish compulsory up to GCSE and German or Latin compulsory in Years 8 and 9. Mandarin recently introduced, which chimes with head's stated aim of giving girls a more global perspective. AS/A2 subjects include theatre studies, product design and psychology (distance learning). No plans to offer IB, as it is beyond the scope of a school this size, but head thinking hard about introducing some core strands, e.g. the extended project qualification is currently available to all students. Parents feel school already quite good at this.

A few girls do not have English as a first language, and school makes provision for this, as it does for a handful with mild dyslexia, but that's about it. Dedicated learning support teacher deals with any referrals from staff and school cites experience of various SENs, even if in-house expertise is seldom called on.

The school has to compete with four local independent schools, including the enormous co-ed metropolis of Portsmouth Grammar School (over a thousand pupils), but, as the head says, a 'healthy tension' exists between them; the offer and appeal of each school is quite distinct and 'relations are friendly – lots of brothers go there'.

Games, Options, the Arts: With a new 'Sport England' standard sports centre and a relatively new director of sport, the subject is thriving. Younger girls take part in a rolling programme of at least six sports and not all team games; from year 10 onwards they choose. School has shared ownership of the University of Portsmouth's local floodlit MUGA and synthetic turf pitch, allowing the introduction of athletics to the curriculum, though track and field events are still the poor relation, some girls think. Rounders on Southsea Common and tennis at the junior school. Good at water sports despite a lack of a pool (school uses nearby Navy facilities) – an Olympic swimmer and a world class solo yachtswoman listed amongst its Old Girls. Gym has a sprung floor – good for dance, aerobics and gymnastics.

The art building generates stunning work, as demonstrated by the annual summer show in fabulous atrium exhibition space and displays around school. DT now very popular – newish well-equipped workshop and studios plus whizzy new teacher combine to make this a real strength. Drama prominent at all levels, with productions transferring to local theatres and at least one to Edinburgh Fringe.

Music wing has welcoming practice rooms, and department boasts many accomplished players and singers from the 35 per cent of girls learning an instrument. School cites performances at the Cardiff Millennium Centre, Blenheim Palace and Winchester Cathedral, as well as local venues and overseas tours, live radio performance and National Choir finals at the Festival Hall, plus workshops with visiting luminaries in school. One parent said 'a phenomenal amount for a small school', though others mention a lack of opportunity for middle-ranking ensemble players. Convention wins over innovation, perhaps: no sign of any budding rock stars or DJs, though parents reckon any talents emerging in that direction would be strongly encouraged (and indeed pupils have recently won recognition in national song writing competitions).

Background and Atmosphere: Founded 1882 and truly a town school – in the best sense. Historically not a thing of beauty: a mish-mash of architectural styles. The interior reflects its urban setting – wedged in and multilayered, with lots of staircases and unusual passages. Slightly down at heel in places but extensive building programme has had modernising effect, revamping and making the best use of the site. Newly done up dining room and café proving very popular, where girls buy lunch if they do not bring their own. Good IT teaching and provision: ICT GCSE compulsory. Small, mainly girl-run library (librarian supervises) very pleasant and heavily used. Careers department lodges in a cubicle in the corner. The school has a warm family feel with the teachers knowing all the girls – even those they don't teach. 'Friendly, without being quaint or smothering', as one mother put it. Much made, by the head at least, of the wider benefits of GDST membership.

Approach is very down to earth and unfussy. Short school day: 8.30am–3.40pm – suits girls who travel long distances to be here. A fleet of coaches, minibuses and ferries brings girls from distant spots like Chichester, Southampton and the Isle of Wight, and some come from miles away by train.

Girls in sixth form mature and confident – look adults straight in the eye, treated like adults and most live up to expectations. Greatly helped in this by young dynamic new head of sixth form, who has smartened up the girls and their lovely sixth form centre, a sympathetic conversion of a listed Victorian dwelling house (designed by local notable architect Thomas Ellis-Owen), encompassing living areas (sofas, TV, kitchen) and hi-tech teaching space for small groups. Sixth formers may come and go freely from site and enjoy many other privileges. Headgirl elected by peers. All girls allocated to one of four houses on entry, which feature as a basis for intra-school competitions but not much else – e.g. no physical base. Relationships (balls, fashion shows etc) with co-ed St John's and Portsmouth Grammar.

Pastoral Care and Discipline: Works well in this relatively informal and egalitarian school environment. Huge emphasis on smoothing transition into Year 7, where girls are allocated a Year 11 mentor. The sixth form provides much support and leadership to the younger ones, attached to forms as helpers and to head the houses they once belonged to below sixth form. Girls register twice a day with their form tutor and confirm always 'someone to help you out'. High praise on all sides for welfare officer in particular, despite off-putting title. School day too short for issues of drugs and drinking to raise many problems.

Pupils and Parents: Parents mostly on the middle side of middle class: educated, professionals, academics and some Services families. Many with humble backgrounds in on bursaries etc and quite a few first time buyers. Girls generally mature, hard-working and glad to be there. Head describes them as 'too insular and modest' – something she is determined to change. We found them delightfully outgoing and unpretentious, and parents like the diversity amongst the pupil body.

Entrance: Three form entry at 11, about 50 per cent come from the junior school. Growing number of girls joining in Year 9 prompted the school to offer a 13+ academic scholarship from 2009; head keen to encourage Year 9 entry for academic reasons – previous experience informs her view.

Girls also welcome at sixth form. At 11, girls sit maths and English papers based on the national curriculum, meant to be user-friendly for girls from the state sector and to discourage coaching. 'Average ability or better' is the watchword. Entry at sixth form requires seven GCSEs at grade C or better, with Bs in future A level subjects, plus interview.

At the junior school, four to seven year olds attend an individual assessment session. Older juniors attend school for a morning, during which they are tested in story writing, reading, spelling, comprehension and maths.

Exit: Forty per cent of girls leave after GCSE, with majority going to local sixth form colleges – 'Hampshire is full of them'. Girls and parents who stayed with PHS are glad they did, reckoning that the narrower range of subjects is more than compensated for by the opportunities for leadership at school. They appreciate its small size, high standards and the close, nurturing relationships between teachers and students. Leavers tend to go on to universities in the south, Southampton and Cardiff in particular, but an outpost in Durham and a clutch to Cambridge and London. Gap years less common than at most schools.

Money Matters: A bargain. Always does well in charts evaluating value for money. Still awards a good number of scholarships (whose value never exceeds ten per cent but whose kudos still counts) and bursaries (even including uniform and travel in cases of extreme need) for such a small school: one-quarter of girls are recipients.

Remarks: A super no-frills choice: big enough to appeal to almost any girl, but not at the expense of the personal touch. Prestigious local reputation and a member of the GDST sisterhood.

Prior Park College

Linked to Paragon School (The) in the Junior section
Linked to Prior Park Preparatory School

Ralph Allen Drive, Combe Down, Bath, BA2 5AH

• Pupils: 310 boys, 270 girls (75 boys board, 235 day boys; 50 girls board; 225 day girls); boarding Year 9 upwards • Ages: 11-18 • Size of sixth form: 190 • RC • Fees: Boarding £18,897-£23,583; Day £11,736-£13,077 pa • Independent

Tel: 01225 831 000
Fax: 01225 835 753
Email: admissions@priorpark.co.uk
Website: www.thepriorfoundation.com

Head: Since 2009, Mr James Murphy-O'Connor MA PGCE (early forties). Educated at St Benedict's, Ealing, before reading history at Greyfriars Hall, Oxford, and then PGCE at Peterhouse, Cambridge. Began career at Stamford where he taught history, thence to Sherborne, where he was a housemaster before appointment to headship of brand new Sherfield in Hampshire. Father, Jim, played rugby for Ireland and was eldest of five brothers who attended Prior – most illustrious of them being (Cardinal) Cormac. Previous career experience was commendably outside the Catholic fold.

He is fourth lay head since Christian Brothers left in early '80s. Early signs are encouraging. Married to Ali, they have four children (two at senior school and two at The Paragon). 'Has worked really hard to get to know everyone,' say parents, who find him 'extremely easy to communicate with'. Acknowledges pupils' achievements in all areas (writes them personal, handwritten letters) and has won their respect. Parents like the way 'he looks you in the eye' and have been impressed by how quickly he has learnt names. Has not been slow to start making changes: building up the boarding side, going for a sports hall and moving the school forwards with IT. Makes no excuse for pushing sport, particularly rugby, but is also keen on the arts: fan of F Scott Fitzgerald and Thomas Hardy plus Picasso's 1920s' art. Enjoys mountain climbing and surfing when able to get to family house at Mayo in Ireland. Intuitive understanding of Prior's mission; loads of energy, a firm faith and refreshingly open-minded.

Academic matters: Over 75 per cent of passes at A level are at grades A and B (a fifth of candidates gain three or more A grades). Mathematics, at A level, currently outshines sciences, philosophy is outstanding but humanities and modern languages more than hold their own. Strength in depth and wide choice of subjects on offer are healthy signs. Head keen to consider new sixth form curricula but disinclined to embrace IB. 40 per cent of pupils gained 10 A* or A grades (most pupils sit 11 subjects) at GCSE and two pupils managed 11 A* grades. We witnessed a lively A level philosophy session based on Nietzsche's ideas on property. Theology is compulsory throughout. Well established PSE programme also reflects Catholic thinking and the resident school chaplain ('He's fab,' said one non Catholic mum) plays a central rôle.

Vast majority take separate sciences for GCSE. Smartboards commonplace and some innovative teaching: we also watched an interactive Year 8 maths class (pupils all had separate white boards to work out their answers) with a teacher (ex-PWC accountant) who was more hip than his pupils, with cool lines such as, 'I'm loving that answer – it's beautiful', to encourage even the most innumerate. D&T suite works well with lively staff: textiles area alongside well resourced workshop and classroom areas. Maximum class size 20 in Years 7 and 8; 24 in Year 9. Staff to pupil ratio is 1:10 overall, with a good balance between experienced long servers and high octane younger blood.

Highly experienced learning support team (one full-time and two part-time teachers) – heavily over-subscribed area (accounts for around seven per cent of 11+ entry each year). Applicants need psychological report; school now includes non verbal test in entrance exam; thorough screening of all entrants for SpLD. Learning support situated alongside library and sixth form centre (some seniors help with paired reading). Open door policy; main emphasis on dyslexia and supporting literacy, but copes with range of specific learning difficulties including dyspraxia and mild Asperger's. Sixty-five pupils currently have individual learning plans. EAL is provided by two members of staff to overseas pupils – one of whom won last year's English essay prize: enough said.

Games, Options, the Arts: Sport, music and drama all impressive. Sport, though strong, doesn't dominate and achievement in the arts is equally recognised. Younger pupils get plenty of exercise (timetabled PE and games) and a good tradition of seniors helping to coach juniors. Recent appointments include top rugby coach from head's alma mater. More flexibility with sports options from year 10 upwards. Extensive playing fields plus Astroturf are all within jogging distance from the main school buildings. Strong fixture lists in all sports with plenty of local rivalry. Basketball players use military facility at Colerne. Lots of representative athletes from district to national level. Sports tours are affordable – rugby tour to Portugal latest venture. Major sports field ten teams weekly; host of 'activity sports' plus Ten Tors, ski trips and D of E activities. Dance (offered to GCSE) has been a great hit: popular annual show features both sexes. Traditional Fisher road relay involving staff and pupils winds up Lent term enthusiastically.

We discovered some keen sixth form artists (they enjoyed showing off their eye catching folders) in suitably bohemian, basement studios, working on a variety of approaches under inspired direction. Not huge numbers for A level but plenty of passion and variety of work on display around the school.

Cracking music department fields three teachers with well established director, Roland Robertson, whose reputation goes before him. Over half the pupils take instrumental lessons and standards vary from grade one to diploma level. Aim is to 'take pupils musically where their interests (and talent) lead them' – seems to bear fruit. Exquisite John Wood chapel provides venue for lots of concerts – we attended an informal ('get up and have a go') lunch-time one, following on from a junior brass practice which belted out a recognisable James Bond theme inter alia. Music to suit all tastes: high level of participation with several choirs, bands and orchestras. Opera every other year, annual musicals and a choral society which includes staff and parents – recent performances include Handel's *Messiah* and Verdi's

Requiem. Many pupils participate in Mid-Somerset Festival. We liked the whole ambience of the music department (once we had panted up seemingly endless flights of stairs to reach it) – recording studio, class and individual practice rooms plus split level area for music technology (limited numbers who take it seriously at AS and A level here) taught by a muso housemaster. African drumming group especially popular with international pupils. Over fifty per cent of chapel choir are day pupils – incredible, given requirement to turn out every Sunday.

New sports hall would definitely plug a gap in sports provision, though carpeted gym fulfils need meantime and recently completed Mackintosh dance studio is up to professional standards. Planners prevented extension of indoor pool from its present, quirky 19 metres to 25, but it provides a well used space. Old fives courts another area ripe for imaginative conversion (planners willing).

Julian Slade Theatre provides a small but cutting edge theatrical environment. Three drama teachers and one theatre technician all have a professional background and it shows: no end to the number of productions (well, twenty-three actually in current year) from musicals (head of science directs these) to Ibsen and Beckett. Recent production of *The Crucible* got rave reviews. Parents 'brilliantly supportive' when it comes to meeting late night returns from theatre trips to Bristol etc.

Prior has gone overboard when it comes to activities: over sixty on offer each week with main slots on Saturday mornings (140 boarders and day pupils turn up for this) and Tuesday afternoons. Activities range from a Leith's cookery course and Padi scuba diving. Prior Concern for those in sixth wishing to get involved in community service. We enjoyed seeing one sixth former going through a Tai Chi form as his alternative to the prescribed Tuesday choices – 'Quite acceptable here,' confided an assistant head. Majority join CCF at start of year 10 in either naval or army sections; well organised alternative programme caters for the non combatants. Compulsory residential course early in Year 7 and team building day for Year 8 pupils make for better relationships from the junior end upwards. Lots of educational visits including history trips, school exchanges with France and Germany, plus study visits to Spain. Recent pupil exploits include participation on polar andUgandaexpeditionsandnationalyouthchoirmember.

Background and Atmosphere: Founded in 1830 and run by the Christian Brothers until 1981, Prior Park is now the largest independent co-educational, Catholic day and boarding school in the UK. This position owes much to the successes of the three previous headmasters, who guided the school into the modern educational age. With about one third boarding and thirty per cent practising Catholics, PPC does not feel like yet another largely day school with token boarders or nominal religious affiliation. Seven senior houses (three mix day pupils and boarders and four have day pupils only). Unmistakably co-educational, with fairly even numbers of boys and girls throughout. Magnificent Georgian architecture of the 'mansion' provides backdrop for an unsurpassed vista over the grounds (much of which are now National Trust property, including the famous Palladian Bridge) and Bath beyond.

Imposing chapel accommodates whole school for weekly assemblies (impressive level of pupil and staff involvement). Mass for whole school roughly once each half term plus particular feast days. Compulsory mass on Sunday mornings for boarders.

New ICT centre and is networked throughout school; well organised library has 20 laptops which can be signed in and out. Pupils' use of fiction, reference and study areas speaks volumes for the self-regulating approach here. Day pupils have nominal workspaces in their rather crowded house accommodation, where prep is supervised between 4.50 and 5.50pm. Junior pupils split into small vertical groups, which counters the risk of year eights dominating within Baines House (recently upgraded) where juniors are registered.

Roche and Allen are relatively civilised boarding houses for boys on the upper floors of the mansion, whilst girls are accommodated in enviable surroundings in St Mary's House, which occupies the nearby 'Priory'. Some day pupils opt to be in boarding houses because they prefer the ethos; weekly boarding is popular. Sixth form centre (located above theatre which is used for assemblies) comprises classrooms, a large commonroom and well resourced careers suite.

Pastoral Care and Discipline: Catholic approach 'looks at whole child,' insists head. Lots of help and advice from all quarters: 'Staff at Prior (compared with her son's previous school in Bath) are superb at following things up,' we were told by one mother, whose son transferred at lower sixth level. Reward system (head's distinctions doled out for all kinds of worthy endeavours) breeds a positive approach. No evidence of a punishment culture. Pupils are generally well turned out without being ostentatious. Strong counter-bullying policy and all sixth forms shoulder some responsibility through a variety of committees; pupil hierarchy survives in terms of a head boy and headgirl together with heads of house. Pupils are 'at ease with the staff,' say parents.

Half-terms are of sensible length (ten days in Michaelmas term) and don't exploit guardianship arrangements. Central but not overly accessible medical centre. Suite of dining areas copes with peak periods and provides good choice of menus to suit most tastes.

Pupils and Parents: Most from within an hour's drive. Half of the leavers from own boarding prep school at Cricklade transfer to Prior at 13. Nearby Paragon (acquired relatively recently) provides good co-ed intake at 11. Six daily mini-bus and coach routes transport day pupils from a 30 mile plus radius. Boarders generally come from further afield, including a mix of overseas boarders (most of whom are Catholics). Good environment for language learning, insisted our Chinese guide, who spoke impeccable English. Former pupils and current parents are very supportive, with a range of fundraising and social events and pages on the school website.

Majority of pupils are non Catholics. Religion is packaged sensitively for all persuasions. Former pupils gaining selection for England and Scotland under 21 rugby teams also on master's degrees at Royal Academy of Music (choral and composition). Famous Old Boys include Cardinal Cormac Murphy-O'Connor (see above), former archbishop of Westminster, famous musical producer, Sir Cameron Mackintosh, international rugby player Damian Cronin and television presenter Hugh Scully, as well as, more recently, Charlie Holt (2009 president of Oxford Union).

Sense of mutual respect between pupils and staff: 'No horrible teachers,' confided pupils. 'A school you have to immerse yourself in,' explained one new parent. Sixth formers have a particularly open and relaxed manner without being laidback. Pupil mentoring now under way.

We liked the idea of information evenings for parents prior to each term's personal development programme (for pupils in Years 7–11), which includes topics such as 'sex and responsibility' and 'respect for life'.

Long-term link with Catholic archdiocese of Songia, Tanzania, where gap year students spend five months teaching in local schools. Student run charities committee raised over £11k last year through all kinds of activities (main focus is annual charities week and former head's performance of 'Show me the way to Amirillo' dressed as Elvis at the 'Staff in Your Eyes' show apparently 'brought the house down'); worthy causes range from Searight Hospital to Aid for Albania. Parents join Saturday activities (e.g. Leith's cookery class). Active parents' group hosts range of events (e.g. annual quiz served with curry and pud).

Entrance: Register at least eighteen months before entrance. January entrance tests for 11+ with majority of entrants coming from own 3–11 prep and about 20 per cent from state primaries. Non verbal reasoning score used as baseline for assessment. Lists close at least a year in advance for LDP (see above) applicants. About 40 pupils join at 13+, with about half of them from the junior school at Cricklade, Witshire. November interviews for entrants into lower sixth, who need a satisfactory reference and a minimum of 6 A*–C grades at GCSE with higher grades in chosen AS subjects.

Exit: Very small numbers leave after Year 11. Almost all to universities (lots take a gap year) with Cardiff and Liverpool recent popular choices, plus art and music courses. Regular successes at Oxbridge entry.

Money Matters: Extensive range of scholarships (academic, art, music, all-rounder and sport) and bursaries, with good academic scholars typically gaining 30 per cent remission of fees. Services bursaries. Currently around 150 award holders (normal range between 5–50 per cent). Drama awards at 13 and 16. Some continuity scholarships from preparatory school. Discounts for siblings. Bus services charged monthly and quite pricey. Music tuition fees represent excellent value for money.

Remarks: Full school which suits parents looking for deeper values and an ethos which 'enables rather than prescribes'. Unusually successful at nurturing, encouraging and stimulating its pupils. Gentle Catholicism in the broadest sense within an inspiring setting and atmosphere.

Prior's Field School

Priorsfield Road, Godalming, Surrey, GU7 2RH

• Pupils: 395 girls; 125 boarders (full and weekly), rest day • Ages: 11-18 • Size of sixth form: 60 • Non denominational • Fees: Day £14,205; Boarding £22,980 pa • Independent

Tel: 01483 810 551
Fax: 01483 810 180
Email: office@priorsfieldschool.com
Website: www.priorsfieldschool.com

Head: Since 2006, Mrs Julie Roseblade, MA (forties). Educated at Pate's Grammar School and has moved up the teaching ranks both at home and abroad, reaching deputy head at St Helen's, Northwood before her current headship. Calm and businesslike and also refreshingly open, she is moving the school on and energising the curriculum, without compromising the spirit of Prior's Field. As one parent said, 'She has definitely raised the standard and has shaken things up a little in a good way'. Parents think she is good news for the school and all those we spoke to hoped that the school would not become increasingly competitive academically. Mrs Roseblade is, in fact, adamant 'that the school will not go down the hothouse route'. She also believes very strongly that the single sex nature of the school allows the girls to make choices that they might not otherwise make – 'They can be as free as they like in a single sex environment; courses are not gendered, the girls can do it all'. She has a very open door policy and regularly sees groups of girls for coffee or informal lunches.

Academic matters: Academics are not the be all and end all here but results are improving – A*/B grades make up 76 per cent of A level results and 63 per cent A*/A at GCSE. The school is also in the top six per cent nationally for value-added. It is undoubtedly mixed ability, but some parents are now positively choosing the school and their bright daughters want to come here despite winning places at more academic schools – the lack of pressure and the small size are particularly appealing reasons. Strong subjects include, unsurprisingly, the arts, with drama and English language scoring well; however the sciences are some of the highest rated subjects with 65 per cent achieving an A/A* at GCSE. Modern languages also feature, with both French and Spanish popular and successful subjects. The small size of the school allows differentiation all the way through – setting in maths, English, sciences and modern languages but 'no fixed approach and huge flexibility'.

An impressive choice of subjects at both A level and GCSE – 22 at A level, which is quite something for a school of this size. PE is available unusually at both GCSE and A level. The most popular subjects at A level include English, maths and chemistry, economics/business studies, photography, art and textiles. Offers some of the trendier subjects such as media studies, music technology, psychology and critical thinking, which may be a real impetus for girls to stay on and study at sixth form – it's certainly something of a problem these days for girls' schools to hang on to their pupils after 16. The head says they try and combat this tendency by providing 'vibrant' options at 16+, superb surroundings and opportunities for community service overseas. One sixth former told us, 'I wasn't particularly academic when I started here but they've done so much for me, I really wanted to stay on.'

Mrs Roseblade is also keen to enliven the curriculum lower down the school and introduce a more lateral way of learning and thinking with cross-curricular links – 'We provide a curriculum which we hope will ignite a spark'. Currently debating is very strong at the school, reinforced by the introduction of the study of philosophy and debating for all girls in the first two years. Also a chance to flex the brain by learning Japanese; the number of overseas girls means there is an enthusiasm for language and, laudably, the school uses this natural resource to give more choice in modern languages – even if only one girl wants to study it. In addition, touch typing has been introduced at this stage as a useful tool for life. Pat on the back for Mrs Roseblade, who has cleverly tapped into what motivates girls these days: incentive schemes – for example Top Shop vouchers – on offer for the best effort grades. All the girls' homework is now on the internet, so they have no excuses if they forget.

Very flexible and inclusive approach to SEN, although anything more than a mild learning difficulty is unlikely to be catered for. If it is just a case of extra help in a particular subject, a 'whole school' approach where subject teachers can provide support where needed. Where it is clear that more specialised support is required then, in consultation with, and paid for by, parents, it is available on a one-to-one or small group basis. Pupils are not withdrawn from timetabled subjects and, if a clash, 'interests and hobbies are given a high priority'. Support for about 10 per cent of girls with English not their first language. All departments include extension work for gifted and talented. Scholars have an enrichment programme, which other girls can also join.

Games, Options, the Arts: Strong sporting tradition where PE is compulsory for Years 7–13. Girls in Years 11–13 can choose their sports. Options include swimming, self defence, dance, basketball, football, gym, cricket, yoga and even individual fitness programmes.

Art is of a very high standard and a popular subject – a relatively high number go on to art colleges. Music is important, with 183 individual lessons a week – standard up to grade 8. Lessons in orchestral instruments as well as pop and rock instruments, singing and music theory. In addition four choirs – one performed with Russell Watson and the Royal Philharmonic Orchestra, as well as a recording session for Russell Watson's CD. Chamber choir competes in Farnham, Woking and Godalming music festivals and has won for several years on the trot.

Superb range of extra-curricular activities (47 at the last count) and lots of opportunities to 'have a go,' as Mrs R says. Photography is a popular activity and is also offered at A level; the standard is very high and the school boasts its own darkroom. Participation is essential to the spirit of Prior's Field and girls are encouraged to join in as much as possible – a kind of freshers' week at the beginning of the autumn term gives an opportunity to find out more about the clubs and activities. One mum said that although her daughter could have stayed on at her prep school until she was 13, 'she felt that the opportunities at Prior's Field were too good to miss out on,' so joined the school at 11.

Background and Atmosphere: Founded in 1902 by Julia Huxley, the granddaughter of Thomas Arnold of Rugby and mother of Aldous (the only boy ever to attend the school). Lovely Arts and Crafts buildings – the main school building was designed by Charles Voysey and has an air of faded gentility. The school has developed over the years, and fortunately the buildings are listed, so it all looks as if it hangs together beautifully. Very rural feel, though only minutes from the A3 – for parents who live within the M25, the place must feel like the sticks rather than the almost-suburb of Guildford it really is. Cosy entrance hall and lovely panelled living room outside Mrs Roseblade's office looking out on to the charming rose garden where super wicker statues (made by pupils) grace the lawn. One could imagine a more genteel time when tea was taken looking out on the view. For a small school it has a buzzy atmosphere – staff use the word 'fizzy' a lot to describe the girls and the bustle of the place. Jaw-dropping new science block has the identikit Voysey Arts and Crafts exterior, but once through the door, you are catapulted into the 21st century – really superb facilities with wireless broadband, multi interactive whiteboards and every gadget and gizmo available.

Very enthusiastic science teacher was on hand during our visit and keen to demonstrate all the fabulous bits of equipment, but she did admit, 'Sometimes the girls have to show me how to use it'. New library is an excellent facility – huge glass windows and a very modern feel. Super art room – bright and airy with lovely views; standard of art and textile design really high and excellent examples adorn the walls. Huge modern sports hall superbly equipped with hairdryers and well designed lockers so that hockey sticks fit in easily. Recently refurbished dining room, with a very good standard of food.

Boarding facilities are generally excellent and the popularity of boarding is testament to this (the school is usually at full capacity) – super dorm rooms (the maximum is four to a room lower down the school) and lovely kitchens; even the first year pupils have their own rather swish kitchens – it's all so grown up. Flexi-boarding is available (even individual sleepover nights – apparently 'great for parents who want a night out'), and boarding taster weekends for those who want to try it, including girls who are considering joining the school. Two thirds of boarders are weekly boarders. The sixth form is housed in a separate building which is really superb – fabulous common room with sofas, café area, enormous plasma TV, kitchen, as well as 20 en suite rooms. It's like a rather posh hall of residence and is again a huge magnet for staying on at the school. The downsides of the facilities are the lack of Astroturf and the tiny practice swimming pool (they use Charterhouse just down the road if they want to have a decent swim).

Uniform is fairly innocuous – green jumpers and tartan skirts. Sixth formers can wear their own clothes but are expected to be 'reasonably tidy and uncontroversial'. How many times have we heard that? The fashion sense in the sixth form is a bit WAG, but when the sixth form girls were suited and booted for open day, they did look very smart.

Pastoral Care and Discipline: A cosy feel to the place. Excellent pastoral care, headed by the dynamic deputy head (pastoral) who has her finger on the pulse of all the modern issues facing today's young women. PSHE is part and parcel of every day life from the top down. Form tutors meet all girls regularly and sixth formers have a one hour session every week. The close-knit community of the school means an individual profile of each girl can be built up. They do not baulk at talking about any of the nastier aspects of growing up such as eating disorders and drug issues; sensibly, the school involves parents for talks at 'pastoral focus evenings' – for example, bringing in a recovering addict's mother to talk to parents. The catering manager also comes to regularly talk to the girls about food. Middle class Surrey this may be, but they have no fear of the real world and all the good and bad it has to throw at them. Sixth formers go on a residential drug education course and then present their experiences to the younger children. The approach to pastoral care is one of the strengths of the place and is one of the main reasons parents and girls choose the school.

Wide catchment locally – increasingly the word has got around and the school has a growing local intake. 10 per cent overseas contingent, currently from nine different countries, the majority being in the sixth form, but they comprise less than one third of the 16+ pupils. Numbers of boarding pupils live around the A3 corridor and south west London. Not a school with huge snob value so wide range of parents and backgrounds – a down to earth bunch ranging from landscape gardeners to solicitors and GPs etc. As one mum says, 'I chose the school partly because of the mix of backgrounds of the children – i.e. state sector etc – so my daughter would be surrounded by people who were "a bit less Surrey".' Many people choose the school on recommendation, which may explain why one mum said, 'It's one of Surrey's best kept secrets'.

Pupils and Parents: Notable OGs include novelist Enid Bagnold (*National Velvet*), crime writer Margaret Yorke, moral philosopher Baroness Mary Warnock, actresses Jill Bennett and Victoria Hamilton, Mary Conan Doyle, daughter of Sir Arthur.

Entrance: Very popular and increasingly so – early registration is advised, as the date of registration may be taken into consideration. Main entry points are 11+, 13+ and 16+. Entry is not a huge hurdle but it is becoming tougher to get in. Girls are invited to the school's open day as a precursor to a day of informal testing and interviews in November. They then complete the school's own entrance exam in January (maths, English and science). The school also asks for a report from the current head. The admission policy says that 'the head is entitled to take into account any particular attribute of the girl that suggests she may benefit from the general ethos of the school'. According to Mrs Roseblade, she is positively looking for girls who are 'quirky, sparky and passionate about learning'.

Huge range of feeders, both state and independent – quite a high proportion from St Hilary's in Godalming, but also from loads of other schools both near and not so near. At 16+, offers of a place are based on predicted GCSE results and an interview.

Exit: More than 25 per cent of girls leave at 16+ and tend to head for sixth form colleges – where there are boys. After A levels, they all go on to higher education, ranging from economics, chemistry and engineering to performing arts, photography and art foundation courses. Institutions are varied and can be anything from traditional universities to art colleges or occasionally Oxbridge.

Money Matters: Scholarships are available at 11+, 13+ and sixth form. Academic scholarships are worth up to 20 per cent of fees. Academic exhibitions are awarded up to 10 per cent of fees. Several art, drama, music and sport scholarships at 11+, 13+ and sixth form up to 20 per cent of fees. As part of widening access, bursaries are available at all points of entry and may be up to 100 per cent fees. The school also offers means-tested sixth form bursaries to local girls – applicants will need top GCSE grades in chosen A level subjects.

Remarks: Prior's Field used to be known as the choice for girls 'who couldn't get in anywhere else,' as one local mum said. But times have certainly changed and the school is now a strong contender rather than an also-ran. In a high-flying, girls'-school-rich part of the world, this is a school which is sensibly carving its niche away from the very top echelons of the league tables. For parents who are turned off by an overtly academic environment and seek a more balanced approach to life and learning for their daughter, Prior's Field provides a refreshing option.

Purcell School

Linked to Purcell School Junior Department in the Junior section

Aldenham Road, Bushey, Hertfordshire, WD23 2TS

- Pupils: 185 boys and girls (60 per cent girls). Three quarters board.
- Ages: 9-18 • Non-denom • Fees: Boarding £30,762; Day £24,054 pa
- Independent

Tel: 01923 331 107
Fax: 01923 331 166
Email: info@purcell-school.org
Website: www.purcell-school.org

Head: Since 2007, Mr A Peter Crook MA BMus FRSA ARAM (mid-fifties), studied at The Royal Academy of Music, the Universities of London and Durham. Previously director of music at, first, Loretto and then Rugby, where he was also coordinator of performing arts. Married to Elaine, another musician. The school had been run benignly but, perhaps, not energetically before his arrival and much to be done when he arrived – some of it radical, much of it of crucial importance to its continued health. In particular, boarding – once almost peripheral to the place – he saw, at once, to be essential and convinced the governors to refocus their development plans dramatically to improve the boarding provision. This, along with other swift and determined changes, has been controversial and he has not enjoyed the full support of all staff – many of whom are very long-serving and pre-date boarding – nor the complete understanding of the school community as a whole.

Not an easy man to read, in his splendid Edwardian drawing room and impeccable pinstripes, he seems, at first sight, at odds with his environment in which pupils wear their own clothes and rigour seems mostly imposed from within the driven temperaments of these young and gifted musicians. But this would be profoundly to misjudge and underestimate the man. He has an impressive focus on what needs to be done to provide the optimum environmental and educational support for his pupils and clearly has the confidence and preparedness to risk unpopularity to see it done – in the short and long term interests of the school. His dedication to music and his musicians is unquestionable. His enthusiasm for what they do, earnestly expressed and demonstrated in, for example, his efforts never to miss a lunchtime concert – and they happen daily – is ample evidence. The Purcell represents a huge challenge – the scale of which is hard for outsiders to gauge – and he has embraced it with courage – 'I was excited by the prospect of working with all these extraordinary young people'. It is, perhaps, not surprising that he comes across as intense and unrelaxed. Anyone in doubt about the man himself should Google him. The results are revelatory. Denizens of Rugby, mourning his departure, formed The Facebook Peter Crook Appreciation Society. The comments – some of which are enthusiastically unprintable here – may inspire you to entrust to him your future Young Musician of the Year. Possibly only Mr Crook himself would be unmoved by the affection and gratitude he has inspired.

Academic matters: Music predominates – academic work seen by everyone as secondary. However, not everyone who enters, keenly scraping or blowing at eight, finds that, by 18, they still want the life of a professional musician, and one of Mr Crook's challenges is to up the profile and provision of the academics so that university is a possible alternative to one of the conservatoires for some. Everyone takes GCSE music, usually in year 10, and virtually all get A*/A. Everyone takes maths and As, again, predominate. Other results also often remarkably good – 2009 saw 81 per cent of subjects getting A*/B, 94 per cent getting A*/C. French and German results are excellent, as are results in the individual sciences for those who take them. A levels are offered in only 11 subjects. Around 47 per cent of subjects taken get As. Again, everyone takes music but only around two thirds get As. Music tech is big and getting bigger (see below), but no other academic subject startles one with the excellence of the results. But then that is not, really not, what the Purcell is about. All parents rave about the extraordinary, exceptional wonderful music teaching – 'and that's what they're there for'. Most academic teaching gets similar praise – 'I'm loving my subjects'. And some of the pupils not destined for music college leave after GCSEs for more traditional education.

Everyone in the GCSE years takes music, maths, English lang and science but, in general, they take no more than seven or eight subjects. Small classes for everything. Specialist music library. Much individual help and support, especially for musical prodigies who arrive playing perfect Paganini but with no English. SENs supported by SENCo and all children identified with such needs have an IEP. All very much on an as needed basis, especially with organisational issues, so important in busy musical lives. Some older pupils feel they need more help in preparing for the life of a professional musician – more practising musicians from outside, for instance, just to tell it like it is.

Games, Options, the Arts: At present, one compulsory weekly PE lesson – which is as likely to be table tennis as something more robust: a controversial issue. Many parents and numerous pupils complain that more sport is needed – firstly because musicians need to be healthy and, to be so, one needs to be fit. Also because sport relieves tension, breeds cooperation in a place where individual achievement is the raison d'être and is just jolly good fun. Others, for whom music is the be all and end all and who resent any time spent from it – even on academic work – throw up their precious hands and remonstrate. Even Mr Crook asks, 'When? When could they do it?' – a good question when pupils' daily régime starts with an hour's pre-breakfast practice at 7.00 am and finishes at 11.00pm. Most boys will kick a ball about – extensive playing fields and rudimentary additional facilities, e.g., a very old gym, but plans for a new sports centre had, rightly, to take second place behind the building of a new boarding house.

However Mr Crook has instituted a new activities programme which includes walking, running, swimming, golf, netball, circuit training and hockey – all timetabled and all optional. So, complainers have things to do, but it does not answer the cry of those for whom everyone should be made to participate – for their own sakes as well as those of the school community. Other activities are bowling, shopping, board games and Sunday evening church. Art is surprisingly varied and good. We really enjoyed what we saw – much vitality and colour in ceramics, painting and printing.

And then the music – all-encompassing and involves a range of activities for everyone. Choir, for example, is compulsory for all – though resented by some as an intrusion into their own practice time. Some few demonstrate this resentment, spoiling it for others. Most of the staff teach at the RCM or RAM and all are of that professional standard – they have to be. We are told the head of keyboard knows how many pianos are in the school, but we lost count and we didn't even see the one played on by Liszt (school has a unique collection of Liszt memorabilia) which is in storage. Professional accompanists work with the pupils – a real and special privilege. Undertakes loads of outreach activities, taking music everywhere, nationally and internationally. Likewise, inreach – pupils from local schools come in to be inspired. And performances. These happen every day on a small scale but throughout each term on a big scale and often – for groups and individuals – on a professional stage. Some of these children have recording contracts.

Music provision is superb. In additional to the concert hall, a new music centre, the outer walls of which are painted a rather startling green. Music tech is state-of-the-art and comes with a delegate each year from the prestigious Surrey University Tonmeister dept, adding massively to the quality of the teaching, as these people are the groundbreakers in the field. Recording studio and excellent facilities for not only soundtrack making but actual film-making to boot. Absolutely beautiful recital room, dozens of practice rooms, from which concert quality playing seeps, and nice little architectural touches everywhere. A thoughtful, sensitive building – maybe apart from the green! – which Mr Crook inherited just after its opening.

Background and Atmosphere: An interesting history. Founded as recently as 1962 by Rosemary Rapaport and Irene Forster, nonetheless the UK's oldest specialist music school. It began life as The Central Tutorial School for Young Musicians, at Conway Hall, then housed for a while in Morley College, from where it moved to Hampstead. In 1973, it was renamed The Purcell School – perhaps reflecting the new enthusiasm for 'earlyish' British music and, in 1998, relocated to the site of the former Royal Caledonian School in Bushey, Hertfordshire. The main building is an attractive low-rise Edwardian pile with wide corridors, good-sized concert hall, assorted classrooms, stark stairwells and a mix of boarding facilities – some now smartened up, some definitely dodgy, but all this set to change with building works now very much in progress.

Boarding top priority for Mr Crook's modernising on all fronts – staff provision and actual housing. Currently, the best of boarding comprises single study bedrooms – spacious and imaginative with the bed on a kind of upper mezzanine above the living area. The worst is cramped, stuffy rooms for four – hard to imagine what it must be like when everyone is trying to get ready at the same time. Girls' rooms attractively girly – beads and boas; boys' room show little sign of much time spent there. Boarders can choose their room-mates. Good, relaxing common rooms with sofas, kitchens, games. Some horribly scruffy but these are set to go when the new boarding opens. Day pupils also have their own space, but this also subject to imminent rehousing. No shortage of space here and more building will follow.

Pastoral Care and Discipline: Unusual issues here, e.g. 'We have to be very careful with things like RSI,' and 'It's the only school where I have had to tell a pupil they've done enough practice for today'. Mr Crook says, 'We have to be extremely alert to pupils showing lack of self-esteem or self-worth – some will need lots of cajoling and encouragement; all are highly individual. They are not easy to look after.' And we met several girls who told us, 'The boys can be very naughty.' So pastoral care being beefed up with new head of boarding and more staff onsite in general. Many parents and pupils have nothing but warm praise for the pastoral care, though we heard this from more girls and their parents than boys and more from older pupils. New small tutor groups, the hope being that the pupils will have the same tutor throughout their schooling. School nurse universally praised. The food now also praised – if not universally.

However, this side comes in for much the loudest criticism – from both parents and pupils – and Mr Crook's innovations and renovations not yet convincing everyone, especially parents of younger pupils. A few expulsions since his advent – for use of alcohol or cannabis. 'I have rigorously tightened up on discipline,' says Mr Crook.' I felt I had no choice. Essentially what I am trying to do is keep them safe.' The message has stuck, but pupils complain of inconsistencies in disciplinary matters – 'The rules seem to change every day' – between boys and girls – 'Girls' issues go straight to the head, boys' issues are dealt with in-house' – and between the various houses. Hard to pin down precise causes – we heard, for example, from some that boys were treated more harshly and from others that girls were, and a great range of comment about house staff – from 'delightful' to 'appalling' – but, although all say that boarding has much improved under Mr Crook, a palpable discontent persists and much remains to be done.

Boarding in new-build set to become wonderfully flexible and will enable day pupils to stay over when they have a concert or other overload. Will also enable offers to be made on musical merit alone rather than a set number of boys' or girls' places. Boarding, especially for the younger pupils, of whom very few, can be a lonely affair – this, too, will improve when can accommodate more and in better surroundings. Currently the junior house has eleven girls in Years 6 to 9, only six girl boarders in Year 9, and friendships can be hard to form. The new junior boarding house will be mixed and will help give the flexibility needed to implement the new policy of admitting purely by music audition. Many boarders go home at weekends and those from abroad need to be robust and driven if they are to cope. Many boarders come in at sixth form level. Pupils enthuse about their fantastic camaraderie – 'We all encourage each other – everyone is so supportive of everyone else,' and you feel this as you see them greet each other in the corridors. However, not all want to work – 'People who want to do very well,' an enthusiastic sixth former told us, 'but not everyone does – those who aren't motivated don't; it's what you put in really'.

Pupils and Parents: Children of exceptional musical talent from the UK and the world – especially, seemingly, Korea. Also from London and the SE. Many with perfect pitch. All pupils are re-auditioned at Year 9 and Year 11 to make sure they are still keen and committed – they have to be able to handle very long and strenuous days. As for Old Purcellians, research needs to be done to trace them as noone is entirely sure which of our musical celebrities went through the school. However Robert Cohen, Oliver Knussen, Nicholas Daniel, Julius Drake, Catrin Finch, Janice Graham, Yevgeny Sudbin and founder members of the a capella ensemble, Miranda Sex Garden, among notable alumni. Will the rest please own up!

Entrance: Via musical audition, held weekly throughout the year. Children come for a preliminary audition and then a majority return for a more thorough going over. Quite a lot come from being home educated – such is the musical focus of many of the families whose children come here.

Exit: Of the 31 leavers in 2009, eleven to The Royal Academy of Music, four to The Royal College of Music, three each to The Guildhall and Trinity College of Music. The rest mostly to other music courses hither and yon, one most spectacularly to an immense scholarship at The Curtis Institute of Music in the US. Oxbridge now beginning to feature more prominently in destinations.

Money Matters: The most expensive school in the country barring Eton and Harrow, but most on some kind of financial support – under the government's music and dance assisted places scheme, school bursary or scholarship. An amazing opportunity for the brilliant but broke – some pay nothing – though tougher for those on average incomes. However fees include a generous allocation of individual instrumental/singing tuition – pupils get more individual instrumental or vocal tuition than they do at conservatoires. Overseas pupils sometimes helped through embassies and other outside bodies or by corporate sponsorship. Works very hard to raise funds for scholarships as well as for much needed building projects.

Remarks: Not for the fragile – an astonishing opportunity for the driven and the robust. 'This school changes people's lives,' a parent said. 'It's Christmas come early,' said an ecstatic pupil.' It's just exactly what I wanted.'

Putney High School

Linked to Lytton House, Putney High School Junior Department in the Junior section

35 Putney Hill, London, SW15 6BH

• Pupils: 560 • Ages: 11-18 • Size of sixth form: 150 • Non-denom
• Fees: £12,063 pa • Independent

Tel: 020 8788 4886
Fax: 020 8789 8068
Email: putneyhigh@put.gdst.net
Website: www.gdst.net/putneyhigh

Headmistress: Since 2002, Dr Denise V Lodge (fifties). She has an absolute army of impressive letters after her name, too many to list – obviously a very learned soul. Previously headmistress at Sydenham High School (also in the Girls' Day Schools Trust stable), deputy head at Sheffield High, and before that head of curriculum, sixth form and chemistry at Sir Roger Manwood's School, Kent. Former finalist in Salters' Prize chemistry teacher of the year. Is definitely not one of the touchy feely, we must bond sort of heads. 'She's not a PR person,' says one mother. 'Better one to one than with big groups.' She may not talk the talk, but on the plus side she is credited with being quite progressive, promoting a fantastic breadth of opportunity for the girls and injecting a real international feel to the place by introducing exchange scheme programmes with schools in China and India. Seen to prefer the older girls, with whom she enjoys discussing current affairs and how events may impact on them and their chosen careers. Married with a son and a daughter, both late 20s. In her spare time enjoys jazz, theatre and the gym, and by all accounts is a mean cook.

Academic matters: Very academic place – some seriously bright girls here, working very hard, but not too pressured. Excellent results – at GCSE (2010) 100 per cent A*–C (an impressive 91 per cent at A*/A). Good performances in sciences, history, music and art. At A level an equally impressive 75 per cent A*/A grades. Fantastic to see in a girls' school that maths is the most popular choice at A level – by a long way. Parents happy school holds its own against St Paul's and Godolphin and Latymer, though the feeling on the outside is that St Paul's is still a jump ahead.

In year seven, when girls are mainly taught in form groups, they average (a large) 28. School is quick to defend the numbers – 'One third of lessons in Year 7 are taught in groups of 21/22 – maths, art and science. Furthermore, DT/ textiles is taught in half classes of 14. By Year 9 only PHSE (lifeskills) is taught as a group of 28'. For sixth formers, the average class size is eight.

Good to see that girls are not over-burdened with lots of homework – theory is that they work hard enough during school day. No setting in year seven, but in year eight they will be set for maths. The setting is more a matter of pace than ability – all can still aim for A grades by the end. Studies all based around a considerably developed national curriculum which is pleasingly broad and flexible. Sciences all taught separately from year eight, when Latin also makes an appearance. Nice to see Mandarin on the list of modern foreign languages – available as a GCSE subject from 2010. School happily retains minority subjects.

No testing for SEN, but specialists on the staff, though the impression from the school is that it is not a huge specialist area, so not a first choice school for a girl with SEN problems. Extra-curricular activities for the exceptionally gifted and talented.

Games, Options, the Arts: A great place for all-rounders as games and music are very well done here. 'Would be a shame to come here as a pure academic – you would miss out on so much,' sums up one parent. Storming sports results lately – school has produced GDST champions in netball, lacrosse and tennis. Playing fields are off site (but close by) – the downside of London location.

Great music – choir tours are legendary and colossal, orchestras and ensembles abound. 'I just cannot get over the music here,' says one mother to a chorus of agreement. A mixture of planning and fortune has seen the music department refurbished, with all the toys necessary for GCSE and A level composition. Lovely to see 15 girls a year take music GCSE – higher than the average elsewhere. Art also very good – average of 20 go on to A level, with eight or nine then to art school. Tons of extra-curricular stuff on offer – too numerous to mention (includes life drawing and medical society). Almost everyone does Duke of Edinburgh.

Background and Atmosphere: Set up in 1893 with 54 pupils in five scattered houses, coming together as one on its present site in 1918. Typically of London schools, the site is relatively small, but it really makes the most of what it has, with some beautiful gardens, and is something of an oasis off uninspiring Putney Hill. Just a few steps from this busy London road and you are in a far more rarefied atmosphere – parallels with Narnia and Mr Benn abound. And of course the upside to this urban location is fab transport links – short walk from tube and BR trains and streams of buses stop right outside.

Inside some super-smart facilities – spectacular library, swish new drama studio and language lab, but overall facilities won't blow you away with glitz and glamour. Doesn't matter, though, as everything under-pinned with great teaching and wide-ranging opportunities. New sixth form centre opens in 2011.

Pastoral Care and Discipline: Parental praise for pastoral care – knows the girls well and understands all the ages and stages they go through. Worthwhile life skills programme is used to discuss bullying, eating disorders et al. 'We pride ourselves on spotting problems early on,' says Dr Lodge. 'Obviously there are occasional issues, but we address them fast and in a supportive way.' Happy, well motivated girls with things to do and places to go are unlikely to spend much time in detention. The usual system of praise and punishment in place as and when necessary – house points, detentions, that sort of thing, but overall a happy ship. Good teacher/pupil relationships make formal sanction the exception rather than the rule. 'When a school is working well like this you can afford to be a bit relaxed,' says Dr Lodge.

Tough rather than tender, no nonsense rather than nurturing – but the bright and robust will thrive. Can be rather rigid about rules and regulations – parents complain about a lack of a personal touch with standardised responses to their queries and of secretarial/admin staff at times not being as helpful as parents would wish.

Pupils and Parents: The hard-working middle classes abound and are really supportive of the school. Perhaps not surprisingly, as they are discussing their own daughters and her friends, most parents describe the girls as 'down to earth' and the place as 'not snobby or élitist'. Pupils are largely a full-on bunch, full of attitude and ideas – and might overwhelm those who don't shine in anything in particular, so not the obvious place for the shy or unconfident. School is proud of its girls and their 'can do' attitude – when confronted with a minor inconvenience, they just get on with it. Pupils are a reasonably smart, normal bunch with no wacky hairstyles, jewellery etc.

Parents very welcome to contribute – preferably via parents' association – rather than helping within the school itself: 'They prefer to keep us out of the way a bit,' says one mother. The parents' association is thriving, seemingly a great place for a night out and one of the few we've come across who make special mention of welcoming single parents who might otherwise find some school events a little daunting. Newcomers will be swept up and supported. Generally the school is big on fundraising.

OGs bear witness to the wide range of talents encouraged at the school, e.g. newsreader Sophie Raworth, fashion designer Edina Ronay, gardening broadcaster Pippa Greenwood, author Sophie Kinsella, politicians Virginia Bottomley and Baroness Elizabeth Symons, journalist

Melanie Phillips, sculptor Emily Young and entrepreneur Calypso Rose, a London young business person of the year.

Entrance: Selective, at 11+, described by the school as 'by competitive examination (papers in English and maths, each 1hour 15 minutes) and friendly interview'. If an average selective school is looking for the top 25 per cent, Putney is after the top ten. Don't struggle and coach to get your daughter here – school knows exactly the girls it wants and you either fit or you don't. 'They'll need to have been well-taught,' is the only hint we could glean for you. Competitive, lots of interest – 2000+ at open day, 400 will sit entrance exam, and bear in mind that almost 50 per cent of the places will go to the about 44 possible arrivals from linked juniors (less than a handful of the junior school brigade won't qualify). Register by November the year before admission. Lots of locals, but as girls are older and travel independently, net cast slightly wider than for juniors.

At 16+, girls need six GCSEs at A*/A, with A*/As in subjects they want to study at A level. Used to have a reputation for 'weeding out' at this stage, i.e. booting out those of their own who do not make the grades, but Dr Lodge insists this is no more – a major relief for parents. Newcomers will need references and informal interviews with Putney staff.

Exit: At 16+ majority move up to the sixth form, though some do head off to co-ed or boarding elsewhere. At 18+ most to redbrick universities of their choice, including about 17 per cent to Oxbridge.

Money Matters: Academic scholarships awarded on merit – all 11+ candidates automatically considered. Music scholarships via audition. At 16+ academic, music, art, drama and sport scholarships. Travel scholarships in modern languages and science for internal candidates only. Means tested bursaries available.

Remarks: Super school best for very bright and diligent all-rounders who enjoy a busy life. An impressive and substantial offering.

Putney Park School

Linked to Putney Park Lower School in the Junior section

Woodborough Road, London, SW15 6PY

• Pupils: 180 girls and 40 boys; all day • Ages: Boys 4-8; girls 4-16 • C of E
• Fees: £10,281-£11,745 pa • Independent

Tel: 02087 888 316
Fax: 020 8780 2376
Email: office@putneypark.london.sch.uk
Website: www.putneypark.london.sch.uk

Head: Since 2005, Mrs Ruth Mann BSc PGCE DPSE (school management) (fifties). Extremely able, first joined as head of maths in 1975. After periods as deputy head, head and bursar, left for an administrative post at Ibstock Place School in 2003. Back two years later to retake the reins as head and has no intention of relinquishing them again for at least another eight or nine years. Still an enthusiastic maths teacher, she is undoubtedly popular with staff and pupils, full of concern for their wellbeing and determined to get the best out of them all – the captain of a much loved, well organised ship.

Academic matters: A small school offering excellent teaching in small groups, maximum 22 per class in the lower school, averaging ten to twelve in the upper school. Traditional teaching with, initially, an emphasis on reading. For children who need gentle nurturing, the perfect school – 'Shy girls flourish'. Lots of bright children here who would find life difficult in a more pressurised environment or who are using the lower school as a starting point, moving on at the end of Year 2 (boys) or Year 6 (girls).

All classes are mixed ability; exam results are an indication of the high standard of teaching and adherence to the school motto, 'E labore praemia manant' ('rewards flow from hard work'). 95 per cent got five or more A*–C grades, nearly 27 per cent A*/A at GCSE in 2009, and five Year 2 boys got places at Colet Court in 2007.

Discipline is strong and good manners are deemed important – all the younger children got to their feet and chimed, 'Good morning,' as we entered their classrooms. Every child we talked to was eager to show us what they were doing or to discuss what they had just been taught. Staff dedicated, enthusiastic and imaginative – the under the sea theme in the reception classes even extended to the children's loos. Interactive whiteboards in all classrooms and the use of computers is much encouraged. For the older children, a brand new computer room, with a keen head of ICT who encourages pupils to explore and experiment with all aspects of technology, believing strongly that 'IT skills are caught not taught'. Parents and future schools are particularly pleased no slacking off once February exams are over, when the curriculum continues to be followed and children are kept up to speed. French taught from reception, Spanish from Year 3.

At the moment 30 children on the SEN register, two of whom are statemented. Concern for a child's wellbeing is of the essence here – those with mild to moderate dyslexia etc fit in well and thrive. However because of the highly disciplined nature of the school, children with behavioural problems would be unlikely to survive long. The SENCo, who came from Ibstock Place with Mrs Mann, is extremely experienced and currently re-vamping the whole of the SEN section. Parents were quick to praise the school for its ability to nurture children who are 'quirky individuals who all look after each other'. An informal link with The Dominie School in Battersea where, if necessary, a move for a couple of years is suggested for any girl who is finding it particularly difficult to cope, after which they are happy to take her back for the remainder of her schooling. EAL is catered for with individual lessons by one of three specialist teachers.

Games, Options, the Arts: Several specialist PE teachers, all female – much use made of the Bank of England sports ground and Putney leisure centre, both close by. Strongest points probably athletics and swimming. Fitness and rowing are taught in Year 11 and PE can be taken as a GCSE subject.

Very strong in music, art and drama, all regarded as extremely important – choir is timetabled for Years 6–9, all children learn the keyboard, about half learn an additional instrument, working up to grade 6. Productions at all levels are put on throughout the year and drama has become so popular it is now offered as a GSCE option.

Lots of outings for every age group – children in reception were eager to talk about their visit to the London Aquarium, trips to France and Spain an integral part of those subjects for the older girls.

Background and Atmosphere: Founded by Miss Jean Tweedie Smith in 1953, still very much a school with a strong family feel about it. Has a strong management base and is secure. The four houses in which it is located are all owned by Miss Tweedie Smith's niece and nephew and the latter, Brian Tweedie-Smith FRICS, has become the school principal. This is purely administrative, but he likes to be involved and has moved to London so that he can be on the spot full time.

The four houses, two on either side of the road, have been excellently adapted for school use yet retain a homely atmosphere. Enormous gardens have been turned into great play areas – those in the upper school include a netball court and special seating sections. When we visited, a large marquee complete with stage had been erected in part of the lower school garden in readiness for end of term productions and activities. A school hall, where Christian assemblies are held twice a week for juniors and once a week for seniors, but not enormous.

Classrooms all light and airy, in the upper school subject based. Physics, biology and chemistry laboratories up in the eaves. Specialist art from Year 5 is regarded as very important – in the artroom the students were proud to show us their folders full of varied and fascinating projects.

Pastoral Care and Discipline: A strict code of conduct and sensible school rules – kindness, tolerance and politeness are expected of everyone. Any problems are swiftly identified and well handled – 'All our little niggles have been addressed really quickly'. Teachers are always available to talk to parents and genuinely concerned with the wellbeing of each pupil – 'When our daughter needed help settling in, they found the perfect solution'. Again the family feel prevails, with everyone looking out for everyone else.

Pupils and Parents: Mainly from Putney, Barnes, Wimbledon, Sheen and surrounding areas; mixed backgrounds, a variety of nationalities (at the moment several Japanese and Australians); all parents keen to see their children do well in a non-pressurised environment. Several children originally destined for the state system but whose parents felt they needed, and would do better in, a more protective environment.

Entrance: Non-competitive entry into reception – prospective pupils registered and invited to visit the school and reports solicited from any previous school. Places are then offered on a first come, first served basis with priority being given to siblings. For Year 7 entry, girls spend a morning at the school when they sit exams in maths, English and non-verbal reasoning. Girls moving from the lower into the upper school also sit these exams. At this stage several girls come in from local state primaries.

Often room for a new student at any stage – the head will always try to help with alternative suggestions should there not be.

Exit: All boys and some girls at the end of Year 2 or 3, mainly to London prep schools – Colet Court, King's College Wimbledon, Tower House for the boys, Bute House, Latymer Prep, Lady Eleanor Holles for the girls. Those girls not moving into the upper school at the end of Year 6 tend to go to the high schools – Putney, Wimbledon, Surbiton – for what is felt to be, by some, a more rigorous education. At the end of Year 11 some still move to the high schools or maybe St Paul's Girls' School for their A level years, some go on to board and others go to colleges, Esher and Richmond perhaps being the most popular.

Money Matters: Bursaries and scholarships are available at the principal's discretion.

Remarks: A small family school filling a definite gap – perfect for the girl who needs her confidence building and who would probably sink in a larger, wilder environment. What it lacks in facilities it gains hugely in enthusiasm, good quality teaching and care. As one parent said, 'I just love everything about it – it celebrates everything that's fabulous in our daughter.'

Queen Anne's School

6 Henley Road, Caversham, Reading, Berkshire, RG4 6DX

• Pupils: 365 girls; 50/50 day and boarding • Ages: 11-18 • Size of sixth form: 100 • C of E • Fees: Boarding £23,385-£25,935; Day £17,595 pa • Independent

Tel: 0118 918 7333
Fax: 0118 918 7310
Email: admissions@qas.org.uk
Website: www.qas.org.uk

Head: Since 2006, Mrs Julia Harrington BA NPQ (fifties). Previously deputy head at Prior's Field School, Godalming, a school with a similar feel to this one. She was educated at Lydney Grammar School and read history and politics at Exeter. In the 1980s she joined the Independent Television Companies Association, the trades association which represented the interests of the, then, 16 independent television companies. Buckets of enthusiasm, much of it directed towards getting the girls to aim high and believe in their ability to make a difference – was saying, 'Yes, we can!' years before anyone had heard of Barack Obama. Married to an IT director; her two daughters are studying at Oxford and her son at Durham.

Academic matters: It's all about personal best here. Not a hothouse, not part of the academic super-élite, but does well by the girls, whatever their ability. In 2010 80 per cent achieved A*–B grades at A level, with one in three gaining three or more A*/A grades. At GCSE 89 per cent gained A*–B grades with one in two girls achieving seven or more A*/A grades. Maths, sciences and Latin are very popular and the range of subjects on offer is ever growing, and are added on demand from the students.

Impressive octagonal two-tier library well-stocked and constantly updated with hardbacks, softbacks and software. Two dedicated IT rooms fully equipped with latest technology. Small classes for all – standard size 16–18. Swish £3m science block, modern languages block and performing arts centre opened in 2006. Mild dyslexics catered for – no specialist teacher. Prep sessions scheduled during the day help procrastinators to stay on track. We're told Saturday morning lessons have been replaced with an 'optional programme of exciting activities' including sports, drama and music and creative options.

Games, Options, the Arts: Focus of huge investment in recent years. Superb sports centre opened in 2000 by Princess Royal. Multi-functional hall (international competition standard) plus squash courts, dance studio, a climbing wall, 25-metre indoor pool and a gym. Great reputation on lax field (arch rivals: Downe House) – current student is one of the youngest players ever to be selected for the senior England lacrosse team. Tennis, rowing and golf have all celebrated recent success. Netball, athletics, squash and swimming also hotly contested; riding, gym and dance. No hockey ('But no one minds,' said our guide, 'because lacrosse is so much better!').

New art and design studio, opened by old girl Posy Simmonds in 2008 – lots of space and light and the school is experimenting with an artist in residence; girls' work has been displayed in professional galleries. Drama a particular strength – the purpose-built performing arts centre, incorporating fabulous 250-seater theatre plus music practice rooms, is well used (three full dramatic productions a year). Two GCSE students were among the top ten candidates (2008) who achieved the highest overall marks out of 60,878 Edexcel entries. One QAS girl played a role in Sky One's drama series *Hex*, another in the recent film remake of *St Trinians*. Public speaking a serious extracurricular and QAS hosted the International Independent Schools' Public Speaking Championship last autumn. Music getting a lot of attention lately: the deputy head is deputy chief examiner for the IB music course and the school now offers IGCSE music. The music department runs a series of subscription concerts and workshops as well as informal/formal concerts and choir tours; recent performance at Westminster Abbey. D of E, Young Enterprise, Team Challenge etc. Lovely room for cookery lessons. Fundraising for numerous charities.

Background and Atmosphere: Dates back to 1698 when the Grey Coat Hospital was founded for children of Westminster. In 1706 Queen Anne granted it a charter and the governors decided to use part of the endowment to found a country boarding school, ultimately creating QAS in Caversham in 1894. The school still has Queen Anne's favourite flower, a deep red rose, as its emblem. Girls' traditional capes (now only used for special occasions and the triennial service at Westminster Abbey) are also red, while their more up-to-date replacement, the humble fleece, is navy. Set in charming red-brick assortment of original and modern buildings up hill from the Thames in 35 acres. Grey Coat Hospital (girls' state comprehensive) remains a sister school.

Reading is a tricky market for a school of this kind, with so many other good girls-only options just down the road, including state ones. But QAS is something special. Drive through the school gates and you forget the busy roads and parking hassles: you could be at any rural girls' boarding school. Indeed, the boarding is an important ingredient of the ethos here and the school gets it just right. Girls sorted into houses on arrival – two for boarders, three for day girls and two for sixth form. Super dorms (largest sleep five), with attention to things like showers that matter to girls. Lots of space, but never feels like too few girls knocking around in too much room.

Sixth form accommodation especially fab, with boarders sharing rooms with day girls. Upper sixth house has wall of lacrosse sticks parked on hooks outside the entrance – says so much about the school – and its own car park. These oldest girls eat supper in their house – Wednesday night is wok night. Loads of space, sofas, sitting rooms ('sits') – luxury. Male guests allowed. Sit and Café 6 – the funky purple and green sixth form snack bar/café/games room created out of the old school gym; school socials with Shiplake, Oratory and others.

Some lovely, feminine touches, e.g. tea which rotates between bread and jam (Mon and Wed), cakes (Tues and Fri) and choc spread (Thurs). Home economics and ballroom dancing sit comfortably alongside chemistry and further maths. While girls more likely to be found poring over their personal statements for university applications than sewing machines, the sewing machines still get some use (as the brilliantly beaded and coloured cushions scattered around registrar's office amply demonstrate).

Pastoral Care and Discipline: Twenty minute worship every morning (female chaplain) in charming chapel. We didn't see much makeup being worn – what's the point when no boys around? Girls allowed (in groups) into Caversham, where the Waitrose is about the height of excitement, on Wednesday afternoons. Older girls can go into Reading – 'We give the sixth formers quite a lot of freedom – this is not a cotton wool school'. No alcohol to be consumed at school, except for a few sixth form events. No permanent exclusions since the current head arrived. Drug offences warrant immediate expulsion. Sliding scale of punishments for smoking.

The head is keenly interested in the differences between how girls' and boys' brains work, reads widely in the field, trained as a psycho-dynamic counsellor and referred knowledgably to assorted experts (none of whom this poor ignorant editor had heard of) throughout our conversation. In short, she knows a thing or two about the cliques, friendship group nightmares etc that frequently bedevil girls-only schools and takes care that the school avoids the situations from which such tensions spring, e.g. girls are not allowed to 'save seats'.

Pupils and Parents: Bright eyed, well-spoken girls. Sixth formers allowed to wear home clothes for lessons but must look businesslike when acting as ambassadors. Uniform, compulsory for everyone else, comprises red and white striped shirt with navy skirt and jumper sporting red band on cuff. Mixed family backgrounds, we were assured – does not have quite the cachet of some of the more famous girls' schools, so does not attract the flashest of parents. Broadly middle class, professional and well-heeled, from within an hour and a half radius. About 15 per cent from overseas (China, Hong Kong, Spain and Nigeria top the list, but quite a lot of exotics including two Mongolians and a Kazakh) – almost too many, but not quite. Plus large handful of expats (FCO, Services etc). Famous OGs include Posy Simmonds, Jenny Seagrove, artist Brenda Rawnsley, T S Eliot's second wife Valerie Fletcher (not the crazy one) and Joan Hunter Dunn – John Betjeman's 'muse and fantasy love'.

Entrance: Assessment days are held in November for 11+ entrants. They sit pre-entry exams in English, maths and verbal reasoning, followed by 11+ Common Entrance in January. 13+ entrance exams take place in January. Papers in English, maths, science and humanities (either geography, history or RE) and a choice of French, Spanish,

German, Latin or Greek. Sixth form entry: minimum of five GCSEs at grade C or above and Bs for subjects to be studied at A level. Applications require English and maths entrance exams and predicted grades. Long list of feeder schools includes preps and state primaries.

Exit: Handful lost to sixth form colleges, art colleges or mixed independents after GCSEs. The rest to good universities absolutely everywhere; one or two most years to Oxbridge. Lots to business/marketing/management courses, also sciences/medicine, and three girls last year went on to read international relations, underlining Mrs Harrington's claim that the girls are developing a political consciousness. Few gap years.

Money Matters: Academic, drama, music, art, sports and all-rounder scholarships at 11+, 13+ and sixth form. Help on hand in cases of hardship.

Remarks: A super little school, within easy reach of London, that deserves to be better known. Suits girls who might wither under the remorseless pressure of some of the better known girls' boarding schools. A feel-good school which keeps its eye on the future without losing sight of the past. Don't let proximity to Reading put you off!

Queen Elizabeth Grammar School (Penrith)

Ullswater Road, Penrith, Cumbria, CA11 7EG

• Pupils: 835; 400 boys and 435 girls; all day • Ages: 11-18 • Size of sixth form: 230 • Non-denom • State

Tel: 01768 864 621
Fax: 01768 890 923
Email: secretary@qegs.cumbria.sch.uk
Website: www.qegs.cumbria.sch.uk

Headmaster: Since 2004, Mr Christopher Kirkup BA PGCE NPQH (late forties). Read history at Queen Mary College, University of London, taught at Torpoint School, Cornwall; Bourne Grammar School Lincolnshire; deputy head at Devonport High School for Girls, Plymouth. A serious, approachable, focused man, ambitious for the school; has pushed its maths/IT specialist status – with spectacular results in classroom provision – but has also improved status of performing arts (he directs the annual stage show). Committed to high academic standards.

Academic matters: Results at GCSE and AS/A2 are very good and, in view of the school's ability range at entry ('wider than most other 163 UK grammar schools'), they are remarkable.

Expectations are high and targets consistently challenge pupils; they seem happy with this and there's a real sense of academic purpose about the place. Average class size up to GCSE is 28, without noticeably damaging effects on achievement (independent schools take note). Broad banding and setting in English, maths and science at KS3, minimum nine subjects per student at GCSE. All do French and German to Year 9, then one of them for next two years. No classics. Over 80 per cent do separate sciences. Usual prescription of four AS plus general studies in Year 12, then three A levels. A level results excellent: 56 per cent A*–B in 2010. No big take-up for modern languages (4 from year group in 2010) but good geography, history, economics, English and maths (half sixth form do maths in one form or another). Extra lessons for Oxbridge. School now has special maths and computing science status; head reports big boost to teaching morale – not that it was low before. SEN catered for in-house and working in partnership with outside agencies.

Teaching is broadly traditional without being rigid. Well qualified and very experienced staff – they tend to stay, Cumbrian quality of life being very attractive. Well-developed programme sharing expertise with feeder schools; evening classes in maths for local Year 6 too.

Games, Options, the Arts: Good range of team games for boys and girls; cross-country (both) and rugby (boys) particularly strong: over 200 runners in Junior Great North Run every year, organised by charismatic head of geography. Playing fields on site and now vast sports hall extends games options. They breed them hardy up here but boys sing in the choir too. Instrumental music and drama strong (students in National Youth Orchestra and Theatre). Dance outstanding. All Year 8 have a 'residential experience' in the Lake District Borrowdale valley. Otherwise the usual run of clubs and societies, trips abroad and theatre visits – the school is a long way from most urban centres and knows it has to work at this. Much fund-raising by students (especially green/Fairtrade variety). Young Enterprise popular.

Background and Atmosphere: Founded by Royal Charter in 1564, moved to present site in 1915, changed from 13–18 comprehensive to 11–18 selective grammar in 1993; now a foundation school which means that governors have control over finance and buildings. Games pitches on site, plenty of grassy areas and some wonderful trees. Not an architecturally striking school, some rooms in the main building a touch cramped, but school works hard at upkeep. Since 1995, a continuous building programme has provided fine IT, technology and science facilities, classrooms for the English department and an impressive sports hall.

What sells the place is the pupils' demeanour – cheerful, confident, purposeful and courteous; they are happy to be here and show it. Last Ofsted report justly drew attention to behaviour and development of social conscience. Rated by Ofsted in April 2009 as outstanding in all categories. Sixth form centre in refurbished former primary school across road from main site; students treated as if at college (no uniform, but 'smart and appropriate' formal dress) and live up to responsibility.

Pastoral Care and Discipline: Pastoral unit is form-based up to Year 11, then tutor groups. Parents generally happy with school's attitude; minor incidents quickly and effectively dealt with. Big city wickedness (drugs, alcohol etc) not really an issue, says head; in many ways, the North really is a different country. Small-town life may lack urban buzz but there is a lot to be said for old-fashioned virtues and a strong school/home common interest.

Pupils and Parents: Enormous catchment area of 400 square miles; half of pupils live in Penrith, half in surrounding country. 28 buses a day carry them in and out.

Whole range of wealth and status, quite a few from low-income families. Most are white British, reflecting local population. Parents very supportive; still a strong desire for self-improvement, especially in rural areas.

Entrance: Almost entirely from primary schools, by September entrance test; usually about 260 candidates for 120 places. Five GCSE A*–C qualification for sixth form entry – high grade (A*–B) expected for some subjects at A level.

Exit: About 12 leave after Year 11 each year, more than balanced by sixth form joiners. Well over 90 per cent post-A level to higher education, a few to college diploma courses. Steady trickle to Oxbridge every year, otherwise to predominantly northern universities. A few take gap years.

Remarks: The only selective grammar school in Cumbria and proud of it, but it works hard at self-awareness and outward vision (e.g. cooperation with primary schools and neighbouring comprehensive). Remarkably successful at sustaining academic ethos and responsibility to local community. Pleasant location, happy and business-like students. World-weary parents moving from the south will appreciate its uncomplicated sense of purpose – if their children can get in, that is.

Queen Elizabeth Grammar School (Wakefield)

Linked to Queen Elizabeth Grammar Junior School (Wakefield) in the Junior section

154 Northgate, Wakefield, West Yorkshire, WF1 3QX

• Pupils: 745 boys • Ages: 11-18 • Size of sixth form: 200 • Inter-denom • Fees: £9,705 pa • Independent

Tel: 01924 373 943
Fax: 01924 231 603
Email: admissions@qegsss.org.uk
Website: www.wgsf.org.uk

Head: Since 2010, Mr David Craig MA MEd (forties). PGCE at Birmingham University and MEd in Educational Leadership with the Open University. Previous head of department posts at Edgbaston High, Birmingham and Wolverhampton Grammar School and deputy head at Merchant Taylors' School, Crosby. He aims 'to cement QEGS as one of the best boys' schools in the north of England.' His outside interests include cricket, rugby, choral music and Derby County FC. Married with two children.

Academic matters: High. 81 per cent A*–B at A level, 57 per cent at A*/A. 68 per cent at A*/ A at GCSE and 100 per cent five passes. IGCSE in maths. 'Boys come here knowing that academic expectation is placed upon them.' Not tempted to push students into different subjects just to help the results tables. 'We have worked hard to improve our academic standards, but some of the results that give me most satisfaction are those achieved by boys who you might not have expected to shine so well at a particular subject,' said the previous head.

A parent told us, 'at QEGS nothing is looked at as impossible. You might not become the best but if you put in the effort, push yourself, you can succeed.' Strong across the board especially maths, sciences, English and humanities. French and German on offer to all, plus Spanish, business French and Latin. Business studies and some languages, drama, studied with the Girls' High across the road.

Max 24 per class, 10/12 in sixth form. Work clinics available at lunch-time. No streaming. Conscious of rising expectation. Not convinced by International Baccalaureate but embracing new A* grade at A level. 'It is getting harder to get into the best universities and we have to be aware of that and prepare our boys accordingly.'

Computers throughout and interactive whiteboards. Good remedial help on hand for mild dyslexia and the like, can 'cope' with mild Asperger's. Children are automatically screened and additional help can be organised, usually at lunch-time, laptops allowed. Recent improvements include new learning resource centre, 240 seat theatre, library, sixth form centre and English department.

Games, Options, the Arts: Emphasis on sport, music, drama, with Duke of Edinburgh (300 take), chess, bridge and trips/expeditions favoured. Art is very strong, aided by art department in the top of the school with masses of light. Screen printing, photography, etchings. Great music, regular scholarships to the Royal School of Music, finalists in the National Festival of Music; Outstanding Performers at National Festival for Youth Music. Brass section wins prizes, over 300 individual players, swing band (played in front of the Queen during her Jubilee) and junior swing bands (available for hire). Concerts often held in Wakefield Cathedral, where the junior boys provide choristers, joined by girls from the High School. Music and drama often joint with High School girls e.g. *Grease*, *Guys and Dolls*. Regularly places students on best drama courses. 'My son had never picked up a musical instrument until he went to QEGS – now his life seems to revolve around music,' said a parent.

School has use of over 27 acres of playing fields, pavilion and new sports hall with special 'resilient' flooring hired out to locals. Training pool for junior school only, seniors use the pool in town. Proud of its sporting heritage, especially rugby – including old boy Mike Tindall. Produced England U19 cricket captain, England U18 rugby cap etc. Masses of sporting trips to South Africa, South America, Australia, Canada, West Indies. Plus cultural tours and exchanges to France, Germany, USA and expeditions to Costa Rica, Borneo and Tanzania.

Background and Atmosphere: Founded by Royal Charter in 1591 and moved to present site in 1854. From 1944–76 it was a direct grant school and reverted to fee-paying in 1976. Imposing Victorian Gothic façade hides mish mash of good, bad and ugly extensions. Junior school also on site, and they play games on the grass in front of the school. Boys all smart in grey uniforms (think boy band in blazers). Modernisation is removing any sense of stuffy grammar school and proud of friendly, all-inclusive atmosphere. Impressive new entrance is very grand. Motto is Turpe Nescire – 'It is a disgrace to be ignorant' – fat chance of that here. Ethos is of boys 'Doing their best and fulfilling potential'. Inspection speaks of 'dedication and humanity' of staff. Great sixth form centre with popular café. Sixth formers drop uniform in favour of a smart suit (think boy band in suit and tie).

Pastoral Care and Discipline: Tutor-led pastoral system with boys encouraged to treat each other with respect. PSE and pastoral care fosters good behaviour by encouraging informed choice by the boys. 'To try to pretend society is not as it is would be wrong. Different challenges face the boys – drugs, sex etc. Through PSE, our pastoral care, assembly and careers education we educate them, give them advice and guidance and help them arrive at their own choices and pathways.' Seems to work, parents report good relationships, camaraderie and 'help each other along' attitude.

Record book incorporates the school rules, inspected by staff and must be signed by parents at preordained levels. Punishments include detentions and suspensions for most serious misdemeanours. Drug possession gets automatic expulsion. Smoking equals detention, three detentions equals suspension. Suspensions and exclusions for bullying, vandalism and aggressive behaviour. Poor academic performance can also find you the door.

Pupils and Parents: Great motorway and rail links give it a wide catchment area and it is seen as the only acceptable alternative to the state system for miles around. Boys come with strong work ethic and parents and pupils must make a 'positive choice' to come here. Fair assortment from ethnic minorities, 'a broad, UK social mix'. None with EAL requirements. Good breeding ground for bishops, Lincoln and York; plus John Scott, former director of music at St Paul's, latterly at the prestigious Saint Thomas Church NYC; and a tranche of internationalists.

Great links between home and school and parents are fulsome in their praise of school. 'We have found even the slightest issue or concern we have had is resolved within 48 hours.' 'QEGS gives the boys the tools but also gives them the blueprint and the instructions to follow – other schools just provide the tools.'

Entrance: Most (60 per cent) from QEGS junior, if their results are up to scratch (only two or three a year don't). Others from Sandal Endowed and Willthorpe feeders. Entrance exam and interview required. Latest inspection said school's induction process was 'excellent'. Always over-subscribed and academic achievement is obligatory – baseline qualifications for entry at sixth form are six GCSEs (but most come with seven or eight) with at least two As in subjects to be taken at AS/A level. Occasional boy comes into the school at other times, subject to academic OK and space.

Exit: Few leave to art courses or employment post GCSE. Most destined for good A levels and heading to good universities – a handful to Oxbridge, Sheffield, Durham, Newcastle, Leeds and London. Medicine and law popular.

Money Matters: Ogden Trust can get the lucky few a 100 per cent bursary. Must be key stage 2 shiner and parental income of less than £40,000 per annum. Sprinkling of other scholarships and bursaries (which are awarded post exam and reviewed annually) plus music and sixth form schools. Bursaries for choristers in junior school, paid 50/50 by school and Cathedral, but only whilst boy is in the choir. Ogden Trust sixth form science scholarships available (worth up to 100 per cent of fees) each year for a student wishing to study maths/science at A level. Parent told us: 'It is a fee paying school and of course you cannot help but think of the other things you could have used the money for – but it is the best investment a parent could ever make.'

Remarks: Great results and great facilities but not a sweat shop. Very traditional feel and loved for it, but very aware of changing society and ensuring boys are ready for those changes. Downside? Tough to get in, expectations high.

Queen Elizabeth High School

Whetstone Bridge Road, Hexham, Northumberland, NE46 3JB

• Pupils: 1,270; 620 boys, 645 girls. • Ages: 13 to 18 • Size of sixth form: 480 • Non denom • State

Tel: 01434 610 300
Fax: 01434 610 320
Email: admin@queenelizabeth.northumberland.sch.uk
Website: www.qehs.net

Head: Since 2008, Mr Neil Morrison (fifties), MA MEd PGCE. Studied economics at Cambridge and postgraduate educational qualifications at Newcastle University and North Staffordshire Polytechnic. Previously head of Whickham School and Sports College, Gateshead.

Academic matters: Good results achieved in friendly, non pushy atmosphere. 85 per cent five A* to C at GCSE. At A level, 97 per cent of entries overall passes with a third of entries at A*/A. Full GCSE and A level curriculum, including Latin up to A level, vocational courses and some BTecs. Also offers NVQ in Hotel Services in swish, fully-fitted restaurant, open to and popular with the public. Flexible curriculum to meet individual needs. Pupils work hard. Further maths centre for Northumberland and pilot school for Science for the 21st Century. Good IT provision, pupils can access and work at home. 'But teachers are the most important resource that we have got.' Awarded High Performing Specialist School Status in 2007 and became a Specialist Science College in February 2008.

Games, Options, the Arts: Strong on extra-curricular activities (70 per cent take up) from music, theatre and sports to clubs (art, environmental, amnesty, Christian Union, fair trade etc). Performing Arts College. Wants more facilities for sport 'to cover all the bases.' Already has Sportsmark along with Artsmark Gold.

Range of sports offered for all abilities. 'We have clubs as well as teams so if you want to get involved there will be something available.' Girls' netball teams county champions at U14 & U18 last season. Particularly strong in rowing with former pupil Matthew Wells returning from the Beijing Olympics with a Bronze Medal in the men's heavyweight double sculls. First fifteen won Rugby World Team of the Year in 2004. The girls' senior rugby squad are Northumberland 7's champions with former pupil Juliet Short playing for England U19 last season.

Usual foreign links/trips with France, Germany, Spain, Italy, Greece, ski trips etc. Has link with a Tibetan monastery and school in India and plans for students to visit.

Background and Atmosphere: Established 1599. School split between traditional '60s build and 19th century former hydropathic hotel. Hydro building houses a mix of subjects but has a genteel, arts and music feel to it. Stroll down steep but beautiful grounds, where wild rabbits and pupils play, to reach bustling corridors of the '60s buildings. Unassuming '60s buildings constantly surprise – uninspiring corridor suddenly opens onto shiny new NVQ hotel services restaurant. Imposing hydro building and its fabulous grounds are a delight. Hustle, bustle in main school.

Sixth form has different atmosphere, no uniform and common room in splendid Victorian glass winter garden in hydro building. 'The atmosphere is nice, staff are helpful and everybody gets on well with everyone else. There are lots of places to chill.' School at heart of community education, gives impression of being open 24/7 – youth service, adult education, classes during holidays etc. 'Education doesn't stop at 3.20pm or at age 16 or 18, it continues for life and we try to make provision for that.' Each year involves around 2,000 adults in courses or activities organised through school.

Pastoral Care and Discipline: Year group and tutor group system provides pastoral stability throughout school. Electronically-monitored SIF system tags poor behaviour, student achievement records recognise the good. Emphasis on peer support and recognition. Behaviour support and learning mentors on site. Rewards healthy eating as well as learning.

Pupils and Parents: Oversubscribed. Intake from Hexham, Corbridge and surrounding villages. Reasonably affluent area with pockets of deprivation. Commuting distance to Newcastle. Almost half are bussed in. Overwhelmingly white British, reflecting catchment area. Small number with special needs. Average class size 25, pupil/teacher ratio 17:1. 'My parents moved to this area because of the good reputation of the school' – sixth former. 'People advertise in the local paper for houses in the catchment area.' – head.

Entrance: Based on LA catchment criteria. Three feeder middle schools: St Joseph's, Hexham and Corbridge. Big effort to ease transition from middle to high school, led by head. Retention into sixth form extremely high and pulls in around 30 a year extra from elsewhere.

Exit: Majority of students go on to higher education with a handful – four in 2010 – to Oxbridge each year. Rest go into higher education, training, apprenticeships or work. But head says, 'our role is also to give them the skills and personal qualities that they need in life.' Over past few years a number of students have won places at National Youth Theatre.

Remarks: Achieves in a relaxed manner. No 'hot house' philosophy but strong sense of purpose. A school confident in its ability but at ease with itself. Probably a rare quality.

Queen Elizabeth's Girls' School

High Street, Barnet, Hertfordshire, EN5 5RR

• Pupils: 1,150 girls, all day • Ages: 11–18 • Size of sixth form: 250
• Non-denom • State

Tel: 020 8449 2984
Fax: 02084 412 322
Email: office@qegschool.org.uk
Website: www.qegschool.org.uk

Headteacher: Since 2001, Mrs Kate Webster BA PGCE MA (education management) (fifties). Studied geography at Sheffield University and taught at Furze Platt School in Maidenhead and Herschel Grammar School in Slough, before joining Henrietta Barnett as deputy head. No children; likes walking, music, theatre and art. Amiable, competent and straightforward; excellent manager. Teaches where needed geography, RE and PHSE.

Academic matters: Some at the top end are creamed off by Barnet's selective and semi-selective schools, but this is a comprehensive with a full ability range, achieving commendable results because of good teaching and high expectations from the start. Around 87 per cent of girls get 5+ A*–C grades at GCSE (79 per cent 5 A*–C including English and maths) with some 40 per cent A* and A grades. Geography, history, maths, RS, media studies, psychology and sociology are all popular and successful A level choices, alongside English and biology. The 20 subjects available include vocational courses in ICT and business studies.

The school's media arts specialism means a focus on English, drama, art and media studies. 'It's about teaching and learning styles which use IT and the media as much as possible. But this does not deflect us from a broad and balanced curriculum and we don't allow over-specialisation.' A good selection of computers around the building – 'though you are always running to catch up with IT, it's a priority to keep updating our provision'.

Setting for maths from Year 7; all pupils now study French and Spanish in Years 7–9, with setting from Year 8. All other subjects are taught in mixed ability groups – 'We tried setting for science but the results didn't improve'. Ofsted comments that most teaching caters well for the whole range of abilities. Maths has, historically, been one of the weaker subjects, 'But we've made lots of progress at KS3 and the school now has a high performing specialist school second specialism in mathematics and computing' (since April 2009). This has allowed increased investment and focus on maths, producing strong results at GCSE and A level.

Good SEN support, mostly within the classroom. The school's split-level site is unsuitable for children with physical disabilities, but around 10 per cent of pupils have special educational needs, including specific learning difficulties, dyslexia and dyspraxia. The gifted and talented co-ordinator identifies very able girls, who are encouraged to take on extension research projects – 'But we don't want to be exclusive, and others can join in too'. Masterclasses in, e.g., music and history. Good careers advice – has Investors in Careers status, recently renewed. 2007 Ofsted judged school to be 'outstanding'.

Games, Options, the Arts: As befits its media arts specialism, drama GCSE is very popular, involving regular showcases to parents. A second drama studio was opened in 2007, together with new media editing suites, kitchen and dining room. Music is also strong, though relatively few take it to GCSE or A level, where it is available through Barnet Music Centre. Senior and junior orchestras, a jazz band and various ensembles depending on the strengths and numbers of musicians. Links with the ENO, Wigmore Hall and various orchestras. Several art studios and plenty of innovative art on display. Good sports facilities – a newly refurbished swimming pool, sports hall, gym and several tennis/netball courts; girls compete in county football and cross country tournaments. Girls doing PE GCSE often organise dance and games tournaments for local primary schools. Trips abroad include skiing in the Alps, watersports trip to France, language trips, art/drama trips to New York and history trips to the battlefields of France.

Background and Atmosphere: Opened in 1888 as a grammar school; has been comprehensive since the 1970s. Hilly site on the edge of London's green belt. Buildings range from Victorian to 1960s. Looks rather tatty round the edges and could do with a major influx of cash for refurbishment. The loos, however, were revamped at a cost of £150,000 at the request of the school council when the head first joined. 'We've done what we can in terms of improving the environment, but we have no space to rebuild.' Relaxed atmosphere with confident, articulate girls, used to speaking up in public.

Pastoral Care and Discipline: The school is renowned for making new girls feel at home quickly. The dedicated head of Year 7 'puts lots of time and effort going to feeder schools and getting information on the girls who will be joining us'. High expectations of good behaviour and discipline do not appear to be problematical – only two permanent exclusions in the last four years. Clear policies on drugs and bullying. 'Obviously girls are exposed to drugs outside, but inside it is not an issue. Our PHSE programme is very good and we put a lot of effort into equipping girls to make informed decisions on all aspects of life. The form tutor or head of year is the first port of call if a girl is troubled, but they are not fazed about coming to find me if they feel strongly about something.'

Pupils and Parents: This is not a purely middle-class school – it has a higher than average percentage of girls on free school meals. But neither is it a gritty inner-London comprehensive – plenty of nice, confident Barnet girls. OGs: Elaine Paige, actress and singer, and Stephanie Beacham, actress.

Entrance: Generally around three applicants for every place. First in line are girls with a statement of social or medical needs specifying the school; then siblings; then those living closest – which in practice tends to mean within about two miles. Girls entering the sixth form – about 18 do so each year – are asked to have five grade Cs or above at GCSE, though many A level courses specify a B grade in the A level subject.

Exit: About a third leave after GCSEs, with some high achievers moving on to selective sixth forms, some to co-ed sixth form colleges, others to FE colleges to pursue vocational courses. Some return when the grass elsewhere proves to be less green than it had appeared. Most sixth form leavers go on to higher education, to do courses ranging from medicine to audio-visual production at old and new universities, including one or two a year to Oxbridge.

Money Matters: Not a rich school. Low down in the queue for government cash for refurbishment but does its best with available funds. Loyal parent body works hard at raising money.

Remarks: A successful comprehensive with high expectations that caters well for all abilities and produces self-assured girls used to discussion and debate.

Queen Elizabeth's School, Barnet

Queen's Road, Barnet, Hertfordshire, EN5 4DQ

• Pupils: 1,150 boys • Ages: 11-18 • Size of sixth form: 280 • Non-denom • State

Tel: 020 8441 4646
Fax: 020 8440 7500
Email: molivestone@qebarnet.co.uk
Website: www.qebarnet.co.uk

Headmaster: Since 1999, Dr John Marinkowitz BA PhD (late fifties). A quietly spoken but formidable figure, entirely at home in an academic gown. Dr Marinkowitz attended St John's College Johannesburg (the 'Eton of South Africa'), then did his undergraduate studies (in history) at Aberystwyth and teacher training in South Africa, where he taught for seven years before completing a doctorate in history at SOAS. From there, directly to QE in 1985 to teach history. 'I was averse to spending my life in the isolation of the archives. I'm a people person. I delight in young people's development.' Dr Marinkowitz is unashamedly elitist and feels that clever children are under-provided for in the state system. A perfectionist and a detail man, he's spent the past ten years in a relentless pursuit of excellence and Queen Elizabeth's is now regarded by Ofsted as outstanding in every respect.

Very much a figure from a pre-Labour universe, Dr Marinkowitz believes that education is a tool for enlightenment ('I battle against a utilitarian view; it's much more important to study for a love of learning') rather than purely a ladder for personal advancement. 'I want to fight against rampant materialism and consumerism, which is so destructive. I want the boys to understand that they are part of a broader society. I want them to take responsibility for others, to stand up for themselves and for causes greater than themselves. I want them to make the world a better place, not just have a successful career'. Married to a university lecturer, with two grown children (one of whom attended QE). Hobbies include sailing, classical music, jazz, reading and watching international rugby.

Dr John Marinkowitz is to retire in July 2011.

Academic matters: Consistently top of the academic league tables, rivalling most schools, independent or state, in its exam results. Definitely not a school for slackers. You work hard here and you work consistently hard, which can be stressful for some, particularly in the early years. Testing is very much part of the modus operandi. Base-line assessment in Year 7, then setting in all subjects, with half-termly tests thereafter. 'It's quite nerve-racking at the beginning,' says one sixth former, 'but it does mean by the time we get to GCSEs we don't find exams a problem.' Certainly not. A*s the norm at GCSE (average 10A*s). All take at a least two languages (French and German) with Mandarin offered as an extra. A level choices are decided by tests in Years 10 and 11 designed 'to tease out' aptitude. 'GCSE grades are not a good indicator,' says the head. 'Of 180 boys here, 165 will get A*s in maths, but not all will be good enough to do maths.' 70 per cent of boys do 4 A levels, most get 4 A grades; 60 per cent take maths, two thirds some science, many do a mix. No fluffy options whatsoever. 'We don't want to dilute the curriculum,' say the head.

Most departments and most teaching is very strong – 'so many departments get all As'. Boys enthuse particularly about geography and history. Homework load is strenuous (one and a half hours in Year 7, one hour per subject per night at A level), but few problems with hungry dogs here. 'We don't need to whine and cajole, it's a culture of achievement.' The school has recently extended its extra-curricular enrichment with the Williams Society's weekly tutorials in informal logic, literary theory and analysis of concepts. 'We talk to them about the social sciences and concepts such as liberty,' no doubt helping to up the school's Oxbridge success rate to an all-time high last year.

Class sizes, 30 in Year 9, 18–23 in year 10, 17 at A level. All the latest gewgaws throughout with up-to-the minute ICT and all labs refurbished in the last 10 years. 'Special needs' at this school tends to be on the gifted-and-talented end of the spectrum, but every department runs a clinic to support the struggling and challenge the most able. School says it can accommodate mild autism, Asperger's and dyslexia.

Games, Options, the Arts: This is a school where competing is important and a big part of the competition takes places on the sports field. All play rugby in Year 7. 'Rugby serves boys so well,' says the head. 'It has a gentlemanly ethos, of which I enormously approve.' England under-16 head coach coaches the rugby squad and the school fields up to D teams on a regular basis. (Sport, however, is setted from Year 7, and it can be difficult to move up the scrum, according to one pupil). Swimming, water polo, Eton Fives, tennis, cross country and fencing also popular. Plenty of county and national representation in sport, bridge, chess. (Old Boy Tim Aggar recently won a gold medal for rowing in the Para-Olympic games.) New eight-lane swimming pool, all-weather tennis courts, multi gym and plenty of neatly trimmed green fields for team sports.

School has specialist music status, with three full-time music teachers, 12 peripatetic teachers and a music suite where boys can study A level music technology with all the latest recording equipment. Big band, jazz quartet, north and south Indian collection ensemble. 'We are in the vanguard of international music development. It epitomises a strength of the world, the dialectic between different cultures. It's beautiful to listen to a group which includes the sitar, the sax and the violin.' Visual arts take place in open-plan, light-filled art rooms but plenty going on elsewhere, with a daily art club held in the lunch hour, an exhibition space for displays of work and field trips to arty destinations like St Ives and Paris for A level candidates (as well as occasional life drawing-classes). Growing national reputation for chess. Outside the classroom, the school has invested heavily in infrastructure. This year sees the launch of a dramatic, architect-designed new hall, which, as well as drama productions and debating competitions, will host recording sessions for professional orchestras.

As one might expect, careers advice taken very seriously. From Year 7, pupils have half-termly meeting on their future. 'We want them to ask early on: What do I want to do in life? After the age of 14, they won't do it for their parents or teachers; they do it because they believe it themselves.' Decision making is aided by extensive work experience from year 10. Loyal old boys, too, come back for an organised meeting with sixth formers to chat about university and subject choice. Some act as Oxbridge buddies for the next generation. Boys also do voluntary work related to their career aspirations.

Background and Atmosphere: Founded in 1573 by Robert, Earl of Leicester, with a charter from Elizabeth 1, the school was rebuilt in 1931–32 by Hertfordshire County Council in a noble civic style with terrazzo flooring, parquet and panelling, all kept in spick-and-span condition. Still relatively well endowed with land held in perpetuity and its own Foundation Trustees, QE went comprehensive in the '60s, reverted to grant-maintained status in 1989 and became a grammar school once more in 1994. 'It was a highly unusual choice to re-introduce selection,' says the head. Difficult to imagine a more orderly and focused environment. Even in traditional chatty art, boys work with heads down, quiet as mice. Significant increases in responsibility from Year 11, when own suits are allowed. 90 prefects voted for by staff and students, monitor lunch (fresh food produced daily), playgrounds and classrooms. 'They lead the school in so many ways.' School captain and house captains appointed from on high.

Pastoral Care and Discipline: Boys motivated by reward and praise with loads of 'celebratory occasions'. (Homework diaries with merit stickers for every subject in the early years; hand-written notes home later on.) Certainly not a school where misbehaviour is the norm. 'I will expel a boy for violence on the premises aimed at staff or other boys, consciously creating racial disharmony or bringing drugs into school, but I haven't expelled a boy in ten years,' says the head. Occasional fixed-term exclusions, however, for persistent 'failure to carry out school protocols' or misbehaving in lessons. Registration twice a day and homework diaries are also monitored for extra-curricular activities. 'If a boy is not sufficiently engaged in extra-curricular activities, that's often the first warning sign.' If concern is felt, the year head will be involved, then, depending on the issues, parents, special needs or an ed psych.

Pupils and Parents: Defies the traditional middle class grammar school profile in its diverse student body. Over sixty per cent of boys come from ethnic minorities, predominantly Asian. Most are first generation, most speak English as a second language. 'Our boys come from very ordinary backgrounds,' says the head. 'In our last Oxbridge intake, many boys had parents who hadn't gone to university, one was a refugee from Rwanda.' The head feels the school 'contributes massively to social mobility and social cohesion. Here, they have to interact across the divides, whether they're scrumming down on the rugger field or playing chess.'

Entrance: 1,300 apply for 180 places. First round tests in non-verbal reasoning (set and marked externally) held in December, when numbers are reduced to 600. Second round in maths, English and verbal reasoning. Places are then offered on a strictly hierarchical basis. 'If you don't get past the first round, you would struggle here,' says the head. 'But we could take all 600 and it wouldn't make a jot of difference to our results.' Indeed, those on the waiting list often end up in top sets. Pupils come from around 90 primary schools, but the ability range is narrow, most are in the top ten per cent nationally. Head is against the 'industry of preparation' that leaves children trembling in the exam queue. 'It's a waste of time stressing children out.' Parents, however, wouldn't necessarily agree. Boys who have passed the first round of the entrance exam are eligible to audition for 30 music places. Occasional vacancies between Years 7 and 10, offered to those on the waiting list. No sixth form entry for external candidates. 'This is a seven-year education and I don't want to tread on any of my colleagues' toes.' Automatic transfer to sixth form for virtually all but pupils have to be recommended for individual subjects. Further maths is particularly hard to gain access to.

Exit: About 30 boys leave at GCSE. Some prefer mixed sixth forms or are looking for subjects the school doesn't offer (law, psychology, media studies). Some win scholarships to independent schools. Other just prefer a more relaxed environment. The odd one or two don't make the grade. Virtually all who stay go on to top universities. 37 Oxbridge offers last year – more than almost any other boys' school, state or private – in every subject from classics to medicine. Otherwise primarily to Nottingham, Imperial, UCL and Warwick. Economics most popular degree, 20 plus to medicine and medical-related degrees. History and law also popular. The school gives excellent UCAS guidance.

Money Matters: State aid is minimal and the head has to put up with the fact he gets less money than many local comps. Gaps are filled with funds from the Foundation and with carefully husbanded donations from parents, old boys and friends, which underwrite school trips and new buildings. Most parents contribute £60 a month, though this is entirely voluntary. 'We say to them, if you want to have a sound education and provide the polish for boys to go to the best universities, you can't do it on state funding.' The head has managed to raise £10m during his time at the school. His next large-scale project is a new library.

Remarks: An extraordinary school that offers the able, the diligent and the aspiring, whatever their social or ethnic origins, an education hard to rival in the state or private sector. You do, however, have to be the right boy. Not a good option for those who would struggle with the workload, rebel against the discipline or dislike competition.

Queen Elizabeth's Grammar School

Linked to Queen Elizabeths Grammar Junior School in the Junior section

West Park Road, Blackburn, Lancashire, BB2 6DF

• Pupils: 520 boys, 110 girls, all day • Ages: 11-18 plus junior school (see below) • Size of sixth form: 130 • Inter-denom on C of E Foundation • Fees: £5,355 to £9,459 pa • Independent

Tel: 01254 686 300
Fax: 01254 692 314
Email: plloyd@qegs.blackburn.sch.uk
Website: www.qegs.blackburn.sch.uk

Headmaster: Since September 2007, Mr Simon Corns MA (fiftyish) following retirement of enthusiastic previous head, Dr David Hempsall. Read modern languages at Gonville and Caius, Cambridge. Taught at Arnold School, Blackpool, before 12 years teaching at St Albans School, first as head of languages, latterly as second master. Also enthusiastic, pragmatic and with a reputation for being firm but fair. Says he is greatly enjoying being back in the North-West (he was educated at Merchant Taylors' School, Crosby) and loved leading QEGS (pronounced 'Quegs') as it celebrated its quincentenary year in 2009.

Married, with two school age sons.

Academic matters: Head says 'realising potential is our aim'. Science particularly strong, with maths and chemistry most popular subjects in school, but other areas such as art also delivering excellent results. Exam results good: 61 per cent A*/A/B grades at A level in 2010 (from a cohort that was not the strongest, but exceeded predicted grades); over 14 per cent of students got at least three grade As. At GCSE, 93 per cent got 5+ A*-Cs in 2010, with two pupils getting all A* grades. Class sizes of around 20–25 in main school and 8–10 for A levels. Pupils take ten GCSEs, including English, maths, at least one modern foreign language (French, German or Spanish), a combination of sciences (core plus additional award or separate sciences on offer – IGCSE courses now being taken) and a short course in ethics and philosophy. Latin and Greek available too. School has now moved from six-day revolving timetable to a normal five-day cycle, with eight 35-minute lessons a day. Loads of computers (four networked IT suites) and state-of-the-art science and language labs. No remedial help but less able taught in smaller sets. Staff very impressive bunch – average age 42 and around one-third have been at school for more than 10 years. Half of staff are women.

Games, Options, the Arts: Dazzling games reputation. QEGS awarded Sportsmark Gold award for third time in 2005, 'with distinction'. Historically a soccer school, it won the Independent Schools FA Cup in 1996, 2001 and 2004 – the first school to win the cup more than once. Close links with Blackburn Rovers – old boy James Beattie (now with Celtic) started his professional career with them, as did England U21 goalkeeper Frank Fielding. Rugby, cricket, swimming, athletics, golf and cross-country all good too: in cricket, the school has defeated the MCC for three consecutive years in the annual fixture. House system enables pupils of all abilities to play competitive sport. Trickier for girls because of smaller numbers but sports department organises combined year teams and U16 netball team highly successful. Splendid six-lane swimming pool with electronic timing system – used outside school hours by appreciative locals.

Around a third of pupils play musical instruments. Drama is popular too. All pupils get opportunities to sing, speak, act or perform in front of an audience, whether it's singing in a choir or taking part in the annual school play and/or musical. Academic trips galore, Young Enterprise, Duke of Edinburgh award scheme etc, plus an array of lunch-time and after-school clubs. Art a growing strength in recent years: two students accepted into top London Art schools in 2010, without the usual requirement for a foundation year.

Background and Atmosphere: School founded in 1509 by the second Earl of Derby, granted Royal Charter by Queen Elizabeth I in 1567. Moved to present site in leafy Blackburn suburb in 1884. Went direct grant in 1944 and returned to private sector in 1976. Traditionally admitted girls in the sixth form but took the plunge and opened doors to girls of all ages in 2001. Girls now in every year throughout school. Staff reckon girls are integrating well and confident numbers will build, though it may take a while. Early Years department, catering for ages four to six, opened in 2002 and was extended to include nursery for ages three plus in September 2005. Original school building, with stunning stained-glass windows, known as 'Big School' and used as school dining hall. Portraits of previous heads, school silver, team photographs and press cuttings proudly on show.

Campus comprises five acres (not counting playing fields) and numerous buildings. Bit of a hotchpotch, some purpose-built, some converted houses, and on a sloping site so lots of steps. Games fields and sports hall 20 minutes away at Lammack – pupils travel there by minibus. Grounds and buildings immaculate – not a scrap of litter or graffiti in sight. Light airy library with 17,000 books and panoramic views across Blackburn and surrounding countryside on top floor of Queen's Wing. Pupils can use it for private study at break and lunchtime. Sixth form housed in purpose-built Singleton House. Has own café, common room (complete with table football, comfy chairs and music blaring out of the stereo system), careers suite and private study room. Pupils wear uniform – distinctive royal blue blazers – for under-16s. 'Business suits' dress code for sixth form introduced in September 2007, opted for by pupils themselves (after a similar proposal was rejected five years earlier).

Pastoral Care and Discipline: Previous head felt that school had lost its 'rough and tough' reputation in recent years – 'We are a much more caring society, more family orientated and able to poke fun at ourselves a little more,' he told us. Staff rightly proud of pastoral care at QEGS. Problems, great and small, relayed via form tutors and heads of year to deputy head (pastoral) and head. School nurse and head of complementary studies (PSHE) often involved too. Punishments range from pink referral slip sent to form tutor and detentions through to temporary or permanent exclusion. School rules succinctly outlined in 14-point code. Hot policy on bullying, verbal abuse, smoking, alcohol and drugs.

Pupils and Parents: School open to 'anyone with ability'. Pupils bright, industrious and confident without appearing complacent or alarmingly sophisticated. Very mixed backgrounds – parents range from wealthy Ribble Valley families to those who make huge financial sacrifices to send their sons and daughters here. Just over one-fifth Asian. Massive catchment area. One third come from Blackburn with Darwen, but rest from 20-mile radius, including Preston, Colne, Burnley, Bolton and Clitheroe. School bus service covers 12 routes. Former pupils are an eclectic bunch, including the late Russell Harty, scientist Sir Ernest Marsden, businessman Sir Kenneth Durham (who died in 2005), designer Wayne Hemingway, film director Michael Winterbottom, professional golfer Nick Dougherty and Krishnan Guru-Murthy, the Channel 4 news presenter/reporter.

Entrance: At 11, school test in English, maths and verbal reasoning, plus school report and interview with the head, who looks for 'character, spark, sparkle and potential.' Boys and girls come from huge array of state primaries and local preps, including Clevelands, Highfield Priory and Park Hill St Joseph's. Virtually all QEGS juniors move up to main school. Sixth form entrants need minimum of five Bs at GCSE. Ogden Trust sixth form science scholarship available to highly qualified student joining from maintained sector (maths and physics essential) and Blakey sixth form languages scholarship now available, introduced in 2009, to highly qualified linguist.

Exit: Handful leave after GCSE, mostly for local FE colleges offering subjects like law and media studies that are not available at QEGS. Over 95 per cent of sixth form go on to university – including a handful to Oxbridge most years. Medicine usually the most popular subject to read, though several each year now going on to engineering degrees. Manchester – 25 miles down the road – currently the favourite university, though Newcastle and Liverpool are also popular.

Money Matters: Head says, 'we live off our fees and use our money wisely'. School previously had large number of assisted places (about a third of the intake) – their loss has affected pupil numbers. One scholarship (one third remission of fees) offered to best new main school entrant each year, plus one Ogden Trust science scholarship for a sixth form entrant from a state school. New sixth form languages scholarship (means-tested) introduced September 2009. There are also over 20 main school and sixth form bursaries (up to one third of fees).

Remarks: Very impressive school. Have been huge changes in recent years and will take a while yet for girls' numbers to build but a stimulating place with friendly, articulate pupils. New head inherited a golden crown and is working hard to maintain and deepen the shine.

Queen Elizabeth's Hospital

Linked to Queen Elizabeths Hospital Juniors in the Junior section

Berkeley Place, Clifton, Bristol, BS8 1JX

• Pupils: 530 boys • Ages: 11-18 • Size of sixth form: 150 boys
• Non-denom • Fees: £10,380 pa • Independent

Tel: 0117 930 3040
Fax: 0117 929 3106
Email: headmaster@qehbristol.co.uk
Website: www.qehbristol.co.uk

Head: Since 2000, Mr Stephen Holliday MA (forties), educated at Batley Grammar School, Yorkshire, then Jesus College, Cambridge (where he obtained 1st class honours in history). Spent two years with British Rail before shunting himself to Dean Close, Cheltenham for six years (including three as housemaster), followed by four years at Giggleswick as head of history before deputy headship at Queen Elizabeth's Grammar School, Blackburn. Wife is head of geography at Colston's Girls' and has two 'sporty' sons at QEH. Teaches PSHE to all of Year 7 and GCSE history. Methodist lay preacher but 'doesn't wear religion on his sleeve,' say staff. A 'straightforward man', welcoming and a good listener – 'What you see is what you get,' say parents. Loves QEH and likely to stay a while. Aware of the political and other pressures in the city but confident that QEH will hold its own in face of massive investment in local state provision. Strong business streak – currently savouring success of joint development with Bristol City FC on Failand sports field. He enjoys skiing and 'escaping' in holidays.

Academic matters: Results consistently outstanding: Over 80+ per cent average A*/B grades at A level over past three years and 60+ per cent A*/A at GCSE (harder IGCSE for English and maths included). Emphasis on quality rather than quantity – maximum nine subjects sat at GCSE and generally three at A level (though 'one boy currently being asked for five A grades to read economics at UCL,' we were told). Sciences and maths very strong; drama and theatre studies outstanding; Spanish appears most successful foreign language. Popularity of government and politics doesn't seem to have detracted from success in history. Large numbers also take geography. Design and technology is only taught to GCSE. Success in Latin and economics point to school's academic breadth. Individual achievements recognised and valued across all year groups. Regular target setting for boys and frequent reporting to parents leave little scope for backsliding. All do three sciences to end of Year 9 and after that choose dual or triple award at GCSE. GCSE options include Latin (compulsory in Years 7 and 8), drama, art, ceramics, Greek and Spanish. Lots of ICT. General studies programme in sixth covers topics such as finance at university. Boys generally rate their teachers highly – 'especially some of the younger ones'.

New SENCo – learning support seen as increasingly important in this selective school. NFER screening for SpLD. A few overseas boys have ESL support; other special needs include hearing impairments, several ADD, mild cerebral palsy and Asperger's.

Games, Options, the Arts: Very sporty. Main off site activity at Failand – QEH sports field with changing and pavilion some ten minutes away (depending on time of day) by coach. Enviable facilities developing apace in partnership with Bristol FC. All boys play rugby to end of Year 9, then some choose football. Diversification of sports as boys move up school. A2 boys not forced to continue games but most do. Cricket and athletics strongest options in summer. Lots selected for Bristol rugby and/or Gloucestershire cricket teams with some rugby players competing nationally at U16 and U18 levels. Swimming and tennis have to be played for time being at outside facilities. Plans for new sports hall and swimming pool on site of present gym complex, currently used for PE, basketball and badminton plus squash (two courts), fitness and weights.

Wide range of extra-curricular activities and clubs at lunchtime and after school. Boys not discouraged from pursuing own outside interests (e.g. pistol shooting, cycling, rowing etc). Impressive programme of visits abroad, from visiting Roman Pompeii to the choir in the United States and rugby players just about anywhere you'll find an oval ball. D of E popular and 150 boys involved in outdoor pursuits, e.g. three teams in Ten Tors (to our amazement, school bursar can be found leading these boys across Dartmoor: 'No-one has ever dropped out,' he asserts proudly). Hugely successful at local and national debating and public speaking competitions. Flourishing Young Enterprise teams and past winners of European Youth Parliament competition. Strong links with local community enhance work experience scheme.

Music is important: many boys playing instruments (a lot also have lessons outside school). Suite of practice rooms and three classrooms including music technology; largest space used for informal (e.g. jazz and acoustic) concerts. School rated locally for its contribution to choral music (one boy in national youth choir); regular slot in Lord Mayor's chapel; sell-out events in Bristol and Clifton cathedrals; regular overseas tours with Red Maids. Trickle of boys to music at universities,

Drama is hugely popular – productions of all kinds throughout year. On-site theatre ('the most vibrant in the west') seats 220 – heavily used by school and touring companies. New drama teaching space being created in main building. We visited during reading week – homework for younger boys is suspended in favour of literature with follow-up activities. Good library, and adjacent careers room is well maintained. Art department housed in former gym: lofty main studio; separate ceramics area. Apple Macs and digital photography replacing older dark room; sixth form achieving high standards – scope for more art to be displayed around school.

Background and Atmosphere: Only all boys' independent school left in Bristol. Motto: 'Dum tempus habemus operemus bonum' ('Whilst we have time let us do good'). School charter and grant of arms given by Elizabeth I. Enviable tradition of scholarship established over four centuries. Strong competitive edge – Crispin Shield for sport most coveted trophy, according to boys we met. Main building (grade two listed) towers (literally) on slope below posh Clifton and close to university. Sense of foreboding on approach – boys love the 'Hogwarts' feel of the place. Within, an impressive stone staircase rises to 'headmaster's landing' – huge flagstones and ubiquitous archive material. Original 'schoolroom' little changed from 1840s and used for supervised study periods through day. Scary, until you talk to friendly boys and staff. School has thankfully moved with times (the 'dungeons' now house refurbished classrooms including ICT). Plasma screens linked to school intranet brought us abruptly back to 21st century. Smartboards everywhere.

New sixth form centre (modern space to work, relax and eat plus discrete IT facility) an obvious privilege for older boys. Purposeful atmosphere created by boys themselves; comfortable relationships built on mutual respect; lots of younger staff and about one third are female. Exciting plans for redeveloping site (outworn science labs) as part of new complex to match wow factor of school's theatre.

Traditional bluecoat uniform now limited to choir members. Blazers and school tie up to Year 11 and suits thereafter. Firm guidelines on appearance (no long hair, jewellery etc) and staff chivvy where necessary. Active school council meets regularly. Plenty of joint activities with girls' schools – especially Red Maids. Most boys dig into honest grub (good choices and boy sized portions) at lunch-time in baronial hall (includes gallery and organ loft) with house shields and honours boards; doubles up for whole school assemblies twice weekly. Theatre used for sixth form assembly. Knockabout area in centre of school known a 'the yard' where boys can let off steam. Generous lot – raised over £10K in a year for various charities.

Pastoral Care and Discipline: Pastoral care underpinned by tried and tested tutorial system. Part-time school counsellor very involved and offers 35 minute slots during day or an hour after school in homely sanctuary. Separate room for highly valued peer support and mentoring schemes (overseen by a sixth form tutor and counsellor). 'Drop in' arrangement every day after school manned by selected seniors – ideas 'have evolved from boys' own suggestions' and so are accepted. Sixth formers are trained and take work seriously – involvement 'makes them good at listening to others when they reach university,' claims counsellor. E-buddying and timetabled group activities also form part of scheme. PSHE (one lesson a week) covers issues such as binge drinking and drug awareness. Induction for new boys includes enjoyable residential expedition.

Parents impressed by way school responds quickly to any problem they raise – 'Staff always have time for me,' said one mum. Sanctions, when imposed, are seen as fair. School rules are few and straightforward. No expulsions in recent times. Long-serving staff help to uphold ethos whilst younger ones give lots of energy. Inspired multi-faith 'quiet room' recently installed for those who need 'time out' for reflection.

Pupils and Parents: Academically selective but not socially exclusive – very mixed bunch. Parents more affluent than in past but many choose QEH to 'steer sons away from more socially exclusive places' and feel it is 'a better preparation for the real world'. Parents 'delighted' with relatively small size – 'Teachers really know the boys,' they report. Close involvement of parents is encouraged and 'Friends' association raises money for small improvements – currently 'greening' a hitherto neglected part of school site. Termly newsletters and school intranet help keep parents informed. Unpretentious boys – friendly, open and polite. Thriving OBs society; former pupils include film star Hugo Weaving; BBC soccer commentator Jonathan Pearce; Ashley Pharoah – writer and creator of TV's 'Life on Mars' series; William Friese-Greene – pioneer in cinema, portrait photographer and inventor; Mike Smith – director of Columbia records.

Entrance: Selective – exam taken in January for entry to Years 7 and 9 (about 15 enter at latter stage – mainly from prep schools). Two applicants for every place at 11 and draws from about forty schools across Bristol area. Popularity soared after decision taken to dispense with Saturday lessons. Red Maids' siblings tend to favour QEH.

Exam comprises VR test (multiple choice) – 50 minutes; 50 minutes non-verbal reasoning test (multiple choice); 30 minutes maths; 30 minutes creative writing exercise; 20+ minutes interview. Nice of them to let one know – many don't. Entry to sixth form – at least six grade Bs at GCSE plus headteacher's reference. Picks up a few from comprehensives at this stage.

Exit: Nearly all Year 11 pupils go into sixth form (a few leave for financial reasons) and most go on to higher education. Number to Oxbridge varies annually; plenty to medical schools and Russell Group universities.

Money Matters: In a city which had the highest takeup of the former government assisted places scheme, QEH has always sought to help the less fortunate. About 15 per cent of boys benefit from school's own (means tested annually) assisted places scheme. A very few receive 100 per cent support. Academic (six) and music (four) scholarships awarded at 11 and 13. Ogden sixth form scholarships. Historically, frugal when it comes to spending, but new development plans set to change that.

Remarks: An academic school with 'plenty of heart'. 'Open, honest boys who work and play hard,' say staff. Atmosphere reminded us of bygone days, though school has moved with the times. Teachers 'go the extra mile' in terms of extra curricular involvement. The importance given to boys' welfare strikes us as exceptional and parents we spoke to had 'no regrets' about choosing QEH.

Queen Ethelburga's College

Linked to Chapter House Preparatory School in the Junior section

Linked to Collegiate Foundation (The) in the Senior section

Thorpe Underwood Hall, Ouseburn, York, North Yorkshire, YO26 9SS

• Pupils: 480 girls, 515 boys; 665 boarders, 330 day • Ages: 3-20 • Size of sixth form: 345 (295 board) • Inter-denominational • Fees: Day £4,518-£9,960; Boarding £20,250-£28,536; International Boarding £24,690-£34,605 pa • Independent

Tel: 01423 333 330
Fax: 01423 333 310
Email: info@qe.org
Website: www.qe.org

Headmaster: Since 2006, Mr Steven Jandrell BA (early fifties), married to Margaret, with a young son at home. Warm, friendly, genuine and approachable, he understands education and enjoys discussing it. Well-respected and liked by staff and pupils, he's part of the furniture, having been here for many years as head of music and deputy head. Long-standing parents describe him as 'the best head so far' – 'he's a good listener who doesn't bat you away with standard answers'. A successor to more commercial heads here, he's a breath of fresh air.

Academic matters: Small classes, unashamedly setted, with regular testing for all – pupils say 'it's good for us.' Sixteen maximum per class for A levels. Choice of 20 A levels or IB Diploma in the College, and the Faculty also offers BTEC in business, fashion and clothing, music technology, performing arts and sport. Many do very well with a third getting four or five straight A grades and a pleasing absence of lower grades. French from nine, Spanish and German for all at 12, Russian and Chinese all on offer. No classics. Single science available – and fab modern labs with spectacular views. High percentage of overseas students means that science and maths are a strength with many A grades. This is a school that is very happy to be judged by its positioning within school league tables.

Dyslexia help available. All children tested on arrival in the prep school during the first half term, ed psych's report if necessary, usually individual lessons for free once a week, if more needed then extra charge. Dual teaching at the bottom end with two and a half dedicated accredited British Dyslexia Association staff on site i.e. SENCo plus. EFL free throughout the school.

The Faculty, a separate school-within-a-school that allows students wishing to follow a less academic and more vocational route, is small but growing and creating its own identity. Serious mentoring here, which pupils value. Sixty per cent of the Faculty are international students.

Games, Options, the Arts: Horses are an important part of QE – clearly, in Yorkshire, where there's (horse) muck there's definitely brass... and large numbers are accommodated in the new outdoor Equestrian Centre. Impressive outdoor manège and masses of pony paddocks are available, pupils may (and do) bring their own animals. Pupils get up to muck out at 7.30am but full livery is available at £3,105 per term, indulgent fathers please note. QE horses are available to borrow free of charge. BHSAI on offer in the sixth form and riding is timetabled, Karen Dixon gives free tuition to students with Karen Dixon Scholarships.

Music (for all) on the up under 'fantastic' head of music with frequent opportunities for performance. The old refectory (now the Phoenix Centre) contains no fewer than four practice drama and dance studios – though the pupils tell us they would 'really like a dedicated theatre please,' school tells us it's on the cards. Art good and strong, with sewing machines in the art dept. Enthusiastic home economics and Leith's food and wine course for sixth formers (no more than two sets of eight per year group) with the smashing kitchen used for grown-up classes in the holidays.

There are 10 acres of floodlit pitches for hockey, soccer, rugby, high jump, volleyball etc. and brand new Astroturf. CCF popular and clubs for IT, archery, fencing, golf. A new swimming pool has just opened as part of the giant sports centre. D of E with plenty of gold participants. Lots of extra-curricular activities, the list is (almost) endless, but some are costly.

Background and Atmosphere: Founded in 1912, QE was the intellectual doyenne of the Northern Circuit, rivalled only by St Leonard's in Scotland. However, falling numbers and threatened closure precipitated the move to Thorpe Underwood, conveniently situated 15 minutes from York and Harrogate and a ten minute drive from the A1. Owned by the Martin family (who still live on site), Thorpe Underwood dates back to the Domesday Book where it is described as Chirchie, Usebrana and Useburn, before becoming part of the monastery of Fountains Abbey in 1292. (The stew pond used by the monks to supply food for the passing travellers has been meticulously restored, though now boasts a fountain which might surprise earlier travellers and has been reinforced with trim stones round the edges). The hall itself was rebuilt in 1902 in best Edwardian Tudor style and the extensions have been sympathetically carried out with leaded paned windows to match the original. The place is a complex mix of old and new – in style and attitude – and full of surprises. Modern facilities sit comfortably alongside a trad country house setting, and modern teaching sits (less comfortably) alongside old-fashioned notions of a 'no trousers' policy for female students and staff.

Impressive newer office facilities include a vast dining room (The Undercroft) that doubles as an assembly hall – though the acoustics are pretty grim and mealtimes can be a deafening experience say some staff. Huge solid oak tables fill the room with comfortable seating on the balcony above, alongside exciting sculptures courtesy of Mr Martin's brother. Fruit available at all times with good salad bar, home-cooked food with a veggie option, all served on monogrammed crockery. Self-service queuing system moves around barriers like a busy post office. A lift has been installed for wheelchair users, a stair lift is also available. Very popular internet café sits alongside the dining room.

The original Hall – previously the home of the Martin family – houses a traditional library and the Phoenix Centre. Some of the blue flock wallpapered classrooms and corridors are a tad surprising, not to mention the excess of taxidermy and hunting trophies around the place – look out for the crouching tigers, might upset small children or anyone sensitively – or pc – inclined, though they remain one of the most photographed parts of the school.

Modern boarding accommodation consists of smart and well-equipped bedrooms, the majority now with private bathrooms, all with flat screen TVs (in fact two TVs in some twin rooms – just in case these lucky pupils wish to watch different programmes ...), DVD machines, telephones with voice mail, fridges, electric kettles, microwaves, air conditioning, trouser presses, room safes and ice-makers – pretty much everything except a mini-bar in fact. Great attention to detail and, it would appear, no expense spared, new boarding houses have fantastic limed oak doors, skirting boards et al. A classy medical centre that resembles a private hospital and oodles of huge common rooms – all with leather sofas, toasters and TVs. Houses for the younger ones surrounded by squidgy playgrounds filled with serious kit. Boys' and girls' accommodation is separate. Day pupil centre for day children plus B & B available if needed. Pay phones on almost every corner, mobile signal dodgy but improving.

Leased for a peppercorn from a charitable foundation (originally the brain child of Brian Martin) QE has benefited from squillions of quids' worth of investment. Good, if not lavishly stocked, library, banks of computers, teletext business info displayed around the school, free internet available to all boarding houses, with wifi covering the whole 100 acre estate as well. Regular formal dinner parties with silver service and speaker for sixth form 'to give them practice in the real world.' Almost 50/50 boy/girl mix, boarding numbers up, though still relying heavily on the overseas market (37 different countries represented here), and a clever move back in 2006 in reducing day fees has brought a considerable rise in day pupils too.

A car park for which most schools (and parents) would give their right arm, an apparently endless building programme and growing numbers – all in a quiet little backwater between York and Harrogate. The school describes itself as a 'broad church' – and it's certainly that, though all faiths and none are welcome. In fact anyone who can afford it (with or without a horse) is welcome really – with little academic selection and a determination to meet all needs, the place could be in danger of becoming a jack of all trades, but its current level of success in doubling pupil numbers in six years is due, they say, to 'painstaking and careful design' and they are enormously proud of their 'very real and rapid progress.'

Pastoral Care and Discipline: According to one parent, the pastoral care here is really good – 'can't plug it enough.' Tutorial system, tutors change yearly, no more than twenty tutees to each. Discipline is described as 'sensible' – exclusion for violence and selling drugs, possibly also for taking drugs 'depending on what it is'. The school reserves the right to search boarders' rooms and to test for drugs and alcohol – and does. Bullies are confronted head on and the bully box, where notes, either signed or not, can be deposited for scrutiny by the head or his deputy, is rarely used. Charming 'leavers' letter' inviting any former pupil (until they 'leave university, or their 21st birthday, whichever is the later') to contact the college or Mr Martin – reverse charge – at any time – if they have got into a scrape and need help or (free) legal advice. (A GSG first). 'One or two take up the offer,' says Mr Jandrell.

Houseparents occasionally express concern that individual facilities are so good that pupils, particularly senior (Chinese) boys are loath to leave their bed/study rooms and join in communal activities. No Saturday school, but full range of activities on offer during weekends, trips to Whitby, the latest cinema preview. After their first term sixth formers can nip into York or Leeds on a Saturday night but must meet the pick up by 10pm at the local station (or be in by 10.30 if they miss the train).

Pupils and Parents: No longer so fiercely middle class, lots of first time buyers, pupils come to board from all over – Scotland, Wales as well as East Anglia and locally on daily basis. Expect a mass of regional accents, as well as 'real foreigners' from abroad – Chinese, Germans, Russians, Scandinavians et al, most of whom come via educational agents or the internet, with a number just coming for the sixth form. Eight buses collect day pupils from all over Yorkshire (not cheap – one parent said it was cheaper to call a cab), buses collect from local station. Parents talk of 'exponential growth' at the school with a mix of pride and delight at being part of that success and the improved facilities, and some regret at both the loss of the small-time old school and the change in student profile.

Entrance: Either via Chapter House but generally aged 11, As and Bs at GCSE for potential A level candidates at sixth form. External candidates come from other independents, local state schools or out of the area. Pupils below year 10 accepted at any time during the school year 'if places available'. The school promotes itself heavily locally, nationally and internationally. There are regular pop-outs from *Good Housekeeping, Horse & Hound* and the like. Informative CD which plays in Chinese Simplified + Traditional, English, German, Japanese and Russian. The heaviest prospectus bundle that we have ever encountered, though fear not, it is fairly repetitive.

Entry to The Faculty is four C grade GCSEs. More a matter of state of mind and wallet than qualifications.

Exit: Most, who want to go to university, go to the university of their choice – these tend to be Edinburgh, Durham, Liverpool, London and Nottingham, with a steady four or five a year to Oxbridge.

Money Matters: Provost Brian Martin FCMI, FFA, FinstD, Executive Trustee of the QE Charitable Foundation hasn't lost his Midas touch. A true businessman, he masterminds the marketing of the school and drives the development of the site. The school is well underpinned financially but quite expensive and 'you pay for absolutely everything,' say parents. Countered a little by masses of scholarships, oodles of awards, 30 per cent corporate body awards (boarding fees only), rebate if you move to QE from another independent school; 20 per cent discount for Services, diplomats and professional bodies. Add to that list sports, art and music scholarships and many, many more – including a Karen Dixon scholarship for equestrians. 'You can also pay by Barclaycard or Amex' but it costs extra to spread the payment over several months. Very streetwise management and 'all awards granted will be repayable in full, if the school fees bill is not paid 7 days prior to the commencement of each term, and, or, if a pupil does not complete their education with us for any reason, regardless of commencement age, until the completion of the end of Year 13'... etc etc. Read the small print. Carefully.

Remarks: QE has come a long way, not just in its facilities but also in its academic provision, and is quietly and deservedly gaining more respect amongst its competitors.

Queen Margaret's School

Escrick Park, York, North Yorkshire, YO19 6EU

• Pupils: 310 girls; more than 85 per cent are boarders. • Ages: 11-18
• Size of sixth form: 120 • C of E • Fees: Day £15,456; Boarding £24,393 pa • Independent

Tel: 01904 728 261
Fax: 01904 728 150
Email: enquiries@queenmargarets.com
Website: www.queenmargarets.com

Headmaster: Since 2009, Dr Paul Silverwood MSc PhD (late thirties). Educated at Queen Elizabeth Grammar School, Wakefield and read Natural Sciences at Cambridge followed by a PhD in Nuclear Chemistry at Manchester. Initially worked in industry but then landed a teaching post at North London Collegiate School, followed by head of chemistry at St Edward's School, Oxford. Prior to this appointment he was assistant head and director of studies at Benenden. Married to Rebecca and has two young daughters.

Academic matters: Although entry is not particularly selective, academic success matters but not too much of a hothouse atmosphere. Fine GCSE results: 70 per cent plus A*/A, the rest B or C. At A level, French, maths, chemistry, art, history, biology and history of art popular, but no weaknesses. Overall performance very good – 93 per cent plus at A*–B in 2010. Special needs department (one full, two part time), and one teacher for EFL.

Games, Options, the Arts: Lots of healthy outdoor life, a flag-bearing sports department with games keenly played in glorious surroundings and stunning facilities: nine-hole golf course, lacrosse (long journeys for fixtures), hockey (floodlit all-weather pitch), two swimming pools (one indoor, one outdoor), sports hall, tennis courts etc – hard to find something they don't have. Riding popular (private riding school on campus); some girls bring ponies, school keeps 15. Good art, but not an 'arty' school. Home economics for all. Strong choral music, and lots of drama in wonderful theatre. Stunning modern chapel, Catholics go to nearby Thicket Priory for Mass. Extra-curricular activities too numerous to mention but include clay pigeon shooting, driving remote control cars and braving climbing walls.

Background and Atmosphere: Founded in Scarborough in 1901, moved to this fine Palladian house (by John Carr), with later 'rustic timber' purpose-built classrooms in 1949. Lovely setting in 60 plus acres of parkland (more leased from nearby estate). Sweeping drive, glorious on approach with fields as far as the eye can see. School has a large yet tight and cohesive campus with a number of Victorian additions, clever conversions; most recent are the award-winning centenary theatre and chapel and indoor swimming pool. Superb library – wood panelling everywhere, open fire, huge windows looking out on to lawns – but not too precious to be used; the range of books is impressive. Circular dining hall (once an indoor lunging school), with somewhat noisy acoustics. Food much improved in recent years, say parents and girls, with school rarities such as a cappuccino machine and balsamic vinegar; younger girls envious of the privilege of pain au chocolat delivered to sixth form houses for breakfast, all very civilised.

Feels more traditional and structured than some of its Yorkshire competitors (more focused?) but manages to be relaxed and remarkably civilised at the same time. Welcoming, homey boarding house for 11-year-olds with bedtime hot chocolate around the Aga. Girls live in year-groups all the way through (though keeping the same tutor for two years); 'prevents them from growing up too fast', observed one pleased parent, though other views are possible. School claims the strong vertical house system and house supper nights on Fridays, encourage girls of different ages to mix. Year 5 have had the luxury of a new custom-built boarding house named after old girl, Winifred Holtby; lower sixth boarders are housed nearby and enjoy the special privilege of being able to sit and walk on the Cloisters lawn – they do because they can. Upper sixth form have increased independence in attractively converted cottages on site; Head Girl has the first pick of houses; all have large kitchens 'great for entertaining' and communal sitting rooms; cottage life has the feel of a college campus.

Girls are kept 'pretty busy' all the time – new girls are monitored to check they aren't overdoing it and taking on too much in the early days. Uniform is an attractive tartan and charcoal; own clothes worn after tea – don't provide anything that you wouldn't want boil-washed. Smart dress code rather than uniform for sixth form, jackets required.

Pastoral Care and Discipline: The pace of life in this attractive rural idyll (and you don't get more rural than N. Yorks) is inevitably slow and there is a noticeable air of protectiveness towards the girls. 'There are no silly rules,' say parents and girls but it is by no means light on discipline. 'We are pretty old fashioned about smoking and drinking' – though senior girls do have their own club serving limited quantities of alcohol. Apart from school, there's not a great deal to do around here so a trip to the village shop is an exciting treat – a shock for girls with serious shopping habits. Sixth formers can go into York during free time on Wednesdays and Saturdays; they are usually careful not to abuse this freedom.

Pupils and Parents: Friendly pupils, less touched perhaps by the world than some of their contemporaries (many parents will not complain about this), enjoying the many benefits of living and learning in such a lovely environment. Parents mainly upper and middle class: landowners, farmers, professionals, a small Hong Kong contingent, many from Scotland ('it's the first real boarding school you hit driving south'), Cumbria, East Anglia, and of course Yorkshire. OGs include Winifred Holtby (author), Ann Jellicoe (playwright), Sarah Connolly (Opera Singer), Mrs Justice Eleanor King, High Court Judge.

Entrance: Own exam at 11, 12 and 13. Additional intake into sixth form (minimum eight GCSEs, with at least two As and three Bs including English language, maths, a modern language and a science).

Exit: Virtually all go on to higher education, northern universities remain popular but girls do go nationwide. Three or four a year to Oxbridge. A few leave for co-ed sixth forms, e.g. Rugby.

Money Matters: Scholarships at 11, 12, 13 and sixth form; Academic, art, dance, drama, music and sport scholarships. Some bursaries.

Remarks: Ex-posh girls' boarding school shifting up a gear over the last few years into the top rank, academically and socially. A boyfriend at Harrow is apparently de rigeur (or at the very least the name of someone's brother's best friend's cousin you can email) – but beyond that the girls have aspirations of higher things and expectations of self and others are high. Confident yet not brash in any way, girls are fiercely loyal, hardworking and committed, and the school earns many approving noises from parents as well as envious glances over the wall from its competitors, with good reason. A hugely attractive and successful school, where the individual girl matters.

Queen Mary's School

Linked to Queen Mary's Prep School in the Junior section

Baldersby Park, Topcliffe, Thirsk, North Yorkshire, YO7 3BZ

• Pupils: 244 girls; 55 boarders, mostly weekly, a dozen or so stay at weekends, plus flexi-boarding • Ages: 3-16 • C of E (Woodard school) • Fees: Day £5,640-£13,515; Boarding £16,020-£17,835 pa • Independent

Tel: 01845 575 000
Fax: 01845 575 001
Email: v.robeson@queenmarys.org
Website: www.queenmarys.org

Headmaster: Since 2003, Mr Robert McKenzie Johnston MA (Cantab) (fifties), known as Mr MJ (as in emjay). Previously joint head with his wife Kate at Hanford, he was educated at Rugby, read economics at Cambridge, and taught at Shrivenham. No PGCE, grandfather's rights. In a former life he was Lt Col in the Queen's Royal Lancers, though he no longer uses the title and can't believe how lucky he is to be at Queen Mary's. The MJs live in the house, he teaches a number of maths classes each week, and his wife Kate, an occupational therapist, assists in the nursery, 'such fun, a perpetual three-year-old's birthday party'. The MJs' daughters come and go, living in the school when they are at home. With so few full-time boarders, the MJs treat the weekending girls as an extended family, looking like a von Trapp family day out as they lead an ever-increasing number of girls on 'jolly trips all over the place.' As they work every weekend they take Wednesdays off and go hunting locally. Twiggy is a much-loved lurcher, often amongst the children. Ebullient, charming and immensely dedicated, Mr MJ believes he works at 'the most comprehensive school in the country,' a reference to the range and scope of both pupils and parents.

Academic matters: No sixth form and therefore no A level stream though some girls are venturing into AS levels a year early. This is a very mixed ability school and all take English, maths and the sciences, nearly all take French as well; French starts early. French email exchange with school set up by previous French assistante. 'It is good because you can practise your grammar. It makes it a lot easier in exams!' seems to be the general opinion of the pupils. Excellent showing across the board at GCSE, with a pleasing number of As and A*s. Classics on offer at 11 and the classics-teaching chaplain has enthused the girls and some are now learning Greek. German results consistently good and the humanities well represented.

Streaming and setting, tiny classes. Good and sensitive dyslexia help. Buzzy library with sagbags. Classrooms in the main building and converted outhouses, plus attractive new build for tinies. Science department boasts a greenhouse and freshwater pond for hands-on experience. A goodly supply of computers throughout, plus dedicated IT rooms, many of the girls also have their own laptops; internet OK, but girls not allowed to use chatrooms. Senior girls do coursework online. Tinies have computers too and good basic three Rs in the lower school. Thirty-five staff on hand plus 12 part-timers. School never closes and girls can be found wandering around in the Easter holidays having been 'doing extra workshops' with dedicated staff, who never seem to take holidays either.

Games, Options, the Arts: Music is very important and the place hums with junior and senior choirs and delicious concerts open to the general public as well as for inmates; impressive for a school of this size. Chapel choristers wear much-coveted green sweatshirts and give regular performances both home and away. Stunning art in the attics including creative textiles and ceramics, sewing machines in the DT room. Home grown art all over the place. Drama good and popular, cooking timetabled and enjoyed by all.

Trad sports, with lacrosse, athletics and tennis teams all doing well, own tennis courts and all-weather pitches. Superb equestrian facilities, children can and do bring their own ponies and ride daily, girls enjoy mucking in – and out – in the stables at weekends, after lessons and occasionally before breakfast. Outdoor manege of Olympian size, as well as rides across the local landowner's fields, Mr MJ in constant negotiation with his neighbours to increase riders' scope, cross country course on site. Tadcaster polo club is nearby and looks like becoming the next horsy activity. Small indoor swimming pool and the adjacent River Swale is popular for canoeing and the occasional swim (hardy girls up north). Climbing frames. Superb selection of expeditions for all, plus D of E.

Background and Atmosphere: Baldersby Park is a grand Palladian mansion (Colen Campbell 1721, Jacobethanised following a fire in 1902) and was converted into residential flats in a previous existence so the girls have a rash of good sized dorms with private bathrooms, all incredibly tidy and well-organised and with great views all round, mostly well-furnished with just a few old Victorian lunatic asylum beds remaining. Glorious main hall used for daily service, with the girls sitting on the carpet, Mr MJ sitting in front of the stairs, the choir ranged behind him in serried ranks. When not being used for formal occasions, girls can be seen walking the trapeze from balcony to balcony high above the main hall, wisely harnessed; it's not compulsory but, as with most things here, girls encouraged to 'have a go'. School uniform evolves over the years with girls graduating from beige to green jerseys and royal hunting Stewart tartan kilts, slight pressure currently to change the uniform but neither the MJs nor the girls can see the point. School food is good quality wholesome home cooking and girls generally approve though 'would enjoy a visit from Jamie Oliver' to liven things up.

Staff and girls are happy with the relaxed atmosphere – like an extended family – all ages mix – with a mass of sisterly teasing. Younger girls like to play and build dens in the woods, 'benign supervision' allowing a sense of freedom with a nod to health and safety. Charming chapel, a peaceful haven for all, school has its own chaplain; Mr MJ is keen that religion should be 'part of the school routine' but not rammed down the throat. The early assumption of seniority (at 16 rather than 18) gives girls confidence and maturity – a great balance with the younger girls happily staying young and the older girls demonstrating early maturity and grace. All pupils have to play some part in keeping the school neat, clean and tidy.

Pastoral Care and Discipline: Like home. No petty rules and others which are bendable but there is an underlying sense of organisation. 'Suspension,' says Mr MJ, 'is a sign of failure on the part of the school and not the pupil.'

Parents' requests granted when reasonable. Not a sophisticated place, no obvious sin, just an occasional ticking off for a girl wearing make-up but it's few and far between and there's an acknowledgement that 'girls like to rebel – and better make-up than vodka.'

Pupils and Parents: Local as opposed to county school, combination of first time buyers, local farmers, landowners and professionals – 'not as *Tatler* and *Vogue* as some of its competitors.' Relaxed 7.30am drop off time for working parents. Quite a lot of army families – Catterick is just up the road – some of whom pop their daughters in the school 'whilst they are based in Yorkshire' and are so pleased with the place that they leave their daughters there, younger sisters often joining them, when they are posted elsewhere. Plenty of flexi-boarding, with some full-time boarders living closer than some of the day girls, ditto the flexi-boarders, 'girls come to escape'. If girls regularly stay three nights a week they get their own permanent space; no charge for extra meals, only for bed. Boarding mainly from 11, and day girls often opt to stay at least on a weekly basis. Parents and pupils can use school facilities in the holidays. No real overseas presence, one or two ex-pats, but boarding is now pretty full and the school has no wish to change its nature by overloading. Parents run a website and are delighted to answer any queries.

Entrance: At any time, middle of term if needed. At all ages. Entry test but, places permitting, only those with special needs beyond the school's capability are liable to be turned away.

Exit: At all ages. Some take common entrance at 11, and a small number at 13. Girls have previously mainly gone to Queen Margaret's Eskrick, with one or two to Tudor Hall, Heathfield or co-eds, Uppingham, Millfield, Rugby. Senior girls go on to do A levels at Ampleforth, St Aidan's, Ripon Grammar, Oundle, Queen Margaret's Eskrick, St Peter's, Uppingham etc. etc. Good collection of scholarships, music predominates, plus academic and sports.

Money Matters: Not a rich school and not endowed, though has benefited recently from generous donations. Scholarships for academics, music and art plus bursaries for clergy daughters, sisters and Services discount.

Remarks: Useful, popular, small, girls' – predominantly weekly – boarding school without a sixth form. Fierce competition locally but this school has no intention of being 'the one to fall off the edge' and the recent increase in numbers would suggest the place in is safe hands. A home from home, with muddy wellies on the doorstep, smiling cheery girls and a predominance of four-wheeled drives in the car park, it provides a good solid education focusing on creating girls with a 'have a go' mentality. It's possibly too cosy for those at the sharp end – but exactly what many need and the girls say they 'wouldn't change a thing.'

Queen Victoria School

Dunblane, Perthshire, Dunblane, Perthshire, FK15 0JY

- Pupils: 270; 140 girls, 130 boys – all children of Services personnel
- Ages: 10-18 • Church of Scotland • Independent

Tel: 01786 822288
Fax: 0131 310 2926
Email: enquiries@qvs.org.uk
Website: www.qvs.org.uk

Head: Since 2007, Mrs Wendy Bellars MA PGCE (late forties), born and educated in Glasgow. With an English mother and Scottish father, holidays with relatives in Somerset and Thurso were the norm so that it was only when she moved to England (for work) and north Wales (to live) in 1988 that the real cultural differences dawned on her.

Mrs Bellars taught English in Renfrew High School for two years then moved to Gordonstoun. Since then she has taught in virtually every type of school, day, boarding, independent, state, mixed and single sex (both girls and boys) in a variety of roles including a spell as head of St Leonard's in Fife when it was undergoing cataclysmic change and as a housemistress at Cheltenham Ladies College. She returned to Scotland in 2004/5 and worked for the Open University, developing the then new-to-Scotland OU PGCE etc.

She has been involved with ATC and CCF cadets and held a ten-year Volunteer Reserve Commission in the Royal Air Force. Theatre, reading and walking two large pupil-friendly dogs – sweeping long-skirted with an elegant greyhound reminiscent of nineteenth century paintings – occupy her leisure. As an enthusiast for both playing and listening to music, one of her dreams for the school is to extend its fantastic tradition in military music to a wider field and to establish a full orchestra. She and QV seem to be on duck and water terms: she exudes deep and knowledgeable concern about the minutest aspect of school life bringing a wealth of relevant and well-balanced experience.

Academic matters: A very firmly Scottish school using only the Scottish curriculum. Services children often find themselves moving from school to school – the known record is eleven and the average four or five – so P7 (approximately half way between top primary and first year secondary in English terms) – is used to assess and consolidate. The very occasional pupil may have to repeat a year at this stage. After the entry year spent consolidating in three streams (red, green and blue) carefully not labelled by ability, pupils are setted (by ability) for maths, English and sciences. Curriculum is trad but flexible, classes not more than 20. German and/or French compulsory to Standard grade, Spanish only as a club so far. Advanced Highers, despite small numbers, achieved with help from Dunblane High School. Down to earth labs (new ones on the way as part of a complete classroom rebuild planned by the MoD for the middle term future) and lots of computers in class and available in houses at night, including impressive Macs for the enterprising art department (better for photography and image manipulation).

Learning support flexible and pupils say 'really supportive', with in-class help, withdrawal, extra tuition in groups or one-to-one etc as appropriate. Good rapport between SEN and teachers. School prides itself on 'holistic' education. Results pretty good – though wholly MoD funded, QV competes and compares with independent rather than state schools in style (both academic and pastoral).

Games, Options, the Arts: Games staff assert proudly that as a small school QV 'punches above its weight' in both girls and boys sports. Football, rugby, hockey, netball and athletics strong: tennis less so. Spacious terraced pitches, huge multi-purpose sports hall with free access to smashing fitness training for older pupils and ancient but serviceable swimming pool often on loan to neighbouring primaries. Military music is king of the activities curriculum. The pipe band has played for every home rugby international since 1922 until last year's ban on health and safety grounds! QV pipes, drums and dancers (PDD) are renowned throughout Scotland and perform in the Edinburgh military tattoo and all over the world. Every pupil must learn one PDD skill. Marching is also compulsory and during our visit pupils joining after S2 (Year 10) were doing daily catch up marching practice. The head girl reckoned that her brother's role of drum major was as iconic as her own. Pupils said that almost everyone enjoyed and felt a sense of pride in the military identity the school gives them. Masses of tours abroad, mainly with band but also recently to Malawi on a school building project. Pupils choose own charities and recently raised £1,700 for Help for Heroes as well as doing a sponsored walk to help themselves (the school development fund). There are about 80 clubs in all ranging from skiing to jewellery making and some participation is compulsory.

CCF plays a strong part with units for all three forces with myriad activities extending into holiday time and D of E is much in evidence. The friendly dogginess of school, spearheaded by Mrs Bellars' Dash and Ginger, is highlighted by girls doing D of E service at a stray dogs' home and completed by Molly the IT department dog.

Background and Atmosphere: With a mission 'to provide stable and uninterrupted education for the children of Scottish service personnel' QV has to balance an imposing site steeped in military history with the need for a 'home from home' environment for children with parents on inaccessible active service. Founded by public subscription as a memorial to Scots who fell in the South African wars, the school has been co-ed since 1996. The magnificent chapel is dedicated to Queen Victoria and its splendour, enhanced by modern audiovisual equipment and comfy seats, typifies emphasis placed on service to Queen and country. Pupils confirmed that this gives most of them a sense of purpose and identity. The school chaplain cares for all denominations though children can go to Dunblane for mass etc.

The granite cliff of a main building, opened by Edward VII in 1908 is maintained, like everything else on site, by the MoD – hence the brilliantly polished but battered floors, doors etc. Public gifts from, for example the MacRobert Trust, have provided a smashing and recently refurbished, up to date and very fully used library, plus (much earlier) pool, and sports hall. The accretion of buildings each in the style of the current MoD (War Office) has made a hotch potch of buildings over the years but the more recent boarding accommodation is well thought out and comfortable. A particularly telling touch in Trenchard (junior house) – the common room with clocks showing the time in Afghanistan and Iraq. Older pupils volunteer to spend a term or so in Trenchard to act as mentors for new arrivals.

The development fund has taken over from the centenary appeal. Its planned new theatre/auditorium had to be abandoned because MoD requirements were escalating the expense. Priority is now a major upgrade of the existing theatre, still hidden under wraps/tin hats.

The san, shiny with new pastel paint and a 'chill out area' complete with relaxation tapes, candles and every kind of health information leaflet, retains its 'hospital ward' since QV, unlike other boarding schools, cannot ship pupils home at the first sign of an epidemic. Efficient looking bedsteads sport teddies and pretty bedspreads. Someone was in for a bit of space and motherly care on the day we visited.

One of the few schools where pupils really do look smart and seem to enjoy it! Formal dress is real military red, high collared jackets, with hunting Stewart kilts and Lovat tweed for everyday, plus some fantastic ceremonial gear – nylon bearskins and the like! MoD supplies, so cost not a problem.

Food looks good; no one complained though not all were entirely complimentary.

Pastoral Care and Discipline: This is full boarding, seven days a week for all, though weekend leave is allowed except for parade days. Sixteen and over can visit cinemas etc in relatively sleepy Dunblane. Not many real problems bar the occasional smoker and, 'surprisingly', no drugs. Very structured disciplinary system including categories of offences, a behaviour management group and punishments such as litter picking days or clearing tables. Strong PSE and careful discussion of problems. Medical services much involved here. Observable loving attention to the real underlying needs of children away from home underpins pastoral care. Impressive! Pupils claimed to like the training of a military style discipline ('teaches you how to manage your things') but evidently also enjoyed a bit of teenage squalor in their bedrooms without undue interference.

Pupils and Parents: By definition, parents are serving members of Scottish Forces or are/have been stationed in Scotland (e.g. Ghurkas in Glasgow). Founded for NCOs, but officers' children are eligible: so a real mixed bag. Oddly the MoD don't fund a past pupils' database but voluntary help is starting this – with a huge reservoir of Scottish history to tap! Strong parent network and generations of same families. Liaison group welcomes new families and supports children. No guardian system needed because most have relatives or close colleagues ready to help.

Entrance: Applications deadline 15th January and admissions board sits in Feb/March. School is full but tries to keep a few places for emergency postings/ compassionate need etc. School's purpose is to take orphans and needy (in that order) and parents meet the high powered but 'not too scary' admissions panel, while children are assessed for academic and emotional suitability. Mrs Bellars wonders if info on the school actually reaches those who most need it.

Exit: Increasing percentage to university (now about 50 per cent) though still low in view of its academic record. A few go straight into the Services. Others to local colleges or nursing. Most have a gap year. No notice required since MoD posts are instantaneous.

Money Matters: No fees and all uniform and books provided (MoD) but 'parental contribution' of £1,050 pa expected (to cover cost of travel, activities etc). There is a benevolent fund for 'hardship cases'.

Remarks: Thriving. An amazing opportunity for those who qualify!

Queen's College (Taunton)

Linked to Queens College Junior School in the Junior section

Trull Road, Taunton, Somerset, TA1 4QS

• Pupils: 770 boys and girls (150 boarders, 585 day). • Ages: 11-18 • Size of sixth form: 155 (65 boarders). • Methodist foundation • Fees: Day £11,940-£14,100; Boarding £18,150-£22,305 pa • Independent

Tel: 01823 272 559
Fax: 01823 338 430
Email: contact@queenscollege.org.uk
Website: www.queenscollege.org.uk

Head: Since 2001, Mr Christopher J Alcock BSc FRSG (late forties). Graduate of Durham University (geography and anthropology). Taught at Stamford School where he was boarding housemaster and rugby coach before going on to be deputy head at St Edward's, Witley. Friendly, approachable, amusing and deeply committed to his charges. Not a pin-striped suited, jargon-spouting managerial head but a get-in-among-the-troops-and-love-them head. Study is full of 'significant' photographs. He singled out one in particular: a boy who had written to thank him for his time at Queen's. 'No one else would take me but you did and now I'm at university.' 'Lowly grades but he really fought for them' added the head, 'that's what I delight in. Literally and metaphorically the winning pass in a 4th XV match is as important as anything in the 1st XV.' That's not empty rhetoric, he really believes it. Always looking out for opportunities to praise and encourage all round efforts. Waxes lyrical about holistic all round education. His monthly letters to parents are not couched in flowery prose but, for the most part, lists of individual achievements. Parents love that. 'If I had a son of school age,' said a successful prep school head, 'I would send him to Alcock, whatever the distance.' There is evidence that others are doing just that. Numbers have increased by over 100 since his arrival. Wife, Linda, teaches French in the Junior School and they have two sons at Queen's.

Academic matters: 'What I really love about Queen's,' a mother told us, 'is that they go for potential rather than force-feeding. If your child is A grade material, that's what he will achieve; if he's D grade, he won't be made to feel stupid. He'll be congratulated on his achievement and made to feel good about it.' GCSE results are sound with good performances from the brighter pupils and gutsy performances from the less able. Average pass rate 95 per cent. There are 23 subjects to choose from at A level. 100 per cent pass rate over the last three years. But this is not a school overly bothered with statistics. Get back to good teaching and potential. Wonderful support from the SEN department with super-caring staff. The designated area is presided over by a brilliant lady who combines compassion with common sense and expertise. Careful screening and individual follow up for the 10 per cent who are dyslexic. Help and encouragement for those with ADHD. 'They often make good rock climbers or swimmers. The important thing is to find something which will engage their interest.' Not just a learning support area, an overall support area. 'My daughter's not bad at maths but she goes for individual help because it increases her confidence.' 'I love coming here,' said a bright and engaging girl, 'it's a comfort zone.'

The school has invested in computers in a big way and pupils are very proud of their proliferation. They are skilfully woven into lessons and there is much clever use of interactive white boards. Classrooms are functional with a good but not outstanding library. Very helpful librarian, though. There are no lessons on Saturday mornings and it isn't just the inspectors who have noted an improvement in academics since that decision was taken. 'It's a question of charging batteries,' says the head. 'They really do arrive fresher on Monday mornings after a break.' No lessons does not mean that nothing happens. Three hour rehearsals for plays, expeditions out into the country, hobbies and activities abound.

Games, Options, the Arts: Sport is compulsory up to year 10 but most continue beyond that because this is not just a 1st and 2nd team school. Everyone has a chance to play in a team – there are up to four teams in each sport. Beautiful cricket and rugby grounds and masses of floodlit, all-weather pitches and tennis courts. Good swimming pool with notable successes (Matt Clay, near Olympic swimmer, is an old boy) and shoals of pupils representing the county and beyond. National and international successes at rugby, cricket, cycling and fencing. Talented games players thrive; less talented have a go and love it. 'Everyone finds an activity they can enjoy,' said a charming girl who had experienced six schools. Some 50 per cent of the pupils play a musical instrument and the facilities are encouraging with bright airy practice rooms in the theatre complex. When we were there, pupils were queuing up to practise (sic). Bags of opportunities for playing in orchestras and ensembles and indulging in music of all kinds.

Large and well equipped theatre doubles up as an assembly hall and chapel. Drama of all kinds is very popular with pupils and parents and eagerly looked forward to. School reviews have been known to include a memorable performance on the spoons by the head and the four notes he can play on the sax. 'Was it as many as four?' asked a boy. Wonderful and sympathetically designed new art school overlooks the cricket pitch (how suitable it should have been opened by Jack Russell) and is full of exciting work. Every year there is an arts festival where artists visit and exhibit, evidence of which can be found in the beautiful stag and imposing giraffe which guard the buildings to the front. Much emphasis is placed on inculcating leadership (the head does not have a senior management team; instead he has a leadership group. A subtle and genuine difference). Lots of D of E with rock climbing and expeditions to say nothing of community service. The cross-curricular approach encourages self-esteem and confidence as well as a strong sense of community

Background and Atmosphere: Founded in 1843, the first independent school in Taunton, Queen's is one of nine schools owned by the Methodist Church. The main building, fine educational gothic, is impressive without being threatening and as you look at it you're surprised you haven't approached it by a long tree-lined drive. Instead you slip in off a pleasant suburb. New buildings crowd around the back, and they do crowd, before giving way to acres of beautifully mown playing fields. 'This is a Christian name school,' said the head groundsman – groundsmen are always a useful indicator of school's morale. 'It's very, very friendly.'

Indeed that is the over-riding atmosphere of the school. The pupils we met were marvellously forthcoming and fun and clearly used to chatting with alleged adults. 'We're suave, sophisticated bachelors,' said one boy. The last word is probably true; the other two, mercifully, not. In more measured tones, the inspectors commented on the pupils as 'open, tolerant, friendly and self disciplined.' Boarding houses have been, and are being, refurbished and are brightly coloured and comfortable. We were interested to see pin ups of handsome RC priests in a girls' house. Lovely, ebullient house staff, including matrons who care.

The sixth form centre is 'a school within a school' housed in its own building with restricted access to ensure greater privacy. There is an impressive learning resource centre with banks of computers and shelves of books. Downstairs are good chilling out facilities, including television and music systems, and a snack bar. Boys and girls were very enthusiastic about it and seemed to enjoy the monthly meetings of the Sixth Form Society when a variety of guest speakers come and entertain and there is opportunity for discussion. It certainly acts as a good bridge between school and university.

Pastoral Care and Discipline: Thanks to the excellent Parents' Handbook which tells them everything they need to know, and thanks to the very detailed but not overly fussy school rules, clear courts are laid out within which pupils know where they stand and are the happier for it. Reins are held lightly but never dropped. Prefects are selected through sixth form ballot and consultation with staff. There is ongoing training with opportunities to discuss their responsibilities and any problems they may encounter. Parents we spoke to described the pastoral care as 'brilliant.'

The house system is the spring of tutoring and sets the tone. Each pupil is assigned a tutor with whom they have regular meetings. There are clear guidelines on drugs (zero tolerance) and bullying is swiftly confronted, though 'there is very little of that.' There is a calm, peaceful atmosphere permeating the busy bustling, an indication that pupils are happy, know where they stand and appreciate the genuine interest shown in them. All schools are very fond of trumpeting 'family atmosphere/values and a sense of community.' It isn't always easy to detect that on a visit. At Queen's those qualities are obvious.

Pupils and Parents: Parents come from a cross section of society, a number making considerable financial sacrifices to send their children. Boarders are drawn from the Services, particularly the Navy and the Marines; others from abroad. A feature of the school is the loyalty and involvement of parents.

Entrance: Seventy per cent come from the prep school. Others come from local prep schools and a few from state schools. Entrance requirements are broad and generous. Pupils at 11, 12 and 13 sit school's entrance papers in English, maths and verbal reasoning or Common Entrance. 'I find it very hard to refuse anyone,' said the head, 'though, very occasionally, I am forced to conclude this is not the right school for an applicant.'

Exit: Regular handful to Oxbridge, otherwise to a wide range of universities. Difficult to detect any pattern in courses read but as wide a range as you would expect from such a school.

Money Matters: Scholarships for the usual things and discounts offered to Service parents.

Remarks: Not a swaggering school; not a showing off school. Nor does the apparent happiness disguise anything. It enlivens and invigorates a wholly unpretentious school.

Queen's College London

Linked to Queens College Prep School in the Junior section

43-49 Harley Street, London, W1G 8BT

• Pupils: 340 girls, all day • Ages: 11-18 • Size of sixth form: 90 • C of E
• Fees: £14,475 pa • Independent

Tel: 020 7291 7000
Fax: 020 7291 7090
Email: admissions@qcl.org.uk
Website: www.qcl.org.uk

Principal: Since 2009, Dr Frances Ramsey MA DPhil (Oxon) (forties). Completed doctorate in medieval history before starting teaching. Taught at Westminster School where she was head of history and director of studies. Discovered the importance of the pastoral side when she became Master of the Queen's Scholars. Cerebral and professional, she is determined to lead the school onwards and upwards. Says it has the same feel and ethos as Westminster and parents and staff feel familiar. All the latter have full lives beyond day to day teaching, which she thinks is important. Very much likes the all girl set up 'no distraction in the classroom'. Initially some uncertainty amongst parents over the direction the new Principal would take: 'The school has a certain quirkiness and it is important that this is not ironed out'. However prospective parents are impressed with 'the buzz of the school and the direction it is going in'. Mixed reactions from current parents to the introduction of uniform for Years 7 to 9, mainly because don't want general informality of the school to change. But, as Dr Ramsey is a firm believer in 'evolution not revolution', we don't feel they need to worry. She misses having the time to teach but makes sure that she is as visible as possible, taking assembly twice a week, having coffee/tea meetings with the senior girls and congratulating younger ones who bring her their 'Show Principal' reward cards. Is also seen at all school performances. As she says, one of the most difficult things, when taking over, is getting to know all the parents of 300 girls but she does interview all those of new applicants and the school maintains a continuous open door policy. (Parents tell us that they can go in and go anywhere any time they like). So she is not inaccessible. Married to an Oxford academic, with two young children in central London schools. We think that Queen's College is lucky to have her.

Academic matters: Excellent results across the board, with a curriculum that covers a broad range of subjects and is as strong on the creative side as the academic. Parents say 'well structured but girls don't feel it is rigid and therefore thrive on it'. 'Art is taken as seriously as maths'. Dr Ramsey has upped the academic ante, increasing the number of subjects taken as IGCSE and bringing in triple science for the top set. She says, despite the school not being super selective, the girls are all able and ambitious. Parents say the school 'embraces a girl's whole brain'; is 'sympathetic, understanding and supportive'. All agree that the school is not a hothouse, that the atmosphere is relaxed, yet it manages to bring out the potential in all girls, academic or artistic. Teachers praised for their dedication and support. The deputy head, one of the good proportion of males on the staff, apparently 'always goes the extra mile and always listens to parents'. Appears to cater well for different types of children guiding them towards opportunities. No EFL tuition but will give support for EAL if necessary. Small classes in the sixth form (average eight), are, a parent said 'the jewel in the crown'. A huge range of subjects available to be studied, including several languages. Maths, English literature, history and biology seem the most popular. Normal pass rate 100 per cent; in 2010 78 per cent were A*, A and B grades.

Popular, fully trained and experienced SENCo two days a week. Can cope with the milder end of the spectrum. All children assessed in Year 7 and extra tuition given where necessary. One-to-one charged as extra. Senior mistress says head of English superb at finding any problems, in fact, all teachers good at spotting and communicating concerns. 'Nobody gets through the net.' Classroom assistants not needed as class sizes small (15–20 in Years 7–11) and varied. Parents kept fully in the picture, communication lines are good.

Games, Options, the Arts: As in many town schools, physical activity an ongoing problem but one they do seem to have cracked here. Recently-appointed head of PE has completely re-organised the system and all girls have at least one sport type session four days a week. Could be gymnastics, in a beautifully re-furbished, fully equipped hall, ballet, seasonal games in Regent's Park, swimming or anything else that demands physical activity. In fact, when we were discussing the school uniform issue, one parent suggested that they didn't really need to bother as 'my daughter seems to wear her sports' kit most days!' Lots of matches played against other schools and the Duke of Edinburgh award is a popular option. Senior girls can go to the Westminster Gym for exercise or pilates and yoga type classes. Very grown-up!

Wonderful pictures on display everywhere. Well equipped art room up in the eaves, (north lit of course), showing coverage of all aspects of the subject. We were fascinated by a huge sculpture made of wire coat hangers. Talented head of art develops ability and encourages imagination as is evidenced by their results. Music from beginner to grade 8. About fifty per cent learn an individual instrument or have voice tuition. Several concerts, formal and informal, and musical ensembles each year, as well as musical theatre productions and opera. Enthusiastic head of drama finds many different ways to stimulate and stretch her students. 2010 will see *The Crucible* being performed in the round. An exciting first. This school is not scared of experiment or innovation.

Clubs abound and take place in the middle of the day as well as at the end. Each day is jam packed with activity. Senior girls even stay late on Fridays for self-defence sessions. There is no excuse for any girl ever to sit twiddling her thumbs. Plenty of outings making use of all London has to offer. Regular trips home and abroad both educational and social. Lots of charitable involvement and fund raising activities.

Background and Atmosphere: Founded in 1848 and given a royal charter in 1853, a pioneer in education for women, this was the first institution in Great Britain to give academic qualifications to girls. Still on its original site in four elegant, well proportioned Georgian houses, internally it has often been altered through the years in order to provide the best modern education possible. Wouldn't those early Victorian students be amazed to see the state of the art glass computer room, 'the goldfish bowl', so cleverly integrated, science and language laboratories beyond their imaginations, the wonderful libraries and the great hall where modern lighting and sound equipment helps to enhance perhaps almost recognizable costume dramas? They would certainly enjoy the more relaxed atmosphere and the idea of learning through discovery rather than rote. Teachers that really care and want to help their pupils to learn and discover in an informal way. There is a happy atmosphere in the school today that gives girls confidence and helps them find their own way to go forward.

Two of the earliest students, Miss Buss and Miss Beale, went on to found the North London Collegiate School and Cheltenham Ladies College, respectively. Katherine Mansfield and Jacqueline du Pre also stand amongst the long list of distinguished old girls as well as, more recently, Daisy Goodwin and Imogen Lloyd Webber. A distinguished tradition and history in the making.

Pastoral Care and Discipline: Dr Ramsey has added a layer of pastoral staff giving, she believes, better co-ordination and consistency. Girls have a year tutor as well as a form tutor, so should always have someone to talk to if necessary and should not slip through the net if difficulties arise. Has also introduced midterm mini reports in every subject, 'a quick reality check' as she calls them, which should help highlight potential academic problems. Apparently, the girls have responded well to this idea. Strong anti-bullying policy. Would not hesitate to exclude an offender.

Pupils and Parents: The usual cosmopolitan London mix of nationalities and backgrounds. About ten per cent don't speak English at home.

Entrance: Mainly at 11+ via the North London Consortium exam. Must also have reference from previous school and be interviewed by the Principal or a senior member of staff. A good percentage from Queen's College Prep, about 30 per cent from local state primaries, the rest from other private preps. Another intake at 16+ subject to GCSE results and letters of recommendation from their previous schools. All prospective entrants at this level will be interviewed by the head of sixth form.

Exit: Mostly after A levels to top universities to study everything from art and design to science subjects. A few each year to Oxbridge and the London colleges, the rest all over. Manchester, Leeds and Nottingham popular in the last couple of years.

Money Matters: Several means-tested bursaries available at 11+ and 16+. Academic, music and art scholarships, for up to twenty-five percent of fees, for both internal and external candidates. Funded by the Old Queen's Bursary Trust Fund. Would hope to always be able to find a way of keeping a pupil in need.

Remarks: A happy, rounded school where girls are encouraged to be individuals in an informal, unstressful environment; where nurturing teachers bring out the best in them and help them to find their own paths; where they develop confidence and a desire to succeed. Where being yourself is respected and really matters.

Queen's Gate School

Linked to Queens Gate Junior School in the Junior section

133 Queen's Gate, Kensington, London, SW7 5LE

• Pupils: 300 girls; all day • Ages: 11-18 • Size of sixth form: 60
• Non-denom • Fees: £14,550 pa • Independent

Tel: 02075 893 587
Fax: 02075 847 691
Email: registrar@queensgate.org.uk
Website: www.queensgate.org.uk

Principal: Since 2006, Mrs Rosalynd Kamaryc BA MSc PGCE (late forties). Born and brought up in Ballymena, Northern Ireland, Mrs Kamaryc won a first in maths at Queens University, Belfast, before sailing seamlessly through schools in the British Isles. Her first teaching post was in Scotland (St Leonards). She then went to London (Forest School), on to Suffolk (Woodbridge School, where she was deputy head and then acting head), from there to Hampshire (Wykeham House School in Fareham, where she was head for ten years), before returning to London as principal of Queen's Gate. Married to an engineer who works for Reuters, she now commutes each day from Guildford, 'I can be home each night by 10.' A keen sportswoman (tennis, hockey and horse riding) she is also highly intelligent, organised and feminine. Her lilting Northern Irish (or is it Scottish?) accent can be hard to keep up with.

Her predecessor Mrs Angela Holyoak, said one parent, ruled the place with a rod of iron for nearly twenty years. Not an easy succession and we heard a number of reports of disciplinary turbulence, with a high turnover of staff, following the change in leadership. School defensive about this and Mrs Kamaryc says she has already met one of her aims, namely the reduction in staff turnover. Whereas Mrs Holyoak, we were told, 'could silence a room on entering it,' Mrs Kamaryc adopts a more gentle, (perhaps modern?) tactic. Extremely approachable, she is respected by her girls but not feared. She teaches maths to the GCSE year (the lowest set as it happens). She also has frequent visits from the girls (they can book an appointment or simply knock on the door of her comfortable and pretty study). It might be because they need the go ahead for a junior disco they've organised (to raise money for one of their many charitable causes you understand) or simply because they want to air a grievance.

Academic matters: Going from strength to strength, reflected in the high number of people who choose to move up from the junior school. Maximum class sizes 26 (A level classes vary between one and 10). Streaming in maths, English and science as well as some streaming in languages. Half-termly tests, girls move up and down. Pupil:staff ratio of 7:1 – impressive.

Fair number of teaching chaps in evidence. Sciences 'strengthening all the time' says principal. The junior school's move down the road has allowed for three more shiny labs in the new building. Three separate sciences taught from 11. Geography, biology and art popular. Languages stronger at GCSE level than at A. French, German, Italian and Spanish offered, all taught by native speakers with masses of hands-on and trips abroad. Ancient Greek as well as Latin. Regular Monday maths clinic. Interesting collection of specialisms: sociology, graphic communication/products and information studies, as well as psychology and philosophy.

Tellies, interactive whiteboards and computers in most classrooms, serious computer suites and wireless network. All learn word processing and do touch-typing in the junior school. Girls screened after entry into senior school. Dedicated SENCo for those who have learning difficulties ('nothing terribly serious' – dyslexia, and mild cases of dyspraxia). Help given (including EFL) as required before and after school, during lunch as well as during some lessons. Gifted and Talented programme.

Games, Options, the Arts: Girls looked quizzically amused when we asked about games. Not that keen perhaps? The gym in the basement looks as if it is used for everything but sport. Mrs Kamaryc is on the case, devising ways of whetting their appetite for exercise, especially the sixth form for whom sport is no longer compulsory. Fitness First membership for the sixth form (they can even go during free periods), trampolining, life saving courses, climbing and kayaking.

Further down the school girls are more enthusiastic about the traditional sports – tennis, rounders and hockey are played in Battersea Park. Swimming happens at the Kensington Sports Centre, fencing offered, 'wish they'd done cricket' said one parent, but it's the basketball team that shines – recently reaching the finals of the All England Championship.

Plenty of enthusiastic noises about art, drama and music, on the other hand. Fantastic roof conversion for art suite, with fabric design, screen printing, CAD-CAM and a clever vinyl cutting machine, lots of real hands-on stuff. Good strong work on show, much of it research based. Good use made of local museums, art galleries and theatres.

Drama vibrant. The girls do everything – play every part and design the sets. Regular end of term house plays in impressive hall. Most take the LAMDA exams in acting and the speaking of verse and prose. Terrific music, chamber orchestra, individual lessons and popular singing; girls join the W11 choir and take part in West End musicals, as well as frequently visiting the West End for opera and musicals. Clubs for almost everything at lunchtime; girls must go to two a week. The range is huge, everything from debating, yoga, aerobics and jewellery making to Japanese and Mandarin. Hot on charity, with regular fund-raising events, and particularly keen on cancer research – sponsored readathons, spellathons and fashion shows.

Background and Atmosphere: Founded in 1891, the school is housed in three large Victorian mansions in South Ken. Civilised and elegant with considerably more room now the junior school has relocated. An extensive refurbishment programme has resulted in music practice rooms, a drama studio, and LAMDA room as well as a comfy sixth form centre complete with plush leather sofas, study, and dining areas. The school spreads into the mews behind and all but one of the rooms have at least two fire exits – some of them about five feet high. New pupils should probably be issued with a map, compass and bits of chalk for orienteering practice in their first few weeks. Two libraries, still not snazzy enough as the last inspection report commented. School says it's on the case – major refurbishment planned. Well-used careers library. Lots of the old features still remain, imposing marble fireplaces, ornate cornices and fire doors make curious companions. Walls filled with photographs, children's work and notice-boards, and a sense of calm prevails.

Girls remarkably well behaved, stand up when the principal enters. Sadly, they no longer curtsey or wear white gloves (haven't for years) but instead are colourfully and casually dressed. No uniform, 'how can you say you encourage individuality when you make them wear the same thing?' is the oft quoted line of the founder of the school. Expressions of individuality do not stretch to facial or body piercing, however. Food excellent. Mrs Kamaryc working her innovative magic here too. Panini – with a choice of meat or vegetarian fillings – introduced at lunch time. More girls opting for school lunch since her arrival but they may bring packed lunches which they eat in their classrooms, otherwise the whole school eats in two sessions in either the white (glammed up since our last visit) or the black (still the grander) dining room.

Pastoral Care and Discipline: Mrs Kamaryc has been busy setting up new 'firm but fair' systems to tackle discipline. Section heads and the director of pastoral care have recently been exercising a policy of zero tolerance. Detentions given for almost everything ('after verbal reminders, order and conduct marks,' school asks us to add). When the girls were coming in for Saturday detention they started to get the message. Section heads will stop girls from dressing inappropriately with the ignominy of being forced to wear a 'granny skirt' instead (we saw one or two skimpily clad unfortunates being taken aside in assembly). On the more nurturing side, two of the sixth form girls are attached to each of the younger forms as 'sisters' – 'often easier to confide in than a member of staff, after all,' said our informant, 'they leave.' We were also told by one of the girls of the unique trusting relationships that are frequently formed between staff and pupils. In a small school that can happen. Not many rules. Three roll calls daily, in the morning, after lunch and before they go home, 'we are in loco parentis'. Tutor system for all (they meet twice a term). Good PSHE system in place, outside counsellor, health adviser, vigilant for anorexia.

Pupils and Parents: We would stick with our previous comment, 'pretty upper class'; from a range of ethnic backgrounds, though principally of Sloane extraction. We were regaled by a number of accounts of 'Camilla's' visit to open the new building. The principal's angle was that the girls just carried on afterwards as if nothing out of the ordinary had happened, 'I suspect a number of them knew her socially.' Pupils, parents and staff all frightfully discreet and unassuming, 'everyone welcome'. Girls are fiercely loyal, delightfully mannered and very pretty. OGs: HRH the Duchess of Cornwall, Redgraves, Sieffs, Guinnesses, Amanda de Souza, Jane Martineau, Nigella Lawson, Lucinda Lambton, Tracey Boyd, Aurelia Cecil, Trinny Woodall and Imogen Poots. The former head of MI5, Eliza Manningham Buller, used to be on the staff.

Entrance: From junior school – at least three quarters of junior girls come on to the senior school – and a huge variety of other schools, confirm entry for the January exams the November before you want to come. Above all priority given to sisters and OGs' children. New arrivals throughout the year, but preferably in September, though pupils who have left and have then been unhappy at their new school often re-join again mid-term. School holds four open days a year for potential parents and it is not unusual to have 800 parents attend. Girls take London day schools' exam for entry at 11 plus interview, assessment and test for entry at other times. For sixth form entry, at least six As at GCSE, essay and interview. Usually over-subscribed, but, because of the volatile nature of London, places do occur.

Exit: Some to Oxbridge (approximately five each year), some take a gap year, otherwise to various universities – Durham and Leeds popular – some to art school. Small leakage after GCSE to (mainly) boarding schools, normally because they have been at Queen's Gate since they were five and want a change.

Money Matters: Four internal scholarships for sixth form entry.

Remarks: Plus ça change. Charming popular school, with a mixed intake, which does jolly well by its girls. Touch of the Miss Jean Brodies. Brings out the best in girls who enjoy the intimacy and security of a small school where they are encouraged to think for themselves. Mrs Kamaryc is breathing fresh life and ideas into the place, guiding it gently but firmly into the 21st century.

The Queen's School

Linked to Queens Lower School (The) in the Junior section

City Walls Road, Chester, Cheshire, CH1 2NN

• Pupils: 570 girls; all day • Ages: 4-19 • Size of sixth form: 110
• Non-denom • Fees: £10,350 pa • Independent

Tel: 01244 312 078
Fax: 01244 321 507
Email: jtaylor@queens.cheshire.sch.uk
Website: www.queens.cheshire.sch.uk

Head: Since 2010 Mrs Sarah Clark (foryish) MA in history and classics from Newnham College, Cambridge. Came here from deputy headship at Wellingborough School in Northampton after teaching history, classics, politics and critical thinking at Tonbridge Grammar School for Girls (qv) and Rochester Grammar School for Girls. A whizzing whirlwind, her energetic enthusiasm leaves one breathless but her GSOH and serious sense of fun are infectious and uplifting. Mad keen on Chelsea FC since falling for Zola in 1992. She's married with two children. In her first half term she's enjoyed joining girls on mountain expeditions and hearing them sing in St Asaph Cathedral but a minibus trip to Cambridge with the classicists really hit the spot, 'a Greek play in ancient Greek – oh, my gosh'. Keen to encourage a sense of community and generous spirits, 'that girls should cheer each other on' she's also determined to strengthen school links with both the city and its Cathedral, to value their proximity. Away from school she cycles, swims, paints in her spare time and is a novice bell ringer.

Academic matters: Traditionally academic; small class teaching and hard work rewarded with excellent grades. Few results below B at both 16 and 18. A level results – pass rate 100 per cent, 84 per cent A/B, grades A–C 96 per cent. GCSE 55 per cent A*, 81 per cent A*/A. Timetables at both levels created round girls' choices. Spanish now the core language, Mandarin and Latin on timetable for Years 7–9, Greek a lunchtime club.

Sixth formers study four AS levels, most reducing to three A2s, and general studies has been replaced with critical thinking at AS, 'a more useful skill especially for medicine or law entry.' Full-on support for each girl to realise future dreams. Few special education needs though school has dyslexia specialist. Gifted and talented co-ordinator beavers to stretch able girls. Of note is wide-ranging library open from 8–4.15 spread through suite of ground floor rooms, each with own character. Plenty of fiction, widely borrowed, papers, journals. Enthusiastic librarian runs charity readathons, author visits and a monthly sixth form book club for 'ladies who literary lunch' with hot meal and book discussion in library. Lots of work spaces here, plenty of IT access during and either end of school. Five other modern computer labs; with equipment and books over three years old recycled to Africa through a charity. State-of-the-art newly refurbished science labs loved by science orientated girls and staff alike. Every mod con, whiteboards, projectors, prep rooms, and air conditioning; 'the top floor rooms of these old buildings can fry,' say girls.

Games, Options, the Arts: Stunning individual sporting achievements just go to prove it's not down to acres of facilities; although the playing fields and courts squeezed into a wedge of land across the road, below the city walls, do boast an exciting new pavilion with changing rooms, spectator space and kitchen, opened by GB gymnast and old girl, Beth Tweddle, in 2006. Not to be outdone, present pupils include GB, national, north and county players in several fields. Successful swim squad regularly reaches national relay finals. Ski team are northwest champions and third in England. Lots of other sports offered for fun and fitness at lunchtimes.

All Year 7s encouraged to try different instruments for a term each and almost 80 per cent of girls have subsequent individual tuition. 11 groups perform in school and cathedral where Christmas and Commemoration Day services are held. Some cathedral girls' choir members. Bright, airy art studio in Victorian eaves with views, light, lots of easels, new stools and tables. A new drama studio has recently been created – lack of one was one of recent inspection's very few criticisms of school. Performing arts thrive and trips include Stratford and open air Ludlow castle. Lots of other travel opportunities, near and far, and photo memories of these are continually shown on two electronic screens in school. ISC inspectors particularly praised the staff's 'extensive contribution to extracurricular activities and trips'. Sports, language, music, science and other clubs abound; debating, drama, equine, creative writing, art, 'clubs are almost at saturation point,' says head, 'there are so many to choose from'. Christian Union has annual weekend away. Many Year 12 girls join Young Enterprise, lots across school D of E, many golds.

Background and Atmosphere: Founded in 1878, the school moved to the Victorian Tudor-gothic style building on its present site in 1882 and expanded over the years as neighbouring houses and a hotel were bought. Changes and development still bring the necessary headache and delay of archaeologists hunting down Roman remains before builders can move in. The school opens as part of Chester's annual heritage trail. Space is at a premium but the charming, leafy upper garden offers oasis for girls, if not escape from ring road traffic noise. History meets 21st century here; stained glass windows in the hall look down on a new sound system and hymn words projected on a screen but the blocked off ceremonial door has been reinstated for high days. New head has introduced blazers and allowed girls to let their hair down. Uniform is pale blue with deep fuchsia, moving to navy for Years 10 and 11 and suits for sixth form. Four houses across the ages compete to earn merit marks in sport, newspaper production and photography. Catering committee includes girls who praise 'grab a bag' system with boxed hot meals for those on activities. £3 a day for good and healthy choice. Teachers enjoy civilised and sociable staff dining room. Annual magazine, now glossy, *Have Mynde,* first produced in 1887 for the sake of the 'noble industry of thought'.

Pastoral Care and Discipline: Something of a maze for Year 7 girls initially but, 'there's always someone to ask the way', they say. Other new girls (and staff) teamed with a peer buddy. Recent inspectors observed, 'excellent relationships exist between staff and girls of all ages who feel secure, happy and confident in a caring environment'. More succinctly girls say, 'we love the teachers'. Biggest behaviour challenge is misuse of phones and computers for inappropriate messaging. Sixth formers trusted with freedom to pop into town during frees and lunch break; they seem equally happy tucked away in their own study and common rooms with kitchenettes. Lots of encouragement. Head describes herself as, 'a great believer in praising and rewarding merit'. Weekly assemblies termly newsletter celebrates achievements including music exams taken through home.

Pupils and Parents: Noticeably cheerful girls look up with a ready smile and cheery hello at every turn. Founded by the Dean of Chester 'for the education of the daughters of the middle classes', nothing much has changed. Lots of professional parents, under nine per cent ethnic minorities, reflecting catchment area, less than two per cent for whom English isn't first language. Gathered from 40 mile area across Cheshire, the Wirral and North Wales. ISC inspectors said girls are, 'polite and well mannered and demonstrate very good social courtesies'. Active Christian parents' group. Parking nightmares eased since re-jig of yellow lines for buses and a deal with council so parents can wait in cars for free in pay and display car park beside playing fields. Some girls and staff come early to avoid

Chester jams. School bears cost of parking for evening events. Notable OGs include Vivienne Faull, Dean of Leicester Cathedral, Ann Clwyd MP and GB gymnast, Beth Tweddle.

Entrance: A third from Queen's juniors leaving some 50 over-subscribed places from which Queen's creams the top achievers. English, maths and verbal reasoning tests, head teacher's report, all candidates also interviewed. Sixth form requires seven Bs with A or A* in proposed A level subjects, 'there's no point in girls coming here if they're going to struggle,' says head.

Exit: Ambitious girls aim high. Queens has spectacular success chasing medicine places; over ten per cent choose and succeed with this. A regular handful make Oxbridge too, the rest to a widely varied range of courses, many in the north or Midlands.

Money Matters: Some means-tested bursaries and a variety of long standing, smaller scholarships and travel bursaries.

Remarks: On a distinctly bijou campus right by city where traffic can be chaos but petite enough for every girl to be individually known, valued and empowered to be all that she can be.

Queenswood School

Shepherd's Way, Brookmans Park, Hatfield, Hertfordshire, AL9 6NS

• Pupils: 400 girls: 205 boarders, 195 day • Ages: 11-18 • Size of sixth form: 130 • Christian/non-denom • Fees: Day £19,200-£20,985; Boarding £24,915-£27,165 pa • Independent

Tel: 01707 602 500
Fax: 01707 602 597
Email: admissions@queenswood.org
Website: www.queenswood.org

Principal: Since 2006, Mrs Pauline Edgar BA PGCE (early fifties). Educated at Dudley Girls' High School, read history at London University. Previously head of sixth form, teaching and learning co-ordinator and head of history and politics at Francis Holland School. Married to Hamish, a maritime lawyer who's currently working in Gibraltar: 'I've quickly learned the benefits of texting.' A proud parent to three children; two sons out of university and a daughter just starting. Loves teaching but doesn't teach any more, confesses to missing the interaction with the girls.

Only the seventh head in the school's history and she feels privileged to be in shoes of previous head. She is taking a softly-softly approach, spending time observing and absorbing; has introduced a few tweaks such as celebration assemblies. Some staff surprised by lack of tangible changes thus far, others comment she has brought some of the London buzz to the school. Admits to a love of London, especially wandering around art galleries and visiting the theatre and cinema, 'I'm a normal person, resisting falling into a headmistress persona.' A petite, elegant, well-spoken, cheerful principal. Passionate about history, politics and music, enjoys running, swimming and sailing holidays but acknowledges she hardly has a life outside school. Says biggest eye-opener since she started has been boarding, 'I thought I knew what boarding might be but now I know what it is, it's a revelation. I can't believe how much fun the girls have, how much they can fit in and all without stressing out exhausted parents. I'm an absolute convert.' Girls are happy with her – 'she's really interested in us and wants to get to know us.'

Academic matters: Results fluctuate between good and very good – 93 per cent A/B at A level in 2005, 82 per cent in 2006, 91 per cent in 2007 and 90 per cent in 2008, 85 per cent in 2009 and 86 per cent in 2010. Particularly good results at A level in English literature, history – but the star of the show is drama & theatre studies, reflecting both popularity and strength. Good GCSE results – 80 per cent A*/A in 2009 and 76 per cent in 2010. Broad intake, coupled with commendable performance, places school at pinnacle of Hertfordshire's value-added tables. Girls often do two modern languages at GCSE and continue with at least one in sixth form. Options in Italian, Japanese and Spanish; girls encouraged to continue studies in their own native languages. No child is refused a go at a GCSE. Teaching mainly traditional with ICT increasingly used by all – every girl has a laptop. Set in maths, French, English and science; class sizes not larger than 24, many smaller. Refurbished library chock-a-block with books, many purchased in recent times.

Currently piloting enrichment activities for gifted including timetabled session of critical thinking; masses on offer for talented. Oxbridge hopefuls encouraged to attend sessions run by staff on range of subjects including decision making, philosophy, interview techniques and subject specific enhancement. 'We're not an academic hot-house but you can be extremely academically successful if that's your thing.' Approximately 10 per cent have EAL needs. Support available for those with moderate dyslexia or other, mild SEN, 'but not as much as we'd like to offer.' Some 96 on register, many monitored, far fewer receive one-to-one (max two lessons a week) from helpful and enthusiastic learning support coordinator. Most have SpLD type difficulties but odd ones with mild ADD, ADHD or ASD. Earnestly insist parents matter, 'they're the ones who know the girls, what makes them tick, what causes them to crumble, so we're always keen to discuss issues, strategies and ways forward.'

Games, Options, the Arts: A school for budding international sports stars – 'I love watching sports and it's a joy to be principal of a school that wins,' comments the head. Lots of successes at regional and national finals. National hockey players include members of the England junior squad and a recent leaver is now a promising player on the international tennis circuit. School is a national LTA clay court centre and hosts the annual National Schools Championships. The Lawn Tennis Association suggests it for would-be tennis stars. With 27 courts in all – 12 clay, 13 all-weather and two indoors – 'you can play tennis at any level,' and at almost any time. Budding stars carefully mentored; help given with diet, fitness, training, fitting in competitions etc. Masses of inter-school competitions, ensures sport for all. Facilities include large, modern indoor swimming pool, Astroturf hockey pitch, weights room, aerobics room and huge sports hall. Girls now learn to cook in posh new practical cookery room. Very little they'd change. Long-lunch affords opportunity for girls to participate in clubs and activities; relax in the grounds or have fun in the adventure playground.

Keen on music, strong choral, masses of ensembles, loads of inter-house competitions. Good drama, several productions a year. Annual trip to Edinburgh festival; a couple of students are members of the National Youth Theatre. Fabulous art and ceramics; housed in 70s 'rot house' which has now received TLC. DT soared in popularity and professionalism over past few years; a Year 9 display received accolades from a visiting AS assessor. Textiles important. Regular art history trips to Europe. Model United Nations, Young Enterprise, debating society, plus charity works. Thriving D of E, some 25 working on gold, 45 recently achieved bronze. School awarded silver level 'eco-school' status, September 2006. Trips galore, 13 Year 9 girls spend up to a term in schools in either Australia, New Zealand, Canada or South Africa and their counterparts come to Queenswood. Numerous other trips to range of destinations including Austria, Alabama, Costa Rica and New York.

Background and Atmosphere: Founded in Clapham Park in 1894, school moved to purpose-built neo-Tudor building in 1925 with masses of later additions. Splendid grounds, glorious gardens open to the public at end of May; 120 acres of sports fields and woodland two miles out from the M25, a 'commutable hour' from London. First-rate Audrey Butler Centre (aka the ABC) houses lecture theatre, language labs and masses of classrooms. Spanking new theatre and associated facilities, a jewel in the crown. Science labs functional, but two recently refurbed reassures parents that academia matters.

Cosy boarding houses divided by year for youngest (Trew), with some resident lower sixth on hand to help. Lower sixth have 27 brand new rooms. Upper sixth have own houses, with modern single or double study bedrooms. Rest of school lives in mixed age houses, with each house having a comfy common room, where other houses can visit. Sixth form centre looks like and known as the Pizza Hut. Boarding breaks and sleepovers on hand for day girls, who are, anyway, at the school for a very full day, lots of stories of impromptu dance and gymnastic sessions suggest boarders just want to have fun. Some fixed 'in school' and 'home weekends', otherwise boarders can spend full weekend at home with choice of Sunday evening or Monday morning return. A few traditionalists would prefer a return to full boarding but most appreciate this is a move to meet twenty first century family needs and preserve the boarding ethos. Girls wear purple and lilac uniform, blazer-wearing recently reinforced; sixth formers wear 'smart own clothes'.

Pastoral Care and Discipline: Methodist foundation with non-denominational Chapel services, an important part of school life, girls frequently leading the services. All divided into houses each run by teaching housemistresses with assistants and a team of academic tutors with around ten tutees per tutor; sixth formers choose their own. Pupil-teacher and parent-teacher relationships relaxed but respectful. 'We work in partnership with parents; we want them to take an active interest in the school and their daughter's education.'

Range of visiting speakers use personal experiences to raise awareness of hard-hitting issues such as drugs, sex, HIV and alcoholism. Girls taking drugs 'lose their right to be a member of the school.' Recently introduced a rewards and sanctions system which aims to reward girls for contributions to school life and help them overcome any problems they may have with that. 'Academics used to be described as 'boffs', but now all the girls achieve good grades at GCSE. We've made a concerted effort to ensure it's cool to be clever.' Postcards of praise, gold badges and stars reward pupils; demerits and detentions aim to deter miscreants, parents involved at early stages. Food a highlight, masses of mouth-watering choices, some even cooked to order, with option of outdoor eating in new picnic/BBQ area when weather permits.

Pupils and Parents: Lots of first time buyers, with both partners working, masses from London. 17 per cent from abroad, fair proportion from Hong-Kong and mainland China, with some ex-pats; EAL taken seriously. Strong, parent supported, Queenswood Fellowship much involved with social activities throughout the year and made generous contribution to new practical cookery room. Very much a 'sleeves rolled up' school, for community minded doers, happy to get stuck in. Refreshing to find pre-teen girls as excited by camping out and hide-and-seek, as they are by beauty and make-up sessions. Sixth formers articulate, poised, feisty but sensible; we commented on the numbers who, in the leavers' magazine, said their ambition was to find and marry a rich man. 'They don't mean it, it's all tongue in cheek,' said the head with a steely stare and wry grin, and we didn't for a minute think they did – but it's refreshing to see girls not taking themselves too seriously – humour, it seems, is a fundamental part of school life.

Girls recognise they live in a Queenswood bubble, realise life on the outside may not be smooth so are determined to get as much out of school life as possible. Parents firmly believe school suits different people, with pastoral care, friendliness and focus on family at the fore and 'parents in partnership' message pervading many areas of school life. Old Queenswoodians' Association is arguably one of the largest, with branches in lands near and far. Oldest OG is 98 – 'I shook hands with her as she skipped out of the car, typifying the Queenswood spirit,' said principal. Old girls include Georgie Thompson (Sky Sports presenter); Helen McCrory (actress); Prof Alison Richards (Vice Chancellor, Cambridge University); Carol Thatcher (journalist); Naomi Cavaday (tennis player).

Entrance: Early registration advised, but entry into most years if vacancies permit either by CE or by own entrance exam. Broad ability intake but should be capable of gaining good grades at GCSE. Strong sixth form intake, candidates must get six GCSEs at B or above, with As in the subjects they want to study at A level. Visits welcome by appointment, many current parents act as tour guides. Pupils from a number of schools including Stormont, St Mary's (NW3), Lyonsdown, Beechwood Park, St Hilda's (Harpenden), Heath Mount, Maltman's Green, Duncombe, Edge Grove and Palmers Green High.

Exit: Steady trickle leave at 16, usually for co-ed education, 'not a cause for concern, but we certainly can't be complacent. Need to ensure sixth-form is a cool and exciting place to be,' says school. At 18 majority to wide range of universities, a couple to Oxbridge. Many do gap years, organised by the school.

Money Matters: Academic scholarships honorary, bringing glory and support rather than cash, though bursaries available in cases of need. Very much looking at what they can offer that will foster girls' talents rather than offering financial sweetener. Music (including organ scholarship), drama, tennis and sport scholarships. Occasional bursaries – means-tested. New discount for Services families introduced. School has picked up some financial disasters with parents who have been upfront about the problem.

Remarks: A happy, healthy, haven for bright, busy, unpretentious girls keen to embrace life. A good place for future Wimbledon wonders. Popular with locals, increasingly a boon for city parents seeking sanctuary from the cut-throat competitiveness of inner London hothouses.

Radley College

Radley, Abingdon, Oxfordshire, OX14 2HR

• Pupils: 685 boys; all board • Ages: 13-18 • Size of sixth form: 270
• C of E • Fees: £27,345 pa • Independent

Tel: 01235 543 000
Fax: 01235 543 106
Email: warden@radley.org.uk
Website: www.radley.org.uk

Warden: Since 2000, Mr Angus McPhail MA (fifties), educated at Radley's local rival Abingdon School and read PPE at University College, Oxford. Previously head of Strathallan School in Perthshire and started life as a banker before switching to teaching ('far more satisfying'). He taught first at Glenalmond, followed by Sedbergh, where he was housemaster. A delightful man with ease of manner, many talents and interests. Someone to whom you could feel entirely confident entrusting your rosy cheeked 13 year old son for the next five years. Years ago we called him a keen cricketer and all-round sportsman; with the passing of time, he now suggests 'active golfer and occasional cricketer'. The years have been kinder to his musical talents. The warden has reunited with the members of his university rock band and, although not ready to give up the day job, they perform '60s, '70s, '80s covers (they 'try to cover five decades'). Wife, Elizabeth, and three university age children; he's fond of children – 'you can't be a good teacher unless you like children – and I've met lots of people in the profession who don't like them'.

Academic matters: If it ain't broke, don't fix it. Not a school constantly striving to reinvent itself or pilot the latest educational strategies (sat tight while the IB and Pre-U were adopted at similar schools). But in its rigour, it has become something of a maverick. Teachers under pressure to deliver and results are frankly astonishing given the entrance criteria. All A levels – AS and A2 – are sat at the end of upper sixth. Hadn't realised this policy would mark them out as different from almost every school in the UK. Their reasoning? 'We're boys only,' says the warden with a dismissive gesture, referring to the masculine gender's late development, 'and it frees up weeks of time in the lower sixth that would have to be used for revision.' The school's outstanding A level results – over half of the 128 entrants at A level in 2010 got three A*/As or above – indicate they're getting it right. Virtually all boys sit four full A levels, with the fourth in a contrasting subject. One reason for not adopting the Pre-U is the school's reluctance to go back to only 3 subjects in upper sixth: 'We get boys who choose three sciences and history ... and then go on to read history at university. And our experience is that their ability to get a university offer is enhanced by doing four subjects.' More than half of sixth formers take part in Edexcel's Extended Project scheme – a 6000 word essay.

Languages outstanding, no mean achievement at a boys' school. First years do French, Latin and a choice of Spanish, German or Greek. Russian also available 'if you're good at languages,' said a pupil. A locum comes in to teach some Mandarin. Up to 50 boys take Latin for GCSE plus a healthy handful of Greek – with exceptional results. French (and maths) IGCSE can be taken a year early, with boys then sweeping straight on to AS. No separate sciences at GCSE – only dual award – something of a surprise at a school that values the basics. History enormously popular and almost every boy chooses to do it for GCSE. History and maths the two most popular A levels with super results year in, year out. Politics and economics also draw A level crowds. Sciences less so.

Not SEN pioneers but learning support dept (SENCo plus several part timers) provides help for 120 'able boys whose progress may be held back by a learning difficulty'. A school where things like beautiful handwriting still matter – if your son's fingertips are soldered to his laptop, you may wish to look elsewhere (boys not allowed to bring own laptops to school during their first year).

Games, Options, the Arts: A vigorous dollop of games a key ingredient in the Radley recipe. Rugby, hockey, cricket and rowing soar over all lesser games. Also hot on racquet sports: tennis (boys say the coaching is 'now' very good), squash, racquets, fives, badminton and, since 2008, 'real tennis'. Thursdays set aside for these and other minor sports including golf, cross country, polo, swimming, basketball and (limited) football. Immaculate playing fields and generally wondrous sports facilities including 5 star cricket pavilion with 360 degree view, 9 hole golf course, superb track. Boys explained earnestly that the rugby posts are the tallest in England – they aren't, but please don't tell them. Rowing taken very seriously with amazing new rowing machine, like a Torchwood facility out of Dr Who, housed in its own building. Rowers consistently among the top British schools VIIIs at Henley and in the National Schools' Regatta over the past five years.

Beautiful theatre and Silk Hall recital room (formerly the main theatre). Music tech room and plenty of practice spaces. A level musicians thin on the ground but their results (including music tech) are first rate. Radley's legendary 'Piano Extravaganza' involves more than 50 boys of all musical abilities. Some 21 pianists play on 7 pianos in a sort of piano orchestra – the school commissions special music for it each year. Fabulous art exhibited far and wide throughout the school, though the art rooms themselves strangely tidy and almost bare. Parents gush over the quality of the dramatic productions. 'Central Hour' 1.30–2.30 daily set aside for 'music, culture and creative activities' i.e. orchestra, choir, drama rehearsals, music lessons, but also sailing, sub-aqua, debating.

As we so often find in boys only schools, chaps dip their toes into streams they wouldn't touch with a bargepole at a co-ed establishment. So here we find first year pupils taking French cookery and Pilates as part of their Wednesday afternoon carousel of activities. Lots of grand visiting speakers; one parent mentioned her son's creative writing being reviewed by OR Andrew Motion and later Carol Ann Duffy. Annual expeditions to help children in Romania and build homes in Southern India. D of E, goes without saying. CCF compulsory in year 10 to most boys' regret.

Background and Atmosphere: Boys only, all boarding, traditional – but half as many boys as you'll find at Eton, so a very different product. Understated rather than flash – a fine wine rather than overpriced bubbly. Website three years out of date, but who's counting? Signage to arriving visitors unfathomable – one parent told us he stumped around for ages before stumbling upon reception. Navigation tricky for new boys too, with the mixture of old and new e.g. 'The Donut' – a futuristic round structure built in 2000 (handsome, useful ... and at odds with the rest of the architecture). New boys allowed to be late to lessons their first 8 days at school before the fist comes down.

Tucked safely up a drive on the suburban outskirts of Abingdon, 'away from temptation – a bit like a prep school,' said a mum. The serenity can be an irritant to some sixth formers but permission to go into Oxford helps satisfy their urges to slay dragons (and meet up with Downe House girls). Featureless entrance drive (school disagrees: 'the avenue of horse chestnut trees lining the front drive is much admired by visitors') reminiscent of the dismal approach to Disneyworld before you reach the Magic Kingdom. Emerge through the castle-like entrance archway though, and a hidden world is revealed. Swathes of mellow red brick (1720) and Victorian Gothic overlook 800 acres of prime Oxfordshire, totally self-contained and away from the rest of the world.

School founded in 1847 by the Revs William Sewell (don at Exeter College) and Robert Congleton Singleton on Oxford college model – with cloisters, quads and dons (teachers). Boys look like mini-undergraduates circa 1962 in their black gowns. The gowns, much like burkhas, are 'weird at first but then you hardly notice them'. Individuality and status marked by style of school tie – there are about 80. Hyper-traditional school tuck shop where pupils have their own 'jam account' – also sells uniform and other necessities.

Pastoral Care and Discipline: Much emphasis on 'character', values, decency, leadership – and it's not just talk. Boys live in one of ten Socials (from Latin socius, meaning companion, since you asked) inventively named by the letters of the alphabet, so we have A, B, C, D, E, F, G, H, and two newer ones – J and K (what's wrong with 'I'?). Shells (first years) in cubicles, but single rooms with hotel-style safes (and fridges in upper sixth!) from then onward. We hear that G is currently 'sporty' and H 'academic'. 'Cocoa' is both a drink and a formal part of the Radley timetable – all boys in the house gather at 9pm 'to gel' over the warm bevie. Privis (exeats) each half term, but boys can go out any Sunday after chapel. Saturday nights made special in socials with pizza etc. Youngest boys kept very busy on weekends, older boys given more rope. Whole school squeezes into lovely chapel four evenings a week at 7pm – 'chapel was quite important to my son,' a parent told us, 'never a nuisance'. Vast majority of staff live on campus in school accommodation – helps attract the best and the brightest staff.

Junior Common Room (school bar) serves limited alcohol with a meal for 17 and 18 year olds, and housemasters may share a beer from time to time with their sixth formers. Abuse of these privileges leads to punishments ranging from £30 fine plus 4 hours 'labour' (hit them where it hurts) up to losing some holiday time. Boys adamant that drugs not a problem here, and Mr McPhail agrees. 'More difficult is the boy who repeatedly offends in small ways.' School works hard to encourage boys to be nice to one another: 'It's not easy!' Parent after parent praised this aspect of the school ('110 per cent brilliant' said one). Two boys expelled for bullying not long ago, according to our guides: 'it's treated more seriously than ... than ... anything,' they told us, with a touch of awe. Much care taken with youngest boys. Boys in lower sixth are mentors (previously 'nannies') for two or three 13 year olds – old and young both benefit.

Pupils and Parents: Mostly British 'because of the entrance system' says the warden (they come along too late) and because it flies under much of the overseas market's radar. Wealthy but unpretentious: reverse snobbism more than a small part of many parents' choosing this school. ORs include Andrew Motion, Sir (now Lord) Richard Wilson of Dinton (former Cabinet Secretary), Lord Scarman, Lord Craig of Radley, Lt Col Rupert Thorneloe, Clive Stafford Smith, Ted Dexter, former world rackets champion James Male, England captain Andrew Strauss, Chairman of John Lewis Charlie Mayfield, Chief Executive of Next Simon Wolfson and Sandy Nairne, Director of the National Portrait Gallery.

Entrance: Names down at birth still the wisest £100 you'll ever spend. One of the few remaining first come, first served schools where it really does make sense to phone the school from the delivery ward. When your son is ten you'll be asked to cough up an acceptance fee (£700 at the mo) if you really want the place (55 per cent pass required at CE, though some flexibility in individual subjects). From the Warden's List, 20–25 latecomers are cherry picked. The bar is higher for these laggards, with the school looking for clever all-rounders – 'go-gettery-make-the-most-of-the-school-types', specifies the warden, whose talents are established via a 20 minute interview; no exams ('we do give them a verbal reasoning test to keep them occupied on the day, but it's not that important – the recommendation from the prep counts for more'). Genuine talents and geniuses can of course apply in the year before entry via scholarship exams. No 11+ exam ('a lot of boys haven't got going yet at 11 – or even at 13!') or pre-testing annoyances. No open days – senior staff meet parents all year. Boys applying from state schools sit Radley's own entrance papers instead of CE. More places available at sixth form than in past – now up to around eight boys join at 16+ including one via the HMC's scheme for pupils from Eastern Europe.

Exit: Lose only a couple of boys after GCSEs. At 18 a minority of boys go straight to university. More take a gap year, with or without resits. Leeds the most popular destination (why Leeds?) followed by Bristol, Exeter, Edinburgh and Newcastle. 15–18 to Oxbridge most years.

Money Matters: Mainly honorific scholarships (up to 10 per cent, but often less) awarded each year at 13+ for academics (10 years of past papers cheerfully supplied on the Radley website), art, drama, music and sport prowess. Can be topped up by means-tested bursaries. Foundation Awards of up to full fees available for a few extremely gifted boys of modest means. Academic, music and organ scholarships available for boys joining at 16.

Remarks: The most traditional of schools but also intimate, academic, robust, kind. The connoisseur's choice saunters into another decade riding high.

Reading Blue Coat School

Holme Park, Sonning Lane, Sonning on Thames, Reading, Berkshire, RG4 6SU

• Pupils: 615 boys, 55 girls in sixth form (all day) • Ages: 11-18 • Size of sixth form: 205 • C of E • Fees: £12,390 pa • Independent

Tel: 0118 944 1005
Fax: 01189 442 690
Email: vmf@rbcs.org.uk
Website: www.rbcs.org.uk

Headmaster: Since 2008, Mr Michael Windsor BA, previously deputy head, Royal Grammar School, Guildford. A graduate in modern languages from Durham University, worked briefly in publishing before teaching English in Italy for three years. On return to UK, took a PGCE (Institute of Education, London) before teaching French, German and Italian, also in London. 'I am passionate about education and hope that Blue Coat pupils will develop their intellectual curiosity and be enthused and excited by their studies.' Married with two young daughters and also has a broad range of interests outside the classroom. Enjoys sport and as a Bristol Rovers supporter he has learnt how to deal with adversity. Plays the double bass in classical and jazz groups.

Academic matters: Not revolutionary, but solid. Maths and sciences lead the way, both in terms of uptake and results. Almost half the A level students take biology and about a third do physics, chemistry or maths (each). That said, English and geography also have strong followings and super results. Languages improving – all modern language students gained A*–B grades at A level. School recorded its best results in 2010 – at GCSE 98 per cent of pupils gained grade C and above with 63 per cent being A*/A grades. At A level 80 per cent achieved A*–B grades, better than at many similar schools. School enthusiastic about the value of languages and has reintroduced Latin and classics. Geology and history of art are two of the more unusual A levels on offer with music technology added in 2007 and psychology in 2010. School tops the Wokingham area's value added scores – ahead of all the local grammar schools – though school would rather be judged on 'more meaningful' criteria than VA scores. Some setting in English, maths, sciences and languages. School offers help to its pupils with learning difficulties but not a school you would seek out in this regard.

Games, Options, the Arts: Sport strong but some boys we spoke to would have liked more of it in the weekly schedule. Currently one main games session a week plus a double lesson of PE. Many boys supplement this by joining out of school teams (and head points out there are substantial after school sporting activities and a full fixture programme in major sports). Soccer and rugby coming on strong, U13 and U14 rugby teams were both County Cup winners. Rowing on the up with the first eight qualifying for the Henley Royal Regatta consistently over the last four years. Less mainstream, the school's golf team is making a name for itself in the south of England. Rugby, cricket, hockey and golf offer international tours. New climbing wall in the sports hall and fully equipped gym suite. A new cricket pavilion was opened in 2009 and a cover added to the school pool to enable use all year round. D of E on offer and the school has a strong CCF with over 100 boys and girls in the various sections.

Big on debating with several awards for public speaking including best speaker at recent International Public Speaking Championships in Canada. Over a third of students receive instrumental lessons with guitar being the most popular (followed by drums we would guess by the sound of things when we visited the music department). School choir and instrumental musicians give performances to the local community. Music fares well at GCSE but, at A level, results are surprisingly wobbly. Music department has just been updated to include a suite of iMacs for music tech and the IT dept has been refurbished with new eco-friendly computers. Plans afoot to update DT accommodation but for now the somewhat outdated space has an old-worldy charm.

Old hall used for theatrical productions and concerts – there are plans for it to become a swish theatre one day. School offers A level in performance studies – with some splendid results – but no GCSE or A level in drama or theatre studies. Art a world unto itself under direction of department head who has been here since 1988. Housed in utilitarian modern block but inside the messy rooms positively buzz. 20–30 pupils opt for art GCSE each year, hand chosen by the department: 'we're very selective – we don't allow boys to take the GCSE if we don't think they will thrive.' A few take it up through A level (many girls) with mostly good results.

Background and Atmosphere: Founded in 1646 by Richard Aldworth, a merchant of London and Reading who was also a Governor of Christ's Hospital, the school moved several times before finally settling in 1947 in its current site in Sonning. Boarding ended 2001. In keeping with its foundation as a school for the indigent, RBCS remains down-to-earth. Not a school to wow you with pomp – its main competitors are in the state sector. The drive up to the school from the main road sets the scene: unpretentious, almost austere – it was used as a set for '70s cult horror movie, *Unman, Wittering and Zigo,* in which a teacher at a boys' public school finds himself threatened by the strange and sinister pupils. Handsome late Victorian Gothic main building somewhat lost among newer additions, some more aesthetically pleasing than others. More of a whiteboard and projector school than a smart board establishment ('by design'). The girls we spoke to were happy and there are enough of them to gel and to make a mark. Formal teaching day finishes at 4.10pm.

Pastoral Care and Discipline: Good. The academic tutoring is organised across year groups with e.g. pupils from Years 9, 10 and 11. This newly introduced system appears to be working well and creates positive vibes between year groups. School has grip on behaviour. The pupils come across as neat and polite. None have had to be asked to leave in recent years. Super refurbished very modern sixth form centre opened in 2010 – pool tables, cafe, seating area and plenty of lockers on the ground floor. Upstairs is a study area equipped with computers. Director of sixth form's office is here.

Pupils and Parents: From within a twenty mile radius. Many from 'down the A4': Maidenhead, Marlow, Ascot, Camberley. Sixty per cent of boys come from independent schools and 40 per cent from state schools creating a social melting pot. Not a school for social climbers. Parents welcomed into the school by various social evenings organised by active PTA.

Entrance: Has stopped taking boys at 13, creating a brouhaha among some heads of local preps. Intake at 11+ by school's own examination consisting of three one-hour papers: general verbal and numerical reasoning, English composition and comprehension, and maths. Main feeders are Crosfields, Holme Grange, Caversham Primary, Ridgeway, St Piran's and Waverly School, but many other schools regularly send boys. A further competitive intake at 16+: around 30 girls and five boys enter the lower sixth each year. Entry at this age requires verbal and non-verbal reasoning tests plus a minimum of seven GCSEs grade C and above with at least Bs in the subjects to be studied at A level.

Exit: Most to university – absolutely everywhere, e.g. Southampton, Nottingham and Exeter. A number of pupils take gap years. Half a dozen to Oxbridge. A few leave after GCSEs, mainly to sixth form colleges.

Money Matters: Cheapish, as Basil Fawlty would say – fees lower than at a few prep schools in the area. Scholarships for art, music, academics – up to 25 per cent of fees. Two foundation scholarships awarded annually on merit and are means-tested – could amount to 100 per cent of fees.

Remarks: Has carved out a unique niche meeting the strong demand for a no-frills private education in the heart of the Reading/Bucks grammar school belt.

The Red Maids' School

Westbury Road, Westbury-on-Trym, Bristol, BS9 3AW

• Pupils: 470 girls, all day • Ages: 11-18 • Size of sixth form: 75
• Non-denom • Fees: £10,005 pa • Independent

Tel: 0117 962 2641
Fax: 0117 962 1687
Email: admissions@redmaids.bristol.sch.uk
Website: www.redmaids.co.uk

Head: Since 2001, Mrs Isabel Tobias BA PGCE (forties). Read English at New Hall, Cambridge. After five years in publishing trained as a teacher and began career at Henrietta Barnett, London. Head of English then deputy head at Royal High School, Bath prior to present post. Well into stride at Red Maids', seen as a good manager who brings out best in her staff. A moderniser with a sense of tradition. Proud of girls' achievements and hugely supportive of worthwhile endeavour. Much respected by girls and parents. Focused head with a light touch and firm grip.

Academic matters: Over 85 per cent of A level candidates achieve A/B grades at A level; a few pupils are entered for advanced extension awards with most achieving distinction. Strong results overall; average class size of eight at A level with preferences varying from year to year. IB introduced as alternative in 2009. Choice of languages includes Russian and Italian. Fairly academic menu with a wide choice of subjects; most girls pursue creative options through extracurricular programme. Art has recently taken off with innovative, (male) head of department. Extended project introduced in 2008 and all students who entered got A* or A GCSE grades. Lots of A level top grades and similar story at GCSE with over 63 per cent A* and A grades. School hosts junior national maths challenge. AS subjects cover a wider choice including psychology. Two written reports and one parental consultation evening per year group each school year. Impressive ICT suites and new science laboratories. Only seven per cent of girls have special needs; those who require extra support receive it by withdrawal. Large percentage of gifted and talented with some being sent on grant-funded special courses. School says, 'ISI inspection report in 2009 rates the school outstanding.'

Games, Options, the Arts: Excellent sports hall and Astroturf – year round facilities on site for wide range of sports. Lots of teams and matches with sport continuing into sixth form. Fifteen girls currently playing county level hockey and netball. Options include fencing, basketball, gymnastics and swimming at Bristol University. Strong music department includes state of art music technology for composition. Over half the girls learn a musical instrument from beginners' to diploma standard. Three orchestras plus choirs, ensembles etc. Regular musical events within and outside school. Frequent musical productions on stage. Chamber choir tours abroad and won HTV's Sing Out competition. Joint tours with QEH. New performing arts centre has strengthened drama: joint productions with QEH and annual whole school festival alternates between drama and dance. GCSE drama, AS and A level theatre studies with some girls proceeding to drama school. Considerable public speaking successes include geographers who won recent global issues competition. PSME course covers wide range of health, moral and other issues. Two careers libraries include one specifically for sixth formers. Events like Business Skills Conference in year 10 and The Real Game in Year 9 plus frequent wins for Young Enterprise teams in sixth. Well resourced library includes good DVD section.

Background and Atmosphere: The Red Maids' School (founded in 1634 at the bequest of Bristol mayor and MP, John Whitson) is oldest surviving girls' school in the country and moved to its present twelve acre site from inner Bristol at beginning of 20th century. Celebrated its 375th anniversary in 2009, with a science and technology conference for girls and a grand ball. The school has outgrown its purely altruistic beginnings (to provide destitute girls with the essentials of good home management) and is forward thinking in all respects. Non-denominational with assemblies covering all kinds of issues and head supportive of individual religious observance. Great sense of community but head also encourages girls to make friends outside school. Close links with QEH boys helps to break down sex divide with joint academic and cultural activities (e.g. choral tours to Europe and USA, timetabled sixth form enrichment programme and philosophy club) as well as social ones. Differs from its two neighbouring independent schools – Badminton (mainly boarding) and St Ursula's (co-ed) – but shares favoured location on northern fringe of Bristol. Surprisingly spacious and green site for a city day school with old and new blending comfortably. Good proportion of male teachers plus blend of youth and experience on staff. World War II air raid shelter draws plenty of visits from Bristol primary children. We thought catering arrangements were much better than in most day schools; breakfast club runs every morning before school, catering staff reached final five in a national 'Cook Off' organised by Waitrose.

Pastoral Care and Discipline: Girls meet form tutors twice a day. Head of Year 7 oversees transition from wide range of state and independent feeder schools; heads of joint years thereafter with director of sixth in charge of recently refurbished sixth form centre which breeds a more varsity type atmosphere.

Pupils and Parents: Friendly, open girls from a wide social and ethnic background. 'Not just for academic girls' though they are in the majority. Traditional dress (including bonnets and capes) reserved for a select few at special occasions. Founder's Day procession through Bristol city centre is a high point, especially for older girls who love it. Otherwise, girls wear simple red jumpers over a white blouse with red skirts for ages 11–16 with a sensibly interpreted dress code for sixth formers. Parental discussion group meets regularly with head. Former pupils include novelist Susan Lewis, TV anthropologist and presenter Alice Roberts and Helen Marsden, winner of 2004 WISE (Women into Science and Engineering) excellence award.

Entrance: Year 7 intake has increased recently to around seventy per annum. Candidates (including those at junior school) sit joint Bristol schools' papers in English, maths, verbal and non-verbal reasoning. Brief interview with headmistress for all. For sixth form entry, minimum five GCSEs with Bs in chosen IB or A level subjects plus interviews with headmistress and director of sixth.

Exit: Some leave after Year 11 for colleges or co-ed sixth forms but majority stay. All sixth formers proceed to higher education; regular flow to medical schools and five per cent annually to Oxbridge.

Money Matters: Three major academic schols plus two music and one sports per year group. Discretionary head's awards for outstanding achievement in particular areas of entrance examination. Four sixth form scholarships annually. Discretionary 13+ entrance and further scholarship. Means-tested bursaries up to 50 per cent of fee and two additional John Whitson bursaries for 100 per cent of fees. New IB bursary. Books and domestic school trips included in fees.

Remarks: Not a stuffy school despite its historical cachet and strong academic record. 'Staff care hugely' and 'girls are genuinely proud of their school,' say parents. Modernising head seeing numbers build from lower years upwards.

Redland High School

Linked to Redland High Junior School in the Junior section

Redland Court, Redland Court Road, Redland, Bristol, BS6 7EF

• Pupils: 420 girls, all day • Ages: 11-18 • Size of sixth form: 100
• Non-denom • Fees: £5,760-£9,600 pa • Independent

Tel: 0117 924 5796
Fax: 0117 924 1127
Email: admissions@redlandhigh.com
Website: www.redlandhigh.com

Head: Since 2006, Mrs Caroline Bateson BA MA PGCE (mid-forties), a historian. Previously deputy head down the road at Badminton where she rose from her post as head of history. She is also an Independent Schools Inspector. One half of one of the dream teams seemingly becoming more commonplace these days – her husband is deputy head at Queen Elizabeth's Hospital, down the road the other way – she has a daughter at university.

Academic matters: Some 28 A level subjects on offer. In 2010, almost 30 per cent of A level entries achieved the coveted A* grade and 82 per cent were at grades A*- B. Three students took the Extended Project Qualification, two achieving A grades and one gaining an A*. At GCSE the overall pass rate (A*–C) was 99 per cent (highest since 2005) with 27 per cent A*/A.

Little feeling of academic hothouse despite results. Top set take separate sciences with physics coming out best though girls subsequently shy away from it; majority take GCSE dual award. Latin and Greek survive well at GCSE, small numbers continue beyond. Lively teaching in modern languages reaps glut of top grades in French and German with Spanish still building up its following; department craves specialist area – link with La Baule has led to performances of *Le Petit Prince* on either side of channel. RE is unusually strong and offers short GCSE course as well as A level: popular trips to experience religions and other cultures in far flung corners of globe.

Individual programme for dyslexic pupils co-ordinated by SENCo who is also junior school deputy head.

Games, Options, the Arts: Music the dominant extra-curricular activity and overall strength of school; two thirds of girls play an instrument; frequent low key lunch and tea time concerts plus bigger events for choirs and orchestra. New music school opened in 2006. Drama very popular; performances highly rated by audiences. 2010 saw a group take *Trojan Women* to the Edinburgh Fringe, gaining excellent reviews. Public speaking, debating and Model UN encouraged. Half Year 12 get involved in Young Enterprise scheme which lets loose hitherto untapped entrepreneurial skills.

Hockey now taking off at the school due to the relatively new and excellent facilities, particularly the all-weather pitch. Some girls reach county standard; majority probably not desperately sporty though hockey, netball and cricket have been successful. Dance popular outside timetable with biannual show; likewise fashion with highlight for girls on catwalk at end of year.

Wonderfully creative vibe strikes visitor from top to bottom of separate art building with a wide spiral staircase providing vantage point from which to relish offbeat feel. Shame that profusion of artistic talent cannot be splashed more around school. Good range of lunchtime and after school activities on offer; D of E scheme from year 10 with expeditions; house system centre of high volume charity giving. The school has just built a state-of-the-art climbing wall in the gymnasium which will be the focus for a brand new climbing club. PSHE to Year 11 termed 'education for life' becomes enrichment programme in sixth including life skills such as student cookery.

Background and Atmosphere: Founded in 1882, school moved to 18th century Redland Court in 1885 where it still dominates one of Bristol's classier areas. Motto: 'So Hateth She Derknesse' engraved in wood over doorway from assembly hall reminds girls of characteristics of daisy (school emblem). Current girls struck us as unlikely to shrink from limelight anyway.

Limited outside breathing space includes pond area, vestige of formal Dutch garden plus newly created 'peace' garden; good hard tennis courts below main mansion for more energetic. Development here suffers double whammy of cramped city site and trying to overcome listed building restrictions. We overshot entrance to only parking area and wondered how everyone coped on parents' evenings. Teaching areas housed in mix of architectural styles; refurbished laboratories show what can be done.

We really liked content and layout of library with quiet area for swots open until 5pm. From 8am, the 48-station ICT suite opens for business so girls can always clear their inboxes before lessons. Well-resourced careers suite shows how seriously RHS takes preparing girls to hold their own in world of work. Mary Crook Sixth Form Centre across road from main site, where teaching and social areas sit cheek by jowl in altogether comfortable and civilised surroundings.

Pastoral Care and Discipline: Rapport generally excellent and builds up through school. Lacking in social areas for younger girls who were observed huddled in classrooms during breaks. Popular, healthy school lunches on an 'eat as much as you like' basis.

Pupils and Parents: Girls see absence of boys as 'definite plus' for their short-term academic achievement but don't doubt that they'll cope at university and beyond. A few still slope off after Year 11 but looks as if head will counter with increased opportunities for mixed activities. Bustling, purposeful atmosphere with no danger of remoteness in this multi-cultural and commercial city.

Noticeable growth in girls' confidence towards upper end; very little posturing or bitchiness; loads of co-operation and positive innovation. Senior girls have open and relaxed approach to adults. Famous old girls include Dame Elizabeth Hoodless, chairman of CSV, and Geraldine Peacock, charity commissioner.

Entrance: Exam at 11 with about one third coming from junior school (qv). Remainder mainly from Bristol state primaries.

Exit: Virtually all to higher education with about 10 per cent to Oxbridge. Wide choice of courses at leading universities. Increasing numbers to drama schools.

Money Matters: Scholarships at 11, 13 and 16 include academic, art, sport and music. Means tested bursaries available for entry into all years from Year 5 upwards.

Remarks: Few frills and short on wow factor in terms of facilities, it nevertheless has impressive record of sustained academic success. Girls work hard, support one another and take full advantage of what's on offer outside classroom. Looks set for a good spell.

Reeds School

Sandy Lane, Cobham, Surrey, KT11 2ES

• Pupils: 580: 520 boys, 60 girls (in sixth form). 90 boarders, rest day • Ages: 11-18 • Size of sixth form: 160 • C of E but all denominations and faiths are welcome. • Fees: Day £14,913-£18,654; Boarding £19,884-£24,675 pa • Independent

Tel: 01932 869 044
Fax: 01932 869 046
Email: hm@reeds.surrey.sch.uk
Website: www.reeds.surrey.sch.uk

Head: Since 1997, David W Jarrett MA (fifties), educated at Oxford (classics), followed by PGCE at Cambridge. Married with two children at university, his wife works in the City but is involved in school life. Mr Jarrett is passionate about sport (cricket and hockey blue), enthusiastic cheering rather than taking part these days. The classics and English lit are his other great loves, when he has time, which isn't often. A friendly, good humoured chap. He is fiercely proud of the school and takes his position very seriously. Describes himself as 'hands on' (confirmed by parents and pupils), he knows the names and backgrounds of all his students. Pupils like him and they can knock on his door if they need to but they know he is not a fellow to cross. Parents describe him as very professional, friendly and approachable, but 'not matey' – he balances relations well. Staff confirm he is genuinely across everything (possibly too much so for his own sake) – he teaches, runs the gifted and talented programme, and is out and about around the school. Dislikes it when paperwork keeps him in his office too much. Academia is not his only goal; believes it is more important to nurture and inspire those children with potential than to hothouse them – 'much more a have-a-go school than a sink or swim one,' he says.

Academic matters: Caters for a broad range of abilities – an all-round school rather than an academic powerhouse. Potential matters more than results when the pupils join the school, once in situ they are expected to knuckle down and do their best. The school 'doesn't pressurise, it enables,' said one parent. The lack of pressure is confirmed by pupils – a sixth form girl said her previous school was 'hellishly pressurised compared to Reed's.' Traditional teaching and hard work, and the results have improved significantly over the years – in 2010, 60 per cent GCSE A and A* grades, 81 per cent A*, A and B grades at A level – increasingly impressive results for a mixed intake school. Broad curriculum. Maths and foreign languages setted from Year 7, English and sciences from Year 9. Pupils select two from French, German, Spanish and Latin. Most popular subjects at GCSE are history, geography, DT, art and PE. At A level, history, economics, English, biology, maths, geography, psychology, art, graphics and PE. For the more adventurous, GCSE astronomy, Dutch at GCSE and A level and photography are on offer.

Lessons are quiet and quite formal, a mix of teaching from the front and interactive, experiments and group work, videos being watched and discussed, children up at the board answering questions, drawing diagrams. One pupil said all his lessons have an element of fun, teachers know how to 'grab our interest,' especially in science, plenty of gruesome experiments. Loads of computers everywhere, three huge ICT suites, more in the large, peaceful library. Classrooms are large, light and airy, many built within the last few years, with up to date equipment everywhere.

Graphic design – a real strength here – with cutting edge, industry standard software. Stunning displays of work in the design block, students have been in the top five in the UK at A level. Impressive website upgraded in 2010.

SEN provision is very good. The school caters mainly for dyslexia and dyspraxia – mild to moderate. Screening on entry, educational psychologists' reports requested if appropriate. A fully equipped English Language Support Centre where pupils have a structured teaching programme devised for individual needs, using a multi-sensory approach. One-to-one help available, mainly for dyslexia, two dedicated staff. A parent described SEN as 'impressive,' pupils she knew with SEN requirements have absolutely flourished with lots of individual help.

Average class size 20, maximum 22/23. Teachers are youngish, average age 35, 15 have been at the school for more than 10 years. Staff recruited for 'inspiration and enthusiasm,' they have to be prepared to 'go the extra mile'. Pupils confirm their approval with a thumbs up for the teachers and no complaints about the amount of homework (must be the first time we have heard this in a private school). Parents/pupils kept fully aware of progress/problems.

Games, Options, the Arts: Sport is huge here – numerous teams, far-flung tours and loads and loads of triumphs. Rugby, hockey and cricket compulsory in junior years but vast range of sport on offer in and after school; everything you would expect plus fencing, riding, skiing etc. Tennis and skiing are particularly acclaimed – National and World School Tennis Champions – talented skiers spend three to four weeks annually in the Alps, their academic curriculum tailored around their talents. Sports facilities superb and wide ranging – too numerous to list, but parents confirm they are 'great and match the commitment they show to sport here.' Aim is for the dedicated athlete and the not so sporty to find aptitude in as many sports as possible. There are teams and lots of fixtures for the serious and for those who'd rather give it all a miss. The non sporty are encouraged (only encouraged, never forced, according to an 'absolutely not sporty' boy) to give it all a try. The same 'not sporty' pupil said hearing the fourth or fifth team match results read out at assemblies shows you don't have to be that sporty to be part of a team – 'really it isn't all about the first team here.' Commitment is all, whatever team you're in – school teams come first (if your child plays sport for a non-school team and fixtures clash, school always takes priority). In the sixth form, there is specific provision for girls' sport.

Pupils have to do three after school activities a week from a 40+ list, which includes astronomy, Celtic folk band, Mandarin and toastmasters. Outward bound scheme for third form, CCF, community action throughout the school, and D of E is much encouraged and popular. In the sixth form, the emphasis is on charity work, also a programme of practical 'survival skills' including cookery, laundry, driving lessons etc – no doubt as much appreciated by parents as the pupils.

Music and drama are a notable focus of the school – 200 learn an instrument, regularly to grade 8 and beyond. One pupil said 'if the musical instrument exists, you can learn it.' Four full-time, ten visiting music teachers. Music block is very state-of-the-art with recording studios. Recently refurbished theatre with lighting and sound.

Background and Atmosphere: A genuinely friendly atmosphere, 'like a nice village,' one boy said. Mr Jarrett describes the school as having real 'soul', due in no small measure to its history of caring for and nurturing those who need help. Founded in 1813 to educate children whose fathers had died, the school still takes pupils on foundation awards – if they have lost one or both parents, if their parents are separated or divorced, if they come from a single parent family, or, if for some special reason their home life has been unhappy or unsatisfactory. Mr Jarrett believes that the 'foundationers', usually about 60–70 pupils, are the cornerstone of the school's caring ethos. He cherishes the memories of many boys whom he has met at entry who've had a rough time at home, can't make eye contact, have little to say and who are transformed by life at the school.

Much community action, charity work etc. Genuinely friendly and caring, pupils and parents feel they are being looked after. Fifty per cent of the staff live on site, which is much encouraged, and enhances the family feel.

The school feels big (number-wise it isn't), set on a sprawling 40 acre site, dominated by the main Edwardian old school building, beautifully kept, and surrounded by playing fields. Newer buildings spread out around the old main building, all built within the last few years and surrounding pretty gardens which, in good weather, are full of pupils.

All children are assigned to a house on entry, 'a sense of teamwork, and belonging'. Dorms, all refurbished, quite smart, common rooms and bed-sits of up to six pupils. Most fifth formers have single rooms. Day pupil centre where day boys and boarders (all mix freely) hang out at breaktimes. Sixth formers have their own building, where they can 'study and chill' and live if they board. Well equipped – computer suite, seminar room, kitchens, bar and common rooms with sofas, TVs etc. Sixth formers love it, 'freedom, with security, good transitional place before uni.' Bedrooms for the boarders are singles and large (some boarders live close by, but want to try boarding for the experience).

Uniform is fairly standard, strictly enforced – shirts tucked in, ties and top buttons in place, or punishments follow. Sixth formers dress in 'office wear.' Food is excitedly commented on and looks good, especially the 'fantastic' breakfasts, day pupils regularly turn up long before lessons for breakfast at school. Lots of options, salad bar, veggie meals, hot and cold, all highly praised.

Pastoral Care and Discipline: The school prides itself on caring for the individual – not lip service either – pupils and parents all give pastoral care the thumbs up. House and tutor system keeps a close check on pupils' welfare. Occasional bullying incidents but it is not a big issue.

Emphasis on prevention through the PSHE programme, confidential surveys every term monitor the situation. All students are encouraged to tell immediately if they have a problem. Any incidents are dealt with firmly, if all else fails, exclusion is on the cards for bullies.

No problems with drinking. Drugs, not a significant problem, a couple of issues in the last dozen years, but very firm rules: counselling and random drug testing a possible condition of remaining at the school. Exclusion and police involvement a possibility for the most serious. Very anti-smoking, anyone caught lighting up gets a letter home, a recurrent problem can result in suspension. Again, strong emphasis in PSHE against drink, drugs, smoking etc. All staff involved in pastoral care, nursing sister on site, a number of staff especially trained to catch the early signs of problems, such as eating disorders. Parents also encouraged to be on the ball re everything that goes on at school and parents say school communication is very good.

Pupils and Parents: A mix of parents: the very wealthy, the wealthy and the quite wealthy – mostly professional and entrepreneurial but the chunk of foundationers successfully redresses the financial balance and stops the school being elitist. Parents have to be 150 per cent committed to the school – they are expected to attend and to make sure pupils attend school events, music practices etc. One parent said she feels the only accepted excuse for missing a major school event would be 'being dead'. Can be an 'all consuming school for the children and for you,' is how another parent described it, not as a criticism, more of a gentle warning. School bus service covers a wide area of Surrey.

Entrance: Entry requirements favour the all-rounder. Relatively lenient selection process – 55 per cent entry exam pass mark. If a pupil misses the pass mark but has potential, a place can often still be found. The school is a useful repository for those who cannot cope with more hard core academia elsewhere. Entry at 11+ tests in English, maths, VR and NVR in January, interview, and report from current school. 13+ common entrance and report from prep school. Approx 25 students join at 16, mostly girls. Need 16 points at GCSE and there is an entry test in two likely AS subjects, general paper, interview and report. The main feeder schools at 11 are Surbiton Prep, Donhead, Westward and local state schools, at 13 it's Parkside, Feltonfleet, Danes Hill, Shrewsbury House, Ripley Court, Cranmore and Hoe Bridge.

Exit: About 20 per cent leave at 16 for local sixth form colleges. In 2010 popular universities included Loughborough, Bristol and London. About 10 candidates a year apply to Oxbridge, usually two or three get in. Several pupils go to art college each year.

Money Matters: Scholarships, bursaries and foundation awards available – very generous provision. Scholarships include those for all round sporting excellence, special scholarships for skiing, tennis and golf.

Remarks: Not an academic powerhouse but parents and pupils are very happy with all the school offers. Ideal for hard working, outgoing, ambitious all rounders, especially if they are sporty.

Reigate Grammar School

Linked to Reigate Saint Marys Preparatory and Choir School in the Junior section

Reigate Road, Reigate, Surrey, RH2 0QS

• Pupils: 495 boys, 385 girls; all day • Ages: 11-18 • Size of sixth form: 230 • Non-denom • Fees: £13,824 pa • Independent

Tel: 01737 222 231
Fax: 01737 224 201
Email: hlg@reigategrammar.org
Website: www.reigategrammar.org

Head: Since 2001, Mr David Thomas MA (forties), educated at Magdalen College School, Oxford where he was a chorister and later an organ scholar at Queens College, Oxford. Followed a musical teaching career and was previously deputy head at Trinity, Croydon. Married to Andrea, an historian, who also teaches part time at the school; they live in a beautiful house adjacent to the school. 'One of the main attractions of the job,' he jokes. Very business-like but friendly and easy to talk to, he enthuses about his school, 'I'm a big fan of co-ed and I love the atmosphere of this place.' Mr Thomas is very visible around the school and the children respect that – 'he comes to loads of sports matches,' said a pupil. 'A top man,' said one parent. 'The kids really like him and he's turned the place around,' said another.

Academic matters: Strong. 88 per cent A* to B grades at A level, GCSE results equally good with 73 per cent A*/A grades. Head believes the school is about more than just academic work. Generally good standards of teaching and super IT facilities with networked classrooms and interactive whiteboards. The aim is for all pupils to leave with IT qualification from the Microsoft Academy – very useful in the real world. Mr Thomas is a big fan of IT and it shows throughout the school – electronic registration is very efficient and the staff even have their own IT trainer. Well-stocked library stays open after school for homework and private study.

About 40 students with a range of needs receive help from two part-time SEN teaching staff. School is happy to discuss whether it can provide the right support for those who need it. But careful consideration needed as to whether an SEN pupil would be happy here as there is quite an academic pace. Those who receive extra tuition do so at extra cost to parents.

Games, Options, the Arts: Sports teaching is exceptional. A new indoor pool at the main school site is complemented by stunning 32 acre sports complex at Hartswood (about two miles from the school), complete with Astro pitches, cricket field, athletics track, golf course and pavilion. All pupils are bused there to spend at least one afternoon a week taking part in a variety of sports. Netball, hockey and rounders for the girls, rugby, cricket, hockey for the boys. School is renowned on the rugby pitch and proudly claims to field up to 18 teams on match days. Most matches are played on Saturdays, the school is mega competitive and always up there at inter-school sporting competitions – the high numbers who take part are expected to show a huge level of commitment. Surprisingly little complaint from the less sporty souls as swimming, tennis and visits to the local leisure centre for badminton and squash are also on offer.

Music, art and drama receive a lot of praise from parents. Art building has an impressive range of facilities, students' work is frequently exhibited within the school and often achieves some of the best exam results. Music teaching is excellent; good facilities, opportunities for all to join in. The head continues to teach some A level music classes. 'It's my haven in the week,' he says, 'and it's a good reminder of the staff workload.' Super drama department led by 'an inspirational teacher' according to parents, puts on several productions each year. Lots of individual drama successes including seven students who have won places at the National Youth Theatre. Numerous after school activities including all the usual; CCF is well supported as is DofE.

Background and Atmosphere: Founded as a boys' school in 1675 and became a grammar school in the nineteenth century. Girls in the sixth form from 1976 when it became independent and fully co-ed from 1993. Located minutes from Reigate town centre, school is housed in 'hotch potch' of buildings – some very old and in need of replacement but many newer and very attractive. Outside space is at a premium. Quite a walk from class to class and to different buildings. Our pupil tour guides were none too keen on the footpath by the cemetery in the winter!

'The food is good,' say pupils and staff alike. Lots of choice. All meals served in a light airy building – 'the best place in the whole school,' said one pupil.

Pastoral Care and Discipline: Head only gets involved in really serious issues and readily involves parents. Sixth formers apply each year to become mentors to the younger ones through their first years at the school. 'My mentor's lovely,' said one pupil, 'she even bought me a Christmas present!' 'It's a very good idea,' commented one parent, 'although I'm not sure they get involved in serious problems – it seems to be more about going bowling and having fun.' New pupils are invited to an admissions evening in June when they are formally welcomed to the school by Mr Thomas in full cap and gown. 'Parents love it,' commented staff, and 'it's an excellent photo opportunity,' said one proud father.

Comprehensive parents' handbook of school life and each term parents are invited to a parents' forum to discuss issues such as bulimia, exam stress, drugs etc. Pupils discuss the issues during the day and parents are invited in the evening. Parents find these very informative and useful – but several comment that they would like more time to discuss their child's progress on an individual basis.

Discipline fairly relaxed, pupils are given space to 'get it right' and are encouraged to feel they can talk to teachers about any problems they have. Clear alcohol, drinking and smoking policy – the head and staff have dealt with occasional breaches swiftly. Very little evidence of bullying – in fact quite the opposite – but staff don't pretend it doesn't happen. Bit of a crackdown on uniform recently but generally not overly strict – 'life's about more than uniform,' says the head. On the whole pupils look smart – a few need reminding to tuck their shirts in and Mr Thomas does so quite regularly. More relaxed for sixth formers but still within guidelines – quite unusual but popular especially with parents. Sixth formers wear their own suits with sixth form tie for the boys.

Pupils and Parents: A very unpretentious place – parents say it is just like the state grammar schools they used to attend. Pupils are a likeable bunch – confident but not full of themselves and very honest. Pupils mainly from the affluent Reigate and Redhill area and the surrounding Surrey towns. Parents from a wide variety of backgrounds: professionals, former pupils, but also plenty of first time buyers. Mega cool rating for its former pupils with many notable Old Reigatians: Norman Cook (aka DJ Fat Boy Slim), Ray Mears, Kier Starmer (Director of Public Prosecutions) and BAFTA winning writer and comedian David Walliams the most famous. Many old pupils return to the school to talk about their careers and experiences – a recent visit from David Walliams and his Little Britain co star Matt Lucas was very popular with pupils and staff alike!

Entrance: Selective but not excessively so, although two applicants for every place in 2010. Majority enter at 11, small number at 13. The school sets its own entrance exam in verbal reasoning (this is now computerised with sample questions on the school's website), English and maths. Interview is given equal importance as is the report from previous school. The school places emphasis on academic achievement but wants to give more children an opportunity to apply, so a new test has been designed in consultation with several local state primary schools who gave it the thumbs up. Approximately 50 per cent of the pupils come from state schools, particularly Reigate Priory Junior. The rest from local preps including St Mary's Prep, which is now amalgamated with Reigate, although admission is by no means automatic. Other regular feeders include Mickelfield and The Hawthorns.

Exit: About 10 per cent leave after GCSE, usually to attend the large local sixth form college. Of those who stay, around 98 per cent go on to traditional universities e.g. Durham, Edinburgh, York and Exeter; five to 10 students each year to Oxbridge.

Money Matters: Scholarships have a fixed value of £1,000 pa but parents can apply for a means tested additional fee reduction up to 100 per cent. In addition, the school operates its own Assisted Places Scheme for gifted children whose parents cannot afford the fees; again this is means-tested.

Remarks: A good all round school with a strong head. Not at all posh.

Rendcomb College

Linked to Rendcomb College Junior School in the Junior section

Rendcomb, Cirencester, Gloucestershire, GL7 7HA

• Pupils: 255; 55 boys board, 80 day boys; 45 girls board, 75 day girls
• Ages: 11-18 • Size of sixth form: 70 • C of E • Fees: £13,275-£24,495 pa
• Independent

Tel: 01285 831 213
Fax: 01285 831 121
Email: info@rendcomb.gloucs.sch.uk
Website: www.rendcombcollege.org.uk

Headmaster: Since 1999, Mr Gerry Holden (fifties), educated at St Augustine's High School, Edinburgh then St Andrew's, where he read history before PGCE at Oxford.

Grew up in Edinburgh as one of four working class boys – 'my primary school teacher would never have imagined me here,' he smiles wryly. Started career at Wolverhampton GS for Boys then head of history at Forest School. Ran large department at Millfield before promotion to deputy headship at Frensham Heights. Turns his hand to most things: cooked breakfast when school was snowed in, did a job swap for a day with head of maintenance ('I got all the rotten jobs but it did wonders for staff cohesion'.) Knows everyone by name and clearly loves the place. 'Very approachable,' say parents. Qualified soccer referee – takes an interest in all sport and latterly a convert to real tennis. Churchwarden in Cirencester. Enjoys teaching PSHE classes. Head of smallest HMC school, has edited four lively publications for SHMIS and chairs that organisation's professional development committee. Married to friendly Liese, who looks after marketing in the school and helps out with riding. Son Alex was at Rendcomb before reading music at Cardiff University. Avuncular and unpretentious; goes down well with everyone it seems, though pupils rib him over his penchant for corduroy trousers.

Academic matters: Consistent if not trail blazing results in recent years. Small numbers overall but 66 per cent A*–B at GCSE and 31 per cent grades A*/A at A level still creditable. May not match high flyers in Cheltenham but delivers as much if not more than Rendcomb parents generally expect. Small groups at GCSE a definite advantage; some tiny ones at A level may be viewed differently by some. Wide range of subjects made possible by part-timers offering psychology, business studies etc alongside traditional subjects. Art shines at both GSCE and A level with a regular crop of top results. A third of each year group takes double science instead of single GCSEs. Versatile D & T department is drawing more pupils into its stimulating environment. We witnessed some effective lessons in English, maths and theatre studies: lively discussion in sixth form groups and hands up everywhere in lower years. Pupils assessed for effort and achievement every three weeks. Library a good place to work (complete silence when we visited) but looking a bit tired, we felt.

Support for mild dyslexia and a range of other mild specific learning disabilities: all pupils screened after entry and help offered either on 1:1 or 1:2 basis. Pupils needing support are generally withdrawn from tutorial lessons rather than main curriculum. Director of studies looks after most able with encouragement to participate in maths Olympiad, other similar national competitions as well as relevant talks, visits etc. Parents say that school is good at celebrating any success (single or multiple) achieved by pupils. Two EFL teachers support regular batch of overseas students, including five annual Japanese students. End of the school day is blurred, making it easy for day pupils to slide into prep alongside the boarders.

Games, Options, the Arts: School is a six-day a week – long days too – some potential parents may be put off but for others it's just what they want. Fifty or so, mainly sporting, extracurricular activities on offer – most take three or four but two is the minimum. Sport is a big deal, enthusiastically supported by staff and pupils alike. School teams generally play 'one down' when they face numerically larger schools but otherwise punch above their weight. Facilities are excellent, with grass pitches and Astroturf, squash and badminton courts, a heated outdoor swimming pool and a large sports hall. Team competition only on sports day though 'this might be extended,' we were told. Individuals regularly make it to the county teams. School offers traditional country pursuits of clay pigeon shooting (highly successful to national level), riding and polo. Four hole golf course on site, while the nearby Cotswold Water Park hosts windsurfing and fishing. National small schools' lacrosse champions.

Very popular art run by extremely enthusiastic head of department. Most play a part in annual fashion shows, almost all at least embark on individual music lessons and the choir is highly rated. Ambitious productions in the school's theatre, once the orangery of the Victorian main house, include large scale musicals – most recent was *We Will Rock You.* Lower School pupils recently staged The Demon Headmaster, also regular performances by GCSE and A level drama students. MAD (music, art and drama) festival at end of summer term includes professionals and a whole range of activities ranging from circus skills to mosaics. Music department is very strong: eighteen peripatetics, one girl currently in national youth choir and five students working beyond grade 8. Variety of ensembles and choirs as well as rock and contemporary music group (whose recent concert featured John Cage's Water Music). School hosts popular world music day for local junior and prep school pupils. 'Performing arts centre is top of my wish list,' says head. Recent visits have included art students going to Barcelona, geographers to Iceland, a battlefields trip and regular local trips by minibus.

Background and Atmosphere: Founded in 1920 when a member of local, land-owning (fags-to-riches) Wills family bought this vast Italianate pile after the First World War from its previous Jewish owners whose legacy (a rather large and incongruous statue of Saul) greets visitors on arrival. Impressive parquet flooring in main house and gracious 'reading room' provides an elegant backdrop for many a function. Noel Wills was inspired by the notion that 'the only aristocracy is the aristocracy of brains and character,' offering an antidote to traditional public schools of the time (a wreath laid annually on founder's grave in Miserden churchyard honours his memory). School has kept aspects of its original philosophy though current market forces operate here at least as much as anywhere else. Rendcomb committed itself to building a one-school ethos since the opening of the junior school in 2000. 'Facilities generally not very swish but natural setting provides wow factor,' explained one mother. No CCF and a lack of strong inter-house rivalry hark back to the idealism of the founder. School Council has increasingly given pupils a greater say in decision making and is listened to by head.

If ever there was a 'school with a view' this is it: looks out over rolling greenery in all directions. Victorian main house sits cheek by jowl with the junior school enabling lots of interaction both formally and informally. Sixth form and other boarding houses are separate as is the stable block which has been modified to provide a range of laboratories and classrooms. Shared bedrooms of younger boarders have refreshing air of light and space, while seniors' rooms are bright, compact and practical. High standard of cleanliness and orderliness reflect well on pupils and boarding/domestic staff.

The grounds spill seamlessly into the village of Rendcomb – the village post office (school was at forefront recently of saving this threatened local facility) doubles as the school tuck shop; village church and its incumbent also double up though post was vacant when we visited.

Old Rectory provides great boarding house for boys in Years 7 and 8. Large, well equipped games room can transform into cinema with projector and screen for favourite movies. Girls' equivalent (Godman) has a pink, fluffy common room complete with disco lights. Friday night challenges (e.g. building the tallest paper tower with help from sellotape) popular with 11–13 year olds. Events for this age group have included a 22 mile cycle tour, a big sister evening and an adventure weekend – a tremendous programme rolls out week after week. Boarders move on at 13 to more senior accommodation. Boys' and girls' common room is a refurbished stable (named 'the barn') – just right for this age group. All sixth formers have their own study bedrooms in dated but flexible co-ed house. Takeaways are restricted during the week; seniors make good use of own kitchen facilities especially after prep. At weekends, boarders can taste town life in Cirencester provided they are back on time. Flexi-boarding popular with day pupils who like best of both worlds.

Pastoral Care and Discipline: School succeeds at being inclusive. All staff appear in school photo – from the head to the maintenance team (who run some sports activities as well as keeping the grounds beautiful). Real sense of caring abounds with a quarter of staff living on site. Seasoned house parents on hand for support as well as medical staff and part-time counsellor. 'Any instances of bullying are dealt with impeccably,' said one parent. Achievement, whether good results or a small kindness, rewarded by praise in assembly or commendation from the head. Rules enforced vigorously by deputy head. Smoking is forbidden but treated more as a problem than a crime. Sixth form 'cellar' club operates within law and serves food plus alcohol carefully regulated by senior staff. Rendcomb's experiment with independent living – via sixth form house in village where a single sex group of pupils lives for a week, manages a budget, cooks meals etc – has drawn national media interest.

Pupils and Parents: Low density of pupils of all ages on such a vast site makes for an unusually civilised atmosphere for a school. Pupils grow to be all-rounders; family feel (enhanced by growth of junior school) attractive to prospective parents. New uniform and sixth form dress code 'will smarten pupils up' we were told. 'Not too much,' we hoped. Most boarders as well as day pupils come from within a thirty mile radius. Unexpected contingent (20+) of Americans from Fairford now part of special link with US defence department. Not swamped by overseas pupils: a few Chinese and German pupils and its annual quota of Japanese in third form only. Children are smiley, polite and quiet. Staff skilled at 'raising the bar' in all areas to avoid excessive cosiness. 'Rendcomb has found my daughter,' said one satisfied mother who was not at all put off by higher proportion of boys: 'relationships tend to be fraternal,' she concluded. Formerly a secluded bastion for farmers' sons and Services' children, now there are many more 'first-time buyers' discovering the school via much improved road link between Gloucester and Swindon. 'Many parents sacrifice holidays abroad to send their children here,' says head.

Meaningful and well-established link with Lords Meade Vocational College in Uganda: school has been helped with whole range of projects with visits by ORs etc – opening privileged eyes to need in developing countries. Lively, glossy magazine splurges pupils' doings in colour photos across its 100 or so pages. Pupils really committed to greening the school across the board from recycling to tree planting. Not many big names amongst alumni – jockey Richard Dunwoody is best known.

Entrance: Selection by own examination at 11 and/or Common Entrance at 13. Interview, report and GCSE grades at 16. Majority from own junior school though good numbers from Prior Park and other local preps at 13. School considers each application on individual basis. Not solely concerned with exam aptitude but also ability to try hard and function as part of a team.

Exit: Most get into university of choice across HE spectrum – art, acting as well as academic subjects. Generally one a year to Oxbridge.

Money Matters: Good value, particularly boarding. Almost everything included in price. Individual music tuition extra but ensemble lessons free. EFL teaching and learning support are charged to parents. Generous academic, choral, music and art scholarships on offer. Bursaries supported by Wills family and Dulverton Trust, plus Noel Wills full bursary annually to one local state primary pupil.

Remarks: Developing the junior school has brought real benefits – numbers have risen overall and the interaction between older and younger pupils seals the family atmosphere. Never an academic hothouse, Rendcomb offers a complete education whilst ensuring that pupils achieve their best academically. A good place to make friends for life.

Repton School

Linked to Foremarke Hall (Repton Preparatory School) in the Junior section

Repton, Derby, Derbyshire, DE65 6FH

• Pupils: 665; 380 boys, 285 girls; 470 board, 190 day. Plus prep school 'Foremarke Hall' • Ages: 13-18 • Size of sixth form: 285 • C of E (other faiths welcome) • Fees: Boarder £27,150; Day £20,145 pa • Independent

Tel: 01283 559 200
Fax: 01283 559 223
Email: registrar@repton.org.uk
Website: www.repton.org.uk

Headmaster: Since 2003, Robert Holroyd MA (mid-forties). Educated at Birkenhead and Christ Church, Oxford. First in modern languages. Previously head of department and housemaster at Radley College. Wife, Penny, also a teacher but now fully involved in life of school community. 'We function very much as a team,' he says. Devoted to Repton and all it stands for. Delights in having raised its profile since his appointment. 'I inherited a terrific ship and we have tried to maintain the core values of the school,' he says. 'But you won't catch us standing still.' Fervent believer in co-education. Good cricketer at Oxford, still enjoys choral music and drama. Big plans for the future. Repton Dubai opened in 2007, 'a Sister School in the Gulf that will provide outstanding opportunities for pupil exchange'. Has two daughters at Repton.

Academic matters: Strives to extract the best from its broad intake – and frequently succeeds. Sound but unexceptional past exam results well and truly put in the shade by more recent year-on-year improvements. 2010 results include 82 per cent A*–B grades at A level with 55 per cent awarded an A/A* grade. GCSE results also strong, with 28 per cent of all entries at A* and 64 per cent of all entries at A*/A. Lots of As taken a year early too. Most subjects setted according to ability. Traditional teaching methods with all teachers living on site or in village – key to the success, says head, of the all-round boarding experience.

Good blend of ancient (library in Old Priory building) and modern (all pupils have free internet access and own email address). School's first ever full-time librarian actually has brought the library into 21st century after school inspectors twice highlighted it as weakness. 'I was surprised at the state the library was in when I got here in 2003,' head told school magazine, the *Reptonian*. Extensive million pound refurbishment now completed 'to make it a more welcoming place where students will want to spend some time to read or study' with new ICT and DVD technology suites combining with traditional ambiance of city club rooms. Computers currently located in other areas and pupils encouraged to bring own laptops for use in boarding house studies (all linked to school network). Wide choice of subjects on offer with business studies, PE, theatre studies and politics more recent additions.

Appointment of an academic 'tsar' has seen more outside involvement in school curriculum with top business names invited to lecture students. Has also introduced electronic reporting on pupils' progress. Parents get usual end of term reports as well as mid-term updates on effort and achievement. Learning support for dyslexics. Two hours plus extra tuition a week can be given in most serious cases, though might be at the expense of French classes. Information and strategies passed to subject teachers to ensure support continues in class. Good teaching environment, new classrooms with state-of-the-art interactive whiteboards under construction, staffed by dedicated team. Students report tutors will 'go the extra mile'. Head can't speak highly enough of them! Those we saw appeared to have boundless enthusiasm and energy to spare. Prep 7–9pm each evening for both boarders and day pupils – only youngest supervised, rest work independently in house studies.

Games, Options, the Arts: Sport now in league of its own. At time of visit school celebrating huge national success. Girls' 1st XI hockey champions (U-18s) and boys victors in U-18s tennis. Repton has long been an outstanding tennis school, recommended to parents by the LTA. Played all year round on outside and indoor courts. Now equally strong in hockey, much thanks to vast sports hall and similarly vast Astroturf pitches. Cricket is no slouch either with county and test cricketers regularly produced, and last year the 1st XI were Twenty20 national champions. And whereas most independent boys' schools still favour rugby as the major winter sport, Repton remains among the handful to stay faithful to football – again with considerable success. (Girls also play football here and this year won the ISFAG national tournament.)

Large indoor pool (also used by locals). Popular extras include D of E, while CCF is compulsory for all for some time. Three half days (Tuesdays, Thursdays and Saturdays) leave time for matches and non-curricular activities. Drama thriving at all age levels. Great competition between houses. Two theatres; a studio theatre and a more traditional school hall to be given a multi million pound facelift in 2010. Music also flourishing, with regular choral performances and trips abroad, orchestra and variety of bands from string ensembles to rock. Best bands even get chance to record. Immensely impressive art studios. Work on show was of extremely high standard and shown prominently all round school as well as at some local businesses. (Money made from hiring out pieces goes into pot to fund foreign trips for art students.) From fine art to sculpture to wall hangings – so big, bold and brilliant. Also plenty of scope for budding photographers and architects. Old squash courts have been transformed into new textiles school. Where will it all end?

Background and Atmosphere: Found on the banks of the River Trent, it's absorbed into the village of Repton rather than dominating it. Boarding houses can be found up leafy lanes, art department tucked down a side street, sports centre and games fields alongside another. Pavements regularly populated by throngs of well turned-out boys and girls making their way from one part of school to another. With a busy B road running through the middle, Repton was never going to be a sleepy idyll, but the school lends a certain vitality. Founded under the will of Sir John Port who died in 1557, school celebrated its 450th anniversary in 2007 with a Son et Lumiere production. A Bloody Mary Foundation, with a long and interesting history dating back to the medieval monastery, the peaceful heart of which still exists (minus the cloisters). Chapel a key part of weekly routine with evensong and Sunday services. Head says, 'all faiths come along to chapel and they love it. If someone from another faith wants to be excused they can be but no-one has asked me yet.' School once boys only, fully co-ed since 1991. Boy/girl ratio roughly 55/45. There are six boys' boarding houses to four girls'. House system still very strong – all pupils return to houses for both lunch and tea. All food cooked in-house and given big thumbs up by regular diners. Small two- to four-bed dorms, sixth formers have own study bedrooms. All-age mixing in communal areas but separate common rooms for juniors and seniors 'just to give us our own space'. Emphasis on homely with mistress/master in charge seen as 'house parent'. As one girl told us, 'it's so nice to be able to take a break from whatever's been happening during the day and be with the family in your house. It's very special.'

Pastoral Care and Discipline: House system again all important. All new arrivals (whatever age) given a 'buddy' (existing Reptonian) to show them the ropes. Pupils encouraged to turn to more senior students, house parents or matron with problems. Plenty of 'motherly' input in both boys' and girls' houses. Miscreants dealt with severely though. Zero tolerance of drugs, demonstrated with five expulsions. 'My first and hopefully my last,' says head. Smoking and drinking both yellow card offences. Bullying (yes, there is obviously some but we are never complacent, insists head) is handled more sensitively with all parties getting involved. Parents encouraged to get involved in school activities at every level and contact with staff can be as often or infrequent as they want. Three exeats by arrangement. Some local pupils allowed to nip home on Sundays – after chapel. Good relationship between teachers and students seems based on mutual respect.

Pupils and Parents: Overall a very down-to-earth bunch. Pretensions go un-nurtured. Hard work is rewarded and with 97 per cent getting the five + B grades at GCSE needed to gain entry to the sixth form, is, more often than not, delivered. Uniform is compulsory – dark suits for Sixth formers, dark trousers and blazers for the boys, grey plaid skirt and blazer for girls who can also accessorise with their own choice of one-colour V-neck jumper 'for that bit of individuality'. Pupils are polite, easy-going, confident. Past OBs and OGs include author Roald Dahl, columnist and TV presenter Jeremy Clarkson, and Lady Carole Blackshaw, Lady Mayoress of London. No one particular type of parent here. Some good northern hard-graft, others from the Cheshire corridor and a good smattering of professionals as well as plenty from overseas.

Entrance: Largely from own prep (sited nearby and co-ed since early 1970s). Rest from growing array of other prep schools. Head says recent good exam results making Repton first choice further afield. Common entrance pass mark required around 50 per cent but can be flexible. Takes those with special needs who can cope with the curriculum. Majority are dyslexic but can cater for others, including dyspraxics and those with severe hearing impairment. Considers needs on individual merit. As well as five Bs at GCSE, potential sixth formers also need at least Bs in chosen A level subjects. But again, rule not written in tablets of stone and other strengths will be considered.

Exit: On average, 11 students to Oxbridge, bulk of rest to redbrick universities, but business, drama and art all have their followers at various destinations.

Money Matters: Scholarships a-plenty. Offered as academic awards, also art, drama, music and sport. Also exhibitions of around 10 per cent of fees. Open to pupils at 11, 13 and sixth form. We are assured that school's five year development plan (including new classrooms, new science centre, reworking of library, large theatre and music school and new textile school) will not mean big hike in school fees.

Remarks: No bargain but value for money. So much on offer, such an all-round experience. Repton is impossible to pigeon hole. Why would anyone want to send their child here? 'We have a strong emphasis on the whole person,' says the head, 'It's standards without snobbery. They come out of Repton proud of their schooldays but able to look out beyond the school.' A feel-good school filled with real youngsters happy to be themselves.

RGS Worcester

Linked to RGS Springfield in the Junior section

Linked to RGS The Grange in the Junior section

Upper Tything, Worcester, Worcestershire, WR1 1HP

• Pupils: 920 pupils; mixed • Ages: 11-18 • Size of sixth form: 290 pupils
• Non-denom • Fees: £9,450 pa • Independent

Tel: 01905 613 391
Fax: 01905 726 892
Email: office@rgsw.org.uk
Website: www.rgsw.org.uk

Headmaster: Since 2005, Mr Andrew Rattue MA PGCE (forties). Educated at Bishop Wordsworth's Grammar School and Brasenose College, Oxford, where he read English. Taught English at Mill Hill School and The Haberdashers' Aske's School, Elstree, before becoming head of English at Highgate School in the early 1990s and then second master at RGS Guildford. Also taught in Thailand and the USA, where he was a Fulbright Exchange teacher at Greenhill School, an independent co-educational school in Dallas, Texas in 1990–91. Married to Jacky, four children. Interests include all sports, American culture, France and the French, the Victorians, hill walking and cooking.

Academic matters: In a challenging environment, Worcester and its environs are well provided with independent schools e.g. King's, Malvern and Bromsgrove and there are some good state grammar schools as close as Stratford. The ending of assisted places in 1997 cost the school 35 pupils in each year (one of the highest proportions of any school in the country), which forced it to look closely at its potential market and the sort of school it wished to be. RGS Worcester is now committed to co-education; over 40 per cent of its pupils are girls after the merger with Alice Ottley. Not as selective as it was, and with excellent provision for dyslexic pupils (although there are not a great number of them).

Given the loss of pupils on assisted places (who were generally the more able part of the intake) the continued impressive academic showing is remarkable. No obvious curriculum weaknesses in most subject areas, having a 100 per cent pass rate at GCSE and, at A level, A and B grades have not dipped below 60 per cent. The school has a particular reputation for its science and maths teaching, which will doubtless be strengthened by recent improvements in laboratory facilities. Engineering in design is strong and the school has some wonderful examples of winning go-karts built by the pupils. The introduction of textiles from Alice Ottley brings in more D and T options.

Dynamic new head of music has raised the profile of music within the school. Art and drama also gaining ground. There are several choirs, orchestras, a cappella, jazz and rock bands and other ensembles.

Games, Options, the Arts: Traditionally very strong in the boys' team games – rugby, soccer and especially cricket. In recent years has much extended its range and will do so again with the influx of girls. Lacrosse and netball very strong as are gymnastics and trampolining. Delightful complex of city-centre pitches, playable all year round, within easy access of the school plus over 40 acres at the junior schools all serviced by four pavilions; two sports halls, dance and fitness studio plus a brand new all-weather floodlit pitch with new pavilion at RGS The Grange. Rowing is increasingly successful with the junior quad sculls crew national champions two years in succession; six pupils selected for national rowing teams in 2002. Cricket remains the pre-eminent sport and it is perhaps significant that the two most famous old boys, Imran Khan and Tim Curtis, both made their name as cricketers. The head is very supportive of games – 'he is at every match,' comment parents, 'we don't know how he finds the time'.

Wide range of activities on offer both at lunch time and in the evening up to 5.30 pm; 'an incredibly committed staff,' commented a parent. CCF seems to be especially popular. However, after school activities are limited by the fact that 250 children have to catch buses rather promptly at the end of the day. Full fixture programme on Saturdays (there is no Saturday school).

Background and Atmosphere: RGS Worcester proud to point out that it is the oldest scholastic institution in Worcester – its foundation pre 1291 (and descent from an episcopal school dating from 685) makes it rather older than the vast majority of leading public schools – notably Eton and Winchester. Alice Ottley School had been established in Worcester for over a century and a half. The merger of these two establishments has created a school with unrivalled facilities, talented teachers and a fully co-ed student body.

Occupies a site on the Upper Tything, perhaps not the most attractive part of Worcester, yet its campus is particularly charming with largely Georgian and Victorian buildings clustered around attractive and well-maintained gardens and lawns. Many of the buildings, including Perrins Hall, were designed by an Old Boy, Alfred Hill Parker, and were funded by Charles William Dyson Perrins, Worcestershire Sauce owner. It even has the ruins of the old medieval convent chapel to add a further air of antiquity to the landscape. The only unattractive building is the English block, built by the LEA in the days when the school was a voluntary aided grammar – it became independent in 1983.

RGS has suffered from being seen as the second choice to King's. In part this is because of the obvious cathedral links and consequent status of its rival. Has the ethos of an old fashioned grammar school, with none of the pretentiousness so often associated with minor public schools. Merger changes ethos and culture completely and we await with interest the overall impact on results and reputation.

Pastoral Care and Discipline: The school's ethos is firmly reflected in its pastoral system and discipline structure. It retains a traditional prefect system which gives real authority to senior pupils, closely monitored by a year tutor system – a structure very clearly set out in easy-to-understand guidelines. The head takes bullying very seriously and much emphasis is placed on good manners, as was obvious when we walked round the school. The boys and girls were delightfully relaxed, charming and very welcoming. The impression was of young people who were genuinely proud of their school and had an easy relationship with each other and the staff.

Pupils and Parents: Most of the children are from local middle class commercial and professional families; lots of first-time buyers. Wide catchment, with buses going as far afield as Tewkesbury, Evesham, Droitwich and Tenbury Wells. Good train links to Malvern, Kidderminster, Bromsgrove and Birmingham.

Entrance: Many from the school's own junior schools RGS The Grange and RGS Springfield; many, too, from local primary schools by test at 11. Some come at 11 from local prep schools and a few at 13 by CE (head quite happy to see more of them coming in at this age). Selective, but not excessively so. Highly regarded by local heads, seen as very good value for money.

Exit: Head is aware of the growing threat from sixth form colleges, especially attractive to some of his financially challenged parents. Virtually all sixth form leavers attend university. Most of them to pretty sound establishments, not too many to the University of Nether Wapping. A solid core of around eight a year make it to Oxbridge.

Money Matters: There are a few scholarships but more emphasis is placed on providing bursaries. It is clear that the head is keen to help able children from poorer backgrounds. 'RGS Worcester tries to keep fees reasonable and not load them in order to entice new pupils with scholarships.' Music and art scholarships are offered at 11+ and 13+.

Remarks: Unpretentious and on the way up. Offers great value for money and will become a larger player in the local independent scene. Merger with Alice Ottley offers scope and space.

The Ridings' Federation Winterbourne International Academy

High Street, Winterbourne, Bristol, South Gloucestershire, BS36 1JL

• Pupils: 1,880 boys and girls • Ages: 11-19 • Size of sixth form: 368
• Non-denom • State

Tel: 01454 252 000
Fax: 01454 250 404
Email: offfice@trfwia.org.uk
Website: www.trfwia.org.uk

Head: Since September 2009, the new principal, Mr Rob Evans (fifties), who should know the school better than anyone – he has never taught anywhere else. A former geography and economics teacher, he was promoted to the top job after being acting principal since February that year. 'Hands-on and business-like', affirm both staff and parents. Long attachment to the school doesn't seem to have stopped him being keen to implement big changes.

Academic matters: Prents enthuse, 'They're not shy of trying new things'. First in the region to offer the International Baccalaureate, now relaunched as an academy (September 2009), and from September 2010 a federated sixth form with the nearby Yate International Academy. The Winterbourne campus looks after the more academic side of things, with the full range of A levels and the IB, with much smaller Yate due to cater for the less academically inclined with more vocational courses, including BTECS.

About 10 to 20 per cent of sixth formers take the IB, including six subjects, a compulsory foreign language, community work, and an extended essay – often seen as good for bright all-rounders and arty types rather than would-be specialist scientists, but the principal is keen to emphasize that the IB is not just for arts and languages students. In one recent year, two leavers went on to study veterinary science at Bristol, one with A levels, one with IB. Even the less linguistically talented can take the IB, with the option of taking Spanish at a more basic level as one of their minor units. IB pass rate is over 80 per cent.

Some of the 'extra bits' of the IB curriculum now standard for all sixth formers, including 'creativity, action, service', and the school has also expanded the critical thinking element of the syllabus to include A level students.

Academy status has given the school freedom to pursue the IB Middle Years curriculum in lower years. Languages a priority, in keeping with international school status – nearly everyone takes at least one language at GCSE, but only small numbers at A level as keener linguists tend to opt for IB. Most popular A levels general studies, psychology, biology and maths. At least one non-European language, most likely Mandarin, on the menu soon.

Classes are setted by ability in some subjects from Year 7 onwards. All types of SEN are catered for, but the numbers are fairly low – 20 or so with SEN statements in the whole school, with another hundred or so getting some support from the SEN team and teaching assistants. Only a handful of EAL students.

Specialist technology school status has now been dropped, but the high-spec DT and ICT suites remain, along with links with industry, notably Airbus (nearby at Filton) and CISCO.

Results above average for a non-selective school: around two-thirds make it over the crucial benchmark of five A to C grades including English and maths at GCSE, and the overall pass rate is around 75 per cent. At A level, nearly 80 per cent get A*s-Cs.

Games, Options, the Arts: A very sporty place, especially since the opening of the shiny new sports 'village' in 2010, including new sports hall, all-weather pitch and refurbished swimming pool. Some of the gym rooms not yet fully equipped, but the main sports hall is a vast improvement. Full-size pool popular with pupils, their families and locals, who can use it out of school hours.

Rugby is the biggest thing here, and not just due to the Welsh head's influence. The 'rugby academy' offers training to all, and produces strong players for the school teams and beyond: one former pupil, is a Gloucester player recently selected for the England rugby squad. Other sports are not neglected: several footballers are training with professional teams, and school teams for just about everything do well in local leagues.

Drama, music and debating standards are high – the academy gives the local independents a good run for their money in regional competitions, and often comes out on top. Art and drama have plenty of space and enthusiasm – lots of school productions, and some impressive art displays around the school. Library disappointingly small for the size of school, but at least they still have one.

Overseas trips limited, as not everyone can afford to go, but video conferences with an imaginative range of partners (from astronauts to school children in Afghanistan) help make up for it. The international outlook pays off for some students with gap year plans – the school has had five leavers over several years picked for the Prime Minister's Global Fellowship, which awards funds for work in developing countries.

Background and Atmosphere: Formerly known as The Ridings High School, the school shook off local authority control in September 2009 and became Winterbourne International Academy, part of a new Ridings Federation with the smaller Yate International Academy. Not many visible signs of change, apart from the new head, and smart new blazers and ties on Years 7 to 11 (sixth formers must dress as 'young professionals' – open to quite broad interpretation, but most seem to have got the idea that it is not jeans and hoodies). The former head, Dr Rob Gibson, is now chief executive principal of the federation.

The modern red-brick office-style building at the entrance to the school campus hides the rather dilapidated core of 1950s classroom buildings lurking behind it. Much-needed classroom refurbishments promised soon. Dining facilities also rather cramped for the large numbers.

International status seen as a big positive by some parents, others not bothered about the languages and extra bits but like the good results and the sports.

Pastoral Care and Discipline: A big school (intake is 302 a year), and possibly a bit daunting for the younger ones. To ease the newbies in, Year 7 tutors start visiting feeder primaries from Year 5 onwards to get to know the likely applicants. Year 6s come to school taster days and even the annual panto.

A part-time in-school counsellor is on hand, and other referrals can be arranged. House system introduced from 2010, but most pastoral care organised via tutor groups. Vulnerable students have older students assigned as peer supporters, and sixth formers are attached to each year group to provide more general support.

Behaviour expectations clearly laid out in personal planners, and parents and pupils have to sign a home/school agreement. Principal says exclusions are down since the school became an academy, and there is low tolerance for disruptive behaviour. Disciplinary measures include detentions and referral to an in-school behaviour unit. The pupils working at desks outside the principal's office on our visit didn't look pleased to be there, but they were quiet and getting on with their work.

Repeat offenders get referred to the Behaviour for Learning Centre (set up in 2005) – an alternative to exclusions, with specialist staff, where troubled and troublesome pupils follow the same curriculum as their classmates as far as possible. The aim is to reduce outright exclusions and eventually reintegrate pupils into the rest of the school.

Pupils and Parents: Cover the whole range from well-off families in commuter villages to those getting the bus in from some more deprived areas on the fringes of Bristol. Comprehensive intake, but on the bright side. Not many non-native English speakers, and the few there are tend to catch up quickly. An international touch comes from engineering staff at nearby aerospace companies, which have strong French links and some overseas workers.

Entrance: There are good reasons why so many Bristol families move to the other side of the M4 when their children are nearing double figures. Many Bristolians would love to get their children into this place, but if you don't live in a small corner of South Gloucestershire – namely Winterbourne, Frampton Cotterell, Coalpit Heath, Frenchay and Hambrook – you are most likely out of luck (unless you have a sibling already there or a special educational need). The academy is heavily over-subscribed, and catchment-area based admission rules haven't changed with the shift to academy status. No entry tests for banding as used by other local academies. Applications through South Gloucestershire council in October before year of entry.

For the sixth form, minimum B grades at GCSE expected in A level subject picks.

Exit: Growing numbers in the sixth form – well over half stay on, but some leave at 16 for work, training or more vocational courses at local colleges. Sixth form leavers go anywhere and everywhere, the majority to some form of higher education, including Oxbridge and Russell Group universities, but a few straight to employment or training.

Money Matters: New freedom from local authority control means the academy now manages its own budgets and can shop around for better-value outside services. Parents' association has active fundraising programme – lotteries, quiz nights etc – and partners in industry have helped out with equipment and some funds in the past.

Remarks: Deservedly popular commuter-belt comprehensive turned academy, with big ideas and an eye on the wider world. Good results and a strong sporting tradition keep its feet on the ground.

Ripon Grammar School

Clotherholme Road, Ripon, North Yorkshire, HG4 2DG

• Pupils: 845 boys and girls; day and boarding • Ages: 11-18 • Size of sixth form: 230 • Non-denom • Fees: Boarding £7,485-£10,395 pa; Day - free • State

Tel: 01765 602 647
Fax: 01765 606 388
Email: admin@ripongrammar.co.uk
Website: www.ripongrammar.co.uk

Head: Since 2004, Mr Martin Pearman (pronounced Pierman), late forties. Read chemistry at Oxford, taught previously at Bristol GS, Stamford and Woodhouse Grove, where he was deputy head. Three sons, one still at his school. Staff positive about their head and his method of gradual, thoughtful change. 'It's the atmosphere in this school which sets it apart; the quality of relationships between staff and students is better than in any school I've worked in.' Has attracted significant funding since award of specialist engineering status in 2006. A very approachable, unpretentious man, who brings a wide experience of schools and a clear vision of his school's purpose: 'to serve the local community with a high quality education, increasing the life chances of ordinary boys and girls.'

Academic matters: Exam results consistently very good – 70 per cent A*- B at A level in 2010 including over 23 per cent A* grades at A level; over three times the national average. Almost 60 per cent A/A* at GCSE. Specialist engineering status has brought astronomy, statistics and product design into the GCSE curriculum. A level science and maths unsurprisingly strong; roughly equal numbers of girls and boys take chemistry and maths, though physics remains a male stronghold. Complete lab refurbishment recently. Elsewhere some evidence of 'girls' subjects' in e.g. English literature and French (compulsory at GCSE). Sociology, psychology (popular), government and politics, theatre studies also available. German (declining in many schools) still on offer, and Latin, originally started as a twilight subject, appearing by popular demand at GCSE. Law offered at nearby Ripon College, though see below for new sixth form centre.

School does a very fine job over value-added (1015 between Key Stages 2 and 4, near the top of the tree nationally). This is all the more remarkable, given that RGS is not as highly selective as some grammar schools in e.g. Kent and Essex, being unable to draw pupils in great numbers from outside its defined catchment area. SEN support very good; SENCo teacher oversees provision for e.g. visual and hearing impairment and a range of special needs.

Games, Options, the Arts: Over ninety different clubs and activities, ranging from the greenpower electric car to dancing – something for even the most reluctant sportsman or woman to get involved in. Compulsory sport: rugby and cricket mainstay for boys, hockey for girls. Football popular for both sexes (girls were Yorkshire junior champions), also mixed hockey, lacrosse, karate, swimming. Brand new sports hall paid for by independent fundraising campaign, will be available for local use too. Astroturf in the pipeline. New music block due to appear, plus performing arts facility in the new sixth form centre. Lots of enthusiastic musicians – big band performs frequently in Ripon Cathedral, even entertained the Queen. Vocalists encouraged to join one of the two choirs. Superb art on display.

Background and Atmosphere: School originally housed in Ripon Cathedral, granted a royal charter by Queen Mary in 1555. Moved to present green and pleasant 23-acre site in 1874. Original Victorian buildings added to over the years, not always sympathetically, though previous air of impermanence is slowly disappearing, and sports hall, sixth form block and girls' boarding house have more of the dignity one expects in a school of this kind. Boys' boarding house (School) is integral, girls' (Johnson) stands on its own; both (especially the boys') were in need of refurbishment, and a rolling programme was completed in September 2009. Weekly boarding popular; pupils come from North Yorkshire and beyond, some from Europe, N Africa, Dubai and Hong Kong. Boarders (room for 100 out of 800+) do well academically and the few in residence over the weekends are well catered for. Demand for boarding places (14 available a year) outstrips supply, especially post-GCSE.

New sixth form block will serve both RGS and nearby Ripon College, making a reality of head's ambitions to serve the community; there were a hundred applicants for the first thirty places. It will be interesting to see how it all works out, as traditional sixth form governance and organisation are adapted to new circumstances.

Pastoral Care and Discipline: Good pastoral system in operation; in addition pupils look after each other, sixth formers are trained as peer listeners, and teams of form tutors ably support heads of school. Genuinely good relations between staff and students throughout the school; friendly and compassionate house staff create a relaxed boarding environment. Exclusions are rare.

Pupils and Parents: Boarders from abroad, Yorkshire Dales and London, some from armed services, day pupils from Ripon and around. Wide range of parental backgrounds and wealth (or lack of it). Pupils a friendly, courteous, grounded bunch of individuals, proud and privileged to be at the school; little sign of the pushiness and fake sophistication often found further south. Former pupils include fashion designer Bruce Oldfield, rugby international Peter Squires, William Hague MP, David Curry MP, Guardian journalist Katharine Viner, TV presenter Richard Hammond.

Entrance: Mainly from local primaries but a smattering from prep schools. Heavily over-subscribed at 11+. Selection by verbal and non-verbal reasoning tests administered by LEA; school takes top 28 per cent of cohort. Sixth form entry has been minimum six B grades at GCSE, will presumably change when arrangement with Ripon College comes into force. Increasing number from local independents highlights excellent cost-free A level education.

Exit: Very few leavers at 16+, vast majority get first choice universities; a handful each year to Oxbridge. Medicine, law, sciences, engineering popular, also art and psychology.

Money Matters: Yorkshire's only state boarding school, free for day pupils, boarders charged on a sliding scale, but still much cheaper than independent alternatives.

Remarks: An unashamedly academic school, exemplifying much of the traditional English grammar school tradition, though certainly not an exam factory; even so, those with an IQ of lower than 120 could eventually find the pace too hot. A school that gives the impression of being happy with itself and its aims, sitting comfortably in its community – clearly wanted by the people of Ripon, who helped to fight off a challenge to its status in 2000.

Robert Clack School

Gosfield Road, London Borough of Barking and Dagenham, London, RM8 1JU

• Pupils: 1,965 boys and girls • Ages: 11-18 • Size of sixth form: 450
• Non-denom • State

Tel: 020 8270 4200
Fax: 020 8270 4210
Email: office@robert-clack.bardaglea.org.uk
Website: www.robertclack.co.uk

Headteacher: Since 1997, Sir Paul Grant MA PGCE (sixties), famously promoted from head of humanities when the school was at its lowest ebb, and who has since transformed it into an outstanding success story. He is the eldest of seven children from a working-class Liverpudlian family. A keen football fan, he once hoped to turn professional. He went to the Salesian Grammar School in Bootle, where an influential teacher inspired him to study history at Hull University. He completed a PGCE at Durham and an MA at London University, and taught in North Yorkshire, Australia and Newham before joining Robert Clack in 1990.

At this point the school was sliding downhill. Weak leadership meant a lack of support for those teachers who did try to keep order and behaviour was deteriorating rapidly. There was a serious gang culture, children smoked in the corridors and caused chaos in the community at lunchtime. Pupils rode bicycles inside and it was commonplace to set off fireworks indoors. In 1996, only 17 per cent of pupils gained five or more A–C grades at GCSE and the school was on the verge of special measures. The humanities department, however, was going from strength to strength. Sir Paul was appointed headteacher with an emergency plan of action which included a tough, transparent code for bad behaviour and a new system of rewards. He suspended 300 troublemakers in his first week.

'He led by example,' says a deputy, who had then just left the school as a pupil. 'I saw him stopping a bus outside the school and talking to passengers about how the school was going to change and inviting them to phone the school if they had any problems with Robert Clack pupils.' Most teachers were delighted by the new regime but some parents were outraged. Sir Paul insisted on meeting every one and gradually won them round. Changing behaviour was a gradual process which included driving around picking up truants and talking to local shopkeepers, local councillors, council employees such as housing officers, and police.

Sir Paul was knighted in 2009 for services to education, a few weeks after the school received an *Evening Standard* award for excellence in challenging circumstances. Larger than life in build and character, and described by Ofsted as 'tireless', he is married with three daughters. The school has been his life's work, he says. 'I wanted to prove that the children in this school could be excellent and my colleagues could be excellent. I'm incredibly proud of the children, parents and staff.'

Pupils are proud too. 'He always works hard to make us succeed in life.' 'He's strict but fair. You know not to get on his wrong side but he always congratulates you when you do well.'

Academic matters: The school is one of 12 outstanding secondary schools feted by Ofsted for excelling against the odds. Some 40 per cent of pupils are on the special needs register and 40 per cent have free schools meals but results have improved steadily from the 1996 nadir: in 2010, 75 per cent of pupils got five or more good GCSEs (56 per cent including maths and English). Top A level students head for Oxbridge, Durham, Imperial College and most Russell Group universities.

Alongside a strict disciplinary procedure, high quality teaching from a mostly young staff has helped the school achieve outstanding status. The 'Robert Clack Good Lesson' is a template devised by staff which involves explaining to pupils the objective, content and process of each lesson. We met one teacher who was off to Suffolk, appointed to help a school there achieve outstanding status by using his experience at Robert Clack.

The school is a specialist science, maths and computing college, and has recently added a modern languages specialism – a bold move in a strongly working-class school. Although everyone takes French and Spanish for the first three years, at present only 15–20 per cent continue to GCSE. However, the department plans to increase this considerably over the next few years and hopes to introduce Spanish A level alongside the new French course. Everyone takes double science, with some opting for the vocational applied science option and a hundred or so taking three separate sciences. Other vocational options include health and social care, business studies, catering, beauty and ICT.

'We have got where we are because all the children feel there is a pathway for them. They're not finding themselves stranded in set 11 for everything.' The school sets right from the start for English, maths, science and languages. 'We're auditing progress all the time, and a significant number have worked their way right up through the sets.' Other subjects, such as history, geography and RE, are taught in mixed ability groups from year 10 onwards. The ability range is massive, from those aiming at A*s to those who joined the school with a reading age of five or six. 'Teaching a huge range is possible if the behaviour is excellent and class sizes are small, so we make sure that they are.'

There are learning support and mentor rooms where children can come to catch up on literacy and numeracy, perhaps because they have had time off sick or are middle-of-the-road and tend to be overlooked in class. Or they may come here because they are upset because of family problems and can't cope amongst their peers. 'If children are in the wrong place they will disrupt the lesson. We want to be proactive and avoid problems if possible.'

But the 40 per cent on the SEN register – including partially sighted and deaf children – are mostly integrated into the classrooms. We saw a boy with cerebral palsy putting his views across forcefully to the class, despite speech problems. 'The children are very protective of each other.'

The sixth form is part of the North East Consortium with three other local schools, offering over 40 courses at different levels. There are over 800 sixth formers in the consortium, including some 450 at Robert Clack. There are no minimum entry requirements, as courses range from a certificate in motor vehicle servicing to further maths, though students who want to take A levels must have at least five grades Cs at GCSE. 'Many of these students are the first in their families to stay on at school after 16. We don't want to set the benchmark too high – despite the risk of being marked down by Ofsted – because we want to give these children a chance.' Media studies and general studies are the most popular A level courses; maths, further maths, physics and chemistry the most successful. BTecs in business, IT and sport are popular too, as is beauty therapy, taught in a state-of-the-art on-site beauty salon. 'We give everyone the opportunity to be successful here.' In 2009, six students got three or more A grades at A level, and 63 per cent of passes were A to C grades.

Games, Options, the Arts: Sport is hugely important here and the school is frequently borough champion at athletics, swimming, rugby and cross-country. It has also been county champion at rugby and netball, a huge achievement against the Essex selective schools. A rugby academy attracts talented players to the sixth form. Pupils have competed nationally at sports ranging from netball to ski-ing, and their team shirts are displayed proudly alongside photos and trophies. 'If you're good at something we'll encourage you and give you recognition,' said a deputy. 'Paul is very good at reinforcing our successes and using them to motivate pupils.'

A plush leisure centre includes a sports hall and fitness suite, open to the local community outside school hours. There are also tennis and netball courts and a large playing field which includes an all-weather pitch. Numerous sports clubs before, during and after school, and even on Saturday mornings, range from hockey to dance to girls' boxing.

The girls' and boys' choirs performed movingly in assembly during our visit, and one pupil has starred in a West End musical. Instrumental lessons are free, and there's an orchestra and a jazz group. Sixty pupils are studying for music GCSE, and a few each year move on to music technology A level. The school puts on major performances of e.g. *Oliver!* and *High School Musical.* Plenty of high-quality art displayed around the school, and DT is another popular option at GCSE. The school debating team recently won 'best delegation' at a Model UN conference.

School trips range from French exchanges to sports trips to Canada and Barbados and a conservation expedition to Egypt. Few parents could afford to pay for these trips, so the school raises funds from e.g. the Worshipful Company of Chartered Surveyors, and children fund-raise enthusiastically too. 'We believe these trips are vitally important to our children's development, and our wonderful staff will always go the extra mile to make sure they happen.'

Background and Atmosphere: This is a huge, split-site school, named after local legend Bob Clack, who was mayor from 1940 to 1942. The lower school site, which houses Years 7 and 8 and most of Year 9, opened in 1935, the upper school buildings – half a mile away – in 1953. The tower blocks of the Becontree Estate – one of the largest in England – bear down on the school like a fortress. It is one of the most deprived areas of the country, and has been a BNP stronghold. Staff and pupils alike express delight that the BNP was routed in the last election, and credit the school with considerable influence. 'The school is the centre of the community.' 'You can't be racist here.'

The buildings range from shabby prefabs put up 'temporarily' in the '40s to the bright new science block and the media block with facilities for drama, music and media studies, as well as the pristine beauty salon. There are plentiful computers and whiteboards, but the planned rebuild now seems to be receding into the far distance as government funds are cut. The school now plans to cope with expanding numbers – particularly in the sixth form – by importing more temporary classrooms.

The school was the highest placed education establishment in the 2010 *Sunday Times* Best Hundred Companies to Work For list, and winner in the medium-sized company section. It also came first for the quality of its leadership, for personal growth and for its employees' pride in working there.

Pastoral Care and Discipline: This is one of the smartest and most ordered schools we have ever visited. Children are immaculate in blazers and ties, orderly in corridors and attentive in lessons. 'People know not to mess about,' say pupils. 'But it's all fair – punishments are fair. The rules are good ones.' The school works on a combination of iron discipline and plenty of praise. There are colours for sport, music and performing arts. During the assembly we attended large numbers of children lined up to receive merit awards. They approve of their uniform. 'It makes you feel proud to wear our uniform, when you see pupils from other schools prancing around in polo shirts and trainers.'

Children feel very safe here. 'If something happens here they get straight on top of it. This school really does hate bullying – they don't tolerate it.' There's a close bond between pupils and teachers. 'They're always really cheerful. They'll make a joke out of things if they can. And they treat us like grown-ups. They respect our feelings.' Staff are stationed in corridors between lessons and outside the school when pupils leave at the end of the day. No-one below sixth form is allowed out at lunchtime. Sir Paul tours classrooms daily, greeting pupils with words of praise or good-natured censure.

The pupil referral unit handles children who have disrupted lessons, breached the uniform code, started a fight or played truant. 'We get in quickly – we're proactive – and so we've only had two permanent exclusions in the last ten years.'

Pupils and Parents: Largely from the surrounding estates, though proximity to the school puts a premium on the prices of the few houses for sale in the area. Large numbers of single parent families and those with several generations of unemployment. The school employs a parental adviser who visits families under stress and helps with housing, clothing and food allowances. Around 20 per cent Afro-Caribbean families, the rest mostly white working class: Robert Clack was the only London school on Ofsted's 'excelling against the odds' list with a preponderance of children from such typically under-achieving backgrounds

Entrance: Takes 300 children into Year 7 but there are over 200 appeals every year, so the intake invariably increases. Looked after children get priority, as do those with special educational needs, then by distance from the upper school site – generally within a mile or so. Some 2000 applications for the 300 places. Large numbers from other schools join the sixth form.

Exit: About 80 per cent of pupils move up to the sixth form, up from around 20 per cent ten years ago. Some hundred or so students go on to university, to read economics at Cambridge, perhaps, sports coaching at Bath, or primary education at Anglia Ruskin. Excellent careers advice and encouragement to aim high. The school has links with Oxford, Cambridge, Essex, York and East London universities, with visiting speakers, university visits and summer schools.

Remarks: Outstandingly successful comprehensive in one of the most deprived areas of the country. Excellent leadership by a tireless head has transformed a failing school into one that is a source of pride for staff, parents and pupils. 'This school gets you ready for the future,' said a pupil.

Robert Gordon's College

Linked to Robert Gordons College Junior School in the Junior section

Schoolhill, Aberdeen, AB10 1FE

• Pupils: 1,090 boys and girls, all day • Ages: 11-18 • Size of sixth form: 325 • Inter-denom • Fees: £9,765 pa • Independent

Tel: 01224 646 346
Fax: 01224 630 301
Email: p.skingley@rgc.aberdeen.sch.uk
Website: www.rgc.aberdeen.sch.uk

Head of College: Since 2004, Mr Hugh Ouston MA (Oxon) DipEd (fifties). Educated at Glenalmond, he read history at Christ Church (aka The House), Oxford and DipEd from Aberdeen. Previously deputy head of George Watsons, head of history at Beeslack High School in Penicuik (under the 'headmastering genius' of Sir Richard Staite), and assistant head at Dunbar Grammar. An SQH boy. He runs the school with a deputy head of College plus four deputy heads (not quite the same thing) plus Mrs Mollie Mennie MBA DipEd who is head of the junior school and two deputy heads of junior school. 'Would love to teach' but 'impossible', 'not fair to the children'; however he (and some of his senior staff) make a point of watching every member of staff take an entire lesson, 'a good insurance policy'.

A wandering head, 'though I am liable to get to the end of the corridor and then be called back.' 'I inherited (from Brian Lockhart) a tightly-run school, superb' and enjoys the tremendous academic achievements of his pupils, 'boasting like mad', 'tops in everything', 'absolutely nothing to do with me but I get all the credit.' Says 'greatest strengths of the school are its co-educational and cosmopolitan community, the work ethic of its pupils and the fact that a quarter of senior school pupils are on bursaries.' Own four children Gordon's educated, one now at university, three in secondary. Wife 'terribly happy here'; she comes from Aberdeen and her mother lives close by. Relaxed, confident and out-going. Mr Ouston is very much in control, an iron fist in the velvet glove perhaps but riding on a serious high.

Academic matters: Unashamedly academic. 'Top passes per pupil, top passes per candidate; essentially very strong.' Follows the Scottish system, traditionally very strong on maths and sciences, 'science strong, exceptionally large number of excellent results and consistently good on languages,' says the head, which more or less echoes the majority of parental careers (oil, business). School thrilled to have pupils achieving top marks in Scotland in Advanced Higher science subjects over past few years. Five Highers the norm in fifth year (lower sixth) – in 2010, 47 pupils gained at least five A Grades. Huge choice of subjects, 30 on offer and masses of add-ons: philosophy, psychology, cooking, plus pre-med courses, Scots law course, university skills, Chinese and Japanese. An educational triumvirate with Aberdeen University and The Robert Gordon University.

ICT strong and internet connection sourced through the university (i.e. = free), computers throughout, from nursery up. Email for all. Computer-based projectors in every room, plus a quorum of interactive whiteboards (they must be used), including in every classroom in the brand new junior school building.

Eight or ten parallel classes throughout, max 22, two classes of mixed ability in each of the four houses, French for all, Latin for all, Greek for the bright (up to higher). Mandarin Chinese for the ambitious. Setted at 12 for English and maths, but otherwise 'continuous assessment'. German a popular option with Italian and Spanish – the latter to advanced Higher level. Spectacular biology room groaning under the weight of various heads and skulls of horned beasties. The support for learning dept now 'straddles' junior and senior school and is linked into guidance. Actual hands-on assistance plus dual teaching in class, mainly from specialists. School doesn't really do dyslexia per se, though any pupil who hits 'either a temporary or a permanent barrier' will be given as 'much help as is necessary' to overcome that blip. 'Learning and teaching and support for learning definitely comes into that.'

Games, Options, the Arts: Art school at the top of one of the many wings; variety of disciplines, and particularly keen on photography; graphic communication now on stream. Drama now timetabled throughout junior and senior School and is a Highers subject, good and thriving with three new staff and three new studios added to the department.

Magnificent 45-acre sports ground at Countesswells with artificial pitches for tennis/hockey et al; the amazing water-based hockey pitch (gets hosed down at half-time to keep it super smooth) is used by the international squad. The ground at Countesswells is also used during the hols both for junior sports camps and international hockey practice. Historically, school fields strong rugby but also hockey, cricket and golf. Internationalists in all disciplines as well as trips abroad for fun as well as for rugby (Canada, Italy, Australia) hockey (Prague, Ireland) skiing (USA). Well-used swimming pool (water polo, canoeing) on site. Two gyms.

Music department recently refurbished, and strong. Masses of instruments on offer, and the recent trip to USA was a tour de force. Enormous (brass) oompah band of over 200, plus pipe band, part of the CCF (army and RAF sections only).

Hugely popular D of E, 'biggest in Scotland' says the head, with oodles of basic, plus silver and gold galore. Zillions of clubs and societies.

Background and Atmosphere: 'Robert Gordon was born in Aberdeen in 1668, he spent most of his life as a merchant in the Baltic ports, building a significant fortune in the process. He always had the idea of building a Hospital for maintenance, aliment, entertainment and education of young boys and, when he died in 1731, that was his legacy.' Magnificent William Adam quadrangle in the centre of Aberdeen. The school currently occupies the northern side, with masses of modern add-ons behind a fabulous front. The Governors' Room still visibly W Adam. Originally occupied by Hanoverian troops under the Duke of Cumberland on their way to Culloden; the first 14 boys did not take up residence until 1750 and The Hospital changed its name to Robert Gordon's College in 1881, went co-ed in 1989, and added a nursery unit in 1993 (popular after-school club for nursery and junior pupils until 5.30 each day, where they can either play or do supervised homework). Thus endeth chronology. To date.

The school currently shares the quad with The Robert Gordon University to whom it sold the lion's share in 1909, but the uni is off to amalgamate its entire campus down by the riverside at Garthdee and RG governors have agreed to buy back the rest of the quad for £10.4 million (out of 'housekeeping'; no special fund needed). The school took possession of the Blackfriars building and the engineering workshop in 2008 which has now been transformed into the modern junior school with glass walls and specialist rooms for anything you can imagine from art and music to languages and video conferencing. Also houses various 'relocated and refurbished departments' including English, maths, technology and drama from the senior school. The move has drastically reduced class sizes, adding an extra class in each junior school year group as well as extra sets in the Senior School.

The final tranche falls in (technology building and total control of the quad) between 2012 and 2015 when the school will be able to spread back into its wings, demolish the excessively nasty 'temporary' buildings which were going up in the playground during our last visit, and equip itself for the 21st century.

The engineering workshop will be converted into an expressive arts building incorporating a theatre, and the final phase of the technology building will be absorbed by the science department. This is exciting stuff; few inner city schools get such an opportunity though some of the plans are so grandiose that they may not all fit into the current footprint, and the school has no thought of expanding its actual roll.

Sixth formers who help with school meals are spared paying for lunch, though from 14 onwards they can (and most do) go into the town for food. The (upmarket) Olive Garden on board for school meals – and 'food fantastic,' said the head (whose girth we shall examine with interest at our next meeting). Girls wear rather jolly Dress Gordon kilted skirts. The whole school processes behind the pipe band down the streets of Aberdeen to St Nicholas Church on Founder's Day.

Pastoral Care and Discipline: House system recently reinforced, with class captains at all levels plus sixth form assistants at 11 to help those newly arrived in the senior school feel more at home. Guidance system in operation – tutors – as well as good PSHE. Fairly sin-free school – pupils allowed out for lunch and 'no bad reports'. No smoking on the premises (campus too small), one expelled for drugs during head's reign. Strong anti-bullying programme, would be suspended for booze, which is a bit obvious out of school; ditto smoking.

Pupils and Parents: This is THE school in Aberdeen. Lots of university parents (easy to drop off), oodles of professional and oil-related ditto, plus farmers etc. Day starts early at 8.30 and children often come from as far away as Montrose i.e. 35/40 miles away. Parking at drop off and collection times hideous. Vast and increasing number of first time buyers consistent with the vagaries of the oil industry, and strong global ethnic mix. Good *Quadrangle* newsletter bi-monthly and parental involvement. Parents love the school so much that often, having spent years in the oily wilderness, they buy a proper house, and at the next placement maw and the wains stay behind, leaving paw to travel the world alone.

Entrance: Interview for nursery and five year olds entering junior school; test for those over nine and exam for senior school. Fewer leave post Highers than arrive: usual strictures for entry plus test. Pupils either come up from primary school, or from local state schools, hugely over-subscribed – particularly in the junior school and S1, but Aberdeen has a fluid population and it is worth applying at any time – school can cope with a short period of 'overlap' if they know a family is about to be re-located. Rather jolly in-house instruction manual for S1s (i.e. first year senior school).

Exit: Coming and going with relocation, otherwise (95 per cent) to universities all over, the odd gap year, 'few don't go to university'. Still fairly conservative in choice, majority choosing either Aberdeen or RGU followed by Edinburgh and Glasgow Universities; trickle – penny numbers – down south, ditto Oxbridge. Medics, lawyers and would-be scientists and engineers top the wish-list, almost all got into their first choice uni, 'but then we have no delusions,' said the head.

Money Matters: Huge number of endowments – Robert Gordon's expectation that 'those who came to the Hospital and did well in later life would plough back some of their gains'. In 1816 'a generous bequest by Alexander Simpson of Collyhill made it possible to extend the accommodation' and Gordonians and FPs have continued to do so ever since. 185 children on some form of bursary, with 100 per cent help available to those in real need with bright kids. Plus The Aberdeen Educational Endowment provides extra bursaries. Around 20 means-tested free places in Secondary 1 available each year. With a mega appeal for more dosh (as ever) and, guess what, there will be an appeal to help convert the newly re-acquired bits of quad.

Remarks: Very strong co-ed day school with a far-sighted head relishing the unique challenge of masterminding the transition into such a happy acquisition. If you want to keep the little darlings at home, and you live near enough, you couldn't do better. Not a school for social climbers and probably rather intimidating for gentle souls.

Roedean School

Roedean Way, Brighton, East Sussex, BN2 5RQ

• Pupils: 375 girls, all board except for 85 • Ages: 11-18 • Size of sixth form: 175 • C of E, but all faiths are welcome • Fees: Boarding £26,100-£29,025; Day £14,580-£16,800 pa • Independent

Tel: 01273 667500
Fax: 01273 676722
Email: info@roedean.co.uk
Website: www.roedean.co.uk

Madame (as the rest of female teachers): Since 2008, Mrs Frances King MA MA MBA (forties), previously head of Heathfield, Ascot (qv). Educated at Ashford School, Kent, did a gap year in Israel where her parents were on secondment (and where she improved her Hebrew) and read theology at Oxford, followed much later by a part-time degree in philosophy and religious ethics plus an MBA in international leadership (i.e. headship) in the independent sector. Must be coming in useful. Previously taught RS at Lady Eleanor Holles, Francis Holland (CG), Guildford County School and Tormead. Married, two grown-up children.

Mrs King has cornered the market in heads who arrive at a school and then find themselves expected to chew up and digest another school called St Mary's. At Heathfield she oversaw the meal that was made of St Mary's Wantage, an event that turned out to be more of a snack than a banquet once the candles were snuffed and the dishes cleared away, Heathfield numbers being only mildly inflated by immigrant Wantagees. She had no sooner arrived at Roedean when St Mary's Hall, half a mile into Brighton – a school with a long and honourable tradition but which had subsisted on meagre fare for too long – arrived with cap in hand and begging bowl and asking for 'a merger'. Mrs King's predecessors had long striven to convince sceptical Brightonians that their school was a local as well as an international one and that they should taste for themselves. Roedean's numbers being, therefore, hardly buoyant, this was manna from heaven. The acquisition of St Mary's with its new, fresh junior school will, at last, give Roedean a firm foothold in Brighton proper and, it is to be hoped, a regular feeder.

The merger, while exciting and full of potential for Roedean, comes at a cost and much heartache. While the St Mary's junior school has been swallowed whole and with relish, the senior school has been closed. The loss is deeply felt among past and present alumnae. For the second time, Mrs King found herself on a panel which saw her staff competing with St Mary's' staff for their own jobs. This is under the TUPE system which ensures parity between staff when mergers occur. Howling and gnashing of teeth is inevitable though some of this has been attenuated by staff agreeing to take early retirement or finding places elsewhere.

Mrs King herself is clever, straightforward, immensely likeable and looks a bit like Kate Moss might a few years on, if she's lucky. She is tautly energetic, visionary, different. She has a huge amount to do and, in time, will get it all done. The right person in the right place at the right time.

Academic matters: At A level, a maths and science powerhouse – partly due to the intake of girls from the far east at the upper end of the school and partly due to the setting of a maths entrance test for post-16 applicants – something Mrs King is now, wisely, 'looking at'. In 2009, 63 takers for maths A level, of whom a stunning 49 achieved As. In physics, out of 30 takers, 19 got As. On the other hand, only one taker each for German and Latin. Says Mrs King, 'I want to work on the languages. It's "an area of development"'. Economics a popular option. Overall, in 2009, 85 per cent of subjects taken achieved A/B grades, 64 per cent got As. Now taking IGCSE in maths and science; physics dept has opted for the more demanding AQA syllabus.

At GCSE, 96 per cent A*–C grades, 64 per cent A/A*. Exceptional results in German, Latin and art suggest that girls are selling themselves and the school short by not pursuing these subjects into the sixth. Mrs King plans to expand the academic opportunities. 'I want philosophy and ethics. I'm determined to bring in an ethical dimension to science.' This is Roedean but not as we know it. IT whiteboards etc all much more in evidence now, plasma screens with latest news, good school intranet – further signs of Mrs King's modernising energy.

EAL taken by many although a good level of English is a pre-requisite for all candidates for places here – around 100 have one-to-one language/learning tuition which includes good support for a wide range of mild SENs. Group lessons to prepare for the IELTS exam. School's location and sloping site make wheelchair access virtually impossible though a range of other physical disabilities e.g.

mild visual or hearing impairments catered for. 75 on current SEN register, of whom two thirds are dyslexic to some degree. School copes well with dys's, Asperger's, ADHD etc. IEPS where needed. Small group and one-to-one help (extra charge) but no withdrawal from curriculum subjects. Gifted and talented stretched as befits need. Good careers centre and good library with first-rate full time staff.

Games, Options, the Arts: Around 30 sports available here including riding at Ditchling riding school and very active polo club, popular with girls from all types of backgrounds. Multi-purpose sports hall and additional fitness suite for older girls, inviting indoor pool and plenty of outdoor space – fields rolling seawards and robust attitude to go with it – 'we don't stop because it's raining a bit,' we were told. Girls return from matches envying the Astroturfs on offer elsewhere and school currently managing doughtily without, though, 'in due course there will probably be one' and they do borrow a couple at nearby sports centre. Everyone takes dance for the first two years and many thereafter. Successes in many sports, notably netball. Yoga and scuba diving now offered. Lovely adventure playground for younger girls (money raised by parents) and a great attraction to visiting prospective pupils.

Arts flourish though in rooms of varying sizes and much work in many media delights the eye – super textiles, ceramics and very lively DT – all witness to clever and inspirational teaching – as are excellent results. Music is strong in good size class teaching room and many smaller spaces. Music tech 'there if you want to' but, as yet, not many do, though fab new music tech room in the ensemble room should change all that. Concerts in the wonderfully atmospheric Edwardo-Romanesque chapel or the hall or theatre – an exceptional asset with wholly flexible staging, allowing for theatre-in-the-round or an orchestra pit and seating 320. 'Team' plays, one senior and two junior productions a year. No shying away from grittiness – *Our Country's Good* tackled in 2009. All looks professional, well-supported and enjoyed with no hint of flashiness. D of E, Young Enterprise and masses of highly enjoyable and very effective charity work. Each year thousands of squids raised for various charities. More extra-curricular opportunities than you can fit into your week.

Background and Atmosphere: You drive out of Brighton heading east, the huge marina clinking below between you and the open sea and there, in front, bolted to the hillside and above the cliffs, you see a vast, twin turreted, red-roofed pile and, if you don't know, you wonder what on earth it could be. This is Roedean of unique (and largely outdated) reputation but no longer with the stern aspect of yore. Its recent makeover with six washes of custard limewash – 'applied', says Mrs King, by 'teams of gorgeous Aussies who come and do it in the hols' – has restored it to the hue of its youth. Now, most attractively, it changes colour according to the light and time of day and no longer looks determined to outface invaders and marauders, especially those of the opposing sex. The school was designed in 1898 by the architect of the former Wembley stadium – hence the trademark twin turrets – Sir John Simpson. And the sign says, 'Welcome' and welcome you feel in this relaxed, orderly, spacious and warm – in all senses – school. Signage, overall, however, needs improvement. It is perfectly possible to drive out of Brighton with Roedean on the cliff above and get lost trying to reach it.

Having begun at the end of the 19th century as a school with 10 pupils and three mistresses, 10 minutes' walk away in Lewes Crescent, the school rapidly expanded and the present building bears witness to the confidence, solidity and durability its redoubtable founders felt about girls' education. The building has a medieval baronial feel with huge high windows, vast tiled fireplaces and many pretty massive rooms. One feels the place could take twice the number of pupils and be far from crowded. Corridors and many other areas are cheerily decorated in a bright primrose yellow and smart new blue carpets giving a fresh, warm feel. Clearly it's a nightmare to keep up and the battering of the elements visible not just outside, as patches of bubbly damp on many walls, but the place is attractively and not skimpily furnished and it feels like home. A few atmospheric rather Gothic corridors and staircases and a lovely cloister area on the way to the chapel – for quiet and repose. Girls in 'French navy' uniforms seem relaxed and friendly and keen to give of their best.

The 'merger' with St Mary's is a major event and one felt acutely throughout the school community. The news was greeted with much anxiety among current parents who feared, 'we would be swamped with less able girls, our classes would be huge, we would lose our lovely teachers' and so on. Panic has died down; in reality only small numbers have joined each year from St Mary's and Roedean can accommodate them with ease. Roedean parents also much soothed by Mrs King's assiduity in keeping them informed. Roedean girls now contemplate with cries of 'sooeeet' the prospect of junior school tots coming up for PE etc. Likewise, the potential ex-St M's pupils were trepidatious. Would Roedean be snobby and posh, full of an international elite, all cleverer than them? Four St M's governors now on the Roedean governing body, the acceptance by Roedean of St Mary's' historic obligation to the clergy and their daughters, and the efforts made by Roedean – girls and staff – to be friendly, mean we anticipate few problems for St M's girls in settling in and finding happiness. 'They have been very welcoming,' a St Mary's girl told us, 'even to those of us who aren't joining them'.

Pastoral Care and Discipline: Discipline is never a problem. No drugs or similarly serious incidents in recent times but 'there would be no alternative to exclusion' if anyone were endangering herself or another member of the community. Integration of overseas pupils is more successful here than in many comparable schools – far less struggle in getting everyone to join in after the first few weeks – though Mrs King has yet to enforce her predecessor's wise stipulation that English alone was to be spoken in day time and in public places.

Strong pastoral system and all staff on the alert for a long face or other signs of unhappiness or disturbance. All girls have open and wholly confidential (except in cases of actual danger) access to a counsellor. Active peer-listening scheme. Pride taken in caring for each other and family atmosphere. 'My daughter finds it a very nurturing environment,' said one parent, 'and she's very happy there'. All female teachers are called 'Madame' but this does not imply a stilted formality in the relationship. 'The pastoral care is amazing,' a sixth former enthused. 'If you ever need to you can chat to anyone. They really want you to do well. Because they live here, they're with you all the time – you become really comfortable with them. You know there's a line you don't step over but we are really relaxed with them.'

Boarding accommodation undergoing rolling programme and best upper school rooms now quite large and with en-suite bathrooms. We saw some much improved since our last visit. Younger girls share in rooms of two to four but all have space and all rooms are quite cosy. All upper sixth in Keswick House in single rooms with proper sized beds, good kitchen and common room. Nice touches like hot choc and coffee on tap all day. Food, in general, excellent, complete with dietary warnings/info where necessary and special needs catered for. Special help given on occasions like Ramadan fasting. Boarders are full boarders though a new flexibility is on the cards, especially for older girls, which would surely add appeal. Currently 225 girls in school over weekends. Roedean more helpful than many schools when it comes to booking travel arrangements etc.

Excellent main hall in the sixth form house used for outside speakers, careers talks, house meeting etc. Sixth Form girls do their own laundry – good practice! Other houses linked by 'bunnyruns' so you don't have to go outside from one to the other. Good support for overseas boarders includes escorted service to/from Victoria and taxis to airports. Some belongings can stay at school over hols. A new café for visiting parents, girls and staff – Horizons – incorporates the excellent shop which sells everything including uniform. Everyone has email and wireless internet throughout the campus. Help for day pupils includes buses which take girls away from school late into the evening, after the extra-curricular activities no-one wants to miss. There is a very flexible approach to boarding and girls are free to go home any week-end provided they do not have commitments at school.

Pupils and Parents: From 30+ countries and every continent. 55 per cent from UK. Chinese, but also Thai, Russian, Korean, African and Europeans of all sorts. Also more than half British, most from the south of England and school busy recruiting in this area. Clientele not the stiff upper class and diplomatic types of yester-year but everyone – and it's hard to imagine a girl who would not feel welcome here. Happy parents in an interview said that they saw their daughters as 'children of the world'. Lots of famous ORs include Baroness Chalker, Verity Lambert, Sally Oppenheimer, Jill Balcon, Katherine Whitehorn, Adele Geras, Tanya Streeter, Honeysuckle Weeks, Rebecca Hall, Philippa Tattersall and Dame Cicely Saunders of blessed memory.

Entrance: Hitherto no main feeder schools. Now own junior and entrance from there more or less a given (see junior school review). Entry at 11, 13 and 16 is via Common Entrance, scholarship or the school's own entrance exam. All entrants are required to visit the school for interview and may spend a couple of days at the school prior to joining. Candidates should be registered as early as possible in the academic year prior to their entry in school to ensure the availability of a place. In reality, school is not currently over-subscribed though this may not last under new regime and with new source of pupils from local junior.

Exit: Very few leave before 16; several do go, post-16, to local sixth form colleges. Some – as elsewhere – return, gratefully, after a few weeks outside. Recent leavers in large numbers to the London University colleges and the LSE; others, mostly, to Bristol, Nottingham and Durham. Courses in everything from cosmetic science to veterinary medicine, German to law.

Money Matters: Lots of scholarships – academic, music, sport, art or performing art – competed for at 11, 12, 13 and 16 by exam and audition – worth up to 10 per cent fees – with additional bursaries if necessary. Sixth form scholarships also by exam in A level subjects and a general paper. Three new 100 per cent bursaries, the Brighthelm Awards, for entry into Years 7, 9 and 12 should increase awareness of the school amongst potential day pupils of high ability. These fully funded places are means-tested and cover the day fees for the duration of the student's stay at Roedean. Roedean has taken over St Mary's Hall's historic commitment to provide generous bursaries for the daughters of clergy. This should be better known.

Remarks: School has a healthy spirit and much to offer. Adoption of St Mary's as its own presents an immense challenge but a bigger opportunity. The impressive Mrs King is relaxed – 'confidence is strengthening', she says. Bin your old prejudices about the place. Go and look.

Rossall School

Linked to Rossall Junior School in the Junior section

Broadway, Fleetwood, Lancashire, FY7 8JW

• Pupils: 620-240 boarding, 380 day with 65 in the International Study Centre • Ages: 11-18 • Size of sixth form: 75 • C of E • Fees: Day £9,510-£11,700; Boarding £14,850-£29,220 pa • Independent

Tel: 01253 774201
Fax: 01253 772052
Email: enquiries@rossall.org.uk
Website: www.rossallschool.org.uk

Headmaster: Since 2008, Dr Stephen Winkley, (mid sixties). Originally from Norfolk, won scholarships to boarding school in Oxford, and then to Oxford University. 'Dropped into teaching by accident in 1969', and has never regretted it. No commuting, wonderful surroundings, astonishing children, magnificent holidays. He even gets paid! Has four children (two boys, both teachers, one girl at school, another at university). Has almost always avoided playing games but made up for it by singing and water colour painting. Spent 16 years at Cranleigh School in Surrey, then six years as deputy head at Winchester College, 'looking after the brainiest children in England'; and then 15 years as head of Uppingham School in Rutland, during which time he was also Chairman of the Boarding Schools' Association. Bubbles over with enthusiasm for the job: 'The great joy of boarding schools is the chance to see the whole child: the hopeless mathematician who is wonderful at rounders ... the undistinguished academic who is an absolutely vital agony-aunt for her year group.' A physical presence, sees and is seen by students, who hold him in obvious affection. Regarded as inspirational by new senior management team. First two years certainly challenging but he's definitely made his mark, will be a very hard act to follow!

Academic matters: Acceptable and improving results given the range of pupil intake. As Dr Winkley says 'Rossall is a broad church'. Over 50 per cent of IB pupils achieved 30+ points, two thirds of A level grades were A/B and 45 per cent of GCSE grades were A*/A with 94 per cent achieving 5 grades A*–C including English and maths (71 per cent in 2009). Improvement underpinned by much more support from EAL department. Widening subject choice at A level though increasing number of overseas sixth formers looking for IB.

Excellent art facilities and outstanding DT workshop and design room. Recent investment in IT infrastructure and evidence of new hardware (with more to come). Outdated science laboratories and some tired classrooms and public areas tell of recent difficult times.

International Study Centre (ISC) in existence for 13 years – overseas students from over 30 countries, China, Hong Kong, Korea, Taiwan, Thailand, Vietnam, Germany, Poland, Spain, Turkey, Switzerland and Dubai. Intensive English language courses lead to International GCSE or a transfer to main school (about 30 a year).

Transition to senior school is through Middle School (Years 7 and 8) newly heralded as Dragon, and housed in a stand-alone building at the front of the school. Pastoral continuity assured through over sight of Junior School Head, whilst academics come under senior school auspices.

Games, Options, the Arts: Traditional team sports of rugby, hockey and cricket for the boys, with regional and national competition success. Hockey and netball for the girls. New floodlit Astroturf opened September 2010 makes a statement. Swimming pool, fives, eight courts recently renovated by the Rossall Foundation, and basketball in gym, make over recently completed, popular additions. Recent staff appointments strengthen specialist coaching available but sport optional from year 10.

Famous for Rossall ('Ross') hockey, played on the beach, tides permitting, and very popular – invented in 1860s, with esoteric rules, providing fierce inter-house competition. Keen CCF (all three arms) includes girls; leads to BTec in Year 11. School has its own outward bound award; Lake District and Yorkshire Dales used.

Plenty of opportunity to make music, in individual tuition or joining choirs and ensembles. Full music, dance and drama programme from weekly informal performances to overseas summer tour.

Background and Atmosphere: Founded in 1844 on the windswept north Fylde coast overlooking the Irish Sea, an easy tram ride from Blackpool. Unprepossessing entrance to the campus eclipsed by the Oxford-type quad which opens up with mellow redbrick buildings and a handsome chapel to one side. Healthy sea air, pretty brisk in winter and, according to Dr Winkley, 'The sea air banishes asthma and eczema and hay fever and promotes complexions of which French beauticians would be envious". However not so kind to window frames and an overdue programme of refurbishment is underway.

The ISC obviously looms pretty large – an influencing factor in the surge in recruitment of international boarding students? Redressing the balance of overseas to UK students and ration of girls to boys, particularly for sixth form, is high on the school's agenda. Senior houses mix day and boarding students to encourage friendship, respect and understanding of different cultures. The success of this is evidenced in social groups seen around the campus. 'I've had the opportunity to make friends from across the world and I am sure I will stay in touch with them when we leave here' said one sixth former.

Church of England foundation, whole school chapel every Friday morning. Large dining hall, seating at traditional long tables and benches, informal seating with staff and pupils happily sharing tables. In-house catering, cafeteria style service, lukewarm pupil comment on food (forever thus?), improvement plans underway.

A full programme of events, activities and field trips runs each weekend.

Pastoral Care and Discipline: Strong anti-bullying ethos 'spotted quickly and dealt with quietly and effectively' said one sixth form prefect. Not a druggy school. Blackpool a temptation, but head says whole-school vigilance pays off. Overseas pupils 'often set our boys and girls very fine examples'. Discipline set on positive values. Expectations of a high standard of pupil behaviour are seldom disappointed. Excellent staff/pupil relationship.

Pupils and Parents: UK pupils from local catchment area, predominantly day, though with some flexi-boarding. Parents are mainly business people, often first time buyers with little or no understanding of boarding. Growing number of Services children amongst the boarders though 80 per cent from overseas.

Socially at ease, confident without arrogance, courteous students, happy to be at Rossall. Lots of smiles, eye contact and deference at doors as you walk around. Cultural breadth encourages tolerance and respect, making it easier for pupils 'to be themselves'.

Entrance: Non selective but 11+, 13+ and 16+ entrants required to sit an entrance examination. Otherwise two latest school reports and reference from head.

Exit: Some 95 per cent go to a wide range of universities, across the UK; some to Oxbridge. Gap years are popular.

Money Matters: Twenty academic, music, sports and all-round scholarships awarded annually.

Remarks: A happy co-educational school with a successful International Study Centre providing a cosmopolitan experience in north west Lancashire. Sweeping reforms at a critical time under Dr Winkley's inspired leadership now bearing fruit with improving academic results and a surge of overseas students. Restoring the balance of pupils, particularly in the sixth form, may prove a more difficult matter.

Royal Grammar School (Guildford)

Linked to Lanesborough School in the Junior section

High Street, Guildford, Surrey, GU1 3BB

- Pupils: 900 boys; all day • Ages: 11-18 • Size of sixth form: 240
- Non-denom • Fees: £13,023-£13,305 pa • Independent

Tel: 01483 880 600
Fax: 01483 880 602
Email: j.cox@rgs-guildford.co.uk
Website: www.rgs-guildford.co.uk

Headmaster: Since 2007, Dr Jon Cox BSc PhD (early forties). Educated at St Mary's College, Southampton, then studied physiology and bio-chemistry at Southampton University. Postgrad course at Royal College of Music (his instrument is the French horn) and toyed with becoming a professional musician. Opted instead for PhD in biochemistry and to keep music as a hobby. Unusual route to headship – began teaching biology at Whitgift School in Croydon in 1992, 'just really to try it out,' never dreaming he would be bitten by the teaching bug and stay there 14 years, rising through the ranks to deputy head. He was appointed to RGS in November 2005 and spent a year as headmaster-in-waiting before replacing the popular and long serving Tim Young – a hard act to follow. So far so good, Dr Cox has made no waves and is enjoying a honeymoon running-in period. One of his first actions was to write to all parents canvassing their views – he says the main message was 'don't change' and he is treading carefully, no wholesale changes so far. But he is already tinkering around the edges, with a few changes to the pastoral system, and is 'looking at the curriculum', particularly Pre-U and IB. 'As the new boy I'm in a great position to instigate these discussions,' he says.

In such a big school, he's still something of an unknown quantity to a good number of boys and their parents. One who has met him several times describes him as 'the chalk to Mr Young's cheese'. Hasn't yet perfected Mr Young's instant recall of names to faces, 'but I'm working on it,' he says. A personable fellow. Laughs a lot in conversation, nice friendly manner, welcomes discussion, 'but in the end I make the decision'. Can obviously be tough when it's needed but is also sensitive – impressed parents at his first prizegiving with a great speech following the school's sad loss of a pupil and governor. Parents feel he and his (inherited and experienced) deputies make a good team. Married with three children, he still plays the French horn and is a keen amateur magician! A chap worth watching to see what tricks he has up his sleeve for the future.

Academic matters: Outstanding teaching plus selective intake equals superb results. Boys come in expecting to work hard and most do. Reputedly and actually strong at maths and sciences. Maths is the most popular option at A and A/S level and over 80 boys take the maths IGCSE a year early. Economics comes second, with physics, chemistry and biology close behind. (The school has moved to IGCSE in maths and sciences). Still, boys praise the English teaching and A level results from the minority who opt for the subject are super. Modern language compulsory to GCSE. Choice of French or Spanish at age 11. German and Greek become options at age 13. Each year a number of boys take Japanese, Chinese and Russian GCSEs. Sixth formers join up with two local girls' schools (Tormead and Guildford High) for weekly general studies programme. All homework done at home. No streaming but setting in French and maths from Years 10–11. No ESL provision. Handful of dyslexics.

Games, Options, the Arts: Perceived as less sporty than bevy of heavyweight public schools that surround it but RGS more than holds its own (two boys last year selected for England U19 rugby team, Surrey U16 hockey champions, Surrey U15 tennis champions). Outstanding sailing (boasting the current British and World Champions) and athletics and wide range of minor sports. Rugby, hockey and cricket each get their own term and the school turns out 27 rugby teams, 15 hockey teams, 12 cricket teams, plus tennis and athletics teams. Competitive soccer is restricted to the sixth form. The 15-minute drive to the school's luxuriant games fields south of Guildford is not the boys' favourite interlude – the travel eats into the once a week two-hour games session. But a £6 million indoor sports centre and all-weather pitch have improved the school's games facilities dramatically.

High standard of music with huge array of opportunities including concerto consort, chamber ensembles, big band and a jazz group. Top musicians or singers can join the high-powered Guildford Sinfonia or the Chorale, along with the cream of other local schools. Good drama – now offered through to A level. Small but useful drama studio. Performance auditorium opened in 2005. Annual musical production also incorporates girls from Tormead and Guildford High. Art school opened 2006 and a sixth form centre in 2007. Big on brainbox activities, e.g. chess, the School National Quiz Competition (finalists for several years) and Olympiads.

During period eight every Monday afternoon, boys are obliged to participate in CCF, Explorer Scouts or D of E. The school day ends at 4pm and, although a few boys stay on for team practices and clubs, most extracurriculars take place at lunch to allow transport connections to be made.

Background and Atmosphere: Ancient and historic, dating from first decade of the 16th century. Mouldering 1552 charter from King Edward VI kept behind glass in head's study and the school's official title is still King Edward VI's Grammar School. Tall white 450 year old building on one side of busy Guildford High Street oozes charm. Shame about the huge main teaching block on the other side which is strictly 1960s, but plans are afoot for redevelopment and adjacent land has recently been acquired for this. Was run as a state school for 30 years after the war but went independent again in 1977. Class sizes reasonable – 21–22 up to age 14, then 16–17 during GCSEs and an average of 10 in sixth form. Space at a premium wherever you go. Cramped library but with spacious computer equipped study area tucked above. Cramped lunchroom (excellent food) with boys queuing down the hall. Breakfast service for early risers. All classrooms equipped with interactive whiteboards.

Pastoral Care and Discipline: A continual challenge as the school stands smack in the centre of Guildford town centre (sandwiched between Argos and McDonald's) but the school manages it well. Boys maintain that this urban location is the school's greatest strength, teaching them how to manage – and excel – in the real world. Head agrees, 'It's real life. The boys see guys selling *The Big Issue* as they walk to school from the station.' Shops out of bounds until age 14 and even then access is a privilege, not a right, and boys learn quickly to be responsible to safeguard that privilege. Littlest boys are well looked after and boys joining the school at 13 are put in lessons as a group so they can all be new together. Each boy's tutor checks him in twice a day. Sixth formers all have a chance to be prefects and mentors to younger pupils. Much more freedom in sixth form when boys may go off campus when they choose. Uniform to fifth form only – all sixth now wear suits. Social life abounds in the High Street and on the trains and buses where there is no shortage of contact with young ladies from the local girls' schools.

Pupils and Parents: Clever, mature, hard-working boys. Parents committed to education and high standards. Many educated by state grammar schools and overwhelming majority have university degrees. About 15 per cent of mothers are teachers. Large numbers join from own prep, Lanesborough. Other main feeders: Cranmore, Danes Hill, Hoe Bridge, Yateley Manor and state schools South Farnham, Busbridge, Holy Trinity and Waverley Abbey. Many boys travel from as far as south west London, Portsmouth and Reading as the school is close to main Guildford train and bus stations. OBs: Terry Jones of Monty Python and cricketer Bob Willis.

Entrance: Selective but not impossible (two and a half applicants for every place). 75–100 boys enter at 11, after attending entrance exam in January before the September of proposed entry. Tested in English, maths and verbal reasoning, plus short interview. Weight also given to report from current school. Further interviews in English and maths for borderline cases. 50–75 boys enter at 13 after having spent a day at the school for pre-CE assessments at either 11 or 12. On the basis of this they will get an offer conditional on satisfactory performance on CE or scholarship papers. 12+ exam similarly involves English, maths and VR. Small number join at sixth form – GCSE As required in all subjects that will be continued to AS. This school is a bargain and many thankful parents, who could never afford more expensive schools, can scrape together one set of fees for RGS. Bursaries are available to fund free or reduced fee places for deserving, needy state school pupils.

Exit: Around 30 a year to Oxbridge and big clutches to Bristol, Exeter, Nottingham and Durham. Large numbers reading medicine, economics, engineering, physics, chemistry. Very few trickle out after GCSEs to local sixth form colleges.

Remarks: Thriving top notch grammar school, which happily whips in the brightest 10 per cent from its juicy catchment area and, on the whole, does them proud.

Royal Grammar School (Newcastle)

Linked to Royal Grammar School Junior School (Newcastle) in the Junior section

Eskdale Terrace, Newcastle upon Tyne, Tyne and Wear, NE2 4DX

• Pupils: 1,250 pupils in junior and senior schools. 25 per cent girls. All day. • Ages: 11-18, juniors 7-10 • Size of sixth form: Approx 380 including girls • Non-denom • Fees: £9,747 pa • Independent

Tel: 0191 281 5711
Fax: 0191 212 0392
Email: admissions@rgs.newcastle.sch.uk
Website: www.rgs.newcastle.sch.uk

Head: Since 2008, Dr Bernard Trafford MA PhD (in educational management), early fifties; previously head of Wolverhampton Grammar School from 1990. Married to Katherine, two daughters post-university. Educated at Downside and St Edmund Hall, Oxford, taught briefly at RGS High Wycombe, went to Wolverhampton in 1981 as head of music, then head of sixth form, finally head. A former chairman of HMC. Has a fine voice, noted for organising a choir at HMC conferences; has been known to sing and blow his trumpet in public at RGS Newcastle. Has particular interests in inclusion and accountability, has written widely on democratic school management.

An urbane, approachable and talented man, with an avuncular air that somehow calls Stephen Fry to mind. No dilettante, though: he led WGS from the front through stormy waters during the end of assisted places and the advent of co-education, and knows what he wants for a school; very clear-sighted and experienced. Has his own website, where you can read all about his jazz band and compositions. Left our meeting (by pre-arrangement) to go and read Humpty Dumpty to a junior form. It's said that Newcastle parents haven't quite made up their minds about him yet.

Academic matters: Impressive; outstanding results, always up there with the best. All take three sciences at GCSE; ten subjects the norm, seven core plus three options, ranging from Latin and Greek to music. Enormous enthusiasm for economics, history and politics at A level; in 2010, just under 70 per cent A*/A grades, 89 per cent A*–B across all subjects. Following introduction of girls into sixth form in 2001, wider choice of subjects at A level; psychology the latest addition. Sciences strong boosted by impressive science and technology block with state-of-the-art labs running off wide corridors filled with home-grown art.

School is keen on local partnerships and runs practical courses on Saturdays and in the summer with local comprehensives on genetics and the like (the Newcastle Science Enrichment Programme). Computers everywhere, email for all. 'ICT not currently offered as an exam subject.' Computer-based language lab, and grand new modern languages suite; Spanish and German on offer, plenty of takers at GCSE but few at A level. Mandarin non-exam course in sixth form. School does well by SEN pupils it takes, but head observes they could do better. They now have a member of staff in charge of learning support.

Games, Options, the Arts: Rugby unbelievably strong, beating all contenders, with regular trips abroad – runners up in the national *Daily Mail* cup in 2010. Vast array of sport on offer – football, cricket, athletics and gymnastics – currently national champions at two out of the three age groups – plus hockey, netball (reached national finals), basketball, swimming, tennis and squash. Girls do well; new director of sport is a woman (there's also – relax, chaps – a male head of rugby). Enviable new sports hall. Own rugby pitch on site, and outfields rented nearby, much use made of local facilities for minority and individual sports. 50-year lease on magnificent Newcastle County Cricket Ground, five minutes' walk from school.

Huge variety of clubs, chess meets three times a week and bridge is popular. Outstanding debating, regular prize-winners. Technology club equally successful. CCF for both boys and girls as well as involvement with local community – the Inner City Partnership, where pupils work with deprived children on a one-to-one basis. Strong charity commitment. D of E flourishing.

Music does very well, not unexpectedly; new £10 million development includes performing arts centre with 300-seat auditorium, recording studio, recital room, drama/dance studio, ten rehearsal rooms and percussion studio. Masses of orchestras, bands and ensembles. Regular concerts; most recent ones well attended, encouraged no doubt by swish new accommodation. Choir recently sang Mass in St Mark's basilica and other cathedrals throughout Europe. Drama important here; performance studies and film studies now added to A levels. Masses of take-up in all disciplines of art, e.g. screen printing and 3D, plus frequent trips abroad; pupils' work exhibited in local galleries. Trips to battlefields for historians, to Greece and Italy for classicists, as well as World Challenge (recently to Kyrgyzstan, Argentina).

Background and Atmosphere: Foundation dates back over 450 years, current buildings much revamped with stylish glazed arches linking the main buildings and making the whole place look more put-together and elegant. Redbrick 1906 Queen Anne style frontage conceals a mass of add-ons round the impressively large, five-acre sports grounds (remember this is a city centre school); more new build planned. School surrounded by inner ring road motorways and a hundred metres from Jesmond metro station, used by vast majority of pupils. Well-used handsome old hall, with organ. Lecture theatre with fine stained-glass windows. Sixth form centre flourishing. Libraries recently upgraded and a certain amount of re-jigging in the classroom area. Junior school extended and refurbished in recent years.

School a buzzy, busy place; sets high expectations in and out of the classroom. 'Students' natural curiosity means they constantly surprise themselves – and their teachers – with how much they can do and achieve, being willing to try out new ideas without fear of ridicule even when they get things wrong.' Plenty of North-Eastern can-do in evidence. Success in just about anything celebrated and applauded in assemblies.

No specific provision of G&T (many will fall anyway into this ill-defined category), but school willing to 'make space', e.g. with special programmes, for the very clever. Value-added statistics treated as amber light, especially for lower middle group as they approach GCSE. Girls admitted to sixth in 2001, school now completely co-educational.

Pastoral Care and Discipline: Pupils are allocated a personal tutor who stays with them throughout; weekly meetings. Vigorous anti-bullying policy, PSHE for all. 'Tackled bullying head on', says school, loads of help from prefects; 'on the whole it appeared to be careless insensitivity rather than malicious bullying'. Out for violence and drugs. Smoking not tolerated and no particular problems with drinking or smoking off-site. Crack cocaine now appearing in certain parts of the north east and head and staff are constantly vigilant.

Pupils and Parents: First choice for clever and lively-minded boys and girls from every corner (inner and outer) of Newcastle and Sunderland, Durham and County Durham, and also from far-flung rural corners e.g. Berwick, Wooler, Alnwick. Broad social mix, new uniform and stricter enforcement has minimised previous scruffiness. Popular with local bigwigs in industry, the professions, academics from the universities. Fifteen per cent from ethnic minorities. Closer relations with parents now fostered. Pupils keen to succeed and 'don't feel life owes them a living,' observed a master with memories of working in a famous public school further south. Old boys include England winger David Rees, Lord Taylor, Brian Redhead, composer and saxophonist John Harle.

Entrance: Tough and competitive via the school's own entrance exam at 11 (Year 7); Year 9 has ceased to be an entry point since 2008. About 75 from the junior school, as long as their work is up to scratch. Very healthy entry post-GCSE, far outweighing 16+ leavers; minimum six GCSEs at A/B required plus report from former school. Entry from over 80 different schools throughout North East.

Exit: Recent average of 22 a year to Oxbridge, otherwise to Newcastle, Leeds, Edinburgh, Manchester, Nottingham and London, mainly to read hard traditional subjects. Small coterie to art or music colleges, though the latter are more likely to read music at university and then go on to conservatoires. Two recent professional footballers (how they need them at St James's Park). Six pupils left after recent GCSE, either for financial reasons 'or because the RGS sixth form was inappropriate for them.' Gap year gaining in popularity.

Money Matters: Has weathered the loss of assisted places. Four bursaries now available under aegis of the Ogden Trust for 'above average children with limited or no parental means from a state primary school'. Big current drive to raise cash for bursaries, school keen not to be seen as socially divisive; in 2009/10, 100 pupils helped financially, 58 of them at a level of 90 per cent of fees or above. All bursaries means-tested, i.e. no traditional scholarships. Some new sixth form subject-specific awards.

Remarks: Powerful traditional grammar school, with high morale under dynamic and civilized head, and an obvious choice for ambitious locals. Not a results factory; pupils avid for – and get – all-round opportunities.

The Royal Grammar School, High Wycombe

Amersham Road, High Wycombe, Buckinghamshire, HP13 6QT

• Pupils: 1,290 day boys plus 70 boarders • Ages: 11-18 • Size of sixth form: 400 • Christian foundation but inter-denominational • Fees: Boarding £10,899-£12,288 pa; Day – free • State

Tel: 01494 524 955
Fax: 01494 551 410
Email: admin@rgshw.com
Website: www.rgshw.com

Headmaster: Since 2006, Mr Roy Page BSc PGCE NPQH, married to Marilyn, who teaches at nearby Wycombe Abbey; two children, one of whom is an old boy of RGS. Did his teaching practice here in 1972 and stayed, rising through the ranks via second in maths, boarding housemaster, head of sixth and deputy head. An active Rotarian and keen sportsman; enjoys cricket, golf, hockey and rugby. Compassionate, calm, popular – the governors were incredibly thorough when appointing the current head. He probably had to jump through more hoops than usual, but his calm demeanour is just what the school needs,' said one parent. Another added, 'The school has always been a huge part of his life. He cares deeply, and thoroughly deserves to be head.' Is vice chairman of the National State Boarding Schools Committee and has been to No 10 to collect a 'gong' for running an outstanding school. Worries that boys may not fulfil their potential – 'It's a boy thing' – but adds he wants 'happy boys who feel secure and enjoy their time at school'.

Academic matters: Average of 11 GCSE passes per pupil and 65 per cent graded A/A*; no weaknesses. Students prepare for four AS levels and continue with four A levels to average 75 per cent A/B. Results for modern foreign languages and mathematics are amongst the highest nationally and, parents note, useful website (ideal revision aid) www.languagesonline.org.uk has over 25,000 hits daily. Host to one of the largest sixth forms in the country; impressive list of languages: French, German, Spanish, Italian, Japanese, Russian and Mandarin. Critical thinking is taught and is supplemented with an array of external speakers. School recently awarded, as a high performing specialist school, maths and computing specialist status to add to its main specialism as a language college, with much needed added funding to replace worn out facilities. All take part in accelerated reader programme with additional enrichment opportunities, e.g. writers' bloc and headstart science for those identified as gifted and talented. Abundance of help for Oxbridge hopefuls.

Six children have statements of special needs with a number of others on the SEN register, mainly for mild dyslexia or Asperger's. Largish teaching groups, very low staff turnover – 'We get young ambitious staff, some of whom have now moved into positions of responsibility'. Parents and pupils full of praise for staff: 'They're committed, inspiring and approachable'.

Games, Options, the Arts: Rugby, cricket, hockey, athletics, rowing, basketball and fencing are the main sports with opportunities in many others, including Eton fives. A very good music department ensures something for all and when girls are required for stage productions, they are 'borrowed' from nearby high schools. A myriad of clubs from astronomy to world wise quiz, plus CCF, community service, D of E, Young Enterprise and World Challenge all well-subscribed to. Trips galore start with familiarisation in Buxton before branching out – everything from learning Mandarin in Shanghai to helping in Mongolia plus work shadowing and opportunities for work experience at home and abroad.

Background and Atmosphere: Founded in the 12th century and received its Royal Charter in 1562. Red brick Queen Anne style building with various additions in similar style built around a quadrangle. Good facilities on the whole – odd tired corner, hence fundraising. Comfortable, well-planned, purpose-built boarding facilities (few posters or personal touches – a boy thing?) offer smart en-suite rooms with good range of communal facilities including IT, table tennis etc. Interactive school prospectus available on website – lots to watch.

Pastoral Care and Discipline: The school expects high standards and boys adhere to them – parents kept well informed. Takes transition seriously with programme starting in Year 5 and continuing throughout Year 7: 'They come here bubbly and enthusiastic, we have to be careful not to flatten that'. Bullying taken seriously, dealt with promptly; those deemed vulnerable supported in constructive ways. Works closely with parents and local award winning PRU if pupil behaviour or other issues require additional support. Assemblies are well received, particularly those with multicultural themes – 'It helps us appreciate and understand each other and respect differing beliefs'. Odd grumble about food, though it is improving. Boarders can opt to take all meals in the boarding house or eat with friends in school during the day. Plenty of activities through the week but nothing planned for the weekend ('some activities,' says school) save a fixture list for the sporty – 'Most who stay do their own thing'. Full care from matron, housemasters and tutors.

Pupils and Parents: An abundance of professional parents, a handful of pupils with ESL and a little over one per cent who qualify for free school meals. Approximately 15 per cent are non Caucasian. Matches and other functions strongly supported by parents. OBs include Professors Roger Scruton, Michael Zander; Henry Sandon of *The Antiques Road Show*, Richard Hickox, conductor of the LSO, Lawrence Power viola player, England cricketer Philip Newport and England rugby players Matt Dawson, Nick Beal, Nick Duncombe and Tom Rees, GB hockey captain and Olympian Jonathan Wyatt, professional golfer Luke Donald, Commonwealth gold medal gymnast Ross Brewer, rock stars Howard Jones and Ian Dury, BBC news commentator Fergus Walsh, Lord McIntosh of Haringey, Lord Ashcroft, Chris Grayling MP, Jimmy Carr and Ian Fraser VC.

Entrance: Selection subject to Bucks criteria and VR score in 11 plus exam. Now over-subscribed within catchment area. Equal preference system used by local authority: if a child doesn't get into their first choice school they have to be considered equally with all others for their second school of choice (including those who put that school as their first choice). School's own selection procedure adopted if places become available further up the school. Boarding worth considering if outside catchment area but definitely not convertible to day places. Independent school candidates attracted to the 25 places available at sixth form, and EU students with good English are considered for full boarding then.

Exit: 100 per cent into higher education, approximately 20–25 to Oxbridge but remainder to other established universities; Warwick, Nottingham, Birmingham, London and Leeds perennially popular.

Money Matters: 'Money matters?' we queried. 'Yes, it does,' admitted the head, who put the school back in the black. Continues on a massive fundraising campaign to build a much needed new maths block, fitness suite and sixth form centre. Some company sponsorships but parents and old boys in the lead, seeking commitments for the coming years.

Remarks: Turns out intelligent, confident, hard-working, community minded individuals with a spirit of adventure. Breadth and depth of opportunities give rivals, near and far, a run for their money.

The Royal High School (Edinburgh)

East Barnton Avenue, Edinburgh, EH4 6JP

• Pupils: 1,250; 625 boys and 625 girls, all day • Ages: 11-18 • Size of sixth form: 140 • Non-denom • State

Tel: 0131 336 2261
Fax: 0131 312 8592
Email: admin@royalhigh.edin.sch.uk
Website: www.royalhigh.edin.sch.uk

Rector: Since 2009, Mrs Jane Frith, previously acting depute rector. She succeeded long-serving and highly-regarded Mr George M R Smuga who, in February 2008, started a two year secondment as adviser to the schools directorate to the Scottish government to work on curriculum reform.

Academic matters: Max class size 30, going down to 20 for practical subjects and much smaller in higher years. Regular turnover of staff, with younger and more numerous common room. Usual subject suspects: maths, English and modern languages set in S1/S2, other subjects set in S3 where necessary. Strong on humanities; modern studies popular. Least hot on geography and biology but other sciences holding up well. As ever, nigh on impossible to get detailed marks by subject for national exams: Ofsted report varies from above average to consistently above average ... which isn't too helpful. Academic dux each year. Only one pupil sat Advanced Higher French, German or history in 2009, though history said to be popular with over-subscribed library lunch-time club (library lunch-time clubs generally over-subscribed anyway). On the other hand, eight candidates studying Advanced Higher drama. Careers advice on Tuesday in the library. Clubs for almost everything, often curriculum related: maths, chess etc plus Tai Chi or Japanese. Pupils wanting to follow more esoteric subjects can often be accommodated in other Edinburgh schools ('we go by taxi'). Good take up in national competitions, with gratifying numbers in ribbons: in every discipline.

Computers everywhere. Number of pupils with 'record of needs': variety of strategies available: one-to-one, plus support teaching, (and, a first as far as we know) a family support group for those with special needs. Head of learning support, plus two trained staff plus two assistants on hand; strategies in place, too, for the brighter pupil. Curricular support for the staff; advice on how to differentiate work sheets and the like (aka staff training). Sixth form involved in mass of extra-curricular activity ranging from paired reading for younger members, plus befriending and 'helping in subject departments across the school' (slavery perhaps?). Recognised fast track for primary pupils, who may combine studies in both places. French and German, plus optional Spanish, with Urdu on the side. Masses of trips abroad in every discipline. Year tutor stays with that class for their time at school. Classrooms and facilities used by adults and locals out of hours – this is a community school in all but name.

Games, Options, the Arts: House system (nations) in place for pastoral care, interhouse competitions and assemblies, as well as games. Terrific new games set up with games hall, fitness room, swimming pool and gym, much used and former pupils (who have a rather posh sports pavilion on campus) use all the sporting facilities (car parking a bit tight). Myriad of rugby/football pitches, including bright green Astroturf; the school does well on the games front with masses of individual and team activities; athletics, badminton, cross-country, fencing and curling, sailing and water sports. Rugby and football for both boys and girls, plus basketball. As ever, problems with those who think it cool not to play the game (any game).

Exotic trips abroad: skiing in the States, rugby to Barbados to name but a few, and participants run a daily blog home to keep parents and class mates in touch, the battlefields of France proved very popular. Music strong. Long-established pairing arrangement with Munich and Italy where school orchestras perform in each others' home towns in alternate years; outstandingly popular concert, choral and orchestra, which used to be in the Usher Hall. Jazz, woodwind, but no pipe band. Mass of choices. The Keith Thompson 'KT' singers are much in demand and contribute a sizable amount to the Sir Malcolm Sargent Fund for Children at Christmas each year. Drama on the up, strong links with the Edinburgh Festival fringe. School entered a musical show in the Edinburgh Festival Fringe – first school to do so, followed up by another the following year. Lottery funding. Dance in all its disciplines. Art dept perched on top floor: imaginative stuff, flat plus ceramics, but gosh it must be tough to be creative in a blue box. Home Economics popular but apparently not that good (according to Ofsted – our guides disagreed), fabric plus design technology (computer linked with state of the art engineering software).

Background and Atmosphere: Unique history: dates from 1128, the school 'provided education for 60 boys'; the site most people associate with the school is on Calton Hill, a site much loved by the telly news cameras (think overnight vigils, think home rule for Scotland). Girls admitted in 1974. Established on the current site in 1968, (were it not for the name: we could have been looking at Davidson Mains or Cramond High) the school buildings have been revamped (50 per cent refurb, 50 per cent new build) over last five years. Holding up well, we noticed one tiny square of scuffed carpet in the library and one bit of missing trim, but still incredibly uninspired: three storeys (plus basement where sixth form study area was locked) of blue covered passages with assorted square class rooms interspersed with prep rooms round under-used (i.e. not) courtyards. Not nearly enuff public space, break was a logistical nightmare – with a disused adjacent courtyard unavailable to the milling masses – why not a temporary roof – or parasols? One constant however, is the memorial door, out of which each graduating student steps, to be greeted on the other side by the president of the FPs' club. The huge marble door is a memorial to those who died in the First World War and the west-facing stained-glass windows to FPs who fell in the second. 'Significant prize-giving.' Highly vaunted end of school leavers' dance, often held in Edinburgh City Chambers, strong charity commitment.

Uniform worn by all, though you might not recognise it as such, current craze is leggings and the shortest of skirts – pupils can be sent home for inappropriate dress. We bounced through the door of a dedicated SEN room hoping to quiz with the nattily clad occupier of the teacher's chair, only to find a fully made-up Barbie-doll who was obviously about to go on a photo shoot, until she confessed she would 'rather be in class' and it was 'too difficult to go home'. Quite. Variety of sports and club ties, 'they work their way up towards the neck as the owner goes through the school', our charming guides had ties about three inches below their top shirt buttons, whereas some of the youngest members wore theirs at tummy button level. 'Bonding' week in the first year, when the whole class plus class teachers take off during November/December for a week's residential at an outdoor pursuits centre.

Pastoral Care and Discipline: Regular assemblies, good, strong PSE programme, school has to follow City of Edinburgh 'guidelines', so difficult to exclude, but will do so in the case of drugs, bullying, physical or otherwise, and abuse. Strong prefectural presence. Very few 'refusers'. 'Civilised guidance strategies in place'. Regular school assemblies. Pupils who misbehave in class are sent out of the room, we found two or three all looking fairly sheepish. Counsellor on site.

Pupils and Parents: Strong PTA and parent council organisation (this is a new name following change in legislation in Scotland), basically 'affluent middle class, but a very wide intake – with a whole range of social and ethnic backgrounds', the catchment area covers Davidsons Mains, Clermiston, Blackhall and Cramond. The school is capped at a 220 pupil intake and there is always a waiting list. Range of grub available, school has its nutrition group, SNAG.

Entrance: Automatic but see above. Some join the school from other state schools post standard grades, otherwise, 'penny numbers' arrive on a re-location basis.

Exit: 90+ per cent of all pupils generally stay for fifth year (i.e. Highers) and some 75 per cent for sixth year. Trickle to Oxbridge, masses to the Scottish universities (financially it makes sense for Scots go free in Scotland) or tertiary education. Bias towards engineering, architecture, creativity of design courses. FPs include Sir Walter Scott, Alexander Graham Bell, Lord Cockburn, Ronnie Corbett, Sarah Boyack (MSP) and the principal of St Andrew's University, Fraser Docherty (aka Superjam).

Money Matters: Current building has been revamped under the aegis of the PPP. Regular PTA fund-raising including discos and jumble sales, tranche of endowments (including Mary, Queen of Scots) provide tiny scholarships for pupils who have done well at the school; not a lot, 'just a nice wee extra'. Below average number of free school meals: social profile of school rising.

Remarks: This is a high school in the old fashioned sense – strong discipline and work code, good results, masses of extra-curricular activities – which also doubles as a local centre with adult learning classes and much use of the sports facilities. You can't get much better for nowt.

Royal High School, Bath GDST

Linked to Royal High School, Bath, Junior School GDST in the Junior section

Lansdown Road, Bath, BA1 5SZ

• Pupils: 630 girls (approx 520 day, 100 boarding) • Ages: Senior school 11-16, girls only. Sixth form college (co-educational) • Size of sixth form: 180 • All faiths welcome • Fees: Boarding £16,914-£19,050; Day £9,627 pa • Independent

Tel: 01225 313 877
Fax: 01225 465 446
Email: royalhigh@bat.gdst.net
Website: www.gdst.net/royalhighbath

Head: Since 2009, Mrs Rebecca Dougall, internally promoted – formerly deputy principal and director of the co-educational sixth form college. Mrs Dougall gained a 1st in English from Bristol and before coming here she was deputy head and acting head at Oxford High (GDST). Has firm views on the benefits of single sex education for girls between the ages of 11–16 – free from the 'gender agenda'. Her aim is 'to stimulate students to reveal for themselves the delights of learning and lifelong curiosity.'

Academic matters: GCSE and A level results are consistently good (overall pass rates of 99 per cent) across the board. Sciences are strong and popular at A level, with impressive new laboratories and separate facilities for sixth form. GCSE students can choose between double science and separate subjects. Excellent language teaching reflected in the results, and a good choice too – French, German, Spanish, Greek, Latin, Italian, Chinese. Several teachers as well as the assistants are native speakers. Art department has an outstanding record of getting students into top art colleges and won a Good Schools Guide Award in 2006. Good provision for individual needs, in particular dyslexia and English for non-native speakers.

The co-educational sixth form college offers the International Baccalaureate as well as A levels. Major current developments in teaching facilities include the issue of laptops to all sixth form students and the creation of a completely wireless zone in the college building. A new art school building, with four studios has recently opened.

Games, Options, the Arts: Students are encouraged to be themselves and 'aim for excellence' in whatever field appeals. Drama is very strong, and the Memorial Hall is well kitted out for performances, of which there seems to be a continuous programme. Second performing arts space refurbished 2009. Everyone does PE, lots of outdoor sports. Well-equipped sports hall with dance studio. Sporting achievements reflect the diversity on offer – diving, showjumping, rowing. About a third of pupils take individual music lessons, there are choirs, orchestras and a swing band. 'We don't shout about the music but it is of very high quality.' Art is valued within the school and there are interesting, and often large, pieces of work displayed. Although it is only compulsory up to Year 9, and technology subjects get more timetable time, art is popular at GCSE and A level. There is a programme of activities on Saturdays, and outings on Sundays, which are open to all.

Background and Atmosphere: Impressive but somehow austere Gothic architecture in the main school, not welcoming but doesn't seem to bother the students. Huge overwhelming internal spaces and corridors seem to suppress rather than magnify noise, and the school feels cool and calm. Plenty of space, and the many common rooms encourage mixing and 'the opening up of friendships'. Lovely boarding facilities (female students only), on two sites according to age, girls sharing rooms of generous size between two or three. Sleepover facility and provision for friends to stay for tea, or to do homework, is an added bonus for working parents. Boarding is popular and usually over-subscribed. No house system for boarders – prefer vertical pastoral structure for boarders 'to promote a sense of one community', all very friendly. Four day houses, with fine names – Austen, Du Pre, Wollstonecraft and Brontë – for competition purposes.

Two girls' schools – Bath Royal and the High School – merged in 1998. Now the Girls' Day School Trust, to which RHS belongs, the treasured pioneer of education for girls, saw fit to introduce the new co-educational sixth form college in place of the traditional all-girls, sixth form. Whether this stems the relatively small outflux of girls to local sixth form colleges or to boys' schools which take girls into the sixth remains to be seen. Parents committed, for very good reasons, to all-girls education, may well wonder at the apparent lack of confidence this move suggests, and be less than delighted by it. The school's own consultation exercise with parents showed overwhelming support, in excess of 80 per cent, for the introduction of the IB and co-education in the sixth form. While we wish it well, we rather wonder too and will watch with considerable interest.

Pastoral Care and Discipline: Manners and courtesies are taught and expected, with a very strong emphasis on self-discipline and self-sufficiency. Smart dress code, the uniform with tweedy skirt, often worn quite short, perpetuates the 'Angela Brazil' image that the school has, in reality, moved away from. Sixth form college students, depressingly, wear suits. Jewellery and pierced ears are discouraged and therefore decidedly low-key or absent.

Pupils and Parents: In the main, girls come from professional families where both parents work, living in the city of Bath or surrounding villages; could do with its own school bus – and parents are beginning to lobby on this front. Wide social mix; students are confident, polite, sure of themselves and instilled with 'can do' ethos. Small numbers from overseas, the school has a policy of only two from any one country in each year group in order to encourage integration and English language learning.

Entrance: As selective as possible, by school's own exam at 11, with just under 50 per cent coming up through junior department. It is also possible to enter at Years 8, 9 and 10, subject to passing exams in English and maths, but there are no formal dates for these. Entry to sixth form is dependent on a minimum of six GCSEs with top grades for subjects to be taken at A level or as part of the International Baccalaureate diploma programme.

Exit: The opening of the co-educational sixth form college lead to an increase in sixth form numbers and retention of nearly all current Year 11 students. Nearly all go on to higher education with the overwhelming majority getting places at their first choice university.

Money Matters: The GDST has its own means-tested bursary scheme, maximum value is the full day fee. There are also a number of Trust Entrance Scholarships awarded on merit for a few Year 7 entrants; these offer reduced fees (up to 50 per cent) for duration of school career. Services discount. 20 per cent of all pupils have an assisted place.

Remarks: A good, solid, GDST school. Not too flashy, emphasis on providing good value, all-round education with an emphasis on the academic side but no hothousing. Introduction of the IB now offers students alternative pathways into higher education and employment. Parents feel that the school offers good value for money – 'you might get a bit more elsewhere but you'd be asked to pay for it'. Co-ed sixth form college is a major departure.

Royal Masonic School for Girls

Linked to Royal Masonic School For Girls Prep And Pre-prep in the Junior section

Rickmansworth Park, Chorleywood Road, Rickmansworth, Hertfordshire, WD3 4HF

• Pupils: 805 girls, including 150 full/weekly boarders • Ages: 2-18
• Size of sixth form: 160 • Non denom • Fees: Boarding £12,870-£22,020; Day £7,380-£13,770 pa • Independent

Tel: 01923 773 168
Fax: 01923 896 729
Email: enquiries@royalmasonic.herts.sch.uk
Website: www.royalmasonic.herts.sch.uk

Head: Since 2002, Mrs Diana Rose MA (early fifties). Educated at Channing, one of the first women to attend King's College Cambridge, read history and social and political sciences. Spent 13 years in Bucks Grammar Schools, became a schoolteacher fellow of Merton College Oxford in 1988. Spent six years as head of sixth at St Helen's Northwood before moving to become deputy head at Oxford High. Married to Stephen Nokes, head of John Hampden Grammar; has two sons, both at Oxford Brookes. Loves family life, wasn't prepared to sacrifice at all costs, bided her time to find a suitable, local headship. Says she gets a real kick from daily walks with her two dogs across the school's wild perimeters, adding, 'the beauty of the site is truly restorative!' Enjoys cycling and keeping fit too, all of which help her look a good ten years younger than she actually is. Snappy dresser, admired by the girls, who love her business acumen coupled with approachability; 'she's interested in me, not what I can do for the school.' Parents say she has a good attitude to the school and the girls; she is focused and has vision but that doesn't mean the school has to be the most academic – staff agree. Staff who disagreed with rapid changes – improved focus on teaching and learning and overhauling of standards – tend, by and large, to have voted with their feet and moved on.

Head loves the fact the school is inclusive rather than elitist but adds, 'no child is short-changed here, be she ever so bright or ever so average; she will fulfil or outperform her potential!' Wicked sense of humour, surfacing from under the professional front. Girls say, 'she's simply a brilliant role model and knows everyone by name.'

Academic matters: Results commendable and improving; very good value-added. Average 77 per cent A/B grades at A level; Over 80 per cent of GCSEs graded A/B with 55 per cent A*/A. Class size maximum in low 20s, setting in key subjects with fewer than 10 in lower sets. Lots of dedicated teachers, happy to give up free time and go the extra mile, numerous clinics and help always on hand – whatever the girls need. That said, occasional pupil and parental grumbles about calibre of odd teacher; also rue the fact that some of the many young, dynamic staff who come along and inspire the girls fly, too rapidly, to pastures new; school says many young, dynamic staff have been appointed over recent years who inspire the girls. Sixth formers have tailor-made timetables to suit individual requirements. Odd A level class runs with only one student, girls take two, three or four A levels, whatever is appropriate. Have own large multi-purpose common room and separate boarding houses.

A tidy environment, facilities good, well kept and constantly upgraded. Library is housed in a splendid, light rotunda, complete with librarian who is so knowledgeable about the school's history she's written a book about it. However, the library and ICT were pinpointed as areas for development in latest inspection reports (despite ICT having best value-added score). Much has been done to address the issue: whiteboards activated in teaching, plenty of computers about, on-going wireless networking and boarding houses are now networked and cabled. Laptop use, a double-edged sword, limited in comparison to other schools.

School claims to cater for all – the sporty (some training for 2012 Olympics), the gifted (Arkwright scholars and recipients of Gray's science bursaries), linguists (Mandarin from Year 8, Italian in sixth form, classics, home languages and all usual), those into theatre arts, plus those with mild to moderate special needs. Most SEN on 'dys' strata or similar (all girls screened). OK EAL, mild ADD, Asperger's; have dealt with OCD and elective mutes, processing difficulties but not MLD, girls must be at least of average ability. Not the place for those with behavioural difficulties but looks after those who may have emotional or health problems. Team of nine offer individual/small group support for two or three lessons a week; approximately 60 girls identified as in need of school action plus, none have statements. No in-class TA support, though teachers encouraged to use visual, auditory and kinaesthetic approaches within their teaching. Enrichment and special classes for gifted and talented too.

Games, Options, the Arts: Fantastic sporting facilities – new, purpose-built, all singing and dancing sports hall, with fully kitted out multi-gym plus five squash courts but swimming pool is at best functional; Astro and floodlights on girls' wish list. A raft of girls play representative sports both in and out of school, individually and in teams. Recently reached national schools final for swimming and commendable second place in hockey nationals. Some parents feel it's incredibly difficult for girls to make it into highly competitive teams, but accept that recent injection of young sports teachers has done wonders for the place and opened up sporting opportunities, which include rugby football, pilates, golf, fencing and synchronised swimming (girls win medals at championship level) as well as all the regular offerings. School says they aim to find a sport for every girl that she can take into adult life. Perhaps with this in mind sports day provides ample opportunity for girls to be truly sporting – day consists of all regular sports plus sudoku challenge, countdown, fashion show, nature trail, creative drawing etc.

Plenty of trips and tours – for teams, choirs, curriculum and fun. Full activities programme offered, girls as animated about bridge as sports and drama. Art popular and diverse, with vibrant and inspiring textiles and photography. Drama improved dramatically in past couple of years; own productions. *Les Mis* a recent offering plus ample opportunity to perform with local boys' schools. Music on the up, lots learn an instrument, regular mini-concerts, plus termly productions and annual choir trip to Europe.

School has a wonderful sense of tradition – perhaps the only school in the country still to do 'drill'. Places in the drill squad are highly sought after with masses of girls volunteering to be reserves. We were treated to a DVD of drill 2006, a wonderful spectacle with pinafored girls, hair pinned back, looking much younger than when in mufti.

Background and Atmosphere: Founded in 1788. The current 315 acre site, built in the 1930s, is the school's fourth home. Mainly single storey, smart, red-brick school buildings with wonderful sense of symmetry and flow; the whole school centres round two quadrangles and boasts the longest teaching corridor in Britain. Indeed this editor felt she might be in a 1930s hospital, half-expecting pristine nurses in crisp white uniforms to march purposefully past. No surprise then, that when the school opened it was run by the head and chief matron who jointly looked after and educated petitioners – the children of Masons, who, for whatever reason, had hit hard times.

School changed its status in 1978 to become an independent school, open to all regardless of background, but still fulfilling its charitable obligation. Today some 50 children are petitioners but they're not marked out in any way; even staff don't know who are petitioners. There's a gloriously serene chapel in the heart of the school, magnificent but with, alas, poor acoustics – particularly when only half-full. Generally very good facilities throughout – 'seductive' said one parent. Only real grumble from girls is about toilets, not enough and not pleasant enough.

Pastoral Care and Discipline: Takes all sorts, including lost sheep, and finds them again, great at developing confidence and self-esteem. Works hard to find something a girl can excel at. Good manners and communication skills are valued as highly as academic prowess. Good pastoral care, head proud that, when OFSTED inspected, over 92 per cent of girls had not seen or experienced bullying. School points out, 'in OFSTED terms and compared to other boarding inspections this is an exceptionally positive figure. We are known for the quality of our pastoral care.' Recognises cliques develop and girls can have niggles and fall-outs. Some girls feel there are definite in-crowds but acknowledge that with so many activities even misfits usually manage to pair up; head says population is diverse and so school is able to play to that diversity. Odd complaint that school focuses on petty rules, wearing correct colour hair-band or shoes; staff explain that there was an initial clamp-down as new uniform introduced but later relaxed as girls got the message – add general policy is a light touch and gentle reminders.

Well kept and kitted out boarding houses, homely feel, lots of pinks and lilacs. Rolling programme of refurb but we didn't notice any particularly rough edges. Most girls have plenty of space, with many senior girls in rooms that would be expected to house two or three in other schools. Staff-student relations relaxed, happy and amicable. Staff vigilant for usual teenage problems as well as anorexia and self-harm – 'problems arise and if needs be we will call in expert help but most things are sorted out from within the staff.'

Full-time Chaplain; boarders of other faiths do not have to attend Sunday Communion but many do – celebrate non-Christian festivals too – very much a Christian background and spiritual foreground.

Pupils and Parents: Ethnic and, to an extent, social mix; some expats, some overseas. A number well heeled, some flash, some discreet, though generally not a competitive group. Large number of first-time buyers, boarding popular with Services families. Girls are generally grounded but savvy, chatty and confident. Vast majority enjoy a full-on extra-curricular life, whether at home or in school. Few eggheads or bookworms but those who are usually find a groove.

Entrance: In an area well served by good, independent and mainstream schools, RMS is no longer the poor relation; parents now place RMS high on their list of desirable schools. Entry is competitive, particularly at 11 when 200 girls compete for approximately 45 places. Once you're in, at any stage, you are guaranteed a place in all future stages; siblings too have priority, so no worries if second and subsequent children not quite up to scratch academically – admirable in these league table driven days. Don't take less able but otherwise have a fairly comprehensive intake. Selection process consists of one day of exams – computerised tests devised by the University of Durham, which test maths, English and reasoning. Also creative writing, a group activity and group interview, Also look at KS 2 performance and report from current school. Positive reports back from selection process – 'my daughter enjoyed a conversation with the head and felt relaxed after the selection process; it was very different to the more formal interviews elsewhere.'

Exit: Approximately 70 per cent to Russell Group universities. A trickle to Oxbridge, rest either take gap year or study wide-ranging, vocationally orientated degrees – psychology and business popular. As the head points out, traditional intake has not been overly academic so expect the exit picture to change in next few years, as new blood filters through. School adds the courses chosen reflect curriculum diversity and the non-elitist philosophy of the school.

Money Matters: Healthy. An endowment, set-up by the Masons, underpins capital expenditure. School is a tenant of the 315 acre estate. Automatic five per cent reduction for sisters; means-tested bursaries available; academic, music, sport and all rounder scholarships; places for RMTGB beneficiaries and Foundationers. 10 per cent reduction for Services families.

Remarks: Just the place if you want to sing, dance or skip and experience academic success. Happy to take rough pebbles and smooth into pearls. On the up, now being taken seriously by local competition.

Rudolf Steiner School (Kings Langley)

Linked to Rudolf Steiner Junior School (Kings Langley) in the Junior section

Langley Hill, Kings Langley, Hertfordshire, WD4 9HG

- Pupils: 410 girls and boys • Ages: 3-19 • Size of sixth form: 30
- Fees: £5,265-£7,965 pa • Independent

Tel: 01923 262 505
Fax: 01923 270 958
Email: langleyc@rsskl.org
Website: www.rsskl.org

College of Teachers: Like all Steiner schools, does not have a headteacher but is run on a non-hierarchical basis by a College of Teachers, which also forms smaller committees called mandate groups to advise on different matters such as staffing and finance. The main initial point of contact for parents is Steffi Cook, the Admissions Secretary.

Academic matters: One of the few Steiner schools in the country that goes right through from three to 19, covering GCSEs and A levels – albeit a year later than most mainstream schools. But exam results are far from being the school's raison d'etre. It shares a common curriculum with some 900 Steiner Waldorf schools worldwide, aiming 'to nourish each child's innate curiosity and love of learning'. The curriculum is organised according to the Steiner philosophy of three phases of child development.

In the kindergarten, the children learn 'through activity and through interpreting impressions'. Three to six-year-olds play together, making boats or shops or houses from chairs and tables, baking and modelling, dressing up and listening to stories. They spend lots of time outside, and all their play-things are of natural materials – wood, cotton, silk. Reading and writing are not on the agenda at this stage but rhythm and repetition are important.

At the age of six they move up to the lower school, where they meet the class teacher who will, ideally, remain with them for the next eight years. At this stage, in Steiner philosophy, they learn through feelings and memory. They begin to learn the alphabet through stories and pictures and come to reading through writing. They learn poems and recite times tables. Each morning there is a two-hour main lesson, studying a particular topic in depth for three weeks. Art, craft and drama are all important. French and German, taught by specialists, are also on the curriculum. No computers in the lower school. 'All learning takes place by human contact and artistic activity'.

At 14, in Steiner philosophy, they move into the 'thinking' phase of learning. At their most questioning and critical, they have specialist teachers for each subject, and begin to prepare for GCSEs, but cramming is not on the agenda. GCSE results – from a limited selection of subjects that includes German, history and drama but not at present geography – are creditable, particularly when one considers that these are the first exams Steiner children have experienced. More than 85 per cent of candidates got five or more A*–C grades in 2010, with 38 per cent of grades A* or A. At A level the subject range is still more limited: maths, biology, chemistry, French, German, drama, English literature, art and photography.

Plenty of class trips to galleries, museums, concerts and theatres. Residential trips have included a class 9 journey to create a forest pathway in Switzerland and a class 6 visit to Hadrian's Wall.

Children with special education needs who are not coping at conventional schools often gravitate towards a Steiner education, with its emphasis on the practical and creative and on learning through experience. The school can cope with dyslexia, dyspraxia and dyscalculia, but not behavioural difficulties – 'unless the bad behaviour stems from frustration with academic work, when we will consider it'. Since Steiner children do not begin to learn to read and write until they are six, most can cope in the mainstream class until they are nine or so. They may have one lesson a week with learning support, and the movement and co-ordination work often helps them academically. But since the classes have around 30 pupils, teachers cannot give individual children large amounts of one-to-one attention.

In 2005 the school opened the Tobias class as a pilot project for 9 and 10 year olds who need specific extra help. The plan is for them to spend up from a few terms to a few years in the class, then integrate or reintegrate into the appropriate mainstream form, preferably before the start of the upper school at 14, so it is not suitable for children with severe difficulties. In this class, run by a trained dyslexia specialist, the emphasis is as much on bodily co-ordination as on academic skills. The children do plenty of maths and English, but also learn circus skills, have massage therapy and curative eurythmy – a harmonious dance therapy that is believed to help with learning and co-ordination. They also go riding, and join in gym, gardening and music with mainstream classes. 'Their progress has been phenomenal,' says their teacher. 'Not only academically, but in their whole beings. They are much happier and more confident.' 'It's been fantastic for my daughter,' said a parent. 'She has improved so much.'

It is not suitable for children on the autistic spectrum. 'They like to know exactly what is going to happen next, but we are creative and unpredictable. I have no assistant, so I can't spend my time dealing with one child's behaviour.'

Games, Options, the Arts: Arts and crafts are an integral part of Steiner education. The walls are lined with paintings in the classic 'wet on wet' Steiner technique. The school has separate studios for fine arts, woodwork, metalwork, pottery and modelling, and photography. Pupils bake bread, tend their allotments. Everyone does art to GCSE, and art and history of art are the most popular A level subjects.

Music and drama also play a large role. Everyone plays the recorder and has singing lessons, can try playing the violin in class 3 and continue if it suits them. Many learn other instruments. There are class, middle and upper school orchestras. Every year the orchestras from the Steiner schools in Kings Langley and in Ottersberg, Germany, exchange places to perform a prepared programme in the other school, which means, on alternate years, students from Kings Langley stay with local Ottersberg Steiner families.

There's a major upper school musical every other year, and many other productions by different classes. The theatre, equipped with fly-tower and full lighting, seats 450 and hosts cabarets and concerts as well as plays. 'Our children are used to appearing in public from an early age.'

Gym/sports hall and extensive playing fields. But while the older children play inter-school volleyball and basketball matches (with considerable success), competitive sport is peripheral to the Steiner curriculum. Eurythmic dance and outdoor activities in general are integral, however. The younger children play non-competitive, co-operative games, go for nature walks, garden. They plant Christmas trees, cut willow for lime kilns, dig clay to make tablets. Class 5 visits the Michael Hall School in Sussex (qv) together with class 5 students from all the other UK Steiner schools to recreate the Ancient Greek Olympics.

Background and Atmosphere: Opened in 1949 in 10 acres of grounds on the site of a 13th century royal palace. Peaceful, harmonious atmosphere with trees and grass, climbing frames and tree houses. Parental involvement vital. Parents run the school shop and cafe, which also provides simple school lunches. They help to run the huge fundraising event, the Advent Fair, which has approximately 3,000 visitors, the Midsummer Market and the Fireworks and Bonfire Night display. They share their expert knowledge – of architecture or embryology or philosophy – with pupils. They can apply for an allotment in the school grounds. They also decorate classrooms, make curtains and help with camping trips and class outings.

Pastoral Care and Discipline: Rewards more important here than punishments, but this is not a free-for-all. The atmosphere is quiet and ordered. Misbehaving youngsters are given warnings, then moved to a seat close to the teacher, then sent to the staff room to get on with some work. Detentions in the upper school. Strong sanctions against those found smoking or using drugs or alcohol, 'but we are very unwilling to expel unless absolutely necessary.' Great attention to individual needs. 'The level of pastoral care is exceptional,' said a parent.

Pupils and Parents: Many families have moved to King's Langley to be part of the school community. Others come from a wide catchment area, including a number by school bus from north London. These are not, on the whole, carefully mannered, diligent, respectful, public school children. They are lively, questioning, active. 'They can be a wild bunch,' said a parent. Quite a few have failed to thrive at more conventional schools. The school limits the number of SEN pupils it accepts in order to keep a balance of abilities within each class.

Entrance: Families who want their child to attend the kindergarten are encouraged to go to the pre-school parent and child group. These get more-or-less automatic entry; next in line are siblings, those from another Steiner kindergarten and local families. Applicants are interviewed by two kindergarten teachers.

For entry into class 1 and above, children are asked to bring a copy of a report from their previous school, and some examples of their maths, writing and drawing. They will have an interview with the class teacher for an hour or so, but no formal test.

Exit: Around half the class generally moves on after GCSEs. They may have had enough of long journeys to school, or want to study subjects the school doesn't offer. A few join the sixth form, mostly from other Steiner schools. Most of those leaving after A levels go to university or art college, some directly into usually craft-related professions.

Money Matters: Has recently appointed a bursar and handed over school fee collection to an agency, to combat a tendency amongst some parents to view fee-paying as voluntary. Fees are in any case very low by independent school standards, and many parents benefit from reduced fees. These factors have led to a lack of funds for capital expenditure. The school is embarking on a tightening up of financial matters, including a major fundraising drive.

Remarks: Friendly, caring school in idyllic surroundings with a focus firmly on the needs of the child, which nevertheless produces creditable exam results. A haven for some children with specific special needs and for refugees from the exam-driven culture of most mainstream schools.

Rugby School

Lawrence Sheriff Street, Rugby, Warwickshire, CV22 5EH

- Pupils: 800 pupils; 645 boarders, 155 day pupils. 445 boys, 350 girls
- Ages: 11-18 (day pupils only at 11 and 12) • Size of sixth form: 350
- C of E • Fees: Boarding £28,050; Day £17,475-£22,815; Juniors £10,299 pa
- Independent

Tel: 01788 556 274
Fax: 01788 556 277
Email: registry@rugbyschool.net
Website: www.rugbyschool.net

Head Master: Since 2001, Mr Patrick Derham, MA (late forties). At 11 was sent to live and study on the naval training ship Arethusa, run by the children's charity Shaftesbury Homes to prepare young men for the navy. His potential was spotted and he was transferred to Pangbourne College, where he eventually became head of school. Read history at Pembroke College, Cambridge and began his teaching career at Cheam School. Moved to Radley, where he was head of history and a housemaster, and joined Solihull as headmaster in 1996. Says he was 'bowled over by the atmosphere' at Rugby when he visited for the first time. Still teaches four periods a week of A level history. 'It's terribly important,' he says. 'It's what I came into the job to do.' The week we visited he'd switched an A level lesson about William Pitt the Younger's rise to power to a Sunday evening to fit it into his busy schedule. Dynamic, level-headed and caring. Very popular with parents. Says it is 'a huge privilege' to be head of a school that 'strives for excellence in everything we do' and is 'so unpretentious, friendly, busy and purposeful'. He lunches with pupils in different houses each day, goes to as many matches as possible and loves watching 'really skilled classroom practitioners' in action. 'It's nice for pupils to see you taking an interest and you can always do your paperwork at night,' he declares.

Delights in the fact that he's sitting in Thomas Arnold's study – complete with a portrait of the great man, Arnold's own (surprisingly small) desk and the spiral staircase in the corner where pupils could come and go if they wanted to see him privately. Their modern-day counterparts still use it before chapel to show good work to present head and pass on the school's latest sports results.

This isn't a highly-selective boarding school but a broad church where everyone is encouraged to achieve their full potential. Head rightfully proud of Arnold Foundation which he set up in 2003 to provide fully-funded boarding places (plus uniform, essential books and trips) for talented youngsters whose parents could not afford to send them to the school. 'Rugby has always provided bursaries for day pupils and I wanted to replicate those opportunities for boarders,' he says. School aims to increase number of funded pupils to ten per cent of the school – figure currently stands at 8.5 per cent (boarders and day pupils) – and recently launched a £30 million fundraising campaign. 'One of the problems for all boarding schools is their increasing social exclusivity,' he adds. 'Something like this helps to make the school more diverse and representative of society.'

Married to Alison, who is head of learning support at Bilton Grange, the prep school down the road. They live in a house in the grounds (head cycles virtually everywhere) and have two grown-up children – a son and a daughter, both of whom were pupils at Rugby.

Academic matters: A Level and Pre-U results in 2010–64 per cent A*-A grades at A level. GCSE results up on the previous year with 80 per cent A*/A at GCSE.

Rugby has always prided itself on its 'pioneering' approach to the curriculum – it was, for instance, the first school in the country to teach science as part of the formal school curriculum in the 1850s – and this continues apace. School now offers IGCSE in seven subjects, plus the new Cambridge Pre-U, an 'academically more rigorous' alternative to A levels where pupils write traditional, essay length answers. It has ditched the AS in favour of a two-year linear approach to A levels – 'with no AS takes or retakes to interrupt the educational experience,' explains head, who says it will also 'win back valuable teaching time'. Meanwhile the school has piloted and developed Perspectives in Science (now accredited by Edexcel). Led by Dr John Taylor, formerly head of physics and now director of critical skills, this is a new course in the philosophy and ethics of science and helps pupils develop high-level research skills. Over one or two years, sixth form pupils (around 95 this year) produce a 6,000 to 7,000-word research project on a topic of their choice – everything from quantum mechanics and black holes to animal welfare and witch hunts so far. One Rugby pupil called it 'a refreshing break from the narrow confines of the A level syllabus,' while another said it was 'an amazing course, not just for learning about what you're interested in, but also for transferable research and writing skills'. The quality of work produced played a key role in encouraging the QCA (Qualifications and Curriculum Authority) to promote the development of extended projects, now available to all schools as qualifications equivalent to A level.

Wide range of languages on offer – French, German, Spanish, Russian, Japanese, Chinese and Italian. Lots of exchange trips – to Paris, Vienna, Madrid. New state-of-the-art language labs, with computers and software in every language. Pupils are setted for all subjects from day one. Three separate sciences at GCSE for top five out of seven sets – others take double award. Class sizes max 24 or less. Stunning 'Science Schools' about to be opened by Earl of Wessex when we visited – Victorian building imaginatively refurbished to provide lecture theatre, seminar rooms and labs. Learning development department (with five-strong staff) offers support to those who need it, on regular or more informal basis. Schools caters for pupils with mild to moderate learning difficulties. EFL programme in situ. Enrichment programme for academic scholars (110 currently). All pupils have their own laptops – supplied by school and charged to parents. Virtually all classrooms have interactive whiteboards.

Games, Options, the Arts: Huge investment in sports facilities in recent years. School boasts the only listed gym in the world. And, of course, the famous Close, where William Webb Ellis first ran with the ball in 1823 (the first XV very proud to play on it, along with leading players and teams who visit from all over the world.) Immaculately-maintained playing fields – with 12 rugby pitches and five cricket squares. Locals use school's Astroturfs, tennis courts, 25-metre indoor pool etc. New sports centre, with squash courts, polo pitches and fitness centre. Boys play rugby, hockey, soccer, cricket, tennis and athletics while girls get hockey, netball, tennis, rounders and athletics. Lots of other sports on offer too – from golf to polo.

Art flourishing and photography too. When we visited, pupils were busy building push carts in school's design centre – ready for a hotly-contested push cart race round the Close that weekend. New Lewis Gallery opened in 2006 – light, airy space cleverly converted from old squash courts, with programme of exhibitions by pupils and outside artists. Drama very popular. All singing and dancing Macready Theatre. Pupils stage major school play and a musical every year, along with a house drama season and 'Arts Festival' too. Recent school productions include Stoppard's *Arcadia* and *Pirates of Penzance.*

Fabulous media studio with all the gear for pupils to practise making videos, CDs etc. Music is magical. Masses of orchestras, choirs, ensembles, rock bands – everything you would expect from a school of this size and importance. Keen voluntary CCF, D of E, Young Enterprise and lots of community service and other charity input.

Background and Atmosphere: Founded as a grammar school in 1567 by Lawrence Sheriff, purveyor of spices to Elizabeth I, it moved to its present site 200 years later. Home of the famous Dr Arnold of *Tom Brown's Schooldays.* School situated on imposing site in centre of Rugby. Feels rather like north Oxford, with school houses scattered all over the place. Glorious Victorian library, the Temple Reading Room, has had facelift and provides quiet, inspiring place to work. Total of 37,000 resources – books, DVDs, periodicals etc.

Pupils attend chapel at 8.25am three mornings a week and on Sundays. Chapel – Thomas Arnold is buried beneath chancel steps – is breathtaking. Walls boast tablets in memory of famous Rugbeian writers like Lewis Carroll and Rupert Brooke. Whole school sings heart out. Upper chapel choir runners-up in Songs of Praise School Choirs of the Year competition in 2008 and again in 2009 and again in 2010.

Weekend leave-outs every three weeks or so. But school buzzes at weekends – buzzes all the time, really. More than 30 societies – law, medical, philosophy, debating, science forum – and everyone seems to be involved in masses of things. In one of the girls' houses helpful sixth formers had posted useful tips for new pupils on unmissable events. School went full co-ed in 1993. Boy/girl ratio is now 55/45, with eight houses for boys and seven for girls. All eat in their own houses – despite cost head 'wouldn't dream of changing it'. It encourages 'real family community,' one parent told us. 'Social' eating in each other's houses by invitation. Girls' houses very civilised. Rooms vary from singles for sixth formers, to dorms of four to six for younger pupils. Housemasters and housemistresses all live in (many with their own families) and see pupils as they come and go during the day. Youngest have to be back in houses by 9.30pm (lights out half an hour later), while sixth formers return by 10.15pm (don't have to be in their rooms till 11pm though.) Boys' houses less ritzy in past but huge amount of dosh put into upgrading them. Two day houses.

All wear smart uniform for lessons. Girls sport distinctive ankle-length grey skirts, now redesigned so they can run in them. Girls say they really like them – you can wear woolly tights and leggings underneath to keep warm in winter, they told us. Prefects – or levée in Rugby-speak – get to wear different ties and gold buttons on dark blazers. Four buttons for heads of school (boy and girl), three for head of house and two for school prefects!

Pastoral Care and Discipline: Forget the fagging of *Tom Brown's Schooldays.* School has put enormous amount of time and effort into its pastoral care. PHSE programme tackles issues like bullying, relationships, even safe driving. Each pupil is given a copy of the school's *Guidelines for Life,* which details everything from bedtimes to fast-food carry-outs. The standards expected are made very clear. If you are caught dealing or with drugs in your possession you are out. If name comes up in an investigation, then random drugs testing for duration of time at school. No smoking at any time – counselling for smokers. Boozing in school hours has a variety of sanctions – four sins and pupils are out. At Saturday evening Crescent Club, sixth formers are allowed maximum of two drinks (wine or beer) with food.

Public displays of affection (PDA) between pupils banned – anything that might cause embarrassment to others, says school. New pupils mentored by older pupils and the levée are assigned to look after each year group.

Pupils and Parents: Pupils come from all over, from Orkney down to Cornwall. Lots from London, Oxford or locations within two hours' driving distance. Around ten per cent from overseas – France, Germany, Russia, US, Hong Kong, mainland China, Taiwan etc. Some ex-pats too. Wide social range but pupils say school isn't 'snobby'. Many are sons and daughters of ORs – nearly 16 per cent at last count. Parents very supportive of school and say there's a real sense of community. 'I just don't know of anywhere else I'd want to send my child,' said one. Illustrious former pupils include Rupert Brooke (who has girls' house named after him), Lewis Carroll, Robert Hardy, Tom King, Salman Rushdie, Anthony Horowitz – and of course Harry Flashman and Tom Brown.

Entrance: Oversubscribed. Admission at 11 is open only to day pupils from local state schools or independent schools finishing at 11. All join Marshall House, a small day house for Year 7s and 8s. Entrance exam consists of computerised test, interview and report from current school. Pupils starting at 13 sit aptitude pre-test and interview four to five terms before entrance. CE pass mark 55 per cent. Boys and girls come from more than 300 feeder schools across the country, including The Dragon, Bilton Grange, Packwood Haugh and St Anselm's. Around 40 new pupils (mostly girls, but some boys) join in the sixth form. UK candidates need six Bs (existing Rugbeians pupils need the same). They sit two academic tests in subjects of their choice and have a house interview too. Potential scholars are invited back at a later date for scholarship interviews. Keen competition for sixth form places – three applicants for every place.

Exit: 13 (9 per cent) off to Oxbridge in 2010. Leeds, Manchester, Edinburgh, UCL popular too. Good spread of subjects.

Money Matters: Huge numbers of scholarships (academic, music, art, design and sport) and bursaries on offer. No limit on number of scholarships. 'We make awards to all those who show the requisite skills and potential,' explains school. Rugby led the way in 2003 by limiting scholarships to ten per cent of the school fees – although this can be augmented to 100 per cent if family need can be shown through a means test. 'It was the obvious and right thing to do,' says head.

Remarks: Famous public school that continues to go from strength to strength. Prides itself on treating everyone as an individual, with boys and girls encouraged to develop their talents and initiative and make the most of their time at the school. One of the most popular co-ed boarding schools in the country, and deservedly so. Just as we said last time round, it is friendly, hard-working and fun. Genuinely innovative too – both on the academic front and with the launch of the Arnold Foundation.

Ryde School with Upper Chine

Linked to Ryde School With Upper Chine, Junior School in the Junior section

Queen's Road, Ryde, Isle of Wight, PO33 3BE

• Pupils: 515 boys and girls, 60 board (mostly weekly), rest day
• Ages: 11-18 • Size of sixth form: 110 • C of E • Fees: Day £10,215; Boarding £19,665-£21,000 pa • Independent

Tel: 01983 562 229
Fax: 01983 564 714
Email: admissions@rydeschool.org.uk
Website: www.rydeschool.org.uk

Head: Since 1997, Dr Nicholas England MA DPhil, previously at Wellington College for some 19 years. A physicist, he still teaches, using his own textbook, *Physics Matters*. Energetic and punchy, keen to be seen to be running a good school and with exacting standards. The numbers in the school have increased during his time and there has been some impressive new building. The fact that half his catchment area is in the sea, and that his school is on an off-shore island, he sees as positive advantages in terms of the variety of pupils who come to him and the less pressurised island environment in which they find themselves.

'We are very impressed with him,' said a parent. 'He's always approachable, always available,' said another. 'Since he's been there the pastoral side has taken off and he's well liked and respected by the pupils.' Both his children moved to Ryde School when he became head. 'It was wonderful to see them enjoying it and exceeding my expectations.' Many of the other staff have children at the school. An extremely capable deputy recently arrived from Warwick School.

Academic matters: A non-selective school. 'Our profile is about half-way between a typical state comprehensive and a selective independent.' Some very high-flyers – 'and it is as good as any mainland public school at the top end,' said a parent of one – and about 15 per cent receiving learning support (mainly dyslexics but a couple of children with Asperger's), plus the whole spectrum of ability. Nearly all get five A*–C grades at GCSE. A previous bias we noted towards greater success in the practical subjects seems to have been addressed in the 2009 and 2010 results, with strong science results and 49 per cent As and A*s overall. Twenty-four A level subjects, including environmental science, government and political studies, psychology and theatre studies. 'And the school is very flexible about A level choices,' said a parent. 'If you let them know your options in time they will do their best to accommodate them.' 73 per cent of the A level grades A*–B – but girls get twice as many A grades as boys.

Class size is around 15 or 16, divided into four streams for most subjects. Two ICT rooms, plus a trolley with 20 laptops; all classrooms have PowerPoint and most interactive whiteboards. In 1997, Ryde took over Bembridge School, which specialised in learning support. As a result, that department is particularly strong, housed in its own unit with pictures of famous dyslexics (e.g. Einstein) on the wall alongside photos of its own pupils and their achievements. But the head emphasises that, while he wants the school to cater for any Island children with special needs – though not behavioural problems – who want an independent school education, he does not intend to expand the department. 'We have a good balance of children and I do not want to upset that.' High calibre, committed staff. 'Hard work is rewarded and respected,' said a parent. 'The children are motivated and set their sights high.'

Games, Options, the Arts: Excellent music, with four choirs, an orchestra and a jazz combo (and good exam results, with virtually all candidates getting A and B grades at GCSE). 'The standard is higher than I would have thought possible,' said a parent. Music tours abroad every year to e.g. Barcelona and Verona. The annual school musical, performed in Ryde Theatre to an audience of paying public as well as parents, 'is reckoned to be the best amateur dramatics on the island,' says the head; parents agree. Recently they performed the musical *Crazy for You*, while plays have included *A Servant of Two Masters* and *A Midsummer Night's Dream*. The school has taken part in Global Rock – understandably, a pupil-led undertaking – and did extremely well, with African Sanctus a big hit. The art department produces excellent work in limited space and regularly exhibits at public galleries on the island. DT also popular and imaginative, with pupils working in any medium from stained glass to concrete.

A variety of sports played on the school's 17 acres of playing fields with a rifle range, tennis courts and a sports hall on site, plus an Astroturf hockey pitch a mile away. Teams play Island state schools and mainland independent schools; the girls' hockey and netball teams are particularly successful. Swimming at the public pool down the road – 'it's far cheaper and easier to use someone else's pool'. The school has four houses, mostly for sporting and other competitions. 'The younger ones are very competitive over the Citizenship cup.' CCF is available in year 10 for one afternoon a week, with air force or navy options. 'My children loved it for the sailing,' said a parent. 'They didn't take the parading terribly seriously but there were lots of opportunities to go on exciting camps for amazingly low prices.' Reports of these camps fill several pages of the school magazine. One pupil at 15 became the youngest person to sail across the Atlantic (and has now made it round the world). 'His parents asked if it would disrupt his GCSEs. I said of course it will but it will look very good on his CV.' D of E popular.

Background and Atmosphere: Founded in 1921 and moved to its present site in 1928; in 1995 it merged with Upper Chine girls' boarding school and, in 1997, took over Bembridge School, which had a large number of overseas pupils. The Bembridge site now houses Ryde School's boarding department in a companionable house atmosphere, and a combination of school transport and the occasional taxi ferry the boarders backwards and forwards. The boarding house is highly distinctive and spacious and the site still has all the old Bembridge facilities (100 acres of playing fields and woodland) and is right on the cliff edge, which is tremendous for the boarders. Friendly houseparents oversee and the only slight fly in the ointment is the sharing of the very large site with a holiday club company.

Ryde School is now more-or-less the only independent school on the Island. Atmosphere is ordered but relaxed with a considerable stated emphasis on pupil initiative and on their growing up in an environment which lacks, because of its island situation, some of the pressures of teenage life on the mainland. Dr England stresses this factor and relishes the lack of sophisticated worldliness of many of his pupils. Pleasant situation at the top end of Ryde, a 10 minute walk from the esplanade where hovercrafts and Seacats dock; at least one family commutes from Portsmouth every day. Buildings range from the Georgian admin and sixth form block to the light, galleried library block which was built in 2000. The science block was refurbished many years ago; the head has hopes for a cantilevered gallery addition to the 200-seater theatre. The new dining hall under construction will create more space in the existing buildings. The junior school has been newly expanded and is housed in pleasant, half new/half old buildings with a sympathetic and child-centred headmaster. Much evidence of purposeful and creative activity in a structured environment which does not weigh heavily on the pupils' shoulders. Parents were unstinting in their praise. Most go on to the senior school at 11+. Five Ways, where the nursery to Year 2 pupils are taught, is a delightful place with new buildings, excellent facilities and a great head.

Pastoral Care and Discipline: 'I was impressed that the head wanted to show us round at breaktime,' said a parent. 'That's when a lot of heads want to keep you clear. But the children were very courteous.' Discipline firm but low key. 'We don't have institutionalised bullying; we do have personality differences. We use a no-blame policy and we tend to be successful by sorting it out without making it a huge deal. Calling in the parents is usually enough.' Very few pupils have been expelled since Dr England arrived, but he reserves the right to do so over serious issues such as drugs or theft. 'PHSCE is superbly taught,' said a parent. 'It addresses real issues.'

Pupils and Parents: About half of the boarders are from Portsmouth naval families; a few full boarders from overseas. The day pupils, from a wide cross-section of families, come from all round the Island, with one or two from the mainland. The school runs buses from different points of the Island. Some parents agonise over the lack of choice of independent schools on the Island, which means that Ryde School's fortunes are linked to those of the local state schools rather than other independents. But all we spoke to were impressed by the standards of Ryde School. They liked the staff and found them approachable (reports every half term), innovative and interesting, on the whole, although there were a few worries about the possibility of difficulties in recruiting staff to the Island backwater. These were rejected by the school, which maintains that the pleasant environment and the affordability of housing ensures that Ryde School holds its own in competition for good teachers.

Entrance: Non-selective but all are interviewed by the head, do some maths and English and an IQ test. 'We want to ensure that they're of a standard to fit into the school. The tests are to look for discrepancies between their IQ and their maths and English standards.' Five Bs 'represents a sensible starting point for A level' but occasionally those on lower grades will start AS courses if parents and the school think that they can succeed. Three or four a year turned away, mostly for misbehaviour. Most go through to the sixth form. The school has open days but prospective parents can make an appointment to look round at any time.

Exit: About 95 per cent to university, mostly redbrick. Trickle to Oxbridge.

Money Matters: Some means-tested assisted places, plus a few external scholarships worth 10 per cent of fees, which can be added to an assisted place. Because the Isle of Wight has a middle school system, the senior school's main intakes are into Years 5, 7, 9 and 12, and its awards are available at all these times.

Remarks: A mixed, non-selective, school that aims to cater for any Island child that wants an independent education, plus a few mainland boarders and a few foreigners. Academic strengths and a strong commitment to all round education both in the classroom and outside it. Character and initiative come strongly to the fore as priorities for the development of pupils. 'My daughter has been very well taught and has developed a real love for nearly all of her subjects,' said a satisfied parent. Numbers on the up.

Ryedale School

Gale Lane, Nawton, York, North Yorkshire, YO62 7SL

• Pupils: 555 boys and girls • Ages: 11-16 • Size of sixth form: Although Ryedale School does not have sixth form status, it is part of a consortium arrangement serving the Ryedale Area Sixth Form Partnership, and is developing Sixth Form provision further. • No religious affiliation • State

Tel: 01439 771 665
Fax: 01439 770 697
Email: admin@ryedale.n-yorks.sch.uk
Website: www.ryedale.n-yorks.sch.uk

Headteacher: Since 2010, Mr Richard Crane (thirties) MA (history), NPQH. Previously worked in a variety of schools and was deputy headteacher at Ripon College. Very keen on building upon the undoubted strengths of Ryedale to move it into a new phase of development. Believes in a strong focus on teaching and learning to ensure that each learner receives a personalised approach to their education. Married with three children. Wife also teaches.

Academic matters: Broadly average intake, well above average results. Pledge to parents that 70 to 80 per cent of pupils will gain at least five A* to C GCSEs each year. Good results with special needs and no-one leaves without at least one GCSE. School achievement award for excellent results. The secret? Hard work. Lessons rattle along at a cracking pace and students are fired up for learning. Good thing, too, because this is no school for shirkers. Regular diligence reports grade pupils not on what they're achieving but how hard they're trying. A-grade pupils can be in firing line if more effort would mean A*s. Across the board slacking leads to monitoring by the school – and a chat with parents.

Games, Options, the Arts: Ryedale's undoubted speciality. No such thing as a lunch break in this hell-for-leather school. No-one goes off-site at lunchtime – not least because there's nowhere to go – so Ryedale crams its lunch hours with all manner of extras, from sport to drama, dance to jazz band. All voluntary, but volunteering is this school's forte. In one morning alone, 87 children out of a year group of 116 spotted a notice for the Duke of Edinburgh award and signed up for more info. These kids are up for anything – orienteering, fund-raising, entertaining at a pensioners' party. Mother Theresa would have loved this school.

Success breeds success. 'What we have noticed is that those who get involved in the most activities also achieve the most academically,' said previous head. 'There's a fine balance between getting the best out of children in exams and squeezing them so hard that they have no chance to do all the other things that children need to do as part of growing up.' Already a specialist Performing Arts College,with excellent community links and a reputation for sporting excellence. Performing arts facilities have been extended to offer A level music technology, and creative and media courses. No doubt enabling a whole new raft of opportunities for these eager beavers to volunteer for.

Background and Atmosphere: Fifty-year-old school in the middle of nowhere. Draws pupils from nearby Helmsley, Kirkbymoorside and a vast chunk of the glorious North York moors. This isn't just school for many of the pupils, it's their entire social life. Some have an hour-long journey so be prepared to join the chauffeur rota if your child and his pals like after-school sport. Head has pupils up on stage for a pat on the back for any achievement. We arrive unannounced in an English lesson where children are writing poetry. A 13-year-old is asked to read his work aloud. It's good, very good. His peers spontaneously applaud. We feel like we're in Narnia.

Pastoral Care and Discipline: Step out of line in this school if you dare. Sliding scale of punishments keeps children on the straight and narrow. Lots of support on discipline for teachers. Students like feeling of security, 'you don't ever feel excluded or picked on here,' says 15-year-old pupil. 'You feel safe.'

Pupils and Parents: Supportive parents speak of a happy school. Ofsted surveys suggest significantly high levels of satisfaction in both parents and pupils. PTA provides many new resources and organises events.

Entrance: Oversubscribed in Years 9, 10 and 11 but the demographic dip now allows students from primary schools outside the area to join, without fear of a lengthy appeal process. No longer the case that you have to move into the area and keep your fingers crossed for a place.

Exit: 80 per cent go into further education all around the county and many ultimately to university. School's involvement in the Area Sixth Form Partnership and improving results over the last few years should ensure even more students progress to further education.

Money Matters: Core budget modest but the school has worked hard to achieve additional funding streams.

Remarks: A school that believes there's more to life than GCSEs and still comes up with the goods in exams. Pupils leave with secondary school qualifications and primary school enthusiasm.

Sacred Heart High School (Hammersmith)

212 Hammersmith Road, (Entrance Bute Gardens), Hammersmith, London, W6 7DG

• Pupils: 795 girls, all day • Ages: 11-16 • RC • State

Tel: 020 8748 7600
Fax: 020 8748 0382
Email: info@sacredh.lbhf.sch.uk
Website: www.sacredhearthighschool.org.uk

Head: Since 1992, Dr Christine Carpenter BA PhD FRSA (late fifties). A hard-working head, known for having a keen interest in her girls and all their activities.

Academic matters: A well-respected and committed team of teachers, majority are Catholic. Now a Specialist and Training school, helping other schools in the borough with good practice and to develop the skills of newly qualified teachers. GCSE results well above the national average – 48 per cent of all results graded A*/A. 94 per cent of pupils achieved 5+ A*–C, 51 per cent of pupils achieved five or more A*/A grades. A selection of A/S subjects are offered.

Games, Options, the Arts: A better than average sports programme, with tennis and netball as firm favourites though, as with many inner-city state schools, the sports facilities are not very extensive. Annual activity weeks, D of E. Some talented artists; not much music; drama and dance are popular.

Background and Atmosphere: The convent is built on an historic site with a long Catholic tradition, four different orders of nuns have taught girls here for the past 330 years. Formerly a grammar school until 1976 when it became comprehensive.

Pastoral Care and Discipline: A strong Catholic ethos. Many parents feel the school's size, which is smaller than average for a London state senior, is of particular benefit in promoting a friendly and supportive atmosphere. Girls all have year tutors. Links within the local community are given particular attention, girls are encouraged to want to live purposeful lives, think about and include others. Discipline is strict and a very high standard of behaviour is expected at all times.

Pupils and Parents: An inner-city multicultural mix, most live in Fulham, Hammersmith or neighbouring boroughs. OGs Pauline Collins and Patricia Hayes.

Entrance: First priority to practising Catholic girls from practising Catholic families. Parents must be supportive of the school's ethos. After that, priority goes to looked-after children, sisters, those with special needs and those who have had a primary RC education. Only then is distance from school taken into account. School maintains ability range by banding entrants into three bands 25:50:25.

Exit: At 16 most go on to take A levels at local sixth form colleges or other Catholic schools, a popular choice being St Charles sixth form college. A few to the private sector.

Remarks: Traditional school aiming to promote the education of women and academic success. Doing a goodish job with pupils of all abilities but perhaps resting on its laurels.

Sacred Heart High School (Newcastle)

Fenham Hall Drive, Fenham, Newcastle upon Tyne, Tyne and Wear, NE4 9YH

• Pupils: 1,350 • Ages: 11 to 19 • Size of sixth form: 235 • Roman Catholic • State

Tel: 01912 747 373
Fax: 01912 751 939
Email: admin@sacredheart.newcastle.sch.uk
Website: www.sacredheart-high.org

Head: Since 1998, Mrs Patricia Wager BA PGCE. Previously head teacher at King James the First School, Bishop Auckland, deputy head at Queen Elizabeth High School, Hexham, deputy head Wycliffe School, Leicester and at three other schools as a teacher. Friendly, justifiably proud of her school. Her philosophy is pursuit of Sacred Heart tradition – give girls best opportunity for greatest personal and spiritual fulfilment and academic achievement. Married, two children, husband Richard, retired head.

Academic matters: For results, best state school in Newcastle. In The *Times* top 450 state schools and top schools for A levels. Newcastle's Centre of Excellence for Music and the city's 'music hub'. Some 79 per cent GCSE A*–C, A level; 99 per cent pass rate. Science strong at KS3, GCSE and A level. Single sex 'avoids stereotypes coming to the fore. So here science and maths are more popular than they are in mixed schools because traditionally boys dominate in those subjects,' opines head.

Children are tested and placed in ability groups in four tiers, two classes in each tier. Standard curriculum is flexible to meet individual girl's needs. English, maths, science, technology and religious education are core – science stays right up to 16 'to give the girls a balanced diet'. 'We tailor the curriculum to the gifts of each child, to play to children's strengths and enjoyments.' Progress closely monitored and curriculum altered if necessary. Desire to see girls achieve excellence in subjects they take rather than push for huge lists of GCSE attempts. 'We give them the time to excel in what they are studying.'

Pupils appreciate teachers giving up time to provide extra help. 'They put in a lot of extra effort at lunchtimes and it is great that it is there if you want or need it.' ASDAN Youth Award Scheme is taught along with BTecs/GNVQs etc. Head wants to extend these to provide much greater range. 'We pride ourselves on excellence across the curriculum because students have a right to expect that.' Great store placed on developing and recognising staff achievement too. 'I want fresh and energetic teachers.' Each month a teacher is presented with a 'thank you' by his/her peers for particular achievement/efforts. Sharing of skills/ideas is key. Teachers have visits home and abroad to learn and develop new ideas.

Twelve SEN statemented children. Average class size 28. Teacher:pupil ratio 1:16. Web-based virtual teaching environment went live in autumn 2006, providing staff, parents, students, partner schools, organisations with a phalanx of school information from statistics, curriculum, performance, preparation material, email, library system, management information etc.

Games, Options, the Arts: Full range of sports available from the usual – hockey, netball, badminton etc, to the unusual – kick boxing, tairobics, tag rugby. National finalists for girls football. Extra-curricular visits include theatre, lectures, concerts, museums etc and holidays/exchanges to France, Germany, ski trips, exchange trips to other Sacred Heart schools. D of E Awards. Girls encouraged to pursue charitable work, each tutor group adopts a project for which to raise funds.

Background and Atmosphere: Education for girls at Fenham founded in 1905 by Sisters of the Society of the Sacred Heart. From 1920 scholarships, since 1977 comprehensive. Previously on two sites. £10m spent on the school in past few years: £1.3m on sixth form study centre; £8.7m on new build and re-modelling to bring everyone on to one site. New building is in keeping with old. Plans to create vocational studies centre to extend current provision, and enlarge sixth form.

Great pride in being 'a Sacred Heart girl'. One sixth former told us, 'at the open day Mass you meet people who had been to the school in the past and get the feeling you are part of something special. There is a real sense of community'.

Catholic faith and Sacred Heart ethos are important – prayer and worship are integral part of school life and each day begins with morning prayer. Group of Sisters live nearby and one is a governor. Religion not forced upon pupils. 'It is a personal thing and everyone takes from it what they want.'

Pastoral Care and Discipline: Journey through school is a key to Sacred Heart success. Pastoral care is spearheaded by deputy head, year heads and personal tutors. Each girl will have the same year head and personal tutor from Year 7 to Year 11 to provide continuity. Buddying system teams up trained sixth formers with Year 7, 8 and 9 pupils to provide a listening ear. Peer mentoring gives year 10 and 11 pupils regular access to sixth formers for advice. A full-time counsellor is also available while school chaplain is faith presence in school providing support to students, parents and staff.

Up to sixth form, merit system rewards good work – 15 merits earns bronze certificate, 30 silver, 40 gold, 50 platinum. Warnings and ample opportunity to correct poor behaviour precede any detention or exclusions. Total exclusions are rare – the last was three years ago. 'Exclusion goes against our ethos of welcoming each child and taking them through the ups and downs of school life.'

Pupils and Parents: Bulk from 13 Catholic feeder schools in north and west of Newcastle. A third come from further afield, Newcastle, Northumberland, Durham. All social and academic backgrounds. Just eight or nine per cent where English is second language. 12 SEN statemented children. Average class size 28.

Entrance: Over-subscribed. Catholic applicants have priority, followed by other faiths. 80 per cent are baptised Catholics, 10 per cent Muslim background and 10 per cent other Christians.

Exit: All stay on to 16, usually 70–80 per cent stay to sixth form. After sixth form, three quarters to university, rest to foundation courses, employment or gap year. School excellent in making sure girls make the right choice after sixth form.

Remarks: A lovely school. Every classroom visited was alive with inspired and inspiring teaching. Harnesses the latest technology and ideas to provide stimulating lessons. Continuity provided by pastoral system is outstanding. Efforts to develop teachers and teaching, and going that extra mile to help girls make the right choices after Sacred Heart, both set the school apart. Adopted the 'Every Child Matters' ethos long before it was de rigeur and it shows.

Saffron Walden County High School

Audley End Road, Saffron Walden, Essex, CB11 4UH

• Pupils: 1,950 boys and girls, all day • Ages: 11-18 • Size of sixth form: 500 • Non-denom • State

Tel: 01799 513 030
Fax: 01799 513 031
Email: prussell@saffronwalden.essex.sch.uk
Website: www.saffronwalden.essex.sch.uk

Head: Since 2004, Mr John Hartley MA (fifties). Born Leeds, educated Oundle and St Catharine's College, Cambridge. Taught physics and was head of Notley High School, Braintree prior to this appointment. Enjoys fell walking, photography, social and local history.

Academic matters: Children are setted for maths in Year 7. Broad setting is introduced for English and languages (all children study French and German in Key Stage 3) in Year 8, and for science in Year 9. Otherwise they are mainly taught in mixed ability groups right up to GCSE. Results well above the national average. Children with special needs well integrated in the school.

Sixth formers follow one of three routes, route one being for the most academically able pupils and requiring a minimum of five GCSEs in grades A*–B. Route two is for those with five GCSEs at grades A*–C. Route three is open to pupils with five GCSEs at grade D or above. Course options are determined by route. Sixth formers have the option of doing work experience in Germany, France and Romania.

Games, Options, the Arts: A strong emphasis on traditional team games, such as hockey, netball, rugby and cricket, with between 50 and 60 sports teams playing regularly, depending on the time of year. Artsmark Gold and Sportsmark Gold. Plenty of musical opportunities – 700 children learn an instrument – and there are numerous choirs, orchestras, bands and ensembles. Many staff help lead the well established D of E programme, which is enormously popular, and there are plenty of other extra-curricular activities.

Background and Atmosphere: Set on the edge of the very pleasant town of Saffron Walden and surrounded by rolling countryside. Grounds are unusually extensive, including a grass cricket square, pavilion and tennis courts. Typically unimaginative 1950s architecture, although recent additions, particularly the new music block, have been thoughtfully designed. Very well-equipped sports centre. The school continues to invest heavily in its premises. 2005 saw the opening of a new multi-purpose hall (the Boatman Centre, which doubles as the town's cinema), classroom block and library extension. Investment continued with the opening of a new sports pavilion in January 2009 and a multi-million pound project to extend the sixth form and provide a world class auditorium for music and drama performance is planned for 2011.

Pupils are generally happy with the school with few gripes apart from the usual – they have too much work and the uniform policy is too strict.

Pastoral Care and Discipline: The emphasis is on establishing relationships between staff and pupils. In Years 7–11 each year group is headed by a year co-ordinator who moves up the school with his or her year group and oversees academic and pastoral care. Each form also has a form tutor who remains with that form from Years 7–11. Relatively few formal rules but pupils are expected to exercise self-discipline. Few permanent exclusions but there is no hesitation in taking this step if required.

The only worry expressed by some parents is that the school is so big that it can be difficult for children to settle in, especially as many of them are moving on from very small primary schools; however, most children settle in well, assisted by a wide ranging induction programme and very well established partnerships with feeder schools. The school has established some systems to ensure every pupil feels they are known as an individual.

Pupils and Parents: Catchment area is predominantly middle class. A small number of pupils come from ethnic minorities, reflecting the make-up of the local population.

Entrance: Heavily over-subscribed. Siblings first, then residents of twelve listed parishes. There are a further three criteria but the vast majority of places are offered on the first two. 'To be sure of getting a place here, you do need to live in the catchment area,' says head.

The majority of pupils go on to the sixth form but there are around 70–80 places for newcomers, including some from the independent sector.

Exit: Many students go on to leading Russell Group universities and, in recent years, a few to Oxbridge.

Remarks: Highly regarded locally. A co-ed comprehensive with high academic standards and well-behaved children.

St Aidan's Church of England High School

Linked to Saint Aidan's and Saint John Fisher Associated Sixth Form

Oatlands Drive, Harrogate, North Yorkshire, HG2 8JR

• Pupils: 1,935 boys and girls • Ages: 11-18 • Size of sixth form: 735 plus 380 in association with St John Fisher RC High School • C of E but welcomes children from all Christian traditions • State

Tel: 01423 885 814
Fax: 01423 884 327
Email: admin@st-aidans.co.uk
Website: www.st-aidans.n-yorks.sch.uk

Headteacher: Since 1989, Mr Dennis Richards OBE MA BD FRSA (mid sixties). Winner of the national Ted Wragg award for lifetime teaching achievement 2007; OBE in Queen's Birthday Honours 2007. Educated at Queen Elizabeth Grammar School, Wakefield, read modern languages at Manchester University and later in his teaching career obtained two (part time) degrees in theology and religious studies from London and Leeds Universities. He taught modern languages in two Yorkshire (state) high schools, then at a London school, followed by a deputy headship at Bishop Stopford C of E High School. His wife, Kath, is a social worker and they have three adult children.

Not a head who stands on his dignity (he has spent a night in prison to raise money for charity) – during my tour he was asked the way to a science lab by a new Year 7 child and by another pupil the results of a cricket match (cricket is a passion – he plays and is Chairman of Yorkshire Senior Schools Cricket); a boy with SEN came over to shake his hand; he discussed a competitive fell runner's evening run with her – I could go on: he had a personal knowledge of an impressive number of his charges, including very new Year 7s.

He teaches RE to GCSE and sixth form students and has a gift for obtaining the services of old pupils, before or after university – 12 work as teaching assistants (TAs) with SEN children and contribute their talents to extra-curricular activities. His financial astuteness enables the provision of an unusually high number of TAs as well as the impressive level of regular upgrading of facilities and resources. He delights in the wide range of outstanding (within and outside of school) extra-curricular achievements of his students, from the international fencer to the special needs student training for the Para olympics; parents say he takes a great interest in students of all abilities. Other pursuits include football, rugby, golf, writing for *The Times Educational Supplement* and *The Church Times* and reading.

He wants RS lessons and assemblies to be 'models of excellence', so students are prepared for life in a multi-cultural society, understanding and respecting those of all faiths, with an ethic of social responsibility and self worth.

Academic matters: Students' attainment at entry is well above average and the school has been judged 'outstanding' (in all respects) in three Ofsteds. Average class size well below average (23 in Years 7–9, 20 in years10–11). Relationships between students and teachers are excellent – students spoke appreciatively of how helpful their teachers are, to the extent of coming into school on a bank holiday before public exams. It has science and maths plus modern languages specialisms, with high uptake and achievement in these areas. Members of the science department produce textbooks and CD roms and students are successful in national competitions; French, Spanish, German, Mandarin Chinese, Arabic and Italian are available, with very effective use of video conferencing; every year has eight annual language trips, e.g. week long visits to language schools in Spain and Germany and work experience in France.

Key stage three results are very good, especially maths, science and art. Year 7s start with one modern foreign language (MFL) and several take a second in Year 8. Year 9s do separate sciences. At key stage 4 all take a MFL and RS (Islam is an option). The very bright can sit maths and French early and then AS.

GCSE results are amongst the best nationally, with a steady improvement in the level of grades obtained over the last few years: 60 per cent A/A* and 82 per cent A*/B in 2010; almost all students obtain five A*-Cs at GCSE or equivalents (89 per cent including maths and English). All three sciences, RS (notably starry), Spanish, music and food technology stand out.

The associated sixth form with St John Fisher RC High School, the largest school based sixth form nationally, offers a ecumenical environment, each preserving its own identity via separate pastoral systems; a small number join from other schools. High praise in the most recent Ofsted report: 'terrific' progress, 'superb' attitudes to learning, 'exceptionally high quality' teaching, 'excellent relationships ... founded on mutual respect and trust', 'a family feel'. Steady A/B at around 60 per cent at A level – 168 obtained three As in 2010 and 108 A*s. Forty three subjects offered: sciences (very popular), maths, history, ancient history, English lit, German, Spanish, psychology, government and politics, RS, art, design and technology, drama and theatre studies and performing arts particularly successful. Students benefit from links with three Yorkshire universities' RS and science departments. Other less usual subjects include dance, engineering, law, geology, plus vocational courses, e.g. health and social care, travel and tourism, music technology. All do RE – very successfully – as part of the AS general studies programme (Buddhism as well as Christianity studied), then non examined RE in Year 13. The AQA baccalaureate is being piloted – A levels plus extended project and community service. Advanced extension awards for the most able. Also a one year intermediate course – IT, leisure and tourism, maths, English and a certificate in career planning.

SEN and disaffected students progress well too. The latter can do the ASDAN vocational course and a diploma in digital applications; they may follow individualised workplace and further education college related programmes. The independent learning centre, with walls covered with motivational quotes, provides a safe space with one to one support. Provision is made for school refusers outside school in a local church. The very well resourced learning support department, deliberately placed by Mr Richards at the heart of the school and given an excellent ranking by the education service for inclusion and dyslexia, has a highly qualified, flexible, very thoughtful and innovative head. All are tested on entry – in Years 7 and 8 statemented students receive individual or small group support outside the classroom. Other children needing support are also placed in small teaching groups for a number of subjects, for as long as seems necessary. Inside class support is provided too, in a sensitive way, and teachers have a lot of communication with the department. Parents of dyslexic students are given training so they can do reading work with their children at home.

A small, purpose built, fitted kitchen helps autistic students to develop life skills; a lunchtime games club enables them to develop social skills and provides a refuge at a time of the day they find stressful (a shed with a model railway layout developed by an autistic boy is another refuge for vulnerable students); a special rest area has been created for three Down's Syndrome children who are worn out by 2 pm. We have heard reports of a few past parents feeling the school was unwelcoming to new dyslexic students, perhaps a result of its renown proving a drain on restricted resources, but current SEN ones speak with great appreciation of the school's attention to individual needs and quick response to their concerns: 'You can't fault the support ... the school is very flexible and innovative'; 'prepared to do everything to meet his needs'; 'A city wide autism specialist (contacted by the school) came to our house for tea and got him back on track'; 'a very open door policy'; 'The teachers provided fantastic extra backup on all his expeditions'. A parent support group meets regularly for information sessions.

Games, Options, the Arts: Described by Mr Richards as a 'sports mad school – indeed the day we visited all outdoor facilities were in use after the end of school. All the main sports plus basketball, cycling and equestrian clubs, aerobics, rowing, tag rugby, dance, fitness and weight training. Lots of success in regional and national competitions plus some outstanding individuals, e.g. martial arts, gymnastics, an international fencer ('Teachers are very supportive about helping me catch up with work I've missed for competitions'). Football tour to Holland, leadership awards, every school year from Year 8 has an outdoor education residential, including a winter mountaineering weekend.

'The school fizzes with music, sport and drama' (Ofsted) – unsurprisingly, has Artsmark Gold. Stunning music in huge quantities, with a high regional and national reputation – twelve ensembles, including the wittily named brass quintet, No Strings Attached, and various choirs; lots of public performances, e.g. at the Labour party conference, the Birmingham Symphony Hall, the Albert Hall, and regular 'outstanding' awards in regional and national festivals; ambitious programmes, e.g. Karl Jenkins' *The Armed Man*; concert tours to Canada and Europe. The big sixth form chamber choir (50 per cent male) has been in all possible finals of the BBC's *Songs of Praise* School Choir of the Year competition (the only choir to have done this) and can often be heard on Radio 4s daily service. The world music group gives African drumming workshops in local primary schools (using their own set of African drums); the worship band, Aidan's Flame, is much in demand for local services.

Drama also of a high standard and ambitious – *History of Tom Jones*, *West Side Story*, 1950s rock and roll version of' *Twelfth Night*, their version of *The Comedy of Errors* was one of only three chosen for The Royal Shakespeare Company's schools festival; regular successful applicants to the National Youth Theatre; tours, theatre trips, workshops, drama clubs, plays produced by sixth formers; a community theatre project takes workshops and performances to local primary schools. A considerable amount of framed, excellent, very original art by present and past students on display throughout the school – fine art, graphics and photography on offer; art trip to Paris.

Students very enthusiastic about the huge range of extra-curricular opportunities (some run by older students), with high uptake – eco club, chess, organic gardening, signing, enterprise clubs for all ages, debating (the mock election was won handsomely by the Lib Dems – 83 per cent turnout), science and technology competitions (regional and national successes), D of E (several golds), cooking events and competitions. Lots of new fiction in the well resourced library – reading very popular with boys as well as girls, says the librarian ('I can't keep up with the demand!'); authors visit during the annual Book Week; creative writing workshops with writers and a residential course in Wales. Has international school status – links with schools in Morocco, China, Uganda, Tanzania, Sri Lanka, Australia (Year 9s do a 6 week exchange), Canada, France, Germany. Impressive sums raised for a great range of charities (£56,000 one year); several students do third world voluntary work in their gap year. Year 12s do a leadership course and modern language students teach local primary school children at an annual languages day.

Background and Atmosphere: Founded in 1968 on a large greenfield site bordering the Harrogate Stray. Pleasant modern front, only two or three levels high. Very thoughtfully and attractively designed throughout, e.g. a cafeteria with a low ceiling to absorb noise, a convivially arranged staffroom. Well maintained throughout (no graffiti), steady programme of development – recent new classrooms, dance studio, second chapel with lovely stained glass windows, deli bar for sixth, careers area and learning resource centre.

The Christian ethos is central, expressed in the thorough going concern for individual needs and tolerance of difference, and assemblies play a big rôle, but sixth formers say it isn't 'very churchy'. Newcomers (some have moved from schools where they haven't been happy) feel welcomed. Academic success is not embarrassing, but neither is it seen as an all consuming goal, we were told – an attitude of 'everyone is good at something' is supported by the wealth of extra curricular activities. A senate of ten elected sixth formers makes suggestions the school responds to – 'It's always trying to improve what's on offer'.

Recently awarded *The Times Educational Supplement* award for the best school dinners in England. Everyone enthuses about the – decidedly up market – food: a sixth form boy (sixth form has deli bar plus separate cafeteria, Year 7s have one and Years 8–11 another) declared, 'The food is fantastic – I could sit here and eat all day!' Parents come in to sample the lunches and praise the 'lovely, varied menu', 'The children get to try new food', 'I don't need to cook a main meal in the evening'; an amazingly cheap (50p) healthy breakfast on offer for early arrivals.

Pastoral Care and Discipline: Parents (and Ofsted) talk glowingly about the 'caring ethos' and attention to the individual needs of students of all abilities and needs – 'The pastoral care is second to none; all staff are extremely approachable and any problems are dealt with straight away with kindness and consideration' (usual structure of form tutors and heads of year, plus a 'very supportive' school nurse). Thoughtful transition arrangements – all (65–70) feeder schools are visited in Year 6. The behaviour policy shows understanding of the need for a flexible approach to discipline, taking developmental stages into account – behaviour rated 'excellent' by Ofsted. Rewards policy includes badges for 'being special', award evenings, postcards to parents.

Mr Richards has a traditional attitude to uniform, admitting to being 'a bit OCD' about boys having their top button done up (which the boys would agree with). His recent controversial decision to ban skirts for girls up to year 10 (Year 11s can chose whether to wear a skirt or trousers; no uniform for sixth formers) was intended to 'take the pressure off a discipline issue that was impeding relationships' and to protect the younger girls from outside school risks. Some grumbles from girls, but parents were consulted.

Pupils and Parents: Mostly white middle class parents, reflecting Harrogate's social composition – only a few ethnic minority, EAL and looked after students. Pupils present as open, articulate, thoughtful and happy, valuing what the school provides.

Entrance: After SEN and children in care, takes local children, extending out to the whole archdeaconry. A big waiting list decided on by an elaborate points system based on regular church attendance by children and parents, siblings at the school and service to the church (or faith equivalent). About 200 from other schools join the sixth form – five A*-Cs needed.

Exit: Very few leave at 16 – almost all to further education college for a course not offered by the school. Most sixth formers proceed to a great range of universities, including several top ones, e.g. Oxbridge (12 in 2010) and the best London University colleges. Several do foundation art courses and degrees; medicine popular.

Two dedicated careers officers give one to one advice; Year 12s attend a three day careers conference after their AS exams – 'An amazing careers department,' enthused a sixth form student.

Remarks: Regularly ranked in the top 12 comprehensives nationally and always striving to improve – 'Children can grow in every direction', 'a fantastic school', 'everything we hoped it would be'.

St Albans Girls' School

Sandridgebury Lane, St Albans, Hertfordshire, AL3 6DB

- Pupils: 1,165 girls; all day; boys in the sixth form since 2007
- Ages: 11-18 • Size of sixth form: 270 • Non-denom • State

Tel: 01727 853 134
Fax: 01727 831 157
Email: jacky.jenkins@stags.herts.sch.uk
Website: www.stags.herts.sch.uk

Head: Since 2010, Mrs Margaret Chapman BSc NPQH (mid forties). Previously deputy head at The Priory School, Hitchin. Studied at the University of Wales, Aberystwyth and went on to teach geography, geology and ICT. Was head of geography and pastoral director of Key Stage 4 at Mill Hill County High School, becoming assistant head. Married to Lewis, project manager, with two children of secondary school age. Believes that teaching is a real vocation and is enjoying the challenges and rewards of a new headship in a super school environment. Passionate about teaching and empowering the next generation to have high aspirations and enthusiasm for learning.

Academic matters: Consistently very good results despite the increasingly mixed intake. 86 per cent five A*–C grades at GCSE in 2010. Maths strong and popular. Average of 62 per cent of A levels grades A*–B; popular subjects include English, maths, psychology and media studies with strong showing in languages. Class sizes 27 max. All take French and most study a second language although some girls with basic skills difficulties benefit from extra English. Some refurbished science labs and whiteboards though not at cutting edge of technology. Well stocked library with computers and separate sixth form study area plus sixth form common room refurbished thanks to friends of STAGs.

Good teaching – with a couple invited to teacher of the year awards. A few 'old school' find the breadth of ability and the challenge of less able pupils difficult to deal with but school are working on this. Currently reviewing the curriculum; working on specialist diplomas and trying to ensure variety of learning pathways open to all girls. For those who find a full GCSE programme too demanding ASDAN and COPE provide freedom and challenges, while working on basic skills and presentation – 'these programmes really build self-esteem and confidence.' Gifted and talented Co-ordinator is developing a range of curriculum extension opportunities including Italian, maths clubs, master classes and the opportunity to take GCSEs early.

SEN improving, learning support staff have a 'can-do attitude' which is slowly cascading through the various departments – head openly supportive and keen to improve. Approximately 100 students appear on the SEN register, every type of learning difference: dyslexia, SEBD, physical difficulties (no lifts), HI, VI aspergers etc. Five have statements, three for speech and language – 'we seem to have developed expertise in helping those with speech and language difficulties.' There are some pupils with high levels of need and no additional LA funding but school does put support in place. There's a whole school push to ensure best practice re accessibility and disability equality. 'It's not about ticking boxes but attitudes and perceptions, there is a spectrum of ability and of disability; simple things such as good manners, holding doors open, can make a difference to everyone.'

Games, Options, the Arts: Strong in sport, music, drama and dance. There are nine tennis courts, three hockey pitches, a cricket square, athletics track, outdoor pool, gym and new sports hall. Teams are very successful at district, county and national level; rugby a recent but successful innovation. Plenty of extra-curricular opportunities including trips, tours, D of E and World Challenge. Dance groups practise on a regular basis and take part in local productions with some girls taking part in national productions and others running their own shows. Three choirs and a chamber orchestra keep the musicians entertained. Girls love collecting for charity, the entrance regularly ablaze with news of the latest good causes and events including, when we visited, a 'no talent show'.

Background and Atmosphere: Founded in 1920, STAGS now occupies a large, modern site towards the north of the city. On the whole facilities aren't fab but most are functional, a few are past their best but there are notable improvements including a superb new sports hall complete with up to date equipment and a smart, bright entrance exuding warmth and light. 'We do spend money upgrading but the reality is we chip away; a little has to go far.' Grounds in good nick, no litter problems externally but some problems internally particularly in afternoons as limited space means packed lunch brigade have to eat in classrooms. Parents frantically fund-raising to provide covered picnic areas. Dining room and snack shacks appreciated – 'the food is fine, tasty and with plenty of choice.'

Pastoral Care and Discipline: The house system is big news, helps enormously with pastoral issues if only by preventing girls from being too cliquey. Houses named after influential women: Austen, Hepworth etc. House points and commendations reward good work and behaviour. Oodles of house events including competitions, challenges, parties, pantos, playwriting etc. Care and academia go hand in hand – 'it's not just about ability, some girls come to school with a lot of baggage, and we have to help them with this if we are to engage them as learners'. Parents' clinic every half-term, appointments needed and head likes to be informed of issues beforehand; 'if parents are giving their time to come to school it's important I can provide the appropriate information or help and advice when they get here.' Senior pupils take on considerable roles of responsibility not just as prefects; 'Hear 4 U', a support group run by sixth formers, led the assembly during our visit. An attention grabbing pass-the-parcel game gave the message that however big a problem there is help on hand to unravel it.

Thoughtful transition programme involving parents and pupils. New pupils do enterprise exercises with the emphasis on team building rather than typical taster day. All Year 7 forms have prefect assigned who acts as a befriender. Seldom exclude but do get tough when necessary – 'the majority of girls want to learn so we will take steps against anyone who disrupts others.' Have good links with police, the community support officer is a regular and popular visitor, appointments available for anyone wanting to chat; similarly school counsellor available for anyone needing an independent ear. Sixth form part of a consortium so depending on subject choices girls may spend only part of their time at STAGS, which means monitoring and mentoring of students can be problematic.

Pupils and Parents: Mainly from St Albans and surrounding towns. Wide range of socio-economic backgrounds, including some affluent families who opt for STAGS rather than the private sector. Was originally a grammar school but intake has broadened. Predominantly girlie-girls. Tend to divide into groups, and the school is very aware of (and deals well with) the resulting potential for singling out of individuals or of bullying. Uniform not the sort you'd readily associate with a business and enterprise college (a number with short skirts and handbags) but proposed new uniform may change that. Since 2007, boys filtered into the sixth form. Sixth form dress is smart casual but sometimes open to interpretation. Head keen for pupils to have their say – imaginative *Dragon's Den* approach to recent school council issues ensures just that.

A very strong Old Girls' network spanning the age range up to 80!

Entrance: Possibly the most over-subscribed school in Hertfordshire with admissions by lottery if there are several applicants for any subsequent vacancies arising. At 11, from a wide range of primary schools in the area, administered by Hertfordshire County Council 'in accordance with the county's admissions criteria'.

Exit: Vast majority (over 80 per cent) goes on to higher education. Some Oxbridge entrants every year despite the lack of coaching and preparation oft found at other schools.

Money Matters: Has an excellent PTA known as Friends of STAGS which raises considerable amounts of money.

Remarks: A sunny school, determined to get the best out of all. In the words of the girls, 'it's fun and cool here and importantly staff listen to you and try to be flexible.' And so long as results remain good it will remain a perennially popular choice with parents.

St Albans High School for Girls

Linked to Saint Albans High School For Girls Preparatory School in the Junior section

Townsend Avenue, St Albans, Hertfordshire, AL1 3SJ

• Pupils: 940 girls, all day • Ages: 4-18 • Size of sixth form: 170 • C of E
• Fees: £9,330-£11,865 pa • Independent

Tel: 01727 853 800
Fax: 01727 792 516
Email: info@stalbans-high.herts.sch.uk
Website: www.stahs.org.uk

Headmistress: Since 2009, Mrs Rosemary Martin (fifties) MEd NPQH FRSA, formerly head of Combe Bank School, Sevenoaks. Previous head, Ms Jacqualyn Pain, went to head Northwood College.

Academic matters: At 11, girls are put into four parallel forms. Class sizes 24, reducing to 20 at GCSE and 15 at A level. Four sets for maths – many succeed in maths challenges, number of Olympiads annually. Popular subjects include modern languages, geography – excellent results and school leads the way in ICT. French, German, Latin and Spanish offered. At GCSE, excellent results – 100 per cent A*–C, (86 per cent got A*/A grades). At A level 92 per cent A*–B; art particularly strong – good facilities. All Y12 take ECDL. No place for the pusillanimous; encourage girls to develop their thinking skills, plan ahead of lessons and appreciate what's required.

No statemented children though some with ADD, Asperger's, sensory needs, dyslexia and dyspraxia. Additional curricular education (ACE) available, no more than one lesson a week. Wheelchair access difficult but have adapted timetables to meet specific needs. Enthusiastic careers staff stress importance, not just of Oxbridge liaison but whole gamut; lots of debates, interview practice, visiting speakers and educating of parents. Wants to encourage ambition to look at exit strategies, and ensure girls plan their futures. Keen to get them to think outside the box and consider more unusual choices such as chemical engineering and management science.

Games, Options, the Arts: Sports fields a ten-minute walk away; state of the art indoor pool and leisure complex with dance studio and fitness suite. Strong sporting tradition: lacrosse, netball, tennis, gymnastics, modern dance, badminton (lots of successes), football and athletics; a number played to county standard. Drama and theatre studies a popular GCSE and A level choice with performing opportunities via school productions and house plays produced and directed entirely by the girls. Plenty of trips: skiing, sports tours, drama etc. Have raised money for mosquito nets, water supply etc for sister school in Mtwara, Tanzania; girls say it makes them realise how fortunate they are. Music strong, separate music block, half learn a musical instrument (a good number beyond grade 8); performing opportunities via four orchestras, three bands, five chamber ensembles, four choirs and a choral society. Refreshing sense of 'giving it a go', 30+ clubs, ensuring something for everyone regardless of level. All encouraged to take a creative GCSE, with an interestingly large uptake for food and textiles at A level.

Background and Atmosphere: Founded in 1889, about half a mile from the centre of St Albans, referred to as The High School by locals to distinguish it from St Albans Girls' School. School sprawls across the suburban street, minutes from the centre of town, most buildings purchased by school but a few residential properties remain. Preparatory school based in Wheathampstead. School entrance feels like a school of yesteryear, solid wooden floors, long corridors, but, for most part, tradition has yielded to modernity. Sixth form have own purpose-built centre, with seminar style teaching rooms, common room, kitchen, work areas etc. Facilities fine but head keen to improve saying it's what the girls need and deserve. The main school has seven bright science labs, two computer rooms, a technology centre, a newly refurbished and fully-equipped food technology room and two well-stocked libraries. Maintains close links with the diocese of St Albans through the Bishop and the Dean; voluntary weekly Eucharist.

Pastoral Care and Discipline: Fairly traditional pastoral care links closely with PSHE and house system (girls stay with same housemistress); firm belief pupils must be happy to achieve. Girls given lots of freedom and say they value head's philosophy of 'do no harm but impress with your intelligence and wit'. Head girl and four deputies are elected by teachers and pupils after each has submitted a manifesto and spoken at 'hustings'. All Years 7–9 have form prefect assigned; school council a recent addition. Good food, healthy tuck shop with goodies such as home-made bio yogurt. Keen to celebrate all achievements and encourage girls to rejoice in the success of others.

Pupils and Parents: Girls polite, confident but not arrogant, come from as far as Bedfordshire and north London, courtesy of some 14 coach services. Old Girls include Dame Anna Neagle and Isobel Lang.

Entrance: Very over-subscribed; by assessment and interview, at 11 and 16 for the senior school; and at four, five and seven to Wheathampstead (some parental perplexity at nature of selection procedure – group tasks, no individual interview or discussion of hobbies). Most progress from the preparatory to the senior school; occasional one may be advised, well in advance, to look elsewhere. Minimum of five As at GCSE for sixth form entry (regardless of whether already at the school or not), underlines that girls must be able to keep up.

Exit: Though most meet stiff sixth form requirements, 15 to 20 leave post-GCSE, primarily for boarding, boys or simply a change of scene. Popular destinations include Oundle, Rugby, Cheltenham or local sixth form colleges. Otherwise post A levels to a wide selection of universities – good handful to Oxbridge.

Money Matters: Academic scholarships available at 11 and post GCSE; music scholarships and fees assistance for those less fortunate. Keen to increase the number of cases of fees assistance based on need; don't want to be an exclusively middle class school, keen to attract those who lack financial means but meet other criteria.

Remarks: An organised, well-run, school that sets high standards and achieves them. Caring, compassionate, but unashamedly first and foremost an academic school with an academic pace; middle of the pack better off elsewhere, tail-enders wouldn't feature, but great for front runners.

St Albans School

Abbey Gateway, St Albans, Hertfordshire, AL3 4HB

• Pupils: 785, all boys except for 65 girls in the sixth form • Ages: 11-19
• Size of sixth form: 285 (65 girls) • Multi-faith • Fees: £13,290 pa
• Independent

Tel: 01727 855 521
Fax: 01727 843 447
Email: hm@st-albans-school.org.uk
Website: www.st-albans.herts.sch.uk

Headmaster: Since 1993, Mr Andrew Grant MA PGCE FRSA, mid fifties, a Cambridge English graduate. Chairman of HMC 2009-10, Mr Grant is the perfect example of what a difference can be made to a school by a professional head with a sustained long-term commitment. He has overseen an impressive revival in his school and shows no signs of flagging. Relaxed, energetic, chatty and with appropriate toughness when required, he is good company and visibly 'hands-on'. Mr Grant communicates a buzz which permeates the place as a whole. 'I feel very personally identified with this place,' he says, enjoys life 'outside the magic circle of the M25' and says of St Albans, 'it's a great place to be.' Mind you, he also modestly describes it as, 'a small cathedral city on the outskirts of our school playing fields' – but with justification! (See below.) His own two boys have been pupils – one as head boy by popular choice and this, too, says a lot for the popularity and democracy of his regime. A good, solid head running a solidly strong school, now getting some of the acclaim it deserves.

Academic matters: Everyone does GCSEs in core subjects plus three options chosen from a pretty standard range. In 2009, 88 per cent of all grades were A*/A, placing school 7th nationally in The Independent's GCSE ranking and 7th boys' school at GCSE in The Times. In 2010, A*/A grades topped 80% for the third year in succession. Top performers were art, maths, history, geography, RS, design technology, science and classics and the minority languages, but results in all the other major subjects not far behind. History, geography and religious studies the most popular options. IGCSE offered in English literature. A levels, in a total of 23 subjects offered, similarly strong, with 90 per cent of grades at A*- B. Big numbers in maths and strong showings in all sciences, geography, economics, PE, DT, RS, history, ancient history and English. Results good across the board.

Languages, as is often the case in boys' schools, have been less popular but interest in both ancient and modern languages is increasing – over 70 sixth form students are studying at least one MFL. French, German and Latin are on an equal footing in Year 7; pupils choose any two to continue into Year 8; top sets take French in year 10 and AS in Year 11. Big recent investments in IT – school now well-equipped with PC suites here and there and interactive whiteboards – used effectively and enthusiastically by those staff who like them and eschewed by others who don't – a sensible policy.

Unobtrusive but efficient SEN provision with those who 'appear to need it' informally assessed by SENCo; ed psychs pulled in if necessary, pupils are assessed termly. 25 currently get some form of help (none with a statement of needs), usually one-to-one, rarely withdrawn from lessons and if they are, then they are rotated on a six weekly cycle so that no boy misses too much of the same subject. Extra help at lunch time, post-school popular. OK on dyslexia and dyspraxia, plus the occasional ADHD and those who find exams threatening. This is old fashioned proper back up, good for confidence and building self esteem: no tricks, just patient ground work. Costs £25 per child per hour, 'works well for the school, works well for me,' says the SENCo who works four full days a week and is chocabloc. School not really good for wheelchairs.

Games, Options, the Arts: In 2003, after a nine-year planning battle and two public enquiries, school finally opened 'Woollams' – 'the best school playing fields in the country.' School sold a 12-acre plot plus planning permission inside the purlieus of the city of St Albans and bought a 400-acre farm two miles down the road with the proceeds. Letting the rest, they then proceeded to level 75 acres to make 19 winter pitches for football and rugby, an all-weather hockey pitch, seven cricket squares and two blocks of tennis/netball courts. Two elegant and impressive pavilions, one 'boyproof' and the other belonging to the energetic Old Albanians. A 15-minute bus ride from the school but well worth it and pupils become gooey-eyed when they talk about it – as does the long-serving head groundsman and who can blame him? Twenty sporting activities are on offer here including all the major games but you can also try sailing, squash, badminton, aerobics, golf, cross country, athletics and table tennis. 2011 will see construction of a new sports hall and swimming pool commence on the main site.

The facilities are matched by the achievements. National and international honours, including, recently, three athletics internationals, an U16 England rugby cap, a Cambridge double blue in athletics and cross-country, one in hockey, two in cricket. 'Too numerous to mention' are school's representatives in county teams in many sports. In the English Schools AA national cross country championships, half the county senior team come from St Albans. You get the picture. Younger, less sporty pupils feel that 'there's not so much to do for us' on the extra-curricular side but this apparently picks up as you move through the school in the shape of more, less physically demanding, clubs etc.

In case you think it's all sports, drama is strong and benefits from recently acquired house across the road from main school into which have been built teaching spaces and a good studio with top-class technics – a real boost for the subject. There is a large, well-equipped school hall which acts as a theatre for major productions as well as – how nice – a small outdoor theatre. School publishes *The Albanian* – one of the most intelligent school mags we have seen. John Mole has been resident poet here for yonks – again a sensible and novel idea. Music is also strong – though music tech isn't big here – and lots of ensembles flourish. Annually, a huge tour taking many groups of all sizes goes to e.g. Barcelona, Paris, New York – Tuscany in 2009. Annually also an oratorio concert, jointly with St Albans High, takes place in the cathedral. The school choir, which sings at school services twice weekly in the cathedral, is 60 plus strong and professional in approach and sound. We were treated to a Scarlatti motet – a privileged start to a morning for the whole school as well as for those who sing. School does not provide the choir for the cathedral – that is made up of boys and men (there is a girls' choir too) from all over the area but five pupils here are also in the cathedral choir – a double and challenging commitment, but those we met who made it were articulately proud of the their involvement.

DT in first-rate new robotic suite, CDT is impressive and creative. D of E is popular and begins with the silver award. CCF also strong. School owns Pen Arthur, a rugged farmhouse in rural Wales and everyone goes there for a variety of activities and field work – a rare and well-used resource.

Background and Atmosphere: School founded in 948 making it one of the country's oldest. It is next to the cathedral and has inherited many of the foundation's buildings and some extraordinary rooms and nooks. It is not, however, the cathedral school, and relations with the great building and its foundation are, says head, 'cordial, loose and ideal, with all the advantages of being thought a cathedral school and none of the disadvantages.' We know what he means. We visited lessons in the old dungeon building and the library (well-stocked) is housed in a super ancient hall with Gothic windows and yard-thick walls. Busts and memorials to the school's venerable history abound and sit comfortably with all the accoutrements of a thoroughly modern educational environment. Other buildings nestle amid beautifully kept gardens and school is reached by many via a walk over the cathedral green. A privileged setting. Strong involvement with the local community including excellent work on local conservation projects and links with local maintained schools.

Boarding went in the 1950s, the direct grant in the 1970s – 80 per cent had been on free places – and girls arrived in the sixth in 1991. Of the 40 or so new pupils into the sixth, most are girls but this still means that, proportionately, their numbers are small. The attitude of the school to them is healthy and we did not detect any of the cattle market mentality observable elsewhere. The girls, many from STAGS, the local state girls' school, clearly love it and, despite – or because of? – their small numbers, thrive. A third of the staff are women. Perhaps this, together with the few girls and the sensible, unmacho attitude of the staff, makes for the relaxed, cheery and comradely atmosphere we observed throughout.

Pastoral Care and Discipline: Carefully structured tutorial system, prefects and a, now full-time, school nurse make for effective pastoral care. 'Anyone who brings drugs on site is too stupid to be here so they have to go,' says head, refreshingly. Random testing used 'on good grounds' and in coordination with home. Head has expelled for drugs and would again but no incidents for two years. School feels orderly but not oppressively so. A sense of self-discipline prevails. Food 'very good', enthuse pupils.

Pupils and Parents: Many come in on good network of school buses. 70+ per cent from local Herts area and about half of those from St Albans itself. The rest, including a good number of Jewish pupils, from north London, mostly from Enfield. Parents mostly professional/business/commercial and a large proportion new to independent education. A smaller number from other ethnic minorities or families where the first lang is not English. Very strong Old Albanians many of whom send their sons here and, later, their daughters. Many siblings so a strong family/community feel. Notable former pupils go back to the year dot but recent ones include Sir Tim Rice, archaeologist Lord Renfrew, film producer Mike Newell, General Sir Richard Lawson and Prof Stephen Hawking.

Entrance: At 11 years old, 260 apply for 72 places. Tests in English, maths and VR and interviews all on the same day. Average IQ of 128 of those who make it. At 13, 90 applicants for up to 48 places. Tests as above plus three interviews and entry dependent on CE results. Around 70 applicants for 20+ places at 16 – predictions of A*–C at GCSE with As in A level subjects. Increasingly school is the first choice and can afford to be choosy.

Exit: A very impressive list of subjects and destinations. All good solid stuff e.g. large numbers in 2009 to read philosophy, economics or history at places such as Bath, York, London; equally large numbers in 2010 to read maths, engineering, sciences at Warwick, Durham, Bristol et al. A sprinkling of Oxbridges in a spread of disciplines – all testament to a broad and serious education.

Money Matters: Variable numbers of schols worth 10–50 per cent of fees awarded on the basis of performance in the entrance tests at 11 and by separate exam at 13 and 16. Choral scholarships by audition at 11+. Also means-tested bursaries up to 100 per cent of fees. Special bursaries for instrumental tuition from 11 and for art.

Remarks: If the glitzy north London heavyweights or the big boys in the shires are not your thing, quietly relocate to a spot on the St Albans bus route – and then gloat over your friends.

St Aloysius' College

Linked to Saint Aloysius College Junior School in the Junior section

45 Hill Street, Garnethill, Glasgow, G3 6RJ

• Pupils: 830 boys and girls in senior school, all day; roughly 50/50 boys/girls • Ages: 11-18 • Size of sixth form: S5 and S6: 250 • RC • Fees: £8,469-£8,748 pa • Independent

Tel: 0141 332 3190
Fax: 0141 353 0426
Email: admissions@staloysius.org
Website: www.staloysius.org

Head: Since 2004, Mr John Stoer BA PGCE (forties) who was educated at Douai School, read theology at Bristol and originally went down the accountancy road, but rapidly changed to teaching, taking his PGCE at London University. A committed Catholic, he is the first lay head at St Aloysius and has always taught in the Catholic sector – starting at St Thomas More School in Chelsea, followed by being head of RE at St Philip Howard School off the East India Dock Road, thence Gunnersbury Catholic School in London where he was director of sixth form, followed by deputy head of The Campion School in Hornchurch. He comes to St Aloysius after ten years at St Joseph's College in Staffordshire where he was also the first lay head ('Steadily moving north'). A thoughtful man, entertaining and interesting, with a puckish sense of humour, Mr Stoer applied for St Aloysius because of its links with the Jesuit tradition which he first encountered at The Campion School (though it was, by then, out of Jesuit control). A theologian and a born teacher, he couldn't resist giving this editor a quick history lesson on Jesuit education via his (heavily marked in turquoise) copy of *Ratio Studiorum*, the Jesuit handbook, first published in 1586.

Mr Stoer arrived with a wealth of experience, a confidence to change and a subtle way of persuasion. The school, which had previously eschewed Standard grades, is now opting for the stronger Intermediate II (in the Scottish system) with music and religious studies taken as GCSEs (with the only exam board with a Roman Catholic syllabus). Highers and Advanced Highers in S5 and S6. 'Real change doesn't happen quickly – you need to change hearts and minds.' No mass staff evacuations which might be expected to follow such radical surgery – just two or three who were of an age to retire. Mr Stoer and his wife, who have two children in the school, live in the West End of Glasgow.

Academic matters: Year sizes of 140, S1 = mixed ability, but expect some setting further up the school into classes of around 20; pupils can move up and down. School has five one-hour lessons daily, with ten minutes added on to the working day – five in the morning and five at the end. Curriculum now settled – no Standard grades at all, with pupils expected to aim for five Highers in S5 and at least two Advanced Highers in S6. Recent results show that twice as many pupils took Higher Latin than Italian, with French and Spanish the only other languages on offer. French, Spanish, classics and the sciences the strongest kids on the block. English and maths perhaps a tad sad – we might expect more than 57 per cent getting A in these subjects and, frankly, five failures in maths is too many. IT computing et al less than brilliant performers but new computing block should produce miracles ere long. Some of the classes are tiny – four in Italian and Greek. The overall pass rate at Higher was one of the top in the country.

The school has returned to a traditional head of department system. Impressive new computer suites used for straight IT and class learning with open access – staff not so keen on this as new Clavius building is vast and needs quite a lot of patrolling, and there is no staffroom, though admittedly that was part of the original design. Dramatic chemistry labs with interesting clusters of really quite high tables round six dedicated work areas with gas and water access. Well-used library. School keen (very keen) on homework for all ages and has a dedicated learning website which children can access from home or wherever and carries lesson notes and homework assignments; homework club for all plus after-school club for extra help – no stigma about popping in at any time.

Huge strides in the additional support for learning department – Mr Stoer was having a planning meeting with the head of additional support during our visit (and so of course we asked to stay). Number of pilot schemes afoot: laptops (and growing), mentoring (which is proving highly successful with four mentors now on staff), scribing, reading (team readers' practice); this is a school aware of SEN disabilities and which is taking serious steps to facilitate learning. Asperger's, ADHD, dyslexia, dyspraxia, OK for the visually impaired ('We work with guidance from the eye hospital' – which includes using coloured lenses and overlays. NB Apart from the dedicated Old Rectory, this is the first time this editor has come across coloured lenses being treated with anything other than lip service). Learning support either for the individual or small groups of pupils. The two new-builds have lifts, with braille on the lift buttons, but the slope is such in the primary school that it would be impossible without hefty carriers to get a wheelchair into the classroom currently used for music.

Games, Options, the Arts: For an inner city school there is a surprising amount of playground space (this includes car parking for important visitors – like this editor; otherwise it is hideous round here), and young were fooling around on the all-weather surface in a serious Glasgow rain at breaktime during our visit. Games are important in the Jesuit culture – 'Sport helps pupils learn to accept both success and failure graciously' – and team games for all (at least once a week). The dedicated playing fields are down the M8 towards Stepps (our guides hadn't a clue where – they just 'slept on the bus'). Old-fashioned gym on site and impressive looking weights room. Quite good representation in rugby and regular winners of the Scottish Schools' Cup plus local and national caps in rugby, hockey and athletics. Annual rugby tour to Ireland, regular joint hockey/rugby tours abroad to e.g. Australia and South Africa. Girls' games important too. Full time co-ordinator of outdoor education and D of E just appointed, so expect masses more expeditions: kayaking, climbing, sailing – all good hearty stuff. The whole senior school decamps for a week's brisk outdoor education between S1 and S4, and post the public exams there are more jaunts and tripettes: walking the West Highland Way, film making, trips to London and the like.

Glorious, light, sunny art department at the top of the elegantly stained-glass Mount Building – nice line in flat painting, one or two jolly sculptures and some terrific fabric design, plus a wizard Roman helmet made out of ring pulls from cans (our guide had been photographed in it and made sure we had seen quite how cunningly it had been made).

Music important with a vast range of instruments on offer and compulsory weekly lessons up to S2. Vibrant school orchestra, terrific and popular choir. This is a school where music really matters. Strong drama throughout the school – we were kicked out of a junior rehearsal with alacrity. Enthusiastic inter-house music as well as sport. Keen debaters; mass of clubs – chess, debating and film making popular, ditto D of E and YE. Regular school links with other schools, 'especially Jesuit ones', for exchanges and the like give pupils a 'broader outlook on life'.

Background and Atmosphere: School founded in 1859 to educate the Catholic community in the west of Scotland and is run still very much on the Jesuit principles that God is in all things and that human excellence and service to others, and the 'fullest possible development of all the God-given talents of each individual', are paramount. St Aloysius (St Aloysius Gonzaga 1568–91) was the patron saint of young people and the school is part of a network of over two thousand Jesuit seats of learning 'educating over two million students in sixty-five countries' – one of the principal missions of Jesuit teaching is education. Charming tiny little chapel in the main building, voluntary mass for all at 8.30 every morning – well attended by parents, pupils and staff and 'over by the time school starts'. Crowded during Lent and the run-up to exams. Crucifixes in every classroom, two Jesuits still on staff.

The school is based on not quite the apex of Hill Street, opposite the convent and next to the splendid Victoria Baroque Jesuit church, which the school uses for whole school mass and regular assemblies (about three times a week) – very much in the centre of Glasgow, just off the M8; brilliant for public transport and well-nigh impossible for car-bound visiting editors to find. The Hanson and Mount Buildings are red brick, serious Victoriana and have withstood the test of time well; however the two newer buildings, one housing the junior school and the Clavius Building, which is home to the IT and scientific world, are already showing their age. The junior school is lovely, full of jolly hanging pics and tiny chairs in groups of six. It is fully self-contained but adjacent (and too many steps). The Clavius Building, however glam it is, causes problems – the staff think it is too big to patrol, the pupils think it is 'pretty weird' to have form mass in the atrium surrounded by blocks of lockers, and the bright blue paint on the doors and cupboards is already chipping off (it has been repainted once); also passages and stairs are horrendously narrow. Both new-builds are prize-winners with Clavius top of the pops, but neither look particularly clever next to the Rennie MacIntosh Glasgow School of Art, which is apparently just what the planners wanted.

Pastoral Care and Discipline: New chaplain appointed. Jesuit principles pervade – formation in all things important including theology, philosophy, a commitment to ecumenism, and the resistance of atheism, materialism and consumerism, with an emphasis on 'service to others even as a lawyer or a doctor' (think UCAS forms). In the real world this means strong anti-bullying dogma in place and sin and wickedness treated with the contempt they deserve. Expect to be dismissed for trading in drugs at school, otherwise subjected to the expected scale of punishments – 'We would gradually raise the ante, but ensure that support programmes were in place to try and solve all problems in a positive way'. The school has recently begun a new sex education programme (Called to Love) authorised by the RC bishops, that is proving a great success.

Pupils and Parents: Predominantly middle-class core, almost exclusively RC, which, in the west of Scotland, historically means predominantly Scots, Irish and Italians, plus a tiny minority of others. Strongly supportive of the school, pupils come (in the main) from the wealth of suburbs that surround the city. Tranches of FPs who seem to accept that the school is progressively changing to lay staff. Fair number of first time buyers. 'Wide diversity'.

Entrance: School claims 'to admit pupils in the top half of the general population. 75 per cent of our pupils come from the top quarter of the population' – we are talking academically here. Priority given to practising Catholics and those who 'share the aims and values of Jesuit education'. More or less automatic transfer from the junior school. Active sibling policy. Assessment by tests but previous school reports, school reference (and preferably one from the parish priest) are all taken into account. If pupils transfer from another independent school, St Aloysius checks that there are no outstanding fees as well as getting a reference!

Exit: Fair number leave post Highers with university entry in the bag – a bare 70 per cent stay on. (Mr Stoer was surprised by this, but it is the nature of the Scottish university entrance system and high time it was changed.) Some 95 plus per cent go on to tertiary education, the school provides a regular (tiny) trickle to the priesthood (some 15/20 pupils are serving in the local diocese), slightly larger trickle to Oxbridge. Deep reluctance to strike out from familiar territory – fair number seem to end up at Glasgow and Strathclyde universities, but they are getting 'progressively more adventurous'.

Money Matters: The school receives no state funding – not even apparently for classroom assistants for those with a record of needs, which is odd. The original Jesuit concept was that their role was to educate free and the school has a certain amount of funding available. Parents are asked whether they need bursarial help at the time of application, almost automatic for families on income support, plus family discounts, but no named or dedicated bursaries. School does what it can to help. Will also try and help out if family hits financial crisis but with the usual strictures – parents must be upfront about the extent of their problems.

Remarks: A traditional and unusual school which has served the local community well – dedicated to providing 'improvement in living and learning to the greater glory of God and for the common good' (St Ignatius Loyola 1491–1556). St Aloysius has adapted well to the twenty-first century; it will be interesting to watch the developments in the exam department. So much better to get some exam practice at 16 rather than go straight to Highers as previously.

St Bede's College

Linked to Saint Bede's College Prep School in the Junior section

Alexandra Park, Manchester, Lancashire, M16 8HX

• Pupils: 825 co-ed • Ages: 11-19 (plus prep 4-11) • Size of sixth form: 255 • RC • Fees: Prep £5,814; Senior £8,646 pa • Independent

Tel: 0161 226 3323
Fax: 0161 226 3813
Email: enquiries@stbedescollege.co.uk
Website: www.stbedescollege.co.uk

Head: Since 2008, Michael Barber MA, MSc (Oxon). No newcomer to the school having been head of maths here for six years before deputy headships at two Benedictine Monastic schools; St Benedicts in Ealing and Downside in Somerset. After a maths degree from St Peter's College, Oxford he worked as a systems analyst at ICL before entering teaching. His MSc is in aeronautical engineering from Manchester university. Like his predecessor, he has a deep rooted faith with the aim that pupils will leave St Bede's College, 'as highly qualified young men and women whose core values are those of the Gospel,' nearly all going to university and on to 'take up responsible positions in society, and make a positive contribution to their communities, always mindful of their duty as Christians to put others before themselves.'

Academic matters: Strong academic results; pupils are expected to work hard. Class size 26 maximum with an average of 20, smaller in the sixth form. Setting in maths and statistics to stretch the more able (with IGCSE introduced in 2010). At GCSE, 52 per cent A*/A in 2010 and 70 per cent A*–B grades at A level (16 per cent A*). Broad range of subjects includes classics, politics and business studies; religious education is compulsory throughout the school though, in the sixth form, the approach is less formal and pupils enjoy discussion groups. A healthy age and gender mix of staff.

DT (the proud recipient of many awards) and art have excellent facilities and display impressive creations. Science labs are being gradually updated and nevertheless produce robust results. The multimedia language lab is impressive and fully computerised. IT facilities good, computers abound, linked to the school's intranet. Impressive, newly refurbished, Maher library with approachable and knowledgeable librarian. Open after school and during the holidays in the run up to exams.

Games, Options, the Arts: Games compulsory throughout the school. Football achieves notable success, being previous finalists in the Boodle and Dunthorne Independent Schools' Football Association Cup and Greater Manchester county champions. Netball is strong but rugby, hockey, cricket, athletics and tennis are also offered. Floodlit all-weather surface.

Plenty of extra-curricular activities from chess to robotics. Sports and studies are enhanced by foreign tours, field trips, pilgrimage to Lourdes etc. Lower than expected uptake of individual music tuition possibly due to costs involved for many. Nonetheless there's an orchestra, a concert band and choirs.

Background and Atmosphere: Founded in 1875 by Cardinal Vaughan, the school moved to its present site in 1877, taking over the buildings of the Manchester Aquarium, and has since expanded onto an adjoining site separated by a quiet road. Originally a boys' Catholic grammar school, it became direct grant but reverted to independence in 1976. Girls were admitted from 1984. Traditionally, the school served the local inner city area but now draws pupils from a 25 mile radius encompassing a wide social spectrum. The Christian spirit is omnipresent but not, according to pupils, repressive; there's an atmosphere of mutual respect and warmth with excellent pupil-teacher interaction.

Pastoral Care and Discipline: Pupils comment on the excellent provision of pastoral care. All pupils have a member of staff to whom they can turn and peer support is available, though this is not formalised. Clear moral framework; pupil behaviour is good with very little bullying, theft etc.

Pupils and Parents: Majority white British or Irish with a number of first and second generation African children who have settled in Manchester. The social mix is broad, in line with the school's ethos. Pupils are courteous to each other and staff, polite and hard working. Uniform is worn throughout the school, with 'office wear' in the sixth form.

Entrance: 11+ selection is by examination and interview. The interview is of particular importance for those children from inner city state schools who have not been 'prepped' for the entrance exam and is aimed to spot potential. Sixth form admission requires seven GCSEs.

Exit: On average eight per year to Oxbridge. Other top redbrick universities are the most popular for the remainder, to follow a broad spectrum of courses.

Money Matters: One third of pupils receiving financial assistance from the bursary fund.

Remarks: An excellent choice for committed Catholics seeking an academic education within a Christian environment. 'I cannot recommend St Bede's too highly,' comments one such parent. A fantastic opportunity for bright young Catholics from underprivileged homes.

St Bede's Senior School

Linked to Saint Bedes Preparatory School in the Junior section

The Dicker, Upper Dicker, Hailsham, East Sussex, BN27 3QH

• Pupils: 560 boys, 345 girls. About half board. • Ages: 12-19 • Size of sixth form: 320 • Inter-denomination • Fees: Day £15,450; Boarding £25,725 pa • Independent

Tel: 01323 843 252
Fax: 01323 442 628
Email: sally.wellings@stbedesschool.org
Website: www.stbedesschool.org

Head: Since 2009, Dr Richard Maloney (late thirties) MA in theology, PhD in educational management. Previously deputy head at Sutton Valence. Married with two children – four and two-years-old who attend the nursery and pre prep. He succeeds Mr Steven Cole who has gone back to his native New Zealand.

He looks very much younger than his years, an energetic, articulate and a caring man who spent the first couple of terms anything but idle. He is already putting his management studies into practice. 100 per cent committed to the aims of the St Bede's Trust which is proudly non-selective and the pupil population is inclusive and diverse. He wants to actively address the middle ability range. This will appeal to parents who feel that, while their children were happy, they could achieve more. The head is wasting no time in tightening the mesh by appointing a director of academic performance who will oversee the setting of motivational targets and monitor pupils' work, with IT systems to track performance.

His aim is 'to maintain the energy, breadth and diversity of the curriculum whilst ensuring students exceed academic potential.' The reputation and huge success of the school has been built on its open door policy. Can he protect this core philosophy of non-selection and up the game academically? 'Absolutely! I am also ensuring that the systems are in place and no child slips through the net.' He feels now is the time to cap the intake. He believes in pupil involvement – during our visit students were involved with the tours and interviews for teaching posts for drama and PE. Most parents feel this is a good appointment.

Academic matters: Headed by John Tuson who has been here since 1993 but took a two-year gap to do voluntary teaching and zoo keeping abroad. He is worthy of mention as the pupils laud him as an excellent and inspirational teacher. Certainly he was enthusiastic as he told us of the work he is now doing under the new head and occasionally came up for breath. VA scores revealed that the middle range in Years 9 and 10 were below national average and their intention is to double these scores within the next three years. Has put in systems for tracking pupils' performance. New dedicated tutor time to underpin an already strong pastoral system so that staff can keep abreast with individuals' targets. Although this focus is necessary as some of the middle range of ability were too happy to coast, it would be a shame if St Bede's became yet another league table climber given their remarkable success as a school open to all.

Vast range of subjects on offer at GCSE and A level. GCSEs achieve a spread of results across the grades as you would expect of a school which proudly takes children of a far wider range of abilities than elsewhere. The number of D grades at GCSE – something less than half the number of As – often reflects the considerable achievement of both pupil and school. A high proportion of Cs. However, at A level the scores read differently with lots of As and Bs. Science department offers nine different courses for GCSE including land and environmental studies – they are perfectly positioned in the heart of east Sussex farmland. A pre-sixth form year is offered for international students to prepare them in English and for the maturity needed at sixth form. Pre-university courses in maths and English for clever clogs but no plans to introduce the IB. Individually tailored learning programmes are central to the success of the school and the flexible curriculum allows for the quirky and boffins to achieve at their own pace.

Well established special needs dept – and this is the school of choice for many children who have SEN – dyslexia, dyspraxia and children on the Aspergers spectrum. Drop-in area where everyone is welcome for help or a chat. Much time spent producing IEPs tailored to pupils who struggle as much as for the Oxbridge pupil who needs extension work.

Games, Options, the Arts: Facilities are nothing short of spectacular. New multi-hall would put most commercial leisure centres in the second league – huge sports hall, squash courts, national size swimming pool. Outside boasts new tennis courts, Astroturf, nine rugby and football pitches, netball courts etc. Some serious sport here especially soccer where the team are holders of English schools' national trophy from a starting field of 2400 schools. Also Old Pupils – Clare Wood, Julie Salmon (tennis) Rob Buchanan (rugby), Luke Wells (cricket).

An extraordinary range of choice for their activity programme ranging from the thrilling to the more cerebral and all pupils are involved four or five afternoons a week. Elite sportsmen and women have top-notch facilities and a tailored curriculum. The Harlequins use their indoor fitness centre for strength and conditioning.

We could be forgiven for running out of superlatives when viewing their art department. They consistently win our top gold award for best school in this category. A real productive buzz in the studios; awash with new quality light studios and outstanding student work. Everything done to the top of the game, ceramics, fine art, photography, graphics, textiles, design technology, sculpting, pottery. Recent new extensions provide a dedicated workplace for each discipline. Music soon to be housed in a new extension. The musical diary is full of recitals and performances for the choir, jazz band, orchestras at various venues including the village fete, the mansion house etc so that they share their talents with the community. A healthy mix of choirs, a samba band, rock and traditional bands. Music accessible for all, regardless of ability. Drama also a vibrant part of each child's life, either as performers, stage crew or audience. Ten or more annual performances to very professional standard with exciting special effects! Dept regularly places pupils with RADA, Central School of Speech and Drama, East 15 and the Guildhall.

Background and Atmosphere: In the heart of Sussex countryside and continuing to expand by buying more fields from surrounding farms. Has enjoyed healthy growth over the last ten years and the infrastructure is expanding to accommodate this although the dining hall in the main house is not coping and plans are afoot for an extension by 2011. School presents as a higgledy piggledy mix – the traditional main house extends to elongated, painted, beach huts parallel to an impressive new science block with large labs, spreading to new dance and drama studios and finally to fabulous boarding houses. Relaxed, playful feel with no-one running around telling students to tuck their shirts in or tighten their ties. A strong multi-cultural mix with an open and tolerant attitude.

Pastoral Care and Discipline: Some of the most stylish boarding we know. The entrance is approached via an arched wooden bridge over a pond of carp. This is more like a three star hotel than a boarding house with the relaxing sound of running water from an indoor feature, an open plan set-up with no corridors, no noticeboards, all rooms coming off a large central lobby and upstairs housing flat-lets for the sixth form. Everyone passes matron's room on entry and there are plenty of smiling personnel around for a chat any time. A hint of the exotic with African lanterns, Tuscan coloured walls, lots of pouffes; all chosen by the pupils on their last African trip (as you do). Two new boarding houses opening in 2011. Each house has three residential staff and one matron. During the weekend, fifty to seventy-five per cent of boarders stay and around eighteen per cent are an international mix of German, Spanish, Russian, Bulgarian and Chinese. Students are obliged to attend a spiritual meeting of their choice on weekends. Pupils praise the relaxed and caring pastoral staff. Zero tolerance of boys in girls' rooms although communal living area divides the girls' section from the boys'. Drugs would normally result in an expulsion and they will test if a pupil is suspected of drug abuse.

Pupils and Parents: An incredibly large fleet of green minibuses transport pupils across Kent, Surrey and East and West Sussex. Parents come from a range of backgrounds, theatrical, city, farming and popular with families from surrounding countryside. Lunch with a selection of sixth formers provoked a spirited debate about educational liberalism versus traditional education leaving one in no doubt that this school fosters enquiring minds.

Entrance: Non selective. Admission by interview with the headmaster and reports from previous school. International students have to provide evidence of their English language ability. At sixth form, students are expected to have a minimum of five Cs at GCSE. A large proportion comes from the prep school at Year 9.

Exit: A handful to Oxbridge, many to universities here and abroad, presently not a large cohort to the Russell group. Many leave for careers in media and the arts.

Money Matters: St Bede's invests in excess of ten per cent of its annual income in scholarships and means tested fee remission. Academic, art, dance, drama, music and sports scholarships. Parents of children applying for scholarships have three options: a) to accept the scholarship without fee remission and as a recognition of excellence; b) apply for means-tested fee remission up to a fully funded place; and c) apply for a small non means-tested award which will not exceed twenty per cent of the full day fee. Prospective students who wish to join outside the scholarship process are able to apply for means-tested fee remission.

Remarks: The new head has a 'can and will do' approach that is infectious and influencing the SMT to set more aspirational targets for all students, particularly the middle range. A very popular school with huge opportunities for pupils – both the quirky and the conventional. Blissfully un-neurotic about where they sit in the league tables.

St Bees School

St Bees, Cumbria, CA27 0DS

• Pupils: 177 boys, 127 girls; 118 board (23 weekly), the rest day • Ages: 8-18 • Size of sixth form: 109 • C of E • Fees: Day £6,300-£14,559; Boarding £14,460-£24,528 pa • Independent

Tel: 01946 828 000
Fax: 01946 828 011
Email: mailbox@st-bees-school.co.uk
Website: www.st-bees-school.org

Head: Since 2000, Mr Philip Capes, previously deputy head of Warminster School; engineering degree from Exeter, married to a primary school teacher; three children, one of whom attends St Bees. Safe, experienced pair of hands; an approachable head, clear about school's future. Many new staff since he arrived; planned retirement scheme for some long-servers.

Academic matters: Broad range, from special learning unit to top scores at A level. Not a hothouse and doesn't claim to be. Much satisfaction over Ds and Es turned into Cs and above. 'Everyone is stretched,' says one satisfied parent, whose two sons' indifferent junior school achievements were turned into three As at A level – attributed to confidence instilled by being treated as an individual. Usual small school constraints on A level choices but Latin, Greek and further maths available. GCSE – over 40 per cent at A and A*. IT, French and Spanish taught in innovative Management Centre (see below). Year 10 do some OU foundation courses. Very committed staff who insist on hard work and high standards.

Games, Options, the Arts: Games fields everywhere in stunning 150-acre site. Rugby strong (tough fixture list), girls' sport also good. Large sports hall, squash and fives courts. Much PE teaching mixed. 60-acre nine-hole golf course on headland, shared with locals. Proximity to unspoiled part of Lake District has led to development of distinctive and successful tradition of outdoor activities. CCF for all aged 13–15. Artwork in evidence everywhere, drama lively, music very good; refurbished music school – many instrumental groups, choir sings in chapel and village priory, tours abroad with chamber orchestra every other year.

Background and Atmosphere: Founded as a grammar school in 1583; original schoolroom now a dining hall with past pupils' names carved on wall panels. Handsome Victorian additions in local sandstone spread over fine site 'between the sea and the sheep', and well integrated with St Bees village, where pupils wander freely. Girls admitted since 1976, so a proper co-educational school. Girls' houses in attractive terrace on the far side of useful local railway (footbridge), senior boys in two houses, one in the same building as the head. All new staff do boarding house duties. International Centre offers specialist EFL plus general courses for one year for up to 18 overseas students aged 11–16 – doubtless a useful boost to numbers. Many now from mainland China. Some join St Bees after basic course, some return home. All international pupils integrated into existing boarding houses. Management Centre, opened in 1992, is an unusual and successful joint venture – used commercially as a conference centre in the week, and by the school in evenings and at weekends.

There's a general air about the school of unhurried but purposeful activity. Working day ends for all pupils at 5.45 pm – 'a boarding school with day pupils'. Various efforts to overcome inescapable sense of isolation, e.g. trips abroad, visits to Stratford, lecture programme, Oxbridge taster visit. Leavers' ball (with parents) a high point of social calendar.

Pastoral Care and Discipline: Tutorial system plus housemaster/housemistress. Staff: 22 male, 17 female. Claim that in a small 'family' school no one slips through the net seems reasonable, e.g. kitchen staff notice if someone isn't eating properly. 'Centralised matrons', husband-and-wife GP team, counsellor on call. Not much real naughtiness in this quiet backwater; pupils seem content with traditional discipline, reputedly tightened up by head. Drug supplying or sex mean the sack.

Pupils and Parents: Many local, though an increasing number from the north east (parents seeking a secure environment?); foreign nationals more in evidence further up the school. Extensive private bus system ferries day pupils to and fro, boarders picked up at nearest airports. Pupils refreshingly old-fashioned, perhaps a touch unsophisticated – neatly dressed in formal uniform, frank and unaffected in manner. Many bright boys and girls attracted to St Bees, says head, because of greater chance of representing school in multifarious activities.

Parents very supportive (some allow their names to be used in prospectus for potential parents to telephone – what a good idea); Cumbrian farmers and professionals, local industrialists (Sellafield – still – a huge employer). Very efficient marketing department; its boss goes on frequent recruiting trips abroad.

Entrance: Not very competitive – though International Centre students have to show realistic level of competence. Two-form entry, mainly from state schools, topped up at 13 and 16. Possibility of extension downwards into prep and nursery departments.

Exit: Nearly all to higher education (very little fall-out after GCSE); a sprinkling to Oxbridge, mainly to a wide range of old and new universities. Leavers' list shows a broad balance between arts and science subjects.

Money Matters: Bursaries for children of clergy, Services and former pupils, and a few for deserving cases. Up to 50 per cent academic and music scholarships; art and sports awards post-16.

Remarks: Good local school, strong reputation, not averse to change; palpable atmosphere of security in beautiful surroundings. Endless care taken over individuals.

St Benedict's School

Linked to Saint Benedict's Junior School in the Junior section

54 Eaton Rise, Ealing, London, W5 2ES

• Pupils: 985 pupils, all day. Fully co-ed since September 2008 • Ages: 3-18 • Size of sixth form: 180 in Sixth Form. • R C • Fees: £7,050-£12,030 pa • Independent

Tel: 020 8862 2000/2001
Fax: 020 8862 2199
Email: enquiries@stbenedicts.org.uk
Website: www.stbenedicts.org.uk

Headmaster: Since 2002, Mr Christopher Cleugh (rhymes with rough) BSc MSc (late fifties). Read chemistry at Hull. Resonant Liverpool accent ('I prefer Everton' he says), he grew up and taught on Merseyside until he came here. Educated at St Mary's Crosby where he returned as a teacher for seventeen years (by the time he left he was deputy head). Went on to become head of St Anselm's in Birkenhead for eight years, before moving south to run St Benedict's, which felt fated: 'I remember the day I saw the advert,' he says. Married with two sons and two daughters – his wife is head of a Catholic primary school in Acton, his first grandchild is a pupil in the junior school here. Utterly unpretentious and forthright, Mr Cleugh is a keen sports fan and loves his cricket and football. Warm and humorous, one nevertheless detects steel beneath the avuncular surface.

Only the second lay headmaster since the school was founded, Mr Cleugh is a practising Catholic and a firm believer in co-education – 'in the modern world it's the right way forward. It's a co-ed world out there and this is the natural preamble to it,' he says, adding that there's 'all sorts of nonsense about which environment produces the best academic performance but at the end of the day it's nothing to do with single sex or co-education – it's the way they're taught and how you instil confidence and self discipline.'

You know where you are with this head who is not afraid to risk unpopularity for the good of the community and is a man of quiet but total conviction. Knows, and knows about, all his pupils, and has a sensitive understanding of their concerns.

Much loved by parents and pupils alike – 'he's always around'; 'easy to talk to'; 'makes time for everyone'; ' you can talk to him about anything – he never makes you feel uncomfortable' is the resounding message. Mr Cleugh unequivocal too about his favourite thing about the job – the children.

Academic matters: Respectable results, especially bearing in mind the school is not highly selective academically. 70 per cent achieved A or B grades at A level in 2010 – a new high for the school. However a starry place in league tables is not what they're about, Mr Cleugh is keen to point out, and what he cares most about is that each child fulfils his or her potential. Among the 70 per cent who got As and Bs there would have been a number who would have fallen by the wayside in a more pressured environment and he is quite happy if a child gets Ds at A level if s/he has worked hard and has fulfilled her/his potential. A good range of GCSE subjects on offer with everyone taking RS. RS curriculum largely RC in content and other faiths learned about in PSHE. History, maths and chemistry most popular subjects at A level. Modern languages reasonably popular and takes place in swanky new language labs in the new £6.2 million development.

Wheelchair access throughout the school (lifts and ramps) means they have been able to accommodate a number of children with severe physical disabilities. Three children in the school currently have statements including one with cerebral palsy and one paraplegic. 'As long as I feel they would be happy I will take them,' says head who is keen to emphasise his inclusive approach. Full time SENCo who occasionally withdraws pupils from lessons but prefers to provide in class support as well and extra time pre and post school. Lots of support given to children with their organisational skills and the SEN room provides a useful base for children who need more help. Very positive noises from parents about the caring and supportive approach of the school to a whole range of special needs. At the other end of the spectrum a Gifted and Talented Coordinator runs a programme through the curriculum but also does a lot outside the curriculum including summer schools at the Warwick Academy – part of Warwick University.

Excellent ICT facilities. The subject is well taught and IT skills used extensively in other areas including art and music.

Games, Options, the Arts: Rugby is huge here. It's the main winter sport (they don't play football, nor do they row, and it's not the place for your son if he's mad about ballet) and school recently ranked the top rugby school in the country (currently slipped to fourth but we suspect not for long). Tours to Dubai, Japan and New Zealand. Girls as keen to perform as well as the boys. Netball tours to Sri Lanka. Astroturf pitches due to be completed. Cricket, athletics, rounders and tennis in the summer. School uses 14 acres of playing fields in Perivale about a mile away and plays hard, winning more than losing. Games staff everywhere – proper professionals in their matching coaching kit.

Onsite sports hall, sparkling multi gym and fitness centre as well as fencing salle and dance studio. Fencing a major sports option with regular fixtures against other schools. Basketball, volleyball and yoga are also offered.

Less than world-class pupils appreciate the school's attitude to sports – 'everyone's given a chance,' said one in heartfelt tones, having experienced the 'if you're not in the first team you're nobody' syndrome elsewhere.

Music strong and there's a huge variety – a symphony orchestra, lots of singing – four choirs (strongly influenced by the Abbey choir), jazz band, big band, swing band, string ensembles and brass groups. (Almost) everyone gets involved at some stage and one parent remarked on how well talent is spotted and nurtured. Excellent facilities, three grand pianos and lots of uprights in tip top condition. An IT lab is dedicated to music, posters of Led Zeppelin and the Beatles decorate the walls, lots of computers equipped with piano keyboards.

Exciting art. Intensely imaginative, disciplined and creative sculptures are dotted around the school and spectacular oil paintings adorn the reception area. IT facilities dedicated to art in the attractive one-storey modern art/DT block. Before – and after – school study supervision in the library on offer, and over 80 clubs which include karate, history society, CCF, D of E, Saint Vincent de Paul charity fund-raising, debating and current affairs. One boy keen to point out that if you want to do something new, school will make it happen.

Background and Atmosphere: Founded in 1902 by the monks of Downside Abbey, St Benedict's is the only Benedictine day school in the country. Its sister schools are Worth, Downside and Ampleforth which, like St Benedict's, have all recently started to take girls all the way through. (There have been girls in the sixth form here since the 1970s, from Year 7 since September 2008). The Roman Catholic faith is evident in every aspect of the atmosphere and the environment of the school, its publications, its ethos, yet almost half the pupils in the senior school are not Catholic. Eighty-fiveish per cent are Christian including those from other denominations and you will find Muslims, Sikhs, Hindus, and Jews. The only condition is that they must respect the Catholic faith and take part in the regular Masses that take place throughout the school year.

The buildings are a mix of un-gloomy Victorian redbrick and various twentieth century extensions, additions and blocks – some of which are wearing better than others. The Cloisters, a stunning development costing £6.2 million, is the first thing you come to as you enter the school and has the same contemporary feel as some of the underground stations on the Jubilee line. Smooth concrete walls, aesthetic balconies, quadrangles and colonnades, an imaginative foil to the glorious Abbey which is situated across the playground and adjacent to the junior school. Whole school Mass is said in the warm and totally unforbidding Abbey but smaller class Mass is said in the intimate Chapel in the modern Cloisters development – stunningly light and bright with a large window in the shape of a cross taking up most of the ceiling.

The Benedictine ethos of respect for each other genuinely informs life here and the school has an unquestioned local reputation for quite exceptional pastoral care. Parents pay tribute to the trouble taken over the smallest worry, and pupils feel supported and secure. Monks are always available for individual counselling and support and many are much loved permanent fixtures.

Pastoral Care and Discipline: Very strict – until the sixth form all children carry around a yellow card – reminiscent of the traditional satis cards (short for satisfecit – has he done enough?) in order that their behaviour – good and bad – can be constantly monitored. Parents are kept in the loop, they sign it each week and House points are affected. However, it's not inflexibly strict – 'first and foremost I'm a parent – I know children can get it wrong sometimes,' is Mr Cleugh's humane approach. Regular parent forums on, e.g. the dangers of ICT at home, 'I would ban Facebook if I had my way,' Mr Cleugh exclaims. He likes to keep the sixth form in at lunch time (though they can go out) 'there is so much to do here' he says 'plus there are a few too many muggings in Ealing'. He sits as a local magistrate – he should know.

Pupils and Parents: 'Pupils in state schools think we're posh but Latymer kids think we're common,' a sixth former told us. You don't get many posey trust fund kids here. Solidly middle class but a genuinely wide range of parents, a number of single mothers and families who have made huge sacrifices to get a good education for their children. A number of parents talked of how supportive the school was – not just of their child but of the family as a whole. One boy commented on how no one is arrogant about money – the influence of the Abbey means that everyone feels welcome. Mostly local. Some come from as far afield as Barnes or Holland Park. Just over 50 per cent are Catholic – though this might change as school fills up and is forced to become more selective.

One girl we spoke to was keen to mention that girls are not treated as second class citizens, attributing it to the fact that there have been girls in the sixth form for over thirty years. There are good inter year relationships. Mentoring schemes where the older ones help out with the juniors and whole school involvement in drama and music. Pupils here are extremely courteous and mature. Old Priorians (the official title for former St Benedict's pupils) include Julian Clary, Lord (Chris) Patten (who also sits as an advisor on the governing board), Peter Ackroyd, Declan Donnellan, Andy Serkis, Professor Denis MacShane MP and poet, songwriter Labi Siffre as well as plenty of rugby players, including Hugo Ellis and Joe Simpson of Wasps.

Entrance: (Practically) all start at 11 – though school will still take the occasional few at 13. Ninety-six places, forty of which will go to the children coming up from the junior school (almost all transfer automatically). Entrance exams in maths, English and verbal reasoning. Most interviewed. Looking to discover what the child will give back to the school. Sixth form requirements – a minimum of six GCSEs at B or above and Bs in A level subjects. A number of people join in the sixth form from local girls' schools looking for a more inclusive approach.

It's no longer true that if you don't get in anywhere else you will get a place at St Benedict's. Although Mr Cleugh is keen not to be too selective, as numbers rise priority will have to be given to Catholics and siblings.

Exit: Virtually all to good universities and to an impressive range of courses – no stereotypes here. Half a dozen to Oxbridge in any given year. A tiny few leave after GCSE to go to e.g. Latymer Upper, Catholic state schools or sixth form colleges.

Money Matters: About half a dozen on 100 per cent bursaries, lots of others get help. 'Once a child is in if a parent falls on hard times we will do our best to help them,' says Mr Cleugh. Limited number of academic scholarships at 11+ and at sixth form – up to 50 per cent fees and can be augmented by bursaries.

Remarks: A wholly unpretentious, good solid school with sound values that is never going to squash your child into a box. Exactly the school for your brightish but quietish child who would sink in a larger, or tougher, environment. An honest, hard working place with a gentle and loving approach.

St Brendan's Sixth Form College

Broomhill Road, Brislington, Bristol, BS4 5RQ

• Pupils: 1,500 boys and girls • Ages: 16-19+ • Catholic • State

Tel: 0117 977 7766
Fax: 0117 972 3351
Email: info@stbrn.ac.uk
Website: www.stbrn.ac.uk

Principal: Since January 2010, Ms Ann Barrow (fifties), who joined St Brendan's nine years earlier as vice principal. Ms Barrow taught chemistry in various state schools, then, after a brief spell at Foster's School for boys in Sherborne, she moved to Strode College in Street as head of maths, science and engineering. Finally, before coming to St Brendan's, she was head of general education for GCSEs and A levels at Strode.

Academic matters: College offers three levels of post-16 study: as well as level three (A levels), a small number of level one courses caters for the most educationally disadvantaged; fifteen level two courses in a wide range of subjects provide the equivalent to four GCSEs at grades A*–C. We met one girl who had completed the DIDA course (an ICT based course using eight different software packages) and was now doing three A levels, having joined college with poor GCSEs from a failing Bristol secondary. The City and Guilds CAD course provides a back-up for A level design students whilst other level two courses including BTec First Diplomas in art and design, business, health and social care, media, music technology, public services.

Much wider range of AS and A2 courses (currently approaching fifty) than you would find in a school sixth form, with every opportunity to mix and match. Principal commented on how even medical schools now appreciate entrants with unusual subjects alongside the expected ones. A and AS results above national average with growing number achieving four or more A grades. In 2010, 45 per cent A*–B grades overall. Good A/B percentages for science and maths and in German and Spanish too.

Annual visit to 'Your Future in Europe' conference in Paris for honours students who are expected to study a minimum of four AS and A2 subjects; take AS critical thinking as an additional AS level plus advanced extension awards. Now offers the AQA Bacc, which includes an extended project and personal development, e.g. community service, alongside A levels and AS critical thinking.

Being taught the 'spiritual journey' and 'preparation for working life' aspects of the core programme in 'honours' groups is making a marked difference to student performances and aspirations, claim staff.

Growing learning support team helps in or outside classroom and includes 18 LSAs. All students have access to learning support and almost half of the student population take up the opportunity in some way. Two hundred of these students have regular support or exam entitlements. Stair lifts also installed. Recognised by Connexions as preferred post-16 centre for learning support. High percentage achieve better grades than predicted. Students praised support they've received – one African girl we met explained how she is now able to progress properly after getting extra English through the ESOL programme.

Games, Options, the Arts: The football and rugby pitches in front of the college may hark back to former days but college still fields strong teams in football and rugby. A new building containing sports hall, fitness suite and dance studio provides modern facilities where participation in health and fitness is encouraged.

Lots of demand for creative courses such as photography, fashion and textiles with some stunning displays. Lots of studio space for art and design with more excellent work and a newly refurbished design and technology suite has extensive computerised facilities. State of art music department caters for all styles and levels as well as production and studio engineering. Drama students were fully involved when we visited and share studio space with dance. Lots of dynamic overlap, especially for productions. Film students very innovative and even have their own 'Oscars' evening at college.

Activities, visits and sports rely heavily on student organisational input. Surprisingly varied programme given the logistical difficulties of getting people together outside lesson time. What runs is well supported but students here also get to enjoy hanging out with peers. Atmosphere encourages making new and lasting friends – more like what students will experience at university. Active student union organises parties and charity fund-raising and has a voice on the college's governing body.

Background and Atmosphere: Founded in 1890 as a boys' independent school run by the Christian Brothers, it later achieved direct grant status before emerging as a co-educational, Catholic sixth form college in 1979. Currently a hodgepodge of buildings – some date back many years (about to be demolished) others (such as social sciences and creative studies) already state of art, purpose-built facilities. Building programme 'will lend a new coherence' says principal and reconstruction was planned not to impede the working life of the college.

First names used throughout college; dress varies widely but errs on side of comfortable. We were impressed by the self-imposed silence in library area which includes a lot of computer spaces and remains open until 5pm. There is an internet café/IT work area adjacent to student canteen where a staff member is on hand whenever there is a need; other ICT suites around college. Increased numbers are placing a heavy demand upon these work stations. Flexible auditorium with raked seating for about two hundred provides performance and lecture space. Assemblies held here to celebrate Christian festivals with extra masses in chapel for Catholic students.

Pastoral Care and Discipline: Parents rate highly pastoral system which keeps a tight rein on attendance and progress. Role of student support managers is pivotal: each has five tutorial groups (about 150 students) whom they see for three 45 minute periods a week. In cases of poor work or behaviour students can be placed 'on contract'. Retention over year is 94 per cent which is high compared with FE institutions. All follow core programmes in life skills and a 'spiritual journey' course (non-sectarian and popular with students as an opportunity to explore their values and beliefs). Careers form important part with a rolling programme of fairs, visits, speakers etc as well as HE advice and an excellent resource base. Qualified counsellors also on hand to meet both referred and self-referred students. Catholic chaplain's role is separate from spiritual journey course; chapel is used for a wide variety of purposes.

Airy student canteen spoilt by failure of majority to clear up after themselves. Healthy options available but no salad bar yet and many go for greasy spoon choices it seems.

Pupils and Parents: Only about thirty per cent are Catholics but college is favoured choice of a number of other Christian churches in Bristol. Fifteen per cent ethnic minorities ('more Muslim girls would come if there were a direct bus,' says principal). Being part of Bristol's southeast area partnership alongside City of Bristol (FE) College has opened the doors to many more non-Catholics. Usual choice for Catholics from Bristol and Bath Catholic collegiate for which it is the only denominational post-16 option. Increasing uptake from ex-independent school pupils. Decision by First Bus to offer a student ticket which can be used for any journey in city has proved extremely popular.

Entrance: Impressive, university style prospectus makes task of selecting courses much easier. About 27 per cent of entrants come from Catholic collegiate schools where they are interviewed prior to admission and meet student ambassadors from St Brendan's. Parents generally like to attend these meetings and are welcomed. Remainder are interviewed at college. Over seventy feeder independent and state schools covering area between West Wiltshire and North Somerset.

Exit: Majority proceed to wide range of degree courses including seven to Oxbridge in 2009. Many to vocational and arts related courses. Some into employment.

Remarks: Welcome to the real student world! More of Bristol's young adults see this as the right compromise between school and university or work. Staff in tune with this age group and whole place buzzes. A great place to make friends and learn independent study skills. University would be less of a cultural shock after two years here.

St Catherine's School

Linked to Saint Catherines Preparatory School in the Junior section

Station Road, Bramley, Guildford, Surrey, GU5 0DF

• Pupils: 630 girls; 160 boarders, rest day • Ages: 11-18 • Size of sixth form: 160 • C of E • Fees: Boarding £23,595; Day £7,050-£14,340 pa • Independent

Tel: 01483 893 363
Fax: 01483 899 608
Email: admissions@stcatherines.info
Website: www.stcatherines.info

Headmistress: Since 2000, Mrs Alice Phillips MA (forties). Followed a traditional teaching career and was previously deputy head at nearby Tormead. Married with a young daughter, very smart and businesslike, a proud Yorkshire woman – 'I know what is right for my school.' A hands-on teacher, she gets huge enjoyment from teaching and not just being office bound – 'if I can't teach, I can't do my job properly and anyway it helps me know what's going on.' A dynamic head ('with lots of stories about her wonderful girls,' said a parent), but parents and pupils find her very approachable. 'A true professional, who really cares about her school and her pupils,' sums up the opinion of many.

Academic matters: Very impressive – a tip top local and national player in the academic league. In 2010, 95 per cent grades A*–B at A level – many girls with three or more grade As. At GCSE, results equally praiseworthy with 85 per cent achieving A*/A and 99 per cent A*–B grades. In recent years, several students have achieved the highest national A level and GCSE marks in a number of subjects including English literature, politics, geography and textiles. High standards of teaching throughout with Good Schools Guide Awards going to the chemistry and classics depts in recent years. Science, technology, maths and languages very popular – numerous science and language labs in the school – and full marks to the increasing number of girls studying Latin and Greek. After school Mandarin. IT facilities are state of the art and would put many companies to shame. DT dept has won a large award to enhance CAD facilities. Each pupil has her own email address and PC access and increasing amounts of homework can be submitted online – 'very handy,' commented one pupil. The sixth form is wireless networked. Well stocked library – with library stock on the web.

The head is very keen to fine tune independent study. All girls in the first year of the school have lessons in 'Grey Matters' taught by Mrs Phillips, covering learning methods, emotional intelligence etc. Bit trendy, think some, but probably useful in higher education. All this could translate into academic pressure, but most parents agree that the girls are stretched rather than pressured. Some parental grumbling that the focus at the school is always on academic achievement but, as entrance standards are high and girls are very bright, only a few struggle and those who do are supported and encouraged. All girls are tested for SEN on entry particularly for literacy. There is a 'very good' learning support department which covers both the prep and senior school. About five per cent of the girls have extra help at extra cost. Provision is made for dyslexia but a girl must have the IQ to support the required level of learning, says Mrs Phillips. Not a first choice school for girls who cannot easily keep up with the rigorous academic regime.

Games, Options, the Arts: A brand new sports and performing arts complex is due for completion in 2010–11. PE teaching is very strong – netball, lacrosse, swimming, rounders, athletics and gymnastics are all compulsory in games lessons until year 10. Several girls have played lacrosse and netball nationally. The school is very competitive and always up there at inter-school sporting competitions – those who take part are expected to show a lot of commitment – pupils often practise netball and lacrosse before school – even in January! Some parental disquiet that there is little opportunity for sport outside PE lessons if you are not part of the 'sporty set'. Mrs Phillips disagrees – 'the school often fields four teams for lacrosse and netball giving every girl who wishes to play the opportunity to do so.'

Art building has a stunning range of facilities. Students' work is frequently exhibited both within the school and outside – one piece displayed at Guildford Cathedral received a bid of several hundred pounds. Musical children thrive at the school – teaching is excellent and practice rooms are housed in a purpose built block. There are a number of choirs, orchestras and ensembles providing opportunities for all to join in – not just the talented ones. One parent commented how proud her daughter was of her musical ability – it was not 'cool' at her previous school. Lots of music tuition available – girls are taken out of lessons (not all parents approve but they never do in any school) on a rotational basis so they do not miss the same subject each week. New performing arts centre will benefit all budding musicians, actresses and directors along with an exciting art exhibition space. Enthusiastic drama department puts on several productions each year. Older girls take on the main roles but there is usually a part for everyone who wants one – a group of students took a play they wrote, directed and performed, to the Edinburgh Fringe. Numerous after-school activities – 'there is a club for everything here,' said one pupil – some parents worry there is just too much and it is difficult to choose.

Background and Atmosphere: Located in a beautiful Surrey village only 10 mins from Guildford, the school is housed in attractive buildings – mix of old and new – within extensive grounds. Lots of space and a very rural feel. School has gone through an extensive redecoration and refurbishment programme in the past year. School chapel nothing special on the outside but beautiful tranquil interior. Used every day for services and assemblies and for girls to just sit and reflect.

Redecorated sixth form centre is well planned and cosy with quiet study areas for day girls. Sixth form boarding popular – it is good practice for university, commented one pupil. Two share a typical teenage bedroom. 'We get lots of privileges,' and there is plenty to do. Pilates classes in the evenings. Weekend activities include trips to rugby matches and West End shows (weekly boarders can go along too). Occasional social events with boys' schools at weekends. Younger boarders' houses comfortable but certainly not plush, up to six to a room. Most boarders go home at weekends. Flexi-boarding for those parents who have to work away for periods – space permitting. Girls can also have supper at school when competing in sport or music activities in the evenings – very useful. 'The food is fantastic,' comment girls and staff alike, and all meals are served in a light airy building more reminiscent of a restaurant than a school dining hall. Lots of choice, healthy options, popular salad bar and more traditional school fare. Very lively atmosphere but pupils are well behaved. Uniform enforced fairly strictly with sixth form in suits on specific occasions such as start and end of terms and St Catherine's Day. Very active St Catherine's Association to which all members of the school, including pupils, staff, parents, past and present, automatically belong.

Pastoral Care and Discipline: House system. Lots of interhouse activities and a fun day for new girls at the beginning of each year to get to know new house members. The house system is more light hearted than competitive, thought one parent – girls may think differently as there are lots of inter-house events such as drama and even Pop Idol competitions.

Communication between home and school is frequent. Discipline fairly strict – although Mrs Phillips prefers to describe it as 'firm'. System of rewards and sanctions operates linked to the 'Traditions of St Catherine's' – basically the school rules. Clear alcohol, drinking and smoking policy – breaches are rare according to staff. The girls take an obvious pride in the school. Very little evidence of bullying – nothing more than usual school banter said parents. As a C of E school, everyone attends chapel once a week. Services are led by a local chaplain who is 'really good' – a refreshing remark – acute boredom is the more usual comment from pupils in other schools.

Pupils and Parents: Thought by many outsiders to be 'very posh', St Cat's is upmarket but not intimidatingly so. Pupils mainly from the surrounding affluent Surrey towns Guildford, Farnham, Godalming, Esher, Oxshott and increasingly from the homes of the chattering classes in south west London – the school has become very fashionable in recent years. There is also an international flavour particularly among the boarders. Parents are largely professional – lawyers, bankers, doctors, diplomats etc. Obviously intelligent and necessarily wealthy, there are a number of first time buyers. Parents who chose St Cat's say they are looking for an alternative to the sophisticated, 'city centre' atmosphere and freedom of the other nearby academic schools of Tormead or Guildford High. Notable old girls include actress Juliet Stevenson and poet Ursula Fanthorpe. Many old girls return to the school to talk about their careers and experiences – much appreciated apparently by the pupils.

Entrance: At 11+ by exam in verbal reasoning, English, maths and science (and the report from the previous school is also very important). School places emphasis on academic achievement and 'they are looking for the brightest girls,' said one parent. A useful tip – several parents checked how well their daughters had done in the entrance exam before accepting a place – they were worried whether an average girl, who just passed the exam, would be able to keep pace in the future. About 40 per cent come from own prep school, although admission is by no means automatic, with a growing list of other regular feeders which include St Hilary's Godalming, Rowan, Halstead, Amesbury and Waverley Abbey. Prospective pupils have a taster morning followed by a sleepover for girls considering boarding. Increasing number of requests to enter at sixth form – boarding is very popular. Seen as a good opportunity to 'enrich the mix,' entrance requirements are an IQ test, general studies paper, interview and a minimum of six GCSEs Grade C or above – though in reality applicants have much higher scores.

Exit: 10–15 per cent leave after GCSE mainly to mixed sixth form colleges locally (the temptation of more freedom and boys no doubt). Of those who stay, most go on to traditional universities e.g. Durham, Bristol, York, Exeter and about 10–15 per cent to Oxbridge.

Money Matters: Four academic and one music scholarship offered at 11. In the sixth form, there are also up to ten internal academic scholarships, one sport, one music, one art and three external academic scholarships. The first Jennifer Bate Organ Scholarship was awarded in September 2007 in conjunction with Guildford Cathedral. Amounts range from one sixth to one third of the fees.

Since 2008, there are a number of means-tested bursaries covering up to the full cost of fees.

Remarks: An increasingly fashionable, upmarket school with superb academics and facilities. Ideally suited for the clever and the outgoing.

St Charles Catholic Sixth Form College

74 St Charles Square, North Kensington, London, W10 6EY

• Pupils: 1,000 pupils, roughly 58 per cent girls • Ages: 16-19 • RC, but other faiths welcome • State

Tel: 020 8968 7755
Fax: 020 8969 1061
Email: dse@stcharles.ac.uk
Website: www.stcharles.ac.uk

Principal: Since 2002, Mr Paul O'Shea BA PGCE (fiftyish). Educated at Maidstone Grammar, got a scholarship to read history at St John's College Oxford and did a PGCE at St Mary's Strawberry Hill. Taught history at Woodhouse College for 14 years, some as head of department, and joined St Charles in 1994 as vice principal. Married with two teenage children; is keen on sport and music. His mild-mannered and unassuming exterior masks his educational brilliance and strong managerial capabilities – 'he is a mover and shaker and has his finger on the pulse,' said an insider. 'He is brilliant with both the staff and the kids.' He is passionate about the inclusive nature of his college and its Catholic mission to provide a leg-up for those who did not succeed at school. 'We believe in the redemptive power of education.'

Academic matters: Tucked away in a quiet square in Ladbroke Grove, this college has been hiding its light under a bushel. It takes students from all over London, most from ethnic minorities and many who have failed to achieve much academically so far, and adds huge value. Whilst its results are more-or-less average for a sixth form college, 'there are very few ... with similar levels of deprivation among their students,' said Ofsted. It is almost always amongst the top five per cent on an added value basis.

The college is largely open access. About 70 per cent take A levels or advanced vocational courses; those without the requisite GCSE grades can take foundation or intermediate level vocational courses, or re-take GCSEs. About half of these move on to advanced courses and many end up at university. English literature, media studies and psychology are, as elsewhere, the most popular A level choices. Around 3 –40 per cent of A level grades are generally A or B – a significant achievement for many students. English and business studies were both rated outstanding by Ofsted, with the vast majority of lessons very good or outstanding. The college also has some very able linguists – many from bi-lingual families – and is the largest national provider of Portuguese.

High-achieving students are in the minority but, almost invariably, come out with top A level grades. The college runs master-classes for them in partnership with universities such as King's College and Imperial and gives intensive guidance and support on making successful university applications.

Plenty of SEN support for those who need it, individually and in groups. Some have designated sessions; others can drop in for help with learning skills. The college is wheelchair accessible and has welcomed students with cerebral palsy, muscular dystrophy and Downs Syndrome but students must be capable of following a mainstream curriculum.

Games, Options, the Arts: Wednesday afternoons are reserved for extracurricular activities. There is a superb £6 million sports hall, complete with fitness suite. The football, rugby and basketball teams play enthusiastic matches. Lunchtime running club. Quite a few students train as mentors and coaches for the Greenhouse Schools Project, which runs weekend sports and drama programmes for deprived local children at private school sports pitches and theatres. D of E, Young Enterprise and drama performances are also on the agenda, and the college runs study trips to Rome and Barcelona. High quality art – and indeed art and design is one of the most popular university courses. DT is one of the less successful departments, and academic music is low profile: few students play an instrument, and those who want to study music A level do so next door at Sion Manning School. However, there is a thriving gospel choir, talent shows and musical productions each year.

Background and Atmosphere: Founded in 1990 by Basil Hume, the college is named after St Charles Borromeo, a 16th century archbishop from north Italy who believed firmly in the redeeming power of education. The aim was to act as the sixth form for local 11–16 Catholic schools. Around 60 per cent of students are Catholic but all must 'be positive about the Catholic identity of the college.' A peaceful chapel is at the physical and spiritual centre of the college. Mass is not compulsory but everyone does a general RE course. 'I think it is important that students of different faiths sit together in RE lessons and learn about each other's perspectives.'

St Charles Square is often referred to as 'The Little Vatican'; alongside the college it houses the Catholic Children's Society, Catholic primary and secondary schools, St

Pius church and the Carmelite Monastery. Harmonious atmosphere – several staff who won promotions elsewhere have found the grass less green and returned. 'It's the best place I've ever worked,' said one teacher.

Pastoral Care and Discipline: Very strong pastoral system combined with strong discipline, 'that is the secret of our success,' said an insider. Students see group tutors every day and personal tutors once a week. 'We work hard to get to know names, faces and stories as soon as possible. We want them to feel they're part of a community, that they're known and looked after.' Underachievement, lateness or absence is picked up rapidly, and the college keeps closely in touch with parents. 'We want the same strength of relationship with families as a school would have. We have a strong culture of encouraging any teacher to pick up the phone on any issue where they need parental support.' There is a range of strategies to bring miscreants back into line but, eventually, those who consistently fail to turn up regularly or turn in work are likely to find themselves out on the street. Similarly, there is zero tolerance for smoking on site and for the occasional drinking or drug taking in the vicinity.

Pupils and Parents: A huge range from across London, with many travelling from the East End and from south of the river – aided by Ken's cut price travel for 16 and 17 year olds. Some 80 per cent are from ethnic minorities, most from families with no history of higher education. 'We have lots of inner-city students with high motivation to make their families proud of them.'

Entrance: Students from the four partner Catholic secondary schools get first priority, and make up about 30 per cent of students. As long as they are supported by their school and do well at interview they will get a place. Catholic students get second priority but, in practice, the college welcomes anyone who applies in time – by the end of April – and is serious about staying on in education. They must explain on the application form that they are happy to fit in with the Catholic identity of the college.

Those with several grade Cs or above at GCSE can choose A level or advanced vocational courses, or both, with perhaps some GCSE retakes if need be. Those with at least four D grades can do intermediate vocational courses or GCSE retakes. Those without several D grades can take a foundation level vocational course.

Exit: About three-quarters of Advanced level students go on to university. The vast majority stay in London for financial and cultural reasons. Kingston, Westminster and London Metropolitan are particularly popular, alongside King's College and UCL. A strong minority gets places at Russell Group universities elsewhere, including one or two a year to Oxbridge. Business and finance, art and design, media studies and psychology are all popular courses.

Money Matters: The college has plenty of experience at administering access funds and educational maintenance awards to give students extra financial support.

Remarks: Students, many from deprived backgrounds, are happy to travel long distances to study at a college where high-quality, enthusiastic teaching combines with strong pastoral care to transform often mediocre GCSE grades into creditable A levels and university places. 'You really feel that you have helped to transform lives,' said a teacher.

St Christopher School

Linked to Saint Christopher School Junior School in the Junior section

Barrington Road, Letchworth Garden City, Hertfordshire, SG6 3JZ

- Pupils: 345 boys and girls in senior school, including 32 boarders
- Ages: 11-18 • Size of sixth form: 80 • Non-denom • Fees: Junior £8,700-£10,800; Senior £14,505-£25,470 pa • Independent

Tel: 01462 650 850
Fax: 01462 481 578
Email: admissions@stchris.co.uk
Website: www.stchris.co.uk

Head: Since 2006, Mr Richard Palmer BEd (Nottingham Trent), FRSA. Mr Palmer has deep roots at St Christopher. First came in his gap year, then did his teaching practice here. After a mild flirtation with the idea of going into PR, took a job setting up the IT system and teaching DT and science. Became resident tutor in a boarding house, then, after meeting his wife, Jenny, warden of the sixth form boarding house, moved to St John's College School, Cambridge, as a housemaster. Spent six years there as deputy head, before returning to St Christopher in 2004 as head of the junior school. Took over as acting head during a troubled period and was eventually asked to fill the job permanently. When the news was announced the children cheered. Jovial, energetic and warm, Mr Palmer knows even the tiniest nursery child by name. Feels school should be fun – 'examinations are important but not mutually exclusive from enjoying yourself.' Despite the first-name, own-clothes regime, Mr Palmer wears a suit and tie and is clearly capable of setting boundaries. 'Sometimes it's important to say I'm the head and we're doing it this way.' Has a son and daughter at the school. Enjoys travel, music and cooking.

Academic matters: The academic range is quite broad – 'average and above' – but this is no longer a school for all comers. It now carefully edits out those who won't fit in, though every effort is made to ensure the right children pass through the admissions net. 'When my son sat his entrance test he came out after five minutes in tears,' recalls one mother. 'The school just led him into another room and gave him one-to-one support throughout.' There is a definite a St Christopher's type. 'If you're "not bothered",' says the head, 'it would be dishonest to offer you a place.' If you are, the school will go the extra mile. Don't, however, expect your child to be militarily drilled into As and A*s. 'If they want to do it, they can do it here,' says one parent, 'but if they don't want to work, the school is not going to make them.' Generally strong teaching (though some recent parental concerns about curriculum monitoring, particularly in IT, now, according to head, 'resolved'). About 25 per cent of the intake has some kind of learning difficulty and receive excellent support from a specialist team. Copes well with dyslexia and dyspraxia at mild to medium levels and operates a counselling service. Some pupils have one-to-one tuition (at extra cost); others are helped by a learning support assistant. Everyone takes nine GCSEs but with a wide choice and only five compulsory subjects (two English, double science and maths). Generally good results, considering the intake. Ninety per cent A*–C, 31 per cent A* and A at GCSE, 57 per cent A and B at A level. Small classes – 13–20 up to GCSE, 5–7 in the sixth form – mean every pupil gets plenty of attention. Curriculum, too, is unusually tailor-made with almost any mixture of subjects accommodated. 'If you want to study art, drama and photography, we'll create a timetable for you if we can,' says the head, 'though we'll make it clear it may limit your options later on.'

Games, Options, the Arts: Strong and vibrant art department offering pottery, ceramics and photography. CDT also important with much emphasis on craftsmanship. Decidedly buzzy atmosphere, with energetic teaching and energetic work. Possibly not the most aggressively sporty school but growing reputation for and commitment to team sports (football, rugby and cricket) and much has been done to expand the range of available games and fixtures list. Wonderful climbing wall, skateboard park and outdoor pursuits club, which has weekends of surfing, climbing, potholing, white water rafting, etc. Good facilities – extensive playing fields, sports hall, indoor pool and plenty of enthusiasts. Philosophy, team spirit, but also high-level representation in basketball and rugby. Letchworth tennis club next door.

Plenty of performance opportunities from major school musicals to orchestral concerts and fashion shows, jazz, a capella choir. Unusual for a co-ed school, too, there is an all-boys singing group. 'They appreciate others taking risks.' Drama, too, highly thought of. Community service plays a major role and pupils have the opportunity to work on an international project working with an NGO in India and/or Kosova visiting schools and development projects with which the school has had considerable involvement over the years. Excellent range of extra-curricular activities, with 'Thursday afternoon' options – 'everything from archery to jewellery' – as part of the curriculum.

Background and Atmosphere: Set up by Theosophists in the middle of the WWI, the school was then at the extreme end of radical – a co-ed boarding school, with no uniform, no prescribed discipline, teachers called by their first names and sofas in the back of the classroom for any exhausted pupils. 'Essentially, the founders were New Age forward thinkers,' says the head. Though the sofas have been excised from the classrooms, the underlying liberal, family-based roots still permeate the school like writing in rock. Nowadays, it's not the first-name terms or own clothes that strike you but the fact that pupils are genuinely treated with respect, not merely as exam statistics. 'People can voice an opinion,' says one boy who moved here from a comprehensive. 'You can be who you want to be; you're not just put into a box.' There is more than lip service, too, paid to the notion of community and caring for others. One sixth former, showing me round, pointed out the work of a fellow pupil, not because he was the star in the class but because he'd had the courage to start art A level from scratch and was doing well.

The school still welcomes all faiths and none, still calls for Quaker silence in morning assembly and lunch hours and there is still a very strong family feel – 'I sometimes think it is an extension of my family,' said one mother. 'I can ring up and interrupt the head when he is eating dinner to find out where my son is.' A small school, just 150 from reception to Year 6, 350 in the senior school, everyone knows everyone well. Founded in a beautiful purpose-built building in the same Arts & Crafts style as the surrounding garden suburb, all the later additions – including a RIBA-award winning IT and English block and a sensitively updated Montessori nursery (the childhood home of Sir Laurence Olivier) – have the immaculately swept and polished appeal of a private home. The manicured flower-filled grounds are another glory, plus allotments for pupils and staff. Food is vegetarian, freshly cooked in the morning and enthusiastically consumed at lunch time.

Small boarding element – 32 throughout the school, 13 in the sixth form – is cared for by residential tutors and supervised by an academic tutor.

Pastoral Care and Discipline: 'We have the usual problems with young people who make mistakes,' says the head. 'We exclude for damaging the school, supplying drugs or persistently disrupting lessons.' 'About six children have been excluded over the time my son has been here,' said one mother. 'But they do it in the best way possible. They always try and help find another school and don't blacken the child's reputation.' Huge amounts of discussion and debate when get things go wrong and individually tailored punishment. 'We may ask a child, "is this the best you can do?"' says the head. 'Since children are inherently honest, they often say no and decide to try again. It's much better than a detention.' Pupils are expected to get involved; recognise what they are not good at and do something about what they're not, have fun and enjoy themselves. A strong sense of discipline coming from within. A bell is struck for silence at lunch and immediately there is not a whisper. Some issues that would be disciplinary matters at another school are school-wide issues here. One boy, for example, accessorised with an empty cartridge belt, found himself the centre of a whole-school debate. The head will intervene when lines are crossed. 'One day, we just got fed up with 'sagging' and told everyone they had to pull their trousers up. They haven't slipped yet.'

Teacher-pupil relationships are notably good, eased by the informality of first-name terms and teachers here are very willing to go the extra mile. 'Classes are so small that you can go and get help from a teacher that you are not assigned to,' said one sixth former. Plenty of opportunities to take responsibility. Head boy and girl, plus eight major offices. Lively school council.

Pupils and Parents: You won't find many bankers or those whose idea of discipline is short back and sides here. (Indeed pupils picketed the poor army officer who tried to come and talk to them about military life.) Parents are mainly liberal media and professionals – 'who are genuinely interested in their children's development,' says the head. Americans, too, tend to identify themselves with the lack of uniform and strong student voice; one or two overseas students from Hong Kong, some Europeans. The students are articulate and responsible and unusually supportive of each other. Pupils are given a clear sense of the harsh reality of the world outside the gates, leaving with a higher than average sense of social and political idealism. Quite a large contingent (about 25 per cent of the senior school) commute from north London, the rest are mainly from local Hertfordshire towns and villages. School bus operates from the station and from north London, including a late run at 5.30.

Entrance: Entrance is by a test of cognitive ability and an extended piece of writing. Head then interviews the parents and the deputy interviews the children. They also talk to the head of the child's current school. Parental interviews are as important as those of the children. 'We will take someone if we feel we can support their needs, they can access all parts of the curriculum and won't be a detrimental force or unbalance a class or year group,' says the head. 'This is a particular style of school, however. We want to ensure parents understand what we're about and not suddenly come in and decide they want blazers and boaters.' With rare exceptions, all the junior school transfer to the senior. Generally five Bs minimum for entry to sixth, though reasonably flexible. 'We'd pause if it was all Cs and Ds.' Capacity for about 50 boarders full boarding throughout, including in the sixth form, though the majority are weekly boarders.

Exit: About 50 per cent leave post-GCSE, mainly to the state sector. 'A lot of parents here are not particularly rich,' said one mother. 'They've made sacrifices to give their children the kind of education St Christopher offers and I think a lot of children, too, who need the kind of environment the school offers are better able to cope by the time they reach the sixth form.' To a wide range of universities. One or so a year to Oxbridge.

Money Matters: Scholarship and bursaries out of school income. Separate bursary fund in the sixth form with two bursaries a years on reasonably complex means-tested basis. Ten per cent discount for siblings.

Remarks: A very unusual school which still works largely against the grain of our current obsession with exam statistics, and you certainly have to be both the right child and the right parent to be able to make the most of the school's philosophy. 'It can be a difficult school in which to hold your nerve if you have a child who'd prefer to play video games, but it does produce profoundly – not merely superficially – confident young adults with a genuine concern for others and for the community in which they live.' For those who want this type of education, it also makes most children very happy. 'Neither of my children has ever said they don't want to go to school. They love it.'

St Clare's, Oxford

139 Banbury Road, Oxford, Oxfordshire, OX2 7AL

• Pupils: 235 boarders, 20 day students, mixed • Ages: 15-19 • Size of sixth form: 200 • Non-denom • Fees: Boarding £28,548-£28,868; Day £17,846 pa • Independent

Tel: 01865 552 031
Fax: 01865 513 359
Email: admissions@stclares.ac.uk
Website: www.stclares.ac.uk

Principal: Since 2005, Ms Paula Holloway MSc PGCE. Educated at Cowbridge High School for Girls in Glamorgan and the LSE, where she read geography. She began her career in banking but started teaching when she moved to Hong Kong and has never looked back. 'I just knew I had found what I wanted to do for the rest of my life,' she recalls. On her return to the UK did an MSc in Educational Studies by research at Jesus College, Oxford, and became deputy and then head of Latifa School for Girls in Dubai. Head of Ashford School in Kent from 2000 to 2004. Married to management consultant and lives close to college. Friendly, inspiring and very focused. Likes working with older teenagers and greets everyone by name as she walks round. 'They're a huge amount of fun,' she says. 'I love running a place with such an international ethos.'

Academic matters: St Clare's prides itself on offering students from all over the world 'an international education' and succeeds admirably. Has been running International Baccalaureate Diploma programme for more than 30 years – longer than anyone else in England. Around 260 students (including 30 from the UK) are currently studying for the broad-based IB Diploma, which involves taking six subjects for two years – three at standard level and three at higher level. The six subjects include the student's native language, a second language, a humanities subject (history, geography, economics etc), a science, maths and an arts subject (e.g. visual arts, music or theatre arts). The IB culminates in exams at the end of the two-year course – there's also an extended essay and compulsory Theory of Knowledge course to complete. Average of nine students to a class, and maximum of 16.

St Clare's has a strong academic track record, with an average IB score of 34.5 in 2010 and three gained maximum score of 45. Principal describes the IB as 'an outstanding qualification in terms of the breadth and depth it offers' and says she would have loved to have taken it instead of A levels. But she admits it isn't for everyone, adding, 'it requires great commitment. You have to hit the ground running and work consistently for two years.' College also offers a Preparatory IB course for students who want to prepare for the IB Diploma (this involves studying academic subjects, study skills and additional support in English where necessary). Well-equipped classrooms – the majority look more like high-powered boardrooms – labs, art rooms and study areas. Banks of computers with WiFi and stunning library and resources centre stocked with 35,000 books.

College doesn't have SEN department – but help with dyslexia and EFL available.

Staff are a very impressive lot. Many have been here for years and quite a number relocated from abroad – which enhances the college's international outlook. St Clare's insists that all students continue to study their own language so makes a point of finding staff who can teach them – everything from Mongolian to Albanian so far.

Games, Options, the Arts: The IB Diploma includes CAS (Creativity, Action and Service) – a programme of sports, artistic and cultural activities and voluntary service to help others. College uses local playing fields and sports centres and offers huge range of sport, from football, basketball, volleyball, rugby and netball to yoga, aerobics, swimming, rock climbing and horse riding. Activities on offer include D of E, Young Enterprise, Model United Nations and international affairs discussion groups. Noticeboards covered with details of what's on – everything from Latin funk dance to dragon boat racing! Art, music and drama very strong and, perhaps not surprisingly given its international viewpoint, debating hugely popular. When we visited, college was about to host IBSCA (International Baccalaureate Schools and Colleges Association) conference on Africa for 250 students from other IB schools and colleges across the UK. Service element of CAS includes working for local charities like Oxfam, helping the elderly and disabled and getting involved in recycling and conservation projects.

Background and Atmosphere: Founded in 1953, the college's main buildings are stunning conversions of Edwardian houses lining north Oxford's Banbury Road. Pots of daisies either side of front door and all buildings immaculately maintained. Most IB students board and live in one of 15 supervised college houses. Most of them are a stone's throw from the college, either in Banbury Road or one of its side streets. First years are allocated to a house but second years get a choice of where they'd like to live. When we visited, 143 Banbury Road (no fancy names for boarding houses here) was being renovated for students – its en suite bathrooms, hairdryers in bedrooms and automated heating are sure to go down well. Weekly and full residential boarding, although day students are allocated to a house too and encouraged to play as full a part as possible in college life.

Light, airy dining room with conservatory and tables on the terrace. Loads of choice – hot, cold, vegetarian and salads. The Sugar House, the lively student café, is popular too, offering coffee, buns, pizza and loud music. Students pay for meals with electronically readable cards topped up to a certain daily amount – they have to use their allowance by 10.30pm everyday so they can't simply stockpile it! 'We are trying to get them to eat healthily without being draconian,' says principal.

Informal atmosphere pervades college, with students addressing principal and teachers by first names, but education taken very seriously. Staff describe St Clare's as an excellent stepping stone between school and university, with students being nurtured and guided but also encouraged to be independent and given 'freedoms appropriate to their age.'

Pastoral Care and Discipline: Excellent. St Clare's has relatively few rules but they are firmly implemented. Students are expected to show respect and consideration for themselves, fellow students and the college community as a whole and know exactly where they stand. Each pupil has a personal tutor whom they meet weekly. All college halls of residence have wardens who act in loco parentis and hold weekly meetings to discuss the running of the house. Students have to be in their rooms by 11 during the week and 12 at weekends.

Very firm rules on smoking, alcohol and drugs. Alcohol banned on college premises (unless wardens give permission) and parents informed if there are 'serious concerns about misuse of alcohol.' Students using drugs are automatically suspended, though not necessarily expelled. Dealing brings instant expulsion. Overt displays of sexual nature discouraged – even students walking round hand in hand.

Teachers say bullying and racism aren't issues here. 'But if they were we would jump on it like a ton of bricks,' says principal firmly. Students describe houses as friendly and welcoming and say college is good at helping them to settle in. All new IB students take part in a special four-day residential course at the start of their two years at St Clare's – to help them get used to their new environment and make friends.

Pupils and Parents: Pupils come from 42 different countries around the world – so the college is truly international. Students we met during our visit were enthusiastic, outgoing and confident, but not alarmingly so. Most said they and their parents had chosen St Clare's because of its international outlook and the wealth of opportunities it offers – and were thrilled to be there.

Entrance: St Clare's recruits 'from scratch' every year. No entrance test – 'we have never had one and don't intend to,' says principal, who relies on prospective pupils' previous reports, references and interview. 'We are looking for young people who are mature and self-disciplined and have made a conscious decision for good reasons to study for the IB.'

Exit: Virtually all St Clare's students go to university – mostly in the UK (University College London and LSE very popular) but a handful to universities in the US and elsewhere. College has very dynamic full-time higher education adviser, as well as a US university adviser.

Money Matters: Around eight scholarships available a year. All means-tested and offered on basis of financial circumstances, school record, references and exam and interview at St Clare's. Scholarship applications considered in February of year of entry and range from full to partial awards.

Remarks: A truly international place – right in the heart of Oxford. Vibrant, inspiring and gets impressive academic results. The perfect stepping stone to university for bright students who want to take the IB and gain a little more independence along the way.

St Columba's School

Linked to Saint Columbas Junior School in the Junior section

Duchal Road, Kilmacolm, PA13 4AU

• Pupils: 735 boys and girls; all day • Ages: 11-18 • Size of sixth form: 95 pupils • Non-denom • Fees: Nursery £2,380 - Senior VI £9,450 pa • Independent

Tel: 01505 872238
Fax: 01505 873995
Email: kzhang@st-columbas.org
Website: www.st-columbas.org

Rector: Since 2002, Mr David Girdwood BSc PGCE MEd SQH (fiftyish and newly into specs). SQH = Scottish qualification for heads – which was the latest wheeze from the Scottish education boys, and about to become mandatory from 2005, and which – alas – has now (like so many bright ideas) been abandoned, but makes Mr Girdwood a fairly rarefied beast amongst independent heads. He was educated at Alva Academy followed by St Andrews University, Jordanhill, Stirling and Edinburgh universities and comes to St Columba's from Stewart's Melville where he 'taught chemistry for fifteen years' and is now a governor. 'I went to Stewart's as head of chemistry, rising to become head of science and head of upper school and part of the management team', as well as doing his day release in headmastering. A man o' pairts then. Married to a solicitor wife who works in Edinburgh, he has two children in the school, which he first visited as part of an HMI team and was 'enchanted that pupils gathered for assembly should be so numerous that transitus sat on the stage in front of the rector'. Not so the boss of the HMI team and, as we reported previously, the transitus 11–12 year old class is now banished – apart from forays to the art and music block – to the (admittedly all singing and dancing) junior dept.

Several years into Mr Girdwood's Renfrewshire experience, he has tackled 'the lack of policies', setting up committees 'to develop anti-bullying policy, ditto health and safety, child protection' et al, as well as encouraging staff appraisal weekends (cor!), combined with 'an explosion of staff going on courses' as well as studying for their SQH. (Keen to involve both management and governors, as well as staff, in decision making, Mr Girdwood has produced a raft of questionnaires and analysis documents. 'Firm policies' having now settled into practice, the man himself comes over as caring, gentle with only the faintest hint of a rod of iron, and full of really quite sensible ideas.

Ambitious and stylish plans were afoot to improve dramatically the senior school. The head's schemes for major development, providing 'fantastic' increased facilities in three adjoining plots (much needed – particularly in the science departments) – have been knocked on the head by planning and again at appeal. Mr Girdwood remains determined. This temporary setback aside, parents are pleased with the way things are going and 'numbers are racing upwards'.

Academic matters: Little change. Only Scottish curriculum on offer – highly structured learning with masses of parental encouragement. French very popular, 'Spanish booming' with ten pupils currently following the normal Higher course this year, and ten others doing a 'crash course' of Higher Spanish in one year. Three languages possible at Higher level 'but not simultaneously' – head of lang dept writes text books. German 'holding its own remarkably well' – some native speakers. Latin for all, Greek 'on demand' but minimal take-up for either at sixth form. Results 'fantastic' and St Columba's is consistently in top six of the Scottish league. Mod langs and the sciences particularly strong, though this could not be verified as the school could not produce subject specific results tables. Revamped labs, classrooms and pupil space now increasingly urgent.

Support for learning headed by a SENCo at deputy rector level, has three dedicated staff (including the head of guidance) covering both the senior and junior schools; help on hand for dyslexics and for those who find some subjects particularly difficult. 'Can cope' with ADHD and Ritalin. No problem with pupils with disabilities (but no lifts in the classroom block) though parents of any child needing a dedicated teacher would have to underwrite the cost of that teacher (though this can often be met via LEAs). Comprehensive measures to check that St C's is doing well by its pupils, including testing which picks up problems as well as monitoring progress. ICT strong with pupils 'taught on computers rather than taught computing'; using trolleyloads of laptops rolled round each floor of the labs (also liftless).

Class size 20, three classes per year, and pupils setted from 12 (transitus) for English, French, and maths; larger numbers have allowed a fourth set which is often a small group that helps strugglers. Exciting newish library above former gym; old library now a business study centre. Pupils can work in the library in their free time (with fabulous views to the south to distract them). Staff common room younger after 'lots of retirements' with recent head of department posts in maths, music, physics 'attracting high calibre from good schools'.

Games, Options, the Arts: School is sportier than it looks and sports taken seriously here. Good and enthusiastic rugby team won Scottish rugby plate in 2001 and reached the final in 2008: not bad for a school with only 210 chaps? Hockey team has won the South West Cup (again!) Regular rugby and hockey tours to Canada. Astroturf pitch near senior school for hockey and tennis though most rugby games are played on local park opposite the junior school which has a vast games hall, tactfully curtained off for little ones so they're not overwhelmed, and a fearsome looking fitness room. Loos and showers in new primary building are next to the sports hall and the boys' showers have the controls outside, which could – but doesn't – cause hours of entertainment. Tennis is at the Kilmacolm tennis club adjoining Shallot (as the junior school previously the girls' boarding house, is known). The school is proud of having pupils competing at national or UK level in seven or so different sports. D of E hugely popular.

Impressive art and music in the Cargill Centre opened by the Princess Royal in 2000, and beginning to look a little tired. So much creative energy: music and pipe band popular, for girls as well as boys, as is choir (lots of travel), jazz band, Calamity Jane, art, fabric design (stunning), photography, etc, etc. All makes for wear and tear! Biennial exhibitions with real artists as well as pupils and local art club clubs. The self-contained ground floor houses a technology department with serious equipment but fun teaching. Home economics for 11s, 12s and the usual pre uni stuff for sixth form but no pottery or sculpture noticed. Exchanges going out of fashion (inhibited by health and safety); recent links with St Petersburg and a one-way Russian exchange! Debating a real wow with victories in Scottish and international competitions – school has its first ever member of the Scottish debating team (Rector's daughter!)

Regular revision classes, weekends, evenings, and classes for all locals, from seven to seventy-year olds, everything from computers, to languages, to bridge. Very popular and good for the community, classes run from September to May.

Background and Atmosphere: Originally part of the Girls' School Company, the school was founded in 1897 and went co-ed (in the face of falling numbers) in 1978 (the junior department) and 1981 (the senior department). The junior department is a long half mile from the senior school. As a result of the fantastic new build and the subsequent shuffling round of classes, transitus, the youngest class in the senior school, is based down here. Healthy amount of walking as juniors visit senior school for music, art, IT, home economics and the sciences, but Shallot is otherwise self-contained.

Juniors hit the jackpot in the building stakes: airy suites of classrooms round a common space for each year group, gleaming pale wood floors, gym/theatre as well as the sports hall, and acres of grassy play space seething, on our visit, with contented and very helpful children. Gorgeous ornate dining room (serving food all made on the premises though packed lunches are OK) in the Edwardian elegance of Shallot, which, sadly, seems at the bitter end of the three-quarters of a million rolling repair programme. Seniors visit for PE and games.

Fair amount of tinkering with senior school fabric under the previous (impressive) incarnation but whilst the original red-brick building is still 'just' recognisable, it seems to have a lot of space dedicated to cloakrooms and passages; the dining hall doubles as assembly, with fold up stool/tables that stack in a cupboard.

Imaginative architectural over-view badly needed here since 'planning blight' is definitely in evidence in the older spaces. Both lab building and the original school are groaning under the impact of modern equipment, school bags and lively teenagers. (It's a pity the planners didn't appreciate what an asset Kilmacolm has in St C's, gaining, like many Scottish villages, business turnover, young professional families, shared culture, sports etc, from a thriving independent school. Rannoch state primary closed when the school went down!) They have been refused planning for new labs/maths development ... classrooms here very dilapidated – unchanged since the union. The senior school campus is pretty cramped, with little space, mostly rather dreary, tarmac.

Pastoral Care and Discipline: Four houses (sibling and FP tradition) and inter-house everything. Zero tolerance – drugs/theft means out. 'No significant problems with bullying,' said the Rector. Juniors address potential bullying via a week of stories and activities in assembly, six 'golden rules', all 'do's' not 'don't's'. The junior head, Mrs DL Cook (a 'Hutchy' girl who was depute in Glasgow School) has a 'button' system allowing her to seek and find anxious children and makes herself available daily to children and parents at arrival times.

Pupils and Parents: Although pupils come from a 30km radius, very much a Renfrewshire school, with about 80 per cent from within a 8km radius, but regular bus comes from north Ayrshire, and a small nucleus from Dunoon 'across the watter'. Pupils catch the 7.30 am boat and join up with the Greenock/Port Glasgow bus. Juniors and seniors can stay in school until 6pm. Kilmacolm, a popular sprawling suburban village, once served by the railway, is booming: first time buyers, a tiny wide ethnic base as well as the traditional Kilmacomics (sic). FPs Lord (Ian) Lang, and Eleanor Laing MP. Don't get it wrong, this is not a toffs' school by any means, just good and sensible; pupils 'are not terribly street-wise'.

Entrance: Own test and interview to transitus and senior school. 'People fail it,' Rector says, and siblings/FPs' children not necessarily accepted if below standard but automatic entry from junior school. Waiting lists all over and fifteen vying for the dozen places available at other ages. Otherwise places only available as pupils leave.

Exit: Small trickle (very small trickle) leave to go to trad prep schools at eight or public schools at 13, plus occasionally after they have got university entrance qualifications – i.e. first year sixth transfer (latest wheeze is to opt for the local state school and apply to Oxbridge – or Bristol – from there) or even for a final year toughening up in a boarding school. Otherwise approx 97 per cent to university, usually in Scotland, two or three to Oxbridge on occasion, one or two to art school.

Money Matters: Means-tested bursaries now available! The school can be hit hard when one of the local companies goes down (and suffered badly on the demise of the local sugar company.) Fees remarkably reasonable, but all parents must cough up £350 for a debenture when their child is accepted; this is returned at the end of the child's time at school (without interest or increase in value). There is a fifty per cent penalty if a place is accepted and not taken up, and a levy of £50 is charged per pupil per term for the Development Fund. Discount of 25 per cent for the third and subsequent children but the Development Fund levy remains the same. Blazers (about £80 depending on size) and summer/winter uniforms for all girls. Juniors have waterproof jackets (£40) and little ones wear fetching green overalls for lunch.

Remarks: Huge waiting lists, academically outstanding, very middle class, thoroughly sound rather than setting the world alight! 'Still a local school' with local attitudes and virtually no ethnic mix. Victorian values, terribly popular, and may be the reason that houses in boring old Kilmacolm (and this editor once lived there) change hands at a premium, and, to quote a local landowner, 'they actually move into the village because of the school'.

St David's College

Llandudno, Conwy, LL30 1RD

• Pupils: 240; 180 boys, 60 girls (120 boarders) • Ages: 10-18 • Size of sixth form: 70 • Christian (all denominations welcome) • Fees: Day £7,680-£13,527; Boarding £16,950-£20,787; SEN: Day £8,850-£16,263, Boarding £18,450-£24,150 pa • Independent

Tel: 01492 875974
Fax: 01492 870 383
Email: hmsec@stdavidscollege.co.uk
Website: www.stdavidscollege.co.uk

Head: Since 2008, Mr Stuart Hay, BEng PGCE (late thirties). Mr Hay joined St David's as deputy head from Warminster School, where he was head of electronics and product design. After gaining his electronic engineering degree and PGCE at Bath University, he taught in both the independent and maintained sectors; he is married to Lucy and they have two children, Ben, four and Milly, two. Mr Hay's main interests are mountaineering, road cycling, mountain biking and racquet sports. Took over at short notice when the previous head departed and his appointment to head was confirmed in 2009.

Academic matters: Academic results are significantly above the national average but the emphasis is not solely on classroom work and, in terms of added value, achievements are spectacular. The school was one of the first schools to implement a multi-sensory teaching policy. Support programme enables some pupils to have individual lessons at the Cadogan Centre, a specialised unit within the campus. These pupils have an individual learning plan appropriate to their needs.

IT provision is first class. The school offers NVQs in CAD and technology. We were shown some space age designs that were both impressive and practical. Pupil:staff ratio is less than five to one.

Games, Options, the Arts: The school believes that outdoor activities can build both teamwork and individual confidence. What is available would challenge Indiana Jones. Sailing, climbing, fell running and kite-buggying are among the large range of activities on offer. The pupils have pride in the skills they have acquired and are determined to continue these activities when they leave school.

Art is popular. We viewed some photographic projects which caught the beauty of the surrounding countryside. About three-quarters of the pupils learn a musical instrument and there is ample practice space.

Background and Atmosphere: Founded in 1965 by John Mayor. He felt that there was a need for a school that could help those who might sink in the mainstream system. A late medieval mansion with 39 acres was leased on the outskirts of Llandudno, near the Snowdonia National Park. The oak-panelled rooms are still used and fireplaces provide a cheering blaze. Additions have been made over the years, including new boarding houses. The head would like to see a further new boarding house when funds allow. While some of the buildings could benefit from some TLC, they are welcoming and well used. Staff and pupils seem at ease with each other, a feature that is mentioned in the latest CSSIW visit.

Pastoral Care and Discipline: Housemasters, tutors and other staff are available to support pupils. Open door policy. During our visit to the Chaplain a number of pupils came in and were given space to take time out. Sixth form boarders were housed separately but they have since been reintegrated into the boarding houses. This move has been welcomed by house staff.

Pupils and Parents: From a wide range of primary and prep schools. Day pupils from across the whole of North Wales. Boarders from all over the UK, a small number from overseas. Inclusive entry helped by quite a number of pupils being funded by their local education authorities. Apart from those with special educational needs many parents chose the school because of its broad all round education and its small class sizes.

Entrance: The majority enter at 10. Selection by interview and school report.

Exit: A few leave at 16. The majority moves on to university with technical subjects being more popular. Pupils are usually successful in being accepted to their further educational establishment of choice.

Money Matters: Given the staff:pupil ratio the fees represent good value.

Remarks: A school that transforms the lives of young people who, when they enter, have both low expectations and low self-esteem. The all round support gives them the skills and confidence to achieve and move forward.

St Dominic's Sixth Form College

Mount Park Avenue, Harrow-on-the-Hill, Middlesex, HA1 3HX

• Pupils: 900; just over half are girls • Ages: 16-19 • RC but other faiths accepted • State

Tel: 0208 422 8084
Fax: 0208 422 3759
Email: registrar@stdoms.ac.uk
Website: www.stdoms.ac.uk

Principal: Since 2004, Mr Patrick Harty BSc PGCE MA (Ed) NPQH, early forties, a scientist and engineer, open, relaxed and positive. Previously taught at three schools, then a first deputy headship at Parmiter's School in Watford, a second at Nicholas Breakspear RC School followed by his first headship at Marlborough School – both in St Albans. Mr Harty spent between two and four years in all his previous posts but is clearly in no hurry to move from St Dominic's about which he is infectiously enthusiastic and has plans! Faith is the common denominator here – 'our faith base is just as important as our academic performance,' he stresses, and these two factors come up again and again. 'The fundamental mission for the college is to provide education for the Roman Catholics of Harrow – in a multi-faith community ... one of the reasons for our success is that we provide an academic atmosphere.' The job has its challenges and its frustrations but the rewards are palpable too and Mr Harty has the energy and the humour to take it all on. He is impressively and vigorously supported by his vice principal, Mr Mark Nicholls – they were colleagues in St Albans – and clearly enjoy working as a mutually supportive team.

Academic matters: Teaching is good here. Staff are efficient and pupils warmly praise their dedication and care. Expert help is given to prospective pupils about their subject choices and to existing pupils about their future courses and destinations. A very good range of courses and subjects offered – A levels include art history, business studies, classical civilisation, further maths, four modern languages, PE and Latin – in addition to all the ones you'd expect. Results are impressive. More than 60 per cent A-B pass rate for the last three years. Biggest cohorts by far in biology, chemistry, mathematics, economics and psychology – results impressive in all three. Large numbers also taking the other sciences, maths, Eng lit and economics and average over 80 per cent A–C in most. Applied A level in ICT with, again, respectable results or better. BTecs taken in business – results high. Increasing number of takers for modern languages and results pretty good and outstanding in Italian – most langs taught by native speakers.

SEN is good here and individuals' physical as well as educational needs can be met. Everywhere is accessible by wheelchair. Everyone is assessed on enrolment and individual learning programmes are constructed where necessary. A 'Study+' manager, i.e. a SENCo with add-ons, organises support in class or one-to-one. Little EAL required. Average class size of 16 with max 22.

Games, Options, the Arts: A new sports hall with a fitness suite and new netball and tennis court opened in July 2010. Games not compulsory but football, basketball, cricket and rugby are options in the Wednesday 'activities' slot. Sport and access to the fitness suite available to students throughout the week. New building opened in June 2006 offering facilities for science, ICT and music. Art and design and DT taken by small but significant numbers with creditable results. One small trapezoid drama studio – theatre studies taken by 17 students in 2010 with 82 per cent achieving A–C. Space is at such a high premium that the school's few larger rooms cannot be spared for large productions – however, in the summer outside performances take place under a large canopy. The refurbished chapel has flexible seating and now provides an auditorium for concerts. Work experience, trips, lectures, opera visits, talks, conferences – there is plenty going on, though some students feel that more could be done and that peers elsewhere are offered more on the extra-curricular side. Space, again, is a factor. However, in 2009–10, a politics group went to New York, history of art to Rome, a history trip to Paris, and 20 students visited a link school in China. In keeping with the ethos there are annual visits to the Holocaust museum at Auschwitz and an annual pilgrimage to Lourdes. You wouldn't come here on account of the extracurricular but there are more opportunities here than immediately meet the eye.

Background and Atmosphere: It's like a mini mini university campus – with the stress on mini. A cluster of buildings of different ages and styles sits on a leafy bit of Harrow-on-the-Hill, surrounded by some of the priciest bits of residential north-west London. Private schools are all around – John Lyon, Orley Farm and, of course, the local Big Brother. It's quiet, attractive, enhanced by the super chapel – a 1920s bit of retro Arts and Crafts – but none of the buildings are unappealing and the site has been developed with sensitivity, since giving up being a convent school in 1979. The new four storey block is taking up outdoor space the college can ill afford to lose but needs must when you are over-subscribed three to one and teaching and IT rooms are essentials. It took seven years to get planning permission so no-one should expect the college's enviable reputation to lead to a rush of new-build to meet demand.

We visited on a sunny spring day so students were gathering everywhere, especially on the few grassy patches. On wintry days there are few places to go and the canteen, in which lunchtime sittings are, of necessity, staggered, was refurbished and extended in 2007. This was in conjunction with a much-needed improved menu. There is no common room – nor plans for one – but the canteen serves as a social space and an attractive canopy provides an outdoor area. Off-site there is nowhere much to go either so everything is conducive to work – and these are, in the main, highly motivated students. The atmosphere is harmonious and cooperative and discipline – mostly in the firm-but-fair hands of Mr Nicholls – is enforced, much as you'd expect at any well-run school. There may not be anywhere much to go in non-lesson time but he will make sure you go there. One such resort is the excellent, well-stocked and recently refurbished library, another is the ICT room and since 2006, the new building has greatly increased workspace. Considering the number of people packed in here it was surprisingly orderly and tidy – we have seen far more mess in far more august and spacious establishments.

Everyone in this very ethnically mixed college looked happily integrated and 'there is no racism here', though we did hear regrets from a few that the ethnic groups didn't mix as much as in students' previous schools. The principal was mystified at this and, certainly, the visual evidence didn't support it. Staff and students seemed on good – first name, in fact – terms and there is a feeling of mutual respect.

Pastoral Care and Discipline: The faith base of the college is crucial and homogenising although 50 per cent of students are Roman Catholic. What counts is faith: 'I will expect the young person to talk about their faith at interview,' says the principal. There is a chaplain and a weekly, voluntary, mass. Everyone has two lessons weekly of Religious and Moral Education. The staff monitor attendance very carefully and there is a biometric registration system at each lesson that picks up unauthorised absence very quickly but absenteeism isn't a problem here. Students realise how prized places are and don't want to jeopardise theirs. Tutors monitor all aspects of a student's life and progress. Many staff stay for 10 plus years – stability counts. Student council and a peer listening system. Progress grades are issued half-termly. Zero tolerance of violence and drugs.

Pupils and Parents: There are seven boys to every nine girls because more girls meet the academic entrance requirements. Of the 50 per cent who are non RC, 25 per cent are Hindu, 12 per cent Muslim and the rest a mix of everything else. Most live locally in Harrow but they come from more than 80 schools in five other boroughs as well as from Berks and Bucks. A commitment to religious faith is the common denominator as well as, increasingly among the non-Catholics, academic ability.

Entrance: About a third come from the Salvatorian College and Sacred Heart on unconditional offers. The rest must meet various criteria based on verifiable religious commitment and academic predictions. Criteria vary depending on courses applied for but, for example, for a full A level course in four subjects, seven GCSE passes are required + at least Bs in the A level subjects. All are interviewed.

Local i.e. the various London University colleges and Brunel predominate here but there's a good crop of other redbricks etc notably Manchester, Southampton, Birmingham and so on. Lots of law, business and medical courses but there are fine arts students and teaching students – they go everywhere to do everything. It's a very impressive list and notably lacking silly courses at exploitative institutions. Students from here clearly mean to have proper careers.

Money Matters: Free if you're under 19. Excellent and enlightened system of bursaries for students and staff to fund specific projects and trips.

Remarks: Measured against its peers on academic achievement, St Doms outscores virtually all the local competition. If the serious work/faith combination does it for you and outweighs the space and facilities other places offer, get onto your priest/imam/rabbi pronto and get those grades.

St Dunstan's College

Linked to Saint Dunstan's College Junior School in the Junior section

Stanstead Road, Catford, London, SE6 4TY

• Pupils: 515 boys and 320 girls, all day • Ages: 3-18 • Size of sixth form: 140 • Anglican foundation • Fees: £7,467-£13,140 pa • Independent

Tel: 020 8516 7200
Fax: 020 8516 7300
Email: hhardy@sdmail.org.uk
Website: www.stdunstans.org.uk

Head: Since 2005, the stylish and keen Mrs Jane Davies BSc (early forties) with a grown-up daughter. She joined the College in 2000 as deputy head having been head of maths (still teaches it now) at Trinity School in Croydon and was promoted after the previous head left after a year. Wary of being probed about her (briefly appointed) predecessor (Mrs Cordeaux seems to have been expunged from history, 1984-style), statistics or the mixed intake her school has. She has a good team around her – including a deputy who was a pupil at the school, has taught there for 38 years and has seen his son pass through – and is looking forward to the USP that the IB gives St Dunstan's in south east London.

Academic matters: Recent examination successes include 65 per cent of GCSE exams being awarded A*–A grades, 91 per cent of exams graded A*–B and 98 per cent graded A*–C. 100 per cent pass rate at A level with nearly half of exams awarded an A grade, and over 80 per cent graded A–B. IB Diploma students also achieved a 100 per cent pass rate and more than one third scoring 37 points or above out of 45.

So good stuff but not as results-focused as local competition Alleyn's, JAGs or Dulwich College. The number of pupils with SEN has risen to 155 and there is a head of learning support who screens all pupils and issues an IEP if necessary. As always, the school is wary of being swamped by pupils who need extra attention, but once you are in, the support is there.

Maths is strong with opportunities to take masterclasses from Year 9, the chemistry labs are state-of-the-art after refurbishment in 2003 – taught as part of general science up until Year 8. Biology is popular; Spotlight Science based course from Years 7 to 9 and apparently half sixth form choose to continue to A level or IB. French is taught using all that ICT can offer without neglecting culture – croissants for breakfast, trips to Montpelier and Paris. German and Spanish students also get to practise languages on trips. Classics department is thriving, with the head doubling as editor of the comprehensive *Chronicle* – separate sections on each form throughout the school! History study is based on concrete examples ranging from the urbanisation of Catford to Bolshevism in Russia. ICT is used throughout the school and St Dunstan's was the first school in England to become a European Computer Driving Licence test centre. Lots of creative options in all academic subjects – chemistry camp, RS students visiting the Hindu temple in Neasden, a reading group shadowing the Carnegie Medal and a trip to Thorpe Park to study physical forces and motion!

The school began the International Baccalaureate in September 2005 and they did their research and training thoroughly. Nearest independent schools that offer it are Sevenoaks and KCS Wimbledon.

Games, Options, the Arts: Co-curricular activities rather extra-curricular – politics, Japanese, sailing, street dance and debating (reached final of the Oxford Union debate). Sport is important, with representation at county and country level, although if you're not sporty you'll still get along OK. Up to 20 sports available with a full fixture list and tours for all ages, games afternoons are compulsory for seniors. Playing fields and newly refurbished swimming pool onsite (new floodlight netball and tennis courts) and a fitness suite as part of the purpose-built sports hall.

Fine art is impressive, hung from every available space in the department (would benefit from more room) and through some of the school. There is an electronic workshop for learning theatre production and interhouse drama competitions as well as 'blockbusters' and more informal productions. With specialist tuition from 21 visiting teachers, two school orchestras, concerts at St John's Smith Square, Southwark Cathedral and All Hallows, smaller choirs and ensembles and tours abroad, music is also taken seriously.

200 pupils involved up to gold award of the Duke of Edinburgh scheme; Fun Fizzical (a club for children with physical and mental disabilities) and a chance to go with kids from a local special needs school on a week's holiday make sure pupils are part of the local community – they also do a talking newspaper for the blind and visit local elderly. The bursar is ex-army and very involved in the burgeoning CCF which is enlivened by young staff.

Background and Atmosphere: Originally built as a boys' school in 1888, went co-educational in mid 1990s. The old building, fondly described by some as Hogwartesque, is dark and imposing, but children streaming through make it feel alive. Wide warrens of passages lead through to spacious classrooms, with pockets of calm like the enclosed garden by the bursar's office. Dining room, purpose-built in the '50s, has plate glass windows with a curved roof (like a Pringle crisp!) and no pillars – an amazing space where the staff have a choice to eat on a platform above the pupils' tables. This does not make them unapproachable; on the contrary the sixth form kids seem particularly at ease with adults and options available to them in the future. Great Hall, where assemblies take place with prefects sitting on stage, has a recently restored stained glass window. A real mixture of tradition and modern life – a large LED screen displays school events at reception, in the staff room and one more to come in the sixth form common room; intranet available from home.

Busy inner-city site next to a road junction is not enviable, nor is tangling with the South Circular a joyful way to spend your mornings – parents and the coaches drive inside the gates to drop the children off. However, this is no ivory tower school; it lives with Catford's busy life on its doorstep and enjoys it.

Pastoral Care and Discipline: Pastoral care is excellent, 'Cannot be faulted,' according to parents, a real strength of the school with a lot of effort and manpower invested in it. 'St Dunstan's picked up instantly on a special educational need for my child, which had not been noticed in two independent prep schools. They were extremely supportive and my child was not singled out in any way.' Friendships made here really last, girls particularly supportive of one another and relationships between sexes are exactly what you would hope for from a co-educational school – realistic and not primarily hormone fuelled!

Four house system is vertical and inter-year mixing is encouraged through older years producing and directing younger ones in house drama. There are heads of year, heads of section, a prefect system and mentor if needed. A strong and successful drugs education policy – the school takes a harder line than the rest of society on misdemeanours. Bullying is not tolerated and is picked up as soon as it occurs.

Pupils and Parents: Very aspirant parent group; lots of first time buyers. Huge multi-cultural mix reflects local society – Chinese, Japanese, Asian, Afro Caribbean and Anglo Saxon – and is not an issue at all, although RS programme and attendance at assemblies (broadly Christian) is not optional. St Dunstan's Family Society is active and has been successful in raising money for minibuses, D of E tents and travel bursaries.

Parents are professional but in no way snooty – would consider Alleyn's to be stuffy, Dulwich College to be overwhelming; school suits a more laid-back, happy-go-lucky child. Advent of IB has drawn international interest from parents moving to London – 'Can we come for a term?' – such requests considered very carefully on an individual basis. Children come from all over south east London; coaches daily from Blackheath, New Cross, Clapham, Streatham, Farnborough and Bromley; Catford train stations just five minutes away. After-school clubs and learning resource centre are available until 5.30pm.

Entrance: By assessment at pre-prep, prep, 11+ exam (with prep sessions available on Saturday mornings in November to January), CE at 13; at 16+ you need seven B grades at GCSE with A grades in subjects to be studied at AS level – and a successful interview. The school is becoming more academically selective and is over-subscribed – half the intake is from the prep school.

Exit: Most pupils go to their first choice of university and 10 to 15 per cent of pupils take a gap year. At least four or five a year go to medical school, study dentistry or veterinary medicine. About the same number go to Oxbridge and the rest to top tier universities like London, Durham, Bristol, Sussex, York, Leeds and the Slade.

Money Matters: Academic, music, drama, sports and art and design scholarships at 11. Foundation (bursary) places after means testing – up to 90 per cent of fees can be awarded to households with incomes under £30,000. At sixth form a range of bursaries and scholarships are awarded at the discretion of the headmistress and head of sixth. These include a number of means tested IB scholarships, worth up to 100 per cent of tuition fees. A separate application is required for an IB scholarship. Awards are made on the basis of GCSE performance, interviews with heads of department, school report, reference from current head and examination or assessment.

Remarks: A happy co-educational school. The ethos of the IB really suits St Dunstan's. Focuses on what is best for individuals and prepares them to move into all areas of society.

St Edmund's College

Linked to Saint Edmunds Prep in the Junior section

Old Hall Green, Ware, Hertfordshire, SG11 1DS

• Pupils: 640 boys and girls of whom roughly 130 board, full, weekly, occasional • Ages: 11-19 • Size of sixth form: approx 160; about a quarter board • Roman Catholic but all faiths welcome • Fees: £12,870-£23,100 pa • Independent

Tel: 01920 824 247
Fax: 01920 823 011
Email: admissions@stedmundscollege.org
Website: www.stedmundscollege.org

Head: Since 2004, Mr Chris Long BA PGCE APDipLCE (fiftyish). Married to Nuala, ex-head of history at Alleyn's, they have two young children and live on site. Appointed as deputy head in 2001, Mr Long was made acting head and then head in 2004. Mild, genial and quietly impassioned, Mr Long is a safe pair of hands in a school which needs careful and determined upgrading if it is to take its place as a serious option for Catholics and supporters alike. Mr Long, a geographer, previously at Culford, St Benedict's and Alleyn's, has the right credentials and a sense of mission.

Academic matters: Academic results have risen substantially from an unimpressive base over the past few years. Crucially, however, this does not mean league table chasing and ratcheting up entry criteria. 'I won't ever sit and dream about the children we haven't got – we take a wider range of ability than our competitor schools and that will stay but I want a school that's buzzing with all kinds of intellectual activity – not an exam factory.' And, in fact, the school does pretty well by its intake – evidenced by its far more impressive showing in the value-added tables as measured by MidYIS and ALIS. While there is much to be done, the less starry pupils may well fare better here than at the pushier competitors.

Once B/C grades the norm at GCSE but results are steadily improving and 2010 saw the best results yet with 70 per cent A*–B and 95 per cent A*–C. A levels improving with 60 per cent A*–B in 2010. Of the major subjects, maths is strongest player and RE and biology don't slouch. Maryvale diploma in RE is well-established and recent additions include economics and business studies at AS and drama at GCSE. Girls currently outperforming boys – except, oddly, in English. Class sizes range from around 20 in lower years to 14 in GCSE years and seven in the sixth.

ICT – slammed in the 2004 inspection report – now dramatically upgraded with new three computer suites, mobile laptops and whiteboards plentiful and multiplying – along with staff training in how to use them. School now totally wireless and on three-year updating cycle. Well-stocked (a whole shelf of philosophy books) and beautifully refurbished library though on the small size in comparison with everything else. Library the main venue for imaginative book week which includes workshops and talks from writers who know their stuff. SEN supported by full-time SENCo and learning support assistant; pupils withdrawn for support in rotation as with music lessons and 'carefully monitored'. Ninety-four on SEN register at time of our visit. Individual help paid for as extra. Prospectus actually says, 'students with special educational needs and/or disabilities are welcome to apply.' EAL is important here as school takes significant numbers of international students – Bulgarians love it here – and supports them well.

Games, Options, the Arts: 440 acres to play with and games pitches surround the main buildings. Rugby is main boys' sport – about half games are won – and girls play hockey and netball on floodlit Astro with the younger years outperforming the older ones. New coaching partnership with the Saracens provides enthusiastic approach to rugby coaching for the boys. Lots else on offer including athletics and tennis on good new courts. Fitness gym has good gallery with the latest multi-gym equipment. Slimmish indoor heated pool but school's biggest asset is space, space, space. CCF compulsory in Year 9 and an option thereafter.

Music not huge here but quality is good and in this, as in so much else, plenty of room for growth. Super recital room. Drama also lively and again house loyalties important when it comes to competitions but main college hall only performance space at present. Art and DT are strong and we were impressed with the quality of the drawing we saw around the college as well as in the art rooms. Very impressive ceramics made in well-equipped studio.

Extra-curricular activities are not optional. All pupils are expected to develop their skills and interests outside the classroom. Over 60 different activities are offered.

Background and Atmosphere: 'England's oldest Catholic school' says the blurb and this will come as a surprise to many. 'How many schools can list 20 canonised saints and 133 martyrs in their old registers?' it asks. Well, this one can. Founded in 1568 when Catholic education was prohibited at home, the college started life in Douai in Flanders. Then when the Revolution had much the same effect in France, the college moved to the village of Old Hall Green just north of Ware in Hertfordshire and took over the small school there already. Part of the Old Hall (1620s) still stands and now houses the school infirmary and uniform shop. The college more or less is the village of Old Hall Green and the sense of an inclusive, self-contained community is what strikes one when walking around the extensive site with all its clusters of buildings – much of it accommodation for staff.

The A10 used to pass just beneath the college's frontage but was diverted a few years ago to half a mile away providing a view of uninterrupted fields and conversation newly unmixed with traffic growl. The five storey main house is large and imposing, with the look of the austere seminary for men and boys it once was. To one side is Pugin's splendid chapel and on the other is St Edmund's Prep, the on-site junior school, also built by Pugin. Everywhere are wide corridors and lots of rooms – many large and grand with wonderful ceilings and used for meetings, house common rooms, quiet study. Splendid refectory with monkish tables and benches and good food. 'Sometimes it even almost manages to get close to my mum's,' we were told. The sense of there being space for everyone adds greatly to the feeling of calm. The parkland stretches away on all sides and the college's position atop a gentle hill adds to the sense of seriousness and prominence lent by the building.

The seminarians left in the 1970s though one splendid specimen remains in the person of sparkly Fr Pinot de Moira who has been part of the place for more than sixty years, though you'd hardly believe it, and who still visits each new pupil at home (unannounced) just before they join the school. Girls arrived in the sixth form in 1974 and the college became co-ed throughout in 1986. The college celebrates its history and memorials of all kinds abound. The main corridor is lined with excellent pencil drawings of college buildings; in glass cases, robes worn by various popes and archbishops are reverently displayed and the grand, stone-flagged 'ambulacrum' is hung with oils of eminent college patrons opposite a Victorian frieze in good nick depicting saints and martyrs.

The college is overseen not by a specific order but by the Archdiocese of Westminster. The Roman Catholic ethos is central to life here though members of other faiths who share the values are welcome and the college had around 20 such pupils when we visited. College also has many pupils from other Christian denominations. The ISI criticised the college's curricular 'appreciation of other faiths' and, again, this has been acted on. There are prayers each morning and at the start of each lesson. Communion and evensong are held in the chapel and open to folk from outside. Its prized relic, in one of the side chapels, is a fibula from St Edmund's left leg, presented by Cardinal Wiseman in 1853.

The school years are named here. We have: Elements, Rudiments, Grammar, Syntax, Poetry and Rhetoric 1 and 2 – the sixth formers being referred to rather grandly as 'rhetoricians'. The houses, more predictably, are named after prominent Catholics. There is a pervasive sense of plainness and straightforwardness about the place, evidenced in one of the clearest, least tricky and most informative websites we have seen as well as in the excellently produced school literature.

Pastoral Care and Discipline: Zero tolerance for anyone dealing in drugs though it hasn't happened here yet. Smoking dealt with by detentions. Pastoral care universally acknowledged to be excellent and recent ISI and CSCI inspections gave unstinting praise. House system main source of pastoral care with each pupil having a tutor and head of house. Boarding exceptionally well-staffed and so many staff live in school or in the houses around the site that there is always a choice of mentors when needed. Rhetoricians cared for by head of sixth form. Bullying felt to be simply not an issue (though with a caveat that if it were an issue it would be dealt with sensitively and swiftly by the deputy head). Pupils feel confident here, 'it's very accepting of who you are,' we were told. 'You feel safer and better here.' The pupils we saw seemed relaxed and happy and we wondered whether simply having so much space to live in – wide corridors, lots of rooms, no crowding – makes for harmony of all kinds.

Boarding accommodation good – everyone in rooms for one or two and rooms are relatively spacious, well-equipped and many have good views. Common rooms and kitchens all spacious. Much refurbishment has happened but more remains to be done. There is a full programme of trips and facilities which has developed significantly since the appointment of a director of activities two years ago. No Saturday school apart from sports fixtures. Weekly and full boarding available and college has space to take quite a few more weekly boarders from roundabout without anyone feeling crowded.

Pupils and Parents: Largely day pupils bused in by excellent network of 17 different routes all over Herts but also from Finchley, Woodford and Enfield. Around 20 pupils come up from St Edmund's Prep each year into Year 7, with the rest (60) from a wide range of preps and primaries. At present 90 international students mostly from eastern Europe, nearer Europe, Africa and Asia. College also runs an international summer school and some students from this feed into main school. Some trad Catholic families used to independent education but most are first-timers and intake covers the social range. A distinguished list of Old Edmundians includes perfumiers James and Robert Floris, the sandal designer William Scholl, Battle of Britain pilot Sq Leader Jocelyn Millard, clerics Cardinal Vaughan, Dr Bruce Kent and Archbishop Derek Worlock CH, along with Mgr Ronald Knox, Sir Ralph Richardson and several notable sportsmen.

Entrance: By competitive exam at 11 in maths, English and non-verbal reasoning. Head or his deputy interviews everyone with their families. 'I never send the child out. I'm interviewing the family,' says the head. In reality, around two children apply for every place which is good odds given how many will disappear elsewhere. Preference always to Catholics and then to siblings.

Exit: Leavers mostly to Russell group with by far the greatest number to London (Imperial, Kings, UCL and Queen Mary). Few go on to the new universities and most take traditional subjects such as maths, law and economics.

Money Matters: 'Douay Academic' scholarships at 11, awarded on performance in the entrance exam. Music, art, sport and all-rounder scholarships also available at 11.

At 16+, academic scholarships are awarded by open competition using the results of a specially set exam. Music, sport and art schols may also be offered through competitive test. Reductions for siblings who attend at the same time and for Services children. Bursaries available at 11+.

Remarks: This sleeping giant has recently shown signs of stirring. Much potential and much still to be realised here.

St Edmund's School

Linked to Saint Edmund's Junior School in the Junior section

St Thomas Hill, Canterbury, Kent, CT2 8HU

• Pupils: 175 boys, 105 girls; 80 board. • Ages: Ages: 13-18. • Size of sixth form: 140 • Christian foundation but all faiths welcome. • Fees: £15,999-£24,900 pa • Independent

Tel: 01227 475 600
Fax: 01227 471 083
Email: seniorschool@stedmunds.org.uk
Website: www.stedmunds.org.uk

Head: Since 2005, Mr Jeremy Gladwin (late forties). Educated at Whitgift School, Croydon and Durham University where he read geography. Spent 15 years at Shrewsbury where he was head of geography, ran the CCF and spent seven years as a housemaster. Spent six years as deputy head of Royal Hospital School, Ipswich – came in as a 'stepping stone' and saw in the new head during his last year. Married to Nicki, they have two children, one at university and one still at St Edmund's. Approachable and welcoming. Very enthusiastic and proud of everything that is St Edmund's – academic and otherwise. Feels that beauty should be an important part of everyone's life. Well liked by parents and children – has taken great trouble to develop good communications with parents and operates an open door policy – not one to lock himself in his office, he is always out and about in the school. He teaches PSHE to some year groups so gets to know the children in the classroom. Sees himself as very much part of a team and hates hierarchy. He is leaving in the summer of 2011 to become headmaster of Bishop's Stortford College, Herts. When he announced this, some members of staff were shocked into silence – and tears – high praise indeed. New head will be Mrs Louise Moelwyn-Hughes, currently senior deputy head at the Perse School School, Cambridge.

Academic matters: A levels: 74 per cent As and Bs. A levels much improved in 2009 over 2008. GCSEs: 93 per cent pass at grades A–C. Recent introduction of IGCSE in maths and separate sciences at GCSE. Introduction in 2009 of AQA English Baccalaureate has brought new challenge to able sixth formers by adding a unit of critical thinking to A levels and a research project in their last year and includes a service element. 16/75 have opted for this. Wide range of A levels offered including psychology, music technology, PE, photography and theatre and film studies. Food technology a popular option for boys as well as girls at GCSE. Native speakers able to take GCSEs in their own languages e.g. Chinese, Russian and Polish. Little difference between performance of boys and girls in national exams.

Wide ability range – 'a private comprehensive,' as one parent put it. About 65 with some form of SEN mostly mild dyslexia, dyspraxia, Asperger's and ADHD. Good one-to-one support. One statemented pupil funded by Medway. Around 50 pupils have English as an additional language, most of whom receive help.

Good communication on curriculum matters between junior and senior schools – some teachers work across both sites. Average class size 12 with a max of 18 and smaller class sizes in lower sets. Very dedicated team of teachers. A number of staff have retired recently and new young teachers have reinvigorated the Common Room. PSHE includes careers' guidance as well as sex and relationships education.

Games, Options, the Arts: The usual mix of sports – football, hockey, cricket, netball etc. Rugby recently introduced as an option. Team games compulsory until GCSEs. More flexible in sixth form but all continue with sport. Small numbers mean that everyone has a chance to play in a team. Under 19 Kent County Cricket Lemon Cup winners 2009. County and National representation in sports ranging from hockey and cricket to martial arts and Ultimate Frisbee.

Lots of trips and outings – New York for drama, Paris for French and art, exchanges with a Polish school and visit to Auschwitz-Birkenau. Annual Middle Fifth Afloat, a four day sailing trip to the Solent – effective team building and bonding exercise always great fun even for those who thought they hated sailing. Work experience compulsory at end of Year 11.

Purpose-built music school with practice rooms, a Steinway grand piano and well equipped recording studio. About 40 per cent of pupils play an instrument. New director of music has brought a new vitality to department – very persuasive and encouraging. One or two recent pupils to Oxbridge to read music. A few pupils attend Royal Academy lessons in London and several pupils selected for National Youth Theatre and National Youth Choir. Two finalists in the Marlowe Young Musician of the Year 2009. 12+ Grade 8 students per year, 6+ at Diploma standard. Invite primary school children into school to take part in East Kent Youth Orchestra. Lots going on – a major concert each term and one in the Cathedral once a year, plus lunchtime concerts and smaller chamber concerts and an active choir and jazz choir.

Strong art department – plenty on offer, ceramics particularly impressive. Large well equipped 450 seat theatre – apparently the largest in East Kent. One major play every year and plays every term. Senior school pupils gain valuable technical experience by helping behind the scenes at junior plays. Occasionally St Edmund's productions have transferred to the Marlowe Theatre in Canterbury and to the Edinburgh Festival.

They have a lot of fun as well e.g.: St Edmund's Got Talent. Most boys and girls do CCF because it's fun – compulsory for Middle 5th (year 10).

Background and Atmosphere: Established in Yorkshire in 1749 as the Clergy Orphan School, school moved to Canterbury via London and settled in its present location in 1855. Centred on school house, an impressive ecclesiastical high Victorian building with chapel attached, set in 50 acres on St Thomas Hill overlooking the Cathedral. Most of the classrooms are in separate blocks around the campus – some quite scruffy and shabby, although plans are afoot to refurbish them – but that is not what the school is all about.

Great emphasis on good works and the wider community and St Ed's have picked up Kent awards for service to the community e.g. the school has its own Rotary Interact Group with a pupil president who coordinates all fund raising and charity work and fosters international links. St Ed's' pupils have helped paint a local primary school and have dug two ponds for Kent Wildlife Trust. They have also set up a one-to-one reading support scheme with a local primary school and adopted a beach on the Kent coast and taken responsibility for keeping it clean as well as fundraising for charities in Tanzania and Eastern Europe.

Pastoral Care and Discipline: Tight-knit community with a nurturing ethos and emphasis on developing individual talents and interests and with the aim of making education fun. One parent said, 'the school has transformed my son's life and has made him feel good about himself for the first time in his life'. The division of pupils into four houses means that everyone has a sense of belonging and children integrate well and get to know other year groups. Small classes and tutor groups mean that pupils and staff get to know each other well and even the most retiring have the chance to have their voice heard. The boarding houses are very comfortable and the lucky ones have a fine hilltop view over the city to Canterbury Cathedral. Girls all have single or twin rooms with en suite bathrooms. Younger boys are housed in dorms, older ones in single or twins with en suite bathrooms. New common rooms with Sky TV and pool tables where they can make toast and tea and where girls and boys can meet in the early evenings. Saturday school for the moment but might well be phased out within the next few years. Weekend activities organised but pupils often happy just being at school. Whole school meets in the Chapel three times a week.

Pupils and Parents: Local professional families, lots of first time buyers who are prepared to make sacrifices to send their children here – discerning parents who are interested in education but not looking for status. Very supportive bunch – good relationship with school and staff. Head takes a lot of trouble to maintain good relations with parents and have them on side – plenty of feedback about the school's work and children's progress. Various handbooks plus comprehensive website – 'Parents' Zone' keeps everyone up to date. Foreign nationals – 40 per cent of boarders – from a range of countries integrate well. Regular parents' mingling events – coffee mornings and Saturday breakfasts. Old Boys include actor Orlando Bloom, writer Lawrence Durrell, pianist Freddy Kempf and ex England cricketer Robin Jackman.

Entrance: Accept a broad range – not really selective in terms of ability but keen to take pupils who will thrive and school takes trouble to get this right. Every child interviewed and personality and character considered very important. Most children come up from the Junior School but also from local prep schools – Northbourne Park, Junior King's, increasingly from Wellesley House, Marlborough House, St Ronan's and Dulwich Prep at Cranbrook. Those from local primaries will spend two years in the prep school before transferring at 13+. About 20 a year join in sixth form, some from the grammars and some from overseas – all seem to settle in well. Sixth form entrants need 6 A*-Cs at GCSE and Bs in the subjects they wish to study at A level.

Exit: About 6–8 out of a year group of 65 leave after GCSEs mainly to grammars and sixth form colleges – mainly for financial reasons. High proportion to university or further education – a couple to Oxbridge every year plus Russell Group, former polys, art foundation courses, drama school, music conservatoires – the whole spectrum.

Money Matters: Many give up a lot to send their children here. Significant numbers receive help through bursaries and scholarships. Not a rich school – bursaries out of fee income and help is given to see children through to next set of exams. Means-tested fee concessions can be provided for children of the clergy, members of the armed forces, diplomatic service and to the third and subsequent children of the same family in the School at the same time. A foundation has recently been set up to secure scholarship and bursary funding and to fund future developments.

Remarks: Warm welcoming, nurturing school, feels like one big family where everyone has a strong sense of belonging – and not doing badly on the academic side either.

St Edward's Oxford

Woodstock Road, Oxford, Oxfordshire, OX2 7NN

• Pupils: 660; 60 per cent boys, 40 per cent girls. 80 per cent board, 20 per cent day • Ages: 13-18 • Size of sixth form: 260 • C of E • Fees: Boarding £28,659; Day £22,929 pa • Independent

Tel: 01865 319 204
Fax: 01865 319 202
Email: webmaster@stedwards.oxon.sch.uk
Website: www.stedwards.oxon.sch.uk

Warden: Since 2004, Mr Andrew Trotman MA (mid fifties). Educated at Alleyne's Grammar School, Stevenage and Balliol College, Oxford (English). Previously headmaster at St Peter's, York and also taught at Radley College, Abingdon School and the Edinburgh Academy (deputy rector). He is off to pastures new in July 2011, a new venture in the offing and one with a hint of philanthrophy but very much 'under wraps' at present. Relaxed and charming he has enjoyed his time at St Edward's being proud of many achievements including the expansion of the bursary scheme – believes that pupils on bursaries are often the best, establishment of peer support, the drive to improve academic results including the introduction of the IB. A strong advocate of co-education and passionate in maintaining the breadth of learning. He leaves the school in good shape with increasing demand in a difficult market and further development planned. Married with two grown-up children he lives across the road and, we're told, can oft be heard in the evening practising his bagpipes.

His replacement is to be Mr Stephen Jones, currently head of Dover College.

Academic matters: Make no mistake, St Edward's is changing. A concerted drive on the academic front is reflected in recent results. Described in one of the earliest guides as 'brawny not brainy' it has long been a haven for those unable to meet the high academic selection of the local boys' independents. This reputation has been slow to change but, with the rising intake bar, is one which will need to catch up with reality. Given the current intake ability the results are impressive – in 2010, 60 per cent of GCSEs were A*/A. At A level, 44 per cent of grades were A*/A and 73 per cent A*–B. The IB was introduced in 2008 and tends to attract the more able pupils. In 2010, 83 per cent achieved levels 5–7 with 25 per cent achieving an overall score of 38. Value added scores are good – pupils exceed predicted results by 10 per cent – i.e. should achieve a grade higher in each subject than expected. One parent pointed out that there should be two league tables, as the equivalent cohort at St Edward's does just as well as the highly academic local independent schools.

All the usual subjects are taken including Latin (or classical civilisation for the less able) and Greek alongside the less academic subjects of PE, DT and drama. Nine or ten GCSEs taken with the more rigourous IGCSEs taken in core subjects. No English lit GCSE. Instead, compulsory non-examined English literature plus ethics and political literacy – should be invaluable holding one's own at Oxford or elsewhere dinner parties. English lit popular and successful at A level, together with maths, sciences, history and geography but reasonably low uptake in languages (although a significant number take these to university level). Breadth of learning outside the curriculum enhanced by the scholars' societies – OX2 for lower school and The Woodstock Group for the senior students – topical/philosophical debate in a pupil led forum with all encouraged to participate. Scholars are taught in their own classes to allow adequate stretching but outstanding work or effort is praised in all pupils – a meeting with the Warden and email home to parents much appreciated. All pupils are screened on entry for learning difficulties and are assessed by an in-house educational psychologist. Currently 15 per cent of pupils receive learning support – timetabled and free of charge – 'all part of education' says the Warden – what a relief to those of us who fork out extra on top of school fees.

Games, Options, the Arts: Despite the academic drive, St Edward's remains a sporty school with fabulous facilites – 90 acres of prime north Oxford. While still winning plenty of acolades – boys' hockey was undefeated last year and girls' hockey have been national finalists three out of the past five years, it is perhaps a little more balanced than yesteryear, with 'teams for everyone' said my guides who seemed to think that a non-sporty boy or girl would be at home here – 'and there's always art, drama and music'. Esporta sports centre – the hub of middle class Oxford mummies working off their lunches – is shared with, and leased from, the school providing a fantastic gym, indoor and outdoor pools, indoor tennis courts and fitness and dance studios. Pupils have their own entrance and exclusive sessions. Add to that outdoor courts, cricket pitches, a new cricket pavilion and a 9 hole golf course ...oh, and a boat house futher up the river. Even that non-sporty boy or girl may be tempted.

Art is fabulous and with excellent results especially at A level. Look out for a teetering column of pottery cups and saucers which my guides assured me was indestructable. Oodles of space and equipment including facilities for jewellery making, ceramics and large fine art displays. The school acquired the North Wall Arts Centre which boasts exhibition galleries, drama studios and an amazing 250 seat theatre – originally built in a Victorian swimming pool, the seating, tiered within the 'pool' can be arranged to suit the production. The North Wall is enjoyed by the local community and hosts visiting artists and theatre groups.

Music is undergoing a transformation. The latest addition to the school is the former Lemon Tree restaurant next door which, as we go to press, is being converted into a rehearsal space and practice rooms. Music not terribly popular at A level or GCSE but nevertheless gets good results. Over 400 timetabled music lessons per week over a huge range of instruments. St Edward's singers involves parents and the community who join together to form an impressive choir performing twice a year. Drama is much praised by parents. 'Fantastic facilities and impressive school plays.' One current pupil now a principal actor in the cult television series,'Skins'. Excellent extra-curricular provision with Duke of Edinburgh and CCF popular. In the first year (Shell) the 'circus' offers the opportunity to try an enormous variety of activities which continues well into the evening – no teens in front of playstations/facebook here.

Background and Atmosphere: St Edward's (known as Teddies) is broad both in academic intake and philosophy.

Less grand than its public school contemparies it incorporates 20 per cent day pupils who are fully integrated into the school – 'we often can't tell who is day and who boards,' say pupils. Co-ed for well over a decade the girls make up 40 per cent of pupils and seem relaxed and confident in their minority role. Situated in leafy north Oxford the setting is privileged indeed. Much akin to an Oxford college the main buildings surround a lawned quad. The site has been developed and facilities improved including a eco-inspired life sciences building – solar powered with 'more technology than you could wish for' housing the science labs. IT everywhere, interactive whiteboards and computer rooms in every block and staff make full use of electronic teaching. Simple peaceful chapel – compulsory on Sundays for boarders and although C of E all faiths participate. Music is currently the recipient of new facilites but next on the wish list is refurbishment of modern language facilities.

Boarding houses are Quad side or Field side (two sites connected by private underpass beneath the Woodstock Road) each with their own feel. Carpeted corridors and simple but homely rooms. Share three to a room lower down the school and single study bedrooms for sixth form. Unusually day pupils have a bed in the boarding houses and often stay over if they're too busy to go home. A long day for day pupils until 9pm so that they can fully participate although there has been some relaxation on this – parents can request an ad hoc early finish at 6pm. 'Day pupils are important to us. They are often the most academic (this is Oxford after all) and they provide valuable links through their parents to the university.' Day parents' support highly valued.

Pastoral Care and Discipline: Highly praised in latest inspection report – 'outstanding'. Peer support introduced under current head. Fines for smoking on a sliding scale according to number of times caught though some parents feel the fines are not high enough. Alcohol a perennial problem with teens but head is absolute that he will pusue any institution that has sold alcohol to a pupil, involving the police if necessary. Drugs – out, no question and if a pupil is in the company of another with drugs, they're out too. Election of prefects is meritocratic – each hopeful applies with a CV and undergoes shortlisting and two rounds of interviews plus a vote from the pupils – 'we've worked hard for these badges and we wear them with pride.' Cohesive boarding houses provides support for the pupils and fosters inter-year friendships. Many staff live in in addition to the housemasters/mistresses. Pupils can go into Summertown and into Oxford at the weekend. Curfew at 11pm for sixth form – no clubbing then. Cheese and biscuits with the housemaster/mistress on return in the evening provides a homely touch.

Pupils and Parents: A local reputation for privilege and from time to time pushing the boundaries – Teddies' girls in particular, yet the pupils we met were grounded and down to earth. Yes, of course, as with any public school, the parents are affluent – second and third homes abound, some parents say. Yet this has its upside 'I've had lots of lovely free holidays,' said one pupil. A sizeable number on bursaries 'often the most able' says Warden and these pupils fully integrate and are not made to feel inadequate. Parents a mix of academics, professionals and business. Nine per cent from overseas from a huge variety of countries. Only four pupils needing English tuition. Most boarders are from London and the South East and most day pupils from the Dragon. Notable former pupils include Laurence Olivier, Jon Snow and Kenneth Grahame.

Entrance: The bar is rising. CE now expected to be 55 per cent and likely to rise further. Non CE candidates take the school's own exam. A handful sit an exam at 11+ in order to guarantee a place. In a drive to attract the brightest, new scholarships have been introduced – see below. Outreach programme – academic challenge day for local Year 6 pupils who can take part in a day of philosophy, Arabic, economics, architecture and politics to spot scholarship potential and encourage applications.

Exit: Huge number of courses undertaken – no clones at this school. Geography, engineering of all sorts and modern languages popular. Eight per cent to Oxbridge. Popular destinations include Manchester, Leeds, Newcastle, Durham and London Imperial.

Money Matters: Recent expansion in scholarship provision in line with drive to improve academic standards. 'Attracting bright pupils is good for the school, good for the teachers and good for results.' At 13+ entry two academic scholarships of 50 per cent fees and two of 25 per cent plus six for 10 per cent. All pupils are considered anually for promotion into a scholarship. At 16+, academic schols for 10 per cent and exhibitions for 5 per cent. At 13+ and 16+, music, all rounder, art, drama and dance and sports schols for 10 and 5 per cent.

All academic and sports scholarships can be means tested to a maximum of 100 per cent.

Remarks: All round broad education with plenty of nurturing. 'They bring you up a notch on all fronts,' said a pupil. Good for self-esteem. A school on a mission to drive academic standards up – get in quick before it's too selective.

Saint Felix School

Linked to Saint Felix School Junior School in the Junior section

Halesworth Road, Reydon, Southwold, Suffolk, IP18 6SD

• Pupils: 260 boys and girls; 95 boarders • Ages: 11-18 • Size of sixth form: 70 • Non-denom • Fees: £12,900-£22,800 pa • Independent

Tel: 01502 722 175
Fax: 01502 722 641
Email: schooladmin@stfelix.suffolk.sch.uk
Website: www.stfelix.co.uk

Head: Since 2004, Mr David Ward (late forties). Taught DT at Kimbolton then deputy at Cokethorpe. An ex-rugby international and an immensely practical man who's fulfilling a lifelong ambition to be a head. Has worked tirelessly to get the school back onto terra firma (bumpy patch before his appointment) and make it fully co-educational. In between breathless promotion he bubbles with inventive ways to get things done including 'sponsor a window' scheme to restore some of the school's 1,000 windows. Present goals are to expand boarding provision and meet high expectations – 'good isn't enough, I want excellence'. Definitely not an ogre – parents see him as optimistic, affable, approachable. According to a pupil, 'nothing seems to faze him.'

A committed Christian. He and physio wife Jane, often seen around the place with watering can in hand, have two daughters at the school. Finds anything outdoorsy, including taking his girls riding or walking Digby the black lab, a perfect way to unwind at the end of the day.

Academic matters: Mixed ability intake and dedicated staff who encourage rather than wield the stick. Small, sometimes tiny teaching groups (especially in the sixth) and above average value-added. Three stage science for the more able and alongside German and Spanish the option of taking Latin. All study French up to Year 11 either in conversation (two native speakers on the staff) or for GCSE. 82 per cent got 5+ GCSE grades at A*–C in 2010. At A level 72 per cent A*–C. No Saturday school but lessons finish at 5pm every day except Friday (4pm).

For those who find the going tough, good support from the maths department. SENCo now full time and qualified (dyslexia specific). Learning support is now delivered in a number of key ways: advice and planning with class/subject teachers, teaching assistance within the mainstream classroom, small group teaching and one-to-one individual lessons. 'Parents are fully consulted and are often involved in helping to set out individual education plans for their child.' SENCo charged with getting the staff up to speed on anything needs-related, she works with two part-time classroom assistants.

Games, Options, the Arts: All appreciate the sporting provision. Weekday fixtures give pupils the chance to play for local clubs at the weekend. No hockey for the boys but all the other majors with a wider range of options for the sixth. Generous modern sports hall, swimming pool, fitness suite and squash courts – also used by parents and the local community. Swimming is a big thing – 'our son hated the water but they taught him to swim and laugh,' enthused a mum. Two coaches (one GB) work with elite, youth, junior and development squads, which includes children from other schools, state and private. Swimmers take part in county and national championships and hold a number of county and national times. Pupils can train as life guards and if they wish work for the school – 'a good way to earn a bit of pocket money especially if they're boarders.' Extra-curricular activities cater for a variety of tastes – sailing, canoeing, climbing wall (very popular), CCF, D of E, sewing, cookery.

Displays of interesting photographic images and cheerful artwork (created in the north-lit, spacious studio) are everywhere – stuck to corridor walls or perched on ledges. Popular drama department puts on at least one good, serious play a year. Inclusive approach gets almost all involved – if not in the limelight, back stage or making props. 'Caring' head of music. Just under half the pupils learn an instrument. Oodles of practice rooms.

Background and Atmosphere: Queen Anne-style purpose-built redbrick buildings dating from 1897 plus well-crafted modern additions are set in a breezily expansive site a brisk walk away from the quaintly old fashioned seaside town of Southwold. Originally a school for genteel girls. Come the late 1990s a new direction was needed and it's now fully co-ed with numbers on the up. Pleasant, positive atmosphere. Essentially a day school with a growing dollop of flexi and full time boarders – the majority of whom are in the sixth. Politeness and courtesy are encouraged – the head believes manners and academia go hand in hand. Girls are well turned out and charmingly friendly – as yet boys aren't as polished but the girls appreciate their sense of fun.

Classrooms are a trifle lacklustre but the Scandinavian-style wood-clad dining hall, which offers standard fare plus chirpy bonhomie, is inviting. The library has been given a preliminary facelift with the introduction of squishy sofas and the removal of tired tomes but shelves are crying out for new books to fill the gaps.

Pastoral Care and Discipline: Everyone knows everyone and the school really scores when it comes to confidence-building. Consideration for others is encouraged and problems are dealt with promptly and sympathetically. The deputy (who's been there for ever and remembers teaching some of the present cohort of mothers) isn't someone to cross – 'she's a real role model and gets lots of respect.' Kindly house mistress keeps a weather eye on sixth form boarders.

Pupils and Parents: Active PTA and supportive parent body. All sorts from entrepreneurs to old brigade who remember when cucumber sandwiches had no crusts. Largely from north Suffolk, south Norfolk and the A12 corridor. School has organised an impressively comprehensive bus service to cover the wide catchment area. Significant number of overseas students (mainly from the Pacific rim) in the sixth form.

Entrance: At 11 and 13+. Not difficult but signs of sifting as numbers grow – progression from the junior to senior school isn't guaranteed. Two day entrance procedure for outside applicants – behaviour and academic ability are assessed. For the sixth, five A-Cs with B or above in subjects taken at A level. Interviews for outside applicants.

Exit: Variety of courses with a smattering of top universities.

Money Matters: For entrants 11–16 academic, performing arts, music, tennis and swimming scholarships (up to 50 per cent) and exhibitions (up to 25 per cent). For sixth form entrants academic, music, sport, art and drama scholarships. Bursaries in cases of need. Services discount.

Remarks: The head has succeeded in getting the school back on track and is moving it forward. Friendly, not overly pushy place giving an all round education – suitable for those who might flounder in a larger pond.

St George's School (Ascot)

Wells Lane, Ascot, Berkshire, SL5 7DZ

• Pupils: 280 girls • Ages: 11-18 • Size of sixth form: 80 • C of E • Fees: Day 17,985; Boarding £27,675 pa • Independent

Tel: 01344 629 900
Fax: 01344 629 901
Email: rlloyd@stgeorges-ascot.org.uk
Website: www.stgeorges-ascot.org.uk

Headmistress: Since 2005, Mrs Caroline Jordan MA PGCE. Educated at St Helen and St Katharine, she went on to St Edmund Hall, Oxford to read earth sciences. After a period of running her own business, she took her PGCE at Manchester University before taking her first teaching job at Wycombe Abbey. Ten years later she left there for St George's, having taught both physics and chemistry. She gained boarding experience as a housemistress and latterly joined senior management as head of sixth form and deputy senior housemistress. Married with one son.

Academic matters: In 2010, 100 per cent pass rate at A level and 81 per cent A*–B at GCSE. Single sciences for those who are capable but double for the weaker brethren. Maths 'surprisingly good,' said the last head, 'and popular'. Various languages on offer and school helps foreign nationals take exams in their own language which boosts results of course!

Personal laptops can be connected to the system. Keyboarding skills are important here and girls get CLAIT and RSA qualifications.

EFL and good dyslexia/dyspraxia cover plus study skills for all, provided by the Helen Arkell Centre.

Games, Options, the Arts: Art, textile and design strong as ever. Super fashion and rather natty corsets on show in the entrance to the art block. Fabulous music, joined-up concerts with Eton (popular), lots of own CDs, masses of instruments – and lessons can be arranged for any instrument. Drama and public speaking popular with regular awards for the former, LAMDA exams. Photography popular, own dark room.

Thirty acre campus, multi-purpose building – very versatile – the hall can be used as a lecture theatre, auditorium, dance floor and for exams. Funds from the sale of Queen's Hill paid for the stunning sports hall, with enviable dance and fitness centre (indoor swimming pool is next on the agenda). Games important here, especially lacrosse and tennis.

Background and Atmosphere: Founded in 1877 as a boys' prep school and converted to girls at the turn of the century. This is rhodie-land. Mega rebuild following sale of Queen's Hill, with purpose-built dorms, and classrooms – incredibly narrow claustrophobic staircases and passages everywhere – single file only. Guides said careers advice and university suggestions tiptop.

There is a certain amount of B&B (currently £55 per night) and flexi-boarding on offer. Day boarders often move to becoming real boarders further up the school. Boarders move from dorms of six/four to dorms of one or two (always called dorms even if it's only one). Common rooms, pay phones (mobiles OK but only in dorms) and kitchens for each year group. Sixth formers can take driving lessons and go out one night a week. Increased privileges come with age, no uniform in sixth – though our guides were wearing very smart black suits (skirt or trousers à choix), plus trips to Windsor (Eton next door) etc. Cookery club popular and sixth formers often cook their own supper.

No timetabled lessons on Saturdays, but all girls start with an hour's prep, juniors then do games, riding, drama lessons and, with the exception of four closed weekends a term, can go out from lunch time on Saturday till Sunday evening. Complaints that there was 'not enough to do' at weekends were refuted by our guides who said there was masses to do, lots of activities organised by the girl-led school council.

Pastoral Care and Discipline: Good pastoral care via house and prefectorial system; day girls are assigned to boarding houses where they have work stations surprisingly cocooned off from each other with gloomy grey screens. Shadows for first year pupils, form deputies and year tutors for all; all girls have a personal tutor and the sixth formers choose a director of studies. School operates school code, enforced on the seven deadly sins – 'girls are in big trouble' if they get involved with drugs, sex (boys in bedrooms), booze, fags, bullying, going out without permission, or theft. 'Straight out' for drugs; fags = chores, fine and gating; booze ditto and contract, strong bullying policy and 'quick follow-up'.

Pupils and Parents: From the south, increasing number from London and masses from further afield, around eight or nine per cent foreigners. Some first time buyers.

Entrance: From lots of different schools – basically the toffs' prep schools: Coworth-Flexlands, Upton House, Windsor, Maltman's, Garden House, Pembridge Hall, Thomas's etc plus local primary schools. CE at 11 and 13, pass mark 50/55 per cent plus previous head's report. Plus interview. Sixth form entry, standard six GCSEs at A*–C. B or above recommended for A level subjects.

Exit: A few do leave after GCSE, going to Wellington, Stowe, Bradfield or sixth form colleges, otherwise 98 per cent to tertiary education. Small tranche to Oxbridge.

Money Matters: Academic, art and music scholarships on offer at 11; academic, art, drama, music and sport at 13 and 16; which can be further means-tested, plus bursarial help (means-tested annually) for those already in the school.

Remarks: School increasingly popular locally (i.e. day boarders), good for the less academic, with impressive results. Arguably, still a bit Sloane.

St George's College, Weybridge

Weybridge Road, Addlestone, Surrey, KT15 2QS

• Pupils: 890 all day • Ages: 11-18 • Size of sixth form: 215 • RC but others welcome • Fees: £12,435-£14,310 pa • Independent

Tel: 01932 839 300
Fax: 01932 839 301
Email: contact@st-georges-college.co.uk
Website: www.st-georges-college.co.uk

Headmaster: Since 1994, Mr Joseph Peake (fifties), educated at Oxford (degree in chemistry), previously director of curriculum at Millfield and taught at Manchester Grammar School. Married, with three children who have been through the school. Having been a chief examiner in A level chemistry and chairman of SHMIS (Society of Headmasters and Headmistresses of Independent Schools), he is now chairman of the Catholic Independent Schools Conference and a member of the Independent Schools' Governing Council. A strong leader, sits erect and upright, knows what he is doing is right and knows exactly what he expects from his staff and pupils. Very confident and hugely ambitious for the school (particularly to make it more academically selective), 'I want us to be the best in the country, an exemplary Christian role model for a 21st century co-ed school.' Parents generally speak well of him – 'he is doing a great job – we don't see enough of him because he is so busy'. Some niggles about him being 'self-assured' and 'somewhat intimidating'. When asked to describe himself, he says he is 'still enjoying life to the full'.

Academic matters: Solid. Caters for most abilities with noticeably improving exam results (67 per cent A*/A GCSE), but not a real academic powerhouse (although one feels Mr Peake would like it be). Academia has (rightly or wrongly) always been perceived as secondary to the stunning sporting/extra-curricular side of the school but the academic souls do get some very good results and Mr Peake is obviously on a mission for the school to rise up the academic league tables. Pupils are setted in maths and French from Year 1. Latin is also taught from Year 1. ICT taught in the first three years with the additional option of ECDL (European Computer Driving Licence – a certificate to verify computer skills and competence. Max class size 22; bright, quite large classrooms – some in need of modernisation. Library well equipped and ICT has recently been improved. Academic support is provided for those with mild dyslexia and dyspraxia – one dedicated teacher. However, check thoroughly before applying whether the school would be right for a SEN pupil. Mr Peake says, 'we do not face issues with academic support since our entrance exams are so highly selective. About 25 students (three per cent) receive extra help and they have been able to pass the entrance exams'.

Games, Options, the Arts: Much praised in all areas. A sporty soul's delight particularly for tennis, hockey and rowing. Tennis facilities are mega impressive – jaw-droppingly extensive courts the envy of any school. Rowing is also high profile. Huge grounds, lots of pitches, the school oozes sport (though very surprising that no swimming pool). National and regional sports cups and awards ad infinitum, and justifiably proud of its sporting achievements. Not the ideal school for couch potatoes or those only able to bumble around on the sidelines but the glowing example of others might gee them up. Music is another strength (much praised music department), one deputy head boy from the recent past snapped up an organ scholarship to Cambridge. New theatre just completed. Drama productions are 'amazing' according to a happy parent. Art department – excellent facilities and about 40 per cent take GCSE art. Extra-curricular – a vast range from the usual to the more unusual e.g. African drumming, public speaking, video club and Scrabble.

Background and Atmosphere: School originally opened by the congregation of Josephites in Croydon in 1869. Moved to its present breathtaking 100 acre site in 1884 and continued to be primarily a boarding school for RC boys until 1992 when it became a day school. Has become fully co-ed (with 40 per cent girls) and increased in size dramatically within the last 10 years. Multi-million development is on the cards including replacing some of the 'shabby' classrooms. A new centre for drama and a water-based Astroturf pitch have been opened recently. Mr Peake's aspirations come to the fore again with his aim 'to have top-class facilities, the best in the country'. School day starts at 8.40am and ends at 4pm, but pupils can be dropped off from 8am and clubs tend to go on till quite late – useful for working parents. RC ethos is paramount (although 50 per cent of pupils are not Catholic). Mr Peake is the first to admit that families from other faiths might feel fazed by the RC influence of the school. He does, however, encourage an atmosphere where the pupils learn tolerance. 'A very real environment. I could not be happier with the school,' commented a mother.

Pastoral Care and Discipline: It is a large school on a very large site and 'not for the faint hearted!' says one parent. However, much parental praise for pastoral care and nurturing atmosphere, 'although my child's tutor is not the greatest, I am quite enamoured by the teachers' carousel system.' Strict rules when it comes to discipline. Detentions seem to be handed out on a regular basis. The head has no problem admitting that he expelled four children from the sixth form. Has no tolerance of drugs and drinking. Smoking seems to be less of a problem – perhaps these sporty teenagers are more aware of health risks. Bullying has raised its head but has always been swiftly stamped out.

Pupils and Parents: Almost all Christian, white and middle class. Quite a few American and Irish. Pupils smart yet stress-free – some imaginative hair styles and slightly relaxed ties but not messy by any means. School says parents include those who 'work in the City' and 'high achievers'. OBs and OGs include Lisa Tarbuck and Sir Clive Sinclair.

Entrance: Entrance exam at 11, many come via their own junior school. At age 13 feeder schools include Bishopsgate, Cranmore, Feltonfleet, Hall Grove, Hoebridge, Lambrook-Haileybury, Ripley Court, St Andrew's Woking, St John's Beaumont and St George's Windsor Castle. Pre-testing is required for entry at age 13. Entrants at 16 must achieve specified GCSE grades.

Exit: Around 10 per cent leave at 16, usually to various sixth form colleges. Those who stay on go to a variety of universities, including Leeds, Warwick, Oxford Brookes and Loughborough, with four or five a year to Oxbridge and a large percentage to Russell Group.

Money Matters: Academic, music, art, drama and sport scholarships for entry at 11, 13 and 16 ranging from 10 to 25 per cent. Lunch and a number of clubs are not included in the fees, neither are academic support lessons; a direct debit system is available though!

Remarks: An all-round school with a very strong RC ethos (though 50 per cent non-RC pupils). Head on a mission to raise the profile of the school, academically and otherwise.

St George's School (Edinburgh)

Linked to Saint Georges Junior School in the Junior section

Garscube Terrace, Edinburgh, EH12 6BG

• Pupils: 790 Day, 60 Boarding • Ages: 2-18 • Size of sixth form: 190
• Non-denom • Fees: Secondary £9,705-£10,860; Boarding +£11,175 pa
• Independent

Tel: 0131 311 8000
Fax: 0131 311 8120
Email: admissions@st-georges.edin.sch.uk
Website: www.st-georges.edin.sch.uk

Head: Since 2010, Mrs Anne Everest BA, (fiftyish), a classicist. Originally a Yorkshire lass, she has lived in Scotland for 30 years and taken the Scottish education system on board. Formerly deputy head of Robert Gordon's College, Aberdeen (qv) and head of St Margaret's School, Aberdeen (qv) for the past 3 years. Mrs Everest was educated at St Mary's Grammar School in Hull and taught classics and ancient history at Beverley High School for Girls in her native Yorkshire. She lectured in ancient history, Latin and new testament Greek at her alma mater, Hull Uni. Married 'very early' to a husband in oil, she 'had three babies instead of finishing a PhD' (on Cicero and his women – Latin and women's education seems a recurrent theme), taking six years out before returning to Aberdeen as acting head of classics at St Margaret's in 1991.

Academic matters: School no longer narrowly academic, the courses are much broader, with girls taking units of Intermediate I and II, as well as following the English or the Scottish system as appropriate. A choice might therefore be Standard Grades, followed by a unit or two of Intermediate in lower sixth (Intermediate studies incorporate a much wider range of options than the regular exams) as well as Highers, followed by further Highers or Advanced Highers. Again extra Intermediates can be added in the Upper Sixth (geddit?). Equally, girls can opt for the English system after Standard Grades and switch between Highers and Advanced Highers, and ASs and A2s. Oodles of As and Credit 1s in both disciplines, and 'lots of flexibility' in course selection. School employs VLE – Virtual Learning Environment – to allow students to access course work, collect work or refer to notes provided by staff online. Top school in Scotland for A Levels and Advanced Highers.

Pupils help with scientific research with the universities, share seminars with staff and undergraduates and take part in an impressive outreach programme which encompasses both the academic and the appreciation of the wider world. No particular bias – English, maths, languages, the sciences and the humanities all outstanding. The very popular Chinese centre has girls studying Mandarin and parents enthusiastically join in too; but otherwise French, German and Spanish make up the modern language options, though the school boasts some 36 languages spoken. Good general studies and careers advice. Joint seminars in a plethora of subjects with an eclectic collection of schools, the state sector as well as other independents (in all disciplines: sport and music as well as academia).

Comprehensive learning support, pick up early, can deal with most of the dys-strata and ADHD; SENCo on site, plus rash of assistants. Drop-in centre for instant problem solving. School not totally wheelchair friendly but will make allowances and change class rooms if necessary.

School is split into three distinct departments – Junior, which encompasses the Nursery, Lower (where Mrs Everest has her office) and Upper. Good learning support throughout, four specialist teachers in all. Small ESOL department to help with non-nationals.

NB league tables are meaningless in this school, given that two systems are followed.

Games, Options, the Arts: Fabulous Centenary sports hall with imaginative viewing area over hall and squash courts; much used lacrosse pitches (recently upgraded) plus a brand new floodlit all-weather pitch, all trad games played with a vengeance. Recently embarked on a tennis academy (with Merchiston Castle School) where future Scottish tennis champions need not be disadvantaged. Magical Robertson Music Centre houses untold numbers of choirs, ensembles, three orchestras, over 600 musicians. Vibrant art department, plus pottery, textiles, sculpture et al. Drama and theatre good. D of E popular, as is CCF – no longer with Merchiston – the girls wage their own wars; sixth formers join forces with Merchiston for sport, art, music etc. Zillions of after-school clubs that offer everything from keyboarding to extra IT. School has a global outlook with girls as young as 13 whizzing off to spend a month or so in Canada, Chile wherever.

Background and Atmosphere: Founded in 1888, St George's is Edinburgh's foremost school for girls. Purpose-built 1912 complex, much altered and expanded, is still home to the school. Long corridors with classrooms but also fab recent add-ons. Lower school now in converted earlier boarding house; primary school much expanded and classrooms totally refurbished late 2005. Stunning dining hall (exit bridge known as Bridget) with entertainment area below has released valuable space for extra libraries and study areas. Parents can (and do) use the dining centre as a coffee shop. Magical new extension too, for the Junior School, complete with dance studio, cantilevered out, with bungee surface below, much used for get-togethers for more senior pupils as well as providing a useful undercover play area for tinies. Enterprise Centre houses a working RBS branch, 90 current accounts currently, girls can pay money in but need to go to a 'proper' bank to take it out.

Pupils have a purposeful air, mufti in sixth form. Skirts incredibly short. Boarders occupy a couple of converted Edwardian mansions with a purpose-built bungalow for sixth formers, singles and twins, all very jolly, lots of extra activities though latest Inspectors' report says they could do more at weekends – programme of events looked pretty busy to me. Long-running romance with the Edinburgh Academy fractured by EA's decision to go co-ed though school tells us that links with Merchiston Castle are still very much still alive!

Pastoral Care and Discipline: Miscreants are given very heavy hints that they 'move elsewhere'. 'No need to break out, this is a liberal environment.' 'No sniff of drugs.' Good PSE, positive behaviour policy which incorporates the best of human rights legislation.

Pupils and Parents: Boarders from the Highlands and Islands and from the Borders; some from 'abroad', links and exchanges with schools over four continents. Otherwise, good straight Scots parents, some with Charlotte Ranger background, incomers and some first time buyers. Unashamedly elitist, lots of parent/pupil forums – on every subject under the sun; Friends of St George's for social events.

Entrance: Selective. Interview via nursery and elsewhere at four and a half. Otherwise, assessment, school report and interview. Entry to sixth form is more or less automatic for home-grown pupils; external pupils by interview and school report. Demands on Sixth Form places very heavy.

Exit: Usual (but rare) trickle down south at 8 and 13, a few leave after GCSE/Standard grade to go co-ed; otherwise gap, degrees, and higher education of all sorts – Scottish law popular, as are the sciences and medicine. Around 50 per cent opt for Scottish universities, Aberdeen, St Andrew's plus Edinburgh and Glasgow.

Money Matters: Means tested bursary scheme now replaces assisted places; 'mustn't let the really bright down'. Sibling discounts. Joint discount with Merchiston Castle School.

Remarks: The top girls' school in Scotland, particularly in the academic field; much more liberal than previously and offering a broad sweep of academe – the main building still looks archaic but this is not a school to judge by its exterior.

At regular intervals this editor is asked for advice by parents who have had their little darlings here since they were three and are looking for a change of scene post-Standard grades (teenagers being what they are) and we have to say that, in all honesty, if it is a change of scene they need then they must go South, for there is nowhere in Scotland that can hold a candle to St George's, be it in the realm of academe or of global awareness.

St George's School (Harpenden)

Sun Lane, Harpenden, Hertfordshire, AL5 4EY

• Pupils: 1,315 boys and girls (including 130 boarders) • Ages: 11-18 • Size of sixth form: 370 • Non-denom Christian • Fees: Boarding £9,900 pa; Day – free • State

Tel: 01582 765 477
Fax: 01582 469 830
Email: admin@stgeorges.herts.sch.uk
Website: www.stgeorges.herts.sch.uk

Headmaster: Since 1988, Mr Norman F Hoare OBE MA. A historian, married to a PE teacher, with two sons who attended St George's and are now in the police and teaching. Kind and sincere, Mr Hoare is determined to provide chances for all in a school based on Christian principles and traditional values. He has an impressive educational CV as a founder member and former chairman of STABIS (now the State Boarding Association), a former chairman of the Boarding Schools Association ('a glorious period in my career,' he says) and a governor of Welbeck College (Quad Services sixth form college) and holds an OBE for Services to Education. These days, though, tries to avoid too many commitments outside school because his work is cut out overseeing the large school and completing a £7.5m refurbishment and, in any case, he 'misses the day-to-day interaction with the pupils – standing in the dining hall on a wet and cold February lunchtime you see how the school family really works together – it's such a pleasure'. Parents value his 'good-humoured praise and encouragement,' and describe him as 'a great head at the heart of a great community'.

Academic matters: As a high-performing, yet totally non-selective, comprehensive, school, value-added is the watchword at St George's. Whatever their merits on arrival, more than 98 per cent of St George's students leave with five A*-Cs at GCSE, and up to 90 per cent with a clutch of top-grade A levels opening the door to university. 'It's hard to exceed that because after all we are an all ability school,' says the head, but he puts this success down to 'dynamic teaching staff who want to teach, and children who want to learn', backed up by a supportive faith-based family environment arranged in houses, which are 'schools within a school'.

A marked absence of pressure, so no early GCSE and AS entry. 'School should be a fulfilling experience, not a race for examination results,' says the head, who eschews students collecting exam passes 'like postage stamps' and instead recommends whole-hearted participation in sport, drama and art and time spent on charity and community work.

Ofsted inspectors recently judged the school 'outstanding' in all categories and, in Key Stages 3 and 4, students from every level of prior attainment – including both genders, all ethnic groups, day students, and boarders – now exceed the result expected of similar students nationally. Any former inequalities between subject departments have now been ironed out so that the head is confident St George's offers the same high standard of teaching whatever the student's choice of subjects. Year 7 is taught in mixed ability groups although setting kicks in after the first three months. French is taught from Year 7 with German offered the following year. English and history are both successful options at A level and the vast majority of maths takers come out with an A or a B. A Level theatre studies and music technology also popular.

Careful analysis of children's needs and strategies to help, even if only short term. Learning Support ranges from extra spellings to a tailor-made timetable. Christian ethos means 'there's no stigma to having a learning challenge here,' says the head, 'everyone is valuable'. More than a quarter of pupils are identified as gifted and talented and they are extended both inside and outside the curriculum with Science Olympiads and Maths Challenges, for example, and the school's re-designation as a Technology College and the award of a second specialism in languages has meant more support for pupils completing controlled assessment and preparing for exams. Parents impressed by the teachers' extra revision sessions and their capacity to mark as much extra work as the students can churn out.

The International School Status – thanks to pioneering cultural and educational exchanges with China – develops pupils' cultural awareness and their Mandarin.

Games, Options, the Arts: Rugby is the main sport for boys and lacrosse for girls – this is the only maintained school in the south of England to play lacrosse so all fixtures are against independent girls' schools – and St George's has turned out some fine lacrosse teachers.

Cricket, netball, rounders, basketball, tennis and athletics are popular and, in common with the many other activities on offer – such as cross-country, football, chess, art, drama, music, dance and sailing – there is some healthy competition between the school's long-established houses. The annual inter-house music competition shows off the best musical talent and there is a range of choirs, orchestra, jazz and wind bands. A major drama production every year and smaller events. 100+ clubs and societies and more for boarders. CCF is well attended. World Challenge Expeditions to Madagascar, Argentina, India and Mongolia and the connection between St George's and Gansu Province, China, has seen exchange trips and a visit by a small team led by the head to lecture at the University of Beijing.

Background and Atmosphere: 'St George's is like an orange,' says the head, 'the school is in segments, and the skin holding it all together is our Christian foundation. We do all we can to keep that interior together.' Founded 1907 by the Rev Cecil Grant, St George's is a non-denominational Christian foundation with its own Anglican Chaplain and Sunday chapel taking place every week – all pupils, day and boarding must attend at least three a term as an requirement of being awarded a place. Many come as families to swell congregations to a maximum of 400. It is one of the longest established fully co-educational independent boarding schools in England and, in 1965, it became voluntary aided. The school has retained many historic connections and traditions, and, while some may see them as idiosyncratic in the modern age of state schooling, pupils at St George's genuinely love them. 'They revel in the house competitions, the formality of chapel, speech days, commendations, and all the different ties awarded,' says the head. 'We try to encourage individuality, which is part of our ethos and Christian belief.'

The original buildings, in a leafy lane on the edge of the modern commuter town of Harpenden, date back to the 1880s and are in the Victorian Gothic style, but there have been various extensions and additions, particularly over the past decade or so and more recently with the recently completed £7.5m refurbishment programme. 'It's a constant battle to maintain the site and attract as much support for the school, which is still short of adequate specialist accommodation,' explains the head.

As a Voluntary Aided School, St George's buildings are owned by the school's Foundation, which has to find 10 per cent of the cost of all capital projects and on-going building maintenance from very limited funds. 'There is a lot of do-it-yourself work here,' reports the head who enlists the assistance of parents, who give willingly of their time, skills and knowledge – and also cash.

State-of-the-art technology centre, drama studio and several computer suites around the campus and those top-notch facilities have recently been joined by a new languages block and sports hall. Work is underway on the refurbishment of the science labs. A new music department and sixth form computer study area opened in 2010 with parents' fund raising and support from the Foundation. Despite the necessity of this upgrading, the landscape at St George's is very peaceful and welcoming. Pupils are credited with the flower planting that is everywhere and the thriving vegetable garden – a gardening club is run by a parent with a passion. 'Quality of life here is important,' says the head. 'Children feel safe and valued, and they have fun.'

Pastoral Care and Discipline: Parents choose St George's for its 'traditional values and caring Christian ethos' and the school is built on a system of praise and reward that recognises students who demonstrate the school's core values of courtesy, integrity, manners and good discipline. Parents support these values wholeheartedly, along with the discipline policy for those who transgress on rare occasions. The four houses give the school its shape and these are presided over by a head of house, assistant and a team of tutors for a close-knit family feel. Tutor groups arranged in lower, middle and upper school groups give students time to develop a rapport with the member of staff responsible for them. Such close attention leaves very little room for bad behaviour and a well-supervised site means truanting is extremely difficult to pull off.

Pupils and Parents: Harpenden and environs provides the majority of St George's day pupils, with the addition of boarders mainly from overseas. According to the head, any child of a Christian faith who is prepared to try hard and be fully involved in the St George's lifestyle will thrive at the school. The head describes the parent body as 'articulate', which sounds like a euphemism, and certainly there is a definite parental contact procedure to prevent the teaching staff from being inundated. Parents demonstrate their loyalty to the school at fund-raising times and it is not unusual to see over 100 parents on the touch-line at sporting events. Sunday services are very well attended by families, as is the termly Catholic mass held by the local monsignor, who brings his parish to join with those of other faiths at the school. Parents from different Christian churches also preach at family services. Families are kept informed thanks to regular contact from staff and the head's traditional end-of-term letter, originally aimed at boarders' families, which has grown into a substantial magazine and now goes out to all. OBs include Kenneth Horne, Patrick Heron, Michael Oakeshott, Sir Maurice Drake, Andrew Hunter MP and Rex Warner.

Entrance: There's no academic selection and the school is still over-subscribed despite the provision of 30 new places in Year 7. Admission is by a complicated system of priorities, but those with siblings and or living locally and attending a recognised church for at least two years (a minister's letter is required) are most likely to be successful. Parents have been known to resort to underhand methods to get their offspring in – but be aware that the school is wise to this. Boarders are totally integrated into the school and potential candidates need to provide a good reference from their previous school and apply at least a year in advance to be in with a shout. A state grant for new accommodation – a sixth form house with en-suite rooms – has recently boosted boarder places to 135.

Exit: About 80 to 90 per cent to university – impressively high for a comprehensive – often with gap years.

Remarks: One of the most successful non-selective schools in the country, welcoming students into a secure, Christian community where academic achievement and altruism are encouraged in equal measure.

St Gregory's Catholic College

Combe Hay Lane, Odd Down, Bath, BA2 8PA

• Pupils: 815 girls and boys; all day • Ages: 11-16 • Catholic • State

Tel: 01225 832 873
Fax: 01225 835 848
Email: stgregorys_sec@bathnes.gov.uk
Website: www.st-gregorys.bathnes.sch.uk

Headteacher: Since 2004, Mr Raymond Friel MA NPQH (mid forties). First class degree in English from Glasgow University in 1987; PGCE from University of Wales, Aberystwyth. As head of English introduced A level English to new sixth form at St Augustine's, Trowbridge, after 'good start' to career at St Charles Sixth Form College, London. Two and a half years as head of St Joseph's, Salisbury which he took from 'challenging circumstances' to receiving a 'good' Ofsted rating. Then 'too good to miss' opportunity arose at St Gregory's. Thoughtful and caring head who follows long-serving predecessor. Good listener and fits St Gregory's academic and Catholic profile. 'Has handled changes with sensitivity,' say parents. Married to Janet Anne, an artist and teacher, with three sons at local Catholic school. Interests include sport, literature and performing arts. Former co-editor of Southfields literary review.

Academic matters: Outstanding results in core subjects, especially English (with GCSE results in both language and literature more than 20 per cent above national average). In 2010, 30 per cent of all GCSE entries achieved A*–A and 80 per cent of all pupils gained five or more A*–C passes at GCSE, with 64 per cent including English and mathematics. Religion compulsory to GCSE. A modern foreign language compulsory for nearly all; we were particularly impressed by quality of teaching and range of languages offered. Second specialism in languages granted by DfES from September 2006 after excellent Ofsted. Most other subjects are also strong and drama, music and dance more than justify the college's specialist performing arts status.

Children streamed and setted in maths from the beginning of their second term. At key stage 4, pupils follow courses in one of three 'pathways', stretching the most able, providing qualifications alongside appropriate experience for small vocational group, and giving mainstream pupils a sensible compromise in terms of breadth and workload. No sense of 'second class' or disaffected pupils. Class sizes vary according to subject and ability.

All Year 7 children are screened on entry. Six statemented children and 29 with IEPs. Early morning reading programme and a lunch club for vulnerable pupils. Close liaison with range of outside agencies. SENCo works with staff to support pupils with SpLD and other special needs largely within normal timetable; learning support assistants work alongside mainstream teachers. High ranking for value-added at key stage three attributed in part to success of support programmes.

Games, Options, the Arts: Active sports department organises range of after-school fixtures across the major games. Pupils spoilt for choice when it comes to performing arts. 220 pupils receiving instrumental tuition in school and another 100 outside. Annual tour for musicians of all kinds and many play in county bands. Parents 'really grateful' for trips abroad organised by staff. New music suite opened in 2006 with state of the art technology, rehearsal space and practice rooms. New music technology offers twilight tuition to AS level for those who can manage extra workload, likewise after-school dance and language options.

Strong drama with school productions involving dance and music too. Purpose-built dance/drama studio opened in 2003 in addition to main stage in school hall. When we visited, one of two professional dancers in residence was inspiring a creative class of uninhibited Year 7 pupils. Annual Artsweek in July has performances every day and draws up to 500 key stage 3 pupils; stunning choice of workshops with local artists and performers volunteering their time. Artists, writers and poets, theatre visits and cross-cultural exchanges add to the heady creative mix here. Children prove resourceful in getting themselves home and many stay after school. Rave reviews for College production of *Les Miserables* (school edition) and *Bugsy Malone* (KS3 only).

Background and Atmosphere: Motto: In Christo floremus (In Christ we flourish) expresses the Christian core of the school. Every day begins with collective worship in tutor groups plus extra masses through year and voluntary mass in school's small chapel which also provides a sanctuary where some pupils have left touching prayer dedications in an open book. Each year group can experience a retreat and there are all kinds of good works for charity. Non-Catholics 'don't feel left out,' confirm parents.

School located on attractive 12-acre site on 'socially mixed' southern edge of Bath; extensive playing fields, new Astroturf for hockey and soccer plus hard tennis courts and gym. Modern 12 classroom block for mathematics, geography and modern languages in spacious, purpose-built accommodation. Well-resourced and airy library; interactive whiteboards, overhead projection and plenty of computers around without being techno crazy. Pleasant bistro area for Year 11 lunches with healthy food options and smart card payment system. School day begins at 8.55am and ends at 3.35pm with many getting back to far-flung homes by bus ahead of those crossing congested Bath. Strong PTFA runs fund-raising events through year.

Pastoral Care and Discipline: Deputy head (former LEA adviser and Ofsted inspector) pioneered peer counselling here; truancy almost unknown with attendance monitored closely. 'Name and praise' assembly and rewards system plus clear sanctions where necessary. Well established House system.

Pupils and Parents: 80 per cent Catholic; very active PTFA. Parents receive three progress reports plus full written report at end of year. Homework set by all and journals for parents to see and sign. Quite a few refugees from private sector and many staff have children here. Strong sense of community; pupils appear relaxed, confident and tolerant of each other. Those who showed us around were articulate and sensitive. Moral values and full of good works for disabled, homeless etc. Smart, green uniform has replaced dreary brown predecessor still worn by older year groups. College Senate has representatives from across years and has influenced uniform and catering changes including introduction of popular breakfast club.

Entrance: Oversubscribed. Prides itself on transition arrangements into Year 7; children come from 200 square mile catchment area and preference system for Catholics operates. Since September 2007, partial selection on the grounds of aptitude in the performing arts has been introduced: up to 10 per cent of places available after Catholics, adherents to other Christian faiths and siblings. Pupils mainly from six linked primary schools (St Benedict's, Midsomer Norton; St John's, Bath; St Joseph and Teresa, Wells; St Mary's, Bath; St Mary's, Chippenham; and St Patrick's, Corsham) plus siblings. Apply through Bath & North East Somerset LEA for admission into Year 7, but apply direct to school if moving into the area.

Exit: Around 50 per cent to St Brendan's and increasingly to school sixth forms in Bath; 25 per cent to further education; 10 per cent to training and employment. A few to Oxbridge via St Brendan's or other colleges. The school has plans to open its own sixth form, depending on funding and planning permission.

Remarks: Much sought-after and dynamic 11–16 Catholic comprehensive which combines creativity with academic success.

The School of St Helen and St Katharine

Linked to Saint Helen and Saint Katharine Junior School (The School of) in the Junior section

Faringdon Road, Abingdon, Oxfordshire, OX14 1BE

• Pupils: 620 girls, all day • Ages: 9-18 • Size of sixth form: 170
• Anglican foundation • Fees: £11,220 pa • Independent

Tel: 01235 520 173
Fax: 01235 532 934
Email: info@shsk.org.uk
Website: www.shsk.org.uk

Head: Since 2008, Miss Rowan Edbrooke (mid-forties), formerly head of St Margaret's (Exeter). Started her teaching career at Queen Elizabeth's Girls School, Barnet. Progressed to senior teacher and head of department at South Hampstead High School then moved to Haberdashers' Aske's School for Girls as head of sixth form; promoted to deputy head. Has promoted students' interest in sport since her arrival; gets to know the children quickly and remains in contact with them. Enjoys theatre, music, literature and outdoor pursuits. A charismatic lady, believes in the encouragement of leadership, independence and initiative. Values extra-curricular activities for the development of a good all-rounder. Her enthusiasm and energy has rubbed off on the school.

Academic matters: Excellent GCSE/IGCSE and A level results that just keep getting better. Girls were bubbling with enthusiasm to tell us how good their school was and where they were excelling. Strong in sciences, although good performances too in geography and history – good teachers. Choice of languages varies with the strong state-of-the-art department offering anything a pupil would like to study from the more mainstream French, Latin, Greek and Spanish to German and Italian. If a girl wants to study a language the school will do their best to organise it. Joint teaching with Abingdon makes offering low take-up subjects or unusual combinations of subjects increasingly possible and, indeed, co-operation between the two schools is now quite widespread.

Amount of homework a surprise at first but girls soon work out how to spread the load. A dozen or so girls with special needs (mostly dyslexia) have a SENCo to look after them. A focused environment where pupils are encouraged to think independently and take responsibility for organising their own work.

Games, Options, the Arts: Sport hugely improved since our last visit, helped not only by the new sports centre but a noticeable emphasis on improving its availability. Being part of a squad means everything to the girls and they are keen to give up their lunchtimes to practise. Sailing increasingly popular, with teams competing in a number of national school events. Many compete at county level in lacrosse, netball, tennis and athletics. Several ranked nationally in lacrosse and squash. Now offering less traditional girls' sports such as football, rugby, basketball, fencing and cricket. Hockey has been successfully introduced with impressive take up. Swimming pool small, elderly, outdoor and uninviting. Ultra modern fitness suite.

Music is central to school life; the performing arts centre provides a first class environment. Vast range of instruments, various scholarships. Amazing choice of ensembles organised by the senior girls and lots in county orchestras and above. Choirs, of course, and lots of foreign tours.

Drama very popular, with boys from Abingdon joining in the productions in the wonderful theatre. More than half doing D of E, with several expeditions in increasingly difficult terrain taking the students to new heights of independence. Young Enterprise. Debating and public speaking very popular, with noticeable success, and community service actively encouraged.

Background and Atmosphere: Founded in 1903 to provide a benunned but 'liberal and advanced' Christian education for young ladies in Abingdon. On the outskirts of the town; the distinctive redbrick buildings are surrounded by beautifully kept gardens and fruit trees. Newly rich – a large donation by the son of a late teacher and governor of the school has led to an expansive building programme. The performing arts centre – an amazing building that houses the music department with its high tech recording studios, art display space, dance studio and theatre – was followed by an exciting new library opened in 2010, incorporating a study area to promote more independent learning and effectively double the school's ICT resources. A further eleven acres of land developed for additional sports fields in 2009. Everything is, and is expected to be, well organised.

Pastoral Care and Discipline: Christian values underpin everything. School exudes an air of intellectual spirituality. Girls very focused on fellowship and a willingness to commit themselves to the school and to their education. Form tutor responsible for day to day welfare, with full time school chaplain, nurse. Doctor and counsellor available as needed. Upper sixth take positions of responsibility in form, charity or sport – younger girls encouraged to do the same.

Pupils and Parents: A school for inspired girls. Focused, motivated, well mannered girls, full of the joys of spring and their school. Not particularly socially mixed – but at least the school bus service (with girls coming from a twenty-five mile catchment area) is comprehensive. In the early years, school goes out of its way to group girls by post-codes to facilitate friendships. Strong parents' association. Alumnae include Jane Tranter, BBC Drama Commissioner; Mary Allen, past CEO of the Royal Opera House; Hattie Dean, British Cross Country Champion; author and journalist Alice Thompson; Jess Harrison and Julia Allan, international triathletes.

Entrance: Entry is at age 9, 10, 11, 13 and 16. Large numbers apply for approximately 60 places at 11 from both local state and private feeders. Entrance based on exam, headteachers' reports and interviews conducted with prospective pupils before exams. Entry at 13 has developed and changes to tutor group organisation for Year 9 help facilitate early integration. Girls with good GCSEs and a positive report join the sixth form to replace leavers. Head prides herself on never denying access to the sixth form to existing pupils, even those with relatively poor GCSEs, regarding exclusion for academic reasons as an unfair way of bumping up A level results.

Exit: Most to further education, with fifteen going to Oxbridge in 2008. Bristol and Cardiff popular choices, a good number of medics and a few overseas. Sciences, English, psychology and languages especially popular.

Money Matters: Fees low but there's a host of extras to pay for – add the cost of the bus, lunch, etc and it soon mounts up. Small number of academic and music scholarships and bursaries for those needing financial help.

Remarks: A vibrant, high achieving school with motivated pupils. Strong (and, some would say, compulsory) ethos, which the school describes as 'encouragement of excellence'.

St Helen's School

Eastbury Road, Northwood, Middlesex, HA6 3AS

- Pupils: 1,125 including junior school and Little St Helen's; all girls
- Ages: 3-18 • Size of sixth form: 160 • C of E but all faiths welcome
- Fees: £8,826-£12,828 pa • Independent

Tel: 01923 843 210
Fax: 01923 843 211
Email: admissions@sthn.co.uk
Website: www.sthn.co.uk

Head: Since 2000, Mrs Mary Morris BA PGCE (fiftyish). A geographer who taught at Dr Challoner's High before coming to the school in 1998 as deputy head. An internal appointment then and, unlike many such, received with popular acclaim which no-one has since regretted. One of the most engaging heads we have encountered – voluble, smiley, relaxed and frank. It's a bit like talking to your best friend except that Mrs Morris is, clearly, a wholly professional head. So many girls' schools still seem to be run on the 'we're-ever-so-nice-really' principle without the forward-looking, cutting edge taken for granted in the boys' equivalents. Not so here.

Mrs Morris is an inspirational head who is also huge fun. She knows her girls, her staff, her stuff, her school and her market and underpins the lot with a profound belief in spiritual and moral values. Conducted an 'audit' of the spiritual content of the academic curriculum – 'we need to be moral in lessons – there should be social, spiritual, moral and cultural elements in every single lesson.' Unashamedly partisan about single sex education for girls, she parried a question from a potential (male) parent who asked why he should send his daughters to a girls' school rather than to a co-ed, 'this is not a girls' school – it's a school and, unfortunately, we don't have room for any boys.' Clearly still thrilled about her appointment, she says, 'this is an incredibly moral job. Above everything else, we are role models.'

We learn at time of going to press that Mrs Morris has announced her retirement as from July 2011. She has been an admirable head and done much for the school.

Academic matters: School moved to the IB in 2004 and, taught in parallel with A levels, it is now taken by around 25 per cent of sixth formers and growing. Excellent range of subjects available in the sixth including two history syllabuses, English lit and lang and economics. The overwhelmingly popular subjects at this level – A or IB – are the sciences and maths. Results outstanding – practically all A level grades are A*–B and very few GCSEs lower than B. Teaching strong across the board but pupils drool over sciences – 'the department is absolutely amazing,' said one.

Main curriculum includes art history, psychology, business studies, lots of languages – school's support for and involvement in langs, especially given the scientific bent of so many pupils, is a joy. Head says, 'I don't want people who can speak French – I want linguists.' Hooray! So, Japanese, Mandarin Chinese, Italian, Russian – along with Latin for all and Greek as an option – available alongside the more predictable lingos. Lots of trips and exchanges abroad.

Head is 'passionate' about IT and there can be few girls' schools – and not many boys' schools – which are as far ahead and well-provided for as St Helen's. 100 Mb per second broadband recently installed – 'it's very fast' – it's wireless now throughout the senior school and everyone can access everything from everywhere. School has a partnership with Toshiba and is now the UK Centre of Excellence in Mobile Education i.e. there are stacks of laptops for girls and staff to be used wirelessly everywhere; two rooms using the Virtuoso multi-media system which facilitates, for example, language learning, enabling the teacher to talk individually to each pupil and each pupil to talk whatever lang it is, individually without disturbing – or waiting for – anyone else – extraordinary! And it's not that IT is an end in itself – 'it's teaching them to use that enormous resource as well as we teach them how to use their books and their teachers and everything else,' reassures head.

Everyone is screened at seven and 11 for potential educational difficulties. 'We then discuss with parents how we can make it better.' One qualified SEN teacher with lots of help. School can and does support autistic spectrum difficulties, mild dyslexia and dyspraxia, mild speech difficulties and children with hearing impairments. EAL also taught and some children have extra help with maths. One-to-one is given to all those with SENs and school has a positive and helpful attitude to these girls. 127 children currently identified as Gifted and Talented and supported with 'differentiated work schemes and activities'.

Games, Options, the Arts: The huge surprise for anyone visiting St Helen's and who, perhaps, has only seen it behind its sedate hedges and modest perimeter walls, is the unbelievable amount of space it has. Acres of playing fields, courts and pitches extend in all directions and you begin to realise that most of this end of Northwood is St Helen's! Vast new sports complex and superb, seemingly endless pool, in stunning new building, already in enthusiastic use. Lacrosse, netball, tennis, athletics, badminton and rounders all popular and many other games and activities available including pilates, aerobics, fencing and trampolining. Lots of success – representation in lacrosse, swimming, cross country and netball county teams and much success for school teams in all these sports plus athletics and rounders at impressive levels.

The school's extensive landscape accommodates numerous blocks and houses, often purpose-built. One such is the Leader building, named after school's outstanding, and aptly named, head of recent years, June Leader – the great builder of the school, both in physical terms – numerous new blocks rose up in her 16-year tenure – as well as in terms of the quality of education and values promulgated here under her uniquely humane regime. This block houses art, DT and drama – all spacious, well-equipped , bright and inviting and matched by the excellence of what is achieved here. We saw much classy wooden furniture – clever designs, beautifully crafted and finished; imaginative ceramics, good painting and drawing – life drawing taken very seriously here. Art is varied, witty and serious. Very good drama studio but main productions happen in good old-fashioned huge school hall – good light and sound systems recently installed. Lots of plays – some in the Founder's Arts Festival. Lots of collaboration with Merchant Taylors' boys up the road – the annual musical now a tradition and very professional.

Music less glamorously housed in one of the older and grimmer buildings still remaining – but it's cosy inside and has a large and inviting recital room. Orchestras, choirs, bands. The jazz band has made a CD, the huge choir tours abroad but possibly fair to say that music is not school's strongest suit. Dance is popular and strong. Loads of extra-curricular opportunities – masses of charity work especially PHAB very much part of school's ethos. Collaboration with Merchant Taylors' also in CCF. D of E and Young Enterprise also popular. Visits from profs, writers and theatre companies. Successes in debating, maths and physics Olympiads, technology competitions. Lots of trips – Ypres, Kew, Rome, House of Commons, Paris, British Museum, galleries – you find it on a map, they've been there.

Background and Atmosphere: The site is everything. Unbeatable in its generous, green space, its trees and gardens. The buildings have sprouted all round the site and none of it feels crowded, although the main senior school blocks are, for the most part picturesquely, at the main entrance end of things. Most subjects taught in own blocks or in main, extended building. One of the joys here is looking through the windows of whichever building you're in – stunning views over the school from every one. St Helen's was founded at the end of the nineteenth century with a vision and ambition for its first pupils which has informed its ethos ever since. It does not aim at league table stardom – that seems to be a happy spin-off.

The junior school (see below) is an integral part of the whole. Situated centrally, it is natural for girls here to stay the course – now from three to 18 – and continue to feel that it's all in the family. Equally natural here is the happy co-existence of girls from one of the most diverse ethnic and cultural mixes anywhere.

More significantly, around 33 per cent of the school's population is Asian – (mostly Hindu) – and a further 25 per cent is Jewish – these stats reflecting, of course, the local population. There can be few stronger arguments for heterogeneous school populations than to see the unqualified friendships between these groups. A sixth former we quizzed looked baffled by our questions – 'from when I was four I've been friends with people from every kind of background – they're just your friends.'

Staff tend to stay – 44 with 10 or more years in school – but lots of young teachers and NQTs as well – average age 38. Staff/student relationships palpably cordial. 'A lot of our teachers are role models,' said one sixth former. 'They are so kind and helpful and it doesn't just stop in the classroom. They will keep helping you achieve what you want to achieve.' A younger pupil agreed, 'and', she added, 'you just have to be friendly here because everyone is. The teachers are so sweet – they really look after you – there's always someone to talk to and problems are sorted out really quickly.'

School has several special places. The chapel is one – now used as a quiet place during Ramadan as much as for services and Christian prayer – a beautiful, tenderly cared-for room with a particular atmosphere which should be cherished. The school library is also special though not as quiet as, perhaps, it might have been. Another asset is Longworthe – a former day boarding house now used for before and after school care in which pupils with busy parents can spend a long day – breakfast and tea included and quiet places for prep and recreation. Younger members of staff live above – this adds to the lived-in feeling of the place. When we visited on a leafy October day, a vast bonfire – mostly old desks, tables and prunings – was being assembled in the centre of the parkland. You could anticipate the fun of bonfire night just looking at it.

Pastoral Care and Discipline: Civilised behaviour the norm here. No rule book but a 'Code of Conduct' and a Behaviour Policy which are called upon if – rarely – anyone needs reminding. Clear sanctions policy. System of warning and detention cards. MP3s/mobiles illegal in schooltime. No drugs incidents in Mrs Morris's time – or in living memory. The occasional foolish smoker is dealt with individually but, in the head's words, 'sanely. It's never public, it's not about humiliation – ever.' Food looked appetising and reasonably varied though we were perturbed to see successive nine-year-olds carrying off plates of pasta and chips with never a word said. Otherwise, pastoral care very good. You're allowed to slip here. Head says, 'they have to be able to fall down and you have to pick them up again because it's safe in school.' Quite.

Pupils and Parents: Couldn't be more ethnically and culturally diverse though the school no longer takes boarders. The families of junior school pupils alone come from 40+ countries. Northwood is prosperous, with lots of large detached houses – no shortage of dosh in most cases. Parental occupations just as mixed – as you'd expect. Girls come from wide area – good coach service covers Beaconsfield, Elstree, Barnet, Amersham, Ealing, Hemel

Hempstead and points between. Old Girls' network huge and devoted. St Helen's inspires a, perhaps unique, loyalty. Alumnae include Patricia Hodge, a great supporter, Vanessa Lawrence (director general Ordnance Survey), Lady Lowry, Luisa Baldini and Penny Marshall, Maria Djurkovic.

Entrance: School part of North London Consortium which shares tests at 11. First point of entry is at three into Little St Helen's (see below). At 11, exams in English, maths and VR; around 300 apply for 50 places – not too terrifying as lots apply elsewhere but school is increasingly candidates' first choice. At sixth form, around 40 apply for about 15 places. You need seven + GCSEs at B+. Few leave along the way – around 10 leave at 11 for state system, boarding or (few) other local independents. Very few leave after GCSEs.

Exit: Everyone to higher education. Everything from medicine to maths, fashion to finance. Everywhere from the LSE to Leeds, St Andrews to Sussex. Half dozen+ to Oxbridge annually.

Money Matters: Range of scholarships and means-tested bursaries. Bursaries awarded annually and are either awarded to girls whose parents could not otherwise meet fees or to girls whose families are experiencing temporary difficulties.

Remarks: So what is this extraordinarily unsung haven – unaccountably neglected by us till now? A poor man's Habs? A refuge for NLCS refuseniks? We don't think so! Get in at three if you can and crow over your neighbours for the next fifteen years.

St James Independent School for Senior Boys

Linked to Saint James Junior School in the Junior section

Linked to Saint James Senior Girls School in the Senior section

Church Road, Ashford, Surrey, TW15 3DZ

• Pupils: 305 boys, all day except for 15 weekly boarders • Ages: 10-18 • Size of sixth form: 60 • Inter-denom (but see below) • Fees: Day £11,895; Weekly boarding + £4,650 pa • Independent

Tel: 01784 266 930
Email: admissions@stjamesboys.co.uk
Website: www.stjamesboys.co.uk

Head: Since 2004, Mr David Boddy, a New Zealander, (mid-fifties) with an unusual pedigree for a head. After a career start as a journalist, he took up a post here with Thompson Newspapers in the early 1970s. In 1976, he joined the Press Office at the Tory HQ and in 1979, was Mrs Thatcher's Press Secretary during the election campaign. He stayed on until the 1983 election – resigning on election night! Mr Boddy spent the next decade running his own consultancy and lobbying company and, in 1997, began a new venture working with graduates in multi-nationals, helping them develop leadership and managerial skills. He founded a trust based in Italy providing leadership training to young people from all over the world and became concerned that 'something was missing at the secondary age level.' This change of focus and direction was inspired by the training in philosophy he had been receiving for many years at The School of Economic Science in London.

The SES runs a number of schools on its philosophical principles and Mr Boddy's own three sons had been pupils at both St James' junior (qv) and senior schools, during which time he became familiar with and supportive of their very individual educational approach. While he speaks the inspirational and heart-lifting language of this group of schools, he is also refreshingly realistic, admitting that 'the ideal and what's actually happening on the ground are not always connected'. It is this brand of realism, honesty and aspiration which has helped to re-energize the St James schools and restore the confidence that, in many eyes, had been sorely endangered. Mr Boddy has the satisfaction of moving his school to its splendid new accommodation in Ashford and of seeing it become, it is to be hoped, firmly established there.

Academic matters: Academically selective but academic promise is not everything – see below. Thus the intake is mixed ability and deliberately so. One might expect the curriculum to reflect a mix of head and hand but this is an unashamedly academic curriculum and, remarkably, many of the boys who seem to promise less on the academic front achieve highly in exams. Whereas the boys' school is not, at present, achieving as starrily as the girls' school, its results are respectable and, in the case of some pupils, startlingly good. 'Recent years have seen steady improvement in academic standards.' In 2009, 94 per cent of GCSE grades were A*–C and, at A level, 90 per cent of passes were at A–C grade. One student recorded 12 A* GCSEs. Two A Level students returned five straight A grade passes. Popular options are history and the sciences. Several take Sanskrit. Recent A level results represent a sprinkling across the range, maths being the most consistent high performer. School takes the sensible view that nine GCSEs is ample for anyone.

All subject teaching is underpinned by the philosophical principles espoused by the school and the ethos is inescapable throughout curricular and extracurricular life. It influences, among other things, the subjects offered. In the school's early days there was no geography, but this was introduced in 2006 and now has a thriving department with the subject taught right through to A level. Sanskrit – the Indo-Germanic language pre-dating even Greek and Latin – is introduced to all Year 7 entrants and continues for those who can manage it until Year 9, becoming an option thereafter – and it is heartening to see Greek and Latin as relatively popular GCSE options, though only minute numbers continue to A level. Minute numbers also for modern languages beyond GCSE. There is art – and what we saw was studious and colourful if not especially lively – but nothing in the way of DT, ceramics, photography etc. If you want a school that will develop the tactile or visual creative skills this ain't it. However, unlike so many schools that rigidly insist on 'breadth', this school sensibly recognises that pupils have natural bents and will allow them to pursue individual routes, specialising in certain areas e.g. humanities, classics. Year 7 setted for maths, French and Sanskrit.

ICT suite is modern and well furbished with 48 new networked Apple computers across two classrooms with wireless access throughout the school. The Cambridge

International ICT is taught throughout the school with a computing option in the sixth form. One of the ICT classrooms is dedicated to the IT teaching, while the second one is for subject teachers and cross-curricular work.

SENs are well supported and use interesting innovative techniques such as 'The Art of Science' – a way of making difficult scientific concepts visually accessible. School will take pupils with a range of special needs including ADHD and, as far as possible, support them in class. All pupils are allowed four 'units' of support free of charge, the value of a unit depending on whether it is individual or group support but anyone who is perceived to need more than four has to pay extra.

Games, Options, the Arts: Music traditionally the strongest of the arts subjects and school is especially keen on singing which 'is part of our philosophical approach, opening hearts and minds and hearing the sound of one's own voice.' Major music and drama productions in collaboration with the girls' school in Olympia and everyone makes light of the considerable amount of inter-school ferrying this involves. Performance is important, as is speech itself. 'If you have not mastered speech by the time you leave here, then those who have will master you,' is a maxim quoted at the boys.

School lays much emphasis – too much for some but, say others, entirely justifiable – on its extracurricular programme of activities. They are able to do kayaking on the school lake and sailing on the nearby reservoirs. Members of the sailing club go further afield. They go climbing and love it and around a quarter enthusiastically take up the cadet force and do all the adventurous things that offers. A popular D of E scheme attracts others. Around three-quarters of the school take up one or other of these outdoor options. Parents enthuse about the opportunities, 'my son loved the cadets ... he felt totally safe with the cadet master – ex SAS, you know,' we were told. 'My boys went on lovely trips abroad – lots of climbing in the alps and sailing across the Channel. They've had such a happy time.'

The school now has all major sports facilities, such as rugby, hockey and football and cricket within its grounds but there are lots of minor sports and opportunities for even the least sporty to find something to do.

Mr Boddy's idealistic leadership programme in Lucca, Italy, presents an unusual and scenic opportunity to all boys twice in their school career to develop all kinds of personal skills. At home there are guest speakers and sixth form dinners hosted at home by the head – a broadening and inspirational programme. Twice yearly lectures at the RSA given by everyone from eminent physicians to ambassadors. Also, the Ficino Society – a programme of academic talks designed to foster and care for potential Oxbridge candidates, which add to the intellectual life of the school and thus meet its requirement to nurture the gifted and talented.

Quiet time for all is a major feature at the beginning and end of every day, silent pauses before and after lessons with benedictions, grace before meals and expressions of thanks in Sanskrit are embedded in the daily life of all pupils.

Background and Atmosphere: The philosophical background is the ethos of the School of Economic Science, founded in 1937, which aims to explore through the study of the world's great religions and philosophies what it is to be fully human in a spiritual way and, in so doing, what goes to make a spiritually healthy and prosperous community. The schools were founded in the 1970s on such idealistic principles and many have found the experience of being educated there rewarding and inspiring. However, in 1970s and 1980s, a too-rigorous application of the discipline and control aspects of the SES ethos resulted in much unhappiness. This came to the surface in 2004 to such an extent that the schools courageously instigated an independent enquiry, under the chairmanship of a QC, into the allegations of physical abuse made by former pupils. This enquiry reported in early 2006 and its findings can be read on www.iirep.com.

The senior boys' school is a happy, settled community. Its head is confidently frank and upfront about the school's background and philosophy. There can be little doubt that the school's defensiveness and protectiveness about the SES philosophy, its influence on curriculum and ethos, the clubbishness of some of its membership and the 'brick wall' some have felt they've encountered when they have attempted to understand what they have signed up to, have contributed to some of the disquiet and misunderstanding. In a sensible attempt to counter this justifiable accusation that the schools have not always been open about their background, they published in spring 2006 an excellent booklet 'Answers to Frequently Asked Questions' and this, we were told, is sent to all prospective parents, thus wisely eliminating the frequent complaint that parents 'weren't told' about the schools' distinctive approach. You may want to ask for the booklet if it is not volunteered, as, on occasions, it isn't.

Mr Boddy is a modernising head and there has been much to modernise and, despite an immense amount done – over 30 initiatives have been put in since his arrival – not counting the vast labour involved in a wholesale move of his entire school! – much still remains to do on several fronts. Despite the physical distance between Ashford and Olympia, he works closely with the two other heads. The new Ashford site is large and offers all kinds of new opportunities and the school hopes to develop its curriculum as it settles in to take advantage of the generous space. The local community, with whom the school now works closely, also enjoys the facilities now on offer.

Pastoral Care and Discipline: The ethos of the school is its principal defence against misbehaviour and anti-social behaviour of all kinds. Yellow/red card system is employed here, designed to foster the use of reason – a graduated system of points for misdemeanours resulting, finally, in detentions/suspensions/temporary exclusions etc. Little bullying, no serious drugs incidents since Mr Boddy's advent, and all other problems dealt with through talk and parental involvement on an individual basis. The prefect system, class representation on the school council and the form masters pick up the rest. 'Manhood', 'character' and 'character-building' are terms much in evidence here. Parents who like good discipline are keen, 'they are strict but very cheerful,' we heard, 'it's very orderly.' Boys whom the school's ethos suits – and there are many – feel it has given them a 'foundation'. We were told by one, 'in a tough situation I find that I can fall back on some base of reasoning.' Another paid tribute to the staff – 'teachers are your friends – they help you along' – and we saw much that bore witness to this degree of cordiality and trust.

School food is vegetarian and organic and is largely composed of fresh and dried fruit, nuts, cheese, home-cooked soups, pasta and rice dishes and quiches. It all looked, and was, delicious and entirely wholesome. Meat is out – 'second-hand food' – and everyone looked as fit as fleas on it. It's all laid out on tables, staff and pupils together and you are supposed to serve your neighbour. It does work – sometimes! The drinking fountains actually work too.

Boarding – weekly only – is under the care of a young boarding master plus a friendly resident couple who live on site and who entertain the younger boys each evening in their home. All junior boarders in two 5-bed dorms, all older boys i.e. from Year 8 upwards, in pairs or singles. Common room with sofas, kitchen area and TV and, in the evenings, the boys have the school's other facilities to themselves. School talks of the 'extended family' nature of the boarding and this feels appropriate where so few – now only 20 – board and where it feels, despite the lack of facilities compared to a regular boarding school, quite privileged. Older boys take much responsibility for younger ones – felt to be a privilege but also something of a restraint.

Pupils and Parents: Ethnic and social mix is typical of the area. A remarkable seventeen faiths were represented in the school at the time of our visit, the families of around a quarter of the boys originate from the Indian sub-continent and are, perhaps, particularly drawn to the basis of Indian philosophy which inspires the school's teachings. There is some minimal need for EAL in the school. Typically, parents are very supportive of and involved in the school.

Entrance: Selection is on the basis of entrance tests in English, maths and verbal reasoning plus interview with the prospective pupil and his parents. Interview can outweigh the entrance test if it is felt the boy has 'character' or other gifts which the school feels would benefit from its distinctive educational approach. Most of the junior school boys, apparently, make the transition to Ashford, despite the distance. School runs various buses. Entry into the sixth form depends on a minimum of six B grades at GCSE plus interview with the head of sixth form and headmaster. This requirement extends to the boys already in the school and some are encouraged to look elsewhere or helped into more vocational areas if the school feels that A levels are not appropriate.

Exit: Those – the vast majority – who go on to higher education follow a wide range of courses, though there is less of a science bias here than in many boys' schools.

Money Matters: Not a rich school, the fees are lower than average and the pot for schols and bursaries is also small. Schols in academics and the arts are mostly for glory rather than cash but the school will support with means-tested bursaries those who could otherwise not come or who have financial problems once accepted.

Remarks: Distinctive, different and, in many ways, special and valuable. Not for the narrowly religious nor those for whom a liberal creative freedom is everything. Acquaint yourself thoroughly with the ethos.

Now successfully moved from its long-established Twickenham home to its new location in Ashford, Surrey. It has taken over the former St David's School – an independent all-girls school – with its magnificent Victorian/Gothic stone building set in 32 acres of grounds. St James has spent £3.6 million on refurbishment, redevelopment and redecoration over the past year and the school was formally opened by Tony Little, the headmaster of Eton in September 2010. It is a bold move and one we will watch with interest.

St James Senior Girls' School

Linked to Saint James Junior School in the Junior section
Linked to Saint James Independent School For Senior Boys in the Senior section

Earsby Street, London, W14 8SH

• Pupils: 290 girls • Ages: 10-18 • Size of sixth form: 50 • Non-denom
• Fees: £12,165 pa • Independent

Tel: 020 7348 1777
Fax: 020 7348 1717
Email: admissions@sjsg.org.uk
Website: www.stjamesgirls.co.uk

Headmistress: Since 1995, Mrs Laura Hyde MEd Cert Ed (fifties). Mrs Hyde trained as a primary school teacher and taught at two London schools before joining the St James Junior School (qv). She became PA to the founder of the St James schools and of the School of Economic Science (see below). After some years at home bringing up her children, she became assistant head at the St James Senior Girls' School in 1994, assuming the headship a year later. Mrs Hyde is an ISI inspector.

None of which prepares you for the charm of the woman herself. Quietly spoken, measured and exuding calm, Mrs Hyde exemplifies the qualities she hopes to develop in the young women she sees into the world. She answers questions thoughtfully and frankly in her cheerful, elegantly furnished study and inspires trust. A subtle, gentle moderniser, she has, while maintaining the core ethos and traditions of the St James family of schools, done much to bring her branch into the twenty-first century. Parents enthuse – 'she's fantastic – she's my current heroine – she has created a gentle, loving, caring atmosphere.' Mrs Hyde's already lengthy tenure has given the school the stability and confidence it needed.

Academic matters: A good example of a school that should not be judged on the league tables. Girls here take the IGCSE in maths and all three sciences – for greater rigour – and, as this is too complicated for the tables to cope with, the school's ranking is skewed as a result. At GCSE, almost everyone gets A*–C. Stunning success in physics, history and English and at least respectable everywhere else. In 2010, 65 per cent A*/A and in general, the quality of teaching is praised. At A level the twenty subject options now include theatre studies, Spanish and art history. Results creditable in most subjects – few grades below B – and English and maths impressive. School also offering the new AQA Bacc – seeing it as recognising much of what they already do in terms of critical thinking and an extended project.

But this is not a school to think of solely in these terms. The school's culture largely determines the extended curriculum. Sanskrit is continued for those who join from the Junior School and available as an option at GCSE. Singing, dance and philosophy are taken by all and everything is taught from the philosophical perspective which underpins the St James schools' ethos. Philosophy is taught all through the school; Mrs Hyde teaches Years 6–7 and 11–13. This approach extends to the LDD provision which is managed on the basis of an individual's needs, although the hope is that most pupils can work independently by the end of Year 8. Thereafter, the SENCo – the deputy head, pastoral, in this case – sees girls individually or in small groups according to need – no withdrawal from academic lessons. The staff monitor progress with care. Strong gifted and talented provision.

Games, Options, the Arts: This is a compact city site so anything involving running takes place at the Chiswick playing grounds, a bus ride away. On site, they cram in netball, fencing, aerobics, gym, health-related fitness and dance etc and off site lacrosse, netball, athletics, rounders and tennis are the main sports. They have their own adventure club – the St James Challengers – and D of E. One good art room in which, largely, the trad skills are taught by much admired staff. Visiting instructors add to the core curriculum and the school now has a kiln but no dark room. And no DT. One of the best schools we know at actually displaying its own pupils' art – everywhere and with style. Music is big here – again under charismatic leadership – everyone sings – we heard it everywhere – the whole school sings together twice weekly. Music seen as part of the spiritual education provided. Lots of individual lessons and good collaboration on concerts and productions with the boys' school – despite the distance. Drama popular and lively. The 'art of hospitality' is taught to years six and seven – cookery but not as you might have known it elsewhere – the thrust here is on sharing food and using it as a way of nurturing relationships. The sixth form cook for each other, have formal dinners with high profile guests etc. In year 10, all go on a residential week which focuses on 'becoming an adult' – life skills, presenting oneself at interview and being a responsible citizen etc. Much emphasis on community service.

Background and Atmosphere: Founded, along with its sibling Junior Schools and Senior Boys' School, in 1975 by The School of Economic Science (see the review of the Senior Boys' School for background and history), the girls' school and junior schools moved to their impressive modern accommodation in 2001. The outside is daunting. The main gate, within sight of Olympia down a quiet side road, is encased in uniquely secure architecture – grilles, grids, gratings and entry phone. If you happen to be a billionaire or high profile political refugee, you will deposit your daughter here in the mornings, confident that the bad world will be kept firmly outside.

The two schools co-exist happily and it is rather nice – if surprising – to come across classrooms full of six year-olds as you cruise around the corridors. Nonetheless, the schools are finding, as was inevitable, that both need more elbow room. New building started in 2010 with a balcony in the Assembly Room and further extensions will be built over the next two years. The place is in good nick – lots of white-painted corridors, blue carpets, good wall displays and useful noticeboards. The sixth form have a good sized common room and study room attached. They also have privileges – eating in the staff dining room, for one – and responsibilities which are taken seriously.

Classrooms, while not quite providing the 'beautiful environment' aimed at, are orderly and well-kept and all now have whiteboards. The library is clearly too small and a new library is part of the building plan. Outside space is limited though care has been taken to provide little trellised alcoves for quiet chat around the tarmac playground. A sense of cheery collaborativeness abounds – girls look relaxed and happy and appreciate their unusual school. Staff, according to parents, 'always smile and are friendly'. 'Silence, stillness and meditation' are important – everyone has a few moments for these at the start and finish of each lesson. The food is vegetarian and the tables are laid invitingly – hot home-cooked food plus fresh fruit, salad, bread and cheese.

Major news to affect all potential – and present – pupils is that the St James boys have moved from the Twickenham site to what was formerly St David's Girls' School in Ashford, Surrey. This will provide much needed expansion space for the St James boys in a very attractive position. But while the arrangement presents opportunities for the St James schools, there may well be difficulties now that the family of schools is spread over a wider geographic area. How families wanting the St James brand of education for their boys, girls, juniors and seniors will adapt remains to be seen.

Pastoral Care and Discipline: Highly praised. Pupils like the mentoring system and the 'strong bond' they feel to many teachers. Younger pupils are assigned sixth form prefects as mentors, older ones have teachers. 'Your mentor is your friend – they always give you someone who doesn't teach you – you go to her with any problems – not just academic ones.' Head relies on the 'very strong programme of education' to guard against the usual teenage problems. 'We emphasise strengthening a girl's social conscience and confidence ... if you present with difficulties we will help you so long as you are not harming the rest of the community.' On bullying, 'we keep working at it ... stressing the importance of unity and not harming each other.'

The school's strong spiritual ethos underpins the disciplinary side but girls don't feel it's thrust down their throats. A parent expressed the general view – 'we like the way they approach education – they believe strongly in the spiritual side of it – it doesn't invade life but they look at the whole development of the girl and believe that the academics will follow.' A sixth former confided, 'Mrs Hyde wants us to be great women – she doesn't want us just to stay at home.' She herself says, 'my emphasis is on creating responsible citizens.' Who wouldn't fit in? 'Someone who is only out for themselves wouldn't find themselves in their natural environment ... our girls are gentle on the outside but inwardly strong and independent – they are women of some integrity.'

Pupils and Parents: Mixed as befits its west London location. Unsurprisingly, given the influence of 'the wisdom traditions of east and west', the school has an appeal to families with Asian backgrounds who make up around a quarter. Some of the staff are members of the School of Economic Science, some are ex-pupils, but a large majority of the pupils are now from families who have no direct connection with the SES. Pupils come from great distances – at least for the first five years – though most are relatively local. Former pupils include actresses Emily Watson and Sasha Behar and novelist Laura Wilson.

Entrance: St James Junior pupils move seamlessly through – NB at Year 6 – and, at present, given that they share the site, this is much easier for girls than for boys who head off to Ashford. Main feeders otherwise are Falcons, Ravenscourt Pk, Avonmore, Orchard House, Kew Green, Pembridge Hall and Barnes Primary. A few join at Year 6 but main intake into Year 7 when around 112 apply for around 25 places. School now part of the North London Consortium so tests in maths and English. School's own reasoning test day also includes activities in baking, art, drama, dance and chemistry. Few come in at Year 12. NB how small the school is. Head says, 'I'm looking at the character of the girls and whether what the school is about resonates with her and her family.'

Exit: Currently a quarter leave after GCSEs; some to co-eds, often to colleges, occasionally to board or to nearer home. A pity as the sixth form classes are small – one-to-one in some cases – the teaching is good and nothing beats the continuity of staying where you are known. This foolish fashion of moving for doubtful gains is on the wane, one hopes. Some gap years. Thereafter, many to the south of England Russell Group or the 1994 group and new unis. An increasing number are pursuing science degrees and over the last three years a third have left to study science of some kind. Many pursue careers in which they contribute to the community.

Money Matters: The school operates a means-tested bursary scheme. All current and future parents may apply. Future parents need to be registered with the school. This is not a rich school so don't look for masses of help.

Remarks: If the high moral tone appeals and you enjoy the repetition of words such as 'fine' 'wise' and 'beautiful' you have achieved Nirvana here. A tiny, peaceful school offering what many parents dream of.

St John Fisher Catholic High School

Linked to Saint Aidan's and Saint John Fisher Associated Sixth Form

Hookstone Drive, Harrogate, North Yorkshire, HG2 8PT

• Pupils: 645 boys, 755 girls • Ages: 11-18 • Size of sixth form: 1110 (in association with St Aidan's C of E High School) • Roman Catholic • State

Tel: 01423 887 254
Fax: 01423 881 056
Email: office@sjfchs.org.uk
Website: www.sjfchs.org.uk

Headteacher: Since 2001, Mr Paul Jackson MA (mid fifties). Educated at St Bonadventure's School (where he taught initially), then read natural sciences at Cambridge. Also taught at The Campion School, Hornchurch and All Saints Catholic School, Dagenham, first headship at St Mary's Catholic School, Bishop Stortford. Dynamic, cheerful, relaxed – seen as 'very approachable and friendly' by pupils and parents, and very 'can do'. Astute and realistic – comfortable with the demands of the post, which he enjoys and handles in a very balanced way, e.g. lets the heads of departments make their own decisions in their subject areas. Strong commitment to the school's Catholic ethos and spiritual life, but not in a narrow fashion. Teaches science to Year 7s and RE to the sixth form, for two to three hours a week, and 'writes a number of sentences on every pupil's report,' enthused a parent. Married with two adult children; enjoys walking and travelling in his spare time.

Academic matters: Has humanities and performing arts specialist status, so these subjects are especially carefully monitored and the latter used to develop creativity across the curriculum. Constantly striving to improve its very good results by systematic target setting and use of data. Calm, purposeful atmosphere in classrooms. Lots of computers regularly upgraded; all classes have electronic whiteboards and all teachers laptops. Pupils and parents see the teachers as helpful and generous with their support at exam time. A parent described the teaching as 'dynamic' – 'The children have a lot of fun along with learning'.

The associated sixth form with St Aidan's C of E High School offers a ecumenical environment and each preserves its own identity via separate pastoral systems; a small number join from other schools. High praise from the most recent Ofsted report: 'terrific' progress, 'superb' attitudes to learning, 'exceptionally high quality' teaching, 'excellent' relationships. Steady 60 per cent A/B at A level. Offers 43 subjects: sciences (very popular), history, ancient history, English lit, German, art, maths, psychology, government and politics, RS, design and technology, drama and theatre studies and performing arts particularly successful. Others include photography, dance, engineering, Spanish, law, geology, sociology, plus vocational courses, e.g. health and social care, travel and tourism, music technology. All do RE as part of the AS general studies programme (Buddhism as well as Christianity studied), then non examined RE in Year 13. AQA baccalaureate being piloted – A levels plus extended project and community service. Advanced extension awards for the most able. Also a one year intermediate course – IT, leisure and tourism, maths, English and a certificate in career planning.

Very strong GCSE results – 80 per cent 5 A*–C including English and maths, 40 per cent all A/A* – reflecting a steady rise over the last decade. Art, sciences, geography, history, drama, music and DT do particularly well. Wide range of subjects: all kinds of science – separate, combined or science for the twentieth first century for the less able; the biology lab houses two live snakes – which we declined to view. Has a developed citizenship programme leading to GCSE in year 10. Also does very well by the less able/academic or disaffected students, who can take a wide range of practical qualifications more commonly offered by further education colleges, e.g. all the available Diplomas, BTec engineering, NVQ French, digital applications (ICT), health and social care, music technology, business and performing arts, even if the take up is small.

In 2008, the school moved to a GCSE course starting in Year 9 'to avoid the Year 8 dip, offer challenge and enhance the curriculum,' said Mr Jackson. This enables teachers to go beyond the curriculum (hurrah!), has improved behaviour and is popular with teachers, parents and pupils. Strong KS3 results obtained at the end of Year 8. Only maths setted in Year 7, then English, French and maths in Year 8. Follows SEAL programme (social and emotional aspects of learning).

Very enlightened and thoroughgoing SEN provision: the department has its own IT suite and provides in and outside class support. Weak Year 8s are given one-to-one tuition in English and maths, SEN and reluctant learners have individual programmes – they can chose vocational courses at college and/or work experience. Learning mentors and good EAL support. Performing arts used to promote inclusion, e.g. of less academic KS4 students.

The gifted and talented can do additional GCSEs via independent learning (with an e tutor), e.g. the Cambridge school Latin project in Years 8–10; separate sciences and additional maths.

Games, Options, the Arts: Three soccer and one rugby pitches, four tennis/netball courts, an oldish gym and more modern sports hall, plus a big field with lots of trees. Also offers cross country, cricket, lacrosse, golf at a local course, cheer leading and hoop fusion for girls, self defence, junior sports leader award, leadership academy. Success in regional, county and national (football and cross country) competitions; strong tennis.

Big focus on the performing arts: has Artsmark Gold and a modern performing arts area; plays tend to be musicals, e.g. *Kiss Me Kate* (seniors) and *Mulan* (juniors, with partner primary schools); theatre trips to Leeds and London. Very strong and diverse music includes jazz orchestra, steel pans, strings, Dixie band and a full set of African djembes (drums) shared with the community; the concert band reached the finals of the National Festival of Music for Youth; students who opt for performing arts GCSE get a free term of music instruction. Also music technology equipment – a recording studio, video editing suite, lots of computers. Dance is a special feature: links with the Ballet Rambert, e.g. a master class workshop from its artistic director; students belong to the North Yorkshire Dance Company; a twilight dance GCSE class for Year 9 gifted and talented boys (urban funk favoured).

Offers a huge range of activities: D of E, a winter mountaineering course, fundraising for, e.g., CAFOD and a linked school in Ghana which sixth formers will visit to do teaching and build classrooms; aiming for Fairtrade school status. Sixth formers help the staff run activities and with lessons, as well as managing their own facilities via elected committees. York University lecturers and students work with history and politics A level students and debating is strong: the school belongs to a local league and has taken part in an Oxford based competition. A representative selection of politicians gave talks before the last general election – in the school's mock version, the Lib Dems won by a large majority, with a strong showing by the Greens. International trips to France; Greece and New York (performing arts); Barcelona (art); Germany (history). All do a team building outdoor activity at the end of the summer term. As an extended school it offers sport and community based activities in the evenings and on the weekends, including an arts programme.

Background and Atmosphere: Voluntary aided; situated on the outskirts of Harrogate – originally a convent school built in 1904, with an attractive 1970s sandstone extension supplemented by seven recent mobiles. The main problem is lack of space – some of the passage ways are narrow, which can cause shoving, but students soon adapt, according to a parent; Year 7 classrooms, which have largest numbers, seem cramped and some areas need decorating (we would have liked to see more artwork displayed). A small cafeteria for Years 7–10, a bit drab and with obstructed light – conventional hot food, sandwiches and fruit or a packed lunch for, e.g., those who want to eat on the large front lawn; the school has healthy school status. Also a huge plasma screen for menus, school and national news – a number of these in entrance halls. Years 11–13 share a modern, larger and lighter space with a small work area equipped with a few computers; the sixth form common room, painted maroon, is rather functional and well worn. Quite a good size library with a wide selection of newspapers and excellent stock of modern teenage fiction, but small adult fiction section.

The traditional chapel plays a central part in the school's spiritual life: one chapel assembly a week for separate year groups, to which various teachers contribute – the one we visited was lively and the students seemed engaged. Each year goes on a retreat, either one day or residential (year 10s visit Lourdes) and Year 8s have trips to non Christian places of worship.

Pupils have a say on school life and learning via the school council and surveys and participate in lesson observations to identify the best teaching and learning practice. Individuality is allowed: girls wear some of the shortest (plaid) skirts we have ever seen (but Mr Jackson says they are working on uniform now and skirts are longer) or trousers, with blue shirts, ties and jackets; boys wear blue shirts, tucked into or outside black trousers – and some of the shortest ties we have ever seen.

Pastoral Care and Discipline: Very thoughtful and comprehensive policies, e.g. the sensible advice issued to pupils on how to cope with bullying. The focus is more on rewards than sanctions. Planners are used by form tutors and parents to get problems resolved quickly and effectively. Year 7s are looked after very well, said a parent: they are encouraged to join clubs, take responsibility and belong to the school community – 'It's a happy, friendly and embracing place that develops confidence'; 'There's an ethos of mutual respect and lots of individual care,' said others.

A very up to date electronic system records data – attendance in all lessons, behaviour, academic progress – which teachers, form tutors and parents can access and enables tracking and monitoring to identify vulnerable students and children with emotional difficulties. Pupils who need support or time out can visit a reflection area in a secluded part of school with a space for prayer, The Oratory; a quiet room with a snooker table and access to an approachable, young lay chaplain. Year 13s and adults provide mentoring and the learning support centre is open at lunchtimes. The number of exclusions is going down, but zero tolerance of 'inappropriate language to staff' prevails.

Pupils and Parents: The majority are practising Catholics – white, middle class professionals from Harrogate and Wetherby and the surrounding district. Also a wide range of ethnic groups, the largest EAL one being Poles. Pupils are lively, outgoing and enthusiastic about the school. Parents are kept well informed via termly newsletters and a parent focus group reviews new systems.

Entrance: Over subscribed: 335 applicants for 195 places. Has its own complicated admissions system – baptised Catholics get preference.

Sixth formers: up to 30 from outside the two main schools; 5 A*-Cs with at least one B needed. Deadline for applications: mid March.

Exit: The great majority continue into the associated sixth form. The school is justifiably proud that scarcely any students become NEETS (not in education, employment or training).

Most sixth formers proceed to a great range of universities, including several top ones, e.g. Oxbridge and the best London University colleges.

Money Matters: The Hayra Educational Trust provides a fund for help with extra-curricular activities, including gap year projects, for sixth formers.

Remarks: A deeply impressive school in all respects, apart from the limitations of its accommodation – deservedly researched by Ofsted for a report on the features of outstanding state schools.

St John's School (Leatherhead)

Epsom Road, Leatherhead, Surrey, KT22 8SP

• Pupils: 550 • Ages: 13-18 • Size of sixth form: 240 of whom 80 are girls • C of E but other denominations accepted • Fees: Day £18,495; Boarding £23,430-£25,425 pa • Independent

Tel: 01372 373 000
Fax: 01372 386 606
Email: admissions@stjohns.surrey.sch.uk
Website: www.stjohnsleatherhead.co.uk

Headmaster: Since 2004, Mr Nicholas Haddock MBE MA FRGS (forties). Read geography at Oxford followed by a distinguished career in the army where he was a major in the Royal Green Jackets. An adventurous Captain Cook type of chap – passionate about wilderness expeditions, mountaineering and exploring and keen on all sports (played hockey for Oxford and is a former Welsh player). He now also manages to squeeze in time for more leisurely pursuits such as reading biographies, fly-fishing and being married with four children! Former house master at Cranleigh School, this is his first headship – has been very well received by parents and students alike and it is easy to see why. Demonstrates great leadership (not surprisingly with his military background); never takes his eyes off the bigger picture while managing to pick up on the small things.

Not one of those pompous military types – in fact quite the opposite. We would describe him as sincere and charming in a relaxed and understated way, a friendly and warm chap. Very careful and considered when answering questions (a bit like a lawyer) – he answers thoughtfully, factually and truthfully but doesn't elaborate with masses of details or funny stories (with some exceptions). He describes himself as, 'believing in people, considered, understated and having a sense of purpose (and humour).' Very much in the modern head mould – he views staff as the greatest asset of the school and doesn't believe a head's role should be 'the be all and end all'. He says, 'it is all about serving the individual (student)' – though hopefully the pupils will not take him too literally.

Academic matters: Definitely on the up. Traditionally viewed as the poor relation to some of its neighbouring academic high flying schools, academia has taken on a new lease of life particularly reflected in the A level results. Still not premier league but the school is certainly rising up the tables at a rate of knots. In 2010, 73 per cent A*–B at A level (compared to 43 per cent A-B in 2002) with no great disparity between girls' and boys' results.

The school and head are not known for blowing their own trumpets – so it will take a bit of time for the new rise in academics to become common knowledge, but needless to say the head is clearly pleased. Typically, he does not want the school to become a hothouse – 'we will continue to be a school of mixed abilities in a caring environment.' Mr Haddock has taken advice from the Russell Group of Universities (top 19 in UK incl Oxbridge) in an attempt to improve students' career prospects and to make sure the school offers the correct curriculum and subjects. He reckons, 'nine or 10 GCSEs and A levels in core subjects' is the recipe for success, therefore he doesn't 'see any reason to offer subjects that are too alternative'. Extremely impressive maths department – stretching even the most able. Parents boast about popular and strong science department with well equipped new chemistry lab, biology housed in adjacent specialist block. School rightly proud of its IT facilities – needless to say computers feature heavily in all teaching. Some muttering that school not as strong in humanities – more mixed results, which deter some prospective sixth formers notably humanity-loving girls. Changing though – 80s per cent A*–B grades in both geography and history at A level in 2010.

Majority of lessons take place in the classroom block, originally built in post war years but superbly renovated and extended in 2002. Up to six 'sets' in some subjects – with plenty of coming and going among sets. One parent, whose son is in the top set in all subjects says, 'maybe he is not stretched in all subjects all the time but there is a sense of balance.' Plenty of rewards for those who work hard and extra school for those who don't. Atmosphere in classrooms varies according to teaching style from quiet and focused to debating and vibrant – lots of keen hands in the air. No departmental libraries. Huge number of outings, visits and field-trips organised by most departments. School caters for those with dyslexia, dyspraxia, ADD and ADHD – appears well organised and managed. Pupils are screened for SEN on entry. Around a third of those with SEN attend individual lessons with SENCo – extra charge.

Games, Options, the Arts: Very good – certainly no shortage of modern facilities and equipment. School has acres of sports fields – main games are rugby, football and cricket for boys and hockey, netball and tennis for girls. In addition, a whole array of other sports can be chosen in indoor swimming pool complex (with squad) and large indoor sports hall as well as many other outdoor pursuits including Eton Fives. 'Sports for all' held throughout the week, plus team fixtures on Saturday afternoon. Judging by the number of silver trophies on display and ecstatic parents emphasising 'participation by all' – sport is enjoyed by most with also notable competitive success.

Art and DT some of the best we have seen – not just the outstanding facilities (open most of the time and now enhanced even further in the new classroom block) but also the extraordinary work produced – the portrait work was quite stunning. About 50 per cent of all students play a musical instrument (up to diploma standard); all may join the choirs – plenty of opportunity to perform. Drama is important with heaps of productions and trips – at the time of our visit, drama students were busy preparing for a tour to California performing *The Tempest*. School has separate multi-media studio for films, smaller plays and concerts. CCF very strong and is compulsory for four terms;

many boys and girls are also involved in D of E and the BTec Diploma in Public Service; trips include expedition to Norway to take on the Nordic Challenge.

Parents give mega praise to the super choice of extra-curricular activities and the positive contribution they make. Mr Haddock is genuinely committed to the importance of character building: 'we offer as many activities as is practically possible in an attempt for each individual to find out who they are and what their passion is.' He is confident of the impact on motivation and academic results, 'once the students have a goal – hard work usually follows.' One sixth form parent unintentionally sums up Mr Haddock's vision when she talks about the change in her previously 'quiet and not so academic' daughter – 'she threw herself at all the activities on offer at St John's (drama, debating, singing and CCF), she discovered new found confidence, leadership traits ... her academic results dramatically improved – she blossomed and was really happy.'

Background and Atmosphere: Founded in 1851 in St John's Wood to educate the sons of poor Anglican clergy – moved to existing 50-acre campus site in 1872. Set in a leafy residential area in the commuter town of Leatherhead; super first impressions – architecturally splendid buildings in mellow Victorian red brick, stunning cloister surrounding large central quad. Imposing cathedral style dining hall on one side, others surrounded by original boarding houses, classroom block and frequently attended chapel. Classrooms are light and modern – firmly in the 21st century with all mod cons: interactive whiteboards, flat screen computers, new desks and chairs. Impressive £3m performing art centre comprising the music school, huge auditorium and a social centre for the sixth form. Social centre is a great success with both boarders and day students – in particular, the bar, for those 18+ (strict supervision and limits) and parents delighted their teenagers have somewhere safe to meet. 2010 has seen the opening of a new £7 million classroom block housing a new library, workshops for design and technology, art studios, IT suites and classrooms. This created space for a new girls' house, Haslewood, to accommodate the arrival of girls in the fourth form (age 13) in 2010.

Boys' boarding facilities have been much criticised in the past. Major renovation of all the boys' houses 2007. School says that all dorms and double/single rooms now have adjacent bathrooms with showers. Smart new boarding house for upper sixth girls, single rooms with en-suite facilities – envious boys liken it to a 'five star hotel'. The older boarding accommodation for lower sixth form girls is nothing like as glamorous – cosy and well-loved are useful (i.e. polite) adjectives to describe it.

All meals are taken together in the wood panelled dining hall. Students confirm that food has improved – nevertheless an interesting assortment of condiments and spices could be seen in most boys' bedrooms (all have a fridge). One sixth form boy confirmed that they are allowed to go to a nearby supermarket (for provisions?). Most boarders go home after sport on a Saturday afternoon. Mr Haddock says, 'twenty or so stay on and activities are put on when demand is there'. In reality, it is very much a day school with weekly boarders, not really the first choice for parents or pupils wanting full boarding.

Pastoral Care and Discipline: Strong pastoral care. On entry all students join a house – they get to know housemaster/mistress and their allocated form tutor who, together with popular chaplain, form the foundation of a wide net of pastoral support. 'There are so many adults on hand should you wish to speak to someone,' said one boy. Bullying taken very seriously and dealt with promptly – it is not seen as problem by parents or students. Parents differ as to whether Mr Haddock is a disciplinarian – all agree, though, that his deputies are very strict indeed.

Like many schools, drugs, booze, cigs and sex can be a problem. Nonetheless school rules clearly outlined and all pupils (and parents) know what punishment applies for offences. The forthcoming Mr Haddock frankly admits, 'we are reinforcing a culture of discipline' – can be a bit of a culture shock to some boys coming into the school and it is not an ideal place for the free spirit. Indeed grumbles from a couple of parents of 'non-conformist' boys – that school seen as heavy on detention for petty misdemeanours. Another parent takes a different view – 'the strict routine and discipline really suits my son ... his organisational skills have really developed.'

Pupils and Parents: The majority from professional middle class families. A relaxed, down to earth bunch of pupils, who are surprisingly neat and tidy, and display confidence without arrogance. 'Certainly not all clones from rich families,' comments one parent. Another parent adds, 'my son has a broad range of friends regardless of their academic ability or success in sport.' It is very much a local school – many pupils live within 20 miles. Notable OJs include architect Lord (Richard) Rogers, novelist Sir Anthony Hope and archaeologist Sir Leonard Woolley.

Entrance: Selection is made principally on the basis of recommendation from a pupil's current head, as well as an assessment when the pupil is in Year 6 and taking into consideration his or her co-curricular strengths. A conditional place will be offered subject to a Common Entrance pass mark of 55 per cent. Head emphasises that he wants pupils who can 'engage fully in what the school can offer'. Boys (and girls from 2010) mostly come from prep schools in Surrey and SW London. Entry at 16 for boys and girls based on an assessment, interview, predicted GCSE result and a report from current school. Approx 40 girls each year come into the sixth form mostly from Manor House and St Teresa's with 10–15 boys, mainly from overseas.

Exit: Number of those leaving at 16 varies from year to year. Broad academic intake and wide range of core A level subjects means at 18 no distinct favourite universities or courses – pupils exit to a huge selection of both. Usually one or two to Oxbridge.

Money Matters: Long list of scholarships offered – worth up to 25 per cent. Bursaries available for those in need. School has separate funds to educate sons of Anglican Clergy. Discounts for siblings at the school and for Old Johnians.Two Albany Awards are available each year – free places for disadvantaged families.

Remarks: A local school in the ascendancy – academia is improving notably, excellent new facilities and huge number of activities make it definitely worth a look for an all round non-pressured education. Don't think of sending hooray Henrys (or Henriettas) here – they would not be happy bunnies.

St Laurence School

Ashley Road, Bradford-on-Avon, Wiltshire, BA15 1DZ

• Pupils: 1,170 boys and girls • Ages: 11-18 • Size of sixth form: 210 • C of E • State

Tel: 01225 309 500
Fax: 01225 309 572
Email: jane.rodway@st-laurence.wilts.sch.uk
Website: www.st-laurence.wilts.sch.uk

Headteacher: Since 2004, Mr James Colquhoun LLB PGCE (fifties); educated at Kelly College, Devon. Read law at Bristol before 'a few years in the wilderness'. First teaching post in Swindon followed by charge of sixth form in Devon, to deputy headship in Wimborne and headships in Market Harborough, Kettering, Bishop's Stopford and the north east. Married to former special needs teacher with grown-up family. Appointed to restore St Laurence's fortunes after predecessor's sudden departure; follows two year spell in noteworthy DCFS 'Fresh Start' headship in Newcastle-upon-Tyne. Track record of raising academic standards, a hands-on manager with clout and business acumen. Energetic and determined to see school back amongst top state schools. Generally liked by parents and respected by pupils; keeps banging out mantra of three core values: commitment, creativity and community. Has dispensed with bursar, privatised support services and restructured staff. Some parents unhappy about shorter teaching day but, overall, reforms have been well received with improved results at Key Stages 3 and 4.

Academic matters: Academic strengths across the board with science and modern languages strong. Provision for exceptionally able. A levels one third A grades in 2009. At GCSE, 75 per cent achieved five or more A*–C; 65 per cent including maths and English. Setting progressively from Year 7. 'Oxbridge awareness programme' in sixth form.

Games, Options, the Arts: Grass athletics track; playing fields provide enough space for cricket, tennis, hockey, rugby and football. Some athletes at county and national level. A Sportsmark School. Riding once a week for SEN students. A hits-you-between-the-eyes art department where dynamic and dedicated team nurtures each pupil to locate the ceramicist, sculptor, textural artist, colourist or draughtsman they didn't know they were. Strong on drama, dance and music – close links with Theatre Royal in Bath. One in five take an instrument. Two choirs – linked to a school in Japan, several string groups, two jazz bands and an orchestra. An Artsmark Gold school. Foreign exchanges to Sully (France) and Norden (Germany), and recent sixth form trips to Paris, Berlin, Romania, Gambia and Kenya. Participated in Model United Nations. A DCFS International School. Each year timetable is collapsed for a week of special projects/outward bound/challenge programmes for all years. Drama and dance trips aplenty.

Background and Atmosphere: The prosperous Italianate town of Bradford-on-Avon spawned rich merchants in the wool trade. In 1860, a freethinking philanthropist, Lord Fitzmaurice, set up a technical school with the radical aim of educating young people for the 19th century. In 2002, archaeologists unearthed a vast Roman Villa on the playing field and uncovered a rare mosaic in almost perfect condition. Fitzmaurice Grammar merged in 1980 with 250 year old Trinity Secondary Modern on a site above the picturesque town. The marriage was St Laurence, blessed with enough land to offer a slice for the Wiltshire Music Centre, built three years ago on £2.8 million lottery and local sponsorship. Although independent, the 300-seat auditorium, recording studio, music technology suite and nine workshop spaces are used for pupils as well as by 2,000 visitors a week for concerts/jazz and voice workshops/dance/lectures/filming. The Schubert Ensemble, The Orchestra of the Age of Enlightenment, Howard Skempton, Jason Rebello, Pee Wee Ellis hold workshops for the school. This fairy godmother has done much to glamorise the image of St Laurence's fast improving environment. Enthusiasm from staff is infectious. Rock star Midge Ure recently visited – 'I wish I'd been to a school like this!' 250 seater restaurant serves healthy options and gives the kind of lift to the place that the head is keen to see generally. 120 seat lecture theatre and plans for a new Independent Learning Centre (library).

Pastoral Care and Discipline: No rebels given reins here. Discipline achieved through reward and sanction system. Hot on parent-staff rapport. Inter-personal skills highly valued – sixth formers taking part in two different mentor schemes and getting certificate of recognition as part of record of achievement. School counsellor and nurse on staff. Tutors and year heads provide continuity of care from Year 7. Clear behaviour management policy including response to bullying. Clear policy on dealing with drugs and other substances, parents are involved and they work in close co-operation with police and other agencies. Tries to lure students into dining room with imaginative sandwiches. Also – excellent idea – breakfast from 8 to 8.45am. Why, oh why, cry pupils, do only Year 7s and sixth formers get lockers, forcing the rest to troll around with books, PE kits, props for drama and kitchen sink from class to class?

Pupils and Parents: Large contingent from affluent villages of Freshford, Westwood, Winsley, Limpley Stoke. Most from middle class catchment area. Professors/teachers/county hall bods/self-employed media/musicians/actors/architects. 'All our teachers send their children here which is a good sign,' says old-timer. Students willingly swap from private schools like Sherborne to endure the mundane uniform of navy sweatshirt with logo, navy trousers/skirt. Body piercing or dyed hair is out. For sixth form, nets are cast wider than catchment, and casual dress allowed. Parent who dumped a 100 per cent bursary from a private school in Bath to send girl here instead say, 'every child in private education needs to come to a place like this to get ready for the real world'. Former pupils include recent stars of small screen Charlotte Long, Emma Pierson, Michael Rouse, singer Mike Edwards, Joe England (Royal Shakespeare Company).

Entrance: 205+ places at Year 7 but anyone in catchment area automatically gets in. (The school's cachet has driven up house prices by 10 per cent.) Induction days for sixth form in June and September.

Exit: 90 per cent to higher education e.g. Cardiff, Nottingham, Liverpool, Sheffield, London. Five to Oxbridge in 2009. Small tranche to art/photography colleges.

Remarks: Stimulating environment which can take just about anybody and get magnificent results. Good relationships between teacher and parent; teamwork and creativity to the fore with current head likely to put St Laurence back where it was in terms of local reputation.

St Lawrence College

Linked to Saint Lawrence College Junior School

College Road, Ramsgate, Kent, CT11 7AE

• Pupils: 330; 210 boys, 120 girls; 185 boarding, 140 day • Ages: 11-18
• CofE/Christian • Fees: Day £14,682 Boarding £25,485 pa
• Independent

Tel: 01843 572931
Fax: 01843 572901
Email: ah@slcuk.com
Website: www.slcuk.com

Headmaster: Since 2004, The Rev Mark Aitken (early fifties). Educated at St Edward's School, Oxford; read geography at Durham followed by theology at Cambridge from where he entered the Church and held curacies in London and Hertfordshire before becoming vicar of a large parish in Norwich. After attending a prestigious course at St George's Chapel at Windsor he became chaplain at Sherborne School for Boys. Here he continued his passion for coaching rugby, ran the school's Roc Soc which produced Chris Martin of Coldplay fame and sat on the senior management team. He says that running a school is very similar to running a parish. A very welcoming and approachable man, sees himself as an intuitive headmaster. Well liked by parents and pupils and has breathed new life into the school. Does not teach but does know the children and makes sure he sees every child individually twice a year before they sit their public exams. His wife Kim, who is charming and enthusiastic, teaches in the junior school and they have two sons, one at Cambridge and one who works as a legal editor.

Academic matters: In 2010, 87 per cent A*–C at GCSE (27 per cent A*/A) and 50 per cent A*–B at A level with 25 per cent A*/A – good results for an unselective school. As well as the usual subjects, psychology, music technology, drama and theatre studies and PE offered at A level. Religious studies GCSE taken early with good results. Everyone (boys and girls) does home economics in Years 7 and 8; further up the school it is a popular option e.g. making Christmas cakes and 'cooking on a student budget'.

Sixty pupils with EAL requirements; strong emphasis on integration from the word go and sixth form intake must have adequate English to be allowed to join. Lots of support individually tailored to needs and will run an intensive course for those who need it, but reluctant to separate them from the mainstream as keen to build an integrated community. Class sizes start at 20, reducing as you go up the school.

Forty need some sort of AEN (SEN) support, mainly for mild dyslexia and there is one statemented child. Two specialist teachers. Children withdrawn from class where necessary, usually from Latin or French. New specialist SENCo appointed 2010.

Games, Options, the Arts: Boys play rugby, hockey and cricket and girls play netball and hockey. Tennis a major feature. Good balance between desire to win and inclusion of all. The major sports are compulsory until sixth form when pupils may give up organised games but are encouraged to take some sort of exercise e.g. aerobics in fitness suite, basketball etc or swimming. Astroturf, all weather tennis courts, indoor swimming pool etc.

Community service encouraged and aimed to give pupils a sense of social responsibility – service being very much part of the ethos of the school. Kent Institute of Art and Young Enterprise provide pupils with contact with the realities of life in the big wide world. The Chapel band visits local churches and the award winning 'Chemical Magic' show is enthusiastically received in nearby primary schools. Trips to Calais and Boulogne plus foreign sports tours. CCF popular with boys and girls, Duke of Edinburgh popular – several children attain their gold award each year – impressive in so small a school.

Music compulsory for Years 7 and 8. School has its own recording studio. Choirs, orchestra, jazz club musicals, concerts, visiting professional musicians. Annual Arts Week with a play, poetry readings, a book fair etc. House plays and singing competitions. Drama not timetabled until sixth form. Various societies e.g. maths and creative writing – debating society recently set up.

Background and Atmosphere: Founded in 1879 as a boys' boarding school to provide a first-class education based upon sound Christian teaching, it went fully co-ed 1983. As you drive through the arch and enter a 150 acre oasis in the middle of Ramsgate – a remnant of high Victorian muscular Christianity with imposing Virginia creeper clad buildings dominated by the chapel – it is easy to imagine the sons of the Empire going forth from here to all corners of the world. The calm, slightly other-worldly feel belies a thoroughly modern and creative approach to education.

The school has recently sold a plot of land for building so has money to spend. A new ultra modern middle school building opened in 2007 and most class rooms, boarding houses and the sixth form centre have been refurbished. There are two specialist computer suites and plenty of networked computers throughout the school and in the boarding houses.

Pastoral Care and Discipline: The strong evangelical tradition of the school underpins its religious and spiritual life. Daily chapel and Sunday services for boarders are based on a strong Christian ethos but an open minded approach is encouraged and alternative provision is made for those who do not want to attend e.g. Jewish pupils can attend the synagogue in Ramsgate and Muslim pupils observe Ramadan. Good interaction between the year groups and international pupils well integrated (the Chinese, as always, find this more difficult than most) – the recent appointment of a director of international students has helped this process. Multi-ethnic nature of the boarding community helps pupils understand the needs and aspirations of others. Strong sense of community and personal responsibility. Pupils have clear sense of right and wrong and moral issues are discussed in lessons e.g. world health and poverty in geography and fair play in sport. Great emphasis on teamwork.

Very low staff turnover – 24 have been in the school for over ten years and a number have children in the school.

Pupils and Parents: Day children from Thanet and East Kent – the school is on the wrong side of the Pfizer site from the traffic point of view, so catchment is limited. Boarders from around the world. Lots from Europe, about 14 per cent Hong Kong Chinese. Sixth form popular with the Germans. The pupils we met were spontaneously friendly and helpful and unassumingly self confident. Parents encouraged to participate in school activities and all parents are invited to a dinner in the autumn term. Well known old boys include General Sir Richard Dannatt, Sir John Stevens, McDonald's Chief Executive Peter Beresford and Gordon Edington.

Entrance: Most children join at 11 and entry is through an interview and testing (not too strenuous) where appropriate. Entry at 13+ is via CE. About half come up from the junior school, the rest from small independent schools and primary schools – the inevitable fallout from the Kent Test. 15–20 pupils join in the sixth form – they are assessed on GCSE performance (normally five passes) and an English test for those from abroad.

Exit: To a wide spread of universities old and new plus a few to art school and a trickle to Oxbridge. A few leave after GCSEs, some to go to the grammars and others to vocational courses.

Money Matters: Academic, music, art, sport and all-rounder scholarships offered at 11+, 13+ and 16+ plus various bursaries.

Remarks: A charming and warm school, openly Christian but open to all. Coming out of a long period in the doldrums (as an 'all right' school for those missing out on grammars or more selective independents) under a popular head.

St Leonards School

Linked to Saint Leonards – New Park in the Junior section

South Street, St Andrews, Fife, KY16 9QJ

• Pupils: 515 boys and girls (roughly 50/50) of whom 165 are in St Leonards-New Park, the preparatory school of St Leonards. 119 boarders. • Ages: 16-19 sixth form (125) 12-16 senior school (225), 4-12 junior school (165) • Size of sixth form: 16-19 sixth form (125) • Non-denom • Fees: Day £7,653-£10,554; Boarding £25,128 pa • Independent

Tel: 01334 472126
Fax: 01334 476152
Email: info@stleonards-fife.org
Website: www.stleonards-fife.org

Headmaster: Since 2008, Dr Michael Carslaw BSc MBA PhD (early fifties). Glaswegian by birth, is 'still delighted to be part of such a vibrant school community with so much going on.' After some pretty cataclysmic changes and a period of consolidation under previous head, Dr Carslaw feels 'that the reeling stage is past now, as exemplified by the strong growth of the last two/three years.' He is 'now looking very much to the future' with extra classes in Years 8, 9 and 10. He adds, 'the students are very lucky to be part of such a historic yet vibrant and forward-looking school and I am enjoying sharing the experience with them.'

He attributes quick recent growth in numbers to the huge positive impact of introducing the IB (International Baccalaureate – not to be confused with the more watered-down new Scottish Baccalaureate) 'as well as the positive buzz about the school as St Leonards re-emerges into the mainstream of Scottish education.' 'Co-ed' he says 'is fully bedded in' (!) with 50/50 all through. Dr Carslaw feels that the long established status which St Leonards enjoyed as Scotland's most academic girls-only school should now be equalled by its distinction as a co-ed IB school. Sensibly, realising that the sixth form college image is a mixed blessing, he is working to bring the three sections of the school together, giving the juniors in St Leonards-New Park (formed following the merger with local prep school, New Park in 2005) the bonus of lots of help from sixth formers required to do 50 hours of 'service' as part of the IB.

Academic matters: School prides itself on 'high quality education right from the preparatory school through to the senior school.' Scotland's only all-IB sixth form – focuses 100 per cent on the IB. 'We haven't taken any half measures with the qualification by offering alternative post 16 options, we have dedicated ourselves to it and we believe that's to the great benefit of our students.'

In 2010 IB Diploma leavers achieved an average of 32 points, equivalent to 435 UCAS points or 3 A*s at A level and 5 As at Highers. Eight made the minimum entrance requirements for Oxbridge. 30 candidates got bilingual diplomas.

GCSE results also impressive with 58 per cent A/A*. Head says 'the IB is probably the least tinkered about with qualification in the world – its basic philosophy of keeping a breadth of subjects going into the sixth form but also studying three to a level comparable to Advanced Higher or A level has remained.' 'Native lang' for IB may be English, Russian, German, French, Mandarin (currently on offer) or whatever, while Latin qualifies as a foreign language, as well as French, Spanish, German, Italian (from scratch). UCAS is now giving points for individual subjects studied under the IB system which means that non linguists/mathematicians etc, previously disadvantaged in the overall IB grading, can now get full credit for their strong subjects.

Max class size 20. Links with St Andrew's Uni are still strong and progressing, Dr Carslaw assures us. (Lots of Profs' children and consequently no dearth of academic governors or visiting speakers.) Norm is 2/3 langs with all doing French from Year 1 and Spanish and /or German from Year 5. Latin flourishes.

Dyslexia/dyspraxia support – 'no statemented pupils accepted' – mostly provided for 'a small proportion of pupils' in mainstream teaching but a good programme with some withdrawal for learning support and, more prominently, for EAL (English as an Additional Language). About one fifth of non English (native) speakers need it to start with; all the overseas IB pupils have to pass an English assessment and they don't need any EAL support. Good IT but rather in the wings (still).

Games, Options, the Arts: Full range of sporting options – chaps' sports fixtures have taken off in recent years. First ever home rugby matches in school's history last year with rugby pitches on the main school site and a growing fixture list for all ages, and increasing number of football fixtures. Girls' sports still strong, with usual mass of international lax players. Rugby good at junior level (parents agree!) and head has high hopes for senior school. Otherwise loads of individual sports: judo, trampoline, skiing, badminton, swimming – university uses pool for water polo – rock-climbing, snow boarding and surfing; in 2008 there was a rock-climbing expedition to the Alps.

It being St Andrew's golf reigns supreme with about a third of the school playing; all lucky boarders can and do become youth members of the St Andrews Links Trust (as residents in St Andrews) so they can play the Old Course. Great new all-weather pitch, despite prolonged problems with Historic Scotland about floodlights. Sports hall probably on the wish list, though school has quite a lot of spare cash after some judicious sell-offs, but talk of lottery funding and community type use.

Outstanding art department, attracting pupils outside normal lessons as well as curricular – huge range of alternative media, dark rooms etc. Gigantic sculptures much in evidence in dining room and about school. Spectacular 'body casts' making Gormley-style figures. Artists in residence doing printmaking etc. Music strong in fabulous Bob Steedman (husband of four heads ago) designed centre. Drama on the up; school performs twice a year in the revamped nearby Byre theatre in St Andrews (and this is popular with both school and public) plus D of E etc. etc. Trips (one per subject per year) with major ones like a drama visit to New York planned on a two year cycle.

Background and Atmosphere: A curious mixture of gracious living, with house 'drawing rooms' reminiscent of Country Life plus lawned courts nestling among old stone building in 'dreaming spires' style combined with faintly scruffy corridors, classrooms, common rooms etc with a distinctly old fashioned (and none the worse for that), schooly feel. Founded and purpose built in 1877, St Leonards inhabits a notoriously windswept corner of Fife, on the sea, bracing air, bone chilling easterly gales, track suits popular for games. Golf, riding and the beach all great draws, as well as trips up town and forays to the surrounding countryside. Mega library and selection of 'Maryana' in Queen Mary's House (oddly flanked by a boys' loo). Individual research emphasis in IB has made library a popular place again with a really helpful new librarian thrown in.

School praised for high standard of pastoral care for boarders by the Care Commission. Weekly and termly boarding but the emphasis is now more on day; numbers have risen since day fees were reduced by 25 per cent to align more with local day schools than with higher day fees for full boarding schools. Boarders have comprehensive facilities, mostly single rooms and down-time freedom appropriate for 21st century to visit the town, dress informally and decorate (or litter) their own living space. Day pupils in the sixth form included in house system with 'day rooms' in boarding houses.

Buses for day pupils: Dundee, Kirkcaldy, Auchtermuchty, Perthshire. Juniors can be dropped off early (8am) and collected late (5.30). This represents a reduced school day but incorporates time for activities, which has 'settled down well and parents appreciate it.' Sixth formers now wear suits during the working day. The few boys visible during an exam time visit looked suave and sophisticated young professionals; the girls less so. Since January 2009, trad but machine washable blazers (£80) and blue tartan kilts for girls are senior school uniform. There is a second hand shop run by the 'bullish' PA which also organises family fun tennis etc.

Pastoral Care and Discipline: School rules feature punctuality, security and civilised behaviour; the student handbook has a rash of rules, most of which are sheer common sense: L-drivers may not drive other pupils and the like. But members of the sixth form have a mass of privileges – can visit some (some definitely out of bounds) local pubs (some are out of bounds), smoke off-campus ('but not if I feel they are bringing the school into disrepute and are identifiable as St Leonards pupils,' says head) and are generally expected to behave like grown-ups. No smoking on campus, no under-age drinking and absolute zero tolerance of drugs. Parents like the drugs policy – random drugs testing and testing on suspicion, out for pushing, forfeit right to remain in school for using – depends on individual and other factors and for how long, and pupils may be allowed back under fairly arduous conditions – and the like. Suspension for continued failure to observe the booze rules. Police are called for theft. No chaplain but team of local ministers who regularly preach.

Pupils and Parents: No boarding in junior school, hence strong Scots contingent up to senior school; small number of UK boarders but most from abroad, particularly at sixth form level, when incomers swell the ranks to follow the IB course – this is encouraged as the internationalism of the college is seen as one of its strengths. Still a few nobs but huge mix of foreign and first time buyers. Fifers beginning to see school as a good option again. St Leonards has a strong Old Girls' network and many at the school are offspring or grand offspring of Seniors. Some concern recently among seniors about school's new direction though others welcome its possible new impetus. Famous seniors include Betty Harvey Anderson, Dame Kathleen Ollerenshaw, the previous President of St Leonards, Gillian Glover of the Scotsman (who didn't last the course), Stella Tennant (ditto), Baroness Byford (current President) and Anji Hunter.

Entrance: Accept CE, but usually own entrance assessment (English and maths) or scholarship exam. Six GCSEs or equivalent for sixth with As and Bs in subjects to be studied at higher level in the IB. 'We usually pick up 30/40 at sixth from entry' for IB.

Exit: 'Minimum' drop out at transition from St Leonards-New Park to seniors and a dribble away post GCSE, (only accept good English speakers to sixth form). Around 90 per cent to universities – a regular 8–10 per cent to Oxbridge. University destinations in 2009 included Oxford, Cambridge, Edinburgh, Brisbane and Toronto. 2010 university destinations included Cambridge, St Andrews, Edinburgh, Glasgow, Munich and Boston. Most do a gap year, armed with addresses of welcoming seniors throughout the world (a boon for worried parents).

Money Matters: A means-tested, Assisted Places scheme in operation; open to application from existing parents in financial difficulties. Currently restructuring scholarships (all means tested) and bursaries to satisfy Scottish charitable status requirements. Serious – though only of nominal monetary value – collection of scholarships, ranging from academic through music, drama and sport – golf scholarships very popular (as you might imagine).

Remarks: St Leonard's hit back at the spate of Scottish elite 'public' schools going co-ed to fill up the gaps in their budgets and academic records with clever girls by going co-ed itself. Dr Carslaw is determined to make St Leonards a cohesive and mutually supportive school community rather than three separate parts. Some revolutionary upheavals in style and leaderships have produced (three heads later) a school that is just beginning to gel into a whole with the potential to become greater than the sums of its parts. Seizing the IB niche gives it an academic edge with an international flavour – visionary, certainly, but not for the fainthearted!

St Leonards-Mayfield School

The Old Palace, High Street, Mayfield, East Sussex, TN20 6PH

• Pupils: 400 girls; about 200 board/flexiboard. • Ages: 11-18 • Size of sixth form: 120 • RC (but non-RCs welcome) • Fees: Day £16,050; Boarding £24,390 pa • Independent

Tel: 01435 874 600
Fax: 01435 872 627
Email: enquiry@mayfieldgirls.org
Website: www.mayfieldgirls.org

Headmistress: Since 2008, Miss Antonia Beary (late thirties). Read English at Trinity College, Cambridge, and has an MPhil in Catholic Education. Two years at The Leys, Cambridge where she became assistant housemistress of the sixth form house, followed by six years at Ampleforth where she started as an English teacher and ended up in charge of the first girls' sixth form house. Two years as head of sixth form at New Hall before joining Mayfield in 2006 as pastoral deputy. Thoughtful, approachable, charming. Likes to help girls develop a sense of perspective and the confidence to make the right decisions. Humphrey the spaniel, always by her side, offers a comforting paw to any nervous juniors who need a cuddle.

Academic matters: A level results good – 61 per cent A*/A grade and at GCSE 59 per cent A*/A grades. Average class size 14 for GCSE and about 10 for A level. Good mix of teaching staff: some NQTs, some more venerable. Everyone to have a laptop connected to school intranet – some financial assistance where necessary. 24 girls currently doing City & Guilds GCSE in cooking, a practical, hands-on course taught in a big, light, airy kitchen – leads to Diploma. A level home economics introduced 2009. Cooking clubs and Saturday workshops well attended. Library a bit dated but a popular, quiet place to work. Plenty of help with personal statements and UCAS forms.

Learning support department very much in the centre of the school where girls can go for help and reassurance 'a real haven' as one dyslexic girl put it. One full-time and two part- time teachers. 10–15 per cent need some sort of extra help mainly for mild dyslexia – girls given coping strategies and learning support closely linked with teaching (first six lessons (35 mins) free; subsequently charged at £18 per lesson). All girls do baseline tests on arrival and staff quick to pick up any problems. Good ESOL department – 8 periods a week – girls taken out of English and PE. Generally high scores on IELTS (average of 7.5 over the past four years) very good reputation with universities.

Games, Options, the Arts: Spectacular ceramics department. We were there when the GCE and A level exhibits were on show in the cloister and it was like walking through a museum – we would have happily bought the lot. Enthusiastic and inspired art and textiles teacher. Lots of flexibility for girls to do what they want at after school workshops four nights a week. Life drawing studio, jewellery, silversmith plus resins and plastics.

The usual sports but no lacrosse. Plenty of sporting opportunities for those who want. Riding a major feature – have won the National Schools Championships for the past 3 years and have a 2012 show jumping hopeful. A recent leaver rode at Badminton in 2009 and 2010. Girls can keep their own ponies at a nearby farm. Outdoor sand school and cross country course within the school grounds; small indoor sand school available locally. Strong fencing – U15 champion 2008. 17 girls represented their county in 2008 and two girls represented England at rounders. About 10 girls do Duke of Edinburgh Gold each year. School very supportive of what the girls do outside school. Sport seems to tail off a bit in sixth from with a focus on top teams but school is trying to engage other girls in different sports e.g. sailing. PE offered at GCSE and A level.

Strong and very experienced music department. Singing particularly good – school's premier choir, the Schola Cantorum, recently performed evening Mass in the Basilica di San Marco in Venice. Chapel choir often asked to sing at weddings. Good orchestra plus classical, musical theatre and rock band. Supervised practice after school. GCSE and A levels offered in music. 2–3 drama productions per year – girls get involved in all aspects of production, direction, lighting and textiles department make the costumes in-house. A group of girls took a production up to the Edinburgh Fringe Festival in 2008. All performed in wonderful concert hall as are fashion shows and various musical events. Theatre studies taught at A level and drama at GCSE. Annual inter-house performing arts festival – sixth form write, choreograph and produce a range of pieces and hone their people management skills. Dance is compulsory for Years 7–9 and is a popular option further up the school with ballet and salsa being taught by qualified visiting teachers.

Background and Atmosphere: Founded in 1846 by Cornelia Connelly, foundress of the religious congregation for the education of Catholic girls, the Society of the Holy Child Jesus; a woman ahead of her time. In 1872 it moved into the The Old Palace of the Archbishop of Canterbury. Stunning medieval chapel which is central to school life and can seat every pupil and where 'The Live Crib' is performed each Christmas with a real donkey and real baby. All classrooms and facilities on one site; four boarding houses split by age. Lower school have their own separate building and their own dining room in the main school. Three separate dining rooms – sixth form eat with staff. Girls in Years 11–13 have study bedrooms and can opt for single rooms. Approximately half of pupils board (including weekly and flexiboarding) and there is no school on Saturday. Strong Catholic ethos but over half now non catholic. Chapel is very important and central to school life. Everyone has to go and girls organise some of the liturgies. Encouraged to question everything and not take anything for granted.

Pastoral Care and Discipline: The first lay head was appointed in 2000. Nuns are still involved in pastoral care and are active in school community. Very supportive school – both girls and staff. 'Be yourself but be aware that you are part of a community.' 'Actions not Words' programme takes girls outside the classroom to serve others and raise their awareness both of the needs of others and of ways in which they can all make a difference. A school of individuals – girls are encouraged to think independently and develop a strong moral awareness and sense of perspective. Not a hothouse. Compulsory mass on Sunday mornings and compulsory liturgy during the week for all year groups as well as occasional whole school masses throughout the term. Christianity rather than Catholicism at the centre of school. A lady chaplain recently joined the school and has livened up the weekly liturgies.

Pupils and Parents: Mostly local, London and South East. Eclectic bunch from a wide range of prep and primary schools – currently working on building relationships with local and London primary schools. Hold masterclasses to bring in prep and primary school children for art and music taster days. Up to 10 per cent foreign nationals: a number of Hong Kong Chinese, Spanish and Mexicans but no one group dominates. School maintains good links with parents. Strong old girl network – Holy Child link helps. Old girls include dress designer Lindka Cierach, journalist Dame Ann Leslie, author Maeve Haran, French actress Anouk Aimee, screenplay writer Olivia Hetreed and immeasurable numbers of barristers, physicians, etc.

Entrance: Two thirds take school's own exam at 11+ and one third take 13+ Common Entrance. Entrance exams double as academic scholarship exams at 11+ and 16+; at 13+ there is a separate academic scholarship route. Entrance in other years by school's own exam. Not highly selective but do not want someone to struggle academically as they would not have time to join in other things and have fun. Look for potential. 10–12 per year come in sixth form, often from schools which finish at 16. Tend to settle in well – tutor groups mixed at this stage which helps. Looking for girls who will be open to opportunities and engaged with the ethos of the school.

Exit: Some leave after GCSEs to go to co-ed schools. Many find this quite a culture shock and some even come back – the door is always left open for anyone who changes their mind. Most girls go on to a wide range of universities to read a huge variety of subjects – several to read medicine. A few to Oxbridge each year. One girl in 2009 had to choose between Trinity College, Cambridge and Harvard – poor love!

Money Matters: Means-tested bursaries for up to full fees. Awards made at three stages – for Year 7, Year 9 and Year 12 and means-tested every year. Academic and gifted & talented scholarships (creative art, drama & physical theatre, music and sport) – max award is 20 per cent of day or boarding fees.

Remarks: A cosy, happy, caring school with something for everyone. Some can find this cosiness a bit limiting and leave for the co-eds after GCSE. Produces well-rounded girls who are expected to roll up their sleeves, get on with it: 'sew on a button, bake and cake and change a fuse' as one mother put it. Has settled well under new head.

St Margaret's School (Exeter)

Linked to Saint Margaret's Nursery, Pre Prep and Junior (Prep) School (Exeter) in the Junior section

147 Magdalen Road, Exeter, Devon, EX2 4TS

• Pupils: 215; all day • Ages: 11-18 • Size of sixth form: 60 • C of E
• Fees: £9,750 pa • Independent

Tel: 01392 491 699
Fax: 01392 251 402
Email: mail@stmargarets-school.co.uk
Website: www.stmargarets-school.co.uk

Head: Since 2008, Mrs Sheila Cooper MA PGCE NPQH LTCL (early fifties). Educated at Carisbrooke High School, Isle of Wight then at St Anne's College, Oxford where she read classics (gaining a double first). Impressive list of teaching posts: King Edward VI, Southampton, Boston High then The Perse Girls' (where she produced three Greek tragedies: in Greek of course) before Norwich High (head of classics and key skills coordinator) and six years as deputy head of St Edward's, Cheltenham before making it to headship at St Margaret's. Engaging 'in a slightly quirky girls' school sort of way,' remarked one mother. Younger girls respect her and know she cares but have not all necessarily been her greatest fans for laying down the law. Parents have welcomed the tightening-up. Astute when it comes to management, she also teaches Latin (which she has re-introduced) to new entrants (helps her to get to know them) and 'Greek as a Treat' for year 10 upwards. Great believer in value of extra-curricular activities in making a whole person. Leads by example – occasionally plays cello in school orchestra and is currently trying to learn Mandarin. 'Really going for it,' confirm parents who praise her 'high level of commitment.' Fair amount of re-structuring since she took hold of reins: spotting holes in the local market by admitting boys into prep and offering nursery places. Softly spoken, has settled into rôle – parents expect she will be there 'for the long term'. Encourages girls to 'believe they can do anything if they try.' Lives opposite the school with husband, Iain. No children of her own but she takes a keen interest in her nine nephews and nieces plus gardening and cello playing.

Academic matters: Sixth form results (80 per cent A and B grades at A level) are a credit to the teaching and dispel the urban myth that 'bright girls go elsewhere.' Surprisingly broad range of (17) subjects for a small sixth form with results in arts and sciences evenly balanced. Physics and business studies departments have broken down former sexist prejudices. Many girls we met gave special thumbs up for the creative subjects. Even wider choice (22 subjects) at GCSE where results (45 per cent A* and A) belie the wide ability range. Performance in maths has improved since introduction of two software packages to improve numeracy:

'Mathletics' and 'My Maths' – parents have been encouraged to participate in a 'triangle of support' and say the teaching in English as well as maths is 'spot on'. Most classes below GCSE average 15 girls but twos and threes are not uncommon in sixth. Girls continue with at least one foreign language to GCSE; RS is taken compulsorily as a half GCSE so the total sat by most is 10.5 subjects.

Learning Success department is staffed by two SpLD specialists and co-ordinated by a music and maths teacher who is committed to teaching lower sets, has a special interest in dyscalculia and is happy 'to work with weak girls'. Fifty-seven girls receive support of some kind with one girl with cerebral palsy currently assigned a learning assistant (provided by parents). All year seven pupils are screened for dyslexia – one mother raved about an approach called 'toe by toe' which had re-programmed her daughter's reading ability. Laptops for those who need them; support sessions are worked out individually and don't necessarily involve withdrawal from lessons. Pupil mentoring programme includes 'study buddies' – sixth formers who helper younger girls with numeracy. High flyers are monitored and encouraged 'to go the extra mile' through activities at school as well as attendance at extra courses, events and competitions outside. Good use is made of school intranet to keep teachers abreast of individuals' needs and sessions on 'what if feels like to be dyslexic' have been run for parents.

Games, Options, the Arts: Limited site (small gym and only two outside hard surfaces for netball or tennis) necessitates use of neighbouring university and other sports facilities including access to new playing fields belonging to Royal School for the Deaf. Young PE staff teaching to GCSE and A levels. School is strongest at netball and swimming but also fields teams in hockey, rounders etc. Sports day is an annual focus for inter-house competition. At sixth form level girls get to take yoga, pilates etc as a break from team based sport. School backs those who participate in outside clubs (e.g. two SW rowers; one girl in SW team on cricket tour in India). Not overrun with full-on gamesy types – rather it's creative juices that flow at St Margaret's: music, drama and art are all real strengths. Full scale, biennial musical (last up was a production of *We Will Rock You*); lots of participation in national and local music festivals; 'Seraphim' trio of sixth formers sing for public at various events e.g. in Exeter Guildhall at Lord Mayor's Charity Concert), four other choirs including chamber choir and chapel choir which sometimes sings evensong at Exeter cathedral. Over fifty per cent of girls have instrumental or singing lessons with team of 20+ peripatetic teachers. Impressive results in music exams and loads of musical activity: full wind band, string chamber orchestra plus informal flute and brass groups. Music offered to A2 but not music technology though good use is made of Sibelius software in all years for composition in keyboard laboratory. Lots of concerts include recent joint one with St Peter's. Energetic head of drama enthuses girls (one is currently in national youth theatre) and oversees full range of productions including small scale plays (e.g. *Be My Baby*) as well as participation in Schools' Shakespeare Festival. Aptly named 'Arthouse' is highly innovative area under long-standing, male direction. Girls increasingly take ownership of their ideas – recent projects we saw included decorative use of a Mini Cooper S and of a garden shed turned war memorial to a lost grandfather.

Unexpectedly, one of only four all girls CCF contingents in the country. Tough stuff with about thirty going on annual camp to Penhale. Amazing record in D of E – school has just celebrated winning 100 gold awards – boosted by successful trips to India to support goodwill village for destitute children in Tamil Nadu. Innovative and well supported schemes for getting girls to visit France. School also puts out two 35 and one 45 mile team for annual Ten Tors Challenge on nearby Dartmoor – 'half the school is out on the moor some weekends,' quipped the head.

Background and Atmosphere: Founded in 1902, school became a charitable trust and one of the Christian based Woodard schools in 1968. Occupies an imposing Georgian house (formerly owned by the Barings banking family) with additions in a scholastic enclave of the city (Exeter School and The Maynard are close by). Long-serving staff member acts as chaplain; termly Eucharist is valued part of Christian tradition here. Senior school worships collectively twice a week and on other days in smaller groups. Beautiful stained glass window embellishes St Margaret's chapel in middle of school. School participates in ICE (Initiative in Christian Education) with outsiders helping to run 'Lighthouse' – a Christian Union for Years 5–7.

Fabric of school appears well maintained: pleasant, light filled classrooms with plenty of display material, modern science laboratories (opened by Princess Anne in her rôle as patron of WISE) and lovely home economics area. 'PAC' – performing arts centre includes music teaching areas and a versatile drama studio. Open planned library is at centre of school; well used by all and private study base for lower sixth. School hall doubles up as an excellent dining area (food is 'amazing' said girls as they 'mixed and matched' their selections) – girls can add as much salad, veggies or fruit as they want (within reason). Breakfast club operates before school and healthy snacks are on offer at break – even via the vending machine. Art department occupies a creative outpost on the eastern fringes which meets its offbeat needs perfectly. School has greened up considerably and holds the eco bronze award. Some of the male staff we met turned out to be dynamic HODs (e.g. physics, art and RS) as well as a deputy head.

Pastoral Care and Discipline: Pastoral heads emphasise value of a team approach and meet weekly with form tutors who are the first port of call for girls and parents. Christian youth worker active in school and some girls are genuinely committed Christians. PCCE course covers personal development, citizenship and careers – parents get a summary leaflet at the beginning of each school year to explain the content. Work experience for Year 11 girls relies on their input but with some help from local Connexions team. First aid centre looked so inviting girls can't mind too much being sent to the full-time matron if unwell. Parents we spoke to all ranked pastoral care as 'the biggest plus' for the school.

Pupils and Parents: Gentle, friendly girls who actually greet their teachers spontaneously. Year group not a bar to friendship – 'our year 10 daughter has lots of friends in the sixth,' explained one mother. Not a rough and tumble place but not prissy either. 'No smell of bitchy competitiveness,' said one parent. All ages more than ready to talk about themselves and what they enjoy. Girls have 'really taken appearance of nursery aged children on site to their hearts,' says head. Active school council is fighting the eco battle amongst others. 'Amazing' carol service held in Exeter cathedral. Week's work experience for year eleven after

GCSE exams gives them a taste of life in business etc. Sixth formers incredibly mature and easily mistaken for staff members. Lovely facilities in new sixth form centre at top of school which offers panoramic views over the city and beyond to 'lift their spirits' says head. Active parent staff association successful at fund-raising through a variety of events. In addition to local bus services parents organise three private buses to serve outlying towns and villages. OGs include broadcaster Mary Nightingale, Royal Ballet musician Emma Granger, Archers' actress Hedli Niklaus.

Entrance: Internally set tests for entry to senior school at 11 (including year six who normally all proceed to year seven) in English, maths and verbal reasoning plus interview with headmistress. Taster days for those who want them. Girls come from a wide area: state primaries as well as local private schools. Some enter at 13 from preps (principally Exeter Cathedral and St Peter's, Lympstone). Small entry into sixth from elsewhere (growing trickle from St Peter's High School – local state Woodard schools member). Homestay arrangements made for any international boarders.

Exit: Few leave after Year 11 – 'girls are more loyal now,' claims head. Some to top academic courses including law, medicine and veterinary science with destinations including Russell Group and sometimes Oxbridge; regular places at Central St Martin's and Wimbledon for art; wide range of choices and many girls proceed into creative careers.

Money Matters: Bursaries up to fifty per cent; academic scholarships from age 11 may be awarded on merit at any time; other scholarships awarded for art, music and performing arts are tested in January. Sixth form scholarship candidates sit a one-hour paper in the GCSE subject of their choice in January.

Remarks: Provides a lively, challenging preparation for adult life having left its old 'finishing school' legacy far behind. Punches above its weight academically and is commendably nurturing. Has a well-earned reputation for all the arts. Any shortcomings are more than compensated for by its quirky uniqueness. Not one to be written off as a second choice without visiting.

St Margaret's School (London)

Linked to Saint Margarets Junior School (London) in the Junior section

18 Kidderpore Gardens, London, NW3 7SR

• Pupils: 135 girls • Ages: 4-16 • C of E foundation; all faiths and none welcome • Fees: £9,042-£10,419 pa • Independent

Tel: 0207 435 2439
Fax: 0207 431 1308
Email: principal@st-margarets.co.uk
Website: www.st-margarets.co.uk

Principal: Since 2008, Mr Mark Webster, previously deputy head of the Royal School in Hampstead (many girls followed him here). 'He's a lovely man,' we are told. 'Both children and parents adore him. He's very sane and solid and an excellent teacher – all the children blossom under his tuition.' Parents say, 'he is available and approachable; he's open minded and receptive to ideas. Everyone feels listened to.'

Academic matters: This used to be the last resort for girls who had failed to get in anywhere else. No longer. Now it is often chosen for its cosy, family atmosphere as a haven for girls who would sink without trace in its larger, more pressured and impersonal neighbours. But they will most probably get very good GCSE results: it is one of the top schools in the country on a value-added basis. 66 per cent of grades were A* or A, with more than a third achieving straight A* or A grades. Most girls achieve consistently better than predicted. Languages are strong; most girls take Spanish or French GCSE.

The school is selective, but not unduly so, and the ability range is wide. All teaching is mixed ability, except for maths in the top two years. With class sizes ranging from 10 in the infants to a maximum of 20 in the senior school, it is, as a parent commented, 'like getting one-to-one tuition'. Can cope with mild dyslexia, and with teaching English as a foreign language to pupils from overseas. 'It is part of the deal – teachers give up their non-contact time and their lunchtimes to help.' This is included in the fee unless outside help is needed.

Ranked top small independent school in the country for the second year running by *The Sunday Times* in 2009/10.

Games, Options, the Arts: Compact, so all sports take place off-site at the nearby St Luke's church hall, at West Heath tennis courts, Hendon sports centre and the South Hampstead High playing fields in West Hampstead. The netball teams often thrash much bigger schools. Clubs include football, cross-country, self-defence and yoga. Girls can do the bronze D of E Award, and take part in the activity weekend each spring. There are visits to theatres, museums and galleries, French and Spanish exchanges, and Year 9 spends a week in Normandy. 'For a small school, they organise lots of activities,' said a parent.

The airy top-floor art studio displays sculpture and silkscreen prints as well as painting and drawings. In 2009, all art GCSE grades were A* or A. DT is not a GCSE option, but outside experts come in to run design-and-build DT days. Everyone does drama to Year 9, and quite a few to GCSE. Girls can learn a range of instruments at school, and play in one of the ensemble groups or the newly-formed orchestra.

Background and Atmosphere: Founded in 1884, it moved to its present site in a quiet, suburban Hampstead road in 1943. Senior and junior schools both occupy the same building and have the same head with different uniforms but little separation between them. The school has three houses where pupils of all ages work together to raise funds for charities of their own choice, and compete at sports. It is small, cosy and friendly; a parent commented, 'It allows the girls to achieve whatever they can – but in a safe, non-confrontational environment.'

Pastoral Care and Discipline: Neither drug nor alcohol abuse looms large here. Bullying does inevitably happen, and it is cyber-bullying that concerns the school most. One parent whose daughter found a larger school overwhelming says the school has been a 'lifesaver'. 'They have been prepared to do whatever it takes to make it work here for her. All the teachers really communicate with each other. There are other girls here with problems too, and they give them as normal an environment as possible. They really look at the individual and try to bring out the best in every girl.'

Pupils and Parents: Mostly local girls, from the sort of social and ethnic mix you would expect in North London, and quite a few from the state sector – 'so it's not as precious as some private schools,' commented a parent. Refugees from more pressured environments value the very safe and protected ambience.

Entrance: Entry into Reception is more-or-less first come first served, with an informal assessment designed to spot major learning difficulties. Another intake into Year 3, mostly from local pre-preps, on the basis of maths and English tests. The school runs its own 11 plus exam in English, maths and verbal reasoning, and applicants for places higher up also do maths and English tests. But while it is selective, and won't take girls with severe learning difficulties, it is less rigorously so than many North London schools. It is generally prepared to be flexible, and will often take girls who want to join Year 5 or 6 in order to opt out of the 11 plus circus. Others come into year 10 because they have not been making progress at state secondaries, and are welcomed despite the likelihood that their GCSE results will not match those of the rest of the cohort.

Exit: School has no intention of opening a sixth form despite parental requests. 'By then it really is time to move on.' Many who could not have coped at 11 with St Paul's Girls or Henrietta Barnett or Highgate transfer happily to these at 16. Woodhouse College, La Swap and St Marylebone are amongst other recent destinations.

Money Matters: One scholarship of half fees awarded at entry into Year 7. Limited numbers of means tested, full and part-fee bursaries are available to existing pupils across the age range.

Remarks: A safe, protected, family environment that can be a haven for girls who have not thrived elsewhere. Small classes and good teaching bring excellent GCSE results, and most girls gain enough confidence to move on happily to more challenging sixth forms. 'My daughter has blossomed here,' said a parent.

St Margaret's School for Girls (Aberdeen)

Linked to Saint Margaret's School for Girls Junior Department (Aberdeen) in the Junior section

17 Albyn Place, Aberdeen, AB10 1RU

• Pupils: 390 girls, all day • Ages: 3-18 • Size of sixth form: 60
• Non-denom • Fees: £5,580-£9,735 pa • Independent

Tel: 01224 584 466
Fax: 01224 585 600
Email: info@st-margaret.aberdeen.sch.uk
Website: www.st-margaret.aberdeen.sch.uk

Head: Since 2010, Dr Julie Land (fifty) BSc (maths) PGCE EdD. Educated at Dame Allan's Girls' School, Newcastle and Manchester and Newcastle universities. Taught maths for nine years before taking 10 years out to look after a young family and did most of her doctoral research during this time. Returned to teaching in 2000 and joined St Margaret's in 2003, becoming deputy head in 2004.

Intends to lead and support staff through a period of educational change and oversee new buildings such as a new school hall and classrooms together with improvement of games facilities.

Married with two grown up children she enjoys walking and gardening as well as table tennis (an accomplished player in her youth).

Academic matters: Academically strong across the board, results are high in the Aberdeen independent sector, offering 21 subjects at Higher and 17 at Advanced Higher. Best at sixth year Advanced Highers, (fifth in Scotland in 2007 with 50 per cent As, and better in 2008). The previous head made some scholarly tweaks to the curriculum, dropping administration and adding economics and PE for the final year, together with a crash courses in higher philosophy, 'though, of course, one does it informally from primary, but it's more appropriate as an exam at the top.'

Not really a formidable selection of subjects, though business management and both information studies and computer studies ('because some prefer it') stand out among all the usual suspects. French and German, plus Latin, compulsory from top primary level. Growing number of classicists get top grades, though the Greek club has not as yet bred that rare bird, a Greek examinee. All can be taken to Advanced Higher level. Excellent results in maths, music, English, mod langs and sciences. Head keen that girls should have the advantage of 'learning independently' and enjoy their lessons. Three newish ICT suites, all intranetted, lots of laptops around.

Strong support for learning throughout the school with help for the most gifted as well as the underperformer. Dyslexia, dyspraxia, ADHD and mild Asperger's all catered for, both individual and group teaching, plus support in class if needed. No automatic testing on entrance for additional needs but 'everyone has a spelling assessment which is a good indicator.' Each department keeps detailed notes of problems that might be 'just around the corner.' Impressive paired reading initiative where girls in senior school 'trained in specific reading techniques' work with younger pupils in their free time and help in lots of other subjects too. Apart from fostering community spirit, senior readers also get brownie points through 'certification from the Institute of Management'.

Games, Options, the Arts: Impressive netball and tennis teams. School keen on team games, especially hockey, but loads of individual sport too; swimming important, (one Scotland swimmer and all juniors have regular dips in a local pool), athletics, tennis, rounders, etc etc. New snow boarding and curling had huge take-up. School keen not to have a 'precious' image, so food technology only up to second year but it reappears as preparation for living in sixth. (School stresses that these facts are not interrelated.)

Art and design department is 'fantastic', with a stunning panorama of urban Aberdeenshire providing part of the flexible natural lighting. A formidable battery of skills available: ceramics, printmaking, metal jewellery-making, sculpture (not much because there is no room for storage), as well as the usual drawing and painting etc. Art and music taken to Advanced Higher level – good results. Lively drama – excellent results. With three major musical productions last year, pulling in art dept for scenery/costume etc, it's hardly surprising that there is a 'resurgence of drama as an academic subject'. Music vibrant, school boasts a collection of orchestras: string, chamber, jazz plus outstanding 'travelling' choir with regular trips. Number of current pupils and FPs in the national youth orchestra. St Margaret's schools worldwide band together for choir tours, heads chit-chat electronically. 'Gives the school a global dimension.'

Masses of activities: twenty plus clubs and classes include ballet, highland dancing, eco, wildlife, film, choi kwangdo, tennis, French, dance, chess and very strong debating/public speaking. Prioritising problem of huge take-up in a small school makes staff flexible over practices in squabbles over musical games players. Strong D of E, regular golds. YE (local finalists in 2008) and masses of charity input. Good global awareness from international pupil mix.

Comprehensive careers department: every girl a member of Futurewise; business dynamics and YPI for fourth years and a week's work experience for fifth years.

Background and Atmosphere: Founded in 1846, St Margaret's is the only all girls' school in the north of Scotland. Based in a hotchpotch conversion of Victorian merchants' houses (and Albyn Place and the adjacent Queens Road in Aberdeen are home to some six or seven various schools). The deep gardens at the back have been neatly filled in with massive new-builds and recently refurbished art studio and resources centre. Charming well-equipped library. Corridors everywhere but walls drip with bright artwork, photos of pupils, productions, school trips, press cuttings etc – it feels friendly and buzzing. Wizard adventure playground on refurbished lawn.

Cooked lunch available, with girls ordering main dishes in advance, in a pretty cramped room in the basement which doubles as after-school club for tinies, adjacent to the recently revamped and very posh loos. Girls eat by class, own sandwiches OK. School is wheelchair friendly. Early drop off from 8 am, with special provision in the nursery for tots to stay up till 5.30pm, though it costs extra if after school's official closing time. Holiday activities club run during the Easter, summer and October holidays. Nursery staff/children – and the nursery is called Daffodil – wear charming yellow tops and black tracksuit bottoms for PE. Senior blazers (expensive) are worn only on the way to/from school but there is a good second-hand shop (well, this is Aberdeen).

Pastoral Care and Discipline: Strong moral background with joint PSE and RME syllabus. Some Muslims in the school, headscarves and longer skirts OK, and pupils made to feel inclusive with Ramadan respected and a special prayer room can be available. Ecumenical assemblies. All join in the Easter service and Christmas concert and the whole school troops off to the cathedral for St Margaret's Day when the smallest have to be restrained from trying to find St Margaret's shield on the roof and falling over in the process.

Girl-support available from form teachers, a dedicated head of guidance, and they can go 'to anyone if in difficulties'. Worry boxes for juniors. Strong anti-bullying programme. Detention for the few and far between 'naughty girls' replaced by a pc 'extra learning opportunity to brush up their skills' (sometimes after school). Whole school family feel with full assemblies most Fridays, pupil council and charity reps meetings include juniors and seniors. With 30 school prefects plus form prefects, sport and activity captains etc, most pupils get a chance to lead. Social life is active with PTA dances and discos and a friendly eye kept that 'someone's brother will arrange partners.'

A change of emphasis in sixth form helped by the new post of sixth form head, and a realistically tidy sixth form flat, refurbished this year. The sixth formers prepared for the world beyond Aberdeen with their own out of school conference: this year 'Being the Best You Can Be', led by past pupils and specialists: Chris Fenn on nutrition, a doctor and former pupil of St Margaret's back from frontline Basra etc.

Pupils and Parents: Large number of first time buyers, large number of non-Brits, strong parent association. And very strong FP links. Charming. Polite and well-mannered. Tessa Jowell is an old girl. Girls come from all the surrounding areas, as well as the city itself.

Entrance: Assessments for all, mini test for tinies where they play in groups and are surreptitiously assessed by experts. Siblings not usually turned away.

Exit: Regular trickle to Oxbridge and (from a quick poll of off-duty sixth formers) more are braving the wider world of English, even south of England universities, studying an astonishing variety of subjects. There is the usual small bleed to Scottish universities after Highers, inevitable before a four year degree.

Money Matters: Means-tested bursaries up to 100 per cent. Will keep a child to next public exam if parents have problems but with the usual caveat about parents being upfront and realistic.

Remarks: Jolly nice old fashioned school with proper values and the best of modern teaching methods. Some of the fabric is a bit sad, although recent inspectors said it was 'very good' and there is a newly-laid lawn in the tiny (school says it isn't) play area. But if single sex education is what you want, St Margaret's is a school which does its girls exceeding well.

St Mary Redcliffe and Temple School

Somerset Square, Redcliffe, Bristol, BS1 6RT

• Pupils: 1,500 boys and girls • Ages: 11-18 • Size of sixth form: 450
• C of E • State

Tel: 0117 377 2100
Fax: 0117 377 2101
Email: enquiries@smrt.bristol.sch.uk
Website: www.smrt.bristol.sch

Head: Since 2005, Mrs Elisabeth Gilpin, formerly head of St Augustine's RC/CofE Upper School in Oxford.

Academic matters: Exam results well above national average for GCSE (norm 10 per pupil) and in line with it at A level. Pupils' individual achievements recognised and valued. Curriculum balance carefully maintained and complemented throughout by a wide-ranging enrichment programme. Special needs resourcing 'adequate but not generous'. Art department linked with local community creative projects; many other departments involved with visits, exchanges and links abroad. Specialised status in humanities awarded 2004.

Games, Options, the Arts: On-site facilities for games surprisingly good given city-centre location, with courts, an all-weather pitch ('the arena') and indoor pool. Further sports facilities out of town. Many pupils compete at local, county and national levels in a wide range of team sports (rugby, soccer, hockey, netball, basketball and others) and individual activities such as athletics, judo and aerobics. The list is long. Music vibrant and encouraged. Orchestral and choral concerts held in adjacent and outstandingly beautiful church of St Mary Redcliffe, a superb historic setting, very inspiring, which also serves as school 'chapel'. Drama offered as a GCSE option, and regular ambitious productions involving large numbers of pupils.

Background and Atmosphere: In the typically 1960s purpose-built and now very over-crowded buildings, space is a problem, particularly in the communal areas such as the dining room and the corridors. However, the school functions in a civilised and orderly manner. (What better way to pass the time, while waiting patiently in a long lunch queue, than to stop one's head teacher and tell her a joke?) School scheduled for re-build as part of Building Schools for the Future project. Parents are kept up to date about all aspects of the school's life via the monthly newsletter.

The close relationship with parents and their underpinning of the school's Christian ethos create positive attitudes to the development of each pupil's potential.

Pastoral Care and Discipline: Impressive system of mixed-age tutor groups reflects the powerful ethos of the extended Christian family. Warmly appreciated – 'a strength' – by parents and former pupils. Valued by staff despite its demanding workload. Enables older students to know and mentor younger ones. Year 7 spend a year in separate house to establish their own year-group relationships before moving into the senior houses; These provide the cornerstones of very good discipline, based on exceptionally effective tutoring. Quick response to any anti-social behaviour, offender withdrawn from class and supervised by, would you believe? – 'Behaviour Manager'. Problems, academic or other, generally detected at an early stage. Parents involved and feel confident about it.

Pupils and Parents: Pupils come from all areas of Bristol and beyond as this is the only C of E VA school in the diocese. The educational provision is explicitly Christian with daily worship, much of it pupil-led, a distinctive feature at its core. The broad social and cultural mix is absorbed comfortably and the close involvement of parents is encouraged, including in worship. Attendance well above national average. Pupils friendly and open. Firm guidelines issued about uniform, and recent reminders to staff, parents and pupils. Girls comment that the grey sweatshirts are 'itchy' but like the option of trousers or skirts. Boys must wear ties for most of the year and always tie and blazer when travelling outside. Tucking-in of shirts appears to be a good-natured battleground. Pupils as cheerful as they ever are about school meals.

Entrance: Comprehensive intake, admissions policy based on family church attendance history and other priorities (siblings, residence). Some pupils of other faiths admitted. Oversubscribed. Applications for Year 7 close in October of the previous year – must also be made to the Local Authority. Sixth form admission based on academic performance at GCSE and 'agreement to respect the faith of others'. Applications close in January of each year.

Exit: Nearly all Year 11 pupils go into the sixth form. 75 per cent go on to universities or other higher education institutions – a few to Oxbridge. Some gap year students go abroad on scholarships and as community service volunteers.

Money Matters: Generous enabling fund supports those from disadvantaged background for school visits etc.

Remarks: 'If only we had qualified ... ' the cri de coeur of many parents in Bristol and the surrounding area. This is a school born of faith and led with conviction. Its atmosphere is purposeful but also welcoming and considerate. Parents and staff did not need Ofsted (June 2007) to tell them that the school is 'Good with outstanding features'. Not over-focused on league tables, but undoubtedly able to hold its own, academically.

The St Marylebone C of E School

64 Marylebone High Street, London, W1U 5BA

• Pupils: 785 • Ages: 11-18 • Size of sixth form: 160, including around 50 boys • C of E • State

Tel: 020 7935 4704
Fax: 020 7935 4005
Email: stmaryleboneschool@yahoo.co.uk
Website: www.stmaryleboneschool.com

Head teacher: Since 1993, Mrs Elizabeth Phillips OBE BA MA AKC (sixtyish). Smart, professional and highly experienced, including sixteen years spent working in education abroad. She educated her three children privately. Mrs Phillips, as befits someone of her doyennerie in the business, is very, very busy. We spoke to several parents who had never met her: 'Don't know what she looks like'; 'I suppose she exists – I've never never set eyes on her. The school is run by her deputies'; 'I'm often there at performances and so on but I've never seen her'. Sadly, we didn't either – she was too busy on the three occasions we had appointments and clearly keeps her staff busy too, as no-one had time to answer our questions.

Fortunately parents are both visible and voluble, and we can report that those who have met Mrs Phillips are wildly enthusiastic: 'She's a very strong leader'; 'She believes in discipline but in a positive way'; 'She does masses of very successful fundraising'; 'She is hugely respected in Westminster'; 'Redoubtable'; 'The children come first and PR second'. Quite. More importantly, she is highly visible to her pupils. She still teaches (RS and history), comes to daily assembly and is, reportedly, in and out of lessons, 'checking'. A fellow professional says, 'Tough cookie, professional, knows her stuff, takes no prisoners – but admirably so. Some say she's a bit ruthless but I think she simply likes competence and professionalism. She keeps staff on the ball.' Mrs Phillips is clearly an outstandingly successful, respected and popular head.

Academic matters: St Marylebone's offers a lot of subject options – 'an amazing variety' enthused one parent. Dance, health and social care, Latin, and business studies canter alongside the front runners at GCSE and all are in the ribbons. 96 per cent 5+ A*–C grades in 2010 (88 per cent including maths and English) with some outstanding performances. 100 per cent A*–C in several subjects. RS results are knockout – all the large cohort got A*–B and the curriculum is praised for its earnest inclusiveness. The Englishes are good, so are the single sciences though most take the double award. Maths more than respectable. Good to see German holding its own but no other lang apart than French, which does pretty well too. Art and history strong and popular. School has policy of taking some subjects – langs, ICT, RS – early to excellent effect. RS and German especially successful.

At A level, English by far the most popular – most results B/C. Psychology, sociology and economics among the options – the first much the favourite with a spread of results. Dance, drama and art are the real stars. Low take up for German and French – more support for modern langs seems needed here. Some parents wonder how the results are achieved with so little homework. Relatively good teacher:pupil ratio and school spends money on retaining good staff.

KS3 SATs are taken in Year 8 and school then uses the time that frees to be 'inventive' academically – much appreciated by girls and parents. Gifted and talented programme. School caters for a range of SENs, has a SENCo, a full time SEN teacher, Learning Support Assistants and specialist centres for students with learning difficulties. It is a centre of excellence for severe emotional and behavioural difficulties and can provide for ASD, ADD and Down's – if not severe. Can provide for moderate physical difficulties too.

Games, Options, the Arts: By all accounts it's the arts that flourish here and sports come a very poor second. 'Sports are useless,' said a parent, 'they just don't bother apart from the regulation double period.' 'You can do it if you feel like it,' said a pupil. 'We get our fitness from dance and drama. There are after school clubs for people who are good' – open to all, says school. And there are – netball, football, trampolining, rugby and tennis as well as before school sessions in fitness, running etc. Underground sports hall – more than many so urban a school could muster. Nonetheless, St M's is a performing arts college and this is evident whomever you speak to. Dance and music are outstanding and production values are high. 'The girls take huge pride in their performances,' we were told, 'even if not everyone can take part. It is inspirational.' The inspiration is further fuelled by the long-awaited £6m performing arts centre. This makes a huge difference – not least to the amount of space it frees for other curricular activities. In all respects the arts reign here. You can make everything from jewellery to ceramics and print your own photos. Debating, dance and musical performance of all kinds thrive.

To an extent these options are only available for the brightest and best. Parents who rave about the musical standards – 'the concerts just blow you away – it's like going to a serious musical event' – acknowledge that only the best will get in on the act. Opportunities like GCSE photography work in the highly professional Metro Studios only available to the three or four girls whose applications to take the course are considered sufficiently impressive. This is the reality of a state-funded school but it must be trying for the also-rans and would-bes.

Background and Atmosphere: Unique city setting – off Marylebone High Street with Regent's Park over the (horribly busy) road. Victoriana with some attractive features – high ceilings, gothic windows and plenty of light. Radical building plans now completed. Cramped and crammed – though the performing arts building makes a big difference, as does the new sixth form centre on Blandford Street; every nook has something educational squashed into it. No space for lockers so girls are adept at carting their lives around with them and being organised about what they need for each lesson. Lunch is eaten in form rooms though year 10 examinees and upwards are mercifully allowed out to settle in the numerous cafes round about at lunchtime.

The admissions policy (see below) dictates that active membership of the C of E is the main criterion for entry and this also influences the ethos. Parents are, in general, impressed. 'I trust it,' said one, 'to give my daughter a good education.' 'It's highly organised,' said another. 'Very efficient, there's plenty of notice about everything. They're very attentive to detail.' Far better equipped and resourced than most such schools largely due to the head's incessant and skilful fund-raising and the band of supportive parents.

Pastoral Care and Discipline: Discipline reportedly 'fearsome' and 'slightly on the petty side' but generally felt to be effective and well understood by pupils. Not a whisper of drugs or even smoking being 'issues'. Links with home are excellent, say parents – and not only when there are problems. 'They write and tell us if our daughter has improved at something or just made a big effort,' nodded a parent. Much appreciated are the proper, old-fashioned termly reports which don't just parrot at you what the class has done but actually talk about your own daughter. Good, realistic and collaborative target-setting also works. House system. Pastoral care and support seen as very good overall on both academic and personal matters and many teachers seen as good and dedicated – but a few glaring exceptions and some just felt to be uninspiring.

Pupils and Parents: About sixty-five per cent from ethnic minority backgrounds and from 90 different countries. Over fifty per cent of pupils are bilingual. More than sixty languages spoken at home. Sixty per cent C of E members, the largest second religious group is Muslim. Some feeling among parents that little is done to encourage friendships between the different ethnic and religious groups. Others reported that, 'The school is big enough for girls to make real choices about friendships and there's a very open environment.' School clearly tries hard – has an annual World Culture Day among many other initiatives – and attracts fierce loyalty. Active parents' group works hard though has problems involving all but the usual – mostly white, middle class – suspects

Entrance: Absurdly and maddeningly over-subscribed – something like 1,000 applicants for 125 places. School no longer allowed to interview applicants – 'they hate that,' said a sympathetic parent. Admissions criteria are primarily that you have to be C of E – sixty per cent are – though looked after children and those with statements have priority. Thirty per cent of places are 'open', with distance the only criteria. Twelve places annually given to those with outstanding aptitude in an aspect of performing arts. Selection also on basis of ability – school takes twenty-five per cent from top ability range, fifty per cent from average band and twenty-five per cent from the below average band. Tie breaker of how near to the school you live. 275 places in the sixth – priority to existing students though they have to fulfil requirements (minimum of five A*–C GCSEs). Boys are taken into the sixth and, again, more apply than there are places for. School receives five applications a week for occasional places.

Exit: Some leave after GCSE and go to sixth form colleges, the independents, e.g. Latymer Upper, or other state schools, e.g. Camden, largely for a greater range of A level objects or for boys. Most stay though entrance to the school's own sixth form is not a given, even for their own. Sixth form leavers to good universities and a range of courses.

Money Matters: National funding programmes such as Excellence in Cities ended several years ago so bidding for extra money from various sources takes up a lot of the head's time and she agrees, 'fund-raising is my nightmare – it's what I do. It's cost me five years of my life.' The result, however, is a school that is well-staffed and well-equipped, if not to lavish private school standards.

Remarks: Exceptional, successful inner-city school serving a diverse community with a strong middle class core. Combines best traditional values with best modern practice.

St Mary's Calne

Curzon Street, Calne, Wiltshire, SN11 0DF

• Pupils: 325 girls; over three quarters board • Ages: 11-18 • Size of sixth form: 105 • C of E • Fees: £6,790-£9,650 pa • Independent

Tel: 01249 857 200
Fax: 01249 857 207
Email: office@stmaryscalne.org
Website: www.stmaryscalne.org

Headmistress: Since 2003, Dr Helen Wright MA EdD PGCE FRSA MIoD (fortyish). Educated at James Gillespie's High School, Edinburgh and Lincoln College Oxford where she read mod langs and earned a Doctorate in Education with a thesis entitled 'Understanding Moral Leadership in Schools'. Taught languages at Reed's School, was head of German at Bishop's Stortford College, then head of German and deputy housemistress at St Edward's Oxford. Came to St Mary's from Heathfield School where she was an exceptionally young head (the youngest ever at the time). She was head there for two years, having arrived as deputy, and then catapulted into acting headship after one term.

Variously described as 'a human fireball', 'academic Mrs Tiggywinkle' etc, Dr Wright actually comes across as warm, energetic and 'in love with education'. She is clearly energised by the learning community she has created for her girls and sees the school as an extended family dedicated to guiding girls though the 'transition of teenagehood'. Totally immersed in providing a first class and highly academic education, she sees the excellent exam results her pupils gain as only a part of the process of enabling them to identify and choose wisely among the paths that St Mary's opens for them. She hit the headlines for being in school seven hours after giving birth to daughter number two. She and her husband Brian, an IT consultant who works from home, also have a son and elder girl. She wants St Mary's girls to see that they need not choose between joys of motherhood and an exiting career. She sees St Mary's as 'a leading girls' school' with the advantages of being small – flexible curriculum, tailor made courses, individual attention. She is totally convinced of the effectiveness of single sex education and passionate about helping young people to find their way through the pressures of growing up. Hence she is extending her influence to the extent of being president Elect of the Girls' Schools Association.

Academic matters: Sees itself as distinctly academic! – though girls clearly take academic success in their stride rather than seeing it as the only objective of education. Dr Wright points out that the impressive results at GCSE and A level – called 'sensational' in one starry-eyed school guide – scarcely do the girls justice as the many subjects taken early at both levels do not actually appear in the league tables.

Girls appear to work very hard and to enjoy doing so, yet the atmosphere at exam time (which coincided with the GSG visit) was definitely more of excited anticipation than of exam nerves. At A level in 2010, 34 per cent grades at A*. GCSE results remarkable as well, with ten or eleven for most with compulsory RE (taken seriously, to judge by the results). Most girls take triple science and a modern language. In the first three years, girls are mainly taught in form groups but setted in maths and French. German, Spanish. Latin, Classical Greek and Japanese on offer; Chinese and Russian on demand. Everyone does two lessons of Chinese in first year. Latin compulsory up to 14 and some hang in till A level while Greek A level scholars enthusiastically promote it to younger girls. The school encourages girls to 'find their own path' through exams allowing them to take subjects early (maths GCSE, drama A level etc) thus freeing up the curriculum for real preferences as well as necessities.

Sixth form lecture programme much enjoyed – politicians, poets, pop promoters et al. The school has good links in every field. Three libraries: senior fiction (rather quaintly called the Oratory), junior fiction and reference. State of art IT taken for granted though no Apple Macs. Not the ideal place for severe dyslexics but does have a learning support department for mild dyslexics etc. Everyone does Critical Thinking. Key to education at St Mary's are the enrichment weeks – when in-depth non-curricular study ranging from a week in the Belize rainforest to philosophy workshops or 'Shakespeare from scratch' allow girls to immerse themselves in a topic or project. 'These are the moments,' says Dr Wright, 'when real deep learning takes place.'

Games, Options, the Arts: Sport not just about winning though school has a star spangled record. Multiple teams in all main sports – 'everyone should have a chance' – with masses of success including numerous county players; girls go on to play for university etc teams. 'If they don't do it now,' Says Dr Wright, 'when they leave school, it's too late.' Riding (local stables) increasingly popular; a current pupil's clear round recently ensured a win for Great Britain's John Whitaker International Pony Team. Super indoor pool with fitness suite upstairs much used by staff, pupils and the people of Calne. D of E flourishing with nearly sixty going for gold this year.

Truly amazing drama in purpose-built theatre putting on one annual, grand, all embracing production, often a musical which has transferred to the London stage (*Royal Hunt of the Sun*) through RADA connections. RADA lays on 'Speak Out', an advanced 20-week communications and skills course, unique in the school world, covering presentation techniques for business, finance, media, politics etc. Sir Tim Rice (former parent) regularly visits. LAMDA and drama A level very popular and St Mary's regularly takes productions to the Edinburgh Fringe.

Stunning music building and pretty stunning head of music too. Edward Whiting, a Queen's organ scholar, still with a role at Queen's, has the skills and contacts to have produced a first class recording of David Bednall's new Requiem, played on BBC radio. Tons of concerts and tours (Tuscany, New York) Fourth form music competition a fun event 'even if you're no good', said a girl. Music exam results for singing are outstanding. Girls clearly love singing and say that they will join choirs at uni and later.

Chaotically creative art department, (with artist in residence) happily producing a spectacular range of sculpture, textiles, paintings. We saw a particularly striking series of clever political cartoons done for A level. (Both art and art history get smashing results). Weekend and other activities range from practical: cookery club (plus occasional sessions with a Michelin starred chef), wine club, dance club, gardening, Alexander technique, fitness, first aid, Young Enterprise etc, to spiritual: the Alpha course started by a sixth former; and intellectual: debating, young medics etc. Weekends are pretty full but girls say there is time for just chilling out with friends.

Background and Atmosphere: Functional, practical, purpose-built rather than gracious, St Mary's was founded 1873 by Canon Duncan (Vicar of St Mary's Church, Calne) in 25 acres of central Calne, a pleasant but undistinguished little Wiltshire market town. Buildings have been added haphazardly forming a mishmash of styles divided by prettily planted and grassed areas. Spectacular new sixth form centre with ensuite study bedrooms and a disconcertingly bouncy rubber path leading to it across the grass playing field. Uncluttered, refurbished minimalist chapel and curious octagonal glass fishbowl reception area. Everything spacious, light and scrupulously clean with girls' bedrooms stuffed with personal icons and surprisingly tidy for teenagers. Each year group has its own house called after women (saints etc); pupils move each year while remaining throughout in multi-age 'companies', called after English bishops, which accumulate 'red points' for good deeds, including tidiness! Inter-company competition in drama, music, sport, general excellence etc and each company has an annual black-tie dinner. Pets' corner, said to house a menagerie of animals from guinea pigs to ducks was almost deserted on our visit, though the newly hatched chickens, Buff Orpingtons etc – one named appropriately after Dr Fowler, the school's first male 'housemistress' – were much cooed-over. Charitable fundraising – good fun which brings in respectable sums for organisations chosen by the girls – is on both a house (year group) and a company basis. The school takes its religious foundation seriously with attendance at chapel or local Catholic church compulsory on Sunday (with twice termly visits to the parish church) and sees religious education as an integral part each girl's journey towards a confident personal world view.

Pastoral Care and Discipline: Plenty of sensible adults around. A housemistress and day housemistress plus a team of five house tutors for each year group so every girl can have a personal tutor. Staff keep a careful watch – 'we are well aware of social pressures' – for anorexia, friendship wrangles and other teenage pitfalls. Letter home and serious talking-to for smoking, suspensions (occasional) for alcohol and straight out for drugs. Dorms (first 2 years) recently refurbished and futons introduced in all the houses for the day girls to sleep over. All girls from age 14 up have their own study bedroom – even day girls have two-girl study rooms. Girls seem well aware of and responsive to the facilities and care given and say proudly that this school does not have cliques or exclusive 'in' groups: 'Everyone knows everyone'. Nice touch – making individual named cake for each of a very big confirmation group. Girl friendly food, delicious with really good salads and plenty of choice – for supper sixth formers can eat in their new dining room or in the main refectory or cook for themselves.

Social Services praised Dr Wright's 'self-harm policy' which takes a firm line with behavioural issues while seeking to resolve any underlying crises. Quite strict on mobile phone use, though some wiseacres try to outwit system by bringing two. Systems and polices up and running for bullying/cyber bullying, complaints etc but girls say that the supportive atmosphere with teachers and older girls mentoring and caring for each other means these policies are seldom used in anger. Girls at all levels take an integral share in the daily running of the school with all sixth formers having a particular responsibility. They feel involved in school decisions and 'almost on equal terms' with the staff. No sixth form uniform but smart black suits 'for formal' with some fabulous footwear! No make-up and only one stud per ear allowed but girls pretty elegantly turned out.

Pupils and Parents: Largely establishment intelligentsia, in strong C of E ethos. 'They are demanding but in a very positive way,' says the head. Many girls from Wilts, Hants and Glos (within hour and a half drive) plus London. 12–14 per cent overseas pupils – must have fluent English when they arrive. Dedicated travel office – its necessity emphasized by the recurring volcanic ash cloud. Medical centre (will do travel jabs) has 24 hour health cover, three beds, a counselling service and two weekly surgeries. Amazing network of celebrity past pupils and parents extremely well used by the school. Parents tend to know each other. Past pupils include David Cameron's sister Clare, Dame Suzi Leather, Jade Jagger.

Entrance: At 11, 12 or 13 plus a few at sixth form. Visit (an absolute requirement), then register. In the summer before entry, girls attend Taster Day. Assessments take place on Entrance Day in October and these together with references from current school and discussions with parents and heads are designed to let St Mary's give a firm indication of whether the school will suit, subject to CE or entrance test performance. Many pupils from the cream of London preps and also from Farleigh, Daneshill, Leaden Hall, Beaudesert and St Francis Pewsey plus some local primaries. Usually a largish bunch from own prep, St Margaret's (which shares site, governors and lots of the facilities but is co-ed, sending boys on all over the place and girls mostly but not exclusively to St Mary's). Siblings encouraged. Sixth form entry (very few places) more straightforward and based on good GCSEs.

Exit: Tiniest trickle post-GCSE; a strong sixth form. Lots make blue chip unis – Bristol, Edinburgh, Durham etc with a handful to Oxbridge thanks to tiptop preparation. Music, art etc popular. Sprinkling of gap years (some really philanthropic) and post-A level applications.

Money Matters: Selection of academic, music and all-rounder scholarships at 11 and 13. At sixth form, three academic, one art, one drama and one music scholarship. Scholarships (can be up to 40 per cent) all are means-tested and only the first five per cent is automatic – parents are invited to apply for the remainder of the award. Foundation scholarship, which could be full fees, for a highly gifted girl who couldn't otherwise come.

Remarks: Certainly cutting edge among the small, rural, academic girls' boarding schools but also very homely. Dr Wright is busy putting it more prominently on the map as a national treasure regarding it as 'Elite' in the best sense of the word. Long seen as a good place for well-bred brains to mix with their own kind but it's a bit more than that – truly educative on every level.

St Mary's Catholic School

Windhill, Bishop's Stortford, Hertfordshire, CM23 2NQ

• Pupils: 940 boys and girls, all day • Ages: 11-18 • Size of sixth form: 175 • RC • State

Tel: 01279 654 901
Fax: 01279 653 889
Email: j.heath@stmarys.net
Website: www.stmarys.net

Head: Since 2001, Mr Anthony Sharpe BA MMus NPQH MBA. Educated at Cardinal Langley High School in Greater Manchester and University of Liverpool, where he studied music and divinity. Taught music and RE in Liverpool before taking up post of deputy head at Loreto RC Girls' School in St Albans. Music is a passion – his liturgical compositions have been published and broadcast; recently demonstrated a lighter side by playing guitar in a school rock band. Married with three children. Is very involved in parish life, 'faith is very important and permeates through all we do.' Staff welcome changes introduced by the head which have upped the pace and expectations.

Academic matters: Pupils are taught in mixed ability groups in Year 7, with setting only for maths, additional setting later. GCSE results are good with year on year improvements – 91 per cent achieved five grade Cs or above in 2009. Around half of A levels graded A/B; sociology, film studies and English literature popular options. Alternatives to traditional A levels include applied courses, BTec performing arts and NVQ business.

SEN well-looked after with successes celebrated via a 'caring to achieve' board. Nine children have statements, plus others on SEN register. Range of SENs catered for including children with ASD, SpLD, medical needs, MLD and VI; have technicians and support staff to help as required. Work on self-esteem through circle of support programme etc. Some grumbles from pupils that they don't always get individual attention particularly in larger classes. School says, 'in part, our drive to increase standards has raised the demands and aspirations of our pupils, but as 91 per cent gain GCSE and all pupils leave with at least five qualifications we feel we meet all needs'. Sixth formers happy – 'we have small teaching groups, it makes a real difference, you get to know the staff really well and they, you.'

Games, Options, the Arts: Plenty of trips to theatres, exhibitions and places of interest and opportunities for travel abroad including rugby to Italy and netball to Jersey. Wide-ranging extracurricular activities include D of E and plenty of sport. Regular music and drama performances involving large numbers of pupils in everything from Cabaret to Coldplay liturgies. Have jazz band, choir, orchestra, brass group etc. First class new sports centre complete with under floor heating, cricket nets, climbing wall, brand new kit etc. GCSE dance group works in partnership with nearby St Elizabeth's special school. Pupils are encouraged to help in the community through various activities, head stresses importance of interacting with the community, including non-faith.

Background and Atmosphere: Established by an order of nuns in 1896 as a girls' convent but co-ed since 1976. Situated near the centre of Bishop's Stortford on a large and pleasant site. Near to bus routes but about a 15-minute walk from the rail station. A mixture of old and new. The new include a modern library and sports hall plus recently built sixth form centre offering plenty of space for both study and relaxation. The old is scruffy and past its use by date; there is a big current building/refurb programme, aiming for first class facilities, but not there yet.

Pastoral Care and Discipline: Praise from all quarters. Pupils say school is incredibly caring and any problems are swiftly and effectively dealt with. Discipline straightforward, firm. Staff have high expectations; recognise they have a duty to educate pupils to be the citizens of tomorrow. Work hard to keep and support students but not afraid to exclude temporarily or permanently when needs must. Recent innovations include peer mentors trained by Childline and an inclusion unit to prevent exclusion. Prospective sixth-formers have a team building/induction week with taster lessons at end of Year 11. Very strong Catholic ethos. There are regular lunch-time Masses and residential retreats; chapel always open, chaplain visits frequently.

Pupils and Parents: Predominantly white Catholic families. St Mary's serves the Lea Valley Deanery, which stretches from Bishop's Stortford to Hoddesdon, Cheshunt and Waltham Cross and many pupils travel significant distances across Hertfordshire and Essex.

Unlike some local schools, St Mary's does not practise backdoor selection so has, the head stresses, a truly comprehensive intake. Serves a fairly affluent area so pupils tend to have relatively few social problems. Very enthusiastic support and fundraising from parents through the PTA.

Entrance: Has expanded to five form entry. Heavily oversubscribed – even practising Catholics may miss out on a place. First priority goes to Catholic children with a brother or sister in the school. Next in line are Catholic applicants with no sibling connection. Places are awarded according to where applicants live, with 40 per cent going to children in Bishop's Stortford and Sawbridgeworth, 40 per cent going to children in other parts of the Lea Valley Deanery and 20 per cent to those living in another five surrounding Essex parishes. Next come any other Catholic applicants who don't fit the above criteria. Criterion four offers places to those with a non-Catholic sibling in the school. Contact the school for full admissions information.

Entrance to sixth form is dependent on GCSE grades. 'If students are not able to sustain the level, we ensure that they leave that course and take up alternative provision.'

Exit: A few pupils leave after GCSEs to move to other sixth forms in the area, a few go straight to work. The majority of those leaving the sixth form go on to further education, with a quarter going directly to employment. One or two a year head for Oxbridge but the head hopes to see this figure increase with the introduction of a new Year 12 extension studies programme.

Remarks: Aims to produce well-rounded youngsters with values they can defend. Ideal for Catholic parents who are keen to have their children educated in their faith, in a happy and academically successful environment.

St Mary's Music School

Linked to Saint Marys Music School Junior School in the Junior section

Coates Hall, 25 Grosvenor Crescent, Edinburgh, EH12 5EL

- Pupils: 72 in total; 18 are choristers; 24 boys, 48 girls • Ages: 9-19
- Size of sixth form: 10 • Non-denom • Fees: individually assessed
- Independent

Tel: 0131 538 7766
Fax: 0131 467 7289
Email: info@st-marys-music-school.co.uk
Website: www.st-marys-music-school.co.uk

Head: Since 1996, Mrs Jennifer Rimer BMus LRAM DipEd HonARAM (sixties), previously head of academic music, career guidance and guidance in the school and, before that, was principal teacher of music at St David's High School in Dalkeith. Educated at Buckhaven High School, she read music at Edinburgh University. Married, with three children; she and her husband live in Edinburgh and all have a high involvement in music.

The school has close links with the four specialist music schools south of the border; musical excellence is a priority but academic results are also consistently excellent and the school is regularly at the top of the Scottish schools' league tables.

Certain amount of hanky panky (of a serious kind) has resulted in staff being given free accommodation by HM Government; all currently seems quiet and peaceful, but possibly a lack of judgement on staff appointments recently (and not so recently).

Academic matters: School follows normal Scottish National Qualification exam syllabus, Standard Grades followed by Highers and Advanced Highers. A pleasing number of A passes in all disciplines (music tops though). Small classes as one might imagine, and no problem with staff, grades are pleasingly high with 100 per cent passes in 2010 at Standard Grade and Advanced Highers and 95 per cent at Highers. A level music also on offer again with 100 per cent passes. At Standard Grade all pupils must take English, maths, a social subject, a science and are advised to take a modern language. All pupils study Music and bypass Standard Grade Music to take Higher Grade Music in S4. 'Support for learning' available.

Games, Options, the Arts: School has an all-purpose games court on site. Swimming club popular, busy art classes, debating, plus regular workshops, masterclasses, rehearsals and concerts. Dedicated staff in every discipline – this is a centre of excellence and if a pupil's music specialism is not normally covered, then a specialist will be pulled in. Music libraries and practice rooms all over. Rooms full of clarsachs and harps; pupils practising in the quaintest corners. Pupils are occasionally joined by musicians from other local schools.

Saturday morning music classes are non-selective, where senior pupils act as class assistants, along with professional staff. Huge variety of choice, from the very basic to quite complicated string ensembles, chamber concerts et al. 'Classes are non-selective and waiting lists are in operation'. Over 200 local children attend.

Background and Atmosphere: Encouraged by Lord Yehudi Menuhin, the school was founded in 1973 in the grounds of St Mary's (Episcopal) Cathedral, and moved to the present site, previously a theological college, in 1995. Delightful if slightly scatty building, the chapel is used for school assemblies, concerts and rehearsals and staircases seem to run in every direction. Some classes held in the 'principal's house' or the 'fives court' in school grounds. 28 boarders who mostly share rooms and can go out with '16-year-olds at night and with two or three of our own age during the day,' said our charming junior guide. Flexi-boarding if space permits. Weekly assemblies include 'praise time'. School uniform for choristers, junior pupils, otherwise tidy dress and the most elegant and put-together collection of teenagers we have ever come across.

Pastoral Care and Discipline: Tiny numbers, not a lot of sin. 'No drugs – as far as I know,' says the head; no obvious smokers. Good guidance system from year staff and the career staff. All of sixth form have some sort of responsibility, either head of school, or deputy head of school or head of library; but all are prefects in one way or another and contribute to the running of the school.

Pupils and Parents: Primarily from Scotland and the north of England, with a trickle from overseas; these are all dedicated pupils, from every corner of society. The school has an equal opportunities policy but the physically handicapped might find the building a challenge.

Entrance: By vocal audition involving the master of music at the cathedral for choristers: aged 9–13 (though a boy may leave earlier if his voice breaks early). Instrumental pupils, composers and singers are also chosen by audition, involving the head teacher and the director of music, plus two or three specialists. Each child is assessed differently; a successful musical audition is followed by a two-day assessment. Auditions are held throughout the year. Part-time Pathways to Specialism scheme is available for post-Higher pupils wishing to apply for music courses at university or conservatoires. Part-time Pathways pupils can attend for up to 12 hours per week, either while still at their own schools or in a gap year between school and university or music college.

Exit: Choristers leave at 13, though some may re-apply for an instrumental place. Almost all pupils go on to tertiary education, be it to conservatoires or music departments in universities. This is a focused school with excellent career guidance for musicians. Good history of music scholarships.

Money Matters: School is basically fee-paying, but with 'aided places' i.e. parents pay according to means, supported by the Scottish Government under the St Mary's Music School Aided Places scheme. Government funding (up to 100 per cent) available and Cathedral bursaries.

Remarks: One of UK's nine MADE (music and dance excellence) schools. For a musical child, there could be no better start in Scotland or thereabouts; outstanding musically and educationally and, possibly, financially.

St Mary's School Ascot

St Mary's Road, Ascot, Berkshire, SL5 9JF

• Pupils: 370 girls; 360 board, 10 day • Ages: 11-18 • Size of sixth form: 110 - all board • RC • Fees: Boarding £28,230; Day £20,100 pa • Independent

Tel: 01344 623 721
Fax: 01344 873 281
Email: admissions@st-marys-ascot.co.uk
Website: www.st-marys-ascot.co.uk

Headmistress: Since 1999, Mrs Mary Breen BSc MSc, a physicist, (mid-forties) via teaching at Wellington and headship of physics at Eton; married to James, a master at Wellington. Stylish, girlish while being tip-top professional, trim and energetic, Mrs Breen must be the dream head for this dream job. She is the first lay head of this much-loved Roman Catholic institution, was young to get it, and few would question the wisdom of the choice. She is smiley, genuinely open and friendly while being totally clued-up on facts, figures and the acronyms heads reel off these days. She clearly takes an immense pride in school, staff and girls and this is made palpable in the sense of contentment which pervades the place. 2007 ISI inspection included more 'outstandings' than we can recall seeing before.

Academic matters: Impressive by any standards. This is a small school, its first criterion for admissions being Roman Catholicism and it is genuinely comprehensive in intake. It has more girls in the third quartile of ability i.e. below average for independent schools than in any other. Yet – gosh – the results! In 2010, 91 per cent A*–B grades at A level. At GCSE, 56 per cent A* and 88 per cent A*/A grades.

How is this done? – chiefly by small classes, individual tuition where needed, carefully streamlined system of targeting in individual subjects, a sense that it's cool to work and a, perhaps, narrower choice of subjects than bigger schools could accommodate. That being said, the head claims that she will find a teacher for any language someone wants to learn and there are currently students of Russian, Mandarin, Japanese, Polish, Italian et al in the school. Latin and Greek are available and survive to A level standard – again a rare thing in a small school. Staff have generous timetables and many live on-site – it all helps. Library impressive for so small a school, complemented by further stock in subject areas.

All are screened at entry for SEN. Dyslexics seen twice-weekly and many others get supported for organizational problems and the like. No designated area and SENs certainly not high profile here.

Games, Options, the Arts: School has splendid sports centre – opened by Darcey Bussell – with everything schools twice its size can boast – dance studio, gym with all the machines, squash courts etc – and this has given sport a considerable boost. Lovely playing fields all on site plus Astroturf and girls play hockey, rounders, netball and tennis (very popular). On site is a 25m swimming pool. Of the extras, modern dance attracts largest numbers. Also on offer are wine tasting and ballet/tap classes. D of E is big here.

Most girls study a musical instrument or two and all learn singing. Concerts mostly in chapel and music seen as outstanding. Drama is innovative and impressive and all are looking forward to new performing arts centre, for which at time of our visit, the earth was being moved. Art is simply stunning. We saw professional quality work in many media but were specially knocked out by the textiles and the ceramics. Again, the range and variety of work is what astonishes, in addition to the amount of space the girls have for the various disciplines – privilege indeed.

Lots of visits to lectures and lots of top quality speakers come – the day after our visit Mary McAleese, the President of Ireland, popped in for a talk. Collaboration with boys from Eton on talks, confirmation classes, socials etc. Some grumble about boring weekends and head's eyes widen at this. Many staff, parents claim, disappear at four o'clock – not unreasonably, perhaps – and there isn't the range of organised activities a larger school could lay on. Nonetheless, girls have the run of all the sports and arts facilities and it's hard to see that they could really be bored.

Background and Atmosphere: School is located in deepest South Ascot – all large detached houses in their own grounds, gated drives, lots of trees in deep, rural-seeming, peace – and only minutes from Heathrow. The site has wooded areas, gardens and green spaces and its buildings are, mostly low-rise and subject-based. None impress by their beauty except the original main school building which is large and a somewhat bewildering architectural gothic-Flemish-Norman-arts and crafts confection. Care has been taken over recent building especially the new courtyard area housing the sixth form – a major recent asset. The site is enhanced by such jeux d'esprit as posts made of ceramic dolly mixtures and ceramic plaques on walls. The site is leafy and delightful to walk around, despite current building and there is an air of serenity hardly familiar to Guide writers.

Founded in 1885 by the Institute of the Blessed Virgin Mary (IBVM), a religious order begun by Mary Ward (1585–1645), an extraordinary Yorkshirewoman who saw that women could serve God in a way comparable to that found by the Jesuits – not an easy path to follow or an idea many found acceptable in the seventeenth century. She insisted girls were 'capable and fit to do God's service' and the school's aim is to 'remain faithful to that mission.' St Mary's is one of the many Mary Ward – or its sister, Loreto, – schools worldwide and there is a sense of a family of schools related by faith and a common mission.

Central, therefore, to the site and the ethos is the gorgeous chapel and its much-loved, long-serving chaplain. The chapel accommodates the whole school and its stained glass, carved stations of the cross, splendid altarpiece and spaciousness cannot but impress and induce a sense of reverence and peace. It is clearly prized by the girls who, comfortably, make it their own. There is a basket of sweets before the altar, collected by all girls and taken by those who make the annual, optional, pilgrimage to Lourdes to share with children with disabilities. Immensely touching small and modest cemetery in the heart of the grounds – resting place of the nuns who spent their lives here and who taught the many Old Girls who remember them with deep affection.

Pastoral Care and Discipline: The sixth form confided their sinfulness to us – 'Water fights get cracked down on like nobody's business.' A haven for druggies, topers and fag-ash Frannies this ain't. 'We call ourselves "a telling school",' says head and girls confirm that anyone upset by teasing or troubles at home would be quickly picked up. 'There's undoubtedly a little smoking in the grounds,' acknowledges head – confirmed by girls – but this is as far as sin extends, bar the occasional incident with alcohol resulting in a week's suspension. One exclusion for drugs in head's eight years and girls look bemused as to why anyone would risk their life here by contravening rules seen to be sensible and reasonable.

Discipline clearly underpinned by Catholic ethos – 'we take our spirituality very seriously but we wear it lightly,' says head and girls concur, 'the fact that everyone is Catholic makes us more of a community.' Efforts also to make this full-boarding school feel home-like – e.g. Pets' Shed, a residence for pupils' rabbits, gerbils etc. Resident house staff, mostly teachers, are popular but most feel that popular Aussie gappies are more likely to be privy to problems or confidences.

Girls live in year groups overlaid by school houses. Entry button system for all buildings. Year 7s in rooms of two, four or eight – girls with older siblings are seen as having more familiarity with the school and share with just one other. Year 8s in cleverly segmented old dorm – now in 'cubies' – separated nooks with bed, desk, basin and shelf – good mix of togetherness and privacy. Rooms – and school as a whole – not specially tidy so no obsessiveness here – some might like a bit more of it. Refectory is bright and functional and girls say food has improved 'out of sight'. Upper sixth can cook for themselves – and do – in excellent kitchen in their courtyard domain – seen as one of many privileges accorded to their superior status. Older girls given freedom to go out and about and take taxis to Windsor, Reading, Ascot etc or trains to London for lectures etc.

Pupils and Parents: No longer the exclusive preserve of the old RC families though many still send their daughters here and, as Old Girls who are current parents told us, 'the underlying ethos hasn't changed.' The Old Girls' list includes Antonia Fraser, Marina Warner, Sarah Hogg, Princess Caroline of Monaco, along with Olga Polizzi, and journalists Lady Celestria Hale (Jennifer's Diary) and Katherine Bergen (*The Times*). Old time watchers of the school recognise the increase in numbers of girls from London and from the US – 'they can afford it,' we were told, ruefully. Vast majority comes from the south-east and around 12 per cent from Catholic Europe. Hugely supportive parents and Old Girls.

Entrance: You have to be Roman Catholic – or, by a convincing accident of birth, a near-miss. Most come either through ancient connections or friend's or prep school head's recommendation. Some put girls' names down at babyhood. Over-subscribed by eligible candidates, around two per place, so many, of necessity, turned away – 'we do it very courteously'. Assessment by interview and testing over which much time and care are taken. Forty places at 11, around twenty at 13.

Exit: It is rare for a girl to leave before A levels – a clear and welcome bucking of the trend. The subjects taken at university cover a remarkable range – medicine, lots of art history, engineering, languages. A good sprinkling annually to Oxbridge and to lots of redbricks, especially in the north. Few plate glasses and former polys here.

Money Matters: Several scholarships worth five per cent of boarding fee which can be augmented by further 25 per cent – assessed by means-testing. Expensive but one can see why.

Remarks: Worth converting for.

St Mary's School, Cambridge

Linked to Saint Mary's Junior School (Cambridge) in the Junior section

Bateman Street, Cambridge, Cambridgeshire, CB2 1LY

- Pupils: 505 girls including 70 boarders (full time and weekly)
- Ages: 11-18 • Size of sixth form: 105 • RC but all faiths welcome
- Fees: Seniors £12,465; Boarding £23,100-£26,862 pa • Independent

Tel: 01223 353 253
Fax: 01223 357 451
Email: admissions@stmaryscambridge.co.uk
Website: www.stmaryscambridge.co.uk

Head: Since 2007, Ms Charlotte Avery (late thirties) BA MA PGCE. Read English at St Anne's Oxford. Began teaching in South Africa at a politically tense time when some of the older boys carried AK47s to school. Back in the UK and several professional moves later – two via

GDST schools – became deputy head at Highgate, where she met her French husband, now a teacher at Sevenoaks School. (Pupils may only address her as Madame Pillet as long as their pronunciation is correct).

A palpably determined bundle of energy and breathless, almost unstoppable, advocate of St Mary's, with ambitious plans to squeeze more space out of a cramped site. Equally passionate about Lourdes – where 'our girls rose to the challenge in true St Mary's spirit' – and food. 'Dining is an important experience and I'm enjoying eating my way socially through each year group.' Everyone's pleased she's taken on board requests to learn cookery and that a perfectly formed, albeit compact, cookery suite has been installed. Pupils appreciate her up-to-date approach and, as a committed communicant member of the C of E, she wholeheartedly supports the ethos and values of St Mary's. An arty background makes visits to a gallery or the opera a must, whilst membership of the Ministry of Defence Ethics Committee ticks the public duty box and 'provides a chance to inject some commonsense into proceedings.'

Academic matters: Not fantastically pushy but competitive in a 'nice way'. Considering the broad intake, good results at GCSE – 66 per cent A/A* with hardly any slippage below C. Abundant encouragement plus drop-in surgeries for girls who need help – school says there's value-added across the board in spadefuls. Relaxed dialogue and mutually respectful relationships between staff and pupils. Parents are full of praise for the teachers and are convinced the bright do as well here as they would at the stratospherically academic institution round the corner. Recently introduced two-week timetable seems to be working well – head has her finger on the pulse in case tweaks are needed. French plus Latin in Year 7 with German and Spanish in Years 8 and 9. At GCSE option of dual award or individual sciences but full RE course for all – the RE teachers are an 'incredibly sane and dynamic lot', according to the sixth, who love the discussions on every sort of issue.

Strong support network in the sixth. Reasonable spread of A level subjects has been maintained because school offers subjects to groups as small as one or two. High A/B rate – around 80 per cent – with results getting a big boost from impressive performances in maths and the proportionally high number of Chinese nationals, not surprisingly, getting As in their own language.

All Year 7 pupils are assessed on entry in English, maths and reasoning. Needs, including those of the gifted and talented, are monitored and sensibly handled – ethos that all have something to offer isn't just prospectus speak. School reckons it's 'dyslexia friendly' but not CReSTed or likely to be despite 2008 appointment of experienced head of individual needs/language/ learning who has an MA in specific learning difficulties. Three part-timers to hand, access to Ed Psych and EFL teaching for international students. Differentiated activities enable most to stay in class but, if necessary, withdrawal during a second foreign language lesson. Usually groups of four. One-to-one tuition outside the normal timetable incurs an additional charge. Small teaching space, laptops as teaching aids.

Games, Options, the Arts: No practices at dawn but the sporty aren't held back – a number of girls play for the county. Enthusiastic staff and older girls happy with the range of options including rowing, touch rugby, yoga and kali – a seemingly ache-making series of movements with long sticks. Limited space so only two netball/tennis courts and smallish first floor gym on site. Hockey pitches a short minibus ride away. Hired pool and Astro nearby.

Drama and music (just over a third learn an instrument) are in fine fettle – conventional orchestras for instrumentalists and samba band for those who fancy something more lively.

Slightly cramped art department but the personal 2 and 3D work is liberally displayed and sixth formers have their own space. For the creation of something more practical there's D and T textiles with its large bright classroom filled with sewing machines.

School is hot on events for charity and, amazingly, given the number of pupils, raises around £25,000 every year. In the summer hols sixth formers join the popular pilgrimage to Lourdes, where they help the needy.

Two-weekly timetable has freed more time for extracurricular activities, and an Arts Council sponsored award scheme (includes journalism, dance, digital film work, music and drama) is taking root with awards beginning to roll in. D of E is hugely popular and an impressive percentage get gold every year. Visiting speakers and debates, to celebrate the 400th anniversary of the founding of Mary Ward's Institute, precursor of the St Mary's schools – a year long series of talks from an interesting mix of eminent women.

Background and Atmosphere: This former convent – the nuns moved out in 1989 – is sandwiched between terraced houses and an edge of the Botanic Gardens. Although there's nothing remarkable, apart from the maze of corridors and staircases, in the diverse collection of dull buildings from the '60s, '70s and '90s which have been tacked on to an early Victorian structure, a sense of safety and warmth pervades this well loved, tidy place. Sizeable classrooms and science labs. Standard gadgetry. Full library plus good range of newspapers and magazines (a sixth former has been appointed as newspaper scanner and daily poster of interesting articles on a corridor noticeboard) and fresh librarian who looks set to shift some of the dustier tomes. Sixth have a separate house where they can browse in the careers library or escape to a somewhat lacklustre commonroom – as one of the girls put it, 'not the tidiest in tidyville ... but it's ours.' Noisy bonhomie in the spacious diningroom, which doubles as part of the hall. Consultant has transformed the lunches and, much to everyone's relief, there's a wide choice of tasty dishes and tropical rainforest of a fruit bar.

Virtually all boarders from abroad. Ordered, typically personalised accommodation is neatly housed on the upper floors – single rooms for all the sixth and some GCSE students. Commonrooms are welcoming, with the slightly quirky junior being especially homely. Likeable and eminently sensible housestaff set great store on trust – sixth are allowed out by arrangement until 10pm on Fridays and Saturdays as long as they let the school know where they are – which, by all accounts, gets the hoped for response from the girls.

Pastoral Care and Discipline: Catholicism with a small c but charitable Christian Ethos in capitals – there's an understanding that all belong to a wider community and behaviour is expected to be, and is, supportive. At the heart of the school is the universally popular chaplain who's often found sitting on the radiator at the foot of the main stairs. Parents say he's a gem. He knows everybody and is a source of comfort and solace.

Open, unspoilt girls at ease in this secure environment. They're allowed to develop at their own pace and 'aren't pushed or shoved into a box.' New pupils settle quickly – parents appreciate promptly established lines of communication by phone or email and the way staff are on the ball with problems including difficulties at home. (Some moans though about the patchy website and we agree it's not the best advert for the place – school says it's going to be given a facelift).

Pretty well behaved lot – the pragmatic policy re banned substances is rarely implemented. 'We need to think about the wider community so out for dealing. In cases of possession we look at circumstances.'

Pupils and Parents: Day pupils are very local whilst others commute by car (absolutely no parking in the vicinity) or train (station is a healthy 10 minute walk away). All sorts – about a third are Catholic – make up the loyal and supportive parent body. Majority of boarders are from overseas – international spread with a fair number from the Pacific rim.

Entrance: Mostly at 11 from own prep or local schools. Small number after GCSE. Informal chat with the headmistress then an application when she ascertains whether child is of 'sufficient calibre to benefit from a St Mary's education' – not hugely difficult as school draws from '60 per cent of the ability range' – bit ambiguous but we think we know what they mean. 'Bottom line is girls need to be enthusiastic about learning and committed to the wider community.' No surprise policy and basic expectation that those from the prep will join the seniors. Any not up to the mark can repeat Year 6 (fine if the child stays in the private sector but problematic if, pre 16, there's a transfer to state education where child must be in the correct age banding and may have to 'jump' a year).

Exit: After GCSE many of the locals to Hills Road. As a strand to its career guidance, school has produced a collation of career stories from alumnae – oodles of advice and thoughts including the balance between work and family. Good stuff. Sixth move on to a broad range of courses and unis. Respectable number to Oxbridge and the heavyweights.

Money Matters: Academic, music, art, textiles, drama, performing arts and sports scholarships at 11, 13 and 16. Mary Ward scholarships for those in Years 8 and 10 who make a positive contribution to the school and wider community.

Small number of 100 per cent bursaries for Year 7 and sixth form entry. Possibility of help, usually to the next public exam, for those who fall on hard times.

Remarks: Energetic head and loyal staff with a positive outlook. Level of pastoral care and awareness of social responsibility give this place something extra special.

St Mary's School (Gerrards Cross)

Linked to Saint Mary's School Gerrards Cross Junior House in the Junior section

Packhorse Road, Gerrards Cross, Buckinghamshire, SL9 8JQ

• Pupils: 325; 220 in senior department • Ages: 3-18 • Non-denominational • Fees: £11,010-£12,405 pa • Independent

Tel: 01753 883 370
Fax: 01753 890 966
Email: registrar@st-marys.bucks.sch.uk
Website: www.stmarysschool.co.uk

Head: Since 2010, Mrs Jean Ross BA (French, Manchester) NPQH. Previously deputy head at St Albans High School. Her educational philosophy is one of identifying the individual talents of each and every child and giving them the tools and motivation to reach beyond their best.

Academic matters: Good results, given broadish church, thanks to good value-added across all subjects. Approximately 70 per cent A/B at A level; almost all pass all their GCSEs with just over 50 per cent awarded A/A* – commendable. All usual subjects offered at A level, plus theatre studies, PE, media studies and health and social care. Lots of loyal, long-serving staff; head comments, 'they're not stick-in-the- mud; they're very proactive, keen to stay ahead of the game'.

50 girls benefit from learning support with 10 or so receiving ESL help. The team copes with a range of mild SEN – mainly mild/moderate dyslexia and some medical/sensory needs. Focus is very much on the individual, regardless of where they are on the learning spectrum. Small classes and attention to learning styles and individual needs ensure all have the opportunity to achieve. Has various events for gifted and talented plus French verse speaking competition open to all. Some of the brighter girls do the 11 plus but it isn't their raison d'être – 'we encourage enjoyment of education, not the confines of cramming'.

Games, Options, the Arts: Girls enjoy their sports – plenty of netball and tennis plus football, cricket, gymnastics etc. Success on the sports pitches doesn't feature as regularly as hoped for but they don't get hung up on 'the games that got away'. Flexibility and support offered, plus allowances made, for those with talents such as ice-dancing, horse-riding etc, which require time out of school. Musicians entertain via school band and orchestra; lots of singing with recognised success for some choirs. Plenty of trips and tours, near and far. A number of girls are D of E Award holders. More dance was the only thing on wishlist of girls and their parents and they're hopeful that will come when the eagerly awaited, state of the art sports hall, a welcome addition to a good range of outdoor sports facilities, is completed.

Background and Atmosphere: Originally an Elizabethan manor house, the estate has shrunk over the years but number of buildings has grown. Founded in Paddington in 1872 as a school for girls, run by Anglican nuns, it moved to its current premises in 1938. Very much a school where girls are known to each other and to staff. There's a real sense of community, a feeling that everyone matters, 'people don't get left out; it isn't cliquey,' insisted senior pupils, adding, 'there's a real big sister, little sister feel'. Facilities wouldn't win prizes; all are well kept but they're more Hennes than Harrods, though there is a decent smattering of gadgets, including whiteboards, laptops, data-logging kit etc. Purpose-built labs and specialist tech areas, two functional libraries (we like the 'donate a book on your birthday' idea), a multi-purpose hall, small teaching classrooms and clinical corridors.

Pastoral Care and Discipline: The school sits just outside the M25 but is a refreshing contrast to many within the zone. Nurturing not pushy, nor highly pressurised; believes the best way to get the most out of the girls is via gentle encouragement, unstinting support and a bit of oomph. Indeed, the school's reputation for caring about the girls and the way the girls care for each other have tempted many a parent through its doors. Drink, drugs and other unhealthy options seem to bypass these savvy girls. A strong house system ensures girls, and their work and efforts, are valued and rewarded. Good careers preparation – work experience in Year 11, community service in Year 12 plus self-evaluation and mock interviews etc.

Pupils and Parents: A broad(ish) social mix – some struggle to meet the fees, others very affluent. This may be 'des-res' land but it's not 'debs' res'. Girls are confident and caring but unfazed by brands and labels. Odd moan – middle school would like an indoor breaktime area, some older children would like a more varied lunch menu (though parents say it is improving) and some grumbles, not about quantity of homework but spasmodic way in which it's sometimes set. Parents would like to see improved facilities for sixth form, citing current Portakabins as less than ideal. Active school council has negotiated recent changes to uniform and additional subjects at A level. Parents kept informed via parent-mail and active parents' association welcomes anyone who wants to get involved.

Entrance: Majority from Gerrards Cross and environs; not league table driven but keeps a canny eye on performance and improvement. Getting harder to get into but, if there's space, girls are welcome and welcomed at any time. Takes all-comers at 3, many stay for the duration; odd one or two who won't make the grade asked to leave prior to 11. In junior school, some come with an eye on a grammar school place at 11, others because they want an all-through school. Selective entry at 11, ideally seeking a VR score of 110+ but does have a number of average children who will benefit from all the school has to offer. Many feeder schools including Maltman's Green, Chalfont St Peter's and High March.

Exit: Steady trickle due to moving away from the area but generally fairly stable. At 16, most stay on into the sixth form (varies year on year); a few enter the grammars or opt for co-ed boarding or local sixth forms. However, as sixth form numbers are small (usually five or fewer girls per subject) they get lots of individual attention. All move on to university, range of courses, occasional one to Oxbridge.

Money Matters: Not a rich school but academic scholarships available at seven, 11 and 16, plus a music scholarship at 11. Offers a small number of means-tested bursaries to those in need.

Remarks: One contented youngster remarked, 'I think this school is wonderful, every single bit of it.' A good choice if you want a school that will nurture, add academic value and care as much about your daughter as you do.

St Mary's School (Shaftesbury)

Linked to Saint Mary's Junior School (Shaftesbury) in the Junior section

Donhead St. Mary, Shaftesbury, Dorset, SP7 9LP

• Pupils: 310 girls; 195 board, rest day • Ages: 9-18 • Size of sixth form: 85 • RC • Fees: Boarding £22,650; Day £15,570 pa • Independent

Tel: 01747 852 416
Fax: 01747 851 557
Email: admin@st-marys-shaftesbury.co.uk
Website: www.st-marys-shaftesbury.co.uk

Head: Since 2006, Mr Richard James (forties). Educated at Kirkley High School in Lowestoft before training as a musician at the Royal College of Music (piano, violin and conducting). Was director of music at Cottesmore Prep for ten years before moving to St Mary's Ascot where he became a head of house with his wife Becca who taught art; later director of music. Composed choral music, mostly for the Campion Singers (chapel choir). Arrived as deputy head at St Mary's Shaftesbury in 2005. Became acting head (six months before an ISI inspection!) and then head. First male head of any Congregation of Jesus (CJ) school. Teaches composition and jazz history at A level; pursues his love of music when time permits. Very down to earth, easy to talk to, clearly loves the place. Three children – one son at university, one at Gillingham and a young daughter at St Mary's.

Academic matters: Results outstanding for mixed ability intake. Almost half the girls do A level English; RS, French and art/history of art popular too; very large up-take of sciences for a girls' school. Separate sciences for all at GCSE and rather whizzy science labs with just the whiff of Dr Strangelove about them, GCSE results also very impressive. Languages – exams usually taken by native speakers, otherwise Spanish, German and French. A level options broadening with recent introduction of AS photography, further maths and sports science. Trained staff stretch the most able 'through our gifted and talented programme'. 'Girls being pushed more and harder these days'. Good calibre of staff and increasing numbers of them. 'We won't give in over little things' – homework must not be late, poor work is not accepted. All girls screened for SEN on entry, five part time and one full time co-ordinator in the SEN department; good links with preps and can cope with mild dyslexia etc; no ADHD or Asperger's. SEN lessons usually take the place of a language.

Games, Options, the Arts: Strong on netball, tennis and hockey, Astroturf, 25m indoor pool, oodles of dosh spent on the sports side, polo popular, but new art department on the way – expect it in a couple of years. Old art rooms burgeoning – lots of textiles. Stunning music dept, with practice rooms and concert hall. Jazz, rock, orchestras, choirs, trips abroad. Envy making. Keen drama, LAMDA. Fab drama studio with seating for 130. Strong on extra-curricular activities – self-defence, modern dance, masses of clubs for just about everything and stunning cooking facilities. Duke of Edinburgh Award taken to Gold level. Retreats, pilgrimage to Lourdes (that well-known smart European marriage bureau) etc.

Background and Atmosphere: Sister school to St Mary's Ascot (the choicest of the three) and St Mary's Cambridge (the most street wise), founded by IBVM (now CJ) in 1945. School tucked down wooded drive; hidden among the moss and pines it feels almost like one is arriving at The Beast's enchanted palace. Charming converted late Victorian house with hotch potch of architectural mismatches. Fifty-five acres of rolling grounds, wonderful views and – for the boarders – a strong sense of 'being out in the sticks' but girls can walk into Shaftesbury. Recent building includes bright new junior school, infirmary and library. Boarding throughout whole school. Boarders graduate from larger bedrooms (never dorms) to individual bedrooms – upper sixth house gives girls much independence and is a significant factor in sixth form retention. Day girls may go home at 4:45pm but most stay later for activities and study. Long flowing wrap-around kilts for all and full length for the sixth form: quite a sight. Strong community happy-family feel. Masterful prospectus.

Pastoral Care and Discipline: All newcomers (even the head) have a mentor for the first term and welcome cards abound. Pastoral care improved and improving with increased numbers of staff per house; pupils meet with their tutor each morning. Palpable RC ethos throughout, 'it underpins everything we do', says the head, 'and that will not change'. Quite a number of C of E girls, Anglican priest comes once a week and celebrates eucharist in the chapel. Head notes the girls are given a bit more freedom than those at Ascot. 13 year olds can walk into Shaftesbury, two miles away, in groups of three; older girls can visit Salisbury and sixth formers may stay out till 10pm at weekends. Weekend activities considerably boosted in the last few years. Girls allowed cars in the sixth form. Fierce anti-smoking policy – fine and letter – suspended – expelled. The odd suspension for overindulging in alcohol (three incidents in last two years).

Pupils and Parents: Only 10 per cent first time buyers. More local than in past: 80 per cent live within an hour of the school. Good mix from overseas (but not more than 10 per cent non-nationals) – Mexico, Spain, Germany, Hong Kong. Unspoilt, jolly nice, articulate, uninhibited girls – and relatively unsophisticated. Just over 50 per cent RC. Quite a few refugees from the hurly burly of London.

Entrance: At 9 (one small combined junior class of 9 and 10 year olds – the two year groups join for art, PE, etc, but are separated for core academic subjects), 11, 13 and into sixth form. Scholarships in all disciplines, music, art and sport as well as academic with the option of bursarial top-up. Minimal testing for those who come into the junior school to go up to senior school. Numbers currently steady and school says registrations rising fast.

Exit: Tiniest trickle to trad girls' or co-ed senior schools, stronger trickle post GCSE to sixth form elsewhere. Of those who remain, almost all to university, every year Oxbridge candidates (head sez: 'special Oxbridge preparation classes. Each year we have at least two Oxbridge offers'), loads to various art courses – foundation or history of art plus medics and chemical engineers.

Money Matters: Not a rich school but does its housekeeping well. Bursar an acknowledged genius.

Remarks: Jolly nice girls' Catholic boarding school, from the same stable as St Mary's Ascot, unpretentious and good at bringing out the best. A safe harbour. School has come a long way from the days when locals used to ride to school and leave their mounts in the stables during the day.

St Michael's Catholic Grammar School

Nether Street, North Finchley, London, N12 7NJ

- Pupils: 760 girls, all day. Boys admitted into sixth form • Ages: 11-18
- Size of sixth form: 280 • RC • State

Tel: 020 8446 2256
Fax: 0208 343 9598
Email: office@st-michaels.barnet.sch.uk
Website: www.st-michaels.barnet.sch.uk

Headmistress: Since 1995, Miss Ursula Morrissey BA PGCE (fifties), educated at Queen Mary College and Institute of Education, London University. She has been at St Michael's for her entire career, joining in 1971 to teach history and rising through the ranks to become deputy and then head. Charming, approachable, excellent leader. 'She's immensely committed and that shows in the school's ethos,' said a parent. 'She's very human, very caring,' said another, 'She really listens to you'.

Academic matters: Described in its 2005 and 2008 Ofsted reports as 'an outstandingly successful school', St Michael's is less ferociously selective than other north London grammars because all applicants must be practising Catholics. However, its results put it not just in the top five per cent of schools but in the top five per cent of grammar schools. In 2010, 89 per cent of GCSE grades were A* or A which places the school in the top 5 state schools. Most girls do 11 GCSEs, including RS, DT and one or two foreign languages; everyone learns French in Year 7 and has a taster of Spanish, Italian and German. Latin lessons start in Year 8. This can result in a crammed timetable – 'we work at a bit of a gallop. The girls are bright and keen and that compensates for having less time for each subject.' Maths is setted from Year 9; everything else is mixed ability. There is no SEN department but heads of key stages are responsible for the few girls with sight or hearing problems or dyslexia.

The sixth form collaborates with Finchley Catholic High School, a non-selective boys' school ('and there are plenty of grammar schools that would be sniffy about linking up with a comprehensive,' commented a parent). It is not a joint sixth form but students from each can study one or two subjects at the other school, which helps to avoid timetable clashes. St Michael's offers 31 A level subjects, including theology, economics, government and politics, and PE. At A level, 83 per cent of results were A*–B in 2010. Classics is a popular A level choice, as are psychology, maths and biology. School expects more students to study foreign languages as a result of achieving specialist schools status as a language college. Ofsted describes the sixth form as 'first class.' Many sixth formers go to Europe for two to four weeks' work experience. It is compulsory for linguists but non-linguists can work in Sweden.

Games, Options, the Arts: On-site are netball/tennis courts, a grassy area for athletics field activities and a new sports hall opened in Spring 2009; girls swim in the Finchley lido in Year 8. 'We are usually vying to be borough champions in netball, cross country, badminton and athletics.' Football, dance, tennis, cheerleading, trampolining, yoga and cricket are popular extracurricular activities. There are Outward Bound and skiing trips, plus field trips and language exchanges. Year 12 is a 'year of service', with girls organising clubs and events and running committees. Sixth formers also help with reading in local primary schools. A very enthusiastic sixth form arts and cultural committee organises dance and music performances.

Background and Atmosphere: Founded in 1908 by the Congregation of the Sisters of the Poor Child Jesus as a prep school for boys and girls, it became a girls' grammar in 1958. Sandstone lower school building, once inhabited by the nuns, including a chapel with bright stained glass windows, also used for assemblies and dance classes. Nineteenth century sixth form centre, plus new sixth form study centre; the rest is mostly 1950s buildings, mostly refurbished. State-of-the-art technology block produces very strong DT GCSE results. The top floor science labs have views to Mill Hill; modern maths rooms; plenty of computers.

Traditional, ordered atmosphere; very welcoming. 'The head has an absolute care and love for the school and this permeates the atmosphere of the whole place,' said a parent.

Pastoral Care and Discipline: Year 7s are each allocated a Year 13 'Guardian Angel' to help them settle in. A parent commented, 'everyone knows each other and the sixth formers look out for the younger ones inside and outside school.' The school's strong spiritual underpinning shows in its pastoral care. 'We have parameters but we work first and foremost on forgiveness.' 'When my daughter had emotional problems, they were so supportive,' said a parent. 'And they dealt very fairly with it when she had a clash of personalities with a teacher.'

No bullying or drugs problems to speak of. 'Because we're a traditional school we probably over-react on the small things. This sends out a message that certain things are unthinkable – the girls probably think we'd have apoplexy if they took drugs.' Some, reportedly, find it a little on the stifling side. Very strict on uniform.

Pupils and Parents: A big mix of Catholic families from a large area of north London. Pupils tend to be keen and motivated and parents relieved they have found such a high quality education in such a sane school. The sixth form offers a broader experience of life by taking in non-Catholics and linking up with Finchley Boys' High. OGs: Jill Paton Walsh, Jessica Martin (actress), Vanessa Gearson – prospective parliamentary candidate for Cheltenham, Julia Stokes (Channel 4's The Mummy Diaries).

Entrance: Only girls from practising Catholic families (letter needed from priest) may take the entrance exam, which consists of English, maths, verbal and non-verbal reasoning. The four sections are given equal weighting and girls ranked in order of merit. The school no longer interviews. Generally around 300 girls after 96 places.

Students after sixth form places – about 50 join Year 12 – do not have to be practising Catholics but do have to attend services and play a part in the spiritual life of the school. NB boys admitted since September 2009. The minimum entrance requirement is six GCSEs at grades A*/A with at least a grade A in the subjects most closely related to those they want to study to A level.

Exit: A few leave after GCSEs to pursue vocational courses or join co-educational establishments. The school has a target of 10 per cent of leavers applying to Oxbridge and about half of those – usually six or seven – are generally given offers. Other students go on to a wide range of mostly old-established universities, to read anything from Italian and management studies to forensic science.

Money Matters: Government pays only 90 per cent of refurbishment costs, so the school is constantly fund-raising. Parents' committee runs international evenings, summer barbeques etc.

Remarks: Small girls' grammar school which gets impressive results as well as being universally popular with pupils and parents. 'My daughter has blossomed and grown in confidence there,' said a parent, 'It's a very human, very caring place.'

St Ninian's High School

Eastwood Park, Rouken Glen Road, Giffnock, G46 6UG

• Pupils: 1750 Co-ed • Ages: 12-18 • Size of sixth form: S5/6 550 • RC • State

Tel: 01415 772 000
Fax: 01415 772 037
Email: headteacher@st-ninians.e-renfrew.sch.uk
Website: www.ea.e-renfrew.sch.uk/stninians

Rector: Since 2005, Mr John Docherty (early fifties), who spent much of his early teaching career at St Ninian's, (and his daughter was a pupil), later becoming assistant headteacher. He was then appointed head of St Andrews, Clydebank, where he 'served his apprenticeship' as a head, 'learning that what goes into making a good school is, above all, not being a one man band'. On moving back to St Ninian's he felt that, despite its good reputation, standards could be better; the school had reached a plateau and both senior pupils and departments needed to be given more opportunities to take responsibility and initiative. His watchword is teamwork and parents are part of his team. As a result, reports are issued termly, parents are invited in to discuss education, 'not just be told about it'. In a radical approach to parents' evenings, one teacher collates information on a particular pupil and then spends a useful amount of time in discussion with parents ('not the usual two minute slot').

Mr Docherty, meticulous in attention to detail, is highly critical of the standards everywhere, from mealtimes to maintenance. If his super modern halls and wide corridors look miles better than most school buildings, it was only achieved 'through constant nagging'. Similarly, every aspect of school information is at his fingertips to the extent that he appeared to know the name and current concerns of each of his 1750 pupils that we met during our visit.

Academic matters: In 2009, St Ninian's had the best SQA results of any Scottish Catholic maintained school. East Renfrewshire schools have such good academic results that families are queuing up for places. (St Ninian's is so popular that East Renfrew Council are running a consultation into the places problem.).

All pupils take a full range of subjects including French and Spanish but (unlike most schools) select their subject choices for Int I or II (rather than Standard Grade) before entering S2. 'This focuses them on the subject area where pupils are strongest and most interested, cuts time wasted in subjects which pupils do not wish to study and avoids timetable pressures and subject rotations.' Emphasis on modern langs with some distinguished results. French, Spanish, German and Italian on offer together with Mandarin – open to all year groups with a real Chinese teacher. Amidst great flourishes of Chinese dragons the school has just been inaugurated as a Confucius Hub – the initiative for Mandarin Chinese in Scotland. No Latin or Greek but an impressively high uptake of English, maths and sciences at Higher and a swathe of technical/admin/business subjects. Learning support has five teachers and St Ninian's can and does provide for profoundly disabled. Easter holiday revision courses to the fore as well as Mass for exam candidates just before Easter (belt and braces?).

Vocational options not forgotten with access to courses in sport, engineering, beauty, cookery, childcare, fashion, nautical etc some with Glasgow Caledonian or other higher/FE colleges, including some courses leading to possible full-time employment.

Games, Options, the Arts: Sport provided for within the curriculum though 'there is never enough room for everything' so bags of it as extra-curricular. St Ninian's has no all weather facilities for rugby or football. The depressingly muddy sand pitch is frankly uninviting in a Scottish climate and badly needs updating. Football strong (girls and boys), rugby less so, hampered by rain and mud. Netball, tennis, badminton and athletics all boast school teams and have access to local clubs, but hockey 'has not really taken off'. A few 'talented athletes' excel in golf, football, karate etc. Activities are available in school until 6pm run by the school or East Renfrewshire but after that the buildings are open for public activities.

Drama, art and music feature strongly in the academic curriculum with all three getting sound grades up to Higher. The school benefits from a site which includes the Eastwood Park Theatre and Sports Centre, as well as having its own drama studio and sports hall. Did 'The Crucible' last year. Art seems popular with lots using the department after school. The Eastwood Park Centre recently displayed a fantastic life-size and life-like sculpture (paper pasted over a cane frame) of a rhinoceros made by St Ninian's pupils for their performance of Ionescu's *Rhinocéros,* helped by county visual arts co-ordinator who also had taken pupils to be part of the 'Streetwise' exhibition and the Burrell Collection. Masses of music, typified by the 60 strong and jolly tuneful string orchestra rehearsing at the GSG visit. Pupils get into Scottish national youth orchestra etc. Endless after school clubs: ceilidh bands, public speaking, language clubs, string quartets, choirs, fashion etc and lots of outdoor education though not D of E.

Oodles of holiday activity (something of a crusade in East Renfrewshire!) and term time outings and projects: London, Kitzbuehl (skiing) Ardeche, Alton Towers, Wimbledon, law courts, lots of theatre etc plus a good smattering of pilgrimages and a pretty sophisticated scheme of retreats and spiritual experiences (moral theology, medical ethics etc); for this is a Catholic school through and through.

Background and Atmosphere: Founded and built in 1984, St Ninian's is part of a civic complex of council offices, arts and sports centre surrounded by grassy banks and urban forest. Huge and spectacular '90s additions by Jarvis cunningly provide an all purpose, open plan dining and performance area – a lofty central space set between three wings with acres of wall space. Potentially a bit bleak but light, airy and full of activity. This is tacked onto the back of the original school, joined seamlessly to the now dwarfed original octagonal hall (rather elegant ceiling) which opens into the newly refurbished library. Further extensions house large well-equipped classrooms, (interactive whiteboards and computer projection now goes without saying) and some state of the art new labs (and some less so – teachers have to work hard – and do so – to keep them up to scratch). The various extensions enclose a large oblong of 'patio' pregnant with as yet undeveloped possibilities. Catholic ethos much in evidence, not just in a rather startling Lenten display but also in the strong sense of the Catholic community. Not exclusively Catholic with quite a few headscarves in evidence though Mr Docherty reports no withdrawal from religious activities. Pupils polite but no tidier than most, ('It's a challenge to raise dress standards'), majority look pleased to get to the end of the school day, though one or two incredibly dapper prefects set a high tone in their maroon blazers and sharply knotted ties.

Pastoral Care and Discipline: All round care of pupils is managed in 'families' (rather than houses) by eight 'pastoral' teams. 'Pastoral' being more catholic terminology than the usual Scottish 'guidance'. These have 'a strong handle' on issues like bullying. Apart from accessible policies, such problems are dealt with, when necessary, by the 'focus for the week' which has included topics like 'mobile phone bullying', 'anti racism', and the more mundane 'using your planning diary', 'lost property' or 'Advent charities'. The pastoral team also manages personal and social education in the curriculum and provides individual supervision which Mr Docherty would like to systematise further. Lots of parental contact and a view that, the better the school does things, the more supportive parents will become. The programme for careers and life skills uses speakers and visits covering every aspect from 'modesty is elegance' to 'gap year projects' and' world development'. Responsibility for the state of the world is encouraged by fundraising and awareness raising for both international and local charities.

Sanctions mainly as a last resort (because the chief weapon is 'high expectations') but include exclusion. Mobile phones switched off inside the building. Intranet bullying – 'dealt with immediately and not really an issue'.

Pupils and Parents: Supportive PSA (Parents Staff Association) does massive fundraising and entertainment for school. Parents work in groups based on the pastoral 'families'. Pupils use public bus service.

Entrance: School is inundated with demand for places and the catchment includes parts of Glasgow as well as East Renfrewshire. This may change, as limiting the catchment may be a means of keeping numbers at manageable level.

Exit: 90 per cent stay on to S5 and of those 85 per cent stay for S6. Last year had the highest percentage of UCAS entries for any Scottish (maintained) school. Seventy per cent to uni, mostly Scottish/Glasgow but a smattering to Oxbridge. Nobody in 'negative destination' (unemployed or not in a training, further ed or somewhere useful). Some gap year uptake.

Remarks: Very big but after negotiating the usual palaver of entryphones, locked doors and office corridors, does not feel impersonal. Clearly a dynamic school with a dynamic head and a consequently dynamic team of teachers and parents. Aims for 'all pupils to aspire to university and college without becoming singularly focused on academic results'. They achieve their aspirations and also focus on fun.

St Olave's and St Saviour's Grammar School

Goddington Lane, Orpington, Kent, BR6 9SH

• Pupils: 860 boys, plus 105 girls in the sixth form, all day • Ages: 11-18
• Size of sixth form: 360 • C of E • State

Tel: 01689 820 101
Fax: 01689 897 943
Email: office@saintolaves.net
Website: www.saintolaves.net

Headmaster: Since 2010, Mr Aydin Önaç BSc BMus ARCM FRCA. Educated at Lady Manners Grammar School, Bakewell followed by The Royal College of Music and UCL. Previously Head of Tewkesbury School and Fortismere in north London. A concert pianist and former student of Cyril Smith and Phyllis Sellick, he has a first in Maths from UCL and is passionate about both maths and music. Keen interests in rugby, chess, rock-climbing and languages; favourite books: *Tess of the D'Urbeville's*, *Anna Karenina*, *Our Mutual Friend*. Two grown-up children.

Academic matters: An outstanding grammar school by any standards, over-subscribed and hugely sought after – 'a traditional education for the academically able'. All pupils assessed on entry, thereafter school's own Individual Pupil Monitoring Scheme ensures every pupil has their own challenge grades set. Broad range of subjects taught, with all the traditional bases well covered. Languages include French, Spanish and Latin. No one here just teaches the syllabus, pupils actively encouraged to think for themselves. Forward-thinking homework policy – one subject per night, a godsend to the 47 per cent of pupils who live more than half an hour away, leaving them more time to pursue the mind-boggling range of extra-curricular activities – 'crucial for extending students' confidence and knowledge,' says head. Pupils confirm that the workload is 'just right'.

Academic results are outstanding, culminating in 2010 with 96% of A level results at A*–B grades, placing the school 3rd best state school in the national league tables. It was also named State Secondary School of the Year in 2008 by the *Sunday Times*.

Excellent facilities in every department – beautiful libraries, a brand new sports/drama hall, state-of-the-art computing suite, airy and spacious classrooms. High calibre, lively staff, and pupils enjoy lessons – 'even the subjects you don't like are interesting,' enthused one Year 8 boy. 'They teach you above and beyond the curriculum,' added a confident and well-spoken sixth former. The girls who join the school in Year 12 are equally positive – 'coming here was the best decision I've ever made,' 'I've gained so much confidence,' 'everyone's been really friendly,' were the verdicts of a group of girls'-school refugees. Small number of SEN pupils are well supported by the SENCo, with individual assistants for statemented pupils.

Games, Options, the Arts: Strong and diverse, with outstanding tuition and facilities available – the only state school to play Eton Fives at national level. A few lament the lack of soccer below Year 12, but rugby is extremely popular, with opportunities for all boys to play, and top players going on to local and national success. 'Our son loves cricket and rugby here, he's incredibly happy,' reported one parent. Sixth form netball also strong; girls have been selected to play for the Kent Netball Academy and the London and South East Region. New multi-purpose sports and drama hall on the way, which should up the game even more. Music equally strong – large number of orchestras and ensembles, and tuition available on any instrument. Pupils can learn blues and African drumming as well as the more classical repertoire – even organ is taught, on the magnificent instrument in the main school hall. School provides choristers for the Queen's Chapel of Savoy, and it's not uncommon for pupils to win choral and organ scholarships to Oxbridge. Theatre studies AS introduced in 2009 but we reported that drama for the younger years was somewhat lacking. School says that this is now offered as part of the KS3 curriculum with three annual productions drawing casts from all age groups. Art and design are well represented, with lots of excellent work on display around the school.

Background and Atmosphere: Originally located in Southwark, St Olave's received its Royal Charter in 1571. Forward-looking school with a strong sense of history – reception area contains a magnificent watercolour of 'St Olave's Grammar School, Tooley Street' hanging alongside a thoroughly modern Infoscreen, which pairing seems to sum the place up. School moved to its present green field site in 1968, in quest of more space and its own playing fields – also, perhaps, to get away from ILEA and the threat of being turned comprehensive. School buildings are lightsome and airy, combining the best of 1960s architecture with postmodern additions – lots of gardens, sloping roofs and quadrangles. Pupils and staff move about the site with calm determination and seem courteous and respectful.

Pastoral Care and Discipline: Praised by parents and pupils alike, a 'do as you would be done by' approach. Heads of year and their tutor teams oversee the pastoral system, and form tutors stay with the pupils throughout each key stage. Ofsted commented on the 'particularly good' staff/pupil relationships and pupils' comments bear this out. 'I really felt looked after,' one said to us. 'Looking back, you appreciate all the care you had,' said another. Older students very much involved with younger ones, running clubs, arranging outings, helping with tutor groups. School has refused to expand beyond the point where the whole community can fit into the hall for assembly, and we were struck by its friendly family atmosphere.

Pupils and Parents: All boys come from families where education matters, otherwise very diverse both socially and culturally – gilded youth and council estate boys all in the scrum together. 'There's a real mix of people here,' observed one sixth former. School's catchment area is massive, but applications particularly encouraged from its original boroughs of Southwark and Lambeth.

Entrance: At 11 by competitive exams in November. Hundreds apply for the 112 places, which are awarded, without interview, to the highest achieving. For sixth form, competitive exams plus at least eight Bs at GCSE. Well over 400 girls and boys apply for around 70 external places.

Exit: At 16+, almost all boys stay on to the sixth form. At 18+, all students go on to higher education. In 2010, 31 were offered places at Oxbridge and almost everyone gained a place at their first choice university. Strong contingent to all the top places – Oxbridge, Bristol, Durham, Imperial, UCL, etc. Consistently high numbers take medicine, law and engineering.

Money Matters: The whole outstanding package is free, thanks to its grammar school status. State funding supplemented by its own foundation, which ensures funds for new buildings and additional teaching staff. Very active PTA raises money for all kinds of projects, while sixth form runs a charity week and raises an impressive amount for various good causes. OBs include John Harvard, Abba Eban, Lawrence Durrell, Wing Commander Andy Green, Baron Hill of Luton, Roy Marsden, Sir Roger Sims, Sir John Smith.

Remarks: One of the finest schools in the country, and a testament to the grammar school system. A superb, inspirational place. As one parent put it, 'All of our expectations have been not just met, but exceeded.'

St Paul's Girls' School

Brook Green, London, W6 7BS

• Pupils: 730 girls, all day • Ages: 11-18 • Size of sixth form: (known as VII and VIII forms): 230 • Fees: £16,302-£17,526 pa • Independent

Tel: 0207 603 2288
Fax: 0207 602 9932
Email: admissions@spgs.org
Website: www.spgs.org

High Mistress: Since 2006, Ms Clarissa Farr MA PGCE, (fiftyish). Ms Farr was an experienced head before her assumption of this most coveted – and exposed – of headships, having spent ten years as the highly successful and popular head of Queenswood (qv). Prior to this, she spent four years as deputy at Queenswood and her career to then had been as a teacher of English in Hong Kong, in a Bristol comprehensive and in a sixth form college in Farnborough. She is married with children.

The highest profile post in girls' education, this headship has been filled by the esteemed, redoubtable and charismatic since the school's foundation in 1903. Ms Farr looks set to further enhance the role's reputation – the post-holder is known as 'the high mistress'. She is elegant, svelte, very pretty and clearly possessed of a fearsomely sharp, though unparaded, intellect. She listens. She has succeeded in winning over, in surely record time, a formidable, dedicated, and – in many cases – long-serving staff. She inherited from her predecessor, the respected and well-liked Elizabeth Diggory, many new initiatives, in particular the project to build an ambitious extension to the theatre block – now complete. She was also bombed by an ISI inspection in her first year which she, characteristically, saw as 'an opportunity'. 'She exudes a sense of calm,' we were told by a teacher. Staff and parents see her as an outstanding communicator – she has a rare fluency of expression – 'her assemblies are touched with brilliance,' we are told – a rare enough attribute.

Devoted to the cause of women's education, she is clearly wise to the pressures on girls' schools from the London co-eds and is not complacent. 'I won't take my eye off that ball – ever,' she affirms. She quickly established herself as an expert administrator and consultative in her approach. She demonstrated this throughout our conversation by paying tribute to 'the very able team I have here. We have a climate in which people, including the girls, are very ready to take on responsibility – they just get on with it – it's my job to make that happen.' The girls think 'she's cool ... she's able to joke, have fun ... she's warm, she's approachable.' We doubt whether we have ever before been able to quote this from a pupil on a head: 'I just love her. She's so pretty and funny. She's my role model.'

Academic matters: Second to none. Since, overall, girls-only education at the top end consistently outdoes any other kind, we have no hesitation in saying this. No school has a better record in league table performance but to stress this is invidious. While the school is assiduous in preparing its girls for the exams, the education on offer here is broad, deep and independent in the best senses. No-one here 'teaches to the exam'. GCSE results in 2010 saw 84 per cent of subjects taken getting A*s and 99 per cent getting A*/As. So no point in mentioning individual subjects. Unsurprisingly, the examined curriculum is narrow – school prefers 'academic' – and traditional – no psychology or business studies here. But Greek had 12 takers at GCSE (all but one got A*, the other an A) and A level economics and history of art are offered. At A level, the most popular subjects are biology, chemistry, history, English and maths. Numbers for modern langs are, perhaps disappointingly, small.

School sees no incompatibility between its academic prowess and the numbers of girls with identifiable SENs – 'there is no stigma here,' asserts the high mistress. Around three a year are dyspraxic or dyslexic or have other difficulties. School has adapted to being accessible for a pupil with mobility problems. Support is 'completely individually based', most with a 'dys' will have two or three individual lessons a week with 'superb' SENCo who, head says, 'is particularly skilled at dealing with these problems in children of high intellectual ability.' In-class support also given when needed and close links with tutors maintained.

School has an enviable library which would do credit to an Oxford college. It contains venerable volumes to give depth and breadth and is well-funded so new books for new modules can be supplied. In the main room, the only computer is used by the librarian (senior girls can bring in laptops). PCs can be found in the upstairs gallery of the newer library room – also most impressive with spiral staircase, fiction and periodicals. It is in its extra-curricular programme that the school excels. This complements and enhances the academic curriculum and earns most praise. Typical is the – compulsory for sixth formers and now open to their parents – programme of Friday lectures. Speakers range from the academic on subjects esoteric e.g. Prof Robin Cormack on 'Why Look at Old Icons?' or Lord Selborne on 'Water management in the UK', to the political e.g. George Osborne MP to the journalistic e.g. Ruth Gledhill, Leo Hickman, Iain Martin, to the artsy e.g. Nick Hytner, Peter Hall, and the seriously fun Richard Curtis on weddings, funerals and Bridget Jones. School's own academic staff contribute assiduously to the broader education of pupils and are described as 'inspirational'.

Games, Options, the Arts: Main games are lacrosse, netball, tennis, swimming, athletics with sizable numbers taking dance. On site are three grass, yes, grass, tennis courts, two netball courts, two table tennis tables and a vast new sports complex with dance studio, multi-gym and sports hall. Round the corner in Bute Gardens and shared with Bute House (qv) in three and a half acres, are two lax pitches, four tennis courts, netball courts and a pavilion. Here athletics and a range of fun sports take place e.g. five-a-side and touch rugby. Matches and tournaments against schools all over the country with notable successes and some county players – these girls exercise far more than their brains and achieve comparably.

Music is famous. Gustav Holst taught here and successive directors of music have maintained highest of standards. Music takes place in the Holst wing, adjacent to the main building which includes an excellent recital hall and umpteen practice/teaching rooms. Two thirds learn at least one instrument in school. Results are as you'd expect and, say parents, concerts are astoundingly good – to professional standards, somehow also managing to be inclusive of even the less than starrily gifted. This also said of art and drama – though not of sports which are seen by some to rely too much on always the same girls. Drama blessed by a large refurbished theatre in a splendid block – the Celia Johnson building 2007 – which includes teaching accommodation. Also has excellent smaller studio. Standards very high and productions large and small entered into with the same zest as is palpable everywhere here. Art and DT are not only skilled but witty – we enjoyed mobiles made from crockery and casts of crockery, a lamp with an umbrella-derived structure, clever wooden toys. Everyone does DT for their first three years. Pottery and lino work on offer as well as CAD.

There are trips galore – D of E expeditions, WWI battlefields, skiing in Colorado, maths competitions in India, music in New York, Iceland, Costa Rica – everywhere where something interesting can be seen or done. 'Staff are outstandingly generous with their out-of-school time,' we were told.

Background and Atmosphere: John Colet, dean of St Paul's, in 1509, founded a school 'for the children of all nations and countries'. He didn't mean girls. The guardians of Colet's estate, The Mercers' Company, a little slow to respond to the cause of women's education (the Girls Day School Trust had, after all, been founded more than thirty years earlier) made up for its tardiness by, in 1903, buying a house in a prime site in west London (Henry Irving had lived there) demolishing it and building the impressive and imposing school which still accommodates the Paulinas. One look at the facade makes plain the aspirations enshrined in this foundation. There are three plaster reliefs – two women – one artistic with book and pen, the other scientific with a far-away meditative gaze – and over the entrance sits the Maid of the Mercers, the Worshipful Company's historic and emblematic figure of a seamstress.

The entrance hall is also impressive – wood panelling, marble flooring and a bust of Colet in a niche. There is the Great Hall and the library is a place of gravitas but elsewhere, though everywhere is freshly painted, the school wears a more workaday air. This is enhanced by the no uniform policy – a sense that this business of being educated is everyday life and we get on with it. Four plasma screens keep girls in touch with the day's programme. The more modern buildings are crowded in and all is overseen by the true head of the place, the groundsman, Don, a 'fixer' held in awe and affection by the girls – 'he's famous, amazing – he gets cross if we leave mud around – in a friendly way.' The school as a whole is five minutes walk from the lead-poisoned, concrete hell that is Hammersmith Broadway but, as soon as that is left behind, the streets are quiet and lined with Victorian two and three storey terracing – expensive, well-maintained, very middle class. Brook Green is a green eyot slipped into an envelope of modest Victorian respectability. Those who pump exhaust into the two arteries at either end probably have no idea it's there.

The atmosphere is lively, friendly, relaxed, and there is a palpable sense of collaborative enthusiasm in all areas. Remarkably few leavers post-GCSE partly due to jolly good and sensible sixth form centre in 'The Forum' – good common room areas, table football, PCs, sofas and rugs and a cafe. Every parent we spoke to used the word 'happy' of her daughter. St Paul's has a formidable history and a considerable mythology on which many consider themselves expert. As so often, the myth long outlives the modern reality. 'One of my missions is to reshape the image of the school in the public mind,' declares the high mistress. High time, we say.

Pastoral Care and Discipline: Pastoral care, not always seen as a strength, is now almost universally commended. Heads of year now have charge of it under the overall supervision of the deputy head and, though some will always slip though a net, however fine, there is a general confidence now that girls are properly cared for. 'Sister system' matches girls in different years in relationships which persist throughout time in school and girls want to extend this to a more 'family system'. To matters such as drug abuse and anorexia, high mistress takes the same approach – 'educational. We are not moralising. We try to educate the girls about the risks they face on a daily basis. We talk very openly and maintain high vigilance.' No incidents of drug/alcohol sin within memory and head very conscious of risks of eating disorders. 'I'm keen to have fantastic food here and a very relaxed attitude about eating and eating well.' Girls say food is 'fantastic' and it looked it – loads of choice and things you actually want to eat. No-one brings food from home.

Pupils and Parents: The brainy and talented. Mostly from west London though increasingly from further north – a commute from Hampstead is not uncommon. From a vast range of backgrounds – the global executive, the literary, arty or scientifically academic, the professional, the relatively humble and from every kind of ethnic and religious origin. We were quoted one current A level group of 12 which included an Iraqi Muslim, an observant Jew, a middle-eastern Christian, a Rumanian, a Chinese, a Pole and a French-speaking Finnish-Mauritian. A walk round the school sees all blending into a visibly comfortable community where any distinctions vanish.

Parents have long-standing reputation for competitiveness and pushiness but this seems to be a thing of the past or, if it persists, it seems to be dispelled pretty quickly in Year 7 when, according to a teacher, 'they relax – realising that there is a narrow range of outcomes here – the girls nearly all end up at the same five unis and they are amazingly supportive of one another.' It's not for the meek or wobbly – but then they probably wouldn't come anyway. The selection process is meticulous. 'School helps you build a big personality,' said a sixth former. 'You have an easier time if you're outgoing though calm studious people do fine here too.' 'Girls come out,' a parent told us, 'with a real sense of self-belief.' Notable past Paulinas include Helen Alexander, Gillian Ayres, Shirley Conran, Rosalind Franklin, Harriet Harman, Celia Johnson, Kathleen Kenyon, Onora O'Neill, Jessica Rawson, Imogen Stubbs, Shirley Summerskill, Salley Vickers, Rachel Weisz, Antonia White, Shirley Williams etc ...

Entrance: Most from west London preps. Around 16 per cent from state primaries. Around four applicants for each place. Online cognitive testing reduces numbers for examination in maths, English and science and an individual interview by high mistress or senior colleague – current or recent. Reports from current schools sought. Highly, highly competitive, as few who aren't up to it even apply and school could probably take many more without lowering standards.

Exit: Most stay the full seven years though three or four are tempted post-GCSE by Westminster or boarding. High mistress says, 'I know Westminster is a vibrant intellectual community – almost as vibrant as this one.' But very few go. 'The education they have here cannot be matched,' says head – 'the opportunities for creativity and leadership cannot be replicated. They grow to become very committed to the community.' When they leave after A levels, their attainment is unique. Of the 96 leavers in 2010, 26 went to Oxford, 25 to Cambridge and nine to Ivy Leagues. The rest mostly to London University colleges, Bristol or Durham, and subjects cover the academic range. Head sympathetic to applications to the best in the US – 'a lot of girls who are broadly intellectually interested aren't ready to specialise.'

Money Matters: Around 12 per cent have some sort of financial assistance with fees. Scholarships are mostly for the honour of the thing but sensible bursaries help the bright but cash-strapped. Remission for those with three daughters at the school.

Remarks: For the bright, talented, motivated and confident girl, there can be no more exhilarating start to the big adventure.

St Paul's School

Linked to Colet Court in the Junior section

Lonsdale Road, Barnes, London, SW13 9JT

• Pupils: 860 boys, majority day; one boarding house • Ages: 13-18
• Size of sixth form: 355 • C of E • Fees: Day £17,928; Boarding + £8,631 pa • Independent

Tel: 020 8748 9162
Fax: 020 8746 5353
Email: reception@stpaulsschool.org.uk
Website: www.stpaulsschool.org.uk

High Master: Since 2004, Dr Martin Stephen BA PhD (fifties), educated Uppingham and Leeds University (English and history), PhD at Sheffield. Taught at Uppingham, housemaster at Haileybury, deputy head at Sedbergh. Head of The Perse, Cambridge 1987–94, High Master Manchester GS 1994–2004. Wife Jenny is head of South Hampstead HS, coming from The Grange, Northwich; three sons.

Arguably the brightest and most experienced head in the independent sector, but affably modest with it. Enormously energetic, great talker, well-tuned sense of humour. Passionate advocate of top-quality education for all, irrespective of family wealth (see below). Recently fought his way back from serious illness, now firing sparkily on all cylinders. Likes drawing and painting as well as writing – has published 15 books on English literature and naval history, plus four historical thrillers (where does he find the time?). Gives very able management team a lot of responsibility.

Major surprise and upset in July 2010 when Dr Stephen stood down – to take effect from July 2011. Dr Stephen was quoted as saying, 'Any decision to leave a school like this is the result of a complex of reasons, some of which are professional, some of which are personal.' Top class independent education can appear as smooth as a mill pond. This is a hefty rock to break the surface and could stir up some sizeable ripples. New appointment awaited with great interest.

Academic matters: As ever, superb in all subjects, with an especial sparkle about maths results. Most recent inspection praised all areas with only minor qualifications about a lack of timetabled 'spiritual' guidance (but head feels it's inherent in many extra-curricular aspects of school's rich life). Overall teaching, as one would expect, is top drawer, with very few exceptions. Head positive about AS exams, backed up by pupils. Enlightened general studies options for Year 12. Five resident language assistants (native speakers): French, German, Spanish, Italian on offer, all sit French GCSE at end of year 10. Science now teaches the more rigorous International GCSE, school having concluded (unsurprisingly) that GCSE is 'an inadequate basis for the future study of science.'

Maths and geography have gone the same way. Successful classics, English and history. Boys readily own up to intellectual curiosity, regarded as a natural activity (co-ed schools please note); but fierce selection means there is a strong identity of interest, and few academic passengers. School wonderfully equipped in all areas scientific, technological, electronic. New streamlined floor dedicated to geography, science and electronics, including data-logging lab and IT control lab. SEN supported, but probably not the place for more than mild cases. Library tastefully revamped in soothing wood invites quiet study. Staff tend to stay long term.

Games, Options, the Arts: Again, superb. School has impeccably kept playing fields, large swimming pool, offers 30 sports including rackets, taught by pro, housed in new court – funded by single benefaction – which hosted recent world championship. Notable successes in fives, basketball, seriously strong in rowing, cricket and rugby. Music in world-class new Wathen Hall; practice rooms designed for specific instruments and an exhilarating concert hall seating 316, in demand by professional groups for rehearsal, recording and performance. Half pupils on roll learn at least one instrument. Drama well provided for in versatile theatre and smaller equally flexible studio space – both well used. Art also impressive. School capitalises on near-central London location and accessibility of celebrated locals.

Background and Atmosphere: Perhaps too much has been made of the 'hideous' 1968 buildings. School now on its fifth site since foundation by Dean John Colet in 1509; foundation now run by the Mercers' Company. Some Old Paulines still lament move from Waterhouse building in West Kensington but few can regret acquisition of this superb 45-acre site between Thames and chic Barnes residential streets. Peaceful, almost rural site well kept and humanised by rose beds and trees. Increasingly, relics from former buildings coming out of store and being integrated on site. Boys' sculptures and canvases also break up starker areas and the place is mellowing nicely.

However, it's been decided that 75 per cent of buildings need replacement over the next 25 years. Current wide-ranging consultation exercise will lead to master plan involving three independent construction phases, hopefully with minimum disruption to daily life. Appeal for this launched in 2007; 'fees won't rise extravagantly'. School tells us £29m has been raised and they expect to start building a spanking new science block, library and junior music school in the very near future.

Head balances idealism with practicality, hence CCTV in new locker room to guard against petty pilfering (not a major problem), also huge new Common Room for final year pupils as well as splendid commemorative millennium sundial.

Between 20 and 30 boys board; some capacity for emergency need. Dormitories (four to a room for younger boys) graduating to individual study bedrooms – small, functional but not spartan. Boarding, though used by minority, seen as central to school tradition.

Pastoral Care and Discipline: Vertical tutorial system, whereby a boy and his tutor build up a close and easy relationship over five years, crucial to community's wellbeing: a Pauline glory, according to Dr Stephen, and he's right. Tutors visit pupils' homes; boys expect them to be on their side and 'look out' for them as the 'prisoner's friend'. Pupils consulted over curricular decision-making, parents increasingly involved in many aspects of school life; hence integrated pastoral care. Tough but realistic drugs and smoking policy relies on parental cooperation, as ever balancing individual's against school's needs. Dress code exists in theory but in practice is imposed with difficulty, though boys are relatively kempt. Atmosphere is generally orderly but not constrained.

Pupils and Parents: Boys come from all over London. Cosmopolitan, multi-faith community, strong US, Asian and European contingents. Parents mostly ambitious middle class professionals, supporting solid work ethic. Boys are independent-minded, articulate, the most mature aware of their privileged lot. Two pupil comments: 'To succeed here you need to be smart, competitive, able to do things under your own steam'; 'It's not so much a hothouse as a free-range academic farm'. Most appreciate the challenge and rise to it. Heavyweight Old Boys list includes Milton, Halley, Marlborough, GK Chesterton, EH Shephard, Compton Mackenzie, Edward Thomas, Field Marshal Montgomery, Paul Nash, Isaiah Berlin, Sir Alexander Graham, Eric Newby, Lords Janner, (Kenneth) Baker, McColl and Renwick, Sir David Rowland, Sir Jonathan Miller, Oliver Sacks, Peter and Anthony Shaffer.

Entrance: 45 per cent come from Colet Court, the rest from assorted prep schools. Registration, accompanied by non-returnable fee, should be five years before entry at 13+. External 13+ candidates are interviewed at age 11 once a satisfactory reference from head of prep school has been received. CE taken at prep school. 70 per cent required in every subject at CE. A few join school at 16+; minimum eight GCSEs, all grade B or above expected, with As at least in proposed A level subjects.

Exit: Vast majority to good universities, reading hard subjects. A quarter to Oxbridge and, a dramatic new phenomenon, about twenty a year to US universities, including Harvard and Princeton. Old Paulines feature prominently in professions needing brains and enterprise.

Money Matters: Means tested bursaries where needed. Scholarships awarded by exam taken in May by candidates under 14. Compulsory papers in all CE subjects + optional Greek. About 30 Foundation scholarships awarded each year. All scholarships are now honorary (£60 per annum). Means testing can mean remission of full tuition fee. Overall number of scholars in the school fixed by John Colet to match the number of fishes caught in the Miraculous Draught. Music scholarships competed for by candidates with at least grade VI on main instrument. Further scholarships – academic, music and art – available in later years. Some remission for families who send three or more children to the school.

Part of the new Great Plan is ultimately to make the school 'needs blind', in the modish unlovely word, i.e. you pay only what you can afford. Colet would have approved, one feels.

Remarks: Remains one of the top two or three London boys' schools, and unlikely to take girls. Pupils bright, inquisitive, unstuffy. Big changes ahead, but in line with school's original principles. Dr Stephen (in a typical rhetorical flourish): 'Our immediate target is to rebuild the school, and our medium to long term target is to return John Colet's foundation to its meritocratic roots.' It appears, now, that he won't be there to see it through.

St Peter's School (York)

Linked to Saint Olaves School in the Junior section

Clifton, York, North Yorkshire, YO30 6AB

• Pupils: 320 boys, 210 girls • Ages: 13-18 (Pre prep and Junior school 3-13) • Size of sixth form: 230 • C of E (but other faiths welcome). • Fees: Day £14,094; Boarding £22,692 pa • Independent

Tel: 01904 527 300
Fax: 01904 527 302
Email: enquiries@st-peters.york.sch.uk
Website: www.st-peters.york.sch.uk

Head Master: Since 2010, Mr Leo Winkley MA MEd (forties), previously managing head at Bedales. Read theology at Lady Margaret Hall, Oxford. Taught at Ardingly College and The Cheltenham Ladies' College as head of religious studies. Still teaches religious studies and contributes to the global perspectives programme for sixth form. A keen runner and follower of sport. Married to Jules (a medical oncologist); they have three young children. Committed to the breadth and all round nature of independent education as lessons for life – says 'school should be serious fun. A good school should offer a safe but challenging environment in which its pupils learn about themselves, develop resilience, confidence and a sense of where they want to go in life.'

Academic matters: Strong work ethos, normal to try hard, lots of aspirational children. Say some do bumble along in middle sets and B teams but hope they get something out of the curriculum – very positive value-added suggests they do. Believe good results are down to having really good teachers as well as selective but not highly selective intake; no weak subject areas. Had several top students in GCSE languages, art and drama in 2010 and pupils with top 10 marks in UK for politics and maths A level. Class size averages 18, in the middle school (maximum 24) and 12 in the sixth form. The occasional D or E grade creeps in but all pupils pass at least six GCSEs at grades A* to C with 77 per cent of passes A/A* in 2010 – best ever results. IGCSEs being taken in maths and languages. Equally impressive performance at A level where 21 per cent achieved the new A* and a very commendable 85 per cent of all entries graded A*–B.

Some support for the handful with mild dyslexia – must be bright and able to cope. Part-time dyslexia specialist. Approximately ten per cent have an Ed Psych report; five per cent qualify for extra time in exams. Ritalin not a problem, very mild Asperger's okay. Third modern language replaced by extra English and study skills for some. Gifted and talented programme in place but don't target top ten per cent. 'All the children here are bright, it would be wrong to concentrate on a handful.' Olympiads and similar challenges stretch those with real talent. Global Perspectives an additional course for sixth form with Horizons being introduced in 2010 for middle school. Do not allow students to take GCSE early and introducing more IGCSEs.

Classrooms, a mix of ancient and modern, are generally well cared for with informative displays, some areas looking tired but rolling programme of improvements in place. Recent additions include four bright new biology labs together, a sixth form microbiology lab, a new chemistry lab and a new Design and Technology room with Cad Cam technology. Three computer rooms are complemented by clusters of computers throughout the school and houses – new virtual learning environment set up in 2010 with WiFi throughout the campus.

Games, Options, the Arts: Sport is compulsory for all. Facilities include two sports centres, one with super climbing wall, new multi-surface pitch, re-furbished fitness centre, new indoor swimming pool, extensive well-kept playing fields, boathouse and tennis and squash courts. Rugby popular and strong, rowing crews regularly pick up national honours and awards, boast 20 international rowers in the last eight years. Hockey, rowing and netball are the most popular girls' sports but tennis, athletics, fencing, squash, swimming and all usual suspects on offer for all. Generally put best coaches with best teams but playing opportunities for all via B teams and house competitions. Competitiveness a prominent feature of the school and success universally applauded at weekly assembly. Duke of Edinburgh and CCF flourishing. Plenty of trips including expeditions to Morocco, battlefield tours, language exchanges and music tours to the USA, Prague, Italy as well as singing in York Minster.

Very good art facilities, including super gallery. Art department appears in the Guinness Book of Records for a remarkable 100 per cent A*/A grade pass rate achieved four years running, though recent years have seen lower grades creep in – 'we were pleased, it took the pressure off, allowed the pupils to experiment, be more creative rather than formulaic,' said one art master. Many learn a musical instrument or two, 300 individual lessons each week with professional specialist music staff, 160 strong choir and plenty of opportunities to perform. Each boarding house has a practice room with piano. Over 100 pupils involved with Community Action projects and all participate in charity fundraising.

Background and Atmosphere: The school was founded in 627 AD by Paulinus, first Archbishop of York, and is one of Europe's oldest schools. In 1844 it was established on its present, attractive, green, grade two-listed site in Clifton, with 47 acres, river access and all within walking distance of York Minster, the city centre and station. The acquisition of the former Queen Anne's Grammar school allowed reorganisation and expansion of the campus, providing purpose-built accommodation for the prep school, St Olave's, which has since undergone major refurbishment.

Pastoral Care and Discipline: Pupils are members of one of the six day or four boarding houses. Boarding received an Outstanding rating in a recent Ofsted inspection. Boarding houses are well equipped with a selection of common rooms, games rooms and a kitchen for snacks (all eat in school dining hall). Improvement programme well underway. Pupils and staff share a healthy mutual respect and relations are good. Houses are headed by husband and wife teams and supported by resident and non-resident assistants. Good pastoral care, head says teachers quickly get the tenor of a pupil and work out what needs to be done. Staff vigilant for problems – invariably have one or two they're watching for eating problems etc. When problems arise advice, help and support may be sought from tutors, house staff, health centre staff or the school chaplain.

Pupils are allowed to visit town twice a week (more in older years) and for younger ones a timetable of supervised events is on offer. All eat in the modern dining hall. Menus offer a wide choice with mixture of typical school meal fare, continental options, salad bar, sandwiches, fruit and healthy eating options. Strong Christian ethos, pupils meet thrice weekly for collective act of worship in school chapel with assemblies at other times.

Pupils and Parents: Day pupils mainly from North Yorkshire, Harrogate, Leeds conurbation, York, and surrounding villages. Majority of boarders live within an hour's drive but others from wide area in the UK. Parents in business and the professions, a popular choice for Services families, small minority from overseas, mostly Hong Kong. Uniform, uninspiring, disliked by pupils: brown blazer, grey trousers for boys, and brown checked skirt for girls. Sixth form wear business suits. Old boys, Old Peterites, include Guy Fawkes, Alcuin (8th century scholar), Greg Wise, John Barry, Laurence Eusden (poet laureate), C Northcote Parkinson (inventor of Parkinson's Law) and Clare Wise (director of the British Film Commission).

Entrance: Automatic entry from Clifton pre-prep to St Olave's (own prep school) and from St Olave's to St Peter's. Eighty per cent follow this route, rest by CE and school's own entrance test at any age including 13 or 16 (minimum six GCSE grade B passes). Assessment and filtering takes place in prep and pre-prep to weed out those who won't cope with the demands of St Peter's. Generally entry to St Olave's requires a child to have a reading age at least a year ahead of chronological age (sympathetic to siblings). Will take pupils who pass exam at any time provided a place is available. Other main feeder schools: Terrington Hall, Bramcote and Minster School.

Exit: Approximately ten pupils leave at the end of Year 11, 'usually because they're sick of us and we're sick of them,' said one master. Ninety per cent of those leaving after Year 13 go directly to university, vast majority selecting Durham, Edinburgh, Manchester, Newcastle and Nottingham. Ten per cent to Oxbridge, seven per cent take a gap year, a few to employment.

Money Matters: Not a rich school but bursary awards based on need are available. Means-tested bursaries available at 11, 13 and at sixth form regardless of previous school. Qualification criteria for bursaries – for those who will need more than 50 per cent of fees funding and if household income less than £45,000. Subject scholarships are awarded but are honorary i.e. no dosh. Music awards available for tuition and instruments.

Remarks: Loved by the sporty academics but plenty on offer for others. Aims to develop confident youngsters who'll have a go at anything.

St Swithun's School

Linked to Saint Swithuns Junior School in the Junior section

Alresford Road, Winchester, Hampshire, SO21 1HA

- Pupils: 470 girls; 255 day, 150 weekly board, 70 full boarding
- Ages: 11-18 • Size of sixth form: 120 • C of E • Fees: Day £14,970; Boarding £24,690 pa • Independent

Tel: 01962 835 700
Fax: 01962 835 779
Email: admissions@stswithuns.com
Website: www.stswithuns.com

Headmistress: Since 2010, Ms Jane Gandee MA (forties). Read French and Spanish at Girton College, Cambridge. Had a brief spell as an accountant before moving into teaching. Has taught in a number of schools and was previously director of studies at The City of London School for Girls (qv).

A keen sportswoman, she represented Cambridge at athletics and cross country and captained the university's women's football team. Married with three children. She intends 'to continue to build on extremely sound foundations and to listen to, and learn from, all members of the school community.'

Academic matters: Incredible exam results, up in the dizzying thin air at the top of the league tables. How a relatively unselective school like this one manages it is mysterious and must drive the London hothouses – with their exacting entry testing of pupils from the age of four – around the bend. Famed for its hotshot sciences (especially chemistry) and maths – so much so that some parents of bookworms have been hesitant to send their girls here. No need to worry, given that English is just as impressive even if pursued by fewer girls. In this heartland of blue stocking education, it is nice to find lady-like subjects like food tech and art history offered at A level (though take-up is low – cookery not seen as a golden ticket into Oxbridge). Compulsory GCSE subjects are English language and maths plus a foreign language and a science. Setting in maths and modern languages. French and German both studied to the end of Year 9 when Spanish enters as an option. All take (only) nine GCSEs and no-one takes any early – a strategy that produces hardly any results below a B. 6–8pm study period for boarders, with social time afterwards. The learning support department gives one-to-one help to some 50 girls who may have dyslexia or dyspraxia or just need help with planning their work. Hillcroft, the newest boarding house, is wheelchair accessible, as is most of the school (one girl currently uses a wheelchair).

Games, Options, the Arts: Plenty of lacrosse fields, tennis and netball courts, 25m swimming pool 'with Olympic springboard standard facilities' and a newly enlarged sports hall with gym upstairs. Hot on lacrosse – often dispatching arch rivals Downe House and Godolphin – and swimming and netball strong, but no hockey. Games follow a compulsory rota until GCSE years when choice kicks in including judo, fencing, and volleyball. Music high profile and high quality, with a range of orchestras, choirs, bands and ensembles. Over 70 per cent of pupils learn a musical instrument and 170 candidates are entered for external music exams each year. Senior choir sings evensong each term in the Cathedral and tours overseas every other year. The performing arts centre provides a wonderful hub for music and drama in the school (and doubles as the venue for morning assembly). Drama studio backs on to the main stage and is used for lessons. Annual mega musical – much excitement on the day we visited as the watertight news embargo on choice of musical for the forthcoming year was lifted – not even the head knew!

Art very popular at GCSE, less so at A level, but fab results all round. Textiles (part of art and design) involved in a project with high street shop Accessorize. Brill cookery room – everyone does food tech for the first three years. There are also after school clubs and a food hygiene certificate course, in addition to A level and GCSE work. DT – splendidly housed – holds its own at GCSE but only one girl did it for A level, two the year before. Our guides made a point of detouring to proudly point out the laser cutter. Overseas trips – Borneo was a destination this year plus skiing and battlefields trips to France, lacrosse players to Prague (!), classicists to Germany (!!). Eleven rather earnest sixth form societies, all with some fund-raising element, from Amnesty International to debating to Young Enterprise. Almost 150 girls take part in D of E.

Background and Atmosphere: Founded as Winchester High School in 1884 by Anna Bramston, daughter of the Dean of Winchester, who remained as school secretary for over 40 years. Changed its name to St Swithun's in 1927 and moved to the present 45 acre site in 1931. Vast, intimidating, red brick, Queen Anne style building with polished wood, long corridors and large windows – sends some parents off screaming before they even make it up the drive. Those who persevere will find smiling faces and some wonderful teaching beyond the imposing exterior. An 'intense footprint' said a teacher describing the school's impressive buildings all bunched in a cluster while the glassy games fields and grounds radiate outward, unbesmirched.

Has always been a 'local' school and weekly boarding for girls whose homes are within an hour's radius is where it really shines (St Swithun's started as a day school and only later tacked on boarding). 'It's so nice not to have guys around during the week – you can get on with your work and meet up at the weekends,' said one studious sixth former. 'I didn't want an isolated convent – I like it that our daughter could get into town, use her mobile phone and come home on weekends,' her mum concurred. Full boarders herded together in one house – mainly from overseas ('and one from Scotland,' explained our meticulous guide). Boarding houses we visited were very high quality and well kitted out with loos, showers and common rooms. But younger girls had curtains instead of doors (noisy?!) and there was an impersonal feeling, a bit like a Travelodge.

Pastoral Care and Discipline: Alcohol more of a problem than drugs (despite Winchester being the drugs capital of Wessex). It is allowed only at a few senior bashes, otherwise, 'if they are caught drinking in school I will send them home.' Not hugely pioneering when it comes to managing friendship group problems and other irritants of all-girl communities. However, its 'cluster groups' have been held up as a model by the Boarding Schools Association – small vertical groups of boarders representing the full age span who meet for suppers once a month. They plan the menu to a budget, do the shopping, cooking and eating, all with the eldest girls as the leaders. Girls do their own washing and mending – good preparation for life we think, although a few parents grumbled that boys are not expected to do the same at their schools.

Girls kept busy on weekdays. Lessons finish at 4.10pm with sport and activities thereafter, then prep. Sixth formers allowed into town two afternoons plus on weekends. Younger girls have more restricted access. In common with every other girls' school in the south-west of England, St Swithun's speaks of its 'links' with Winchester College (though St Swithun's definitely 'out-links' its rivals). The two schools work together on occasional plays, societies and musical endeavours, along with more informal social interaction. Activities at weekends tend to be sporadic – or as school prefers, 'specific to their needs'. All meals taken in the dining hall and girls report good food.

Pupils and Parents: Not a place oozing with social cachet. Middle class, middle-of-the-road, Wessex girls with mostly professional parents. 'Our girls are not natural rebels or rule breakers.' Any of these will tend to leave after GCSEs for more free-spirited establishments. Girls not swamped by make up, Jack Wills or Ugg boots (though all are here).

Entrance: Entry at 11 and 13. Everyone must pass CE (whether from state, private, or school's own junior school) and produce a report from their previous head, but are accepted in order of registration. Staff repeatedly stress that the entrance requirements are not high. A few join the sixth form, generally with A grades in their chosen A level subjects.

Exit: About a quarter leave after GCSEs, bound for the local sixth form college or for other co-ed sixth forms. Almost all the others go on to university, mostly the old-established ones, with Oxbridge, Bristol, Edinburgh, Durham and Exeter being the top destinations (in that order) over the past five years. Sciences unsurprisingly popular, but also classics.

Money Matters: About one in five pupils has a bursary, an academic scholarship or a music award (available at 11 and 13). Academic scholarships range from 10–50 per cent of school fees and are based on the calibre of the applicant, rather than need. Music scholarships pay up to 30 per cent of school fees and include free music lessons. School working to plump up a bursary fund to fight off Charity Commission bullies.

Remarks: Academic powerhouse taking in a relatively wide range of abilities, working its magic, and producing a shimmering set of academic results year after year. Not as scary as it looks, but still not the place for rebels or slackers. On the cusp of change as leadership moves into new hands. Weekly boarding specialists.

St Teresa's Senior School

Linked to Saint Teresas Nursery And Preparatory School in the Junior section

Beech Avenue, Effingham Hill, Dorking, Surrey, RH5 6ST

• Pupils: 380 girls, including 90 boarders • Ages: 11-18 • Size of sixth form: 90 • Roman Catholic but all faiths welcome • Fees: Day £13,080-£13,440; Boarding £21,030-£23,160 pa • Independent

Tel: 01372 452 037
Fax: 01372 450 311
Email: info@stteresas.surrey.sch.uk
Website: www.stteresasschool.com

Head: Since 2006, Mrs Lesley Falconer BSc, previously, for seven years, head of More House in London. Studied microbiology at London, then combined research with teaching at a sixth form college. Teaches some biology and science.

Academic matters: The school is selective but not hugely so, priding itself on developing the whole girl. Girls of all academic abilities. Good and improved results from such a cross section: in 2010, 73 per cent of A level grades were A*–B, with 46 per cent A*/A at GCSE (100 per gained five or more A*–C). Languages are strong – French, Latin, German, Spanish, Italian on offer and Japanese as an extra. Unanimous thumbs up from parents for the language teaching – 'a huge asset to the school'. Girls are setted in maths, French, science and humanities. Computers and interactive facilities used in the classroom in all subjects. Classrooms are large and colourful and the library offers a very wide range of books and resources. There is a cross section of ages amongst the teaching staff. One SEN teacher on site full-time and one part-time. The girls are regularly assessed – parents have to pay extra for SEN support.

Games, Options, the Arts: Sports facilities aplenty! An indoor heated swimming pool complex and all-weather hockey pitch, hard tennis courts and a multi-purpose sports hall means that the girls are spoilt for choice. Strong in netball and hockey, says a mother. At least 50 per cent play an instrument and the school choirs beaver away preparing for a main concert every term with lots of other musical events, both informal and formal. There are 22 opportunities in the year for girls to perform musically and professional musicians are invited to perform to the music society. An impressive performing arts theatre hall opened in September 2005. It is fully equipped with a 750 seat theatre, sound recording studio, two large interconnecting drama studios, dressing rooms and two music teaching rooms as well as five music practice suites. 'Much needed,' according to a satisfied mum. Photography, art and textiles are impressive. 'The girls produce work of professional standard,' commented one enthusiastic mother and the artwork we saw was of gallery standard. Textiles, photography and small metals classes are popular – taught in a relaxed atmosphere with the radio playing in the background – you feel as if you are walking into a gallery or a workshop rather than a classroom. 'I can't even sew a button, my daughter can make dresses!' says a parent. School is constantly buzzing – 'there's always something going on' – with lots of clubs; even the astronomy and lifesaving clubs are popular.

Background and Atmosphere: St Teresa's was founded in 1928 by the Religious Order of Christian Instruction on what was originally part of a manor site recorded in the Domesday Book. The present house, dating from 1799, is the centre of the senior school set in 48 acres of parkland – the small buildings where the classrooms are located and the gravelled walkways give the feeling of a small, self-contained town. Boarding girls comment that it is like 'a home away from home.' (Girls have the option to full board, weekly board or simply stay one night a week – useful for the odd nights when parents are short of baby-sitters). Full boarders are taken out to London, nearby Kingston or Guildford at the weekend. They certainly seem to enjoy their time. Boarding girls are very down to earth – older girls do a great job taking care of the younger ones. Boarding facilities are very clean, spacious and recently refurbished. A nice touch for those who board occasionally (e.g. once a week) – they get the same beds and do not have to play musical beds changing every time. Non-boarders say that 'sometimes we wish we were boarding' – day girls can be left till six or seven in the evening. The school has a pleasing, almost family atmosphere and environment. As one parent says, 'it has a feeling of old-style establishments.' Many new refurbishment projects since the new head arrived and living accommodation is smarter but it will always be a homely school rather than grand. And everyone is very approachable and friendly. 'Focused and happy' is the general feeling amongst parents.

Pastoral Care and Discipline: As one ex-pupil with a daughter at the school said, good pastoral care is one of the main reasons for choosing the school. Strong RC ethos based on 'the unique value of the individual,' but girls from all faiths are embraced. Teaching staff are respected and liked. Discipline well-managed, structured, strict but fair. Drugs have not surfaced and the few smoking and bullying incidents are swiftly sorted. Parents are kept in close contact generally, and are encouraged to approach staff with any concerns.

Pupils and Parents: A noteworthy number of pupils are daughters or even grand-daughters of ex-pupils: 'I went there, my mother went there, my daughter is there and hopefully, one day, her daughter will too.' Also popular with the Far Eastern community, and 15 per cent of the girls are from overseas. Pupils are smart, skirt lengths are decent, one or two unnatural blondes in the school but not enough to call the highlight brigade! Some experiment with fashionable hair styles and makeup in the sixth form but nothing too worrying. Local parents are a mixed bunch – professional mums and dads as well as first time buyers. The school seems sheltered from the growing 'Surrey Mums' syndrome – the atmosphere at sports days and school events is still quite relaxed with no obvious competition between the mothers.

Entrance: Many enter via the junior school after sitting the entrance examination in Year 6, but a large number also come from other schools including Hoe Bridge, Halstead, Danes Hill, Downsend, Feltonfleet and Rowan and from local state primaries. Tested in English, science and VR – not too onerous. Increasing numbers of girls join at 16 for the sixth form. Special exam for entry from overseas.

Exit: Fewer, we're assured, now leave at 16 to sample co-ed independent schools, sixth forms or specialist colleges. Others finish their A levels and head for a variety of universities which include Bristol, LSE, York, Birmingham, Leeds,

Warwick, Bath, Durham and one or two to Oxbridge. Girls are regularly offered unconditional places to Central St Martin's, Chelsea, Camberwell and all other Colleges which make up the University of the Arts, London.

Money Matters: Academic, music, sport, drama and art scholarships are available and can amount to 50 per cent of the fees. Good to see that tuition fees include lunch and before and after school care facilities.

Remarks: An ordered, friendly, all round school with strong religious ethos and good pastoral care.

St Thomas More Catholic School

Croftdale Road, Blaydon-on-Tyne, Tyne and Wear, NE21 4BQ

• Pupils: 1,500; boys 715, girls 785 • Ages: 11-19 • Size of sixth form: 290; boys 125, girls 165 • Catholic • State

Tel: 01914 990 111
Fax: 01914 141 116
Email: pellis@stthomasmore.org.uk
Website: www.stthomasmore.org.uk

Head: Since 2005, Mr Jonathan Parkinson (mid-forties) BSc physics (Leeds University) PGCE. Previously deputy head, assistant head, head of science, head of physics, all at St Thomas More. Previous schools: Carre's Grammar School, Sleaford; All Saints High School, Huddersfield. Cheerful and witty with easy but respectful relationship with pupils. Places emphasis on development of staff and sees 'classroom excellence' as the way to keep the school moving forward. Believes in a culture of change. A teaching head who gets a buzz from 'seeing the lightbulbs go on in little brains, watching children grow and go out into the world as young adults and to know you have had an impact on them.' Not driven by results. 'We do things here for the right reasons – the needs and abilities of the pupils, and our results grow from that.'

Away from school a keen, but slow, runner; has his own ceilidh band.

Academic matters: Technology College (first in north east); Leading Edge School. Full GCSE and A level curriculum, along with GNVQ and BTecs offered and matched to pupil's ability. Pupils banded on ability from Year 7 with scope to alter as abilities change.

In 2009, all of the students achieved five or more passes at grades A*–C at GCSE or equivalent qualifications, 72 per cent of the pupils achieved 5+ A* to C grades including GCSEs in English and maths. Year 13 take a wide range of qualifications – about two thirds do A levels and the rest vocational qualifications. In 2009, 46 per cent of the grades at A level were A or B and the vocational students all completed their courses, with large numbers gaining Distinction and Merit grades. School reckons they are in the top 25 per cent nationally.

Games, Options, the Arts: Growing reputation for music, drama and dance. Plethora of bands, choirs, orchestras. Also excels in sports, particularly team games, with a list of county and national sporting honours. Wide selection of clubs and societies – from sports to chess and Scrabble; enjoys exchange/educational visits to French/German-speaking countries and outward-bound weekends.

Background and Atmosphere: Catholic faith is strong in school, evidenced in worship and also in teaching of mutual respect and in charitable works. Believes that Christian ethos binds children and staff and encourages all to give of their best. 'We are quite old-fashioned in what we do, but whatever trends come and go, our belief in respect, behaving well and being civilised will never change ... when we go on outward-bound weekends the people who take us are astonished at how well behaved the children are.'

Evidence of 1960s, '70s and '80s buildings chart the school's growth. Sport England helped fund most recent acquisition of new sports hall/fitness room and library.

Pastoral Care and Discipline: Pastoral system sets this school apart. Works on four house system which develops allegiance and competitive spirit. House acts as surrogate family. Houses mixed on gender and academic ability. Parents know house heads – house heads know parents. Tutor groups stay the same until Year 11 for continuity. Pastoral system dedicated to ensuring each child feels secure, confident and valued. Programme ensures tutors look after social, emotional and academic needs. 'It is important that children enjoy school and our pastoral system helps ensure they do,' says head. Target setting, supported by pastoral mentors, assists development. Strong on discipline and maintaining standards e.g. inflexible uniform policy, litter picking duties. Good behaviour, manners and attitude to work are paramount.

'School is not just about qualifications; it is also about making children better people, equipping them for work, college, university or wherever they next go in life,' opines head. Complex merit system based on academic and social achievement and contribution to the life of their house and the school. Certificates/Head's commendation much sought after by pupils. Pupils look up to sixth formers and aspire to be one. Competition for head boy and head girl posts is stiff. Pupils taught respect for others and their school environment.

Pupils and Parents: Bulk of children come from nine Catholic feeder schools, mainly in West Gateshead. Predominantly British white with some from other backgrounds. Comprehensive intake, above average KS2 results. Pupil/staff ratio 15:1. Seventy per cent stay for sixth form. 'Everyone here gets on really well and there are opportunities to get involved in everything, music, sports the lot. I never thought I would say that I love coming to school, but I do.'

Entrance: Oversubscribed. Priority to Roman Catholic children from feeder schools, then youngsters with siblings already at school; other Roman Catholics; other faiths. 'People come here partly because of our results but a lot is down to our reputation for setting high standards of work and behaviour.'

Exit: Majority of A level students go to university with regular Oxford/Cambridge places.

Remarks: Great emphasis on teaching the teachers pays dividends. House system and sound pastoral care have created a school where children are clearly very positive and proud of their school. Work hard, play hard school. A gem.

Sale Grammar School

Marsland Road, Sale, Cheshire, M33 3NH

• Pupils: 1250, boys and girls, including 320 in sixth form • Ages: 11-18 mixed • Size of sixth form: 320 • Non-denominational • State

Tel: 01619 733 217
Fax: 0161 976 4904
Email: office@salegrammar.co.uk
Website: www.salegrammar.co.uk

Head: Since 2010, Mr Mark Smallwood MA (fifties). Previously headteacher of Fearns Community Sports College in Rossendale, Lancashire. Educated at Manchester and Lancaster universities. He describes himself as a family man who strives for excellence. Delighted to be appointed – 'it is a real privilege and an honour to lead such an outstanding group of pupils and staff.'

Academic matters: Described by Ofsted as an 'outstanding school' with an 'outstanding sixth form', and has since been allowed to add science as a secondary specialism after the visual arts. Named as high performing specialist school in 2008 by DCSF. Takes up to the 35th centile of ability range through the school's own entrance exam yet consistently in top ten per cent nationally for A level results – 24 subjects offered with 65 per cent results A or B. At GCSE, over 50 per cent of grades are A* or A with at least 50 per cent of pupils achieving 5+ A*/A and 98 per cent A*–C with most pupils achieving nine or ten at these grades. Fantastic results in art and strong across the board although French and German tend to be inconsistent weaker links – 'we're working on them' – and we're told German has improved. Pupils study compulsory Design and Technology subject to GCSE as part of school specialism; some academically minded parents grumble at Year 9 choices time. Parents and pupils agree school's 'not overly pushy or as competitive as some other schools', tending instead towards lavish encouragement with commendations and awards. Library has ranks of laptops to borrow, nevertheless older students say it's a scrum to beat the queue for one and that work is hampered by overly tight net filtering. Staff monitor all IT work and younger pupils talk of 'serious consequences if you're just playing games'! Go-getting attitude towards academic competitions, Olympiads, maths challenge and inter-school quizzes with plenty of successful high fliers celebrated in the glossy, student-produced newsletter and monthly bulletins. Refurbished science labs and specialist college status for science since April 2008. Thirty-nine on the school's SEN register with a designated learning support room and full time SENCo.

Games, Options, the Arts: Specialist College for visual arts since 2003. Exciting modern art and technology department with resident artist and ceramicist as well as teaching staff. Light boxes exhibit senior student work in corridors. Joined up thinking means art crosses curriculum boundaries so most other subjects use art creatively with impressive resultant displays. Easter and summer art, music and science schools and Gifted and Talented workshops hosted here. Great emphasis on community involvement; partnerships with other schools, businesses and the local NHS Trust leading to art exhibitions and patient art therapy work in local hospital. 'We try to move citizenship beyond a paper exercise,' says head, 'and our community programme is seen as a model of good practice'. Year 9 has restored a Romany caravan in collaboration with local travellers. Annual joint drama performance with nearby Special School which 'promotes a positive attitude to inclusion'. In-house yearly drama production enormously popular involving over 400 pupils and a nightly sell-out. Performing arts exam results excellent, especially at GCSE, despite very basic facilities. Head of music is described by parents as, 'dynamic and inspirational, if strict'. School is home to the Trafford Youth Orchestra and has over ten music groups of its own.

Wide ranging sport played with national level players in basketball, synchronised swimming, tennis, archery, martial arts and a rash of county level players across all sports. Plenty of indoor and outdoor courts and pitches with further facilities available through partnership with nearby Brooklands Sports Club. A sport co-ordinator works with five partnership primary schools and older students take a Junior School Leadership Award in PE. Two minibuses facilitate sport and other trips including D of E; 150 students up to silver level. Other trips and activities include World Challenge, Young Enterprise and a Fair Trade group. International School Award in 2006 for links with Uganda and re-awarded in August 2009 for work with South African schools. Charity fund raising here is excellent, at least £5k annually. Extensive range of extra-curricular activities at lunch and after school.

Background and Atmosphere: Once the home of Sale Girls' Grammar, the current buildings have evolved, piecemeal fashion, round a series of quads where students chat at break under wooden shelters amongst chain-saw sculptures. Each department has its own livery with green paintwork on the new English block and, surprisingly, the school colour purple for the main old heart of the school. Most notable are the ultra modern art, IT and maths buildings of white breeze blocks with brick herringbone flooring, red paintwork and silver ducts humming with air conditioning. Some sixth form teaching happens at Claremont, about a mile away. Everywhere is neat and tidy, but not stuffy. Pupils are repeatedly told to tuck shirts in and do up top buttons, and they do, temporarily. The place seems relaxed and happy, a hive of activity with a one way system on stairwells. Uniforms are black and grey with purple trim, and blazers for the last two years, 'so we can carry everything'. All cooking is on-site; lunches pay as you go, '£2 a day is enough and it's much healthier since Jamie Oliver,' with an option to order a packed lunch to take to activities, or to bring your own. Staff turnover is low with a mix of experience and young enthusiasm including a handful of ex Sale students. There's fun to be had here, as the student-produced DVD prospectus proves.

Pastoral Care and Discipline: Through form tutors and a staff hierarchy. School nurse has an open door with drop in sessions and there's a Relate trained counsellor and 'storyteller' counsellor on site, as well as a peer mentoring scheme using older pupils. Year 7 outward bound induction for three days and one parent said, 'my son didn't know anyone but the school put us in touch with someone else during the summer before he started, and then helped him with a personal plan when he struggled to be organised at first'. Everyone has a locker with a combination padlock on loan from school. Mobile phones, iPods etc are forbidden on school premises, although off and out of sight seems to be the order of the day. School premises protected by CCTV and thanks to yet another community partnership a community officer is based in school with police trainees who sometimes use pupils in role play incidents. Pupils describe school as 'clean but you can sometimes smell smoke in the toilets'. Sanctions start with slips and weekday detentions; head's Saturday detention is a dreaded threat, and exclusion a very rare ultimate step.

Pupils and Parents: South west of the Greater Manchester conurbation, in the middle of Trafford Borough with its wealthy south and less affluent north. Mostly solidly middle class but significantly fewer personalised number plates than some competitor schools and notably more reasonably priced trips; a Canadian ski trip stands out as an oddity and a quarter of over 16s here are eligible for EMA. Below average ethnic minorities. The intake is academically broader than many other selective schools but as pupils say, 'there's nobody in this school who's not smart'. Pupils travel on school and public buses and Manchester's tram system with Brooklands Metro station a half mile walk away.

Entrance: Currently, selection based on school adminstered entrance examination results drawing from 45 primary schools with just seven per cent of pupils from outside Trafford Borough. Year 7 consistently over-subscribed.

Entry to sixth form at needs at least two As and three Bs at GCSE but most exceed this by some way. About 78 per cent stay on to sixth form leaving 35 places offered to external applicants – always over-subscribed with waiting list; no wonder with Ofsted's 'exceptional' across the board.

Exit: Over 95 per cent to higher education, mainly universities in the North and Midlands; a few to Oxbridge.

Remarks: Relaxed and happy but first and foremost a go-getting school with impressively strong community links, a huge range of opportunities for pupils, and much broader horizons than just academic success.

Seaford College

Lavington Park, Petworth, West Sussex, GU28 0NB

• Pupils: 610; 130 boarders (95 boys, 35 girls), 480 day (315 boys, 165 girls) • Ages: 7-18 • Size of sixth form: 135 • C of E • Fees: Juniors £6,858-£15,900; Seniors £15,600-£24,075 pa • Independent

Tel: 01798 867 392
Fax: 01798 867 606
Email: jmackay@seaford.org
Website: www.seaford.org

Head: Since 1997, Mr Toby Mullins (mid forties), quick-witted and engaging – this and his background in economics (MBA at London Business School) have had much to do with the boost to Seaford's reputation and bank balance over the past decade. His wife agreed to act as his PA a couple of years ago and has not looked back since; his two children are still in the school. Previously deputy head at Churcher's College and before that houseparent at Framlingham.

Teaches economics and business studies and is keen on hockey and golf – the school's golf course came about when the head was looking for a new way to use the land and stables were ruled out because of a neighbouring stud's exclusion zone. Governors have learnt to trust him as they've seen his decisions on the fabric of the school pay off.

Academic matters: Non-selective, with 40 per cent SEN but still a mainstream school – one which does dyslexia teaching better than others. No longer seen as 'a collecting house for kids who couldn't get in elsewhere.' GCSE A*–B 27 per cent and 62 per cent A*–B at A level but school's ethos is definitely not about being top of the league tables – 'that's like measuring driving ability by the power of the car; the driver of a Ferrari may do no better job that than of a family saloon – he just gets more attention!'

Campus is arranged by subject area marked with smart blue and gold signs. Wireless network throughout means everyone's laptop can be online everywhere – Skyping home especially useful for international boarders; also two ICT suites with 20 desktops. History has a passionate and very popular HoD, maths and science taught in beautiful new labs/classrooms with interactive whiteboards and scope for exciting experiments. Bright murals painted on the walls of the language department and popular school trips.

Sixth form size is creeping up to full capacity; entrance guidelines are 45 points at GCSE but no stipulation as to whether any need to be C or above – this means places for all who work hard. Crafty three for two offer on GCSE retakes encourages application for A levels.

Learning Support Unit housed in a central flint cottage which it shares with careers – definitely not a broom cupboard under the stairs. Eight staff deal with mainly dyslexic and dyspraxic on a release basis, pupils are never taken out of core subjects or ones that they particularly enjoy. One-to-one class each week and each teacher has been trained to deal with dyslexics within class and invites comments from LSU on improving delivery.

Games, Options, the Arts: The waving golf flags mark this out as a sporty school from the moment you drive in the gates. Hockey (the head often umpires) is the top game but rugby, golf, tennis, cricket, squash, athletics and swimming are all popular and successful. External membership of the Golf Academy; the rugby coach, an ex-Scottish International, has excellent contacts with inspiring guest speakers/coaches; and the football coach is an Aston Villa scout as well as a classicist! The small outdoor swimming pool is due to be replaced by a new complex. Competitors whose chosen sports can't be practised on campus are encouraged, with recent success stories in riding, sailing, polo, judo and skiing – some representing England at a school level.

Woodwork, DT, ceramics, textiles, photography and fine art are all taught in the purpose-built arts faculty around a central gallery used for temporary exhibitions – plenty to encourage individual talent and the evidence is on display. Art trips to London galleries and to foundation exhibitions in the summer.

Graphics (now with 20 new machines) is the only option currently not available up to AS, Inventor software has been introduced recently. Electric cars have been in the Greenpower races at Goodwood for the past three years, with steadily increasing handicaps to keep Seaford's success in check! Pupils' imaginations caught by this competition and even those not directly involved in construction pop in for an update from the DT department.

The music rooms are based around a courtyard set apart from the main school – this is covered over for events such as the sixth form prom. The choir practises for its performances (Eaton Square, Chichester Cathedral, St Mary's Shoreham etc) both here and in chapel. House music encourages competition for excellence internally and inspiring organ teachers have groomed at least two pupils for scholarships at Oxford.

School production, 'Seaford Stock' (like 'Woodstock' ...) and a sixth form play each year – the hall has a stage at one end and floor to ceiling windows on either side – with the Festival Theatre in nearby Chichester providing inspiration.

Background and Atmosphere: Main building is a gracious Georgian house set in 400 acres with stunning views of the South Downs – if you arrive on a sunny afternoon you'll definitely want your child to grow up here. A campus feel because of distinct departments and boarding houses but the local flint has been re-used in some of the new buildings so much is in keeping. The chapel was mentioned in the Doomsday book but, more recently, assemblies held there at least twice a week as well as regular eucharists and evensongs. In the summer everyone is outside (football on the terrace behind the Mansion) as much as possible, but big common-rooms for each year provide table football and tennis, pool and lounging space when the clocks go back.

Wilberforce, the junior school, has its own dorms (10–15 per cent weekly boarding), classrooms, library and a different sitting for mealtimes to avoid the little ones being intimidated. Gap students help look after the dorms and preps here and the house parents are sensible and experienced. The kids seem happy, busy and communicative. Pupils and parents appreciate the enthusiasm and support provided by the staff – 60 per cent of them live on site and a fair few have children in the school, many of whom have held positions of responsibility recently.

Younger girls sleep upstairs in the Mansion House – as ever, their rooms are more personal than those of the boys, the new furniture with lockable drawers is particularly welcome. The '60s boys' boarding houses are functional; a new one is under construction. Most popular feature is the upper sixth's common-room with its bar (home brewed beer is planned ...) and full size snooker table. The boys' houses appear to run on well-founded trust in the kids, which makes for a happy environment. Girls need permission to relax next to the fireplace in the lower sixth boys' area but boys are not allowed vice versa.

Pastoral Care and Discipline: Each child changes tutor every year (15–20 per group) until you share a personal mentor in the upper sixth with just five others. Prep sessions are less supervised the further up the school you rise. Good manners and consideration for others is expected, very much three strikes and you're out. Bullying – letters home, warning of suspension next time around. Out for serial wickedness – drugs usually equals out. Beautiful grounds for hiding behind a bush and smoking, but apparently it is mostly the foreign students who do this. Science department is using a new breathalyser to demonstrate the levels of carbon monoxide in a smoker's exhalation, hoping education 'will hammer home the message better than short-term disciplinary action'.

Pupils and Parents: Lots of local farming families and those who have created their own businesses, a few lawyers, doctors and dentists. Many choose to send all their children here, confident that the school will educate a wide range of academic abilities. Fundraising support for the school through tables at the summer ball etc. Most boarders are weekly, a handful of full from Asia and Eastern Europe, few British ex-pats. Old boys include a more recent winner of the same *Daily Mail* award as Dyson, music scholars to Oxford and the de Haan brothers.

Entrance: After trial day and ability tests. Lots from Haslemere schools, also a handful of preps – Windlesham, Amesbury, Prebendal, Westbourne House, Dorset House, Great Ballard. About 30 per cent internally from Wilberforce. New entries at sixth form are often hard workers who were strained out of other sixth forms because of range of GCSE grades.

Exit: A third leaves after GCSE to take more vocational courses at sixth form college. Practically everyone who goes through sixth form goes on to university, two or three to Oxbridge (good links with Jesus, Oxford, through music), also Exeter, Bristol, Warwick, Loughborough, Durham, UCL and Imperial. Good relationship with selection boards – since this is a non-selective school, if the children get great grades, they've done so through hard work.

Money Matters: Small scholarships (maximum discount £500 per annum) at 11+ – choral and music only. At 13+ and 16+ in art, music, sport, academic and DT. Bursaries available through means-testing.

Remarks: The happiness of the children is this school's greatest strength – they're great fun to be around; academic successes are celebrated but certainly not the only ones. The staff are really approachable; parents say, 'a visit to the school can feel like a social event!' Everyone seems to be appreciative of opportunities Seaford affords and snob value is not an issue.

Sedbergh School

Linked to Sedbergh Junior School in the Junior section

Sedbergh, Cumbria, LA10 5HG

• Pupils: 310 boys, 130 girls; 430 full boarders; 9 day • Ages: 13-18 • Size of sixth form: 205 • C of E • Fees: Day £19,350; Boarding £26,265 pa • Independent

Tel: 015396 20535
Fax: 015396 21301
Email: enquiries@sedberghschool.org
Website: www.sedberghschool.org

Head: Since 2010, Mr Andrew Fleck MA (mid-forties), formerly head of Ashville College, Harrogate. Educated at Marlborough College, he read geology at Nottingham and has an MA in education from Sussex. Member of HMC Professional Development Committee, a Governor of Westville House Preparatory and a Fellow of the Royal Geographical Society. Interests include sailing, canoeing and cycling – canoed around Ireland, Newfoundland,

Japan and Arctic Norway to the Russian border. Cycled the east/west European border and with his wife Anne, cycled the deserts of central Iceland and the northern Sahara on a tandem! Has 11-year-old twin daughters, both at Sedbergh Junior School.

Academic matters: GCSE averages 99 per cent A*–C passes, 50 per cent A/A*, not bad for a school with a comprehensive intake and a policy of entering all pupils for exams, very good value-added. 99 per cent pass rate at A level. Some learning support is offered for those in need, principally children with dyslexia. Average class size is 15 with a ceiling of 25. Pupils have good relationships with the helpful, caring and dedicated staff. Many classrooms, language labs and laboratories have had much-needed refurbishment. Modern technology is now weaving its way throughout the school, boarding houses and many curriculum areas. Departmental libraries are well stocked. Main library, housed in a super conversion of Georgian building on the site of Lupton's original school, is rather frayed round the edges but has just had new IT facilities put into the gallery floor and the new librarian has revamped the reading stock.

Games, Options, the Arts: Renowned for its sporting prowess (34 sporting activities on offer) with many pupils winning representative honours, especially in rugby, cricket, hockey, sailing and shooting. Brand new cricket facilities plus sports hall and 25-metre indoor pool. Famous for its Wilson Run – a 10-mile fell race open to ages 16+. All pupils participate in CCF in Year 9 but involvement is optional after that, though many continue. Magnificent conservatoire style music school with recent £1m expansion. Many ensembles; the CCF band recently performed at the Chinese New Year Night Parade in Hong Kong. Lots of good drama with regular productions each summer at the Edinburgh fringe. Numerous trips and tours abroad in all fields of School life. Many clubs and societies available including D of E award scheme. A Sedbergh group climbed Everest and reached the highest point ever by any school team.

Background and Atmosphere: Founded in 1525 by Roger Lupton, a provost of Eton. School lies in the centre of a small, picturesque town surrounded by magnificent fells, in the heart of the splendid (if often wet and cold) Yorkshire Dales National Park but only a short drive from the M6. Departments housed in several separate buildings which gives rise to a mature, campus feel appreciated by pupils. Each pupil is assigned to a house where they live and eat (excellent food, lots of choice, special diets catered for). New entrants quickly develop keen house loyalty and rightly see the system as pivotal to the success of the school. New girls' boarding houses are bright, modern and well furnished. All the boys' boarding houses have been refurbished over the last three summers.

With the arrival of girls in 2001 and reverting to a 13 to 18 school in 2002, the school is now better placed to serve its population. Younger children are catered for at the newly established prep and pre-prep school developed on the old Bentham Grammar School site, 30 minutes drive away. At the start of the fourth year of the co-ed intake the 118 girls form a significant, vibrant and impressive part of the school. Smart and business-like in appearance (super navy uniform with tartan skirt) the Sedbergh females are a force to be reckoned with, very much keeping the boys and staff on their toes. Look out for improving results in the coming years and famous Old Girls in the not too distant future.

Make sure to check out the *Sedberghian*, the school magazine, for well reported information on every facet of the place and the students who populate it.

Pastoral Care and Discipline: Effective house system with strong, popular and caring housemasters and mistresses heading up dedicated teams. Well thought-out punishment system. Bar available at weekends to sixth formers, school encourages a sensible attitude to alcohol. Over-familiar relationships between boys and girls actively discouraged.

Pupils and Parents: Mostly northern professionals but some from Scotland and increasingly from the south. Traditionally a school for landowners, industrialists and farmers' sons (Wordsworth was a parent) but now an eclectic mix including Services, expats and a few foreigners. Pupils are confident, sparky and generally, though not universally, sporty. A straightforward bunch admirably demonstrating many typical northern values. Not afraid to get their hands dirty, they might call a spade a spade but willingness to help others, loyalty and compassion are values universally to the fore. This is a very happy school, lots of laughter in and out of lessons. Still not a place for the timid or loner but anyone else, especially those who appreciate the fantastic surroundings and teamwork, will love it here. Old boys include Simon Beaufoy (Full Monty), Will Carling, Will Greenwood, Lord Bingham (Lord Chief Justice), James Wilby, Sir Jock Slater (First Sea Lord) Sir Christopher Bland (Chairman BT), Robert Napier (Chief Exec of Met Office, Ex Chief Exec WWF and Chairman of Governors).

Entrance: For most, CE is the normal route, others applying in Years 9–11 sit exams in English and maths. A current school report is required. Sixth form requires a minimum five GCSEs at C or above. Main feeder is Sedbergh Junior School but significant proportion come from prep schools across the north of England and beyond.

Exit: Mostly to university, many choose to stay in the north. Steady trickle to Oxbridge (traditionally strong links with Cambridge). A Sedberghian won one of the coveted Morehead Scholarships to the University of North Carolina. Several opt for a gap year having secured their university place. Handful embark on vocational courses or careers at 18, trickle leave at 16. In 2006 saw the first girl from Sedbergh to get a first at Cambridge having joined in the sixth form five years before when the school went co-ed.

Money Matters: Several scholarships: academic, all-round, sport, drama, DT, music and art. Awards vary but may be up to half-fees. Couple of index-linked major scholarships. Exhibitions and bursaries also available.

Remarks: Sedbergh has faced up to the demands of the 21st century but managed to retain traditional values and ethos – increasing numbers especially for boarding indicate parents very much approve. It rightly retains its reputation as a formidable force on the sports field but, away from there, provides a happy and caring environment for all its pupils regardless of ability or sports prowess.

Seven Kings High School

Ley Street, Ilford, Essex, IG2 7BT

• Pupils: 1,400 boys and girls, all day • Ages: 11-18 • Size of sixth form: 500 • Non-denom • State

Tel: 020 8554 8935
Fax: 020 8518 2975
Email: enquiries@skhs.net
Website: www.skhs.net

Head: Since 2000, Ms Tracy Smith BA PGCE (forties). Educated at St Martin's School, Brentwood. Read history and sociology at Warwick, PGCE at Goldsmith's College, London, then taught at Barking Abbey School for seven years. Moved to Seven Kings as head of sixth form in 1995, then deputy head to former head Sir Alan Steer and a key player in the team which transformed this east London school into one of the country's most successful comprehensives. Before taking over the headship, she led a project on Assessment for Learning carried out by King's College, Cambridge and the Institute of Education and continues to sit on a number of influential committees, including the SSAT London Headteachers' Steering Group. Energetic, level-headed and good-humoured, she's undoubtedly a safe pair of hands to keep this school top of the form. Married (to the vice principal of an FE College), with two teenage children. A keen West Ham supporter, she spends down time watching football, going to the theatre, hill walking and travelling.

Academic matters: If academic matters are uppermost in your schooling choice, then you have very little to fret about at Seven Kings. Despite its 'very average' intake, Seven Kings seems to sail effortlessly to the top of the league tables. Over 80 per cent of the GCSE candidates in 2010 achieved 5 A*–C, including English and maths, and the large sixth form produced even more dazzling results, particularly in the school's specialist subjects of science and maths. As were evident in abundance. 64 students had a least three As and there were 64 in chemistry (out of 103), 61 in maths and 39 in biology, as well as plenty in psychology, sociology and art. Teaching is vibrant and committed – 'the quality of the teaching manages to challenge every student,' said one parent' and teacher-pupils relationships strong. 'Teachers know you well and know how you are feeling,' said one boy. 'You can ask them anything.' One of the reasons for the school's success is its tailor-made approach to learning and certainly no one here gets lost at the back. 'You won't find a pupil we haven't spoken to in the past three weeks about their learning,' says the head.

Success is down to monitoring, tracking and a can-do approach. A wealth of information (interim report grades, Cat score, pastoral data) are fed into a central computer to keep staff, parents and pupils up to speed with progress and an academic co-ordinator identifies those needing additional focus, whether that's one-to-one tuition, intensive intervention from the SEN or access to Gifted and Talented master classes. 'They don't give us grades, they give us comments,' said one pupil. 'They tell you what you can do to improve and what you've already done well. They know what you need to do to get better.' Every student is also given two one-to-one interviews annually about their academic progress. 'We track, interview and talk.' But as well as talking the school is thoroughly au fait with what's demanded. 'This isn't an exam factory,' says the head, 'but we do know the syllabus and the exam requirements.' And not only can they distinguish their Pre-Us from their A levels, they know how to prioritise a UCAS form, with a large chunk of the high-powered sixth form going on to all the country's top universities.

As well as science and technology, the school has specialist status both as a Training School and for languages. So three languages on offer (French, Spanish and Mandarin) and well over half the pupils keep on at least one language to GCSE. Science newly energised by a 'skills-based' approach and bangs and smells part of the fabric of school life. 'Pupils now say science is their favourite subject,' says the head, 'there are about 50 experiments going a day.' After-school clubs include the academic as well as the just for fun, providing support with homework and coursework.

Games, Options, the Arts: Art and DT strong, with enthusiastic staff and pupils who proceed in largish numbers to study art, architecture and design. PE increasingly popular under a dynamic sports department. 'Everyone used to compete, now we also win,' says the head. But even those who don't are not allowed to sit idly by. 'Our kids do two hours PE a week and even on days when they don't have sport, we make sure they get off their bottoms,' says the deputy. Football, cricket, netball, running and athletics all core to the curriculum. Rugby a new offering, for girls as well. One basketball superstar recently won a scholarship to a top US university. Facilities, sound rather than state-of-the-art – usual sports hall and gym, cricket pitch, netball courts, full-size third generation pitch – but the spirit is strong and the school has taken cricket tours to Barbados and Malta.

Music and drama perhaps less of a priority with pupils in this very career-focused school but plenty on offer for aspiring performers with a yearly whole school musical. Purpose-built music centre with soundproof rooms. Plenty of extra-curricular enthusiasm, too, for spiritual, social and cultural nourishment with out-of-lessons activities including Amnesty International, chess, model airplanes, astronomy and a film club. Pupils while away the lunch hours playing chess with giant chessmen out of doors in quiet courtyards. 'When we introduced it,' says the deputy head, 'we thought no one would play, but they do.'

Background and Atmosphere: The school started life as a leafy suburban girls' grammar in the 1930s and still has as strong feel of the inter-war years with an expansive spread of low rise brick buildings and a Betjemanesque assembly hall ideal for listening to the clock ticking away the exam minutes. Inside the tall-windowed classrooms, the focus is on learning, helped by full range of thoroughly modern additions from a new lecture theatre and a spacious, glass entrance hall to a wheelchair park and interactive whiteboards. The motto is 'friendship, excellence, opportunity' and most pupils (and parents) believe the school more than delivers. 'I think the school lives up to its motto very, very well and I think it exceeds it,' said one student. 'The kids know we really care about them,' says the head. Seven Kings is particularly noted for its SEN provision and has a national reputation as a centre of excellence for disabled children. As well as the specially adapted entrance and well equipped medical centre, all classrooms bar one are accessible by wheelchair. SEN department has six full-time staff and 42 statemented pupils. 'Disabled kids are an asset,' says the deputy.

Pastoral Care and Discipline: Seven Kings sits in a neighbourhood that is certainly on the less affluent side of the rich-poor divide but, despite its relatively stark surrounding streets, the school itself is a haven of purposeful calm. Discipline is assumed, corridors are quiet, classes orderly. That's not to say of course that every child's an angel. 'We have 1500 hormonal kids,' says the head, 'of course we have discipline problems.' But few that aren't sorted out rapidly. 'We haven't excluded anyone permanently since I've been head.' Short sharp shocks for fighting or cheeking the teacher. 'Expectations are very clear, as are sanctions, but we try and apply them sensitively. This isn't a zero-tolerance environment.' Positive peer pressure is a definite help keeping potential bad boys on the straight and narrow. 'We often look back and think, that's someone who might have drifted into something,' says the deputy head. 'Some kids are definitely from challenging homes and we do our best to keep them going.' No-one let off site between Years 7–11, but not too much in the way of local distractions so many stay in too in the sixth form. All pupils have a form tutor, year leader and academic co-ordinator. Prefects appointed in Year 11, with head boy and girl. Student council. Timetabling, too, used constructively. 'How you timetable the school day has a massive impact on behaviour,' says the deputy.

Pupils and Parents: This is a local community school in a primarily Asian area and over three quarters of the pupils come from Indian, Pakistan or Bangladeshi backgrounds. Parents here want their children to do well and give their full backing to the education on offer with nearly all seats filled at parents' evenings. They aren't, however, a cake-baking, raffle-holding crowd and the school has no PTA. The kids themselves support their parents' aspirations, work hard and behave well. 'The kids are bright and ambitious,' says the head.

Entrance: Vastly over-subscribed with 1800 eager candidates queuing for the 180 Year 7 places. The waiting list, even the year after entry, extends well into the hundreds. 'Fortunately, that's all done by the Local Authority,' says the head. Strict catchment rules apply, though those with statements automatically go to the top of the admissions ladder. The majority of pupils proceed to the sixth form, which expands to about 240. Minimum grade requirements at this point for all pupils is 6A*s-C with Bs in proposed A-level subjects. 2000 apply for 90 additional places, generally awarded to those with the highest predicted grades, which means the sixth form is definitely skewed to the higher end of the ability spectrum. This trend is underlined by a primarily academic curriculum, with only a handful of vocational courses.

Exit: About a third of upper sixth to Russell Group universities: Imperial, Kings, UCL, LSE, Manchester, Warwick, Essex. Three Cambridge offers for maths in 2010. Most of the rest to the older unis, including a large chunk to Queen Mary's College, London. Excellent university guidance with a specialist Saturday programme, Oxbridge Access Scheme, mock Oxbridge interviews and links with Newnham College, Cambridge and the LSE. Twenty off to study medicine or dentistry in 2009, over 100 to take maths and science related courses. All in all, a considerable achievement considering the majority of parents have not themselves been to university.

Money Matters: A school where the generous funding of the past decade has been effectively used to keep all facilities thoroughly up to date.

Remarks: An inspiring place, where any parent could feel confident their child's need would be met and where every child will reach or exceed expectations.

Sevenoaks School

High Street, Sevenoaks, Kent, TN13 1HU

• Pupils: 510 boys, 510 girls; 165 boys and 175 girls board • Ages: 11-18 • Size of sixth form: 420 • Non-denom • Fees: Day £17,070-£19,392; Boarding £27,378-£29,700 pa • Independent

Tel: 01732 455 133
Fax: 01732 456 143
Email: regist@sevenoaksschool.org
Website: www.sevenoaksschool.org

Head: Since 2002, Mrs Katy Ricks MA (fiftyish). Educated at Camden School for Girls (to which she attributes her feistiness) and Balliol, where she took a first in English. Taught at Latymer Upper, King Edward's Birmingham and St Paul's Girls, was head of English at St Edward's Oxford and deputy head of Highgate. An impeccable, co-educational, academic and quality school cv and one which made her, possibly, uniquely qualified for this job. And that's just what's on paper. Vivacious, articulate, deliciously enthusiastic and hugely appreciative of her luck in having charge of such a school, her pleasure in it all is palpable and infectious. We canvassed masses of parents and heard not a word against her. 'My children think she is wonderful'...'she comes to everything'...'she speaks brilliantly'...'she's a brilliant ambassador for the school'... 'she's very thoughtful'. 'She's an outstanding head,' an old hand claimed, 'and in a different league.' She, likewise, pays tribute to her staff and her pupils. 'People here think all the time about what they are doing. I have an incredibly clever staff – both in their intellectual expertise and passion for their subject and in their relationship skills. They talk to pupils and parents like proper people – which, of course, they are!' We know what she means. Wisely, she sees the recruitment of top notch staff as her main responsibility and she pays great attention to the 'feel' of the school. 'I do really believe very strongly that environment shapes character.' The school feels smiley – and she is a very smiley head. Her pride and excitement in the school permeates the place. We felt it in everyone we met.

Academic matters: Sevenoaks is best known for pioneering the IB and for being a strongly international school – not just in its intake but in its outlook. All take IGCSEs in many subjects though GCSE survives in Ancient Greek, Russian and some arts subjects. Everyone does a MFL, everyone takes all three separate sciences. And, in the sixth form, when everyone takes the IB, the language options are exceptional – seven are on offer as part of the IB curriculum and tuition is available in at least 8 more for native speakers and others. Greek and Latin thrive, economics, psychology, philosophy, history – med and mod – it's all here. The results are terrific – in 2009, 14 students gained the maximum 45 points at IB and a further 15 gained 44. At (I)GCSE in 2010, 24 pupils gained 10+ subjects with all A* grades. Over 90 per cent of exams taken got A*/A. That is pretty amazing. You won't find Sevenoaks in league tables – the IB/IGCSE combination make them meaningless. Virtually all teaching praised, virtually universally. Staff seen as assiduous – 'they're concerned, caring, tough'. A seriously impressive library – would grace an Oxford college – 30,000 books and 70+ periodicals – good blend, here as everywhere, of old and new – the august portraits of Edwardian and Victorian headmasters overlooking the gallery of PCs. Up to 10 per cent on Learning Support register with, mostly mild, dyslexia/dyspraxia/dysgraphia. Some with ADHD and visual impairment. Wheelchairs not a problem. Everyone has to have excellent English though school will support EAL if necessary but with no more than one weekly lesson.

Games, Options, the Arts: Huge amounts of space, all the impressive facilities you'd expect including sports hall (2005), pool, dance studio, indoor climbing wall et al. The usual sports are compulsory but range of super options includes trampolining, judo, yoga and fencing. Regarded as the top sailing school in the country and outstanding success in both tennis and shooting. And both sexes play football. Sport no longer the Sevenoaks Cinderella – 2009–10 saw impressive wins in athletics, hockey and rugby and numerous individual successes and county colours.

Brand new 2010 performing arts centre surely unrivalled in its Pamoja (Swahili for 'togetherness') Hall which seats 450. Built according to sustainable principles from locally sourced wood, matched by the pale gold fabric seats and heated via solar panels, with water from a bore hole, it is vast, light and provides a venue of international quality. The stage can accommodate a full orchestra and the two grand pianos we spotted there looked, from the back of the auditorium, like dolls' house instruments. Building also full of practice rooms, a recital room, recording studios, theatre – you name it – and it feels good. And productions to match – arts, visual arts, theatre and musical events to high standards. Virtually all involved in something arty – a large number learn at least one instrument and ensembles for everything. Not too much pupil art on display as you go round – could do with more, perhaps, though head's extraordinary minimalist study has a vast, meticulous, charcoal representation of the huge tree outside her vast window. Stunning range of awards and prizes in arts, public speaking and representation in National Youth Orch/Theatre etc. They pop up everywhere there's a competition in which to shine and it's their intellectual and expressive skills which most impress. 'Fantastic' outside speakers who are 'really inspiring – especially when they are Old Sennockians'. Internationalism translates into trips abroad – less of the glam skiing and snorkeling and more of the DT trip to Toyota's assembly line in Japan and Model United nations in The Hague.

Background and Atmosphere: You'd pass it without noticing as you drive out of sleepy Sevenoaks on the road to Tonbridge. You might notice the sign to Knole (think Sackvilles, Sackville-West and sofas) on your left but you wouldn't realise that the path to Knole bisects the 70 acre site of Sevenoaks School and that the glories of that Jacobean pile and park abut the playing fields and are a considerable resource to the school. The school's foundation is almost as old as that of its illustrious neighbour. And in some respects it eclipses it. Sevenoaks (1432) is the oldest lay school in the UK and this liberal, unallied, ethos underpins the exuberance of its intellectual and social life today. There is no one imposing main school house but a collection of 33 buildings from the last two hundred and fifty-odd years – the old and new all generously conceived, stylish and attractive in their own ways and somehow blending to make a welcoming gesamtwerk. The ambience is much assisted by the ubiquitous greenery – gardens, imaginative planting and the disposition of the houses hither and yon. The head's house – perhaps the least inspired architecturally – is plumb centre and reflects the current incumbent's involvement in everything.

A proper co-educational school. Boarding provision is good everywhere and exceptional in the sixth – the international students are housed in separate buildings – the boys in a state-of-the-art building – a stunning design with views and provision to match and the girls in a Queen Anne period house with comparable facilities. We were struck by the zest with which pupils from everywhere share information about their homes and countries – a true global community, literally in the making. Years 7 and 8 housed in Lambardes – much-loved as is the current housemaster – 'he's ex-army – excellent fun but he knows how to keep discipline,' a parent enthused. 'Even at this stage, there are enough boarders for you to find a friend. We have a battle to get our children to come home at weekends though sometimes it's so full-on at school they like to just flop.' Much praise, too, for the way younger and older pupils mix and collaborate. Some houses e.g. Park Grange a delight and with a big and enviable, communal kitchen in which 'everyone gets to know everyone'. This school understands about sofas, carpets and big TVs. Huge dining room with vast choice of truly tempting food. One pupil who vouchsafed little in answer to our questions, broke out with, 'I'm so pleased I came here – the food is so good!'

Pastoral Care and Discipline: Few problems here. No house system. Sound and well-established pastoral system in years and boarding houses. You stay in the same boarding house from 13–18. No drugs incidents in recent years, no exclusions, few minor misdemeanours mostly sorted by detentions. No-one wants to be kicked out of this place. No drinking allowed anywhere and boarders under 16 not allowed to go to day pupils' parties if alcohol is offered. Nonetheless, lots of integration of day and boarding pupils and those who can bear to forgo all the weekend activities often invited home by locals. Universal feeling among parents that you are expected to be independent, take responsibility for yourself and if you forget something or don't do your homework, no-one will cosset, prompt or mollycoddle you. 'It's a very grown-up school – it expects you to be grown-up,' we were told. 'Sometimes,' another parent felt, 'the boarders are just left to get on with it.' But this seen, again, as part of the self-reliance the school builds and not as a deterrent. 'Strongly secular' ethos, as one parent described it, 'very hands-off, no spoon-feeding.' However, one international sixth former, clearly ecstatic at his good fortune, breathed, 'it's the support – it's flawless – after two years I still haven't found anything wrong'.

Pupils and Parents: A truly – and uniquely – global clientele. Possibly nowhere other than our elite universities accommodates such an international crème de la intellectual crème, blending them so successfully, and creating such a rich and enriching mix of cultures. Around a quarter from overseas – but from a bigger range of home countries than any other school – 31 in 2010 – no cliques or sects here, though Germans and Italians are relatively numerous. The majority of overseas students join for the sixth form and are given an unbeatable education in the roundest and broadest sense. The rest from the UK – and two thirds are day pupils reflecting the strong local commitment to the school, despite strong competition from Kent grammars. And local can mean right up into London and into Surrey. Pupils are open, unpretentious, clever, thoughtful and hugely appreciative of their luck in being here. Parents describe them as independent, confident but not arrogant. Also as individuals, 'they don't go into tweed jackets and stay in them for the rest of their lives'. Parents, likewise, and mostly just grateful for their children's chances here. Some feel that home-school communication could be better but this, as everywhere, varies from house to house and teacher to teacher.

Entrance: Around 190 apply for the 65 places in Year 7. Candidates sit the school's own exam, are interviewed and prep/primary reports are considered. The odds against getting a place are not as high as they look as there is strong competition at this stage from the Kent grammars and many who get places here will opt for the state sector. At 13+, around 180 apply for 80 places – again exam – or CE – interview and report. Lots of feeders including Holmewood House, New Beacon, Hazelwood, Windlesham, Dulwich Prep. Stronger competition for the sixth form which really is an elite institution. Over 400 apply for 80 places. Required with the application are a personal statement, 3 exams in their likely 'higher' level subjects and school references. All must have taken the school's pre-test/interview – this can, if needed, in some cases, be conducted in the applicant's home country or on Skype. 'We want people with above average academic ability, strong co-curricular interests and an enquiring spirit,' says head, 'someone who will enjoy their time here.'

Exit: Truly impressive in the quality and diversity of the courses and institutions. In 2009 saw 26 to Cambridge (including 3 on choral schols) and 19 to Oxford – that's a quarter of the year. Large numbers to Bath, Bristol, UCL, Durham and the LSE. A dozen to Ivy Leagues or close to. And studying everything from aeronautics to zoology. Notable alumni include musicians Emma Johnson, Mathew Best; journos and writers Plum Sykes, Olivia Cole; academics Francis Everitt, Jonathan Bate, Oliver Taplin; sportsmen Chris Tavare, Anthony Roques, Dan Caprice; and in the arts Daniel Day Lewis, Charlie Higson, Simon Starling, Paul Greengrass, Geoffrey Streatfeild, Emma Hope; also spook Jonathan Evans (DG of M15). To say nothing of William Caxton.

Money Matters: Not a rich school but offers bursaries up to 100 per cent of the day fee following means-testing. Scholarships worth up to 20 per cent of day fee awarded for excellence in academics, sport, music, art and drama. One big sports scholarship on offer.

Remarks: Tough for any university not to be an anti-climax after Sevenoaks. Hard to imagine a Sennockian not being an asset to any uni they grace. 'It feels,' one sixth former confided, 'as if I'm an apprentice and the whole school is one big teacher.'

Sexey's School

Cole Road, Bruton, Somerset, BA10 0DF

• Pupils: 525 boys and girls; 250 boarders (majority board in Years 7-11) • Ages: 11-18 • Size of sixth form: 170 • C of E • Fees: Boarding £7,950 pa; No day fees • State

Tel: 01749 813 393
Fax: 01749 812 870
Email: jfairhurst@sexeys.somerset.sch.uk
Website: www.sexeys.somerset.sch.uk

Head: Since January 2008, Mr Ray McGovern MA (late forties) educated at St Thomas Aquinas School, Glasgow then via apprenticeship with British Leyland and nine years' service as an RAF engineer technician to a lectureship in computer aided design and aeronautical studies at West Thames College, Isleworth. Completed certificate in education at Brunel in 1992 and began secondary teaching career at Charles Darwin School, Biggin Hill where he became deputy head of sixth form whilst studying for OU Master's degree in education. Five year spell at Christ College, Brecon saw him become a housemaster as well as head of technology. Moved to deputy headship at Sexey's in 2001 then promotion to headship after seven years. Carried a lot of responsibility under previous head and now 'shaking things up' according to parents.

Chairman elect of State Boarding Schools' Association and heavily committed to promoting the boarding side of Sexeys. Teaches citizenship to year seven in order to get to know pupils – 'works well,' say parents who like the family feel of the school. Married to Rachel with two sons and a daughter. Sings tenor in St Mary's, Bruton, church choir and also plays clarinet. A forthright head with a commonsense approach based on a wide experience beyond the classroom. Clear views about putting others first: 'has a vision for the school,' we were told from different sources.

Academic matters: Consistently good A level (57 per cent A*–B grades) and GCSE results (92 per cent 5+ A*–C grades including English and maths). Amongst best value-added results in Somerset. 25 subjects on offer at AS, slightly fewer at A2. Specialist humanities college (quite a battle to gain this status) with new facilities and initiatives in these subject areas. Recent results indicate strengths in art, DT, maths, sciences, sociology and business studies. Outstanding GCSE results in history may presage things to come. Head keen on AQA baccalaureate (extended sixth form project) involving two hours a week spent outside main taught curriculum. Buzz word is 'personalisation' – means taking time from year seven upwards to consider each pupil's needs. Relatively small classes helps and fortnightly timetable with five one hour long lessons per day (doubles where required for science etc) reduces chaotic lesson changes. Flexibility offered in DT choices and we were pleased to see food technology carried through to AS level. Religious studies and citizenship figure at both

GCSE and AS level. Good level of ICT with smart boards throughout school; many students use own laptops.

Clued up learning support provided for around 10 per cent of pupils. Improved base also acts as sanctuary for more vulnerable. Expanded team with four LSAs and teaching assistants attached to specific pupils. Sexey's claims for special needs funding are probably hampered because of its relatively affluent social profile but SENCo maintains system is fair. Pupils screened (CATs) on entry; voluntary support given to pupils until 5.00p.m. Some pupils receive three or four hour long sessions a fortnight. Lots of computer games (e.g. number/word shark) to help. 'It helps being such a happy school,' we were told. Less able placed on IFP (individual flexiblility programme): involves small number who spend time at FE college in Years 10 and 11. Assistant head very focused on getting gifted pupils in all year groups onto relevant extra courses and activities – about half are on school's NAGTY register. School also benefits from being link school for Exeter university teacher training programme.

Games, Options, the Arts: Promotes sport (house rivalry includes sport, music and drama); enthusiastic participation in main games and teams with fixtures against state and independent schools and success in various inter-school competitions. Representation at county level in cricket, rugby, athletics and badminton. Karting team have reached national finals two years running; equestrian team now competing in inter-school events. Ideal terrain for cross-country; heated indoor swimming pool; good pitches, no Astroturf but easy access to Bruton girls' facility; sports hall and four hard tennis courts which double up for netball.

Strong on drama: 'new HoD has done wonders,' say parents. Good studio space for smaller productions plus traditional hall for bigger performances. Music department has come on 'by leaps and bounds' also under new HoD – 130 pupils currently play instruments; boys have joined school choir (featured recently in BBC 2 series) – who has transposed concerts into a jazz café format – 'goes down well,' we were told. Former head's house provides a good atmosphere for music making: large classroom, recording studio and individual practice rooms on three floors. Good uptake at GCSE but small numbers to A level. Performance groups include choir, wind band and soul band. Separate, cramped two storey art department (new dual purpose art/DT area in new building will alleviate this) achieves success at all levels in a suitably bohemian ambience.

Wide range of extra-curricular activities and after school learning. Range of visits abroad: Paris, Berlin and Egypt plus trips to plays, House of Commons etc to broaden horizons. Established link with German school through annual exchange – with visitors dividing time between boarding houses and host families. Public speaking, Ten Tors challenge and D of E (four currently doing gold) all well supported. 20–30 pupils participate as cadets in ACF from 13 onwards. Eco School bronze award. Good level of charity fund raising through variety of student led initiatives.

Background and Atmosphere: Named after Hugh Sexey, who rose to become auditor to Elizabeth l and James l. He established Sexey's Hospital, which still provides care in Bruton for 30 elderly people. In 1889, trustees founded a trade school under guidance of Hon Henry Hobhouse who drafted the 1902 Education Act. Unremarkable original buildings stand behind an attractive small garden; front entrance leads into a pleasantly modernised reception area. Sexey's has metamorphosed through boys' grammar, voluntary controlled, grant maintained (when school became cash-rich and improved facilities) to voluntary aided. Went co-ed in early 80s, took its first 30 day pupils into Year 7 in 2003. We encountered a lingering resentment from some Bruton villagers that day places remain so difficult to obtain but head is walking this political tightrope with some skill. No day versus boarding issue as far as pupils we spoke to were concerned. School is a 'victim of its own success locally,' said one mother.

Expansion over years has resulted in a mishmash of architectural styles squeezed into narrow site between main road and cliff edge, but the glorious countryside that bounds up on three sides makes up for its shortcomings. Some overdue developments – e.g. junior science labs and smart design/humanities centre (opened in September 2009) spelled end of shabby huts and mobile classrooms: a vast improvement all round. Head aims to create a new social area for lower school pupils on site of former DT workshop.

One way system through buildings helps ease congestion at lesson changes. Relatively small but workmanlike library with study carrels on mezzanine floor for independent learners. Sixth formers 'feel comfortable' wearing their own clothes and mostly heed dress code. 'Some stuffiness over dress rules for younger pupils,' thought one mother who then endorsed the school's insistence on good manners. Attractive, purpose-built sixth form centre provides necessary social focus for Sexey's large body of 16–18 year olds – includes small IT suite plus tutorial offices (e.g. for careers/HE advice); plenty of space to relax and snack bar facilities available throughout day.

Pastoral Care and Discipline: Emphasis on boarding ethos influences whole school; vertical tutor groups (20 minutes' tutorial time each morning) led by heads of houses plus head of lower school responsible for Years 7–11. Head keen to participate in Pathfinder scheme to offer boarding places to children in care of social services but little uptake by latter to date. Code of conduct set out in school diary exhorts courtesy and consideration. Pupils generally understand school's uncompromising line – few need to be hauled over the coals it seems. Staff trained in restorative justice – provides forum for all parties to explain their feelings and to express regret. Only sixth formers allowed mobile phones during school day but not in lessons. Girl we spoke to had lost her father whilst on tour of duty in Iraq: she could not praise the school enough for the consideration and support she had received through a difficult and upsetting time of her life.

Chapel part of new building; school pays more than lip service to its Christian foundation – witness appointment of a lively Christian youth worker to raise profile of this side of school life. Some lovely houseparents and assistants (strengthened by post A level Aussie gappers and two foreign language assistants) help to make boarding at Sexey's highly enjoyable. Minimum of four staff resident every night. Boarding houses vary in layout, tidiness and social provision; we were impressed by fantastic set-up for Years 11–13: range of facilities allowing students to socialise or retreat as required. Young staff (average age is 35) though 19 teachers have served over 10 years. Some sixth form prefects attached to each of lower school houses plus peer mentoring scheme – younger pupils really appreciate this. Students' common room also put to good effect during day as a lecture hall. Good medical arrangements with 24 cover by qualified staff and adequate sick bay. Head aims to add to staff accommodation and to rationalise boarding for younger pupils so they no longer have to come and go beside busy Wincanton road. Traditional approach – leaders (head prefers this term to prefects) first chosen from Year 11 pupils and then responsibilities shared higher up. Head boy and girl plus heads of house retain importance. School has 'healthy plus' status; meal arrangements work well in modern dining area and 'food has improved,' say pupils. We saw good choices on offer at lunch: salads as well as hot veggie and meat dishes. Sittings at supper work on house basis; day pupils can also sign up for tea.

Pupils and Parents: Generally bright eyed, cooperative and well turned out – blazers and ties in lower school for first two terms then polo shirts in summer. Sixth formers provide leadership and want to do well; organise own social programme. Easy relationships between staff and students as well as between year groups. Active school council and environment committee. More boys than girls but not patriarchal. Annual meeting (two in year ten) with parents before exeats; loads of e-mail contact at all levels between staff and parents. Former pupils include Alex Tew (creator of the 'Million Dollar' website; BBC wildlife film maker, James Brickell, John Bryant – consultant editor of *The Daily Mail* – and broadcaster, the late Ned Sherrin.

Entrance: Parents can visit year round – usually on Tuesdays. Separate interviews with head and head of boarding. Head will ask if child wants to board and refuse a place if they don't – he places priority on child's welfare and happiness. Not much hope of a day place at 11+ if you live more than a mile away – blame Somerset CC not the school. Some further afield may qualify on church or sibling grounds. Popular choice for boarding within county – can usually accommodate more boy boarders at 11+ than apply; some girls usually turned away – plans to increase accommodation for them. Good number of army families and navy from RNAS base at Yeovilton. Large transfer from other Somerset comps for sixth form plus some from independents. Minimum GCSE requirements spelled out in prospectus. Interviews for all applicants. School operates two minibuses to pick up students in addition to those who come by other means.

Exit: Small leave at 16+ to vocational courses; one of the broadest portfolios of university destinations we've seen in terms of spread of courses and variety of institutions. One or two a year to Oxbridge.

Money Matters: Boarding fees only for British passport holders and EU citizens.

Remarks: Look no further for value for money: all the advantages of boarding in a small school without the enormous price tag or social pretentiousness. Since admitting day pupils from Year 7 has tidied itself up and broadened its appeal. Perennially popular at sixth form level. Lots of good teaching here and a genuine sense of community.

Shapwick School

Linked to Shapwick Prep School in the Junior section

Shapwick Manor, Shapwick, Bridgwater, Somerset, TA7 9NJ

• Pupils: 105: 80 boys (60 board), 25 girls (15 board); 20 in sixth form.
• Ages: 13-19 • Size of sixth form: 20 • Non-denom • Fees: £14,652-£21,000 pa • Independent

Tel: 01458 210 384
Fax: 01458 210 111
Email: office@shapwickschool.com
Website: www.shapwickschool.com

Joint heads (Director of Studies; Pastoral Head): Since 1983, Mr David Walker BA CertEd (fifties), director of studies and since 1981, Mr Jon Whittock CertEd (forties), pastoral head – a veteran team. When David Walker began teaching science at a comprehensive he noticed 'bright' pupils (one boy was a county chess player) dropping off the academic radar because of poor reading and spelling. Robust with a soft centre, he is seen as 'strict but fair' by pupils and has demonstrated long-term commitment to helping children overcome dyslexia. A former rugby club captain and veteran of five marathons, he is married to Annette who teaches maths at Shapwick. Jon Whittock, a PE specialist, is married to Sandra with four children from six to twenty-five, has been here since the school's inception. 'The most important thing here is the positive peer support,' he explains. Also a former rugby captain and member of Somerset County RFU as well as leading adventure expeditions of all types. Both men hugely respected.

Academic matters: Percentage of pupils achieving five or more GCSEs at grade C or above has risen from forty to sixty-nine per cent over last four years. A tremendous achievement with so many statemented SpLD pupils – eight per cent above the national average. Figures including maths and English are less impressive and have actually worsened over the same period though pupils are entered in Years 9 or 10 for maths if they are ready to achieve grade C or better. GCSE English remains the battleground for these pupils and recent reductions in proportion of coursework in the syllabus (with a corresponding increase in functional skills and technical accuracy) have made things even more difficult for dyslexics. A good reason for staying here beyond 16 is to have a second or third crack at GCSE English – with some success it seems. No setting in English throughout school ensures mixed literary abilities though 'word attack' (spelling) groups are set. CReSTeD Category A (the highest level of provision) for the last ten years.

Many pupils receive occupational and speech and language therapy. 'Parents are glad when they hear that there is something we can fix,' explained guardian angel and senior therapist, Cynthia. Health Professions Council (subsumed RCSLT with whom Shapwick was only UK school to have accreditation) 'has already praised school's degree of ownership of language problems,' she adds. Tip top therapy centre is very much at core of school's success: three speech and language plus three occupational therapists. THRASS picture chart used throughout the school to reinforce spelling. Lots of cross-curricular work and encouragement of joined-up thinking. SCAEP (social competence enhancement) introduces pupils to problem-solving and negotiating skills. Emphasis given to improving short-term memory. Tremendous range of help in public examinations: pupils often able to request amanuensis they know and virtually all receive extra help of some kind.

Pupils take core science in year 10 and additional science in Year 11. Most take four of five optional GCSE subjects: resistant materials technology combines with product design and engineering to provide two GCSEs. Surprisingly, no food technology but geography, drama, photography and art all do exceedingly well with 80 per cent of grades at B or above. Lots of ICT and most pupils have own laptops provided by LAs. Maths taken 18 months early – 70 per cent achieve grade C or above. Traditional boarding timetable: nine thirty-five minute lessons per weekday, two supervised preps and no escape from lessons on Saturday mornings.

Until twenty years ago, post-16 students simply stayed on for re-takes or moved away to sixth form colleges. Without continued specialist support even those who had done brilliantly at GCSE floundered or panicked and fled – 'crash and burn' in SEN-speak. Scheme between Bridgwater College and Shapwick has created a dyslexia-friendly sixth form, which enables pupils to have all the advantages of the wide choices offered for A level and GNVQ by a large college without losing the multi-sensory teaching and speech and language therapy back at their familiar base where they still spend two days a week. Learning to get the correct bus and find their way round Bridgwater prepares them for life in the world outside Shapwick.

Games, Options, the Arts: Sport compulsory for all until sixth form. County level players in badminton, athletics and rugby. Semi-finalists at ISA rugby sevens tournament. Walled garden has been converted to provide floodlit, all-weather surface. More than adequate sports hall is well used with extra facilities (including swimming) available at Strode College in nearby Street. Teams play state and private schools. D of E generates much enthusiasm and bronze awards. Annual ski trip to France combines junior and senior schools; improves co-ordination, listening, confidence, high level organisation while they learn to bum-board, snow board and ski. Recent art trips have included to Egypt and Normandy.

Stunningly lively art studio run by charismatic HoD who masterminds Summer Arts festival – local artists workshopping tapestry, painting, willow-weaving etc. Pottery and photography particularly strong. Drum, guitar and keyboard taught to a handful but no music classes in senior school as 1:1 tuition has been found to work better. Pupils showcase talent at end of year concert. Loads of activities (from potholing to go-karting) everyday after lessons. Ten Tors challenge and D of E ever popular. Fleet of five minibuses to shuttle pupils between outlying houses and Manor. Year 10 have work experience at end of year; good careers database and links; mock employment interviews for Year 11.

Background and Atmosphere: School motto 'The same road by different steps' says it all. The sense of relief at having gained a place here amongst these dyslexic pupils is almost palpable – 'I have to pinch myself to be sure I'm here,' said one. One teacher said pupils 'were a pleasure to be with and a pleasure to teach.' Staff are hugely experienced and many come from state sector.

Shapwick Manor, previously owned by Lord Vestey, is the hub of the school and dates from sixteenth century. Fifteenth century dovecote sits rotundly on front lawn. Tuscan style stables have been converted into therapy centre but retain their unique external appearance. Shared foundation with Millfield – remained in ownership of Atkinson family until Easter 2008 when it passed to Kedleston UK who currently own four specialist schools in UK. No town distractions here to detract pupils from work – school sits comfortably in this quiet, pretty village. Has retained former Millfield model of outlying boarding houses including The Lakes (currently houses 24 boys) in Meare and sixth formers on prep school site in Burtle. Originally a boys' prep school, has grown into a co-ed senior with an expanding sixth form (about 50 per cent stay beyond 16). Classrooms and laboratories (biology was the largest and pleasantest we saw) are scattered around split site with DT centre in old village school. Pleasant dining area: food given thumbs up by pupils.

Pastoral Care and Discipline: Tutor groups based on three houses. Mentoring system for incoming year nine pupils works well. School council meets regularly with senior management. Small boarding houses run by houseparents (some even cook for pupils at weekends). Games room beside sports hall provides on site space for relaxation with pool tables and easy chairs. Some Year 11 pupils act as prefects and have separate room in the Manor. Staff bring a new meaning to the word dedication – many have family members and children who have suffered with dyslexia or dyspraxia, so their compassion and zeal does not stop when the bell goes. School offers parents opportunity of up to twelve meetings a year with staff and 'we can ring any member of staff at any time,' said one mother. Strong parental involvement contributes to its success. Discipline is firm but fair with well established procedures for bullying (virtually none here) or drugs which rarely have to be activated.

Pupils and Parents: All pupils are dyslexic/dyspraxic – come from all over UK and a few overseas. Many arrive feeling 'crushed' but soon begin to flourish. Uniform and the routine of boarding come as a shock for many – 'none of our pupils are natural boarders,' says Jon Whittock, 'but they generally cope better with boarding than their parents.' Percentage of girls has crept up and they seem to fit in well. School prides itself on close contact with parents and up to twelve parents' meetings throughout the year. Summer Diary has replaced newsletter and is published annually to illustrate breadth of activity. One mother told us, 'the difference it makes to our whole family's life is incredible.' For day pupils, another parent said, 'it's no problem now getting them to school.'

Entrance: One third of younger pupils either have or are in process of seeking LA financial support. Process usually takes up to eighteen months; nearly all applications from state schools pupils go to tribunal and can involve costs up to £10K (though occasionally more). About one half of pupils are privately funded. School offers 'taster' days or even 'taster weeks'. Open Days generally spread over Friday and Saturday and include opportunity for applicants to be assessed to ascertain level of need. No admissions, apart from lower sixth, allowed after first term of Year 10.

Exit: About fifty per cent stay into sixth; remainder go mainly to variety of FE colleges.

Money Matters: Parents pay for trips and uniform but everything else is included in fees.

Remarks: Parents full of praise: 'Staff are miracle workers,' says one. 'Our son is a different child,' confirms another. No doubting benefit for dyslexic boys and girls whose self-confidence grows by leaps and bounds here. We encountered a staggering volume of positive testimonials from parents past and present who had given up hope for their children until they discovered Shapwick.

Sheffield High School

Linked to Sheffield High School Junior Department in the Junior section

10 Rutland Park, Sheffield, South Yorkshire, S10 2PE

• Pupils: 1000 girls; all day • Ages: 4-18 • Size of sixth form: 190
• Non-denom • Fees: Senior £9,531 pa • Independent

Tel: 0114 266 0324
Fax: 0114 267 8520
Email: enquiries@she.gdst.net
Website: www.sheffieldhighschool.org.uk

Head: Since 2004, Mrs Valerie Dunsford, BA Hons (forties). Mrs Dunsford read French and did her PGCE at Manchester. She taught at Ryburn Valley HS in Halifax, Benfield in Newcastle and then was head of modern languages, head of sixth form and deputy head at Durham High School.

Academic matters: Strong A level results – steady growth to 76 per cent A*–B have meant the school consistently outperforms all other schools in South Yorks; almost all sixth formers get into their first choice universities. Seven years 100 per cent pass rate at A level. A good range of subjects including sports studies, Russian, psychology, government and politics, with some very small sets; all take either general studies A level or critical thinking, AQA Bacc available. Strong GCSE results – 99 per cent average pass rate over last five years, 76 per cent A/A* with only a small proportion below B.

Four modern languages offered. Only setted for maths. Experienced, hard-working, enthusiastic staff who use very up-to-date teaching methods integrating ICT into classes, are generous with their time and enjoy good relationships with girls. Average class sizes of 20 in senior school and 8 in the sixth form (there are only two private all-girls schools in Sheffield and only one with progression from 4–18). ESL teaching available. Excellent IT provision and use in teaching, particularly in modern languages, science and music; qualifications are taken at GCSE and in the sixth form. Library well-stocked and pleasant – despite its origin as a gym – with computer facilities. Strong careers education – has excellent links with local industry and commerce providing a broad range of work experience opportunities.

Games, Options, the Arts: SHS was awarded the title of UK's Best independent School for Sport in 2005 by *The Daily Telegraph*. Highly successful mainstream sports teams in hockey and netball but with wide ranging opportunities in trampolining, badminton, cross-country and skiing. A well equipped sports hall with a dance studio; all-weather courts and an Astroturf hockey pitch. Music is strong, including choirs and orchestra with a swing band that performs annually in Europe; converted stables with recording and drama studios. Yamaha C5 grand piano inaugurated with a recital and masterclass by Benjamin Frith.

Wide range of extra-curricular activities with local, national or international successes in Young Enterprise, public speaking, chemistry, technology, maths and creative writing competitions; Duke of Edinburgh Award Scheme very popular. Several do LAMDA exams. Trips to Mongolia and Argentina (World Challenge), Ecuador, ski trips to Europe and Americas, Russia plus homestay residential visits to France, Germany, Spain and USA. Sports tours to Australia, South Africa, New Zealand and China and Barbados. Excellent art, e.g. ceramic work, fabrics; new extension to art suite has provided excellent modern facilities. Trips have been organised to France and New York.

Background and Atmosphere: Founded in 1878 by The Girls' Day School Trust. A city school on a cramped site, it has undergone considerable development and extension and is located in a leafy residential area. Architecturally very mixed, including a church that housed the original gym, a graceless but now refurbished 1960s science block with an extension from 2005, a converted old lodge with an elegant ex-billiards room, and separate infant, junior and sixth forms located in large Victorian houses on site. The classrooms are well-resourced; the decoration has been upgraded with interactive whiteboards. Relatively new dining hall with a popular breakfast club.

Pastoral Care and Discipline: Clearly a virtue of the school. A strong pastoral support system with a sensible code of conduct written by staff and the student council and a successful merit system. Sixth form tutor groups formed by combining self-selecting friendship groups. Exclusion for repeated unacceptable behaviour, e.g. drugs, smoking, theft, intransigence – the whole picture is taken into account. A thoughtful Year 7 induction; they have all their lessons in classrooms off one corridor for the first year. Focus on moral/spiritual development rather than religion.

Pupils and Parents: From Sheffield, south Yorkshire, north Nottinghamshire and north Derbyshire. Most come from professional and business families but a social mix because of the large number of Trust bursaries. Well-motivated, confident girls who feel happy and secure and speak appreciatively of their teachers.

Entrance: Tests in English and maths plus an interview at 11; 50 per cent from state schools. Entry to sixth form: girls need seven GCSEs at A–C with A/B in AS subjects and they are coming in increasing numbers from outside. Scholarships available in subject areas. Entry to the junior school is through observation during a child-friendly day – they are looking for bright, lively girls who are ready for school. Most proceed from the junior school to the seniors. It caters for average to above-average ability, 'sparky girls who want to learn and are interested in their own development'.

Exit: Retention into the sixth form is higher than at several sister schools. Nonetheless, 12–18 leave after GCSE, for local state schools, other independent day schools (e.g. co-educational ones) and sixth form colleges. Almost all the rest go into the sixth and on to a range of universities, most students go to their first choice university; about 10 per cent to Oxbridge. Many do a range of science/medically related courses; business courses are also popular.

Money Matters: 20 per cent have Trust bursaries or scholarships which can amount to a significant proportion of fees; anyone who passes the entrance exam can apply. Two full fee HSBC/Trust scholarships. Scholarships based on academic ability are also available at sixth form entry plus a sixth form music scholarship awarded through a music exam.

Remarks: A successful all-round city school, especially suited to academic, musical and sporting high flyers. Excellent value-added, staff especially proud of lower ability girls who achieve outstanding grades at A level. Must be prepared to work for it, though.

Sherborne Girls School

Bradford Road, Sherborne, Dorset, DT9 3QN

• Pupils: 405 girls; most board, 30 day • Ages: 11-18 • Size of sixth form: 150 • C of E • Fees: Boarding £29,760; Day £20,109 pa • Independent

Tel: 01935 818 224
Fax: 01935 389445
Email: enquiry@sherborne.com
Website: www.sherborne.com

Headmistress: Since 2006, Mrs Jenny Dwyer BEd, formerly head of Prior's Field. Educated at Bradford Girls Grammar and then read maths at Homerton College, Cambridge. First job at Benenden (teaching/housemistress), then went on to Queen Anne's School, Caversham, where she was deputy head responsible for pastoral care. 'Glad to be back in full boarding,' and plans to turn the school, 'from good to great'. Has increased time-tabled sport, beefed up the range of extra-curricular activities, brought in some young staff and given the girls a bit more rope. Married to a 'very supportive man', they have two sons (educated at Charterhouse and Milton Abbey). Keen on maths and hockey and maintains that pastoral care is her particular passion. Comes across as friendly, but reserved: more of a listener than a talker. Enjoys dinghy sailing at her home on the Norfolk coast.

Academic matters: Has, in tandem with Sherborne School, joined the swelling ranks of schools offering the IB. Only 25 pupils involved this year, but this will grow. Head says staff return from IB training courses full of enthusiasm which filters down to everyone. 2009 A level and GCSE results were very good and the first cohort of IB results were excellent with the average point score just under 36 and equivalent to AAAA at A2. It's hard to fault a single department. Maths and English come through with flying colours year after year. At A level, modern languages are particularly strong (v swish language lab, chock full of computers). Art and design, and history of art, produce high flyers. Catering and home economics both offered as GCSEs. Though much made of joint teaching between the schools in the sixth form, only a small fraction of girls attend lessons at the boys' school (and even fewer boys come to the girls' school). Theatre studies are, however, a genuine joint enterprise between the two schools. Lessons have recently been stretched from 35 to 55 minutes resulting, they say, in better teaching ('a teacher can wing a 35 minute lesson, but not a 55 minute one!'). Much setting and streaming from 13. No form tutors; girls meet individually with a tutor all the way up the school. School currently investing in SEN, to improve resources. Less than 20 per cent of pupils have mild special needs. Any extra lessons are at a time agreed: girls are not withdrawn from lessons or key activities. In recognition of need for more careers and university advice/support, a director of sixth form has now been appointed as well as a Careers Co-ordinator.

Games, Options, the Arts: Much emphasis lately on beefing up extra-curricular offerings, with good effect. Has revamped sports e.g. making sure all levels of players have access to top coaches, shifting some games sessions to mornings, reintroducing netball(!) and offering more choice. L4 and U4 have sport every day, L5 to U5 have at least three sessions per week, plus activities. New-ish Oxley Sports Centre with indoor pool, fitness suite, gym, dance studio plus floodlit Astro, plenty of grass pitches and 27 tennis courts (eight floodlit). Girls proud of school's lacrosse record – 20 Sherborne girls currently in the Dorset/Wilts County lacrosse teams (NB Sherborne Girls is reputedly the only school in Dorset to play lacrosse). Hosted ELA Lacrosse finals for 1st and U15 teams throughout UK and holds pop lacrosse tournaments for prep and primary schools. Hockey also fearsome. 17 girls currently in the Dorset/Wilts teams. Second equal last year in National Schools' Show Jumping competition at Hickstead.

Serious about music – this year, every A level and GCSE music exam received an A*/A. The school takes part in the Sherborne Schools' Symphony Orchestra which skims off the cream of musicians from Sherborne Girls, Sherborne Boys and nearby Leweston to produce two joint orchestras. Singing particularly illustrious. Sherborne Choral Society runs jointly with boys' school. Chamber orchestra, jazz band, senior choir, elite madrigal choir etc etc. There are 45 pianos, all tuned(!), including new Steinway grand (a gift to the school). Some girls complain about the music building's slightly depressing breezeblock design, with extra, 'temporary' music huts alongside. But a new circa £3.5 million project was launched this year to build a new performing arts centre. Plans also afoot for increased music technology.

Stunning art, well taught in inspiring – if slightly cramped – art and design centre. Head of art is an A level examiner. Each A level candidate has her own fenced-off studio space in the large general art room. Some keen artists appear to virtually live here. Weekend workshops offered on juicy topics e.g. book-binding, stained glass and paper or jewellery making. Overseas trips, jointly with history of art dept. Computer-aided design and manufacture suite opened 2003. 100 pupils participated in D of E award this year – 20 winning gold. Many girls do the Leith's Cookery course starting in lower sixth: four distinctions awarded last year and school has now introduced the Junior Leith's course. Joint musical theatrical productions with Sherborne School.

Background and Atmosphere: Founded in 1899 – large architecturally undistinguished conglomeration on a 40-acre site on the edge of the town, looking out over open country. The school trades heavily on the perceived benefits of close co-operation with the boys' school nearby – 'the best of both worlds'. Parents, pupils and teachers are all very enthusiastic about the concept, to the annoyance of similar girls-only schools in the area. Town location another selling point: SSG feels less isolated than many other girls' boarding schools. Girls have quite a bit of freedom to go out of school and a quiet backwater like Sherborne is a wonderful place for them to gain a little independence. Younger girls can go into town at weekends. Lower sixth can go as far as Yeovil, Exeter, Salisbury. Upper sixth girls allowed into the sixth form bar at Sherborne Boys. Parents like the school's strong boarding ethos ('we wanted a proper boarding school that didn't empty out at the weekend,' said a mum). Day girls may go home at 6pm though some stay to do prep until 8pm.

Pastoral Care and Discipline: Head has reduced 28 pages of school rules to ... four. Exclusion for dealing drugs; experimenters can 'expect' to go. One exclusion in past couple of years (drink). Boarding done extremely well, with housemistresses taking immense pride in their enterprises. Much refurbishment to the boarding houses which are lovely. If you are worried about your 11 year old fragile flower taking to boarding, then this is the school for you. All 11 and 12 year olds start off in West House: charming and homely, with fabulous pastoral care. While we were there, several older girls popped in to have a natter with their 'old' housemistress. Girls sleep in cubicles (partitioned compartments in a dormitory – day girls have a bed too); vast majority are in at weekends. Supervised prep in the evenings. Thereafter, girls disperse into five mixed-age houses (Wingfield Digby said to be sporty, and is flavour of the month). Food a serious deal here. Each house has own kitchen and dining room. Formal lunches (sixth form devises seating plans, with a member of staff at each table), but cafeteria-style suppers. Seating plans change frequently to avoid cliques forming. Some nice touches e.g. girls get to choose the menu on their birthdays. In the upper sixth, girls move into the hotel-like Mulliner – less cutting edge than it used to be now that so many other schools have opened similar versions, but its individual study bedrooms and air of independence are still a draw.

Pupils and Parents: Girls smarter and more worldly than we remember them being last time we were here. Sixth form dress code has been radically relaxed with predictable results – probably the right thing to do though. Many Services families, diplomats, Londoners with south west connections (Sherborne station quite near, and service good). Also 17 girls from Hong Kong and 30 from elsewhere abroad (numbers from Germany on increase since IB introduced). Around 25 girls require EAL support of one lesson per week. Recently awarded the DCSF International School Award in recognition of the international dimension being a key part of school ethos. Old girls – aviatrix Winifred Spooner, tennis player Shirley Bloomer, Camila Batmanghelidjh (founder of Kids Co and 2006 Woman of the Year), soprano Emma Kirkby, violinist Ruth Rogers.

Entrance: Visit, registration, 'at work days', taster weekends, deposit paid, then scholarship exams, common entrance papers or own entrance exams. One small form enters at 11, a few girls join at 12 but the majority (three forms) enter at 13. Mainly from Hanford, Port Regis, Hazlegrove, Knighton House, Sherborne Prep, Leaden Hall, Perrott Hill, Cheam, Bute House, Newland, Thomas's, Mount House and Sunninghill. About 20 join for sixth form – at least five grade B or above GCSEs required (to do A level or IB).

Exit: Some ten per cent leave after GCSEs, mainly to sixth form colleges. After A levels, practically all go on to university to read a wide variety of courses (modern languages topping the list). Bristol, Leeds, Durham, Oxford Brookes, Newcastle, Edinburgh and Manchester have led the pack in recent years. A few to Oxbridge most years. Half a dozen to art schools last year.

Money Matters: Fees steep (ouch!) but scholarship provision generous for a girls' school. Range of academic, art and music awards pay up to quarter of fees, plus bursaries based on need. Music scholars entitled to up to three lessons per week – more than at most schools. At any given time, nearly 100 girls are receiving some sort of award or bursary.

Remarks: Going strong academically and just about every other way. Now one of the sturdier pins in the glut of Dorset/Somerset/Wilts girls-only boarding.

Sherborne School

Abbey Road, Sherborne, Dorset, DT9 3AP

• Pupils: 600 boys; all but 55 board • Ages: 13-19 • Size of sixth form: 245 • C of E • Fees: Day £22,725, Boarding £28,065 pa • Independent

Tel: 01935 812 249
Fax: 01935 810 426
Email: registrar@sherborne.org
Website: www.sherborne.org

Headmaster: Since 2010, Mr Christopher Davis MA (fifties). Previously a housemaster at Eton where he went to school. He read English at Cambridge and before moving to teaching, he worked for the Bank of England International division and was seconded to the Cabinet Office for two years. He is married with two school age daughters.

Academic matters: Welcome to the new improved Sherborne. There has been a big effort – driven from the top – to make sure that brainy boys have the opportunity to push out the inside of the envelope. 'The brightest,' said previous head, 'will almost do better than they would at Winchester.' The challenging IB has been on offer alongside A levels since 2007, in conjunction with the girls' school; IGCSEs have been introduced in some subjects (more straightforward than GCSEs – less jumping through hoops); an 'Intellectual Enrichment Committee' helps boys to expand beyond undiluted exam preparation. Lessons have been extended from 35 to 55 minutes and supper delayed to help academic societies flourish and to create a calmer environment with less hoo-ha and wasted time trotting between lessons. The school has been following with interest the development of the Cambridge Pre-U – an alternative to A levels for the brightest pupils.

Mere mortals doing fine too. Sciences and maths results particularly stand out. All boys are required to take separate sciences to GCSE (a few lab-coat-challenged lads are allowed to do dual award) and high numbers continue with sciences to A level. History, economics and – extraordinarily – Spanish (famously good here) also woo large numbers though results more varied. Two modern languages plus Latin compulsory during first year and all boys must study a language of their choice to GCSE (French, Spanish, German or Chinese). Greek available at GCSE and A level. Philosophy and ethics and politics are new A levels. Languages setted from the start, other subjects in both arts and sciences streamed. ESL help available. A number of sixth form courses are offered jointly with Sherborne School for Girls.

SEN provision not cutting edge (head not keen to be viewed as a magnet for learning support cases) but successfully supports those who are already here (approx 80 boys). New shape to the day means these pupils no longer need to miss lessons to receive help – most welcome.

Games, Options, the Arts: Games are important here, full stop. Most boys have a games session four times a week (though confirmed geeks may be able to wangle twice plus PE – less in the sixth form) and many do more. The classic Sherbornian is an all-rounder – very good at several sports, not exceptional at one. Rugby is number one, but cricket more successful, said the boys we spoke to. Rob Hill, who captained England's hockey team at the Barcelona Olympics, coaches hockey and cricket.

Recent termly newsletters feature fives, shooting, golf, tennis, squash, basketball, riding, cross-country, swimming, hockey, skiing and the Ten Tors hike. Not much they don't do, although swimming is low key and rowing non-existent. Polo blooming via the Taunton polo club, with three teams and a full fixture card in the summer term. Squash and fives also very popular. Boys free to opt for soccer instead of hockey. Fifty acres of playing fields, all-weather pitch, 20 tennis courts, fives courts and sports centre comprising 25m indoor pool, squash courts, fitness centre and sports hall. Lots of overseas tours.

Musicians also seeing the world – joint symphony orchestra (with Sherborne School for Girls and nearby girls' school, St Antony's-Leweston) recently toured France and the Czech Republic, the strong choir sings abroad (Rome! Venice! Tuscany!) every second year and instrumental ensembles also get off the ground (e.g. the jazz band to Cuba, the swing band to Grenada). Rock music given a stage e.g. an 'Unplugged' concert and the more raucous 'Concert in the Courts'. Beautiful recording studio for music technology. A new £3.5m Music School opened in 2010. Two thirds of pupils learn an instrument and over 100 learn more than one. Drama a particular strength. A dozen dramatic productions each year, often in co-operation with Sherborne Girls', Leweston or The Gryphon – the local comprehensive school – staged in the Big School Room (seats the whole school) or the diminutive Powell Theatre. Directors in residence a big success.

Art continues to thrive with several visiting artists to invigorate proceedings. DT department has recently been completely revamped – now fabulous, with mega-spending on the technology side. Upmarket glossy brochure lists and describes the school's (many) extra-curricular activities (20 pages) e.g. golf, sailing, canoeing, rock climbing, excellent boy-run debating club, sub-aqua, D of E, CCF. Weekly extra-curricular activity session (ACE), undertaken with the girls' school – compulsory for 13-year-olds but optional thereafter. Lower sixth pupils may apply for travel grants to fund overseas visits relevant to their studies.

Background and Atmosphere: Glorious mellow-yellow stone wonder, set in charming, safe country town, in shadow of ancient abbey. Founded by Edward VI as grammar school in 1550, though origins go back to 8th century and subsequent arrival of the Benedictines in 998, who were removed by Henry VIII. One of the few schools that has managed to keep its new additions aesthetically pleasing, decade after decade – Pilkington science block is particularly well-designed. Splendid library with hammer-beam roof, now completely computerised.

Loveliness of setting and collegiate atmosphere brings in nice little income from visiting film companies. Many parents choose the school for its town setting – not too big, but has its own Sainsbury's. Boys of all ages may go into town in their spare time outside of lessons. School also trades heavily on its proximity to Sherborne School for Girls and Leweston Girls' – the best of both worlds etc. Good food, all cooked here – no Sodexho or other industrial caterers – dished up in big recently refurbished central dining hall. Worship takes place twice a week in lovely chapel, plus regular services at glorious Sherborne Abbey (which shares a wall with the school). Popular chaplain (boys: 'a legend'). Forty RC boys bused up to Leweston School for Mass.

Pastoral Care and Discipline: Eight boarding houses, each with some 70 boys – School and Green said to be 'in' at the moment. All in very good nick – a rolling programme of refurbishment. Biggish dorms to start but individual study bedrooms for some of fifth form and all of sixth (though even this was not enough for the chap whose parents recently rented him a flat off-campus so he could swot for A levels undisturbed!). Each house assigned at least six members of staff as tutors. Boys and girls may visit one another's houses, during certain hours, so long as they sign in. Sixth formers from Sherborne Girls' and Leweston frequent the boys' sixth form bar. Though girls are frequently around, it still feels extremely masculine – very much a boys' school. A few misdemeanours in recent years resulted in suspensions. As almost everywhere, alcohol more of a problem than drugs. School continues to hammer away at bullying – head calls it a 'drip, drip, drip method'. In common with many boys' schools though, there is still work to be done. Some 'minor bullying' reported and some less than 'minor'. Most, but not all, parents are satisfied that it is quickly dealt with. We still find the occasional Sherborne refugee at neighbouring schools.

Pupils and Parents: Pupil numbers back up. Well-mannered boys capable of holding their own in a conversation, but not screaming of public school. Boffins and loners can do well here, but you need a good brain. Boys come from Sherborne Prep, Sandroyd, Hazelgrove, Port Regis, and then in ones and twos from 50 or 60 preps in the south of England plus a batch from Edinburgh via Bristol airport. Forty foreign pupils, mainly Chinese and Thai; some via Sherborne International College (qv) who tend to keep to themselves; 30 overseas Brits. Some rather groovy Old Boys: Chris Martin of Coldplay, John Le Carré, Jon Pertwee (Dr Who), Jeremy Irons, Cecil Day-Lewis, John Le Mesurier (Sergeant Wilson in Dad's Army), Alan Turing

(Enigma code breaker), Lord David Sheppard, Sir Christopher Chataway, Nigel Dempster, Sir David Spedding (former head of MI6), Sir Alastair Pilkington (glass) – not to mention womanising landowner Brian Aldridge from the Archers.

Entrance: Some 115 boys enter at 13 via CE, scholarship exam or school's own papers. Two years before proposed entry boys visit the school for a working day. Deposit required 18 months before entry. About 15 join at sixth form; five A-Cs required at GCSE, with a minimum of B grades for the subjects being studied at A level. Sherborne boys have been asked to leave after GCSE when they've not made the grade. Currently booking five years ahead, full three years ahead. An unusually informative prospectus, worth a read.

Exit: Highest numbers to London, Birmingham, Bristol, Nottingham and Newcastle. Oxbridge entrances down over past few years which school says is the result of fewer pupils choosing to submit Oxbridge applications. Up to 50 per cent of boys opting for gap years.

Money Matters: Sherborne Foundation, set up in 1998 as a 'permanent fund-raising vehicle', seems to be doing the trick. OBs coughing up large donations including through assemblages of overseas OBs e.g. American Friends of Sherborne. Scholarship programme has been overhauled: a variety available at 13 (academic, music, art, DT, sport), fewer at 16 (academic, music and sport only), but all give a maximum of 25 per cent off fees, often quite a bit less.

Remarks: Strong, traditional public school in delightful setting, working hand in hand with neighbouring girls' school. Excels at producing confident, well-rounded young men. An invigorating, intellectually sound and multi-faceted environment but not always gentle – though school says 'always fair'. New head, new direction?

Shiplake College

Shiplake Court, Shiplake, Henley-on-Thames, Oxfordshire, RG9 4BW

• Pupils: 345 pupils, mostly boys (30 girls in sixth form). 225 boarders • Ages: 11-18 • Size of sixth form: 105 • C of E • Fees: Day £13,260-£16,536; Boarding £24,525 pa • Independent

Tel: 0118 940 2455
Fax: 0118 940 5204
Email: info@shiplake.org.uk
Website: www.shiplake.org.uk

Ester Pastmore
lorna.

Head: Since 2004, Mr Gregg Davies BSc Cert Mgmt (mid forties). Mr Davies studied physiology, taught at Haberdashers' Askes, then moved to Fettes as head of careers, became deputy head and finally head of the prep. Wife, Alison, has a beautiful Scots lilt and teaches in the Learning Development Department. They have a daughter at a local independent girls' school. Mr Davies who, despite his name is a patriotic Scot, greeted us sporting spectacular trousers in St David's tartan (vivid green and crimson, since you ask) in recognition of the trouncing his rugby team had given England the day before. He is ebullient, humorous, clearly on excellent terms with staff and pupils but the banter and bounce rapidly gave way during our post-tour conversation to earnest communication of the profound commitment he feels for his charges and for the unique ethos of Shiplake. 'I love teaching,' he confesses, ' I know every boy and I still tutor.' Not the suavest, not the glibbest head we have encountered, and he doesn't go down well with everyone, but you feel damn sure he'll pull out every stop to give your child the best schooldays he can.

Academic matters: 'We're academically non-selective,' explains head, 'but we select those pupils who we feel will benefit from being at Shiplake – that's our ethos. But it doesn't mean we can't do really well by the academics.' Wonderfully small classes. Each of the first three years divided into four sets for different subjects. Sets one and four are the smallest so that the brightest are seriously stretched and slowest are seriously supported. Learning is almost a subject in its own right here and school publishes enlightened and illuminating booklet full of practical common sense and acknowledging, for example, that 'we all learn in different ways'. School uses a range of tested, practical ways of supporting individuals and their own learning styles – reviewing, revision, reinforcement etc.

Just under fifty per cent of pupils perceived to have some sort of learning difficulty – so that means that the majority hasn't! Mild dyslexia, as ever, the most common but school takes much else in its stride including ADD/ADHD but not including Asperger's. Wise and wonderful learning development team demonstrates a commitment to the all-round welfare of their pupils that is rare and accounts, in part, for the loyalty pupils feel for the school. Hard to fall through the net here as monitoring is built into all stages and aspects of life though reports that, somehow, a very few still do. Learning development sensibly timetabled against langs and is given to those who need it individually or in small groups. Other support given flexibly, sensitively and as needed, without withdrawing from sports or activities. Gifted and Talented programmes also supported. School couldn't accommodate severe physical disabilities and no statemented children at time of our visit but they have had them before and would again. EAL support given one-to-one where necessary.

Exam results not on a par with premier league but exemplary in value-added terms especially between GCSE and A level. At A level, 73 per cent A–C pass rate. BTEC business offers an opportunity for a modular, hands-on, vocational course, assessed 100 per cent by coursework and practical activity – no exams! One budding entrepreneur importing raw materials from China. Nine GCSEs the maximum here which allows more time for the basics – English, maths, sciences – than elsewhere. Who needs 11 GCSEs anyway?

ICT coming along – much of the school is now wireless. Somewhat worryingly, there is no main library though individual subject areas have their own stocks. Plans to turn the Great Hall into a resource centre when the new dining hall is built. In the meantime the Great Hall is used for supervised study for senior pupils during the day. Increasingly, research and study done using the internet but the lack of a library – especially for the pupils with academic inclinations and aspirations – does seem extraordinary despite the wonders of Google.

Games, Options, the Arts: Sport is big here. Not rolling acres but plenty of pitches and courts including three with Astroturf, a good gym and sports hall, though this no longer top of the range, a smallish outdoor pool (a good indoor one on everyone's letter to Santa). Enthusiastic D of E. CCF 'it's great fun', we were told, and, above all, a wonderful bend in the river below school's terrace and grassy slope with boat house and island for adventure/rafting/camping exercises. We longed for our wellies and rowlocks! Rugby main winter game, hockey and rowing later in the year. Girls play netball, hockey and tennis. Visiting dance and aerobics teacher. Lots else available and intense house competition in many sports. Good sports tours abroad. Lucky cricketers went to Barbados early in 2006, hockey players late in 2006. Overseas rowing tour to California in 2008 and rugby tour to South Africa in 2009.

DT popular and proficient music. Good range of work in many media. Workshops for metal and woodwork looked enticing. Lovely studio theatre in old tithe barn scented with woody smells. Performing encouraged and not just for budding professionals. One film star and one stage star on the books in 2006. Music dept annexe housed in old water tower and includes a rock music studio and a recording studio. Various ensembles. Lots of picturesque outdoor productions including a prestigious invitation to perform at the Oxford 'Alice' festival, held in the Oxford University Botanical Gardens in 2009.

Background and Atmosphere: Shiplake Court, an attractive red-brick house overlooking the Thames five minutes from Henley, was built in 1895 as a family home and farm. Not grand, it has some highly attractive features, notably the gothic Great Hall currently used as a very upmarket dining room. Much used by film companies for location work – you may spot it in repeats of *Midsomer Murders* etc. Various adapted old farm buildings dot the site along with attractive and sensitively incorporated newer buildings – boarding houses and subject blocks – and, though the main area is not crowded, one no longer has the sense of limitless space into which the school could grow. All the buildings here are on a comfortable, domestic and human scale. Lots of staff live on site and the odd play space in a house master's garden with slides and swing add to this. Housemasters have partners/spouses and children also contributing to the family feel.

The allocation of houses based on whether you are to be a full or weekly boarder or day pupil. Much flexibility built into the boarding system – helpful, of course, to all. Since 2006, boarding for sixth form girls, and much interest in the few places. No plans for further moves to co-ed – largely for reasons of space. Visiting potential pupils want to come on account of the friendliness they find here – this felt equally by girls and boys.

Pupils like the food and there is choice, fruit and salad on offer along with careful meeting of dietary needs. Healthy eating has a major emphasis within the school – perhaps less of the heavy duty carbo diet than hitherto.

Pastoral Care and Discipline: Several layers of pastoral care and the head of pupil development oversees the lot and steps in to deal with anything academic or otherwise if needed. Everyone has a tutor and housemaster, houses have day matrons and there is always someone to go to – including older pupils who have much-prized positions of responsibility. The school chaplain plays a central role and the school has a strong Christian tradition. Gorgeous twelfth century parish church is onsite and shared with the local community. Boarding accommodation varies – some younger boys in rooms of up to five, all older pupils in singles with basins. Nothing glitzy here but proper sized beds and everything functional rather than posh. Rooms reassuringly untidy. Good provision of games rooms, kitchens, common rooms etc.

A bullying incident had happened over the weekend before our visit and had been robustly dealt with – suspensions of various durations. Some unease still palpable and some acknowledged problems still around – we still hear of disturbing incidents and look forward to a longer period when no such reports reach us. Good to learn from pupils how quickly overseas pupils fit in – not so everywhere. Most popular member of school? – the Davies's bearded collie, Darwinnie the Pooh.

Pupils and Parents: Majority from local preps and primaries and south London. Few Services children, fewer yet from overseas and those are from all over. Not a smart or fashionable school though no obvious reason why not. Notable former pupils (aka Old Vikings for most implausible reasons) include Sydney gold medallist Ben Hunt-Davies; Entrepreneur of the Year – Soho House owner Nick Jones – and Starbucks UK CEO Phil Broad.

Entrance: For entry into Year 7 or Year 9 boys visit the school for a taster day. There are now short tests in English and maths 'designed to give the school additional information on pupils, not as a pass/fail exercise' and participation in discussion groups and outdoor activities. Prospective pupils are interviewed during the taster day by the head or deputy head and a housemaster. Entry to sixth form for incomers requires 5+ GCSEs with English and maths at, at least, C grades 'though we will always make exceptions' for those they feel will fit in. 'We will let our own boys stay on if we can find something useful and enjoyable for them to do.'

Exit: Around eighty per cent to degree courses, largely of the newer types in the newer places, but a few more to trad academics each year including Cambridge. A few to vocational further education courses and the rest into interesting gap year activities or employment. Clear emphasis on real work in the real world.

Money Matters: Art, music and sports scholarships; however money is small and schols' main worth is the prestige they bring. Sixth form schols awarded on test results on two subjects to be studied at A level and general aptitude test. Means-tested bursaries awarded at the school's discretion and school digs into its small pot to help existing pupils with short-term financial problems.

Remarks: Most frequent word heard here is 'confidence'. 'We are a small school,' says head, 'good for those who would fail to cope or not play a leading role in a bigger place. Here they emerge as leaders – everyone has the opportunity to flourish.' 'It's given me so much confidence,' we were told, repeatedly. 'I love it here.'

Shrewsbury High School

Linked to Shrewsbury High Prep School in the Junior section

32 Town Walls, Shrewsbury, Shropshire, SY1 1TN

• Pupils: 685 girls, 80 boys • Ages: 2-18 • Size of sixth form: 125
• Non-denominational • Fees: Senior £9,627 pa • Independent

Tel: 01743 494 000
Fax: 01743 494 039
Email: enquiries@shr.gdst.net
Website: www.shrewsburyhigh.gdst.net

Head: Since 2000, Mrs Marilyn L R Cass BA MA (in education management) (fiftyish). Educated at Royal School, Bath. Six years in WRAC – recruitment, PR, intelligence officer. Travelled all over world with husband, a former naval officer, who now works for charity. Two sons, twenties. Did her degree at Exeter, after children arrived, and went into teaching. Previously deputy head at Redland High, Bristol. After ten years in post says she could be good for another ten! Unstuffy, articulate, energetic, enthusiastic, no-nonsense and an excellent communicator. Prefers to enthuse and motivate rather than drive, but has strong expectation of hard work and good behaviour. Expects to know her pupils well and does a small amount of teaching. With her husband, takes the annual ski trip to the Alps – both are keen skiers and are qualified instructors. Girls say that she has 'sharpened up and modernised the school, with a new uniform, a wider curriculum which includes psychology.' It is now more formal and structured but also more flexible and broadening.

Academic matters: Robustly academic, top level, but with three-form entry the senior department aims for a broad intake, with lots of middle of the road girls. Takes great pride both in its impressive academic results where four out of five are expected to gain A*/A (GCSE) or A/B (A level), and in the number of pupils placed at popular universities, but staff are also genuinely concerned for the under-performers, who are supported sympathetically. A small number of dyslexic children – 30 with Individual Educational Plans – who are helped to cope with normal classroom life and the school will 'see them through'.

The academic routine is lively and stimulating and the result is interested, excited children all striving to fulfil their potential. Girls report 'unpressurised but as academic as you might want it'. 'Challenging at the top end but does well with the less able.' 'Lots of after school help from the teachers.' 'Doesn't worry about league tables.' 'Brilliant teaching atmosphere.' French, German and Spanish available. Superb IT facilities, and music and art and particularly drama (super drama studio) are clearly strengths. On the value-added side, the ALIS assessment suggests that it is up a full grade from GCSE to A level. Class sizes can rise to 26 but the average is below this. A level forms average 14. So, who wouldn't fit in? 'Someone who wasn't enthusiastic about learning.'

Games, Options, the Arts: Space for sports has improved with the recent development of the prep, with thirteen acres of grounds. The GDST has invested in a new gym and classroom block at the prep, opened in 2008, enabling more activities to take place after school. While it could not really be described as a 'gamesy' school, more sport is planned for the sixth form and they do have up to 30 county players in a variety of sports. Also holds its own with the best at tennis. Superb sports complex, the Kingsland Centre, opened at the senior department in 2005. Uses fine facilities at Shrewsbury School: Astroturf, rowing, swimming pool.

Background and Atmosphere: A GDST school, it was opened in 1885 in much older premises along the old town walls, with grounds running down to the river Severn. The buildings are a pleasing mixture of old and new, largely concentrated within one site, but with a sixth form centre and music school on other parts of the campus. The head has a strong vision for the school and the Cass effect is visible nearly everywhere. It is losing its hitherto rather institutional feel, with brand-new labs and lots of cheerful paint, and there is a brand-new library and resource centre, though some of the classrooms and displays await attention. Two new classrooms have been incorporated in the new sports complex, the Kingsland Centre. The school is joined by the Kingsland Bridge to nearby Shrewsbury School, across which there is much to-ing and fro-ing, and also the pre-prep just a few minutes' walk away. In 2007 Shrewsbury High School acquired Kingsland Grange Prep, close to the other two sites. A new teaching block on this site was completed in September 2008, and the prep offers single-sex classes for boys and girls across the core curriculum.

Staff, of whom several have been there ten years plus with no sign of staleness, include quite a few twenty- and thirty-somethings to take the culture of the school forward. All like working there. Clearly a good working environment with inspiring and enthusiastic management.

Pastoral Care and Discipline: Not only do all pupils have form tutors but, in the GCSE years, they are also individually mentored by other teaching staff. In addition, there are pupil mentors, drawn from the sixth form, who are attached to every form group. Strong house system right through from pre-prep to sixth form. The head stresses importance of communication with parents and talking through problems which are handled firmly but sympathetically. She says, 'Children need to expect anything in life and to cope – to persist and not give up: a culture of achievement.'

Pupils and Parents: Pupils are confident, outgoing, assured, friendly, cheerful, with a strong sense of community and greatly supportive of each other. A wide social mix, with children drawn from the county set, professional classes, business and farming and new industries in Telford. It is a very popular option for staff at nearby Shrewsbury School and the headmaster's two daughters attended. Girls come from wide radius – Ludlow, Telford, Market Drayton, Bridgnorth, Wolverhampton and Whitchurch.

Entrance: Its popularity locally ensures a good stream of able girls in the senior department and it can afford to be selective, though projected increases in numbers give a chance for the not-so-academic. Largely fed from its own prep (a certain amount of filtering here). The rest of the intake at Year 11 comes from other prep schools and some thirty odd state schools.

Exit: The sixth form is thriving, though some leave at 16 – to sixth form college and co-ed and girls' boarding schools. All go on to some form of higher education at 18 and the large majority ends up at university, with at least half a dozen going to Oxbridge. Boys at the prep take Common Entrance at 13 and go on to a variety of senior schools including Shrewsbury School, and each year a number of boys gain scholarships there.

Money Matters: Fees – extremely modest and wonderful value and, unlike most except other GDST schools, include almost everything (exam fees, personal insurance, external careers advice etc). Bursaries available.

Remarks: A strong academic school, but with plenty of time and space for the ordinary mortal as long as they are enthusiastic about learning. Inspirational head doing great things.

Shrewsbury School

The Schools, Shrewsbury, Shropshire, SY3 7BA

- Pupils: 675 boys; 545 boarding, 130 day. 70 girls in sixth form
- Ages: 13-18 • Size of sixth form: 285, including 70 girls • C of E
- Fees: Boarding £27,300; Day £19,125 pa • Independent

Tel: 01743 280 552
Fax: 01743 351 009
Email: registrar@shrewsbury.org.uk
Website: www.shrewsbury.org.uk

Headmaster: Since 2010, Mr Mark Turner MA PGCE (forties). Educated at Rossall School (qv) where he was head boy, followed by Mansfield College, Oxford where he read geography. Served with the Royal Artillery for four years before completing a PGCE at Cambridge. This is his third headship after Kelly College and Abingdon School and yet he is still in his forties! Married to Elizabeth who is a teacher of religious studies. Two sons.

Academic matters: To spend time here and talk to teachers is to be aware of a depth of commitment which far supersedes systems designed for monitoring and tracking and recording – though they have those too, of course. The teachers have a football team, The Ramblers, which plays boys' teams. It's just one example of how developed their relationships with their pupils are. They share a lot of their lives with each other and a lot of fun. They know each other very well; it's this that makes the difference. Yes, they are very bright pupils they teach but they're not the brightest in the land, not all of them. These latter they make the best of. As to the brightest, the sky's the limit because these teachers are bright in their own right so, shortly after hearing a girl singing Puccini exquisitely we were not a bit surprised to bump into a sixth former playing rather good clarinet who, together with fellow members of the Astronomy Society, has just won a contest to design an experiment which will fly in a British-built satellite. Sums it up. Results show excellent teaching in all subjects, with typical boys' school strengths in maths and the sciences tempered with popular English, RS and languages (French, German and Spanish but including non-examined Russian, Mandarin and Arabic) and a very strong showing in art. Business studies and classical civilisation show good results for academic and less academic boys alike. A multitude of superb trips and visits, cultural, sporting and academic, at home and abroad, are also on the menu.

Study resources are superb – check out the library on their website. There's also an ancient library full of all manner of delectable incunabula. Typical of the school, they bought Principia in its first edition.

There's learning support for those who need it, mostly mild SENs (dyslexia, dyspraxia et al; OK too for the mild wild (ADHD, Asperger's)), free for the first year. About 15/20 per cent of school has some form of help, one-to-one and regular drop-in clinics. No big deal. Moderate OK for disabled, new house wheelchair friendly, but still stairs. 'The odd disabled child not a problem,' can cope with visually and hearing impaired, with assistants if necessary. SENCo plus six fully trained staff plus one dedicated EFL teacher.

Games, Options, the Arts: Truly terrific sport on all fronts, rowing, football and cricket especially. Rowers are coached by a man from Harvard; cricketers have an indoor school in which the county pros come and train. All ability and enthusiasm levels catered for; if you're less than top-notch there's always the Ramblers to play against.

Music is superb, brilliantly led, in its purpose built, Prince of Wales approved music school and its acoustically perfect performance space. Annual performances in St John's, Smith Square and the Edinburgh Fringe. Annual summer term rock concert under canvas followed by classical fare – 'One day it's Glastonbury, the next, Glyndebourne'. Drama similarly strong. Links, musical, too, with Moreton Hall, Shrewsbury High and Shrewsbury Sixth Form College. Prestigious lecture programme.

Art spectacular, backed up by trips to everywhere including Italy and USA. Photography notably popular.

Proximity to Wales inspires all manner of outward bound activities, plus D of E. Strong community links with Shrewsbury House, a youth club in Liverpool. This school goes flat out at weekends.

Background and Atmosphere: Founded in 1552 by Edward VI, the school throve, faltered, then revived in 1882 when it moved across the river into the old workhouse-cum-lunatic asylum. What you see today is the original workhouse poshed up a bit. It's a stunning setting looking out across the Severn, a proper Huck Finn sort of river, over to the town, which pronounces itself differently. Shroo, they say, not Shro. It's the sort of thing that could be the stuff of town-gown bickering but, as Shro-speakers point out, the only people in the country who say Shroo are those who live in it. School buildings, well-made Edwardian buildings, mostly, gird the playing fields which act, someone suggested, like a village green. It's the biggest village green you ever saw at 100 acres but, d'you know, there's truth in the observation, you can stand and watch the school go by, beaks on bikes and all. Heartstealing stuff.

It's the sort of place that has its own slang, of course, a slang as rich as the street slang in some of our more no-go 'ends'. Top Schools, they call homework; brushers, they call teachers, though one of them bristled when we put this to him; he said that had died out. A great deal of recreational ping-pong is played. For all that, pupils mix easily with the world outside, they're a markedly normal lot. The advent of girls in the sixth form has raised smiles, not eyebrows.

Pastoral Care and Discipline: It's the customary house system here. Choose your housemaster. 82 per cent of pupils board, and there's none of yer flexi here, or weekly, for that matter, so quality of care is of crucial importance. The calibre of housemasters is high, their commitment bordering on humbling. Six hours' sleep a night is what they reckon to get by on, that's what they're like. All teachers play a pastoral role so there's plenty of backup. Relationships between older and younger pupils observably relaxed and friendly. Scrummy new girls' boarding house.

Pupils and Parents: Though this is one of the great, ancient public schools, Shrewsbury pupils have none of the eyewatering conceit of some of their ancient public school counterparts. There's a cheerful, engaging unaffectedness about them, a very notable agreeableness – as an ex-state school sixth form entrant testified. There's a healthy tradition of merrymaking irreverence which stems from Ingrams, Rushton and Foot, and which finds expression in mischievous rags, *The Public Nose* and, latterly, *The Falopian.* It says a great deal about the confidence of the regime that these are not forced underground, and it says as much about the pupils that their iconoclasm is tempered by so much affection for those who have dominion over them.

Pupils come here from all corners of the island. It's a fast road from the motorway.

Entrance: By CE at 13. If your boy's not up to it they'll tell you in good time. At 16+ according to GCSE results plus special school entrance exam. Girls, boarding and day, at 16+. Very prepared to consider the less academic if they've other strengths. Not quite so academically selective as some of the other big beasts, but the top end is as good as it gets. Applications handled by the registrar, the wholly delightful Mr Robin Case. You'll find the website excellent and invaluable. The prospectus eschews the narcissism of most and they'll send it to you with a booklet describing some of their most famous former pupils. It's a most impressive collection.

Exit: University. Around 20 a year to Oxbridge.

Money Matters: The school's grant making policy is described in great and complicated detail on its website. Broadly, there's lots available but most is either tied up in bequests with specific rules or available as means-tested bursaries – and it is expected that even the 'extended family' will have been tapped first: visiting the fees of the sons upon the fathers unto the third and fourth generation.

Remarks: What you get here is a unique blend of wholeheartedness, humanity and down to earth decency, a place where hard work and fun are indistinguishable. If you like what you see, look no further. You've found it.

Sibford School

Linked to Sibford Junior School in the Junior section

Sibford Ferris, Banbury, Oxfordshire, OX15 5QL

• Pupils: 410 boys and girls; 60 board, the rest day • Ages: 4-18 • Size of sixth form: 75 • Quaker • Fees: Boarding £20,079-£21,990; Day £7,050-£11,319 pa • Independent

Tel: 01295 781 200
Fax: 01295 781 204
Email: admissions@sibfordschool.co.uk
Website: http://www.sibford.oxon.sch.uk

Head: Since 2004, Michael Goodwin BA PGCE. Educated at Bury Grammar School, followed by University of Nottingham, where he read history. Vastly experienced – taught in state system for more than 20 years and previously head of Sheringham High School, Norfolk. Married to Veronika, who lectures in Spanish at Oxford and Cherwell Valley College, down the road from Sibford. They have four children – the youngest is a pupil at Sibford. Energetic, approachable and seems unfazed by most things, even the sudden power cut on the day of our visit. Drawn to Sibford because of its Quaker ethos – he and his family became Quakers several years ago. 'I was bowled over by Sibford when I came to look round,' he says. 'There's something very special about the atmosphere here.' Throws himself into everything with gusto, whether it's kneeling on the floor to inspect proofs of the new prospectus or guiding a couple of new juniors to the lunch queue.

Academic matters: Known as a 'gentle, nurturing school,' Sibford prides itself on letting individual talents flourish – rather than simply treating children as statistics. Wide range of abilities but head exasperated by what he calls 'myth' that the school isn't academic – 'if you look at our exam results, we do very well,' he declares. School is by no means an academic hothouse but gets respectable results and good value-added scores. In 2009 it beat its own record with 95 per cent of pupils gaining at least five A*- C grades. At A level the school recorded a 100 per cent pass rate with 42 per cent A/B grades. Most pupils take English lang (and usually lit), maths, double science and religious studies at GCSE, then choose at least another four subjects from a raft of options including French, Spanish, history, geography, business studies, art, PE etc. Good choice of subjects at AS and A2, with media studies, music technology, ICT and textiles currently in vogue. School also offers BTec qualification in countryside and environment and countryside management.

Committed staff – average age 45 and half have taught at school for more than ten years. Class sizes average 12–15 up to GCSE and are often as tiny as four or five in the sixth form.

Sibford is well-known for its strong SEN department, though no more than a third of its children need additional help – for dyslexia, dyspraxia, mild Asperger's, maths difficulties etc. School makes it quite clear from the outset that youngsters must be able to cope in a mainstream environment, but there's lots of help going for those who need it. SEN pupils offered small group classes (up to five sessions a week), either before or during the school day. Touch-typing classes and voice recognition software also available in dyslexia department. Well-equipped IT room, computers in most classrooms and many pupils use laptops.

Games, Options, the Arts: All traditional games – rugby, football, cricket, hockey, netball, rounders etc – played, with sport compulsory for all up till sixth form. Massive gym, two squash courts, weights room, dance studio and ultra-swish 25-metre swimming pool (very popular with locals too).

Music very impressive. Nearly half the school plays an instrument (many play more than one) and there are recitals, concerts, festivals galore. Art and DT are stunning and shown off to splendid effect in school's own art gallery. School has resident potter, Richard Phethean, who teaches all age groups.

Background and Atmosphere: Sibford was founded as a co-ed boarding school by the Quakers in 1842. Originally housed in splendid Cotswold stone manor house, it expanded into a hotchpotch of buildings over the road (known as 'The Hill') in the 1930s. The manor was sold to developers several years ago and the proceeds have been astutely ploughed back into state-of-the-art music and art blocks. Three boarding houses (one for boys, one for girls, plus mixed sixth-form house). Boarding facilities a little on the spartan side but gradually being smartened up. Junior department is based in its own modern self-contained building within the main campus. New sixth form study centre opened in September 2008.

School encourages pupils to make the most of its extensive 50-acre grounds. Guided by enterprising head of environmental science and horticulture, youngsters have created a stunning three-acre garden on a windy south-facing hill overlooking lush rolling countryside. Everything grown here is organic and surplus fruit, vegetables and flowers are sold to appreciative visitors and staff on open days. There's an orchard, woodland, pond and even picnic benches where students can write up their horticulture notes. All Year 7 children get to plant their own trees – oak, lime, beech, Scots pine and rowan – soon after they arrive in the senior school.

Pastoral Care and Discipline: Sibford is one of only seven Quaker schools in England and has a very strong Quaker ethos, with firm emphasis on self-discipline and treating others with courtesy and respect. Whole school meeting for worship twice a week – ten minutes of silence plus opportunities for children and staff to stand up and share thoughts or good news. Pastoral care good, with teams of tutors who see pupils twice a day. House system and selected sixth formers, including head boy and head girl, sit on student management team.

Bullying rare and firm rules on alcohol, smoking and drugs. Head is vehemently anti-smoking and took the radical decision to allow outdoor 'smoking compound' outside school hours for boarders aged 16 and above to help phase out smoking. 'It might look like a liberal policy,' says head, 'but it's actually the opposite of that.' The campus is now smoke free.

Pupils and Parents: An eclectic bunch. Fewer boarders than before but weekly and flexi-boarding available too. Small tranche from overseas (including China, Hong Kong, Japan, Thailand, Germany, Russia and Iran) but numbers capped at 10 per cent. Most pupils come daily, by school bus or car, and from as far afield as Warwick and Oxford. A handful are from Quaker families but most not. Pupils charmingly self-confident, but not arrogant – a well-mannered, yet sparky lot, unafraid to offer ideas, make suggestions and ask questions. On our tour of the school a chirpy Year 7 girl flummoxed the head by suddenly inquiring which school house he belonged to.

Parents come from wide range of backgrounds and income brackets. Many very involved in school. 'They are very keen on academic results but not at the expense of their children's mental well-being,' says head. He has introduced a weekly 'surgery' for parents who want to see him as well as half-termly parent forums – these discuss everything from sex education to the complexities of modern maths! Notable old pupils include the late Paul Eddington, Guy Ritchie and Charlie Boorman.

Entrance: 'We are looking, above all, for children who want to be here,' says head. 'We don't have a little box we are trying to squeeze them into.' Prospective pupils sit literacy, numeracy and non-verbal reasoning tests, plus interview and an ed psych's report where appropriate. Youngsters entering sixth form from outside (around 12 or so a year) usually need five GCSEs at grade C or above.

Exit: Most junior pupils go through to the senior school. Up to 25 leave after GCSE, mostly for further education colleges, independent schools offering different subjects at A level, apprenticeships or training. Nearly 80 per cent of sixth-form leavers go on to higher or further education – many to their first-choice destination.

Money Matters: Head has hired ex-Thames Valley Police business manager to oversee financial side. Not a rich school by any means but offers a number of academic, music and art scholarships, plus means tested bursaries to both Quaker and non-Quaker families. Sound financial management means the school is currently embarking on new building programme.

Remarks: Mainstream school that caters for wide range of abilities and learning styles. Great for raising self-esteem, spotting talents that might have been missed elsewhere and getting the best out of pupils in nurturing and friendly surroundings.

Sidcot School

Linked to Sidcot Junior School (The Hall) in the Junior section

Oakridge Lane, Winscombe, BS25 1PD

• Pupils: 525 • Ages: 3-18 • Size of sixth form: 155 • Quaker • Fees: Day £5,850-£13,725; Boarding £21,300-£22,800 pa. • Independent

Tel: 01934 843 102
Fax: 01934 844 181
Email: marketing@sidcot.org.uk
Website: www.sidcot.org.uk

Head: Since 2001, Mr John Walmsley BSc PGCE (early fifties). Educated at a comprehensive in East Yorkshire before reading geology at Leeds then PGCE at Lancaster. Began career at nearby Churchill School in North Somerset teaching geology and ICT for ten years, then two years at Greengates School in Mexico and a further eight years on career ladder (including three years as assistant head at Simon Langton Girls' Grammar in Canterbury) before joining Sidcot in 1998 as academic deputy.

Popular appointment with staff – approachable, straightforward and caring; hugely respected by pupils; parents think he's 'great' and say 'his heart is completely in the school' though some feel he could be more proactive. Believes passionately in what Sidcot represents – father was a Quaker and he is an 'Attender'. Married to ex-teacher, now stonemason and carver, Barbara, and they have six children – four at Sidcot junior and senior schools, plus two elder daughters who now work in Bath. Enjoys Octopush, scuba diving, cinema, cooking, music. Sees staff-pupil relationships which place everyone 'on the same side' at heart of Sidcot's uniqueness. Believes in 'taking the time to listen and explain.' Not your self-important kind of head; pupils feel 'able to discuss anything with him'.

Academic matters: Traditionally holistic but academic results have improved greatly in recent years – Maths and science strong with 92 per cent A/B at maths A level. Good Schools Guide Award for the best further mathematics A level results for boys in the country. School has made strong play for overseas students whose work ethic has had positive influence overall. Staff:pupil ratio of 1:7 in sixth form and 1:15 lower down. Head doesn't like AS exams at end of lower sixth and has offered IB ('breadth with depth') alternative since 2007, alongside A levels. 2009 IB entries gained an average of 32 points, two points above the national average and equivalent to three grade As and a B at A Level. 50 per cent of IB students gained the equivalent of five A-Levels, four at grade A and one at grade C or above. GCSE results have also improved with 96 per cent 5+ A* to C which, given significant number of dyslexic pupils, suggests any pupil can fulfil his or her potential here. SATs have also gone – head wants pupils to 'like thinking about things' and prefers them to be 'happy and creative' away from the constant exam treadmill. Pupils with special needs are well catered for by specialist staff. Dyslexics especially well supported. Not unusual for dyslexics to get top GCSE grades.

Light, airy classrooms with well equipped practical areas; lots of ICT, interactive whiteboards with LCD projectors etc but not techno crazy. Some dedicated and charismatic teaching. Seemed appropriate that RS group we saw was learning about Gandhi. Pupils enthused about DT which also covers product design (quite a few choose this at uni having enjoyed it here), fashion, textiles and food. Head working hard to persuade more day pupils to stay for sixth rather than get a free 16+ education nearby. GCSE choices include Latin; able mathematicians add statistics. New arrangement for science taken at end of Year 10 with additional science a year later. Boys do as well as girls at GCSE here – attributed to lack of peer pressure problems. Day pupils can stay for supervised early prep (5 to 6pm) but no Saturday lessons.

Academic English School accommodates about 20 overseas entrants in refurbished and discrete area of school with fast track and one year induction programmes. IGCSE, plus three levels of Cambridge English and mother tongue exams with visiting Chinese teacher to support A level candidates. ICT and GCSE subjects also offered; lots of cultural visits and full use of Sidcot facilities though some resistance towards early and full social integration say indigenous sixth formers.

Games, Options, the Arts: Quaker emphasis on involvement before competition or compulsion; sport is 'not a vigorous and pump thing' in the sixth form according to some students. However, there are three houses for internal competition and school produces winning teams in traditional sports plus representation at all levels. Cullis Centre (named after OB donor) boasts large sports hall plus awesome 25 metre swimming pool now properly managed by sports graduate to give pupils plenty of access outside lesson time. Sixth formers were eyeing squash court as a possible disco venue when we visited. Sports choices include lively table-tennis tournaments, Octopush, canoeing, fencing, riding, dry slope skiing and golf. Three short tennis/netball courts close to school; 20 acres of playing fields (reached safely via bridge over A38) for hockey, rounders, rugby, football and cricket.

Huge range of mainly weekday activities caters for all tastes and interests from aerobics to pottery; chess to guitar construction. How many other schools make life drawing an 'open' activity from Year 7? 'Younger pupils can really get into the drawing once they get used to the idea,' commented a committed sixth form artist. Public speaking and UN club encourage pupils to engage with peace issues whilst environmental action group is also 'up for it' and plans to 'green' areas of the school. Lots of D of E to encourage self-motivation with community service, overnight expeditions on Quantocks etc. Cultural/educational trips; visits abroad include skiing and to USA; non-Quakers can join annual Quaker schools' pilgrimage (affectionately known as 'Foxtrot') to Pendle Hill in the Lake District.

New arts centre officially opened in 2009. Successful art department (check out their on-line gallery) is well resourced and includes animation and computer graphics as well as facilities for ceramics and sculpture, screen printing, painting and drawing. Lunchtime concerts for parents and locals feature choirs, jazz group and band. DJ academy run by a peripatetic has led to home grown, student run discos. Music technology will expand with new facilities and drama studio will no longer have to cope with acoustic nightmare of acting under a tin roof. Full orchestra and over one third of school play an instrument with many reaching diploma level.

School has own horses plus limited stabling for mainly boarders' horses; working livery arrangements; preparation for British Horse Society certificates; hacking in local countryside. Great for boarders who can't bear term-time separation or any who want to learn to ride.

Background and Atmosphere: Founded in 1699 by tolerant Quakers in West of England to spread a liberal educational ideology, but still not well known. Equality of sexes and critical enquiry valued from year dot and the 10 per cent of pupils with SEN issues have high self-esteem, know they can achieve and that they are valued. Meeting Hall used for daily assemblies and weekly 'meeting for worship' run by two sixth form 'elders', Sidcot's serene 150 acre location close to Cheddar Gorge is just off busy A38 and near Bristol airport. Onside parents commented, 'the Quaker atmosphere hit us immediately we entered,' but for most of us it would take a little longer, especially as there are few overt Quaker symbols. Smaller than most independent schools with no far flung boarding houses and its teaching accommodation all within close proximity. Parents have kept faith with school despite some upsetting media allegations regarding a teacher no longer on the staff.

Environmentally aware. Catering mantra is '25 per cent organic, 25 per cent locally produced and 50 per cent unprocessed,' but there wasn't a carrot or apple to be seen at the tuck shop. Superb, light dining area with great veggie options, salad and pasta bars; breakfast club free to early comers. Mounting pupil pressure for outside play areas likely to upset erstwhile 'peaceful' atmosphere of school's well-kept gardens. Inside, stunning library on two floors with stained glass cupola based on pupils' own designs. Well appointed sixth form centre with networked study spaces, careers and conference facilities. Corridors display pupils' art work well and also highlight contemporary issues.

Five sensitively run, if largely forgettable, boarding houses vary a lot in lay-out and accommodation. Personal expression extends to students choosing furnishings in common rooms and cooking own meals; local Chinese take-away predictably faring much better than its Italian predecessor. Generally alcohol free; health education an initial response to illicit smoking. Lesson-free weekends allow day leaves to Bristol giving plenty of freedom to boarders, but many stay on site. As you'd expect, lots of fund-raising through year for worthy causes with famine lunches etc.

Pastoral Care and Discipline: Pupils care for each other with uncommon empathy in this 'community of individuals'. Vertical grouping in boarding houses encourages everyone to mix easily and juniors are in and out of senior school during day. Strong sense of fairness and honouring individual differences; recognises a child with a prestigious talent may not be straight down the line, won't fit in neatly or think as majority do but will make own way with help, support and guidance. Believes some aspects of SpLDs are an advantage – help a child think outside the box. Won't write children off, use role models where they can, including parents. Bullying an anathema here. College of Teachers confers on important decisions. Twenty sixth formers called 'office holders' organise various events. Female pastoral deputy co-ordinates all aspects of discipline with horizontal year heads and houseparents in the front line. Usual mix of sanctions and rewards but you'd need to be beyond the pale to get expelled. Most problems sorted out with gentle rather than authoritarian response from staff.

Pupils and Parents: Only 10 per cent Quakers; most day pupils come from affluent local area for whom Sidcot is seen as socially preferable (at least to 16+) plus progeny of Bristol's more liberal illuminati who are transported to and from the city by coach; weekly boarders from M4/M5 corridor; international students currently represent 23 countries with strong oriental contingent. 'Could fill a second school with special needs children,' remarked one teacher, so school selects those 'who'll give something back'. One third board with over half from overseas (more in sixth). Quaker attitudes seem to rub off on those who stay into sixth; pupils described by teacher as 'predominantly justice seekers.' Pretty scatty lot (to judge from volume of lost property waiting to be claimed in sports centre) but it's 'safe to leave stuff lying around,' insisted pupils we met.

Smartly uniformed pupils up to sixteen in blue and white striped shirts, ties (for boys), neat hair etc, whilst sixth formers wear what they like within reason. Sixth formers dress smartly, however, for weekly meeting for worship, which mystifies Quaker old hands for whom it's not important.

Week's pow-wow for former pupils every Easter when pupils put on concerts/theatricals/art exhibitions. Old Scholars include Sir George Trevelyan, Robert Shackleton, George Palmer (Huntley & Palmer), historian Edmund Ashby, Justin Webb and some of the younger Dimbleby clan, Zoe Wanamaker, Tim Bevan, Deborah Warner (RSC director) et al.

Entrance: Automatic entry from junior school. Entrance test at nine and 13 can be taken at applicant's present school. Common Entrance a possible alternative to school's own entrance exam in February. An overnight taster day can be arranged. Entry to sixth form requires minimum six C grades at GCSE or equivalent. EAS students accepted at any time of the year. A genuinely mixed ability school but not usually for severe SEN cases, though everyone is given a fair chance. Handful of students have a range of special needs: exceptionally bright, gifted and talented, dyslexia, dyspraxia, dyscalculia, Asperger's, ADD, ADHD and physical disabilities (improved wheelchair access on cards). Looks at every single child, takes those who'll benefit from school and give a bit back; only has room for occasional child requiring a learning support assistant.

Exit: After GCSE some join local sixth forms or college in Bristol etc but majority stay. Geared to finding right course at right institution, however talented a student. Recently helped a very bright dyslexic student who wanted to study medicine find a course with a practical bias (a great comfort to those of us who'd rather be opened up by a surgeon with a steady hand and good eye than a whizz at spelling!). At 18, seventy per cent proceed to wide range of universities and degree courses. Significant number take a gap year. Twenty per cent to art foundation/art colleges; some to drama colleges; usually one or two to Royal Academy of Music; a couple to Oxbridge.

Money Matters: Variable boarding fees hit non-EU students harder so Russians pay more than Bulgarians or Poles. Day fee higher than QEH and Bristol Grammar but compares favourably with other independents in area. Means tested bursary support is available and non-financial scholoarships are awarded in accademic and non-academic subjects. With six other Quaker schools in UK offers up to 100 per cent remission of fees for Quaker families.

Remarks: A school which serves a wide constituency both locally and internationally; draws strength from its Quaker foundation and generally walks its talk. Singularity of style lays it open to misinterpretation but pupils become its best ambassadors. A rare breed of school which values individual worth above corporate success.

Sir John Cass Foundation and Redcoat Church of England Secondary School

Stepney Way, London, E1 0RH

• Pupils: 1500 girls and boys • Ages: 11-19 • Size of sixth form: 560
• C of E foundation • State

Tel: 02077 906 712
Fax: 02077 900 499
Email: sirjohncass@hotmail.co.uk
Website: www.sjcr.net

Head: Since 1995, Mr Haydn Evans (fifties), who arrived in Stepney after deputy headships in Tonbridge and, briefly, at a large rural comprehensive in Bridgend. His then school-age children failed to settle in Wales and he returned happily to commute in from Kent to the headship of this inner-city church school. Praised as a strong, determined, strategic thinker and very successful head ('exemplary,' said Ofsted), he has overseen the opening of the sixth form and the upward trajectory of the whole school, transforming it from an under-subscribed comprehensive with exam results on the minimal side to one with over 1,200 applicants for 180 places in 2010. For September 2011 the school will have increased capacity with extensions to buildings through the Building Schools for the Future programme increasing the accommodation considerably.

A hands-on head, he teaches chemistry to A level and is frequently out and about in the school with other senior managers, helping to police the comings and goings between lessons as 1,600 pupils move round a school built for 800. 'We act as an unobtrusive presence – we rarely have to say or do anything.'

Academic matters: Consistently near the top of the value-added tables and has three times been ranked the most improved school in the country. Most pupils come in with lower than average achievement but around 80 per cent get at least five A* – C grades at GCSE or equivalent. This falls to about half if you include maths and English, unsurprisingly since English is a second language for around 80 per cent of the pupils. They come from a huge range of primaries and many have difficult home lives. 'Our first focus is on behaviour, on creating a climate for learning. Then we engage them with exciting teaching.'

The latest Ofsted report, which rated the school 'outstanding', praised its very high expectations of all pupils. New Year 7s are tested and placed in sets for maths, English, science and RE. These are fluid and there's plenty of scope to move up as one's English improves or down should the maths start to prove tricky. There are vocational as well as academic courses at KS4, for example in science and IT. The school keeps a close eye on pupils' progress, targeting those who need extra help to ensure that everyone gets the grades they need to move on to the next stage. 'They have very high aspirations for my daughter,' said a parent. 'They push the children very hard to succeed.'

It is a specialist language college and everyone studies two languages for the first three years, from a choice of French, Spanish and Bengali, continuing at least one to GCSE. There is also a choice of 11 languages in twilight classes (for parents as well as pupils), and many pupils take a GCSE in their own native language before Year 11. Many go on French or Spanish exchanges. The school has links with one in rural Spain and children who had rarely left the East End of London have found themselves travelling to school by horse and cart.

It also has a business and enterprise specialism and good links with Canary Wharf and City firms, with some offering work placements, scholarships to cover university fees and jobs after graduation to talented students. Sixth form business studies students can have mentoring from business partners, visits and seminars, lectures and summer internships. One pupil recently spent the summer in America, having won a coveted place on a Student Leadership programme.

The large sixth form, with some 600 pupils, has its own new centre, including a library, IT suite, mixed and girls' only common rooms (the latter with pink net curtains) and a popular café. It offers a variety of vocational courses alongside A levels and GCSE retakes, and is piloting the new IT diploma, with business and finance and society, health and development diplomas to follow. Many students come in from elsewhere to join those moving up, and quite a few have relatively low qualifications. Some start with intermediate level courses then move up to higher levels en route to university. Science and maths A levels are particularly popular and successful, alongside psychology, RE and sociology.

About ten per cent of pupils have some kind of special need. 'We have an elaborate academic support team. The governors have decided to invest heavily in this and it is a very worthwhile investment.' Gifted and talented pupils are also identified for extra support. Learning mentors and assistants work through teachers and directly with pupils, helping to track their progress and ensure they know what they need to do to improve. There are regular extension and catch-up classes. Staff recruitment is not a problem, with over 60 applicants for a recent RE vacancy. 'We have a high profile and we attract high quality applicants.'

Games, Options, the Arts: Sports facilities include a swimming pool (everyone learns to swim by the end of their first term) and a sports hall with space for basketball, badminton, football and cricket. Football and basketball teams play enthusiastic and successful matches against other schools. Table tennis, boxing and fencing are also on the agenda. A level sports science students coach younger pupils. Girls and boys have separate PE and sports lessons, as well as separate entrances and playgrounds – an innovation that is very popular with pupils and parents.

Actors perform at the Mile End Theatre and the steel band has played at the Albert Hall. Guitar club and a gospel choir and many pupils have individual music lessons. Trips to operas and musicals. A school ski trip in the Easter holidays, D of E, ice skating, rock climbing and canoeing trips. Sixth formers organise societies, including Christian Union and Muslim Students' Society.

Background and Atmosphere: Formed in 1964 by the governing body of Red Coat School (established in 1714 for boys born within Mile End Old Town) and the governors of the Sir John Cass Foundation (a charity set up in 1710 by Sir John Cass for poor children in the East End of London). The school is owned by the Foundation, one of

London's oldest educational charities, and Founder's Day in St Botolph-without-Aldgate church is one of the highlights of the school year. Its present site, with its pleasant red-brick buildings, dates from 1965. It is right in the middle of the East End but in a deceptively rural-seeming setting with a city farm opposite, a park next door and the school church and its tranquil graveyard beyond.

The school has been refurbished to include up-to-date science labs and learning centres stocked with computers. These are open before and after school and on Saturday mornings, with learning mentors around to help. Many pupils have no computer at home, nor quiet space in which to do homework. The great hall with stage and balcony doubles as a lecture theatre and can accommodate the entire school for assemblies. 'These are important for setting the behaviour tone for the school.' Lower school pupils wear a traditional uniform including a blazer, which becomes more informal higher up the school. Honours boards line the reception area. Although this is a C of E school, the vast majority of pupils are Muslims and they have their own prayer room.

Pastoral Care and Discipline: An orderly atmosphere is central to the ethos of the school. 'Security and mutual respect are very high priority. First of all we make them feel secure and safe, then we start to cultivate respect for all. A feeder primary school may be less traditional than we are but we're confident that when they come here we'll get them into our ethos by the end of the first half term.' The atmosphere is indeed calm and orderly, with some exuberance in the corridors between lessons but quiet concentration in the classrooms. There are CCTV cameras throughout, which, say staff, discourage vandalism and add to students' sense of security. Staff check on the destinations of those wandering the corridors between lessons.

By all accounts very little racial tension and very few exclusions – only one in the whole of 2009–10. 'We do very occasionally have some challenging behaviour but it doesn't threaten the learning environment. We try hard not to exclude if we can possibly avoid it.' Two qualified counsellors on the staff. 'It's a very happy school,' said a parent, 'but the kids are expected to knuckle down and achieve.'

Pupils and Parents: About two thirds of the pupils are Bangladeshi, the rest from a variety of ethnic minorities, including many Somali refugees. Parents mostly very supportive of the school and its high expectations for their children. They join in maths workshops and twilight language classes and become involved in the numerous community projects. Pupils form strong peer groups. 'There's a very strong ethos of care for one another,' said a parent.

Entrance: Some 1,200 applicants for 180 places in 2010. Everyone is placed in one of four ability bands, assessed by the standard Tower Hamlets primary school test, with equal numbers of places offered from each band. This is a C of E school, so it does allocate a minority of places to committed Christians. Thirty-six places go to worshippers in a recognised Christian church, with looked-after children, social and medical needs, living in one of the listed parishes and then siblings in order of priority. The other 144 places have a similar priority order but 20 are offered to first-born children. Families in the area tend to be large and siblings would otherwise monopolise the intake. Distance from the school is the tie-break.

The sixth form is also highly over-subscribed, with over 1,000 applicants for 300 outside places. Most advanced level courses require five or more A*–C grades at GCSE including English and maths, with some higher stipulations e.g. an A in maths for maths or further maths A level. But those with lesser qualifications can take lower level courses, and the majority of pupils from Year 11 go through to the sixth form.

Exit: Those who leave after GCSEs – about 15 per cent of Year 11s – mostly go on to another sixth form or straight into a job. All Year 13 leavers for the past three years – and some of these may have spent several years in the sixth form improving their qualifications – have gone straight to university. For social and cultural reasons, the vast majority choose London universities, but some venture further afield. The first successful Oxbridge applicant started classics at Cambridge in 2008 and three had offers in 2009. 'I am confident that once they start coming back to tell our students about it we'll have more applicants.' Some students return to the school as teachers or learning mentors.

Remarks: A beacon of excellence in a deprived area of London, which takes in students with low levels of attainment and sends the majority off to university with commendable exam results. A strong head and committed staff insist on good behaviour, provide expert teaching and inspire high aspirations. 'It's gone from strength to strength,' said a parent. 'It's a great school.'

Sir Roger Manwood's School

Manwood Road, Sandwich, Kent, CT13 9JX

- Pupils: 915 boys and girls, mostly day but 55 board • Ages: 11-18
- Size of sixth form: 275 • Non-denominational, Christian tradition
- Fees: £8,190 pa • State

Tel: 01304 613 286
Fax: 01304 615 336
Email: head@srms.kent.sch.uk
Website: www.srms.kent.sch.uk

Head: Since 1996, Mr Christopher Morgan. Read history and a tennis blue at Fitzwilliam College, Cambridge. Previously deputy at King Edward VI Five Ways Grammar School, Birmingham, prior to that head of history and then head of sixth form at Leicester Grammar. Relaxed, down to earth, efficient – 'good on paper work and supportive' say the staff. Accurate in his appraisal of teaching staff, 'no glaring weaknesses', all very competent – this borne out by a warm, open atmosphere and cheerful ambience in the staff room. His three children were all educated at local grammar schools.

Academic matters: Excellent academic record – 63 per cent A*/A/B grades at A level, 54 per cent A*/A at GCSE. All study French in Year 7, and an alternative is offered in smaller groups thereafter – either Spanish or German. All pupils encouraged to take two languages. Good take up of German at AS; Italian popular with the sixth form, 20 to 30 pupils, and Mandarin going mainstream soon. Partnership with a school near Beijing – pupils do an annual three-week exchange and the Chinese Government sends a specialist teacher every year to live and teach at the school. The German exchange is to a similar type of school in North Rhine Westphalia, and a clutch of German sixth formers board at the school. Exchanges with schools in Provence, France and the Veneto region of Italy. Japanese and Russian also offered in lunch-time and after school sessions.

Games, Options, the Arts: Plenty of acreage and more than adequate sports facilities so a very good standard in a variety of sports. Pupils play at county and national level. Lots of extra-curricular, including golf (they're next to Royal St Georges). Vibrant art; brings in a mix of practitioners e.g. film makers, potters etc, and they spark creative ideas with students – maths is brought alive.

Parents happy with drama – plenty of productions in drama studios and main hall and photos displayed in the main hall. Music has a new and industrious head who is deemed a fantastic asset and a tireless worker, bringing a fizz to the frequent concerts, brass band, jazz, rock, solo artists – and all levels of competence and participation are encouraged. Frequent trips to Italy, Hungary and Spain for the choir and orchestra.

CCF for both sexes; usually about 120 pupils involved with adventure training weeks, annual camps etc. D of E, public speaking, Manwoods Medics, chess club etc etc.

Background and Atmosphere: In 1563 Sir Roger Manwood founded a Free Grammar School to educate the local townspeople of the Cinque port of Sandwich – a quiet small town inhabited generally by retired people and retired Admiralty. Architecturally pleasing buildings, old and new dotted around the site. Off the beaten track, nestled between the quaint Kent village of Sandwich, surrounded by the trickle of the river Stour, and on the outskirts of Royal St Georges. Sounds and is idyllic. A stress-free zone and safe environment, especially for boarders, who are free to hop on their bikes and explore the river trail into the town or the golf course. A no frills environment.

Boarding a mix of overseas (NW Europe and China) and British (Londoners). Spacious; plenty of large individual rooms. A happy atmosphere with very good and approachable housemistresses and staff. These are old houses with creaking polished oak floors, mullioned windows, and grand staircases. The Grange, however, has some very Dickensian baths and uninviting showers with a décor to match, but these are due for refurbishment. The boys didn't seem to notice anyway, they happily were occupied with a busy school life. A lot of boarders are musicians.

Pastoral Care and Discipline: Staff feel the pastoral care is strong and caring. The sixth form operates a buddying system that gives an opportunity for junior children to discuss their problems.

Pupils and Parents: The children are a friendly open, normal bunch of teenagers.

Entrance: Pupils take the 'Kent test' or, from Year 8 onwards, a test administered by the school, and need a letter from their current head teacher. While still locally competitive, the standard is marginally lower than e.g. the region around Tunbridge Wells. Sixth form entry needs six GCSEs A–C with at least B grades in chosen subjects. For boarders this could be more flexible and each place is granted on individual merit. If the boarding places are not all taken up the places are offered to day pupils.

Exit: A good cluster to Oxbridge; typically most achieve the university of their choice. A wealthy old Manwoodian, who amazingly supports every student studying medicine through university to the tune of £1,000 annually, set up the Claringbold scholarship. Not surprisingly, a healthy few study medicine.

Remarks: One of a handful of grammar schools in the country offering boarding education. A relaxed, unfussy school with very good teaching across the curriculum.

Sir William Borlase's Grammar School

West Street, Marlow, Buckinghamshire, SL7 2BR

• Pupils: 1,005 boys and girls; all day • Ages: 11-18 • Size of sixth form: 360 • Inter-denom • State

Tel: 01628 816 500
Fax: 01628 816 501
Email: enquiries@swbgs.com
Website: www.swbgs.com

Head: Since 1997, Dr Peter Holding MA BA MA(Ed) (late fifties), studied both in the United States and back in United Kingdom. Married with no children. Approachable – his dog certainly is – although some parents say he can appear a little distant. Sits on various educational committees and praised for implementing the latest thinking at a good pace and with a firm grip. Values international experience. Seizes on opportunities to enhance individual achievement and develop young people in the wider community. Few successes seem to pass him by or go uncelebrated.

Academic matters: Selective intake with consistent performance well above average, with parents and pupils loath to pinpoint particular areas of strength or weakness. Some references to truly fabulous teaching and one or two to weaker staff members, most of whom appear to move on of their own accord. Cross-disciplinary collaboration an increasing focus. 'We want creative physicists and mathematicians.' Well up in the top ten state schools across the country for A level results, but also lauded for wider personal and leadership development.

No-one rests on their laurels, the school included. It is seeking specialist status in additional subjects, subscribes to a commercial IT-enabled virtual learning environment, reports to parents online and allocates learning mentors from amongst staff and sixth formers to ensure all on track and sufficiently challenged. Not considered overly pushy – but could some lower down the school be pushed more? Some think so, but a very minor criticism and one which the school seems to be addressing. Recently it has introduced an accelerated two-year Key Stage 3 programme to create opportunities for extended project work, independent thinking and wider spread of subject areas. Most pupils take 12 GCSEs. Very few SEN pupils but when problems emerge responsive to parental concerns and, of late, general agreement that getting better in dealing with them effectively.

Games, Options, the Arts: Croquet matches in progress in the quad at lunch time, with aspiring players waiting patiently in the wings, but the school offers much more than that on the sporting front. Around 20 at any one time form the Borlase Elite Sports Team (BEST). Strongest are rowing and hockey with two full international girl rowers, and 40–50 county hockey players. Through the School Sport Partnership pupils flex their leadership and other muscles, organising extra clubs and competitions in cheerleading, dance, table-tennis and girls' rugby, to name but a few.

The school's specialist performing arts status is well-deserved. Ex-pupil Ben Smith who appears in Disney Channel UK's comedy sketch show *Life Bites* is a source of considerable pride in the community. Another sixth form student popularised dance at the school through hip-hop. There is little resistance to it being compulsory from year seven to nine. The hugely impressive Technology and Performing Arts Centre hosts regular productions involving pupils from all years, again with an eye to reinforcing different aspects of the curriculum and individual achievement. There is even an annual 'Boscars' complete with red carpet and bronze statuettes. Marvel at the recording studio and equipment and huge range of musical talent. Musicals, hip-hop, jazz, rock, choral performances – talent abounds and gets due recognition within the school and local press. Varied activity weeks and excursions organised throughout the year and fantastic opportunities to prepare for life beyond school including the Engineering Education and Young Enterprise Schemes, foreign language exchanges and fund-raising for a month-long World Challenge over the summer for 20 plus students in Years 11 and 12.

Background and Atmosphere: Founded as a boys' school in 1624 by Sir William Borlase in memory of his son. Some of the original flint and brick buildings are still in use, alongside modern additions housing up-to-date facilities more in line with today's less austere and expanded education system. Great café and outdoor areas populated by relaxed and happy-looking pupils with lots of socialising outside school too. Ample opportunities for parents to get involved but virtually non-existent parking must be a disincentive at this main street site. On track to provide full disability access throughout the school.

Pastoral Care and Discipline: 'Your skirts are much too short for our school,' read the headline in the local paper. Staff do not shy away from reminding parents and pupils of the perils of showing too much leg. Walking around there is an honest, ordered and respectful attitude in evidence. Rooms containing expensive equipment left open and five pound note found outside a classroom handed in promptly. Extensive PSHCE could well be a contributory factor to low levels of bullying and other troubles at the school, but also strong is its commitment to developing pupil voice, leadership and team skills, particularly amongst prefects. They speak highly of mentor training and encouragement to take on real responsibility.

Pupils and Parents: A moneyed and ambitious parent body and children with aspirations to match. Suits doers, the enthusiastic and keen. Unsolicited testimony from member of the public regarding good behaviour during a London theatre trip pinned in reception and general reputation for being pleasant and positive members of the community.

Entrance: Catchment area shrunk in recent years but still heavily over-subscribed at 11+ with entrance by county exam. 40–50 enter sixth form from outside, both from within Bucks and further afield, selected on GCSE results and school's assessment of their general enthusiasm and commitment to chosen field of study.

Exit: A week-long masterclass in Year 12 exposes pupils to a wide range of professions and careers through presentations and workshops and helps them build their leadership skills and prepare for the university application process. Some pupils groan about leadership overkill but some parents certainly see its value. Whatever, many go on to top level universities and colleges, Oxford and Cambridge amongst them. Popular destinations are Birmingham, Exeter, Nottingham, Oxford Brookes and Warwick. Wide range of disciplines chosen from science, business, ICT, management and sport.

Money Matters: 'Build a Better Borlase' highly successful in mobilising financial and other support for the school from current and past parents and pupils, resulting in outstanding facilities. Voluntary contributions invited to make school funds go further and few miss out on broad range of activities offered.

Remarks: Strong focus on creating and celebrating confident and responsible individuals who will do well in their chosen fields. Far from detached from the outside world and yet there's a feeling of being an oasis from many of the worries and problems that typically beset teenagers. Deep sense of appreciation amongst pupils and parents alike.

Sir William Perkins's School

Guildford Road, Chertsey, Surrey, KT16 9BN

• Pupils: 560 girls, all day • Ages: 11-18 • Size of sixth form: 120 • Non-denom • Fees: £11,769 pa • Independent

Tel: 01932 574 900
Fax: 01932 574 901
Email: office@swps.org.uk
Website: www.swps.org.uk

Head: Since 2007, Mrs Del Cooke BSc MBA NPQH (early fifties) married with three sons. Maths graduate with MBA in educational management. Her broad experience covers the comprehensive system, sixth form college, adult education and boarding at Cranleigh, where she was head of maths, housemistress and finally deputy head. A very likeable, relaxed lady, her mathematical bent fell into conversation a couple of times – obviously an analytical soul. She had almost lost her voice the day we visited; however she was very willing to talk even though it was in a whisper! Parents describe her as approachable – which we would echo. She is a great advocate for the school's ethos of a caring and supportive community and plans to build on these strengths. Interested in music, she plays a number of instruments, including self-taught bassoon – not many heads can boast that accomplishment.

Academic matters: Academic standards are consistently good; Mrs Cooke describes the flavour of the school as 'highly academic but not a hothouse' and 'full of motivated, busy, happy girls.' Parents very much agree – 'academically rigorous – they expect success and help you achieve,' and 'a well rounded school,' are among the typical parental comments. Most girls gain a string of A grades – 89 per cent A*–B grades at A level, 78 per cent A*/A at GCSE in 2010 – but the aim is to receive a balanced education developing their personal and leadership skills. Popular subjects at GCSE include English, sciences, maths, foreign languages and history. Maths is particularly strong, results very impressive (a refreshing change for a girls' school). Critical thinking is now a regular part of sixth form studies.

Form sizes below the sixth form average 21 but can get up to 24; teaching group average is smaller. In the sixth form, class sizes of eight. An individual education plan (IEP) is drawn up for each pupil with any special educational need in consultation with the special needs coordinator, the pupil and the parents, and these are reviewed regularly. Strategies are agreed to help each pupil and the information is circulated to all the relevant teachers who then take steps to support the pupils as appropriate. About four per cent of pupils have IEPs. 'A lot of pupils have one-to-one help from teachers for a period at one time or another but no pupils are withdrawn from lessons,' says Mrs Cooke. She is refreshingly open about SEN at the school. 'We are delighted to take any pupil who will thrive at the school and this includes pupils with quite a diverse range of special educational needs. If pupils need specialist SEN teaching then they are referred externally to experts.' A large number of pupils are gifted and talented and 'there is endless provision for high achievers both within lessons and outside lessons in our extensive extracurricular programme.'

Facilities are good, notably the language and science labs, and the design and technology facilities are out of this world – another unexpected delight in a girls' school. The ground floor houses loads of machine tools for wood, metal and acrylic work and the first floor has a laser cutter, drawing tables and computers dedicated to CADCAM work. Parents comment that the 3-dimensional work the girls produce is 'fantastic'. The clean and modern home economics room was refurbed in summer 2007. There are two air-conditioned IT suites – modern and airy and all pupils have their own email accounts.

Games, Options, the Arts: A great selection of sports on offer, from netball, hockey and rowing to orienteering, football, volleyball, fencing etc etc. A new extention to the Sports Department will be completed by summer 2011. Clubs after school and at lunchtime. 'Girls have a go and enjoy most things and get included in matches, even if they're not very good,' say parents. Really strong D of E – usually 50 per cent of the sixth form do gold award and the scheme has its own training room and office.

Drama prominent; the performance hall has been impressively refurbished to include electrically operated, retractable seating and smoke machines (much to the delight of the drama students). Also a large drama room. The performing arts centre has good acoustics, a private drama room and seven music practice rooms, all with pianos. Music very strong, loads of after school groups (swing band popular). Artwork is bold, bright and creative and very much reflects the girls' own characters. There are three lovely, big, bright and airy art rooms, a kiln, and printmaking facilities with a resident printmaking artist. Head of art encourages lots of different types of media.

Background and Atmosphere: Founded in 1725 by Sir William Perkins, a wealthy Chertsey merchant. Started with 25 boys but a decade later added 25 girls. Moved to present site in 1819. 12 acres of gardens and playing fields. Original 1905 redbrick building imaginatively extended to form a figure of eight of interlocking buildings with two pleasant courtyards – a tranquil oasis in the red brick.

Lots of energy and enthusiasm about the place. Mrs Cooke says, 'we try to ensure that girls achieve academically but not in an environment that makes them think that only academia is valued.' Very friendly school with good teacher/pupil relationships – 'the teachers are always willing to help; they're concerned, friendly and very welcoming.'

Pastoral Care and Discipline: Head places strong emphasis on pastoral care with rigorous policies, which parents like. No problem is ignored and staff deal with issues quickly and sympathetically. Fully accessible to physically disabled pupils – stairlifts on all short flights of stairs where a lift is not available.

Discipline is good. Girls comment that you could get a detention if uniform rules are not adhered to, but there's still the odd ladder in tights, scruffy shoes and skirts rolled up. No summer dress – the girls lobbied for this through the school council and also agreed that the uniform should be updated: out with ties and white shirts and in with striped open neck blouses.

Pupils and Parents: Large school bus network. Girls are lively, fairly boisterous, individuals, down to earth, friendly and enthusiastic. They like to 'get involved'. Parents are a cross section – as one commented, 'there's a good mix of cars in the carpark. It's not all Porsches and Mercedeses. Some parents are obviously making sacrifices.'

Entrance: Forty per cent come from surrounding state schools, the rest from a wide range of independents. Lots of care is taken over the selection process. (A pat on the back for the school as it will accept girls who are out of year.) Parents need to register their interest in the October before the pupil is admitted. Entrance exam is based on key stage 2. Maths and English tested, backed up by report from current school. Girls need to be academically inclined – it is not for the non-motivated. Entrance for sixth form needs at least five GCSEs at grade B or above including English language and maths, and interview.

Exit: A few want the experience of mixed schooling after GCSEs but most stay on to sixth form. Majority then leave for top of the range universities where maths, science and languages are popular choices. Eleven per cent went to Oxbridge in 2007 (it was a good year).

Money Matters: Fees 'good value for money'. Means-tested bursaries available to deal with personal hardship are re-evaluated each year. Two Perkins bursaries available each year up to 100 per cent of fees for local girls who would otherwise be unable to come here. Some scholarships – academic, art and musical.

Remarks: A friendly school with very good academic standards – ideal for unstuffy girls who enjoy healthy competition and getting stuck into what is on offer. Not for hooray Henriettas, who would stick out like a sore thumb.

Skipton Girls' High School

Gargrave Road, Skipton, North Yorkshire, BD23 1QL

• Pupils: 795 girls, all day • Ages: 11-18 • Size of sixth form: 215 • Non-denom • State

Tel: 01756 707 600
Fax: 01756 707 613
Email: sghs@sghs.org.uk
Website: sghs.org.uk

Headteacher: Since 2002, Mrs J Renou BA PGCE ATD NPQH, previously vice principal at Landau Forte College, Derby and head of sixth form and design at Djanogly City Technology College, Nottingham. Highly professional and businesslike yet warm, welcoming and unassuming; two daughters. Originally from North Yorkshire coast. DT background, clearly focused on taking the school forward as befits its new spin – 'Engineering the Future'. Encourages girls in the belief that they 'can do anything', readily challenging gender stereotyping. Led the school to specialist status in engineering (first all girls' school to achieve this) to some surprise from staff but support from governors. Proud of the girls, wants them to 'know how to behave in any given situation'.

Academic matters: Academically selective on intake; girls competitive and hardworking, GCSE and A level results highly impressive. Regular position in top 50 best state schools. Top 25 per cent for value-added (this, given the selectivity, is a crucial measure). Average class sizes vary – 28 in lower school to 18 post-16. All academic subjects strong – no surprises in science/DT focus (girls buzzing with knowledge and interest while making complex lighting circuits); home economics still surviving here and art vibrant. French and German taught as standard, Russian available as extra-curricular. Post-16 collaboration with nearby boys' school has widened A level options in minority subjects. Some provision for special needs. ICT has been significantly upgraded with new computer suites, laptops, data projectors and interactive whiteboards. Homework club popular, mainly for research tasks, as internet access can be a problem for those living in the outer reaches of the dales.

Games, Options, the Arts: Not the school for your highly sporty girl, team games and competitive sport limited mainly due to lack of facilities (no sports fields or sports hall on site). Several tennis courts, small gym; aerobics and dance popular. D of E Awards also popular with North Yorks national park on doorstep. Music is strong, majority of girls play an instrument; drama popular (in the Judi Dench Drama Studio, opened in 1996 by the good dame herself) and increasingly so since scheduling joint activities with the boys' school down the road. Centre of excellence for dance; lectures, workshops and professional performances. Overseas visits popular and encouraged.

Background and Atmosphere: Founded in 1886 as a girls' boarding school. Tight, cohesive campus, space limited; mix of buildings works well and is tidy, attractive and welcoming. Original Victorian and Edwardian houses; sixth form centre housed in recently refurbished large Edwardian house complete with 'bistro' courtesy of IKEA and a rabbit warren of small but useful cubby holes for private study. Extensions include hall, gym, labs and classrooms; current embargo on further building. Parking and access restricted and therefore troublesome, hairy at 4pm.

Healthy mixture of long established staff and new young teachers, even a few Old Girls of the school, who can tell a tale or two about the changes they have seen but remain loyal to the cause. Teachers here have to be of 'high calibre and secure in the knowledge of their own subject', otherwise they are in danger of being severely tested and possibly tormented by these confident, articulate girls – expectations both of self and others are high. Austere portraits of previous headmistresses are a bit of a surprise in modern surroundings but remind the school community that, despite recent innovation, long-standing traditions and history of success are to be maintained.

Rolls Royce plc is a key sponsor of the specialist status but this is not a Rolls Royce school. The academic engine is undoubtedly first class but it lacks the flamboyance and frills. More of a Volvo.

Pastoral Care and Discipline: Communication between home and school quick and efficient thanks to web-based communications package. Parents/staff given access to each other for discussions on progress and homework and extension tasks posted on site for students. Code of conduct and drugs policy rigorously enforced; small amount of bullying especially amongst younger girls, with 'wicked tongues' taken seriously and dealt with. Unusual and reassuring lack of lockers – coats, belongings left in cloakrooms, stealing very rare. Active student council requested healthier lunches and the removal of the soft drinks machine in favour of water.

Pupils and Parents: Full range of social and cultural spread on intake. Shy and confident girls do equally well. Girls are delightfully enthusiastic and eloquent with a genuine social conscience – charities, anti Iraq war demo ('allowed but with strict parameters' i.e. school grounds only). Pupils fully supported engineering status spurred on after hearing from the charity Water Aid how engineering had changed the lives of African women. The best thing about the place? A spontaneous and unanimous 'the teachers ... because they listen to us'. And the worst? They struggled to come up with one but, when pressed, 'the pressure'. From whom? 'Ourselves – it's the way we all work here but we thrive on it'. These are the offspring of liberal quirky 1960s roots – only the hairstyles and clothes have changed – parents are very vocal, demanding, yet supportive and 'know what they want'; a real mix of middle class professionals, university staff and sheep farmers – free-thinking people who encourage their daughters to challenge, investigate, accomplish something, with open minds and hearts and are quick to leap on the school should it attempt to over-restrain. Local house prices high as parents move to secure a place in catchment area.

Entrance: For entry at 11, LEA testing procedure – verbal and non-verbal reasoning tests. Coaching for selection discouraged as less able will struggle here. Priority given to girls living in catchment area, greater competition for those out of catchment.

'How bright does a girl have to be to get in?' is apparently a question that no one ever dares to ask (or answer) – it would be easier to obtain classified information from the Menwith Hill spy base up the road than to get an answer to this question. We would say (though the school might not) that girls should have a high pass at 11+, with the ability to attain nine or 10 GCSEs at A or A* and three or four top grade A levels. Anything else would be a real disappointment to all concerned.

Exit: 99 per cent stay post-GCSE. Favoured universities – Newcastle, Leeds, Edinburgh, half a dozen to Oxbridge. Notable Old Girls Elizabeth Harwood, opera, Ruzwana Bashir, Chair of Oxford Union 2004.

Remarks: The press loved this school's move to engineering status because the 'blend of girls with engineering' was seen as 'sexy' – forcing a wry smile in this unpretentious market town sandwiched rather quietly between industrial West Yorkshire and the Dales. Won't turn heads but it's as sound as it comes – will get your daughter safely from A to B (or rather from B to A*).

Slindon College

Slindon, Arundel, West Sussex, BN18 0RH

• Pupils: 100, all boys, about 50 per cent board • Ages: 9-16
• Non-denom • Fees: £14,490-£24,660 pa • Independent

Tel: 01243 814 320
Fax: 01243 814 702
Email: registrar@slindoncollege.co.uk
Website: www.slindoncollege.co.uk

Headmaster: Since 1999, Mr Ian Graham MA BEd Cert Ed, (late fifties). Formerly a teacher of history and PE with 25 years service at Rugby School under his belt, Mr Graham had lots of experience at housemastering and heading numerous depts including General Studies and Activities before taking up his headship at Slindon – different, eh? Perhaps not so different for a teacher clearly committed to giving the best to and getting the best out of each individual. This challenge and the attractions of the college's stunning site and buildings convinced him and his tenure so far has overseen the development of a school with a clear focus and direction. At Rugby, he tended to take on the boys with problems or who were struggling and he has a natural touch, together with the required toughness when appropriate. Now with a staff who see things the same way – 'we know what we are about, we know what we are doing and we get on with it.' He is realistic and honest – 'it doesn't always work. I do have to move people on. It's unethical to take people's fees if a boy really doesn't want to learn.' However, it clearly does work for the vast majority who stay. 'I know every boy in the school and I know what makes him tick,' says the head. Of a current leaver he says, 'he'll be a success in life and that's what we want.'

Academic matters: 'Not a special but a specialist school', says the literature. 'It specialises in helping pupils whose needs have not been met in larger schools despite extra support because of insufficient individual tailoring.' The key to this approach seems to lie in school's 'holistic' approach and in its constant stressing of the need to create and bolster self-esteem in everyone. Helpful are the small classes – none bigger than 12, the use of individual learning plans and a highly flexible, undogmatic approach. Some boys might even be encouraged to repeat a year so that the basic skills are reinforced, allowing for a more confident step into Year 10. Some make such good progress that, by Year 10, they no longer need individual support and are wholly reintegrated into class.

Slindon children may well be dyslexic, dyspraxic, have mild Asperger's syndrome or mild autism, ADD, ADHD or Semantic Pragmatic Disorder or be school refusers, but often specific labels won't do and the history is one of simply not thriving educationally in the mainstream world. Hence, a special school isn't called for and a rigid approach is inappropriate. Asperger's children, for example, aren't treated to 'serious behavioural modification – we're creating the right atmosphere and then tweaking things'. SEN education at Slindon is highly sophisticated but confident enough to allow the staff to pick and choose which bits of which approach will best assist each individual. In this, the Learning Support Dept and its impressively committed head – himself a successful dyslexic – are central, together with the extensive use of trained learning support assistants in Years 5–9, to strengthen the work of the specialist classroom teachers. There is an emphasis on the basic skills, primarily reading, and a range of techniques is used to help each pupil achieve in the best way for him. 'We're wrapping our education around the individual pupils,' says head. Lessons are an hour long – sensibly allowing for the disorganized to get organized and the careful conclusions to work that some such students need. Even breaks are supervised by SEN-trained staff.

Everyone does double or single science at GCSE. Everyone does ICT and takes either a GCSE or the CLAIT exam. Food technology is popular and all Years 6–9 do cookery. School has a little observatory – no light pollution here – and GCSE astronomy is a recent innovation for the more able students – such a good idea. In that, as in other areas, school making good use of its assets. There is a small farm allowing for animal husbandry – school lovingly cares for ducks, geese, hens, a goat and four sheep – as well as crop growing. Super Victorian conservatory already used for growing fruit and veg – students will be able to take a GNVQ in environmental studies. Those boys for whom a hefty clutch of GCSE subjects is not on are allowed to drop some and are assigned to grounds/maintenance staff and learn electrics, plumbing, painting and decorating, mowing and so on – useful for many who move on to college vocational courses – and good for self-esteem.

Not everyone here has a specific learning difficulty. In particular, the younger brothers of existing pupils, who themselves would have no problems in mainstream education, often choose to come. In addition, there are those few able but socially less robust individuals for whom Slindon is a safe and comfortable learning space. So – a wide range of results at GCSE. Some here gain grades from C–G and this represents a notable achievement. Others may gain mostly Cs and the odd A or B. PE and Food Tech score well. Art and photography sometimes get A*/A. Efforts clearly made to involve the practical in the theoretic to encourage interest in everyone. We watched a bunch of boys with small circuit boards, soldering irons, mini loudspeakers and batteries making tiny electric organs. School built two racing cars for the annual Greenpower event at Goodwood and won The Spirit of Greenpower award in 2004. This and other activities encourage both individual skills and team-building.

Games, Options, the Arts: Huge, super fields on which football and rugby are played, a floodlit court, purpose-built squash courts, archery, golf, tai kwondo, basketball, tennis, mountain biking, cross country etc with an outdoor heated pool – open from Easter to late October, along with the Duke of Edinburgh Award Scheme – no shortage of things to do even though there is, as yet, no sports hall. Some worthy achievements here – especially in cross country.

Lots of extra-curricular opportunities, mostly of the outdoor type but also car mechanics, stagecraft and various musical activities. Music is popular, especially the recording studios where boys can record and then cut their performances into CDs or mini-discs. Lots of guitars and drumming here. Many learn individually with peripatetics; there is a jazz band, choir and other impromptu bands. Music is taken at GCSE. Appealingly messy art room full of primary colours, mobiles, ceramics and purposeful work. Purpose made 'White room' for graphics, two dark rooms for photography. School's principle is to display everything everyone does and there is plenty of space to cover. New skateboard ramp in the gardens possibly the most popular innovation yet.

Background and Atmosphere: The site and buildings are owned by the National Trust. The house itself is Tudor Sussex flint and is an imposing grey three-storey pile on top of a superb site overlooking the south Sussex landscape – fields and woods, down, on a clear day, to the sea and the Isle of Wight. Most rooms, including dorms, look out over this deliciousness but it is probably never taken for granted – just too special. Up here you hear nothing but birdsong and a distant mechanical saw. School celebrated its sixtieth anniversary in 2006. It's not all in perfect nick but it's impressively well-kept for a school of such a size and in such high-maintenance accommodation. Boarding is good – a choice of a 2/3 or a 5/6 bedder for juniors and 2/3 for senior boys except for the top year who have single study bedrooms of good sizes. Good common rooms and bathroom facilities. Belongings not, for the most part, kept in rooms – to help boys learn about organization – but stored in loft rooms to which access is allowed twice daily or by pleading with matron at other times. Welcoming surgery with san next door and ensuite bathroom – not too scary if you're ill away from home. General atmosphere is very relaxed and friendly – no-one could feel threatened here.

Pastoral Care and Discipline: Clear pastoral system – academic staff being also tutors with pastoral responsibilities but a strong sense of general caring for each other pervades. Resident boarding staff, houseparents and matron supported by evening tutors oversee the boarding side. Rewards and sanctions system all maintained by the head who manages it all by much walking around and being visible. Erratic behaviour, so often part of the frustrations attendant on SENs, is accepted and treated with compassionate firmness but head will exclude a pupil if misbehaviour becomes a problem to others. Credits and prizes abound and head keeps a drawer full of cash (used to be chocolate!) as rewards – so much nicer than a sticky star! Food mostly cooked on site by much-loved resident cook who will even make sandwiches on demand if main menu – which looks good – doesn't appeal. Many boys on regular medication regime – Ritalin is common and seen as a very effective tool – so no-one bats a proverbial. Summer term sees as much going on outside as possible including lessons, once-weekly each bbq and picnic.

Pupils and Parents: Boarders from everywhere in the UK; a few from Hong Kong – only English allowed to be spoken during the school day – and one or two from elsewhere. Day boys from as far south as the sea and within 20 miles or so around. Social mix but very few supported by LEAs so a self-limiting cohort. Small but busy PTA making a big contribution both in fund-raising and in actual physical work. Every Friday is a tea-party to which all staff go and all parents are invited – an excellent chance for a quick word about Edward's homework/chilblains/lost bat without a palaver.

Entrance: By interview with head, current school report plus ed psych's if any and assessment by head of learning support. Taster days – and nights for prospective boarders – are popular and useful. No actual tests – refreshingly enlightened.

Exit: Mostly to local colleges for vocational courses or for A levels. 'By the time they get to post-GCSE, they need to be exposed to all the things we've been protecting them from,' we were told – sensible enough.

Money Matters: 10 per cent reductions for Service families and siblings attending concurrently. Some bursaries available on application.

Remarks: School started taking from Year 5 from 2005 – a good idea and they could start even younger as, by the age of 8, most problems are apparent and parents at their wits end. Slindon is a happy answer to the sort of boy for whom mainstream – whatever the in-class/out-of-class support – simply isn't right. Slindon parents exhale relief, gratitude and hope and the boys come here and no longer feel different, dim or excluded.

Slough Grammar School

Lascelles Road, Slough, Berkshire, SL3 7PR

• Pupils: 1,240; mixed, all day • Ages: 11 to 18 • Size of sixth form: 350 equally boys/girls • Non-denom • State

Tel: 01753 522 892
Fax: 01753 538 618
Email: office@sloughgrammar.berks.sch.uk
Website: www.sloughgrammar.berks.sch.uk

Principal: Since 2010, Mrs Mercedes Hernández Estrada MA (philology). Born and educated in Spain (Oviedo university), Mrs Hernández Estrada has worked in English schools for the past twenty years in Haringey, Swindon, Bath, Southampton and as a deputy headteacher at Tonbridge Grammar School for five years. For the last three years Mrs Hernádez Estrada has been a lead practitioner for curriculum design for the Specialist Schools and Academies Trust, supporting schools all over the country to design and successfully implement forward thinking and innovation. Mrs Hernández Estrada believes in the power of education to change the world. Standards are important and the school should provide a calm environment where respect is the key to productive learning.

The school has, under the previoius head, developed over years strategies to support the learning. Boys and girls, for example, are taught separately in some subjects for the first three years – and achieve more as a result. 'We have driven up the performance of girls doing physics ... . boys prefer fact to fiction – we choose girl-friendly and boy-friendly books e.g. *Treasure Island* and *Jane Eyre*.' They have separate drama lessons – 'young men will not perform in front of girls.' The 2004 Ofsted inspection report, one of the most lyrical we have read, noted that there is 'very little difference between pupils of different ethnicity or sex' in terms of their achievement.

Academic matters: In addition to a full National Curriculum programme, school offers a vast range of other options and opportunities. Food technology is popular – 'everyone learns how to make a samosa,' as are textiles and languages – modern and ancient – both Latin and Greek are taught here. 15+ other languages also available as extra-curricular options though, perhaps surprisingly, the majority of pupils in the school – those whose families originate from the Asian sub-continent – mainly choose to study the languages and the music of their culture outside school. The sixth form offers both A levels and the International Baccalaureate. 'It's a really good course, it helps you to think creatively and it offers opportunities to those who don't want to specialise,' School also offers AVCEs in travel and tourism and in business studies – useful qualifications and results are a spread across the grades. School works to a fortnightly time-table facilitating a more-or-less free choice from the huge range of options.

Results in core subjects show a spread, mostly across the A/C grades, with a good sprinkling of A*s, notably in English lit and maths. Very few grades below B in the sciences. In the optional subjects, RS is very popular and the results are exemplary. Food and nutrition also does well – for both sexes. 15 A levels are offered and results seem pretty evenly spread, some subjects being vastly more popular, e.g. biology, chemistry and psychology, than others. Languages and RS have tiny groups at this level.

Overall, results are more than respectable and indicate a serious and successful approach to learning and preparation for professional life. The plan is for every child to have his or her own Individual Learning Plan – i.e. a programme and plan of work tailored to their own abilities and aptitudes. This is a dream elsewhere – here it is close to being realised. SEN not a big deal here – few with SpLD – and a SENCo and teaching assistants give, mostly, in-class help. Physical disability catered for though there is no lift but visually and hearing impaired students are supported as are wheelchair users and few autistic spectrum pupils. Extra support and masterclasses for those identified as gifted and talented.

Smallish library with helpful full time librarian who works closely with the academic departments. Limited but well-chosen books and extensive fiction section – again well-chosen and well-used, as is the library as a whole. Library also houses UCAS handbooks though there is a good careers library and staff elsewhere. IT is impressive – 'the equivalent of 13 computer rooms' – and the school is 'wireless' so that anyone can access anything anywhere. A system of wall-mounted screens in the corridors keeps everyone in touch with school information.

Games, Options, the Arts: Wednesday afternoon is spent on diverse 'activities' such as 'Out and About in historical Slough', digital photography, music composition, bell ringing, health and beauty, first aid, football refereeing, cycle proficiency and sports and languages galore – this is serious 'enrichment'. The 17 sports on offer include all the usuals plus badminton, 'new age kurling', and cricket at which the school is more-or-less unbeaten. School has a good, large, on-site field, several courts for tennis and netball and buses pupils to the Thames Valley Athletics Centre in Eton. Buses also go to the nearby municipal pool, the Montem Sports Centre.

Instrumental music is not huge here but there is a choir and an orchestra and five rock bands. Drama also is not high profile but major productions happen in large school hall. Art is strong and painting, drawing, sculpture, cartoon animation, ceramics and textiles all produce lively and attractive results. Super aboriginal work on 'self-identity' on display when we visited. Good woodwork and DT. Artists and writers come and give masterclasses. Provision for all these subjects was described as 'good' in the recent Ofsted. In all these areas, though, as with staff and office accommodation, school suffers from a lack of space. The abilities and enthusiasm are there – more space and facilities could make a huge difference. Projects with local companies, e.g. GSK, provide training and experience in problem solving and the world of work. Young Enterprise students were taking orders for Valentine's Day roses when we visited. They'd been up at Nine Elms at 4am to get them!

Lots of trips all over the place – in and out of the country – many linguistic but also scientific and geographic as well as cross-cultural. School has links with another in China and one in Norway. School participates in the British Council's Comenius project to encourage such links.

Background and Atmosphere: The main, two-storey, long building is a classic 1930s design, brick, unbeautiful but practical. Pupils do not admire it nor its add-ons but it is well-maintained and kept in good order. In a quiet, prosperous residential road, lined with well-spaced detached houses – hardly the Slough of unfair repute. Two minutes from the M25 intersection with the M4 and just off the A4 but it feels safe, suburban and very respectable.

We saw far less litter inside the school and roundabout and fewer heaps of back-packs than in most comparable schools. Orderliness is the theme and it is palpable in every class you pass and in the disciplined and purposeful movement of pupils around the place. Some, inevitably, find the regime too rigid but most appreciate it and feel what it does for them. We met two prospective sixth formers hoping to be offered places partly because 'there's no racist fighting here' – unlike at their existing schools.

School institutions are democratic and important. Houses – Herschel, Hampden, Brunel etc – count in the school structure and cultural life as does the exemplary school council which, as in another place, has committees for such concerns as health and safety, learning and teaching, bullying, the school environment and so on. These committees research questions of importance to the school community, report back and their findings and recommendations are implemented. This is impressive democracy and is also part of the school's citizenship programme.

Sixth form centre in converted squash court. Lunch here would not delight health campaigners – a high proportion of pizzas, pies, sandwiches and crisps and a very small salad bar. The least impressive thing we saw on our visit, though the school says this is no longer the case.

One of school's major successes is in the happy co-existence of students from such diverse backgrounds. Many children are bi-lingual and you hear odd snatches of other languages as you move around. School is keen to unite them in a common British heritage and 2005 saw everyone making trips to Portsmouth to learn about Nelson in the bi-centenary of his death at Trafalgar. 'I said they could have their money back if they didn't enjoy it and no-one asked for it.' School has British Council's International School Award and is now also accredited as an Initial Teacher Training provider – high level stuff.

A high-flying institution with an atmosphere of high standards and aspirations. School elects 'honorary fellows' – people with no direct connection but who help in different capacities e.g. in careers advice or support. Ex-head of Eton – across the river – Sir Eric Anderson, came to give the prizes and, when you wait in the school's entrance foyer, a large screen shows the occasion, with staff in gowns all sitting on the platform. Screen apart, this could be a scene from fifty years ago.

Pastoral Care and Discipline: Pupils rise when a teacher enters the room. Lessons are orderly, disciplined, quiet. Pupils move along the corridors in a civilised manner and treat each other and staff with respect and courtesy. There is a daily assembly. Everyone wears uniform. Zero tolerance of drug-taking and stealing but only two exclusions in recent years – for drugs. For stealing – 'I will call the police,' says head but 'we're a pretty honest community'. Ofsted commented, 'the pupils' spiritual, moral, social and cultural development is outstanding, resulting in, and from, a school ethos of racial harmony, mutual respect, tolerance and personal dignity.'

Pupils and Parents: Pupils come from Slough but some from Ealing, Chiswick, Twickenham and Harrow and some from as far away as Paddington and Reading. Considerable ethnic mix but the majority is of Indian and Pakistani origin and the rest mostly white Brits. Once you're there it becomes an irrelevance. Most people's first language is English, Punjabi a not-close second. Sikhs, Muslims and Christians in more-or-less equal numbers. Very supportive parents. 90+ per cent turn up to parents' evenings and many support school in diverse ways e.g. work experience. Former pupils include novelist Susan Cooper, Lord William Bradshaw, transport expert, ophthalmologist Prof Anthony Moore, Olympic swimmer Philip Hubble, Andrew Watts, opera singer.

Entrance: Via Slough 11 plus NFER exam. Highly competitive – it's about five children trying for each place at 11 and about three for each sixth form place. School can afford to be highly selective – 'we're educating people who are going to be the bedrock of the community,' said previous head, citing the numbers of lawyers and doctors produced during her time there. Intake comes from some 60+ primaries. For entry into Year 12 students will need 5+ GCSEs at C+ for vocational subjects and for A levels 6+ good GCSEs with, at least, B in their A level subjects.

Exit: Most to study scientific or business courses. Most to London, Brunel, City, Westminster or other local universities. However, others to everywhere from Stirling to Southampton to read everything from languages to aerospace engineering, from history to drama. A few to Oxbridge.

Remarks: Impressive at all levels. Head's stated aim is 'to be better than we are'. School motto is 'Ad Astra'. Watch out, solar system!

South Devon Steiner School

Linked to Rudolf Steiner School South Devon; Early Childhood Dept in the Junior section

Hood Manor, Dartington, Totnes, Devon, TQ9 6AB

• Pupils: 300 boys and girls • Ages: 7-16 • Christian foundation; non-denom • Fees: £3,885-£5,475 pa • Independent

Tel: 01803 762 528
Fax: 01803 762 528
Email: admissions@steiner-south-devon.org
Website: www.steiner-south-devon.org

Head: None. Steiner schools don't have them and it's one of their distinguishing features. At SDSS monthly 'mandate circles' provide a first level of discussion for teachers, key admin staff and parents. Teaching vision, strategy and direction arise from the weekly 'collegiate' and departmental meetings. Principle is that fuller discussion leads to better long term outcomes. Prospective parents are advised to do their homework beforehand if new to structure of Steiner schools.

Academic matters: From class 1 (six year olds) each day begins with a two hour 'main lesson' on themes which follow Steiner curriculum but which allow for individual interpretation by class teachers. Main lesson in classes 9 and 10 (Years 10 and 11) are taken by specialists. Lower and main school class teachers follow same children through four or eight year cycle – often broken for a variety of reasons but concept of keeping same class teacher is central to Steiner philosophy – when it happens, results can be astounding. Everything is done to encourage self-directed learning so tiniest sparks of interest are fanned into passionate flames of enthusiasm. Class themes run for three weeks and cover topics such as Norse myths, house construction or geology. When we visited, class 2 girls were all dressed as native American Indians whilst class 3 were starting to look after animals, grow their own food and learn about forestry. School uses unconventional approaches e.g. class 6 pupils get to understand principles of levers by making baseball bats. You won't fall over computers and tellies here and books only make a gradual appearance. Writing and 'feeling' shape and sound of letters precede reading. Main lesson (exercise) books provide record of what has been learned with standard of presentation all important as is ability to recall earlier topics. We saw class 4 enjoying storytime ('Little Grey Men') while class 5 were building model Trojan towers out of clay to 'storm' later. Creative writing is encouraged at all levels.

Children get engrossed in whatever they are doing and there is a productive buzz wherever you go. Artistic learning is central to what happens – children learn colour blending (using a palette of primary colours) in classes 1–3 then appreciation of form grows out of that. Class 9's 'science of agriculture' lesson included learning about medicinal herbs then finding and drawing them on site; felt work, growing crops (school has an area marked out for larger scale agriculture) and investigation work in small but adequate laboratory. Science of lime cycle involves constructing, firing and manufacturing from a lime kiln.

No SATs here and senior pupils only take four GCSEs – English language and literature plus maths and a foreign language. Academic results (around the national average) not seen as be all and end all by parents; staff seek to instil genuine thirst for knowledge. German (chosen for its sound quality and closer relationship to English) is introduced from class 1 with French as an optional extra in classes 7–10. Self-assessment is seen as important though teachers do grade older pupils for content, presentation and effort. New wooden hall (previous one burnt down whilst parents were rehearsing Macbeth) is a fine structure comprising five classrooms plus specialist music and handwork rooms.

SENCo has brought valuable experience from state sector and benefits from help of two LSAs. Learning support with groups of two or three pupils covers range of needs from SpLD to Asperger's. SENCo says that Steiner approach offers those with learning difficulties many more opportunities to work from gross to finer motor skills and 'keeps children in touch with their bodies' preventing them from being 'sensory deprived'.

Games, Options, the Arts: The 'new' concept of the 'outside classroom' is old hat here. Much of the land is given over to growing produce and keeping animals. Pupils literally 'make hay' here plus logging and other outdoor skills. We watched class 6 harvesting organic produce to sell at their weekly food stall. Class 10 students had just returned from two week ecology trip (staying with staff at Trevose Head near Padstow, Cornwall) and had put on an exhibition for parents in the marquee (used for games, wet breaks etc). One boy had whittled a fishing rod out of driftwood and another had created a human shaped sculpture out of garbage collected on the beach. Parents clearly appreciated how the sculpture 'said it all' about human impact on the environment. We caught up with class 10 in the garden caravan (another of RSSSD's 'temporary' structures) as they returned in full protective gear from a bee keeping session. Earlier we had watched weekly class 9 music class (singing challenging Georgian song 'Batone Bo' in four-part harmony). Impressive for fifteen year olds but we were told that the same group had produced an opera based on life of St Francis (written by a teacher at Wynstones in Stroud) whilst in class 7.

Main hall also serves for assemblies and eurythmy (origins of this dance-like form lie in Greek temples – movement is related to specific sounds and is central to Steiner education). There is a specialist music room in same building plus individual practice rooms for lessons with peripatetic music staff – some pupils graduate to Torbay youth orchestra. Class 7 have formed own orchestra thanks to parents who include several professional musicians. Hall had just witnessed a class 9 production of Romeo and Juliet (school stages a Shakespearean play every year and most productions run for three nights). Emphasis is upon a combined effort rather breeding prima donnas. Class 10 complete their time here with a major production. Moving on, we saw some of class 8 doing 'handwork' – natural fibres (wool comes from school's own sheep) and dyes are de rigueur and manual dexterity ranks high in the Steiner taxonomy of skills. Boys and girls were equally engrossed in making hats and hand puppets. Across the site another part of class 8 was carving heads for the puppets in the small but perfectly adequate woodworking hut. There is also a forge where a local blacksmith comes to lead practical sessions. The upper school art rooms (one is a uniquely shaped wooden structure) are immersed in creativity and show what pupils achieve artistically. In other, less impressive huts we discovered a dark room for photography, a pottery and (well hidden) a small ICT base.

Competitive sports not a big deal here though class 6 pupils recently won a regional gymnastics tournament. Sports include hockey for boys and rugby for girls. After school clubs include basketball and volleyball. Older pupils go to sports facilities at Dartington College and Ivybridge but own sports hall is on wish list. Cycling is a structured activity from year seven upwards; there is a cycle path from Totnes to the school.

Trips away from school are vitally important – these grow in duration and scope as children get older so that, by class 7, pupils are canoeing and exploring down the Wye and in class 8 they go abroad for three weeks. Recent destinations have included Hungary, Romania and Portugal. Foreign cycling trips have included Brittany, Holland and Germany. Class 9 have a term of intensive outward bound activities and begin with a fortnight on a working farm in Scotland. Class 10 trips includes surveying on Dartmoor and art history in Germany.

Background and Atmosphere: School founded by local parents as a kindergarten in 1979 before moving to present idyllic eight acre site between Totnes and Dartington. Main school (classes 1–8) divided between Hood Manor (formerly the dowager house on Dartington estate) and the new hall and classroom block opened in 2007 – new classrooms have colour washed walls and enjoy plenty of natural light. Senior school (classes 9 and 10) housed in disparate, idiosyncratic collection of temporary classrooms, huts and shacks whilst Early Childhood Department enjoys a discrete, purpose-built area. Classes 1 and 2 also have a separate play area at front of Hood Manor.

School retains an 'alternative' feel but an extremely safe one – a gentle approach to all that happens – and it is reassuring to see so much mutual respect. Steiner educational movement has worldwide influence but has only recently (2008) achieved final state recognition in UK with granting of foundation status to a hitherto independent Steiner school in Hereford. Plans are afoot at SDSS to add a sixth form to the senior school and planning permission has been granted for the necessary extension as well as a sports hall. Now it is simply a matter of raising huge amounts of money. Parents are amazed though at how successful school has become at fund raising.

'Outside classroom' is of prime importance here as well as the creative life. School is fully involved in delivery of honours degree course in Steiner education run from Plymouth university – brings up to 15–20 undergraduates on site to interact with staff, parents and pupils, but unfortunately course now set to close. School day starts at 8.30am for all ages and ends at 3.00pm or 4.00pm for main and upper schools respectively. Staff:pupil ratio is 1:12 but with LSAs and other adults on site this ratio is often much less. When we visited children were dancing around the maypole which had been erected for May Day – one of the festivals celebrated annually. Relationships between pupils and staff are quite different from most schools – first names are used throughout and there is an obvious two-way feeling of trust. We also liked the balance of ages and gender amongst the staff.

Pastoral Care and Discipline: From the outset, children learn tolerance, respect and reverence. There is never a sense of pupils being talked down to and they are really 'heard' by staff. Anti-social behaviour or bullying would be anathema to pupils as much as teachers here. Each new class 1 is adopted by class 8 pupils. Pretty basic veggie catering; parents make pizzas and pasties on Wednesdays (half day for lower and main school pupils) otherwise food taken round to classrooms. Majority bring own lunch. Nothing is swept under the carpet and emphasis always on getting the emotional, physical and spiritual balance right in each individual. School comes down heavily on smoking; possession of alcohol or drugs can lead to immediate expulsion.

Pupils and Parents: Mostly local. Some pupils cycle to and from school (new cycle path between Totnes and Buckfastleigh facilitates this). Strictly for parents who are prepared to get involved and kids who want to discover and express all aspects of themselves. Some escapees from state sector but most home grown. Few schools involve parents as much as SDSS – parents attracted (about 75 per cent have relocated) by what school provides. Relatively few parents are anthroposophists, however majority find Steiner philosophy fits their value system – especially how it develops creativity alongside ecological and spiritual awareness. We met one parent mandate holder who explained how parents have a real say (they even have own room, used for study, school shop, tea breaks, meetings etc). Parents volunteer in all kinds of ways: hearing readers, gardening, serving food and cleaning classrooms on a rota basis. Parents' evenings are not at all conventional but still provide for one-to-one chats as well as group interaction. You notice a difference right away – children are focused and involved in a freer, warmer environment than in mainstream education.

Quite a lot of giving to charity – e.g. class 8 made and sold toys for school in South America. Always some European students who attend upper school for one or two years and who are found host families in area. Oldest former pupils barely thirty years old but are beginning to send second generation to SDSS. Many have achieved academically as well as in arts and drama.

Entrance: Most children enter through over-subscribed Early Years Department but gaps appear infrequently further up school. Three day visits for older children ensure they and parents know what school is about before signing up. Class teachers have an eye on dynamics of whole group which can have positive or negative consequences for individual applicants. Parents of children with special needs must produce educational psychologist's report. Lots come through attending an event at school – a play, concert or perhaps one of two main annual public functions – Christmas indoor market and summer fair. At end of Year 9 parents and pupils have to recommit to upper school (Years 10 and 11) which involves an interview and review of work.

Exit: School's local reputation and reference enables students to move from Year 11 to join 16+ colleges in Totnes, Plymouth or Exeter for A levels or appropriate vocational training.

Money Matters: Parents don't pay fees – they make 'contributions'. Discounts for siblings and bursaries for needy cases. Like most Steiner schools SDSS started out trying to be wholly inclusive but financial realities soon began to bite. Still comparatively affordable though parents we spoke to would love school to acquire foundation status to remove financial burden.

Remarks: Just brilliant. 'A lovely environment where emphasis is not on cramming knowledge,' say parents. Stands educational claptrap on its head, defies conventional wisdom and produces confident, creative and genuinely independent thinkers. Not for bookworms perhaps but a wonderful antidote to left brain overload we find elsewhere.

South Hampstead High School

Linked to South Hampstead High School Junior Department in the Junior section

3 Maresfield Gardens, London, NW3 5SS

• Pupils: 575 girls, all day • Ages: 4-18 • Size of sixth form: 140
• Non-denom • Fees: £12,006 pa • Independent

Tel: 020 7435 2899
Fax: 0207 431 8022
Email: senior@shhs.gdst.net
Website: www.shhs.gdst.net

Headmistress: Since January 2005, Mrs Jenny Stephen BSc (early fifties). Mrs Stephen, a scientist, came with impeccable credentials – three previous headships – in Bedford, Leeds and, latterly, for eight years, at The Grange in Cheshire, a co-ed HMC school – during which period her husband, Martin Stephen (High Master at St Paul's Boys), was head of Manchester Grammar – a high-flying dream team, clearly. Prior to headships, she had five teaching posts which included a spell at an 'adolescent sin bin' in Hertfordshire as well as experience at Sedbergh and Haileybury. She also has three sons and you might well wonder how it's all been possible especially given that – tall, impossibly chic and elegant – (she is putatively 50+ but you can't believe she's over 35) – she is immaculately, in fact, perfectly, turned-out. Her vehemently and winningly expressed educational principles and her clear ambitiousness (somehow so much harder for some to swallow in a woman than in a man) excite a rare diversity of responses from parents, staff, girls and fellow heads. Though many in the school community feel they don't yet know her, there can be little doubt that she brings the right combination of professionalism, dedication and vision for this school.

She inherited a flagship school with a rare record of achievement but one which had had a rocky few years culminating in a surprisingly grudging inspection report, the precipitate departure of the head and a very happy term in the in loco magistrae care of Miss Lusk from Oxford High, (now head of Abingdon (qv)) – much enjoyed by all but not necessarily easy for her successor. All pay tribute to some of the changes Mrs Stephen has introduced since her arrival – especially the house system (it was abolished 40 years ago in a fanfare of sixties anti-competition fervour, but the girls seem to love it), the much-improved pastoral care and so on. The words 'systems' and 'brand' occur frequently in her conversation – as do acknowledgements of the human frailty which make such things fail more often than they should. There can be no doubt of her commitment and devotion to the school – a job she is clearly delighted to have. 'The girls are captivating ... this is a gorgeous school which I adore to bits.' Her latest project – see Background and Atmosphere – is a planned major redevelopment of the whole school site. Her biggest tasks are to halt the fashionable exodus of girls at both 11 and 16 and to create an environment in which confidence, warmth and relaxed relationships can flourish long term in this highly academic and creative institution.

Academic matters: Hard to beat. Famous high-octane teaching and intellectual atmosphere – well, this is Hampstead – the school is always in the 'premier league' in lists of results whichever way you look at it. Things had slipped a bit in the last few years – a somewhat demoralised staff and a high turnover – but Mrs Stephen has, by all accounts, beefed up the staff considerably and 'made some terrific appointments' – there is a new buzz about the place. 'One thing we cannot compromise on at all is quality of staff.' 2010 A level results in 22 subjects taken saw 79 per cent at A*/A grade, 94 per cent at A*–B. At GCSE in 2010, 25 subjects were taken with 93 per cent at A*/A and 100 per cent at A*–C.

Well-resourced IT. Philosophy recently introduced and a range of supplementary langs available though German struggles – here as elsewhere. Good programme of foreign trips and exchanges. Well-structured and interested PSHE. DT cheeringly impressive and school won GCSE 1st and 2nd prizes for Young Inventor of the Year and 2nd prize for Young Engineer of Year and, at A level, 1st and 2nd prizes in Graphics Young Inventor of Year along with 2nd and 3rd prizes for RM Inventor of the Year. We saw some of the prize-winning pieces – wood and perspex – and marvelled at the coupling of inventiveness and style.

SEN not a major feature here though five or six girls in each year on school's SEN register with, mostly, dyslexia, dyspraxia or ADHD. A SENCo and both the head and deputy head 'have SEN knowledge'. Staff have been trained in dealing with LDD requirements. IEPs where needed.

Games, Options, the Arts: A good sports hall on site but otherwise no space at all so girls are bused here and there, most importantly to the school's own sports ground minutes away where they have a multi-gym and facilities for all the usual sports as well as dance, trampolining, yoga. Football and cricket both popular. Sport compulsory for all including the sixth. Swimming pool on most people's wish-list. In 2006, a sports tour with the boys of UCS to Australia and Hong Kong and to South Africa in 2008. More planned. Some parents feel that sporting opportunities for the less than Olympian are limited – not so, says school.

Drama excellent – there is a super studio theatre – not just a dark poky box room with lights as so often – amazing how they found room for it here – which is well used for all kinds of productions – some in collaboration with nearby University College Boys' School. Music is strong – over two thirds learn at least one instrument and we counted around twenty ensembles of all kinds. Good new music tech room feeds enthusiasm. There are concerts, festivals, competitions and innovative things like commissions from established composers, masterclasses and so on. Lots of tours and trips too e.g. a recent jazz band tour to Amsterdam and a choir trip to New York. Collaboration with UCS a long-established and much-valued feature – possibly now under threat as UCS sixth form is now co-ed. Art is unusually colourful, varied and energetic – annual fashion show, good textiles, graphics, photography.

All kinds of extra-curricular activities, recently shot in the arm by the new houses which inspire energetic, friendly rivalry. D of E is popular and successful – many leave with silver D of E and a couple with gold – and the list of clubs – mostly held in lunchtime – includes football, philosophy, health and fitness, knitters and theatre. Annual visit to the Llangollen Eisteddfod. Some parents feel there could be more, especially lower down the school but school tell us there are over 100 extra-curricular activities available across the junior and senior Schools. Girls enthuse, 'there are fantastic activities – especially in the sixth form ... I didn't realise how much there was to do.' 26 girls went on World Challenge trip to Costa Rica and Guatamala in 2009. A more than usually interesting school magazine.

Background and Atmosphere: South Hampstead was one of the first schools of the, then, Girls' Public Day School Company (which first lost the 'Company' becoming a 'Trust' and then lost the 'Public') – now the GDST. Set up on enlightened principles in the 1870s to educate girls, it has, largely, since then stuck to those principles and has been responsible for educating over 250,000 girls who have gone on to make a unique contribution to all aspects of life, especially in the professions.

South Hampstead is typical in that its approach has been based on fine teaching rather than frilly facilities and typical of the London GDST schools, until recently, in that it has always been cramped. The school has expanded hugely and imaginatively, acquiring, demolishing, building, rebuilding and now boasts considerably more space and resources but the core of the place is still its Victorian redbrick original building, complete with smallish classrooms and parquet corridors. Substantial further developments are proposed: the school put in for planning permission for a more-or-less total redevelopment of the school site, including dedicated art and music schools and a sports hall. This was intended to start in 2009 and take two years; however, Camden has refused planning permission. Mrs Stephen has publicly refused to give up on her ambitious plans, and the position is at present stale mate.

The school is on a leafy, quiet road lined with substantial redbrick houses just above the hum of the Finchley Road and within walking distance of the civilised pleasures of Hampstead, Belsize Park and Primrose Hill, but its reputation is such that girls come from all over north London. Around a third of the staff is male.

Pastoral Care and Discipline: Form teacher has main responsibility, backed by heads of year. Trained school counsellor; the deputy head has overall responsibility for pastoral matters. Few behavioural problems though proximity of local and West End fleshpots offer usual temptations. Parental complaints about poor communication with staff and less-than-satisfactory follow-up of queries. Head acknowledges the danger – 'if anything goes wrong in a school it's communication' – but is on the case. Recent innovations include a Leavers' Dinner – a civilised and imaginative idea – and a garden party for those who stay on into the sixth form – ditto. An orderly, relaxed and cooperative feel about the place.

Pupils and Parents: 'The pupils' background reflects the cosmopolitan diversity of North London and the intake reflects the policy of the Trust to have competitive fees which allow for an interesting cross section,' says school, ponderously. Traditionally a good mix of the first-time buyers, the local Hampstead big-brains, the liberal and arty, the moneyed and those who struggle – common denominator being a valuing of a sound academic education. Old Girls include Angela Lansbury, Antonia Forest, Fay Weldon, Anne Karpf, Julia Neuberger, Diana Preston, Amanda Harlech, Joanna MacGregor, Helena Bonham-Carter, Olivia Williams, Freya North etc etc.

Entrance: School is part of the north London consortium group 1, which shares its entrance procedures to avoid children sitting half a dozen exams. Exams can be taken at any school in the consortium and 'girls have equal consideration by all the schools in the group' – though common sense tells you that the school in which you sit your exam may be assumed to be your first choice. The head then scrutinises the results and chats to the heads of the primary schools to get further information. Interviews for the higher achievers – with the head or a colleague – then offers are made. A very difficult process to get right as girls may have applied for any number of schools. Somehow, each year, it just about works but – there must be a better way.

Exit: Girls from the sixth go on to all top courses in top places. 2010 saw over 10 off to Oxbridge. Lots take gap years and return to a particularly impressive range of courses – mostly serious subjects in Oxbridge/London. The few who go for art do it at the best places e.g. Chelsea, Camberwell, Wimbledon.

The fashion is to leave post-GCSEs although the school points out that more and more pupils are now staying on. Of those who leave many go to Westminster – must be a tribute to the teaching at SHHS though a doubtful one from the school's point of view – some to co-ed boarding and some to good local state comprehensives. No obvious reason why there should be such an outflow when the school is doing well.

Money Matters: Top quality education at a value-for-money price. Some academic and music schols – even up to 50 per cent of fees; for the music schol high, high standard expected. Means tested bursaries available in case of need.

Remarks: 'I've always had very good teachers,' we were told and this sense of across-the-board quality is pervasive. School doing well but with the potential to rival all-comers still to be realised. Needs to be valued, as the only high-achieving, girls' independent in the area, for the gem it is.

South Wilts Grammar School for Girls

Stratford Road, Salisbury, Wiltshire, SP1 3JJ

• Pupils: 980 girls, all day • Ages: 11-18 • Size of sixth form: 350
• Non-denom • State

Tel: 01722 323 326
Fax: 01722 320 703
Email: head@swgs.wilts.sch.uk
Website: www.swgs.wilts.sch.uk

Head: Since 2003, Mrs Frances Stratton BSc (fifties). Read geology at UCW Aberystwyth, before embarking on teaching at Luton Sixth Form College where she spent 24 years. Moved for five years to Corfe Hills School near Poole before coming to South Wilts. One grown son now working as a project manager. A veteran builder, she has overseen big construction projects in every job she has had, sometimes drawing up the plans herself (speaks of the new mathematics hub here as 'my third maths block'). Has no plans to tinker with the curriculum – 'it's too good as it is'. Together with the head of boys' grammar, Bishop Wordworth's – also a geologist – Mrs Stratton has introduced geology as an A level subject. Parents of girls in the lower years of the school describe her as 'fair' and are delighted to be here.

Academic matters: School covered in glory, as you would expect given the selective intake. School points out that its value-added scores are excellent and that its exam results are on a par with far more selective grammars. Academic pressure can be intense, with 12 GCSEs not unheard of for girls in the top sets. Don't coach your academically average daughter to get through the 11 plus or she is likely to wither here. GCSE results so good it is impossible to fault any major department. No language compulsory at GCSE and only French and German on offer at that level. Separate sciences studied at GCSE. At A level, the range of subjects (and abilities) broadens and some subjects e.g. Spanish are offered jointly with Salisbury's boys' grammar school, Bishop Wordsworth's, a 20 minute walk away (the schools have synchronised schedules to allow sixth form pupils to get to and fro). Biology, chemistry, maths and psychology, are the most popular subjects. Communication studies has been popular and the results are good, especially at AS level for which it received a Good Schools Guide A level award, as did technology. Economics (offered at Bishop's), which often attracts the intellectually challenged like wasps to a honey pot, managed A*/As for six of its eight entrants in 2010. Class sizes look big and feel big, with up to 32 girls per class in Years 7 and 8, and up to 22 in sixth form. SEN barely figures here, though the school has taken steps to improve wheelchair access.

Games, Options, the Arts: Well tried, as the many outside coaches would say. The quality of extra-curricular activities is now higher, with the largest programme ever involving over 300 girls. PE said to be a 'happy department', especially for the younger girls; sport is less vigorous as girls move up the school. Good range offered, including tag rugby, football, gymnastics, cross country, hockey, basketball, volleyball and self defence. Girls say netball and tennis are strong, football increasingly so. Also cricket – school won a national six-a-side indoor cricket competition at Lord's. Some county and even national representation, especially at athletics and lately at specialist sports like sailing and orienteering. Equestrian teams take part nationally. Generous games fields, plus all-weather athletics track used out of hours by community.

Music famously good. Head of music was one of Classic FM's five national finalists one year for the 'Music Teacher of the Year' and promotes inclusiveness ('music for all') rather than elitism (focusing on the most talented). Choral music especially hot, with 140 girls singing in the senior choir. Usual range of orchestras and bands, plus guitar ensemble and quite a few girls go on to music college or to study music at university. Music block opened in 2006 with state of the art technology. Art thrives. New 'theatre' (more of a studio, really, with seating for 70) is a well-used resource. Much of Year 7–9 drama, as well as music and other activities, run by sixth form pupils (pros and cons ...). Quite a lot of uptake for D of E at all levels, and has won awards for Young Enterprise. Scores of lunchtime clubs (bring a packed lunch to save time) but after school the place tends to empty out.

Background and Atmosphere: Opened in 1927 with 207 girls. Imposing brick main building with constantly improving additions, all in a jumbled heap at one end of the school's large property. Girls beadle along the maze-like paths between buildings – ('it took us ten minutes to get from one lesson to another when we were new!'). Building programme has done wonders and the new sixth form block is a tour de force, its computers gleaming and its 'study centre' awash with comfy sofas. Super new maths block. All science labs refurbished to a high standard, improbably interspersed among language classrooms. Good technology – the place is certainly not short of computers. Girls spoke with enthusiasm of their DT projects and we admired the glistening food tech kitchens. Fantastic music block with plenty of practice rooms and music technology. Much recent staff turnover (mainly retirement, says head). New Learning Resources Centre completed in September 2009 and dining room extension in 2010.

Pastoral Care and Discipline: Girls say they feel 'trusted' and relish the freedom they are given. Younger girls in Years 7 and 8 seem to be kept out of main school fray (our young guide did not know where the sixth form centre was). School currently winning battle on skirt length.

Pupils and Parents: Not a hotbed of ethnic diversity. Girls come by bus and train from over 50 primary schools – some from up to 40 miles away – plus from a few local preps. Unlike the boys' grammar, which stands alone as the premier boys' school in the area, South Wilts has plenty of local competition from the independent sector, especially from the Godolphin School which narrowly pips it in the A level league tables most years. The sorts of parents you will find at the two schools are almost indistinguishable, a few will have one girl at each.

Entrance: Girls take tests in VR, maths and English in November before year of entry. Some 350 girls sit the 11 plus and up to 128 are offered places, some through the border zone and review process (e.g. girls who performed below par on the exam, but whose primary schools can vouch for their indisputable academic ability). A small handful enters at Years 8, 9 and 10. Up to 70 girls join at sixth form, mainly from local 11–16 schools; entry requires six A–C grades, with a B usually required in subjects to be studied at A level.

Exit: 10 per cent leave after GCSEs, mainly to sixth form college, often because they are tired of commuting a vast distance to school (60 per cent travel more than five km to get to South Wilts, many much more). Five to Cambridge and seven to Oxford in 2010. Top university destinations, by far, are Cardiff and Exeter, followed by Southampton, Surrey, Bristol. Surprisingly high numbers into sciences, technology, medicine, engineering etc. Also many to read modern languages.

Remarks: A superb, free education for clever, self-motivated girls. Lacks the imposing atmosphere of Salisbury's boys' grammar but most parents consider that a plus.

Southbank International School (W1)

Linked to Southbank International School (W11) in the Junior section
Linked to Southbank International School (NW3) in the Junior section

63-65 Portland Place, London, W1B 1QR

• Pupils: 315 boys and girls; all day • Ages: 11-18 • Size of sixth form: 105
• Non-denom • Fees: £20,100-£22,200 pa • Independent

Tel: 020 7243 3803
Fax: 020 7727 3290
Email: admissions@southbank.org
Website: www.southbank.org

Chairman: Since 2007, Mr Terrence Hedger BA (fifties) who has been in education his entire career. He has had posts in Jamaica, the Cayman Islands and Madrid and was Principal at the International College Spain in Madrid before arriving in London. Married for 35 years; wife also in education. They met while Terry was working for the VSO (Peace Corps) in Jamaica; their three children live in the London area.

He is passionate about the IB and he feels that he can make the Southbank one of the best IB schools in the UK. He has an open-door policy and he seemed to know the names of everyone. He sees talent and ability in all the students and he feels the atmosphere at Southbank encourages these talents to flourish. He affirms that with his team he 'can get good average students to overachieve.'

Academic matters: Southbank follows the IBO system and is run on 'international lines'. Divided into Primary Years 3–11, Middle Years 11–16, and Diploma 16–18, the school is spread over three campuses: Kensington and Hampstead house the Primary Years and Westminster has all the Middle Years and all Diploma students (in a dedicated IB Centre opened in 2007). The Primary and Middle Years focus on the IBPYP and IBMYP methods, 'what do I want to know?'

The Diploma Program is a demanding two year course preparing the pupils for university. The students choose one subject from six subject groups, of which two are languages. They must also write a 4000 word extended essay, complete a theory of knowledge course and do 150 hours of activities outside the classroom including community service (CAS). Results in 2010 saw 51 students achieving an average score of 35 points. Nine students scored 40 points or higher and one student achieved 43 points. 16 students were awarded Bi-lingual Diplomas.

Classes are small, never more than 16, and teachers are available to parents and students by email or in person (teachers devote three hours each week to the parents). Full reports are sent each semester and mid-semester evaluations are made, so any problems are caught early and dealt with (at primary school campuses, full reports are sent twice a year, with conferences held twice a year and student-led conferences once a year). Students who have completed four years of high school are awarded 24 credits and given a US high school honours diploma in the US tradition in recognition of their IB coursework.

Computers are everywhere; the school has a progressive IT curriculum and is considered an innovator in the world of e-learning. Students can bring their own computers or use the many on campus; interactive whiteboards in most classrooms.

Languages are important. Spanish is started at the Primary level and French is introduced at the Middle level. Each child is encouraged to continue to learn his or her mother tongue. There are 17 languages taught and if the language isn't on the books, all you have to do is ask for it (will generally incur additional fees).

Teachers are dedicated and enthusiastic. The turnover is low but hiring young teachers is difficult, given the London housing prices. The student:teacher ratio is eight to one.

A full-time SEN teacher serves all three campuses to help with light to medium dyslexia, bi-lingual learning problems and some other special needs. The school gives a chance to kids with these problems. But sometimes if it becomes clear that Southbank cannot grapple with more severe problems adequately, then the school and parents work together to find alternative solutions. Those who need to learn English as an additional language are supported by EAL lessons as part of the standard program. They eventually mainstream into the normal classes.

Games, Options, the Arts: Art is everywhere, the music practice rooms are full, buses are waiting to take kids off to PE (no gyms on the Westminster campus; at Kensington and Hampstead, off-campus facilities supplement the multi-purpose halls), and, when we visited, there was a drama class in the cafeteria. The school participates regularly in the International Schools' Theatre Association (ISTA). The pupils learn violin and cello at the Primary level with the Suzuki method, and music carries through to the Diploma level with rock bands and choirs. The senior girls recently won the ISSA volleyball championships.

After-school activities are heavily subscribed. 'London as a classroom' might as well be the school mantra. The head said it was hard to keep track of all the classes that are visiting museums, galleries or learning events around the capital at any one time, although some parents say there is less of this now than in recent years, and – having been drawn to Southbank for that very appealing aspect – there is some disappointment that their children have had only one or two field trips around London in a year. Reporting inconsistent here – seems to depend on the year group, from almost no trips in one year to children's toes barely touching down on school property in other year groups ...

Model United Nations is a popular activity and every one at the Middle and Diploma level goes on a five day adventure trip as a team building exercise. Community service at all the schools is 'cool'. The three campuses are sponsoring tsunami orphans in Sri Lanka, building a community centre and sports ground, sending teachers and grade 12 volunteers out to help build the facilities and making a five year commitment to the orphans. Each campus will develop its own programmes of support for the orphanage and other projects. The school has a long-standing relationship with a school in Tanzania.

Background and Atmosphere: The school opened its doors in 1979 on the Southbank. It was an idealistic concept of the 'city as the school' and a 'school without walls'. After many moves and growing pains, the IB was adopted in 1984 and the current campuses established (Kensington in 1988, Hampstead in 1995 and Westminster, Portland Place in 2003). Campuses are all over the map, but the school provides great bus transportation to catchments all over London.

The Kensington Southbank campus consists of two houses and a garden with a large assembly room. The classrooms are small but the atmosphere is great. Art is on the walls and there is an IT space. Hampstead is a purpose built school behind an Edwardian facade. There is even enough room for a gym (multi-purpose room). Westminster Southbank is a grade II listed Regency building which has been refurbished with classrooms and labs. It currently houses the 11–16s. No outside space; small cafeteria. In September 2007, Westminster opened an annexe on Conway Street (eight minute walk from Portland Place), fitted with classrooms, a library and labs; primarily for the Diploma students (16–18). This has allowed Kensington and Hampstead to concentrate on the Primary Years (3–11), feeding the Middle Years to Westminster.

The Southbank recently sold a majority share of the school to Cognita, a group that owns and manages independent schools and is headed by Chris Woodhead, former UK Chief Inspector of Schools. Cognita has promised the parents and staff that they will let the current administration run the school, because they want to 'preserve [its] established ethos'.

The headmaster retired in the summer of 2007, and that role has been replaced by the Chairman of the Education Board, which is made up of the the Westminster, Hampstead and Kensington principals and other senior administrators.

Pastoral Care and Discipline: Although no official school rules, there is zero tolerance for drugs, alcohol and chewing gum! Staff are trained to recognise the signs of substance abuse and even though the older kids have exit privileges, there have been no recent problems. Bullying is not an issue as everyone is so different; in fact the school celebrates difference, encourages independent thinking and responsibility for oneself and for others. They are expected to work hard and get results.

Pupils and Parents: Many Southbank students are ex-pats, children of diplomats or business people. There are 66 nationalities represented. Although there is no dress code the kids look good. They are sharp, friendly and not intimidated by teachers or visitors. Classroom exchanges are lively yet respectful. Parents are very welcome here. There is an active PTA and the school is very family friendly. They have access to teachers any time, directly or with email.

Entrance: Students are admitted based on availability and level of preparedness. Candidates must be able to cope with the demands of the IB. Transcripts, teacher recommendations, a statement from parents and a profile written by the student are considered. While academic achievements are important, Southbank tries to attract pupils who are open-minded, motivated and enjoy learning. English is essential for passing the IB. Applications are accepted all year. Waiting lists depend on the class but, as with most schools with such a large ex-pat population, students do come and go, so don't give up on finding a place eventually.

Southbank is an 'international school', priding itself on a diverse student body and staff. It understands the problems of kids who have moved frequently and knows how to make them welcome. Extra support is given to families arriving during the year, the school website links up with useful contacts. The PTA is active with the administration as well as fund-raising, so there is scope for a newly arrived parent to get involved.

Exit: Since September 2007, the guidance department has had two dedicated advisers; one for US universities and one for UK and non-US universities. A careers survey is taken by all students in Grade 10 and a university course survey is taken in Grade 11. Information evenings are held for the parents who might be unfamiliar with the application process. A careers day is organised for the students.

All Diploma students go on to university – mostly in the UK or US. Duke, Brown, BU, Parsons School of Design were some choices, as well as Oxbridge, King's College, LSE and St Andrews.

Southbank's IB program makes it easy for mobile families to find a common curriculum world wide. Transfers during the two year IB Diploma programme are not encouraged, and may even require starting the Diploma programme over again rather than picking up half way through. However, Southbank tries very hard to make transitions work .

Money Matters: Some bursarial help is available for those Southbank families who are suddenly in reduced circumstances. The Milton Toubkin Scholarship awards scholarships to outstanding, motivated students at the Diploma level.

Remarks: Good family-orientated urban school with international flavour. Well geared for the smart, curious and self motivated student, but the average student would do very well here. Wait and see how the new administrative triumvirate will work and what Cognita will do with the school they claim will be their international flagship.

Stamford High School

Linked to Stamford Junior School in the Junior section
Linked to Stamford School in the Senior section

St Martin's, Stamford, Lincolnshire, PE9 2LL

• Pupils: 625 girls; 35 board, rest day • Ages: 11-18 • Size of sixth form: 180 • C of E • Fees: Day £11,796; Boarding £16,308-£21,540 pa • Independent

Tel: 01780 484 200
Fax: 01780 484 201
Email: headshs@ses.lincs.sch.uk
Website: www.ses.lincs.sch.uk

Head: Since 2003, Mrs Dyl Powell BEd NPQH (fiftyish), a PE and maths specialist, and a football enthusiast who supports Barcelona but likes 'good football' whoever plays it – including her own girls. Mrs Powell came from The King's School in Peterborough where she'd been deputy head for nine years. Sensible, practical and down-to-earth, Mrs Powell is clearly a 'doer' rather than an administrator or ivory tower-dweller. 'Involved' – i.e. she involves herself – is the word most often used of her. She teaches, she sings in the chapel choir, she is a member of the schools' CCF, she is a hockey umpire and, working comfortably with the other two heads of the Stamford Endowed Schools (SES) and the principal, she has been busily changing, renewing, updating. 'Our school song begins, "Within these walls of grey ... " and that's exactly what they were,' she admits. 'I set myself to lighten the atmosphere – new colours, refurbishment, signage, plasma screens, redecoration of the hall, an honours board, a new house system and, well, it seems to have worked.' Parents agree and all talk of the friendliness in the school and its new sense of confidence. Something good is happening here and Mrs Powell is at the heart of it.

Principal: The three schools in the Stamford Endowed Schools foundation are overseen by the Principal, Mr Stephen Roberts, who arrived in September 2008 from Felsted School of which he had been head for fifteen years – a safe pair of hands then. This was a clever appointment and Mr Roberts sees eye to eye with the three heads of the individual schools over the aims – near and far – of the foundation. 'He comes to all events,' we were told.

Academic matters: Given that the school has a pretty comprehensive intake, the curriculum and the results are impressive and value-added in particular is notable. In 2010, at GCSE, 100 per cent of girls gained at least 5 A*–C grades and a remarkable 71 per cent achieved A*/As. Particularly successful were DT, drama, RS and music. At A level – which is taught coeducationally with the boys of Stamford School – 28 subjects are offered. Most popular are biology, business, chemistry, Eng lit, geog, history, RS, business studies and maths. Exceptional maths and RS results. Stamford School's (the boys' school) head is a modern linguist and this ensures that langs more than hold their own – good to see French, German, Russian and Spanish on offer though numbers not huge. Chemistry is very popular, with the number of girls taking science bucking the national trend. GCSE French is fast-tracked for top two sets and taken early. Setting in English, maths, langs and science to GCSE.

Good learning support dept for those with SEN. LSAs in class, individual help given in lunch and morning breaks and no withdrawal from lessons. School eager to support all-comers – 'we look at the individual'. Wheelchairs users would have difficulties because of the site – and its spread over the town – and especially in the main high school building which is listed so modifications are a problem. But head says, 'we look creatively at what we can do within the internal structure.' A positive attitude overall. Head has inspirational new initiative – RiFTT – 'Reaching for the Top' – which aims to encourage girls 'to think outside the syllabus and expand their horizons' – especially important for the G and T and those who might take Oxbridge. Currently 14 need EAL but no-one accepted who can't deal with the curriculum. Weekly EAL lessons for those who need it, mostly one-to-one, sometimes in groups of two or three. The EAL teacher liaises with subject staff. More support given in boarding houses. Sixth form EAL students sit IELTS examination.

Games, Options, the Arts: One parent summed up what everyone told us, 'there is a good balance between the importance the school gives to academic achievement and the rounding the girls get from doing other things.' There are lots of other things but sport and music, perhaps, stand out most. Excellent sports facilities – all three schools benefit from excellent spread of shared facilities and no big posh independent school can offer more. Much success – girls unbeaten in badminton in 2008–9 and equally successful across the range. 'You can pick what you enjoy,' we were told – if only it had been like that we were at school, we mused. Masses of after-school activities – too much to choose from for many. CCF is especially popular.

Music is 'really big' and is mostly in collaboration with the boys' school – the same head of dept oversees all three schools which makes sense but must be a huge job. The dept occupies an ancient building opposite the High School. There is every kind of ensemble – orchestras, choirs of various types and sizes, bands and chamber groups – among the most energetic music set-ups we have met anywhere. Girls pay tribute to their teachers – 'you can learn any instrument you like – they'll always find you a teacher' ... 'there's so much music on offer here'. Even the non-musical feel the effects and walls we passed trembled with drum-beats, piano rhapsodies and brass clarions. Music tech popular but more so with the boys, we were told. Lovely art – precise and imaginative – excellent DT and clever textiles – a sense of enjoyment pervades all. Speech and drama also 'big' and successful with girls carrying off prizes at local and national events.

Background and Atmosphere: Though less venerable than the boys' school, the High School is no Joanna-Come-Lately and it occupies a stunning Georgian building on a broad and elegant street in this stunning Georgian town. Stamford, for those who think they don't know it, will be familiar to all as the ready-made backdrop to most of the eighteenth century costume dramas you've drooled over – not least *Pride and Prejudice* – yes, that version. It is simply delicious – especially out of traffic-snarly periods – and one can understand an occasional gentle smugness and unwillingness-to-look-outside quality in its denizens. The High School occupies a fine position next to Burghley House and its estate, a splendid Elizabethan pile built by Elizabeth's Lord Burghley and helped along in the following century by Capability Brown who didn't half get about. A useful resource to have next door.

And the new has most definitely arrived here too. Whiteboards everywhere, IT bristles around the place, plasma screens hither and yon announcing the events of the day – both internal and external. New lang labs – school very proud. New and excellent dance/drama studio and another drama studio – well-equipped – elsewhere. New spectroscopy suite – this was explained to us and we left feeling erudite and impressed. Nice to see Rosalind Franklin honoured in its naming. The arts rooms have recently been refurbished, creating a hub of artistic endeavours and beautiful, spacious studios. In other ways, it still feels very much like a trad girls' school – narrowish corridors, smallish classrooms and a bit of a rabbit warren ('they give you maps when you arrive,' we were told) full of happy bunnies in long skirts. Two good sized rooms for home economics – which is very popular. Excellent library – especially well stocked in English. Good displays everywhere and they have much that merits it.

The SES was formed in 1997 and now works well – all the administration managed centrally and overseen by the principal. The coed sixth form is a popular and unqualified success and works well on academic, social and economic grounds. In effect, rather than the sexes being entirely mixed in the sixth form classrooms, timetabling more frequently results in the pupils of each school sharing their teachers. This is partly because there's a ten minute walk between the two schools and you can't have the pupils belting across the town and back all day. Parents applaud the single sex tuition in Years 7–11 and the co-ed sixth with all the shared opportunities it brings. Girls clearly approve, 'it's great being all girls until you're sixteen but it's also great being mixed in the sixth form,' said one. There is every sense that the three heads and principal like each other and collaborate fruitfully, though communication between the two senior schools and the staff – and opportunities for cooperation – still need work, as many acknowledge. There is the potential for a constant stimulating dialogue and sharing here – it's not fully realised yet.

Pastoral Care and Discipline: Friends in Stamford High School – 'FISH' – is school's mentoring system in which Year 10 girls keep an eye on Year 7s – around 80 per cent of the older girls take part. Form tutors pick up most other problems and parents enthuse about the pastoral side. 'It's one massive big tick,' a current dad assured us, 'they are very good at handling the business of being a young kid in a community'. Surprisingly, to this addled urban writer, all the High School girls, including the sixth, wear uniform and an eccentric one it is – the younger girls wearing long – ankle-length in some cases – skirts. 'We love it,' we were assured and it is attractive in an Edwardian kind of way.

House system ensures vertical mixing and is popular and it makes the girls very competitive. Over-competitiveness and cliqueyness were the only two common grouses we heard – but we did hear them quite a lot. On the other hand, everyone told us, 'it's very friendly – the teachers help you a lot – all my teachers have different teaching styles – they're all great characters.' Boarding in big old house – used to be the junior school – girls in Years 7–11 in twos, threes or fours and sixth formers in en suite ones and twos in a separate building. Boarding is cosy and small and, unlike in so many other places, rather on the increase here – mostly due to the school's wonderfully flexible policy about girls staying for a bunch of nights as and when. Boarding rated as 'outstanding' in latest Ofsted report.

Pupils and Parents: Mostly local though some day pupils from up to an hour away. Some few parents commute the hour's train journey to London – well worth a ponder if this is the sort of school you want. Useful school bus system. Most boarders are from Services families though a few come from overseas and are helped with EAL if needed, though their English must be good enough for them to cope with the academic demands. The County Scholarships have long ensured a good social mix – within the meaning of that in rural Lincs/Rutland – but in truth, this is a pretty homogeneous, and exceptionally pretty, we thought, bunch of girls. They were also open, unpretentious, highly articulate and warm – of great credit to the school. Lively and supportive PA but some complain – of all three schools – that they need to be more ambitious and promote the foundation more vigorously. The new principal and his dept will probably address this – early days yet – but it is interesting that the Stamford parents, conscious of what a treasure they share, feel that the wider world could – and should – take note. Lots of famous Old Girls e.g. Eleanor Turner, Sarah Outen, Sara Cawood, Bishop Maureen Jones, Lucy Cohu, Daphne Ledward-Hands and Susannah Ivens 1998 Dressmaker of the Year for wedding dresses!

Entrance: Most come in from the junior school. 125 sit exam for the school's 90-odd places – quite good odds overall, given that many will have also applied elsewhere. They come from Copthill Prep, Malcolm Sargent, St Gilbert's, St Georges, Uffington, St Augustines, Bluecoat. At 13, applicants from Orton Wistow, Laxton Junior, Brooke Priory, The Bythams, Ketton and Witham Hall. 60 candidates for the 12 coveted County Scholarships (see below). Entrance to the sixth form requires five B+s at GCSE and school advises with candour and compassion those few of their own who are unlikely to cope to look elsewhere. 20+ come into the sixth from all over – some from quite far afield – and all are quickly integrated.

Exit: The move to a co-ed sixth stopped the outflow after GCSE and only a few go now – far fewer than hitherto to the local independents. Those who do leave after GCSE go mostly to the local sixth form colleges. The vast majority at 18 to further/higher education – a good spread of mostly Russell Group universities – Birmingham, Sheffield and Leeds currently the faves. Impressive range of subjects too – no pigeon holing here. No Oxbridge in 2007, 2008 – are these bright,delightful girls selling themselves short? But school assures us that six went to Oxbridge in 2010.

Sixteen County Scholarships, awarded by Lincolnshire CC in lieu of grammar school places as, although Lincs is still a grammar school county, Stamford doesn't have one. These awards currently cover the whole fee but they are gradually being phased out during the coming decade and will mean that the last scholars under this scheme will arrive in 2019. Thereafter, both SES senior schools hope to supply the gap with their own means-tested bursaries. Much highly successful fund-raising among alumnae. Boarding fees not covered by this scholarship.

Money Matters: Remarks: This school and the foundation of which it is a part offer rare opportunities and at a more than competitive fee. In the words of one sixth former, 'the teachers put so much into helping us – there's nothing they wouldn't do,' and a fifth former, 'it's a school for anybody. I don't know anyone who doesn't enjoy it.'

Stamford School

Linked to Stamford Junior School in the Junior section
Linked to Stamford High School in the Senior section

Southfields House, St Paul's Street, Stamford, Lincolnshire, PE9 2BQ

• Pupils: 680 boys, 70 board • Ages: 11-18 • Size of sixth form: 195 • C of E
• Fees: Day £11,796; Boarding £16,308-£21,540 pa • Independent

Tel: 01780 750 300
Fax: 01780 750 336
Email: headss@ses.lincs.sch.uk
Website: www.ses.lincs.sch.uk

Head: Since 2005, Mr Stuart Burns MA, a modern and medieval linguist (late thirties). Previously, Mr Burns was senior master and i/c boarding at Brighton College, prior to which he taught at Dulwich College. He was a Cambridge rugby blue and began his working life as a city bond dealer but his competitive instincts are now directed to tennis, golf and sailing. Very much a hands-on head, he is credited with having made 'big improvements' in a short time and gains a thumbs-up from the close-knit local community which provides his core market. 'I have been rationalizing the site,' he says. 'It had been rather ramshackle but full of heart.' Walking around the town one sees evidence of this more coherent thinking all over the place – and of the 'heart'. In common with his fellow heads in the Stamford Endowed Schools (SES), Mr Burns manages to teach – he takes the weakest GCSE French set and beginners' German – and works closely with the SES principal and his two peers in the programme of renewal and development that is in rapid progress. Candid, sensible, brisk and likeable, Mr Burns has much to build on here and, still, much to do.

Principal: The three schools in the Stamford Endowed Schools foundation are overseen by the Principal, Mr Stephen Roberts, who arrived in September 2008 from Felsted School of which he had been head for fifteen years – a safe pair of hands then. This was a clever appointment and Mr Roberts sees eye to eye with the three heads of the individual schools over the aims – near and far – of the foundation. 'He comes to all events,' we were told.

Mr Burns will be leaving at Easter 2011 to take up the position of director on the board of Palatinate Schools – a company which owns several schools in London.

Academic matters: More than respectable results. 53 per cent of subjects taken at GCSE in 2010 achieved A*/A. Exceptional showings in all three sciences, maths and RS. RS (compulsory) seems to be exceptionally taught across the three schools. Popular options at this level are geog, hist, PE and DT. At A level – taught coeducationally with Stamford High School – 76 per cent A*–B grades in 2010. Of the mainstream subjects, languages, maths and history achieve most highly with exceptional results in maths. Mr Burns is a linguist and this ensures that, unlike in so many boys' schools, languages are properly supported and successful – hooray!

School good at liaising with junior/primary schools over pupils with SEN and also good at picking up those who arrive without a diagnosis but who need support. Learning support dept helps with weekly and drop-in classes and works closely with teachers to develop strategies tailored to individual needs. 'We really support those with physical disabilities,' says Mr Burns, 'they need looking after and special attention but fundamentally they just need stretching rather than being hived off.' A sense of care and attention to individuals here.

Good provision for the most part though latest inspection report (2005) commented on the need for improvements to the library. The new Research and Learning Centre is the school's somewhat tardy response and integrates 10,000 books with 'online learning suite'. 'Tardy' may be unfair. It has taken a big effort and time to save the £1.6m required. This facility places a modern, spacious and well-equipped study and research centre at the heart of the school and is well-used by students. We do wonder why the word 'library' is verbum non gratum anywhere these days!

Games, Options, the Arts: 'Sport has come on hugely,' everyone told us, because of the new director, an ex-London Irish player. Cricket has been given a boost with the recent addition of Dean Headley – the former England international cricketer – to the coaching rostrum. Some of the most stunning playing fields we've seen anywhere. Good Astro provision and the sharing of facilities across the three schools makes every kind of sense. Good open air pool – used by boarders whenever – and covered pool too. Planning permission has now been granted for a new sports centre, which will house a 25m pool. CCF is huge here – the indoor shooting range supports highly successful shooting team which wins everything going. School sports generally very good – opportunities and successes and something for everyone.

Art impresses wherever you go. Excellent displays of boys' work; we rejoiced to see evidence of the trad skills – e.g. painting and drawing, to a high level as well as applied work of various kinds. Fine portrait work here and good use of small art library though art history not offered. We loved the DT and craft work e.g. clay profiteroles (looked scrummy) and a pizza which we nearly took away. We admired the exam work – the wine rack, the shoe locker – simple, imaginative and deft work. Music – here as in all three schools – exemplary – rich, various and dazzling. Music not for the geeks but an integral part of life and overseen by the same head of dept for all three schools. Pupils positively fizz when they talk about the sheer fun of all the opportunities they have, ensembles, tours etc – and doing much in collaboration with the girls clearly doesn't hurt. Music tech is big news here too. Good, lively drama – again popular, especially when the two schools work together. Work will soon begin on a Performing Arts Centre so that more parents and people from the town will be able to enjoy the large-scale productions.

Background and Atmosphere: Stamford is an eighteenth century aficionado's bit of heaven and any such visitor will virtually know their way around as so much of the town has been used in costume dramas over the years. This is Georgian, honey-coloured elegance not yet ruined by constant traffic – though they're working on it.

In 1997, the governors of Stamford School and Stamford High School decided that 'the two schools should work more harmoniously together' and brought in new structure overseen by a new principal of all three schools, including the junior school. The idea was that the three schools should 'maintain their individual character but that the foundation which would then comprise all three schools would be able to educate the school population from 4–18, girls and boys, day pupils and boarders'. 'It's been huge for us,' says Mr Burns. 'The co-ed sixth form has been, perhaps, the most profound change – it's like a mini university,' he says and it does have a flavour of that. In effect, rather than the sexes being entirely mixed in the sixth form classrooms, timetabling more frequently results in the pupils of each school sharing their teachers. This is partly because there's a ten minute walk between the two schools and you can't have the pupils belting across the town and back all day. Parents applaud the single sex tuition in Years 7–11 and the co-ed sixth with all the shared opportunities it brings.

There is a substantial programme of renewal going on. As so often happened, twentieth century architects here clearly felt under no obligation to design in sympathy with the existing glorious school buildings and Stamford is saddled with a number of edifices from Grimsville, notably the old gym, the bridge – clearly inspired by Motorway chic – and the central quad – but the well-funded and sensitive renewal programme is doing its best to conceal or enhance where they can.

Boys and parents alike feel that, not just in the sixth form, the 'merging' of the school with the girls' school has 'really raised our game'. However, some boys' school parents also feel that the school could be better organized and there is a palpable difference between the efficiency of the girls' school in this regard and the boys' – as several parents of children at both confirmed. 'The girls' school staff are always quick to get back to us – sometimes you never hear back from the boys' school.' Other parents, however, express themselves happy with both schools in this respect. Some parental feeling that the SES schools don't 'court' the locals enough. 'Oundle, Uppingham and Oakham really promote themselves – in the local preps and so on – the SES should do far more,' we were told.

Despite its laudable upgrading and new sense of pride, the SES is not at pains to 'up the academics' (i.e. position in the league tables) which would result in doing itself out of much of its loyal traditional market. Nonetheless, the schools deserve to be far better known and appreciated. This writer can see little reason why some locals might choose the big three, relatively close-by, independents given all on offer here. The principal, Mr Roberts is affable, forward looking and a true educationalist. It is, in part, his job to up the school's confidence, boost the cooperation between the schools and to bruit abroad the excellence of his foundation. Stamford's pride should be more than just a smug local secret.

Pastoral Care and Discipline: Parents praise the pastoral care – 'they are extraordinarily nurturing,' we were told, 'and boys with problems get wonderful support'. Mentoring of the young by the older and 'we don't accept bullying,' says Mr Burns, 'we go straight at it – we work with parents, we don't wait for it to sort itself out.' Yes! In general, the pupils – especially in the sixth form when, of necessity, they have to be able to move around the town unsupervised, are trusted to behave and they do. 'We live or die by our reputation in this town,' says Mr Burns. Few major incidents – no physical contact allowed (a 'six inch rule' obtains, we were informed) between six formers, and misdemeanours of the drink/smoke nature are few and petty. Two recent exclusions for drugs.

Slight sense among some parents that the 'shut-up-and-get-on-with-it' boy can get overlooked. However, others told us that the school's students are 'not just cardboard cut outs' and very much seen as individuals. Some parental feeling that the discipline 'could be better' and that there is rather too much variation in behaviour deemed acceptable by different members of staff. 'Sports stars seem to get away with stuff others never would', we also heard – but there may be a tinge of jealousy here? And school strenuously refutes the idea. Most parents feel the school has a 'very good atmosphere' and that the boys are prepared to 'be able to mix with anyone'. There is a 'lot of banter and lots of respect – a balance that wins boys' interest. But they know there is a line.' 'The good education gives them choices but they also learn the life skills to work with others and motivate themselves and other people.'

Boarding is tiny – in relation to the overall numbers – and cosy – surprisingly good for so few and rated as 'outstanding' in the recent Ofsted inspection. Four resident tutors and two matrons in houses, all sixth formers in single rooms – mostly en suite – Year 11s in singles/twins and younger boys in twins. Around 15 per cent from overseas – Hong Kong, China, Russia etc. Excellent common rooms and facilities, good kitchens in boarding houses, WiFi all over, rooms small but sensible. Good healthy food eaten by all.

Pupils and Parents: From a good thirty miles around – sometimes more in the sixth. Families mostly local and professional and as you'd expect – people who value the education, location, good social mix and very reasonable fees more than the name of a glitzy, famous public school. It's only one hour by train to King's Cross – some parents commute and you can see why. Boarders often from RAF families with a sprinkling from overseas. The boys we met were some of the most unpretentiously impressive and charming we have met anywhere. This particular writer has visited over 150 schools for The GSG and cannot remember more open, articulate, and delightful boys anywhere. They do the school great credit. Famous OBs include the Lord Burghley and various later ones, Alfred Harmsworth (Viscount Northcliffe), also musical knights Malcolm Sargent and Michael Tippett, various literati including Colin Dexter and his most famous creation, numerous military men including Sir Michael Jackson, many divines, industrialists and sportsmen of note.

Entrance: Over 130 external applicants for 60 places at 11+ – tests in English, maths and reasoning – junior school pupils transfer more or less automatically. Also from Copthill Prep, Witham Prep and local primaries. 5+ B+s required at GCSE for entrance to the sixth. Not huge hurdles. Perhaps seemingly too easy? If they made it harder, maybe people would value more what is on their doorstep?

Exit: Penny numbers each year to Oxbridge, clutch of medics, chemists, engineers. Popular in the large mix of destinations are London University colleges, Newcastle, Leeds, Loughborough and many of the newer universities. Impossible to select favourites from the vast range of subjects undertaken. Clearly no sausage-making going on here.

Money Matters: In addition to the County Scholarships (see entry on Stamford HS), school offers numerous academic, music and art awards at 11,13 and 16. A special scholarship fund for Poles – result of strong local Polish community from WW11. Also means-tested bursaries for the bright broke.

Remarks: Impressive on all fronts. A privileged – but not spoiling – start in life for all but snobs. Why pay more?

Stanbridge Earls School

Stanbridge Lane, Romsey, Hampshire, SO51 0ZS

• Pupils: 180 of whom 140 are boarders. 140 boys, 40 girls • Ages: 10-19
• Size of sixth form: 45 • Inter-denom • Independent

Tel: 01794 529 400
Fax: 01794 511 201
Email: admin@stanbridgeearls.co.uk
Website: www.stanbridgeearls.co.uk

Head: Since 2010, Mr Peter Trythall MA (late forties). Previously head of boarding and sixth form at the troubled Bolitho School. Educated at The King's School, Canterbury he read history and politics at Stirling University and spent nine years in the army. He is married to Beth, a teacher and nurse and they have four children.

Academic matters: This is a CReSTeD category SP school, and whilst a mainstream curriculum is (more or less) followed and children take A levels, Stanbridge Earls has long had a good reputation for catering for specific learning difficulties. Learning support is offered to all pupils in varying degrees, from supporting the 'fragile' pupil to help for many specific learning difficulties, including dyslexia, Asperger's, dyspraxia, dyscalculia, dysphasia and dysgraphia. Mrs Edwina Cole runs the SEN (Special Educational Needs) department with a large dedicated staff. Tiny classes, staff/pupil ratio of 1:6, max class size 12, but mostly eight or nine. SEN classes are either for children withdrawn from class on a one-to-one basis, or for small groups; many subjects are also taught with a support teacher in class. An occupational and two speech therapists are on call and their time greatly over-subscribed; this is a school which treats the whole child. Impressive.

80 pupils currently statemented, of whom most are wholly or partly are paid for by their LEAs (often after tribunal). GCSEs, A levels, NVQs, Certificates of Achievement are the norm though most take the exam at modular level. English lit, English lang, maths and science are the core curriculum subjects for GCSE. Ahead of time they have chosen to omit the obligatory foreign language – often a nightmare for the SpLD pupil. Courses are tailored to the child's interest and ability. They gladly embrace behaviour problems that derive from an SEN – from the low self esteem which results from all that early years drubbing – but they draw the line at problems that display obduracy – there are vulnerable souls here who need space to grow. Stanbridge pupils exhibit all the jolly loquacity you expect from, especially, dyslexics and, they say, 'they develop quickly, behaviourally and emotionally, because they're so grateful and relieved to be here.' We saw this for ourselves – we were shown around by a boy declared unteachable and disruptive two years ago by his previous school. As sensitive and personable a fellow as you'd ever meet, he's just bagged a quiverful of A*s in his GCSEs.

Accelerated learning centre with an all female staff of 20–15 literacy specialists, two speech and language, two English as a second language and one occupational therapist (for dyspraxics). A busy, happy hub of a place, where to stand and chat is to be thoroughly in the way. There's a separate department, seven strong, for numeracy skills – the only one of its kind. For lots of these pupils, here is where it happens. They like it. Most have regular one-to-one and you can swap tutors on the rare occasions you don't get on with each other.

Tiny classes, most eight or nine, many fewer. Entry Level Certificates, GCSEs, A levels, NVQs and other vocational, creative and practical subjects – see their website. English, maths and science are the core curriculum subjects for GCSE. Courses are tailored to the child's interest and ability. The accent is on studying conventional academic subjects. Prep supervised in small groups and all assignments published so no one can 'forget'.

Pupils rave about the teachers. Many of these children are victims of that inability of mainstream schools to work with any but conventionally intelligent children and endured misery before coming here. They say they are never, ever, treated dismissively or with impatience – quite the reverse, 'they simply can't do enough for you'. Observable also, and vital to the efficacy of the regenerative elixir, pupils are notably supportive of each other. Teachers irrigate them with praise. One pupil said, 'I'm sure they've got one of those psychologist's reports in my file somewhere, and they may even refer to it sometimes, but the point is they know me as an individual and treat me as I am.' SENs here are addressed not clinically but holistically – emotionally, intellectually, physically and socially.' You've got to say, it works. Teachers picked for quality of heart – 'they've got to give, give, give.' Very low turnover. 'If they still love it after a year, they stay forever.'

Performance table results used to be dismal in the bad old days when exams taken a year late – as are many here – were not counted. Now they are, and in 2008 school just squeezed into the Times top 450 independent secondary schools list. School says the MidYIS value-added scoring system shows Stanbridge is in the top 10 per cent.

Games, Options, the Arts: Usual collection of games on offer; excellent and well used swimming pool, sports hall, plus riding, judo, archery etc. Forty different activities on offer after class – pupils must opt for five, of which three must be of a physical nature. D of E, leadership training, no CCF.

Home economics popular and fabric design. Drama strong, music good – on Tuesdays all the staff listen to any child who wants to perform anything, even if it's only a one-finger exercise on the piano. One of the lakes is well stocked for fishing, and a tributary to the River Test runs through the grounds. Art very strong and popular, CDT well supported; lots of successful entrants in all subjects at national competition level.

Background and Atmosphere: Founded in 1953 by refugees from the London world of creative arts as an 'alternative to the conventional public school'. Became renowned for its early recognition of specific learning difficulties. Charming, much altered sixteenth century manor house set in 50 acres of delightful parkland, with streams and lakes and mature trees. The campus has a spacious feel, the low rooflines abetting this. Just as well because, though the old is giving way to the creditable new, a lot of these buildings have a less than semi-permanent look to them. The pupils loyally say it's because the school spends its money on people not architecture, and they proudly showed us the WW2 theatre – ENSA would have been at home – and said, very fondly, 'this place sums the school up' – which, in many ways, it most agreeably does. This is not a rich school but it is adequately resourced. The welcoming and helpful telephone receptionist deserves a beacon award in her own right.

Pastoral Care and Discipline: You move up a house year by year. They describe it as 'multi-layered', meaning you have a housemaster/mistress, plus the couple who are in charge of your living quarters. So easy are relationships here between staff and pupils that it's straightforward to find someone to talk to. They like to talk to the 'gappies' – the gap year students, too. Pupils call teachers 'Sir' and 'Miss'. Normal school rules apply: smoking = fines, drinking = breathalyser, counselling and gating as a last resort. Drugs testing, random after first offence. Pregnancy only ever among married staff. The atmosphere is very mainstream – prefects, etc. Blazers from Year 9 on, own suit and tie for sixth formers.

Brilliant regime for Years 7 and 8. They inhabit an anxiety-free zone of their own. Minimal organisational expectations of their short-term memories, so they only have to get themselves to class – everything they need is waiting for them. They go into meals first, in front, even, of the prefects. Once their self esteem has begun to grow they are ready to embark on a gradient of responsibilities as they move up the school. Sixth formers notably self reliant.

Most board and it works. They don't get out much, even the oldest, and they don't complain, and you wonder if they are learning enough about the beastliness of the world. It's a fine line the school must tread between putting them back together and pitching them out too soon. Around half the school in at weekends. Sixth form bar where staff drink, too – hugely approved of by the students. Food decidedly good.

Pupils and Parents: Growing number from abroad where SENs are apparently more believed-in than acted on – small handfuls from France, Germany, Middle East, Far East, Africa, India. Predominantly English, countrywide catchment, with an equal number from state and independent schools. Guy 'Two Smoking Barrels' Ritchie was here.

Entrance: The interview's the thing. Ed psych report, of course, but they reckon the scores are often skewed by disinclination or despair – 'if we judged by the Wechsler scores we'd never let our best in.' They reckon IQs span 90–150. Main intake at Year 7 with more in Year 9 and then if places become available. Significant increase in Year 10s kicked out of other schools cravenly fearing for their league table places.

Exit: Around 40 per cent post-GCSE to sixth form colleges, though this number is falling because more than ever are staying on. Post-sixth form they go on to 'the conventional range of options'. They remind you – 'a SpLD simply occludes a conventional intelligence'.

Money Matters: Some bursaries and scholarships available.

Remarks: A parent sums it up nicely, 'if you'd told me when my son was nine that he'd get these GSCE results, I wouldn't have believed you'. To its long track record of expertise, Stanbridge brings a quality of rigorous kindness, and it's this that makes all the difference.

Stephen Perse Foundation/Perse Girls

Linked to Stephen Perse Sixth Form College (The) in the Senior section
Linked to Perse Girls Junior School in the Junior section

Union Road, Cambridge, Cambridgeshire, CB2 1HF

• Pupils: 470 girls, all day – co-ed sixth form college on separate site
• Ages: 11-18 • Size of sixth form: 110 • Non-denom • Fees: £11,190-£13,155 pa • Independent

Tel: 01223 454 700
Fax: 01223 467 420
Email: office@stephenperse.com
Website: www.stephenperse.com

Principal: Since 2001, Ms Patricia Kelleher MA (late forties), read history at LMH Oxford, followed by MA at Sussex. Taught at Haberdashers then Brighton and Hove GDST before deputy headship at Brentwood School. Absolutely perfect in her role as the 'face of the Stephen Perse Foundation' (rebranded, discrete educational entities comprising the Perse Girls junior and senior schools and the Stephen Perse Sixth Form College) – an engagingly sagacious, forward thinking principal who readily thinks outside the box. Actively promotes add-ons to the traditionally strong academic provision – says a pupil. 'Discovering an inner ability' is the most rewarding aspect of her job. Much time is spent charming potential punters and managing the foundation (areas needing development or fine tuning are collaboratively resolved) so day to day headmistressy business in the senior school is handled by the approachable Dr Stringer – fantastic and clearly visible, according to parents.

Academic matters: How is it done? 96 per cent A/A* with the vast majority taking 11 GCSEs and some even managing 12. And about a third play an instrument. Answer – very able pupils plus a combination of high quality teaching ('we appreciate just how bright our teachers are'), an examy environment, excellent reporting ('they really know and understand the girls'), maximum class size of 24, plenty of homework ('we're all geeks – we work so hard') and expectations. The latter is all pervading – from home ('it's the Cambridge mentality,' mused one pupil), school and most importantly the girls themselves. Arty or sciency pigeon holing is minimal and all areas shine, from single sciences to languages – a goodly clutch including Greek and Latin. Fine facilities; a recently refurbed 'designer' library where books can be ordered or computers accessed, science labs aplenty and a funky, circular IT suite with two spot lit computer topped concentric work stations – the 'mother ship' according to our guides. No EFL or SEN unit in the school – only the mildest of learning difficulties are manageable in this environment.

Sixth: from 2008 marketed as the co-ed Stephen Perse Sixth Form College. Slightly out on limb – a mile away from the senior school – but shuttle buses are provided for those who need to be there for lessons. Laptops for all with class sizes no more than 14 although this is likely to increase if college grows as intended. Some 73 per cent grade A*/A at A level with IB now on offer – haemorrhaging after GCSE not nearly so acute as this clever move provides something previously unavailable in the city. Fresh faced head of college 'wants to encourage thinking' and is tremendously enthusiastic about compulsory TOK (theory of knowledge programme) – much discussion and blogging of ideas – he says unis approve.

Games, Options, the Arts: Over the years, netball and hockey teams have enjoyed county successes – but some parental wizzles re games; from the sportier girls too. It's not a lack of staff, facilities or choice; it's time. For younger ones it's reasonable but, once GCSE courses start, something has to give. Of course, the less sporty are perfectly happy with the one hour twenty minutes a week (minus ten mins there and ten mins back from the Astroturfed sports field) – and there is plenty of support for those who want more and can shoehorn a practice or club (dance, basketball, football, badminton, rowing or anything else the girls can initiate) during the lunchbreak or after school. Sixth have access to nearby sports/fitness centres.

Music flourishes – three orchestras, bands, choirs, chamber groups and concerts abroad. Broad choice of instrumental tuition and plenty of practice rooms. Well endowed visual arts centre opened in 2008. Tidy general studio with trendy back lit lettering proclaiming 'ARTS' in 'post feminist pink' (q. the principal), a print room and huge atelier for sixth formers. Not much work on show round the school but what we saw was carefully considered with some interesting use of materials in textiles. Annual drama production for every year group plus speech and drama lessons in preparation for LAMDA examinations.

No shortage of extra-curricular activities – some before school. Recently reintroduced gold and silver D of E and annual trip to the Gambia for sixth formers who can find the air fare – they take money raised for projects and give help. Long list of foreign visits and collaborative ventures – school has an EU Comenius award in recognition of international activities.

Background and Atmosphere: Founded in 1881 as a sister school to the much older Perse Boys. Association now firmly at an end – they've gone co-ed and the SP foundation is taking boys in the sixth. Main school tucks into narrow streets near the centre of Cambridge and is a 10 minute walk from the station. Understated dark blue front door in a characterless brick wall belies what's beyond – much money spending coupled with bold design statements has made a warm, comfortably stimulating place of learning (same goes for the sixth form centre even though it's in a bland ex-office block). Sparkle comes from the brightly lit and imaginatively designed dining-cum-common room, which pleasantly buzzes as girls happily spend time together, and a courtyard area where there's a large flower power mural created by pupils and a local graffiti artist. A secure, well ordered environment filled with conscientious pupils who have a clear sense of direction – greater freedom in the sixth form centre produces more of a bustle.

Pastoral Care and Discipline: Ethos which builds self esteem – 'they're good at making the girls feel good about themselves,' said a parent. Steady encouragement to be independent and give reasoned opinions – 'they're not "yes women" – but that does make for an interesting time at home.' Pupils speak of positive relationships with staff – for help or advice it's the year head or form tutor. If that doesn't suit there's a choice of school nurses – for the sixth an off-site counsellor.

School lunch for all except Year 11, who are allowed out twice a week. Ample choice with lasagne a firm favourite. Apparently, girls now spend longer in the dining area where the relaxed atmosphere has led to a healthier relationship with food – an unexpected and positive spin-off from the refurbishment. Light snacks are available for the sixth who are allowed to do their own thing.

Biddable, well-behaved lot so no real discipline issues – but just in case there's a code of conduct which has been drawn up by the student forum. Year 11 take on roles of responsibility and, after the autumn term, are allowed to wear their own clothes – greatly appreciated. Competition between the six 'houses' (house talent contest is highly popular) but form loyalties are the strongest.

Pupils and Parents: Pupils mostly local. Articulate and mature. Loyal parent body – quite a few academics who come for a year and a high proportion of working mums. Old girls include author Phillippa Pearce, archaeologist Jacquetta Hawkes, broadcaster Bridget Kendall and Olympic gold medalist Stephanie Cook.

Entrance: Exam and interview at eleven – latter is the clincher. About half from Perse Junior – entry is more or less automatic. Rest from local prep and primaries (according to one mum 'a great deal of testing with no let up with the teaching' can be a shock for those used to a state school regime). A number also join in Year 9. For the sixth, A grades in subjects to be studied at AS/A or IB. 'We like international diversity but not dominance,' so cap of 10–15 per cent on students from abroad. 'We're looking for the brightest and they must have at least an IELTS (International English Language Testing System) score of 6.5 in writing ... 7.5 to 8.5 is typical.' Universities want 7.5 so Stephen Perse is being pretty picky.

Exit: Number staying on for the sixth on the up (approximately half) but Hills Road SFC remains a popular alternative. Impressive list of university destinations – around a third to Oxbridge. Good showing for medicine and other heavyweight subjects.

Money Matters: Scholarships at KS3 and for the sixth (up to 25 per cent). Means-tested bursaries. Nuffield bursaries awarded annually for science.

Remarks: First rate selective school with a forward thinking head who is working hard to make it much more than an academic hot-house.

The Stephen Perse Sixth Form College

Linked to Perse Girls Junior School in the Junior section

Linked to Stephen Perse Foundation/Perse Girls in the Senior section

Fitzwilliam Building, Shaftesbury Road, Cambridge, Cambridgeshire, CB2 8AA

• Fees: £12,600 pa • Independent

Tel: 01223 488 430
Fax: 01223 467 420
Email: admissions@stephenperse.com
Website: www.stephenperse.com

Head: As for Perse Girls/Stephen Perse foundation.

Remarks: See full entry for Perse Girls/Stephen Perse foundation.

Stewart's Melville College

Linked to Mary Erskine School (The) in the Senior section

Linked to Mary Erskine and Stewart's Melville Junior School (The) in the Junior section

Queensferry Road, Edinburgh, EH4 3EZ

• Pupils: (SMC) 730 boys (almost all day), (MES) 735 girls (almost all day) • Ages: 11-18. (Separate entry for junior school) • Size of sixth form: Joint: 220 boys and girls • Non-denom • Fees: Day £8,916; Boarding £17,790 pa • Independent

Tel: 0131 311 1000
Fax: 0131 311 1099
Email: principal@esmgc.com
Website: www.esms.edin.sch.uk

Principal: Since 2000, Mr David Gray BA PGCE (fifties), who was educated at Fettes, read English at Bristol, where he did his PGCE. Taught English in a Bristol comprehensive, before moving to a language school in Greece, then taught English and modern Greek at Dulwich and was head of English at Leeds Grammar, before heading Pocklington School in East Yorkshire, for eight years. Since the Stewart's Melville vast conglomerate forms the largest independent school in Europe, it is not surprising he feels he is in a position here 'to give something back to Scotland having been away for almost a quarter of a century.' Brought up in Inverness, he is proud of his Scottish roots and sees himself and Stewart's Melville/Mary Erskine as at the 'most exciting cutting edge of Scottish education' and stresses that he's the first overall principal who is actually Scottish. Mr Gray spends part of the week in each school. We visited him at his base in Mary Erskine, where he was busily involved in compiling a history of the school for his teaching contact with the girls.

Very much a hands-on head, the principal reckons to keep sane (and fit) by swimming and jogging at 7am each morning, and is a familiar sight as he cycles between the two campuses. He also 'works the room' quite beautifully, 'we all think we know him well and that he knows our children almost as well as we do,' said one father (a gift no doubt inherited from his politician father?). Keen on promoting self-confidence in his pupils, he sees himself as an 'educator' and is teaching English and coaching cricket at Stewart's Melville. After eight years he feels pleased that the school has 'become a gentler place' and that the 'children are wedded to our ethos of reasonable, sensible behaviour.' No need for draconian action on the discipline side recently and, when there is silliness, 'the student body can be very conservative on behaviour,' while parents 'don't want to be ashamed of the school.'

Mr Gray runs the twin senior schools with two deputy heads, and the head of the co-ed junior school, Bryan Lewis, who is also vice principal. Mrs Linda Moule took over as deputy head of The Mary Erskine School in August 2009; she was previously vice principal of New Hall School in Chelmsford. Mr Neal Clark, depute head of Stewart's Melville for the last 10 years describes himself as a 'grammar school boy, in tune with Scottish social culture.' All school facilities have been upgraded in the last 10 years 'so future plans are for maintenance rather than development.'

Academic matters: The principal and three heads have agonised together over the pros and cons of single-sex v co-ed. All four speak with the same passion – and often the same phrasing – of their 'best of both worlds' system. Boys and girls educated together at junior school, separately from age 12–17 – gains for girls (being able to get on with learning) and boys (feeling free to talk about poetry etc) – then the social etc. plus factors of co-ed for sixth year and all activities. 'Not a highly selective school,' however, described by an educationalist as a 'grade one academic machine.' Classes of up to 25 (20 for practical classes) setted, with groups subdivided to extend the most able. School has embraced the new Advanced Higher in depth – greater analysis, independent study, projects and dissertation. Mr Clark – though pleased that this years SMC sixth year averaged two AH passes – would like three to be the norm. Recent results show a pleasing number of As and Bs across the board in both schools, with some outstanding successes in history, sciences and maths. Higher results impressive, particularly at MES 'on the languages front' and for SMC in history and geography. French, German, Spanish and Latin on offer to Advanced Higher Grade.

Since 2002, Standard Grades phased out (except drama) in favour of Intermediate 2, (which is based on the same assessment pattern as Highers). Results pretty impressive here too!

Very good links (still) with the Merchant Company who do masses of business breakfasts and links with professional firms around Edinburgh. Single IT network across all three schools with 'massive schools' intranet', interactive whiteboards galore and close on 1000 computers. Biology dept links with the horticultural dept of the world famous Edinburgh Botanic Gardens. Impressive careers structure across both schools and excellent library facilities. Pupils can sign in for private study.

Schools combine for sixth form, most extras, and pastoral structure. In the interests of integration sixth formers have to take academic courses from both schools – a feat resulting in limitless (almost) variety of course permutations, miraculous timetabling and a quite a few bus journeys. Outstanding back-up for those with learning difficulties; school has its own educational psychologist; 'some on Ritalin'; 'will never abandon anyone.'

Games, Options, the Arts: Big is beautiful; providing a list of over 75 different clubs for all – from goldsmithing to Greek, costume design to curling and cross country – lunch time and post school. Popular. Major sports have separate clubs for ages/stages and 27 rugby teams. Good at football too! Girls prefer hockey and basketball, still better at shooting than boys and both sexes join the voluntary CCF (trillions of girls, over 400 members in all). A second super new floodlit Astroturf at MES, 'so everyone gets a chance,' dramatic wavy roofed swimming pool (at Stewart's Melville) with co-ed sixth form slump-out room adjacent, new gym (at MES), cricket pavilion (MES again). FPs and current pupils share sporting facilities at MES; extra games pitches at Inverleith. Needle matches in almost all disciplines, with FPs representing both county and country across the board. Smart dining room complex serves all juniors and 80 per cent seniors opt in. Sixth form coffee bars with stunning overview of school and pitches.

Incredibly strong drama – regular performances at the Edinburgh Festival and throughout the year at the Playhouse etc. Masses of every sort of orchestras. Pupils can learn to fly, ski (Hillend and the real thing, the Alps, Canada); brilliant debating team (regularly the Scottish Debating Champions, European Youth Parliament finalists) and SMC has represented Great Britain abroad all over the shop. Good home economics. Arts spectacular. Dramatic art room atop MES (with adjoining pottery and greenhouse). New £2.5m performing arts centre's opening splash was Snowman composer, Howard Blake and Scottish Chamber Orchestra. Centre took 12 years in the planning – seats 800 with a 'retractable' stage and dividing walls, replacing the old assembly hall – which was huge and impressive – and jolly nice in its way.

Background and Atmosphere: Stewart's Melville campus is based round the magnificent David Rhind-designed Daniel Stewart's Hospital which opened in 1885 and merged with Melville College in 1972. Fairy-tale Victorian Gothic with a cluster of necessary modern additions surrounded by ever decreasing games pitches and car parks. The old chapel is now a library complete with organ and stained glass windows. Stewart's Melville is also home to the senior department of the junior school – see separate entry.

Mary Erskine was founded in 1694, as the Merchant Maiden Hospital, moved to Ravelston in 1966, changing its name to The Mary Erskine School, and amalgamated with the boys' school in 1978. (Girls wear charming Mary Erskine tartan kilts) MES clusters in decidedly 1960s architecture with, now, quite a lot of more modern extensions, round the pretty but sadly overwhelmed Ravelston House (1791): swimming pool, tennis courts, games pitches, Astroturfs etc. The last much used by FPs. The nursery department and the youngest classes of the junior school are also based here – see separate entry.

Two boarding houses, Dean Park House and Erskine House, furnished like large (and very well equipped) family houses and based on the edge of the Stewart's Melville campus. Tremendous family feel, boarders are encouraged to invite friends home, caring house parents and only 60 boarding places.

Regular buses from East and West Lothian and Fife service both schools, which operate as one, under the auspices of Erskine Stewart's Melville Governing Council. Each school, though, is fiercely proud of its individual heritage.

Pastoral Care and Discipline: Both schools have a tutorial system for the first year, followed by house system in Upper Schools. Houses are common to both schools and House competitions have mixed sex teams. Good links with parents. Brief is that 'all children have a right to be happy here.' Code of conduct established by consulting pupils so 'they know exactly where they stand.' Excellent anti-bullying policy: wary pastoral staff and peer-support group 'with professional training' stop 'children slipping through the net.' Sophisticated PSE programme right up the school, including study skills. Buddy system for those coming up from junior schools. Automatic expulsion, 'zero-tolerance,' for those bringing in illicit substances – 'those on the periphery of the same incident will not necessarily be excluded but can come back in as long as they agree to random testing.' Fags 'unacceptable and pupils suspended.' Booze 'not an issue in school.'

Pupils and Parents: Edinburgh hotch-potch of New Town and suburbs, with many first-time buyers and lots up from England. Siblings and FPs' children. Taking over a third of Edinburgh's independent secondary pupils, it's less elitist and perhaps less dusty than some city schools. Children living far out can spend the night when doing evening activities. Parent-teacher group ('the red socks brigade') slightly better organised into a Friends of the School group, fund-raising, ceilidhs, 'good cash cow.'

Entrance: At 11,12, 13 or sixth form – otherwise 'by default.' Automatic from junior school. Entrance assessments held in January but can be arranged at any time. Waiting lists for some stages but just go on trying. Entrance to upper school is by interview, plus school report plus GCSEs/Standard grades (five credit passes for S5 entry.) Numbers up overall.

Exit: Minimal leakage pre Highers, most sixth year (96 per cent) go on to university (gap years growing in popularity, especially for girls), most opt for Scottish unis but a few Oxbridge, London, Bristol etc. SATS (for American Colleges) not a problem. Art college, music/drama are popular alternatives.

Money Matters: Scholarships/bursaries available, some linked to the Merchant Company, others sibling directed. 'No child will be left wanting in a (financial) crisis.'

Remarks: A glance at the school mags, *Merchant Maiden* and *The Collegian*, sums it up: bags of boys' poetry, multiple hockey, rugby and cricket teams, nine Oxbridge places, fabulous art, photos and writing plus fascinating glimpses from boys and girls reporting on the same activities with subtly different views.

An outstanding school; happy pupils, happy staff – focused on self-development with impressive results!

Stockport Grammar School

Linked to Stockport Grammar School Junior School in the Junior section

Buxton Road, Stockport, Cheshire, SK2 7AF

• Pupils: 1,030, all day; 50/50 boys and girls • Ages: 11-18 • Size of sixth form: 245 • Secular • Fees: £8,883 pa • Independent

Tel: 0161 456 9000
Fax: 0161 419 2407
Email: sgs@stockportgrammar.co.uk
Website: www.stockportgrammar.co.uk

Headmaster: Since 2005, Mr Andrew Chicken BA (early forties), head of Colfes (qv) since 2001. He read history at London, trained as a teacher at Oxford, followed by a career in both state and independent schools, notably Cheadle Hulme and before that Manchester Grammar. Married to a teacher, no children. A straight-talking northerner who faces problems head on, he would be the first to make a joke of his name. Parents warm to him. Places a strong emphasis on academic matters. At Colfes he was difficult to track down as he was either on PGL camp, coaching cricket or teaching students – but parents put up with the inconvenience for the sake of the involvement. Knows students, from first year upwards. Prepared to go the extra mile – sees parents at weekend if there's something that needs sorting out.

Academic matters: Particularly in past five years, results have been excellent, with almost three quarters of candidates gaining A* and A grades at GCSE in 2010 and never less than 90 per cent gaining B grades or above. Likewise, impressive A level results. Head feels that obsessional national emphasis on GCSEs is misguided, but clearly his own reservations do not prevent him from ensuring pupils score top marks. Pupils take nine GCSEs. Pupil/teacher ratio is 1:12. Years 1 to 3 have 25 maximum class size, narrowing down to a maximum of 24 (more often 20 or fewer) in GCSE year groups, and in sixth form general maximum target is 12. Average age of staff is 40, half of whom have been at school for ten years or more. No statemented pupils in school, although several have dyslexia, which does not, however, prove a barrier to learning or to acceptance into school in the first place.

Games, Options, the Arts: Sport very popular and important. Everywhere you look there's a sports pitch. School has own swimming pool. New sports hall. Lots of sporting activities and matches. Rugby popular, extra-curricular lacrosse teams are given special coaching by US coach. Football hockey and netball too. Saturday morning practices and fixtures provide opportunity for pupils and staff to build good relationships in less formal context.

Music another strength. About half of pupils learn at least one musical instrument, mostly in school. Lots of choirs, orchestras, bands, performances at Manchester's Bridgewater Hall and on TV. In drama, there are usually three school productions a year. Lower sixth stage own production in the few weeks at the end of the academic year. Art, whilst valued, does not have particularly good facilities. Walls of corridor leading to head's office are testimony nonetheless to high standards.

Background and Atmosphere: Founded in 1487 by Sir Edmond Shaa, for boys, 'to teche allman persons children the science of grammar'. Became co-educational in 1980 (girls insist there's no sense of being add-ons at a boys' school). Continues to have links with The Worshipful Company of Goldsmiths. Atmosphere purposeful but not pedantic. Pupils happy, positive, proud of their school. Friendly, generous spirit pervades. Parents find school accessible. Their views are taken into account and they are kept properly informed on a regular basis.

Pastoral Care and Discipline: Pastoral care primarily the concern of form teachers. Peer mentor system and 'first form friends' system in place. Pupils rather vague about procedures in the event of bullying – perhaps a sign of its scarcity? Discipline, and self-discipline, important to school, part of its package of traditional values.

Pupils and Parents: Drawn from Greater/ South Manchester and from further south through Cheshire into Derbyshire, as well as from Stockport itself. Year 1 intake represents 50 per cent from own junior school and rest from between 50–75 primary schools.

Famous Old Boys/Girls so far: Professor Sir Freddie Williams (inventor of the first stored program computer), John Amaechi (basketball player), Sir Victor Blank (chairman of the Mirror Group) and Gordon Marsden, MP for Blackpool South. Association of Old Boys and Girls (Old Stopfordians) going from strength to strength. Parents reflect solid ethos of the school.

Entrance: By full day examination, encompassing maths, verbal reasoning, English and comprehension. Followed by interviews, which provide opportunity for school to get to know pupils a little and vice versa.

Exit: Almost without exception, to university, often the more prestigious. Pupils tend to do well, achieving upper second and first class degrees. Regular Oxbridge offers.

Money Matters: Fees very good value. Bursaries available at 11+ and 16+. Music scholarships also available each year.

Remarks: Safely square, gentle school. A good bet for a solid, traditional style of education in a caring environment. As the school's motto – 'Vincit qui patitur' – suggests, this is a school where the value and the rewards of hard graft are recognised but not to the exclusion of 'a balanced diet' of interests and activities.

Stonar School

Linked to Stonar Preparatory School in the Junior section

Cottles Park, Atworth, Melksham, Wiltshire, SN12 8NT

• Pupils: 300 girls; 160 board • Ages: 11-18 • Size of sixth form: 80
• Non-denom • Fees: Boarding £22,440; Day £12,735 pa • Independent

Tel: 01225 701 740
Fax: 01225 790 830
Email: admissions@stonarschool.com
Website: www.stonarschool.com

Head: Since 2010, Mrs Elizabeth Thomas BA PGCE NTQH (fiftyish). Read English at Lancaster University followed by a PGCE at the University of Bath. Wide experience in education initially in maintained schools in Somerset and Berkshire then 10 years at Luckley-Oakfield School, Wokingham as head of English, head of sixth form and assistant head. Acting head at Leighton Park prior to this post. Married with one daughter at university.

Academic matters: Scores well at value-added. No risk of becoming an academic hothouse, exam grades improve each year. English, maths, psychology, art, German and PE all strong performers plus bonus Chinese. School admits about 15 per cent overseas students and percentage rises in sixth form; head points to positive influence on work ethic and there's no doubt they fit in well here. Favourable staff: pupil ratio of 1:8 overall and small class sizes. In 2010, 44 per cent A*/A grades at GCSE and 73 per cent A*–C grades at A level. Successful GCSE short courses run in ICT and RE. Four girls reached top five nationally in Spanish, geography, English lit and French.

Excellent food technology with lower sixth following Leith's course of high repute. Extension studies cover life skills and ethical issues. Lots of career and HE advice. ICT well integrated.

SENCo teaches textiles and history of art in addition to running learning support programme. About 15 per cent of girls on SEN register. Dyslexic pupils receive one-to-one help as an 'extra'. Pupils all screened using Dyslexia Institute tests; aim is to see girls predicted two Ds at entry achieve five Cs or better by GCSE. LSA support in classes where needed (e.g. in set three maths). In such a mixed ability school, support with study skills and better approaches to match different learning styles is paying off across board (including most able – 10 girls currently on NAGTY [gifted and talented] register). EAL support given through languages department and overseas girls take IGCSE English to avoid cultural bias. School really goes extra mile to help disadvantaged (e.g. blinds have been fitted in classrooms to help girl with rare eye condition affected by sunlight) but not yet wheelchair friendly.

Games, Options, the Arts: Heaven for any young horsewoman – a third of the girls ride; stabling for about 60 horses; equestrian facilities second to none and riding integrated into school day; all runs like clockwork from 7.00am till late. Charts for feeding horses and turn-out into fields etc maintained with military precision. Sparky former international eventer in charge with support from good yard managers plus gappers and girls on BHSAI course who also teach younger girls. Expert tuition for competitive riders from resident and visiting staff gives girls edge at huge annual Inter-Schools One Day Event (ISODE) hosted by Stonar and at mini ISODE for 9–13 year olds. Good sized covered indoor arena for 'flat' lessons plus newly extended 80 x 40 metre Martin Collins floodlit outdoor school. Facilities booked solid by pony clubs during holidays who like to be photographed by famous 'Stonar' jump on own mini Badminton cross-country course; about half the horses 'belong' to school (many loaned by former pupils) with remainder brought by pupils from as far afield as Malaysia. Another huge equestrian centre within hackable distance provides additional opportunities for dressage and cross-country; trips to nearby Badminton (where school has own trade stand) and horse of the year show very popular.

Director of sport has turned PE and games around; now joined by a current member of the Welsh women's rugby squad. As well as the traditional sports, soccer and rugby are becoming popular activities. The absence of Saturday lessons allows more flexibility for games as well as riding. Older students make good use of fitness suite (they helped raise cash for extra equipment) and dance studio. Heated 20 metre indoor pool, tennis courts, modern sports hall and floodlit Astroturf. Several county hockey and netball players; some athletes train at Bath university; judo, dance (Year 11 had just staged multicultural dance show) and gymnastics popular. D of E expeditions plus loads of trips away including sixth form spending sixteen days under canvas in American national parks before ending up hitting the town in Las Vegas.

All girls participate in drama in some way. GCSE and A level performances, enjoyable senior school productions, including musicals such as *Fiddler on the Roof* and some more contemporary material, plus some student-directed pieces. Lots of performance successes at the 2010 Mid-Somerset Festival.

Largely trad but successful music department; during lunch break we witnessed high volume chamber choir practice and jodhpur-clad girls working hard on pieces in practice rooms. Nine pupils currently on grade 8 piano. Spring concert held at Wiltshire music centre and girls participate annually in Mid-Somerset Festival. Recent successes include choral scholarship to Cambridge. Digital recording studio provides music technology to A level and allows for recording of pupils' work – composition and song writing encouraged. Lively art (and photography) department now re-housed and with superb dark room facilities. Brand new gallery opening soon to display material including girls' own take on Jackson Pollock and some pleasing 3D textiles.

Background and Atmosphere: Cottles Park (former home of influential Fuller family) is a pleasing Strawberry Hill Gothic house built of Bath stone. Forgettable classroom blocks and fabric rather tatty in places. Brand new sixth form centre incorporating new social centre, art facilities, study centre and seminar room, completed in early 2009. Horses and horse boxes everywhere (must be murder at end of each term).

Nice surroundings and pleasant walkway to outlying houses in converted farms; sweet house for youngest girls. Prep school on site (most girls move to senior school); loads of space for everyone. All dorms comfortable and well maintained; good study bedrooms for sixth formers. Computers everywhere for work not games but girls can keep up with emails. Non-denominational but religious themes included in the afternoon assemblies. Inviting fiction library well stocked with readable titles and separate reference library with study tables and computers. Dining arrangements suit all ages with tasty meat and veggie choices for hungry horsewomen.

Pastoral Care and Discipline: Discipline not a problem (nor eating disorders) with so much activity around the place; some social links with Milton Abbey boys. Older girls can get leave to Bath and village shops nearby plus trips for younger ones. School nurse plus two female doctors on call from Bradford-on-Avon. Girls see Stonar as a lifestyle as much as a school.

Pupils and Parents: Girls quick to point out that, despite school's obvious horsiness, a large number of pupils don't ride and still think Stonar offers a good deal. Riding is a bonus rather than a 'must' for majority of parents who choose place for variety of reasons: small classes, care, special needs, rural setting, single sex or just 'its lovely feel'. Friendly, self-confident girls – neither stand-offish nor hugely adolescent. About half sixth form boarders from overseas (fewer lower down school) but no evidence of cliques. Girls are super organised (horse owners up at crack of dawn to feed animals) and buzz around the place. A lot of mums would probably like to be here too – not uncommon for them to stand chatting for hours after dropping off daughters.

Former pupils include actress Romola Garai and controversial author Gitta Sereny, plus several accomplished international event riders.

Entrance: Half enter aged 11, the rest over the next two years with quite a big intake at 13. Entrance exams in January in maths and English with high scorers invited back to sit scholarship papers. Informal interviews with the head or formal for scholarship candidates. Separate assessments for sports, music, drama and riding scholarships. Range of feeder preps and local primaries for some day girls. Growing numbers from Services. Entry into Year 10 by school report. Separate entry papers for overseas candidates in English and maths. Many come through horse world or recommendation rather than advertising.

Exit: Wide variety of degrees and universities including Oxbridge. Music and art courses popular and some follow equine careers.

Money Matters: Scholarships at 11, 13 and 16 including music, art, drama, sport and riding. Services bursaries available. Day fee includes lunches but termly extras include riding, peripatetic instrumental and singing lessons, speech and drama, dance, D of E, dyslexia support and EAL.

Remarks: Long-time GSG favourite, going full out, we hope, with the new head holding the reins and spurring it along.

Stonyhurst College

Linked to Saint Mary's Hall in the Junior section

Stonyhurst, Clitheroe, Lancashire, BB7 9PZ

• Pupils: 460: 320 boys, 140 girls; 300 boarders • Ages: 13-18 • Size of sixth form: 140 boys, 65 girls • RC but enquiries welcome from all Christian denominations • Fees: Boarding £21,960-£25,659; Day £15,003 pa • Independent

Tel: 01254 827 073
Fax: 01254 827 135
Email: admissions@stonyhurst.ac.uk
Website: www.stonyhurst.ac.uk

Head: Since 2006, Mr Andrew Johnson, previously deputy head of Birkdale School. Mr Johnson is a Catholic and married to Dawn, with two children aged 13 and 11. He was educated at the Skinners' School, Tunbridge Wells and Bristol University, where he read French and Spanish. He has a postgraduate diploma in Education Management from Portsmouth University. Mr Johnson was deputy head at Birkdale for four years, prior to which he was at Winchester College for nine years where, for his final four years, he was head of modern languages.

Academic matters: Broad curriculum including astronomy (up to GCSE if demand) – own observatory for this. Average class size 17, 10 in the sixth form. Some setting. RE compulsory to GCSE, thereafter theology. Pupils are assigned a personal tutor whom they meet three times a week to discuss progress. Broad ability intake and thus not the academic powerhouse of city day schools but a genuine wish for each pupil to fulfil their potential. Average results over a three-year period show 42 per cent A*/A at GCSE, 63 per cent A and B grades at A level. Maths consistently popular at A level, achieving good results. Ten per cent of pupils have special needs and receive extra help – majority of these are dyslexic. Plenty of computers around linked up to the school's intranet and all pupils have their own email address. Pupils do 'a quick GCSE in IT' at 14 years. Terminals in sixth form study bedrooms and at the study work places for younger pupils.

Games, Options, the Arts: A 'sport for all' policy. Compulsory sport throughout the school achieving notable success in rugby, golf, hockey and netball. Super indoor swimming pool and new all-weather pitch, the latter used by athletes training during the 2002 Commonwealth Games. School is divided vertically into four 'lines' for sporting competitions. Music is highly valued. Free instrumental tuition on an orchestral instrument is available to all pupils and maintained if satisfactory progress is made. Three pupils were recently selected for the Halle youth orchestra. The school is the proud owner of a Steinway, a Bosendorfer and a Bechstein and other facilities include a keyboard lab and practice rooms looking like mini greenhouses. Good DT department with plenty of scope for those artistically inclined. Outdoor pursuits in abundance – fishing, canoeing, sailing, fell walking, clay pigeon shooting, CCF etc. Further afield pupils participate in world challenge trips, pilgrimages to Lourdes, D of E expeditions, to name but a few. In the second year the cadet corps is compulsory. School runs the Arrupe Programme – sixth form pupils give a period of voluntary service each week in the local community.

Background and Atmosphere: Founded by the Jesuits at St Omer in what is now northern France for English families forced to pursue a Catholic education abroad. After a succession of moves the school was given refuge at its present site in the Catholic part of Lancashire by Thomas Weld, who later donated the property to the school. The magnificent buildings are set in a 2,000-acre estate, most of which is farmed. 'I arrive each morning and cannot believe that this is my school,' comments one pupil. Each year group is termed a 'playroom' with its own common room and boarding facilities, cared for by a married couple. The girls have separate accommodation and are looked after by a housemistress. Recent developments include a magnificently refurbished and equipped library and study centre in the heart of the school and Years 9 and 10 boys' dormitories have been transformed. Other parts of the school are truly splendid; huge staircases, wood panelling, polished stone, works of art, brimming with history and tradition. Some formerly hidden treasures are now exhibited in a millennium display for all to enjoy. Shared boarding accommodation (four or five per room), lower down the school, makes way for smart study bedrooms for the sixth formers. A brand new sixth form boarding house with ensuite rooms opened 2010.

This is essentially a full-time boarding school, 'no mass exodus at weekends' but exeats are readily approved, according to pupils. Sunday afternoon appreciated by some as their only free time to do as they please, as much of the weekend is consumed by prep, excursions and church, though there is now a boarding activities co-ordinator who makes sure there are activities available on a Sunday afternoon should the pupil choose. Religion is taken seriously but is not oppressive. Now co-ed and feels as if it has always been so. Girls 'have improved communication at all levels'.

Pastoral Care and Discipline: A family handbook sets out clear expectations of conduct and behaviour. Cases of bullying are dealt with by playroom staff and general policing by the pupil-run playroom committees. A few suspensions in the past for drug offences but 'not a drugs school'. Discipline not a major problem. The Jesuit school chaplain is singled out for special praise by pupils. Being a former pupil, but widely travelled in the interim, he is highly valued for his pastoral care and general availability.

Pupils and Parents: 'Broad mix'. More socially mixed than equivalent schools – being in Catholic Lancashire. Catholics make up over 70 per cent of the total. Southern parents cite one reason for their choice being the school's lack of consumerism and the social competitiveness of some southern schools. Rich mix of accents – regional and international (25 per cent pupils are non-Brits). International links are highly valued and there has 'never been a problem with racism'. Confident, articulate and mature pupils praise the community feel of the school, which is enhanced by the playroom system. 'Looking at the whole picture,' comments one pupil, 'the school works extremely well.' Day pupils are encouraged to stay after school for studies and activities – a facility valued by parents – and may feel left out if they choose not to do so. Alumni include twelve martyrs, seven VCs, also Arthur Conan Doyle, Charles Laughton, General Walters, Paul

Johnson, Peter Moorhouse, Bishop Hollis, Bishop Hines, Charles Sturridge, Hugh Woolridge, Jonathon Plowright, Bill Cash MP, Bruce Kent, Mark Thompson, Lords Chitnis and Talbot, Kyran Bracken and Robert Brinkley.

Entrance: From own prep (St Mary's Hall), St John's Beaumont and a variety of other schools, both here and abroad. Broad ability intake – 'for some, six GCSEs will be an achievement'. Academic entrance exam but other factors taken into account, particularly family connections with the school. Six GCSE passes, plus interview, for entry into sixth form. Those unable to attend for interview e.g. overseas pupils, write a 500 word essay explaining why they wish to come to Stonyhurst.

Exit: All over. London popular. Numbers vary to Oxbridge, but average 10 per cent over recent years. Art foundation, medicine, management and business courses currently look popular. Plenty of international links and scope for travel through the Jesuit community with many students taking a gap year.

Money Matters: A variety of scholarships; academic, music and art and design to a maximum of 50 per cent of fees. Some bursaries are available up to 50 per cent of fees for those in need.

Remarks: Distinguished Jesuit boarding school, steeped in history and set in beautiful surroundings, now comfortably co-ed and at capacity. A genuine concern for the individual pervades.

Stover School

Linked to Stover Preparatory School in the Junior section

Stover, Newton Abbot, Devon, TQ12 6QG

- Pupils: 475, girls (55 board), 180 boys (some stay with host families)
- Ages: 3-18 • Size of sixth form: 55 boys and girls in mixed classes
- Christian • Fees: Day £9,990-£10,185; Boarding £17,490-£20,850 pa
- Independent

Tel: 01626 354 505
Fax: 01626 361 475
Email: fwhite@stover.co.uk
Website: www.stover.co.uk

Principal: Since 2005, Mrs Sue Bradley BSc CBiol MI Biol PGCE (early fifties). No stranger to Stover, Mrs Bradley and her husband, a senior lecturer in micro-biology at Plymouth University, arrived from teaching in London in 1986. Quickly worked her way through the ranks via head of science, director of studies and deputy head. A restructuring of the hierarchy saw her emerge as principal. Approachable and reassuring, she enjoys good relationships with staff and pupils, and clearly loves the set-up. Realistic about the school's position in the market-place. Conversation enlivened with bursts of common sense. Thoughtful and compassionate. 'If the boys and girls are happy, they'll thrive.' A safe pair of hands with a clear eye on future developments.

Academic matters: At GCSE nearly 60 per cent gain A*/A grades and 89 per cent gain five or more A* – C, a strike rate that compares very favourably with local schools with bigger names. A level results are good and bright pupils achieve very good results, while not so bright achieve their potential. Given the non-selective intake this is impressive. 'Children enjoy their lessons and like their teachers,' said a mother. 'Nobody is made to feel a failure.' 'We are guided by a programme of assessment for learning rather than of learning,' says the principal. 'It's important that pupils are at ease with themselves and realistic about their abilities.' As far as is possible the school builds timetables around the pupil's choice of subject. Daily help is available for children with special needs. From Years 7–11 boys and girls are taught in separate classes but mix for extra-curricular activities, the sixth form is co-educational.

Games, Options, the Arts: Good facilities in the beautiful and extensive grounds with six all-weather floodlit tennis courts, football, rugby, netball, tennis, hockey and cricket pitches. Good record at county level. 'Everyone finds a sport they can enjoy,' says a happy girl. Cross-curricular activities are important to the school. 'We are looking to educate the whole person.' Astronomy and public speaking, home economics, and riding. Busy Music Centre with about 200 learning musical instruments. Wide variety of concerts; choral, orchestral, jazz, ensemble, given all over the county. Duke of Edinburgh and Ten Tors Competition on Dartmoor. Lots of good art, photography and media studies in the attractively designed Millennium Building, opened by HRH The Princess Royal in 2001. Charismatic art master, also head of sixth form, believes strongly that the beautiful surroundings encourage creativity.

Background and Atmosphere: Founded in the grounds of Stover Estate by two sisters in 1932, the object was to help girls lead independent lives. Boys and girls have been in the prep school since it started in 1996. From 2005 they have continued into the Senior School. The sixth form building is a homely study centre where pupils talk of knowing the staff well and discourse openly and naturally about the pleasure of being at Stover. 'I know it sounds a bit cheesy,' said one elegantly attired girl, (uniform in the sixth form is 'smart for work') but it's the feeling of living in a community which makes it all such fun.' A number of pupils like it so much that they can't leave; instead they come back for a gap year to help out with the younger pupils. It's a school for friendships.

Lovely entrance through Arcadian fields brings you to a great fist of a house built of granite ashlar, with an incongruously huge portico with double flight of balustraded stairs. Inside, beautiful plasterwork and elegant fireplaces. The school looks after the building well and pupils commented on how proud they felt to live in such surroundings. The refurbished boarding accommodation retains interesting features which contribute to the homely feel. Intimate rather than dominating. Boarding – for girls only; boys may be housed with host families – is much appreciated, and girls often opt to stay on over weekends. Indeed, we met one girl in the sixth form delighted by the prospect of staying on for another year.

Pastoral Care and Discipline: Courtesy and common sense seem to be the watch words, and with the genuinely good relations that exist between staff and pupils, and boys and girls, there aren't many discipline problems. 'Surely, you must get up to some mischief?' we asked. 'We have a lot of fun,' replied a girl enigmatically. House parents, school nurse, tutors are all involved in keeping an eye on the pupils and overseas pupils are made to feel at home with, for example, Stover's special Chinese mid-autumn festival and the American fourth of July celebrations! The school appears open and honest.

Pupils and Parents: Day pupils from Newton Abbot, Exeter, Woodbury, South Hams, Torbay, Bovey Tracey, Plymouth. Boarders from as far as Aberdeen, or overseas. Parents are mostly in professional occupations.

Entrance: By examination in English, mathematics and non-verbal reasoning, together with school report and interviews.

Exit: 75 per cent stay on for sixth form, the others move on to non fee-paying alternatives. Popular university choices are Bath, Sheffield, Warwick, Cardiff, Exeter, York. All sixth formers who stay go on to university.

Money Matters: Academic, music, art and sport scholarships available at most ages up to 25 per cent of day fees, a small number of bursaries for existing pupils. Stover has introduced two means-tested scholarships at Year 10 and sixth form entry, the Maurice Key and Laurus Scholarships offering up to 100 per cent of day fees.

Remarks: An attractive, well-run school embarking on new challenges with justifiable confidence.

Stowe School

Stowe, Buckingham, Buckinghamshire, MK18 5EH

• Pupils: 760; co-ed • Ages: 13-18 • Size of sixth form: 335 • C of E
• Fees: Boarding £28,125; Day £20,400 pa • Independent

Tel: 01280 818 323/ 818 205
Fax: 01280 818 181
Email: admissions@stowe.co.uk
Website: www.stowe.co.uk

Head: Since 2003, Anthony Wallersteiner MA PhD, a thoroughbred academic, Cambridge history scholar and art historian (his PhD at the University of Kent was partly on theory of art). He is married to Valerie and has three young children. Previous two posts were at St Paul's Boys and Tonbridge – strong academic stables. Appointed at 38 to this Grade One post, his first headship, he is, as you would surmise, impressive and this is the word most frequently applied to him by current parents. Which did not prepare us for the reality. Think sired by Stephen Fry out of Nelson's Column with a trace of HRH the P of W and Boris Johnson somewhere under the blanket. He is frank, relaxed, confident, charming and unstoppably chatty. He has ice-blue-green eyes but this is the only icy thing about him. He's rather a man on a mission – and whether or not one agrees with the direction in which he is determinedly driving Stowe, it's certainly going to be worth watching carefully, laying some cautious bets and being there at the finish.

Academic matters: Hitherto traditionally (but not historically, as head reminds us) seen by many as the home for the less bright but otherwise worthy sons of families whose abler offspring might find natural stabling at Eton or Harrow, Stowe's reputation in this regard is now on the line. The CE pass mark has been upped to 50 per cent and, related or not to this fact, the school now has a waiting list for the first time in living memory. The head had a brief to boost the academics and points out his pedigree – 'what would have been the point of appointing me,' he asks, legitimately, 'if that were not what was wanted?' Where new pupils are concerned, he wants the 'best as well as the rest'.

The rest don't do badly. A level grades in 2009 showed the second highest percentage of A and B grades in the last five years. Thirty pupils gained three A grades or more. 2007 GCSE results were the school's best yet and 2009 saw particularly good GCSE grades in art and religious studies. English, drama, art, design, economics all popular and doing very well. The curriculum has no surprises at this level but it's nice to see Greek hanging in there – especially in these classically-inspirational surroundings. Religious studies is a good option but it's sad to see it set against Latin.

Teaching reported by parents and pupils as 'patchy'. Head did some early weeding out of weaker teachers. Some teaching is clearly 'fantastic' and some teachers dedicated well beyond reasonable expectation. However, more individual support and guidance was felt to be necessary by some pupils at exam time – in response to this academic clinics are now held four evenings a week in each department specifically for pupils who require extra support.

IT gathering strength. Interactive whiteboards are now used in all classrooms. Six new classrooms opened in 2007 fully equipped with the latest technology. School now intranetted and laptop stations are everywhere. Rather neat lockable laptop housing now behind the beds. School arranges a laptop purchase scheme which provides an option on a range of laptops which come fully loaded with all the required educational software and are fully supported by the school's ICT department and they are now developing programs in some areas which they export elsewhere. We heard about IT's use in demonstrating chemical reactions and almost stayed to watch, it sounded so interesting.

Most children with SEN are identified before they arrive though school picks up a few en route. All are helped in the Skills Learning Centre housed in the most dismal of the buildings on site. 15 per cent have some sort of help at some stage but the hope is 'to wean them off it.' On the other hand, head concedes, 'we need to acknowledge that people learn in very different ways.'

Games, Options, the Arts: The grounds are, of course, extraordinary and cross-country runners and casual joggers have miles of glorious woods, parkland and gardens to canter through. Unless you happen to have a ducal estate of your own, this is something to make the most of while you can! Likewise, playing fields, a legendary golf course, courts and pitches cover a huge area. There is a sports hall and pool – frankly, everything you'd expect and more. School says, 'all pupils are expected to represent the school in a team' – unusual and encouraging. Winter sports are rugby, hockey and lacrosse; summer sports are cricket, athletics, and tennis supplemented by numberless others. 'We have more than our fair share of polo players', successful sailing, popular golf etc etc. Fairly recently, three sixth form leavers secured professional county level contracts – two in cricket, one in rugby. Two U19 cricketers recently selected for national U19 squad. Everyone does CCF or D of E. School keeps pack of 60 beagles (30 couples) and pupils we met walking them knew them all by name. 'We're trying out aniseed now, since the new law came in,' we were told. 'Drag hunting, you know. But (wistfully) of course, it's not the same ... ' Sounds of merry shooting echo through the woods and school has its own fishery.

Art is strong, DT is very strong. Textiles are varied and lively. Music reportedly similarly strong and parents lyricise about concerts, especially, jazz evenings which attract large numbers of insiders and outsiders alike. Roxburgh Hall is main venue – too wide to be ideal performance space – but several other spaces including fabulous state rooms in 'the mansion' and wonderful chapel. Annual arts festival inaugurated in 2005 included classy visiting lecturers and musicians and performance events of all kinds – in-house and out. The festival has now grown to encompass science and sport as well as numerous workshops in dance, music, art, drama.

Stowe recognises that it is set in a truly magnificent work of art and design and makes good use of it. Landscape drawing/painting unsurprisingly popular. And school publishes series called Discover Stowe, encouraging pupils to engage with their surroundings from historical, aesthetic, classical and architectural points of view.

Background and Atmosphere: The school must have the longest, straightest approach of any in the world. It's a bit like driving into the ancien regime – you almost expect to see Louis XIV and retinue galloping by, wigs afly. The main school building – 'the mansion' – is a splendid palace, largely modelled by Robert Adam in the mid-eighteenth century and benefiting from the respective geniuses of Sir Johns Vanbrugh and Soane, William Kent and 'Capability' Brown among others. It is breathtaking – all the more so if you are not expecting quite this expanse of grandeur. The Marble Saloon, the Music Room, the library – most tours for prospective parents boast nothing like this. The grounds match the house in conception and scope. They include woods and waters, temples and gardens and the privilege of five years living and education in such surroundings could hardly be equalled. The gardens are open to the public and maintained by The National Trust and, consequently, pupils get used to bumping into visitors and cheerfully volunteer information as impromptu guides.

Boarding houses, courts and other facilities nest in sylvan wilderness provided by 750 acres of landscape garden and parkland. It became a school only in 1923. The house is undergoing massive renovation and restoration – paid for not by the school but by the Stowe House Preservation Trust. The art-historically-minded head is, of course, hugely conscious of the privilege and responsibility of running a school in such a place and reminds pupils of their role in keeping up their side of the trust – 'gave a talk about litter this morning,' he grinned, ruefully. Restoration and refurbishment on a rolling programme, of course, and taking in boarding houses. Accommodation ranges from homely, tasteful and inviting to some few remaining tattier areas – lots of upgrading has happened – more to come. Younger boys can find themselves in a room for 12, all sixth form now in small but adequate bedsits. And all views to sell the semi for. Girls' houses attractive and welcoming though some rather far-flung and can feel isolated. Big change in 2005 was the move to co-ed throughout – girls long established in the sixth but younger girls a Wallersteiner innovation and, seemingly, taking off with lots of interest. Two new girls' boarding houses recently added, the first opened by HM The Queen last year – house is named Queen's House in her honour. The second opened in January 2009, called Stanhope House (following a tradition of using names linked to Stowe).

Not all buildings touched with glory. Recent boarding houses architecturally unexceptional and one or two minor blocks frankly dire. An environmentally friendly, girls' boarding house opened in 2007, sensitively designed by Rick Mather. We marvelled at the sorry housing for careers and 'learning skills' but then landed in the library – previously, lamentably, used for detentions but now taken seriously and properly used and resourced. It is sadly overheated, though, and must be drying out the priceless eighteenth volumes in the gallery something chronic – as well as inducing torpor in its readers. Since our visit, we are told that the library has been revitalised with central working areas, all with network connections and a quieter reading area developed in the Ante-Library. We just hope it's cooler now!

Dining mostly takes place overlooked by three Knellers in the fabulous dining hall and overlooking unrivalled landscape. Food was described by one parent as 'appalling' but it looked pretty good to us – salad and fresh fruit here and elsewhere, a decent choice and not unappetising and, as a seasoned Stoic pointed out with a shrug, 'it's school food, made en masse'. Weekly menus on the school's website to assure loving parents that their babes are equally well-nourished in all departments. A brighter servery, 2008, with easier access and, in addition to the previous menu, options of a full hot meal, a salad bar, desserts, fresh fruit and hot drinks. Also now a popular pasta bar with a range of sauces and toppings each day.

School nerve centre in 'Plug Street' – stone-flagged, below-stairs basement in which all admin offices housed, including head's breathtaking study – 'Sir John Soane in gothic fantasy mode' – a mini replica of Henry VII's chapel in Westminster Abbey with fabulous fan vaulting, lead canopies, brass screens and tracery. And that view. Plug Street named, deliciously, after the village of Ploegsteert south of Ypres, at the southern end of a famous series of long tunnels. Major Howarth's Lancashire Fusiliers were based near there during the Great War and 'The Major' was the first housemaster of Chandos at the eastern end of Plug Street for its first 24 years.

Pastoral Care and Discipline: 'This is now the most draconian school I've been in,' says head, implying that times since the school gained its free-and-easy reputation in the alcohol-drugs-gosh-we're so-liberal days have a-changed indeed. Chucking out was a feature of Wallersteiner Era Year One but had appeared unnecessary since then until, in May 2010, two pupils were arrested after another boy was injured with a craft knife in a fight in one of the boarding houses. Police were involved and one boy was taken to hospital. Dr Wallersteiner was quoted as saying, 'aggressive behaviour will never be tolerated here'. Ghastly story which made all the papers, of course, and which no school needs. We hope it indicates no general slippage of grip.

Houses very important here – both in physical terms and in terms of loyalties, rivalries and who you are. Houseparents, then, as essential for happiness here as anywhere and the houses are very well staffed. 'My son's housemaster is fantastic,' we heard over and over. 'My son's housemaster doesn't communicate with us,' we heard a bit. Head now appointing older, more experienced, house staff who are likely to add stability and not move onto higher things after five minutes. Shrewd thinking. Carefully developed and well-structured careers programme begins more or less when they do. Dress code is dark suits for the sixth form, blue tweed blazer for third to fifth forms – and is pretty unexceptionable. No plans for weekly/flexi-boarding – don't bother to ask. Head sensitive to criticism that the parents don't know him yet. 'They're not asking me out,' he points out. 'I love going out. I'm awaiting their invitations ... '

Pupils and Parents: 'So,' we asked disingenuously, putting the point of view of the anxious traditionalists, 'you don't see Stowe as having a natural constituency?' He's not falling for that one – 'I'm not going to alienate our traditional constituency but how could I justify the pursuit of mediocrity to guarantee places for their challenged off-spring? What sort of head would I be? We're getting art dealers, lawyers, bankers, barristers who are now beginning to think that Stowe can be trusted to provide a wonderful environment for learning alongside strong pastoral care. But I'm not going to turn it into a sausage factory. We don't need another Winchester or Eton but I don't want to lose out to Oundle, Oakham, Uppingham or Radley because people think we're academically not up to it.' So he's looking for a gallop up the league tables? Not so. 'I'd rather sacrifice pole position in the league tables for a more interesting school but I think we can improve academically so that the very able are stretched while also providing a rich menu of extracurricular activities which brings out the best in those who do not necessarily shine in the classroom.' If that gives you the jitters, he is reassuring. 'If you haven't got the academic ability to get to the best university, we'll look after you.'

Parents crow over the unspoiled, un-arrogant behaviour of the pupils and the ones we met were articulate and friendly. We saw some reading *The Telegraph*, some chewing gum and a tall boy wearing a hairband. Stoics come from all over with a 'significant number' from London and the south-east. 'My son has a huge range of friends from all over the country ... all with terribly nice parents,' we were told – repeatedly, by, naturally, terribly nice people. Around 60 overseas nationals – mostly from eastern Europe and the far east but only 28 need any EAL help – which is administered according to need. Notable OBs and OGs include David Niven and Sir Leonard Cheshire, Richard Branson, Howard Goodall and actors, Miranda Raison and Ed Stoppard.

Entrance: Fifty per cent at CE and it's mostly done through a good working relationship with the prep school heads. Largely from Winchester House, Swanbourne House, Beachborough, The Dragon, Cheam, Ashdown House, Beeston Hall, Lockers Park, Papplewick, Sunningdale, Windlesham. The advent of girls, of course, will also have an impact on boys who 'traditionally' might have expected a place by right.

Exit: To a huge range of everything everywhere. In 2009, they bagged six Oxbridge places. Diverse spread of other courses – quite a number to Oxford Brookes for everything from business to land management to more hist of art. A lot to Leeds and a considerable number make it into good art schools too with some going to highly acclaimed music schools.

Money Matters: Academic, art, sport and music schols and exhibitions ranging from 10 per cent to 25 per cent of fees available to candidates at 13 and 16. Bursaries also available to award winners according to need, a small number of fully funded places for exceptional candidates, where there is proven financial need. Additionally, Roxburgh schols (named after Stowe's revered founding headmaster) awarded to outstanding all-rounders nominated by the heads of their previous schools. Stephan schols available for bright day pupils from the state sector – worth up to 25 per cent of fees, with further support from bursaries as with other scholarships.

Remarks: Nowhere better for a child who is sensitive to and will be appreciative of the place itself. Most parents reported blissfully happy children. Beyond that, the school has a head who wants to drive it up the educational quality stakes and there is no reason why he shouldn't see it rapidly closing in on the leaders. Whether anything is lost in that pursuit depends on who is watching.

Strathallan School

Forgandenny, Perth, Perthshire, PH2 9EG

• Pupils: 310 boys, 240 girls; 360 boarders; 185 day pupils; 105 in Riley (the junior house) • Ages: 9-18 • Size of sixth form: 200 • Non-denominational • Fees: Day £11,325-£17,262; Boarding £18,141-£25,440 pa • Independent

Tel: 01738 812 546
Fax: 01738 812549
Email: admissions@strathallan.co.uk
Website: www.strathallan.co.uk

Headmaster: Since 2000, Mr Bruce Thompson MA (forties), educated at Newcastle High, thence New College where he read literae humaniores (classics to the rest of us) and came to Strathallan via Cheltenham College, where he was head of classics, and Dollar Academy – he wanted to 'try the Scottish system'. 'Loves Scotland, and loves Strathallan,' as does his wife, Fabienne, (French, teaches at a local prep school, worked in travel and tourism, expert skier – coaches it and most likely to be found whizzing round the campus on her bike). The Thompsons have two young daughters (in the school, they were 'desperate to come') and were delighted to find young staff with similar aged children on their arrival. No change here. Head teaches classics and coaches rugby; the pupils enjoy finding him practising weights alongside them (and he takes the odd coaching session on Mondays and Thursdays). He has a reputation for calling into houses – unannounced as far as pupils are concerned – for the odd chat on their own ground and has lots of informal brainstorming sessions in the evenings. ('Great fun, got to kick 'em out'.) Though, alas, the increasing burden of headmastering (HMC Sports Committee, Boarding Schools' Council – busy boy!) 'gets harder and harder as one gets more involved in things' means that he has less time for the 'pupil stimulation' he so enjoys.

Academic matters: Not tremendously academic (school says 'strong academic record') – but you can reach the heights from here. School reports it was top Scottish A level school in 2009 and 2010 with 23 per cent A* grades and 100 per cent pass rate. Twenty A levels currently on offer, pleasing number of As and Bs in science based subjects, ditto maths, with a couple of glitches in further maths. History fairly lamentable: no As at A level in the preceeding three years and one A grade achieved 2009. Pathetic number of entries in French over last couple of years but school says a good number in 2009 with 70 per cent A; we suspect the Chinese candidates may be native speakers. School plays the system, both Scottish and A levels. Some 75 per cent take A levels, the others opt for Highers (over two years). School tries to please parents but the choice between A level and Highers is always a contentious one.

Top two sets take single sciences now, rest do double award science at GCSE. No subject much stronger than others and exam grades are generally good across the board. DT continues to be excellent. Sophisticated computer design equipment, pupils work here in spare time. Intranet access all over. Four computer rooms and a £1 million ICT Centre 2006 (known as the Royal Bank – it is all steel and glass). We met 'a lesser member of the team' with one of his labradors in situ: 'if you've met one, you've met all three,' said our guide. Mixed age common room: discrimination 'even to raise the subject of age.'

School has always had a welcome reputation for picking up weaker brethren and has a small but effective learning support system which had a smashing HMI report with talk of 'systematic identification', 'sensitive support', 'informative advice' (yawn yawn). All pupils screened on entry with ed psychs brought in where necessary. One-to-one, small groups, plus after-school clinics in various disciplines which act as drop-in centres. Two full-time trained staff, plus three others, and a dedicated full-timer for 9–13-year-olds in Riley who has strong links with the senior school. Extra time for exams. Regular assessment orders for all – i.e. reports (these are becoming more commonplace). 'Rarely costs extra.' School can cope with mild Asperger's/autism and the dys-stream, physical infirmity not a problem, most classrooms on ground floor.

Games, Options, the Arts: Fantastic state-of-the-art art school over three floors with marvellous light and inspired work; very much in use, a rather cumbersome painting was screwed onto the window sill of the top floor blocking a fair amount of light from the north when we visited. Two pupils were amongst the top ten in A level results in art in 2008. Art/history combined field trips to Venice etc graphics, camera and screen printing. Good music (Copeman Hart manual organ) including keen traditional Scottish music group. Popular pipe band plus jazz and choirs and Cathedral choir in St Ninians, Perth (choir gets paid by cathedral), plus concert in Perth Concert Hall which holds a thousand and has always been full (freebie) aka Headmaster's Music. Lots of drama and small theatre, a clever conversion of a former dining hall, the insides cleverly scooped out (theatre doubles as an examination hall).

Swimming pool revamped with the swimming team developing under new outside coach – has two national champions, a national record holder and one of the top teams in the country. Sport taken seriously, two synthetic pitches, rugby, football, cricket, hockey, netball, own golf course, skiing, CCF (boys and girls, voluntary), flying, sailing. Shooting, clay and small bore. Sports hall with climbing wall and old fashioned gym. School has eighteen national champions and twelve national representatives. Former member of SRU also qualified in weights takes classes in either general fitness or elite sport. Some rather unhappy girls were about to go for a serious run in the rain during our visit. Masses of charity work: grannie bashing now more likely to involve teaching them computing than listening; help in charity shop. D of E.

Background and Atmosphere: School founded in 1913 by Harry Riley, based in 19th century red sandstone country house with masses of sympathetic additions, set in 150 acres. Two fantastic double-deck libraries, one with the carpet reflecting the plaster work in the ceiling; adjacent media rooms – cosy and useful. Fairly utilitarian chapel (children quite rude about it) and recently refurbished dining room, million quid – ceiling dropped, new floor – though not sure it is that good for dancing. Main classrooms 150 yards away beyond the old stable building which has been converted into a splendidly cosy junior house, Riley, boasting a most amazing atrium plus library and music practice rooms etc. Classroom blocks undergoing programme of refurbishment, latest improvements including three new state-of-the-art chemistry labs. Houses new and newish, boys and girls have own study bedrooms for their last four years, lots of kitchens and common room area on each floor. New girls' house now completed and as a consequence there has been an increase in girls. Much general to-ing and fro-ing, but co-ed works well here; girls' houses out of bounds to boys on Sunday mornings so that girls 'can laze around in their dressing gowns if they want.' School facilities much used by groups during holiday period. Over 70 staff live on site in school houses, lots of young and good family feel – 'nice place for a family – a complete way of life.' All the houses are quite close together – with the new girls' house being perhaps the furthest away, which gives a cosy air of friendliness. Not an overwhelming school. School council operates under aegis of head girl and boy.

Pastoral Care and Discipline: Houseparents live on site with two staff on duty in each house every night. Academic tutor attached to each pupil and tutorial team in every house. Tutors often using the time available for informal chats. Mr Thompson 'aware that things happen' and talks of rustication and drugs testing 'in case of suspicion'. Will suspend; automatically out for drugs and contact police. Head works hard on bullying awareness, lots of briefing – expectations, ownership, relationships, 'be reasonable'. 'Like running a huge great family,' with a 'good cross age group.' Boy/girl relationship 'works well'. Punishment system for misdemeanours of 'fatigues' – jobs around the buildings and grounds – 'no shortage of them'!

Pupils and Parents: A quarter of the pupils from overseas, mostly ex-pats, plus 80-odd foreign pupils from Spain, Russia, Africa, China, Eastern Europe, Hong Kong, Germany et al. School is popular with Scots (regional accents of all kinds) well-placed, an hour from both Edinburgh and Glasgow, plus a small contingent from south of the border. (School claims it is 'two hours from London': three from Heathrow or Gatwick more like). Day pupils allocated to one of the houses; daily buses to and from Perth, Kinross, Auchterarder, Stirling, Crieff and Dundee. FPs Dominic Diamond (computer games whizzo), Colin Montgomerie (golfer), Sir Jack Shaw,(Bank of Scotland), John Gray (former chairman of the Hong Kong and Shanghai Bank). Not a toffs' school, despite brief showing in the fashion stakes when David Pighills took the school co-ed. 'Very good relationship with parents,' says the head.

Entrance: At 9, 10, 11 or 12 for the junior house (entry day and aptitude report-tests) then automatic entry, otherwise by CE. Not a high hurdle but popular. Later entry by report and interview if space available. Excellent route map for parents unfamiliar with public school entry procedures – complete with CD which is currently jammed in this editor's lap top.

Exit: More than 95 per cent to an enormous range of universities (Glasgow, Aberdeen and Edinburgh are popular). Trickle to Oxbridge, ('where they often get firsts'). Services popular.

Money Matters: School financially strong. All the recent revamping and building has been done without appeal or fundraising – impressive. Junior scholarships, open scholarships and sixth form scholarship plus academic, all-rounder, sport, music, cathedral and art scholarships. Parents can also apply for means-tested help with fees – 'moving towards bursaries' for all.

Remarks: Outstanding head – tops in Scotland. The school is in fantastic heart and at ease in the local community. PS bet there will be some sort of appeal to celebrate 2013. Any takers?

Stroud High School

Beards Lane, Cainscross Road, Stroud, Gloucestershire, GL5 4HF

• Pupils: 900 all day girls • Ages: 11-18 • Size of sixth form: 255 girls in mixed sixth form, Downfield, formed jointly with next door boys' school Marling • Non-denom • State

Tel: 01453 764 441
Fax: 01453 756 304
Email: admin@stroudhigh.gloucs.sch.uk
Website: www.stroudhigh.gloucs.sch.uk

Headteacher: Since 2007, Mr Tim Withers BA MA PGCE (late forties). Married, with one son, two daughters. Stroud High's first male head, Mr Withers is an English teacher. He taught in Spain and Turkey, was head of English in Somerset and Gloucestershire and joined Stroud High following deputy headships in North Somerset and Bristol. His interests are continuing professional development, self-evaluation 'and – above all – teaching and learning'. Friendly and straightforward – 'We want to be an outstanding school', his style is not obviously showy. 'He's very calm, deep-thinking, and keeps a clear view of the big picture,' says a colleague. One parent calls him, 'a rock; he's the foundation'. He says: 'We're very values-driven. Education is important, but it's not just about a nice collection of GCSEs and A levels. We're about personal best, respect and fun. It's really important this is an enjoyable place – it's fun that colours our memories of school.'

Academic matters: Selects bright girls at entry and does well by them. Results are excellent, despite staff's constant refrain, 'We're not an exam factory.' Pupils take 10 compulsory GCSEs from a range of some 30 subjects. Less mainstream subjects include astronomy and photography. 98 per cent of pupils achieved 5 or more A*–C at GCSE in 2009. 100% of pupils take a science subject and some 20 per cent of leavers go on to study a variety of science subjects. modern foreign languages specialist status: good recent A level results for French, Spanish, Russian, more mixed at GCSE for German and Spanish. Staff go to great lengths to offer flexibility. 'The more unusual the subject combinations, the better I like it,' says one pupil. 'We don't do columns of subjects here.'

The school forms part of the Stroud District Partnership, a collection of nine local secondary schools and Stroud College that between them offer a wide range of subjects and diploma courses, though in practice just a handful of students seem to cross over. Specialist Science and Maths Status in 2003, which helped provide funding for an army of interactive whiteboards, and opened up new initiatives: a recent project involves building a plane from scratch. English, maths and psychology are currently the most popular subjects in sixth form, with very good results. Joint sixth form teaching with the boys has not affected girls' results, and the verdict seems largely positive. 'It has made things more chilled and sociable, in and outside school' says one sixth former. 'The boys bring a lot of fun to everything.' Another confides: 'At first, we all mill round the new sixth form block being social, then gradually – usually after the boys have a bit of a shock with their ASs – everyone gravitates upstairs to study.'

Very dedicated staff: about half are early 40s and under. 'Staff don't just go that extra mile, but two or three,' remarks a parent. Year 7 is taught in 4 tutor groups of around 32. Year 8 onwards divides into smaller groups of 24–6, up to sixth form. You can hear a pin drop, walking round during lessons. 'My brothers teased me I was off to school with the nerds,' says one girl, 'but everyone just wants you to do your best – it doesn't matter what sets you're in.' 'No stigma' for the school's 20 or so pupils on the SEN register. SENCo works alongside all members of staff. Pupils can have one-to-one mentoring. Some who find coping with a whole school day difficult due to their medical conditions are on reduced timetables. Other SEN students say they feel so supported by their peers and teachers they cope without Teaching Assistants. A few use laptops in lessons and examinations.

Games, Options, the Arts: Lots of sports on offer, from netball, athletics, hockey, rounders, tennis to football and basketball. Large, well-equipped sports hall and newly renovated gym. Girls compete at national level in athletics (including one tipped for potential Olympic stardom); cross-country, rounders and swimming. Recent overhaul of the tennis courts seems to have paid off, with the school reaching national finals of the prestigious Aberdare Cup for past two years running. School represented at regional level in netball and hockey, plus county level. 'There are lots of fun sports as well as team sports,' says one girl. Recent attempts to boost numbers for fun sport clubs.

Around one-third of girls take a musical instrument, with singing lessons very popular. Regular school concerts open to all ability and a range of choirs, orchestras, ensembles and groups. Gospel Choir performed recently with Mica Paris, the Senior Choir sings at Cheltenham Festival. Wide range of clubs available within school day: popular ones include badminton, street and contemporary dance. Notices are posted on in-house plasma screens dotted around school, in assemblies and the fortnightly newsletter. Art and drama good and very popular. Terrific – and well-used – photography room.

Success in national competitions – Investment Challenge, Young Consumer of the Year – and local ones: the High School Food Team won at an enterprise day at Calcot Manor. Lots of trips, plus visits, exchanges and work experience in France, Germany and Spain. Foreign trips seem to be expanding: recent destinations include New York, St Petersburg and China. (One girl quick to point out: 'Not everyone has the money to do things but there's enough going on that you don't feel you miss out'). Very strong ICT department, which permeates all levels: as a tool for staff to track pupils' progress, and giving girls excellent access to computers, plus a range of music technology and software and state of the art multi media equipment. 'Nothing's ever locked up and we have no vandalism,' says a teacher.

Background and Atmosphere: The school was started in 1904 by far-sighted local dignitaries to give girls an education similar to that enjoyed by boys at Marling School. In 1911 the school moved to its present site beside Marling, set just off the main road into town (mayhem at drop-off/pick-up). The school's first fourth generation pupil started recently, and the School Birthday remains the celebratory highpoint of the school year, with everyone bringing in cakes. The original red-brick, creeper-clad main building can feel cramped inside, but is sunny, both in aspect and atmosphere. Some old pre-fabs remain, and the school remains divided from its former junior school site by a car-crammed residential street, but there has been a feverish programme of building and refurbishment over the past few years, and the school is justly proud of the smart new sixth form block.

'The school's come rocketing into the 21st century,' says one parent, and there is a real sense of a good school sharpening up still further. This shows in various ways, from a smart new uniform, introducing burgundy jackets – 'not "blazers",' the girls explain – although pupils voted to keep their distinctive candy-striped shirts; to an overhaul of the way the school tracks and monitors pupils' and teachers' progress throughout school, to the building programme, and removal – both physical and psychological – of walls between the girls' and boys' schools.

Pastoral Care and Discipline: Lots of support systems in place. Girls struggling, for whatever reason, are mentored by designated staff, whom they can choose. Girls think buddying system and peer mentoring work well. Active whole school council, with all senior pupils eligible to be termly prefects. Separate sixth form council. 'We're encouraged to be independent in improving the school,' says one girl, e.g. some Year 11s set up their own informal homework club, The Space (known as 'the Biscuit Club'), which has become a focal point for other year groups too.

'I like to think we're nurturing the next generation of eccentrics,' says one teacher. 'The girls are very eco-minded, always checking my recycling bins,' says another. Stroud High girls are continually described as 'quirky', 'original', 'vocal' and 'feisty' by parents and staff alike, and so they are, although not dauntingly or overwhelmingly so. This is Stroud, after all, and the school reflects the town's liberal-minded, arty/artisan ethos – what one teacher calls 'the Stroud effect'.

Which is not to say discipline is airy-fairy. 'It's about recognising things can go wrong and positive behaviour management,' says Mr Withers. School adopts a graded approach to discipline (which wasn't in place before), starting with a warning, then room detention: 'usually that's sufficient,' says Mr Withers. 'I've not made a permanent exclusion. The ratio of praise to sanctions is about 6.1. It's not about hanging people out to dry.' He uses the fortnightly newsletter to 'nag' (his word) on anything from no eating lunch in classrooms, to getting down to revision.

Pupils and Parents: Interesting, fun and fair-minded girls have a touching sense of their good fortune, and a strong sense of the world around them. They raise huge amounts for charity, and are 'always coming in with fund raising ideas.' Pupils predominantly white British with high proportion of middle-class. 'But it's not all ponies in the paddock,' says one teacher. 'There are some poor pockets locally, which makes for a good leveller.' School has instigated a hardship fund. Some pupils travel from as far afield as Ross-on Wye, Malmesbury, and the fringes of Bristol, but majority are from Stroud and surrounding area. Energetic Parent Staff Association and strong governing team.

Entrance: Approximately three applicants to one place. (In 2009, 299 entered for 120 places). School has own exam, two Verbal Reasoning tests, usually in October. Pupils come in from over 50 partner schools which vary from year to year. Additional places at sixth form, with minimum requirement of five A*–B at GCSE.

Exit: 'We're definitely encouraged to apply for university,' says a sixth-former. Almost everyone goes on to higher education, all over the country, and doing a huge range of subjects. Anything between 2–6 go to Oxford and Cambridge.

Remarks: Really warm, vibrant school that offers bright, sparky girls a combination of single-sex education and co-ed. Girls go it alone up to sixth form, then join forces with the neighbouring boys' grammar to form the Marling School and Stroud High School sixth form.

Summerhill School

Linked to Summerhill School (Junior) in the Junior section

Westward Ho, Leiston, Suffolk, IP16 4HY

• Pupils: Around 70; roughly half girls, half boys; majority board but also a small number of day pupils • Ages: 5-17 • Size of sixth form: No sixth form • none • Fees: Boarding £8,160-£14,181; Day £3,558-£8,505 pa • Independent

Tel: 01728 830 540
Fax: 01728 830 540
Email: office@summerhillschool.co.uk
Website: www.summerhillschool.co.uk

Principal: Since 1985, Zoë Readhead (a very youthful sixty-ish) daughter of school's founder AS Neill. Literally born, bred and educated at Summerhill. Not a teacher – more akin to a head of state. Has been a staunch guardian of school's core values when lesser mortals would have been tempted to allow their dilution. Inspiring and uncompromising but not everyone's cup of tea. Can sometimes come across as intimidating or defensive and, at times, seems a bit outside the day to day rough and tumble of the community. Married to Tony, a farmer, with four grown-up children all educated at Summerhill, two of them teaching here. Son, William, serves as a second in command.

Academic matters: Of secondary importance here. In fact, the word 'school' is barely appropriate – community is more fitting, or even 'kibbutz'. Summerhill is a 'free' school run on the principle that children have the same rights as adults and should be able to choose their own educational goals unfettered by the interference of nervous parents. Lessons are optional – some children will not attend a single lesson for a number of years. Play is considered as valid a part of a child's development as formal teaching. 'Many kids just need to play until they are ready to learn,' a teacher told us. As the parents' handbook emphasises, 'remember, at Summerhill your kid could theoretically NEVER go to a lesson – they have that right. Staff members are not going to persuade, cajole or bully your child about lessons.'

All that said, the school has had to change with the times. Effort is made (through e.g. mock exams to hone test-taking skills) to help pupils who wish to take exams to leave with several GCSEs under their belt. The school's ex-curriculum manager (left 2007) who arrived in the aftermath of the infamous 1999 Ofsted report (see Background) tightened up the academic offerings and helped to produce a less chaotic school (head says it was never chaotic). Some teachers offer younger children small prizes for attending lessons with some regularity. Prime emphasis is put on reading and writing. Beyond that, eight full-time, live-in teachers, together with peripatetics, offer normal range of subjects plus environmental management, German, Chinese and Japanese. Pupils are entered for Cambridge International O levels for some subjects rather than GCSEs; the school finds the former more straightforward (no coursework, no Byzantine marking schemes).

Science lab is rather good. We observed a physics lesson which consisted of one seated pupil soberly facing a whiteboard where the teacher was instructing – curiously alternative and traditional all at once. It struck us as a great environment for independent learners – the school brings this out in many of its pupils – but less ideal for those who thrive with a collegiate buzz and, dare we say it, constructive competition from likeminded pupils.

'Special needs' are not recognised here – 'we don't like labels – a lot of the pathologies that pupils bring here are contextual. In this healthier context, many of their problems melt away.' Pupils with ADHD do particularly well. Parents report miracles as youngsters are free to fidget, to come and go from lessons and to burn off as much energy as they wish playing in the grounds. A few autistic spectrum children and plenty of 'individual' types who were miserable elsewhere.

Games, Options, the Arts: Lots available but not too lots. At Summerhill, boredom is considered an important ingredient of education. The parents' handbook warns, 'on non-lesson days it is important that your children are at the school and you do not pick them up just because they are bored ... Boredom leads to creativity!' Well, y-e-e-e-s, up to a point, but we can think of plenty of other things boredom leads to. Sports not high on the agenda for folks who choose this school. No games in the conventional school sense, but pupils can play tennis of sorts, football, basketball, volleyball, table tennis, badminton, and Summerhill's very own 'tork'. Swimming for the bold in unheated outdoor pool and for the meek at the Leiston Leisure Centre. Dance is an option and performance of all kinds is valued here. Music very important with some excellent teaching and good facilities for music technology and studio recording. The school holds a 'Summerhill Woodstock' complete with outdoor stage. Similarly, drama is big among these arty kids and the school has a refurbished small theatre. GCSE drama teacher visits the school and there are plans to hold an annual drama festival. Woodwork taken seriously, in lovely and orderly premises, operating on same footing as English or maths – except it is probably more popular. Other activities include riding, crafts, life drawing, metalwork, photography (there is a darkroom), writing for the school newspaper, film-making, cooking in the café, camping in the grounds, making tree forts etc. Some parents grumbled to us that many areas of the school are locked when not in official use, making it hard for pupils to use facilities and study areas in their own time (school says children just need to make arrangements for access).

Background and Atmosphere: Founded in 1921 by AS Neill near Dresden, Germany as a response to the 'children should be seen and not heard' mentality of the day. Settled in Leiston in 1927, where it became one of the most famous and controversial schools in the world. The school has been threatened with closure on several occasions, most recently in 1999 after a damning Ofsted report that called the pupils 'foulmouthed' and accused the school of failing the children educationally. Summerhill chose to contest the notice of closure in court and four days into the hearing – in the face of enormous protest from current and former parents and pupils – the government's case collapsed.

So much has been written about it that it is hard to discuss Summerhill as a living entity rather than as some kind of experimental education dissertation. Constant flow of visitors from around the world with clipboards in hand has no effect whatsoever on proceedings. Extremely low-key 11-acre setting consists of large Victorian house, many single-storey additions, staff accommodation (some in 'their beloved', pretty squalid, hippy-style caravans – you've got to see it to believe it), wooded grounds. Spectacular beech tree for climbing, rope-swings and general play – a 'Summerhill thing', the pupils told us. Little gardens, ponds and an orchard planted by pupils. Fab spider-web climbing frame constructed by visiting artist. Atmosphere informal to point of jaw-dropping (we saw one class working on a group art project while a five year old pupil sat sprawled across the table on which they worked). Long holidays – five weeks at Christmas, five weeks in the spring and nine weeks each summer, but no half-terms – works well for overseas pupils.

Pastoral Care and Discipline: Far from being a place where you can do anything you like, Summerhill has more rules than any school we have ever visited. However, there are few fixed rules (other than the laws of the land). Everything is voted on at 'the Meeting', held three times a week. All children, from age 5 to 17, have an equal vote, as do the teachers. There is absolutely no special authority invested in adults, indeed quite the contrary as they are vastly outnumbered! The Meeting is chaired by pupils and will sometimes make outlandish decisions e.g. to abandon bed-times. The children will stay up all night, every night. Sooner or later a glassy-eyed pupil will suggest that bed-times be reinstated and the Meeting will eagerly support the measure. Misdemeanours are 'brought up' at the Meeting and an appropriate 'fine' is decided upon. The Meeting we attended was calm and thoughtful, with older pupils looking out for their younger peers. The proceedings were surprisingly formal, with older pupils serving as chairmen on a rotating basis after first attending training sessions – all in all a fabulous educational experience. As a former pupil told us, 'what Summerhill does give you is an ability to communicate with people, and it teaches you to just be nice.' We could do with more of that in our schools. Pupils not afraid to voice complaints about their peers; bullying is rare and when it happens it is dealt with calmly and swiftly. NB: Special rules apply to the pupils when they visit Leiston village e.g. no swearing.

The school makes much of its claim that it allows kids to be kids. To us, however, at times it felt that it allows kids to be adults, in some ways robbing them of their childhood rather than celebrating it. Summerhill's freedom and democracy can extend into unsettling areas. There is absolutely no filter on internet access. And, except for the very youngest children, there is no restriction over what videos pupils can rent. Sex is not officially allowed, but there is no effort made to discourage it. The school will assist pupils with contraception 'when it is thought necessary' and parents will not be informed unless the child requests it. Drug taking or drinking will get a pupil sent home for four to eight weeks, but a child would only be asked to leave if they consistently made clear they could not fit in e.g. for extremely disturbed behaviour or consistently failing to follow the community's rules.

Pupils and Parents: Having seen the Channel 4 documentary showing the pupils swimming in the nude and beheading a sick rabbit with a machete, we were immensely relieved not to be greeted by pupils with pitchforks dancing naked on the lawn or similar. Indeed, the pupils we met were straightforward and interesting people, not whacked out problem kids (the school does not take pupils older than 11 so is not a dumping ground for disturbed teenagers). In common with home-schoolers, parents at Summerhill tend to be over-zealous advocates of the school, born, no doubt, of having continually to justify their choice of this kind of education. Several parents expressed the belief that a happy childhood was simply not possible at any other school. The school is well-known abroad and almost two thirds of children come from overseas, especially Japan, Korea and Taiwan. Also currently Holland, China, Sudan, Germany, France, Poland, The Netherlands etc. Around 50 per cent of pupils are receiving some sort of EFL help (if they choose to turn up).

Parents here have taken the decision to 'let go' for the benefit of their children. Keeping them at arms length so that children can develop free of parental anxiety and interference is a key tenet of the school. There are no formal end of term – or even end of year – reports and parents will not be informed if their child transgresses. The school becomes a sort of alternative family for the children and it is common for pupils to tell parents that they 'cannot understand' Summerhill because they do not live and breathe it. The school's literature says, 'what happens at school is usually considered to be the kid's own business, not necessarily to be shared by parents. Accepting this, is part of learning to accept your new independent, free child.'

Entrance: Takes children ages 5 to 11 – older kids are enrolled only in rare circumstances. There are day places, but it is basically a boarding school with children going home twice a term for weekends (although they can ask at the Meeting and usually get away more if they want to). Weekly boarding is an option for the youngest children or as a settling stage for pupils who will become full boarders later. Pupils may enter the school at the start of any term and, as they seldom start with a cohort, it is common for them to take several terms to fully integrate. Interested parents are encouraged to read about the school, and then to visit.

Exit: A few leave at 14 to attend a more traditional GCSE course elsewhere. The majority stay until 17. Most end up with several GCSEs and go on to some kind of further education. Many proceed to sixth form colleges (and then to university) although entering a normal school can be a jolt. Some end up working in skilled craft jobs. Children's writer John Burningham (The Snowman) attended the school, as did several well-known actors, musicians, artists and scientists – others are off making tepees in the Welsh hills. AS Neill said, 'I'd rather produce a happy street sweeper than a neurotic prime minister.' And judging from the many ill-spelled, non-punctuated, but joyful letters we received from ex-Summerhillians keen to contribute to this review, his goal is being met.

Money Matters: Mega-cheap but then they do not have the overheads of keeping up historical buildings, state of the art sports centres, interactive whiteboards etc etc. The whole place runs on a shoestring with an air of frugality. Teachers' salaries are lowish. Food is good and choices include the usual vegetarian options. Ten per cent discount for children of Ex-Summerhillians. Some subjects – like Chinese – charged as extras, plus riding, dancing and music lessons. School squirreling away funds for the AS Neill Summerhill Trust which will eventually be able to provide limited bursaries.

Remarks: Thank goodness something like this still exists in 21st century Britain where exams and paper qualifications are almost a religion. While we cannot agree with the school's claims that this kind of education would suit all children and that most children in mainstream schools are unhappy, for many of those who choose it, the school works. Other schools seek to incorporate watered-down elements of the Summerhill philosophy, but none provides such an uncompromising, full-on, 'free' education – accepting the good (enlightenment) and the bad (illiteracy) that may result. Inspiring, fun, risky, profoundly educational and, often, unsettling: a national treasure.

Sunnydown School

Portley House, 152 Whyteleafe Road, Caterham, Surrey, CR3 5ED

• Pupils: 70 boys; 30 weekly boarders • Ages: 11-16 • Non-denom • State

Tel: 01883 342 281
Fax: 01883 341 342
Email: head@sunnydown.surrey.sch.uk

Head: Since 1982, Mr Moore Armstrong. His wife Jill also teaches history at the school – 'I did not appoint her!' Smiley, caring and respected – fierce when necessary, obviously loves coming to work. 'I could be accused of failing in ambition in not moving to another job but this is a very interesting place ... ' Not complacent, yet shows endless delight in boys' achievements.

Academic matters: All the boys have very severe dyslexia and arrive at the school streetwise – albeit with behavioural and communication difficulties – but with their only academic experience one of failure (e.g. 11 years old with a reading age of 5). Immediate assessments of reading, comprehension and spelling set challenging targets for each boy, which are achieved and rewarded with the focus and encouragement of form teachers and learning support staff. About 8 boys and two adults in each class; outgoing yet disciplined behaviour with laughter, practical examples of subjects and peer evaluation holding the kids' attention. Mainstream curriculum from Year 7, good range of GCSEs; mainly focused on work related skills. Entry Level Certificates mean everyone leaves with a qualification. Effective and well-used IT room, ditto library. An excellent working environment where fear of failure does not exist; 'if they don't make it here, they won't make it anywhere.'

Games, Options, the Arts: Games and outdoor activities recognised as immensely important for 11–16 year old boys. Lunchbreak lasts an unfashionable 80 minutes, giving everyone time to let off steam before more lessons – the basketball court is very popular, the London Towers professional team come and coach 24 boys each week. Swimming takes place in the pool at the neighbouring mainstream state school – and snowball fights between the two when the weather is right! Astroturf area enables all-weather football. Sunnydown competes with the 70 other members of Surrey Special Schools Sports Association – trophies displayed in the school hall. Duke of Edinburgh Award Scheme, Ocean Youth Trust South, Army, Sea Cadets, St John's Ambulance – the biggest problem is not enough days for all the available options. Many of the activities stem from pupils' suggestion books. Music is part of the curriculum but there is also an opera workshop each week. Art is of a mainstream standard – pupils recently took part in a national sculpture competition and were ranked by the V&A as one of the top ten schools in the county.

Background and Atmosphere: Friendly atmosphere as soon as you enter and are given a bright visitor's badge. Each individual's needs are known without looking them up in a file. Boarders love it here – not just because of the range of evening activities – rooms are clean, bright and there are obviously no problems with stealing, since I saw mobile phones lying around and a dorm's safe box wide open. Zero tolerance to bullying means that everything is reported – including complaints such as 'so and so is not talking to me' – if that is seen as bullying then communication has to be pretty important here! The care staff is dedicated and perceptive, 6 ½ in total; 1 of the 2 men is an ex-pupil. Couple of whole school assemblies each week; no group religion outside RE syllabus. Two dogs (pets of care staff) and a part-time cat (belonging to head's daughter). Form tutor and care staff are the first points of contact for concerned parents yet head operates open (truly) door policy. Written report at Christmas and in July, three parents' meetings a term and pupils' statements are reviewed every year.

Pupils and Parents: From all over Surrey (weekly board available for those with long commute) and families have moved into the county to attend.

Entrance: Surrey LEA SEN panel meets each November and examines statements – the youngest with the most severe SEN come to Sunnydown. School does not really want to dilute effective size but may stretch to 80 pupils with extra facilities in the future. Open mornings for parents alone.

Exit: Around 95 per cent stay in education, mostly to local colleges for vocational GNVQs.

Money Matters: State financed, parents and friends contribute to extra fund-raising; a few eyebrows were raised at letter proposing a collection for Guinness – the name of the often sick – now deceased – school cat!

Remarks: A remarkable school with a family feel, effective and inspiring for the visitor and obviously for the pupils too – old boys return to visit, normally around lunchtime ... Sunnydown builds boys' self-esteem fast; one applied for a job as a apprentice at a hairdresser's and ended up cutting hair on national TV.

Surbiton High School

Linked to Surbiton High Boys' Preparatory School in the Junior section
Linked to Surbiton High Junior Girls' School in the Junior section

Surbiton Crescent, Kingston Upon Thames, Surrey, KT1 2JT

• Pupils: all girls; 675 + 200 in the sixth form; all day • Ages: High school 11-18, junior girls' school 4-11 and boys' prep 4-11 • Size of sixth form: 200 • Christian ethos (but all denominations accepted) • Fees: £12,246 pa • Independent

Tel: 020 8439 1309
Fax: 02085 470 026
Email: surbiton.high@surbitonhigh.ucst.co.uk
Website: www.surbitonhigh.com

Principal: Since January 2008, Ms Ann Haydon BSc (Hons) (early forties) here styled as principal. Arrives with an excellent reputation from Guildford High (Surbiton's sister school) where she spent five years as deputy headmistress and therefore already au fait with school's owners UCST. Previously she was at Sutton High for seven years, having joined as youngest ever head of department (geography), and before that she was at Putney High.

Has been quick to make her mark on the place, showing dynamism and commitment to change, but without making great waves. Already homed in on music and sport – which our previous review identified as in need of some oomph -significantly raising the profile of both. Has also expanded the extra-curricular side. Girls like her, parents seem pleased and consensus is that she will be good for the school. 'Supremely professional,' says one parent. 'She's very charming,' says another, 'Personable, but formal,' declares a third. Always around and has made great efforts to get to know the girls – teaches Year 7 geography, holds form captain lunches, sees girls with especially good reports – which helps her put names to faces. She describes herself as 'passionate about the whole child – it may be a cliché but there really are only visible children as far as I'm concerned.' Hobbies include sport, theatre and music, while her real love is to travel – especially to Africa where she has set up, and continues to run, a children's charity.

Academic matters: Though not the crème de la crème, the girls are generally above average on entry and the school does well by them, delivering solid results with very good value-added. More nurturing than a power house. High quality teaching and learning – girls are pushed to their ability in appropriate sets for core subjects. At GCSE (girls generally take nine or ten) more than one third of all results are A* and 95 per cent of all results are A* to B. Good place for linguists – wide breadth on offer at Key Stage 3 including French, Spanish, German and Latin – even Mandarin available through enrichment programme. Also separate sciences at KS3. At A level, 54 per cent of girls achieve a grade A; 86 per cent A-B. Less common offerings include Italian and Russian. Critical thinking and further maths also available. Average UCAS points 400 and most students get places at universities of their choice including nine per cent (handful) to Oxbridge. Ms Haydon is keen to improve on this and has appointed a coordinator to promote the idea to the girls a bit more, with potential candidates identified in Year 10 and supported with special lessons and master classes. Parental perception that Oxbridge places are coveted above all others has put a few noses out of joint.

Lessons are pacey, taking account of different learning styles, and the girls are well challenged. Excellent monitoring systems in place. Nice emphasis on encouraging pupils to organise themselves – good note-taking skills drilled into them from the off, so that by Year 10 it is automatic. Well resourced, the school makes excellent use of technology all round – one neat example is via Active Expression handsets, linked to software and interactive white boards, which the girls use to answer questions during lessons. Means that no-one can be anonymous and teachers can analyse the information later to identify anyone in need of support. The technology moves lessons along more quickly and is proving a powerful tool.

Healthy mix of male/female, young/older teachers and pleasingly not much use of supply staff. No SEN screening on entry but screening for literacy difficulties in Year 7. Supported learning section provides individual and small group tuition as needed, literacy booster groups if required and EAL. Parents pay extra towards SEN but cost is subsidised by school – currently eight per cent of the girls receive such help. There is gifted and talented programme for the most academically able girls, involving master classes, mentoring and a range of challenging learning opportunities.

Games, Options, the Arts: Great tradition of high quality art – school won 17 top candidate awards at GCSE – with girls flourishing in gorgeous open plan art studio. The artwork on display in reception is so good that a visitor might think it was professional – it is all by pupils! Budding thespians be aware that drama could be stronger – it's there but not as high profile as some places. Music is emerging from a bit of a dip and has been reinvigorated by a new director of music ('he's outstanding,' say parents). Although there appears to be lots going on and school points to a number of individual stand out performances, parents generally don't recommend the place for a very sporty daughter. All could be about to change as Ms Haydon is determined to turn this around and wants all girls to have more opportunities to participate and perform. Initiatives include overseas hockey and netball tours, tennis development programme and a fitness suite for sixth form. In any event it's not at all bad – outstanding skiing (school produces champions on plastic and snow) with strong rowing and gymnastics and there's an existing gifted and talented programme for sport. Strong emphasis on extra-curricular clubs since new head arrived. There are over 70 options, from Bollywood films to word games – new ones include riding and astronomy – and breadth of interest is encouraged; girls are not encouraged to specialise academically or otherwise. Numerous examples of individual successes with girls winning places and competitions in all sorts of areas from music to design to literacy. Put some money aside for some enviable overseas trips – recently France, Spain, USA and Iceland.

Background and Atmosphere: School celebrated its 125th anniversary in 2009 – it opened at the same address in a large Victorian house in 1884. Still owned by the United Church Schools Trust, an independent Christian educational charity. But few other clues to such heritage these days. Newcomers searching for the place would easily mistake it for a corporate headquarters. School fills one suburban block, 10 minutes walk from main shops of suburban Surbiton and is surrounded by assorted housing stock and wide, but car-choked, avenues. Recent years have seen tremendous investment and expansion – all good, but new buildings and layout involves girls in a fair bit of walking to different sites for different lessons – including crossing a main road, albeit with a permanent crossing warden. Refreshing exercise on a summer's day, more miserable in the winter and it does put a few families off.

Classrooms are light and bright, and facilities first class. Only real minus is a lack of outdoor space on site. (Off site there are extensive sports grounds at Hinchley Wood.) Sixth form has its own building with good IT and private study facilities and a common room. Overall a purposeful, business-like atmosphere with pupils and parents alike raving about how friendly the school is. 'There's a lovely feel to the place,' sums up one.

Pastoral Care and Discipline: High praise for pastoral care. When talking to one prospective family visiting with their (generally) sweet 11 year old, school staff assured them that, 'we'll still like her when she is 15!' 'And they do,' says that mother; 'the pastoral care is really very good.'

Most parents report an immediate and effective response to any issues. Generally a well-behaved bunch – largely complying with the zero tolerance policy on drugs, drink and cigarettes. Smokers hauled before Ms Haydon even if they were caught out of school hours and uniform. School nurse on site, doctor available weekly. Good induction routines for Year 7s, followed up with 'big sister' mentoring programme. Healthy culture of 'telling' about problems and school quick to support anyone in difficulty and any of their friends who may have been involved. Not a bitch-fest – girls say their classmates are supportive of them. Parents pleased that school somehow manages to keep cliques and queen bees under control.

Pupils and Parents: Townie mix – English middle-class predominate. Some families pay the fees without a thought, while other families work extra shifts to afford the place. 'We're a fairly down to earth bunch,' says one. Parents delighted when their unconfident 11 year olds emerge five years later completely self-assured. Several mention how their daughters have blossomed under the Surbiton High watch. Not the smartest set of girls and several parents said they'd like to see tighter monitoring and control of standards – usual problem of creeping hemlines. Sixth formers wear their own clothes – no 'business-dress' requirement. Street-wise, the girls are by and large dedicated and hardworking and can't get away with coasting as involved parents and caring school marshal them in an effective pincer movement.

Entrance: New initiative allows 'natural progression' from the junior to the senior school. 'We know our girls well and there is no need for them to have the stress of an exam,' says Ms Haydon. The 'handful' who may not make the grade are given fair (Year 5) warning. Newcomers are assessed in English and maths and will write a personal statement which they are encouraged to consider beforehand. Word on the street is that the exams are not as hard as others taken on the entry exam round. The school says that 'interest in the school is such that we have become increasingly selective.' Six forms of 24 – though occasional one-off years of 7 form entry (e.g. 2009). There are isolated parental moans that the school and classes are too big with such a substantial new intake every year – it is a large school so make sure your shrinking violet would not feel lost in the crowd. Head says there is no such thing as a 'Surbiton girl,' but they are all 'interesting girls'. Intake from south-west London and north-east Surrey. Main feeder schools are Fern Hill Primary, Holy Cross Prep, Rowan Prep, St Michael's C of E, St Paul's C of E, Thames Ditton Junior and Twickenham Prep. For sixth form entry, offers are based on interview and GCSE predictions.

Exit: Some fall out at 16, mainly to co-ed sixth forms (there's a good mixed state 6th form nearby). From sixth form most to good universities of their choice – new emphasis on Oxbridge (see above).

Money Matters: Parents happy they get value for money – it's not the dearest in the area. Some recent parental disquiet over reports that fees go towards subsidising other schools in UCST group – but the school says there is absolutely no truth in this statement. Help with fees available three ways: from scholarships – academic, music, art, sports; Church Schools Foundation Assisted places (dependent on family income) and bursaries for 'daughters of the clergy'.

Remarks: A large school with a good local reputation – it is not elitist nor a school that treats you as if you are lucky to be there. New head is forward thinking and full of plans. Parents recommend heartily. Friendly place with happy girls who are achieving academically and progressing personally.

Sutton Grammar School for Boys

Manor Lane, Sutton, Surrey, SM1 4AS

• Pupils: 835 boys, all day • Ages: 11-18 • Size of sixth form: 240
• Non-denom • State

Tel: 020 8642 3821
Fax: 020 8661 4500
Email: sgs@suttonlea.org
Website: www.suttongrammar.sutton.sch.uk

Head: Since 1990, Mr Gordon Ironside MA PGCE (fifties). Read physics at Cambridge. Joined the school in 1983 as head of maths, then deputy head in 1987. Comes across as a generally good egg and proud Northerner. Very much a man's man rather than a smooth charmer – no bad thing. His out of school interests include sport, particularly golf and tennis and Rotarians. 'And, like everyone, family life takes up a lot of my time,' he says. Highly rated by parents who describe him as 'friendly' and 'effective.' 'He's a great role model for the boys and a very strong figure but friendly rather than frightening,' says one mother.

Academic matters: Very impressive – a selective school with excellent GCSE and A level results. 'It's not a hothouse like some state grammars, although the results are on a par,' says one pleased parent. Head says boys are picking up prizes all the time (top GCSE score in geography, design awards and Arkwright scholarships – offered to A level students intending to go on to university to study for careers in engineering). Popular optional GCSEs include history, geography and business studies and, at A level, maths and physics (by a mile). Mathematicians thrive here. Science is another real strength. Plenty of homework but parents feel the pace is right. 'You probably would not enjoy it here if you just scraped in after being heavily coached as standards are very high,' said one parent.

There are EAL students but their success in passing the entrance test shows that this is not a major issue. The school has a part-time SENCo – as a selective school there is only the occasional statemented pupil but dyslexia and dyspraxia and Asperger's are more common – though not exactly loads of it – and the school advises staff how to handle these conditions in their classrooms.

Games, Options, the Arts: A high achieving sporty lot. Parents at pains to point out how good the sport is here – several feel the school underplays its sporting card for fear of not being taken so seriously as a strongly academic school. Fantastic sports grounds – 27 acres of playing fields, pitches, cricket squares and athletics track – three miles from school in Cheam and the boys make the 15 minute journey in the school's own coach. On the main school site there is an old faithful, heated, 25m open air swimming pool (in regular use) and a recently built sports hall. 'Lots of football – which makes a nice change as you usually get rugby at selective schools,' says a mother. School also supplies ball boys for Wimbledon – the envy no doubt of many a private school boy.

The old gym now converted to a drama studio – drama gradually getting stronger and offered at A level. Lots of the music and drama is produced in conjunction with Sutton High School for Girls. Usual mix of Young Enterprise, D of E and CCF is popular here – we did a double-take as boys in camouflage sat in lessons – they wear their CCF uniforms during school hours if they are meeting afterwards.

Background and Atmosphere: School has been around in various incarnations for over 100 years and is now on a small compact site, rather hemmed in by the popular Sutton shopping centre which has grown up around it. (Pupils are allowed off-site at lunchtime from Year 10, which eases pressure on space and the limited canteen facilities). Main building is circa 1928, and looks it, with associated wood panelling in places and the odd old-fashioned lab still surviving, but lots of new bits have been added as part of a major modernisation programme. A couple of the science rooms have roof gardens housing outdoor experiments.

IT facilities are all around the school, with three main classrooms for full-class teaching. Corridors are narrow and warrant a 'one-way' system as the boys navigate the school. Overall facilities are workmanlike rather than flashy – but it's all there. Scruffy in places – these are boys after all. A traditional grammar school environment where the boys appear to work and play hard. 'It's a lovely, lovely place,' says one mother. Boys we saw were fully engaged in what they were doing. Purposeful atmosphere. 'It's formal and old-fashioned in a good way,' say parents. Long standing staff – over a third have been there more than 10 years and turnover is low.

Pastoral Care and Discipline: 'Very happy and caring,' says one mum. 'There's an emphasis on everybody participating in everything,' adds another. Buddy system exists for new boys. School acts quickly if any problems occur. A parent we spoke to was very impressed with the fast and effective way her son's experience as a victim of bullying was handled. Form tutors, heads of year and pages of policy are in place – but in fact all staff take responsibility for the boys' welfare. Parents feel their sons have a healthy respect for the head and his staff and the staff get to know their pupils well. Head says he prefers to inspire self-discipline but he doesn't think twice about imposing it where necessary. A boy was sent home on the day of our visit for arriving with streaks in his hair after a study break. Zero tolerance of smoking, drink or drugs. (School feels a strong line on smoking makes the latter vices less likely.) Strictly upheld standards for uniform, hair and behaviour. Sixth formers dress for business in suits. Basically, you have to toe the line here.

Pupils and Parents: Good cultural mix (over a third of the boys are from non-white ethnic backgrounds), a confident and polite bunch. Majority are local but others travel from homes along the main transport links to Sutton, including Epsom, Cheam, Worcester Park, Kingston, Surbiton, Merton and South Wimbledon. Most from state primaries. There are about 60 feeder schools with none sending more than about four boys in any one year. Parents are mostly 'middle class and middle aged,' jokes one mother. Lots of professional parents and supportive PTA. OB network very strong – David Bellamy is one of the better known and is a regular visitor.

Entrance: Overwhelmingly in Year 7. School sets its own exam covering verbal reasoning, literacy (including a piece of 'free writing') and numeracy. 'I felt it was a fair test,' said one mother, 'it's based on what they will have learned in Year 5 rather than necessitating lots of extra coaching.' Hugely over-subscribed – now between 1200–1500 boys apply (from about 60 feeder schools) for 120 places. The places are allocated in rank order; there is no longer a catchment area. For the sixth form, the minimum entry standard is four A grades and two Bs at GCSE. Existing pupils take most places, with only a small number (five to ten) joining from elsewhere.

Exit: Each Year 5–10 boys leave at 16, mostly for FE colleges: some have not made the grade for the sixth form, others are looking for different A level options or more freedom. At 18, most go to university, with approx 10 a year to Oxbridge.

Remarks: A friendly, disciplined school with high academic standards and good pastoral care. Not for free spirits or rule breakers.

Sutton High School

Linked to Sutton High Junior School in the Junior section

55 Cheam Road, Sutton, Surrey, SM1 2AX

• Pupils: 710 girls, all day • Ages: 3-18 • Size of sixth form: 85
• Non-denom • Fees: Senior School £12,006 pa • Independent

Tel: 020 8642 0594
Fax: 020 8642 2014
Email: n.new@sut.gdst.net
Website: www.suttonhigh.gdst.net

Head: Since 2003, Mr Stephen Callaghan BA NPQH (forties), a linguist, formerly deputy head at Guildford High (also a girls' school). Approachable and down-to-earth, an easy communicator and a great advocate for the girls. Married with two children (son and daughter); his wife is also a teacher.

Academic matters: Academically strong across the board – a good first division school. In 2009, 66 per cent got straight A*/A at GCSE. IGCSE maths offered and 100 per cent pass rate to date. 88 per cent of A levels A/B. Traditional range of subjects on offer, very good results in English, history and French but most encouraging is take-up and success in less typical areas of study for girls – physical sciences, maths. Much is made of IT as both an examined subject and as a cross-curricular educational tool. State of the art ICT suites and all girls in Years 12 and 13 take CLAIT.

The head, as a modern linguist, has raised their profile: French, German and Spanish all offered at GCSE, and the last now also introduced in Year 7. Extensive and imaginative programme of field trips/exchanges.

Only nine subjects are compulsory at GCSE as head keen to have space for e.g. further challenges/subjects for stretching the most able, or support for SEN or EAL students – a genuinely bespoke support system. Head doesn't weed out weaker candidates post-GCSE and his approach of supporting all pupils in their progress through the school is refreshing and praiseworthy, particularly in this academic environment (other heads take note). 'Endless support is there if you need it but you have to want to help yourself too,' acknowledges a sixth former.

Class sizes start off quite large (an average of 24 up to KS3) falling to 15 by A level.

Games, Options, the Arts: Vast, aircraft hangar style gym and fabulous 25m heated indoor pool. Both facilities much used (also for after school clubs) and help the inclusive feel at the school by being open to pupils and their families at weekends. Outside sport not so much available – a few hard tennis/netball courts (some girls in national netball squads) and one hockey pitch used by Year 7 only, everyone else is bused out.

Large, light and airy hall for performing arts, with staging and lighting equipment. Girls are often joined by boys from Sutton Grammar for drama productions. Lots of music – particularly impressive music technology rooms – active orchestra, chamber choir and mixed choir – again with Sutton Grammar. Large art department, but housed in different buildings, includes ceramics/pottery/photography suite (although has no pretensions to offer such specialities as separate A level subjects) – evidence of talent and hard work on display throughout.

Background and Atmosphere: The original school is a lovely Victorian building which now mainly houses the headmaster's office, reception, etc. The rest of school comprises several large buildings and a few smaller ones (some more attractive than others) built at various stages of 20th century. This gives a cramped first appearance but large open areas at the centre of the site create a more spacious feel. Some grassy areas for girls to enjoy on warm days. Sixth form block (Dene Centre) is a delight with plenty of space and extra facilities (it even has its own gym!) including the much appreciated careers centre with its own dedicated laptops for pupils' research. An ideal place for the sixth formers to spread out and feel independent from rest of school.

Pastoral Care and Discipline: Head (with plenty of support from form tutors, heads of year and school council) places particular emphasis on pastoral care and discipline – it is a great source of pride to the school. Very clear strategies for dealing with anti-social behaviour and for nurturing a feeling of community. Successful 'buddying' arrangement between Year 7 and Year 13 encourages vertical friendships and a sense of belonging for new pupils. House system in junior school has been extended to senior school to develop vertical integration through the school. Strong on discipline with subject detentions held during lunchtime, and headmaster detentions after school followed up with a letter home.

Pupils and Parents: Wide ranging in every sense. Geographically – from Wimbledon to Reigate and everywhere in between. One reason for the geographical spread is the local state grammar schools – many pupils travel in from beyond their catchment areas. (These highly respected state schools also account for loss of some of brightest local pupils from the junior school at 11+.) Socially – daughters of local business people and City mix. Lots of first time buyers with ethnic mix representative of the area, especially popular with Korean families. Belying outward appearances typical of their age, girls are polite, mature and well informed; seem to know exactly what they want out of life and where to look for it. OGs of note include novelist Susan Howatch and Sue Littlemore, BBC correspondent.

Entrance: At 11, 70+ per cent from junior school, others from wide range in both state and independent sectors, including some from international schools. Entry test in January before admission – English, maths and verbal reasoning and interview. At 13+, occasional places are available each year. Sixth form candidates need 'good GCSE results' and usually A or A* in chosen A level subjects together with passes in general and verbal reasoning papers. Occasional places do arise at other stages, so definitely worth a try.

Exit: About 90 per cent stay on to sixth form. Loss of some, due to girls having been in same place from age four, 'so feel time to move on' and to others wanting to take a less traditional range of A levels. Most to top universities to read traditional subjects – wide range of sciences, medicine and law recently popular. Around 10 per cent to Oxbridge. Some opt for the more vocational, for example, QTS courses, physiotherapy and art schools. Careers advice much praised and is taken very seriously, with many outside speakers and an in-house ISCO adviser – 'we do feel up to date and well informed about our choices,' comments a sixth former.

Money Matters: Scholarships and bursaries for senior school pupils only. Bursaries are means tested. Scholarships at 11 and 16 for those who excel in entrance exam. Head is able to 'flex amount of money available' and awards can be made for music, drama, sport as well as academic prowess at 11 and 16.

Remarks: Happy, purposeful school with good results and grammar school feeling and strengths. Head keen to continue 'maintaining high standards but the challenge comes with retaining flexibility too.'

Sutton Valence School

Linked to Sutton Valence Preparatory School in the Junior section

North Street, Sutton Valence , Kent, ME17 3HL

• Pupils: 510; 375 boys, 135 girls. 95 boys and 30 girls board • Ages: 11-18 • Size of sixth form: 140 • C of E • Fees: Day £12,840-£16,800; Boarding £20,190-£25,620 pa • Independent

Tel: 01622 845200
Fax: 01622 844 103
Email: enquiries@svs.org.uk
Website: www.svs.org.uk

Headmaster: Since 2009, Mr Bruce Grindley MA Cantab (organ scholar) MusB FRCO. Previously director of music at Christ's Hospital, Horsham. Started his teaching career at Christ College, Brecon followed by a move to Bedford

School where he was director of Chapel music and a boarding house master. His wife Lilla is an English teacher and they have two young children.

Academic matters: A school which looks for good for all-rounders who will work to the best of their abilities and benefit from the wide extra-curricular programme; the emphasis is on joining in and getting involved. Selective intake but not hugely. Strong science and maths; 30 per cent enter international maths challenges. Also good English, drama and media studies. Four languages taught and foreign exchanges arranged. Computers everywhere, access at any time, pupils run the school website and newsletters. Peaceful, well stocked library. Recent additions of 'twenty-first century facilities' for ICT, languages, science and Design Technology.

Good quality staff, with purposeful approach; average age is 40. School likes to have teachers who have their own families, many of whom live on site. Results are good given the broad intake – most take eight or nine GCSEs; most go on to A level. Popular subjects at A level include ICT, business studies and economics, history, geography and maths; media studies and psychology have lost their grip on higher numbers. At GCSE, highest concentration of results in the B/C bands with DT and geography bucking the trend with more As than Bs.

Both group and individual teaching is available for mild dyslexia/dyspraxia, the principle being that strong support at the right moment leads to independence. Parents feel that staff have a good awareness of children's difficulties. EFL well-resourced, with specialist teachers on hand to help with language, settling-in and customs; the school gets more applications from foreign students than they can accommodate. A good choice of outings, theatre trips, sports/music tours and foreign travel is arranged for pupils.

Games, Options, the Arts: Sports are strong, main games are rugby, tennis, athletics, netball, and cricket; enormous sports hall, contains full-sized indoor hockey pitch, sprung floor, cricket nets, gym, changing and teaching facilities. Girls have been hockey and netball county champions. School has links with professional cricketers Richie Richardson and Brian Lara; girls' cricket is growing in popularity. Outdoor swimming pool – some parents would like to see this updated. High quality music and drama, a third of the pupils play an instrument, splendid concerts and plays that are welcomed by parents and staff. Also jazz group, concert and chamber orchestras, big band, girls' choir, chapel choir.

The art and DT departments have expanded in recent years to offer wider scope. Now housed in the village a few minutes walk away, art in a converted chapel complete with sculpture and photographic studios and lecture room, DT in a converted gymnasium; everything appears to be on offer from metalwork to pottery. Sixth form DT pupils have the opportunity to enter the 'Audi Young Designer of the Year' competition.

A very busy extra-curricular programme includes many sports, games and arts. Pupils choose between community service and CCF (army, navy or air force – some of these groups interestingly are run by female teachers). Community service pupils get involved with environmental projects, old people's homes, tending graves and helping in local primary schools.

Background and Atmosphere: One of the oldest public schools in the UK, founded by William Lambe in 1576; a portrait of the gentleman hangs in the school, no longer atmospherically draped in cobwebs. The original school building was demolished although some Tudor almshouses still exist now converted into classrooms. Uninspiring but bearable buildings. Extensive grounds with beautifully kept gardens that help to create a tranquil feeling about the site. Part of the Westminster Schools Trust – other members include Emanuel and Westminster City Comprehensive – they still meet for traditional annual inter-school sporting events.

Pastoral Care and Discipline: Solid support, the traditional 'house' system has been replaced by tutor groups – each pupil will attend their tutor group twice a day, and will have access to their tutor at any time if they need it. There is set of clear school rules to follow – fair but firm, detention for persistent offenders. Prefect system. New school council just established. Boarding houses are well kept and homely, particularly the girls' where there is a very friendly matron. Lots of flexi-boarding – aims to meet parents' and pupils' many different needs.

Pupils and Parents: Parents mainly from the professional classes; popular with foreign parents – 12 per cent from abroad, Hong Kong Chinese predominate. Pupils are relaxed and friendly. Alumni Ben Brown TV journalist, Mark Benson cricketer, Stephen Hopkins film director, Prof Allan Hobson professor of psychiatry Harvard, Terence Cuneo painter, Sir Charles Groves conductor.

Entrance: 11+ exam, looking for those who have A level potential; also 13+ and 16+. 40 per cent come from Sutton Valence's prep school, and then a radius of 15/20 miles – Hastings, Sevenoaks and Weald of Kent from both state and independent sector.

Exit: Over 95 per cent go on to university; popular choices are Leeds, Bristol, Durham, Bath, Oxbridge and Nottingham. 97 per cent gain entry to their first choice university.

Money Matters: A quite well-endowed school; up to 10 scholarships and bursaries each year including music, art, drama, D&T, sport, all rounder, academic and some sixth form. Can also help some pupils with fees whose family circumstances change, at the head's discretion.

Remarks: School gets good results both academically and socially. 'Both my sons left the school confident, feeling they had achieved well in a number of different areas and went on to university. Most of all, I appreciated the fact the they had a sense of reality about the world, something that not all public schools manage to achieve with their leavers.' Much to build on, much to do for new head.

Sydenham High School GDST

Linked to Sydenham High Junior School GDST in the Junior section

19 Westwood Hill, London, SE26 6BL

• Pupils: 705 girls, all day • Ages: 11-18 • Fees: Senior £12,006 pa
• Independent

Tel: 020 8768 800
Email: d.hogarth@syd.gdst.net
Website: www.sydenhamhighschool.gdst.net

Head: Since 2002, Mrs Kathryn Pullen BA MA PGCE (mid-fifties). Educated at Llanelli Girls' Grammar School. Studied English and American Studies at Warwick followed by a drama PGCE at Phillippa Fawcett College London. Appointed headteacher after spending 12 years as deputy. Says it was beneficial to already know girls and their parents. Recognised and appreciated academic strength but wanted to add a caring dimension too. Changed management systems – sought to empower staff.

Smart and fashionable, an inspirational role model for the girls, worked hard to get to where she is today, still very hands-on. Says work and learning should be a challenge not a pressure and each child should be happy in their own skin. Lovely Welsh lilt exudes genuine warmth, big hit with girls and parents alike.

Academic matters: An academic school currently soaring up the league tables. All usual suspects on offer with additions of classical civilisation, government and politics, philosophy and theatre studies in sixth form. Languages and sciences ever popular, there's even a Japanese club. Classes average 20 in senior school, much smaller in sixth form. All pass A level with 70-ish per cent graded A*- B. GCSE A* to C pass rate a commendable 95 per cent with no subject 'letting the side down.' Excellent well-stocked library. Lots of ICT; all classrooms have interactive whiteboards – 'they make lessons fun, bring things to life, teachers use things from the internet, computer documents and drawings – much better than blackboards.' Email links for help with work on tap for sixth form soon to be extended school-wide.

Mix of traditional and modern teaching styles plus specials such as science week. Emphasis now on how learners learn; believe it's important to teach to learn, not just to pass exams – must look ahead to demands beyond GCSE. Girls say they get very involved in lessons and are encouraged to ask questions; the ones we spoke to were able to intelligently and enthusiastically discuss their work. Even homework was manageable and if it isn't 'you can always talk to the teachers, they're very understanding.' Girls take GCSE ICT in Year 9, brightest go on to do a further nine but frees up time for those who'll benefit from extra English or additional study time.

A few pupils have SEN – dyslexia, dyspraxia – but on the whole mild-moderate. Head of learning strategies in place since 2005, beefing up support. 'Some of our brightest girls have dyslexic tendencies and may be disorganised, occasionally eccentric.' Pupils who need a little extra support can swap Latin for communication studies (mind-mapping, organisational skills, additional literacy etc).

Games, Options, the Arts: Hockey, netball, cross country, trampolining, volleyball, badminton all popular. Modern gym block houses a large sports hall and fitness centre. There isn't a swimming pool but there is a decent Astroturf on site with playing fields a coach ride away in lower Sydenham. Girls spoke highly of PE staff – saying department transformed in recent years. Emphasis changed too from one of taking part to one of winning – sport seen as a good area to build in a competitive spirit – 'you need a competitive edge to make it in life'. Expressive arts thrive, plenty of opportunities to perform: wind band, jazz, percussion group, orchestra, choir plus numerous drama productions. Excellent performing arts complex, incorporating a theatre, a recital room and a new school hall. 'We have the talent and expertise; now we can show it off in our own environment not perform in someone else's facilities.' Indeed a recent leaver was one of only four successful applicants out of 40 accepted for Royal College of Music. Super 2D and 3D artwork – the clay fruit looked good enough to eat. Stacks of after-school activities: music, sport, D of E, sign language, puppetry, Amnesty, ballet, speech and drama, subject orientated and much more – all timetabled so pupils can plan extra-curricular life carefully.

Background and Atmosphere: Set in open leafy grounds, the original Victorian mansion was built as the home of a diamond merchant and, despite the many redbrick additions, the splendour of the day still seeps through. Indeed the eclectic mix of traditional and modern is very much a hallmark of the school. Separate sixth form block, small classes, dress code – casual smart (former prevalent) – must be ready to meet parents so jeans permitted but not with holes. Parents comment on lovely fresh faces. School says no make up but girls we interviewed said, as long as it was discreet like theirs, that was fine – and it looked jolly pretty too.

Pastoral Care and Discipline: Pastoral care is supportive and academically enabling, caring but not cosy. 'Girls are presented with opportunities, they must grab them and run.' Much tracking and monitoring takes place to identify girls who are under-performing. Children here are known and valued with parents involved whenever necessary. Excellent pupil planner, full of useful curriculum pointers and targets as well as places to record successes and misdemeanours. Thriving house system revived under current head along with introduction of a student council (in lesson time) – wanted to give girls opportunity to take on responsibilities. Lots of photos of Year 6 visits displayed on walls – helps new girls feel part of the school prior to entry. Several joint social ventures with local boys' schools. Lunch a mix of healthy and the devilishly tempting, hot food also available before school and at breaks.

Pupils and Parents: Wide catchment area – south-east London as far as Peckham and into Kent. Handful from north of the Thames, especially if brothers go to Dulwich College. Parents a wide social and cultural mix of professional and blue-collar workers, half are first time buyers of independent education. Achieved aim of being academically selective but not elitist makes school an approachable option for first timers. Head candid, says they're in a highly competitive market so have to work hard to get people through the doors. 'Lots of schools get pupils nine GCSEs so we have to add in something else, give parents value for money.' Famous old girls include Margaret Lockwood, Philippa Halben (scientist), Dame Rosemary Rue (scientist), Winifred Gerin (critic), Elizabeth Anstruther (philosopher), Emily Joyce (actress), Sandie Powell (Oscar winning costume designer).

Entrance: Entrance for all, including Sydenham High Junior School pupils, is via interview and exams in maths, reading/comprehension and writing, in the January prior to September entry. Notification given to those placed on waiting list. Majority of pupils enter at beginning of Year 7, a few places occur at other times. Sixth form places available, keen to attract more. However, not a bums on seats exercise – if girls don't come up to scratch they won't get a place.

Exit: Lose quite a few post-GCSEs – some to co-ed schools; some because they've been at Sydenham for 12 years and want to broaden experience before a move to University; many for financial reasons. School competes for entry with super selective local state schools, girls may not have been offered a place at 11 but do so well at Sydenham that state schools are happy to take them for A levels. Popular moves are to St Olave's and Newstead Wood. Sixth formers to a wide range and mix of universities and courses, traditional and modern. Handful to art colleges, occasional one to Oxbridge.

Remarks: Staff say, 'girls are a pleasure to be with'. Suits capable, compassionate but confident girls who get results but have interests too – heavily coached could come unstuck. May not compete on quite the same terms as some of its flashier rivals but has no problems producing an equally desirable end product.

Sylvia Young Theatre School

1 Nutford Place, Marylebone, London, W1H 5YZ

• Pupils: 75 boys and 155 girls; 27 board, rest day • Ages: 10-16 • Fees: £8,850-£18,800 pa • Independent

Tel: 0207 258 2330
Email: info@sylviayoungtheatreschool.co.uk
Website: www,sylviayoungtheatreschool.co.uk

Headteacher: Since 2005, Ms Frances Chave BSc PGCE NPQH (early forties), previously deputy head of Overton Grange comprehensive school in Surrey. Educated at Putney High, universities of Exeter and Southampton, she's a mathematician who still teaches maths, mostly to Years 10 and 11.

Helped to set up Overton Grange from scratch, and then felt the need for a completely new challenge. With no theatre school background, she is not perhaps the most obvious choice for a new head but, with principal and founder Sylvia Young firmly in charge of the vocational side of the school, her own remit is academic and pastoral. Unassuming on the surface, she is not to be outdone by her students on physical fitness terms. She is a qualified aerobic dance instructor and lists numerous outdoor activities amongst her interests.

Academic matters: Upping the ante on the academic front has been a high priority over the past few years and academic study and exam results are now very important. In 2008, came 17th in *The Times* list of top independent secondaries without a sixth form. Also scores extremely well on a value-added basis. Does not select academically – written tests form part of the entrance process only to provide a baseline. 'If they're talented, we'll take them unless they really couldn't cope with the work. And they need to be able to do it in three days a week, alongside performing.' Quite a few pupils have special needs such as dyslexia – 'it tends to go with the territory' – but while the school will give specialised help it emphasises that this is not its main aim.

The curriculum has necessarily been slightly limited, though there has been an emphasis on broadening this in recent years – everyone does English lang and lit, maths, science (core and additional), expressive arts and drama to GCSE. Other GCSE options include music, art, media studies, history and Spanish. Years 7–9 also study humanities and ICT. Very few results below C; maths results have improved considerably in recent years with 96 per cent of students gaining grade C or above in maths in 2010. Overall, 93 per cent of students achieved five or more GCSE grades A*–C including English and maths in 2010, with most students gaining 8 or 9 GCSEs at these grades. 45 per cent A*/A grades in 2010.

Pupils are frequently off performing in plays or making films; their teachers set coursework for them while they are away. 'It can be a big organisational problem but we have a clear system of getting academic work to them.'

Games, Options, the Arts: On Mondays to Wednesdays the school is heavily disguised as a traditional one, with neatly-uniformed pupils sitting at desks in classrooms. During Thursdays and Fridays, pupils in tee shirts and leggings sing, dance and act with gusto. This is the raison d'être of the school and the pupils' passion. The talent, enthusiasm and sheer professionalism is palpable – even in the youngest classes. Everyone studies drama, music and dance, with classes on subjects ranging from voice production to recording technique to tap, and everyone takes LAMDA speech and drama exams. All pupils are represented by the in-house Sylvia Young Agency, and the school is arbiter of which jobs they are allowed to accept. 'It depends on how they keep up academically. Of course, if it's their big break then we will bend over backward to help them but we might say no to routine work. And of course they have to accept that some get lots of opportunities and some don't.'

The school does not go in for big theatrical productions – students are so often away performing that getting everyone together for rehearsals would be almost impossible. In any case, when your child is starring in *Chitty Chitty Bang Bang* in the West End, the prospect of watching them perform in the school play must lose its lustre. But pupils represent the UK at many international events and Royal Gala performances in venues such as Buckingham Palace, the Royal Albert Hall and the Queen Elizabeth Hall.

Sport is more-or-less non-existent, though younger pupils go swimming, and of course everyone dances – even in the corridors, on occasion, whilst waiting for classes.

Background and Atmosphere: In 1972 Sylvia Young produced a charity show at her daughter's primary school. The children were so keen to learn more that she began giving part-time drama classes. In 1981 she opened a full-time school in Drury Lane, which then moved to the site of an old Marylebone church school in 1983. In September 2010 the school moved into much larger premises in Nutford Place in Marylebone which have been purpose built within an old church building. There are 10 purpose built studios and 12 specialist classrooms for academic subjects. The increased space means that the school will be able to fulfill its desire to have a sixth form eventually, but no date has yet been set for this.

Pastoral Care and Discipline: Discipline problems are rare – 'every single student wants to be here. They don't want to jeopardise their place.' Team work is an integral part of the curriculum and, though one might assume there is infinite potential for prima donna-esque behaviour, the head is clear that this is ultra mores. 'They're remarkably unassuming considering their talent. Sylvia is adamant that you don't go making a big song and dance about auditions and they don't – most people don't even know if someone's got a lead part in *Les Mis.*'

Pupils and Parents: Some (from Year 7 upwards) board with local families; the rest travel from up to an hour away – which can be quite some distance, since the school is close to Marylebone and Marble Arch stations and many tube and bus connections. Not by any means your average private school crowd; many use theatrical earnings to help pay the fees. Some are aiming at *Mamma Mia* or *EastEnders,* others aspire to the Royal Shakespeare Company or the National Theatre. Alumni include – amongst many – Denise Van Outen, Emma Bunton, Billie Piper, Matt from Busted and Daniella Westbrook.

Entrance: The school has expanded to two form entry from Year 7 upwards but retained one form of 20 students for Year 6. Another 22 are taken into Year 7, then places as available when someone leaves. As mentioned, the academic test is merely a baseline one – it is the audition that counts. Students must show special potential in one or more of drama, dance and singing.

Exit: Some go to local state or private sixth form colleges, often with scholarships, usually to do A levels in drama-related subjects. Many then apply to drama colleges at 18. Others go to schools' sixth forms such as the Arts Ed or straight on to to diploma courses at dance colleges such as Laines, London Studios and Millennium.

Money Matters: Hundreds apply for what is officially two full and two half scholarships, though plenty of others get places assisted in one way or another, such as subsidising school fees from earnings. Fees are low-ish by private school standards.

Remarks: Children with a passion for theatre are likely to be ecstatically happy here. And they'll almost certainly get decent GCSEs too.

Talbot Heath School

Linked to Talbot Heath Junior School in the Junior section

Rothesay Road, Bournemouth, Dorset, BH4 9NJ

• Pupils: 380 girls in the senior school. Mainly day, but 30 girls board, weekly and full, from age 11. 215 in the junior school. • Ages: 3-18 • Size of sixth form: 80 • C of E • Fees: Day £10,458; Boarding + £6,648-£6,960 pa • Independent

Tel: 01202 761 881
Fax: 01202 768 155
Email: office@talbotheath.org
Website: www.talbotheath.org

Headmistress: Since 2010, Mrs Anghred Holloway MA (fortyish), previously Director of International Baccalaurate Programme at Royal High School, Bath (qv). She read German and Italian at St Anne's College, Oxford and is married with two small daughters.

Academic matters: Traditional teaching + high standards = fabulous results – much better than the relatively broad intake might lead one to expect. 2008 was a weak year for A levels (and 2007 not great for AS results, so we suspect it was a limitation in the cohort, not the teaching) but 2010 an improvement with 62 per cent A*/A grades and 83 per cent at A*–B. Maths and science very popular – all take dual award GCSE science and a number go on to study medicine and veterinary science at university. Setting by ability for French and maths the term after 11 year olds start – 'we give them time to get settled,' says head – and for science at GCSE level. In 2010, 99 per cent GCSEs at A*–C with 73 per cent A*/A.

Plenty of computers. Staff tend to put down roots – 29 members of staff have been here for more than 10 years. One teacher who did move on is local Liberal Democrat MP Annette Brooke who taught economics here. Class sizes range from 20 at lower end of school to 15 at GCSE stage. School has EAL teacher and caters for those with dyslexia, dyspraxia and ADHD. 25 girls currently receive some help for SEN – the school is quite meticulous about this and girls can be given a reduced schedule if necessary. Still, this is first and foremost an academic school and, helpful as staff may be, probably not one to seek out for a child with anything more than mild learning difficulties.

Games, Options, the Arts: Gym, dance, hockey, netball, swimming, tennis, rounders and athletics, plus lacrosse, volleyball and badminton from Year 9 on, and even more choice as girls move up the school, including golf. The school now even offers a Tennis Academy – a joint venture with the West Hants tennis club – providing full-on tennis coaching alongside a specially designed academic curriculum. Not cheap, incidentally, but less costly than moving to Florida. Talbot Heath was named Dorset Tennis School of the Year by the LTA. Many individual sporting and team successes nationally and even internationally (these are competitive girls). Heated outdoor swimming pool used from May till October for lessons and lunchtime clubs. Large sports hall (check out the lovely wooden ceiling), playing fields across road, netball and tennis courts, new Astro. Almost three hours a week of sport in Year 7 decreases to an hour and 25 minutes in Year 11, an hour in lower sixth, and sport can be dropped altogether in the final two terms. Not enough activity for several parents we spoke to – 'it's a shame they don't do more, given the wonderful facilities they have. It's all available but there's no one pushing you to find your sporting niche.'

Music is a particular strength – cellist Natalie Clein, a former Young Musician of the Year, is an old girl as is soprano Kate Royal, winner of the 2004 Kathleen Ferrier Award (interestingly both of these students left the school briefly but came back!). Some 250 girls have instrumental lessons in the well-appointed music school and there are loads of choirs, ensembles and orchestras to join. Bournemouth Symphony Orchestra's education department works from an office here and the BSO's contemporary music group, Kokoro, rehearses in the music school. Drama also gets a big tick. Between ages of 11 and 14 every form produces a play for the annual drama festival – 'every girl takes part, even if it's just pulling the curtain.' Two drama studios, loads of LAMDA exams and some girls go on to take theatre studies at AS and A level. Art impressive, though elbow space in the department is limited. Domestic science room a 1980s marvel but does a great job with lots of space and cookers.

Background and Atmosphere: Founded as Bournemouth High School in 1886, its first head, Mary Broad, believed girls should have same opportunities in education as boys and shocked locals by teaching her pupils cricket and gymnastics. School moved to eerie 24-acre purpose-built site in Talbot Woods in 1935, when it became known as Talbot Heath – school birthday is still celebrated every May. Senior school is built round two dated quads which have been vastly added to over the years. Not a school that bowls you over with charisma, the words 'forbidding' and 'drab' (as well as 'charming' and 'efficient') came up several times among the parents we spoke to – all of whom were fans of the school. 'The first time I came up the drive and saw the windswept pines, I almost put the car in reverse,' said a mum who sent both her daughters to Talbot Heath and never looked back.

Girls wear navy blazer, skirt, blouse and tie; sixth form girls given more freedom – no uniform (but no slobs), more free periods, and sixth form common room. Many take part in Duke of Edinburgh Award scheme and Young Enterprise. Local employers have praised Talbot Heath girls on work experience post-GCSE for being reliable, competent, able to shoulder responsibility and work as a team. School monitors the girls' extra-curricular commitments – including those outside of school – to check they are not taking on too much (or too little?)

Pastoral Care and Discipline: School has system of sanctions – order marks, detentions etc – for unsatisfactory work or behaviour. Parents always informed. Each form has two form leaders, voted for by peers each term, and there are two head girls, two deputies and a raft of prefects. Assemblies, often with outside speakers, every day but Thursday. Like any girls-only school, friendship group problems surface but the younger girls say they can talk to the older prefects about any problems. In severe flare-ups the head has been known to interview every single girl in a class individually to get to the core of the problem. 'I'm not saying I've never had a complaint,' said a parent we spoke to, 'but when I have, it's been resolved quickly.'

Small number of boarders enjoy loads of flexibility at St Mary's boarding house, a short walk from main school building. Dormitories for younger girls and cubicles for older ones. Full-time housemistress (not a teacher). Boarding judged outstanding by Ofsted (2008).

Pupils and Parents: Girls come from enormous catchment area – some cycle in from close by while others travel from as far afield as Beaulieu to the east and Weymouth and Portland to the west (good train service and the school runs several buses and minibuses). Wide range of backgrounds, including people who never expected to be paying for private education. Most, but not all, boarders come from overseas, particularly Service families. Sixteen overseas pupils when we visited, mainly from Hong Kong and Korea. Not a snobby school – very down-to-earth. Notable old girls include Dame Shirley Williams, Caroline Gledhill (first woman to receive Young Engineer of the Year award), Frances Ashcroft (first woman to receive Fellow of Royal Society award), Natalie Clein and Kate Royal (see above).

Entrance: Senior school holds entrance exam in January for the following September. Most Talbot Heath juniors progress through to senior school but all must pass exam. At 11 girls sit papers in English, maths and verbal reasoning and at 12, 13 and 14 there is a French exam too. Not too horrific a hurdle: despite its reputation as 'academic', the ability range is wide. Girls come from local preps The Park, Castle Court, Dumpton, Talbot House and Durlston Court, or from 'local church primaries'. Lately quite a few have come across from Wentworth College. Entry at sixth form requires a minimum of five A–C grades at GCSE and at least Bs in subjects to be studied at A level. Entrance to the tennis academy is highly selective.

Exit: Three quarters of girls stay on for sixth form – those who don't tend to move on to Brockenhurst Sixth Form College or the Bournemouth or Poole grammars, often to do subjects not on offer here. Virtually all sixth form go to university – Exeter, Birmingham, Surrey, Bath currently popular choices. Few gap years (three last year).

Money Matters: Academic, all-rounder, music and sport scholarships available at 11+, 12+, 13+ and sixth form, plus bursaries (currently received by 23 per cent of girls in the senior school) including one fee-free place each year. Discounts for Services children and clergy.

Remarks: With two girls-only state grammar schools within 20 minutes' drive, Talbot Heath needs to offer something above and beyond. And it does: a wholesome and sheltered environment, academic rigour, musical excellence, reasonable fees, and a safe landing pad for girls who didn't quite make the grammar school cut. Lots of good things going on here.

TASIS - The American School in England

Linked to TASIS - The American School In England (Lower School) in the Junior section

Coldharbour Lane, Thorpe, Surrey, TW20 8TE

• Pupils: 730 boys and girls • Ages: 3-19 • Size of sixth form: 240 (135 are boarders) • Non-denom • Fees: Pre-K £4,475; K-13 £7,625-£9,325; Boarding £15,300 pa • Independent

Tel: 01932 565 252
Fax: 01932 564 644
Email: ukadmissions@tasisengland.org
Website: www.tasisengland.org

Headmaster: Since 2010, Mr Michael McBrien BA MA, previously head of Baylor School in Chattanooga, Tennessee – an independent, co-educational day and boarding school. He has twenty-four years of experience in education and has worked as an administrator at the University of California, Berkeley, Babson College and the Frontier Academy in Colorado. Married to Betsy, they have two daughters and two sons – the youngest a junior at TASIS.

Academic matters: The academically demanding IB Diploma programme is proving popular with students and their families. The 34 IB candidates in 2010 averaged 33 points. The AP (Advanced Placement) results also reflect academic success: in 2008–9, 87 per cent of all 138 students taking 300 AP tests in 21 subjects made a passing grade of 3 or better (31 per cent 4s and 34 per cent 5s). The middle 50 per cent range of SAT scores achieved by students graduating in 2009 were: maths 550–690; critical reading 540–680; writing 560–670. NB 21 per cent of the students that took the SAT tests speak English as a second language.

Students are expected to meet the challenge of a tough academic regime and are given great support through frequent advising and daily opportunities to see teachers during the tutorial periods. Class sizes are small (average 12) taught in bright open classrooms. Computers are everywhere and students can connect to the wireless network anywhere on campus. As reflected by their outstanding results, students are well prepared and classroom interplay is definitely on an AP level. The faculty take their jobs very seriously and the kids take up the challenges. Wallflowers beware!

Special Education Needs: No specific programme but dedicated Learning Resource teachers access and bolster those with mild specific learning problems (fee based). Language Support: ESL students can join the international section in the Upper School; ESL support is done privately in the Lower and Middle Schools (fee based). Classes in history, science and literature are closely linked with those of the mainstream courses and the aim is to cover the same content, while meeting the needs of the international students. As their skills improve they may move into the mainstream classes.

Games, Options, the Arts: A beautiful new gym and endless playing fields host a very dynamic sports programme. Many of the sports found in the US are offered. The under-14s through the under-18s participate in International Schools Sports Tournament competitions throughout Europe and even set the standard in volleyball and basketball. Intramural, after school and Saturday morning sports are popular and even though they are not mandatory, it seems everyone plays something.

Art is everywhere and when you are in the arts wing you can feel, see and hear the energy. The kids are enthusiastic about what they are creating and are good at it too. The staff, be it music, theatre or art, are definitely doing a good job. All arts programs are performance based – plays, musicals, art shows and recitals are all student led and supported. The Travel Study Program takes the students outside the classroom around England and Europe. Daytrips to the London theatres, galleries and museums, weekends in Paris and one-week study trips to Spain, Greece and Austria are among those on offer.

Background and Atmosphere: The school doesn't look like a real school, rather the school you always imagined. The 34-year-old campus is an enchanting jumble of cottages, gardens and a manor house, all overlooking a pond, in the ancient village of Thorpe. Boarders live in un-dormitory like rooms and mix easily with day students.

The lower and middle school students eat in their own lunch room, well supervised; the staff and upper school students share a light filled dining room overlooking the gardens. The food is healthy, tasty and varied. New buildings are well designed and blend easily with the historic buildings.

Pastoral Care and Discipline: Responsibility for yourself and for others is stressed from the lower school on up. Tolerance is a given with a student body so diverse. Bullying is not a problem and, if it occurs, the staff and students work it out right away, with counselling support available if needed. The students are expected to work hard and they try not to disappoint their teachers. An open door policy with the heads of all three divisions and regular brainstorming with faculty means that problems are tackled early. Community service is important, from supporting the local Salvation Army to fundraising and hands-on work in an orphanage in Romania or sponsoring a Tibetan school child for a year.

Pupils and Parents: Easy-going, sophisticated and self assured, largely American, but over 50 nationalities are represented, even some Brits. The dress code (uniforms) is respected. Classroom exchanges are lively, no one is afraid to express his or her ideas; in fact here it is 'cool to be smart'. The kids are motivated and focused.

Parents, for the most part American and international families (usually diplomatic and corporate) looking for a college prep curriculum, are a big part of the school. Spouses are often not here long enough to get involved in their careers so they focus on the school, and the school is delighted. Saturday sports, classroom support, welcoming committees just to name a few of the activities available. As the head of the Upper School said, 'the school is a better place because of the parents.' They can even use the very well equipped fitness centre. Nationalities mix well; this group doesn't have time to lose, so they take advantage of an up and running social scene.

Expat Issues: As arriving families usually choose the area for the school, the Admissions department gives great support with housing and neighbourhood information or just settling in. The Parents' Council takes over with events like 'Mid-year Orientation for New Families' or 'Navigating the College Application Process'.

With such a mobile student body, kids ease into the routine, be it mid-year or at the beginning of term. Since the admission process is competitive, the pupils catch on very quickly; if not, the staff deals immediately with adjustment problems. Students transferring out do well at other schools but sometimes choose the boarding option when in the Upper School, rather than leave. The IB Diploma programme and the ESL programme are attracting more international families, giving the school a more worldly flavour.

Entrance: Selective – they are looking for children who are consistent, motivated and well rounded. About a 30 per cent turnover due to a population of corporate and diplomatic families, but mostly during summer break.

Exit: College counselling actively starts in Grade 11 but awareness starts earlier. An eight-week course helping with the ins and outs of the application process provided for juniors. Dedicated college counsellors and the staff stay abreast of the US and British universities and are successful at guiding the students and parents to a well thought out range of schools.

Graduates go to the top and second tier colleges (Brown, Duke, MIT, Princeton, Stanford, Tufts), from small liberal arts schools to large state universities across the US as well as the best universities in the UK (55 per cent go to the US, 25 per cent go to the UK and 20 per cent go to universities across the globe). In the lower years the students stay unless the family is transferred, and even then if they are old enough (14 or over), some switch to boarding.

Money Matters: School originally owned by a private family, now owned and governed by a not-for-profit Swiss foundation with an executive board based in the UK. Fees cover tuition, books, IT, some materials, lunch and the cost of most curriculum related activities and field trips, and in the case of boarders, weekly linen service, travel insurance for school sponsored trips and the Fall travel week. A one-time only development fee of £750 towards an ongoing building and maintenance programme.

Remarks: Academically challenging American and international boarding and day school. Caring and committed staff producing great results all set in an Arcadian setting; what more could you want?

Taunton School

Linked to Taunton Pre Prep And Nursery in the Junior section

Linked to Taunton Preparatory School in the Junior section

Staplegrove Road, Taunton, Somerset, TA2 6AD

• Pupils: 500 pupils; 200 boarders. 295 boys; 205 girls • Ages: 13-18 • Size of sixth form: 225 • Inter-denom • Fees: Boarding from £24,495; Day from £15,000 pa • Independent

Tel: 01823 703 700
Fax: 01823 703 704
Email: registrar@tauntonschool.co.uk
Website: www.tauntonschool.co.uk

Head: Since 2005, Dr John Newton MA PhD FCollP DipMS(Ed) (early forties). Educated at The Manchester Grammar School and Merton College, Oxford. Has a doctorate in organisational culture in independent schools (more interesting than it sounds). Previously director of studies and housemaster at Eastbourne College and head of modern languages at Bradfield. A teacher of French and Russian, involved in the CCF, has sung in school choirs, coached rugby, hockey, cricket, fives, rowing and football. Four young children, all at Taunton; wife Catherine a trained primary school teacher and musician.

A fizzing, rather than a bubbling head, his tour of the school was punctuated by fist-smacking soundbites and energetic press releases. Keen to emphasise the genuinely co-educational nature of the school. 'This is proper co-education: after all we've taken girls since the 1970s not the 1990s and it takes years to integrate fully.' Keen, too, to banish the idea that girls choose girly subjects and boys macho ones. 'The boys are in competition with some very powerful girls,' he continued. 'That's what it's like in the 21st century: boys have got to match the girls. Our best DT pupil last year was a girl, as was our best competitor in the Ten Tors. Girls are very significant in the CCF, too, and our CCF is the biggest in the south west.' But the image of gun-toting, metal-chewing, walking-booted Amazons is easily dispelled. The girls are stylish ('the most stylish in Taunton,' said one), open and friendly – as well as competitive. When asked about those 'powerful girls', admittedly in mixed company, one charmingly languid boy answered, 'I dare not argue the point.'

'Our marketing is aggressive,' said the headmaster. 'It has to be.' Taunton is a cauldron of schools, though the head doesn't see them as rivals. He is justifiably proud of the extended and improved DT centre and is excited by the planned extension to the music department. Clearly a healthy and vigorous man himself, he is pleased that all his SMT go on regular runs. That is not a condition of the job, though. The word 'dynamic' is unavoidable when meeting this youngish and ambitious headmaster. He knows his pupils and cares about them; above all he cares about the school and where it is going. 'He tries very hard,' said one appreciative pupil; 'he's SO energetic,' said another.

Academic matters: The school does not see itself as overtly academic but claims to set much store by value added. That they have maintained at A level a respectable 70+ per cent A/B grades over the last decade and a 99 per cent pass rate supports their claim. Bright children are given the opportunity to flourish; not so bright are carefully nurtured. Last year's 48 per cent results at A*/A in GCSE are significantly up on the previous year.

Has recently introduced the IB which is proving increasingly popular. Mandarin also introduced – in the prep school, in general studies and ab initio at IB level. Plans afoot to adapt an undistinguished example of 1960s architecture into a Learning Resources Centre. School aims to encourage more independent learning. Potential Oxbridge candidates are identified in lower sixth and prepared. One sixth form boy told us that the history department was 'brilliant' – the results bear him out.

Help for mild/moderate dyslexia. EFL assistance available. A thriving International Study Centre adjacent to campus brings 65 foreign students and crucial cash flow.

Games, Options, the Arts: Art department with four studios equipped to art school standard. Innovative head of dept, trained as sculptor, says half of each year group ends up at art foundation courses. Music taught in core curriculum from third form. One third of pupils learn an instrument, many two or more. The orchestra, jazz band, wind and advanced vocal ensemble perform regularly outside school. Management is keen to bring the arts to the school as well as teach and perform them. Boys and girls spoke enthusiastically of drama and public speaking. Careers are taken seriously – much input from OTs who give 'Horizon Lectures' and offer work experience as far afield as Hong Kong.

A wealth of sports facilities which turn out dozens of county and several international champions in hockey, rugby, swimming, aerobics, tennis, wake-boarding(!), athletics, cross-country and National Schools show jumping. This astonishingly high calibre explained by the school's effort to put county fixtures before school matches – 'inter-school results may suffer but it's worth the pupils getting exit routes for later,' says a sports coach (from an England squad). Nevertheless, games flourish at all levels and it is only the lack of opposition which prevents more matches for 4th level teams.

Background and Atmosphere: Founded over 150 years ago for sons of dissenters (non-conformists) and moved to its present site on spacious campus (eclectic buildings surrounding a purpose-built one) in 1870 on edge of Taunton, with London train track at bottom of 56 acres of sports pitches. The enormously long corridor of the handsome main building disappears into the distance but is lined with pictures of sporting heroes, past dramatic productions and original art work. Despite its potentially intimidating length, it is a corridor of celebration. Pupils, bustling along between lessons, smiled in a friendly manner as we approached.

The original intention of the founding fathers has been subsumed by a variety of religions but has been preserved, in the words of the headmaster, by having 'no snobs and no yobs'. Friendly, active atmosphere and sixth formers say they are treated with respect and are allowed a degree of freedom. Their sixth form centre, The Guvvy (repeated efforts by the authorities to change the name failed), is brightly decorated with an area for serious study and one for lolling about. Relaxed boys and girls, and one sixth form entrant from a state school said that joining the school was the best thing he had ever done. 'It was nothing like as difficult as I feared it might be.'

Pastoral Care and Discipline: Houseparents primarily responsible for each pupil's progress and hold two tutorial meetings a week to monitor both academic and pastoral. Every year group is allocated a year tutor within each house. Tremendous rapport between students and staff, thus bullying gets reported instantly and dealt with. Head recognises that a few sometimes experiment with cannabis and he acts accordingly but anyone caught dealing or doing hard drugs is out. Average age of staff 40; 20 of them have been here over a decade.

Pupils and Parents: Not a county-set school and glad of it. Recent survey showed that large proportion of OTs use it for second and third generation, also that 94 per cent of pupils would recommend the school. Parents are professionals, farmers, local businessmen. Ten per cent London émigrés. Day pupils arrive from Sidmouth, Exeter, Minehead, Yeovil, Bristol and beyond in school's own buses with encouraging slogans clearly painted on the sides saying the school 'offers more' (other schools must love that!). Pupils from 20 countries. Old Tauntonians: Mark Getty, Vice Admiral David Blackburn, Sir Robert Malpas (MD of BP), Michael Willacy (advisor to Mrs Thatcher), Nicholas Prettejohn (chief exec Lloyds), Peter Westmacott, Sir Peter Wallis, Dr Christopher Gibson-Smith, Sir Michael Milroy Franklin.

Entrance: Around 60–70 per cent enter via own prep at 13. The school is next door to its main feeder, and as a result of constant communication between the two very few applicants are turned away (see entry in junior school section). Otherwise CE or entrance assessment but particular attention paid to report from previous head. 'Above all we are looking for potential,' said the head. Over 60 (in 2010), enter at 16 on minimum five grade A*-Cs, again interview more important than academic, and 'we always take a sibling'. About 15 other prep schools on their books.

Exit: Over 96 per cent to universities or colleges (half a dozen to Oxbridge, ditto to medical school). 10 or so leave at 16 for sixth form colleges or employment.

Money Matters: Scholarships at 11, 13 and 16 for academic, music, art, sport and an all-rounder.

Remarks: Parents speak highly of the energy and commitment in the community and a sense of 'happily expended energy'. Numbers rising, and the school is becoming better known and beginning to appeal to a wider audience. Sportsmen, musicians and artists can flourish in a mutually encouraging environment. Oh, and the food is outstandingly good, presided over by an excellent chef who once kept MCC members happy in their pavilion. A school on the up.

Tavistock College

Crowndale Road, Tavistock, Devon, PL19 8DD

• Pupils: 1,630 boys and girls, all day • Ages: 11-18 • Size of sixth form: 300 • Non-denom • State

Tel: 01822 614 231
Fax: 01822 612 030
Email: a.thomas@tavistockcollege.devon.sch.uk
Website: www.tavistockcollege.devon.sch.uk

Head: Since 2010, Ms Helen Salmon BA (English), the first female principal. Has previously been a deputy head in North Somerset, an associate head in Bristol and the head teacher of St James School in Exeter. Under her leadership, exam standards rose rapidly and St James was in the top 10 most improved schools in the country.

Academic matters: 61 per cent of students gained 5+ A*–C GCSE grades in 2010. Maths and science results in particular have improved across the ability range. Has left an unsatisfactory curriculum behind, now with a great spirit among students, with revision sessions being organised not just by teachers but also by students for their peers. 'It is really good to realise that hard work can lead to the results you want. It makes it worthwhile,' said a pupil.

'The Japanese is excellent here,' say parents. Largest centre in the country for teaching Japanese – some 130 GCSE candidates. Nottingham University has adapted its

Japanese language degree programme to cater for the outstandingly high levels of knowledge that Tavistock pupils enter with. Tavistock College is proud of its links with Momijigawa High School in Tokyo and was the only school in Britain approved for inclusion in the programme of events for the 2005 EU Japan Year of People-to-People Exchanges. Other links are with France, Germany, Uganda, USA, Spain and India.

SEN pupils helped to gain in self-esteem by being encouraged to play part in active life of school so all leave with qualifications and life skills. SEN provision is responsibility of all staff and The Learning Support Team has a range of specialisms. The college is wheelchair friendly and equipped with lifts and a centre complete with bed and washing facilities for disabled students.

Games, Options, the Arts: Art and drama are very strong here. Jazz, soul, classical and contemporary music regularly performed. On Friday nights the college drama hut is transformed. Professional arts practitioners pass on their theatre skills to prepare the students for the Trinity Guildhall Board exams. Duke of Edinburgh and Ten Tors are also popular. Successes in football, netball, table tennis and rugby. £3m development of outdoor and indoor sports facilities including fitness suite, dance studio, floodlit all-weather football pitch and separate athletics track.

Background and Atmosphere: Biggest local employer. Only state senior school for Tavistock. The college traces its origin to a 10th century foundation known as the Abbey School, restored in 1552. Turned from grammar to comprehensive in 1959. Funding for a £3 million investment programme makes this an attractive school inside and out with garden courtyards, a leisure centre open to the public, six-lane athletics track, an all-weather pitch, fitness suite, new dance studio, changing rooms, squash courts, disabled access, public reception area. Parents say, 'the children are certainly encouraged to make the most of themselves.'

Pastoral Care and Discipline: Tavistock has a good reputation for nurturing all individuals' talent. Bullying or behavioural problems are dealt with quickly. Temporary expulsion faces anyone using abusive behaviour. Support for any necessary punishment is expected from parents.

Pupils and Parents: Tavistock's affluent reputation tends to mask any underlying social problems. Wide social range – some discussing choral recitals, sports results and swapping pleasantries with the headteacher, others socialising in the corridor and chatting on mobile phones but, whatever their demeanour, there is a pleasant atmosphere and a good sense of camaraderie between pupils and staff. Parents comment on how enthusiastic and well motivated the pupils are, especially in sport and music.

Entrance: 15 feeder schools, covering a 400 square-mile catchment area.

Exit: Approximately 75 per cent of Year 11 students progress to Tavistock's sixth form, others head for City College Plymouth, Plymouth College of Art and Design, employment-based training and Kelly College. Universities include Oxbridge, Bath, Nottingham, Marjons and Plymouth.

Remarks: An up and coming school.

Teesside High School

Linked to Teesside Preparatory School in the Junior section

The Avenue, Eaglescliffe, Stockton-on-Tees, Cleveland, TS16 9AT

• Pupils: 145 Girls, 80 Boys • Ages: 11-18 • Size of sixth form: 80 • Non-denom • Fees: £10,242 pa • Independent

Tel: 01642 782 095
Fax: 01642 791 207
Email: abullen@teessidehigh.co.uk
Website: www.teessidehigh.co.uk

Headmaster: Since 2006, Mr Thomas Packer BSc MSc CPhys FInstP FCollP NPQH, educated at Kimbolton School and University College, Durham, where he read physics and maths. His main interest is in musical acoustics on which he wrote a thesis in 1991. He began his career at Hereford Cathedral School – taught physics, maths and music and was i/c CCF, moving on to Downe House as head of science. Then to Victoria College, Jersey, as deputy head including a spell as acting head. Then head at Stover School where he introduced boys. Wife, Janet, a PE teacher. Introduced boys into the high school in 2008.

Academic matters: Good. 92 per cent of GCSE grades in 2010 were A*–C and 35% A*; 65 per cent grades A/B at A level. Traditional academic curriculum. Option of three separate sciences at GCSE or taking a dual award science course. All 11–13 year olds take (inter alia) separate sciences, three languages (French, German and Latin), RE, music, home economics and IT (everyone takes CLAIT in Year 9). Free access to IT suite during school hours and each pupil has own email address at school. Normal class size 16. Experienced staff – over half have 10 or more years experience with the school. Very low turnover. Some mixed ability teaching for 11-year-olds but, from Year 8, pupils are setted for maths, science and languages.

Homework ranges from 90 minutes a night for 11-year-olds through to three hours a night for sixth form. Pupils get report of some kind every term with full report sent out at end of year. Special needs co-ordinator – support for dyslexia and dyspraxia. A few pupils come from families where English is not the first language but don't usually need support with English as an additional language.

Games, Options, the Arts: All now take part in wide range of activities – these include public speaking, market gardening, chess, sign language and, a very popular recent innovation, football. Most Year 10 pupils take Duke of Edinburgh awards. Music and drama very strong. The majority play a musical instrument and there is a variety of orchestras and choirs. Pupils were rehearsing for performance of *Daisy Pulls it Off* when we visited while recorder group were recording a CD in school hall, padding around in slippers to avoid making a noise in between takes! Large number take Guildhall speech and drama awards. Art is very popular – 50 per cent take it at GCSE and paintings and sculpture on show everywhere. Sport is strong and compulsory for all – several county standard hockey and netball players. Other sports include athletics, tennis, football, hockey, rugby and badminton.

Background and Atmosphere: School founded as a girls' school in 1970 when Queen Victoria High School and Cleveland School amalgamated. Set in 19 acres bordering the River Tees. Extensive woodland used for forest trails. The first boys were admitted to the prep in 2005 and in 2008 boys entered the high school and the sixth form. Follows the 'diamond' model of education where boys and girls are educated together up to Year 5 and in the sixth form and separately in between. Site has stunning views of the Cleveland Hills – 'brilliant for teaching perspective,' say art teachers, appreciatively. Classrooms are newly decorated, bright and cheerful. Smart dining room with cafeteria system, trendy blue tables and murals painted by girls, offers choice of hot and cold meals. Even though this is a day school, breakfast and tea are available too if wanted. Sixth form has self-contained building – 'a stepping-stone to university' says the head, with shared studies (students are given a free rein how they decorate them), kitchens and common room. Atmosphere everywhere is bubbly, enthusiastic and busy. Work is important but emphasis on fun too.

Pastoral Care and Discipline: The school prides itself on being 'a community in which everyone is treated with respect and understanding and where all talents and gifts are nurtured and valued.' Form tutors play very important role in guiding pupils. School sets a lot of store by community projects – Christmas parties for OAPs, charity quizzes, visits to local hospice etc. Dialogue and discussion are strongly encouraged. Head pupil and deputy head pupil run school council – each year group has three reps and recent innovations include chilled water supply and napkins in dining room! Buddy system introduced to encourage older pupils to befriend and help younger pupils. There is also open forum for parents to raise issues once a term. Behaviour is good – no vandalism, graffiti or discipline problems, says head, just occasional high spirits in corridors. School has introduced extended day to help working parents – now open from 7.45am till 6pm. Also runs popular Megakids holiday clubs for 3–13 year-olds during school holidays.

Pupils and Parents: Pupils come from wide range of economic and social backgrounds and from rural as well as urban areas. 'A lot of parents make real sacrifices to send their children here.' Many travel in by bus (organised in house) from 25-mile radius, from as far afield as south Durham and north Yorkshire. Delightful girls and boys who take pride in their school and brim with enthusiasm. Old girls include broadcasters Shiulie Ghosh (of ITN) and Pam Royle.

Entrance: At 11, all pupils (including those from the prep) sit verbal reasoning paper and emotional intelligence questionnaire. Two thirds entering senior school come from prep, a third from primary schools. Boys and girls entering sixth form need at least six GCSE passes (preferably grade B and above).

Exit: About ten per cent leave post-GCSE. Almost all sixth form leavers go to university. Durham, Nottingham and Edinburgh are currently popular choices.

Money Matters: The school offers up to eight means-tested bursaries every year on a first come, first served basis.

Remarks: An attractive, happy, unpretentious school that prides itself on turning out well-educated, confident and compassionate young men and women. Environment is safe and nurturing yet encourages boys and girls to have a go.

The Thomas Hardye School

Queen's Avenue, Dorchester, Dorset, DT1 2ET

• Pupils: 2,300 boys and girls, all day • Ages: 13-18 • Size of sixth form: 920 • Non-denom • State

Tel: 01305 266064
Fax: 01305 250510
Email: admin@thomas-hardye.dorset.sch.uk
Website: www.thomas-hardye.dorset.sch.uk

Head: Dr Iain Melvin BA PhD OBE retired in December 2010 – having tried a couple of times before but was found to be irreplaceable! The school's senior management team were holding the fort as we went to press at the end of 2010 and a new appointment was expected early in 2011.

Academic matters: Creditable results here with 85 per cent A*–C grades at A level (34 per cent A/A*) and nearly 30 per cent A*/A at GCSE. Maths particularly strong and far and away the most popular A level subject here. Head points out that there are more pupils doing A level maths here than in all the schools in the rest of the county combined. Science popular but results a little disappointing for a school that became a science college in 2002 although school remarks that science results have improved significantly and the school has the 2010 UK Young Scientist of the Year. It is now a High Performing Specialist School and has just been granted two other specialisms – humanities and SEN. Ofsted report so over the top with gushing praise that it makes embarrassing reading. Has been given every award going: Charter Mark, Schools Curriculum Award, Investor in People, Arts Mark Gold, Leading Edge School, Education Extra Award, School Achievement Awards ... you get the picture.

Being so large allows the school to provide some unusual subjects, including Latin and dance at GCSE, and sociology, dance, electronics, food technology, travel & tourism and accounting at A level. Also offers the CACHE diploma in nursery nursing. On top of all this, Hardye's is a teaching training school, working in partnership with Exeter and other universities. IT a sore point for some pupils: though well-equipped with swarms of new boxes, monitors, interactive whiteboards etc, pupils speak of perpetual printer problems down on the shop floor – while the head's printer purrs like a dream ... 'we believe that our printer options have improved significantly – much now centrally linked – and my printer is very old!'

Some 180 pupils take advantage of SEN provision here, ranging from moderate learning difficulties (the majority) to a handful of pupils in wheelchairs. The school has a physiotherapy room, a unit for the hearing impaired, two large SEN rooms and several specialist SEN staff. And for pupils who just need a boost, there are after-school homework help sessions – well attended 'and no stigma attached,' said a pupil. A few parents of kids with minor problems (e.g. poor handwriting, organisational issues) felt the school could do more.

Games, Options, the Arts: Super sports facilities – floodlit Astro, sports hall with climbing wall, fitness suite, verdant playing fields, plus use of the facilities at the Dorchester Rugby Club and neighbouring leisure centre (two swimming pools). New swimming pool opening in 2011. Rugby keenly played, along with football (boys and girls), cross-country, netball, athletics, traditional cricket and swimming. Vast numbers of pupils to choose from means the school's 'won' column contentedly exceeds its 'lost'. A good range of minor sports e.g. water polo and kayaking, plus outward bound activities. Drama, music, art and dance are all buzzing. Music department stands out, with recording studio and music tech room. Music tours, two orchestras, school music festival, lots of rock bands, annual joint concert with Imperial College, steel band, chapel choir – 'you name a cathedral, they've sung in it!' says the head. Drama in own theatre, RSC visits every second year. Small museum area displays some excellent artwork. THTV, the school's in-house television channel, shows pupil-produced programmes on a plasma-screen TV in the heart of the school, known as the Spine. Lots of charity do-gooding and recycling.

Background and Atmosphere: Thomas Hardye founded the first free school in Dorchester in 1569 (the school has nothing to do with Dorset novelist Thomas Hardy who confusingly attended school in Dorchester in the 1850s, in case you were wondering). Doubled in size in 1992 when amalgamated with local girls' school. Is now enormous, heaving, multi-layered campus. Feels more like a small university than a comprehensive – owing partly to the absence of 11 and 12 year-olds, a key element of Hardye's uniqueness. Sixth form immense. 'We think it is the largest of any comprehensive in the country,' says the head, which gives you some idea. Just in case any other school is plotting to eclipse them, Hardye's is in the process of expanding its sixth form further still, until they will be the ... SUPREME ... MASTERS ... OF ... THE ... UNIVERSE. A gigantic sixth form means better funding which 'percolates down through the rest of the school.' It also allows them to offer their good range of A level courses.

School's swish office and reception area immediately radiates a school that has its act together. Lots of new building including £2.7 million English and modern languages block with central glassed-in atrium housing 50 computers. A new learning centre, nursery and sports hall. Beauteous sixth form centre, with own mini-canteen, well appreciated by the students. Class sizes pushing the boundaries in the sixth form.

Pastoral Care and Discipline: The few local parents who do not choose the school mainly cite pastoral matters (will my child be lost in the vastness? Will he suffer peer pressure?). But parents who have taken the plunge are almost all happy here. The head points out that, by breaking the school down by year group, they have created five manageable-sized groups of children. Pupils coming into Year 9 keep the same tutor for three years – helps enormously. Appearance a constant source of skirmishes, with the pupils' guerrilla tactics usually overpowering the administration. Barber shop visits have not greatly troubled the boys. However, the school outflanked the pupils in the battle of the neckwear, introducing clip-on ties for new pupils in 2005.

Behaviour otherwise OK, if informal. No uniform in sixth form. Out if caught in possession of drugs but head says he is 'a realist' and there have been no permanent exclusions in the past eight years – 'easily the lowest temporary exclusions in Dorset.' Area where sixth form pupils store their bags is guarded by CCTV (a good idea). Library well used and quiet – a sea of heads earnestly down. Bullying low on list of concerns – 'it's uncool to fight here,' said a pupil.

Pupils and Parents: School is the pinnacle of Dorchester's Schools Partnership, a cohesive 4–19 educational pyramid. Hardye's has traditionally been able to count on this mainly homogeneous, middle income, non-urban catchment to provide reasonably wholesome kids with a good work ethic. Sadly, some negative aspects of youth culture are reaching even here, and Hardye pupils are not quite the bushy-tailed, fresh-faced youngsters they were when Dr Melvin first came to the school. Negligible sprinkling of ethnic diversity – most with English as their home language.

Entrance: 475 pupils at 13+ mainly from Dorchester's three middle schools. Some fifty pupils come from outside the area, from as far away as Sherborne and Blandford. Handful from local prep, Sunninghill, settle in just fine. Number seeking entry roughly matches places available, although this is changing. All candidates for entry to the sixth form are interviewed, including the school's own pupils. 180 new pupils enter at that stage, a few from Poole and Bournemouth's grammars, attracted here by wide range of A levels, less authoritarian sixth form and lure of the opposite sex.

Exit: At least 80 per cent to higher education. 20 per cent leave after GCSEs, most of these to further education elsewhere. Head says that none are pushed out, but that the less able tend to leave, some looking for more vocational courses. UCAS a Herculean labour here, with Dr Melvin reading every single application. Half a dozen pupils to Oxbridge most years – sometimes more, eight in 2008 – but also students to UCL, RVC and LSE. First IB results in 2008 were excellent and this element of the sixth form continues to grow – it was the first (and only) school to introduce the qualification in Dorset.

Remarks: Bulging metropolis, humming purposefully under twenty years of efficient head. Exactly what educationalists had in mind when comprehensives were first invented and going from strength to strength. Now needs new head to help it carry on surging forward.

Thomas Mills High School

Saxtead Road, Framlingham, Woodbridge, Suffolk, IP13 9HE

• Pupils: 525 boys, 605 girls. All day • Ages: 11-18 • Size of sixth form: 290 • Non-denom • State

Tel: 01728 723 493
Fax: 01728 621 098
Email: inmail@thomasmills.suffolk.sch.uk
Website: www.thomasmills.suffolk.sch.uk

Head: Since 2005, Mr Colin Hirst, a biologist with considerable teaching and management experience (and knowledge of the area; he taught at East Bergholt High). Previously head of Noadswood School in Southampton.

Academic matters: Impressive results across the board at both GCSE and A level and superb value-added scores. A specialist school for technology since 1996 – the then new head used the funds to improve provision for science, maths (a whole new block) and IT, which is impressive in every area. Now a language and arts college too. Express streams in maths and science take GSCE in Year 10, and there is setting in maths, science and languages at KS3/4. Developing opportunities for able students to take AS qualifications in Year 11. 'Key players' used to teach the, mainly male, middle sets – aims to bring boys' performance more in line with girls'. 2010 A level results showed 57 per cent A*–B grades and 77 per cent A*–C. Very few linguists at this level. At GCSE in 2010, 76 per cent got 5+ A*–C including English and maths. Around half A* grades for each single science. Latin taken by a handful in Year 10 though none take it further.

Humanities and arts subjects also do very well. A language is compulsory at GCSE and all pupils do French and German at KS3. Latin is taught as an optional extra-curricular subject and is increasing in popularity. Some 26 subjects at A level – take-up is variable so some, like languages, have small groups, whereas maths and biology nets 50 or so at A level. Not that results seem adversely affected by group size. Provision for learning support is excellent, and the department has its own cheerful area.

Games, Options, the Arts: Bought back a lost games field, so facilities are good and shared by the public after hours. A thriving house system, dating from grammar school days, means that large numbers are involved in competitive sport, much encouraged as part of the school ethos. On Sports Day, there is an 'open mile', in which around 300 children take part.

Art department a haven of creative chaos, producing bold, quite avant-garde results. Music is superb. Orchestras, choirs and instrumental groups abound, catering for all tastes and providing frequent concerts. Drama is on the curriculum in Years 7/8, and the new performing arts studio with its dramatically sweeping black curtains is every young thespian's dream environment. Every member of staff is involved in one or more of the wide range of extra-curricular activities, visits and foreign exchanges.

Background and Atmosphere: This is one of the 18th century Mills schools, a grammar school from 1902 to 1979. The campus is large, in a semi-rural setting on the outskirts of Framlingham, and consists of a hotch-potch of buildings. The main block is a bit battered-looking, with rather oppressive long corridors, but new building in the last ten years lifts the spirits. A much needed new canteen was recently completed, as was a new gymnasium. There are some nice touches; two air-raid shelters preserved on site provide a WW II museum and an experience of the blitz, complete with terrifying sound effects. The general atmosphere is exceptionally studious and disciplined. In the large, well appointed and modernised library, even when it is full, you could hear a pin drop. Pupils are relaxed, courteous and well behaved. The head is keen to promote a sense of pride and the site is peppered with plaques celebrating this or that achievement or new development.

Pastoral Care and Discipline: System of form tutors appears to work well, with sixth formers involved in befriending and counselling younger pupils and also helping those with reading problems. Traditional values and individual responsibility. A real feeling that the highest of standards of behaviour and effort are expected. The house system, which permeates many areas of school life and is entirely run by the sixth form, promotes a strong sense of pride and belonging.

With so many pupils on a crowded site, noise levels are surprisingly low and unauthorised absences are well below national average, although this is probably to be expected in a school with an essentially problem-free intake and few inherent issues with discipline.

Pupils and Parents: Pupils are all from the surrounding region and from a broad spectrum of social backgrounds but there is very little ethnic diversity. Both pupils and parents are highly complimentary about the school and tend to express only minor complaints about, for example, the untrendy design of the girls' trouser option (you have to look hard to see any girls in trousers!). Parents are very supportive and everyone seems extremely proud of the school's outstanding achievements.

Entrance: About 70 per cent come from the catchment area of surrounding villages, plus 30 per cent from out of catchment (quite a few more apply in this category than can be accommodated). There is an influx of 25–30 per cent into the sixth form, from other high schools and even from independent schools.

Exit: Vast majority go on to higher education and a wide range of courses, including a good number to top universities. A few to vocational training or directly into employment.

Remarks: One of the best comprehensive schools in the country; a real community school. Judged by Ofsted to be 'outstanding' in 2006.

Thomas Telford School

Old Park, Telford, Shropshire, TF3 4NW

• Pupils: 1,240 boys and girls, all day • Ages: 11-18 • Size of sixth form: 400 • Non-denom • State

Tel: 01952 200 000
Fax: 01952 293 294
Email: jdavis@ttsonline.net
Website: www.ttsonline.net

Head: Since 1991, Sir Kevin Satchwell BA (early fifties). OU education degree plus a diploma in educational management. Taught PE, ran his department in two schools, then deputy head in Kirkby and head of Moseley Park in Wolverhampton, before being appointed as TTS's founding head, with the brief 'to raise educational standards in Telford and Wolverhampton'. This he has unequivocally done, hence the superhead gong. The school is very much his creation and he's proud of it, as he is of fighting his way out of his limited background to current fame. Likes media attention and the range of visitors it brings (many turned away), but keeps closely in touch with pupils (is part of the personal tutor team, holds regular working lunches with students of all ages, runs a football team – on the day of the GSG visit was seen after school boarding a minibus with them for an away match).

A quiet, modestly confident man, down-to-earth and direct in manner. Married, with two children. Sometimes sounds like the head of a successful trad independent grammar school – which indeed the school resembles in many ways. Prides himself on innovative approach to running a school, e.g. day divided into two three-hour periods – a long day, especially if pupils stay for a third session (up to 5.40) for sports and activities – but no one seems to complain. Also flat management structure for staff – nine deputy/departmental heads have responsibility for the curriculum and for appointing their own teachers; Sir Kevin claims that this releases cash for everyone else (teachers have a lightish teaching load and get overtime for extra duties).

Academic matters: Very important (the head's first sentence in the prospectus), and very successful. The claim to be 'England's top comprehensive school' gives rise to lively and intermittent argument about how they do it – and how the exam statistics are worked out – but there is no doubt that drive towards achievement and celebration of success are hot-wired into the place. Some A level students recently wrote to the press in answer to a disparaging criticism of the school (see below), 'our school and students are competitive and we make no apologies for that. We do not accept mediocrity and why should we?'

Pass rates at both levels are high and rising (vocational qualifications included in the calculation); science, maths and technology A level are strong (as one might expect), also English literature, history and business studies. Languages feature pretty well at GCSE though few take them in the last two years. Still, this is a wide-ability school and clearly something in the air makes the pupils work hard and want to do well. 'Students should feel good about being successful.' Sir Kevin would say it's all to do with an ethos of high standards, secure surroundings, staff commitment and strong parental involvement; now where have we heard all that before? Bags of encouragement and reinforcement underpins all this.

The school pioneered the use of IT early in the 1990s and is still at the leading edge in the production of educational software – so much so that it sells its curriculum and allied material to schools nationally as part of an outreach programme. The whole curriculum is planned in July for the following year; the claim is that it can be accessed in school or from home at any time. Quite what 'curriculum' means here is not clear – it sounds as if teachers are expendable – perhaps 'schemes of work'; but in context it has to be a bright idea, handing initiative to pupils to learn and releasing teachers from some drudgery. 'It may sound mechanistic', says the head, 'but it's very productive'.

Average class size is 24 below the sixth; groups range from four to 23 in Years 12 and 13. Around 88 pupils on the SEN roll, four of them statemented.

Games, Options, the Arts: Enormous range of games played (Sportsmark 2007 awarded), much student representation at every level up to national: football (boys have link-up with Wolves, one girl played for England), cricket, hockey, athletics, swimming etc etc. Inter-house competitions taken seriously; excellent facilities, including floodlit pitches. Over a hundred pupils currently involved in D of E at all levels. Performing arts are strong, especially dance and music.

Background and Atmosphere: Founded in 1991 with attractive purpose-built campus; the use of space underpins the head's philosophy. As a CTC, the school is sponsored, notably by the Mercers' Company and the Tarmac Group, who have plenty of influence on the governing board. This means the head has great freedom of action – and no anxieties because no fees to garner.

Plenty of open spaces, including open areas where two or three classes are taught simultaneously; an interesting reversion to the old schoolroom idea, which appears to work well, and certainly suits the three-hour periods. Generally there is an impression of quiet and purposeful study, with elements of both focus and relaxation. Everywhere is carpeted, and noise levels are impressively low (no bells). Reception area could belong to a corporate HQ, with (silent) TV screens giving the latest in news and sport, and a monitor for visitors to access the school's very professional website – and indeed much of the building looks like a modern open-plan office. Neatly uniformed boys and girls (they even have TTS lab coats).

Parents encouraged to become involved in the school's life, through an advisory council and through constant monitoring of their children's progress: they get a report every four or five weeks, and are invited to comment on e.g. whether they are satisfied with their child's work. Much contact with personal tutors, who are encouraged to draw the diffident into the educational process; they even visit housebound parents on their own initiative. The very hard-working can be rewarded by becoming Parent of the Year.

Pastoral Care and Discipline: Vertical tutor-group system (like St Paul's London – another Mercers' school), two to three from each year in one 'family'; meets every day for 20 minutes. 'Students can see the headmaster at any time to discuss issues of concern.' Zero tolerance over bullying and use of harmful substances, inside or outside school. Uniform rules strictly enforced.

Pupils and Parents: From Wolverhampton (ten coaches ferry pupils to and fro), or from Telford town. Obviously a wide span of social backgrounds – some families on income support and some middle class parents who, elsewhere, might have avoided comprehensives but can sniff out a successful middle class school. Ideologically-driven observers like Roy Hattersley have sought to explain academic success by accusing the school of a socially skewed selection policy, a charge vigorously countered by Sir Kevin, who points out that all CTCs have to pick in fixed proportions from the standard distribution of ability bands. The argument will doubtless continue.

Entrance: Entrants at 11 come from a defined catchment area; no preference for siblings. Selection is 'from the full ability range ... in accordance with the criteria embodied in the funding agreement between the school and the Education Secretary', which is different from LEA schools. Within each of the nine ability bands 'places will be allocated as far as practicable over the full range of ability. The headmaster will select students ... and in exercising his professional judgement will take into account the range of ability admitted, geographical dispersal of intake, and competence in science, technology and maths.' So the head has some freedom within broad parameters. (Note carefully – applications usually have to be in by 30th September for the next September. Check with Admissions Office at the school). Our translation of this for eager parents would be – underlying ability is no barrier or advantage but do interest your child in something technological or mathematical. There will be geographical patches where the chances of success are higher because the level of applications is lower. This is one of the few good schools where moving to a cheaper house may give an advantage! Enthusiasm for the school, a real interest in education and an obvious willingness to get stuck in should be on display at visits; this applies to your child too. There may be a few places after GCSE.

Exit: Increasingly to higher education, mainly in and around the Midlands; 87 per cent in 2009, including two students taking a gap year, the rest to employment or training. About a third of leavers to older universities, three to Oxford and Cambridge. Numbers staying on to the sixth are steadily increasing (now over 90 per cent). The school claims a low drop-out rate at university (two per cent).

Remarks: A remarkable school, proof (for some) of what a comprehensive – albeit a special one – can achieve under strong and visionary leadership. Whatever you think about the overtly competitive drive towards academic success, you can't be unaffected by the pupils' all-round confidence, and their pleasure in belonging to an institution which stimulates them in the classroom and appreciates them for what they can offer outside it; not new values by any means, but all the better for being asserted here. If you're moving to this part of the West Midlands, get your form in in good time.

Thurston Community College

Norton Road, Thurston, Bury St Edmunds, Suffolk, IP31 3PB

• Pupils: 1,435 boys and girls, all day • Ages: 13-18 • Size of sixth form: 375 • Non-denom • State

Tel: 01359 230 885
Fax: 01359 230 880
Email: admin@thurstoncollege.suffolk.sch.uk
Website: www.thurston.org.uk

Principal: Since 2005, Miss Helen Wilson BSc MBA NPQH (forties). Studied applied physics with chemistry at Durham, followed by a PGCE in science and PE at Bristol. Previously assistant principal at Comberton Village College and vice principal at Thurston. A dynamic, clear thinker whose enthusiasm is palpable, as is her fervent support of the comprehensive system – she means it when she says she's not just interested in exam results. Despite managerial load is still 'passionate about teaching' and lessons with Year 9 provide some of her happiest moments. Definitely a team player who works hard to make staff and pupils feel valued – Ofsted says her management and leadership are outstanding. Sport offers a safety valve and way to maintain a 'healthy work- life balance'. Captains a local hockey team. Also enjoys skiing and wind surfing.

Academic matters: Approachable staff who're always there to help. Some 'outstanding' teaching – to address inconsistencies the principal has instigated a collaborative learning scheme for staff. Wide range of subjects at GCSE including separate sciences, business studies, engineering and dance. Above average value-added with 68 per cent getting 5 or more A–C grades. Sixth form caters for a broad spectrum of abilities with BTec courses in sport, hospitality and catering. A level results have steadily improved with 72 per cent scoring A–C. Fair amount of prodding in the main school but, once in the sixth, according to one of the students, 'it's your responsibility to get the work done'.

Most of the time those with SEN are supported in class by one of the large team of teaching assistants. There's also a 3+2 scheme – two days in school, three days working on vocational courses at the local college. No fast tracking for the extra bright – 'we extend rather than accelerate'.

Games, Options, the Arts: Strong emphasis on taking part with most club activities at lunchtime (four out of five pupils come to school by bus or coach). Not overly competitive but sporting achievement is recognised and there's friendly inter-house rivalry on the games field. Success in sport with numerous teams and individuals participating at local, county and regional level.

Individual music lessons and selection of musical activities – 'They really go to town on the annual productions,' said a parent. Large, recently refurbished art and design studios. Textiles is popular and the unusually sophisticated work well worth a look – in 2008, five of the top ten GCSE candidates nationally.

Sixth formers are encouraged to get involved with extra-curricular activities -at the last count 16 were going for gold D of E. Lots of fundraising and committees who organise anything from social events to the installation and management of recycling boxes in every classroom.

Background and Atmosphere: Airy, pleasant setting in dormitory village on the outskirts of Bury St Edmunds. Spacious, seventies single storey main school with interconnecting pods – has something of the hospital about it – and newer, self-contained sixth form centre. All softened with attractive landscaping and colourful planting. Good IT provision, two libraries – one is used by the local community – and large playing fields at the back of the site. Smiley, exuberant crowds of pupils (no smaller ones to dilute the considerable physical presence of year niners and their elders) teem in the corridors, but once in class attentive calm appears to be the norm. For many the positive relations with staff and a friendly atmosphere are the best things about the place.

Pastoral Care and Discipline: Because of its huge size the school is divided into four houses each with a team of tutors. High priority is given to welfare and support – ranked as outstanding by Ofsted. Good lines of communication with parents and according to a pupil 'always someone who looks out for you'. Sixth form mentors who are given specialist training before working with Year 9s/10s, plus an effective inclusion policy which identifies and supports kids who are in danger of exclusion (one to one or small group teaching in a dedicated area) helps keep almost all in main stream education.

Ethos which rewards rather than chastises. All sorts of endeavour (academic, sporting, good deeds etc) are rewarded through the hugely popular points system.

Points mean prizes – a few points will earn a non uniform pass but serious savers can aim for goodies like a Top Shop voucher, a day at Alton Towers or a DVD player. How things have changed! Head is refreshingly firm but fair and, on the odd occasion when it's necessary, will stand her ground on permanent exclusions.

Pupils and Parents: Largely from surrounding rural area, predominantly middle class with a tiny number from ethnic minorities. Informal uniform (pale blue polo shirt, navy sweat shirt and black trousers – girls rarely wear skirts) is strictly adhered to in lessons but customisation seems to be fair game at break and lunchtime.

Entrance: Heavily over-subscribed. Catchment rules are stringent and at times oversubscription criteria may have to be applied. Important to check out the County Council admissions policy for Suffolk maintained schools.

Exit: 60 per cent stay on to the sixth and a good proportion go on to higher education.

Remarks: Large rural comprehensive where all are valued. Forward-thinking head who looks set to take this lively school to the top of the ladder.

The Tiffin Girls' School

Richmond Road, Kingston Upon Thames, Surrey, KT2 5PL

• Pupils: 895 girls; all day • Ages: 11-18 • Size of sixth form: 290
• Non-denom • State

Tel: 020 8546 0773
Fax: 020 8547 0191
Email: tiffin.girls@rbksch.org
Website: www.tiffingirls.kingston.sch.uk

Head: Since 2010, Mrs Vanessa Ward, previously vice principal at St Philomena's Catholic High School for Girls. She read English at Edinburgh University and qualified and practised as a solicitor before going into teaching.

Academic matters: Outstanding. Regularly tops GCSE, A level and value-added league tables and holds its own against the independent sector. Gained a Grade One ranking in its latest Ofsted inspection. Among the highest performing state schools in the country at GCSE with a 100 per cent A–C pass rate, the majority at A*/A grades. Maths and French may be taken early in Year 10 – about 20 girls a year are offered this option and generally go on to achieve an A* grade. Maths and science are particularly strong (the school is a specialist maths and computing college). Girls average nine or ten GCSEs and a few take an AS level in Year 11. Most popular optional GCSE subjects are history, geography and art.

Similar success at A level – impressive 64 per cent of subjects taken get A grades, 90 per cent get A/B. Maths, biology and chemistry are popular A level choices (lots of Tiffin girls go on to study medicine and science). Teaching staff impress – combining the energy and new ideas of the younger members with the experience of exam preparation and extension work coming from a solid, longer-serving bunch. There is a fair degree of staff movement – partly typical of this part of the country and also because experience at Tiffin Girls is a significant career boost. However, parents and girls all mention the 'special relationship' between teachers and pupils. Girls work very hard during their lessons – all bright, co-operative and eager to learn, there is very little messing about. Teachers capitalise on this enthusiasm and endeavour to make the work as much fun as possible. Lots of lively lessons and great interaction between teachers and pupils – girls formed a human graph in maths, love using the 'show me' boards and, according to one mother, 'they are forever dressing up; staff too – the science teacher was dressed as a battery pack the other day.'

Years 7–9 follow the National Curriculum with the addition of Latin, Spanish and drama. Homework generally surprises the Year 7 girls by not being too onerous – starts at about an hour each evening. Not too pressured – but largely because these carefully selected girls are bright enough to be able to work and play. Teachers have more problems reining in their tendency to over-work than encouraging them to work harder. Limited provision for SEN. There is a lift in the new wing. Girls with EAL requirements – generally for written English – receive extra help from sixth form pupils. School holds a well-deserved clutch of awards – and has just gained Arkwright Trust status.

Games, Options, the Arts: Certainly not 'all work ... ': there's plenty going on here. Masses of music – school has a 'Musician in Residence'; three or four girls a year go on to take music at university, including Oxbridge choral scholarships. Orchestras, smaller ensembles and choirs abound – including a choir for parents. About 200 girls take individual music tuition as a (paid for) extra. Similarly good drama on offer with several productions each year – cast boosted by Tiffin Boys as necessary. Drama studio completed 2007 and music suite opened in 2009. All funded by the school's own charitable fund raising. Dancers not as well catered for. Striking displays of work festoon the art rooms, with additional workshops and clubs running after hours.

Sport very strong; good sports facilities on site (unusual for schools in urban areas such as this) – hard tennis courts, Astroturf, gyms and an impressive sports centre used by the local community after hours. Hockey and netball in winter, and tennis and athletics in the summer are the main sports and girls are successful at borough, county and national levels – school has built up a sparkling silverware collection.

Lots of overseas trips on offer across all subject areas, plus all the usual jaunts to London and surrounds. Overall facilities and resources are good – nothing mega-flashy but it's all there.

Background and Atmosphere: The school's roots are back in the 17th century when prosperous brewers, Thomas and John Tiffin, established a charitable fund for the education of the poor. Boosted by other benefactors, by the 1870s the fund could afford to establish two new schools – one each for boys and girls, both taking 150 pupils. Originally both were housed in the same new building by the Fairfield in Kingston. Today the girls' school is in what was once a boys' secondary modern school building, set back on a main road linking Kingston with Ham and Richmond.

A good 20 minutes trot from the centre of Kingston – and not really near anything much (save a bus stop for the one route along here) so no danger of the girls nipping out to the chip shop at lunchtime and nor should they need to. The school food looks yummy and is varied enough to tempt adolescent appetites. The older school buildings are rather dreary and old fashioned but the £4 million Holdsworth wing is much more cheerful and fit for purpose. This was built to replace the old classrooms and offices lost in the 2003 fire – the school had been crying out for refurbishment for years but it took the fire to propel them to the top of the list for a grant. Centred on a striking atrium, the building has an open staircase and nice wide corridors. Lots of natural materials – wood, glass and concrete and an 'intelligent' building management system controlling light and temperature. Pink and purple colour scheme and rather smart loos attest to the pupils' close involvement with the plans. A definite happy atmosphere abounds. Separate sixth form building is a bit sad and tatty but also obviously well loved and actually quite homely. Usual set up of those teenage necessities – microwaves and coffee cups.

A swim or sink place; the pool is so much bigger and brighter here that many girls who were big fish in their small pond junior school quickly have to get used to being surrounded by equally clever (if not even cleverer) clogs. Girls need to get their act together – homework is expected promptly, strict standards of appearance are required and punctuality is imperative. The school is difficult to get to on public transport, yet staff will have no truck with lateness. To be fair, prospective parents are all warned to consider the journey their daughter will make before choosing the school.

Form groups are strong – girls are taught in these groups – and each form (all of equal standing) belongs to one of four houses, named after previous headmistresses. There is terrific house spirit, lots of inter-house competition and friendly rivalry. Even the older girls seem positively childlike in their enthusiasm for the place – they happily sing the school song and get quite excited about the school's birthday when they all bake cakes to be covered in the 120 plus candles lit during a special assembly. There is room for the whole school to meet together several times a week which may help explain this good community spirit. The girls are also fervent charity fundraisers – sometimes led by their teachers – but also getting up to lots of things off their own bat.

Pastoral Care and Discipline: Pastoral side seems to have continued to improve in recent years with many parents reporting sensitive handling of any difficulties. Girls are encouraged to 'tell' if they are worried about a friend and a school counsellor is on hand. Self-discipline and consideration for others are the watchwords upon which the rules are based. No make-up allowed – and not even a stud earring permitted until Year 10. A few moans that the uniform is expensive – no picking up a skirt in Tesco or the like but, we're told, uniform is responsibly sourced from English factories with high employment standards. Despite this emphasis on appearance in the early years, there is no smart dress code for sixth formers. Usual system of sanctions and rewards apply – although one mother did mention that there are rather more sticks than carrots here. 'It's simply that good work and behaviour are expected, so the girls are never heaped with praise,' she says. All the usual no-nos re drink, drugs and bullying apply. Although conformity is rather a given, the previous head confirmed that she never needed to exclude a pupil for drug use during her 16 years in post.

Pupils and Parents: Phenomenal social mix of families – from C2 white collar where the girls will be first generation graduates in their families, through to professionals saving on school fees. It's a broad church, yet the mix appears to work well. Head says the girls are conscious of each other's abilities rather than backgrounds and that the place is racially harmonious. A quite charming and hard working lot, who listen in amazement at their friends' tales of fighting and bullying at other schools. Certainly it's one of those places where being an ace mathematician is cool rather than nerdy. About 40 per cent are from ethnic minorities – lots from Korea and Sri Lanka – and about one third are bilingual. Tiffin girls are quite distinctive – a very cosmopolitan bunch, keen and confident and generally wearing their intelligence lightly. Head is the first to acknowledge that the school is in partnership with the girls' families as well as with the pupils themselves. Good feedback and email contact from school to home. There are some top-notch events for parents including celebrity appearances to boost fire-fund coffers. Old girl Lynne Truss proved a riot apparently.

Entrance: Tough and hugely over-subscribed – at 11, parents almost fight to get their daughters a place here and most shell out for coaching in the verbal and non-verbal reasoning tests which form the entrance exam. School at pains to stress it does not consider coaching necessary and says that girls can run through the practice papers available in WH Smith. This may have been true years ago, but few families take the risk these days, believing that coaching is essential to ensure their daughters learn technique and time-management. 'You can't turn a child around but you can improve their performance by around five per cent and ensure they enter the exam calm and well prepared,' says a parent.

An average of 1200 girls sit for Tiffin, with places offered to the top 120 scores. There are no distance criteria and the school draws girls from a wide area beyond its borough's borders – though head suggests all try the journey by public transport before accepting a place. In practice, most come from within about six miles, though there are always a few outriders. At 16, the school offers additional 20 or so places to newcomers. Entry requirement is eight GCSEs A*–C including maths, English and science, plus A*/A in subjects to be studied at AS level.

Exit: At 16, most move up to the sixth form – a handful choose elsewhere or win a scholarship to the private sector. At 18, it's university for all. Average of 18–24 to Oxbridge and 15–20 to medical school. Others to Russell Group and good redbricks. Head reports early milk round in place – predominantly banks and accountancy firms coming in to cream off some of the talent pre-university.

Money Matters: 'Leafy green Kingston' is apparently the richest borough in London but funds still a problem. Parents good at fund-raising and pay £30 a month voluntary contribution by direct debit to boost finances. Recently they raised £80,000 for computers and the like. Fire Appeal raised over £180,000.

Remarks: A top class education and a tremendous range of opportunities in this highly sought after (even by parents who could afford to pay elsewhere) school. A shining example of the very best the state has to offer and indeed there is undoubtedly a certain cachet attached to being 'a Tiffin girl'. Suits competitive, hardworking, high achievers whom it will engage, entertain and challenge.

Tiffin School

Queen Elizabeth Road, Kingston Upon Thames, Surrey, KT2 6RL

• Pupils: 1,060 boys; all day • Ages: 11-18 • Size of sixth form: 350
• Broadly C of E, all faiths admitted • State

Tel: 02085 464 638
Fax: 02085 466 365
Email: hedwards@tiffin.kingston.sch.uk
Website: www.tiffin.kingston.sch.uk

Headteacher: Since 2009, Miss Hilda Clarke, a history graduate (Sussex), formerly head of Langley Grammar School near Slough. She replaces Mr Sean Heslop, head since 2004, who departed sooner than expected to head a new academy. His departure coincided with the revelation of a financial deficit: Tiffin had been running down reserves to finance projects, and found itself running at a loss too, which resulted in the need for a financial recovery plan worked out in liaison with the Local Authority. Mrs Pauline Cox, head of the Tiffin Girls' School, held the fort until Hilda Clarke took up the post.

Academic matters: A hot ticket in these parts – its academic reputation precedes it. The Ofsted inspection in 2007 stated 'Tiffin School is an exceptional performing arts college that provides its students with an outstanding quality of education'. Parents often have their sons coached the year prior to the exam (sometimes more in hope than expectation) and private preps also work hard to get their boys in. Once in situ, consistently strong academic results – in 2010, 86 per cent A*/A grades at GCSE. Boys take 10 GCSEs. Half of the students take dual award science at GCSE with the other half taking the option of triple science. History and geography most popular optional subjects. Among the top 20 grammar schools in the country for A level results (does even better when compared solely with other boys' schools) – in 2010 it was the 4th best boys' state school – 90 per cent A*–B grades. Pupils usually study three A2 levels, an additional AS level and critical thinking – idea being to leave them time for sport and other extra-curricular activities. Sciences and maths attract the most takers, followed by history and English.

School became a Performing Arts College in 2003 and attained its second specialism in Languages in 2009. Dance is on the curriculum from Year 7, available as a GCSE option. School also has links with the Royal Ballet School and several parents have been surprised by how well their sons have taken to dancing – 'Billy Elliot has helped a lot,' acknowledged one mother. Otherwise the school does well in the traditionally 'masculine' areas of maths and science. There are no social science options at Year 10 or at A level (except economics), Latin compulsory in Years 7 and 8, Greek available at GCSE and A level.

Not a school for slackers – hard work and high achievement are on the agenda. A good number of boys score in the top 10 of all exam entrants in various subjects. Average class size is 30 – in line with most state schools. In the main, teaching staff rate well with parents – average teacher age is mid 30s and plenty of female faces around the place. 'They all seem to be of a high standard,' says one father. 'And I notice that most senior teachers who leave are going on to take up deputy headships elsewhere.'

Selection is by ability – any SEN identified subsequently is addressed via additional needs support teacher. School tests pupils in Year 7 – most needs tend to be dyslexia or dyspraxia. Currently less than five per cent of boys receive extra help, no extra charge. 'I had super help for my son, they are very aware,' said one mother. Disabled access in place via ramps and lifts. Boys with EAL requirements receive additional booster classes. Generally English competence is high.

Currently KS3 boys have two subjects of homework per night of 20 minutes each and KS4 have two subjects of 40 minutes each. 'There is the expectation of 30 minutes per night spent on independent study.'

Games, Options, the Arts: All done well – school places strong emphasis on a rounded broad-based curriculum to counterbalance the heavy academic workload. Good sport – 12 rugby teams and 11 cricket teams, playing matches most weeks during their competitive seasons. Old boys include former England cricket captain Alec Stewart, who still supports the school and came back to open on-site nets. One of the few state schools to offer rowing in a big way and is regularly successful in national competitions. Some moaning from parents about the lack of football on offer – serious players have to look outside school for a game. Large, modern sports hall on site, with full disabled access. Outdoor sport played at Grist's sports grounds in Hampton Court, 'they're a bit of a trek away but great once you get there,' says one father.

Music very strong – head says second only to cathedral schools. 'It's phenomenally good,' agrees one parent. School has a history of sending boys to Oxbridge on choral scholarships. There are some 29 different musical groups – everything from the main choir which sings regularly at the Royal Opera House and on international tours, through all sorts of instrumental ensembles. Over 450 boys learn an instrument. Drama productions regularly appear at Edinburgh Festival. Old Boy, Jonny Lee Miller, recently starred in lavish BBC adaptation of Jane Austen's *Emma.*

Background and Atmosphere: Nestled at the centre of Kingston's notorious one-way system, the school and its surprisingly spacious grounds are largely screened from view by high brick walls offering some respite from the traffic noise, urban bustle, and a nearby needle exchange project for drugs users. 'We are vigilant about security,' says head. CCTV cameras at each of the three entrances, visitors and all staff (including head) wear ID badges at all times. Upside of locality is successful green transport policy – 85 per cent of the boys walk, cycle or use public transport to get to school.

Main school block dates from 1929 and is behind a small, early 18th century school house called Elmfield, which houses Tiffin Broadcast Network studio and some teaching rooms. This building is listed for its staircase, so school's hands are tied, but looks a bit sad and in need of some TLC. Generally the school is workmanlike rather than beautiful and looks a little tired and knocked about in places. Much more appealing is the Dempsey centre opened in 2004 – a great facility and a nice piece of architecture. A huge downstairs library sits below a circular balcony-style learning resources centre – all open and light. Next to this is a smart lecture theatre. Art and technology and IT suites are functional and modern. Good careers facilities. A new sixth form cafe gives sixth formers an informal social space, providing coffee and food throughout the day. Definite sense of fun and enjoyment around the place. School's stated mission is 'to inspire a love of learning and build a learning community.' Huge range of enrichment activities including D of E scheme – long lunch break is packed with activity. Healthy and very competitive house system. Tons of trips – locally and abroad. Limited links with nearby selective Tiffin Girls – some shared teaching in sixth form for general studies.

Pastoral Care and Discipline: Parents come up with countless examples of how the school has sensitively and smoothly dealt with all manner of issues – from friendship problems to rule-breaking. 'Any school of this size is bound to have a few bad apples – but bullying and bad behaviour are not tolerated,' said one father. 'There are plenty of staff and procedures in place to nip things in the bud. They understand boys and are realistic. There's a good atmosphere.' Another mother had particular praise for the relationship between the boys and the staff. 'The teachers have a nice way of relating to the boys – it's very noticeable.'

Smoking banned (for adults too) – more serious misdemeanours could lead to permanent exclusion but generally are handled through detentions and liaison with parents. Overall, school seems to achieve good control with a light touch. Strong moral thread runs throughout. 'If you choose the school for your son you have to buy in to all of it,' says one father. This includes ensuring the boys' availability after school and at weekends to represent the school when asked – 'we like them to commit to a five and a half day week.' Similarly don't even think of heading off for some cheap winter sun in term time – such holiday requests will be refused.

Pupils and Parents: Obviously attracts professional families with high expectations. Just under 50 per cent white middle class, the rest comprise large contingents from Indian sub-continent and Korea. 'I find the hard-working culture prevalent in these communities is pervasive and generally a good thing,' says an English mother. 'Relationships between the boys are good and my sons have good friends from all over the place,' says another. Parents are generally happy that their sons achieve results on a par with the private sector – for free. Seems an accommodating place; has a few eccentric boys who gain acceptance and cope well. Dizzying array of ties and blazers differentiate houses and year groups. Boys not super-smart but all in correct uniform. Head boy, deputies and prefects gowned. Some leeway allowed on hair length and style but no dye permitted. Vibrant parental support e.g. in music, rugby and PTA, and fundraising a priority, as ever in the state system. Car boot sales are legendary. In addition, parents are asked to fund the school to the tune of £10 a week. 'Nobody minds,' says one father and many pay.

Entrance: Heavily over-subscribed – typically 1,400 plus applications for 140 places. Applicants take two tests at 11+ – verbal and non-verbal reasoning – results are age weighted and places offered to the top 140 (tied positions are offered). No interviews – test results alone win a place. No linked schools. Over 40 per cent of pupils come from the Kingston area, others from Richmond, Hounslow, Sutton and other parts of Surrey. School advises against applying if a boy's journey to school would take more than one hour. Percentage arriving from prep schools is declining (now around 12 per cent). School is keen on forging links with local primaries through its specialisms, especially music and languages. For sixth form, some 45 additional places are available. Requirement is four A and two B grades at GCSE.

Exit: At 16+ less than three per cent go elsewhere, usually to a mixed college. Not too much turfing out by school between Years 11 and 12. 'It's not a brutal place – the boys are helped to try and make the grade,' says one parent. Post sixth form almost all head to the better universities – 18–24 to Oxbridge each year and 15 to medical schools.

Money Matters: State funded, free for all. Manages well on limited budgets and is hot on the trail of any opportunities for extra government cash. Fund-raising activities are rife, weekend car-boot sales have become something of an institution in the area. School shop retailing a dizzying range of varying ties and blazers, must turn in a fair profit. Well-supported alumni association also lends financial muscle.

Remarks: Certainly the best boys' 'free' education to be had in these parts – and academically it gives the private schools more than a run for their money. A buzzing place which likes its high-calibre boys to see beyond pure academia and provides plenty of opportunity for them to do so.

Tonbridge Grammar School

Deakin Leas, Tonbridge, Kent, TN9 2JR

• Pupils: 1,090 girls plus 45 boys in the sixth form; all day • Ages: 11-18
• Size of sixth form: 385 • Non-denom • State

Tel: 01732 365 125
Fax: 01732 359 417
Email: office@tgs.kent.sch.uk
Website: www.tgs.kent.sch.uk

Head Teacher: Since 2005, Mrs Rosemary Joyce BA MA PGCE NPQH. Read religious studies and history at Stirling, followed by a PGCE and MA at London. Previously deputy head of Nonsuch High School for Girls at Cheam; senior teacher at Clarendon School, Trowbridge; head of religious studies at Aylesbury High. Charming, approachable, businesslike, combines professionalism, warmth and genuine interest in the pupils and the school and is prepared to fight her corner for the school when necessary. Has 9-year-old twin girls.

Academic matters: Consistently at the top of the league tables – they take their rating seriously. A good range of languages including German, Italian, Latin and Spanish – an exceptional department praised by all. Regular cognitive ability tests (CAT) to measure progress against ability and to help with subject choices. Children encouraged to try out range of different learning styles and develop a love of learning and independent thought.

Flexible curriculum which allows the girls to take some GCSEs and AS levels early. Some take French and drama, some GCSE maths and complete AS by the end of Year 11. A levels and IB: first batch of IB candidates took their exams in 2006 with very impressive results. In 2009, two students, of only 65 worldwide, scored full marks and school was ranked the top IB state school in the UK that year. Emphasis on students learning to manage their work patterns with independence and confidence and take responsibility for themselves.

Broad range of links with other schools and businesses. Staff a healthy mix of young NQTs and experienced staff; calibre is top notch and kept on their toes with very effective monitoring of stats both internally and externally. Extraordinarily dedicated team who give up huge amounts of their own time to run clubs and sporting fixtures. Any shortcomings quickly surface and mentors always on hand. Setting in maths and French from Year 8 but generally there is no streaming or fixing of labels as this does not tally with the culture of being respectful of others' different and diverse strengths. Very good science, ICT integrated into every subject.

Curriculum designed to stretch the gifted and talented. A group of pupils recently went to Holland to teach a school how to run its own maths challenge. Particular attention given to individual learning needs; pupils can progress at their own pace – the girls we spoke to were particularly enthusiastic about this. One brilliant mathematician had completed her maths A level by the end of Year 9 and has been given individual tuition for further maths. Very keen to keep exceptionally talented students socially in their own year.

Good dyslexia support – students tested throughout school career. Part time specialist dyslexia teacher – students taken out of lessons.

Games, Options, the Arts: Corridors are decked with students' work in a nice higgledy-piggledy way, showing a full range of abilities; increasing amounts of work presented digitally. Art very popular as a club, inspiring textiles course – the most popular choice at GCSE. Music technology studio and spectacular graphics software. Plenty going on – rock bands, three choirs, two orchestras etc etc. Currently 300 students learn a full range of musical instruments. Plenty of students involved in county and national youth orchestras as well as choirs and bands. BBC Choir of the Year Finalist 2007 and winners Barnardo's Choir of the Year 2009. Lots of drama, some joint drama with Tonbridge School who have professional theatre complex – together they stage about 30 plays a year. Students are encouraged to direct and are able to train as theatre technicians.

Usual games on offer. PE compulsory to Year 13. Hockey and netball teams have distinguished themselves at national level and participated in tournaments in Europe. Intermediate cross-country team got through to national finals. Gymnastics and dance very popular with annual competition and display. Playing fields on site waterlogged for much of the winter, and wide craters appear in summer, hence most matches played at Weald of Kent Grammar down the road and hockey training on Astro at Tonbridge. D of E popular at all levels. Lots of trips and outings – China, Singapore, Paris. Developing links with a school in Sri Lanka. World Challenge expeditions to Borneo in 2009 and Chile in 2010. (Students expected to earn their own money for this).

60+ clubs at lunchtime and after school – podcasting to jewellery to life drawing to human rights discussions and 'computer club for girls'.

Background and Atmosphere: Tonbridge Grammar School (known locally as TGS) was founded in 1905 and perched on a hill on the edge of Tonbridge, overlooking the town. The main red brick buildings date back to 1913. The age of the buildings does not dampen the pupils' enthusiasm and pride in their school which has recently benefited from major refurbishment. New building completed (2009), 35 classrooms, library and learning centre, drama studios, dance studios and sports hall. Main school building refurbished (2010) for music, art, new sixth form centre and new dining facilities. Overall this represents a £10 million investment in the infrastructure of the school.

The introduction of boys in the sixth form has proved good news, particularly in debate; the large common room is a very friendly place. Girls often return as classroom assistants in their gap years – we're unsure whether to read that as a fine advertisement for the school or a lack of get-up-and-go. Not a school to rest on its laurels, constantly assessing itself and striving to do things better.

Assemblies mainly Christian but non-denominational in character – students encouraged to reflect on a range of spiritual and moral issues. Pupils contribute and lead assemblies as do many teaching staff.

Pastoral Care and Discipline: Pastoral care seen as a whole school responsibility. Parents very impressed with the confidence and level of maturity the girls achieve. Sixth form students play a major role in the running of the school and have initiated a peer mentoring one2one system whereby each student takes responsibility for a topic, e.g. anorexia; they receive counselling advice and provide confidential support for junior girls. Great emphasis on preparing and welcoming new students.

Discipline is hardly an issue as girls are motivated. 'Perhaps one downside of being so selective is that pupils can feel they have failed if they achieve a B grade. We work very hard with their self worth and perception,' says one deputy head. Great emphasis on respect: for each other and selves, for hard work and scholarship, for diversity of achievement and for the community and environment. Bullying is rare and the school takes effective action if it does occur.

Canteen offers good food with salad and pasta bar and two main meal options but about half of pupils bring in their own lunch. Breakfast is available every morning.

Pupils and Parents: They have the pick of the bunch who make the most of every minute. Pupils come from up to 80 different schools both maintained and private, mainly from the surrounding areas of Tonbridge, Sevenoaks and Tunbridge Wells with some from Surrey and East Sussex . Small numbers from other European countries, Middle East, America. About 13 per cent come from an ethnic minority background. Large majority are middle class (with their fair share of 4x4s), supportive of the school, friendly with no pretensions. Active and effective PTA. Good Old Girl network – Victoria Hislop (novelist and travel writer); Felicity Aston and Jo Vellino (polar explorers); Rebecca Stephens (first British woman to climb Everest and Seven Summits); Linda Taylor (author); Hayley Allen (Olympic diver); Jacquetta May (actress); Cathy Gilliat Smith (Bronze Commonwealth medallist Hockey 2005).

Entrance: Places are hard fought over here. Most students join at the age of 11 via the Kent 11 plus selection procedure. No allowance made for siblings. No geographical limit to the catchment area, but proximity to the school will be taken into account where there are two girls of equal ability. A minimum of 35 'Governors' places' are reserved for able pupils from outside the area but the same criteria apply as for Kent selection.

Sometimes place further up – children have to sit school's own test. Entry to the sixth form – 'where ability is appropriate': a minimum of 30 places offered annually (male and female). Confidential reference from present head teacher plus guidance interview. Must be capable of studying four subjects to AS level and must demonstrate an aptitude for their chosen subjects. Minimum requirement is 6 GCSEs at grade B or above, generally expected to achieve grade A in subjects they wish to study.

Exit: Diverse choices – mainly to higher education through university, studying anything from the traditional, e.g. classics, medicine, law, psychology, through to film and French, chemistry and forensic science, politics, early childhood studies, textile and fashion, sports science etc. Increasing numbers to Oxbridge, including choral scholarships. Specialist preparation and guidance for Oxbridge entrance linked with Tonbridge School. Good tradition of specialist art, music and drama college places.

Money Matters: State funded. Music bursaries available and awards in sixth form. The school co-ordinates a fund, administered exclusively by the headteacher, to assist in cases of financial hardship.

Remarks: A remarkable school. Pupils exceptionally confident and mature without being pushy, utterly natural and appear to have great sense of social responsibility and awareness of what is going on around them. Compassionate and considerate and outward looking. Has a bit of a local reputation for being a hothouse, but girls insist that this is not the case and the school seemed a relaxed and happy place.

Tonbridge School

High Street, Tonbridge, Kent, TN9 1JP

• Pupils: 770 boys; 445 board, 325 day • Ages: 13-18 • Size of sixth form: 335 • C of E • Fees: Boarding £29,913; Day £22,335 pa • Independent

Tel: 01732 365 555
Fax: 01732 363 424
Email: hmsec@tonbridge-school.org
Website: www.tonbridge-school.co.uk

Head: Since 2005, Mr THP (Tim) Haynes BA PGCE (early fifties), a historian, married with two school-age boys. After a post-university stab at stockbroking, Mr Haynes sensibly moved into teaching, beginning with QEGS (qv), Hampton (qv) and then a thirteen year spell at St Paul's (qv), where he rose to be surmaster. Ten years as head of Monmouth (qv) gave him lots of experience for this higher profile job in which he followed the fifteen year tenure of the much-respected Martin Hammond. So not a school which needed pulling up by boot-straps. 'I came here and found a fantastic school so I don't wish to turn the place upside down,' he acknowledges. 'I want to build on the strengths my predecessor developed, particularly its balance and breadth.' It's almost a pity so much has so recently been done here as the man has abundant nervous energy and dashes about all over the place, involving himself in a way everyone appreciates. 'He's very willing to chat,' say boys, 'he wants to get people's opinions about things – to hear it directly from them.' Parents are generally enthusiastic – 'he's approachable, a good communicator,' we are told. He's certainly smiley, rangy, open, chatty and immensely proud of his school, its staff and boys. A sound man for a blue chip school.

Academic matters: Truly excellent. In 2009, the average GCSE candidate achieved one A* and nine As. 93 per cent got all A*/A and 98 per cent – think about it! – got all A*–B. Modern language results especially pleasing – unusually so in a boys' school. Whizzy multi-media centre for langs surely helps. Everyone starts the first year taking two langs and they must do at least one to GCSE. Mandarin now a curricular option and can be taken to A level. 57 per cent who took French got A* and most of the rest got A. All 19 of the Italian takers got A* and German also holds up well here. Most popular A levels are maths, economics, physics, chemistry, geog, history and English. Results pretty breathtaking – 100 per cent A in both Latin and German and as near dammit in Spanish, politics, further maths and chemistry – (astounding, given the numbers). No weak areas. Languages notably popular and successful. Subject choices are trad rather than trendy – no psychology or tourism at Tonbridge – and sports are played not studied.

Mild dyslexia and dyspraxia the likeliest SENs here and boys may be withdrawn once weekly by top-notch SENCo for one-to-one help in developing strategies for self-reliance later on. A few with controlled ADHD or mild ASD might make it through the entry procedure – 'mild' being the key word here. No specific G and T programme but masses of enrichment and stretching across the curriculum and the extracurricular activities – along with setting and streaming in the younger years – will challenge your nascent Isaac Newton.

Staff universally praised, and what struck us when we barged into lessons was the sheer enthusiasm of the teaching. Good library with quiet, workful atmosphere and good stock of books – older and newer – though most boys were typing away rather than turning pages. School up-to-the minute in home-school intra-netting and work, tutors, news all accessible from home PCs or terminals in boarders' rooms, houses etc. Large screens about the school also update everyone on news and activities.

Games, Options, the Arts: If you don't love games before you come here, you will after a week or two: or if you really really won't this is probably not the right school for you. A vast choice of sports. Miles of fabulous pitches tempt the most firmly-couched potato – and various county teams who practise here – and the wonderful sports centre has every imaginable facility – you'd happily pay a couple of grand a year for membership if it was in London. School's new water-based Astroturf used by 2012 potential Olympians.

School offers 20+ sports – lots of choice. The most popular are cricket, rugby, hockey, soccer, tennis and athletics. Teams at all levels means that if your idea of rugger is a gentle chat during a slow canter you won't feel threatened. They don't win everything but they compete fiercely and give their all. Several individual stars in rugby, fencing, athletics and cricket. CCF is big and there are gentler alternatives – community service being especially strong, popular and useful locally. Boys feel encouraged to use their own initiative to start pet projects and many do.

Famous for music – excellent facilities include two impressive recital rooms and seriously good staff. Art and DT are lively though it would have been nice to see more boy-work around the place. Indeed there is no guiding sense of beauty about the place: each department does its own thing, from history's inspiration to science's expiration. Masses of applied arts and crafts. A knock-out theatre – perhaps the best we've seen – seats 375 and would grace any lively provincial town – a real privilege in a school. Lively music, theatre and arts programmes involve girls from two local schools. Week-long annual arts festival brings in professional companies and artists but also a staff play and school-run productions, exhibitions and concerts.

Tonbridge reaps benefit of being only 35 minutes from Charing Cross yet in unsophisticated setting in which there is an appreciative buzz at so many good things. Outstanding programme of visiting speakers – as good as anything a top London school could lay on – lectures, debates and discussions – to stimulate, challenge and involve.

Background and Atmosphere: Founded in 1553, school moved to its present privileged site in the mid-nineteenth century and the main buildings are splendid, but not opulent, Victorian gothic. School's chapel burnt down in 1988 and its replacement, rededicated in 1995, is huge, simple and dignified. We thought it a great waste of money at the time – cost about £10 million – but it is a place of great beauty and calm, and beyond price. Its massive organ was a vast investment and, on its own, would justify the school's pride in this confident and determined rebuild. Chapel accommodates the whole school three days a week and boys value opportunities to read and speak in such a place. Later school buildings are imaginative and represent the better aspects of twentieth century architecture. Short-term expediency has not dictated building here. DT and the arts especially imaginatively housed in 1996 building. Excellent lecture theatre.

Boarding mostly in solid Victorian houses abutting the playing fields. Younger boys in functional four-bed dorms, older ones in one or two-bed rooms. Nice touches like little TV rooms with tiered carpeted stair-seating and dozens of cushions – great for communal heckling during football matches etc. Healthy eating has taken off in the last two years and food is substantial but sensible – fizzy drinks etc off the menu. Boarders eat in houses – relaxed and homely atmosphere. Fierce house loyalty in general. 'It's an incredibly happy school,' a grateful parent of three happy boys told us.

On a 150 acre site adjacent to Tonbridge's main street, this is an ideal position – private, secluded and in the middle of things at the same time and boys are sensibly allowed into town so no monastic seclusion found elsewhere. The site is beautifully maintained – though some of the boarding still to benefit from the rolling refurbing and we saw some fairly scary carpets and wall-peel here and there. It's all very boy-friendly though and the boys themselves were about as well-turned out as anywhere – in nice grey jackets for the first three years and inoffensive suits for the sixth. A sense of order without repression prevails – evident in a fairly relaxed range of hair-styles but no eyesores or nose-rings. Boys happy with things as they are – don't miss girls as lots of interaction in co-productions etc. 'It's a real boy atmosphere – I just love it,' one alpha male sixth former told us, rather sweetly.

Pastoral Care and Discipline: Little to worry about – the school's culture simply doesn't encourage transgressing. Successful house system seen as crucial to overall care and watchfulness. Lots of male and female staff in each house, close relationships between tutors (half a dozen attached to each house) and tutees, well-structured prefect system and a clear policy on disciplinary matters. Head will test on suspicion of drug misuse but no incidents in recent memory. Boys really value what they have here – 'we don't really like the idea of smoking or drugs,' said one, 'it's something to do with the sports culture and people know it's incredibly bad for you.' Over-18s allowed into pubs for a drink or two but no drink in school. Nowhere is immune to temptations, especially where cash abounds, but it's hard to imagine real problems here. Likewise, little talk of bullying – a sense that boys 'look out for each other' and a real trust in the pastoral system. Especially in the houses. 'The pastoral care is there when you need it but not in your face,' a parent felt. Likewise the disciplinary side – 'it's firm but fair – they're tough when they have to be.'

Perhaps not the best school for boarders from over-the-hills-and-far-away or overseas who want the full-on 100 per cent boarding school experience – and particularly so if they are not dedicated sportsmen. Even loyal parents admit that 'not enough goes on at weekends' and one complained that his boy 'rattles around in the house on Sundays with no-one to talk to – not even the housemaster'. However, school now upping weekend activity programme but makes no claim to provide what, say, Harrow would. 'We're not a weekly boarding school – the culture here is boarding,' says head 'but with so few boys (around a third of boarders) here over the weekends we can't offer what a school with 100 per cent boarding could.'

Pupils and Parents: 90 per cent from the UK. Most – day and boarding pupils – live up to one and a half hours away – this is a very south-east England school. However, some from up north and lots of boarders from overseas – popular in Hong Kong though not yet in Russia. Around ten per cent speak English as a second language – most are fluent. School sensibly separates entrants from the same prep schools into different houses so everyone has to make new friends. Usual problem of sixth form entrants from HK who come to work and can be a bit cliquey – though perhaps less so here than elsewhere. A Tonbridge boy is unpretentious, un-ostentatiously 'can-do' and a thoroughly good chap – often not from a traditional boarding family. Parents are sensible, supportive, appreciative and increasingly now involved – unobtrusively rather than bawling from the touchline. Have their own flourishing arts club. High-achieving Old Boys include Colin Cowdrey, E M Forster, Derek Barton, Frederick Forsyth, Sir Patrick Mayhew, Dr William Rivers (he of WWI fame), Vikram Seth, Sidney Keyes and 'Keane'. A touching plaque commemorates George Austen – Jane's pa – who was second master here.

Entrance: Oversubscribed three to one. Applicants register at start of Year 6 and school report is sought. All candidates seen for non VR-type test – so don't bother with coaching – it won't help! It does, however, mean that applicants from state primaries are not disadvantaged. Conditional offers made thereafter and an acceptance allows you to express a preference for a house. Head reserves a few places for special circumstances or late-comers. Academic scholarship exam happens one month before CE – your bright son's best bet for a means-tested bursary – see below. Recent scare stories about soaring CE required grades are rubbished by head. 'Aim for 65 per cent' Applicants with possible SENs seen at early stage by school's SENCo to aid assessment and develop strategy. Around 15 taken into the sixth – minimum of six Bs at GCSE required but 'minimum' means you'd be better off with a clutch of As.

Exit: Virtually no-one leaves after GCSE. In 2008, 27 went to Oxbridge – around double that apply. In fact, in The Sutton Trust's ranking – based on five years worth – Tonbridge ranked third best boys' boarding school nationally and the best in the South East at getting pupils into the top two. The rest to good universities – London, Durham, Bristol – to read solid subjects – medicine, engineering, accounting, and proper arts/humanities. They go on to be sound citizens who contribute.

Money Matters: Exceptionally well-endowed. Some 22 academic schols awarded to new entrants – 10 per cent but top-uppable on a means-tested basis. Up to 100 per cent remission schols/bursaries – academic or musical – for the deserving but impoverished. 220 boys on some kind of fee remission – 30 have over 80 per cent remission and 15 have 100 per cent remission. Take a careful, serious look.

Remarks: 'It's like a beautifully made watch,' a delighted parent enthused, 'it just works.'

Tormead School

Linked to Tormead School Junior School in the Junior section

27 Cranley Road, Guildford, Surrey, GU1 2JD

• Pupils: 545 girls, all day • Ages: 11-18 • Size of sixth form: 120
• Interdenom • Fees: £11,910 pa • Independent

Tel: 01483 575 101
Fax: 01483 450 592
Email: registrar@tormeadschool.org.uk
Website: www.tormeadschool.org.uk

Head: Since 2010, Mrs Christina Foord MA MPhil PGCE, previously deputy head and head of boarding at St Catherine's, Bramley. Prior to this she taught English and history in a number of schools including The Queen's School, Chester.

Academic matters: One of the high fliers in Surrey (and way beyond). Excellent academic results across a wide range of subjects – 84 per cent of GCSE passes are A*/A with particularly good performances in maths, English, sciences and languages (mostly As). Plenty of scope for choice in languages at both GCSE and A level including Spanish, German, Greek and Mandarin. Art is exceptionally strong here – 98 per cent of GCSE and 100 per cent of A level students attained A*/A; wonderful examples are on display around the school.

Ten GCSEs is usually the maximum allowed. Refreshing to see that risk-taking is also encouraged – pupils who are keen to pursue a subject which may not be their academic forte are still encouraged to follow their dreams. Pupils do not feel unduly under pressure academically ('not as pushy as other schools,' says a parent), and any worries about exams are sensitively handled by the school. Grade sheet system introduced where pupils are marked for effort as well as attainment throughout the school year, so the less academic still get plenty of credit for trying hard and 'you feel on top of how your daughter is really doing,' says a parent.

SEN provision is there for those who need it on an individual basis and no stigma here for anyone having extra help. Some parents feel that those with learning difficulties might struggle with the pace – one parent chose to send one of her daughters who has dyslexia elsewhere.

Games, Options, the Arts: A school known for its gymnasts ('we're hot on gymnastics here,' says one pupil, proudly); there's an excellent complex (one of the newer buildings on site) with sports hall, specialist gymnasts' training hall with sprung floor, strategy area with teachers' rooms leading off and viewing gallery. All sport is played keenly and to a high standard – including hockey, netball, rounders, swimming and tennis. Enthusiastic uptake of a new system of 'development squads' for the keen but less naturally able players. However, 'there should be more fixtures for the B and C teams,' says a parent.

It's a small site and space is at a premium – hockey teams have to practise off site ('It used to take us the whole lesson to get there and back,' says a pupil). Tennis on two on-site all-weather tennis courts but swimming is at the Spectrum Centre in Guildford. Some parents find the sports facilities limited but 'what they do, they do well'. Tormead has sporting success at county level and nationally, especially in swimming, gymnastics biathlon and sports acrobatics – a lack of facilities isn't holding them back.

Big tradition of music – borne out by high number of individual instrument players (325 individual lessons a week), two senior school orchestras, jazz band (which tours Europe biennially), multiple ensembles and choirs. A programme of events throughout the year, including the inter-house music competition in which every girl takes part. Provision for music and drama was lacking in the past, but all this changed with the opening of an all-singing, all-dancing performing arts centre in 2007. Drama teacher described by pupils as excellent – 100 per cent of GCSE students attained A*/A. LAMDA speech and drama awards are a popular extra-curricular option and several girls each year get gold medals.

More extra-curricular opportunities were requested by parents and school responded. Now a huge range of sporting, language, film, art and craft activities – including the more unusual choices of fencing, Japanese, classic movie club, cake decorating, origami and debating (another school success story). Some are selective (mainly the sports and music clubs) but there is something for everyone and there is a palpable 'have a go' attitude. Also D of E Award Scheme (multiple gold awards achieved each year) and community work – three pupils in past four years have received Diana, Princess of Wales awards for service to the community. School is one of only a handful nationally to have been awarded Star status by the British Schools Exploring Society. Pupils also able to participate in World Challenge expeditions, in the past to Costa Rica and Bolivia; next one to China.

Background and Atmosphere: Founded in 1905 and is now a mishmash of old and new tacked onto the original and once lovely Victorian building in relatively small grounds. It feels quite intimate and is divided into four sections, each with its own head reporting to Mrs Foord – junior, lower, upper and sixth form; parents commented on how 'sensible' this arrangement is. New areas of the school are quite impressive, old parts rather dark and confusing – cramped corridors and Hogwarts-style staircases appearing out of nowhere. Daunting names like 'the Maths Corridor' could be a bit off-putting, with apparently endless number of classrooms in dark hallways. New pupils 'get lost all the time', but there is always someone to ask and new, colour coded floorplans help too.

Well-equipped science labs, design and technology room and super textiles room (inspiring stuff going on in there) as well as the impressive art department. Two libraries, one small and intimate and a larger, brighter one, which is used for some lessons, quiet research etc. You might get trampled in the rush at lunchtime – pupils from the junior department as well as the seniors use the refectory; luckily lunchtimes are staggered. IT provision is good with plenty of the latest computers and internet connections. The sixth formers have their own department (revered and envied by the younger girls) and no uniforms in the sixth form either so girls can let their hair down a bit – and they do, but nothing to frighten the horses. The sixth form commonroom fulfils the cool quotient with comfy chairs, kitchen area and stereo system. A family feeling throughout the school. Various socials with the Royal Grammar School boys very popular. Sixth form curriculum includes a joint general studies programme with the RGS boys. Also quite a social life with other Guildford schools via the daily train journeys, but they are 'a nice crowd,' says a parent.

Pastoral Care and Discipline: A strength of the school is its nurturing environment. Various problem-solving options that start with the form tutor. A trained counsellor on hand. System of 'aunts' whereby every new girl has another girl assigned to her to help through the first few weeks. Good career counselling and advice.

Pastoral care programme unanimously praised by parents as being superb – for some parents the deciding factor in choosing the school. Less confident girls undoubtedly benefit from the caring and positive ethos – 'the greatest gift anyone can get is self-confidence,' says the head. Pupils leave the school with good social skills, self-confidence and a dash of worldliness.

Parents 'have no hesitation' in getting in touch with the school on any issues – dealt with swiftly and effectively. PSHE lessons start in the junior department – including moral and social discussions – and, by the time the girls are in the sixth form, debates on, e.g., substance abuse, personal safety, relationships and childcare. Assembly is an important part of the schoolday, and an emphasis on care and respect for others apparent throughout the school. Tough line on all transgressions including smoking, with expulsion for persistent offenders. Drugs possession likely to lead to instant expulsion. Out, too, for persistent misbehaviour. Bullying is tackled head on, with open debate and a school policy drawn up in consultation with pupils – no whitewash here. Pupils and parents are clued up on the reality of bullying – these days via email and text – and report back accordingly to teachers. When it does happen, 'it's stamped on pretty quickly,' says a pupil.

Pupils and Parents: Pupils are a self-confident lot without being arrogant, friendly, and sociable – also pleasingly noisy as they wander from lesson to lesson. Neatly dressed on the whole, hair tied back, although a few customised uniforms in evidence. No ties – pupils requested this through the school council and their pleas were heard.

Parents from a mix of backgrounds – old girls, first time buyers, professionals, with a wide catchment of the Surrey stockbroker belt from Esher to Haslemere. Excellent coach service takes the hassle out of the school run.

Entrance: Entrance exam at 11 – pupils selected on the basis of academic potential (reasoning, maths and English tests), extra-curricular interests and current school reference. No interview apart from for those applying for scholarships. Places are very competitive as junior department girls get priority – 95 per cent of the juniors sit the entrance exam and go on to the senior school. Only the cream of students from other schools get the remainder of places – main feeders are: Rydes Hill, Rowan, St Hilary's Godalming and Halstead. 'You wouldn't want to scrape in,' commented a parent. Sixth form entrance requirement described by the school as 'modest': seven GCSEs, A*–C with a minimum of four Bs in the subjects to be studied (Tormead students usually far exceed these requirements). Girls entering the sixth form from other schools will also be interviewed.

Exit: Majority of girls stays on for sixth form – on average less than a quarter of students go elsewhere. About eight a year to Oxbridge, other popular university choices Nottingham, Exeter, Durham, Leeds, Birmingham, Cardiff, Bristol, Imperial, University College, London, also various medical schools. Recent places at London College of Fashion and Wimbledon Art School a testament to high standard of art.

Money Matters: Several parents remarked on the 'good value' represented by the school. Five each of academic, music and art scholarships, worth up to a third of the tuition fees. Scholarships are also available for sixth form entrance.

Remarks: High standards, superb academic results and commendably keen to winkle out any sparks of talent elsewhere – whether it's art, sport, drama, music. Not the ideal place for girls who are bookish without any other strings to their bow, or for the rebel who may find it hard to toe the line (although the all-embracing approach might just win them over).

Torquay Boys' Grammar School

Shiphay Manor Drive, Torquay, Devon, TQ2 7EL

• Pupils: 1,050 boys • Ages: 11-18 • Size of sixth form: 300 • Non-denom • State

Tel: 01803 615 501
Fax: 01803 614 613
Email: enquiries@tbgs.torbay.sch.uk
Website: www.tbgs.co.uk

Head: Since 1987, Mr Roy E Pike BA BEd FRSA (fifties). Progressed from head of history at old Torquay Boys' Grammar School to deputy head when school moved to present site in 1983 until appointed head four years later. Energetic, dedicated and personable. Parents cannot sing his praises enough – see him as 'the heart of the school' and say that 'his experience and clarity have been crucial for the school's success.' Not one to rest on his laurels but clearly revels in school's achievements. Totally effective at publicising school locally and in recruiting excellent staff. Visionary head who has raised TBGS to top rank of state grammars. Stickler for detail and exacts highest standards. Boys say 'he knows everything that's going on' and respect him hugely. Has had number of staff move to headships elsewhere and has a healthy regard for staff development. Likes to unwind on his smallholding in the country with his family. Married with six children. Both boys have gone through the school. Will be quite an act to follow when time comes.

Academic matters: Over seventy per cent A*–B grades at A level and A*/A at GCSE. Maths, English and science have all scored extremely well. Interesting choices abound at A level. 22 subjects on offer including some taught to mixed classes with girls from neighbouring Torquay Grammar School for Girls – optimises available resources and a good way of mixing. Fortnightly timetable gives more flexibility and allows for one hour lessons. Boys encouraged to take AS critical thinking; A level RE is also popular across the board (course focuses on philosophy and ethics). History is rated highly by parents. Number of further mathematicians indicates strength of the subject – 'fabulous' teaching said one parent – noteworthy successes in national maths challenge (made top one per cent and has represented UK internationally). IT suites in each department and no shortage of interactive smartboards. Aspiring medics given lessons looking at ethical issues.

Former school policy of two compulsory languages to GCSE recognised as counter-productive and now option approach is generating far better take-up. At a time when MFL are suffering a decline nationally TBGS is offering Spanish, French, German, Japanese and Chinese. Spanish and Chinese are emerging as front runners. Amazing range of exchanges, visits, links (including one with Jiaxing university in China), work experience abroad etc. Joint winners of Spanish embassy's school of the year award. Spanish head of department is taking Chinese herself and reported that it is 'very challenging' but that 'boys are picking it up remarkably well'. School's second specialism is in business and enterprise sponsored by HSBC. Boys meet for lessons in 'wow factor' boardroom atmosphere with 25 computers with dual flat screens 'churning out economic information.' Reuters link enables boys to simulate city financial dealing. HOD (ex-London independents) wanted TBGS boys 'to have a taste of what is second nature for many in London area.' Boys in Year 9 get an introductory lesson per week.

Recently became an academy in partnership with three other leading grammar schools in South (Bournemouth, Colyton and Poole). As school has increased in size, head has created two new houses enabling class sizes to be reduced to 25 in lower school. Library is well stocked: a good place for boys to work during free periods. Set to become learning resources centre in next revamp. Now also an IB school; first cohort (30 boys and girls) started the programme in September 2009.

Panel for individual needs for pupils who are dyslexic or have problems with numeracy etc. Opportunities galore for gifted and able.

Games, Options, the Arts: Dedicated staff, talented athletes and good facilities provide recipe for success. Boys all get two hours of games and one hour of PE each week. Matches are generally played on Wednesday afternoons or after school. Reputed to be a football school but also has strong tradition in swimming and water-polo. Rugby, soccer, cross-country, hockey, athletics, cricket and tennis (full time coach). Every sport has regional or county championship teams and all four Torbay Hockey Club teams are stuffed with students from here. When we visited, U16 team had just become national football champions – no mean feat. Fifty boys in Year 10 take sports leaders award. Astroturf shared with TGGS next door plus new half size one. Sports hall large enough for three basketball courts. Boys pay £10 a year to enjoy benefits of heavily used fitness suite. Ten Tors (school holds 45 mile record time) and D of E Gold Award plus demanding Three Peaks Challenge and World Challenge expeditions. All students are treated to potholing, canoeing, rock-climbing, orienteering plus special rates with local sailing club for all.

Lots of visits further afield: economics conference in Paris, twenty-seven art students going to Barcelona and A level biologists spending ten days in Costa Rica. Strong house system includes novel ways of charity fundraising. Music is especially strong with whole range of activities from trad to modern. New block includes five individual practice rooms. Over thirty boys play in wind band and a dozen or so in strings orchestra. Twenty strong jazz band recently played at Montreux Jazz Festival. Director of music forms ad hoc orchestra for one-off events. School choir for all ages plus full scale musical each year at end of spring term. Individual successes include national youth choir and distinctions in grade 8 music exams. Boys often make Devon orchestra.

Drama has benefited from new theatre in addition to well equipped studio. Number of productions set to increase with new theatre; GCSE well established and A level in pipeline; lots of co-operation with TGGS. Lively media studies department – film making, local radio, podcasts, blogs etc; excellent school intranet is kept up to date by students. Innovative art department involves upward of 30 boys in each sixth form year – includes digital design and sculpture work. Will benefit from relocation to Manor. DT staff also enthusiastic and workshop area well resourced with CADCAM suite and latest production software to capitalise on boys' creative designs and ideas.

Whole range of clubs and activities at lunchtimes and after school; local ATC has HQ on site – some boys belong to this or in larger numbers to school's own scout troop. 250 participate in house chess championship and top players go on to win at national and international level. School has a 19-inch Newtonian telescope, one of the largest in the south-west; members of the after-school astronomy club undertake deep sky photography and video imaging of the moon and planets. Not surprisingly, the school's patron is famous astronomer, Sir Patrick Moore, and Chris Lintott, 'Sky at Night' presenter, is a past pupil. Dartmoor society extremely active. List is endless.

Background and Atmosphere: A fine site of 40 acres situated 15 minutes above Torquay town centre. School benefited from former grant maintained status and continues to be successful at attracting investment. Sixty classrooms well arranged in different subject areas. Entrance foyer juxtaposes past glories and present day achievements. Purposeful atmosphere and dedicated teachers (parents testify to this). Works closely with neighbouring Torquay Community College to help raise standards and academic aspiration of pupils. New plans will see the refurbishment of the Manor as an art centre allowing further expansion of science laboratories and a resource area for maths. Head believes that keeping things constantly on the move raises morale generally.

Pupils rave about the food. School's nutrition action group (including community dietician, school nurse, parents and pupils) recently won award for promotion of healthy eating; 'boys only get chips once a year,' said chef, but at least one mum thought boys should still be allowed doughnuts 'which they loved' as a treat. Good value. Newly branded 'bistro' operates in former school hall.

Pastoral Care and Discipline: Evident respect between pupils and teachers. Consultative approach to rules. Participatory and co-operative culture among pupils. Bullying dealt with sensitively – where possible would try to turn the bully around; instant punishment is not preferred route. Strong house system through school with seniors encouraged to take leadership roles. Year 13 boys mentor Years 7–9. Active school council: junior and senior sections meet regularly to voice boys' ideas – recent successes have included the new Astroturf. Parents approve of school's hard line on drugs etc and praise work of heads of houses. Appearance is mainly tidy without being rigid. Uniform cards operate if things get too sloppy. No stone left unturned.

Pupils and Parents: Parents come from a large area stretching from Plymouth across to Exeter; many move to be near school. Recent establishment of Metereological Office in Exeter has brought fresh influx of professional families. Notable past pupils too numerous to mention but include Chris Read (Nottinghamshire captain and former England wicket keeper), former Wimbledon tennis player, Mike Sangster, newspaper mogul Sir Ray Tindle, Marcus Bateman (world champion rower) and six times British swimming champion Malcolm Windeatt; Professors Simon Whittaker (St John's, Oxford) and David Southwood, Director of Science at the European Space Agency. One former languages graduate, Marcus Richardson, now fluent in Serbo-Croat, became interpreter at the War Crimes Tribunal at The Hague, and Tom Ewing is one of the UK's top fund managers. Chris Lintott, old boy and Cambridge astronomer, works alongside Patrick Moore.

Not much ethnic diversity but school has grown links with a school in London through the Beacon initiative. As long as they have the ability, all types of boys excel here, from slightly-built budding masterminds to burly rugby types. Student of the week award recognises every conceivable kind of achievement. Younger pupils seem relaxed and happy, while older ones are extremely polite and incredibly mature. All seem modestly proud to be here. 'Phenomenal,' say parents. One father had turned down a job elsewhere to keep his son at TBGS. No regrets.

Entrance: 'Not super selective,' insists head. Takes from up to 70 primary schools, with some coming in at 13 and some at sixth form. Exam includes NFER verbal reasoning, plus maths and English set by the school. Candidates have to pass at least two of the three elements. Numbers have risen from 750 to 1,000+ in last five years; head trying to resist further expansion. Boys not admitted to sixth form with fewer than six GCSE successes at B or above.

Exit: More than 95 per cent to university including a dozen to Oxbridge. Other preferences are Cardiff, Bristol, Bath, Southampton. Medicine is popular as is science, followed by maths, law, business and sports studies. Various scholarships and awards.

Remarks: Achieves fantastic results compared with far more selective schools. Produces career-driven, well-presented boys who work hard and play hard. Amazing that Torquay should be able to boast a school of this calibre.

Torquay Girls' Grammar School

30 Shiphay Lane, Torquay, Devon, TQ2 7DY

• Pupils: 870 girls • Ages: 11-18 • Size of sixth form: 270 • Non-denom • State

Tel: 01803 613 215
Fax: 01803 616 724
Email: admin@tggs.torbay.sch.uk
Website: www.tggs.torbay.sch.uk

Headmaster: Since 2007, Dr Nicholas Smith MB BS PGCE NPQH (early forties) practised medicine for only two years before realising where his true vocation lay. Worked as a keeper of penguins at Regents' Park Zoo – great for a teaching career, before completing PGCE course at London Institute. Taught biology and science in London before moving to South West where he climbed promotion ladder rapidly, ending up as deputy at Devonport High for three years before appointment at TGGS. Early indications are that he is rattling enough cages to move school onward and upward. Hands-on, modest and a good listener – 'more involved,' say girls who rate his assemblies and like his approach. Parents say that he is 'extremely personable' and 'quietly confident'. Married (wife is a teacher) with two children at school in Cornwall. Previously a keen marathon runner we were informed – he'll need that skill to go the distance here and raise TGGS to 'the next level' as he intends.

Academic matters: The last three years have seen significant improvements in exam results with 68% A*/A grades at GCSE and 78 A*/A/B grades at A level in 2010. This places the school amongst the top performing schools nationally. Over 22 subjects offered at A level (a handful in tandem with TBGS). Specialist humanities college with geography the flagship subject. Rigorous assessment procedures through out the school are bearing fruit. Parents are hopeful the girls will be stretched without sacrificing the happy atmosphere which they enjoy. The school has recently joined a Trust with seven high performing south coast grammar schools including Torquay Boys and Colyton to further improve their teaching of bright students. Year 12 students take four AS levels. Huge numbers take biology through to A2 level with psychology another firm favourite: three groups currently at A level. Parents comment on the 'dedicated staff in English and religious studies departments' which turn in good results. Short course in citizenship gives nearly all girls an early GCSE qualification in Year 9.

Core subjects strong at GCSE but longer than expected 'tail' in foreign languages. Keen linguists participate in exchanges in Nantes and Bavaria. A level French and German results are good. Formally organised clinics in maths where older girls help younger ones at lunch-time. Keen participation for all ages in a range of maths challenges and a clutch of further mathematicians at A level. Main school classes number thirty girls (fewer in Years 10 and 11) but small groups in sixth form where girls enjoy discussion based approach. Fortnightly timetable with most lessons 55 minutes; double lessons where needed for practical subjects. Time for movement between lessons no longer such an issue now girls have stopped commuting to and from far flung Manor building.

Media studies suite (with high tech editing facility) for sixth formers and substantial improvements to ICT provision (including 100 new PCs) have plugged gap spotted previously by Ofsted. Classrooms kitted out with latest technology including some fixed head data projectors. We were impressed by competent exploitation of VLE (virtual learning environment) software in a geography lesson. Success in AS critical thinking and extent to which sixth form girls have contributed through community studies have prompted TGGS to be first Torbay school to embrace new British Baccalaureate. School has ditched initiative to make more radical move to IB with TBGS on grounds it is too costly and not suited to the many girls who prefer wider choices offered by A level.

SENCo is a psychology teacher: learning support is delivered by LSAs (recently received SEN training). There are 90 students on the SEN register with a range of needs some of which are complex learning and physical difficulties. Lots of girls qualify as 'gifted and able' and head is keen to provide better for their needs.

Games, Options, the Arts: Own Astroturf (plus second shared with TBGS) providing all-weather facility for range of outdoor sports. Head sees sports hall as next major project. Broad programme of fitness/sport available for girls to find out what's right for them. Lots of participation in team games with fixtures at all levels both after and during school lessons. Girls arranged into four vertical houses for sports and activities with some keen rivalry. County representation in hockey, tennis and netball; a few girls reach national level in a range of sports – currently in swimming, judo and archery. Use of nearby facilities includes English Riviera Fitness Suite for squash and swimming.

Music and drama boosted considerably by new facilities and theatre studies is progressing from GCSE to A level standard. Fifty junior girls now participate in drama clubs and more productions are planned. Choirs, school orchestra, flute and jazz bands perform at West of England festivals and special school events and also help raise money for charities such as Devon Air Ambulance.

Clubs and activities include Dartmoor Society with keen participation in Ten Tors challenge and D of E both led by dedicated sports staff. Body combat and aerobics have proved popular activities for sixth formers. School's work experience initiatives have won awards – Years 7 and 8 go on industry days at places such as Paignton Zoo; business enterprise week for all Year 10 girls places them in local businesses and sixth formers compete keenly in Young Enterprise. Co-ordinated approach to HE and careers advice: tutorials and community studies sessions as well as chance for sixth formers to attend popular HE fair at Exeter university plus usual milk round of open days etc. Plenty of trips and visits (to all five continents in 2009/10): annual ski trip; Years 10 and 11 recently toured battlefields of Ypres and the Somme; Year 11 RE students visiting 'Jewish London' and Year 13 girls were hosted by school in Croatia as part of their A level geography course with special interest in Adriatic dolphins (school has now adopted one). School also owns splendid residential centre in Brittany (used for cross-curricular studies) where all Year 7 and 9 girls spend a week with teachers on a rota basis.

Background and Atmosphere: Founded in 1915, school moved to present site in 1939. First four headmistresses (whose names live on in the names of four houses) spanned an impressive sixty years – their photos lend an air of gravitas to the reception area where displays of art, a plasma screen (broadcasting school's intranet information) and other bits and pieces provide an informative focus for visitors. Art deco features and erstwhile shiny white exterior have suffered over years and original buildings cry out for eventual replacement. Long radiating corridors are hardly a feature but we liked the triangular lawns in the centre of the school which give girls a chance to breathe and relax. Main school hall was being used for public examinations when we visited but serves for half school assemblies during week.

School managed to make the most of what it had but has now thankfully added some impressive new buildings designed to bring it into the twenty first century. These upbeat additions include light and airy dining hall – also used for assemblies as well as dance and drama performances. Impressive new music suite with ample space for individual lessons plus recording studio integrated with both classrooms. Girls use Sibelius software and Apple Macs for composition work. Fine new drama studios and greatly heralded sixth form centre (to be funded by sale of Old Manor to TBGS) includes common room with kitchen. Extensive, attractive grounds include expanse of grass shared with the boys' grammar next door – this (and laudable open access to sixth form common rooms in both schools) does a lot for breaking down social barriers whilst leaving the sexes to benefit from totally separate learning environments.

Pastoral Care and Discipline: Strong management team includes deputy with 18+ years of experience at TGGS plus another deputy and two assistant heads – one of them oversees PSHE and work of heads of year who are generally parents' first point of contact. Strong anti-bullying policy; code of behaviour sets out rights and responsibilities for girls. Discipline is 'hardly an issue' say parents. School has done well in healthy school awards and we certainly enjoyed lunch when we visited. Surprisingly high take-up of meals; school also runs breakfast club from 7.30am daily. Active school council and head girl team come up with a lot of bright ideas. School is keen on eco issues and is working to become more sustainable. Sixth formers take mentoring younger girls seriously; qualified counsellor is available two full days a week.

Pupils and Parents: Relaxed and friendly girls who exude natural self-confidence and seem to enjoy their school life. Head wants to place more emphasis on developing leadership skills for seniors and is concerned that girls often undervalue themselves. Senior girls we met loved the place and thought it had served them well. Head girl's team make real impact and organise fund-raising events for charity – a Traidcraft stall is run regularly by senior girls whose other recent initiatives have included painting themselves red for Comic Relief and baking over 600 cakes to sell during annual charity week.

Neat appearance at all levels: navy blue blouses, jumpers (with school logo) and skirts for girls in main school and a smart black and white dress code for sixth formers. Wide social cross-section from Torbay and beyond (e.g. Newton Abbott, Paignton, Teignmouth and Exeter). Most girls stay into sixth where new social and work facilities are a bonus. PTA now strong and organises regular events for the school including quizzes, pamper nights, talent shows, car boot sales etc. Old girls include Professor Tanya Parish – professor of mycobacteriology at Barts and London Queen Mary's School of Medicine, a range of other professionals as well as Rachel Innes-Lumden who won a BAFTA for her documentary series, *The Tower*, and Jane Cox who plays Lisa Dingle in Emmerdale Farm. Siblings follow and parents often move nearer to school to make commuting easier for daughters.

Entrance: Heavily over-subscribed. Became Foundation school in 2002 and a Trust school in 2009. Admission purely ability based and school handles own admissions procedures. Some 120 places available at 11+ on basis of written exam comprising verbal reasoning, maths and English papers in two sessions. No other selective girls' school in area; about 45 girls join sixth form annually from other state schools and some German students also come to study AS or A level English.

Exit: Ninety-five per cent of girls remain for sixth form. Increasingly, girls like to choose universities within relatively easy striking distance of Torbay (e.g. Exeter, Bristol or Bath). Some further afield to Russell group and an impressive average of seven girls annually to Oxbridge.

Remarks: Great to have this choice for bright girls in South Devon and time for TGGS to get a bigger share of the limelight – new head has helped achieve this. Parents optimistic that school is 'set on right course' for future and have high expectations. Definitely one to watch.

Tring Park School for the Performing Arts

Linked to Tring Park School for the Performing Arts Preparatory School in the Junior section

Tring Park, Tring, Hertfordshire, HP23 5LX

- Pupils: 320; 230 girls, 90 boys. Three quarters board. • Ages: 8-19
- Size of sixth form: 135 • Non-denom, but traditionally Christian
- Fees: Day £18,135-£19,710; Boarding £26,505-£28,350 pa • Independent

Tel: 01442 824 255
Fax: 01442 891 069
Email: info@tringpark.com
Website: www.tringpark.com

Principal: Since 2002, Mr Stefan Anderson MA BMus ARCM ARCT (fiftyish). Attended Carleton University, Ottawa, the Royal College of Music and Emmanuel College, Cambridge. Previously director of music at King's Canterbury for seven years and prior to that assistant director of music and organist at Wellington College. The first man – and, we assume, the first Canadian – to be principal of Tring Park. For someone with a background in the most traditional of traditional public schools, he brings a surprisingly light touch, a dash of eccentricity and buckets of enthusiasm to this very special job. 'He's got exactly the right balance,' one parent told us, 'between holding the line on discipline and gaining the trust of the children.' The trad background probably helps keep feet on the ground, order intact and the mundanity of things like GCSE revision cracking on, in a place where the airy fairy is always whispering temptingly from the wings.

Academic matters: Academic work takes up half of each day and 'vocational' work, i.e. dance, drama, music theatre and music, takes up the other half. Given that, and the fact that pupils are selected only for their performing abilities, the academic results are more than creditable. A smaller number of subjects available here than elsewhere – 17 A level options (and several of those are 'vocational' e.g. dance, theatre studies and film studies) and BTEC National Diploma in performing arts. Popular subjects are all the vocational ones plus art and design. Few other subjects get more than a handful of takers at A level. This makes for small classes and a range of decent results mostly in the A–C bracket. French and German on offer but only one can be taken at GCSE. Newish science labs. SEN is big here – a quarter of pupils are dyslexic – something to do with people with aptitudes in drama and musical theatre having a tendency in this direction, apparently. No statemented kids when we visited but 56 at School Action Plus and 34 at School Action. 1.2 full time equivalent learning support staff. No Saturday lessons per se but some extras are bunged onto this spare day, e.g. preparation for RADA exams and Spanish classes.

Games, Options, the Arts: Well, that's what this place is all about – minus the games. We have previously said that 'you simply wouldn't come here if sport matters much to you,' but sport is keenly missed by many, especially by the younger pupils ('but if they have the time or the energy to do sport, after everything the school throws at them, then they're not working hard enough!') a parent insisted. Of course dancers can't afford sports injuries and everyone expends huge energy and develops high-level fitness with the rigours of dance training. Everyone dances, including drama students who may never have done a step before coming here. 'Dance' covers classical ballet, contemporary, tap, jazz, musical theatre, notation and choreography, dance medicine, dance journalism etc etc. The top dancers are a joy to behold. A former pupil, now in Matthew Bourne's Company, was making a film involving 11 Tring students on the day we visited. Lots of rigour, but perhaps not with the hardcore, blood-on-the-toe shoes ferocity you find in the specialist ballet schools? Musical theatre students study acting, voice and speech, singing – and dance. Drama students do all the above plus more extensive theatre training in many technical areas. Energy levels are dizzying – no shrinking or self-consciousness here – everyone gives their all.

There is some confusion over the role of music in the school: while this is a musical place – with over 200 individual music lessons a week and much emphasis on singing and choral music – music in not offered as a specialism in the way it is at the specialist music schools (despite what some school literature suggests). There is no school orchestra (at the moment) and, aside from singing, the standard of music is no higher than at other mainstream independent schools. Everyone takes art to GCSE and a good range of media available. Super, purposeful art studios – not too tidy. Classes in film take in camera technique, story-boarding etc – all very practical and seriously undertaken. Debating society competes against other schools.

Background and Atmosphere: Founded as the Arts Educational School in 1919 in London, Tring Park was bought from the Rothschild family in 1945 to be used as a second location overseen by the same principal. Over the years, the two locations grew apart and in 1994 formally separated. In 2008 the school decided to change its name to Tring Park School for the Performing Arts: a mouthful, but a more accurate and better name. The director of dance, who has been at the school for 25 years, wrote a brilliant article in recent school magazine describing the school when she first arrived: 'Tring was rather like a parallel universe where the strange 'matrons' in white coats ruled the school, and the dormitories were so cold that the girls (we did not have boys until 1992) used to wear all their home clothes over their PJs to keep warm and scrape ice off the inside of the windows to see outside ... and 'hair-washing' featured on the timetable ... '.

The main building is as knock-out and as OTT as its denizens. Few schools can boast an atrium, staircase, wallpapers and ceilings of this quality. We peered through 'the biggest piece of glass in the world' to watch the girls-only chamber choir sing like angels. All this said, the school is in need of more teaching space and a variety of upgrades. We thought we'd seen every possible permutation of temporary classroom until we saw Tring's marquees in the garden. They've been used for the past two and a half years to house overflow dance lessons: we shudder to think what they feel like in mid-January although they are coming down any day as phase one of the new build is completed. The Markova Theatre, seating 170 and built in 1990 when the school was still girls only, would be brilliant in a normal school but feels a bit poky here. What was once a covered swimming pool has been filled in and is now a weird, but wonderfully large, space for singing and dancing. Tring has already received a grant from the DCSF towards an ambitious development plan and the school has planning permission for a three-phase development including studios, a new art block and sixth form study centre and finally a new theatre. Phase I, which consists of five new purpose-built performance studios, is due for completion in October 2010.

Music and movement resounds from room after room. Costumes for the English National Ballet's Nutcracker summer in the hallways, waiting to be unleashed each winter when pupils from the school take part. Only the quiet corridors where the academic lessons take place, the newly expanded library and the conventional uniforms, strictly regulated e.g. no trainers, remind a visitor that this is a real school where coursework, prep and curriculum successfully co-exist with everything else. 'Below stairs' – mostly white-tiled and with narrower corridors – as much in use as the grander areas – for classes, dining, everything. 17 acres of super grounds in which the buildings sit comfortably and lots of huge mature trees make for a very pleasant, established feel. Reach4Dance, the school's outreach programme, offers dance workshops to primary schools in the area, a boys' coaching scheme and other projects.

Pastoral Care and Discipline: You might think that with this amount of general artiness and hyper-activity, discipline would be a real problem here – but it isn't. A sense of self-discipline is palpable as you go around. Everyone seems to understand that, as the head says, 'they can't mess themselves up,' without risking everything they work so hard for. So only a few incidents of smoking and drinking and three exclusions for drugs since Mr Anderson's arrival.

Boarding accommodation variable but some in splendid grand rooms and all is homely and cosy. Upper sixth girls live in Victorian houses down the road – much appreciated until you're ill and have to trek up to the san (bus whisks girls from the house at 7.15am for breakfast in school at 7.30). Upper sixth boys live a short walk from school. San a large, important hub – counselling available as well as a breathing space and a quiet moment for television-assisted recovery. The school feels like a healthful place – very good salad bar, fresh fruit everywhere. If pupils get below a certain weight, they are taken off dance; if they get thinner, they are sent home.

Pupils and Parents: From everywhere. Forty from overseas – in ones and twos, and from some pretty unusual places e.g. Mexico, Egypt, Cayman Islands, UAE and Ukraine. Ten get EAL help. Otherwise from North Yorks to Cornwall. High proportion, of course, from Herts, Bucks and Beds. Girls outnumber boys throughout – 2.6 to 1 – but boys are an important ingredient in the mix and the school is a haven for some boy dancers who may not have met another boy who danced before they came here. Diversity of backgrounds – many first time boarding families, some experienced public schoolers, some new to the whole thing, on full bursaries. Around a fifth from some kind of performing background. What unites these disparate spirits is the common purpose, the commitment and the energy. Eyes sparkle everywhere and everyone smiles. Ex-pupils include Jane Seymour, Thandie Newton, Caroline Quentin, ballet dancer Tyrone Singleton, Amy Nuttall (*Emmerdale*) and Anna Carteret. Current pupils are performing in the West End's *Sound of Music* and *Oliver!*, *Inherit* *the Wind* and *Angelina Ballerina* with the English National Ballet.

Entrance: By audition in your chosen specialism and, for under 16s, a 'very straightforward academic test' used for setting only. Entrants up to age 13 opt for either dance or theatre arts specialisms. In sixth form, theatre arts pupils must choose between musical theatre or drama.

Exit: Recent past students have done everything from read physics at Imperial College to study Film at NYU in the States. A few stars straight into major companies e.g. English National Ballet. Some to university courses in anything from drama to physics. Many to drama or dance schools e.g. Laine Theatre Arts, The Place and the Bristol Old Vic. Some gap years, some to employment. The school is not particularly rigorous about cataloguing leavers' destinations. Tring has recently introduced a 'third year' sixth form, so far only available for dance, but may extend to musical theatre. Last year a half dozen stayed on for this. Straight-talking career guidance ('we're gently realistic with them') and several pupils mentioned that they saw coming here as a 'low risk option': they could pursue their love of performing without jeopardising their academic opportunities.

Money Matters: One third are on 'funding of some kind', but it is a complex mosaic. Forty-one dancers, who enter at 11, 12 or 13, are funded through the government's means-tested Music and Dance Scheme (NB if you are aiming for this pot of funding, it's probably easiest to win for entry at age 11). 37 dancers enter at age 16 on non means-tested DADA scholarships. Some 20 musical theatre and drama pupils received means-tested scholarships given by the school itself. One of the increasing number of schools to charge a higher fee to pupils who enter in the sixth form.

Remarks: No sacrifice on the academic front if you send your young dancer or actor here – they'll get a pretty balanced regime but masses of what they love best.

Trinity School

Shirley Park, Croydon, Surrey, CR9 7AT

• Pupils: 890 boys; all day • Ages: 11-18 • Size of sixth form: 230 • Christian (respectful of other faiths) • Fees: £11,940 pa • Independent

Tel: 020 8656 9541
Fax: 020 8655 0522
Email: jef@trinity.croydon.sch.uk
Website: www.trinity-school.org

Head: Since 2006, Mr Mark Bishop (forties). Educated Charterhouse and St Edmund Hall, Oxford, PPE moving to theology. Previously deputy and acting headmaster for a term at Caterham School. Brisk, frank, easy to talk to and very determined. Parents and prep heads agree that he is friendly, welcoming, knowledgeable about individuals and focused on getting his school right. Took time out to work in business (as a headhunter for senior leaders; good training, he says) before coming to Trinity, and has an MBA from Henley Business School. This background shows in much of what he has done at Trinity and he has a vigorous, business-like approach. The organisation of his impressively thought-through three year development plan is stiff with mission statements, key objectives, detailed plans and mild management jargon – and none the worse for that. Performance management and staff development is the key, he believes, to moving the school forward. He thinks that schools and businesses have much in common in management terms, provided one remembers that 'schools are ultimately about children and not the bottom line'. Trinity, he says, was a good school before he arrived but he is keen to make his mark and says that the place lacked sufficient ambition. This he is anxious to instil in teachers and in boys. He wants staff to share good practice, to reflect on what they do, and to have feedback, including from the boys if they are happy to do so. The school councils (boys) have discussed both teaching and learning and he has offered to video teachers teaching. All this could be quite alarming for those in a comfort zone and anxious to remain there, but one gathers that the staff are enjoying the new wind of change blowing through the place, and squaring their shoulders for the advance into the middle of the 21st century.

But Mark Bishop is not a business automaton. His theological degree led him to prioritise pastoral care in his career and he spent a year in Australia and New Zealand on a Churchill Fellowship studying their approach to pastoral care and moral development. Well, people do say that the moral tone of *Neighbours* is second-to-none. He has spoken at numerous conferences on pastoral care, and now his mission statement at Trinity is 'the rigorous pursuit of excellence balanced by compassionate concern for individuals'. He wants to achieve 'real balance' for his boys, academic ambition coupled with all-round and varied extracurricular experience. Parents all mention how good Trinity is at bringing out individual aptitudes and talents, and every parent surveyed said how happy their sons were at the school. Brothers with very different interests have thrived and, for a day school, the list of clubs and societies, the activities on offer and the opportunities available are impressive.

Academic matters: Trinity's results rank highly in the very competitive atmosphere of south London. Mr Bishop is insistent that Trinity is, and will remain, an all-round school with strong extracurricular emphasis, but this is not to be at the expense of academic excellence. In 2009, 63 per cent As at A Level, 91 per cent A/B, but Bishop still has some particular departmental targets. He has brought in outside inspection, new teachers, and individual development plans to liven up departments. This brisk approach should pay dividends and results will be worth watching in the next few years.

The subjects offered are on the conservative side – a solid sciences/humanities/modern languages mix. But Mandarin and electronics spice up the curriculum to GCSE and A level respectively. Three boys took Chinese at university in recent years and there is a Chinese exchange programme. Impressive photographic successes and facilities enrich a more traditional approach to art and a local artist has taken up residence. Electronics is on offer at A level and modern foreign languages have received a boost with an influx of new blood recently. Theatre studies and classics have enthusiastic followings with Latin taken to A level by a few, and others taking it in addition to their GCSE loading lower down the school. Mr Bishop is keen to introduce Greek as soon as he can and politics also likely in the sixth form.

Most staff teach with their doors open, which is a good sign of their confidence. Their average age is 40 and they are a relatively stable group with 41 having been in the school for more than 10 years. Older classrooms are traditional in layout and in their wood finishes but the new classroom wing is impressive and airy. Class size averages 22 in the first three years, descending to 10 in the sixth form but pressure on numbers is pushing this a little higher (see Entrance below). Electronic whiteboards abound and ICT facilities, language technology and equipment generally are impressive. IT is taught in 'chunky' sessions outside the timetable, to allow for the introduction and practice of new software techniques in sustained session. Boys conduct virtual operations and dissections in the biology labs, and lessons seen were lively and full of interchange between boys and staff. Parents and boys say that relations between pupils and their teachers are respectful but very friendly, with appropriate familiarity as the boys become more mature in the sixth form. Many departments lead days out and trips to support the curriculum, including a recent physics trip to CERN in Geneva (but see the school magazine for the good times had by all). There are a good few women in evidence in this all-boys school, although it would be good to see more in management and a few more on the governing body (the Whitgift Foundation with a Trinity Committee). Some sixth form lessons (General Studies) are taken with girls from Croydon High School, as are some extracurricular activities and trips.

Special needs are handled sensitively with a new SEN head possibly in the offing but Trinity is not the school for any other than those with mild difficulties. Lunchtime clubs support both the less able and the gifted.

Games, Options, the Arts: One of Trinity's greatest strengths is the music. The website and school magazine are stuffed with references to wonderful musical events, such as the junior choir's fully-funded trip to Osaka courtesy of the Huddersfield choir, and other professional appearances at The Royal Opera House and Glyndebourne (as fairies – but make no mistake, these fairies were definitely boys!). There are numerous orchestras, ensembles and choirs. Boys confirm that it is really cool to be a musician at the school. But it is not just for the specialists; music involves all the new boys when they first arrive and one parent commented how impressed he was that his son took up singing as a result of the encouragement he gained from the junior choir at Trinity, when he had only mimed at his previous school. The music school is a modern, dedicated space. Some have ambitions to continue with musical careers, others see it as a fund for enjoyment in their future lives. Over 500 individual music lessons take place weekly, carefully organised not to impact on academic studies too much.

Trinity has numerous theatres and halls, of varying sizes and architectural impact, and drama benefits accordingly. Drama productions at all levels abound, from the junior self-produced efforts to the high standards of the boys of the sixth form. Examples recently include *The Wind in the Willows, Murder in the Cathedral, Oliver!* and involvement in professional productions. There is an impressive TV/video mixing production facility, partly run by an enthusiastic old boy now working in TV in London. PSE is taught through drama, which must be more effective than a classroom approach to bullying, relationships and the other pitfalls of adolescent life that form the curriculum.

Art has a fairly new, purpose-built building in which to spread itself, with exhibition space and generous classroom facilities. Light floods in to some areas but it is disturbingly gloomy in others. Traditional photography produces boys who understand about dark rooms and chemicals and computers are plentiful. The design department has CAD facilities and their stylish work is evident from the school's magazine. Trinity boys are pretty vocationally focused (see below Exit) and this may be why art does not seem to attract the numbers one might see elsewhere, although one parent specifically cited the art dept as the reason her son had chosen Trinity above other local schools. Conversely perhaps, design has a considerable fan club, and extra-curricularly extraordinary Greenpower F-24 cars take their designers and drivers (junior boys who weigh less) to the finals of competitions in this esoteric field of motor racing.

Sport has received a boost through the recruitment of a number of international sportsmen to the staff and there is clearly the intention to raise Trinity's sporting profile amongst the boys and the local opposition. Parents have noticed a considerable increase in expectations of staff in this area since the arrival of the head, and all the senior managers take games sessions. The standard boys' school sports, rugby, hockey and cricket, are augmented by an interesting and wide array of alternatives, including soccer, sailing, and sub-aqua, and water polo in the school's newly refurbished swimming pool in which boys reach top levels nationally.

In addition to these three main areas, there is a host of clubs, societies and activities in which to get involved: Duke of Edinburgh Award, CCF, community service (ecstatic great-grannies at the Christmas party), mountaineering, electronics, dance (the cha-cha, with girls from Croydon High – very useful in the clubs of Croydon) the Hard Sums Club, to name but a few.

The extra-curricular provision at Trinity is overseen by a recently appointed director whose function it is, amongst others, to reconcile conflicting demands of the timetable for individuals.

Background and Atmosphere: Trinity School was founded by John Whitgift at the end of the sixteenth century, as the middle school for Whitgift School. It has branched out on its own now, and occupies a large site in Croydon with generous playing fields augmented by extra pitches half a mile down the road. There is a grass running track, four tennis courts, two Astroturfs and a cricket pitch delightfully positioned outside the school's windows with a pavilion. The buildings are perhaps not the school's greatest asset but, in fact, the white concrete materials, the wide corridors and delightful fountained courtyard are all rather appealing. It is certainly functional rather than beautiful but plenty of green around – grass, trees, shrubs and climbers. Boys opt for the light and airiness of most of Trinity over the more hallowed buildings of other local rivals. Smart new teaching block and plans to refurbish the main assembly hall.

Pastoral Care and Discipline: One of Trinity's main selling points, often reiterated, is its emphasis on pastoral care. Parents make frequent references on how good the school is at responding to individuals. The main emphasis for tutors is individual academic monitoring and boys commend the friendliness of staff and the generally happy atmosphere in the school. One parent commented on how the boys from diverse backgrounds 'all come together; all are equally valued'.

Discipline is firm but explained rather than simply enforced and the impression is of boys being allowed to mature into responsibility rather than of a straightjacket. Uniform is mostly neatly worn on the school campus – black with white shirts and school ties. Attitudes to bullying are clear in the PSE programme and the excellent parents' handbook, and the rule on drugs is that anyone who brings them into the school will be asked to leave.

Pupils and Parents: Trinity School 'never forgets you have a choice', and parents have many schools within reach to choose from, some independent, some good state. The chief reasons for choosing Trinity are its lack of stuffiness ('Trinity is not precious, it does not have delusions of grandeur' said a parent), its happy atmosphere, its relatively wide cultural and social mix, its academic record, its music, its activities ('there is something for everyone, it is very diverse,' another parent). The teachers are praised for their care of individuals and their quality of teaching, and their encouragement of weaker brethren. One parent whose son had previously been at a state primary school thought the day was overlong, including activities, with homework on top, but others were delighted that their sons were being challenged (which is a word Mr Bishop uses a good deal too) and broadened. Many parents comment on the good friends their sons have made at the school and that Trinity boys are nice – 'girls want to date Trinity boys,' said one mother whose son has recently left. Certainly one reason for choosing a school!

Entrance: Entrance exams in verbal reasoning, English and maths, and an interview by which the school sets considerable store, particularly for boys not coming from prep schools. Boys need to be at about level 5 in SATs in most subjects to be sure of a place. They come from local prep and state schools and those who do well in entrance tests are automatically assessed for an academic scholarship. Sixth form scholarships are awarded on the basis of GCSE performance to those entering the school (honorary ones for those already in the school). While boys are being examined the parents have the opportunity to meet the headmaster individually. Boys can come at 10+, 11+, 13+ and 16+ with the majority arriving at 11+.

Exit: Most boys go on to university, usually without taking a gap year. They choose vocationally-orientated subjects in the main, rather than the humanities or modern languages, such as engineering, accountancy and medicine, maths and law. They choose all the universities one might expect, mostly Russell Group; about ten or so get into Oxbridge every year.

Money Matters: Generous bursary fund where help with fees is awarded to parents on a sliding scale. Will always try to help boys on bursaries and scholarships when it comes to expensive trips which augment the curriculum or the extracurriculum and they are often free. Scholarships awarded for academic performance, music, sport, drama, art and design technology.

Remarks: Definitely one to watch if you want a forward-looking, diverse community which puts the individual and his needs first and offers a sufficiently wide range of opportunities to be able to do so. The staff now need to match their pastoral focus to the academic élan to get the school to where Mark Bishop wants it to be.

Truro and Penwith College

College Road, Truro, Cornwall, TR1 3XX

• Pupils: 5000 full time • State

Tel: 01872 267 000
Fax: 01872 267 100
Email: enquiry@truro-penwith.ac.uk
Website: www.trurocollege.ac.uk

Principal: Since 2010, Mr David Walrond MA MBA PGCE. Previously worked at the college for seven years as director of curriculum and quality. Has worked in further education institutions in London, Hampshire and Cheshire and has been an associate Ofsted inspector. Early on in his career he lived and worked in Italy where his work ranged from driving a fork lift truck in a scaffolding warehouse to lecturing in English and linguistics at Padua University and believes that living and working abroad provide invaluable experiences. Recently introduced the Academic Academy which offers additional sporting and academic programmes for talented students. He is a passionate follower of cricket and has a keen interest in classical music and literature.

Mr Walrond believes that the college has a reputation for innovation and initiating change rather than just responding to it. 'Above all we focus on giving students the best possible deal. That has to be the pattern for the future and I'm looking forward to working with all staff and students to take forward the remarkable success story of this college.'

Academic matters: You can research courses on the college's excellent website, written in admirably plain English. International Baccalaureate. Sixty AS/A2s to pick from and you can do them in any combination. 'We are always trying new things. With this range of courses you can definitely find the right ones for you.' Class size 17, though this is likely to be exceeded in faddy subjects like psychology. No small classes in the interest of efficiency and good educational experience. Some 27 National Diplomas on offer, 12 sporting academies and one academic academy. Re-takes in maths and English. Determinedly not deselective at any stage, they say, but the proof of the pudding lies in what they call internal progression – the numbers allowed to stay on from year to year. Figures show that the college does not protect its results by deft weeding. You can fail your AS and still go on to do A2 so long as you failed for a good reason. Considering the amount of roguish stats-mongering that goes on in this sector the college's 9th place in *The Independent* 2009 league tables is all the more admirable, on this count at least, and testifies to its loyalty to the needs of the people of Cornwall.

Wonderfully resourced at every turn, this is the sort of place that would tempt any fee-paying parent to toss their chequebook gratefully aside. Quite simply, state-of-the-art everything down to the underground soundproofed bunker in which rock musicians thrash their stuff. Quiet study rooms liberally scattered where you can hunker down or have an impromptu tutorial with your lecturer.

Close relationships with all local schools so as to manage the transition to this big and potentially (initially) bewildering campus. On starting, they'll set you minimum target grades based on your GCSE results, after which regular monitoring won't let you forget them. National stats show good value-added in A level performance. Special needs provision a matter of pride. In this notably adult environment where students must take responsibility for their own learning, many who chafed in what they felt to be a pestering school setting take wings and fly.

Games, Options, the Arts: Sport a matter of excellence here because of the strength of the sports academies, most of which welcome participation by the student body. 'You'll find the most able sports people in Cornwall here.' What they call Study Plus is your way in to all manner of sporting, creative and recreational activities, some 50 of them. It's a Wednesday afternoon thing and it looks good on your cv. Some courses carry accreditation. Art, music and drama all seriously top notch.

Background and Atmosphere: Architecturally stunning but also humane. Ever expanding (fast but sustained) as HE takes off. The college stands in the western suburbs, well served by buses from everywhere which arrive in wave upon wave. The inspired quality of the building makes sense of the college's mission statement in a way that other colleges' retail park architecture dully doesn't. The feel is that of a university campus (which it now partly is), decidedly adult and also conspicuously friendly. Not a place where you'll feel lost – plasma screens in every building carrying latest info and what's on. It's a buzzy place, everyone looks happy to be here. Ne'er a graffito to be seen – that's what they think of it. Broad range of students of all sorts and ages from the PMLD (profound multiple learning difficulties) group to the growing band of HE students (this is a Plymouth University satellite), bright young things and a sprinkling of grizzled codgers gearing up for a career change. Almost all daytime students are 16–18 year olds. Student satisfaction surveys posted visibly and you can see why. There's less close monitoring than you get in some schools, of course, but doing your A levels here has to make the transition to university easier. Parents universally report satisfaction with the way their sons and daughters were looked after but there's a caveat: only if you can hack this level of responsibility.

Pastoral Care and Discipline: Your little world within the big world is your 15 strong tutor group; your tutor is someone who teaches you. Parents' evenings, termly report, instant tip-off in case of bunking off. Student services helpdesks where you can bring worries about everything from a lost bus pass to HE guidance. Counselling for graver problems. 'If you need help at any time,' says a student, 'they're really open and I've found they really put themselves out for you. As far as the work goes, I think they've been quite strict at keeping me on track.'

Pupils and Parents: They come from all over the county. Not ethnically mixed, as isn't Cornwall. Just a few from abroad.

Entrance: Interview at which you get to discuss and choose courses best suited to you. For A levels you'll need five GCSEs at C to get in; for the IB, As or Bs for those areas you want to study.

Exit: Twenty a year to Oxbridge and around a thousand to other universities. Or you can stay on here and do an honours degree (small selection) or one of a growing number of vocational foundation degrees.

Money Matters: Pay for your meals and transport. Tuition and textbooks are free.

Remarks: A really inclusive place where you can come with nothing and leave with a degree. Wonderful opportunities in all zones. A level and IB students the majority. People here are more important than glittering statistics – hence, probably, the glittering statistics. That's a win-win.

Truro High School

Linked to Truro High School Preparatory Department in the Junior section

Falmouth Road, Truro, Cornwall, TR1 2HU

• Pupils: 305 girls (40 board) • Ages: 11-19 • Size of sixth form: 60 • C of E
• Fees: Day £6,435-£10,320; Boarding £18,717-£19,617 pa • Independent

Tel: 01872 272 830
Fax: 01872 279 393
Email: admin@trurohigh.co.uk
Website: www.trurohigh.co.uk

Headmistress: Since April 2009, Mrs Caroline Pascoe BSc MSc PGCE NPQH (forties). Educated at Tiverton Grammar before reading microbiology at Bristol then opted for a PGCE in physics and science at Roehampton. Completed her MSc in educational leadership at Leicester and followed this with study for a doctorate in education at Exeter. Has also fitted in useful qualifications in youth training and mountain leadership. Began career teaching physics at a Twickenham girls' secondary school before moving to Elliot School, Putney as HoD (whilst there she rowed for GB at the Barcelona Olympics – a finalist in the women's VIIIs). A spell as head of science at Ibstock Place School was followed by six years running her own trekking and climbing business in India: founded Burua School for poor 'hill' children (now 140 strong) and climbed three unnamed peaks in Ladakh. Came to Truro from Wellington School in Somerset where she had been a successful deputy for five years.

Mrs Pascoe whirled into Truro High not a moment too soon. Girls think she's great and it's clear that she means to carry on as she's started: leading from the front. Married to Brian whose work commitments now limit his involvement in the boarding house. Son, Kiran, is at Truro School. A boarding dad said that his daughters 'like seeing the head in a family mode away from her office responsibilities'. Extra-curricular opportunities for boarders 'have increased greatly,' he added. In addition to headship duties and running boarding (numbers at long last on the up), Mrs Pascoe teaches science to two out of three year seven groups and recently led expedition from school to climb in the Himalayas and help at Burua. Plans to row Cornish gigs across to the mainland from the Scillies as a fund-raiser in summer 2011. Loves what she's doing, exudes purposefulness and trumpets girls' achievements.

Academic matters: Recent results show 65 per cent A*–B at A level and 60 per cent A*/A at GCSE. Head believes in value of the A2 extended project which now overlaps lower and upper sixth years thus avoiding clash with summer AS papers. 21 subjects on offer in the sixth: maths and chemistry very strong (all girls take separate sciences at GCSE plus a large number take additional maths). English consistently good at both A level and GCSE. Latin holds up very well at GCSE and is still there at A level (even Greek exisits as a twilight subject as do astronomy and geology). Difficult to make direct comparisons with competitors when class sizes are so small but the 'long tail' in a number of A level subjects suggests that some girls are pushing the limits of their academic comfort zone.

Teachers are committed to getting the best out of every pupil – and the small class sizes allow miracles to happen. We noticed how the girls don't hold back in giving their views: no fear of censure by male peers here. We enjoyed watching a Year 10 group locked in discussion in their religious philosophy and ethics lesson (compulsory to GCSE with great results). The teaching we saw was enthusiastically delivered and thorough.

Classroom accommodation is generally refurbished, some smartboards and sufficient computers without being a cyberdrome. Some exteriors are short on aesthetic appeal but generally the site works well; juniors, boarders and sports facilities all within easy reach. We were particularly impressed at sixth form level where the atmosphere was relaxed but academically rigorous. Some groups would be considered unviable elsewhere but girls see the sometimes 1:1 ratio in the sixth as a big plus. Just one girl was taking A2 textiles but she certainly wasn't complaining and her work was top standard (as was the teaching room). Parents think their daughters have improved academically by leaps and bounds since joining the school.

Learning support is free on a one-to-one basis for an hour weekly in any girl's first two years. Experienced and well qualified staff; friendly ed psych called in to observe and test as required. Roughly thirty girls currently require support. Sessions are timetabled carefully to minimise losing ground in key subjects; extra help before and after school as well as at lunchtimes. EAL help as required for overseas pupils. Staff have been made increasingly aware of special needs issues. Over sixty enrichment activities – from study trips through digital animation competitions to work experience and a chemistry camp.

Games, Options, the Arts: School punches above its weight in most sports. Staff include top flight hockey and netball players, school is rightly proud of its reputation for sporting success (two Year 11 girls representing England – netball and high jump plus Welsh fencer and two top national pentathletes). School defended seven county team titles in 2010, twenty-five girls represent county and nine play either hockey or netball for West of England. Increasingly popular girls' football and tag rugby now included in broader sports spectrum. Around fifty per cent of Years 7–9 attend extra-curricular sports practices, fewer in higher years. 25 metre heated indoor swimming pool is well used (open some evenings for boarders). Full sized Astroturf, extensive playing field and two good netball/3 tennis courts provide ample outdoor sports facilities. Head's current wish list is topped by sports hall to transform indoor PE provision. Double award GCSE on offer for top athletes.

Music is joint top dog here with loads playing instruments and singing – we watched a lunchtime choir rehearsal with 140+ girls. Carried off main choral accolade at recent Cornish music festival. School orchestra is fifty strong and rehearses after school. School acts as centre for its own diploma candidates, many play in Cornwall youth orchestra. A few have played in national groups and some proceed to music colleges. Director of music regularly leads tours abroad with girls, staff and parents – Belgium and Hong Kong in 2010–11. She is a tower of strength and encourages budding talent where she sees it – even writes parts for beginners to be able to play in the orchestra.

Not much in the way of co-ed collaboration apart from annual concert bash with Truro School. Performing arts centre provides an alternative indoor space to the main hall. Sixth form lesson we saw in Agutter drama studio was quite edgy: 'helps girls to find themselves,' said talented HoD. Lots of performances including major annual production ('Scrooge' in 2010). Strong art department sends plenty of girls to prestigious Falmouth foundation course; experienced, male HoD predates school's ownership of the studios; Kensey group formed to provide exhibition opportunities for former students; technician a well qualified illustrator. Charity fashion show organised by girls who also went to the NEC for Clothes Show Live. Seventy girls involved in D of E – sixteen at gold level. Recent trip to India included community project at Burua school and twelve day trek in the Himalayas (including 5000 metre Bhaba pass) plus some sightseeing. School's first ever team in 2010 Ten Tors challenge on Dartmoor – two teams in 2011. Foreign exchanges, work experience for AS French students as 'mini assistantes', choir trips and loads of excursions at all levels to broaden horizons beyond the peninsular (recent destinations include The Scillies, Malta and Greece). Girls are keen on debating and participate in competitions organised by the ESU and the Cambridge Union. Large numbers take LAMDA qualifications and take part in Rotary public speaking competitions.

Background and Atmosphere: Founded in 1880 by Bishop (later Archbishop) Benson (first Master of Wellington College) who built Truro cathedral and gave Henry James the idea for 'The Turn of the Screw'. School motto: Luce Magistra (With light as my teacher) has been stridently transposed into 'Girls First' as its modern logo. Not very churchy despite its origins and we couldn't see why girls who love music wouldn't want to sing hymns in their assemblies. Friendliness between staff and pupils is tangible though school's earlier grammar school incarnation haunts corridors and honours boards. Original school building is relatively small and lies closer to the city centre than its main competitor. From the befittingly Cornish granite (partly castellated) entrance we proceeded towards what is otherwise a hodge podge of buildings stretching back and across a deceptively large site (which includes the useful, if somewhat tired, remnants of a former girls' secondary school) and up the hill to sports pitches. Cross-country can be fitted in without leaving the site we were told. Some building replacement has already happened and super new modern languages suite has shown what can be realised on this site. Ten year development plan to rationalise the rest.

Highly experienced staff includes significant male teachers and some young blood but high property prices 'make it difficult to recruit newly qualified teachers,' says head. Main hall doubles as a gym space but not used for dining (there's a pleasant and spacious refectory which provides yummy lunches for day girls plus breakfast and supper for boarders). Well stocked library (33,000 volumes plus networked pcs) at heart of school is a welcome haven for private research and study – one girl we spoke to with three noisy siblings at home said she preferred to work there after school. Recent authors visiting have included Cornish children's novelist, Ann Kelley.

Sixth formers have their own recessed study area in addition to individual carrels in their own centre: not ritzy but sensibly planned to allow for leisure or study. Separate boarding houses: Dalvenie for girls in the prep through to Year 8 and Rashleigh for girls in Year 9–13. Links with Scillies now include offering boarding accommodation to islanders studying at Truro College – 'great PR and a valuable service,' said one islander we spoke to. Both houses offer refurbished accommodation with loads of ensuites plus comfy sitting rooms with all the gizmos. They also interconnect with the dining room so no getting wet on the way to brekky. Actually, there is no brekky on Sundays – girls have opted for lie-ins and inhouse brunch instead. Yawn.

Pastoral Care and Discipline: Relatively small numbers mean that pastoral deputy has direct leadership of the form tutors who move up with their groups within an overall 'care plan' approach: tutors deliver the PSHE scheme of work and combine pastoral and disciplinarian rôles. Robust anti-bullying policy operates at all levels. Sixth formers (allocated to girls in Years 7–9) receiving mentoring training for scheme they call CHAT from Red Cross and the Samaritans. School has been at forefront of National Healthy School Programme with fresh air, healthy food, PSHE and general well-being championed alongside well honed substance education policy. 'Bonding' residential weekend held at beginning of year seven for staff and girls at the Penzance or Fowey youth hostel. Everyone here is very accommodating and friendly so individuality can blossom. Discipline problems are rare. Mobile phones were banned under a previous head and no-one seems to mind.

Pupils and Parents: Girls we met were fun and loyal: 'every teacher knows who we are,' they beamed. Self confident girls who communicated with us readily and happily. Appearance (Balmoral tartan skirts and green pullovers up to Year 11) is neat but not in a stiff and starchy way. Sixth formers take the dress code sensibly and are somewhat difficult to differentiate from staff. Middle-of-the-roaders do particularly well here. The hoped for increase in sixth form numbers would help lift things even more. Head is working at bringing parents and old girls into closer working partnership to support school. Old girls include Dame Lynne Brindley (CEO of British Library), TV presenter Hannah Sandling and mezzo soprano Anna Burford.

Entrance: Mainly from own prep plus Polwhele House, Roselyon, St Piran's, Bolitho and Truro prep. Good sprinkling from state primaries – particularly in Truro. Boarding numbers are finally on increase: majority from UK (some come from Scillies), fifteen currently from overseas. Good rail link to Paddington and air (from Newquay) to Gatwick. Applicants for senior school invited to spend a day with appropriate year group then usual round of exam and interview before admission. For sixth form entry, GCSE grade A*/A looked for in proposed A level choices plus interviews for UK candidates (test papers and school assessments for overseas).

Exit: Some (probably too many in recent years) leave at 16 to go to (free) Truro College up the road, Truro School or co-ed boarding elsewhere. Those who leave appear to do so as a change from what they've known since they can remember, rather than as a negative reaction. Art foundation at Falmouth, medicine at Bristol and Cardiff plus wide range of other courses and destinations beyond the Tamar (including two on average each year to Oxbridge).

Money Matters: Full range of scholarships (academic, music, sports,art) and means-tested bursaries at year seven entry and into sixth form. Boarding (all-rounders') scholarships at 13. Extra bursaries occasionally for those suffering from special or temporary pecuniary hardship. Maximum fifty per cent remission of fees.

Remarks: Flying the flag for girls' education in Cornwall. Look beyond the exterior for a Cornish treasure that performs beyond expectations. Under its inspiring head looks set to raise its game across the board. 'Small, family school with lovely relationships,' say parents. A 'must visit' for those seeking an academically challenging yet emotionally nurturing environment for their daughters.

Truro School

Linked to Truro School Prep in the Junior section

Trennick Lane, Truro, Cornwall, TR1 1TH

• Pupils: 850 boys and girls • Ages: 11-18 • Size of sixth form: 250
• Methodist foundation • Fees: Day £10,770-£11,115; Boarding £18,195-£20,595 pa • Independent

Tel: 01872 272 763
Fax: 01872 223 431
Email: jeg@truroschool.com
Website: www.truroschool.com

Headmaster: Since 2001, Mr Paul Smith MA MEd (fifties). Educated at Aylesbury Grammar and Cambridge. Rugby blue, played cricket for the university. Geographer. Taught at Royal Grammar School, Worcester and St John's, Leatherhead before winning the headship of Oswestry School in Shropshire. Far nicer in real life than his photo on the website, definitely not one of those heads who plays high status and freezes the blood. Very much at ease with both himself and this school, which he truly embodies. Warm, agreeable, funny, he clearly thoroughly enjoys being here. Parents and pupils like him a lot. Teaches a spot of geog to the youngsters and retains a keen roving eye for balls chased by chaps with muddy knees. Married to Kathy, who coaches cross-country runners, does a bit of one-to-one maths and supervises the entertaining of visiting VIPs like us. Two daughters.

Academic matters: Mr Smith describes the school as 'Cornwall's grammar school' and this accurately describes the down to earth, meritocratic feel of the place. It's cool to work hard, it's a busy little campus and you can easily see that there's a whole lot of achieving going on. If you haven't done your homework, your fellows will ask you disdainfully, 'Oh? Why not?' For most parents, results are not at all the be all and end all – you don't live in Cornwall to adopt an exclusive focus unless it's for surfing or painting. They want good stats, oh sure, but they also want everything else, all the extra-curricular stuff. The word most apply to the desired end product is 'rounded' by which they mean enriched rather than supersized.

But, yes, results are good across the board. We could find no weak areas, just the odd misfiring teacher (well, everywhere has some of those). Science and maths, though, are particularly strong and popular, with a good many going on to be medics, engineers and – a quirk of this school – geologists (it's an old tin mining thing). Pupils speak very approvingly of the staff and a notable feature is the collaborative way teachers work with the boys and girls – you can watch for yourself as you go around. Relationships are informal, personal and mutually respectful, you can see how it brings out the best, which is why one pupil told us 'no way do they let you get away with being cheeky.' It's all rather grown-up, even more so in the sixth form where uniform yields to smart business suits, a move which has goaded some of the tattier teachers hurriedly to get their sartorial act together.

The curriculum is recognisable to any parent of a certain age – bog or gold standard, whichever you will – the core academic subjects unleavened by anything faddish or vocational. There's theatre studies, a strong department, and art, of course, superbly taught. And there's design technology taught in a proper workshop by proper teachers with oil under their fingernails and machines that make proper things out of proper materials. You get the feeling you could knock up a pretty handy railway carriage in a month of lunchtime sessions. This being Cornwall, they like to make (you guessed it) boats, but they've built an aeroplane – oh, and flown it, too.

Special needs catered for only if your reading is good enough to pass the entry exam – which doesn't leave a lot of room for special needs. A lesson a week for those who need tweaking but, understandably, there's not a lot of call. Gifted and talented programme for the 25 per cent who need it. For sixth formers needing to be taken through a puzzling topic once more, there are drop-in clinics offered by all departments on Wednesday afternoons. Critical Thinking and EPQ also on offer.

It's a buyer's market down here, with the superb FE college up the road offering unbelievable facilities, all the courses you could ever want in any combination and, above all, that chimerical thing they call freedurm. The temptation to take a two-year fees holiday post-GCSE and put together a stash for university must be strong but parents and pupils stay loyal to the school in droves. Great effort has been made to make the sixth form different, interesting and fun. There are enrichment activities you'd expect, like Young Enterprise, and there's a local initiative, ACHE (advice, care, help and empathy), which trains pupils as listeners (think Samaritans), who then make themselves available to their younger fellows. Very nice café where they can buy healthy snacks and natter and a newly refurbished sixth form centre (opened September 2009). New dining room too, with a separate staff and sixth form seating area which has transformed the old heart of the school.

Games, Options, the Arts: Sport is important and, Cornwall being a county where cauliflower ears are more numerous than cauliflowers, rugby is king. The top players are looked after by the England Under-18 coach and Bill Shankly would approve of the spirit in which they set about it. A new football coach, who is also very involved with the local City team, has now also been appointed. Non-combatants have to do rugby up to GCSE but not in a bloodletting way. Girls' sports growing in stature as numbers rise and the hockey and netball teams now accompany the 1st XV on annual tours abroad – major, let us tell you, highlights of the school year. Sailing strong, of course, Optimists the boats of choice. Annual inter-house surfing competition. Indoor swimming pool, sports hall and all-weather pitches. Regional and national representation not at all unusual, testifying to good coaching – 'we tend to monopolise the county in terms of excellence.'

Art is superb, local artists drop in and do masterclasses, and the school has an excellent gallery of work by local luminaries, Terry Frost et al. Drama top notch, marvellous theatre, highly professional direction, one play in 2006 through to the finals of the Shell Connections National Theatre drama festival. Lots of top class music of all sorts, and they embrace the Cornish windband tradition. Sixty-piece orchestra and jazz band. The choir sings at St Paul's and, in 2006, sang at Festival Mass in St Mark's, Venice. Whatever they do at this school, they like to get out and about and do it.

They like lungfuls of fresh air, too. D of E Award exceedingly strong – 40 going for Gold this year says it all. Ten Tors expedition team places are hotly contested at all three levels. There's an outdoor centre on Bodmin moor where the youngest go and get back to muddy basics.

Wednesday afternoons are for clubs and activities – they operate in lunchtimes, too. There are plenty to choose from. Chess strong, as is fencing. Parents say there's so much to do they have to curb their children's enthusiasm or risk watching them frazzle.

Background and Atmosphere: Gloriously situated looking over the River Truro and down onto the cathedral. A Methodist school founded in 1880 and Methodist values infuse the ethos. Original Gothic building in local stone much added to behind making it, in the words of a parent, 'a bit of a warren'. Co-ed since 1990 and feels co-ed for all that many locals still reckon it to be essentially boyish. The only HMC school in Cornwall.

Pastoral Care and Discipline: Expectations are clear and personal. Nothing heavy-handed and prefects are trained to fill a big brother/sister role vis a vis the younger ones. Yes, some uniforms can look a little louche but we're hardly talking about the dressiest county in the UK. Parents express themselves perfectly happy and rejoice in the way the school really does address itself to the individuality of each and seek to discover peculiar talents. 'He/she just loves going to school,' is something of a refrain. The school motto encourages pupils 'to be rather than to seem to be' and when you've worked out what that means it has to be said that the school remains absolutely true to this.

There's a house system, but it's not characterised by strong local patriotism. Your tutor is your first port of call and your significant other. Parents say they can ring teachers at home in the evening and encounter no terseness – 'the staff really put themselves out'. The chaplain gets rave reviews. Food is cooked by a chef lured from a local hotel. Uptake for lunch has soared from 35 per cent to 80.

Around 55 board, boys and girls, separate houses for each. They're a minority but they don't feel like one – this is definitely not one of those schools where the tide goes out leaving you beached and mateless. There is much praise for houseparents, for close family feel and for ease of contact. Parents with daughters absolutely feel they're safe, we checked this carefully. A good deal for parents living in further flung parts of the county.

Pupils and Parents: Parents from all over Cornwall, some from the Scillies, professional folk and a growing number of incomers who've turned their back on serious rat racing to work in the knowledge economy. Prosperity levels are rising fast hereabouts. Very nice, unaggressive lot and it shows in their children. Nothing flash or lah-di-dah here.

Distinguished alumni include former chair of M&S Paul Myners, actors Robert Shaw, John Rhys Davies and Nigel Terry, baritones Benjamin Luxon and Alan Opie, triple Olympic Gold sailor Ben Ainslie, chess grandmaster Michael Adams and Queen drummer Roger Taylor.

Entrance: At 11, 13 and 16. For 11 and 13-year-olds exam in Jan in English, maths and verbal reasoning or, where appropriate, CE performance. Around 160 compete for 120 places. At 16, predicted GCSE grades plus school report plus interview. Prep pupils make up about 35 per cent of the entry. Up to 25 per cent of sixth form newcomers.

Exit: Good universities, mostly not too far up-country. Exeter, Bristol, Cardiff especially popular. Falmouth College of Art, too.

Money Matters: Decidedly good value for money. True to itself, the school has its own Assisted Places scheme for the deserving indigent, means tested and up to full fees. Not a rich school – no endowments – so must rely on prudent husbandry. Strives to be as inclusive as it can afford to be.

Remarks: Not at all the sort of school that looks over its shoulder but operates according to its own dynamic, its own values. Makes the most of all sorts and everyone seems to find their own niche.

Tudor Hall School

Wykham Park, Banbury, Oxfordshire, OX16 9UR

• Pupils: 325 girls; 250 boarding, 75 day • Ages: 11-18 • Size of sixth form: 100 • Anglican but makes provision for RCs • Fees: Boarding £25,500; Day £16,539 pa • Independent

Tel: 01295 263 434
Fax: 01295 253 264
Email: admissions@tudorhallschool.com
Website: www.tudorhallschool.com

Head: Since 2004, Miss Wendy Griffith, BSc PGCE (early fifties). Educated at Queen Elizabeth Grammar School, Carmarthen and the University of Wales where she read zoology. Previously head of sixth form, Tormead School, then director of studies, St Catherine's, Bramley. This is her first headship. Married to a history teacher, they have a daughter.

Parents speak of her 'can do' attitude – 'an excellent role model for the girls' – bold, bubbly, attractive and driven – you get the sense there is nothing Miss Griffiths won't tackle. Large, warm green eyes – a compassionate head as well as a 'savvy' one (her word). Clear sighted and thoroughly committed to her staff, her girls, her school as well as her profession. She inspects other schools and networks like mad – knows everyone in the industry but marketing has to be done in the 'Tudor Hall style – with subtlety and discretion'. Still finds time to teach biology several times a week – 'it's my treat,' she says, 'a good lesson can turn your day around'. Knows every girl by name and is prepared to run with any ambition the girls might have – whether it's to be a national shot putter or an Oxbridge candidate (with less than perfect credentials). 'What matters most, whatever the outcome – is that they try and we nurture their confidence. Too few women appreciate what they are capable of,' she says.

Academic matters: Once known as the school for toffs' daughters without academic aspirations, but this is not the case now. Performs well in value-added terms and Miss Griffiths is firmly focused on the academics. Respectable results – in 2009, 98 per cent A* – C at GCSE with girls taking an average of nine subjects and 94 per cent A–C at A level. 20 subjects offered at A level. Still a strong preference for arts subjects – particularly English, history and French but enthusiasm for sciences from the top is filtering down and more girls are choosing biology. Junior and senior science clubs, science festivals and field trips including a physics trip to European Centre for Nuclear Research, and the lure of eminent scientists (recently Professor Jocelyn Bell Burnell) as well as Etonians at the joint Eton and Tudor Hall science lectures.

Small number receive help with e.g. mild dyslexia or learning difficulties. Withdrawn from prep periods and given one-to-one help – for a fee. School has SENCo as well as a Gifted and Talented co-ordinator to stretch the brightest.

Inspiring library, well used and brimming with books and computers as well as comfy bean bags and sofas. Devoted librarian forever changing attractive displays, entering school into book-judging competitions and promoting unusual reading material. Current favourites (among these girls and practically every other of this age) *Twilight* series and Malorie Blackman.

Lots of fresh blood among the staff as well as a few devoted and long serving. Average age 36. Average class size is 16, maximum 20.

Games, Options, the Arts: Sports strong – significantly improved since the arrival of Miss Griffiths, say parents. Lots of fixtures in hockey, lacrosse, rounders, tennis and netball. Girls exude fresh-faced enthusiasm in their tartan games skirts and cheery red socks. Stunning green house-style swimming pool – the walls can be removed in summer. In sport, as in everything else, if you show signs of talent you run (or jump) with it – currently one national high jumper. Sports day happens at Radley; 'it's so much more convenient,' gushes one girl, without making it clear precisely why – as you would expect, playing fields stretch away into the distance here.

Textiles department fizzes with talent and originality. Poky but busy design tech dept where we saw girls designing model radio controlled cars to enter the Formula Schools' Racing at Silverstone (a far cry from the flower arranging of an earlier era!) and a beautiful oak folding dining table – 'the kind of thing my parents would buy,' said one.

Relaxed art room where senior girls listen to the radio as they work on perspective – the fresh Oxfordshire air pouring through the double doors from the balcony. Energetic cookery department with excellent kitchen – large, bright and squeaky clean. Full of eager girls in blue aprons, hair tied back, assiduously making pastry.

Vibrant music – good quality pianos in every music room – and people playing them. 85 girls play at least one instrument; choirs, orchestras and bands perform concerts throughout the year. Pupils frequently win festivals and occasionally local musician of the year comp. Dance strong – you can choose dance as a GCSE – lots of enthusiastic noises from parents.

Strong debating and public speaking tradition, with girls taking part in Model United Nations. Lots of trips – gritty as well as glamorous – to Auschwitz and the WWI battlefields as well as to schools in India and Canada.

Background and Atmosphere: An imposing, beautiful and immaculately kept school, Tudor Hall presides over the 48 acres of Wykham Park where it's been since 1946. Founded as an Anglican girls' school in 1850 by the Reverend and Mrs John Todd, it's one of the oldest girls' school in the country. You sense the tradition from the moment you enter the large iron gates, negotiate your way past sheep along the long drive and arrive at the fine former manor house in honey coloured stone, smelling of freshly polished wood floors.

An army of discreet (and uniformed) staff industriously tend fine gardens, clean well equipped and comfortable boarding houses, and maintain solid Cotswold buildings old and new. A lucky few of them live in the grounds. A magical walled garden – with a mass of purple wisteria when we saw it – surrounds tennis and netball courts. An enchanting place to watch your daughter in her matches.

A mix of buildings. Some more tasteful than others. From the inappropriately named cowshed (it couldn't look less like one though, legend relates, this charming boarding house once housed cattle) to the exciting circular dining room with floor to ceiling glass known as the spaceship, and the delightful cottage where the first year (Todds) live. Here the young ones can enjoy an (even more) sheltered existence. A short walk from the main buildings, girls breakfast in the cosy dining room and at the end of the day play on the swings or tend their own patch of garden. It's as if you had sent your daughter to stay with a friend in the country rather than to boarding school.

Each year group lives in a separate building which, we were told, makes for strong, lasting friendships. Cheerful dormitories splashed with colourful Cath Kidston duvet covers and walls of photos of parties and holidays. Upper sixth girls have rooms of their own, many with fabulous views.

Civilised behaviour and values permeate the place. Girls can help themselves from a large choice of food ('the fewer issues that surround food the better at this age,' remarks the head, sagely). Flowers on individual tables in the dining room and no benches. A sober uniform (no hoisted up skirts here) until they reach 15 when it's gradually dispensed with as the girls earn their 'privileges'. By the sixth form no one wears a uniform but girls look a lot neater here than in many other places we've seen with more unforgiving dress codes.

Quirky traditions befitting of such a small community. The whole school departs on a jolly (e.g. to Stratford-upon-Avon, The Globe, Kew or World Music) to celebrate the school's birthday. Lots of weekend activities and trips to Oxford, London etc. This is a full boarding school; until the sixth form they are here to stay – with organised exeats twice a term.

Pastoral Care and Discipline: Tudor Hall's forte. Praised by all – girls, their parents and the official reports. Firm line taken on smoking (drugs and drink are off the radar – fingers crossed) – the aim is to educate rather than punish but if you're caught red handed then you go home, with all the ignominy that entails.

School's motto is habeo ut dem – I have that I may give. Strong emphasis on courtesy, manners meetings held twice a term where each girl is awarded marks for conduct, kindness, helpfulness etc. Grade A denotes 'an outstanding member of the community' whereas grade E is 'unacceptable behaviour'.

Head girl 'rotates' every term – chosen from upper sixth for one term and then lower sixth for next two terms. Lots of other highly regarded positions of responsibility – e.g. Music Prefect, Public Relations Prefect. Group prefects for each of the year groups. Privilege system provides incentives to encourage good behaviour – girls earn the right to dispense with uniform or to go into Banbury. Strong, positive relationships between girls and the staff that last well beyond their school days.

Pupils and Parents: Thoroughly well bred girls, polite, courteous and discreet. They know how to behave and seem to be in control – assured and confident – whilst being natural and open. An apparent sensitive awareness of their privileges. Recent effort to raise money for a local homeless project involved a few girls sleeping in cardboard boxes in various sheltered spots around the school. Even with the hot chocolate and biscuits brought to them by Miss Griffiths in the middle of the night they said how much it reinforced the 'horror' of being without a roof over one's head.

Largely rural families from all over the UK. A few from London who want their daughters to experience the freedom of the countryside and enjoy being young for longer. Not many from abroad but nor are there large numbers from down the road. Some come from as far as Scotland. High proportion of mothers are Old Tudorians. Notable old girls include Artist Tessa Campbell, Financier Nicola Odey, Sculpter Candida Bond, Serpentine Gallery director Julia Payton-Jones.

Entrance: Register early. Entry at 11 and 13. Selection process includes school report, common entrance and interview with the head who looks for that 'special spark'. Occasional vacancy in the sixth form – minimum of seven GCSEs with grades A*–C in subjects to be studied at A level.

Exit: Some to art college, a tiny few to Royal Agricultural College or Cirencester (no longer popular for Tudor girls), most to university or to the 'new universities' – popular destinations are Leeds, Bristol and Edinburgh where they read combinations of philosophy, politics, languages or other arts subjects. More choosing medicine and veterinary science than ever before. Head keen that we point this out. One or two to Oxbridge each year.

Money Matters: Scholarships for excellence in anything (academic, music, art, dance, drama and sport) but you won't get a huge amount of money. Bursaries available but this is not a particularly rich school despite an impressive building programme funded from income.

Remarks: No longer the automatic fall-back for your less bright child but still a safe and beautiful place for young girls to grow up away from the pressures of the real world where they can discover the important things in life and build strong friendships. The wide range of opportunities, high level of support, and small size means your daughter will always feel special and, whatever her strengths, is unlikely to be lost in the crowd.

Twyford Church of England High School

Twyford Crescent, Acton, London, W3 9PP

• Pupils: 1,345, boys:girls 160:130 • Ages: 11-18 • Size of sixth form: 395, mixed • C of E • State

Tel: 020 8752 0141
Fax: 020 8993 7627
Email: lwelch@twyford.ealing.sch.uk
Website: www.twyford.ealing.sch.uk

Head: Since 2002, Ms Alice Hudson MA, (mid-forties) educated at Slough Girls' High and Leighton Park, then St Hilda's, Oxford, where she read English. Previously deputy head at Brentside HS, also in Ealing, and prior to that taught at Central Foundation Boys', Islington and Maria Fidelis, Euston. Joined Twyford in 2000, first as deputy then as acting head. Married, four young children. This was a failing school, financially, and seriously underperforming academically and socially, when Ms Hudson arrived, and one needs to visit the school to believe the extraordinary turnaround she has achieved in her tenure, so far. It is a unique experience for this particular, hardened, Guide editor to see so much change in every aspect of a school's life, effected with such irresistible enthusiasm, focused and intelligent rethinking, authority, conviction and energy – all articulated in an entirely disarming and infectious manner. Very much faith-inspired vision of what the school should – and could – be.

Our meeting was delayed and then punctuated by fallout from an incident before school – pupils set upon by a child from another school – and Ms Hudson was hot on the case to identify the culprit and ensure via a meeting between perpetrator and victims that it wouldn't be repeated. 'She gets involved ... you see her about ... she makes people take a pride in themselves'. Somehow she manages to teach nine periods weekly. Her idea of a 'career break' was to have three children in four years and to do an MA in education policy. Hm! 'Profoundly', is a key word in her vocabulary. Staff pay tribute – 'she is an absolutely delightful person to work for'. Lucky school.

Academic matters: Hugely improved results in this, academically, non-selective school. Three Bs average at A level; maths results exceptional. Choices include economics, music tech, photography (very successful), psychology, sociology. Biggest improvement in sixth form – head's especial baby – 'it's a reliable place for your high-achieving child ... we chase them much more in the sixth form', but the less academic well supported too.

ICT (we saw loads of computers) a developing area though head refreshingly cheery when asked about interactive whiteboards – 'almost nothing.' Head sees wisdom in routeing the less academic to the practical which 'can be studied alongside A level', so double AVCE in ICT popular along with other more vocational subjects. 12 per cent have SLD or SEN (65 have statements) and are well-supported, either by regular staff or from outside. 'They will be valued and survive here,' says head, 'and parents are very well supported – we have very good home-school links.' 280 pupils have EAL – first languages in this very ethnically mixed area Gujurati, Punjabi, Arabic and Urdu – but no-one needs additional help in English. Proactive on modern languages – 'we identify potential linguists in Year 7, accelerate them in French and, in Year 8, give them a choice of German and Spanish.' RE always a feature of school life and supported by two conferences each year, often with outside speakers on moral or spiritual topics. Curriculum taught on an alternating two-week cycle which some find confusing at first but they get used to it.

SEN dept does not always pick up strugglers as fast as it should nor provide the continuous support needed. We wonder whether the major advances at the upper end of the ability range are sufficiently matched by rigorous attention to those who struggle to realise their potential.

Games, Options, the Arts: Remarkable playing fields, well-concealed along this urban high street site. Netball especially strong here but hockey, tennis, football, cricket, basketball too. Dance and athletics popular. Rugby coached by pros from London Wasps. Consistent successes in many sporting areas and representation in borough and regional levels. Thriving art, drama popular and lively though restricted to one well-used studio. Good and well-used music and music tech facilities, especially now with new block and state-of the-art audio-visual recording studio. Good work placement programme. Pupils enthuse about the number and quality of trips and expeditions – everywhere from St Petersburg to the New Forest for every activity imaginable – photography to water skiing. Lots of charity work.

Background and Atmosphere: School tucked behind rare bit of green along the Uxbridge Road. Main building, Grade IIA listed 'The Elms', an elegant, early Georgian house, built 1735, now well-preserved and sensibly painted in blues, houses the admin and offices side of things. A diverse mixture of less distinguished and pretty scruffy later blocks, A, B, unaccountably then D and M, house rest of school – not too much room for growth and development – but, we are told, there has been much recent building resulting in a sixth form centre, learning resource centre, café, maths and science rooms, refurbished modern foreign languages department, state of the art performance centre, new chapel, creative media suite with radio station and refurbished music areas.

Black uniform with white shirts creates somewhat sombre impression but most pupils look tidy (head strides around, not averse to pointing out, amicably, 'shirt!' to any wearer of stray shirt tails) and overall impression of a good-humoured, confident, mix of the boisterous and the purposeful. No uniform for the sixth. Huge ethnic diversity –

52 per cent from non-white British backgrounds, of whom the largest number from Afro-Caribbean families; Asians make up next biggest group. Christian principles in practice evident in staff's approach to all aspects of this richly diverse community. While Anglicanism predominates, all churches and faiths are celebrated and explored here and everyone feels part of the school.

Two minutes' daily silent reflection before lessons – everyone is quiet', said a sixth former. 'Faith has a big profile here', says head, 'we place a high premium on formal acts of worship.' Everyone attends a termly Communion service and there is a weekly voluntary one. Assemblies are inclusive but have an unashamed Christian bias. 'The key to inter-faith issues,' believes head, 'is to be clear about what one's standpoint is.' She talks of the validity of each individual's own 'faith journey'. 'Spiritual matters are neither embarrassing nor taboo here' – a big claim but it feels legitimate. Pupils, though seldom deferential, respect teachers here – there is a good working relationship between staff and pupils at all levels. 'They stretch you as far as you can go – but not beyond what you can do,' reflected one sixth former.

Pastoral Care and Discipline: Well established system of form tutors – first resource though pupils able to talk to whichever member of staff they choose. Heads of year back up the tutors and pupils have regular meeting with tutors to check on targets, progress, happiness. Chaplaincy team also available. Interaction between ages encouraged – actively by sixth form mentoring of younger pupils and system of form reps. School Council much appreciated – 'it has a lot of power over changes and we can meet the governors,' we were told. Few serious problems – most pupils feeling that offending in school time and on school property 'not worth it' and seemingly a bit immature, though usual crop of minor misdemeanours.

Pupils and Parents: As above, huge ethnic mix, Christianity being the unifying principle though 30 places reserved each year for those from 'other world faiths' and Christianity itself taking in Russian/Serbian/Eastern Orthodox along with other denominations. Pupils come from wide geographic area – Brent, Hounslow, all over Ealing and further into town. Most, though, from Christchurch junior school, half a mile away, and nearly 50 other primaries. More boys than girls though this not generally perceptible. Princes and paupers here – all social strata represented and cheerfully interrelate.

Entrance: Hugely over-subscribed and getting ever more so. School already stretches its capacity. Complex pecking order based on family's attendance at and commitment to church, along with home's distance from school. Worth checking this out in detail before losing your heart to the place. No-one is fooled by rapid conversion when your child is in Year 6 – though it is still – widely and unsuccessfully – tried. Thirty places for pupils from other world faiths where the family is committed to the idea and principles in practice of 'faith'.

Sixth form, hitherto less stringent, now over-subscribed 11:1. They must be getting something right. The criteria for external places in the sixth form:

1. Students must meet individual entry criteria for courses as set out in the sixth form prospectus (minimum requirement for each course is usually a B with one or two exceptions)

2. Places are available on individual courses following first allocation of internal students.

3. Students must be in sympathy with aims and objectives of a C of E school.

Exit: Vast and creditable range of courses and universities – three to Oxford in 2009 and everywhere else from Exeter to Newcastle. Pupils encouraged to aim high and have aspirations while remaining realistic and practical.

Remarks: This isn't a smart school and the head's priorities have been to get straight the finances, the staffing, the ethos – this has been triumphantly achieved but a lot remains for this dynamic regime to accomplish.

University College School

Linked to University College School Junior School in the Junior section

Linked to Phoenix School in the Junior section

Frognal, Hampstead, London, NW3 6XH

• Pupils: 750 boys, plus 30 girls in the sixth form; all day • Ages: 11-18
• Size of sixth form: 220 • Non-denom • Fees: £15,495 pa • Independent

Tel: 020 7435 2215
Fax: 020 7433 2111
Email: hmsec@ucs.org.uk
Website: www.ucs.org.uk

Headmaster: Since 1996, Mr Kenneth Durham MA (fifties); educated at St John's School, Leatherhead, and read PPE at Oxford. Taught economics at St Alban's School (qv), then became director of studies and head of economics at King's College School, Wimbledon. Writer of several books on economics education. A big, bearded, relaxed and affable man who seems universally popular. 'Utterly fantastic ... We love him,' say parents, who describe him as approachable, kind, full of compassion. Was concerned, during our visit, to make sure that a boy was invited to his study to celebrate his birthday – a UCS tradition. By all accounts an excellent public speaker, skilled at fund-raising (as evidenced by the multi-squillion pound developments that have been arising apace on the site over the past few years); leads from the front. 'He's very good at running things without seeming to do so,' said a pupil. Married to the head of Francis Holland School NW1.

Academic matters: Says it does not measure success by exam league tables – can afford not to, with an impressive 85 per cent of GCSE grades A or A* and 91 per cent of A levels graded A*–B. An unusually wide GCSE choice – two English, maths, a science and a modern language are compulsory but boys have a free choice of their other five subjects. 'The kids do the subjects they enjoy and we achieve good results in every subject.' There is guidance to ensure that, for example, someone with an inclination toward medicine does not end up doing only one science.

But the numerical bias is undoubtedly towards the social sciences – economics, government and politics and history are particularly popular A levels and around a third of leavers go on to do social sciences at university. 'This says more about the families; the boys are encouraged to talk and discuss and think a lot from a young age, so they tend towards the discursive, argumentative subjects.' Having said that, plenty take maths A level and the sciences have a good minority showing.

Everyone is assessed when they enter the school and those in need can get extra help outside the classroom and can e.g. use laptops. 'But they must be bright enough to cope with the classroom work.' At this liberal school the emphasis is on self-motivation and some north London parents find it insufficiently pushy. It is stricter, say pupils, in the early years. 'As the workload increases you develop an instinct for getting on and doing it.' Undoubtedly, some develop more of an instinct than others but there are safety nets. 'We have huge rafts of processes in place to help them develop their own motivation,' says the head. 'But we want to get them off those systems as soon as possible and get them self-supporting.'

Teaching styles vary from the military to the liberal but tend toward the latter. 'The relationship between teachers and pupils here is very individual,' said a sixth former. 'You can disagree and question their views. But it is disciplined in the classroom because we respect the teachers. If someone you respect is talking you'll listen to them.'

Games, Options, the Arts: The swish new Sir Roger Bannister sports complex includes a swimming pool, sports hall, multi-gym and dance studio – and a Costa Coffee bar. Small Astroturf pitch on site and sports fields a couple of miles away in West Hampstead. Most people play twice a week and sports include hockey and basketball as well as rugby, soccer and cricket. The teams win reasonably often but it is fair to say that macho ultra-competitiveness is not a UCS characteristic and the captain of rugby is equally at home giving a camp starring performance in the school play. 'We're not triumphalist,' says the head. 'We like to do things for the hell of it.'

A range of orchestras, choirs and ensembles, including a joint symphony orchestra with South Hampstead High School. Plenty of concerts including a lunchtime classical series in the great hall and jazz evenings in the Lund Theatre. But UCS is best known locally for its rock groups, including Bombay Bicycle Club and Cajun Dance Party, formed to play in assembly and now signed up for the Reading Festival. The annual Battle of the Bands showcases talents like these to a boisterous audience of north London teenagers.

Excellent art, DT and modern language facilities are housed in the recently completed Jeremy Bentham Building providing fully equipped studios, workshops, classroom and two language laboratories. Drama strong too, with a large variety of plays from *West Side Story* to *Macbeth*, including some joint performances with South Hampstead High School. Plenty of opportunities for those with a technical bent to get involved backstage.

Numerous extra-curricular activities: Ten Tors challenge, skiing in Colorado, cricket in Florida, language trip to Hamburg. Raises £20,000 – £30,000 a year for charities, some of which goes to linked schools overseas – one in Uganda, run by an OG (Old Gower), schools in India and Sri Lanka and an orphanage in Romania. Pupils go out to work there during holidays and gap years and many find it a life-changing experience. The annual Beyond Words festival – rated amongst London's top cultural attractions of the week by *Time Out* – includes well-known authors, journalists, actors, musicians, economists and many more.

Background and Atmosphere: Founded in 1830 by the University of London as the 'Godless College' of Gower Street, it was one of the first schools to teach modern languages and sciences, and one of the first to abolish corporal punishment. It moved to Hampstead in 1907 and maintained its liberal and secular outlook. There are no school bells, no religious observance and technically no religious education – though a few boys each year, nonetheless, do take RS at GCSE. 'It develops free-thinking, self-assured and entrepreneurial boys,' said a parent. 'It fosters independent thinking and makes the boys feel that they are very clever.'

The main building – including the panelled great hall with organ – is a notable example of Edwardian architecture. Recent developments – now complete – include a sports centre, art, DT and modern languages block, and refurbishment of classrooms, administration area and play spaces.

The Independent Schools Inspectorate commented on a 'lack of clarity about the required standards of dress and appearance' and there is certainly a feeling that uniform is a somewhat voluntary matter. 'They're intelligent young men,' says the head, 'and they understand what the school's priorities are. If they've worked hard and are getting on well but don't tuck their shirts in, we know what is most important.'

Pastoral Care and Discipline: Renowned for its friendly atmosphere and caring attitude. The Lower School, Years 7 and 8, is organised largely apart from the rest of the school, with its own building and pastoral staff. In Year 9 boys join one of five Demes – roughly like houses – and are looked after by Deme wardens and form tutors.

Boys report that bullying is virtually non-existent. The tolerant and open-minded atmosphere reaps good relationships between pupils and between staff and pupils. 'There's no set code of conduct except that you behave responsibly,' said a sixth-former. Boys feel that it is very hard to get punished: 'The gardener is the only one who's strict when it comes to discipline. You don't mess with his flower beds.'

'Boys do get punished,' says the head, 'but we don't have a tariff of offences. We try to treat each offence and each pupil as an individual. So some kids spend a lot of time talking to teachers about what's going wrong. Most north London boys like talking about themselves, so they don't see it as a big deal.'

Pupils and Parents: Mostly wealthy families from a relatively small area. The school does not record the ethnic or religious background of its pupils but they mirror fairly accurately the inhabitants of the Hampstead/Garden Suburb/Hendon/Finchley catchment area, with around half Jewish and a good sprinkling from various ethnic minorities.

Pupils tend to be confident and self-opinionated. 'They go through an arrogant phase,' said a parent, though the school feels that most teenagers do so, and prefers to say, 'we at UCS are quite good at developing assurance rather than arrogance.' Another parent commented, 'you need to be the life and soul – to throw yourself into things. It's probably not ideal for a quiet, bookish boy. They like you to get involved.' Students say, 'you have to be open-minded and accept other people and their views. And it helps if you have an in-built inclination to do well. There's space for all here – but the UCS type does tend to be out-going.'

OGs include Sir Chris Bonington, Sir Roger Bannister, Sir Dirk Bogarde, Alex Garland.

Entrance: About two thirds of 11-year-olds come from the junior school in Holly Hill. They move up without needing to take an entrance exam. Another 30 or so come from outside – mostly local state primaries. About 200 applicants take maths, English and non-verbal reasoning tests, and about half are called back for group activities and interview. Another 30 come in at 13, mostly from local preps. They are assessed during the summer term of Year 7 in maths, English and non-verbal reasoning, with half invited back for interviews, with offers conditional on common entrance.

A few boys and some 30 girls join the sixth form. 'I feel that a co-ed sixth form will offer a better educational experience,' says the head, 'and a better preparation for what's coming next. I want the sixth form to feel like the start of something rather than the end.' The school sets its own assessment test, which is not subject specific but measures thinking skills, problem solving, interpretation of data. It takes GCSE forecasts into consideration but offers are not conditional on achieving particular results.

Exit: Nearly all end up at university, around half after a gap year. Around 15–20 a year to Oxbridge to do a range of subjects, though classics, English and languages probably most popular. Social sciences, as mentioned, particularly popular elsewhere, alongside humanities and languages.

Money Matters: Offers the equivalent of 15 full-fee bursaries a year and is on target to continue to increase this number each year through successful fundraising. There are also various scholarships, though the head regards these as 'basically pat-on-the-back awards', feeling that they should be means-tested rather than handed out to those who can well afford the fees.

Remarks: Achieves impressive exam results with a relaxed atmosphere. An ex-pupil insists that we describe it as 'the top liberal public school' and says, 'I look on my time at UCS as a golden age.' Certainly parents and pupils are uniformly happy – 'My son is having a fantastic time. If you're enthusiastic, there's so much scope to do what you want to do.'

Uppingham Community College

London Road, Uppingham, Rutland, LE15 9TJ

• Pupils: 850 boys and girls, roughly split 50:50; all day • Ages: 11-16
• Non-denom • State

Tel: 01572 823 631
Fax: 01572 821 193
Email: principal@ucc.rutland.sch.uk
Website: www.ucc.rutland.sch.uk

Principal: Since 2007, Mrs Jan Turner MA Cert Ed (fifties). Mrs Turner began her teaching career in schools in Lancs and N Yorks, then moved to the East Midlands, becoming head of dept, pastoral head, assistant head, deputy principal and, briefly, acting head all at Robert Smyth School in Market Harborough where she stayed for twenty years. So she knows the territory from the bottom up and she knows UCC of old as her own daughters were pupils. Svelte, pretty, relaxed and on the ball, Mrs Turner is popular with everyone. 'She gets things done,' we were told. 'She responds promptly to questions and she makes sure the staff do too.' 'She's smartened up the children – the new blazers were a good idea.' We found her delightfully disarming. 'I've never done this before,' she twinkled when we sat down to grill her. Her office is light but stark – nothing here to distract the eye or mind. One reason, perhaps, why this clear-sighted, articulate principal seems so naturally and deftly in charge.

Academic matters: UCC is a Technology College, specialising in DT, maths and science. It works in a collegiate system with two other local schools that have Business and Enterprise and Visual Arts specialisms. Lots of ICT integrated into and underpinning the curriculum includes four banks of laptops and a proper home/school communication system. Everyone takes a core of nine subjects at KS4 and they then have a choice of three 'pathways' from which to choose one. Blue is a diploma course in either ICT or 'creative media', red is trad GCSEs of which they take four, and green is vocational courses in e.g. motor vehicle mechanics, hairdressing or construction. Also young apprenticeships in e.g. catering. A true 'comprehensive' mix on offer, then.

While most (especially girls) opt for red, the vocational and diploma courses are popular and successful. Much praise for day release sessions in Stamford and Melton – felt to be valuable and well-organised. 78 per cent of pupils got 5+ A* – C GCSE grades in 2009. Geography more than usually popular among the options and DT notably successful. Much praise for head of mod langs, the lang exchanges and the recent introduction of Spanish. More boys than girls opt for the green pathway but this does not disguise the fact that girls seem significantly to outperform boys in their GCSEs here though, interestingly, the value added tables tell a different story. Head expresses interest in the IB – could be significant developments then – watch out.

School is especially well-supplied with Teaching Assistants who play a number of important supporting roles, especially on the pastoral side. They are essential to the progress of pupils with SEN – more than 10 per cent of the school population. 21 statemented pupils at the time of our visit plus 120 on School Action or SA Plus. In-class support, withdrawal for individuals or small group help. Sensibly, the SENCo liaises with all the main feeder primaries so that all children with identified SEN are known before they arrive and everyone is screened on arrival anyway. Good team of specialist teachers. G & T pupils under the care of the impressive head of DT dept who sends them on courses, works with the other two schools in their local 'family' who offer art and enterprise courses and special awaydays. But parents of the super-bright feel the work needs to be more challenging on occasions. Also some feeling that 'it's the middling pupils who don't get all the attention they need'. Much parental concern about the irregularity of homework setting, especially in the first three years.

Games, Options, the Arts: Lots of space outside but limited inside. One largish sports hall but not enough for a school this size, especially when there is no separate hall or assembly space. A timetabling nightmare, one imagines.

Good Astroturf a real asset. 'Session 6' allows pupils to stay for an extra hour after the school day, which otherwise ends at 3.00pm, and choose activities e.g. Chinese, cooking and badminton. Parents, while praising Session 6 as an idea, complain that not all staff take it seriously and that the popular options e.g. sport get over-subscribed too fast. This is a general complaint – not enough sport. Swimming is a session 6 option – otherwise, there is no swimming. However, we gather that changes are afoot. Existing sports do well – a good range of games played here including athletics – school has numerous county winners. Equestrian team competes around the country and there are hopes to extend access to this to those who can't provide their own mounts. Lots of outward bound and subject-based trips. 'My Berlin history trip? – loved it! Brilliant.' Popular Don Bosco sporting exchange to Belgium.

Good-sized drama studio but this is the only sizeable space other than the sports hall and it is very well used, including for lunch when music is played. Drama and music both popular minority pursuits – no orchestra yet, though a good concert band and a new choir under teacher from outside. School hosts annual music festival for local primaries. Art and DT are exceptional – we were knocked out by the skill and craft of the pottery, the individuality of the work and the professionalism of the approach. A choice at GCSE between product design – taken by 5/6 of the year – textiles, graphics, ceramics, wood, metal, plastics, art, electronics on offer – or food tech, taken very enthusiastically by those who do. 'They're making things of marketable quality,' we were told. Yes. A real school triumph.

Background and Atmosphere: A mile south of the sleepy little town of Uppingham, high on a hill overlooking classic British countryside sits UCC, a medley of less than stunning buildings dreamed up in the 1960s and 1970s, not exactly the Golden Age of school architecture. It is surrounded by space and, apart from the lamentable lack of a hall, feels pretty spacious inside too. (There had been a hall but it became the dining room with fixed seating – not a good idea!) One's first impression is of open skies, one's second is of dull buildings and one's third is of smiley faces. This is one of the smiliest schools we have visited. Classes are orderly and quiet, we saw no litter and the place is kept in good nick. Pupils are taught to look after their surroundings and they appear to do so. Nice features include a gallery space with glass cases in which DT work is properly displayed – though we felt the exhibits could be changed more frequently. Outside there are several good places to sit, picnic and chat – little courtyards and gardens – someone has thought about this and, inside, the buildings are airier and more congenial than their outsides suggest. Nice library with 17 PCs but, except in fiction, pitifully small stock for a school of this size. Library used for socialising in break.

Three screens around the place announce the notices and events of the day and pupils look purposeful and focused. Mrs Turner has initiatives to make them more involved in school decisions – despite their youth and the lack of a sixth form – and this is yielding good – and appreciated – results. For example, she allots them a 'bursary' with a choice of what to spend it on – they chose between a rock climbing wall and more staging for the drama studio – sensible, mature choices. Nonetheless, uniform is an issue and staff swoop, hawklike, onto infringements. Most pupils look pretty orderly to us though we are told of staff who keep make-up and nail varnish remover in their desks. What we felt, though, was summed up by a party of school nurses who were just leaving as we arrived. 'It's been a lovely atmosphere,' they said which, considering they'd been administering jabs, is pretty good! And everyone smiled at us.

Pastoral Care and Discipline: Good relations between staff and pupils. School tries to keep classes with same form teacher for the five years. Year 11 mentoring scheme with younger pupils. 'If you do something well the teachers really appreciate it,' a Year 10 girl told us. 'They stay after to school to help you if you need it.' Disruptives are put on report or sent to cool off to the Remove Room where staff sort out the problems. The rest report that the system works well. 'In Years 10 and 11, you're not kids any more. It's your learning and the teachers say they'll help you in every way but if you're here just to be disruptive they don't want you here – you're not going to ruin the learning of others.' Atmosphere generally healthy – includes eating – good food – though only eaten by around half the school, and three vending machines selling only healthy drinks. Little serious sinning.

Pupils and Parents: Most pupils from seven local primaries but also increasingly out of catchment as reputation grows. Seen as an alternative by some to Oakham School (qv) which is 50:50 day:boarding – but not so much to near neighbour Uppingham School (qv) which is virtually all boarding and which, while more or less occupying the town of Uppingham itself, seems a little reserved in terms of finding opportunities to collaborate with its sparky neighbour. Many rural families, some from local regiment at Edith Weston, and head says that some Service families now apply to that regiment on account of UCC. Some from Corby, Market Harborough, Melton. Real social mix from the area.

Entrance: Oversubscribed but not vastly so. Well worth applying even from out of catchment and recent record of successful appeals too.

Exit: Few to employment but vast majority to sixth forms, sixth form colleges or to FE. Quite a choice available – in Stamford, Peterborough, into Leicestershire or local colleges. School cries out for its own sixth form though practical matters make this a non-starter. However, with collaboration, investment and an imaginative strategy? Some each year to Oakham School for the sixth and UCC has a stunning recent record of providing Oakham Oxbridge successes. More mileage for the sixth form idea?

Remarks: A well-run, friendly school, doing well and set to do better under excellent leadership.

Uppingham School

High Street West, Uppingham, Rutland, LE15 9QE

• Pupils: 770; 455 boys, 315 girls. Virtually all boarding, apart from 19 day pupils • Ages: 13-18 • Size of sixth form: 365 • C of E • Fees: Boarding £28,401; Day £19,890 pa • Independent

Tel: 01572 822 216
Fax: 01572 822 332
Email: admissions@uppingham.co.uk
Website: www.uppingham.co.uk

Headmaster: Since September 2006, Mr Richard Harman, MA PGCE (late forties). Uppingham's thirty-first headmaster. Educated at The King's School, Worcester (he was a King's Scholar), followed by Trinity College, Cambridge, where he read English. Spent two years working in sales and marketing for academic publisher Harcourt Brace Jovanovich, then 'literally woke up one morning and realised that I ought to be teaching at a school.' He was offered a job at Marlborough and taught English and drama there for five years (with a sabbatical half way through to do a PGCE at Exeter University). Spent twelve years at Eastbourne College, progressing from head of English to housemaster of sixth form girls' house to member of the senior management team. Then became head of Aldenham, where he oversaw major expansion in both pupil numbers and facilities.

Energetic, approachable and charming (also slightly bashful at previous edition of The Guide referring to his 'film star looks'). Says being headmaster of 'such a wonderful school is an amazing privilege.' Firm believer in benefits of co-education. Taught English AS level during his first year at Uppingham (most of his students got As) and now teaches drama to new 13 year olds. 'It's great because drama is an "on your feet" subject and it means I get to know them all very early on,' he says. Married to American wife Karin. They met at Marlborough – she was a teaching fellow from the University of Virginia and he was assigned to be her mentor. They live in a house on the school site and have a grown-up daughter.

Ghastly fracas in May 2010 when Mr Harman expelled seven sixth formers for bullying and two thirds of the school marched out of classes in protest. Reportedly, one of the expellees had 13 GCSEs at A* to his credit.

Academic matters: Not an academic hothouse but results are good and teachers confident they deliver the best for the individual. School says curriculum is, 'sufficiently challenging for us to need to insist on a certain level of academic ability in the pupils we take, but the emphasis is upon identifying and bringing out the strengths of all pupils – in whichever field they may shine.' One in three pupils – 68 out of 170 – received straight A's in 2010 with 91 per cent A*–B. Around 28 subjects on offer at A level, with history currently the most popular subject, followed by maths, English, geography, politics, RS and art. Refreshingly un-hung up about league tables but 62 per cent A* and A grades at GCSE in 2010. Most take 10 or 11 GCSEs. Triple and dual award science on offer, plus French, Spanish, Italian and German. IT lessons for all. Average class sizes of 16 and 9 in sixth form. Learning support department for pupils with mild learning difficulties offers help 'according to individual needs'.

Games, Options, the Arts: All very strong. Music as superb as ever. School was first in the country to appoint a director of music – in 1865! – and still leads the way. Music groups galore, including two orchestras, chamber groups, jazz, wind and swing bands, chapel choir, chamber and close harmony choirs etc. Around two-thirds of pupils learn an instrument and there are more than 60 music scholars and exhibitionists. Chapel choir is much in demand and has performed all over the place, from St Paul's Cathedral to Hong Kong and China. Third music school opened in 2006, with 100-seat recital room and recording studios. Total of 80 practice rooms in school. Lots of lunchtime concerts, annual music festivals and breathtaking carol service.

Stunning glass-fronted art block designed by old boy Piers Gough. Walls hung with vibrant artwork and there's also a film studio and photo lab (complete with 3D printing). Pupils encouraged to try their hand at everything from fine art and ceramics to photography, sound and video. Drama very popular. Two venues – 300-seat main theatre and smaller drama studio with foyer, two drama classrooms, workshop space etc. Major school production every year, ranging from *Habeas Corpus* to *Sweeney Todd*, along with sixth form and lower school productions, junior drama club and performances by visiting professional companies.

Sport very good. 'Our teams do pretty well but you don't have to be brilliant,' say pupils. Sixty-five acres of playing fields (apparently the largest playing field in England), sports centre (with gym, weights room, swimming and diving pools), three Astroturf hockey pitches, a separate all-weather pitch, plus reams of tennis and netball courts, squash courts, five courts and a shooting range. Fabulous state-of-the art sports centre opened in 2010. Vast range of sports on offer. Rugby, hockey, cricket for boys and hockey, lacrosse, netball for girls – along with tennis, athletics, squash, badminton, swimming, basketball, cross-country, shooting, fencing, dance, aerobics, golf and sailing (on nearby Rutland Water). Rugby excellent. Links with Leicester Tigers and Northampton Saints RFCs. Lots of pupils play county sport, and some regional and national. A 15-year-old girl won a silver medal at the 2008 European pony championships. D of E and Young Enterprise popular. CCF or community service (visiting the elderly, helping in primary schools, working for Riding for the Disabled) for fifth and sixth formers.

Background and Atmosphere: Founded in 1584 by Archdeacon Robert Johnson. The school's handsome, honey-coloured buildings are dotted throughout the pretty market town of Uppingham. Pupils are much in evidence scurrying along picturesque streets but some places are out of bounds and only prefects (or 'pollies,' as they are known in Uppingham-speak) are allowed in tearooms like the popular Baines' Cafe.

There are 15 boarding houses on the school's 120-acre site, six for girls and nine for boys. All have their own character and ethos. According to their location, they are 'town,' 'country' or 'hill' houses. Boys' house, Brooklands, for instance, is situated up the hill in a rambling Victorian mansion, complete with its own swimming pool and flood-lit tennis court. The downside is that it's a good ten minutes' walk from lessons – 'but it keeps us fit,' one

14-year-old told us enthusiastically. Meanwhile Samworths' is a modern, purpose-built house (also created by Piers Gough) for 60 girls aged 13 to 18.

Around 45 new girls enter the sixth form each year and they are assigned to one of two sixth form girls' houses – The Lodge or Johnson's. New fourth formers (Year 9s) are mainly in dormitories (they have individual partitions, known as 'tishes' to give them privacy), with separate cabin-like studies, while sixth formers get bedsits. All pupils have their own school-provided desktop computer in their study or bedsit. Parents and prospective pupils are encouraged to look around the houses and make their own choice, though some have waiting lists. Pupils eat breakfast, lunch and supper in their houses – 'not the most economic way to do it,' says school, 'but it encourages friendship within a family setting.' One parent told us, 'it makes for a real home from home atmosphere – none of this awful going into a main hall and worrying whether you will have anyone to sit with.' Visitors are frequently invited to lunch in houses and youngsters take a pride in looking after their guests.

Pupils attend morning chapel five times a week. Atmosphere everywhere is busy and purposeful. Girls very well integrated – have been here since 1975 and school went fully co-ed in 2001. There's a tuck shop (known as the buttery) selling fruit, sweets, yoghurt and drinks, and a club for upper sixth pupils (tightly-restricted hours/consumption of drinks). Grey/black/claret school uniform for all till 6.20pm most days. Some parents grumble about pupils' 'scruffiness' but no sign of this when we visited. Loads of different house and prefect ties. So many, in fact, that a new pupils' handbook features a tie spotting guide! It also includes a list of dos ('when emailing a teacher make sure the email is polite') and don'ts ('don't use your mobile phone or iPod in the street'). Two school captains (boy and girl) and raft of prefects.

Pastoral Care and Discipline: School prides itself on its pastoral care. Each boarding house is run by husband and wife team (often with own family) who live in. At one house girls regularly troop into the housemistress's drawing room to play the piano while at another the housemistress's two black labradors are an integral part of pupils' lives. Lights out for youngest at 9.45pm while sixth form have to be in their rooms by 11pm. All boys and girls have a house tutor whom they meet once a week to discuss academic progress. New pupils get slightly older mentor to help them settle in and there is a wide choice of possible confidantes for youngsters – housemaster/housemistress, chaplain, matron, tutor, independent school counsellor etc. All pupils have life skills lessons – covering sex education, personal relationships etc. Rules are crystal-clear and outlined in the school's invaluable 'white list,' a prep diary containing maps, house lists and details of everything from uniform to exam timetables. Everyone gets a copy. Head takes firm line on drugs (expulsion), drink and smoking but says he can count the number of pupils he's asked to leave 'on the fingers of one hand'. Pupils told us school is 'strict but fair'. Detention system mainly for academic matters but also used for cutting a lesson or inappropriate behaviour. No exeats but parents welcome to visit and, by arrangement, take their children out on Saturday afternoon or Sunday (provided they have no school commitments). School passionately anti-bullying – 'persistent bullies must expect to be required to leave,' say rules.

Pupils and Parents: Pupils come from far and wide – Scotland down to Kent and Sussex, but many live within two hours' drive. Around 100 feeder prep schools but regular arrivals from Maidwell Hall, Old Buckenham Hall, Winchester House etc. Only four per cent from overseas but some children of Brits working for multinationals abroad. Around eight per cent are children of former pupils. Old Uppinghamians an eclectic lot – including Rick Stein, Stephen Fry, Carphone Warehouse founders Charlie Dunstone and David Ross, former health secretary Stephen Dorrell, Jonathan Agnew, Johnny Vaughan and John Suchet. A smattering of musicians too – Charlie Simpson (ex-Busted), Harry Judd (McFly) and two members of up and coming band Elliot Minor.

Very friendly, well-mannered pupils who are outgoing and confident but not arrogant. Most throw themselves into the myriad different activities on offer, from beekeeping and cookery to salsa and building go-karts. As one girl told us, 'it's cool to be involved'.

Entrance: Apply at any time from birth – but ideally more than three years before proposed entry. Head says lists looks 'pretty full' for next couple of years but it is always worth talking to the school. Pre-assessment and interview when prospective pupils are 11, plus report from present school. Provisional offers are made at this stage and deposits taken but youngsters still have to sit CE at 13 (head has upped baseline CE mark to 55 per cent), scholarship exams or tests/reports for those who haven't been prepared for CE. All pupils, whether they've been at Uppingham since 13 or are new at 16, must get six Bs at GCSE to progress into sixth form.

Excellent information pack for prospective parents, stuffed with detail. Information even includes contact details of parents of current and former pupils who are happy to talk about the school. High contentment rating among those we spoke to.

Exit: Virtually all to higher education – a number to Oxbridge each year, with Leeds, Durham, Newcastle, London very popular. A few to Cirencester and one or two to US universities. A large percentage of leavers take gap years.

Money Matters: A wide range of academic, music, art, design and technology and all-round scholarships (known as Thring scholarships after 19th century headmaster Edward Thring, who transformed Uppingham from a small grammar into a large public school) awarded at 13. Some at 16 too (but not all-rounder). Means-tested bursaries scheme for able children whose parents might not otherwise be able to afford it (up to 95 per cent of the full fee and much of this financed by former pupils).

Remarks: A wholesome, positive, happy place – both traditional and forward-thinking. Benefits from being a real seven-day a week boarding school, with lots to do at weekends. Pupils, whether they're academic or sporty, musical or artistic, seem to love it and results are good too. The previous head told us that children 'aren't "sent" to boarding school any more – they come because they wish to'. It's still very much the case here. Recent fracas seemingly wholly out of character – for both the place and its head – but has left a bitter taste for the moment.

Wakefield Girls' High School

Linked to Wakefield Girls' High School Junior School in the Junior section

Wentworth Street, Wakefield, West Yorkshire, WF1 2QS

• Pupils: 730 girls, all day • Ages: 11-18 • Size of sixth form: 170 • Inter-denom • Fees: £9,705 pa • Independent

Tel: 01924 372 490
Fax: 01924 231 601
Email: admissions@wghsss.org.uk
Website: www.wgsf.org.uk

Principal: Since September 2009, Mrs Gillian Wallwork BA (Manchester) English Language and Literature, previously deputy head of Cheadle Hulme School. Likes the theatre, a good book, the coast, family get-togethers, her spaniel, plants and Pre-Raphaelite art.

Academic matters: Over the last four years, 70–82 per cent obtained all As and Bs at AS/A2. Excellent results in all subjects and a wide range on offer, even if it means groups of only two or three at A level. Most take three A2s plus general studies. Art and design is very popular; the AQA external examiner the day we visited said that the work was the best he had ever seen. It's very well resourced; girls are allowed a lot of freedom and respond with remarkable creativity, using a variety of media. Biology is popular too, and very strong, as is chemistry; maths, politics, psychology and Spanish also stand out. Boys from QEGS can join a number of subjects, e.g. theatre studies, ICT and RS. There are no hurdles for existing girls to enter the sixth form (but if it's clear a girl will struggle with the pace, she will be encouraged to go down a less academic route elsewhere) and no AS to A2 hurdles.

GCSE results are also consistently excellent, around 76 per cent getting all A/A*; virtually 100 per cent A*–C. Superb results in 2009 in art and design (18 A*s and 32 As); German, Spanish and RS all A*s. Large numbers do separate sciences; dual award also offered. Textiles are done by all in Years 7–9 and girls make all the clothes for a fashion show. In design and technology the projects are tailored towards girls' interests and creativity, and product design is offered at GCSE. Lots of PCs and several interactive whiteboards; all girls do the ECDL in Year 9 and learn keyboard skills in the junior school. Class sizes are around 24 for Years 7–9, 5–25 at GCSE and 2–16 at A level. Setting for maths and French only from Years 8/9.

The well-staffed special needs unit, unusually, can be accessed easily by junior and senior girls, which reduces any sense of stigma. It's modern, bright and comfortable, catering for around 150 girls with e.g. dyslexia, dyscalculia, Asperger's – but not children with statements who, the school considers, would be better served in the state system. Support is given outside lesson time.

Games, Options, the Arts: The sports facilities are very good and exceptional results are achieved in local and national competitions in the usual range of sports as well as cross-country; netball and hockey are particularly strong, probably because they are started at the age of 7. Nearly half the school takes part in teams. Self defence and various kinds of gymnastics are also available. Very good drama facilities – a drama studio and access to a purpose-built theatre at QEGS. Lots of productions – mainly conventional choices, apart from the drama comp for Years 7–9 where girls write their own plays. Masses of music – a great range of choirs, some enjoying success in local competitions, and music groups for all ages, some in combination with QEGS, plus a wide choice of instrumental lessons (over half the girls learn) including jazz piano and bass guitar, with lots of very good exam results. Concerts, as well as plays, are put on with the boys' school (the Advent Carol Service is held in Wakefield Cathedral) and there is a recording studio funded by the PTA. Girls in Years 7–9 create their own dance routines in an inter-form dance competition. The library is generously resourced and fiction reading actively encouraged at all ages; a major extension is being planned. Plenty of school trips, in England and abroad, e.g. a swing band tour of north Italy, a hockey and netball tour to Hong Kong, Australia and Singapore, visits to France, Spain, Rome. Year 7 girls have a residential at the start of their first term to help them make friends, which they greatly value. A very wide choice of clubs and societies, including hamster care, Fun with Food and a gardening club that cultivates a vegetable garden and has a wormery. Huge numbers achieve D of E awards.

Background and Atmosphere: The school belongs to the Wakefield Grammar School Foundation, which offers 3–18 education to both sexes. It occupies a number of buildings in a conservation area near the centre of Wakefield, one-time town houses, the focal point being the original Georgian Wentworth House, with some attractive and thoughtfully designed modern additions, though some areas are drab and in need of re-decoration. Subjects are located in zones, e.g. creative arts, embracing music/drama/English/textiles and food tech, with a common, well-equipped computer suite.

There is an immediate buzz as soon as you enter the school. Girls come across as well-mannered, happy, confident and eager to learn. They appreciate the understanding and support they are given by teachers if they have any difficulties, work hard and have fun, too, e.g. the sixth formers have a fancy dress day in their last week at school, and there is a Christmas review performed by girls with guest appearances by staff. Lots of marvellous artwork and photos of girls' activities on display. Girls' birthdays are highlighted on big TV screens in three locations and all are given a teddy both on entering the junior as well as leaving the senior school – the latter dressed in a school hoodie! There is a strong sense of community, which the girls value; they see the school as friendly and safe.

Huge amounts of money raised for a broad range of charities (£18,000 in 2007–8), with the girls doing all the organisation, and there are links with a sister school in Tanzania, where girls teach on visits, as well as state school partnership events. The school council's views, e.g. on food, charities and qualities wanted in the new headmistress, are taken on board; its eco committee is aiming for the 'Green Flag Award'. The sixth form have their own building, an old house (due to be refurbished) with a café, kitchen and common room well supplied with battered sofas – the clutter is all very homely and they are allowed to entertain boys and enjoy a degree of independence there. There are three lovely memorials to old girls who have died young – a stained glass window depicting a rainbow, an indoor fountain and a small garden with wooden animal sculptures – that illustrate the school's humanity and thoughtfulness.

Pastoral Care and Discipline: Pastoral care is very good – girls are well known to staff, who soon spot signs of unhappiness. Girls see teachers as taking any upsets or arguments seriously and say there is no real bullying. The very good bullying policy was re-drafted by girls and there is a very sensible, realistic sixth form handbook. The transition from junior to senior school happens easily, as junior girls are able to use some of the senior school facilities. The girls are given freedom and clear limits (a code of conduct that 'gives guidelines for acceptable behaviour rather than rules') which they rarely breach, allowing a relatively relaxed atmosphere. A very strong line is taken with drugs and smoking.

Pupils and Parents: Some wealthy parents but most are professional/middle class. This is not a prosperous area and about a fifth of the girls currently receive assistance with fees – 'No one knows who's on an award; money is not an issue'. The catchment area is extensive: Wakefield, Huddersfield, Barnsley, north Sheffield and south Leeds. Parents organise bus services to fill in any gaps left by public transport. Half of Year 7 come from the junior school, the rest from local schools. Ethnically very mixed – one year had a Muslim head girl 'clearly the best person for the job', so the school decided to adapt the post's duties to accommodate her religious beliefs.

Entrance: 11+ by exam in English and maths, with verbal and non-verbal reasoning (110 in verbal reasoning is the cut off point, as 'they must be able to cope with the work – it's an absolutely basic requirement') plus primary school report and reference. The school provides clear, detailed information on what needs to be covered. Almost all junior school girls continue but it's not automatic. Girls can join at other years (preferably not in the middle of exam courses, though). 20–30 leave after GCSE and up to 12 enter at Year 12. These need a minimum of 440 points from their nine best GCSEs in a wide range of subjects and A/B in their proposed AS subjects.

Exit: To a wide range of universities – lots of Russell Group, steadily increasing numbers to Oxbridge (an impressive eight Cambridge offers in 2008), some to art/veterinary college; almost all achieve their first choice. The most famous old girl is Barbara Hepworth (head's elegant study contains two of her sculptures, as well as an interesting collection of model owls); other Old Girls are writers Helen Fielding and Joanne Harris, and Katherine Kelly and Priya Kaur Jones from the media world – plus Claire Young, the runner up in the 2008 *The Apprentice!*

Money Matters: Fees are all inclusive – no extra charge for learning support or exam entries. There is a pot of money for means-tested Foundation Awards, from 25–90 per cent, where parental income is less than £35,000, which funds about 14 bursaries in each year group with additional ones available in the sixth form. Also a 100 per cent fees scholarship awarded at entry in Year 7, with possibly another to come. There could be 100 girls on bursaries out of the 730 total. In addition, there is a 100 per cent Ogden award for the sixth form (reserved for state school applicants who want to take science/maths) and 12 other scholarships of 25/50/75 per cent.

Remarks: A very impressive and attractive school, offering a great range of opportunities for girls to develop talents and win respect for them, affording all the advantages of single sex education combined with plenty of interaction with nearby QEGS. It has the feel of a very stimulating, high achieving and caring family, where all the members are known and appreciated for who they are. Girls find it almost impossible to think of anything they would like to change – 'You just grow to love the school as it is,' said a Year 12 girl. 'You're not judged on your cleverness; you're seen as an individual – everyone's got their own strengths,' said another. Also outstandingly creative – witness the school mag, packed with stunning art and very strong writing.

Waldegrave School

Fifth Cross Road, Twickenham, Middlesex, TW2 5LH

• Pupils: 1,000 girls, all day • Ages: 11-16 • Non-denom • State

Tel: 020 8894 3244
Fax: 020 8893 3670
Email: info@waldegrave.org.uk
Website: www.waldegrave.richmond.sch.uk

Headteacher: Since 2006, Mrs Philippa Nunn BSc from UCL in Cell Biology, MA in Educational Management from Greenwich, PGCE and NPQH. In her early forties, married with two daughters at the local primary school. Was previously head of the Holt School in Berkshire, an all girls comprehensive. She started teaching science in 1987 and has only ever stopped for maternity leave. Currently teaches science and IT. Has a calm, measured and courteous manner and is content not to be too much of a new broom. Believes in stability and continuity and in taking the long view. Some staff have been at the school for more than twenty-five years which 'adds strength to the ethos of the school'. Aims to develop the curriculum by offering vocational qualifications in addition to the traditional curriculum. Introduced a house system (2009) to promote a greater sense of loyalty and belonging and to enhance student leadership opportunities.

Academic matters: Consistently achieves good results in English, maths and science GCSEs. French, history, art, drama always good too. The success rate in A–C grades is well above the regional and national average. Mrs Nunn strives to give every pupil the widest possible access to a variety of subjects as she is determined that they will leave the school intending to continue education. Virtually all do, so her determination is paying off. Quality of teaching is excellent. Teachers and support staff are committed to the school and urge the pupils to enjoy success and savour the rewards that accompany it. Achievements are recognised at assemblies throughout the year and at Celebration Afternoons at the end of the year. High academic standards are expected but provision is made within the curriculum for all abilities and modest acts such as helpfulness to the school or to others are duly acknowledged and rewarded. Lessons are given in broad ability tutor groups initially but setting for maths, science and languages occurs early on in the first years. In subsequent years setting in other subjects if appropriate. All are entered for 6–10 GCSEs, some do 13 after discussion with parents and staff. Short course subjects such as ICT, RE and PE well subscribed with good results.

The specialist schools status provides extra funding for science and maths including new ICT suites installed in 2006. Designated area in an independent learning centre for gifted and talented girls and those with other special needs. With an incredible cultural diversity, (43 different languages), EAL support is strong, even offering a lunchtime club for all age groups. On the subject of lunchtime, a great deal is compressed into a very short thirty-five minute break: careers advice, ICT, rehearsals for choirs and bands, puzzle club, homework clubs. Similarly, lots of before and after school activities. A breakfast club at 8am every morning with badminton on offer at the same time for the more energetic. After school up until 4pm – choice is much more varied with a high take-up rate.

Games, Options, the Arts: Good range of sports offered from the more traditional – rounders, tennis, volleyball, athletics – to the somewhat bizarre – Gaelic football. Classes in the new fitness suite, cricket, rowing (linked in with Walbrook Rowing Club) and table-tennis. Hidden from view from the road is a huge outdoor green area with tennis courts and marked out running track.

School regularly wins regional netball leagues and was recently the Middlesex hockey champion. Also borough winners at rounders. Head positively oozes enthusiasm listing her school's sporting achievements. Another of her aims is to improve participation in sport. Gymnastics is strong – both a multi and traditional gym on site. A dance studio, funded through the national lottery, 2006. Extra opportunities include bridge, drama, study skills, chess, art, music theory, ICT, choirs, rock bands and full orchestra. Art and music are both strengths. Beautiful displays throughout the school testimony to the high standard of work. In Year 11 the school offers a business mentoring system whereby girls are allocated someone from outside the school who comes in to see them on a regular basis over their last year. This is a forward-looking scheme, well organised by welcoming staff, which helps develop their social and business skills and gives them a timely introduction to outside world experiences.

Background and Atmosphere: Strange mix of building styles with the newer ones added on to the original (1930s) creating a bit of a hotch-potch. A 'temporary' cabin put up in 1948 still serves as the school canteen. Food cooked on site and those who bring packed lunches can either eat in there or in their form rooms. Space is limited and recent years have seen a new dance studio and fitness suite squeezed in. However, the major project completed September 2009 was the overhaul of the outside play area transforming it into an outdoor theatre with landscaped surroundings. The money for this raised by the extremely supportive PTA. They also maintain three small internal quadrangles which echo different themes – pond area, bamboo garden and the vegetable patch. Touches such as these add an element of style to the otherwise uninspiring architecture.

The girls themselves give this school a buzzy atmosphere. A former pupil remarks that 'all girls is a positive rather than a negative.' Uniform is worn by all, albeit often customised as has ever been the case in girls' schools. The end result is not unpleasing to the eye.

Pastoral Care and Discipline: No real behavioural problems. Room 16 is their room 101 and no-one wants to go there. First years are invited to spend a day in the school to find their way about and practise their journey to and fro – puts a stop to later excuses about buses being late. They also start the term a bit earlier before the older ones arrive. Prefects help out with the younger ones, organise charity events, welcome visitors and play an important leadership role in the school. Each tutor group elects a representative to attend the school council, which in turn represents the school at the Richmond School Student Council. All good training ground for debating and public speaking.

School is honest about bullying and admits that, like the poor, it is always with us. However, stringent efforts made to put an end to it. Girls, staff and parents exhorted to report any incident straight away and assured that something will be done.

Pupils and Parents: Although the school has no religious affiliation, the majority of the pupils are Christian. Twenty-five per cent are from an ethnic minority and the school rules stipulate that whilst permissible to wear the hijab (for religious reasons) the niqab should not be worn to school. All come from the surrounding borough of Richmond, which is known nationally for its high level of professional parents. A local parent declares it to be the sort of school where 'decent folk will be prepared to break all sorts of rules to get their daughters in.' Its lack of a sixth form does not deter as no state school in Richmond has one. 'I had no problems undertaking coursework and I was taught how to take exams at Waldegrave, so I felt confident about my A levels and about my degree course,' is the view of a former pupil. They're an ambitious lot and they have a very strong PTA to back them up.

Entrance: Fully comprehensive intake. It is the only all girls' state school in Richmond so is always over-subscribed. Much to the head's relief, all admissions are dealt with by the education authority. Despite clear and rigid guidelines about admissions policies there are always appeals. Sibling policy includes stepsisters, half sisters and adopted sisters living in the same household. A percentage of their intake includes those with special needs and those in public care or who are deemed by the LA to have a particular need. Most girls will have attended local primary schools in the borough.

Exit: Majority to Richmond Sixth Form College, some to Esher College and others to sixth forms of co-ed independent schools, day or boarding.

Remarks: A lively, happy school with pupils to match. Mrs Nunn strikes one as a slow burner who will move this school forward. Her enthusiasm and her demand for high standards are already reflected by the staff and students. A very good choice for those lucky enough to meet the entry criteria.

Wallington County Grammar School

Croydon Road, Wallington, Surrey, SM6 7PH

• Pupils: 890 boys, all day. Girls in the sixth form. • Ages: 11-18 • Size of sixth form: 225 boys and 45 girls • Non-denom • State

Tel: 020 8647 2235
Fax: 020 8254 7921
Email: admissions-wcgs@suttonlea.org
Website: www.wcgs.org.uk

Headteacher: Since 2009, Mr Peter Smart, following the retirement of Dr J Martin Haworth who had been head for 19 years. Mr Smart has been at the school for over 32 years, was deputy head for four years and then acting head.

Academic matters: A top notch, academic, selective state school. Pupils take up to 12 GCSEs – 75 per cent A/A* grades – 100 per cent five or more passes including English and maths (2010); consistently very good results. 82 per cent A*–B at A level in 2010; lots clock up four or more straight A grades – English lit and maths particularly impressive with religious studies attaining all A grades in 2009. Inclusion of girls in the sixth form has not distracted the boys from their studies – in fact, one parent claims that it promotes a slight rivalry to do well; one of the few schools where boys get better results than the girls. Extensive investment in DT, IT and music depts – now state-of-the-art. Interactive whiteboards all over, all teachers have laptops. Class size averages a hefty 30 in the lower years and 25 in Years 9–11. Pupils start GCSE studies in Year 9. Sixth form classes average 14–17. No specialist teachers for SEN – not really an issue here.

Games, Options, the Arts: Heaps of outdoor space for sports with a large field for rugby and 30 acres (owned by the school) at the Clockhouse for rugby and hockey. New sports hall opened Spring 2010. Sport seen as extremely important and there is an extensive fixture list against leading schools in the south east, many from the independent sector, including athletics, cross country, tennis, cricket, hockey and, in particular, some impressive rugby.

Music and drama taught extensively but, again, there is a lack of space for music practice (although group performances take place in the school hall). Music now higher profile with new director. Orchestra, wind band and choir. Recent drama productions include Animal Farm, Bouncers and Antigone. Excellent artwork is proudly displayed, predominantly in the main hallway outside the head's office. Art is strong, with several spacious art rooms. School clubs include chess, Warhammer, D of E, debating, Fair Trade, Christian Union, Islamic Society and many more.

Background and Atmosphere: Red-brick building c1935 houses the main school (founded in 1927), and encircles a superb courtyard garden – 'the Quad' – which is used only by teachers; pupils gain access on rare occasions. Inside, wooden floors, a pleasant entrance hall and the impressive oak panelled main hall create an impression not dissimilar to that made by an independent school. Overall, the school is a good size and not overcrowded. Different playgrounds are allocated to various year groups, which must be a relief for new pupils in particular, who have their own separate space. Large-ish cafeteria with a wide range of hot food. Overall, a studious atmosphere in which pupils seem relaxed, friendly and polite. To quote one parent, 'When we visited, the first thing we all noticed was how lovely the atmosphere was.'

Pastoral Care and Discipline: New buddying system – kindly sixth formers take a small clutch of Year 6 pupils under their wings just before the school summer holiday. New pupils get a good feel for the school prior to the start in September and (unlike other schools) this initiation lasts for four days – the newcomers can really get to know their new environment and teachers, as well as their 'buddy' sixth former. They then have the summer holiday to mull it all over and there is a friendly face to say 'hello' when they start school. According to Ofsted, this is one of the best induction programmes in the country – more than seven opportunities for pupils to get together before they arrive, including the four induction days. Parents are extremely happy with the results – 'my son settled down really well, he has found the school to be very friendly ... a few teachers are on the strict side however! Luckily, he was used to having a lot of homework at his previous (independent) school, so homework was not a problem and the buddying system really helped him feel at home.'

Bullying dealt with swiftly and severely. Smoking is forbidden on the premises for teachers and pupils alike and there are very few instances of smoking, drinking or drugs. House system a focus for loyalty and competition. Badges and ties awarded for sports and other school achievements.

Pupils and Parents: A big mix, well-integrated. Pupils are smartly turned out in uniform – sixth formers wear suits. Pupils are expected to be involved in sports and drama and with the local community. Parents can be as little or as much involved as they like. Good information flow from the school. Excellent PTFA who organise an extensive range of events – quiz nights, international evenings, balls – and support many school functions with refreshments, including parents' evenings.

Entrance: Selective at 11 – entrance exam prepared by the school – English, maths and a short verbal reasoning paper. There is no catchment criteria and places are almost all awarded in rank order. Competition is stiff for the 120 places with typically well over 1,600 taking the exam. Not surprisingly, private tutors earn a good living with many children being coached, though school discourages this – 'we work hard to ensure tutored children are not advantaged,' says admissions manager. Wide geographical intake – from south-east London, Croydon, Sutton, and Surrey, from numerous primary schools, including a few independents. Entry to sixth form no problem to most pupils who are rarely denied their chosen subjects. Each year there are typically 350 external applicants for 30–40 places in the sixth form; although the minimum requirement is lower, those offered places in 2009 achieved a minimum of 6A*s and two A grades, and in 2010 5A* with 3A grades (taken from their best 8 grades.) Places offered in rank order of GCSE results.

Exit: Many pupils elect to stay on to the sixth form, only a few leave for other further education or sixth form colleges. University choices are varied, many to London colleges. Between six – 12 to Oxbridge each year and quite a few students studying law and medicine. Very few take a gap year.

Remarks: A friendly, welcoming, academic school with excellent results and much praise for the pupil/teacher relationships. A real alternative to private school if your child is bright enough to get in.

Wallington High School for Girls

Woodcote Road, Wallington, Surrey, SM6 0PH

• Pupils: 1,300 girls, all day • Ages: 11-18 • Size of sixth form: 400 • Non-denom • State

Tel: 020 8647 2380
Fax: 020 8647 2270
Email: wallingtongirls@suttonlea.org
Website: www.wallingtongirls.sutton.sch.uk

Head: Since 2002, Mrs Barbara Greatorex (fifties) BSc in molecular science from Warwick University MA (in educational management from the Open University). She came to Wallington from Wolverhampton, where she was a deputy head for five years (previously held posts as a science teacher). A relaxed, very friendly and down to earth lady, she likes to teach but doesn't do too much – 'It's not fair to the students as I am away so much.' She describes herself as understanding, patient, supportive and caring. Her compassion is for all to see but she also has vision, aspirations and high expectations for all. Has been driving force behind recent changes as well as fantastic new facilities. She is a head who is not afraid of change – 'I want continuous improvement. I have high expectations.' She strives for 'excellence in everything' and hopes she can pass on a 'life-long love for learning' to her students. Parents describe her as 'very approachable – always surrounded by smiling girls when she walks around the school'.

Academic matters: Academically impressive – in 2009, 81 per cent A/A* grades at GCSE and 74 per cent A/B grades at A level. Particularly refreshing to see a girls' school so heavily promoting and succeeding in the science subjects. Sciences form the backbone of academia here (and there are remarkable facilities). Students take up to 12 GCSEs and, not surprisingly, popular subjects for both GCSE and A level are the sciences, maths, and technology – 70 per cent of girls take at least one science subject for A level. Recently awarded High Performance Specialist School Status and adopted languages to complement and contrast with engineering specialism. Head originally chose engineering to steer girls towards problem solving, creating and designing, as well as pushing engineering up to the same status as medicine (an extremely popular career choice at the school, especially among the girls from ethnic minorities). Strong maths department. Amazing IT facilities with three IT rooms equipped with state-of-the-art flat screen monitors. School has been kitted with thirty interactive whiteboards and every teaching member of staff has a laptop (top of the range!). A parent who moved to the school from the private school sector said she was 'amazed to find equipment I had never seen in my daughter's previous school!' Needless to say computers feature heavily in teaching of most subjects – students can access topics and their homework from computers at home. Good choice of languages, English and humanities very sound. Much praised teaching throughout the school, with staff delivering exciting multi-activity lessons. Students enjoy their learning and teachers enjoy teaching them.

Classrooms are reached through a warren of corridors displaying girls' work and posters from school trips (Morocco, Vietnam and others). Bang up to date classrooms, buzzing science labs, art and technology rooms – all impressive. Students are focused, neat and happy – lots of keen hands in the air. Library is very small but in full action at lunchtime. School's intake of students with dyslexia is very low. SENCo and teaching assistants are on hand. Study support groups offered major subjects.

Games, Options, the Arts: Sport is strong and girls take part in the sports leadership programme where they help out pupils from feeder schools. Attractive grounds offer surprising amount of outdoor space; huge concreted area used for tennis and netball, acres of playing fields. Next on head's wish list is new indoor sports facilities – currently the school hall doubles as sports hall, and there is also a very cramped gymnasium: building work started Autumn 2010.

Very impressive art displayed in classrooms as well as reception – not surprising, being an Artsmark gold status school. Fabulous designs by the textiles students. Drama also very impressive. The girls do everything from producing, directing, acting and lighting to costume design. One parent happily said, 'if I did not know any better, I would have thought I was in the West End!' Girls who take part in a production are immediately set to train the girls who get involved in the following year's play. Music lessons on offer for groups as well as one-to-one tuition. Sixth formers introduced to variety of leadership programmes and from Year 9 upwards work experience is on the agenda.

Background and Atmosphere: Very large school with vibrant and professional feel. Established in 1888 but moved to its current site in 1965. Houses the 1,300 girls as well as staff without making you feeling claustrophobic. Archetypical 1960s school building wih recently refurbished entrance hall. The head feels that her aspiration to teach her girls 'excellence in everything' can only be attained by providing the girls with a friendly happy atmosphere – 'Life is about enjoying what you do and if you do not, then you need to reflect' (parents feel this depicts Mrs Greatorex perfectly). Huge amounts of money have been raised by the school and parents alike, to bring to life the music block (which opened during head's first year at the school) followed by the major development of the new Link building with six classrooms, two offices and lifts. School day starts at 8:25am and ends at 2:50pm. Girls can be dropped off as early as 7:30 and after-school clubs like drama, sports and chess clubs are run by sixth formers until 4 IT suites are also available for use during these times. Independent catering company offers freshly cooked meals with lots of choice and variety. Also a breakfast club.

Pastoral Care and Discipline: High on the agenda. Very little bullying. 'You have to be realistic,' says Mrs Greatorex. No drugs problems faced. The head feels that punishment does not work in all cases and support can be more productive, she is very much in control of her girls – kind but firm. Anorexia and self-harm (a growing problem in many girls' selective schools – who said that academically bright girls don't have personal issues?) were 'major problems' in the past. Mrs Greatorex has since employed full time counsellor – 'virtually no cases since!' she says, with a real sense of achievement and care. Counsellor has proved to be a huge success generally – 'My daughter's friend lost her father and the support she received from the counsellor was just amazing.' Parents are kept informed regularly with newsletters, reports and parent/teacher meetings. Mrs Greatorex also runs a drop-in session on a monthly basis should anyone wish to see her personally – a super idea, particularly in such a big school.

Pupils and Parents: Lots of ethnic minorities, with parents who want their daughters to achieve highly – particularly those looking to study medicine. Very harmonious and friendly, it is an outgoing place; quieter less motivated souls may struggle a little despite being given individual support. Girls are very polite, happy and extremely smart. Hair neat and skirts of a decent length. Sixth formers (who do not wear the school uniform) range from smart dressers to followers of fashion.

Entrance: From over 60 feeder schools – private and state. Highly over-subscribed for entry at 11 – over 1200 girls compete for 180 places. Entrance is via exam – verbal reasoning and maths papers. 'Apply via common applications process and put us as one of your schools of preference,' stresses Mrs Greatorex. Entry into sixth form – six passes grade B or above, with an A or a B in subject chosen for A level as well as its supporting subjects.

Exit: Between 10 and 12 girls leave after GCSEs. Around 98 per cent go on to higher education after A levels. Some 11 students went to Oxbridge in 2008 – head is pleased that the number is rising. Others to London, Reading, Loughborough, Warwick and many more. Popular degree courses are medicine, engineering, law and dentistry.

Money Matters: Fundraising is high on the agenda – 'Unless we raise the funds ourselves nothing would improve,' says Mrs Greatorex. Parents work very hard to help fundraise and support the school.

Remarks: Energetic, happy and positive place with top academic results and a switched on head. Ideal for academic, confident girls (particularly for aspiring medics and engineers) who have a clear aim and are up for a challenge.

Warwick School

Linked to Warwick Junior School in the Junior section

Myton Road, Warwick, Warwickshire, CV34 6PP

• Pupils: 1165 boys, mostly day. Around 50 boarders. • Ages: 11-18 • Size of sixth form: Approximately 250 boys in the sixth form. • C of E • Fees: Day £10,107; Boarding £10,107 - £11,460 pa • Independent

Tel: 01926 776 400
Fax: 01926 401 259
Email: enquiries@warwickschool.org
Website: www.warwickschool.org

Head Master: Since 2002, Mr Edward Halse, BSc, FRSA (late forties). Brought up in Welsh mining valley and educated at Garw Grammar School and University of Wales, where he read economics. Vastly experienced in both state and independent sectors – first job was at Brynteg Comprehensive in Bridgend and later became senior housemaster at Kelly College and second master at Dauntsey's before being appointed head at Kent College, Canterbury in 1995. Played for British students' rugby team in his 20s. Down to earth, dedicated and ultra-professional – 'it's my job to discover in every boy a seed of genius by giving them a massive range of opportunities.' Keen advocate of single-sex education – 'fewer distractions in the classroom,' he reckons. Married, with two grown-up children at university. Jean, his wife, very involved in school too – teaches English as a foreign language and sixth form cookery. Family lives in part of the main school. Head knows most boys by name and hosts series of birthday parties for new Year 7s.

Academic matters: Good performance at all levels. Head says Warwick is 'first and foremost an academic school in which all pupils are encouraged and motivated to give of their best,' and they certainly do. 75 per cent A/A* grades at GCSE in 2010. 39 boys achieved a clean sweep of A/A* grades. Good A2 results too, with 89 per cent A*, A and B grades. 16 boys achieved three or more A* grades.

Year groups divided into six forms. Average class sizes of around twenty up to GCSE and ten at A level. Setting by ability for most subjects. Boys take Latin for first two years, French for first three. German, Spanish, Russian, Arabic and Mandarin also on offer and everyone takes at least one modern language at GCSE. Science hugely popular throughout school. At a time when sciences are declining in many schools, half the sixth form at Warwick take sciences at A level (physics is number one choice, followed by chemistry, then biology.) Lots of boys go on to do science, engineering, medicine, dentistry etc at university. A state-of-the-art £6 million science building opened in 2007, with 14 new labs and 120-seat lecture theatre. Dr Mo Afzal, former head of science at school, founded the Science for the 21st Century Initiative to promote contemporary science to sixth formers from state and independent sectors and Warwick boys very involved in project. School has number of pupils with mild or moderate dyslexia, dyspraxia, dysgraphia and Asperger's. Around 24 come out of lessons for extra help from specialist SEN teachers, either one-to-one, in pairs or small groups. Cost is £32 an hour for individual help and £16.00 for group work. Similar number of boys, mainly from Hong Kong, China and Korea, get EAL support (maximum charge £520 a term).

First-rate library, with 20,000 books. ICT networked throughout school and two-thirds of classrooms have interactive whiteboards. Team of 100 staff, around 20 per cent of them women. Teachers dedicated and energetic – and all expected to help out with extra-curricular activities. Very hot on study skills too. Head of upper school's tips for GCSE pupils include use Mind Maps, switch off the music and don't leave work till last thing at night. Sensible advice!

Games, Options, the Arts: Sport plays a key role in school life. All boys take part, with 23 rugby teams playing in matches on winter Saturdays. Main sports are rugby, hockey, crosscountry, swimming, cricket, athletics and tennis, but everything from rowing to rock climbing available too. Lots of county players and recent sporting triumphs include winning the national schools' championships for waterpolo, claypigeon shooting three times and in rugby, Daily Mail Cup winners in 2007.

Music is top-notch. Very dynamic director of music keen to get as many boys involved as possible and succeeds. All 11-year-olds given instrument and free weekly music lesson for a year to inspire them. Imaginative approach that pays dividends – 450 instrument lessons timetabled every week in school. Concerts galore throughout year – everything from full orchestra to big band and rock groups. Chapel choir sings at school every Sunday morning in term-time and at packed candlelit advent service in December. Three music bands were awarded the highest accolade, platinum, at the National Concert Band Finals in 2010.

Lots of drama opportunities – *Titus Andronicus, Chicago,* you name it – take place at school's 300-seat Bridge House Theatre, which is used for school productions, lectures and concerts as well as shows by professional companies. Art and DT popular, with boys' work proudly displayed throughout school. All pupils get double period of art and design a week for first three years and can then opt to carry on to GCSE, AS and A2. A school production, *Victims of Duty,* was selected for the National Student Drama Festival in 2007 (the only school to be selected) and won two awards.

Astonishing range of clubs and societies to try – cryptography, car mechanics, robotics (national champions 2006 and 2007), fantasy football, even ultimate frisbee (whatever that is!). Boys can also sign up for D of E, Young Enterprise and CCF. Dizzying array of trips, foreign visits and sports tours as far afield as Cuba and New Zealand. Highlight of the year for youngest boys is the lower school sleepout, where they get to sleep in cardboard boxes in the playground to raise money for charity. Head and his wife do their bit by pushing soup trolley round at midnight!

Background and Atmosphere: The oldest boys' school in the world (they claim) – reputedly established in 914 and moved to present 50-acre site bordering picturesque River Avon in 1875. Facilities include very couth sixth form centre, 25 metre indoor pool, two Astroturf pitches and playing fields as far as the eye can see. Senior school is a maze of buildings, old and new, but maps posted at strategic points to guide lost visitors. A Church of England foundation, school accepts boys of all denominations and faiths. Head boy and raft of prefects in place, all voted in by peers and staff. Boys belong to one of six houses and there are lots of interhouse events. School uniform strictly adhered to – no loose ties or untucked shirts.

Around 50 boys, many from Hong Kong, China, Eastern Europe and Russia, board in comfy rooms on upper floors of main school building (maximum of three boys to a room). Boys can board from seven but when we visited all boarders were senior school age. Scope for weekly and flexi-boarding too, plus after-school homework club.

Pastoral Care and Discipline: Huge emphasis on pastoral care. Boys are polite and helpful – 'it's ingrained in the system,' says head. 'We don't have to drum it into them.' Peer support system in place where younger boys can talk to prefects if they have any problems. Boys say school is 'relatively strict', but know where they stand and are happy with it. Firm stance taken on smoking, drinking and drugs. Head says, 'I'd be naïve to think that none of our boys do those things but we have no evidence of it happening in school.' Very strong anti-bullying policy in place – 'We believe that everyone has the right to be who they want to be,' says a senior master. Although school is all-boys, lots of joint activities with King's High, the girls' school up the road – drama, music, debates etc.

Pupils and Parents: Area has excellent transport links so boys arrive by bus, train and car from huge catchment area – as far away as Oxford, Northampton and Solihull. Just under half of each 140-strong year group comes from Warwick School's own junior department. The rest are from state primaries and preps like Arnold Lodge, The Croft, Eversfield and Abbotsord.

Warwick boys are a purposeful, friendly bunch who appreciate the myriad of opportunities on offer. One busy sixth former told us, 'this place never closes. It's a seven-day a week lifestyle and I'll be very sad to leave.' Notable old boys are an eclectic lot, including the celebrated poet John Masefield, England cricketer Neil Smith and millionaire entrepreneur Denys Shortt.

Entrance: School is selective but not rigidly so. Head says that if boys can cope with standard and pace of work they are likely to be offered a place. Usual entry points are 7, 11, 13 and sixth form. Youngest boys take maths, English and non-verbal reasoning tests and head interviews scholarship candidates. Fewer places available at 13 but still worth a try. All boys entering the sixth form need at least five Bs at GCSE, including Bs in their chosen A level subjects.

Exit: Most pupils stay on to do A levels at Warwick. Virtually all boys go to university, with 10 to 20 a year heading for Oxbridge.

Money Matters: Range of scholarships (academic and music) on offer – usually up to 20 per cent of fees (means-tested above that). Other awards and bursaries include Warwick Foundation places (restricted to boys living in town of Warwick) and a sixth form science scholarship for an outstanding student from a state school.

Remarks: An impressive school, offering countless opportunities. Perfect for boys who relish throwing themselves into everything under the sun. They seem to have fun while achieving excellent academic results. 'Whatever we do we like to do it well,' says head, and it shows.

Watford Grammar School for Boys

Rickmansworth Road, Watford, Hertfordshire, WD18 7JF

• Pupils: 1,250 boys • Ages: 11-18 • Size of sixth form: 350 • Non-denom • State

Tel: 01923 208 900
Fax: 01923 208 901
Email: brownc@watfordboys.herts.sch.uk
Website: www.watfordboys.org

Head: Since 2000, Mr Martin Post MA FRSA (early fifties). Former head prefect at WBGS in 1976. Started his career at King's, Rochester, moved to Mill Hill County High and then Richard Hale School in Hertford before joining WBGS as deputy head in 1995. Read English and related literature at the University of York. Teaches some English and PSHE. Married, with one son who, he hopes, will join the school when he is 11. Popular with parents – 'he has a strong presence. We think very well of him' – and Ofsted – '...outstanding leadership and management ... ' He says, 'I've got the best job in education'.

Academic matters: An unashamedly academic curriculum. Everyone tries three languages, and takes at least one to GCSE; talented linguists can take Italian GCSE in Year 9. Latin and classical civilization are important departments. Around two-thirds take separate sciences at GCSE and many continue to A level. 'Outstanding' maths department. Huge numbers take it at A level and most get A grades. Overall, the percentage of A/B grades at A level is generally in the high 70s.

The only 'studies' on offer are business, religious and sports – the latter popular at A level as well as GCSE. The intake is undoubtedly skewed in favour of the top of the ability range, but since nearly everyone gets at least five good GCSEs, those who are less academic are evidently lifted by the same rising tide. 'There is plenty of mixed-ability teaching at KS3, so low-ability pupils are not ghettoized. They have their aspirations raised and it can be very liberating.' The school works with other providers where necessary – one boy learns basic skills at WBGS and construction elsewhere. 'You don't succeed with a broad range of students unless you are prepared to be flexible. We're very proud of the fact that boys with autism, dyslexia or dyspraxia succeed very well here. But they must want to work and to have their aspirations raised. With boys for whom this is not the appropriate school, we give them all the support and use our best influence to find the best place for them.'

Games, Options, the Arts: 'This is not an exam factory. It's about music and drama, sport and debating too.' Sports high profile here, particularly rugby, cricket and hockey. 'We're the best state school in the country for hockey. They can pick it up at 11 and take it to international level.' Football is not on the curriculum – although, said our guide, 'it can be difficult to get from one end of the playground to the other because of footballs flying about.' More individual sports like cross-country, athletics and sailing also popular, and the school houses a table tennis academy.

Eighteen places a year are awarded for musical aptitude and there are lots of music groups and ensembles, including a joint orchestra with the girls' school. The stunning new music centre has a 200 seat concert hall as well as many practice rooms, a recording studio and a music technology suite. Very few take art GCSE or A level, 'though it's interesting how many keep doing art even though they're not working for an exam.' Food tech, a new addition, 'has taken off hugely', and there is a sixth form survival cookery club.

Plenty of clubs – from chess to debating – and trips away: sports tours, World Challenge, language exchanges, field trips, creative writing courses. Lots of work with charities e.g. Mencap.

Background and Atmosphere: Has its origins in the Watford Free School, founded in 1704 by Mrs Elizabeth Fuller, which split into separate boys' and girls' schools in 1884; these were renamed the boys' and girls' grammar schools in 1903. Has the feel of a '50s grammar school – and indeed, *The History Boys* was filmed here and at the girls' grammar. Polished wood, cream panelling, stone stairs, honours boards, oil paintings of previous heads. The long neo-Georgian main block and adjacent Master's House are grade two listed buildings. The add-ons of various architectural pedigrees culminate in the award-winning Clarendon Muse music building on the front lawn, splendidly clad in blue/green glass, which is also used by the Watford Music Centre.

Pastoral Care and Discipline: Has a critical mass of pupils who want to work hard. 'It becomes a virtuous circle – our boys tend to want to succeed, so exceptions become isolated.' Boys say: 'They're strict when they need to be strict, but they try to make it as fun as possible.' One who had moved from an independent school was happy to find it freer and more relaxed than his previous school. There are around 15–20 short term exclusions a year, but few of these become permanent. 'This is a very ordered environment. They take responsibility for themselves, and we can trust them to do so.'

Pupils and Parents: Wide social and cultural mix; about a quarter have English as a second language. Those with specialist places come from up to five miles away, though the third or so who get in on distance usually live within about a kilometre. OBs include actor and comedian Terry Scott; pornographer, publisher and chairman of West Ham United David Sullivan; England rugby international Josh Lewsey; and poet Michael Rosen.

Entrance: Don't bother to apply for one of the 180 places unless you live in the right WD or HA postcode. Forty-five academic and 18 music places, 60 per cent allocated to those who live in the nearest Watford postcodes ('Watford Area') and 40 per cent to those in the 'Rest of Admission Area'. Then eighteen places to those who live nearest and haven't got a specialist place, then priority to siblings. In 2008, and to much parental angst, the schools' adjudicator ruled that the two Watford grammar schools may no longer give priority to siblings of those at the other school – so boys with sisters at the girls' school don't get preference. After siblings, the remainder of the places are allocated by distance – usually less than a kilometre. A few join the sixth form, with a minimum of six B grades at GCSE.

Exit: A few – usually less than 10 per cent – leave after GCSE, some because they didn't get the six grade Bs needed for sixth form study. 'It's rare for people to leave on bad terms. We tell everyone it's a seven year programme; the assumption is that everyone goes through to the sixth and everyone goes to university.' Most years 30–40 have a go at Oxbridge and 7–10 get places. Medicine, economics and business all popular courses, a large proportion at Russell group universities.

Remarks: Very popular, high performing, partially selective school with a grammar school ethos. Boys work and play hard with results to match.

Watford Grammar School for Girls

Lady's Close, Watford, Hertfordshire, WD18 0AE

• Pupils: 1,260 girls; all day • Ages: 11-18 • Size of sixth form: 360 • Non-denom • State

Tel: 01923 223 403
Fax: 01923 350 721
Email: head@watfordgirls.herts.sch.uk
Website: www.watfordgrammarschoolforgirls.org.uk

Head: Since 1987, Mrs Helen Hyde MA (early sixties, with no intention of retiring). Educated to degree level in South Africa; moved to the UK in 1970 and did a Masters at King's College London. She started her teaching career at Acland Burghley in Camden, then moved to Highgate Wood as curriculum deputy, before taking up the Watford headship. Married to a consultant paediatrician, she has two adult daughters, one of whom went right through the school during her headship. 'It was mind-blowing. I'd get the thumbs down during assembly if she didn't like what I was saying. We had girls from the school in and out of our house all the time, so I've got very close to them.' Has a South African lack of ceremony and breaks off our interview to go and hug one daughter, up at the school for a violin lesson.

Her aims are to make Watford 'the best girls' school in the country' and to produce confident girls who are willing to take risks. 'Instead of "every child matters" I would say that "every teacher matters". If you make sure that your teachers feel confident to teach, they will make sure that every child learns.' The school motto, Sperate Parati – 'Go forth with preparation' – is translated by staff and girls as 'I can do it and I will do it'.

'I don't do hierarchy.' She views the school as a team effort, welcoming suggestions from governors – 'we come up with phenomenal ideas together' – and viewing teaching and non-teaching staff as all part of the team. Her PA is 'a proper partner', and the business manager – who spent most of his working life in Tenerife – assesses the Spanish level of applicants to cover a maternity vacancy in modern languages. 'They are all fully accountable. Trust goes all the way down. We work as a team to drive up academic standards.'

Her aunt and other family members were murdered in a death camp in Nazi-occupied Poland, and the school is a centre for Holocaust studies. 'If we don't look at the Holocaust in depth and find out how it came about, we won't be able to explain why Rwanda, Darfur and other tragedies happened.'

High praise from parents. 'She's a brilliant head…very strong, very dynamic…She wants girls to be aware of their wider moral responsibilities…She pushes everyone to do their bit for charity.' Indeed, she leads the way, climbing Ben Nevis in 2009 to raise money for the Anthony Nolan Trust, and cycling to Paris to raise funds for the new maths building.

Academic matters: Watford is one of only five UK training schools for De Bono thinking tools, and the head teaches all new staff and Year 7 pupils to use these skills. 'I tell them that this is a no mistakes zone – that a mistake is just a little opportunity to try something else.' Staff and girls use these in conjunction with Mind Mapping. 'A combination of the two programmes makes them look at a subject from all angles.'

Certainly, it seems to pay dividends: well over 90 per cent of girls get 5+ A*–C grades at GCSE including maths and science, and generally over 80 per cent of A level grades are A or B. There is an expectation that everyone will work hard and do well, and most do, though some feel that the academic pressure can get too strong. Ofsted talks of 'an almost relentless drive to ensure that everyone achieves her very best'.

The school has two specialisms: visual arts, and maths and computing, which mirror its mix of academia and creativity, tradition and innovation. 'We teach the solid stuff – what history is, what geography is, French grammar – and then creativity.' The girls all study traditional subjects but they also do Young Enterprise, enter the Bank of England and *The Times* Interest Rate Challenge, win prizes in the Taylor Woodrow Art Competition.

Maths is a particular strength, with huge numbers taking it and further maths to A level. 'It's an amazing department,' says the head. 'I'd never seen maths taught like this before.' About two-thirds do three separate sciences at GCSE, and biology and chemistry are consistently amongst the most popular A level choices. The head of physics fancied studying GCSE astronomy, so he enrolled a group of girls who learned alongside him. Now several take the GCSE each year, studying at lunchtime.

Everyone studies two languages – 'we teach them grammar, which is not part of the curriculum, but it helps them to speak better and write proper essays' – and takes at least one language to GCSE. 'As a linguist and a head I said no to allowing them to give up languages at 14.'

Offers the Extended Project Qualification in the sixth form, enabling girls to pursue an extended study of any subject that fascinates them. 'We get some weird and wonderful projects.'

There are a few girls with SEN statements, some with dyslexia or dyspraxia, and the school has accommodated special needs ranging from blindness to a girl with spina bifida. 'We're not wheelchair accessible, but she got on her crutches and made her way round the school.' Girls can get extra help within the classroom but no-one is withdrawn for special classes.

Games, Options, the Arts: Two playing fields, an indoor pool, tennis and netball courts, gym and sports hall including a fitness suite, dance studio and weights room, open to members of the public outside school hours. Teams play in galas and inter-school matches, and some make district and county level swimming, hockey and netball teams.

In keeping with the school's visual arts status and its Artsmark Gold, art in its different forms is high profile here. Highly original paintings, photos and textile designs line the corridors and a sculpture garden shows off sixth form work. 'My head of art is so original and so zany.' Fine art, 3D art, photography and graphics are all GCSE options, alongside graphic products and textiles. 'DT's great,' said a pupil. 'We're taught how the machines work then left to get on and use them.'

Large numbers have instrumental lessons, and there is a huge range of choirs, groups and ensembles, including a joint orchestra with the Boys' Grammar. Drama is important too – 'it's really good,' say girls – with some joint productions e.g. *Wizard of Oz*. Plenty of clubs – in Year 7 girls are encouraged to try three, including one music and one sports. Lots of field trips, theatre and museum visits, ski-ing and sailing trips, expeditions abroad.

Background and Atmosphere: Founded in 1704 by Mrs Elizabeth Fuller, the school originally taught girls to read, knit and sew, as well as recite the Church of England catechism. It moved to its present site – handily just down the road from Watford High Street station – in 1907, and has been expanding ever since. The History Boys was filmed here and at its brother school, Watford Grammar School for Boys, and the original buildings have a traditional feel with polished wood floors and cream panelling. 'It's like a 1950s grammar school, in a good way,' commented a parent. Lessons are orderly, but pupils are encouraged to show their exuberance outside class. 'I like my girls to let off steam at lunch time.'

Recent additions include the bright and airy Food Factory (designed by one of the head's daughters) with its café-style tables – 'everyone loves it,' say girls – and the new Hyde House maths block – 'it's our pride and joy. We all worked hard to get it.' This was completed in double-quick time by a triumvirate of the head, business manager and site manager, who side-stepped the lumbering government Building Schools for the Future programme by raising their own funds and organising their own design and construction.

Year 7s have their base in Lady's Close House, reached by a bridge over a public footpath from the main part of the school, which originally housed the prep school until it closed in 1944. The latest fund-raising project aims to refurbish it into a vibrant teaching area for the English Department.

Pastoral Care and Discipline: Firm and fair. 'I have some very naughty characters, but I won't allow a child to disrupt learning. If someone is seriously disruptive I will remove them.' No-one has been permanently excluded for many years, however. 'If you're very firm and everyone knows your expectations, most will live up to them.' Strong emphasis on building up girls' confidence and self-esteem. 'I believe passionately that the school is like a jewellery box. I tell the girls that they are my diamonds, and that we're going to polish and polish them. Alongside academia, we stand for respect, tolerance, caring and kindness.'

Pupils and Parents: Good racial and social mix – bright, well-motivated girls make up a good proportion of pupils. 'There's a nice multi-cultural feel,' said a parent. Parents tend to be very supportive and join in the fashion shows, fairs, discos, indulgence evenings and aquathalons. Notable OGs: Geri Halliwell and *EastEnders* actress Rita Simons.

Entrance: Don't bother to apply for one of the 180 places unless you live in the right WD or HA postcode. Forty-five academic and 18 music places, 60 per cent allocated to those who live in the nearest Watford postcodes ('Watford Area') and 40 per cent to those in the 'Rest of Admission Area'. Then eighteen places to those who live nearest and haven't got a specialist place, then priority to siblings. In 2008, and to much parental angst, the schools' adjudicator ruled that the two Watford grammar schools may no longer give priority to siblings of those at the other school – so girls with brothers at the boys' school don't get preference. After siblings, the remainder of the places are allocated by distance. Thirty or so join after GCSEs, bearing at least six good GCSEs, with A or B grades in their A level subjects. Those already at the school get first choice of subjects.

Exit: All GCSE students are advised to investigate alternative sixth forms in case they don't make the grade to stay on. Around 30 students a year leave after GCSEs, some because their results aren't up to it, others because they fancy a sixth form college experience. 'Brilliant' advice for sixth form leavers. 'The careers adviser knows everything there is to know about universities,' say sixth formers. A dozen or so a year to Oxbridge; a large proportion of the rest to Russell Group universities. Plenty of budding pharmacists, dentists and medics, and a good crop of engineers.

Remarks: Very popular semi-selective girls' school with a dynamic, determined head who ensures that it continues to go from strength to strength.

Wellington College

Linked to Eagle House School in the Junior section

Duke's Ride, Crowthorne, Berkshire, RG45 7PU

- Pupils: 990 pupils, including 350 girls. 205 day pupils, the rest board
- Ages: 13-18 • Size of sixth form: 340 • C of E • Fees: Day £21,570-£24,450; Boarding £28,785 pa • Independent

Tel: 01344 444 013
Fax: 01344 444 115
Email: admissions@wellingtoncollege.org.uk
Website: www.wellingtoncollege.org.uk

Master: Since 2006, Dr Anthony Seldon MA PhD MBA FRSA FRHistSoc (fifties), who was the making of Brighton College in his nine years there. Educated at Tonbridge School and Worcester College, Oxford. Author of many well-regarded books, including biographies of John Major, Tony Blair and Gordon Brown (2010). Capable of rattling off books at a tremendous speed – his history of the Foreign Office was written in three weeks – and ploughs all the profits back into education charities. Charismatic, enthusiastic, strong social conscience (sponsoring an Academy in Tidworth, Wiltshire, strong army connections). A star. Wife, Joanna (Oxford double first and DPhil) is an oasis of calm, teaches English; three children.

An historian, piles three lives into one and needs two secretaries to keep up with him. During our visit to the school – our itinerary was changed three or four times – Dr Seldon interviewed for a new head of dance ('five minutes is sufficient, I can tell just by looking at them; I'll see them all together'); had lunch with a dozen brand new 13-year-old girls at his home, The Lodge, (rather underfurnished and ruled by a tee-shirt wearing dog called Toby) and met with a potential new head of mod langs (or there may have been two of them). He also left us with the girls in his dining room whilst he whizzed off to chair a governors' meeting ('knock on the door when you go'). The previous day he had been at Gordonstoun and was flying off to China the following morning and emailed us four days later from Princeton. Seldon has lunch and/or dinner with pupils every day. Phew. 'An inspired appointment', 'Wellington was lucky to get him' are regular comments from peers and colleagues alike.

The man is a workaholic and, indeed, even before he took up the mastership, was writing to prep school heads inviting them to visit the following term; he currently visits three or four a week. Conferences are now a feature of Wellington life, leadership, head boy/girlship et al. Seldon churns out regular serious hefty articles on education – his current passion is happiness. Skills of well-being (in conjunction with the Cambridge Institute for Well-being) are part of the PSHE curriculum; Seldon himself has given up coffee, tea (he drinks a milky brew that his staff call sludge), meat and booze – all of which gives him 'more energy ... to become a better person'. His disapproval of smoking is a given.

Described as 'the most quoted head in living memory', Seldon's mastership has done Wellington nothing but good. A rash of new houses have sprouted over the last couple of years, and a huge amount of revamping and consequent movement interhouse under way – heaven forfend if contractors are late in delivering. Over 70 new staff and a number of new housemasters have been appointed. The school is now fully co-ed and both day and boarding numbers are up, with places heavily over-subscribed and the school roll now the highest in its history. IB introduced in September 2008 and its first IB results, average point score of 35, are in line with similar schools that have already been running the IB for a decade or more. Seldon has brought Wellington 'well out of the third division and into the first' – a claim we'd agree with wholeheartedly.

Seldon wants Wellington to be the most innovative school in Britain. He has set up an Academy modelled on Wellington; put well-being ('happiness') at the heart of school; modelled the curriculum and co-curriculum around eight aptitudes; established the first Festival of Education there; offers leadership programmes to all pupils; has given an international focus to the school; and innovations in the classroom include the use of Harkness tables (see http://en.wikipedia.org/wiki/Harkness_table – holding classes round a large table) and appointing a thinker-in-residence (Tony Buzan), a philosopher-in-residence (Julian Baggini) and the introduction of the Middle Years Programme of the IB to complement the IB Diploma. By his own admission he is 'a stickler for detail', 'not remotely complacent', 'driven – everything looking good at the moment'. Do not be deceived by appearances, this is a very iron fist in a gossamer glove; think Puck, think Ariel: this man is a legend in his time, hopefully purity of diet will prevent early burn out.

Academic matters: A school which many parents consider alongside Eton and Radley, it is good to report that exam results have improved substantially. Wellington has traditionally emphasised breadth over swotting but is becoming increasingly selective. Maths is the most popular A level subject, followed by economics and biology, the latter taught by an enthusiast who keeps a tank of enormous snapping piranhas in his classroom. Fantastic biology expeditions to Malaysia and Madagascar in conjunction with geography department. Learning support is low-key and pupils describe the SENCo as wicked.

Setting from the start in most subjects. Free choice of modern languages, with Latin 'almost compulsory' (six out of eight first year sets learn it, with the remainder doing classical civilisation), plus Mandarin and Hebrew. All pupils are taught well-being, philosophy, history of art and thinking. Now offers International Baccalaureate Middle Years Programme alongside GCSEs and the IB Diploma alongside A levels. All the usual suspects for IB and A level; graphs and statistics show dramatic rise in results over the last three years. 93 per cent A*–B at A level.

Games, Options, the Arts: Spectacular, invincible sportsmen, particularly good at rugby and hockey where they do almost nothing but win, win, win. Everyone is involved in something (the school turns out 24 rugby teams and 17 hockey and cricket teams, plus teams in 17 other sports). Rugby for all boys in the early years but those who want to go on and do other sports like shooting, do so pretty quickly. Regular school polo champions, riding available for all and has now moved up a gear with an eventing course within the grounds. Good shooting and rackets. Golf course a thing of wonder and beauty (one of the top 18 courses every golfer should play before they die according to *Country Life*), 'better than Eton's!' boasted a staff member and we agree. Over 400 boys immediately signed up for golf after the course was built; it and the fitness centre are open to the public. The 'Field Gun Run' a popular, if eccentric, pastime. Girls' sport now a real factor with girls moving up the inter-schools ladder; hockey and netball well embedded (with a significant number of girls competing at county and national level) and no longer (says school) restricted by small numbers. Success in girls' sports now rivals the boys. Multigym. Pool available, whenever.

Art better than impressive, energetically taught in beauteous new building. Textiles an exam subject, part of art, sewing machines etc available for use in free time. Dance on tap. Keen drama with the school taking a play to the Edinburgh Festival each year and last year's *Othello* tour to China a particular highlight. Music on the up ('fantastically strong', says school); a very good place to have a go at a music scholarship.

Background and Atmosphere: In 1852, when the Duke died, plans were in place to erect his statue in every town in England. Happily it was decided to build a school instead on a distant end of the old Windsor estate. HM remains the school's official Visitor. Immaculate, formal grounds reached via imposing avenue of oaks, Wellingtonias and Andean pines. Five lakes, endless lawns and abundant green space, three gardeners have been spotted simultaneously raking the gravel outside the Lodge. Huge building programme: the changes have resulted in seventeen houses, with 50–65 girls or boys per house, plus a complicated arrangement for day pupils (20 per cent of pupils) – who may be collected at 6pm or 7pm, or later, if they have in-house/school activities. There is a fee differential, depending on the type of house a day pupil joins. Two houses are for sixth form only and two for day pupils only. New boarding houses for the boys, more girls' houses. The names remain the same, only the locus changes. Rooms cheerfully unkempt. Most popular/ sporty houses: Benson and Beresford. Most academic: Stanley and Lynedoch. Glitzy new central social area.

Currently three houses have own catering for breakfast and supper but the rest eat in formal, grand dining hall. More funds recently awarded to the catering department and our lunch was excellent, good salad bar and selection of hot meals with fruit an option to trad puds. New servery opened, which means even wider choice (though there appeared to be no complaint). Beautiful chapel, tranches of memorials to the fallen now updated. Charming quads, quite a lot of relaxed use of space – dedicated exam room for example. Delightful library with two full-time librarians and CCTV scanning nooks and crannies, soon to be substantially redeveloped. With such abundant loveliness, the gloomy Queen's Court teaching block, opened by the Queen in 1974 and described by staff as built in 'neo-brutalism', is an unfortunate sore thumb. It does, however, house a well-equipped theatre (doubles as a cinema). A number of new classrooms, with interactive whiteboards and PC keyboards for all, cost the school a fortune. Current big investment in new modern languages building and in pitch-side pavilion. New two-week academic cycle is easier to manage. Tidiness has obviously not yet been tackled from on high and books were scattered outside the dining room door.

Pastoral Care and Discipline: The 'Basic Courtesies,' published in school diaries, sets the high standard for behaviour (how many schools still have rules like, 'If you are wearing any kind of head-gear, you should raise it – or at least touch the brim – to all adults'? And, our favourite, 'In our culture, it is considered discourteous – and probably a sign of weak character – not to look directly into the eyes of the person who is talking to you'). Member of the Round Square since 1995 (international family of schools, associated in this country with Gordonstoun, Kurt Hahn and bracing fresh air and exercise). The organisation provides endless opportunities for fund-raising for impoverished schools in the southern hemisphere and ready-made destinations for school trips. It also runs team-building weekends, international conferences and exchanges, leadership training course for sixth form. New honour code introduced by Seldon to combat previous bullying problems, and all the pupils to whom we talked agreed that there was no discernible bullying.

Girls now 35 per cent of pupils – previous problems with social interaction have been resolved, says the school, and first head girl in 150 years just appointed. The girls' houses offer better visiting areas, the boys' common rooms are thought to be somewhat 'intimidating'. New V&A social centre, with sofas, flat screens and Starbucks-style coffee counter, is a huge hit with the pupils. Enterprising pupil-led entertainments committee. Jackets now for all, with suits for those in sixth form; girls wear pleated check skirts with somewhat unforgiving boxy jackets – they say the bulky shoulders make working difficult (too much fabric under the arm and deeply unflattering for the bigger busted, with jolly awkward internal pockets). Vast number live quite close, spending most weekends at home but, for those who remain at school, there are activities enough to satisfy: trips to the cinema, skating, sailing, kayaking, riding. No bar whatsoever, 'but of course sixth formers will be offered a drink when they come to dinner,' said Seldon. 'One whiff of drugs and you're out'. Full stop. New housemasters/housemistresses deeply beady eyed.

Pupils and Parents: Turns out nice, unsnobbish, decent chaps, popular with their girlfriends' mothers. Similarly for girls and fathers. Four per cent from British families abroad and 13 per cent foreign – Germany, Russia, Asia and China the main suspects (few are receiving ESL tuition but the school requires very good English for entry). Around 10 per cent of pupils' fathers were here. Still some Services children, though numbers dwindling. Some well-known sporting families. Girls coming with pre-existing links to the school (brothers, fathers, uncles) now increasingly joined by fresh intake without connections. OBs include Sir Harold Nicolson, Robert Morley, Sebastian Faulkes, Rory Bremner, Peter Snow, Sir Nicholas Grimshaw (architect of Eden Project), Pop Idol winner Will Young and 15 winners of the VC.

Entrance: Registration for 13+ entry by June 30 two years in advance. Pre-testing at 11+ (first term of Year 7). 180 pupils at 13 through scholarship, or CE (around the 60 per cent mark), or school's own test. Main feeders: Caldicott, Crosfields, Elstree, Feltonfleet, Eagle House (a mile away and owned by Wellington – 50–75 per cent of its leavers come here), Hall Grove, Highfield, Lambrook, Papplewick, Shrewsbury House, St John's Beaumont, Thomas's Schools, Twyford and Yateley Manor. Three or four girls and boys may find places to join at 14 for GCSE/MYP courses and beyond; about 20 boys and 30 girls join at sixth form. Huge and recent amount of interest – particularly from the London prep schools. Three applicants for every place. Over 1,000 potential pupils visited open days last year.

Exit: Largest numbers to Bristol, Newcastle and Leeds. Then Durham and Oxbridge; much more Ox (classics, history and PPE) than Bridge (sciences). Sixty per cent to gap years.

Money Matters: Reckons to 'get child on to next stage' when parents have fallen on hard times, though this is not always possible. Number of scholarships and exhibitions for academic, sports, arts, music and all-round talent, and bursaries are available. College's charter allows for children of deceased Army officers (and, latterly, other Services and civilians who have died in acts of gallant bravery) to be educated here on a means-tested basis – a fast, efficient, generous and friendly system. New fresh blood in governing body.

Remarks: Anthony Seldon has worked miracles, and Wellington has been established as a leader in the field of education. Fingers crossed that copious quantities of sludge (herbal tea, says school) will keep his energies unbounded.

Wellington School

Linked to Wellington School Primary in the Junior section

Carleton Turrets, Craigweil Road, Ayr, KA7 2XH

• Pupils: 570 boys and girls 50/50; 60 in nursery • Ages: 3-18 • Size of sixth form: fifth form 50; sixth form 35 • Non-denom • Fees: £9,735 pa • Independent

Tel: 01292 269 321
Fax: 01292 272 161
Email: info@wellingtonschool.org
Website: www.wellingtonschool.org

Head: Since 2006, Mr Mark Parlour BSc BA PGCE MMBA FIAP FRSA (fiftyish) who took over after a convoluted interregnum. Born in Calcutta, educated at the University of Wales, Trinity College Oxford and the Open University, with degrees in zoology and applied zoology, then computing, maths and electronics. An IT whizz, he was head of computing at Bloxham, Gordonstoun and Robert Gordon's College, with a short stint in the computing industry in between. He came to Wellington from The High School of Dundee where he was a deputy head of the senior school. Married, with four grown up children, his wife is also a computer whizz, and co-ordinates the ICT side of Français! Français! – 'a dynamic interface' language programme which is rapidly spreading throughout the education world and includes 'raps and songs'.

The Parlours have bought a house five miles from Ayr, though he gets back late, having spent his 'whole life' helping children. He used to be 'deeply involved with the boarding and the sports side' at his previous schools and can't help popping into post-school clubs. In an earlier life he represented Oxford University at rugby and was a serious coach – he has a rugby ball balanced to the right of the fireplace in his study – he also coached cricket, kayaking, scuba diving and swimming, played national league octopush and water polo, yomps over hills, and canoes. His knees now prevent him from super activity, though he has 'cured them' by cycling. Quite a coup for sleepy Ayr to find such a star – and he is dishy to boot – (local mums were queuing up to ask random questions during our toot round the school – with designer jeans tucked into their high heeled boots a la Mrs Beckham). Though still fairly new, Mr Parlour is pushing ahead with improvements in the pupil welfare system, sixth form experience, curriculum balance, transition between nursery, primary and senior, extra-curricular involvement and learning and teaching.

Academic matters: Max 18 per class in primary, with slight expansion in size at age 10 and 11; basically two parallel classes to S1 when increased numbers mean three or four classes; setted from senior school with a max class size of 20. Numbers capped 'naturally' – by building and room size. Head working on 'sixth year experience'; though most stay on after Highers anyway. New ICT and web site on starting block (as you might expect given the head's speciality) network manager recently appointed, and we saw nothing but Dell flat screens and interactive whiteboards in every classroom. Languages particularly strong, with Prestwick just down the road it's a natural; long term exchanges with Germany and France; deeply involved with Comenius and sent 12 pupils to the UCAPE conference in Italy last year – where they debated 'The Europe of Tomorrow' – in French. 'If it's on the doorstep, go for it'. All do French from primary and can elect to do German at senior level but results not all singing and dancing at any level and minimal take-up at Advanced Higher level.

Tiny classics stream but impressive results. Awards in the UK Junior Mathematical Challenge, which is not entirely reflected in the maths results; impressive numbers but too many Bs and Cs; applied maths now offered at Advanced Higher level. Accountancy and finance, admin and business management available at Standard and Higher Grade for the latter. Humanities very strong, ditto sciences with well equipped labs; few results of lower than C (which in GSG parlance = fail). Media studies dropped recently in favour of proper academia.

Despite having a non-selective intake, Wellington's S5 Higher results have put it in the top ten of Scottish schools the last two years. In 2008 the school enjoyed the headline of 'top performing independent school in Scotland', with a 98 per cent pass rate at Higher in S5. Five staff retirements recently, with 126 years' service between them; teachers 'top notch', according to Parlour and eager to serve on the many working groups he has set up. No problem in getting new staff, 12 applications recently for heads of both art and physics. New phonetic reading programme should go some way to improving literacy; SENCo and a team of dedicated staff. Pupils assessed in primary, and individual lessons where necessary, will pull in ed psychs as needed. Drop in centres to hit problems on the head asap, auxiliary (i.e. dual teaching) in primary school, with perhaps 20 pupils receiving 'serious help' throughout the school.

Games, Options, the Arts: There is a 20 acre sports ground ten mins away at Doonside in Alloway, a new pavilion with changing and reception facilities has just been completed, with Astroturf and floodlighting completed this month. Mr Parlour, a sports guru, is sad that rugby, though strong, doesn't quite have the numbers to thrash all comers. Terrific hockey, with hockey sticks kept in wheelie bins. Fair showing of Scottish caps – particularly in tennis, semi-finalists in the U14, building links with the Prestwick tennis academy – both short and conventional. Swimming in the nearby Citadel pool in Ayr, head keen to use the sea more – it is, after all, quite literally on the doorstep. So expect kayaking, canoeing, (sailing?) – 'it takes time', but links on the horizon with local clubs. Skating, riding, golf growing in popularity, karate post school in junior dept – huge take up here. Cycling plus lots of individual sports and head keen to build on the outdoor aspect; expect miracles shortly. Strong local partnerships, D of E and leadership expeditions all thriving.

Spectacular music but space limited simply because of the number of simultaneous activities and the orchestra was practising in the dining room while the choir was in the music room when we visited. Nicola Benedetti a former pupil, mass of choirs and orchestras and school shows – down to P1. Michael Foyle, leader of the Scottish Youth Orchestra was head boy last year. Jazz band. Can't fault it. New head of art is into jewellery and art rooms buzzing with pupils post-school, fabric design and stunning silk screen printing, as well as conventional flat art and three dimensional stuff. Art & Design results healthy but surprisingly little take up in music even at Standard grade. Vast array of post-school clubs, with science on

Wednesdays when the 'whole school hums'. No cooking though these days.

Background and Atmosphere: Originally founded in Wellington Square in 1836 by the wife of an Ayr teacher for 12 young ladies (think dame school), the school moved to Carleton Turrets on the leafy outskirts of Ayr in 1923, dropping boarders and moving to co-ed 14 years ago. After a certain amount of logistical re-organisation, the senior school now occupies the Carleton Turrets, with the more recently acquired Craigweil House home to the music school, the lang dept and the dining room – the latter operates on a fairly tight timetable. The primary and nursery school are accommodated in Drumley, just across the road (they have their own dining facilities). A number bring packed lunches and it is a removable privilege to eat these in form rooms. Drumley has a bright and jolly extension in the nursery leading directly onto a dedicated play area for tinies. A recent development is the nursery garden.

The three turreted Victorian grade B buildings (splendid stained glass windows) on the sea front have obvious limitations on expansion; the gym at Carleton Turrets doubles as assembly hall with a proper weights room strategically placed to one side, but this editor couldn't help feeling that better re-organisation of the office space might lead to more efficient use of the ground floor. School looked in jolly good heart, only one tacky classroom that we saw though it still feels a bit dameish. Books in every classroom as well as on all the landings – with a shelf labelled 'for oversized books'. Stunning library, most of the classrooms on the top floors have stunning views over to Arran and Goatfell, which must make concentration difficult. Fairly restricted play areas round the actual buildings but expansive (flat) links and beach opposite for informal footie and the like at break times. New sixth form centre under construction.

Enthusiastic parental input, particularly at weekends, Ayr is proud of the school – this editor had to stop at Morrison's supermarket (not so close) to ask the way and the cashier at the petrol station and a goodly proportion of the customers were all keen to put me on the right road, and to tell me what a smashing school it was.

Pastoral Care and Discipline: School works closely with parents, efficient tutorial system throughout senior school, reports twice a term followed by parents' meeting to discuss the report. Strong inter-house competitions, siblings in same houses. Not a lot of sin, green indiscipline slips for minor sin, three green slips and letter home, red slips for more serious sin, automatic letter home. All slips count against the pupil's house 'Conduct Shield'. Detention at lunchtime or referral to behavioural timetable if pupil consistently sinful. Ultimate deterrent is expulsion. PSHE and anti-bullying strategies (anti-bullying email and strategically placed anti-bullying boxes), plus seminars on healthy eating et al.

Detailed clothes list (including hair clasps) and handy parental book of rules; delightful handbook/prospectus with jolly pics could have the words tweaked a trifle, no mention of email alongside the address either. Newly formed pupil-led school council. Recent HMI report thought more God would be good – 'I would hope our assemblies are meaningful,' 'huge moral dimension,' muses head. Increasing number of pupil-led assemblies. Visiting chaplain. Active and helpful board of governors.

Pupils and Parents: Strongly middle class, parents (and grandparents) who may have gone to more trad schools elsewhere hold The Wellie in high regard; fair number of first time buyers, professionals, builders, company directors, refugees from 'London and Manchester'. Nice well behaved pupils, not obviously that street-wise. Parent organised buses locally.

Entrance: Via nursery; P1 – P7 children spend a morning in school, thereafter school's own test in English and maths, usual entry stage to senior school S1 but pupils accepted at any time if space available. Very occasional entry post Standard for Highers or Advanced Highers.

Exit: Most stay the course; occasional one or two leave to go to trad public schools, some may go to state system post primary. Mainly to Scottish universities, vets, medics, biologists, mathematicians.

Money Matters: Sibling discounts and bursaries available. Not a poor school.

Remarks: Smashing useful local school for Ayrshire, if limited in facilities by its site – sports/dining/assembly hall needed, a redundant church would be nice. No feel that it is still a girls' school with boys tacked on – it is properly co-ed throughout. Not (yet) a member of the HMC though watch this space.

Wells Cathedral School

Linked to Wells Cathedral Junior School in the Junior section

The Liberty, Wells, Somerset, BA5 2ST

- Pupils: 570 in senior school; almost evenly split between boys and girls. 40 per cent board (120 girls, 105 boys) • Ages: Junior School: 3-11; Senior School: 11-18 • Size of sixth form: 195; 80 day, 115 boarding • C of E
- Fees: Boarding £22,929-£23,820; Day £13,770-£14,250 pa
- Independent

Tel: 01749 834 200
Fax: 01749 834 201
Email: admissions@wellscs.somerset.sch.uk
Website: www.wells-cathedral-school.com

Head: Since 2000, Mrs Elizabeth Cairncross (fifties), married with three children. Formerly deputy head of Christ's Hospital, Horsham, where she had been a mistress since 1986. The first female head in the history of the school, obviously delighted to be in such beautiful surroundings. 'Such a wealth of history and tradition that we can get on and do modern things.' Has a tough job, juggling a bewildering number of balls in the air while dropping none. Oversaw Wells' participation in the Channel 5 documentary *How the Other Half Learns.* Three of her pupils swapped places with three kids from a sprawling Wembley comprehensive for two weeks – sensitively handled and a learning experience for all. Enthused by recent government vote of confidence (2008): a grant of £3.5m to be used – along with £1m already received – towards new classrooms and a music building (see below).

Academic matters: Flexibility without disorder. Maths the most popular subject, with brilliant results, especially among musicians. Began offering maths IGCSE in 2007 with able pupils taking it a year early. Sciences lacking quite the same pzazz (though A level marks in sciences consistently very good and many pupils go on to read medicine). Broadish range of A level subjects including geology, Italian, Latin, psychology and politics. Law through video conferencing and distance learning, but not much take-up. Leisure and tourism a GCSE option. Some hotshots take GCSE music two years early and power straight on to AS. Pupils we spoke to raved about the English teaching. Setting for French and maths from Year 7. Specialist musicians throughout the school have adjusted timetables and curricula to integrate music and, especially, practice. They may take only two A levels, but most take three. Not a school where pupils are buckling under academic pressure – much emphasis on learning to work independently and be responsible for one's progress. Information on SEN provision not supplied.

Games, Options, the Arts: One of five independent schools in the UK with government-funded specialist music provision. So the music, of course, is fabulous. The prospectus lists over 50 music staff, with departments of strings, keyboard, woodwind, brass, percussion, vocal and choral studies, music technology and composition. Possibly a notch less hard-core and tunnel-visioned than the other specialist music schools. Lots of practice? Yes. At dawn? Probably not. Forty choristers (half boys, half girls, in separate choirs). Rehearsal five mornings a week before school and alternate Friday afternoons. They sing in the cathedral most Sundays during termtime, plus evensong every day except one. Opportunities for music extend throughout the school and are not limited to the specialists.

A strong tradition of drama and fine art and, as would be expected in a school where performance is important, standards are high. The only specialist music school to allow its musicians to play in school games teams – in fact, the only specialist music school to have games full stop. Sport does not share the high profile of the arts but is well provided for – rugby, hockey, netball, cricket and tennis. Shooting triumphant at the moment: three members of the school's shooting team were recently selected for the Great Britain under 21 rifle and pistol squad. Newly renovated and now covered swimming pool. Newish dance studio used by all ages. D of E and CCF. Alexander Technique for the musicians (and others).

Background and Atmosphere: Traditional on the outside, progressive on the inside. Celebrated its 1,100th birthday in 2009; Wells is one of the world's oldest schools, rambling through the ancient heart of one of England's loveliest towns. Buildings a mixture of the sublime (half-timber, cobblestones and mellow stonework) and the – less sublime – 'temporary' classrooms slated for extermination. The cobbled Vicar's Close, surely one of the loveliest lanes in England, is home to several school buildings. The lovely 'Stable Yard' is home to a diminutive but homely library (a bit short on quiet space for work), sixth form centre and classrooms. The music department is centred on the medieval buildings down the road. Somewhat 'bitty' in feel: you need to negotiate a rather dicey roundabout to find the strings department and a boys' boarding house. Much new building work in the pipeline, including a new classroom building to ease incremental expansion of pupil numbers. Plans also for spectacular new music building, with architecture inspired by Elmhurst School for Dance and maximising opportunities for peer observation and learning (= glass walls). Junior and senior schools adjacent provides a family feel and also means that siblings can see each other in the day. Has not skimped on marketing – do bring along a wheelbarrow to carry the mountain of (beautifully produced) bumf with which you will emerge. School difficult to get through to by phone and can be hard to make an appointment to visit – perhaps marketing needs to shine its beam in this direction.

Pastoral Care and Discipline: The emphasis is on 'mutual consideration, respect and courtesy'. Drug testing 'on concern'. No school bar – never has been one. Drinking allowed at sixth form events where meal served and at certain pubs. Much emphasis on learning to support one another and biggest sanctions reserved for 'betraying trust within the community'. Head points out that it's easier to teach children to be independent when you have space and the safe rural environment of a town like Wells. More pupils per dorm than at most schools we see nowadays, with two or three sharing even in the upper sixth. No scheduled exeats after Year 9 but school relaxed about pupils going home on weekends. Years 10–13 allowed into town after school day and on weekends. Day pupils assigned to boarding houses where they register, have lockers and flop. School day formally ends at 4pm (4.30 on Wednesdays). Wells Cathedral involved in the governance of the school but keeps a light touch. The whole school gathers for a service there every Monday. Female chaplain was previously the British Army's first female chaplain and was stationed in Iraq for six months. Black uniform worn to age 16, with 'dark suits' acceptable thereafter.

Pupils and Parents: Large local catchment area for day pupils, boarders from far and wide but mostly south west. Good balance of overseas pupils (about 10 per cent) – some for music, some not – enriches but does not swamp. EFL available and Chinese and Japanese feature in the A level results. Web of school bus routes includes villages towards Bristol and Bath. Pupils confident and articulate, interested in each other and in the community of the school, including the juniors. Old Wellensians (or Old Wellies even) include businessman Roger Saul (founder of Mulberry), opera singer Sarah Fryer, portrait painter Justin Mortimer, Bruce Parry of BBC2's *Tribe*, Olympic gold medallist Danny Nightingale, and Glastonbury Festival founder Michael Eavis and his daughter, Emily.

Entrance: Formally at 11 and 13 (assessment tests are held at the school on a Saturday in late January), but 12 and 14 will also do nicely. Entry to sixth form is subject to interview and at least six grade C passes at GCSE, with grade B or better for subjects to be taken at AS level. Auditions for music places held in November, for sixth form, and January, for all age groups. A few prospective parents of musicians put off by the fixed date for auditions (other music schools hold them on a rolling basis throughout year).

Exit: All expected to go on to higher education with Cardiff currently popular; about a quarter take gap years. Most, but by no means all, musicians go on to music colleges – a wider than expected range including Royal Scottish in Glasgow and Royal Welsh in Cardiff. A couple read music at Cambridge and four or five to Oxbridge most years for other subjects.

Money Matters: Not a school with a big endowment, so money is tight. Over 90 'specialist' musicians (72 government-aided music places – means-tested but can amount to full fees) plus 18 non-funded pupils (often from abroad). Seventy 'special provision' pupils take part in a programme similar to the specialists but – crucially – without funding; a moderately talented musician might do better financially, though probably not musically, to try for a music scholarship at a mainstream independent school. Choral scholarships, but NB boys are entitled to up to 25 per cent off fees and girls only 10 per cent off day fees. Means-tested academic, music and all-round scholarships available for entry to Years 7, 9 and sixth form (worth a five per cent minimum). Sons and daughters of clergy and Services may qualify for a 10 per cent bursary. Day fees a bargain, but watch out for annual music 'capitation fees' of £152.10 (or more), on top of music lessons charged at £40.45 per hour.

Remarks: Tranquil and cultured from afar but a bubbling cauldron once you get up close, with a very tasty stew sizzling within. Few schools – perhaps none – so successfully weave together so many strands: boys and girls, senior and junior (and nursery!), day and boarding, mainstream and music specialist, ecclesiastical and lay, old-fashioned and modern. If you have trouble making choices, you need look no further. But make sure to nail down funding questions in advance.

Wellsway School

Chandag Road, Keynsham, Bristol, BS31 1PH

• Pupils: 1,330 boys and girls • Ages: 11-19 • Size of sixth form: 275 • Christian • State

Tel: 0117 986 4751
Fax: 0117 916 1039
Email: headteacher@wellsway.bathnes.sch.uk
Website: www.wellsway.bathnes.sch.uk/

Head: Since 2005, Mrs Andrea Arlidge BA.

Academic matters: Specialist Sports and Science College. Fine results for a non-selective school in a not solely middle class area. In 2009, 82 per cent got five or more A*–C GCSE grades. 60–70 per cent stay on for sixth form – achieved 46 per cent A/B grades in 2009. Sixth form study centre opened 2008. Investors in People awarded 1998 and re-awarded 2006. Very strong departments led by specialist staff. Sound provision for statemented pupils.

Games, Options, the Arts: Sportsmark Gold in 1997 and re-awarded 2000, 2004 and 2006. Heaps of teams in all sports. Artificial pitch. Annual French trip for Year 7, ski trip, water sport trip. World Challenge expeditions have been to Ecuador, South Africa and West Canada. Currently running 'Wellsway Challenge' introduced in 2004 to destinations in Europe.

Innovative and fabulous art department. Dedicated staff stay long after school hours to keep facilities open. Mad on musicals – staged *Return to the Forbidden Planet*, *Barnum*, *Grease*, *Guys & Dolls*, *Billy*, *Cabaret*, *My Fair Lady*, *Animal Farm* and *Oliver!*.

Background and Atmosphere: A once thriving market town between Bath and Bristol, Keynsham is a town of churches – five Anglican, one Baptist and one Methodist, denoting its past trade wealth. A spacious campus amongst green fields is cheek by jowl with Chandag Junior & Infant Schools. Highly motivated staff aged 22 to 60; seem far less frantic than most at large comprehensives. Many of them have own children here and the relationship between staff and pupils is that of a close-knit village school. Bulletin boards bursting with news or press cuttings of ex-pupils making local headlines.

Pastoral Care and Discipline: Policies on everything from asthma to child protection. School rules insist that anyone being bullied report it. Comes down ton-of-bricks on anti-social or violent behaviour and nips any incident in the bud by locating pupil's parent instantly. A counsellor is on staff. Sixth formers become 'buddies' to any Year 7 who request one and may coach sports/share lunch and chat/solve bigger problems.

Pupils and Parents: Local business folk, many Old Girls'/Boys' kids, every class and creed. Very loyal. A weekly newsletter keeps parents well-informed and asks parents to monitor homework and control absence. Excellent, informative website. Uniform of green blazer/black trousers/skirts. Strong on community service and raising funds for charities.

Entrance: Over-subscribed. Wellsway serves Keynsham (to the east of the River Chew), Chelwood Village, Compton Dando, Corston, Marksbury, Newton St Loe, Priston and Saltford. Children from within this area whose older sibling will be attending the school on the admission date come first, followed by other children from the area, then other siblings. Five Cs at GCSE preferred for sixth form entrance.

Exit: 60–70 per cent of GCSE pupils continue on to sixth form here, 20–30 per cent to education elsewhere. After A levels most go to universities e.g. Cardiff, West of England, Plymouth, Bristol, Exeter, Cheltenham, Birmingham, Leeds, Loughborough, Manchester, Nottingham, Oxbridge, Warwick. A few to a gap year or employment and a sprinkle to art foundation or drama school.

Remarks: Confident pupils with high expectations well prepared for life. Loveliest bunch of teachers in the county.

Westbourne School (Junior and Senior)

60 Westbourne Road, Sheffield, South Yorkshire, S10 2QT

• Pupils: 360 boys and girls, all day • Ages: 4-16 • Non-denom • Fees: £7,185-£10,020 pa • Independent

Tel: 0114 266 0374
Fax: 0114 263 8176
Email: admin@westbourneschool.co.uk
Website: www.westbourneschool.co.uk

Head: Since 2004, Mr John Hicks MEd. Educated at Archbishop Holgate GS, York, Exeter University, Masters at Kingston University. Previously head of upper secondary and head of campus at International School of the Regents, Thailand, which taught the UK National Curriculum. Before that deputy head of Durston House in west London and senior master at Parkside. Still teaches senior maths and coaches sport. Forthright, businesslike, ambitious for school. Very committed to needs of individual child.

Academic matters: School has non-selective intake; aims to develop those who find learning difficult as well as the talented. Two in-house dyslexia teachers who work on a 'federal basis' i.e. the parents pay; otherwise dyslexia support across the board (and free). Will 'never ask a child to leave' but may not take on one who needs more learning support than that year and class teacher can handle, i.e. if it alters 'the balance of a particular class'.

Recent excellent GCSE results in all subjects. Drama, music and media studies recently added. Tiny classes, max 15, often smaller. Maths and English setted from age nine and science from age 11; accelerated learning and scholarship group from age 11. Computers all over the place – no one afraid to put their hand up.

Outstanding French language teaching throughout; starts at reception and by the time children reach the French department in the senior school they are taught in a typical café, complete with little round tables and bentwood chairs, though naturally no Pernod. Spanish at age 11, specialist science teaching from Year 6 in impressive dedicated labs in three buildings, taken as either single subject, dual or triple award at GCSE. Ten subjects the norm. History, geography, music, drama, art, DT, sports science, business and media studies are options. Head claims state of art ICT, school linked to Oslo University providing the virtual learning environment for pupils aged from 10 yrs up. Emphasis on individual child achieving his/her own potential is achieved by very small class sizes. 2009 cohort had excellent GCSE results; 30 out of 32 students obtained five or more A-Cs grades and in 2010, 100 per cent A*–C grades.

Games, Options, the Arts: Several playgrounds, one covered, make do for in-house games, otherwise much use made of local facilities: Abbeydale, Don Valley, English Institute of Sport, HSBC, Hallam University Astro, Ponds Forge, Hallam cricket/football/tennis clubs and Rother Valley Country Park for water sports. Rugby, football, cricket, athletics for boys; netball, hockey, athletics and rounders for girls. Hockey, basketball, dance, sailing, canoeing, etc available to all. School hires coaches though they have a smaller clutch of their own. Many fixtures against other schools, internal house competitions encourage participation by all. Stunning art in both sectors, excellent drama in wonderful outdoor theatre – think Bryanston and Dean Close.

GCSE music started in 2005–300 per cent increase in individual lessons in last few years. Lots of school trips over the place at most age groups. Excellent use made of locality; recent visits to Bishop's House, Kelham Island, The Sheffield Cathedral, Worksop College and further afield to Rua Fiola and Barcelona.

Background and Atmosphere: Founded around 1885 by a Mrs Whitfield as a boys-only prep school in leafy Sheffield 10; actual date uncertain, as Gaffer Johnson (head in 1941), terrified that Hitler was about to invade, burnt all the school records. (He also used to quell unruly youngsters by taking out his glass eye and polishing it with his hanky!) Took girls in 1998 and went up to age 16 in 2000. Original prep school was composed of three Victorian buildings – very nooky and cranny, with staircases everywhere, much revamped, with good tinies' wing, and sensible classrooms for every discipline further up. Senior school is a beautiful late Georgian building opposite, with a garden to die for (well, it was an offshoot of the local Botanic Gardens). House has been totally rearranged, with brand new staircase leading everywhere. Major expansion completed in summer 2007, following acquisition of fine nearby house (Ashdell Grove) – more room, opportunity to restructure internal organization of classes. Breakfast for all on arrival (cooked on Tuesdays and Fridays as special treat). Late waiting for younger pupils until 5.45pm (end of prep).

Pastoral Care and Discipline: School claims mutual respect reinforced daily. PSHE taught throughout. School strict on behaviour, drugs and smoking; if difficulties and trouble persist, previous conduct goes into the balance – if OK, a spot of leniency, if not then curtains. Drugs equals out anyway.

Pupils and Parents: Mainly middle class, not a huge number of ethnic minorities, so no overt facilities for Ramadan, no halal fare in dining room. Charming uniform for girls, boys equally smart. Pupils incredibly polite, much standing up and saying sir.

Entrance: Children taken at any time and at any age if places available but waiting lists now the norm. Non-selective intake into junior school, first come first served. 'However, we may refuse entry, even to bright children, if they are disruptive and uncooperative.' Assessment into senior school via tests and a day's trial; after visit both child and school say what they thought of each other. Nearly all juniors go through to seniors, more join at 11 or 13.

Exit: Not all stay on after age 13, but progressively more do. As Westbourne started life as a prep school, there is still a slight trickle to Oundle, Uppingham, Repton and Trent. This will probably dry up. 'Girls are, so far, staying,' and others from local schools joining at senior level. Post-GCSE almost all into some form of further education mainly to Birkdale, Tapton, Silverdale, High Storrs.

Money Matters: Scholarships taken in Year 6; bursaries available on request.

Remarks: Prep school ethos still important but non-selective principle and fine new senior school represents a niche market in the area, especially in care for individuals of all abilities, which seems to be much more than lip service.

Westminster School

17 Dean's Yard, London, SW1P 3PB

• Pupils: 615 boys; 125 girls all in sixth form; 465 day boys, 145 boy boarders; 95 day girls, 30 girl boarders • Ages: 13-18 (but a few Westminster Assisted Places from 11, see below) • Size of sixth form: 370 • C of E • Fees: Day £20,364-£22,080; Boarding £29,406; Queen's Scholars £14,703 pa • Independent

Tel: 020 7963 1003
Fax: 020 7963 1002
Email: registrar@westminster.org.uk
Website: www.westminster.org.uk

Head Master: Since 2005, Dr Stephen Spurr DPhil, an Oxford and Sydney classicist (mid-fifties), married, one son, one daughter. Dr Spurr was previously head of Clifton College for five years, prior to which he was at Eton for sixteen years, successively as head of classics and as housemaster. Dr Spurr holds one of the most coveted posts in independent education, one regarded with awe, even wariness, by some. It can be a high profile job but the elegant and quietly spoken Dr Spurr has been assiduously keeping out of the press. His headship involves daily interaction with, possibly, the most erudite, stimulating, challenging and entertaining community of pupils, staff and parents in the business. In measured, almost laconic, tones, he speaks of the excitement he feels at doing the job. His thoughtful, understated, manner of expression leads some to finding him 'inscrutable', even 'humourless' but the manner conceals a deeply felt commitment and warmth of feeling. 'I feel more attuned here than anywhere I have been,' he asserts and, manifestly, the Westminster ethos of the pleasure and value of learning for learning's sake is safe in his hands. 'We will, whatever it takes, stick with the intrinsic good of the academic life'.

Since his appointment, Dr Spurr has set about streamlining and tidying, intending to sharpen, rather than dilate its focus on the life of the mind. His is a scholarly and purposeful vision – 'we will continue to innovate, expand, look outwards – not withdraw into Fortress Westminster ... Westminster is on the crest of the wave and we all know what happens to waves.' There is the sunbeam flash of a rare smile. 'Our job is to prepare young people as well as possible so that they are flexible for an international future – to be individuals without being individualistic, yoking their high intelligence to social responsibility'.

Five years into his tenure, Dr Spurr's assiduity and dedication continue to impress.

Academic matters: Second to none. Always in the top five of any league table but that is a by-product of what goes on here. Syllabuses can be almost incidental, to the extent that a check needs to be made near exam time to ensure that the actual requirements of the course have been attended to as so much else has. Teachers teach from immense depth and breadth of knowledge of their subjects and far beyond. Many are acknowledged experts in their fields. This enthusiasm is met by that of their pupils who may not all be boffins but who have lively, questioning minds, turned on by the general buzz of the intellectual life on offer.

If you want convincing, in 2009, at GCSE, 98 per cent of subjects taken got A*/A. In the previous fourteen years, 100 per cent of subjects achieved A*–C in all but three years (it was 99 per cent in those). All GCSE subjects, and some others, can be taken to A level and A level results are equally impressive. In 2009, 90 per cent of subjects taken achieved A, 98 per cent getting A/B (nearly all take four A levels, and many five). Most popular are maths (massive), history (nearly so), sciences, English and economics. There are equal numbers of Latin and French takers and languages are always strong. German, so sadly moribund elsewhere, taught in part via poetry and song. Theatre studies, electronics, music and RE are taken by minorities as exam subjects but all have lively profiles on the extra-curricular side of life.

Everyone does DT and electronics in year nine and school owns an electron microscope in its up-to-the-minute labs. Computerised projection system in all classrooms, whiteboards for mathematicians. Each dept has a supply of laptops available on demand. The library – in a stunning set of rooms – is open until 9pm and has its own much-praised website. Overall teacher:pupil ratio of one to eight. Recent injection of young teachers appreciated by Westminsters who also revere their sages. Some teachers seen as 'wacky and inspirational' rather than efficient but, of most, we are told, 'nothing is too much trouble'.

Dr Spurr looked bemused at the thought that anyone with the right kind of intellectual capacity might be denied a place because of an SEN e.g. mild or moderate dyspraxia – 'there's no problem'. Study skills coordinator sees all who need support, whether the super-bright but chaotic or those with a dys. All pupils provided for on a case by case basis. 'I believe that as you go through the academic life you move from one level of learning to another,' says the head. 'Our study skills co-coordinator helps everyone think about the skills needed to empower their learning at different stages.'

Games, Options, the Arts: The Westminster extra-curricular programme, extraordinary by universal consent, is impossible to encapsulate here and is much enhanced by the contribution of the academic staff who offer activities founded on their private enthusiasms. It is further embellished by a unique list of outside speakers. Recent visitors include Rowan Williams, Simon Singh, Martin Rees, Christopher Ricks, Colin Thubron, Tony Benn, David Ramsbottom, Margaret Hodge, Oliver Letwin, George Galloway, Robert Fisk. There are evening concerts given by the like of Ian Bostridge, Imogen Cooper, Felicity Lott. If Westminster parents sometimes niggle that their children do not go out into London sufficiently that is because London comes to them. There are esoteric trips everywhere – to Iceland for plate tectonics, to New York for art, to the Crimea for rock climbing, Venice to row in the regatta and to Chios for classicists and on and on.

The arts are privileged and more so since the acquisition, in 2002, of the Millicent Fawcett Hall, now an excellent flexible studio theatre and, in 2005, the opening of the Manoukian Music Centre – an ex army drill hall with recital room, teaching and practice rooms and recording studios. Outstanding music and drama and school mounts productions of e.g. Mozart and Weill operas to professional standards. Drama taught throughout school. Art, too, is breathtakingly good – four studio areas, a traditional printing press and much emphasis on the traditional skills – people can draw and paint here. Other options, reflecting the staff's eclecticism, include bookbinding, Warhammer, languages, board games, D of E, jazz, philosophy, carpentry, comic films etc. Debating is famously strong. PHAB, like other community service projects, gets enthusiastic participation.

Games (known as 'station') played vigorously and joyously and with stunning success in, particularly, rowing (winners of the Fawley Cup at Henley in 2009), cricket (winners of the London Schools' Cup in 2008 and 2009) and cross country (London Schools champions). There have also been successes in football, fencing, netball and fives. Sporting opportunities are multifarious but no-one would claim world class sportiness for Westminster overall. Games mostly played on the surprisingly large field in nearby Vincent Square.

Background and Atmosphere: The history of Westminster reads like the history of England and its list of Old Westminsters is a list of main players in that story. The thousands of tourists who tramp the precincts of Westminster Abbey must be startled to see knots of vaguely uniformed teenagers comfortably chatting round about Dean's Yard – the adjacent grassy square. They would need to peer through the inconspicuous archway that leads into Little Dean's Yard – the school's central quad – to find the hotch-potch of houses that form the nucleus of the school.

Westminster began in 1179 and has been in continuous existence since the fourteenth century. Elizabeth I bestowed royal patronage upon it in 1560 and is celebrated as the school's official foundress. The abbey is its chapel – an astonishing privilege in itself. Many meals are eaten in College Hall – a medieval room with coats of arms, portraits of former heads and wonderful painted corbels under a beamed ceiling – in which the abbots and monks gathered to eat in the early years of the abbey. It is an integral part of the deanery and adjacent to the Jerusalem Chamber. School has, of course, its own argot and it can be mystifying. Also its own traditions – ask about 'The Greaze'.

The school buildings have been built, acquired and developed over the centuries, most of them abutting Little Dean's Yard, the houses named after revered and redoubtable former housemasters and Old Boys. They include a series of rooms in the beautiful Ashburnam House which make up the library – a national monument in itself. The quiet streets round about provide outposts, all only minutes away. These include the girls' boarding house, in the Georgian silence of Barton Street (opposite T E Lawrence's former house), the Robert Hooke Science building on the far side of Smith Square, the theatre and music centres and, most recently, the Weston Building on Dean's Yard which provides airy, spacious new teaching rooms in a very Westminster mix of modern technology, cornicing, panelling and parquetry.

Girls arrived in the sixth form in 1973 and are much valued though there are no plans to include them lower down the school. Dr Spurr appreciates how a Westminster sixth form works for both sexes – 'the girls' results are the highest nationally, they thrive on our debating style of teaching and the boys pick up on their work ethic'. The Westminster sixth form life is relaxed and collaborative. A pupil told us, 'people make their own relationship with the school which the teachers respect ... problems are worked out through a kind of bantering interaction with the teachers'.

Boarding recently upgraded. All rooms are now comfortable and most are well-appointed. Many are surprisingly spacious and, of course, have views over the abbey, school or college buildings and gardens. Younger boys in rooms of between two and eight and all pupils have their own rooms in the last three years. Thumb print recognition or key pad entry systems. Good kitchens, common rooms, games rooms and sensible, relaxed discipline maintained by resident housemasters (male or female are called this), many of whom have young families on site. All boarders in the lower school (up to the age of 16) go home every weekend. Some sixth form boarders stay at school at weekends but the school is very quiet on Saturday nights.

Overseas numbers remain small though Dr Spurr sees Westminster in a global context in interesting ways. 'We're not dragging in pupils from abroad but we need to see ourselves as a world-wide school competing with the best pupils from everywhere. I'm interested in links with the top academic schools worldwide and in learning what they do educationally. That's where our future competition for university places will increasingly come from – rather than from UK schools.'

Pastoral Care and Discipline: Famously relaxed and liberal as has been felt appropriate in a school which thrives on the individuality of its members. Dr Spurr has undertaken to smarten up his charges, much as he has restructured the school's top management – on similar principles – 'my belief is that there is some link between form and content ... management should take care of things to allow housemasters and teachers to concentrate on their core activities ... I like pupils to show a little more respect for school dress and I like them to look reasonably tidy in Abbey'. To our seasoned eye, however, Westminster pupils look much as they have ever done and shirts seem not to stay tucked in for long. Girls have a dress code – plain colours, no denim, jackets rather than jumpers since '08, etc. Some staff grumbles about meetings and 'directives' and a less-than-accessible head. Times are clearly changing – our guess is for the better, overall.

No serious drugs-related disciplinary incidents in Dr Spurr's reign thus far. 'I'm probably more concerned with alcohol than drugs but I believe in taking a firm line.' The approach is very much to educate and to involve parents, establishing a collaborative and supportive home/school relationship. 'We have a disciplined system which, if it is to be fair, has to be consistent ... you've got to keep talking to your young but, whereas we would look at infringements on a case by case basis we can't be individualistic at the expense of the school community'.

Maybe not individualistic but individuals really count here and great efforts are made to support and nurture those taken into the school fold – sometimes at unconventional times in their careers. Pastoral care, not always the school's strength, now impressive and it's hard to fall through the net. Some parents feel that, for girls, the pastoral side 'has a bit of a hole in it'. One said, 'I don't think they really take on board that girls have certain issues' and some take longer to settle in than others, though the boarders have a cosy nest in their homely house. The tutor system, at its best, is supportive and comradely though 'some tutors are not really involved and are pretty useless,' we were told. 'People who are thought likely to get into trouble are allocated to really good tutors.'

Pupils and Parents: 'We are more metropolitan and cosmopolitan than most public schools,' says Dr Spurr. Most pupils come from moneyed and clever families resident in London but originating everywhere so many languages spoken at home. Only a quarter boards and most of those are Londoners with busy-busy families. Very few from really far away – Russia, China etc. Pupils are quirky, sparky, irreverent, natural sceptics, though seldom 'cynical' as reported in the rhapsodic 2006 ISI inspection report. They are articulate, endlessly intellectually curious, creative, individual, challenging in the best sense. Their parents, many of whom are active in supporting the school, know exactly what it is they are paying for and love it – 'it's fantastic'.

Former pupils (Old Westminsters) include some rotters, for example most of the officers in command during 'the disaster in the Crimea' such as Lord Lucan. Also Kim Philby. But then there are also Ben Jonson, George Herbert, John Dryden, John Locke, Christopher Wren, Robert Hooke, Henry Purcell, Charles Wesley, Earl Howe, Warren Hastings, Edward Gibbon, Jeremy Bentham, GA Henty, AA Milne (who vastly endowed the school), Adrian Boult, John Gielgud, Angus Wilson, Norman Parkinson, Andrew Huxley, Peter Ustinov, Flanders and Swann and, still with us, Tony Benn, Peter Brook, Nigel Lawson, Roger Norrington, Corin Redgrave, Andrew Lloyd Webber, Stephen Poliakoff, Helena Bonham-Carter, Ruth Kelly, Imogen Stubbs, Louis Theroux, Dido and Mika etc etc.

Entrance: Register your son up to two years before 13+ entry. He will be screened in Year 6 or 7 – tests in maths, English and VR and interview – places conditional on CE performance offered thereafter. At least 70 per cent expected. Further interview at 13 – 'we like it as it opens the teacher/pupil dialogue'. Alternative method of entry is the Challenge – a competitive exam for scholarship places. Those who don't win scholarships may be offered places with other financial help if they do well enough. Around 350 are seen at 11, around 175 offers are made for the 120 places. It works. Boys and girls applying for 16+ places must register by the October before entry. Offers based on interview, tests and meeting GCSE requirements.

Exit: Some 45 per cent annually to Oxbridge and, now, about 5 per cent to Ivy League, though pupils stress, 'they make a big deal about not going to Oxbridge if it's not for you – they try to educate the parents that it's OK if we want to go somewhere else.' Most of the rest to Bristol, UCL, Imperial, LSE, Edinburgh, Warwick, Durham. Principal degree subjects history, economics, PPE, management, maths, languages, medicine. But they go everywhere and study everything to distinguished levels.

Money Matters: Eight Queen's scholarships annually worth 50 per cent of the boarding fee and scholars must board. Music scholarship worth 25 per cent of the day or boarding fee at 13+. Means tested bursaries of up to 100 per cent of fees. Expensive trips highly subsidised by school when appropriate.

Remarks: For the right boy or girl, simply the best.

Westminster Tutors

Linked to David Game College

86 Old Brompton Road, South Kensington, London, SW7 3LQ

• Pupils: Between 30-100 depending on course and time of year
• Ages: 14-19 • Fees: up to £19,200 pa • Independent

Tel: 020 7584 1288
Fax: 020 7584 2637
Email: info@westminstertutors.co.uk
Website: www.westminstertutors.co.uk

Head: Since September 2007, Ms Virginia Maguire BA MLitt (late thirties). Previously director of studies at David Game College and founder of Uniprep which prepares candidates for admission to highly competitive universities. Read English at UCL, gained distinction in her MLitt in English Studies from Strathclyde University and lectured at a Thai university for five years, publishing articles on sociolinguistics and aspects of Thai culture. Ms Maguire's own mother took her A levels at Westminster Tutors!

Entrance: By interview

Remarks: Founded in 1934, this tiny (by London standards) tutorial is a very personal crammer and A level college. All ages and courses catered for, especially Common Entrance, GCSE and A levels. Staff are pulled in to teach the esoteric as well as the mundane. Easter, Christmas and half term revision courses, and after school assistance all year round. Max class size six (usually much smaller), plus lots of one-to-one and smaller seminars. Hours can be long, from 9am to 8pm if need be. Specialist preparation in admissions tests for medicine, law and oxbridge, and university-level tuition can also be provided. This is a really helpful, friendly crammer. Students from all over, usually, but not exclusively from the independent sector. No history of drugs or school drop-outs. Jolly bright rooms opposite Christie's, South Ken, with a good library, IT facilities and common rooms with running tea and coffee.

Westonbirt School

Linked to Rose Hill Westonbirt School in the Junior section

Westonbirt, Tetbury, Gloucestershire, GL8 8QG

• Pupils: 245 girls; 160 boarders, 85 day. • Ages: 11-18 • Size of sixth form: 90 • C of E • Fees: Day £15,645-£18,816; Boarding £22,992-£27,990 pa • Independent

Tel: 01666 880 333
Fax: 01666 880 364
Email: office@westonbirt.gloucs.sch.uk
Website: www.westonbirt.gloucs.sch.uk

Head: Since 1999, Mrs Mary Henderson MA PGCE (mid-fifties). Educated at Berkhamsted Girls' then read French at St Andrews and played lacrosse for Scotland. PGCE from Durham before teaching French at Cheltenham Ladies' where she became a housemistress. Four years at co-ed Warminster School before appointment to Westonbirt in 1996 as head of modern languages. Since our last visit, she has consolidated numbers and raised standards: still oozes savvy whilst remaining wholly approachable. Champions single sex education for girls and loves working in such inspiring surroundings. Married to retired senior lecturer from Bath University with whom she sings in local choirs and tours Europe. No children of her own but 'really knows every girl in the school,' said one mother. Keen on music and all things Scottish (particularly dancing – which she teaches the girls). Has proved an effective and successful head: setting high standards for girls and staff alike. Popular with girls for the right reasons, parents rate her as 'passionate about the school' and are amazed that 'she seems to be at every event.' Admits to being 'very competitive,' enjoys seeing girls motivating each other 'to perform beyond reasonable expectation.' Respected as 'traditional without being old fashioned.' Clearly pleased by how girls' work ethic has improved: 'It's in their soul now to do well,' she says.

Academic matters: Rigour has taken hold across the curriculum but still lots of nurturing: plenty of 'late bloomers' thanks to small classes throughout and a 'tried and tested' learning support department. Inevitable seepage (for a variety of reasons) at 16 is more than counterbalanced by increasing numbers of girls arriving for sixth. Numbers opting for harder subjects have grown in recent years. Notwithstanding, the percentage of A and B grades at A level has levelled out around a respectable 60–70 per cent. Flexible timetable allows for unusual subject combinations. Sciences doing particularly well – biology and chemistry (75 per cent A grades) lead the way but English and maths more than hold their own. Art continues to flourish, Latin survives to GCSE with the occasional candidate at A level; languages have regained some popularity – Year 9 girls recently wrote and performed their own French plays. Saturday lessons survive here though Year 13 get weekends for revision from the Lent half-term onwards.

Most parents thrilled at daughters' progress. In past four years, the percentage of girls achieving 5 or more A–C grades at GCSE (including English and maths) has increased from 71 per cent to almost 100 per cent – quite an achievement given the numbers receiving learning support. We observed an English lesson with some strident Year 11 girls who were articulate and mature in their analysis of each others' contributions to a commendably interactive lesson. Teachers appear 'on side' here, giving plenty of praise and encouragement. Displays are better than in many senior schools and help to create a positive learning environment. A level historians we observed looked set for good results and knew their stuff as did the sixth form geographers we saw studying the effects of monsoon climate (except that the 'stuff' of geography is no longer about knowing where places are). By the time we reached the professional looking chemists we were completely out of our league so we didn't try our luck with questions.

Twenty per cent receive some form of learning support. Close liaison with prep school SENCo. Initial screening to ensure none escape radar. Many come with psychological report and range from a very few 'almost non readers' to girls needing relatively little individual help. Four in successful, caring department; dyslexia trained staff deliver up to four thirty-five minute lessons a week according to need. Emphasis may be on reading, spelling, short-term recall etc. School can handle mild Aspergers or dyspraxia within limits. Girls are not taken out of mainstream lessons for learning support and therefore feel no stigma. All staff trained in differentiation which includes stretching gifted and talented in all lessons.

Games, Options, the Arts: Highly successful in sport especially lacrosse (coach is ex-international); all girls enjoy superb outdoor and indoor facilities. Early morning training demonstrates girls' greater commitment. Triennial lacrosse tour to USA a highlight for many. All play lax to year nine then around fifty seniors continue and generally reach national finals; similar numbers opt for tennis (year round coaching available). Netball, rounders and hockey all get a look in. Swanky new sports hall includes heated 25 metre pool and fitness/aerobics suites upstairs with viewing gallery – facility plays host to several hundred locals each week which helps to finance its high overheads (offered free of charge to local state primaries thereby earning charity status brownie points). No stabling for horses here but polo (girls play by arrangement with Beaufort Polo Club) is a particular favourite.

Art department boasts two large studios and makes its creative presence felt around the school. When we visited, Year 10 were inspired by van Gogh (having just visited the Royal Academy exhibition). Westonbirt was one of the first two schools to pioneer the Leith's Food and Wine course and its popularity is as great as ever – nearly all sixth formers participate over five terms to gain the coveted certificate which provides access to jobs (particularly useful for gappers) on the Leith's list. 'Inspirational' director of music (escapee from banking but with PhD in music) 'takes the girls with her' and is certainly making waves: musical participation in all areas has leapt up since she took over the reins and the full-on samba band has also helped to stir things up. Some outstanding musicians here and a really impressive programme of orchestral and choral concerts – 'it's cool to be in the choir now,' say girls. 'I never knew my daughter could sing,' cooed one mother. Drama also very strong but HoD on maternity leave when we visited. Lunch-time current affairs sessions for sixth formers help to broaden political horizons. D of E is popular and is offered at bronze and gold award levels.

Background and Atmosphere: Few schools match the setting of Westonbirt: a magnificent neo-Renaissance pile built for ludicrously wealthy Holford family (who also founded nearby arboretum) at height of Victorian expansionism. Belongs to Allied Schools group (includes Stowe and Harrogate Ladies' amongst its five members). Girl Guides a strong influence in early years and some traditions survive: e.g. vespers sung whilst stood around edge of Great Hall. Christian life important but not dominant – Sunday chapel (on site) is still compulsory for boarders. Imbued with excellent taste, Robert Holford spared no expense here and since the school opened in 1928 they have been worthy custodians of the grade 1 listed building and ornamental gardens not to mention 250 acres of parkland. Library has recently been renovated (thanks to deep pockets of some worthy old girls) with exquisite pelmets re-fashioned at Royal School of Needlework and wall fabric hand-dyed to match original colour. Adjacent reading room is next for the top drawer make-over. Some dorms are exquisite with plum billet in Lady Holford's boudoir: individual dressing tables here not just wardrobes. Girls' lasting memories tend to be of delightful gardens rather than of marble columns or frescoes. All sixth formers have personal study bedrooms and their boarding provision has been much improved by a recent Cotswold stone fronted (shame about the rear side) addition. Classrooms in the converted stables are adequate but showing their age; newer Francis Rawes building accommodates science, IT, art and D&T not to mention the multi-use lecture room. Camelia House has been exquisitely refurbished (period drama producers please note) and provides a pre-Raphaelite backdrop for informal concerts. An appeal has been made to replace eyesore of a music department – not before time and a project close to the head's heart.

Friendly atmosphere throughout; good balance of male and female teachers who put up with a cramped staff room – 'money goes to the children,' quipped one colleague over coffee. More girls studying in sixth has definitely improved the work ethic since we last visited. Lots of trips and activities for all ages with special events thick on the ground – head (doyenne of the school's Caledonian Society) particularly enthusiastic about those with a Scottish flavour. Some girls would like more contact with boys' schools but sixth formers were preparing for a dinner debate with Abingdon when we visited and had just been to Eton for Scottish reels.

Pastoral Care and Discipline: Former is effective to a level where latter is now a rarity. Senior girls tend to defuse potential difficulties in many cases. Beaufort house provides haven for girls in Year 7; three houses for 12–16 year olds with designated (mainly non-teaching) pastoral staff. Housemistresses often assigned other responsibilities and parents praise 'mature approach' of house staff and parents say that moving girls around helps to ensure there are no major friendship issues. Academic tutor makes up trio of carers for each girl. Sixth form includes prefects ('Study One') who operate from summer term in Year 12 until start of A levels. Counsellor comes regularly to lend confidential support; 'star' of a chaplain whom girls 'really trust'. Active approach to Christianity involves girls taking a lead but religion is not rammed down throats. Qualified nursing staff operate sanatorium 24/7. School likes ISCO careers support and believes in girls getting a wide range of work experience: 'ten different sorts if possible,' said head of careers. Fines for rare instances of smoking (part of growing up); glass of wine permitted to sixth formers on special occasions but never spirits; tough on drugs. Night-time high jinks avoided by alarmed doors and night watchmen who patrol the grounds. Parents say that any problem is 'dealt with properly.'

Pupils and Parents: 'Turns out polished and lovely girls,' beamed one parent. 'Not immaculate' and more down to earth than you'd expect – no riffraff but many families are making 'huge sacrifices'. Appeals to a broad cross-section of girls mainly within a two hour travelling radius but increasing numbers of Londoners board here and other enclaves of boarding families have sprung up in Cornwall and Wales; fewer overseas pupils these days (ceiling is now twenty-five per cent we were told which belied some parental observations but, says school, is absolutely true). Sociable, hearty girls in the main who enjoy the atmosphere and sporting opportunities. Some shrinking violets (present head girl admitted to having started in this category) who blossom over time. 'No naughtiness now,' claimed senior girls who 'get cross' if girls step out of line. Reading is part of the culture as is throwing oneself into all aspects of school life. Percentage of boarders increases as girls move through school. Day girls can 'sleep over' once a week for free and some buy extra nights to be with friends. Many 'convert' as a result of trying out boarding this way. Girls who leave at 16 sometimes live to regret their decision (and even return). Overseas pupils benefit from effective ELT teaching and bring an extra dimension; many short-term German pupils want to stay longer if it can be arranged. Famous old girls include children's author Georgia Byng (Molly Moon series), TV's *Hotel Inspector* Ruth Watson, TV producer Patricia Llewellyn (Two Fat Ladies, Jamie Oliver), and socialites Lady Emily Compton, Lady Sybilla Hart and Lady Natasha Rufus-Isaacs.

Entrance: Common entrance at 11 and 13; own exam for those outside CE system and for sixth formers outside of GCSE system (otherwise minimum 5+ GCSEs at A–C are needed). Most Rose Hill Westonbirt girls proceed here at 11+; local primaries also provide some day girls. Beaudesert Park and St Margaret's, Calne have been favourites alongside Leaden Hall and Godstowe but net is being cast wider and wider it seems. Head regularly visits Garden House to recruit from 'the smoke'. Daughters of clergy still receive a 30 per cent bursary. Educational psychologist's report if special needs – girls are only turned away if really unable to cope. Overseas pupils increasingly from Europe rather than Far East with German and Spanish girls coming for between one term and two years.

Exit: About half the sixth form leavers take a gap year. Most sixth formers proceed to reputable universities (including medicine and veterinary science). Good HE advice ensures sixth formers make realistic choices and advice continues after they leave.

Money Matters: Scholarships and exhibitions offered at 11, 13 and 16 include academic, art, drama, sport and music. 5 per cent sibling reductions; more for services, diplomatic and clergy daughters. Extras include ballet, learning support and golf.

Remarks: Has got even better since our last visit with a more viable sixth form and greatly improved recreational facilities. 'If you want a small boarding school you can't beat it – miles ahead of others we looked at,' said satisfied parents of a Year 8 boarder. 'My daughter has found it brilliant,' said another mother. Head runs a tight but happy ship and girls flourish in a setting which is second to none.

Whitgift School

Haling Park, South Croydon, Surrey, CR2 6YT

• Pupils: 1,175 boys; all day • Ages: 10-18 • Size of sixth form: 205
• Non-denom • Fees: £13,731 pa • Independent

Tel: 020 8688 9222
Fax: 020 8760 0682
Email: office@whitgift.co.uk
Website: www.whitgift.co.uk

Head: Since 1991, Dr Christopher A Barnett MA (Oxon) DPhil (Oxon) (56), who has 'no intention of retiring at sixty ... take another generation of youngsters through ... love it'. He runs the school with an eight strong senior management team. An historian, he read modern history at Oriel, followed by a somewhat esoteric doctorate (also in history) whilst acting as research assistant for Nigel Fisher (then MP for Surbiton). By age 21, Mr Barnett was lecturing at Brunel University in economics, thence to teaching: nine years at Bradfield where he became head of history, followed by Dauntsey's as second master. He lives with his psychotherapist wife, who works at nearby Mayday Hospital, in the grounds behind the Tudor wood. They have three sons, all educated at Whitgift, and one daughter.

Tall, commanding, full of initiative (addressing a complaint that 'he was often away,' he said he was 'pretty much ever present but sometimes away with large groups of Whitgift students'). He has both raised the intellectual bar and increased numbers in the school and his building/re-building programme is unlike any this editor has ever seen. New gym, new magical swimming pool, old gym being turned into drama-zone with linking walkway, huge fencing salle. The school hosted the Mary Rose exhibition during the summer with over 32,000 visitors, and the car park was a bit muddly when we visited 'but (this was second week September – referring to the car park) all this will be changed next week'. Keen racing man (sticks and flat – often buys yearlings); his colours echo the school yellow and blue and nags are named Whitgift Rose, Whitgift Rock etc – has been known to bring Phar Too Gifted and Quick Whitted to school a la Red Rum. Charming, less extrovert than you might imagine, his educational vision should be cloned and marketed.

Academic matters: GCSE for all until first form sixth, when pupils opt for A levels, IB (straight or bilingual) or BTech after mega consultation. Three sciences, maths, two English for all and two langs for most at GCSE: pleasing numbers of As and A* at all levels; occasional glitch in geography; French surprisingly underwhelming; classics (and to A level), Spanish, German, Italian, Arabic, Mandarin and 'the biggest Japanese dept in the country'. Russian on the cards. Bi-lingual programme – French, German and Spanish: Jstore and Factiva (French and Italian newsmags) available in the library plus on line foreign lang news throughout). Foreign langs dept based in 'rue de Folkestone and Rheinstrasse'; native speakers, oodles of trips and exchanges. Enormous and vibrant science dept linked to DT and some rather trendy goodies on display – the dildo-like attachment to the life jacket is apparently a torch – (more Arkwright Design Technology Scholarships have been won by Whitgift than by any other school). Computer rooms all over, linked in every dimension and lap tops for all. IB results well above 'global average'; bold decision, seems to be working. Regular trickle doing PE at all standards.

Class sizes average 18 (10 in the sixth form) with 25 maximum, some setting in maths, science and langs. Staff mostly young(ish) – said to 'be under thirty' – though not the ones we met, with 40 per cent women, 130 staff, plus 'peries' and 60/70 on the support side; heads of departments 'have a say in staff appointments'. School is serious about special needs, and particularly hot on dyslexia. SENCo, plus three assistants, either one to one or groups, well used drop-in centre, with after-school clinics: 'teachers especially helpful during exam time,' said our guide. Help for the ablest as well as those with problems (no bored boys here). No charge. School has open access, currently none in wheelchairs; staff wear special mikes when they teach two profoundly deaf students (and head mutters darkly about the embarrassment of 'forgetting to take the mike off and discussing something scurrilous outside assembly'). Links with Hungary and Japan and two year scholarships offered to 'outstanding pupils' of whom seven currently board with a member of staff in the grounds. New boarding house under consideration, hopefully built in time for the Olympics, to house up to 150.

Games, Options, the Arts: Sport exceptional: with 27 rugby sides – including an E team – 20 cricket teams and 16 hockey teams. Win county and national competitions in rugby, cricket, hockey and fencing, and are local honchos in athletics, swimming and football. Cricket strong, with expert coaching, and possibly the longest nets in the country. Surrey CC holds a Cricket Festival Week and four-day, first-class game at the school. Table tennis, golf, water polo and pentathlon all produce champions. Fabulous £9m sports complex – for many years a pipe dream – now open: 'one of the wonders of the educational world!' says head. Development includes indoor pool, four squash courts with moveable walls, fitness centre, conference room, kitchens, classrooms, plus vast sports hall (seating for 1600). Eton and Millfield eat your hearts out: this is truly international stuff and will be used during the Olympics – modern pentathlon, swimming, fencing. Astro pitch on site. Sports department open at 6.45 am (breakfast said to be worth it) and the list of sporting achievements legendary.

Exciting music with mass of orchestras, choirs, chamber groups, bands plus Whitgift's own Corps of Drums. No pipes. Free compulsory lessons for all their first term – no particular bias: 'if we need strings, they learn strings, if we are short on brass they learn brass'. Some amazing success stories. The gifted attend Saturday lessons at Trinity College of Music or the Royal Academy of Music and are members of the National Youth Orchestra. Whitgift hosts the Croydon Music Festival, the London Mozart Players are regulars: organising masterclasses, commissioning music and providing performance opportunities for pupils. Carmen for all this year. Drama dept now relocated in old swimming pool – ginormous space (with massive storage underneath).

We were taken to task for admitting that we felt art was less 'in yer face' than we had expected – given the superlatives we use elsewhere, and indeed the art room had a strong and purposeful air, but stuff on show was more mundane than some we have seen – though it was the second week of term. History of art apparently not constrained by the nanny net (think Titian, think Botticelli). Pottery and photographic facilities are super, with textile design an add-on.

Regular Arts Festivals with an impressive collection of performers, plus political conferences; and, last year, a Bilingual conference 'under the auspices of the French Presidency of the European Union and co-hosted by the French Ambassador'. Overseas expeditions for musicians, linguists, sportsmen and adventurers. CCF for all, outdoor pursuits and D of E on offer. Many and varied community service projects. Bonding trip for all lower firsts (ten year olds) for a week in Lake Garda which includes culture (Verona, Venice et al as well as mountain walking and sailing). Every three years 800 boys go to the French Alps, the Italian Lakes on an international study programme during term time. No charge.

Background and Atmosphere: Founded 1596 by John Whitgift, Archbishop of Canterbury in the time of Queen Elizabeth I and endowed with, apparently, most of the land in the centre of Croydon (including the Whitgift Centre). The school has had a chequered career, changing name and location several times over the past 400 years before moving to Haling Park, (one-time home of Lord Howard of Effingham, Lord High Admiral of the fleet sent against the Armada) in 1931. The immaculately-groomed 45 acre oasis is bordered by seriously posh pads on one side and gritty central Croydon thoroughfare on other. Glorious red brick (think Basil Spence) with panelled interiors and old masters and school photographs in almost equal measure. Grounds contain a three acre 'site of scientific interest'. Some eccentric touches. Prefects range around in royal purple gowns. Legendary central quad has topiary in shape of red squirrels (their furry counterparts are bred in cages here – they were due to be released into the wild in 2009, but the dreaded squirrel virus put paid to that scheme and more resilient Asian version is currently being bred) and rampaging peacocks (soothing to look at until they open their mouths: 'they can be a pain during exams,' said one boy: and one particularly vicious hen had a bash at this editor's face – glasses protected a full frontal assault). Fantastic new Water Gardens, replete with pink flamingos and albino wallabies, opened by Sir David Attenborough, two or three local junior schools visit each week for a touchy-feely experience. Junior section separated from main school buildings. Compact dining room serves the boys who eat in two shifts and about to be greatly increased.

Huge charitable commitment, including SNAP – in-house respite care – which operates at Whitgift during the summer holidays, plus charity comedy night and a musical extravaganza.

Pastoral Care and Discipline: This is an Anglican Foundation, complete with in-house Chaplain. The headmaster must be a confirmed member of the Church of England and the Archbishop of Canterbury is, ex officio, head of the Foundation, however all faiths welcome, with a 'bungalow' (aka the Spirituality Centre) set aside for prayers, no apparent lip service paid to other faiths' holy days. 'We are a light touch Anglican Foundation,' said the head. Zero tolerance of drugs. 'Head is big on discipline,' said the boys. Bullying, alcohol, dyed hair, 'excessive laziness' – all forbidden. Pro-active bullying strategy. Boys tend to arrive early (breakfast served from 7.30am) and leave at 3.45pm, unless they have sporting commitments at school, though the gates have been 'known to be open well after midnight'. Complicated house/tutorial system: eight Senior Houses and eight Junior Houses, tinies allocated a house on arrival, ditto a tutor, and there is a mentoring system. Heads of Year cover two years, with assistant heads and tutors. Next intake doubles size of year, also allotted houses. Sixth form common room an expanse of exposed steel and grey floors. 'They don't give us that much stuff because we'll just wreck it,' explained a pupil solemnly. Theft equals out.

Pupils and Parents: Pretty good social mix thanks to bursary scheme but funds no longer doled out as liberally as they once were (see Money Matters). Around 25 per cent ethnic minorities; help with extra English. Most boys fall within the London day school species homo boffinus – this is not a hive of eccentric creative rebels – many are jolly grown up and focused. Astonishing geographical range for a day school – some from across the road, others via rail (South or East Croydon Station) from Surrey, (Brighton!), Kent, West and East Sussex, north London. Eight school buses. Senior boys can drive to school, staff maintain that pupils' cars are smarter than theirs! Strong parents association. OBs include cricketer Raman Subba Row, actor Martin Jarvis, Professor Sir Bernard Crick, WWII heroes Lord Tedder and 'Cats Eyes' Cunningham.

Entrance: Via report, interview and examination, with emphasis on the latter (taken in January in maths, English and verbal reasoning). Five applicants for each place. Commitment matters – places are most likely to go to persistent, keen, bushy-tailed families who make Whitgift their first choice. Takes up to 100 ten-year-olds and slightly more 11-year-olds. Another 30 boys cobbled on at age 13, and there is an intake at 16. Not on radar screens for many trad preps where all boys stay on to 13. Head not a fan of 13+ entrance, 'when they come at 11, they are a long way from public exams and have time to stretch themselves'. Half the pupils come from state primaries, half from preps. Main feeders are Elmhurst, Cumnor House (in Croydon, not the E Sussex prep), Downsend, Homefield, Oakhurst Grange and several strong local primaries. Dizzyingly large catchment area of more than 1,000 square miles.

Exit: Up to 25 per cent a year to Oxbridge – history and Japanese the top subjects. Then London, Nottingham, Sheffield and Birmingham, in that order. A few pupils leave after GCSE 'to pursue more career-orientated options'.

Money Matters: Once the primary beneficiary of the Whitgift Foundation's largesse, with up to 40 per cent of pupils receiving financial assistance, the school has had to share with nearby boys' school, Trinity and, more recently, with the girls at Old Palace. Bursaries now more competitive, but this is still the biggest bursary programme in the country, and thanks to the Whitgift Foundation, Croydon remains an excellent area in which to be clever but poor. Scholarships for candidates of outstanding merit also on offer for boys entering at 10, 11, 12, 13 or 16. All boys automatically entered for scholarship and bursary schemes when they sit entrance test. Awards also for music, drama, art, technology, sport and all-rounders. School does have 'particular' sponsors; Chelsea Football Club sponsored a boy here, and the social services occasionally suggest prospective pupils.

Remarks: Superb cosmopolitan boys' school, with outstanding facilities, reasonable prices and a strong academic reputation – an example of what education is really about.

Wigmore School

Ford Street, Wigmore, Leominster, Herefordshire, HR6 9UW

• Pupils: 470 boys and girls, all day • Ages: 11-16 • Non-denom • State

Tel: 01568 770 323
Fax: 01568 770 917
Email: admin@wigmore.hereford.sch.uk
Website: www.wigmore.hereford.sch.uk

Head Teacher: Since 2005, Mr Andrew Shaw BSc PGCE NPQH (forties). Previously worked in Worcester, Gloucester, Jersey and Staffordshire. Originally a PE teacher, he retains a very strong interest in sports – to which a number of muddy footballs in his office bear witness! Genuinely friendly and enthusiastic, he has vision and energy for innovation and excellence in all areas of the school from the skirting boards upwards. Proud of the high quality of his staff, says the school's greatest strength is its ethos of community and shared responsibility. Keen to grow international links for the school and broaden its curriculum. Designated as a National Leader of Education.

Academic matters: Very good GCSE results. Over 95 per cent achieve five or more A* to C grades, 89 per cent five A* to C including English and maths. Children are tested on entry and there is setting for all core subjects in KS3 and KS4. All pupils study for an applied course in ICT worth four GCSEs, regarded by the school as vital in preparing pupils with skills for life in the 'information age'. Pupils still have a good range of choices at KS4 and are encouraged to choose a broad and balanced curriculum, supported by the excellent careers guidance service and work experience programme offered by the school. Now a specialist maths and computing college. This is improving its resources and its links with local businesses, as well as increasing access to IT resources for the local community. It is developing plans for an improved art room, library and careers area.

Special needs support well organised, with weekly reviews of progress, and a team of 'high level teaching assistants' dedicated to supporting those children who need individual care. An active reading recovery programme led by older pupils. Staff are particularly aware of the potential for cultural isolation: ethnic minorities are practically non-existent in this corner of Herefordshire, and great effort is made to ensure that the children are acquainted with the full spectrum of faiths and cultures, with visiting speakers, trips to mosques etc. Residential trips every year for each year group and a high uptake of French exchanges and other extra-curricular offerings. The school is a designated National Support School providing support and guidance to other schools and is recognised by Ofsted for its innovative and successful approaches to learning, leadership and quality assurance.

Games, Options, the Arts: Over 80 per cent of pupils participate in after-school activities – dedicated parents do a great deal of ferrying in this deeply rural area.

Games provision is impressive, with a huge, pristine sports hall, fitness room, cricket nets, 400m track and a large hard play area. A high level of participation in all sports, and staff ensure that all who show enthusiasm get a chance to represent the school. This inclusive approach is no barrier to excellence. A number of children participate at county level and where some allowance is needed to get to externally run practices (e.g. swimming) the school is flexible about making this possible. A great food technology room, buzzing with activity and enthusiastic chefs. Has Healthy Schools status, and with the combination of excellent sports facilities and switched on thinking about food both in the classroom and the dining hall, you can see why. The school has also been awarded Artsmark Gold, a recognition of the very good work it does with sometimes limited facilities.

A lot of extra-curricular drama – from Shakespeare to home-grown. A well equipped music room, plenty of school bands and orchestras and a popular singing group. A good range of instruments taught by peripatetic staff, although the school could do with more practice rooms. IT provision is very good, with lots of networked PCs which the children are encouraged to use across all subjects in the curriculum. The design technology workshop is well equipped, with a good deal of interesting kit for the children to get stuck into.

Background and Atmosphere: In a pretty village in a pretty corner of Herefordshire with fantastic outdoor spaces. The building itself is not an architectural gem and not as well maintained as it might be. There are some fairly scruffy areas, but plans to improve them. A new SEN extension has improved rooming provision.

Despite the lack of polish, the atmosphere is one of happy, calm, purposeful hard work and a proper pride in the high standards that are achieved. No lockers and charity collection jars are not chained down. Pupils appreciate the opportunities and care that they receive at Wigmore. Who wouldn't fit in? Not for those attracted to ivory towers or wedded to their cucumber sandwiches.

Pastoral Care and Discipline: Members of staff keep their tutor groups for the whole of the pupils' five year progress through the school, so get to know each child. A strong policy on bullying is posted in every classroom. Staff say the calibre of the senior management team means any problems of this sort are dealt with immediately and effectively. Relationships seem positive and co-operative. The head says he expects and gets a high standard of behaviour from the children – 'we have a few pupils with problems but they aren't a problem in school.' Peer pressure underlines the strong sense of mutual responsibility and community. Pupils say that they feel comfortable with the rules and are treated fairly.

Pupils and Parents: The catchment area is predominantly agricultural land and the pupils and parents are mainly of farming stock, although some from the professional classes and some from the much more deprived end of the social spectrum. Many parents attended the school themselves and are very supportive of the staff. The children may not have given much thought to the tucking of shirt tails into trousers or to standing up when you come into the room, but they are friendly, enthusiastic, responsible and hardworking – even coming into revision classes during the school holidays.

Entrance: The school is part of the Wigmore Hard Federation which offers an all-through education from Wigmore Primary into Wigmore Secondary. It is wholly non-selective (80+ with special needs of whom approximately 25 per cent are statemented), accepting pupils on the traditional LA criteria of catchment area, siblings in school and so on. The school is over-subscribed, with a waiting list for each year group and a substantial number of disappointed parents on appeal to the LA. It is essential to be within the catchment area, but this is quite large and, generally speaking, being in catchment gives a good chance of a place.

Exit: Most go on to take A levels at Hereford Sixth Form College (very good academically) or Hereford College of Technology (more vocationally based – and not as strong), others go on to sixth form in Ludlow, some to apprenticeships in horticulture, farming or engineering. All benefit from the school's outstanding careers advice and work placement scheme in Years 10 and 11. The majority of A level pupils consider university – the school says approximately 80 per cent moving on beyond A level.

Remarks: A really nice school. Relaxed in terms of etiquette – not the place to 'finish' Isabella, but an extremely successful, friendly and happy school where children are encouraged not only to learn but to take responsibility for themselves and one other. Pupils leave as rounded individuals with a positive outlook and high expectations.

William Ellis School

Linked to La Swap Sixth Form in the Senior section

Highgate Road, London, NW5 1RN

• Pupils: 870 boys, all day • Ages: 11-18 • Size of sixth form: 1,250 in a consortium of four schools, 'La Swap' • Non-denom • State

Tel: 020 7267 9346
Fax: 020 7284 1274
Email: info@williamellis.camden.sch.uk
Website: www.williamellis.camden.sch.uk

Head: Interim head for the 2010–2011 school year is Ms Jill Hislop MA in Education and NPQH; formerly head of Woodhouse Business and Enterprise College in Tamworth, and experienced in helping schools in troubled circumstances. She has over 30 years experience. Ms Hislop was appointed after previous head, Mr Robbie Cathcart, left suddenly at the end of the summer term in 2010 after suffering prolonged ill-health. He had joined the school in 2008 at a challenging time, with a half million pound deficit, a barely tepid Ofsted report and demoralised staff and pupils. Fiona Millar, highly effective and outspoken chair of governors and the vice chairs 'have worked really fast to get a really good temporary replacement, in order to get things moving ... and also give the governors time to make a good new appointment,' said a parent.

Academic matters: A huge ability range here, with large numbers at either end of the academic spectrum. Camden is consulting on whether to introduce ability banding into the admissions process throughout the borough, so in future the intake may be more evenly spread.

William Ellis is a language college – the only boys' comprehensive with this specialism. Everyone starts French in Year 7 and adds German or Spanish in Years 8 and 9, continuing at least one to GCSE – hurray – with the top set taking French in Year 10. 'Fantastic' Mandarin club gives boys the opportunity to write and perform a Chinese play and visit Beijing. Latin GCSE is a new after-school class; the previous head hoped to bring it into the mainstream curriculum. Evening language classes for parents; language staff teach at feeder primary schools. Science refreshingly available as three separate subjects (very popular), as well as a dual award and a single applied science.

Most lessons for the first two years are in mixed ability groups, with languages setted from Year 8 and maths from Year 9. It is fair to say that many boys find the school more convivial once they reach Year 9 and join tutor groups organised largely by ability.

GCSE results are rising after a sharp dip a few years ago, and are back up above the borough average for boys. Mr Cathcart worked to regain parents' confidence in the school. He beefed up the senior management team, with deputies who have responsibility for overseeing what is taught and how. 'We're focusing on making lessons more interesting across the board. Our big priority is raising standards and expectations.'

Parents have complained for some years about massive inconsistencies in teaching standards and expectations. Some still feel that whether homework is set, completed or marked can be somewhat random. Mr Cathcart commented: 'I have spoken to heads of year and told them that we have a homework policy and they must stick to it. The senior management team have done spot checks on homework planners to see what is being set. I'm acutely aware that parents want to support the school and I want to make sure we're meeting our side of the bargain. We have a new programme of teaching and learning development for all staff. It's about sharing good practice and making sure that every lesson is a good lesson.'

The school is looking at its KS3 curriculum and considering the Middle Years IB programme. 'From day one it encourages independent learners and global citizens. It makes us think about learning and about our place in the world.'

Bright boys do regularly achieve sheaves of A* grades. Gifted and talented Year 7 and 8 boys are invited to a summer programme including trips and booster activities. 'My older son had a brilliant career at William Ellis,' said a parent, 'and his brother is having a great time there. He's enjoying the work and has a lovely tutor group – friendly, supportive and bright.' 'They get the measure of the boys,' said another. 'They don't underestimate the bright kids.'

The school runs a popular joint sixth form with Parliament Hill School, which is also part of La Swap consortium with Acland Burghley and La Sainte Union schools. This offers a huge range of courses including several vocational options at different levels. There tends to be a strong humanities bias with English, history and sociology much the most popular courses, and an average of around 20 per cent A grades at A level. It is discussing offering the IB, 'but there are lots of alternatives'.

The school has its fair share of boys with special educational needs and behavioural difficulties. It lost the dedicated learning support unit when government funding came to an end, coinciding with the budget deficit, 'but we're looking to put staff back, at least in reduced numbers'. The head of Year 7 visits every feeder primary school and gets information about the boys about to join the school. Those who are likely to need extra support are invited to a summer school before they join, where they get help with literacy and with settling in to their new school. There is plenty of targeted support for those in need, though as with most comprehensives the SEN department is stretched thin. The building is mostly wheelchair accessible, with stairlifts giving access to the upper floors.

Games, Options, the Arts: Sport is improving. The sports hall includes basketball and badminton courts, and the school is enviably situated on the edge of Hampstead Heath, with running track, cricket nets and football pitches nearby. Football, basketball, cross country, cricket and rugby teams compete against other schools and in borough events, 'though there's only one team for each year, and my son has never been picked,' said a parent sadly. Boys following the sports leadership qualification help to coach Year 7 football teams.

Music is also on the up. There are 12 music places – which must be awarded in future for aptitude rather than ability, but have so far brought in talented musicians who play in the orchestra and ensembles. There are 'interesting concerts,' say parents, with 'flashes of brilliance'.

This is not a school that puts on large-scale school plays but it has excellent connections with hallowed establishments. Pupils might find themselves working on a version of the *Magic Flute* with staff from the Young Vic, or seeing their script performed at Hampstead Theatre.

The school owns The Mill residential field centre in Surrey. All Year 7s have an outdoor pursuits week there at the end of the summer term. It is also used for master classes in music and drama, for study and revision weekends and for field trips. There are language trips to Europe and China, ski trips, field trips to Morocco and Spain, study tours to Russia and the USA.

Background and Atmosphere: Founded in 1862 in Gospel Oak by businessman William Ellis, who wanted children to be taught 'useful' subjects like science instead of rote learning. In 1937 it moved to its present site on the edge of Hampstead Heath, as a voluntary aided grammar school. It became comprehensive in 1978.

Smallish but leafy site – many boys walk to school across the Heath – with buildings and facilities that are gradually being upgraded, including swish sports hall and library, and a rather cramped tarmac playground. Planned major building works now kiboshed by Coalition cuts. Parliament Hill School is next door and La Sainte Union across the road, so lunch times and end of school can see a veritable swarm of pupils socialising.

Pastoral Care and Discipline: A robust school, with some low level disruption in class and a certain amount of jostling in corridors and playgrounds. Some boys take this in their stride; others find it more challenging. Simple measures have helped: the school has successfully reduced friction between lessons in its small building with narrow corridors by cutting down on the number of bells and giving more leeway at change-over times.

Mr Cathcart said: 'The biggest challenge any school faces is consistency of expectations. One of our priorities is behaviour for learning. We're focusing on consistent sanctions, so that boys know that if they do x the consequence is y. But we also know that one of the main ways of combating disruption is making lessons more interesting across the board and we're working on that.'

There are points and prizes for good referrals in the lower years as well as sanctions for bad ones. No head boys or prefects, but boys are encouraged to enter public speaking competitions, to become involved in the school council and outside organisations such as Camden Youth Council.

Exclusions are likely for dealing drugs, for extreme violence or for possessing offensive weapons. The school, like most others in Camden, has 'safer schools police officers' around most of the time. 'Part of their role is to educate children on what is the law so that they don't break it inadvertently. Far more actions are against the law now than there were 20 years ago – carrying a penknife, for example. Even a cricket bat could be classified as an offensive weapon. We don't want to criminalise behaviour unnecessarily, and we want to support students at risk to avoid them getting on the wrong side of the law.'

Pupils and Parents: From a huge range of different countries, ranging from Kosovo to Somalia, from the council estates of Gospel Oak and the million pound houses of Dartmouth Park and Belsize Park. 'There are some really nice parents,' said a mother. 'Interesting, diverse and charming.' OBs include Len Deighton, Sean French, Richard Thompson, Toby Young, Andrew Sachs and Fred Titmus.

Entrance: Some 600 applicants for 123 places at 11. Admission criteria: (i) looked after children (ii) siblings (iii) 12 music places – now chosen for aptitude rather than ability, by aural tests rather than references from instrumental teachers (iv) location – in practice, up to about a mile and a half.

La Swap sixth form: About 200 new entrants join the 450 or so moving up from the four constituent schools. Applications by early February; most students who apply on time will be offered a place. Qualifications vary from D grades and below at GCSE for introductory diplomas, to at least eight GCSEs including two B and three C grades for A levels and advanced vocational courses.

Exit: About two-thirds of Year 11 students move on to La Swap, the rest mostly to further education colleges or other local sixth forms e.g. Camden School for Girls. About 90 per cent of leavers with advanced qualifications go on to higher education, with about 20 per cent to Russell Group universities and six or eight a year to Oxbridge.

Money Matters: Has done well out of the DCSF for building funds, and is voluntary aided by the William Ellis and Birkbeck Schools Trust, but otherwise is as hard up as most other state schools.

Remarks: Small boys' comprehensive which has had a rocky few years and now faces choosing its third new head in a short space of time. But parents are still optimistic. 'There are some really talented boys here,' said one. 'It has got massive potential.'

Wilson's School

Mollison Drive, Wallington, Surrey, SM6 9JW

• Pupils: 1060 boys, all day • Ages: 11-18. • Size of sixth form: 270. • C of E (but pupils of all denominations and none accepted on an equal basis).
• State

Tel: 02087 732 931
Fax: 02087 734 972
Email: office@wilsonsschool.sutton.sch.uk
Website: www.wilsonsschool.sutton.sch.uk

Head: Since 1999, Mr Damien Charnock BD MTh (in theology and philosophy from University of London), (early fifties). Came to Wilson's from The Latymer School in Edmonton where he was deputy head (previously head of middle school in King's School, Tynemouth). Assertive head who knows exactly how he wants to run his school, which he does with authority as well as dedication. Happy to talk about the school, but is not interested in revealing anything about himself or his personal life. Pupils describe him as 'strict,' and 'very respectable and runs the school like clockwork,' adds a very satisfied parent. Mr Charnock believes that all pupils in his school are capable of extremely high achievements and 'Wilson's will provide them with every opportunity to achieve those goals.'

Academic matters: Academically very impressive. Boys take an average of 11 GCSE subjects. At A level, maths, sciences and economics/business studies dominate in the sixth form – not surprising for a school with specialist status in mathematics and computing. Hence no shortage of facilities, labs or latest equipment for the boys to use. Almost every classroom in this vast school has an interactive whiteboard and a laptop – if not, then an up-to-date projector and a PC. There are four PC suites, all equipped with up to date computers and flat screen monitors (around 30 in each room). A number of students take AS ICT in Year 11. Ten science labs 'and we still need more!' says head. However, he is keen to stress that the school is not a one trick pony – 'it has a huge range of subjects on offer in the sixth form and we invest heavily to ensure that small subjects like Latin, music, art, philosophy etc can be taken by students.' In 2006, the school took on a second specialism of the creative arts, with an emphasis on media and English.

Choice of languages is abundant. All boys take French or German and Latin in Year 7, with an option to take up a second modern language in Year 9; Ancient Greek is also on offer for GCSE. Teaching is highly praised by parents – although some comments that there is a constant movement of staff and new teachers are brought in on a regular basis. 'Not sure why teachers do not like to stay here,' added a mother. 'I feel Mr C likes to have new blood. Either that or they cannot keep up with his pace. Whichever it is, we are happy!' Mr Charnock denies staff turnover is an issue – 'turnover is in fact pretty much in line with other London grammar schools and better than some,' and he attributes many of the changes in personnel 'to the significant growth of the school and reducing class sizes.' You might want to check the situation when you visit.

Classrooms are bright and very spacious with an average of 25 pupils per class. Corridors are filled with photos of school activities and impressive trips to Cuba, Greece and Italy as well as World Challenge visits to Zambia and Peru. Pupils are focused and excited to be learning. 'Every boy here is here because he wants to achieve,' says the head. 'They are serious about their work yet at the same time they are well rounded and happy. If you nourish the pupil with sports, creative activities and challenges, then he will automatically flourish academically.' Classrooms, labs and language suites are all buzzing. Library is of a good size and full of keen students. No SEN department, provision is made on the basis of assessment of individual needs. Students are not tested for SEN on entry, and very few receive one-to-one help.

Games, Options, the Arts: Sport is very prominent and compulsory through to lower sixth form. Football, cricket, badminton and athletics are most popular. School runs a badminton academy and has national championship teams in badminton and water polo amongst others. Super fields on hand for the boys, as well as new indoor facilities and gym. Very impressive and striking art displayed in classrooms as well as corridors and even more impressive DT creations. Drama very strong – parents highly praise performances such as Macbeth and Amadeus. Shock Tactics, the school's drama society, is very popular with the boys, who get involved in all aspects of production, acting and directing. Music at Wilson's is a strength with numerous entries into the school's young musician of the year competition. 'Music teachers are great,' says one happy parent, 'they make sure that most boys either play an instrument or are part of the choir or the jazz or Latin bands – not something you find in many grammar schools.' CCF and Duke of Edinburgh Award on offer.

Background and Atmosphere: Founded in 1615 as a grammar school in Camberwell, the school moved to Wallington in 1975 into an archetypal 1960s building with a deceptively small entrance opening up like a maze – to rooms, corridors, halls and fields. New Foundation Building. Mr Charnock is very passionate about renovating every corner of the school and modernising it. He feels that students need to be inspired, not only by teaching but also by being in a welcoming environment. Boys can arrive as early as 7:30am and, after school, IT rooms and the library remain open and clubs including debating, drama, sports and chess as well as homework run until around 5pm.

Pastoral Care and Discipline: Very strong pastoral care team who deal firmly with any issues. 'Any head who tells you that bullying or smoking do not happen is lying to you,' affirms Mr Charnock. 'The important thing is how to tackle such problems.' Parents assure that racism is non-existent and bullying is very rare but, if issues arise, are well handled. 'My son has a goal to succeed and so do his friends – they know why they are at Wilson's and that is why they do not waste their time being awful to one another,' comments a mother.

Pupils and Parents: Fifty per cent of boys from ethnic minorities. Buzzing atmosphere with smart boys. The odd ponytail or spiky hair on a sixth former but nothing too scruffy. Parents vary from those who move their boys from private schools to reap the rewards of a super grammar school to others who move from the state sector. Old Wilsonians include actor Michael Caine and fashion designer John Galliano.

Entrance: Vastly over-subscribed for entry at 11: about 1,450 applications for 150 places from about 70 feeder schools – private and state. Entrance is via exam – verbal reasoning, maths and English. 'Competition for spaces is huge,' stresses Mr Charnock. 'Our main intake is Sutton and Croydon which account for 70 per cent, then 20 per cent London and the rest is from around Surrey.' Entry into sixth form – about 20 to 25 students. At least eight GCSEs required with grades A* to C and must include maths, English and a science. 'In practice, they will need A*/A in any subject they wish to study at A level. Places are offered in rank order of GCSE point score.'

Exit: Hardly any boys leave at 16, 'unless parents are relocating,' says a parent. Majority go on to university, with 12 to 15 to Oxbridge. Others head for London, Warwick, Leeds as well as other universities, to study a variety of subjects.

Money Matters: 'We are very grateful for the voluntary funding we receive from parents. They are very generous,' says Mr Charnock. 'May the money keep coming,' adds a parent. 'We are in an area where it is needed.'

Remarks: An extremely impressive, busy school, perfect for high achievers with a clear goal (especially budding mathematicians). Not for the faint hearted, the rebel or those who want to take life easy.

Wimbledon High School

Linked to Wimbledon High School Junior School in the Junior section

Mansel Road, London, SW19 4AB

• Pupils: 605 girls • Ages: 11-18 • Size of sixth form: 155 • Non-denom
• Fees: £12,063 pa • Independent

Tel: 020 8971 0900
Fax: 020 8971 0901
Email: info@wim.gdst.net
Website: www.wimbledonhigh.gdst.net

Headmistress: Since 2008, Mrs Heather Hanbury MA Edinburgh, MSc Cambridge in geography then land economy (late forties). A breath of fresh air with experience in the 'real world' prior to teaching – spent nine years working in various management consultancy roles in the City, then as a corporate fundraiser. She was always told she should teach ('and resisted it because I don't like to do the expected'), eventually had a change of heart and took a PGCE with the express ambition to become a head. 'I always wanted to run things,' says Mrs Hanbury. 'I like making organisations efficient, effective and happy.' Began her teaching career at Blackheath High School in 1996, quickly rising through the ranks to head of sixth form, before moving on to Haberdashers' Aske's School for Girls 2000–3. Was deputy head of Latymer Upper School from 2003–8. She hums with energy, is quick to smile and laugh and is intent on injecting some fun into this highly academic school. 'This is a great school but my first impression was that it needed to lighten up a bit to make sure the girls enjoy all that they do,' she says. Gets things done: persuades rather than dictates – but gets her way anyway. Has hit the ground running with three big projects already underway: a curriculum review, 'Six is the Best' – to make the sixth form the best in London – and Learning to Learn – aiming to foster courage and confidence in the classroom.

Warm and welcoming (makes her own tea for visitors) she's a bit of a dynamo, small and neat with auburn hair to match her Irish lilt. Really mucks in – she delighted the girls who had organised a pyjama day for Red Nose charity by joining them in assembly, barefoot and wearing pyjamas. Married. A keen ('but rubbish') bridge player, loves the theatre (hasn't missed an Edinburgh Festival in 20 years) and enjoys cooking ('entertaining friends and generally showing off!'). Huge hit with both pupils and parents. Parents are delighted that their daughters so happy; she has made great efforts to know them all and turns up to watch teams and performances in the evenings and at weekends. 'My daughter absolutely loves her,' said one mother. Another said that her daughter described Mrs H as 'just the perfect head teacher.' Other compliments too numerous to mention.

Academic matters: An academic place – but not pressured. Each girl encouraged to reach her own potential, whatever her personal ambition. New 'Learning to Learn' project aims to encourage risk taking in the classroom and ensure intellectual and emotional robustness. 'I can't bear to hear a girl say 'do we need this for the exam,' says Mrs Hanbury. 'I want to make sure our girls are very good learners with wide interests.' Good scope for this via a broad curriculum including Latin and Greek, design and technology and textiles. Popular options at GCSE are history, geography and French. 52 per cent A* grades, most girls get a full set of A*–B – a C grade is rare. At A2 high take-up of maths, biology and chemistry, results good across the board, again 90 per cent A*–B grades. Nice to see history of art option here. Good preparation for Oxbridge, but thankfully not a feeling that candidates are better than the rest.

Class sizes are initially large for a private school at an average 28 for Years 7–9 (except for maths which is streamed, science, art and DT), but down to 22 for GCSE classes and 15 (or often fewer) at A level. In sixth form (Years 12 and 13) pupils are in mixed tutor groups of about 14. Experienced staff have very high expectations. 'They are largely a most dedicated bunch,' said a parent – 'great mentors'. All pupils are screened for SEN on entry and learning enrichment coordinator (SEN specialist) supports those with specified needs, advises girls and parents on study methods and offers timetabled 'Learning to Learn' lessons in Year 7. Gifted children offered regular extension activities. School is active in London Challenge, bringing together the gifted and talented from neighbouring schools to participate in special projects.

Games, Options, the Arts: Lots going on both in the classroom and after hours. Doesn't attract the uber-sporty, one parent feeling strongly that expectations are not high enough in this area, but school has produced junior national representatives in skiing, three-day eventing and gymnastics. Usual compulsory sports and from Year 10 upwards girls can select additionally from further offerings including aerobics, circuit training, squash, horse-riding, badminton, basketball. Wow-factor pool and sports hall on site. Girls go off-site to playing fields, games pitches and courts a few minutes' walk away on the site of the original

All England Lawn Tennis Club. Years 9 and 10 girls do duty as ball girls during Wimbledon championships.

Drama and music strong and enhanced further with the opening of very impressive Rutherford Centre for the performing arts, which is now at the heart of all performance work. (It's named after old girl, actress Margaret Rutherford). About 80 per cent of the girls learn a musical instrument. Autumn and spring concerts are highlights – fathers and staff join as tenors and baritones, while at the informal summer soirée the girls' own compositions are showcased. Drama department stages many productions over the year, culminating in a summer musical.

Mrs Hanbury a strong believer that most pleasure in life comes from hobbies and passions – and so is keen for her girls to learn how to be passionate about something. 'They need to learn to use a hobby to help them to unwind and relax without resorting to blobbing in front of the TV. They need good habits for life,' she says. To this end girls take their pick from a pleasingly long and varied list of clubs, which as well as the usual offerings include niche interests e.g. music for shy performers, 'knit and natter', mah jong, and cryptic crosswords (solving and compiling) School's aim is for every girl to find her niche, however unusual or unlikely it may be.

Background and Atmosphere: Owned by the Girls' Day School Trust, the school celebrated its 130th birthday in 2010 – so great heritage and knows exactly what it's about. Like many London schools the site is relatively small, on the plus side its urban location has the benefit of excellent local transport links with tube, train, tram and bus terminals all within eight minutes' walk. Don't be put off by first impressions: Victorian red brick building fronts the place, surrounded by a rather grey site and unwelcoming (almost prison-like) entrance lobby – Mrs Hanbury has plans to remedy this and 'much else besides.' Inside there are some super-smart facilities, but these vie with some old-style labs, smallish classrooms, peeling radiators and a few grim corridors where a slick of gloss paint wouldn't go amiss. But more importantly the place is friendly, the girls very happy and free to play to their strengths. Sixth formers busy with 'Six is the Best' project, which includes new accommodation and furniture for their common room – working party of pupils was sent off to Ikea to choose it themselves!

Pastoral Care and Discipline: Happy, high achieving pupils in no great need of discipline, but for the five per cent or so who do require correction it is described as 'firm'. Teachers, though approachable, are strict and there is a head mistress detention every Friday. 'I am aware that parents are paying good money for a good education at this school and we do everything we can to provide it,' says Mrs Hanbury. Strong head of year system. Sixth formers very good at helping to run house system and peer counselling. From Year 7, girls have 'behaving nicely' drummed into them, zero tolerance of bullying. Problems such as eating disorders taken very seriously. 'We don't hesitate or pussy-foot around,' says Ms Hanbury. 'We are straight in once we come across anything like this to support the girl involved and all her friends who undoubtedly will have been worrying themselves.' Less serious issues, e.g. uniform niggles, nicely handled – girls have worked with staff to draw up acceptable guidelines including deciding the maximum distance above the knee for skirts!

Pupils and Parents: Exuberant live wires and timid flowers will all find a happy home here – the school is very tolerant, even encouraging, of individual types and unusual characters. Good sense of community from a diverse bunch. English middle classes, mixed with Korean and East European families joining the longer established Indian and Chinese communities. OGs include children's author Michelle Pavers, journalist Rosie Millard, investment banker turned Hollywood actor Amara Karan and Professor of Experimental Pathology, Harvard University, Lynne Reid. A chunk of parents from financial and legal worlds. Thriving parents' association.

Entrance: Selective at 11+ tests in English, maths and verbal reasoning. Typically between 350–400 applications for 50ish places, depending on exactly how many of the 48 possible arrive from juniors (only a handful don't make it). Extra form intake in Year 7 every five years e.g. 2009. Register from Easter the year before entry, interview in autumn term and exams the following January. School references and interview notes decide borderline cases. Attracts families from Wimbledon and wide surrounding area. Feeder schools include The Study, Holy Cross Prep, with other applicants coming from various state and independent schools. At 16+ girls need GCSE grade A in subjects to be studied at AS level.

Exit: About 85 per cent move up to the sixth form. Mrs Hanbury will have to work hard to keep the percentage up – some pupils may be swayed as nearby King's College School for boys (qv) opened its doors to sixth form to girls in 2010. At 18+ most to good universities of their choice including six or so to Oxbridge each year – the school is working towards increasing it to 10–15.

Money Matters: Academic and music scholarships available at 11+ and academic and science scholarships at 16+. Some bursaries are on offer.

Remarks: Terrifically purposeful place with super new head and tons going on – think Richard Scarry's Busy Town. Suits bright hardworking girls prepared to muck in and have a go. All the activity is underpinned by hefty academic foundations, so a girl who would just scrape in or who doesn't like to knuckle down may want to look elsewhere.

Winchester College

College Street, Winchester, Hampshire, SO23 9NA

- Pupils: 680 boys; 680 boarding • Ages: 13-18 • Size of sixth form: 280
- C of E • Fees: Boarding £29,970 pa • Independent

Tel: 01962 621247
Fax: 01962 621 106
Email: admissions@wincoll.ac.uk
Website: www.winchestercollege.org

Headman: Since 2005, Dr Ralph Townsend MA DPhil, an Australian with no trace of it in his voice, (mid-fifties). Dr Townsend taught briefly at Dover College and Abingdon before proceeding to Oxford where he was first a senior scholar at Keble then a junior research fellow, tutor and dean of degrees at Lincoln, teaching theology. In 1985, he became head of English at Eton, leaving in 1989 to head Sydney Grammar School. In 1989, he returned to England to become head of Oundle – thus sixteen years headmasterly experience before his arrival in Winchester. He is urbane, direct, clever, serious. He is married to Cathy, a musicologist, who is involved in everything and is warmly liked by everyone. They have two children in their twenties.

Dr Townsend's appointment followed one of the more troubled periods in the college's illustrious history. Clearly now, the school has rediscovered its energy and confidence. Dr Townsend is assured, lucid and purposeful. His commitment to the school's fundamental ethos, its unique traditions of scholarship and teaching through dialogue, is manifest and resolute. Parents are palpably relieved – 'a good egg ... .excellent ... decisive'. One of his headmagisterial colleagues told us, 'there are very few great heads but I think he will be one of them.'

Academic matters: Winchester has arguably the finest tradition of scholarship of any school in the country. An uncompromising approach to standards has resulted in, for example, the dropping of GCSEs in preference to the IGCSE and a move to the Cambridge Pre-U examination in most subjects. 'There's more stretch and content,' says Dr Townsend, 'and it's assessed by final examination not coursework.' Subjects can be taken early to allow boys to progress at their own pace. Results always outstanding and remarkable as much for the subjects chosen as the grades awarded. Around three-quarters of sixth formers study maths. Also popular are all three sciences, English and economics. Few candidates achieve lower than B (94 per cent of A level grades A/B in 2009). Stunning successes in national academic Olympiads.

In 2007, Winchester took the decision to abandon A levels (excepting ancient history, Design Technology and biology) in favour of the Cambridge Pre-U examination from 2008. The Cambridge Pre-U has no coursework and opens up sixth form study as a two-year programme with examinations at the end, much as A levels were before successive reforms of the last 25 years. The idea is to enhance Winchester's intellectual distinction yet further and it will be interesting to see whether the few schools of comparable academic standing follow their lead.

GCSE results average 98 per cent A*–B. Refreshing to see German, Russian, Italian and Spanish flourishing at this level. This is not the place for the more modern subjects and no-one would expect to find them here. What one gets instead is 'Div' – the unique and highly-prized complementary programme at the heart of the Winchester ethos. It aims to instil a knowledge and understanding of British, European and world history and culture and, as such, is a true, liberal education. 'The boys and dons love it,' says Dr Townsend, 'it's the one bit of this over-structured world in which they can pursue their own intellectual interests.' As one parent told us, 'Winchester sets out to be a centre of excellence in learning. It has unique individuals there and does not fail to bring out highly educated, intellectual boys. That's what you're paying for and it does not disappoint.'

College on message with special needs and has 160 boys on its register, mainly for dyspraxia or dyslexia but it can deal with other difficulties if the child has the requisite general intelligence and intellectual curiosity. Housemasters assess candidates as part of the pre-admission process and all are screened on entry. Reassuringly, school affirms, 'continual vigilance is necessary since coping strategies often disguise learning skills problems'. Pupils are given individual learning plans and assistance, taken out of lessons – but not sports or activities – as needed. Support is organised and efficient.

Games, Options, the Arts: Main sports are soccer, Winchester College football (read the rules) and cricket but these supplemented by everything from aikido to water polo. Fabulous playing fields and sports facilities of all kinds. Games played to high levels but, head concedes, 'while we believe we provide a good experience of sport, we have a relatively liberal discipline when it comes to those who aren't particularly interested or who have no talent'. Some parents feel he could support games more – 'it's not top of his list' – but he is now spotted at matches and races. Lively CCF – compulsory in Year 10, after which it can be replaced with Community Service. Music famously strong – around three quarters learn at least one instrument – more than 50 specialist teachers (including five for singing) and a separate music school with designated recital, concert, percussion and rock rooms. Vast range of musical ensembles and performance opportunities – weekly Tuesday concert and many more throughout the year – open to the public. Music tech now popular and modern music sits easily with the conventional – Mozart and James MacMillan. Chapel central to this as to other aspects of college life. Very lively drama and art and standards commensurate with everything else.

Background and Atmosphere: A little bit of Oxford fell to earth one day, It landed in Winchester – not so very far away. That's what it looks like and feels like. Founded in the fourteenth century by William of Wykeham, Bishop of Winchester and Chancellor to Richard II, it began in 1387 with a Warden, ten fellows, two schoolmasters three chaplains, seventy scholars and sixteen quiristers – the Winchester version of choristers. The Bishop also founded New College, Oxford, with which the college maintains strong links. The quiristers have since moved down the road to the Pilgrims' School (qv) but continue to sing in Chapel. So this is a quiet land of flinty walls, leafy quads, a venerable Chapel, many other buildings of ancient date and visible history. Later foundations, e.g. Eton College, seem like modern upstarts by comparison. Not that the college hasn't kept building and acquiring. There are ten boarding houses in adjacent streets, and buildings for all major disciplines. And space.

The atmosphere is donnish – the masters are called dons here and the college has a language of its own (called Notions) for almost every aspect of daily life. Booklet devoted to this makes fascinating reading. The downside is a tendency to inwardness and separation from educational and social advances on the outside. Dr Townsend admits that, in the fifteen years or so before his advent, this sense of removal from the big, bad world had become somewhat entrenched. A real effort to improve the boarding arrangements, which had decidedly not kept pace with progress elsewhere, is now in evidence. So too with the food, which used to be described as 'diabolical'. 'The cooks don't know an aubergine from a courgette,' a parent told us and 'no-one's heard of nutrition'. Boys have accounts at the local M & S and Chinese. Again, Dr Townsend is onto this and change is in the air – and on the plates.

Housemasters much praised individually but the system is bizarre by outside standards. They have immensely more autonomy here than elsewhere, though rules and restrictions now differ less widely house to house than they used to. Some parents like the variations and see this as resulting in each case being dealt with on its merits while others grouse about it – rather more than boys who seem to accept it, much as they would that some parents are more liberal than others. Of the many parents we spoke to, no-one said anything less enthusiastic than, 'my son loves it'. Staff morale, sadly damaged by latter-day difficulties, now felt to be high again and the all-important housemasters are clearly more comfortable with the new regime.

The upside of the Winchester, male-dominated, scholarly world is a wonderful freedom of expression. We had lunch with the head, Mrs Townsend and a bunch of boys and everyone shared views on all aspects of school life with complete frankness and a sense of equality. 'He listens to us more than to the dons,' we were told by one boy, 'almost too much really,' and democracy and mutual respect built in to the college community. What there isn't, as parents and boys attest, is any sense of elitism, snobbery or social cachet. Boys are proud of their school and touchingly conscious of how privileged they are to be there. They would, however, appreciate more 'socials' – both between houses and with, particularly, girls. College consulted widely about going co-ed in Dr Townsend's first year and decided against.

Pastoral Care and Discipline: Of bullying, the head says, 'we have a real handle on it' and he got a grip in his first year, expelling three. On drugs, 'zero tolerance – they live in a world in which drugs are normal – in a boarding school you cannot do it because it endangers other people's children'. On alcohol, you get one major warning if you're caught, 'and it works'. Boys have more freedom to organise their own time in and out of school than in most schools – some even meeting local girlfriends in spare time. Housemasters run most aspects of a boy's life – pastoral and academic – but major matters end up with the head.

Pupils and Parents: From a vast range of preps covering the UK but mostly from the southern half. Overseas pupils principally from Hong Kong, Japan and India but also Europe (increasingly the eastern bit), USA and Africa. Very few day boys – always local and for exceptional reasons. This is not a day school and no-one leaves before 9pm. Families who come here know what they are coming for and specifically opt for this style of unashamed intellectual life because it suits their individual boys. Not a school for social climbers. There is a general feeling – acknowledged as just by the head – that school is not sufficiently parent-friendly. Says Dr Townsend, 'I rather agree. It's a totally boy-oriented world. The dons will do anything for the boys but it rarely occurs to them that parents have an opinion on anything.' This may well change – slowly.

Entrance: Register your son from the age of eight. Admissions for 'Commoners' are via the housemasters who see twenty-five to thirty sets of parents when the boys are 10–11, test them, get reports from existing schools and offer places to around half. It helps to have an idea of which houses you are interested in – ask around – it matters. Head then invites all those offered places a year in advance of entry to meet him. College sets own entrance exam in all usual CE subjects. Scholars and Exhibitioners selected by exam which includes 'logical reasoning'. Scholars live in 'College' – a separate house pulsating with hyperactive brain cells. Entrance also possible for the sixth via exam and minimum of six GCSE A grades.

Exit: In 2009, 33 to Oxford and 18 to Cambridge, and it wasn't an especially glittery year. The rest to a predictable spread of the best redbricks. They distinguish themselves in all areas but, perhaps, more in the humanities, politics and social reform side than in sciences and there are surprisingly few of the biggest names in British letters or history in the list of Old Wykehamists. However, famous OWs include Sir Thomas Browne, Sydney Smith, Thomas Arnold, Anthony Trollope, Lord Alfred Douglas, Richard D'Oyly Carte, Hugh Dowding, Stafford Cripps, A P Herbert, Oswald Mosley, Douglas Jardine, Hugh Gaitskell, Richard Crossman, Kenneth Clark, Mansoor Ali Khan Pataudi, Geoffrey Howe, Tim Brooke-Taylor, Hugh Dancy.

Money Matters: In 2008, Winchester announced that its scholarships will be reduced from 25 per cent to 15 per cent of the fee in 2009 and to five per cent in 2010. Parents of boys who win scholarships who need more financial assistance can apply for a bursary. From 2011, all scholarships, academic and music, will be means tested from zero, with bursaries awarded up to 100 per cent of the fee where necessary.

Remarks: Uniquely civilised. Academically, comradely and architecturally privileged boyhood most Wykehamists treasure throughout their lives.

Windermere School

Linked to Windermere Preparatory School in the Junior section

Browhead, Patterdale Road, Windermere, Cumbria, LA23 1NW

• Pupils: 260, even mix boys and girls, day and boarders with 30 % international • Ages: 11-18 • C of E, all faiths recognised
• Fees: Boarding £19,482-£26,130; Day £11,598-£13,086 pa • Independent

Tel: 01539 446 164
Fax: 01539 488 414
Email: ws@windermereschool.co.uk
Website: www.windermereschool.co.uk

Headmaster: Since 2009, Mr Lavender, previously senior housemaster at Gordonstoun and therefore experience in the Round Square ethos embraced by the school. After a chemistry degree from Oxford he spent time in management consultancy and served in the TA before starting teaching. At Gordonstoun his interests included membership of the mountain rescue service, cross-country, and running the Rwanda International Service Project – a particularly challenging responsibility, being the first school group to work in Rwanda since the genocide of 1994. Since his appointment he has assigned a personal tutor to each student so that work is overseen daily, and students benefit from individual tuition. He has also embarked on a campaign to prepare the school for its 150th Anniversary in 2013. His wife, Jacqui, is a GP and they have three school age children.

Academic matters: Hard-working pupils, taught in small classes (15–20 up to GCSE). Intake is broad, so results don't compare with selective schools, often middling, though in a good year there have been plenty of top grades and few Ds and Es at A level. Now an IB World School offering the IB Diploma for sixth form, reinforcing the school's international dimensions. The introduction of the IB brought a sea change – a focus on academic rigour and a new energy in the commonroom with staff encouraged and rejuvenated by up to date training and an increase in pupil numbers. Conscious of their broad intake, they are piloting an IB Career Certificate (IBCC) which, in addition to academic teaching, adds one day a week on the water or in the mountains, leading to formal qualifications, to cater for the more practical minded student and to allow access for all to the IB.

All the usual subjects offered, plus occasional exotic languages (up to 25 nationalities in school at any time); around 20 per cent overseas students, mainly European with a scattering from the Far East. Efficient learning support on hand; integration into classes favoured. Exchange programmes encourage students to spend time overseas broadening horizons. Good mix of male and female staff, average age 42.

Games, Options, the Arts: Extensive use made of beautiful surroundings – school has its own jetty and boats on Windermere, competes at a high level in sailing. Also D of E, expeditions, 'Swallows and Amazons weekends', outdoor pursuits of every type. Hockey and tennis the main sports for both boys and girls and played all year round on all-weather surface; some rugby also for boys and netball for girls. Athletics popular. Currently 29 county sports champions in school, smaller number competing at national level. Impressive dance studio and excellent facilities for music produce high standards. Vigorous drama, too, backed by theatre visits. Art impressive throughout school, DT also popular. Service project expeditions take pupils to South Africa, Borneo and Iceland.

Background and Atmosphere: Founded in 1863 as St Anne's High for girls, moved to Windermere site from Lytham in 1924. Called Windermere St Anne's thereafter and co-ed since 1999 and has achieved a well-balanced boy/girl mix – no former girls' school feel about the place. In 2010, school decided to drop the 'St Anne's' moniker – a popular move, especially with the boys. Much building in 1970s and 1980s (sports hall, science block, performing arts centre, sixth form house). Buildings are spread out around original Victorian house on steep wooded site, with newly refurbished girls' dorms and common rooms. Lots of movement between buildings in all weathers; pupils here need a degree of resilience but insist that it's 'not a problem' – tough cookies without being hard-faced – an attractive combination. Stunning views all around, this is a school that encourages one to look outwards, in every respect.

Boys and girls, seniors and juniors, live in remarkable harmony, making a reality of the 'family atmosphere' cliché. Sixth formers live in single-sex flats with joint common areas and their own bistro/coffee bar. Boarding provision is good, with real effort in supporting the younger students – boarding staff happy to 'play mum' – and allowing independence in the older ones – who do their own washing and ironing. Everyone seems keen to make things work smoothly and humanely. Teachers expected to devote a lot of their time to running activities, which is certainly appreciated by the young. Great play made of the Round Square movement, founded by Kurt Hahn of Gordonstoun, dedicated to service and internationalism; students understand and value the ideals of this philosophy and it runs deep through everyday school life, from moments of reflection to start the day, to international flags hanging in the dining room.

Pastoral Care and Discipline: Pupils do need a fairly high level of self-discipline since the site is almost impossible to police effectively. However the culture is such that it appears to work surprisingly well; staff keep their eyes and ears close to the ground and it is 'understood' that pupils will behave responsibly and the consequences are made very clear should they fail to do so. The school's ethos precludes a heavy-handed approach but the light touch appears effective and ensures that, whilst encouraging independence, pupils are made aware of their personal accountability.

Pupils and Parents: Forty per cent of pupils are from the immediate local area. Weekly and full boarders from the locality, also West Cumbria, Yorkshire, Scotland, Manchester conurbation and 30 per cent from abroad – perhaps more evidence of a parental desire for low-temptation and wholesome surroundings. Many parents of day pupils in hotel and tourism business. You're struck by the pupils' unaffected but courteous directness – not unusual in the north – and they are, perhaps, a touch innocent compared with the Thames Valley, but a good thing nevertheless. Parents are appreciative and supportive and express genuine regret that the school's strengths are not measured or recognised in league tables.

Entrance: Most pupils come directly from the school's own prep, others from local primaries and preps further afield. Entrance exam not too taxing – school does not aim to be selective, prides itself on being a broad church, though all applicants vetted by head, who likes to get a feel 'not only for their academic abilities but also their enthusiasm, passion and interests.' Two streams at 11 usually growing to three at 13. Five GCSEs A*–C (or equivalent) for entry to sixth form.

Exit: A few leave after GCSE but outnumbered by incomers. Post sixth form most go on to a range of higher education institutions home and abroad – the majority to their first choice, a few gap years and Services.

Money Matters: Scholarships available in the academic, performing arts, visual arts and sport categories and are not means-tested. Means-tested bursaries available.

Remarks: A genuine phoenix, thriving on the opportunity to reinvent itself and has done so a number of times now, surprising all by its ability to bounce back. It offers something different in what is often a 'one size fits all market' – strong on service, challenge, adventure and internationalism, and now daring to be different by widening its appeal with the IB. Not for the urban sophisticate but perhaps attractive to the city dweller looking for a rural education in a school with a good soul.

The Windsor Boys' School

1 Maidenhead Road, Windsor, Berkshire, SL4 5EH

• Pupils: 1015 boys • Ages: 13-18 • Size of sixth form: 325 • Non-denom • State

Tel: 01753 716 060
Fax: 01753 833 186
Email: windsorboys@rbwm.org
Website: www.wbsweb.org.uk

Headmaster: Since 2010, Mr Julian Clauson (fiftyish). An unusual career – in his 20s he travelled to Tibet, Zambia, Nepal and Zimbabwe reporting back to Amnesty on the problems facing children there and didn't go into teaching until he was nearly 30. 'The first time I went into a classroom to see a teacher at work in quite a challenging school, I thought "this is it. This is what I want to do."' Later he worked for London Challenge which was set up to help failing schools. Life at Windsor Boys should seem like a chug down the Thames by comparison. Mr Clauson hopes to forge closer links with Windsor Girls' School, which makes up the other half of the town's comprehensive education provision.

Academic matters: In 2002, 60 per cent of pupils gained five or more grades A*–C at GCSE. This was before the school became a Specialist School in the Arts. This has risen to, in 2010, 93 per cent (68 per cent including English and maths). Similarly, at A level, 72 per cent of all grades were at A*–C – not bad for a full comprehensive in an area where the many well-regarded local grammars – to say nothing of one or two well-known independent boys' schools nearby – cream off the very best. Over 100 students gained their first choice place at university. School now in the top 10 centile of all schools and colleges in the country. This is now the school of choice for many and not just on account of its famous sporting prowess.

A level subjects are a trad mix plus psychology, sports studies, theatre studies, DT. New computer-controlled, digital language centre with satellite/video links – this is high-level stuff – allows individual and distance learning but French is the only modern language to survive to A level here and few takers. ICT now better-resourced than hitherto and used intelligibly and appropriately. GCSE subjects include PE, electronics and graphics. Applied and vocational courses in IT taken in Year 12 and advanced in Year 13 with impressive results. When asked about performing arts college status, last head said it enables them to 'use performance, music and dance to stimulate achievement across whole school.' SENCo and team of twenty, either on site or at local 'Achievement centre', where first-rate, creative work in learning support takes place. School being adapted for the less physically able. In general, Ofsted reports ('Outstanding', 2008) well above average results in comparison with similar schools. Parents report good teaching across the curriculum. This is a school where, if you work, you can reach the heights, but there are opportunities for everyone.

Now offering the IB alongside A levels.

Games, Options, the Arts: Famous for sport, above all, rowing. School has a boat house on the nearby Thames and, by 2003, its under 18s had won the coveted Fawley Cup at Henley five times in the previous nine years. Pictures of boats and crews everywhere and a stack of upturned boats in the car park. Similarly impressive rugby teams tour internationally – Australia and Canada in 2008. Financial help for those who need it. Athletics and cricket also strong and everything else you'd expect played hard here too. As well as rowing. School has 1994 sports pavilion, extensive on-site fields including a large Astroturf pitch. Plays cricket against the MCC! School has a Sportsmark and previous head felt that sport is, overall, school's strongest suit. Especially rowing.

When not rowing, boys remember that theirs is a specialist arts college and gained an Artsmark gold award for the fourth time in 2008. Drama is famously good and ambitious. Lord of the Flies and Berkoff's Agamemnon among recent productions – some with girls from Windsor Girls' School. Excellent drama studio. New performing arts, exhibition hall and sixth form block in 2004. Imaginative cross-curricular work e.g. a languages and drama collaboration praised by Ofsted 2003. Music is formidable – every kind of instrumental tuition and bands including a full orchestra, jazz band, close harmony singers and a 'junk band' – instruments made out of old plastic bottles etc. Their very successful band (famous for playing at the marriage of Prince Charles to Camilla Parker-Bowles) enjoyed a first in playing at the International Network of school leaders in Beijing, September 2007. The boys were the first UNESCO students visiting Beijing, staying at Chinese homes, visiting a series of schools. WBS has a very good music technology resource including a good recording studio. Annual themed arts week each summer provides opportunities for experimentation of all kinds and visits from celebrity writers and musicians. Art is imaginative and varied, and boys actually learn to draw here. Lovely, lively and thoughtful work here and around the school – critical Ofsted report of 2003 clearly bonkers and re-judged as Outstanding in 2008. New completely refurbished and re-equipped art rooms with state-of-the-art ICT facilities were added in 2005. School has excellent 'artists in residence' scheme and benefits from charismatic and inspiring on-site sculptor in addition to dedicated regular staff. Lots of local, national and international trips – sporting, artistic, linguistic, cultural. Lots of extra-curricular options – Young Enterprise, public speaking, debating, clubs for riding, philosophy, chess etc – and then there's always rowing.

Background and Atmosphere: Main, almost handsome, redbrick building dates from school's foundation as a boys' grammar in 1908. Later blocks of various vintages and degrees of attractiveness at rear make for a somewhat cluttered and amorphous site but no building more than two storeys so a human-scale, unthreatening, almost domestic ambiance overall. Subjects taught in all redbrick faculty blocks. School became a comprehensive in 1977. Chronic lack of investment makes for a general interior shabbiness – oh for some floors without chewing gum blots! – and exterior neglect but no more here than in comparable schools elsewhere and made up for by ubiquitous worthwhile displays of work and evidence of achievement.

Inescapable distant roar of the motorway at the end of the road punctuated by traffic in and out of Heathrow a couple of miles away; nonetheless, the school feels peaceful and purposeful. Surrounded by genteel if not affluent Victorian sprawl on the way to Maidenhead, it's easy to ignore the vast regal edifice down the road if you choose to do so. Litter is a feature here but school is used by the local community until late most nights and all weekend so it's a lost battle though gamely joined by previous head. House system important in all school activities. About a third of teachers are women.

Pastoral Care and Discipline: Previous head believed in permanent exclusion for anyone who brought drugs into school in most circumstances – not the fashionable view perhaps but the conviction of a clearly humane man. 'Traditional' is a word he used, and mostly as a term of approbation. Assemblies 'with me in my gown' used to celebrate school successes but 'if you talk during assembly in our hall you're in detention for an hour.' Would sound familiar to – and go down well with – many parents. Atmosphere is relaxed and civilised – boys look you in the face and smile at their teachers.

Pupils and Parents: Boys come from all over Windsor, Slough and surrounds. Intake is strictly according to catchment area so applying from further afield is a waste of time. Socio-economic backgrounds greatly varied as demographics would suggest. Despite several good local grammars, this is increasingly the school of choice for the less-than-loaded parents of the less-than-brilliant prep school leavers – and there are a lot of prep schools in Berkshire. About a fifth of boys from a variety of minority ethnic heritages, predominantly Indian and Pakistani. Very few need substantial EAL help. Pupils mostly from four local middle schools and various preps.

Entrance: Via local authority registration and application. See note above about catchment areas. This school is now seriously over-subscribed. Since 2006, 10 per cent of students selected by aptitude in the performing arts.

Exit: After GCSEs school loses 10 per cent to other educational establishments and 15 per cent to employment or training. The rest stay on for sixth form studies. A further 10 per cent of those will leave for employment after one year in the sixth. Of those who complete the sixth, around 90 per cent go on to higher or further education – Oxbridge (three in 2009) to vocational courses of all kinds. A good record.

Remarks: 'Success' is a word you read a lot as you go round the school. 'Achievement' is a word the previous head used frequently and there is, throughout, a sense of realistic aspiration. Parents put a lot into this school – it has a true sense of community and a pride in being what it is – not glitzy, not flash nor trendy. Quietly, carefully and with dedication the last head 'built on our traditional strength with an eye to the future' and achieved impressively across the board. And on the river. Mr Clauson takes over a school in good heart if not in great nick.

Withington Girls' School

Linked to Withington Girls Junior School in the Junior section

Wellington Road, Fallowfield, Manchester, Greater Manchester, M14 6BL

• Pupils: 650 girls, all day • Ages: 7-18 • Size of sixth form: 170
• Non-denom • Fees: Seniors £9,300; Juniors £6,930 pa • Independent

Tel: 0161 224 1077
Fax: 0161 248 5377
Email: adsheada@withington.manchester.sch.uk
Website: www.withington.manchester.sch.uk

Headmistress: Since 2010, Mrs Sue Marks MA (early fifties). Moved from a nine year headship of Tormead School, Guildford (qv) where she also taught economics. Read PPE at Jesus, Oxford, bagging blues for rowing and athletics. Before teaching she had a career in the City. She is treasurer of the Girls' Schools Association. No stranger to Manchester, her teenage years were spent in Wilmslow; she still has family nearby and of her move says 'it's bringing me home'. A mother of four, although her eldest daughter died suddenly in 2002 aged just 17. Her second daughter now teaches at Downe House School (qv) 'which gives me great pleasure and makes me enormously proud'; her younger two are at university and school. 'It's an extraordinary privilege to be given the chance to lead Withington, one of the very few schools in the country I'd have left Tormead for,' she says. A great believer in knowing every girl, probably through teaching from Year 7, time permitting, and in 'educating the whole girl and not just the bit that sits exams and gets certificates.'

Academic matters: Off the scale with almost all GCSEs awarded an A or A*, 97 per cent in 2010, and at A level 36 per cent A*, 84 per cent A*s or A grades, 97 per cent A* to B grades. It goes without saying that they're strong across the curriculum here and know how to advise girls to tackle exams but a Withington education is so much more than that. At the entrance to the new sixth form centre an LCD notice board incorporates a BBC news feed. During our visit a sixth form girl exclaimed at the breaking news of Obama receiving the Nobel Peace Prize. The head of sixth came out of her office, girls gathered round including several who uncurled themselves from the new cerise and burgundy sofas, and a discussion ensued about the merits and implications of this news. Beyond 'academic matters' for sure, but that's what it's like here. 'The teaching's fabulous, our daughter's completely engaged' parents tell us, 'it is a steep curve from a state primary but it's not the hothouse we expected.' *Sunday Times* Independent Secondary School of the Year 2009.

Classes aren't dramatically small, up to 28, although much less for many A level courses which will run for just a single keen student if need be. Very strong science, as stipulated by the founders, producing lots of medics and scientists. Links with university and lots of national academic Olympiad achievers, although there are no internal school prizes in line with the founders' diktat of 'the pleasure of learning being its own reward'. Very strong foreign languages, very strong everything really. One teacher told us 'girls do work hard here, they get a lot of homework and the pace is very fast yet I still see them running around singing, and enjoying sport, music, drama and looking beautiful in the fashion show.' Drama recently introduced at GCSE as well as A level.

Games, Options, the Arts: Something for everyone and a can-do attitude to help girls with lots of interests fit everything in. Astroturf pitch for hockey, grass for lacrosse, county and country players in both and county in netball. Strong lacrosse tradition, reaching national finals, also tennis. Community service in local nurseries, schools and residential homes for the elderly. Charity fundraising, links with schools and a hospital in Kenya, Uganda and The Gambia. Recent trips to Uganda, Berlin, Mongolia, France and Wales. Over seventy D of E bronze each year and increasing numbers of silver and gold. Young Enterprise, Ogden Trust business game, public speaking competitions, strong Model United Nations and Mock Trials. Drama Studio and hexagonal hall/theatre in the round for assemblies, concerts and drama, including some joint productions with Manchester Grammar (qv) boys who also join girls for a combined Philsoc. Three orchestras, wind band, jazz group, several choirs. DCFS-sponsored art and music partnerships with local state schools. Contemporary art collection initiated in 2006. Lots of other extra-curricular clubs including cheer leading and mosaic club. Girls look stunning in annual fashion show and are joined by boys from MGS, 'but,' they giggle, 'they're not usually very good'.

Background and Atmosphere: Unprepossessing but neat and tidy site in suburban Withington south of Manchester with Tardis-like add-ons at the rear and compact playing fields, courts and an all-weather pitch behind these. Building projects in 2002, after a major fire in 2003, in 2005 and in 2009 mean most subjects now enjoy suites of classrooms round a departmental office. Carpets and blinds, Velux windows and open ceilings in the refectory, and in the sixth form centre huge windows, new sofas and lockers with cornices give the place a classy, comfortable but executive feel. Four houses carry the names of the founders who, back in the late 1800s, wanted the same educational opportunities for their daughters as for their sons. 120th anniversary celebrations in 2010. Girls seem naturally and spontaneously helpful to visitors and the mixed ages, from 7–18, mean it's a gentle place. Staff conversation buzzes over lunch with varied choices in their own dining room.

Pastoral Care and Discipline: The air is thin at these giddy academic heights so a main pastoral care issue here is helping those with a predicted B grade retain a 'global perspective and not lose their self-esteem ... to remember that low in the top five per cent is still high in the other ninety-five per cent.' Girls speak of 'phenomenal help from teachers in school' including a SENCo who's 'really great' and even help over the summer, and whilst laziness is frowned on, both groups are adamant no-one's edged out for under-performance. One recent parent told us he felt the focus is on the brightest girls but when asked how his daughter fared in the end had sheepishly to admit, 'ah, she did rather well actually'. Otherwise the care structure is strong and includes an approachable full-time nurse in a super new sick bay. The last ISI inspection said 'the pastoral care of pupils is excellent across the school. Relationships between staff and pupils and amongst pupils is very warm and mutually respectful.' Older girls mentor younger girls and it's a small school with zero tolerance for bullying. Everybody knows everybody so the 'respecting other people and respecting self' guideline seems to be pretty much enough. Apart from no midriff on display and no shorts allowed, sixth form dress is 'up to us to act on our own responsibility, to bridge the gap between school uniform and uni.' Lower years are getting used to a blazer and a skirt designed so it can't be rolled over at the top.

Pupils and Parents: You have only to look at the governors' page of the school website to see that the good and the great both use and support this school but pupils aren't all super wealthy by any means. Battered old family estate cars arrive alongside glitzy 4x4s and one in five pupils receives some sort of means tested bursary. It's a diverse community from varied ethnic and faith backgrounds with opportunities for all groups to meet alone and together in assemblies, societies and with visiting speakers. 'The Christian Society comes and goes, it's pupil led, but we do stand for mutual tolerance and understanding,' says head. Girls come from all points of the compass and often travel long distances on buses or with parents, some of whom therefore become long distance taxi drivers at weekends. Pupils describe a Withington girl as 'ambitious, determined, articulate, caring, well-mannered and intent upon an excellent career' and Withington as 'the Rolls Royce of schools'. Notable Old Girls include TV's Judith Chalmers OBE, opera star Christine Rice and pianist Katherine Stott.

Entrance: Head personally greets everyone arriving at and departing from January exams, two maths, two English, with drink and biscuit break. The standard is high, way beyond NFER 11+ tests, so a bit of extra prep is a good idea using sample papers available from school. Two apply for each place and roughly a third of places will be filled by school's own juniors (who also have to sit exam), a third come from independent preps and a third from state primaries. Selection also depends on previous school report and a 15 minute interview, including a few minutes with parents. A 'spark' and potential are key and the amount of primary hothousing, or lack of it, is taken into consideration. Sixth form entry needs six A* or As at GCSE with A*s in chosen A level subjects and considers report from previous school and interview.

Exit: A few leave for sixth form elsewhere to join boys or for an end to fees, but there's always an influx too. All sixth form leave for university, mostly to top institutions on top courses. Some dozen to Oxbridge, ditto medicine. Head gives final individual supervisions before UCAS applications are sent and MGS and Withington swap teachers to make mock uni interviews more realistic. Gappers can apply for a £100 travel award on leaving.

Money Matters: Cheap at the price for such excellence; you could pay a lot more for a lot less elsewhere. Almost a hundred girls on means tested bursary support. No scholarships. Termly £6 charge for insurance. Lunches £156 per term.

Remarks: Excellence on all fronts with very intelligent girls being very intelligently taught. Some might say it's a privileged and academic bubble – it's certainly a place where love of learning and avid interest in all things are inculcated and nurtured; and who'd prefer the 'real world' to that for their daughters' girlhoods? Change of head will be interesting.

Woldingham School

Marden Park, Woldingham, Surrey, CR3 7YA

• Pupils: 530 girls; 300 board, 235 day • Ages: 11-18 • Size of sixth form: 145 • Roman Catholic, but girls of all faiths welcome • Fees: Boarding £26,805; Day £16,617 pa • Independent

Tel: 01883 349 431
Fax: 01883 348 653
Email: registrar@woldingham.surrey.sch.uk
Website: www.woldinghamschool.co.uk

Headmistress: Since 2007, Mrs Jayne Triffitt, MA PGCE (early fifties). Educated at Truro High School, read chemistry at St Hilda's College, Oxford. A committed Catholic, (both she and her husband converted), most of her career has been spent in Catholic schools, 17 years in the state sector (La Sainte Union, Highgate, St Michael's Grammar School, North Finchley) before becoming head of the sixth at St Mary's, Ascot and then head of St Mary's, Cambridge.

A direct, pragmatic, highly principled and serious soul, she can initially seem rather reserved but soon warms up. Even so, there is no spin and gloss to Mrs Triffitt. Following the glamorous and charismatic Diana Vernon, Mrs Triffitt brings something completely different to the place. Her brief included tightening up the academics and bringing more structure and discipline to the timetable. This involved changing the structure of the day, raising expectations and introducing setting and banding into most subjects in Years 7, 8 and 9 as well as setting tight boundaries – met with exasperation from some girls! Like all good boundary markers, however, she also knows when to relax them. Her maternal commonsense won her the accolade of being the coolest headmistress, when she was witnessed giving two senior girls money for a cab back to school, rather than forcing them to leave a party early with her. Her motive for making any decision is a practical and principled conviction of what is the right thing to do. She does have a sensitive awareness of the feelings of the girls, but 'I am not a panderer,' she says.

Some parents wonder whether she will see the big picture and bring enough flair and vision to the school. Thus far she has focused keenly on the detail. 'I had a lot to contend with in my first year, with an inspection in my first term,' she says, 'it's now that the school really starts to feel my own.' She would like more parents to feel that they can just drop in to see her.

After more than three years her family has also become part and parcel of the place – her husband teaches history part-time, her daughter is a pupil and her dog is a high profile character around the school. She would like more parents to feel that they can just drop in to see her.

Academic matters: Impressive, given relatively broad intake. A parent sums up the academic ethos, 'there is a clear understanding at the school that these girls will have to earn a living.' Setting in many subjects – from as early as 11. Average number of GCSEs is at least nine, with 98+ per cent of grades C or higher – 70 per cent get A* or A. RS compulsory for GCSE, as are maths, English lang and lit. Geography popular and most take double award science. Nice to see for a change that girls can do Japanese at GCSE. Currently in the top ten per cent in the country for value-added performance at A level, where over 85 per cent of all grades are at A*/A or B with over 27 girls achieving three A*/As or more – maths, business studies and art the most popular. Courses available at AS and A2 include politics, textiles, Japanese, design, music technology and psychology.

Handful of girls per year identified as having mild specific learning difficulties (dyslexia, dyspraxia, Asperger's) needing one-to-one attention. Full-time SENCo appointed by Mrs Triffitt. Extra support made available to everyone, not just those on the SEN register. One or two pupils with statements. Perception has always been that the school suits a wide range of ability from very bright downwards, but will this continue? As part of the drive for academic tightening, Mrs Triffitt is implementing a number of changes including careful monitoring of special needs at entry to ensure the school can accommodate a girl's requirements. Although it would be very unusual to refuse to accept a sibling, 'we would do so if we couldn't offer the support they needed.' Gifted and talented provision includes an Oxbridge programme led by the head and a team of three other members of staff. 'Oxbridge has not been a major focus – I want to change that.'

Games, Options, the Arts: Almost every parent we spoke to enthused about the attention given to renovation, innovation and refurbishment. Facilities 'truly excellent' ('for a girls' school') seems to be the general consensus and one of the reasons they chose Woldingham for their daughter. Sport, drama and music are rolled out in first class accommodation. Terrific grounds hold everything you would expect including a floodlit all-weather pitch. All major games played. Compulsory sport for all. One girl commented on the wide choice of sports available, 'you aren't forced to play netball if you can't stand it.' A tired acceptance among some parents (we hear this at virtually every school we visit) that their enthusiastic daughter never gets picked for matches – but 'that's just life'. Polo offered and body combat as well as dance club run by professional dancers. Three golf courses available nearby and riding at local stables, either with or without your own horse. Smaller animals can be accommodated at Hamster Hall and Guinea Pig Gallery.

Saturday morning weekend programme (Saturday Active) – run by professionals to a very high standard – includes claypigeon shooting, yoga and fencing. Drama happens in a splendid 600 seat auditorium, with a hydraulically raised orchestra pit no less, which would grace most towns, and studio theatre with computer-controlled sound and lighting system. Also dressing rooms and a costume workshop of a professional quality. Frequent theatre visits. Not surprisingly, A level theatre studies results have been good over recent years, with typically over 92 per cent of candidates gaining A or B grades. Music teaching accommodation very high standard and senior choir go on frequent concert tours including performing Mass at St Peter's in Rome. Annual musical hugely popular with girls and performed to an (almost) professional standard. Fifty per cent of the girls learn at least one musical instrument, but few take the subject for GCSE or A level. Art strong, with art and history of art popular at A level – sixth form have their own desks in the art building, which also has a sculpture room, kiln and darkroom. Excellent careers programme mentioned by everyone – parents, girls and inspectors alike. Girls very well prepared and clued up about the opportunities available to them. Regular careers/university admissions sessions both for girls and parents. Girls can consult the careers officer at any time and regularly do.

Background and Atmosphere: Idyllic rural setting in 700 acres in Area of Outstanding Natural Beauty, much of it let as agricultural land. As you approach the school after travelling up the long drive (10 minutes by car) it feels as if you have arrived on a BBC drama set. Mellow chateau-style house with wide sweeping balustraded steps to the front door. A statue of Christ stands on the perfectly manicured lawn opposite. Yet it is so close to London. Woldingham railway station is within the grounds and a free minibus shuttles girls to and fro – central London 35 minutes and East Croydon 15 minutes by train. The school has organised a bus from Keston, Hayes, Redhill, Nutfield and another from Sevenoaks and the Purley area.

Formerly a Convent of the Sacred Heart (has links with other Sacred Heart schools throughout the world and does a week's exchange if desired with some European ones). Overall impression is one of space, with some truly impressive modern building on site. Recently renovated chapel, suffused with the calming smell of incense and tranquil light from stunning stained glass windows. As well as compulsory Sunday Mass, girls attend prayers here one night a week in their dressing gowns.

The head is looking to increase the number of boarders. Boarding is structured according to year groups. Own room from Year 10 onwards. Girls delighted with separate new upper sixth form block, Shanley, or 'the Hilton'. Not only does it have university-style study bedrooms with ensuite bathrooms, but also a lift to get to the second floor. CCTV surveys the site and most buildings have linked TV screens displaying the day's activities, menus etc. Head of year is the equivalent of a housemistress and the first point of contact for parents. Some parents complain that they don't get the opportunity to build a long term relationship with one individual as they would do in a boarding house that operated on a vertical rather than horizontal system.

Saturday morning attendance compulsory for boarders (until the sixth form when things get more flexible) but they can then go home for weekends. Day girls can stay overnight, arrive early or stay late (a Godsend for working parents who also want the occasional night away together), they can also come in on Saturday mornings and some Saturday attendance is compulsory for them. Annual Day of Reflection compulsory (on a Sunday), when the girls go into retreat and contemplate issues such as 'friendship' or 'image'. Typical weekend activities for the boarders as well as the usual visits to art galleries and museums are the (very popular) shopping excursions to London or Bluewater, Millennium Wheel, ice-skating, paintballing with Worth School and group treasure hunts around London with Worth. Socials at weekends with boys' schools for Years 7–11.

The pupils seem a grounded bunch, their friendships relaxed and uncompetitive. Strangely, no pressure from sixth form to wear own clothes (can wear their own dark suits instead of uniform with pastel shirts) – apparently the absence of boys and any nearby town means that girls feel under no pressure to be mega-cool. Both RC and Anglican parents appear to feel comfortable with the religious ethos of the school – one Anglican mother said, 'we are not in any way made to feel second-class citizens.' Alternating C of E and RC confirmation years. Parents consistently praise the very happy atmosphere.

Pastoral Care and Discipline: Parent after parent comment that the pastoral care is the best aspect of the school – a feature highlighted by the latest inspection. Staff generally regarded to be 'a tremendous bunch of dedicated and caring professionals'. The same form tutor generally stays with the girls the whole way through from Year 7 to Year 11 and girls can in addition choose their own personal tutor. 'Buddy' scheme run by lower sixth girls to counsel Years 7 and 8. Sixth formers can become Ribbons (prefects). Those who make it proudly wear their broad blue band across their black suits. They have special responsibility for the wellbeing of others and for promoting the spirit of the school – election is initially by democratic process. Parents praise the way the school introduces the girls to levels of responsibility, with lots of opportunities for leadership. The sixth form are given a good dose of independence during the week to counteract the effect of being cloistered in a valley, as well as leaving for the weekend on a Friday night (an upper sixth privilege), back on Monday morning. A coffee bar, complete with comfy leather sofas and coffee machine, in one of the smart rooms in the main building, where the sixth form can mingle with staff, adds to a sense of privilege. Some girls remarked that the removal of their freedoms was a valuable disciplinary weapon – a sign of how much they value them. No make-up or nail varnish allowed, use of mobile phones permitted (if you're lucky enough to get a signal) but not during the school day.

Pupils and Parents: Over 35 per cent of pupils are RC, a higher percentage are Church of England, also several other non Christian religions, including Muslim, Hindu and Buddhist. 60 per cent board (of these about 18 per cent live overseas, the other 45 per cent are from London or the Home Counties). When we visited, the head was about to go to Hong Kong on a marketing tour (school prefers we call it by its official title 'top schools UK' organised by Academic Asia). Keen to recruit able international students. Parents from professional backgrounds – bankers, company directors, Foreign and Commonwealth Office, lawyers, accountants. A number are undoubtedly posh (as are their offspring), but by no means all. Famous OGs include dress designer Caroline Charles, Caroline Wyatt (BBC defence correspondent), Clarissa Dickson-Wright, writer Victoria Mather and novelist Louise Bagshawe, Lady Isabella Hervey, Lady Caroline Waldegrave, actresses, Dillie Keane, Carey Mulligan (TV and film actress), Lady Marsha Ryecart, Princess Theodora of Greece and UK water-skiing champion Sarah Gatty-Saunt.

Entrance: Specialist Woldingham entrance exams taken at 13+ in the November before entry and at 11+ in the January before entry. Mrs Triffitt has ditched CE – 'I wanted to broaden the access and make it fairer for those schools who don't prepare for CE.' Candidates take papers in English, maths and science. The girls also see the head, or a senior member of staff, for a short chat. After the assessment day, school identifies any high-flyers to sit for the academic scholarship exam a few days later for sixth form entry and in February for 11+ and 13+. Girls come from a variety of schools in London and home counties. Also overseas pupils from the Far East, Spain, Africa and Mexico. Siblings (no longer quite so) automatically accepted – only if they can cope. About 15 taken into sixth form at 16. Minimum entry requirement for sixth form is currently six Bs and two Cs at GCSE – a contentious area – school keen to get the message across that each case will be considered individually. Applicants sit the school's own entrance exam.

Exit: Mostly to Russell Group universities, especially London, Newcastle, Nottingham, Manchester and Warwick. A fair number go onto the 'new' universities – Oxford Brookes, West of England and Manchester Metropolitan being the most popular. Wide variety of subjects – some go down the traditional path of medicine and law, a lot do business studies, also geography, philosophy, politics and sociology, and economics. Drama courses and art school also popular. A few leave after GCSE, mostly unable to resist the sixth forms at schools such as Charterhouse, Wellington, Worth and Hurtwood House – though girls we spoke to said they couldn't wait to get to the sixth form at Woldingham and all the privileges it held.

Money Matters: Four academic scholarships at 11+ up to the value of 20 per cent of tuition fees. Drama, music, art and sport scholarships up to the value of 15 per cent of tuition fees available at 11, 13 and sixth form, for the duration of a pupil's time at Woldingham. Music scholars receive free tuition on one instrument in addition. In the case of need, means-tested fee remission may be available.

Remarks: Super flexible in its approach to boarding – Woldingham provides best of both worlds for boarders and day pupils – and their parents. It turns out girls who are not prissy but resourceful and fun. Doesn't have the edginess of more City-type schools but, to compensate, there is a hugely supportive and cooperative atmosphere. A beautiful, safe environment for your young girl to grow up in away from home.

Wolverhampton Grammar School

Compton Road, Wolverhampton, West Midlands, WV3 9RB

• Pupils: 620; 375 boys and 250 girls, all day • Ages: 10-18 • Size of sixth form: 150 • Non-denom • Fees: £8,208-£10,995 pa • Independent

Tel: 01902 421 326
Fax: 01902 421 819
Email: wgs@wgs.org.uk
Website: www.wgs.org.uk

Head: Since 2008, Mr Vincent Darby BA NPQH (mid fifties). Married to Susan, a community midwife. Educated at St Thomas Aquinas Grammar School and Lancaster University. Spent thirty years at King Edward's Grammar Schools in Birmingham, twenty-four at King Edward's Aston – twelve as deputy head. For six years was head of King Edward's Camp Hill School for Boys, State School of the Year 2006.

Described as an 'inspirational leader' by Ofsted, Mr Darby is a dynamo with a light touch. Credits success to his colleagues and pupils but his energy has driven WGS forward, with improved buildings and facilities; a tightening up of procedures; the success of 'Big Six' – a Year 6 intake of 30-odd children who follow a different curriculum based on 'learning to learn', avoiding SATS (introduced by his predecessor) and – most ambitious – a new junior school, scheduled to open autumn 2011: 'The need was there,' he says.

'We ought to be challenged and expand. I see my job as taking the school to the next level: what do we need; what haven't we foreseen? If I were to sum WGS up in three words, it would be "busy, happy, successful" – happy being the most important.' Considers teaching 'a fantastic job – we should talk it up more.' Gives excellent assemblies. 'He puts a lot of thought into them,' say pupils.

Academic matters: Not particularly selective but is an academic school, producing good, solid results. GCSE and A level results have improved steadily over past 5 years, with 2010 GCSE results best to date. Years 7–9 study Latin, French and German (with option of Italian in Year 9) alongside usual subjects. Strong languages, maths, science (taught as three subjects), history. Recent improvements – more consistency in approach to marking, better co-operation between departments – seem to be paying dividends.

'We're not statistically driven,' says Mr Darby. 'Weighing the pig doesn't make it any heavier. Youngsters are constantly measured and assessed, it's a harsh world for them. We're often asked 'will it be in the test?' but we don't teach to tests. We have room to be experimental, go off at tangents, while being thorough and professional. We pick out initiatives that suit us. An issue for everyone now is the myriad of qualifications: IB, Cambridge, pre-U. We look at the best combination for us at that particular moment.'

WGS is aspirational and hard-working but not unduly pressured. 'Not a hothouse – they try hard to get a balance between work and life,' said a parent. 'It's very relaxed; they trust us to go and do the work,' says a sixth former. School at forefront of the OpAL programme (Opportunities through Assissted Learning) which started at WGS in 1998. A nationally recognised model of support for academically gifted students with dyslexia, some 50 WGS pupils, supported by six teachers with one-on-one teaching; small groups, maybe doing 9, rather than usual 10, GCSEs. Cost is additional term's fees each year (usually reducing to 50 per cent after first three years). OpAL well supported throughout school by pupils and staff, who use OpAL inspired initiatives for all their pupils and has become school's academic Research and Development department. First OpAL pupils graduated recently, with range of good degrees from good universities, and are working in media, theatre design, teaching English and, most recently, winning a Saatchi apprenticeship over 10,000 other applicants.

Games, Options, the Arts: Football, rugby, cricket, tennis (a recent re-introduction) for the boys; hockey, netball, rounders, tennis for girls; mixed hockey, athletics and cross country for all. Strong football teams in a competitive region for football – first team acquit themselves well against bigger schools in independent schools cup, considered one of the toughest national trophies to win. WGS fortunate in its grounds, with pitches and Astroturf on-site. School big player in local, highly competitive games scene. For the adventurous, there is a popular climbing wall and the 24-hour Coast to Coast run. Year 10 pupils plus staff run in relay through the night across the country. Very popular, ambitious expeditions programme, from Duke of Edinburgh to climbing trips, Cotopaxi and Peru's remote

Cordillera Blanca. Colourful photo-displays of pupils grinning in goggles and down jackets look like adventure travel company ad, an impression enhanced by particularly vibrant geography displays, with any available surface plastered with maps and quirky facts – feels a long way from Wolverhampton.

Pupils take part in range of local and national competitions, quizzes and debates. Drama popular, with whole-year productions in professional 200-seater theatre. Lovely, well-used library that would shame many public ones. Art strong: all WGS pupils have scored straight As at art A level eight years running. More choirs, groups and ensembles throughout school than one might expect. Ambitious choral society programme – singing Shostakovich in Russian. Recital room (opened by local Led Zeppelin legend Robert Plant) and recording rooms particularly appreciated by band-nuts. Annual Jazz Spectacular is highlight for pupils and parents.

Background and Atmosphere: School founded by the Merchant Taylors' Company in 1512. Moved to its present imposing building in smarter suburbs of Wolverhampton in 1875. Mellow red-brick towers and open green spaces, where pupils relax, gives school a collegiate feel. Buildings mix traditional and new – old-fashioned science labs crammed with specimens; snake skins (Monty the school python is a draw); smelly cockroach tanks and menagerie of creatures. School takes workmanlike approach: new arts and drama complex was fashioned from a local car workshop; the old school gym will be new junior school's main hall. WGS is a small oasis: head says 'we could feel rarefied', but whole atmosphere is unpretentious. Effort made to 'put the school back into Wolverhampton's life, in terms of its status and relationship with the town'. Upcoming 500th Anniversary should help this.

Pastoral Care and Discipline: 'It's a cliché but there's a real warmth and community feel here,' says Mr Darby. 'No school is perfect but we've found them quick to address concerns,' said one parent. Pupils say they feel 'listened to', and relations with staff notably respectful and friendly. Friendly air between year-groups: psychology A level pupils pounce on Year 6s for experiments ('because they're so malleable at that age'). Pupils encouraged to take responsibility for themselves. Lively school parliament is consulted on whole range of issues although, in practice, not many pupils feel actively involved – something head is keen to change.

Pupils and Parents: Pupils represent a fair cross-section, some travelling up to 20 miles to attend, including some from Birmingham, with its wealth of high-powered schools. One Shropshire based parent chose WGS above local schools because of its social/cultural mix. Not a 'smart' school, but friendly and confident, turning out good citizens (Governor of the Bank of England, Mervyn King, is an Old Wulfrunian). Reporting on school netball tour, a pupil writes: 'Most young people will never get the chance to have a holiday in the Caribbean, let alone go there on sports tour with their friends'.

Pupils have more clear-eyed view of their futures than some – could hardly fail, given head's passionate belief they know about the world beyond school (giving the children chocolate bars on their birthdays, he updates them on take-over at nearby Cadbury's). Pupils are notably polite and orderly, though may partly be an effect of their very dark uniform which lends air of seriousness. (Splashes of scarlet have been added to lift the sombre black).

Entrance: Pre-junior school opening, mostly from local primary schools and handful of prep schools, with around 30 coming in via the 'Big Six'. (Local primaries were not all thrilled by start-up of Big Six, nor prospect of a WGS Junior School, but school has worked on relations, with WGS pupils volunteering in local primaries). Own entrance test at 11 and 13.

Exit: Nearly all go to university, almost everyone to first choices in recent intakes. A few to Oxbridge, a good proportion locally – Birmingham, Warwick, Nottingham – but also Durham, Leeds, Manchester, Exeter.

Money Matters: Social base may narrow with arrival of fee-paying junior school (many parents say they would have come to WGS earlier had there been a junior school) a matter school is aware of. Sense of not just paying lip-service but real commitment to school's original purpose, 'educating poor boys'. Fees are competitive and school building up and rejigging its scholarships and bursaries to make them better suited for needier pupils.

Remarks: A fine school offering good education and value in highly competitive area. Particularly good for bright pupils with dyslexia. Pretty sure we'll hear more of WGS in run up to school's 500th anniversary in 2012 and beyond.

Woodbridge School

Burkitt Road, Woodbridge, Suffolk, IP12 4JH

• Pupils: 960 boys and girls, all day with some sixth form boarding
• Ages: 4-18 • Size of sixth form: 200 • C of E • Fees: Boarding £22,332-£22,998; Day £12,351-£13,017; Junior £7,164-£10,743 pa • Independent

Tel: 01394 615 000
Fax: 01394 380 944
Email: admissions@woodbridge.suffolk.sch.uk
Website: www.woodbridge.suffolk.sch.uk

Headmaster: Since 1994, Mr Stephen Cole (early fifties), married with grown-up stepdaughter. An Oxford educated scientist, previously taught at Wellington and at Merchant Taylors', where he was housemaster and head of science. Is also an experienced schools' inspector. Has kept boarding to maintain a bit of multi-culturalism (two thirds of the boarders are from abroad) in an otherwise very Anglo Saxon, East Anglian community. Charming and approachable, extremely proud of the school, he has resisted the lure of more prestigious job offers.

Academic matters: Results very sound, with plenty of top grades at GCSE and A level, and a bulge around the A/B area in both. Mostly academic curriculum, although psychology and philosophy are A level options. Pupils are banded from Year 7 (two bands) and from Year 8 there is setting in various subjects. The top band does Latin from Year 8 and Latin, Ancient Greek and Italian are on offer in the sixth form. One language is compulsory to GCSE. Class sizes maximum 22. The head feels the school is underrated and that league tables don't reflect either the excellence at the top end or the sterling work done with middle of the road and less able pupils (despite being selective at 11, there is quite an ability range). Nor do they give an inkling of the stunning extra-curricular achievements. School has recently introduced IGCSE maths and due to this, school says, it no longer appears in league tables. Classrooms and labs are well equipped – there is, for example, a state-of-the-art language lab. The library is well-stocked and managed and a pleasant environment. Densely packed nine period school day (there is no Saturday school) with every pupil involved in extra-curricular activities on a Friday afternoon. About three per cent of pupils need learning support for which there are full-time teachers who like to integrate their work into mainstream lessons. A charge is made for those needing more concentrated support. Highly resourceful EAL teacher.

Games, Options, the Arts: Fine games fields and courts, a superb sports hall (best viewed from the inside – outside it looks like an alien spacecraft), and an outdoor swimming pool. Local schools must tremble when Woodbridge features on their fixture list, as school teams regularly trounce the opposition at all levels. Wide range of sport and pupils are frequently selected for county and national teams. School has new 'sports development programme' for the most talented sports students, but sport is regarded as essential for all and all are encouraged to participate. On Friday afternoons the entire school stops lessons for the 'Seckford Scheme', with everyone taking part in an amazing carousel of non-academic activities, including work in the community. CCF figures prominently in the scheme, as does D of E. In addition, school has a full-time chess grand-master; teams are county champions at all levels and pupils represent England at international level.

350 seat state-of-the-art theatre allows the drama department to rival the outstanding music department. Over half the pupils learn an instrument and the standard of the vast range of choirs, orchestras, groups and ensembles make the school a magnet (especially in the sixth form) for parents wishing to further their children's musical ambitions. A proliferation of links with other countries, with many visits and exchanges developed throughout Europe, Australia, South Africa, Oman, India and China. Charity fund-raising is a real feature.

Background and Atmosphere: Founded in the 17th century, the school moved to its very pleasant, beautifully kept, 45 acres in the 19th century and became co-ed and independent in the 1970s. It is part of the Seckford Foundation, which owns almshouses in the town, and whose members form the governing body. A mix of buildings dates from Victorian times to the present. New sixth form centre and Belstead Centre (teaching block) recently opened. There is a very good and busy feel about the place and no visible litter. The atmosphere is relaxed, pupils are courteous and friendly and walls are cheerfully covered with artwork and photographic evidence of what goes on outside the classroom.

Pastoral Care and Discipline: Excellent pupil care through the vertical tutoring and house systems. Sixth formers involved in the welfare of younger pupils. Boarders from 13+ have their own large Victorian house and, because there are not many of them, are completely integrated into the school, often, informally, spending weekends with friends. The head doesn't like a formal prefect system so sixth formers apply for jobs, the most sought after being school charity organiser. Few discipline problems.

Pupils and Parents: Day pupils often come from far afield in Essex, Suffolk and even Norfolk, in fleets of buses. Varied social backgrounds (professional, scientific, artistic, musical), as a result of the proximity of BT on one side and Aldburgh on the other. Foreign students from far and wide, either for long or short stays. The majority of pupils is still solidly East Anglian.

Entrance: By testing and interview at 11 and 13 and by GCSE results for the sixth form. In Year 7 about half the intake is from The Abbey, the preparatory school, the rest from local schools. About three-quarters of tested applicants gain a place. Many join the sixth form from nearby independent and state schools. Waiting lists at all ages and much interest from Londoners moving out.

Exit: A few leave after GSCE for vocational courses elsewhere. Exit after the sixth form is nearly always to university (98 per cent), with a good number to Oxbridge and other good universities.

Money Matters: Academic scholarships worth up to 50 per cent of fees and up to 100 per cent means-tested bursaries for the needy. Music scholarships which include a proportion of the fees and instrumental tuition, an art, sports and even a chess scholarship.

Remarks: A very positive and ebullient school for wide variety of tastes and quite a wide range of ability. Even the lunches are good.

Woodford County High School

High Road, Woodford Green, Essex, IG8 9LA

• Pupils: 855 girls, all day • Ages: 11-18 • Size of sixth form: 255 • Non-denom • State

Tel: 020 8504 0611
Fax: 020 8506 1880
Email: head.woodfordcountyhigh@redbridge.gov.uk
Website: www.woodford.redbridge.sch.uk

Headteacher: Since 2010, Ms Jo Pomeroy MA MEd PGCE (forties), previously deputy head at Nonsuch High School for Girls, Cheam. Studied English at St Andrews and has taught in schools in Scotland, Essex and France. Enjoys hill walking, literature, theatre, music and travel.

Academic matters: Since this is a selective grammar school you'd expect good exam results and you'd be right. About 80 per cent A*/A grades at GCSE and A*–B at A level. Languages offered include French, German, Italian and Latin. Results are equally good in humanities and the sciences. The most popular choices for A level are mathematics, chemistry and biology, with economics, history and politics some way behind – quite an unusual profile for a girls' school. Staff training days include special needs issues – not that there are many such here. The school also operates a mentoring system in which sixth formers give academic support to younger girls if needed.

Games, Options, the Arts: Sports include netball,hockey and rounders. Cross country, gymnastics, dance, athletics and trampolining are popular and there are successful extra-curricular girls' football and cricket teams. The school has fairly extensive playing fields. A sports hall and aerobics/dance studio, funded in part by a successful lottery bid, opened in recent years. There are several orchestras and choirs and regular concerts and recitals. House drama and dance competitions and an annual school play – *Guys and Dolls* 2010 – all parts played by girls, of course. The Asian Society also puts on an annual drama/musical production. Recent visits include France, Germany, Russia and Italy as well as expeditions to Mongolia, China and Ghana.

Background and Atmosphere: The school building was formerly a country manor house, Highams, built in 1768, with landscaped gardens added in 1794 by Humphrey Repton. There's a small Greek open-air theatre in the grounds which, sadly, isn't used much, except that girls sit on the steps to eat their lunch in the summer. It's been a school since 1919 and the school birthday, 29th September, is celebrated every year. It's an attractive setting but the listed building requires urgent repair and the school admits that it is expensive to maintain and they don't have that kind of money. Indeed, shortage of money is the main problem here.

All classrooms are equipped with computers and some with interactive whiteboards. There are now three IT rooms with 20 networked computers apiece and another on the way to provide for the 853 girls. There is a shortage of space – the school does feel decidedly crowded. The atmosphere, though, seems happy and supportive. Some pupils report that there's quite a competitive atmosphere; one girl said that there was occasional teasing for being a boffin but added that it 'wasn't too bad because we're all boffins here, really'. Woodford is the only girls' grammar school in Redbridge; there is a brother school, Ilford County High for Boys (qv), and the two schools link up occasionally for debates and discos.

Pastoral Care and Discipline: Discipline provided through form tutors. There is a peer support system in which sixth formers help younger girls with problems or worries. They are specially trained for this. It's a pretty well-behaved school. Detentions are held once a week but don't tend to be very crowded – usually only one or two girls. No pupils expelled in the last 19 years and only a couple of fixed term exclusions. The school's policy is to nip problems in the bud. Bullying (teasing or cold-shouldering rather than physical violence) is dealt with swiftly; the school brings those involved together to talk it out whenever there is friction. Rarely, if ever, is there need for action beyond that.

Pupils and Parents: All pupils are drawn from the borough of Redbridge or very nearby, so that's where you'll have to live if you want your daughter to come here. Cultural diversity contributes to the richness of the school. There are flourishing faith and cultural groups such as Asian Society, Jewish Society and a Christian Union.

Entrance: By 11 plus style exam, with verbal reasoning and non-verbal reasoning papers. Competition is intense: 800 candidates for 120 places.

Exit: Nearly all pupils go on to university. Around eight a year to Oxbridge.

Remarks: Traditional girls' grammar school and parents love it. One said, 'The best thing is the way the older children look after the younger ones – the academic success is a bonus.' Main drawbacks – lack of space, lack of money and it's fiendishly hard to get into.

Woodhouse College

Woodhouse Road, North Finchley, Finchley, London, N12 9EY

• Pupils: 1,080 pupils, slightly more girls than boys • Ages: 16-19 • Non-denom • State

Tel: 020 8445 1210
Fax: 020 8445 5210
Email: enquiries@woodhouse.ac.uk
Website: www.woodhouse.ac.uk

Principal: Since 2008, Mr Keith Murdoch BA MSc, who took over from Ann Robinson OBE.

Academic matters: Consistently near the top of sixth form college achievement tables. 67 per cent of A level grades were A*- B in 2010. Biology, chemistry, English literature, maths and psychology are consistently the most popular subjects from a choice of over 30, 'in almost any permutation', which include business and ICT applied A levels. A few students retake GCSEs, mostly maths and English.

Does well in value-added terms – 'Learners consistently achieve beyond predicted grades,' said the latest Ofsted report, which graded the college 'outstanding' in every category. Excellent training for staff, with a 'rigorous lesson observation scheme'; strong target-setting and tracking system to ensure no-one slips behind.

Students are asked about special educational needs on the application form and at interview. The learning support co-ordinator can help with assessments and extra support, including one-to-one help where necessary.

Games, Options, the Arts: Plenty of impressive artwork and DT designs on display. Extra-curricular activities are important here – 'If you want to do five A levels, we probably won't let you, because we think you should be doing other things too. You'd have to persuade us really hard.' Everyone has to take part in at least two six-week enrichment courses in, e.g., sport, music, drama. There is a four badminton-court-sized sports hall, dance studio and fitness space on site including a flood-lit all-weather pitch. Students play for the College at badminton, football, hockey, netball etc. Annual autumn term musical, with large numbers acting, singing, playing, dancing or working backstage. The College band plays at in-house events. Also photography, debating society, Islamic society, Christian Union, field trips, foreign exchanges, 'highly effective' work experience etc. The Woodhouse Challenge is a series of talks, debates and workshops led by guest speakers.

Background and Atmosphere: Pleasant position in North Finchley based round an 18th century manor house, extended in the 1920s and 1930s and again in 1997 and 2000. The website shows grassy expanses but we could not verify this as we visited on a dark November open evening – along with most of North London (don't even think of going by car; a long way from the tube, too, though buses pass the door). 'A lovely atmosphere and a nice lot of students,' said a former staff member.

Pastoral Care and Discipline: This is a half-way house between school and university, with informal but strong discipline. 'Sensible behaviour is what we do – we try not to fall back on rules.' The previous head felt that because her students had already experienced the transition from school, 'Doing it the next time is so much easier. Our students are less likely to trip themselves up in the big wide world at 18.' Good pastoral care – each student sees their personal tutor every day for registration and for an hour's group tutorial each week. Also allocated a senior tutor, who can help with long-term difficulties. Underperformance should be picked up quickly. Student support manager operates a drop-in service with advice about health and welfare issues and discussions of personal problems. One of the lowest drop-out rates in the country – 'It's very hard to escape from Woodhouse once you get here. We'll stagger along with you until things improve. We have an ethos of looking out for each other.'

Pupils and Parents: Good social and ethnic mix with around 30 per cent Asian and 40 per cent white pupils, travelling from a wide area including Haringey, Enfield and Harrow as well as Barnet. 'It's very important that young adults learn about diversity. We come from all different backgrounds, from all over North London, but we all are part of one community.'

Entrance: First in the queue are students from the 11–16 partner schools, Compton and Friern Barnet. These usually take around a quarter of places, and get first choice of subjects, but must meet the same entry requirements as everyone else. Different courses have different specific requirements, but A level students are expected to average B grades and applied A level students C grades. Everyone is expected to get at least C grades for maths and English. Applications close in late January, and include a confidential report from the student's present school. The College interviews as many applicants as possible and says it takes into account 'academic potential, ability to contribute to the College by participating in activities beyond the classroom and the availability of the course.'

Exit: About 95 per cent to university, including usually double figures to Oxbridge, and several to art foundation courses.

Money Matters: Asks for a £100 deposit for books and materials, repaid at the end of the course.

Remarks: Caters firmly for those aiming at higher education. Competes with three grammar schools in the borough, to say nothing of successful comprehensives, but is perennially popular with students from independent as well as state schools. Excellent teaching, good pastoral care, strong on arts and drama and enrichment activities. Go to an open day and judge for yourself.

Worth School

Paddockhurst Road, Turners Hill, Crawley, West Sussex, RH10 4SD

• Pupils: 525 pupils; 435 boys, 90 girls; about 60 per cent board • Ages: 11-18 • Size of sixth form: 225 • RC but others welcome • Fees: Day £16,587-£18,981; Boarding £22,386-£25,626 pa • Independent

Tel: 01342 710 200
Fax: 01342 710 230
Email: registry@worth.org.uk
Website: www.worthschool.co.uk

Head Master: Since 2007, Mr Gino Carminati BA MA (forties) who was previously head of the Methodist Kent College, Canterbury. Catholic and educated at St Aloysius London, he read history at Bedford College, University of London, whence to the London Institute of Education. Started his teaching career at Forest School, followed by Sir Roger Manwood's School, was deputy head of King Edward VI Grammar in Chelmsford and head of Queen Elizabeth's Grammar School, Faversham, Kent. A wealth of experience then and, whilst he would love still to be teaching, he has been busy fronting the move to co-education which started at Worth in 2008.

The decision to take girls was made 'just before Christmas 2006' after much soul searching and, although it had originally been decided that Mr Carminati would take a sabbatical term before arriving at Worth, he wanted to get to grips with the new regime and so swapped places with the previous head, Mr Peter Armstrong, who had been in place since 2002 and who took up the headship of Aiglon College in Switzerland. The decision to go co-ed was taken on a philosophical level. 'The school did not need to open up' – true – we have checked previous Guides and indeed pupil numbers have been steady around the 440/450 mark for about five years or more – but increased numbers will allow for increased choice.

Married with two children, not a proselytiser, and great fun (we have been taken to task before for describing heads as giggly – but he is and he does). He is relishing his appointment – 'Benedictine values important, that's what we are all about.'

Deputy head Dr James Whitehead joined the school in 2007 in preparation for the intake of girls into the sixth form in 2008 and the rest of the school in 2010; previously director of studies at Downside, which went co-ed in 2005, he is expert on the complexities of fitting girls into the monastic Benedictine way of life.

Academic matters: All do GCSE followed by either the IB which was introduced in 2002 or trad A levels/AEA; punches well above its fighting weight – particularly as Worth has a non-selective entry. Fair number of pupils from Germany (who arrive in sixth form to do their IB in English); good German and French results, strong results in Chinese. Not bad results either in the mathematical/science world, large numbers doing economics at A, and maths in both disciplines. English strong, but little take-up in the classics, Greek is available at IB. The boys comment that 'a real strength of the school is the high quality teaching', the staff are getting younger.

Massive funding put into a campus-wide ICT network, all classrooms have smartboards – pupils confident using

IT for research, laptops OK, and school network holds any info put on the smartboard during a lesson so that if in doubt during prep or whatever, pupils can go online and see exactly what was on the board.

Pupils on learning support can and do use laptops in class. SENCo plus four dedicated staff deal with learning hiccups, be they on the dys-strata, mild Asperger's or ropey English (that being said, good basic English is a pre-requisite for admission). All assessed on arrival at the school, referred to ed psych if need be (ditto those who come with ed psych's reports). £28 to £40 per hour for pupils who need either one-to-one help or EAL. Around 10 per cent have some form of IEP and back up, and the centre – at the top of one of the myriads of staircases which was filled with boys and girls doing various assignments – is open to all. Study skills and typing for all.

Games, Options, the Arts: Games important. Rugby pitches are across the (not very busy) road; a major sport (ex head boy capped for England schoolboys) but not compulsory. Move to co-ed has prompted additional sports such as hockey and netball since 2008. Multi sports programme of badminton, squash and fencing. Good success at the latter – both foil and epée – students compete at national level. Eight hole golf course. Large, well equipped sports hall and multi-gym, cricket nets, weights, trampolines etc. Trad green wellie sports; shooting, both team and individual. Stables. No pool as yet.

Handsome oval theatre with excellent squashy seats to match any commercial one, and serious theatre involvement for young would-be thespians. Two or three proper productions per term – with recent old boys and girls (Worthians) and current pupils putting on plays during the holidays. Debating popular, ditto music and choir; trips abroad and regular choral and organ awards to Oxbridge. 'All singing and dancing', battle of the bands, gigs for charity. Art the poor relation, three dimensional stuff on offer – art and technology compulsory for one year only. Minimal showing in exam results, with penny numbers doing art or music, but school tells us increasing uptake for art, with 100 per cent A* and A grades at A level in 2010. Recent staff recruitment in the art department to increase breadth. NB No history of art. Centre of excellence for D of E.

Background and Atmosphere: Founded by the Benedictine order in 1933, Worth was originally based in a late Victorian mansion, once part of the Cowdray estate and set in 500 acres of rolling Sussex parkland. Fantastic views and now surrounded by a motley collection of purpose-built slab classrooms and dormitory blocks. The Patrick Lamb Centre – aka Gervase, 2002, the new upper sixth form house – is stunning – en suite study bedrooms for all, with snooker tables and a vast exposed beamed common room, the unused bar sitting forlornly in a corner (booze no longer allowed unless with a plated meal), Sky TV (football, you see) and a strong smell of toast. Called the Hilton by pupils and described by one youth as an Ikea showroom, it feels somewhat under-used. Good senior house (Years 9–12) boarding accommodation, recently refurbished at vast expense. Years 9–10 have four or five to a room, Year 11 share and Year 12 have their own rooms, frescoed cornices and wood panelled/pillared living rooms with views across the countryside. No official b & b, but school can accommodate the 'odd pupil in an emergency'. Housemasters live in – for actual sickness or real emergencies pupils have to go to the infirmary a couple of hundred yards away. Certain amount of unused bedroom space, the head explained this by saying that years differed in size, but there appears to be no problem in accommodating the influx of girls in the sixth form and those who arrived into Years 7 and 9 in 2010. St Mary's House has been developed as the new girls' boarding house and St Anne's as the new girls' day house. Girls' places are oversubscribed. The monks in particular are supportive 'We believe that by welcoming girls into the school community, we will be able to enrich our ethos and further develop Worth's special qualities,' to quote school president Abbot Kevin Taggart. On the shop floor there is much talk of uniform designs, hair dryers, horses and mirrored practice rooms for dance and aerobics. This educational volte face may well change the school's reputation locally of being a 'very social' school (girls are bused in from Woldingham, Burgess Hill, Ascot and then firmly bused out).

Certain amount of minor titivating in the class room blocks. Former outbuildings have been pressed into good use: the recently refurbished labs seem to be based in the former stables; whilst the music school looks as though it was once a series of potting sheds. The gardens themselves are a delight. And whilst the monks no longer play any part in the academic life of the school, they run the chaplaincy with each house having its own chaplain.

The Abbey is one of the most exciting modern religious buildings this editor has ever seen. A vast light dome, acoustically almost perfect, capable of seating over 1400 – 'though it is a bit of a scrum', said my guide, a 'PR' prefect (and jolly good he was too), 'particularly for the candlelit service at the end of the Christmas term'. Does duty as the local parish church, all are welcome at the Sunday service. The monks worship here six times a day; the school once a week on Thursdays (compulsory), though pupils may join the monks if time permits.

Around 60 per cent of pupils are Catholic, 35 per cent Anglican and five per cent 'other'. The relationship between pupils of all ages is relaxed, all queue for lunch – even the staff and your editor – and the head joined us at an ad hoc table – eating at breakneck speed whilst sorting out a couple of problems on the run. The only discordant note came from a slightly OTT gap year student who was firmly ticked off by the Spanish mistress who looked barely older than he. Fairly basic current shopping experience about to be expanded to ensure some form of inhouse retail therapy for the girls. New café in the new social centre very popular. New website much more involving and constantly updated and now includes protected parental access to academic reports. Cars at 18, day pupils can drive themselves to school.

Pastoral Care and Discipline: Parents (and inspectors) say this is a major strength – boys and girls allowed to be and accepted as individuals. Chaplaincy team and tutors deal with problems – no reports of bullying have reached us. Daily prayer in boarding and day houses, whole-school assembly weekly. No real discipline issues, pupils clear about boundaries, suspension for smoking indoors, zero tolerance drug policy but supportive of testing.

Pupils and Parents: Still has a big appeal to Catholic Europe – Spain, Gibraltar, Italy, Germany (particularly in sixth form) plus the Chinese. Parents like the fact that it is only 15 minutes from Gatwick airport and has a traditional feel. Basically a middle class professional lot – plus first-time buyers – often from London, who send their little lads here (because it IS close to London and CE is not really perceived as an intellectual challenge) and then promptly buy a nearby cottage to be on hand at the weekend – an expensive experience in this neck of the woods – think Cowdray Park, think polo. Pupils a cheerful and open lot, though Worth's isolation can't be relied upon to breed independence.

Entrance: Mainly at 11, 13 and 16. Exams at 11 and 13 involve maths, English, verbal reasoning plus interview. 50 per cent (fairly relaxed) at CE. Interview for sixth form plus report from current school and at least six GCSEs grade A*–C, with at least three at Grade B or above. Would not turn away a pupil just on exam results – effort and attitude to work is more important.

Exit: Almost all to university, impressive proportion to Oxbridge, generally business, economics, science, agriculture, engineering, humanities, art, the Services. Some leave at 16 – academic reasons.

Money Matters: In extremis will 'keep to the next public exam, throughout if possible'. Academic scholarships up to 40 per cent, music scholarships up to 40 per cent (two instruments, one of these often choral), all-rounder scholarships up to 40 per cent and art awards – more accolade than monetary.

Remarks: Jolly nice caring school in fantastic surroundings. The nuts and bolts are all in place, and with new appointments, new buildings, the IB on offer and improving results, you can't fault it. The chaps are not particularly streetwise but the advent of girls should liven things up.

Wychwood School

74 Banbury Road, Oxford, Oxfordshire, OX2 6JR

• Pupils: 135 girls, of whom 45 weekly or full boarders • Ages: 11-18 • Size of sixth form: 35 • Non-denom but Christian foundation • Fees: Day £10,980; Boarding £16,995-£17,865 pa • Independent

Tel: 01865 557 976
Fax: 01865 556 806
Email: joanna@idnet.com
Website: www.wychwoodschool.org.uk

Head: Since 1997, Mrs Susan Wingfield Digby MA PGCE, mid fifties. Educated at North Foreland Lodge School, Hampshire and Somerville College, Oxford (French and Italian). After various posts in Oxford and London, became head of Year 7 at Wychwood and rose through the ranks thereafter. Teaches French to Year 7; 'unfair to teach further up the school' as headship duties can take her away from her teaching commitments. Quite reserved and not terribly forthcoming, she keeps her cards close to her chest, but 'does well by the girls and is hugely proud of them,' says one parent. 'Spot on with the girls and talks a lot of sense; quietly in control,' says another. Disappointed to hear the word on the street is that the school is good for SEN; 'there's so much more to Wychwood than that.' Likens schools to the road network – 'some schools are motorways all the way but at Wychwood we take a mixture of routes to the same end point tailored to the girls' needs.' Thinks art dept is a microcosm of the school – every girl comes in with different ideas and abilities and, through a variety of means, produces work of which to be proud. Aiming for stability, her ten year plan is to maintain the school's friendly atmosphere and achievement to date. Married to Rev Wingfield Digby with three adult children, she enjoys homemaking, reading and ski-ing.

Academic matters: Good range of subjects on offer considering the size of the school. Core subjects at GCSE include compulsory RS in addition to maths, English, one science, one humanity and a modern language for most (some dyslexic pupils and pupils where English is not their first lang are excused). IT facilities have improved – pupils taught in split year groups so each now has a computer terminal.

Not as academic as some of the Oxford schools but given the ability intake the results are very good. The ethos is non-competitive, all the head asks of the girls is that they try to improve on their previous result. English, maths and sciences are popular. An average of 97 per cent A*–C grades at GCSE, 70 per cent A*–B at A level. Class sizes average 18 in the lower years with a max of 25, down to an average of 10 at GCSE and four at A level.

'Non competitive,' say parents, echoing the head, 'but they get the results' with much tailoring of teaching to the individual by 'enormously dedicated staff' who are prepared to go the extra mile for the girls. Extra lessons are offered by teachers to those who need/want it.

Good SEN policy. Girls are admitted with special needs as long as these are compatible with the education on offer. SEN are picked up through monitoring; all screened on entrance in Year 7. Currently seven girls have Ed Psych's report, one girl is statemented and an additional six receive special support for which there is a fee. At any one time there may be additional girls being monitored for areas of concern. SENCo is the deputy head who is also head of English. A number of girls (eight at present) have English as an additional language. These pupils have extra tuition according to individual need.

Games, Options, the Arts: All girls play sport, including the sixth form who have one timetabled lesson per week. Limited sports facilities due to the location. On site tennis/netball courts and a multipurpose school hall which doubles up ably as a gym. Further courts/pitches are a short walk away through leafy north Oxford and the school has use of the university swimming pool. Some difficulty with achieving success on the sports field – 'difficult to pick a good hockey team from only 15' – but not a problem in the higher years, say pupils, as you can choose from a wider age range.

Enthusiastic and thriving art department. Popular choice at GCSE and A level with the options of photography and textiles with very good results in the former. Older girls are able to work in their own area dedicated to A level. A fair number go on to art foundation courses. No DT.

Half the school have individual voice or instrumental lessons and participate in the orchestras, jazz band, chamber choir etc. Chamber choir recently gained distinction in Oxford Music Festival. Multi-purpose school hall has tiered seating for concerts which concertinas against a wall when not in use.

Range of extra-curricular activities with almost all girls achieving Duke of Edinburgh bronze and many going on to do the silver award and a few to gold. Boarders in the lower years have organised activities including compulsory (unless parents object) church on Sunday morning. Older boarders are free to choose their weekend activities. Fairly early curfews in the evening. 'If you want to go out clubbing, you stay with friends overnight.' Once a term there is a whole day out to London, Cadbury's world and the like to which day girls are also invited.

Day girls can stay for prep until 5.15 or 6.45 – great for working parents, for a fee.

Background and Atmosphere: Founded in 1897 by Miss Lee, an Oxford academic who trumpeted the individual education of girls and individuality. Her legacy lives on. School housed in a large Victorian house on the main Banbury Rd; 'great location,' say girls who can walk into town very easily. Warren of staircases interlinking different parts of school. Gardens behind the school surround the courts and bridge to further school buildings and boarding facilities. Classrooms are small, ditto labs, reflecting the size of the school. Christian foundation with weekly religious assembly.

Cheerful, impressively tidy, boarding bedrooms, three or four to a room in lower years with individual study bedrooms in the sixth form. Mixed age groups in each bedroom with the oldest girl being head of bedroom – encourages peer support. Half the boarders are full boarders. Occasional boarding is possible. Help is given to parents in arranging transport, booking of flights etc. No resident matron but doctor's surgery nearby and a weekly visit to school by the doctor.

Pastoral Care and Discipline: Good. Very relaxed relationship between staff and pupils allowing good communication. Good peer support. Each new girl is allocated a house mother who is an older girl to whom she can turn. Later entrants are also allocated a house sister – a girl in the same year for support. Through this system girls say they can spot potential problems. Not a huge problem with discipline. Bullying stamped out early. Drugs have not been a problem nor alcohol but any case would be looked at individually. Elected school council of staff and pupil councillors has real clout, say parents. Pupils feel they are listened to.

Pupils and Parents: Mix across the board from university dons to self-made men and first time buyers. Come from all over. Most within 20 miles. Choose school for small size. Just under half the boarders are from overseas. Pupils polite and relaxed and not overtly rebellious; notable lack of microskirts here. Notable alumnae include Vicky Jewson, film maker, and Joan Aiken, writer.

Entrance: Takes girls of average/above average ability but head will consider every case on an individual basis and cites a girl who came in at level 3 maths and went on to win the maths challenge. Usual entry point at Year 7 though entrance at other ages possible. Entrants come from local primary schools as well as prep/independent junior schools. Sixth form entrants need a minimum of five GCSE at C grade or above with the minimum of a B grade in the subjects to be studied.

All candidates interviewed by head – looks for their passion. Asks about reading matter, current events, what makes them tick. Tests in maths and English within a day's visit and participation. Entrants at later years tend to be those who are struggling ('looking for a change,' says head) at the more academic day schools in Oxford or those from the maintained sector.

Exit: Almost all to higher education. Some leave post GCSE, 'mainly to maintained sector,' says head, 'for boys,' say others. A few come in at A level. Sixth form leavers to a range of universities both new and established. Huge mix of subjects with art being a popular choice. Occasional Oxbridge entrant.

Money Matters: Middle of the road fees plus usual extras. Three scholarships at 11+, three at 16+ of which one is for science. Music scholarships and creative art scholarships also available.

Remarks: Small, intimate, nurturing school where the individual is valued, within a highly supportive atmosphere. 'They never lost faith in me,' said one former pupil. 'Not a place for prima donnas,' says another. Look elsewhere for a high-tech, buzzing, competitive and highly academic atmosphere; this school promotes education in a relaxed, friendly environment and, according to parents, achieves results unachievable at other schools.

Wycliffe College

Linked to Wycliffe Preparatory School in the Junior section

Bath Road, Stonehouse, Gloucestershire, GL10 2JQ

• Pupils: 420, two thirds boys, one third girls; two thirds board. • Ages: 13-19 • Size of sixth form: 195 • Inter-denominational • Fees: Day £14,925-£16,320; Boarding £24,795-£26,730 pa • Independent

Tel: 01453 822 432
Fax: 01453 827 634
Email: senior@wycliffe.co.uk
Website: www.wycliffe.co.uk

Head: Since 2005, Margie Burnet Ward (early fifties). Invited initially to run the overseas development wing of the school and then became deputy head. She had been head of an international school which had without warning been sold off for development. 'I had to tour the country in a minibus full of overseas students, trying to find places for them. When I came to Wycliffe, they were by far the most helpful and sensitive school I had dealt with. Next day on my return I was telephoned and asked to join the staff.' Two years later through unexpected circumstances she was invited to become the first female head of Wycliffe. Universally popular – 'by far and away the best head since I've been here,' said a groundsman who has been trimming the lawns since the last century. 'The thing is, she's so incredibly fair,' a senior pupil told us. 'It isn't just that she knows the names of all of us – anyone can do that if they take the trouble to learn them – it's that she really understands us. She knows our hopes, our anxieties, our parents.' The latter is important to this universal mother, with two children of her own who experienced the Wycliffe adventure and who are now at university. 'You can't deal with a child without engaging with parents.'

Conscious that many mothers of boarders are married to serving officers who are frequently away, she offers genuine friendship and support. Parents we spoke to were hugely appreciative – 'she absorbs everything at meetings and is warm, approachable and shrewd.' Doesn't play the grande dame, though she could; instead she is involved and active, bustling about reminding people to tuck in shirts (with lightness and humour), congratulating pupils on recent performances and engaging with sincerity and interest. She has restructured the senior management team who spoke of a 'real sense of leadership'. 'She's injected a new sense of purpose,' said a local head. No plans to go anywhere else – 'besides, no one else would want me. I'm not from the traditional background of heads. I've had an exciting life of travel and adventure and I love it here.' It shows.

Academic matters: Not a demanding school in terms of entrance requirements 'though absolutely not a dumping ground,' growls the head. GCSE and A level results are very respectable. What the school really prides itself on is value-added. Last year's results put them in the top 5 per cent of all schools in terms of the government's contextual value added performance tables. There is a range of nearly 30 subjects at A level with seemingly no limit on the various permutations available. Plenty of guidance and advice on choosing the best options. 'We aim to find the right subjects for individuals, rather than shoe horn them into rigid blocks.' Japanese, for instance, is very popular and the school enjoys excellent relations with its sister school in Japan. Exchanges and visits abound. This school travels.

Supporting and encouraging individual and community progress is the compulsory life skills programme, a wider-ranging version of PHSE. Each year group is involved, the aim being to develop skills beyond the merely academic: thus there are courses on working as a team, problem solving, creativity and 'learning how to learn'. The pupils we asked were very appreciative of the programme. The school offers a Development (third) Year in the sixth form. Primarily designed for pupils from abroad (see Pupils and Parents) to get their English up to scratch for A levels but also used for pupils who will benefit from building deeper foundations. Pupils will only sit GCSEs and A levels when they are ready for them, not because they're the right age.

Very good remedial and special needs programme with lively, sensitive and fully qualified teachers who help and support . Pupils are automatically assessed on entry to the school. This is as much to identify Gifted and Talented (the school is the only independent school with an accreditation with NACE) as well as those with learning difficulties (the school is much praised by CReSTed).

Classrooms and laboratories have been revamped, repainted and in some cases redesigned. There is a light and spacious feel about it all. Computers are everywhere. They appear and disappear on the desks in the excellently laid out library which is also a fabulous multimedia resource centre, very popular with the pupils. In the delightful music department computers aid composition and musical appreciation; they appear alongside work benches in the DT department. Everywhere. Interactive whiteboards are in all the classrooms and are used to engage involvement and interest in ways which seem imaginative and effective. ICT is clearly very important at Wycliffe and the school has invested nearly a million pounds over the last few years.

Games, Options, the Arts: We hear mixed opinions on the standard of games at Wycliffe though clearly squash is good, with frequent tours to Europe and even as far as Peru. But there can be no doubting the excellent facilities. Floodlit Astroturf hockey pitch, an attractive cricket square, masses of squash courts with people queuing to play when we visited, an excellent sports hall: it's all here. Rowing, particularly sculling, is popular and successful as is girls' hockey and basketball. Not a hearty school but one where pupils are encouraged to participate and expected to take part in Saturday afternoon sporting commitments. Plenty of scope for outdoor activities with D of E and CCF along with plenty of opportunities for caving, climbing and adventure. An active, doing place. Music has always been important and the arrival of two new musical whiz kids heading the department has seen a deepening and broadening of musical possibilities. A huge number learn instruments and both the house singing and drama competitions contests are tremendously popular. Interesting theatre. Theatre studies is very popular. Judging by the pupils' work on display all over the school, Art flourishes. Indeed we had the feeling that this is a creative community. We heard much enthusiastic talk from pupils about debating and the Model UN with students going as far afield as Istanbul, Dublin and Chicago, where there's another sister school.

Background and Atmosphere: A busy campus with friendly staff and pupils strolling purposefully around. Some interesting buildings, particularly the original listed building which now houses the head, admin staff and the advanced learning centre. Since the school's foundation in 1882 the powers that govern have chosen their architects with sensitivity and good sense, combining aesthetics with practicality and blending old and new into a pleasing and interesting whole. A feature of the overall layout of the place is the number of sofas and benches dotted around the buildings and grounds, inviting conversation with a sense of reasonable privacy. The dining room is delightfully airy – there's a lot of glass about at Wycliffe – and serves delicious food with a tantalising variety. Sunday brunches 'are to die for.' It's good to witness the easy relationships between cookers and eaters.

Accommodation has much improved. The mixed day house with generously broad corridors, brightly painted studies and common rooms with balconies over looking the green sward is very pleasant and clearly much appreciated. 'We're like boarders who don't have bed and breakfast,' one told us. Flexi-boarding is a possibility. The new sixth form boarding house built round three sides of a quadrangle is miles better than much student accommodation. All rooms en suite and, we were assured, the boys have a sauna and Jacuzzi. The school has been fully coeducational for more than 30 years and feels absolutely right. There's a lovely atmosphere.

Pastoral Care and Discipline: The school revolves around the house system for day pupils and boarders, each presided over by a house master/mistress, supported by a matron, house staff and a team of house tutors. Prefects and responsible sixth formers provide invaluable back up and conduits. Those to whom we spoke impressed us with the seriousness of their approach and delighted us by their lack of pomposity. One told us that consideration for others is deeply ingrained. The pupils' handbook is admirably clear about the school's zero tolerance of bullying and via two splendid pieces of writing from the founder and a later headmaster, the current head establishes clearly the expectations and ethos of the school, while demonstrating that decency is timeless. There are clear guidelines to follow if any pupil feels aggrieved or threatened in any way. Pupils praised the (female) chaplain and appreciated the introduction of the school council. The head approves of pranks and high spirits (providing they are not unkind or thoughtless) and acknowledges that pupils will take risks and make mistakes. 'That's what they learn from.' All very civilised. Assemblies and church services in the delightful chapel, built in the 1950s by pupils and staff incorporating wood from a pier on the Isle of Wight and stone from a bombed church. All faiths are catered for, though many assemblies are forums for discussion rather than 'exclusively religious'.

Pupils and Parents: Friendly, open, relaxed pupils who seem healthily proud of Wycliffe and grateful for the experience. We didn't encounter a whiff of arrogance or affectation: the pupils seemed secure in what they were doing and were uniformly and naturally polite. Instinctively. Parents to whom we spoke were pleased to feel included and though there were some wrinkled brows over the question of extras, expressed satisfaction bordering on affection for the school. A number told us that they enjoy the opportunities for involvement and appreciate the parents' council. A lot of pupils come from abroad, some 30 per cent from 27 different countries, so it's something of an international experience. That needs to be taken into consideration. As many from Europe as from the far east. Also a number of Services children.

Entrance: The majority of pupils joining in Year 9 come from the school's own prep school, though recently increasing numbers come from other prep schools as well. Pupils from the prep sit scholarship exams or the CE; pupils from outlying schools sit either CE, scholarships or tailor-made exams. 50 per cent at Common Entrance is acceptable – or less, if there is clear evidence of specific strengths. (Remember their pride in value added). Entry into the sixth form usually requires at least five GCSEs at grade C or above but they do consider, more carefully than many, the question of potential.

Exit: Over 95 per cent go on to university with six Oxbridge places in the last three years. Nottingham, Cardiff, Birmingham and Bournemouth remain popular, as do Sussex and Exeter. Some Art Foundation courses and drama school, otherwise business related subjects and law are favourites. About 12 per year post GCSE move on to vocational courses and sixth form colleges.

Money Matters: The school is not particularly wealthy though the head stresses that it is 'strong financially.' Scholarships are available at 13 and 16 for academic excellence, art, music, DT, ICT, drama and sport. Maximum value up to 50 per cent but in exceptional circumstances the school may make up the difference. Much depends on school reports and financial circumstances.

Remarks: Strong on breadth and individual tailoring. 'I have three very different children: very bright, very sporty and very dyslexic. Wycliffe was the only school which could cope with them all. It's been wonderful for all three,' said a mum. An Old Boy told us that a few years ago he had the impression that Wycliffe had become a bit dull and dry and 'lost its way. Now it's established its own identity again.' Fair comment.

Wycombe Abbey School

Abbey Way, High Wycombe, Buckinghamshire, HP11 1PE

• Pupils: 570 girls, all board except for 30 day girls • Ages: 11-18 • Size of sixth form: 175 • C of E • Fees: Day £21,930; Boarding £29,250 pa • Independent

Tel: 01494 520 381
Fax: 01494 473 836
Email: registrar@wycombeabbey.com
Website: www.wycombeabbey.com

Headmistress: Since 2008, Mrs Cynthia Hall (fifties). Educated at North London Collegiate and St Anne's College, Oxford, where she read English. Previously head of St Helen's & St Katharine's for 15 years, and before that head of English at St Paul's Girls. A former president of the GSA, and co-chair of the HMC/GSA university sub-committee, this is her first experience of a full blown boarding school (it was she who closed down boarding at St Helen's). Much involved with the government's Independent/State School Partnerships Forum, Wycombe Abbey works closely with nearby Cressex Community School. Was at first worried that Wycombe Abbey was so tip top that there was no room for improvement but is making her mark. Has improved the quality and quantity of advice on higher education (see below) and introduced new tutorial system – girls seen in groups of 8–10 from each house. Now keen to beef up work experience, 'both the impressive kind, for law and medics, but also the less glamorous jobs in which girls experience what work is really like'. Described as 'shy', but the girls like her. Parents say she's dragging the school into the 21st century – and none too soon. Married to Tony, with two adult children, one in university and one now working.

Academic matters: The school's raison d'être. Over 50 per cent of A level exams were awarded the new A* in 2010 and, out of 76 candidates, 27 achieved A*s in 3 or more subjects. Nothing to speak of below a B. Girls setted for most subjects 'but even the bottom sets get As on their exams,' a parent pointed out. All subjects superb but classics deserves special mention: thirty girls took GCSE Latin in 2010 – a massive number for a smallish school – and every single one earned an A*. 12 sat the Greek papers, and, you guessed it, all A*s. Maths the most popular A level, followed by history. Modern languages being beefed up under newish head of dept.

Generally small class sizes, and the teaching is superb: 'the girls buzz with it', a parent said, 'and they love bouncing ideas off one another'. Homework schedule 'mind boggling' according to parents. 'They work terribly hard but seem to thrive on it.' Prep hour each evening in each house's study area; other prep times individually timetabled. Girls normally do 5 AS exams including critical thinking (though nearly a third are currently taking 6) and between 3 and 5 A levels.

Games, Options, the Arts: Music recital hall lovely with brill acoustics. Music very important here, though exam results – as in art, DT and drama – are a micron less phenomenal than in the straight up academic subjects. Brass and sax particularly hot according to girls (school says violin and piano are tops). Acres of practice and teaching rooms, though a few grumbles from girls that there is not enough space to practise in some of the houses. Something for everyone from the most able to the tonally challenged e.g. two orchestras, string, wind and brass ensembles, choral society and three choirs (chapel choir tours overseas every two years). Over three quarters of girls play an instrument – there are lots of informal lunchtime concerts – but are never taken out of lessons for a music lesson. Three girls currently excused from Saturday school to attend London music colleges, part of the school's recognition that exceptional specimens may require external nurturing (a few hard feelings among their peers).

Drama taken seriously – they have a full time wardrobe mistress! Very swish theatre with alarmingly sloping seating – do bring your oxygen tank. Art receiving attention – it has 'become more important' and girls are able to work in the evenings and on weekends. Very high quality output on display, especially the textiles. School has set its sights, if not yet its pocket-book, on a new DT and Art centre.

Fabulous sports centre, opened 2004, with huge pool and brill gym, squash courts, climbing wall, sports hall, dance studio with sprung floor. Don't let these bluestockings fool you – this is a sporty school packed with girls who are used to winning. Lacrosse their 'signature' sport and the most important game here 'by far' (with some top coaching); Downe House the arch rivals. Netball also played hard, plus girls' football, swimming, hockey, trampolining, gymnastics, fencing, golf, tennis, rowing, dance, skiing – you name it. Bit of riding for the 'little ones' and the school has a polo team, but this is not a horsey school regardless of the photos on the website. Parents of un-sporty girls also commended the provision here: something for everyone. Debate unusually energised for a girls' school. Model United Nations, Young Enterprise, D of E – all here. And leave it to Wycombe Abbey to offer something truly unique: the Sir Adrian Swire Flying Scholarship offers 15 hours of flying instruction with the aim to going solo in a light aircraft.

Background and Atmosphere: High voltage. Girls literally running from place to place like the female employees of a Japanese bank. Unlike most schools where we are shown around by pupils, the idea of girls missing lessons to guide us was dismissed out of hand. More international, outward looking and cosmopolitan than most of the other academic girls' boarding schools – this is not middle England. Approached via an awkward sharp turning off a suburban roundabout near a Staples and collection of sixties architectural monstrosities. Main building a rather grey, grim Gothic structure – initially feels more like a London day school than a boarding idyll. But the school gates successfully shut out the sprawl, one feels safe and sheltered within the campus walls, and as one hesitantly ventures into 166 acres of exceedingly hilly, but pleasant, grounds, things start to look up. School founded in 1896 by Miss Dove, later Dame Frances Dove, whose aims to develop students' talents, foster awareness of God and understand others' needs are still upheld today.

No weekly boarding – for those thinking Wycombe Abbey is a halfway house between real boarding and a London day school, think again. Closed the first and last weekends of term. Other weekends girls can go home after morning chapel on Sundays, and every 3 weeks there is exeat or half term. Weekend activities 'improving' and you can never please everyone. Most girls potter into the Eden Centre in High Wycombe for a spot of shopping on Saturday afternoons. Girls attend short, simple service in school's rather austere chapel every morning, often led by the girls.

Pastoral Care and Discipline: Some boarding houses crammed to bursting. 8 girls in one dormitory may be fun for 11 year olds, but is unacceptable for 14 year olds working towards GCSEs. Yet this is the norm in the Abbey Houses – Pitt and Rubens. The junior house for 11 year olds, by all accounts a happy place where the youngest girls learn to organise themselves and make friends for life, has one room of 16 girls (with partitions), another of 12. Meanwhile, the three state-of-the-art Dawes Hill Houses ('the place to be' say parents), already benefitting from the most spectacular facilities in the school, are expecting further renovation. Outhouses – Airlie, Barry, Butler and Campbell – vibrate to the hum of traffic noise but are otherwise very pleasant, with nice kitchens and lounges. The obvious discrepancies between the houses can spill over into status issues for some girls, according to parents, with girls in the Abbey Houses the lowest on the totem pole. School is aware of the discrepancies and is raising funds to eventually replace Pitt and Rubens. Houses also vary in terms of rules (e.g. on TV viewing).

Boarding is 'vertical' so girls sleep in rooms with the full age range from 12–16. Helps to build friendships across the years and punctures cliques. Lower sixth girls get smaller rooms of 2 or 3 (Abbey Houses) or singles (Dawes Hill). Bullying not a problem – 'they're kept too busy and there's a 'we're all in this together' mentality, a parent expained. No drugs. Occasional girl suspended for alcohol. Smoking punished by fines etc. Housemistresses excellent, but as overworked as their charges. Much emphasis on 'work/life balance' – this is a school where girls frequently have to be leant on to work LESS hard. Clarence House for upper sixth designed as preparation for university. Wycombe parents ooh and aah over the single study bedrooms and adult ambience (own clothes, self catering, fewer rules) but it's pretty standard girls' school upper sixth modern. Sixth formers allowed out Saturday nights until 11pm. Lots of socials, debates etc with Royal Grammar School High Wycombe (state grammar), Eton, Harrow, and the like. Food outstanding – huge variety – reflecting the school's international outlook.

Pupils and Parents: Not for the faint hearted – stamina the number one requirement, even above brains. Introverted shrinking violets look elsewhere. Enormously popular with overseas families, especially from the Far East, who value its academic league table standing above all else (Wycombe Abbey always comes top of the boarding girls' schools). Proximity to London also a big tick. And the famous name seals the deal. 16 per cent of girls have non-UK main addresses. Lots of brothers at Eton but the schools bear no resemblance. 30 day pupils – the number is capped by the governors. List of old girls contains surprisingly few recognisable names for a school of this age and pedigree – draw from that what you will. Includes judge (Baroness) Elizabeth Butler-Sloss, actress Rachel Stirling and (Baroness) Elspeth Howe, life peer and wife of Geoffrey.

Entrance: 11+ and 13+ entry very different beasts. The former attracts mostly London parents who will also be applying to the top day schools. 'If they get a place at St Paul's,' says the head, 'chances are they'll take it.' 13+ entry is smaller and candidates are coached to the teeth by prep schools, or are top brains applying from abroad. To be blunt: it's easier to get in at 11 ('we don't have to disappoint many girls at 11,' says the school), but not a doddle. Children wishing to enter at 11 are assessed at age 10 – no exam, just 3 hours of activities ('lots of puzzles', recalled a parent whose daughter was unsuccessful) – plus report from primary/prep. Provisional offers then made with CE merely a formality ('they never fail'). 13+ entry process similar but pre-tests more exacting.

Exit: A quarter regularly head for Oxbridge, most of the others to top universities like London, Edinburgh, Bristol, Durham. Timetabled university entrance preparation sessions start at the beginning of lower sixth. An hour and a half of interview practice, entrance test practice, talks on the application process (from visiting university representatives) etc. Now we know what universities mean when they say applicants from top girls' schools are 'over-prepared'! Help for girls applying to US universities better than we've seen at any other school and the results speak for themselves with girls admitted not only to the usual suspects but to some real powerhouses less frequently chosen by UK applicants (UC Berkeley, Stanford, University of Chicago) and to superb but lesser known establishments. A Princeton graduate, now a post-grad in the UK, comes in to train the girls to excel on the American college entrance exam, the SAT.

10 per cent of year group leaves after GCSEs, some having chafed at the rules and regulations, others finding the work and pressure too much for them, a few simply seeking change. Replaced by chunk of overseas girls – only top brains need apply at this age.

Money Matters: Scholarships at 11+ 13+ and 16+ for academic prowess though their financial value continues to decrease. Music awards available to girls under the age of 14 provide free music lessons, but nothing off the school fees. No awards currently for sports, drama or esoterics. One internal sixth form art scholarship. School aims to target ££ toward those 'who really need it' so scholarships can be topped up with bursaries. Hoping to provide one full fees bursary, not necessarily to a scholar.

Remarks: A school for intellectually curious, outgoing, self-disciplined, ambitious girls. One parent summed it up: 'A tough school, and you have to work very, very hard, but the rewards are tremendous.' Select your house carefully (school says parents have no say in choosing a boarding house).

Wymondham College

Wymondham, Norfolk, NR18 9SZ

• Pupils: 1,120 boys and girls; about 50 per cent board (both sexes) • Ages: 11-18 • Size of sixth form: 320 • Non-denom • Fees: Boarding £8,010-£8,550 pa • State

Tel: 01953 609 000
Fax: 01953 603 313
Email: admissions@wymondhamcollege.org
Website: www.wymondhamcollege.org

Principal: Since 2007, Mr Melvyn Roffe BA FRSA (mid forties). Read English at York, studied Education at Durham. Previously head of Old Swinford Hospital, another state owned boarding school. Married with a son and daughter who are at the college.

Hints of public school, a residue of teaching and directorial stints at Oundle and Monmouth, are just the ticket for someone in charge of this state owned but decidedly middle class day and boarding hybrid. Personable, patient and calmly in control – one can't imagine him being in the least bit intimidating – he comes across as a clear thinker; also determined – a tightening of belts hasn't deflected efforts to raise money needed to upgrade the sports hall and antique language facilities. Links and exchanges with far flung schools in exotic places are pet projects – 'pupils need perspectives other than their own especially if they're in a field in Norfolk' – and he's well on the way to making them a College feature. (On the basis of interests or performance at the College students are invited to join exchanges as 'ambassadors' and have most costs met by the College). Still manages to teach a little – English to the sixth – and has been chair of the Boarding Schools Association. Run of the mill interests apart from, as gamely admitted, a 'rather sad fascination with public transport.' Driving a decommissioned Routemaster bus from London to his old school fulfilled a boyhood dream.

Academic matters: Class sizes are on the large side but this doesn't seem to be a major issue; instead parents talk of the way effort and independent learning are encouraged and how, as one mum put it, children are 'nicely challenged'. School points out that class sizes are are 21 per group in Year 7 and 24 in Years 8–11. There's a general sense that pupils are keen to do well and a recognition of the hard work put in by staff – 'teachers have a vested interest in us and will help us after school.' Given the comprehensive intake, good results and noteworthy value-added – twelfth highest 'contextual value-added rating' (government speak) of any secondary in the country. Almost 90 per cent 5+ A-Cs including maths and English. Definite academic slant in the sixth – only four vocational courses in the long list of subjects offered. Virtually all pass at A level with recent improvements at the top end – 60 per cent A/B.

Large SEN room with soft seating area and fair number of computers. Parental perceptions that this is a school for clever kids and that those with special needs would struggle to keep up go some way to explaining the relatively low number of statemented pupils or those needing additional help. Pragmatic approach ('I'm dyslexic so I'll have to develop strategies to cope and work harder') coupled with maintenance of self-esteem ('I'm clever because I'm at Wymondham College') seems to work. Paired reading with sixth form volunteers, SENCo and LSAs on hand at lunch time and for those with statements, withdrawal during second year (yr 8) language lessons. College has specialist language status and all have to take languages up to Year 10 regardless of statements etc – powers that be won't budge on this. Also has a technology college status.

Co-ordinator to support the Gifted and Talented. Head isn't a fan of fast tracking but he has overseen the development of an interesting pilot scheme. 15 students, selected in Year 10, spend two periods a week, plus their own time, on an extension programme comprising a research project (findings are presented in yr 11) and a course from one of the following – literature and ideas, space science, Russian, Latin, government and politics. Visiting staff from the UEA give 'additional academic clout'.

Games, Options, the Arts: All the mainstream, seasonally adjusted, team games plus wide choice of options for the sixth who are 'encouraged' to include some sport on their timetable. School has a couple of Sportsmark awards – also an Astroturf and vast sports hall – and the sporty have plenty of opportunities to shine, especially if they make it to the 1st or 2nd teams – parents say it's less zippy for those lower down the pile.

High standard of textiles and art (chunkily assured) produced in the spacious 'Tech Block' where large studios, IT suites and technology workshops radiate from an airy central atrium.Inclusive approach towards music with 30 per cent learning an instrument – no full orchestra but parents say the jazz band is excellent. After falling by the wayside, D of E now has a co-ordinator who's on a mission to get the scheme running again. According to the head, CCF has been 'revived and reinvigorated'.

Background and Atmosphere: Founded in 1951, this state maintained boarding school, the largest in Britain, is unusual in that it provides a good co-ed comprehensive education coupled with trad boarding provision – and they have a well-resourced sixth form centre. Generally, the tremendously tidy pupils and students come across as mini adults rather than revolting teens – as if they're preparing for the world of work. There's pride in the place and talk of a special sense of community amongst pupils and staff. Calm behaviour in and out of lessons and at lunchtime a cheerful buzz. Apparently food is getting better – 'we don't get awful meals any more.'

The 82 acre site – virtually in the middle of nowhere – has ample space between an assortment of disjointed blocks. The legacy of a US air force hospital is still just visible with a small memorial garden and one surviving Nissen hut – now listed – which, with its curving roof and well tended interior, makes for a surprisingly reassuring chapel. School officially non-denominational but chapel once a week with confirmations. Pre-ark 'modern (ha!) language centre' and drably utilitarian boarding houses offset by good access for the disabled and newer builds. The most recent, a state of the art award winner, is a plush sixth form centre unfairly referred to by the students as the 'Travel Lodge'. Generous communal spaces and single, ensuite rooms for all upper sixth boarders – the move to university accommodation could come as a shock.

Pastoral Care and Discipline: House-based tutor groups with tutors overseeing academic and extra-curricular activities. Year 7 boarders and sixth are in age grouped accommodation. The rest in four mixed age houses – apparently some are more relaxed than others. Peel (Year 7) is pretty strict – 'it gets you ready for when you move up' said one aficionado – and the adjustment to boarding can be hard especially if the previous school was cosy. That said, when the chips are down, help is sensitively and readily given – but on a more day to day basis parents have sometimes felt sidelined. Head first to acknowledge that historically communication with parents hasn't always been good – 'it was dealt with as if we were simply a day school.' New parent support office – one mum said, 'it works like magic' – likely to put this bugbear to rest.

Two counsellors, recent appointment of a 'dean of students' whose role is 'to provide the support kids need to thrive here' and peer mentoring programme – children are encouraged to (and do) look after each other in a spirit of co -operation. Very little evidence of bad behaviour or bullying – sensibly no complacency here and the student council is working on a revised anti-bullying policy. Strict adherence to local authority code on banned substances.

Pupils and Parents: Most are politely assured without the slightest whiff of arrogance. Value of education is clearly understood with Saturday school weeding out the less than serious punter. East Anglian/London bias – a few from overseas. MOD presence (officers and ranks) has shrunk to 10 per cent and only a handful from ethnic minorities. Predominance of 'professional' backgrounds.

Entrance: Main intake at 11+, very few thereafter except for the sixth form. High pressure on day places – boarding increasingly over-subscribed. Applications need to be made a year in advance.

For day places: applications through the LEA. Admissions criteria in order of importance: looked after children, sibling, musical or sporting aptitude, distance from school – in one year once all the other categories were dealt with it was down to 0.6 of a mile. (Check carefully as this is a bit of a minefield). Approx five applicants per place.

For Boarding: applications through the LEA and College. This year 100+ applicants for 81 places. Admissions criteria in order of importance: looked after children, boarding need, sibling, musical or sporting aptitude. Distance isn't a factor and at this point selection is 'random' – literally out of hat. NB potential boarders have an informal 10 minute 'interview' to see if they can cope with boarding.

Most stay for the sixth but some day and boarding places available for external candidates. Minimum of four Cs and three Bs at GCSE doesn't seem to be much of a hurdle but, because of exponential growth of applicants, the final entry criteria after 'looked after children' etc has become rank order of GCSE results for day students from outside the College. Boarders' places are allocated randomly after priority criteria.

Exit: Majority on to higher education. Healthy mix of courses and institutions but lowish numbers to Oxbridge. Head wants to raise its profile but quite rightly doesn't want to make it a fetish. College now has an 'Oxbridge escalator' and they're on the look out for potential candidates through the Gifted and Talented scheme.

Money Matters: College supported by LEA. Fees are only for the cost of full or day boarding provision – fantastically good value. Funds for large initiatives raised by letting buildings. Academic, sporting and music scholarships available in the sixth form.

Remarks: A flagship school with the reputation it's long deserved. Positive vibes from local parents who see beyond the lack of frills and know a good thing when they find it – an alternative for those who'd like the benefits of a public school education but have a problem with the associated ethics or, perish the thought, cost.

Wymondham High School

Folly Road, Wymondham, Norfolk, NR18 0QT

• Pupils: 1630 boys and girls • Ages: 11-18 • Size of sixth form: 380 • Non-denom • State

Tel: 01953 602 078
Fax: 01953 605 518
Email: office@wymondhamhigh.norfolk.sch.uk
Website: www.wymondhamhigh.norfolk.sch.uk

Head: Since 2008, Ms Victoria Musgrave MEd FRSA. Head of Crompton House C of E High School from 2006 to 2008, and before that principal of Wymondham College from 2000. Consultant Leader for NCSL, part-time consultant for ASCL in leadership courses. Four grown-up children, youngest two are at university. Hobbies include: theatre, foreign travel, family and reading. One of the best in the business and an interesting move back to Wymondham – down the road from the College where she made such an impact.

Academic matters: A true community school without hidden filters. At GCSE, around 72 per cent get 5+ A*-Cs. Short course RE for all. Three sets, known as rivers, for academic subjects and fast track for those who shine in art, music and maths. Average class sizes are 25–26 although they sometimes creep up to 32. Parents speak of fantastically supportive, approachable teachers who go the extra mile – particularly in the maths department where 'they have a good way of getting kids on board.' Governors provide late buses for pupils from outlying villages who want to stay for extended school activities or use after school 'helplines' – all subject areas provide a member of staff to give additional help at least one afternoon a week. Pretty pushy sixth form with strong academic bent – 'outstanding' says Ofsted. Every student takes five ASs and is interviewed after the first term in the sixth to see if they've done enough to come off probation. No wandering off site in between lessons – 'they don't have free periods – they have study periods,' said the jolly but no-nonsense head of sixth. Virtually all stay for the full two years.

Support department for those with special needs and an enthusiastic assistant headteacher who's responsible for inclusion – she's overseeing a pilot scheme to give support through the family. Specialists based in the excellence centre (also caters for the gifted and talented and those who are falling by the wayside), differentiated work and classroom support given by assistants. Laptops and additional time in exams. In Year 11, ten youngsters, the majority of whom are statemented, are given the opportunity to join a two year course – 'pathway two.' This involves spending a day at a local college, a day on work experience and three days in school where they are taught as a discrete group. As yet zero drop-outs – all credit to the school.

Games, Options, the Arts: Modern sports centre shared with the town and additional activities for the sporty – they've managed to spawn several English schools' athletics and judo champions. Designated a specialist school for the arts in 2004 – art, drama and music get an extra boost. In 2009, a science specialism was added, with new modern labs being created. Recording facilities, two orchestras, timetabled practice sessions and a small studio theatre which becomes a community arts venue in the evening. Recent rap workshop with an evening performance for parents 'went down a storm,' according to a participant. Productive art and DT departments where kids are happily engaged. After-school activities include Japanese club and African drumming – late buses every day so no one misses out.

Background and Atmosphere: School is comfortably nested on the edge of Wymondham, a picturesque country town. Straightforward buildings, the majority of which hail from the 1950s onwards, are well maintained. Clutch of grim mobiles still in use but a recent extension has much improved the library and sixth form study area. Degree of separation between the main school and sixth who don't perform prefectorial duties (that happens in the fifth form) don't have to wear the uniform and are based around a generous quad to one side of the main school. Immaculate lawns – the school groundsman used to work at Royal Windsor polo club – and large playing fields provide ample space to spread wings and let off steam.

The 'snack shack' – a centrally plonked brown shed – is a popular way to beat the lunch queue. Serving jacket potatoes and soup it's been so successful there's another in the pipeline. Sturdy picnic tables – supplied after a request from the school council – are dotted around for outside meets and eats.

Pastoral Care and Discipline: Good rapport between staff and kids plus vertical forms affiliated to one of four houses make this very large school a civilised place to be. Pupils settle quickly and support each other. Parents speak of an atmosphere of friendliness and well being – 'they're good at treating the kids as individuals rather than fitting them into a box.' Well structured school council gives a voice to all and encourages a sense of partnership. The new head is focusing on dress and behaviour with a slightly modified uniform. The Head's Council, made of elected upper sixth students, meets weekly as does the Head's House Captains' Council.

Pupils and Parents: Affluent Wymondham and surrounding villages are attractive to those who work in Norwich – easy commuting distance. Wide social mix with a high proportion living in the town – tiny number from ethnic minorities. Sixth formers come from an extensive catchment area including Norwich. Hugely supportive parents with high expectations and chirpy, good humoured pupils who enjoy being at school. Trad uniform until the sixth, who have to wear 'business dress'.

Entrance: Over-subscribed. Stringent catchment rules for yrs 7–11 (Wymondham and satellite villages. Check current precise locations with the LEA advice centre – an absolute must). No preference for siblings. For the sixth, seven GCSEs (including English and maths) at C and above with no lower than a B for subjects to be studied at AS.

Exit: After GCSEs, those more suited to practical courses to local sixth form colleges. Post A level nearly all to university.

Remarks: Popular, successful community comprehensive with strong, academic sixth form. They are lucky to get Ms Musgrove and should perform even better from now on.

Yarm School

Linked to Yarm Preparatory School in the Junior section

The Friarage, Stockton on Tees, Yarm, Teesside, TS15 9EJ

• Pupils: Senior School 680, Prep School 320, Yarm at Raventhorpe 100 • Ages: 11-18 • Size of sixth form: 190; 125 boys, 65 girls • Multi-faith with a Christian tradition • Fees: £10,317 pa • Independent

Tel: 01642 786 023
Fax: 01642 789 216
Email: dmd@yarmschool.org
Website: www.yarmschool.org

Headmaster: Since 1999, Mr David M Dunn BA PGCE (mid-forties). Previously deputy head at Stewart's Melville College in Edinburgh; head of Year 11 at Bolton School. Cheerful and welcoming, happily balancing traditions of grammar school with modern, forward-thinking attitude. Big on pastoral care – 'happy children have better self-esteem, learn better and have a go at anything. Treat every child as an individual and celebrate all their achievements.' Two daughters in school and wife is PE teacher and in charge of girls' welfare. Announced early 2010 that prep and senior school are to have a £20m redevelopment scheme.

Academic matters: Up with the very best, with 100 per cent five or more A* to C passes at GCSE, 60 per cent at A*/A. IGCSE for ablest mathematicians. Similarly, 100 per cent passes at A level, with 54 per cent grade A*/A, 78 per cent A*–B. Top Teesside school. No magic wands here. Take cream of the local catchment area, add excellent facilities and great, committed teachers and the results speak for themselves. Strong across the curriculum – design technology particularly eye-catching. Traditional academic curriculum, no vocational. Willingness to tailor courses to suit the individual (only one girl taking Latin A level but it happened). In maths, brighter pupils take International GCSE. Pupils are in forms for first, second and third year but in same ability sets for maths and modern languages from first year. More setting is introduced in the third year and by fourth year forms vanish.

Pupils take 10 GCSE subjects. Teaching begins straight away in the morning with assembly. Less academic subjects (sports etc) kept for afternoons. 'Children are most receptive in the mornings,' affirms head.

Games, Options, the Arts: Yarm seems to excel at everything, from sport to music, as its heaving trophy cabinet is testament. Next to River Tees so rowing is strong – three national golds in past year. Also strong in rugby, hockey (boys and girls), netball and tennis. Very inclusive and runs teams for all ages/skill levels to foster team spirit. Regularly provides sportsmen and women for county and country.

Strong choral society and school choir sings Evensong in Durham and Ripon Cathedrals. Amadeus Quartet is national semi finalist. Breathtaking breadth of extra-curricular activities – 52 offered each week with every member of staff offering at least one. Drama to debating, technology club to rock climbing, horse riding, golf. Lunchtime and after school clubs and thriving D of E.

Good opportunities for foreign travel. How many schools could offer a summer's trek through the mountains of North Eastern India at 4,996m and a winter trip to Cambodia? There are plenty of trips to Yarm's partner school in Werther, Germany, each year and typically trips to places like Holland (hockey), Northern Ireland (rugby), Cambodia (cultural), Berlin (languages), Austria (skiing), Normandy, France (history and French), Barcelona (business studies), Italy (skiing), Lisieux, France (French exchange) and Belgium (battlefields tour). In 2008 leavers visited the jungles of Borneo and there have been recent trips to China and Russia. Closer to home there is plenty of opportunity for outward bound/adventure trips.

Background and Atmosphere: Badge features a phoenix and the school has risen from nothing. Lacking a 'proper' grammar school for some years, executives at nearby ICI wanted a good school to send their boys to – so they started their own. They bought the old Yarm Grammar School building and started a new school with 50 boys in 1978. Pictures and TV footage of parents helping fit out the classrooms with begged and borrowed furniture are shown annually to new pupils! School bought the nearby Friarage (18th century stone-built mansion) in 1980 and by 1996 the whole of the senior school was based there, allowing Prep School (opened in 1991) and Early School use of the old grammar school building.

School has grown rapidly since. Girls came in 2001. Major £14m redevelopment of facilities is underway, commencing with new all weather, floodlit netball and cricket facility. Major new performing arts facilities due any time now. Striking art and design technology work festoons the corridors.

Parent power continues to hold sway and flexibility to their (and their children's) desires drives the school. Atmosphere is of a modern school with traditional grammar ethos, discipline, high expectations and achievement – gowns at assembly, compulsory Latin to Year 8.

Pastoral Care and Discipline: Majors in pastoral care. Each student is allocated a tutor who is key to boy/girl's happiness at school. Programme of personal, social and health education is led by tutor and he/she is first point of contact with parents. Heads of year and head of sixth form co-ordinate work of tutors and monitor academic progress. Home-school links are strong, helped by regular reports, parents' evenings and a weekly newsletter. Tutor groups belong to one of four houses – Aidan, Bede, Cuthbert and Oswald – which promotes mixing of age groups for social, sporting and fund-raising events. Sixth formers 'take a lead' on some house activities to assist younger pupils.

Pupils and Parents: Takes pupils from wide catchment area – Sunderland in the north, Thirsk in the south, Catterick in the west, Saltburn in the east. Runs twelve private daily coaches to bus pupils in. 90 per cent from white, middle to upper management family background, remainder split Asian, American, African. 10 per cent helped by school bursary. Also Ogden Sixth Form Science Scholarships. Just one per cent have EAL requirement and eight per cent SEN – mostly mild dyslexia. Maximum class size in senior school is 22, sixth form just 16 (average is 9). Teacher/pupil ratio of one to ten.

Pupils exude confidence and are aware of great opportunity time at the school affords. 'It is a privilege to be a Yarm student and I am grateful for the fantastic time I have had here, particularly the amazing opportunities to travel,' one sixth former told us. Parents closely involved and Yarm School Association well supported for social activities. Regular personal contact with parents allied to weekly newsletters, photo books, IT link-ups etc.

Entrance: For senior school, entrance exams in maths and English held January before September entry. Good school reports and interview also needed. Scholarships available and also possibility of a bursary.

Exit: Youngsters mostly head off to university with about 10 per cent a year to Oxbridge. Medicine very popular. Several others to veterinary or dental courses. For the rest, northern universities – Durham, York, Leeds, Teesside, Newcastle, Northumbria seem favourites, mostly to study traditional degree courses.

Money Matters: Reliant on fee income. Invests mainly in staff, books, IT.

Remarks: Opportunity oozes from every pore at Yarm. From the chance to achieve well academically to the life-enhancing opportunities to travel the world. The push to achieve is not explicit but it is tangible, from nursery to sixth form. Little things count – school dinners are fantastic and the quality of the school's literature for parents is outstanding. You wouldn't judge a school on these but they are indicative of the attention to detail that runs through the school. A great school that will doubtless get even better as ambitious developments come to fruition.

Yehudi Menuhin School

Linked to Yehudi Menuhin Junior School in the Junior section

Stoke d'Abernon, Cobham, Surrey, KT11 3QQ

• Pupils: 70 boys and girls; mostly boarders • Ages: 8-19 • Size of sixth form: 7 • Non-denom • Fees: Boarding £41,106; Day £40,044 'for those not on music and dance scheme'. • Independent

Tel: 01932 864 739
Fax: 01932 864 633
Email: admin@yehudimenuhinschool.co.uk
Website: www.yehudimenuhinschool.co.uk

Headmaster: Since 2010, Dr Richard Hillier MA. Previously headmaster of The Oratory Preparatory School in Oxfordshire and, before that, head of classics and housemaster at Repton. A former cathedral chorister (at Peterborough), he read classics at St John's Cambridge, where he sang in the choir, then teacher training and doctorate (on Arator: an obscure late Christian-Latin author!) at Durham, where he was also a lay clerk in the cathedral choir. He still sings as a baritone soloist (when asked!) and continues to be actively involved in academic research. He is married to Elaine, who is currently engaged in the task of making sense of the mounting archives of the school as it approaches its half-centenary in 2013. They have two grown-up sons and a parson russell terrier.

Academic matters: The most specialised of the country's specialist music schools, the Yehudi Menuhin School provides tuition on strings (violin, viola, cello, double bass and guitar only) and piano. 'We operate on a plane above the other music schools,' said one proud pupil. How much practice is expected? Hold onto your seats. For 8–10 year olds the school organises a mere two hours of daily supervised practice. By ages 11–15 the school expects 3–4 hours. In sixth form, 5š6 hours of practice per day is the norm. On top of practice, pupils will be spending a minimum of 11 hours, scattered through the week, taking part in organised music – from orchestra and chamber music ensembles to lessons in composition and music history. All pupils must study two instruments, except the pianists.

Alongside music, pupils study traditional academic subjects and most emerge with at least five good GCSEs (usually seven), three AS levels and two A2s (though some geniuses cram in more). The range of subjects is small – English, French, German, Russian, Japanese, maths, science, music and history – as are class sizes – between six and twelve pupils. Academic ability varies. Some YM pupils are gifted all round; others shine only at music and struggle in an academic setting. GCSE and A level results usually very, very good. School offers special tuition in English for foreigners but overseas pupils we spoke to said that remedial help had consisted largely of having been moved down an academic year (in some cases temporarily) and briskly thrown in at the deep end. Small computer suite with Sibelius software for composition and other computers dotted around. Many pupils have own laptops and take advantage of school's wireless network. Music library stacked floor to ceiling with sheet music and CDs. Also traditional library for other subjects and fiction.

Games, Options, the Arts: Physical fitness valued. Sport of some kind twice a week. Lots of table tennis but also swimming, running, tennis and football, though not against other schools. A bit of Alexander Technique for all. Art compulsory and of high quality. Very popular for evening relaxation after all that music. Drama also big here – these are not kids who shun the limelight.

Background and Atmosphere: Lord (Yehudi) Menuhin founded the school in 1963, 'to create the ideal conditions in which musically gifted children might develop their potential to the full on stringed instruments and piano.' Some four plus decades later, little has changed. While numbers have grown, the ethos remains the same as does the great man's posthumous presence. Buried in the leafy grounds of the Victorian Gothic 'Music House' – (once owned by a member of the Hansard family) – his portrait still oversees all young performers in what used to be the school's main recital hall, before its fabulous new concert venue, The Menuhin Hall, was completed in 2005.

Lunchtime concerts held daily in this wonderful wood and glass edifice (though not at time of visit due to chandelier cleaning so we all squeezed into the old hall – full school attendance assured by three-line whip). New hall also available as public venue. Standard of musicianship we witnessed was truly breath-taking. Very few fidgets in the young, appreciative audience during the hour-long performance. Something extra special for our visit, we wondered? Absolutely not, head insisted. Just regular fare. Air of quiet intensity pervades whole school, only interrupted by what sounds like excerpts from Classic FM which head informs us is lessons and practice sessions.

No noisy huddles of gossipy school-kids – even lunch was a relatively sober affair. Basically they know why they're there, they want to be there, and if that means an amount of isolation to get in their two to six hours' practice, then so be it. 'In a normal school they don't feel part of that community. They feel excluded as they're not like other children,' says head. 'They're perfectly normal kids but what makes them different is they're interested in music.' Understatement. Self-discipline is key to making what head admits is an 'unbalanced curriculum' work. New buildings alongside original white house have created peaceful college-style quad.

Pastoral Care and Discipline: Caring but relaxed. For a school that requires such rigorous self-discipline, YM gives its charges an unexpectedly loose rein. School day finishes at 6:30pm. Saturday morning school for all, except the 8–11 year olds. Currently around eight day pupils. Age is not the boundary that it is at most schools and YM prides itself on functioning like a family, with older pupils looking after the younger ones and all working and playing together. Discipline not a big problem, though adolescence throws up the usual issues and the occasional pupil has been suspended. Fab new boarding house for 11–19 year olds with a piano in every room (most are doubles). Pupils live in 'pods' rather than along corridors. Handful of the very youngest maestros live upstairs in the main house, over the dining hall. School beefing up security since the opening of its new concert hall, which draws in members of the public. Teachers take pains to keep competition in check. It may come as a surprise to some that the effete world of classical music can be more brutally cutthroat than heavyweight boxing. School tempers this by, e.g., rotating positions in the school orchestra (there is no one leader and even hotshots may have a turn at the back of the second violins). The pupils support one another and provide an enthusiastic audience. Still, for children who have been used to being big fish in less august ponds, the adjustment to a school where everyone is of a towering calibre cannot always be easy.

Pupils and Parents: Totally non-denom, very broad mix of backgrounds (no parents pay full fees – everyone grant assisted in some form or other) and countries of origin. Pupils must have three Cs in common though – concentration, commitment and co-ordination. The instrument 'must be an extension of the body'. Explains head, 'It's that quality that makes the hair on the back of your neck stand on end.' Esteemed alumni include Tasmin Little (violin), Nigel Kennedy (violin), Nicola Benedetti (violin) and Paul Watkins (cello).

Entrance: We don't want to dishearten you, but here are the facts: for 500 enquiries received each year, the school makes offers to between five and ten young musicians. The offer of one of these precious places depends on a sequence of auditions designed to spot the real McCoy. The first one (which can be in person or submitted on video, DVD or CD) determines if the candidates 'are even in the ballpark'. If they pass this hurdle, they then spend a day at the school, during which personal qualities like motivation are assessed. Pupils whose prowess owes more to Mummy's ambitions than to their own are rooted out. At this second stage applicants are asked to play two contrasting pieces from different stylistic periods and undertake sight-reading and aural/oral tests. The last hurdle involves spending three days living at the school. School says it is looking for potential rather than achievement but we suspect that these come together as a package. Also strives for a cultural and international mix. A lack of academic aptitude is not an obstacle to entrance. Nor, apparently, is being an oddball. There a perpetual waiting list of qualified youngsters.

Exit: Head initially said all go on to music college, later amended this to 95 per cent as, occasionally, some pursue academic courses at university if they plan to compose rather than perform. But entry to best British musical academies and overseas conservatories pretty well guaranteed. Very few fail to make the grade and regular termly assessment quickly identifies pupils who are 'unsuitable or not interested'.

Money Matters: All UK pupils qualify for an aided place under DCFS Music and Dance Scheme. Government funds places on sliding scale according to parental income. Eight pupils funded by school bursaries, aid also available for overseas pupils.

Remarks: If you are in doubt whether your child is talented enough to come here, then he or she probably isn't. This is no environment for the faint-hearted or the over-ambitious parent. Don't be tempted unless this is something your child desperately wants. Having said that, it's lovely, refined and nurturing within a harmonious conservatoire setting but with a large dollop of eccentricity thrown into the mix. Of those talented enough to be offered a place, most would grab it with both lithe, sinewy hands. This school is, quite simply, something else.

JUNIOR SCHOOLS

Abberley Hall

Worcester, Worcestershire, WR6 6DD

• Pupils: 115 boys, 55 girls; 70 per cent board, the rest day. Also pre-prep/ nursery with 50 boys, 35 girls • Ages: 7-13, pre-prep 2+ -7 • C of E
• Fees: Boarding £18,195; Day £3,990-£14,490 pa • Independent

Tel: 01299 896 275
Fax: 01299 896 875
Email: gill.portsmouth@abberleyhall.co.uk
Website: www.abberleyhall.co.uk

Head: Since 1996, Mr John Walker BSc who was educated at Bradfield, and took his degree (in psychology from Surrey) on the wing. He went straight into schoolmastering from school itself, with stints at West Hill Park, Edgeborough and Sunningdale, before going to Pembroke House in Kenya, where he became head of studies (retains strong links – a rugby team was visiting when we were at the school). He also spent four years at Bramcote. His wife, Janie, is 'fully involved with the school, particularly on the pastoral side'; she also supervises the school ponies. A charming and delightful couple, with three grown-up children, they love being in the 'people business'. Head comments that the 'golden thing about a small school is small classes – not only can you see the problems but you can always get on top of them'. He teaches maths to scholars and the bottom rung of the CE ladder and monitors work cards – both the good and the bad.

Entrance: Informal interview, no exam as such but children are tested before their interview to give the school some idea of their strengths and weaknesses. All ability intake, a few means-tested awards on offer 'for nice children who need boarding, who will fit in and for whom the school can do something'. This is not a scholarship award and, often as not, will go to a single parent. Main entry in September but can and will take at any time.

Exit: Historical links with Winchester and still sends a regular supply; also to Shrewsbury, Radley, Cheltenham, a few to Eton, Malvern, Marlborough – all over. Girls to Cheltenham Ladies', Malvern Girls', Haberdashers' Monmouth, Cheltenham College, Malvern College, Tudor Hall, Rugby, Marlborough etc. New Malvern day house popular with locals.

Remarks: This is predominantly an English school (check the number of green wellies in the cloakrooms) so 'no need for EFL', despite the 'odd Spaniard or two who come for a couple of terms' (via the Astec agency in Madrid). Mixture of parents, mostly from Shropshire, Hereford, Warwickshire, Worcs and Derbyshire with a trickle from London; trad families and quite a number of first time buyers and, strangely enough, a growing number of ex-pats and Services personnel. Excellent feedback and regular reports to parents. Super parents' book too, with alphabetical lists of subjects of possible concern e.g. 'Teddies. These are a delightful feature of boarding school life and most pupils' beds are awash with them' (they were). School only offers full boarding with all-in and all-out weekends, plus some optional outs. No weekly boarding. Top two years have their own bedside lights. Fabulous dorms carved out of stable lofts, old drama studio and bachelor quarters.

The school is housed in a remarkable Grade II listed Victorian country house, complete with fine crumbling stucco and a ceiling to die for in the main drawing room. Outstanding conversion of existing buildings and sympathetic additions make this one of the most pleasing schools this (incredibly fussy) editor has visited in many years. A delight. School was originally founded in 1889 at Blackheath in south London – then called Lindisfarne after the monastery – and moved to Worcestershire in 1917 under the aegis of the remarkable Ashton family, who eventually endowed the place when it became a charitable trust. Mostly quite jolly extensions, enlivened by a giant chess board which slightly suffers from courtyard cricket; plus peacocks and a guinea pig club. Fishing lake, 'the ink pot', popular with children. School digging own bore hole during our visit, sadly out of bounds, could have provided hours of pleasure, rather like the somewhat bizarre clock tower, popularly used for abseiling.

Wide range of abilities, so fairly tight academic standards; no prep; lessons and homework are combined and, after the first two years, school runs on a 29.5 hour week. Reading encouraged, library has £750 worth of new books each term, pupils read in chapel, and once a year they prepare and give a speech. Great for self-confidence. More than 40 per cent have some sort of learning support in super suite of rooms in the old lofts (there may be an extra charge). French from eight, with newspapers, telly programmes and articles as important as text books. Regular study trips to France, with their own chalet near Bourg Saint Maurice in the French Alps; groups of nine- and 10-year-olds spend three weeks there during the term learning 'to speak French but also to discover the mountains and to learn about the French way of life'. Latin on tap for all, with Greek option for the brightest; school has its own Latin course: Disce Latinum. Older children must spend 18 months doing German and Spanish – 'no choice'. Tiny classes, 12 the norm, usually streamed and set where necessary. School has abandoned key stage 2 tests in English, maths and science – 'they were a waste of time', head asserts, 'they disrupted teaching' – and embraced modern technology plus all the usual suspects, touch-typing for all at eight and a huge recent investment in machines and networks. School proud of its interactive white boards. 'We only bought them where they could be of use'. Class names vary according to form teacher.

No problems with staff either on the academic or the pastoral side, 'they like our way of life'. The entire span of British history is taught over three years. Extremely competent academic briefing booklet. Art, design, music and drama all important with stunning new music dept underneath the octagonal Ashton Hall in the former shooting range. Ambitious woodwork, DT and art rooms open each evening. Own kiln and good pottery. This is a keen sporting school, pupils regularly qualify for regional and local championships. Ricochet court (sort of mini-squash – not a lot of 'em around) plus Astroturf, huge sports hall which is used by the local cricket club, climbing wall, super 25-metre indoor swimming pool and a proper manege. This is a terrific child-inspired school, no uniform except for 'formal', lots of visits, with firm discipline, jolly high standards producing self-confident, articulate pupils with a fair number of scholarships and an enviable CE record.

The Abbey Junior School

Linked to Abbey School Reading (The) in the Senior section

30 Christchurch Road, Reading, Berkshire, RG2 7AR

• Pupils: 350 girls; all day • Ages: 3-11 • C of E • Fees: £7,470-£10,620 pa • Independent

Tel: 0118 987 2256
Fax: 0118 987 1478
Email: schooloffice@theabbey.co.uk
Website: www.theabbey.co.uk

Head of Junior School: Since September 2008, Mrs Carol Ryninks BA MA HDE. Came from The Kingsley School, Leamington Spa, where she was deputy head. A hands-on head-warm and genuinely interested in all the girls, passionate about providing an exciting curriculum and enrichment opportunities for pupils of all ages.

Entrance: Informal one-to-one for youngest and tests plus interview for older girls.

Exit: Almost all to the senior school, a tiny handful to free grammars. Those who might struggle at the senior school picked up and gently redirected in good time.

Remarks: No curricular eccentricities. The tinies inhabit an Alfred Waterhouse villa surrounded by a fairytale 12-foot yew hedge. The juniors in their own big house with late 20th century extension. A luxurious new upper junior school building has just been built to house Years 5 and 6, includes classrooms, performing arts studio, music suite and common room, all done to eco-schools standard – sun pipes, wind-powered lights etc. Great care taken to spark up every brain cell, rave Ofsted report on the early years centre, efforts made to inspire intellectual curiosity – encouragements to read, speak in public, lots of trips of all sorts. Wide ranging extra-curricular programme. It's all strong.

While the atmosphere is anything but laid back, these bright-eyed girls are infused with gusto, excited by what they're learning. The social tone is set by the ladies at reception, where everyone gets the same big welcome – all parents remark on this, so do we: it's special, and they say new girls feel at home almost at once. Relationship management canny, clique formation discouraged by mixing up classes. Buddy system, school council. You don't have to be brilliant at everything, so it's sport for all and, at concerts, squawkers do their happy bit. One mum summed it up, 'It's just the way you'd want your child to be looked after.' Thoughtful touches like all correspondence on instantly identifiable yellow paper. Thriving PTA, second-hand uniforms, fundraising, social events, gadding off with daughters on trips.

Intensely purposeful, in no way remorseless. Peace of mind for those who get angsty about senior schools – the first part of an attractive 3–18 package.

Abbey Lane Primary School

Abbey Lane, Sheffield, South Yorkshire, S8 0BN

• Pupils: 385 • Ages: 4-11 • Non-denom • State

Tel: 0114 274 5054
Fax: 0114 274 6708
Email: enquiries@abbeylane.sheffield.sch.uk
Website: www.abbeylaneprimaryschool.co.uk

Acting Head: Mrs Maxine Stafford (previously deputy head) is acting head of the school whilst it recruits for a permanent one.

Entrance: Non-selective and over-subscribed. Apply to Sheffield LA by end of February of the year due to start. Priority given to SEN, then catchment area children, then siblings. Most children come from the Beauchief and Abbey Lane area.

Exit: Most go to Meadowhead Comprehensive, a few to other state schools with sixth forms, e.g. Silverdale, High Storrs, All Saints.

Remarks: Very strong SATS results, especially at KS2; KS1 results are less exceptional but improving. Little gender difference in achievement. Thinking skills work done in small groups with four of the years, a particular strength of the school. An LEA Foundation lead teacher has developed an individual approach to learning with reception children based on their interests, which encourages independence and allows very bright ones to be stretched, and now speaks on it at conferences. Class sizes 28–30 but may go down in future. Strong on SEN support, especially for dyspraxia ('fantastic support staff'). A recently acquired computer suite with 20 computers plus one in each classroom, as well as eight interactive whiteboards.

Staff ('very supportive of the children and the parents') are very dedicated and talented and were encouraged by the previous head to develop their talents, even if it meant losing them to higher level jobs. The children run some of the extracurricular activities and there is a well established school council.

Extracurricular cricket, football, athletics. A generous amount of outdoor space, a small playground with a climbing wall, a small garden area and a very large playground facing onto a wood, allowing the older children plenty of space to play cricket and tennis and just run around. Good variety of clubs: choir, gardening, art, drama as well as sports. A lot of emphasis on outdoor play: 'It's like a well-run nursery with academic development'. School food improvements are under way and mental health problems are addressed in collaboration with a child psychologist. Healthy child accreditation is a target.

The day we visited, the school was humming with creative activity, independent and adult-led, with elaborate, larger than life-size pinatas being completed in preparation for leading the Lord Mayor's parade that starts the annual Sheffield Children's Festival. The Year 1s have a wedding each year, with a church service and reception at school, attended by parents in formal dress, as part of the RE curriculum. The school is light and bright, with walls covered with interesting displays and some excellent artwork, e.g. Tudor houses and robots, in the corridors, one of which has an interactive beach scene painted on it by a classroom assistant in her spare time. The main drawback is the lack of space inside the classrooms, especially in the top years.

Mainly home-owning/professional families; lower than average SEN, EAL and free school meals figures. Parents are very involved – they help inside the classroom, raise funds and cleared an orchard area, now sporting picnic tables and a nature trail. Polite, friendly and well-behaved children who get on well together and are very enthusiastic about their school; parents say their offspring are very happy here and enjoy learning. The chief motivation is by reward, e.g. certificates; Golden Time at the end of the week (half an hour's free choice activities, forfeited for poor behaviour).

All together an impressive school that enjoys a strong reputation locally.

Aberlour House the Junior School at Gordonstoun

Linked to Gordonstoun School in the Senior section

Gordonstoun School, Elgin, Moray, IV30 5RF

• Pupils: Day 60, boarding 50; boys and girls 50/50 • Ages: 8-13 • Fees: Day £11,040; Boarding £16,497-£17,958 pa • Independent

Tel: 01343 837 829
Fax: 01343 837 808
Email: admissions@gordonstoun.org.uk
Website: www.gordonstoun.org.uk

Head: Mr Robert McVean

Entrance: By assessment and interview. Report from previous school also requested.

Exit: Most to senior school.

Remarks: Rather jolly, purpose-built junior school in the grounds of Gordonstoun itself with self-contained classrooms and dorms all in the same building. Children all use the main school facilities and dorms are strategically placed on the second floor with glorious views and somewhat incongruous work-station type beds. A large extension to the existing school was opened two years ago to accommodate the extra demand for boarding places. The new extension houses additional classrooms and recreation areas as well as residential accommodation and a large assembly hall. The boarding facilities are now nearly full; siblings of children already in the school are flocking in. Parents appreciate the convenience of having all their young in the same place and flexi and weekly boarding have also been introduced.

Abingdon Preparatory School

Linked to Abingdon School in the Senior section

Josca's House, Kingston Road, Frilford, Abingdon, Oxfordshire, OX13 5NX

• Pupils: 250 boys; all day • Ages: 4-13 • Christian • Fees: £9,270-£11,355 pa • Independent

Tel: 01865 391 570
Fax: 01865 391 042
Email: registrar@abingdonprep.org.uk
Website: www.abingdon.org.uk/prep

Headmaster: From Easter 2011, Mr Crispin Hyde-Dunn (thirties). He read history at St Catherine's College, Oxford. Currently deputy head of King's College School, Cambridge; was head of history at New College School in Oxford. His wife is a research fellow at St Edmunds College, Cambridge. Acting head during the spring term 2011: Mr Mike Rees.

Entrance: Head says pupils are 'keen, enthusiastic and confident' and likes the fact that there isn't a particular Abingdon Prep 'type'. Boys come from a wide range of backgrounds (lots of medical families) and mainly from Abingdon, Oxford and surrounding villages. Many parents choose the school on recommendation, attracted by its single-sex, day-school ethos, good results, cosy atmosphere and link to the senior school. Main entry points are reception and Year 3. At seven, most boys come from local primaries. Prep isn't as selective as its senior counterpart – but prospective pupils have maths and literacy tests and also come in for induction day. Waiting lists in some years and school says 'interest continues to be good and solid'.

Exit: After CE, three-quarters go on to Abingdon School at 13. A handful choose schools like Radley, Magdalen College School, St Edward's, Bloxham, Millfield and The Oratory. In 2010, 14 boys won scholarships to their next schools.

Remarks: Previously known as Josca's, school was founded by Evelyn Farrell in 1956. At first the school was based in an out-building in Mrs Farrell's Oxford garden and had five pupils, three of them her sons. The eldest, Julian, was nicknamed Josca – which is why the school took the name Josca's. School has been based at present site in pretty village of Frilford on outskirts of Abingdon since 1970. Move was masterminded by former head Tony Savin who, with strong support from pupils' parents, transformed former home for the elderly into a vibrant, working school. In 1998 school merged with Abingdon School (see entry in Senior School section) three miles up the road. It changed its name to Abingdon Preparatory School in 2007.

Main school building is a rambling country house situated in 50 acres of grounds. Has been vastly added to over the years – latest developments include new sports hall, swish changing facilities, new classrooms and music practice rooms. Loads of interactive whiteboards and computers everywhere. School also uses Abingdon School's facilities for concerts and drama productions and the two heads meet regularly. One class per year group in pre-prep, two classes (each of 18) per year group in prep.

Unusually for a prep school, all teachers known by their first names. Custom dates back to founder's day and 50 years on, school sees no reason to change it. French from Year 1 and Latin from Year 6. Setting for maths, science and languages. School follows standard foundation year programme in reception (Ofsted judged its early years provision to be 'outstanding' in 2008), national curriculum in Years 1 to 6 and CE syllabuses in Years 7 and 8. Scholarship set in Year 8 for potential scholars.

Pupils are very chirpy, confident boys who jump at the chance to show off their school. Keen on games – football, rugby and cricket are core sports – but they can also do hockey, tennis, golf, judo, shooting, fencing and athletics. Indoor swimming pool, adventure playground and acres of outdoor space to run off steam. Plenty of opportunities for music and drama. Boys very enthusiastic about art too. When we visited, the school's dynamic head of art was so pleased with the Year 5s' artistic endeavours that she played Abba's Mamma Mia as a treat at the end of their lesson. Seeing a group of nine and 10-year-old boys uninhibitedly dancing their hearts out was a joy to behold. Lunchtime and after-school activities range from eco club and word games to gardening and jazz band.

Boys belong to one of four houses – Dragon, Griffin, Phoenix, Unicorn – and there are lots of inter-house competitions. Pupils very clear about what is expected of them. School values, clearly laid out in boys' diaries, include 'be guided by common sense at all times' – wise advice! School very parent-friendly. School minibuses bring boys to school from surrounding area and there is a breakfast club (8–8.15am) and after-school club (not run by school itself, but open till 6pm). No Saturday school, although Year 8s attend Saturday morning revision classes between CE mocks and real thing.

Abingdon Prep is clearly a happy, successful place, small enough for everyone to know each other but big enough to offer first-class, all-round education. Not only that, it encourages boys to enjoy lots of fresh air and fun along the way too.

The Academy School

3 Pilgrims Place, Rosslyn Hill, Hampstead, London, NW3 1NG

• Pupils: 70 boys and girls, all day • Ages: 6-13 • Fees: £14,550 pa
• Independent

Tel: 020 7435 6621
Fax: 020 7435 7457
Email: office@academyhampstead.com
Website: www.academyschoolhampstead.com

Head: Mr Garth Evans BA (forties), who started the school with Chloe Sandars in 1997. Taught English at Trevor-Roberts (qv) for two periods of five years each, as well as private tutoring, and started the Academy School partly at the request of clients. 'They liked the way I taught – their children were inspired and given confidence – and suggested I set up a school along those lines.' Relaxed, informal and completely dedicated; at the end of a phone 24 hours a day, even for pupils who have moved on to secondary school. 'For a whole term I used to ring him up every day,' said a parent. 'He was totally involved.'

Entrance: Most come in at seven or 10 years old but applications welcome at any time. Some pupils move on from pre-preps, others transfer from any of the local prep schools, a few from state primaries. Most have failed to thrive in more traditional and inflexible environments. Children spend a morning at the school, taking part in lessons, to see if they will fit into the group socially and educationally.

Exit: Girls usually leave at 11, boys at 13, to selective London day schools ranging from Mill Hill to Westminster, Queen's College to St Paul's Girls.

Remarks: The school was set up to fill the need for a small, nurturing, co-ed environment. 'Children need emotional security and to feel good about themselves. Then work falls into place.' Classes of up to about 14 pupils, but often fewer, meet in small rooms in two adjacent cottages, in the adjoining Unitarian chapel, complete with stained glass windows, and in its hall. The science teacher heats a solution over a portable Bunsen burner to a rapt class in a basement classroom. Another teacher sits on the steps in the sun marking books. 'It feels like going round to your favourite teacher's house for tea, only there happen to be other teachers and children there too,' said a parent.

Classes are not strictly by school year (they often encompass an 18-month age range) but similar abilities. Specialist teachers for every subject, including French and Latin. Lessons start at 8am, and continue with a short break till (packed) lunch at 1pm. As far as possible, academics take up the first part of the day, with art, music and sport in the afternoon. The school is mixed-ability, the teaching rigorous and lively. High praise from parents for the dedication of the staff, which includes several charismatic young men. No scholarship classes, though children do sometimes get them. 'We want to make very little of the differences in ability. You can't improve the intellect but you can praise the endeavour. There's lots of praise here.'

Parents value the breadth of learning, 'My 10-year-old has astounded us with his general knowledge'. As 11+ and Common Entrance exams approach, the level and pace of learning increase. 'They really work the kids hard – but the teachers work hard too,' said a parent. 'They'll stay till seven at night and give up their holidays if necessary.' Computers are the weakest link. 'All the children have one in their bedroom, so we don't use them overtly. But it would be desirable to teach them to touch-type if we could find the time.'

Not a school for a special needs, though it can accommodate mild learning difficulties and behavioural problems provoked by more rigid environments. Children must be able to sit down and learn at an appropriate level. The small class sizes mean they get plenty of individual attention, with some one-to-one help where necessary. 'But our curriculum is flexible. We can help children catch up and improve their performance skills, but they must not disrupt the group and they need to function as part of our community.'

Two afternoons a week of sport plus extra PE periods. Swimming and, e.g., badminton at the nearby Royal Free leisure centre; football and hockey on Hampstead Heath when weather permits; PE in the hall next door. The school does on occasion put together a team to play a match, but its small pool of players means success is a bonus. 'We were excited to lose by only 5–4 to Westminster

Under School – until we found out we had played their 12th or so team!'

Art, however, is strong, with a specialist pottery teacher and – unlikely as it seems in such a small space – a kiln. Co-proprietor Chloe Sandars was trained at the Royal Academy of Music and teaches singing plus another music lesson every week. Children can also learn the violin, clarinet and saxophone, and there is a small orchestra. Rehearsals for the big school musical take over the school for several weeks of every summer term. 'The standard is phenomenal,' said a parent, 'and we're used to the performances put on by the big senior schools.'

Informal environment – everyone is on first name terms and rules and regulations are minimal. 'Everything is based on mutual respect. Our children get plenty of freedom but they have to meet their responsibilities. It's a far more sophisticated concept than having a list of rules. You put the mirror up in front of them and let them look at themselves. That's far worse than any punishment.'

'The main ethos of the school is that we really care for the individual needs of each child. They feel completely safe and secure emotionally.' Parents concur, 'My son, who felt alienated at his previous school, loved it here from the start. It's small, cosy and very nurturing. They steer a steady course between being too strict and too lax, and they get the most out of every child.'

Families are mostly wealthy, from Hampstead and environs. Most have already tried the more conventional prep schools. 'I just had a gut feeling my son wasn't happy at his old school. As soon as I walked in here I knew he would adore it and he did. It gave him the confidence to feel he could succeed.'

ACS Cobham International School (Junior section)

Linked to ACS Cobham International School in the Senior section

Heywood, Portsmouth Road, Cobham, Surrey, KT11 1BL

• Pupils: 100 girls and boys; all day • Ages: 2-11 • Fees: £8,480-£18,650 pa
• Independent

Tel: 01932 867 251
Fax: 01932 869 789
Email: cobhamadmissions@acs-england.co.uk
Website: www.acs-england.co.uk

Lower School Principal: Ms Lacy Chapman

Remarks: For further information, see senior school.

ACS Egham International School (Junior section)

Linked to ACS Egham International School in the Senior section

Woodlee, London Road, Egham, Surrey, TW20 0HS

• Pupils: all day; boys and girls • Ages: 2-11 • Fees: £8,480-£18,410 pa
• Independent

Tel: 01784 430 611
Fax: 01784 430 626
Email: eghamadmissions@acs-england.co.uk
Website: www.acs-england.co.uk

Head of school: Mr Jeremy Lewis. Lower school principal: Cindy Blanes

Remarks: For further information, see the senior school.

ACS Hillingdon International School (Junior section)

Linked to ACS Hillingdon International School in the Senior section

Hillingdon Court, 108 Vine Lane, Hillingdon, Middlesex, UB10 0BE

• Pupils: 200 boys and girls; all day • Ages: 4-11 • Fees: £8,480-£17,760 pa
• Independent

Tel: 01895 259 771
Fax: 01895 818404
Email: hillingdonadmissions@acs-england.co.uk
Website: www.acs-england.co.uk

Principal: Michelle Eriksen

Remarks: For further information, see senior school.

Akeley Wood Junior School

Linked to Akeley Wood School in the Senior section

Wicken Park, Wicken, Milton Keynes, Buckinghamshire, MK19 6DA

• Pupils: 145 (85 boys, 60 girls); all day • Ages: 12 months-11 years
• Independent

Tel: 01908 571 231
Fax: 01908 265 726
Email: enquiries@akeleywoodschool.co.uk
Website: www.akeleywoodschool.co.uk

Head: Since 2008, Mrs Clare Page BEd (forties). Educated at Ancaster House in Bexhill, then Chelsea College, Eastbourne, where she did PE and science. First teaching job at Haberdashers' Aske's School for Girls in Elstree. Later moved to Akeley Wood senior school as head of girls' games and then to Beachborough School, a local prep.

Returned to Akeley Wood Lower School in 2001, first as Year 6 teacher, then as head of Year 5. Smiley, energetic and enthusiastic. Teaches handwriting to Year 5s and says that despite her head's workload, 'I wouldn't like not to teach'. Her door is almost always open and children pop in to chat. Husband Michael teaches PE and is head of Year 11 at senior school, and they have two daughters – one a former head girl at Akeley Wood, the other in the sixth form there.

Entrance: Prospective pupils come for a low-key assessment day and school says it looks for pupils who are 'well-behaved, well-mannered and enthusiastic'. School has a reputation for its special educational needs provision, which is widely praised. Head says school is happy to offer any child a place 'if we feel we can meet their educational needs and that they will be happy at the school'.

Exit: At 11, more than three-quarters go on to Akeley Wood's senior school. Others leave for local grammars – like The Royal Latin School in nearby Buckingham, Aylesbury High and Aylesbury Grammar.

Remarks: The junior school is housed in the Georgian-style Mansion School, set in a dozen acres of games fields and gardens – fantastic for running off steam at breaktime.

Subjects like science, French, IT, music and PE taught by subject specialists while all class teachers teach English and maths. Maths lessons start with quick-fire mental maths session. French taught from word go in Year 5 and introductory Latin course offered to more able. Setting for maths and phonics. All children get a 35-minute library session each week, when they can choose what they want to read – Anthony Horowitz is a big favourite. IT suite of 12 computers (28 across whole school). Lots of cross-curricular work in IT and all IT lessons start with ten minutes of touch-typing practice. IT club very popular – children make their own animated films and create stories. Teaching staff mostly women but two male Year 5 teachers, plus a male PE specialist. Head says there is a wide spread of ability among pupils but the school is 'particularly good at finding children's strengths and nurturing what they are good at'. No Saturday school or late finishes. Head reckons that parents' lives are so busy these days that everyone 'values family time together in the evenings and at weekends'.

House system in place. Four houses – like senior school, Hillcrest, Pilgrim, Stuart and Thompson. House captains showed us round when we visited and were very proud of their badges and new house ties. Housepoints awarded for good work and being helpful. Head also chooses a 'class star of the week' in each class and posts children's names on board outside her study. When we visited, results eagerly awaited by our guides. Pupils wear similar bottle-green uniforms to senior school but are distinguished with jaunty red and green tartan skirts. Self-service family-style eating with staff at end of each table and variety of appetising dishes, including yoghurt, fruit and vegetarian option. Manners important and children must show staff their plates (hopefully scraped clean) before they leave table.

Sport for all. Boys play rugby, football and cricket while girls get hockey, netball and rounders. Like its senior counterpart, lower school has its own equestrian team. Music is strong. Up to two-thirds of children learn an instrument – regular big productions, complete with brass, string ensembles and choir. 'They like jolly singing, with lots of actions,' the music teacher told us with a smile. Children very enthusiastic about art – everything from leaf prints to self-portraits when we visited. Lots of clubs – Warhammer, mah-jong, Scrabble etc – and school trips to places such as the National History Museum, Northampton Museum. Annual ski trip and week-long expedition to Devon activity centre for Year 6s.

Akiva School

80 East End Road, London, N3 2SY

• Pupils: 296 • Ages: 5-11 • Jewish • State

Tel: 020 8349 4980
Fax: 020 8349 4959
Email: admin@akivaschool.org
Website: www.akivaschool.org

Head: Since 2008, Mrs Susy Stone (fifties). Formerly head of Bell Lane Primary in Hendon. Possibly more a teachers' head than a parents' head, Mrs Stone inspires loyalty and affection for her thoughtful approach to the curriculum. 'She's quite visionary,' said one member of staff. Friendly and down-to earth with pupils and teachers, she may not be the sort constantly seen about the playground, but all the complex bureaucracy now required to run a modern state school is firmly in place. Married with university-age children.

Entrance: A maths PHD would certainly help when it comes to estimating your child's chances in the entrance stakes for this heavily oversubscribed school. Suffice it to say that, if you're not a looked-after child or a sibling with parents who've attended a Reform or Liberal synagogue for at least 18 months, your best chance of a place lies in regular synagogue attendance for as long as you can muster, five years prior to entry minimum. Sixty places currently on offer in reception, though Akiva hopes eventually to increase the number to 90.

Exit: The great majority to Jewish secondary schools, either to the long-established JFS or to the recently founded JCoSS. A handful to grammar schools, such as Henrietta Barnett, or to the private sector, Mill Hill, Francis Holland, UCS, etc.

Remarks: Parents who choose Akiva are looking to provide their children with a nurturing foundation to their education and a strong Jewish identity. 'The teachers are very caring,' said one, 'and the children love coming to school.' Academically, Akiva is one of Barnet's highest-performing primaries and, in 2009, not only did the vast majority of its pupils reach the government benchmark in Year 6 SATs, but over 50 per cent also achieved the highest grade possible. This is partly due to thoughtful (though sometimes patchy) teaching and partly to the intake of committed parents and kids, many of whom come into the school with above-average ability. Indeed, some of the most able are not always stretched to the limit. Classroom discipline, too, can sometimes be an issue. 'There's quite a lot of off-task chatter,' said one parent. Those with moderate learning difficulties are well supported.

The curriculum is rich and broad and the government basics are interwoven with a substantial additional offering of Jewish studies, including Jewish history and ethics and modern Hebrew taught from reception. 'The school gives pupils a real sense of Jewish identity, without thrusting it down their throat or being dictatorial,' said one parent.

Jewish life is important to all aspects of the way the school operates. Prayers are held every morning, thanksgiving said after meals and pupils welcome the Sabbath on Fridays (as well as leaving early when the season demands). Meals, freshly cooked on the premises, are kosher. The Year 6 trip to Israel is a highlight.

Other faiths, however, are certainly not neglected. 'The school is progressive in its thinking,' said one parent. 'There's a huge interest in other religions.' Recent visitors have included an Anglican bishop and pupils from a Catholic school.

Plenty of cultural stimulation of a more general sort, with trips and talks that have included an Olympic athlete and children's author Henry Winkler, the Fonz. Out of lessons, there's an abundant array of well-run clubs, including chess, choir, drama, yoga, dance and film (where participants learn to review as well as create their own masterworks). In-hours sport is perhaps not unduly impressive, but those looking for greater mastery can sign up for post-lessons 'Enjoy a Ball'.

Named after a second-century scholar Rabbi Akiva, the school started out in 1981 as a small independent school, the first progressive Jewish primary school in England. In 2007, it doubled in size and transferred to the state sector. Parents feel there have been pluses and minuses. 'It's less homey, less personal, more official,' said one. One undoubted win is the accommodation. In 2008, the school moved into a brand-new two-storey building on the site of the Sternberg Centre, the largest Jewish community in Western Europe, which includes a rabbinical training college, a synagogue and the headquarters of the Jewish Reform Movement. The well-equipped modern space is light and airy, with plenty of surrounding greenery and all the requisite IT. 'The facilities are excellent,' commented a parent, and security, also a key concern, is well attended to.

Following the teachings of Rabbi Akiva, the school places a firm emphasis on humility, kindness and forgiveness. 'It's very social, caring and uncompetitive,' said one mother. Some find it a bit too uncompetitive. 'It allows pupils to be who they are, but not necessarily to shine.'

Charitable activities are important and have included fund-raising for Haiti and singing in an old peoples' home. 'My children have gained a strong moral sense, which I think will last them their lifetime.'

All pupils here – including a number of rabbis' children – are from Progressive Jewish homes, and as well the local population, families come from four continents, with a plentiful sprinkling of Israelis and South Africans. Parents tend to be deeply committed to their culture.

Albyn Lower School

Linked to Albyn School in the Senior section

17-23 Queen's Road, Aberdeen, AB15 4PB

- Pupils: 170 girls and 115 boys; 40 toddlers doing various sessions
- Ages: 2 years-11 years • Fees: £5,985-£8,645 pa • Independent

Tel: 01224 322 408
Fax: 01224 209 173
Email: information@albynschool.co.uk
Website: www.albynschool.co.uk

Remarks: For further details, see senior school.

Aldenham Preparatory School

Linked to Aldenham School in the Senior section

Elstree, Borehamwood, Hertfordshire, WD6 3AJ

- Pupils: 85 in prep, 60 in pre-prep plus 35 in nursery
- Ages: nursery 3-4; pre-prep 5-7; prep 7-11 (boys and girls) • Fees: £7,299-£10,593 pa • Independent

Tel: 01923 851 664
Fax: 01923 851 605
Email: marketing@aldenham.com
Website: www.aldenham.com

Head: Since 2007, Mr Jason Whiskerd BA PGCE (fortyish). Prior to Aldenham, deputy head of the King's Junior School, Chester, having previously taught at Alleyn's Prep. Wife teaches at the school, three young daughters. Clearly thrilled with his new, purpose-built domain, its location and its community, exudes enthusiasm and commitment and seems to know everyone's name – even the tots in the nursery.

Entrance: Two-form entry at three to nursery. Assessment-based one-form entry for places in reception at 4+ for which 50-60 apply. A few more at 7+ for which tests are set. Occasional places thereafter.

Exit: Most into the senior school – otherwise mostly to local state selectives, to Haberdasher's Boys' or Girls', North London Collegiate etc. Increasingly, and for good reason, however, they stay.

Remarks: Two buildings house the 3–11 year olds. Woodrow House, a modern, low-rise building, is home to Years 3–6. It has a large entrance atrium and a corridor off to the right with classrooms and further classrooms to the left. Rooms have an orderly feel but not too much – some reassuring blobs of clutter here and there. Very impressive IT suite. ICT taught as a subject in its own right but also used widely in the cross-curricular sense; masses of huge interactive whiteboards (clearly adored), nice little library and very good outside area – green space, Astro, excellent play equipment, safe surface and a wonderfully safe-feeling leafy garden all round. Prep children can use the senior school's sports facilities and fields. Good displays, e.g. 'The View From My Window', complete with framing curtains, and life-enhancing features like Mr Whiskerd's 'Question of the Week', e.g. 'Who is your hero?' and 'What is mankind's greatest achievement?' – that is, questions that Google cannot answer for you. From Year 3 everyone is in one of four houses – good preparation for the importance of houses in the senior school. All Year 2s learn the recorder and all in Year 3 learn the violin – excellent. Lots of small group work and clubs. Lots to stretch the most able, not all of whom go on to the senior school – as seems to be generally accepted.

Pre-prep and nursery in Wilson House, an older building, a little like a cottage in the woods. Again, super outside area with wild space, play area and bird boxes on trees. Good, lively orderly classes, a relaxed feel. In the nursery, all food is cooked on-site by chef using fresh ingredients. Nice touches like pretend doctor's surgery in reception. A sense of productive and comfortable activity. Parents enthuse, 'A very good school in terms of bringing them on', 'It's a happy school', 'A really good balance in terms of social interaction and academics', 'The teachers take no nonsense but they treat them with respect, even though they're children'. Parents of the super-bright seem, mostly, to look outside Aldenham for the next school, but most talk about 'the balance' wisely provided here. And it is for that that most decide to stay.

Alderley Edge School for Girls Junior School

Linked to Alderley Edge School for Girls in the Senior section

Wilmslow Road, Alderley Edge, Cheshire, SK9 7QE

• Pupils: 120; girls • Ages: 3-11 • Independent

Tel: 01625 583 028
Fax: 01625 590 271
Email: admissions@aesg.co.uk

Head: Since 2009, Mr Lawrence Groves (mid-fifties). Came 'with some trepidation' from twin headship of co-ed Forest and Forest Park Schools in South Trafford. Speaks of girls with both affection and pride admitting, 'it turns out my first all girls school experience has in fact been wonderful'. Teaches history and PHSE to Years 5 and 6 and enjoys a weekly half hour reading to nursery. First changes were reconfiguring rooms and adding a fun play area for nursery and reception, changing merit system and dropping SATs in favour of InCAS assessment. Describes his staff as 'supportive, forward thinking and very open to change' and they're certainly smiley. Originally from New Zealand (you wouldn't know it) he has two grown children and a grandson and commutes from Lymm, arriving by 7am staying until early evening 'when traffic's no problem'. Describes himself as a 'not hugely active Christian, preferring hill walking and mountain climbing in the Lakes and Peak District at weekends' but 'I wholeheartedly support everything that goes on here'.

Entrance: No assessment for entry to nursery (minimum two days or three half days from three plus) or infant school, nor any religious requirements bar sympathy with Christian ethos. Indeed a few Muslim and Hindu girls co-exist happily with Christian and non-church girls. Places in junior years offered after a taster day in school, not sitting papers as such but including some reading, writing, numeracy during a normal school day. Looking for 'behaviour, attitude and a focused work ethic' from the bright to middle ability ranges, 'girls who're likely to get into the seniors' but keen to protect happy atmosphere; 'we have absolutely no disruptive elements in our classes'. Spaces in some years.

Exit: About half the top twenty senior school exam results are from prep girls 'even though we don't cram for the exam'. Almost all move on up. A few (in 2010 three girls, or ten per cent) move to high flying Manchester High, Withington or elsewhere.

Remarks: Happy eager girls cosseted in lower years, gradually blossoming and integrating with seniors for seamless integration at eleven. Girls share senior hall, dining room, ICT suite, sports facilities and as they advance up the years a stair well, the new dance studio and the senior library.

Large 'learning enhancement unit' with SENCo's office, mainly helping dyslexic pupils. Class size average is 15, maximum 22. Maths sets from Year 4, reading age and spelling assessed yearly and summer tests. Netball, hockey and cross country popular, swimming at Wilmslow leisure centre. 'Best thing here is the after school clubs,' said one girl; lots of extra-curricular including LAMDA exams and popular art club. Individual music lessons for many instruments and voice. Residential trips for top three years, lots of day trips. Library with pile of bean bags and huge armchair for newly introduced parent reading helpers. Celebratory assembly gives out weekly star awards, certificates for successes outside school and presents chosen by captains from box in head's study for weekly house champions. Two reps from each class on council, only grumble is rickety loo locks. Every Year 6 girl has a job.

From the 'golden rules' corridor girls selected 'do be honest, do not cover up the truth' as most important. Friendship Council encourages girls to be friendly and work things through. 'It was the anti-bullying council but there wasn't any bullying so we didn't have anything to do and it was changed to the friendship council,' say girls who describe the way they're treated as 'firm but fair' and say 'it's a fun community'. Head adds 'no school can say they don't have bullying but any problems are mainly about falling out with friends'. He has introduced a mediator – 'a gentle, sensitive lady who gets all parties involved' – and finds parents turning to her for other advice. School prayer, written by a pupil and said daily, ends with 'dear Lord, help us in all we think, do and say'. Weekly colour bulletin packed with info and news. Toast and milk free for early birds from 8am and a charged after school club runs until 5.45pm with extra levies for late collections.

Aldro School

Shackleford, Shackleford, Godalming, Surrey, GU8 6AS

• Pupils: 220 boys; 185 day, 35 board • Ages: 7-13 • C of E
• Fees: Day £13,491-£14,991; Boarding £17,784-£19,284 pa • Independent

Tel: 01483 409020
Fax: 01483 409 010
Email: hmsec@aldro.org
Website: www.aldro.org

Head: Since 2001, Mr David Aston, BA PGCE (forties). Formerly housemaster at Shrewsbury and before that taught at Monkton Combe Junior School. PGCE from Cambridge. Charming, friendly, down to earth chap with clear enthusiasm and approachable nature. Likes children and thinks this is a particularly interesting age group to teach. Wife, Sue, teaches Latin and they have two children – a boy and a girl; their son is currently at Aldro. The school's warm family feel is due in no small way to the Astons who make an excellent leadership team. Head very popular with parents and pupils alike – 'He's made some good changes which have made our lives easier,' said one admiring pupil. Parents say he is 'dynamic without being intimidating'.

Entrance: Very early registration advised for day places – a hugely popular school locally. Boarders receive priority and can often be accommodated later in the day. The main intake is into form 3 (7+) and the January entrance test sees 45 to 55 boys competing for 32 to 34 places. Some spaces available for older boys, particularly boarders – Mr Aston says usually more demand than places available. Wide range of feeder schools, St Hilary's in Godalming providing about a third of 7 year olds. Head says Aldro is 'not like a London school – we're not ruthless academically', but boys who are going to struggle in the classroom may find it isn't the place for them. Entrance exam not a rubber stamp – some do fail; academia aside, the school is also looking for boys who 'love to get stuck into many things'.

Exit: Almost all to topnotch public schools. Charterhouse (five minutes away) is the most popular, closely followed by Eton and Wellington, then a couple each to Winchester, Cranleigh, Harrow, Marlborough, Sherborne, Shiplake. There were 33 scholarships won since 2007 including awards at Charterhouse, Eton, Radley, Sherborne, Shrewsbury, Wellington and Winchester.

Remarks: Academically very impressive – the school starts very softly, softly, but do not be deceived – those impressive destination senior schools do not come without a lot of hard work later on. 'Children aged seven or eight should not be put under pressure – they should be little boys; they should have a lovely time. We crank up the pressure later on,' says Mr Aston. A fountain pen and paper environment (although IT facilities are good and whiteboards are the norm), with tried and true teaching methods. Core subjects are English, mathematics, French, science, scripture, history, geography, drama, art, music, ICT and design technology. Boys taught in their classes from seven and then separately for each subject at nine. Boys also streamed from nine, with the most academically able going into the scholarship stream for all subjects – this can be hard work if you are not a star in every subject, said one pupil. Latin also on the curriculum from aged nine – a popular subject.

Hard work is recognised – boys are given industry grades four times a term, which reward effort rather than attainment; Mr Aston felt that the previous system of publishing form orders was counter-productive. The boys' progress is monitored by regular twice-yearly exams so it becomes part of the norm – the prospect of exams seemed like water off a duck's back to the boys we spoke to. Certainly a challenging environment – not a place for anyone who would struggle, including those with anything more than a mild learning difficulty (boys are tested on entry for learning problems). Help available for these – around 10–15 per cent of boys have extra help. Specialist SEN teachers are on hand and parents pay extra for one-to-one sessions. One parent of a boy who has a mild learning difficulty says that he has 'blossomed' since coming to the school.

An unintimidating and calm atmosphere – Mrs Aston describes it as 'gentle' – certainly the impression one gets. Set in an idyllic Surrey village (five minutes from Guildford) in 30 acres of fields, woodlands and lake. A lovely old country house at its centre and superb purpose built facilities – architect has sympathetically designed the newish teaching block known as the Centenary Building and no jarring 1970s prefabs anywhere. This also includes a very well equipped modern library (with more than 5000 books). Superb science facilities, huge ICT room with latest PCs and excellent music centre.

Wonderful art and design complex, including light and airy artroom (some very impressive artwork on the wall – hard to believe it was created by boys of 13) and design and technology room which inspires creativity and problem solving. Lovely atmospheric chapel. New dining hall (serving a choice of home cooked food at lunchtime – very good it is, too) and a flat for headmaster added, again in keeping with surroundings. Mr Aston has super view of playing fields and grounds from his balcony, so he can feel in touch with goings on at every moment.

A definite boarding feel to the school, despite the fact that day pupils hugely outnumber boarders, the vast majority of whom are in the last two years. Head says, 'There is no expectation of boarding but it makes huge sense if the senior school they are attending is a boarding school – one less adjustment to make at senior level.' Dorms feel warm and friendly – most bright with lovely views and boys not packed in like sardines. The TV we spied in one dorm was special privileges only. The notice on the dorm wall says it's Bible reading from 8.30pm till lights out at 8.50. However, 'we are allowed to read other things,' say the boys. Boarding much praised by parents and boys alike. 'The boys do love it and even my nerdy, oddball, loner son adored boarding there,' said one ex-parent (who shall remain nameless, not least to preserve her son's identity!). 'Boys whose parents are overseas are really well looked after – it is popular with Foreign Office families.'

The school day is relatively long – seven and eight year olds finish at 5pm, older boys work until 6.30pm. Prep done at school, however, so parents can breathe a sigh of relief that it is all taken care of. Also Saturday school, with one Saturday off every half term.

The Christian ethos is at the heart of everything that goes on at the school and particularly central to the pastoral care. Head has introduced a strong anti-bullying policy in consultation with the boys – each boy carries a 'red card' that details the anti-bullying code. The role of the prefects is an important backup – 'The prefects can be where teachers aren't, such as the changing rooms,' says Mr Aston.

Has an enviable reputation as a formidable sporting opponent. Main sports are rugby, soccer, hockey, tennis, cricket, athletics – all 'absolutely compulsory', the head says. All played from age seven but several teams so the less able have a chance to shine and fixtures at all levels. Five tennis courts, huge gymnasium that also doubles as a music venue and theatre with an impressive stage area. Heated swimming pool – the fact that it is outdoors doesn't seem to be a problem for pupils or parents. Team swimmers use the pool at Godalming leisure centre nearby. Sporting activities include rifle and pistol shooting, judo, badminton, golf, fishing, rowing on the school's lake and the sailing club, which regularly sails on nearby Frensham Ponds. The afternoon we visited there was a sense of purposeful busyness with boys getting ready to play matches or go exploring in the woods.

Plenty on offer in terms of extra interests and activities. The less sporty can enjoy model railway, fossil hunting, bottle digging, drama, photography, fly tying and animation, amongst other things. The school also has very active and popular cub and scout groups. Head keen to encourage boys to develop 'niche interests' – something they will carry with them through adult life. Chess hugely strong with seven national championship winning teams in 2004–5 and five boys representing England at various levels. Chess really is a big deal here and strapping sporty boys who you would never imagine playing chess often get involved. Expert coaching as well: 'I know boys who have transferred to Aldro from a different prep specifically for the chess,' says one mum. Lots of healthy competition generally among boys – six 'squads' (houses to you and me) curiously named after bits of the Commonwealth and squad marks awarded for a wide variety of achievements, leading to treats ranging from watching a DVD to trips out.

Music flourishing with about 75 per cent of boys learning an instrument. Music scholarships and exhibitions abound – music scholarships to Winchester, Charterhouse, Eton and Radley. A variety of orchestras and ensembles including a jazz band and brass group. The choir also very popular, with both senior and junior versions. Drama well supported – timetabled for younger boys and drama workshops available as an extra activity for older ones. What is delightful here is that it is equally 'cool' to be in the choir or on the rugby pitch – no stigma for the perhaps less obviously manly pursuits. Head thinks the fact the school is single sex has much to do with this – 'The boys can behave like little boys and they are happier to do the girly things; it's been great for the choir!' No plans to go co-ed – head very keen to point this out – but room for every kind of character and personality type: Mr Aston very against forcing boys' personalities into a 'dreadful mould', as he puts it. Boys a charming, sociable and happy bunch. On the whole a well turned out, unselfconscious lot – no doubt the lack of girls means that experiments with hair gel etc are kept to a minimum.

Aldro does not have the snob value that other preps have, although many parents are relatively moneyed, as one would expect in this wealthy corner of Surrey. It is an extremely successful, in many ways traditional prep school, unassumingly going about its business in its own way – a real gem if you don't want production line education. A somewhat eccentric world with some delightfully eccentric teachers that makes a welcome home for boys of every variety, it is very popular (though some parents hate the place almost on sight) and, according to one ex-parent, 'is not afraid to strike out in its own directions and is not like many preps that are basically glorified versions of a state primary'.

Alleyn's Junior School

Linked to Alleyns School in the Senior section

Townley Road, Dulwich, London, SE22 8SU

• Pupils: 230; 115 girls, 115 boys • Fees: £11,538-£12,015 pa • Independent

Tel: 020 8557 1519
Fax: 020 8693 3597
Email: juniorschool@alleyns.org.uk
Website: www.alleyns.org.uk

Head: Since 2003, Mr Mark O'Donnell BA, PGD Des MSc (Arch) EdM PGD ES, (mid-forties). Previously deputy head of Thorpe House School, Gerrards Cross. Educated at Stonyhurst and St Ignatius College, New South Wales. Married to Esther with three sons of school age. A quietly-spoken but intensely committed and dedicated head who has his finger on every detail of his super school, its management, assets, achievements and plans. Clearly assiduous, though almost disconcertingly earnest, Mr O'Donnell is a prize catch for the school and has an excellent working relationship with Dr Diggory (head of the senior school) and the other senior staff. He will put himself out to a perhaps unique degree to help a child or family with a problem.

Entrance: Around 180 applicants for 18 places in reception. Days are spent assessing hopeful four-year-olds; immense care taken and candidates given a range of developmental exercises. As the school is reluctant to say a final no, children are regularly invited back for re-tries. Lots of helpful feedback to parents.

Exit: Almost all to the senior school (automatic right of entry, though they all sit the exam). Some go for scholarships elsewhere.

Remarks: The 'two schools within one school' format really works here, for the benefit of all. A safe routes scheme funded by £250,000 of local authority cash has made a green path for safe travel around the site from the main school to the junior school end, at the far end of the main site, behind the music block but with the benefit of a huge field for outdoor play. A special science garden with a wildlife pond and herb, flower and vegetable plots. Two adjoining semis newly acquired will provide an inviting garden entrance just for the tinies – a lovely and imaginatively thought-up way to enter your school.

The building itself, purpose-built in 1992, is a model of what a junior school should be. School day begins with an enlightened 40 minutes of time for chat, administration and 'warm-up' and then a smooth transition into a 'calm and orderly' day. From Year 4, all subjects are taught by specialist teachers. Spaces are big enough to allow a sense of freedom but not overwhelming – bright, stimulating, but not over-busy classrooms, a first rate IT room with passionately committed specialist staff (when we visited pupils were peacefully absorbed at individual PCs to the sound of evensong from St Paul's Cathedral), excellent library – 'the hub of the school' – and a good, multi-purpose hall/gym. A sense of purposeful, pleasurable work pervades the whole – super textiles and excellent artwork everywhere, rooms have French names, everyone has two years learning a string instrument and around a third take it further. Lots of other music, individual and collaborative, plus drama, including a major production annually. Splendid new Edward Alleyn building houses new theatre and lots of practice rooms. Plenty of sport and games to suit everyone. SEN have exceptional resources for a junior school – two super roomlets for individual help, after careful assessment, and bright, dedicated and expert support. As in the main school, loads of clubs – 45+ for chess, gardening, judo, drama and everything else you could imagine.

There are other super junior schools in the area – ones you'd practically reproduce for – but you'd be hard put to find a happier, more secure environment than this and one run with more dedication, vision and enthusiasm. The result is a homogeneous bunch of eagerly collaborative, exploring and creative learners in a comfortable and stimulating atmosphere.

Allfarthing Primary School

St Ann's Crescent, Wandsworth, London, SW18 2LR

• Pupils: 445 boys and girls, all day; 54 part time and 12 full time places in nursery • Ages: 3-11 • Non-denom • State

Tel: 020 8874 1301
Fax: 020 8870 2128
Email: info@allfarthing.wandsworth.sch.uk
Website: www.allfarthing.wandsworth.sch.uk/

Headteacher: Mrs Claire Boag (fifties), married with two teenage children. First degree in English; PGCE from University of Surrey; Diploma in Mathematical Education; MA in Educational Leadership – University of Surrey. Has been a teacher since 1982 and taught the whole primary age range from nursery to Year 6. She has worked as an independent consultant in the state and private sectors and as an advisory teacher for Kensington and Chelsea. This is her third headship. In her previous headships she worked with staff in low-achieving schools to turn them around. The early years and the teaching of mathematics are particular interests.

Her outside interests are walking, being with friends and family, reading, cooking and eating good food.

Her intentions: 'Children thrive and achieve well at school when they are happy and have encouragement, fairness and excellent teaching. It has always been my aim to give the best possible education to all children, whatever their background. A good school can change a child's life.'

Entrance: At three into nursery, or at four into reception (re-application necessary even after attending the nursery). No tests or interviews; siblings and then shortest distance to school take precedence, then first-come-first-served and the waiting list. Spaces sometimes appear further up the school; ring to check availability.

Exit: Has partnerships with Graveney (for ICT), Burntwood (for science), Southfields (for PE) and Elliot (for modern languages), meaning that experts from these come into Allfarthing and raise the profile of a particular subject, offering out-of-school masterclasses in the latter case. Pupils move on to these schools, to the Tiffin grammar schools in Kingston, and to private ones: Alleyn's, Emanuel, Dulwich College, Latymer and Wimbledon High. Also Whitgift, Putney High, James Allen's Girls'.

Remarks: The 1920s building is sandwiched between the affluent homes of re-vamped Wandsworth and council estates, and the children at Allfarthing reflect this mix of society, ethnicity and language. They are confident and aware that they are lucky to be at this school. Parents who have moved out of the catchment area send younger siblings back, one mother pulled her son out of a private school when an Allfarthing place became free and some families are on their second generation of learning there.

The teaching is obviously very effective (see results and 'particularly successful' accolade by Ofsted) and fires imaginations way beyond the lessons. Children spawn trout in their classroom, go on a flight to Ghana in a classroom converted to a plane for the day, worry that the recycling bins might not be emptied often enough, sing at the Queen Elizabeth Hall and sleep overnight on The Golden Hinde. Much of this happy success is due to the management team and their keenness to listen to and act on the fresh ideas of parents, pupils and staff. A recent school play on Beowulf morphed swiftly into a film with a premiere at the Curzon Soho, an aftershow party and a DVD with special features available shortly. The PTA raises lots of money and it is used creatively.

Over 400 places are available at after-school clubs each term, with activities to cater for all tastes, including lots of sport, cine club, Spanish, art, ICT and textiles.

SENs are catered for effectively with booster sessions available to all so that attention is not just marked for those with statements. A calming area to help deal with the statistical rise of autism is housed separately from the main building. Rugby on the Common, swimming in Tooting and canoeing in Wimbledon Park help the kids let off steam outside the two large playgrounds, where a friendship stop is used to combat loneliness.

The ICT centre and library is in a hall, and the impressive deputy, who has already got the pupils involved in the termly Allfarthing News, will soon wind the children into the website – really worth a look – full of information, links and a detailed and up-to-date school calendar. The key to Allfarthing's buzz is the recognition of everyone's contribution, whether that be during Good Work assemblies, by putting art up on every available wall or by letting the school council talk directly to the contractors about meals. An exciting and very inclusive school.

Altrincham Preparatory School

Marlborough Road, Bowdon, Altrincham, Cheshire, WA14 2RR

- Pupils: 300 boys; all day • Ages: 3-11 • Non-denom
- Fees: £5,970-£6,630 pa • Independent

Tel: 0161 928 3366
Email: admin@altprep.co.uk
Website: www.altprep.co.uk

Head: Since 2000, Mr Andrew C Potts BSc PGCE. (an unbelievable 60), genial and prone to chuckle but serious about the ethics of education. Has steadily piloted school from former elitist, pressure cooker reputation to mellower, more caring times where SENCo is key. 'It's not just about academic success but about that rounded young man who's polite, courteous, confident to talk to you, able to empathise with others and establish good relationships,' says head, 'because that, ultimately, is what'll make him happy'. Father of five, married to Marilyn a modern language teacher at Chetham's School of Music, his youngest is on a music scholarship at Uppingham and another's still at university so 'retirement's a while off yet'. 'His assembly speeches are quite long,' say boys, 'but we like him, he can even make comprehension enjoyable.'

Entrance: Thirty non-selective nursery places with a waiting list. Entry further up depends on assessment in school and parent interview with Head; less about seeking geniuses, more about ensuring school can meet a boy's needs in a balanced year group.

Exit: Traditionally strong performances in 11+ entrance exams mean many can choose between Altrincham Boys' Grammar across the road and Manchester Grammar in town. Cheadle Hulme School always features on the leavers' list along with North Cestrian Grammar nearby and the odd one each year to King's Macclesfield. Head prides himself that 'all the boys go to the right school for them'.

Remarks: Welcoming boys' prep with sunny, open disposition where the strong chance of success at 11 is just a small part of the story. Articulate boys fall over themselves to share their school telling of the lamb's heart they just dissected in science (Year 5), and (Year 6) how studying cartoons leaves them thinking they don't know much in French, 'but then the teacher asks a question and your hand automatically goes up, the answer pops out of your mouth and you find you do know it after all'. After our meeting they spontaneously tidy away the chairs, restoring order without prompting.

Maximum class size 24, smaller in lower years with classes divided into smaller groups for much teaching. A full time SENCo, a speech and language specialist and English as a second language specialist serve the 20 or so who need extra help. One has a statement of SEN, and eight have English as an additional language. 'We're very well qualified to help boys with difficulties and our ethos is that we help boys achieve their potential across the spectrum of levels' says SENCo. So it's no longer just rarefied academic air here but the ample places bagged at top secondary schools suggest this doesn't hold the brightest back, partly thanks to gifted and talented co-ordinator. Homework rises each year. 'It's too much in Year 6, even after the entrance exams, and they're pretty harsh if you don't do it, you have to miss playtime,' say boys who do however, reluctantly accept it might be good preparation for senior school. The latest ISI inspection (2010) called behaviour here 'exemplary', praising excellent pupil staff relationships, pastoral care, academic achievement, almost everything in fact.

Specialist teachers for French, science, sport, art and tech in a bright airy studio, and for music. Parents describe music teacher as 'amazing'. 'He encourages everyone,' boys say, 'even if you're not very good you get a solo, he lets everyone have a go at everything'. Orchestra of 75, all boys sing, check the website videos. Participation in sport isn't optional either, 'every boy has to represent the school at sport even if he doesn't like it; we want the boys to feel valued but also to know they have a valuable contribution to make'. Both sports teachers came straight from college, one has been here for 30 years. Links with Bowdon Cricket and Hockey Club nearby and sessions in the Grammar sports halls across the road, enhance PE and provide facilities should ambitious proposed development of APS Marlborough Road site go ahead. If so the junior school should then have an all-weather pitch of its own, bespoke music and ICT rooms, science and language labs, and a modern kitchen and dining hall. Hot meal at lunchtime compulsory, 'wish they'd bring back curly fries'. Nursery at end of junior block with own playground. Infants in homely refurbished Victorian building a mile away. Car park chaos despite staggered finishing times. Lots of clubs, some after school. Active website with videos of recent events, up to the minute information for parents, even remote learning when school shut for snow one recent winter.

Boys compete for house points and merit badges. Colours ties for special achievements worn with great pride. School council expected to bring ideas to the table and everyone in Year 6 has a job. Links with an inner city mission and local residential care homes for charity and community work. Partnership with youth worker from nearby St Mary's. Trips to Lakes in Year 5 and France for Year 6. Uniforms and bags in burgundy and grey.

The American School in London Junior School

1 Waverley Place, London, NW8 0NP

- Pupils: 400 girls and boys; all day • Ages: 4-10 • Fees: £18,600 pa
- Independent

Tel: 020 7449 1200
Fax: 020 7449 1350
Email: admissions@asl.org
Website: www.asl.org

Head: Coreen R Hester

Remarks: For further information, see senior school.

Amesbury School

Hazel Grove, Hindhead, Surrey, GU26 6BL

• Pupils: 190 boys, 135 girls. All day • Ages: Ages: 2-13 • Christian non-denom • Fees: £7,890-£12,105 pa • Independent

Tel: 01428 604 322
Fax: 01428 607 715
Email: enquiries@amesburyschool.co.uk
Website: www.amesburyschool.co.uk

Head: Since 1994, Mr Nigel Taylor (fifties). An interesting teaching background – he began his career at Stowe, then St Andrew's School, Buenos Aires, Cheltenham College and then finally deputy head of St Paul's, Sao Paolo. Friendly and business-like, he doesn't come across as your average posh head of a Surrey prep school – he's a much more streetwise character. In some ways his approach is quite laid back – 'There are more important things than an untucked shirt'. However, don't be fooled – he still insists on being, 'Mr Taylor' or 'Sir'; none of that Christian names business; and there is a steely edge lurking underneath that soft exterior. Keen on continually moving the school forward and has raised the bar academically. One parent commented that he has 'surrounded himself with a young and motivated common room,' and he is happy to credit his staff as 'vital' to his success. Married to Caroline 'for 20 years of bliss'. According to one parent he is 'a surrogate father' to all the children in the school; he refers to the pupils fondly as 'the kiddies'. He was clearly on very friendly terms with our two pupil guides; when they arrived a little early he invited them to 'make yourself at home, sit down, have a glass of wine,' which they thought was hilarious.

Entrance: Main points of entry pre-nursery (2+), reception (4+), and Year 3 (7+). The school wants siblings to study together and so the intake is quite broad. However, according to the head, 'Our intake is above the national average. We are not looking for everyone to be the brightest and best but our ability range is much narrower than it used to be – does that sound really brutal?' No entrance test for those coming into the pre-nursery and nursery or, in fact, for any child entering the prep school from the school's own pre-prep department. A child entering reception up to Year 8 will be assessed during a day visit – 'A number of tools are used to help assess whether a child would be likely to thrive at Amesbury, based on their academic potential and emotional and physical development. The key is a detailed questionnaire parents are required to complete prior to a child's visit'. Usually oversubscribed for entry in Year 3; eight places available at this stage with a 'wait list'. The system is flexible: too many girls in a year may result in that year being closed to girls to ensure a good balance and vice versa. Tip: the best bet by far for entry is into reception.

Exit: Wide range of day and boarding schools in the immediate area and beyond. One parent told us that the head 'has very strong views on where the kids go on to and he may disagree with your choice, but he is always supportive of the decision'. Fifty per cent of girls leave at 11 for girls' day schools in the area, the most popular current choice St Catherine's Bramley; according to Mr Taylor it has the most similar feel to Amesbury, 'The Amesbury girl is not a prissy girl'. Parents have felt much supported, even when leaving at 11. Girls also to Prior's Field and St Swithun's. Boys who leave at 13+ for single sex schools choose Charterhouse and Royal Grammar Guildford among others. Huge list of co-ed boarding school choices at 13 which includes everywhere from Bedales to Canford to Rugby and a host of others in between. Big increase in the number of scholarships across the board in the last few years – 53 in the last six years including Royal Grammar Guildford, Winchester, Downe House and St Catherine's.

Remarks: A forward-thinking yet, in many ways, traditional prep that manages to combine a purposeful approach with a relaxed atmosphere. Mr Taylor has taken a school which he describes as 'days away from closure' when he took it over and turned it into a major player in this area. Hottest competition (particularly in the fashionable Londoners exiting to the Surrey countryside stakes) comes from Highfield (qv) but, as one parent said, 'it has a very different feel to Highfield – it's not a better school, just different'.

Amesbury was founded in 1870, and is now housed in a beautiful Lutyens-designed main building – our charming pupil guides were a fount of knowledge on the whole history of the school and positively revelled in all the historical details. This main building is for Years 1 and 2, the lucky devils. It has pleasing wide corridors with child-height windows, painted in sympathetic National Trust colours. The dining hall is also within this building, again lovingly maintained with the infamous stuffed bison's head on the wall (of which more later). The littlies (two- to five-year-olds) are housed in their own purpose-built modern block, which is lovely and airy with practical, light classrooms, and superb indoor castle in the nursery area. Year 3 and above have another modern building all to themselves. All of the buildings have undergone a major overhaul (most of the key buildings are new) and really there is very little left to do – the last couple of eyesores are due to be bulldozed soon and a new extension added to the main academic building, along with new visual arts department. The library is fairly new and very swish. The new buildings don't jar too much with the Lutyens original. Newly kitted out san would be the envy of many a GP.

Academically, Mr Taylor is ambitious for his pupils without academia being the be-all-and-end-all. Fairly traditional and rigorous approach with emphasis on a wide education, broadly following the national curriculum. No setting in Years 3 and 4 though from Year 5 there is a first set and two equal second sets in some subjects. Innovative system of small group 'intervention' teaching' in English and Maths from Years 3–6 is helpful particularly for the 'quiet, compliant, more average child who can easily be missed,' according to the head. Mr Taylor is also keen to stress the whole-school approach. There is none of the traditional pre-prep / preparatory school division. Amesbury is one school. This is reflected in the leadership, timetabling, curriculum and use of resources. Great emphasis on using assessment data (it was one of the first schools in the country to use Durham University's PIPs programme) to ensure work is being pitched at the right level for each child. True to the head's word on being tougher 'with the lower ability range,' if any pupils are struggling with the academic curriculum, parents 'are encouraged to seek more appropriate schooling options'.

Learning support is provided for within the school fees 'in just the same way that we provide scholars with additional support within the fees,' says Mr Taylor. Three learning support teachers provide 'withdrawn' and 'in class' support. As the school is selective, we feel it probably isn't the best place for anything more than mild dyslexia. However, one parent of a child with a more severe learning difficulty said they had felt 'incredibly supported' and that the school had been 'very realistic and ready for the challenge.' There is also support for those at the top end of the academic spectrum.

The performing arts centre is the venue for all music and drama lessons and performances – a thriving and important part of the school, the 540 individual performing arts lessons a week attest to this. One parent said the standard of the performing arts is 'mind-blowingly good' and one of the major strengths of the school. Head of music, Lotte Lush (we couldn't have made up such a wonderful name if we had tried), is universally praised for her enthusiastic approach, and ensures that rappers as well as classical musicians are all part of the musical experience here. Annual 'Party in the Park' performance, lots of tours, ensembles and CDs. Tiny little chapel, which is rather sweet and still used regularly for choral performances, but sadly too small for the whole school to fit into. The self-contained art room is stuffed to the gunwales with super artwork, models, masks and still life. Sport is important here, the teams more than hold their own and, according to Mr Taylor, the school 'punches above its weight in sport' with a raft of successes under its belt. Massive sports hall and lovely grounds with a nice complement of pitches and hard courts. Nearly all pupils play tennis, which is very strong. No pool – the children use the leisure centre in Haslemere, but that doesn't seem to bother most people. All sports are compulsory and there are fixtures for everyone including the B and C teams. Huge choice of extra-curricular activities including all the usuals and many more, including funky modern dance and big band.

Pastoral care generally has been complimented by parents as 'a natural part of the way things are at Amesbury'. Teachers are on hand to talk things through and Mr Taylor is universally praised for his availability if there's a problem. He happily gives out his mobile number if parents need to chat – and 'the kids aren't scared of him,' added one dad. The children seem to be on very good terms with their teachers and Mr Taylor says one of the values the school cherishes most is 'mutual respect' – this certainly comes across. Tutor group system is felt to be good and meaningful, discipline is also palpable – the head told us that one boy who was a keen sportsman was told that he would be banned from matches unless his behaviour improved, a mind-sharpening experience by all accounts. Self-discipline and at the same time 'no overt discipline' are the mantras of the approach here – i.e. responsibility is placed on the pupil for their own behaviour, and the approach seems to work. Bullying and the other nasties of school life are out in the open and discussed as part of a positive PSHE programme. Mr Taylor says, 'when bullying happens, the victim doesn't necessarily want the bully to be punished, they want the bullying to stop – the child in real need of real help is usually the bully.'

Innovative house system whereby the house names change every year (the children think of the names, for example, the white wolves and the raging bulls – you get the picture) and pupils are mixed around each year also so that there isn't a sense that they are always in the losing house, which may become a self-fulfilling prophecy. The houses compete for the bison trophy, modelled on the dining hall's stuffed version (as above), which is legendary and one of the school's icons.

Amesbury is now a hugely flourishing place. Parents tend to be more low key and less ostentatious than at some other schools (but make no mistake, there are oodles of parental money here). There are the ubiquitous Chelsea tractors (a number owned by the exiting Londoners), but they vie for places in the car park with beaten up Volvos owned by parents who could run around in 4x4s but choose not to do so. As Mr Taylor says, 'they want to be discreet and not to define themselves by their wealth or by the fact that they send their children to an independent school'. And (illustrating he can take our comments in good spirit) he concludes, 'probably due to the head being "streetwise" rather than "posh".'

Appleford School

Elston Lane, Shrewton, Nr Salisbury, Wiltshire, SP3 4HL

• Pupils: 70 boys, 15 girls, most boarding with limited day places • Ages: 7-14 • Inter-denominational • Fees: Day £15,081; Boarding £22,131 pa • Independent

Tel: 01980 621 020
Fax: 01980 621 366
Email: secretary@appleford.wilts.sch.uk
Website: www.appleford.wilts.sch.uk

Head: Since September 2009, Mrs Lesley Nell, formerly head of Orchard Close, junior school to Sibford school. Trained at Bedford College of physical education, Homerton College Cambridge and University of East Anglia. She is a former Scottish lacrosse international player.

Entrance: At any age from 7 to 14, from anywhere, but must have English as a first language. Very occasionally a pupil will start in last term of Year 2 (age 6+) and a few pupils stay on into Year 9. They will then repeat the year at their senior school. Prospective pupils asked to spend whole day at the school (overnight if planning to board) during which they attend lessons and are informally assessed in reading, spelling and maths while their attitude to learning and to their peers is also checked. A wide range of abilities and needs: some with severe dyslexia, others may end up performing above their chronological age in some subjects. All new entrants are internally assessed and each child is given their own multi-sensory Individual Education Plan. Currently 12 pupils with statements but only six funded by their LEAs. No pupils with special physical needs but the school would strive to accommodate.

Exit: At 13 the majority of pupils return to mainstream education at schools such as Clayesmore, Milton Abbey, Shiplake, Millfield and St David's College. Some pupils who still need whole school provision move on to e.g. Mark College, Shapwick, More House or Northease Manor. Appleford hosts a Schools Day every two years to assist parents in making decisions about future schooling.

Remarks: Small, specialist school for boys and girls with dyslexia and associated learning difficulties e.g. dyspraxia and ADHD (CReSTeD Category now SP). Full national curriculum – core subjects taught before lunch every day by specialist teachers with SpLD qualifications. This same staff teaches other subjects after lunch, so the specialist approach reaches across the curriculum and even into the pastoral care and boarding. Teacher:pupil ratio is approximately 1:8 supported by a team of classroom assistants, an educational psychologist, speech and language and occupational therapists – on site. Prep sessions are built into the day, supervised by the teacher who set the work. Two further sessions in the evenings for seniors. All pupils take SATs tests annually for information only – results not submitted. School reports issued in December and July provide parents with their child's national curriculum levels. Appleford received very good 2006 OfSTED report.

Every child participates in the school musical production and more than 60 per cent learn a musical instrument in free time, mainly drums, which work a treat for co-ordination problems. In 2006, school took part in Devizes Eisteddfod. Good art area with particularly impressive pottery and ceramics. Carpeted (!) sports hall also used for assembly. Lots of games and sports: rugby, soccer, cricket, netball, pop lacrosse, trampolining, tennis and swimming; judo and riding as extras. Teams are fielded against local preps – this can be thorny for the girls given their numbers; as at most schools for dyslexia, boys outnumber girls 6:1. Loads of special theme days, school trips, outward bound, camping experiences etc add sparkle to the curriculum. Daily activity period between 4 and 5pm for extra sport, art, gardening, computing etc. Conversational French is taught to the older children and there is a day trip to France each year.

Founded in 1988 in outskirts of tiny Wiltshire village – will never make a bundle on drive-by trade – but Salisbury only 12 miles away. Mellow grey stone main house with sympathetically designed additions. The small assemblage of buildings feels homey and almost picturesque, with red phone box in foreground. Traditional feel, with rules clear and firm, and children not hurtling towards adulthood. Not a school that falls prostrate before technology. Pupils may use laptops in upper years, but not a lot do. Two good computer rooms and four interactive whiteboards; teachers focus on helping youngsters develop their handwriting as well as their typing speed. Inviting, well-stocked library. Appleford is curiously low profile but new website and literature – all very good – are helping to put this school on the map.

Happy boarders and the boarding side is a definite strength of the school. Rooms kept beautifully tidy and orderly – all part of the programme and there are photographs on the wall to help children visualise how their things should be arranged. Dormitories a bit stuffy though – fresh air would help here, as in much of the school. Majority of boarders are weekly and may go home at 4pm on Friday and come back on Monday morning (or Sunday night). Some local flexi-boarding. Around 10 full boarders – NB mainly boys – are taken on major outings on Saturdays but mooch around after church on Sundays.

The parents we spoke to had all washed up at Appleford in a state of desperation, having tried various mainstream and specialist options. All of them gushed with praise for the school, particularly citing the confidence it had given their youngsters. A fine school all round and, for many children, the answer.

Ardingly College Prep School

Linked to Ardingly College in the Senior section

Haywards Heath, Haywards Heath, West Sussex, RH17 6SQ

• Pupils: 240 in the Prep school and 110 in the Pre-Prep • Ages: 2.5-7 in the Pre-Prep and 7-13 in the Prep school • C of E • Fees: Day £9,975-£12,660; Weekly Boarding +£3,750; Pre Prep £6,960 pa • Independent

Tel: 01444 893 200
Fax: 01444 8932001
Email: registrar@ardingly.com
Website: www.ardingly.com

Head: Since 2007, Mr Chris Calvey BEd (late thirties), educated at Bearwood College, then (now defunct) Westminster College, Oxford. Comes from a family of teachers but initially worked in the world of finance. Housemaster at Feltonfleet School in Cobham, then deputy head at Bishopsgate Preparatory School, Englefield Green. Married to Nicola, who teaches English and French in the prep school. They have two boys aged seven and four. Interests include running, squash, golf, photography, cooking and reading.

Head of Pre-Prep: Since 2010; Mrs Nawrocka BSc (Hons) MSc (late forties), started her career as a radiographer and worked for many years in higher education as a university lecturer before taking a PGCE in primary education. Taught in both the state and private sector before joining the pre-prep this year. Is a passionate reader and dog walker.

Entrance: Interview with the head and an assessment during a taster day.

Exit: All pupils sit Common Entrance in Year 8. They proceed to the senior school.

Remarks: Lower school actually in two: pre-prep 'Farmhouse' in old farm buildings takes from two-and-a-half to seven, prep school in wing of main building, from seven to 13 – all integrated into one 'college'. Prep has excellent performing arts studio, strong music and much specialist subject teaching. Uses main school sports, music and other facilities but pretty self-contained otherwise. Weekly boarding and casual flexi-boarding available. Daily games, very secure site, parents met at end of day by head. Good, popular after-school activities, some until 7pm to help busy parents. 'My school,' announced unprompted 11-year old, 'is exceptional. They have helped me hugely even though I'm not sporty, and it's very good academically and musically too.' Parents agree, 'They produce all-round individuals rather than hothousing them.' This school is on the up.

Ardvreck School

Gwydyr Road, Crieff, Perthshire, Crieff, Perthshire, PH7 4EX

• Pupils: 150 (90 boys 60 girls); 100 board, 50 day. No weekly or flexi boarding; 9 in pre-prep department • Ages: 4-13 (including Little Ardvreck) • Inter-denom • Fees: Boarding £16,995; Day £11,310; Pre-Prep £5,298 pa • Independent

Tel: 01764 653112
Fax: 01764 654920
Email: office@ardvreck.org.uk
Website: www.ardvreckschool.co.uk

Headmaster: Since 2008, Mr Peter Sutton AKC BD MTh (forties); has had a whizz bang career since leaving Fettes where he was head of school (he started life at New Park Prep School and still holds the British Prep Schools' 400 metre record). Post Sandhurst he was commissioned into the Black Watch, thence to St Andrew's University via King's College London, to read divinity on an army scholarship, thence chaplain to Loretto, head of department at The Perse, followed by Gordonstoun in 2000. Married to Dr Isabelle Crawford BSc MB ChB MRCGP (a French Californian who ended up at Marlborough College – she is known as Mrs Sutton); they met whilst undergraduates at St Andrew's. He proposed on the end of the pier and was accepted 'on condition that they had at least six children'! Three of his five daughters are at Ardvreck with the eldest at Fettes. Very keen skiers, often to be found carrying out the winter locum chaplaincy at St Bernard's Church in Wengen. A Fellow at Trinity Hall, Cambridge, uses his research into children's spirituality to lecture nationally and in the States and currently advises the Scottish executive on how to deliver good corporate worship in the maintained school sector, but is actually quite well-balanced, despite all the above. As a Fettesian, he finds the strong bonds with Glenalmond slightly stick in his craw. He teaches general studies to third and fourth formers and reads 'the weekly story to the pre-prep on Friday afternoons'. Late news November 2010 was that Mr Sutton had announced his resignation.

New deputy headmaster appointed, Richard Harvey, from St Mary's Melrose. Ex-head of Belhaven School also welcomed onto the staff.]

Entrance: Via pre-prep but most come at eight. Boarding in the last year no longer compulsory but great majority do. Prospective pupils visit school, meet head and get a pupil tour, then spend a taster day in school (or overnight if boarding) wearing school uniform 'so they don't stick out'. Each child is issued with a 'school brother or sister'. They arrive at 10.30 and leave after lunch the following day. Head reports back to parents after feedback from staff.

Exit: This year a third went to Glenalmond with the rest to Eton, Fettes, Gordonstoun, Harrow, Kings Canterbury, Merchiston, St Mary's Calne and Strathallan. Impressive collection of awards and scholarships. Not really perceived as a prep for Eton, though currently 'four at the place', with a couple of others about to take their assessments.

Money Matters: Selection of academic scholarships on offer and bursary support available, subject to means test.

Remarks: Jolly popular. School founded in 1883 by former housemaster from nearby Glenalmond. Purpose-built with swimming pool (rather grand but in a polythene tent nonetheless) and a fairly ad hoc collection of classrooms (some a lot better than others) perched on 75 hilly acres (woods etc). Littlest Ardvreckers all together at one end of the hog's back – rows of green wellies. Younger boarders live in main house (different floors) in a motley collection of cosy rooms; top two years live in his'n'hers chalets 'to prepare them for public school'. Fairly scruffy common rooms, selected television only, no Wiis for the younger boarders, whose mobiles are handed out when needed. Older girls can and do their own washing, stay abed late on Sundays – boys apparently watch Match of the Day at 8am ... Dorms filled with climbing boots and rucksacks, school does three mini Barvicks each summer term. Fixed exeat every third weekend, Friday noon to 10.15 on Mondays (but school 'not inflexible' to requests). Parents particularly pleased that this is a proper boarding school and not a day school with weekly sleepovers, consequently popular with the army, diplomatic core as well as traditional parents (though some find the Friday and Monday collection and delivery a tad tiresome). Day pupils stay till 6pm and usually try to board eventually (their choice).

Impressive weekend programme (parents and pupils confirm that there 'isn't time to get bored'); bonfire building practice the Sunday before our visit, which coincided with grandparent day (a tough, fairly toffish lot, some of whom fill in for expat parents). We spent 20 rainy minutes in mid-March hearing notices, observing the flag being raised and listening to the junior pipe band (senior boys on a rugby toot to Oundle) play Highland Cathedral followed by croissants, choccy spread and coffee. The young were in (their family) kilts and green jerseys. Not really a first-time buyer school and really quite Scottish. Parents 'a close-knit group of families', with pupils 'tending to remain friends well into middle age' and beyond.

A splendid child-oriented school. Class sizes 15/16, no streaming, though maths is taught in sets. Two parallel CE classes in sixth, plus scholarship class and lots of scholarships and awards, but no honours board ('the only honours board we have is our war memorial'). Head of learning support plus three pick up both the bright and those with dyslexia et al, three student teachers help in class. One hour at one-to-one, plus one hour group sessions are free, thereafter £20 per hour. Keyboarding skills on offer and computers for teaching maths and English as well as more traditional teaching; French from five, lyrical artroom. Latin, Spanish a post CE option. New Expressive Arts Centre opened by Turner shortlisted Scottish artist Nathan Coley. Seriously strong orchestra – 40 play at assembly each Friday. Singing and drama outstanding – school regularly features in the ribbons at the Perth Festival, and orchestra now plays on a Thursday assembly. Outstanding on the games front-all sports, all comers, though parents from other schools have been heard to mutter about trying too hard (still). Head wants us to add that he is a 'keen sportsman, but equally keen that all pupils get a chance to collect team kit from matron, welcome visiting teams and host them at match teas'. New sports inclusion policy introduced (not sure what that means) and going down well – 'School continues to thrive on games field but not at the expense of sports for all'. Our earlier comment is unchanged. Games pitches fairly well scattered on the flatter areas. New combo-hall, with carpentry below, all singing and dancing above, cunningly perched on really quite a steep slope. Four tennis courts, three netball courts, hockey pitch, Astroturf and shooting range.

Arnold House School

1 Loudoun Road, St John's Wood, London, NW8 0LH

• Pupils: 250 boys, all day • Ages: 5-13 • C of E, but all are welcome
• Fees: £14,700 pa • Independent

Tel: 020 7266 4840
Fax: 020 7266 6994
Email: headmaster@arnoldhouse.co.uk
Website: www.arnoldhouse.co.uk

Head: Since 2006, Mr Vivian Thomas (early fifties). Educated at University College School, Hampstead, where he excelled at sport, then on to St Luke's College Exeter, to specialise in PE and history. Taught PE and maths at UCS, then at the Caracas American International School in Venezuela. Returned to England as head of maths and senior master at Arnold House, followed by five years as head at Keble Prep, Winchmore Hill. A soothing and confident presence, still keen on history and sport, regularly joining in football practice to get to know the younger boys. Married to Rowena.

Entrance: Register between first and second birthday, followed by a viewing at one of three open evenings held in the summer term. Parents who wish to proceed are invited in for a chat 'to find out what they're hoping for'. Boys assessed on an individual basis at rising four. 'We're not interested in creaming off an academic élite,' says the head, 'but we do try and assess whether we'd like to teach the child. Once we've taken on a boy, as long as he's happy and making progress, that's our commitment.' Reasonably broad ability range. 'We're not just sending boys to the London day schools but to top-flight and other boarding schools as well, which means we choose not to be overly selective.' Around 250 families register for entry each year. Typically, 150 sets of parents will see the admissions process through to its conclusion for one of the 38 places available. Siblings given preference, Old Boys' offspring looked on favourably. Some space later on for boys 'who'd fit in comfortably'.

Exit: Sixty per cent to London schools – St Paul's, Westminster, Highgate, UCS, City of London, Mill Hill – the rest to boarding. 'It needs to be the right fit and we spend a lot of time finding a school where the boy is going to thrive.' Fairly broad intake means fairly broad exit. 'Some will have to work hard to get a Common Entrance pass of 50–55 per cent, but overall last year 83 per cent were awarded As and Bs in scholarship and Common Entrance.' Still very much a 13-plus school. 'Our parents are comfortable with what we're trying to achieve.'

OBs include Sir Jonathon Porritt, Sir Jonathan Miller, Sir Crispin Tickell, Sir John Tavener, Lord Ackner and Lord Wolfson.

Remarks: Housed in three decorative, neatly-kept buildings behind secure gates in a quiet St John's Wood side street. Founded in 1905 in the existing buildings, but renovated and re-designed in 1999, so has an airy, modern feel inside. The school is small and intimate and the head knows all boys by name. Very strong sense of community and the desire to produce all-rounders. 'Yes, of course we're driven by academics but there's an equal emphasis on what they're like as people.' Lively house system, with points gained for effort, attitude and industry as well as courtesy, conduct and politeness. 'It's a very nurturing environment with the accent always on the positive,' enthuses one mother.

Thirty-six boys in early years, with two parallel classes of 18. Numbers tend to shrink over time with London's peripatetic population and Year 8 can be as few as 24. Juniors from Years 1–4, seniors from Years 5–8, when all teaching becomes specialist. Three teaching assistants, including specialist maths support. French from Year 1, Latin from Year 5. Setting in maths from Year 4, in Latin and French in Years 7 and 8. No scholarship form but scholarship potential identified in Year 7 and given appropriate extra sessions. First class teaching, particularly in the senior school, and a common room that seems to get on unusually well.

Good special needs department, which has moved from pulling out those who need help to offering support within the classroom. Will also suggest outside help if that's the most appropriate way to go. Two homeworks a day, but head very anti homework stress. 'We have a very, very busy day and there's no point getting in a terrible tizzy of angst and fear. We want boys to go home, do their homework and still have time to themselves.' Music a great strength – 'the best in London,' commented one parent, 'especially the jazz' – with music scholarships aplenty. By Year 3, 85 per cent studying one instrument, by Year 4 many have added a second. Two music lessons a week, with music technology, composition and recording technique taught in a modern recording suite. Orchestra, jazz band, woodwind ensembles. Splendid art room, with proper studio skylight. Thriving after-school clubs from Chinese and Ju-jitsu to digital photography and chess, with each member of staff making a contribution each term.

On-site sports facilities limited to decent-sized London playground and smallish gym, but the school also owns a fabulous seven-acre site – 'Arnold House in the country' – at Canons Park in Stanmore, used for sport, field studies, and performances. A recent £1.8m refurbishment created new changing facilities, a field-study room and 180-seat theatre for music, concerts and plays. Younger children go by coach, Years 7 and 8 by tube. Two games periods a week. Football, hockey and rugby in the winter; tennis and cricket in the summer. Also regular 'Canons Park days' to plant trees or have snowball fights.

Discipline based on kindness and courtesy. 'We appeal to the boys' better instincts. They know very clearly what we expect and that we will follow it up if they fall below that. You don't want 233 rules. You treat others as you wish to be treated – everything follows from there.' Christian values, assembly and traditions – grace said at lunch – though all welcome. Parents mainly local, and then from Islington, Hampstead and west London. Significant number of Old Boys' offspring.

'It's a fantastic little school,' says one parent, who has seen three boys go happily through. 'Old-fashioned, but in a very nice way. It seems the opposite of so many London schools, which test all the time. It's very relaxed, but they still get a very good education.'

A calm and nurturing school with a rich education, which brings out the best in most pupils.

Arnold Junior School

Linked to Arnold School in the Senior section

Lytham Road, Blackpool, FY4 1JG

• Pupils: Kindergarten: 45, 20 boys, 25 girls; Infants: 70, 35 boys, 35 girls; Junior: 155, 80 boys, 75 girls • Ages: 2-11 • Non denom but with Christian ethos • Fees: £6,831 pa • Independent

Tel: 01253 346 391
Fax: 01253 336 251
Email: info@arnoldschool.com
Website: www.arnoldschool.com

Head: Since January 2010, Miss Kate Wright, previously deputy head of Cheadle Hulme Junior School.

Remarks: Enters children for internally assessed tests at KS2: 94 per cent reach level four or above in English, 100 per cent in maths and 98 per cent in science. The kindergarten has a mix of activities and learning. Very young children (under three) follow the nationally established foundation stage curriculum, which is play-based. Particular attention is given to matching activities with differing abilities and starting points of learning.

Infant pupils follow the national curriculum. A specialist ICT teacher provides dedicated lessons; the usual history and geography topic-based study as well as art and design, music, PSHE, PE and French, again taught by a specialist. At junior level, the emphasis is on English, maths, science and ICT, and in two of these – English and maths – the pupils are put in sets based on ability. Other subjects covered include history, geography, design technology, art and design, music, French, PSHE, religious education and games.

Little Arnold pupils are in uniform (albeit a simple one) from their arrival. Class sizes are small: around 20 in infant classes and 23 in juniors. In juniors they have a wide choice of after-school and breaktime clubs – from brass ensemble to cross-country to gardening. Many trips in this country and abroad – skiing in the Alps, history trips to Normandy and exchange trips to a French school in Lyon. Great emphasis is placed on making children in the infant and junior schools feel part of the Arnold 'family'.

Ashdell Preparatory School

266 Fulwood Road, Sheffield, South Yorkshire, S10 3BL

• Pupils: Prep: 90 girls, all day; Snowdrops: 25 boys and girls • Ages: Prep: 4-11; Snowdrops: 2-3 • C of E • Fees: £7,770-£8,295 pa • Independent

Tel: 0114 266 3835
Fax: 0114 267 1762
Email: headteacher@ashdellprep.co.uk
Website: www.ashdellprep.co.uk

Headteacher: Since April 2008, Mrs Anne Camm (fifties), educated at Princess Gardens School, Belfast, Trent Park College of Ed (now Middlesex University) and Bristol University. Taught at Kirkinriola Primary School, Co Antrim, class teacher and housemistress at Cabin Hill Prep School, Belfast and Edgarley Hall, Millfield prep school, before becoming head of Birkdale School's pre-prep, Sheffield. Married to Peter, in property; Lisa (18) and Olivia (16). Does some teaching.

Entrance: The school looks for confident, mature girls of at least above average IQ. Initial pre-prep entry by informal assessment; maths and English tests after that. 12 per cent have bursaries.

Exit: Mostly to Sheffield High with a small number to local state schools.

Remarks: Attractively decorated Victorian houses with well-tended small-scale gardens, including a lily pond, and thoughtfully designed asphalt play areas – pre-prep has three wendy houses and prep a climbing wall. Classrooms spacious, bright, light and well equipped, particularly for practical subjects; plenty of displays of good work and photographs of school activities in the corridors. Well-stocked library; all girls learn to touch type; 'Fabulous IT,' commented a parent.

Academic standards high, classes small (maximum 18, can be as low as 11); regular testing and an atmosphere of enthusiastic, disciplined learning in the classrooms; specialist teaching builds up over the years and offered throughout in ICT, sport and creative/practical subjects. The very able receive a separate stimulating programme delivered by staff specialists for half a term/year. Special needs girls receive extra support (no extra charges; all pre-prep children screened for dyslexia) and care taken to nurture every pupil's self esteem – emotional intelligence taken seriously, as is awareness of different learning styles, encouragement of creativity and independent learning and girls taking responsibility for enterprises. Woodwork, textiles and cookery timetabled. School dinners (made on premises) excellent.

Lots of music, in the lunch hour and after school (though girls mostly encouraged to use the lunch hour for outdoor play) – all learn the recorder and keyboard; orchestra for all plus choirs and instrumental groups. Other after-school clubs popular and plentiful. Girls compete against local schools in a variety of sports; everyone has a chance to play in a team.

Only a few obviously ethnic minority children but girls come from a mixture of cultures/countries and levels of incomes, three per cent having bursaries. Pupils confident, happy and enthusiastic. The uniform – dark red blazers, summer boaters and winter grey felt hats, and even red schoolbags – bespeaks the school's traditional leanings, but it has been brought tactfully into the 21st century. Teachers know the girls well and talk openly to parents. A protected, very well-endowed little world for bright responsive girls, but not so much for those of a less conventional or tractable turn of mind.

Ashdown House School

Forest Row, East Sussex, RH18 5JY

• Pupils: 70 boys, 75 girls; some day in the early years; nearly all board for last three but very few hold out that long • Ages: 7-13 • C of E services but with wide ecumenical base • Fees: £14,550-£21,570 pa • Independent

Tel: 01342 822 574
Fax: 01342 824 380
Email: secretary@ashdownhouse.com
Website: www.ashdownhouse.co.uk

Headmaster: Since 2009, Mr Dominic Floyd, previously deputy head and director of studies at Polwhele House, Cornwall. He and his wife Maria were in charge of boarding at Cothill House before that. Grew up at The Dragon School – the fourth headmaster in his family, going back to his great grandfather. Maria oversees the pastoral and domestic side here. Two children (eight and six).

Entrance: At seven by meeting child and parents – everyone participates in 'an honest appraisal'. At 10–11 some testing in core subjects, but the main assessment is still by interview and the applicant may be invited to spend 24 hours at the school.

Exit: All children to first choice schools, which are rarely local – Benenden, Eton, Downe House, King's Canterbury, Radley, Tonbridge, Wellington, Harrow, Marlborough, Winchester and Wycombe Abbey are particularly popular. Mr Floyd sees it as vital to find the right school for each pupil – he knows the head and the registrar of each school and also has a useful resource of friends teaching at boarding schools throughout the country.

Remarks: The main house is Greek revival, designed in 1793 by Benjamin Henry Latrobe – a year later he moved to the US where he was responsible for the building of the Capitol and White House ('It looks just like Ashdown,' commented a pupil's friend as they drove through Washington – she'd apparently no idea of the architectural link!). It's elegant but looks well-loved and well-used (architecture buffs would be attracted to the nearby and more accessible Latrobe building, Hammerwood Park) – the duty master's bike propped by the portico, kids' pottery on shelves between the graceful columns and little legs racing out through it to play on the (huge) 'Patch' of grass in front. This easy freedom is one of the defining features of Ashdown, but there is also a formal structure, well padded by the characters of teachers and pupils – and confidence is not bred at the expense of manners.

'Academically very robust and they are getting the kids to do it themselves, to become independent thinkers' – the results back up this parent's judgement. Scholarships won every year to chief public schools. A newly catalogued library with an open fire and quiet time after lunch every day – the whole school settles down and sits in the theatre for half an hour, to rest and read. Dyslexia and dyspraxia fine, but these coupled with a low IQ would be a no-no. Everyone does Latin here. SEN provided in the Log Cabin with one full-time and two part-time staff, some EFL, and laptops for dyslexics. The three science labs in The Jungle Block are brilliantly equipped (and have table footie and tennis on the ground floor) with a huge pond (between the jungle and the block) for collecting and exploring. Guinea pigs, a goat pen, rabbits, fish, chickens, a newly planted orchard, more vegetable plots and a wild meadow, to encourage awareness of the environment and sustainability. Input from Natural History Museum experts. A five mile speed limit on the drive for fear of 'children the size of Yorkshire terriers tearing out of bushes and swinging down from trees'! With the stunning grounds to race about in and sport on the timetable every day, the children are fit enough to ski from nine to five on their family ski holidays!

The staff are really committed here – many of them live on site (very convenient for London and southern England exploits) and those who don't still devote an enormous amount of time in loco parentis to these children – sport, plays, mucking around. One teacher, who's been there 18 years and came from a local grammar school, comments, 'Here I can teach, which I love. There's such great feedback.' Activities are often unstructured – a teacher might join a group in their choice of play – 'What time is it, Mr Wolf?', firemaking, an expedition to the heffalump trap, showing off his snakes after prep – we also heard of a fantastic outing to Plumpton races where everyone had a flutter! Every year will go on a residential trip to broaden their education, e.g. the little ones to the Lake District (reading Swallows and Amazons), the leavers to survival training on a Scottish island. Under the governance of the Cothill Trust, every child in their penultimate year spends a term at Château Sauveterre soaking up Pyrennean culture, markets and skiing, with lessons entirely in French.

Sports teams are very successful – e.g. football, rugby, netball (three senior teams in the National Championships), hockey, cricket (barn with indoor nets as well as carefully rolled pitches), rounders, athletics, swimming – but you don't need to be brilliant to have a go; the same goes for music and drama. About nine drama productions a year, so every child will get involved –'They're very good at rejoicing in each other's achievements,' say parents. (Lots of friendships across years, not just because of siblings.) You can practise music all around the school – drum kits and pianos on landings and in lecture theatres; a creative head of music – performances designed to tweak interest (Für Elise on bells?).

Discipline is relaxed on the small things (bookbags in tidy piles etc) but with a core of moral courage – children will own up to misdemeanours, mostly because of peer pressure and guidance from the elder children (dorm captains, heads of school, heads of patrol, prefects). In the back of every calendar are the guidelines for boys and girls, which begin, 'All rules are dictated by commonsense and the need to look after each other well, living together as we do in the same community'. Add to those the head's three rules, 'Be kind, be kind, be kind'. Enough said. Breaking into the computer system or being hideously unkind to another child might be punished by suspension; this and anything less serious would be worked out between parents and staff.

Five boarding 'landings' (these don't correspond to the patrols – Elks, Hippos, Kangs and Rhinos) upstairs in the main house, each with computer for emails and TV for DVDs, with dorm captains, house parents and nurses. These landing staff are crucial – parents will trust the school on academic matters, although some would welcome more frequent informal communication about current subjects to allow them to ask questions of children and arrange linked activities out of school. However, it is their children's well-being that they're most concerned with. The pastoral side is exemplary – if you can use that cold adjective to describe the friendly, relaxed and flexible care – from nosebleeds, through phonecards (no mobiles) to Sunday evening letter-writing. Homesickness is fleeting. Relationships and experiences prioritised over facilities, which is a defence against charges of old-fashioned and well-worn dorms.

One third local (within an hour of school), one third London (hedge-funders, management consultants, bankers) and one third ex-pat children (Hong Kong, Cayman Islands, Singapore – lots of Foreign Office); no weekly or flexi-boarding. Lots of word of mouth recommendations, especially in Hong Kong and Cayman Islands. Many locals come in from Fonthill Lodge – mothers (including Maria Floyd) with younger siblings share a school run before the older ones board (they want to as soon as possible). Affluent but relaxed families – parents turn up to matches, plays and to experience the leavers' Fairy Liquid foam slide! Ex-pupils include Boris Johnson, Rachel Johnson (Daily Telegraph), Damian Lewis, Nicholas Coleridge and Viscount Linley.

The children are obviously happy here and the local community find them really nice as well – no ivory tower. 'Ashdown is like the real world – you've got to get stuck in and experience things,' says a parent – we wish the real world was more like Ashdown ...

Ashfold School

Dorton House, Dorton, Buckinghamshire, HP18 9NG

• Pupils: 250 (150 boys, 100 girls); 5 weekly boarders but 80 per cent of 9-13 year olds board some nights every week • Ages: 3-13 • Christian • Fees: Pre-prep £3,285-£9,405; Prep £12,900; Weekly boarding £15,075 pa • Independent

Tel: 01844 238 237
Fax: 01844 238 505
Email: katrina.hartley@ashfoldschool.co.uk
Website: www.ashfoldschool.co.uk

Headmaster: Since 1997, Mr Michael Chitty BSc (late forties). Educated at Clifton College, Bristol, then read economics at Exeter before following father and grandfather into army. During nine years' service travelled extensively, reached rank of captain in Queen's Royal Irish Hussars and appointed equerry to Prince Philip. Bitten by the teaching bug when posted to Sandhurst as officer instructor. Resigned commission and moved to Stowe, where taught politics and economics and was housemaster.

Head-hunted to reverse failing fortunes at Ashfold and has had huge impact on the place. Energetic, enthusiastic and caring. Hits floor running when faced with new challenge. Great supporter of co-education (girls now make up 40 per cent of pupils) and benefits of boarding. Firmly believes that school should 'develop every child's potential'. No longer teaches (taught maths when first arrived) but highly visible around school – on games pitches, in classrooms and chatting to staff and pupils. Commands respect throughout school. Well-liked by parents – he's even introduced a room where parents can wait for their children and chat over a cup of tea. Clearly loves the place. 'Why would I leave?' he asks. 'I'm here to stay.' Married to barrister wife Louise, with daughter and son at university. Like many of the staff, lives in house on school site.

Entrance: Non-selective. Prospective pupils invited to visit school for assessment only. 'It's important that the child is placed in the right form and that parents are sure they've made the right choice,' says head. Waiting lists for pre-prep places, so best to get names down early.

Exit: Head puts a lot of time and effort into helping parents choose children's next schools. At 13, pupils leave for a wide range of destinations, with Magdalen College School, Rugby, St Edward's, Stowe, Headington, Bloxham, Rye St Antony, Abingdon consistently popular. Over a third of form 6 gain scholarships regularly (39 per cent in 2010). A few to local grammars too.

Remarks: School originally founded in 1927 and moved to present site in rolling Buckinghamshire countryside in 1956. Stunning Jacobean mansion set in 30 acres of grounds (lots of space for children to run off energy). School has flourished since arrival of present head and pupil numbers have almost doubled, although head 'wants to stay small and won't go above 290'. Pupils don't sit SATs so school won't be found in national league tables, but most recent ISI inspection (2006) found levels of attainment at the ages of seven and 11 were above, sometimes well above, the national average. As head declared during our last visit: 'How do you measure confidence, kindness and enthusiasm?'

Class sizes small. Average is 14 and never more than 18. No setting till the last two years. All pupils do ICT (there are 100 networked PCs across school), French from age of seven and Latin from nine. New science block opened in 2008 and pupils clearly very enthused by the science teaching. Lots of interaction in lessons. When we visited, one group was acting out the water cycle (complete with rainbow-coloured costumes) while another class watched with bated breath as a teacher demonstrated the principles of static electricity using balloons and a sprinkling of sugar. Library in main building has been refurbished and stocks 6,300 books. School has just introduced innovative reading groups for children and their parents – so young and old can discuss books together (Michael Morpurgo's *Why the Whales Came* one of the first choices).

Junior department housed in wing of main house while most senior department lessons take place in recently-renovated courtyard classrooms and whitewashed, single-storey building known as the 'Shippon'. Classrooms have own computer and interactive whiteboards. Limited number of scholarships (up to 30 per cent of fees) available for pupils 'who show outstanding academic, artistic, sporting, musical or all-round ability'. Screening at age seven for dyslexia and other learning difficulties – both for new and existing pupils. Around 27 pupils with mild SpLD, dyslexia or dyspraxia. In-class support and small group work with a learning support assistant free. One-to-one lessons with one of school's two SEN specialists £31 per hour. No Saturday morning school.

Around 80 per cent of pupils learn a musical instrument or take singing lessons. All Year 1s and 2s learn the violin. Three choirs, two string and one brass, clarinet, flute and guitar ensembles plus school orchestra. Chapel choir trip to Rome in 2008 ('We sang in St Peter's,' one chorister told us proudly). Art fantastic – everything from pastoral landscapes to surrealism adorning the walls of the busy first-floor art studio. 'By the end of the year you can't see the walls at all,' smiled the head of art, who teaches every year group. Lots going on in drama too – recent productions of *The Pirates of Penzance* and *Twelfth Night* for the older pupils, Roald Dahl's *Goldilocks and the Three Bears* for the younger ones.

Impressive new pre-prep building, with light, airy classrooms opening on to outside play areas, opened two years ago – with dynamic department head at helm (she began her teaching career at Ashfold and the present head invited her back). 'The fabric of the building has changed but not the atmosphere,' she says. 'That's what brought me back here. My philosophy is that if pre-prep children are having fun and enjoying school, they will learn.'

Prep children play sport every afternoon – hockey, netball, rounders, athletics, swimming and tennis for girls and rugby, hockey, football, cricket, athletics, swimming and tennis for boys. Facilities impressive for a school of this size – full-sized Astroturf, heated outdoor pool, adventure playground. New (and very wholesome) changing rooms alongside the large, bracing sports hall. School holds its own on the sports fields, even against much bigger rivals – runners-up in national clay shooting for last three years and one pupil is member of England's under 13 squash team, as well as ranked in top five players in Europe.

Strongly Christian but accepts other denominations. Rightfully proud of its pastoral care. Bullying taken very seriously by staff but children say there isn't any safe boxes posted around school so pupils can flag up anything that's worrying them. House system in place – Lions, Dragons and Gryphons – with lots of eagerly-contested competitions. Pupils win credits for good work (and debits for misdemeanours). House with most credits wins cup and treated to a feast. Sixth-form prefects, with head boy and head girl appointed in the autumn term. Traditional burgundy and bottle green uniform, with different ties for scholars, choir, prefects etc.

School day starts with assembly in impressive wood-panelled 'saloon' or the pretty village church, which is in the school grounds. Pupils sit at long wooden tables for lunch, each with a teacher, who encourages good table manners and conversation. 'There is nothing worse than nagging about table manners,' says head, 'so we focus on one thing at a time.' School day ends at 5 or 6pm for prep pupils (they do homework before going home), 3.15pm for pre-prep (although crèche facilities available for working parents till 5pm). You certainly can't miss the start and end of lessons – Ashfold has the loudest school bell we've heard in a long time.

Boarding has made a real comeback here, with weekly boarding on offer from age of nine. School only has three pupils who board every night of the week but large numbers stay one or two nights a week to take full advantage of popular evening clubs and after-school activities – from drama and cookery to nature detectives and five-a-side football. Total of 40 beds for boarders. Average of 36 pupils a night board, signing up a term in advance. 'Ninety per cent of the children try boarding,' says head. 'We don't force boarding on them. It's a positive choice to opt in.' Husband-and-wife team – wife teaches at school – live in with their small daughter and look after boarders. Freshly-painted dorms on first floor of mansion – boys one end, girls the other, with a landing of creaky floorboards in between. Boarders aren't allowed to bring in mobile phones, iPods, PSPs etc – very popular move with parents. TV carefully monitored and lights out at 9.30pm. Boarders' cooked breakfasts a particular hit.

Ashfold pupils come from wide variety of backgrounds – some old money, some new. Most live within 30 minutes' drive of school. ISI report in 2006 commented that the children are 'a real credit' to the school – 'pleasantly self-confident, behave very well and are responsible members of the school community'. Praise indeed – and still very much the case. Ashfold continues to be a very happy, wholesome place. Not fiercely academic, but balanced across the board and gets good results. 'It's a warm, friendly, family, purposeful school that turns out nice, well-balanced, confident children,' says head. The pupils agree.

Ashford Friars Preparatory School

Linked to Ashford School in the Senior section

Great Chart, Ashford, Kent, TN23 3DJ

• Pupils: 175 in the pre-prep on the Ashford site. 165 in the prep school at Great Chart. 50:50 boys:girls • Ages: 3-11 • Christian, but all faiths welcome • Fees: £6,081-£10,290 pa • Independent

Tel: 01233 620493
Fax: 01233 636579
Email: ashfordfriars@ashfordschool.co.uk
Website: www.ashfordschool.co.uk

Headmaster: Since 2001, Mr Richard Yeates (fiftyish). Joined Ashford as deputy head in 2000 and became headmaster a year later. Educated at Exeter University and The Royal College of Music. Previously director of music at King's Hall, Taunton and a housemaster at King's School, Taunton as well as being master in charge of the first XI cricket. His wife is head of the nursery at Ashford; they have three children, all now at university. Unassuming but quietly in control. Popular with parents and respected by the children; seen as very fair and good at including all the children.

Entrance: All children attend an assessment day but generally non-selective. Most join for the nursery or reception class, a few into Years 1 and 3 and whenever there is a space.

Exit: Most to the senior school at 11, admitted on recommendation (they expect children to have the potential to go to university). About 20 per cent a year to the grammars (parents and children given guidance on the Kent Test but not intensive tuition).

Remarks: Housed in the Old Rectory at Great Chart, a few miles outside Ashford. Spacious and comprehensive facilities of its own as well as those shared with the senior school. Generally does everything right and turns out sensible, well-balanced children. On-site playing fields, indoor heated swimming pool with learning pool, sports hall, tennis courts, theatre, science labs, technology lab, music room and modern learning resource centre.

Interactive whiteboards throughout. Injection of cash as a result of the merger – all classrooms refurbished a year ago and plans afoot to build more.

Attracts children from a wide range of backgrounds: local children, some from the maintained sector, others who have recently moved to the area, some children of foreign nationals – mostly European – who are working locally, plus some African families who have relocated from London.

Full time SENCo – early intervention policy; about 10 per cent of children need some sort of learning support, mainly through withdrawal from lessons for specialist help. Three parallel classes per year with an average class size of 14 and a maximum of 16. The children are setted from Year 4 in maths and English.

All the usual sports – boys do rugby, football, cricket, hockey and athletics; girls play touch rugby, netball, hockey, rounders and athletics. Biathlon a particular strength – an Ashford Friars team recently won the silver medal in the National Biathlon Championships. Triathlon recently introduced. The girls are particularly successful at cross-country running.

Lots of musical events – termly concerts, singing very strong. A big play once a year and smaller ones for year groups – each year group does something every year. Full range of lunchtime and after-school activities: windsurfing, fencing, chess, computer club – 35 activities in any one term. Activities are optional but most children participate in about three per week. Years 3–9 have cooking and healthy eating lessons which are tied in with science and PSHE.

No boarding on the Ashford Friars site but children from the age of 10 can board on the main school campus and come over on the shuttle bus. Good food cooked on site with a choice of hot meal and salad option. Cafeteria system – teachers sit amongst children to supervise manners etc.

Some matches and tournaments/sports day on Saturdays but no lessons. Over a third of children get involved in voluntary Saturday morning activities. The school day ends at 4pm followed by prep and activities; children can be looked after from 8am to 6pm to help working parents. Active parents' association – lots of social and fund-raising activities, e.g. fireworks, quizzes, Christmas fair.

Ashville Junior School

Linked to Ashville College in the Senior section

Green Lane, Harrogate, North Yorkshire, HG2 9JP

• Pupils: Prep: 160 boys and girls; pre-prep 90 boys and girls; boarding and day • Ages: Pre-prep: 4-7; prep 7-11 • Methodist • Fees: Pre Prep £6,435 pa; Prep £7,725-£9,345 pa • Independent

Tel: 01423 724 800
Fax: 01423 870 318
Email: v.birk@ashville.co.uk
Website: www.ashville.co.uk

Head: Since September 2008, Mr Jonathan Dolman, previously head of middle school and housemaster at New Hall School, Chelmsford. A geographer, keen cricketer and rugby coach; married to Clare, they have four daughters. Teaches geography and games across the school. Is particularly keen on the extra-curricular and is often seen running the cross-country club.

Entrance: Entry to pre-prep and junior school is by interview and assessment with the head of the school.

Exit: Majority to Ashville College, some to local state schools, handful to other independent schools.

Remarks: A cheerful and cosy environment. Pupils taught in form groups with specialist teaching in Spanish, French, music, science and ICT. All Year 4s learn the violin and interactive whiteboards bring a new dimension to lessons. More than 30 clubs from art, gardening and chess to dancing, orienteering and karate. The school council gives children an opportunity to make decisions sensibly on behalf of their peers. Recent push on academic standards, together with an innovative programme for gifted and talented children, having a good impact on results but no room for complacency – the competition from local state schools is fierce.

Pre-prep a purpose-built, happy, vibrant school. Pleasing inspection. Used to be popular with those unable to secure a place in the local high-achieving primary schools but now over-subscribed, with small class sizes a real draw to parents – no more than 15 children in reception.

Auchtergaven Primary School

Prieston Road, Bankfoot, Perth, Perth, PH1 4DE

• Pupils: 110 boys and girls; all day • Ages: 3-11 • State

Tel: 01738 787 227
Fax: 01738 787595
Email: headteacher@auchtergaven.pkc.sch.uk
Website: www.auchtergaven.pkc.sch.uk

Head: Since 2006, Mrs Frances Dean, who comes from North Muirton in Perth.

Entrance: The school is all-embracing, so children coming up from the nursery – as long as they are in the right catchment area – plus all-comers. Slight problems when children arrive in the area and their particular age group is full, but composite classes (i.e. more than one age group) are OK.

Exit: Usually at 11 to Perth Grammar or Breadalbane Academy (the two are equidistant). A very occasional pupil will head off to the independent sector.

Remarks: A stunning school – an earlier Victorian building which was much extended in 1999, with new windows and a totally modern feel. Max class size is in theory 24 – but it might be 25 or 33; SEN on board, but currently no problems. The school follows national guidelines. IT is rampant, wireless throughout, with two interactive whiteboards, masses of computers everywhere – even in the nursery – where we found a small girl totally engrossed, with ear-phones, on a serious computer. Flat screens abound, and there is a trolley of lap tops which motors round the school. The ICT programme includes keyboarding. French from ten, currently Gaelic at six; good sciences, school is piloting the new Perth and Kinross maths initiative. Strong, positive personal social development.

Has the occasional glitch with city (i.e. Perth) pupils being a trifle 'cityish', but bullying firmly sat upon. Weekly assemblies, where God is not totally omnipresent. Good parent back-up. Much involved in charity, collection boxes everywhere. Strong games ethos, with more than the regulation one period a week of PE. The netball team won the rural schools league. Loads of parental support, and a 'jolly supportive school board'. School is keen on eco-education and they are currently building a bog-garden, much use is made of the (very) local Scotswood for environmental studies. Cooked lunch comes in from Stanley, buffet-style, good dining-room. Loads of care. What more can you ask? Numbers noticeably down in 2006 – change of head?

Aysgarth School

Newton-le-Willows, Bedale, North Yorkshire, DL8 1TF

• Pupils: 125 boys in the prep school, 60 boys and girls in pre-prep and nursery; 90 per cent plus board in the prep school • Ages: 3-13 • Christian • Fees: Boarding £18,750; Day £14, 610; Pre-prep £5,880-£7,650 pa • Independent

Tel: 01677 450 240
Fax: 01677 450 736
Email: enquiries@aysgarthschool.co.uk
Website: www.aysgarthschool.com

Head: Since 2002, Mr Anthony Goddard (fifties). Mr Goddard went from Cambridge to ICI and thence to Accenture. Successful manager and marketing expert; no teaching experience but was an Aysgarth governor for 10 years. So this was an imaginative appointment and numbers have risen by 20 per cent, while the boarding focus has been enhanced and teaching facilities have been developed and improved. Charming, friendly and approachable, Mr Goddard teaches geography and some games and is very involved on the pastoral side. His delightful wife, Caroline, is also busy on the pastoral side, where she is much appreciated, especially by new boys and mothers. She also teaches RS, craft and DT. They make a great team and, along with their dogs, are the lifeblood of the place.

Entrance: By interview and assessment to look for boys with a 'willingness to get stuck in'; no exam, 'we try not to turn anyone away'. A few scholarships and some bursary help. Siblings and Services discounts.

Exit: Excellent record to public schools: Harrow, Eton, Ampleforth, Uppingham, Radley, Sedbergh, Shrewsbury, Stowe and Winchester. Good sprinkling of academic and music scholarships.

Remarks: Grand, purpose-built 19th century school, including splendid tower and gem of a chapel. Quiet, beautiful rural setting with glorious views in 50 acres of parkland; feels remote but only a short drive from the A1. Described as 'a place where boys can be boys', though girls are welcomed into pre-prep. Very much focused on full boarding – in fact, north of Oxford, the only all boys' boarding prep in England and parents come from both north and south of the border and say 'it's worth the journey'.

Day boys certainly in the minority and they follow the boarding routine. Traditional and demanding curriculum with streaming and setting and extraordinary continuity of tradition over the years in gaining places at top public schools. SEN provision improving all the time as the school becomes 'a broader and kinder place'.

Sports facilities to die for, especially cricket field and swimming pool. The Aysgarth game of COW – 'Cricket Off The Wall' – is a love of Aysgarthians old and new, the real challenge being to hit the ball from the playground into the head's garden. Sport is high profile and they play to win, whilst still managing a well done and a slap on the back for the chap who comes last. Rugby, football, shooting, fishing, sailing, riding, golf and climbing all on offer. After-hours activities for boarders include both pillow and water fights (though not at the same time) and it's fine to get down and dirty and build dens in the grounds as well as engaging in debating.

Art is strong and technology is popular in well-equipped rooms where the boys can get their hands on serious equipment and tools. Four new classrooms were completed last year which provide light, stimulating spaces for the first year of the prep school and Latin. Music at the school is outstanding and boys – both the very musical and the less so – can be seen enthusiastically practising their musical instruments in dorms and classrooms at break times. They can play anything here, including bagpipes if they so wish, and the choir is a joy to hear. Good to see boys enjoying reading sessions in the library after breakfast and lunch.

Many of the boys look as though they are about to take Eton in their stride; happy, confident and courteous, yet without being arrogant, they are both charming and endearing. They enjoy occasional socials with nearby girls' schools (though are coy about which schools/girls they prefer ...) but the boys clearly relish this boy-friendly atmosphere where you can 'be your own man'.

Food is ample, is prepared in-house using fresh ingredients and 'not bad for school food' (though the boys did say they would like a little more salmon and duck on the menu please), served in a pleasant if slightly old-fashioned Dotheboys Hall-style dining-room with long tables and benches where good old-fashioned courtesy and table manners count.

Staff know the boys well and, although the phrase is often over-used, there really is a 'family feel' about this place, thanks chiefly to great enthusiasm and care from the top. Boarding accommodation includes serried ranks of sinks where boys have to be reminded to wash occasionally, and cheerful dorms where caring staff keep a close eye, tidying up after them and providing a homely feel.

Clientele mainly solid (upper) middle class from the north (including Scotland) and Midlands, and strong support from the Service families at Catterick. Governors very active and close to headmaster, and a lively Old Aysgarthian association. Families are a mix of old school and new; many first time into boarding, including some who, interestingly, say they had previously neither considered boarding nor single sex. Whilst initially a little reluctant to let go, these parents place huge value on all that the school has to offer, both in and out of the classroom, the end result being that their sons are then 'prepared, and then some' for the next school.

Badminton Junior School

Linked to Badminton School in the Senior section

Westbury Road, Westbury-on-Trym, Bristol, BS9 3BA

• Pupils: 100 girls; a few board • Ages: 3-11 • Non-denominational
• Fees: Boarding £18,120; Day £6,900-£10,200 pa • Independent

Tel: 0117 9055 271
Fax: 0117 962 8963
Email: admissions@badminton.bristol.sch.uk
Website: www.badminton.bristol.sch.uk

Headmistress: Since January 2010, Ms Emma Davies, previously deputy head of the Lower School of Bristol Grammar School.

Entrance: The school is very popular so early registration is recommended. Girls are invited for the day and observed by Mrs Davies and her staff. Of course they are looking for bright, inquisitive girls, but how they interact, how easily they become involved and caught up in it all is equally important – this is not a school for those who hang back. Girls applying aged seven, and older, are given tests in maths, English and non-verbal reasoning.

Exit: The expectation is that all girls will move up into the senior school aged 11, usually automatically, though all girls are examined in their last year to confirm potential. 'Moving up wasn't a problem at all,' a senior school girl told us. 'That's what I had been prepared for.' Boarding is available for those who want it.

Remarks: Has recently enjoyed a complete makeover and the whole place is bright and welcoming. Downstairs is dedicated to the younger girls (known as Acorns, aged 3–6); the older girls go upstairs. Tremendous science room complete with a range of live exhibits for observation – science is taught properly – and all the apparatus. Homely and well stocked library, where budding young scholars snuggle into beanbags and devour books; airy rooms with small classes of girls who are monitored and encouraged by their form teachers. Tutor groups are structured vertically to break up cliques and broaden experience. An efficient-looking medical room.

All girls are encouraged to learn musical instruments and join in various musical groups and the choir. Out-standing musicians have the opportunity to join in music-making with the senior school. In fact the proximity of the senior school is a great bonus: girls use the swimming pool, tennis courts, Astroturf, gymnasium and other sporting facilities; they become familiar with the senior school without losing their own safe identity and may attend concerts and plays. But for drama, it seems, nothing to beat the annual Acorn and Junior productions, with every child involved. This really is a school for involvement: history days, for instance, are inclusive and fun, be it Agincourt, Roman, mediaeval, where clothing, appropriate food and language are explored with great gusto. Much is learned almost without the pupils knowing. Visits are made to country houses and castles, museums and adventure parks.

Though the academic expectation and standards are high, not a hothouse school but one where learning and experience go hand in hand with having fun. Girls with special needs are helped at the nearby dyslexia unit. Family-style lunch lends itself to old fashioned courtesies gently instilled and the food is 'brilliant', 'scrumptious', 'really delicious'. Over a neat little bridge, spanning a sunken footpath, girls trip lightly on their way to an attractively laid out adventure playground. There's a mediator 'bus stop' and 'buddy bench', where girls can quietly signal that they could do with some extra friendship – staff are alert to that.

Financial assistance is available for daughters of parents in the Armed Forces, siblings and those with demonstrable need. New Foundation Awards worth up to 100 per cent off fees available for Year 5 in 2011 entry. Arrangements can be made to arrive early (breakfast is an option) and post-school activities are available up to 6pm. Increasing junior boarding with very busy flexi-boarding.

A fizzing school where the girls are busy without being stressed, academic rigour is instilled, but not at the expense of fun and talents, and interests are nurtured. It encourages independent thought and individuality, ideal preparation for the excellent senior school, a confident stroll away.

Bancroft's Preparatory School

Linked to Bancrofts School in the Senior section

611-627 High Road, Woodford Green, Essex, IG8 0RF

• Pupils: 250 boys and girls (equal numbers), all day • Ages: 7-11 • C of E but other faiths welcomed • Fees: £9,840 pa • Independent

Tel: 020 8506 6751
Fax: 020 8506 6752
Email: prep.office@bancrofts.org
Website: www.bancrofts.org

Headmaster: Since 2005, Mr Christopher Curl MA BEd TEFL (mid forties). Approachable, efficient and thrilled to be part of the impressive system that is Bancroft's. Previously head at Ferndale Prep and before that resident housemaster/head of English/drama at senior and prep schools, most recently Junior King's Canterbury, his old school. A family man, both his children now attend Bancroft's; his wife (a dentist – this does not stop head giving out Curly-Wurlys as rewards!) concentrates on being a mother rather than the headmaster's wife. He loves the opportunity to teach myths and legends, current affairs and after school football. Produced the first ever whole school musical, *Oliver!*, in 2007, which ran for four nights to packed audiences, and put on another major production in 2010. He is now overseeing a major expansion of the school including a significant new extension (performing arts studio, science room, three new classrooms, reception and waiting area and other offices) and an increase in the total number of pupils from 200 in 2008 to around 265 by 2012.

Entrance: Register by 1st December of the year prior to entry. Possibility of means-tested bursaries. Over 175 applicants for 66 places – part of the huge local competition that is getting a place at Bancroft's, Chigwell and Forest. In September 2008 the school began a four-year expansion taking an extra 16 children each year. Selection takes place through interviews (chats with six-year-olds) by head and deputy, who both see every child in groups of four. Tasks set include maths, non-verbal reasoning, reading aloud and writing a story – all aspects of the child's personality are considered and it is not just the smartest who get in.

Exit: Automatically to Bancroft's – the main reason for getting your child into the prep; few parents pass up this chance. Scholarships available at 11 plus.

Remarks: Airy yet compact, purpose-built, to the south west of the senior school, separated by a games pitch and the new sports centre. Entry is right next door to the well-stocked library, with sporting awards at the top of the bookshelves and beanbags on the floor for wet-weather lounging. All the walls (inside and outside classrooms) covered in work and art – e.g. silhouettes of the pupils, a project on the Owl and the Pussy Cat going to sea; the children run into the skylighted art room to show their peers and visitors their work. Respect is important here – pleases, thank yous and doors being held open are automatic.

Early morning supervision available for busy parents and the little ones troop up to the new dining room in the senior school for lunch. DT days involve the senior school staff and pupils in a more formal way. SATs results were outstanding – best mixed prep and in the top five in the country. The school has now abandoned SATs, which the staff believe has allowed for a richer and broader curriculum. Form teachers (about 22–25 children in each class) and specialists are supported by two or three floating classroom assistants, ready to skim off the quick pupils or ones who are struggling.

No heads of school, responsibilities assigned to particular children – the school council successfully lobbied for an adventure playground to join the giant chessboard. IT now taught with two trolleys of portable laptops. Games practices, rehearsals and other activities (swimming, buses to 15 acres of sports grounds at West Grove, choir and recorder groups, over-subscribed trampolining and mixed cub scouts, to name just a few) take place at lunchtime or after school, mostly on site. Homework diaries, curriculum summaries and regular newsletters keep parents in the loop and they are encouraged to help with reading, school trips and the PA.

A confident, friendly and busy school, shadowed and protected by the brilliant facilities and reputation of the senior. Vitally successful in introducing tolerance, initiative and curiosity to these youngest Bancroftians.

Barnardiston Hall Preparatory School

Barnardiston Hall, Nr Haverhill, Suffolk, CB9 7TG

• Pupils: 115 girls, 135 boys (50 boys and girls board) • Ages: nursery and pre-prep; 2-7; prep 7-11 • non-denom • Fees: Nursery to Pre Prep £4,305-£8,925; Prep School: Day £11,430, Boarding £15,810-£17,145 pa • Independent

Tel: 01440 786 316
Fax: 01440 786 355
Email: registrar@barnardiston-hall.co.uk
Website: www.barnardiston-hall.co.uk/

Headmaster: Since 1990, Colonel Keith Boulter (late fifties), married with three grown-up children. Cambridge theology graduate, hockey blue and keen musician who joined the Royal Army Educational Corps in 1973 and administered five Gurkha schools in Hong Kong and Brunei. Also worked at the MOD briefing four-star generals. Infectiously enthusiastic – a whirlwind who's not in the least bit blimpy and is involved in every aspect of school life. He teaches maths to older pupils (something he particularly enjoys), umpires hockey matches, trains the choir (delightful recording can be heard if you ring and have to hang on – much better than ubiquitous Mozart muzak), drives the mini bus for surprise outings and guides children up mountains abroad and at home. But that's not all – when there's time he also deals with admin. Parents confirm this is someone with an astonishing work ethic. A great deal is expected from pupils and staff who, if they aren't already, become 'boulterized' – cheery and ready to enter into all sorts of extra-curricular activities.

Entrance: Children spend a day attending lessons and are observed and tested by subject teachers. Where appropriate the school's ed psych is used to assess a child's particular needs. Bursaries at the BSA rate for Service personnel. Limited scholarships for Hong Kong-based pupils.

Exit: Most to local independent schools of their first choice. Good smattering of scholarships. A few to local state schools.

Remarks: Firm belief that there's more to education than pushing to get through exams. Children quickly get involved in all sorts of activities. Sleep-overs start early, as do Enid Blytonesque night time expeditions; according to one mum, 'Barnardiston children are well-rounded and pretty resilient. You can throw anything at them and they can take it'. Traditional teaching styles and old-fashioned values – good manners, hard work and community spirit – plus spontaneous fun (staff appearing at the end of a school play with water rifles or dressed in tutus for the end of term netball match) and D of E-ish exploits make a 'school where life goes at 100 mph.'

Gently rural property, set in 35 acres, bought by the Colonel when he left the army in 1990 and now the core of a family business. His tremendously jolly sister teaches little ones whilst sunshiny daughter is head of the pre-prep and down to be principal when he retires. NB: there's no board of governors but Colonel Boulter is keen to point out that there is a senior management team. Also owns Riddlesworth Hall, where he teaches one day a week, and Broadlands Hall (for autistic children) which is run by his son. Rambling main house is home to Boulters and boarders but the distinction between its comfy domesticity and the school is blurred – carefree children, smiley staff and two friendly retrievers mill between the two. Both are stuffed with an eclectic collection of objets trouvés, including full sets of armour and three half-scale wooden giraffes which Colonel Boulter couldn't resist – transportation from Cambridge with their necks protruding from car windows led to one acquiring a prominent bandage.

Initial 50 pupils (no boarders) has grown to 250 (50 boarders) and several major building projects have been completed – purpose-built pre-prep department, new prep extension with classrooms, language lab and well resourced SEN department. Plans are afoot for further developments – although nothing yet to replace the semi-permanent marquee which is an adequate sports hall.

Broad intake. Those who might struggle in less accommodating institutions find areas where they can shine, and parents say the solid, not too hot-housey academic approach 'gets everyone to where they want to go'. Streaming starts early. French from the nursery and Latin from Year 3. History continues to be a firm favourite – according to one insider 'because the gory bits aren't left out'. Good IT provision and a fully computerised weather station. No academic elitism or stigmatisation here – school has a holistic approach and the Colonel positively glows when talking about those who, with the know-how of the friendly and highly-regarded support department (The Bridge) have 'been turned round'. Help, given to about a quarter of the school by up to 12 staff including two fully-trained SEN teachers, is usually one-to-one or from classroom LSAs. Needs range from an extra boost to identifiable conditions (mild aspergers/autism, Tourette's, dyslexia and dyspraxia. Colonel B won't take children he knows he can't help, but a few have statements – fees are state-funded). Gifted children also attend the unit, as do those needing TEFL provision.

Parents are happy with art, drama and music (over 50 per cent learn an instrument) and chirpily, respectful children readily enthuse about school sport (national prep school orienteering champions from 2006 to date). They also enjoy letting off steam in the adventure playground or pedalling round the mini two-way road system with its roundabouts and T junctions. Long hoped for Astroturf (one in Haverhill is used at the moment) is due to be installed on a recently-acquired field, but date of materialisation not yet clear.

We've heard that over-anxious or inflexible parents won't last long, but those who can cope with the Colonel's expectations and laudable desire to do what's best for the child are devoted to the place and often return long after their children have left. A school which isn't constrained by petty regulations – wonderfully happy and well worth consideration.

Bassett House School

60 Bassett Road, London, W10 6JP

• Pupils: 175 boys and girls, all day • Ages: 3-11 • Non-denom
• Fees: £6,300-£12,996 pa • Independent

Tel: 020 8969 0313
Fax: 020 8960 9624
Email: info@bassetths.org.uk
Website: www.bassetths.org.uk

Head: Since 2003, Mrs Andrea Harris BEd Mont Cert CEPLF (fifties). Previously spent eight years as deputy head at Denmead School in Hampton, and in pre-motherhood days worked in comprehensive schools. Married to another headteacher and has two grown-up sons, both in the civil service. Immaculate, professional and articulate, she is popular with parents and passionate about her school. 'It's heaven on earth here. They are such lovely children.'

Entrance: Come and have a look round before signing up. Most parents arrive soon after the birth, though 'we never close the waiting list – we don't like to close the door on anyone'. Takes around 20 three-year-olds into The Den and another 20 four-year-olds into Lower One. Many parents sign up for both lists. No assessment; more-or-less first come first served, though siblings signed up in time get preference and the school does try to balance the genders. Inevitably autumn-born children tend to be at the top of the list, but it is fluid, with some families moving out of central London or taking up other options, leaving enough space for spring and summer children. Occasional places higher up, subject to an informal assessment to check that 'the child will be happy and successful here'.

Exit: Some – mostly boys – leave at seven or eight for e.g. Colet Court, Latymer Prep, Sussex House or The Harrodian. 'We're disappointed if parents want their daughter to sit for Bute house, for example, because we believe we can do just as well, but we will always be supportive of the process.' Most girls, and now an increasing number of boys, stay on till 11, nearly always getting an offer from their first choice of senior school – including South Hampstead, both Francis Hollands, Latymer Upper, Notting Hill and Ealing, More House, St Marylebone, St Paul's Girls, Godolphin & Latymer, Queen's College, Queen's Gate and the Harrodian. 'Our parents are very reasonable. We have a lot of conversations about suitable secondary schools. Some do have unrealistic expectations, but we encourage them to weigh up the consequences for their child of trying for inappropriate schools.'

Remarks: Set up in 1947 by Sylvia Rentoul, a Montessori-trained mother of three young boys who lost faith in the education at the local state school and decided to teach her sons at home. The school grew 'like Topsy' and is still expanding; the three sons are still part of the governing body. Shares governors and plays sports matches with sister schools in the group, Orchard House in Chiswick and Prospect House in Putney.

Just north of the Westway off Ladbroke Grove in a Victorian family house, the school was substantially rebuilt in

2001. It now includes St Helen's church hall some 100 metres away, which houses the two youngest year groups, an assembly hall with a stage, which is also used for gym and dance and as the dining room, a kitchen and a small garden where the younger ones can learn and play outdoors. Friendly, welcoming feel throughout. Some of the classrooms are undoubtedly compact but everywhere is brightly decorated with children's work and artwork. Small playground used by different classes in rotation.

Smartboards in every classroom; ICT is important here. 'We're happy to spend money on IT. We use it for management and assessment for learning as well as for teaching.' The children are assessed regularly and 'we diagnose what each needs as an individual'. Studywhiz learning platform enables children to access any of their work from home over the internet, and helps to keep parents in touch with what they are doing.

The stairs up to the top floor are lined with (clothed) life drawings and there is a bright art and DT room full of imaginative work – 'our head of art is very talented and we win lots of prizes'. There are tortoises – and, on occasion, chicks – wandering round the science room, newts and stick insects in tanks. A tropical zoo comes to visit with salamanders and scorpions, and children sleep over at the science museum.

Early years teaching is based on Montessori principles, and the school also trains Montessori teachers. 'We're not purist – we're a little more structured than a classical Montessori school, and we also follow the national curriculum and do SATs. But it encourages the children to feel responsible for themselves and for one another.' French for everyone and Latin from Year 4 – 'the teachers really bring Latin to life'.

SEN and EAL help available (at extra cost if one-to-one), though the latter is not usually a problem as most of the foreign children are bilingual. 'We're very good at differentiation – our teachers prepare at least three levels of work.' Parents are asked when they are offered a place to disclose any learning difficulties, 'but so far we haven't had any we can't cope with'.

A Tuesday Club gives extra help to Year 2, 3 and 6 children preparing for entrance exams. 'They might practise a comprehension, or perhaps go over decimals or fractions, if that's what they need. But everything required is incorporated into the syllabus.'

Despite the school's lack of outdoor space immediately to hand, there are plenty of opportunities for fresh air and exercise. All the older children play cricket, netball, rounders and football, with early morning clubs and matches against other schools. The Westway sports centre – five minutes' walk away – has all-weather football pitches and netball and tennis courts, as well as an indoor climbing wall. After school clubs range from Myths and Mysteries to Funky Street Dance.

Music is high profile, with an orchestra and choir – winner of the 2009 Wetherby Prep Choir competition – and a summer music concert which includes as many budding musicians as possible. Most year groups are involved in drama productions, and all the classes take it in turn to do form assemblies. 'They get used to performing in public and realise that no-one minds if they make mistakes. They gradually become aware of their own achievements and set out to improve upon their last best performance.'

High expectations of behaviour – 'someone once crayoned on a toilet door' is the worst crime the head can remember – within a relaxed and informal atmosphere, which includes permission to eat and drink in class. 'We're lucky to have staff who are so committed to the children's happiness. They are treated with great warmth and affection.' Staff and pupils eat a cooked lunch and chat together, and on occasion parents are invited too. 'It is a very important time of day.'

Occasional scholarships for children coming in from state primaries. Parents are lawyers, writers, accountants, journalists – the BBC is nearby; about 10 per cent are European, some American. They are 'hugely supportive', keen to come in for social lunches, for concerts, plays and assemblies. 'They're confident the school will do a good job. We have a shared vision for their child's future.'

The Beacon School

Chesham Bois, Amersham, Buckinghamshire, HP6 5PF

• Pupils: Approximately 455 boys including up to 24 in the nursery
• Ages: 3-13 • Fees: £4,500-£12,465 pa • Independent

Tel: 01494 433 654
Fax: 01494 727 849
Email: admissions@beaconschool.co.uk
Website: www.beaconschool.co.uk

Headmaster: Since September 2009, Mr Paul Brewster, BSc in Maths/IT from London University. Formerly head of Foremarke Hall for seven years before helping Nord Anglia Education establish a school overseas. Married to Debbie, a teacher; they have three grown-up children.

Entrance: Key entry points at age three (nursery), age four (reception), age seven (Year 3) and age 11 (Year 7). Non-selective in early years, assessment for entry to Year 3 and above, primarily to ensure child will fit in with existing cohort; looking for good progress within the national curriculum.

Exit: All to guided first choice school. A number of scholars – music, art, sport and academic – annually, including most recently Berkhamsted, Merchant Taylors', Millfield, St Edward's Oxford and Winchester. A number of boys leave at the end of Year 6 for Buckinghamshire grammar schools. At 13, boys move on senior independent schools including Abingdon, Berkhamsted, Eton, Harrow, Marlborough, Merchant Taylors', Shiplake, St Edward's Oxford, Millfield, Oundle, Wellington and Winchester College.

Remarks: Taught in mixed ability to Year 5 (set for maths), thereafter streamed and setted. Class sizes reduce from approximately 20 to 14 in upper school. All usual subjects plus French from Year 2 and Latin from Year 6. Eight per cent of pupils have recognised special needs, a further 10 per cent receive some support from the team of four. Currently, one statemented pupil for physical needs; school is wheelchair-friendly and accessible. Speech and language therapist and a number of peripatetic specialist support teachers visit weekly (additional charge). Good home-school liaison.

Head believes qualifications are a mere currency and, once banked, qualities and skills matter more. In Years 7 and 8 boys are prepared to sit for the Beacon Certificate of Achievement (BCA), Common Entrance or scholarship examinations to leading independent senior schools. The Beacon Certificate of Achievement has gained acceptance by a number of top-flight academic schools. The certificate is designed to preserve academic prowess and incorporate key skills fundamental to 21st century Britain, principally: the intellectual embracing of enquiry, analysis, evaluation, interpretation, inference etc; team skills encompassing communication and collaboration; and high level IT competence ensuring transferable skills.

From the busy road in this leafy commuter heartland you'd be forgiven for thinking this is a small suburban prep. As with the Tardis, a few steps and you realise it's a sizeable school with big ambitions. Founded in 1933 with just five boys; the current site, at the time a derelict 17th century farm, was acquired in 1952. Former barns now house the Harry Potteresque beamed dining hall and enticing library. Facilities are very good indeed: large modern sports hall (with cricket nets and automatic bowling machine), outdoor pool, floodlit Astro, fantastic sportsfield (housing manicured cricket pitch, pavilion, athletics tracks etc), plus lots of specialist teaching rooms with good kit. Moreover, this is possibly the whizziest ICT prep school we've seen. Not just the usual Smart and Promethean whiteboards and dedicated ICT suites but abundance of well-utilised technology in all areas – cutting-edge in music (recording studio, keyboard technology for composition). No real need for personal laptops, though some used by those with learning needs.

Separate buildings for nursery and pre-prep ensure thoughtful transition and increasing independence. A vibrant, happy nursery for the little ones aims not to hothouse or push but nurture and develop. Importantly, parents are not expected to have three-year-old Freddie proficient in anything. For those who come in at four, useful if they can dress and undress but no need for the three Rs – they work from premise that too much pressure, too young, can scar for life. With this in mind you may be surprised to hear, or perhaps understand why, children in the lower school are cheerfully producing high quality work, in a thoughtful and purposeful environment. By the end of key stage 2 most (a wide spread of ability) attain level 5 of the national curriculum in the basics.

Teaching matches, if not exceeds, the facilities. Parents comment that teachers go the extra mile: 'It's not about ticking boxes – they really seem to enjoy their work and get a buzz from it'. According to parents even the homework is interesting! One boy said the history teacher was really strict but he'd learned a lot from her. Boys say lessons are a mix of styles: 'Sometimes in science we seem to make a lot of notes but other times it's experiments, bangs and stinks.' We chanced on a superb science lesson, with each boy not only designing his own creature, based on knowledge of habitats and adaptations, but also presenting and justifying the choices to his peers. Hands stretched, scraping the ceiling, eager to quiz the designer, or even catch him out, but most knew their stuff, sharp enough to think on their feet. Differentiation, revision, enquiry, assessment – all the teaching boxes ticked, and for the boys, one fun-filled journey of discovery – uplifting stuff.

Parents say boys are stretched but not pressured and that school is inclusive and supportive, celebrating success and achievements of all, not just top dogs. Lots of extracurricular opportunities, a strong sport-for-all policy with every boy representing the school in a team. Head says, 'It's important we remember they're children – we know what's in their pockets and heads, what makes them tick. We must ensure there is a balance, offset those things they find tedious.' Lots of fabulous art, many media including digital photography, sculpture and video (produces own weekly news bulletin posted on the web); scholarships won annually. DT (with latest addition of a food technology centre) and drama strong. Four choirs, concerts and performing opportunities galore and most play instruments from Year 2. Jury still out on food (found in favour, according to school) but boys appreciative that concerns addressed via experimentation.

With a real zest for life, boys lap up the breadth of activities on offer. Few incidents of boisterous or brutish behaviour, though occasional occurrences and how dealt with were cited. Clearly head and parents do not always concur; unafraid of ruffling feathers, the head's speech day oration included, 'Every parent would claim to support the school's discipline, but for an increasing number that means supporting the school to discipline other people's children.' Adding, 'I see teachers increasingly frustrated because they do not receive support from some parents and, incrementally, more parents seek to interfere in the decisions made by the school.' Parents we spoke to agreed with the head's perceptions.

Discipline tends to focus on support and encouraging the boys to think about their actions, with withdrawal of privileges for repeated offences. Pupils au fait with anti-bullying policy and some brave enough to tell how school had taken appropriate action – universal agreement that issues dealt with promptly and effectively. All spoke very highly of the school's counsellor, a mother-figure to troubled boys – emotional health and well-being taken very seriously here: 'It underpins everything – a stable emotional base is essential'.

A forward-looking school, seeking to preserve traditional values, well worth discovering; suits a broad range, including those considered different. Education with an edge: expanding minds, pushing the bounds of learning but ensuring the adage 'boys will be boys', is not forgotten.

Beaconhurst Junior School

Linked to Beaconhurst in the Senior section

52 Kenilworth Road, Bridge of Allan, Stirling, FK9 4RR

• Fees: £6,510-£9,456 pa • Independent

Tel: 01786 832 146
Fax: 01786 833 415
Email: headmaster@beaconhurst.stirling.sch.uk
Website: www.beaconhurst.com

Remarks: See main school.

Beatrix Potter Primary School

Magdalen Road, Earlsfield, London, SW18 3ER

• Pupils: 230; all day, 50/50 girls and boys • Ages: 3-11 • Non-denom • State

Tel: 02088 741 482
Fax: 02088 719 416
Email: Info@beatrixpotter.wandsworth.sch.uk
Website: www.beatrixpotterschool.com

Head: Since 1988, Mr Stephen Neale MA DipEdTec (mid fifties). Popular, easy-going, very hands on. Dedicated. Attends every PTA event, takes charge of wall displays throughout the school, deals with all IT problems. A bit of a computer whiz. Has taken on the role of SENCo himself, with support from LSAs. Married to a Polish opera singer with one, now grown-up, son. Variously described as chaotic, friendly, relaxed, cynical – certainly a bit of a maverick.

Entrance: Strict admission policy, detailed in the school's joining letter. Those living closest and siblings are the first priority. Children who gain a place in the nursery are not guaranteed a place in the junior school. However, Wandsworth, like most London boroughs, does have a high mobility rate and parents moving to the area should always give it a whirl. Fifteen places per year come up on average in the different year groups. Perceived as a middle-class school, it is, in fact, totally non-selective and is merely defined by its location. Now in the second year of two-form entry, so a wider catchment area than before.

Exit: Forty per cent to private secondaries: Wimbledon High, Thomas's, Emmanuel, Dulwich, JAGS. Large number to Burntwood Secondary and Ernest Bevin (especially since the opening of their new sports centre). Other state secondaries are Wilson's, Southfields, Willington, Graveney and Wallington Girls'.

Remarks: Some schools just stand out when you visit them – like buying a house, you know immediately if you like it. BP positively fizzes with energy and enjoyment. The corridors may be crammed with books and toys and apparatus, but they just add to the atmosphere of a place where children are encouraged to use every tool available to gain knowledge. Each pupil has their own individual computer housed in a separate IT suite. Not an effete centre of learning following government guidelines and ticking all the boxes all of the time – here the children's education comes first. An Ofsted inspection mildly baulked at some of the teachers' recording of pupils' progress but could not fault the behaviour, enthusiasm, personal development, enjoyment and positive attitude to learning which BP pupils display.

Sports coaches are brought in for lacrosse, cricket, netball, rugby and football. Dance lessons happen from Year 1, music, singing and percussion all very popular, with drama classes every day. Large play area outside with a vegetable patch and pond to tend. Adjacent is a sports field belonging to Wandsworth, so available for the school's use. Also has links to schools in US through the Fulbright Project. Links to schools in Denmark, Germany, Holland and Poland are promoted by group projects using Skype and email. Each year the top two classes enjoy trips to Arran or Plas Menai, personally escorted by Mr Neale himself. Something for everyone at this school – 'It's a very happy place'.

Beaudesert Park School

Minchinhampton, Gloucestershire, GL6 9AF

• Pupils: 375; 200 boys, 175 girls, including 90 pre-prep. Up to 110 boarders, 90 flexi board, 20 weekly board • Ages: 4-13 • Mostly C of E • Fees: Day £6,825-£13,350; Boarding £15,225-£17,460 pa • Independent

Tel: 01453 832 072
Fax: 01453 836 040
Email: office@beaudesert.gloucs.sch.uk
Website: www.beaudesert.gloucs.sch.uk

Head: Since 1997, Mr James Womersley BA PGCE (early fifties), educated at St Edward's and Durham where he read 'economics, history and rugby'. Previously at Eagle House, then Emanuel (London) before spending seven years at The Dragon School, Oxford, as a housemaster. Humorous, charming, straight-talking, e.g. 'Pre-testing for CE really screwed things up for everyone'. Teaches Year 6 PHSE, referees, and reads to pre-prep children (jumps onto piano at exciting points, to delight of little ones). 'I'd like to do more but, sadly, the days when the head took lessons, then whizzed round on the tractor mower have gone,' he confesses.

Beaudesert has nearly doubled in size during Mr Womersley's headship. 'He's raised the school's profile,' says one parent. 'Before, it was a local Gloucestershire school. Now people know of it in London.' Makes an impressive double-act with wife Fiona, who is right at the heart of Beaudesert. She comes from a prep school family: 'You either love it or resent it,' she says. 'I love it. Something makes you laugh every day.' 'They really complement each other,' adds a parent. 'She's brilliant on the pastoral side. You feel there's nothing they haven't seen before.' They have three sons who all went through Beaudesert. Their eldest is at Loughborough; their middle just leaving, and youngest still at St Edward's. Head's name cause of intense focus – 'It's very funny hearing the little ones trying to say it,' says his wife.

Entrance: Not selective. Fed by independent local nurseries. Children transfer from pre-prep automatically via basic assessment. Pupils come mainly from within 30 miles.

Exit: To wide spread of senior schools, from Milton Abbey to Ampleforth, though most go locally. Big clutches to Marlborough, Cheltenham College, Eton, St Edward's, Cheltenham Ladies', St Mary's Calne.

Remarks: School perches on top of Minchinhampton Common, overlooking one of Stroud's 'Golden Valleys'. Main building imposing mock-Tudor Victorian, with Cotswold stone wings. Mr Womersley has overseen a steady programme of building during his tenure, with clever use of space providing new classrooms, science labs, art and design studios. Thirty acres of wooded grounds and grass terraces step down to games fields and Astroturf. Friendly, straightforward and happy children are an active, tree-climbing, den-building lot. (An onlooker at the Cheltenham Literary Festival complimented staff on their children looking 'so fit'.)

Three class groups per year, pupils setted for maths, English, languages (French, Latin from Year 6) plus science in top forms. Approximately 60 children receive learning support, on withdrawal basis. Strong maths, Latin. 'A child in pre-prep who, we feel, would struggle with Common Entrance would find the prep stage difficult,' says Mr Womersley. 'It's a quite demanding curriculum.'

Smiley staff, average age of 40. Interactive whiteboards throughout and Apple Macs. Parents are invited for talks on cyber-bullying and internet safety. Great emphasis on effort and encouragement in all fields: Mr Womersley (who sets great store by people being 'purposeful') hands out weekly certificates. Prizes awarded for wide range of achievements besides academic. Parents get three-weekly reports on top of termly ones.

'Sport for everyone' taken very seriously – school regularly sends out 20 teams on match days. Children yomp over the airy common to rugger pitches ('You need an extra sweater watching matches here, but we never cancel fixtures,' says Mr Womersley). Sporting activities include golf, sailing, fly fishing and polo – school polo team particularly strong, thanks to keen polo-playing parents.

Strong music (senior choir recently sang Evensong at Worcester Cathedral). Good art (lovely old-fashioned pottery room) and drama: 'My daughter, a real drama fiend, loves having plenty of opportunities to perform. The school seems to get particularly good LAMDA results, too,' says one parent.

School has very flexible approach to boarding – can do occasional nights, flexi or weekly. Virtually all children board before going on to senior school. Children, including weekly 'regulars', think flexi boarding works very well. 'It can mean the difference between having to employ a nanny or not,' says one parent. Boys' dormitories in particular pretty packed, but homely. Friday nights hugely popular for the football league: children raise their own teams, the more wackily dressed the better. Wide range of activities for daychildren and boarders, from crochet to bushcraft skills (wildly popular). Recent innovation is the 'Beaudesert Badge', a programme of evening activities ranging from bread-making and shoe-polishing to pitching tents and moth-catching. 'It's not for every child, but those who do it love it,' says one parent. Food is good and plentiful. Dining room self-service, but with emphasis on manners – no eating off trays. An earlier Good Schools Guide report described Beaudesert children as 'not streetwise', which head takes as a compliment. 'We've found the school is approachable, and any problems are dealt with quickly,' says one parent.

Families comprise solid Gloucestershire and environs, with a mix of Bristol professionals and, recently, more Londoners relieved to find 'a country bolthole' for their children. A sociable place, for parents and children alike. Many families are related or know each other, and it really does arrange leaves around Badminton Horse Trials ('Only because many parents are involved'), though one parent comments, 'People joked we'd need ponies and labradors to come here, but we've found everyone to be very friendly'. A happy, country prep school, where friendly, uncomplicated children enjoy being children.

Bedford Girls' School Junior School

Linked to Dame Alice Harpur School (Senior School) in the Senior section

Linked to Bedford High School For Girls in the Senior section

Cardington Road, Bedford, Bedfordshire, MK42 0BX

• Pupils: 250 girls; all day • Ages: 7-11 • Fees: £7,398 pa • Independent

Tel: 01234 361 903
Fax: 01234 361 909
Email: juniorschool@bedfordgirlsschool.co.uk
Website: www.bedfordgirlsschool.co.uk

Head: Corinne Royden, Head of Bedford Girls' School Junior School.

Jo MacKenzie, Head of Bedford Girls' School.

Entrance: At seven, girls have a group interview and an assessment day.

Exit: Junior School girls transfer to the Bedford Girls' School Senior School.

Remarks: Based in Howard House opposite the senior school. A former Barnardo's Home – delightful gardens and brightly decorated accommodation. Strong links with the senior school – girls from the sixth form, for example, often pop over to Howard House to help with reading.

Bedford Preparatory School

Linked to Bedford School in the Senior section

De Parys Avenue, Bedford, Bedfordshire, MK40 2TU

• Pupils: 450 boys; day and boarding • Ages: 7-13 • Fees: Day £9,915-£12,990; Boarding: £16,101-£20,058 pa • Independent

Tel: 01234 362 271
Fax: 01234 362 285
Email: prepinfo@bedfordschool.org.uk
Website: www.bedfordschool.org.uk

Headmaster: Since 1997, Mr Chris Godwin MA (late forties). Educated at comprehensive school in Gloucestershire. Read geography at Loughborough University, then master's degree in Middle East studies at Durham. Second master and director of studies from 1993 until he took over headship four years later. Gentle and unassuming, obviously popular with the boys, loves his school. Keen and active sportsman, particularly rugby, which he now coaches rather than plays. Has recently taken up indoor rowing. Also interested in photography and 20th century art and design. Parents find him relaxed and easy to talk to. Very excited about latest building project – they have taken over part of St Luke's Church and are transforming it into classrooms for Years 5 to 8 and, in particular, for the teaching of geography. Also thrilled that they will be running a pilot programme for mini laptops in the near future. No plans to move on yet.

Entrance: Mainly at seven, eight and 11. Classroom visits in the Christmas term prior to entry, followed by assessment tests and an interview in January. If a place is not achieved in the first year, don't despair – could be one on the next time of trying.

Exit: Most move up to the senior school, via an internal test.

Remarks: Everything a small boy could possibly want, with academic excellence that more than satisfies his parents. Some specialised staff cross over with the senior school but predominantly a separate teaching team.

Situated in a southern corner of the campus, whilst it does share some facilities with the senior school, has its own entrance, own buildings and own all-weather games pitch. Good combination of old and new, the library and English and history classrooms being in the oldest building, the Inky – from 'incubator for fledgling Bedfordians'. Lots of light and space in the main Wells Building (mid 1990s), well-equipped science labs and great art facilities. Plenty on display everywhere. Music and sport mirror the senior school. Good pastoral care. Lovely and cosy for the first two years, own building, own class teachers, own library.

Modern purpose-built boarding house for 30. Foreign Office and overseas residents roughly 50 per cent. Homely, house-parents popular with boys and parents alike. Each boy has his own sleeping area for personalisation but is still in the security of a dorm.

A happy school full of cheerful, confident boys. A great place to start the serious educational years.

Beechwood Park School

Markyate, St Albans, Hertfordshire, AL3 8AW

- Pupils: 500 boys and girls, flexi-boarding and day • Ages: 2.5-13
- Inter-denom • Fees: Day £8,844-£12,096; Weekly boarding £15,375 pa
- Independent

Tel: 01582 840 333
Fax: 01582 842 372
Email: admissions@beechwoodpark.herts.sch.uk
Website: www.beechwoodpark.herts.sch.uk

Headmaster: Since 2002, Mr Patrick C E Atkinson BSc MIBiol PGCE (fifties). Deputy headmaster at the New Beacon School, Sevenoaks, followed by 11 years as head of Lochinver House School. A tall, smart marine biologist, with a lively, thespian air and love of the arts; married to Claire, an educational psychologist; two children soon to fly the nest. Says job is all-consuming but occasionally finds time for skiing and water sports. Has tightened things up – made staff more accountable. Parents warming to him: 'He is a doer,' commented one. Most children say he is into everything – watches matches, attends concerts, sees good work etc. One child thought the head reclusive (perhaps he was too engrossed in all that's on offer to even notice the head!). Head says he is impressed by children who are great thinkers, interested and engaged.

Entrance: Register early. Assessment and interview, to ensure child ready for next stage. Stresses every child must qualify but entrance is non-competitive. Priority is given to siblings, then date of registration is used. No scholarships but means-tested bursaries may be available.

Exit: Co-ed choices anywhere in the country: Rugby, Haileybury, Oundle, Mill Hill, Uppingham and Berkhamsted. Girls, at 11, tend towards St Albans High, Abbot's Hill, Haberdasher's Aske's and Queenswood; more staying to 13 than previously. Boys also choose St Albans, Haberdasher's, Aldenham and Bedford. Regular academic, music, art scholarships

Remarks: Maximum class sizes of 20 reduce to eight or fewer in some senior sets ensuring individual attention for all. SATS results usually at level 5 for key stage 2; lots of help and support given. Low staff turnover but healthy injection of new blood keeps all on toes. Thanks to fizzy teaching, languages – French, Latin and Spanish and Mandarin clubs – top the popularity poll. Odd grumble about RE but all cut it at CE. Setted in maths from Year 4; more setting and subject specialisation as progress through school. Sets are flexible, 'My son moved across from the scholarship set to one where he could gain extra help; the sets are flexible and it's about what's best for the child at the point'. Science is strong; the subject benefits from bright and well-equipped science labs and some enthusiastic, investigative teaching. Pupils are continuously assessed and parents appreciative of improved communication including detailed termly reports: 'They really know the children well'.

The school takes special needs seriously – and (others please note) includes support in fees: 'We don't charge for specialist rugby coaching or for master classes for gifted, so why charge for SEN?' However, it looks carefully at what needs they can cope with, though they are willing to put training/resources in, if school is a good fit for the child. All children are screened for learning difficulties and those with special needs (dyslexia, dyspraxia) are given extra help from three SEN teachers – lots of successes, input as flexible as pupil need. Trial of laptops for dyslexics proving successful. Places equal emphasis on the additional needs of the academically gifted and talented (some of whom have SEN too). There's a special scholars' group in Years 7 and 8 and a 'sparklers' group' for academically gifted children lower down the school. It's not just the extremes that sparkle – we were invited into classes (of our choosing) and had great fun in discussions and with challenges; lively, enquiring minds, keener to discover than to be spoon-fed. Not surprising then, that this is the first school where a child asked us what we thought of the head, before we had chance to ask that very question of them!

Small tutor classes of 10 ensure children's welfare attended to. Main grumble from parents concerns the length of school day, particularly for those who travel a distance, have prep to do and younger children in tow. However, after-school club for younger ones being introduced and youngsters undoubtedly relish their busy, active and entertaining days. Popular breakfast club, a unanimous hit with busy parents and somnolent youngsters, alleviates tensions at the start of the day. Boarding (weekly/flexi), bursting at the seams and for boys, waiting lists operate. Tidy dorms (thanks to competitive points system), warm colours but few posters or personal effects, no hot-bedding. Good facilities but snooker tables, air hockey, old play station, modern bistro-style kitchen and cosy communal areas pale into insignificance amid the fun to be had, for staff and pupils, when school becomes a playground for well-loved games: Murder in the Dark, Stuck in the Sahara, Escape from Colditz etc.

Once the home of the Saunders Sebright family; set in 37 acres of designated outstanding natural beauty on the Hertfordshire/Bedfordshire borders just outside Markyate. The original, splendid grade 1 listed building has been carefully maintained with new buildings housing the junior/middle departments, sports hall and performance hall. The stable block has been converted into a music school. Original parkland designed by Capability Brown and film buffs will recognise the drawing room from The Dirty Dozen. Impressive, traditionally well-stocked, wood-panelled library complete with leatherbound volumes, possibly a bit imposing for a young child. Montessori nursery for children aged two and a half to five years recently acquired. Daily bus and coach services pick up from surrounding towns and villages.

As well as outdoor playing fields including Astro, facilities include an indoor sports hall, squash courts, swimming pool (permanent cover on pupil wish list), and tennis courts, though too few areas available for breaktime ball sports, moan some boys. Inter-school sporting fixtures on Saturdays. Very strong music, art and drama; some 250 children learn a musical instrument and we were treated to a resounding, harmonious, early morning choral fest – terrific! Five choirs; the best are excellent and regularly perform in local parishes at St Alban's and in festivals; 'Choirs set a tone for parents,' proffers the head. The new theatre stages many concerts and drama productions, but expect a four week burst of frenetic activity rather than protracted rehearsals.

One child remarked, 'It's a very good school with great facilities and excellent teachers, offering the best value for money in the region.' We sense a future in marketing? Confident youngsters, full of the joys of learning. A caring school, with a warm family feel and high expectations, but be warned – the children may just prefer school to home!

Beeston Hall School

West Runton, Cromer, Norfolk, NR27 9NQ

• Pupils: 140 co-educational (boys:girls 5:3); 60 boarding and 80 day, 'daily boarders' free at weekends • Ages: 7-13 • Mainly C of E, but provision made for RCs. • Fees: Boarding £18,750; Day £14,025 pa • Independent

Tel: 01263 837 324
Fax: 01263 838 177
Email: office@beestonhall.co.uk
Website: www.beestonhall.co.uk

Head: Since September 2009, Mr Robin Gainher (forties), married with three daughters. Degree in government at the LSE – might be useful! Prior to this, Mr Gainher was deputy head at Cranleigh Prep, (acting head for one term) also director of studies, head of history, coached the first XI hockey and cricket. Also had stints as a boarding housemaster and director of sport. He and his wife Alison, who plays an active supporting role, have three young daughters and 'are strong advocates of family values'. 'School should be about inspiring moments where the spirit is well and truly lifted'.

Entrance: Candidates seen in spring prior to entry and assessed via informal tests, and new children invited for a 'fun day' in summer term before entry. Potential boarders invited to 'try it out'. Boarding numbers strong and most children opt to board before they leave. Entry not a foregone conclusion.

Exit: Wide spread of good schools, including Eton, Harrow, Oundle, Uppingham, Rugby and, locally, Gresham's – several with academic and/or music scholarships here. Large number of awards in recent years – on average, 30–40 per cent of leavers get them, in academic, music, art, all-rounder and sporting fields, to schools as diverse as Queen Margaret's, Tudor Hall, Radley, Harrow, Oundle, Downe House and Uppingham. CE results good even for children in lower sets – extremely rare for children not to get into their first choice schools.

Money Matters: New means-tested bursaries for talented children and school has own in-house charity for parents who 'fall on hard times'.

Remarks: A very different ethos and atmosphere from, for example, home counties preps. Few video games, PlayStations or even TVs in evidence here. Children less sophisticated but open, natural, spontaneously friendly. Head stresses the pleasure children take in outdoor play – in the woods and extensive fields around school site, on the nearby beach in West Runton. School benefits from its position a couple of miles from north Norfolk coast, surrounded by farmland, National Trust woods and heathland. Full-size Astro pitch and a new large outdoor pool. Most pupils come from trad country families but also now attracting families from very different backgrounds too. Shooting a popular activity here, as are sailing, golf and archery. School recently bought own fleet of Toppers. National champions in several sports at this level in recent years, as well as many children gaining county, regional and national recognition.

Main school building a super Regency hall, sensitively adapted and beautifully maintained, extended and transformed. New buildings fit well into the site, being small-scale and inviting. Super music school, DT and IT rooms and a larger library and SEN facilities completed in 2008. Newly refitted labs, wonderfully civilised dining hall with conservatory extension looking onto putting-green, surrounded by traditional Norfolk flintstone walls. Plans for new performing arts centre, as next stage of development plan, in next few years. Loads of money spent on constant refurbishment and everywhere beautifully decorated and kept in very good condition – remarkable given the age of the residents! Children encouraged to keep their habitat orderly and given various duties and responsibilities – seen as part of their general education. Attractive boarding houses – recent ones like 'real' houses in scale. Rooms for 10, eight and four, dependent on age; a senior pupil in each room for younger children acts as a kind of 'room parent', for which they are given extra privileges in compensation. Boarding rooms not huge but colourful and snug, with home duvets and toys, photos etc. Recent inspection praised pastoral care.

School rich in activities and clearly scarcely time enough in the day to do everything on offer. Superb, imaginative, witty and highly-skilled artwork of all kinds, taught by teacher 30 years in post who clearly gets the best out of the children – beyond expectations. Pupils' art is everywhere, deservedly, in the school and a good thing too. Also everywhere are sofas – in the library, in the common room etc – giving lovely relaxed, civilised feel. Music also good – 80 per cent learn instruments, a huge variety offered, including bagpipes and harp. Ensembles of all kinds flourish, as does solo work. Strong SEN department supports 15 per cent of children, mostly with mild dyslexia. Most children, against national trend, come from traditional boarding school families, though few parents will have experienced comfort and care on this scale. Parents travel considerable distances to support weekend activities, although most do come from Norfolk or surrounding counties.

One of the very few full-boarding prep schools in East Anglia. Its small size creates rare family atmosphere. It does well by its pupils and turns out friendly, eager, purposeful and confident children who have been taught to take a pride in their school and in themselves.

Belhaven Hill School

Dunbar, East Lothian, EH42 1NN

• Pupils: 65 boys, 55 girls; 105 board, 20 day • Ages: 7-13 • Non-denom
• Fees: Day £12,585; Boarding £18,150 pa • Independent

Tel: 01368 862 785
Fax: 01368 865225
Email: headmaster@belhavenhill.com
Website: www.belhavenhill.com

Head: Since 2009, Mr Innes MacAskill BEd (fifties), who was previously head of Beeston Hall School, Norfolk, having spent 17 years at Caldicott, ultimately as deputy head. Educated at Bedford Modern (a Harpers Trust school) he specialised in history and sport and still – for his sins – runs the first XV. Married with three daughters, all now up and away, he is a hands-on head, and really enjoys knowing each child well and taking a fatherly interest in their concerns. Believes that school has to be 'homely and comfortable'. Popular; supported by wife, Sandy, lively and fun – this is a partnership. A fellow head says he 'has all the best bits of headmastering under his belt and actually likes the children' – not a universal characteristic. We thought he was splendid, but came across a couple of dissenters recently, but then Michael Osborne always was going to be a hard act to follow.

Entrance: No test, but register as soon as possible. Children spend a day at Belhaven the term before they come. Informal test when they come in but no official screening.

Exit: About three a year to Eton, Ampleforth, Oundle and Queen Margaret's, York. Otherwise Glenalmond, Harrow, Loretto, St Mary's Ascot, Downe House, Fettes, Radley, Rugby, Winchester, Sherborne, Shrewsbury, Strathallan, Uppingham, Marlborough, Benenden and Stowe, Bryanston.

Remarks: Numbers still as high as ever before and lists full for the next few years. 'Rash of new younger staff employed recently – they really care,' said one mother of three. School has 'a good combination of experience and enthusiasm' and 'brilliant house staff, matrons and learning support teacher'. Pupils not assessed on entry but glitches picked up early, tame ed psych, plus qualified SENCo, ditto assistant as well as two further assistants (one the husband of a housemistress in the midst of a career change who, as a trained engineer, is a whizzo at maths). The learning support base, 'The Hut', has now been fully revamped (to the envy of some non learning support pupils). Withdrawn from class, one-to-one, small groups, dual teaching – all disciplines covered – at no extra cost; though if a child has severe and particular difficulties school is relaxed about parents employing additional help.

Scotland's school for toffs, (head prefers traditional families: dearie me), which specialises in sending the little darlings to public school in the south. Dubbed 'Hogwarts for Muggles' by 'Edinburgh Evening News'.

The school went co-ed in 1995. Boys based in late 18th century sandstone house (surprising long interlined flowery curtains in window seat in hall), and imaginative additions; tower, eight new classrooms, music school et al, but still a bit of a rabbit warren. Dorms recently revamped with carpets and pinboards, alas bunks now a thing of the past (and round the world ditto).

The snazzy girls' house has a spit new circular rumpus room, known as the Rosie room (after the much loved but probably only a distant memory for older members of staff of Rosie Conran Smith who died – of cancer – at the school some twenty years ago) with plasma television and plenty of brightly coloured beanbags to snuggle up in. More long double interlined rose patterned curtains. No books or newspapers spotted in either the boys' or the girls' common rooms, though head assured us there were libraries aplenty just steps away, but bored children are good at instant literary grazing.

All pupils on-line, two computer rooms. Own laptops not a problem. Pupils setted in core subjects – maths, English, science and langs for final three years, but lots of toing and froing. Tutors for top two years, otherwise classroom based, with form teachers and class sizes down to 10/14. No scholarship stream as such, but more a case of 'children extended through setting and provided opportunities for further support in activities and prep' etc. Vast choice of extra-curricular activities, bright creatures steered towards the more intellectually challenging.

Occasional Greek on offer (but not a lot recently, though all this may change as new classics enthusiast on staff) drama and dance increasingly popular; magnificent sports hall which adapts for school plays. Piping much encouraged and well taught with FPs the core of pipe bands in English public schools and much in demand at weddings and funerals; eight chaps and two chappesses were in Edinburgh playing for the Pope at the time of our visit (as was the head). Manicured grounds including two cricket pitches, new cricket nets, six tennis courts, masses of Astroturf, a putting course and an 18-hole golf course 'over the wall'. Head plays too, though the clubs in his office belonged to one of the boys. Bracing sea air. Streams of unbeaten teams in almost every discipline. Regular trips to Hillend artificial ski slope. Young encouraged to have their own bit of garden in which they take great pride: current competition is for the biggest sunflower. One member of staff, along with the children, uses all the apples from the orchard to make one big brew of apple juice for the children and staff to drink (head suspects this has something to do with cider making), but expect home made apple pies, dumplings and crumbles. Grub for all in the dining room – benches and tables – with quartered oranges on offer during our visit.

Last HM Inspectors' reports could have been written by the previous headmaster himself. Happy social parents and children, with masses of input from locals – tranches of farmers/Charlotte Rangers from East Lothian, plus the usual quota of quite grand children from the North and an increasing gang from south of the border, usually with Scottish connections. Girls fully absorbed. School is flourishing.

Belleville Primary School

Belleville Road, Battersea, London, SW11 6PR

• Pupils: 725 boys and girls • Ages: 3-11 • Non-denominational • State

Tel: 02072 286 727
Fax: 020 7228 8070
Email: info@belleville.wandsworth.sch.uk
Website: www.belleville-school.org.uk/

Head: Since 2001, Mr John Grove (forties) BEd MA, previously head at West Hill and deputy head at Fircroft. Awarded national leader of education status 2008; school is a national support school. Married with two teenage children. Very well thought of by staff, pupils and parents, who comment that he has a wonderful combination of enthusiasm and foresight, an inspiration to the school community. A keen sportsman and traveller, he promotes a whole-school approach and is interested in developing the talents of his staff as well as his pupils.

Entrance: At 3+, 52 places; at 4+, 120 places; always over-subscribed, some occasional places in the older age groups. Wandsworth admissions' criteria: special requirements, siblings and those living closest to the school.

Exit: To a range of good local state and independent schools – Graveney, St Cecilia's, Elliot, Wilson's, Dulwich College, Lycée, Emanuel and Alleyn's.

Remarks: A larger than average primary school that aims to give each child confidence and stimulation plus a varied arts and sports curriculum. SATs results above average and progress monitored regularly. Teaching and results in core subjects have improved over the last two years; has an extension programme for more able mathematicians. Year 6 classes reduced to 18 pupils, enabling more individual attention in preparation for secondary transfer.

A large Victorian building with lots of space and many stairs. Recently redecorated in contrasting colours – a little bright for some tastes but creates a cheerful atmosphere for the children. Well maintained with imaginative displays of awards, competitions, photographs and impressive art throughout the corridors and halls. Has full-time specialist art and music teachers; actors come in to run drama workshops. All pupils learn recorder, flute and African drumming; individual lessons on a range of instruments also available. Annual culture week with carnival. Has just been awarded gold Artsmark. A full-time dedicated sports teacher ensures a good range of sports – football, netball, athletics, swimming; also a gym coach.

Pupils come from a variety of backgrounds; very popular with the French community – has an after-school class to teach the French national curriculum. Very good selection of clubs including flamenco dancing, yoga, four foreign languages and many sports. Two part-time specialist teachers for SEN, plus a gifted and talented programme. Aims to ensure curriculum is inclusive and accessible to all; also a learning mentor scheme. Committed and enthusiastic teachers. Graded as 'outstanding' in recent Ofsted.

Belmont House Junior School

Linked to Belmont House School in the Senior section

Sandringham Avenue, Newton Mearns, Glasgow, G77 5DU

• Fees: £4,116-£7,725 pa • Independent

Tel: 0141 639 2922
Fax: 0141 639 9860
Email: admin@belmontschool.co.uk
Website: www.belmontschool.co.uk

Head: Ms Linsay McDonald.

Remarks: See senior school.

Belmont Mill Hill Preparatory School

Linked to Grimsdell Mill Hill Pre Preparatory School in the Junior section
Linked to Mill Hill School in the Senior section

The Ridgeway, Mill Hill Village, London, NW7 4ED

• Pupils: 415-42 per cent girls, 58 per cent boys • Ages: 7-13 • Fees: £13,806 pa • Independent

Tel: 020 8906 7270
Fax: 020 8906 3519
Email: office@belmontschool.com
Website: www.belmontschool.com

Head: Mrs Lynn Duncan.

Entrance: By entrance test, reference and interview.

Exit: Nearly all go on to the senior school.

Remarks: Popular prep with few adverse comments.

Belmont Primary School

Belmont Road, Chiswick, London, W4 5UL

• Pupils: 470; boys and girls equally; all day • Ages: 3-11 • non-denom • State

Tel: 020 8994 7677
Fax: 020 8742 7866
Email: office@belmont.hounslow.sch.uk

Head: Since September 2010, Ms Verity Coates, previously deputy head.

Entrance: Preference given to those who live within the Primary Admissions Area – 'catchment' to you and me. In recent years, even living in the catchment has not guaranteed a place at the school. Second come siblings, who also now find it very difficult to join their brothers/sisters at the school. Children with SEN and medical/social needs who fit these criteria come higher on the admission list. After that – don't even try. Very over-subscribed, despite head's telling all-comers from outside the area that really, really no chance. Parents are known to rent property within the area just to qualify, and then ... ? However, although the area is largely made up of quiet Victorian streets with large Victorian semis in private ownership, it's not all like that – a sizeable proportion of pupils comes from non home-owning families, those on temporary contracts and those who need EAL support. Inclusion policies help to level these differences – no appreciable differences in achievement between those of such diverse backgrounds, much to the school's credit.

Exit: Around half to two-thirds to Chiswick Community School. Some to other local state comprehensives such as Twyford C of E or The Green School. The rest to the local independents, e.g. Godolphin and Latymer, Notting Hill and Ealing, Latymer Upper, City of London. Does nothing extra to prepare children for such schools so many do have outside coaching. However, education levels such that fairly recently one child won a top scholarship with no outside help at all.

Remarks: Housed in a large, three-storey, London brick building and celebrated its centenary in 2004. Thanks to a very extensive refurbishment programme with the support of both public money and funds raised by parents, it looks pretty good for its age. It has a decent amount of outside space too and all ages have their own designated play areas with equipment and surfaces appropriate for their needs and capacities. No green anywhere apart from a small nature garden with pond – certainly no playing fields – but no feeling of being cramped or choked here, as with so many schools in comparable urban situations. The locality is certainly urban – it's on a crossroads with Sainsbury's and Starbucks opposite, lots of residential streets and light industry all around, near the tube and on a bus route but, once inside, the environment feels safe, comfortable and peaceful and the outside world is decidedly outside.

The ground floor is home to the nursery, reception and Year 1 children and is remarkably spacious. The nursery in particular – 26 children – has three large rooms and a hall – few chic little independent nurseries provide as much as this. The quality of work, as demonstrated by the classroom displays, is exceptional. In one nursery room we saw 'The Belmont Hospital', with a very expert game of doctors and nurses in progress aided by real X-rays of hands, skulls, chests and ankles suspended over the enthusiastic patient's bed; we saw work on textures, water play, construction toys and individual reading – this with one of the army of parents who help with many aspects of class work. Reception was similar – very orderly classrooms with everyone at a table for five to six and working away at a variety of topics between which they swap during the course of a morning. Parents come and help with cooking – everyone wears a 'Belmont Bites' apron and a deliciously slurpy strawberry fool was developing when we visited.

The first floor houses Years 2 and 3 and is the 'transition floor'. Again, a good hall for PE, with £8,000 worth of new equipment paid for by the parents' association. A designated music room in which everyone has two class music lessons weekly – singing and composition – and, we are told, few children leave the school unable to read music. We witnessed a Year 6 class, all armed with instruments, mostly percussive, and singing away with gusto. 'Music permeates the school,' said Ofsted and, in addition to class music, many learn individually. Annually, Year 6 puts on a Shakespeare play – Twelfth Night and Macbeth in recent years; The Dream was in rehearsal as we visited. Photographs on display suggest a high level of production, again much supported, especially with costumes, makeup etc, by parents, many of whom are 'in the arts'.

Teaching up to the end of Year 2 is mixed ability. Setting in maths and English arrives in Year 3. Two sets – the higher being slightly the larger and having, therefore, around 33 children to the lower set's 27-ish. The upper set has just one teacher, no classroom assistant being needed with these children because, of course, they are motivated and keen to learn. We couldn't see much problem with the lower sets either. Years 3–6 are on the top floor and, again, all classrooms are orderly and full of displays you want to stop and look at – both of the children's own work and of materials from outside. Years 3–6 have 40 minutes of French weekly. Libraries – well-stocked (parents again) for both infants and juniors – and two excellent IT suites – 15 PCs for the younger children and 30 for the older ones – intelligently used by specialist staff; when we visited, a Year 3 class was concentratedly working on a maths programme about 'capacity' – well beyond ours! Interactive whiteboards also now in use and Ofsted's one and only quibble about ICT being under-used now decidedly out of date. Everyone has two hours of physical activity weekly and it was especially pleasurable to see a dance class with budding Billy Elliots clearly not at all embarrassed to be dancing – quite balletically!

Belmont does very well academically: SATs results in all subjects are at least 10 per cent above local and national averages and are far higher by Year 6. The achievement and value-added results from those from ethnic minority groups especially remarkable. SENs of all kinds are well-supported here. Hounslow borough has a well-established language service and those with EAL needs are seen individually or in small groups for up to a year until they are up to the general standard. A SENCo gives three full days to individuals, pairs or groups. A 'reading recovery' teacher sees individuals who, by Year 1, are falling behind – with 'fantastic' results. School has children with a large range of physical disabilities – lots of asthma but also cerebral palsy, Down's Syndrome, cystic fibrosis – and parents clearly grateful for the care and individual attention their children are sure of here. Staff 'very highly committed – they go that extra mile; we work as a team'. When we visited, no staff changes for two years.

Outside, in the extensive playground areas, lots of bike sheds, a covered stage with costume boxes, all kinds of different trails, apparatus, a super climbing wall painted by parents. Inside is cheerily decorated in a rich yellow and aqua blue and feels cosy and bright. The rooms are all good sizes, the furniture is in good nick and everywhere are thoughtful, orderly displays in a stimulating, orderly environment. The uniform – seemingly strictly adhered to – is attractive: navy and, again, orderly and neat – we saw not one scruffy child. Three male teachers – always a bonus; six staff have been in school for 10+ years and staff covers the whole age range. Two-thirds of children bring their own lunch. The local borough delivers the hot lunches – we saw the menu rather than the real thing: a clear emphasis on starch, though tasty starch, and a sad lack of fresh fruit and vegetables, though the children are offered a salad bar every day. Everyone eats in the canteen – possibly not the most attractive area in the school, two rooms being given over for lunchbox eaters.

A transformed school. Head is greatly aided by a posse of 'liberal middle class' parents only too eager to help in all areas of school life, including giving unobtrusive financial support when needed for the disadvantaged pupils who wouldn't otherwise be able to take part in trips etc. She is aided, too, by an excellent governing body, as well as by a good relationship with her local authority. A number of exclusions in previous years, but none in the two years preceding our visit. A proper and well-understood system of sanctions. Also an established homework system with extension work on the school website for those who want to push their offspring further – this school is working on all fronts. 'We got the systems in so pupils could learn,' says school.

The 2003 Ofsted report concluded, 'The school ensures that all children do as well as they can ... The leadership of the headteacher, in partnership with the governing body, is excellent ... An imaginative and innovative curriculum promotes high levels of achievement. Partnership with parents is very good. The school provides very good value for money.' Find the Primary Admissions Area and move in.

Belmont School (Dorking)

Feldemore, Holmbury St Mary, Dorking, Surrey, RH5 6LQ

• Pupils: 170 boys, 70 girls; 40 weekly boarders Sunday – Thursday night (or flexible), 215 day pupils. • Ages: 7-13 main school, 5-7 pre-prep, 2-5 early years • C of E • Fees: Day £6,288-£10,689; Boarding + £5,040 pa • Independent

Tel: 01306 730 852
Fax: 01306 731 220
Email: schooloffice@belmont-school.org
Website: www.belmont-school.org

Head: Since 2006, Mrs Helen Skrine, BA PGCE NPQH FRSA (forties). Educated at St Albans High School for Girls, Exeter and London universities. Taught at Wrekin College, Greenacre School, Chinthurst Preparatory and Highfield School, Liphook, before taking up headship here. Met her husband, John, at university; they have two sons, Henry and Giles, both at Marlborough. Enjoys lacrosse (laments absence from Belmont fixtures), has a passion for music and enjoys watersports and sailing (currently restoring a yacht); loves walking her three dogs. Two were parked in the homely study (squidgy sofas and something of a busy thoroughfare) when we arrived. 'They're good for breaking the ice and excellent pastorally: children tell them their troubles,' ventured the head.

Children approve of the 'good-strict' head, saying she's brought a lot of new ideas, improved the school and can act too. Popular with staff and parents – 'She's tightened things up but kept the family feel that is so important to Belmont'. Shrewd and efficient but with a wonderful blend of care and compassion. We were about to meet with the head when a worried child came along: child was prioritised. We waited. Would you have wanted it any other way? Teaches and feels it is essential to do so – 'That way I really get to know the children'.

Entrance: Main points of entry: 2+, 7+ and 11+. Broad range of ability and keen to maintain this. Pupils assessed during whole day spent with appropriate teaching group (the two 'on trial' when we visited thought the place amazing). Year 5 expands from Year 4 and breaks into two forms. A year later, a third form joins in Year 6, many of whom come from Moon Hall (qv) and form a specialist dyslexia stream, offered additional support needed for CE or a senior school's own assessment procedure (these children take all lessons bar English, and sometimes maths, at Belmont). Girls leaving at 11 has become increasingly unpopular over the past three years, and only one or two now leave, with the majority staying till 13. 'I wanted my daughter to stay at Belmont until 13. Once a couple of us committed to staying here, others followed suit,' said a parent. Sibling policy, but no fee reduction until third child, and a good many travel long distances. Bursaries (up to 100 per cent) available from Year 3.

Exit: Most to schools in south, e.g. RGS Guildford, St John's Leatherhead, Epsom College, Cranleigh, City of London Freemen's, Reigate Grammar, Millfield, St Bede's Hailsham, King Edward's Witley, Reed's Cobham, Hurstpierpoint, Bedales, Lancing, Box Hill, Manor House and Roedean. Approximately a quarter of pupils gain awards, mainly to local senior schools. One or two academic awards annually. Head a great fan of boarding and keen to encourage parents to look further afield at 13+. All Belmont pupils sit Common Entrance in Year 8 but a handful of Moon Hall children do not, following the KS3 curriculum in self-contained set; all enter a guided school of choice.

Remarks: Normal Common Entrance curriculum alongside KS2 and 3, to make sure those moving into state sector are catered for (no Latin). Two sets for maths and English in Years 5–6 with general streaming for science, humanities and French. This develops into three sets in Years 7–8. Smallish classes throughout, maximum 20, many with fewer. Science (refurbished lab), French, games, PE, music, art and DT (called Studio 4) taught by specialist staff in specialist rooms. Bright and breezy pre-prep, good indoor and outdoor facilities. We discovered a class of wee ones delighting in the humour of 'Shampooed and Cinderburg', and others dressed as pirates, not for a special day but to help their stories come to life. New nursery opened in 2007 – 'A godsend,' added one hopeful parent. Recent inspection sounds promising.

Music not yet as head would like: three choirs and an orchestra but still room for growth. Sufficient keyboards for whole class teaching. Major musical production at end of spring term sees 80 children on stage and numerous eager hands helping with everything else. Christmas productions involve all; form assemblies turn into major events and it's okay for boys to dance – some even do tap. Fabulous drama produces young pros – one pupil acted with Derek Jacobi, another on the West End stage with the Von Trapps. Sports teams compete against those from local schools; good offerings in art with art scholars most years.

Very good provision for dyslexics and other SpLD. Assessments carried out on anyone flagged up, at any time, either by parents or staff – so no worries if five-year-old Freddie develops his dad's dyslexic traits. If extra help is needed youngsters can be supported in English and maths at Moon Hall – a separate but co-located school that utilises some of Belmont's facilities. Indeed we love the way the two schools play off each other's strengths: instant help for any child at Belmont who may need an SpLD assessment or support at whatever level is reciprocated via Moon Hall pupils using Belmont for lunches, PE, boarding and some extra-curricular activities. 'My daughter was bright but struggling with spellings. 40 minutes a week for two terms at Moon Hall put her back on track – a real bonus to be able to get timely specialist help for those odd hiccups.' (Note that there is no link with Moon Hall's more distant offshoots, Moon Hall College and Burys Court).

An idyllic setting. Bit of a sat nav nightmare to get to (seriously hairy roads) but 65 acres of woodland and outstanding natural beauty soften the blow. All-weather floodlit pitch, sports hall and outdoor heated pool (cover on the wish list), go-karting track, low-ropes, high wire and two adventure playgrounds keep youngsters busy in free time. Making Celtic round houses in Celtic style when we visited: 'Typical Belmont,' commented head. Sports fields rented from local country estate across road as school's 65 acre site is on a fairly steep hillside. Variety of clubs. Boarding offers flexi and weekly options. Boarders stay in main house with separate wing for girls (currently 10). Parents a mix of first time buyers and old hands. A good number find fees from income. Headmistress is available at any time, except when teaching. Informal opportunity for all parents to talk to staff over tea on Friday when collecting pupils. A refreshing honesty about the children: 'Oh, are you from the book?' one asked. On hearing the affirmative he ventured, 'And how many pages does it have?'

A secure, happy prep school experience lets children be just that. If the child's got it – the school will bring it out; if the child doesn't quite cut it, school will stand by and put everything in place until they do. Second chances not a problem here. On the up.

Bentley Church of England Primary School

School Lane, Bentley, Farnham, Surrey, GU10 5JP

• Pupils: 215 boys and girls, all day • Ages: 4-11 • C of E • State

Tel: 01420 525 010
Fax: 01420 525 011
Email: admin.office@bentley.hants.sch.uk
Website: www.bentleyschool.co.uk

Head: Since 1991, Mr Phillip Callaway (fifties). Previously six years as deputy head at a primary school in Farnborough. Appears very easy-going, but underneath is determined to fight hard for his school. His enthusiasm for the children and the school is obvious and he encourages everyone to have a go and do their best. A well-liked chap by pupils and parents, he is also highly regarded by the LEA – he was recently seconded to another Hampshire primary for half the week. 'This happens from time to time,' he explains, 'but I am confident the school is left in good hands and it brings more vital money into Bentley.'

Entrance: Always over-subscribed. Pupils from in catchment get a place and so far out-catchment siblings have been successful, but last year school received 20 out-catchment applications and only a few gained places.

Exit: 70 per cent to Eggars (local state secondary) in Alton. Rest to local independents such as Royal Grammar Guildford, Lord Wandsworth, Churchers and Alton Convent.

Remarks: A one-form entry, typical village primary school full of happy children who want to learn – worth moving to be near, particularly if you are a hands-on parent. A relaxed atmosphere with children always busy, on task and enjoying their work. Academically very strong and consistently outperforms national and LEA key stage averages – often achieves 100 per cent in English and maths. Always in the Sunday Times Good Primary Schools Guide. Children enjoy their learning and always encouraged to succeed. Average class size 32 in junior and 30 in younger classes but pupils often work in smaller groups. About 10 per cent with SEN (two statements) taught mainly with the class or in groups by one full-time SEN teaching assistant. Very recent Ofsted categorised the school as outstanding.

Super ICT facilities with new equipment and interactive whiteboards in all classrooms – very impressive for a state school. Funded by the LEA; however, the PTFA makes a significant contribution of around £15,000 pa. Staffing a high priority – pupil:teacher ratio excellent for a state school. Parents feel much of the strength of the school lies in the (mainly female) staff 'They are so dedicated'.

Brand new hall completed in November 2009 which allows for greatly enhanced PE and many opportunities for after-school sports clubs. Assemblies and drama productions can now be easily accessed by the whole school community. New kitchen, opened in January 2010, serves hot meals to nearly 150 children (75 per cent of the school – highest take-up in the county) on a daily basis.

Prides itself on opportunities offered to children including day trips and residential visits. Ethos of school is: 'Never turn away an opportunity – give it a try'. All children from Year 3 upwards go on a residential trip each year, usually to various nearby outdoor activity centres. Often the first time away from home – 'The children love it, especially when they get really wet and muddy,' said one mother. Head feels these trips are vitally important to the children's development and a great chance. More than half of children learn an instrument, lessons held mainly at lunch-time or after school – 'Music tuition is wonderful'.

Sport a high profile with a wide variety of before- and after-school clubs, e.g. cricket, football, netball, cross-country, judo, dance, gym, swimming (at nearby Treloar School; early bird swimming club before school for the keen) and rounders. Teams compete regularly against other local schools in a variety of sports with considerable success. The football team has won several local competitions and the KWIK cricket team is one of the best in Hampshire. 2010 was an exceptional year on the sporting field for the school. The six-a-side football team reached the national finals at Ewood Park, Blackburn, the Year 6 team won the Hampshire County Cup and the Year 5 cricket team emulated this feat on the cricket pitch. Opportunities always taken to enter other sporting events.

Other extra-curricular activities run by staff or privately organised – a veritable hive of activity: 'If we have a failing it's that we take on too much,' says head.

Pupils a lively, well-behaved bunch, encouraged to act in a sensible and mature way and care for each other. Problems dealt with efficiently and thoroughly by teachers – head confident nothing more serious than playground squabbles, which are quickly resolved, and the children are taught the importance of respect for each other in regular circle time discussions. 'They are totally absorbed in the life of the school,' comments one parent, 'and so are we!' Parents help in the classroom, on day trips, with sporting events and generally around the school. PTFA very active both socially and for fund-raising activities.

Berkhamsted Preparatory School

Linked to Berkhamsted School in the Senior section

Kings Road, Berkhamsted, Hertfordshire, HP4 3YP

- Pupils: 425 girls and boys; 50:50 • Ages: 3-11 • Christian
- Fees: Pre prep £3,375-£7,200; Prep £8,475-£11,325 pa • Independent

Tel: 01442 358 201
Fax: 01442 358 203
Email: admissions@berkhamstedschool.org
Website: www.berkhamstedschool.org.uk

Head: Since 1998, Mr Adrian Taylor BA Cert Ed (London) (mid-fifties). His third headship, having been at St Joseph's Pontefract and Barlborough Hall. On coming to Berkhamsted he led the merger of the two single sex prep schools and maintains his enthusiasm more than 10 years on. Clearly very excited by current plans for further infrastructure investment. Has now seen his own children move up and through the school; gives the impression that the pupils are still his family and the school his home. His wife also teaches here. Lots of direct eye contact and ebullience as pupils strain out of their seats to tell him what they like most and good humour as he hears their replies. Reputedly a kind man thought to have their interests very much at heart, keeping a good eye on them while ensuring he himself is very visible to parents. Warm relationships all round and close collaboration with the principal and senior management. A trained school inspector, he also takes an active interest in supporting other heads and keeps up to speed with new developments by serving on national education committees.

Entrance: Children observed by experienced teachers at play and undertaking fun activities to determine their readiness to enter pre-prep. Skills and abilities also tested at 5+. Interview with head/deputy at 7+ and 10+ along with English and maths tests linked to key stage two national curriculum. The main feeders are local primary schools including Christ Church C of E, Butlers Court Combined School, Bridgewater School and St Thomas More RC Primary School, though pupils also come from Francis House Prep School and a variety of other independent preps.

Exit: Vast majority – about 70 – go on to senior school, where the boys and girls study separately from 11–16 – a major attraction for many parents. Very few do not gain entry and appropriate warning given to those who might not. The school does not provide help for those seeking grammar school entry.

Remarks: Tucked away amidst leafy residential roads, a stone's throw from the high street, offers much in terms of convenience and happy seclusion. Opened in 1998 as a result of a merger of the former single sex boys' and girls' prep schools. It shares many of the facilities of the adjacent senior schools, but retains a more playful atmosphere. Climbing frame and swings opposite the headmaster's office and a colourful dining room with encouragement to eat your greens and be healthy. The food gets high praise indeed from the pupils, but lots more they like. 'The school should open every day. I get so bored at the weekend,' laments one girl. Busy calendar of trips and activities designed to drive greater independence and skills for life. The Skern Lodge residential trip in Year 6 particularly popular, but on a more day-to-day basis much to keep the pupils at school and relieve pressure on working parents. The prep offers Years 3–6 day boarding until 6pm Monday to Thursday and until 5pm on Friday, and a wide range of after-school clubs until 4.30pm, and for pre-prep until 4pm.

Suits the sporty with ample opportunities to take part in external and inter-house competitions. Further up the school grounding in cricket, football, rugby, hockey and lacrosse pays off with regular success at regional and even national level. Music is encouraged with free lessons in groups of three to four in Year 3 and lots of opportunities to perform in the orchestra and choirs.

Ofsted recently ranked the pre-prep outstanding. It provides a good basis for learning and being part of a community, as does the rest of the school. Pupils are proud of it and parents comment that its value system, and that of the linked senior school, is particularly strong, making for a caring environment and happy children. A lone boy was fair smothered with female concern during break. The school chapel hosts regular assemblies, services and concerts, which reinforce the sense of unity, allowing a wide range of children to perform and drawing in parents. They also enjoy regular communication with class representatives and invitations to participate from the Friends' Committee. It caters for a wide range of abilities with setting in maths from Year 3. Results at the end of key stage 2 place the school in the top five per cent nationally (ISI inspection report). Parents are confident that all children are challenged and supported as appropriate. Report diaries are completed on a weekly basis and open lines of communications maintained between parents and staff. SEN provision exists but not fêted.

Learning support team deals with all specific learning difficulties throughout the school. Children are assessed regularly with extra help provided where necessary. However some concern that class sizes have a tendency to creep up, diluting individual attention and making some classrooms cramped.

BGS Infant and Juniors

Linked to Bristol Grammar School in the Senior section

Elton Road, Bristol, BS8 1SR

• Pupils: 45 Infants boys and girls; 175 Juniors 115 boys and 60 girls
• Ages: 5-11 • Non-denom • Fees: £5,700-£7,017 pa • Independent

Tel: 0117 973 6109
Fax: 0117 974 1941
Email: admissions@bgs.bristol.sch.uk
Website: www.bristolgrammarschool.co.uk

Head: Dr Alison Primrose – who departs in July 2011.

Entrance: January 2010 saw new pre-prep with Years 1 and 2; reception class opened in September 2010. Entry by informal assessment. Entry to junior school – mostly into Years 3 and 4 but also a Year 6 entry for those aiming at the senior school – by reading, writing and reasoning tests.

Exit: Many to the senior school – but you have to pass the exam.

Remarks: For further information, see senior school.

Bilton Grange School

Rugby Road, Dunchurch, Rugby, Warwickshire, CV22 6QU

• Pupils: 340 boys and girls including 135 in pre-prep (Homefield); 45 full/weekly boarders, lots of flexi • Ages: 4-7 pre-prep; 8-13 prep • C of E (all faiths welcome) • Fees: Day £7,968-£15,255; Boarding £18,735 pa • Independent

Tel: 01788 810 217
Fax: 01788 816 922
Email: rlb@biltongrange.co.uk
Website: www.biltongrange.co.uk

Headmaster: Since Sept 2003, Mr Peter Kirk BSc, FRSA (fifties). Read maths at Edinburgh, then Royal Naval officer for five years before three-year teaching stint at Welbeck College (British army's sixth form residential college) launched current career. Previously taught at Marlborough College and Glenalmond College, first headship in 1996 at mixed prep Bramcote School, Scarborough, taking up BG reins seven years later. Inherited strong prep but rigorously building on firm foundations with subtle changes to day-to-day running and pupil participation in school affairs (new school council). Takes pride in offering children 'a balanced diet with opportunities to do everything'. Considers the school's one strength to be 'all-round excellence'. Wife Rosemary closely involved in school activities, two university student daughters. Mr Kirk is a devotee of mountaineering and skiing 'when time allows, but our lives now are boarding school lives.'

Entrance: Pre-prep bulging so parents must get names down early. Roughly 60:40 boys to girls. Non-selective ('Not sure how to select academically when they're only four,' comments head) but placement test and interview for candidates. Academic potential looked for. Also wider interest in music, sport etc. 'We take our sport seriously,' says head. Pupil numbers still rising – lack of vacancies has meant some being turned away. Book early to avoid disappointment, he advises.

Exit: Up to 85 per cent of leavers go to senior boarding schools. Exams twice a year prepare pupils for Common Entrance. Top academic scholarships bagged in last two years to Wycombe Abbey, Rugby (five), Oundle and Repton, and several music scholarships to same. Other popular destinations include Eton, Cheltenham Ladies' College and St Edward's, Oxford.

Remarks: Magnificent Victorian mansion on raised plateau with far-reaching views across Warwickshire countryside. Main school rather imposing with large entrance bordered on two sides by high redbrick walls and chapel on third. More welcoming once inside thankfully and electronic flat-screen notice board keeps pupils, parents and staff on top of the day's events or recent sporting success (showing pictures of U10s winning rugby team at time of visit). The blend of old and new is extraordinary. Wood panelled halls, acres of windows, tiled floors and creaking floorboards are brought bang up-to-date with computer suites and interactive whiteboards.

This may be a traditional prep in its most traditional sense (boarding ethos, Saturday school, staff all Sir or Miss, loads of rough, tumble and rugby) but it's also at the cutting edge of 21st century technology. BG claims to be the best-equipped prep school for ICT in the country, the army of electronic whiteboards is in constant use, there's a school intranet for all to use and linked laptops. High tech isn't confined to prep pupils, though – pre-preppers at Homefield are taught touch-typing and digital cameras are regularly used as part of lessons. Teachers insist none of it replaces good old-fashioned teaching – it adds to it, improves it, makes it more effective. Neither do electronic research aids replace books. Reading is taught to be enjoyed at the pre-prep, there are book rooms at every stage of school and a huge library for reading or study in the mansion house. Class sizes inevitably small with setting for subjects by ability.

Older children take three separate sciences in modern labs. ICT taught as subject in its own right, then incorporated into all lessons for last two years. Wide curriculum for little ones too, including drama and dance in hall (which doubles as dining room for lunch) and computer studies. French compulsory; Latin started by all, though some later drop it in favour of life studies (i.e. revision techniques, current affairs etc). Learning support for around nine per cent of pupils with some form of difficulty. No limit to help received – judged on individual basis. New director of music has boosted already very good music provision. Children taught to compose as well as play. Around 75 per cent take instrument lessons as well as class music. Daily sport for all – indoor pool means swimming all year round. Also large sports hall in addition to acres of playing fields. Facilities certainly are second to none. Drama consistently strong (productions have been to Edinburgh Fringe in past years) led by a small team of enthusiastic and (by all accounts) talented teachers. Large school hall with 300 seats has everything needed for both stage shows and concerts.

Stunning little chapel designed in the mid 1800s by Augustus Welby Pugin (as is much of the school). This is where school starts every day with a service/assembly (non C of E pupils also asked to attend). Chapel for boarders too every Sunday. Year groups (both day and boarding children plus their parents) take it in turns to attend one Sunday a term. Religion clearly still an important part of school life. Fine old organ – the original on which old boy Sir Arthur Bliss learned to play – now fully restored and used constantly by organ scholar from Birmingham Conservatoire. Head calls BG a 'broad church' (in the secular sense) with children taken from vast spread of backgrounds – professional, self-starter, old money – as is more than adequately illustrated by its list of former pupils. As well as Bliss, it includes humourist Miles Kington, actor Alexander Hanson (Baron von Trapp in the latest West End's Sound of Music – he apparently played one of von Trapp's daughters when it was put on at school) and film star Rupert Evans.

Form tutors responsible for pastoral care but that also extends to house-masters and mistresses. Sanctions (for such things as bullying) can include removal of privileges. But head says they rely heavily on talking and working problems through together. Boarding houses light, bright and comfortable. Top bunks in dorms kept for flexi-boarders. Girls' accommodation cosier than boys' but all made more homely by children's own belongings and family atmosphere created by house-parents. School set in 150 acres of gardens, woods and fields – all used by school and for pupils' exploration. Head says, 'We give children the freedom to climb trees and really enjoy the grounds. But I believe what's different here from other schools is that pupils at the top of the school get a tiny bit more independence and free time. They develop confidence without arrogance.' The pupils we watched in class and met as we went around certainly upheld that belief. They were a lively, happy bunch that seemed to revel in their surroundings and the self-belief BG has given them. Social interaction is as much part of the curriculum here as maths and English. 'We make time to talk and get to know each other,' says head. The result? Well-developed, adjusted youngsters ready for the next chapter in their lives.

Birkdale School Preparatory School

Linked to Birkdale School in the Senior section

Clarke House, Clarke Drive, Sheffield, South Yorkshire, S10 2NS

• Pupils: 260 boys; all day • Ages: 4-11 • Christian • Fees: Pre-Prep £7,203; Prep £8,520 pa • Independent

Tel: 0114 267 0407
Fax: 0114 268 2929
Email: enquiries@birkdaleschool.org.uk
Website: www.birkdaleschool.org.uk

Head of Preparatory School: Since early 2009, Mr Christopher Burch BA PGCE (mid thirties). Previously deputy head of Great Walstead Prep.

Entrance: At 4, by interview and at 7, by interview and exam held at the start of the Easter term – English, maths and reasoning. Boys come both from the independent and maintained sectors and from as far away as Retford, Doncaster – huge catchment area.

Exit: All but a handful on to senior school, rest to other independents or into the state sector.

Remarks: Elegant, late-Georgian house, overlooking the Botanical Gardens and once home of the Osborn family, he a master cutler. School acquired building in 1988 and did a spot of adapting. Now works well – servants' quarters house the computer room. Hall was probably purpose-built when the buildings housed either the grammar school or the nurses' training establishment – some slightly surprising alterations giving rooms glass windows onto corridors. Gloriously cosy tinies' wing with sandpits and a dedicated play area. All immobile items labelled in large letters – door, printer, computer, desk.

NB This is not a school with a nursery and is academic, starting French at four, science right through, specialist teachers from seven when boys are setted in maths. Sets in English and science at nine. Strong learning support, both withdrawn and dual teaching in class, no problems with dyspraxia, ADHD, ADD, all boys screened. Good library and boys decide which books they would like to read. Christian foundation, act of worship four times a week; about 12 Muslims and Hindus, no-one feels indoctrinated and indeed, non-Christians prefer to be at a school with a 'living faith'. Appropriate religious texts all over. Halal meat on request and vegetarian options, 'We like kids to finish their veg but we don't insist'.

Loads of first-time buyers, not all middle class by any means – 'Parents beggar themselves to come here'. IT throughout, oodles of computers, ICT lessons from seven. Computer-linked piano, and masses of music and theory of music, drums and percussion and other instruments (everything except the harp). Good orchestra and choir. Drama vibrant. Significant liaison between staff at senior and prep schools; older boys and girls come and help out on a one-to-one basis, and future plans for staff from the senior school to visit the term before boys move up and teach the relevant classes to ensure continuity. Uses big school games field and cricket nets and shares the extensive playing fields 10 minutes from the campus. Hopes to develop building here, with enlarged classrooms, particularly in the pre-prep department. Masses of post-school clubs, late waiting till 5.30pm and children can be left at 8.15am. Jolly, academic prep school. Zinging.

Birkenhead Prep School

Linked to Birkenhead School in the Senior section

57 Shrewsbury Road, Oxton, Birkenhead, CH43 2JA

• Fees: £6,522-£7,194 pa • Independent

Tel: 0151 652 4114
Fax: 0151 651 3091
Email: Enquire@BirkenheadSchool.co.uk
Website: www.BirkenheadSchool.co.uk

Bishop's Stortford College Junior School

Linked to Bishops Stortford College in the Senior section

Maze Green Road, Bishop's Stortford, Hertfordshire, CM23 2PH

• Pupils: 450: 240 boys, 210 girls; 50 boarders. Plus up to 120 in pre-prep. • Ages: Junior School 7-13, pre-prep 4-6 • Non-denominational • Fees: Day £6,750-£11,553; Boarding £14,181-£15, 894 pa • Independent

Tel: 01279 838607
Fax: 01279 306110
Email: jsadmissions@bishopsstortfordcollege.org
Website: www.bishops-stortford-college.herts.sch.uk

Head: Mr John Greathead BEd (early fifties), read education at University College of Wales, majored in English. Married with one grown-up son; he loves sport in general, golf in particular, and enjoys reading, travel, music, natural history and photography.

Entrance: Entrance to the pre-prep department is by a day's assessment; for the junior school by entrance exam.

Exit: Vast majority to senior school, a few to local state schools; those unlikely to make the grade warned in good time.

Remarks: Co-located with the senior school; has its own well-furnished and equipped classrooms, kiln room, art facilities, science labs and outdoor space, but also shares some of the senior school facilities. Academic streaming starts in Year 4 plus setting for maths. All pupils study Latin from Year 5; Saturday school for everyone above pre-prep. Common entrance not offered but does follow the CE syllabus.

Heads work closely together to promote the same work-hard, play-hard ethos. Sporting success aplenty: U13 national rugby champions (strong links with local rugby club), and boys' and girls' U11 and U13 teams are county hockey champions. House system popular: lots of competitions, challenges, high profile visiting speakers etc. Junior boarding house offers the same boarding options as the senior school, including weekly boarding. Plenty of good work on show; lively and interesting displays, changed frequently, ensure latest achievements celebrated. Tuesday and Thursday afternoons dedicated to wide-ranging activities, with all pupils sampling photography, bridge, origami, cooking, golf and a whole lot more. Oldest pupils spend the first week of the year under canvas, team-building and developing leadership skills; trips and tours for others.

A happy, lively school that encourages curiosity and creativity; ideal starting point for anyone intending to hot-foot across the tarmac to the senior school.

Blackheath High School (Junior Department)

Linked to Blackheath High School GDST in the Senior section

Wemyss Road, Wemyss Road, London, SE3 0TF

• Pupils: 300 girls, nursery part time and all day, 4-11 all day • Ages: 3-11 • Non-denominational • Fees: £7,212-£9,342 pa • Independent

Tel: 020 8852 1537
Fax: 020 8463 0040
Email: info@blj.gdst.net
Website: www.blackheathhighschool.gdst.net

Head of Juniors: Since 2007, Alison Cordingley PGCE NPQH. Enthusiastic, energetic, comes from a family of teachers. Taught violin while at Trinity College of Music, then joined West Lodge School in Sidcup where she stayed for 20 years, latterly as deputy head. Loves her new job and feels herself very lucky to be working in such an excellent, forward-thinking school. Parents are happy that she threw herself straight into immediate improvement of the school. The changes that she made, and is still making, are entirely child-centred, 'totally focused on the girls'. She has also made herself visible to all and is accessible to everybody, standing at the school entrance every morning to welcome her pupils.

Entrance: By interview prior to entry at nursery level. Individual assessment at other stages.

Exit: Most move on to the senior school but some move into the state system or, occasionally, to other local schools.

Remarks: The original purpose-built structure, in which the whole school started in the 1800s, is now thoroughly refurbished but still retains a lot of charm. The parquet hall with its classical subject frieze, busts, columns and elegant double staircase is a delightful memento of days gone by. Yet the classrooms surrounding it are all large, light and airy and the specialist rooms – science, art, music, IT (several) etc – are all bang up to date. A great gym which is also used for class assemblies, a brand new drama studio and a friendly, welcoming library – everything a girl needs for a good broad start to her education can be found here.

The nursery and reception areas are big, bright and enticing, with their own well-equipped playground outside. The bigger girls' play section is divided into several areas where they can experience different sorts of fun, and an excellent buddy system so no-one ever feels left out. Lovely art displayed everywhere; computers and interactive whiteboards in every class; enthusiastic music – choral or instrumental; everyone gets to join in. French taught from nursery and Mandarin in Year 6. Bi-weekly use of the sports ground and swimming lessons locally.

SEN policy the same as the senior school. Children are all carefully watched and potential problems quickly identified. Communication with parents good. An excellent SENCo and lots of classroom assistants ensure that children get the help that they need. Any possibly difficult issues are dealt with quickly and sensitively.

A house system that works, with housepoints available for everything from being in a winning sports team to writing a good story to just being kind. A school council where girls have to apply for specific jobs provides them with a good feel of responsibility for others and a taste of things to come.

The two girls who took us round were relaxed, confident and enthusiastic – good ambassadors for their school, eager to explain everything that was going on. In fact, all the children we saw seemed well-behaved and happy, attentive in class and chatting away 19 to the dozen outside.

Parents have nothing but praise for a school that they feel is a happy place with a sensible approach to work and play. Not a hothouse but somewhere with a strong work ethic. 'My daughter works hard on her SATs in the morning and then really enjoys the play rehearsals in the afternoon.' Another parent was keen to stress the ability to build up a child's confidence – 'The teachers were very responsive, flexible and willing to work with me'. 'The bottom line is: how is your child performing? Here they really do get the best out of them.'

The Blue Coat School

Somerset Road, Edgbaston, Birmingham, West Midlands, B17 0HR

• Pupils: 560 (including pre-prep), 60:40 boys:girls; all day • Ages: 2-11 • C of E, but respect shown to many other faiths • Fees: £6,405-£9,855 pa • Independent

Tel: 0121 410 6800
Fax: 0121 454 7757
Email: headssec@bluecoat.bham.sch.uk
Website: www.bluecoat.bham.sch.uk

Headmaster: Since 1998, Mr Alan Browning (mid-fifties). Married to Helen, who is very much involved in school life; three boys, one at Cambridge and one at King Edward's School, Birmingham. Educated Clifton, Trinity Cambridge and Oxford. A musician, started career as a lecturer at Leicester University, thence to Blue Coat as director of music in 1982 and then deputy head and director of studies in 1993. 'He is someone who has lived and breathed the school for most of his professional career,' remarks a parent. This is of course both a strength and a weakness. A devout evangelical Christian, sees his faith as central to his role as headmaster. A man who is deeply committed to the interests of the children. 'This is a school that really cares about its pupils,' says a parent – a reflection of the head's most important priority.

Entrance: Usually at two into pre-prep or seven into prep. Test and interview at seven. Most children sign up at or near birth. The vast majority of the pupils enter the nursery (Buttons), then move through the school. Head keen to ensure that the girl/boy balance is maintained. Some places (dependent on natural wastage) at all levels but especially at seven. The vast majority of the children are recruited from the local Edgbaston and Harborne areas but the school is expanding its catchment area.

Exit: Blue Coat copes well and in many ways prospers in the demanding educational environment of Birmingham. The aspiration of most parents is to get their child into one of the super-academic King Edward VI schools or one of the many fine selective maintained schools in the area. Bearing in mind that the intake is an academically wide one, the school does well to get the largest single group into the King Edward schools. Others to schools such as Solihull, Edgbaston High and Old Swinford Hospital.

Remarks: The school was founded in 1722 by the Reverend William Higgs as a co-educational charity school (making it one of the oldest co-ed schools in the country) and now occupies a truly beautiful site in 15 acres of playing fields and gardens. Moved here in 1930 and the buildings, nearly all of which were erected at that time, are clustered around well-manicured lawns, giving the impression of a cloistered antiquity that would not be out of place in a public school. This is a true oasis of peace and tranquillity just outside the bustling heart of inner city Birmingham.

One might suppose that the avowedly Anglican tone of the school might fit uneasily within the modern multi-ethnic West Midlands community. Yet it all seems to work remarkably well and the school has retained its Anglican tradition – with its own lay chaplain – and lovely collegiate-style school chapel. At the same time it has a school roll of which about 50 per cent are from an ethnic minority background, and only some of the rest are in any sense strictly Church of England. Whilst there is no doubt that the Anglican voice is the dominant one, the school has gone to great lengths to invite visiting speakers from other Christian denominations and to introduce discussion of the Muslim, Hindu and Sikh traditions. This is a school where tolerance and mutual respect are taken very seriously indeed.

It has an innovative approach to language teaching, with all the children having the opportunity to taste Italian and Spanish before focusing on the main language, French, and Latin in Year 6. Science and art both flourish conspicuously, helped by some quite outstanding facilities. The success of so many pupils in the demanding King Edward VI entrance examinations says much for the quality of the teaching of the core academic subjects. As you would expect with a musical headmaster, music is especially strong, and the school has well-established links with Birmingham Cathedral and Birmingham Conservatoire, no doubt one reason why Sir Simon Rattle sent his children here. Chapel choir and four other choirs, numerous orchestral ensembles and 220 children learning at least one musical instrument. A notable recent addition is a Steinway concert grand piano. Lots of wonderful concerts, most notably special events at Symphony Hall (conducted by Rattle), St Paul's, Hockley and the CBSO Centre.

Boarding a thing of the recent past. The house system, originally designed for a predominantly boarding population, has been imaginatively reorganised to meet the needs of a day environment. Every prep school child is designated a house, uses its common room facilities and is under the care of a particular house parent. This ensures that pastoral support is especially strong and each child has a very intense sense of belonging to a small, intimate unit. It also means that the school is able to offer very effective and well organised out-of-school care until 6pm – a great boon for working parents. Happy, well-motivated children.

A great deal of emphasis is placed on a wide range of games, and the hugely impressive sports centre (incorporating a 25 metre pool) enhances this sporting tradition. The school organises its own sporting tournaments, which are enthusiastically attended by preparatory schools from far and wide.

Blue Coat's enormous strengths make it a natural choice for parents looking for a traditional preparatory school education within this city.

Blundell's Preparatory School

Linked to Blundells School in the Senior section

Milestones House, Blundells Road, Tiverton, Devon, EX16 4NA

• Pupils: 250 pupils • Ages: Two-and-a-half - 11 • Christian • Fees: £6,600-£9,000; Kindergarten/Nursery £5,175 pa • Independent

Tel: 01884 252 393
Fax: 01884 232 333
Email: prep@blundells.org
Website: www.blundells.org

Head: Since 2000, Mr Nicholas Folland. Previously taught at Blundell's Senior School for 11 years, including six years as a housemaster. Teaches both sport and geography in the prep school and is a member of the Blundell's School senior management team.

Entrance: Prospective pupils spend a taster day in school, during which an assessment in English and maths is carried out.

Exit: Some 85 per cent of pupils join Blundell's; however children are prepared thoroughly to take entrance exams for the school of their choice.

Remarks: The school links with some Blundell's Senior School facilities but is autonomous and run separately.

The Bolitho Junior School

Linked to Gems Bolitho School in the Senior section

Polwithen Road, Penzance, Cornwall, TR18 4JR

• Ages: infants 5-6, juniors 7-10, middle 11-13 • C of E • Fees: Day £5,850-£8,790; Boarding £15,930-£18,090 pa • Independent

Tel: 01736 363 271
Fax: 01736 330 960
Email: enquiries@bolithoschool.co.uk
Website: www.bolithoschool.co.uk/

Remarks: For further information, see senior school.

Bolton School Boys' Division Junior School

Linked to Bolton School Boys Division in the Senior section

Park Road, Bolton, Lancashire, BL1 4RD

• Pupils: 185 boys; plus 200 boys and girls in the pre-prep (Beech House); all day • Ages: 7-11, 4-7 in pre-prep (Beech House) • Fees: £6,879 pa • Independent

Tel: 01204 522669
Fax: 01204 410 073
Email: juniorboys@boltonschool.org
Website: www.boltonschool.org/juniorboys

Head: Since September 2008, Mr Stephen Whittaker (fortyish), BEd from Chester College, part of Liverpool University, and an NPQH. Taught at St James' CE school in Lower Darwin for six years before becoming deputy head of St John's CE/Methodist Primary School in Brinscall, then head of St Peter's CE Primary, Chorley. Came to view job and school for a fresh challenge and something different and knew immediately from the welcome and life in the place that this was the school for him. Big fan of the 'tweak to transform' concept, of taking something that's already good and making small changes to keep on improving it. Married to an infants teacher, with two children settled in other schools. A vicar's son, he leads Leyland Methodist Church's music and drama group, co-writing and producing an annual musical involving over 80 youngsters in his spare time. Into music, he's a drummer in a band and has delighted boys, junior and senior, by enhancing school performances with his backing.

Entrance: Assessment by English, maths, VR and non-VR exams and interviews with head and deputy, looking at academic ability and extra-curricular passions. Only slightly over-subscribed so bright applicants should bag a place; feedback given. Children from infants have rite of passage into juniors; they've already entered after assessment.

Exit: Junior boys have to sit same entry for seniors as outsiders but almost all pass, and in fact they tend to sit in the top quarter of the overall intake's ability. One or two to MGS (qv) instead and a few to state secondary schools.

Money Matters: All junior places full fee-paying.

Remarks: Busy, bright boys bound along at speed here in super setting with great atmosphere. Two classes of 25 boys in each year in a spacious, three-storey, whitewashed building known as Park Road, newly extended and refurbished in a £1.5m project. It's just down the road from the senior schools and next to the infants' division in its own brand new, state-of-the-art Beech House. Lessons are pacey with specialist teachers and bespoke classrooms from the off; in some areas their work's a year ahead of other schools. No shortage of fun though; during our visit one class was knee-deep in a muddy flower bed planting bulbs, having learnt about sowing and reaping during harvest festival. Beyond them a full-sized games pitch lies beside an adventure playground with a climbing wall. Head meets every class for a weekly session in the library, 'I'm a great believer in sharing stories'. A reading award scheme encourages even the reluctant to get reading for bronze to platinum-plus awards. There are stick insects galore in the science lab, 'and sometimes out of it, just look at this spider plant, or what was this spider plant,' laughs head from the corridor. There's an ICT lab, an exciting DT room buzzing with busyness, fabulous landscape paintings adorn the entrance hall and outside the music department (there are three practice rooms as well as two classrooms) lots of violins stand to attention in home-made racks. Older boys also stand to attention when head enters room, in preparation for senior school manners. Four houses mean boys can earn house merits, and dreaded demerits where you lose ten points just like that, and after three demerits it's a report card, 'for bad behaviour for, you know, whacking someone with a recorder or something'. There's not much time for that sort of thing though, with lunch time and after-school clubs from jujitsu to brain games and play reading. Two representatives from each class take boys' ideas from the listening boxes to school council; a cookery club is starting as a result of this. The refurbished dining room is furnished with the same traditional refectory tables and benches as in senior school, 'ah no, we couldn't lose the benches' and there's a further main hall for assemblies, concerts and indoor PE. Juniors share some senior facilities, most notably the swimming pool. A SENCo helps with minor learning difficulties.

Bolton School Girls' Division Junior School

Linked to Bolton School Girls Division in the Senior section

Chorley New Road, Bolton, Lancashire, BL1 4PB

• Pupils: 200 girls in the main school; infant department (Beech House) 215 boys and girls; all day • Ages: nursery 0-4, infants (Beech House) 4-7, juniors 7-11 • Fees: £6,879 pa • Independent

Tel: 01204 840201
Fax: 01204 434710
Email: juniorgirls@boltonschool.org
Website: www.boltonschool.org/juniorgirls

Head: Head of infant school, Mrs Deborah Northin. Head of juniors Mrs Ruth Brierley.

Entrance: Entry to infant school by short interview, with automatic transfer to junior school. Test for outside applicants to junior school in Year 3. Occasionally spaces are available in Years 4, 5 and 6.

Exit: Most girls transfer to the senior school via tests.

Remarks: Housed in its own state-of-the-art school, which was completed in the summer of 2010. Like the senior school, there are a wide range of popular lunchtime clubs and activities. Assessment tests mainly held in January, although arrangements for assessment can be made at other times during the year. Headteachers' reports from previous school and KS1 results taken into account.

Infant department (Beech House) on same site as senior school and is also housed in purpose-built state-of-the-art premises (completed in June 2009). Entry in September following fourth birthday via short individual interviews during autumn term of previous year. No formal skills required but readiness to listen, concentrate and adapt to school life essential. Nearly all children go on to junior school. Progression is automatic for pupils moving through from Beech House.

Nice department with evidence of much industry and happiness – takes traditional harvest festival seriously, with proper little baskets of fruit and vegetables; none of your cash donations and a token tin of baked beans! After-school care until 6pm.

Nursery school a modern, purpose-built nursery close to senior school. Excellent Ofsted report. No automatic transfer to Beech House but majority do. Lively programme of activities.

Bootham Junior School

Linked to Bootham School in the Senior section

Rawcliffe Lane, York, North Yorkshire, YO30 6NP

• Pupils: 150 girls and boys • Ages: 3-11 • Fees: £2,760-£8,520 pa • Independent

Tel: 01904 655021
Fax: 01904 651666
Email: junior@boothamschool.com
Website: www.boothamschool.com

Head: Ms Sue Ratcliffe.

Remarks: For further information, see senior school: Bootham School

Bousfield Primary School

South Bolton Gardens, Old Brompton Road, London, SW5 0DJ

• Pupils: 215 boys, 215 girls, all day • Ages: 3-11 • Non-denom • State

Tel: 020 7373 6544
Fax: 020 7373 8894
Email: jennifer.selmes@bousfield.rbkc.sch.uk
Website: www.bousfield.rbkc.sch.uk

Head: Since 1998, Ms Connie Cooling MA DipEd. Studied education management and the teaching of maths, has taught in a number of London schools. Has built up a good team of teachers, assistants and SEN support; a very stable staff. Very keen to reflect the school's international nature, both socially and culturally – the head sees this as a real strength.

Entrance: Over-subscribed. Nursery place does not guarantee entry to reception. Priority given to children who live nearest the school. One nursery class of 30, two reception classes of 30 each, all admitted in September. Lots of European ex-pats. Broad social mix. Despite location, 15 per cent of children are eligible for free school meals.

Exit: A number of leavers go on to private schools, including the Lycée. State favourites are Holland Park and Chelsea Academy.

Remarks: As popular as ever. Very successful Ofsted inspection in 2008, which they are rightly proud of. On the site of Beatrix Potter's childhood home. Built in 1956, this post-war building is listed. The large playground has been revamped, making the site more secure and colourful. Parents have painted a huge mural with Quentin Blake characters – the artist has close ties with the school. Classrooms are light and airy and full of creative artwork. Library well stocked and used. Since our last visit, ICT has been developed considerably with interactive whiteboards and computer linked projectors in every classroom.

English is not the first language of about half of the pupils, with 35 mother tongues (Arabic and French chief among them). No school uniform but children look bright-eyed and tidy. The school ticks over efficiently; it's in good condition and spotlessly clean. Food is cooked on site, using organic fruit and vegetables. A member of the National Fruit Scheme – every infant has a piece of fruit or carrot at breaktime. Lots of parental involvement both in school and with fundraising. All classes have homework.

Fosters the creative arts and has gained an Artsmark Gold award, in recognition of its high quality music, dance and arts. Work in visual literacy well used as a starting point for creative writing. Children will eventually make their own films using special child-friendly cameras. Sport is taught on site to targeted year groups, with matches taking place off site with local schools. The school's busy diary includes a round of plays, concerts, museum visits, themed curriculum weeks. After-school clubs are oversubscribed and offer a range of subjects – Spanish, French, Chinese, football, chess, guitar, creative thinking.

Head is keen on achievement across the board, good manners and discipline. It obviously works – walk into a classroom and you will find earnest faces and busy activity. An active school council made up of two elected representatives from each year reports on issues affecting pupils. They recently conducted a survey on how children travelled to school, resulting in the purchase of more bicycle racks.

An oasis in the middle of London, this school has something to sing about.

Bradford Grammar Junior School (Clock House)

Linked to Bradford Grammar School in the Senior section

Keighley Road, Bradford, West Yorkshire, BD9 4JP

• Pupils: 205: 155 boys and 50 girls; all day • Ages: 6-11 • Fees: £7,985 pa • Independent

Tel: 01274 553 742
Fax: 01274 553 745
Email: chsec@bradfordgrammar.com
Website: www.bgsjuniorschool.co.uk

Remarks: For further information, see the senior school.

Brambletye School

Lewes Road, East Grinstead, West Sussex, RH19 3PD

• Pupils: 290; girls and boys • Ages: 7-13; Pre-prep/Nursery two-and-a-half - 7 • Anglican • Fees: Boarding £19,830; Day £7,710-£16,170 pa • Independent

Tel: 01342 321 004
Fax: 01342 770 197
Email: registrar@brambletye.com
Website: www.brambletye.co.uk

Headmaster: Since 1997, Hugh Cocke (pronounced Coke) BA CertEd (fifties), appointed with his wife Lucy. She was in primary education in Peckham while he taught history at The Old Malthouse in Dorset (is no more) and then joined him there when he was made second master (at 26!). So they've had plenty of experience as a pastoral team – Cheam in North Hampshire and then the headship at Old Buckenham Hall in Suffolk for six years. Got on the property ladder as soon as they could in Dorset (lots of teachers at boarding schools are less canny because of the accommodation provided) – this organised foresight is characteristic of Mr Cocke. Tall and trim (squash, golf and cricket coaching), wielding a boldly-patterned handkerchief to blow his nose, he implements a smart schedule of daily and weekly communication with his (strongly developed) common room, ensuring that issues are flagged up and dealt with promptly.

Mrs Cocke, as the figurehead of the pastoral side, appears less regimented with her time, although she is outside the front of school greeting every morning with a notebook for parental queries. 'You get to know the children's grannies, sisters and dogs – I love that aspect of prep school life.' Their house adjoins the girls' dormitory wing and she cures homesickness with the help of Monty the labrador.

Head still teaches history (in the middle of the school), RS and the headmaster's lesson (for scholars and potential scholars on current topics) and is judged by pupils to be 'tough but fair'. Has overseen two major building projects, and the latest – the seven-classroom Blencowe Centre – was completed in 2009.

With two adult daughters who boarded away from their parents' teaching roles, this couple are a thoughtful and experienced team, making sure Brambletye's traditional stance is effective and tempered by compassion.

Entrance: No exam but questionnaire with searching questions on literacy, numeracy and extra-curricular character to be filled out by form teacher or head, 'To make sure our curriculum is suitable – we have a two-year CE syllabus'. If SEN concerns are raised, child will be invited down for informal assessment, mild dyslexia is fine. 50 per cent from pre-prep, 50 per cent external, some entrance at 11. Majority local boarders (Oxted, Forest Row, East Grinstead, Turner's Hill), some from London (school coach at exeat weekend), 10 per cent from abroad (Gatwick is very close) – USA, Spain, Thailand, India, Hong Kong, Russia, Ukraine. The opening of the pre-prep (2000) has gradually increased the local contingent throughout the school, since the jump from local primaries to Brambletye's schedule is large. London parents appreciate the growing local peer group – it 'keeps them from cruising King's Road for another couple of years'!

Exit: Not a feeder, instead to a range of about two dozen (mostly boarding) schools: Charterhouse, Radley, Stowe, Eton, Winchester, King's Canterbury, Marlborough, Bradfield, Benenden, Downe House, Harrow, Wycombe Abbey. The head visits at least four schools a term to maintain up-to-date contacts and information, also often invites a chaplain to preach at chapel on a Sunday and then stay for a coffee or a glass of wine in his study afterwards and then a meal – a great opportunity for parents to do their own research. Scholarships (strong on art and music) awarded are listed in gold on a board in the old gymnasium hall. Old boys range from the actor Ben Cumberbatch to the current Admiral of the Fleet.

Remarks: Founded in 1919, moved from Sidcup to this old hunting lodge near Ashurst Wood in 1933, and since then the rolling grounds have been semi-deforested and developed to make room for athletics, tennis, cricket, football and rugby pitches, a modern sports hall, a purpose-built pre-prep building and the new classroom block. Much of the main building is still panelled with dark oak, which makes for an atmospheric entrance hall (the boarders sit on the stairs and local oldies come in for carol singing accompanied by the piano in the corner) and dining room (three sittings for lunch, led by the little pre-preppers).

Evidence of proud tradition faces you on the walls – not just oils of previous heads, but the weighty house shield, the colourful house boards (children are quick to explain their stereotypical characters by reference to Hogwarts' houses), the original PE lockers under the seats in the gymnasium hall where everyone lines up before chapel three times a week. The children look charming in their uniform (pink and grey, right down to the stripy socks), pay attention both during school notices and the lesson in chapel and greet teachers politely in the halls with a 'Hello Sir' or 'Miss'. Parents set store by these confident and respectful manners.

So much on offer here that the announcements of various auditions and rehearsals made in chapel call up are always prefaced by 'as long as you've got no clashes'. An emphasis on children managing their own time, and at least one teacher advises his pupils not to schedule anything on a Sunday so that they have some time for unstructured play. Despite all the amazing activities (every staff member offers something once a week – canoe polo, wildlife club, extra art or music, squash, trampolining ...) the children say that it is the summer term that makes day pupils want to board – after high tea at 6pm, no activities and most people just race outside and play until bedtime at 8pm (lights out at 9pm). An assault course with a climbing tower and balance pole (built by an ex-Royal Marine), plenty of trees, time to catch up on 'the goss' and the latest crazes (diabolos, remote control cars etc). Parents recognise the invaluable contribution that residential staff (there are a lot) make.

The girls' dormitories are warm and in a modern wing, while the boys have a better view (one is the old master bedroom of the hunting lodge) but are chillier. Dorm captains, Australian gappies and matrons form part of the pastoral team with Mrs Cocke. As ever, the girls are speedier at making their space homely, the boys are more likely to stick to a football club branded duvet set and then concentrate on working out the correct trajectory of a tennis ball to the next door dorm. Dorm raids are very popular but only happen at the very end of term – when the stars and minuses lists are closed. You get your post at lunchtime (and a chance to post it in a red pillar box donated by some old boys), payphones for calling home (no mobiles permitted), access to the ICT room for emailing directly after breakfast and parents can visit on a Wednesday or a Saturday to watch sports matches. If you're around at the weekend there's plenty laid on (10 pin bowling, campfires, Scottish dancing, trips to see club rugby matches) and local children go out to horse riding or Stagecoach schools.

One big school production each year (e.g. *Oklahoma!*) is staged in the multi-use theatre (art exhibitions and exams when the orchestra pit is covered over) with jobs for everyone both on and backstage. The music department has well-used practice rooms and school instruments, with parents investing in their own when the children are definitely interested – the most talented musicians play in the Alpha Orchestra. They perform in concerts (some for charity, alternate years local and international ones) with renditions of modern classics such as Spider Pig (from The Simpsons Movie – pupil suggestion) and other more conventional pieces. The art department has moved to fresher premises with new site development and remains a hub of creativity (ceramics, drawing and painting, oils, an artist in residence) with external trips and full use of ICT. The summer holiday art course is so popular that children have begged their parents to shift their family trips abroad so as not to miss it.

New classroom block and two redeveloped science labs – inter-disciplinary competition rubrics include a croquet playing machine, parachuting eggs from the sports hall gallery, a soapbox derby. Practical learning is facilitated by destinations ranging from the Centre for Alternative Technology in Wales to Kenya.

Bullying and discipline are discussed in class and sometimes in assembly, ideally nipping issues in the bud through good communication. The form tutor is a kind of thermometer but the disciplinary system is heavily biased toward reward – 25,000 stars as opposed to 98 minuses given out per term. A pupil left recently after repeated breaking and stealing of other people's possessions – 'He used to get over-excited at competitions and kick out'. School works with two local educational psychologists, as well as the full-time learning development coordinator who takes an English set as well as teaching one-to-one. 'If they struggle in the classroom they're sure to be doing well in other fields. Pastoral support is so good we can help those who are a little unusual.' Lots of happy siblings here; welcoming of differing levels of academic and sporting skills.

Tries to give each child the space for a simple childhood full of opportunities while avoiding becoming an anachronism. This popular aim, coupled with the school's proximity to central London and international airports, makes it a great choice for busy commuters and international parents looking for quality time with their children when they return.

Bramcote School, North Yorkshire

22-30 Filey Road, Scarborough, North Yorkshire, YO11 2TT

• Pupils: 75 (full, flexi-boarding and day children) • Ages: 3-13 • C of E
• Fees: Day £9,906, Pre Prep £6,531 pa Boarding extra • Independent

Tel: 01723 373 086
Fax: 01723 364 186
Email: office@bramcoteschool.com
Website: www.bramcoteschool.com

Head: Since September 2009, Mr Andrew Snow (late forties), previously deputy head of the school, his own children attended the school some years ago. Teaches science at the upper end of the school and PSHE throughout – 'a great way to get to know all the children'. A considerable vote of confidence and well able to hit the ground running after a number of years teaching at the school, and not afraid to make necessary changes. Mrs Snow is in charge of the domestic arrangements and they present a strong and immensely caring and committed team at the top of the school. There is a welcoming friendliness and confidence here, yet without a hint of arrogance, very refreshing, and those same admirable qualities are there in the pupils too.

Entrance: By interview, non-selective. Some scholarships available. Children come from all over UK and abroad, but predominantly from Yorkshire and Humberside. Several Services families.

Exit: 100 per cent go on to the secondary school of their choice. Excellent record of Common Entrance success and scholarships. Pupils go regularly to Winchester, Oundle, Harrow, Uppingham, Shrewsbury, Eton, Ampleforth, Repton and St Peter's York. Queen Margaret's York, and Wycombe Abbey are favourites with girls when they leave at 13.

Remarks: Founded on Yorkshire coast in 1893 on Scarborough's South Cliff only 15 minutes' walk from the beach with sweeping views to the sea, the school sadly lacks a bit of kerb appeal but is definitely worth exploring further. Set in its own self-contained seven acre site, main school is a row of Victorian houses, but they hide a well kept secret that sometimes surprises even the locals. Behind the school lies an impressive array of additional facilities, including the delightful nursery and pre-prep department, extensive playing fields, tennis courts, a sports hall and swimming pool.

Busy road at the front and no car park, fortunately the side roads adjacent to the school are a relatively easy drop-off point and pleasingly, there is even a growing trickle of children who walk to school. Tedious travel time slashed for longer-distance parents with daily escorted buses taking children to rendezvous points north and south. Despite a raft of excellent facilities, with a large competitor on your doorstep and half your catchment area in the North Sea, it's a recruitment challenge, even for the committed and long-established teaching staff who clearly love the place. Time and tide in a period of change mean that it's now definitely a day school that also takes boarders, but there is a wide range of activities after hours and the school works very hard to accommodate the needs of all parents, being just about as flexible as it's possible to be. You can stay late, or leave on time; eat at home or eat at school, board occasionally or every day, the permutations are endless – an admin nightmare for the school but a real boon for today's busy parent. And incidentally it is often the children themselves who work hard at persuading their parents to allow them to stay, such is the fun to be had.

Parents of leavers and Friends of Bramcote are very generous – previously funding refurbishment of music block and tennis courts and more recently buying a greenhouse – in appreciation of the good work of the school and the care given to the children during their time there. 'It's going to be very hard to leave, I'll miss this place,' said one boy. Academic success features highly at the school, scholarships are proudly displayed in the main hall and the school works hard to prepare the pupils for entrance to any school, anywhere in the country.

Just as the school gives extra exam preparation to pupils heading for top academic schools, so it gives additional help to pupils finding learning a struggle. A full time learning support specialist helps pupils with all kinds of difficulties – dyslexia, ADHD, dyspraxia, Asperger's – at no extra charge. There is no stigma at all here for pupils who need learning support. Full curriculum of maths, science, English, languages, classics, ICT, history, geography, religious studies and PSHE.

Boys play rugby, football and cricket, mixed hockey and tennis also feature. Girls enjoy traditional activities – like dance, hockey and netball – but also join in football and cricket with gusto. School boasts a very busy programme of extra-curricular activities. For its size, it enjoys an embarrassment of riches in terms of indoor and outdoor sports facilities and it also has a dedicated art and music centre, a good-sized multi-purpose school hall and a small gym. Music is a proud tradition and the full range of instrument tuition is available. The successful choir goes far and wide to entertain – including Rome, Venice and Salzburg.

Prides itself on feeling like home and indeed it does. Children trot happily between dorms and classrooms, make hot chocolate for themselves after school and love the fact that it's into home clothes straight after prep and tea. The headmaster, his wife and several other staff live in and all are involved in evening and weekend activities.

Meals are cooked inhouse – good old-fashioned fare served in a good old-fashioned dining room, to staff and children with good old-fashioned manners and grace in Latin. Weekend entertainment, after Saturday school and sports matches, includes trips to cinema, ten pin bowling, clay pigeon shooting, Flamingo Land theme park and, of course, the beach. More opt to board as they move up the school, often in preparation for senior school, even a number who live in Scarborough.

Parental involvement and links are important. On top of the weekly effort grades given in assembly, parents receive reports every few weeks detailing progress in each subject, with comments from a tutor and the headmaster. Many teachers have email addresses and these are available to parents. Other evidence of encouraged involvement includes five-a-side football for dads and the hosting of a grandparents' day. Parents can visit, particularly on Wednesdays and Saturdays, and relish what is known as 'the Bramcote community' where they enjoy post-match drinks in the headmaster's study and 'meet up with old friends'. Long-standing parents acknowledge the school's evolution from a boarding school to being predominantly day, but insist that the school's strong spirit remains and that whether boarding or day, pupils are in a very special place and lucky to be here.

Very successful school, highly regarded with a record of sending out confident youngsters to the school of their choice. Bramcote knows its pupils well and achieves a wonderful balance of warmth and care whilst maintaining academic rigour. A banner outside school reads 'New Head, New Day, New Fees'. New Head now firmly ensconced and making his mark; the new day emphasising the increased flexibility for all; and the new pay-as-you-go fee structure has, for many, meant a blissful reduction in fees. Prospective parents should be queuing outside.

Bramdean Preparatory School, Kindergarten and Pre-Prep

Linked to Bramdean School in the Senior section

Richmond Lodge, Homefield Road, Exeter, EX1 2QR

• Pupils: 80 boys and girls; all day • Ages: 3-11 • Inter-denom • Fees: £4,950-£7,620 pa • Independent

Tel: 01392 273 387
Fax: 01392 439 330
Email: info@bramdeanschool.co.uk
Website: www.bramdeanschool.com

Entrance: Children are admitted to kindergarten and pre-prep on understanding they remain in prep until 13.

Exit: Pupils usually move into the senior school subject to satisfactory Common Entrance results at 13.

Remarks: The transition through the school to full-day pre-prep after at least one or two terms of five mornings in the reception class is seamless. All parts of the school are close to each other, coming under the same Bramdean umbrella. Siblings are never far apart and by staggering the various activities, children are able to share the facilities; indeed, one of the bonuses for children in the junior school is being able to enjoy so many opportunities. Scholarships available for a variety of skills. Sibling discounts and a 15 per cent reduction for sons and daughters of clergy – do ask.

Busy, well-stocked classrooms with lots of bright pictures, posters and home-made creations. Well equipped. 'Teachers are successful in fostering pupils' personal development and their enjoyment of school. As a result, pupils' attitudes to learning and life are very positive,' says the 2007 Ofsted report (do read it). 'It's brill and we have fun,' said a rather more succinct tiny. Happy-looking children in smart uniforms. Lunch in the dining room at different times to the senior school. A school well worth a visit.

Brandeston Hall Preparatory School

Linked to Framlingham College in the Senior section

Brandeston Hall, Brandeston, Suffolk, IP13 7AH

• Pupils: Boarders 50, day 200; pre-prep 50, nursery 25; day and flexi-boarding • Ages: 2.5-13 • Church of England; all other faiths welcomed. • Fees: Boarding £18,693; Day £6,681-£11,625 pa • Independent

Tel: 01728 685 331
Fax: 01728 685 437
Email: office@brandestonhall.co.uk
Website: www.brandestonhall.co.uk

Headmaster: Since 2007, Mr Martin Myers-Allen BSc(Hons) PGCE. Joined school in 1989 as house tutor, teaching chemistry, biology and sport, having been in stockbroking and IT worlds. Coached rugby, hockey and athletics, ran the CCF (still does) and D of E. Organised overseas expeditions (still involved) and in charge of sixth form. Housemaster for eight years from 1994 – senior master for six years. Wife Helen teaches ICT and biology. Three school-age boys.

Entrance: Scholarships available for 11+ entrants who wish to continue to the senior school, Framlingham College (music, academic and sports and all-round Albert Memorial Scholarships).

Exit: All students are prepared for Common Entrance. The majority to Framlingham College.

Remarks: Nursery in a purpose-built building with separate garden and play area, next to pre-prep department. Pre-prep (up to seven years) has specialist teaching in French, music and games. Good modern facilities: science and technology laboratories, design and technology centre, well-equipped ICT centre and language lab, library, arts studio and ceramics centre, specialist music room, music practice rooms and a generous recreation area for boarders. Latin is taught in Years 6–8. The school uses the parish church, which stands in the grounds. Large multi-purpose hall for concerts and plays. Sport, music and drama very strong. Sports include rugby, hockey, netball, cricket, tennis and athletics major games, plus activities including swimming and golf. Well supplied with golf course, eight tennis courts, pavilion, indoor and outdoor cricket nets, covered swimming pool, full-size floodlit all-weather pitches. Numerous sports tours available. Also use of facilities at Framlingham College including the indoor swimming pool, theatre and Astroturf pitch.

Two boarding houses warm and homely. Girls share dormitories in a purpose-built wing and boys have comfortable dormitories in the heart of the old manor house.

For further details see Framlingham College.

Bredon Junior School

Linked to Bredon School in the Senior section

Pull Court, Bushley, Tewkesbury, Gloucestershire, GL20 6AH

• Fees: Day £8,085-£11,835; Boarding £17,070-£21,615 pa • Independent

Tel: 01684 293 156
Fax: 01684 276 392
Email: enquiries@bredonschool.co.uk
Website: www.bredonschool.org

Brentwood Preparatory and Pre-Preparatory School

Linked to Brentwood School in the Senior section

Middleton Hall, Middleton Hall Lane, Brentwood, CM15 8EQ

• Pupils: 145 boys and girls in pre-prep; 245 in prep. All day • Ages: 3-11 • C of E • Fees: £10,251; Nursery £5,130 pa • Independent

Tel: 01277 243 333
Fax: 01277 243 340
Email: prep@brentwood.essex.sch.uk
Website: www.brentwoodschool.co.uk

Headmaster : Since 2005, Nigel Helliwell MA BEd(Hons) (mid-forties). Attended grammar school in Yorkshire, then university to train as a teacher. MA in curriculum studies at Institute of Education, London University. Formerly head of Colfe's Preparatory School, Blackheath, London (2000–2005) and director of studies at Holmwood House Preparatory School, Colchester (1992–2000). Taught at Ipswich Prep (1986–1991) and Ilkley Grammar School (1985–1986). Main subjects are maths and sport. Former county player in cricket and rugby. Currently plays golf and tennis. Involved in education at a national level – qualified schools' inspector and elected to IAPS National Education Committee. Strong educationalist, keen to emphasise academic standards as well as importance of all-round education. Caring headmaster who knows all the children personally.

Wife, Jane, plays an active role, particularly at social occasions, sports matches and major events, and is very approachable to parents. One son who has been through the independent school system. They live on site with their long-haired Jack Russell dog called Mollie, who is very popular with the children.

Mr Helliwell is leaving in July 2011 to become head of St Faith's, Cambridge.

Head of pre-prep: Mrs Sarah Wilson.

Entrance: Pre-prep takes two classes of 18, chosen after an informal assessment of child's language, dexterity and competence in a range of skills. 'And we meet the parents to ensure we are in tune with their expectations.' Preparatory pupils must also pass the English, maths and verbal reasoning exams taken by outside applicants before they move up to the prep, which has three classes of around 21 pupils. More-or-less automatic entry for siblings.

Exit: Large majority goes on to the senior school but must pass the entrance exam. For those who aren't going to make it, 'We flag up problems early and help the family look for alternatives'. A few move on to the local grammar schools.

Remarks: The prep and pre-prep buildings have their own site, across the road from the main school, and use its facilities. The 1995 pre-prep building sits harmoniously alongside the gracious Middleton Hall, the heart of the prep school, with its stained and leaded glass and stucco ceilings. Art and science rooms in the old stable block, top floor drama suite also used for lectures and house meetings, lashings of computers. Bright and spacious classrooms in the pre-prep, which has its own walled garden area and playground with wendy house, climbing frame and toys. Happy, busy children listen to story tapes, paint, use the interactive whiteboards.

Academic standards high and improving. Class average 20. French and drama both on the prep curriculum, taught by specialists, as are DT, science, art and music. Learning support for both ends of the spectrum. 13 different music groups, teams for 20 different sports, over 50 clubs including fencing, basketball, ballet, French and Spanish, trips abroad. Recent ISI inspection report praised 'caring ethos' that prevails throughout both schools and good relationships.

Brighton and Hove High Junior School

Linked to Brighton And Hove High School in the Senior section

Radinden Manor Road, Hove, BN3 6NH

• Pupils: 260 girls, all day • Ages: 3-11 • Non-denom • Fees: £6,876 pa • Independent

Tel: 01273 505004
Fax: 01273 505006
Email: enquiries@bhhs.gdst.net
Website: www.bhhs.gdst.net

Head of Junior School: From January 2011, Mrs Sian Cattaneo, formerly head of St Ives school, Haslemere.

Entrance: By varied tests and observation.

Exit: Almost all to senior school.

Remarks: Situated further into the suburbs and half a mile away from the senior school, on a good-sized site with excellent facilities for a junior school – netball courts, full sized Astroturf and grassed areas for, amongst other things, tomato growing. Light rooms.

Two parallel forms in each year group, unstreamed and often brought together for social events, trips etc. The children are taught by their form teachers, who are specifically appointed for their all round strengths including music, art, drama – plenty of craft/art displayed around the whole school. Netball teams do well; PE and French specialists from senior school visit junior school.

The girls do SATs, and understandably shine. Numerous clubs. School menu looked appetising, all fresh produce cooked on the premises – salad bar, vegetarian option, very healthy eating. Parents remark how sociable the girls are.

Brighton College Prep School

Linked to Brighton College in the Senior section

Walpole Road, Brighton, East Sussex, BN2 0EU

• Pupils: 300 in prep school (170 boys, 130 girls) ; 200 pupils in pre-prep, all day. • Ages: 8-13 in the prep, 3-8 in the pre-prep • C of E
• Fees: £11,292-£14,406 pa • Independent

Tel: 01273 704 201
Fax: 01273 704 204
Email: registrar@brightoncollege.net
Website: www.brightoncollege.net

Head: Since 1999, Mr Brian Melia MA (Cantab) (early fifties), a slim and energetic Yorkshireman who believes humour is vital in his job. Married with two sons, who both moved to Brighton College with him. Previously head of prep at Broadwater Manor in Worthing and before that spent nine years at a comprehensive in Angmering. He still teaches geography or history or RS to one exam class and greets each child by name, with a smile that often quickens to a shared laugh. The head of the pre-prep school is Sue Wicks.

Entrance: By assessment in maths, English and verbal reasoning plus observation. Special arrangements for dyslexic pupils.

Exit: Most to the senior school – but they have to take CE on a par with outsiders.

Remarks: This school seems such a fun place to be – the corridors are bright and buzzing, the children are engaged and talk nineteen to the dozen. Just one block to the east of the senior school; the two are very closely linked – the little ones troop across to eat there, go to the dyslexia centre, play tennis, netball, rugby, swim and do performing arts; both schools have the same shape of the day.

The pupils come in on the same buses that serve the senior school – a third of the prep school children live in town, a third from Hove and the rest come from Lewes, Worthing, Shoreham, Hassocks etc. Pupils come from the maintained sector and from private schools (lots of the girls from single sex schools) and the staff also have experience of both. This means that no one is complacent, everyone knows how lucky they are and fresh ideas are always bubbling up. Many enter at 8+ and over 90 per cent go on to the senior school. Increasingly the parents have moved south from London.

The children are taught by class teachers initially, working up to being setted in Year 6. The bright and well-used library (author visits documented by handprints on the wall) is housed in the converted chapel. Music is impressive and well-enjoyed with bands, orchestras, percussion ensembles and musical theatre performances. Examples of cross-curricular learning abound, art being particularly integrated and exciting. Mandarin was made compulsory for three- and four-year-olds in 2007. Sport is high profile, the school regularly winning county titles and fixtures available for all levels of ability. Activity holidays and field trips are very popular; a huge number of clubs.

Four houses compete against each other in drama, sport, debating etc. House captains of both genders are appointed and the school council is also influential – the water dispensers in the corridor were their idea. Awards given each year for effort, achievement and consideration – the latter is particularly important since, as the head says, 'There are a lot of successful people in the world but some are very unpleasant!'

Bristol Steiner School

Redland Hill House, Redland Hill, Redland, Bristol, BS6 6UX

• Pupils: 235 boys and girls • Ages: 3-16 • Non-denom • Fees: £5,160 pa
• Independent

Tel: 0117 933 9990
Fax: 0117 933 9999
Email: reception@bristolsteinerschool.org
Website: www.bristolsteinerschool.org

Head: As in other Steiner schools, a 'college of teachers' replaces the headteacher. The school's management group comprises trustees and staff representatives.

Entrance: Fewer than hoped for progress from kindergarten; no shortage of applications from special needs children, but school wants to attract more of those who support Steiner educational principles.

Exit: Some to Wynstone's (a Steiner school near Stroud with a sixth form) but most proceed to mainstream state schools where they reportedly do well.

Remarks: A highly distinctive education. For any parent in Bristol looking for a broader, deeper philosophy of education we would recommend investigating this Steiner alternative. Throw away your preconceptions about what you expect a school to offer materially and take this parent's view to heart – 'I'd sooner have my child sitting in a bog and come out of it with a love for learning than going to some over-funded, over-resourced school without a work culture'.

No SATs here: academic results not seen as 'be all and end all' by parents; staff seek to instil genuine thirst for knowledge and feel that too many children are 'damaged' in assessment-driven mainstream schools. Steiner viewed childhood as integrating the developing personality in three successive seven-year stages.

Having said that, now has an upper school for 14–16-year-olds, which does prepare children to take GCSEs in English, maths, science, French and art. In 2010, 14 students sat 72 GCSE exams between them: 82 per cent of their grades were A-C and 40 per cent were A or A*.

From its origins in 1919 as education for the children of tobacco factory workers in Stuttgart, the Steiner educational movement has grown to influence progressive education worldwide. To the uninitiated some of what takes place seems quirky and parents will agree that it's 'off-beat' compared with mainstream schools. We came away wondering why so many sacred cows remain in the model from Steiner's early days, but nonetheless uplifted by the atmosphere of the place.

Bristol Steiner typically places creativity and emotional security ahead of early intellectual achievement. We spoke to parents whose children had been 'late starters' in reading but who had gone on to shine in GCSEs after leaving the school at 14. We saw lots of highly-creative work being done by pupils, but relatively little of it is displayed. However, classes give imaginative performances to parents incorporating themes from their lessons. Children hear, re-tell and enact stories before reading them from their own workbooks: text, reference and fictional books are thin on the ground here compared with other schools. TV/VCR/DVD and computers are all eschewed as being counter-creative for young children.

Each day begins with a main lesson which lasts two hours: this covers a range of activities both within the classroom and outside. Class teachers aspire to work as 'artists developing enthusiasm for learning', but we observed some being challenged by the evident wide range of ability and motivation. Children here spend about an hour at 'play' outside in what looks much like an adventure playground on a sloping garden behind the school. Even the main lesson includes periods outside: letting off steam or learning maths through movement such as 'tag', finger clicking or skipping. Children learn to read through walking the shapes of letters on the floor and drawing – the underlying aim being to 'approach through the feelings' and 'never go directly to the concept'. The younger classes we saw engaged in the main lesson were lively and very self-expressive whilst senior classes impressed by their concentration and involvement. A lot of time is spent in class discussion, and recall of previous lessons is seen as important. The content derives mainly from what Steiner laid down, so children are immersed in the wonders of ancient civilisations, which the school sees as an appropriate preparation for understanding our contemporary world.

The college of teachers will share and disseminate information about children in a way that focuses on individuals. In addition, a qualified SENCo coordinates the special needs programme. There are currently no statemented children but a number require support for SpLD. Pupils are screened for dyslexia at class two and four stages. Children are withdrawn either individually or up to three at a time. The building and site are unsuitable for physically-challenged pupils.

Gym and games are taught separately and an outside area close to the school is used for a variety of informal sports; excessive competitiveness is frowned on. A basketball area in front of the school was proving popular with older boys when we visited. Eurythmy is central to Steiner education: origins of this idiosyncratic, dance-like art form lie in Greek temple dances, and link movement to specific sounds; sometimes copper rods are used in the movements. The teacher we observed was highly skilled and succeeded in winning the cooperation of all pupils, who weaved mesmeric shapes across the floor. We couldn't help wondering what the children might have done with freer or funkier forms of movement and the extent to which they were really sold on eurythmy. Art here also includes recitation and drama as well as painting, plus modelling in beeswax and clay, as the traditional divisions between subjects are constantly blurred.

We witnessed a 'magical' music lesson for class two: it involved a fairytale sung to a lap harp accompaniment, as well as puppetry and the use of both imaginary pencils and real wax crayons; pupils sang as they passed a drumstick around to decide who got to choose an instrument to play (from a good choice of simple instruments available in the middle of the circle) each time the music stopped. Older children have individual music tuition and opportunities to perform together. Another outstanding lesson was handcraft (a key aspect of Steiner schools is to instil motor skills) where the teacher had inspired girls and boys to produce highly original sewing, knitting and crochet work (having first made their own knitting needles out of natural materials). Much thought is given to materials as well as to the colours used. Older children also make their own clothes in this way. French is the only foreign language taught at present but we were unable to witness a lesson or any display related to languages. Some parents agree that the menu gets 'a bit thin' in upper classes, with only five GCSE subjects offered. School benefits from Steiner students on placement plus regular in-service training for staff (six of whom have served for over ten years).

Founded as Bristol Steiner Waldorf School in 1973, it occupied crumbling premises on the former site of the city's Roman Catholic cathedral before moving to the present Georgian building in Redland when vacated by UWE in 2002. One of 25 Steiner schools in the UK, Bristol has struggled financially since its inception, controversially abandoning its sliding feescale in 1998 in favour of a standard charge for all. Staff are all paid substantially below national scales and come via Steiner teacher training courses (two of which are validated by UK universities). DfES has recently conducted research into UK Steiner schools and looks set to grant the first instance of Waldorf School academy status with Steiner Waldorf Schools Fellowship as sponsor. Questions remain as to how much educational freedom would be sacrificed in return for state financial support (not a problem in Germany, it seems) but Bristol Steiner School clearly suffers from under funding. School compensates for its shortcomings through committed staff, pupil goodwill and parental support. Average class size is sixteen and staff: pupil ratio is 1:11. Children celebrate a variety of Christian and other festivals, whilst the spiritual aspect of Steiner's philosophy is implicit rather than overt.

Stylised introductions and endings to lessons seem rather quaint but suggest a deeper, spiritual significance. No catering facilities but children are happy enough bringing home nosh. Class teachers move each year with pupils so parents can relate to same person throughout their child's school career (OK if you like the teacher). All the staff exude commitment and a genuine care for their charges. One parent said 'curative' eurythmy (used on a one-to-one basis with younger children) had 'worked wonders' for her 'withdrawn' daughter but had no idea why or how.

Lots of mainly middle class free spirits here in a secure setting with a few from ethnic minorities. Children 'love going to the school' and clearly trust their teachers. First names throughout and no uniform, of course. Staff skilled at engaging each child in learning process. An interesting blend of liberalism and old-fashioned values. Some parents fall into Steiner education faute de mieux (especially in Bristol where choices tend to be polarised) whilst others promote its virtues strongly and have made it their conscious choice.

Brockhurst and Marlston House Schools

Marlston Road, Hermitage, Thatcham, Newbury, Berkshire, RG18 9UL

• Pupils: 240 boys and girls (split roughly 60/40); weekly/flexi-boarding • Ages: boys 6-13 (Brockhurst), girls 6-13 (Marlston House), mixed 3-6 (Ridge House pre-prep) • C of E • Fees: Boarding £18,300; Day: Pre-prep £8,250; Prep £12,990-£13,800 pa • Independent

Tel: 01635 200 293
Fax: 01635 200 190
Email: info@brockmarl.org.uk
Website: www.brockmarl.org.uk

Head: Since 2000, Mr David Fleming MA MSc (mid-forties). Has been at Brockhurst man and boy. Recalls taunting matron as a naughty pyjama-clad 12-year-old in early schooldays – amazingly, she's still here too, though about to stand down as housemistress after so many years! So poacher turned gamekeeper as ex-pupil becomes head and is part of family that also owns school. How much more involved could he be? Hugely ambitious. Wants school 'to be the best'. Never happier than when a new building project is underway. Lots of impressive additions since our last visit. Head cuts clean and businesslike figure. No-nonsense approach but pupils seem to respect that – 'sirs' drop thick and fast. After Brockhurst, educated at Radley College, read natural sciences at Trinity College, Oxford, medicine, then land management, before appointed Brockhurst bursar, science and geography teacher. Married with two daughters at the school.

Marlston House (girls' school) has own head, Caroline Riley MA BEd Cert Ed (forties), appointed 1999. Previously head of mixed school in Hazelgrove, which grew enormously under her reign. Similar plans for Marlston House. Educated at West Country girls' school. Has taught in both single sex and mixed schools. Quietly efficient, very focused, allowed free rein despite coming under 'Brockmarl' school umbrella. Married with two grown-up children.

Entrance: Majority from school's pre-prep Ridge House, previously short distance away but now within school grounds. Non-selective but aiming for average and above-average intelligence. Prospective pupils interviewed and assessed for level of ability only; parents also given the once over.

Exit: Wide and wonderful array of 'big' schools. Latest set of 13+ academic scholarships to Cheltenham Ladies' College and Downe House (the girls), and Bradfield and Marlborough (the boys), plus music exhibition to St Edward's, Oxford. But last decade has seen pupils go to Radley, Eton, Stowe, Charterhouse, Wellington, Millfield and Queen Anne's, Caversham, to name but a few.

Remarks: Two schools (three including pre-prep) with one passionately beating heart. Brockhurst and Marlston House, a mixed prep with a difference, but one that seems to work in perfect harmony. Brockhurst founded as boys' prep in 1884, moving to current Hermitage home in 1945. Set in 60 breathtaking acres, mock-Jacobean in style, with girls first taking up residence in listed Marlston House a relatively recent 12 years ago. Once boys and girls leave Ridge House at six, they part company – boys to Brockhurst and girls to Marlston House. Small classes (average 17) of single sex teaching from then on, only remerging for music and drama. Any further merger totally ruled out by head. It works for staff, works for parents and (most importantly) works for pupils. They comment, 'We see enough of each other outside lessons. We don't feel we're missing out on something just because we don't sit next to each other in maths or English or whatever. That's the way it is.'

High flyers can be accelerated a year. Some also creamed off into scholarship sets. Able to cope with some learning difficulties but 'We are not a school for special needs,' says head. Staff can give extra literacy/numeracy help and, where needed, encourage pupils to retake year to give them a better start at chosen senior school. Formal eyes-front teaching for main academic subjects but no stiffness apparent from staff or children in lessons. Pupils encouraged to speak out; free interaction of ideas. There's a visible pride in hard work and a job well done. Usual range of subjects, also French taught from age four, German in top two years, introduction to Russian and classical Greek for scholarship students, Latin for Common Entrance and scholarship. Spring fortnight in France for Year 7 in school's own fabulous chateau – regular lessons in the morning, activities and excursions in the afternoon. Truly an annual highlight for all concerned.

Impressive ICT facilities, networked computers, and new reference library (thanks largely to parental effort) with state-of-the-art thumbprint scans for added security. Food technology (i.e. what's in it and how to cook it) being launched soon as curriculum subject and activity. New art and DT centre wonderfully productive – a real buzz to the place. Selection of best work goes on show at Stowe. Also lovely indoor 25m pool now means all year round swimming, with recently appointed director of sport running entire complex. New buildings well-designed and cleverly landscaped so no aesthetic clash with existing listed buildings. Fine use of school acres with extra activities including golf, fishing in school lake, and giant chess. Pupils can also stable own ponies for riding during termtime.

Large musical uptake – between 80 and 90 per cent have individual tuition as well as class lessons for all, mixed choir and orchestra and various ensembles. Composition suite with electric keyboards and drum kit. Drums growing fast in popularity (so future project might have something to do with better sound-proofing). Weekends busy whether day or boarding – Saturday morning school for Year 6 upwards, activities for younger ones. Afternoon often involves school matches – both boys and girls fare well. Girls still basking in glory of first netball tour to South Africa where they lost just once in two weeks. More trips to follow, sports staff hope.

All pupils allocated house (four for boys, three for girls) where tutors responsible for pastoral care. Fairly basic boys' dorms, girls' more homely (as usual). Boarding facilities likely to be top of head's to-do list. Respect for others and discipline high on agenda. Misdemeanours quickly dealt with through detention, loss of breaks etc.

Stripes for minor offences, stars reward good work or behaviour – seen as fair by pupils.

Wide mix of backgrounds – professional, nouveau riche and old money. Bursaries and scholarships, plus hardship fund. Pupils academically driven – no-one would pretend they're here for an easy ride – but the school motto, 'No reward without effort', says it all. And as one boy commented, 'I've really enjoyed my time here. I'll be sad to go.'

Bromley High School (GDST) Junior Department

Linked to Bromley High School (GDST) in the Senior section

Blackbrook Lane, Bickley, Bromley, Kent, BR1 2TW

- Pupils: 310 girls; all day • Ages: 4-11 • Broadly Christian
- Fees: £9,342 pa • Independent

Tel: 020 8781 7001
Fax: 020 8781 7003
Email: admissions@bro.gdst.net
Website: www.bromleyhigh.gdst.net

Head: Since 2009 Mrs Ellen Hill (fifties) BEd(Hons), previously head of Derwent Lodge, Kent, her specialist subject is maths.

Entrance: 4+ competitive entry assessment, always oversubscribed, thereafter waiting list for occasional vacancies.

Exit: Majority transfer to the senior school.

Remarks: Strong academics, arts and sport, the junior school benefits from being able to share a fantastic range of sporting and musical facilities at the senior school. Year 5 and 6 pupils are able to link with subject specialist teachers in the senior school. Tuition is available on any instrument. Wind and string ensembles and training orchestra prepare pupils for the variety of orchestras that the music department run. Drama and dance also play an important role in the curriculum. Purpose-built site is rather utilitarian, softened by numerous imaginative art and project displays which offer an insight into the broad curriculum. Dedicated, mostly long serving class teachers run a full range of extra-curricular clubs and activities. Lots of hard work going on, crisp orderly little girls present as purposeful and happily engaged.

For further details see the senior school entry.

Bromsgrove Preparatory School

Linked to Bromsgrove School in the Senior section

Worcester Road, Bromsgrove, B61 7DU

- Fees: Boarding £17,685-£21,885; Day £8,880-£11,580 pa • Independent

Tel: 01527 579679
Email: admissions@bromsgrove-school.co.uk
Website: www.bromsgrove-school.co.uk

Brookham School

Linked to Highfield School in the Junior section

Highfield Lane, Liphook, Hampshire, GU30 7LQ

- Pupils: 110 boys, 100 girls all day • Ages: 3-8 • Non denom
- Fees: Day £8,250-£10,200; Boarding £15,300 pa • Independent

Tel: 01428 722 005
Email: headteacher@brookhamschool.co.uk
Website: www.brookhamschool.co.uk

Head: Since 2003, Mrs Diane Gardiner MA(Ed) (fifties). Previously deputy head of Eagle House, Sandhurst. A very charming, friendly and approachable lady, parents say she is 'determined and not at all wishy washy' and 'has done great things for the school'. Always on the look out for improvements. A modern educationalist very in tune with her colleague at Highfield, Phillip Evitt, and has a very similar ethos of good academics within a caring environment. Warm relationship with the pupils: her open door policy ensures they're always in and out of her office (for positive reasons) – one little girl came in while we were there to get a sticker from Mrs Gardiner because she had just finished her reading book.

Entrance: Non-selective. Most children enter the nursery at 3 but a recently built section for rising 3s will, in future, cater for younger children. Others entering the reception class can visit for a day to acclimatise. Also intake in Year 3 (seen as a true transition year for Highfield): about 10 a year, who take NFER tests after they arrive, with time being spent at both schools so that they get slowly geared up for the change.

Exit: Vast majority to Highfield.

Remarks: A modern purpose built pre-prep school; shares fantastic grounds with its big sister Highfield (qv). Owned by William Mills whose grandfather founded Highfield. A very well designed building which envelops you as you enter. You are 'buzzed' in for security purposes, but no gimlet-eyed receptionist behind a glass wall here: the head's office is literally in the middle of everything. Classrooms open out from the central library area, which gives a cohesive feel to the whole place, with the older children upstairs to give them a sense of independence from the litties down below. A map of the world in the hallway together with photos shows where pupils have taken the school teddy bear on holiday – he's even been on tour with one of the dads who is in a well known band. Many of the superb facilities of Highfield are also used by the pupils at Brookham. Lunch is eaten at Highfield: pupils feel part of the greater whole.

Very forward thinking on academics and educational policy – head has introduced Thrass system of phonics, which is begun in the nursery for those who are ready. Traditional subjects but refreshingly taught – head is also keen on a multi sensory, creative approach which involves being outside as much as possible to appreciate the fabulous setting – 'Our ethos is "think outside first" or "have visitors in",' she says. Forest School is now an integral part of all the children's experience with a dedicated member of staff to lead the sessions. While we were there one class was creating a newspaper documenting the fire of London, the previous day it had been re-enacted by a visiting theatre group and the teachers had dressed up too. A broad based curriculum; children are taught by their class teachers in the main, but subject specialists are slowly introduced higher up the school including for sciences, French and some sports. No SATS, but on-going assessments. The opportunities are there for the brighter kids, but one mum felt that if you had a child prodigy on your hands, Brookham might not suit.

The good standard of academics is backed up by an excellent SEN team – one full time special needs teacher plus one part time. There is also a bank of therapists who can help (for a fee) with dyslexia, dyspraxia and speech and language difficulties. At the time of our visit, a pupil was having a one-to-one occupational therapy session in the open space at the centre of the school, so it is obviously very much part of the life of the school and not cloistered away in a corner. The SEN team also supports individuals or groups who may not have an identified SpLD but still need extra help – strugglers with reading or handwriting are given help in groups called Shooting Stars.

Rugby, football, netball, hockey and rounders, plus use of the wonderful pool at Highfield (this includes the tinies in the nursery, which is nice to see). Sport is less formalised than some would like – lack of netball teams until Year 3, for example – but head has responded to the parental mutterings by recruiting a head of sport. A more formal sports day, which encourages a bit more healthy competition, has also been put in place. Housepoints can be won for anything from sporting prowess to being helpful, 'So everyone has a chance to shine,' said one mum.

Art is super with plenty of lovely displays of work – the fabulous Viking longship was a group project. Music is a big deal here – individual lessons start in Year 1, and there are numerous concerts and musicals throughout the school year. The extracurricular activities on offer are impressive for this age group and include magic, art, judo, fencing, tennis, swimming, dance and chess.

Full marks to head for the pastoral care – very well thought out and original. 'Bubble time' works well – in each classroom there is a cardboard 'bubble' and each child has a peg with their name on it. If a pupil wants to have some quiet one-to-one time with anyone (head included) they put their peg on the appropriate teacher's 'bubble'. The head said they can come and chat about anything – from telling her about their pets to more serious issues at home. Another innovation is the 'golden table' at lunch time, for pupils who have exhibited particularly good behaviour throughout the week. However, one parent told us that the school had struggled with her admittedly less than easy child, although the school 'tried its best'.

Parents are encouraged to be involved with the school at all levels, with numerous opportunities to help out, including Forest School. The school is popular with those exiting London and as such has a more sophisticated feel than other preps in the area, but parents are from a genuine mix of backgrounds (although presumably none are short of money) and a wide catchment from Godalming to Petworth and beyond.

In a nutshell, broad based academics tempered with a touchy-feely gentle approach.

Broomwood Hall (Garrads Road)

Linked to Broomwood Hall (Ramsden Road) in the Junior section

Linked to Northcote Lodge School in the Junior section

Linked to Broomwood Hall School (Nightingale Lane) in the Junior section

3 Garrads Road, Tooting Common, London, SW16 1JZ

• Pupils: 140; girls and boys • Ages: 4-8 • C of E • Fees: £11,490 pa • Independent

Tel: 020 8682 8800
Fax: 020 8682 8858
Email: b.goddard@northwoodschools.com
Website: www.broomwood.co.uk

Head: Principal: See Broomwood Hall (Nightingale Lane). Head: Since 2010, Mrs Sarah Graham.

Entrance: As for Broomwood Hall (Ramsden Road).

Exit: As for Broomwood Hall (Ramsden Road).

Remarks: A large detached Edwardian mansion less rambling than the SW12 parts of this school. Beautiful large, airy classrooms and a bit more evidence of technology. A comfortable library with a computer suite. A huge garden with lots of room to play in, which adds to the homely, relaxed feel. The children even grow their own vegetables. Tea parties and other gatherings held here in the summer term so that the girls from both lower and upper schools can get together. Everything is done to help the transition to the next stage; constant communication between not only Broomwood and Broomwood but Broomwood and Northcote.

The same syllabus is followed as in SW12 and the organisation is equally detailed and efficient. Bookbags hang on the backs of chairs in the classrooms and each child's reading folder contains loads of information.

These are all very well-run schools with a strong adherence to philosophy. Children are introduced to education in an organised, sympathetic way, acquiring a solid grounding and having lots of fun as well. Teachers are young, mainly local and very caring. Excellent documentation and an informative website. According to a soon-to-start parent, the school uniform shop, which provides both new and used items, is efficient and friendly.

What more could you want?

Broomwood Hall (Ramsden Road)

Linked to Broomwood Hall School (Nightingale Lane) in the Junior section

Linked to Broomwood Hall (Garrads Road) in the Junior section

Linked to Northcote Lodge School in the Junior section

The Old Vicarage, 192 Ramsden Road, London, SW12 8RQ

• Pupils: 265 • Ages: 4-8; girls and boys • Fees: £11,490 pa • Independent

Tel: 020 8682 8820
Fax: 020 8682 8824
Email: b.goddard@northwoodschools.com
Website: www.broomwood.co.uk

Head: Since 2004, Ms Diana Mardon AVD Dip Tchg TTC, a slightly reticent, brusque New Zealander. Taught here in the early '90s then went back to her home country to teach and to train in special needs until returning to take up this headship. Takes daily assemblies but no longer teaches regularly: 'there is no time'. According to parents, very approachable and quick to sort out any problems.

Entrance: A strict one-mile policy so all children really local and not a huge ethnic mix, but fairly multi-cultural. Non-selective. After registering your child, you are invited to an open meeting in October where the principal and lower school heads speak; then later, after a tour of the school, parents meet the head individually. Children are assessed for school readiness at three. Siblings are given priority and they try to keep the boy/girl mix as close to 50:50 as possible and a range of birthdays across the year.

Exit: Most of the girls go on to the upper school and the boys move to Northcote Lodge, King's Wimbledon or Dulwich with a smattering to boarding preps: Ludgrove, Sandroyd, Cheam for instance. Wherever they go, they are certainly well-grounded and fully prepared both academically and socially.

Remarks: School in two buildings – The Vicarage, a rambling Edwardian house, for the first two years and 50 Nightingale Lane, another Victorian building, for the third and fourth. Both houses carpeted throughout, the tartan theme predominant, with lovely bright classrooms and generally good facilities. Good outdoor play area.

The four-year-olds are divided by age, then mixed together when they move into the second year and are setted in phonics and maths. Lots of gap year students to help the class teachers. French from five and recorders for everyone from the beginning. There is a learning support teacher for one-to-one sessions if necessary, 'judged on merits and what's best for the child'. The pastoral care is reckoned to be excellent.

Broomwood Hall School (Nightingale Lane)

Linked to Broomwood Hall (Ramsden Road) in the Junior section

Linked to Broomwood Hall (Garrads Road) in the Junior section

Linked to Northcote Lodge School in the Junior section

68-74 Nightingale Lane, London, SW12 8NR

• Pupils: 180 • Ages: 8-13; girls • C of E • Fees: £14,085 pa • Independent

Tel: 020 8682 8800
Fax: 020 8682 8805
Email: admissions@northwoodschools.com
Website: www.broomwood.co.uk

Head: Principal is Ms Katharine Colquhoun BEd (mid fifties). Somewhat aloof, rather formidable, started school from scratch in 1984 with 12 pupils in local church hall. Now three schools, three heads and over 600 children, together with a boys' prep school for another 200, all due to her drive and ambition. Although she is no longer involved in the day-to-day nitty gritty, it is still very much her school under her direction and she takes assembly and teaches literature. Her husband, Malcolm, is in charge of the financial and administrative side of things and takes care of the school's expanding portfolio of property in Wandsworth. It is very much a family concern – the school board consists of the Colquhouns, the four school heads and one outside director, no governors. They have two almost grown up children.

Head is Ms Carole Jenkinson BSc PGCE. A bright, bustling former parent who has, according to parents, had a very positive influence on the school. 'She manages the girls fantastically and there is no stress.' Her enthusiasm and real understanding of the children is clear and every parent we spoke to was keen to emphasise how easy she is to talk to and how no problem is too small (or large) to discuss with her.

Entrance: Most come up from the lower schools. For the occasional places remaining at eight and 11, and the very rare ones cropping up at other times, an interview with Ms Jenkinson and an ability test to make sure that the girl will be able to keep up with the work. Otherwise non-selective, so first come first served. No settling in problems – all teachers and children work hard to make anyone new feel at home.

Exit: About 30 per cent leave at 11+, mostly to south London day schools, JAGS, the High Schools, etc or to good boarding schools, Downe House and Benenden seeming popular at the moment. 70 per cent stay on to take 13+, the majority to board, more often than not at co-ed schools, Stowe, Cranbrook, Marlborough, Wellington, Bradfield, St Edward's, Wycombe, Benenden, St Mary's Ascot amongst others, with a trickle to day schools depending on availability of places.

Remarks: Three large Victorian houses combined to create a warm, welcoming school. Carpets everywhere, many of them tartan; bright, if not particularly large classrooms, a friendly, happy atmosphere. An excellent, spacious, outdoor play area in the huge garden behind the houses. Places to play and climb and a wonderful amphitheatre where class plays are performed and imaginary scenarios can be acted out. Each year group has its own classroom where they start each day. The youngest girls' classrooms are close together and they have the comfort of at least three lessons with their home teacher each day. Classrooms are subject-based, so a certain amount of moving around. However, surprisingly (and noiselessly) no bells dictating changeover – clock-watching is regarded as part of time management. Each classroom houses all necessary books and materials, so only pencil cases have to be carried around. Setting in English and maths throughout, and in French and Latin from Year 7. All homework is done in school after a tea-time carbohydrate snack.

Good teaching in small classes. The decision to keep girls on to 13 so that they can move to co-educational public schools such as Wellington and King's Canterbury has proved successful – girls are joining from other local schools at 11, or, increasingly, at eight, in order to be sure of a place. Ms Colquhoun has spotted the trend and managed to move ahead of everyone else.

No particular SEN policy. Individual special support lessons are available to children with mild problems such as dyslexia and dyspraxia. EAL lessons for children who need them.

A school with traditional values where good manners are paramount. Christian school with compulsory daily assembly – hymns, prayers and a Bible story – and once-a-week service in local church. Smart red and blue uniform for the girls and a dress code for staff as well – no jeans worn here. Bad behaviour is not acceptable and rarely occurs – these are well brought up little girls. Each girl is part of a tutor group of up to 10 and, as well as a group meeting once a week, also has an individual session with her tutor. The house system also encourages competition amongst pupils and staff alike, another good means of promoting loyalty and building confidence. A resident matron.

Plenty of interactive white boards and a good IT room where they all learn to touch-type and use email, and two computerised laboratories. The DT room was about to be refurbished when we visited. A lovely old-fashioned library where we met the principal taking a literature group. She was quick to assure us that she had read and chosen all the books herself – so nothing unsuitable to be found there.

Sports every day except Friday, either on the premises (they have their own hard courts) or at Trinity Fields. Matches played against local schools and inter-house – 'Everyone gets a chance to play in a team'. Cross-country and swimming teams as well. After-school clubs cater for other sports – for instance, they have had competitive successes in karate and fencing. Lovely art and good music facilities. About 70 per cent learn an instrument, for which they are withdrawn from class on a rolling timetable. Choir, orchestra, chamber choir. Lots of singing goes on in church. Class excursions, field trips to France and Devon, outward bound courses for the top years. Plenty of drama – a class play a year and a whole-school production. Everyone will take part, on the acting or production side. LAMDA exams available for those who want them.

An exciting innovation is their cookery school, a great stainless-steel heaven, affiliated to Leith's. The 10-year-olds all have a term of cookery and the 11-year-olds have a special Leith's-designed cookery course built into the curriculum, which culminates in an exam that involves cooking a whole dinner party for their parents. Out of school hours and in the holidays, the school runs courses here for adults and children alike. What fun!

A traditional school, with its values in the right places – the parents we talked to all love it. Unsophisticated and in many ways old fashioned, it provides an excellent education and produces well-rounded, confident girls. If you and the school agree that it is the right place for your child, then she will grow and flourish here, acquire lots of similar friends and get into the right senior school.

Bruern Abbey School

Chesterton House, Chesterton, Bicester, Oxfordshire, OX26 1UY

• Pupils: 85 boys, most board • Ages: 7/8-13 • Inter-denom • Fees: Day £15,837; Boarding £19,233 pa • Independent

Tel: 01869 242 448
Fax: 01869 243 949
Email: secretary@bruernabbey.org
Website: www.bruernabbey.org

Headmaster: Since 2002, Mr Philip Fawkes MBA CertEd (fifties). Educated at Embley Park (where he returned to teach and establish junior school) and Keele University. Previous posts include headships of Lathallan Prep, Scotland and Twyford, Winchester. Tempted out of semi-retirement on Channel Islands to take up current position and salvage sinking ship. Quickly doubled pupil numbers through inspirational leadership. Now runs buoyant outfit but maintains firm grip on rudder. Boys see him as strict – Fawkes prefers 'firm yet fair'; either way, he's praised and respected by pupils and parents alike. Still teaches 'a little bit of RS', referees rugby and umpires cricket – 'I don't like the boys to think of me sitting all day in my ivory tower'. Passionately keen ornithologist, evidenced by wall clock in head's study which chimes hour in birdsong. Boys see him as approachable – a head whose door is never closed. Mr Fawkes and his wife Jane insist they're very much a team. Principal and founder, Sterling Stover, continues to oversee the development programme.

Entrance: As this is a school for boys with specific learning difficulties, entry is necessarily extremely selective. Parents must provide recent (less than six months old) educational psychologist's report. Boys have to show that despite their mild to moderate dyslexia, dyspraxia or dyscalculia, they're intelligent enough to cope with the demands of the curriculum. School looking for IQ of at least 110 but talent in music, art and sport also welcomed. Young hopefuls invited to spend a day and a night at school for informal interview and assessment.

Exit: 100 per cent pass Common Entrance to get into first choice senior schools including Winchester, Rugby, Stowe, Tonbridge, St Edward's, Wellington, Canford, Uppingham, Shrewsbury, Charterhouse (recent Exhibition), Bradfield, Gordonstoun, Oratory and Milton Abbey.

Remarks: On the site of a Cisterian Monastery, the current yellow stone building dates from the late 19th century with some more recent sympathetic additions. To all intents and purposes, looks like traditional single-sex prep

– a grand country house set in 23 acres of grounds and woodland tranquillity. But because of its mission to overcome learning problems and prepare boys for CE to major English and Scottish public schools, it claims to be 'unique in the market place'. 'The main difference is the method of teaching,' says Fawkes.

Each boy has an individual learning plan tailored to his specific strengths and weaknesses. Staff decide on the best approach and design timetables to include a variety of oral, aural, visual and practical skills. All new boys are taught touch-typing on arrival and must supply laptops they can take to every lesson. Work is emailed to the relevant teacher, marked and emailed back to the boy. A wireless system means they can use them anywhere and at any time they want. Head adds, 'Bruern Abbey is a dichotomy in many respects. On the one hand you've got a prep school stuck in a 1950s time warp where boys can climb trees and build dens in the woods and, on the other, we are at the cutting edge of technology.' Money still being ploughed into improving teaching areas, with plans to convert outbuilding into design technology complex.

Small classes – 10 maximum – mean plenty of individual attention. Speech, language and occupational therapists on hand when needed. Strong focus on English and maths – 10 periods of each a week – but not at the expense of anything else. 'Children don't have the stigma of being withdrawn from a history lesson to do extra English or whatever,' says head. 'It's built into the curriculum. That's the strength of the school.' French a must (except in very exceptional circumstances), art, music and drama all thriving. Sports cover usual rugby, football and cricket with Bruern able to hold its own against tough opposition – like The Dragon, albeit their fifth XI. Small heated outdoor pool and tennis courts, also nearby golf course much in demand. Fawkes admits their sports facilities aren't the best. 'To a certain extent we're still playing catch-up,' he says. 'We don't have an indoor gym or Astroturf like other preps in the area.' So makes full use of local countryside with riding, shooting, fishing and cross-country.

Pastoral care hugely important as confidence often at very low ebb when boys arrive. Though intake starts at seven, most boys join at nine or 10 after being 'let down' by educational system elsewhere. Said one boy, 'It's totally different from my last school. There I was made to feel stupid, I was always coming bottom and I got bullied a lot. But here the teachers listen to me and take the time to explain.' Another added, 'Other schools will try and change you. Here you can be who you really are. You are free in this school but there are boundaries and even when we think we're on our own, we know someone's keeping an eye on us.' Pastoral side shared mostly between housemaster, matron and head's wife. Bad behaviour or bullying speedily dealt with. Apart from detention, severest punishment often means missing one of school's twice weekly formal dinners – a splendid candlelit affair which is so popular parents must book in advance. Good food seen as central to school life – smashing chef delights in cooking the best fresh produce. All faiths, intolerances and allergies catered for. Boys boast, 'Chef used to cook for the Queen.' It's true! Chapel attended weekly in converted orangery – readings seen as crucial to boys' growing self-esteem.

Handful of day boys. Majority of pupils board, full or weekly with some flexible. School buses in large number from London, one or two arrive by helicopter. Former parents include a rock star and best-selling novelist, current crop includes actresses and directors. But plenty of 'ordinary' boys too. Very much a boys' school, with activities to match. Those we spoke to were impressively polite, confident, articulate, enthusiastic and outgoing. Bruern's certainly not a cheap option but for some it's their only hope. One boy summed it up, 'I actually look forward to school on a Monday morning now.'

Burgess Hill School for Girls Junior School

Linked to Burgess Hill School For Girls in the Senior section

Keymer Road, Burgess Hill, West Sussex, RH15 0EG

- Pupils: 200 girls; plus 30 boys and 55 girls in the nursery; all day
- Ages: 4-11 junior, 2.5-4 nursery • Size of sixth form: girls only
- Non-denominational • Fees: £6,180-£10,860 pa • Independent

Tel: 01444 233167
Fax: 01444 243538
Email: jsoffice@burgesshill-school.com
Website: www.burgesshill-school.com

Head of the Junior School: Miss Fenneke Fulleylove.

Background and Atmosphere: Very new nursery and infant building providing excellent facilities for the students at the lower end of the school.

Entrance: Nursery (boys and girls), flexible entry criteria. Junior school (girls only) via entrance assessments or entrance assessments combined with taster days for possible mid-year entry if a space is available, informal activity sessions for entry to reception and key stage 1 classes, and previous school's report.

Exit: Automatic entry for girls from nursery to reception and from junior school to senior school, as long as pupils can cope and are comfortable with the work ethos and general pace of the year group.

Remarks: Occupies a separate house next to the main school, the twain overlapping very occasionally, but the facilities of the senior school are available. A few subjects taught by subject specialists from senior school, e.g. French, but generally taught within their own age group. No more than 18 to a class. New and improved IT suite with specialists on hand with smartboards – most classrooms now have this technology. Strong music tradition with four or five music periods per week. Orchestras in Years 4, 5 and 6 plus flute, clarinet ensembles, choirs – high percentage learn an instrument. Good art clubs and renowned stamp club – very popular. Happy, happy children on a wet, wet day.

Burys Court

Linked to Moon Hall School in the Junior section Linked to Moon Hall College

Flanchford Road, Leigh, Reigate, Surrey,
RH2 8RE

• Pupils: 50 • Fees: £6,300-£16,500 pa • Independent

Tel: 01306 611 372
Fax: 01306 611 037
Email: enquiries@buryscourtschool.co.uk
Website: www.moonhallcollege.co.uk

Bute House Preparatory School for Girls

Bute House, Luxemburg Gardens, London, W6 7EA

• Pupils: 310 girls, all day • Ages: 4-11 • Non-denom, predominantly Christian, currently 15 different religions represented • Fees: £11,505 pa • Independent

Tel: 0207 603 7381
Fax: 0207 371 3446
Email: mail@butehouse.co.uk
Website: www.butehouse.co.uk

Head: Since 1993, Mrs Sallie Salvidant BEd CertEd (fifties), an English graduate. Previously Mrs Salvidant was head of the pre-prep in Holmewood School from 1985 to 1987 and then head of Rupert House School, Henley-on-Thames, 1987–93. She is relaxed, comfortable, loquacious when enthused and knows her job inside out. She believes in 'education not schooling' and this philosophy underpins every aspect of this remarkable school. Parents crow, 'she's wonderful.' 'She has such spirit.' 'She really knows about children and education.' A staff member took us aside when we visited and confided, 'It is wonderful here and it is all Mrs Salvidant, you know. She made the school'. It would be a greater tribute to say that she has created a unique school with a precious ethos – strong enough to outlive her own tenure because its inspired children, past pupils, parents and staff will ensure that it does.

Entrance: 22 children enter the school in reception. Around 400 children apply and they are picked by ballot. No point in coaching your three-year-old then. Even less point if your child is not a sibling. The 2008 intake included 18 siblings of existing pupils! This, we are assured, is not usual but it might rather lessen the odds. 38 children enter Year 3. Around 140 girls apply for these places and places are offered on the basis of tests, interview and reports from current schools. No sibling preference at 7+ assessment but school 'looks very carefully at sisters'. Occasional places thereafter are competed for by test and the school has a waiting list for each year. This, then, is to a considerable extent, a mixed-ability school. Girls come from the local boroughs and as far as Barnes, Ealing, Kew, Putney, Wimbledon and north London. Vast diversity of backgrounds and a number are bilingual in French/Mandarin/Italian/German to name but a few. Read the Bute prospectus for the sheer pleasure of it then use their website for facts.

Exit: Around a quarter each year to Godolphin and Latymer, a further third/quarter to St Paul's Girls' School. The rest go to other good London day schools e.g. Putney High, and the Francis Hollands, or to Latymer Upper – the local co-ed. A few to the best boarding schools – Downe House, Wycombe Abbey. Interestingly, around the same proportion of those who enter at 4+ as those who come at 7+ go on to the top schools. Bute girls trail scholarships – in 2010, the 54 leavers were offered, between them, 15 schools – and not just brainbox schools either – music too.

Remarks: This is not the prep school for St Paul's Girls' School – let's get that clear right now. It happens to be round the corner and it used to be called St Paul's Girls' Preparatory School but, since 1958, there has been no formal link between the two schools and NB Bute girls have no right of entry or preferential treatment when it comes to the entrance exams for its venerable neighbour. So, if your idea is to get into Bute so that your daughter can be pruned, clipped and polished for St Paul's, by way of drilling, testing and hothousing, you are looking at the wrong place, my friend. For a start, Bute has no exams. What! I hear you cry. Neither do its staff put marks at the end of pupils' work – they re-mark i.e. write copious helpful comments And, yes, there are no form lists or end-of-year placings. And yet, no other prep in the country is so successful at getting places for its alumnae at the best schools.

How can this be? Bute has a culture of learning for learning's sake. The girls are well-motivated anyway and love being at the school. The use of IEPs where needed, the practice of re-marking work rather than marking and of not squandering time on exams and tests means that each child competes only against herself and learns from her own efforts and the teachers' comments. It also ensures that no-one is complacent. Progress is assessed frequently and carefully but not overtly or wastefully. The proof of the pudding is in the girls themselves. We have never been escorted by such happy ones – they strive to outdo each other in enthusing about every aspect of the place – even the teachers – 'she's so nice – I want to hug her!' cried one of one and when we looked at the photo of all the staff, each one seemed somehow special to the girls. These are happy girls who love their teachers though the day is so full of stimulation, greedy learning and excitement that, although all the right pastoral care systems are in place, one wonders how a minute might be found if anyone actually needed a quiet space and time to share a problem.

The Bute building itself is a surprise – a somewhat futuristic 1950s neo-greenhouse farrago with add-ons in pine, pink render, louvred glass and warm-toned brickwork in a quiet Victorian terraced street just off fashionable Brook Green, five minutes from the Hammersmith jungle. It has a splendid 2006 atrium with the reception and offices and big screens with the news of the day, timetable changes etc – even the day's birthdays – rather nice. We blushed to see our own visit prominently announced but it did mean that everyone knew who we were which has its advantages. There is a wall on which all Bute pupils are represented by a little ceramic tile which they make and which remains as a record of their time in the school. The school, thereafter, in the head's words, 'is a bit of a Tardis' and one is not prepared by the hotch-potch exterior for the spaciousness – of each classroom, the immense hall and outside space as well as of the airiness and uncluttered feel of the whole. Outside is a tarmac playground and the girls use the St Paul's Girls' school field for games and their swimming pool. Perhaps the perimeter of the playground could use a few more benches to accommodate the older girls who like to sit and chat.

The classrooms are a feast. Reception is big and there is plenty of space for everyone at the little tables and around the many activities – they'd been cooking banana cake when we got there. Everything is beautifully laid out – pencils in pots, a discovery table with 'new life in spring' exhibits – most remarkable – a canopied and cushioned book corner and lots of lovely dressing-up stuff including some pretty cool shoes. All the children use the garden, complete with lots of climbing things and a real – not a bouncy – castle and sandpit. Reception have their own times when they also use large wheely toys. The Year 3 classroom we visited was similarly spacious and the ceiling was hung with the results of exciting projects – planets, models of polygons, globes, plants and skeletons. Year 6 had done The Plague so we enjoyed NHS-style pamphlets on 'A Guide to the Plague and How to Avoid It' or 'The Plague – how do I know if I've got it?' One nascent epidemiologist called hers, 'Look On the Bright Side!'

This is perhaps the most colourful school we know – everywhere are displays, pictures and models – all bursting with vitality, wit and fun. We giggled over the fish mobiles and the models in DT – caravans made of wood, mostly drawn by horses but one drawn by a mobile muffin and another by David Beckham. Superb library, invitingly laid out and well-stocked, is so popular that the number of visitors have to be restricted. ICT seen as a tool not a subject – hallelujah! – though there is one lesson per week just to learn skills – then laptops available to everyone for help as needed. They were being used, during our visit, in delightful projects by girls who were preparing PowerPoint presentations on their favourite hobby. Grown-up lab hung with inflatable insects almost tempted in this labphobic writer. Girls had just done vacuum-packing which was 'so much fun – you just sat in a bin-bag and it sucks the air out and it was so much fun!'

Many rooms, including the hall, are flexible, and divisible into two. All classrooms have smartboards and – oh joy! – all are air-conditioned. The girls eat in one half of the hall and drool over the food. 'It's just the best' ... 'it's cooked to perfection!' Free cucumber and carrot wedges are served at break and there are water-fountains inside and outside school. Milk, however, has to be paid for, which we thought rather mean.

The teaching is clearly, for the most part, inspired and this is true of the Learning Enrichment programme too, which covers SEN and G & T. 52 girls on the Learning Enrichment register, many needing only minimal support. This support – unlike the milk – is free. Those who don't speak English at home have one weekly support session. Some see the SENCo on a one-to-one basis and some in small groups. 90 on the G & T register. Wonderfully enlightened policy. We enjoyed meeting one mildly dyslexic girl who had made 'amazing' progress with her one-to-one but who was also part of the G & T maths group – 'we learned about the hypotenuse! It was so fun!' – but could she spell it? Another enthused about the 'stretching' she experiences in the group – clearly the highlight of her week – 'this room is heaven for me'.

The curriculum is rich anyway – everyone does French from reception, Spanish from Year 4 and Latin from Year 5. Bute girls excel in sports, drama, dance and music too and win most of the competitive activities in which they engage – Mrs Salvidant sees not the winning, so much as the opportunity to engage in healthy competition, as important. 2008 saw Bute win the London Schools Swimming competition, the British Schools Regional U9 Novice gym competition, the Regional Round IAPS netball tournament, the Ealing Borough cross-country championships and the Thames Valley Harriers cross-country. The arts activities and opportunities are both numerous and classy but you'd better see the prospectus for that!

If your daughter gets in, you're in for a lively, exciting and stimulating time – one she will never forget. And Mrs Salvidant – sane, experienced and definitely to be trusted on this one – will make sure that she leaves for the school to which she is best suited. She knows.

Calder House School

Thickwood Lane, Colerne, Chippenham, Wiltshire, SN14 8BN

• Pupils: 40 boys and girls, all day • Ages: 5-12 • Non--denominational
• Fees: £13,800 pa • Independent

Tel: 01225 742 329
Fax: 01225 742 329
Email: head@calderhouseschool.co.uk
Website: www.calderhouseschool.co.uk/

Head: Since 2008, Mr Andrew Day BEd (early forties) educated at Ysgol Gyfun Ystalyfera (only Welsh speaking comprehensive in West Glamorgan), then University of Wales Institute, Cardiff. Aim of teaching in Welsh medium thwarted by romance: followed wife Helen across Bristol Channel to begin teaching career at Bristol Grammar Lower School for first seven years (maths and ICT plus lots of games coaching), then to be director of studies at Hornsby House, Balham, for next three, where he says, 'I had to rethink my whole approach to teaching'. Subsequently at Wycliffe Prep for three years, then similar period at Cheltenham College Junior prior to landing 'dream job' at Calder House. Hearty Welsh rugby player who is universally liked by pupils: has a real passion for helping dyslexic children realise their potential. Left Cheltenham College Junior as he disliked 'seeing perfectly bright children not making it through to the senior school'. Parents rate way head is 'bringing school up to date' and 'making the right changes'. 'Boys at CH really benefit from head's kind but firm approach,' glowed one satisfied mother. Enjoys getting away to native Wales or Cornwall with wife and two daughters (currently attending Red Maids in Bristol) in 'Daisy', their trusty VW campervan.

Entrance: Full day's assessment to determine extent to which applicants are under-achieving due to SpLD. Parents commented that the assessment day was 'pupil friendly' and gave children 'a good chance to see what lessons were like'. Some referrals through LAs who currently fund 10 per cent of pupils. Frequent approaches via local preps who recognise school's unique contribution. Catchment covers area within 25-mile radius.

Exit: Aim to get pupils up to at least chronological reading, writing and maths age within three years or less before returning to mainstream state or independent education. Amazing success rate. Only a very few continue through special education.

Remarks: Looks more like a country farmstead (which it formerly was) than a school – among the smallest we have visited. Pastoral location on edge of Cotswold hamlet close to Bath, Chippenham and M4 corridor. Lovely grassed area in centre of school (alas, no longer any chickens here since last avian flu scare) gives a sense of calm. Site extends across fields at rear to copses hiding historic World War II air raid shelters: a 'living history' lesson for excited pupils when they are allowed to go there. Calder House founded and owned by delightful Sandra Agombar, who retains title of principal and lives on site with bursar husband – 'He also mows the grass,' we were told. Son, Edward (for whose SpLD benefit the original CH was created in London), works as a teaching assistant and is a living testimony to the school's success. After years at helm, Sandra lets head get on with running the show, though she clearly still looks upon school as her labour of love.

School is approached by gravelled drive with farmland to the side and rear. New classrooms (completed in 2002) and multi-purpose hall were built to replace formerly dilapidated farm outbuildings and connect to original school, which now houses administration, library and some ICT/teaching space. Large, covered barn provides great play and social space (containing purpose-built play equipment) for break and lunchtime use – staff also read to children here. Some activities take place at mid-morning break (we saw some absorbed chess players – some involved in national schools' chess championships) and others (such as drama and gardening club) during lunchtime. Children bring their own packed lunches.

Pupils are a very mixed lot brought together by a common need for urgent remedial support. Unpretentious blue and white uniform – scope for improvement, we thought. Good cloakroom facilities with plenty of loos and space to change in and out of wellies and coats. We watched a captivating Monday morning assembly on the theme of 'learning from our mistakes', in which the head span a moral tale about discovered theft, during which he managed to produce 17 oranges from his jacket and trousers – quite a tour de force and much enjoyed by everyone. On Fridays, classes take it in turn to present assembly.

CH accommodates six classes of maximum eight children, though much of the work is in smaller groups or one-to-one. Each child receives two reading sessions a day when they are listened to and taught to read using specific programmes. A daily spelling lesson and two sub-skills lessons which might comprise one-to-one speech and language, specific dyslexic or gross and fine motor support. Other sessions include working memory (visual and auditory), spatial perception or extra maths support. Daily maths lessons: we saw one Year 7 boy (who had already achieved SATs level 6) making considerable headway in this area. Seven full-time staff plus four teaching assistants and two volunteers. Staff:pupil ratio is 1:4. Whole school approach to SEN ensures all pupils attend mainstream lessons (taught as discrete subjects rather than thematically). Timetable gives way twice a term for theme days – recently including poetry day, maths fun day and Robbie Burns day.

In the morning, children move around with great purpose carrying plastic trays for their materials and checking the colour-coded individual timetables sellotaped to the bottom of each. Pupils know where to go as timetables correspond with the differently coloured floors of each classroom. Afternoon lessons are age group based and the broad range of national curriculum subjects includes RE, PSHE and Italian: chosen to avoid unfair comparison at home with siblings. Art-room displays we saw included pottery, gargoyles and geometric designs in the style of Klimt – 'art has improved recently,' say parents. Music is class-based at present and taught by a peripatetic teacher in the main hall; school choir with annual in-house as well as local events. We hope that school will introduce individual music tuition before long. Lively science classes make increasing use of the 'outside classroom' on the doorstep, and pupils obviously enjoy their forays into the natural world around them. School's new minibus means pupils enjoy four external visits per term as well as going to swimming (own instructor and lifeguard) at nearby army barracks (25 metre covered pool) and away games fixtures, which parents say boys in particular enjoy. Annual activity week is organised on site and includes overnight camping for some. Considerable success in ESB exams including recent distinctions.

Head rates established system of individualised timetables and we were amazed at how smoothly it operates. We saw pupils working with Arrow software to improve auditory memory, others working on fine motor skills and dyspraxic children improving their co-ordination with the physiotherapist by moving backwards between special cones placed in the multi-purpose hall. Pupils use wide selection of word games with the speech and language therapist. Two ICT rooms are in constant use and serviced by an outside technician. Pupils were learning fractions with the aid of BBC Bitesize software; Heinemann maths course used for older pupils, and we watched a beautifully-delivered lesson on symmetry. Care is taken to ensure that pupils do not miss core teaching. We liked the way pupils are organised to work with others of a similar level: this is kept under constant review. Parents speak highly of parent-teacher meetings where they have in depth consultations with key staff. Head has provided email access to all staff, which is 'really helpful'. Teachers re-evaluate each child prior to the start of each new term/half-term. Pupils take key stage 2 SATs with some spectacular improvements in attainment.

One-third of pupils leave each year, but this movement reinforces rather than detracts from school's mission; pupils sense that their time at CH is short and that they must make the most of every minute. Former pupils include PhDs, nurses and even an ice hockey player. This is a happy school where children can regain their self-esteem and learn to trust their teachers. 'Buckets of letters' from ex-parents praise work done here. Parents spoke of how primary schools had failed to deal with their child's dyslexia and how honest school had been in giving an accurate time-scale for putting things right. Short intervention is the aim here, not hanging on to pupils unnecessarily. Pupils are taught to cope with failure and then move forwards. Those we spoke to were eager to say how the school had helped them overcome their learning difficulties and how much they value the opportunity provided to improve. One father said school had 'been an absolute godsend', and he really meant it.

Caldicott School

Crown Lane, Farnham Royal, Slough, Buckinghamshire, SL2 3SL

• Pupils: 250 boys; 115 board (including all in the last two years); the rest are day boys • Ages: 7-13 • C of E • Fees: Boarding £19,227; Day £13,080-£14,148 pa • Independent

Tel: 01753 649 300
Fax: 01753 649 325
Email: registrar@caldicott.com
Website: www.caldicott.com

Head: Since 1998, Mr Simon Doggart BA (mid forties), educated at Winchester and read history at Cambridge. School-mastering is in his blood – his father was a legendary figure at Winchester for many years – and he previously taught history at Eton, where he also ran the cricket. A larger-than-life figure, he has gathered around him an energetic and dedicated staff of young Turks and experienced war-horses. 'He chooses his staff very well,' says a mum. Wife, Antonia, is the very best sort of prep-school head's wife: invaluable at match teas and when entertaining parents, wise and shrewd in counsel and enormously good fun. They are a wonderful couple, much loved by all.

Entrance: The school is divided, though not separated, into three: 7–9; 9–11; 11–13. Two forms, with 15 pupils each, enter at seven with a further form at eight. Inspirational teaching greets the young ones, who are involved in imaginative, colourful and exciting work to prepare them for the joys ahead. In the October before their September entry, registered boys and parents meet the head and his staff, are shown round and the boys then sit a 35-minute assessment. 'All done so gently they hardly notice it,' a senior boy told us. Potential is valued as much as attainment. Families from Windsor, Henley, Amersham, Beaconsfield etc, and an increasing number from London – 'loads' from Notting Hill and Chiswick, where four buses collect and return (homework done) including Saturdays.

Exit: Yes, it's an Eton, Harrow and Radley school but, as staff are keen to point out, not exclusively so: St Edward's, Wellington, Marlborough, Shiplake, Winchester, Oundle – 18 different schools in 2009. The school is not blind to the importance of matching up with the right school, though 'the competition is cut-throat and parents sometimes have unrealistic notions'.

Remarks: The school feels in some ways like the traditional boarding school of 40 years ago in terms of its insistence on 'good manners and playing the game'. But it is much better than that. Most of the staff live on site – the school has built generously and intends to build more houses for its staff. 'We are here 24 hours a day, seven days a week. That's what I joined up for,' says a youngish member of staff. The school sends its most recent inspection report to parents with its prospectus. Prospective parents should read carefully what the head says in his introductory letter about the bland language used on such occasions. Then consider the full significance of the sentence in the report, 'Relationships between boys and staff are excellent'. Every school makes claims for that – Caldicott demonstrates it. 'Spot on,' says a mother; 'They're right,' says a happy boy.

Occasionally parents bleat about the 'relentless setting', but these boys thrive on the competition and in any case the sets are not cast in bronze. 'Children develop at different stages,' said one wise old bird. Nevertheless the scholarship stream (springing from the well of nine-year-olds) is full of bright-eyed boys who, of course, do Latin and Greek and get that extra help towards scholastic glory. Those with learning difficulties are given careful individual treatment – much appreciated. From age 10 boys do an hour of prep every night. 'The academic régime is inspired by enthusiastic teaching and is firm but fair,' said the father of a son recently departed. 'Caldicott boys are well-adjusted and pretty vigorous in their approach,' said a senior school housemaster. Parents appreciate the frequent reports they receive and the staff are said to be 'most approachable'. A recent improvement, thanks to extra classrooms and staff, is to have four sets in the senior school. That gives greater flexibility to move between sets.

Only 20 miles from London, the school is safely lodged in leafy and opulent-feeling Bucks. Founded in 1904 and named after the founding headmaster's new bride, it moved from Hitchin to its present handsome building in 1938. Many sensitively-designed additions: the award-winning centenary hall, a wonderful glassy space for concerts, plays and assemblies of all sorts, and most recently a new science building with cleverly-adapted roof space and state-of-the-art equipment. Two brand new computer rooms, much used and enjoyed.

Bright, cheerful dormitories where a senior boy sleeps in each junior one to ensure peace and happiness. Boys are required to board aged 11 – good preparation for the next stage of the adventure. Junior boarders may go home from 1pm on Saturday until Sunday evening providing they warn the school; senior boarders (11 plus) are allowed out on Saturday nights. Lots of pleasant common rooms and a comfortable dining room with the oldest boys helping to supervise with teachers. It's a nut-free school!

Music is improving – it has, perhaps, been a weakness in the past, at least in terms of music scholarships won. Now practice is timetabled in four times a week and concerts are given by professional musicians who spend a day at the school helping budding performers, many of whom play in the school orchestras, jazz bands, quartets: you name it. The art and DT department is fizzing with colour and creativity and is very popular at weekends. Excellent husband and wife team run it. Annual programme of visits to major London galleries – by the time they leave, boys will have visited six, starting with the National Portrait Gallery, marvellous for linking up with history, and ending with Tate Modern. Other activities include annual declamations for which everyone learns a poem, debating and chess. Life is full and opportunities of every kind abound.

Famous for its rugby and cricket, played on an outstandingly good pitch which has witnessed county and club games. The groundsman is justifiably proud of his work and his beautifully-manicured grounds are the envy of less happy schools. Nowadays Caldicott turns out many more teams than it used to and players who are keen, but not effortlessly gifted, can get into one of the six senior rugby teams or five cricket XIs. The school has given much thought to extending the range of activities for those less team-games-oriented: sailing, cycling, rowing, chess matches, badminton, squash, fishing, tennis, athletics and so on. Of course many of those are pursued by sporty boys, as well. 'You can always find something you're good at,' said a boy who, on his own admission, was not a natural athlete nor a scholar. Boys hurl themselves around the excellent sports hall, splash around in the heated outdoor pool, practise on the golf area. The overall scene is idyllic, with Burnham Beeches over the road and sweeping views from the pitches.

The excellence of Caldicott lies in the way it has combined the best of the past in prep schools with the comparatively modern emphasis on personal fulfilment. 30 years ago, the hope for some might have stopped at survival. Now there is no stopping. Insistence on good manners does not blunt spontaneity and bubbling enthusiasm. Boys rush around happily, greet with open friendliness and are full of zest.

Superb facilities, excellent staff and lovely surroundings. No sense of standing still; instead the feeling that alert minds are constantly looking for areas to improve, to tweak, to alter. This is an exciting and civilised school which offers an excellent all-round education.

Cameron House School

4 The Vale, Chelsea, London, SW3 6AH

• Pupils: 65 girls, 50 boys; all day • Ages: 4-11 • Non-denom but C of E roots • Fees: £13,785 pa • Independent

Tel: 020 7352 4040
Fax: 020 7352 2349
Email: info@cameronhouseschool.org
Website: www.cameronhouseschool.org

Headmistress: Since 2007, Mrs Lucie Moore BEd. School founded in 1980 by Josie Cameron Ashcroft who is the proprietor and, as Mrs Moore puts it, 'is her one and only governor'. A member of the IAPS, she taught at Thomas's and coached children privately before setting up her own school in St Luke's Church, Sydney Street. She remains principal and still keeps a close eye on the ongoing vision and image of the school and knows all the parents as well as the staff.

Mrs Moore, as headmistress, is in charge of the day-to-day running of the school. She started her teaching career in a state primary in Winchester, and then international schools in Italy and Bangkok before settling into the hurly burly of London day schools. She spent seven years at the Hampshire School, where her career took a meteoric rise under the paternal guidance of Arthur Bray: 'he was like a mentor to me'. He soon identified her talents and she swiftly became head of prep and vice principal of the Hampshire Schools before he encouraged her to apply for the post here.

Her husband, the finance director at City Airport, is always by her side at school events. A young headmistress (she was 36 when she started), Lucie (as she is known to everyone, pupils, staff and parents) is attractive and bubbly. She has a huge sense of fun and clearly adores the children. Each sentence is peppered with 'aren't they just so sweet?' She's got a point – children here are very cute – girls clad in fresh blue and white striped summer dresses with cherry jumpers and cardis, boys adorable in blue cord shorts.

Parents gush over her smiling enthusiasm, warmth, excellent communication and understanding of each child. We heard reports of her firm but sensitive approach to the big issues that arise in a child's life, whether it's an instance of unkindness – difficult to conceive of a child being actually bullied here – or problems at home. She also has enormous reserves of energy and is very driven. As well as teaching every class in the school once a week ('it's important that I keep my feet on the ground for the sake of the children and the staff'), coordinating the SEN, and working on the weekly newsletter, she is at the front door every afternoon and morning greeting each child. If any parent expresses an interest in a senior school she doesn't know she will make sure she spends plenty of time there – not only to establish important links with the head but also to make sure in her own mind that the school would suit that child. Highly efficient, 'I'm a Virgo,' she says, 'I need to be organised and to plan ahead.' Not at all concerned about getting her hands dirty, she describes the job as 'fitting like a glove'.

Entrance: All children are assessed at three so there's no need to rush to get your baby onto a list; register up till a year before entry. A popular school – over 200 applicants for 20 places and Mrs Moore acknowledges how difficult it is to choose – 'it's heartbreaking to reject anyone,' she says. Ultimately they look to create a class with a balance of the confident and the shy and some happily in between. They work closely with nurseries and rely on their reports (children come from a wide range including Pippa Poppins, Paint Pots, and Miss Daisy's). Putting school down as a genuine first choice always helps.

Exit: A few boys at 7+ or 8+ to e.g. boarding, or Catholic schools (Ludgrove, St Philip's), but fewer and fewer now. Mrs Moore has fine tuned the 'stepping stones' options for boys who want to do 13+ Common Entrance and sends them for two years at 11 to e.g. Newton Prep, Fulham Prep, Sussex House, Wetherby and the Hampshire School. Lots of advice given to parents from Year 5 onwards.

At 11 girls and boys go to a broad range of schools each year – current favourites are Latymer Upper, St Paul's Girls, City of London girls and boys, Dulwich, Alleyn's, Emanuel, Godolphin & Latymer, Queen's Gate and Francis Holland. They nearly always get their first choice school, we're told (due in large part to Mrs Moore's determination that parents choose the school that suits their child whatever they themselves might prefer) 'and they interview beautifully because they're so confident,' she gloats. One or two girls every year board at e.g. Wycombe Abbey and Downe House.

Remarks: A tiny (one class per year of about 20), cosy, pretty school but don't be misled into thinking it's just chocolate boxy – Cameron House is a serious player in getting children into sought-after London schools. There is a wide range of ability but what all children have in common is that they are confident and very, very smiley. They are given a lot of preparation in the final year. In Year 6, class sizes shrink so everyone gets more attention, compulsory homework club gives all children an extra hour at school and removes the pressure from the parents. 'We shoulder the worry,' says Mrs Moore, 'and the last thing I want is to see 10-year-olds being counselled for stress.' A lot of staff channelled into Year 6 when they do group work, prepare for scholarships, mock interviews and confidence-building workshops. The formula clearly works. They get results but no-one could describe this as a hothouse.

Approximately 15 children are helped with mild to moderate SEN – dyspraxia, dyscalculia, dysgraphia etc. The school takes a holistic approach. Learning support is timetabled and structured with clear IEPs drawn up. Parents pay extra. Mrs Moore herself is the SEN coordinator – another member of staff coordinates the programme for the gifted and talented which is run within the class. In addition a select few are invited to join the Discovery Club and Explorers Club. Mrs Moore explains the cautious approach to the gifted and talented programme. Children are identified towards the end of Year 1 – 'we wouldn't want to have to say, "you weren't gifted after all!"' she says.

A town house with not a great deal of space, but the soft plush tartan carpet throughout the stairwell, lavatories with pretty wallpaper, water filters, attractive blue furnishings and every teacher referred to by their first names – without even a Miss or Mister attached – gives the school a homely, uninstitutional feel. Children have fun here, whether it's enjoying music, drama, sport, watching caterpillars transmorph into butterflies, or playing giant magnetic chess in the playground (a good excuse to see the lovely Lucie to get the chess pieces). Even maths can be made to be an excuse to dress up and laugh. Bubbles the maths clown came to school, the hall was filled with balloons and children came to school dressed as shapes. In Book Week everyone dresses up, even Mrs Moore who is not at all phased when she greets prospective parents dressed as Captain Hook. 'If they don't like to see their future headmistress being able to laugh at herself then we're clearly not the right school for them nor them for us,' she says.

Nearly everyone plays an instrument or has singing lessons – the lessons happen in a little Wendy house-type hut in the playground. Major dramatic productions – The Lion King, A Midsummer Night's Dream among them – take place in a closely guarded secret venue – 'let's just say a theatre off Kensington High Street,' is as far as Mrs Moore will be drawn. 'We aim high,' says Mrs Moore proudly, as she lists the impressive artistic accomplishments for such a small school which include getting to the final for young choir of the year at the Royal Festival Hall. They have an orchestra, string quartet and three choirs.

One of Mrs Moore's challenges has been to stop the boys leaving at 7+ or 8+. There are signs of success. Although previous Year 6 classes have had few boys, some none at all, when we visited there was an equal number of both sexes. 'Parents are starting to realise that they can get their boys into Westminster Under, Colet Court and Latymer at 11,' she says, 'and there are plenty of stepping stone options between 11 and 13.' Boys are kept a lot more active here than at many similar schools. Games takes place three times a week – children can do cricket, football, hockey and netball as well as martial arts in the huge loft space at the Boudokwai centre. Lots of matches (most of which they lose, comments one parent) but the advantage of being a small school is everyone gets to have a go, it's not just the sporty types who do everything.

A lot of expat families from mainly the US, Canada and Australia reflecting the cosmopolitan area. We saw masses of glamorous long-haired mothers off to the gym after drop off. Lots of city types but also more than the usual number of creatives – artists, actors, as well as doctors and art dealers. All parents are very involved and enjoy the open door policy of the school.

A charming school that will discover your child's strengths, nurture and support them.

Cargilfield School

37 Barnton Avenue West, Edinburgh, Edinburgh, EH4 6HU

• Pupils: 310; 7-13 years 215 girls and boys; 60 boarders. 3-7 years 85 girls and boys • Ages: 3-13 • Non-denom • Fees: Day £7,950-£12,600; Boarding £15,600-£16,200 pa • Independent

Tel: 0131 336 2207
Fax: 0131 336 3179
Email: admin@cargilfield.com
Website: www.cargilfield.com

Headmaster: Since 2004, Mr John Elder MA PGCE (fifties), formerly head of Malsis and before that Beeston; he has been a headmaster for 26 years. Educated at Lathallan and Cranleigh, followed by St Andrews and Edinburgh unis, (he changed from history at St Andrews to American history at Edinburgh), and started off by recycling wine bottles in Docklands – and would probably have been a millionaire by now, had he stuck at it. Charming and charismatic, he has given Cargilfield a much-needed boost in continuity and in confidence, and is in charge of both the prep and the pre-prep. Mrs Elder (whom we did not meet on this occasion) very active around the school, particularly at weekends. The three Elder children are up and running – their daughter had her wedding reception at Cargilfield last August (they have a house in Angus and Mr Elder is a Scot).

A giant of a man, Mr Elder teaches maths to scholars ('strong maths staff are the most difficult to find') but no longer coaches, though he does enjoy going on tours with teams.

Entrance: Nursery and pre-prep popular and upper school numbers have grown enormously; places pretty well guaranteed through pre-prep but tests if learning difficulties suspected.

Exit: All the Scottish public schools; Glenalmond and Fettes head the list, but also Merchiston. Kilgraston, less to Gordonstoun, almost none to Loretto or Strathallan – much as you would expect. Huge cohort – around half – head south of the border: Eton (biggest feeder north of Oxford), Harrow, Shrewsbury, Rugby, Oundle, Ampleforth, the odd one recently to King's Canterbury (sports scholarship) ditto Marlborough, Downe House, occasionally Wycombe Abbey. More scholarships than you can shake a stick at – 50+ last three or four years – 'genuine academic awards', including Winchester, Shrewsbury, Ampleforth, Eton and Oundle. Top award to Fettes regularly and top classics to all.

Remarks: School was in decline when Mr Elder arrived: wobbly governors and even wobblier heads had made for wobbly numbers. No longer. The Elders have effected a transformation and Cargilfield is now the 'family school with superb facilities, preparing children for the great schools in Scotland and the south' which the head promised six years ago. Spanish on the curriculum: superb classics results with 20 doing Greek; Latin for all from eight (no exam result less than A) – including Eton and Winchester scholarships). Mass of new-build lately. Sports hall, which impinges a tad on the (much reduced – but not under this regime) games pitch has been joined by couple of cedar-clad (rather grand inside), huts which blend well, but look like early huts for battery hens (or photographs of Bletchley Park) and provide a new teaching centre plus a 10-room (sound-proof) music school with a mini-concert rehearsal room, used for drama too. Magnificent two-storey classroom block for English, ICT and history, with colonnades, cloisters and walkways at the front. Certain amount of internal restructuring, with dorms becoming classrooms (and vice versa).

Pupils setted and streamed. Most year groups divided into three: scholarship stream for the last three or four years plus two mixed-ability classes. Setted for maths from age eight. Fantastic learning support (known as learning development). Assessed on entry, Head of learning support plus two and a half staff. One of the best departments in Scotland combining individual and co-teaching: max 5.5 hours per week. Currently school has a parent underwritten (i.e. they pay school fees and for a dedicated teacher) unit for two pupils who have very special needs. The school will now no longer be able to accommodate many of the weaker brethren, unless they are, in fact brethren. Masses of options and extra-curricular activities – 80 clubs – lots of music, the pipe band is second to none, taster sessions for all in pre-prep, with 240 individual music lessons each term. Strong choir, which tours 'down south', and terrific strings ensemble: 'our top area and they have won major awards at the Edinburgh Music Festival'. Pop group. Hockey regularly in national ribbons, with masses of tours all over the UK.

Founded in 1873, the school moved to its purpose-built site in 1890 (23 acres then, 15 now). The revamped girls' boarding house is full, difficult to find space for flexis. Jolly sitting-rooms on ground floor (along with showers etc) and some of the prettiest dorms we have seen in a long time (Mr Elder chose the curtains). Some space in boys' dorms – the trad old school dorms – huge, with sofas and games tucked into corners – given the choice, chaps preferred more mates to smaller bedrooms. Chaps in bunks, girls have drawers below beds, total replacement of furniture and fittings factored in every three years (popular second-hand shop!) Two-weekly boarding for all. Day pupils regularly join boarders for a huge variety of weekend activities (though all must stay for three nights and can't just pick and choose). Kayaking, shooting, international coaching in fishing, fencing, judo, hockey. skiing both at Hillend and the real thing. Two small Astroturfs. 80 clubs on offer, chess champions with boards set up all over the place (and visiting chess master). Trips all over, both at weekends, and longer ones abroad to Rome and France (headmaster currently threatening to lead a trip to Greece for Greek scholars – much mirth). Much use made of resources in grand Scots cities. 'New' website.

Discounts for MoD children (handy for Scottish Command). The school offers 100 per cent bursaries which are means-tested – five or six pupils at Cargilfield on this kind of bursary (but not necessarily every year), graduated sibling discount. A mixed bunch of parents; grander than previously; and none currently from abroad. Boarders from Yorkshire, the Borders, the West Coast, Aberdeenshire, Angus and Perthshire. Bus on Sundays from Angus and Aberdeenshire, and daily from India Street in Edinburgh, Fife and West Lothian but, as children often stay till after eight, parents must collect them themselves. Serious advertising campaign on local taxis.

Pre-prep and Nursery is based in stunning three and a half million quid building with cherished (quite small) Astroturf and enclosed play area. Individual form takers for each year in the nursery and pre-prep, both housed in the multi-million pound annex to the main school with a dedicated play area, but all share big school facilities. School not keen on folk using the nursery as a springboard for a couple of years and then heading off elsewhere.

Carrdus School

Overthorpe Hall, Blacklocks Hill, Banbury, Oxfordshire, OX17 2BS

• Pupils: 120 girls, 20 boys; all day • Ages: 3-11 girls, 3-8 boys • Non-denom • Fees: £8,145-£8,685 pa • Independent

Tel: 01295 263 733
Fax: 01295 263 733
Email: office@carrdusschool.co.uk
Website: www.carrdusschool.co.uk

Head: Since 1985, Miss Susan Carrdus BA (sixties). Educated at The Carrdus School (her mother Kathleen founded school in 1952) and Banbury Grammar School, followed by Southampton University, where she read English. Previously head of English at nearby Tudor Hall. Has a grown-up daughter and two grandchildren.

Warm, approachable and immensely dedicated. Unusually for a head, she spends a third of her time in the classroom and is responsible for all Year 5 and 6 English teaching. 'I love it,' she says. 'I really like and enjoy the company of children.' Very child-centred and doesn't miss a trick, whether greeting pupils by name as they race around the garden at break-times, searching out pencil sharpeners in the stationery cupboard or crouching down to help a nursery child put her shoes on the right way round. Throws herself into all school activities, even painting, decorating and sorting out the garden during the holidays. 'I drive a mean dumper truck,' she laughs. Enjoys walking and learning to play the piano in her spare time (not that there's much of it).

Entrance: No entrance test. Very broad intake. Majority of pupils comes from Banbury and surrounding villages, with parents registering children up to three years in advance. Most common entry points are nursery, reception and Year 3 but it's worth trying in between too.

Exit: At 11, girls leave for a plethora of schools, including Tudor Hall, King's High, Headington, Rye St Antony, Oxford High, Cheltenham Ladies' College and Bloxham. Good smattering of scholarships over the years. At seven or eight, boys head for prep schools such as Winchester House, Warwick Junior, Cothill and Bilton Grange.

Remarks: School moved to present site in 1970, when Kathleen Carrdus (now in her eighties but still taking a huge interest in school activities) bought Overthorpe Hall for the princely sum of £22,500. Became an educational trust in 1991, with 100 per cent of fee income ploughed back into the school. Main building a rambling 1880s hunting lodge set in 11 acres of grounds. ISI report (2004) says school gives pupils 'a very caring and positive education'. Friendly staff pride themselves on making sure children are happy and secure in 'informal yet stimulating' atmosphere. Place feels straight out of a Mary Wesley novel – lots of fresh air, smiley faces, muddy knees and heaps of praise.

Despite relaxed ambience, pupils work hard and academic record is impressive. Hugely experienced staff (average age 48, around a quarter have been at school for more than 10 years). Maximum class size 24 but in practice more like 18. No setting, but most able get chance to move faster in 'sparkle sessions'. Head of maths holds walk-in surgery first thing every morning for anyone who needs help, including parents puzzled by modern maths! Has number of pupils with dyslexia, dyspraxia and/or learning difficulties who get support from two specially trained staff. No extra subjects apart from instrument lessons – school ethos is that everyone does everything. Children learn French from reception and take Latin for last two terms of Year 6. Homework for all. Reception children take reading books home; Year 3 pupils get prep three times a week, Year 5 and 6 pupils every night. Thousands of books, all colour-coded for different reading abilities – head reckons school possesses virtually every children's book published since her mum was a girl in the 1920s. At least one computer in each classroom and school proud that it now has a fully equipped IT room.

Arts strong, with children encouraged to play instruments, speak confidently in public and take part in concerts. Pupils' work on display everywhere you look. African tribal masks dangling from the main staircase, a collage of moles burrowing underground (using real mud!) and a poll of favourite books in the entrance hall – just for the record, Year 6 voted for Private Peaceful and Holes while Year 3 reckoned Roald Dahl's BFG was tops. Music terrific, with youngest children all playing percussion instruments and everyone from seven upwards learning the recorder. Many older pupils also learn piano, violin, guitar, saxophone or flute.

Daily assembly, as well as weekly hymn practice and bible story. Delightful – and short – list of school rules advises pupils: 'No sticks, no stones', 'Only climb as high as your friend's head' and 'it's only fun if everybody is enjoying it'. No school uniform, games kit aside. Dress code is 'not smart, not scruffy', with parents advised to send children in comfy, machine-washable clothes due to 'lots of mud and trees'. Pupils, mainly kitted out in mini Boden-type leggings and stripy jumpers (no jeans or bare midriffs), approve wholeheartedly. When we visited only one girl said she'd quite like to wear uniform – as long as it was blue.

Sport is compulsory for all. Children do hockey, netball, athletics, gym, tennis, gymnastics, dance, cycling proficiency and swimming (heated outdoor pool set in pretty walled garden). Cross-country a particular strength – pupils have won every cup going. Lots of school trips, to Stratford-upon-Avon, Oxford's Ashmolean Museum, Roald Dahl Museum etc. All Year 6 girls get annual expedition to Normandy – French speaking only from the minute the coach leaves school.

Nutritious, wholesome lunches cooked on-site and served by friendly dinner ladies who know children well. At breaktime youngsters help themselves to cheese, crispbread, raw vegetables and fruit before racing off to play in the garden in virtually all weathers.

Very strong, sociable PTA, with activities ranging from new parents' breakfasts to annual bonfire party, Christmas fair and spring sale. Parents arriving to collect their children in the afternoons gather in the entrance hall, complete with squashy sofas and, in winter, a roaring fire. Way ahead of its time, school launched annual Carrdus At Work day 15 years ago, giving mums and dads the chance to work alongside their children in class for a day during the spring term.

Children have a whale of a time here, while achieving good results. Devoted pupils and parents stay in touch for years after they leave, ringing for advice about everything from university entrance to career choices. Much to head's amusement, old girls frequently implore her, 'Can't you start a secondary school like this?'

Casterton Preparatory School

Linked to Casterton School in the Senior section

Kirkby Lonsdale, via Carnforth, Lancashire, LA6 2SG

• Pupils: 56; 36 girls, 20 boys; boarding and day • Ages: 3-11 • Fees: Day £6,570-£12,252; Boarding £17,949-£19,242 pa • Independent

Tel: 01524 279 282
Fax: 01524 279 286
Email: admissions@castertonschool.co.uk
Website: www.castertonschool.co.uk

Remarks: For futher details see senior school.

Castle Court

Knoll Lane, Corfe Mullen, Wimborne, Dorset, BH21 3RF

• Pupils: 260 boys and girls; all day • Ages: 3-13 • C of E
• Fees: Reception-Year 2 £7,125; Years 3-8 £12,945 pa • Independent

Tel: 01202 694 438
Fax: 01202 659 063
Email: admissions@castlecourt.com
Website: www.castlecourt.com

Headmaster: Since September 2010, Mr Richard Stevenson (early forties), BA (Hons) PGCE. Previously head of Kelly College, Tavistock. Married, with four children; enjoys sailing, walking, IT and wood-turning. Says: 'Children have one childhood and it has to be the best. Under my headship, Castle Court will always be family-centred and a place of fun where children will be inspired to learn a passion for life'.

Entrance: For three- to five-year-olds, first come, first in. Thereafter, informal assessment 'to ensure that children will be comfortable with the pace here'. Mild dyslexia only. They flock from all compass points – Weymouth, Shaftesbury, Burley, Swanage. First choice for Poole-Bournemouth conurbanites. Scholarships from 7+ for those likely to repeat the performance at a senior school. Automatic discounts for brothers and sisters.

Exit: If not Canford, one of a scattering of premiership independents. Impressive numbers of awards. Around a fifth leave at 12 for the excellent local grammars or the equally good comprehensives. Golden alumni include Tony Blackburn, pop singer Amy Studt and rugby sevens hero Ben Gollings.

Remarks: Though held in highest esteem, beguilingly unpretentious. Parents span old and new Dorset – farmers to flashy over-achievers/entrepreneurs. Expect no quirks. Castle Court is the product not of evolution but meticulous planning and it all stems from the top. Everything tickety-boo but never too good to be true. Beautifully-behaved children walk to assembly in marshalled lines, evenly spaced. They sit in rapt silence – contentedly. They listen to the Word as it relates to contemporary events, as it applies to daily lives, the delivery humorous, interactive, thought-inspiring, backed by powerpoint. The objective lies not in the act of worship but in what they call outworking – being kind to each other, raising money for charity. That's why parents like it – no sense whatever of evangelical mind-stealing. Zealous atheists may wince, though.

In the classroom the pace is rapid for this is a blue-chip school. Slower children will puff a bit but are supported, and almost all subjects are setted. The brightest not worked to death, yet mop up scholarships by the barrow-load. Every lesson we invaded was calm and, yes, orderly, but with masses going on – it's that sort of school. They want the children to work well together, and they do; so do the teachers. Marvellously focused, careful as can be. Results are no happy accident because each child is so painstakingly tracked – every building-block is put in place before the next block is added. One mum says, 'Pupils miss nothing academically, socially or extra-curricularly. A child can enter at three and leave at 13 and you can be absolutely confident that there is no chink in what they have learned or experienced.' Those with emergent SENs are pit-stopped and fine-tuned, mostly one-to-one, expertly, and equipped with 'special skills'. The void left by those off to grammar school instantly filled for those who remain, with extra attention from really impressive form teachers.

Does such an environment favour passive conformity? No. At breaktime we saw reassuringly semi-feral high spirits in the rough-and-tumble covered playground and surrounding woods. This really is a school for all sorts where problems are earnestly remedied, never shuffled off. Sport played with exuberance and winning prized – everyone has a go in a team at some level. Pastoral care attentive and personal. Music strong: 75 per cent learn an instrument and performance opportunities of all shapes and genres. Art superb and has wide appeal, including a thriving after-lunch drop in club where children do their own thing. Children urged to try their hands at everything, so the IT suite has outward bound posters above the monitors. Juniors have a go at riding and sailing. From Year 5 children can stay till 6pm for 'tea and prep' and activities – a good range. Camping weekends for Year 3 and up, some at the wonderful Kingcombe environmental centre.

Classrooms and facilities generally sound but not snazzy. Knoll House, the homely Regency mansion, lies at the heart of a roomy 30 acres. Lovely gardens, azalea-smitten in early summer, where we watched weenies playing Grandma's Footsteps before lunch, an Edwardian vision. All-weather pitch. Constantly uplifted IT. Classrooms comely if unremarkable. Building and upgrading under way subject to planning regulations.

A kind, gentle school which inspires in parents admiration and affection in equal measure – as good as they get.

Caterham Preparatory School

Linked to Caterham School in the Senior section

Harestone Valley Road, Caterham, Surrey, CR3 6YB

• Pupils: 290 girls and boys; all day • Ages: 3-11 • Fees: Nursery £4,335; Reception-Year 2 £7,275; Years 3-6 £9,285-£11,157 pa • Independent

Tel: 01883 342 097
Fax: 01883 341 230
Email: anita.noble@caterhamschool.co.uk
Website: www.caterhamprepschool.co.uk

Head: Mr Howard Tuckett.

Remarks: Sharing the senior school site in separate large redbrick buildings set in leafy spaces, both schools are inviting and well away from busy roads. Many shared facilities with main school. Nice touches here and there – a huge aquarium in the prep's main corridor, super displays in the pre-prep's classrooms, masses of space and good libraries. Sensible uniform includes burgundy anoraks.

Central Newcastle High School Junior Department

Linked to Central Newcastle High School in the Senior section

West Avenue, Gosforth, Newcastle upon Tyne, Tyne and Wear, NE3 4ES

• Pupils: 355 girls, including 20 girls in the nursery; all day • Ages: 5-11, nursery 3-4 • Fees: £6,978 pa • Independent

Tel: 0191 285 1956
Fax: 0191 213 2598
Email: cnhsjuniors@cnn.gdst.net
Website: www.newcastlehigh.gdst.net

Head: Acting head Miss Linda Hunter.

Entrance: Assessment and interview.

Exit: Most to senior school.

Remarks: Junior girls are housed in a former convent, set in five acres of grounds, in Sandiford. Younger girls (three to seven) are located in Gosforth.

Centre Academy East Anglia

Church Road, Brettenham, Ipswich, Suffolk, IP7 7QR

• Pupils: 24 of whom 20 are boarders. • Ages: 7-13 • Inter-denom
• Fees: Day £16,650; Boarding £22,950 pa • Independent

Tel: 01449 736 404
Fax: 01449 737 881
Email: admin@centreacademy.net
Website: www.centreacademy.net

Head of School: Since September 2010, Mrs Kim Salthouse BA MEd, previously acting head at the school.

Entrance: See below.

Exit: See below.

Remarks: This is indeed an old rectory, next to the church which is used for daily assemblies, and is set in seven acres of deep Suffolk. The fabric of the school was bought from Mr and Mrs Phillips by Michael Murphy (whose role appears to be that of interested benefactor) in 1999.

Boarding girls live in the Coach House, recently modernised and extended. Boys live in the main house, in immaculate tidiness (can this really be so?!) – most are weekly boarders. Lessons are either taken in a large hall subdivided into four class rooms with folding screens – The Arches, which was opened by Lord Archer – or in Portakabins outside. Lots of English, maths and other trad subjects are taught in small classes (max size eight), according to ability rather than age. The school follows a modified national curriculum, with Spanish rather than French. Dedicated IT room, with children taught touch-typing early, but no laptops; two handwriting lessons a week match the two keyboarding lessons.

Music and drama important. Games on site and masses of extra-curricular activity, including karate, target shooting and fire crew – the school has five fire engines which specially-selected pupils can help 'crew', usually putting out controlled fires only! All the extra-curricular activities are chosen to improve motor skills.

This is a school for the dyslexic, the dyspraxic, those with dyscalculia and the occasional fragile child. The school does not take any child with behaviour problems, nor any child on Ritalin, though there are several on efalax oil, and several wear coloured spectacles in deep pink, mauve or dark blue which are often promoted as remedial aids. The usual age for children coming to the school is 10 or 11, often only for a year or two; they then return either to mainstream schools or to schools offering continued specialist help. Some children are statemented, with a few of them receiving funding from their local authority – others are going through the process of accessing funding via a tribunal. Many of the children do not come from a boarding school background and their parents 'may have sold their house or gone without holidays' to send them here.

Entrance is by an educational psychologist's report and interview after which the child is invited to spend a day at the school so that staff can ascertain where they will best fit in. Plus points for good behaviour, bad points for negative behaviour, really disruptive children can be sanctioned, involving loss of privilege and occasionally suspended or expelled.

Female staff are invariably called Miss and the few men, Sir. No real problems in getting staff but the head feels that it is important to have more than just the very popular groundsman as the token male role model, and takes time to find men with the right qualifications and, if staff do not come with suitable dyslexia training, they undertake appropriate courses. Occupational and speech therapists on hand. This is a helpful little school, which sends children with special needs back into mainstream education. Worth considering.

Chafyn Grove School

Bourne Avenue, Salisbury, Wiltshire, SP1 1LR

• Pupils: 160 boys and 70 girls in prep; 55 boys and 30 girls in nursery and pre-prep. 54 boarders. • Ages: 2.5-13 • C of E • Fees: Pre-prep £6,930; Prep £10,410-£13,755 pa; Boarding +£4,920 pa • Independent

Tel: 01722 333 423
Fax: 01722 323 114
Email: admissions@chafyngrove.co.uk
Website: www.chafyngrove.co.uk

Headmaster: Since 2004, Mr Eddy Newton BA PGCE (forties). Stonyhurst, Jesus College Cambridge (classics). Impeccable credentials – head of classics at The Dragon, deputy head of Pinewood, near Swindon, director of studies and housemaster at Highfield School, then headmaster of Felsted Prep. Liked what he found when he came here but wanted to 'sharpen up' the academics and broaden the range of senior schools pupils progressed to. 'We're more ambitious now – we just had a boy win a scholarship to Winchester. A few years ago the school wouldn't have put him in for it.' Focuses on traditional prep school virtues – 'We're not too pioneering – the core needs to be done well'. Wife, Alison, is in charge of marketing, superintends the nutritiousness of the food and shows prospective parents round. Two young children, both at the school.

Entrance: Interview as much to display school to child and parents as for the school to assess them. Known to do a good job by the brightest, the brain range is broad but the climate is quick-witted, so think hard if it looks as if your child may dawdle. Scholarships of up to 20 per cent available at Years 2 (academic and all-rounder), 4 (those plus music and sport) and 6 (all the above plus drama and art). Sibling and Services discounts. Some bursaries for financial need: head says that half of all prospective parents are currently asking for one! One child on 100 per cent bursary through the Jet scheme. Parents come from a 45-minute radius, mostly from the city and from Salisbury's satellite villages. They're a mixed bunch, professionals, business, around 15 per cent army. Popular with parents of boys and girls who want their children to attend the same school. Sting's children were here.

Exit: Most stay till 13, moving on to a variety of senior schools with Canford and Dauntsey's at the top of the list, then Bryanston, Eton, King's Bruton, Sherborne,

Godolphin, Marlborough and Winchester. Around a quarter leave at age 11 for the Salisbury grammars and girls' independent schools – rather depletes girls' numbers in the last two years but that just makes the lasses bond more solidly, say most parents.

Remarks: The burghers of Salisbury must have been mightily concerned about the education of their young populace because, there's no way around it, Salisbury has too many prep schools. There are four others within a few minutes of Chafyn Grove, and that's without counting the ones just outside of town. But that just makes them try harder. Chafyn Grove is the broadest church of the town preps and comes closest to being the genuine article.

Imposing Victorian school building supplemented by modern, light and bright, purpose-built classrooms. Library buzzing when we saw it, with swish computers and comfy sofas. They work really hard to get the children reading. Latin from Year 5 for almost everyone. Up to 10 pupils a year do Greek CE. Hoping to beef up Spanish teaching, currently one lesson a week in Years 5 and 6. Three full-time equivalent teachers offer learning support, mostly on a one-to-one basis at no extra charge – excellent. Offers ESL currently to one local Chinese boy.

Large sports hall and performance hall, the latter now doubling as chapel (with organ!). Though only 10 minutes' walk from the centre of Salisbury, the school has plenty of grounds with pitches, Astro, hard tennis courts, two good squash courts, an outdoor pool and lovely views of Salisbury Plain. Takes sport seriously. When one talented girl could not arrange transport to a regional sports final last summer, the head drove her himself and nipped them both back to school in time for Sports Day. Much emphasis on 'equality of coaching opportunity' with the top coaches working with athletes of all abilities, not just the top teams. Boys play rugby, hockey and cricket (and football in the lower age groups); girls, hockey, netball and rounders. Lots of success in girls' hockey and netball and the under 13 boys have been Wiltshire hockey champions for the past two years.

Music 'greatly improved' and does jolly well given that Salisbury Cathedral School soaks up many of the ultra-able. Three choirs, orchestra and training orchestra to encourage beginners. One keen pupil played the organ in 10 cathedrals in a recent fund-raising effort. Buzzy art, with DT, claywork and other materials all given lots of time and space. Some setting of the more able artists to encourage potential scholars. Drama has long been a crown jewel, with four or five productions each year for different age groups. Lots of outward-bound type trips e.g. to Dartmoor and Leavers' Camp to Wales. Large computer room for ICT and specialist use in some subjects. Everyone is taught to touch-type.

We enjoyed the names of the houses (they call them Eights) – Wasps, Birds, Frogs etc. Everyone has a proper locker – you'd be amazed how rare this is. Lots of hard work going on to populate the brightly decorated dormitories. Big praise from parents and children, who definitely love being here. They offer flexi-options but expect regularity. Children can go home on Sundays, barring three weekends a term. Food a source of pride – the children don't rate it, what would they know? – but it's proper and prepared by their own chef, not one of those catering outfits. Staff famously flexible – children can be dropped off early and picked up late if parents are stuck.

We can still say there's a 'family atmosphere' and, cliché though it may be, that's how parents still reckon it's best summed up. Lots of emphasis on the pre-prep at the moment: we saw loads of imagination, high standards and some lovely writing. Pre-prep children play in the woods and have their own slot in the charming adventure playground. Not sure what the long-term effect of taking nearby children from two-and-a-half will be as they feed through to boarding age. But we are sure it will remain a very happy school.

Chandlings School

Linked to Cothill House School in the Junior section

Bagley Wood, Kennington, Oxford, Oxfordshire, OX1 5ND

• Pupils: 250 boys, 175 girls, all day • Ages: 2-11 • C of E • Fees: £7,800-£12,060 pa • Independent

Tel: 01865 730 771
Fax: 01865 735 194
Email: annapoole@chandlings.org.uk
Website: www.chandlings.org.uk

Head: Since 2008, Mrs Sophia Ashworth Jones, BSc QTS (science and technology) (early thirties). Educated at Nottingham Girls' High and Ashville College followed by Leeds University. Once qualified, taught exclusively in the independent sector, rising rapidly through the ranks to be appointed as head of Leeds Grammar junior school at the age of 26. Following the long awaited arrival of a baby daughter, a strong desire to find a nurturing environment that would allow her family to thrive drove her southwards. Captivated by Chandlings' family feel, she found the idyll she was seeking.

Not a 'typical' head, she is young, glamorous, friendly, chatty and unreserved. Parents comment on the contrast between the 'calm, steady' previous head and her energy and enthusiasm. A few parents reeling, others embracing the arrival of one so young and vibrant. 'She listens to children,' says one parent. 'When one pupil suggested a race for Haiti, she made sure it would happen, running herself in fancy dress.' 'She loves the children,' says another, 'and is loved by them.'

Since her arrival, she has overseen new buildings and the expansion of early years, revamped the house system and has made several staff changes encouraging full time staff in particular. Plans afoot to introduce flexi-boarding so that her family can live as one big family with the boarders 'snuggled up on the sofa together.' She believes in the individual and and aims to increase the profile of Chandlings.

Married to Andy who gave up his job as head of maths at Leeds Girls' High to follow his wife's quest south – dedication indeed. He now teaches maths at Chandlings. Young daughter in reception.

Entrance: Main entry points are nursery, reception and Year 3. Children may now enter the nursery from the age of two (flexible sessions). Parents put children's names down early and in nursery, it's first come, first served. Reception children come in for an informal assessment while Year 3s and upwards are subject to a competitive assessment. 'We are gently selective,' says head. Behaviour is important too as head is reluctant to take a pupil who would spoil family atmosphere. Pupils travel in from up to 25 miles away – from as far afield as Henley, Newbury and Woodstock.

Exit: Small number of boys at the end of Year 3 to boarding schools but majority leave at 11. Leavers go to a huge array of schools. At the end of Year 5, the head meets with members of staff and each child is discussed, taking into account all their NFER scores, so that parents can be advised of the most appropriate senior schools. St Helen and St Katharine, Headington, Tudor Hall and Downe House are popular choices for girls, while boys head to places like Abingdon, Magdalen College School and Cokethorpe. A good number of scholarships won every year – 'impressive,' comments head, 'considering our broad base intake'.

Remarks: A country prep school with 'all the facilities of a boarding school in a day school setting,' remarks head. A former manor house set in 60 acres of stunning countryside on the outskirts of Oxford, with woodlands, lakes and extensive playing fields. Founded in 1994 by the Cothill Educational Trust as a co-ed day school to complement Cothill House School, the boys' boarding prep up the road. 'The trust gives huge financial security,' head acknowledges. Scope too to use the Trust's Chateau de Sauveterre in France. Head is answerable to the trust and some believe that she has to dance to their tune but she is adamant that she has complete independence from them. Staff a good mix of experience and youth and highly praised by parents, they are committed, enthusiastic and encouraged to develop innovative ideas.

Each year group has four parallel classes (of no more than 16). Classes are changed every year but children fill in a form to say who they'd like to be with. 'By the time they get to Year 6 they are really bonded and know everyone,' says one member of staff. An excellent policy ensuring that everyone mixes and newcomers find it very easy to slot in. Pupils are taught by subject specialists from Year 4. Classes are mixed ability, in the main, but setting for maths and French from Year 3 and English from Year 4. School has introduced synthetic phonics programme to teach pre-prep children to read so they learn the sounds and combinations of letters from the word go. French, impressive, taught by native speakers from the age of two and Latin optional from Year 5. From Year 4, pupils have the opportunity of trips to the Chateau de Sauveterre and Year 6 can even spend their last term boarding at the chateau being totally immersed in the language. SEN provision for dyslexia, dysgraphia, speech and language difficulties.

Interactive whiteboards everywhere and children have one IT skills lesson a week. IT used across all subjects; pupils encouraged to see computers as tools to make learning easier, learning to touch-type in Year 4. Year 6s write and produce their own radio play in their last year. Wonderful library, with giant heart on wall listing pupils' favourite books (Roald Dahl, Philip Pullman and Michael Morpurgo get the thumbs up). Two science labs – science teaching focuses on the practical, like building electronic circuits and writing intergalactic postcards.

All year groups have their own area of the school. Early years provision was upgraded in 2009 and has received 'outstanding' in all areas from Ofsted. It boasts two new dedicated rooms with qualified teaching staff and specialist teachers for French, music and ballet.

Pupils do sport most days. Parents comment on improved PE under new head with new staff appointed and broadening of programme with inclusion of all pupils. Girls play netball, hockey, rounders etc while boys' sports include football, rugby and cricket. Everyone gets chance to represent school in a team at some point. Lovely indoor pool – children swim every week from reception to Year 4; an outdoor pool too. Other activities on offer include golf, riding and ballet. From the age of eight up most children partake in the enrichment programme – everything from gardening club to orienteering.

Music very strong and majority learn a musical instrument. New music department opened in 2007 – concerts and musicals galore – now able to take place in a brand new school hall. Wonderful art on display throughout school, plus DT, textiles and pottery. Perhaps unusually for a prep, food technology is on the curriculum too, the school boasting a dedicated large cookery room.

School rightfully proud of its pastoral care. Children encouraged to be courteous, helpful and responsible, and they are. Pupils have also written their own Chandlings' code of conduct (tenets include caring for others, doing what is right and being a good friend). Discipline not an issue here. The head has re-vamped the house system so that house points are collected or taken away according to achievement or misdemeanour, giving the appropriate reinforcement. Head says she will always ask a child to explain poor behaviour and discuss ways to improve it rather than giving a reprimand. With a C of E foundation, Christianity is important but the head is trying to broaden the experience of the children and introduce them to multicultural Britain with trips to mosques, synagogues etc where possible.

School food very wholesome and organic produce used as much as possible. Three sittings for lunch and member of staff sits at end of each table to reinforce good table manners and chat. School helpful to working parents. Early bird system allows children to arrive from 8am and they can stay to do prep until 5pm.

It's not surprising that this very active, happy school has seen increasing numbers in recent years. The new head is full of ideas to take it forward and further develop it while promoting its family, nurturing values. As one parent said, 'there is never a day when my children are not happy to go to school'.

Channing Junior School

Linked to Channing School in the Senior section

1 Highgate High Street, Highgate, London, N6 5JR

• Pupils: 180 girls; all day • Ages: 4-11 • Fees: £12,375 pa • Independent

Tel: 020 8342 9862
Fax: 020 8348 3122
Email: fairseat@channing.co.uk
Website: www.channing.co.uk

Head: Since April 2008, Miss Louise Tarr BPrimEd (mid-thirties); attended senior school in South Africa, teaching degree at University of Port Elizabeth. Taught in state schools for seven years, then curriculum coordinator and head of prep at Hampshire School, Knightsbridge, where she stayed for seven years. Interested in scuba diving – a qualified PADI divemaster; has strong ties to children's charities in South Africa.

Entrance: By assessment. Parents report finding the process unfriendly and austere.

Exit: Almost all of Year 6 go on to the senior school.

Remarks: Across Highgate Hill from the main school. Elegant old buildings in lovely grounds with plenty of grass and trees and outstanding views. Modernised to include a performing arts studio, music rooms and a computer room. Food still dire (school says, 'A range of hot meals and salads is provided daily, catering for all dietary requirements'). Some rumblings of discontent amongst parents, but valued as a good route into the increasingly popular and successful senior school.

Chapter House Preparatory School

Linked to Collegiate Foundation (The) in the Senior section
Linked to Queen Ethelburga's College in the Senior section

Thorpe Underwood Hall, York, YO26 9SS

• Pupils: 65 girls and 85 boys; boarding and day • Ages: 3-11 • Fees: Day £3,549-£6,456; Boarding £20,250-£20,907; International Boarding £24,690-£25,500 pa • Independent

Tel: 01423 333 330
Fax: 0870 402 2754
Email: pat@queenethelburgas.edu
Website: www.chapterhouseschool.org.uk

Head: Mrs M Pickles.

Remarks: For further details, see senior school: Queen Ethelburga's College.

Cheadle Hulme School Junior School

Linked to Cheadle Hulme School in the Senior section

Claremont Road, Cheadle Hulme, Cheadle, Cheshire, SK8 6EF

• Pupils: 250 girls and boys; all day • Ages: 4-11 • Fees: £6,612-£7,098 pa • Independent

Tel: 0161 488 3334
Email: registrar@chschool.co.uk
Website: www.cheadlehulmeschool.co.uk

Head: Since January 2009, Mrs Barbara Bottoms (late forties). Secondary chemistry teacher until falling in love with primary level while volunteering at her own children's first school. Deputy head at Alderley Edge Girls' School, then head of Bury Grammar Girls' Juniors and has loved coming back to co-ed here. 'I just got a good feeling when I visited – the children are happy and love to come to school, which is not to say we make it easy: we do challenge and push them.' Hugely enthusiastic about pupils, staff, curriculum – everything really, including educational developments, 'It's really important that schools have fresh ideas and are progressive, but as an independent school we can take our time – we don't have to jump onto the bandwagon to adapt too quickly'.

Entrance: By assessment from observation for reception to written tests further up the school, 'But it's a friendly kind of academia, not threatening,' says head. Waiting list for reception with some children registered from birth, and often full in later years, so the capable early bird does get the worm here.

Exit: Most sit and pass entrance to senior school. Those who're unlikely to make it are warned with plenty of time to look at other possibilities.

Remarks: A small school with all the advantages of a big school, contained enough to be a safe place for littlies to start but ideally placed for seam-free transition to seniors and to take advantage of the overall facilities. Class sizes start at 20 in reception, rising to 26 in the top years, split for IT and DT. Lower years beaver happily in light, modern, spacious building where computers, interactive and white boards abound. Story bags hang outside two libraries near a dressing-up station for infants. Rooms for Years 5 and 6 are connected to senior school, along with bespoke music, art and science rooms. Maths and English timetabled for mornings – 'They're fresher' – while afternoons usually involve practicals, sports and weekly visit to school pool. Four houses compete for points and trophies.

French, German and Spanish taught in rotation. No homework on Wednesdays but pupils say 'homework at weekends is harder because there's more time to think then'. Exciting infants' adventure trail and covered play area next to garden overflowing with sunflowers and beans and two play chalets. Work to create similar haven for juniors has been foiled by planning restrictions, but fingers are crossed. Children enjoy dipping in new school pond. Very slightly more boys than girls (who are just as keen on football) and four full-time male teachers. Swipe card for lunches, 'which you have to be careful not to lose as it costs £2 to replace', but you can bring sandwiches. Central hall with lighting for plays is also home to assembly, which includes hymns and a prayer. Head describes pastoral care as a key strength and says, 'I know every child, each family and the siblings,' and the latest inspection report says, 'The strong pastoral care mentioned in the Junior School aims and the caring, family atmosphere are a reality in the school'.

Cheam School

Headley, Newbury, Berkshire, RG19 8LD

• Pupils: 295; 155 boys, 135 girls; half boarding, half day. Plus pre-prep with 110 boys and girls. • Ages: Prep: 8-13, pre-prep (including nursery) 3-7 • C of E • Fees: Boarding £21,990; Day £9,315-£16,275 pa • Independent

Tel: 01635 268 242
Fax: 01635 269 345
Email: office@cheamschool.co.uk
Website: www.cheamschool.com

Head: Since 1998, Mr Mark R Johnson BEd (fifties). A charismatic, enthusiastic, 'preppy' (his own word). Passionate about boarding, having done so himself from a young age and loved it. Educated in the West Country, went straight to Summer Fields post-university and stayed for 17 years. Taught maths, German and rugby. Rose to housemaster and deputy headmaster for five years before moving to Cheam and transforming it. Known by all as Mr J (from his initials), much loved by parents and children alike. Abounds with energy. Full of ideas for the school, now and in the future. Driven by the constant need for a new project: currently the transformation of the old sports hall into an up-to-date design and technology centre. No longer teaches – 'there simply isn't time'. Mad about sport, played cricket to minor county standard while at university and is still a playing member of the MCC.

Lists golf, fishing, shooting, racing, opera and ballet as other enthusiasms. Goodness knows when he finds time for them all. Has been governor of three other prep schools, directed the IAPS New Heads' Induction Course in 2000, represents IAPS on Boarding Schools' Association Executive Committee and was recently invited to sit on Council of IAPS as Boarding Representative. Elected Tatler's 'Best Prep School Headmaster of the Year' in 2007. Definitely believes in keeping busy and his school has the feel of a very busy place. Married to Jane, a bouncy, bubbly, energetic classicist who teaches both Latin and Greek to scholarship and Common Entrance level and designed the tartan seen round the school and worn as part of the girls' uniform. Two daughters now happy at St Edward's, Oxford, having been pupils at Cheam for 10 years.

Entrance: Non-selective into the nursery and pre-prep. Higher up, the headmaster sees all children for a familiarisation day to ascertain their suitability for entry. This is not just based on academic data but rather an assessment of the whole child, games, musical ability, character etc.

Exit: A main feeder to Marlborough but also regularly sends pupils to Radley, Wellington, St Edward's Oxford, Cheltenham Ladies' College, Downe House, Eton and both Sherbornes amongst others on a long, impressive list. The transition to mainly boarding public schools appears to be reasonably easy, according to one parent of girls who loved the place so much she returned to work in the bursar's office when her children moved on. However, we were told by others that some boys seem to find it hard moving into a less-protected environment.

Remarks: A school for active, busy children. As one parent said, 'it's incredibly beautiful'. Set in 100 acres of glorious countryside, for sporty, outdoor loving, energetic types, it is the perfect place to spend their early school days. Anybody who remembers it, as we do, as the rather stuffy, unexciting royal school of the early '90s, would be amazed to walk round it today. One current father, ex-Cheamite, who refused to even look at it until his children went there, is now one of its greatest fans. The focus here is not totally on academia and they get so much more than just lessons. The outcome is a band of happy, confident, well-balanced children who generally get into their chosen schools, often with scholarships (16 in 2010).

A broad curriculum from the start in preparation for Common Entrance to top schools. All children setted for maths and French. Scholarship forms for two top years with Greek introduced to the brightest. Young teachers (average age 35 to 40) have easy, relaxed relationship with pupils. Parents feel Mr J selects staff well. Some bachelor staff accommodation in grounds, 'Cheamville', so less geographical restrictions. Small classes, max 18 often fewer. Books regarded as an essential part of their lives. Silent reading, or 'digest', is timetabled in for half an hour after lunch each day and, for boarders, every evening. Weekly general knowledge quiz encourages them to look things up.

Light, bright classrooms with interactive white boards throughout. Good IT, art, science facilities. Parents say 'music and drama very strong' and they put on 'excellent productions'. One major play or musical each year. Lots of choirs and several orchestras including a jazz band. Most learn an instrument with lessons timetabled differently each week and practice sessions set up for boarders. Anything from beginners to grade six. Masses of art and photographs on display everywhere. Internal news and information computer screens in main halls. Loads of field trips, expeditions and excursions, home and overseas. These really are privileged children.

Perhaps it's sport that's the most impressive and they all love it. Everything is on offer from football, rugby, tennis, hockey and cricket to polo, judo, fencing and golf on their own course. Games every afternoon with matches on Wednesdays and Saturdays. National polo champions, national cross-country champions and cricket and rounders teams reached the National Jet finals in Oxford. Lots of matches against other schools and overseas cricket and hockey tours. The trophy cabinet is proof of their achievements. Despite this, one parent told us 'even non-sporty children are well catered for. One boy even got a scholarship to the Royal Ballet Schoool'.

A long list of extra-curricular activities but 'sadly no woodwork' says one parent. There is even a climbing place called 'Cheam Tops' in the grounds. Indoor sports hall built about six years ago ingeniously provides courts for different games as well as all necessary gymnastic equipment and great changing rooms. Everything has been well thought out. Only parental complaint: 'Why do they have to be sexist? Why can't girls play football?'

Excellent pastoral care and learning support where needed – one or two sessions a week with a specialist teacher on a rotating basis if in lesson time. About 10 per cent have processing problems, there is the occasional statement but nothing seriously major. Gap year students help with games when needed. Gentle counsellor is always there to listen. Believes very much in the importance of building self-esteem, which she feels is definitely one of the school's assets. Specialist EFL help given, often one-to-one in class. Believe it's absolutlely essential to keep parents involved. 'Our children do not have difficulties, they have differences.' G & T register currently being reformed. PSHE is strong, each child has a tutor and anything verging on bullying (probably not the right word) is quickly and sensitively dealt with. 'We want everyone to be happy!' Timetables rigorously watched, so the whereabouts of any child at any time is always known.

Parents have nothing but praise. 'A very happy school', 'the head really has his finger on the pulse', 'sussed out our daughter very fast and gave us excellent advice on her next school', 'children are easy-going, sensitive and supportive of each other', 'very good at involving parents', 'the kids have such fun'. One even told us 'we brought our children over from South Africa where they were a good year behind academically and the system was totally different. Nevertheless, our 11-year-old was quickly assimilated into the system, booked himself into boarding after one term and achieved an all-rounder scholarship to Radley'. A happy parent indeed.

Boarding is either full time or flexi. Children can do just two nights a week if they like. We were assured that this is not at all unsettling and that they seem to love it, opting in and out as and when. The majority of the top year board full time in preparation for their next school. Full time means weekly, they go home after games on Saturday afternoon and return in time for lessons on Monday morning. Most come from within a 15 mile radius of the school although there is a largish London contingent and the occasional child from overseas. Dorms are upstairs in the main building, boys on one floor and girls on another. Homely, welcoming rooms with a variety of duvet covers and lots of teddies. Always one or two older pupils in with the younger ones. Smart modern bathrooms, not at all as we used to know them. Great pile of bags on the landings waiting to be collected by flexis at the end of the day. Recent 'outstanding' boarding certificate from Ofsted. We asked a pupil what she felt about weekly boarding. She replied 'I love it. It's so great to be at home with my brothers on Sundays and to see my horse but it's also good to be at school with my friends'. Bedtime routine pretty regimented with time for reading and talking before lights out but after that, silence reigns.

Quite a large amount of charitable stuff going on. Support for a school in Zambia, a rural school in Johannesburg, the Red Cross children's hospital in Cape Town and the children's wards in the Royal Hampshire Hospital. Hands-on partnership with local primary schools who can apply for funding and use their facilities for free. Some scholarships and bursaries and a fund for suddenly needy children.

Perhaps the oldest prep school in the country, with its origins in the 17th century, there is an interesting archive room containing mementos of past headmasters and pupils. Apart from HRH the Duke of Edinburgh and HRH the Prince of Wales, William Pitt the Younger, Lord Randolph Churchill, Ivo Bligh, 8th Earl of Darnley and Jake Meyer also spent their formative years at Cheam.

A school full of happy, open, confident, polite, exceptionally busy children who are used to living to a rigid timetable and to keeping their shoes done up and their shirts tucked in. One slightly wonders how they will manage to cope with the rebellious, disorganised world outside.

Cheltenham College Junior School

Linked to Cheltenham College in the Senior section

Thirlestaine Road, Cheltenham, GL53 7AB

• Pupils: 400 girls and boys; boarding and day • Ages: 3-13 • C of E
• Fees: Day £6,150-£14,760; Boarding £15,025-£19,665 pa • Independent

Tel: 01242 522 697
Fax: 01242 265 620
Email: ccjs@cheltenhamcollege.org
Website: www.cheltenhamcollege.org

Headmaster : Since September 2010, Mr Scott Bryan, previously deputy head. He took over after the precipitate departure, after only two years, of Mr Adrian Morris, who disagreed with school council plans to redevelop the site. Interesting times for the college with a new senior head in place too.

Entrance: At all ages. Non-selective below age 11 with entry by assessment and interview – all applicants are invited to taster days. More choosy later on as pupils must be able to pass CE at 13. Lots of local interest. Tiny intake from overseas. Popular with Services. Doors opened to girls in 1993. Discount available for third and subsequent siblings. Generous discounts for Service families and bursaries available. 11+ scholarship up to 50 per cent of fees in a variety of areas and valid throughout Cheltenham College.

Exit: Good record of pupils getting into their first choice school. Vast majority move across the road to mixed senior school, Cheltenham College, although they make up just 40 per cent of the overall intake at 13+. CE entry pass around 50 per cent, other schools vary. A number of girls leave at 11 for Cheltenham Ladies' College, despite efforts to hang onto them for another two years. A few also to good local grammars. Parents advised on best senior option for their child. Famous OBs (head calls them OJs as in Old Juniors) include General Sir Michael Rose and actor Nigel Davenport.

Remarks: Known simply as The Junior. Set in conservation area, large Edwardian red-brick purpose-built (in 1908) school house with seamless (and some not so seamless) additions over the decades. Newest building for lower school the best yet and overlooking lake. Second last head's decision to go co-ed caused great ructions but school has never looked back – there were fewer than 240 pupils when Nigel Archdale took over in 1992. Numbers peaked at 450 and are now a strong 380 and growing.

School day action packed – hardly enough hours in it. Lessons start 8.15am for all but youngest (Kingfishers pre-prep department in own well-designed extension) and include daily class music. Not at expense of anything else though. Still finds time to fit in French from age of three alongside staple diet of core subjects. ICT extremely well catered for with annually updated computers, 24-hour internet connection, and school network. Laptops everywhere. Internal email system keeps staff in touch – replaced old-style staff notice-boards. Academically thrusting for a non-selective school but geared up to the individual. Help available (at no extra charge) for mild dyslexics, dyspraxics and other minor learning difficulties. The emphasis is on mild, but a parent with criticisms elsewhere in the school is unstinting in his praise of the help for SEN. Well-run shuttle system boosts youngsters' intake of core subjects in place of occasional French or Latin. Extra charge for EFL lessons. Well-stocked pleasant library with well used mezzanine, used to be school gym.

Artwork on show quite unbelievable (easy to forget you're in a junior school) – large silk painting in library and an outstanding series of murals along one corridor wall, painted in 2000. Justly proud of working scale-model fleet of warships (made by past pupils and maintained by current pupils) which are sailed each year on Junior's own shallow lake. Bags more innovative projects emerging from technology department – great merging of design, woodwork and electronics, as big a hit with girls as boys. Super sports hall and indoor pool (shared with senior school, as are science labs). Lovely cricket pitch, good hockey and rugby tradition, hard courts for tennis and netball, Astroturfs for hockey and several squash courts, plus mini sports hall for indoor games. Brand new assembly hall, attached sympathetically to old school, has transformed the big event, put drama back on the map and given school a unique venue for major productions, concerts and gatherings. Only non-purpose building is music school, a lovely wood-panelled setting for individual lessons and small group recitals. Four choirs (chapel choir regularly tours), various bands and ensembles, regular concerts.

Boarding not at full capacity but allows for sleepovers. Large airy dorms in old building, shared curtained cubicles for older children, all well kept with enough pictures, toys and own duvets to make it homely. Boarders' privileges extend to use of library, computers, art and DT studios at any time of day. Can also use pool for special supervised sessions. Pupils allowed mobile phones though use strictly controlled. Fabulous grounds and lush green setting provide plenty of scope for outside play. Pupils allocated houses for competitive and pastoral reasons. Strict anti-bullying policy rigidly enforced.

Weekly chapel on Saturday, Sunday service three or four times a term. Chapel 'essential but not in an overarching way,' said penult head. Saturday school is optional for Years 3 and 4, compulsory for years above. 'Pupils enjoy a programme of co-curricular activities, such as trips and project work, which has been a resounding success,' says the school. Extra activities include twice-weekly dry slope skiing in nearby Gloucester, squash, trampolining, and paddle-boating on lake.

Plenty of moneyed backgrounds, landed gentry and self-made millionaires, but ordinary folk too – 'We have a very broad parental constituency'. New PTA.

Smashing bunch of children seen around school, no-one apparently at a loose end, and a certain confidence clearly evident from the youngest Kingfisher up. Enthusiastic pupils, staff and 'most parents'. An overwhelming feeling here of purpose and activity. Kids with street cred as well as an appreciation of their privileged circumstances. Recent instability not good but school strong enough to weather it well, we feel. Numbers joining this September are certainly higher than last year.

Chethams School of Music Junior Department

Linked to Chetham's School of Music in the Senior section

Long Millgate, Manchester, M3 1SB

• Pupils: boys and girls, some board • Ages: 8-11 • Fees: Day £23,988; Boarding £30,987pa; Choristers: Day £9,480, Boarding £14,371 pa • Independent

Tel: 0161 834 9644
Fax: 0161 839 3609
Email: chets@chethams.com
Website: www.chethams.com

Remarks: See main school.

Chigwell Junior School

Linked to Chigwell School in the Senior section

High Road, Chigwell, Essex, IG7 6QF

• Pupils: 340 boys and girls, all day • Ages: 7-13 • C of E but welcomes all • Fees: £9,696-£14,532 pa • Independent

Tel: 020 8501 5721
Fax: 020 8501 5723
Email: hm@chigwell-school.org
Website: www.chigwell-school.org

Head: Since September 2010, Mr Simon James BA Hons PGCE, who has a degree in history. He teaches drama and games and says it gives him an opportunity to get to know the pupils. Very welcoming and approachable, his educational philosophy is to 'care for each individual and turn them into well-rounded, well-educated people with a life-long love of learning'.

Entrance: Competition is fierce. At seven, there are three times as many applicants as places and young candidates are put through their paces with an assessment, interview, classroom time and a report from their previous school. At 11, there are nearly 10 times as many applicants for the 40 new places in the thirds, and these are weeded out by an exam and interviews. About 10 academic and music scholarships are offered and bursaries are also available.

Exit: Almost all to senior school with a handful choosing secondaries closer to home.

Remarks: Set on the main school site, the junior school is integral to the Chigwell community and adds to the all-pervading family feel. Its educational philosophy, academic and pastoral structures are the same as those in the senior school, supporting the school's aim to 'provide a consistent approach to education throughout the child's school career'. Joint activities bring juniors and seniors together, easing the passage through the school, and major facilities are shared, including the dining hall and gym, plus the impressive art, music and drama departments.

The juniors' own domain has a dedicated playground, classrooms, ICT lab and a recently refurbished library. The Wilson Building opened recently and houses more bright, modern junior form rooms as well as the modern foreign languages department. The junior school also has a spacious learning support department, offering tuition in small groups to children who require additional input in specific or more general areas.

Pupils generally hail from the local area – many are the offspring of Old Chigwellians. 38 join in lower one, aged seven and move through upper one, lower two and upper two. The number doubles by age 11 for the thirds and fourths, who learn Spanish, German and classics.

The reason for the scrabbling for places is encapsulated by the glowing recent ISI report, which described the academic progress of the juniors at Chigwell as 'exceptional'. It also praised the 'outstanding' personal development of pupils and judged spiritual development 'excellent' – chapel is as central to school life for the juniors as it is for the seniors.

Enjoying school is of great importance here – colourful and creative displays of work and cheery faces attest to this. Clubs include animation and astronomy and there are chances to take part in activities in partnership with the seniors, creating a happy mix of ages and cultures at this small, warm and nurturing school.

Christ Church Cathedral School

3 Brewer Street, Oxford, Oxfordshire, OX1 1QW

• Pupils: 165 boys; 140 day, 20 boarders • Ages: 7-13; 4-6 pre-prep; 3-4 nursery (girls in nursery only) • C of E • Fees: Day £11,436; Boarding choristers £7,875-£7,134; Pre-prep £7,890 pa • Independent

Tel: 01865 242 561
Fax: 01865 202 945
Email: registrar@cccs.org.uk
Website: www.cccs.org.uk

Headmaster: Since 2005, Mr Martin Bruce BA MA (early fifties). Former chorister at All Saints', Margaret Street, London, then at Winchester Cathedral. Won major music scholarship to Wellington College, followed by choral scholarship at Durham University, where he read English. Broad teaching experience in both state and independent sectors and single-sex and co-ed schools. First headship at Bickley Park School, a boys' prep school in Kent, then moved to Christ Church Cathedral School. ISI inspector and former member of IAPS council. An energetic, focused and approachable head, he's passionate about music. Sings with Worcester and New College Chapel choirs, plays organ and has written several musicals and choral works – 'It's good for the boys to see the head engaged in the same musical discipline as them,' he says. His subject is English but currently teaches RS to top two years of school. His wife, KT, is a life coach and photographer (brilliant at capturing school events) and very involved in the school. They have two grown up children.

Entrance: Head says at least 90 per cent of pupils apply on the recommendation of others. Lots of siblings. Ability tests and chat with head for entry at seven but most join in nursery or pre-prep and stay till 13. Some year groups full but worth trying at other entry points too. Some pupils arrive from state primaries, others from local pre-preps. Most live in Oxford but a few travel in from Wheatley, Bicester, Abingdon etc. Parents an eclectic mix, says head – academics, medics and 'hard-working parents who want the best for their children'. Modest bursaries on offer for Worcester College choristers but no other scholarships for day pupils. Four cathedral choristers selected each year by voice trial and aptitude and intelligence tests (they pay only 40 per cent of full boarding fee).

Exit: Leavers go to vast range of schools, including Abingdon, Magdalen College School, St Edward's, Bloxham, Eton, Harrow, Rugby and many more. Fine record of winning music and academic scholarships to top schools – a total of four in 2010.

Remarks: Delightful school tucked down a picturesque side-street in the heart of Oxford. Tiny site but school makes the most of every last inch (last ISI inspection commented on its 'ingenious' use of space). Founded in 1546 when Henry VIII established nearby Christ Church and made provision for the education of eight boy choristers. Main building dates back to 1892 and was the boarding house created by Dean Liddell, father of Alice, the girl who inspired Alice in Wonderland). It houses beautiful panelled dining room, with scholars' names through the ages in gold lettering, ultra-smart IT suite with 20 networked computers and the revamped boarding house – newly-decorated dorms and well-equipped common room complete with comfy bean bags, TV and Xbox.

Next door is the school's new building. Light, airy classrooms, science labs and the stylish Walton Hall, named after illustrious old boy William Walton and used for everything from indoor games and PE to concerts and drama productions. Upstairs are more classrooms, with names like Darwin, Shakespeare and Venn to signify their use. School fully networked and lots of interactive whiteboards. Three libraries – two for fiction, the other a reference library to encourage boys to use books rather than Google. Pianos absolutely everywhere – the head reckons about 20 at the last count. The third school building, once Cardinal Wolsey's house, has been redeveloped to accommodate the Montessori-based nursery and a maze of art and DT rooms.

Music is a core part of school but head emphasises that boys who don't sing or play an instrument thrive here too. Even so, most take individual music lessons – more than 115 timetabled a week for Years 2 to 8. 'If the atmosphere is such that it's seen as cool to sing or play a musical instrument, then nearly all the children get swept up by it,' says head. Lots of orchestras, ensembles and choirs to join, including Worcester College choir, which comprises day boys and sings at two services a week during the university term. The boarding choristers who make up the Christ Church Cathedral choir (usually 16 choristers and four probationers) sing at Christ Church most days of the week during term-time (first practice at 7.25am!), three times on Sundays and also up to Easter Sunday and Christmas Day. Head and his wife soften the blow of staying at school after the end of term with a jolly party and stockings to open on Christmas morning. Christ Church choristers have to be bright and resilient as well as sing like angels – no academic concessions made for three hours of choir practice and performance every day. There are bonuses, though, including singing on radio and TV and recent tours to Germany, Bermuda and Jamaica.

Academic ethos of school is strong. From Year 5, all subjects taught by specialists. French from the age of six, Latin from nine. Class sizes average 16 in the prep and never more than 20. Committed staff – their average age is 45 and a quarter have been at the school for more than 10 years. One-to-one learning support available at £32 per hour. Setting in maths and English from Year 5 and from Year 7 in French. RS taught from Year 3 and assembly, largely Christian, held every day (in school on Monday to Thursday and in Christ Church Cathedral on Fridays).

All boys have school lunch – good manners a priority. Recent school newsletter homed in on table manners – keep lips closed as you chew, no talking with food in your mouth etc. All pupils stand when visitors enter the room. The oldest boys get an expedition to Snowdonia at the start of their last year to encourage leadership and responsibility. Bullying very rare – 'we are very clear about what goes and what doesn't,' says head. All Year 8s appointed prefects and organise their own duty rota. Three houses (Carroll, Sayers and Wolsey), with variety of inter-house academic, sport, music and poetry competitions. Supervised after-school care offered free of charge to prep boys (but charged for pre-prep pupils) till 6pm – a boon for busy working parents.

Head didn't particularly enjoy his own schooldays, which has reinforced his determination to encourage boys' self-esteem and confidence. 'My schooling seemed to be about what you couldn't do,' he says. 'When boys leave here I want them to walk out of the door feeling good about themselves and ready to face the challenges that come their way.' When he arrived at CCCS he abolished Saturday morning school, redrew the timetable and introduced an impressive array of clubs. They range from the cerebral (chess, crossword-compiling etc) to the sporty (squash, judo and fencing).

Despite school's small size, sport is strong. Boys play rugby, football, hockey, cricket and athletics – games mostly take place across the road at the scenic Christ Church Meadow. Busy fixtures list of matches against local schools and head proud of fact that all boys make a school team at some point. Swimming once a week for prep boys at Westminster College. Art is wonderful – lots of Aboriginal designs, totem poles and autumn collages when we visited.

CCCS has a real family atmosphere, good academic results and wonderful music. It's tiny compared to many of its local counterparts but boys, whether musical or not, enjoy themselves hugely here. They are cherished, inspired and encouraged – and seem to have fun along the way too.

Christ Church C of E Primary School

1 Robinson Street, London, SW3 4AA

• Pupils: 210 boys and girls; all day • Ages: 4-11 • C of E voluntary aided • State

Tel: 02073 525 708
Fax: 02078 233 004
Email: info@chch.rbkc.sch.uk
Website: www.chch.rbkc.sch.uk

Head: Since September 2009, Mrs Avis Hawkins, who was previously joint acting head during the summer term.

Entrance: Application by late January for the following September for reception class. All other ages on an ad hoc basis. Priority given to (i) children with siblings in the school (ii) children of families who are regular worshippers in St Luke's or Christ Church, Chelsea (iii) children living in the parish (iv) children of families who are regular worshippers in a neighbouring parish church etc. Complete the school's supplementary admissions form as well as applying through the LA.

Exit: Shene School, Grey Coats, Gunnersbury, Holland Park, Graveney, ADT etc etc and about 20 per cent to independent London day schools – Alleyn's, Emanuel, Dulwich etc.

Remarks: Excellent primary school in super location tucked away in a quiet corner of Chelsea, with – by London standards – lots of space, including good-sized playground and extra area of garden/pond etc. Judged 'outstanding' by Ofsted in every category. Founded 1840, affiliated to local churches (Helen Morgan Edwards is now chair of governors). Cherry-coloured uniform. Newly-refurbished prize-winning buildings. Approximately 50 per cent of pupils from Chelsea, the rest from Wandsworth, Westminster and beyond – very mixed intake.

Good core and cross-curricular and SEN provision; all children have experience with computers. Maths and English very good and Spanish on offer after school; swimming for Year 2 and above. PE in much-used all-purpose school hall as well as local green space. Keen games and music. Even here parents sending children on to fee-paying schools usually opt for a year or two of coaching. Continuing good and happy reports from parents though some would like to see an 11+ class. Oversubscribed for all year groups.

Churchill Gardens Community Primary School

Ranelagh Road, London, SW1V 3EU

• Pupils: 295 • Ages: 3-11 • Non-denom • State

Tel: 02076 415 935
Fax: 02076 416 388
Email: office@cgprimary.co.uk
Website: www.churchillgardens.westminster.sch.uk

Head: Since 1996, Mr Stephen Pye CertEd DipC (SEN) (fifties), previously deputy head of Curwen Primary in Newham. Smiling, unpretentious, a most impressive and committed headteacher, arrived 12 years ago to find the school in a state of disrepair and has transformed it into an exceptional and fully-inclusive learning environment.

Entrance: At three to the nursery or four to reception, then occasional vacancies as they occur in older age groups. Westminster entrance criteria – children with special requirements, siblings, then those living closest to the school.

Exit: Mostly to local Westminster state secondary schools. Occasional scholarship to the independent sector.

Remarks: A popular community primary school, which also has a budget to run a children's centre offering advice and guidance for parents to access other services. Working towards being an extended school open 48 weeks a year from 8am to 6pm, with provision for holiday care and activities. The national curriculum plus, a positive ethos and in the top three per cent for added value. Each child has a personal learning platform to enable them to work at their pace and develop their full potential. Uses ICT well, has its own media suite and will soon have video conference facilities. The children also learn how to use digital cameras in IT. A well-stocked and greatly valued library.

An exceptionally good choice of extra-curricular activities includes theatre club, kayaking, photography, fencing, along with regular coaching in football and in modern languages. Links with The Royal Shakespeare Company, Wigmore Hall and The English National Ballet for music and drama projects. Everyone gets the opportunity to learn the violin in Year 5 and the children have written their own school song. Pupils are also taken on many visits around London and taught about their heritage. Learning mentors, EAL support, and they house Westminster's language provision, providing 40 specialist places for children with speech and language impairments.

Hoping to expand their facilities by redesigning some of their buildings to create a community centre, with a large hall/gym, Astroturf and eco garden. Benefits hugely from imaginative leadership, supportive governors and the local Rotary Club. Has awards for inclusion, Investors in People and an outstanding Ofsted.

City of London Freemen's Junior School

Linked to City Of London Freemens School in the Senior section

Ashtead Park, Ashtead, Surrey, KT21 1ET

• Pupils: 365; 180 boys, 185 girls. All day • Ages: 7-13 • Inter-denom
• Fees: £10,710-£11,277 pa • Independent

Tel: 01372 822 474
Fax: 01372 822 416
Email: admissions.clfs@cityoflondon.gov.uk
Website: www.clfs.surrey.sch.uk

Acting head: Since April 2010, Mr Mark Beach (forties), married with three children. Mr Beach was headmaster of Longacre School near Guildford and before that deputy head at Barfield. As part of City of London Freemen's School, the junior section comes under the overarching headship of the head of senior school, Mr Philip MacDonald.

Entrance: Selective entry at seven and 11 and at other ages as and when available. The tests in English, maths and non-verbal reasoning are the 'first filter'. Results are considered together with feeder school report with an eye for consistency. All candidates are interviewed, looking out for 'a positive attitude to learning, evidence of interests and attributes to contribute to school life or just a spark of something.' The school website gives guidelines and some sample papers for entry tests. Parents report that although it's perceived to be tough to get in at seven, once in it seems easy and not at all pressured. Pupils come from the local area, from Guildford to Kingston. School buses provide transport for both juniors and seniors from East Horsley, Bookham, Esher, Cobham and a shuttle to Ashtead station.

Exit: Overwhelming majority move on to City of London Freemen's senior school in a managed and seamless transition which is clearly expected by the school. No entrance tests for them.

Remarks: CLFS junior has a solid, non-elitist, family feel, but again like its senior school lacks a certain pizzazz. This does not worry the CLFS faithful, for whom the real draw is the through education – once in the junior school, worries about future school choices and entry exams are a thing of the past. It is straight through to 18 – and a family can have all their children at the same place if they are seven or 17, boy or girl. A big headache solved for time-poor working parents. 'Going through from age seven takes away the stresses of 11+ and CE,' says one parent. Another added, 'with progression through the school you don't notice any pressure at any particular point and don't realise the high levels children have achieved as they've got there slowly and steadily.'

The junior school is housed in the purpose-built, modernish Kemp House. It is OK, but couldn't be called inspiring. Painted breeze block walls (which are covered with artwork). Buzzing with well-occupied children, some classrooms can be tight and crowded in use. A couple of newer ones are more spacious and well-equipped with IT.

Impressive art room and lovely, decorative and inspiring artwork displays all over the school.

It is the outside space which is the very, very, big plus. Fantastic, a definite 'wow factor'. The rolling parkland of grassy embankments, shady trees and crested iron railings are shared with the seniors, although juniors have broadly their own area beside Kemp House – it is not sectioned off. A large fenced and well-equipped adventure playground is used exclusively by the juniors during supervised breaks.

Class sizes start at around 12 rising towards a maximum of 20 by age 11. There are three forms per year increasing to four per year in the final two years, when there is a further intake of pupils. Setting in maths from Year 4 and English from Year 7 has recently been introduced, head says 'school is flexible and big enough to do whatever suits the cohort, it may be different for different years'. Watch this space as the experience develops. French, German and Spanish are taught as a 'taster' for a term each in Years 3 and 4. In Year 5, pupils select one language to learn exclusively and then add a second choice in Year 7. No testing for SEN on entry and extra help is limited – not the best school therefore for a child with significant special needs, and check carefully whether the school can cater for minor special needs.

The junior and senior schools are managed as one; each has its own staff but it feels very much one school. The top two years of the juniors (ages 11 and 12) use some senior classroom facilities and are taught by some senior school staff. Parents report 'they are so familiar with everything there is no huge transition when moving into the senior school'. Senior school pupils trained as listeners visit the junior school daily to provide an informal point of contact to help pupils with personal or school issues. Seniors also run some of the huge range of lunchtime and after-school clubs.

The school's ethos is 'getting kids to try things, being open minded and socialising'. Pupils are encouraged to take part in everything on offer. The majority learn a musical instrument. Sports are important and taken seriously, rugby and cricket for boys, hockey and netball for girls and swimming in the superb indoor pool for all throughout the year. Teams have reached national standard in swimming and, more unusually, fencing – one of a number of extra-curricular sports activities. The junior school really benefits from sharing the extensive sports grounds and top-notch sports facilities with the seniors.

Both parents and staff praise the family atmosphere, with lots of siblings across the whole school. Children are caring and help each other, boys and girls mix well: 'they are encouraged from day one to sit and work in mixed groups'. Pupils are a tidy bunch and the pupils we talked to were likeably chatty (shame we were shown round by the marketing manager and not a pupil as we had requested). Parents are a mix of background and social types; the broad cross-section of families reflects this more cosmopolitan part of Surrey. From first-time buyers keen for their children to experience everything on offer to experienced fee-payers who are content to let the school make the decisions and feel it's 'great value for money'. Parents say, 'socially there's a bit of everything, not only the very rich, lots of ordinary families, very much a cross-section'; 'it's not one of the most expensive schools and that adds to the rounded, normal feel of the school.'

City of London School for Girls (Prep School)

Linked to City of London School for Girls in the Senior section

St Giles' Terrace, Barbican, London, EC2Y 8BB

• Pupils: 100 girls; all day • Ages: 7-11 • Fees: £13,131 pa • Independent

Tel: 0207 847 5540
Fax: 020 7638 3212
Email: admissions@clsg.org.uk
Website: www.clsg.org.uk/Preparatory_Department

Head: Miss Jane Rogers, previously the Senior Teacher at the Lyceum, London. She has also been a lecturer at the Institute of Education. Has two teenage children.

Entrance: Assessment consists of a half day of written tests including maths and English and a half day of practical tasks, which may include painting and modelling. Takes into account school report and extra-curricular interests.

Exit: Nearly everyone goes through to the senior school at 11+, taking the same entrance test as external candidates, but not competing against them. One or two occasionally advised to look elsewhere. Academic, music and art scholarships to senior school plus places and scholarships at a range of London secondary schools, UK boarding schools and prestigious schools abroad, especially in the Asia-Pacific region.

Remarks: Broad curriculum, which includes four modern languages, Latin and an academic options programme. Shares senior school facilities, specialist teachers and Monday assemblies. Girls try out French, Spanish, German and Mandarin over four years, choosing which to continue in the senior school.

Aims to have at least one lesson timetabled out of the classroom for every girl every day. All-weather playing surface, netball courts, gym and swimming pool on site. Clubs and squads include netball, rounders, fencing, gym, swimming, football, cricket and cheerleading. Has won the London prep schools' swimming gala for nine consecutive years. Plenty of outings and residentials.

Much recognition of achievements including postcards home and an Excellence Book. No formal sanctions – deals with difficulties through talking. Encourages contact with parents; flourishing and supportive PTA.

Lively atmosphere and good, solid teaching.

Clayesmore Preparatory School

Linked to Clayesmore School in the Senior section

Iwerne Minster, Blandford Forum, Dorset, DT11 8PH

• Pupils: 255 boys and girls; 75 board. 25 in nursery • Ages: 2-13 • C of E
• Fees: Boarding £18,306-£20,064; Day £13,956-£14,901; Pre Prep £7,326 pa
• Independent

Tel: 01747 811 707
Fax: 01747 811 692
Email: prepadmissions@clayesmore.com
Website: www.clayesmore.com

Head : Since September 2006, Mr Richard Geffen BEd. Previously deputy head at Westbourne House Preparatory School, near Chichester. Experience in both maintained and independent schools. First job at Chichester High School for Boys. During his time at the High School, went on exchange to Vancouver Island for a year. Together with his wife, Ann, ran one of Westbourne's boarding houses. Has coached rugby and cricket; Ann is a graduate PE teacher and experienced coach.

Entrance: Interview with HM, report from previous school; all come for a trial day and are informally assessed, with an educational psychologist's report if necessary.

Exit: 'More or less an automatic transfer to senior school – about 85 per cent go on.'

Remarks: A separate school but linked to the senior school, sharing the same 62-acre beautiful countryside campus. Charming, with a delightful combo building on a sort of cruciform shape with dormitories and classrooms dotted around (in a rather more organised fashion than it reads). A fantastic new building was opened in September 2008. This provides four new classrooms for Years 3 and 4, a geography room, two science laboratories and residential accommodation on the top floor. Previously based in Charlton Marshall, the school was sold by its founder to Lt Col Ivor Edwards-Stewart who, when he retired in 1974, 'funded a school of a most modern design' on the senior school campus, with a dedicated play area (hopscotch and climbing frames). It shares senior school facilities – indeed the old squash court, which has a tremendously grand entrance on the school side, is the music department for both prep and senior schools. Each school has its own designated area with plenty of practice rooms, separate classrooms, ensemble room and music technology suite.

Good use made of the sports pitches, big dining room (trails of children, some being carried, skip back from terrific lunch), music school, chapel and leisure centre. Popular arts week runs at the end of the summer term and throughout the year a huge number of music groups rehearse weekly. Major drama production each year and LAMDA lessons very popular. Similar emphasis to the senior school on good pastoral care and the importance of the individual. A very popular school with parents in the area, also has a sprinkling of ex-pat children, some foreigners, fair number of Services children plus siblings of those in the senior school, a number of first-time buyers and London refugees. 70 boarders maximum, day children may stay for a minimum of two nights a week. Dedicated team of houseparents, matrons and the nursing staff, who are known as 'the sisters'.

All are assessed at five, COPS on the computer; each child is monitored and the results held for future referral. A centre of excellence. Pupils have learning support as and when required, may spend an hour or two in the unit daily and then transfer back into the main school for the rest of the day. SENCo, plus fully-trained learning support assistants (not teachers) and gappers help in the classroom, as well as properly qualified teachers. Gym club and OT group, touch-typing, speech and language therapy once a week, sloping desks, special pens – all sorts of tricks brought into play. Register of gifted and able – staff aim to stretch them. Social and emotional needs catered for here, as well as individual educational programmes. Three live-in dedicated assistants, plus two part-timers, though if a child has really severe learning problems, this may not be the school for them.

Traditional school curriculum, strong tutorial system: tutors also responsible for PSHE. Strong music, as per the rest of the school, drama and good art. For the challenged child this could be just the place; for the less challenged, or those who need challenging, this school is all singing and dancing. Continuation scholarships to senior school available.

Clifton College Preparatory School and Butcombe Pre-Prep

Linked to Clifton College in the Senior section

The Avenue, Clifton, Bristol, BS8 3HE

• Pupils: Prep 385 girls and boys; 70 board. Butcombe pre-prep 250 girls and boys. • Ages: 3-13 • C of E. Pupils come from many different faith backgrounds. • Fees: Boarding £19,500-£20,250; Day £12,225-£13,350; Butcombe £4,500+ pa • Independent

Tel: 0117 315 7502
Fax: 0117 315 7504
Email: hwilliams@clifton-college.avon.sch.uk
Website: www.cliftoncollegeuk.com

Head: Since 2008, Mr John Milne (early forties). No stranger to Clifton, he joined the staff in 1994, and in a morning assembly 'one cold Wednesday morning in November of that year' found himself distracted and enchanted by the sight of a new teacher, Helen, a housemistress. Two years later they were married, and after three years of running a house they were off to run the British School in Manila, where their first two children were born, and coincidentally they became involved with helping an orphanage, now adopted by Clifton Prep. Clifton is a hard place to leave and four years later Bob Acheson, the previous head, went out and persuaded the Milnes to return as house-parents of a girls' boarding house and he as director of studies. After he had piloted the school through three different inspections, the governors fully recognised his qualities and he was chosen as head in waiting. The waiting is over.

After attending Montrose Academy he went to Dartmouth College, an Ivy League university in New

Hampshire, where he specialised in British history. On his return he was 'lucky enough' to play professional football for Aberdeen (post-Fergie days) – centre half, no red cards. Then on to Bristol University where he took his PGCE in history. Tall, but not intimidatingly so (unless you are a short centre forward), he is popular with parents and committed to involved teaching and assessment for learning, i.e. pupils learning through sensitively-handled interaction with peers and staff – most importantly, learning to understand themselves. Pupils describe him as 'brilliant'; parents express uniform pleasure. 'We're just so lucky to have him,' is the common response.

The pre-prep, Butcombe, with its own headmistress, Dr Wendy Bowring, operates separately, from the prep but is just down the road. It is an outstandingly good set up. Ask to see its inspection report.

Entrance: Many pupils arrive from Butcombe and everyone is assessed in English, maths and verbal reasoning. The minimum standard required is the expected national SATs level for the relevant age group. Entrance possible at Years 4, 5 and 6, depending on available places.

Exit: The large majority go on to the upper school, sitting the same exam as others.

Remarks: Run autonomously but in close and frequent touch with the heads of Butcombe and the college, many of whose facilities they use. The prep moved off the college campus 75 years ago and in 1932 built the handsome main teaching block. With brightly-painted broad corridors – plenty of room for scurrying school children – and rooms which are spacious but not forbidding, it's an inspired piece of architecture which has adapted marvellously to modern needs. Well-carpeted now and with artwork adorning the walls (note the yummy-looking cakes in the entrance hall) everything is welcoming and encouraging. Computers are everywhere – two rooms designated exclusively for them with thick red carpet in one room and blue in the other.

The music school, opened by Sir David Willcock of King's College, Cambridge fame and an old boy, not only has masses of practice and rehearsal rooms but also an astonishing battery of computers where every child learns to compose their own works, coincidentally learning to read music. Recording studio and the means of writing your own music to films on DVD, like an auditory version of painting. OK, marvellous facilities, but are they used? The answer is a resounding and harmonious chorus of yes – 370 out of 400 perform in various orchestras, ensembles, quartets and groups and 70 sing in the choir.

The newly-updated library is bright, airy and attractive and has literally raised the roof. Computers there, but many more books and an alert and helpful librarian. Museum where aspiring cricketers can gawp in amazement at the original score book which records Arthur Collins' score in 1899 of 628 not out, which remains the highest individual score in the history of the game. The art is absolutely stunning – excellent by any standards, not just by prep school standards. In a smallish, non-purpose-built studio, children learn the importance of draughtsmanship, testified by the busts lining the wall and the rows of white-painted bottles challenging bright artists to master perspective. When we visited, the children were working on Henry Moore's sketches of sheep (they had been to London to see the exhibition). Their sketches were on the wall and they were engaged in creating clay sheep. Brilliant teaching and in addition the school has visiting artists in – most unusual.

Tennis courts and a playground in front of the teaching block remind the hesitating scholar that another world exists. Up at Beggar Bush, the other side of the suspension bridge, a games player's paradise (see Clifton College's entry in the senior section) – at how many prep schools can you play, amongst a cornucopia of sports, real tennis or rackets? The prep has its own sports hall.

Lots of drama – both in the school's own hall and in the College's Redgrave Theatre. Assemblies are held in in the hall, complete with organ; services are held in the justly famous college chapel and the charismatic chaplain is much in evidence. In the state-of-the-art ICT suite budding inventors create working robots and other wonders. The list of activities and clubs is endless. Children talk enthusiastically of the weekend activities. Close by is the Coach House, where skilled and sympathetic staff help with learning support garnished with loving kindness and encouragement.

All children, day and boarding, are attached to a house in one of the carefully-adapted Victorian houses that grace that area of Clifton. Little distinction between day and boarding, other than bed and breakfast, and ample provision for flexi-boarding for children whose parents are out clubbing. The school is divided into two tiers, 8–11 and 11–13, and housed accordingly. Boys and girls don't share houses though they intermingle merrily in every other department. A recent programme of refurbishing has resulted in brightly-coloured accommodation (oh, that pink in the girls' boarding house!) with ample space for lolling and chatting. Lots of computers and cuddly toys. One house, unique in England, can watch sea lions from their bedroom windows and gorillas cavorting about – a favourite joke is to ask on which side of the road the real zoo is.

Parents are ecstatic about the school – 'I thought this was a school for toffs,' said one, 'but it jolly well isn't. I know parents who are really scrimping and saving to send their children here. It's worth every penny because they have fun learning, make friends for life and because the staff really care. It's a blissfully happy school'. That from a mother who looked as if she could really dish it out if dissatisfied. 'I would,' she replied to the question. 'Relationships in the boarding houses are outstandingly positive,' wrote the inspectors – in the jargon of inspectors that's close to ecstasy.

Inspection report in an attractive and informative booklet. Do read the previous head's foreword, noting his comments about the language used. Then read the report and, if you like, count the number of times the word 'outstanding' is used. Then go and brave the traffic – it's well worth it.

Clifton Hall Junior School

Linked to Clifton Hall School in the Senior section

Newbridge, Edinburgh, EH28 8LQ

• Pupils: 270 boys and girls • Ages: 3-11 • Non-denom • Fees: £4,080-£9,255 pa • Independent

Tel: 0131 333 1359
Fax: 0131 333 4609
Email: office@cliftonhall.org.uk
Website: www.cliftonhall.org.uk

Headmaster: Since 2005, Mr Rod Grant BA PGCE (early forties).

Entrance: Non-selective.

Exit: Most to the senior school.

Remarks: An 'independent primary school' based in a magical Bryce house in 50 acres of child-inspiring grounds. Junior school regarded as reliable and steady, nursery streaking ahead. Jazzy young staff blend well with the more mature, but we saw few of the latter. French from three, Spanish and German from eight, keyboarding skills in primary for all.

School games as good as ever, teams often combine year groups. Previous head started the nursery in 1989, since when numbers have risen and risen. Huge growth and conversion of outbuildings. Great facilities, swimming pool, sports hall, networked computers, music classrooms; small classes, learning support both withdrawn and dual teaching. Music and drama are particularly strong.

For more opinion and information see senior school entry.

Clifton High Lower school

Linked to Clifton High School in the Senior section

Clifton High School, College Road, Clifton, Bristol, BS8 3JD

• Pupils: 235 girls and boys; all day • Ages: 3-11 • Non-denominational with a Christian ethos • Fees: £4,800-£7,665 pa • Independent

Tel: 0117 973 8096
Fax: 0117 933 9097
Email: enquiries@cliftonhigh.bristol.sch.uk
Website: www.cliftonhigh.bristol.sch.uk

Head of Lower School: Head of Lower School is Mr Tony Richards, formerly head of an international school in Malaysia. He seems very well liked by parents and pupils. Softly spoken and 'not at all scary', according to one four-year-old. Mr Richards sits on the school executive along with Mr Guy Cowper, director of operations, and Dr Alison Neill, who is head of school and Clifton High sixth.

Entrance: From age three in the pre-reception class, with children accepted at every stage based on informal assessments rather than tests.

Exit: Most girls have historically carried on to the upper school, while in previous years boys dispersed to a wide range of the local independents. Now boys can also progress to the upper school, and most do. Lower school pupils do not take the entrance tests for the upper school unless they are trying for a scholarship.

Remarks: A small, happy and inclusive school which inspires gushing praise from parents, particularly in the early years. Smaller than it used to be – two classes per year rather than three, with a maximum size of 18 – but the school has taken a policy decision to stick with those two rather than keep expanding and contracting numbers. Closer links with upper school, and the option for boys to stay on, make for a smoother transition and a more unified feel.

Broad curriculum, including French and Latin from Year 3 (Clifton High is home to the creator of the Minimus Latin scheme for primary schools). Children seem busy, but not stressed.

Improved support for dyslexia and other learning problems with a newly-expanded learning support team (shared with the upper school), but the occasional child needing more intensive support is gently turned down or advised to move on before the end of junior school, though only after considerable consultation with parents and teachers.

The main lower school buildings are converted from a large Victorian house, with later additions, on a campus shared with the upper school. Buildings and classrooms have been repainted recently and are looking much brighter. Equipment is reasonably new, including a large computer room. Lower school children eat in the upper school canteen, and go to assembly in the main hall twice a week.

Not a huge amount of outdoor space, but what there is is well-designed for play and out-of-classroom learning (evidence of plenty of gardening, creative projects and fun experiments going on). The wide open spaces of the Downs are a short walk away. Children have access to the on-site swimming pool and gym (shared with the upper school), and are bussed to the sports fields at Coombe Dingle for an afternoon's sporting activities once a week. Lots of lunch-time and after-school clubs from French to taekwondo to computers.

Cokethorpe Junior School

Linked to Cokethorpe School in the Senior section

Cokethorpe School, Witney, Oxfordshire, OX29 7PU

• Pupils: 130 boys and girls; all day • Ages: 4-11 • Joint C of E and RC foundation • Fees: £9,885 pa • Independent

Tel: 01993 703921
Fax: 01993 773499
Email: admissions@cokethorpe.org
Website: www.cokethorpe.org.uk

Head of Junior School: Since September 2006, Mrs Christine Cook. Educated Westminster College, Oxford, Brockenhurst Sixth Form College. Formerly director of studies at Chandlings School, teaching houseparent at The

Dragon School, head of year at Peers School, Oxford, and coach for the South Hockey centre of excellence.

Entrance: Mostly from local nurseries including school's own linked nursery, Westfield House, and primary schools.

Exit: Virtually all to senior school. During Year 5, parents of junior school pupils unlikely to make it into the senior school are helped to look elsewhere – 'We have to learn to say no to parents'.

Remarks: Housed alongside the senior school in The Mansion, sharing the idyllic, extensive rural grounds and some facilities. Classrooms are bright, lively, and readily accommodate the maximum 16 per class. Follow national curriculum with additions such as French for all from year dot. Individual subject teaching increases as children progress through the school. Own dedicated art room, library, language teaching room; other specialist facilities – for drama, music, PE, ICT, DT – shared with the senior school.

We visited following a Tudor day and were suitably impressed by the costumes and historical knowledge of the little ones – nothing like experiencing for understanding – even the packed lunch was based on Tudor food! All children remain at school until 5pm – a long day for the youngest, but most seem to thrive and all enjoy an array of activities known as AOBs. Additional help provided by learning support department if needed. All are members of senior houses, following siblings where appropriate.

Lots of happy, lively faces, even at the end of a long day.

Colet Court

Linked to St Paul's School in the Senior section

Lonsdale Road, London, SW13 9JT

• Pupils: 435 boys, all day • Ages: 7 to 13 • Colet Court is a Christian foundation but boys of all faiths are represented at the school • Fees: £14,334 pa • Independent

Tel: 020 8748 3461
Fax: 020 8746 5357
Email: hmseccc@stpaulsschool.org.uk
Website: www.coletcourt.org.uk

Headmaster: Since 2007, Mr Tim Meunier MA PGCE C.Chem FRCS, (very early fifties). Educated at Forest School, London and Trinity College Cambridge. Married to 'lovely, smiley' Sarah (say boys who love it when she covers their lessons – no official role for spouse here). They met doing their PGCE at Homerton and have two grown-up sons. Apart from a spell at The Dragon (Sarah ran a boarding house, he was head of science) Mr Meunier's experience is largely in senior schools – Felsted, deputy head at Clifton College. Quietly humorous, thoughtful and sincere, Mr Meunier is the perfect foil to the dynamic and charismatic Dr Martin Stephen, High Master of St Paul's. Embraces the 500 year traditions of the place and the history of academic brilliance but at the same time working to soften the image. Has already tweaked the entrance procedure to make it less daunting (particularly for parents) and insists that 'we are surprisingly cuddly once you're here'.

Entrance: At 7+, 8+, and 11+. State primary school candidates can sit an exam in Year 5 for a deferred place at 11+ (10 places available). Boys at prep schools that finish at 11 sit the 11+ exam in Year 6 (at least another 10 places available). Very competitive – at least 200 candidates. Looking for innate intelligence – 'we have only one criterion – very very bright boys'. Tailor-made exam and headmaster will interview all boys – as well as parents (school prefers to use word 'chat' with respect to parents – 'to put them at their ease, they are much more nervous than the boys'). Would be naïve, says headmaster, to assume no preparation is necessary – whether it be tutoring, extra reading with granny, or stimulating conversations with a doting uncle.

Will fill the occasional place (very rarely happens but anything possible in this economic climate) but ONLY with boys who have already taken the entrance exams, or couldn't possibly have gone through the system. Strict policy in place to avoid any possible loopholes.

Exit: (Almost) all to St Paul's School. That's the expectation (a shudder at the suggestion that Colet Court is a feeder for Eton). At 13+ boys now sit a mixture of Common Entrance and St Paul's transfer/scholarship papers (Common Entrance in the core subjects of English, maths and science). Others schools e.g. Eton will accept these exams, but the school doesn't – understandably – bend over backwards to give extra coaching for e.g. the Winchester exam, though it will explain to parents what is necessary. 'We feel it is a positive advantage that boys don't have to work towards a lot of different exams for different schools.'

Remarks: It's going to take a lot more than the odd off-the-cuff comment about cuddliness to change the school's prevailing reputation – confirmed by many current parents – that if you want nurture and a flexible approach geared to the individual then find somewhere else. (The school feels that this is unfair and out of date: 'Our teachers go out of their way to nurture boys.') The overwhelming message – whether it be during assembly, in the newsletter, in the school magazine, or on the website, is that Colet Court is about excellence. Unashamedly ambitious about achieving that excellence, boys here know what's expected of them and have an insatiable appetite to keep striving for it. As soon as you cross the threshold as parent or pupil – a surprisingly intimidating experience given the unprepossessing buildings – you sign up to this culture of achievement and you sign up for the long term. Once you're here why would you want to go anywhere else? As one parent put it, you have a pass into a top school (if not the top school as far as they are concerned) on a plate (all being well, very few don't make the grade) and an excellent prep school into the bargain.

Situated in 45 largely green acres – (some shared with St Paul's and so, note – a few lumbering teenagers will be crossing paths with your budding boy), replete with playing fields, a full-size swimming pool, large sports hall, fencing salle, dojo for aikido, rackets court and tennis courts, plus cricket nets, basketball courts, ICT suites, technology workshops, fully-equipped science labs, music school, music hall, large assembly hall, separate dining hall, playground with wood, ropes, and swings. All this so close to the centre of town and on the river too – is unparalleled for a London day school. Latest inspection report littered with superlatives. Sport, music, facilities, exam results 'outstanding', 'excellent', 'exceptional', of the 'highest quality'.

Stunning music, 'ridiculously good' says Mr Meunier, a keen lover of music himself (he and his wife sing in various choirs). Three orchestras, chamber ensemble, string quartet. Piles of distinctions on music exams. Three choirs, full to bursting, with invigorating schedule of appearances. Over 80 per cent of boys learn one or more musical instruments. Art superb, in bright, spacious art classroom overlooking Thames. Excellent chess team; super well-used library, regular additions. Sports abundant. seven-year olds play tag rugby. Higher up the school there is a multi-sports option for boys who do not want to play contact games. Soccer in spring, cricket in summer. Games for two hours, two afternoons a week, plus a session of PE. Loads of teams – most boys (including all of those in the junior classes) can represent the school at some level. One of the few independent preps to take boys on overseas soccer tours. Cricket tour to Barbados, football to Brazil and rugby and football to South Africal. Saturday morning games or practice, for boys in teams. Golf off-site.

A murmur of criticism in the recent inspection – the breadth of education at the top of the school – is swiftly addressed. The decision to dispose of the controversially elitist scholarship form, and to have two-tiered streaming in the final two years (only) with potential scholars drawn from the entire year group, Mr Meunier says was 'pushing at an open door'. The tendency to focus even more on the academics in the final years will now be a bit more balanced with more outward bound activities, art, music, design and drama. Here any change is about tweaking, not about overhaul. On the fundamentals, that is infrastructure, it's another story. A massive multi-billion building project to span the next 20 years is about to get underway. Sixties prefab, never meant to last more than 50 years, will gradually be replaced with 'architecturally exciting, environmentally-friendly buildings using a mix of materials'. In the meantime even the hoardings will be high quality, assures Mr Meunier. Nor will the academic standards be in any way threatened. Strictly no noise during lesson times.

Surprisingly broad intake: although 60 per cent of parents are probably lawyers or bankers, the generous bursaries (quite a few on 100 per cent) funded by the John Colet foundation allow the less well-off to benefit. Help also for extras such as trips and tours abroad. One thing all parents (many of whom are themselves old Paulines and Paulinas) have in common is that they are highly-motivated and ambitious (no surprises there). Quiz night is something to limber up for and one parent confessed that she preferred not to admit to ever getting drunk on the sofa watching Spooks. A broad geographical intake too; although most are from Barnes, Chiswick, Kensington etc, some are prepared to tackle a school run of up to two hours each way to ensure their son experiences what they regard to be London's finest.

Don't gasp – there are those who struggle, The reality is some 30 to 40 boys have a difficulty of some sort, mostly mild dyslexia or dyspraxia but ADD, ADHD (Ritalin okay), and mild Asperger's found among the numbers. Everyone is screened on entry to the school, and at the first sign of trouble (generally quickly spotted because of excellent communication between staff) they are swept up by the universally-praised learning support lady who will teach them to organise themselves, draw up tables of French and Latin verbs, or bring their maths up to speed. Learning support could be for the long term or a short sharp burst, but either way it is readily available, at no extra cost, and enables the boys to carry on sprinting. 'Some of our best and brightest have a difficulty. Ironically, the baggage can help. They have to develop strategies to cope, they think differently and some get to Oxbridge.' Big study skills programme for all Year 8s, who get three lessons before their mocks and further ones in the run-up to Common Entrance/transfer exams.

In a system that boasts outstanding exam performances and is so results-based, you must be wondering how they have time to do anything else. There is very long lunch break when they can do anything from fencing to aikido, bridge, second orchestra or woodwind ensemble. You name it, but they have to go out and find it. Boys here need initiative and plenty of oomph. There are some who prefer to play tag or cards in the copious play areas, but one parent expressed concern as to whether little Johnnie would forget to eat lunch (school insists that there are duty staff who will send boys to lunch). If they forget their mouthguards for rugby they get short shrift – third time without it, that's a detention. Taking responsibility for yourself starts here. In term time you go at full throttle. One parent commented that she was relieved her son was never ill. Sometimes boys won't get home until 9pm after performing in a concert. The holidays are still called remedies. A time to catch up but otherwise total recuperation.

We would have to agree with the inspectors: this is a superlative school for the right boy, but don't be wowed by the brand unless your son is the genuine article, energetic and competitive – brilliant at one thing at least and undeflated by rarely being the best at anything.

Colfe's Preparatory School, Pre prep and Nursery

Linked to Colfe's School in the Senior section

Horn Park Lane, Lee, London, SE12 8AW

• Pupils: 340 boys and girls; all day • Ages: 3-11 • C of E • Fees: £8,730-£10,134 pa • Independent

Tel: 020 8852 0220
Fax: 020 8297 2941
Email: head@colfes.com
Website: www.colfes.com

Head: Since 2007, Mr John Gallagher BA (Carnegie) MBA (Hull) (forties). Taught at Colfe's Senior for 14 years and was director of sport for seven of them. A local lad from Lewisham who went to New Zealand for his gap year and ended up staying for seven. Played rugby for the All Blacks, including the 1987 World Cup Finals, and was named NZ Player of the Year in 1989. After joining Colfe's back in the 1990s, 'I always wanted to be a teacher', continued playing for neighbouring Blackheath until he was seduced by the Harlequins into becoming their director of rugby. Now, even tiny pupils approach him crying, 'Sir, sir, I support Harlequins, sir!' His own sons attend the school and his wife is deputy head of a local academy. His excellent rugby credentials plus his leadership skills endear him to parents (especially the dads) as well as pupils.

Entrance: At age three to the nursery, four to pre-prep and seven to prep. Places may be available in other year groups but, owing to the growing popularity of this school, names should be put down asap.

Exit: Since the arrival of Richard Russell at Colfe's Senior, great majority head straight there. No longer deviations to Dulwich or Eltham or any other independent school, although some will inevitably stray towards one of the excellent local grammar schools.

Remarks: Unprepossessing buildings from the outside but surrounded by green open spaces and interspersed with surprising shady corners revealing nesting boxes and bird feeders. Distanced from the senior school. Has a sense of its own identity. Every window seems to look out over something green so despite its suburban setting atmosphere almost rural. Classrooms full of light and colour: mobiles, artwork, projects hang from the ceilings and adorn the walls. Everywhere movement, energy, purpose. Staff friendly and smiling, happy to talk about their school.

The learning support teacher offers 'preventative medicine where necessary' twice a week for 20 minutes. Music and drama taught and practised most enthusiastically with full-time specialists. Healthy meals cooked on the premises and menus clearly displayed so parents know exactly what the little darlings had for lunch. Easy and attractive school uniform.

Myriad after-school clubs together with an after-school care facility. Clubs offer short tennis, judo, cookery, book making, handicrafts, mandarin Chinese. Whole school projects undertaken involving music, dance, recitals, art. Swimming every week in the senior school for all nursery and reception children. Strong house system with rewards for good work/behaviour.

A thriving, growing, successful school with the added bonus of a senior school on site and some bursaries for arts and sport.

The Compass School

West Road, Haddington, East Lothian, EH41 3RD

• Pupils: 60 boys, 65 girls; all day • Ages: 4-12 • Inter-denom • Fees: £5,142-£7,755 pa • Independent

Tel: 01620 822642
Fax: 01620 822144
Email: office@thecompassschool.co.uk
Website: www.thecompassschool.co.uk

Headmaster: Since 1997, Mr Mark Becher (pronounced Becker) MA PGCE (early forties), educated Queen Margaret's Academy Ayr, Dundee University, (modern history) and PGCE at Craigie College of Education in Ayr (now part the University of the West of Scotland). Previously head of sport and primary teacher at The Mary Erskine and Stewart's Melville Junior School, and primary teacher at Edinburgh Academy.

An enthusiastic head who lives and breathes The Compass (as it's known – symbolic of finding the right direction for pupils), a keen distance runner, teaches sport, Latin and history, team teaching everyone in school. Supported (recently) by a management team of deputy and part-time bursar, he has seen the school through a £1 million building programme and is revelling in the spanking new facilities. Hall classrooms, milling about space and dedicated ICT suite, all jigsaws remarkably harmoniously into the compact spaces around the pretty Edwardian main house.

Twelve years into post, he takes pride in running a successful Scottish primary – 'Not prep/IAPS,' he stresses – based on the philosophy of the Scottish Curriculum for Excellence but with specialist teaching – 'ideal preparation' – allowing pupils to feed the Edinburgh private sector well ahead of the field. 'Four years ahead in French,' one school complained; 'No apologies for letting children work to their capabilities,' says Mr Becher. Previously for ages 4–8 with a composite class for 9–12 year olds, has grown to include a nursery run in partnership with East Lothian Council and seven year groups (class size between 12 and 20). Mr Becher says the confidence gained from representing the school in the extremely successful choir (everyone's in it and it's won the Edinburgh Festival Primary Schools' Choir trophy twice) teams, drama etc prepares children to take a lead happily in large schools at secondary level.

Entrance: Children can (and do) join at any time – they have an informal assessment and begin at any stage of the school year. School uniform is sold in house and in Edinburgh. Can apply for 'financially assisted places' at any entry stage; specific bursaries for forms 6, 7 and 8 plus sibling discounts and parents can ask for help if struck by financial meltdown. Good proportion of first time independent buyers with catchment from east Edinburgh along the coast to Berwick on Tweed and south to the Lammermuirs. No buses but lots of shared driving etc.

Exit: Most leave at 12 for Edinburgh independents or local state school. 'Everyone gets where they want' and few now leave at 8 for traditional prep schools.

Remarks: Small but extremely perfectly re-formed to bandbox smartness in both the old house and the extension, now has room for a grand though gloomy dining room where class tables are supervised by staff and each has a tray of raw vegetable appetisers 'so they nibble and learn to enjoy while they are waiting'; also dedicated music and artrooms with sweeping views of hills and cornfields – 'a great teaching aid for Year 5 doing farming'. The dramatic galleried stairs rising from the elegant hallway with its glowing (gas fired) coal stove cry out for (and get) carols and holly at Christmas. Classrooms all round are full of bright, shiny but practical equipment and staff. Support for learning is run in close consultation with class etc teachers and takes whatever form fits the child, with a blanket overview from the support teacher, who sits in on all classes and observes/helps to make sure she reaches all the needy.

All the usual traditional subjects: French from age four and Latin from age nine. Pupil work on show everywhere and 'visitors tend to be stunned!'. Best of all were the little booklets of good work and 'daily life in class one' scrapbooks in the parents' waiting area.

Started in 1963 and run by Mrs Alny Younger for years, still feels homely with Astroturf lawns for playtimes and outdoor learning space (smart hut). Lots of games and sport, making use of local authority grass and Astro pitches, Haddington Golf Club, local pool, Loreto's theatre and local churches. Rugby, cricket and hockey matches and swimming galas, all with impressive wins 'against bigger schools'. Same goes for music – a huge range of activities packed into a 9am to 3.30pm day with after-school supervision (paid for) and activities (nominal cost only). The atmosphere has a 'good prep school buzz' but feels more fun than frenetic.

Small is beautiful here! Feels like a first-rate, friendly and efficient school deeply embedded in a supportive, tight-knit and ethnically Scottish community. Parents raised £250,000 in last few years and treat school as a social hub.

Connaught House School

47 Connaught Square, London, W2 2HL

• Pupils: 35 boys, 40 girls, all day – working towards 50/50 • Ages: 4-11 but boys leave at 8 • Non-denom • Fees: £12,000-£13,800 pa • Independent

Tel: 020 7262 8830
Fax: n/a
Email: office@connaughthouseschool.co.uk
Website: www.connaughthouseschool.co.uk

Joint Principals: Since 1991, Mrs Jaqueline Hampton (fifties) and her husband, Mr Frederick Hampton, MA RCA. Has been run by the same family since it opened in 1953 with just six pupils. That tradition continues today as the Hamptons' daughter-in-law, Mrs Vicky Hampton, teaches form 1 and is the key stage 1 advisor. She formerly taught at a Beacon school in Clapham and also spent some time at the British School in Cordoba, Spain. Both Hamptons senior are artists and they have two grown-up sons.

Entrance: At age four into reception (here called Junior One) but with the understanding that they will continue into the main school. Preference is given to siblings and to children from local families. Places are offered after a short, informal assessment. Applications can also be made for entry in the upper end of the school. Academic and music bursaries are available to those applying at 7/8+. Quite a few from Dr Rolfe's Nursery.

Exit: All boys leave at eight and tend to go to local prep schools such as Sussex House and Wetherby. The girls stay until 11 and generally opt for London day schools. Francis Holland is currently popular but many also go to Godolphin and Latymer, City of London, Greycoat Hospital, More House, Latymer Upper, Queens Gate and South Hampstead. Those wishing to board choose Wycombe Abbey or St Mary's, Ascot. Despite leaving a very small school to go on to these much larger establishments, none of the pupils seems to be fazed by this – the confidence they acquire in CHS gives them the ability to cope in a broader environment.

Remarks: Such an individual school that you will instantly know whether you love it or hate it – very small, so does not take long to visit. Crossing it off your list because of its size could be a bad mistake. In a world where everything seems to be getting bigger, this little gem offers old-fashioned notions such as pleasure in learning, time to listen and be listened to ('They are all happy to talk to people of any age,' remarks one mother); good manners and courtesy to others; the acquisition of general knowledge; delicious home-cooked lunches; traditional uniforms including boaters for the girls and caps for the boys. Has never advertised but a waiting list. Most of the pupils live locally so a fair sprinkling of EAL pupils throughout, but support is provided, with many specialist therapists coming in to the school each week. In addition, many of the staff have SEN training. 'Very nice parents and lovely children,' says Mrs Hampton. 'We try to support every child. We are not at all ruthless – that's not our way.'

Art and music are the main extra-curricular strengths of the school – 'The art really strikes you,' says one parent. Art displays and individual work cover the walls in and out of the classroom, 'Something for them to absorb even when they're lost in space'. Music welcomes them into school in the morning. A high percentage undertakes piano lessons – violin, recorder and guitar are also taught. The peripatetic music teachers are all successful musicians and performers in their own right but still find time 'for this funny little school'. Teachers and pupils thrive on the feeling that their school is a place of learning. All develop work habits which serve them well when they move on to bigger schools.

No formal PTA, but the parents are very much in tune with the school and are frequently consulted. A recent poll showed 95 per cent were in favour of keeping the traditional look to the uniform. 'Very nurturing – older ones mentor the younger ones. They find that little thing in each person and bring it out. They embrace the individual,' says one parent enthusiastically.

The lack of sporting facilities does not seem to concern the parents nor the pupils. They make full use of the existing outside areas all around them – Hyde Park is over the road, they do yoga on their mats every day. 'Anyhow, it is something London parents are used to. After all, you spend your weekends driving your children around,' claims one of the mothers.

All in all, a very special little school which is loved by parents and pupils alike, where the children feel challenged every day and their parents are constantly amazed by what they know. 'The closest you can get to home schooling,' declares one. If that sounds appealing, take a little trip to Bayswater Road now.

Coombe Hill Infant School

Coombe Lane West, Kingston upon Thames, Surrey, KT2 7DD

• Pupils: 300 boys and girls • Ages: 4-7 • Non-denom • State

Tel: 020 8942 9481
Fax: 020 8949 7496
Email: CHI@rbksch.org
Website: www.coombehilli.kingston.sch.uk

Head: Since 1991, Mrs Sarah Hobhouse CertEd DPSE in school management (fifties). Comes from Somerset, educated at Sherborne School in Dorset and Surrey University. Tall, elegant, previously deputy head at St Paul's Chessington. Describes herself as 'user-friendly,' with an open door policy; described by more than one parent as 'fantastic'. Teaches RE and obviously has a great rapport with the children – all clamouring for her attention with 'Mrs Hobhouse, look at this' and 'watch this, Mrs Hobhouse.' Very impressive the way she knew every child by name and all wanted to show her something they had done or tell her something about themselves.

Entrance: You need to live almost on the school's posh doorstep to get in. Substantially oversubscribed, though in 2008 the addition of an extra class in reception allowed the catchment to widen a little. Priority to children with sibling attending the school or the associated junior school at the time of admission; pupils with a medical or social need and then those living nearest the school. In practice, about a third of places to siblings. One or two have medical or social needs and the rest tend to live within three-quarters of a mile of the school.

Exit: Majority trot off to the junior school next door. A few to independent schools – Kings College School Wimbledon, Surbiton High School, Wimbledon High School, Putney High School, Rokeby and Shrewsbury House.

Remarks: Top notch school in upmarket area, with winning combination of supportive middle class parents, rich cultural mix and good achievement. Located in one of the most prestigious residential locations in the borough and surrounded by substantial detached houses bristling with security alarms and locked gates to their private roads. A most favourable location for any school, so hugely refreshing that the intake is very ethnically diverse, with more than 50 per cent of the children having EAL, a third speaking more than one language and some speaking more than two. Many children from European backgrounds, together with some Korean and Japanese. School celebrates this rich mix of cultures to the full; highly popular international week and international evenings every year for the whole family – they are invited to wear national dress (even the Brits), have national dancing shows and sample many home-made culinary delights. Forms of mixed ability entry – 30 per form. KS1 results are very good but head points out that, with so many children having EAL, the higher grades in literacy are harder to achieve for many pupils. SEN – typical of the national average – 21 per cent.

School recently updated to a very high standard, on a semi-open plan basis with lots of natural light. Amazingly for a state primary school, computerised interactive (and expensive) whiteboards (we have seen many independent prep schools without these), together with a new IT suite. Lovely grounds with far-reaching views. Shares swimming pool with junior school, used by each class twice a week in summer. Buildings adapted for disabled users.

Super school to visit with loads going on and children very absorbed. Great range of after-school activities: clubs for gym, drama and music, art and craft, construction and a dinosaur club – charge of approx £3 per session. Lending library for videos, games, reading and maths schemes. Do look at the super website, a lot of it created by the children. Support from the solid middle class parents is tremendous – ' the parents raise a fortune,' says the head – the school's swimming pool is heated and maintained from proceeds raised by the PTA.

No lunch provided, children have to bring it from home. Parking problematical, as ever, with busy main road outside. No problems dropping off in the mornings – a quick in and out – not so easy in the afternoon when head insists parents park in adjacent side roads and walk to collect.

School has everything going for it – great head, vibrancy, enviable buildings, grounds, location and catchment area. Deservedly very popular, worth moving to be near – or should we say very near – to get a place, assuming of course you have the money to buy in its largely upmarket catchment area.

Coombe Hill Junior School

Coombe Lane West, Kingston Upon Thames, Surrey, KT2 7DD

• Pupils: 360 boys and girls,; all day • Ages: 7-11 • Non-denom • State

Tel: 02089 491 743
Email: chj@rbksch.org
Website: www.coombehillj.kingston.sch.uk/

Head: Since 2004, Mr Chris Hodges, BA PGCE, (mid-thirties). Prior to joining Coombe was deputy head and then head at Sparrow Farm Juniors in Feltham. Has risen through the ranks very quickly, though, in typically modest mode, he claims to have been 'in the right place at the right time'. Has the national professional qalification for headship and has completed the leadership programme for serving headteachers – he's a thoroughly modern man.

Tall, sharp-suited (no tie) with a Grant Mitchell haircut and an amenable, laidback manner which belies his steady finger on the pulse and steely resolve. He 'never stops assessing and looking for improvement', and is bursting with ideas (he seems particularly clued-up on attracting government money to the school). Bounces around the school with Tigger-like enthusiasm, insisting his (female) management team – the deputy head and senior teacher – share credit for the school's fantastic local reputation.

A 'doer' – he makes things happen fast. Has given the management team, year heads and class teachers significant levels of responsibility. But don't be fooled – Mr Hodges has selected his able, like-minded staff carefully (he had to 'lose a few' when he took over, perhaps because they were not committed to the philosophy) and knows exactly what is going on. Not a lover of office life – preferring to grind through his paperwork at home – he enjoys the classroom and fits in an impressive 40 per cent teaching time, including daily Year 6 maths.

Not interested in the trappings of office; his own is smaller than his deputy's and has a less attractive aspect – 'I wanted to be more central, near the entrance and the sick bay,' he explains. Obviously likes children – his door is literally always open to them and he's a familiar figure in the playground, where he mucks in and is frequently called on to sort out any 'domestics'. Not expected to win a long-service award – parents see him as 'going places', though he is adamant he is not going anywhere. Married with one young daughter, he is a busy family man, with all that entails. A chap to watch for the future.

Entrance: Catchment is from Coombe Hill and New Malden areas. Oversubscribed, typically 150 applicants for 90 places, extras go onto a waiting list. Three form entry, with 30 children in each class. The school is always full – key is to get your child into the adjacent, and similarly sought after, linked Coombe Infant School (qv) from whence automatic transfer – 99 per cent of children arrive from here.

Exit: Most stay in the state system, with impressive numbers winning places at Kingston's highly selective Tiffin grammar schools. Well-regarded local Coombe Girls is a popular option. These three schools account for about 50 per cent of Year 6 leavers – others elsewhere in handfuls. Some 10 per cent head off to local independents.

Remarks: A brilliant, buzzy state school which packs a real punch, easily holding its own among its largely private sector competition. In one of Kingston's most upmarket areas, shares a large and attractive site with its partner infant school, both heavily oversubscribed with children from solid middle class families. 'It's a lovely school,' says one parent, 'but it's not the only lovely school in the area so it's not simply that it's an easy option. It does well to ensure it's a positive choice for us all.'

SATs results are consistently top notch – 99 per cent reach level 4, 75 per cent level 5; tremendous value-added too. School very keen on teaching learning strategies. Classes are mixed ability, but with bags of setting and even sets within the sets. This makes for well-paced lessons where the children seem genuinely engaged in their activities. When we visited, noise from a drumming workshop in the hall was reverberating around the place, but no one appeared distracted – it merely served to underline the fact that this is a place where lots happen. French for all.

ICT plays a major role in motivating the children. Interactive boards in all classes, a smart, good size and well-used ICT suite with technician, plus wireless laptops. All learn touch-typing. Alpha Smarts (a type of personal digital assistant) available to the school's 30 or so diagnosed dyslexics and other reluctant writers.

Over 20 per cent of the children have an identified special need (just above the average). School happily caters for a broad range of requirements, including those for dyslexia and dyspraxia. Provision includes social skills groups and vocabulary groups, one-to-one maths, additional and further literacy support, and class brain-gym. Additionally there are weekly 'excellence sessions' and a 'challenge zone' resource area for the 25 or so pupils identified as gifted and talented. The G&T programme is broadened out to include areas such as art, music and sport, not just academics.

The school benefits from detailed and thorough records passed on by the linked infants' school and the SENCo concentrates for the first half term of Year 3 on the identification of any additional needs. Additional SEN specialists are on hand three mornings a week. Such good pick-up and support means SEN pupils here make above-average progress. The mother of one little boy raves about how well he has done since joining the junior school: 'He arrived with minimal reading and writing skills and is now in the middle of his class. They do push and expect a lot of the children, but so they should. They have kept a close eye on him and I am delighted'. Some 27 different languages are spoken by children across the school – plenty of support available

Nice ambiance about the place; recently upgraded facilities include a lift to allow disabled access and one of the smartest staff rooms we've seen anywhere – we mention it only as an indication that the school pays more than lip service to the notion of valuing its staff. Although wide corridors and atrium space create a generally roomy feel, some of the classrooms are actually a little tight. But the total space is flexible and desks are carted around as needed. 'Every cohort is different and we tailor their activities to suit,' says Mr Hodges. Good, effective displays abound.

Staff female – just one male classroom assistant and two learning support assistants. Parents are full of praise for teaching. Art and science both mentioned by several parents as being 'fantastic', but a drizzle of complaint about 'not enough sport' (although this is probably more a criticism of the national curriculum than the school) and Mr Hodges is on the case. Every morning begins with an aerobic session in the playground before school starts. It's optional – but most children badger their parents to be there. Another sporting bonus is the on-site heated swimming pool (shared with infants). Plenty of music on offer. Most teachers are musical and competent enough to take their own music lessons, peripatetic staff teach the 45 or so pupils who study an instrument. Busy choir and orchestra. Year 3 pupils all get the chance to try trumpet or violin in the spring term.

Children have a fairly free rein in the playground. A few diehard couch potatoes may skulk around the edges, but otherwise everyone seems to be having a great time – the fact that the lines need repainting every five weeks bears witness to the many activities that go on here. Children digging up the grassy area with a stick are allowed to get on with it – 'You've got to have a bit of fun,' says Mr Hodges. 'What's life come to if you can't let a child play with a stick? I found someone building an assault course for ants the other day.' Even trading cards, widely banned elsewhere, are permitted as staff believe children learn a life lesson from them – even when in dispute.

Obvious zero tolerance of any aggressive or bullying behaviour – older pupils are trained as peer mediators and head is noted for acting fast if any problems do occur. 'I'm actually very proud of the way children at this school behave towards one another,' he says. A counsellor (not a parent or teacher) is a recent addition to the ranks. Parents agree this is a school which belongs to the children – they are well-motivated and therefore mostly keen to participate in all that's on offer. But boundaries are made clear and there are consequences for 'bad choice'. No-one likes being left to stew, crosslegged, outside the head's office.

Good range of after-school clubs. Only grumble concerned a lack of casual, classroom-door type access to staff – school prefers contact via the office for appointment; 'A bit over the top if I just want to mention that the goldfish died,' says one mother. More generally, school/home communication has been a bugbear for some parents going back several years – but it is felt to be slowly improving under Mr Hodges: 'I totally get what parents want since my own daughter started school,' he says. There is an external blackboard at the front entrance for daily notices, but an email facility is high on parental wish-list.

Children are offered a genuine role in helping to run the school and take it very seriously. The school council is a force to be reckoned with – pupil members temporarily withdrew playground equipment they had chosen and bought with part of their £1,500 budget, because they felt it was not being properly respected. Pupils also play a big part in the school's myriad environmental initiatives as part of a 'green team' facilitated by a teacher.

Parents are viewed as a key resource, and they show tremendous support, over and above the norm. School is overwhelmed with offers of help, and the very active and sociable parents' association raises big money – £30k plus. 'The school is definitely a big part of our community and lots of friendships are based here,' says one mother. Parents also operate a rota to control vehicle access to the school at the beginning of each day – the school drop-off, as ever, is problematic.

Families are affluent and diverse – 27 different languages are spoken. Almost 50 per cent of pupils have English as their second language. This mix of cultures is a plus for many parents – all are made to feel welcome and valued. Mr Hodges is also intent on making school's facilities available to the local community. Adult learning courses (from creative writing through to computer skills and first aid) are open to all, not just parents connected with the school. 'It is simply ludicrous that our facilities can only be used for 12 per cent of the year,' says Mr Hodges. 'We must be a community facility.' He doesn't garner unanimous support for this – one mother vehemently believes he should have let this particular idea gather dust in his intray – not that one seriously imagines anything does. That said, grumbles are few and far between.

Cothill House

Linked to Chandlings School in the Junior section

Cothill, Abingdon, Oxfordshire, OX13 6JL

• Pupils: 250 boys; all board • Ages: 8-13 • C of E • Fees: £20,970 pa • Independent

Tel: 01865 390 800
Fax: 01865 390 205
Email: jane@cothill.net
Website: www.cothill.net

Head: Since 2003, Mr Neil Brooks BA QTS (forties). Educated at Magdalen College School, Oxford, and Warwick University, where he read PE and geography. Spent eight years as army officer (7th Parachute Regiment, Royal Horse Artillery) before deciding to teach. Wrote 112 letters to schools; 'I knew it was the world I wanted to be in,' he says, and was snapped up by Cothill. Ran senior boarding house for two years then took over from Mr Adrian Richardson (now principal of the Cothill House Educational Trust) as headmaster. Married with two sons, who both attend the school; his wife, Tracy, works alongside him and is responsible for much of the practical side of boarding life, particularly the food – all cooked in-house, sourced as locally as possible and pronounced 'yummy' by the boys we spoke to.

Charming and approachable, Mr Brooks is candid, independent-minded and expresses himself enthusiastically with a refreshing absence of 'corporate speak.' Even more important, he has a great rapport with the boys in his charge, whether he's sharing a joke or wiping a grubby nose. His study is at the heart of the school next to the dining hall and the all-important telephones; boys can go in 'whenever we like as long as we knock first' to borrow sports equipment or the much-prized laser guns rather incongruously housed in an antique bureau. He is aware that many boys arrive at the school bearing a weight of family tradition and expectation, assuming at the age of eight that they will be going to Eton, Harrow or wherever their fathers went. The head is equally determined that each boy should go to the school that will suit him best, even if this may occasionally point to a different destination. He has interesting views on the value of pre-tests, 'all they do is pick off the predictable boys rather than looking at the whole child,' pointing out the obvious fact that the difference between a child at ten-and-a-half (the average age at which boys take the pre-test) and 13 years of age can be 'immense'. He is genuinely concerned about where such tests leave the late bloomers, perhaps, he says, because he was one himself.

Entrance: Despite changing attitudes to boarding school, the number of boys who start at Cothill from eight has hardly changed over the years, averaging at about 30; of these only two or three are from families where there is no tradition of boarding, but for most here it is 'simply the norm'. Applications to Cothill have remained immune, thus far, to the economic malaise, and early registration is advisable even if the head's modesty prevents him from saying so directly (his way of putting it is 'nicely busy'). The process begins with a meeting for parents only, after all 'this is going to be their decision', followed by an open day and assessment morning. No great emphasis on academic ability at this stage: the assessment is principally to check that the boy and the school are right for each other. After this, boys are encouraged to visit as often as possible prior to joining.

Exit: The head is very keen that each boy leaving Cothill should go on to the school that is right for him and he sees it as part of his role to advise parents. Happily, school and parents seem most often to be in agreement and the destinations are just as one would expect. Boys depart, often accompanied by scholarships, to Eton, Harrow, Radley, Shrewsbury, Sevenoaks, Charterhouse, Marlborough and other public schools.

Remarks: Charming village location feels comfortably rural, although Cothill is just on the outskirts of Abingdon and six miles south of Oxford. The main building is a large country house with a variety of later additions and 26 acres of grounds and playing fields. Sports facilities include a 19 metre indoor pool housed in a high roofed wooden barn with glass sides, a squash court and six all-weather tennis courts plus a nine-hole golf course where boys are coached by a pro. Parents are welcome to come and watch midweek, as well as weekend, sports fixtures and many do, especially mothers who find boarding 'harder to adapt to than the boys'. Details of recent equestrian successes are pinned up on the head's notice board, but the school does not keep horses and teams are organised by the parents of the boys who do.

Head's family quarters are very much part of the school; boys take cookery classes in the kitchen, an extremely popular part of the timetable, particularly if the recipe contains chocolate. Child gates on open doors are to stop Jem, the beagle, visiting the dorms upstairs. The games room is surveyed by Dexter, the grey parrot, who apparently just arrived in the garden one day and has been known to utter the odd, mild, profanity. The large, comfortable sitting room with squashy sofas has a television for Saturday film nights and important sporting events only. Dorms are tidy but characterful, boys sleep in bunk beds with four or eight to a room and there are plenty of posters, flags, soft toys, family photos and colourful duvets from home. No mobiles or other electronic distractions until the final year when boys are allowed an iPod. In theory small pets are accommodated (nothing further up the evolutionary scale than a ferret); however, a sad little shed full of empty hutches and cages is testament to brief lives and attention spans.

The excellent library, housed on the top floor of a modern teaching block, is light and tranquil with plenty of squashy chairs; if a boy needs a bit of time out he can 'come and be quiet' here, according to our guides. On display was a selection of letters from soldiers at Camp Bastion thanking boys for gifts they had sent. The library leads on to what was described by one boy as the 'temple of fun', in other words the IT suite. Here are 18 shiny iMacs from where boys can email home or talk on Skype, although a proper handwritten letter must also be sent once a week. No Facebook or YouTube here; all is filtered and the head of IT keeps a benign but watchful eye on curricular and extra-curricular internet activities. The school hall is modern with a stage and retractable seating, a venue for frequent concerts and drama productions as well as assembly where boys are graded each Monday according to their work and behaviour. Marks out of 10, or 'weeklies', are read out by Mr Brooks (although anything under five is between the head and the boy concerned); a running total is kept each term and boys with the best scores are rewarded by surprise trips. One trip that isn't a surprise but is equally eagerly anticipated is the term spent at the Chateau de Sauveterre near Toulouse. Total immersion in French language and culture, visits to local schools, French food and sunshine make this a highlight of any boy's time at Cothill.

The timetable is designed to suit boys' learning styles. Classes are small (around 14), lessons are short (35 to 40 minutes) and characterised by 'lots of practical activity' and movement between lessons. There is sport every day and plenty of running around time afterwards. Fairly traditional range of subjects taught in preparation for Common Entrance, lots of excellent music with plenty of opportunities to find the right instrument – not just a few 'try out' lessons but a whole term of class violin for all boys (just imagine ...) followed by other orchestral explorations. Drama is very popular with boys and parents alike and everywhere we went was busy and productively messy.

Out of lessons, boys are free to explore the grounds, build camps and play, but staff are vigilant and know when to intervene if necessary; practical departments such as art and pottery are staffed until 8pm so that boys can use these facilities too. Our delightful trio of guides, picked seemingly at random from the lunch queue, confided that they were going to 'save the best until last'. So, at last, we came to the 'best' – the woodwork room. In a large pine-scented shed full of shavings is the woodwork master, a twinkly, patient ex-police officer who has been at Cothill for 24 years. Just imagine free rein with all your parents' (trying to avoid stereotyping here) tools, an endless supply of wood and someone with the time and skill to help you realise your ambitious plans. Boys really can make 'whatever they want', just so long as parents can transport it home. There are garden seats, bird tables, boot racks, jewellery boxes, guns, book shelves all under construction, and boys work on their creations in lessons and free time. On offer here are invaluable practical skills coupled with a creative freedom that most children can only dream about; the boys know how special it is and love every minute.

High expectations and not much in the way of outside distractions mean that serious disciplinary problems are rare. The head stresses the importance of observation, and a daily meeting for all staff ensures that any concerns about individual boys or tensions between friends are discussed in the round and dealt with sensitively. Boys know that they can confide in whomever they wish, whether it's their tutor, the junior matrons (usually gap year girls) or subject teachers. Staff are very visible, even at lunchtime – we saw plenty outside playing cricket and talking to the boys.

Yes, this is a traditional boarding prep school, but in the best possible way and without being stuffy. Standards of teaching and expectations are high and the Common Entrance results speak for themselves, but that's only part of what the boys who come here gain. There's a real sense of fun and camaraderie, not just between the boys but also between boys and staff. Parents praise the excellent home/school communication; Mr Brooks is, apparently, 'always available' and one commented that on weekends spent at home her son was rather wistful about all the fun he was missing at school! The excellent and unusually readable school magazine seems to capture the spirit of the place rather well. It features letters from boys who have moved on to senior schools as well as some delightful articles by members of staff about pudding etiquette and the like. When asked if there was anyone who might not fit into school life at Cothill, the three guides were thoughtful. 'Everyone is a bit quiet and shy at first,' said one, 'but then you make friends.' Another added rather decisively, 'grumpy people might not like it though'. Enough said.

Cottesmore School

Buchan Hill, Pease Pottage, Pease Pottage, West Sussex, RH11 9AU

• Pupils: 100 boys, 50 girls; boarding and day • Ages: 7-13. Pre-prep 4-7 • C of E • Fees: £7,200-£13,770; Boarding £18,810 pa • Independent

Tel: 01293 520 648
Fax: 01293 614 784
Email: office@cottesmoreschool.com
Website: www.cottesmoreschool.com

Head: Since 2008, Mr Tom Rogerson (mid-thirties). Mr Rogerson is the third generation of his family to run the school, which is owned by the family. His legendary father is still in the background as a benign and wise counsellor. Educated at Cottesmore and Eton and then on to university. Previous teaching posts include Ludgrove, Eaton House and Broomwood Hall where he was head of English and, far more important, met his wife-to-be. 'I winked at her during a beginning of term assembly.' Articulate, entertaining and thoughtful, he is full of sensitive ideas about improving what was good when he took over and determined to nurture the tradition of bringing out the best in every child. 'We aim to ignite the passion in every child; every child is good at something and should leave with that inner confidence that comes from success. We have a number of experienced members of staff who power the place along with some excellent new teachers. Essentially this is a boarding school (90 per cent do board). We don't do flexi-boarding. The word flexi sounds like a particularly unpleasant carpet underlay. Everyone has a bed and most day pupils convert because boarding is such a good option.' Parents are clearly delighted with him, as are the pupils.

His wife, Lottie, is a brilliant addition to Cottesmore, with a good knowledge of schools. A pupil at The Dragon, where she was heavily outnumbered by boys, she went on to Cheltenham Ladies', where she was not. Thereafter, university before teaching at Broomwood and Elstree. She heads the new pre-prep and teaches maths and English to the bottom form in the prep. 'It helps to preserve a sense of continuity.' She is overall responsible for the pastoral side – a universal mum. An outstandingly engaging couple. They live in the house with the pupils.

Entrance: Prospective pupils enter prep via interview, a straightforward ed psych paper and a good report from their previous school. Very occasionally pupils are not admitted but the emphasis is on potential rather than achievement. However the academic pace is brisk ... Most pupils enter aged eight but they may enter later, if places are available. We met a boy who had joined aged 12 and 'the school was brilliant with him,' said his delighted mum, 'I only wish I had sent him earlier'. About 30 per cent come from London, 30 per cent from Sussex and 30 per cent from abroad, including ex-pats, children of diplomats, Europeans and the far east. A good variety of internationals, who all seemed very happy and integrated. Not so much a good school for dyslexics as a school which offers good help to children with dyslexia. Every child is screened for dyslexia on arrival, if parents want that.

Entry to pre-prep at four.

Exit: The usual suspects: Eton, Harrow, Radley, Marlborough, Charterhouse, Winchester, Canford, Cranleigh and girls to Benendon, Downe House, Wellington and King's Canterbury – but not exclusively so by any means. 'We are keen to find the right school for the child.' 'Happy, confident children,' says head of a senior school.

Remarks: Extraordinary late Victorian mansion with turrets, towers, gables and gargoyles, built by a man who originally made his dosh from ostrich feathers and then, after they became less fashionable, from diamonds which he discovered when he found one of his ostriches in South Africa had choked on one. Huge log fire in the enormous hall, fascinating carvings on the staircase and over lintels, tooled leather on the walls of the dining room. The house was built for weekend parties, which perhaps explains why it has adapted so well to the school. It is big but not overpoweringly grand; impressive but fun to live in.

Sensitively-designed classroom block, reminiscent of cloisters, with bright and airy teaching spaces. Superb Sopwith Centre for Art, Technology Design – real design with most impressive results – computers and science labs. Named after Tommy Sopwith, the aircraft engineer, an old boy, with inspirational views over glorious countryside and inspirational teaching going on inside. Art and DT are part of the core curriculum, as is music. No question of dropping them to concentrate on the restrictions of Common Entrance, let alone the challenge of scholarships. Chess is compulsory for the first two years – not in lessons but in the slot between 11 and 12 every morning, a time set aside for charging intellectual batteries in between lessons.

Academic results are very good and the teaching we saw was lively and interesting with pupils enthusiastically involved. Class sizes are small – rarely larger than 14 – and streaming for scholarships is done with sensitivity and tact. This is not a hothouse school, indeed many London parents choose Cottesmore because it isn't, but academics are taken seriously.

A recent Ofsted inspection was so impressed that the school was identified as an 'Outstanding Provider', followed by a letter from HM Chief Inspector congratulating the school on its exceptional provision. Readers of ISI reports with their bland and faintly curmudgeonly language will be amazed to note that the word 'outstanding' was used 17 times. A world record? Nowhere is the excellence of Cottesmore more apparent than in its provision for the individual happiness of pupils. The crucial question of bullying is approached via its 'Happiness Charter' prominently displayed all over the school and its 'Worry Box', into which pupils may post letters expressing any concern they may have. The medical sister with six assistant matrons is clearly actively concerned with the pupils' happiness. 'You can tell how a pupil is really feeling by how they look in the morning. If we're worried we discuss that individual and keep a close eye open.' Pupils confirmed how safe and happy they felt, with lots of people to whom they felt they could talk, if worried, including the excellent ground staff and the kitchen folk. (Cottesmore won 'Best School Food 2009' at the Tatler School Awards. That's out of 225 prep and public schools.) Our lunch and, later, match tea made us feel we were from The Good Food Guide. Six pit stops for food refuelling every day.

Dormitories are brightly decorated in the original bedrooms and dressing-rooms of the original party house – 'it's like having a sleep-over every night,' said one girl – and pupils in dorms are regularly rotated to ensure everyone gets to know each other. Down in the vast cellars is an indoor shooting range, a bowling alley constructed by the head's grandfather and still in excellent nick, a superb model railway and a modelling room – the Airfix sort.

Despite its proximity to London and Gatwick, the school is in 35 acres of its own and surrounded by another 1,000. 'Bet you can't see another house from here,' challenged the head. We couldn't. In the grounds is a nine-hole chip and putt golf course and top golfers can use the adjoining private golf course; the lake provides opportunities for fishing and boating; the orchard for scrumping and cooking and gardening is popular – especially when you can eat the food you grow. Playing fields are expansive and beautifully kept. Football has improved markedly in the last few years and is challenging the more traditional rugby in popularity. Hockey and cricket are also very popular (every two years the first X1 cricket team goes to Dubai) and for the girls it's netball, hockey, rounders and tennis (three manicured courts, three hard with floodlighting). Teams are, by and large, successful and a pleasing feature is that everyone who wishes to play in a team is able to do so. We watched a third X1 match against another school which was played with all the zest of a cup final.

The school appears tireless in its wish to find activities for individual interests. Ask to see the list of hobbies and activities on offer and then realise what a bonus it is to have 99 per cent of the staff living on site. Lots going on at weekends, too. Three choirs – we heard the chapel choir practising and they were eye-smartingly good – and 80 per cent learn musical instruments; enthusiastically performed drama in the ancient, but perfectly functional gym. There are plans to build a theatre in time and presumably it will be called the Olivier theatre, since four generations of Sir Larry's family have attended the school. Lovely chapel, with superb organ, in which daily services are held. Pupils play a leading part. 'Reading in public helps their confidence and encourages them to think about what they are reading.' A tuck shop where you can buy a limited amount of sweets and birthday cards.

Most schools trumpet their 'family atmosphere', that intangible quality which is so hard to define. This school undoubtedly possesses it. Perhaps it's the building and setting, perhaps it's the sense of continuity. Certainly all the parents and children we spoke to commented on the friendly feel of the place. The children give every impression of being happy and confident without precocity. No whiff of snobbishness; no sense of unnatural sophistication. Children allowed to be children with freshness, spontaneity and a sense of purpose. One of those schools where it's very difficult to find a weakness.

The same could be said of the new pre-prep which opened in September 2009. Bright classrooms with engaging activities and fun. We saw lessons involving rubber skeletons from which you could pull teeth ('so it's important to look after them'), an exciting lesson on air raids in WW2, drawing and French lessons. Masses of space for playing around, including an Astroturf area laid by the ubiquitous groundsman. Compulsory recorder lessons and rhythmic clapping to music. A marvellous introduction to the Cottesmore adventure. It is planned to have a maximum of 45 children.

Coworth-Flexlands School

Valley End, Chobham, Chobham, Woking, Surrey, GU24 8TE

• Pupils: 140 girls, 15 boys, including nursery, all day • Ages: 3-11, boys until 7 • Inter-denom • Fees: £3,885-£10,185 pa • Independent

Tel: 01276 855 707
Fax: 01276 856 043
Email: admissions@coworthflexlands.co.uk
Website: www.coworthflexlands.co.uk

Head: Since September 2010, Mrs Anne Sweeny MA DipEd (fifties), previously deputy head of Maltmans Green. A maths graduate from Aberdeen University, her career teaching maths at senior schools and in further education was interrupted by having four children in quick succession. When her youngest child went to nursery, a friend asked her to fill a pre-school vacancy, and she discovered a fascination with how young children learn. 'I realise that the foundations for a life-long intellectual curiosity and love of learning are laid down early and nurtured by teachers who have the interests of children at the heart of all they do.' Keen on spending time on her allotment, and bee-keeping.

Entrance: Non-selective. Places are offered following a meeting with the head and a tour and introduction to the school (together with the receipt of registration fee) on a first-come-first-served basis. Children join the nursery in the term they become three. The result of two merged schools, it is not yet full to capacity, so worth trying for vacancies at other times.

Exit: Papplewick, Lambrook, Haileybury and Woodcote House popular destinations for the boys when they leave at seven. Girls depart to a whole variety of places including St George's, Ascot, The Marist and Luckley Oakfield locally, but some move further afield to Guildford High, St Catherine's Bramley and Cheltenham Ladies' College. On average about five or six each year win scholarships.

Remarks: The school is set in 13 acres of grounds on the edge of Chobham Common and attracts pupils from the local (and very expensive) Surrey/Berkshire area – Chobham, Ascot, Windlesham and Woking. The school is centred on a large old house with later additions – something of a rabbit warren to find your way around, with new classrooms, music rooms, staff-room and ICT suite completed in 2007. Excellent library – well-stocked with lots of new books: pupils use the library during lesson time and are also encouraged to visit at lunchtimes when they can sit and read quietly on one of the comfy beanbags.

Average class size is smallish: 18–20 or fewer in some years as the year group has been split into two where space allows. Year group sizes vary as a result of the merger. Several young and enthusiastic staff members and 'some who have been there for a very long time', according to one parent. Head is very proud that this non-selective school achieves good SATs results and that many pupils go on to gain places (and also scholarships) at some top senior schools – she is convinced they do well because they do not pressurise the children. Pupils are encouraged to be enthusiastic and creative and to follow a broad-based curriculum. School offers SEN assistance readily to those who require it. They can cater for dyslexia, dyspraxia, hearing impairment and physical disability and also offer a gifted child programme. There are two SEN qualified staff members and the school is happy to discuss individual requirements. Maybe not top of an SEN school list, but the relaxed and happy atmosphere combined with lack of academic pressure could make this a good choice.

Sport is compulsory for all and children are encouraged to take part in a variety of activities including netball, rounders, athletics and swimming once a week in Woking for Years 2–6. About half the children play an instrument – they have a free choice; piano is very popular, as is guitar; others learn cello, clarinet, sax and one is even learning the double bass. Music lessons are timetabled mainly before and after school to minimise class disruption, which is a popular move with staff and parents. Pupils take part in the local Chobham music festival and put on a musical production each summer.

Very attractive uniform – blue tartan pinafores or kilts for the girls and the more usual grey shorts or trousers for the boys; the younger ones wear tracksuits in the nursery – 'very practical', commented parents. Lunch is excellent, said the staff, and this was confirmed by pupils. All have a hot meal cooked on site, with a choice of salads.

Pupils are encouraged in areas of decision-making – two representatives from each year are on the school council and attend weekly meetings chaired by a member of staff. A lively place throughout the day, and this continues after school with all the usual extra-curricular activities, including clubs for gardening, science and homework (groan!). The school also has its own Rainbow and Brownie packs. Outside space is good – a fantastic adventure playground and a separate smaller area for the younger children. Pupils have access to the extensive school grounds and playing fields. Security is tight with key pad entry and the front of the school is completely enclosed.

The six 'golden rules' are displayed all around the place. Lovely family atmosphere and the pupils are friendly and polite. Mrs Stephen is keen to send her pupils away confident in their own abilities (whatever they may be) and with high self-esteem. A delightful school with a vision of developing the whole child – an ethos which pleases parents, together with the good results achieved in a relaxed atmosphere.

Craigclowan School

Edinburgh Road, Perth, Perth, Perthshire, PH2 8PS

• Pupils: 285 boys and girls, plus 35 or so in the nursery (it comes and goes). All day • Ages: 5-13, 3-5 in nursery • Inter-denom • Fees: £9,630 pa • Independent

Tel: 01738 626 310
Fax: 01738 440 349
Email: headmaster@craigclowan-school.co.uk
Website: www.craigclowan-school.co.uk

Headmaster: Since April 2007, Mr Andy Rathborne BA (mid-forties). Educated at Latymer Upper School and University of East Anglia (Education – middle years). Returned to Latymer to begin his teaching career before spending 17 years at Caldicott Prep as head of maths, director of games and activities and ultimately as deputy head. A lover of sport, he currently coaches rugby and cricket. Taking over after nigh-on 30 years of a brilliantly idiosyncratic predecessor, he has been occupied with the things a conventional head has to do, though not going 'over the top with health and safety'. No major changes, as 'the school was in very good heart', but improvements: streamlining parental contact (form tutors now deal with educational and pastoral issues), improving parking/drop-off arrangements and school report formats, moving the rocking horse to the waiting area for very young visitors and setting up a committee to revamp the defunct kitchen garden. This is a real eco-schools project with advice from his own and local primary pupils, aiming for pond-dipping, main-school and pre-school play areas and community participation. The mixed age eco-group audits the school energy use and challenges the head on issues such as quality of insulation. His wife, Alex, helps wherever and whenever: hearing the little ones read, teaching SEN pupils and hotting up the 'very traditional Scottish' food to Jamie Oliver's standards (admitting to an uphill struggle). The family lives on site and she finds the activity-crammed Craigclowan week 'as busy as boarding school'. Two sons, one at Craigclowan, the other at Strathallan. They love Scotland and live – when they can, briefly, tear themselves away – in Cornwall.

The Rathbornes report 'no great change in ethos' having inherited a talented devoted staff who are 'embracing change'. There have been some replacements, largely with younger staff. If bullying happens Mr Rathborne believes in dealing firmly and keeping parents informed so there are 'no nasty surprises!' He likes it that Scottish children seem less rushed into adulthood than down south and thinks they have more fun and naturally good manners which flourish when encouraged.

Entrance: Children from all over the northern central belt; usually within 40 minutes travel/30 mile radius, middle-class professionals, plus a toff or two. Large number of first-time buyers.

Exit: 70 per cent go relatively locally – Glenalmond, Strathallan, Fettes, Merchiston, St Leonards, Kilgraston, Dollar and Dundee High. A few down south; trickle to Queen Margaret's York, Harrow, Eton, Oundle. All to their first choice of school over the last three years, 15 or so scholarships a year.

Remarks: Cunning conversion of amazing Victorian mansion set in 13 acres of undulating urban Perth overlooking the M90. It's a wee bit drab inside the main building because it's made of solid concrete which does not encourage picture-hanging. The newly-completed block, which mirrors the rather grand clock-towered classrooms, zings with activity. A jazzy new fully-equipped lab, impressive though not lavish computers, art room full of sound but adventurous work, bright rooms (pictures of the whole class on every door) and books everywhere. Enthusiastic and articulate pupils of all stages chat informatively about their lessons and show errant visitors where to go. New Astroturf for tennis and hockey plus a – very small – artificial ski slope. Tinies work in newish classrooms attached to the sports hall (they love using it), with spare waterproof ponchos and a welly cupboard so everyone can learn outside. Masses of mite-sized indoor equipment, including real carpentry tools and wood to use them on (the Care Commission saw and approved!)

Tartan everywhere. Two classes throughout, some streaming further up, but basically divided alphabetically, with those whose birthdays fall in the spring or summer joining the school the summer term before their fifth birthdays. French from nine (though some earlier exposure) with Latin also on the timetable. Fantastic multi-purpose sports hall, good music room well furnished with instruments, snazzy keyboards and mirrors galore. Learning support for 'any child who needs help for any reason, either for a long or a short term, and for the very able'. Two teachers for every year, plus trained support staff – we saw many children getting one-to-one attention in little work stations all over the main classroom block. Rewards are plus points for juniors, smiley stickers (because they like them best) and 'golden time' (activities of their choice). Sanctions: the sin bin.

Lots of foreign contact as well as regular tours abroad – part of the Comenius project. This is a vibrant, seven-day-a-week, co-ed day school, with classes on five days and a mass of extra-curricular activity. Parents can (and do) leave their young at 7.45am and collect them again at 6pm: nursery from 8.15 to 5.30. Late stayers – not otherwise occupied – finish prep before home-time. After-school time is charged at £4.50 per hour. PTA runs a lift-share and monthly second-hand uniform and sports equipment shop. New prospectus says it all (successfully) in pictures – with a bit of explanatory text thrown in for parents. Lots of involvement with Perth festival; all singing and dancing.

Craigholme Junior School

Linked to Craigholme School for Girls in the Senior section

72 St Andrew's Drive, Glasgow, G41 4HS

• Pupils: 250 girls; all day • Ages: 5-12 • Fees: £7,380-£8,790 pa • Independent

Tel: 0141 427 0375
Fax: 0141 427 6396
Email: admissions@craigholme.co.uk
Website: www.craigholme.co.uk

Headmistress: Junior school: Mrs Jeanette Smart; Nursery manager: Mrs Karen Grant.

Mrs Smart (late forties) has been head since 2005, having previously spent 18 years at The High School of Glasgow, latterly as deputy head. She works 'as a team' with Mrs Stobo (head of senior school – see entry) and was appointed a year before her from the same school, and says Craigholme was one of the few schools she really wanted to go to. Brimming with enthusiasm, she is very much in touch with pupils and their activities: J6's newspaper assignment, the Victorians theme in J5, and the planned J6 visit to the Lake District.

Entrance: Applications welcome from girls at all stages but traditional entry points are nursery and first or sixth year juniors.

Exit: Most to senior school.

Remarks: Upper junior school is attached to the senior school but the nursery (Little Stars), which takes boys, has a separate site on St Andrews Drive. Small classes; specialist French, IT, music and PE from nursery on. Top year takes selected subjects – science, art, home economics – in senior school. Lots of extra-curricular activities and care provided from 8am–6pm as an 'extra'.

Immediate plans include swapping round rooms to provide a library in what was a small classroom. Books and novels feature strongly in learning as 'preferable to the sort of snippets you get in reading books' and children start off with (Jolly) Phonics leavened with other methods as appropriate. 'Riding the crest of a wave', the junior choir and the training choir had won their respective Glasgow music festival prizes, and the cross-country teams came first among the Glasgow schools just before our visit. Successes, even small ones, build confidence, so all children have a personal 'magic moment file' recording their achievements, though Mrs Smart and Mrs Stobo agree that confidence is about being able to cope with whatever comes. This may include the experience of risk-taking and not always being equal to challenges – 'they have to explore their strengths and weaknesses in order to make informed decisions'. Careers advice starts in the juniors, and an impressive collection of professional parents is assembled to give short interviews to J6 reporters. Nursery is run in partnership with Glasgow city council, and qualifying families receive a refund on the fees.

Cranleigh Preparatory School

Linked to Cranleigh School in the Senior section

Horseshoe Lane, Cranleigh, GU6 8QH

• Pupils: 185 boys, 105 girls; 200 day, 90 board • Ages: 7-13 • Non-denom • Fees: Boarding £18,450; Day £11,760-£14,910 pa • Independent

Tel: 01483 542 058
Fax: 01483 277 136
Email: fmjb@cranprep.org
Website: www.cranprep.org

Headmaster: Since September 2008, Mr Michael Wilson BSc (late forties). Raised in Kenya with an early teaching tenure in Thailand, the travelled Mr Wilson can't keep away from Cranleigh – he was a teacher at the school in his very early career, left, returned as a deputy housemaster, left, returned as a housemaster, left to become head of Edge Grove Prep (where we liked him immensely) and is now back again. He's also been a professional tennis coach (Kenyan Davis Cup). Mr Wilson is a direct, yet friendly and good-humoured chap who is very serious about the business of education. He says he 'wasn't looking to move' when the headship of the school came up but sees the role as an opportunity to build on the work of his popular predecessor, Michael Roulston (of whom he is a fan).

Having come from the North London prep environment, it's clear he is delighted to be in Surrey where parents don't feel quite so pressured. Mr Wilson believes strongly that the role of head is one of leadership and being able to think creatively about the curriculum – he's backed this up with a boosted management team so he is freed up from the minutiae of every day school life. Married to Carolyn, an SEN specialist and now the school's SENCo; they have three boys: two at Cranleigh Senior, one at university. He sees himself and his wife very much as a leadership team – she balances his creative thinking with an eye on the paperwork 'I'm the blue sky thinker – she's the paper tiger' as he puts it. Parents say he is very child-focused – one commented how quickly he got to know the children's names. He's tightened up the general running of the place – 'he has plugged the gaps in admin and really improved communications,' says one happy customer. Mr Wilson is also hot on discipline, which has, according to one parent, been noticeably cranked up.

Entrance: Main entry points are 7+ and 11+. Pupils are selected on academic merit, and ability to contribute to the life of the school. However, Mr Wilson feels a flexible approach is important and the door is always open for those who don't get in first time round. At 7+ and 11+ pupils take written and/or oral assessments in English, maths and reasoning as well as assignments in art and sport. At 11+ the pupils also have an interview with a senior member of staff. Prospective pupils spend a day at the school and are observed for their interaction – it's not just about paper results but the whole person and how the Cranleigh ethos will suit them. Even in these straitened times, there is a waiting list, albeit shorter than before. However, Mr Wilson thinks that this can only be a good thing as, realistically, those on it will have a better chance of getting in.

Exit: About 70 per cent (fewer than previously) over the road to Cranleigh School. Mr Wilson doesn't believe it's a done deal that all children will head to the senior school and is very supportive of those who make other choices – indeed, will encourage it if it is the right choice for that child. Other senior schools include, for boys, Charterhouse, Eton, Wellington, Winchester, Marlborough, Tonbridge. For girls, St Catherine's Bramley, Downe House, Farlington, Guildford High, Prior's Field, Wellington and Hurstpierpoint. On average 18 scholarships a year.

Remarks: Dynamic, go-getting prep tempered with a reassuring warmth and friendliness. Ambitious and challenging academics but not at the expense of everything else. Currently Mr Wilson is focusing on driving forward 'the best aspects' of the IB primary years programme and complementing with a more energised curriculum and a more focused approach to Common Entrance in the upper school. Has kept on the universally praised 'fantastic' staff – Mr Wilson is a strong believer in professional development and investing in teachers. Joined-up thinking definitely encouraged e.g. the allotment project which linked WW2 history with photosynthesis, via art, maths and economics!

Curriculum differentiated increasingly as children move through school – children start off with in mixed ability groups with the majority of time spent with their form teacher, and in form 3 (Year 5) are streamed for English and maths. Beyond this, all subjects are streamed, with smaller groups in core subjects. Scholars' set in form 6 (Year 8).

Head believes the real key to success is managing parental expectation. Children whose parents have already decided that they will captain England in cricket may not be happy here, as Mr Wilson believes this can only have a negative effect. 'They wouldn't be happy anywhere,' he says. Parents can expect excellent communication with the school – form teachers are in regular email contact (which is 'much appreciated'), and the website now boasts enhanced revision notes as well as the usual info. Children's progress is closely monitored and communicated. Strong (and much improved, according to one parent) links with the senior school – 'we'd be mad not to use their resources,' says Mr Wilson. Two-way dialogue between the schools a regular thing – the prep school informing the senior as much as the other way round. Prep school benefits from the facilities as well as senior sports coaches, not to mention a 'dovetailed' curriculum.

SEN provision is big news here and very important – as Mr Wilson says 'we can't take every child with a learning difficulty, but when we assess at seven, we think how many we can cope with and do a good job'. He sees huge potential with those he does take and believes there are no barriers to success with the right support – currently 16 per cent have one-to-one support. The approach is fairly flexible and individually tailored, varying from one-to-one sessions up to three times a week (which parents pay for), to support within the classroom. Has beefed up the already strong SEN department, now headed up by Mrs Wilson – a situation which is proving hugely beneficial to all (not least because she has the ear of the headmaster – not something every SENCo can claim!). Mrs Wilson is full time, with one other full-timer plus one part-timer – the very renowned Elizabeth Holtom, author of Study Skills – the Complete Guide to Smart Learning (Galore Park), who also teaches all of the children study skills. G&T / scholars also approached creatively 'We don't just work them harder! We aim to create innovative, creative forward thinkers.'

On a musical note, vast range of activities on offer from singing lessons to electronic music. Lots of individual music lessons (27 specialists teaching 400 lessons a week – 85 per cent of pupils learn a musical instrument). Dance teacher gets a pat on the back for getting boys up on their feet – street dance is very popular with the boys here. Impressive drama and art facilities – director of art believes everyone capable of doing amazing things, which is obviously filtering through to pupils as standard is extremely good and children's art is everywhere round the school.

Sport is very definitely for all regardless of talent; the very unsporty may find this aspect tough but all are encouraged to do their best. One parent commented on the competitiveness for team places, and resultant disappointments. Whole gamut of usual sports; in addition, options for riding, squash, golf, judo, archery and Eton fives. Extra-curricular opportunities abound so pupils are busy, busy, busy all day and beyond – hence encouragement to board so that these can be enjoyed to the full. Boarding is actively on the agenda in the last couple of years: 'at 10 to 13 the children positively look for opportunities to be independent and boarding gives that opportunity – they can flex their wings in a nurturing environment'. No question that the boarding aspect of the school adds another edge to the prep school atmosphere, but this constant go-getting all day atmosphere is not for everyone: Dreamy Douglas, Trembly Tess and the-sit-down-and-read-a-book-at-home types may feel it is all too much. Head has listened to parents on the thorny subject of Saturday school and form 1 (Year 3) are no longer required to turn up on Saturdays, although Saturday school is for everyone else, every alternate weekend.

School located opposite its big sister, Cranleigh, and in the same lucky location of rolling Surrey countryside. Money has obviously been chucked at the place but it has been done with intelligence. Integrity of the original buildings has been kept whilst transforming the interior into a light, bright and breezy welcoming environment. Reception area is full of squashy sofas, giving impression of a swish hotel. Design and technology block impressive. Inventions are created on computers and then made in the workshop which is gadget heaven – every possible piece of machinery is available there. Dorms are light and bright – again with really attractive furnishings. One has a funky living room called 'the Ikea Room' – apparently according to matron because some brave soul went to Ikea and bought all the furnishings in one go. Matrons seem lovely – 'you can always talk to them,' said a pupil.

Pupils are a self-possessed and happy bunch. Parents are mostly local, middle class professionals. The school is currently riding high and is becoming increasingly popular out of the immediate area.

Cranmore School

Epsom Road, West Horsley, Leatherhead, Surrey, KT24 6AT

• Pupils: 450 boys; all day • Ages: Boys 4-13, co-educational nursery 2-4
• RC, but other denominations welcomed • Fees: £8,775-£10,650 pa
• Independent

Tel: 01483 280340
Fax: 01483 280341
Email: helenperry@cranmoreprep.co.uk
Website: www.cranmoreprep.co.uk

Headmaster: Since September 2006, Mr Michael Connolly BSc BA MA MEd (late forties). Formerly 12 years as head of, and credited with giving a big boost to, Barrow Hills School in Godalming. Previously, he gained extensive experience working in several HMC senior schools. String of letters after his name is testament to his sentiment that learning 'doesn't just stop at adulthood but is an ongoing process', a view demonstrated by his commitment to staff development and a keenness to instil a love of learning in the pupils. Reserved but professional – 'his sense of order and discipline was much needed,' approves a parent, though his underlying warmth smashes the physicist stereotype. Knows lots about how boys tick as is married with three teenage sons – one of them provided 'valuable feedback from the ground', spending his final prep school year at Cranmore as his dad started his headship.

Very straightforward and level-headed, he relates well to all the different needs and personalities of a school community. His varied interests (his further degrees are in philosophy and theology) and playing football outside school mean that he can engage with parents and boys on many levels. He appears to have a huge sensitivity to those who, perhaps, would never make first XV or be scholars. Undoubtedly bringing a breath of fresh air to the school, and he is carrying parents with him. Keep watching this space as Mr Connolly has not stopped yet; he enjoys the immediacy of prep schools – 'You can make a difference quickly'. Lives on site and Mrs Connolly also very much involved in school life.

Entrance: Non-selective entry for nursery and reception. Boys entering thereafter are interviewed and spend a day at school, joining a class in their age group. Tests given in literacy, numeracy and receptive vocabulary. For entry from Year 4, also a verbal reasoning test.

Exit: A few leave at 11+ but most at 13+. About a third to the tiptop Royal Grammar School, Guildford. St John's Leatherhead, Epsom College and Cranleigh also all well represented with handfuls to St George's College, Weybridge and Charterhouse among others. Good sprinkling of scholarships, academic, sports and all-rounder – with a sizeable proportion to Royal Grammar.

Remarks: Large, strong, Catholic (which it wears relatively lightly) prep school moving into a new era – continuing to do everything well, but now doing it with more sensitivity. Original Victorian building buried deep within leafy site, with more and more impressive facilities bolted around periphery. Very busy place, positively humming with activity. Nursery boys given refuge in own purpose-built classrooms opening onto colourful play areas, attractive picket-fencing protecting tinies from the exuberance of older boys. 'Their day is more structured here than at most other nurseries,' approves one mother. Joint assemblies make for a seamless transition to juniors. Having started 'school proper', boys move from lower to middle preps, both housed in bright modern classrooms facing terraced play area with glorious views of manicured playing fields and trees beyond. Here they become exposed to subject specialists in music and swimming and have 'golden time', a much appreciated free choice from huge range of activities on Friday afternoons.

Be under no illusion, though – this is an unashamedly academic school. 'Boys are stretched without feeling it (!),' claims a delighted parent. Specialist teaching begins in earnest at Year 4, though school very keen to prevent 'boys getting lost through the gaps'. Scrapping of streaming at age eight – 'Too early to tell,' says Mr Connolly – was among first of his popular changes. Now streaming only for Years 7 and 8 – final CE syllabus where boys are channelled into scholarship class or one of two other parallel classes. Setting for separate subjects further tailors learning to the individual. Separate sciences taught in three huge, well-equipped labs – the envy of many a secondary school. Mr Connolly teaches physics and philosophy (to senior boys), the latter surprisingly popular – 'Really helping to develop their analytical skills'.

Emphasis on academia means 'a rising tide lifts all ships'. Any ships in need of a little extra lifting are well-supported by the progress unit. At extra charge, the highly-praised unit provides small group work or one-to-one tuition for boys with (in reality no more than) mild learning difficulties. Run by one full-time and several part-time specialists; about 20 per cent of boys receive help at some stage.

Amazing sports facilities are what sells the school to many parents, and previous gripes about under-utilisation and lacklustre coaching seem to have been put to rest with reorganisation of the sports department. Now separate masters in charge for main three sports – football with considerable Chelsea FC input, rugby and cricket. School says: 'A real coup was the appointment in summer 2010 of Barry Everitt, of London Irish and Northampton fame – one of the most prolific scorers in premier rugby'. Regularly fields up to 'I' (yes, really I, not just A and B) teams in some sports. The 24-acre grounds are constantly being upgraded and improved – at time of our visit, levelling and the addition of yet more Astroturf pitches were well under way. Athletics track, six-hole golf course, four Astroturf courts, enormous sports hall with cricket nets (used also by Surrey CC for winter training), gym with climbing walls (not just a token – enough for whole class to use at once) and three squash courts in operation with another which has been converted into an outstanding, fully-equipped fitness centre. One of very few prep schools to offer rowing and to use Sandown Park dry ski slope – genuine ski club rather than just the annual school ski trip. With 26 sports on offer it is no wonder that sport is extremely important at Cranmore – proof is in the silverware!

Music, too, very strong. Over 50 per cent of boys learn instruments – standards currently ranging up to an impressive grade seven. Annually, usually two or three boys win music scholarships. Loads of opportunity for involvement in endless list of bands, groups, orchestras and choirs. Concerts, recitals abound – the music department's timetable for lessons/practices is truly mind-blowing.

Parents previously complaining of complacency and staleness appreciate a new vigour in the school. 'His [Mr Connolly's] ideas are the injection the school was ready for.' Improving communication between school and parents has been a priority of new leadership, with more emphasis on pastoral role of form teachers. Also an interesting initiative to prevent jaundice in school life – awareness that many boys by Year 8 will have been at Cranmore for 10 years has prompted black blazers (rest of school wear maroon) swapped on old-for-new basis, which has given recognition of seniority and, by extension, responsibility to older boys. Idea very popular with both pupils and parents. Fabulous new common room for Year 8 with pool table, PlayStation, newspapers, hot chocolate ... will also help to put 'clear blue water between seniors and what has gone before'.

Active parents' association: lots of socials including a few fund-raisers for those little extras and occasionally a big project – last year another minibus to add to the fleet (boys need to get to all those matches somehow!). The buses are also put to good use in mornings and evenings to ferry boys from far-flung corners of Surrey – Dorking, Pirbright, Weybridge, and Wonersh. 'We come here because we like the school, not because it is the nearest,' acknowledges one mother.

A buzzing place turning out charming, happy boys who thrive in this well-ordered environment.

Croydon High Junior School

Linked to Croydon High School in the Senior section

Old Farleigh Road, Selsdon, South Croydon, Surrey, CR2 8YB

• Pupils: 270 girls; all day • Ages: 3-11 • Fees: £6,966-£9,027 pa • Independent

Tel: 0208 260 7508
Fax: 0208 260 7462
Email: info2@cry.gdst.net
Website: www.croydonhigh.gdst.net

Head: Since 2007, Mrs Vivien Sergeant, previously deputy head and an old Croydonian herself.

Entrance: From 3+ into the nursery, then by assessment from 4+ and subsequent year groups.

Exit: At 11+ around 70 per cent continue to the senior school; leavers tend to opt for local grammar schools.

Remarks: Offers plenty of opportunities for children to excel in music, art, sport and academics. Everyone has the opportunity to learn a string instrument in Year 3, quite a few budding cellists look set to impress. Introductory courses in Spanish, German and French to tempt young linguists. Imaginative art displays throughout the corridors and classrooms.

Culford Preparatory School and Pre-Prep

Linked to Culford School in the Senior section

Culford, Bury St Edmunds, Suffolk, IP28 6TX

• Pupils: 230 boys and girls (125 boys, 105 girls); boarding and day • Ages: 3-13; takes boarders from age 7. • Fees: Day £9030-£12,660; Boarding £17,340-£18,600; Pre Prep £7,350-£8,070 pa • Independent

Tel: 01284 385 383
Fax: 01284 385 409
Email: admissions@culford.co.uk
Website: www.culford.co.uk

Headmaster: Mr Michael Schofield BEd (Hons) (mid forties), taught history and games at a boys' grammar school for five years and head of 11–18 day house. Then at a co-ed grant maintained school where he was sixth form master, head of politics and games teacher. Most recently, at Culford Senior School, ran a senior boys' boarding house and was senior housemaster (part of senior management team). Has always taken an active role in coaching all major games along with, most recently, being master in charge of school golf, plus supporting charity work such as the British Heart Foundation, for the past 11 years. Outside interests include dog walking, mountain biking, skiing and reading historical novels.

Aim is to re-affirm traditional values of respect and responsibility in all members of the school community, whilst ensuring an all-round education which is challenging, enriching and fun.

Entrance: Admission at 7+ and 11+: entrance papers in English, mathematics and non-verbal tests, plus satisfactory school reference and recent school report. Entry at other ages consists of similar papers at age-appropriate levels, again with satisfactory school reference and recent school report.

Academic scholarships at 7+; academic, music, sports, tennis and Jubilee (all-rounder boarding scholarships) at 11+.

Exit: Pupils prepared for Common Entrance. The majority proceed to senior school at 13.

Remarks: For further details, see senior school.

Cumnor House School (Croydon)

168 Pampisford Road, South Croydon, Surrey, CR2 6DA

• Pupils: 395 boys in the prep and pre-prep, with 60 boys and 15 girls in the nursery • Ages: 2-13 • Christian • Fees: Nursery £7,425; Pre-Prep £8,010; Prep £9,600 pa • Independent

Tel: 020 8660 3445
Fax: 020 8660 3445
Email: admin@cumnorhouse.com
Website: www.cumnorhouse.com

Headmaster: Since 1999, Mr Peter Clare-Hunt MA CertEd (fifties). Previously at St Dunstan's College and then Northcote Lodge Preparatory School, so experience in both senior and preparatory schools before joining Cumnor House as assistant headmaster in 1998, before taking over as headmaster in 1999. He has a number of years to serve in the school, the retirement age being reasonably flexible. The school was formerly owned by Mr and Mrs Jenkins, but was bought by Cognita in 2008.

Entrance: Boys from the school's Treetops Nursery pass into the pre-prep without examination in order of registration. For entry at reception level the head of pre-prep meets the child and parents and places are offered if the child meets 'fairly basic' criteria. For entry into the prep school an assessment (one-to-one meeting with the heads of maths and English, and the headmaster) but no formal tests. The school recruits at a number of ages – into Treetops at two, into the pre-prep, the lower school and at 11+. Approximately 34 places each year for entry into the nursery and usually 54 places in reception. Occasional places are available in other year groups depending on numbers; around 50 boys per year in 7-11 age classes in the prep, divided into three classes. Usually around 20 boys will leave at 11+ for senior schools. Some boys join at 11+, typically those who have failed to gain entry to their chosen schools, and are prepared for entry to senior schools at 13+, very successfully.

Exit: Mr Clare-Hunt is keen, as are most prep school heads, to keep boys until they are 13 – in his view that is the optimum time to move, when they have matured within the safe surroundings of the smaller school and are ready for the big wide world of senior school. Not all parents agree, and quite a few boys move on at 11+, some to local grammar schools, others to day schools in the area such as Trinity, Whitgift, Wilson's Grammar School and Wallington County Grammar School. Boys planning to do this get a certain amount of good-natured teasing from the headmaster which they take in good part. Those who stay till 13 will go to these schools too, but also some further afield to Charterhouse, Tonbridge, Westminster, Winchester, Eton, Epsom, Caterham and Royal Russell. Most boys pass into the schools of their choice, and Mr Clare-Hunt is particularly pleased that those who join at 11+ will frequently pass at 13+ into schools which failed them at 11. The school wins a number of scholarships every year, and clearly takes considerable trouble to prepare its boys for entry and for scholarship, and to fit each boy to what they believe is the right school.

Remarks: 'Boys will be boys.' Cumnor House has about 360 of them, and is a fantastic mix of cultures as they all rush around the playground, bundle into lessons and sing their hearts out in one of the many choirs. An immediate impression is one of energy purposefully contained within a relatively confined space. The school prides itself on being multi-racial and multi-cultural, and encourages knowledge, understanding and tolerance of all faiths, within a predominantly Christian setting. The boys are incredibly polite and headmaster stresses that good manners, kindness and looking after one another are reinforced all the time. It certainly works on the good manners front – boys leap to their feet, greet the headmaster (who responds by name) and visitors both individually and collectively. No chance of sneaking into this school unnoticed for a quick inspection. The boys relate easily to their teachers, plenty of confidence and, mostly, eye contact, and teachers eat with the boys and are much in evidence at breaks.

Housed in a series of, well, houses, one of which is The Music House, where the music that is one of the school's strengths is created. A maze of classrooms and corridors, laboratories, ICT suite, library, dining room and hall. The site presents its challenges, and 'a quart into a pint pot' springs to mind, but there's a generous playground and boys rush around at breaks walloping balls of all kinds. Cricketers feel particularly at home (Mr Clare-Hunt played good club cricket at semi-professional level and there are some first class cricketers amongst the old boys); the Cumnor House rule is no balls hit above knee height or you are out! Good training for the MCC. Cricketers have recently toured the Caribbean (Trinidad and Tobago/Grenada/Barbados), Dubai and South Africa. Younger footballers (Colts aged 9–11) also tour Holland every year in October.

There is a quiet garden (monitored by boys) for those who don't thrill to the hurly burly, and an enticing indoor swimming pool. Down the road is a tremendous playing field, bought from the local council. The view is splendid, with the Wembley arch in clear sight, although no doubt the boys don't have the time to notice. Ample room for sports, with the possibility of developing the site further. Treetops, Cumnor House's nursery, is shortly to be moved into an extended house on the playing field. Run by a tremendous enthusiast who wants to make hers the best nursery in the country.

The main school has three departments – pre-prep, lower school and upper school. All are housed under the one roof and the rabbit warren of classrooms lead out of one another – easy to get lost. Pervasive air of purposeful activity. Traditional prep school setting, traditional teaching, classrooms traditionally arranged with the desks in rows, occasionally grouped into pairs. An emphasis on academic attainment, endeavour, splendid results. Honour boards line the walls. Mixed ability until Year 6 when boys are streamed across the board by ability, with a scholarship set and one or two others. Uniform – grey with red touches – and while the occasional shirt tail sneaks out, most boys are smart in their red blazers.

Great emphasis on extra-curricular activities. A major drama production every year, numerous concerts, and sport plays a very important part in the life of the school. Refreshingly honest reports as to sporting successes and the lack of them pepper the school's termly newsletter but the school is justly proud of its sporting record, regards sport as one of its greatest assets, and achievement in the sporting area as very important to the school's morale. All boys introduced to orchestral instruments and over 200 take individual music lessons. Brass instruments are most popular and the head of music is an exacting enthusiast who extracts powerful performances. Very proud of having recently won two music scholarships to Westminster School. There are numerous tours and trips (the choir went to Rome in 2007 to sing in St Peter's, cricketers regularly tour in South Africa, skiers go to Alpe D'Huez) and the school tries to help parents who find it hard to afford the costs.

Parents are on the whole very happy with the standard of teaching and with the way the headmaster deals with any problems. Parents say he is a man of principle, one who knows his boys as individuals and is concerned to develop their unique potential. The school's staff are pretty committed and share the same aim. There is a general impression that Cumnor House has come up in recent years – staff turnover has decreased, sporting achievement and the variety of sports on offer have improved. General satisfaction at the standard of teaching, with parents citing some excellent commitment on the part of some teachers and a general commitment to academic achievement and the fulfilling of individual potential. Parents love the school's often-stressed good manners policy, and the only downside of this is that boys entering at 11+ sometimes take a certain amount of training to adapt.

An impressive school for a number of reasons. Boys' energies channelled all day – they rush purposefully around the school and playground. Integrated multi-cultural mix throughout the school but one doesn't have to be a sporting conformist to enjoy Cumnor House; music, art and drama also absorb. Parents stress the happiness of their sons and their achievements. The downside is the site and the buildings, which are not spacious and often rather utilitarian, although the neighbourhood is pleasant. The sports field is a major asset and school has plans to exploit this further.

Cumnor House School (Haywards Heath)

Danehill, Haywards Heath, West Sussex, RH17 7HT

• Pupils: 365: 185 boys, 180 girls (40 boys, 30 girls currently board)
• Ages: 7-13, pre-prep 4-7 • C of E • Fees: Pre-prep £8,100; Prep day £15,315; Boarding £18,210 pa • Independent

Tel: 01825 790 347
Fax: 01825 790 910
Email: registrar@cumnor.co.uk
Website: www.cumnor.co.uk

Head: Since 2001, Mr Christian Heinrich BA PGCE (late forties), educated University of Kent and Westminster College, Oxford. Previously 15 years at Summerfields as housemaster, then head of junior school (1990) and deputy head (1998). Approachable (by children – 'What socks have you got on today?'; parents, 'I saw him this morning as mine were getting out of the car,' and staff, 'Shall I take the staff meeting?') and sensible: he has expanded the school while preserving the homely atmosphere – he knows all the children individually. Married to Belinda (teaches French in the pre-prep) with four of their own, the youngest still at Cumnor and the eldest at Manchester University. He covers different subjects depending on the staff and timetable – at present the bottom set of CE Latin (Latin car names – Audi, Fiat?), previously ICT, history, English, French ... Big believer in the value of inspections (senior management team do not escape) and training (GTTP – proud of deputy head appointments for protégées, now hoping for a headship).

As the chairman of the district and district representative for the IAPS, governor of another prep, an ISI inspector of schools and a trainer of other heads, he's not interested in moving to a bigger and more mainstream prep – 'I've got other greasy poles to climb!' With all these rôles he's well aware of the difficulties facing small schools at present and is keen to avoid aggressive competition in the local area. The five per cent sibling discount has just been removed to provide a full bursary for a local child – he's canny but realistic, empathetic and transparent, very reassuring in these financially strained times. Built new theatre on raised funds – 50:50 school resources and personal appeal (£700,000) – so he's certainly an effective communicator. Numbers are stable at present – a third reception class is an unusual 'temporary' measure to accommodate an influx of siblings.

Holds two parents' meetings per year for each age group – one with canapés, one with a sitdown dinner (very hard-working, creative, effective and popular chef – his home economics class is oversubscribed); friendships develop – 'You'll not find many wallflowers in the car park at Cumnor'.

Entrance: Non-selective at reception – thereafter by interview. Waiting list at present has 25 per cent ex-London parents. No marketing bar word of mouth. Headmaster spends time with prospective parents and pupils 'making sure they are comfortable with the feel and culture of the place'. Many parents are city commuters – the general trend out of London after 9/11 has been a factor in the growth of the school; lots of children come from a London pre-prep. City commuters and local country professionals live mostly within 30-minute radius – a real local (albeit recently local) feel, with 80 per cent of the children at Thursday night cricket in Fletching (nearest village) coming from Cumnor.

Exit: A feeder to no school – pupils head off to an enormous range; could say every pupil gets to their first choice, but that choice is guided by in-depth consultation with head and staff. Head and his wife visit schools continually and try a couple of new ones each year. Over past seven years, leavers have gone to 41 different schools, including Benenden, Tonbridge, King's Canterbury, Charterhouse, Lancing, Eastbourne, Brighton College, Eton, Radley, Wycombe Abbey; high percentage to boarding schools. Record-breaking number of scholarships recently – 27 in one year.

Remarks: Beautiful site – no buildings taller than two storeys and 62 acres of fields, trees, games pitches, sports hall, theatre, children's allotments and an old swimming pond – you get banned from it for a week if you fall off the raft or ropeswing into its grubby waters. The Old Library and the terrace outside it are the main gathering points – snooker and table-tennis tables, bikes, British Bulldogs, cricket nets; no Wii, X-boxes or iPods, some arrangement for Skype for boarders. In the summer the children can run around until 8.30 at night, with a small break for second prep – only the Easyjet flight path breaks the idyll. Once they're in bed it's time for reading (no magazines for girls, boys anything as long as they're quiet!). Yet everyone also learns to touchtype from Year 3 and there's thumbprint recognition in the library – no anachronisms here.

Differentiates itself from local peer preps by being larger and without compulsory boarding, although practically every child in their final year opts to board (full or flexi – two or three consecutive nights per week, no hot-bedding, same group of friends) – a good taster of what is to come at many of their senior schools. Two wings – pine beds or bunkbeds in carpeted dorms with names that change each term; haircuts and strange fears when we visited (arachibutyrophobia – fear of peanut butter sticking to the roof of the mouth?). Residential housemaster and mistress, six Gappers and a nurse (trained in paediatrics) in school from 8am until 6pm and on call locally outside those times.

Originally a small, quirky family-run prep school. Although numbers have grown, it is still quirky – parents hope desperately this will not be lost – and the current head is apparently in for the long haul, although he's not related to the founders. Staff:pupil ratio is still 1:7, all pre-prep classes have teacher and assistant and are capped at 16. Sets from Year 6 upwards for maths, English and science with three mixed-ability classes for PE, DT (all manner of automata being made during our visit), drama and music. The curriculum has been broadened to make sure what you do at Year 3, you do at Year 8 as well, e.g. class music lessons all the way through to the top.

Years 6 and onwards choose their own personal tutor and have 10 minutes of dedicated time with them per week; every five weeks the entire staff go through a list of all the children to check for any issues. A freshly inaugurated anti-bullying committee consisting of five senior boys and five senior girls. The house captains (Red, Black, Blue and White – points tallied for good work, house music, sport and general knowledge) and heads of school change every term – one of their responsibilities is to manage the 'kiss and fly' first thing in the morning, opening doors and rolling young ones out of their parents' cars, avoiding traffic jams, speeding up the flow and encouraging inter-year friendships. Since the pre-prep is housed in the middle of the campus (lovely classrooms in the eaves of converted barns), a lot of caring between across age groups. Compulsory to sit boy/girl throughout prep school, and if everyone manages that ratio in assembly a fairy cake each for break the next day.

Learning support department has a full time SENCo (parents say fabulous, can phone her with questions at any time); main aim is to integrate children as thoroughly as possible so first level of support is help in class. Since reception is non-selective it's no surprise that 35 per cent of school has been screened – 'If we take them in, we stand by them' – and then one-to-one work if necessary (12 per cent).

The head of PE is an ex-professional footballer (rumoured to be still sponsored by Nike?!) who has done away with the traditional aggression of competitions (although school still unbeaten in rugby some years); instead sees training, mindset and enjoyment as being much more important. Very full and successful fixture list, particularly strong in athletics and swimming (new 25m indoor pool certainly helps – local primary kids walk through grounds to use it too). Sports hall with web of indoor pitch lines and all kit laundered onsite (parents love this). Sports tour to Cape Town and new relationship with a South African charity being built. Noticeboard for results by dining room (polite children queuing behind us went ahead while we were peering at them) and four screens around school detailing events, weather, matches, birthdays, thought for the day and any messages – they seem to be read.

Everyone has to try a musical instrument when they first arrive and few drop out – 95 per cent of the prep take individual lessons and the first orchestra is 45 strong. Parents particularly enjoy the yearly jazz day where the children learn from external musicians and perform in the evening. A school trip to Cothill House's chateau every summer also gives them a chance to perform at the local cathedral. Keyboards used a lot post-scholarship for Garage Band – a Mac application for composition. Most recent development is a dedicated barn for music recording and technology.

Art takes place in another converted barn, all manner of creations hanging from the roof and cursive script (tradition of winning competitions) being practised under teacher's beady eye. 'Occupations' are a series of after school activities and range from cricket through Lego to make-up – stories of very convincing cuts and bruises eliciting sympathy from matron.

Drama in spanking new public school-standard theatre (time capsule buried underneath) with pupil-operated sound and lighting room (parent and actor James Wilby was a consultant and performed two-hander recently) – acts as a cinema every Wednesday and Saturday evening, children bring duvets; big TV in main house is other venue. Shakespeare play performed yearly in outside Greek Theatre. Impressive performer alumni – Rebecca Hall, Simon Williams, Tyler Butterworth, Piers Morgan. A gem of a school.

Dame Allan's Juniors Fenham

Linked to Dame Allan's Juniors Forest Hall in the Junior section
Linked to Dame Allan's Girls School in the Senior section
Linked to Dame Allan's Boys School in the Senior section

Fowberry Crescent, Fenham, Newcastle upon Tyne, Tyne and Wear, NE4 9YJ

• Pupils: 85 boys, 50 girls; all day • Ages: 8-11 • Christian foundation
• Fees: £7,467 pa • Independent

Tel: 0191 275 0608
Fax: 0191 275 1502
Email: enquiries@dameallans.co.uk
Website: www.dameallans.co.uk

Head: Mr A J Edge, MA (St Andrews).

Remarks: For further details see Dame Allan's Boys School.

Dame Allan's Juniors Forest Hall

Linked to Dame Allan's Juniors Fenham in the Junior section

Linked to Dame Allan's Girls School in the Senior section

Linked to Dame Allan's Boys School in the Senior section

72 Station Road, Forest Hall, Newcastle upon Tyne, Tyne and Wear, NE12 9BQ

• Pupils: 120 boys and girls • Ages: 3-11 • Christian foundation
• Fees: £5,388 pa • Independent

Tel: 0191 266 2943
Email: fhjuniors@dameallans.co.uk

Remarks: A prep and pre-prep for Dame Allan's (qv).

Dame Bradbury's School

Ashdon Road, Saffron Walden, Essex, CB10 2AL

• Pupils: 270 girls and boys • Ages: 3-11 • C of E • Fees: Reception £7,065-£8,850 pa • Independent

Tel: 01799 522 348
Fax: 01799 516 762
Email: info@damebradburys.com
Website: www.damebradburys.com

Head: Since 2004, Mrs Jane Crouch MA NPQH (forties). Previously deputy head at Ashford School and Great Walstead. Has a strong sense of duty to all in her charge, but not in the least bit stuffy, and seems younger than her 'early forties'. Well liked by pupils and parents – professional, caring and approachable are common epithets – she's brought the school forward without denting its ethos. A believer in being 'out and about', she spends time in classroom taking PSHE lessons or listening to early readers and (following pleas from pupils) runs an after-school Lego club (having first introduced Warhammer, now run by the IT technician with assistance from a toy shop and two sixth formers at the local comprehensive). In her spare time she's involved with church youth work and for pure relaxation loves photographing wildlife, walking coastal paths or watching films with her husband – the in-house Father Christmas.

Entrance: Waiting list with sibling preference. For the nursery/reception, informal 'chat' with Mrs Crouch. Later entrants, depending on age: chat/observation in the classroom/tests in reading and writing. School purports to be non-selective but head says children are accepted on the basis that it 'can cater for their needs without detrimental effects to others' – pragmatic get-out clause.

Exit: Ready help from the head – if parents are particularly keen on a school that's new to her she makes it her business to visit. Healthy mix of destinations with The Leys, Perse Girls and Saffron Walden County High heading the list.

Remarks: Dame Johane Bradbury is named after its founder – the sister of an early 16th century rector of Saffron Walden. Today the school is situated in a quiet suburban street not far from the town centre. Slightly dour late Victorian edifice, plus new-builds tucked round the back, contrasts with the cosy, welcoming interior. A few tired bits (including the library) and a couple of rooms doubling as through routes – but on the whole the place is well maintained and improvements are ongoing. Look out for the inviting adventure equipment – a big draw in the playground.

Although school not considered overly pushy on the academic front, pupils are streamed and the most able stretched. Parents like the formal approach to learning and are impressed by the level of support from teachers (predominantly female) who 'don't see children as part of a herd' – 'They're tuned to the needs of each individual'. Good rapport between staff and pupils with plenty of questioning and encouragement at all levels. ICT (unusual but inspired choice of Macs instead of PCs – 'Fosters creativity,' said a member of staff) and French (native speaker for the older ones) right from the start. Classrooms lower down the school bulge with bright, visual stimuli and work is readily celebrated through display. Dedicated art and DT rooms with plenty of technically-proficient work on show.

SEN department, three teachers all with SpLD qualifications, caters for a range of needs – Asperger's, dyslexia, dyspraxia, speech and language development. 'Tracks' literacy scheme – 'It really works,' enthused one of the specialists – and sensible help for those who could do with the occasional boost – up to 10 per cent at any one time. 'They didn't let my son sit at the back but encouraged him to do his best – lots of extra help with English and writing twice a week before school,' said one grateful parent. Basic fees cover additional help (including motor skills sessions) of up to an hour a week – any more is charged.

Usual clutch of games on offer with girls getting a chance to opt for some traditional boys' sports. Large, purpose-built sports hall is a huge asset and parents are pleased the head has boosted boys' sport with the recent appointment of a boys' sport co-ordinator.

Number of yearly awards on offer. Note: packed lunches aren't an option. School lunches compulsory – no bad thing – but costs aren't included in the fees.

Children are well-behaved but not subdued – they're keen to explain and confidently venture opinions. One parent commented, 'They're studious in a relaxed atmosphere' – spot on. Manners and consideration towards others are high on the agenda – all have to shake hands with their teacher on leaving at the end of the day – and enlightened schemes encourage self-confidence coupled with a caring approach. Year 6s help in the nursery – 'I love it. They're soooo sweet,' said one girl – whilst all in Year 5 are trained as play leaders and each assigned to a pupil in Year 3 whom they hear read once a week. Music is on the timetable – just under half the juniors have instrumental tuition; four big productions a year which bring a tear to parental eyes – 'It's quite amazing what what they achieve – the standard is so high'.

Mixed bunch of parents – goodly proportion of professionals and 'lots of resourceful businesswomen'. Healthy PTA, with two parent representatives in every form, organises socials and promotes improvements – lunches are now wholesome and include home-grown fruit and vegetables from the PTA-funded teaching garden.

A flourishing place providing a safe, traditional education with plenty of emphasis on the skills needed to cope with life.

Danes Hill School

Leatherhead Road, Oxshott, Oxshott, Surrey, KT22 0JG

• Pupils: 465 boys, 400 girls, all day • Ages: 3–13 • Christian non-denom
• Fees: £9,585-£13,512 pa • Independent

Tel: 01372 842509
Fax: 01372 844452
Email: registrar@daneshillschool.co.uk
Website: www.daneshillschool.co.uk

Headmaster: Since January 2007, Mr Willie Murdock BA, PGCE (late forties). Studied classics at Queen's Belfast. Arrived at Danes Hill in 1984 to teach Latin and French and has been here ever since. He worked up through the ranks: year head, assistant head and five years as deputy head, before taking over after the untimely death of the previous head. Personable, calm and considered, he knows every aspect of the school, particularly his market – affluent, confident and driven – and ensures the school ticks all the boxes. Sees his role as 'managing continuous development', and adds 'we can't tolerate complacency'. A hands-on chap, he likes to get around the school every day, teaching Latin and German to Year 8s and PHSE to Year 5s. He takes the annual skiing trip, a Year 5 trip to France every summer and, when we visited, was about to take a group of Years 6, 7 and 8 to Berlin. This way he gets to know everyone and parents agree that he is 'very friendly and approachable', 'the kids like him', 'quietly getting on with things and doesn't make a big song and dance about it'. His appointment has obviously been good for continuity and the whole Murdock clan are Danes Hill through-and-through – his wife, Glynis, provides learning support at the school and he has two teenage daughters and a son, all of whom have been pupils here.

Entrance: Waiting lists are not generally an issue but they do exist for some year groups (although they do not operate more than two years ahead) so get names down early. Various entry points including at 3–4 and at 7–8, when they are tested in English, maths and reading. In such a large school, worth ringing at odd times to see what is available. No longer offers scholarships – Mr Murdock says, 'but we do offer bursaries'. New registrar is Carolyn Ward.

Exit: Boys and girls theoretically both leave at 13 (although about 20 per cent of girls exit at 11). Pupils go on to City of London Freemen's School, Epsom College, Royal Grammar School Guildford, King's Wimbledon and Guildford High School amongst others. Impressive list of school awards, particularly academic and sports, from a wide range of schools including St John's and Cranleigh. Last year, 29 scholarships into senior schools were awarded, including St Paul's, Brighton College, Epsom College and City of London Freemen's School. All children received offers from their first choice of senior school.

Remarks: A very large school with traditional values and a strong feeling of discipline and achievement. Academically strong with a broad curriculum and a very good level of general education. Main aim is to prepare children for CE and public school scholarships with a high success rate in both. Some parents feel not as much importance is put on 11+ and that the focus on girls leaving at 11 is lost.

So what about the school's reputation as an academic hothouse? Yes, academia is extremely important, yet there's a real sense of pride in helping the less able to achieve their best. According to the head, as long as your child shows 'enormous compassion and imagination' then their achievements are valued. On average, 20 pupils in each class but children are placed into small sets from Year 2 and scholarship streams from Year 6. Class groups are mixed at various stages, so children get the opportunity to make new friends. There is controlled discipline in the classroom – children stand automatically as you enter – and this is well balanced by 'friendly teachers who help to bring fun to the lessons.' Lots of hands-on experimentation and practical work. Computerised whiteboards in every classroom. Two noticeably impressive computer suites.

Unanimous parental comments that there are no weak teachers. Languages very strong – all introduced to three languages – more if they study the classics! – French throughout the school, a 'taster' course in Spanish and German (half a year each) in Year 4 and then either Spanish or German as the second modern language in Year 5. Works well – a very high pass rate for language GCSE at age 13 (all candidates scoring A* in 2009 and 2010). Lots of residential trips with very intense language study whilst abroad. Latin and classical Greek – about twenty 10 year olds studying this option.

Significant learning support unit that works hard to provide additional help. The unit also plucks out the very bright, gifted and talented children and enjoys bringing them on. Some parental feeling that 'there's not such a focus on the average child – who must be self-motivated to succeed.'

Great emphasis on the arts, many arts scholarships to senior schools – three separate art rooms (three-dimensional, graphic design and general). Some beautiful and very mature 3-D work and extremely enthusiastic specialist art teachers. Artwork adorns the walls in the most unexpected places and children use visual work in all areas of study. Design technology, drama, dance and music equally strong. Every year group presents an annual drama production involving every child in the year. A high percentage of pupils learn a musical instrument (up to grade 8) and many play more than one. Practice takes place at home although orchestra and ensembles, as well as choirs, rehearse in timetabled sessions at school. Vibrant jazz band and orchestra of 50+ players. Performances recently at Guildford Cathedral and St Margaret's, Westminster. Pupils also in the National Children's Orchestra and the National Children's Choir.

Sport flourishes, helped by the school's extensive grounds, and sporty children really thrive here. Grand display cabinet full of sporting trophies in the reception. Lots of tournaments. Rosslyn Park seven-a-side semi-finalists and finalists, and national biathlon champions. One parent comments, 'there's a huge focus on rugby. It's given so much priority each year that football peters out.' Despite this, there's such a variety of sport on offer that any child should find something to suit.

School site is large and wooded with many areas for the children to play and explore. Lovely natural feel, with beautiful sculptures and building names – The Rookery, The Ark. Tidy and litter-free. A real feel of history and tradition about the place – the school has only existed since 1947, but the Victorian buildings and choice of décor in reception areas make it appear more long-standing. New buildings have been sympathetically added to the main house, some temporary classrooms. Bevendean (pre-prep) site has been remodelled and includes a new double storey classroom block.

There's a feeling of strict order and control. Children don't mill around but move along with purpose. A large school. 'Without the size', the head says, 'Danes Hill would not be able to offer such a wide and well resourced curriculum with so many specialist teachers'. On the negative side, parents feel that the management structure stops them from talking directly to the head about day-to-day matters. Parental opinions vary from the disgruntled – 'It's hard to see the head. You are referred to the head of year or head of school' to the more positive, 'If you want to see the head he'll make time for you'. But it's often better to deal with the head of year 'because they know your child better'. Unanimous thumbs up for the head of the upper school – 'He is excellent. He's very in touch with the children' and 'lots of help when discussing where your child should go next'.

Pastoral care is much praised. Children taught to be responsible for their own actions from an early age. 'The school makes children very independent,' says one parent, 'They're very responsible. There's sex education and puberty education!' Good home cooking with plenty of healthy choices.

The large number of international children creates a unique atmosphere (there's even a specialist EAL teacher). The school is the only factor that binds all these disparate people together – may explain why there is such a strong sense of community. Parents are corporate chieftains and the like, and mostly rather wealthy. They put in a large amount of effort and commitment to the school and this is strongly encouraged by the head. A few comments that the parents form cliques. Drop-off and pick-up times are a nightmare – the entrance to the school is on the brow of a steep hill. School runs a bus service from and to the immediate surrounding areas (Walton, Weybridge, Esher, Claygate and Bookham).

Suits bright, confident, sporty children happy to get involved in school life and who would not get lost in the crowd.

Dean Close Preparatory School

Linked to Dean Close School in the Senior section

Lansdown Road, Cheltenham, Gloucestershire, GL51 6QS

• Pupils: 255 boys and girls, 65 board; pre-prep 145 boys and girls • Ages: 7-13; pre-prep 2.9-7 • C of E • Fees: Day £9,315-£15,240 pa; Boarding £15,555-£19,695 pa • Independent

Tel: 01242 258001
Fax: 01242 258 005
Email: dcpsoffice@deanclose.org.uk
Website: www.deanclose.org.uk/

Head: Since 2004, the Reverend Leonard Browne MA, educated at St Catharine's College, Cambridge where he read history and then theology. Won blue at both rugby and athletics. Began career at Clifton College where he taught history and RS. Subsequently ordained and entered parish work but still found time to coach schoolboy rugby. Initially chaplain and head of RS at senior school before taking up present appointment. Much-liked Christian rôle model with strong beliefs that fire his approach to pupils. Married to Alison, they have three children and a golden retriever. Loves sport, good literature, music and international food.

Entrance: Own exam (English, maths and VR) plus interview and current school report. Most of Year 3 entry from pre-prep but a third more pupils added at Year 7 from local preps and state primaries.

Exit: Possibly a few girls to Cheltenham Ladies' at 11+ but 90-95 per cent proceed to Dean Close School.

Remarks: Pre-prep, now well into its second decade. Enviable facility on Lansdown Road opened by Professor Robert Winston in 2004 (a pre-prep pupil featured in his TV Child of our Time documentary). Thoughtfully designed: large, multi-purpose hall, impressive ICT suite, super library and ground floor classrooms link via common creative areas. Sports facilities shared with prep. All Year 2s learn recorder; 20 currently learning piano or violin and informal concerts held twice per term. Visual environment and multi-sensory approach to early learning help 'squirrels' to get a good start.

Prep has distinctive combination of Georgian and modern buildings. Separated from senior school by extensive playing fields. Christian ethos kicks in more obviously at this stage but 'staff don't have to be tambourine-carrying Christians to work here'. Nevertheless, school has its own chaplain, three Christian unions and many committed Christian staff. 'We don't foist Christianity on any pupil,' insists head but Dean Close makes no apologies for 'walking its talk'.

Strong academic basis laid down in prep with emphasis on preparation for CE. Separate sciences and second foreign language introduced from Year 7. Oxford Latin course for brainboxes or combined Latin and classical civilisation for the rest. ICT well-embedded in all areas and two ICT suites (one of which curiously resembles US Starship Enterprise thanks to head's Trekkie predecessor). Constant upgrading of buildings: modern teaching facilities show up weary old assembly hall (apparently next on list for replacement). Covered play area for inclement weather where children are served extra drink and snacks twice a day. Pupils benefit from sharing first-rate sports facilities with senior school including super dance studio. Impressive art studios with wide range of work on display.

Lots of sports and all pupils will play for a team at least once a term: rugby, netball, hockey, cross-country, squash and athletics. School now incorporates choristers for Tewkesbury Abbey (Schola Cantorum) plus three other choirs. Eight girls in national children's choir; two boys in national children's orchestra. 80 per cent play instruments and pupils take exams up to grade 8 practical and grade 5 theory. Regular in-house performances plus plaudits and success at Cheltenham Festival of Performing Arts. Musical plays and annual concerts for ensembles, swing band etc plus emphasis on speech and drama.

School not one to embrace moderate or severe needs but individual and group support offered for numeracy, curriculum needs and mild dyslexia (only pupils allowed individual laptops). Good deal for EFL pupils. Strong pastoral care. Three day houses placed for easy pick-ups. Cosy, co-ed junior boarding house for youngest with lots for them to do; two separate boys' and girls' boarding houses (with own kitchen/common areas and roomy dormitories). Up to four day boarders allowed in each boarding house. Discipline firm but fair for all with easily understood credit and debit system. Boarding routine 'helps shape the week' says head with Saturday chapel, lessons and games a must. Own cafeteria provides healthy choices.

Communication with parents includes 'Hermes' (informative weekly newsletter), bi-annual reports, meetings and social groups. Range of academic awards and bursaries available from 11+. Former pupils include unfortunate former Rolling Stone Brian Jones and the late Bishop Jim Thompson, latterly Bishop of Bath and Wells.

An integral and successful part of the Dean Close brand with impressive facilities, strong teaching and a caring, Christian environment.

Derwent Lodge School

Linked to Somerhill Pre-prep in the Junior section

Linked to Schools At Somerhill (The) in the Junior section

Linked to Yardley Court in the Junior section

Schools at Somerhill, Tonbridge, Kent, TN11 0NJ

• Pupils: 140 • Fees: £11,910 pa • Independent

Tel: 01732 352 124
Fax: 01732 363 381
Email: office@schoolsatsomerhill.com
Website: www.schoolsatsomerhill.com

Remarks: See The Schools at Somerhill for write-up.

Dollar Academy Prep and Junior School

Linked to Dollar Academy in the Senior section

Dollar, Clackmannanshire, FK14 7DU

• Pupils: boys and girls; boarding and day • Ages: 5-11 • Fees: Boarding £18,702-£19,908; Day £7,335 pa • Independent

Tel: 01259 742 511
Fax: 01259 742 867
Email: rector@dollaracademy.org.uk
Website: www.dollaracademy.org.uk

Remarks: For further details see the senior school.

Dolphin School

Waltham Road, Hurst, Reading, Berkshire, RG10 0FR

• Pupils: 240, all day; 140 boys, 100 girls • Ages: 3-13 • Liberal humanist
• Fees: £7,545-£10,350 pa • Independent

Tel: 0118 934 1277
Fax: 0118 934 4110
Email: omnes@dolphinschool.com
Website: www.dolphinschool.com

Head: Since 2008, Mrs Veronica Gibbs BSc PGCE (fifties), degree in pure maths with history and philosophy of science from University College, Cardiff. She has been at the school since 1990 and before that taught maths in state secondaries. Still teaches Year 3 and above, once a fortnight. Both her children, now adults, went through the school and still come back and visit the place. Husband works in IT and is a keen amateur archaeologist and walker who often helps on school trips. Watch out for walking and trips, they feature prominently in this report.

Mrs Gibbs is not your typical head but then this is not your typical school. Her office, very much not a study, is small and functional with a desk, a couple of chairs and some family photographs and school memorabilia. It is not designed to overwhelm prospective parents, indeed, those who consider grand architecture to be a desirable backdrop to their child's education should look away now. Like her office, Mrs Gibbs is modest and unpretentious, her focus is the school and she radiates quiet pride in its uniqueness. The founder and owner, Nancy Follett, still lives next door in the Tudor Manor where the school was born in 1970 as a Montessori nursery. It grew with its pupils and now occupies a sylvan site with well-designed modern and less than ideal older buildings. The family still governs the school via a trust assisted by advisors, many of whom are former pupils.

Entrance: This school offers a very different approach to education, best described by that over-used word 'holistic'. Parents are academics, visiting Europeans, artists and others who approve of the free-thinking ethos but equally expect their children to gain places, if not awards, at top independent and grammar schools. Pupils entering from age five upwards are invited to spend a day at the school that includes tests in maths and English. There is no formal assessment for children entering the nursery. The school, as the head puts it carefully, is best suited to the 'academically able', but that should be taken as a broad definition of the term.

Exit: About a third of pupils leave at 11 for local state and independent schools, the rest stay on until 13 for Common Entrance; according to the head all get places at their first choice school. Dolphin children were awarded the top Harrow scholarships in 2009 and 2010 and in recent years an average of 30 per cent of those going to independent schools were awarded some sort of scholarship. Recent destinations include Bradfield College (qv), Reading Grammar, Abingdon School (qv), Wellington College (qv), Eton, The Abbey and many to Leighton Park.

Remarks: What is the secret of Dolphin's success? Seemingly independent of any rigid educational ideology (and that's a good start), the ethos of Dolphin is hard to define, and yet a visitor soon becomes aware that something very special is going on. The reception area, complete with grey cat purring on a visitor's chair, sets an informal trend that is true to the whole school. The lack of a uniform, the comfortably-dressed staff, the easy, open relationships between teachers and pupils (most address each other by first names), the creative untidiness, all this and more may be your first impression, but do not mistake it for 'anything goes'. Here is the total immersion approach to learning – the polar opposite of spoon-feeding pre-chewed lumps of facts that can characterise the national curriculum at its worst. In every classroom we visited children were busy, engaged, doing and teachers were enabling and encouraging independent learning. In not one case did our visit interrupt a lesson because the pupils did not have to wait for their teacher to finish talking to us in order to continue with a task. Teaching here can't be easy but it must be rewarding; several members of staff who had joined from other schools said it had restored their faith in their vocation. The ability to wander productively in the outer limits of one's subject (and a few others besides) while covering all the usual areas is not given to all. As one teacher expressed it memorably, 'we follow a subject's tangents but not its red herrings'.

Children join at rising three where they follow the early years' curriculum 'plus', lots of good mucky hands stuff inside and out. On the day we visited the three- and four-year-olds were out on safari in the sports field, just a taster of adventures to come. From Year 1 there are at least three trips a term, all of which are 'threaded' into every subject plus a residential walking expedition. As if this weren't enough, Years 8 and 9 can go to Italy or Normandy for 10 days at the end of August for a romp through art, classics and history ancient and modern. It's a lot to take in for 12- and 13-year-olds but 'the teachers make it really fun'. Our impressively mature Year 8 guides were approaching the literal and metaphorical peak of their school career as they prepared for nine days camping, climbing, walking and swimming in the Alps. In order to reach these heights children (and parents are welcome too) must start on the South Downs and ascend year by year through the Black Mountains, the Lake District, the Brecon Beacons, Snowdon and so on. It is necessary to 'pass' each successive challenge if one is aiming for the Alps. A wall of photos in the assembly hall provides encouragement along the way. All trips except foreign ones (where parents pay about half) are included in the fees.

Bolstered by trips, the usual range of subjects is taught beyond the usual boundaries. In addition there is French from the nursery, classics for Years 2 to 5, Latin from Year 6, German, Spanish and Greek from Year 7. Maths is very strong and juniors and seniors regularly arrive home counting awards won in the UK maths challenge. Likewise drama and music and, perhaps not surprising among such confident children, pupils often gain drama scholarships to their senior schools. Chess is taught as a discrete subject in Year 4 and the school plays an active and successful part in local, regional and national leagues. Other 'extra' subjects include architecture, astronomy, traditional games and construction games and the aim is that up to Year 6 each year group should sample at least one of these a year. Great IT suite and, wonder of wonders, touch-typing is taught from Year 3, 15 minutes at the start of every session. Another wonder is SQUIRT (silent quiet uninterrupted individual reading time) – heads in books for 15 minutes every day for children and staff alike.

Subject specialists teach in dedicated rooms and from Year 2 pupils, armed with timetables (and maps!) make their way from lesson to lesson – the aim is to foster independence and senior schools benefit from notably well organised newbies. Pupils are given every encouragement to take the scenic route down their own 'avenues of thought' but, lest this engender wooliness, individual weekly goals are set and expected to be met. Special needs, including the extra bright, supported by INCo – individual needs coordinator. An anchor in this sea of learning is the form tutor, who stays with the same group all the way through the school. Pupils in Years 6, 7 and 8 also have a mentor to whom they can bring any concerns. Parents and children are positive about pastoral care. This a small school and the pupils all know each other well, older children buddy up with their younger peers and bullying, though rarely encountered, is 'not tolerated.'

Science labs are still state-of-the-ark and, to be frank, much of the older fabric of the school is shabby rather than chic. The swimming pool is just about indoors but only used in the warmer weather because it lacks changing rooms and not even these intrepid children fancy a bathing suited dash across the tarmac in February. And finally there is (or in this case, is not) the catering. On a summer's day staff and children picnicking outside has a certain pastoral charm but lunchboxes in the classroom is considered a bind by parents ('you just try not to think about it,' sighed one), although our guides claimed they always made their own sandwiches. None of the above seems to impinge on the quality of teaching or learning, which just goes to show that in the end it's about the teaching, not the technology.

Sport is more about cooperation than competition. This is not to say that there are no losers, just that anyone who wants to be in a team or play in a tournament may do so, and mixed teams are encouraged. Punching above its weight as usual, the Dolphin teams are strong opponents on inter-school fixture lists and it has produced county players for most mainstream sports. Claire Taylor, England number one female cricketer of the year, is an ex-pupil and returned recently to give a cricket workshop. 20 after-school clubs supplement the timetabled sport along with the gentler exertions of yoga, gymnastics and dance.

An unwavering and confident cross-curricular approach to learning is what distinguishes the school from others, the intention being to develop a self-motivated child with a love of learning and an enquiring mind. We saw about 250 of these on our visit. All this and traditional academic rigour is what Dolphin does, but even the head can't pinpoint exactly what the magic ingredient is – apparently one of the challenges at the annual teacher conference is to define the difference. The word that comes up again and again from teachers, parents and pupils is 'freedom' – a dangerous idea in conjunction with education some might say but, as the head is at needless pains to point out, Dolphin is no Summerhill. Pupils are carefully selected; the school is looking for the type of child who will 'thrive' there and some would not. For instance, a child who needs a strong routine, the same teacher every day and the security of a familiar classroom would not respond to the delphic way.

Parents are enthusiastic bordering on evangelical about this school. One, whose three 'very different' children have all attended, was already anticipating with real regret the day that her family's contact with the place would end. 'I wish it could go on forever,' she said.

A rare school. All schools say that they treat every child as an individual but it can be difficult to see this working in practice. To encourage each child to blossom academically while not producing a bunch of prima donnas is quite a challenge, but pupils leave humane, mature and thoughtful with a life-long love of learning ahead of them. This Dolphin, naturally, is swimming confidently and successfully ahead of a conformist tide.

The Dominie

55 Warriner Gardens, Battersea, London, SW11 4DX

• Pupils: Pupil capacity: 30 • Ages: 6-12 • Non-denominational • Fees: £22,800 pa • Independent

Tel: 020 7720 8783
Fax: 020 7622 4357
Email: info@thedominie.co.uk
Website: www.thedominie.co.uk

Headmistress: Miss Anne O'Doherty – BA (Hons), University of London; DipSpLD (Barts); Montessori Diploma, St Nicholas Montessori Training College, London. Became owner and principal in 2007, having been the director for six years. Married, has always used her maiden name for her work. Has been involved in teaching children with specific learning difficulties for 30 years – extensive experience in mainstream and special needs education. Previously co-director of The Dyslexia Teaching Centre in Kensington, where she worked for 14 years. Before that taught and head of lower school at Thomas's London Day Schools, Kensington, before joining The Dyslexia Teaching Centre.

Aim is to secure the pupil's confidence and help them to re-discover the joys of learning and succeeding. Believes learning in small groups alongside others with dyslexia and dyspraxia dispels the idea that they are alone and unable to achieve.

Entrance: Entry can take place at any time if a place is available – a two-day assessment which encompasses both class and one-to-one assessments. Copies of any existing reports required to provide as much information as possible of the child's learning profile.

Exit: To a range of schools, the majority of which are mainstream. Recent leavers to The Harrodian, Putney Park, Windlesham House, The Moat and Stonar.

Remarks: An independent co-educational school which specialises in providing education for pupils with dyslexia and dyspraxia. Housed in attractive premises close to Battersea Park. The classrooms are bright and informative with frequently changing displays of exciting artwork and examples of pupils' achievements.

The National Curriculum is followed, but is carefully adapted and modified. Specialist provision is an integral part of the approach in delivering a broad and balanced curriculum. Offers a wide range of after school clubs and numerous educational visits to galleries and museums. The day is divided, mornings concentrate on literacy and numeracy whilst the main focus of afternoons is on practical and sporting activities. Pupils are generally allocated to forms according to their age and taught in groups according to their strengths and weaknesses. Dedicated and talented teachers are supported by experienced learning support assistants.

The distinctive difference is that it is small, which is capitalised on by the head, teachers and learning support assistants in that they develop a deep understanding of each and every child. Pupils say learning is fun – 'I couldn't take away [i.e. subtract] until I came here,' said one child, 'but the teachers worked with me and showed me new ways. I can't believe it's so easy or that I learned so quickly – they really cheer you up'.

The pupils are happy and articulate. They recognise and champion the benefits of the school, especially the way everyone cares for each other. The pastoral system is not a structure – it is a continuum that involves everyone the whole of the time. Formal recognition of pupil achievements takes place in the weekly assembly, when merit badges are awarded and pupils often present special pieces of work to the rest of the school. The communication between school and home is open and regular feedback is given to parents about their child's progress. Homework is an important and integral part of school life with appropriate and carefully considered amounts allocated.

Does not have any outdoor facilities of its own – however pupils visit nearby Battersea Park daily and use local sports facilities for swimming, football and PE. All bring a packed lunch – school encourages healthy eating.

A delightful, heartening oasis for children with dyslexia or dyspraxia who require an intimate, dedicated and caring environment.

Dover College Infant & Junior Department

Linked to Dover College in the Senior section

Effingham Crescent, Dover, CT17 9RH

• Pupils: 80 boys and girls, all day • Ages: 3-11 • All faiths welcome • Fees: £5,940-£8,850 pa • Independent

Tel: 01304 205 969
Fax: 01304 242 208
Email: registrar@dovercollege.org.uk
Website: www.dovercollege.org.uk

Head : Mrs Heather Miller.

Entrance: All prospective pupils need to attend a taster day, following which an offer of a place may be made.

Exit: Most to the senior school. Some to local grammar schools.

Remarks: Opened in 2001 and accommodated in a house in the grounds. Wonderful themed art and photographs of all the children all over the walls. Small classes. Specialist teachers for music from pre-reception, French from Year 1 and Spanish from Year 3. Setting in maths and English. Keen eye kept out for any children who might have any learning difficulties – one-to-one dyslexia support. Fully integrated part of Dover College and pupils make use of wider college facilities (Astroturf, playing fields, ICT centre, music schools, dance studio, refectory). Sport is played against other schools at U11 age group and after-school club is provided for all year groups. Most pupils move on to the main school at 11 but will prepare children for the Kent Test.

The Downs, Malvern College Preparatory School

Linked to Malvern College in the Senior section

Brockhill Road, Colwall, Malvern, Worcestershire, WR13 6EY

• Pupils: 190 girls and boys; boarding and day • Ages: 2-13 • C of E but ecumenical • Fees: £5,568-£17,700 pa • Independent

Tel: 01684 540 277
Fax: 01684 540 094
Email: enquiries@thedowns.malcol.org
Website: www.thedowns.malcol.org

Head: Since September 2009, Mr Sam Cook, previously head of Pembroke House in Gilgil, Kenya. An Oxford graduate, this is his third headship. He is married with three small chilldren.

Entrance: Entrance is by informal observation during taster days supported by information gained by interview and discussions with parents.

Exit: Common Entrance or Common Scholarship is the focus, in the same way as other aspirants for Malvern College. At least 90 per cent move up, some move by choice to other local schools. Occasionally a pupil does not make the academic grade. Pupils' progress is monitored closely and parents would be told at an early stage if it is thought their child will not do well enough to move up.

Remarks: The merger of The Downs, Colwall with Malvern College Prep has gone extremely well and the aim of combining the best practice from both successful schools has largely been achieved. Of Malvern Prep we said: 'Useful little trad co-ed day/boarding prep which feeds both Malvern and elsewhere.' For the new school, joiners are welcome at any time, some financial support available. Small classes, Montessori early years, Forest School and World Challenge experiences add to the school's diversity.

Children streamed at top end. German or Spanish in Year 7 and 8; French starts in pre-prep. Science taught as independent disciplines from Year 6 and design and technology linked with very good ICT provision throughout. Has its own sports hall, Astro hockey surface, outdoor swimming pool and steam railway. Uses the College chapel, theatre and 25m indoor pool.

Boys play rugby, soccer, hockey, cricket and athletics, girls netball, hockey, lacrosse, rounders and athletics. Strong teams at U9, U11 and U13. The opening of a brand-new sports centre will allow badminton, basketball, gymnastics and dance. A partnership with a local, highly-successful cricket club develops young cricketers throughout the year through use of the indoor cricket lanes.

Popular locally; foreign pupils tend to come at 11 to top up their English. School operates its own bus service, after-school club and holiday club. If you couldn't fault it before, you most certainly will not be able to now!

The Downs School

Charlton House, Wraxall, Bristol, BS48 1PF

• Pupils: 165 boys, 85 girls; all day • Ages: 4-13 • Christian ethos • Fees: £8,100-£12,600 pa • Independent

Tel: 01275 852 008
Fax: 01275 855 840
Email: office@thedownsschool.co.uk
Website: www.thedownsschool.co.uk

Head: Since 2001, Mr Marcus Gunn MA(Ed) BA PGCE (fiftyish). Went to Bloxham, then Liverpool, followed by South Bank and an OU postgraduate degree in education. A cheery traditionalist who believes in children developing old-fashioned virtues such as 'opening doors for others, shaking hands and looking adults in the eye'. Career began at now defunct Marton Hall before deputy headship at Mowden Hall in Northumberland. Didn't quite realise what he was walking into as fourth head at The Downs within two years. After some much-needed hatchet work in the staff room precipitated by a critical ISI report in November 2000 and substantial withdrawals by unimpressed parents, he has now managed to turn the school around. Has established a 'happy, talented staff' encouraged by a positive follow-up inspection in October 2002 and an even better one in 2006 and seen through some major changes. With wife Valerie very much involved and three children (Joshua, Olivia, Henrietta, who've all been through the independent school mill) the Gunns are clearly seen as good news by the parents whom they have gone out of their way to get on side. A former windsurfing buff, Mr Gunn likes to snatch quality time with the family or perhaps dabble in a bit of painting or photography.

Entrance: Candidates above reception are assessed informally for a day and offered places if they are in line with the school's expectations of at least average ability. Low ability candidates are accepted provided school's learning support department can meet their needs. Former nursery, now run independently, located near the entrance off the B3128. Pre-prep now free to recruit four year olds from various local nurseries with encouraging results. Ratio of boys to girls nearly 3:2 in the pre-prep and 2:1 in the prep. Girls appear confident and are increasingly making their presence felt. Two or three scholarships offered annually with academic scholarship worth up to 15 per cent of day fee.

Exit: A number move on to Clifton, QEH, BGS and Badminton in Bristol. Other popular choices have recently included Blundell's, Bryanston, Sherborne, King's Bruton and Millfield. A few to Marlborough and Winchester. All in recent years have been accepted by first choice school. Impressive scholarship success rate continues. Very few now go off to Bristol day schools after 11+ entrance exams so majority, including girls, stay to 13.

Remarks: Founded in 1894 overlooking Clifton Downs; school 'escaped' from Bristol in 1927 and was tenant on late Lord Wraxall's estate until 2002 when Charlton House, along with assortment of other school buildings, 60 acres of playing fields and parkland, were bought by governors 'for a song'. 30mph speed limit on mile long drive is a first challenge for visitors; unsympathetically rendered exterior to mansion finally comes as anti-climax. Entering the matrix (Hugo Weaving is an old boy), Victorian gothic interior with magnificent fireplace and spooky staircases more than compensates.

Experienced staff exact high standards in what still feels like trad prep; has woken up to unpopularity of Saturday lessons and scrapped them; boarding ended in 2006. For parents who don't want their children to leave home before 13, The Downs offers as full a programme as you can find in a day prep. Attracts broad social mix and now that school has accepted the inevitable (though Saturday afternoon matches continue most weekends) demand is likely to rise further. Accessible from quite a wide area, being close to junction 19 on the M5 and only 10 minutes' drive from Bristol's western edge. School now has a 'stunning' pre-prep – a significant investment.

Pre-prep department recently refurbished and extended. Teenies taught to read phonically with a number of schemes (not just Jolly Phonics) in use. Children not hemmed in by formality and come across as lively but respectful. Music at this level includes recorders, violins and choir; plenty of creativity though thematic work would benefit from more imaginative displays.

School is retaining positives from boarding régime with older ones mostly staying for after-school clubs (ranging from Warhammer to cookery) or supervised prep until supper at 6pm, despite formal day ending at 5.10pm. After-school care for pre-prep children also runs until supper. Saturday matches off menu every third weekend. Workaday uniform is low key and practical but children don garishly striped blazers (which they refused to have scrapped) for all travel to and from school as well as functions.

The curriculum from Year 5 is geared to demands of CE, with all subjects, including Latin, French, Spanish and science (separate sciences in Years 6, 7 and 8) taught by specialists. A new art department but not much provided for DT as yet. New library, which would benefit from a CD-ROM (let alone DVD) facility – school begs to differ – is a long overdue bonus.

Sporting tradition is paramount but head has worked at improving creative and performing arts. Music department is particularly strong with 75 per cent being taught one or more instruments; a 35-strong chamber choir plus variety of concerts and productions. Boys' and girls' sports teams perform exceptionally well. Has won the prep schools' rugby sevens at Rosslyn Park more than any other school, and the girls are currently national rounders champions and runners-up in hockey, and won four national titles in three sports over the last five years. Also an imaginative alternative to games for the less sporty known as The Downs Award Scheme, which concentrates on more individual and outward-bound type activities and in which everyone participates on Thursdays.

Three specialist teachers support pupils with special needs; department has experience of a range of learning disabilities. Targeted support in literacy and numeracy working well to raise pupil performance.

Year 8 has own common room – children in Year 8 have at least one school responsibility so no-one gets left out. 'Tiffin' is provided for all mid-morning and afternoon; tasty nosh served up for a fairly formal lunch with staff in the dining-hall, which ends in pin drop silence while notices are given. Plenty of places outside to let off steam; two floodlit Astroturf pitches and plenty of tennis courts. Science laboratories adequate. Now two ICT suites, interactive whiteboards in many classrooms, all site networked. Not a laptop school but thankfully still a mobile phone free zone. More than adequate sports-hall somehow got past planners 15 or so years ago; bears external scars inflicted by hockey sticks in rowdier days. Heated outside pool has failed repeated attempts to get it covered but remains popular through summer months. Recently refurbished theatre with retractable seating and new staging.

In a school where manners still matter, we felt that most children would be happy and do well. Not an obvious stomping ground for city slickers but parents from nearby Bristol might be pleasantly surprised at the benefits for children of regular exercise in fresh air.

Downsend School

1 Leatherhead Road, Leatherhead, Surrey, KT22 8TJ

• Pupils: 570 • Ages: 6-13 • Non-denom • Fees: £9,360-£11,355 pa • Independent

Tel: 01372 372 197
Fax: 01372 363 367
Email: admissions@downsend.co.uk
Website: www.downsend.co.uk

Head: Since September 2008, Mr Floyd Steadman Cert Ed (fifties), married with three teenage sons. He commutes as his family are settled in west London. Previously head at Salcombe Prep, Southgate, and before that deputy head at Belmont School (Mill Hill prep), and head of games and seniors at Colet Court. His subjects are geography and sports and he is currently studying for a MEd in leadership and management. A top class rugby player who captained Saracens and Middlesex in the pre-professional era.

Outwardly quite relaxed, Mr Steadman is a pleasant chap who is keen to show he knows what is going on around the school and is familiar with the schools the children move on to. He expounds on all the positives at Downsend. Parents find him accessible and open-minded, 'he's maintained the status quo, but it's early days yet'. He has 'big shoes to fill' taking over from the previous head who had been at Downsend for 40 years.

Entrance: Vast majority enter Downsend into Year 2 from the pre-prep Downsend 'Lodges', where they take children from two years old. Transition is smooth with no tests, though parents say 'they would tell you if they thought your child couldn't cope'. In Year 3, a further 20 to 25 pupils join, mainly locally from St Giles in Ashtead (state C of E infants) and St Christopher's in Epsom (private nursery and pre-prep). Entry assessment is relatively low key, short tests in reading, writing and maths, described by school as 'designed to assess ... not be overly challenging,' echoed by parents who mostly see it as easy to get in. The head tells us 'there is an entry requirement – pupils must perform well in the assessment tests. These are basic tests in English and maths to see where pupils will fit into the system.'

Currently a waiting list for Year 2 entry, priority is given to registered siblings and then order of registration. No scholarships, but head tells us bursaries were introduced in September 2008. He is reluctant to give details describing them as 'means-tested and individually based' and 'some bursaries have been awarded.'

Attracts families from across all of this part of Surrey, nearby Ashtead and Leatherhead and further afield to Dorking, Epsom and Reigate. About 150 pupils use school transport covering East and West Horsley, Banstead, Chessington, Dorking and stops in between.

Exit: Head tells us proudly 'our children go on to the best local schools'. Most go to Epsom College, St John's Leatherhead and City of London Freemen's School. A smattering to the Royal Grammar School Guildford, Guildford High School, Reigate Grammar School, Reeds, Manor House and St Teresa's. Parents say most of the girls leave at 11 (Mr Steadman says it is not most, but 40 per cent of girls); increasingly boys too. One parent adds, 'Obviously they want to keep you until 13 but give support for those sitting 11+ exams and help with mocks and verbal reasoning papers'. Many parents, and presumably the school, are delighted that nearby St John's School – previously all boys – now takes girls from 13, which should help keep a few more girls at Downsend for the two senior years. In 2010, 25 of the 13-year-old leavers won a scholarship to their next school.

Remarks: Downsend has good facilities, solid academic results and pleasant, easy going children – 'a school for children who enjoy life' is the motto. And the school does just as it says on the tin (which is particularly valued by working parents). What is missing is the wow factor, something to make you sit up and say 'here is something different'. Mr Steadman is quick to rush to the school's defence and feels 'the broad curriculum and the enjoyment and fun children have every day set Downsend apart from other schools'.

Cognita, which took over the school in 2004, owns and manages a rapidly expanding group of schools across the UK, plus a few in Spain, Singapore and Thailand. Officially they provide financial governance, personnel and training, strategic and development planning plus 'specialist support and expertise in education', leaving the head free to run the school with the senior staff team. Some parents feel there is a whiff of big business which isn't always comfortable, variously complaining 'it's bums on seats,' 'there's no dialogue with parents,' 'Cognita is very guarded,' 'you don't get answers from Cognita, there are grey areas'. However, the school staff are seen by parents as separate from Cognita and children are not affected by any of these 'business issues'.

Downsend is on a site next to the M25, not the most glamorous of locations (the morning traffic locally is horrendous – but parents in the area no doubt get used to it). The school is large, with about 570 pupils. It is organised into three sections, which the head explains is 'to make it more personal and to give the opportunities of a larger school within a smaller community.' There is a junior section for Years 2, 3 and 4, middle for Years 5 and 6, and senior for Years 7 and 8. Each section has its own head, style of classes and playground areas. Junior school pupils are largely taught in their own classrooms by form teachers and some subject specialists, middle school is subject-teacher based – all are in bright and modern buildings. Seniors move from room to room for lessons in the more traditional, original '1891' school house. Staggered breaks, lunch and leaving times also help to make this big school seem not too crowded.

Generally, parents are not looking for hot-house academics but for a friendly, happy school. Academically pupils are streamed in Year 4 into two groups: three B classes and two A classes. By the time they reach the senior school, when pupil numbers have decreased (some 40 per cent having left at age 11), there are four classes: one for scholarship, one A stream CE and two B stream CE. Parents are aware of their child's position and do stress about it. Mr Steadman tells them that children are taught in different styles and pupils will prepare for scholarship or CE exams in Year 8. Parents feel the school is 'not too pushy, there's room for different characters and abilities'. Some, however, did remark on the differences as their children progress through the school, feeling the focus is on the scholarship stream in the senior section. Most feel their children have a dynamic and positive relationship with teachers and are 'fired up' in class.

A very good school for an SEN child. SEN help for mild, specific learning difficulties on offer, pupils are screened from Year 2 using standardised tests. One of the aims is 'to identify and support even those with a low level of need in order to help each child reach his or her potential'. Consequently about 20 per cent receive extra help, but parents pay extra for this – anything up to £60 per hour – depending on what's needed. The SEN team is managed by two part-time SENCos with referral access to qualified literacy specialists, an occupational therapist, a speech and language therapist, plus trained specialist assistants who help dyslexic children with a lower level of need. Brain gym sessions help children with co-ordination difficulties. A gifted and talented co-ordinator offers additional stretch and challenge sessions for the brighter children.

Some parental muttering about staff turnover with comments about too many newly qualified (and consequently inexperienced) teachers – Mr Steadman says 'there were only two newly qualified teachers appointed in September 2009 and one appointed in 2010'. Other parents have no complaints about teaching. Bullying also – its existence and the school's action against it – provokes a variety of responses. There were comments from parents with children who have been '100 per cent happy' to others whose children have been made anxious by bullying. One parent told us her daughter was bullied and 'the school didn't handle it well – nothing was done until we threatened to leave,' another whose son was harried continually found 'the school doesn't act quickly enough, they could nip it in the bud but they don't'. Mr Steadman tells us, 'Bullying is not a major issue. Children are not afraid to report unkind behaviour'. He stresses the importance of identifying the difference between unkindness and real bullying: 'there are sanctions if needed', and explains they are 'rarely used'. House points are awarded for kindness, politeness and good acts as well as good work.

Lots of sport for both boys and girls. Facilities are good, including a large sports field bordered by high fences and trees alongside the M25, plenty of netball courts and an Astro pitch, plus a pool described by one parent as 'the best school pool in the area'. Parents tell us, 'The A teams are kept busy, not so much going on for the Bs, Cs and Ds,' with the usual variety of views – some want their children to play in more matches, some are pleased the pressure is not on the weaker players, whilst others are delighted their less-sporty children get a place in a match. Everyone does get a chance to compete including inter-house matches. The trophy cabinet includes silverware for boys' and girls' biathlon from U10 through to U13, both team and individual, plus swimming and various athletics trophies. Squads have bi-annual international tours for cricket, netball and hockey and there is a popular, annual skiing trip.

About 50 per cent of the pupils learn a musical instrument, from beginners up to grade 6. Peripatetic music teachers offer instruments ranging from harp to drums and electric guitar, there's also a singing teacher. Three orchestras and choirs – one for each junior, middle and senior section – perform informally and occasionally formally to a large audience. Parents report the choirs are more active than the orchestras.

Drama is available via extra-curricular clubs with annual productions in the middle and senior schools. Art is part of the curriculum, but not seen as a particular strength by parents. Nice to see the old-fashioned skills of cooking, sewing and woodwork (timetabled in a rota of food technology, textiles and DT) – practical and participatory activities which both parents and pupils value. The aim is for every child to be successful in something; the head feels that 'success in one thing leads to confidence in other areas.' Parents support this view, telling us 'the children all believe they will be good at something' and 'all are made to feel important'.

Parents describe themselves as 'not like traditional old prep school types, it's more of a mix here' and 'down-to-earth people'. Some are 'quite modest and here because they really want to be, working hard to earn the fees,' others are wealthier, but no 'local celeb set' types. Heaps of help for working parents – there are lots of them. After-school clubs keep juniors busy until 4.10 pm when the older pupils finish. An extended day programme starts at 8am and finishes after tea at 5.45 pm. During the school holidays 'Downsend+' provides day care with lunch, all very flexible and run by familiar teaching staff. It's widely praised as 'a fantastic resource' and 'very popular with working parents'; children can be cared for here for up to 50 weeks of the year if required. Downsend+ lists a genuinely exciting range of activities including scuba diving (PADI courses), dry slope skiing and even driving for Years 7 and 8 at nearby Mercedes Benz World. Super to have on offer, but by no means free: it would in theory be easy to notch up a bill of £250 for a child per week, though Mr Steadman says this figure would be unusual.

Overall, parents and their children are happy here; even those with concerns and gripes still extol the school's virtues. Pupils are busy throughout the day having lots of fun whilst also cutting the mustard academically.

Downside Junior School

Linked to Downside School in the Senior section

Stratton-on-the-Fosse, Bath, Radstock, Somerset, BA3 4RJ

- Pupils: 55 girls and boys; boarding and day • Ages: 10-13
- Fees: Boarding £20,037; Day £12,285 pa • Independent

Tel: 01761 235 103
Fax: 01761 235 105
Email: registrar@downside.co.uk

Remarks: For further information, see Downside School.

Dragon School

Bardwell Road, Oxford, Oxfordshire, OX2 6SS

• Pupils: 545 boys, 295 girls, of which 175 boys and 80 girls are boarders, and 131 boys and 84 girls are in the Dragon pre-prep, Lynams • Ages: 8-13, pre-prep 4-8 • Non-denominational • Fees: Day £16,320; Boarding £23,370; Lynams £8,850-£11,700 pa • Independent

Tel: 01865 315405
Fax: 01865 311 664
Email: admissions@dragonschool.org
Website: www.dragonschool.org

Head: Since 2002, Mr John Baugh BEd (forties), educated at Aldenham School, followed by St Luke's Exeter, where he read education with geography and still does the odd spot of teaching – 'Takes occasional cover lessons when staff are away for some reason'; taught RS last year. Started his teaching career at Haileybury, previously head of both Solefield Prep School in Sevenoaks and Edge Grove – an experienced head, then. Found the school 'in fantastic shape', 'The children are terrific, getting on with things from day one', regularly praises 'the wonderful quality of the staff-room' and mentioned dozens of times 'the sheer buzz and excitement'; 'I get up in the morning excited to get on with the job'. A 'people person,' said our guide; has instigated open days for parents 'so that they can find out exactly what (and how much) the school has to offer'. 'Every single child has to believe that they are part of the school.' Caring, thoughtful, GSOH (thank goodness!), has the support of staff, parents and pupils and keen on promoting parent-school partnership. Married to Wendy, who is fully involved in the school; two daughters – both were at Haileybury.

Entrance: By early registration – nothing has changed, though immediate places available in exceptional circumstances. A seriously intimidating double A4 sheet of instructions for parents of would-be pupils. No tests for 4+ entry to Lynams but non-competitive assessment for all for entry to the main school. Easier to board than day, takes occasional refugees from London hothouse preps – worth a try at any time.

London day refugees buying up the neighbourhood, pushing dons even further out. School is keen not to stray too far from the traditional parent base (bussing under consideration). New boarders have taster sleepovers before they come. 20 per cent from abroad, both foreign nationals and ex-pats. One of the selected Eton continuation scholarship schools, where pupils from the state sector are underwritten at prep school before going on, but not many of these recently.

ODs: Sir John Betjeman, Dame Naomi Mitchison and Sir Jack Smyth VC. Bursaries and more offered (in the pipeline) in memory of Nicholas Knatchbull who was killed with his grandfather, Lord Mountbatten. Prince Charles recently unveiled a commemorative plaque.

Exit: To 95 or more different schools over the past few years, but many to St Edward's Oxford and tranches to Eton, Radley, Marlborough and, more recently, Rugby, plus Abingdon, Magdalen College School, Headington and Oxford High, otherwise all over the public school shop from Ampleforth to Wrekin. Regularly wins squillions of scholarships for everything – 38 last year.

Remarks: Still one of the best, most exciting and charming academic prep schools in the country. A genuine co-ed: head has taken great steps 'to get girls part of the whole set-up', give them a 'much higher profile' and improve their lot – moving their games programmes alongside the boys has done wonders for their self-esteem. Boarding houses broken down by age – four for the youngest two years, three for 10 year olds, and three for the top two years. Girls' houses charmingly full of Barbies and ponies, boys' with table football and rugby posters. Excellent house-parents on all fronts. Noticeably easy though respectful pupil/staff relationship – some staff still called by their nicknames; female teachers and house mothers called Ma (e.g. Moira Darlington is Ma Da).

Certain amount of tinkering with the tutorial system in the final two years which 'now involves many more staff', integrating boys and girls, day and boarding in the same two-year group. The school projects an image of informality – scruffy cords, the scruffier the better (and only day pupils wear bomber jackets), blazers for best; girlies wear jolly yellow shirts and tartan. Even scruffier casuals after school. All meals taken in main dining room, and food 'much better', bun break and tea still in houses.

This laissez faire attitude to outward appearances charms the children who feel that someone somewhere is on their side. Underneath, however, the school is very disciplined with rigorous academic timetabling and absolutely no messing about allowed in class. Maximum class size 23, average 19. Seven streams in each year after the junior school with pupils moving up and down (within their age group) where necessary, even in the middle of term. Maths, French and Latin setted separately, top two streams do Greek, German or Spanish in their last two years, and much more setting at this time. Japanese and Mandarin available as extras. Strong scholarship streams – 'It is quite common for people to take scholarships whilst still being in the second stream'.

Six state-of-the-art science labs, with six lab technicians (more than many public schools) and five ICT suites. Impressive library, dead efficient with trillions of computers, and more scheduled plasma screens have replaced noticeboards throughout the school – duty staff can change them from their laptops. Laptops around the place too. Classes often taught in the computer suites. Intranet, interactive white boards, and 'computer operated telephoning' – all singing and dancing. Learning support fully integrated, with four full-time and several part-time staff, pupils either withdrawn or certain amount of team teaching in class; pupils with problems greater than school can deal with encouraged 'to go elsewhere', though siblings are often allowed to come on a trial basis. PSHE increased and strong anti-bullying ethos in place – 'The old culture of not sneaking has now gone – it is a child's right to say "I am unhappy"'; 'Good system of checks and balances in place'.

Superb music, with choirs, orchestras, jazz bands, etc; terrific art and three heavenly art-rooms above the swimming pool. Cad Cam in place as well as traditional drawing and painting – children crouching on the table to 'get a better angle' when we visited. Good (once state-of-the-art) assembly/multi-purpose hall, with professional sound box and lighting, much used for daily assembly, service on Sunday, regular talks (both during and post-school hours) and all sorts of entertainment. Jolly drama, regular hysterically-funny traditional staff pantomime. No prep on Fridays: school has instituted a cultural evening known as 'Spectrum' and has a selection of lectures and performances, open to day pupils and parents too – popular.

Masses of options, trips all over, parents often go too. Links with school in Tokyo, with pupils and staff doing regular exchanges and attending school there. Masses of sport and good at it – traditional rugby, football, hockey, tennis etc, extra land recently acquired for more tennis courts, Astroturf everywhere. Children must still swim two lengths of the pool before playing by the river; girls now proficient at sculling. Health and Safety regulations mean specialist staff employed for climbing wall and canoeing. Teaching days end at 4.15, but masses of activities both before and after; school will field all day pupils till 6pm.

Conglomerate of purpose-built blocks mingling with Victorian North Oxford. Planning rules will prevent massive expansion. School runs own very busy pre-prep (Lynams) about a mile away. Lots of Dragon traditions; Christmas fair attracts ODs back for Chrissie present-buying – they return anyway at regular intervals 'to see what's happened now'. A very exciting school to be at and a place which ODs are proud to have attended.

DUCKS (Dulwich College Kindergarten and Infants School)

Linked to Dulwich College: The Junior School in the Junior section

Linked to Dulwich College in the Senior section

Eller Bank, 87 College Road, London, SE21 7HH

• Pupils: 240 boys and girls • Ages: 6 months - 7 years • C of E
• Fees: £3,294-£10,590 pa • Independent

Tel: 020 8693 1538
Fax: 020 8693 4853
Email: DCDUCKS@hotmail.co.uk
Website: www.dulwich.org.uk/ducks

Head: Mrs Heather Friell, previously head of JAPPS, the James Allen's Pre-Prep.

Entrance: Takes babies from six months; put your name down whilst pregnant. More children join the nursery and reception classes, ending up with two reception classes of 22. More-or-less first come first served but priority for children of College staff members. Tries to take roughly equal numbers of boys and girls, but boys tend to predominate as some girls go off to e.g. JAPS in reception. A few Year 1 places, but at this point children must be able to 'communicate, socialise, be part of a working group'.

Exit: Many, but not all, of the boys move on to the junior school. Preference for siblings and sons of staff members. Other children go to e.g. Dulwich Prep, Rosemead, JAPS, Sydenham High, a few to Alleyn's.

Remarks: A homely wood-clad building in spacious grounds surrounded by playing fields, a short walk from the main College site. 'It's a lovely place to take your children,' says a parent. Large outside segregated play areas for different age groups, including ride-on toys, slides, climbing frames, play-houses, sandpits. There is a verandah for wet days and the older classes have an all-weather playground, plus use of some of the extensive College grounds. The College pool is just down the road and everyone learns to swim before they leave. PE and music are particular strengths, with teaching from specialist staff; very able children can join junior school groups. Senior College boys visit Ducks to help with lessons as part of their community service. Lunches are prepared on site by Ducks' own chef.

'The children are all very happy here,' say parents, but we do get reports that there has been discord amongst management and staff, and of a lack of continuity between the different age groups.

Ducks copes with various degrees of SEN including Asperger's, ADHD and dyslexia, sometimes in one-to-one sessions, with varying degrees of success. 'We have a great variety of ways of delivering the curriculum. And sometimes there are helpful changes that parents can make at home, such as ways of communicating.' The school has 'never had behavioural difficulties we can't cope with.'

Inevitably, preparing for entrance to the next school looms large in parental viewpoints. Ducks is not a hothouse and does not cram for 7+ exams. 'We try to develop their confidence and skill base so they're ready to try new things and engage with other people. We give them increasing levels of responsibility, starting with class duties and moving on to showing parents round and appearing in school plays.' Generally, all but around four or five of the boys who apply get places at the College junior school, but girls and other boys must apply to an increasingly wide range of schools to ensure an offer. 'Some are not ready for the experience,' says the head, and parents agree.

The College is now looking at the issues that have been raised and we are confident that the new Master and his team have it all in hand.

Dulwich College Preparatory School

42 Alleyn Park, Dulwich, London, SE21 8AT

• Pupils: 805 boys and 25 girls; mostly day but up to 20 weekly boarders
• Ages: Boys 3-13, girls 2.5-4 • C of E • Fees: Day £4,500-£14,025 pa; Boarding extra • Independent

Tel: 02086 703 217
Fax: 020 8766 7586
Email: registrar@dcpslondon.org
Website: www.dcpslondon.org

Head: Since 2009, Mr Michael Roulston, following the long-serving and exemplary Mr George Marsh.

Entrance: At three to the nursery, and at four, five, seven (large intake) and eight. Registrar closes lists when the school is heavily oversubscribed. Informal interview for all 'to assess potential, not what they've been taught'. The registration fee is £50.

Exit: Around one-third to Dulwich College; rest to other top boarding and day schools. Scholarship class produces a regular clutch of academic and music scholarships – 40 last year – to e.g. Eton, St Edward's, Winchester, Dulwich College, King's Canterbury, Westminster, Tonbridge, Marlborough.

Remarks: Maintaining its place as one of the top London prep schools. However, not the prep for Dulwich College, as its misleading name suggests – no automatic transfer to that institution. Ongoing impressive building programme has provided new library, ICT suite, artrooms, classrooms and entrance hall and four-court sports hall, cheering it up no end. Set in the middle of prosperous tree-lined Dulwich, parents are mainly solid (slightly anxious?) professionals with a sprinkling of foreigners here on secondment. The grounds are large (for London) and sport is big, with boys and staff strong on main games – rugby, football and cricket, although competition for teams is stiff. Plenty of other sporting options for the less team-minded. High-quality artwork everywhere and head of art producing some inventive installations, with boys drawing for fun at lunch times. Science strong – very enthusiastic head of department runs lots of extra-curricular clubs (as do other department heads).

Over 80 per cent of boys take at least one musical instrument. Orchestra plus jazz, brass, swing bands and several choirs. Drama department produces annual plays in all sections of the school that are always of an extraordinarily high standard. Games, swimming and music tours recently to South Africa, UK, Strasbourg and Italy; regular skiing trips and language groups to France and Germany. Lots of bright, precocious types, full of ideas and used to having their opinions taken seriously – not a place for wimps or those with special needs, although pastoral care taken very seriously, one parent saying, 'It's as good as it gets'. Some rumbles that only the brightest and best get to use the facilities fully and have the lion's share of the best teaching – school, deeply hurt, disputes this.

Boys divided into houses (Native American tribal names). Brightlands, the newly-refurbished weekly boarding house, set in five acres of grounds, provides good practice for boys off to board at 13 – has space for 24 boys, very useful for parents who travel often. The housemaster, who teaches sport, and his wife have a young family. Parents run minibuses bringing in some boys from Wandsworth area and many others use buses from all over south London run by Foundation Schools' Coach Service. Virtually all boys stay to 13.

Dulwich College: The Junior School

Linked to DUCKS (Dulwich College Kindergarten and Infants School) in the Junior section

Linked to Dulwich College in the Senior section

Dulwich Common, London, SE21 7LD

• Pupils: 200 pupils, all boys • Ages: 7-11 • Fees: £14,184 pa • Independent

Tel: 020 8299 8432
Fax: 020 8693 6319
Email: junioradmissions@dulwich.org.uk
Website: www.dulwich.org.uk

Head: Since 2009, Mrs Alison Fleming, previously deputy head at Highgate Junior School.

Entrance: 48 boys join Year 3, around a third from Ducks, the pre-prep. Applicants take maths, English and non-verbal reasoning tests and everyone is interviewed. The college takes into account reports from their previous schools and quite a few boys come from state primaries. 'We understand that they may not have covered all the concepts. We don't expect perfection: the college has an exceptional understanding of boys with a "spiky profile". I want good all-round boys who are academically able.' Siblings and children of staff members have particularly sympathetic consideration but no automatic entry. 'I need to see academic potential. They must be able to cope with the curriculum. If I take them and they don't progress sufficiently it's grim at 11 plus time.' Those who don't get in at seven can try again when they are eight or nine. 'August-born boys in particular may be on track by then.' Small entries at 8+, 9+ and 10+, after maths and English tests, may well take the numbers up to 60 boys in Year 6.

Exit: Nearly all to the senior school. This is no longer automatic, but 'subject to satisfactory progress'.

Remarks: It is fair to say that, in the past, Dulwich Junior was seen as a stepping-stone between Ducks and the main school, noted more for its sporting than for its academic prowess. The new head is keen to give the school its own identity – a prospectus is in production – and to shine the spotlight on academia. She has brought with her from Highgate Junior School – which has followed the same path towards greater academic rigour – a culture of assessment for learning. 'We explain to the boys what it takes to be successful and try to get them to evaluate their work for themselves. We're keen on developing reflective thinking.' Happily, there is no need for exam preparation to dominate the curriculum. 'We don't have to train them up to hop through all the different hoops that senior schools wave around.'

Learning support help for individuals or small groups of boys with a suspected or diagnosed learning difficulty. 'The difficulties often arise from a short-term visual and auditory memory deficit,' says the school website, 'and the work is usually to help with the way these difficulties affect spelling, organisation, maths, creative writing and comprehension.'

Boys take part in house conkers, chess, art and academic competitions as well as sports matches. They put on performances, such as Joseph and the Amazing Technicolour Dreamcoat, in the Edward Alleyn theatre, play in ensembles and orchestras, sing in choirs. 'We have elite opportunities for very talented boys but we also have a culture of providing opportunities for all.' Everyone tries out a stringed instrument in Year 3 and a brass instrument in Year 4. The boys have access not only to the senior school's groomed acres of playing fields, the theatre and concert facilities, but also to high level sports and music coaching and tuition.

Plenty of lunch-time and after-school clubs ranging from Lego to Chapel Choir and Mandarin. All the boys get a trip to the school's field centre in the Brecon Beacons to do 'non-London things' such as hiking and canoeing. They can also join the school scout troop in Year 6.

The head's aim is to provide 'a compassionate education for boys – not just a rough, tough rugby-playing world'. She aims for a 'relationship of mutual respect' with boys and parents. 'I like to feel they can come and talk to me or other staff.' Exclusion is rare and a last resort. 'We will work to keep the boy if we possibly can. I'd only exclude permanently for something like persistent real defiance, or someone who is not safe to have around.'

There are some 10 per cent academic scholarships for boys joining Year 3, and quite a few are on means-tested bursaries. 'It looks like a very privileged public school from the outside but I love the fact that it represents the ethnic and social diversity of south London.'

Dulwich Hamlet Junior School

Dulwich Village, London, SE21 7AL

• Pupils: 360; 50/50 boy/girls; all day • Ages: 7-11 • Non-denom • State

Tel: 020 7525 9188
Fax: 020 7525 9187
Email: office@dulwichhamlet.southwark.sch.uk
Website: www.dulwichhamlet.southwark.sch.uk

Head: Since 2007, Mrs Sonia Case BA PGCE (fifties). Previously deputy head of Greenstreet Green Primary, she has had number of years' experience teaching in Bromley schools. Married with two grown-up daughters and with her broad artistic background, Mrs Case is ideally placed to helm this primary school. Originally trained in theatre, she worked in performing arts and marketing, before turning her attention to education and leading this unique school with its truly enhanced curriculum. She is supported in her work by a diverse and committed team of teachers and specialists. Her enthusiasm and cheerful personality are much appreciated by staff and parents who feel children just love being at the Hamlet. Mrs Case appears to be something of a wizard when it comes to the school budget.

Entrance: At 7+, 90 places; entry is via the Southwark admissions policy. Parents are advised to apply on time. Pupils come from many local primaries, particularly Dulwich Village Infants. Always oversubscribed, but don't let that put you off applying.

Exit: At 11+, usually about two-thirds to state sector – The Charter, Newstead Wood, Haberdashers, Lewisham, Kingsdale. One third to independent schools – Alleyn's, JAGS, Dulwich College. Pupils regularly win scholarships and awards for music and academics.

Remarks: Probably Southwark's most sought-after primary school. The Hamlet continuously develops and updates its spacious site which consists of several Victorian and modern buildings skillfully blended and connected. Most recently, a fabulous space has been redesigned to create a multi-purpose hall, dining room, design and technology suite, and children's cookery area. Adventurous and inspiring curriculum has ensured the school remains a top performer both academically and artistically. Classrooms are attractive and well-resourced with traditional equipment alongside all the latest technology. Class sizes are mixed ability and large, usually about 30 pupils, setting for all year groups in maths.

Undoubtedly the most distinguishing feature is the arts curriculum, particularly music, which is almost unheard-of today in the state sector. Nearly all pupils learn an instrument and structured music lessons are part of every child's education. Impressive range of instruments, anything from euphoniums to Gamelan gongs. Choirs, woodwind, strings and brass groups and ensembles regularly entertain parents, and the children are invited to many public performances and festivals. A variety of dance and drama projects run and children have 100 per cent pass rate for LAMDA exams. Several art exhibitions in-house and in local galleries and school is involved in community art projects. Musicians, actors, artists and writers regularly invited to the school to talk to the children and run workshops.

Technology is embedded across the curriculum; everyone has the opportunity to learn touch-typing, Apple Macs for animation, art projects and of course music technology. French is thriving, Year 5s are taken on annual residential trip to France. Sports Active Mark, pupils take advantage of the local sports facilities, a number of sports specialists visit the school to coach gymnastics, netball, cricket and football. Other young athletes represent Dulwich in swimming and athletics competitions. Enrichment afternoons run during the summer term giving children the opportunity to explore all kinds of activities and discover new interests. Around 15 after-school clubs to choose from, amongst the most popular are cookery, magic and table tennis. A full-time inclusion manager is responsible for running additional support programmes, and specially-trained teachers for those requiring SEN provision. Speech and occupational therapists work with the school as necessary. ESOL can also be arranged.

Pastoral care is organised through the PSHCE curriculum, producing confident, articulate and responsible pupils who come from a wide variety of backgrounds. Healthy eating is important here; lunchtime is a social event in the new dining room or outdoor picnic area. Monthly menus are on the website and all food is freshly made. The Hamlet Herald keeps the school community up-to-date with all the current happenings, also an excellent user-friendly website. Parents are asked to make a small voluntary contribution each term to school activities and an enthusiastic PTA and governors run a variety of social and fund-raising events.

As you might imagine, judged outstanding by Ofsted in all areas. The school continues to play an important role in supporting trainee teachers working with Southbank and Goldsmith's Universities. An educational treat.

Dulwich Preparatory School

Coursehorn, Cranbrook, Kent, TN17 3NP

• Pupils: 535; 50:50 boys and girls. Mainly day with some (up to 70) flexi and occasional boarding • Ages: 3-13 • Broadly Christian but all denominations welcome • Fees: Nursery - Y8 £4,548-£13,365 pa; Boarding £35.50 per night • Independent

Tel: 01580 712 179
Fax: 01580 715 322
Email: registrar@dcpskent.org
Website: www.dcpskent.org

Headmaster: Since September 2010, Mr Paul David BEd (early forties). Attended Exeter University. Housemaster and maths and games teacher (head of cricket) at City of London Freemen's School prior to moving to Colet Court, St Paul's Preparatory School, as deputy head, where he coached rugby across all age ranges and taught mathematics at St Paul's School. For the last eight years has been a successful headmaster of Eaton Square School, a co-educational nursery, pre-prep and preparatory school in the heart of central London. An active ISI inspector, his interests include skiing, playing tennis and music (former member of Surrey Opera and a competent trumpeter). Married to Nicky, also an experienced prep school teacher, with particular interests in art and drama. Two children, nine and four, who have joined the school; Mrs David now works there too.

Firm believer in the benefits of preparatory co-education. Believes 'every single child has the capacity to excel. Our challenge is to identify a child's abilities and work out how to motivate, how to inspire, when to be firm and when to let things coast along'; and 'education must be fostered from within – it stems from connecting not directing'.

Entrance: On a first-come-first-served basis, with the only priority being given to siblings. Non-competitive assessment tests from age 7+ – very rare for a child to fail but school doesn't want to take someone who can't cope. Intakes in nursery, reception, Years 3 and 5 (and in-between if space). Another intake in Year 7 when some children leave for the grammar schools and others come from local primary schools to prepare for Cranbrook entrance at 13+.

Exit: Up to half to Cranbrook at 13+. About 10 or 11 per year (of 72) move on to the grammars at 11+ – the school will prepare the children for these exams. Otherwise, the most popular schools are Tonbridge, King's Canterbury, Sevenoaks, Sutton Valence, Eastbourne, St Leonard's Mayfield and Bethany, with a few going further afield to, e.g., Charterhouse, Bedales and Winchester. Variety of scholarships each year ranging from major academic awards to Tonbridge, King's Canterbury and Cranbrook to art, design technology, sport and music scholarships; 13 scholarships in all in 2010.

Remarks: Evacuated from London to Cranbrook in 1939, the school began life as a series of huts. These are long gone and have been replaced over the years by modern buildings. In spite of the historical links, the school is quite separate from Dulwich College, London.

Set in 50 acres of grounds, playing fields etc, has a campus feel to it. Divided into three self-contained sections: Nash House (3–5 year olds), Little Stream (5–9 year olds) and Upper School (9–13 year olds). Children from the age of six are split into four Tribes: Chippeways, Deerfeet, Mohicans and Ojibwas – lots of inter-house competitions. Whole school has a theme for each term, e.g. 'Look smart, be smart'.

Nash House is set away from the main school in its own building, all very up-to-date with interactive whiteboards; climbing frames and sandpit outside. The nursery now offers flexible sessions. Open door for parents to come in and see how their children are learning. Great emphasis on building children's social confidence; they are encouraged to stand up in front of an audience on a regular basis, whether relating their news in assembly, taking part in form plays or participating in class showing times when parents come into the school to hear what the children have been doing (shades of Calvin and Hobbes). Music and PE taught by specialist teachers; a member of the special needs department teaches any children who need extra help. Structured but relaxed atmosphere. Lots of theme days. Every child has work on the wall. Wonderful music.

Little Stream has specialist teachers for science (taught in a lab), music, PE and French. Classrooms very colourful with children's work all over the walls. Each has its own computer linked to a network system; also an IT suite plus set of laptops for classroom use. Well-used library with its own librarian. Outings, talks and workshop days a major part of the curriculum, particularly in history and geography.

Upper School feels more like a public school than a prep school – superb facilities. Children are (where possible) setted for academic subjects, but not streamed, apart from a separate scholarship form in the final year. The average class size is 18 with a maximum of 20. IT top notch: all classrooms have interactive whiteboards, overhead digital projectors and video-recorders and monitors; separate computer room with 24 computers plus computers in every classroom. Much use of the internet. Education outings a major feature of school life, and include theatre trips and visits to sites of historical interest. Geography field study trips, visits to France and an adventure training week for the final year pupils after their exams.

Fantastic library – masses of books, and computers linked to network. Authors visit every term. Twice-yearly book fairs. Library competitions. Audio tapes in library for those not so keen on reading.

About 20 per cent of children have some sort of learning support, individually and in small groups – no extra charge. Provision for the physically disabled, one or two statemented children.

Older pupils choose a member of staff to keep an eye on their academic progress and general well-being. Strong anti-bullying policy – school intranet can be used for children to email worries in confidence. Democratic structure – no prefects or head boy or girl. Every leaver is a 'senior' with a specific area of responsibility.

Regular parents' evenings. A curriculum summary is provided for parents so that they can see the work being done by their child's year group. Each term parents are invited to attend a subject evening at which they can sample the lessons given to their children.

Strong musical tradition. All children can read music by the time they leave Nash House age five or six. Separate music department with a director and three full-time music specialists. All children have two or three class music lessons a week. About 280 learn an instrument – 19 peripatetic teachers. Over 15 extra-curricular groups including an orchestra, two wind bands, six choirs, a jazz band, pop groups plus a number of smaller chamber groups. Small informal concerts two or three times a term after school and more formal evening concerts twice a year. Lots of music exams and children take part in music tours of Italy, Germany, Holland, Paris and Austria.

Drama incorporated into weekly timetable. Drama clubs for the enthusiasts and children can take the English Speaking Board examinations each year. Each section of the school produces annual play. Wonderful John Leakey Hall with fixed seating which can be moved electronically. Art clubs held after school plus extra tuition for those taking art scholarships (usually win a couple of these each year). Lots of artwork displayed around the school.

Strong tradition of cross-country running for both boys and girls. All the usual sports, with teams in most; as many children as possible are included – up to four teams per age group and the school tries to have an inter-school or 'Tribe' fixture every week for each age group. Opportunities to have trials and play for Kent teams. Good sports facilities.

Boarding: boys at The Lodge and girls at The Manor. School very accommodating (when they have room) if parents need to go away for a few days or on holiday. School day for boarders ends at the same time as for day children and the boarding houses are very much 'homes from home'.

Parents include lots of local business people and farmers as well as City commuters; most children live within about 15 miles of the school. No Saturday school, but children expected to be available for Saturday matches.

Just about everything you could possibly want here – its size means that the facilities are superb. Some parents who avoid it say children can get lost in the system but, as one parent put it, most children are very happy and do well, though it particularly suits those who are up-front, determined and capable.

Dumpton School

Deans Grove House, Deans Grove, Wimborne, Dorset, BH21 7AF

• Pupils: 140 boys and 70 girls in prep; ages 8-13; 90 in pre-prep, 40 in nursery; all day • Ages: 2-13 • Christian • Fees: Pre-Prep £6,960; Prep £12,465 pa • Independent

Tel: 01202 883 818
Fax: 01202 848 760
Email: secretary@dumpton.com
Website: www.dumpton.com

Head: Since 2005, Mr Andrew W Browning BSc PGCE MA CChem MRSC (forties). Educated at Farnborough Grammar School in Hampshire, read chemistry at Southampton University, followed by PGCE, thence a Master's in education at the Open University whilst at Canford where he spent 22 years, becoming head of chemistry at 27, housemaster at 35 and registrar thereafter (winning the coveted Salter's prize for chemistry teaching on the way). He 'always wanted to teach' and still teaches an hour a day to 12- and 13-year-olds, blaming Mrs Sharpe, the head of science at Dumpton, for 'sending him on courses to improve his skills'.

Mr Browning took over from the much-loved Garth Watson (27 years at the helm), who left him 'the best staff I have ever had' and they are still there today; he was a regular visitor to Dumpton before taking over and the deputy head 'has been a great help' – he also coaches rugby and hockey and seems to turn his hand to most things. A gentle man, thought a 'good egg' by his pupils, has a quiet self-deprecating sense of humour, does his share of coaching and blesses his governing body for providing 'every form of backup – legal, financial or just straight backup'. His wife, Jo, who taught at Castle Court for eight years, runs the mums' and toddlers' group on Thursdays (which is free), is child protection officer and 'totally involved with the school'. They have two young children, Jacob, who is in the school, and an enchanting daughter, Esther, who was privy to some of our interview (and wore toning clothes to her mama's).

Entrance: Via toddlers' group, nursery – no test; gentle test thereafter, though those who are not up to scratch and apply aged 11 or 12 may not be accepted. Pupils can come at any time, presuming space available, mid term if necessary (fair amount of Service personnel locally).

Exit: For the most part to local schools: either into the state system, to Canford (the closest) or Bryanston, Clayesmore, Wentworth etc; a minority opt for boarding. Horses for courses, but an impressive diaspora. Trillions of scholarships in all disciplines all over.

Remarks: School moved from Kent (where they were at Dumpton House) to Dorset during the second world war, and then had a peripatetic trip round local stately homes, arriving at Deans Grove House (previously the headquarters of the Dalgety piggery) from Gaunt's House in 1986. They now boast 26 acres of playing fields (with a splendid oak in the middle of the athletics track across the road) dedicated to a combination of blue and green Astroturfs, hockey/netball et al and bordered by the most magical of eco trails – proper ponds and pontoons with a hefty input from the Ecology and Hydrology Centre at Winfrith. The eco-project has garnered loads of medals, with 'real' scientists working alongside pupils.

Ecology important: the paper police paid a call on the head and solemnly removed his wastepaper basket – school normally expects to raise two-and-a-half grand each year through recycling – and yes, pupils do expect to carry on the good work at home. Allotments for all on a house system, which head has done much to encourage (though they sound rather like a bus timetable) – Sussex, Kent, Hants and Dorset, with prefects (house captains) chosen from amongst the top form on an election system. Wizard adventure playground for tinies, complete with pirate ship. Campsite in the offing, ditto an orchard – a couple of boxes of apple trees arrived during our visit. School is all on site, with complicated arrangements of gates to keep cars away from pupils. Certain amount of tinkering with the fabric and lots of developments – new science and maths blocks, library, art and extended ICT centres plus refurbished kitchens.

Good assembly hall has impressive new lighting and sound kit – drama and music very important here, with only 40 not learning an instrument or two. Dedicated music school; the drum practice room is in a separate building. The school sings locally at the Minster and in Sherborne. Proper games hall with what looked to us like an apology for a climbing wall (but is in fact a fiendishly expensive traversing wall 'allowing safe lateral climbing to develop upper body strength') and was commissioned by the Friends of Dumpton. One or two miscreants had obviously been wearing black-soled trainers – a fair number of nasty marks – and we visited the second day of term! Games for all each day for an hour, open-air pool which is heated and usually runs into the autumn term. House meals, with salad bar option – staff sit more-or-less at random amongst the pupils and Mrs Browning was happily feeding her two-and-a-half-year-old in a high chair at the tinies' lunch, with another small creature on her lap. The school is nut-free – so no Mars Bars then.

Jolly Phonics taught from scratch; classes are tiny – no more than 18, with two (or occasionally three) parallel forms in any one year. PSHE from age eight. Certain amount of streaming at the bottom and very serious scholarship classes at the top. Latin, but no Greek, and French early (photographs all over of jolly japes on school trips to French-speaking Switzerland – indeed trips all over). Dedicated classrooms; only one computer suite (we usually like to see more) – but in fairness, there was a maths lesson in progress at the time. A couple or so of interactive whiteboards and great use made of the latest technology: e-beam, which turns every whiteboard into a more-or-less active whiteboard via a magic pencil (at 400 quid they have to make sense and can be moved from classroom to classroom – with the aid of a wodge of blu tac).

Continuous assessment picks up early problems in the dyslexic stream, with pupils visiting the Eyrie either for one-to-one (costs extra) or small group lessons. Rather more pupils in the regular spelling lesson during our visit than there were getting specialist help, but four dedicated staff doing the business in the Eyrie, which also acts as a drop-in centre for those needing immediate help.

School ceased boarding some time ago and Saturday school shortly after. Pupils come a fair distance, their parents often moving to Dorset (cheaper than Gloucestershire with good fast trains to Waterloo from Poole) to benefit from the local independent school network. School organises buses to Blandford, Parkstone, Poole and Ringwood – 'The A31 is a boon'. Not really a green wellie school. Shorts for chaps until age 11 and pretty check skirts and elegant dark blue trimmed blouses for girls (Mrs B runs a secondhand shop). Number of first-time buyers – probably more numerous than the old boy network, who are relentless in their fundraising via the Friends of Dumpton.

Can't fault it.

Dunhurst (Bedales Junior School)

Linked to Bedales School in the Senior section

Petersfield, Hampshire, GU32 2DP

• Pupils: 190 boys and girls in Dunhurst; 55 board (full, weekly or flexi); 90 in pre-prep Dunannie • Ages: pre-prep (Dunannie) 3-8 prep (Dunhurst) 8-13 • Fees: Boarding £19,050; Day £14,910; Dunannie £6,630-£8,100 pa • Independent

Tel: 01730 300 200
Fax: 01730 711820
Email: jjarman@bedales.org.uk
Website: www.bedales.org.uk

Headmistress: Since 2004, Mrs Penny Watkins (late fifties), previously deputy head at Bedales, prior to which she was senior mistress at Whitgift and then head of English at Latymer Upper. Coming back to the Bedales schools was for her 'coming home'. It also brought to Dunhurst a much-needed stabilising presence after several years of disruption and unhappiness resulting from a series of short-lived heads and public dissent about the school's structure and direction. Now all but forgotten, thanks to Mrs Watkins' highly competent hand on the rudder. Parents think her sound, sensible and entirely trustworthy. Children love her. Authoritative, relaxed and highly experienced, she will be hard to replace when she leaves in July 2011.

Head of Dunannie: Since May 2010, Ms Jo Webbern, Froebel CertEd, (fiftyish) previously class teacher and then head of kindergarten at Ibstock Place for 26 years. Newly in post when we met her, she was clearly full of enthusiasm and excitement. 'I feel these are my roots,' she exclaimed. 'One can deliver that special ethos and creativity here while teaching children all the important skills of life.' She has lots of plans – especially 'to develop the outside classroom'.

Entrance: No selection in nursery – and the school has a crèche which takes staff babies and others – except to try and balance boys/girls. Healthy waiting list. Otherwise, applicants to Dunannie – 15–20 – places and to Dunhurst – 45 places for applicants from outside – spend a day in school before having a more formal assessment. 20-odd places at 11+ – very over-subscribed. Much depends on whether the school and families like each other – understanding of and sympathy with the ethos is all-important.

Exit: 95 per cent of Dunhurst leavers move to Bedales. Of course.

Remarks: Nursery, for the 2 ¾–4-year-olds, is in a fabulous old barn nesting in trees, full of activities worth getting on your knees for. We liked the owl's tree-top house and the Brio train. Thence to Dunannie – the purpose-built and super school for the tots – cunningly housed under six overlapping and interlocking colourful roofs with big windows and home to the pre-prep years. 'It's a nice school,' an eight-year-old told us. 'It's very comfortable – you feel more free than in most schools. People don't mess about because the teachers are very calm and don't say "Do This! Do That!"' Much to enjoy here – the super wall-hanging – 'we weaved it and felted it with Steve-the-Weave, one of those workshoppy people' – the Year 3 enchanted forest illustrating A Midsummer Night's Dream, the super seasons project with outsize drawings of pomegranate seeds. Every inch is covered with displays, book boxes and hangings – creativity drips off the walls. Outside is garden and space, space, space. We loved the 'Celtic hut' in the orchard, the 'sound garden' and the musical fort. Children everywhere, in tiny classes, are absorbed, relaxed and happily occupied.

Up to Dunhurst at eight. Boarding begins at this stage and most children spend some nights each week in school, though hardly anyone is in over the weekend. Outdoor work also features importantly now – masses of woodwork, gardening and animal care. Woodwork – in yet another old barn (see Bedales entry) – uses lots of different materials and techniques – soldering, circuitry – and the children make toys, automata, bird boxes, lamps, guitars, chairs and library steps. We loved the sound-operated cars and toys. They design on paper using pencils – hooray! They make textiles too and pottery – witty stuff – observant pieces on parts of animals – a crocodile's jaw, a turkey's eye, an elephant's trunk. Other lessons are likewise creative and collaborative – in art they study colour while in science they cover primary colours and the spectrum. Not rocket science – why can't other schools do this? 'We like our science room,' we were told, 'we have to invent or discover something which would make a difference to us or to the world.'

Subject areas are traditional but informed by the Bedales ethos and a consistency between the three schools – as well as a welcome cross-curricular approach. See the Bedales entry for a fuller description of this. SEN teacher supports those who need it. 'She's a miracle worker,' one bright little button told us. A family therapist works with parents and children when appropriate.

Saturday school until 1pm. Many staff and some facilities shared with Bedales. All eat (toothsomely) together in dining room decorated with African mural and wall-hangings. The older children are very teeny – floppy fringes, low-slung jeans and mini minis or shorts over tights – the Bedales uniform. All are relaxed and chatty – this is a school where people smile spontaneously. Relations between staff and pupils are open, friendly and mutually respectful. The first-name business doesn't seem odd after you've been here five minutes. Mrs Watkins has her sights firmly set. 'We're working terribly hard to move those academic standards up a notch without losing what is special about this school.' The three heads are clearly in harmony and share values and goals. This informs continuity in academic, ethical and pastoral matters. The school feels in good heart.

Durand Primary School

Hackford Road, Stockwell, London, SW9 0RD

• Pupils: 860 boys and girls, 50 full time and 60 part time places in nursery • Ages: 3-11 • Non-denom • State

Tel: 02077 358 348
Fax: 0207 793 0605
Email: headteacher@durandprimary.com
Website: www.durand.lambeth.sch.uk

Head: Durand has recently restructured the management, creating a director of education in addition to the headteacher position, as the school continues to grow and the governors look to the future. The director of education is Mr Greg Martin BA Hons (fifties), who has been at the school since 1986. Focused, committed and full of far-sighted initiative, has four children, three of whom have been through Durand; he commutes weekly from Kent to live on site. When he moved from his deputy headship at Sudbourne Primary in Brixton (previously taught at St Mary's in Clapham), Durand had a separate junior and infant school – 'A disaster!'. In 1988 he moved from the headship of the junior to leading the new amalgamated school.

The headteacher since 2007 is Mr Mark McLaughlin, who has been at the school since 1988. He has a BA Hons from Durham University, is in his forties with one child and has lived in south London for 20 years. He has seen and been involved in the transformation of the school for 20 years, and with the director of education is looking forward to the next stage of the school's development.

He has an experienced leadership team which compensates for and accommodates the high turnover of newly-qualified teachers (NQTs): an acting deputy head, a home-grown assistant head (originally an NQT) who has responsibility for the day-to-day running of the Mostyn site, and 10 team leaders responsible for the development of teachers within their year group.

Mr McLaughlin feels strongly that the current 19th-century school structure is outdated and ineffective and that the extra resourcing given by this government has not solved the problem. Too many of the 190 teaching days are lost to teacher sickness and training, schools should be open from 9am to 6pm for 52 weeks a year and teachers should book five-week holidays in advance like the rest of the work force. The morning should be dedicated to rigorous academia, with sport and drama in the afternoon, providing childcare and keeping children off street corners. Parents could take their children on two-week holidays when they liked, by prior arrangement. Teachers would be responsible for the same curriculum content over a longer period, theoretically reducing their stress.

However, in the absence of any politician risking their neck on such a radical change, Mr Martin and Mr McLaughlin continue to implement their own version of accountable and rigorous teaching and management at Durand, and their legal and moral contract involving public money and children's lives has made them popular with pupils and parents, but not with Lambeth LA. This philosophy has been explained to other head teachers and the national press but the former are not bold enough to follow this example as yet. 'I see it as my job to speak for the silent majority, the children. If you don't give them leadership, they will provide it from within their ranks via a strong personality or a bully, and these have no accountability.'

Entrance: At three into nursery (main point of entry), or at four into reception. No tests or interviews; siblings and then shortest distance to school (Durand site) take precedence, always over-subscribed. No choice as to attendance on Durand or Mostyn site.

Exit: 60 per cent stay in Lambeth for secondary schooling (some return after trying elsewhere), 40 per cent go to Wandsworth or Southwark. Popular choices include Dunraven, Graveney, Burntwood, St Martin in the Fields, London Nautical and Bishop Thomas Grant.

Remarks: A beacon school and one of the largest and best-equipped state primaries in western Europe, fiercely independent, has its own sports centre and sparkling indoor swimming pool! These facilities are subsidised for family use – 80p per week for parent use of the sports centre. Instead of selling off its land when it became grant maintained in 1995, Durand developed it and built an accommodation block for NQTs and students, and did it again after the GM period was over in 2000. The rental accommodation and the sports centre each turn over about £300,000 per year; the sports centre does little more than pay for itself, but the accommodation blocks provide a healthy profit, ensuring that the school never lacks money (they save £400,000 on the budget yearly) which, in turn, leads to many successful matched-funding applications. Lambeth LA does not feel comfortable with this and there has been a history of antipathy between the council and Durand. One of the results of this may be the lack of SEN statements granted to pupils in the school, despite repeated applications.

Eighty per cent black Caribbean and African pupils, many from single parent families with more than one job. There are three SENCos to deal with 35 per cent SEN and 30 per cent of the pupils have English as a second language. Class size is 20 or under and children are screamingly happy and courteous. This primary-painted, well-kept school has an all-weather sports pitch and creative playground. The original building is 1886 but the old school York stone gates are now arches in the dining room. Subsidised food (40p per meal and 50 per cent free school meals) is heading towards gold star organic standard.

Durand is a training centre (one of 16 in the UK) and takes on three or four graduates and 20 NQTs each year. Management team makes it extremely clear that rigour, direction and purpose are vital. Pupil and teacher progress is monitored constantly and 28 teacher assistants (many parents themselves) help this. Pupils are aware of the high turnover of NQTs (normal in an inner-city school) and accept it as a cycle, although they do wish some teachers would stay longer. Unfortunately, the discipline and strategies taught to these primary age children are often unsustainable in the local state secondary schools. The management observes that there is a gap around Year 7 where state education could be called 'child-minding' and the children's focus and concentration lags until GCSE prep begins. A Durand secondary might combat this apathy.

The strategies obviously work; Durand results are 20 per cent above other Lambeth schools and 14 per cent above the national average, and the school is in the top five per cent for value-added. The community votes with its feet for this school – local people are employed here, former pupils bring their children and there are no graffiti or break-ins. The after-school club was set up in 1995, breaking an NUT picket line to do so, and now there are 250 children who use it for a subsidised 63p per hour to explore French, Spanish and other topics.

Fifty per cent of the children come in below national expectations for their age and, after streaming from the age of eight, they leave very engaged, 90 per cent having achieved at least the national average. From this age to until six they are taught, in groups of about 15 pupils with a teacher and TA, to 'access education', to sit still, concentrate and follow directions – nursery is not all about racing around and riding bikes! The children are formally assessed on entry using the early years' assessment process and then their progress is tracked using monthly assessments (and ongoing teacher and TA assessments continually through these two or three years). By Year 1 they are sitting at desks and start the national curriculum, in Year 2 they do SATs, and in Year 3 they're streamed. By this time there is a body of information on each individual and the least able are put into classes of 12 (according to the kids, there is no stigma attached to this at all) who each have a full-time teacher and two part-time TAs.

Streaming continues to Year 6 – changes are normally marginal and they always involve difficult decisions. Should a child be at the top of least able class or bottom of the average? Which are they temperamentally better suited to? Every child has a target set in first month of the new academic year; these can be academic or about coming to school on time – any behavioural issue which impacts on their education. These targets are communicated to the parents and they are reviewed at Easter, Christmas and end of year. The body of information is built from a sampling of work, formalised assessments, SATs, reading assessments, teacher observations, pieces of evidence – usually pieces of work. There is a huge range of evidence and it is as independent as possible; a teacher other than the form teacher will carry out a reading assessment to ensure the test is done to a particular standard. The school is aiming to avoid polluted results in assessments since, often, form teachers will say they know the child and take that into account. Of course, there is space for that knowledge, but the independent view is vital and the head is secure that the school's assessments are fair.

At key stage 2 there is a real focus on targets, with reviews with the parents at least three times a year. At these, parents go through targets with teachers to ascertain the success of the child. The constant feedback means that the school knows within weeks if there is a problem and then the question is: why? If the kids are not meeting the targets, the school will often look at the teacher and the classroom; they assess teacher knowledge and teacher performance too, e.g. planning, marking and classroom practices. Has the child had a change of circumstance? Thankfully, only a small percentage does not make their targets. If there is a five or six per cent discrepancy between the target and actual performance, the school revisits the initial assessment. Sometimes the teacher will undervalue child's ability in order to get them moving. The causes of target failure could be child ability, planning or not completing work, but quite often the problem is the teacher, in particular the small percentage of teachers that fail.

The school's problematic relationship with Lambeth LA means that at present only three children have a statement. Durand now encourages and supports parents to take the LA to court in order to get their child the necessary statement.

The parents' main beef was with the Mostyn site, which was taken over as a failing school in 1999. In three weeks 90 per cent of issues were resolved, but the facilities were shabby compared to Durand's until the 2009 renovation. This and the other successful projects would not have been possible without the consistent support of the governors. There are curriculum meetings for English, maths and science and for SATs preparation. Children who bully are sent home immediately. Murals, and children's work is hung on a 'good work board' and other walls; the children are tidy (no jewellery or chewing gum) and their favourite teachers are those that are 'strict, nice and funny'. Pupils are sparky, intelligent and good company. A really impressive and effective school. One of the first primary schools to become an academy in September 2010, and will no doubt make the most of the freedoms this brings.

Durham High School For Girls Junior School

Linked to Durham High School For Girls in the Senior section

Farewell Hall, Durham, County Durham, DH1 3TB

• Pupils: girls; all day • Ages: 3-11 • Accepts all faiths and none
• Fees: £6,090-£7,215 pa • Independent

Tel: 0191 384 3226
Fax: 0191 386 7381
Email: juniorhead@dhsfg.org.uk
Website: www.dhsfg.org.uk

Remarks: For further information see senior school entry.

Eagle House School

Linked to Wellington College in the Senior section

Sandhurst, Berkshire, GU47 8PH

• Pupils: 340 boys and girls; 50 board • Ages: 7-13, plus nursery and pre-prep 3-7 • C of E • Fees: Boarding £18,375; Day £13,695 pa • Independent

Tel: 01344 772 134
Fax: 01344 779 039
Email: info@eaglehouseschool.com
Website: www.eaglehouseschool.com

Headmaster: Since 2006, Mr Andrew Barnard BA PGCE (early forties). Educated at Christ's Hospital and Sheffield University, where he read archaeology and pre-history. After PGCE at former King Alfred's College, Winchester, began his teaching career at Eagle House. Spent five years as head of English and drama at Heath Mount and five more as deputy head at Winchester House. Enthusiastic, focused and very happy to be back at Eagle House – 'It's a lovely school and a lovely part of the world'. Teaches six periods of English a week to Year 7s – 'I was determined to keep my hand in'. Very keen on drama and sportingly got cajoled into playing an Ugly Sister in the staff panto at the end of his first term. Married, with three children, two at Eagle House, one at Wellington. His energetic teacher wife, Sarah, is very involved in school life – everything from organising match teas to helping out in the nursery. Family lives in house 100 yards down the school's leafy drive.

Entrance: Broad intake. Most children live within 10- to 15-mile radius of school and come from myriad of nurseries, pre-preps and state primaries. No entrance test (which some London parents find odd) but previous school report requested and children visit for informal assessment before entry. 'We aren't just striving for academic success,' says head. 'We pride ourselves on being a very rounded school.' Main entry points are nursery (called The Nest and housed in separate building on school site) and Year 3. Pretty flexible, though – worth trying at other ages. Increasing numbers are arriving at 11 to do two years before public school. Handful of pupils from abroad – Spain, Italy, Nigeria, South Korea and Japan etc. An amazing display of clocks was on show in the vast hall when we visited – each clock set to boarders' home time zones.

Exit: Dr Anthony Seldon's arrival as master of neighbouring Wellington College (the two schools share a boundary) has created a huge spark of enthusiasm. Nearly three-quarters of Eagle House pupils go to Wellington College at 13, with rest heading for schools like Winchester, Eton, Bradfield, Shiplake, Downe House and St Swithun's. Now Wellington has gone co-ed most Eagle House girls stay on till 13 rather than leaving for girls' schools at 11.

Remarks: Founded in Hammersmith in 1820, moved to Wimbledon in 1860 and has been on its present 40-acre site between Crowthorne and Sandhurst since 1886. Owned by Wellington College but run independently. Uses many of Wellington's facilities and the two heads meet regularly. Main building is a rambling redbrick house surrounded by well-tended lawns, playing fields and woods (den-making a very popular pursuit). Grounds also boast adventure playground, athletics track and school's very own thatched Tudor house, built by staff and pupils and opened by Prince Charles in 2003. Boarding facilities have been updated with new common room plus various computer stations for emailing home.

Classes are small (maximum 18 but more likely to be around 15). Well-qualified and friendly staff – average age 42. Traditional curriculum, plus extra one-to-one provision at £22 per lesson for children with SEN (dyslexia, dyspraxia, ADD, SpLD, EFL, Asperger's Syndrome). Most subjects taught in forms but older children setted for maths, English, science and French. Scholarship group in Years 7 and 8 – school wins a good smattering of scholarships each year. All children learn French, with Latin from Year 5 and Greek for scholarship group.

School assembly held every Monday morning, with chapel and other assemblies for small groups on other days. Music strong. More than two-thirds of prep school pupils learn musical instrument. School concert held every term and lots of informal recitals, competitions and tours. When we visited there was huge excitement about the school's forthcoming E-Factor talent competition (with performances by pupils and teachers) to raise money for charity. Drama popular – 10- to 13-year-olds put on major production each year. Children's artwork on show everywhere – bustling artroom boasts everything from pottery piggy banks to self-portraits.

Big emphasis on sport. Boys play rugby, football, hockey and cricket while girls play netball, hockey and rounders. Cross-country, athletics and swimming (in school's own indoor pool) for all. Recent sports tours to Argentina, South Africa and Australia. All children join a 'section' when they start at Eagle House – Merlins, Ospreys, Harriers and Kites – and sports matches between them are fiercely contested.

Happy pupils who are friendly, polite and keen to show off their school. 'I want to come back and work here during my gap year,' one of our young guides told us. Children are very proud of their school council, which is made up of elected representatives from each year and meets twice a term. Recent triumphs include the installation of water coolers and hopscotch in the playground. Pupils' behaviour is good and reinforced by system of stars and stripes – stars handed out for work, sport, music and being helpful while too many stripes mean a headmaster's detention.

School rightfully proud of its pastoral care, overseen by the deputy head (pastoral). Day master greets children in person every morning and even acts as a postman for parents, dropping off notes for teachers. Each year group split into three or four tutor groups and one tutor appointed pastoral year head. Head boy and girl, along with raft of prefects. New pupils are given a 'guardian' to guide them through their first fortnight. The school also has a buddy system linking Year 3s up with Year 6s – to encourage a caring approach and help younger children make friends higher up the school. Head very interested in Anthony Seldon's decision to put happiness lessons on the Wellington College curriculum but feels that children's well-being is well looked after in PSHCE, citizenship and life skills lessons.

The week is long (compulsory Saturday school and 6pm pickup for oldest day pupils, after prep) but children get a 90-minute lunch break and are encouraged to make the most of it. Whole host of activities on offer, from street dance and trampolining to food technology and choir (known as the Chapel Chamber Choir, or Cha Cha Ch for short). Head likes children to keep at least one lunchtime free – 'It's important that they get the chance to play too,' he says. Recent ISI inspection report very impressed by the school's imaginative Golden Eagle programme, which teaches Year 7 and 8s responsibility, initiative and team-building through activities like first aid, camping skills and bushcraft.

Children say food is 'amazing' (praise indeed!), with lots of choice. Cafeteria system, with dining-room decked out in jolly blue and white checked tablecloths and a teacher sitting at each table, along with a mix of year groups. Small number of boarders housed in main school building – boys at one end, girls at the other. Head would like to see boarding numbers grow to 70, but says occasional and weekly boarding becoming increasingly popular.

A happy, successful school that is firmly on the up. Anthony Seldon has created a real buzz at neighbouring Wellington College – no doubt that Eagle House is feeling the effect too.

Eaton House Belgravia

Linked to Eaton House The Manor Schools in the Junior section
Linked to Eaton House The Vale in the Junior section

3-5 Eaton Gate, Eaton Square, Belgravia, London, SW1W 9BA

• Pupils: 220 boys, all day • Ages: 4-8 • Non-denom • Fees: £11,925 pa • Independent

Tel: 020 7730 9343
Fax: 020 7730 1798
Email: admin@eatonhouseschools.com
Website: www.eatonhouseschools.com

Headmistress: Since 1998, the energetic and enthusiastic Miss Lucy Watts (thirties), previously taught at a co-ed Montessori prep school before moving to Eaton House Belgravia in 1990. Joined as a class teacher, then head of science and deputy head before working her way up to lead the school. She does just that – providing calm, considered and efficient leadership coupled with a sense of fun. Feels strongly that the Eaton House group of schools is an inclusive family – pupils, peripatetic and admin staff, cooks and teachers – which is caring and hard-working, with good manners. Very keen on upholding tradition while innovating; open to new suggestions from parents and staff (e.g. staggered leaving times for seniors and juniors to avoid congestion on stairs) but will weigh pros and cons carefully before implementing. Committed (four godchildren through friendships formed at Eaton House) and full of good ideas (seniors discuss daily headlines in current affairs group for 15 minutes while lunch queue dies down). Covers absences and currently teaches handwriting to the little ones, maths to the Year 3s.

Entrance: Preference for siblings, children of staff, ex-staff and old boys, otherwise first come first served. With a waiting list – most parents put names down at birth. £50 for definite registration, £30 to go on the waiting list. Deposit of term's fees, two terms before pupil starts – credited in full against final term's fees.

Exit: Top London day schools are most popular (85 per cent of leavers): Westminster Under, Colet Court, Westminster Cathedral Choir, Eaton House The Manor, Sussex House. Also boarding schools: Summer Fields, The Dragon, Ludgrove. Westminster Cathedral Choir and Eaton House The Manor run specific open days for this school, also good relationships with heads of feeder preps for Eton, Radley etc.

Remarks: Cheerful, hard-working, well principled pre-prep, with delight in learning obvious as you walk in the door and are faced by a display of photographs documenting the worldwide travels of Percy the school bear. Two-and-a-half buildings just off Sloane Square mean that the school is vertical rather than horizontal (lift available), but colourful art and awards cover all the available wall space. Boys are bussed to Hyde or Battersea Park every afternoon to let off energy/play sport, or to the Queen Mother Sports Centre to swim – all made aware of the school sports motto, 'Win with grace, lose with dignity'. Inter-house competitions encourage 'friendly rivalry'.

Indoor hockey, football, cricket and climbing take place in a hall which is also used for assemblies – the whole school troops in daily with the head boy and deputy holding the door open politely.

Manners are taught early here, with prizes for a tidy class and smart pupils -a 'visitors' boy' in each form shakes the hand of any stranger who enters the door. Each pupil is taught peer responsibility, every senior who is not a head of house/monitor has mentor duties for a younger boy. Usual curriculum with great science lab, drama, French and IT – while not neglecting handwriting skills. Class exams get children used to formal tests each term and termly written reports back up more informal contact with class teachers (available in their forms for parents at the beginning of every day). No formal PTA but each class hosts information evening every September and a Christmas newsletter is sent out as well at the annual issue of 'The Column' (covers all the Eaton House group of schools' news) and regular updates on the school's website, www.eatonhouseschools.com.

Head provides extended help to parents – these are largely local and bankers, lawyers and MPs – when choosing next school. Most parents are confident of their sons' long term prospects and see the future involving schools such as Eton or Radley and then perhaps Harvard. Eaton House is part of the Boys' School Coalition whose other members are chiefly from the US and Australia. Exchanges with NY schools particularly popular. Approximately 30 per cent of the boys have one non-British parent but on the whole these boys stay through the school – less transient than neighbouring pre-preps.

Lunch is served in two sittings in the basement, small rooms but a choice of healthy, fresh food daily. The five music rooms are also below street level; experienced and long-lasting part-time music staff teach the boys piano, violin, guitar, recorder, voice and cello. Performances in assemblies and choirs outside school encourage confidence.

School trips take advantage of all that London has to offer and extra-curricular clubs are popular, karate especially. Guest speakers also visit; the local vicar (St Peter's), local policeman, charities and parent volunteers.

'Since we are non-selective we need a good team', and SEN is particularly well supported here, a tradition for Eaton House ever since dyslexia was called 'word blindness'. A family feel about this school: each individual, pupil or member of staff is cared for – encouraged by the Harper family (principals of the Eaton House group) who began their association when Mrs Harper was a teacher at the school in the 1960s. In the past this pre-prep has been referred to as an academic hothouse, but no doubt that the boys are enjoying themselves enormously as they learn. 'An "us" school in a "me" area,' comments a parent. The boys are exuberant – it is the responsibility of both parents and staff to make sure their confidence does not stray into arrogance outside the school door!

Eaton House The Manor Schools

Linked to Eaton House Belgravia in the Junior section
Linked to Eaton House The Vale in the Junior section

The Manor House, 58 Clapham Common Northside, London, SW4 9RU

• Pupils: Prep 150, pre-prep 180, nursery 60; all day • Ages: Prep: 8-13 (boys only), pre-prep 4-8 (boys only), Girls' School 4-11 (girls only), nursery 2.5 to 4.5 (co-ed), • Non-denom • Fees: £11,925-£14,745; Nursery £2,655-£5,130 pa • Independent

Tel: 020 7924 6000
Fax: 020 7924 1530
Email: admin@eatonhouseschools.com
Website: www.eatonhouseschools.com

Prep: In September 2010 Mr Jeremy Edwards became Headmaster of Eaton House the Manor Prep School and a member of the Board of Directors of the Eaton House Group of Schools. He was previously Master (headmaster) at Westminster Under School for 10 years.

He was educated at Monmouth School and is an English graduate from the University of London (Royal Holloway College). He took his PGCE at King's College London and in 1993 he completed a two-year course for an MA in educational management at the Institute of Education in London. He has worked in the secondary sector as well as the prep school world and was head of English and deputy head at Emanuel School in Battersea before moving to Westminster Under in 2000.

Mr Edwards was an international oarsman many moons ago, representing Great Britain in the World Rowing Championships of 1977 and 1982. After hanging up his oar, he coached British junior crews. He is married to Alexa, who is managing director of her own medical public relations company. They have three children – one at university and two in the sixth form of their respective schools. He lives near Clapham Common, loves all kinds of music and is a keen theatre-goer.

Pre-prep: Since 2008, Mrs Philippa Cawthorne MA, BA, PGCE. Previously head of studies at Halstead with two grown-up children.

Nursery: Since 2004, Mrs Roosha Sue (early thirties).

Girls' School: Since 2010, Mrs Sarah Segrave, formerly head of the pre-prep who returned from maternity leave to head the girls' section.

Entrance: Put names down early (at birth for the nursery) – entry at four on a first-come first-served basis. At seven or eight by assessment (English and maths are what matter) and school report. No automatic entry from the school's own pre-prep but most go through. Academic, music, sport, art and design and all-rounder scholarships for eight-year-olds.

Exit: At eight over three-quarters move to the prep, the remainder boarding at Ludgrove, Summer Fields, Sunningdale, Windlesham, Cothill and The Dragon. At 13, 50 per cent move to day schools and 50 per cent to boarding via CE or scholarship routes – Westminster, St Paul's, Dulwich, City of London; Winchester, Radley, Eton, Harrow and Marlborough.

Remarks: Younger brother school of the older established (1857) Eaton House School, Belgravia near Sloane Square (pre-prep only, for boys ages four to eight): boys at the Eaton House schools wear the same holly green and red uniform. Mrs Harper is the owner of and principal at both these schools (Eaton House The Vale, in Elvaston Place, is also part of their group). Eaton House The Manor schools were set up in 1993 and quickly established themselves. A popular first-choice school, well-run and happy, with prep, pre-prep, girls' school and super nursery school all on site. Distinguished main Georgian house, with Victorian additions plus newly purpose-built block behind, with attractive courtyard. Previously part of South Bank polytechnic (i.e. lots of teaching devices already in place) and before that a prep school. Acres of green with Clapham Common Park just across the road. Children mainly from Wandsworth, Clapham, Stockwell; the school runs a bus service to/from Eaton Gate, another to/from Parsons Green.

Pre-prep uses the same excellent teaching methods as its older brother school across the Thames – children are taught in small groups within the class according to their ability (which is mixed). Girls' school, boys' pre-prep and nursery (both super) are round at the back of the school, the latter smelling deliciously of baking the day we visited.

At eight, boys are put into sets for English and maths, two parallel classes per year group, Latin for all at eight, specialist subject staff from first year in prep. Small special needs department. Lots of male teachers, average age of staff 35 (several with public school teaching experience). Thorough teaching throughout, big emphasis on reading. Supervised homework option from 4pm until 5pm every day. Light, bright classrooms and good equipment, big gym, theatre. Keen games. Busy extra-curricular programme, with lots of clubs (including air rifle shooting) – a work hard, play hard school. Boys appear industrious and cheerful and not over-pressurised – but it is a competitive place. House system, cups galore. Popular with parents – 'Just the right balance of tradition and spark,' according to a father.

Eaton House The Manor Girls' school is built on an adjacent site and opened its doors in September 2008.

Eaton House The Vale

Linked to Eaton House Belgravia in the Junior section

Linked to Eaton House The Manor Schools in the Junior section

2 Elvaston Place, London, SW7 5QH

• Pupils: 50 girls, 40 boys; all day • Ages: 3-11 • Non-denom
• Fees: £11,925 pa • Independent

Tel: 020 7584 9515
Fax: 020 7584 8368
Email: admin@eatonhouseschools.com
Website: www.eatonhouseschools.com

Head: Since 2008, Mr Robin Greenwood FTCL ARCM BSc (forties). Educated in South Africa, then studied biological sciences at London University. Was a teacher at the Eaton House group of schools before headship at Wetherby Prep.

Entrance: At aged three to the nursery or aged four to the pre-prep school, entrance is on a non-selective, first-come-first-served basis. Also at aged seven and eight (mainly girls), an occasional place with an informal assessment day.

Exit: Boys at eight go to Sussex House, Colet Court, Westminster Under, Westminster Cathedral School, Eaton House The Manor. Some to boarding schools. Girls at 11 go on to all the major London day schools or boarding – Woldingham, Westonbirt, Tudor Hall, St Mary's Calne are popular choices. Some scholarships.

Remarks: Traditional school with emphasis on the abilities and talents of each individual; class sizes reflect this. Part of the Eaton House group of schools. Accommodated in a large six-storey town house just off Queens Gate and Gloucester Road; some of the older children's classrooms are on the smaller side; well-stocked library, science lab and an ITC room. Staff committed and mostly long-serving, good mixture of age groups and experience. Classes mixed ability, no streaming; the curriculum 'all good solid stuff,' commented one parent, along with interesting projects and a range of outings, the premises being ideally located for easy access to all the London museums and galleries. No playground – for morning break each class goes for a walk followed by snack time in the hall, where pupils are encouraged to interact with other age groups. After lunch, pupils taken to Kensington Gardens for playtime. Lunches home cooked by a long-serving cook – unanimous vote from pupils was 'Pretty yummy!'

Interesting drama and music – the head keen on children developing self-confidence and learning through drama. Varied choice of individual instruments and music lessons. Regular plays and concerts performed at nearby Baden-Powell House. Sports in either Kensington or Battersea Parks, swimming and gym also on offer. From 7, pupils taken on multi-activity weeks so they can try their hands at canoeing, abseiling, raft building and the like. After-school clubs include dance, art and touch-typing – becoming a must for today's generation. Homework club four nights a week.

Sympathetic approach to minor SEN difficulties: individual help can be arranged and children who need to can use a laptop, but not able to cope with more severe difficulties.

Active parents' group – many live within walking distance of the school – who run the library, listen to readers and fund-raise for the school and charities. Whilst not for the really rumbustious, The Vale provides a happy learning environment for most.

Ecole André Malraux

Linked to Ecole Charles de Gaulle - Wix in the Junior section

Linked to Ecole de South Kensington (Primary School of the Lycée Français) in the Junior section

Linked to Lycée Français Charles de Gaulle in the Senior section

44 Laurie Road, Hanwell, London, W7 1BL

• Pupils: 260 girls and boys; all day • Ages: 7-13 • Fees: £4,608-£9,111 pa. • Independent

Tel: 020 8578 3011
Fax: 020 8575 0191
Email: contact.malraux@lyceefrancais.org.uk
Website: www.lyceefrancais.org.uk

Remarks: For further information see senior school, Lycee Francais Charles de Gaulle.

Ecole Charles de Gaulle - Wix

Linked to Lycée Français Charles de Gaulle in the Senior section

Linked to Ecole André Malraux in the Junior section

Linked to Ecole Marie d'Orliac Linked to Ecole de South Kensington (Primary School of the Lycée Français) in the Junior section

Wix's Lane, Clapham Common North Side, London, SW4 0AJ

• Pupils: boys and girls, all day • Ages: 4-11 • Independent

Tel: 020 7738 0287
Fax: 020 7223 9128
Email: contact.wix@lyceefrancais.org.uk
Website: www.lyceefrancais.org.uk

Remarks: See senior school.

Ecole de South Kensington (Primary School of the Lycée Français)

Linked to Ecole Charles de Gaulle - Wix in the Junior section

Linked to Ecole Marie d'Orliac Linked to Lycée Français Charles de Gaulle in the Senior section

Linked to Ecole André Malraux in the Junior section

35 Cromwell Road, London, SW7 2DG

• Pupils: Boys and girls: all day • Ages: boys and girls: all day • No religious affiliation • Fees: British Section £8,472 pa • Independent

Tel: 020 7590 6845
Fax: 020 7589 7041
Email: webmaster@lyceefrancais.org.uk
Website: www.lyceefrancais.org.uk

Remarks: Three outlying annexes: Ecole Charles de Gaulle-Wix on Clapham Common North Side, Ecole André Malraux in Ealing and Ecole Marie d'Olriac in Fulham.

Edgbaston High School for Girls Preparatory Dept

Linked to Edgbaston High School For Girls in the Senior section

Westbourne Road, Edgbaston, Birmingham, West Midlands, B15 3TS

• Pupils: 400 girls; all day • Ages: 2 ½-11 • Fees: £5,925-£8,613 pa • Independent

Tel: 0121 454 2401
Email: prep@edgbastonhigh.co.uk
Website: www.edgbastonhigh.co.uk

Head: Since September 2010, Mrs Sally Hartley, previously on staff in the prep department at Haberdashers' Monmouth School for Girls. Married to a teacher, she studied at the College of St Paul and St Mary, Cheltenham.

Exit: Most to senior school.

Remarks: For further details see senior school entry.

Edge Grove Preparatory School

Aldenham Village, Hertfordshire, WD25 8NL

• Pupils: Prep: 175 boys and 75 girls; 75 board, the rest day; Pre-prep: 70 boys and 50 girls • Ages: 3-13 • C of E • Fees: Day £10,800-£13,395; Boarding +£3,900-£4,890; Pre-prep £4,575-£8,985 pa • Independent

Tel: 01923 855 724
Fax: 01923 859 920
Email: admissions@edgegrove.com
Website: www.edgegrove.com

Headmaster: Since January 2009, Mr Michael J Davies (forties), friendly and avuncular former head of Perrott Hill School in Somerset and deputy head of Ashdown House. He comes as a package with his charming French wife Isabelle and their three children, who are all at the school.

While Mr Davies has made some popular tweaks to academic and organisational matters since his arrival, Mrs Davies has absorbed herself in the more homely aspects of prep school life. She has already revolutionised the food – now most ingredients are locally sourced and the vast majority of dishes are made from scratch – and she has grand plans to redecorate the dorms to make them more cosy and replace the televisions with more traditional toys. She deliberately distances herself from the academic life of the school and focuses on the 'family' touches, including magnificent birthday teas and getting to know everyone – she regularly invites groups of boarders, teachers and parents to eat with her in her kitchen – and even provides a shoulder to cry on for homesick gap students. A real lynchpin.

'Parents are learning that Mike and Isabelle are very approachable,' says a parent. At break-time, Year 8s flock to the head's garden gate to pet the family's guinea pigs.

Entrance: Head worried that Edge Grove was a boys' school with girls, and is keen to even things up. Edge Grove is 'relatively speaking, non-selective,' he says, and he only turns down applicants if he feels the school can't do a good job for them – 'at age three or four, if they sit down and smile and the parents smile and I think we're going to be friends, then they're in.' Something of a contrast to previous policy, where evidence of an academic bent was winkled out at interview. Edge Grove is generous with bursaries and there are a few 100-per-centers. Parents thrilled with the decision to do away with scholarships at age seven, which they felt were divisive. No specific scholarships – they're just offered to the children the head feels would bring something to the school and gain from it.

Exit: Recommended to parents looking for a boarding prep for their boy before joining Harrow, so exit mainly to there and Haileybury, plus Eton and Uppingham, with girls to Downe House. Locally Merchant Taylor's, Haberdashers' Aske's are popular. The vast majority stay until 13 and up to half win scholarships to top senior schools.

Remarks: A lovely country house boarding prep, set in delectable grounds just a stone's throw from the buzz of North London. A new emphasis on individual nurturing has given an already successful prep a discernibly more caring and relaxed atmosphere, and makes it an ideal springboard for the area's top boarding schools.

The main building, formerly the home of JP Morgan, is all polished wooden floors and panelling with a superb entrance hall. A red-carpeted sweeping staircase leads to the boarding department. Other buildings are a mixture of 20th century with a few temporary-looking classrooms that are actually bright and spacious inside. 25 acres of glorious grounds, including a field for cricket and rounders, an outdoor swimming pool set in a walled garden, and a lake.

There has been a notable lightening of pressure in the school day since the arrival of Mr Davies. Breaks have been doubled to 40 minutes and lunch sittings have been concertina'd to create more time for play. To this end, the current library is to become a larger dining hall and the books are to be moved to a new library. Kitchen Agas are to be complemented by combi ovens to speed up cooking at mealtimes. Exams are being moved to before half-term rather than after to give scope for family time in the holidays.

Also a subtle but noticeable change of direction. The head's focus is on finding potential in each individual, be it academic, sporting, musical, or any one of the other pursuits on offer – or perhaps 'just being a lovely child'. Telltale change of syntax in school documentation from 'children' to 'every child' to emphasise the way ahead, which has prompted cheers from the majority of parents. 'We can stop panicking,' says a mother. Head agrees, 'We don't want to be in the situation where we're great with the round pegs and the round holes – there are plenty of square pegs and we have to do the best for them too.'

Despite the non-selective approach, exits are impressive. There is no setting in the junior part of the school, but with classes maxing 18, and averaging no more than 16, this is not necessary, according to the head. Specialist subject teachers and streams are brought in at 11 but only A, B, B, so no C to have an adverse effect on morale.

Sporting success is also notable, especially in hockey, despite not having a proper hockey pitch, and there is a very strong tradition of cricket, supported by some big names. Junior county cricketers are among the pupils. The head intends to maintain the quality but also to offer more opportunity to those of lesser ability.

Art is staggeringly impressive; leavers win art scholarships every year. Music is strong and very inclusive – 90 per cent learn an instrument, and there are several grade 8 certificates adorning the walls of the music school, although there are also concerts for those who are new to music making.

Languages are also a forte. Annual French exchange trip with a school in Cannes is a huge hit, and there's a French assistante. Year 8 leavers are invited to the head's own home in Brittany for a relaxing holiday.

A handful of children have EAL requirements. SENs are well catered for with individual lessons.

The result is happy, smiling pupils who are polite to a fault – visitors are met with a deluge of 'good mornings' at every turn. A small handful of children are from overseas, but most are local north London. Some Services, based at Northwood. Parents are of the traditional boarding prep variety and no shortage of applicants from London and the suburbs.

The Edinburgh Academy Junior School

Linked to Edinburgh Academy (The) in the Senior section

10 Arboretum Road, Edinburgh, EH3 5PL

• Pupils: Prep school 350 boys and girls; nursery 105 boys and girls. Fully co-ed since September 2007. • Ages: Prep 5-11, nursery 2-5 • Non-denom • Fees: Junior School £6,390-£7,980; Nursery £1,980-£6,450 pa • Independent

Tel: 0131 552 3690
Fax: 0131 551 2660
Email: enquiriesjs@edinburghacademy.org.uk
Website: www.edinburghacademy.org.uk

Acting headteacher: Acting head since October 2010 is Mr Ben Dean, previously deputy head, who took charge when previous head Mrs Caroline Bashford moved to Grantown-on Spey primary school.

Entrance: Primary 1 assessments held in early January. Primary 2–6 assessments can be arranged at times to suit parents – also one main assessment afternoon in late November. Waiting lists operate where demand exceeds supply.

Applications for nursery can be made at any time. Places formally offered in the autumn for the following school year. If space available, places also on offer during the year.

Exit: Children move on to the senior school aged 10 or 11, to 'Geits' (the equivalent of primary 7 in the Scottish system).

Remarks: Co-ed since September 2007. The school roll (excluding nursery) has increased gradually since 2007 (from 270–350) and nursery has been full for the last two years and has a waiting list. Children from nursery get priority entrance to the junior school. Original, recently refurbished, '60s school building was extended in 1980s to house growing pupil numbers. New purpose-built home for nursery, designed by award-winning Edinburgh architect, Richard Murphy, with 100 girls and boys, two to five years. New all-weather play surface used for hockey and netball as well as children's breaktime play. Huge dining hall, with 'proper lunches for all'; staff can cater for any kind of diet and no packed lunches allowed.

School buzzes with energy and enthusiasm. Junior school in general very good – the old gang have more-or-less gone, and a new influx of whizzy young teachers gladden the eye. Maximum class sizes are 20 in primary 1 and 2, increasing to 24 for primary 3 to 6. Parallel classes throughout, though set for maths at eight. No Latin. French taught from primary 5 and Mandarin from primary 6. Computers and Smartboards everywhere. Art-room gratifyingly exciting and art all over the place. Ambitious music and plays, lots of games and sports hall. A small team of pupils from primary 6 won the Junior Euroquiz championship held at the Scottish Parliament, which earned them a trip to Brussels and a tour round the European parliament.

After-school club and holiday club (various holiday activities, mostly based at the sports centre) which operates every day 3–6pm during term-time and all day during the holidays, available for children from three years. Early birds' club for all – school open from 8am. Huge variety of after-school activities – sporting and non-sporting (drama, chess, bridge 'on the horizon') taken by the teachers and outside specialists.

Edinburgh Rudolf Steiner Lower School

Linked to Edinburgh Rudolf Steiner School in the Senior section

60 Spylaw Road, Edinburgh, EH10 5BR

- Pupils: girls and boys; all day • Ages: Kindergarten 3.5-6yrs
- Fees: £3,663-£6,693; Kindergarten £1,611-£3,114 pa • Independent

Tel: 0131 337 3410
Fax: 0131 538 6066
Email: erss.management@steinerweb.org.uk
Website: www.steinerweb.org.uk

Head: Ms Astrid Maclean.

Remarks: Lower School flows seamlessly into upper, certain extra responsibilities, but essentially no change. Kindergarten has parallel classes, depending on numbers, but not divided by age. Tinies learn by copying and each has their own job – raking the gravel, doing the compost, tidying the classroom etc. Drop off at 8am. After-school club.

The Elms School

Colwall, Malvern, Worcestershire, WR13 6EF

- Pupils: 70 boys, 60 girls; 80 per cent board; plus 70 children in pre-prep
- Ages: 3-13 • C of E • Fees: Boarding £19,665; Day £18,315; Pre Prep £6,945-£11,655 pa • Independent

Tel: 01684 540 344
Fax: 01684 541 174
Email: office@elmsschool.co.uk
Website: www.elmsschool.co.uk

Head: Since September 2010, Mr Alastair J L Thomas. Mid-thirties and married with a young daughter, who is in the early years department at the school. A degree in French from Kings' College, London was followed by a brief stint at John Lewis before he joined Kingshott Prep School, where he embarked on teacher training and became head of French. Moved to The Downs School as head of French and Latin before becoming deputy head at Lambrook in Ascot. When the position of headmaster became available at The Elms, he jumped at the opportunity and is keen to maintain the traditional ethos of The Elms whilst updating the boarding facilities and promoting the arts.

Wife, Hannah, throws herself into the life at the school, especially on the farm and in the gardens.

Entrance: Over-subscribed, but not excessively so. Entrance into pre-prep as early as three, regular intake at seven and eight. A few children from local state schools but the majority from very traditional independent school families. Most children from Herefordshire, Gloucestershire, Monmouthshire and Powys but a significant number from other parts of the country – notably London.

Exit: A few girls still leave at 11 but increasingly rare, says school. The largest number goes to Malvern College or Shrewsbury School, but over the last five years pupils have moved on to 23 different schools including Cheltenham College, Eton, Winchester, Marlborough, Monmouth, Uppingham, Rugby, Cheltenham Ladies' College and Tudor Hall. The majority of girls still seem to go on to single sex schools. Respectable scholarship list; about 25 per cent of leavers get some kind of award, but one needs to bear in mind that a number of awards over the last few years have been for art, drama, sport etc, reflecting the school's aim to provide a breadth of education. This is not an academic hothouse.

Remarks: The oldest prep school in England, founded by Humphry Walwyn in 1614. In the middle of the attractive village of Colwall, just outside Malvern. Not immediately impressive, the main school buildings abut the main road, yet to walk through the gates is a revelation. The school backs onto 150 acres of pristine gardens, beautifully maintained games fields and a small working farm complete with pigs, cows and horses. Perhaps unique amongst prep schools in having rural studies as part of the curriculum. The animals are not just here for show, one is assured – 'We eventually eat the pigs, chickens and cows' (not the horses!). The farm is a wonderful asset for all the children but especially for the less sporty and the academically challenged, who can get a real sense of achievement from helping with the animals. Riding and shooting are important parts of the activity programme, with children having achieved success at national equestrian events – school is said to provide, in one way or another, half the Ledbury hunt. Winners of the prep school national shooting competition in 13 out of the last 18 years.

Remarkable number of new buildings including a vast sports hall, indoor swimming pool and brand new changing facilities. Plans to build a new girls' boarding house and further classroom to start in the next 12 months. There cannot be many small schools with equivalent facilities. Remarkably, so successful has the financial management of the school been that all this has been achieved without an overdraft. A factor in this is, no doubt, the somewhat high fees, with little distinction made between the charges for boarding or day. Charges the highest termly fee of any prep school in the area but, perhaps, this just adds to its exclusive appeal.

The least impressive part of the school is the children's dormitories (although one is assured that this will be addressed in the new development programme). Every child in the prep school (not pre-prep) has a designated bed; there are rest periods after lunch every day. This means that day children can board when they want, provided it is not more than four nights a week, when they must convert to full boarder and stay over the weekend. However, this policy has meant that the dormitories are overcrowded and not very homely.

Academically sound with many long-serving staff (very low staff turnover). Inspection imminent. Traditional curriculum which includes a strong classics department. Follows a traditional prep school policy of moving children through classes as the need appears – this the school describes as the ladder system – which can mean that the brighter sparks might spend the last two years in the top class. However, it is quite clear that the school is very sensitive to parental concerns and there is a certain flexibility in the system. The determination to maintain this structure cocks a snook at current educational theory – it will be interesting to see what the inspectors make of this. Groups are very small and no class is larger than 13, the smallest just nine. It seems to work well and both parents and children seem happy with it.

Delightful, well-mannered, cared-for pupils. School places great emphasis on developing polite, confident children and in this it is very largely successful. Very few foreign pupils, fewer than half a dozen. Very conventional school uniform – boys wear corduroy shorts until they leave at 13. Wonderful cosy family atmosphere – not only the farm animals but lots of friendly dogs wander around the school; children are even encouraged to bring in their own (smaller) animals. Difficult to imagine much problem with homesickness here. The small size means that each child is known as an individual.

A wide range of activities which are well chronicled in very full termly newsletters (the school does not have an annual magazine). It is nice to see so many children involved in a wide sporting programme with the emphasis on participation rather than producing a sporting elite. Very strong art and drama, but the school is refreshingly honest in admitting music is not especially strong, although nearly 60 per cent of pupils learn at least one instrument

In many ways an idiosyncratic and very unusual school, offering a traditional prep school experience increasingly rarely found. Not everyone will care for it, but those who do have nothing but good to say of it.

Elstree School

Woolhampton, Reading, Berkshire, RG7 5TD

• Pupils: 185 boys plus 70 boys and girls in pre-prep (Home Farm). 45 full boarders, 65 regular flexi-boarders, rest day. • Ages: 7-13, pre-prep 3-7. • C of E • Fees: Day £15,900; Boarding £20,475; Pre-prep £8,925 pa • Independent

Tel: 01189 713 302
Fax: 01189 714 280
Email: secretary@elstreeschool.org.uk
Website: www.elstreeschool.org.uk

Headmaster: Since 2008, Mr Mark Sayer (early forties). Read classics at Fitzwilliam College, Cambridge; previously popular housemaster at Wellington College. Parents and boys speak highly of him. 'He has made thoughtful changes after careful consultation,' says one parent; 'You can talk to him about anything,' said an appreciative young boy. He certainly comes across as friendly and approachable with an excellent sense of humour and a firm grasp of what is going on. Indeed, he's something of a perfectionist 'giving a thousand per cent to the school' as another parent put it. Particularly appreciated are the Powerpoint presentations he gives to new parents explaining how the school works and what is expected of them and their children. 'Excellent communications with parents.'

Numbers joining are significantly on the up. Very keen on boarding and well versed in explaining his support for boys' only education at prep school, even though he was at co-educational Wellington. Genuinely interested in the 'ways boys' minds work. I believe they progress via experiment, which is why we have separated physics, chemistry and biology. This is a paradise for boys.' Visits the pre-prep regularly to read to them ('it's about the only time I have to read books'). Predecessor was much admired but the general feeling seems to be that the new head is 'shaping up very well.' Enjoys getting into the classroom wherever possible. Ably supported, and occasionally delightfully teased, by his wife, Sarah who was 'one of Seldon's babes' at Wellington, who teaches modern languages and has started a French club in the pre-prep, which is very popular, as we saw. Lively and good fun, they make a splendid team.

Entrance: Non-selective. 98 per cent from the pre-prep (a significant increase on a few years ago). Boys can join at any stage, providing there is room in the year group, and a number of boys in Years 5, 6 and 7 join from London day schools to prepare them for boarding at their public schools. 'A benign assessment' and a report from their previous schools to ensure a sensitively handled transition. Mostly local and a few from abroad with a regular crop from Spain and Korea. Not, perhaps, as many from London as there used to be, but they're always welcome and the excellent registrar is on the case.

Exit: Boys go on to the country's leading public schools – the usual suspects – Eton, Radley, Marlborough, Harrow,

Winchester, and Bradfield has become popular for those considering the day option. There has been a great craze for Winchester recently with awards and places. In fact, Elstree broadcasts its seeds very wide and parents are appreciative of the help they receive in selecting the right school for their sons.

Remarks: The Georgian house and surrounding grounds of 150 acres are elegant and beautiful without the intimidation of grandeur and pomposity. The very obvious fire escape at the front signifies the use to which the house has so effortlessly been adapted; the grounds offer exciting opportunities for building dens and generally mucking about. The bark on the giant redwoods at the front of the house is worn smooth by generations of Elstree boys who have run up the sides and delighted in the size and splendour of such magnificence. What tales those trees could tell since the school moved from Elstree, Herts, at the beginning of the war and then wisely decided to stay put!

Inside, the hall is impressive with its intricate carvings and panelling, a delightful background for the impressive art work on display and the flowers, arranged by the ubiquitous Mrs Sayer. When we arrived, boys were happily tripping along to lessons, not 'creeping like snails,' but bouncy, happy and ebullient: certainly not fazed by their surroundings though, as we discovered during our tour, appreciative. Proudly they showed us the carved wooden pillar that swivels round, allegedly opening a nearby trap door, now nailed down; proudly they showed us the elegant and functional library with painted pillars, nothing like as big as it looks in the prospectus but terrific all the same. Elstree takes its library seriously and the delightful librarian is keen to promote the joys of reading. Upstairs – and, yes, the boys do tear up and down the very fine staircase – there are brightly coloured dorms, one with a magnificent stuccoed ceiling in a vile colour – there are problems with inhabiting a listed building – but, nonetheless, fun to be in; there is an exciting rabbit warren feeling about the corridors upstairs but 'we quickly find our way around and it's exciting to explore,' our guides told us. The old building plays an important and lively part in their lives.

Elstree is keen to maintain its boarding tradition and under the hugely energetic and hugely everything master in charge of boarding and his wife, it's hard to understand why everyone doesn't want to board all the time. There's a devilishly difficult putting course on the landing with local rules that defy the smoothness of the carpet, there are feasts and cocoa parties, socials with Downe House (very popular) – but not in the dormitories – even a lively and informative paper, The Boarding Times, with amusing insights into the joys of boarding. For anxious, nervous parents with thoughts of Tom Brown's Schooldays there is helpful and reassuring information published in booklets, along with one for the boys themselves. The friendly new boarding master and his charming wife, who live in the thick of it all, are responsible for the senior boys and for weekend activities which are numerous and varied. A housemistress is in charge of the juniors and other matrons and a tutor live in. There is a very real atmosphere of adventure coupled with comfort, in every sense. No wonder even the curmudgeonly worded Ofsted report glows with praise. Elstree does all it can to be flexible about boarding: there are a number of permutations available and on Friday nights up to 110 board. Not surprising.

For full time boarders, indeed for every boy at Elstree, parents are encouraged to visit as often as possible and keep in contact. Boarding is not seen as separation; it's an extension.

Academically, Elstree has had many successes in the scholarship stakes and prides itself on well balanced and inspirational teaching. Of course, the main focus is on Common Entrance, and very seldom will a boy fail to get into his first choice school. Potential scholars are creamed off to be stretched and challenged. Those bright eyed, would-be scholars we spoke to at lunch over delicious fish and chips (it was Friday) and in the marvellously-designed dining room, enthused about their intellectual aspirations without a hint of smugness, let alone arrogance, while above their heads the names of previous scholars on the honours board beckoned. A good variety of scholarships won, with music awards being particularly noticeable, along with academic awards to serious schools. But scholarships are not pursued at the expense of those with learning difficulties. All new boys are screened and plenty of support is available with regular confidence-building being the key. Excellent teaching facilities. Bright and functional classrooms, very good ICT room with masses of terminals; computers involved in all lessons. Everyone, including the top year of Home Farm, is taught the skills. Much music and good drama, with plenty of orchestras and ensembles and a very active choir. Popular geography trips to Dartmoor and trips to France. Academic involvement is treated seriously but this is no hot house relying, as it does, on the notion that happy boys are more likely to reach their potential. Every school claims to be happy. Elstree certainly is.

A fascinating and attractive feature of the hall when we visited was an exhibition of beads, clothes and other articles sent from a school in Afghanistan with which Elstree has developed links. This includes writing to their counterparts, generally making friends and raising money. It's not a gimmick. It's for real and the hope is that one day exchanges may be possible. Strong, but not stifling, Christian upbringing with regular prayers and 'bible bashing.' 'It's rather fun,' said one boy. Parents are involved – there is a prayer group for parents, too – and speak appreciatively of the sound moral guidance given to the boys. This includes the excellent PSHE programme run by form tutors in small groups. It's not too fanciful to say that the results are visible and delightful. The boys are open, friendly and genuinely courteous with good manners that rest like cloaks rather than strait-jackets. They assured us that there was no bullying and no shortage of people they could talk to if they were worried or upset. Interesting that a number spoke of 'the excellent ground and maintenance staff', always an indication of a happy community and, incidentally, of good management. More than lip service is paid to leadership, leadership in its many facets. Senior boys are all given the opportunity for responsibility, whether it is for the discipline and happiness of a dormitory or for trying to ensure that consideration and generosity abound. The Elstree Award, their version of the D of E Award, is very popular with first aid courses, helping with the Home Farm pupils, site work and a number of team building activities from raft building on the lake to camping. The culmination in a demanding 24 hour camp in the grounds. There is also, in the holidays, an immensely popular week of camping.

All the usual games are on offer and facilities include a jumbo sports hall, a new all-weather playing area and masses of pitches. A feature of sport at Elstree is that attention is paid not only to the top teams but to everyone who wants to play. Every age group, it seems, has at least five teams playing. 'I love playing against Elstree,' said a master from a rival school. 'They always play with the right attitude and are good fun to talk to at square leg'. We met a swimmer who is honing himself (modestly) for swimming in the Olympics but no-one was making a great fuss about it, least of all the boy himself. Not a hearty school. Hobbies and clubs abound. One boy, when asked for a criticism of the school, offered the comment, 'We don't have much free time'. 'Yes we do,' said another, 'we have 35 minutes and more on Wednesdays.' A splendid argument ensued with all concluding that 'anything is better than being bored.'

As we left, after talking to a group of young boys about to set off for a run and who told us that it was fun running in the rain, we just had time to hear the master in charge say, 'or we could play ping pong inside'. The cheering shook the redwoods. There's lots to cheer about at Elstree say parents.

'It's a very glitzy part of the country with lots of other schools around', said one. 'We looked at several but chose Elstree because, in our opinion, it has the freshest atmosphere. Not a whiff of arrogance, just cheerful happy boys.' Clearly, with so many other schools in the area, not everyone agrees; nonetheless, it's certainly worth checking out.

Home Farm School (the pre-prep) head, Mrs Kay Markides graduated in science, and was married with a family (including a son who attended Elstree) before deciding to train for teaching young ones. Thrilled to be involved with Elstree and it shows. Warm and at ease with the children ('I love them') she is clearly not only very competent but also exudes calm dependability. Presides over a talented young staff who clearly relish the company of their young charges, patiently explaining things and then rushing around with them in the grounds of the prep school. Home Farm is where the Elstree adventure begins, and what a place to start. Between the ages of three and seven, boys and girls are housed in a splendidly rambling old farmhouse, complete with old oak doors and unexpected fireplaces. There is a lovely feel about it. Very close to the farm house is a well-designed bright new block for the absolute tinies. Masses of child-friendly and subtly educational toys ('this is wonderful for improving their balance and giving them confidence'; 'they don't really know that they are learning to count when they're playing with this'.) What looks like Macadam below the swings and slides is actually rubberised and virtually incapable of causing scratches, though a carefully controlled programme encourages investigation and adventure.

We saw (and heard) French being enjoyed, maths and stories, music and laughter. Serious teaching through fun and quiet professionalism. There are regular PE sessions and plenty of scope for games within the attractive walled garden, to say nothing of the larger grounds of the prep. Lovely, cosy library in the old dairy. Lots of books and some computers 'but books and reading come first'. There is a rolling programme of activities constantly changing, offering variety and challenge. Non-selective and recognised by the local authority as an example of best practice. 'People are sent here to see what a good school is like'. Confirmation of their belief in the school is that the local authority is going to build them a Wendy house in the adventure garden of trees, where they can play (and learn as they do so.) Happy children; happy staff. A place that makes one long to be young again. 'Impossible to fault,' said a young mum. 'The best possible start my children could have.'

Eltham College Junior School

Linked to Eltham College in the Senior section

Mottingham Lane, Mottingham, London, SE9 4QF

- Pupils: 190 boys; all day • Ages: 7-10 • Inter-denominational
- Fees: £10,800 pa • Independent

Tel: 020 8857 3457
Fax: 020 8851 7160
Email: ts@eltham-college.org.uk
Website: www.eltham-college.org.uk

Master: Since September 2010, Mr Edmund Cavendish, previously deputy head of the senior school.

Entrance: Selective and competitive. Approximately 80 boys at 7+, trying for around 40 places. Saturday activity morning in school followed by assessment by head and testing of reading, maths and language skills, in small groups. A few more spaces at 8+, so always worth retrying if 7+ doesn't work.

Exit: The majority to the senior school, 25 per cent with scholarships. Others mainly to local schools.

Remarks: Situated in its own corner of the main school grounds, with own entrance and playing fields, here is a mini version of the senior school. Redeveloped about five years ago and when we visited then, we got the impression of lots of light, glass and bang up-to-date facilities. Great glass-roofed art and DT room, science lab with a particularly lively teacher, ICT suite where other subject lessons can also take place, well-stocked library, bright interesting-looking classrooms. Assemblies held every day in main hall; our youthful guide pointed out with glee the fact that hymn books are no longer necessary as the words descend on a special screen! Use is also made of senior school facilities, particularly the sports hall and swimming pool, the chapel, the dining room (where the food is apparently 'yummy') and the theatre.

The usual broad curriculum with one unusual innovation: Mandarin Chinese is now taught from day one instead of French. They believe that this is the way forward and that it has many, much wider, educational benefits and cross-curricular links. Certainly when we visited, the school was right into the Chinese theme. But then it was not long after the annual China Now! Day. Parents seem to have mixed views: some think it is an excellent idea and that it is what the future is about, others feel it is gimmicky and they would rather stick to European languages for now. We think it could be very good move but only time will tell. All boys screened for dyslexia in Year 3. Class teachers and tutors are constantly on the watch for any other learning problems that might develop. Sympathetic and knowledgeable learning support co-ordinator, who parents say is 'wonderful', 'easy to talk to' and 'always available'. If a boy is not particularly good at one thing, they encourage him to shine somewhere else. 'All children have something and will find their niche somewhere'.

High quality music. Every child in Years 3 and 4 learns an individual instrument, initially free of charge. Three choirs, an orchestra and several specialist groups. The variety is huge. Masses of sport, extra-curricular activities, internal and external competitions. An impressive number of trophies on display. In fencing, epee British School Team Champions in 2009 and foil runners up. Two boys selected for the England under-11 chess squad and two more played for Kent in the victorious under-nine team. Concerts, plays, and lots of outings home and abroad. Really, there should be something for everyone here. Only possible niggle is that it tends to be always the same children selected to lead and star; does this totally fit into 'giving everyone a chance to shine'?

Ease of contact seems very much the culture of both halves of the school. Good pastoral care. Peer mentoring certainly helps and form teachers and tutors are always there to talk to. Any problem is usually dealt with quickly and sensibly. Boys are 'treated as individuals for both strengths and weaknesses'. 'We try to look after all the boys and give them the best experience we can'.

Eridge House School

1 Fulham Park Road, Fulham, London, SW6 4LJ

• Pupils: 200; 50/50 boys/girls; all day • Ages: 3-11 • Fees: £12,450-£13,200 pa • Independent

Tel: 020 7371 9009
Fax: 020 7371 9229
Email: admissions@eridgehouse.co.uk
Website: www.eridgehouse.co.uk

Principal/Headteacher: Since January 2007, Mrs Janie Richardson (late thirties), previously deputy head. Attractive, warm and impressive, reassuringly unheadmistressy. Like the rest of her staff, known by her first name. She arrived from Australia in her early 20s and has worked in education here ever since, mostly in independent schools and nurseries. Head of infants at Eaton Square Schools before arriving at Eridge House in 2003. Married to a children's author, her two daughters are at the school. Parents enthuse about her hands-on approach, 'She's very visible'. She knows all her children (even siblings who are not at the school yet, commented one parent) and is at the front gate every morning so she 'can tell who's here and how they're feeling'.

The previous head and founder, Mrs Lucinda Waring ('dynamo, bombshell, sage and mother') is still around ('we work very well together') but tries to remain in the background, concentrating on the long-term development of the school. Not that there's any need for her to keep a tight rein: Mrs Richardson is devoted to the school and is determined to maintain the convictions of her predecessor. The aim is to find for all the children the round holes they slot into – no-one is pushed too far too fast: 'They start reading when they're ready and we know when that is'. Not afraid of standing up to the pushy parent who confuses what's best for them with what's best for their child – 'We are not a school that suits the helicopter parent'.

Entrance: Non-selective, i.e. first come, first served. Number of registrations increasing as word spreads. Now you need to put your child's name down at birth if you want to be sure of a place at three or four. Nursery children given priority for entry at four. Occasional places do crop up further up the school.

Exit: Still untested. The aim will be to continue the round hole policy rather than to prepare all children for the swankiest or most academic next schools. Mrs Richardson will make sure they progress to the school that best suits them – she knows the children well enough. At the moment she is busily building up networks with a mix of London day schools and boarding schools. Regards Ibstock Place, The Harrodian and Latymer as natural successors, 'Our parents are likely to want a school with a similar ethos to ours and won't want to go too far for it, but it will depend on the individual child' – of course.

Remarks: The aim of founder, Mrs Waring, was to create 'a village school in the middle of Fulham'. Impossible? You'd have thought so and she waited till she found the right property to try out the idea. School housed in handsome former lodge to Fulham Palace, a generously-proportioned Victorian house, comfortably on a corner in leafy, residential Fulham. A modern extension makes it feel like the Tardis. Excellent multi-purpose hall where they do drama, dance, music, gym and eat freshly cooked food at lunchtime. No cramming into tiny rooms – here there is space to move, to play, to feel relaxed. And that's not just inside. The former lodge must have had large and leafy gardens as school has an extraordinary amount of space around it. An Astroturf pitch (carefully cut round mature trees) and several outdoor adventure playgrounds thoughtfully designed to develop little arm muscles ('good for handwriting') as well as to allow their imagination to fly. Matches happen here but they also walk two streets to Hurlingham Park with tennis, netball and athletics facilities. Few preps in this part of London could compare.

Emphasis is on providing an all-round education. The school cherrypicks the best of three education systems – the Montessori (for nursery and transition), the national curriculum and the French programme. Attracts a wide international mix of pupils, particularly French. A small – but significant – number is taught a carefully planned version of the CNED by school's resident French native speaker and highly experienced teacher, which is co-ordinated into the main curriculum. All children have French twice weekly. Syllabus varied with much specialist teaching including music, sports and dance. Lowest class has 'lots of structured play' but can run in and out of the garden at any time. Plenty of fresh air had by all. Parents are not shooed off the premises at drop off as in many schools. Quite the contrary – if you watch your child's assembly you can stay for coffee, croissants and a chat afterwards. Useful after-school clubs until 4.30pm, from fencing and Mandarin to cooking and board-games.

School's prospectus states it welcomes children with SEN. Head reiterates that they would always see what they can do to accommodate special needs and would never automatically say no. All good stuff but no evidence of much experience yet. The Year 2 teacher doubles up as SENCo and has a few people on her books needing help with handwriting and organisation. Otherwise only one dyslexic pupil. Gifted and talented pupils are catered for in the whole class. Very mixed ability classes but 'classes are small enough to be able to cater for each individual's needs,' assures Mrs Richardson.

Children encouraged to take responsibility for each other as well as themselves. When we visited, a French boy was helping a fellow French speaker who was struggling with his English. House system fosters good relations among children in different years. On the eagerly anticipated 'House day' each term, normal lessons are off; instead everyone works together on activities – whether it be building something out of newspaper in total silence or designing a house flag. The reward: highly-coveted house points. They are big on certificates and rewards here – each week in assembly prizes are awarded for a range of achievements, e.g. we saw a desperately shy girl win the headteacher's award for being chatty. Everyone gets a chance to shine. One parent explained why she chose Eridge House, despite the school not being on the dinner party gossip list – 'I needed a school where my daughter would be noticed, and she is'. Sports teams are circulated so everyone gets a chance. 'Although they want to win, it's not the only important thing. We also keep a watchful eye on each of the houses to prevent one from becoming too strong in every area,' says Mrs Richardson.

Laughter and happiness are key. If that means allowing your daughter to wear her fairy dress over her uniform, so be it. 'The important thing is to get them running through the door in the morning.' This is not a place where you'll see ordered children filing through the school. 'We like our corridors to be filled with chatter,' says head. The focus is as much, if not more, on how they learn rather than what they learn. Absolutely no SATs, 'But we do inform parents regularly of where their child is according to the national curriculum'. If parents want to see written evidence of how their child is doing, they are shown on-going assessment and self-assessment forms filled in by the children, with targets set by themselves as well as by their teachers. 'Some of our parents need educating,' admits Mrs Richardson. Be prepared to be given a lump of playdough at a parents' evening and come up with bright ideas on what you might learn from it.

Many heads – and parents – claim to be against pressure early on. This is the real thing. 'We are not the soft option – there are some very academic children at the school,' asserts the head. However those who aren't will not be pushed; otherwise they risk ending up somewhere where they can't cope. All pupils come from minutes away. Many can – not all do – walk to school so the place has a real local feel. It's a bit of a gem. Can it preserve its ethos while continuing to expand? Tough one, but if you live in Fulham and are not paranoid about league tables, it could well be for you.

Exeter Cathedral School

The Chantry, Palace Gate, Exeter, Devon, EX1 1HX

• Pupils: 170 boys and girls (including pre-prep); 30+ boarders • Ages: 3-13 • C of E • Fees: Day £5,367-£9,078; Boarding +£5,127-£7,269 pa • Independent

Tel: 01392 255 298
Fax: 01392 422 718
Email: reception@exetercs.org
Website: www.exetercs.org

Acting head: Mr Simon Carder is acting head, following the early retirement due to ill-health of Mr Brian McDowell. The new head from April 2011 Mr Stephen Yeo, is fresh from the headship of Lyndhurst School in Camberley.

Entrance: Entry by interview plus taster day. Voice trials for choristerships. Full academic range here – SENs mild to moderate.

Exit: Almost all stay to 13, then on to sou'westerlies, mostly: King's Taunton, Exeter's Maynard School, Exeter School and St Margaret's, Torquay Boys' Grammar School, Blundell's, Wellington. Two-thirds win music scholarships. Former pupils include Coldplay's Chris Martin and, they claim, 14th century theologian Boniface. Hit and myth!

Remarks: Origins lost fancifully in the mists of time, like all these cathedral song schools – goes all the way back to a henge where the choristers kept pet pterodactyls. Main school building up by the cathedral, access a bit of a nightmare. A huggermugger place of thundering stairs, classrooms, dorms, common rooms. We didn't dare go down to the cellar. Retro vibe all-pervasive – old millennium chic down to the smell of the polish; many desks accommodate inkwells. You look out of an upper window down onto the playground and the children morph into a Lowry painting, then into an engraving from Great Expectations.

A bling-free zone and it clearly filters out the WAG set, because parents here are an unaffected, unpretentious lot, bookish-looking, from quite a range of backgrounds, for whom this school is an affair of the heart. 'It's as far away as you can get from a SATs machine,' they say. When they talk about things that matter, they mean values and the way people treat each other. When you talk about facilities, they ask tartly, 'At this stage, do they really need so much equipment?' Fees are attractively non-exorbitant.

A well-worn place with a cheerful, slightly doolally feel and the children love it, only wishing they had their own green space to play in, as they wistfully gaze into the overgrown garden next door in the old deanery. They do have masses of green space all round the cathedral. When they go to the other school buildings, none of them more than a hundred yards away, children are escorted or, if old enough, walk in pairs – it's a perfectly safe environment. And it's easy to feel that the lack of mod cons is compensated for by the ancient cathedral, in whose chapter house the children meet every morning for assembly.

Games fields have they none or, to phrase it the school's way, 'We have jolly good facilities but by no means all on site'. It's a short ride by minibus to a selection of sports fields, including the university's – judging by the jollity of those we watched embarking, social value in the ride. Hockey is the pick of the bunch.

Musically, the school tests parents' superlatives. Exceptional director of music has been here 20 years. A hard life for choristers, of course – 'Friday evensong's the real killer' – but they feel they are part of something extraordinary – and they get to go on great tours abroad. All the music-making you would expect, all classically based. Not just a chorister thing – in tune with the spirit of the place, almost all children get caught up in music-making, instrumentally or vocally. Boy choristers get 25 per cent scholarship, girls 20 per cent – because they sing fewer services. Means-tested bursaries available and they do their best to find the money. 'We want music here first, parents who can afford to pay second.' Non-choristers do not feel they are there to make up the numbers – no way.

Academically, parents like the breadth, the quality, the way teachers make their child think creatively and ask 'ridiculously difficult questions'. Above all, they like the relationships between teachers and children. A fair number of heritage prep school teachers here, a retro touch a lot of parents would travel a long way to get: characters, eccentric certainly by the standards of the wide world but, in their own world, remarkably effective, funny, caring and unforgettable – legendary. Parents say: rigour and 'a realistic sense of what each child can do'. They praise responsiveness to problems, speed of communication and the ever-helpful admin staff. A school where parents get very stuck in – membership of the PTA comes with registration; an unusually strong sense of belongingness in everyone.

For those with special needs, a team leader and four specialist teachers, who also dispense EAL as necessary to overseas pupils.

Art taught in a room in which a profusion of work is in progress, so it's definitely not tidy – so it's a real art-room. Drama thrives, a bit old fashioned some say, but the teacher's lovely. Good number and range of after-school clubs.

Discipline isn't really an issue in a school in which the personal touch plays the leading part. Parents talk of 'moral and spiritual growth' – just a posh way really of saying their child is growing up to be a very nice person with a strong sense of self, and having masses of fun while doing so. This is what small schools can do best and where this school, having little in its purse, directs its efforts. Really, really nice lay chaplain who supports children and families. Boarding is well done – the children feel looked after and flexi-boarding is popular. The IT's just been revamped, a matter of gigantic pride to the children (though nothing to make a rocket scientist swoon), and now at last boarders can email home.

Popular pre-prep in its own building and walled garden.

Parents wanting a prep school hereabouts have just two very good schools to choose between. It's no dilemma – ECS has to try terribly hard to make up for what it lacks, which gives it its special quality, though it doesn't paper over the lacks. It is remarkable how many parents we spoke to had rejected the other when they found ECS – it's all down to your value system and what you reckon your child needs most.

Exeter Junior School

Linked to Exeter School in the Senior section

Victoria Park Road, Exeter, Devon, EX2 4NS

• Pupils: 95 boys and 65 girls; all day • Ages: 7-11 • Fees: £8,940 pa • Independent

Tel: 01392 273 679
Fax: 01392 498144
Email: admissions@exeterschool.org.uk
Website: www.exeterschool.org.uk

Head: Since 2006, Mrs Alison Turner BA (early forties). Previously assistant head in two maintained primary schools and head of a Devon primary school for three years.

Entrance: Entry can take place at 7+ and 8+, but applicants may also enter at other ages where places are available. Selection is by informal assessment and a report from the pupil's current school. During the assessment pupils will be given an opportunity to demonstrate literacy and numeracy skills as appropriate for their age.

Exit: The majority of pupils continue at Exeter School until aged 18. A trickle of junior pupils lost to Colyton and Torquay grammars.

Remarks: Modern and bright, well-stocked and plenty of room thanks to major extension. Next to the senior school – the playground is possibly frustratingly close for senior pupils trying to concentrate in the French rooms above. School dinners compulsory.

Nice, bright and cosy atmosphere for little ones and lots of scope to develop visual displays. Final year makes use of senior facilities. Lots of activities available. The junior school choir leads the singing at the weekly chapel services throughout the year.

Fairfield Preparatory School

Linked to Loughborough Grammar School in the Senior section
Linked to Loughborough High School in the Senior section

Leicester Road, Loughborough, Leicestershire, LE11 2AE

• Pupils: 500 girls and boys; all day • Ages: 4-11 • Non-denom • Fees: £7,506 pa • Independent

Tel: 01509 215 172
Fax: 01509 238 648
Email: admin@lesfairfield.org
Website: www.lesfairfield.org

Head: Since 2001, Mr Roger Outwin-Flinders. Great sense of humour and a drive for his pupils and staff to succeed.

Entrance: At four (selective) and at seven (tested).

Exit: Most children go on to either Loughborough High School (girls) or Loughborough Grammar School (boys) – but it's competitive and not automatic.

Remarks: A very active, busy school with excellent facilities for science (own lab), music, ICT, art and gym. Run along traditional prep school lines. A happy place; plenty of opportunities for children to excel in academics, music, drama and sport.

Fairley House School Junior Department

Linked to Fairley House School in the Senior section

220 Lambeth Road, London, SE1 4YJ

• Independent

Tel: 020 7630 3789
Email: ps@fairleyhouse.org.uk
Website: www.fairleyhouse.org.uk

Remarks: See main school.

Falkner House

19 Brechin Place, London, SW7 4QB

• Pupils: 150 girls, all day. Plus co-ed nursery for 50 • Ages: 4-11, nursery 3-4 • Christian non-denom • Fees: £13,200 pa • Independent

Tel: 020 7373 4501
Fax: 020 7835 0073
Email: office@falknerhouse.co.uk
Website: www.falknerhouse.co.uk

Headteacher: Since 1999, Mrs Anita Griggs BA PGCE (mid-fifties) – formerly head of economics at St Paul's Girls, she is married to a city lawyer and has four grown-up daughters, all educated at London day schools (St Paul's, Godolphin and Latymer, Francis Holland). Her mother, the flamboyant Flavia Nunes, now in her nineties, founded the school in 1954 and is still principal. Always to be seen at sports days etc, frequently carrying her watering-can handbag, she no longer takes part in the actual running of the school. Since taking over, Mrs Griggs has done this with every ounce of her boundless energy and enthusiasm. At the gate each morning, smart and focused, you can talk to her about little Molly's project on Greek heroes, share a joke or discuss a serious illness in the family. Rarely to be found in her elegant study at the top of the school, she hot-desks in the ground-floor office so that she can be in the thick of things. If you can't see her she may be unblocking a lavatory – 'I wouldn't ask anyone to do something I wouldn't do myself. It's essential that the girls understand that no one is too grand to do anything'. Unashamedly ambitious for every one of the girls, she says her hands still shake when she is opening the letters from the senior schools. She understands pushy parents – 'I am one too'. Parents, like their daughters, should have grit and determination – help them choose the poem to learn (they have to do this every two weeks), make sure they get to their exams on time, fever or no fever. She prides herself on producing independent, 'can do', confident girls who get to where they should be going with minimum stress.

Entrance: It's as hard to get into as you'd expect when 120 girls compete for the precious 22 places. For a nursery place, put her name down at birth, but this won't guarantee you a place in the main school. Nursery children assessed along with everyone else, for an hour in groups of six with three adults – 'Above all we're looking for an ability to focus'.

Exit: 'Like the stock market,' says Mrs Griggs, 'past performance doesn't guarantee future performance,' but currently most girls are going to the top girls' schools. Many to St Paul's, Godolphin and Latymer, Queen's Gate, fewer to Francis Holland (south), Latymer Upper and Putney High. Some to board at, principally, Wycombe Abbey, Cheltenham Ladies' College, Benenden, Downe House and St Mary's Ascot. Two or three academic and music scholarships won annually.

Remarks: 'If the school were a bank it would be an investment bank,' observed a parent (harking back to the days when investment banks could be trusted!). Fleet of foot, decisions are made quickly and problems dealt with immediately. Mrs Griggs is always a 'phone call away' and never afraid to tackle anything. This is a small, family-owned school, with no governing body, where red tape can be – and is – kept to a minimum (except on the important issues – girls with allergies are given a red plate at lunch). There is no PTA – 'I don't want alpha mothers jousting for position,' says Mrs Griggs, who will instead ask someone on the gate in the morning if they would like to organise, say, a cake-bake. Any fundraising is always for charity, never for the school – 'That's what the fees are for'. Parents find the very close, personal community where everyone knows what's happening all the time 'incredibly reassuring'.

Despite the limited space and lack of on-site playing fields, they punch above their weight in sport and the netball team is currently clocking up particularly impressive results. Music is strong, lots of informal concerts which give the opportunity for girls to 'break a string on their cello and realise it's not the end of the world'. Head girl and prefects rotated every term so that everyone gets a bit of the limelight.

All in two, joined, seven-storey Victorian houses in a quiet side street off Gloucester Road. It doesn't smell like a school: elegantly decorated, combining rich displays of girls' work alongside real and reproduced 'serious' pictures and artefacts, demonstrating the wisdom of surrounding children with good things. Good IT facilities, interactive white boards throughout and a lovely big bay-windowed room for assemblies and dance. A small playground which backs onto the street gives them a chance to get some fresh air.

Food cooked to at least home standards – no restriction on helpings here! No bells and no rules contribute to the naturally self-policing, civilised atmosphere in the busy 'home-at-school' environment, and pupils have an engaging openness, directness and courtesy. 'We like them to have ability and oomph,' says Mrs Griggs, 'but not to be sassy or precocious.'

This school will go every inch of the mile for its girls, who are bright, articulate and responsive. A girl here will want to share her news from the weekend with the whole school in assembly, whether she found a hedgehog or her mother ran the marathon. The few who do have SEN will need to be able to keep up – support will be given but only in the mainstream. As for the gifted and talented, 'They're routine!' says Mrs Griggs. A complaint that their daughter was bored would be the worst possible insult. Girls cite the warm friendliness of the place and the excellence of their teachers as main assets.

Early- and late-bird systems – a godsend for working parents. Multinational clientèle, though, almost entirely Londoners – even if they're 100 per cent Italian, this is their home.

The grounded, non-glitzy, mend-and-make-do values of Mrs Griggs and her staff make the school a rare gem in what can be the rather precious world of prep schools in this chic and expensive area.

Farleigh School

Red Rice, Andover, Hampshire, SP11 7PW

• Pupils: Kindergarten: 17 boys and 5 girls; pre-prep: 48 boys and 51 girls; prep: 168 boys and 118 girls (of whom 48 boys board plus 26 flexi-boarders and 63 girl boarders and 9 flexi-boarders) • Ages: 3-13 • RC
• Fees: Day £15,135; Boarding £16,740-£19,695; Pre-prep £8,325 pa
• Independent

Tel: 01264 710 766
Fax: 01264 710 070
Email: office@farleighschool.co.uk
Website: www.farleighschool.com

Head: Since 2004, Father Simon Everson (forties). Brought in to hold the fort during an interregnum, became a permanent installation by popular acclaim. His life journey has taken him from low to high. Educated by non-conformists at Caterham, he became a C of E vicar and ministered to indigent souls in Bermondsey, Kennington and other low joints. Converted to Catholicism, despatched to be chaplain at Farleigh and ascended without trace. The school has been counting its blessings ever since – 'The parents would have revolted if he hadn't been appointed'. Hugely popular, you can't chat to anyone for more than a few seconds before Father Simon assumes a starring role in the conversation. Praise veers to extravagance: 'He is the glory of the school'; 'Great leadership, very clear principles'; 'Firm finger on the pulse'; 'He tells you what you don't want to hear'. Bucked by this, we calibrated our expectations for mind-rocking charisma. In the event, it turns out he doesn't do that. Don't be wobbled. 'He can be distant with adults but he knows exactly the right thing to say to each child.' 'You've got to get to know him.' His acts of kindness are legendary. He visited a homesick girl in her public school twice in her first term. The weekly mass overflows the chapel. He is a Good Thing with, it seems, no holds barred. Lives on campus with his wife Gail, who 'supports him and keeps an eye on him', and does all sorts of jobs around the school from learning support to flower rota. Two daughters, who have both moved on to their senior schools.

Entrance: Kindergarten at three, pre-prep at five, both non-selective. Assessment (not too rigorous) at seven if coming from outside. Oversubscribed, so priority given to RCs, boarders, siblings and children of former pupils. Presently 50 per cent RC. Boarding nurtured and thriving.

Exit: The customary diaspora – most to boarding schools: Ampleforth, Downside, Eton, Winchester, Radley (you get the flavour). The westerlies flavoursome, too – Sherborne, Marlborough, Bryanston, Cheltenham. For Catholic girls any of the St Mary's popular. Hardly anyone leaves at 11, just a handful for senior girls' boarding schools or for state grammars – boys to Bishop Wordsworth, girls to South Wilts. Around 10 scholarships won per year (eight in 2010). Notable former pupils include actor Rupert Everett, journalist Craig Brown, Lords Stafford (pro-chancellor of Keele University) and Hesketh (Formula 1), rugby player Hugh Vyvyan and Hampshire cricketers, James and Edward Bruce.

Remarks: Formerly a Catholic boys' prep, now co-ed boarding with lots of day. Swanky Georgian house in the Test Valley in the midst of 60 acres of well-bred parkland and haughty trees. Lovely new kindergarten and pre-prep department where all do dance and ballet up to age seven and Year 2 learn French, the recorder and optional violin free of charge. Well-equipped theatre with tiered seating. Stunning new art and design block. New indoor heated 25m pool and large sports hall. New treehouse construction known as Fortress Farleigh built in the woods close to the school – an adventure play area containing walkways, swings, climbing ropes, fireman's pole etc. Close by, a new and very realistic Anderson shelter to give the children a taste of what life was like during an air raid in the Second World War with genuine WWII air raid siren and gas masks. New and flourishing school garden tended by pupils. No way is there anything down at heel about the hardware. The head praises financially-astute governors. Results speak well of the teaching but they tell only part of the academic story. Non-selective, they assert, with the customary caveat about SENs beyond their ken. 'We'll never break up a family unless we can't meet a child's needs.'

The pre-prep, in the words of a parent, is 'cosy, well run, faultless'. In the prep they seek to stimulate self-motivation. Self-exiled Londoners greet remission from force-feeding with relief – 'Farleigh is very nurturing' – and all parents agree that children are 'not overly pushed'. Children setted according to ability in a gradual process over Years 4 and 5. Max class size 18, most 15. Fair amount of cross-curricular learning. Latin from Year 6. Art and design just terrific and very well-resourced. Attitudes to special needs astonishing. We are shown round by the most personable fellow in the world who talks about his dyslexia with no trace of a hangup. How rare is that? Strong learning support with four qualified staff. They are quick to spot SENs as they reveal themselves in the pre-prep. They'll have a go at dyslexia, dyspraxia, mild social/communication difficulties and nervous examinees. There are 69 pupils on the learning support register and 44 on the gifted, able and talented register.

Teachers feature high in the pantheon of pupils' heroes and several, to their mild bewilderment, are summoned from the staffroom by our pupil hosts so that we can scrutinise them. Mr Butt is absolutely not to be missed and, by jingo, are we glad we do get to ambush him on his way to coach cricket! Here is a dyed-in-the-wool, ancestral prep school master whose colourful nature defies the greyness of our times. That he thrives here speaks highly of his habitat. Number one school hero is Andy. Andy is the chef and he leads a great team. He listens and he tries his best. He plays football with us after prep. He sources his food locally – organic where possible, free range chicken and eggs, and only British meat. He cooks big breakfasts and, twice a term, themed suppers or dinner nights. There's always fruit all day long. He's well wicked is Andy! In a new initiative, and very popular with the children, junior boarders help cook supper on a Friday evening for the whole community, and senior boarders (Years 7 and 8 in groups of six) prepare a three-course meal with their houseparents every Wednesday.

Boarding is perfectly comfy. You have to remind yourself that at this age they don't much mind having not much territory. There's a junior boarding house for boys and girls aged seven to 10, one boarding house for senior boys and one for senior girls (run by a husband and wife team) in dormitories, some parts of which have been sub-divided, with improved recreational spaces. There's flexi-boarding for the littlest if that's what they want, but in the summer of Year 7 most sign up for weekly at least, giving them four terms to get ready for five years of serious porridge at boarding senior schools, which are very popular with Farleigh parents. Everyone spends two weekends per term banged up. Lots of staff around in the evening, including the five gappies. Third-degree interrogation of children punctuated by incredulous snorts reveals nothing but kindness and, behind that, more kindness. Housemothers rated very highly.

There's unquestionably masses to do, including jolly jaunts to nearby pleasure domes. Special feature is the drawing room, where the children divert themselves before bedtime. It's so nice you'd think children would be barred from it. The social atmosphere of the school is decidedly warm – bullying rated 'nauseous'. The Fr Simon influence is strong here. Children from a school for special needs come on Tuesdays and the Farleigh folk play with them unselfconsciously. Senior schools note that friendships forged at Farleigh keep their shape. Discipline is all about self-regulation but, this being a full-on, action-packed place, exceedingly shrinking violets may stay shrunk.

Moral and spiritual values rated high – religion is 'a warm breeze'. Attitudes to sport are liberal. 'Everyone has the right to be coached in any sport. There's no hierarchy. Anyone can play for the school if they want to.' Those who sidestep hard knocks swim some of the time instead. It's perfectly okay not to be sporty but, if you're a boy, probably better if you are. Nevertheless, parents say, 'It's not all about winning and success like other schools.' Oh yeah? 'That comes back in the language the children use.' There are many incentives and awards for effort, and colours for academic work, music, art, drama and sport.

Music is strong – two-thirds learn an instrument. Decidedly inclusive – 'There are some awful voices in the choirs but no one seems to mind'. School says that senior and chapel choirs are more exclusive – the latter by audition – 'the former enters competitions regularly and the latter sings all over the place'. Much choral singing and all the ensembles you'd expect. The Jazz Band, recently renamed The Thundering Herd, performed at the Edinburgh Festival in the summer. Drama good. After-school activities numerous, mostly sporty. Lots of romping in the woods, of course – dens, that kind of thing. Very few pupils from abroad, but there's a Spanish connection, so usually a couple from there plus a handful of overseas, mostly Services, Brits. Parents the usual rural cross-section plus a swelling inpouring of Londoners, commuters and weekenders, for whom Farleigh has become the country boarding school of choice. It shows in the cars. Some of the locals resent their flash metrocousins who, they reckon, look down their blingy noses at them but, deep as we dug, we found very little of this. Good social life for parents, the Friends of Farleigh are dedicated to organising pleasurable events – bonfire nights, family funday, tennis, touch rugby, football, including annual staff v parents football and netball, that sort of lark. This is a smart, successful and engaging school, no doubt about it, whose dynamic reflects some fast-paced, high-achieving parents. The influence of the head is pervasive, rooting the school in values of right thinking and right conduct.

Felsted Preparatory School

Linked to Felsted School in the Senior section

Braintree Road, Felsted, Essex, CM6 3JL

• Pupils: 460; 55 in reception, 15 full boarders and 75 flexi-boarders, boarding 8+ • Ages: 4-13 • C of E • Fees: R-Y2 £6,390; Y3-Y8 £10,620-£13,965; Boarding £17,850 pa • Independent

Tel: 01371 822 610
Fax: 01371 822 617
Email: rmw@felstedprep.org
Website: www.felsted.org

Head: Since 2004, Mrs Jenny Burrett BA MEd (Cambs) (late forties). Educated at Birkenhead High School and Durham University with a degree in modern languages, which she teaches at the school. Recently completed a Masters in educational leadership and school improvement. Formerly head of department and house-mistress at Felsted School. Married with three children in their early 20s. A larger-than-life figure, hugely popular with staff, pupils and parents alike, who works in harmony with the head of senior. Demonstrates utter dedication and enthusiasm – 'not unusual to be on the email at four in the morning' – and very much in evidence at all events. Recently spotted polishing shoes at the school gate at drop-off time. Absolute dynamo with a Cheshire cat grin and boundless energy which infects all about her. Not many at her age would cavort in a tutu, but all in the spirit of fun.

Entrance: Various entry points with big intake at 11+ when prospective pupils submit a confidential report from their previous school and undergo interview and written tests in English, maths and verbal reasoning. Scholarships and outstanding talent awards are available and some bursaries. Entry lower down less stringent but interview and reports still a must.

Exit: Most move seamlessly from prep to senior, often to join older siblings. 'Caters for all types, so why look elsewhere?' Some help available for those moving outside the Felsted world.

Remarks: Four 'schools', which move the pupils on towards greater self-reliance, focus and specialisation. Extension lessons for very able in subjects where they have particular strengths. Personalised learning approach for SEN; strong on dyslexia; learning support pupils members of the Smart Club.

Leadership weekend for Year 8 – most skill-building activities within the main school day. Football and swimming academies – regular fixtures for A-G teams in many sports. Day starts at 8.15am and finishes late, with Saturday school from 9+. Flexi-boarding from 8+ popular option. Food good. Lots of parental involvement and communication.

Feltonfleet School

Byfleet Road, Cobham, Surrey, KT11 1DR

• Pupils: 370 girls and boys. 45 weekly boarders, rest day. Nursery and pre-prep (Calvi House) 70 boys and girls. • Ages: 7-13, pre-prep 3-7 • Christian ethos • Fees: Weekly boarding £18,825; Day: Pre-prep £9,345, Prep £13,695 pa • Independent

Tel: 01932 862 264
Fax: 01932 860 280
Email: office@feltonfleet.co.uk
Website: www.feltonfleet.co.uk

Head: Since 2000, Mr Philip Ward BEd (mid-forties, but looks younger). Educated at Reigate Grammar School and Exeter University. Spent 17 years at Uppingham (he is a huge fan) working his way up the ranks to senior housemaster. Married to Sue, who plays an active wife-of-the-headmaster role, as well as running junior department and having overall pastoral responsibility for girls. Two children – both of whom were pupils of Feltonfleet. Clearly passionate about his school; a charismatic, family man who enjoys a chat. Full of energy, he says he wants 'fizzy-buzzy staff' – fresh faces and fresh approaches. Very approachable – 'Cares greatly that this is a place where children feel at ease'.

Entrance: Waiting list for entry into pre-prep on a first-come-first-served basis – get names down early. Most join at age seven into Year 3; 18 from the pre-prep and about 30 from many feeder schools including Emberhurst, Glenesk, Hurlingham, Milbourne Lodge Junior, Weston Green and Wimbledon College Prep. Tested in English and maths but it's a 'gentle approach' to pupil evaluation. Head says they're looking for long-term commitment and potential, known as 'headmaster's eye test'. Entry possible higher up as odd gaps appear – always worth a try.

Exit: Mainly at 13 after Common Entrance. A few leave at 11. Leavers go all over the place: local schools Cranleigh, Epsom College, St George's Weybridge, St John's Leatherhead, Priorsfield, Reed's and Wellington get a chunk, but popularity goes in peaks and troughs. Increasingly to co-ed schools and weekly boarding is popular. Number of scholarships increasing – more to all-round schools than to real academic hothouses.

Remarks: Family feel, love-of-life atmosphere, an incredibly energetic and sporty school. Suits active kids who like to be busy – as one parent says, 'Not for the child who needs stillness and downtime as pupils are always on the go'. Has come a long way in recent years and established a premier league appeal. Demand for places very high.

Buildings centred on a large Edwardian house, hidden from view behind woodland and high fences. Centenary Building houses 'super-duper' new library and spacious classrooms for geography, history, French and Latin, networked wireless laptops and interactive whiteboards. Lots of space outside for free play and a new purpose-built tree-house provides outdoor learning area for lessons as well as play area accessed by climbing wall and fireman's pole. Well-maintained and tidy, but the school is next to the A3 which gives a constant background hum to the otherwise peaceful surroundings.

Total refurbishment of pre-prep department, Calvi House, run by Mrs Jan Preece, in 2008. Large extension now provides dedicated sports and dining hall plus resources area with ICT suite, as well as landscaping of play areas and gardens and introduction of a new, more practical uniform for pre-prep pupils. Most children still join the school at 7+ and above, though.

Academic standards are high, but a broad range of children is accepted and not a school for parents who want hothousing. Staff believe happy kids flourish – every class has circle time to help build their self-esteem. Teachers are young and friendly, although the ever-youthful Mr Ward says, 'The average age of staff is 40 – we have several wise and energetic ones too.' Progressive style of teaching – mixture of few desks facing forward and desks in circles. School reckons that a variety of different teaching styles gives children more chances of success. All-roundedness celebrated – 12 scholarships to public schools in music, sport, art and drama recently.

Average 16 children per class from Year 3 upwards; setting in English and maths begins in Year 3. From Year 5, teaching is by subject specialists, with setting in French (starts in the nursery and very well taught) and science. Scholarship streams in Year 7. School fully supports 11+, though one isolated parental comment that 'They do as much as they can to prepare for 11+, but are limited by majority continuing to CE'. Languages strong: Spanish from Year 6, Year 8 scholars do some Italian and Greek, Mandarin and other exotic languages taught online. Science, ICT and DT together in a newly-refurbished building.

Pupils with moderate learning disabilities welcome. School has full-time SENCo and team of peripatetic learning support staff. Also a gifted and talented co-ordinator.

Music has seen a revival in recent years. Own music technology room where pupils experiment with melodies. Lots of positive changes, and loads of new music clubs including pop bands. 180 children learn a musical instrument and there's an annual Party in the Park every May. Drama also strong and taught in newly kitted out performing arts centre. Productions are taken to the Edinburgh Festival and every department puts on a production during the academic year. Art is strong and trips organised annually to Paris, Rome or Granada with the MFL department.

Sport is an incredibly important part of a Feltonfleet child's life. There's a well-used covered swimming pool, a large leisure centre with two squash courts, a small Astroturf pitch and loads of space for rugby, hockey, cricket etc. Matches every Wednesday for pupils in Year 5–8 in school hours and Thursdays for Years 3 and 4. Girls have a super games mistress who also takes on role of 'big sister'. Lots of overseas tours and national tournaments. Girls strong in netball and hockey, boys in rugby with first XV qualifying for national prep school finals again last year. Recent squash scholarship to Millfield. Head very involved with sport – he referees, runs golf and senior girls' tennis.

Massive choice of clubs – pupils encouraged to be busy. One parent felt too much is expected of their child – 'I get the impression they spend a lot of time dashing about'. Long school day with flexible finish times. Weekly boarding is part of the ethos – 29 boys and 15 girls. Boys and girls get along very well and mix at activity time. Dorms are cosy and homely. Boarding master and mistress have built boarding up to a very high standard and there's a good feeling of closeness. Flexi-boarding very popular for occasional use.

Pupils are a happy, active and lively bunch. Boys outnumber girls so 'girls get lots of opportunities to play in teams because there are fewer to choose from'. But several year groups are equally co-ed and the demand for girls' places at 11+ is very high. Some recent uniform changes have softened things up and a certain amount of individuality glimmers through.

Pupils get lots of praise and encouragement from staff, especially from the head, who opens his doors to a queue of children every morning to show him good work for 'headmaster's initials'. Thumbs up from the parents for the school's pastoral care – 'It's a caring, nurturing and supportive environment'. Mix of parents, lots of first time buyers and professionals. Growing number from SW London. The school is perceived as full of moneyed souls – the usual convoy of suburban 4x4s does little to allay this. Plenty of parking for drop off and pick up, but allow time in the morning to battle with the rush-hour congestion. School bus runs from Wimbledon, Putney, Esher, Cobham and The Horsleys with more routes planned.

Fern Hill Primary School

Richmond Road, Kingston Upon Thames, Surrey, KT2 5PE

• Pupils: 415 boys and girls in main school, all day (52 half day places in the nursery) • Ages: 3-11 • Non-denom • State

Tel: 0208 247 0300
Fax: 0208 247 0309
Email: FHP@rbksch.org
Website: www.fernhill.kingston.sch.uk

Head: Since the school opened in 1994, Miss Diana Brotherston BEd Hons DipEd Science MA (fifties). Previously deputy head at Coombe Hill Infant School. A self-contained person, who prefers to talk about her school rather than herself, but she is welcoming and very polite to everyone – acting as a role model for her pupils. Parents say she is straightforward, responds well to problems, knows her stuff and gets parents fully involved in school life.

Entrance: School is hugely popular and heavily oversubscribed. Two-form entry with 30 in each class. Children who attend the nursery do not have priority, but siblings do, then proximity to school comes into play. Children come from a more and more local area – pretty much white middle class. Frantic housemoving by parents to get into the perceived catchment area: which road you live in and even which end of the road is becoming more and more important! Parents who live half way between Fern Hill and the other local in demand school, Latchmere (qv), may find themselves counting the metres between home and school to work out which school is more likely to offer them a place.

Exit: To a wide variety of schools including all the local state secondary schools. Head is sanguine about children being privately tutored for grammar or independent school entrance, but is quite happy to offer parents her opinion as to whether a child will be able to cope in a highly academic school. Private tutoring (a booming industry in this part of the world) can pay off with pupils going to some of the best local secondary schools including Tiffin Boys and Tiffin Girls and independents, particularly Surbiton High, Kingston Grammar and The Hall, Wimbledon.

Remarks: The school of choice for parents who like a formal (school prefers 'friendly and well focused') atmosphere where it is easy to see learning happening: a private school feel, traditional, conservative, with homework, concern about children's appearances etc etc. A school with structure – in its buildings, organisation and attitudes.

One of the best academic schools in the borough. Very good SATs results and pupils look as though they are enjoying their work in an organised environment. They sit still in class in an attentive way (fidgeters and daydreamers could find it rather too ordered). Head says, 'We are also developing a more creative way of learning.' Staff very aware of their able pupils' policy – they feel that setting high standards for the brightest raises the achievements of everyone. About 25 children with SEN needs – SEN coordinator four days a week, and Miss Brotherston says, 'We constantly self review to evaluate the effectiveness of our approaches and we keep abreast of any new studies and programmes. We adopt a "dyslexia friendly approach" (including brain gym, multi sensory teaching and learning, IT) and we are regularly advised by the excellent support services in the local authority. Each pupil presenting with reading difficulties is carefully screened to find out exactly where their difficulties lie'. Pupils who have EAL have a teacher to support them and the teaching staff one day a week.

Very light, bright and busy place and quiet. Quietness will appeal to some parents; others will feel a lack of vibrancy. Children wear a neat uniform, strong emphasis on politeness and courtesy: this shows itself in a very detailed home-school agreement to be signed by parents, pupils and the school, which is augmented by a seven page behaviour partnership document.

Buildings feel much more spacious than many primary schools and security is strong. Corridors are wide with some open plan areas off them – used for small group activities like reading. Classrooms bright and airy with masses of artwork on display. Super music and drama room, with a music teacher who works two days a week to teach music throughout the school (but under-used according to one parent), a dedicated SEN area and a computer suite with 30 terminals in addition to the terminals in the classrooms. Classes named after trees and flowers, which reflects the importance attached to nature in the school. Classrooms look onto an attractive courtyard, which allows easy access to the outdoors in the summer.

Nursery, infant and junior classes are also easily accessible to each other, helping to promote a sense of community. Communication between year groups is encouraged via a buddy system and pairing of classes for certain projects. Lovely gardens where parents and children work regularly – they grow vegetables which are eaten later by pupils. The school has the Green (top) standard in the Eco Mark, Gold Mark for Arts, Gold Award for Sustainable Travel Plan and also is recognised as a Healthy School.

Grounds are well maintained with reasonable outdoor sports facilities for football and netball. Pupils take part in matches against other schools and after school sports clubs are available, but not a strong feeling of a competitive sports ethos (no sports photos obviously on show) and swimming is only available in Year 4. There is, however, a celebration of sports in the weekly newsletter and in the sports diary displayed in the entrance hall, and the school has just been awarded the national Kite Mark for PE and sports provision. You get the impression that academia rules the roost here, and a few parents feel that the school is happy merely to fulfil the requirements of the National Curriculum for sport rather than make use of the good facilities available. Drama is regarded as a strength with some kind of production every term. Peripatetic teachers come into school to give individual lessons in a range of musical instruments and all pupils get a chance to learn the recorder and guitar in Year 6. No opportunities yet for playing in an orchestra or band within the school, despite the large dedicated music and drama room, though there is a large choir. Again the impression is that there is potential for more than is actually provided. Annual art exhibition for parents to enjoy.

Praise for the pastoral care, communications with parents are also excellent – the head and/or her deputy (an ebullient soul much praised by the parents) are at the school gates every morning, and parents are encouraged to speak to teachers about any concerns.

Parents are hugely loyal to the school; it is judged by many to be the best school in North Kingston (and in the whole borough?) although the Latchmere parents (much undisguised rivalry with this neighbouring school) would ferociously disagree.

Fettes College Preparatory School

Linked to Fettes College in the Senior section

East Fettes Avenue, Edinburgh, EH4 1QX

- Pupils: 95 boys, 85 girls; 25 boys and 30 girls board • Ages: 7-13
- Fees: Boarding £18,735; Day £11,955 pa • Independent

Tel: 0131 3222976
Fax: 0131 3224724
Email: PrepSchool@fettes.com
Website: www.fettes.com

Headmaster: Since 2003, Mr A A Edwards BA London (mid-forties). Formerly a housemaster at Gresham's School, Norfolk. Married to Jill; three young sons and one young daughter. A history graduate and a talented sportsman.

Entrance: By assessment test and interview.

Exit: Internally set exam for entry to senior school.

Remarks: With 180 pupils during the seventh year of its life, this newest addition to Scotland's prep schools is shaking other prep schools – particularly Edinburgh prep schools – rigid. In a previous incarnation this was a junior house and before that a junior school, in each case taking children from 10 (now takes from seven). Tiny classes, excellent remedial, super facilities and plumb in the centre of Edinburgh. Latin early, computers everywhere. Possible drawback would be the lack of stimulation for children spending 10 years in the same place. 'Edinburgh's best kept secret'; huge expansion on the way.

Finton House School

171 Trinity Road, London, SW17 7HL

- Pupils: 110 boys, 195 girls; all day • Ages: 4-11 • Non-denom
- Fees: £10,950-£11,880 pa • Independent

Tel: 02086 820 921
Fax: 02087 675 017
Email: admissions@fintonhouse.org.uk
Website: www.fintonhouse.org.uk

Headmaster: Since 2005, Mr Adrian Floyd; came from Newton Prep, where he was head of upper school. Previously taught at Tower House, East Sheen, as head of English. Prior to working in London, taught at Summer Fields, Oxford.

Entrance: Much sought after. Non-selective, first come first served – put names down early. Places appear in later years, always worth checking – children very welcoming to newcomers. At least three special needs places per year for children with significant but not severe needs. LEA funding may be available for statemented children – very oversubscribed; following educational psychologist's assessment places are offered to children with the greatest need that can be met by the school's resources. Siblings have priority. Comprehensive academic ability ranges from gifted and talented to SEN, with some children appearing on both registers.

Exit: Some move to 'the country' before 11. Some boys leave at eight for boys' prep schools: King's Wimbledon, Westminster Under, Northcote Lodge, Eaton House, Dulwich Prep, or go on to board at Summer Fields, Windlesham, Ludgrove etc. At 11, guided choice to wide variety of day and boarding schools: Putney High, Wimbledon High, JAGS, Alleyn's, Francis Holland, Downe House, St Mary's, Ascot, Woldingham, Benenden, Dulwich, Wycombe Abbey etc.

Remarks: Achieves excellent results for pupils of all abilities across a broad curriculum. Lessons interactive and exciting with a strong emphasis on creativity and self-expression. Interactive whiteboards, used by pupils and staff, add a new dimension to already sparky teaching and learning. Even assemblies deemed great fun: 'Especially the trust one where a teacher pretended to be late, then ate cat food – which was actually Mars bar and jelly'. School walls burst with fantastic displays of work by all pupils. Plenty of theme days (India, Romans, Vikings ...), lots of project-based work and trips throughout but especially for Y6 once exam pressure removed – 'It's important to educate in the broadest sense, not just to pass exams,' insists the head. All usual curriculum subjects offered including French from reception and Latin and Mandarin as clubs. Pupils successful in gaining places to their first choice senior schools plus scholarships and awards.

All pupils actively encouraged to participate in wide range of after-school clubs and activities. Some, such as brain gym, target SEN; others 'super siblings' – the brothers and sisters of children with SEN. Boys play football, rugby and cricket, girls play netball, hockey and rounders. Two games lessons a week, plus weekly PE and swimming. Regular fixtures against other schools in the area and a particularly strong swimming team. Frequent successes in local competitions; inclusive policy means every child has the opportunity to represent the school in matches.

Warm, friendly atmosphere due in part to its inclusive ethos and the degree to which parents are involved with the life of the school. Headmaster and staff friendly and approachable. Discipline firm but fair with plenty of rewards and relatively few sanctions. Strong emphasis on good manners and consideration for others, well-supported from home – excellent relationships with parents. Plenty of family events throughout the year, and parents welcome to attend assemblies, plays and fixtures. Most families live within walking distance of the school; a strong social network which makes newcomers very welcome. Parents encouraged to get involved by volunteering to help in school or helping to run events.

Children local to smart Wandsworth. Smallish school accommodated in two handsome and well-proportioned Victorian houses sensitively adapted for school use. Light rooms – gym (doubles as dining hall), specialist science, art, ICT (new, state of the art) and DT rooms, purpose-built music block (plenty of extra-curricular music and opportunities to perform), good library, lots of stairs (would be difficult for children with physical disabilities). Purpose-built reception block opened 2005. Decent-sized playground packed with equipment including wendy houses, friendship bench, climbing frame and much used barrels – great for rolling on and in.

School fizzes with enthusiastic youngsters – comfortable with adults, look you in the eye and clearly love school: 'It's fun and we do loads of sport,' (fixtures from Year 1). Respect for teachers (all called by first names prefixed with Miss or Mr) and sensitivity to each other are virtues to the fore.

Not a special needs school but the school's team, including speech and language and occupational therapists with special needs assistants (a staggering 14 full-time and eight part-time) means that children with learning difficulties can be helped on site on a one-to-one basis (many schools claim this, few actually deliver). Some help is free but one-to-one specialist support outside the classroom incurs a cost – 'kept to absolute minimum, we don't want to make a profit out of SEN'. The head of special needs is assisted by two SENCos: one for the 10 per cent of children who arrive with more complex needs, the other for children with specific learning difficulties who may require monitoring or intervention. Caters for wide-ranging SEN: profoundly deaf (must have some form of communication), Down's, Asperger's, speech and language disorders, SLD etc. An early-intervention programme has been established to identify mainstream pupils who require additional support. Keen to stress all gain from having SEN children in the school and happy co-existence in a non-patronising environment where differences don't matter, also that even the most able, outgoing and ebullient child needs nurturing and care.

Emphasis on inclusion, individuality and results without pressure its forte.

Foremarke Hall (Repton Preparatory School)

Linked to Repton School in the Senior section

Milton, Derby, Derbyshire, DE65 6EJ

• Pupils: 455 boys and girls (390 day, 65 boarders) • Ages: 3-13 • C of E, other faiths welcome • Fees: Day £7,101-£13,743; Boarding £18,249 pa • Independent

Tel: 01283 703 269
Fax: 01283 701 185
Email: registrar@foremarke.org.uk
Website: www.foremarke.org.uk

Headmaster: Since September 2010, Mr Ian Elliott BA (sixties) has been acting head following the departure by mutual agreement of previous head, Paddy Watson. Acting head is widely respected and experienced (he retired as head of Orley Farm School in Harrow in 2006 after 16 years in the post). Known to Foremarke parents already, as he stood in as head for a term in 2007. 'I know schools pretty well,' he says. 'I didn't like retirement and knowing the ethos of this place so well meant that it was easy for me to come back and seamlessly fit in.' Married to former teacher Clare, with two grown-up children and five grandchildren. From April 2011, Richard Merriman, currently headmaster of Birchfield School, co-ed prep near Wolverhampton, takes the reins at Foremarke.

Entrance: Youngest need only enrol for pre-prep and attend for day visit before starting. Virtually all pre-prep children progress through to prep. From age of seven, prospective pupils are assessed in English and maths. School takes 'broad range of ability,' although keeps sights on Repton's academic requirements. When it comes to special educational needs, school says it takes a 'thoughtful and sensitive approach' and each case is decided on individual basis. One to one and group support is available for those who need it. Three learning support teachers on prep staff and four learning support assistants.

Exit: At 13 around 85 per cent go on to Repton. Others leave for schools like Denstone College, Radley, Rugby, Eton, Oundle, Abbotsholme and Cheltenham Ladies'. Foremarke is officially Repton's prep school but pupils bound for Repton must still take Common Entrance or scholarship exams to get there. Level playing field for all. Brightest children go into scholarship class for more intense tuition and school regularly wins a clutch of awards.

Remarks: Foremarke Hall's setting has the real 'wow' factor, with long drive sweeping up to stunning 18th Century Palladian mansion in the wilds of Derbyshire. Once a grand country house, it later became a WW1 hospital, then a WW2 cadet training unit and finally, in 1947, a school. Grounds stretch as far as the eye can see (55 acres in all) and are a fabulous mix of woodlands, walks, sports pitches and even a lake. Plenty of room, as we said last time, to stretch legs, lungs and imagination. Head of history told us that when he arrived for his interview he gazed in wonder at the grounds and thought 'can I really be this lucky?' He certainly could.

High proportion of staff live on school site. Major £6 million building programme underway (following close consultation with English Heritage), with revamped music facilities, new classrooms and new art and DT block to come. Aside from the main house, a very mixed bag of buildings, from ancient to modern. One of the newest is the purpose-built pre-prep, a light and airy building opened in 2006. Pre-prep has 114 pupils – in spacious nursery, reception, Year 1 and Year 2 classes. Facilities include library, computer room and ultra-posh cloakrooms that have lights and water activated by sensor – so no floods! Pre-prep very keen on 'Forest School' approach, with all children spending an hour and a half in the woods every other week, building dens, counting leaves etc. Nursery children eat lunch in pre-prep hall but reception classes, Year 1s and Year 2s walk across to prep's dining hall with their teachers. Whilst pre-prep day finishes at 3.45pm children can enrol for activities till 6pm. Staying for pre-prep activities costs extra but it's a boon for working parents.

The school is busy, busy, busy. Even the acting head says, 'I don't think I've been in a school that tries to do as much as this one'. The school day consists of 12 25-minute lessons, with one of the loudest bells we've heard in a long time signalling the end of each class. From Year 3 day pupils can either go home at 4pm or stay on till 5pm or 6pm after activities, tea and supervised prep. School offers French from Year 1 and Latin from Year 5. Setting by ability for maths, English and French from Year 5. Pupils in upper school (Years 5 to 8) taught by subject specialists.

Lower school (Years 3 and 4) and upper school (Years 5 to 8) are in self-contained parts of the school. Average class sizes of around 16 and none larger than 20. Saturday school for Year 5s upwards but Year 3s and 4s can sign up for Foremarke Plus, a Saturday morning activity programme with pursuits like film-making, swimming, football, hockey on offer. Large, well-stocked library, both print and electronic. All computers on school network for security. Children's work (academic and art) on display everywhere you look. 180-seat theatre refurbished in 2000, with fold-back seating and large stage. In constant use for music and drama. Music is key to Foremarke life, with loads of concerts, competitions and choir trips. Several current pupils are members of the National Children's Orchestra and National Youth Choir. As acting head says, 'there is a staggering amount of music here – 408 instrumental lessons a week.' When we arrived a visiting string quartet was encouraging young violinists in grand, high-ceilinged entrance hall.

Foremarke is a very sporty school and teachers reckon sport is 'an integral part' of the school. In recent years, pupils have won national football, hockey and rounders trophies and cricket, netball, swimming and fencing are all strong too. Large sports hall, football and hockey pitches, astro and hard courts and 25m indoor swimming pool used all year round. Sport for all philosophy, with dedicated games staff supplemented by academic teachers. Extras include sailing, canoeing, horse riding, dance and golf. School also rightfully proud of its Greenpower programme. Run by the go-ahead DT department, Year 7 and 8 members of school's engineering club design and build their own electric cars and Foremarke's Racing F-24 team (supported by parents) competes all over country in them. Autumn term starts with Outward Bound trips for Years 5 to 8 – camping, team-building exercises etc. Outward Bound instructors on most recent trip so impressed by the children's energy and enthusiasm that one said 'I've never seen a group of children who are so up for it.' To which a Foremarke teacher replied: 'What do you expect? They're Foremarke for goodness sake!'

Boys account for 58 per cent of pupils, girls 42 per cent. Day pupils come from 20 mile radius (one or two from as far as Solihull and Sutton Coldfield – quite a trek.) Parents a mix of local business people, farmers and some from county set too. A few boarders from abroad, including three Russian orphans who come to Foremarke for a year, financed by the Foremarke Trust (set up by former head Richard Theobald.) Boarders live in one of four boarding houses – two for boys, one for girls and one for flexi boarders, who can book in for certain days every term or on an ad hoc basis. Some even do 'home and away' boarding, going home on Wednesday nights but boarding the rest of the week. The boys' boarding houses and flexi boarding house are all part of the main school building but the girls are housed in a converted stable block. Dorms range from two to eight pupils and houses are run by houseparents, mostly with young children of their own. Family atmosphere, with houseparents testing children on Latin vocab and serving 'M-n-B' (milk and biscuits) before lights out. Youngest in bed by eight, then quiet reading for 20 minutes, Year 8s in bed by ten past nine and lights out at nine-thirty. Loads of organised activities for boarders – swimming, dodge ball, craft, gardening etc but in summer they're off riding bikes and playing in the woods. Weekends a whirl of action too – anything from 30 to 50 boarders most Saturday and Sunday nights.

Pastoral care excellent. Anti-bullying policy clearly stated in school's invaluable 'blue book,' which lists everything from Foremarke's sports code for pupils (and parents!) to the school's daily routine. Assemblies held three mornings a week and there's a weekend service for boarders at nearby St Saviour's Church or in school. Day pupils aren't allowed to bring in electronic games but boarders can use iPods and mobiles (no internet-enabled phones though) in their free time. Games rooms for boarders equipped with Wii, table football etc and computers for boarders to email home. Overseas boarders are now allowed to use Skype to talk to their families (a suggestion made by the boarders' council and agreed by staff.) No prefects or head boy/head girl system. Instead children apply for and are interviewed for specific roles – pre-prep, assembly, music helpers etc. Badges for academic excellence awarded too.

Parents kept informed of children's progress with face-to-face meetings and termly reports giving grades for effort and attainment. Weekly Foremarke Flyer newsletter keeps parents updated on everything from drama productions to sports results. Parents' group, Friends of Foremarke, runs regular social get-togethers.

Foremarke allows pupils the time (and space – acres of it) to grow up in their own time. Pupils are encouraged to have a go at the myriad of activities on offer, whilst being supported and nurtured throughout. As the head of boarding told us, 'It's a great place for children who like doing things and being busy'.

Forest Preparatory School

Linked to Forest School in the Senior section

College Place, Snaresbrook, London, E17 3PY

• Pupils: 225 girls and boys; all day • Ages: 4-11 • C of E foundation with a sizeable proportion of pupils from other faith groups
• Fees: £8,475-£10,116 pa • Independent

Tel: 020 8520 1744
Fax: 020 8520 3656
Email: prep@forest.org.uk
Website: www.forest.org.uk

Head: Since April 2006, Mrs Elizabeth Garner.

Entrance: 16 places at 4+ and 28 at 7+. By play assessments or maths/English tests according to age.

Exit: Nearly all to the senior school.

Remarks: Co-education in the pre-prep, then single-sex classes. The prep school is situated between the girls' and boys' schools, with its own playground. Light, bright building with lots of work proudly on display. It makes use of the senior school facilities and its football, cricket, netball and rounders teams play matches against other schools. Inter-house tournaments give nearly everyone the chance to compete. The band and choirs perform in concerts and assemblies and plenty of opportunities for budding thespians. Specialist music, modern language, drama, ICT, DT and PE teachers. Everyone learns a musical instrument for at least a year.

Forres Sandle Manor School

Sandle Manor, Fordingbridge, Hampshire, SP6 1NS

• Pupils: 280 boys and girls, 100 board • Ages: 3-13 • Broadly C of E
• Fees: Boarding £19,380; Day £14,205; Pre Prep £3,150-£7,785 pa • Independent

Tel: 01425 653 181
Fax: 01425 655 676
Email: office@fsmschool.com
Website: www.fsmschool.com

Head: Since September 2010, Mr Mark Hartley, previously deputy head at Winchester House, Brackley and before that house master at Mount House School, Tavistock. Wife Beth and three children have joined the school as well. A Westcountry lad and privately educated, Mark returned to Plymouth for his PGCE after a degree at Worcester. He cut his teaching teeth at Fowey Primary School and progressed to housemaster at Mount House School, Tavistock with five years.

The Hartleys have come full circle taking up the reins of FSM, as Beth is a local girl with a love of the New Forest and keen to involve the children in all things earthy. Mark is keen to develop ICT within FSM with the aim of making it a beacon school. Green issues are another concern. The Hartleys are definitely an outdoorsy family, enjoying activities from kayaking to climbing, so they should fit in well at FSM.

Entrance: Most at age three or eight. Boarders at eight only 'if the headmaster is satisfied that the child wishes to board'. Non-selective and they get the full rainbow. The superb learning centre for those with SENs a draw. Day children bypass perfectly good schools in a 25-mile radius – Winchester, Poole, Salisbury. A good crowd from the New Forest, Avon Valley and environs of Cranborne. Boarders a 50-50 mix of ex-pats, mostly Services and locals. Around 50 per cent of parents first time buyers. Geography is against ethnic mix but there's always a wodge of migratory Norwegians (a quirky historic link) and a handful of Spaniards. Start when you like, if there's room. Lists of day children wishing to convert to boarding run years ahead. No schols or bursaries, but 10 per cent off for Services' children.

Exit: Canford a staple. Then the full gamut of locals – the Sherbornes, Bryanston, Marlborough, Blundells, Millfield, Wells. For the less conventionally academic, Milton Abbey, Clayesmore, Grenville. Impressive numbers of schols in everything. 80 per cent stay to 13. At 11, 20 per cent to single-sex girls, grammars or comp. Eminent outcomes: Michael Foot (Forres), Alec Guinness (Sandle Manor).

Remarks: It feels good and it looks good – the Jacobean manor, the bosky grounds, the engorged rhododendrons – but reality matches it. The educational idea is simple enough: 'Happy children succeed' – children thrive when they feel good about themselves. This is the exclusive focus and all achievements are reckoned a by-product. No SATs. Parents don't call for regular benchmarking 'because they trust the school'. Expectations must be high because academic results are boastworthy and rising. Annual Headmaster's Prize to each year group for the child who has worked the hardest.

The school does not apply a play-safe policy to staff appointments, preferring passion, character and kindness. Teachers must be 'up for it'. Plenty of that: avant-garde music teacher has the children playing fruit – even bicycles. Lots of new young faces and a reassuring leavening of wise ones.

The flagship learning centre for children with information processing difficulties – average to above-average IQs only – has no whiff of casualty about it. The brightest are tweaked there too and none are hived off; it is integral to mainstream learning, and the techniques in use have pervaded all classrooms. Teaching methods accord with up-to-the-minute thinking. Impressively led.

Boarding well done and a matter of some vanity. Over half the 7-13s do it. The secret lies in the supervision – always from seven to 10 adults on duty and 10 sleep in the main building. Rooms amusingly painted in colours children delight in. Plenty to do, Wednesday fun evenings the biggest hit. Always around 50 in at weekends, and rising. Genuinely humane – parents say the children look after each other. Sports facilities now good – Astroturf, heated outdoor pool, four hard courts for tennis and netball as well as rugby/hockey/rounders and cricket pitches in the stunning grounds.

For all the equal emphasis on everything, music transcendent under inspirational teacher. Here, democracy of opportunity defers to a little light élitism and the less able are less indulged. They do the lot, from hip-hop to holiness. We heard the jazz band (breathstopping) and delighted in the number of girls playing sassy brass. More than three-quarters learn an instrument and they perform, perform, perform. Ensembles of everything and choirs too. Demand the CD with your prospectus pack.

An un-snobby, unselfconscious school apparently too busy to bother with narcissistic PR or bigging itself up, which it could frankly do more of. Manners work on a democracy of respect basis, with the staff holding doors open for children. Discipline intelligent – errant Year 8 children may be dispatched to devise their own punishment – and extends to parents, too: strict rules of courtesy and self-restraint govern their conduct at sports events. The excellent parents' handbook both informs and requires – with no shred of bossiness or hauteur. The children themselves are delightfully at ease with everyone – we recall three slightly smudged girls out sketching – but live, reassuringly, in a child's world. Parents tell us they always feel welcome and listened to. Those whose children had problems say they were dealt with quickly and expertly.

This is a school where, clearly, most of the children and staff have a lot of fun most of the time, but the philosophy of fun is underpinned by strong seriousness and rigour. Parents who prefer FSM do so over schools they reckon 'too precious' – the sort where toil is tightly focused. The prospectus and website give you the flavour of the place and act as an effective filter. Take it from there.

Fox Primary School

Kensington Place, London, W8 7PP

• Pupils: 315 boys and girls, all day • Ages: 4-11 • Non-denom • State

Tel: 02077 277 637
Fax: 02072 294 628
Email: info@fox.rbkc.sch.uk
Website: www.fox.rbkc.sch.uk

Head: Since 2006, Mr Paul Cotter BA PGCE (forties). Previously deputy head at Avondale Primary in North Kensington. Bringing much of what he learnt there with him, including his young, extremely bright and capable deputy, Miss Emma Madden. They make a formidable team.

A strong dynamic teaching staff, average age less than 30. Larger number of women than men. They bring fun and lots of motivation to the daily curriculum. Parents enthuse about the cohesive staff. By all accounts Mr Cotter has built a team of excellent teachers. Makeover of buildings, playground and learning space too. Cotter is savvy. He knows how to access funding and use it to the max. Energy saving schemes (they are aiming for green flag system and have an 'eco team' of pupils to help them do it) and clever organisation has resulted in his being able to employ more staff and ensure the school is extremely well equipped. Delicious lunches cooked by their own chef (no imported catering service here) allows for every penny to be put back into the menu. Staff eat with pupils in the school hall. They don't need persuading to eat fresh Greek salad. One of his cleverest achievements has to be the class sizes – reduced at every opportunity. Currently only 22 in two classes in reception, Year 1, and Years 4 to 6 with an ingenious scheme to allow for differentiation according to age and stage in Years 2 and 3. Rightly proud of this innovation, 'standards have shot up as a result' he observes.

Entrance: Heavily oversubscribed. Over two hundred applicants for forty five places. Priority (rather than catchment) area is mainly to the south towards Kensington rather than the North to Notting Hill where there is greater density of state school provision. Lots of mobility, however, so places do crop up and further up the school they have admitted children beyond this area. Siblings have priority but no one else. Entrance procedure is administered by the borough and the head can exercise no preference. Children come from over 40 different nurseries, but parents we spoke to mentioned Strawberry Fields, Rolfes, St Peters and Kids Unlimited.

Exit: About half each year to Holland Park, several recently to the spanking new Chelsea Academy. About a third to independent schools – a wide range including Latymer Upper, Godolphin and Latymer, City of London Boys and Girls, St Paul's boys and girls, some board at e.g. Christs Hospital and Cheltenham Ladies College, some win scholarships to e.g. Charterhouse. 'They can go wherever they want,' said one parent. Mr Cotter meets all secondary heads – 'they generally like Fox children,' he says proudly. Parents notice that he sees this as an integral part of his job – makes no judgement about the choice other than finding what's best for each individual.

Remarks: A buzzing local primary with a liberal, funky feel to it. A sea of colour greets you as you enter the well secured gates. Brightly clad children (no uniform) playing noisily (as you would hope) in the imaginatively and tastefully decorated playground. As well as the main area for football and netball, there is a quieter arbour with wooden tables, canopies and lavender, the gentle rushing of water running around the perimeter. A popular place to trade Match Attacks and Go Gos on a Friday and for parents to discuss their next fund-raising project after drop off. A giant chess board and climbing wall in the far corner while, behind the school, in the younger years' playground, there are allotments (where the children tend radishes and chillis as well as lychees) – and a woodland trail. Dedicated play area with sand and water for reception children with beautiful mosaics on the walls.

The school is housed in a large 1930s building and has all the hallmarks of being purpose built. Wide corridors and staircases. Large windows into bright, spacious airy class rooms. Every inch of space is used to benefit learning. The deputy head's office also has an interactive white board and desks. There are music rooms, dedicated learning rooms for smaller groups, an IT room with thirty flat screen computers, a large hall with a huge white screen. IT is used to liven things up at every occasion, particularly the assemblies (which happen at 3pm when 'everyone has had enough rather than first thing which is prime learning time' says head sensibly). We saw the house (named after four different species of fox) spellathon conducted like a prime time quiz show. Everyone had fun and everyone learnt something. This is clearly key to the ethos here.

Music and dance are central to the school day. Years 2 and 3 all learn the recorder in key stage 1 with over half the school going on to learn an instrument in key stage 2. There is an orchestra with regular concerts, jazz and dance throughout the year. Science week happens in the autumn term, arts week in the winter term and sports week (where they canoe and climb, do archery and judo as well as the sports you might normally expect) in the summer. Over 38 clubs are offered either before or after school – children can choose almost anything from Chinese to table tennis, sculpture to archery.

Academic standards soaring. Fox rates as one of the top three primary schools in London, seventeenth in the whole country. Everyone achieves here – the bright ones as well as those with special needs. High ratio of staff to children in each class and the SENCo teaches smaller groups of up to 10 who have learning difficulties (PTA funded laptops for this). About 14 per cent of children are currently on the SEN register. Some have statements. One or two reports that it took a bit of prodding before school diagnosed e.g. dyslexia (school deny this 'we have rigorous monitoring systems' they say) by all accounts once any problems are discovered school gives tremendous support. English is the second language for about one third of children. They catch up quickly. School accepts child as he or she is and work enthusiastically with what they've got, say parents – they don't try to iron out the problems and pretend they're not there.

Very supportive and active PTA raises significant sums of money each year, helping to fund e.g. the stunning areas of the playground. One parent described the parent body as having 'a can-do attitude that you find in some private schools.' A number of parents were at Fox themselves – always a positive indicator. High number of professionals – barristers, journalists, diplomats, authors as well as artists and muscians, and 17 per cent of pupils are on free school meals. One parent spoke of the relief she felt that her daughter wouldn't grow up thinking everyone had a second home in Barbados.

A school with a strong, very positive identity (witness the 'mighty Fox' anthem, sung by the whole school at every successful achievement). One parent described it as mini UN – can be up to 15 nationalities in one class. School thrives on multiculturalism and diverse influences but 'doesn't see that as an excuse for poor performance' emphasizes one parent. School quick to point out that bilingual pupils outperform their monolingual peers. Bright eyed, confident, articulate and above all happy children who enjoy coming to school. A rare and precious jewel showing real life at its best – not to be overlooked in this super affluent patch of London.

Francis Holland Junior School, Sloane Square

Linked to Francis Holland School, Sloane Square in the Senior section

Graham Terrace, Belgravia, London, SW1W 8JF

• Pupils: 160 girls; all day • Ages: 4-11 • Church of England
• Fees: £12,060-£14,205 pa • Independent

Tel: 020 7730 2971
Fax: 020 7823 4066
Email: education@fhs-sw1.org.uk
Website: www.fhs-sw1.org.uk

Head: Since September 2010, Miss Sarah J Styles BA (Hons) MA (London) in philosophy of education. Previously director of studies at Wheathamstead House, and was a member of the Women's Royal Naval Service before she took up teaching. Took over after the immensely long and distinguished reign of Mrs Bown.

Entrance: Very competitive entrance at age four. School is the flavour of the month and has been for some time. Children are 'tested' in January for the September term. 200 seen for 24 places. Maturity, ability to relate to others, memory and coordination are assessed – 'Are they ready for school?'

Exit: 50 per cent (ish) to the senior school (via London Schools Consortium exam). A number choose to board – at, e.g. Cheltenham Ladies' College, Wycombe Abbey, Downe House – and a fair few (often the brightest) to other London day schools – St Paul's, Godolphin and Latymer Upper.

Remarks: Strong, academic pre-prep and prep school near Sloane Square. Remarkable building for Central London, the site being shared with the senior school. A quad in the middle serves as playground for all years but plenty of games (either on site or Battersea Park four days a week). Ballet very strong (although some mutterings among parents about the sidelining of mediocre children). Highlight of the annual calendar is the Princess Margaret classical ballet awards day. Music also strong with at least 80 per cent of girls learning an instrument.

Parents very social – banking, diplomats, lawyers, media types, some royalty and celebrities, although everyone frightfully discreet. Mostly from Chelsea, Fulham, Pimlico. Old Girls include Lady Sarah Chatto, Vanessa Mae and Jemima Khan. Vigorous science department under buzzy Scottish head who has lots of clubs (doing all the experiments you'd rather they didn't do at home) and an annual 'spaghetti and marshmallow' day where families compete (some fathers taking it very seriously indeed) to build the biggest structure.

Specialist teachers brought in from the senior school in science, ICT, art, PE and also French, which is taught from eight. Strong 'helping others' ethos with girls raising money for charity at home and abroad. Bright and airy library shared with the senior school.

Not a school for the faint-hearted – that's the parents, not the children; 'The children are used to being stretched,' says the head. Homework is very demanding and a lot of support is required. It pays off because girls do outstandingly well here. High standards, wholly committed approach, and individual attention mean that very few don't succeed in some capacity. Girls here are neat and articulate and enthuse about their 'marvellous' trips to Cornwall and Canterbury 'where we dressed up as knights'.

From the highly dedicated staff through to the bright orange worry bags in each classroom (which are not just on display) and the regular contact with the girls from the senior school (they read to them once a week), girls here are well-adjusted and can be stretched without becoming neurotic. Miss Styles inherits a celebrated junior school and we will watch with interest as she makes it her own.

Frensham Heights Lower School

Linked to Frensham Heights School in the Senior section

Rowledge, Farnham, Surrey, GU10 4EA

• Pupils: boys and girls; boarding from 11 • Ages: 3-13
• Fees: Day £5,340-£14,655; Boarding £20,550 pa • Independent

Tel: 01252 792561
Fax: 01252 794 335
Email: admissions@frensham-heights.org.uk
Website: www.frensham-heights.org.uk

Headmaster: Mr Andrew Fisher. Head of First and Lower School: Mr Nic Hoskins.

Remarks: New, lovely, bright First School houses three- to eight-year-olds. Confident, busy six-year-olds rushing about calling teachers 'Sue' and 'Caron'. Seven-year-olds get specialist teachers for French, drama, ICT, music and PE.

For further details, see senior school.

Friends' Junior School

Linked to Friends School in the Senior section

Mount Pleasant Road, Saffron Walden, Essex, CB11 3EB

• Pupils: 160 girls and boys • Ages: 3-11 • Quaker ethos
• Fees: £6,330-£8,850 pa • Independent

Tel: 01799 525 351
Fax: 01799 520681
Email: adminjs@friends.org.uk
Website: www.friends.org.uk

Head: Mr Andrew Holmes BA BEd.

Entrance: By individual assessment.

Exit: Most to senior school.

Remarks: See senior school entry.

The Froebelian School

Clarence Road, Horsforth, Leeds, West Yorkshire, LS18 4LB

• Pupils: 190 boys and girls; all day • Ages: 3-11 • Christian, non-denom
• Fees: £3,945-£6,030 pa • Independent

Tel: 0113 258 3047
Fax: 0113 258 0173
Email: office@froebelian.co.uk
Website: www.froebelian.co.uk

Headmaster: Since 1991, Mr John Tranmer MA PGCE (fifties), read history at St John's, Cambridge, PGCE at St Martin's Lancaster. Taught at Bolton School, HMS Indefatigable (nautical school), Parkside School, Cobham (ran history, RE and games). A friendly, almost reserved, manner hides a very determined head, who is taking the school forward on all fronts. Recent chairmanship of IAPS helped raise his and school's profile regionally and nationally. His role as a schools inspector also helps keep him aware of best practice. Despite increasing calls on his time he remains a teaching head and also has an eye on further educational qualifications himself, 'I like to learn new skills and get a buzz from the children learning new things'. Shares that ethos with staff: 'If we have a love of learning it is easier to understand why it is important for the children'. Seeking to create an extended community feel for school, he works closely with parents whose 'expectations are high and rising'. These expectations are met partly through greater individualisation of education 'right down to individual spelling lists per pupil'.

Very aware of increasing need for children to gain transferable skills and looks to instil a love of learning to prepare children for secondary school. 'I am trying to give them a thirst for learning, an understanding that my whole life is going to be more fulfilled if I am a more educated person'. But while education moves forward (greater use of ICT, individual learning etc), head is also keen to retain traditional value: 'We need to stimulate children and educate them to be their best – provide the best teachers, the best resources; the chemical formula for success doesn't change'.

He is liked and respected by parents, 'He is someone we knew from the outset we could have confidence in'; 'He is very personable and spends a lot of time in the playground getting to know the children'.

Entrance: Almost exclusively at three; first 24 to register invited to spend some time in school, where they are informally assessed by staff. One-form entry of 24, perpetual waiting list of between 10 and 30. Places occasionally available for older children.

Exit: About 80 per cent to Bradford and Leeds independent grammar schools (boys and girls). Harrogate Ladies' College, Ashville and Woodhouse Grove also popular, Ripon Grammar. Occasional entrant to Eton, Wycombe Abbey or reputable maintained (e.g. St Aidan's, Harrogate).

Remarks: Happy little children dash about in bright red uniforms and t-bar sandals, almost harking back to a bygone age. But this is no retro school. Founded in 1913 and proud of its history, it is very much a forward-looking and progressive school. Lots of ICT, laptops, whiteboards, crammed into modest school footprint. Recent years saw two large additional classrooms, a multi-purpose studio and enlargement of the playground. Opportunities for more expansion or relocation are limited but watch for internal shift around to open up space to coincide with school's centenary in 2013. 'In an ideal world you would have a big playing field and more car parking, but that's the way it is and as a city centre school it copes very well,' says a parent.

Pulls in affluent families from Leeds-Bradford area and, thanks to bursary scheme, a sprinkling of able, less-well-off children. Parents expect a lot and excellent ('top 30 in the country') SATs results ensure they get very good value. Doesn't sweat over SATs but uses them to 'keep a watchful eye on where we are' – head.

Average class size 22, but early years have classroom assistants. Exposure to IT from the start. Supports gifted and able and offers learning support for SEN (possibly at extra cost depending on level of need). Set apart by specialist teaching as marked as in most secondary schools. Pre-prep has specialist support for music, ICT and PE and specialist teaching increases year on year until a full range of subjects is taught by specialists by Year 6. Children get used to different teachers, different locations, just like secondary school. 'Plus it plays to the teachers' strengths' – head. 'I want able teachers who can stretch some very able and gifted children, in their own specialist subjects.'

Strong on encouraging idea of learning skills for life, aware that many people now go on to change career many times. 'Achieve your best' is a mantra spread throughout the school, nowhere more prevalent than in sport where, despite limited facilities (school uses nearby fields and pool) the emphasis is on taking part. Deputy head has received Sports Teacher of the Year award from the National Council for School Sport. Music and drama very strong – 'almost all' juniors learn at least one instrument, school famous locally for its musicals (e.g. Mary Poppins, Oliver!). Also field trips, outings, juniors' week in France; Three Peaks trip for Year 6 particularly loved. Close contacts with parents, via e-mail or text, plus traditional letters home and homework diaries. Parents like 'lovely, friendly family feel to the school'.

Clear school code and anti-bullying policy. Emphasis on children allowing each other to be happy in their school lives, and older boys and girls supervise smaller pupils' lunchtime. Has embraced extended school idea with busy breakfast club (includes opportunity for computer games) and after-school club to 6pm which offers supervised homework or play and activities.

Fulham Prep School

Linked to Fulham Pre-prep School

200 Greyhound Road, London,
W14 9SD

• Pupils: 585 boys and girls; all day • Ages: 4-13 • Non-denom
• Fees: £12,225-£13,575 pa • Independent

Tel: 020 7386 2444
Fax: 020 7386 2449
Email: prepadmin@fulhamprep.co.uk
Website: www.fulhamprep.co.uk

Headmistress: Since 1996, Mrs Jane Emmett BEd (fifties). Original founder of the school. Jolly, enthusiastic, friendly, hands-on approach, really loves her job and her school. Started her teaching career at small school in Buenos Aires. On returning to England after birth of her sons, did her DipEd and taught in a country state school until coming to London. After a brief involvement with child-based charities, she joined Cameron House, where she remained for 13 years, including six as head. The school is very much a family concern. Her husband is the bursar, one of her sons is the school's project manager, the other runs his own company but is also on the school board. When we mentioned the R (retirement) word, the reply was very definitely not yet and anyway, the school is and always will be a family company, with some external shareholders, but the family have a controlling majority. Everyone we spoke to emphasised that her leadership and enthusiasm are the essence of the school.

The head of the pre-prep, under Mrs Emmett as principal, is Miss Di Steven BEd University of Glasgow (late thirties); lots of teaching and managerial experience and now a proud new mother. Also enthusiastic head of ICT.

Entrance: Non-selective in reception, first come first served, with priority always given to siblings. An informal assessment, a day in the school for Years 1 and 2, mainly to reassure child and parents that it is the right place to come to. Then by examination and interview at 7+ 8+ and 11+. Usually places in other years if necessary.

Exit: Girls mostly at 11, though some do stay on and Mrs Emmett would dearly like to encourage more to do so; boys at 13. All to a wide range of day and boarding schools, including Eton, Winchester, Stowe, Dulwich, King's Wimbledon, The American Community School, Cheltenham Ladies', Downe House, Francis Holland, Queen's Gate, Putney High and Lady Margaret's. 'We believe it is more important to find the right school for each child than to be a feeder.'

Remarks: A school which has grown at enormous speed since its humble beginnings 10 years ago. Some say it is now too big but admit that without the size the breadth of facilities would not be there. An academic school that nurtures rather than pressurises and does not like 'pushing'. A local school producing 'nice, unprecocious children' and mainly happy, satisfied parents.

Excellent traditional teaching across a broad curriculum. Adheres roughly to the national curriculum with adjustments to cater for 11+ and 13+ Common Entrance exams, plus extras such as French, starting from reception, with Latin and philosophy being introduced in Year 5. From Year 4, all subjects are taught by specialist teachers. Lots of young enthusiastic graduate teachers, largely from South Africa, New Zealand and Australia; in the prep about 50 per cent of these are male. We were told the age range was from 23– 60+, but no-one we met seemed to be beyond their 30s!

Up to five classes in each year group, all of which are mixed ability, none with more than 20 children. Until Year 3 all are classroom-based; after that they have a home classroom for domestic affairs but move around to specialist subject rooms and laboratories. Everywhere we went we found children eager to explain what they were doing; nowhere a bored-looking face. The artroom with African-inspired T-shirts, beautiful pots waiting to be fired in their own kiln and fantastic sculptures was just one example of enthusiastic teaching.

Computers and interactive whiteboards in every room in the prep plus a mobile IT lab in a box which can be wheeled to where it is most needed. A well-used exciting library, with an imaginative librarian who likes it all to be interactive, with puppets and special play areas. Years 3 and 4 have a class in there once a week just for fun reading. Not a place for silent reading and homework sessions – that all happens elsewhere.

No real provision for much more than mild dyslexia, dyspraxia, ADD problems; if anything more serious were to develop a school move would probably be suggested, 'We are an academic school and do not feel that it is in the child's interest to keep him if he is not coping. There are places that can do it so much better'. Having said that, there are three rooms for special one-to-one teaching (at extra cost) and the SENCo is exceptionally kind, caring and supportive. She is well-informed and will always go round a suggested alternative school with parents if they want her to. Gifted and talented children are identified and well catered for with extra specialist classes if required. No EAL – children are expected to be able to be able to cope and have pretty fluent English if they join the school beyond Year 3.

One all-weather sports pitch and another planned for imminent construction. Much use made of Fulham Pools, just round the corner, and weekly sessions at Barn Elms Sports Ground. All encouraged to take part in a wide range of physical activities. Teams play against other London schools and in tournaments – everyone gets a chance to represent the school. Sports club on Fridays where the older children are given the chance to try out different things such as sailing, rock climbing, rowing and trampolining. Squash, karate, gymnastics, basketball, girls' football also offered as after-school clubs, plus the current flavour of the month, Mandarin Chinese.

Built in 1870 as a Victorian board school, now a spankingly modern school with high ceilinged, large, bright classrooms and laboratories, wide corridors and bang up-to-date facilities. Externally it looks like a typical purpose-built Victorian school, but the lightness and the colour everywhere present an entirely different picture, and the imaginative teaching to enthusiastic pupils is a far cry from the canes and learning by rote of yesteryear. The main school hall, where assembly is held once a week, is perfect for all sorts of activities including theatrical performances and gymnastic displays. A separate building acts as the dining hall where healthy food is cooked and served – 'Whatever can be home-made is, including yoghurt'. Another building contains a huge indoor play area and currently doubles up as a common room for Years 7 and 8.

The pre-prep is a big, rambling building in two halves: an older Victorian part with lovely large bright classrooms (a computer in each) and a newer part built six years ago. Large hall for PE, school productions, concerts etc: the whole school gathers there for assembly twice a week. Most productions are class-based so that everyone gets a chance to perform. This does mean several different nativity plays, concerts etc, which one parent felt was a bit of a shame. A great artroom, with an enthusiastic, imaginative full-time teacher and a very grown-up looking IT lab – by the time the children move on their computer literacy cannot be in doubt. A dark music room for singing and experimenting with various different instruments. Two tarmac playgrounds but no climbing frames. Lots of toys and equipment ready to be brought out at play time. The older children are creating a garden in the newer play area, wonderful homemade scarecrows and lots of vegetables as well as flowers. All parents seem very happy, although one or two felt that it was perhaps now just a tad too big – 'It's not what we originally signed up for'.

House or class points for good behaviour, but not lost for bad behaviour. Respect and consideration for others, and an ability to fit into the school community, of paramount importance. The anti-bullying policy is sensible and comprehensive and the SENCo, who is a trained counsellor, is always there for children who need to talk to her. The head feels that the fact that the pupils are divided up into houses helps, and Years 7 and 8 are always asked to keep a protective eye on the younger children. Inevitably, in a school this size, there have been odd incidents, but nothing that has led to serious measures having to be taken. All the parents we talked to commented on the general friendliness of the children and the exceptionally pleasant aura of the school. No real problems for children moving from elsewhere: 'Everyone was very helpful and friendly', 'There is a real community feel'; they all seem to settle in fast.

The prep catchment area covers Barnes, Chiswick, Brook Green and West Kensington as well as Fulham, while the pre-prep seems to remain more local, within walking distance, which does include Putney. With the expansion of the school this has broadened; free transport is provided between sites where there are siblings in both sections. 25 per cent of families are ex-pats, from all over the world, mostly bankers but some from big international companies.

The occasional FPS bursary, and they aim to find the means to keep a child with financial difficulties. Scholarships available for Years 7 and 8 for which anyone can apply.

Garden House School

Turks Row, London, SW3 4TW

• Pupils: 455: 185 boys + 270 girls; all day. Single-sex teaching after kindergarten • Ages: 3-11 • Non-denom • Fees: £16,500-£17,040 pa • Independent

Tel: 020 7730 1652
Fax: 020 7730 0470
Email: info@gardenhouseschool.co.uk
Website: www.gardenhouseschool.co.uk

Principal: Since 1973, Mrs Jill Oddy BA. Also runs three pre-prep schools in New York. Girls' upper school head: since 2009, Mrs Kate Simon BA Hons PGCE. Girls' lower school head: since 1988, Mrs Wendy Challen CertEd Froebel. Both heads experienced, knowledgeable and very hands-on. Work well together and create a home-from-home atmosphere for their girls.

Boys' school head: Mr Christian Warland BA Exeter. Garden House old boy (and son of the principal), practised as a lawyer in the City for many years before coming into teaching. Fortyish with three sons of his own (two at the school), originally joined in 2006 as the manager/ coordinator for the move into the new buildings. When the former head of boys left the school, Mr Warland was, as they say, 'in the right place at the right time'.

Entrance: First, go and visit the school. Applications made without a personal visit are discouraged – regular tours for prospective parents (many pregnant with first child!). £120 secures a place on the lengthy waiting list. Children interviewed but not examined, thankfully, at ages three and four. Once a place is offered, a registration fee of £2,000 is payable and the child will start in September. Girls stay on till 11 but many boys leave at eight, so places become available later on. Applications for those places subject to an examination plus interview.

Exit: Boys leave at 8+ and 11+ for top London day schools, including Sussex House, Westminster Under, Colet Court, Latymer, and boarding prep schools such as Ludgrove, Summer Fields, Cothill House, The Dragon. Girls leave at 11 having been prepared for their Common Entrance exam, often achieving academic, art and music scholarships and exhibitions. Current popular boarding options: Cheltenham Ladies', Wycombe Abbey, Woldingham, Downe House. London day schools: Francis Holland (SW1), Godolphin and Latymer, More House, St Paul's and Queen's Gate.

Remarks: Ever a lovely school – the name alone evokes an image of peace, tranquillity, beauty and knowledge. Now it has moved to the new premises in Turks Row just behind Sloane Square, it has become even more delightful and finally acquired a real garden of its own, with a plot in the grounds of the Royal Hospital. In true Garden House style, this will be fully used as a teaching aid as well as providing hours of fun and interest for the pupils. Separate teaching for boys and girls, although they interact during playtime and have joint musical and drama performances. Average class size 15 and unusual subjects such as ballet ('dance' for the boys), Latin, DT, current events, French and fencing are part of the everyday curriculum. (It did originally open as a ballet school in 1950 and the tradition lingers on.)

Sport taken very seriously with football, rugby, cricket, rounders, hockey, lacrosse, tennis, netball every day in Burton Court and Ranelagh Gardens and swimming at the Queen Mother's Pool (all within walking distance). Each class has a teacher plus a full-time assistant (many being old boys/girls), mixed ability with no streaming apart from some later for maths. Any special needs requirements provided by two full-time specialist teachers.

Fine displays of artwork throughout the school. Many art competitions held within the school and with other schools. Science rooms well stocked with weird and exciting-looking equipment; music and recital rooms aplenty. Two-thirds have individual music lessons; also Dawn Chorus and chamber choir on offer. No shortage of space in their new home. Stunning senior library complete with imposing fireplace, vases of fresh flowers, sculptures and superb paintings – almost demands that you take a book off the shelf and lose yourself for a while. Productions put on three times a year at the Royal Court and the Christmas concert is held in the Holy Trinity Church. All festivals eagerly anticipated by staff and pupils alike; no opportunity for dressing up or decorating the school missed as everyone has enormous fun.

The tiny kindergarten is in a separate building attached to the Holy Trinity Church. Morning sessions for 24 children and afternoons for 12. They share a playground with the C of E primary school over the road. Really sweet set-up – perfect for tiny tots: very inviting with tables covered with puzzles, colouring pencils, paints and modelling clay.

A gem of a school. The staff here are a happy mix of long-serving, experienced teachers and young, enthusiastic newly-qualifieds, giving these children the best of both worlds. The PTA is very active and supportive. Lucky indeed are those who reach the top of the waiting list – they will enjoy a brilliant education in beautiful surroundings and have fun along the way.

Gateways Preparatory School

Linked to Gateways School in the Senior section

Harewood, Leeds, West Yorkshire, LS17 9LE

• Pupils: Girls and boys (3-7), girls only 7+ • Ages: 3-11 • C of E foundation, but 'all faiths or none' accepted • Fees: £5,394-£8,127 pa • Independent

Tel: 0113 288 6345
Fax: 0113 288 6148
Email: gateways@gatewayschool.co.uk
Website: www.gatewaysschool.co.uk

Remarks: For further details see senior school.

GEMS Hampshire School (Main School)

Linked to GEMS Hampshire School (Early Years Section)

15 Manresa Road, Chelsea, London, SW3 6NB

- Pupils: 220 all day; 50/50 girls and boys, spread over two sites
- Ages: 3-13 • Non-denom • Fees: £13,134-£13,899 pa • Independent

Tel: 020 7352 7077
Fax: 020 7351 3960
Email: hampshire@indschool.org
Website: www.ths.westminster.sch.uk

Principal: Since 1986, Mr Arthur Bray CertEd MISA (fifties). Came from Millfield Junior where he and his wife were senior house parents. Mrs Bray is school bursar; their two children, now grown up, both attended the Hampshire. Proud of the family atmosphere they have worked hard to create yet determinedly modest – verging on the diffident: 'We rate ourselves average on absolutely everything,' says Mr Bray about his school. An adjective parents, on the other hand, don't readily choose to describe him. They prefer 'tremendous' and 'exceptional', commenting on his devotion to the school and the children, his very visible presence throughout the school (quite a feat, considering that the school is currently spread over three sites) and his availability to talk through concerns of any kind. An experienced head who nurtures his children with good humour and quiet wisdom rather than authoritarian discipline.

Entrance: From 3, an informal interview; older children attend an assessment day – nothing too daunting. School is currently expanding (can accommodate up to 240 in Manresa Road – currently only 160 in this section of the school) so plenty of places at various different levels in both the prep and the pre-prep. As school fills up likely to be entrance points at rising 3, 4 and 5 (kindergarten and reception based at Wetherby Place) only, with the occasional place further up the school

Exit: Handful of boys leave at 8, majority at 13, most girls at 11, very few to boarding schools, most to a (very) wide range of London day schools. 'I can't think of a London day school to which we haven't sent anyone – certainly across the whole range,' says head. Favourites with the girls are More House, Francis Holland and Godolphin & Latymer; for boys Latymer Upper, Westminster, Dulwich, Emanuel and Colet Court. Mr Bray offers excellent individual advice on senior school selection. Nor is he afraid of losing bright boys to more academic establishments at 7 – 'He always puts the best interests of the child first,' commented one parent.

Remarks: Founded as a dance school in 1928 by June Hampshire; on moving to London in the early 1930s became mainstream. Her daughter, Jane Box Grainger, took over as head in the 1960s; another daughter is the well known actress Susan Hampshire. Now part of the GEMS group, has grown from 140 to 220 pupils since the Brays' arrival. Since January 2009 pupils in Year 1 through to Year 8 have been accommodated in impressive premises on Manresa Road (marbled Corinthian columns, no less). Formerly a King's College library and, prior to that, the public library built by Earl Cadogan in 1891, the building is listed and after extensive negotiations with various bodies including English Heritage, Mr Bray and his team have created his dream building for the school.

State of the art technology throughout. Whiteboards that are not only interactive but also move up and down walls (wonderful for children in the early years who still sit on the carpet) and even move around the room (an ingenious way of getting round English Heritage's intransigence about having a whiteboard installed in the grand library). Individual computer desks in many of the classrooms already and more are planned – soon all children from Year 6 through to Year 8 will have their own computer, carefully hidden away inside the smart wooden desks, at which they can also write. ICT a great strength. Children become highly competent with technology and are given the opportunity to learn touch-typing.

Lifts throughout the building – children with physical disabilities can now be accommodated – as well as individual staircases and entrances for different sections of the school – 'I was determined to keep the homely atmosphere and ensure that the younger children would still feel secure. Each area is personal and relevant to each age group,' says Mr Bray proudly. A large kitchen, which can prepare banquets for 160. Children arrive in the morning to the smell of fresh bread, baked daily, and eat lunch with the staff at round tables in the impressive June Hampshire Hall, complete with moveable stage and soundproofed screens. Gym also takes place in here and plenty of space to tuck things away, so you would never know it serves so many different purposes. Space is the overwhelming impression you get as you are shown round – no cramped stairways and classrooms in this central London school (what a welcome change from the norm) and good sized walled garden, where all children can get some fresh air during break times.

Games take place at Battersea Park, swimming at Chelsea swimming baths (younger ones still swim at Fulham pools). Wonderfully atmospheric library which smells of studiousness. Domed window in the ceiling – balcony bursting with bookshelves but treacherous balustrade, too dangerous to use so just for show (Mr Bray filling up the empty shelves as fast as he can with any books he can get his hands on). The downstairs, however, teems with genuine learning – old and new: the hallmark computer desks again, a long wide mahogany table around which a whole class can work, mobile interactive whiteboard as well as doughnut cushions for the younger ones in an intimate space carved out for them between two marble pillars.

Family-based, community-spirited atmosphere; pupils are friendly and encouraged to look after each other. They work hard and are much praised. A wide curriculum, including four languages. During a week in May each year the prep school section closes down and relocates to a chateau in France where they rock climb and canoe etc as well as continue with academic subjects.

Careful assessments of the children at every stage through a combination of PIPs, NFER and CATs testing ('SATs are a waste of time,' says head). Maximum 20 to a class, a watchful eye is kept and special needs are quickly identified. A dedicated SENCo (highly praised by one parent for her direct approach and ability to make her sessions fun) is employed full time, and works one-to-one with children diagnosed with, e.g., dyslexia and dyspraxia. The gifted and talented, after a lengthy and careful assessment, are given a programme of accelerated learning. Visiting speech therapists and EFL is catered for in-house. A lot of demand for this as school is made up of a significant number (though no more than reflects the demographics of the area, insists head) of foreign pupils whose parents are on temporary postings.

Good inclusive arts programme: everyone is in an annual drama production, often a musical. Busy choir and orchestra (more than half the school play an instrument). Children entertain each other over lunch with informal piano recitals. Enthusiastic noises from parents, who are pleased with the breadth of education their children are getting at this stage. A relaxed and secure environment for the normal child who wants to have a go at everything.

George Heriot's Junior School

Linked to George Heriot's School in the Senior section

Lauriston Place, Edinburgh, EH3 9EQ

• Pupils: all boys, all day • Ages: 4-11 • Fees: Day £15,135; Boarding £16,740-£19,695; Pre-prep £8,325 pa • Independent

Tel: 01312 297 263
Fax: 01312 296 363
Email: admissions@george-heriots.com
Website: www.george-heriots.com

Remarks: See senior school.

George Watson's College Junior School

Linked to George Watson's College in the Senior section

67-71 Colinton Road, Edinburgh, EH10 5EG

• Pupils: boys and girls; all day • Ages: 3-12 • Fees: Nursery: £3,654-£6,390 ; Junior £6,078-£7,326 pa • Independent

Tel: 0131 446 6040
Fax: 0131 446 6099
Email: jsadmissions@gwc.org.uk
Website: www.gwc.org.uk

Head of Junior School: Since 2007, Mrs Linda Fleming. Internal promotion, previously director of studies, with responsibility for learning and teaching.

Entrance: Nursery from age three. Early entries up to Primary 3 by interview. From Primary 4 upwards entry is by written test and interview.

Exit: No guarantee of advancement from nursery to main primary school but, once in, majority go on to senior school unless family circumstances dictate otherwise.

Remarks: Learning begins through play in nursery. The Watson's claim is that learning should be fun – even at home; homework given from first year and parents encouraged to support. Specialist subject teaching for the older children, French from age seven with native speakers. Special catch-up classes run for any latecomers. ICT skills taught and used widely to support other subjects. Mixed-ability groups with setting only for maths at the top end of the school. Extensive library, plus audio books and tame librarian.

Good dyslexia support throughout, anxious to get away from any image of having 'a school with a unit'. In yer face drama and music. Four choirs, two recorder groups, chamber orchestra, ensembles and pipes. Oodles of extra activities and clubs. Primary pupils have full use of all senior facilities with hockey for girls, rugby for boys (only) and swimming for all.

No official scholarships but in line with the ethos of the school, financial help given in unforeseen circumstances.

Breakfast and after-school clubs popular with children from professional parents who are pleased to have an 'extended day': 7.45am – 5.45pm. A big school and, at 23+, biggish classes, max 27 currently P5–P7. Plethora of junior school assistants throughout. Manages its size well, taking advantage of its senior school's facilities. Good teaching and good value for money. Pre-school nursery either mornings or all day.

Giggleswick Junior School

Linked to Giggleswick School in the Senior section

Giggleswick, Settle, North Yorkshire, BD24 0DE

• Pupils: 75 girls and boys, including approx 10 boarders • Ages: 3-11
• Fees: Day £6,105-£12,735: Boarding £15,615 pa • Independent

Tel: 01729 893100
Fax: 01729 893158
Email: enquiries@giggleswick.org.uk
Website: www.giggleswick.org.uk

Headmaster: Since September, 2007, Mr M S Brotherton BEd NPQH (38). Trained with PE specialism and is a keen sportsman and coach. Previously director of studies and deputy head at St Hugh's School, Woodall Spa, Lincs. Wife, Heather, teaches languages in the junior school, two children, both in the junior school. Interests include rugby, cricket and golf. Wants children to be 'happy, respectful and confident ... , keen to learn and enjoy opportunities presented to them at school'. Is working to maintain a 'warm and friendly family atmosphere in which children thrive and develop'.

Entrance: Broadly selective. Children from 7 years are offered places provided they have a good basic knowledge of reading and writing. Entrance is via tests, interview with the parent and child and a full report from the previous school. Pupils who are non-native speakers of English may expect to take extra English lessons (EFL) according to need. Children with specific learning difficulties may be accepted provided the school feels able to offer the specialist and general assistance required. Some junior awards may be offered for pupils entering Years 4–6.

Exit: Majority to Giggleswick.

Remarks: School located in purpose built premises containing bright modern classrooms, an early years unit with indoor/outdoor play area, library, ICT suite, learning support tutorial room, self-contained playground and brand new sports hall. Languages are introduced in reception, as part of a cultural programme that runs throughout the school. Younger children spend most of their time with their form teacher, but by Year 6 all lessons are taught by specialist teachers. Children follow national curriculum and take SATS. Separate junior boarding house, opportunities for day pupils to board on an occasional basis at any time, subject to space. Full activity programme for boarders.

The Glasgow Academy Atholl

Linked to Glasgow Academy Preparatory School (The) in the Junior section

Linked to Glasgow Academy (The) in the Senior section

Linked to Glasgow Academy Dairsie (The) in the Junior section

Mugdock Road, Milngavie, Glasgow, G62 8NP

• Pupils: 70 boys and girls • Ages: 3-9 • Fees: £6,690-£7,395 pa • Independent

Tel: 0141 956 3758
Fax: 0141 955 0874
Email: atholl@tga.org.uk
Website: www.theglasgowacademy.org.uk

Head: Ms Jean McMorran.

Remarks: See senior school.

The Glasgow Academy Dairsie

Linked to Glasgow Academy Atholl (The) in the Junior section

Linked to Glasgow Academy Preparatory School (The) in the Junior section

Linked to Glasgow Academy (The) in the Senior section

54 Newlands Road, Newlands, Glasgow, G43 2JG

• Pupils: 75 boys and girls • Ages: 3-9 • Fees: £6,690-£0-£7,395 pa • Independent

Tel: 0141 632 0736
Fax: 0141 632 1302
Email: dairsie@tga.org.uk
Website: www.theglasgowacademy.org.uk

Head: Mrs Shona S McKnight.

Remarks: See preparatory school.

The Glasgow Academy Preparatory School

Linked to Glasgow Academy Atholl (The) in the Junior section

Linked to Glasgow Academy (The) in the Senior section

Linked to Glasgow Academy Dairsie (The) in the Junior section

Colebrooke Terrace, Colebrooke Terrace, Glasgow, G12 8HE

• Pupils: 540 boys and girls • Ages: Prep 3-11, Atholl and Dairsie 3-9; all day • Fees: £7,275-£9,465 pa • Independent

Tel: 0141 342 5481
Fax: 0141 337 3373
Email: enquiries@theglasgowacademy.org.uk
Website: www.theglasgowacademy.org.uk

Head: Since 2007, Mr Anthony M Brooke BEd, previously head of Sutton Valence prep (qv).

Assistant Head, responsible for Atholl: Miss Jean McMorran DCE PGDip in Leadership and Management Dip TEFL.

Entrance: Through nursery up via kindergarten. Some come straight to kindergarten.

Exit: Some 'local' parents may simply use the toddler groups and go into the state system, but most go on to junior school at Colebrook Street, followed by senior school. Very occasional pupil may leave at eight to go to trad prep schools, ditto some may go to junior depts of trad senior schools at 11.

Remarks: All three sites operate a terrific nursery school with toddlers sporting tracksuits, heavily-staffed with different staff for lunch. Atholl and Dairsie provide local pre-prep facilities both north and south of the river (Clyde) with all youngsters moving to Kelvinbridge aged nine and joining up with those already there. French from seven for all. Tiny classes: 12 in Dairsie, up to 18 at Atholl and a whopping 20/22 at Kelvinbridge, but numbers here coming down. All pupils at Colebrook use senior school facilities as in labs and dining room etc. Terrific child-care facilties. Drop off at Kelvinbridge and Atholl and Dairsie from 8am; Mini Cool Kids' Club from 3.10-3.50pm at all three sites, plus short after-school care 3.50-6pm and full after-school care – depends on age of pupil, homework supervision if necessary. Holiday Club for those up to 14 based at Kelvinbridge throughout most of the holidays and half terms, costs £28 per day, children bring their own lunch and the school offers a comprehensive and varied programme including visits to the beach, Kelvingrove etc. Themed holiday weeks too: circus, film, sports. And parents have to fill in the most complicated permission forms: to have their photographs taken, to have a medical plaster if skin is broken in an accident, to have a snack ... Well thought out, incredibly useful. Impressive set-up, cradle to grave, can't fault it.

Glebe Primary School

Sussex Road, Ickenham, Uxbridge, Middlesex, UB10 8PH

• Pupils: 300 boys and girls + 60 in the nursery • Ages: 3-11
• Non-denom • State

Tel: 01895 671 951
Fax: 01895 674 143
Email: glebe@hillingdongrid.org
Website: www.glebe.hillingdon.sch.uk

Head: Since 2006, Mr Nick Alford BA PGCE NPQH, (fortyish). Prior to his appointment at Glebe, Mr Alford had been deputy head at West Lodge Middle in Pinner and had taught previously in Hayes and Weston-super-Mare, with specialisms in maths and PE. Immediately likeable – open, chatty and capable – Mr Alford is making something special of this school. Only a year into the job when we visited, he had already made sensible innovations e.g. bright red sweatshirts in which the children looked great and proud and a new house system. The physical future of his school is uncertain as we write (see below) but, if the move currently under discussion is made and Mr Alford has the site and facilities his children deserve, we feel Glebe will become a much sought-after school.

Entrance: Currently easy. For all but places in the special unit for the deaf (SRP) Glebe is currently undersubscribed and if you apply you should get a place. The reasons for this undersubscription are largely historic and demographic. A visit to the school should dispel pre-conceptions.

Exit: Virtually all to the nearby comprehensive, Vyners, where there is also an SRP for the deaf and hearing impaired.

Remarks: Glebe is in a quiet bit of Outer Suburbia – the village of Ickenham, leafy, settled, disturbed only by the planes from the local airports. The school on its current site is blessed by plenty of space – inner and outer. A huge green field and a large tarmac playground frame the light, single-storey main building with its decent-sized classrooms, bright and lively displays. The children have room to move and breathe here – not least because the school is, in most years, still undersubscribed – but also because of the sensible use of space, blinds, furniture. The school, built in the 1950s, though needing work, is in visibly better nick than many. Many staff – especially on the SEN side – are long-serving – the school clearly inspires commitment.

The complicating factor is that a move is in the offing. Glebe is in an area with many Air Force and Army bases, some of which are being decommissioned. This is freeing a larger school nearby on a larger site into which Glebe may well move in the next two or three years. So, uncertainty is in the air and limiting development on the current site which Mr Alford, otherwise, would be energetically undertaking. On the other side, no move would take place until the new school is properly refurbished and kitted out so there would be no intermediate half life in mobile classrooms. Either way, Glebe is a lively, relaxed and happy community.

Pupils are largely a mix of white English, Eastern Europeans, Asians and around 50 per cent are very local. Others come from Uxbridge, Ruislip or further from Hayes and Harefield. Discipline is barely an issue. We saw nothing but happy, orderly classes and friendly, well-behaved children. The results have been good and need to be better, as Mr Alford admits, though school twice won the Brains of the Borough Competition in 2006/7. Also given Healthy School Award in 2007 – and the drinking fountains work! The population is a mix of the local and settled and the transient and this has not helped SATs in the last couple of years. Parents very involved in all kinds of imaginative and practical ways. School has gained an increasing reputation for being able to handle special needs of various kinds better than others and the SEN dept is understated but quietly impressive.

The SRP – Special Resourced Provision – for the deaf and hearing impaired has been in existence since 1982. It is staffed by one full-time specially trained and vastly experienced teacher of the deaf. She is aided by a speech and lang therapist who comes in one day week and another for half a day. Between them they have over 30 years of experience. They – assisted by trained nursery nurses – support the children in both mainstream classwork – most children are in mainstream classes most of the time and are completely and happily integrated – and in the designated two teaching rooms and separate speech and lang therapy room. Support is all needs-based and flexible.

The SRP teaching rooms are carpeted and acoustically treated with ceiling tiles. School has a Soundfield system in all rooms and is aural rather than signing though signing is used when needed – especially for the newer children. Currently they work with nine children, though there is room for a few more. They come from all over the borough – this is the only such provision in Hillingdon for primary pupils. The children who access the SRP are all statemented and their hearing levels vary from severe to profound. The profoundly deaf children have cochlear implants, the others are all hearing aid wearers.

Other SENs also well-catered for. SENCo is welcoming, sensible and on-site three days a week. There is a support room for all SENs well-stocked with e.g. Tracks, Toe-by-Toe, Springboard, Spotlight etc. School is fully accessible to wheelchairs and has one current user in school. All children are assessed in Year 1 – if not before – and school aims to support whatever it can. ' If we can meet their needs we will do our very best,' says SENCo, 'wherever possible we would never turn anyone away.'

Glendower Prep School

87 Queen's Gate, South Kensington, London, SW7 5JX

• Pupils: 210 girls, all day • Ages: 4-11 • Inter-denom • Fees: £14,820 pa
• Independent

Tel: 020 7370 1927
Fax: 020 7244 8308
Email: office@glendower.kensington.sch.uk
Website: www.glendowerprep.org

Headmistress: Since 2004, Mrs Rosamond Bowman BA Hons PGCE (fifties), a modern linguist. Previously taught at Colet Court, ultimately as assistant head, then head of juniors at The Hall, Hampstead and two years as head of Willington prep in Wimbledon. Immensely likeable, quietly spoken but transmitting intense enthusiasm and enjoyment, this is a head who makes you want to hand over your daughter that instant. Mrs Bowman speaks of her girls, her staff and her school with the confidence of a round peg in the right hole. During her reign the school has speedily recovered from the hiccup and minor haemorrhage of pupils that occurred towards the end of her long-serving predecessor's tenure. Common sense and a genuine concern for each individual now prevail and a relaxed Mrs Bowman presides, supported by a loyal staff and a governing body which includes some of the biggest brains in the city – most current or ex-parents. It also includes the former head of Godolphin and Latymer which can't hurt. Mrs Bowman has a gentle determination of her own and there can be little doubt that considerable changes are on the way – recent reports of some excellent new appointments.

Entrance: The applications of 150 tots are taken for the 36 places at the age of four, but this degree of competition is normal anywhere good in this area and no-one should be deterred from having a go. After that the list is closed. 90 children are assessed by careful observation – mostly for their 'social maturity' – and any parents who think that coaching at this age is a good idea need to forget it now. 'I don't want them coming here reading the FT,' asserts Mrs Bowman. The notional 36 places may, in the event, be diminished by the school's sensible sibling policy. Unsuccessful applicants for 4+ entry and later applicants to the school will be placed on a waiting list for consideration for entry should an occasional place arise. Assessment is by way of a morning spent on reading, writing, maths and generally socialising. No particular feeder schools. Occasional places occur but school unlikely to fill them after Year 5 – the cohesion of the year being seen as paramount. It's worth a call though.

Exit: Unusual not to get into your first choice from here. Most to the top London day schools with biggest contingents to St Paul's and Godolphin and Latymer. Far more offers than the pupils can take up, this school is maybe uniquely successful in placing its girls. Some to board, with places taken up at Wycombe Abbey, Cheltenham Ladies College and St Mary's Ascot, amongst others.

Remarks: An elegant 1830s white building – Cubitt? – on Queen's Gate occupying a large corner plot facing Stanhope Gardens. Since January 2010 part of the adjacent building intergrated with the school through a major development and refurbishment programme. The present six storey building is remarkably spacious. An airy, panelled and white-painted entrance hall complete with wonderful large Quentin Blake originals greets the visitor and is also used, with the doors opened to the adjacent library, as an assembly space. Library attractive and well-stocked. Super staircase, excellent displays of work everywhere, lots of up-to-the-minute equipment in all rooms and all rooms remarkably orderly with inviting and interesting-looking work and resources everywhere. A good mix of the formal and instructive with the creative and inspirational. Classes are light and bright, but some were pretty airless on our visit and we longed to open windows, notwithstanding the street noise, which isn't very great here. Rooms are good sizes and, though some passages are very narrow, this school feels less cramped than some of its local competitors. One teacher/assistant to 11 girls and a class maximum of 18 in the upper school.

Not a school for those with serious SENs but school will pick up and support those with mild difficulties and make individual learning plans for those who need them. Some five per cent come needing a little extra help with English – many, given the South Kensington population, are European – and EFL is given in small groups or one-to-one as needed. French is well-supported with three weekly lessons for everyone and taught by native speakers. Years 5 and 6 participate in an annual activity trip which alternates between France and the United Kingdom. Latin is taught in Year 6 and there is one, newly refurbished, all-purpose science lab. The full academic programme includes DT and ICT and, despite having no grounds to speak of, the school is famously sporty. They seem to win more than two-thirds of their matches and excel in tournaments of all kinds, especially in swimming and netball. They are bussed everywhere – 'we keep Impact in business', says Mrs Bowman – and sporting activities take place in local parks and sports centres, with the timetable adapted to take traffic problems into account. Many of the academic staff are involved in the sporting side and, somehow, it all seems to work.

Drama is creative, they write and produce their own plays. Lovely, varied and imaginative art taught by professional illustrator/teacher. We saw clocks and mazes and silhouettes and papier-mâché creatures and wanted to get stuck in. Music is busy – lots of individual lessons.

Lunch is unusual. All vegetarian and cooked in the basement kitchen. From January 2010, due to the development, the School has its own dining room. Crudités and fresh fruit with every meal and meals have names such as 'cowboy stew' (veg bangers and beans).

Girls come from high-achieving, well-off families as you'd expect in this area. Parents are heavily involved and many live round the corner. A family atmosphere is what Mrs Bowman is after. The expansion is to facilitate the school becoming a two-form entry from 4+ instead of taking an extra class at 7+. 'I don't want to lose sight of our ability to cater for the individual,' she says, and she is clear about the sort of girl who will do best here. 'We look for a Glendower girl – with enthusiasm, curiosity, a love of life, a willingness to fit in and be part of the group, and we have an ability to build up her self-respect. By building on their individual strengths you can give children a sense of their individual self-worth. We 't have any arrogant girls here.'

School keen to quote ISI inspection report of June 2005: ' ... small, happy and very caring environment ... good standard of attainment across a broad and challenging curriculum which prepares them very well for success in entrance examinations ... high level of pastoral care ... '. You can read the rest yourself online.

The faces we saw were happy and attentive and it felt harmonious and purposeful. Places here are rightfully prized and not just because of the admirable record of placing pupils in their next schools. Mrs Bowman impresses with her quietly articulated but strong and clear-sighted vision of the school in its entire community.

Overall, an outstanding school in many respects but probably better for Brunnhilde than for Mimi – though school would disagree!

Godolphin Preparatory School

Linked to Godolphin School (The) in the Senior section

Laverstock Road, Salisbury, Wiltshire, SP1 2RB

• Pupils: 75 girls, all day • Ages: 3-11 • Fees: £5,319-£10,278 pa
• Independent

Tel: 01722 430 652
Fax: 01722 430 651
Email: admissions@godolphin.wilts.sch.uk
Website: www.godolphinprep.org

Headmistress: Since 2005, Mrs Paula White, formerly head of Burghclere Primary School, Hampshire.

Entrance: Assessment day and head's report.

Exit: Girls are prepared for Common Entrance, a range of 11+ examinations and scholarships; about 75 per cent go on to the Godolphin School, a few to the local grammar school, the rest to St Mary's Calne, Wycombe Abbey, Dauntsey's and Leweston.

Remarks: Has good access to senior school facilities.

Godstowe Preparatory School

Shrubbery Road, High Wycombe, Buckinghamshire, HP13 6PR

• Pupils: 90 boarders, 290 day girls. Also pre-prep/nursery 95 boys and girls, all day • Ages: 7-13, pre-prep 3-7 • C of E
• Fees: Day £8,340-£12,990; Boarding £19,080 pa • Independent

Tel: 01494 529 273
Fax: 01494 429 009
Email: headmaster@godstowe.org.uk
Website: www.godstowe.org

Headmaster: Since 2006, Mr David Gainer BEd (forties). Educated at Claires Court, Maidenhead, and Belmont Abbey in Herefordshire, followed by St Mary's, Strawberry Hill, London, where he studied mathematics and drama. Began career at Llanarth Court Prep in South Wales, then housemaster of junior house at Belmont Abbey, followed by three years at Forest Grange Prep in Horsham where he was deputy head, before becoming young head of Belmont Prep near Dorking in 1991. Friendly, jovial, approachable and vastly experienced. Ideas bubble, and he is determined to continue to raise the profile of boarding. On arrival announced he did not want to live in traditional head's house, preferring to be 'in the thick of the action', where he is now. Married to Cathy, who teaches PHSE and works hard as registrar. They are a wonderful double act and their influence is apparent both in terms of rising numbers and the overall happiness of pupils and staff. 'We take happiness seriously,' says the headmaster. 'I want the girls to jump out of the car because they want to be here.' Visits pre-prep pupils regularly. Has two children, one at university, one a recent graduate. Just what this school needed after a rocky patch.

Entrance: Not a selective school. Entry at 7 for the main school. Academic scholarships at 8+ and 11+. Sibling discounts as well as reduced fees for clergy and parents in the Services. Girls can have a guest day (and night) in the school. The way things are going it's advisable to apply early.

Exit: Pre-prep boys usually go to traditional boys' boarding at seven – Caldicott, Papplewick and Summer Fields particularly popular. Girls to major senior schools, including Wycombe Abbey, Cheltenham Ladies' College, Downe House, Haileybury, Rugby, Badminton, Benenden, Wellington, Oundle. Most take CE at 13, with scholarships and exhibitions on all fronts. In 2010, 21 girls departed with 23 scholarships, awards and prizes. Small trickle to state sector at 11 – getting smaller and smaller. Girls enjoy an excellent reputation at their senior schools. 'They are happy, well adjusted and hard working without being cloned,' said one experienced registrar.

Remarks: The first girls' boarding prep in the country, purpose-built in 1900. Delightful, virginia creeper-clad buildings (with later extensions). Fabulous new reception building and recently built music school with inspiring head of department, serious re-vamp of the dining room (food 'terrific') and other buildings, particularly the boarding accommodation. Here the head has changed the old system – now a junior house and two senior houses. Bedrooms are bright in pinks and blues, chosen and painted by the girls with space for treasured possessions. A popular innovation is that instead of wake up calls or strident bells, boarders may choose the music by which they like to be woken (heavy rock was not selected). Boarding very popular and nearly full up.

Brilliant use of very hilly ground on outskirts of High Wycombe: assault course and outdoor activity areas. Amazing new food technology kitchen just opened by Raymond Blanc. Masses of activities at weekends (rarely fewer than 50 girls in) plus free clubs and options – two hours per day from 4.30pm. Early drop-off plus breakfast (7.30am) and late pick-up plus supper (6.30pm) for 'a few pounds'. Excellent PSHE in place and girls get lifestyle course after CE which includes self defence classes, hair and beauty day, charitable works, trips out and visiting lecturers.

Pre-prep has expanded hugely and is now housed in separate buildings deliciously close to the all weather playground. French from age four, Latin or Spanish at ten. Classes in prep school 'subtly' streamed. Maximum class size 18. New IT equipment, art, marvellous textiles and ceramics, fantastic music. Over 130 soloists on a variety of instruments with masses of girl-inspired concerts. Dyslexia help on hand, with one-to-one sessions where necessary; regular spelling and reading help available. EFL also available, though only about 5 per cent overseas (not counting expats). Some MoD parents.

A parent said to us, 'The atmosphere is so much more positive now. The teachers' morale has shot up and the atmosphere is full of buzzing happiness. This is a first class nurturing environment owing much to the husband and wife team – brilliant. My daughter can't wait to board.'

Godstowe is treading the sunny uplands of girls' education. Well worth a visit – and not just for the teddy bear that every prospective pupil is given!

The Grammar School at Leeds Junior School

Alwoodley Gates, Harrogate Road, Leeds, West Yorkshire, LS17 8GS

• Pupils: 430 junior, 295 nursery and pre-prep • Ages: 3-11 • Non-denom • Fees: £7,092-£7,731 pa • Independent

Tel: 0113 229 1552
Fax: 0113 228 5111
Email: admissions@gsal.org.uk
Website: www.gsal.org.uk.

Head: Since September 2009, Mr Robert Lilley, former head of Silcoates Junior School in Wakefield, West Yorkshire. He is supported by three deputy heads.

Entrance: Selective, by observed activities and tests appropriate to the child's age. The usual points of entry are 3+ for nursery, 4+ for reception, and 7+ for junior school, although applications can be made at any time for any age.

Exit: All pupils transfer at 11+ to senior school unless they are obviously going to struggle; parents consulted well in advance.

Remarks: Same site as senior school, sharing some facilities yet sufficiently distinct from it to allow younger children to grow up in secure surroundings. Atmosphere is happy, positive and purposeful. Year 5 on average one chronological year ahead. French or German studied from Year 4. Unusually for this age group, half staff are male.

Leeds Grammar and Leeds Girls' High Schools finalised their merger, to form The Grammar School at Leeds, in September 2008. This brought together girls from LGHS Ford House and boys from LGS junior department into one, co-educational junior school.

The nursery and pre-prep for The Grammar School is Rose Court, based in Headingley. This caters for three to seven year olds. Most progress to the junior school at seven.

The Grange Junior School

Linked to Grange School (The) in the Senior section

Beechwood Avenue, Hartford, Northwich, Cheshire, CW8 3AU

• Pupils: 175 pupils in kindergarten to prep 2; 290 in prep 3 to 6; all day • Ages: 4-11 • Fees: £6,525-£7,050 pa • Independent

Tel: 01606 77447
Fax: 01606 784581
Email: office@grange.org.uk
Website: www.grange.org.uk

Head: Since January 2005, Mr Stephen Bennett. Previously principal of Saudia SAS School in Jeddah, Saudi Arabia.

Entrance: Main entry point is at four. Informal assessment in small groups. Pupils can join the school at all ages if places available.

Exit: Majority, but not all, go on to the senior school.

Remarks: Idyllic setting for friendly, homely junior school. Very much a rural, rather than a street-wise/urban feel. 'Early birds' and 'Sundown' clubs provide before and after care for pupils. Relaxed but watchful staff.

The Grange, Monmouth Preparatory School

Linked to Haberdashers Agincourt School in the Junior section
Linked to Monmouth School in the Senior section

Hadnock Road, Monmouth, Monmouthshire, NP25 3NG

• Pupils: 110 boys, with some boarding in Year 6 • Ages: 7-11 • Anglican • Fees: £8,736 pa • Independent

Tel: 01600 715 930
Fax: 01600 710 915
Email: thegrange@monmouthschool.org
Website: www.habs-monmouth.org

Head: Mrs Elaine Thomas.

Entrance: Entry at seven though other stages considered if places available.

Exit: Most to Monmouth School – but they have to take the entry exam on the same terms as outsiders.

Remarks: Part of a family – the Haberdashers' Monmouth schools. The co-ed pre-prep is Haberdashers' Agincourt School. The preps are separated into boys' and girls' schools, ditto the senior schools, Monmouth School being the senior school for boys.

Subject specialist teaching throughout, flourishing choir, orchestra and band and full sports fixture list. Moved to brand new purpose-built premises in February 2009, sited next to large new school sports complex, all weather pitches, playing fields and brand new sports pavilion.

Gresham's Preparatory School

Linked to Gresham's School in the Senior section

Cromer Road, Holt, Norfolk, NR25 6EY

• Pupils: Co-ed - 130 pre-prep; 250 in prep. Boarding and day - 60 boarders. • Ages: 3-13 including pre-prep and nursery
• Fees: Boarding £18,525; Day £14,085 pa • Independent

Tel: 01263 714 600
Fax: 01263 714 060
Email: prep@greshams.com
Website: www.greshams.com

Head: Since 2003, Mr James Quick (late forties) BA and PGCE from Durham. Taught at The Dragon, Oxford, where he was a housemaster, then at St Edward's. Teacher exchange at Geelong College, Australia, before coming here with wife Kim, who teaches English, history and Latin – she's a motherly presence and at meal times checks that sensible choices are made. They have four daughters – all educated at Gresham's. He's an approachable, intelligent educator who's 'visible at everything'. Big on charity and keen to get the pupils to recognise their good fortune. Teaches RS and classical studies to Year 8 and is well liked by the children – the headmaster's weekly challenge is eagerly awaited and those who want to answer questions, which often require research, visit his office at the end of the week; those who do well are rewarded with a chocolate 'Freddo Frog' bar. Also a marathon runner – his best ideas often come when training.

Entrance: Waiting list for some pre-prep year groups. Generally first come first served, although they try their best to offer places to children with siblings in the school. At seven – no formal assessment. Quite a few at 11 – entrants take national standardised maths and English tests plus verbal and non verbal reasoning tests. Some from the state sector. Some of the less able follow specific French and English courses leading to a different exam for the senior school.

Year 7/8 follow the CE syllabus – its significance is slightly downgraded, as most know, after Year 6, in that as long as appropriate progress is made, they have a senior school place.

Exit: Most to the senior school – advice on alternatives has to be sought.

Remarks: Unalloyed parental praise for this virtually autonomous, happy, prep school – a mini bus ride for litties or healthy walk away from the senior school, where a pool, sports hall and squash courts. Enthusiastic staff (they clearly enjoy working here) and 'wonderful atmosphere – children are allowed to be children but they know and respect boundaries'. Not a hot-house but languages from six, Latin from 11 and dedicated classrooms including science labs.

Well-respected educational support department (two full-time and three part-time assistants). Dyslexia etc and mild degrees of Asperger's – charges in line with senior school. All round, inclusive ethos – 'They seem to have concerts all the time' and play masses of sport; 'passionate coaches' and squillions of winning teams. Nothing lacking in the facilities department (although head says he wouldn't mind another large hall) – what they have ranges from homely and well tended (boarding houses: one extended to cater for extra demand – full, weekly and flexi) to exceptional (art room and acres of play space, including robust adventure equipment).

Everything one would expect in a well-run school. Add in creative flourishes and it becomes something more: a red telephone box discreetly nestling in a boarding house from where the off-site independent listener can be phoned (although it seems as if the 'terrific house parents' and matrons are the first port of call); music practice rooms named after composers; a welcoming library; a house master who looks out for rail deals for those who need to take the train home; the door of the RE room festooned with wonderful philosophical quotes; a music lesson (two a week) with pupils busily developing a composition based on train sounds; colour coded food stations in the dining hall – greens, carbs, protein: pupils must have something from each; flowers on all the dining tables; annual performances at the Edinburgh Fringe and large scale artistic mementos from leavers – one year group painted famous images on the backs of all the chairs in the art room and another produced huge, wonderfully bold replicas of modern paintings which have been framed and now cheer the dining hall.

Pre-prep and nursery – separate entities – provide a happy and secure start. We loved the bustling playground – even though bitterly cold when we visited, convincing horse mimics happily cantered whilst scooters scooted and boys with miniature plastic hockey sticks played something close to a proper game.

Grimsdell, Mill Hill Pre-Preparatory School

Linked to Belmont Mill Hill Preparatory School in the Junior section
Linked to Mill Hill School in the Senior section

Winterstoke House, Wills Grove, Mill Hill, London, NW7 1QR

• Pupils: 150 girls and boys; all day • Ages: 3-7 • Fees: £5,226-£11,361 pa
• Independent

Tel: 020 8959 6884
Fax: 020 8959 4626
Email: office@grimsdell.org.uk
Website: www.grimsdell.org.uk

Remarks: For further details, see senior school.

Guildford High School Junior School

Linked to Guildford High School in the Senior section

London Road, Guildford, Surrey, GU1 1SJ

• Pupils: 290 girls; all day • Ages: 4-11 • Fees: £7,560-£10,314 pa
• Independent

Tel: 01483 562 475
Fax: 01483 537 611
Email: Guildford-Admissions@church-schools.com
Website: www.guildfordhigh.surrey.sch.uk

Head of Junior School : Since 2005, Mrs Sue Phillips. She took over from the redoubtable Marian Shepherd, who had been in situ for 13 years and under whose aegis the school won Prep School of the Year 2004. 'Have there been any changes,' we asked, 'since you took over?' 'Well, the KS1 results have gone up.' No flies on Mrs Phillips, then – this is obviously a go-getting environment and the only way is up. A charming and approachable lady, she is head of the junior school, although overall head is Fiona Boulton at the senior school. Like Mrs Boulton, she is a quiet storm with a similar take on education – the ethos is one of continually developing and pushing forward the boundaries of academia and how it is taught.

Entrance: Selective. At 4+, pupils are assessed individually using standardised games and puzzles. However, as Mrs Phillips says, 'Academic potential may not be recognised at four, so we ask parents to come back again,' if the pupil doesn't quite make the grade first time round. At 7+, prospective pupils take papers in English, maths, verbal reasoning. But, be warned: heavily oversubscribed, with two pupils applying for each place. Only the brightest will get in and so they should – not for the just-scraped-through-the-test bunch, who would flounder around at the bottom and not be happy.

Exit: Intended to be the ideal preparation for the senior school, where the vast majority (maybe less one or two a year) trot with automatic entry.

Remarks: Other schools often glibly comment on fostering a love of learning, but here it is really engendered naturally as part of the educational process. This may be intimidating for some and downright daunting for others but, if this innovative approach to education appeals to you and your very bright daughter, then this school (and its big sister) is worth moving heaven and earth to get into.

Academically top of the pile, not just locally, but nationally. At KS2 tests, more than 90 per cent of pupils attain level 5 – with 98 per cent in science. Mrs Phillips is particularly proud of the curriculum which, she says, is 'hugely broad for a junior school'. Core subjects including English, maths, science and humanities are taught thoroughly and well, as you would expect from a top notch prep, but it is going the extra academic mile that adds an edge and is so refreshing. 'Thinking skills' sessions are taught from reception on a weekly basis. As the head says, 'Girls are taught how to think, not what to think – we want to inspire them to think creatively.' Activexpression handsets engage all the pupils in lessons and activities throughout the curriculum. The virtual learning environment enables pupils in Years 5 and 6 to access many subjects from home.

Spanish is taught from age 5 to 11 with French added for girls 7 to 11 – and the learning process here looks like a bundle of laughs. Interactive whiteboards are everywhere and nowhere are they used with more aplomb than in language lessons, when a cartoon hedgehog helps pupils learn. Resources are used to teach songs and dance, simple mathematics and even humanities in both Spanish and French via the interactive boards. Science lessons are timetabled six times a week at the junior school.

Provides information booklets for each year which give parents a thorough idea of the curriculum and also how they can help their daughters at home. These are vital tools to any parent, with information on which words need to be learned and by when, in terms of the spelling or reading. Homework is given, but in the early years it focuses on spellings and reading practice. Further up, up to an hour a night, but teachers are careful to monitor quantity and the homework focuses on consolidating work in the classroom. SENCo arranges support for any SEN pupils (in 'a small minority', according to the head) within timetable if necessary – this extra tuition is paid for by parents; also provision for gifted and talented pupils.

Music is strong with more than 85 per cent learning a musical instrument and various choirs and ensemble groups. Lots of clubs on offer, including gardening, library, story, dance, swimming, creative writing, Mandarin, Italian and Latin. The list gets ever longer as you move up the school, although clubs are not encouraged in reception where, 'girls need to spend much of their unstructured time playing'. Sport is a very important part of school life – pupils have competed internationally at fencing, been national swimming champions and also national big shots at biathlon. All the other usual school sports are played.

Nice modern building shoe-horned into the centre of the senior school campus and, while no getting away from the shortage of space (not a school for claustrophobics), much has been made of what space there is both internally and externally. No grotty bits as far as we could see, just well designed, modern and airy classrooms, with busy little bees participating like mad in lessons. Excellent library with comfy beanbags and very well equipped science and ICT rooms; also lovely art room, where girls were painting a still life with inspiring classical music playing in the background. Lessons seem involving with a good degree of fun.

The playground is small but perfectly formed, with giant coloured pencils providing a novel space divider. The girls have access to the new property acquisition next door at Nightingale Road, judiciously purchased recently by Mrs Boulton to add extra classrooms and rather nice green space, currently laid out with attractive teak furniture and adventure playground for the junior girls. The junior school also regularly uses the facilities at the splendid new sports centre with its stunning swimming pool, indoor sports halls and, most importantly, café area for parents in need of a reviving cuppa during chilly fixtures.

Pastoral care is regarded as paramount, with numerous opportunities for pupils to talk to teachers about any problems and encouraging mutual care and respect for each other. Mrs Phillips has a 'worry box' for any concerns that individuals may wish to raise. The fact that the junior school is located within such close proximity to the senior school means that all are seen as part of the whole rather than a separate entity – sixth formers often drop by and read with the younger ones.

Pupils are confident and chatty, tidy and well presented in their uniform, which veers towards the practical with pale blue tops and navy skirts. Parents are mainly professional/academic who expect the best that private education has to offer, both from their daughters and the school.

Haberdashers' Agincourt School

Linked to Inglefield House in the Junior section

Linked to Grange, Monmouth Preparatory School (The) in the Junior section

Linked to Haberdashers' Monmouth School For Girls in the Senior section

Linked to Monmouth School in the Senior section

Dixton Lane, Monmouth, Monmouthshire, NP25 3SY

• Pupils: 125 girls and boys • Ages: 3-7 • Fees: £3,600-£5,919 pa • Independent

Tel: 01600 713 970
Fax: no fax
Email: enquiries@agincourtschool.org
Website: www.habs-monmouth.org

Remarks: For further details, see senior school.

The Haberdashers' Aske's Boys' Pre-Preparatory School

Linked to Haberdashers' Aske's Boys' Preparatory School (The) in the Junior section

Linked to Haberdashers' Aske's Boys' School in the Senior section

Hazel Road, Park Street, St Albans, Hertfordshire, AL2 2AH

• Fees: £10,641 pa • Independent

Tel: 01727 873 632
Fax: 01727 873 662
Email: admissions@habsboys.org.uk
Website: www.habsboys.org.uk

Headteacher: Since 1997, Miss Yvonne Mercer BEd Dip Ed. Keen interest in travelling and sport. Plays hockey for successful St Alban's Ladies vets' team (currently national champions). Chatty, sociable, good rapport with pupils, of whom she is clearly very proud.

The Haberdashers' Aske's Boys' Preparatory School

Linked to Haberdashers' Aske's Boys' Pre-Preparatory School (The) in the Junior section

Linked to Haberdashers' Aske's Boys' School in the Senior section

Butterfly Lane, Elstree, Elstree, Hertfordshire, WD6 3AF

• Pupils: 205 boys; all day • Ages: 7-11 • Fees: £14,103 pa • Independent

Tel: 020 8266 1779
Fax: 0208 266 1808
Email: admissions@habsboys.org.uk
Website: www.habsboys.org.uk

Headteacher: Since 1997, Miss Yvonne Mercer BEd Dip Ed. Keen interest in travelling and sport. Plays hockey for successful St Alban's Ladies vets' team (currently national champions). Chatty, sociable, good rapport with pupils of whom she is clearly very proud.

Entrance: All who apply by registration date are assessed, with a short list invited back for further assessments and interviews. Boys bussed in from all over.

Exit: Rare for boys at 11 to be directed elsewhere.

Remarks: A popular choice as a way into the senior school, over-subscribed. Pleasant building, light, airy classrooms, superb well-kept outdoor space. Mostly use own facilities but share swimming, music, some ICT and canteen facilities with main school; abundance of choice, smart-card system so no losing lunch money. After school care facility available at additional cost for those who need it.

All follow national curriculum and take SATs. French from Year 6. Confident, articulate, courteous, busy boys, stand when adults enter the room. All are placed in one of four houses for competitions and merits. Many extracurricular activities including Pythagoreans, Warhammer and highly successful chess – currently England under 11 champions (national players too). Sport for all: cricket, soccer, table tennis, swimming – a selection of offerings. Plenty of opportunities for music – all must play an instrument for at least one year and most have performing opportunities in choir, orchestra or recorder groups, some even performed at the Barbican. Drama productions throughout the year offer chance for everyone to be involved. Artwork adorns the corridors and classrooms. Trips both at home and abroad, e.g. ski trip to France, activity weekends, as well as the usual language and field trips. Plenty of opportunities – difficult to be bored.

Haberdashers' Aske's School for Girls, Junior School

Linked to Haberdashers' Aske's School For Girls in the Senior section

Aldenham Road, Elstree, Hertfordshire, WD6 3BT

• Pupils: 300 girls; all day • Ages: 4-11 • Fees: £9,468 pa • Independent

Tel: 020 8266 2400
Fax: 020 8266 2403
Email: juniors@habsgirls.org.uk
Website: www.habsgirls.org.uk

Head of Juniors: Since September 2010, Mrs J Charlesworth, previously deputy head. A career spanning education for all age ranges from 4 to 84. Originally a lecturer in mathematics in a college of higher education, she decided to carry on the adventure into secondary education and then into primary. 'Nothing is more exciting than learning, nothing more infectious than doing so with children as your companions in thought. Haberdashers' Aske's School for Girls Junior School is alive with enquiry and a zest for embracing all life has to offer. It is a huge privilege to work with such enthusiastic staff and girls and with such supportive parents. The school is a very special place.'

Entrance: Assessment is careful and scrupulous. At four, girls are seen in small groups with other applicants whose ages are as close as possible to their own – within a month, usually. They are observed and talked to and, out of the 250-odd who apply, around 80 will be called back for one-to-one interviews and aptitude tests for the 22 places. Much the same process takes place the following year and around 80 girls apply for the 22 places. At seven, six or eight applicants out of the 60 or so who apply, will be given places. They are assessed via written tests in English and maths and reasoning.

Exit: An occasional girl will be advised to look elsewhere by Year 5. The rest move, via the entrance exam, into the senior school. A very few might leave for the state sector of co-ed schools.

Remarks: A beautiful, new spacious, light and welcoming building – special in its own right even if it didn't lead onto its exceptional older sister. Occupying a central place in the huge school site, it is only two storeys so not daunting, but it has big, airy rooms and good displays everywhere. Orderly classrooms with plenty of room to move, even for the oldest girls, very impressive art room with quite stunning art, own gym and own music room with, again, very impressive work taking place here.

Languages are important here. Everyone learns Japanese from Year 1 to Year 6. It is optional thereafter but school sees a start in this difficult language as a way of teaching the girls to be linguists from the earliest possible age. 'Transferable skills,' we were told – French must be a doss after this. A sense as you walk around of learning and thinking being seen as great fun. The walls are papered with interesting questions posed by pupils: ' I wonder why people have freckles', 'I wonder where God came from', 'I wonder why our tummies rumble'. It gets you wondering too. We witnessed the visit of 'Saxon visitors' – a group of actors who arrived with helmets, animal skins and spears for a bit of 'historical re-creation' – a bit more fun than learning dates, this! Lots of cultural visits, e.g. to The Henry Moore Foundation nearby, and links with the Japanese school in Acton which occupies the site left by Habs in the 1970s – good for language, culture and fun.

All the classes we saw were quiet, relaxed and purposeful and all the faces happy and absorbed – everyone has room to move freely, which makes a huge difference. Adventure playground in leafy surroundings and ample playground space. Reception girls have their own garden with safe surface. Overall, a super start to educational life and a privilege to learn and be nurtured in such surroundings.

Hale Preparatory School

Broomfield Lane, Hale, Altrincham, Cheshire, WA15 9AS

• Pupils: 190 boys and girls • Ages: 4-11 • Inter-denom • Fees: £5,625 pa • Independent

Tel: 0161 928 2386
Fax: 0161 941 7934
Email: mail@haleprepschool.com
Website: www.haleprepschool.com

Head: Since 1980, Mr John Connor (sixties). Down to earth, old fashioned, genial disciplinarian. Previously senior teacher at Xaverian College, Manchester, and head of Hillcrest Grammar, Stockport. Founded Hale Prep in 1980 to be his own boss; now owns buildings too. Has 'no intention of retiring', two of his four children work at the school. Puts school's success down to high expectations, small classes, help when needed, instilling self discipline and ability to work independently. Ultra-available – head or deputy (head is magistrate one day a week) stands at school gate morning and afternoon and positively encourages parent interaction. Children describe him as funny, 'He can make lessons we don't really like enjoyable', 'We like his jokes and stories', 'He doesn't like dangly earrings or children leaving others out'.

Entrance: Non-selective, strictly by waiting list. Most of 22 places in reception go to those registered before birth, but classes grow in juniors and people move, so worth signing up. Late entrants do take a 'happiness (IQ) test' to ensure they'll integrate successfully.

Exit: Outstanding for a non-selective intake – almost all to top rate secondary schools. Lots to Manchester Grammar, also Withington Girls' School or the grant-maintained Altrincham Grammars.

Remarks: Beavering, happy but ordered atmosphere with enthusiastic teachers on four floors of Victorian mansion, plus extra classroom blocks. All academic teaching in half classes, so maximum size at top of school is 16. 'We do offer a lot of help, a lot of one-to-one,' says head. Over 70 per cent 3s at key stage one, over 90 per cent 5s at key stage two, especially strong in maths and science. Designated rooms and teachers for music, art, IT and science lab.

Specialist teachers too for drama, DT and games. LAMDA exams, after-school dance club, choir, individual instrument lessons during lunch hour and after school. Disproportionately (for size) successful in local netball, football, tennis, rounders and cross country contests; also offers lacrosse, athletics, fencing and cricket. Annual ski trip and outward bound in Wales for all, plus diverse day trips.

School lunches compulsory, infants served, juniors self-serve at later sitting, head presides over both. Salad bar and fresh fruit available; pupils say, 'Some lunches are dodgy, some are really nice; we like the doughnuts and fish and chips on Fridays'. Some Jewish, Hindu, Sikh and Muslim pupils. In assemblies, the head says, 'My aim is not to confuse them but to make them aware of other religions and give them a code of behaviour that's moral for all.'

Congested road at drop-off and pickup time. A few parents feel the pressure of homework; maximum expected is one hour a day but pupils want to succeed –'They want you to do well and try your hardest but they make it fun,' they say.

The Hall School

23 Crossfield Road, Hampstead, London, NW3 4NU

• Pupils: 450 boys; all day • Ages: 4-13 • Christian foundation, all faiths welcome • Fees: £11,100-£13,575 pa • Independent

Tel: 020 7722 1700
Fax: 020 7483 0181
Email: office@hallschool.co.uk
Website: www.hallschool.co.uk

Head: Since 2006, Mr Philip Lough (pronounced Lock) MA PGCE (fifties). Educated at Sherborne, he read modern languages (French and German) at Trinity College, Oxford, followed by a PGCE at Durham. Then taught languages for 17 years at Marlborough, where he also ran the cricket team, served as a housemaster and preached. The charming Mr Lough arrived after a successful ten-year headship at Windlesham House School, co-ed boarding prep in West Sussex, and seems to have settled seamlessly into to what some might call a challenging school. Completely relaxed and at home, he is comfortably refining an already successful set-up. Three grown children, one at Oxford, two already working in London. His wife, Christine, who was assistant head at Windlesham, has moved to London with him and now heads South Hampstead High School Junior Department (qv).

Entrance: Competition for entrance is keen and applications restricted to those registering before their first birthday – even so, the school is three times over-subscribed. At three, parents discuss with the head whether a child will enter at four or five (32 places at four, 22 at five). All applicants are tested in the same year – 4+ entrants in January for September, 5+ entrants in late April/May for the following September (school tests close together to ensure the comparison is as fair as possible.) Boys are assessed in groups of six and the school is looking for 'happy, well-adjusted little chaps who want to have a go,' says Junior School head, Kirsty Anderson. 'We want them to be responsive, able to concentrate and integrate with others,' says Mr Lough. 'We're not looking for them to be intellectually precocious, just natural and spontaneous.' Even so, mistakes have been known and though every effort is made to support the strugglers, a child may occasionally be guided elsewhere. Until now, the school has relied solely on its own testing, but is contemplating contacting feeder nurseries for more background. Looks 'fondly' on siblings, but no guarantees – 'It has to be the right school for the individual child'. Occasional places arise at other times, so always worth contacting the school.

Exit: 70 per cent to top London day schools, particularly Westminster and St Paul's, but also largish contingents to City of London, UCS, Highgate, Merchant Taylors' and Mill Hill. Sizeable minority to traditional single-sex boarding schools – Eton, Harrow, Winchester, Tonbridge – but head trying to spread the word about co-ed and three off this year to Marlborough. Strong scholarship form with 10 or so boys looking to take away top honours. Boys carefully guided in their secondary school choice. 'We start talking to parents when boys are in the middle school, suggesting what type of boy would fit what school; we don't like to leave it with a year to go,' says the head. The match is made by annual assessment of verbal and non verbal reasoning - 'We track them over the years on a graph' – as well as day to day performance. Scholarship form in Year 8 for those contemplating the demanding exams of Westminster and Eton, but not all scholarships derive from this form.

Remarks: Remains confidently the top north London prep school for those looking towards the country's top academic secondary schools. A hard core of clever boys is stretched in every direction, producing confident and ever more articulate pupils. 'They're already talking when they come in at 3 and never stop,' said one teacher.

Long-serving, experienced and enthusiastic staff who clearly love their jobs and the school have won the respect of parents. 'The teaching here is wonderful,' said one parent, whose son arrived in Year 5. 'My son just blossomed.' Primarily female teachers in the lower years, predominantly male from Year 5, and younger staff encouraged to stay by the clever recent addition of an on-site crèche.

Specialist French, science, music, sport and ICT more or less from the word go. Latin added in Year 5, Greek in Year 7 for scholarship candidates. Setting in core subjects from Year 5 and Latin from Year 6. Three sciences, one taught each term. Very well-stocked library with library sessions once a week. ICT provision already notable but the head is looking to spend over £300,000 to create a single network for the entire school. Homework starts gently but builds up to a considerable volume in the upper forms, averaging two preps of 45 minutes for Years 7 and 8. No SATs but exams taken seriously with all subjects examined twice yearly in the upper forms.

Housed in three airy and orderly buildings with the Junior School (reception to Year 3), middle (Years 4 and 5) and senior school (Years 6–8) on separate sites all within a short walk. Two classes of 16 in reception, re-shuffled to three of 18 in Year 1. By Year 8, four classes of 12 to 14, with a scholarship form, fast Common Entrance form and two further parallel classes.

Strong special needs support provided gratis with a full-time learning support co-ordinator and four part-time specialist staff. Most difficulties – mainly problems with literacy – are picked up at the earliest point in the Junior School.

On the games front, like most London preps, not overly endowed with outside space, though the Junior

School benefits from a colourful and imaginatively refurbished playground. Rather tired playground for older boys is on the brink of a re-think. Nonetheless, sport taken seriously with the boys dispatched by coach to East Finchley two afternoons a week and rugby, hockey, cross country, gymnastics, fencing and five a side all on offer. All boys get the chance to represent the school at some time in a team game (nine football teams). County and national representatives at chess, fencing and tennis. Cricket tour of Sri Lanka, football tour of Holland.

Music outstanding at all levels, both in the classroom (two specialist music lesson a week) and outside, with a host of peripatetic teachers. More than three-quarters of the boys play at least one instrument and are encouraged to perform in the large orchestra, string quartets, jazz group and choir, leading to an abundance of music awards. Excellent drama with a highlight annual drama in summer term which includes every boy in the final year. Boys throughout the school are encouraged to perform in plays, concerts, and in public speaking. Lovely, bright rooftop artroom, with a potter's wheel and annual exhibition.

Senior school boys enjoy an enviable commonroom, known as the Pit, with a focal snooker table and daily newspapers. Vast range of clubs, including cookery, Mandarin, model making, computer maths games etc.

Far more traditionally religious than many nominally Christian schools. Recently built chapel for quiet contemplation, which includes a corner for Jewish worshippers. Grace said before meals, morning assembly, with hymn practice. House system encourages boys to raise money for charity.

Parents mainly from high-powered, high-income backgrounds in the professions, banking and business, who can be – some would say frequently are – fairly demanding. Most are local but a percentage are happy to make the trek from Notting Hill, Holland Park and Islington.

Undoubtedly a super school for the brightest boys, who take away the best grounding possible and a real intellectual curiosity. 'It's often described as a hothouse, but I don't feel it's like that,' says the head. 'They're not boffins, just normal, cheerful boys, who are particularly enthusiastic about a concert, a play, football or a piece of pottery.' Most parents concur. 'My son suffers from quite serious dyslexia but he still received the most marvellous education,' said one. 'His general knowledge is really astonishing.' For the right boy there can be few better schools, but some have been known to feel a bit left out in the drive to achieve.

Hall School Wimbledon, Junior School

Linked to Ann Margaret House at Hall School Wimbledon, Junior School Linked to Hall School Wimbledon in the Senior section

Stroud Crescent, Putney Vale, London, SW15 3EQ

• Pupils: 250 boys and girls, all day • Ages: 4-11 • Fees: up to £10,470 pa • Independent

Tel: 020 8788 2370
Fax: 020 8788 2121
Email: enquiries@hsw.co.uk
Website: www.hsw.co.uk

Headmaster: Since 1990, Mr Timothy J Hobbs MA (fifties) educated at Eastbourne College and St Andrews, where he read medieval and modern history. He founded the school in 1990 (see senior school entry) and as numbers grew and the school developed a senior and junior section, his brother Jonathan joined as principal of the junior school in 1999.

Mr Hobbs remains head, oversees operations and devotes massive amounts of energy to preserving the original spirit of the place. Entirely child-focused and delighted to leave the detail and day-to-day running of the school to Jonathan. He's based on the senior school site, but visits almost every day and takes assembly once a week. 'Children are very at ease with him,' said one mother. 'Of course there's respect and formality, but they like him and aren't afraid of him.'

Jonathan M Hobbs MA (education management from OU) was also educated at Eastbourne College and then at the British School of Osteopathy. He is married with children; his wife also works at the school. Ably assisted by deputy Susan Harding, who is more parent-facing – his brief is largely finance and management.

Entrance: Interviews during the year by appointment with the registrar. First come, first served for the 44 reception places. Non-selective, but will request a report from nursery school and assess all to make sure the child will fit in. Parents from wide socio-economic spread, a chunk – about 20 per cent – from overseas.

Exit: About two thirds to HSW Senior School (qv) – entry is automatic but the children will sit the same exam as the external senior school candidates to give an idea of where they are. Others to a range of London day schools, just a few to board. Doesn't prepare children for scholarships, although some do win them. 'They all get where they want to go,' says school.

Remarks: Like the senior school HSW Junior School is a very free-thinking place, all about celebrating the individual. The current site, is a former state school – it's been improved and landscaped, Timothy Hobbs himself doing lots of planting. An 'American Garden' was added after 9/11 and serves as a place of reflection and commemoration. Also incorporates a library in a colourful caravan. School backs on to Wimbledon Common and staff take full advantage of this with plenty of expeditions.

Mixed ability classes, each about 22 strong, within which children may be set different work, so treated according to their ability without feeling singled out for special treatment. 'We don't like to take the weaker pupils out and teach them separately because it's hugely important that they gain from hearing what their brighter friends say,' explains Mrs Harding. Huge focus on reading in the early years – they have to 'get it' and school won't rest until they do. Unique homework and monitoring system of senior school called 'flints' begins from Year 3 – it's based on a theory of 'little and often' testing to reinforce what's been taught in school. Most of the schemes of work, methods and innovations of the senior school begin here. Hence it follows components of the Common Entrance and national curriculum, with its own HSW-stamp on it all.

About 30 children need EAL and special needs support. Two special needs support teachers and a new enhanced learning unit. School is happy to take on children with mild learning difficulties, visual impairment, dyslexia and dyspraxia. As with senior school, some perception amongst outsiders that the place includes a high proportion of special need pupils; such views strongly denied by school and dismissed by a parent as 'coffee-morning tittle-tattle – it's not a special school: most of the children are just regular kids'. Within the school grounds is Ann Margaret House (named after the two Mr Hobbs' mother) which caters for children with severe autism. Managed by the school, but really a separate entity, although sometimes the main school children will come in to play with the AMH children.

Parents mention again and again the confidence their children gain at the school and again like the senior school, a huge focus on encouraging the children to think for themselves. 'We want to rein back from too much guidance, noise and teachers' voices,' says Tomothy Hobbs. 'Thinking needs time. We want to challenge their minds.' Plenty of opportunities for the children to have a go at everything – and the academic are valued as much as the artistic or the sporty. Overall the message is: do as well as you can, whatever your strength.

Very strong sport here. Like the senior school, the day begins with 30 minutes of circuit training – even in the drizzle – followed by tons of sporting activities, changing each week, rather than each term, the idea being everyone will do something they enjoy – if gym is not your thing, what about rugby? Hockey is currently flavour of the month and the school is sponsoring Wimbledon hockey club. Children apparently get used to all the running about. No swimming, though – nothing to facilitate it nearby, so travelling and changing times involved make it hardly worthwhile. If your child is not into sport would it be a living nightmare? We asked one of our Year 6 tour guides what would happen if you didn't enjoy all the outdoors activity. 'Tough luck,' he replied grimly.

Major music and drama productions each term, plus children prepared for external LAMDA exams. From Year 4 children can join school choir and orchestra and get lots more of performance opportunities. School provides a solid foundation in art – lots of inspiration surrounds the children in the classrooms and corridors – and they complete varied craft and design projects, everything from basic architectural concepts to costume and set design, bookbinding and mosaics.

Their ICT experience will not be so wide. As in the senior school, it will not be studied for its own sake. The children are taught the joys and frustrations of using books as a resource – 'They need to know that a sparkling new book may yield them very little of use, whereas a tattered old thing may be packed with good stuff,' says Timothy Hobbs. No interactive whiteboards in classrooms or so much as a whiff of an ICT suite.

Longish day – from 8.30am to 3pm for youngest, and to 4pm for years 3 to 6 – a lot to pack in. Outside lesson time the children play beautifully, with all ages mixing together. Particular praise for 'fantastic' field trips. 'I know I'm verging on hyperbole, but they are nothing short of magical,' says one mother. Educational, but also full of great experiences and treats of the kind normally only available to a boy scout these days, as not many parents are prepared to sit in the garden while their children fry bacon over a campfire or abseil down the walls.

Lunchtimes are said to be 'special' – lunch is served in a family way; from years three to six the children say grace and are encouraged to develop good table manners. 'I think children take the lunchtime ritual for granted while they are here, but after they have left they say it's one of the main things they miss,' said one mother.

Pupils' birthdays are celebrated on a major scale with the child in question entertaining their parents and a few chosen friends at their class table for lunch. Then he or she stands on their chair while everyone sings 'Happy Birthday' before they cut and share their Hobbs-baked cake. Even the most retiring soul basks in the spotlight for a few minutes. 'It's a wonderful ritual and the children love it so much,' said one parent. 'Those with summer birthdays spend inordinate amounts of time planning for the school celebration once they get back in September.' And as well as the cake, every child gets a present from school's own Father Christmas – again to show that they are valued as individuals.

The place is boy heavy (60/40, like the seniors), but mothers of girls don't seem to find this a problem – 'Teaches them an early and necessary lesson in how to hold their own in the world,' says one mother. Behaviour is good – no real need for punishments: 'The children quickly get to understand what is expected of them and rise to it,' says the school. Parents are generally delighted that all their children learn good manners, strong morals and simple courtesies almost by osmosis here. Writing thank you letters, standing back for others, saying 'Good morning' as you pass somebody in the corridor – all de rigueur.

Real mix of parents from all walks – bankers, lawyers, media-types, fewer working mothers than at senior school. A bit more sociable than the senior school, with organised coffee mornings for everybody to get to know each other. Parents also help on trips and come into school to share any expertise they may have – recently a Japanese parent delighted with a demonstration of origami. 'I like the fact that the school offers all the best bits of a traditional education, while rejecting the silly stuff that goes on elsewhere,' says one mother. HSW school life won't be for everyone, but definitely worth a look.

Halstead Prep School for Girls

Woodham Rise, Woking, Surrey, GU21 4EE

• Pupils: 200 girls • Ages: 3-11 • C of E • Fees: £8,955-£10,416; Nursery £2,274 pa • Independent

Tel: 01483 772 682
Fax: 01483 757 611
Email: registrar@halstead-school.org.uk
Website: www.halstead-school.org.uk

Headmistress: Since 2001, Mrs Sabine Fellowes BA PGCE (she says jokingly her age is '29 again'). Previously head of St Catherine's Junior School, although began her career as an accountant before retraining as a teacher in 1989 – being able to 'balance the books' has stood her in good stead for overseeing recent building projects. A business-like lady, not one to linger either with her time or with any searching questions: we have never been round a school at such break-neck speed – the whole process was over in less than 40 minutes. With calm enthusiasm she runs a well ordered and tight ship: 'A very good leader,' says one mother, but she can appear defensive to parental input. Clearly pleased with school's growing academic reputation, she knows the girls well and likens her school to 'a home with desks in it'. One mum sums her up nicely saying, 'She is quite formal and reserved, but is good on discipline and the importance of respect for people and property'.

Entrance: Non-selective, on first come first served basis. Main points of entry are nursery and at 7+. (Some parental muttering about class numbers too high in some years, while very small in others.) Girls joining after kindergarten are invited for a day before place is offered, 'to make sure we can meet their needs'.

Exit: Impressive, given absence of academic screening at entry. Most to top Surrey girls' schools – parents convinced exponents of single sex education. Most popular: Guildford High, Sir William Perkins's, St Catherine's, Tormead, Priors Field, Notre Dame, including plenty of scholarships.

Remarks: A very proper and focused, yet happy, small, traditional school with a feeling of ordered industriousness. The nursery now has double the classroom space it previously had. Girls may begin in the term they are three and can choose between three and 10 sessions a week, including pre and after school care. This is often their first school experience and much effort is made to ensure all are happy, including parents, who may be reassured via a two-way mirror! Single form entry for the nursery – girls are taught as one large class (24 children) by four members of staff (three qualified). Specialist teaching is highly valued – begins with music, dance and drama in the nursery and steadily increases through the school.

Glossy pre-prep department is housed in its own building – hard to believe it was purpose built way back in 1996. Immaculate, bright and airy classrooms lead from a central lobby/play area with views of equally beautifully manicured gardens – this could only be a girls' school! From 7+, girls based in original Edwardian building and taught in two parallel groups to a maximum of 18 in each. Here, too, squeaky clean, tidy classrooms with pervasive feeling of space. Smartboards everywhere. Setting for maths and English from Year 5, based on performance in maths only – 'It works particularly well,' says the head. Year 6 girls have their own building, Halstead Cottage, which doubles as a maths centre, while providing a more grown-up base to give girls an increasing sense of independence before they move on.

Though non selective, academic achievement is very important – 90 per cent level 5 SATs don't just happen by themselves. A hard working atmosphere (some parents feel it is becoming more academic) but not as relentlessly academic as some of the other girls' powerhouses in the area. Languages could be taken more seriously – parent mutterings suggest French still has room for more improvement. That said, most parents now much happier with SEN provision (no extra charge made for support given during school time). However, still some reservations – 'I've been very happy with Halstead for my older, academic and laid back daughter – it's been less successful for my younger one, with mild SEN,' said one mum. We got the feeling it may not be a school ideally suited to girls with anything more than mild SEN. Mrs Fellowes disagrees and says the school caters for all ('We currently have one statemented child at the school'). Answer – visit and ask lots of questions.

Sport is on the up – here it appears parental concerns have been addressed: longer school day designed to incorporate more in the timetable. Remains to be seen whether this is enough to satisfy parents with sporty children, who felt too few opportunities/fixtures. All girls play netball, rounders and hockey at school and from Year 2 are bussed to Woking to swim. Fabulous gym/hall, completed in 2004, still smelling deliciously of pine panelling (rather than the usual feet!), provides inspiring centre for indoor sport and performing arts. Cleverly designed, the front of the gym opens to reveal first class staging equipment with dressing/rehearsal room behind.

Famous for its music – 80 per cent of children learn an instrument. The high percentage could perhaps be attributed to 'Music Circus', which allows Year 3 pupils to learn and bring home an instrument from each section of the orchestra for a term. Music lessons are given in small groups and include flute, clarinet, violin, cello, cornet and trombone. Orchestra, string group, four choirs, all busily competing locally and staging at least three productions plus other musical events a year. 'Pursuit of excellence sometimes compromising enjoyment,' says one mum. Terrific art on display everywhere – from Year 3 taught by professional illustrator, Jane Upton, and it shows. Working towards, and will easily achieve, the silver eco award – pond, vegetable patch and now a wormery and compost bin all maintained by the girls. After school activities include cricket, judo and trampoline, with tea and homework supervision if needed.

Pastoral care is very much praised, with no discipline problems. 'We work very hard, teaching the girls independence, and have an active school council for the Year 6 pupils.' Communication to parents on administrative matters, however, is not the school's forte – 'An irritation tolerated because of the school's many other strengths,' says one mum. Working mothers well catered for – daily cover available from 7.30am to 6pm (extra hours charged).

This homely place turns out happy and confident young ladies and is ideal for very good little girls who don't challenge the system and respond well to pressure. Not the obvious choice for the sporty/scruffy/tomboy or tearaway – although Mrs Fellowes challenges our conclusions: 'The school has always welcomed all strong individuals: tomboys, tearaways and scruffs!'

Hampden Gurney CofE Primary School

Nutford Place, London, W1H 5HA

• Pupils: 230 girls and boys • Ages: 3-11 • Church of England • State

Tel: 02076 414 195
Fax: 02076 415 468
Email: office@hampdengurney.co.uk
Website: www.hampdengurneyschool.org.uk

Head: Mrs Evelyn Chua (forties). A firm and fashionably-dressed visionary, originates from Malaysia and has worked immensely hard to transform this inner-city C of E primary to a school with beacon status, recently ranked third in the country. A formidable figure, the children certainly respect her, the punishment of last resort for the naughty, but those who've experienced her teaching also find her an inspiration. No British embarrassment about supporting the gifted and talented, but equally determined that every child in this exceptional school will come out a winner.

Entrance: Twelve of the current foundation stage pupils attend the High Anglican Church of the Annunciation in Bryanston Street near Marble Arch, so if sung mass and ample evidence of the Virgin are not part of your belief system, not the school for you. If they are, don't relax your church attendance once your eldest has secured a place – siblings are only given priority if they, too, are seen on Sundays. Heavily oversubscribed with about 200 applicants for 30 places in nursery (which starts the term before a child's fourth birthday). No automatic transfer to reception and 30 places then available at rising five, with one intake in September. Occasional places occasionally go to non-Anglicans.

Exit: Results to make many a prep-school head weep. Last Year 13 out of 24 pupils went on to the independent sector, three with full-fees places. 'We don't give specific preparation, but we just teach them very well,' says the head, and clearly 'very well' is very well indeed, since many win scholarships and bursaries. Recent awards have taken pupils to Harrow, Eton and all the leading London day schools, UCS, North London Collegiate, City, Latymer etc. The rest largely to schools in Westminster, including Quintin Kynaston, St Augustine's C of E High School, Grey Coat Hospital, Westminster City, Surprisingly few, however, to nearby high-flying St Marylebone.

Remarks: Long-serving head is clearly able to stretch and enthuse young minds but also seems to have the instincts of a property developer. Five years ago the school decided to rebuild its worn-out classrooms to match its league-table-topping position and, working with architects Building Design Partnership, sold off part of its land to fund a new building. Now 'The Beehive', a six-storey dome of steel and glass, has become both a local landmark and an inspiring place to learn, with nursery pupils starting out on the ground floor and progressing to the tent-covered roof as they rise through the curriculum.

Mrs Chua is equally dynamic on the education front and the busy, well-organised classrooms and dedicated staff (three male teachers) are testament to her management skills. Clearly no area of the curriculum here where good is good enough. Half the pupils come in speaking little English; the rest are prosperous middle class, many from international backgrounds, but nearly all those moving on to secondary school attain top marks in maths, English and science. Specialist teaching in PE, art, DT and music, with a rotation system of teachers two afternoons a week. Mandarin taught in Year 2, Spanish thereafter.

Particularly noted for its gifted and talented programme, this is definitely a school where it is cool to be clever. Mrs Chua has high standards and many students reach or exceed them. 'In Year 6, some of the children are doing GCSE maths,' said one mother. But also strong (individual and group) out-of-class support for every child who needs it.

A fairly hefty homework diary, particularly for a state primary: 30–45 minutes a night in Years 3–5, one hr in Year 6, with English, maths and science set nightly and other subjects once a week. Optional holiday homework as well. Well-equipped ICT suite with digital cameras and laptops. Interactive whiteboards in every classroom. ICT taught creatively with an annual ICT week, where even the youngest gets a chance to demonstrate their Spielberg potential. Light and well-equipped rooftop science 'pod'.

Despite its restricted playground space, the school performs sporting miracles with daily sport clubs and specialists provided by the local authority to teach PE, netball, cricket, tennis, tag rugby. Young footballers play for Westminster and regular football competitions with other local schools. Swimming at nearby Seymour Leisure Centre.

Neat and practical red-and-grey uniform. Strong house system with houses named after eminent Brits and points for everything. Ample extra-curricular activity, ranging from sewing and gardening to writing and publishing the school newspaper. Strong emphasis, too, on charitable fundraising. Residential trips to the countryside.

Heavy emphasis on attendance and punctuality (head firmly warns prospective parents against sinful thoughts of mid-term breaks). Escalating punishment system (warning, missing play time, time out, Mrs Chua) but minimum behavioural problems. Indeed, classrooms are a model of well-ordered enthusiasm.

Founded in 1863 by Reverend Hampden Gurney, Rector of St Mary's Bryanston Square, the school's ethos is still strongly High Anglican, with compulsory attendance at weekly sung Eucharist and RE teaching firmly rooted in the Church of England.

Mrs Chua has collected more awards than a Brown Owl, everything from the National Association for Able Children Award to Service Excellence Award. Not unnaturally, most parents are immensely positive: 'You couldn't find a better education in the state system,' said one mother, who'd taken her children out of the private sector. And the articulate, confident and happy pupils are the school's best advertisement. One boy, asked about what he liked about the school, replied, 'Everything.'

Hampton Court House (Junior School)

Linked to Hampton Court House (Senior School) in the Senior section

The Green, Hampton Court Road, East Molesey, Surrey, KT8 9BS

• Pupils: 190, slightly more boys than girls • Ages: 3-16 • Non-denom
• Fees: £9,795-£12,825 pa • Independent

Tel: 020 8943 0889
Fax: 020 8977 5357
Email: sarah@hamptoncourthouse.co.uk
Website: www.hamptoncourthouse.co.uk

Headmistress: Since its inception in 2001, Lady Eliana Houstoun-Boswall ISIT (Paris). For full account, see Hampton Court House Senior School.

Entrance: At three into the nursery via informal interview with child and parents. Eliana looks for families who will be in sympathy with school's aims and ethos and will tell them if she feels they aren't. Into pre-prep via reading and interview. Likewise into the prep – looking for potential, a capacity to think and imagine rather than the crammed and tutored child. At 10, the children are tested more conventionally in English and maths.

Exit: As some come in, some go out. Oddly, you may think, still thinks of itself as a prep and expects its 11 year olds and 13 year olds to sit for other schools at this stage – and several do. As it gains confidence in its new senior school, this practice should wither and die. So they prepare for 11+, 13+ and CE and send pupils to a range of schools. Probably wise to ask to which schools in the last few years but, in 2009, students went on to Eton (exhibition), Wellington (top schol), Marlborough, Kingston Grammar, Latymer and The Brit School.

Remarks: It's a magic place and little children must be wowed to have the run of the stunning old house, its gardens, sizeable pond, outbuildings, and all in one's home clothes too. The educational principles warm the heart – the 3Rs predominate – hooray! – in the early years, but discrete subject teaching starts early too and everyone learns Latin from Year 5 right through to CE. Greek for some from 11. Language learning is a fundamental. French is taught – in French – from day one and by native speakers 'with perfect accents' so all children who go through the prep emerge as competent, if not fluent, communicators in French. One hears it as one passes down corridors – spoken, chanted, sung, from room after room. Spanish also lively and enthusiastic.

Art, drama and music seen as central to education in its broadest and deepest senses and divinity is taught very much with an eye on the art it has inspired. Music seen as exceptional by everyone. IT now well-provided for with a designated room full of Macs with big screens. We watched a class of happy nine year olds working on music animation programmes. Some onsite sport but swimming etc a ride away. The garden a wonderful asset for outdoor play, though 'We have stopped the children climbing trees,' admits Eliana, sadly. The younger children need more designated outside space attached to their classroom, as Ofsted noted in January 2010.

Continental teaching methods are important here – Eliana is impressed by, for example, maths as taught in Hungary and Poland and incorporates principles derived therefrom. The academic staff are multi-national – around half from abroad and many more with overseas experience. Parents have mixed views – the rapid staff turnover is an acknowledged problem, but Eliana feels, 'I would rather have a child taught for one year by an inspired teacher than by the same mediocre teacher for many years'. Hmm. Internationalism flavours the wider curriculum and prep school children learn about major world figures, e.g., Leonardo da Vinci, Dante, Mozart and great European dynasties, e.g. the Hapsburgs and the Holy Roman Empire. Science takes a Socratic approach – discussion is as important as experimentation.

Unusually flexible about keeping children down a year or bumping them up one – in consultation with parents. This can work extremely well, especially in a case of mild bullying, exceptional aptitude or slowness, but can also have adverse consequences and be a problem if the child wants to move elsewhere. SEN provision, previously reportedly 'well-meaning', now tightened up and 'outstanding', as far as Ofsted is concerned – they praised IEPs. Provision for more than mild dyses may need careful enquiry. Not that caring, dedication and attention to individuals are lacking – it's just that in this haven of the love of learning, one can, maybe uniquely, appreciate officialdom's insistence on policies, systems and strategies. Certainly some parents, seduced by the trumpeted ethos, flee after a while, scared off by the realities of the place. Not a school for the conservative, the conventional, nor those who snuggle down of an evening with health and safety reports as bedtime reading.

Hanford School

Childe Okeford, Blandford Forum, Dorset, DT11 8HN

• Pupils: 115 girls; 80 per cent full board; rest flexi or day • Ages: 7-13
• C of E • Fees: Day £15,300; Boarding £18,450 pa • Independent

Tel: 01258 860 219
Fax: 01258 861 255
Email: office@hanford.dorset.sch.uk
Website: www.hanford.dorset.sch.uk

Headmaster: Since 2003, Mr Nigel Stuart Mackay (early fifties). Born and educated in Zimbabwe. Spent his career at a stiff boys-only (latterly co-ed) boarding prep there, rising from assistant teacher of maths to head. Not an obvious choice to be entrusted with the role of running this very special school but, contrary to some expectations, has slotted right in. Hanford has that effect – you don't change it: it changes you. Has worked to keep numbers strong (more professional marketing) and overseen sensitive refurbishment (of IT, decoration, etc), rather than tampering with the ethos. Married to Sarah, who was director of music at Sunningdale School for 13 years before becoming director of music at Ruzawi for 10. She now teaches piano, organises the annual fifth form musical and manages a lengthy list of headmaster's wifely responsibilities. The Mackays have four young children: the boys at Sandroyd, the girls at Hanford.

Miss Sarah Canning MA (seventies), the source of Hanford's spirit and owner of the school, retired from her rôle as headmistress in 2003, handing the school to a charitable trust in 2004. The school remains her home and she still runs the riding, teaches Latin, serves as moral backbone and can be found almost everywhere, like a benevolent ('Not always!' she says) genie.

Entrance: Informal. Girls can come at any time, if space available (and lately that's a big if). Some at seven, the largest number come as eight or nine year olds, and a few at 10 or 11. Locals, Wessex girls, Londoners (regular coach to Battersea) and numerous families posted abroad (popular with Services and FCO families). A sea of fair hair, blue eyes and wellies; a sprinkling of Europeans, usually Spanish, tip up for a term or year to boost their English. A few genuine overseas exotics. Few first-time buyers. Some bursaries.

Exit: Mainly to Sherborne Girls' and Bryanston at the moment but, beyond that, all over, with Leweston, St Mary's Shaftesbury, Downe House, Marlborough and Bedales featuring most years. School strives to find the right niche for each child. Leavers win loads of scholarships (31 academic, art, games and music scholarships won in the last four years; phenomenal for a school of this size). Most girls stay to 13.

Remarks: As the years go by, this school becomes more and more special. It doesn't change, sailing serenely on, while other preps scramble towards identikit purgatory. Has defied the downward trend of girls-only boarding – we note with sorrow that we can now count the number of free-standing girls' boarding preps in England on one hand. Back on track after a wobbly period while the torch was being handed on to new leadership.

Set in 45 acres of rolling countryside (we drove by it three times before spotting the drive, despite having been there before) on the edge of the Stour Valley and surrounded by iron age barrows and Roman fort remains, Hanford House was built in 1620 for Sir Robert Seymer (later Kerr-Seymer). Basically Jacobean with Victorian overtones, it has been splendidly adapted to scholastic life. The magnificent glazed internal courtyard is now the dining room.

We can continue to say this is one of the nicest, if not the nicest, girls' boarding schools in the country, with a gentle, kind, friendly, enthusiastic, gloriously happy-go-lucky, genuine family atmosphere. A place you can feel absolutely confident leaving your ewe lamb in, with the knowledge that the school will probably do a better job of looking after her than you would yourself and, almost as a side issue, give her a thorough grounding in CE subjects, and a fun time with it. Not a flash school. Faded carpets, slip-covered arm chairs, large chilly rooms, dogs wandering down corridors and the bracing smell of rotting manure – the informality can be too much for some parents. No uniform – girls sit happily in class in their riding togs, their (seriously padded) crash helmets on the desk in front of them, working as hard as they can, because the next lesson has four legs. Ponies are important here – the school has 'around' 20 – plus a few privately owned (but used by everyone). 95 per cent of the girls ride, although most didn't when they arrived. Indoor riding school, outdoor arena, jumping paddock. A summer treat is a pre-breakfast ride.

History starts with the Norman invasion and works forward. And the breezily non-PC scripture teacher told us, 'We teach them the Bible because they'll only get comparative religion once they leave.' French from age eight – pupils are usually way past the standard of their senior school by the time they leave (ditto for Latin). 'Native foreign speakers' plus the daughters of British diplomats based abroad are encouraged to continue with their languages. Specialist teachers in all subjects from Year 5 onward. No scholarship set per se, but pupils streamed and potential scholars looked after. Occasionally puts girls up a year. Class sizes tiny throughout the school: nine or ten in each lesson – makes a huge difference. The lessons we watched were so intimate, they reminded us a children's game – 'Oh, I know, let's play school!'

On top of this, 30 girls receive extra help for SEN from a mixture of sources who add up to one full time member of staff. Mostly mild to moderate special needs, but a couple in the 'more severe' category. School introducing new 10-15 minute 'drop in sessions' for quick jolts of extra help. Lots of consistency and stability: average age of staff a youthful 50 and many teachers have been with the school for ages. Classrooms are incredible – some in the converted stables (you go in and out of the window – promise) and some in the most ramshackle collection of what might, in a real world, be temporary buildings.

Music very important – 90 per cent of girls learn an instrument and practice sessions timetabled. Two girls preparing for grade 7 exams when we visited. Girls are auditioned for the chapel choir (only). Also a normal choir, folk group, bands for everything – woodwinds, strings, recorders – and orchestra. Incredibly ambitious art, with ceramics that would not disgrace any senior school; regular masterclasses for gifted artists, plus weekend art club for all. Drama also prolific and good – do ask to see the famously well-stocked costume cupboard. Games (hockey, rounders, pop-lacrosse etc) played on the lawn, adjacent to the outdoor swimming pool. Tap dancing, ballet, year round tennis coaching, even a bit of pistol shooting in the gym. Watch for the magnificent junior cloakroom, a picture of managed chaos with towering heap of rollerblades, riding kit, trainers, wellies, all more or less in their places.

Vast majority board, but loads of flexibility and the line between boarding and day is blurred. All day girls have their own bed and get 20 nights' boarding for free ('They can decide at 6.30 in the evening that they want to stay and, with a quick phone call, it's sorted'). All prep done at school and day girls leave their clobber there. Hanford never closes for exeats – only half term – so perfect for overseas families. Dormitories tidy and feminine – no posters but lots of cuddly toys. Matching bedspreads instead of duvets – now when was the last time you saw that? Not all singing and dancing at weekends – more like a real home, with Sundays spent mooching around the grounds, playing hide and seek, tree-climbing, berry picking, reading. This is a school where time for play is treasured and children are allowed to be children rather than rushed to the nearest shopping centre or games arcade at the first whiff of free time. No TV on weeknights – only on weekend evenings (why do so few schools have the guts to do likewise?).

Time-honoured Hanford extra-curriculars include sewing and dressmaking (the cherished 'Hanford skirts' were much in evidence), pottery, current affairs and art appreciation. In the IT department, upgraded 2007, girls can email whenever – but a school where the post is still keenly awaited. Loads of Hanford traditions, like using a briefcase as a tuckbox, climbing the massive cedar tree (whose branches are each named), early morning rides in the summer, bonfire night entertainments and the marvellously convoluted – and effective – 'manners system', which includes SYRs (serve you rights) for the naughty. Sweets the occasional bribe. School's enormous walled kitchen garden produces veg for the menu plus fruit and the lovely flowers that decorate the main building.

Old Girls include singer Emma Kirkby and Amanda Foreman, author of 'Georgiana, Duchess of Devonshire', on which the film 'The Duchess' was based. And what better example to the girls that they can do anything in life than Peggy, the 82-year-old paddock manager, who powered past us driving a tractor, as we toured the school? No other school like it.

Harrodian Preparatory and Pre-preparatory schools

Linked to Harrodian School (The) in the Senior section

Lonsdale Road, London, SW13 9QN

• Pupils: Girls and boys; all day • Ages: 4-11 • Fees: Pre-Prep £10,965; Prep £12,543 pa • Independent

Tel: 020 8748 6117
Fax: 020 8563 7327
Email: admin@harrodian.com
Website: www.harrodian.com

Head: Since September 1999, Mr James Hooke BSc Hons PGCE, (early fifites). Youthful and subtly effective, headmaster of all three schools (pre-prep, prep and senior) and oversees the day to day running of the prep and pre-prep. The head of the prep school is Mr Matteo Rosetti (early forties) – an Oxford classicist (Balliol), passionate, with a rounded, highbrow approach. He injects still more of an international flavour to the school while being determined to increase its academic profile. Mrs Horan, calm, capable and homely, has been running the pre-prep since 2004. Her previous experience has been in the state sector – Our Ladies of Victories in Putney and deputy head at the Oratory in Chelsea.

Another key player in the management of the whole school is the principal, Mr Peter Thomson. Formerly the surmaster at St Paul's, he ran The Harrodian for a short period until he 'retired' in 1999. A colourfully eccentric individual, he is thoroughly committed to the school but describes his role as largely 'advisory and supportive'. He will do anything that is thrown at him, whether it be showing parents round or jumping on his bike on an errand, but what he clearly loves is leading the tinies in their singing and music assembly on a Friday afternoon. His grandchildren are in the pre-prep and all the children here seem to regard him as a kindly elderly relative.

Entrance: The pre-prep is non selective, but you need to put names down as soon as humanly possible. Siblings welcomed and encouraged. To get into the prep children sit an exam at 8+ and 11+ (and for occasional places). Most are interviewed. It gets tougher the further up the school you try. A good school report counts for a lot. Keen to preserve its balanced approach and attempting not to be seduced by just concentrating on exam results as the calibre of applicants gets increasingly dazzling.

Exit: Almost all continue to the senior school now, but you still get a few sitting CE to trad boarding schools as well as one or two moving onto single sex London day schools. Be ready to put in a lot of extra help if you want your child to go to one of the more academic establishments.

Remarks: The Harrodian was originally founded as a prep school in 1993 by Sir Alford and Lady Houston Boswell since when it has quickly expanded in both directions from 4 up to 18. Their aim was to create a civilized environment where children would learn and grow in a happy, relaxed way, with an emphasis on languages (for a fuller picture see our entry on the Harrodian senior school). Although this is very much one large school with many of the buildings and facilities used by all age groups the pre-prep is self contained in a separate building surrounding a small paved courtyard. Huge classrooms with large bright windows. No one ever feels cramped here. A conservatory at the back where small group work can take place, opens up onto Astroturf where reception can play with fluid access between the classroom and the outdoors. There is a charming allotment complete with scarecrows and dung, as well as the French Garden for quiet contemplation.

The prep school is more integrated into the senior school but cleverly arranged so that they don't seem to get swallowed up by lanky long haired teenagers. Wonderful library – bursting with books of all different genres and a comfortable studious atmosphere. Book club is a surprisingly popular one of the many lunch time clubs on offer (elegant, wide corridors, large windows. You couldn't feel hemmed in here – so refreshing to be able to say that about a London day school. One of the best things about the school is the space – inside and out. Twenty five acres of playing fields, an elegant outdoor swimming pool, charming statues and features in the attractive gardens. Bid farewell to the nagging boarding school question. It's all here on your London doorstep but without the heavy weight of the traditional and institutional.

Unlike the senior school where there is no uniform, the prep school has a (pretty relaxed) dress code. This includes collared shirts but boys can wear the Harrodian hoodie with their collared shirt underneath. The pre-prep wear simple navy uniforms. Discipline is discreet. Children here are given responsibility and respect and are largely self regulating. There are no bells, parents are welcomed and can get as involved as they wish to be.

An effective SEN department run by a highly praised SENCo with a team of ten support staff who work closely with the mainstream staff. Pupils who need extra help (on account of mild to moderate needs – the usual dys-strata etc) will get mostly one-to-one attention. There is an extra charge for this as well as help given before or after school and during lunchtime. High proportion of EAL, a lot of language support is available. Those identified as being gifted and talented are given extra challenges in the classroom and there is a mini chess club for Years 1 and Reception. All pupils learn a modern foreign language and many do an additional language at a lunchtime club.

The school buzzes with creativity. Innovative drama and music with ambitious projects – the prep school recently performed the Magic Flute and the battle of the bands is hugely popular. One boy took a few terms out to perform in the film of Peter Pan. School appreciates the value of the seizing opportunities as they arrive and is flexible in accommodating them. Plenty of sport – as you would expect with such extensive grounds – and a wide choice from the more mainstream, football, cricket, netball etc to fencing, dance and gymnastics. Lots of fixtures both within school and with other schools – some parents commented on the patchy performances but as with everything here what matters most is that everyone gets involved.

A trendy school with some traditional touches, it attracts a lot more creative media types and celebrities and less of the usual lawyer and banking clientele found in most London independent schools. A few first time buyers. Many are local – Barnes, Hammersmith etc but an increasing number from the chic areas north of the river.

A stimulating but relaxed environment – suits an all rounder who isn't ready to be chiselled into a square peg.

Hawkesdown House

27 Edge Street, Kensington, London, W8 7PN

• Pupils: 130 boys • Ages: 3-8 • Primarily C of E • Fees: £11,700-£13,425 pa • Independent

Tel: 020 7727 9090
Fax: 020 7727 9988
Email: admin@hawkesdown.co.uk
Website: www.hawkesdown.co.uk

Head: Since 2010, Mrs Claire Renton Bourne MA (Mrs Bourne to parents), a Cambridge classicist and Nottingham theologian (late forties). Married to a civil servant and has two children, both educated at Bryanston School, now at university. She spent three years at Perrott Hill School in Somerset, tutoring the scholars and heading the classics and RS departments. Moved to Knighton House in Dorset in 2001 as deputy head, became head there in 2004. Remained head of classics, teaching both Latin and Greek. Keen on 'children, education, classics, piano, flute, gardening, sewing' and is a 'passionate believer in single sex education to 13'.

Entrance: Main entry at nursery and reception level on a first come first served basis, and then as places crop up through the school. Boys go for a familiarisation session, normally about an hour, and, if it looks as though their needs can be met and they would thrive in the school, a place is offered. For older boys, places are offered after a letter and report from the previous school (or a conversation with the head, if in the UK) and a day's assessment to see if they would fit in comfortably.

Exit: Most to established London prep schools – Colet Court, Westminster Under, King's College Wimbledon, Wetherby, Latymer, St Philip's, for example; others might board at Caldicott, The Dragon, Summerfields, Sunningdale or elsewhere.

Remarks: A traditional school with traditional teaching. Main emphasis on solid grounding in the basics plus excellent introductions to history, geography and science. French taught from reception and chess in the last two years. Teachers are all young, friendly, enthusiastic and imaginative. Children not pushed but allowed to develop at their own pace. As one parent said, 'They never make any child feel he is useless.' All classes seemed disciplined with boys eager to discuss and explain the work they were doing. Very neat workbooks.

Most teachers also have an assistant, either a student between first degree and PGCE or a qualified teacher from overseas learning how we teach over here. Pupil teacher ratio is approximately 8:1. The majority of classteachers are female but this does not seem to worry the parents – several males around in various other capacities. Interactive white boards and computers everywhere.

Few language problems despite the fact that the majority of the boys come from multinational families. Homework is kept to a minimum and only during the week – mainly reading with just enough written work to instil self reliance and pave the way for the next step. 25 boys are on the high ability list and 33 on the SEN register for a variety of needs including speech and language difficulties, sensory integration problems, dyslexia and deafness. Not able to deal with extremely disruptive behavioural problems nor physical difficulties (because of school's geography). In case of problems emerging, will assess and deal with it – for instance, a boy who was found to have fine motor skill difficulties was taught to type. Good, frequent monitoring with IEPs issued as necessary.

SEN staff are young, enthusiastic and incredibly caring and will look at individual needs – when installing whiteboards, they first checked the equipment would work with hearing aids. Their thirst for information and new ideas is endless – as members of the West London specialist group, one or other of them attends any talks and relays information back to all staff members. Outside agencies support as needed, with extra teaching brought in if necessary. As one parent said, 'To them, SEN children are not a big deal and are not singled out and made to feel different. They soon learn to fit in with the day to day life of the school and their classmates accept them without thought.' An excellent and caring department.

No outdoor play area, but no parent we spoke to seemed to feel that this really matters, although several mentioned it. Daily walk or run around Kensington Gardens and, in good weather, they use Holland Park for PE. Football once a week – older boys play competitively, each child will get to play in at least one match. Perhaps not brilliant for a very physical child but fine for most. Lots of after school activities – art, drama, cookery, ceramics, choir and three classes of Mandarin among them.

Very friendly atmosphere. After a series of confusing doors, you reach a lovely wide hall with an informative parents' notice board. Own kitchen, excellent cooking, compulsory for boys to eat school food (those with eating disorders or special diets are specially catered for and can bring the occasional titbit from home).

Parents pack the main hall on Fridays when awards are given out. Christian ethos, but many other religions are celebrated with parents very much involved. In the hall also wall bars and other equipment available for use in gymnastic lessons and mats for judo, which is so popular that, although it is charged as an extra, it is timetabled for all boys from Year 1 onwards. Loos are all low-level, including mini urinals, all with stickers to be aimed at, and no nasty smells.

Classrooms generally light and airy, some smaller than others but usual maximum number of boys is 15 or 16 in each, so plenty of space. Lots of happy, friendly, well mannered small boys in smart red and blue uniform, with 'just the right mix of discipline and bright cheekiness'. Strict behaviour policy for the boys promoting kindness, thoughtfulness and consideration for others. Complaints system in place but, judging from the parents we spoke to, very rarely needed.

Most live reasonably locally and a large number walk to school. Two thirds expats (American and European mostly) and one third English, the great majority of both from the financial sector. A mixed culture school with a lot of bilingual children – so having overseas teachers helping in the classrooms is useful. Strong parental network, an active PTA and a good sense of community. No scholarships or bursaries but, in an emergency, the head is sure something could be done.

A school that any small boy would love to attend.

Hazlegrove School

Linked to Kings Bruton in the Senior section

Hazlegrove, Sparkford, Yeovil, Somerset, BA22 7JA

• Pupils: 180 boys, 195 girls. 50 boys and 40 girls board. 35 boys and 25 girls, all day, in the pre-prep plus 15 in the nursery • Ages: 2+ -13 • Christian • Fees: Boarding £15,390-£19,635; Day £6,837-£13,854 pa • Independent

Tel: 01963 442 606
Fax: 01963 440 569
Email: admissions@hazlegrove.co.uk
Website: www.hazlegrove.co.uk/

Headmaster: Since 2002, Mr Richard Fenwick MA (forties). Educated at Bishop's Stortford College. Had a misguided shot at banking till his vocation dawned. After that, a rapid rise through the ranks of a number of preps till he reached the summit of St Andrew's Turi, Kenya. Not by any means an everyday sort of head from whom you expect the customary, ever-lulling stream of blah, Mr Fenwick can be intriguingly enigmatic, deceptively sphinx-y. Sentences, at the ends of which seem to hover ghostly question marks, sometimes trail off half-said. Don't be fazed – there's no dark purpose. It's because he's a wonderer – he genuinely wonders what you think. Not a lot of heads, when you come to think of it, wonder what you think. His utterances can be oblique, runic, playful, can raise eyebrows, but stem, actually, from constant cogitation and a passion for what he's about. It's very simple – he wants every day to be the best of every child's life and he wants everything they learn to be useful in their later lives. When he talks about what the school does and how, he often tags on the words 'for the benefit of the children', and you can see it's not for the benefit of the shop window – that's incidental. Here is a man whose mind and spirit have, as he avows, expanded under wide African skies. Steel here – he's an effective force, tremendously ambitious for every child. Parents and pupils cheer him to the echo. Wife Katie deeply implicated, in charge of the boarders. Three children.

Entrance: No academic hurdle to worry about unduly – the full academic rainbow here, but the waiting list is filling.

Exit: The brightest win awards everywhere and every year brings an estimable hatful. No channelling to the senior school, King's Bruton, on to which go around a half. Sherborne and Sherborne Girls are popular, so are any number of others.

Remarks: 'Academically they know what they're about,' says one mum (she's a teacher somewhere else, so there's verification). 'It's a tight ship.' Achievement speaks well of the school, parents declare themselves pleased. The head says, 'Amid all the romantic fun there must be results. Our education must be sound.' They do well by their best – 'There are children winning scholarships who wouldn't have two years ago' – and also by their pretty long tail. The secret lies in the delivery thing, of course, and you'll find no national curriculum apparatchiks here. The head wants only passionate teachers who like children (that's two rare breeds already) and he gets them – almost three-quarters of the staff are his appointments. Any applicant who asks at interview about salaries is out on their ear – 'They've got to want desperately to work here.' You meet big-heartedness wherever you go. Some of the best have been here for years and the new crop are top drawer.

A gifted and talented programme – they work jolly hard to prepare their scholarship candidates. Parents in this area know that King's School, Bruton (the senior school) is good for dyslexia, and that is the expectation they exert on Hazlegrove. An established, highly-rated learning support unit. Diagnostic test on entry, remediation as necessary only for as long as – no dependency creation here. It's cool to go to learning support and at the end of every term the pupil who makes the most progress wins the cockerel (don't ask).

'If a child isn't very good at something, focus on what they can do,' says the head – praise from parents for the way they work out the best way forward for every child, radically if necessary (nothing here is formulaic), giving some their first cloudless experience of school. All individual achievement is pursued and celebrated – if any chance of winning whatever, they go for it. Creativity expresses itself in excellent art and design, and 'fantastic music' – this from a violin-maker father: fifteen ensembles bear witness. Drama is strong, taught to all from Year 3, purpose-built theatre. Sport is win-win, played hard in the right spirit, productive of county and national players. Sports hall, swimming pool, squash courts, Astro – this really is a well-resourced school. Outdoor education is big, taught to all in Years 5 and 6, and camping out in the grounds for the littlest. Pre-prep purpose built, set apart, shipshape. Parents hugely approve of the nursery.

The school day ends at four, when clubs, activities and prep happen, popular with parents who value family life unclouded by homework, so around half the children are still there at six – as, most days, are all the teachers. You can come for breakfast, stay for tea – they'll take your fraught work schedules in their stride right up to the last minute.

The setting is drop-dead gorgeous – early 18th century house fronted by the newly restored Williamite Court, set in lord-of-all-you-survey grounds at the end of a drive halfway up which time stands still. No wonder former pupils remain so fond, 163 of them at the last reunion, some dating back to 1947. Indeed, a lot of present parents did time here. These days children come in minibuses from as far away as Crewkerne; many are brought by their parents 'so we can pick up on what's going on'. Some reckon the school takes a fair bit of motoring to get to but, nestling as it does on the banks of the A303, these are quick miles. Parents a mixed bag – some Services (especially boarders), local farmers and business people, old money, a sprinkling of those metro exiles and quality-of-lifers who are beginning to colonise this part of Somerset. What sort of child wouldn't be happy here? 'An arrogant one,' says the head – and you can see he'll have none of that.

Discipline in this child-centred school is all about good manners and consideration for others – no hiding place for those who don't see it that way. Values are Christian ones. Parents rate the pastoral care. We stayed on till lights out to check out the boarding – excellent staff, very well done. Had to tear ourselves away, actually.

Something good going on here, and it's getting this school talked about.

Headington Preparatory School

Linked to Headington School in the Senior section

26 London Road, Oxford, Oxfordshire, OX3 7PB

• Pupils: All girls; mostly day with some weekly boarders • Ages: 3-11 girls • Fees: Boarding £19,683-£24,945; Day £6,768-£12,885 pa • Independent

Tel: 01865 759400
Fax: 01865 761774
Email: admissions@headington.org
Website: www.headingtonprep.org

Head: Since 2006, Ms Andrea Bartlett, previously deputy at Bute House. She teaches PHSE to all the girls. 'Each girl tells me something that she is proud of achieving in the week before and we keep a record in the Proud Book. We also have a value of the month, such as courage, which gives us focus as a whole school.' Parents comment, 'A very likeable lady. She loves the children.'

Entrance: Takes 16 into the nursery class and another 16 straight into reception. Put name down soon after birth. No selection at this stage, so first come first served, though siblings have preference. Class sizes gradually increase up the school to 24, so a dripfeed of places for older children, with an exam for those aged 7+. Means tested bursaries of up to 100 per cent of fees are available to applicants for entry at age nine, and Services/C of E clergy bursaries also available.

Exit: Nearly all to the senior school. Year 6 girls take the Common Entrance exam and most sail through. 'We start preparing parents at the beginning of Year 5 if there are likely to be problems. Their daughter will probably be having learning support already, so it won't come as a shock. Sometimes we feel somewhere smaller might suit her better. And sometimes we have the conversation, then she comes through well. And because both schools have a broad all-round curriculum, a girl who is not strong academically might be good at other things like sport or art or drama and that makes up for it.'

Remarks: Lovely setting across the road from the senior school. Rambling Victorian building with its own grounds, playing fields and wooded area. Separate nursery and reception building with its own playground and vegetable patch, surrounded by pencil fence. Library, IT suite, music room and science lab with hamster and stick insects.

Sport is 'fantastic, brilliant,' said a parent. 'Lots of matches and they include everyone who wants to play.' Girls swim each week in the senior school pool and the upper forms use the sports hall. Extra-curricular activities include fencing, judo, trampolining and cross-country, and several pupils play or swim at county, national or territorial level. Music is strong too, with an orchestra, jazz band, wind group and chamber choir. Drama includes a play performed entirely in French by Year 4 and a Year 6 musical. Lots of popular lunchtime clubs and after-school care until 5.45pm.

French from Year 3. Three 'flexible' maths groups in the older classes. Encompasses a broad ability range but 'class teachers are good at differentiating the work', and a strong learning enrichment department. Can cope with mild dyslexia and dyspraxia. Means tested bursaries of up to 100 per cent of fees available to girls joining the school at nine years.

Praised by parents as a 'very friendly place. My timid daughter was a different child after being there a year'.

Hereward House School

14 Strathray Gardens, Hampstead, London, NW3 4NY

• Pupils: 175 boys, all day • Ages: 4-13 • Non-denom • Fees: £11,250-£13,050 pa • Independent

Tel: 020 7794 4820
Fax: 020 7794 2024
Email: herewardhouse@btconnect.com
Website: www.herewardhouse.co.uk

Headteacher: Since 1980, Mrs Leonie Sampson BA ('as old as she feels'), formal, lively and chatty. She was previously head of the junior department and was able to purchase the school when it came up for sale. She has presided ever since over this friendly, family school, amassing an encyclopaedic knowledge of north London secondaries in the process. 'She's very kind to the staff and the boys,' said a parent, 'and this permeates the whole atmosphere of the school.' Is ably assisted by 'super' deputy, and intends to stay on for several years yet – 'I get a buzz as soon as I walk in the door'.

Entrance: Sign up as soon as possible after birth (not before, though parents have tried). Tries to close the lists at about 80 but doesn't always succeed. Parents are asked to contact the school about 18 months before proposed date of entry, when they and their son will be invited to come for a chat with the head and to look around the school. 'I suggest that parents tell their son he is coming to see if he likes us. That makes it less nerve-wracking.' The head offers 18 places to those she feels will be most compatible with the school and with each other. Offers are made during the summer term a year before entry, some eight months before other local preps make their offers.

Will always take siblings. Places do come up later on, so it's worth phoning to check.

Exit: Parents are given careful and knowledgeable advice on which senior school will best suit their son and no-one has failed the Common Entrance in 20 years. Westminster, St Paul's, Highgate and City of London are the most popular destinations, alongside, increasingly, boarding schools such as Harrow, Winchester and Uppingham. 2009 academic scholarships and awards to Westminster, Rugby, City of London, Highgate and Aldenham.

Remarks: Not overtly selective, but tends to attract a relatively homogeneous bunch of mostly bright boys from north London professional families. All mixed ability teaching, except for maths and Latin in the top two forms, divided into two groups mostly on the basis on which senior school they are aiming for. This is a moveable feast and late developers can change groups. Plenty of extra individual help for boys who are struggling and no-one is asked to leave – 'You can't get lost here down in the C or D stream – everyone is in the A stream'.

Redbrick house in a quiet Belsize Park road with a soft-surface playground out the back. Space is undoubtedly limited, but the timetable is organised so that academic lessons in formrooms are interspersed with trips to the science lab, music room or artroom across the playground.

Cricket, football and cross-country at Brondesbury Cricket Ground and the Heath Extension, with swimming at Swiss Cottage and a full programme of matches against other local prep schools. 'And because it's so small, everyone gets a chance to be in a team,' said a parent approvingly. Music is particularly strong – around 90 per cent of senior school boys learn an instrument, 43 piece school orchestra. Owns a huge variety of instruments – including a bright yellow piano – so boys can try out any one they fancy. Informal concerts every Monday afternoon and a major school concert every summer.

Artroom filled, during our visit, with papier mâché dinosaurs and clay modelling. Plenty of outings to galleries, museums, concerts and lectures, with field study trips in the UK and France. After-school clubs include chess, karate, fencing and Greek. An annual ski trip for parents and children.

In a school this size, discipline is rarely a problem – 'It's an advantage being a female head in a boys' school. I think the boys believe that it would be too awful to behave badly because it might upset Mrs Sampson. Boys like structure and I truly believe that you can keep order gently'. Parents are always welcome to come in and have a chat – 'They know I have an open door policy and they can always have a quick word, so nothing builds up'. Parents agree, 'She will sort out any problems immediately'.

Valued for its gentle, nurturing, family atmosphere. Not overtly competitive –'They're good at coaxing rather than pushing,' said a parent, who commented that boisterous, pushy boys might be better off elsewhere – but gets good results from all its pupils. 'They teach them to be nice to each other,' said another parent. 'My son absolutely loves it.'

High School of Dundee Junior School

Linked to High School Of Dundee in the Senior section

Euclid Crescent, Dundee, DD1 1HU

• Pupils: 345 girls and boys; all day • Ages: 5-11 • Non-denom
• Fees: £6,930-£7,920 pa • Independent

Tel: 01382 202 921
Fax: 01382 229 822
Email: admissions@highschoolofdundee.co.uk
Website: www.highschoolofdundee.co.uk

Head: Since January 2007, Mrs Gwyneth McLaren, previous deputy head.

Remarks: School scattered around the attractive old Dundee Girls' school buildings on west side of the main school courtyard under the music department. Entrance is attractive stairway with impressive stained glass and a myriad of activities notices for both seniors and juniors. Masses of choice for juniors including earlybird and lunchtime IT and a gardening club (currently providing a wintry courtyard with paper flowers).

A bunch of bouncy young teachers, leavened by the odd older face, take tinies up to senior school. Juniors have own dining area, gym and games space, French from P6, with a P7 trip to Paris eagerly anticipated by pupils. P6 and 7 get lots of lessons in the senior school: computers, art, drama etc. Friendship club cleverly supervised helps spot potential problems and provides cosseting when needed. Classes in early years strictly capped at twenty for L1 rising to 22 for L3, but school will make an extra class when there is the demand though space is tight! Good support for stragglers plus a thinking skills course for every year group – one group was busily doing Su Doku! Littlest start with Oxford Reading Tree plus lots of phonics and multiple reading methods. The class we visited was having a ball – expressively reading aloud. Children happily busy in every corner though an older group caught in a lull had time to talk maturely about the imminent French trip and their huge array of hobbies.

Before and after school care at extra charge from 8–8.30am and 4–6pm, but free from end of school till 4 when buses leave. Places at a premium and Dundee, Perthshire and Fife folk queue up for them.

High School of Glasgow Junior School

Linked to High School Of Glasgow (The) in the Senior section

27 Ledcameroch Road, Bearsden, Glasgow, G61 4AE

- Pupils: 380 boys and girls in the junior school, 50 in the nursery. All day
- Ages: 4-10; plus nursery (kindergarten) 3-4 • Non-denom
- Fees: £5,910-£8,325 pa • IndependentIndependent

Tel: 0141 942 0158
Fax: 0141 570 0020
Email: adminjs@hsog.co.uk
Website: www.glasgowhigh.co.uk

Head: Since 2004, Mr Colin Mair of the senior school, who has ultimate responsibility, but the day to day running of the junior school has been in the capable hands of Mrs Karen Waugh BA DipPrimEd (fiftyish) since 2001. She was educated at Hutchesons' Girls' Grammar, followed by a DipEd at Jordanhill College, and took her BA via the Open University. Her children are in the school. She was previously head of Mearns Primary (700 pupils), deputy head of Carolside Primary (800 pupils) and then acting head; before that she taught at Carlibar, team-taught at Crookfur and taught at the open plan Torrance Primary. Her current appointment is her first in the independent sector. New staff appointments very much a joint activity.

Entrance: 55/65 applicants at kindergarten level (max 54), though this is now 'capped at 50 to allow for the odd beginner at primary 1'. But get in early – school 100 per cent oversubscribed for entrance thereafter. Parents have coffee and cakes and the children are taken to the kindergarten and assessed individually. Social interaction and 'emotional readiness' rather than crammed academics is the yardstick, so children with a reading age of six will not necessarily come up trumps. Interviews are held annually – if you don't get a place the first time round, you may be kept 'on hold' and may be accepted, so don't give up. Recently, 63 applications for two places between primaries 1 and 6. Priorities to siblings, FPs' children and the rest of the field.

Exit: Automatic transfer to senior school and usually all do. P7 (Transitus – i.e. 12 year olds) are accommodated at Anniesland.

Remarks: The Glasgow prep they all – with good reason – fight to get into. Huge number of pupils shoe-horned with enormous skill into tiniest site imaginable (rector doesn't like this description: he would prefer 'restricted site'). But think Victorian villa, think stained glass windows, think very steep site, think 380 odd children, think the impossible. Massive new build since our last visit, positively Swiss engineering to construct a magical new basement, fantastic kindergarten (with its own entrance); masses of light – this is imaginative architecture at its most productive.

Junior school shares senior school facilities, bussed to Anniesland for rugby and hockey, swimming at the Allander centre, not a huge amount of playground on site (a couple of converted tennis courts), but each age group has their own. Small gym (i.e. not a sports hall) and impressive convertible hall/theatre. Excellent and imaginative drama. Superb music, three choirs, orchestra, wind, guitar, chamber, chanter – you name it. Specialist art teacher – the entire complex (building is too simple a word) is covered in child-paintings and models.

One (only) male teacher, dedicated French, drama, music, art and PE teachers, otherwise form teacher throughout. Two parallel classes for each year group, with 'group teaching where appropriate'. Support for learning at both ends of the spectrum with specialised learning support (as in dyslexia, dyspraxia and those whom the rector would prefer us to call 'slow learners') upstairs in main building. No 'problem' with ADHD or children on Ritalin (none in the school at the moment). Sixth formers at senior school act as buddies when pupils move up to senior school. Class size 27 and down, French from the age of eight, IT from the start – IT Works, spread sheets, word processing, data bases. Dedicated computer lab – the works.

Same ethos as senior school – positive relationships and anti-bullying plans. Elected junior school council who have a serious input and recently quizzed the catering manager about the lunch supplied. Trips for everything everywhere – a busy school. Own tartan for children. Mainly middle class parents, some from far away – children can be left early and collected late. Buses link up with senior school runs.

Kindergarten super with dedicated area, children on the academic ladder at four – play learning at its best. All wear badges with their name on it – automatic for the first few weeks, but then, 'The children love wearing them'. Charming, convenient – couldn't do better.

Highfield School

Linked to Brookham School in the Junior section

Highfield Lane, Liphook, Hampshire, GU30 7LQ

- Pupils: 130 boys, 105 girls; 85 boarders/150 day • Ages: 8-13 • C of E
- Fees: Day £13,275-£16,425; Boarding £17,400-£19,425 pa • Independent

Tel: 01428 728 000
Fax: 01428 728 001
Email: admissions@highfieldschool.org.uk
Website: www.highfieldschool.org.uk

Head: Since 1999, Mr Phillip Evitt MA (early fifties). Educated at Kimbolton School and Gonville and Caius College Cambridge (history and PGCE). Taught at Monmouth School and then Dulwich College for 14 years. Very approachable, yet a real dynamo and forward thinking into the bargain. Parents say he is 'really inspiring', 'very well liked', 'knows my children inside out'. Has a genuine pleasure in teaching and is very aware of his role 'in loco parentis' within the school at all levels.

He has undertaken a major staff reshuffle, bringing in much new blood to key positions and slowly but surely making changes – as he puts it, 'There were a few sacred cows to be despatched'. Teaches history and enthuses about the subject, keen to show it's not about 'just the Tudors and the Nazis'. Lives on site in a rather lovely house with wife Joanna and their four children, all educated at Brookham and Highfield. Also keeps chickens and has VW van in which family goes camping. Many comment his speaking voice is disarmingly like Tony Blair's and, like TB, it wouldn't surprise us if he doesn't have his eye on bigger and better things – a prestigious public school headship in the future perhaps? 'Absolutely not,' says Mr Evitt.

Entrance: Broadly non-selective although really weak children, i.e. significantly below national average, may wish to apply elsewhere. Majority of pupils come from Brookham School, the linked pre-prep (see separate entry), from which automatic entry. Interestingly, pupils enter Highfield in Year 4, having done Year 3 at Brookham – Year 3 seen as a true transition year, with time spent at both Brookham and Highfield, so that pupils feel comfortable once they enter Highfield proper at Year 4. Not oversubscribed at present, but it may only be a matter of time as the school is riding high locally and is currently popular with parents moving out of London. When the A3 tunnel is completed (in 2011, so they say), this will open the floodgates for parents north of Hindhead – currently a hideous bottleneck.

Exit: Almost all to top notch public schools. Massive breadth of senior schools, with a strong leaning towards co-ed. Most popular co-eds are Marlborough, Bryanston, Wellington, Canford, Bedales, Cranleigh and Millfield. Senior single sex boys' schools include Winchester, Eton, Charterhouse, Sherborne, Radley and, for girls, Sherborne School for Girls, St Swithun's, Downe House, Wycombe Abbey. Awards and scholarships abound. Mr Evitt keen to stress that he supports all senior school choices including those which take from 11. However, one parent said that, 'Highfield isn't keen to lose pupils at 11,' and another added, 'He is very pro co-ed and boarding.' Mr Evitt hotly denies any bias against single sex schools and says, 'The senior school destinations have much more to do with what our parents want'. He stays in touch with ex-Highfieldians and gets the low-down on all the senior schools. (OBs include Ludovic Kennedy and Terence Conran.)

Remarks: Exciting country prep school storming its way into the big league. Traditional with a twist – good academics with a reassuring touchy-feely element which will endear it to parents who worry about entrusting their little darlings to someone else's care. Mr Evitt is aiming for a modern prep for the 21st century, though Highfield has increasing competition in the 'fashionable' ex-Londoners school stakes with nearby Amesbury – he believes the schools happily co-exist by serving different needs.

Education is broad and rigorous – standards have been slowly cranked up. Excellent results – 'No-one has ever failed to get into their first choice of senior school – certainly in the whole time I've been here,' says Mr Evitt. He is very anti full-on setting and absolutely refuses to have a scholars set, having 'agonised' over the issue. When he inherited the school it was divided into a top, middle and bottom set, encouraging a culture of 'boffins and thickos' which, as he says, became 'a self fulfilling prophecy'. (He gets quite cross with parents who push for unrealistic scholarships – 'You're setting children up to fail'.) Slow build up of setting from Year 4, where 'gentle groupings', setting in maths and English is gradually introduced in Year 5 and other subjects follow. By Year 7 virtually everything is setted, but head very keen to stress plenty of differentiation within the groups and huge flexibility.

Whilst knowledge based education is a vital element, Mr Evitt thinks that 'emotional intelligence', a phrase which he (and other trendy heads) uses often, is as important – 'In practice, it's educating our children for the 21st century – managing relationships, managing anger, the whole development of the child' (much the same as most of us thought education was about, anyway).

Excellent SEN provision – very wide ranging support available for dyslexia, dyspraxia, mild autism and Asperger's. Also gifted and talented provision. Full time SENCo supported by a number of fully qualified assistant teachers who do one-to-one and classroom support. Also classroom assistants in Years 4 to 6. If needs can be addressed in a maximum of two one-to-one sessions per week, 'there shouldn't be any problem'.

A relaxed environment in 175 acres of glorious countryside on the Hampshire/West Sussex/Surrey borders. We were fortunate to see it on a sunny day with endless blue skies and it seemed nothing less than idyllic. Plenty of outdoor activity within secure space – loads of opportunity for, as Mr Evitt says, 'Ray Mears (an adventure aficionado, for parents not in the loop of TV culture) stuff'. Fantastic new indoor swimming pool – nice to see that it's also used by non-Highfield children for swimming lessons.

Fab new music school just completed, dripping with computers. Dear little old fashioned san with charming school nurse, who appears to be the best friend of several girls: at least four were in there in break time -'They like to come in for a chat'. Superb much used chapel. Recently refurbished theatre and DT rooms breathe new life into previously tired areas. Really superb facilities with a nice homely feel. Head says, 'It would be nice to have endless resources to develop new facilities, but for us as a prep school, the range of senior school style facilities is simply not always achievable, and I also feel it important that when our children move on to their senior schools, they experience an appropriate sense of stepping up a gear and enjoying the real wow factor that their new school should provide.'

Sport for all and at all levels – all the children are in a team for something and have a chance to represent the school. Very important to be involved here. 'If someone doesn't like a particular sport, they're encouraged to have a go and usually they end up enjoying it,' said one pupil. Huge range of sports played, with equal emphasis on boys and girls. Nine hole golf course is on the wish list, but a budding Tiger Woods can practise on the golf range. Music increasingly important: loads of individual lessons – more than 200 children learn an instrument. Several choirs, mostly for all, apart from the chapel choir – auditions needed. Art is outstanding: the number of art scholarships attests to this.

Very impressive extracurricular programme, run by a dedicated director of activities: tap dance, fencing, model making, camping skills, felt bag making, mountain biking, to name but a very few. Boarders can bring their bikes, skateboards, scooters and rollerblades into school to make the most of the magnificent grounds. Pupils are clearly privileged but charming and aware of how blessed they are – 'We went to visit another school and said, "Let's go into the woods," and then we realised there weren't any'.

It is an all-go environment, so if you want your little darlings at home early every day and at weekends, this is not the place for you. The school day ends at 4.40pm most days, but with all the opportunities and activities, most day children chose to stay until 5.25. Boarders then do prep, reading and music practice between 5.30 and 6.30. Saturday school for all until 4.00pm, when everyone, including boarders, is usually free to trot off home. Boarding is no longer compulsory at 11, although we get the impression the head is a huge fan of boarding and all that entails. He says, 'Experience shifts perception of boarding,' and that parents who start off saying, 'Over my dead body!' slowly come round to the idea.

Nice to see they are still children at 13 and not (yet) hormonally charged and monosyllabic. Not a scrap of makeup or hair gel in sight, although plenty of posters in dorms of, one assumes, the latest boy bands etc. 'The girls' dorms are a bit messy because they are always changing their outfits,' says one (boy!) pupil. Uniforms are in the main neat and tidy, with attractive kilts for the girls.

Christian ethos underpins everything. Impressive booklets for parents and children coming into Year 4 give a very reassuring picture of the school – 'Even the headmaster had to ask for help when he started at Highfield!' Long list of people the pupils can talk to if they have any problems. Parents are invited to attend all chapel services, matches etc, and boarders can see their parents for 'car park time' on Wednesdays and Saturdays if they are not going home, which they can do on all but the first weekend.

We previously reported the odd complaint about pastoral care, but Mr Evitt is adamant 'our qualities of pastoral care and relationships are absolutely central to what we are about'. Perhaps not the ideal place for oddballs and those who don't toe the line (although Mr Evitt hotly disputes this). But complaints are few and far between and, all in all, the school is one of the most innovative (but still with a sense of tradition) boarding and day preps we have visited.

Highgate Junior School

Linked to Highgate Pre-Preparatory School in the Junior section

Linked to Highgate School in the Senior section

3 Bishopswood Road, Highgate, London, N6 4PL

• Pupils: 300 girls and boys; all day • Ages: 7-11 • Fees: £13,860 pa
• Independent

Tel: 020 8340 9193
Fax: 020 8342 7273
Email: jsoffice@highgateschool.org.uk
Website: www.highgateschool.org.uk

Principal: Since 2002, Mr Mark James BA MA PGCE (forties), previously deputy head at King's College Junior School, Wimbledon and, before that, head of liberal studies in the sixth form at Dulwich College. He has overseen the change from a boys' prep to a fully co-ed junior school – 'It was a significant challenge to ensure that it wasn't just a boys' school with girls grafted on'. (Parents say, 'They've bent over backwards to accommodate the girls.') He is now in charge of admissions to all three Highgate schools and teaches philosophy to the sixth form. His wife is a junior school teacher; he has two daughters in the junior school.

Difficult to find parents with a word to say against him – 'He's such a fantastic fellow. Full of kindness and compassion'; 'He's very approachable, always happy to talk through any worries'. Indeed, during our visit, at 11+ decision time, his mobile phone rang several times – 'I've given my mobile number to five or six prospective parents who are in need of help. It's never wasting my time – it's so important to make people feel that you do understand'.

Entrance: Some 200 applicants for around 50 7+ places, to join those moving up from the pre-prep. They take 45 minute maths and English papers, in a child-friendly setting, with invigilators who will encourage them to keep going or have another try at a question they are finding tricky. About two thirds of them are invited back for interviews in groups of three or four, where they might find themselves with a task such as deciding what items to take with them on an adventure trip, while a teacher observes how they interact, focus and cooperate. Tutoring greatly discouraged – 'I tell parents that if I know a child has been tutored I will take that into account'.

Exit: Year 6s don't have to take the 11+ exam – 'We already have plenty of information on how they are doing' – and nearly all go through to the senior school. One or two may go off to boarding school, a single-sex, highly academic senior school or one that caters for learning difficulties. 'I will start having discussions in March of Year 5 with parents of children who are finding aspects of the core curriculum challenging and tell them about the support we can offer and the strategies they can use. If, by the end of the summer, the child is still struggling, I'll suggest looking at other possible schools and ring up the heads myself. If the parents still think we've got it wrong we'll say okay. But in the end, we don't want an unhappy child.'

Remarks: As the junior section of one of the few co-ed 3–18 independent schools in north London, it has become increasingly popular as a first choice school, and the academic bar has lifted accordingly. But equally important for many parents is its glorious position in a quiet side road near the top of Highgate, with the acres of playing fields, sports centre and art/DT centre it shares with the senior school nearby.

Years 7 and 8 have now moved to the senior school and the junior school has a much more homely feel. The buildings have been redecorated in bright primary shades with colourful displays in classrooms and corridors and beanbags in the library. The playground has a playhouse, climbing frame and slide as well as concrete mushrooms and marked-out games. 'The kids have become young again now they don't have to compete with 12 and 13 year olds,' said a parent. 'They play imaginative games, and they don't feel the pressure to become too organised too young.' The pre-prep nursery classroom leads out into its own playground and playtimes are staggered to ensure no-one feels threatened by large numbers of older children running about.

Learning moves at a brisk pace from the reception class onwards, but the high staff:pupil ratio, with two support staff in many of the pre-prep classes, means scope for faster and slower development. The learning support department gives group and individual help (at no extra cost) to those with needs at both ends of the spectrum. Has accepted statemented children, including those with autism – 'I feel strongly about our moral obligation to keep faith with the children we have admitted. We can cope with special needs at the milder end of the spectrum, as long as the children are bright. Our outstanding head of learning support has worked with me on making it a positive experience'.

'I think it's a brilliant school,' said a parent. 'My children are not particularly academic, but it's nurtured them both very well. The teachers are very kind and committed. My son has always been at the bottom of the class and has often been determined not to learn a thing but they have really encouraged and supported him. Even the teachers he didn't get on with did their best with him.'

Year 6 has its own house with specialist teachers and increasing responsibilities. Children apply to be prefects, mentors or reading buddies, showing round prospective parents, playing with younger children or helping them learn to read. 'They really rise to the challenge,' said a parent. 'They engage with little lost souls and turn their school experience around.'

Links with local state primary schools include teacher exchanges, a gifted and talented maths programme, a summer school organised jointly with UCS, joint concerts and getting together to design costumes for a carnival parade. Primary school children also join in the annual science week. Plenty of emphasis on fundraising for charities too. Says head, 'You realise that the children here are over-fortunate. In our four wheel drive culture, I like to put across to them the principle of optimism and thanks in the face of adversity'.

Highgate Pre-Preparatory School

Linked to Highgate Junior School in the Junior section
Linked to Highgate School in the Senior section

7 Bishopswood Road, London, N6 4PH

• Pupils: 130 girls and boys; all day • Ages: 3-7 • Fees: Nursery £6,555; Pre-Prep £13,095 pa • Independent

Tel: 020 8340 9196
Fax: 020 8340 3442
Email: ppadmin@highgateschool.org.uk
Website: www.highgateschool.org.uk

Principal: Mrs SE Kennedy BA (University of Surrey).

Entrance: Applications should be submitted between March and May in the year before entry – several for each of the expected 32 places offered in the nursery. Gives consideration to siblings but not priority – competitive entry. The practical assessment comprises a series of play-based tasks to assess learning readiness. The child, accompanied by one parent or carer, will spend approximately 20 minutes with a pre-prep teacher where they will be asked to carry out tasks presented in an informal, relaxed way, then meets another teacher and takes part in some further activities, plus an opportunity for free play.

Transfer to the Junior School is not automatic – children have to be considered suitable for Highgate's curriculum. The principal of the junior school confirms acceptance in the November prior to transfer, subject to good academic and behavioural track record at the pre-prep.

Exit: Year 2 children take the same 7+ exam as outside applicants, though they are not competing against them and – despite rumours to the contrary – virtually all move up to the junior school. 'Very occasionally we will say to parents that we don't feel a child should go through to the junior school, but it doesn't come as a shock to them. We flag up problems early and we work with parents to resolve them if we possibly can.'

Remarks: For further details see prep school and senior school.

Hill House International School

17 Hans Place, Knightsbridge, London, SW1X 0EP

• Pupils: 960; 60:40 boys:girls; all day • Ages: 4-13+ • Non-denom
• Fees: £9,000-£12,300 pa • Independent

Tel: 020 7584 1331
Fax: 020 7591 3938
Email: info@hillhouseschool.co.uk
Website: www.hillhouseschool.co.uk

Principals: Since 2002, Mr Richard Townend FLSM (sixties), educated at Westminster and the Royal College of Music, and his wife Mrs Janet Townend Cert Ed. Mr Townend is principal and headmaster and Mrs Townend is principal and director of admissions. He is quirky, humorous, clever and a passionate musician. She is terrifically busy. This is a huge school – just shy of 1,000 children spread over several sites in London, all of which are small town houses and short on space – no wonder little children marching in crocodile in their brown and mustard uniform through the streets of Chelsea is as much a part of the scenery of this chic and expensive area as the Venus statue in Sloane Square. They spread into the space that's available.

Like Prince Charles, an Old Boy of the school, who is still waiting, Mr Townend had a long wait before getting his hand on the job that was always going to be his. The school was founded by his late father, the legendary Lt Col H Stuart Townend, whose image, influence and inspiration persist. The Colonel, as he was known to everyone, was 93 when he died in 2002 and he ran the school as a tight ship right to the end. He died during half term and that's when Richard Townend took the reins. 'I had no idea how to run the place,' he confides, though this has to be a bit of an exaggeration as his wife had been the administrator under the Colonel. However, the impression one gets is that Mr Townend's heart is really in his music – wonderful instruments all over the place, a harpsichord and clavichord in his flat, a splendid 456 pipe wooden organ in the main school and fabulous pianos and harps scattered throughout, 'I couldn't get up in the morning if I didn't play each day,' he says.

They regard their job as being to inspire the children and Mr Townend's disdainful intolerance of petty inspectors who worry more about the site of sick bays and the use of Tipp-ex in the register than the teaching and the evident happiness of the children is unashamed. Some may criticise this as failing to keep up with the times, but his exasperation at how he was questioned about the identity of his wife without a photocopy of her passport on record does invite the question as to which is the wiser approach.

Mr Townend, taking a different tack to his controlling father, is already preparing his second son Edmund Townend, for the eventual running of the family business. Edmund Townend runs the upper school (Years 3 and 4) and has the official title 'Second Master'. His elder brother, William, is given the title of 'Property Bursar'. His father wryly observed that this effectively means he unblocks drains. He is also a full time opera singer. Each part of the school has its own head, known as Heads of House. Another key figure is Mr Donal Brennan, the Undermaster. Mr Brennan takes assemblies, is voluble and high profile. Some pupils apparently think he is the headmaster. Not unreasonably, some parental anxiety as to whether this constitutes an effective leadership.

Entrance: First come, first served at four but the school, famously, will fit people in if they possibly can and if they like them. At six a test in maths and English. Prospective parents are invited to turn up for a tour of the school on any morning without appointments. A pool of children who are regularly on hand to show visitors round. When we visited, the front hall was filled with eager children waiting to show round equally eager, though slightly overwhelmed, prospective parents. Places occur at all stages. This is an international school and a lot of movement.

Exit: A wide and diverse spread. Mr Townend has no truck with parents who don't carefully assess the right school for the child and will not spare them his forceful advice. Nearly all girls leave at 11 to a range of London day schools, including state schools – Marylebone, Grey Coats and Lady Margaret's. The independent schools are those you would expect – St Paul's, Godolphin & Latymer, the two Francis Hollands, Queen's Gate and Queen's College, More House and Latymer Upper. A tiny few stay on to 13 – often to board at Wycombe Abbey, Downe House, Benenden, Millfield or Bedales. Most boys leave at 13, about half to London day schools and the other to board. A few leave at 11, and a tiny few to the Catholic state schools – the Oratory and Cardinal Vaughan. Chief destinations are Latymer Upper, City of London and a few to St Paul's, Westminster, Dulwich College and Highgate. No special boarding favourites, but spread of top schools which includes Eton, Stowe, Charterhouse, Bedales, Winchester, Worth and Haileybury. Most pupils get their first choice of school and always a cluster of scholarships each year. No preparation for any boys to leave at seven or eight – this is not expected nor supported.

Remarks: A tour of Hill House is unlike a tour of almost any other school and you get a real sense of what the hordes of Hill House children do each day. Rather like a line from 'Annie', little children everywhere, scampering around the rabbit warren of buildings. Each of the five sites is cramped and used to the max. The famously conspicuous brown knickerbockers and mustard cable knit woollies were designed as a uniform so that the children didn't need to change for sport – no room for that kind of luxury. On our visit we spent much of the morning stromping around Chelsea, and jumping on and off a Hill House mini bus (the school owns a fleet). The two girls who showed us round were whipped off mid tour to rehearse their end of term play. Mr Townend scooped us up and we then interrupted a class music lesson in the organ room while Mr Townend gave an impromptu in depth tour of each organ pipe.

As soon as you enter the main hall at the senior school in Hans Place you are transported to a 19th century boarding prep school. A smell of faded grandeur – oak panels, Latin mottos, a plethora of gold leaf memorial boards, listing among other things the four principles of the school, past head choristers, various awards and scholarships as well as contributors to the life of the school. A sweeping staircase, piles of silverware and even an Olympic flag (the Colonel was also an outstanding athlete who competed in the 1930 Empire – now Commonwealth – Games and was in charge of housing for the 1948 London Olympics). Hill House was founded by the Colonel in 1951 and his aim from the first was to create a genuinely international school which nurtured each individual child's talents. Glion House in Switzerland, the Hill House chalet, used to be a major feature of the education here and though less so now, it is still used by the school for anything ranging from geography field trips, ski and hiking trips to trumpet tours. The signature oak panels in all the London sites is intended as a reflection of their Swiss residence. Photos plastered all over the walls – lots of smiling children as well as fabulous Swiss landscapes, some dating from the 1970s, vaguely reminiscent of a teenage bedroom.

The classes are unusually small, averaging 12 – just as well, as most rooms are too small for many more. At the top end of the school they get results – several scholarships, recently the King's scholarship to Eton and the top scholarship to Wellington, and almost all getting into their first choice school, partly, no doubt, as a result of Mr Townend and Mr Brennan's shrewd guidance as to which school is right for the child. Boys and girls taught separately from Year 5 (though they continue to do music and sport together); Latin from Years 6 to 8. French from the beginning – teachers are all French ('Preferably not Parisian – they have the wrong attitude,' comments Mr Townend). Girls can do Mandarin in Year 6. Lots of antipodean teachers – 'They are so good,' remarks Mr Townend – though not all parents agree.

Small classes also allow for individual help when needed (we are assured) but no SEN to speak of – nothing more than mild dyslexia catered for here and you would be advised to look elsewhere if this is going to be a problem. When we visited, a potential SENCo was being interviewed – signs that this will change. Rave reports from some parents, on the other hand, about how the gifted and talented fare here. 'My child has been set alight – his previous school just didn't recognise his talents,' commented one parent. The school motto is: 'A child is not a vessel to be filled but a fire to be kindled'.

This ethos permeates the music – a central feature of the curriculum, as you would expect from someone of Mr Townend's pedigree. No grades allowed – 'That's just for the mothers to boast about with each other in the playground,' retorts Mr Townend; instead the school owns more than 300 instruments, from tubas to harps, on loan for individual use: 'If a parent knew what a bassoon costs, they might not let their child play it,' explains Mr Townend. 32 choral scholarships available to existing school choristers which enable them to attend residential music courses, often abroad. Parents enthuse about the whole school assemblies, which burst with music, that take place on Wednesday mornings in St Columba's, the Scottish Church in Pont Street – the only place suitable and big enough to fit the whole school.

Proper freshly cooked food at each site served in a civilised way, all children eating at long tables which magically appear at lunch time in some of the more cramped premises. No catering companies and no contract cleaners – in recruiting all his staff, from the brilliant head of music teacher (a former Durham organ scholar) to the chefs, Mr Townend keeps his ears to the ground, and if he discovers someone good he will poach them. 1950s style menus – no choice or puddings, but well prepared, and very fresh produce bought from Covent Garden market each day.

Lots of exercise had by all – an hour of sport each day; Duke of York Square is their local playing field and where 'Field Day' happens at the end of each summer term, when the four houses compete vigorously. Hyde and Battersea Parks are also used, as well as various local pools, halls and gyms, providing for a good range of physical activity – 24 sports, we're told.

The art teacher is a current parent and canny about entering the children into various art competitions – outside as well as within school. Lots of prizes are won and during our tour we were asked to choose our favourite painting of a flower from a wall where about 40 different flowers were displayed – not an easy task. Finally plumping for one, we were told, 'That child will win the prize this week'.

When we visited, the school had recently achieved an extraordinary coup in securing the purchase of the former Welsh Church in Radnor Walk. One of the advantages of not having governors and no red tape, Mr Townend explained – they could pounce quickly. These graceful premises will be used as a theatre, a gym, an art gallery and ICT centre. They are hoping it will be in use by the time this goes to print. A beautiful lofty space, to Mr Townend's delight, it also came with the Church organ thrown in.

Parents here come from all over the world and from all walks of life – a few Chelsea football stars send their children, as well as a large number of embassy families. They have many more first time buyers than a lot of London preps, primarily because the fees are relatively low (an advantage of having such a large school). Alumni equally diverse, from Prince Charles to Lily Allen. If a family needs help with fees, arrangements can be made but, as with so much here, no formal structures in place. Once you sign up, the deal is that you leave the education and the running of the school entirely to the school. No PTA (Mr Townend is as scornful of the motives for joining one of these as he is about the motives for doing music grades). Quite the contrary – parents are positively discouraged from becoming involved with the everyday life of the school.

For all the apparent chaos, a huge amount of work is put into the children by a dedicated and loyal team of teachers, games staff, music teachers (all real musicians, points out Mr Townend, many of whom are old friends of his), caterers and cleaners, all of whom embrace the eccentric ethos of this family run school. It is a long day so that everything can be packed in. Upper school stay until 6pm Monday to Thursday and 5pm on a Friday. An overwhelming buzz of creativity and energy here, but if you are looking for calm, controlled order, with 'yes sir, no sir' boys and girls, this is definitely not the place for you.

Histon & Impington Infant School

New School Road, Histon, Cambridge, Cambridgeshire, CB24 9LL

• Pupils: 270; boys and girls • Ages: 4-7 • Non denominational • State

Tel: 01223 568 826
Fax: 01223 568 827
Email: office@histonimpington-inf.cambs.sch.uk
Website: www.histonimpington-inf.cambs.sch.uk

Head: Mrs Sharon Honig.

Entrance: For mainstream schooling – within catchment. For the Assessment Unit – LA referral. Not necessarily within the accepted catchment area – parents can and do express a preference.

Exit: Most to Histon and Impington Junior School

Remarks: Histon and Impington are popular, vibrant villages (not far from central Cambridge) which benefit from the through nature of schooling – Impington Village College is close by. Opened in 1912 and most recently revamped in 2005, the Infant School is in a quiet residential cul-de-sac (opposite is its feeder early years centre – an attractive, modern development). Austere exterior gives little indication of the welcoming, child-friendly interior. Modernisation has provided an ample hall, new classrooms and surprisingly spacious library with its own suite of computers. All classrooms have direct access to a playground – cheered up with several purpose-built structures including a jolly, two dimensional, palm tree. Large playing field for picnics and games is across the road.

The school is one of two in the Cambridge area with an in house assessment unit. This specialised unit (a standard sized classroom within the school) is run by a long serving SEN teacher and the deputy head. The unit (in place since the mid '80s) is seen as a 'half way house' – programmes are devised with a view to getting pupils back into mainstream education wherever possible. Up to 10 attend at any one time and most pupils' needs come within the autistic spectrum, with social skills and language development high on the agenda – a visiting speech and language therapist comes in two mornings a week. Integration is clearly important and absolutely no stigma attached to needs – 'Infants don't see differences like adults – they're very accepting,' commented the head, who went on to say, 'It shows all the children how different needs can be accommodated and teaches them to be tolerant'. Every child from the unit – always referred to simply as class 4 – joins the rest of the school for assembly, break and playtime and they're assigned to a mainstream class which is visited regularly (frequency of sessions depends on the individual).

Those in mainstream classes who have special educational needs (approx 24 per cent overall) are supported through timetabled withdrawal and/or designated classroom assistants. The sensible and sympathetic part time SENCo is based in a cosy room in the centre of the school. She also spends one afternoon a week in the assessment unit and liaises closely with the early years centre – all very helpful with the cross fertilisation of ideas and possible referrals to the unit.

School is lucky enough to have a designated room for timetabled music lessons and individual violin tuition is available (provided by the county). Those in Year 2 get to play recorders and a singing club, which includes children from the assessment unit, meets at lunchtime. Also on offer, for a nominal charge, are lessons in French (Years 1 and 2).

The catchment area doesn't include much social housing but the head feels a healthy mix of children. A strong community spirit and plenty of parental help within the school. An active school association raises money for 'icing on the cake' and runs several clubs, including one to encourage kids to love and value books – each week children can buy a stamp, which is saved until the end of term, when there's a book sale: a great idea.

A popular school where the assessment unit is recognised to be a big plus for pupils and teachers alike. A civilised and effective arrangement which respects the needs of all within the community.

HLC Highfield Prep School

Linked to Harrogate Ladies College in the Senior section

Clarence Drive, Harrogate, North Yorkshire, HG1 2QG

• Fees: Day £7,296-£8,325; Boarding £18,900 pa • Independent

Tel: 01423 537 060
Fax: 01423 568 893
Email: highfield@hlc.org.uk
Website: www.hlc.org.uk

Holmewood House School

Barrow Lane, Langton Green, Tunbridge Wells, Kent, TN3 0EB

• Pupils: 420 boys and girls; predominantly day with some weekly & flexi- boarding • Ages: 3-13. • Inter-denom • Fees: £10,245-£15,660; Nursery £5,340-£6,870 pa • Independent

Tel: 01892 860 006
Fax: 01892 863 970
Email: registrar@holmewood.kent.sch.uk
Website: www.holmewood.kent.sch.uk

Headmaster: Since 2010 Mr James Marjoribanks (pronounced Marchbanks), previously headmaster of Chesham Preparatory School, Buckinghamshire. A graduate of Sandle Manor, Cheltenham College, Rennes University (France) and Exeter University (French and education). Head of French at Forres Prep School, head of modern languages at Cothill House, deputy head of Terra Nova, then head of Chesham Prep School for the last nine years.

Entrance: The majority of children enter the school in the nursery, some into reception and some into Year 3, although children can join at any stage if places are available. Entry into the pre-prep is non selective, providing the school feels that the child will benefit from the education on offer at Holmewood following an informal assessment. Standardised tests in maths, reading and spelling for those entering in Year 3 and above plus an interview and report from current school. Very exceptionally, if a child has more learning support requirements than the school can realistically provide, it is agreed with parents that the child may thrive better in a different environment. Means tested scholarships for academic potential and bursaries up to 107% available for pupils from state schools. Bursaries offered once children are in the school for parents who find themselves in temporary financial difficulties.

Exit: Mainly to local schools, with a very good record of getting boys into Tonbridge, often with scholarships. Sevenoaks, Eastbourne, Mayfield (St Leonards Mayfield) and King's Canterbury very popular and occasionally pupils go further afield to, e.g., Eton and Harrow. Emphasis on 13+ Common Entrance and scholarship to senior independent schools, although a few leave at 11+ to the grammar schools – very few go to non selective schools.

Remarks: Top prep school, top fees and facilities to match. 'Premium fees with a premium service,' as one parent put it. Numbers are slightly down from their peak a couple of years ago when the school grew very quickly, but still large for a prep school. Founded in 1945 in a stunning setting just outside Tunbridge Wells, centred on a large country house surrounded by over 30 acres of grounds and playing fields. Most parents from the Tunbridge Wells area – lots of London commuters, medics, local professionals and first time buyers who have very high expectations of the school.

Good work ethic and strong academic ethos – children encouraged to aim high and follow the school motto 'Constantia Praesta', which means 'continually striving to succeed'. Bright children accelerated from Year 5 in special scholarship class. Enviable record in scholarships over the years, not just academic but sport, music, art and DT.

House system allows for plenty of friendly competition and a well developed tutor system from Year 6 ensures that children have someone specifically looking after their interests. Stars for good work, behaviour and courtesy added up for weekly award of the house cup. Children encouraged to follow a strong moral code laid down by the school. A firm line is taken with any bullying – the headmaster deals with it himself. Children from Year 6 do prep at school, and the day ends at 6pm (3–4.30pm for younger children). Weekly and flexi-boarding are options. Self service dining room with good choice of very healthy food – no spotted dick or steamed treacle pudding here. Children unanimous in their praise of the food.

Saturday school from Year 5 – headmaster keen to retain this despite pressure from some parents, as it gives more time for sport and activities during the week. A huge range of opportunities. Sport taken seriously and the school likes to win, but most children who wish to are able to play in a team. Boys' and girls' teams enjoy huge success entering national tournaments in all the major sports. The girls' gymnastics team competes nationally with regular success. Recent awards in national shooting competitions; school has its own 20 metre rifle range. New all weather pitch, 25 metre indoor pool, full time swimming coach. Tennis and squash particularly strong.

Extremely active and impressive music department; children regularly win music awards to their senior schools. Three full time music teachers and a team of peripatetic instrumental staff; 75 per cent of children learn at least one instrument. Playing music together is strongly encouraged and groups include five choirs, three orchestras, wind and jazz ensembles, a swing band and diverse chamber groups.

Art equally impressive with all children producing 'works of art'; new art room just built; pottery with kiln and wheel. DT similarly strong; children learn a progression of skills and by Year 7 make amazing pieces of furniture. Children prepared successfully for art and DT scholarships to senior schools. Drama taught throughout the school and as an afternoon activity. The school is a LAMDA centre and children perform on stage from an early age. A major production every year in the school's fully equipped Jubilee Theatre, as well as junior plays.

ICT very much a cross-curricular skill with specialist software available in all subjects. Two computer rooms each with 20 computers and interactive white boards in most classrooms. Head of ICT, network manager and technician all on hand to help children. Large well stocked computerised library with full time librarian. Strong classics department with both Latin and Greek offered – two very good classics teachers.

Impressive learning support department, recognised as one of the strengths of the school by the inspectors. Problems are spotted early and children are screened annually from Year 1 to Year 8. Two full time specialists and three part time learning support assistants provide individual and class based help. Those with mild physical or learning difficulties welcomed so long as they can benefit from the education on offer. Various learning support programmes in place, ensuring all children can access the curriculum based on their preferred learning style.

Nursery and pre-prep housed in their own purpose-built buildings with their own head and with access to the main school's facilities. Class music is on the curriculum from nursery and many children start an instrument in Year 1. Pre-prep orchestra (unusual for this age group) and choir. Several concerts and drama productions each year. Separate junior department for Years 3 and 4.

First phase of major new development project begun in summer 2010 – two-storey 12 classroom block to house junior department and subject classrooms, ready for occupation in September 2011.

Lots of trips in the holidays – annual French and skiing trips plus music and sports tours. Recent cricket tour to the West Indies; cricket and netball tour to South Africa in 2007. The school has a link with a school in Ghana and has raised money to build a library and stock it with books – five children and two members of staff came to stay at Holmewood for 10 days.

New parents made to feel welcome with coffee, drinks etc. Parental involvement encouraged. Comprehensive 'Annual Information' booklet given to all parents detailing school policies and procedures and what goes on on a day to day basis so parents left in no doubt about where they stand.

Famous old boys/girls include Tristan Gemmell aka Dr Adam Trueman in 'Casualty', who returned to visit his alma mater in 2010, much to the delight of all (particularly the girls!); actors Hugh Skinner and Dan Stevens (of 'Sense and Sensibility' fame); Shane MacGowan of 'The Pogues' and classical tenor Mark Dobell.

Lifelong friendships are made here. Happy, well rounded confident children. An academic, competitive school, yet still caring, nurturing and supportive, which caters to the needs of all its pupils; it may not suit everyone but is a wonderful place for the majority.

Holy Cross Preparatory School

George Road, Kingston Hill, Kingston-upon-Thames, Surrey, KT2 7NU

• Pupils: 265 girls, all day • Ages: 4-11 • RC, but other denominations and faiths welcome • Fees: £9,360 pa • Independent

Tel: 020 8942 0729
Fax: 020 8336 0764
Email: admissions@holycrossprep.co.uk
Website: www.holycrossprep.co.uk

Head: Since 1992, Mrs Kathleen Hayes BEd MA (fifties), studied education at St Mary's (University of London) and Roehampton. First lay head of the school (the Sisters of the Holy Cross own it), blonde, petite, very down to earth and well-liked by parents, many describing her as 'very caring'. 'Very switched on, with a relationship with the girls that I would call one of quiet respect on both sides,' says another. A dynamo, she considers herself to be 'an ideas person' and greatly fond of children. Retiring July 2011.

Entrance: Oversubscribed by about 2:1 for main intake at age four: 40 places available to fill two parallel classes – pupils come from about 12 local nursery schools. Apply to the school as early as you can and by 30th September in the year prior to entry. In effect, a test for admission – children attend an introductory session on a Saturday in November for what the head describes as 'a holistic look' at the child, focusing on attitude and concentration, social and personal skills. Spaces occur periodically in other years and are filled on an ad hoc basis. No scholarships.

Exit: Impressive record of success to the best local senior schools (with a handful of academic scholarship won every year): Surbiton High, Putney High, Lady Eleanor Holles , also Tiffin Girls' School (state grammar) and state girls' schools Holy Cross in New Malden and Coombe Girls' in Kingston. Occasionally to some of the swanky boarding schools such as Benenden and St Mary's, Ascot.

Remarks: Lovely inclusive school in smart location with friendly atmosphere and excellent academic results. School is housed in a wonderful Victorian house complete with carriage sweep and specimen trees, high up on the upmarket private residential Coombe Estate – in arguably the most prestigious road. Formerly the home of novelist John Galsworthy of 'Forsyte Saga' fame. Library is a wood panelled room – easy to imagine Galsworthy, sitting there, pen in hand, gazing out over the eight acres of well-maintained grounds. Modern block houses reception class and Years 1 and 2 – everything bright and cheery, with loads going on. Up-to-date IT.

Academically shines, with sky-high KS2 results across the board. Mild to moderate SEN catered for and an independent teacher provides assistance – extra fees are paid direct to her. Occasional girl has EAL and one member of staff is the nominated support teacher. Class sizes maximum 20.

Sister Ursula, the present deputy head, now the only sister on the staff, hugely popular. 'Every child should have a Sister Ursula – she is quite wonderful with the girls,' said one mother. The RE programme embraces all faiths – 45 per cent of the girls are RC, the remainder being mostly C of E, with a few Muslims and Hindus. Non-RC parents frequently talk to the girls about their faiths and practices – particularly appreciated by RC parents, one of whom commented that he 'would not feel nearly so comfortable with a conventional convent school'.

Terrific artwork on display everywhere, particularly involving textiles. Music important – choir and orchestra open to all, although naturally the orchestra tends to attract those with music exam grades. Unusual clubs include pottery, ecology and German (although not on syllabus).

All sports on site, except swimming. A feeling among parents that grounds could be used for more sport – only one PE teacher for the whole school. Sports teams are selected on merit and girls can be in more than one team – those who don't make the team are encouraged to join the relevant club.

Girls are polite and courteous, individually greeting visitors in the corridors and chorusing 'Good morning, Mrs T,' unprompted in class. Top two parallel classes write letters of welcome to the prospective little newcomers into the reception class and become their mentors for the following year. Girls we spoke to assert that bullying does not exist and that relationships between staff and pupils are tremendous. One said, 'It's a very enthusiastic school which does lots of exciting things. We laugh with the teachers but we also respect them.' Parents heap praise on the pastoral care at the school, said to be very concerned for each and every girl's moral welfare.

Holy Trinity and Saint Silas CofE Primary School

Hartland Road, London, NW1 8DE

• Pupils: 210 • Ages: 4-11 • Church of England • State

Tel: 020 7267 0771
Fax: 020 7916 5881
Email: admin@holytrinitynw1.camden.sch.uk
Website: www.holytrinitynw1.camden.sch.uk

Head: Since 2001, Ms Annie Williams (fifties) – grew up in Wales ('the land of preachers and teachers') and did a BA in English and drama at Bangor before proceeding to Roehampton to train as a teacher. 'Teaching is like acting, but to a very critical audience; you have to be constantly improving your performance.' Taught in North Africa and France, before returning to London as a supply teacher. Then to ChristChurch C of E Primary School, where she was twice acting head. 'I was never interested in management. I wanted to do what I was best at – teaching.' When she took over at Holy Trinity the school was far from the buzzing place it is today. 'It needed quite a lot of remodelling; staff weren't seeing the clearer picture.' Nowadays the picture is crystalline and Ms William and her deputy Mr Brian Welsh make a perfectly balanced management team: 'I'm hysterical and he's calm. Children see it as a partnership'. As do parents – 'They are very good foils to each other,' said one.

If such a thing as a typical head of an inner-city primary, Ms Williams is certainly not it – glamorous and groomed, her ready-for-business trouser suit is accessorised with diamante and her delivery is more grande dame than school marm. In her spare time, she enjoys theatre, opera and reading. Married to a photographer, she has one son at university.

Entrance: After the customary priority for looked-after children, the primary admissions criterion is church attendance, either at The Most Holy Trinity Church across the road or at St Silas the Martyr in Kentish Town. About a third come via this route. When Ms Williams became head, very much bottom of the parental-choice agenda, but the intake has altered – 'Because of our Ofsted, we now get more professional parents'. Not too many, she hopes – 'We have a good social mix and I want to keep it that way'. At the moment, remains a class and ethnic melting pot, with the largest minority being Bangladeshi and Somali families.

Exit: Mainly to the local comprehensives – Haverstock, William Ellis, Parliament Hill, St Marylebone and Camden School for Girls – but Ms Williams has also developed a relationship with the Hall, one of north London's leading prep schools, and some Year 6 boys have gone there with bursaries before proceeding to leading London independent day schools.

Remarks: This, in the words of Ofsted, is 'an exceptional school' and, without a doubt, its exceptional quality stems from the passion and focus of its 'talented and hardworking' head. Ms Williams is a woman who has edited the word 'compromise' from her vocabulary. Over the past nine years, she has built up a team of energetic, often newly-qualified teachers ('We grow our own'). 'I'm very snobbish about teachers – they have to have been to a good university and to have travelled. It gives them a cultural understanding.' The teaching staff is unusually well qualified, with three MAs, two law degrees and three teachers who speak fluent French (so French is taught convincingly from reception), as well as a number of graduate teaching assistants. Ms William's management philosophy includes encouraging staff to take a year-long sabbatical every three years to do voluntary work mentoring and coaching – 'It highlights their own skills'.

Housed in a typical Victorian schoolhouse, a meander from tourist-packed Camden Lock. Inside its pristine, soothing interior, however, you'd never guess where you were – fresh flowers, polished parquet and a big red school bell are all from another era.

Despite the fact that the majority of pupils arrive at Holy Trinity with well below average attainment, the school is at the pinnacle of the league tables, with results in English in the top one per cent nationally. 'Level 4 is ridiculously low,' says Ms Williams. 'Even our special needs children reach that.' Literacy is taught for two hours a day, primarily through poetry and prose. 'We're strong on story-telling,' says the head. On the day we visited, a group of eight years olds listened spellbound as a young male teacher first played the flute, then, in true 'Jackanory' style, announced: 'And now I'm going to tell you a story'.

All the arts are fundamental to the curriculum. Drama 'has a very big focus' – every year, mounts a whole-school Shakespeare play including every pupil and member of staff and has now helped found a borough-wide

Shakespeare festival with five neighbouring primaries. Hardly surprising then that, according to Ofsted: 'Pupils' empathy with the works of Shakespeare is quite remarkable'.

Despite limited square footage, has its own art department and pupils' work is hung boldly throughout the building. Painting even spills out into the large urban playground, where one inner-city wall has been reborn as a rural, summer scene (with a 3D vegetable plot to extend the experience). Music is equally central and Ms Williams insisted all staff learn a musical instrument to perform alongside pupils: 'Some of our pupils are at grade 5 and it does them good to be better at something than we are'. Trips are very much part of the education – visits are free of charge – to the theatre, opera, ballet and museums are planned on a regular basis

Though about 75 per cent of pupils are not Anglicans, the Christian message is strong, with a thoroughly involved parish priest, regular church attendance and class mass held half termly. Grace is said before lunch. Lunch itself is entirely healthy ('we had the smoothie debate,' says the head – 'one person's smoothie is another's fizzy pop') and mealtimes, too, are considered a development opportunity. Music is played and, on Fridays, tablecloths laid. A firm emphasis on good manners. The 'golden rules' dictate: 'don't talk with your mouth full; learn to use your knife and fork correctly'.

Rules elsewhere are equally clear cut. Attentive good behaviour is the norm, but for those who stray, the first offence means displacement to another class; further disruption means an encounter with Ms Williams – 'I use my actress hat and go very over the top'. Badly behaved parents can also find themselves hauled in front of the head.

Standards may be firmly upheld, but the school is also compassionate and warm. Ms Williams keeps an ever open door. On the day of our visit, one child came into recount the details of her special day out, quickly followed by an entire class offering cakes they'd just baked. With mums and dads, the same policy applies: 'You can never let anything fester, otherwise it just goes round the playground'.

Takes a pro-active approach to its parents, offering jewellery classes as an incentive to engage with catch-up maths, and parents respond with energetic fundraising. 'We are very grateful for the wonderful education our children receive,' said one. Ms Williams herself is no ingénue when it comes to fundraising and has won considerable support from charities like John Lyons and the Mercer's Company, who have underwritten school trips and paid for 30 laptops.

'Superb' is Ofsted's summary of the Holy Trinity and St Silas experience and parents agree: 'Children want to come to school. They think it's fun'.

Honeywell Infant School

Honeywell Road, Battersea, London, SW11 6EF

• Pupils: 335 boys and girls • Ages: 3-7 • Non-denom • State

Tel: 02072 286 811
Fax: 02077 389 101
Email: office@honeywell.wandsworth.sch.uk
Website: www.honeywellinfant.wandsworth.sch.uk

Head: Since 2004, Ms Jane Neal BEd NPQH (forties), previously deputy head. Married with two children who attend the school. Her interests include creative arts and early years learning.

Entrance: At three to nursery but this does not guarantee a place in the school at four. Criteria are broadly siblings first, then proximity to the school, but a category for special medical or social applications and children in LEA care. A place in the junior school reserved for each child attending the infant school.

Exit: All to junior school.

Remarks: Infants and juniors share a site, but each has their own accommodation and head teacher specialising in their particular age group. Class sizes 30 max. School Achievement Award for improving SATs results, also Wandsworth quality award for organisation and management development (self-review and evaluation). New library, ICT suite, enlarged and improved playgrounds and organic environmental gardens. SEN specialist support runs for groups and individuals. Discipline is good with a sensible set of rules, but the lack of uniform can make the children look a bit scruffy. A happy, positive and hands-on atmosphere prevails. A super state primary, much sought after.

Honeywell Junior School

Honeywell Road, Battersea, London, SW11 6EF

• Pupils: 360 boys and girls; all day • Ages: 7-11 • Non-denom • State

Tel: 02072 235 185
Fax: 02077 389 101
Email: office@honeywell.wandsworth.sch.uk
Website: www.honeywelljuniorschool.com

Head: Since 1999, Mr Duncan Roberts BEd NPQH (fifties), previously deputy head and married to a teacher. Well liked by staff, pupils and parents, straightforward and approachable with a great sense of fair play. A keen sportsman, he also runs the chess club and swimming team.

Entrance: 3+ nursery, although this does not guarantee a place in the infant school at 4+. Wandsworth criteria special requirements – siblings, then proximity to the school. The infant and junior schools are separate schools; however everyone in the infant school who wishes to move to the junior school is allocated a place. A few places at 7+, then casual vacancies as they occur.

Exit: At 11+, 50 per cent to the state sector including Sutton Grammar, Wilson's, Wallington County, Greycoats, Graveney, Tiffin, Lady Margaret's; other half to independents – Dulwich College, Streatham and Clapham High, Emanuel, Alleyn's, Trinity, Whitgift and JAGs.

Remarks: Long reputation for being one of the most popular primaries in south London. Infants and juniors share a site, each with their own accommodation and head teachers. Class sizes are 30 max, staff:pupil ratio 1:14.

School Achievement Award for excellent SATs results and some 'outstandings' from Ofsted. Healthy schools award, also Wandsworth quality award for organisation and management development, self review and evaluation. In the junior school, Mr Roberts raises funds to improve the school's facilities. They are now able to boast an on-site all-weather pitch, solar panels to reduce the school's carbon footprint, a large ICT suite which, with the help of parents, he decorated, 'so there is more money for equipment and teachers – clever man,' say parents, and a new library opened by author Anthony Horowitz. Beautiful new wooded garden area creating an inspiring learning and play environment.

Great variety of sports, matches with other schools, even lacrosse and cross country, regular winners of the Kwik Cricket and Trinity Fields football tournaments, Gold mark for sports. Specialist teachers provide good music, choirs, orchestras, string and wind sections, individual tuition on the trumpet, cello, violin or flute also available. Annual sell out drama and music show produced at The Rose Theatre, Kingston; they also recently received their Gold Arts mark. Many choices of lunchtime or after-school clubs including drama workshops, yoga and French.

Clientele are a reasonable social mix; 'open door' policy; parents encouraged to support the school through PTFA, with fundraising, as reading or library partners or helping in classrooms. Computers upgraded to enable the children to work with ICT across the curriculum.

SEN specialist support runs for groups and individuals, laptops available for pupils. Discipline is good with a sensible set of rules. No uniform after consultation with entire school community. Happy, positive and hands-on atmosphere prevails in both schools. If you are looking for a good, all-round education and strong leadership, it's definitely here. Pupils could be encouraged to do some litter picking in the front playground, otherwise a super state primary.

Hordle Walhampton School

Walhampton, Lymington, Hampshire, SO41 5ZG

• Pupils: 335 (more boys than girls), 195 in the main school (30 full or flexi boarders), 140 in pre-prep • Ages: 7-13; pre-prep 2-7 • C of E
• Fees: Day £6,690-£13,395; Boarding + £3,885 pa • Independent

Tel: 01590 672 013
Fax: 01590 678 498
Email: registrar@hordlewalhampton.co.uk
Website: www.hordlewalhampton.co.uk

Headmaster: Since 1998, Mr Henry Phillips BA (fifties), educated at Harrow, worked as a stockbroker before doing an Open University degree in English. Housemaster at Caldicott and assistant head and director of studies at Summer Fields before becoming head of Hordle House, which subsequently amalgamated with Walhampton (see below). 'He's larger than life,' said a parent. 'He says what he thinks and doesn't tolerate fools,' said another. Full of ideas for the school and no shortage of energy: 'I ran a marathon when I was 19 stone!' he told us, in passing. Chairman of parochial church council and a governor at Clayesmore School. Voice strangely reminiscent of Ken Clarke. Wife, Jackie, is in charge of boarding, teaches and looks after guests like this editor. Three children who all attended Hordle Walhampton: one grown, one at Bristol University, one at Clayesmore.

Entrance: Non-selective. First-come-first-served entry at two into the pre-prep, with preference for siblings. Nearly everyone goes through to the prep at seven; a few more join at that point. A fair amount of to-ing and fro-ing – a few leave the pre-prep for state primaries, some come in from abroad for a term or two to improve their English, others move into or out of the area. Always worth trying for a place; those coming in higher up are assessed. On a sound financial footing because 'I am very mean,' says the head. 'The governors instruct me to be. We own the 100 acre site outright – no borrowing, no overdraft and a solid rainy day fund.' One or two Services discounts available plus endowment fund for truly needy.

Exit: At 13 Clayesmore tops the list, followed by Canford and Bryanston and then a range of schools in the south-west. A few leave at 11, for, e.g., King Edward VI in Southampton. Occasionally one to a selective state school, e.g. the Bournemouth grammars. Not a hothouse – happy for children to aim for Clayesmore or the local Ballard School, rather than Winchester (although one or two head for the latter plus the likes of Radley or Marlborough most years).

Remarks: From the front it is a splendid Queen Anne/Victorian building with panelled, galleried entrance hall and original cornicing. Tucked round the back are infinite pancake flat lawns, three lakes, lovely views and bracing sea breezes. Somewhat isolated in feel and in reality – although the picturesque town of Lymington, with its Waitrose and two train stations, is reassuringly nearby. Slightly over the top grandeur at odds with what is essentially a cosy, jolly prep school alive with activity and purpose.

Parents are local or have some tie to the area – sailing perhaps, or a holiday home. Many lived in London but have relocated – partly or wholly – to the New Forest. Grandparents in the area is another draw – enough so that the school has introduced an annual grandparents' lunch. A few come for a term or a year from France and Spain – head would like more – and a clutch from the Isle of Wight as boarders, or even daily. Minibuses bring children from the ferry terminus in Lymington, and from all over.

Proud of their flexi-boarding, with the emphasis on the 'flexi'. Almost all arrangements are negotiable. Take Saturday school – it's optional. The 60–70 per cent of pupils who take part in the wide range of offerings – e.g. sport, art, computing, fencing, archery, 'high jump clinic' – show up in jeans and T-shirts. Full boarding numbers have dwindled since Walhampton School (the home of the current school) merged with Hordle House in 1997 – 'It made us look like less of a serious boarding school,' says the head.

Since September 2009 the boarding setup has been revamped and consolidated in the two floors of the main building. All extremely cheery and well-run, parents rave about the pastoral care, and the school would love to encourage more pupils to dip a toe into boarding – much encouragement to do so in the final two years. Strongly Christian ethos. Assembly takes place in the chapel every morning and a service on Friday evenings.

Year 3s get a gentle start – kept a bit separate from the big kids, have classes of 16 max, and can go home earlier (before games) if they wish. No mollycoddling when it comes to setting, though: setted for maths from Year 3, for English from Year 4 and streamed from Year 6. IT provision, mildly criticised in 2008 inspection report, has made a great leap forward. Really lovely library – encapsulates the school's values in a nutshell. Children have one taught library lesson a week, are advised on their reading and have their progress monitored. Brill librarian has painstakingly tagged some books as only appropriate for Year 6 and older, and a few of the more mature works for Year 8 eyes only – why don't more schools do this? Scholars work to a special book list.

Excellent SEN department used by 18 per cent of children (individual and shared teaching at extra charge, plus extra help in class). Good at spotting problems. Will cater for mild Asperger's, ADD, specific learning difficulties (dyslexia unit is registered with CReSTeD). Sometimes pupils are removed from Latin for learning support sessions, but the head is not keen – 'It's very sad; often I'd rather see them miss French'. Now working to improve the gifted and talented side of things.

Games important. Outdoor sport every afternoon run by members of staff. The standard team games are played, plus fencing, shooting and riding. Astroturf for hockey, tennis etc. Outdoor heated 15m swimming pool, small but challenging adventure playground – not for the timid. Revamped and charming, but relatively low key, 'equestrian centre'. Pupils may bring own pony if they are willing to look after it themselves and allow others to ride it. Riding instruction from the school's two specialists can be incorporated into the school day. Awfully nice sports hall, built using the proceeds of the merger – mothers muscle in on it for their Pilates classes.

Lovely performing arts centre with tiered seating – used to be the gym. Four drama productions a year and LAMDA exams are offered. General knowledge quizzes alive and well. Music department continues to be 'up and coming', with steel drum samba band, two choirs and two school pop groups. Years 3–5 learn recorder. Art the jewel in the crown – pottery, textiles, one hour a week of formal art lessons and door open to the keen in evenings, clubs and breaks. Head of art dresses up as a famous artist for a performance each year. Student council elected twice a year and meets several times a term.

Children good all-rounders who can hold their own in conversations with adults. Expressed some gripes about too many outside areas being out of bounds (despite its robust spirit, this is not a 'climb trees and camp in the woods' school). Oddly enough, the head of sport voiced the same opinion, wishing the pupils 'could go onto the games field at break – there's too much health and safety nowadays!' All told, a happy, hearty, outdoorsy place, crammed with the best of prep school joys. January 2009 snow may have flummoxed the London buses and forced most boarding schools to send their charges packing, but Hordle Walhampton carried on serenely – 'We had an interhouse snowball match – one of the teachers measured the throws with his speed gun'. Expeditions week – the penultimate week of the summer term – is prized by all. Head remembers the days when the expeditions involved hitching horses up to a gypsy caravan.

Pre-prep takes children from the day they turn two. Uses main school's art and IT facilities and shares the dining room. Tiny classes of 12 in reception through Year 2. 'Forest school' for getting in touch with the out-of-doors one morning a week. The prize of sitting at the urbane, table-clothed 'café table' goes to the children who have 'eaten most nicely' each week. Lots of optional after school enrichment, e.g. ball skills, speech and drama, 'yoga teddies', ballet and tap, French. A comprehensive start to school life, but looks a bit tired: a blast of fresh air would work wonders. Children in the pre-prep can flexi-board.

Hornsby House School

Hearnville Road, London, SW12 8RS

• Pupils: 355 girls and boys, 50/50; all day • Ages: 4-11 • Christian-based Non-denominational • Fees: £11,130-£11,940 pa • Independent

Tel: 020 8673 7573
Fax: 020 8673 6722
Email: school@hornsby-house.co.uk
Website: www.hornsby-house.co.uk

Headmaster: Since 2006, Mr Jon Gray BA (thirties). Young, quietly confident, delighted to have become a head after only ten years in teaching. Previous experience in boarding and day prep schools together with two years here as deputy head. Is enjoying the further challenge of planning the future development of the school and has lots of ambition and a breadth of ideas. Came with the intention of staying seven years at Hornsby House – is now in his sixth year, loves the school and plans to be here for at least another seven, and probably longer.

Married in 2007 – was thrilled when the school choir put in a surprise appearance at his wedding. A keen cricketer and mountain walker, really likes sport (has taught it previously) and taking children on expeditions. Teaches history throughout the school, bringing lots of humour and fun into his classes. Regularly reads stories to the reception classes. Seems extremely popular, with an easy-going relationship with the children.

Mixed opinions from parents, however – some say he is less approachable than his predecessor, others he is much more visible and easier to talk to. Definitely the latter now, says school. He certainly knows all the children well and is on gate duty every morning to greet his pupils as they come into school. He says that he has increased the focus on academic progress through the school years – each child's development is now carefully monitored. He believes strongly in the balance between work and play and has banned all weekend homework prior to Year 6. He also believes 'that we should be preparing children for the business environment they'll be working in in the future, not purely for academic success'; with this in mind he has introduced a school council for Year 3 up, encouraging teamwork and showing them how to run elections.

Entrance: First come first served at 4+ with priority for siblings. After that an interview with the head and a morning at the school for assessment. Children with behavioural or learning difficulties will also need reports from their previous schools and will be assessed before being admitted to the school. If it is felt that they could be too disruptive, they will probably not get a place.

Exit: Nearly all at 11, mainly to south London day schools – Dulwich, Alleyn's, JAGS, Streatham and Clapham High, Emanuel, with a smattering elsewhere, including boarding.

Remarks: Started by Dr Bevé Hornsby in 1988 with 20 children in a church hall; after moving to this site five years later, has grown significantly – now three classes per year with an average of 18 pupils in each. The Edwardian school buildings have been well adapted for today's use, alongside two purpose-built modern additions, a couple of Portakabins and excellent playground space. Reception has its own building with good sized classrooms and a central play area. The library was disappointing, housed in a Portakabin, but apparently that is likely to change soon – this is not a headmaster who sits back complacently.

Solid grounding in all the core subjects. Young, enthusiastic teachers with an average age of 36; also plenty of classroom assistants comprising gap year students, post university would-be teachers and several older mothers to add balance and experience. Classes are mixed ability with setting in maths (and maybe English soon) for the older children when classrooms become subject-based.

All said classrooms light and bright and soon to be air-conditioned, 'Overheating is not conducive to learning – I don't want to see lots of sleepy children!' Interactive white-boards in every class, including reception, and an interesting ICT pilot project going on at the moment in four classrooms, three Year 3 and one Year 6: each child sits, with four others, at a pentagonal table in front of a work station that drops down when it is not needed. This could be the interactive teaching of the future.

The SENCo works three days a week and has seven 1:1 learning support teachers with her. One state-provided helper for a statemented child. Children who need support are monitored and their parents kept informed; the school itself is a caring, nurturing place. The head feels that most children benefit from remaining in the classroom as much as possible. Extra one-to-one English and maths tuition is provided, when necessary, by part time specialists, and children who need it are given extra EAL lessons.

A very sporty school – teams are fielded at all levels in all the popular sports. Trinity Fields nearby is well used and matches played against all the similar schools locally. Lots of specialist coaching from sports consultants. Tournament victories include the Broomwood Netball and Battersea Football Cups. Boys definitely do not need to leave before 11 – they flourish here. Excellent music – the chamber choir performs regularly and about a third of the children take individual lessons in a variety of instruments. These take place in normal classroom hours, which does not appeal to all parents. Lots of visits to museums, galleries etc and from Year 3 up a field trip every summer, or a 'journey', as it is known.

Mainly local families – the majority live within a mile. As one parent said, 'We are all very down to earth, normal parents who love the school.' Rows of bicycles and scooters line the playgrounds, indicating proximity and the ability to walk to school. Very much a caring for others attitude and seemingly no real discipline problems. Communication with parents excellent and all children are carefully monitored. The school is a charitable trust, run by a board of governors. Bursaries are available in case of genuine need, with individual cases being considered by the head on their particular merits.

All in all, a friendly, welcoming school with a disciplined but informal atmosphere. Happy, relaxed children, all seemingly having a good time. Pity about the Portakabins, but they are necessitated by growth. Some parents feel that the playgrounds can become a bit overcrowded – fine for the sporty children but not so good for those with less confidence. However the school is pretty careful to keep age groups apart with separate playtimes and the children don't seem to mind. A really great local school.

Horris Hill School

Newtown, Newbury, Berkshire, RG20 9DJ

- Pupils: around 120 boys; 115 boarders (compulsory in last two years)
- Ages: 8-13 • C of E • Fees: Boarding £20,640; Day £14,580 pa
- Independent

Tel: 01635 40594
Fax: 01635 39586
Email: enquiries@horrishill.com
Website: www.horrishill.com

Headmaster: Since 2006, Mr Jon Phillips BEd (fifties) educated at Canford, then St Luke's, Exeter, before teaching PE and geography at various prep schools in the UK and Africa. Keen on instilling sportsmanship in boys and loves to watch matches. Spent 15 years as head of The Old Malthouse followed by sabbatical in Kenya, then short spell at Ashdown House before appointed to HH job. Has had a hard act to follow but, with wife, Sally (who looks after youngest boarders 'superbly') has quickly won hearts and minds. Spent first year 'listening to parents' rather than making waves. Inspires confidence and exudes experience – 'Boys know he's seen it all before' – and parents relax, knowing that he'll keep HH on right track. 'He's done brilliantly,' effused one mum, who said the head is 'easy to talk to' and that his wife 'reassures parents' and 'rings up if she's at all concerned about anything'. Mr Phillips' calm and understated manner wins 'enormous respect' from boys 'who like talking to him,' say parents. Two grown-up children went through Bryanston, then university. Couple enjoy travel and theatre, given half a chance.

Entrance: By registration and informal one-on-one test. Takes in around 25 boys each year. School's reputation filters out no hopers; nearby Cheam scoops up local, co-ed day market. Informal interview, NFER non-verbal assessment plus English/maths test for all. Minor fee concessions for up to four brainboxes annually. Around a quarter of boys live in area; further quarters from London, rest of UK and abroad (half expats, half foreign – who fit in seamlessly).

Exit: More to Winchester than anywhere else (some families choose HH because of this historic link). Steady flow to Eton, Radley and then down the list of usual suspects. Former head forged link with Shrewsbury; local parents with daughters favour Bradfield but most parents opt for single sex. Number of scholarships won bobs up and down but enviable record overall; head not keen on entering boys who, he knows, stand little chance. Ten awards in 2007, including two each to Winchester and Radley.

Remarks: Famous country prep school founded in 1888 by ex-master at Winchester to train up boys for admission there. Terrific. Lack of spin refreshing and appealing. Has risen phoenix-like to confound those who believed this breed of prep was near extinction. 'London parents are beginning to realise that early boarding in a caring, busy environment makes sense after all,' said one parent, who admitted to having thought 'long and hard' before sending her son to HH aged eight. 'Small boys like to be organised and at HH they know where they are,' said another, who had had a bad flexi-boarding experience elsewhere. Still a relaxed atmosphere but combs are back under new head, who expects a modicum of tidiness. Unfussy uniform and boys get to choose their own tie, with some hilarious results amongst youngest. Well mannered, down-to-earth boys who look you in the eye and enthuse about all aspects of school life. Former pupils include Max Woosnam (oftimes referred to as 'Britain's greatest sportsman'), author Richard Adams and pop idol turned actor Will Young.

Wonderful driveway leads through woods and grounds and eventually to headmaster's house, where prospective parents will continue to be met even when new main entrance has been completed. 70 acres of grounds provide archaeological (iron age fort) and natural (home to rare spotted orchid) interest for visiting cognoscenti. Youngest boys play in 'junior wood' whilst older ones roam far and wide. Lots of older boys keep bikes at school and use them anywhere on site within reason. Saturday night camping (under effective but non squelchy staff supervision) hugely popular with boys we met. Convenient layout, nothing grandiose, but music school particularly impressive. Swish classroom block with rooms named after schools to which boys move on (Eton, Radley etc), adequate chapel and sports hall. New library (we particularly liked the fold-away computers) and ICT suite have made a huge difference. Central building a square of narrow corridors with labyrinth of junior dormitories above.

Idiosyncratic form system. No year groups – boys are moved up when they are ready. On average, boys spend two terms in each form, but this can be lengthened to three terms or shortened to one according to ability. This 'ladder' system ends in the final year when most 12 year olds go into one of the two CE forms. Scholarship candidates spend the final year in a separate top form. Class sizes average 11–12 with a maximum of 15.

'Teaching fantastic,' say parents, who like the way that 'each boy gets picked up and made to feel special'. Some younger teachers and plenty of old hands with eye for high academic standards. Junior staff get boys humming through maths and English: we liked how lessons (40 minutes long) changed pace while holding boys' interest throughout. Boys taught to think quickly and laterally – lots of mental gymnastics. Super atmosphere in English lesson we watched involving a verbal 'shoot-out' between boys. Maths area alive with wall charts and displays. Boys we saw loved their lesson on probability and seemed to have grasped the concepts well. HH 'gets boys enthused about subjects,' said one parent, and we felt this held true for lessons we watched. French taught throughout; also classics (including some Greek for scholars) in upper years. Senior boys spend a term on each science pre-CE. Labs a little dated, as is DT area, but ICT boasts spanking new suite plus overhead projectors and smart boards wherever needed elsewhere. All boys have double lesson of art plus lots of scope for working in free time. Studio (created from former pre-prep area) includes ceramics with Applemacs for design work.

Experienced part-time SENCo currently supports 13 boys on one-to-one basis with needs ranging from SpLD and dyscalculia through to improving revision technique. All boys screened for auditory problems by staff from nearby Mary Hare School (for the deaf). Half hour supervised prep for juniors increases to an hour at top end of school.

Very sporty school – 'My son is always in the A team at HH,' said one parent, who thought that he 'would probably have missed out in a larger setup'. Recent cricket tour to South Africa hugely successful. Lots of sports practice on new Astroturf as well as games on ample set of pitches. Tennis very popular (with two thirds receiving coaching and first team unbeaten last season). Outdoor, heated swimming pool gets lots of use in summer. Athletics and cross-country; nine hole golf course a favourite and lots of squash. Sports hall-cum-theatre (not ideal) with fold-away stage.

Boys love drama and each section of school gets to stage one performance a year – not a flashy setup but boys and staff achieve good results. Major music production biennially in super, galleried music school which also hosts school assemblies. Great acoustically and aesthetically – 'the icing on the cake,' said one parent. 85 per cent play at least one instrument up to grade 5/6 plus concert band, brass group, various ensembles and two choirs. Generally gets a major music scholarship each year. Choir trips to Normandy where boys go down a storm. School prizes for sports and academics but also less mainstream accomplishments, e.g. general knowledge, current affairs and gardening. A few unusual rooms tucked away include the 'old gym', crammed with table tennis, snooker and drum kits; the model railway room and the modelling room (Airfix and Warhammer model-building a big deal here).

Lovely dormitories for youngest boys (tucked up a narrow staircase) above the Phillips: 'We mollycoddle them,' says head, who reads to them on Fridays. Boys quickly weaned into fending for themselves in central dormitories, then moved into half-way house (still near school) before oldest get to be in further flung, more independent houses. Married staff act as houseparents with plenty of backup from teachers and gappers. Sick bay with resident sister and local doctor on call. Boys get to choose chums and whether they are in single or bunk beds (not many of the latter). Parents like the fact that boys can come home any weekend if they like (once games commitments have been honoured) and that they bring them back on a Sunday evening to a happy environment (the busy Sunday programme having lured half the school to remain). Huge plasma screen in new TV room adjacent to library enables boys to watch rationed amounts of sport on Sky TV, for which they successfully lobbied.

Competitive house system for internal competitions mixes everyone up into different 'colours'. Grub (sweets) handed out three times a week after lunch. No mobile phones or money used here by boys – what a relief! Food is wholesome and varied and boys rate it. Home-made biscuits available three times a day. Head boy and monitors handle responsibilities sensitively – 'No-one throws their weight around,' say others. Rare incidents of bullying taken seriously. Christian ethos generally implicit, though oldest boys take turns leading the Sunday evening services.

Great to know that schools like this are still alive and well. A reassuring antidote to the 'must have', 'me first' society, whose negative influences can be left at the school gates. Boys have a chance to discover their talents here in a happy, inspiring environment.

Hotham Primary School

Charlwood Road, Putney, London, SW15 1PN

• Pupils: 245; 50/50 boys and girls; all day • Ages: 3-11 • Non-denom • State

Tel: 02087 886 468
Fax: 02087 898 732
Email: info@hotham.wandsworth.sch.uk
Website: www.hotham.wandsworth.sch.uk

Head: Since January 1998, Miss Pam Young BA. Graduated from Otago University in New Zealand with a degree in early years education. Came to the UK in 1987 and was previously the deputy head of a school in Camden. Still teaches, taking Year 6 one day a week and offering other classes and booster lessons where needed. Serious and quiet on first acquaintance, but underestimate her at your peril. She is fiercely proud of her school, of its pupils, teachers and parents and will brook no criticism. She knows the name of every child, enjoys the support of her governors, her 'great critical friends', and relishes the cultural diversity of the intake. Running marathons as a hobby might give a clue to her tenacity.

Entrance: 60 children were admitted to the reception class in 2008 and currently full in most year groups. Waiting list for places, which is an indication that someone is doing something right, considering four state primary schools in very close proximity, one of which is virtually next door. Admissions policy is administered by Wandsworth local authority so out of Miss Young's hands. Most start in the nursery at 3 years.

Exit: To a range of 15 different secondary schools. Maybe two or three a year go into the private sector but the majority are predominantly state school bound. Ashcroft (formerly ADT) is popular, but some also to Shene School, Burntwood, St Cecilia's.

Remarks: At first glance this looks like a typical Victorian primary school. It even has the original Boys' and Girls' entrances. The classrooms have high, light, draughty windows and are accessed by corridors and stairwells decorated with those funereal tiles so beloved of that era. The whole cries out for a lick of paint and some TLC. Outside the obligatory grey, hard playground surrounded by a high wall.

However what lies within tells a very different story. Take a closer look at that playground, for example – well tended, well planted flower beds all around the edge, each one the responsibility of one year group. Look further still and you come across a hidden, secret garden containing bird boxes, trees and plants to represent the four seasons, wood piles to provide homes for dozens of creepy crawlies and a quite amazing human sundial which looks very like a mini Stonehenge. All this surrounds a small classroom usually inhabited by the man affectionately known as 'Mr Hotham'. Retired, he then returned part time to give extra help to those in need and seems to embody the spirit of the school.

The classes are large (26–30 on average) but all supported by TAs. Twenty per cent of the pupils need EAL help with full support on offer. Special needs pupils include those on the autistic spectrum, some dyslexic, some have cerebral palsy, some with language delay, some have ADHD. All are supported within the classroom as the head can see 'no point in doing anything else'. She sees the school as a 'place where we all learn from one another' and her greatest wish is to see her pupils become 'independent learners, to use their initiative and solve problems by using their fantastic, inquisitive minds'.

The school hopes to become bilingual in the near future and discussions are in place with the local authority. Four French speakers already on the staff and Years 5 and 6 go on school trips to France. Link with a school in Paris.

Music is very strong with choirs performing in Wandsworth events. All Year 4s learn the clarinet. Swimming is taken seriously in KS2 when all children are taught in four ability groups over a six month period. Teams in football, cricket, netball, cross country, swimming. After school clubs in gym, yoga, photography, art, French. Very active PTA – recently completely refurbished the library. Polite, happy children in smart red, white and blue uniforms. Excellent handwriting throughout (would put many a private school to shame). As one parent remarked, 'Despite the presence of two excellent faith schools in the vicinity, Hotham gives a brilliant start to its kids. Its multicultural mix seems to work well.' In 2006 they won the Green School of the Year Bike-It award and two of the staff are finalists in the annual Teaching Awards.

This is a solid primary school offering a solid education to its local community from the nursery ('the best in the borough', according to one parent) to the final year where discussion groups in the class are animated and passionate. One book which should not be judged by its cover.

Howell's School Junior School, Llandaff

Linked to Howell's School, Llandaff, GDST in the Senior section

Cardiff Road, Llandaff, Cardiff, South Glamorgan, CF5 2YD

• Pupils: 300 girls; all day • Ages: 4-11 • Non-denom • Fees: Nursery £5,982; Junior School £7,113 pa • Independent

Tel: 0290 562 019
Fax: 02920 578 879
Email: mail@how.gdst.net

Head of Junior School: Since September 2006, Mrs Judith Ashill BEd (thirties). Did her degree at Swansea University. Previously head of Redland High School Junior School.

Entrance: Applicants for nursery assessed through play. For reception and Years 1 and 2 assessment is by play, informal activities and unstructured tasks. Candidates for Years 3–6 sit papers in mathematics, English and non-verbal reasoning.

Remarks: Happy and lively atmosphere. Housed in a modern building on the campus but within its own space. Imaginative design of classrooms and specialist areas gives a light and airy feel to the school. Well-designed play areas. Classes we visited had photos of all the pupils up, a nice touch which helps the girls bond as a class. Art and music are strong. Outdoor learning is used in addition to other teaching methods. The girls are energetic and enthusiastic – a palpable feeling that here learning is fun. Nursery and music department housed in Cumberland Lodge, which was Roald Dahl's childhood home.

Hurlingham School

122 Putney Bridge Road, Putney, London, SW15 2NQ

• Pupils: 310 boys and girls • Ages: 4-11 • Non-denom • Fees: £10,716-£11,346 pa • Independent

Tel: 020 8874 7186
Fax: 020 8875 0372
Email: admissions@hurlinghamschool.co.uk
Website: www.hurlinghamschool.co.uk

Headmaster: Since 2010, Mr Jonathan Brough BEd NPQH, previously head of City of London Girls' Prep, before that deputy head at Bute House Preparatory in Hammersmith and head of English in two boys'preps. Now teaches Latin to every child in Years 5 and 6, leads three whole-school assemblies per week (often accompanied by firm favourite puppet, Mischief) and is always to be seen joining in something or other around the school, regularly getting sidetracked by philosophical discussions with reception children. Places enormous emphasis on happiness being central to everything that goes on and strongly believes that all individuals make greatly valued contributions to school life: 'Children at Hurlingham are never just taught, but are educated in the broadest sense of the word, as each day brings fresh opportunities, challenges, discoveries and achievements. As a school, we aim to capitalise on them all and not to waste a single one.'

Claims the next few years of the school's development are 'evolution not revolution', but has already had a significant impact on several aspects of provision, especially the rewards system – very popular surprise postcards home and Excellence Book – and reinvigorated programme for the gifted and talented in all age groups. Outside school, is married to a leading international lawyer and lists interests including reading and writing fiction, multimedia authoring and travel.

Entrance: Non-selective. Actively promotes walking to school so preference given to those living within 1.2 km radius. Under 60 per cent of parents drive to school. Sibling priority. Otherwise it is first come first served. The school is co-educational from ages 4 to 11. A three form intake with 15 to 20 in each class.

Exit: Girls and boys are prepared for entrance to co-educational and single-sex London day schools and boarding schools at 11+.

Remarks: Such an energy and drive about the place that it's almost palpable. The building is truly fantastic (you quite envy the pupils). A wonderful Astroturfed outside play area with every kind of equipment you could wish for, including a horizontal rock climbing wall. Separated from it is a fabulous nature corner complete with herb garden, fruit trees, vegetables, bird table and pond. Head of sports likes children to have structure even at playtime and involves parents in all things sportive.

Similar degree of enthusiasm seen in all the classrooms. The walls are myriads of brightly coloured, beautifully presented pupils' work, each piece carefully named and titled. 'Every child's work is exhibited – no selection.' The school's ethos is 'positive encouragement': house points – 'We now have a house system, which the children think is the best thing ever' – for all. Little ones have 'Stripey' the tiger, who goes home each night with the best behaved or hardest working or most polite.

Music, singing and percussion are noisily enjoyed in class and assemblies. Individual music rooms available too. Ballet teacher is busy three mornings a week in a dedicated mirrored dance and drama studio. Warm and friendly furnishings impart a calm and peaceful aura to the early years department. All new pupils are profiled and the resulting record presented to parents. Children are setted for maths only. The first three years have full time teaching assistants and a full time learning support co-ordinator, who does lots of support work with many of the children and is available for any pupil identified as having minor learning difficulties.

This is a school where children are celebrated, learning is encouraged, successes are rewarded. And, on top of all that, everyone looks as though they are having fun doing it. Hurlingham is looking good. Things can only get better.

Hurstpierpoint College Preparatory School

Linked to Hurstpierpoint College in the Senior section

Hurstpierpoint, Hassocks, BN6 9JS

• Pupils: 245 in the prep; 80 in pre-prep; roughly 2:1 boys:girls in prep school • Ages: 4-13 • Christian • Fees: Boarding £14,640-£15,990; Day £11,070-£12,735 pa • Independent

Tel: 01273 834 975
Fax: 01273 833 957
Email: hurstprep@hppc.co.uk
Website: www.hppc.co.uk

Head: Mrs Heather Beeby BH MA

Entrance: Non-selective at pre-prep. Prep uses standardised reasoning tests.

Exit: 95 per cent of children go on to the senior school.

Remarks: The three-storey prep and the pre-prep are all comfortably on the same site as the senior school, so a cohesive, whole school community. This also allows full use of the senior school's facilities – rare to have a prep and pre-prep with onsite swimming pool, Astro etc. Very full activities programme includes trad games plus boules, karate and ultimate frisbee. The buildings themselves are uninspiring, built on quad lines.

Prep has a cheery atmosphere much supported by humorous and imaginative art and artefacts lining the corridors – great plaster and chicken wire crisp packets, work inspired by 'The Simpsons' and other cartoons, almost life-size plaster of Paris tennis players. The whole is light, bright and relaxed. A good library and the children were bright-eyed and busy. Some boarding in prep. We witnessed boys and girls playing together in the playground – not a common sight at this age.

Pre-prep also fun and lively with, again, good art work on display. Good sporting programme includes yoga. Lots of quiet spaces, good safe, outside play areas. After-school care sessions in pre-prep from 3.15 to 4.30 pm and to 5.45pm. Whole school emphasises centrality of Christian ethos. Worth the car journey for this degree of space, security, inspiration and quiet.

Hutchesons' Grammar Primary School

Linked to Hutchesons' Grammar School in the Senior section

44 Kingarth Street, Glasgow, G42 7RN

• Pupils: 530 boys and girls; all day • Ages: 4-11 • Non-denom
• Fees: £7,427-£8,527 pa • Independent

Tel: 0141 423 2933
Fax: 0141 424 0251
Email: admissions@hutchesons.org
Website: www.hutchesons.org

Depute Rector: Since 2010, Mrs Christine Haughney, BA in psychology from Southampton University, PGCE and MEd (with distinction) at Strathclyde University. Previous leadership positions in Renfrewshire and East Renfrewshire primary schools and latterly head at Calderwood Lodge Primary School. She aims to make Hutchesons the school that parents are glad they could send their children to and children love to belong to. Her outside interests include reading, cheering from the rugby touchline and skiing. Married with two children, both educated at Hutchesons.

Entrance: One intake a year (but see secondary school), all children assessed, 100/120 apply for 60 places.

Exit: Most children go on to Hutcheson's secondary school, having learnt how to work (with a vengeance).

Remarks: An enormous primary school, in the most fabulous original Victorian academy, think green and cream tiles, think fabulous carved oak assembly hall, think huge sunlit classrooms (three of the old ones now converted into two), spacious, full of light. All screened for dyslexia et al on arrival, though the incidence is rapidly declining with the re-introduction of learning to read by phonics.

Hymers College Junior School

Linked to Hymers College in the Senior section

Hymers Avenue, Hull, HU3 1LW

• Pupils: 230 girls and boys; all day • Ages: 8-10 • Non-denom
• Fees: £7,236-£7,641 pa • Independent

Tel: 01482 441 211
Fax: 01482 472 854
Email: enquiries@hymers.org
Website: www.hymerscollege.co.uk

Remarks: See senior school for details.

Ibstock Place School, Preparatory and Kindergarten

Linked to Ibstock Place School in the Senior section

Clarence Lane, Roehampton, London, SW15 5PY

• Pupils: mixed • Ages: 3-11 • Inter-denom • Fees: £11,520-£11,925 pa • Independent

Tel: 020 8876 9991
Fax: 020 8878 4897
Email: registrar@ibstockplaceschool.co.uk
Website: www.ibstockplaceschool.co.uk

Headmistress: Mrs Anna Sylvester-Johnson BA PGCE (fifties) heads a team of three all in their early fifties: the head of Priestman House, Miss Maggie Smith (nursery to Year 1); Miss Diana Wynter(head of Macleod House – Years 2 to 6); and for nearly 20 years Miss Sharon Worthington (director of primary studies).

Entrance: Places in the nursery and lower kindergarten (reception) are offered according to date of registration, with priority being given to siblings. Assessments are held for occasional places in Years 1–6. For places in Years 1 and 2, one-to-one assessments lasting about 30 minutes. Applicants for Years 3–6 sit papers in English and mathematics, with those applying for Years 5 and 6 also taking a reasoning paper. All candidates are interviewed by the relevant head of department.

Remarks: Register at birth – long waiting lists: siblings given priority for entry into nursery class of 24. One more class introduced at age 4 and then two all the way up to age 11 when year size doubles. Parents of pupils who are deemed unsuited after later assessments will be helped with alternatives, i.e. they get a letter when child aged 7+ to warn them they will need to look elsewhere at Year 6. 20 primary pupils need SEN help, mostly for dyslexia or dyspraxia.

Kindergarten's curriculum and approach is based on the principles of the 18th-century German educationalist Friedrich Froebel, whose original concern was to train female teachers and promote the teaching of young children through experience and not just theory. Infant and prep buildings are purpose built and so fit the ethos and pupils of Ibstock Place – 'Wide corridors avoid trouble'. Set away from the senior school on the other side of the orchard with separate entrance on quiet road. Parents love the after-school clubs and holiday art club for primary pupils. Priestman and Macleod House are nearest to the hard courts and swimming pool and use them regularly.

ICT introduced early and integrated successfully, beginning with a PC screen projected on to a whiteboard in reception class. Pupils benefit from specialist teachers for music, dance, art and French. Two male teachers in primary. School is busy with interesting subjects – mind-mapping legends, debates about rural communities. Involvement with the outside world starts with bird spotting in the nursery (including a parent-donated webcam) for the Big Garden Bird Count. Parents help with cookery for kindergarten children. Everyone caterpillars up to the conservatory in the old building for lunch. In Macleod House pupils begin homework and are setted in French and maths and prepared for 11-plus. Transitions of pupils from each of part of the school are celebrated, which provides all pupils with a sense of belonging to the IPS community.

Inglefield House

Linked to Haberdashers' Agincourt School in the Junior section
Linked to Haberdashers' Monmouth School For Girls in the Senior section

Hereford Road, Monmouth, Monmouthshire, NP25 5XT

• Pupils: 110 girls • Ages: 7-11 • Fees: Day £9,150; Boarding £19,203 pa • Independent

Tel: 01600 711 100
Fax: 01600 711 233
Email: admissions@hmsg.co.uk
Website: www.habs-monmouth.org

Headmistress: Mrs Sue Riley BA geography and American Studies from University of Wales (Swansea), PGCE geography and PE (Bristol University). Taught at Sevenoaks and The Banda Preparatory Schools, previously housemistress and head of upper school at The Dragon School. Married to Mark – formerly Royal Signals, worked at The Dragon as reprographics manager and health and safety officer. One daughter at Bristol University. Interests include walking, golf, theatre, travel, wildlife, anything to do with Africa. Aims to create a happy, nurturing environment where girls can achieve on many different levels, in and outside the classroom, working as part of a team and also having an opportunity to shine, where girls and staff feel valued and success is congratulated.

Entrance: Exams at seven, eight, nine and 10.

Exit: Most to senior school after sitting 11+ exam.

Remarks: Lovely, intimate junior school at the heart of main school site. Physical education, science and music lessons taught by specialists, most of rest taught by class tutor. Lots of music, singing and dancing. Separate play area. Newly built mini-amphitheatre provides unusual outdoor performance area. Self-contained facilities, such as art area and well-stocked library, plus ready access to extensive facilities of main school, offer the best of both worlds.

International School of Aberdeen, Preschool and Elementary

Linked to International School Of Aberdeen in the Senior section

Pitfodels House, North Deeside Road, Pitfodels, Cults, Aberdeen, AB13 0AB

• Pupils: 165 boys and girls; 30 in pre-school • Ages: Elementary (5-11); pre-school (3-4) • Fees: £16,205 + £2,000 Capital Fee • Independent

Tel: 01224 730 300
Fax: 01224 735 648
Email: admin@isa.aberdeen.sch.uk
Website: www.isa.aberdeen.sch.uk

Remarks: For details see senior school.

International School of London

Linked to International School Of London in the Senior section

139 Gunnersbury Avenue, London, W3 8LG

• Pupils: 120 juniors, boys and girls • Ages: 3-11 • Non-denom • Fees: £14,250-£15,750 pa • Independent

Tel: 020 8992 5823
Fax: 020 8993 7012
Email: mail@ISLondon.com
Website: www.ISLondon.com

Head: Headmaster Huw Davies, MA (Oxon) PGCE from University College, Worcester. Has extensive experience as a former deputy head, IB Diploma coordinator and higher education advisor, as well as being a governor of a sixth form college in West London. Has taught history and theory of knowledge at Diploma level and is a member of Llafur – the Welsh History Society.

Ipswich High Junior School

Linked to Ipswich High School in the Senior section

Woolverstone, Ipswich, Suffolk, IP9 1AZ

• Pupils: 190 girls; all day • Ages: 3-11 • Non-denom • Fees: £6,978 pa • Independent

Tel: 01473 780 201
Fax: 01473 780 985
Email: admissions@ihs.gdst.net
Website: www.ipswichhighschool.co.uk

Head of Juniors: Since 2009, Mrs Eileen Fisher BEd, formerly deputy principal (Head of Juniors and Early Years) at St Margaret's School in Edinburgh.

Entrance: At 3, assessed in informal play session. Later, at seven, eight, nine, via written assessments in basic skills. Occasional spaces at other ages.

Remarks: One/two-storey school, bright, modern if not the most attractive building on site. Two parallel classes from Year 3, 24 to a class. Well-equipped, good extra-curricular activities especially music, some homework. A lovely safe setting for early school years – space, trees and resident sheep.

Ipswich Preparatory School

Linked to Ipswich School in the Senior section

3 Ivry Street, Ipswich, Suffolk, IP1 3QW

• Pupils: 300 boys and girls, all day • Ages: 3-11 • Fees: £7,971-£8,775 pa • Independent

Tel: 01473 281 302
Fax: 01473 400 068
Email: prepregistrar@ipswich.suffolk.sch.uk
Website: www.ipswich.suffolk.sch.uk

Head: Since 2009, Mrs Amanda Childs MA DipEd BA (QTS). Very experienced in day schools – previously deputy head of Alleyn's Junior School, London and Leeds Grammar School, following a teaching career as far afield as Thailand. Married to Martin (journalist) with two young daughters in the school. Says job is all consuming but occasionally finds time for skiing and scuba diving and would love to get back on the golf course. Time does not often allow for these passions but singing and music are frequent endeavours.

Enthusiastically believes that the Prep School is a place to work hard, try everything and have fun. Pastoral care is at the top of the school agenda, with the belief that if children are happy, with the right opportunities, everything else can fall into place.

Entrance: Into most year groups from nursery (age three) upwards. Entry to prep (age seven upwards) via tests in January in maths, English and reading plus confidential report from current head.

Exit: Most transfer to the senior school but all children are required to sit the entrance test.

Remarks: Since 2006 the prep school (Years 3–6) has been housed in brand-new premises on the same site as the purpose-built nursery to Year 2 accommodation, which was built in 1996. The prep school is next door to the senior school and shares many facilities, such as playing fields, Astroturf, indoor pool, sports hall and theatre. Unusual in that the prep has been going since 1883 – not just a modern addition to pull 'em in early. A well-organised, welcoming school.

James Allen's Preparatory School (JAPS)

Linked to James Allen's Girls School (JAGS) in the Senior section

East Dulwich Grove, London, SE22 8TE

• Pupils: 110 boys and girls in pre-prep; 190 girls in middle school, all day • Ages: 4-7 pre-prep, 7-11 middle school • C of E Foundation, but all are welcome • Fees: £11,472 pa • Independent

Tel: 02086 930 374
Fax: 02086 938 031
Email: Japsadmissions@jags.org.uk
Website: www.jags.org.uk/japs

Headteacher: Since 2007, Miss Finola Stack BA PGCE Mont Dip (forties). Co-founded Finton House School in 1987 and moved to become head of Cameron House School, London SW3 in 1994. ISI inspector, IAPS District committee member. Tall, slender, mother of three sons; very pleasant, gently spoken, straightforward and calm.

Head of the pre-prep, JAPPS, is Mrs Sue Saunders Cert Ed MA, a cordial and kindly Yorkshire lady with 30 years' teaching experience and two daughters. Taught in the maintained sector, then at Dulwich College, then deputy of DUCKS before coming here. Both women impressed us with their blend of intellect and warmth. 'The head is simply great,' said one parent, of Miss Stack. Another described Mrs Saunders as 'warm, calm, very approachable'.

Entrance: Very high number of feeder primaries and nurseries, mostly in Dulwich and neighbouring areas. Entry at 4+ is selective, a process which one mother described as 'horribly stressful. I'm not looking forward to it with my second daughter one bit'. Parents aside, though, the children usually enjoy it, because the tests and interview are expertly disguised as play. At this age the staff look for 'adventurousness of spirit', among other attributes, rather than any kind of attainment, and Mrs Saunders emphasized that the children are not all readers on entrance. No sibling policy, not even for boys. At 7+ things become proportionately more formal: maths, English and reasoning papers, followed by interview. Standards are very high – over-subscribed as it is, it can afford to be unbending in who it admits; girls who aren't strong academically don't stand a chance. Miss Stack comments, 'This may be a parental perception, but there is very good support for girls of all abilities throughout the school.' However one parent praised the JAPS selection process as 'more personal and welcoming than some others round here'.

Exit: At 11, virtually all girls go on to JAGS, the senior school, often with scholarships and other awards; a few decide to try co-ed and effortlessly make the switch to Alleyn's. Girls at 7 all go on to JAPS Middle School.

Remarks: JAPPS is a truly lovely pre-prep, housed in a handsome Edwardian house in the heart of Dulwich Village. In recent years, local independent boys' schools have increased their own pre-prep provision, and the result is that fewer and fewer boys came to JAPPS. The governors therefore decided in summer 2009 to return JAGS pre-prep to providing for girls only. As we passed through the porch, we heard some splendid reading aloud from a confident, strong-voiced little girl of four, which very much set the tone for our visit. The classrooms (18 children in each, 36 children per year group) were full of agreeable buzz and liveliness, but not at all noisy. Children worked with focus under the guidance of young, elegantly dressed teachers – or so they seemed to us – and all seemed kind, knowledgeable and authoritative. Nor do appearances deceive – all the parents we spoke to were extremely happy. 'My daughter's blossomed,' 'She's really happy, thoroughly enjoys her day,' 'She's made really lovely friends,' 'Her teacher's very sensitive to her needs,' 'It's a kind environment, not at all pushy,' 'The teachers are fantastic,' are just a few of the comments we garnered, and the children we met were bright, articulate and adorable.

Teaching focuses on building independence and the ability to solve problems. French programme is impressive, with French lessons but also PE and singing taught entirely in French; science, music, debating, football (yes, indeed) all strong. Excellent academic and art work displayed on the walls. Mrs Saunders keeps a watchful eye on the children's developing characters too: weekly 'gold-leaf' assemblies reward acts of individual thoughtfulness as well as achievement and a 'kindness cup' is awarded every half term.

After browsing around JAPPS's peaceful garden and its inviting little library – Miss Stack adds, 'and well-stocked' – entering JAPS is like suddenly encoutering a charmed world. This is a school that positively glitters with success. Clad in their stylish, practical, and, according to one mother, expensive – where isn't it? – uniform (navy culottes, red polo shirts), the girls here radiate a particularly whizzy kind of confidence. And no wonder – already one of a picked band when they arrive, everything they get from then on is simply the best. French? Immersion programme taught by native speakers. Library? Modern, wonderfully equipped. Sports facilities? Amazing – the girls compete at national level. Music provision? Astounding – not a single instrument they can't learn. DT? The envy of all the local boys' preps, and the girls do electronics too. Clubs and societies? Huge variety. Organization? 'Runs on oiled castors,' said one parent. Staff? The best money can buy. Academic attainment? 'Exceptional', according to the ISI in its recent report. Some of the work we saw was approaching GCSE level in its scope and sophistication. Good SEN support for the few girls who need it, but 'special needs' tends to mean something different here, i.e. what are we going to do about Maria, who has done every sum in the maths course already and she's only in Year 3? Such girls are, of course, nurtured, and no doubt their presence helps to retain those top quality staff.

Last year 'The Times' ranked JAPS the fifth best prep school in the country – which may have disappointed, because the year before it was fourth. The girls are competitive, as Miss Stack has no problems admitting. And indeed, the gales of laughter and eager putting up of hands and very genuine expressions of friendship that we saw were interspersed with wrinkled noses whenever a peer got a question wrong, or so it seemed to us – 'It's great if you're in the top 50 per cent there, and not so great if you're not'. Head says, 'It's just as stimulating whatever your abilities.' If you were offered a place off the waiting list, it can be a struggle,' commented one parent candidly. The pastoral care was rated outstanding in the school's 2008 ISI inspection, but it may not be the gentlest school in the world for all that. How could it be otherwise, given its intake and aspirations? But if your daughter can cope with the pace here, she's made.

Jordanhill School Primary

Linked to Jordanhill School in the Senior section

45 Chamberlain Rd, Glasgow, G13 1SP

• Pupils: 460 girls and boys; all day • Ages: 4.5-11 • State

Tel: 0141 576 2500
Fax: 0141 576 2555
Email: info@jordanhill.glasgow.sch.uk
Website: www.jordanhill.glasgow.sch.uk

Remarks: For details, see Jordanhill School.

The Junior King's School

Milner Court, Sturry, Canterbury, Kent, CT2 0AY

• Pupils: 335 (pre-prep 75); boarders; 25/35 girls/boys • Ages: 3-13 • C of E, broadly Christian • Fees: Boarding £19,830; Day £13,140-£14,610; Pre-Prep £6,075-£8,610 pa • Independent

Tel: 01227 714 000
Fax: 01227 713 171
Email: registrar@junior-kings.co.uk
Website: www.junior-kings.co.uk

Headmaster: Since 2000, Mr Peter Wells BEd (fifties). Educated at Eltham College and Exeter University where he studied art and design. Before coming to Junior King's he was headmaster of Liverpool College Prep and St Hugh's School in Lincolnshire, and before that a boarding housemaster at Dulwich College. His wife, Vivienne, is the registrar and also teaches some RS to Year 5. Very involved in the life of the school. Three adult children. Seen as quiet but doesn't miss a trick; businesslike and professional but approachable. Teaches some art.

Entrance: Looks for children with above average ability. Entry at the pre-prep level is by informal class visits; from 7+ tests in English, maths and non-verbal reasoning. New boarders are invited to spend a night at the school to try it out.

Exit: 85 per cent of children go on to King's Canterbury, others to, e.g., Eton, Harrow, St Swithun's (music and academic scholarships), Millfield (sports scholarship) and Fettes (all rounder scholarship). Half a dozen leave at 11+ to go to the grammar schools – some preparation for this during Activities but the school prefers to keep children until age 13 where possible. Plenty of scholarships to King's Canterbury – art, music, academic and sport (as one would expect).

Remarks: Founded in 1879, spent the first 50 years in the Canterbury Cathedral Precincts and moved to its current home at Milner Court, set in 80 acres of grounds two miles from Canterbury, in 1929. Part of the King's School Foundation, much of what it does is driven by the senior school. Huge amounts of money have obviously been spent over the last 10 years and the facilities are superb. The two boarding houses have recently been refurbished and are currently full. The whole school is networked, interactive whiteboards all over the place, computers in every classroom and laptops trolleyed in when required. Computers around the school have constantly updated school news.

Average class size 15, maximum 18. Children setted in maths from the age of nine and streaming from the age of 11, but children are not put into order. Scholarship children are taught separately for the last two years. French is taught from the age of four, Spanish and Latin from the age of nine and a few pupils learn Greek in the last two years. Emphasis on modern languages. About 30 children in the school with some sort of SEN – mostly for mild dyslexia. Not the school for someone who struggles.

Sport taken seriously – they like to win and the most able children are always picked for the top teams, although most children do get the chance to play in a match. Boys play rugby, football and cricket; girls netball, hockey and rounders: no danger of equal opportunities here. All year cricket coaching from an ex-Kent professional. Wonderful sports hall and floodlit all-weather pitch. Lots of other sporting opportunities from rowing on Westbere Lakes to creative dance and trampolining. Fencing popular. Lots of inter-house competitions for everything – the four houses are all named after parrots. Recently U11 Rugby National Champions

Music is strong – lots of concerts, orchestras, etc. Recent concerts include one with the Dublin Schools Group at St John's Smith Square, a charity concert in Canterbury Cathedral with the Uralsk Symphony Orchestra and an invitation to perform with the Eastbourne Symphony Orchestra and choirs of Eastbourne College in Chichester Cathedral. About two thirds of pupils play one or more musical instruments and all children are taught music in the classroom. Boarders' music practice is timetabled and monitored. Strong choral tradition – the choir leads singing in the carol service held in the Cathedral each year and also occasional evensong services.

Purpose-built art studios and workshop, very high standard of art, often taught by practising artists and designers. Art activities arranged most afternoons and keen artists and potential scholars are encouraged and nurtured with master classes. Wonderful summer exhibition when outside artists exhibit in the gallery alongside pupils. New director of drama started September 2008. Four or five plays a year from different age groups, staged in the Tithe Barn Theatre. Leavers put on a big production post Common Entrance, following a week of outdoor activities. Lots of clubs and activities and children kept very busy – including gardening, orchestra, technology and drama workshops and many more. Special midweek activities for boarders.

Broadly Christian environment with daily prayers in the local church; boarders have their own Sunday services which are conducted by the school chaplain. Children operate within a code of behaviour which has been devised by the pupils themselves. Excellent choice of food in purpose-built, canteen-style dining room – staff eat with children where possible. Saturday school until 3.30pm from the age of nine.

Parents generally well-educated professionals who have high expectations for their children – lots of first-time buyers and some local bling. Most children are fairly local but some from London and overseas.

The school expects very high standards from its children and most achieve this – those who are self-confident and motivated do very well here, but those who need more nurturing sometimes struggle a bit. Famous Old Boys include Freddie Kemp and Orlando Bloom.

The Pre-prep department is housed in a Kentish oast-house in the grounds and was set up in 1986 – bright and airy with its own facilities including a hall and library. They also have the use of the playing fields, Tithe Barn and dining hall. Children can enter from the age of three into the nursery class. Specialist early years teachers. Regular French conversation and activities from age four. Now an accredited Forest School, which means it has an 'innovative educational approach to outdoor learning', and pupils from further up the school are able to participate in 'Forest Park' activities.

Junior Lavant House

Linked to Lavant House in the Senior section

West Lavant, Chichester, West Sussex, PO18 9AB

• Pupils: mixed; girls 3-11, boys 3-7 • Ages: 3-11; boarding from 8+ • C of E • Fees: Day £6,210-£10,410; Boarding £17,085 pa • Independent

Tel: 01243 527 211
Fax: 01243 530 490
Email: office@lavanthouse.org.uk
Website: www.lavanthouse.org.uk

Head: Since 2008, Mrs Zoe Woolley BA (Hons) (Birmingham), very young, energetic, smiley and vibrant, with her own young children in the school. Previously taught here for four years.

Remarks: Head has made it her objective to know the pupils well and be thoroughly versed in the individual needs of each child. When she took over she changed the teaching style from a set national curriculum blanket approach to a focus on each individual, which was doable because of the small classes – 'We cannot expect every child to reach the same standard and so we keep with each child's pace'. She wants the children to feel not just happy but also excited to be there. Children are bright eyed and bushy tailed.

Small foundation stage for three to five year olds and every child leaves with some basic literacy and numeracy skills. High ratio of staff to pupils – the teacher hears every child read every day. Years 1 and 2 are grouped together for lessons. Years 3 and 4 and Years 5 and 6 are also taught together for humanities, PE and music, but the core subjects taught separately, with the senior teachers teaching them science.

Years 3 to 6 have personal tutors. The junior school is invited to the senior school's drama and debates but otherwise considered independent from the senior school, as 'it's important the younger ones feel safe and can be big fish in the pond,' says head.

This is an 'out and about' school, so that you see the wellies and bright mackintoshes lining the classrooms beckoning the next trip. The school is close to the beach, close to the great warrior ships at Portsmouth, goes orienteering and hiking on the Downs, into the Roman town and theatre of Chichester and is great for camping in the extensive grounds. The head says that you might see two girls splashing around in their wellies after a falling out, which is worth more than hours of indoor circle time – 'They're soon the best of friends'. The junior head shares the philosophy of the senior head that the children here can enjoy an extended childhood – in the playground we saw much rôle-play and fun.

Kelly College Preparatory School

Hazeldon, Parkwood Road, Tavistock, Devon, PL19 0JS

• Pupils: 100 boys, 100 girls; 15 board, rest day • Ages: 2.5-11 • Anglican foundation but all faiths and denominations welcome
• Fees: £5,880-£15,300 pa • Independent

Tel: 01822 612 919
Fax: 01822 612 919
Email: admin@kellycollegeprep.com
Website: www.kellycollegeprep.com

Head: Since September 2010, Mr Matthew Foale, previously deputy head, married with three children.

Remarks: Lively head. High academic standards; predominantly feeding Kelly. Broad range of extracurricular clubs from chess to riding. Good sporting facilities, boys playing rugby, hockey and football. Girls playing netball and hockey. Nursery has 25 pupils from age 30 months. Boarding from Year 5.

Kelvinside Academy Junior School

Linked to Kelvinside Academy in the Senior section

33 Kirklee Road, Glasgow, G12 0SW

• Pupils: boys and girls; all day • Ages: 3-11 • Inter-denom
• Fees: £6,090-£8,994 pa • Independent

Tel: 01413 573 376
Fax: 01413 575 401
Email: rector@kelvinsideacademy.org.uk
Website: www.kelvinsideacademy.org.uk

Head: Lesley A Douglas, BEd CMath MIMA SQH.

Remarks: For details, see senior school.

Kensington Prep School

596 Fulham Road, London, SW6 5PA

• Pupils: 280 girls; all day • Ages: 4-11 • Non-denom • Fees: £11,547 pa • Independent

Tel: 02077 319 300
Fax: 02077 319 301
Email: enquiries@kenprep.gdst.net
Website: www.kensingtonprep.gdst.net

Head: Since 2003, Mrs Prudence Lynch MA PGCE (mid fifties). Hails from Guernsey, studied psychology at St Andrews before going to Goldsmiths to do her PGCE. She has two grown up sons and is a proud and committed grandmother. A zany, thoroughly modern head, from her boldly stylish dress sense to her dropped vowels and upward inflection at the end of her sentences. She also brings a wealth of experience to the job – previously head of juniors at Notting Hill & Ealing, a sister GDST establishment, via Colet Court, where she initiated the SEN department, taught study skills, maths and 'thinking', a passion of hers – here she teaches philosophy for children, which is 'too wonderful for words', where they discuss things like 'Is it helpful to have an unrealistic ambition?' or 'Is it ever right to kill someone?' She relishes encouraging them to think and listen to each other. 'Girls need to be as good as men at thinking up fresh ideas and taking risks. Spoon feeding is not going to solve a credit crunch no one has ever experienced before,' she says.

Keen to inject an element of risk to the very safe school she inherited. While she accepts that not every child can achieve anything they want, she firmly believes that it's better to go for the thing you can nearly do rather than the thing you know you can do – otherwise what have you learnt? 'I, too, am a risk taker,' she says.

A touch scatty – efficient administration is not one of her strengths, something remarked on by parents – and she freely admits that she forgets things all the time, while hastening to add that there are enough efficient administrators around her to make sure the school doesn't drop any balls. She is a head with something much more to offer, however: vision, a big heart and a huge sense of fun. 'I love playing,' she says, as she shows us her latest acquisition – a black rag doll that sits – rather incongruously – among the array of toys and clutter on her desk. Determined to counter the intense pressure felt by parents here and elsewhere in the 'ruthless' London day school system – trying to ensure that the girls still have 'dream time' and still enjoy their childhood. How refreshing.

Entrance: At 4+ – over 200 applicants for 44 places. Put your daughter's name down any time up to December prior to entry the following September. Assessments in January. Girls are seen in groups of five or six and assessed during play – 'With a heavily oversubscribed school like this one there isn't an ideal fair way of doing it'. Also an official entrance point at 7+ – register any time up to September the year ahead, but the number of places varies and may be only as few as two. Occasional places do crop up – keep trying. Expects most siblings to join the school, but reserves the right to say no if it is felt to be in the child's interest.

Exit: Almost all to where parents here consider to be 'the top' London girls' day schools – St Paul's Girls, City of London, Godolphin & Latymer, Wimbledon High, Putney High, and a few to the major girls' boarding schools – Wycombe Abbey, Downe House and Cheltenham Ladies'. Lots of scholarships – music as well as academic.

Remarks: Housed in a former Marist convent on the corner of a busy junction of the Parsons Green neck of the Fulham Road, the school occupies a wonderful space. Wide corridors, large windows, spacious high ceilinged classrooms, broad staircases – institutional but brightened with loud colourful murals of, e.g., clowns and kites. A wonderful library in the former chapel, with stained glass windows, high beamed ceiling, some sturdy oak tables softened by comfortable sofas and beanbags – a soulful place to work and read.

The playground stretches into the distance complete with tennis courts, slides, colourful springy tarmac and a snazzy bandstand where they hold popular summer concerts. When the whole school is out here it doesn't look crowded, just a sea of bright colours (Mrs Lynch swiftly replaced the drab grey tunics with the cheerful electric blues and reds – 'I wanted it to be fun for them to get dressed in the morning,' she says). At the ring of the bell all girls freeze in silence before filing obediently into their correct line ups – that's what they're like here, law abiding and conscious of the school values. They couldn't fail to be – they are prominently displayed throughout the school, the positive balanced with the negative, 'Do listen, don't interrupt'. (They sometimes trip up on this one – our guides, a case in point, who were bubbling over in their desire to please and enthuse about their school.)

A GDST with a difference. It stands alone, so doesn't benefit from the resources that come with having a senior school attached. No bursaries at all and fees are a bit higher than at other GDSTs. But the no nonsense high academic standards you would expect, combined with affluent and demanding parents, make this one of London's most competitive girls' schools. 'We are good at fast paced education,' says head. Parents here feel hugely lucky if their daughter makes it through the assessments at three, but we heard reports of a number of children getting tutoring further down the line because they want to ensure results. Our view is that this pressure doesn't necessarily come from the inside. A number of parents here want a seamless transition to schools they regard as being the best and are not always prepared to accept it if they are told their daughter may not be up to it.

Mrs Lynch does her best, and the curriculum is broad – lots of open homework and off piste whole school activities to stimulate thinking skills and collaborative team work through the year groups. 'The big freeze' had the whole school interpreting and creating. The result: swathes of tin foil around the school as well as a smashed mobile phone. Lots of interdisciplinary projects using art, DT and photography. Thursday morning is 'thinking time': 'What would it be like to have legs like jelly?' A whole afternoon dedicated to music and drama, another to music and art. We saw innovative teaching – the younger children on all fours marching round the room barking numbers one to 50. Computers everywhere and laptops widely used in every classroom. Year 6 create TV programmes as well as cook canapés – in addition to doing all the marketing and costing associated with the project.

Resident SENCo manages learning support, which is part of the package until key stage two, from when it's organised on the same model as visiting music staff. Children may dip in and out or have more structured support over a period of several years. It may be just to boost their understanding of maths or to tackle a more serious problem like dyspraxia. However only mild to moderate learning difficulties can realistically be accommodated here. Mrs Lynch abhors the label 'gifted and talented' – 'They're far too young – it implies there's something rigid about who you are'. She infinitely prefers everyone to be stretched through lots of differentiation in class and the open ended activities they do so well here.

French from Year 1 – 'Not mega,' says Mrs Lynch, 'but you get your 'êtres' and 'avoirs' and more formal stuff at the top to help those who go on to do CE elsewhere'. A relaxed taster of Latin in the final year. Class sizes of about 20, maximum 23. Young, (almost entirely) female staff who tend to stay for a long time. Only two or three men, including the recently appointed and much praised head of music, who has introduced a junior orchestra and won't stand for any waiting lists for girls who want to learn an instrument – 'We'll just get more teachers'.

Parents largely local – the Caffè Nero opposite is bursting at 8am with yummy Fulham mummies sipping lattes and testing their pretty daughters on their timetables. Dads very present in the school too, helping with reading and on the parents' committee, 'We like to encourage that,' says Mrs Lynch. Lots of clubs – football run by a Chelsea FC player currently very popular, also bridge, Mandarin, Spanish cookery, craft, lots of music, as well as a host of others. School likes to keep a close eye to make sure girls don't do too much. 'Food amazing,' gushed our guides. Mango and orange red smoothie caused great excitement as we were shown the bright yellow and green dining room in the bowels of the building. Lots of trips – including a choir tour to Belgium, trips to France, Cornwall and the Isle of Wight.

A vibrant place in every respect. Girls here are earnest and keen, immensely privileged with impeccable manners. A quirky eccentric – whether she is fiercely bright or not – could get lost here (school refutes this – 'We are absolutely about inspiring quirky girls as much as the more conformist') but a wonderful start for your robust all rounder.

Kent College Preparatory School, Pembury

Aultmore House, Old Church Road, Pembury, Tunbridge Wells, Kent, TN2 4AX

• Pupils: 195 girls • Ages: 3-11 • A member of the Methodist Independent Schools Group - broadly Christian but all faiths welcome • Fees: Day £7,047-£10,611; Boarding £19,182 pa • Independent

Tel: 01892 820 204
Fax: 01892 820 214
Email: prepschool@kentcollege.kent.sch.uk
Website: www.kent-college.co.uk

Head: Since 2002, Mrs Ann Lawson BEd (Hons) Exeter (forties). Previously spent four years as deputy head at Croydon High and prior to that spent nine years at City of London Freemen's Junior School, Ashtead.

Entrance: From the age of three. Girls may join at any time when spaces and are encouraged to come for a taster day beforehand. Girls joining from Year 3 upwards are required to take entrance tests in English and maths.

Exit: About 50 per cent make a seamless transition to the senior school at 11+, with the majority of the rest going on to the grammars. One or two each year move to other independent schools, e.g. Sevenoaks and Benenden. The school has a good track record in the Kent Test and also prepares girls for the entrance exams to other independent schools and runs a revision course during the summer holidays. Girls coming up from the prep have to sit the entrance test to the senior school in English, maths and verbal reasoning. A requirement of the senior school is that girls must be able to sit nine GCSEs and three A levels, so occasionally it is decided that the senior school might not suit a particular girl. Parents are always kept closely informed of their daughter's progress, so this is always very much a joint decision.

Remarks: Similar ethos to senior school with great emphasis on kindness, respect and emotional wellbeing and a strong sense of community that encompasses everyone. Own purpose built teaching block on the same site as the senior school and with the use of the senior school facilities – science labs, computer suite, sports facilities, music block and theatre. French taught from nursery to Year 6. Sport features strongly – dance gymnastics, netball, swimming in lessons and clubs. U11 netball team recently the runner up in a national tournament for prep schools. Plenty of clubs from classics to cooking and lots of music, singing and drama. Great emphasis on play in the early years and a play therapist comes in once a week to help build girls' self confidence and interpersonal skills. One to one learning support offered at no extra charge – mainly for mild dyslexia and dyspraxia. Only four full boarders at the time of our visit but they seemed happily integrated. Flexi-boarding from the age of 10 a popular option with local children. Breakfast club and after school care very useful for working parents.

Kilgraston Preparatory School

Linked to Kilgraston School in the Senior section

Bridge of Earn, Perthshire, PH2 9BQ

• Pupils: 120 girls + 10 boys • Ages: 2.5 to 13 (day boys 2.5 to 9) • Roman Catholic, but plenty of non-Catholic pupils (including Muslims) • Fees: Day £7,875-£13,050; Boarding £19,050 pa • Independent

Tel: 01738 812 257
Fax: 01738 813 410
Email: headoffice@kilgraston.com
Website: www.kilgraston.com

Head of Prep School: Since 1998, Mrs Audrey Kellaway. In 2003, when Butterstone was absorbed into Kilgraston, she became an IAPS head of Kilgraston Preparatory School. After graduating from Edinburgh University, taught history, modern studies and mathematics in state secondary schools before joining Kilgraston.

Entrance: Generally by interview and school report. Taster days are welcomed.

Exit: To Kilgraston (all girls are able to progress automatically to the senior school) and other senior schools in Scotland and England.

Remarks: Based in the converted stables. Delightful. All girls learn French from seven, physics from 11 and progress automatically up the senior school. All use the senior school facilities, and 11+ year olds share senior specialist staff and visit main school for lessons. Pupils from the age of two, with boys to nine.

King Alfred Lower School

Linked to King Alfred School in the Senior section

Manor Wood, 149 North End Road, Golders Green, London, NW11 7HY

• Pupils: boys and girls • Ages: 4-10 • Fees: £11,310-£13,035 pa
• Independent

Tel: 020 8457 5200
Fax: 020 8457 5249
Email: lowerschool@kingalfred.org.uk
Website: www.kingalfred.org.uk

Head: Mr David Weale BSc PGCE.

Remarks: For details see senior school.

King Edward's Junior School (Bath)

Linked to King Edward's Pre-Prep And Nursery in the Senior section
Linked to King Edward's School (Bath)

North Road, Bath, Bath and North East Somerset, BA2 6JA

• Pupils: 185 in junior school • Ages: 7-11 • Non-denominational
• Fees: £8,670 pa • Independent

Tel: 01225 463 218
Fax: 01225 442 178
Email: junior@kesbath.com
Website: www.kesbath.com

Head Teacher: Since 2008, Mr Greg Taylor, previously deputy head, appointed after a spell as acting head.

Entrance: No formal assessments from pre-prep to junior school. For external candidates, tests in English, maths, reading and non-verbal reasoning plus free writing and interview – details appear on the website. Admits 36 pupils annually into Year 3, small numbers into Years 4 and 6, and up to 20 into Year 5, when it extends to three forms. Flexibility over points of entry has proved popular, with increasing number of parents choosing to move to Bath from London.

Exit: Nearly all pupils proceed to King Edward's senior school via entry examination at 11.

Remarks: The Junior School models itself on its big sibling in terms of its breadth of curriculum and high expectations in all areas. It moved from the other side of Bath some 20 years ago to a purpose-built airy building, which commands the view from the top left corner of King Edward's sloping site. Although separate, it benefits from the amenities of the senior school: the theatre and Astroturf pitches, as well as sharing some of its specialist teachers. An unashamed precursor to the senior school, it makes no bones about catering for the top 25 per cent of seven to 11 year olds, though admissions policy does make clear that children with innate rather than developed ability will be considered.

Lots going on other than work, however, with plenty of sport, music and drama plus loads of clubs. Some of the more ambitious and time-consuming options take place at weekends and pupils have their own activities week each summer term, which takes them away from Bath for a few nights.

King's St Alban's School

Linked to King's Hawford School in the Junior section
Linked to King's School (Worcester) (The) in the Senior section

Mill Street, Worcester, Worcestershire, WR1 2NJ

• Fees: £5,874-£9,381 pa • Independent

Tel: 01905 354 906
Fax: 01905 763 075
Email: ksa@ksw.org.uk
Website: www.ksw.org.uk

Remarks: For details, see associated schools.

King's College Junior School (Wimbledon)

Linked to King's College School (Wimbledon) in the Senior section

Southside, Wimbledon Common, London, SW19 4TT

• Pupils: 460 boys • Ages: 7-13 • C of E (but other faiths welcome)
• Fees: £13,320-£15,030 pa • Independent

Tel: 020 8255 5335
Fax: 020 8255 5339
Email: jsadmissions@kcs.org.uk
Website: www.kcs.org.uk

Headmaster: Since 2006, Dr Gerard Silverlock (fiftyish), previously head at Aberdour, a prep school in Surrey. A historian whose PhD is from the war studies department at King's College London. Before taking over Aberdour, he taught history and politics at Millfield, and was head of history at Lord Wandsworth College in Hampshire. Married with four young children, a sports enthusiast who has coached both cricket and soccer, enjoys reading, cinema and theatre, and is 'totally committed to maintaining KCJS as an outstanding prep school for bright, lively boys'.

Entrance: Difficult. Takes 56 boys at seven and a further 10 at eight, some at nine, 10 and up to 15 at 11. All boys interviewed. Weeds out boys who have been over-coached. Bursaries at seven, eight, nine, 10 and 11. Boys come from mainly local independent and state schools and coaches from all over SW London.

Exit: Boys almost always go on to the senior school, gaining a good number of the scholarships – academic, art, musical and sports – although a small number each year move to major boarding schools.

Remarks: A busy, bustling school. On the same site as the senior school, neatly tucked at one side. Heart of its main building was once Tudory Victorian, brutally destroyed and built over in the 1960s, but softened, face-lifted and altogether improved in the 1980s and 1990s. Corridors are enlivened by pupils' work/paintings/maps/posters. Good library and quite terrific emphasis on reading (lists galore). All subjects taught in subject rooms. Some facilities (art, music, sport, dining hall) are shared with the senior school. Indeed some staff, unusually, teach both age groups.

Acquired Rushmere in 1992, the large handsome Georgian house which backs on to the main junior school building (divided by a garden and now a jolly playground), bought from the sculptor, David Wynne, and the home base for the seven and eight year olds, who have a quiet, low-key start with cosy classrooms and their own dining room, which doubles as the hall. At nine life gets much busier. From 10 onwards boys are setted in French, maths and Latin. Music is extremely strong. Touchtyping in the ICT room for seven and eight year olds. Maximum class size 24.

Lots of clubs – chess and debating keen. Some nice art and wonderful creative writing. Drama hall (shared with senior school) has tiered seats that fold and run to the wall at the press of a button. School does consistently well in rugby, tennis and cricket. Recent first XI tour to South Africa was huge fun. The school holds workshops for parents to discuss any relevant issues. Broad social and ethnic mix. Bright-red blazers. An outstanding prep school.

King's College School (Cambridge)

West Road, Cambridge, Cambridgeshire, CB3 9DN

• Pupils: 60 boys and 50 girls in the pre-prep; 180 boys and 110 girls in the prep. All day except for 35 boarders (including 15 choristers and 10 probationers) • Ages: 4-13 • C of E - other faiths welcome • Fees: Weekly Boarding (boys) £18,465; Day £9,240-£11,910; Choristers £6,165 pa • Independent

Tel: 01223 365 814
Fax: 01223 461 388
Email: office@kcs.cambs.sch.uk
Website: www.kcs.cambs.sch.uk

Headmaster: Since 1998, Mr Nicholas Robinson BA (fifties). Educated at Worth, read English at Anglia Ruskin, PGCE in maths at Goldsmiths. Master, then housemaster, for 12 years at Worth. A bachelor – disarming and a good listener. Doesn't want to be known simply for masterminding building projects (upper school teaching block, ICT and DT wing, music department and squash courts completed 2010 – much needed sports centre planned for 2015) and profile raising of the school (numbers up from 290 to 402 during his tenure) but this is parents' first port of praise. He says he gets to know children when reading to the little ones and through extra-curricular activities – 'always in the front row of every concert and drama production,' said a mum. Also very involved with the choristers, whom he sees as a defining element of King's. Seriously musical (conducts) and more than keen on skiing.

Entrance: Oversubscribed. They say a 'fairly broad intake.' In reality ability range starts well above average – one parent suggested that 'you could lock some of the children in a cave and they'd still get scholarships'.

At four, place offered 12 months before entry. Waiting list but preference given to siblings/children whose parents were past pupils or those who have connections with King's. Date of registration taken into account where a split decision has to be made. Applicants spend an afternoon in a reception class and are observed – they're interested in children's behaviour. Parents ('might not drive Range Rovers but are the V8 engines behind the kids' – lots of ex-Oxbridge) also have a 'chat' with Mr Robinson.

At seven via assessments in English, maths and verbal reasoning – means tested bursaries up to 100 per cent available for those who show musical potential. Occasional entry at other ages via assessment.

Choir auditions twice a year – many apply. Choristers have super demanding schedules and are in the public eye – but, apart from not having enough time to be tip top sportsmen, are well integrated into school life.

Exit: The Perse (co-ed), Oundle and King's Ely are popular. Other destinations include Eton, Rugby, The Leys, Uppingham and Winchester. Respectable clutch of scholarships and awards. Old Boys include Orlando Gibbons, Michael Ramsey, Christopher Tugendhat, John Pardoe, Professor Andrew Wiles (who solved Fermat's Last Theorem).

Remarks: Founded in the 15th century, one of the top Cambridge preps, just a brisk walk away from King's College. Primarily a day school – about 35 boys board. Choristers have to be full boarders and a few places are left for boys who want to board – we hear the dedicated housemaster and wife have created a homely environment and are seriously good news. Hotch potch of buildings, largely of recent vintage, cluster on the edge of a relatively open site where children enjoy being children. Not much 'sirring' (some staff are called by their nicknames) or children being 'scrubbed up to within an inch of their lives' – as far as parents are concerned the emphasis is on more important things. Intimate, family atmosphere with a touch of spontaneity – it's not unusual for impromptu events to be sprung on pupils (and parents) and realised within days: recent talent show raised over £7,000 for charity.

'Absolutely great' teachers. Trad academic approach from the start gives a solid grounding. Subjects are delivered in a 'fun way by lots of different personalities'. Pupils are competitive and want to learn – 'They teach us how to concentrate'. French from day one (taught by native speakers) and Latin from Year 5. Spanish, Mandarin Chinese and German clubs on offer. Positive vibes about DT and science – smart labs wow the children. Thoroughly modern teaching gizmos plus inviting, new library with tempting literary goodies and tremendously enthusiastic, popular librarian – 'They love her'.

High standards are expected and pace hots up in the final two years – scholarship class for Year 8. School tries to stop parents panicking about exams – private maths coaching not unusual prior to CE – but accepts that a small number would benefit from some 1-to-1 help. To make life easier for all, the previous head of maths gives private tuition on site.

Pretty hot on the identification of learning needs – around 20 per cent receive support at some time. Welcoming department caters for mild needs – one full timer (DipSpLD) plus four part timers. For a boost in English another three part timers on hand. Liaison with class teachers, IEPs, useful links with educational psychologists and termly themed open evening for parents – topics include paired reading and home support. Help for pre-preppers in or out of the classroom. Removal from lessons only in the upper school where a language has been dropped (no charge); otherwise sessions, always at the same time to avoid muddling the children, are first thing in the morning, break or lunch time (charges per session).

Angelic choristers aside, music is 'five star' – an inclusive ethos encourages enjoyable involvement. Tuition from the word go – it's quite normal to play two instruments and not unusual to play three. Forty two chamber groups (a prep school record?) and all manner of orchestras – 'If you can scrape a bow across a string, the amazing head of department will find you a group to play in'. School has had a relatively unsporty reputation, but children are happy with what's offered and parents say definite improvement, particularly for girls. Planned facilities, including somewhere for indoor sport, likely to give an extra boost. Tennis coaching, throughout the year, additionally charged. Selection of after school clubs and late stay for homework – good for working parents.

Citizenship awards for younger ones, special tea party at the end of term for the house which has gained the most merits, form based clubs where children get together to air pastoral issues and Little Tea at 4pm where everyone gets a cake ('Impossible to get the children off site till they've had Little Tea – so no quick getaways') typify the caring approach of this liberal school filled to the brim with cheerful, friendly children.

King's Hall School

Linked to King's College (Taunton) in the Senior section

Kingston Road, Taunton, Somerset, TA2 8AA

• Pupils: Prep: 30 boarders, 210 day pupils (50/50 girls and boys). Pre-prep: 90 day pupils. • Ages: 3-13 • C of E • Fees: Day £4,710-£12,444; Boarding £14,403-£18,396 pa • Independent

Tel: 01823 285 920
Fax: 01823 285 922
Email: admissions@kingshalltaunton.co.uk
Website: www.kingshalltaunton.co.uk

Headmaster: Since 2009, Mr Justin Chippendale (early forties), was deputy head at Chafyn Grove, Salisbury, for four years. He attended The Dragon School, from where he won a scholarship to King's Taunton in 1980. He subsequently taught at The Dragon, where he was a popular and successful housemaster, before moving on. A keen sportsman – he captained rugby, hockey and cricket teams at King's – he is supported by his wife, Claire, and his three young children, who are pupils at King's Hall.

Entrance: Pupils join any time after three years old. The Pre-prep runs from 3–7; the Prep from 7–13. Informal assessments in English and maths as well as a chatty interview.

Exit: King's Hall is more than the junior school for King's College, though 75 per cent do go on. Entrance, via Common Entrance, is not automatic but very few fail. 'If we feel a boy or girl is not up to it, we warn parents in plenty of time,' says the head, 'but we do take the Common Entrance seriously: it motivates both pupils and staff and the results are used for setting.' Other destinations include Eton, Radley, Bryanston, Sherborne and others. A number of parents choose King's Hall because they can keep their options open. 'There is no pressure,' said one parent. The last three years have seen children gain over 100 scholarships to many different schools.

Money Matters: Generous arrangements are available for Services families and scholarships, open to all, are awarded at 11+. They continue through the College, subject to annual review.

Remarks: Gazing out across the park and lake at the distant view of Taunton's magnificent cathedral-like church, it is hard to believe the school is only one mile from the station (two hours to London) and ten minutes from the College. The central house – a handsome and homely eighteenth century building – is the focal point around which the school operates. The original stable block now forms part of a delightfully intimate courtyard with rose bushes and inviting benches for chatting in the summer. Over the years brightly coloured and airy dorms have been added with clever partitioning, affording privacy without separation. (Do make sure you see the boys' bathroom, marvellously painted with jungle scenes for aspiring Mowglis and with admonitions on hygiene for young 21st century Stalkys cleverly woven in.)

Separate common rooms for boys and girls are delightfully furnished with areas for more private conversation, while children can munch on the fresh fruit provided. Accessible library in the original house – elegant but functional. Terrific art and very popular drama in the theatre. Well equipped labs and lively teaching. Excellent computer facilities. Riding is very popular and plans for fishing in the recently purchased lake. A wide variety of games are played to a high standard, with success in national and regional competitions. Good modern sportshall, outdoor heated pool, ten tennis courts and three netball courts. An interesting range of hobbies offered on a daily basis. Pupils are kept busy.

Several things make King's Hall special. Taking advantage of their rural surroundings, there is an exciting Forest School in the grounds, complete with leafy huts for pow-wows and areas for cooking over wood fires: a wonderful place for simply mucking around and being children. Also the Pelican Pals, boys and girls in Year 7 sporting their distinctive red caps who go out and play with younger children, really getting to know them and frequently offering comfort, encouragement and advice. We watched some in action with the tinies on the superb Astroturf: it was impossible to tell who was enjoying it more. Prefects have given way to Pelicans – a big improvement, leading to humane and considerate leadership. All of Year 8 then play a part in helping to run the school.

Weekend activities are popular – one mother told us it was virtually impossible to persuade her child to come home on Sundays – and all boarding staff, led by charismatic houseparents, are fully involved. The nursery and pre-prep are delightfully housed in what look like log cabins, adding a sense of adventure and discovery. That is the overall feeling we had about the school. The children are obviously happy with the considerate challenges they are set and the encouragement they receive; that is reflected in their sunny friendliness, on which sit the good old fashioned virtues of courtesy and consideration.

Generous arrangements are available for Services families and scholarships, open to all, are awarded at 11+. They continue through the College, subject to annual review.

Not a slick or sophisticated school – not a county school with over-riding social pretensions, but a place where children can mature at their own pace, enjoy their surroundings, have a lot of fun and know they will be ready for their next school. Indeed we met a number at their next school, who looked back on their days at King's Hall with huge affection and gratitude. One told us she had 'never been happier in her life,' but added thoughtfully, 'Mind you, in those days, I didn't have A levels to worry about'.

King's Hawford School

Linked to King's Saint Alban's School in the Junior section
Linked to King's School (Worcester) (The) in the Senior section

Hawford Lock Lane, Worcester, Worcester, Worcestershire, WR3 7SD

• Pupils: 350 girls and boys; all day • Ages: 2-11 • Church of England
• Fees: £5,874-£10,056 pa • Independent

Tel: 01905 451 292
Fax: 01905 756 502
Email: hawford@ksw.org.uk
Website: www.ksw.org.uk

Head: Since 2006, Mr Jim Turner, previously head of junior school at Sunderland High School, 1997-2006.

Entrance: Entrance is by assessment. This takes place during a normal school day with assessments in English, maths and verbal reasoning for the older children. Younger children can be assessed at home.

Exit: Most move on to King's School, Worcester.

Remarks: For further details, see senior school.

King's House School

68 King's Road, Richmond, Surrey, TW10 6ES

• Pupils: 375 boys; all day • Ages: 3-13 • C of E • Fees: £9,075-£12,255; Nursery £2,700-£5,100 pa • Independent

Tel: 020 8940 1878
Fax: 020 8939 2501
Email: schooloffice@kingshouseschool.org
Website: www.kingshouseschool.org

Head: Since 2002, Mrs Stephanie Piper MA BA (forties), formerly at Durston House in Ealing, Notting Hill and Ealing High School and St Helen's in Northwood. A modern languages expert married to a teacher at Lady Eleanor Holles School, with two grown-up sons and a daughter at Lady Eleanor Holles. The third female to be appointed head of an independent boys' prep in Britain, which is quite a coup considering previous King's House heads were from a very traditional mould – male, bearded, sporting tweed jackets; 'the feminine touch' is generally viewed as a good thing.

Having survived the 'Kevin' stage of her own sons, King's House boys hold no fears for her. Since arriving, she has renovated the front of house area ('Was rather gloomy'), improved security, invested greatly in IT both in admin and the classroom (interactive whiteboards throughout) and has introduced more streaming so that all levels of ability are catered for. She is happy and proud to maintain the tradition of a mixed ability school serving local London day schools and nearby boarding schools.

Entrance: Nursery for both girls and boys from 3+. Most boys enter the main school at 4+ – places are offered a year before entry in order of registration; word has spread re great head so places are harder to come by than they used to be. Some casual vacancies later and a small 8+ entry following a test. Most boys are from the local area – Richmond, Barnes, Kew, Wimbledon, Chiswick. Parents are middle class, professional, university educated.

Exit: It is a given that all boys stay until 13. Twenty five per cent go to boarding schools within the M25. Epsom College (weekly boarding) is popular, Cranleigh, Wellington, Bradfield, Charterhouse the other usual choices. Good relationships with London day schools (Hampton, St Paul's, Latymer, Westminster, King's Wimbledon, Emanuel, Kingston Grammar) – high success rates at screening.

Remarks: What was a rather dull, plodding boys' prep, albeit with a good local reputation, has been rejuvenated. Within the somewhat limited facilities the buildings can offer, innovations support and inspire staff. The new purpose-built theatre with its state of the art equipment can seat 200 – drama department has spread its wings, and all can take part.

Sport is an evident strength – mainly rugby, football and cricket. Head of PE encourages everyone, 'not just the firsts', and A to E teams play regularly and enjoy considerable success. Mrs Piper herself turns up at rugby matches – it helps that she knows the rules and understands the game. Has just obtained the lease on the old civil service grounds at Chiswick, so now has 32 acres of pitches, a pavilion, tennis courts and full changing facilities. Everyone has a music lesson a week and nearly three quarters learn an instrument. Wind instruments are exceptionally good, providing jazz and blues ensembles.

Very strong teaching staff including the legendary and inimitable senior master. How many parents re-live their own school history lessons on hearing their sons relate the latest battle played out on his blackboard, whether it's between the Roundheads and the Cavaliers or the Persians and the Greeks?

Links with parents are excellent – a weekly newsletter ensures good communications between school and parents and a thriving Friends' association which raises money for equipment and charity. Every class has a representative to organise social events within each age group.

New nursery opened January 2009 for boys and girls from age of three, housed in a renovated old school, well equipped and very well subscribed. Boys automatically move into the junior department at King's House and girls go either to the Old Vicarage or one of the other local girls' schools.

A lively, happy, flourishing prep school.

King's Junior School

Linked to King's School Chester (The) in the Senior section

Wrexham Road, Chester, Cheshire, CH4 7QL

• Pupils: 225 girls and boys; all day • Ages: 7-11 • Cathedral foundation
• Fees: £7,797 pa • Independent

Tel: 01244 680455
Fax: 01244 689 518
Email: junior@kingschester.co.uk
Website: www.kingschester.co.uk

Head of The Junior School: Since 2001, Mr Simon Malone BEd (early fifties), deputy from 1993. Friendly and open with a genuine heart for his charges here, 'We look on ourselves as a family'. Actively involved with sports coaching because, 'I really enjoy it and the children and parents see me in a different light'. It's more than just a job – he's passionate about the pupils, the school, King's itself, talking of pupils having 'a sense of worth belonging to this fine institution'. His helming makes it feel like a stable, happy ship in safe hands right through to the chatty cleaning lady caring for the aquarium fish. Unpretentious and approachable, in our book he's a good sort.

Entrance: From seven years into Year 3 (Year 1 here) by examination related to key stage 1 requirements, designed to assess potential as well as achievement. Tests in maths, written English, reading and reasoning, as well as play activity and a talk with staff. We're looking for 'an above average level of competency and the potential to do well – it's not an interview, but you can learn a lot from how, for example, a six year old draws'. Entry at ages eight, nine and 10 is also possible, although head says numbers have increased slightly despite recession.

Exit: Most pupils proceed to the senior school at 11. Entrance is likely but not guaranteed, being dependent on the same entrance exam as outsiders. Very few choose elsewhere.

Remarks: Confident children work and play hard here. 'We are an academic school,' says head, 'but we also emphasise music, games, drama, fun – it's very important the pupils have fun.' Amongst the 'activity lessons' on offer are kite-making, baking and golf. A lesson on aerodynamics we saw involved paper plane test flights into and with the wind on the field.

Peer reviewed books in classroom libraries help others choose books and a central library area has curved seats and shelves. Curriculum includes French for three years, Spanish for one and German as an activity too. Progress is assessed with internal testing and school is trying the externally marked on-line INCAS scheme. Latest ISI inspection in March 2009 described the quality of educational experience as 'outstanding' and said, 'The junior school provides pupils with an excellent all-round education'. Year 4s (top juniors) talk of a daily hour of homework, an hour and a half at weekends, and everyone's keen to earn house points for work, effort and behaviour. Two elected reps from each class sit on school council and a suggestion box for all.

Pupils are fiercely proud of sporting successes, including winning the 'double' of the Association of Junior Independent Schools' (AJIS) cricket and football twice in last three years and being AJIS cricket cup holders for five of the past six years; one captain was a girl. Children can use playing field at break times 'when it's not muddy', but would like more facilities in the playground, although they do have a doodle wall in the art and DT pre-fab block 'for if it's raining or we're bored'. New assembly and sports hall with screen for hymn words, benches for the top year and Friday class assemblies. Christian faith strongly represented with regular visits from local vicar and the cathedral vice-dean twice a term. Many take private music lessons and two annual drama productions. The staff of 20, mostly in their 30s and 40s, includes six full time men. Girl pupils now represent 33 per cent. A private after school club operates until 6pm.

King's Preparatory School

Linked to King's Rochester in the Senior section

St Nicholas House, King Edward Road, Rochester, Kent, ME1 1UB

• Pupils: Nursery 25; pre-prep 115; prep 190; in prep boys outnumber girls 2:1 or 3:1 depending on years; all day except for 3 boarders in top years of prep • Ages: Pre-preparatory & nursery: 3-7, preparatory school: 8-13 • C of E • Fees: Boarding £17,370; Day £8,190-£11,940 pa • Independent

Tel: 01634 888 577
Fax: 01634 888 507
Email: prep@kings-rochester.co.uk
Website: www.kings-rochester.co.uk

Headmaster: Head of Prep School, Mr Roger Overend BA FTCL ARCM FRSA (fifties), a musician and previously head of Westminster Abbey Choir School. Brisk, energetic, enthusiastic and fast-talking. Active in IAPS (the prep schools' association), an experienced director of music and head – his Westminster time an obvious asset in this less spotlit choir school – he is sanguine about the difficulties of maintaining the school's position with so much free and good state provision on the doorstep. However, his results help – 'We have the top KS2 results in Medway for both 2004 and 2005 and we offer so much more on top,' he enthuses. In his six years he has updated the school – though its buildings are possibly the least attractive on the site – and brought in much that is new and innovative – including 'highly-motivated staff'. 'Mr Overend has his own methods,' a parent told us. 'He managed to clear the snow in the school yard by organising a huge snowball fight!'

Since January 2009, the Pre-preparatory head is Mrs Sarah Skillern MA BA NPQH.

Both heads sit on the school's executive board with the head of the senior school, Mr Kevin Jones, and Dr Ian Walker – a unique management structure that oversees all aspects of the life of the school and its community. Within that they are largely autonomous – 'I work under a head who is strong enough to devolve authority,' says Mr Overend. 'The four of us just see eye to eye – I'm in daily contact with the pre-prep and nearly as often with the senior school. We hold traditional values but we're not boring and dull.'

Entrance: Entrance to the nursery offered to 28 children of 3+. Early registration is the key. Pre-prep starts the following year – places awarded after interview with parents and a simple assessment of the child. Most move into the prep at 8+ when a further intake from outside, particularly at 11+. Assessment by examination. Again most, but not all, will move into King's senior school at 13.

Exit: A few leave early, finding the ethos a little too structured for their free spirits. Most move seamlessly through the whole school – and it is very much a whole school – though some leave at 11 for the state sector if they get a place at one of the grammars. Mr Overend is generous in his support of these though, of course, the school does not 'teach for' the 11+.

Remarks: Pre-prep and prep very much part of the whole King's School. Though enjoying their own buildings and facilities, they also have the run of all the senior school offers – pool, pitches and cathedral! The pre-prep in its purpose-built, home is spacious, bright and colourful without the over-displaying and clutter that sometimes unsettles rather than stimulates. Sensible planning allows for reception having their own 'loo block' and air-conditioned PC suite. No more than 18 children to a class, though the building is flexible enough to allow up to four classes to have activities together. Pre-prep is orderly, calm and happy. Children are attentive, absorbed; 'Nobody shouts at children here,' we were told – but we saw a lot of smiling. We went to a reception class German lesson taught by the 'German Teacher of the Year', an award made by the German embassy, and it was huge fun. Kaspar the puppet was packing his case to go off to the World Cup and we helped him in songs and games and all auf Deutsch. Certificates awarded for everything from improvement in maths to kindness and helpfulness.

Prep in less glamorous accommodation – though it shares the pre-prep's super hall – is busy and fun. Still far more boys than girls here – the word that the school is co-ed has been slow to catch on even after 14 years, though the year groups now in the pre-prep will change all that. Much to offer girls here – they love the jazz dancing and trampolining. Value-added is strong – a good school to which to send your borderline 11+ failure who will catch up fast and have his confidence boosted too. Good support for dyslexics and altogether 'a place of learning but a place where people are enjoying each other'.

Good communication with home – all new parents are contacted by an existing parent on a kind of buddy basis. Parents 'very committed' and come from up to 30 miles away. Teachers are friends – 'The staff without exception are very switched on and are genuinely very nice people,' said a parent. Boarding is small but has a real family feeling and the pupils can use all the school's facilities. Says one parent, 'For the boarders to be provided with PE every single evening is something you cannot put a price on in this day and age. My lad goes every evening to the gym for different sports and loves it.' All the heads stress the same fundamental principle – the main priority is that your child will be happy.

King's School Ely, Junior School

Linked to King's School Ely (The) in the Senior section

Barton Road, Ely, Cambridgeshire, CB7 4DB

• Pupils: 210 day boys, 145 day girls; 30 boarder boys, 5 boarder girls. Plus King's Acremont pre-prep with 105 and nursery with 45 • Ages: 3-13 • C of E • Fees: Day £7,155-£11,865; Boarding £17,340-£18,300 pa • Independent

Tel: 01353 660732
Fax: 01353 665 281
Email: admissions@kings-ely.cambs.sch.uk
Website: www.kingsschoolely.co.uk

Headmaster: Since 2008, Mr Richard Whymark BA (Ed) (late thirties), head of Stonar Junior since 2005. Educated at Merton Court, then Eltham College, before obtaining first class honours (combined degree in fine art and education) at Exeter. Parents say that he is 'great at sorting things out quickly.' Committed, friendly and fatherly (own young children – Molly and Bertie). Married to ex-housemistress and part-time primary teacher, Joanna. Managed a ceramics company before starting to teach at City of London Freemen's. Two years at Hazelwood in Surrey followed by seven at Salisbury Cathedral, where he became deputy head. Enjoys painting for pleasure and tinkering with aged Morris Minor Traveller. Lots of creative ideas. A dynamic and well-respected head.

Entrance: Informal assessment at 4+. Most carry on into the prep unless the school considers they'll not thrive – help is given to find alternatives. Informal interview and standard assessment tests for external entrants of 7+ and upwards. Potential choristers have to jump the same hurdles plus, of course, a voice trial. Mild dyslexia, dyspraxia and dyscalculia can be accommodated (a specialist SEN teacher) but children need to be 'able to access mainstream curriculum with minimal support'.

Exit: Nearly all to the senior school – no test but exams to establish sets. Entry isn't guaranteed – plenty of warning if a problem. Uppingham, Oundle and state are other destinations.

Remarks: Although on the edge of the senior school campus, a self-contained unit. Airy classrooms in modern buildings look out across the Fens or into a sunny courtyard with a giant chess set and an expansive awning to give some shade.

Academic subjects are setted from Year 5 onwards but whipcracking doesn't really feature. 'They don't make you work – they inspire you to work. There's some leeway and it's fun,' mused one of the older pupils. Specialist teaching rooms for science, DT, IT and art – the door's always open. Mountains of carefully controlled, neat work – the chatty art teacher is 'a real optimist'. Music is very strong. Enthusiastic and approachable head of department, good facilities and concert trips abroad – around 80 per cent learn an instrument. Plenty of photos trumpeting after school activities – golf, lace making and a junior tennis club where Year 8s coach youngsters, excellent stuff for the development of leadership skills.

Relaxed but respectful rapport between children and staff – according to one pupil, 'There's a definite element of trust – they trust you to do it right'. A secure, friendly school where all have plenty of opportunities to shine.

The King's School in Macclesfield Junior Division

Cumberland Street, Macclesfield, Cheshire, SK10 1DA

• Pupils: 350 girls and boys; all day • Ages: 3-11 • C of E • Fees: Infants £6,390; Juniors £7,275 pa • Independent

Email: mail@kingsmac.co.uk

Website: www.kingsmac.co.uk

Principal: Mrs Caroline Hulme-McKibbin, formerly head of Alderley Edge Junior School.

Entrance: Entrance to the infants is non selective, to the juniors by assessment.

Remarks: Occupies a site integral to the girls' division. Juniors and infants housed in separate buildings. Bright classrooms with every inch of wall space covered by ever changing colourful displays. Pupils have the use of the girls' sports facilities, assembly hall but have their own playground. A happy atmosphere.

Knighton House School

Durweston, Blandford Forum, Dorset, DT11 0PY

• Pupils: 110 girls, of whom 60 board. Pre-prep with 35 children including boys, and nursery children • Ages: Prep 7-13; pre-prep 4-7; nursery 2+ - 3+ • C of E • Fees: Day £14,640; Boarding £19,500; Pre-prep £7,410 pa • Independent

Tel: 01258 452 065

Fax: 01258 450 744

Email: admissions@knighton-house.co.uk

Website: www.knightonhouse.dorset.sch.uk

Headmistress: Since January 2010, Mrs Alison Tremewan, previously deputy head of Sherborne Prep.

Entrance: Any child can come – more or less at any time – so long as space is available. Head likes girls to start in the summer term when possible. Not unusual for girls to start mid-year, sometimes fleeing less happy schools. Families mainly local (within an hour) or from London; very few from overseas (one French, one Spanish when we visited). Not a school bursting with marketing nous, so remains curiously low profile – which only adds to its charm.

Exit: All stay until 13 – Bryanston School has risen to first place among destinations, which makes sense as Knighton House and Bryanston literally adjoin. A few most years to Sherborne Girls' and St Mary's, Shaftesbury, then to anywhere and everywhere – all the top girls' schools, plus a few co-eds. A couple of scholarships won most years – for music, art or sport as often as academics. Pre-prep boys go on mostly to Sandroyd and Clayesmore.

Remarks: Founded in 1950, by Christopher Booker's parents, this delightful, happy, unassuming school is perched on a windy hilltop beside Bryanston's western gate surrounded by paddocks and games fields. Unspectacular old-rectory type house – believed to have been the dowager home of Lord Portman's mother – with usual carbuncular collection of add-ons. However a new building containing two classrooms and a preparation room for the science lab has recently been opened. This is phase one – more new classrooms are planned to replace temporary ones.

Boarding flexible, from a minimum of two nights to full. Almost half the girls in the prep are full or weekly boarders, a few are day girls, and the rest board a few nights a week. Everyone gets her own bed, even the two night a weekers, and anyone who boards at all can stay on the weekend for free (helps to keep the numbers up on Sundays). Nice loos, matrons and gappies. Lovely food cooked by school's marvellous chef and never in short supply. The famed and much-loved red dungarees give way to elegant long grey skirts in Year 8. Now revamped 'best uniform' for any trips or visits off the school premises – red knitted jersey, checked blouse with Peter Pan collar and dark grey kilt; grey cloaks for cold weather. Charming co-ed pre-prep (now named The Orchard) and nursery bring in local families. We defy anyone to sit through the pre-prep's heart-warming promotional DVD and not be champing at the bit to enrol their child by the end.

Small classes, maximum 18, with some setting in maths, science, French and English; French from the early years and Latin from Year 6. Top Latinists do Greek for CE and scholarships. Scholarship classes are arranged as necessary – potential scholars are given an extra infusion of brainy stuff through one-on-one sessions off the timetable. Happily, does not fuss about doing SATs exams, but plenty of monitoring and regular half-termly assessments. Two libraries – reference and fiction. Good computer room where girls are always supervised. DT includes cookery and sewing. Very good SEN department with two staff catering for usual variety of mainly mild learning difficulties. Junior and senior plays produced every year. Art includes lots of innovative 3D work – all 8 year olds design and make their own shoulder bag. Keen games – does well for a small school. Uses Bryanston's Astroturf hockey pitches and swimming pool, as well as riding through their grounds.

Ponies an important ingredient of the school's recipe. More than half the girls ride; many bring their own ponies, which other girls also use. The stables are right there, almost in the heart of the school, and has its own all-weather arena and cross country course. Other extras on offer include pop lacrosse, touch rugby, early morning running, dance, trampolining and speech and drama. Play areas include adventure playground, apple and pear orchard, vegetable gardens and funny little swimming pool perched on hillside. Tree-climbing a favourite pastime – all 'climbable' trees marked with a special dot.

A school with a musical heritage. Music has dedicated red-brick buildings, with recital room and masses of individual practice rooms. Lots of different bands and groups, a serious orchestra, small concerts every Friday to which parents can come. Main strength, however, is singing – head of music teaches individual singing to over a third of the girls and the superb chapel choir recently sang at Mont St Michel.

A school which has weathered and adapted to the changes of a turned millennium; all the pupils are friendly, mutually supportive, many from the country. In this protected nook, they can stay relatively unsophisticated until they go to public school. As a freestanding girls' boarding prep school, it is one of the last of a dying breed – barely a dozen left in the country. 'More like a family than a school,' said one teacher. Last words come from a parent who told us, 'In a world falling apart, there is one corner of sanity and perfection – this is Knighton House'.

Lady Barn House School

Schools Hill, Cheadle, Cheshire, SK8 1JE

• Pupils: 455 boys and girls, all day • Ages: 3-11 • Non-denom
• Fees: £3,462-£5,949 pa • Independent

Tel: 0161 428 2912
Fax: 0161 428 5798
Email: info@ladybarnhouse.stockport.sch.uk
Website: www.ladybarnhouse.org

Head: Since 2002, Ms Sue Yule (fifties). Fast talking, slim, elegant, she was a parent at Lady Barn before coming to teach Years 5 and 6 in 1989 and working her way up to headship. Describes herself as an adventurous outdoors type who likes trekking and is first in to gorge walk or abseil on school trips. 'She's not how you'd imagine a headmistress to be,' say articulate pupils; 'She's nice, but not so nice that she's not strict'. 'I like to treat them as I'd like them to treat each other,' she responds. 'They're not scared of me but they respect me.' Her sons came here and went on to Manchester Grammar School and, she says, 'Quite a few of the staff have or have had children here'.

Entrance: No assessment for entry to two nursery forms at three but be warned, parents register names early and once they have started, school sometimes suggests children might fare better elsewhere, if they have special needs that the school cannot cater for. Entry to further 20 places in third class at four is by informal half day observation with peers. If places become available later, infants are assessed from a half day in school and juniors a full day with standard tests looking for potential.

Maximum class size is 22 but the average 19, as head does not need to fill all places and can afford to select only children she's convinced will succeed here. 'We're very careful who we offer a place to,' she says, 'and after a day's assessment many are turned away, but any decision we make is from the point of view of what's best for the child.' Two open mornings when children run a French café for existing parents and visitors; then an invitation to view the school on a working day when the scrutiny works both ways. The impressive website tells all except the fees.

Exit: Absolutely awesome results at 11. About half the year goes to Manchester Grammar, 30 in 2007, and about half the girls bag an offer from Withington. The other top destinations are Manchester High School for Girls, Alderley Edge School, Stockport and Altrincham Grammars, Cheadle Hulme and King's Macclesfield. Mrs Yule has a strong working relationship with the local secondaries, which speak warmly of Lady Barn, and her references are well respected. 'The worst thing from our point of view would be to get a child into the wrong secondary school,' she says.

Remarks: Founded in 1873 as a co-educational school. Very smart and successful, in leafy suburb two minutes from John Lewis and right under the final approach to Manchester Airport. The royal blue livery is everywhere – the paintwork, railings, minibuses and uniform. A Victorian house, now extended, stands with two further buildings in verdant space against a parkland backdrop. The adorable royal blue swathed three and four year olds can look forward confidently to bagging places at the region's tip top secondary schools and to having a lot of fun along the way.

'We're not a sweatshop,' claims head and, although the results make one wonder, the thorough preparation over years means plenty of time for continued mind stretching education in Year 6, when many prep schools focus boringly on entrance tests. Besides, the timetable here includes so many specialist teachers that it doesn't allow for too many practice papers. The school believes its teaching and 'value-added' should take the credit, but the trick also seems to lie in handpicking children with most potential: 'There's no gifted and talented register here; it would be huge – we cater for these children as a matter of course with extended activities as part of the curriculum,' says head, who describes herself as 'a linguist at heart'. French is taught from the early years in a designated room and used throughout the school for registration, the day and date etc. The ICT suite announces itself as La Salle des Ordinateurs. Mandarin has recently been introduced and Mrs Yule herself runs the Latin club. No streaming, just old fashioned teaching at single lift up desks with smaller group work as necessary. A catchup room for one-to-one help for incoming children or the odd one with very mild dyslexia. SATs are shunned – 'We hate numeracy and literacy strategies that hold them back; we let them fly while consolidating their foundations'.

Lots going on with after school team and open sports, four choirs, orchestra and lots of ensembles, 135 children take private music lessons in school in individual rooms as well as ballet and speech training. Impressive list of clubs includes chess, Spanish, Scrabble, drama, Warhammer, internet, as well as lots of music and sport activities. Library club members enjoy extra time in brand new but characterful library in eaves of old house. Compulsory lunch, cooked on site, is served in several sittings and the head takes her turn at lunch duty to get to know the children. Menus are displayed outside so parents can discuss them too. Snacks must be healthy, 'Crisps are not allowed'. A nurse on duty from 10am–3pm each day.

Children walk ten minutes to Cheadle Baths for swimming. On site they're served by a floodlit, all-weather pitch and the little ones enjoy daily timetabled sessions on their soft surface adventure playground. Indoors a hall with climbing wall and proscenium arch stage, and two music and drama spaces with soundproof dividing screens, as well as bespoke art and technology and science rooms. Pupils describe the atmosphere as 'very happy – the teachers are really friendly; in fact everybody's friends even in different years'. House points are awarded for good behaviour as well as sporting endeavour but the head, who doesn't like shouting at any time, also attributes good behaviour to school's very high expectations: 'It's a dreaded thing to have your name recorded in the discipline book. We have a zero tolerance for bullying, and swearing or disobedience result in a serious detention'.

The pretty much exclusively middle class parents seem to love the place – some want more homework, others less, but all agree the car park's a nightmare at times. School's care starts at 8.10am and paid after school care is available until 6pm. The impressive array of trips includes two family outdoor pursuits weekends and a family ski trip each year. Pupils also enjoy annual trips to the Lake District, south coast or France and the two 17 seater minibuses come into their own for day trips and fixtures. School produces a weekly newsletter and the glossy termly 'Ladybarn Chronicle'. A Year 6 team's newspaper was awarded distinction in the 'Times Educational Supplement' Newsday contest in 2007 and a six year tradition for a Lady Barn pupil to win the Blenheim Palace project competition and be invited to tea with the Duke and Duchess of Marlborough, but this school doesn't have undue airs and graces – rather it's a go-getting place where children (we say bright children) will really take off.

The Lady Eleanor Holles School, Junior Department

Linked to Lady Eleanor Holles School (The) in the Senior section

Burlington House, 177 Uxbridge Road, Hampton Hill, Middx, TW12 1BD

• Pupils: 180 girls • Ages: 7-11 • C of E • Fees: £10,560 pa • Independent

Tel: 020 8979 2173
Fax: 020 8783 1962
Email: junior-office@lehs.org.uk
Website: www.lehs.org.uk

Head: Since 2004, Mrs Gillian Low MA Oxon PGCE Cantab (early fifties). Previously head of Francis Holland School, NW1, and deputy head of Godolphin and Latymer School. (See senior school entry.) With overall responsibility for the school, she takes junior assembly once a fortnight.

Working under her aegis is Mrs Jennifer Adams BA (Hons) Newcastle, PGCE (early fifties), head of junior department, responsible for day-to-day running and the main point of contact for parents. Taught in the junior department 1977–86, returning as head of department in 2002. Considered a solid, safe pair of hands following what had been a rough patch for junior department staffing. The yin to Mrs Low's yang, she describes herself as 'a good listener, fairly relaxed' and has a generally consultative style of working. Nice relationship with the girls – knows them by name – helped by the fact she fits in teaching time (RE and history). 'She is very warm-hearted,' says one parent, 'approachable and very fair.' Married, with triplets away at university, she enjoys reading and sailing.

Entrance: At 7+. Tests in English comprehension and essay and mathematics – described to them by staff as 'doing a bit of work with us'. All are interviewed but it's low key – usually in groups of three. Entry is two forms of 22 – school says two to three children after each place. Main feeders are Jack and Jill, Denmead, Athelstan House and Weston Green.

Exit: Many families here covet a place at the more prestigious senior school – and indeed most do move there – but transfer is not guaranteed. However, since 2009, the vast majority of junior department girls are offered guaranteed places in LEH senior department without having to take the entrance exam. Places are offered at the end of Year 5, following a careful review of a girl's work and progress, and parents of girls who may not be offered guaranteed places are notified 'several months earlier', so they can meet the head of department and discuss possible alternatives. Junior department girls can still apply for academic and music scholarships to the senior department and are also eligible for bursaries.

Remarks: A very good junior school but not in the same illustrious league as its hugely famous senior school parent. That said, the long-held perception that the junior department is a 'poor relation' of the senior school is gradually becoming old hat, confirmed by recent improvements and renovations.

Academically it does the business – curriculum is based on the national literacy and numeracy strategies – although girls generally work in advance of their chronological age. The maths syllabus, for example, is finished by Year 5, leaving lots of time for revision and consolidation and practising working to time. Generally standards are high and the pace is fast – picking up as they move through the school. 'I think the girls are pushed hard academically,' says one mother, 'but they are bright girls and fairly competitive, so up for it.' Parents are happy that it is not a hothouse but still gets impressive results.

Staff appear committed and caring. Good provision of specialist subject teaching, which increases to include nearly all subjects by Years 5 and 6. Lessons we saw were lively, productively so. French taught from day one. Plenty of homework but it's generally considered manageable. Provision for the exceptionally gifted and talented and, at the other end of the spectrum, can cater for mild learning difficulties and EAL. All pupils are screened for any problems in Year 4. One-to-one study skills lessons are available at extra charge for pupils with dyslexia or dyspraxia – currently eight out of 180 pupils are receiving extra help. EAL support includes a lunchtime reading and conversation club – good takeup from Korean and Japanese pupils.

Laid out over three floors but can accommodate some physical disabilities and a lift has recently been installed. The junior department occupies a Victorian building, Burlington House, on the northern side of the main school site. Shares some facilities and space with the senior school. Originally used as the school's boarding house, Burlington House was extended and completely renovated in 2003. Classrooms are large, light and airy and good specialist rooms for many subjects including music, art and ICT. Not a blank wall in sight – no area left uncovered by some inventive display work. And not just the usual selection from the art department – even the maths work had generated some eye-catching pieces using patterns made by Fibonacci numbers. Lovely dining room, decorated in foody, papier-mâché motifs by the pupils, lots of choice and enticing aromas when we visited.

Comfortable, well-stocked library, with dedicated librarian in the afternoons. Little sick bay off the main office where the afflicted can snuggle down under the watchful eye of highly praised school secretary – credited by parents as smoothing out all sorts of tiny day to day issues for them and their offspring. Cosy feel overall. Attractive outdoor area including a trim trail and climbing frame. 'Hedge houses' (little dens carved out of the hedge borders) are very popular areas for unstructured play.

Several parents describe the school as 'well-balanced', with lots of opportunity for sport, music and arts specialists to flourish. Sport and music are particular strengths, with the senior school's facilities, including the pool, available to junior pupils. A thriving orchestra, a choir for which the girls audition and a chorus open to all comers. Around 50 pupils learn an instrument in school – typically to grade 3, with a few achieving grade 4/5. Drama is taught as a class lesson, with individual lessons available as an extra. Sport is strong – particularly netball, swimming and gymnastics, where teams enjoy regional and national success; rounders, tennis and short tennis also played.

Wide range of after-school activities and clubs – all the usual, plus embroidery and hand bell ringing as less common offerings and, since 2006, Mandarin classes. 'There's so much on offer that I have to remind my daughter not to go for everything and just to play sometimes,' says one mum. Most of the after-school stuff is actually at lunchtime to allow for the fact that the school buses leave at 4pm. About 50 per cent of pupils live more than three miles from school, and many use the school coach system from entry – a boon for working parents too. Pastoral care is good – the informal house system allows extra friendships across year groups and all new girls get an older 'buddy' from their house.

Nurturing feel – 'It's a lovely, cosy place with lots of care,' says one mum, who actually prefers the junior to the senior school. 'The pastoral side is very good,' adds another. 'I've never waited more than a day for a teacher to get back to me whenever I've raised anything – email system is superb. I feel I've got the best school/parent partnership at this school.' Mrs Adams says no LEH type and it would be a shame if there were. That said, this is a place for a bright girl and a competitive edge to things. Parents who have chosen it are happy and, more importantly, feel that their children are too.

Lady Royd Preparatory School

Linked to Bradford Girls Grammar School in the Senior section

Squire Lane, Bradford, BD9 6RB

• Pupils: 155 boys and girls; all day • Ages: 2-11 • C of E • Fees: £6,441-£7,632 pa • Independent

Tel: 01274 545 395
Fax: 01274 482 595
Email: registrar@bggs.com
Website: www.bggs.com

Headmistress: Since 2009, Mrs Joanne Jenkinson BA (early forties). Degree in economics at Leicester University, then PGCE, maths co-ordinator at Churchfields Primary School and deputy head here. Married to an architect, has a four-year-old daughter at the school. Very pleasant, competent and committed – makes a lot of use of value added data, termly targets and monitoring; links with the wider early years' world including the LEA; well liked by pupils and parents, who see her as open to feedback.

Entrance: Early years foundation stage (EYFS) children by informal class based–assessments; Year 1 upwards, a maths and English assessment based on the National Curriculum.

Exit: Most to the senior school – automatic entry if at the right standard; a few to co-educational maintained or independent schools.

Remarks: Purpose built in 2006 – smallish, cheerful classrooms with good displays, including a junior science lab with drop-down desks. Attractive, well-stocked library has beanbags, computers and story sacks for parents to borrow. Senior school DT and music facilities also used. Grassed play areas, a sensory garden and little greenhouse; well equipped nursery and kindergarten.

Average of 15 per class (18 maximum). Broad curriculum – French from four years, building up to an hour a week for Year 6s, from specialist teacher; specialists for music and PE too and generally for key stage 2 classes, who also have thinking skills (draughts and chess, study skills, budgeting from an Argos catalogue) plus food and nutrition. Very keen on Jolly Phonics – parents given instruction. Strong results in core subjects at the end of Year 6, well above the national average – no national tests; focused atmosphere in classrooms. Several computers – a parent commended the use of ICT in lessons to engage pupils. Recent ISI report praised 'outstanding individual attention' in EYFS and children's excellent relationships with teachers.

Well led SEN department: three SEN lessons a week if needed plus support within and outside the classroom. Dyslexia Action visits for half a day a week for individual sessions (parents pay it directly) but more systematic provision is needed for gifted and talented children – it depends on individual teachers, said a parent.

Parents receive a detailed guide for the forthcoming year at the end of the summer term, termly newsletters (two kinds) produced by the school and children and sessions explaining educational approaches. They see teachers as very approachable and happy to collaborate with them on all kinds of problems.

Happy and friendly children, from Bradford and the surrounding area, including Leeds, Halifax and Huddersfield. Socially and ethnically varied; several doctors' children. All given responsibilities from Year 3, e.g. Year 6 'Friendship Police' and Fine Dining monitors, who select the best behaved and best eaters for a special end of the week meal with the head (drinks in plastic goblets); school council.

Lots of clubs: sports – teams do well in competitions (table tennis is a school strength); music – almost all do individual lessons, various groups (steel pans, guitar, fifes, trumpets), orchestra, choir, several concerts, the school is working towards Sing Up silver award; LAMDA popular; plays; jazz and street dance as well as ballet; debating, poetry reciting, creative writing and handwriting competitions. Charity work for Africa linked to a Bradford Royal Infirmary skin care research project; several trips – Year 4–6 residentials; theme days, e.g. with staff dressing up too. Breakfast club and after school provision.

Like the senior school, very thoughtfully run, strong on relationships and offering a wide range of opportunities.

Lambrook School

Winkfield Row, Bracknell, Berkshire, RG42 6LU

• Pupils: Prep: 200 boys and 120 girls, 20 weekly board; pre-prep 105 boys and 45 girls • C of E • Fees: Day £8,661-£14,484; Boarding £16,635-£20,784 pa • Independent

Tel: 01344 882 717
Fax: 01344 891 114
Email: marketing@lambrook.berks.sch.uk
Website: www.lambrook.berks.sch.uk

Headmaster: Since 2010, Mr Jonathan Perry, previously head of Kingsmead School in Hoylake. Degree in religious studies and history from the University of Gloucestershire and a PGCE from Cambridge.

Entrance: From local primaries, Montessori schools and own popular pre-prep. Children can and do come at any time – half term, relocation, whatever, 'as long as there is space'. High percentage of first time buyers. All prep school entrants assessed prior to entry. More pupils coming out of London to take up the weekly boarding option, particularly into Year 7 as a gentle introduction to boarding before their senior transition.

Exit: Array of scholarships. Leavers to a range of destinations – Eton, Shiplake, Charterhouse, Wellington, Bradfield, Haileybury, Rugby, Marlborough, Leighton Park. St George's, Ascot draws small numbers of girls who leave at 11.

Remarks: Lambrook and Haileybury separated finally from Haileybury senior school in July 2009 and is now known simply as Lambrook. Flourishing – numbers continue to increase and facilities improve. Mélange of mismatched buildings – the old, new, grand and the ghastly: serene chapel, utilitarian 60s assembly hall. Boarding facilities recently overhauled completely with the girls now occupying the main school building and the boys all in Westfield – both have their own kitchen, games and TV rooms. Terrific grounds: burgeoning blooms, manicured sports pitches, boy-inspiring woods for camping, the all-important Astro, plus squash, tennis, swimming pool, golf, sports hall – something for everyone.

A flourishing purpose built pre-prep, complete with adventure playground and exquisite quiet garden looked after by the children. A speech therapist available should a child require an assessment. Mums' army runs clubs, helps with swimming, fundraising (lots for charity) and socials for parents/staff but isn't involved in helping in the classroom – reading et al very much left to the experts. Classes average 16 (maximum 18) with three or four parallel classes in each year group. Since January 2007 has run a nursery, The Westfield Saplings. The children can enter following their third birthday and can mix and match morning and afternoon sessions, leading to their entry into the pre-prep in the September following their fourth birthday.

Academically impressive, especially given broad-based intake. Believes in offering provision for the whole family, not just the brightest of the brood – 'If a child can benefit from what we offer we're happy to take them on board and put in strategies and support, though we have to be realistic too'. Twenty per cent or so with mild/moderate SEN. Always a good handful of scholars, Greek for the gifted, public speaking practices and lots of options. Drama timetabled and masses of music. Eighty per cent of the children play at least one instrument and the choir is seriously good – they provide trebles for Eton and have produced their own CD; lots of rehearsals (singing lessons subsidised) but trips and fun too. Good work and lively displays abound.

Very comprehensive learning support division, recently rehoused – all staff in the learning development centre are dyslexia trained specialists but deal with a range of difficulties including the dys-strata, EAL, ADD/ADH (mild) and sensory integration problems CP (though must be able to manage stairs). OT and SALT by arrangement. If child boards, matrons will practise any exercises set by therapists, optometrists etc. Recognises SEN no respecter of ability or talent – 'Unit children are often stars of the show: many are very bright, even gifted, but have terrible memories or poor organisation'. Offers study skills and strategies, uses a multi-sensory approach – very à la carte: 'We'll do whatever is in the IEP'. Each unit child has class teaching strategies/targets – passed to all staff for implementation; these bridge the gaps and keep lines of communication open. As a rule of thumb, child must need no more than seven lessons (of 35 minutes each) in the LDC a week, unless for short, sharp shock (as with EAL children). Says, 'We can't wrap children in cotton wool – they'll choke, so we encourage them to cope.' Works on targets, and self-evaluation is so successful, similar being rolled out for all children via new tutorial system.

Run as a boarding school with day children. Occasional boarding flourishing but full boarding numbers are close to single figures. Currently no one in on Saturday evenings, but provision is there if needed and Fridays are oversubscribed. School says, 'There are popular theme and party nights throughout the term and all children are encouraged to give it a go.' Much improved Saturday school a big hit – options extend from theatre studies, fashion design, public speaking through to traditional sport and academic subjects – emphasis on breadth in Years 5–6 and extending or reinforcing in Years 7–8.

Children polite, happy; rescues the odd refugee from hothoused environments. Food tasty and healthy – always a choice. Now very much a co-ed school, on the up, solid, family oriented, not quite 'sale of the century' but getting there.

Lanesborough School

Linked to Royal Grammar School (Guildford) in the Senior section

Maori Road, Guildford, Surrey, GU1 2EL

• Pupils: 350 boys, all day • Ages: 3-13 • C of E • Fees: £7,437-£10,026 pa • Independent

Tel: 01483 880 650
Fax: 01483 880 651
Email: secretary@lanesborough.surrey.sch.uk
Website: www.lanesborough.surrey.sch.uk

Head: Since 2007, Mrs Clare Turnbull BA (Exeter), previously deputy head at the school since 2004. Married to Andrew, who works in charity finance. Youthful, open and chatty, has an energetic presence – teaching of games reluctantly sacrificed on headship (but she does teach PHSE to top two years and French lower down the school). Considers herself fortunate to have taken over a school in such great shape and has no desire to 'make changes for their own sake'. However she is doing lots of improving and tweaking around edges – more cathedral choristers (now 20 in all), installing of pitch floodlighting and ideas for mezzanine in gym to increase performance space are all keeping her busy. She feels atmosphere is very important and is keen that all achievements should be recognised. We don't often see a woman as head of a boys' prep school – but Mrs Turnbull is one to watch.

Entrance: Three main points of entry. For unselective admission to nursery, registration advised between one to two years old. Thereafter, boys joining from elsewhere are given gentle assessment for pre-prep, 'really just to see their levels of concentration and how they respond to instructions'. At 7+ about 18 extra places available. The process then is designed to check similar skills, formalised into English, spelling, non-verbal reasoning and maths papers, interview and reading. This takes place on a Saturday, but only after all candidates have spent an afternoon seeing the school in action – playing games with PE masters, taking part in some music and, most importantly, having a doughnut. 'By including sports and music teachers in the selection system, we hope to achieve a balance of boys beyond the basic academic. Good orchestras and match results matter too.' Main feeder schools to prep are Glenesk in East Horsley and St Hilary's at Godalming.

Exit: About 55 per cent move on to the topnotch Royal Grammar School in Guildford, though far from an automatic shoo-in. Other perennial exit favourites include St John's Leatherhead, Charterhouse, Wellington, Cranleigh and Reeds. Recent 13+ scholarships (2006–2009) include 11 to RGS, 14 to St John's, three to Reed's, two to Charterhouse, one to Winchester, Wellington and City of London Freeman's.

Remarks: Traditional prep school with lots to shout about but with an unusually inclusive feel. New head is seamlessly continuing the good work. Suits those who are either bright or at least want to try their best. Not for the unwilling, disruptive or those with more challenging behaviours. On the whole, happy parents (particularly those who ultimately get a much coveted RGS place) and certainly happy children.

Shares the same governing body as the Royal Grammar School in Guildford (RGS). Care is taken to maintain a level of autonomy and although geographically not close, the two heads and schools' departments liaise on curriculum matters – so much so that Lanesborough sends at least twice the number of boys to RGS than any other feeder school (20 per cent of RGS pupils).

Boys start in the main part of Lanesborough in Year 3, joined by a new intake to make an additional parallel class, and are mostly taught by class teachers until Year 5. Setting for maths only Year 4 and 5, then maths and English from Year 6, though fluidity between sets remains. The very able boys certainly do well in maths, though parent mutterings suggest a more inspired approach could help others. Latin for everyone from Year 5 along with first taste of exams – none before this 'as learning should be an ongoing delight, not an end with a fear of getting things wrong'. No separate scholarship class. Progress monitored via assessment database with grades for effort and attainment pitched against recently fine-tuned 'Lanesborough Scale'. No de-merit or minus points systems, but discipline is managed by red and yellow cards, football analogy proving resonant.

SEN provision particularly praised by parents, but the odd report of severe dyslexics having not coped here in the past. In spite of small proportion of boys needing it, support is taken seriously – up to one lesson a week with specialist at no extra cost, thereafter charged. 'All boys feel really valued and encouraged by their peers and the school,' approves a mother. 'There are no feelings of inadequacy.'

In common with most preps, sport is integral to boys' lives here. The focus is particularly on breadth of activity – all rotate to try 10 different disciplines in any one year. The school is keen to winkle out hidden talent -it has produced two county level fencers from scratch this way. Traditional sports strong and it is sport for all – D and E teams often fielded in football, rugby and cricket. The boys play on the two pitches (grass and Astroturf) at the back of school or walk 10 minutes to Stoke Park – not ideal, though most parents are resigned to this inconvenience in the Guildford suburbs. Pitches also heavily used during lesson breaks on a rotation basis. Swimming is taught to all.

Ideal for music loving boys – famed for its music. It provides choristers for Guildford Cathedral – boys may be invited to join choir at age 8 and receive a bursary which reduces their fees. In the past they've sung for HM The Queen (Royal Maundy), broadcast by BBC. Popular school choir with over 90 boys. Class music lessons taken by all. 145 boys learn musical instruments in school – amounting to 1,700 timetabled lessons per term! And it all starts young with the pre-prep entering the Godalming Music Festival. Recently, a Year 8 boy awarded IAPS Young Musician of the Year. At least two school concerts each term; the carol service at Guildford Cathedral is one of few occasions that the school gets together as a whole.

Sited on leafy, suburban north east edge of Guildford in two converted red-brick Edwardian houses with later additions. Not a hugely spacious place and some facilities are rather cramped, which fazes some parents but doesn't worry others. The pre-prep, in Braganza House, including nursery, is actually accessed from a parallel road through its own entrance. Acting head is now Mrs Shore, who was the senior teacher. (A permanent head is to be appointed.) The pre-prep is spotless and bright with a purposeful hum of activity; that said, it has a gentle almost spiritual feeling too.

Impressive recent artwork everywhere (only two weeks into start of year when we visited) coupled with some new interactive whiteboards. Mrs Turnbull is keen not to fall into trap of many other schools – acquiring 'all singing and dancing technologies to impress the parents', while she is mindful of her responsibility to keep attracting good teachers, as 'most now expect them'.

Picket-fenced area protects nursery boys from general rough (though not very) and tumble of Braganza playground. Boys encouraged to cultivate gardens – these green-fingered souls always do well at Guildford in Bloom displays. Library particularly well stocked and thumbed with colourful murals of fictional characters. All boys, other than in nursery, have cafeteria-style hot school lunches – 'Too many activities going on at lunchtime for all to sit down together'. Across the road at Lanesborough the atmosphere changes – definitely a more serious feel here. Still similar style of well maintained buildings but now with an ordered, almost reverential, hush.

Boys quite a tidy bunch dress-wise – in fact they would look rather out of place if scruffy in such an ordered environment – but, like those at many boys' schools, they are far from immaculate. Parents largely Surrey middle class with all the social trappings that this entails, though not all very rich – sacrifices made by some to be there. Small sprinkling of other cultures, notably Asian pupils.

Very much a carrot rather than stick environment, building the confidences of eager beaver boys.

Latchmere School

Latchmere Road, Kingston Upon Thames, Surrey, KT2 5TT

• Pupils: 680 boys and girls; all day • Ages: 3-11 • Non-denom • State

Tel: 020 8546 7181
Fax: 020 8549 9182
Email: LTS@rbksch.org
Website: www.latchmerej.kingston.sch.uk

Head Teacher: Since 2008, Mrs Julie Ritchie, CertEd BPhilEd MSI SIP (Special). Married with two children. Enjoys music and reading. Aims to ensure Latchmere School is outstanding in all areas whilst developing and growing.

Entrance: At 3+ to nursery. A scrabble for the 52 places (26 each in one morning and one afternoon session). Nursery place doesn't absolutely guarantee main school place. At 4+ 90 places in reception in a three form entry; in 2009 Latchmere gained an extra reception class, bringing the numbers to 120. Nursery and reception entry criteria are the same – looked-after children, a sibling, a special need and then proximity to school gets you in, in that order. Latchmere and Fern Hill (qv) are the two top-notch, over-subscribed schools in North Kingston. They're not far apart and those who live equidistant between the two have an agonising decision over which to choose – 'I had to keep ringing both schools to find out how many parents had applied from which roads, so that I could decide which one to put down as my first choice,' said one prospective parent. We're talking savvy parents in this area – many could afford independent schooling at a pinch but come here instead. 'I want my child to be part of the local community,' says one.

Exit: Majority move on to Grey Court School in Ham, the nearest state secondary school, others to various state secondary schools in Kingston, including Hollyfield and Coombe. Significant number (10+) to selective Tiffin grammar schools. Handful to local independent day schools, mostly Kingston Grammar and Surbiton High.

Remarks: Latchmere infant and junior schools were amalgamated and reopened in September 2007 as Latchmere School – an all-through primary, which has an associated Children's Centre incorporating health and community facilities. Impetus for the move came as part of Kingston Borough's push to implement the government's 'Every Child Matters' vision of creating a joined-up system of health, family support, childcare and education services. Both separate schools were very successful in their own right but, despite the usual 'if it ain't broke ...' maxim, most parents strongly supportive of the change. School says it will allow better continuity across the curriculum from key stage 1 to 2 and help the children mix more across the age range. Cash has been forthcoming for the necessary building work – the two schools already shared a site, so reasonably straightforward.

Ofsted paid a visit in 2009 to inspect Latchmere as a primary school for the first time and pronounced it 'outstanding' in all respects. 'At the heart of the success lies a commitment towards educating the whole child, both academically and emotionally,' they enthuse. 'It succeeds overwhelmingly in both these aims.' No areas of weakness identified, only an edict to ensure that systems, curriculum and ethos benefit both children and staff.

Latchmere scores well in SATs tests well above local and national average, all the more impressive because it has higher than average numbers of EAL pupils. Breadth of learning, says head, is what enables it to do so well by its pupils. Specialist teachers for art, music, social skills and French; more able linguists offered either German or Spanish. Parents are impressed by the professionalism and teamwork shown by staff – pleasing number of male teachers around the place.

Children enjoy lessons and are able to work independently and quietly from an early age. Opportunities for grouping by ability are timetabled into the day, so that all abilities can be dealt with, including the very able and those with special needs. Range of teaching methods employed to support different learning styles. Good provision for SEN and considerable expertise among staff with dyslexia, dyspraxia, ADHD and autistic spectrum disorder. Few children need one-to-one support but group support is widely employed. Large team of teaching assistants support SEN teacher in her efforts with some 70 plus children. Brighter children well challenged with initiatives including science days, citizenship conference and master classes at senior schools.

Art, sport and music are all particular curriculum strengths. Art teacher and artroom help pupils produce outstanding work, of a standard normally expected from older pupils. Numerous opportunities for music, through class teaching from the specialist teacher and instrumental tuition from peripatetic teachers, plus two choirs and an orchestra. Sport is overseen by dedicated teachers of PE. Three sessions a week timetabled. School has its own on-site heated indoor swimming pool (funded by PTA) in use from spring to autumn, large grass playing fields across the road and playground space for hard courts. Football, cricket and netball squads do well in borough competitions – many cups proudly displayed in the hallway. Sports day is a major event – every child's achievements earning points for the team. Indoor sports hall planned, to be shared with the community.

Social skills programme very evident – friendship bench and squad make playtime a happy sociable occasion and pupil-written rules are up in the classrooms. Positive discipline promoted by pupils learning to take responsibility for their own actions through this programme. Makes a real difference, as much for the older child learning to mediate as for the child being helped. School council taken seriously – pupils vie for a place. 'Blue Room' is a fantastic facility characteristic of the ethos of care and support for the children: used for PSHE and as a centre for relaxation for pupils and staff, it features soft, soothing music, blue walls and a magnificent sunset mural; pupils say it helps them cope with any worries.

Outdoor play space divided into several rich and exciting areas for different activities – quiet or active – and includes an 'enchanted wood' area of trees, paths and benches, with a playhouse nestling at the end and some good climbing equipment.

Generally communications with parents are very good. Weekly newsletter and governor's reports written in an informative but informal style. Parents are made to feel valued here and repay the compliment in spades, raising huge amounts of money – a staggering £60,000 some years ago for the pool just one example – and helping out in the classrooms. School would be a poorer place without them.

Working parents delighted by the wraparound care packages on offer – holiday clubs and in term time it's possible to drop off at 7.45am and collect at 5.45pm every day. Choice from more than 30 after-school clubs – fairly varied and including lots of sport. A very health conscious environment and the children learn a lot about fitness and health – in addition to all the PE and swimming, three 'healthy days' a year to promote their understanding of health issues. Water for all, milk for nursery children, fruit for KS1 and pupil-made oat flapjacks available mid morning – children able to explain why the slow release energy of the oats is good for them. Unusually, the school runs its own show at lunchtime, producing hot meals of surprisingly high quality. 'They really seem to care about food here,' says a father in a surprised voice.

A shining star in North Kingston and beyond – good academics, wide ranging curriculum, great emphasis on social skills in the broadest sense and fiercely loyal and supportive parents. New head and new setup make interesting spectacle.

Lathallan School

Linked to Lathallan Senior School in the Senior section

Brotherton Castle, Johnshaven, By Montrose, DD10 0HN

- Pupils: 120 (5-13), mostly day pupils but around 25 opt to weekly or flexi-board (62 max); plus nursery with up to 45 babies and children.
- Ages: 8-13, prep 5-8, nursery 7 weeks to 5 years. • Non-denom
- Fees: Pre-prep £8,565; Prep £10,830-£12,273; Boarding +£3,510 pa
- Independent

Tel: 01561 362220
Fax: 01561 361695
Email: admissions@lathallan.org.uk
Website: www.lathallan.org.uk

Headmaster: Mr Richard Toley is now headmaster of the whole school. Mr James Ferrier is deputy head. See senior school entry.

Entrance: Springboard Nursery: from six weeks, 80 tinies registered but no more than 49 at any one time. Handful of real babes being pushed out in three prams when we visited (good North Sea air). Nappies not a problem. This is a 50 week nursery with two weeks off for Christmas. Magic (and not at all expensive).

Exit: Senior school an unknown quantity in the junior school – some pupils are still opting for traditional secondary schools, as in Glenalmond, Strathallan, Fettes, Merchiston etc, plus tiny dribble down south – St Margaret's Eskrick, but their number is diminishing. Magnificent record of scholarships.

Remarks: Some funds on hand for new development, looking for £2m. Some bursarial and scholarship help available. Nursery goes from strength to strength, ditto junior school. Senior school seems to be settling in remarkably well. Brave new venture – bated breath ain't in it.

Latymer Prep School

Linked to Latymer Upper School in the Senior section

36 Upper Mall, Hammersmith, London, W6 9TA

• Pupils: 165 girls and boys; all day • Ages: 7-11 • Non-denom
• Fees: £12,705 pa • Independent

Tel: 0845 638 5700
Fax: 0845 638 5732
Email: mlp@latymerprep.org
Website: www.latymerprep.org

Principal: Mr S P Dorrian BA (previously head of English and head of Years 7 and 8 in the senior school).

Entrance: Maths, English and verbal reasoning exams at 7+ interview.

Exit: Virtually all go on to the senior school. Very occasionally parents advised to move their child to a less academic establishment.

Remarks: Beautifully-situated building with views over the Thames from one side and lawns from the other side, plus all the senior school facilities. Has broadened the activities available since going co-ed, e.g. circus skills as well as football at playtime – 'We have some very unsporty boys who spend all their time on stilts'. Mixed teams for all sports, dance also available – 'The boys love it'. Curriculum enriched by, for instance, looking at famous women in history. Italian from Year 3 and French and Italian in Year 6. Broad curriculum benefits from not having to work towards Common Entrance.

SEN department liaises closely with the senior school; currently four pupils with statements of needs, any pupils with suspected problems are given 'a battery of tests' to suss out their problems. School can deal with mild to moderate dyslexia et al but, if pupil has 'severe' dyslexia, then parents are advised to get external help. (The school feels that pupils with severe dyslexia benefit from specialist teachers outside school.) Not frightened of Asperger's – one pupil currently with full-time mentor, part paid for by the school and part by the parents. Can deal with moderate physical problems, CP, ADHD, profoundly deaf etc. Pupils who provide educational psychologist's report get 25 per cent extra time in their entrance exam. Two fully trained and dedicated staff, one-to-one help, school will 'pick up and run' with pupils, but must be able to access mainstream.

Laxton Junior School

Linked to Oundle School in the Senior section

East Road, Oundle, Northamptonshire, PE8 4BX

• Pupils: 265; boys and girls • Ages: 4-11 • C of E • Fees: £8,790-£9,630 pa
• Independent

Tel: 01832 277 275
Fax: 01832 277 271
Email: lat@laxtonjunior.org.uk
Website: www.laxtonjunior.org.uk

Headmaster: Since 2008, Mr Mark Potter BEd (mid thirties). Educated at Deben High School in Felixstowe and Liverpool John Moores University. Began career at St Mark's RC Primary School in Ipswich, then moved abroad to teach at schools run by Shell in Nigeria and China. Energetic, enthusiastic and very youthful. Knows virtually every child by name and enjoys chatting to them as he goes round the school. Arrived at Laxton Junior as deputy head in 2007. Six weeks later, when the head's post was advertised, he applied for and got the top job. 'It truly is a fabulous school,' he says, 'and having that year as deputy to learn from my predecessor was ideal.' Loves teaching and in his second year taught mental maths to every year group – an impressive achievement for a busy head. In 2009–10, he ran a polymath club for Years 4 to 6. He's a member of Oundle School's senior management team and meets Charles Bush, Oundle's headmaster, at least once a term. Wife, Lisa, is an early years teacher and they have two young children (their daughter in reception at Laxton Junior).

Entrance: Most children start in reception in the September after they are four (non-selective at this stage). Pupils joining later on spend trial day at school and also take verbal and non-verbal reasoning tests. Every year group has maximum of 40. Waiting lists for several year groups, but not all, so it's always worth talking to the school. Some means-tested bursary provision and an annual award set up in previous head's name for all-rounder entering Year 5 (10 per cent of fees).

Exit: At 11, two-thirds to three-quarters move on to Oundle as day pupils (the occasional boarder) but attending Laxton Junior in no way guarantees automatic passage to the senior school. Oundle's entrance exam has to be passed and as head of Laxton Junior points out, 'We have quite a breadth of ability so Oundle won't be suitable for all the children'. Others to Oakham, Kimbolton, The Peterborough School, Stamford School and Stamford High. Around a quarter of each year group win scholarships to their senior schools. Occasionally a child might head to a traditional prep school like Winchester House or Bilton Grange for Years 7 and 8.

Remarks: Founded in 1973 but moved from its original premises in picturesque Oundle to its new purpose-built home in 2002, when the school roll doubled in size. Fantastic school building is light and airy, with wide corridors and spacious classrooms. School prides itself on its academic achievements – curriculum is based on the national one but 'adapted to suit the requirements of our children and our school'. As head says, 'Learning is at the heart of everything we do.' Two classes per year group and never more than 20 in a class. No setting, except in maths from Year 4. French taught from reception and Spanish available as an after-school activity. Older children taught by subject specialists – science and maths teachers have strong links with their counterparts at Oundle. Everyone gets two ICT lessons a week in suite equipped with 22 computers. Terminals to be fitted throughout school in 2011.

Younger children do an hour's prep a week (letter sounds and reading) while older ones get 30 to 60 minutes a night. No prep set for Friday or weekends and no Saturday school. Those requiring learning support get extra help from four-strong educational support team, either in small groups or one-to-one. When we visited, 68 children were receiving help – no extra fees charged for this. Total of 35 teachers at school – a few are part-time but all form teachers are full-time. Around a quarter of today's primary schools don't have any male teachers at all but 18 per cent of Laxton's teaching staff are men (including a teaching assistant and form teachers in reception, Year 4 and Year 6).

Head firmly believes that all children should get their turn in the spotlight, whether it's for academic, sporting or artistic achievements, being polite or having 'super personal skills'. Music very popular – all Year 2 children learn the violin or cello and from Year 3 those wishing to continue receive group or individual lessons. Around 200 music lessons timetabled a week – everything from piano, violin and drums to the bagpipes. Hymn practice for all each week, plus orchestras, choirs and a brass ensemble to join. The children we met during our visit were very keen on sport – rugby, football and cricket for boys and netball, hockey and rounders for girls. New full-time sports teacher says school does pretty well in matches but he'd like 'our sporting prowess to match our academic and musical prowess'. Chess and swimming particularly strong. All year groups get one swimming lesson a week at Oundle's six-lane pool. Raft of after-school clubs and activities on offer from 3.45 to 4.45 – choices include yoga and flower arranging!

School is C of E (has strong links with St Peter's Church in Oundle) but also celebrates other faiths. Oundle School's chapel used for carol service and end of year service. Two whole school assemblies a week, plus house and key stage gatherings on other days. School encourages children to respect others and the environment and pupils' behaviour is very good. Clear discipline system – poor behaviour is noted in the discipline book and if this happens three times pupils go 'on report', but in the past three years only three names entered. Staff keen on 'positive praise' – as we walked round the school head thanked pupils each time they held a door open. Mobiles, iPods etc aren't banned but teachers say the children 'just don't bring them in'.

Four houses – plenty of inter-house matches and competitions. School is rightly proud of its school council, which comprises representatives from each year group, plus the head boy, head girl and their deputies. Recent suggestions to have been implemented include proper football goal posts and hairdryers in the girls' changing rooms. Pupils give school dinners the thumbs-up (especially the puddings) and say they like walking across to the senior school in pairs for lunch, accompanied by their teachers. When we asked about rainy days, the children told us, 'it just never seems to rain at lunch-time'. Teachers eat lunch with the children, encouraging good manners and conversation.

Head says pupils are polite, well-mannered, can hold a conversation and speak freely – and that's certainly what we found. When we asked school council members if there was anything they'd change about the school, just one grumble – 'I think the Year 4s should be allowed to read "Swallows and Amazons",' requested one boy. The head promised to look into it.

Most live in Oundle and its pretty surrounding villages. The majority arrive by car, although Laxton staff are keen to encourage local children to walk to school. Parents range from those for whom 'fees are a drop in the ocean' to others who have to work flat out to send their children to the school. New parents appreciate the impressively active parent and friends' association, which organises a variety of social events and has a raft of parent reps. 'The parents are very supportive,' says head. 'We look after their babies, and they want them to be safe and secure in an environment where they are going to be successful learners with high challenge and low stress.' Excellent parent handbook details everything from the school day and behaviour code to snacks (fruit provided in morning and afternoon breaks) and uniform (blue and grey).

Last time round we commented that Laxton Junior School might be tough for the more sensitive child, but this is definitely not the case now. Led by a dynamic head, it's a happy, successful place that offers a first-class, all-round education.

Lincoln Minster Preparatory School

Linked to Lincoln Minster School in the Senior section

Eastgate, Lincoln, Lincolnshire, LN2 1QG

• Pupils: boys and girls • Ages: 2-11 • Fees: Day from £7,356; Boarding from £16,638 pa • Independent

Tel: 01522 523 769
Fax: 01522 514 778
Email: lincoln.prep@church-schools.com
Website: www.lincolnminsterschool.co.uk

Headmistress: Mrs Karen Maltby.

Remarks: For details see senior school.

Little St Helen's and St Helen's Junior school

Eastbury Road, Northwood, Middlesex, HA6 3AS

• Pupils: Little St Helen's 225; Junior School 250; all girls • Ages: Little St Helen's 3-7; Junior School 7-11; all girls • C of E but all faiths welcome • Fees: £3,210-£3,360; Nursery £2,942 pa • Independent

Tel: 01923 843210
Fax: 01923 843 211
Email: admissions@sthn.co.uk
Website: www.sthn.co.uk

Head: Since 2000, Mrs Mary Morris BA PGCE (fiftyish). A geographer who taught at Dr Challoner's High before coming to the school in 1998 as deputy head. An internal appointment then and, unlike many such, received with popular acclaim which no-one has since regretted. One of the most engaging heads we have encountered – voluble, smiley, relaxed and frank. It's a bit like talking to your best friend, except that Mrs Morris is, clearly, a wholly professional head. So many girls' schools still seem to be run on the 'we're ever so nice really' principle without the forward-looking, cutting edge taken for granted in the boys' equivalents – not so here.

An inspirational head who is also huge fun. She knows her girls, her staff, her stuff, her school and her market, and underpins the lot with a profound belief in spiritual and moral values. Conducted an 'audit' of the spiritual content of the academic curriculum – 'We need to be moral in lessons – there should be social, spiritual, moral and cultural elements in every single lesson'. Unashamedly partisan about single sex education for girls, she parried a question from a potential (male) parent who asked why he should send his daughters to a girls' school rather than to a co-ed, 'This is not a girls' school – it's a school and, unfortunately, we don't have room for any boys'. Clearly still thrilled about her appointment, she says, 'This is an incredibly moral job. Above everything else, we are rôle models.'

Entrance: At three or four by observation and interview. At seven by tests in English, maths and non VR and interview.

Exit: Usually a smooth transition from LSH to the juniors and from juniors to seniors, but head is clear, 'We do it very carefully. If I genuinely think a girl will struggle, we talk to the parents well in advance – usually by Year 4 – and help them look at alternatives'. Very few to local state grammars, boarding or competition.

Remarks: The nursery, Little St Helen's and the junior school are all housed in buildings around this beautiful site and share many of the facilities of the main school. Some buildings have more inviting exteriors than others; however each has bright, airy classrooms, excellent, thoughtful displays and exhibited artwork, libraries, gyms, good-sized halls or studios and is well-resourced. Heartening posters greet one, e.g. 'Enter with an Open Mind', and we saw an exciting display about pirates complete with huge paper schooner. Lots of ICT, good DT and everyone tries out three languages before they move up to the senior school. All do ballet, PE, music and speech and drama as part of the curriculum. Happy atmosphere, lovely bright uniform, civilised loos and teachers who say, 'Ladies, will you please take off your shoes now,' to a crocodile of receptive six year olds.

A teacher, teaching assistant and gapper to each class in Little Saints, some teaching assistants in junior school. 'I think these girls are so lucky,' sighed the registrar wistfully as we strolled. 'We are the lucky ones', replied a passing teacher.

Lockers Park School

Lockers Park Lane, Hemel Hempstead, Hertfordshire, HP1 1TL

• Pupils: 150 boys; 25 full boarders, 40 flexi and the rest day • Ages: 5-13 • C of E • Fees: Day £8,100-£14,685; Boarding £18,240 pa • Independent

Tel: 01442 251 712
Fax: 01442 234 150
Email: secretary@lockerspark.herts.sch.uk
Website: www.lockerspark.herts.sch.uk

Headmaster: Since September 2010, Mr David Farquharson BA PGCE (forties), previously head of history, deputy head and head of boarding at Beaudesert Park in Gloucestershire. Mr Farquharson has taught at boarding preparatory schools in England and Scotland. He teaches history and is a keen sportsman – a Rugby Football Union and Scottish Rugby Union qualified coach and a Football Association qualified referee. Wife, Brigid, has taught in maintained and prep sectors (the latter for the past 15 years). She teaches English at Lockers Park and is very involved on the pastoral side. They have a daughter and a son, both at university/college.

Entrance: Having resisted the temptation to add a nursery class – plenty locally that do the job well, according to the head – takes boys from five, who join the Year 1 class (known as 'Chestnuts'). A tie-up with nearby girls' school, Abbots Hill, which takes boys in the nursery. After that and spaces allowing, boys can arrive at any time from state or prep schools – the oft-cited reason for the move being that boys find they are not suited to the level of attainment and behaviour set by co-ed schools.

'No entry exam as such,' says school – uses a 'simple academic assessment test' in verbal and numerical reasoning designed to spot 'potential' and an interview. 'We want boys with a spark,' says head. A scholarship day in early February when boys can try out for up to 50 per cent remission in fees according to academic ability, talent in music, art or sport, or all-round. Historically has offered a lot of bursaries and the head is trying to encourage boys living within walking distance to take advantage.

Exit: Generally to top independent boarding schools, e.g. Harrow, Stowe, Shrewsbury, Bedford, Eton; a handful to day schools. Several academic, drama, music scholarships every year. 'Lockers Park really finds the right shape peg for each boy,' says a parent. 'The head and staff know each individual boy so well that they can recognise strengths and weaknesses and advise parents on the best possible next step.'

Remarks: Boys can be boys here – positively encouraged in every aspect of life at this singularly male focused school. From the 40-minute morning break – ringing the bell to signal the end of it prompts a swarm of faces to emerge from the shrubbery and belt across the rolling parkland – to the well considered structure of classes, lessons and activities, purpose-built to bring out the best in a boy.

Founded in 1874 as a feeder school for Rugby, on the train line, red-brick buildings sit in 23 glorious acres of woodland, playing fields and sports pitches that have since been engulfed by one of the less prepossessing suburbs of Hemel Hempstead. But this just serves to emphasise this close-knit 'Boys' Own' world – 'There's no real stress or pressure,' reports a parent. 'The boys work hard when they have to, but there is nothing that gets in the way of them being children.' Certainly, the atmosphere is matey and informal, characterised by the lack of uniform – boys wear blue cords and their own choice of check shirt day to day, with grey flannels, a tie and tweed jacket for 'best' – and the friendly staff, who work with small classes – 14 on average in the lower school and 16 in Year 7 (now has three forms) – giving real attention to each individual.

A long day – up to 12 hours, including breakfast, lunch and supper even for day boys if they want it – and a fifth board full-time, which all helps to cement the community feel. 'If you ask the boys who is a boarder and who is a day boy, they probably won't be able to tell you – there is so much flexibility,' says the last head. Unusually, the boarding house is part of the main school building and is presided over by the history teacher, who is housemaster, supported by three matrons, two living in. The dorms are bright and functional and boys can choose their beds and bring their own duvet covers. Clothes are kept in the laundry room and the matrons lay out each boy's outfit for the day. The good boarding arrangements and convenient location just off the M25 tempt boys from London, overseas and the forces, although many are from local families. Unusual system of exeats – two weekends on and one off, so one every third weekend, from Friday lunchtime to Monday morning. On non-exeat weekends Saturday school until lunchtime, then fixtures in the afternoon.

Although a gentlemen's club feel to the original part of the school – the rather Spartan dining hall is panelled and furnished simply with long tables and chairs engraved with the names of former pupils – the classrooms are bright and welcoming, especially in the main teaching block, where younger classes are taught in their forms; Year 5 up have specialist teachers and are arranged by ability rather than age. Languages a speciality – French and Latin, with the option of Spanish and ancient Greek, and even Esperanto for the Year 8 scholars. Justifiably proud of its academic record – around a dozen secure top scholarships.

Academic lessons make as much use of the grounds and outside space as possible – when we visited, a science class was investigating the speed of sound by banging saucepans.

The inviting library has plenty of space for browsers and the whole school can fit into the chapel at a push. Favourite hang-outs for boys are the so-called 'boys' hall', which has a whiteboard with communications to pupils and is decorated with strewn bits and bobs of sporting paraphernalia, and the old gym, essentially a rec room for snooker and free time.

Boys' pride and joy, though, is the 'train room', filled with a huge model railway layout with numerous engines and complete with scenery, which the boys tinker with.

Although the school buildings are generally in excellent nick, the last head had a plan to revamp the hall, with its sunken seating area and a stage, to create a mezzanine level. However, he departed after only three years so we await Mr Farquharson's take on things. DT has recently been re-housed in a new block at the back of the school and is sensibly divided into a design room and a work room to circumvent the problem of boyish fiddly fingers. Large art room inspires one or two boys a year to gain scholarships to next schools. Good size, modern sports hall.

Outside, plenty of space to roam. Cricket nets at the front of the school and at the back is a football field slightly on the slope, but as the head points out, 'It's a game of two halves'. Rugby matches often field 100 boys – two thirds of the school – but also plenty of inter-set matches that call for every boy to take part. Tucked away are tennis courts and a swimming pool, as well as a nine-hole golf course, which needs some attention, head admits. A plot for vegetable growing, croquet lawn and putting green.

Daily session of games or activities in the afternoons, determined by boys' interest and prowess, which takes in the traditional sports plus jujitsu, shooting and more. 95 per cent of boys learn an instrument, many learn two, while the chapel choir is made up of 20 boys from all years. One major annual drama production and several others besides. Taking part is key here and great efforts are made to ensure that every boy feels he belongs. In particular, great indulgence for the quirks of life at Lockers, which are so numerous that newcomers are issued with a handbook to explain the finer points. Most baffling to the uninitiated is the school's own lingo – 'slatter' is sweets, named after a former master; houses are 'sets'; 'spin the platter' and 'bell and bolster' are traditional games that have been played at the Christmas feast since the First World War. School rules are kept to a minimum – instead an all-pervading ethos of Christian values and good citizenship – and punishments are rarely necessary, thanks to a system of rewards for success and good behaviour.

In all, a boarding prep that has hit on a winning formula of security, activity and motivation designed to prepare boys to continue with confidence and success to major public schools. New head has much to build on.

Lomond School Junior Department

Linked to Lomond School in the Senior section

10 Stafford Street, Helensburgh, G84 9JX

• Pupils: 100 boys and girls, plus nursery • Ages: Prep: 5-10, Nursery: 3-5
• Non-denom • Fees: Day £6,540-£8,850 pa • Independent

Tel: 01436 672 476
Fax: 01436 678 320
Email: admin@lomond-school.org
Website: www.lomond-school.org

Remarks: For details, see senior school.

The London Oratory School Junior House

Linked to London Oratory School (The) in the Senior section

Seagrave Road, London, SW6 1RX

• Pupils: 80 boys; all day • Ages: 7-11 • State
Fax: 0207 381 7676
Email: admin@los.ac
Website: www.london-oratory.org

Head: Since 2007, Mr David McFadden, head of The London Oratory School in its entirety.

Remarks: Not a separate school but a separate wing, the junior house, with four classrooms, a choir room and several practice rooms, as music is everything here. Officially it is part of the senior school but it is the part which takes under-age boys (7-11). Unofficially, it operates rather like a choir school in a cathedral school – only without the boarding. In that respect it is unique – the only state choir school. For potential applicants, who must be of at least average ability, musical promise is the only criterion which counts here, once you have demonstrated your Catholic credentials – all the boys have musical potential. Entrance tests in academic and musical aptitude. Not all boys are in the Schola – some just follow an instrumental course. The Schola sings every Saturday evening in the Brompton Oratory. Junior house boys play every instrument you can name under the care of innumerable peripatetic teachers of high quality and use all the senior school facilities. They tour, record and give stunning concerts. A super start in life for your musical, Catholic, motivated little boy.

For more details see senior school entry.

Loretto Junior School aka The Nippers

Linked to Loretto School in the Senior section

North Esk Lodge, North High Street, Musselburgh, East Lothian, EH21 6JA

• Pupils: 190 girls and boys; boarding and day • Ages: 3-12
• Non-denom • Fees: Boarding £15,465-£17,085; Day £3,210-£12,255 pa
• Independent

Tel: 0131 653 4570
Fax: 0131 653 4571
Email: juniorschool@loretto.com
Website: www.loretto.com

Headmaster: Since April 2009, Mr Philip Meadows (late forties). Head of chemistry at Loretto 1987–96, then housemaster at Sedbergh School and head of Mowden Hall School, Northumberland, and Tettenhall College Junior School, a day school in Wolverhampton. Married to Sylvia, three children, 16 and twins of 13.

Entrance: Entry from nursery (age three) and at all stages throughout the Junior School. Scholarship awards (academic and all rounder) may be offered to external candidates entering Years 6 and 7 and are for the duration of a pupil's education at both the junior and senior schools. A limited number of academic exhibitions are available to current pupils in Year 5 – these recognise achievement and effort in academic studies and are for Y6 and Y7 only. Pupils are assessed for general entry from Y4 onwards.

Exit: The majority of Nipper pupils move up to the senior school at 12.

Remarks: Super school. Historic campus on the edge of Edinburgh, close to East Lothian countryside, just across the River Esk. Newly refurbished and spacious co-ed boarding house, bright and cosy dorms. Parents can drop children from around 8am and collect around 6pm – very popular. Generously staffed; science lab and computer room, linked via cable to the communications and resource centre in the senior school; shares main school facilities – the Astroturf (which, to be honest, is quite a long hike for smaller legs) and theatre. Lots of extra curricular activities. Plus nursery.

Lovell House School

Linked to Nottingham High School in the Senior section
Linked to Nottingham High Junior School in the Junior section

13 Waverley Street, Nottingham, Nottinghamshire, NG7 4DX

• Fees: £7,446 pa • Independent

Tel: 0115 845 2222
Fax: 0115 924 9716
Email: lovellinfo@nottinghamhigh.co.uk
Website: www.nottinghamhigh.co.uk

Remarks: See Nottingham High School.

Ludgrove

Wixenford, Wokingham, Berkshire, RG40 3AB

• Pupils: 185 boys; all board • Ages: 8-13 • C of E • Fees: £20,850 pa
• Independent

Tel: 01189 789 881
Fax: 0118 979 2973
Email: office@ludgroveschool.co.uk
Website: www.ludgrove.net

The Headmasters: Since September 2008, the tradition of having joint heads has continued with Mr Simon Barber BA PGCE and Mr Sid Inglis BA PGCE, both in their late thirties. Mr Barber is the latest in the illustrious line of Barbers who have run Ludgrove. After an 'amusing' spell in the City, he decided that teaching was, after all, the right job for him and he cut his teeth at Ashdown House before joining the staff at Ludgrove. He is married to the delightful Sophie, who is responsible for the day to day running of the school. Together they live in the midst of the boys and closest to the youngest, who seem to share the landing with the Barbers' three young children – a home within a home. They are responsible for the pastoral side, but it really does feel as if they are parents of an extended family.

Mr Inglis, who has taught at Ludgrove for 15 years, is responsible for the academic side but, in truth, they overlap happily. After all, who would wish to separate the pastoral from the academic? Mr Inglis's bright and engaging wife, Olly, with a background in advertising, is overall responsible for marketing the school, though 'the most effective method is word of mouth and the loyalty of the old boys'. The Inglises, who also have young children, live close by, lunching with the boys on Sundays, and are actively involved with parents at match teas etc.

Both heads teach at least 20 periods a week and, between them, aim to teach every boy in the school. They also get stuck into games, coaching with enthusiasm. The two families make the most wonderful quartet of collective involvement and dedication. They are also tremendous fun. Anyone doubting the wisdom of having joint heads should visit Ludgrove – other reasons, too, of course.

Entrance: Being a proper boarding school and with a justifiably good reputation, they have a large catchment area with boys as far away as Yorkshire and Suffolk. A large number come from the London area – 'Boys are relieved to be fully involved seven days a week, rather than sitting in the car bored to tears while their sisters are driven to ballet lessons'. But this is not a refugee camp: it's a school with demanding academic standards, and although no entrance test, much is expected. Early registration is recommended: schools which are boarding only cannot be very flexible with numbers – it's all down to beds.

Exit: Eton, Harrow, Radley most popular destinations with occasional sorties to Marlborough and Stowe. Scholarships are won, of course, but those who like totting up the number of awards should remember that those schools don't award scholarships for having blue eyes.

Remarks: The majority of boys enter aged eight and are sympathetically eased into the school with the help of an obviously very competent team of women teachers. The boys, who expressed unbridled happiness with their lot, are taught in a separate wing of the main building and cocooned carefully before hatching out into the main school, where their 'shadows' lead them around assiduously. They are introduced to various activities to see what they like – judo is very popular – and careful preparation is the key. It shows – from natural good manners to spontaneous pleasure and alertness.

The school's policy on bullying is clearly defined and implemented. 'The heads would rocket down on any bullying,' one boy told us. A new 'listening ear' outsider for those who might require extra soothing and advice; according to one of our guides, the previous one was only contacted once when a boy couldn't find his Fives gloves. Nevertheless, as with all schools, always the possibility of bullying, and staff are not only alert to that but also reminded of the importance of setting a good example. Boys assured us that plenty of people to whom they could talk, including the long serving groundsmen and wise old carpenter who, after all, taught Mr Barber as a boy. In fact the community feeling of the school is most reassuring.

Excellent learning support. Every boy is screened on arrival and dyslexics are given one-to-one help (about 15 per cent) with another 5 per cent who regularly attend for TLC 'to help their self-esteem'. Some cracking good female teachers at this boys' school and not just for the new boys. The impressive head of science, for instance, helps to counter any myth that 'girls can't change light bulbs'.

Mrs Barber, accompanied by three year old Alice, showed us the newly carpeted dorms and landings covering the old lino, mourned by some boys who enjoyed sliding about on it. But the real excitement when we visited was the installation of a splendid new bathroom with showers, baths and everything else you would expect. Indeed such was the excitement that 'The Ludgrovian', a delightful home-grown weekly magazine, featured a huge photograph on the front with the caption, 'Cleanliness is next to godliness', and recording for posterity the name of the first boy to use the new showers. 'Templa quam delecta', as Mr Inglis might say.

Classrooms are well equipped with whiteboards, interactive boards, computers and all that jazz. Well equipped music school with pictures of boys who've achieved grade 5 on the Wall of Fame. Over a hundred boys learn instruments – but 'we could do with some cellists', says the infectiously enthusiastic young director, who recently persuaded the whole school – including cooks and bottle washers – to join in a singathon. Art, pottery and carpentry are timetabled in for all boys, including scholars; everyone is expected to try something extra-curricular. Staff appear young and enthusiastic – for the most part – though it's good to see some wise old heads around. 'It's a funny thing,' said one older boy, 'but staff don't seem to leave Ludgrove.' 'A good thing, on the whole,' commented a parent. Another parent confessed to some initial misgivings about the youth of the headmasters but added, 'Actually, they're shaping up rather well'.

The first three heads of Ludgrove were international footballers and the enthusiasm for sport remains. 'The school is justifiably proud of its sports record,' says Mr Barber, and boys of all abilities are involved in matches. All the usual games are on offer, from fencing to clay pigeon shooting, and more. Two squash courts and two fives courts, a nine hole golf course and a recently built heated indoor pool, a jumbo sports hall and 130 acres of grounds and woodlands in which to build camps (very popular), plot dynasties and indulge in every boy's favourite occupation of mucking about.

Weekends are full – 'It's impossible to be bored with these fabulous grounds,' said one young enthusiast, and every two or three weeks exeats from Friday midday to Sunday evening. (A minibus is laid on to Fulham – revealing.)

For a few – mostly people who haven't visited Ludgrove – 'The school is stuck in something of a time warp'. For others, 'It's a bastion of good manners and courtesy where boys can be boys and, above all, have fun while fulfilling their potential'. Yes, some features which might be considered old fashioned – the carpentry shop, for instance, but it's hugely popular and buzzes at weekends with evidence of excellent (and practical) work; modelling – the creative sort – is very popular, too. The ear-splitting cheers which broke out when Mr Barber entered the dining room holding aloft a batch of recently arrived modelling kits showed that television is not all-pervading; mobile phones are not allowed, but all boys have access to emails, though after chapel on Sunday boys write handwritten letters (sic). If such outdated habits induce thoughts of walrus moustaches and Luddites, look elsewhere or, better still, look more closely.

Not everyone likes single sex schools rather than co-ed – often those considerations blind parents to what a good school is. For those who value a school with lightness of touch but with firmly held principles based on understanding what makes boys tick; for those who aspire to a particular niche and want their sons to be happy with the chance of fulfilment; for those who wish to celebrate the richness of boyhood, this could be the school. Don't go because of the 'Who's Who' of names on the dining room wall – that's not what it's about. It won't suit everyone but it's well worth a visit – surely why no prospectus.

LVS Ascot (The Licensed Victuallers' Junior School)

Linked to LVS Ascot (Licensed Victuallers' School) in the Senior section

London Road, Ascot, SL5 8DR

• Pupils: 95 girls, 115 boys (30 boarding) • Ages: 4-11 • Non-denom • Fees: Day £7,761-£9,315; Boarding £19,875 pa • Independent

Tel: 01344 882 770
Fax: 01344 890 648
Email: registrar@lvs.ascot.sch.uk
Website: www.lvs.ascot.sch.uk

Headmistress: Since 2006, Mrs Helen Donnelly, read education and religious studies at the University of Kent. Previously taught at state schools in London and at Thomas's Battersea. Came to LVS in 2002; married with two young children.

Entrance: Non-selective so no exam. Vast majority of pupils enter reception class in September. One form for reception and Years 1 and 2, two for Years 3 and 4 and three for Years 4 and 5. A maximum of 20 pupils per form.

Exit: Virtually all pupils carry on into the senior school.

Remarks: Separate building a few paces away from the main school in same modern style. All ages housed in one light and airy open plan building with sliding doors into classrooms. Fine hall and computer centre and library. Lunch in main school dining hall with wide choice and excellent menus. Boarding on offer for Years 3 to 7, with separate girls' and boys' corridors but mixed communal areas. Hugely spacious, nurturing, cheery and – again – pleasantly airy. Junior pupils use senior school facilities increasingly as they go through the year groups, including the indoor pool, science labs, food tech room and sports facilities – a big advantage over most junior schools. French and Spanish taught. Lots going on and children well cared for. School day ends at 3.30pm.

The Lyceum

Kayam House, 6 Paul Street, London, EC2A 4JH

• Pupils: 95 boys and girls (including nursery); all day • Ages: 3–11 • Non-denom • Fees: £10,950 pa • Independent

Tel: 020 7247 1588
Email: lyceumschool@aol.com
Website: www.lyceumschool.co.uk

Heads: Opened in September 1997 by Lynn Hannay Cert Ed, now director of curriculum, and Jeremy Rowe BEd, now managing director. They formerly worked in the state sector as head and deputy of a challenging Hackney primary but eventually, fed up with 'endless government interference and a growing mountain of paper', decided to go it alone. Before they did so, however, they wrote a book describing their ideal school and The Lyceum is modelled on that template. Their priorities, then and now, were to create a liberal, progressive, child-centred education where tests and targets are definitely not a priority and creativity very much is. Both continue to teach – Rowe maths, Hannay English. He is passionate about the role of the arts in education, especially music, and is programme director of the Wagner Society. She is particularly interested in environmental studies.

Entrance: The school started with an advertisement in 'The Evening Standard' and just 16 families, but over the past decade its reputation and student numbers have grown steadily and it's now waiting list only, if you don't register early. Parents are recruited via 'dinner parties in Islington' and come largely from Islington, Hackney and, increasingly, the City. Places at three or four are allocated on a first come first served basis with priority to siblings. A few places for seven year olds and the odd vacancy later on, all awarded after assessment.

Exit: A few occasionally leave at seven for schools like City of London School for Girls but the Lyceum is reluctant to prepare children for exams at this point and most parents make the decision to stay till 11. The opposite of an exam factory – though children are carefully prepared for entrance tests at 11, this is not necessarily the ideal place for those looking for the most academic London day schools. A sprinkling each year to Highgate, UCS and City of London, otherwise the majority to Queen's College, Northbridge House and Portland Place. Pupils are particularly successful at winning scholarships for the arts and music – a number go to The Purcell School and St Marylebone School.

Remarks: A short walk from Liverpool Street and Moorgate, housed in a former warehouse, which from the outside looks like an ordinary office block. All classrooms, except for the nursery, in a spacious open-plan space in the basement – 'I prefer everything open plan,' says Hannay. 'That way problems don't arise.' Mornings are predominantly given over to academic work (generally topic-based, though with specialist teaching in French (from reception), Latin, maths and music) and afternoons devoted to creativity (music, painting, dance, drama as well as sport). Though the school has no outside space, it deals with the problem imaginatively with a covered playground for break plus trips to the local TTA training ground for organised games and to nearby Broadgate Centre for skating, where a qualified ice-dance instructor means the children learn to skate remarkably well. Every child does some form of physical activity every day.

Non-selective and has a SENCo, but can feel a child is beyond its range – 'We can cope with minor learning difficulties but have occasionally advised parents they will need more specialist help'. The atmosphere is thoroughly unpressured. No end of year exams until pupils start preparation for 11+ in the summer term of Year 5 (though verbal and non-verbal reasoning taught from Year 3) because it's felt that exams impinge on the 'real' education the school is giving. Year groups are small – largest 19, smallest 10 – and sometimes classes are merged to make up the numbers for games or other activities.

Art and music are both unusually strong – all music teachers are professional musicians – with three productions a year of drama, dance and music. Every child is taught the recorder from the start and also learns to sing; most take a second instrument as well. Dynamic displays of art throughout the building. Lots of residential trips from Year 3, based round subjects – a Year 6 trip, for example, to France to study Monet's garden. Also residential trips for seven year olds (overnight) and 10 year olds (a week).

The approach is generally down to earth with a sensible navy and white uniform. Strong emphasis on traditional manners. Few behavioural problems. One of the school's key benefits is that it is tailored to the needs of working parents. Many parents are City workers (though plenty in the media as well) and hours reflect their working day, so school starts at 8.30am and, for those who wish it, continues to 5.45pm with a wide range of after-school clubs (sport, chess, jazz band, cinema). 'It means, instead of nannies, we often have a very good relationship with parents.' All children bring packed lunch.

Suits those for whom exam statistics are not life's ultimate aim and, for those parents, does a remarkably good job. 'It's not a hothouse but it teaches kids to think for themselves. Not every child is going to get into Westminster, but it's a lot more academic than it was and they undoubtedly bring out the best in everyone,' enthuses one mother of three pupils. 'It's a lovely school.'

Produces well-rounded and enthusiastic pupils, with a mature attitude, who manage the transition to secondary school unusually well.

Lytton House, Putney High School Junior Department

Linked to Putney High School in the Senior section

35 Putney Hill, London, SW15 6BH

• Pupils: girls; all day • Ages: 4-11 • Non-denom • Fees: £9,387 pa • Independent

Tel: 020 8788 6523
Fax: 020 8780 3488
Email: putneyhigh@put.gdst.net
Website: www.gdst.net/putneyhigh

Head: Since 2003, Mrs Jane Stevens BA PGCE NPQH (early fifties). Previously acting head of Wimbledon High junior department, before that various senior leadership posts in maintained sector, including assisting the LEA with targeted inspections. Advocates describe her as 'amazing' and a 'good manager' with 'great integrity', though others find her 'rather remote' and 'rather defensive'. Good with the girls, less so with the parents – she wastes no time schmoozing them, so parents should look elsewhere if they need lots of head teacher tlc. 'She's not a politician, in that she doesn't feel that she needs to service the parents as clients,' sums up one mother. 'But the girls love her and she really seems to care about them all as individuals.' Spends a third of her time teaching. Out of school, likes fast cars, hot places and chocolate – famed for her brownies.

Entrance: Selective at 4+ and 7+. Expansion (from one to two form entry since our last review) has gone well. School says it's hard to put a finger on a 'Putney girl' – 'There are many different types here, all individuals,' says Mrs Stevens. 'But my team worked out the other day that between us we have 250 years of experience in selecting four year olds – that's got to count for something.' Parents feel that the Putney team knows exactly what it's looking for; almost an X factor, with no priority for siblings. 'I don't know how they get it right, but they do,' says one mother whose youngest was rejected several times and now totally supports the decision. 'It wasn't the right place for her – they saw it before I did.' Assessments, described as 'friendly and informal', last 1.5 hours for four year olds and twice as long at 7+, where new applicants will complete papers in English, mathematics and non-verbal reasoning. (At 7+ junior classes increase from 22 to 24, thus a minimum of four extra places.) Existing pupils do not need to sit this test. Girls come from a wide area of south-west London, but most are local, say a five mile radius.

Exit: Vast majority to linked senior school (qv) where they 'qualify' rather than 'compete' for a place. As the girls are monitored so closely from day one, no horrible surprises for parents when the time comes to move to senior school. Year 5 is the latest you'll hear if your daughter is failing to cut the senior mustard. Small exit elsewhere at 11+, though the school probably does not advertise this. An undoubted expectation to go on to the senior school and, although applications elsewhere are not encouraged and other entrance exams are not particularly prepared for, in 2009 two girls to St Paul's, two to Lady Eleanor Holles, one to Godolphin and Latymer and three boarding (Downe House, Wycombe Abbey, Tudor Hall) – all top of the pile destinations.

Remarks: A punchy place full of very confident little girls. Fairly structured from the off – classic girls' prep. Teachers are (mainly) highly regarded by parents – 'absolutely fantastic,' says one – and well supported and managed by Mrs Stevens, thus minimising the high staff turnover levels that can plague London schools. High standards throughout for everything from handwriting to gym squads. Mrs Stevens presides over handwriting classes in key stage 1 – handwriting taken terribly seriously here – and school won 2008 National School's Handwriting competition. Everything taught very thoroughly and then tested and retested (though much of it without the girls realising they are being scrutinised).

Standard national curriculum fare plus French introduced at Year 4, German from Year 5 and Latin in Year 6. As girls move up the school the number of specialist teachers increases. Quite unpushy on homework – school feels quite enough is packed in during school day. Class sizes are the (large-ish) GDST norm – 22 at key stage one and 24 at stage two.

A learning support teacher and SEN coordinator – 'Learning support offered as required,' says school. No SEN testing on entry. Extra-curricular activities for the gifted and talented.

Music is great – 90 strong school choir was runner-up in BBC 'Songs of Praise' School Choir of the Year 2008 and 2010. Parents delighted to spot their daughters on TV. Huge percentage learn a musical instrument – many learn two – and it's not uncommon for them to have reached grade 6 by Year 6. Orchestra of over 50. Lots of performance opportunities; universal praise for first ever junior Gala Concert in 2009.

Sport majors around netball, tennis (Surrey under 11 champions) and gymnastics (second place in UK national floor and vault competition), with addition of swimming from Year 3. A 'sport for all' policy to encourage everyone to have a go. Overall feel is that sport has improved since our last review. Girls are kept busy after hours, too, with good selection of clubs, plus rehearsals and games practice, and lots of trips, both day and residential.

Generally life moves along in a happy fashion. Despite its thorough approach to education, it's not stuffy and regimented. 'I like to feel it's a relaxed place,' says Mrs Stevens. 'I've got extremely high expectations of everyone – myself, my staff, the girls and their parents – but that's not to say we don't have lots of fun.'

The working environment is fresh and smart, with some new building to cope with recent increase in numbers. And what a sensible idea – new classrooms for the littlies have been designed to include loos inside them. Junior department shares small but pretty site with senior school (qv) but has its own playground, one of the nicest we've seen, including a stage and benches, pirate ship, Wendy house, giant chess board and even tables with games board tops – lots to keep them busy at break. Junior department is divided into two – Garden House is reception to Year 2, Lytton House years three to six. Each has a 'secret safe' where the girls can post notes detailing any worries or concerns.

Robust house system – great participation in hustings. Parental involvement encouraged and school advertises a very open-door policy – though some complaints that persistence is needed to get past the school secretary. Parents say fees provide value for money – but expect to write cheques for FOPHS, the parents' association. It's something of a social whirl – Putney parents know how to party while whipping up support for the place. Generally parents are a worthy selection of the great and good of south west London.

Overall school comes very well-recommended by parents as a safe choice. Rather a prescriptive place – it's not particularly exciting or off the wall creative – but it does know exactly what it's about and undoubtedly delivers the goods.

Magdalen College Junior School

Linked to Magdalen College School in the Senior section

Cowley Place, Oxford, Oxfordshire, OX4 1DZ

• Pupils: 100 boys; day • Ages: 7-11 • Fees: £12,594-£13,068 pa
• Independent

Tel: 01865 242191
Fax: 01865 240379
Email: registrar@mcsoxford.org
Website: www.mcsoxford.org

Head: Since 2007, Mr Matthew Coatsworth, previously deputy head of Headington Prep. He studied music at New College, Oxford, followed by a PGCE at Exeter. He taught in state schools in London and Sussex before returning to Oxford with his young family to take up the Headington post. He teaches maths and art and plays the violin and viola in his spare time. 'He's incredibly young-looking,' said a parent. 'He's pretty balanced, pretty nice, very easy to talk to.'

We hear, rather unexpectedly, that Mr Coatsworth is off to be deputy head at a state primary in Kidlington, Oxon.

Entrance: At 7+ by maths and English papers plus a half day of group activities. 'Attention is paid to each child's co-operation, enthusiasm, self-discipline and ability to concentrate.' At 9+ by maths, English and verbal reasoning papers plus interview. Junior school pupils all take the same 11+ exam as outside applicants to the senior school, and virtually all pass. Auditions for choristers in October and January.

Exit: Nearly all to the senior school. Occasional families encouraged to look elsewhere; one or two opt out for financial reasons.

Remarks: Housed in the original 1893 School House just down the road from the senior school, but shares all the senior school facilities. Bright-eyed, bushy-tailed boys perform in 'Charlie and the Chocolate Factory', win national chess competitions, compete in house music events, play football, cricket and tag rugby. Refreshingly, sufficient teams and fixtures to give almost everyone a chance to play for their school. The academic pace can be a shock to those coming in from more relaxed establishments, especially as the 11+ exam looms. They learn French from Year 3 and can go to Spanish and German clubs. Everyone is assessed in Year 5 for special educational needs and can have one-to-one help as necessary. 'I'm glad they're so rounded,' said a parent. 'It's a very happy school.'

Maidwell Hall School

Maidwell, Northampton, Northamptonshire, NN6 9JG

• Pupils: 100 boys; 95 board; girls admitted since September 2010;
• Ages: 7-13 • C of E • Fees: Boarding £21,165; Day £12,975 pa
• Independent

Tel: 01604 686 234
Fax: 01604 686 659
Email: headmaster@maidwellhall.co.uk
Website: www.maidwellhall.co.uk

Head: Since 2001, Mr Robert Lankester MA PGCE (forties). Educated at Elstree School, Charterhouse and Selwyn College, Cambridge, where he read history. Worked as City stockbroker for seven years before deciding to teach. After PGCE at Durham spent 13 years at Uppingham, 10 as a housemaster. Enthusiastic and focused, with no-nonsense approach. Maidwell only had nine girls when he was appointed, so took decision to make school all-boys and full-boarding (with two termly leave-out weekends either side of every half-term). Under his strong leadership the school has thrived with expansion and proper co-ed, launched in September 2010. 'Parents choose us because of the boarding,' says head. 'The place fizzes at weekends.' Despite history background, now teaches geography and RE – 'It's quite fun picking up new subjects,' he says. 'Teaching is a fantastic job – I definitely don't want to be a head stuck in a study shuffling paper and answering the phone.' Married with three older children. Carey, his charming Montessori-trained wife, is very involved in school life – she has a tutor group, teaches swimming and does a host of boarding duties. Family lives in leafy wing of the main school.

Entrance: 'We have a very broad intake,' says head. 'Our target is to get the children into their first choice of school at 13 and we've succeeded in that for the last seven years.' Pupils come from pre-preps and state primaries and visit a year prior to entry for informal assessment – i.e. maths, reading, spelling and relaxed ten-minute chat with head. They also have a 24-hour boarding trial the summer before they start, 'just to get them (and their mothers) used to the idea'. Most pupils live up to two hours away and are from rural areas (Lincs, Notts, Rutland, Leics, Cambs, East Anglia etc). Handful from abroad. Quite a few offspring of old boys. Distinguished former pupils include Earl Spencer and poet laureate Andrew Motion.

Exit: All over but lots to Eton, Harrow, Radley and Uppingham.

Remarks: Eleven miles north of Northampton in a picturesque country village. Founded in 1913 and moved to present 44-acre site in 1933. Main school building an imposing turreted mansion overlooking its own lake (pupils have to pass swimming test before they are allowed anywhere near it). Boys particularly relish the arboretum – known as 'the Wilderness' – where they build camps, climb trees and play old favourites like British Bulldog and hide and seek in their free time. Facilities include indoor swimming pool, shooting range, squash court and acres of immaculate playing fields.

Classes are small (maximum 15 but more likely to be around 12). Two streams in each year group and all taught by subject specialists. Well-qualified and happy staff – average age 30 something and slightly more men than women. Traditional curriculum, plus extra one-to-one SEN provision at £17 per lesson for those with mild dyslexia and dyspraxia. Despite newspaper headlines about reluctant boy readers, most pupils read avidly – they also get 20-minute reading period every day after lunch, either in dorms or, on sunny days, lying on the grass outside. All do ICT and touch-typing. School assembly each morning, with prayers read by a pupil and thought for the day from a member of staff.

All meals cooked in-house. Lunch is a formal affair, with long tables and a member of staff at each end to serve food, encourage good table manners and chat. Pupils allowed one boiled sweet every day after lunch (plastic tub solemnly passed round) and 70p of tuck on Sundays. When we visited, a group of jolly 12 year olds tucked into a lunch of roast beef and Eton Mess and chatted exuberantly about everything from the school food (firm thumbs-up) to their favourite authors (Anthony Horowitz, Celia Rees and Robert Muchamore). House system in place, with head pupil, prefects, house captains too.

Dorms are wholesome and shipshape and all housed in main school building. Younger pupils sleep in dorms of about six, smaller numbers for older ones. Discipline 'isn't a big issue,' says head. 'The children are extremely courteous and well-behaved.' Emphasis on being kind, well-mannered and tidy – the school rules warn to 'make sure Matron checks your appearance every morning before breakfast or you will be sent back and you may miss a pain au chocolat'. Perhaps unusually these days (but very popular with parents), mobile phones, Gameboys, iPods are banned (apart from final year, who are allowed to listen to iPods in their dorms). Children get to watch a film on Saturday nights and see key sports matches but no TV apart from that. 'We're probably a bit of a time warp,' laughs head. 'But we don't think it's healthy or right for people of this age to spend their lives in front of screens. We want them to get out in the fresh air and make the most of our lovely grounds.' Head's wife agrees – 'I love seeing 13 year olds whizzing around on their bikes and playing games that use their imagination,' she says. 'They aren't worried about looking cool here.'

Music, drama and art good. Two-thirds of pupils learn musical instruments and music practice is timetabled. Two school concerts a year and choir sings anthem in church every Sunday. Drama growing in popularity – the light airy artroom is a delight. Works of art on display throughout school – everything from gargoyles to modern art. Strong emphasis on sport – rugby, soccer, hockey, cricket etc. Sport six days a week and, considering Maidwell is usually up against far bigger schools, its teams trail clouds of glory.

Weekends are very busy. Pupils walk to the village church on Sunday mornings (lots of parents attend regularly too), write letters home and then enjoy a wide range of activities, from trips to Blenheim Palace and the Peak District to tree climbing, water polo and cooking. Annual three-day mountain expedition to Snowdonia, Lake District or Brecon Beacons for the eldest. Very chirpy pupils who are friendly and polite and exude pride and enthusiasm for their school. When benefactor Oliver Wyatt was asked about the ideal Maidwell pupil, he described the sort of child who 'was invited to someone's house and was invited back again'. The current head agrees wholeheartedly with these sentiments. A 13 year old about to depart for Harrow watched his form-mates speeding through the grounds on their bikes (a post Common Entrance treat) and said wistfully, 'This isn't just a school for lessons. I'll be very sad when I leave.'

A traditional, full-boarding prep school which encourages pupils to work hard but have lots of fresh air and fun along the way. Small enough for everyone to know each other but big enough to offer good, all-round education. As one satisfied parent told us, 'It punches above its weight both on the sports field and in academic terms.'

The Mall School

185 Hampton Road, Twickenham, Middlesex, TW2 5NQ

• Pupils: 300 boys; all day • Ages: 4-13 • C of E, all faiths
• Fees: £8,865-£10,230 pa • Independent

Tel: 020 8977 2523
Fax: 020 8977 8771
Email: admissions@mall.richmond.sch.uk
Website: www.mall.richmond.sch.uk

Head: Since 2004, Dr Jeremy Jeanes MA DPhil FRSA (fifties). Modern linguist, previously head of lower school (Years 7 and 8) at Latymer Upper School, Hammersmith. Much effort has been made by him to get to know boys and how the school works from their perspective, including becoming a Year 4 boy for the day. 'Great ice-breaker and provided tremendous insight into what it is to be a Mallian and the demands made on my staff,' he says. Urbane and chatty, 'very approachable,' say parents, 'relates well to us and boys alike'. He has gained support from parents by working hard to modernise the school's culture and create a more nurturing environment for all, while trying not to compromise on academic success. Retires summer 2011 – new head to be announced January 2011.

Entrance: Non-selective entry at 4+ in September on first come, first served basis. Waiting list, so apply early. Some places available at 7+ and 8+ by competitive exam, with possibility of major or even full fee reduction after teacher assessment in maths and English (means tested). Feeders vary but pre-schools usually include Jack and Jill, De Lacey Montessori, Pavilion Montessori, Greenacres, Tic Toc, Teddies. For prep entry, boys come from Athelstan House, Sunflower and The Falcons.

Exit: All at 13, the majority to localish academic day schools – ever popular are Hampton, King's College School Wimbledon and St Paul's. Few to board each year at Charterhouse, Wellington etc. Lots of awards including major scholarships to Charterhouse and KCS, other scholarships to KCS, Hampton, Emanuel, St George's Weybridge etc – that's only for one year! 14 sports scholarships in last seven years.

Money Matters: Up to 100 per cent bursaries (means tested) available at 7+ and 8+ point of entry, but hardship bursaries also available to parents who fall on hard times.

Remarks: Happy, vibrantly academic school with traditional values, though not at all in the dusty sense. The Mall is divided into Mall Infants (reception and Year 1) and The Mall main school, which are five minutes' walk apart along same stretch of busy road. Mall Infants is bounded by a high brick wall creating a surprisingly calm oasis away from the traffic outside. In this classic Victorian villa, opened in 2002, two lots of two parallel classes are taught in bright, airy classrooms by a teacher and classroom assistant. Class size of around 20 boys (they are not streamed or set until Year 6).

Boys transfer up the road to the main building for Year 2. They continue being taught by their own class teachers, joined by specialists in Year 3 for science (industrious buzz emanating from suite of spacious, well equipped laboratories), music and French. In the past, some weeding out of academically weaker children has taken place at this stage, much to parents' chagrin. Dr Jeanes has been keen to address this and 'appears to be more supportive of boys of all abilities,' approves a parent.

Particularly impressive French taught from the age of six by two native speakers – 'Very high standards – everyone does well,' comments a mother. Boys seem relaxed and happy to speak only in French in classes after Year 5: 'Helps tune your ear in,' one pupil remarked. Maths, too, is strong (boys in national final of primary maths championships), but a few areas of concern in English and Latin, causing some parents to turn to outside help. Seems not to be, however, a culture of private coaching endemic in so many other academic preps. Reading is important throughout school – sessions timetabled in superbly resourced library including lots of well thumbed papers and French magazines. Walls groaning with scholarship boards remind visitors what it's all for.

Efforts and successes rewarded by system of headmaster's commendations. Credits collected on 'credit cards' carried by boys, that go towards house tally. About 5 per cent of boys (mostly with mild difficulties) have SEN – initial support through in house (no charge) early years intervention programme. Later help appears more tokenistic, although Dr Jeanes does not agree with this comment and says, 'SEN boys (i.e. those with diagnosed difficulties) get help from our in-house specialist (for those with dyslexia and dyspraxia) at an extra charge – normally two sessions a week. The teacher feeds back to the staff about the boy's needs. This is full specialist support'. Full time SENco. It must be remembered that this remains an academically focused school – not really for those with anything other than mild difficulties.

Lots of sport – two full games afternoons a week at nearby Teddington Cricket Club. Rugby, football, cricket, swimming – all compulsory, but very popular with the boys. Fabulous swimming in spectacular indoor pool that is also lent to some neighbouring schools. National Primary Swimming Champions out of 3,000 schools; four boys invited for Olympic training for 2012. Rugby strong and a number of boys achieve county standard in cricket.

Music taken seriously with 120 boys learning instruments in school up to grade 7. Two orchestras, variety of bands, ensembles and choirs perform concerts and recitals throughout year. Rehearsals for big productions often take place at weekends, such is enthusiasm. Boys also currently represented in National Children's Orchestra and Chapel Royal Choir.

Children drawn from Richmond to Teddington, Hounslow to East Molesey, social and ethnic mix reflecting locality. Lots of professionals and first time buyers. Head keen to open new channels of communication with parents and keeps his ear to ground by regularly inviting parent representatives to lunch meetings, visitors eating with boys. Dr Jeanes is (rightly, according to boys we spoke to) proud of healthy, freshly sourced and often organic school food.

A purposeful school with an ordered informal atmosphere, living up to the expectations of many of its parents (who are saturated with local school choices). 'Boys genuinely supportive of each other,' enthuses one mother, 'which makes this hard-working school a very positive place to be.'

Malsis School

Cross Hills, North Yorkshire, BD20 8DT

• Pupils: 75 boys, 40 girls; 35 board, the rest day • Ages: 7-13; lower school 4-7 • Inter-denom: C of E and RC • Fees: Boarding £17,475; Day £13,380; Pre-prep £7,440 pa • Independent

Tel: 01535 633 027
Fax: 01535 630 571
Email: admin@malsis.com
Website: www.malsis.com

Headmaster: Since 2008, Mr Marcus Peel (early fifties). Arrived at Malsis in 2005, formerly deputy head and head of boarding. Married to Louise, a qualified remedial gymnast who is joint head of boarding with her husband; two grown-up children who went through the private system. Educated at Repton, read history and classical civilisation at Kent. Started life in the Metropolitan Police before joining Orwell Park as a teacher; enjoyed success as hockey coach and was made deputy head early on in his teaching career. Mad about adventure pursuits, a canoeist, air rifle instructor, mountaineer; loves music and is often seen tinkling the ivories, surrounded by kids having singalongs. Formerly ran his own adventure company and now runs courses under the school's banner, 'Adventure Malsis', enjoys bushcraft, something of the Ray Mears about the man, happy plucking and cooking pheasants, or anything else actually. Friendly, personable and praised by Malsis parents for bringing boarding into the 21st century, making it exciting, fun and parent-friendly. Teaches history and music.

Entrance: No formal entrance test – interview with the head and tour of the school, 'taster' days encouraged. Scholarships and bursaries considered for children with talent in academic work, music, sport and drama, particularly for entry at Year 6 and 7. Many join in lower school but numerous others along the way, right up to the final year as a 'last push' before senior school, or even to consciously defer entry to a senior school post 11. Parents predominantly city professionals from the length and breadth of Yorkshire, Cheshire, Lancashire and further afield. Fair number of Services families and trickle of expats.

Exit: The usual suspects: Oundle, Shrewsbury, Giggleswick, Oakham, Windermere St Anne's, Queen Margaret's York, steady one or two to Bradford Grammar, Glenalmond, Sedbergh, Stonyhurst, Uppingham, Eton, Rugby, Repton, Ampleforth, Radley and Stowe. Some also into local maintained sector grammar schools – Ermysted's popular. Regular stream of scholarships to all over, including music, sport, art and IT.

Remarks: School founded in 1920, by a teacher from Giggleswick, in a splendid Victorian mansion with gloriously ostentatious ceilings. Forty acres of games pitches and fields; numerous later building additions, some more attractive than others, in a variety of styles.

Not as many pupils as there used to be, the cry of many prep schools in this part of the world, sadly, but projects a dynamic sense of determination and clear intent. The four cornerstones are 'balance', 'purpose', 'style' and 'charm' – an interesting take on the needs of the 21st century pupil, but the children who acted as our guides around the school exuded all four, welcoming smiles and firm handshakes all round. You could also add entrepreneurial spirit to that list (or is just northern thrift?) – 'We've got a great new cookery room, all kitted out, and thanks to parents and generous donations, it didn't cost the school a penny!' pupils tell us proudly.

Classrooms for the youngest children are bright, colourful and cheery – sadly, slightly less so for the older ones, though interactive whiteboards are appearing for staff willing and able to use them. Marvellous John Piper war memorial windows in the chapel, plus the flags that used to hang on the Cenotaph in London. Chapel converts into hall theatre. School holds services and performance slots on Saturday, rather than Sunday, so Sundays are 'free for activities'. Civilised dining room with linen napkins and white tablecloths for Sunday evening roast. Huge range of country-type activities, stacks of sports with twice weekly fixtures and regular tours; as well as the trad prep school type extra-curricular activities also offers mountain biking (British Cycle Federation approved 3km mountain bike track within grounds), bushcraft, hill-walking, canoeing, camping – including camp cooking. A good-sized swimming pool, shooting range, cross-country, nine-hole golf course, and high-octane outdoor thrills with the assault-course style 'Rap tree' for 'confidence-building' – shades of a corporate team-building weekend and a favourite with the pupils. Thursday afternoon's two hour 'PAT' – Protected Activity Time – sees children taking six week courses in falconry, shot guns, fly-fishing and cookery, 'high adventure', dry-skiing and more – the list is endless. Also a selection of activity weeks and camps in holidays throughout the year.

A busy boarding school – day pupils have to be in school by 8.30am and stay till 6.15pm (it's not all work – activities are built into the school day), and many stay later for activities (over 70 of them) – they can stay for supper and enjoy many of the evening activities at no extra charge, a real boon for busy parents with active children. Most 10-13 year olds board at some stage, as well as a number of younger ones – around 30 per cent in all, increasing to 40 per cent in the summer with a probationary boarding on offer to ease children (and parents) into boarding. Much investment into making boarding accommodation homely and appealing – serious about its boarding profile: it's full boarding here or nothing, with compulsory boarding for Year 8. Boarders certainly get a good deal – full and varied activity programme after school and at weekends (including trips to Blackpool pleasure beach, charity abseil, lasertag in the grounds) keeps youngsters happy and entertained.

Predominantly trad teaching styles, strong academically, head sees outstanding work. French from 5, Latin from 9 and Italian and Spanish club very popular. Small classes, max 18 or 20. Excellent learning support for pupils – currently mostly dyslexia/dyspraxia, but range of others considered if they think they can help and child will cope. IEPs for those with needs, one-to-one help, regular additional reading (often with parent volunteers), small group work and setting (including holding back the weakest or advancing the brightest a year, so they get to spend extra time on scholarship work). SEN not seen as a barrier – possible to be getting extra support and be in scholarship classes. A rather grand-sounding enhancing learning coordinator who keeps an eye on all things SEN, including gifted and talented. All staff informed and involved with SEN. Needs across curriculum recognised.

Lots of different sports and opportunities for all to represent the school – building confidence and finding something a child is good at all feature. Annual jaunt to Normandy, annual Three Peaks challenge, three week leavers' programme of numerous activities culminating in a week-long camp in the Lakes or Snowdonia.

Palpable pride in excellent drama, masses of music with seventy per cent of children learning an instrument. Vibrant art and creative DT, plenty of visits to local hot spots: Manchester, Bradford, Halifax, Leeds all have orchestras and theatres. Director of music, James Ashworth, former Huddersfield Choral Society voice coach, is driving forward a desire for the school to become a centre of musical excellence.

Described to us by one parent as a 'fab' school – classes are small, children work hard but are not hot-housed (unlike some other local schools, allegedly); nothing wrong with the place at all, except that it 'could do with a few more children'. This parent was initially wary of prep schools, fearing 'Tom Brown's Schooldays' styling, but on her visit saw a roaring fire in the entrance hall, a large Christmas tree, and muddy boots in the porch – and felt she had 'come home', converted in an instant and remains so. Parents admire sense of etiquette instilled from an early age and the way in which children look after each other; they also love the slightly avant-garde style of some of the teachers who, after a day of heavy rain, will take the children for a walk to look at the effect on the local river – geography and science teaching in action, without the children even realising it. One maths lesson involved learning how to calculate the angles needed to build a bridge over said river. Plenty of serious classroom teaching too, but making the most of the environment, in every respect.

Strong house system, with termly activity days/dinners for winners of duties and house cups and all participate in competitions. Effective personal tutor system for each child. A busy school with a family feel, parents are hugely supportive and contribute much to the value-added life of the school. Former pupils include Simon Beaufoy, who wrote 'The Full Monty', and 'Slumdog Millionaire', Martin Taylor ex of Barclays Bank, Mark Umbers and Sam Riley, actors, and James Whitaker, England cricketer selector.

Maltman's Green School

Maltman's Lane, Chalfont St Peter, Gerrards Cross, Buckinghamshire, SL9 8RR

• Pupils: 400 girls, all day • Ages: 3-11 • Non-denom • Fees: £7,245-£10,635 pa • Independent

Tel: 01753 883 022
Fax: 01753 891 237
Email: registrar@maltmansgreen.com
Website: www.maltmansgreen.com

Head: Since 2005, Mrs Joanna Pardon MA PGCE BSc. Previously head of Gateways Prep school in Leeds. Married to Brian, the school's network manager. Girls say she is kind, caring, wears posh clothes and smiles nicely. Smart, confident, friendly, with a solid background in, and great supporter of, all-girls' schools. Loves the elastic band effect, taking a child or group and stretching them, trying to make a difference. Thinks it's important the girls are happy and confident but not arrogant. Doesn't want to pressurise them (some high achieving parents don't always agree). Believes goals are important but that it's necessary to meet challenges and gain experience to reach them. A genuinely happy person, enjoys working for and organising things with others, but isn't a workaholic.

Entrance: By assessment/visit – mobile local population results in vacancies popping up all the time. Children (with very rare exception) automatically move up the school. Oversubscribed in many years, waiting lists.

Exit: A good area for grammar schools with, e.g. Dr Challoner's and Beaconsfield High – approximately 50 per cent take this route. Rest mainly to, e.g., Wycombe Abbey, Queenswood, Royal Masonic, St Helen's, St George's Ascot, Queen Anne's Caversham, Pipers Corner, Downe House, Berkhamsted Collegiate and Cheltenham Ladies'.

Remarks: Very popular all-day school. Housed in what looks like just another grand stockbroker's pile in ritzy suburban belt of Gerrards Cross but, in reality, started out as a farmstead way back in the 18th century. Tiled floors gleaming with polish – probably the most immaculate school we've ever visited: even the bins are organised and labelled for recycling. Eleven well-kept acres; adventure playgrounds get more so as children progress through school; fantastic, indoor six lane 25m pool, complete with superb viewing gallery – very much venue of choice for all manner of competitions.

Average 14–20 in a class. Subject teachers for everything from eight. Good design technology, which has been flourishing for some time, smart science and technology building and ICT room, separate libraries for junior and senior; French for all. Excellent and enthusiastic sports, notably gymnastics – GISGA U9, 10 and11 national champions (top independent gymnastics school for the 10th year running); U11 Carita House national champions; U11 British Schools' floor and vault national champions); tennis (county and national players); rounders (IAPS 2008 and 2009 U11 champions); and strong showing in national swimming and netball competitions.

Art department an Aladdin's cave – fantastic rainforest display by Year 2. Choir outstandingly successful, winning all manner of competitions – we were treated to a rendition of 'I Feel Pretty'. They certainly looked it, and cheerful and charming too. Plenty of extras – takes sport and competitions seriously. In fact, when head said she was going to watch her girls win (they did) at the weekend, we did wonder if it was more than a Freudian slip!

A busy, happy, bright place, ditto children, who are confident and outward going, zooming about in their smart purple uniform; any sign of arrogance quickly stamped on. Understandably, the girls appear to enjoy everything about the place, from the kind, helpful, amusing teachers to the friendships and fab facilities, even the way the inevitable falling-outs are dealt with. Lively but mannered lessons, even revision is fun. Good, tasty food. Girls can come in early for breakfast and stay late for tea if it suits their families. Good on trips and outings. Outstanding pastoral care, says the latest inspection report and the girls.

Takes from three, so a genuinely mixed bag from the real high flyers – six academic scholarships in 2009 (to St Helen's Northwood, The Abbey School Reading and The Royal Masonic) – to those with special needs, including one girl with a statement for visual impairment. Happy to accept any girl who will benefit from the experience and whose presence will not have a negative impact on the others. Keen to ensure children with SEN are fully included and don't feel different. Will do all they can to improve the environment and make it work for any girl – move mountains, if necessary. Says they aim to ensure all the girls understand how privileged they are – that also means understanding how lucky they are and how important it is to help others. Working on stretching the most able even further but wants to ensure a balance between confidence, competence and connectivity (with others) – suggests need all three in right measures.

A delightful, superbly resourced school. Lots of sparkly girls, each a success in her own right. What more could you want for your daughter?

The Manchester Grammar School Junior Section

Linked to Manchester Grammar School (The) in the Senior section

Old Hall Lane, Rusholme, Manchester, Lancashire, M13 0XT

• Pupils: 100 boys, all day • Ages: 9-10 • Non-denon • Fees: £9,660 pa • Independent

Tel: 0161 224 7201
Fax: 0161 257 2446
Email: general@mgs.org
Website: www.mgs.org

Head: Dr Ray is overall high master of every part of MGS. Deputy high master Stuart Leeming oversees the junior section where the head (one of four in the school overall) has been, since 2008, Linda Hamilton (mid fifties). Educated locally at Stretford Grammar and Manchester University but with a subsequent international teaching career including a spell establishing a pre-school in Nigeria. Taught boys at Altrincham Preparatory School (qv) where she became deputy head and was very popular. Mother of three sons, two educated at MGS, she's also an independent schools inspector. Very happy here describing her task, 'to start something from scratch, with new staff in a new building' as 'glorious, I'm a lucky girl and I do know it'. Very keen to establish traditions; a first was a 'moving on' event when the first Year 6 leavers were waved off by the Year 5 boys and junior section teachers, to parade owl banners through the senior school to a Year 7 lecture. She is also passionate about fostering a love of books alongside internet abilities. Parents are invited to 'tea with the head' and other social events and her direct email address is on the website.

Entrance: Boys admitted to the juniors have guaranteed passage to the senior school so this is an attractive option for leapfrogging the 11+ scrum, and logistically for parents with older boys in the senior school. Selection is based on a stimulating and challenging assessment day which includes written work after teaching on a non-curriculum subject, with much emphasis on drawing out each boy's strengths, and making specific preparation impossible (though we think you might consider a practice session or two with a tutor if your son is unsure how he will cope with the experience, MGS say that this is completely unnecessary). Applicants are given a personal buddy for lunch time. Primary school report also considered. School is looking for potential, aptitude and attitude, 'boys who are sharp, who can pick up an idea and run with it', although they do allow for nerves and shyness. Following the assessment day school is able to give detailed feedback to parents. Recent intake has been half and half from state and independent primary schools and places are hugely over-subscribed. Those who do not make it at this stage are welcome to try again for the senior school at 11.

40 join aged 9+, and another 20 a year later.

Exit: Straight into seniors hitting the ground running and, school tells us, with lengthy care taken over the distribution of junior section boys into senior classes. Senior classes benefit from the presence of experienced pupils able to help new boys settle in. Boys also mixed up in move from Year 5 to Year 6 when new boys join.

Remarks: For the first time in 50 years MGS has, since September 2008, admitted boys of nine and ten years old. So what's going on?

MGS explains it to us thus: Aware of exam pressure at 11+, and admitting competition for its own entrance exam formed part of the problem, MGS started seeking a way to end this 'impoverished diet of being drilled to jump through exam hoops'. MGS explored the possibility of working with feeder junior and prep schools to widely enhance their top junior curriculum, and offering Year 7 MGS places in advance to very bright Year 5 boys. Unfortunately, MGS tells us, parents and boys preferred early MGS entrance, so MGS started a Year 5 entry junior section of its own.

A degree of rumour, confusion and disaffection ensued and of course many preps are unhappy to lose some of their best Year 5 and 6 boys early, plus their accompanying fees during a recession. What had begun as a discussion of enhancement and support had ended up as neither. Year 5 entry is unusual and it is hard for the preps to replace pupils at that stage. We think that the preps must feel like Christians sharing a bed with a lion – warm and cuddly most of the time, but when will he be hungry again? MGS's logic, and much that has been said by the school in the past, points (in our view) towards further expansion of the Year 5 intake, and an evening out of the chances of a bright boy getting to MGS via state schools as compared with preps.

Junior boys are housed in the attractive, purpose built Bexwyke Lodge (pronounced Bezzik) on campus. Made from timber from a sustainable Estonian forest and using automatic lighting sensors, the building has an environment award. The entrance is flanked by a pair of chain-saw owl sculptures from the trunks of two trees removed during the building process; five more trees were planted elsewhere. A new, junior-friendly version of the school owl symbol and Dare to be Wise motto is etched on the glass doors to the junior section. Inside the place feels like a huge, warm Swiss chalet, a cocoon-like base from which younger boys make teaching-assistant-accompanied forays to many facilities in the 'big school'. It's bright and airy with two Year 5 and three Year 6 forms, each of circa 20 boys, and two music practice and instrument lesson rooms.

Boys use traditional individual lift-top desks arranged in various ways, so they need take only the minimum to lessons elsewhere. There's a laptop for use in school for every boy. Classrooms are full of creativity, fun and a happy buzz of boys working together. Some teaching is from senior school specialists and the junior class mistresses also teach their specialist subjects at senior level.

Several parents, though delighted that their children had got in, have been less than perfectly happy with the arrangements made for them. They told us that some teachers didn't readily empathise with younger pupils, that there's too much homework (one described this aspect of the junior years as 'far more pressurised than for the older siblings in the senior school'), that the school 'hasn't sought feedback ... complaints fall on deaf ears'. The school, and other parents, roundly dispute these assertions: 'the intensity is less than in the senior school', 'the school is incredibly supportive if a child struggles with a particular subject', that much homework 'is based around research which is something my son finds interesting and tends to view less like work', and that 'there have been lots of formal and informal opportunities for parents to give feedback'. Given that it's a new venture, and that 9-year-old boys may well find the transition to senior school challenging (it's tough enough at 11), we are not surprised by the complaints. Given the sharpness with which MGS reacted when we relayed them, we will be surprised if their causes continue.

The school day mirrors the seniors', and after school clubs (30 possibilities with lunch time activities) run to 6pm, although circa 45 minutes of homework must be done first. Juniors lunch 15 minutes before the older pupils, accompanied by their teaching assistants and the head who 'enjoys this daily informal interaction'. The advanced curriculum is designed to broaden education not merely advance it, 'they'll be studying Year 7 work in Year 7'. Classical Greek, Portuguese, Italian and German are introduced and, in science, practical work and experiments emphasised. Wednesday afternoons are the preserve of options when MGS juniors are joined by gifted and talented pupils from a local state primary for classes ranging from cookery to business enterprise or photography. An annual Bexwyke lecture and workshops for 300 Greater Manchester junior children also reflects MGS commitment to contribute to the community; space scientist Dr Maggie Aderin led the inaugural day in 2009. On-line InCAS is used for assessing progress; school tells us the Durham based company wondered if its software was faulty when MGS juniors scored so uniformly excellently in its tests.

There are several musical groups, and very talented boys can join groups higher up the school, one is in the senior orchestra. Head introduced a house system so that every boy can represent a meaningful team, and the last sports day included parent races, afternoon tea and a musical background to every race. Year 5 have an outward bound or water sports trip during activities week. Year 6 go further afield – last year to Italy to support their Italian language work. Officially optional, in practice every child went (financial assistance was available, as was an opportunity to pay in instalments). This year there will be a cost-free alternative – helping out on the younger boys' summer camp.

Expensive option at prep level as junior fees are same as seniors, £9,660 pa, justified by juniors sharing senior facilities and specialist teachers. One local competitor charges £8,820 but this includes lunch and other local prep fees are between £5,500 and £6,700. Many would say 'cheap at the price' to bag the early MGS place.

Manchester High School for Girls Preparatory Department

Linked to Manchester High School For Girls in the Senior section

Grangethorpe Road, Manchester, Lancashire, M14 6HS

• Pupils: 220 girls; all day • Ages: 4-11 • Non-denominational • Fees: £6,606-£6,744 pa • Independent

Tel: 0161 224 0447
Fax: 0161 224 6192
Email: administration@mhsg.manchester.sch.uk
Website: www.manchesterhigh.co.uk

Head: Mrs Claire Hewitt BSc PGCE.

Entrance: By assessment during a visit for entry to reception and Years 1 and 2, and by examination in English, maths and reasoning for Years 3, 4, 5 and 6.

Exit: Most girls pass an entrance exam to the senior school and transfer to it. Plenty of support and gentle warning for those who won't.

Remarks: On the same site as senior school but in a separate wing with own entrances and playgrounds. Some sharing of facilities, such as physical education, music and drama, and close links ease transition at 11. Uniform is the same colour scheme, although the gingham summer dresses are left behind. Classrooms are welcoming, informal and bright, with excellent equipment. Lots of clubs and other extra-curricular activities. Before-school supervision and after-school club available.

Manor House School Junior Department

Linked to Manor House School in the Senior section

Manor House Lane, Little Bookham, Leatherhead, Surrey, KT23 4EN

• Pupils: 165 girls; all day • Ages: 2-11 • Christian non-denom
• Fees: up to £9,990 pa • Independent

Tel: 01372 458538
Fax: 01372 450514
Email: admin@manorhouseschool.org
Website: www.manorhouseschool.org

Head: Miss Zara Axton (for details see senior school).

Entrance: Baby and toddler group once a week helps ease children (boys and girls) into Manor House before they can remember anything else. Nursery, for girls only, starts from age two. School proper, with uniforms, at age four in the prep, moving through into the juniors at age seven. Very informal entry assessment on a 'taster day' – reading, sums and chatting to a teacher – simply to judge where a pupil fits amongst her peers.

Exit: Automatic follow-on into senior school. Manor House works hard to be a truly 'through school', there is no distinction between the juniors and seniors. All girls are fully expected to go into the senior years and the vast majority do.

Remarks: Nothing but praise from parents for this gentle and rather sweet introduction to school life. Purpose-built nursery facilities sit alongside the prep classrooms and share an extensive outdoor play area. Junior classrooms are located in the very beautiful main house and girls play outside in the lovely grounds. The whole place has a quiet, country feel and parents feel strongly that their daughters will be safe here.

Girls of all ages mix – Miss Axton, the head of the whole school, describes junior and senior as 'one community'. The prep and junior girls love being with the seniors and greet them with hugs and kisses, parents value the respect and love girls have for each other. Each girl has a 'buddy' from two years ahead, who supports them throughout their school year.

Small classes are full of giggling little girls and kindly enthusiastic teachers. Academically there's the full spectrum, not just high achievers. Parents like this 'healthy mix' and the 'innocence, warmth and friendliness.' Suited to those who want their daughters to enjoy school life without academic pressure, this sets Manor House apart from other highly academic girls' schools in this part of Surrey. Parents feel confident in the teaching, saying 'the lines of communication are very open' and 'they cover the spectrum by extending classroom work for the brighter girls'. Teachers instil a sense of security and growing independence in the girls, whilst making lessons fun and interesting. One pupil described enthusiastically how fractions had been taught by cutting up and eating a large cake! Teachers can refer pupils to the Head of Learning Support if extra help is needed.

Some parents felt Miss Axton had little to do with the junior school girls – Miss Axton hotly denies this and says, 'I visit junior and prep lessons every day. In J5 it is a standing joke that I always appear when they are doing maths (my subject).' There are a number of leading teachers in the prep and junior sections who have been there 'since they were girls themselves' and are very committed to the individual well being of their pupils. One teacher we spoke to had been at the school for many years, and was so wildly passionate about the place, she would probably have talked all day about the joys of Manor House had the bell not rung when it did! In a nutshell, unpressurised and pure fun – a breath of fresh (country) air.

Marlborough House School

Hawkhurst, Cranbrook, Kent, TN18 4PY

• Pupils: 215 boys and girls in prep school; 100 in pre-prep; 20 in the nursery; day and flexi-boarding. • Ages: 3-13 • C of E • Fees: R-Y2 £6,660; Y3-Y8 £13,290 pa • Independent

Tel: 01580 753 555
Fax: 01580 754 281
Email: registrar@marlboroughhouseschool.co.uk
Website: www.marlboroughhouseschool.co.uk

Head: Since 1995, Mr David Hopkins MA PGCE (fifties). Educated at King's Canterbury and Oxford where he was a scholar. Previously headmaster of Streete Court (his old prep school). Married with three children, all now at university. His wife, Emma, is actively involved with the school, particularly with the pastoral care and on the boarding side. Approachable and a good listener and genuinely looks into any parental concerns. Well liked by pupils and parents. Takes a great interest in how the children turn out. Teaches Latin to the top three years and referees football and hockey. A very experienced headmaster, at the top of his game; quiet and unassuming manner but approachable and knows all the pupils well.

Entrance: It is worth registering as soon as possible as oversubscribed, but most people who really want a place usually get one. Informal assessment day plus school report and interview with the head. No formal tests – important that the school is right for the child. Those with mild learning difficulties assessed to make sure the school can cater for his/her needs. Majority of children arrive in the nursery and stay right through until 13, although children can join at any age if spaces. Some children come in from the primaries for the last two years to sit Cranbrook entrance exam. A few move on to boarding preps at 8+. Up to 24 children in the nursery (age 3–4) which rises to 32 per year in the pre-prep (two parallel forms of 16) and 36 in the prep school (two parallel forms of 18).

Exit: Mainly to fairly local schools: up to 40 per cent to Cranbrook plus Tonbridge, King's Canterbury, Bethany, Eastbourne and Benenden. Occasionally further afield to, e.g., Harrow, Winchester, Eton. Good range of scholarships most years. 2009/10 academic scholarships to Harrow, Sevenoaks, Sutton Valence and St Leonard's Mayfield and academic exhibition to King's Canterbury and a music scholarship to Tonbridge and sports scholarships to

Eastbourne, Ardingly and St Leonards Mayfield. Art scholarships most years. Three to four a year leave at 11+ for the grammars – the school will prepare them as much as possible for the Kent Test.

Remarks: Founded in 1874, the school moved in 1930 to a Georgian house set in 34 acres of landscaped grounds on the edge of Hawkhurst. Wonderful setting where everything looks beautiful and is kept immaculately. Purpose built pre-prep and a large sports hall used by all age groups. The nursery in its own house next to the main school with its own garden and play equipment.

No streaming but children are setted in some subjects from age seven. Spanish or Latin introduced as a second language from Year 5. Touch typing taught from Year 3. No special scholarship class; gifted children are given individually tailored programmes within their year group in the form of one-to-one tuition and discussion forums and small extension groups. Good back-up for mild dyslexia – three full time learning support staff for individual or group sessions. Teachers always on the look out for problems.

An exceptionally friendly school where everyone is quickly made to feel part of the community. The Friends of Marlborough House, a parents' group, is very active in welcoming new parents and making them feel part of the school. They also organise social events throughout the year – quiz nights, various parent/teacher friendlies and the biennial summer ball. No full or weekly boarding but flexi-boarding a popular option and most children do a bit of this. No longer Saturday school. Own in-house catering – excellent food with everything prepared on site, justifiably proud of their reputation.

Main sports are football, rugby, hockey and cricket for the boys and netball, hockey and rounders for the girls. Also tennis, .22 rifle shooting; keen golfers ferried to the local golf course for lessons and sailors to the local reservoir. Taking part is more important than winning and most children are given the chance to play in a team. Long list of thriving after-school activities including popular gardening and cooking clubs. For one night a term the dining room is turned into a restaurant and the children who are members of the chef club cook and serve a meal for their parents. Older children stay on at school for prep and may also stay for supper and evening clubs – a popular option with parents. Strong anti-bullying policy and always someone on hand for the children to talk to. Low staff turnover, a number have been part of the school for many years – a dedicated team who are happy and committed.

About two-thirds of prep school pupils learn a musical instrument up to and including grade 8 – a good record of music scholarships. A number of informal concerts throughout the year. Lots of opportunities to get involved with music making. Thriving art department with scholarships most years. Creative pottery workshops for Year 8. Annual art exhibition featuring work from every pupil. Strong IT department. All have a chance to get involved in drama productions during the year – one big school play annually and smaller plays for most year groups during the year, plus the very popular Marlborough House 'X Factor'. Everyone given the opportunity to take part in the annual poetry reading competition. Plenty of trips and outings both locally and further afield – geography trips to Montreuil and Isle of Wight. French and classics trip to Aix-en-Provence and annual winter skiing trip.

Produces confident children who are generally tolerant and respectful of each other. School keen to ensure that children are aware of a world beyond the school gates – emphasis on fundraising and charity work, e.g. the whole school did the Sports Relief mile. Pupils visit the elderly at Bowles Lodge Residential Centre in Hawkhurst to chat to them and the younger pupils visit to entertain the residents with songs and poems. Values for Living Code displayed around the school: Be honest, be kind, be helpful, be polite, listen, do your best. Very charming Garden of Good Manners in the pre-prep reinforces these messages. Calm ordered school where everything seems to run smoothly.

Famous old boys include cricketer David Gower, screen writer and director Stephen Poliakoff and his brother, the chemist Professor Martyn Poliakoff CBE.

A very happy, caring and gentle school where every child is treated as an individual and reaches their full potential, academically and in sport, art, drama and music – always looking for hidden talents.

The Mary Erskine and Stewart's Melville Junior School

Linked to Mary Erskine School (The) in the Senior section

Linked to Stewart's Melville College in the Senior section

Queensferry Road, Edinburgh, EH4 3EZ

• Pupils: 1205 boys and girls. • Ages: 3-11; almost all day • Non-denom
• Fees: Boarding £15,810; Day £5,853 pa • Independent

Tel: 0131 311 1111
Fax: 0131 311 1199
Email: jssecretary@esmgc.com
Website: www.esms.edin.sch.uk

Vice principal: Since 1989, Mr Bryan Lewis MA (fifties), educated at Dublin High School, followed by Trinity College, Dublin, where he read classics. Married, with three daughters, one still in the school, and one of our very favourite heads (we are always slightly surprised – and thrilled – to find him still here). He first came to the senior school in 1974. As both head of the junior school and overall vice-principal of all three schools, he values the latter 'because it make a statement that the junior school matters. Get it right by 11 and secondary is easy'. Charismatic, giggly, fun, he believes, 'Life is too important to take seriously,' adding, 'The least significant thing we do is academic'. The confidence, interest and evident happiness of children such as his 10 and 11 year old tour guides are the key. '10 per cent happier equals 10 per cent better academically,' says Mr Lewis.

Potty about drama (which is absolutely brilliant), he insists that every child who wants to should be on the stage (eight shows annually) or in one of five choirs. He expects and obtains the highest standards and is almost prouder of the life skills and tough training that these activities instil than of the outstanding achievement of SMC's Scottish rugby cup last year – he thinks everyone should have a chance at sport too. Describing himself as a 'benevolent dictator', he insists his staff opt into school values, i.e. find a way to do what's right for children, 'Because it's not fair if teachers are all different'. Even so, 120 or so apply for every teaching post. His 'philosophy', that 'they will never be 10 again', led him to extend last year's classics trip to Italy from the 40 places offered to all 126 applicants, organising three separate expeditions. 'The perfect age for a child is 11 and they should be proud, not hankering for the teens' – so no discos. Boys wear shorts with smashing scarlet socks 'to keep them different from the seniors'. A visiting parent, knowing him as a stickler for formal good manners, likened him to the Pope when boys (actually pulling their socks up) bobbed respectfully as he passed.

Very, very keen on children's self esteem – 'Every child has a right to make mistakes, every child has a right to be happy'. 'Be proud to be good.'

Entrance: Automatic from nursery (where you should register at birth), otherwise by assessment. Oversubscribed: 107 applications for 21 places at primary 1 and 45 for 24 places at primary 4; 80 for 60 places at primary 6. Priority to siblings – as always – but occasional places available at every level. Not quite as tough as Eton to get into – but apply early!

Exit: To senior school; minimal trickle leave to go elsewhere.

Remarks: A terrific school with a young staffroom – the school all other Edinburgh preps look up to. Despite the divided campus, the various parts of the junior school operate as one and, perhaps because of the divided campus, children are not overwhelmed by the numbers.

The fabulous new nursery (£1.2 million), New Ravelston, designed in consultation with parents and children, provides home from home, if necessary all year round, from 7.45am-6pm, for 3–5s. No parent could ever feel guilty about leaving a child in this amazing play paradise, complete with teachers, nursery nurses, play experts and a tantalising array of equipment/activities. A sensory quiet room – moving lights, swimming fish projected over the ceiling, soft music and seating. (Pre exam 6 year girls were allowed a one-off relax.) Primary Start leads automatically into P1, based in the purpose-built Easter Ravelston (tiny classes, can arrive early, stay late). At age 5/6 all move to Wester Ravelston – a very specially constructed part of Mary Erskine site, with charming classrooms all opening onto a dedicated playground.

The school educare system, called e-Plus, gives wraparound care throughout the entire junior school, which includes early birds, lunch club, after school and holiday clubs. Also parent workshops and use of Ravelston sports club for all the family. Coaches to and from school. School is based at Ravelston until the age of seven, when all move to 'big school' at Stewart's Melville. They remain here until P7 (aged 11/12), when girls return to Mary Erskine proper and boys go up to the senior school. Strong anti-bullying programme. Every child made to feel loved – the Lewis touch again.

Emphasis on academics, mainly French from primary 6, ICT, home economics, science from primary 6 and 7 – all with dedicated teachers. Strong emphasis on basics: spelling, presentation etc. Mr Lewis insists on fountain pens as a 'commitment to presentation skills, matching commitment to basic good manners'. Maximum class size 25, 20 for practical subjects. From primary 4 (7/8 year olds) pupils are taught in fairly fluid dedicated ability groups, particularly in maths and language, moving to a subject-based curriculum at the top of the junior school in preparation for senior school. Lots of input from sixth form pupils, who help with reading and classroom support (boys are as much a part of this programme as girls).

Computers all over; excellent library facilities, plus all the other accoutrements you would expect in the junior department of a truly great school: swimming pool, super gyms, massive games options – rugby, football (Scottish champions, tours to Chelsea and Valencia), cricket, hockey etc, with at least ten teams in action every Saturday, plus inspired expeditions and the like.

Magical drama (Mr Lewis again) with major involvement in real professional theatre – over 650 appearances in 21 West End touring shows in last ten years. 'Carousel' with Lesley Garrett was running at the time of our visit and last year relays of children did 67 performances of 'Joseph' at the Playhouse. So lots of workshop contacts with top class professionals – Cameron Macintosh et al. All inclusive music with over 120 children playing in orchestras, 170 in choirs and over 300 instrumental music lessons weekly. Specialist choirs from primary 3. More than enough sport for all who want it. Fabulous art, with a great millennium staircase decorated by all the pupils – Mr Lewis was cross when we used the word 'pupils': 'Never use the word "pupils" – "pupils" are things you teach; "children" are real boys and girls'. Currently streets ahead of any other Edinburgh prep school.

The Maynard Junior School

Linked to Maynard School (The) in the Senior section

Denmark Road, Exeter, EX1 1SJ

• Pupils: 100 girls, all day • Ages: 7-11 • Fees: £8,226 pa • Independent

Tel: 01392 273 417
Fax: 01392 355 999
Email: admissions@maynard.co.uk
Website: www.maynard.co.uk

Head: Since 2006, Mr Steven Smerdon (early forties), educated at Downside School and Exeter University. We last met him as housemaster at Loretto near Edinburgh, so he's certainly travelled a bit to get here. 'Hands-on, caring and enthusiastic,' say delighted mums. 'He has time for each girl and knows everything that's going on.' Super. Teaches RE and drama. He enjoys playing the guitar and all outdoor activities – a keen VW campervan owner.

Entrance: Tests in English, mathematics, reasoning and reading.

Exit: No qualifying examination for entry to senior school at 11, therefore seamless for nearly all.

Remarks: Present building replaced Victorian villa destroyed by fire in early 1970s. Refurbished summer 2009 and plans in train for extension to facilities – juniors will gain enlarged multi-purpose hall and an additional classroom to allow for two form entry at seven. Shares tennis court area with seniors for outside play, but children have to start sprints on sports day at a 90 degree angle to finish – quite a sight apparently.

Super, friendly atmosphere. Experienced and creative teachers plus two LSAs help generate high standard of work throughout. Lovely reading area for Year 3 girls. Exciting displays are changed regularly to keep pace with theme work. Girls mainly with class teachers until Year 6, when they spend more time with senior specialists. We were impressed by girls' written work, both creative and formal. Reading culture and girls get a taste of three languages before they transfer. SENCo screens for SpLD and provides learning support in small library also used for speech and drama.

Extended lunch-times for wide range of activities including drama, art, French club and orchestra. Head keen on digital animation. Older girls join middle school choir, so lots of ways to make transfer to senior school work well. 85 per cent play an instrument – musical talent showcased in concert at end of spring term. Senior girls help out a lot at lunchtimes. Emphasis on inclusion in drama, music and sport so 'every girl can share limelight'. Travel considerations mean not much happens after school and girls get small amounts (10–20 minutes) of homework. Year 6 monitors run weekly fair trade stall selling healthy snacks. Lots of sport using senior facilities. Swimming in spring term. Expeditions in summer and outdoor pursuits. Room for every kind of girl here – definitely a winner.

Mayville High School Junior Department

Linked to Mayville High School in the Senior section

35-37 St Simon's Road, Southsea, Hampshire, PO5 2PE

• Pupils: 300 girls and boys; all day • Ages: 6 months-11 years • C of E
• Fees: £5,481-£6,090 pa • Independent

Tel: 023 9273 4847
Fax: 023 9229 3649
Email: Enquiries@MayvilleHighSchool.com
Website: www.mayvillehighschool.com

Remarks: See senior school's entry.

Merchiston Juniors (aka Pringle)

Linked to Merchiston Castle School in the Senior section

Colinton Road, Edinburgh, EH13 0PU

• Pupils: 120 boys • Ages: 8-12 • Non-denom • Fees: £11,385-£18,570 pa
• Independent

Tel: 0131 312 2200
Fax: 0131 441 6060
Email: admissions@merchiston.co.uk
Website: www.merchiston.co.uk

Head: Mr Nathan Mylin.

Remarks: See senior school, for details.

Merlin School

4 Carlton Drive, Putney, London, SW15 2BZ

• Pupils: 140 boys, 50 girls; all day • Ages: 4-8 • Fees: £10,800 pa
• Independent

Tel: 020 8788 2769
Fax: 020 8789 5227
Email: secretary@merlinschool.net

Head: Since 2003, Mrs Kate Prest BA Music/Ed PGCE (fortyish), educated at Oxford Brooks. Formerly head of pre-prep at The Harrodian, and before that teacher and music specialist at Oratory Primary, Chelsea. Married with three children. Very chatty and enthusiastic, eager to show off the school and seems justifiably proud of school and pupils. Knows all the children well. Parents can discuss any problems easily, and have found her to be 'very approachable'. Sees herself as very open-minded, easy to communicate with and 'always has the children's best interests as heart'.

Entrance: Following an open evening talk and tour of the school, places are offered on receipt of registration (unless a waiting list) on a first come first served basis, with priority given to siblings. However, following a 'fantastic' Ofsted inspection in 2007, school is full and has a waiting list.

Exit: To some top-notch preps and junior schools including Westminster, Bute House, Kensington Prep, Latymer and The Harrodian – which has the same owner. The Merlin is not a feeder school for The Harrodian, although it does have a link at 8+ if The Harrodian is an option for Merlin parents. (Instead of the normal January 8+ exam for The Harrodian, Merlin children have an informal interview plus a report from the Merlin head in November.) Pupils also go off to Colet Court and King's College Wimbledon, as well as other local independent schools. An occasional few to boarding school.

Remarks: Welcoming and friendly school which caters for a wide range of abilities but still manages to get places at some of the best London preps. 'It has never been a hothouse but the children are greatly encouraged,' says a parent. On first appearances, the school is fairly homely (carpeted in most areas) and quite plain, but the classrooms are well equipped with children's work proudly displayed. Good use made of all available space; playground is adequate and has a super Astroturf surface.

Teachers very keen for each child to reach the best of their ability, without cramming – whilst still preparing them for the 7+ and 8+ entrance exams. Smallish classes – average 16. Computers in each classroom and children are encouraged to use them alongside lessons. French is taught from reception. Separate science lab, music room, ICT room and art room used by all classes. Classes divided into small teams for maths and English according to ability but these are not fixed teams – children move regularly within various groups for support as and when required. 'The children here really do strive to do their best,' says a parent. 'Even if they are not academically minded, they are helped along without being made to feel different.'

Support teacher for English and maths for those who need it and an SEN teacher for dyslexia and dyspraxia at an extra cost to parents.

Sports OK. School now has in place new designated sports master, which should lift it. Much emphasis on music, singing, drama and art. In addition to class music teaching, all children are given the opportunity to learn the piano and violin with peripatetic teachers. Drama and music based productions are part of the school year.

Laid back, cosy atmosphere (some teachers are called by their first names and still command respect), quite a large number of male teachers – unusual in a pre-prep school. Children smart in dark blue and green uniform and very well behaved. Has always had a tendency to be boy heavy, 'But the girls are very much in evidence,' says head. Parents tend to be middle class professionals.

Not for those who want acres of outside space to let off steam but a real home from home.

Michael Hall Lower School

Linked to Michael Hall School in the Senior section

Kidbrooke Park, Forest Row, East Sussex, RH18 5JA

• Pupils: boys and girls • Ages: 0-11 • Non-denom: Steiner Waldorf Schools Fellowship • Fees: £7,200-£8,900; Early years £4,900 pa • Independent

Tel: 01342 822275
Fax: 01342 826593
Email: info@michaelhall.co.uk
Website: www.michaelhall.co.uk

Chairperson of the College of Teachers: There is no head teacher. Steiner Waldorf schools are self-governing communities and a 'college of teachers' administers and manages pedagogical issues without a traditional hierarchy supported by the Council of Management (trustees).

Remarks: For details see senior school.

Milbourne Lodge School

43 Arbrook Lane, Esher, Surrey, KT10 9EG

• Pupils: 135; all day • Ages: 4-13 • C of E • Fees: £9,600-£11,115 pa • Independent

Tel: 01372 462 737
Fax: 01372 471 164
Email: admin@milbournelodge.co.uk
Website: www.milbournelodge.co.uk

Headmaster: Since September 2010, Stephen Ilett (early fifties). Educated at Rossall and Lincoln College, Oxford, came to teaching after a career in the City – eight years at Caldicott Prep before appointed here. Reputedly, a big hit with current parents. His wife, Amanda, runs marketing for the school; five children between them, 13–23.

Entrance: Entry to pre-prep on first come basis. Children feed through to the main school, with the rest from local pre-preps, an increasing number travelling out from London (a school bus from Putney) in search of country-style prep schooling. Mostly at seven or eight (a few places available at other times) via maths and English test and a 'chat'. Looking for academic potential (with a view to scholarships) and takes into account previous education. Some feeling among parents that it's easier to get in here than to Colet Court or Westminster but that Milbourne is just as good. Keen to increase numbers, particularly of girls.

Exit: The first thing you see when you enter is the impressive black and gold scholarship board in the hall positively groaning under the weight of names of pupils and their prestigious public school destinations. St Paul's appears regularly and more recently Westminster. Otherwise it's top notch boarding schools: Eton, Harrow, Winchester, Charterhouse and other highly academic institutions, including Wycombe Abbey for the girls. Parental rumblings (that have finally been taken on board) that the school needs to take more account of the preferences and requirements of the London day schools, which are increasingly the destination of choice these days. 'They are getting better at it, but Milbourne has sometimes struggled with the pre-tests for these schools,' considers one mother.

Remarks: If a place can be traditional and unusual at the same time, then this is it. It's an old-fashioned, academically aggressive school with very high expectations of its pupils, by whom it generally does jolly well – assuming your aim is a good public school. Doesn't do anything by the book – and consequently in 2007 received a rather damning Ofsted report which sent some parents into a flat spin. Adding to the turbulence, around the same time Mr Norman Hale, the school's founder, proprietor and headmaster from 1948 to 1999, sold the school to Cognita, which owns and manages a growing group of independent schools all over the country. (Cognita Chairman, Chris Woodhead, was HM Inspector of Schools until 2000.)

The view of Cognita, Milbourne Lodge and its more supportive parents is that the inspectors totally missed the point of the school and that Milbourne and Ofsted are an ideological mismatch. Much of the Ofsted criticism concerned the school's failure to comply with regulatory requirements, including those relating to pupils' welfare, health and safety, behaviour and personal development. Additionally Ofsted required immediate action relating to staff appointments, including insistence that the school take up references and run Criminal Records Bureau checks on staff, of which there had been none. Cognita banged back a six-week action plan almost by return post and is running its own inspections until Ofsted's next visit. School says all the issues raised in this Ofsted report have now been fully addressed and complied with.

Cognita stressed at the time that it had no plans to change the staff or ethos of Milbourne Lodge, so Mr MacLarnon's departure a year later in 2008 caught parents on the hop and aroused a degree of disquiet from a vocal section, with half a dozen families moving their children elsewhere. Still some concern that the original ethos of Milbourne will disappear with the recent death of Norman Hale and that Cognita does not have the experience of running such a top drawer academic institution. Cognita, not surprisingly, is keen to reassure existing and prospective parents that all is well. 'We see Milbourne as the jewel in the Cognita crown,' says Chris Woodhead. 'There was certainly some parental concern initially, but I am constantly talking with and listening to parents and the feeling of the vast majority now is that the school is settling down. I am determined that Milbourne will retain its academic excellence.' Looking ahead, Mr Woodhead added that Cognita has plans to beef up the pastoral care side of things, broaden the curriculum and invest in new resources and facilities. Following a period of Wendy Holland as acting head, a new permanent appointment has been made.

New toilets (previously lacking in number) complete with copious supplies of soap (similarly lacking) have been installed. Parents also told tales of boys left behind after sports fixtures, transport for which was generally just another parent's car, but now coaches take pupils to and from matches. 'The school treats the children almost like adults, so it doesn't line them up and escort them everywhere,' explains one parent. 'There is actually not a lot of supervision, particularly in the playground and in the Dungeon (relax – it's an underground changing room) and that can be quite hard for some children in the beginning, but they do get used to it – it's quite character forming.' So positively no mollycoddling on the curriculum – your reaction to the above will largely determine your suitability as a happy Milbourne parent. A happy Milbourne child will generally be a robust character, very bright, a sporty type who doesn't feel the cold – compulsory outside sport every afternoon, rain or shine, plus necessary moving around between buildings.

The main building is a large, converted, Gothic-style red-brick house. Slightly shabby, although much has been recently redecorated, contains the main admin office, kitchen, all-purpose hall; upstairs in the attic are the art and IT rooms. Other classrooms (the majority) are in what are essentially wooden huts in the gardens. One parent said she found this scruffiness reassuring, 'I like my son being taught in a hut – it shows the school is concerned with teaching, not impressing the parents'.

However, grounds are naturally lovely, with great vistas over woods and neighbouring farmer's fields. This place is very keen on the great outdoors. Behind the buildings is a fabulous playing field incorporating football, rugger and cricket pitches, as well as an eight-lane athletics track. Also an outdoor heated pool, apparently well used. Older boys and girls do cross-country runs, younger ones play a wonderful 'ambush' game in the woods – unique to the school, invented 40 years ago by a teacher and just as popular today.

No theatre or performance space but classrooms now contain computers and three interactive whiteboards. The adjacent Small House, previously the head's accommodation, has been refurbished and is the home of the rapidly expanding pre-prep department. What you get is a traditional, classical education with the emphasis on English, maths and Latin. It aims to prepare children solely for Common Entrance and scholarships and offers a virtual guarantee of a place at a public school.

Even unsympathetic Ofsted agreed the standard of education was satisfactory and that, 'pupils achieve very high standards of academic work' – though more sourly noting, 'This does not provide sufficient opportunities for pupils to apply skills or develop analytic and creative thought'. It was also dismayed to find the school had neither curriculum policies nor subject schemes of work, and teachers had an over-reliance on worksheets – but school counters that Ofsted were in during the last days of the term and attended an unusually high number of cover lessons. More importantly, school is proud that its worksheets are tailor-made by its own teachers for each lesson and class, crafted to take account of how much was understood in the previous lesson.

By now it comes as no surprise to learn that the school does not follow the national curriculum, instead adhering to the requirements of Common Entrance and the passions of the staff. Pupils are streamed from day one into 'A' and 'B' – scholarship stream and Common Entrance stream – but movement between the two as necessary. Pupils are made aware of their place within the class for each subject and strive to improve it. They also have rankings for effort. One result of this is that some parents (insiders estimate the majority) opt for additional outside tutoring when the results are not as high as they think they should be – a tough life for some children, with pressure heaped upon them from all sides. A number of pupils do sport to a very high level and many do extra sport outside school. You have to wonder how they find the time – it's a long school day, with the top three years not finishing until 5 or 6pm and coming home laden with homework. It's a competitive place, be in no doubt.

In addition to the main subjects, Latin for all and Greek for the scholarship stream. Speech and Drama offered as an extra activity, continuing after the exams are finished – always an annual production. Art is a real strength – the work on display is among the best we've ever seen for this age group. Among the highlights is a fantastic 'Toast to Van Gogh' – his 'Sunflowers' reworked in toast slices and crumbs. School regularly features in the Royal College of Art Best School awards. Music is also strong – pupils regularly pick up music scholarships. Large music room; tuition of all sorts is available, with opportunities to play in an orchestra or group.

Inside the classrooms children work hard and quietly. Reference books may have seen better days but beautiful neat work can be seen. Children stand up politely as visitors enter – all very smart in blazers and ties, a few in sweatshirts, which have crept across from sports and are deemed acceptable and warm in winter.

This is traditional teaching by traditional staff (perhaps even eccentric in one or two cases) for bright, motivated and energetic pupils in pursuit of excellence. One parent, particularly pleased with the teaching, felt, 'The teachers make sure my son really understands the foundations before moving on'. She added, 'This might constrict the range of what they learn, but at least it means they can do the homework.' Another said that the children were given the facts, tested on them and later revised them, which ensures a 'sound grounding'. 'The style of teaching imposed here means the kids massively increase their ability to memorise information and are almost blasé about being tested,' adds another parent. 'It certainly fosters a resilient character.'

On the other hand, critics of the place feel the academic success comes at too high a price – reports of teachers treating children in a harsh way, e.g. sergeant-major shouting and books being thrown around – and a few parents voted with their feet and headed off elsewhere. 'The kids are under huge pressure and are continually ranked for everything,' says one ex-parent. 'And so two thirds of them troll up the road to Walton for extra coaching, which seems nonsense. The place is completely out of tune with the times – they're not preparing boys to be fags at Eton any more.' School says staff changes mean severity is no longer an issue. Parents also raise concerns about the pastoral care – although a deputy has now been appointed to strengthen this side of things, plus a new tutor system.

Milbourne is a school that attracts vociferous praise and criticism in equal measure. The question to ask is whether this mentally and physically action packed régime will suit you and your child. Do you both have the energy? Is it hot-housing or simply what a really bright child needs for inspiration? 'I love the school and so do my kids, but when people ask me if I'd recommend it, I have to say no, go and look for yourself ... You will either love it or hate it,' sums up one parent.

Not for the faint-hearted nor the progressive, Milbourne has had stormy times of late, which have undoubtedly increased the criticism from some parents. It is now up to Cognita, and the new head, to finally put a lid on the turmoil. We will be keeping an eagle eye on what happens.

Millfield Preparatory School

Linked to Millfield School in the Senior section

Edgarley Hall, Glastonbury, Somerset, BA6 8LD

• Pupils: 500 boys and girls; boarding and day • Ages: 2-13
• Inter-denominational • Fees: £11,475-£20,655 pa • Independent

Tel: 01458 832446
Fax: 01458 833 679
Email: office@millfieldprep.com
Website: www.millfieldprep.com

Head: Since September 2010, Mrs Shirley Shayler MA BSc PGCE. Educated at Carrickfergus Grammar School, Northern Ireland, degree in biology from the University of Stirling, master's in educational management. Taught at Millfield Senior 1989–2002 – senior tutor, houseparent, manager/coach to the girls' 1st XI hockey team, in charge of waterskiing, parachuting and SCUBA diving, part of the Millfield activities programme. 2002–2006 deputy head of Taunton School, then head of Stonar School, where she led significant development of sixth form experience.

Married to Gary, biology teacher and deputy head of careers at Millfield Senior; a daughter, 11, who attends Millfield Prep. Hobbies include swimming, cycling, skiing, reading and the theatre. Coaches hockey at school.

Entrance: Variety of ways in – many via interview and report from previous head, from prep schools finishing at 11, pre-preps, overseas and local primaries. Others sit scholarship exam in January for September entry. Can be flexible – will always make the effort to take pupils and has been a sanctuary for pupils unhappy or failing to thrive elsewhere: 'IQ not the only arbiter; we need to see the child, not just a collection of data'. Can and will take when space available.

Exit: Vast majority go to Millfield. Transfer not automatic, with good behaviour and a satisfactory academic standard necessities. A small number move elsewhere, almost always to other independent schools.

Remarks: Extensive site spread round a bend in the road outside Glastonbury, facing the school golf course and a boarding house at the foot of the famous Tor across the road (better view if you move a tree or two). Quite difficult to find reception – the signposts are in just the wrong place, and having started in the wrong place, it is quite difficult to locate. An external car park services the stunning games complex.

Appearance of school functional rather than beautiful, with limited attempts to co-ordinate or blend in new and less new with the Gothic Victorian pile at its heart where the head is based, and quite a lot of stuff (as in mantelpieces and the like) looks as though it has come from the Abbey itself (the previous owners used to own both). Lots of unusual touches, though – a huge outdoor chess set has moved from outside the girls' houses at the senior school (where we last saw it) to just in front of the main building, and the multi-coloured climbing wall on the outside of one building gives it the personality much of the architecture lacks. Architecturally the place needs a makeover: an enormous (three storey – why? – in the country?) cruciform classroom block was deeply muddling to this (experienced) editor, but the children seemed quite content, scurrying around like worker bees under the queen's command – well, it was the end of the schoolday and it was daylight, and there were golf clubs everywhere, and we do mean everywhere (golf is the current passion). Two boarding houses opened in September 2003 and a pre-preparatory department, catering for pupils aged 2–7, is now based on campus in the former kitchen garden – stunning, specially made story chair and super, cosy library.

Children coming into the pre-prep are automatically assessed – one-to-one groups and up to three specialist lessons a week for those who need help. The language development centre (LDC) is a centre of excellence, currently more than 180 pupils in this deceptively small building: ten tutors, five part time, and strong liaison throughout – the school all other prep schools recommend when they can't cope (and here this editor speaks from experience).

Pupils come with a range of problems from mild literacy difficulties to those with a diagnosis of dyslexia and/or speech and language difficulties. Detailed assessments are carried out in the main body of the school and the LDC, with ensuing discussions between the department and the heads of year groups regarding individual pupils. If reading or spelling is more than a year behind chronological age, this is flagged up, 'But data is not the only aspect taken into account when determining a pupil's current needs'. Each pupil on the SEN register has a pupil diagnostic profile, which details a pupil's strengths and weaknesses as well as offering support and guidance to class teachers. The head of LDC is also qualified in neuro-developmental delay with the Institute of Neuro-Physiological Psychology. If the programme is thought beneficial for a pupil and after a positive assessment (co-ordination, balance, visual development, laterality and spatial awareness), a 'five to ten minute a day programme, using no special equipment and replicating movements from the first year of life, is implemented, which gives the brain a second chance to develop the reflexes needed to provide a firm foundation for learning'. This programme usually lasts about a year.

Over 120 pupils of all ages are currently attending the LDC on a regular basis, being taught in small groups by specialist teachers. Visual overlay and auditory assessments can be carried out by trained members of the LDC team and referral can be made to a speech and language therapist who works closely with both the prep and pre-prep. Good tie-up with houseparents when children may need extra help. All areas of life here based on efforts to find an aptitude, build self-esteem and develop the potential of every child. Special programme (Potential Academic Curriculum Excellence or PACE) undertaken by super-bright. Help at both ends of the spectrum included in fees.

Pupils follow broad curriculum with setting for maths and languages in all but first year, French taught from the first term and Spanish and Latin added by the age of 10. Plenty of exciting trips out to bolster learning, from nearby basketworks and Hinckley Point power station to London galleries and France. Class sizes small, normal maximum 16. Each child watched over by group tutor, responsible for welfare and progress, and first port of call for anxious parents. Reports are termly, with grades for effort as well as attainment. Scholarships for chess as well as academic, music, sporting and art.

Set in acres of manicured greenery, with a bubble over the tennis court in winter (some houses have their own – as opposed to the school's one). Sport as important as expected: a second sports hall was opened in 2005, an equestrian centre with two maneges (school's preferred word is arena) was built at the same time, a nine-hole golf course just for Millfield prep, a fine 25-metre pool (ditto) and all sorts of courts, pitches and fields to cater for every conceivable sport and activity. Underpinning the school's ethos, finding talent in whatever area and inspiring confidence in its wake, the games list includes Airfix modelling and touch typing, as well as sports from pop lacrosse and indoor go-karting to squad training for swimming, rugby and soccer.

Music is particularly well-supported, with a wide range of instruments, 350 individual lessons, 29 music ensembles and 18 annual concerts. Facilities include 28 music rooms and a light and airy recital hall (currently under wraps); junior baroque chamber orchestra plus the expected choirs et al. Art of all kinds very popular, from printmaking to ceramics via ICT, with critical discussion an integral part of its teaching.

Pupils are chatty, bubbly, confident and clearly have a fun time. The school makes great efforts to preserve pupils' childhood for as long as possible – a welcome air of separation between the school and the town beyond. Boarding houses are particularly cosy, aiming to create homes from home, with bright colours, football team duvet covers and jazzy pinboards a feature of the bedrooms.

Welcoming, cheerful school with pupils treasured whatever their special talent, be it rugby or brass-rubbing. Wonderful facilities in every sphere. Genuinely turning out well-rounded individuals and a centre of excellence for those with serious problems. Couldn't do better.

The Minster School, York

Deangate, York, North Yorkshire, YO1 7JA

• Pupils: boys 85, girls 85; all day • Ages: 3-13 • Anglican
• Fees: £5,274-£8,109 pa • Independent

Tel: 0844 939 0000
Fax: 0844 939 0001
Email: school@yorkminster.org
Website: www.minsterschoolyork.co.uk

Headmaster: Since 2004, Mr Alex Donaldson MA PGCE Cert ICT (mid-forties). Choral scholar at St John's College, Cambridge; professional singer for five years (counter tenor) with, among others, the Tallis Scholars and the BBC Singers. Still helps out in the Minster. A serious musician, but has a wide perspective on education. Joined school in 1988, promoted head 2004. Still teaches history and acts as IT network manager. Warm, relaxed personality; communicates easily with both the very young and adolescents, popular with parents ('dashing new head,' according to one mum). Instrumental in introducing more collaborative style of management, though still in many ways the traditional prep school head, who knows his pupils well and what's going on. Wife Jane runs the pre-prep; three children, two at university.

Entrance: Most come up from nursery, but any age considered if room. Non-selective; would-be choristers must audition at age seven, when up to four of each sex are chosen to join prestigious Minster choir. Boys' and girls' choirs of 20 each are separate, take equal part in Minster worship. Choristers enjoy virtually free education – but work hard for it (as do their parents).

Exit: Most to northern independents at 13: Bootham, The Mount, St Peter's (all York city), Queen Margaret's, Ampleforth. Some to Rutland triangle, occasionally Eton, Fettes, Shrewsbury. Understandably excellent record in music scholarships. A few to local maintained schools.

Remarks: School famously claims foundation in 627 by Archbishop Paulinus; certainly a 'song school' existed then. Refounded 1903, specifically to provide choristers for the Minster; co educational since 1987. Occupies world heritage site slap in the middle of York; small children play unconcernedly in the lee of one of the finest buildings in Christendom. Hence expansion impossible, but most parents like it that way: 'We think of it as the City of York's village school, a small community of families from all walks of life with similar values'. Main buildings date from 1832; school also uses string of earlier town houses and handsome Georgian 'Old Residence' for lower school. Despite confined site, it feels remarkably uncluttered, though must be times when staff and lively children get on top of each other. Perhaps – like, e.g., Hill House in London – they learn a useful lesson about rubbing along together. Parents unconcerned by lack of 'flashy classrooms', appreciate 'wholesome, traditional, caring education – rather like a comfy old slipper'. But no gym, and pupils have to crocodile to playing fields near Bootham (admittedly only ten minutes away).

Most significant recent development has been a broadening of school's identity and purpose. Prospectus says very firmly, 'Musical ability is not an entrance requirement'; in head's eyes, this is more a school which does music than a music school. Well, yes, though most places would give teeth to reach even half its standard. The Minster still requires – and gets – a top class choir, but it's no longer true that choristers dictate the curriculum or shape of the school day. Even so, over 90 per cent of pupils leave playing one instrument, and about half play two or more. The usual offering of games, societies and trips. SEN (mostly literacy) catered for (free). Plenty of computers around, but – as 2004 ISI report noted – the school's great strength is in its top flight teaching. Parents mostly professional and business.

A real gem, combining (often awe-inspiring) visual and musical tradition with a forward-looking attitude to the current needs of all its girls and boys.

Moira House Junior School

Linked to Moira House Girls School, Eastbourne in the Senior section

Upper Carlisle Road, Eastbourne, East Sussex, BN20 7TE

• Pupils: 100; a few boarders, rest day • Ages: 2-11 • C of E
• Fees: Day £6,000-£10,950; Boarding £19,155 pa • Independent

Tel: 01323 636800
Fax: 01323 649720
Email: info@moirahouse.co.uk
Website: www.moirahouse.co.uk

Head: Mrs Linda Young CertEd NPQH, who spent many years teaching in Thailand.

Entrance: Interview and taster day.

Exit: 95 per cent to senior school.

Remarks: For further details, see senior school entry.

Monkton Preparatory School

Combe Down, Bath, BA2 7ET

• Pupils: Pre-prep: 65 boys and 55 girls; Prep: 170 boys and 85 girls of whom 20 boys and 20 girls board and flexi-board. • Ages: 2-13
• Church of England, evangelical • Fees: Day £7,542-£13,794; Boarding £18,366-£19,464 pa • Independent

Tel: 01225 837 912
Fax: 01225 840 312
Email: admin@monktonprep.org.uk
Website: www.monktoncombeschool.com

Head: Mr Chris Stafford (fifties). Educated at Kingswood, learned to wield chalk at Oxon. Geographer. Taught at Bishop's Stortford and St Peter's, Lympstone before taking on St Andrew's, Turi, in Kenya. Accounts himself fortunate to be where he is now and gives every impression of being to the manor born. Filled with warm energy, he's one of those new every morning sort of people, his spirit always pristine. You can tell by looking at him that he's the sort children really like, and, indeed, the epithet they mostly reach for is 'kind'. His innate attributes are irradiated by Christian beliefs of a joyous tendency. Loves his drama, directs plays and musicals, up into which all are swept. Big on boarding, does his bit up there in the dorms of an evening. Married to Jane, who teaches in the pre-prep. Three children grown up children. Swims before breakfast, whacks a squash ball, turns wood. Much involved in his local church.

Entrance: Essentially non-selective and jampacked. Boarding numbers doubled this year – 'We are a boarding school with day pupils'. Given the boarding numbers, the tail is wagging the dog here – in the interest of a big, busy school day. Informal interview for pre-prep. For the prep at age seven, interview plus tests (English, maths and verbal reasoning). Eleven year olds can either join the prep or go direct to the senior school. The only school in the Bath area which does CE and scholarships at 13. Parents mostly local professionals and business folk with a leavening of Services, an easy mix of the churched and the unchurched.

Exit: Most at 13 to the senior school, a smattering to Canford, Bryanston, Marlborough, Sherborne; an egg cupful at 11 to King Edward's, Bath.

Remarks: Dramatic hilltop setting with great downland views. Manor house with much built on rear end, which, unfortunately, you see first.

Academically sound across the board and very much on the ball – 'Teachers getting better,' say parents; first class director of studies. Science and history excel, but why single them out? Two form entry in Years 3, 4 and 5; streaming from Year 5, and an extra scholarship stream added in Year 6. They aim to get children to 'take responsibility for their own education – it's good ground for GCSE'. How? By reducing exam pressure and fostering a culture of working hard for its own sake. Certainly a whole lot of reading going on – maximum credit here to greatly loved librarian who never closes and offers beanbags to flop out on. Learning support detects info-processing glitches as they emerge very early – long established, very competent. Super-healthy meals, and tasty, too. Boarders rate the suppers even better than the lunches, and that's something you don't often hear. It's a long day – day pupils don't go home till 6pm, by which time they're probably done in, but so's their prep, so who's worrying? Saturday morning school for Year 4 and above.

Pre-prep and nursery in a separate converted villa which retains its homey feel. Plans afoot to build an integrated pre-prep as part of the Prep. Bright, cheerful. 'Loving,' parents say, 'wonderfully caring and nurturing.' All the right things. Super play area in the copse outside with a floor of wood chippings and what look a bit like pig huts to den up in.

Loads of music of every genre – a culture of singing and an amazing number learn an instrument: 'You're in a minority if you don't'. Scholarships to senior schools for the best, 'hobby for life' for the rest. Music, says the director, should be 'damn good fun'. Art for all out of this world under the veteran head, for whom the foundation of creativity is discipline and the children always working to the limit of what they can do: 'They're not supposed to find it easy, ever'. They think big and what they do is everywhere you go. Drama good and lots of it.

Much sport, done well, especially hockey, boys' and girls'. Fab swimming pool also open to the public. All-weather hockey pitch in stunning location has just opened, much to school's delight. Nothing for the ungamesy to fear. Heaps of teams. Says one parent, 'My son hates hockey but he still gets to play for the school.' Hm! Lots and lots of after school activities and clubs – in a parent's words, 'I'm always surprised how little goes on in some other schools by comparison'. This is definitely an up for it place which prizes children who give things a go. Those disinclined will feel wallflowery.

Mr Stafford is a boarding man and he wants more of it. The new director of boarding has beefed up what was already a good deal and now weekends are crammed with serious fun. Though boarders are a minority, they assure us they don't feel left behind. When, say, they are invited to a birthday party, someone takes them to it and fetches them back afterwards.

Of greatest concern to believers and non-believers alike must be the influence of evangelical Christianity. Is it the child-stealing, staring-eyed sort? Absolutely not. As in the senior school, the social atmosphere is notably celebratory of otherness so that, in the morning, 'One child can be lying on his bed reading the Bible, his friend 'The Beano', and both are equally respected'. Values here drive dogma into distant second place, making it equally appealing to those of a secular bent, a very difficult balance to achieve. Discipline is unashamedly old-fashioned but never Old Testament – rules are clear and firm. Most of the teachers are filled with faith, which makes the most of their already impressive work ethic – 'The staff work their socks off'. The children told us they feel their teachers are personally interested in them and they reckon them extremely approachable. They talk impressively about how people look out for each other here – it's a Monkton thing, and you can see it for yourself. A nice, natural lot, not a bit cocky.

An engagingly happy, notably humane school, very much its own place, which does it all and does it well. They'll always put character first here, but they darn well butter the parsnips at exam time, too.

Moon Hall School

Linked to Burys Court in the Junior section Linked to Moon Hall College

Pasturewood Road, Holmbury St Mary, Dorking, Surrey, RH5 6LQ

- Pupils: Full time pupils: 40 (of whom 5 are girls) age 7-11. Part time pupils: 40 age 11-13 based in Belmont Prep. 13 board (at Belmont)
- Ages: 7-13 • Inter-denom • Fees: Day £16,875; Boarding + £5,040 pa
- Independent

Tel: 01306 731 464
Fax: 01306 731 504
Email: enquiries@moonhallschool.co.uk
Website: www.moonhallschool.co.uk

Head: Since 2005 Mrs Pam Loré (pronounced Laurie) MA (Ed) BA Hons Dev Psych RSA Dip SpLD (fifties). First came in 1992 to assess pupils, then to teach, becoming deputy head, then head. Has a background in developmental psychology and is a Phono Graphix trainer (runs regular courses). A keen walker and traveller, speaks fluent Italian and French and has lived on most continents and in many countries – particularly loves Italy. Married to Beni. Has three grown-up children and three grandchildren. Reads widely and is particularly interested in the research into the acquisition of reading; not a fan of TV or computer games – believes they remove conversation and command of language.

A wonderful no-nonsense air underpins a can-do attitude. Says it's important to take the reins and feel the bit too, so not only teaches but is also the SENCo. Admits to being frantically busy but stresses multiple roles help her know the children well, a great asset at reviews. We met as she was dashing off to heap praise on an improved class. Feels passionately that to read functionally is key and can be done for anyone. Proud that school always manages to get the children reading, 'It helps that I've a loyal and experienced staff'. Understands the angst of parents as her own son is dyslexic.

Entrance: Takes an ever widening range of ability and severity, as mainstream schools get their acts together for the bright dyslexic. Most, but not all, pupils are of average ability (verbal IQ 100 approx) or above – a good many do not have any reading skills on entry. Report from educational psychologist must indicate dyslexia, though some have additional needs, mainly dyspraxia or dyscalculia. Prospective pupils carefully vetted during half day assessment. For additional fee, assessments include occupational therapy/speech and language needs. Does not accept children with emotional or behavioural problems and unable to help those with severe speech and language difficulties. Currently one pupil has a statement of special educational needs (increasingly difficult to get statements for dyslexia and funding doesn't necessarily follow).

Places in demand, waiting lists for most years, but anyone joining mid-year gets one-to-one help until up to speed. Some latecomers (Years 5 and 6) enter 'Delta' class – created for those who require intensive help with the acquisition of literacy skills – some want a quick fix – CE or bust. Moon Hall Schools Educational Trust has opened Moon Hall College at Leigh, near Reigate, for secondary age children (day only – a budding senior school).

Exit: Pupils usually move across to Belmont Preparatory School after Year 5 (on same site) except for a few Delta pupils who may leave the site after Year 6 or 7. Overall aim for all is to move to mainstream at 13 (or sooner) with minimal support – e.g. Millfield, Seaford College, St Bede's, Box Hill, Shiplake, Milton Abbey or Stowe. A few require more specialist schools, e.g. Mark College and More House, with the newly established Moon Hall College, on site of former Burys Court, an increasingly popular option.

Remarks: This is a CreSTeD category SP School. Founded in 1985 by Mrs Berry Baker in her home, Moon Hall, at Ewhurst, for her son. It relocated to Belmont School site in 1989 when the current, purpose-built building was erected. Mrs Baker is now Principal of Moon Hall School and Moon Hall College, the senior school. A well resourced specialist school with dedicated teaching for youngsters with moderate/severe dyslexia. Most will have fallen behind in previous schools. Teach full National Curriculum aiming for competence in basic language and maths, take SATs at end of KS2, 'a good benchmark of progress and useful for those moving to state sector.' adds the head. Key stage 2 results highly creditable though maths not as good as English and science ('we're working on it').

Specialist morning tuition in very small groups, (maximum seven pupils), for literacy and numeracy. Groupings as flexible as pupil needs – don't have hard and fast rules – it's whatever is needed. Complete class (14 pupils) re-forms in afternoon for remainder of curriculum. English course uses Phono-Graphix method for reading – encouraging results especially with Delta pupils (see below for definition of Delta). Indeed results for the latest intake show, in five months, all had improved their reading age by at least a year with one child adding almost three years to his score. Multi-sensory lessons the order of the day. All teaching staff trained in special needs, and in Phono-Graphix. All pupils taught touch typing from Year 3 with above excellent OCR examination results in word processing. No written French, oral occasionally offered. Homework done at school removes stresses at home.

Has a symbiotic relationship with co-located Belmont School: PE, music, DT taught by specialist staff in Belmont. Games likewise – Moon Hall School pupils may join Belmont teams. Meals and boarding also at Belmont. Some Belmont pupils attend Moon Hall for extra/specialist help (charged as an extra) seen as a bonus even by Belmont parents: 'a good insurance policy' commented one. If required, speech and language and OT help from visiting therapist available. Full time therapy assistant follows recommendations of external specialists (e.g. optometrist and occupational therapist).

Cheerful classrooms, art and DT displayed throughout the school. Individual music lessons available but must not conflict with core subjects. Drama is strong both at Moon Hall and Belmont and a former pupil has appeared in the West end. Comprehensive library including facility for parents to borrow material.

Lively, polite pupils, self-esteem restored, unanimously view Moon Hall as superb, saying the specialist help and support makes a real difference. Equally takes delight in the very many benefits of being able to share in and be part of regular prep school life at neighbouring Belmont. It seems you can have your cake and eat it!

Moor Park School

Moor Park, Richards Castle, Ludlow, Shropshire, SY8 4DZ

• Pupils: 240 boys and girls (55/45); 75 boarding beds: full time, weekly and flexi boarding, plus weekend tasters. • Ages: 2.5-13 • RC but inter-denom • Fees: £12,285-£16,785; Pre-prep £5,055-£9,270 pa • Independent

Tel: 01584 876 061
Fax: 01584 877 311
Email: head@moorpark.org.uk
Website: www.moorpark.org.uk

Head: Since 2008, Mr Jonathan Bartlett, BSc QTS with hons (forties). Graduate of Brunel University where he read PE and history. Keen sportsman and competitive by nature; something of an entrepreneur and visionary; something of an adventurer too, with piercing blue eyes which scan horizons and spot shirt tails that need tucking in. Genuinely passionate about boarding and 'keen to put the fun back' into education, while encouraging pupils to reach their potential. Healthily irritated by the nanny state approach to schools but 'very good on paper', says a fellow professional.

Had an interesting stint teaching in New England at a school near Salem but, after a brief spell working with a newly founded education agency, came back with a bonus: his delightful wife, Lisa. Quite liked the cut and thrust of the world of business but concluded that schools were where he wanted to be. So to Papplewick, where he was described as 'the best deputy head anyone could wish for'. Popular with children and parents – 'a breath of fresh air', 'fair and fun' – he is generally credited with bringing a new energy and vision to the school. Keen to make the most of the facilities and revels in the glories of Shropshire after the rather more manicured Thames Valley – 'Much less television watched here – the outdoors beckons'.

Mrs Bartlett is surely the best of the head's discoveries in New England and has also met with universal acclaim – 'brilliant', 'can't fault her', 'very kind and nothing is too much trouble', 'a total winner', 'much more than just one of those head's wives who smarm and charm over the match teas and shriek on the touchline'. Indeed she is: helping in the sick bay, 'pleasurable duty evening' in the girls' dorms, teaching foreign languages and health education – but not simultaneously, 'nor as much as I would like to'. They make a delightful team. They also have three young children in the school.

Entrance: Broadly speaking, four starting blocks from which to start the Moor Park adventure. Those 'rising three' may continue through the nursery and kindergarten to the transition stage, aged seven, then on to the senior school. (In fact, the school will consider anyone of any age, providing room.) Potential pupils come for a taster day and sit a relaxed assessment. Pupils aged four are screened for learning difficulties and offered help, if appropriate. Children come from a broadish cross section of society : old money in crumbling houses; new money from escaped Londoners; farmers, who cannot escape; Catholics and Protestants – all drawn by the country feel of the school, with its delight in muddy boots and bright eyed pupils. The catchment area has increased significantly as boarding has become ever more popular.

Exit: To an increasingly varied number of schools. Last year 29 leavers went to 17 different schools with 26 scholarships. Proper scholarships, too. An eclectic range of destinations: Shrewsbury, Eton, Winchester, Radley, Oundle, CLC, Tudor Hall, Moreton Hall, Stowe, Bedstone. Art, academic, music and sports scholarships particularly successful.

Remarks: Founded in 1964 as a Roman Catholic school and housed in an elegant Queen Anne mansion surrounded by wonderful grounds, complete with lake, old trees, a winding drive with a lodge at the foot and distant views of Housman's 'blue remembered hills': a paradise for children. The new head is keen to make the most of the grounds and has already overseen the cutting back of the banks of the lake so as to restore vegetation, improve fishing and introduce some boating. Nearby, a classroom has been constructed for outdoor studies and the estate management regularly checks the trees so that this is one of those increasingly rare schools where children may climb trees. Also a boiler suit school where, the head told us with great delight, 'the children often come to lessons covered with mud'. Yes, it's all a long way from the Thames Valley, but that shouldn't detract from the underlying seriousness of academic endeavour. This is not a play school – rather a school which believes that encouraging all round happiness leads to self-realization and success. Most schools trumpet that belief; this one fulfils it.

The main entrance of the house is warm and inviting with a roaring log fire in the winter, an impressive stair case and remarkable tooled leather wall paper. Old photographs dotted around remind us that this is an old country house; splendid art work reminds us that this is a lively and creative school. How well the two blend together. Within the house are the various dining rooms (food excellent, as we can testify), the bright and generously proportioned dormitories, with custom made bunks ('Super!' enthused a guide) and home to twelve members of staff, some married with children. This arrangement must be one of the reasons why such a tangible family atmosphere – really a happy overlap between staff and pupils. The fine library and the chapel, which has adapted effortlessly from being a spectacular ballroom, are uplifting features. Chapel is held on a daily basis and much appreciated by those to whom we spoke. 'I'm not a Roman Catholic,' said one mother, 'but I like the feel it gives. I'm glad it's around.'

The youngest adventurers start off in the old clock house and are referred to as the Tick Tocks. Thereafter classrooms and subject buildings are housed in small buildings, some of them reminiscent of porter cabins but all of them brightly done up and ideal for the purpose. Wonderful art block with paint- daubed atelier for senior artists, who are allowed to work up there unsupervised, another example of the new head's mantra of trust. Lively and spirited art teaching. Fizzing D and T with basic carpentry taught to all before moving on to more modern techniques of creation. Brand new computer block. All these marvellous facilities on offer and enthusiastically taken up during after school clubs and any free time that is available. Art and DT are timetabled in and remain part of the core curriculum; intelligent use of computers means they play an integral part in the whole learning process. We've seen smarter, slicker buildings but none where the teaching was any better as a result. This is a school where teaching really matters and where those with learning difficulties are well looked after.

Boarding is on the increase – partly as a result of the hugely popular weekend activities, partly because of the enthusiasm and involvement of the staff, but mostly through word of mouth. It clearly is fun – 'My child nagged and nagged us to let him board,' said one delighted parent. In celebration of the increase in boarding numbers and as an example of putting into practice what is being taught, has recently built a low cost sustainable house for young boarders. Not only is it an absolutely fascinating example of eco-building with its larch exteriors and oak interiors brought in from Wales, it is also a trend-setting design for comfortable and practical boarding. Twenty boys and girls now live in magical surroundings with house parents, a resident matron, a dog, kitchens for snacks and rooms for chilling out.

Not long ago it was described as a 'gem' – the word remains appropriate. Forty four activities, hobbies and sports on offer, from Swahili to origami, jewellery making to bush craft. 'Fun' is the buzz word – and how the staff throw themselves at it! A number are ex-pupils drawn, they say, by the magical surroundings and their happy memories. All of them appear cheerful and involved. A wonderful place in which to grow up: particularly in these exciting times.

Moreton First

Linked to Moreton Hall School in the Senior section

Weston Rhyn, near Oswestry, Shropshire, SY11 3EW

• Pupils: girls: boarding and day; boys to age 8 (day only) • Ages: 3-11
• C of E • Fees: Day £7,350-£10,350; Boarding £17,070 pa • Independent

Tel: 01691 773671
Fax: 01691 778552
Email: moretonfirst@moretonhall.com
Website: www.moretonhall.org

Head: Mrs Sarah Mostyn-Jones.

Remarks: For details see senior school, Moreton Hall School, Oswestry

Morrison's Academy Junior School

Linked to Morrison's Academy in the Senior section

Ferntower Road, Crieff, Perthshire, PH7 3AN

• Pupils: 85 boys, 95 girls; including nursery: 15 boys and girls
• Ages: Junior school 5-11, nursery 3-5 • Inter-denom
• Fees: £6,393-£9,108 pa • Independent

Tel: 01764 653 885
Fax: 01764 655 411
Email: principal@morrisonsacademy.org
Website: www.morrisonsacademy.org

Head: Mr Alasdair Robertson.

Remarks: See senior school.

Mount House School

Mount Tavy, Tavistock, Devon, PL19 9JL

• Pupils: 110 boys, 65 girls; 80 full boarders in main school; 65 in pre-prep.
• Ages: 7-13; pre-prep 3-7 • C of E • Fees: Boarding £16,065-£18,171; Day £9.321-£13,629; Pre-prep £6,510-£6,900 pa • Independent

Tel: 01822 612 244
Fax: 01822 610 042
Email: office@mounthouse.com
Website: www.mounthouse.devon.sch.uk

Head: Since 2002, Mr James Massey BSc (forties) born in Birmingham and educated at Bilton Grange, then Oundle. Read economics at Reading, whence he cut his business teeth in the city prior to first teaching job at Caldicott, where he became a housemaster and coached a lot of sport in addition to teaching English. Enjoyed a year away at Hereworth School, New Zealand, before five years at Oundle, where he taught economics, coached sport and became a housemaster. Brings an obvious commitment and enthusiasm to the job which hits you right away – parents confirm that 'head is passionate about the school'. Now, seven years into this headship, parents hope he will remain. Seems almost too good to be true: deals with any situation 'with integrity,' relates well to all the children and is described as 'approachable' by parents.

Married to structural and civil engineer wife, Jo(anna) who manages 'front of house' and runs the school shop – relates as a fellow parent, we were told; mums love the Dartmoor walk she organises – parents can 'chat about anything and everything,' they say. Son and daughter both currently at Mount House. Head is realistic about market forces – keen to build on school's strengths but has also steered it into hitherto uncharted waters: a broadening of the curriculum and a radical change to the working week. Loves the outdoor aspect of Mount House; enjoys sailing when he gets half a chance.

Entrance: Wide ability range; tests in English and maths 'more for benchmarking than selection,' says head. Most entrants attend a taster day in February prior to admission. Majority start in pre-prep or at start of Year 3 but growing numbers delay start until Year 7.

Exit: Highly successful record at Common Entrance: range of scholarships (academic, art, music and sporting) to mix of senior schools including Bryanston, Sherborne and Eton. Twelve or so different destinations each year from a leave of 30+. Two or three may leave at end of Year 6.

Money Matters: Bursaries advertised locally when available (two available for whole school). Individual music and learning support incur an additional cost, likewise some activities.

Remarks: Founded in Plymouth – school crest reflects its roots. Motto: 'Ut prosim' ('to be of use') now more relevant than ever. Stunning grounds include a trout stream (ideal for fly fishing) and a beautiful lake (great for science) bordering on Dartmoor National Park. Recent team of inspectors dubbed it 'an inspirational learning environment'. Core of school based in and around a charming, stone-built Georgian manor house with an assortment of additions to the rear. Attractive hall fulfils variety of functions, including regular assemblies and church services; head's oak panelled study leads off on one side and the school dining-hall on the other. Upstairs are all the boys' dormitories plus the sick bay. The original stables have been converted in a variety of ways including the 'giraffe house', which features a climbing wall. Further on we found the modern sports hall (with two squash courts), two large science laboratories and impressive music school (a step up from its previous location in a cellar). Wortham Hall is used for major productions, concerts, exams and drama lessons (ex-TV actress in charge of this).

Most of the classrooms are an extension of the main building: attractive internally – some with stunning displays – and all with high level of equipment (smartboard in every classroom). Eighteen PCs in IT suite and staff are mostly IT savvy. Outside farm/sustainable technology area has grown out from D and T building (workshops and classroom still used in winter) and is a really great initiative: children of all ages fully involved in animal husbandry and crop cultivation.

Pre-prep in purpose-built, low level accommodation (opened in 1996) for sixty children up to end of Year 2 with discrete outside area. High level of care and individual attention – most pre-preppers transfer seamlessly aged seven. Lots of fun and outdoor experience for this end of the school as well as developing strong foundations in the classroom basics.

Pupils are well turned out – variety of dress according to age and season (suits still worn for formal occasions); they come mainly from Devon and Cornwall, a few from London or elsewhere (very few overseas). Professional, farming and service families make up the majority here. 'A lot of Mount House parents are contemplating senior schools further afield,' explains head. Boarding ethos is all important, especially to day pupils.

'Mix of old timers and new blood on staff works well,' commented one father. Ten couples/families live on site and rotate weekend duties. Staff:pupil ratio of 1:10 keeps average class size at around sixteen. Curriculum is designed to allow pupils to go 'off piste' and generate individual enthusiasms – 'Able teachers have given our son a passion for maths,' reported one mother. High quality of written work wherever you look – we were particularly impressed by some highly imaginative poetry folders we saw, worthy of much older pupils. Some infectiously eccentric science teaching and motivational French lessons were other strong points we noted. Director of studies acts as SENCo with thirty-five pupils on special needs register. Pupils are screened for dyslexia and a dedicated education psychologist will develop an IEP if required. Two part-time SpLD staff give 1:1 help where required.

Five days a week sport here – facilities include fine pitches, heated outdoor pool (very popular) and full size Astroturf; national/regional successes principally in rugby, cricket and girls' hockey. Boarders love to play in the nets or swim after prep in the summer. Shackleton Award scheme (loosely based on senior D of E award) fills the only non games afternoon and aims at developing self-confidence through a range of (mainly) outdoor activities – e.g. raft building and scavenger hunts. Horsey pupils get to ride in local hunt and compete at inter-school equestrian events.

Pupils' art work is a credit to HoD (Year 8 pupils were working on 'Op art' project when we visited). Lovely studio in converted coach house and art scholarships are not uncommon – latest to Bryanston. Parents very pleased with music – 'It has changed dramatically for the better,' they say: staggering 90 per cent of pupils have individual instrumental tuition. Music seen as 'cool' and lots happens, from robed church choir to participation in local music festivals. Full orchestra as well as jazz band, woodwind, choir, rock band – all get to perform at concerts throughout year.

Latest innovation is introduction of sustainable design and technology course; each pupil spends two periods a week in farm area. Head is passionate about need for next generation to have hands-on experience. Possible issues for veggies (e.g. Boris the pig going off to the abattoir, then back to the dining table) are 'handled sensitively,' we were assured. 'Whole school's Christmas feast will be home grown from now on,' beams the head enthusiastically; he has little time for 'box ticking eco awards' but wants this side of the school to be seen as vital. Even the tractor runs on re-cycled vegetable oil from the school kitchen and a bore hole in place for the water supply. Next step: solar micro generators.

Pupils badger parents to let them board – many of the latter wait until four terms from senior school to cut the apron strings. Boarding staff very popular (girls we spoke to quoted their houseparents as the best thing about boarding at MH). Dormitories are neat and light; common rooms are places for relaxing after long and busy days. Television limited to Wednesdays and Saturdays but plenty of choice of games etc. Lovely, separate house for up to thirty girls bursting at seams. Reward system includes 'headmaster's bar' – lots of ways of winning this. No-one mentioned punishment. Great choice of food (mainly locally sourced) – some exotic dishes included to widen tastes. Civilised eating where proper conversation is encouraged by staff presence. Parents can drop their charges off early and then they get 'breakfast on the house'; day pupils can also stay for tea.

Head has gambled on folding compulsory Saturday classes and sport in favour of voluntary Saturday excursions and activities. He feels that 'modern' parents will more readily accept a prep school boarding commitment which allows them quality time with their children at weekends when desired. New régime includes Saturday evening pick-up after activities, then low key, on site Sunday programme. Early signs are encouraging with boarding numbers apparently on the increase. Subterranean library has been created out of former storage area – attractive with lovely hideaways for bookworms to self-indulge. Decking area outside library has created another space for relaxation and quietude. All staff stay here until 6pm every day; prep finishes at 7pm for older pupils (younger ones have clubs) and duty team of staff remains until dorm staff take over at 8.30pm. Head loves way that pupils 'spill out' into grounds after prep.

Fun filled leaver's concert is climax of summer term. Twice-termly Oracle lectures tap into parents' know-how – recent outside speakers have included explorer Pen Hadow and yachtswoman Tracy Edwards. Lots of local visits for all ages and regular ski trip to Alps. Head claims to be 'anti flashy sports tours', but recent ones to Amsterdam and Barcelona might gainsay that.

Former pupils include Phil de Glanville (England rugby captain), Adrian Lukis (actor in 'Pride and Prejudice'), former foreign secretary and SDP co-founder Lord David Owen, and explorer, long distance swimmer and environmentalist, Lewis Pugh, to name but a few.

An unexpectedly rewarding find this far west – a thoroughly successful prep school which caters for all needs. More than holding its own by combining new ideas with traditional values.

Mowden Hall School

Newton, Stocksfield, Northumberland, NE43 7TP

• Pupils: 115; 65 boys, 55 girls. 80 boarders, 35 day children • Ages: Pre-Prep and Nursery: 50; 25 boys, 25 girls. • C of E but all faiths welcome • Fees: Day £4,110-£14,370; Boarding £18,570 pa • Independent

Tel: 01661 842 147
Fax: 01661 842 529
Email: info@mowdenhall.co.uk
Website: www.mowdenhall.co.uk

Headmaster: Since 2007, Mr Ben Beardmore-Gray (forty-ish). Ludgrove and Ampleforth educated, read history at Newcastle. Worked in the City for three years before taking a teaching post at Ludgrove, where his father had taught for 20 years. He then moved to Farleigh Prep School in Hampshire and was deputy head there for six years. Wife Sarah and three children.

Entrance: Wide ability range – interview with head, no exam or test, three term entry. Pupils come from all over the north of England and southern Scotland – Northumberland, Yorkshire, Cumbria, Dumfries and Galloway, Scottish Borders.

Exit: Largest numbers to Uppingham, Oundle and Sedbergh, though Eton, Harrow, Rugby, Ampleforth, Queen Margaret's, Glenalmond and Fettes feature, as well as Newcastle day schools at 13+. Forty awards in last four years.

Remarks: Pre-prep unstreamed, maximum of 18 per class; main school streamed, maximum class size 16. Scholarship stream study Greek; French for all from nursery; Latin from Year 5. Good and imaginative teaching at all levels. Light bright classrooms, with plenty of work on display, and heaps of encouragement on hand. Good library, brilliantly converted science, art and technology centre in the stable yard (very busy at club time in evenings and over weekends) and super art.

Keenly sporting – particularly successful at rugby and girls' hockey, with soccer, swimming (own pool) and tennis also popular. Weekend life is kept busy and full, with Saturday school, lots of expeditions, outdoor pursuits of all kinds (madly popular), plenty of staff on hand. Deputy head ensures that Saturday evenings have a clear focus (themed suppers – Mexican night, medieval night etc) and that Sundays are structured. Most boarders opt to stay in for the weekend.

Old country house with many additions and conversions. Splendid setting, on a sixty-acre site with fine views and reached via a sweeping drive, dodging pheasants and sleeping policemen. Far less isolated and much more accessible (just off the A69 and ten miles from Newcastle) than its setting would suggest. Impressive sports fields abound (games every afternoon) and woodland provides a muddy but exciting landscape for den-building competitions and a BMX trail. Recent merger with Cothill Educational Trust has given a sound financial base – dormitories and social rooms are seeing the benefit of a structured investment programme in the fabric of the buildings.

Boarding numbers are growing. All children (however local) encouraged to board early and particularly for their final three years. Response to current market means that flexi boarding remains an option, although the emphasis is on full boarding. Relaxed but busy and purposeful atmosphere, a family school with a healthy balance of discipline and freedom. Pupils encouraged to have a 'broad outlook', be open-minded and prepared to 'have a go', otherwise they may struggle here, at least initially. During break cheerfully grubby boys sport boilersuits and wellies to make the most of the grounds, some girls join in but most prefer to look on.

Good food in agreeable dining room with staff seated at each table, children on rotas to clear plates. Healthy eating is a focus in accordance with the school's enthusiasm for sport, fitness and general wellbeing; add to that the recently ordained school chaplain and this should ensure that both body and soul remain in good shape.

Nursery and pre-prep from the age of three, popular with local families and healthy in number. Parents a mix of long-established Tyne Valley residents, Newcastle professionals, Services, North Cumbrian county set, Scottish landowners and the occasional country squire. Fair percentage of first-time buyers opting for boarding as a lifestyle choice rather than because of any long-standing family traditions.

Good, traditional prep school with lots going on, in good heart and doing well, exuding energy from the top down and concentrating on developing well-rounded individuals, whilst still aiming for those highly competitive top scholarships. Good parental noises.

The New Beacon School

Brittains Lane, Sevenoaks, Kent, TN13 2PB

• Pupils: 385 boys, mainly day with limited weekly/flexi boarding
• Ages: 4-13 • Non-denom • Fees: £8,685-£11,205 pa • Independent

Tel: 01732 452 131
Fax: 01732 459 509
Email: admin@newbeacon.org.uk
Website: www.newbeacon.org.uk

Headmaster: Since 2008, Mr Michael Piercy BA (Hons) (late forties). He read English at university and was previously head of Moor Park, Ludow and Dunhurst (Junior Bedales) and earlier deputy head at Forres Sandle Manor. Certainly the move has been successful on the personal front – he met and married the head of music within 18 months of arrival. Parents find him friendly enough, say he keeps a fairly low profile and are quick to praise some of the practical changes he has introduced without any great fanfare. The new traffic and parking systems have clearly had a positive impact, as well as the after-school clubs. He promises more changes, including encouraging parents to consider a wider variety of senior schools based on their child's particular needs and strengths. He is aided by what he feels is an ideal mix of long-serving and new staff, enabling him to build on the achievements of his predecessor (of 32 years' service) while keeping pace with educational developments.

Entrance: Most put their names down well in advance for reception entry, at which stage, and until Year 2, the school is non-selective. Higher up, places become available fairly regularly with pupils admitted from Year 3 based on academic work and progress to date.

Exit: Most boys enter the school early and stay on to 13, at which point the vast majority gain entry into their preferred senior school. A sizeable number win academic and non-academic scholarships to Sevenoaks and Tonbridge, by far the most popular choices, but others go on to Worth, Caterham, Cranbrook, Eton and King's Canterbury. Under 20 per cent leave at the end of Year 6, when they receive limited support in preparation for the 11+.

Remarks: In the context of a shortage of good boys' senior schools in the area, the school consistently meets its mostly City working parents' aspirations and delivers confident, responsible boys whose impressive CE results – averaging 76 per cent – secure them places at sought-after local day schools and other leading public schools further afield.

The prevailing attitude seems to be that it's a competitive world out there and getting used to it early is no bad thing. 'Let's face it, boys are naturally competitive and the school in addition does a great job of motivating them.' When from Year 4 things begin to hot up, most cope well, though the Year 5 and above scholarship stream does cause resentment amongst some parents – 'We all pay the same but they seem to get superior treatment and better teaching staff'.

Winning and success are openly acknowledged to be important and underpinned by the belief that if you expect a lot, you won't be disappointed. The prospectus is replete with statistics testifying to, in particular, the school's academic and wide-ranging sporting achievements. Lots of trophies to prove it. The head, however, is keen to highlight a move to a more inclusive approach and broader recognition of talents. At the top of the school two headboys are now appointed each term and, from Year 4, all pupils given the opportunity to represent the school at least twice a term, although in sports some grumble that fixtures for all but the top teams can be hard to find.

Academic grades are no longer read out in class and an expanded activities programme has been introduced featuring fencing, judo, skiing, chess and drama, amongst others. This is hugely popular, not least as it extends school hours and reduces pressure on working parents. It can also provide additional opportunities for boys to shine, though, for some boys, not making the football or rugby teams will always be a disappointment.

Another area where many excel is music. Nearly 300 hours of music tuition take place each week and boys regularly perform in bands, orchestras and choirs, locally, nationally and internationally. The focus and concentration required are considered a useful lesson in discipline – while not squashing their sense of fun, it gives boys an understanding of how to behave. All remark on how the school promotes good manners, makes clear the standards it expects and is quick to come down on those few who step out of line. Indeed, unprompted, even the smaller boys step aside in the corridors and cheerfully meet your gaze and interact with staff. A happy and purposeful feel.

Class sizes are kept below 20 and parents praise the school for knowing each child's capabilities. Standards are high and the school is not shy of alerting parents to potential problems as the boys move up it. Parents agree, saying communications are effective and teachers generally highly responsive to concerns. New post of individual learning coordinator created to ensure learning is tailored to individuals' needs, although in this the junior school, in particular, is already considered excellent. All boys receive a really good grounding in all subjects, with ample support for those who struggle and scope for the more able to be moved up a year. Some setting also higher up the school. The new learning coordinator is charged with enhancing SEN provision, refreshihg the school's focus on learning support, the gifted and talented programme and provision for the small number of EAL (currently approximately five to ten families).

Although the school has insufficient indoor space to host whole-school events – the chapel is fairly small, as is the sports hall (though due for expansion) – it works hard to be welcoming to families, encouraging them to attend events and stand on the sidelines at matches. In this and in other ways the parents' association is a great asset. It organises a variety of highly professionally-run social events each year and is successful at fundraising, improving the already enviable facilities. Set in 21 acres of beautiful grounds, the school has a 25-metre pool, well-equipped classrooms, labs and workshops. The junior school building, opened in 2007, provides a particularly vibrant learning environment. Plans afoot to revamp the pre-prep using the same architect.

Flexi-boarding is currently limited to 14 with priority given to older boys likely to move on to full boarding at their next school, though it will expand to meet rising demand. The dormitories are housed in the original school building dating from 19th century. The accommodation is good and the boys reportedly well-cared for and entertained.

New College School

Savile Road, off Mansfield Road, Oxford, Oxfordshire, OX1 3UA

• Pupils: 130 boys; all day • Ages: 4-13 • C of E but welcomes all faiths and beliefs • Fees: £7,413-£11,985; Choristers £4,185 pa • Independent

Tel: 01865 243 657
Fax: 01865 201277
Email: office@newcollege.oxon.sch.uk
Website: www.newcollegeschool.org

Headmaster: Since 2008, Mr Robert Gullifer MA Cantab (fiftyish). Educated at Bristol Grammar School, followed by a choral exhibition at St Catharine's College, Cambridge (English). Previously head of English and under master at KCS Wimbledon, deputy head at The Dragon and deputy head at Bristol Grammar School. Delighted to be appointed and is 'extremely proud of the school and its boys'. Stepped into the shoes of Mrs Hindle, who had a rather formidable reputation – 'I have a different style', clearly one that's an improvement and is proving popular with parents. Enthusiastic about moving the school forward – has developed Saturday morning music, improved pastoral care, broadened extracurricular activities – 'so important for the boys to develop lifelong interests' – and introduced a weekly short service in New College chapel for the school plus parents. Teaches RS to Year 7 and the scholarship class, i.e. philosophy for those tricky scholarship questions.

Married to an Oxford law don and has two daughters, one still at school. Still sings regularly with the Oxford Bach Ensemble and loves drama – directs the Year 7–8 play: 'Murder in the Cathedral' last year. Is aiming to establish New College as an academic school within a small, caring environment. A good appointment, popular with parents and staff. 'Listens,' say parents – a universal comment. Stands at school gates every morning and is available for any concern – 'If a boy's cat dies, we need to know so that we can fully understand that boy on that day'.

Entrance: Put your child's name down by age 1–2 for the pre-prep (entry of 14). Boys invited in for a session of play to check that they will be happy. At 7, a further four to six join – 'gentle assessments' in maths, creative writing and reading aloud to head. Sympathetic to relocaters – vital in a place like Oxford. Not terribly selective, but would refuse a boy they thought would struggle to keep up or who would not be happy.

Choristerships – voice trials for 7 year olds held in the autumn preceding the year of entry by Professor Edward Higginbottom: 'Very simple assessment – he can immediately hear a boy's potential'. Two thirds fee remission for choristers.

Exit: The odd one at 11, though most parents keep their sons here until 13 to reap the rewards of being senior boys. Good liaison between the head and heads of senior schools. Admissions evenings held when senior school representatives can chat to parents. Advice is given to parents on suitable choices for their son and the vast majority grateful to receive this. Majority to Magdalen College School, Abingdon, St Edward's. Others to Leckford Place, Radley and a few to the major public schools. Eight scholarships out of 12 leavers in 2010, seven out of 13 in 2009.

Remarks: School was founded in 1379 to provide an education for the choristers of New College and is governed by its warden and fellows. Tucked away in a quiet corner of central Oxford it is described by a parent as 'a rare gem of a school'. A programme of development has ensured growth and provision of facilities including a fabulous new sports hall with a climbing wall in 2008. Light and airy, it houses a new art room, music room and technology suite on the upper level and received an Oxford Preservation Trust Award. Otherwise the usual motley collection of school buildings – original, '60s and modern, cheek by jowl on the tiny site, but the school is able to spill into New College for use of the chapel and for special events.

Class size is small – average 14 in pre-prep, 18 in prep with max of 20. Pre-prep classes bright, buzzing and cheerful. Years 3 and 4 taught mostly by class teachers, Years 5–8 by specialist teachers. French from reception, Latin from Year 5, optional Greek in Years 7 and 8. SEN tends to be picked up in the pre-prep by experienced teachers. Parents are advised if further assessments are needed and extra tuition is provided at a cost. EAL (6 boys at present) also catered for through learning support department. Classrooms are mainly small and traditional but with data projectors in every room. Multipurpose science lab with interactive whiteboard, IT room with enough terminals for all, DT room, pottery room, small library etc. Head always keen to introduce new blood into the staff room as well as new ideas. Staff encouraged to take opportunities to visit other schools and import fresh ideas.

Music 'phenomenal,' said one prospective parent. This is a musical school and it's taken seriously – 91 per cent of boys play an instrument, 50 per cent two. Some older pupils reach grade 7. Choristers learn two instruments – the piano and one other. Many practice rooms, ensemble rooms, music technology room etc. Saturday morning music for instrumentalists so that more time can be devoted to playing without the restriction of a school timetable. Optional for boys in Year 5 and above, compulsory for choristers. Twenty choristers in school have a schedule not quite as gruelling as some other choir schools – choir practice four times a week at lunchtimes and after school, evensong five times week including Sat and Sun evenings but, surprisingly, no Sun morning commitment. Ditto Christmas or Easter. The choir is world renowned and frequently tours worldwide. Won the Gramophone award for Ludford recording in 2008. Head encourages choristers to share their musical experience with the other boys and bring the music into the school. Extra-curricular opportunities encouraged at lunchtime – fencing, archery, Mandarin. Drama specialist after school for LAMDA awards and many school productions including annual French play.

School uses the playing fields of New College for sports, including tennis courts. Not known for its sporting prowess, boys say it's difficult to win when the team is chosen from so few – keen, though, to point out to me that some have, on occasion, won sports scholarships. Wet afternoons on playing fields (this head's schoolboy memory) now a thing of the past, courtesy of the new gym.

Revamp of pastoral care system under Mr Gullifer. Recent inspection report commented on outstanding pastoral support. New head has implemented clear guidelines on rewards and sanctions – feels rewards are hugely important but boys also need clear boundaries on behaviour. Series of warnings – in reality only 1–2 headmaster's detentions in a year. Any concerns with any boys are discussed at head's weekly meeting with staff – 'Can discuss every single boy if necessary'. No evidence of poor behaviour on our visit, indeed the boys were happy and industrious. Articulate and delightful guides extolled virtues of school. What's the best thing about this school? 'Absolutely everything,' came the answer. Favourite teacher? 'All of them!' – clearly experts in diplomacy as well as model pupils. An 'OK' for food.

Majority of parents academic, medical, business. A few with more limited financial means have been able to send their sons with a choral scholarship. Head points out that the link with New College brings university into contact with many parents who may be otherwise excluded – bridges town/gown divide. Huge parental expertise, as one would expect in Oxford, from which pupils profit, as parents are generous with their time. Parents choose the school for its warmth, family feel and academic reputation. Say head has opened the door to parents – now has parents' committee, parents' choir one evening a week and views are taken seriously. This editor was treated to the short weekly service in the chapel (New College organ scholar provides music) with presentation of achievements and coffee for parents afterwards – 'Love to be able to see my son in the school setting,' says one; 'A time for quiet reflection during a busy week,' says another. Some prospective parents fear the school is too Christian – 'Not at all,' says a current parent. 'It's pretty low key.'

Others put off by small size, but if you're looking for an intimate, family, nurturing school with a good academic reputation and lots of music, this is ideal. Likely to become increasingly popular under enthusiastic new head.

Newcastle Preparatory School

6 Eslington Road, Jesmond, Newcastle upon Tyne, Tyne and Wear, NE2 4RH

• Pupils: 265 day boys and girls (roughly two thirds boys), plus 25 in nursery
• Ages: 4-11, Kindergarten 3-4 • Non-denom • Fees: £7,779-£8,742 pa
• Independent

Tel: 0191 281 1769
Fax: 0191 281 5668
Email: enquiries@newcastleprepschool.org.uk
Website: www.newcastleprepschool.org.uk

Head Teacher: Since 2002, Mrs Margaret Coates (mid-forties), previously head of infants and juniors at Durham High, before that at RGS Newcastle. Studied English at Westminster College, Oxford. Confident, smart, articulate, obviously loves children; insistent on handing over much responsibility to children for creation of their school world and as a counter to potential over-protectiveness; all within a clear disciplinary framework.

Entrance: At ages four and eight; no test, but children spend a morning in school and are informally assessed.

Exit: Boys go on at 11 to Royal Grammar School, Dame Allan's, Durham, King's Tynemouth. Girls leave for Central Newcastle High, Dame Allan's, Newcastle Church High, Royal Grammar School and Westfield.

Remarks: Fairly traditional prep school with nursery attached, long established in city (1885). Firmly entrenched as first choice for parents wanting the two main secondary schools, and successful with it. Three and a half terraced houses in Jesmond near city centre, ingeniously interconnected at various levels, every room crammed with lively work and displays. Cosy feel; inevitably lacks a sense of space, air and greenery – makes up for this by busy sense of purpose.

Broad intake, with two parallel classes of 16–20, no streaming or setting. French starts at age three, Spanish introduced at age nine, German taster sessions take place at ten as well as Latin. ICT provision is good with interactive boards in all classrooms and an up to date computer suite. The well resourced comfortable library is in the centre of school. Many opportunities in and out of classroom, including 11 year olds' philosophy club. Music excellent (professionally run): choir, orchestra, jazz band. Provision for special needs, including gifted and talented. Small playing field and new sports hall on site and sport is taken very seriously. Chirpy yellow and dark grey uniform, and cheerful and courteous children.

Parents are as you would expect in a large city: aspirational, many professionals and first time buyers. Lively and supportive Friends' society.

Newland House School

32-34 Waldegrave Park, Twickenham, Middlesex, TW1 4TQ

• Pupils: 280 boys and 150 girls • Ages: 4-13 • Non denom
• Fees: £9,000-£10,080 pa • Independent

Tel: 020 88651305
Fax: 02087 440 399
Email: admissions@newlandhouse.net
Website: www.newlandhouse.net

Headmaster: From 2010, Mr David Alexander BMus DipN-COS. Previously head of Haden Dene School, Broadstairs.

Entrance: Heavily over-subscribed – it's one of those places where children are registered at birth. Two main points of entry: 4+ and 7+, with occasional vacancies at other times. 40 places available at 4+ when entry is non-selective. At 7+ another 20 places are available, although at this point the children will be assessed in English, reading and maths. Places are offered on the understanding that girls remain until 11+ and boys to 13+. Academic and music bursaries are available – up to 50 per cent of the fees. Ten per cent discount for third siblings, when all are in the school together. Feeder schools include a range of local private and state primary schools.

Exit: A number go off to top boarding schools such as Charterhouse and Wycombe Abbey, but generally pupils aim for the best of the private day sector, including St Paul's, King's College Wimbledon, Lady Eleanor Holles, Hampton, Wimbledon High, Kingston Grammar and Surbiton High – picking up a fair number of scholarships en route.

Remarks: Aptly described by one mother as 'very much the good private co-ed primary school that Kingston lacks', ticks all the boxes for a high quality modern prep despite its old-world values. It's a demanding environment and a school that likes to win. Suits bright sparks who like sport and have good London/Surrey senior schools in their sights. May not be first choice for a quiet, more sensitive soul.

This is an academic school in every sense of the word. Lessons are fast-paced and fairly intense. 'Everything is geared towards getting the children through the Common Entrance,' says a mother. 'It makes for a fairly long and busy day and the children are challenged and stimulated all the time.' Homework is set (and expected to be done) every day – roughly an hour or so for a 10 year old. Class sizes are smallish (for London) with an average of 20 pupils per class – fewer by Years 7 and 8. English, French and maths are setted from Year 6.

Classrooms are spacious, bright and buzzing. Children usually sit in beautiful rows at traditional desks, writing neatly in exercise books, yet equipment is high-tech throughout: laptops and interactive whiteboards. The school is proud of its IT facilities and has a very whizzy, state of the art IT suite with tailor-made desks.

Languages are well catered for – French from Year 3, Latin and Greek are offered later. Separate sciences are taught from Year 4. Some provision for SEN such as dyslexia – around three per cent of pupils currently receive one-to-one tuition, for which they pay extra. One mother was pleased that the school had identified her child's special need in good time and has given good support since – though the general pace of life here would not suit anything severe.

Has a sporty feel and parents all mention sport as a strength, but some grumble that not enough on the timetable – 'Little puppies need a good run everyday,' believes one. Children need to work hard if they want to represent the school – keenness alone won't guarantee a regular team place.

As at many London schools, space is at a premium. The playground is not huge. A reasonably sized sports field on site with two multi-purpose, all – weather courts and four all-weather cricket nets. Children are bussed to nearby Imperial College sportsground and local swimming pools for some lessons. Main sports are rugby, football and cricket for boys and rounders and netball for girls. Other sports are offered as extra-curricular clubs.

Parents enthuse about 'amazing' music – more than 50 per cent of the pupils take additional individual lessons and plenty of ensembles, orchestras and choirs. 'Their concerts are of senior school standard,' says one mother. Similar praise for tip-top art and also drama – both highly valued here. DT is 'second to none', say parents. Daily DT club is very popular and has produced some amazing work, e.g. assembling a car for the Shell Ecomarathon; Newland House – the only junior school competitor – wins over senior school competition almost every year. Plenty of other clubs on offer – from the usual art and chess to the more esoteric African drumming and calligraphy.

A popular and bustling – not for slackers – academic school in the heart of residential leafy southwest London. Founded in 1897, became a charitable trust in 1971 and is now run by a board of governors. Occupies two buildings. 'Number 11' houses pre-prep pupils, while the main school is across the road almost opposite. Plans to move the pre-prep into a purpose built building on a site recently purchased next to the main school. This move, according to the school, is to provide space, rather than to up the numbers significantly.

A school where 'manners' is a watchword. We would describe it as pretty strict with regard to discipline. Tolerance of others, common courtesy and self-discipline are promoted. Extremely polite and well presented children will leap to their feet when an adult enters a room, they hold doors open for others and shake hands with their teacher at the end of the day. The whole place is highly organised. Pastoral care is considered top notch under deputy head, Mr Arnold. Bullying in particular is swiftly dealt with – one mother recalls a small problem for her daughter being dealt with expertly and stamped out virtually overnight.

In the pre-prep, the entirely female staff are likened to 'extra mummies'. As you move higher up the school, it is a pleasure to see plenty of male teachers. Teachers 'walk on water here,' says one mother. 'They all go that extra mile, for both the children and their parents.' Informal contact with staff can be problematic as school life is busy: you are encouraged to contact the school office to make an appointment rather than catch a busy teacher at the classroom door – this system is designed to benefit both parties. Some reports that, like the head, teachers are slightly defensive when challenged – however the school refutes this criticism.

Parents are predominantly professional, the intake mostly white middle class and from local families, although the recently introduced school bus services benefit those from further afield, such as East Sheen, Richmond, Hampton and East Molesey. They are also trialling a walking bus service and have a breakfast club. Very active parents' association raises bags of cash and provides a nice social focus for those so inclined. 'It's very friendly – almost clubby,' says one mother.

Few grumble about money – school is generally seen as good value – but apparently the phrase, 'This will be added in arrears to your account', is a standing joke in the playground. 'Though really it's only the extras you pick up anywhere,' says one mother – trips and outings etc.

Newton Prep

149 Battersea Park Road, London, SW8 4BX

• Pupils: 280 boys, 275 girls; all day • Ages: 3-13 • Non-denom
• Fees: £11,790-£13,590 pa • Independent

Tel: 020 7720 4091
Fax: 020 7498 9052
Email: registrar@newtonprep.co.uk
Website: www.newtonprep.co.uk

Headmaster: Since 2006, Mr Nicholas Allen BA PGCE (mid fifties). Four children (including a stepdaughter) all educated at London day schools. Spent most of his career as a head, initially at Ipswich Prep (seven years), then Arnold House for 12 years from 1994. You can see why he was fast tracked to the top job – he looks and acts like a headmaster. A smart if slightly stiff appearance belies a debonair charm and dry wit. Not short of charisma and authority either – a man whose judgment you would be pleased to seek. Educated at Bedales, where he was also a governor for eight years, read history and archaeology at Exeter. Practical and hands on – 'I do a lot of sorting out' – he's enjoying tightening up the systems that are needed in a large establishment. Maintains a small teaching load in the middle years.

Entrance: Selective at nursery and reception – a gentle assessment which looks for early indications of ability and potential. 'We don't reckon on tears at this stage,' says head, who ditched the process whereby all applicants were sent to a psychologist at parents' own expense. Siblings given priority at nursery; thereafter, while regarded 'favourably', they won't automatically be given a place. Also a competitive entrance at Years 3 and 7, when scholarships are available with top-up bursaries for those who need financial assistance – keen to award more scholarships at these points.

Exit: To many and varied destinations – London day as well as boarding, including Dulwich College, St Paul's, St Paul's Girls, City of London, Westminster, Trinity, Emanuel, Benenden, Roedean, Wycombe Abbey, Cheltenham Ladies', Charterhouse, Wellington College, Winchester College, Bedales, Bryanston, Marlborough, Millfield, Francis Holland (both), Alleyn's, JAGS, Latymer Upper and a range of other schools. Success with arts, music, sports and academic scholarships as well as places at 11 and 13. Increasing numbers of boys stay on after 11 and boys and girls are being recruited in greater numbers each year to join Year 7.

Remarks: This big bustling co-ed school fills an imposing Victorian purpose-built building (high ceilings, long corridors), situated in the no man's land between Battersea and Nine Elms, almost opposite Battersea Dogs' Home. Recent additions are light and spacious, including two new gyms, state of the art auditorium, art studios and humanities suite, three tip top science labs, three ICT labs and an extended and modernised library, well organised and an attractive place to curl up and read a book in; each classroom now equipped with an interactive whiteboard. Unlike many central London day schools, a lot of outside space, with all-weather pitches, two large playgrounds and a garden (plus extensive car parks filled with 4x4s first and last thing). Plenty of room for children to charge around outside letting off steam.

They need to. Although keen to downplay its 'hothouse' reputation, committed to 'offering a challenging education for inquisitive children who are eager to engage fully with the world' and 'inspiring children to be adventurous and committed in their learning', whilst 'providing balance and breadth in all aspects of a child's education: intellectual, aesthetic, physical, moral and spiritual'. Is that all? Four classes of 20 from reception, streaming in, e.g., maths starts as early as Year 1, and specialist teaching from Year 4. 'We do very well by bright children,' says head, 'and one of the advantages of a big school is that it allows you to differentiate in a way that the parents and children can't tell.' French from nursery, Latin from Year 5. Mandarin is offered after school. A lot of inspirational teaching (why have interactive whiteboards when you can have model soldiers and WWI helmets as teaching aids?).

A combined SEN and high ability co-ordinator ensures that 'no one slips through the net'. 'There is no stigma about going to the Resource Unit,' we were told by one parent, 'so many of them do.' It will cater for children in the dys-strata as well as people with physical disabilities, but the special need for a number of them is that they are very bright. School takes a flexible approach, but child needs to be able to 'stand the pace'.

Sport (currently getting much needed attention from head, who is determined to improve Newton's competitive status) now flourishing. More inter house matches programmed and a greater focus on the 'sports we shine in like hockey'. Tremendous art. Lots of wonderful brightly coloured papier-mâché figures floating around the school. Fresh food with a varied menu cooked on premises and eaten in a surprisingly uninstitutional dining room.

Wide geographic intake produces larger social mix than other SW London schools – catchment area stretches into the far reaches of Streatham and beyond, as well as north of the river. Eclectic parents – lots of professionals (both mother and father) – as well as media types and shopkeepers; attracts first-time buyers. Children are confident, articulate, well behaved and refreshingly not overly deferential, communicating with adults like fellow individuals. School is much more down to earth than a lot of the competition. 'Newton is the acceptable face of private education – meritocratic, broad ranging and grounded,' says head. Appeals to parents who would not normally regard themselves as private sector.

Norland Place School

162-166 Holland Park Avenue, London, W11 4UH

• Pupils: 150 girls, 90 boys (boys to age 8 only) • Ages: 4-11
• Non-denom • Fees: £10,008-£12,552 pa • Independent

Tel: 020 7603 9103
Fax: 020 7603 0648
Email: office@norlandplace.com
Website: www.norlandplace.com

Head: Since 2002, Mr Patrick Mattar LRAM MA (forties), a Brummie (though you wouldn't know it), educated at Solihull, one of four siblings all of whom are talented musicians and went to various prestigious music colleges. Came here in 1989 as director of music straight from the Royal Academy of Music. He says if he had gone to an academic establishment he would have been more of an arts/language person than a scientist. A six year interlude at Wetherby from 1996, where he ended up being deputy head before returning to Norland to run the school when he was only 36. Married with two young sons, his wife teaches at Sussex House, where several boys move on to from here each year. Works very closely with his bursar and with proprietor, Sylvia Garnsey, who ran the school for 40 years – 'She gives me a loose rein but needs to know what's going on'.

Since his arrival a huge amount of building and structural systems put in place – it's paid off, he says with some relief, as, despite being delayed by volcanic ash in Australia for two weeks at the beginning of the summer term, the school could carry on seamlessly.

With his background one would expect the school to be heavily weighted in favour of music (he confessed to being secretly delighted when asked by parents to do a recital to a packed Steinway Hall in Marylebone to raise money for an auction) but he stresses that equal weight is given to art and sports – 'I've never been one of those heads who thinks, "I'm musical and therefore want the school to be musical,"' he says.

Very popular with parents, who comment on his approachable natural manner and understanding of the children. He teaches Years 3 through to Year 6 current affairs, reasoning and some Latin in Year 6. He has a good feel for senior schools and which would suit each child, but says he will be as involved as parents want him to be when deciding where their children should go. His quiet confidence brims with integrity. You would think ambition might be making him restless but he clearly loves the job – 'There's never a dull moment – and my favourite part is the children: they're the easiest,' he grins.

Entrance: At four years old: not selective, so you need to get your child's name down as soon after birth as is feasibly possible – preferably on the day. Parents are given forms so they can apply before birth and deliver it on the way back from the hospital! If you don't get it in until your child is a week old, you will end up on the waiting list. Mr Mattar will make sure he sees all parents who have places, so they understand the ethos here and know what they're signing up to. Children come from a number of local nurseries including The Acorn, Miss Delaney's, Ladbroke Square, Strawberry Fields, Rolfes and Mynors – no particular feeder. Siblings won't automatically get places – they still have to be registered and will be given priority on the waiting list, but be warned: siblings of a daughter who has left early to go to, e.g., Bute, is unlikely to be given priority. 'There's no point coming here unless you want Norland and want it all the way,' he warns.

Exit: Boys at 8+ to, e.g., Westminster Under, Colet Court, Sussex House, Westminster Cathedral and Choir School, Wetherby Prep and St Phillips, and the odd one to board at, e.g., Caldicott.

Girls at 11+ to St Paul's, Godolphin and Latymer (head points out that recently nearly half the year got in here – impressive for a non-selective school), Wycombe Abbey, St Swithun's and Downe House.

Remarks: Founded in 1876, situated on bustling Holland Park Avenue in three town houses connected by a maze of corridors and staircases giving it a very up and down feel, but with two smallish playgrounds and a plethora of outdoor toys. Unashamedly traditional – boys are in shorts, girls neat in blue and white checks, berets are worn in winter, boaters in summer. A definite flavour of 'old money'. Parents here are terribly discreet and reluctant to be drawn into talking about the school or each other. Increasingly families come from Shepherds Bush and Hammersmith rather than round the corner, as Notting Hill becomes more flashy. To the casual observer it appears very English – not much evidence of headscarves and only a few brown faces, though school anxious to point out that it does not select on any criteria at all. Families here seem grounded, wanting what's best for their children without being drawn into the competitive London day school fever which is more susceptible to brand rather than ethos. Lots of children here had parents and grandparents at the school. George Osborne and Hilary Benn are among the alumni. We witnessed excellent rapport between staff and pupils, which was confirmed by parents. Senior girls are natural, mature and responsible but humorous and not fawning.

A wide range of ability. Children assessed for SEN from reception, when any concerns are flagged up and watched. Mild to moderate SEN can be catered for, but children have to be able to make the benchmark each year. EAL is dealt with in class, help often given before school. From early in the morning teachers are on hand to support and stretch those who need stretching, but a charge is made for timetabled learning support lessons.

For the more able ('I try to avoid labelling them as gifted and talented,' says Mr Mattar) lots of opportunity to differentiate and split lessons for English and maths in Years 4, 5 and 6, but not setting or streaming. The ethos here is that children support each other – 'Everyone has different talents'. Specialist teaching for English, maths and science from Year 4.

Two forms per year until Year 3 when boys and girls divide. Boys then get their heads down to prepare for the 8+ and one form for girls from Years 4 to 6. French is taught from the start with a smattering of Latin from Mr Mattar at the end. 'We're very good at not pressurising the children,' says Mr Mattar, 'while still getting the results.' Humanities has had an injection of energy with the appointment of the dynamic and greatly loved Mrs Hart, who brings history vividly to the present with dramatic interpretrations of, e.g., VE day. We saw an assembly littered with bunting, every child waving a flag (including the odd German one), a number of them wearing hard hats and forties style headscarves and the whole school doing the Lambeth walk.

Nothing is done on a grand scale but we met with great enthusiasm for what is on offer – only one afternoon of sport a week: football and cricket for the boys, a bus ride away; netball and rounders for the girls. Two PE lessons a week happen in the playground and hall. Swimming from Year 2 at Kensington leisure centre. DT is incorporated into art – we were shown bird boxes that the Year 5s were making for their gardens while others bubbled about growing chickens in incubators. Disappointing library which looks rarely used, understocked and forbiddingly uncomfortable (school keen to point out that the library is very much work in progress – we're glad they agree that something needs to be done about it). The atmosphere of grounded traditionalism is epitomised by the traditional desks in the classrooms which, when opened, not only reveal neat piles of books but also colourful personal displays – photos, glitter, magazine cut outs – decorated by each girl.

A good traditional London day school that prepares each child for the next stage beautifully and punches well above its weight.

North Bridge House Junior School

Linked to North Bridge House Preparatory School Linked to North Bridge House Senior School in the Senior section

8 Netherhall Gardens, London, NW3 5RR

• Pupils: Nursery school: 205; junior school: 185 • Ages: 2 years 9 months - 8 years • Non-denom • Fees: £12,810 pa • Independent

Tel: 020 7435 2884
Fax: 020 7794 1337
Email: junior@northbridgehouse.com
Website: www.northbridgehouse.com

Head: Since 1997, Mrs Robyn Allsopp BEd Cert Ed (fifties). Australian, began here in 1976 as a class teacher, deputy head in 1983, when the building now housing the nursery on Fitzjohn's Avenue was acquired in 1989 became head over there, then head of Nursery and Junior Schools – one has the sense that it is her lifeblood that runs through the veins of the school, keeping it an integral whole. Certainly she knows every inch, floorboard and door hinge, as well as everyone – child, teacher, support staff – one meets. She is also clear about the school's ethos – 'We're a family school' – by which she means that, as a mixed school, with many former pupils' children now attending, and one which does not have an academic entrance requirement, unlike its neighbour opposite, it really can take everyone it has room for. When asked about her guiding principle, the answer is instant – 'Happiness is what we're about. Happy children learn, and we also offer so much for those who are not academically gifted'.

Entrance: Life begins at playgroup level and children are mostly siblings of current pupils. Then the nursery takes around 30 children out of the 120 applicants. Reception, the following year, takes the same number out of a similar number of applicants. Occasional places thereafter, but around 10 children out of 40-odd are taken into Year 3. Criteria are refreshing – first come siblings, then children of former pupils, then families who live closest and finally those who fit the age bracket the school wants to fill. Makes a point of covering the entire chronological year in any class year group. That doesn't mean no assessment – all applicants visit and parent and child are interviewed. So the emphasis is more on whether the child – and family – fit the school's ethos rather than on academic potential. The result is a spread of ability, ethnicity and just about everything other than location – most live within three miles of the school, many near enough to walk. Equal split of boys/girls. Runs a good coach service to obvious areas.

Exit: Virtually all move on from the junior school to the prep school, despite the different location. Those who leave at this stage mostly do so for single sex education.

Remarks: Highly confusing for outsiders. The nursery and junior school are housed in two buildings moments from each other in Hampstead. The preparatory school lives off Regent's Park, sharing the building with the senior school to which, in most other respects, it isn't related (see separate entry.) Life begins in the nursery building – a splendid Victorian house on Fitzjohn's Avenue, used as a nursery school for decades but only acquired by North Bridge in 1989. Classrooms are fill of happily absorbed children – we saw Year 1s engaged in water play and modelling while the parallel class had a friendly 'show and tell session'. Art was fun – we enjoyed Mondrian-inspired collages on the walls and appreciated the principle that 'everyone's work goes up – not just the best'. It's well-equipped – a music room doubles as an eating room, a good gym/hall for concerts and shows – and does not feel as crowded as some similar schools, though we found some of the rooms uncomfortably hot. Everyone learns French from reception and PE is four days a week. Outside space, again, compares well with comparable schools – some safe surfaces, a lovely wooden play train and caterpillar, with some covered nooks for secret conversations and conspiracies.

The Fitzjohn's site houses the playgroup, nursery, reception and three of the Year 1 classes – those with the younger children. The building on Netherhall Gardens is the main site for the junior school and has the rest of Year 1 and Years 2 and 3. This is a quieter corner – a cul de sac overlooking the Finchley Road; the house is a five-storey red-brickery, interestingly sited between the British College of Osteopathic Medicine and the former home of Sidney and Beatrice Webb. It's a corner favoured by independent schools – the South Hampstead Junior School is opposite and nearby, Southbank International (just bought by Cognita, the owners of North Bridge) is up the road, and others not more than a rubber's throw away. Efforts are made to stagger drop-offs and pick-ups. From the top of the main building splendid views – over to Harrow-on-the-Hill one way and to the North Downs the other.

As in the nursery building, every inch is covered in displayed work – much to intrigue and delight the eye. Classrooms are occupied by quiet and relaxed children, clearly engaged and interested. Music, French and PE are said to be the school's specialties – everyone learns music and a third or more learn piano, guitar or violin in school; choirs and bands. Outside space is less impressive, though. A marked out chess board and a climbing frame on the tarmac. Sports mostly at the Talacre Centre in Kentish Town. More could be done to make this a livelier area.

A full-time learning support teacher sees around 25 pupils regularly – up to three times a week – for varying types of support. Despite the manner of entry, nothing more than mild dyslexia/dyspraxia surfaces here. All children are monitored twice-yearly to check progress.

Junior and nursery School parents praise the friendliness and welcome they find here and feel what is offered at this level hardly differs from what the overtly academic neighbours do.

North London Collegiate School Junior School

Linked to North London Collegiate School in the Senior section

Canons Drive, Edgware, Middlesex, HA8 7RJ

• Pupils: 310 girls in the junior and first schools • Ages: 4-11 • Christian foundation, but all faiths welcomed • Fees: £11,472 pa • Independent

Tel: 020 8952 1276
Fax: 020 8951 1293
Email: office@nlcs.org.uk
Website: www.nlcs.org.uk

Head: Since 2003, Mrs Jo Newman BEd (fiftyish). Came from Fairseat, Channing's junior school – parents there still mourn their loss. 'They've got our lovely Mrs Newman,' we were told. She is bustling, bright-eyed, thrilled with her school and proud of her charges, who smile sweetly and confidently at her. Popular with parents and just about everyone.

Entrance: Vastly over-subscribed at 4+, when group and individual assessments (no reading/writing, mercifully) result in the allocation of 40 places. At 7+, maths and English tested, but only eight-ten places for the armies who turn up. Most continue from first school through to lower school until they are 11.

Exit: All but a very few continue into the senior school, though this is not guaranteed. Parents of those who the school perceives might not make the grade are alerted early and helped to look elsewhere.

Remarks: Shares the glorious site with its big sister but has a bright one-storey modern (1995) building of its own, divided into first and lower schools. Good stable staff – 16 have been at the school for more than 10 years – retain their enthusiasm and clear enjoyment of their bright and bubbly charges. Two form entry – first school class size of 20, and 24 in the lower school, each class having its own teacher and TA. Rooms are spacious and airy – room to move, not found in more central London preps.

Our tour was full of pleasures – inside and out. We liked the bright displays everywhere, the sense of orderliness and the little loos – so important – with their fish motifs. We loved the Montgolfier balloons, an imaginative undersea montage with fishing nets, lobster pots and portholes and some lively nascent DT sculptures – thank heaven for kitchen roll tubes and egg boxes! We watched reception miming seed planting to a tape, and saw that not all were fully engaged in this – perhaps still learning to listen? We did wonder whether artistic endeavours might not be over-directed, but the vivid Year 2 Kandinsky–influenced houses seemed more relaxed. We applaud the garden club, Friday's Golden Time and the Three Bears' cottage with bed, kitchen and mirror.

Overall, facilities are good – designated science, IT and artrooms plus a good sized hall and libraries for both parts of the school, the lower school one being particularly inviting, with a lovely display of 'antique book covers' when we visited. The girls also enjoy the senior school's sports facilities as well as the senior girls themselves – several come down to help. Specialist subject teaching from Year 5 and we were impressed by the school's introductory courses to languages: Spanish in Year 3, German in Year 4, Chinese in Year 5 and French in Year 6 – good fun and sensible. No children currently with statements but around five per cent with mild SEN – catered for by school SENCo; most leave for the senior school no longer needing much support.

Parents enthuse – 'It's a lovely school and Mrs Newman and the staff are very kind.' The ethos – of discipline, a non-competitive striving for one's personal best and stimulation which is also fun – is very much that of the senior school, and the junior branch, in every way, equips its young alumnae to seize the opportunities they will be offered in the next exciting stage.

The North London International School Kindergarten

Linked to North London International School Lower School (The) in the Junior section

Linked to North London International School (The) in the Senior section

6 Friern Barnet Lane, London, N12 8SH

• Pupils: 80 boys and girls • Ages: 2-6 • Fees: £7,560 pa • Independent

Tel: 020 8920 0600
Fax: 0208 211 4605
Email: admissions@nlis.org
Website: www.nlis.org

Head: Since 2000, assistant principal lower school (ages 2–6), Mrs Gabriele Weber CertEd (forties), who has been at the school since 1988. Charming, caring and lively. Educated in Germany, where she also studied primary education. Enthusiastic about the PYP.

Overall head of school is Mr D Rose MAEd BA CertEd.

Remarks: Based at Holmewood, a lovely old building that used to be a small boys' preparatory school back in the 1800s. Now a great place to start being educated. Big light rooms. A separate entrance for the two to three year olds. Two amazing playgrounds with some of the most fun equipment we've seen, brightly coloured to capture childish imaginations. Surface made from re-conditioned old tyres, so bungee soft. Year 1 divided into two classrooms in their own section.

The North London International School Lower School

Linked to North London International School Kindergarten (The) in the Junior section

Linked to North London International School (The) in the Senior section

49 Woodside Avenue, London, N12 8SY

• Pupils: 110 boys and girls • Ages: 6-11 • Fees: £11,955 pa • Independent

Tel: 0208 8920 0600
Fax: 0208 445 0835
Email: admissions@nlis.org
Website: www.nlis.org

Head: Mr David Rose, previously head of Montgomery School in Germany and The British School of Houston, Texas, an Independent Schools inspector, Chair of the London International Schools Association and an accreditation visitor for international schools. Lower School principal is Mr M Parkin BEd DipEd, who has taught in the UK, USA and Indonesia.

Exit: Most go on to the upper school but a few trickle elsewhere.

Remarks: Two sites here (Holmewood for kindergarten and Year 1, and Woodside for Years 2–6) within few minutes' drive or 15 minutes' walk of each other – there's a school hopper bus. The epitome of what an international school should be about. Year groups divided into two parallel classes with an absolute maximum of 20 in each. Lots of child inspired batiks, pottery and art help create a vibrant atmosphere. IB principles displayed everywhere. PYP well linked with the national curriculum keeps both inspectorates happy and ensures children are well grounded. All lessons in each half of term based around one aspect of the IB curriculum. Homework important and can be done at school.

Years 2 to 6 have good sized light classrooms with washing lines displaying student work. Each child has his or her own drawer for storage. Computers everywhere. Media resource centres instead of libraries; however individual book sections in each classroom and a well labelled storeroom with student access. A great gym, which doubles up as the dining hall. Healthy food served from the kitchens next to it (where meals for the kindergarten are also prepared). Photos of all the Year 6 prefects displayed in the passage with their personal blogs. Good music room and lovely art room. Year 2 have two classrooms in a separate building easing the move from the nursery.

Strong emphasis on pastoral care and exceptional provision for special needs – Quest again – and good screening for dyslexia and related problems. As in the upper school, the policy is to accept a controlled number of children with learning difficulties but not those with disruptive behavioural problems. Excellent EAL provision with an enthusiastic and dedicated teacher. Children will usually become fluent within a year.

Playground not huge but much use made of local park for cross country runs and scientific experiments plus compulsory swimming once a week at Trent Park. Lots of trips, visits and excursions as well. All Year 6 students spend a week at an activity centre in Normandy (practising the French that they have been learning since they were three) and some of them go on exchange to the Dwight School in New York.

North Primary School

Meadow Road, Southall, Middlesex, UB1 2JE

• Pupils: 435; mixed • Ages: 4-11 • non-denom • State

Tel: 020 8571 7749
Fax: 020 8574 0629
Email: admin@north.ealing.sch.uk
Website: www.northprimary.com

Headteacher: Since September 2010, Mrs R Hastings BSc PGCE NPQH (late forties).

Studied at Leicester University, PGCE at the West Sussex Institute of Higher Education, worked in primary schools in London – Camden, Hackney and Harrow – where many pupils have English as an additional language and come from areas of social deprivation. Assistant headteacher, acting headteacher for two years, associate head in a school facing challenging circumstances. One daughter who has just transferred to secondary school.

Passionate about learning: schools are a place of learning for children, staff and parents/carers – makes extra curricular activities available to children and their families. School has a responsibility to provide quality learning experiences for all children, a curriculum that is engaging, to ensure every child achieves the best they can.

Entrance: Admissions handled by the London borough of Ealing – the usual criteria apply. Main feeder is Grove House Nursery. No one except looked-after children will get into the early years from out of catchment; a waiting list for all years. KS2 applicants may have more luck – entrants (often new arrivals from abroad) in the later years.

Exit: Most go on to Villiers HS, some to Greenford HS, a few to Guru Nanak or Cardinal Wiseman. A handful each year try for the Berkshire grammars or Tiffin schools – around seven or eight get in.

Remarks: We went as sceptics but came away converts – and in love. Twenty-two languages are spoken at home by these children – mostly Punjabi or Gujerati, though significant numbers of Singhalese children and Somalis too. According to social deprivation statistics, school's population is in the top 80 per cent. Also has significant numbers on School Action or School Action Plus, though not huge numbers with many SENs other than EAL. 98 per cent of pupils speak English as a second language but English unifies the school and everyone is open and friendly. We were struck by the clear and helpful delivery of the teachers – they mean children to understand, they back up their words with helpful body language when needed and everyone learns. We were impressed with every class we went into – and we went into them all.

SATs results are astonishing – especially given this intake and the fact that children come at all stages with little or no English. Everyone except a few SEN pupils reaches level 4 or higher in English – this is extraordinary and is achieved, in part, by determined individual catchup sessions with those who fall behind or arrive with little English. In both science and maths, 90+ per cent get level 4. Large percentages at level 5. This puts it way ahead of comparable schools, both locally and nationally. Not that it teaches to the test – teaching has to be good from reception onwards, not just Year 6. This is a lead school for good practice in EAL provision and the induction process for each new child is meticulous. Has translators and resources in all its main languages and works hard at involving parents. We were touched by the care taken to instruct each new child in, for example, how to ask in English for the loo.

So – a modern, purpose-built jewel in Ealing's crown? Hardly. The core is an 1851 schoolroom, still in remarkable nick and surmounted by the original bell tower, complete with pullable bell chain – still used on special occasions. Later add-ons are solid and functional and make for a well-structured, two storey building overall. We have yet to see a tidier, cleaner school. Everywhere is freshly painted in bright but not garish colours and we spotted not one piece of litter in our entire visit. Children are proud of their school and it shows. Outside is just tarmac and apparatus, but well marked out for the younger children and reasonably spacious, with railings separating the older children from the tots. Older children have a tarmac football pitch. The school is in a quiet residential nook at the east end of Southall close to an old village green and with some splendid older buildings round about, reminding one of the village this once was.

In every classroom the children were attentive, engaged and absorbed. Every inch of wall space has excellent displays – pupil and teacher-made – all helping to structure and illustrate the work in hand. Everyone can see at a glance what the term's syllabus and aims are in all curriculum areas. Corridor displays on everything from black history to symmetry, musical notation, bridges and forces. Boards for improvement, achievement and attendance encourage everyone. Community project volunteers have provided imaginative murals here and there – we especially liked the Aztec drinking fountains. Excellent brand new ICT suite is an exciting addition and each class has a whiteboard. Resources are carefully used. The KS2 library is better-stocked than those in many senior schools we know and as inviting and orderly as everywhere else in this welcoming, safe-feeling school.

All classes are orderly and inviting. Most seem well ventilated and comfortable but a few look rather crowded and were decidedly too warm. What goes on in them is consistently impressive. Reception and Year 1 children work purposefully in small groups but all together in a big sectioned room with teachers and support staff and, seemingly, concentrating so busily that they need little regulation or control. We enjoyed a Year 2 French class taught by a native speaker with a mouth-watering unison recitation of the constituents of une salade. A Year 5 class was working on rhetorical questions and a Year 6 class writing 'recounts' of events and being given demanding literary objectives – which they seemed to relish. Both key stages have good-sized, airy halls and we warmed to the way children really spoke out in rehearsal of their Easter assembly.

G and T children are well-catered for by a designated teacher, who provides 'challenge boxes' for each class, brings in graduate volunteers and runs a chess club and newspaper club exclusively for these children. Lots of other clubs for everyone. Most children with SpLD are supported in class. Part time SENCo and TA will take children individually – some have a differentiated curriculum. An Alexander technique teacher comes in on occasions. We saw a lesson taken by a supply teacher with an entirely attentive class. Each child is assessed every half term for progress in reading, writing and maths.

Music is big here: won the local Rotary's Best Ensemble award for 2005, 2006 and 2007 – their ensemble containing instruments from every bit of the globe is a major investment but at the heart of its ethos. Good ceramics and a collection of musical instruments made from re-cycled materials which included a beautiful harp. The little garden is eagerly worked on by the children, who grow vegetables from seed – and then eat the results in the school's canteen. The home-cooked food is a good mix of the trad and the healthy – we drooled at fisherman's pie, Asian pasta and chunks of fresh oranges. Parents are helped to continue the healthy eating approach at home and encouraged to involve themselves in all activities. Many do – the school's annual fête – the mela – along with its concerts and shows are huge events and several parents help in class. Children look good in white shirts, grey trousers and scarlet cardigans.

Mrs Grewal, the last headteacher, has built a first rate school and will leave a lasting legacy. A model for primaries everywhere.

Northbourne Park School

Betteshanger, Deal, Kent, CT14 0NW

• Pupils: 185 boys and girls. • Ages: 3-13 • School of special religious character • Fees: Day £7,395-£13,110; Boarding £15,630-£20,700 pa • Independent

Tel: 01304 611 215
Fax: 01304 619 020
Email: office@northbournepark.com
Website: www.northbournepark.com

Head: Since 2008, Mr Edward Balfour BA (Hons) PGCE (fortyish). Read English at Cardiff University and did his PGCE at Homerton, Cambridge, where he specialised in English and drama. Previously a housemaster at Bradfield College where he directed and produced 'Hippolytus' in ancient Greek. Approachable and immediately puts people at their ease, very popular with parents and staff. Energetic and ambitious for the school whilst believing passionately in building on what is there and retaining its ethos. Believes in a holistic approach to education and wants to break down the barriers between academic work, extra-curricular and pastoral activities. Married to Emma, a Cambridge graduate in French and former teacher. They have two young children in the school and a baby. He teaches English to Year 7.

Entrance: Taster day and tests in English and maths. Almost non-selective – can adapt the curriculum to suit a child with learning difficulties as long as they are not too severe. They look for children who will be happy at Northbourne. Spaces in most year groups.

Exit: Most children go on to King's Canterbury and St Edmund's in Canterbury. One or two a year to Benenden and Kent College and one or two to Sevenoaks and Tonbridge. Occasionally a couple to Eton and further afield. Two or three each year leave at 11 to go to the grammars – the school will prepare children for the Kent test. Good range of scholarships each year – academic, music and sport (nine in 2009).

Remarks: Seems to be a well kept secret. Set in 100 acres of parkland and woods on the Betteshanger Estate near Deal, formerly the home of the Northbourne family. Large rambling Victorian House – a much loved, happy place. Traditional values, a strong work ethic and a belief in and encouragement of service to the community. Not a grand school – great sense of informality and freedom with a cosy family feel. Children are encouraged to climb trees and each year group has a designated area of woodland where they are allowed to play. Some classrooms housed in very well-appointed Nissen Huts in the garden erected by the Canadians during the war and which somehow got listed along with the rest of the house. Lord Northbourne, whose family used to live in the house, is still involved with the school and likes to take the top year to tea in the House of Lords each year.

A broadly Christian foundation with great emphasis on instilling a sense of care and respect for the needs of others both within and outside the school. Boarders attend the local church in the grounds on Sundays. One class per year of about 15 children with a maximum of 18/19. Some setting in the last two years and the scholarship children are taught within the class. The brighter children are extended and the less able are nurtured and encouraged. Lots of building and refurbishment plans afoot – everywhere has had a lick of paint and interactive whiteboards beginning to pop up around the school. Well equipped ICT room. New girls' boarding house with bright airy dormitories and boys' dormitories all refurbished.

The French and Spanish programme is a unique selling point. Northbourne Park is home to two full-time classes of French and French-speaking Spanish children, the equivalent of an extra Year 7 and 8, known as the Sixième and Cinquième. This programme is not actively marketed but is spread by word of mouth in France and Spain. They come to learn English for one or two years, smart French types often from top Parisian schools. The Spanish children tend to be already attending the lycées in France and might then opt for British or American schools abroad – tend to be very European minded. French and Spanish children are taught separately by French staff and follow the French national curriculum in history, geography, French and maths – the exams are ratified by the Lycée in London and monitored by the CNED in France. The deputy head is French and the housemaster and his wife are both French speakers. Children come together outside lessons for sport, art etc. Charming to hear twitter of French/Spanish voices echoing along the corridors. Inevitable benefits to English children, who also spend a few days with an exchange school in Lille and with families in Spain. The children interact well and lots of close friendships are forged here – much to-ing and fro-ing across the Channel during the holidays.

Excellent pastoral care. Girls sometimes have special 'girls' nights in' when matron administers 'beauty treatments' and does their hair. Currently 40 full boarders in the school and others flexiboard several nights a week. Wednesday and Saturday film nights in the old drawing room. The new head is keen to encourage more boarding. Good food prepared on site and served on a cafeteria system. The school consistently gains the National Heartbeat Food Award; the whole school can be seated in the dining room together and staff sit with the children to supervise table manners.

Children enjoy sport and a dynamic director of sport recently appointed. Quite a small pool to choose from, which means everyone has a chance to play in a team and often sporting ability is developed in a child who might be overlooked in a bigger school. Boys play football, rugby and cricket and girls play netball, hockey and rounders. Also cross country, triathlon, tennis, badminton, fencing and archery. Outdoor heated pool; they go to Duke of York's School or Dover Leisure Centre for triathlon training during the winter.

Northbourne gets 2–3 music scholarships each year – recently to Benenden, King's Canterbury, Kent College and St Edmund's. Over 100 children learn an instrument, some to Grade 8. A Northbourne Old Girl returned as director of music in 2009. Lots of encouragement and music appreciation from pre-prep upwards. Lots of opportunities to play in informal concerts and children are encouraged to have a go. Plenty of opportunities to stand up in public too. One junior and one senior play each year – usually a musical – and a French play every two years. Public speaking competition and occasional debates. In-school clubs include electronics, art, pottery, computers and cookery. After school societies include The Sophists, a literary discussion group open to all and held in the head's study, Bilingual society, Greek and Latin society, new science, maths, geography and history societies. Senior children and especially scholars are encouraged to attend.

Busy art department – head of art a sculptress by training, likes big projects, e.g. a tractor for the local ploughing match. The children love getting involved even if they are not very artistic. Lots of art competitions, Christmas card competition, pavement art on MDF. Local artists come and do workshops. Pottery housed in the dairy, which still has the Victorian tiles and marble slabs intact.

Good learning support – one full time and two part time teachers. Mainly dyslexia, dyspraxia and ADHD. A few children in the school with mild Asperger's Syndrome but they are carefully selected and assessed. Northbourne will take statemented children but not more than one per class. The school wants to attract bright dyslexics. A charge is made for the support programmes.

The school day runs from 8.30-5pm and about half the children stay on for prep until 6pm. The pre-prep children can be accommodated until their older siblings are ready to go home. School on alternate Saturdays from Year 4 – lessons, games and leadership course which has been going for years and is a particular feature of the school, like a mini Duke of Edinburgh scheme with lots of den building and campfires in the woods. Very popular with the children – gives confidence and fosters teambuilding and leadership skills. Lots of gutsy stuff – they are encouraged but not forced to take part. The children are put into teams and challenged to build camps in groups. Campcraft skills at the weekends – the children learn how to make a campfire and use penknives to help build the camps. They then spend the night in their camps, are given luxury ration packs and can turn rabbit and pheasant into a stew if they choose. Year 8 children go on an adventure holiday to the Ardèche as part of their leadership programme.

Close links with the French Lycée in London, who send a group down for a weekend each summer – sleeping outside in the camps can be a bit of a revelation for some of them. Northbourne children do a return day trip to London.

Pupils mainly local farmers and businessmen – the local Pfizer plant has boosted numbers of international children. A few from London and some Americans. Some struggle to send their children here – lots of first time buyers and working mothers, quite a cross section of parents and a friendly bunch. The school is growing and going from strength to strength – head does not want it to grow much bigger or it will be in danger of losing its unique character. Very fortunate to have such a loyal and enthusiastic team of staff – some old hands, some straight from college. Friends of Northbourne Park a welcoming and sociable group. Lots of social and fundraising events – wine tasting, quiz, Christmas fair, a major summer event and a ball every other year. Old Boys include: writer Giles Brandreth, composer Sir Richard Rodney Bennett, concert pianist, Freddy Kempf and reporter Giles Dilnot.

The pre-prep is housed in the Old Rectory about 10 minutes' walk away and caters for 3–7 year olds. They eat separately – food prepared in main school. The headmaster takes assembly once a week and gets to know the children. The children are taught French by French nationals every day from nursery upwards. The hall is used for assemblies and PE. Directors of music and sport come over from the main school to sow seeds at an early age. Lots of team sports. Seamless transition to prep school with Year 2 going over once per week for science, games lessons and swimming.

Northcote Lodge School

Linked to Broomwood Hall School (Nightingale Lane) in the Junior section

Linked to Broomwood Hall (Ramsden Road) in the Junior section

Linked to Broomwood Hall (Garrads Road) in the Junior section

26 Bolingbroke Grove, London, SW11 6EL

• Pupils: 195 boys, all day • Ages: 8-13 • Christian non-denom
• Fees: £14,085 pa • Independent

Tel: 020-8682-8888
Fax: 020-8682-8879
Email: northcote@northwoodschools.com
Website: www.northcotelodge.co.uk

Headmaster: Since September 2008, Mr John Hansford BA Hons (fifties). Arrived in 1997 as deputy head, having previously taught at Sherborne. Married with three grown up children. Boys say he is an inspirational English teacher – they particularly enjoy the books he recommends and reads to them. Keen interest in sports – he joins pupils for the odd game of cricket. Parents say he encourages everybody and is definitely a hands-on head. Reputed to have an encyclopedic knowledge of public schools and sees parents and pupils individually to advise and assist with selecting the right senior school.

Entrance: Around half from Broomwood Hall, its sister school under the same ownership, with more or less automatic right of entry. Next priority to siblings (including those with sisters at Broomwood Hall Upper School). Parents must come to an open day, then spend an hour with the head – a two-way interview: 'It's important that parents are supportive of the ethos of the school'.

Assessment, in November of the year before entry, includes English, maths, verbal reasoning and ball skills tests – the latter 'to see their attitude. They will have to play games four times a week, so if they really hate it, this isn't the place for them'. Candidates are also interviewed in twos by the head, and observed playing and eating snacks – 'We like to see how they approach work and play'.

Those offered a place must pay a half a term's fees immediately, rather than waiting to see if they get other offers – 'I'm looking for parents who are positively choosing Northcote Lodge, rather than using us as a back-up if they don't get a place elsewhere,' says head.

Exit: Vast majority to boarding school, favoured ones being Eton, Harrow, Marlborough, Bryanston and Wellington. A few to London day schools, e.g. Dulwich College, Westminster, King's Wimbledon. Head concerned to find 'the right school for the boy', even if this involves challenging parental wishes. Virtually all get their first choice.

Remarks: Opened in 1993 (with 14 pupils) in response to a growing south London inclination not to send one's son off to boarding school at eight. Aims to replicate the feel of a country boarding prep school (emphasised by the uniform of corduroy trousers and tweed jacket), with a school day that runs from 8am to 6.20pm. Games most afternoons, followed by tea and homework, with plenty of afterschool clubs ranging from woodwork to computing. Two great bonuses for parents – the school takes responsibility for washing PE kit and for homework: 'The boys aren't aware of doing prep because it's part of the school day. And we find out what they, rather than their parents, can do'. Optional Saturday morning programme of sports and other activities.

Karate is on the PE curriculum in the first two years, and optional thereafter. Everyone gets to play in teams – cricket, football, rugby – though the A teams inevitably get more matches than the Ds. The school has its own gym; sports pitches are across the road on Wandsworth Common and on nearby Trinity Fields. Plenty of music and drama, vibrant art and DT, tending to tail off in the top two years as Common Entrance preparation eats into time available.

Residential trips each year to, e.g., Isle of Wight, Wales, Normandy – 'These sometimes reveal boys who should not be going off to boarding school'. Inaugural exchange with two South African schools in 2006. Year 7s can – and nearly all do – undertake the Northcote Award, which involves personal, academic and charitable endeavours. Annual Year 8 cricket tour to South Africa.

Public speaking encouraged – whether reciting a poem, taking part in a debate, acting in a play or reading out a match report in assembly: 'We want them to be seen and heard'. Pupil-led school council and food committee – 'Probably about two thirds of what they ask for they get'. School meals were overhauled by a nutritionist a few years back and became much too healthy for the boys' liking; they now look, smell and, apparently, taste good too.

Head believes that most London preps put children under too much pressure – 'We expect high standards but there's more to life than work. We try our best to provide a genuine all-round education'. Setting for maths and English from the first year, and most other subjects from the second. In the top three years, two forms become three, including one smallish group of boys working for scholarships or entry to the more academic senior schools, and two parallel classes. Special needs teacher will provide up to two support lessons a week for mild dyslexia/dyspraxia; those who need more help probably won't be able to cope. However, 'When I had spelling problems they were really helpful,' said a pupil.

Head emphasises that in a recent survey of all current parents, 'The overall score was 4.4 out of 5 for pastoral care and 4.6 for the caring atmosphere'. Full-time matron reportedly very popular with boys. A Christian school, and though other faiths are welcome, they must join in with daily assemblies and the weekly church service.

Virtually all parents have been to independent schools themselves. Occasional families from overseas, but otherwise the intake is solidly from the surrounding SW postcodes, plus a few from central London – the school runs minibus services to Fulham and Chelsea. Boys well brought up, friendly, polite, stand up when a lady enters the room. Not the place for trendy urbanites or eccentrics – traditional families aiming at country boarding schools will feel happily at home here.

Northwood College Junior School

Linked to Northwood College in the Senior section

Maxwell Road, Northwood, HA6 2YE

• Fees: £8,655-£10,635 pa • Independent

Tel: 01923 825 446
Fax: 01923 836 526
Email: admissions@northwoodcollege.co.uk
Website: www.northwoodcollege.co.uk

Remarks: See main college.

Norwich High School for Girls Junior Department

Linked to Norwich High School For Girls in the Senior section

Stafford House,, 93 Newmarket Road,, Norwich, Norfolk, NR2 2HU

• Pupils: 260 girls; all day • Ages: 3-11 • Non-denom • Fees: £7,077 pa • Independent

Tel: 01603 453265
Fax: 01603 259891
Email: admissions@nor.gdst.net
Website: www.norwichhigh.gdst.net

Head: Since September 2010, Mrs Tracey Richmond MA Cantab (classics) PGCE from Leicester University School of Education NPQH (mid forties). Primary maths specialist. Married with three children. Previously deputy head of largest middle school in Norfolk, 2000–2006, and most recently taught maths in a high school in Australia for four years until returning to NHSG after a 13 year absence. Outside interests include reading, cake decorating, dancing, camping and spending time with the family.

Entrance: Selective – they're looking for independent learners with potential. Fairly picky and rarely get it wrong. For the nursery at three – observed play plus interaction with a teacher. Entry at four – playing games and sequencing with Mrs Richmond. At seven, written tests in English, maths and reasoning.

Exit: Nearly all to the senior school with a few to Norwich School or Wymondham College. Plenty of warning if the senior school won't suit.

Remarks: Teachers are enthusiastic and believe that learning shouldn't be a chore, and it clearly isn't – that delicious atmosphere which comes when everyone is purposefully and happily engaged. Eclectic teaching style which is subtly pushy with a healthy helping of the traditional. 'It's clever the way they do it – at the beginning you think you're playing, but now we can see we were learning,' said a perceptive playgroundee. Taster courses in several European languages plus Latin – 'useful as it subliminally supports English grammar' – highlight differences and similarities, whilst three to four sets for maths ensure that 'children in the support group aren't exposed'. Learning strategies and skills from day one with fairly low-key homework until the final year. Academic competition isn't encouraged and girls progress as individuals, but high achievers are well known and encouragement to 'strive harder each time'. According to one mum, 'They don't let the kids slack – they drive them on,' and some parents wonder if their children worry that they 'won't make it'. Basic learning support but works hard to dispel the slightest hint of stigma. Those who'd benefit have individual or paired sessions where coping strategies are developed.

Sport every day – well equipped facilities are shared with the senior school close by. Encouragement to learn an instrument – 60 per cent have individual lessons – plus all pupils learning to play ocarinas before graduating to recorders. Good selection of clubs before, during and after school – touch typing is popular with fencing, art appreciation and German adding breadth.

Charming homely touches everywhere and warm, welcoming classrooms bulging with visual stimuli and examples of children's work. Girls are polite, pleasantly confident and articulate. Tour guides aren't the chosen few – every year sixer plus partner takes at least one set of visitors round the school. Houses named after famous Norwich daughters – Fry, Cavell, Martineau and Mother Julian, who apparently 'got depressed and locked herself in a basement'. Girls have the opportunity, after a maths test and submission of a CV, to manage a mini school-based HSBC: reinforces the 'girls can and do' approach to life and learning.

Norwich School Lower School

Linked to Norwich School in the Senior section

Bishopgate, Norwich, NR1 4AA

• Pupils: 170 • Ages: 7-11 • Fees: £10,560 pa • Independent

Tel: 01603 728 449
Fax: 01603 728 491
Email: admissions@norwich-school.org.uk
Website: www.norwich-school.org.uk

Master of the Lower School: Since 2007, Mr John Ingham BA (forties). Previously head of juniors at Rossall School. His wife Mandy works in school administration and they have a young daughter. Keen to promote opportunities for all and encourages pupils to be fully involved in extracurricular activities. Teaches mostly history and maths. Hobbies are playing fives and supporting England RUFC.

Entrance: Entrance exam and interview mainly at 7+ but any time if space. Takes children of high to average ability and has a 'handful of children with special learning needs'. Cathedral choristers educated here – but must pass the entrance exam before being considered for the choir.

Exit: Entrance to the senior school isn't guaranteed – plenty of warning if a problem – but virtually all move on up.

Remarks: Designed as a coherent whole in the 1970s, sits on the edge of playing fields to the west of the cathedral and a five minute walk from the senior school. Classrooms ring a central hall and accessible library – a well thumbed 'How to Tell a Proton from a Crouton' alongside a full set of 'Horrible Histories'.

Over half the staff are male – lessons are traditional and teacher led. Enthusiastic participation from the pupils – a lively session on the correct use of the apostrophe, with pupils wielding fat marker pens and mini whiteboards. The inter-relationship between academic and extracurricular activities is a feature and pupils are encouraged to (and do) join at least two of the various clubs. 80 per cent learn a musical instrument.

Every available wall plastered with children's work or photos of grinning kids on one of the numerous trips – Year 6 in Paris ('a chance to practise some French'); ten day PGL experience at the beginning of the summer hols right on the Med (over subscribed). Two playgrounds, one with newly installed adventure equipment, and infields in the summer term give plenty of space to run around or perfect skills in diabolo.

A busy school filled with refreshingly normal, bright and happy children.

Notre Dame Preparatory School

Linked to Notre Dame Senior School in the Senior section

Burwood House, Convent lane, Cobham, Surrey, KT11 1HA

• Pupils: 350 girls, all day – including 40 in the co educational nursery
• Ages: 3-11 • RC foundation but all faiths welcome • Fees: £10,215 pa
• Independent

Tel: 01932 869 991
Fax: 01932 589 481
Email: headmaster@notredame.co.uk
Website: www.notredame.co.uk

Headmaster: Since 2001, Mr David Plummer BEd Hons (forties). Previously principal at Latymer Prep. Married with two daughters, both at the senior school, his wife runs IT department. A self-assured, ambitious and likeable Welshman from a boys' school seems an unlikely choice of head in a convent setting, but he's very popular with both parents and pupils.

Entrance: Non-selective by assessment (spend a day at school) backed up by report from feeder school. Girls come from the school's own pre-prep, plus around 20 different feeders including St George's, Weybridge, Denmead, Ripley Court, Danes Hill, Felton Fleet, The Ursuline, Holy Cross, The Study, Hall School, Danesfield Manor, Emberhurst School, Weston Green and local state schools.

Exit: 80-90 per cent move on to senior school. Rumblings amongst some parents that the assumed place at senior school no longer a certainty and a gap is forming between the academic standards of Year 6 prep school girls and the expected entry level for Year 7 senior school girls. Mr Plummer does not accept this criticism and says, 'The entrance to senior school is by formal examination, not the non-selective setting of the prep school'. School tells us the girls are very well prepared and standards remain high, with the majority of leavers accepting scholarships to Notre Dame Senior, Guildford High, Sir William Perkins's, Surbiton High or boarding schools.

Remarks: Nurturing atmosphere and children seem to settle in well; the head is also keen to mention the 'beautiful grounds'. Enthusiasm for maths, science and IT. Great IT department – computers used as a teaching aid and pupils taught to touch type in Year 5. An extensive development programme has taken place over the last nine years, with the new learning resource centre, science building and BlueBelles Nursery. £3.4 million performing arts centre with 400 seater theatre due for completion 2011.

Girls setted for maths in Year 3, in English and science in Years 5 and 6 – sets taught by subject specialists. Average class size 16, although some can reach 18 or 20 – worth checking out when you visit. Lots of new methods of teaching and learning. Head has taken on five male teachers (he used to be the only one) and believes the school is now 'not just cosy but academically exciting, with strong pastoral provision'.

Girls are prepared well for 11+ but classwork is balanced with plenty of extracurricular activities. Music superb, and the music room very well equipped. Loads of opportunities for every girl to learn an instrument or sing in a choir, even a private room away from the main school housing a drum kit for really noisy practices. Head very sporty – an impressive sports hall – and encourages all to take part. He's introduced lots of new sports (golf, swimming, athletics and soccer really strong) and residential trips, including a Daddy and Daughter camp-out – parents see all of this as a real plus.

Notting Hill and Ealing High School Junior School

Linked to Notting Hill and Ealing High School in the Senior section

26 St Stephen's Road, Ealing, London, W13 8HH

• Pupils: 310 girls; all day. • Ages: 4-11 • Non-denom • Fees: £9,387 pa
• Independent

Tel: 020 8799 8484
Fax: 020 8810 9947
Email: enquiries@nhehs.gdst.net
Website: www.gdst.net/nhehs/junior_pages/junior.htm

Headmistress: Since September 2003, Mrs Gabrielle Solti (pronounced Sholti) BA Oxon PGCE Institute of Education (late thirties). Previously deputy head at Primrose Hill Primary. Married to a French lawyer, they have two small children. Always wanted to be a teacher, but was told while reading history at Oxford that she would be head by the time she was 30 and couldn't see the point. 'What then?' she asked. So she headed for the European Commission in Brussels, where she met her husband, then worked in the marketing department at Nestlé in Paris and London, before finally she could no longer resist the lure of teaching and went to train at The Institute ('the gold standard – stands out on the CV; I always appoint graduates from there if I can').

Her first job was at Trevor Roberts, where she did anything and everything, before going on to Primrose Hill. Very bright and driven. Destined for great things, we suspect – this is only the beginning. Parents describe her as knowing her own mind – 'She won't take any nonsense from parents or children' – but approachable and sympathetic to concerns – operates a genuine open door policy. Clear educational vision – 'Our job is to spark an interest in learning,' she says. Wholly committed to single sex education. 'Girls tend to have low self esteem and aren't risk takers' – she is determined to inspire them with confidence and encourage them to learn interactively and independently. A great rôle model for budding young girls.

Entrance: Heavily oversubscribed and fiercely competitive – about 100 applicants for 40 places. Assessed just before fourth birthday – three staff will work with four children for an hour and half. 'We want to see how they play and how they interact – we're looking for inner confidence and self assurance,' says Mrs Solti. 'It's not about knowing your ABC or how to count to two thousand – we can teach them that.' Very flexible before assessment – will reschedule for illness; takes into account what a child's previous experience has been. But no budging after assessment and no sibling policy – it was the talk of Ealing when a child with four older sisters who had been through the school was refused a place. At Year 3 (age seven) eight places and usually 20 plus applicants. They sit papers in English, maths and verbal reasoning, plus interview for those who have done well enough. Other than these two entrance points it's very rare for the occasional place to come up, but it does happen.

Exit: Almost all to senior school – informed in Year 5 if eligible, then do exam in January of Year 6, primarily for the purpose of setting in senior school and to award academic and music scholarships (usually a handful of these). Help is given to the (very) few who are not up to it (these will normally have left at seven anyway) – they are placed at, e.g., Heathfield and Northwood College. Tiny few to St Paul's or Latymer Upper – tends to be for a specific reason – e.g. proximity to home or availability of scholarships.

Remarks: All the hallmarks of a GDST – excellent delivery of the curriculum, thorough assessment of children, down to earth professional parents. Bright spacious classrooms – lots of windows and impressive displays in corridors as well as in classrooms, some of the best (and most genuine) we've seen. Large playground with imaginative places to sit and to play – gazebo with benches, round tables and chairs, assault course, springy colourful tarmac and netball hoops. Separate playground for reception where the little ones can spill out to play with sand, Wendy house and puppet theatre. Funky lavatories decorated in bright girly colours – lots of pinks and purples reminiscent of a Vue cinema. The senior school is hundred yards to the rear, younger girls share their swimming pool, netball courts and dining room and perform the odd concert in the grand 'West Wing' auditorium, but otherwise it's a separate entity.

By all accounts Mrs Solti is upping the ante in terms of academics – the school was fourth in the league tables, since moved to third place, parents suspect she wants to get to the top. Wouldn't suit a child that isn't up to it academically: if she can't keep up she may find herself excluded – even in the playground, reports one parent. (School surprised at these reports and keen to deny them.) Year 2 class teacher doubles up as SENCo – a few on the dys–strata and some with mild Asperger's. They can have extra help at a cost – not the school to send your daughter if she has serious learning difficulties. As for the gifted and talented – 'All girls here would be given that label,' says Mrs Solti – and she clearly knows. The particularly brilliant (about four in each class) are catered for with differentiation and extension exercises – 'It helps that they can bounce off each other'.

Good discipline and pastoral care. Girls are taught right from the beginning to wait their turn and to respect others, but do have fun and are encouraged to participate. Our guide proudly related the teaching behind the catch words, THINK ('Is it truthful, is it helpful, is it inspiring, is it necessary, is it kind? If not, don't say it') and TAG (tell person how you're feeling, ask them to stop, get help from an adult). It clearly sticks.

You can do almost anything from Mandarin and chess to yoga and gardening in spare time but the music is particularly strong. Ninety per cent of girls learn a musical instrument, one third of the school is in the main orchestra. Impressive carol concerts in St Barnabas. Larks and tone deaf given equal attention – the hugely committed head of music holds 8am sessions in the week for the enthusiasts, of which many.

Most parents working professionals – ladies who lunch thin on the ground. Children of BBC types, lawyers and doctors come mainly from the local area, but a fair number prepared to travel the distance from Shepherds Bush and Ruislip – determined to get their daughter an excellent education from 4 to 18.

If your daughter wants to work hard and play hard, this is an excellent choice.

Notting Hill Preparatory School

95 Lancaster Road, London, W11 1QQ

• Pupils: 280 boys and girls at present, all day. • Ages: 5-13 • Non-denom • Fees: £13,440 pa • Independent

Tel: 020 7221 0727
Fax: 020 7221 0332
Email: admin@nottinghillprep.com
Website: www.nottinghillprep.com

Head: Since September 2003, Mrs Jane Cameron BEd (early fifties) who ran the Acorn Nursery in Lansdowne Crescent for 25 years. She had long nurtured the idea of taking pupils in Notting Hill (though not exclusively) up to CE. Married, with three grown-up children, approachable, realistic and respected by parents and pupils alike. Also persistent and fun. Deputy head, David Gee BEd, was previously director of studies at Hazelwood School in Surrey.

Entrance: Already over-subscribed for tinies – waiting lists to 2014. School has filled up from the bottom with Mrs Cameron running a twice-yearly ballot for reception (anxious to avoid fathers with sleepless post-labour eyes racing in asking, 'Am I in time?'). Siblings' entrance is automatic if places available. Mrs Cameron is still principal of The Acorn – many pupils coming on but not automatic. Applicants now come from a range of nursery schools. Advertising has been word of mouth. Assessment prior to entry for Year 2 and above (English, maths and a chat with the head). Developing trend of children joining in Year 7.

Exit: The majority of pupils have opted for London day schools, but as pupil numbers increase, some leavers are now heading for boarding schools at both 11+ and 13+. Parental meetings with headmistress and staff are offered well in advance of final registration dates for senior schools.

Remarks: School grew from local demand – with the impetus coming from experienced teachers and local parents, partnership between parents and teachers is particularly strong. Parent profile mimics that of The Acorn – mostly creative, fashionable and successful. Housed in a former school building (just south of the Westway, corner of Lancaster Road and Ladbroke Grove), purpose-built in 1902, but recently used by Camden Charities and now totally revamped, with a playground at the front where parents gather and chat.

A splendid new building over the road houses Years 4–8 and provides a dining room, science lab, music room and extra facility and practice rooms. Reception to Year 3 children can now spread out in the original building, where space is also available for artroom, computer room and library. This spacious site, comprising the delightful original Victorian building and the exciting new building, reflects the ethos of the school: a combination of the best of old values while looking forward to the challenges and stimulation of the new. In both buildings large bright rooms provide a welcoming environment for children, with lockers in the new building being a source of great excitement – as is the purpose built dining room and kitchen, providing delicious hot meals and a wide variety of options.

The headmistress and deputy head stand at the school gates to welcome the pupils to OB (old building) or JCB (Jane Cameron Building) at the beginning of each day. Parents either walk with their children, each wearing a blue rucksack marked with the pink NHP logo, across the busy intersection, or pile them out of four by fours. School opens at 8.20am and pupils can stay till 4pm for free, followed by clubs till 5pm.

Additional playgrounds at JCB have increased play space, and Linford Christie Stadium, Perkes Field, Westway Sports Centre and Kensington Leisure Centre provide the dedicated facilities necessary to support a comprehensive sports programme and busy fixtures schedule from Year 3 – with after-school clubs for keen ones.

Dynamic head of music composes a new school song with the children every term – most recently a piece for orchestra and choir ('The Eagle', based on the poem by Alfred Lord Tennyson). After a series of audition rounds it has been selected for performance at this year's Schools' Proms at the Royal Albert Hall in November. Art and drama from reception, regular plays and performances in assembly give the children performance confidence and weekly certificates and points are awarded to individuals in each house. These merit marks are popular and not restricted to academic skills – witness a little girl knocking on the head's door to make sure that her points were being registered for putting her head under the water in swimming. School divided into four houses (named after local roads). Headboy/girl team, heads of houses and school council help to support the welfare of the children in school. Worry box available for those who prefer to remain annonymous.

School follows RML (Ruth Miskin Literacy, which is magical – and we mean magical), based on 44 phonological sounds and graphemes (or Fred sounds) – 'my turn, your turn' policy, partner work and small groups: phenomenal. Class teachers in lower school for literacy and numeracy; maximum class size 20, no streaming but maths setted from Year 3. New deputy head (academic) streamlining teaching and learning strategies. Specialists for middle and upper school; Latin for all from Year 5 and Greek on offer. Small classes at the top end, so really all at scholarship level. School follows own curriculum leading to CE and scholarship in Years 7 and 8.

Computers from reception and interactive whiteboards in every classroom. Terrific emphasis on problem solving and study skills. Exam technique and learning strategies taught early and regular exams to practise on, ditto practice CEs, good contact between head and senior schools now established. Regular detailed reports home. Strong parental links – parents and children feel comfortable about 'dropping in on the head unannounced'.

Has a well established learning support centre with full-time SENCo which caters for children at both ends of the learning spectrum – mild learning difficulties, e.g. dyslexia, dyspraxia, mild speech and language difficulties, plus very bright children who meet criteria for gifted and talented. Active programme for the latter involving de Bono, P4C and Mindlab is developing creative, out of the box thinkers. Workshops and programmes available in preparation for external exams, curriculum, study skills etc.

Non-denom but major Christian and other festivals celebrated, carol service in local church. Uses all that London has to offer – oodles of visits: Natural History and Maritime Museums, V & A, plus residential trips for older pupils: Calshot activity centre in Hampshire for Year 5, French trip for Year 6 and geography field trips for Years 7 and 8.

School bedding down nicely – 'Feels like a village school' – in the centre of Notting Hill. Active parents' committee and popular fairs, concerts and fundraising initiatives. We're told that inroads have been made on the previously unproven exit record for older children, with reports from parents of recent leavers that pupils shoot straight to the top sets. Confidence that Mrs Cameron's years of success in shaping confident, happy, creative nursery children would extend to the older age group has, so far, not been misplaced.

Nottingham Girls' High School Junior School

Linked to Nottingham Girls' High School in the Senior section

9 Arboretum Street, Nottingham, Nottinghamshire, NG1 4JB

• Pupils: 290 girls, all day • Ages: 4-11 • Non-denom • Fees: £6,978 pa • Independent

Tel: 0115 9500423
Fax: 0115 9240757
Email: enquiries@not.gdst.net
Website: www.gdst.net

Head: Since September 2010, Mrs Faith Potter (early forties) BA PGCE , studied ecology at Bedford and previously deputy head of an international school in Cyprus. Married with two young children. Approachable, fair and has high expectations of behaviour. Keen to develop every child's full potential both in and out of the classroom, so is a great advocate of a busy school with a wide choice of musical, dramatic, creative and sporting activities.

Entrance: Majority at four and seven, a few places at other ages, especially nine – happy to recruit at all ages. Each child is invited to an informal, enjoyable assessment within the EYFA class and an additional group assessment. Head says school is 'not only interested in what they've done academically – we're looking to see what we can teach a child rather than what she has already been taught.' At seven, children take tests in numeracy and literacy – designed to assess potential, not simply what they have been taught.

Exit: Majority to the senior school. A small number move to alternative schools.

Remarks: Split between a modern purpose-built block and an extended period building. Good facilities: brand new library, additional classrooms, bright classrooms, hall, gym, two ICT suites, artroom, new multi-activity playground, wooden amphitheatre, landscaped gardens and soft play surface.

Takes SATs – all girls get a minimum of level 4 in all subjects and most of the results are at level 5 – but doesn't teach to them – sees them as just one indicator of pupil performance. Enjoys celebrating excellence – has a special achievers' board. Some help for those with specific learning difficulties is offered in class and on an individual and group basis.

Performing arts important and integrated into curriculum. All take part in at least one annual performance. A high percentage of pupils learn an instrument. Extracurricular opportunities include country dancing, gym, steel band and chess – school play, numerous sports matches and has county players. Many girls participate in chess team matches and regularly win the local league. Holds regular themed days where pupils take part in problem-solving activities, e.g. Take One Picture (linked to the National Gallery), Building Aliens, One World and Philosophy. Super examples throughout of pupils challenged to think 'outside the box', such as themed weeks and open homework weeks.

A major building programme was completed March 2009 with a large extension resulting in a new library and learning resources centre, new ICT centre, three additional classrooms, new waiting area and a new main entrance to the whole Junior School. This means it is now accepting two form entry at age 4 and continues with two forms throughout.

A happy, encouraging, child-friendly environment for able girls.

Nottingham High Junior School

Linked to Lovell House School in the Junior section
Linked to Nottingham High School in the Senior section

Waverley Mount, Nottingham, Nottinghamshire, NG7 4ED

• Pupils: boys; all day • Ages: 7-11 • Fees: £8,658 pa • Independent

Tel: 0115 845 2214
Email: juniorinfo@nottinghamhigh.co.uk
Website: www.nottinghamhigh.co.uk

Headmaster: Since 2007, Mr Andrew Earnshaw NPQH, previously deputy head of Beeston Rylands Junior School. Qualified in educational and professional primary studies with physical education practice of teaching at the University of Lancaster. He is married to Julie and they have two sons.

Entrance: Majority by assessment in maths and English at age seven and eight but some join at nine and 10. Need aptitude, school selective, wants children who have a great attitude to life and to working together. Gets very bright kids but Joe Soaps too.

Exit: Most progress to senior school.

Remarks: Modern brick building on two floors, separate DT/art room (with kiln), science lab, library, recently improved ICT room, chess room (a big thing here – lots of county players, trophy winners and even a few international players), hall doubles for assembly and music. All belong to a house – keep house colour when move to senior school. From Year 4 do most of lessons outside of form rooms. Lots of earnest faces say learning is fun and teachers are helpful. Learning support display highlights importance of understanding difficulties some children face. Children speak openly about benefit of having extra help and staff interested in how children learn. Bright displays show emphasis given to investigative learning and theme days such as architecture day – wants learning to come alive. Reading a big thing – aware of problems with boys and reading so introduced an incentive scheme; not only are boys rediscovering the joy of reading but it has helped identify those with problems and extend the gifted and talented.

Music and sport are passions of the school, giving life and colour. All Year 3 play a stringed instrument (no additional charge for tuition). The equivalent of a working day a week is devoted to sport. Plenty on offer: football, fencing, rugby, tennis, swimming etc. Challenges boys to play with good spirit, play to win but lose with good grace.

Enquiring minds couldn't ask for a better start.

Old Buckenham Hall School

Brettenham Park, Ipswich, Suffolk, IP7 7PH

• Pupils: Prep: 170; 65 girls, 105 boys; plus attached pre-prep of 35 pupils and nursery • Ages: 7-13; pre-prep and nursery 3-7 • C of E
• Fees: Boarding £18,885-£19,485; Day £7,380-£14,850 pa • Independent

Tel: 01449 740 252
Fax: 01449 740 955
Email: registrar@obh.co.uk
Website: www.obh.co.uk

Head: Mr John Brett MA CertMusEd, MCollP GCLCM (forties), previously head of St Mary's Melrose. Educated at King's Bruton, studied music at Leeds and London and trails more letters after his name than most. Previously head of music at Thomas's (Battersea). After his appointment in 1998 to St Mary's Melrose he discovered a school firmly entrenched in the trad boys' prep school mindset with a newly-built, barely-used boys' dormitory and rooms shut up all over the place. With 60 children and 'only three in the top year group', St Mary's was a school with a problem. It flourishes now, and Mr Brett happily admits that 'the first two or three years were a rocky ride'. We regard him as an urbane, enterprising head.

Entrance: Interview and report from previous school. No entrance exam, no academic selection (although parents suspect this could change as OBH becomes increasingly popular). Scholarships now offered at 7+, 8+ and 11+ with entrance tests being held in the Spring term. A few children of overseas Brits and a few foreigners (a couple of Spanish pupils come each year) but most from East Anglia, many parents commuting into London. The school provides good dyslexia support for a limited numbers of pupils. A fund is provided for families experiencing hard times and bursaries are offered. Pressure on places in the pre-prep, so names down early.

Exit: All leave at 13. Majority to nearish schools – Uppingham, Oundle, Rugby, Oakham, Stowe, Framlingham, Felsted, Ipswich, Culford – then top schools dotted around the country, including Harrow, Winchester, Eton and Radley. Girls throughout the school, some heading for traditional boarding, e.g. Tudor Hall, Downe House, Benenden, Roedean, St Mary's Ascot.

Remarks: Located in nowhereland, Suffolk, and set in a 75-acre park, this is as tranquil and unsullied as England gets. Founded as South Lodge in Lowestoft in 1862, the school moved several times (fires, wars) before settling in 1956 at Brettenham Park, south east of Bury St Edmunds. If coming to visit, treat map provided by OBH as modern art, but do pay close attention to the printed directions, if you do not want to end up lost forever among tractors, pheasants and organic chicken farms.

Went co-ed in 1998. Before that, well-heeled locals tended to send boys to OBH and girls to Riddlesworth Hall. Lovely old house, with some splendid showpieces, quirky features (prefects have their own staircase up to dormitories) and one or two gloomy corners (the old gym and scattered huts).

Superb girls' boarding house built atop new IT centre. The latter heavily used outside lessons for computer games (provided by school – children cannot bring their own) and emailing home. Lovely art and DT rooms – both open in the evenings. Separate music block with good facilities (most famous OB: Benjamin Britten). Wonderful adventure playground, Rory's Place, named after a pupil who died in a (non-school) skiing accident. 'The Ark' houses the children's pets. In their last year, pupils may bring bicycles to school. Plenty of flat playing fields, hard and Astroturf tennis courts, two squash courts, all-weather netball courts, nine-hole golf course, outdoor pool. Sailing takes place on local lake.

Two forms in each year group with three in the final year. More boys than girls, particularly at the top of the school, but this should slowly even out. Pupils start in mixed ability forms but are later streamed. Some setting in individual subjects during last three years. Less academic pupils also given careful nurturing and do well. Written assessments given every three weeks, plus detailed end of term reports. Usual prep school curriculum including Latin. Exams twice a year – February and summer. Good reports on academic standards from parents with children now at senior schools.

Brilliant sport, with a real effort (not wholly successful) to draw everyone in (when we were there, a talented girl was playing on the boys' hockey team). School claims that, at any time, 80 per cent of pupils are on a school team – the challenge will be to sustain this as the school expands. Games five times a week plus individual tuition in golf, archery, squash, tennis, sailing, riding and clay pigeon shooting.

No flexi-boarding. Weekly boarding available until age 11. Thereafter, pupils are encouraged to be full boarders, particularly if progressing to full boarding senior schools. Headmaster encourages parents to discuss individual family needs. One or two local children continue as day pupils all the way through. Girls housed in extremely pleasant dorms. Boys' rooms also nice and located in the main house. Each dorm has a dorm captain, who looks after the younger pupils, keeping the peace. Exeats every third weekend from 12 noon Friday until bedtime on Sunday. Day pupils' day ends at 6.15pm on weekdays and 4pm on Saturdays (Year 3: 5pm/12.10pm). Phasing out form tutors in favour of small tutor groups which meet weekly, so can really get to know the children. Politeness and good manners strongly emphasised with good results.

Many homely touches. School operates a catering 'dislikes' list – children may register loathing of a particular dish (e.g. curry, lemon meringue pie, prunes) excusing them from the ordeal of having it plopped onto their plate. At Christmas, a dorm decorating competition and the school organises fireside entertainment with songs, pupils' skits and general hilarity. Organised activities on Sundays include archery, horseriding, clay pigeon shooting, plus outings to theatres, museums and cinema. Lots of evening activities, changing each term to cater for indoor and outdoor. Limited tuck – boarders are allowed to spend the princely sum of 35p in the tuck shop twice a week. Glorious feeling of freedom not found at many other preps – 75 acres, bicycles, adventure playground, unfenced lily pond, cavorting pheasants.

Pre-prep and nursery housed in beautiful new building with main house's charming old walled garden as their play area. The pre-prep practically screams with 'enrichment' – cookery, French, gym, drama, music and movement plus new library facilities and computer suite – producing a very high standard of academic work. Big cheery room for the nursery.

Old Palace of John Whitgift School Junior Department

Linked to Old Palace of John Whitgift School in the Senior section

Old Palace Road, Croydon, Surrey, CR0 1AX

• Pupils: girls; all day • Ages: 4-11 • C of E • Fees: £7,626 pa • Independent

Tel: 020 8688 2027
Fax: 02086 805 877
Email: schooloffice@oldpalace.croydon.sch.uk
Website: www.oldpalaceofjohnwhitgift.org

Head: Ms Judy Harris.

Exit: Most to senior school (qv).

Remarks: For details, see senior school.

Oratory Preparatory School

Linked to Oratory School (The) in the Senior section

Goring Heath, Reading, Oxfordshire, RG8 7SF

• Fees: £3,435-£15,825 pa • Independent

Tel: 01189 844 511
Fax: 01189 844 806
Email: registrar@oratoryprep.co.uk
Website: www.oratoryprep.co.uk

Remarks: See senior school entry.

Orwell Park School

Nacton, Ipswich, Suffolk, IP10 0ER

• Pupils: Main school: 150 boys, 70 girls; 55 full boarders, 85 flexible boarders; pre-prep: 40 boys, 30 girls • Ages: Main school 7-13, pre-prep 3-7 • Inter-denom • Fees: Boarding £17,220-£19,140; Day £13,440-14,925; Pre Prep £5,895-£9,090 pa • Independent

Tel: 01473 659 225
Fax: 01473 659 822
Email: headmaster@orwellpark.co.uk
Website: www.orwellpark.co.uk

Headmaster: Since 2009, Mr Rowland Constantine, the long-time and recently retired headmaster of The New Beacon School in Sevenoaks. Sally, his wife, has become very involved in the school socially and with parents. They have three children, two grown up with children of their own and the youngest at university. 'Leads from the front and keeps his cards close to his chest', according to a New Beacon parent. School has advertised for a permanent head from September 2011.

Entrance: By registration and standard assessment tests.

Exit: Impossible to list all the schools nowadays – in fact girls and boys go on to nearly all the major public schools. 2002 saw the highest number of awards and scholarships in the school's history – 19 – and pupils continue to win scholarships, with 14 awarded in 2008 (academic, music, art, design technology and sport).

Remarks: A lovely place. Glorious setting, the main building is gorgeous late Georgian with Victorian additions and the facilities superb. The place has a warm, happy feel to it but still manages to look business-like and elegant. Pupils are mainly drawn from East Anglia (becoming more of a 'local' school) and many have strong London connections. A nice mixture of politeness, informality and willingness to chat in both boys and girls; they are buzzing with keenness and amazingly tidy. Emphasis on academic standards is strong. Streaming throughout the main school, particularly in the final CE year. Plenty of quiet time – e.g. every day begins with a 20-minute reading slot. Maximum class size in the main school is 16, average 12; in the junior school numbers range from 12–16.

Terrifically busy special needs department with SENCo overseeing a team of five or six. Strong support for those with dyslexia, dyspraxia, dyscalculia, mild Asperger's, ADHD, but nothing too serious – must be able to access mainstream. Children with known problems before they come to the school are assessed to see if they will be able to cope with curriculum and problems for those in school are dealt with as they arise: spelling, handwriting, paired reading, maths and prep support. Study skills for a couple of years during run-up to CE. One-to-one, one-to-two, small groups, dual teaching in class. Outside agencies co-opted if necessary – OTs, SALT and physios. At recent speech day headgirl remarked on how well the school had helped her overcome her dyslexia, develop her confidence and self-esteem and make significant strides.

Plenty of adults around – each class in the junior school has a qualified teacher and an assistant – and six gap-year student helpers, including some from eastern Europe – the school has links here through an HMC scheme. Some exciting exchanges and events have come out of this, such as a year's stay by a young Russian concert pianist.

The spirit of competition is far from dead. Children encouraged to take part in verse, public speaking and solo singing competitions and so on, and the list of school, regional and national sporting events that boys' and girls' teams compete in (and win) is endless. The new Astroturf has made a welcome addition to the outstanding sports facilities. A concert or lecture every week, with pupils either participating or just attending. Two thirds of the pupils play an instrument, many to grade 5 and above; plenty of orchestras, bands and choirs. Forty music practice rooms in the basement, now equipped with good pianos. Unsurprisingly, with all this activity, quite a few music scholarships to public schools every year.

Children are kept very busy with a wide variety of activities, from sailing (the school has 10 toppers) to theatre trips, via 10-pin bowling and some very worthy charity fundraising. The school has its own observatory (manned by a local astronomy group) with a ten-inch refractor telescope and radio station. A very flexible boarding system enables children to choose freely what they want to do. Library and IT room are open at all times and no silence rules. Dormitories are airy and bright. Junior school has formal family meals, main school has a cafeteria system. The former has expanded hugely, lately. They have to manage for the time being in Portakabins and although these are beautifully got up, colourful and comfortable, the next major school project will be the construction of a permanent structure for the junior school.

Most headmasters retire at 60. Mr Constantine clearly intends to carry on for several years yet. He ran a fine school at New Beacon.

Our Lady of Victories Catholic Primary School

1 Clarendon Drive, London, SW15 1AW

• Pupils: 195 boys and girls; all day • Ages: 4-11 • RC • State

Tel: 02087 887 957
Fax: 02087 850 450
Email: info@ourladyofvictories.wandsworth.sch.uk
Website: www.ourladyofvictories.wandsworth.sch.uk

Head: Since 1990, Mrs Margaret Ryall, previously deputy at Honeywell Junior School in Wandsworth. A no-nonsense head, very proud of her pupils and staff, will not suffer time-wasters. Sceptical of unproven fads in education, happier to fall back on her extensive experience – however not anti-change, just realistic about the constraints of admission, funding and space on her school.

Entrance: No dedicated feeder nursery although 19 places for RC at the ecumenical nursery at All Saints School, Putney Common. Heavily over-subscribed so first places go to those who live within the Parish of Our Lady of Pity and St Simon Stock and worship there weekly or more often – and have done so for the past three years. Priority given to siblings, then shortest walking distance from school. Admissions are a nightmare for head each year, so criteria and notes are published. Some children (parents working international company placements in London for a couple of years) enter the school near the top when demand is lower, meaning even non-Catholics get a look in.

Exit: To a huge range of independent and state schools, although very rarely in Wandsworth, e.g. Cardinal Vaughan Memorial School, Gumley House RC Convent School, Lady Margaret, Lady Eleanor Holles School, London Oratory, St Paul's and Tower House School.

Remarks: Founded by Mr Simon Harworth in 1923 and given in charge to the Religious Institute of the Poor Servants of the Mother of God. The Sisters handed the school over to the Diocese of Southwark in 1978. In the web of residential streets to the west of Putney High Street; housed in a Victorian ex-convent and modern extension, where the assembly hall, library and ICT room lie. Two playgrounds, the smallest just for reception, rostered play times for the rest of the school. The head would love more space and has a potential building in her sights over the road. The present setup is not very good for disabled access – adaptation is being considered.

A happy and colourfully decorated school, renowned for its music – all children learn notation, music making, appraising, singing and recorder. Violin is optional but many play, and other specialist lessons take place at the Wandsworth Centre. At least two school productions each year, in the summer and at Christmas, well attended by parents and friends – collections at the end of the production go to charities. The community is really that of the parish – 90 per cent of the parents are regular church goers. On a social level, they meet after service (the school choir sings up there on special occasions or feast days) and the kids play in the garden attached to the church. Father Richard, the parish priest, pops into school twice a month providing an alternative male rôle model to that of the PE teachers at Putney sports centre and fathers – the teaching staff at OLV is all female.

Food has improved recently – after the Jamie Oliver campaign, the school elected to employ an independent provider. Nearly all children now enjoy a freshly cooked lunch each day. Very low staff mobility, although pupils do move on – when parents need an extra bedroom, Putney property prices make a move out of the borough more attractive. A lot of French children (no formal EAL teaching) with parents on short term postings mean that French classes have particularly good rôle models for accents. Further developments include an exchange day with the French Lycée in Kensington. The SENCo is in 3.5 days a week to provide literacy and numeracy help in small groups – this level of support boosts the bottom tier in each class, even if nationwide they would not be deemed to need SEN teaching.

Most children walk to school – if they do it for a month on the trot they get a WOW badge; a pupil at OLV has just designed the new logo to be used to encourage walking nationwide. They walk to the swimming pool or take a coach to the playing fields at Roehampton. Relationships within the school are particularly nice – a yellow concerns box on a landing for anonymous complaints, but it has not seen much action since the novelty wore off. Two recent Ofsted inspections have judged the school to be outstanding in all areas.

Our Lady of Victories RC Primary School

Clareville Street, London, SW7 5AQ

• Pupils: 225 (boys and girls including nursery) • Ages: 3-11 • RC • State

Tel: 020 7373 4491
Fax: 020 7244 0591
Email: sarah.mcbennett@olov.rbkc.sch.uk
Website: www.olov.rbkc.sch.uk/

Headteacher: Since 2007, Mrs Sarah McBennett BEd (Hons) from Queen's University, Belfast. Was formerly deputy head of St John's RC Primary in Kent, which boasts an enormous 700 pupil roll. Before that, was head of primary at the International Community School of Amman, Jordan, for five years and 'loved every moment'. Has always been in teaching and has had experience of teaching children from reception through to Year 6. Is now a non-teaching head, only filling in when necessary, but 'loves teaching and loves children'. Well supported by her deputy, who has been at the school for 25 plus years and knows all the families. She is 'very good news', according to the Chair of the PTA.

Entrance: Entry is based on the parishes of Our Lady of Victories and Our Lady of Mt Carmel and St Simon Stock. Places are usually only available to strictly practising Catholics with baptised children. Always very oversubscribed. Where possible, siblings have priority. Children who start in the nursery are not automatically guaranteed a place in reception. All applications must be supported by a letter from the parish priest. Proximity takes precedence.

Exit: To a broad mix of both state and private secondary schools all over west and southwest London. Boys go to The London Oratory, Emanuel, Dulwich, Westminster, Gunnersbury, Cardinal Vaughan Memorial School, City of London Boys' and St Paul's School. Girls to Sacred Heart in Hammersmith, Gumley House Catholic School for Girls or Lady Margaret in Fulham, St Paul's Girls, More House and City of London. Co-educational choices are St Thomas More, Holland Park, St Benedict's and Latymer.

Remarks: A most desirable state primary in a fabulous location just off the Old Brompton Road. Its Victorian building, though wedged between residential streets, has a certain charm with its tall windows flooding light into the classrooms. Very up and down; lots of stairs, but good exercise as little outside playing space. Good sized gym which doubles as theatre, assembly and PTA activities area. Otherwise sports take place in Battersea Park with football and cricket professionals from nearby clubs coming in to coach the pupils. Discipline and uniform (straw boaters in summer), are rigorously maintained, making the children proud of their school and letting them stand out as being different from neighbouring schools. The high standards of appearance and behaviour give it the flavour of a private prep.

On the academic side, standards are similarly high. Children are encouraged to excel with options for the gifted and talented. Specialist teachers provide added value with lessons in French, Latin, music. Large EAL contingent whose needs are met by dedicated staff. Many of the strategies used in EAL are adopted successfully in other areas of the curriculum wherever speaking and listening are involved, so overall results are excellent.

A busy school with after-school clubs offering Italian, Mandarin, Spanish, drama, art, ballet, chess, cooking. Supportive and visible PTA which organises events between the parishes and the school. Any parents who have free time during school hours are encouraged to offer their services to the school either regularly or from time to time on a voluntary basis, helping with class outings, reading and library duties. Strong links with the churches in all the parishes. Daily prayers and family masses are integral. Religious statues, each adorned with a potted plant, can be found in every corridor. For Catholic families seeking an excellent education for their children within a religious framework, Our Lady of Victories must be their first choice.

Our Lady's Junior School Abingdon

Linked to Our Lady's Abingdon in the Senior section

St John's Road, Abingdon, Oxfordshire, OX14 2HB

• Pupils: 90 girls, 45 boys • Ages: 3-11 • Roman Catholic • Fees: £6,480-£9,000 pa • Independent

Tel: 0123 5523 147
Email: officejs@olab.org.uk
Website: www.olab.org.uk

Head: Since 2007, Mr Brendan O'Neill BEd Hons, NPQH (fifties), educated at St Brendan's College, Bristol and Southampton University. Married with two grown up children, both work in education. Has been at the school for 25 years, loves his work, utterly dedicated and a calm but authoritative leader. Still teaches – mainly maths and sport plus 'a bit of geography'. Inspires great confidence in parents – one senses a man with a very strong vocation who knows every child in his care not just by name but also by character. Outside school his interests are coin collecting and football.

Entrance: Various entry points; from Year 4 an assessment including verbal reasoning, maths, English and informal observation. Report from previous school important.

Exit: Majority to senior school, some to other independents. Good that boys can now also move through to the senior school, the destination for the majority of girls (partly as a result of pressure from junior school parents). Prior to 2009, boys would leave at 11 (mostly to local preps, Abingdon, The Oratory) – early days yet and it remains to be seen how many of them do.

Remarks: A great deal of thought has gone into making this a secure, stimulating and enjoyable place to learn. The buildings incorporate the original Victorian convent and the resulting quirky layout, high ceilings and mullion windows are rather magical. The art room is housed in what was the nuns' dining room and children's work is on every wall; when we visited the children had been drawing with a visiting artist.

Nursery and infant classrooms are brightly decorated and comfortable, beautiful displays of themed work – the early years curriculum is followed 'with tweaking'. Juniors have their own entrance and outside space with play equipment; we liked the 'reading shelter' with a box of books – an idea from the school council. Nursery children have a separate area with picnic houses for eating outside.

Real sense of an educational journey as children move up through the school; in one room we saw Year 3 children concentrating on handwriting to the accompaniment of Vivaldi. Year 5 and 6 pupils sit at individual desks as they develop independent learning, making forays into the senior school laboratories for science lessons.

Lots of PE and outdoor sport: boys and girls introduced to rugby and football and swimming for all in senior school pool – even the three year olds have one session a week. Visiting ballet, piano and violin teachers.

For many activities a system of what the head calls 'family groups', consisting of three or four children from different years who take part together. The intention is to build relationships between the different ages, the older children supporting the younger ones; a buddy system pairs up older pupils with the youngest members of the school.

Extremely well run, very child-centred and a warm family atmosphere.

Oxford High School GDST Junior School

Linked to Oxford High School GDST in the Senior section

1 Bardwell Road, ., Oxford, Oxfordshire, OX2 6SU

• Pupils: 335; 10 boys in the junior school (reception–Year 2); all day (boys currently being phased out) – admission Year 1 and 2 only) • Ages: 6-10 at the junior school at Bardwell Road; 3-5 at the junior school at Woodstock Road • Non-denom • Fees: Nursery £2,910; Junior £7,044 pa • Independent

Tel: 01865 515 647
Fax: 01865 510 841
Email: oxfordhigh@oxf.gdst.net
Website: www.oxfordhigh.gdst.net/

Head of Junior School : Since September 2010, Mrs Ellie Stacey BA. Headteacher of Burford Primary School for six years, having taught at SS Philip and James C of E Primary School before that. Completed a post graduate certificate in advance early years practice. On leaving school joined British Airways as cabin crew and saw the world. Husband Derek is a physicist attached to Christ Church, four children between them and five step grandchildren. Likes to spend time in Cornwall, singing and growing things in her garden and allotment.

Has always believed it to be a privilege to work with children. Sees families as essential partners with school to ensure that children fulfil their potential.

Entrance: Although over-subscribed at all entry levels it is worth having a go. Selective after nursery and reception – tests in maths, English, reading and spelling at later entry. External candidates can apply at any age to junior school.

Exit: Transfer from junior to senior school generally automatic.

Remarks: The Junior School is located on two sites within walking distance. See Oxford High School GDST.

Packwood Haugh School

Ruyton XI Towns, Shrewsbury, Shropshire, SY4 1HX

• Pupils: 180 boys, 110 girls; main school 135 boarders, 115 day; pre-prep 40 • Ages: 7-13. Plus small pre-prep department ages 4-7 • C of E • Fees: Pre-Prep £6,135; Day £10,800-£13,926; Boarding £17,406 pa • Independent

Tel: 01939 260 217
Fax: 01939 262077
Email: headmaster@packwood-haugh.co.uk
Website: www.packwood-haugh.co.uk

Head: Since 2000, Mr Nigel Westlake LLB PGCE (early fifties). Studied law and qualified as a solicitor before taking his PGCE at Exeter. Finds his legal training 'comes in useful for dispelling myths about health and safety.' Taught at Sunningdale, The Old Malthouse (deputy head, head of English) and Aldro School, Surrey, before coming here as deputy head in 1998. Married (Mrs Westlake is head of music) with two small sons. Dislikes 'pointless paperwork', likes 'getting out of the office as much as possible'. Takes a lesson with each form every fortnight, coaches rugby 1st XV. Has an easy manner: children cluster round him to chat, parents find him 'approachable'; 'a good listener'. Places strong emphasis on the Packwood Way and Packwood Code, a list of guiding principles posted up at various points around the school.

Entrance: Not selective. Short informal assessment – maths and English. Scholarships awarded: academic, sporting, music, art, all-rounder. Help for the needy. Children come from Shropshire, Cheshire, Wales, Staffordshire, London. Handful of overseas students, particularly from Spain and Japan.

Exit: Most of the boys go to Shrewsbury (where rumour mill has it that Packwood children are noted for an ability to get on with others), but also steady numbers to Rugby, Eton, Harrow, Winchester, Radley, Uppingham, Repton, Sedbergh. Rugby and Cheltenham Ladies' College popular with girls. Moreton Hall and Ellesmere are local choices.

Remarks: Traditional country prep school, a 'proper' boarding school. Head is committed to full boarding, 'otherwise the character of the school changes'. Boarding numbers, which fell in the '90s recession, have risen strongly, are holding up well – resists pressure for more day school places. 'Last year we reached 306, which seemed a little tight in one or two areas,' says the head. 'When the school reaches 285, we will only take boarders.'

Academic but unpressurised. Careful streaming. Has gained more scholarships in recent years, with record number for 2010 and strong Common Entrance results (40 per cent of all grades As). Parents like the broad range of abilities: 'They look after the quirky child, and work hard to find what makes each child tick,' says one. 'A goodish number' of children (around 80) have varied SEN, many physical. Good learning support department. Prides itself on being inclusive and does seem so – one boy in a wheelchair was getting stuck into a vigorous playtime ball game. A recent leaver, born with hemiplaegia, played an active part in the school's sporting and musical life, winning the coveted Character cup.

Good place for children who like the great outdoors. Strong sports – competes successfully at football, cricket, netball, hockey, punches above its weight for lacrosse, and is regarded highly for its rugby. Regularly sends out 3rd and 4th teams. Winter sports programme recently changed so can play bigger schools: 'More travelling, but more – and tougher – matches'. Competitions between houses (known as 'Sixes'). Fantastic new sports hall. Judo and fencing particularly popular. Over 80 children signed up for summer 'Duel in the Sun' fencing competition and several rated nationally. Riding is big – has a cross-country course, runs its own gymkhana and hosts a series of horsey events. Sympathy for the non-sporting, who might do other activities. 'My son hates all sport, but found his niche in a very sporty school,' says one parent. Another avowedly non-sporting boy became a whizz at stage-lighting.

Strong music – 85 per cent of pupils learn an instrument and 120+ take music exams. A recent development has been to introduce more ensembles. Art is good and popular – better facilities have meant greater scope for adventurous projects. A corridor of computers links the art studio and DT room, where shutters close off the scariest equipment so children can work there in free time. Big year-based drama productions. 'I'd say the drama is OK, not the school's strongest point,' comments one parent. Others would disagree.

Around 125 children in school at weekends. Three levels of boarding: occasional (up to two nights on regular basis); a year's transitional, giving children an option of going home at weekends, and full. Boys' dormitories are over four landings in main school, with kind matron on each. Some fittings in boys' dormitories a bit careworn, although boys like the prospect of being in 'Crocodile Swamp' or 'Snake Pit' and love the appropriately themed murals. A move to add bunks has created more floorspace. Generally, the more recently re-decorated girls' dormitories (in a separate building, Park House) look more welcoming (or is that just girls?). Main building comprises original sandstone house and farm buildings dotted with additions – some unlovely 1960/70s, with nicer newer ones, including great theatre. Grounds roll away from the buildings like a green sea. Space (66 acres) is its luxury and it makes the most of it. Lovely grass tennis courts. A big draw is The Spinney, a wooded area with an intricate den system where children – boys and girls – go on Wednesday and weekend afternoons. 'It's like a mini-state: they have their own currency, elections and ruling cabinet," says the head.

Lots going on at weekends. 'Be aware if you have day children – you will come under huge pressure from your children to let them board,' warns one mother. Clubs range from the outdoorsy – clay pigeon and rifle-shooting, fly-fishing and fly-tying – to chess and website building. Ballroom dancing has been the most popular evening club for many years and the Packwood Ball is an annual highlight. No association, but gets a lot of support from parents, who help run events like the popular biannual Dog Show (black labs in abundance). Winter match teas in front of a roaring fire are popular – a sociable place. Lots of traditional country families.

Maybe it's all that fresh air and space, but children seem a particularly cheerful, unprecious bunch, happy to chatter away to adults, and feel no 'them and us' between boarders and day pupils. At time of writing, children and parents expressed sadness that several highly experienced, valued staff members were retiring – 'They have been the backbone of school for so long, it will be interesting to see what happens,' says one parent. A parent at one new appointee's school said Packwood 'had stolen their best teacher': overall feeling seems to be school is in sure hands.

Palmers Green Lower School

Linked to Palmers Green High School in the Senior section

104 Hoppers Road, London, N21 3LJ

• Pupils: 200 girls, all day • Ages: 3-11 • Non-denom • Fees: £7,665-£8,685 pa • Independent

Tel: 020 8886 1135
Fax: 020 8882 9473
Email: office@palmersgreen.enfield.sch.uk
Website: www.pghs.co.uk

Remarks: See senior school.

Papplewick School

Windsor Road, Ascot, Berkshire, SL5 7LH

• Pupils: 200 boys; 130 boarders, 70 day, weekly or full boarding; boarding compulsory last two years and previous summer term • Ages: 6-13 • C of E • Fees: Boarding £22,425; Day £13,350-£17,220 pa • Independent

Tel: 01344 621 488
Fax: 01344 874 639
Email: registrar@papplewick.org.uk
Website: www.papplewick.org.uk

Head: Since 2004, Mr Tom Bunbury BA PGCE (fortyish), who was previously deputy head and has been at the school since 1993. Educated at Woodcote and Millfield, he read law at Durham and worked for four years before turning to teaching. He first taught at Woodcote before attending Homerton College, Cambridge, and has been both housemaster and head of maths at Papplewick. He was 'thrilled at the chance to lead the staff that had evolved during the years that I'd been at Papplewick'; not a weak link in the team, the staff appointed are of a consistently high quality. No immediate staff changes in the pipeline.

Thoughtful, quietly confident and with a laid-back sense of humour, the head runs the school with two deputies and leads a remarkably young common room. He still teaches four periods a week – 'Get to know the little chaps', 'having a lovely time'. He and his wife, Sallie, live on site with four small children. Two thirds of the staff also live on site, Mrs Bunbury holds birthday breakfasts for all chaps (staff sometimes included) whose birthdays fall within the previous week, each birthday boy can bring a friend, and the Bunbury front door was festooned with balloons when we visited. All very jolly and fun.

Entrance: Entry now from age six with a Year 2 class being introduced from September 2010. Waiting lists but suck it and see. First come first served, boys informally screened for setting purposes only and remedial problems often picked up then (in which case they are referred to an 'outside expert' and ed-psyched if need be). One or two from the state sector but most from the local preps – Upton House and Coworth Flexlands – plus quite a growing number come daily from London and school has a daily bus to Chiswick (wow); pupils also from Maidenhead, Henley and points north. Some from Lambrook, St George's and St John's Beaumont recently. About 10 per cent ex-pats and ditto foreigners, EFL on hand. Dyslexia and EFL cost extra. Five scholarships – academic, music, art, sport, all-rounder – available each year. School fields Eton continuation scholarships on a regular basis.

Exit: Streams to Eton, Harrow, Wellington. Stowe, Marlborough, Bradfield, Winchester following and superb record of scholarships in every discipline to top schools (33 scholarships gained to major public schools in the last three years, including four to Eton).

Remarks: Work is important but fun here, boys happily interacting with staff and visitor alike, male staff called 'sir'. We were treated to a serious display of snake charming in the gruesome biology lab with creepy crawlies, snakes, crickets and fish (and made to wash our hands afterwards). Super boy stuff, with the odd rugby ball which mysteriously moved up and down the classroom staircase throughout our visit. Old pound weights used as door stops. Class sizes average 13, max 20, three forms from 10 up, fiercely setted and streamed, boys move up and down as needed. Top form equals scholarship but Latin for all and Greek for scholars for three years.

Brimful of computers, their keys 'blanked out' until boys 'have passed their test', lessons as much on computers as by trad methods. Interactive white-boards. Artist in residence. Whizzy art everywhere and incredible murals all over the school, 3D fish float up the wall by the swimming pool and mosaics on hand for next installation. Ceramics etc. Good strong music – electric guitars, drums, music technology suite (senior stuff this) and strong choral tradition. Head plays the piano. Keen drama, inspired teaching; peculiar combo assembly hall-cum-chapel arrangement which offers endless scope (serious re-organisation on wish list).

Teams for all for everything, plus under-eight fixtures in trad sports – football as well as rugby. Riding popular and school fields a polo team. 15 acre school site plumb opposite Ascot number 7 car park (which the school is hoping to lease for practice grounds out of season) crammed with boy-inspired activities including karate and fencing; chaps scoot madly round the new hard-standing at break time with a great feeling of purposefulness. Covered pool facility so swimming all year round.

New staff flats in the making, plus even more boarding accommodation. All pupils must board their last two years and the previous summer term. Very buzzy boarding, superb houseparents – Years 3–6 have one set of houseparents, as do Years 7 and 8 separately; regular trail of cocoa and buns. Dorms re-vamped, jolly bunks, pine furniture, absolutely no work allowed upstairs, still the biggest and best dorm in the business, though no longer arranged for round the world. Mobile phones allowed between prep and bed time only. New family friendly approach to boarding allows all boarders to go home on Saturdays after matches until Sunday evening on all but the first weekend of each term. Strong programme of Saturday night entertainment and Sunday outings and activities for the many full boarders. Day boys encouraged to enjoy the odd taster aka 'the big sleepover'.

Salad option or set meal each day, boys sit in houses; fruit and biscuits handed out at break time and fruit constantly available. Bullying stamped on at birth – 'It's usually only name calling, but that's enough'; top school award basically for niceness. Positive PSHE in operation. Tuck shop two or three times a week and regular 'socials' for oldest boys when they join forces with Heathfield and Downe House.

Strong teaching, good ethos, smashing little school with trails of glory on the scholarship field.

The Paragon School

Linked to Prior Park Preparatory School
Linked to Prior Park College in the Senior section

Lyncombe House, Lyncombe Vale, Bath, BA2 4LT

• Pupils: 145 in prep school (60 girls, 85 boys), 90 in pre-prep (35 girls, 55 boys) • Ages: prep school 7-11, pre-prep 3-7 • Christian (open to all faiths) • Fees: £7,665; Pre-prep £6,549 pa • Independent

Tel: 01225 310 837
Fax: 01225 427 980
Email: admissions@paragon.priorpark.co.uk
Website: www.paragonschool.co.uk

Headmaster: Since 2006, Mr Titus Mills BA PGCE (late thirties) educated at The Pilgrims' School, Winchester, then Eton, before reading history of art at UEA and PGCE at Westminster College, Oxford. Gap year experience with Tibetan community in Himalayas dramatically rearranged his world view. Overseas dimension broadened further by two years' teaching in Kampala, Uganda (sandwiched between six years in state sector, including four in Lambeth) prior to five years at St George's International School, Rome. Convincing head who looks the part though still a relative novice: high octane energy meets sophisticated unconventionality. 'Fantastic', 'lots of brilliant ideas', 'has moved school up a gear' – the accolades from parents pour in thick and fast. High levels of commitment and sensitivity soon become apparent. We were left wondering whether The Paragon is a stepping stone or whether his love affair with Bath might mean he's in for the long haul. However the cookie crumbles, Titus Mills is just what TP needs right now to hold its own in a fiercely competitive marketplace. He and lovely wife, Jemima, have 'much in common' with other Paragon parents. Cassius, youngest of three sons (Malachi, 6, and Raffi, 4, already at TP) had just been born when we visited and Jemima 'sees herself as a mum' first and foremost. Head is an infectious enthusiast whose own, positive prep school experience and sincerely held Christian faith help to explain why he is 'on a mission' here. Loves football (plays in a dads' five-a-side team), art and drama (which he teaches). Doesn't want school to be 'wishy washy' – not much fear of that, we thought – and has already shown parents and staff that he's not afraid to take tough decisions for the good of the school. On a personal level, enjoys meeting war veterans (whose stories he finds profoundly moving) and worshipping at nearby Anglican church. He is clearly raising profile of TP locally but above all is succeeding in making it a fun place in which to learn.

Entrance: Applicants invited for trial morning (nursery) or day (pre-prep upwards) plus interview with head. Entrance is possible in any year, space permitting. Strict quota operates for those needing learning support. No longer perceived as a 'cheap and cheerful' option in Bath, though continues to undercut competitors.

Exit: Three-quarters proceed to Prior Park via normal admission test at 11+; remainder to local state schools and a few to other independents.

Remarks: Fortunes of this attractive little prep, tucked away up Bath's most beautiful vale, have been restored by becoming junior school of nearby Prior Park College. Seven and a half acre grounds include natural springs and beautiful woodland, now being exploited as part of the 'outdoor classroom' with expert help from 'Swainswick Explorers'. Original Lyncombe House School was a convent whilst The Paragon started as an educational gymnasium in the Bath street of that name. Schools amalgamated in 1983, a charitable trust was formed and the facilities were improved. Conservation area restrictions still an issue but serious improvements to the facilities are envisaged.

A new school crest, bright red striped shirts and a fleet of liveried minibuses signal changes here. Lots of new teachers, visually attractive prospectus, lively wall displays, smart boards and enhanced décor take this a step further. School reception is now much better located and head 'pops up everywhere' to meet parents and sort out any difficulties on the spot. We didn't witness the arrival or collection of children by parents, but a staggered end to the day and a one-way system through the grounds apparently prevent gridlock.

Nursery on ground floor of main building is hugely popular and will soon benefit from upgrading. Pre-prep continues in linked reception classes, located in converted stables at the bottom of the sloping site. Safe and happy feel to the place with bright eyed and friendly faces everywhere. Phonic approach to word building much in evidence as well as Oxford Reading Tree and other schemes; emphasis on practical number work (new Abacus scheme popular) with lots of games and outside activity to keep learning as practical as possible. Lively, busy classrooms throughout pre-prep with some lovely thematic displays. Lots of new play equipment for tinies and a 'buddy bus stop' where anyone feeling lonely will soon find a friend comes along to cheer them up.

Preparatory classes are spread between various buildings with specialist areas for ICT (20+ new computers) and music (with separate rooms for individual practice). New director of studies has helped revamp the curriculum balancing attention to core skills with a more exciting use of topic work – we saw an encouraging improvement in motivation, participation and standard of written work since our last visit. New internal awards scheme which emphasises good work and behaviour is having a huge impact. Staff much more geared up to new teaching methods and resources through in-house training and more focused curriculum management.

Given school's small size, sports achievements are disproportionately impressive – girls were recent runners-up in national schools' U11 hockey finals. Good range of sports and four hours' games per week for older children. Nice blend of inclusion and representative teams. Lots of inter-school matches including Saturday fixtures. Pupils benefit from excellent facilities at Prior Park (including indoor swimming pool) and travel to and fro by minibus; extensive use of external coaches as well as full-time PE specialist who drives things along with gusto. Music is particularly strong with a senior orchestra which includes parents and former pupils. Also a training orchestra and lots of other choirs and instrumental groups, including a samba band. 'Something for everybody,' claimed the ebullient HOD. Lots of concerts and drama performances throughout year. Lively school magazine.

Small library area is well resourced and inviting; children we met enthused about their favourite authors (one of whom was visiting on the same day as us) and parents are amazed at how quickly school has managed to 'turn reluctant readers into avid bookworms'. New junior librarian software allows readers to write reviews on their favourite books. Art room feels creative and is appropriately housed in a second floor garret, but little space for large scale DT work. Science resources are kept in a Year 6 classroom. Head is keen to teach science through practical means and to utilise their 'outside classroom' wherever possible. Parents rate skill and enthusiasm of teachers and even we understood the way that fractions were being explained to a Year 6 class (with expert use of the smart board, it has to be said). Assembly hall at heart of school ideal for performances as well as providing ample space for apparatus work and a pleasant dining area.

Food gets thumbs up from children and parents and TP now has 'healthy school' status. Good, level outside play area used alternately by different age groups plus attractive area of grass in front of Lyncombe House now being put to greater use. A new hide for junior twitchers includes equipment provided through the fund-raising efforts of an especially keen Year 6 pupil. Lovely walk through 'dingly dell' is a favourite with pupils, as is the conservation area in the woods. All Year 6 pupils are prefects and share responsibilities. Parents thrilled by range of extra-curricular activities (from film making to speech and drama) and appreciate way head has listened to their requests to reduce homework for younger ones so that family time is safeguarded and enjoyed more.

Open, friendly staff combine wise heads and new brooms. Part-timers, peripatetics and sports coaches give breadth. All pupils get an hour of ICT per week in computer suite using PCs for creative writing, digital video editing, web site design etc. Plenty of visits including stay in France; popular theme days when children dress up as part of their studies. Contributors to assemblies include local postman as well as regular visits from RC chaplain from Prior Park.

School has strengthened its learning support provision and now has three dedicated specialists including the SENCo and a qualified SpLD teacher; cosy, well-resourced base conducive for bringing on slow starters. Careful assessment leads to appropriate levels of support.

Shuttle bus before school links with Prior Park coaches, which serve a wide catchment area. Head keen to be on good terms with neighbours and to reach out to wider community including local primaries. Charity giving has become a buzz phrase and is taking up worthy causes locally and internationally. As one mum said, 'This is a prep that is beginning to fly.'

Parkside School

The Manor, Stoke D'Abernon, Cobham, Surrey, KT11 3PX

• Pupils: 300 boys; the nursery has 90 pupils, including girls; all day
• Ages: 2-13 • Non-denom • Fees: £7,350-£12,300 pa • Independent

Tel: 01932 862 749
Fax: 01932 860 251
Email: enquiries@parkside-school.co.uk
Website: www.parkside-school.co.uk

Head: Since 1999, Mr David Aylward BEd MA FRSA (fifty-ish). Almost an institution, Mr Aylward (affectionately known by everyone as DA) has been involved with the school for over 25 years. Down to earth, good-humoured and popular, he runs a tight ship without any overt authoritarianism. Educated at Portsmouth Grammar and Kingston University, this is his first headship. He does not give the impression of a tough go-getter, far more of a laid back, relaxed, chap – which must be very refreshing for those Surrey parents more used to heads keen to hothouse their children. Has a genuine fondness for his pupils and does much to ensure a warm and pleasant atmosphere throughout the school. Hands-on approach means he is very visible around the school.

Entrance: Usually boys come via the nursery but places do come up later. Anyone joining at five or older has an assessment day to check academic ability and to see if they fit with the school. Worth checking for an odd place at unconventional times.

Exit: Popular choices locally include Royal Grammar School Guildford, St John's Leatherhead, Hampton, King's College Wimbledon, Kingston Grammar and Reed's Cobham, with boarders going on to Cranleigh and Charterhouse. A handful to other public schools such as Wellington, Winchester, Harrow and Millfield. On average 22 per cent of boys win scholarships – to academic and not so academic senior schools.

Remarks: Happy laid back school providing a good all round education. Mr Aylward says, 'The way we operate is much more low pressure than other schools in the area, but our boys are going on to the same schools as the competition.'

Lovely old building set in bosky Surrey countryside with river frontage. Main house, known as The Manor, is lovely in a faded grandeur kind of way – dining hall atmospheric ('like something out of "Harry Potter",' says head) with the beautiful salon providing the location for the twice weekly assemblies. New classroom block known as The Crescent contains well designed, airy classrooms. New 100 seat performing arts hall, lecture room, refurbished science labs and new art block are the source of much pride. New library and plans to build a new second IT suite.

Pupils a happy bunch who enjoy lessons. 'They're encouraged to have an opinion,' said one mum. Boys are setted from age 9 into three sets. French and Latin are on offer, and every boy will do music, art, PE and DT whether or not they are in the scholarship set. Class sizes on average 16–20. DA comments that 'We're big enough to be flexible with setting and streaming and small enough to be able to value the individual.' Refreshing approach to study – 'I firmly believe setting loads of homework is counter-productive'. This more relaxed style doesn't suit all parents and the head admits that some parents think that the school does not give enough homework. 'It's not regimented enough for some,' commented a parent. 'Parkside is definitely not a place for pushy parents,' said another.

Excellent approach to SEN – very switched-on team providing across the board support with a wide range of experience. About 20 per cent of boys receive learning support. Head says older boys who join are tested on entry, and the school 'will only take them if we can help them'. Must be able to follow the CE course. One parent described how her son's mild dyslexia was 'picked up on quickly and dealt with'. Another said, 'The school's view is that it shouldn't hold you back and that it's not a problem.'

School has an enviable reputation in sport but 'this can be a bit of a drawback,' says DA, 'as that is all people see'. Super sports facilities with playing fields stretching away as far as the eye can see and top notch indoor pool. Not particularly rugby focused, this is more of a football school, which head says is a bit easier and therefore more inclusive. Sport compulsory, but 'There are other things,' says the head, if sport is not a boy's favourite pastime. Many teams in all sports so room for every keen player, regardless of talent. Major sporting successes at national and county level in all sports in U13 and U11 age groups. Music is strong and important – well over a third of boys learn an instrument, there's a choir, an orchestra and various ensemble groups. After school clubs include judo, golf, gardening, chess and kayaking, which takes place on the river.

Strong pastoral care system: room for every kind of talent and personality here – each boy is appreciated for his individual character. Boys in their final year wear white shirts so that the younger boys know who to talk to if they want help. Code of conduct drawn up by a committee of pupils encompasses such values as respect, helpfulness, and sharing. Each half term, a pupil from each class is nominated by his peers to be the keeper of the code, embracing the values of the code 'without being a goody-goody,' says the head. Discipline has improved as a result of these measures – 'The boys feel as if they have ownership of the rules rather than them being imposed'. Zero tolerance for bullying.

A vibrant, happy, atmosphere. Boys polite and well mannered. Parents from a mixture of backgrounds, though most not short of money.

Pembridge Hall School

18 Pembridge Square, London, W2 4EH

• Pupils: 400 girls • Ages: 4-11 • Non-denom • Fees: £14,595 pa
• Independent

Tel: 02072 290 121
Fax: 020 7792 1086
Email: contact@pembridgehall.co.uk
Website: www.pembridgehall.co.uk

Principal: Since January 2010, Mr Barry H Evans, previously principal of the Falcons Schools in West London, where he oversaw the running of the three schools. Prior to this head of a co-educational prep school in London, having also taught at Westminster Under School and in California.

He believes all girls should be treated as individuals to enable them to meet their academic goals and, even more importantly, to ensure that they develop a love of learning, on which to build the foundations for their success in all areas of life.

Entrance: Names down at birth and long waiting lists. Girls join at rising five with no academic assessment, though these take place in the first few weeks and then again at the end of the first year, so parents get an early warning of potential problems and appropriate support/ action can be taken. Dyslexia and dyspraxia catered for, but if your daughter needs dedicated specialist help, she should look elsewhere.

Exit: About 20 per cent to boarding schools such as Downe House, Wycombe Abbey, St Mary's Ascot; the rest to London day schools – Francis Holland and Godolphin and Latymer most popular at present, followed by St Paul's and Latymer Upper.

Remarks: Split between two Georgian townhouses just above Notting Hill Gate, sandwiching Wetherby's (another Alpha Plus owned school – Pembridge Hall was bought by this venture capital group in 2002) between the kindergarten to 8+ at number 18 and the new upper school at number 10. The littlest ones had a hand in selecting the colours for the lower school so bright hues prevail – the decision to paint the upper school in more neutral colours also came from the girls. Some passed on their mothers' wisdom – 'You should live in a house before you decide what colour to paint it'! However Claes Oldenburg inspired papier-mâché objects hanging from the ceiling and art on all walls enliven the space.

Form teachers for the lower school with specialist ones for French, IT, music (orchestra, string group, and recorder ensemble), drama, art, PE and swimming. Small gyms in the upper and lower school (the latter doubles as a dining room, girls can talk after finishing the first course), other facilities at Perks Field, Porchester Baths and Avondale tennis and netball courts. Year 3 walk to the upper school to use the sparkling new science lab. Number 10 also has an impressive sky-lit artroom and a well equipped IT lab. The senior and junior libraries both have thumb recognition pads to register book loans – it must make borrowing books more exciting.

Desk checks are carried out by head in upper school – the headgirl chooses the week's tidiest classroom and is also responsible for collecting house points from each classroom. The four houses meet four times a term – their focuses, apart from points, are the swimming gala and charity fundraising.

Parents live locally and are international. Many are in banking or high flying business and their girls are dropped off at school in tinted Range Rovers, sometimes by chauffeurs. Fewer Notting Hill media types send their girls here than in recent years, but the traditional Pembridge Hall reputation still holds with senior schools. The girls are polite, smiling, well-behaved and love it at PH – they especially enjoy the clubs and trips to Devon and France. One parent noticed a massive increase in her daughter's confidence just weeks after she entered the school. Another felt hers was not stretched broadly in later years – a concentration on maths and English at 11 plus, since these are what the London day schools focus on for entry. Reports of extra tutoring bought in by parents in order to achieve first choices (no school is exempt from this).

A friendly, secure and successful non-selective school. Suits a child of average intelligence perfectly, but could do more to keep the brightest ones active and engaged.

Perrott Hill School

North Perrott, Crewkerne, Somerset, TA18 7SL

• Pupils: 110 boys and 90 girls; 50 boarders - full and weekly • Ages: 3-13
• Fees: Day £4,095-£12,135; Boarding £14,835-£18,345 pa • Independent

Tel: 01460 72051
Fax: 01460 78246
Email: admissions@perrotthill.com
Website: www.perrotthill.com

Head: Since January 2009, Mr Robert Morse BEd (late thirties). Previous incarnations include house mastering at Mount House and deputy head at St Anselm's, where he was extremely popular and much appreciated by parents and pupils. 'Warm, welcoming and wise beyond his years,' comments one experienced head; 'an excellent listener to all ages' – a parent. 'He has had a hugely beneficial impact' – the experienced registrar of a famous public school, adding, 'The Perrott Hill pupils who come to us have retained the wonder of childhood instead of parading themselves as young adults. A traditional prep school of the best sort.' None of this surprised us or the parents to whom we spoke. 'Can't fault him,' sums up their response. 'I'm lucky enough to have worked under great headmasters and if I have inculcated any good ideas, they are borrowed from them,' says the head modestly. But it's the selection that is important. 'I count myself very fortunate to have inherited such a happy and committed staff.'

He is also extremely lucky, as he readily volunteers, to have such a super wife in Lottie. A fine artist (they met at Bedford Modern, where she was artist in residence) she does some team teaching in the art department, produces plays, is a generous hostess to pupils, staff and parents, possessed of a friendly, bubbly personality and fully and sensitively involved in the running of the school. Together they are a wonderful couple and one of the reasons why the school has such a genuinely cheerful family feel about it. Other reasons as well – they are blissfully happy at Perrott Hill. 'We love it here,' they almost chorus. 'A small school like this is like an extension of a boarding house and everyone is so friendly.' Their two young children, Daisy and Harry, are also very happy to be in the school, as is their black labrador, Nell. One parent volunteered how delightful Daisy and Harry are – 'Like their parents – no side.'

Entrance: Pupils may enter aged three, when they will spend two years on the Montessori foundation course before joining years one and two and thence the prep school. In fact boys and girls may join at any stage, providing room. We met a girl who had joined aged 11 and found it 'very easy to settle in'. No formal test but taster days, then, 'Providing we feel we can do a good job with them, we'll offer a place'. Staff refer any concerns to the excellent learning support team and the children are given help and encouragement when necessary. Scholarships and bursaries are available – do ask.

Exit: Currently the most popular destinations are the three Taunton schools, Sherborne (boys' and girls'), Leweston, Bryanston, Canford and King's Bruton, but that list only tells part of the story. Eton, Winchester and Radley have featured, as have many others. Pupils regularly win a good spread of scholarships and the school prides itself on matching children with appropriate senior schools, something appreciated by parents and registrars.

Remarks: Once you reach the pretty village of North Perrott you need to keep a sharp look out for a small sign to the school. Driving down the lane shuttered with branches, do not cease from exploration nor be deterred by the road sign that informs you are following a dead end: remember this is Eliot country, where 'In my end is my beginning' – there is nothing dead about Perrott Hill. Through beautifully kept gardens and past the converted stables, you will then come to what was the manor house, built in 1878 by the architect Thomas Wyatt, described by Mark Girouard as 'tireless and tedious'. The house itself is much of the first and nothing of the latter. It has been adapted marvellously since it became a school during the second world war and the children love it. Wonderful big L-shaped hall which acts as an assembly room/chapel and library – though plans are in process to move the library to the Orangery. Plans for an Astroturf, too, but it's library first. Bravo! When we visited a blazing log fire, much enjoyed by children and staff. A superb focal point, where everyone can congregate and chatter.

Most boarding schools trumpet their 'family atmosphere' – here it is the real thing. Part of the reason is that twelve members of staff live with the 45 boarders (the numbers have just about tripled in the last three years). The headmaster has appointed an excellent head of boarding who is overall responsible. He and his wife look after the boys; a junior housemistress and experienced matron look after the girls. The dormitories have recently been painted and new showers and loos. Each house has a commonroom, more like a family room, with inviting chairs for lolling around, television and facilities for making toast and hot chocolate. Staff, including three gappers, and children mingle happily together all under the same roof – that's family atmosphere.

Full boarding, weekly boarding and flexi-boarding are all available, but the increasing popularity of boarding has made flexi-boarding harder to come by. Exeats from Friday pm to Sunday evening every three weeks; in between family Sundays where the boarders eat with the staff and generally behave as they would at home, sometimes going to the nearby beach, local town for shopping or to the cinema. Also massively popular activity Sundays, themed and varied. When we visited they were gearing up for a circus weekend when they were going to learn juggling and other activities. The children are extremely enthusiastic about them and parents talked of the need for booking up well in advance. From Year 5 all pupils attend Saturday school: morning lessons and games in the afternoon. Matches take place most Wednesdays and Saturdays.

This ambitious programme would be impossible without a fizzy, dedicated staff. We saw some terrific teaching. No interactive white boards – just interactive teaching, supported by projectors and intelligent use of computers.

Extra curricular activities with staff seem boundless and the mutual affection and respect between staff and pupils are extraordinary. One youngish teacher in response to a question about moving on replied, 'This school is a graveyard for ambition. Why on earth leave this?' Too much of a comfort zone? Results and attitudes don't support that suspicion and besides, the head is watching. This is an active and positive school, not a sanatorium for professional skivers. As one parent told us, 'The head is very approachable, but he's also very sharp on detail and doesn't miss much.' 'I'm unashamedly a stickler for good manners and endlessly chip away at the business of opening doors, greeting people with eye to eye contact and encouraging courtesy' – he's done some good chipping: the children (and staff) are friendly and forthcoming, wearing their manners like well worn clothes and not as strait jackets.

Being a small school, everyone gets involved in all the main activities. Sport is for all and results are impressive. Traditional games are played on five afternoons a week and the school regularly punches above its weight. A number of pupils go on to represent the county and some regularly win sporting awards to public schools. Drama, too, is enormously popular, as is public speaking, art and music, with over 70 per cent learning musical instruments. Facilities are good without being flashy – indeed some of the teaching buildings are a trifle scruffy. The science lab, for instance, is very basic, but the children and parents we spoke to were enthusiastic about the education offered there. Plans are in place to upgrade the lab, but that won't improve the teaching. Another area which is distinctly cramped is the art and DT departments, housed in the old hayloft above the converted stables. Being a listed building expansion is restricted, but no restrictions on the creative energy and ingenuity of the young artists. Everyone has two lessons of art a week; scholarships and prizes at local shows confirm the standard achieved in that cramped but lively place with excellent teaching – ask about Captain Pugwash. Most of the classrooms, however, are bright, airy and congenial for their purpose. The music department at the top of the house is well kitted out with practice rooms and computers – music is clearly important.

Two sports halls – as the school grew, the original one proved too small for its original purpose but has been skilfully converted into a spacious and well used theatre; a larger one was opened recently with space for indoor hockey, cricket nets, netball, fencing – you name it. Outside, tennis courts (hard and grass), a heated swimming pool and good games pitches – though ideally more. The house is surrounded by 25 acres of woodland and scrub where children muck about happily in boiler suits (sic), construct dens, invent games and on occasions in the summer enjoy what the pizza cob offers. On the day we visited, a seal would have longed for shelter, but it's not hard to imagine the fun and laughter ('the children in the apple tree') echoing round the gardens and woodlands in this idyllic spot. No wonder Perrott Hill boys and girls 'retain the wonder of childhood'.

But in order for children to feel really happy and fulfilled, they need to be loved and secure within a clear framework. Each child is assigned a tutor who closely monitors work and morale; a clearly defined Circle of Friendship addresses any unhappiness. Staff and pupils are alert to any evidence of bullying (neither of our guides could remember any) and every week the staff discuss the work and happiness of every pupil. In addition to the resident matrons, another matron comes in every weekday afternoon to help with anyone who is feeling ill or 'just feels like a chat' – all part of the family.

For many the start of the Perrott adventure takes place in the pre-prep, safely and excitingly housed in the cleverly converted stable block close to the big house. There, using the Montessori method, they learn to learn, gaining in confidence and, while safe behind the gates, use the appropriate facilities of the prep school. 'It's lovely having them around,' said a senior girl.

Parents whom we asked spoke appreciatively of the coach service (the school runs three minibuses) not only because of the convenience but also because of the personal service. The three excellent groundsmen, who have been at the school for ages, know the children well and will go out of their way to make special and individual arrangements. One father talked of his amused delight at watching one of the drivers delivering his two young sons with one tucked under each arm, an image which in many ways sums up the joy of Perrott.

We have never come across such universal appreciation of a school. It's hard to find fault with this idyllically placed and excellently run 'traditional prep school', and we failed miserably. One parent told us that at the start of each term he murmurs, 'And all shall be well and all manner of things shall be well.'

Perse Girls Junior School

Linked to Stephen Perse Sixth Form College (The) in the Senior section
Linked to Stephen Perse Foundation/Perse Girls in the Senior section

St Eligius Street, Cambridge, Cambridgeshire, CB2 1HX

• Pupils: 140 girls • Ages: 7-11 • Non-denom • Fees: £11,610 pa
• Independent

Tel: 01223 346140
Fax: 01223 346141
Email: juniorschool@perse.cambs.sch.uk
Website: www.persegirls.com

Head: Since 2007, Miss Katie Milne BEd (geography and education). Taught at the school for over twenty years before taking on headship. Pleasantly professional – 'strict but not frightening,' said a parent. Promoting the school is an important part of her role and she's an impressively quick-thinking relayer of information. No longer teaches on a daily basis but says the hall, when she takes assemblies, is her classroom. Keen supporter of international links and eco friendly projects – school recently raised money to fund the planting of twenty trees on a site outside Cambridge.

Entrance: Testing in English, maths and verbal reasoning – plus informal interview. They're looking for lateral thinking, sparky children who have a high interest in school life. (Annual rearrangement of forms prevents fixed groupings and helps those who arrive in Years 5 and 6 to fit in.) Bursaries 'for those who demonstrate particular potential – but whose families cannot afford the fees'.

Exit: Nearly all to the senior school. Plenty of warning if child won't be able to cope – according to the head, when this is the case, most parents intuitively know their daughter would be better off in a less rigorous environment.

Remarks: This place has the same DNA as its big sister round the corner – a blank exterior hides a world of tip-top learning and bright young things. Inside the gate a prominent plaque proclaims 'Welcome' in an abundance of languages – testimony to the school's desire to be outward looking. Parents are happy with the 'traditional but fun approach' to work which, according to one mum, 'just keeps on coming'. Homework, revision and exams are a fact of life – head says they're 'stepping stones for moving through the school'. Preferred learning styles are identified and supportive staff boost self-confidence – an independent approach is encouraged. 'They gave our daughter an enthusiasm for learning and she just loves her work.' Cross-curricular links are central – check out 'Persephone' (school mag) for some impressive examples. French from day one and Spanish from Year 4 – for fun the whole school played a game of bingo, in Spanish. Learning support co-ordinator gives small group or individual support. Only those with the mildest needs will survive.

Music is valued and instrumental tuition is compulsory – offer of free group sessions in violin or cello for Year 3, but if nothing appeals it has to be the recorder. Sport happens but tends to be squished into a full timetable – head says competitive events (sports day and house competitions) and that the number of fixtures has increased. 'Drop in' clubs at lunchtime for the especially keen – philosophy, debating and Latin are alternatives.

Girls are expected to be smart and polite and, according to a parent, are 'very happy in an ordered sort of way'. Plenty of girlishness and steam letting in the playground – hush returns in an instant when the bell rings for lessons. Everyone has school lunch. Break time snack trolley sells only fruit, juice, milk and water – a tad un-eco to sell bottled water but school says it's at parents' request. Pay as you go breakfast for those who arrive early.

A tight site (they use senior school sports facilities and a nature reserve near the Cam) but the school building doesn't feel cramped. Recent refurbishment has given something that's generally light and airy. Well-stocked library (with friendly full time librarian), computer suite, art, DT and food technology room, somewhere for the kiln and a cleverly designed hall which doubles as a dining area. Outside a small playground (head hopes it will be given a makeover), a climbing wall and two delightful courtyard gardens – one for peace and quiet; the other a memorial for a member of staff – this is where cake and juice are shared by those, including staff, who've had their birthday in the month just gone.

The Perse Pelican Nursery and Pre-Preparatory School

Linked to Perse Preparatory School (The) in the Junior section
Linked to Perse Upper School (The) in the Senior section

92 Glebe Road, Cambridge, Cambridgeshire, CB1 7TD

• Pupils: boys and girls • Ages: 3-7 • Fees: £5,547-£10,377 pa • Independent

Tel: 01223 403940
Fax: 01223 403941
Email: pelican@perse.co.uk
Website: www.perse.co.uk/pelican

Head: Mrs S Waddington, BSc (Hons) MA PGCE.

Remarks: Parents cannot speak too highly of the Pelican. Deserves its reputation as one of the hardest schools to get into for the best possible reasons. Lovely, affectionate and happy environment.

The Perse Preparatory School

Linked to Perse Pelican Nursery And Pre-Preparatory School (The) in the Junior section
Linked to Perse Upper School (The) in the Senior section

Trumpington Road, Cambridge, Cambridgeshire, CB2 8EX

• Pupils: 190 boys, 80 girls • Ages: 7-11 • Non-denom • Fees: £12,153 pa • Independent

Tel: 01223 403 920
Fax: 01223 403 921
Email: prep@perse.co.uk
Website: www.perse.co.uk/prep

Head: Mr Gareth Jones.

Entrance: By entrance tests.

Exit: Most pupils will transfer to The Perse Upper School.

Remarks: For details, see senior school.

Phoenix School

Linked to University College School Junior School in the Junior section
Linked to University College School in the Senior section

36 College Crescent, London, NW3 5LF

• Pupils: 140 girls and boys • Ages: 3-7 • Non-denom
• Fees: £8,250-£12,090 pa • Independent

Tel: 02077 224 433
Fax: 020 7722 4601
Email: thephoenix@ucs.org.uk
Website: www.ucs.org.uk/the-phoenix.html

Head: Since 2007, Mrs Lisa Mason-Jones, previously head of the pre-prep at St Columba's College, St Albans. Taught at St Albans High School for Girls whilst completing a master's in education and management.

Entrance: Two main entries, each taking equal numbers of boys and girls. The 'Cygnets' afternoon sessions nursery class takes children whose third birthday falls between September and December. Another 20 (with birthdays at any time of year) join them a year later to make two 3+ nursery classes of 16 each, attending for five mornings and two afternoon sessions. Register in January 18 months before admission. Most places go to siblings or to those with University College School (UCS) connections (e.g. brother or sister at the school). Occasional vacancies at 4+, 5+ or 6+; prospective pupils are invited for a half-day assessment.

Exit: Most boys go to UCS Junior School at seven, subject to passing the entrance exam. Girls are also expected to stay till they are seven and most move on to South Hampstead High's junior dept or Highgate. A few pupils to, e.g., Westminster Under School, North London Collegiate, North Bridge House, Academy School.

Remarks: Was purchased by the UCS foundation in 2002 as its pre-prep and benefits from sharing the funding and facilities. Compact site up above the Finchley Road near Swiss Cottage, which nevertheless includes a hall, art room, music room, library and playgrounds with sand pits, climbing frame and wendy house, as well as classrooms. Children also use the junior branch ICT suite and the senior school swimming pool and theatre and spend an afternoon a week at the UCS playing fields in West Hampstead.

Specialist music, art and PE teachers. Before and after school clubs include ballet, yoga, tae kwon do, Mandarin and art. Plenty of visitors and trips to, e.g., museums and art galleries. Takes part in the UCS literary festival, Beyond Words, with author visits, circus skills and ballet classes.

Can cope with mild special needs, e.g. dyslexia. But though the school is not a hothouse – 'We don't do never-ending practice exam papers' – it has a strong academic focus and prepares well for the next stage.

The Pilgrims' School

3 The Close, Winchester, Hampshire, SO23 9LT

• Pupils: 250 boys. 80 full/weekly board, the rest day and day boarding • Ages: 4-13 • C of E, but all welcome • Fees: Boarders £18,690; Day £14,775; Pre-prep £8,490 pa • Independent

Tel: 01962 854 189
Fax: 01962 843 610
Email: info@pilgrims-school.co.uk
Website: www.thepilgrims-school.co.uk

Headmaster: Since 1997, The Reverend Dr Brian A Rees BA BD DipMin PhD (fifties). A Canadian, he studied child psychology, computing and religious studies at McGill University, then a master's degree and doctorate in church history at St Andrews, Scotland. Trained as a banker and then a priest in Canada, curacy in Canada, then to Bedford School as chaplain, then housemaster, then head of Bedford Preparatory School, where his charm and enthusiasm for PR wowed potential parents.

Wants boys to feel glad each morning and have a sense of accomplishment each evening. Teaches RS to Year 6. Comes across as a little otherworldly and ethereal but is praised by parents as 'superb, kind and compassionate'. Married to Susan and has three children. School owned by the Chapter of Winchester Cathedral; board of governors has representatives from the Cathedral and the College but also from education, business and the local community.

Entrance: Test at 7 for ordinary mortals, in English, maths, perceptual and verbal reasoning, and 'other such tests and activities as may prove helpful in determining readiness to begin at The Pilgrims'. A bit of football, music, art may be thrown in while the little chaps are 'observed'. Says it's looking not only for the most academically able but also for bright-eyed all-rounders and team players. Still, no getting around the fact that this is a very academic prep school (see Exit).

Day places usually oversubscribed and boarding increasingly so. Singing auditions for choristers (who sing in the Cathedral) and quiristers (who sing in the Winchester College chapel) in November or by individual appointment at other times. Boys will be aged seven to 10 (many come at eight when choral foundation scholarships kick in). One audition for both; parental views on the different musical and life styles (public and committed for Cathedral, private for College), and different vocal requirements (bigger, purer for Cathedral, top line in full for College), usually decide who goes where; no difference in kudos. 'It is expected that successful candidates will stay at the school until 13; the first year is regarded as probationary.' Half boarding fees for these, plus means tested bursaries if needed.

Boys come from St Swithun's Prep, Prince's Mead, Twyford and state schools locally, plus from London and abroad. Since September 2007 has had its own pre-prep taking boys and girl siblings from age four, to accommodate demand and provide a 'Pilgrims' style of education' for the tiny tots, so not so much catch-up when they come to the main school. Will also be handy in competing with

Winchester's other main prep school, Twyford, which runs its own pre-prep.

Exit: Up to half to Winchester – some years more than half (40 awards here in nine years). Sends some to Eton, Charterhouse, Sherborne and Canford plus ones or twos elsewhere. Most definitely does not like boys to leave at 11. 56 music scholarships in the last 10 years.

Remarks: Traditional prep school in the most glorious site in the shadow of Winchester Cathedral (tourists milling round). School (and its previous incarnations) originally for the 22 choristers who sing in the Cathedral. Present school founded in 1931 to add 'commoners' and turn what had been a choir school into a 'proper' prep; the 16 quiristers (pronounced kwiristers), who have sung in Winchester College Chapel since 1383, joined the school in 1965. 'A magnificent place,' said an experienced parent.

Music strong – 185 boys learn at least one instrument, and music scholarships are regularly won. Two choirs of its own. Wonderful rooms for class music lessons and music technology. 'They emerge,' said a mother, 'as little professionals.' The boy who showed us around was in the running for BBC Young Chorister of the Year, an award that has been won by Pilgrims' boys several times in recent years. Members of the two professional choirs (except the probationers) do not take part in extra-curricular clubs/activities but do participate fully in sport and regularly represent the school in teams.

Academics strong – French from reception, Latin from Year 6; streaming, setting and differentiation within years and subjects; final years divided into CE, scholarship and Winchester entrance sets. An impressive staff room – a good many young and female, good teaching; head wants teachers to be the best in the UK at their disciplines. The most able boys are encouraged (strongly) to reach the highest academic standards but school is careful not to overcook those not headed for Winchester or Eton. Assessment card filled in for each pupil every three weeks – keeps close tabs on progress. SEN as much for the gifted as for the struggling – one exceptional Year 3 boy was attending Year 7 lessons when we were there. Short term one-to-one support helps boys with academic snags but definitely not a school for boys with true learning or behavioural problems. Class sizes up to 19 or 20 in younger years but smaller at the top of the school.

Sport strong – 12 teams out on the average weekend. Football, rugby, hockey, cricket, swimming/water polo and athletics are the main ones but has full use of Winchester College's sports complex (25m pool, squash, fives, dojo etc). Boys also go 'tolling' (urban cross country running). Parents tell us that, by and large, the luminaries of the school excel in either sport, academics or music. Of course, some boys will be none of these, so for them occasional scope for disappointment.

In previous editions we have said the school had a 'split' feeling between choristers, quiristers and commoners, but we certainly did not find this the case this time – many close friendships across these lines and all the boys are mixed together for most of the day. School day for day pupils: 8.15am to 4.40pm, then hobbies hour (known as 'Commoners', as the singers are singing at this point) till 6pm, then supper and prep. Day pupils can go home at 4.45pm but plenty stay on for activities. Saturday school from Year 4 until noon for juniors and 3.30pm for seniors – unless in a match that goes on later. Half day on Wednesdays plus matches.

Uniform for most is Lovat-green sweaters, grey trousers or shorts, but choristers wear red sweaters and quiristers blue ('so we can easily spot who needs to go where,' says head). Buildings an interesting squashed hodgepodge from wonderful medieval Pilgrims' Hall, in which pilgrims were thought to rest from their exertions at St Swithun's shrine (now the school hall – note the ancient hammer-beam roof) to tasteful modern buildings put up to house classrooms, labs, IT etc. Inviting library and art and ceramics rooms. Glass eight-sided 'Octagon' used for junior assemblies and drama (a junior and senior school play each year). Traditional dining hall with family service. 75th anniversary development opened September 2007 comprising pre-prep, new heated outdoor pool and changing rooms, Design technology and ICT suite.

As the number of boys' boarding preps shrinks year by year, it is a pleasure to see a school where boarding is agreeable, flexible (without being 'flexi') and popular (even at the bottom end of the school). Dormitories in middle of school particularly jolly with 8 or 9 boys to a room – lots of furry animals and nice showers. Twenty-eight also sleep in the 'Q School' just down the road. Boarding numbers plump at moment, especially since Twyford ended full boarding. Most go home on Sundays but a dozen or more boys will be in all weekend – NB not enough to make it an easy school for expat parents. Year 8 boys have own study room – 'Toys' – with individual cubicles. Younger boarders have supervised prep in classrooms. Music rooms and practice cells in what was probably the stables – incredible old oak. River in the grounds – senior boys have fishing rights. Adventure playground and all-weather court floodlit for fun at all times of year.

A fine school all round. Despite rarefied atmosphere, boys lively and jolly, courteous and smart. Culture is one of developing excellence and the talented will go far.

Pinewood School

Bourton, Shrivenham, Wiltshire, SN6 8HZ

• Pupils: 230 boys and girls (55/45) of whom 90 board, 30 weekly (but see below) and 100 flexi (but they must commit to particular days throughout the term), rest day. Plus pre-prep and nursery: 115 boys and girls, all day • Ages: 3-13 • C of E • Fees: Day £7,215-£13,875; Weekly Boarding £15,555-£17,625 pa • Independent

Tel: 01793 782 205
Fax: 01793 783 476
Email: office@pinewoodschool.co.uk
Website: www.pinewoodschool.co.uk

Head: Since 2002, Mr Philip Hoyland BEd (forties), educated at The Downs in Malvern (a prep school started by his grandfather, which he owned whilst there as a ten year old!), followed by Cheltenham College. He read English and education at Exeter and teaches the top set English. Previously housemaster, then a deputy head at The Dragon, he started his teaching career at Ludgrove, where he met and married Henrietta (who was under matron at the time). They have three children, two boys and a girl, the youngest having just left Cheltenham, plus a 'black lab and a mad springer spaniel'. Henrietta is head of girls.

Outgoing and charming, but do not be fooled by his casual red jersey and socks approach. A school with firm discipline but, following his Quaker great grandfather George Cadbury's belief, he is keen 'to allow each child to be an individual'. He arrived following a period of turmoil – the school was failing, with distinct lacks of both confidence and pupils. All that has changed. Difficult to get him out of the pre-prep as a profusion of children hung onto any limb available. Collecting mothers equally insistent on attention in the car park (though fortunately not quite so keen on limbs).

Entrance: Early registration advised, then by assessment ten months out, with waiting lists at most stages. 'Subject to there being no obvious academic or behavioural problems, a firm offer of a place can be made.' Fair number of children comes up via the nursery and pre-prep but also takes a quantity of Shrivenham children (i.e. parent doing officer training at Joint Services Command and Staff College down the road) and early numbers are subject to variation. Occasional refugees from other, larger, nearby prep schools.

Exit: School lists 36 schools, but primarily Marlborough, Radley, St Edward's Oxford, Cheltenham, 'the odd Etonian'. Also St Mary's Calne, Rendcomb, Tudor Hall, Cheltenham Ladies' College, Stowe, Malvern, Downe House, Abindgon, Heathfield and Dean Close (doing jolly well). Not a hot house but average of nine scholarships per year in last three years. Most proud of all-rounder scholarships: two or three a year. Bumper year in 2010 with 17 scholarships in all, including the top music and academic scholarships at Marlborough.

Remarks: Founded in 1875, moved to this stunning Victorian Cotswold stone house, Rab Butler's cousin's former home, in 1946. A delightful conversion, with vast hall for parents' teas (important here, and open to all, whether their children are in a match or not). Elegant 84 acres of grounds, with terraces and child-proof woods to hide in. Nursery and pre-prep in stable block with fantastic play area for tinies in old walled garden. Family chapel in grounds can only accommodate one year group, so school uses local Bourton church 'as much as possible' to help the infra-structure of the village (Mr Hoyland is on the St James Church PCC and Chairman of the Almshouses). Selection of staff accommodation available round the back.

Splendid, bright, if aseptic, modern teaching block attached to main school, with lots of nooks and crannies, each year group cunningly separated, plus classrooms scattered throughout the school. Outdoor classroom and fairy garden hugely popular in warm weather. Stunning new computer room. Stately drawing room and widescreen TV (which children can watch in the evenings) doubles as a conference/class room. Library now rehoused in renovated Orangery – lots of new books. New changing blocks and state of the art science labs opened with great excitement in 2009. Brand new performing arts centre in full use.

Deceptively relaxed attitude to academia and discipline – French from four, Latin from ten, Greek and philosophy for scholars. Year groups up to 42, three sets 'for academia'. Slight hesitation when we asked about dyslexia – Mr Hoyland 'anxious to protect the academic nature of the school', though OK on the sibling front. Busy SEN department from pre-prep through to Year 8: highly qualified staff – two full time and two part-timers. Dyslexia lessons = extra charge; ditto EFL, but no need for the latter at the moment.

The art room, previously described as 'a bit gaunt', has been recently modified and redecorated and new head of music has overseen redecoration of music school – strong music, drama and art. Huge number of options on offer. Additional charge for extras like music, ballet, fencing and polo, though trips during the working week are included. Flourishing sport with new Astroturf and extended pitches. Pupils grow their own organic veggies and much fuss is made when they are served at lunch; dining room now does three sittings; family feeding and strict eye kept on diet. The Hoylands have jazzed up the fabric of the school and changed the school uniform to blue jerseys with (washable and tumble dry-able) tartan skirts for girls.

A 'gentle, non-materialistic' environment where '12 year old girls regard going roly-poly down the bank as the height of fun' and it is 'important not to fall out of the trees when you climb them', and a place where good manners and kindness matter. Firm on discipline, but currently no theft, vandalism or bullying – 'Three strikes and you are out', and yes, they have been sent home 'for a few days'. Mr Hoyland keeps an open door with wife and PA next door. All Year 8 children are monitors – their responsibilities include keeping an eye on the younger girls and boys. God is 'quietly there', but ecumenical in outlook.

School operates a fortnightly system, where every other weekend is closed. Weekends when the school is open are crammed full of activities: caving, trips to the local Water world (day children can join as well – it makes coach travel cheaper) etc etc. But not a school for boarding children without grannies or guardians in the area, though school will step in if need be. All dorms, recently decorated, are cheerful with teddies and posters, boys on top floor, girls the one below.

Local-ish school: popular down the M4 corridor with collection of London refugees plus Shrivenham, Lambourn and the racing crowd and the Wiltshire green wellie brigade – bussing from Marlborough in the mornings; also the occasional first time buyer.

Pupils and parents happy. Popular, and growing ever more so, but the Hoylands have no intention of expanding beyond the current numbers, as they want to know each child individually and to treat them as such.

Plymouth College Preparatory School

Linked to Plymouth College in the Senior section

Saint Dunstan's Abbey , The Millfields, Plymouth, Devon, PL1 3JL

- Pupils: 250 girls and boys; all day • Ages: 3-11 • C of E
- Fees: £6,450-£8,400 pa • Independent

Tel: 01752 201352
Fax: 01752 201351
Email: prep@plymouthcollege.com
Website: www.plymouthcollege.com

Headmaster: Since 2007, Mr Chris Gatherer (forties), previously deputy head for ten years.

Entrance: On application.

Exit: Majority of students automatically migrate to Plymouth College, no examination or interview is required. Others leave for, e.g., the Devonport High Schools.

Remarks: Moved into its £2 million, newly refurbished, premises in 2004. Head says, 'We are part of a happy community and we take full advantage of being on such a magnificent site.' Wide curriculum and lots of extra-curricular activities.

Polam Hall Junior School

Linked to Polam Hall School in the Senior section

Grange Road, Darlington, County Durham, DL1 5PA

• Pupils: Co-ed nursery up to Year 4. Boys and girls taught separately in Year 5 and 6; boarding from 8+ • Ages: Early Steps 2-5, infants 5-7, juniors 8-11 • Inter-denominational • Fees: Boarding £17,355; Day £6,150-£8,550 pa • Independent

Tel: 01325 463 383
Fax: 01325 383 539
Email: juniorschool@polamhall.com
Website: www.polamhall.com

Head: Mrs A P J Foster.

Remarks: For details see senior school.

Port Regis Preparatory School

Motcombe Park, Shaftesbury, Dorset, SP7 9QA

• Pupils: Pupils: 320 boys and girls (55 per cent boys), 200 board, 120 day • Ages: 7-13. Plus pre-prep (around 50 boys and girls ages 3-7) and nursery with 30 children • C of E
• Fees: Boarding £22,350; Day £17,550 pa • Independent

Tel: 01747 857 800
Fax: 01747 857 810
Email: office@portregis.com
Website: www.portregis.com

Headmaster: Since September 2010, Mr Benedict Dunhill, BA, educated at Caldicott and Cranleigh, where he played 1st XI cricket and hockey and captained the school Eton Fives team, then read French and English at University College, London – spent one year teaching in Le Puy as part of his degree.

Joined S G Warburg in the City, then a business partner in an event management company. Started teaching French at Blundell's, where he was a boarding deputy, member of the marketing committee and master i/c overseas exchanges, plus coached cricket, hockey, Fives and clay pigeon shooting. Obtained PGCE at the University of Sussex while boarding housemaster and French teacher at Worth School, where he chaired a full review of the school's timetable to accommodate the advent of the International Baccalaureate, and also served on the School Chaplaincy Committee to oversee the pastoral and spiritual development of the pupils. Headmaster of Moreton Hall (prep) in Bury St Edmunds in 2004.

His wife, Elizabeth, is fully involved in the school, especially on the pastoral side – previously worked for the World Challenge organisation. Three young children.

Entrance: Interview with the head and school reports – no test. But NB 'Those who would prefer a more sedentary school life with mobile phones, computer games and playstations less likely to be offered a place'. Pupils show up at all ages and in every term. New boarders encouraged to join in the summer term. Academically non-selective, 'But can't be so dyslexic or intellectually challenged that they can't deal with Common Entrance'.

Exit: The Sherbornes (boys' and girls') the top destinations in recent years, followed by Marlborough, Bryanston, Millfield, King's Bruton, Canford. One each to Eton, Winchester, Radley each year. All girls (and boys) stay to 13 – 'They have to be dynamited out at 13!' 104 awards to senior schools in the last four years (41 academic) including to Eton and Winchester. Pre-prep children almost all move up to the main school.

Remarks: Still the best-equipped prep school ever covered by 'The Guide' – all 15 editions. Could pass for a full-scale public school – until you catch sight of the midget inhabitants. This is a school where appearance matters – whether tidiness of uniform, architectural elegance or no tolerance for litter. Newest classroom block opens into a flagstone atrium – much like Trump Towers in New York. Ventilation system designed by Cambridge University: sensors measure temperature and CO_2 levels and control air vents. Eco-friendly, and uses geothermal power – they had to bore an 80m hole. The main school 'mansion' dates from 1894, Victoriana at its most exuberant, built for Baron Stalbridge, younger brother of the first Duke of Westminster. Founded in London by Dr Praetorius in 1881, via Folkestone, Broadstairs (where there was an arch commemorating the landing of Charles II in 1683 – hence Port Regis, gateway of the king), Bryanston, Hertfordshire, and back to Wessex, arriving at Motcombe Park in 1947.

Nursery and pre-prep so delightful that one finds oneself thinking that teaching small children might make a rather agreeable career change. Includes a 'secret door' to enchanting grass area; wonderful rustic 'forest school' built in nearby woods with campfire and range of wooden instruments made and used by the young children (unaccountable whiff of 'The Lord of the Flies' in all this rough hewn woodwork). Has been feeding locals into Port Regis for over 15 years with so far no ill effect on boarding numbers higher up the school.

The whole of the campus has something of Disneyworld's Epcot Centre about it, with its infinite space, range of building styles – from traditional to futuristic – central lake, fountain and geothermal heating experiments. Music building's glass walled recital hall affords leafy wide-angle view over the impeccable grounds – an architectural representation of the school's musical excellence. All 7 year olds learn recorder and 8 year olds wrestle with the violin. Practice time is scheduled for all – even day pupils. Art majestically housed and taken seriously, with pottery, art clubs, design studio, computers – pupils absorbed in concentration as we wandered by. DT lavishly equipped and spread over three rooms. Assembly hall with tiered seating and a stage – used for two plays a term. Next project in the pipeline is to take down some old wooden classrooms and turn the area into a play area for older children. The classrooms will then be recycled into building a cottage to accommodate visiting speakers or parents: very Port Regis.

Gymnasium fully dedicated to gymnastics, including sunken trampoline (IAPS holds its competitions here). Second gym, a full blown sports hall, looking a bit tired now – but most preps would still give their right arm for it. Two squash courts, shooting range, nine hole golf course and 25m indoor pool all taken for granted. 'Takes sport seriously,' said a parent with a gift for understatement. The first XV has made grown men weep, winning all its matches for the last five years. So no pressure then. Football and boys' hockey teams are both regional champions. Girls' hockey and netball both feared throughout the county and beyond. Twelve girls in the England U13 rounders squad in the last three years. Piles of national awards in gymnastics and swimming (top swimmers can train at dawn). Girls returned from the 2008–9 IAPS National Championships with the Overall Best School title for the ninth year in a row. At the other end of the fitness spectrum, effort is made to incorporate all children into a school team every term, 'And we get close to achieving this,' says the head. 109 pupils take ballet lessons (not just girls). 'Funky dance' also on offer.

A proudly non-selective school – academic results are superb, but if you are looking for the intensity of a top London prep, you will not find it. Fabulous at bringing on pupils who are struggling when they arrive. Just under a quarter of pupils (80 out of 350) receive learning support, with two one-to-one lessons per week the norm, and support 'woven through all the lessons'. Head not wild about extra tuition seeping into children's free time: 'They need time to play'. Streaming kicks in at Year 4, plus setting in maths. By Year 6 they are set for everything and top sets are 'watched' for scholarship potential. Most pupils taught Latin from age 10 or 11 – scholars top up with ancient Greek. French the default setting, but can opt for Spanish. Some Japanese and Mandarin available. Creative writing an anomalous strong suit in this famously outdoorsy school: has won the National Prep School Poetry award for three of the last five years and was runner-up in the national Pound a Poem competition. Library virtually perfect, if a tad formal – could be said of much of the school. Smallish class sizes, 19 maximum. Parents praise the teachers to the rooftops, and staff seem content – around 20 have been here more than ten years.

Much emphasis on mealtimes, both for pleasure and as 'a civilising experience'. Younger gourmets eat alongside their teachers to help untangle the finer points of wielding fork and knife. Much the same for the older pupils, but looser reins and they can sit where they like. All catering done in-house, with ingredients provided by local suppliers. Light and airy cafeteria affords 180° views of the grounds. Open invitation to all parents to come to any meal at any time. Tuck shop open two afternoons (maximum purchase one item), plus Sunday evening for penny sweets painstakingly selected and taken away in little paper bags.

A centre of excellence when it comes to boarding, with outstanding pastoral care. A whopping 17 gap students help keep the wheels greased, and the majority of staff live within the school, so people around at all hours and the school never feels like the 'Marie Celeste' at weekends. School never closes except half terms. Local boarders can go home from after games on Saturday until Monday morning, often towing along a school friend or two. No official flexi-boarding, but flexibility, e.g. local pupils can 'ease into boarding' three nights a week. Younger pupils sleep in the main school 'mansion'. Mainly large dorms of around ten beds to a room, neat as a pin. Formality punctured by fizzy touches of personality like the Che Guevara and 'Borat' posters on one ten year old's wall. Posh senior girls' houses with beaded entryway and the unparalleled extravagance of 12 individual rooms with basin – in a prep school! (Doors only shut with house parent's permission, though, so operates much like a large dorm.) Senior boys much the same. The 'Day Room' – an inspired dog's body of a room – is manned 8am till 9pm as a sort of communications hub. It's where children are collected, notes handed in and telephone messages passed.

Children mainly confident and competitive. Two thirds of pupils hail from within an hour's drive (many live on the doorstep) with around 25 from London. 25 overseas pupils from a wide range of countries (the States, Korea, France, Spain, Hong Kong, Singapore, Nigeria, Iran) and 65 expat kids ('Cayman Islands lawyers', FCO and Services) plump up the boarding numbers. English taught to 17 overseas pupils – 'occasionally from scratch'. Former pupils: Zara and Peter Phillips, Prince Rashid El Hassan (son of the Crown Prince of Jordan), Jasper Conran, Tim Payne and Nick Greenstock (current and recent England rugby players). Some superfab former parents, e.g. Georgie Fame, Barry Humphreys and the lead singer with Iron Maiden, Bruce Dickinson.

All scholarship winners means-tested: no automatic financial award. Bursaries for poor gifted children but also for the occasional average child who would benefit from a Port Regis education. Hardship fund for extreme cases parcelled out scrupulously.

One or two parents felt that with so many talented children knocking about, it is possible for a good sportsman to end up on a third team or a bright child to fail to make the scholarship set cut. But if any substantial fault can be found – and believe us, it's not easy – it would be that the school is almost too wunderbar – 'Do eight year olds really appreciate the chemical-free swimming pool and amazing Astro?' asked one mother wryly. 'The real problem is that every senior school we've looked at is going to be downhill from what we have here.'

The Portsmouth Grammar Junior School

Linked to Portsmouth Grammar School (The) in the Senior section

High Street, Portsmouth, Hampshire, PO1 2LN

• Pupils: 455 plus 50 in nursery; two thirds boys, all day • Ages: 2 ½ -11
• Christian non-denom • Fees: £7,329-£8,379 pa • Independent

Tel: 023 9236 4219
Email: jsadmissions@pgs.org.uk
Website: www.pgs.org.uk

Head: Since December 2010, Mr Peter Hopkinson, previously head of Arnold Junior School in Blackpool. Read communication studies at Sheffield and was previously head of the junior/infant department of Abbey Gate College, Chester. Married with two young children, enjoys walking with his family, reading and playing the guitar and ukulele.

Entrance: At four children attend a play afternoon to familiarise themselves with the school. During the following week they spend an hour each with the head of the junior school and the head of foundation stage and are assessed, using tests compiled by educational psychologists to identify academic potential. No need to read or write, but does like to see an ability to follow instructions – questions might include, e.g., point to the red square, or put the smallest brick on top. The assessment is not much of a hurdle in securing one of the 60 places, but children are occasionally turned away: 'We are trying to decide if the school will suit the child until they are 18'. January entrance tests at seven (20 places) in maths (no calculators), English and verbal reasoning, plus interview. Places may be available in other years too. A wodge of pupils from Glenhurst Pre-prep and elsewhere enter in Year 3. Children also enter in Years 4, 5 and 6 if space allows.

Exit: 11+ tests in maths, English and VR must be passed in September of Year 6 to gain entry to the senior school. Virtually all pass, but the tests must be worked towards and are no rubber stamp. The rare child who does not pass heads for 'an independent school with lower expectations'.

Remarks: Extremely well thought out programme – ticks along purposefully.

Nursery tucked round the back of PGS is a magical place brilliantly led by Lois Johnson. Assertively play-based with a hint of Montessori. Hugely well thought out, based around 'imagination rooms' that focus on numbers, books, building, craft, plus outside play. Like many of the best nurseries we see, maintains its own powerful identity, quite separate from the main school. Slightly more boys than girls. Outdoor play area not its strong point, but they make the most of the sheltered and roomy chunk of al fresco that they have been allotted.

Reception to Year 4 lives in hived off section of main school site – younger brothers and sisters greet their hulking teenage brethren over the wooden play train that separates the communities. Emphasis on spelling, a 'blitz' on joined up lettering and much work on extended writing. Outside the children enjoy a glorified primary school set up and senior school children wander through the front playground. Extremely nice, sheltered back play area. Years 5–6 in cheery separate building outside main school and over two zebra crossings (home to the entire grammar school once upon a time). No grass but unusually pleasant tarmac. Lunches eaten in main school dining hall.

Three forms of 20 in reception, Years 1 and 2. Expands to four forms of up to 24 in Years 3–6. SATs taken at end of Years 2 and 6 so school can monitor achievement. No quarter given on academics – would prefer to drop to three forms rather than take in children who have not met the academic standard. Daily assembly. Smart uniforms, although there appear to be mechanical problems with the fit of the little girls' kilts. French from Year 3 upwards. SEN provided from lowest level – just keeping an eye on a straggler – to pupils receiving two sessions of learning support per week, to children with educational psychologist's report, for whom outside help may be brought in.

Many extra-curricular activities including girls' football and ballroom dancing club. All Year 3s receive a term's free violin tuition. Year 4s get a term's free tuition on a brass or woodwind instrument and a free week's sailing. Other activities offered for a fee, e.g., ballet, judo, karate and Mandarin. Indoor pool used in summer term up to Year 4. Older children swim off site. Games twice a week – one morning session, plus a Wednesday afternoon schlep out to the school playing fields at Hilsea – plus PE. Upper juniors have fab food tech, textiles, art and DT rooms. IT suite bang up to date, library inviting. Drama ambitious: each year group from reception to Year 6 produces an annual musical. Drama studio very impressive for a junior school. Saturday mornings children from Year 3 up can attend optional morning of activities, sport (and some matches). Time never wasted – optional, but popular, residential trips mostly take place in holidays so as not to cut into teaching time; children arrive at school in games kit on Wednesday mornings to avoid the kerfuffle of changing later in the day.

Portsmouth High Junior School

Linked to Portsmouth High School in the Senior section

36 Kent Road, Southsea, Hampshire, PO5 3ES

• Pupils: 120 girls, all day • Ages: 3-11 • Non-denom • Fees: Juniors £7,044 pa; Nursery £5,820 pa • Independent

Tel: 023 9282 4916
Fax: 023 9281 4814
Email: headsec@por.gdst.net
Website: www.portsmouthhigh.co.uk

Head: Since September 2010, Mrs Philippa Harris-Burland Mont Dip MA, previously head of Rookesbury Park School.

Entrance: By assessment at 3+ and 4+.

Exit: Virtually all to senior school.

Remarks: Junior school (internally known as Dovercourt), in elegant Thomas Ellis-Owen house two minutes' walk down Kent Road. Old-fashioned, spacious feel – complete opposite of the senior department. New early years building and nursery plus main building recently renovated. Four tennis courts (also used by senior school). Grass playground.

Prebendal School

53/54 West Street, Chichester, West Sussex, PO19 1RT

- Pupils: 155: 85 boys (20 boarding), 70 girls (0 boarding)
- Ages: 3-7 pre-prep; 7-13 prep • C of E
- Fees: Boarding £15,516-£16,194; Day £11,976 pa • Independent

Tel: 01243 772 220
Fax: 01243 771 821
Email: secretary.prebendal@btconnect.com
Website: www.prebendalschool.org.uk

Head: Since 2005, Mr T R Cannell MA BEd. Wife involved with the social life of the school, two children at Cambridge University.

Wide experience of prep schools including being a day master, director of studies and housemaster. Has taught maths and RS through to scholarship level in different schools. Still teaches a few periods a week and helps in the boarding house as a house tutor, as it enables him to know the children better. ISI inspector and member of both IAPS and CSA. Interests include music and sport – playing and watching.

Entrance: By registration, mainly at three into the pre-prep, where children are continually assessed and enter the prep school automatically. Children from outside interviewed and take a baseline assessment test to ensure progress throughout the school can be measured. The main entry to the prep is at seven.

Exit: The majority leaves at 13, a few at 11 – Ardingly, Bedales, Bryanston, Cheltenham Ladies' College, Downe House, Eton, Harrow, Milton Abbey, St Swithun's Winchester, Portsmouth Grammar, Lancing, Winchester, to name but a few. Most pupils get into their first choice school; of late, over half of leavers at age 13 have gained scholarships. Perhaps not inclined to over-exert itself on behalf of the less high-flying alumni whose next schools won't reflect quite so much glory on the leavers' lists.

Remarks: The Prebendal School is the oldest school in Sussex and probably dates back to the foundation of Chichester Cathedral in the eleventh century, when it would have been a 'song school'. Girls were introduced into the school in 1972 and a pre-prep was added in 1996.

The main school building, the thirteenth century schoolhouse, is a rabbit warren of passages and stairs. The classrooms are not particularly enticing but a refurbishment is planned for this year – a bit of the old-fashioned boarding school feel to it, although furnishings have recently been updated. However the new Highleigh Building has provided light and airy classrooms for pupils in Years 2 and 3. Also an assembly hall and an art, design & technology room, a modern science laboratory and an ICT room. The atmosphere around the school is friendly and nurturing – all the pupils play together. A friendly and close-knit community, partly because it is a small school, partly because activities mix year groups. Gets the best out of its children without undue pressure or anxiety and they enjoy their work.

Class sizes average 16. Teaching standards are high – most children seem to leave the school about 18 months ahead of their peer group. Good core of young dynamic staff and a few experienced long-standing staff. Special needs teaching has not been a strong point in the past, but now all who have contact with the SEN department describe it as outstanding. About 15 per cent of the school are on the SEN register – mainly dyslexia. Very well qualified staff with varying specialities; all SEN staff are fully supported by the school; good communication – all departments are aware of individuals' needs.

Communication with parents, on the other hand, has not been especially good, but is being addressed. Links with the cathedral remain very strong and, although pupils of all faiths are welcomed into the school, during the daily life of the school an emphasis on Christianity, with school assemblies held every morning and two days a week in the cathedral. Cathedral choristers are all educated at the school, having entered on scholarships. Music is very strong, around ninety per cent learning one or two instruments, but no-one feels left out or pushed into musical activities.

Extra-curricular activities include fencing, tennis, cooking, camera club, gardening club and swimming. Good flexi system of boarding – only the choristers have to board full time, although many higher up the school choose to do so, especially as the boarding area has recently seen a complete refurbishment. Meals in a canteen – the children say the food is good, a choice of hot dishes and also a salad bar.

Pre-prep department is on a separate site five minutes' walk from the main school. Headmistress is delightful, kind, switched on and very approachable, leading an enthusiastic staff. Small, cosy, nurturing set up, wonderful for the littles. The bigger children in Year 2 occupy two classrooms in the recently built Highleigh Building on the main school site, which affords them more space and eases the transition to the prep. Own, small, play area – nearby park sometimes used. Links with the main school are good, including joining in the cathedral based assemblies, the bigger children go swimming and have various other activities in the main school. Some of the prep teachers teach the top year in pre-prep, also helping the transition.

The parental buzz is of a happy atmosphere with perky, chirpy children. One visiting peripatetic teacher, whilst teaching at many schools, still describes this as 'the favourite', due to the pupils being 'well balanced and upbeat'. Head has much to do in this rather special nook and we watch with interest.

Prospect House School

75 Putney Hill, London, SW15 3NT

- Pupils: 190; 50/50 boys and girls • Ages: 3-11 • Inter-denom
- Fees: £12,210-£12,666 pa • Independent

Tel: 02087 800 456
Fax: 02087 803 010
Email: info@prospecths.org.uk
Website: www.prospecths.org.uk

Head: Since April 2004, Mrs Dianne Barratt BEd MEd (fifties); vast experience and knowledge of young children, having taught across the spectrum in UK and USA, from large challenging state primaries and specialist schools to selective independent preps. Previously deputy head at Croydon High Junior School and acting deputy head of JAPS. Her specialist subjects are psychology and language and literacy teaching. Her management has transformed a once rather shaky Prospect House into a thriving school with a number of outstanding features. Parents say she is a mine of information and does her best to help if a problem, big or small. Her smiling face and enthusiasm for developing the school and children's potential are appreciated by staff and parents. Married with two grown-up daughters who were educated in London day schools, she enjoys running and holidaying in Turkey.

Entrance: Mainly at 3+ nursery and a few places at 4+ reception, waiting list first come first served, non-selective, sibling policy. Thereafter telephone to inquire about occasional vacancies in older age groups. Some scholarships available for children from maintained schools from age 8.

Exit: At 11+, some to boarding schools, mostly to London day schools. Mrs Barratt and her staff are always available to discuss appropriate choices for secondary school transfer with parents. Popular choices include King's College Wimbledon, Hampton, Kingston Grammar, Emanuel, Latymer, Lady Eleanor Holles, Godolphin and Latymer, The Harrodian and Ibstock Place. Pupils are significantly successful in gaining scholarships at 11+.

Remarks: Highly organised and well planned, achieves great things for its pupils without being pushy. Considering the intake is non-selective, this is impressive. Pupils do well across the curriculum, particularly in core subjects, with around 90 per cent achieving level 5 in Year 6. All progress is tracked – personal development as well as academic; extra support is available for strugglers and streaming for maths and English from Year 3. ICT is outstanding, embedded into all subjects, thus adding new dimensions to classroom-based learning. Modern server-based network of Apple Mac equipment, interactive whiteboards throughout, and wireless laptops. First independent school in the country to be awarded an ICT Mark of Excellence by BECTA – has gone on to win best school in the UK for primary ICT. Staff pupil ratio is very high, as is the number of subject specialist teachers.

Good choice of games on offer, with a 'sport for all' policy leading to some many successful fixtures and tournaments. Large purpose built hall for dance, drama and gymnastics; all weather sports pitch and local sports grounds are used for team sports. Musical opportunities are outstanding for a small school – inspiring class music for all taught by a specialist teacher. Traditional methods alongside Suzuki teaching, pupils can choose to play instruments with one of a number of specialist instrumental teachers who visit school. Award-winning choir, several ensembles and school orchestra. Terrific variety of clubs to choose from each term – old favourites – tag rugby and handicrafts – run along with the more unusual archery, wii fit and animation.

SEN is forward thinking – qualified and experienced SENCo with three specialist visiting teachers run a well resourced learning support department. Good links with local speech and occupational therapists, who visit the school as required. Some support and screening is included in the fees, an additional charge is made for one-to-one sessions.

Pupils' well-being and pastoral care are thought to be outstanding. 'Getting home-school contact right is not always easy – this school really tries,' say parents. Active PTA works with the head to organise social and fundraising events. Volunteer parents help to run the school's library. Occupies a compact site at the top of Putney Hill which has been cleverly designed and extended to offer just about everything; however no on-site kitchens, so everyone brings a packed lunch. In 2001 became part of the House Schools Group.

A thriving school for the 21st century doing a great job, with added bonuses of fantastic ICT provision and excellent senior management.

Purcell School Junior Department

Linked to Purcell School in the Senior section

Aldenham Road, Bushey, Hertfordshire, WD23 2TS

• Ages: boys and girls: two thirds board • Non-denom • Fees: Boarding £30,762; Day £24,054 pa • Independent

Tel: 01923 331100
Fax: 01923 331166
Email: info@purcell-school.org
Website: www.purcell-school.org

Head: Mr A Peter Crook MA BMus FRSA ARAM .

Remarks: For details, see senior school.

Putney Park Lower School

Linked to Putney Park School in the Senior section

11, Woodborough Road, London, SW15 6PY

• Pupils: 180 girls, 40 boys • Ages: Girls 4-16, boys 4-8 • C of E
• Fees: £10,281-£11,745 pa • Independent

Tel: 020 8788 8316
Fax: 020 8780 2376
Email: office@putneypark.london.sch.uk
Website: www.putneypark.london.sch.uk

Remarks: See write-up for senior school.

Queen Elizabeth Grammar Junior School (Wakefield)

Linked to Queen Elizabeth Grammar School (Wakefield) in the Senior section

Northgate, Wakefield, West Yorkshire, WF1 3QY

• Pupils: 255 boys • Ages: 7-11 • Inter-denom • Fees: £7,047-£7,692 pa • Independent

Tel: 01924 373 821
Fax: 01924 231 604
Email: camilla.field@wgsf.co.uk
Website: www.wgsf.org.uk

Head: Since September 2007, Mrs Louise Gray.

Remarks: See senior school.

Queen Elizabeth's Grammar Junior School

Linked to Queen Elizabeth's Grammar School in the Senior section

West Park Road, Blackburn, Lancashire, BB2 6DF

• Pupils: 110 girls and boys; all day • Ages: 3-11 • Inter-denom on C of E foundations • Fees: £5,355-£6,819 pa • Independent

Tel: 01254 686 300
Fax: 01254 692 314
Email: headmaster@qegs.blackburn.sch.uk
Website: www.qegs.blackburn.sch.uk

Head of Junior School: Miss Alison Wharmby.

Remarks: Junior school housed in separate building on main QEGS site (formerly known as 'Horncliffe') but uses many senior school facilities – dining hall, swimming pool etc. Early years dept in adjacent building – 'Lawn Bank' – now caters for children aged 3–6. Headed by Mrs Kym Marshall, department buzzes with activity. French now taught in dedicated languages room by qualified senior school language teacher through to Year 6. New on-site extended hours provision (7.45am to 6pm) available as an option for working parents.

Queen Elizabeth's Hospital Juniors

Linked to Queen Elizabeth's Hospital in the Senior section

Berkeley Place, Clifton, Bristol, BS8 1JX

• Pupils: 95 boys • Ages: 7-11 • Non-denominational • Fees: £6,783 pa • Independent

Tel: 0117 930 3087
Email: juniors@qehbristol.co.uk
Website: www.qehbristol.co.uk

Head: Since 2009, Mr Martin Morris (early 50s), graduate of Exeter University, plus BA from the Open University. Married with seven children – wife works at QEH Senior School. Taught at Sedbergh School, Cumbria, for 11 years, moved to Reading as houseparent, then head of Catteral Hall School, Giggleswick (co-educational boarding prep). Head of Kingham Hill School (senior co-ed boarding) for 8 years. Interests principally revolve around sport (particularly cricket, rugby, hockey and running), walking and gardening. Enjoys cooking and reads avidly. Passionately believes in the importance of viewing education as more than just what happens in the classroom.

Entrance: Normally at 7+ or 9+, unless vacancy occurs in other years. Tests in English, mathematics, reasoning and reading plus interview.

Exit: Seamless entry to senior school at 11.

Remarks: Super new junior school opened in September 2007. Filled up immediately: unheard of in our experience – 'only boys' prep in Bristol' explained one parent who wanted her son to move up to QEH anyway. Pleasing accommodation converted from former boarding houses in adjacent Georgian row owned by QEH. Split level classrooms with formal and practical spaces. Lovely Georgian features retained but sparklingly modern throughout. Reading ethos important – great library to reinforce this and selection of books geared to boys' interests. School aims at broad curriculum with plenty of kinaesthetic activity (e.g. design and technology). SENCo (shared with senior school) screens boys on entry and offers support for SpLD etc. Boys get to go on frequent visits and expeditions. Bright and airy art room. Lots of games at Failand plus swimming and PE in gym (three sessions a week) to tire them out. Pleasant music room and ten instruments to choose from for individual music lessons – 75 per cent take-up. Boys love classroom assistants who also run popular after school club until 6pm. Given Bristol's traffic problems a major plus for parents is that they can drop and collect boys safely using adjacent NCP car park for free. 'This facility gives us peace of mind,' say grateful parents. Separate PTA formed for junior school. QEH have come up with a winner – looks set to do well in Bristol's competitive market. 'Our son arrives and leaves each day with a broad smile on his face,' say impressed parents.

Queen Mary's Prep School

Linked to Queen Mary's School in the Senior section

Baldersby Park, Topcliffe, Thirsk, North Yorkshire, YO7 3BZ

• Pupils: 114 girls, variable boarding arrangements. • Ages: 2-11 • C of E (Woodard school) • Fees: Day £5,640-£11,205; Boarding £15,105 pa • Independent

Tel: 01845 575 000
Fax: 01845 575 001
Email: v.robeson@queenmarys.org
Website: www.queenmarys.org

Remarks: See senior school entry.

The Queen's Church of England Primary School

Cumberland Road, Kew, Richmond, Surrey, TW9 3HJ

• Pupils: 420 boys and girls • Ages: 4-11 • C of E • State

Tel: 02089 403 580
Fax: 02089 481 796
Email: info@queens.richmond.sch.uk
Website: www.queens.richmond.sch.uk

Head: Since 2009, Ms Susan Pavlis.

Entrance: Regularly over-subscribed (even though a new non-denominational primary school has opened close by). Siblings get first priority, then one or both parents must be a member of one of the three Kew C of E parishes – applications must be accompanied by a reference from the vicar (word on the ground is that the number of siblings per year affects how important the vicar's reference is), then it depends where you live. No nursery on site so children come from a range of local nurseries including Windham, The Studio, Kew Montessori and The Barn. Worth trying for an odd place further up the school, as there is a mobile business community in the area.

Exit: A jaw-dropping more than 50 per cent of pupils regularly go on to independent schools, and not just any old independent. You are talking tip-top academic schools including The Lady Eleanor Holles, Godolphin and Latymer, St Paul's, Surbiton High, Kingston Grammar, Latymer Upper, Notting Hill and Ealing High, Putney High, Hampton and King's Wimbledon. Even more astounding – there are a few academic and art scholarships each year to these schools (no scholarship board, it's not really politically correct in a state school). Equally impressive each year a handful goes to Tiffin Boys or Girls (top-notch grammar schools in Kingston). Waldegrave Girls Twickenham also attracts five or six each year (but its catchment area regularly changes so it's a risky school to rely on). Christ's C of E School (the most improving state secondary locally) in Richmond is the top choice for the rest. Uniform now goes from reception to Year 4 – much smarter!

Remarks: A huge favourite of the well-heeled chattering classes, who want to send their children on to the best senior schools. Yet Queen's feels like a completely normal, happy, friendly, state primary school – it is rather scruffy (though in pretty and spacious grounds), doesn't boast exceptional facilities and is in an international area – 20 different second languages are spoken.

The secret of its appeal (to the many who would be able to pay for primary education if they felt it necessary) is the desire of the whole school community for the children to do well in all areas – academically, in sport, art, computing or socially. Add in the remarkable array of senior schools that the children go on to, and it is no wonder that Queen's is the most talked about school in this area.

The large number of pupils aiming for top notch senior schools does affect the character of the place – one mother described it as her 'free prep school', but this is wide of the mark. There are 30 pupils in most classes and the light homework load differentiates the school from the prep over the road and from any other. In reality, Queen's is a state school where the curriculum is soundly taught by dedicated staff, with lots and lots of parental input – which includes paying for private tuition to get the children into those sought-after senior schools.

The last head insisted that pupils do not all get extra coaching for entrance exams – doubtless true for the exceptionally bright but, in one Year 5, parental chit-chat reckons 80 per cent received private tuition. Much praise also for the school staff – despite the class sizes, 'all children seem to get at least some individual attention,' said one mum. 'The staff stay a nice long time,' remarked another. 'Of course you get occasional less good teachers,' but most parents are so happy that they even want to join the ranks.

Last head introduced a 'thinking skills programme'. 'I've no idea what it means in practice,' said a parent and a pupil looked blank when asked about it. However, 'there's always been plenty of support for special needs,' said a mum. If your child is more middle of the road, they could risk getting a bit lost in an ocean of clever middle-class pupils – 'there hasn't been much special help for my son – he just survives,' was one slight moan – perhaps somewhat harsh.

Music is a strength – how many primary schools can boast two orchestras? Sport is played competitively and with some success. Everyone in the school – staff, children and various parent helpers – are cheerful and busy, with loads of work on display, an enormous world map in the hall, dotted with multi-coloured pins showing the countries of origin of its pupils. A school uniform of school sweat-shirt and grey skirt or trousers is being phased in starting with the younger ones, resulting in the unexpected sight of half the pupils in 'mufti' and half in uniform. This phasing-in was done in consultation with the parents over a long period to achieve maximum consensus, something the head holds great store by. Consensus with the children is also much prized – an enthusiastic school council, discussing matters such as how to deal with bullying resulted in friendship benches in the playground. Discipline doesn't appear to need discussion – there is a foregone conclusion that it is good.

Not a school for parents who just want to sit back and let the school take the strain of educating their little dears. 'There are always loads of parents at curriculum evenings,' one mother said. In addition to the two orchestras, there are recorder groups, a choir, drama, song and dance, touch typing, netball, football, basketball, cricket and rugby all going on before and after school, with many parents helping in the classrooms or with outdoor activities during the day. Weekly newsletter to parents is full of information. The website is one of the best we have seen.

Queen's College Junior School

Linked to Queen's College (Taunton) in the Senior section

Trull Rd, Taunton, Somerset, TA1 4QP

• Pupils: Girls and boys; (15 boarders, 205 day) • Ages: 3-11 • Methodist foundation • Fees: Day £4,920-£9,870; Boarding £10,140-£15,405 pa • Independent

Tel: 01823 272 990
Fax: 01823 323 811
Email: junior.sec@queenscollege.org.uk
Website: www.queenscollege.org.uk

Head: Since September 2010, Tracey Khodabandehloo, educated in Wellington, Somerset, trained at Goldsmith's, London University. Started her teaching career in London, then completed her master's in Bristol whilst teaching in the city centre. Head of two well respected Somerset schools and has also raised a family of three, two of whom were educated at Queen's. Hobbies include horse riding and travel.

Outstanding Ofsted and SIAS reports at her previous school. Passion for providing an interesting, challenging and motivating primary curriculum which focuses on the whole child.

Entrance: Many children come from the delightful pre-prep, a hop, skip and jump across the field. Others come via a day's visit for mutual assessment and a friendly test in maths and English. They are assessed again in Year 5, to make sure they are on track for the senior school and to give them that extra confidence.

Exit: Most make the easy stroll across the grounds to the college to continue the great Queen's adventure.

Remarks: Much lively teaching across the board with involvement from the pupils and much interaction. This is where achievement as opposed to attainment come in. It's rare to find philosophy timetabled into a prep school, but here 9,10 and 11 year olds have one session a week. Cynics may scoff but the lesson we saw was wonderful – children were sitting around in a circle discussing whether the apple that was in the middle was alive or dead. Sounds cranky? It wasn't: what it did elicit was enquiry, evaluation, questioning what seems obvious (even pointless), which leads, in turn, to a healthy challenging of convention. Wonderful assets in a carefully packaged, health and safety, risk-free society. It's around such emotional intelligence that the academic life of the school is run.

Nor are more conventional subjects ignored. The usual subjects are there, taught in bright and airy classrooms, but every class we saw was enlivened by the spirit of enquiry. Good learning support, where children have 40 minutes a week for help in essay planning, study skills and organizing their time. Described as 'excellent' by one parent we spoke to; interesting sculpture and painting in the art rooms; good ICT and creative DT. A real feeling of buzz around the place.

The boarding house has just been completely redecorated. Currently three boys' dorms and two girls': space for 28 with a dedicated couple looking after them, assisted by matron and a resident tutor. Sleepovers are available and increasingly popular. Bags to do in the evenings and boarders may go home at the weekend. On the other hand, weekends are fun: not only is the vast range of the college's facilities available but also frequent expeditions. 'It's brilliant fun,' said one boy, 'and breakfast is later on those days.' (No Saturday school.) Plentiful sport and hobbies: 'They're never bored,' said a delighted mum.

It's good to note the mutual respect and affection between the two halves. Boys and girls in the senior school recall with great fondness the days at their junior school and recognise from where their subsequent happiness stems – it's an essential step to another good school. Scholarships and bursaries are available for talented children in a wide variety of skills. Parents with more than one child in the college may well be assisted – don't be afraid to ask.

Over all, a lovely school where individuality really does seem to be encouraged and happiness abounds. 'One college, four schools' is the advertising slogan for Queen's and the junior school represents the important foundation for the overall package.

Queen's College Prep School

Linked to Queen's College London in the Senior section

61 Portland Place, London, W1B 1QP

• Pupils: 170 girls; all day • Ages: 4-11 • C of E • Fees: £12,345-£13,350 pa • Independent

Tel: 020 7291 0660
Fax: 020 7291 0669
Email: twinthrop@qcps.org.uk
Website: www.qcps.org.uk

Head: Since 2008, Mrs Annie Dempsey BA Cert Ed (fifties). Gentle, softly spoken, smartly dressed, imaginative and passionate about her school. English specialist who graduated from UCL. Married with two grown-up daughters both educated at London day schools. Wide experience at both preparatory and secondary levels having taught at Blackheath High School, been deputy head of Blackheath Nursery and Prep School and, for five years, head of St Dunstan's College Junior School which she apparently took from 'good' to 'outstanding'.

Full of praise for her predecessor who founded QCPS in 2002 and 'created a wonderful school. I am now building one her achievement'. Feels particularly lucky to be in such a perfect position where, 'building on strength, I can embrace the past and incorporate all the great developments of the 21st century'. Doesn't teach but has a weekly discussion session with form 6 and reads stories to each form 3 class, watching and listening. Joins the younger classes when she can and sees forms 4 and 5 unofficially. Believes it is important to know every girl and all parents personally. To that aim, she is in the entrance hall every morning to greet them individually and to maintain visibility. Feels it is important that parents should be given clear lines of communication so that they can talk to the right person to deal with their questions or concerns – she is always available but should probably be the last person that they see.

A change from the previous head who was, according to parents, 'so hands on she even answered the phone. No-one ever saw anyone else'. Has improved leadership by creating a larger, more effective team of leaders and managers who also monitor and discuss each girl's progress regularly. A great fan of Shirley Clark s works on learning through formative assessment. Parents feel that although she had a hard act to follow she is making positive changes to the school.

Entrance: Non-selective at reception stage, September after 4th birthday. All parents interviewed by the head before place offered. Entry to all other year groups involves assessment of child's academic achievement and potential, an evaluation of her social skills and a report from her previous school. No-one is offered a place until the head has met her parents.

Exit: About two thirds to the senior school (no shortcuts here, they have to pass the same entrance exam as every one else). The rest mainly to London girls' day schools, both Francis Hollands, City of London Girls', Godolphin and Latymer being the most popular. Occasionally one or two to board, Cheltenham Ladies' College, Wycombe Abbey and Heathfield have featured in the last three years.

Remarks: A small, traditional school producing well mannered, enthusiastic, happy girls fully aware of the value of a good education and the importance of being nice to each other. Head says, 'not a school for princesses, they have to be able to relate to everybody'.

Well situated, just a short walk from Regent's Park, housed in two tall Adam buildings, where much use has been made of the elegance of the architecture. The result, a lovely light school with good sized bright classrooms and a warm, homely feel. Lots stairs but the littlest girls are at the bottom and the eldest at the top which works well. A parent said 'the girls really appreciate the beauty of the building and treat it with respect'. Good to hear. Good-sized carpeted hall on first floor. This is a C of E school and whole school gathers for assembly three times a week, one of these taken by the head. 'Her assemblies are brilliant,' said a teacher. Also used for films, plays, fencing and other activities. Basement recently redeveloped to include an excellent ballet and drama room, a gymnasium, a common room for the oldest girls where they can loll around on bean bags, chat and listen to cds and an extended dining area. 'Lunches are no longer a bone of contention,' said a parent. 'The food is much improved and a weekly menu comes home every Friday so we can see what they are being offered'.

Broad curriculum including French from reception and Latin from Year 5. Good solid preparation for 11+ CE, North London Day School Consortium and other senior school entrance exams. Small classes, average 16 maximum 20, alongside good mix of experienced and recently qualified teachers, all of whom are enthusiastic and appear to have good relationships with the girls. Head feels it is really important that children should want to learn and be able to respond to challenges. Those that we saw and spoke to certainly seemed eager enough, happy, intent on their lessons and keen to explain what they were doing. A parent said, 'they are encouraged to work hard academically'. Assistant head, who is also head of maths, is a man but otherwise no full-time male teachers and only a couple of part-timers. We were assured that this is more a question of availability than policy. Teaching assistants in all pre-prep level classes. Specialised teachers from then on, so more movement around the school. Setting in maths and, where appropriate, English from form 3. Interactive white boards in every class and, as a parent said and we agree, 'fantastic ICT suite'. Big bright science lab and lovely light art studio on top floor with a great view of the roofs behind. Head of art very enthusiastic, says it is her dream job.

Good music. About 75 per cent learn an individual instrument, 'they encourage girls to make the most of every opportunity. Ours learn guitar and violin'. Up to grade 4 or 5 but school says 'the emphasis is always on enjoyment rather than exam results'. Weekly sessions for mini-strings and string group. Also choir and bands take part in external events as well as school performances. Does sound fun. Drama for all, plus ballet for the younger children and modern dance for the older ones all part of the curriculum. Lots of trips and expeditions; head says, 'we definitely make the most of wider London'.

No outdoor play area so head has adjusted timetable to give more active time in the garden opposite each day for the younger children. 'But don't the residents mind?' we queried. 'Oh no, our girls are so well behaved they are perfectly happy.' Older girls also have active time each day whether it's PE, dance, fencing or just a walk. Use local sports venues and Regent's Park for team games and swimming and play competitively internally and against other schools.

Comprehensive pastoral care policy. Simplified code of conduct on the wall of every classroom. Believe in positive not negative attitudes and the need to 'help children get out of a hole when they make mistakes and misbehave'. New full time teaching SENCo very impressed with observations system put in by the head. All teacher concerns go onto SEN file and if specific learning difficulties are suspected she discusses with assistant head, who is also head of pastoral care, and with parents. She says 'small classes make monitoring easy'. 'This is a school where we all talk to each other and individual tasks and monitoring are possible'. Works closely with the nearby Dyslexia Teaching Centre and two teachers come in twice weekly for one-to-one sessions.

Parents say, 'a fantastic school producing lovely, happy, confident girls'. 'Excellent pastoral care.' 'Brilliant head has provided much more structure.' 'As a girls' school – perfect'.

Queen's Gate Junior School

Linked to Queen's Gate School in the Senior section

125-126 Queen's Gate, London, SW7 5LE

• Pupils: 130 girls, all day • Ages: 4-11 • Non-denom
• Fees: £12,000-£12,150 pa • Independent

Tel: 020 7589 3587
Fax: 020 7584 7691
Email: cstevens@queensgate.org.uk
Website: www.queensgate.org.uk

Head: Since 1997, Mrs Nia Webb BA PGCE, (fifties) educated in Wales, read modern and medieval history at Bedford College, University of London, did her PGCE at King's London. Married with one grown-up daughter, Mrs Webb has been at Queen's Gate forever – she's worked under three different principals. Before taking the helm at the junior school she taught history to the sixth form. This is a bit of a transformation and she is relishing it. Lovely and cuddly, with a Celtic twinkle in her eye, she taught many of the parents of the children she teaches now, 'but I'm not teaching their grandchildren yet'. One rather suspects that she is looking forward to it though.

Entrance: Massively oversubscribed so names need to go down as early as possible. Family connections count for a lot (preference given to grand-daughters/daughters/sisters/nieces of OGs). Mrs Webb sees everyone (approximately 120 applicants for 23 places). They visit, a year in advance, about 10 to 12 at a time, with eight staff on duty for organised 'playtime' and story time. Social skills are important – they are looking for children who sparkle but won't overlook the shy ones, 'this is a school for individuals'. It's absolutely no use little Annie boning up on her reading practice.

Exit: Massive exodus to senior school as academics grow stronger and people see the merit in keeping their daughters in a secure happy environment which can't always be found in larger establishments. Mrs Webb keen to point out that she doesn't push the senior school – it sells itself. Otherwise to other London day schools – St Paul's, Godolphin and Latymer, or to boarding schools (Cheltenham Ladies College and Bedales). Recently some have turned down places, school tells us, in order to stay on at Queen's Gate.

Remarks: In 2007 the junior school moved a few doors away to magnificent new facilities at 125/126 Queen's Gate. Spacious, bright classrooms, impressive hall with original features meticulously restored and only the finest fittings. It's not just tasteful either, facilities are first class – sparkling specialist science laboratories, art and ICT. Much needed new library nearing completion.

One class entry, about 20 per form. Dual teaching in the class room, with every child, and not just those who need remedial help, getting individual attention so no-one feels too special. Differentiated teaching using support teachers and assistants copes with children who do have special needs, though there are specialist SEN teachers on hand should your child need one-to-one help either in or out of class. One disturbing report of learning difficulties being allowed to slip through the net – parents had to go straight to the top. At that point all the stops pulled out. School quick to point out that this was 'one isolated incident and should not be regarded as the norm'. Gifted and Talented are catered for in the lunchtime clubs, many of which are academic (philosophy, art history, science, Mandarin and two maths clubs as well as needlework, chess and table tennis amongst others).

Sparky teaching, computers and laptops everywhere, touch-typing at eight, French from four, Latin from age nine and some ancient Greek during the final year. Italian, German and Spanish introduced from age of eight. Much use is made of nearby museums and galleries, 'the girls must realise there is a classroom beyond the school'. The younger girls eat their cooked lunch in the splendidly restored hall; from eight years all girls eat in the senior school where they can also eat a packed lunch if they wish. This is where they go to do gymnastics but good use is made of Hyde Park and Battersea Park too (girls no longer walk but are bussed there – 'much safer'). A tiny bit of outdoor space in the courtyard. Music strong, two formal concerts a year as well as a number of informal ones and school takes part in Music for Youth Festival have been finalists for two years running. Drama important and very popular, 'HMS Pinafore' was recently performed in Baden Powell House across the road.

Bright eyed, pretty girls all neat in navy blue Harris tweed coats, on their way in to school, with knitted wool hats, blazers and boaters in summer. Their own dresses underneath you understand – too much uniformity goes against the important principle here that everyone is an individual and should be treated as such. Good pastoral care, PSHE starts early, with circle time, and popular bonding weeks in Dorset, the Isle of Wight and York from the age of eight. Strong PTA and parental links, many mums and grandmums are OGs. Day officially 8.30-3.45 (3.00 and noon on Fridays for tinies), but late waiting until 4.00 or 4.30 is OK in a crisis. Collection time a real bore for passing traffic, double parking all over the shop. Recent acquisition of a school bus apparently eases the problem a little. Notable old girls include HRH the Duchess of Cornwall, Lady Gabriella Windsor, Nigella Lawson and Lucinda Lambton. Super, not so little, cosy and popular girls' prep school, where all the girls feel cherished and do surprisingly ('there's nothing surprising about it', says head) well.

The Queen's Lower School

Linked to Queen's School (The) in the Senior section

55 Liverpool Road, Chester, Cheshire, CH2 1AW

• Pupils: 190 girls; all day • Ages: 4-11 • Non-denom • Fees: £7,245 pa
• Independent

Tel: 01244 382843
Fax: 01244 381152
Email: secretary@queens.cheshire.sch.uk
Website: www.queens.cheshire.sch.uk

Head: Since 2004, Mrs Felicity Taylor (fifties). She attended Durham University where she rowed for her College and achieved elite oarswoman status. She had previously been head of pre-prep at The Grange School

Cheshire. Energetic and lively, she has created a strong leadership team with vision and leads a superb staff of excellent and dedicated teachers. She is also a member of the senior school management team.

Entrance: Entrance by assessment and interview; worth checking for availability of places.

Exit: Most move up to seniors.

Remarks: Two attractive Victorian houses with modern extensions in landscaped gardens a mile (busy at peak times) from the senior school. 190 girls, class size variable. Forward thinking, high academic standards and stimulating curriculum. Strong pastoral care. Dedicated music and PE teachers. Indoor heated pool (shared by seniors), own playing field, supervised play park and friendship garden on site. Christian assemblies. Before and after school provision until 6.00pm.

Ravenscourt Park Preparatory School

16 Ravenscourt Avenue, Ravenscourt Park, London, W6 0SL

• Pupils: 260, roughly 50/50 girls/boys • Ages: 4-11 • Christian but welcomes all faiths • Fees: £12,807 pa • Independent

Tel: 020 8846 9153
Fax: 020 8846 9413
Email: secretary@rpps.co.uk
Website: www.rpps.co.uk

Head: Since 2004, Mr Robert Relton BEd (mid forties), previously deputy head for three years and, prior to that, teaching (mostly PE) experience at a range of top schools – Habs Boys, City of London Boys, Ibstock Place and King's College School. A good pedigree. His degree was in history and PE and he still coaches games two afternoons a week – an excellent way of knowing the less formal sides of his charges.

Serious, friendly and with high principles, moral and educational, Mr Relton is clear about the kind of school he wants to run and likes parents to be clear and supportive of the ethos too. Everything he says emphasises each individual child – their aptitudes, difficulties, personalities – and he clearly takes the trouble to have all-round knowledge of each child. This is reflected in the unusually broad range of schools to which he sends his pupils. 'I don't want there to be a Ravenscourt Park clone,' he asserts, 'I want there to be 36 individuals leaving this school, each year.' A nice touch in his 'open door' approach is that children who want to avoid the hectic playground at breaktime are welcome to play quiet games on his study floor – a clutch were happily heads down when we visited, quite at home.

Entrance: This is the bit you need to know. The school has current waiting lists of 100+ in each year. The only, repeat only, way in is to register your child on the day of his/her first birthday. The day after will get you nowhere and if you ring up when he/she is three you may as well save the phone money. In the event of birthdays being in the hols, postmarks are taken into consideration and there is always someone on site to take hand-delivered forms. In the June/July of the year before entry all these are put into a hat and balloted; interviews begin in September. Those who come up are invited to meet the head and staff and entrance is more-or-less automatic. This results in a truly mixed-ability intake with a good spread of, not necessarily mild, special needs. Mr Relton looks undaunted by our mentioning more than mild dyslexia – moderate, severe – all such children will be welcome and are seen as representing the range of any community. Physical disabilities will be accommodated but wheelchairs might be a problem though they'd do their best. They've met ADHD and ADD and Asperger's and will support everything. After entrance at four the waiting lists dwindle, and thereafter it is worth calling if you're contemplating a move to Hammersmith or environs. Many families live close enough to walk; the current remotest commuters slog in from Notting Hill.

Exit: This is the surprising bit. You might expect there to be a subway from here to the two local Latymers but it ain't so. A number of pupils do go to Latymer Upper and Godolphin & Latymer but the school truly does scrutinise each child and starts from scratch in drawing up a longlist for parents to think about. They assess carefully using trusted tools. Parents return with their own shortlists and most children make it into their first choices. Apart from the Lats, they go to Ibstock, St Paul's Boys (via Colet Court) and Girls, St Benedict's, Notting Hill and Ealing and a range of elsewheres including the odd boarder. However, 'there's always a minority who are reluctant – or fail – to take your advice,' says the head, sadly. This would be unwise – he has good relations with heads of all the likely schools and will make efforts if you express an interest in an unlikely one. Trust him. He knows. Don't apply here if you plan to try for somewhere else when your child is seven – they don't prepare for exams before the 11 plus and won't support you if you try to nip down the road to Colet Court or Bute. On the other hand, don't write it off if you're hoping for an eventual place at St Paul's or Westminster – boys sit the 11+ for Colet or the Under School and get in.

Remarks: 'Not a hothouse,' we were told by enthusiastic parents before we went and this was borne out by what we found. It's a school where a child will be taught at his or her own level – there is support for both the strugglers and the gifted and talented – 'we will move a child into the year above for certain lessons if necessary.' There are pressure cooker schools in the area but this isn't one of them. Children here are confident, self-motivated, articulate and cheerful – everyone stresses how friendly the school is – and it looked it, though we were a little alarmed by some fierce ear-pulling in the playground which went unchecked by the only visible supervising adult around – apparently there was another but attending the quiet area – and these things will happen in the best regulated playgrounds.

So, what do you get here? Three buildings – old, rebuilt and new. Good teaching, pretty good facilities all-round – soon to be improved with the addition of a brand new building adjacent to the existing school, due to open in September 2011. This will provide nine new classrooms, a theatre, library, well-resourced science laboratory, music department, art studio (which will include design and pottery) and extra learning support rooms. ICT is burgeoning

– school has an intranet and is working towards a school-home link but not quite there yet. Interactive whiteboards in all classrooms with staff now experienced in how to integrate them into teaching; good IT room with a laptop per child plus one computer per classroom. A school which gives the appearance of being thoroughly well-organised and making good use of precious little space. Excellent displays of art and craft everywhere and some of the best and brightest we have seen in a prep school of this size. Imaginative stuff like weaving on home-made mini-looms, a Tracey Emin-inspired appliqué blanket, super ceramics – we saw a row of houses – and wonderful, life-size, papier maché penguins. You imagine there must be a huge art studio to produce this range and standard of work but art is done in a cramped and uninspiring room – a new arrangement which, along with science also housed in inadequate accommodation, is temporary: both subjects badly need more space – soon to be resolved by the new building. The library – though newly kitted-out and well-stocked – suffers a similar lack of space. Ditto.

There is a smallish but versatile hall/gym/theatre/meeting room in which daily assemblies happen – 'really good' enthuse the children – not something you usually hear. These are topic-based and clearly inspirational. A rather dull dining room but with seriously good food including bowls of fruit for each class at breaktime and scrummy raw veg along with stodgier staples for lunch. 'We like Wednesdays best,' we were told, 'chips!' Plus ça change. Classrooms at all age levels are attractive and well-organised, good display is a feature everywhere. Everywhere, too, is the school's Code of Conduct – you couldn't not know that bullying, racism etc are unacceptable here. The playground, largely tarmac but with a safe-surface quiet area with a slide – is pretty manic in break and, as everywhere, taken over by boys with footballs. However, there are little niches on the perimeter, mostly nested in by girls, and, at morning break, no football is allowed – a blessed relief for the otherwise-inclined! Two games cupboards and the library are open for everyone in breaks. And there's always the head's study!

The curriculum has no surprises but pupils enjoy learning here. Head keeps a close eye on what is taught and everything is carefully considered. Especially sensible is the 'all-round' curriculum from reception to Year 5 and the more 11 plus focused work for Years 5 and 6 but there is a wise and wonderful blossoming allowed after the entrance exams which takes in such things as writing short novels, maths becoming a practical, problem-solving activity, putting on a play and lots more art. Clubs are important – for everything including classics – Latin, Greek myths, architecture – all enthusiastically lapped up. Another is the 'Bloomsbury Group' for literary enthusiasts or those who want to write more sophisticatedly. Choir is popular and music theatre is strong. Head plans to develop music further. There are sports clubs and, wonderfully, all reception children do yoga! Sports take place in Ravenscourt Park which more or less abuts the school and gives a sense of the school having more space than it does. Everyone has two to three hours of games weekly. There is a full programme of outings – cultural and academic – school makes good use of local rich opportunities as well as of residential visits to centres in Surrey and in Devon for study and team-building and so on. There is an annual, optional, trip to France for Years 5 and 6. School invites in visitors – notably, and very popularly, authors in Book Week.

Parents' help is central in hearing readers, supporting French, running the library, fund-raising and accompanying trips. Clientèle is a true London mix – many professionals, media folk, self-employed. Not a huge ethnic mix – odd for this very mixed area – perhaps the first birthday stipulation catches out the less experienced education buyers who may not dream of having to apply so early. School has system of sanctions ('warning' and 'time lost') and rewards and children are pinned to their (very attractive) uniforms with rows of badges for everything you can think of. There is a musician/sportsman/star of the week in each year and awards for improvement etc so that it's not always the same winners. 'Aftercare' available daily at extra charge but popular and well worthwhile for busy parents.

Smiley children and smiley staff make for a thoroughly welcoming, happy school. More space would make it ideal but it's an inner London prep which aims to broaden and develop rather than cram and, as such, is a bit of a gem.

Reay Primary School

Hackford Road, London, SW9 0EN

• Pupils: 250 • Ages: 3+ to 11 • Non denominational • State

Tel: 02077 352 978
Fax: 020 7820 9165
Email: admin@reay.lambeth.sch.uk
Website: www.reay.lambeth.sch.uk

Head: Since 2005, Liz Tennant BEd (Hons) NPQH. Started her teaching career after her children started school and previously taught at Clapham Manor followed by deputy headship at Kingswood School. Her interest in art is evident throughout the school and she is a keen painter herself.

Entrance: 3+ to the nursery, 4+ reception class, thereafter occasional vacancies only. Standard Lambeth admission policy, pupils with special requirements, siblings then distance from the school.

Exit: 11+ pupils are successful in gaining places to the Independent and maintained sector most choose to go on to Wandsworth and Lambeth secondary schools.

Remarks: A welcoming and friendly primary school which caters for a wide range of abilities and provides an outstanding quality education to all. Higher than average numbers of the staff have advanced skills teacher status; quality marks for both literacy and numeracy. Everyone, from the nursery upwards, learns French. There is an annual trip to Paris for eight to nine-year-olds. Artsmark Gold, the school has its own art and dance studios. Children are offered excellent choice of artistic and dramatic activities – several teachers have art degrees. An enterprising barter system is run with artists, dance and drama groups exchanging use of the studios for workshops and teaching services. All age groups are taught music by a specialist part-time teacher and children can have individual lessons on the flute, violin or brass instruments.

School is dedicated to developing a really good awareness among pupils about environmental issues and has been awarded, for the second time, the green flag for eco-friendly schools. Sport is popular. School has its own Astroturf for football and netball matches; pupils are keen to compete in local tournaments and mini leagues. There is a good playground area and small garden with a frog pond. Governors and parents give much support to the school and also organise fundraising events and charity collections. Reay aims to look after the whole child and has it own learning mentor and school counselling service.

Do not be put off by first appearances. The exterior of the school is somewhat austere, particularly in comparison with the imaginative and well run interior. Reay is a little gem in the heart of Stockwell.

The Red Maids' Junior School

Grange Court Road, Westbury-on-Trym, Bristol, BS9 4DP

• Pupils: 140 day girls • Ages: 7-11 • Non-denom • Fees: £6,630 pa • Independent

Tel: 0117 962 9451
Fax: 0117 962 9451
Email: juniors@redmaids.bristol.sch.uk
Website: www.redmaids.bristol.sch.uk

Head: Since 1986, Mrs Gillian Rowcliffe BEd (early fifties), educated at High Wycombe High School and then at Bristol University. Something of a human dynamo who teaches all the girls and is constantly coming up with projects to keep them (and parents) on the ball. School fits her like a glove – she converted a former suburban house ('a home from home,' say parents) in two terms and has run it as a school ever since. Loves what she does and enthuses children, teachers and parents alike. Delighted to have opened the award winning new junior school extension in 2007. She is a governor of 'brother school' QEH (qv)and helped to set up their junior department. Thrilled to discover that neighbours love having the school in their road and plans to involve them more. Ex scuba diver, loves decorating. Married to Neil with two sons who went to QEH.

Entrance: Two main points of entry with 20 places in Years 3 and 5. Headteacher selects pupils into Year 3 by one-to-one assessment and into Year 5 by small group assessment. Girls come from wide range of feeder schools. Recruitment relies on word of mouth and assessment occurs in December and January.

Exit: Normally automatic entry to senior school including scholarships via entrance examination except where head indicates child will not cope. This would be flagged up early on and parents given advice about alternatives. Occasionally to state education or scholarships to other Bristol independent schools.

Remarks: Super school with a homely feel. Girls are keen, lively and friendly. Neat appearance: red and white striped dresses with sailor collars and red cardigans in summer; kilts and white blouses in winter. High academic standard. Discrete site but easy access to senior school. Award winning extension was opened in 2007 to provide large hall, library, art rooms, ICT suite and an additional classroom. Close co-operation between staff and strong sense of common purpose. All classrooms pleasantly light with lively displays and equipped with interactive whiteboards which staff exploit to full advantage.

Entrants screened for dyslexia and given specialist support on site where necessary. We saw a visually impaired girl coping very well alongside her sighted peers. Lots of encouragement to improve reading habits through book club etc; head teaches Latin by popular demand. Mandarin is taught as main foreign language with native speaker. Lots of sports and music with about 60 per cent receiving instrumental tuition. Choral scholarships. Recent winners at Bristol Drama Festival. Girls get to go on loads of visits (including link with a school in Paris) plus activity stays in Somerset and Devon. Plenty of room to play safely at rear of school and access to senior school sports, further specialist ICT and science facilities and senior school teachers. A stretching, happy and creative place which leaves you with a 'lovely, warm feeling'.

Redcliffe School

47 Redcliffe Gardens, London, SW10 9JH

• Pupils: 90 girls, 55 boys; all day • Ages: 2.6-11 (girls) 2.6–8 (boys • Christian (though accepts all faiths). • Fees: £11,625 pa • Independent

Tel: 02073 529 247
Fax: 02073 526 936
Email: apeartree@redcliffeschool.com
Website: www.redcliffeschool.com

Head: Since September 2006, Mrs Susan Bourne BSc PGCE (late forties). Previously deputy head at the Old Vicarage, Richmond, where she taught science for seven years. Also taught GCSE and A level chemistry to boys and girls at Nottingham comprehensives (Ashfield and Kimberley), as well as at a girls' boarding school (St Elphin's near Matlock, RIP). Married with three London day school educated daughters. (Godolphin & Latymer, Queen's Gate and Latymer Upper).

Keen to impress, her bright blue eyes miss nothing. Breathing fresh life and ideas into this traditional but cosy prep and pre-prep. New premises housing the junior end of the school and allowing for two classes per year since 2007. Staff and parents describe her rolling up her sleeves as she swiftly responds to requests, whether it be to make drinking water available in all the classrooms, choosing wall paper to smarten up premises definitely in need of a makeover, or starting a Spanish club. 'If parents see you meeting requests at a micro level then you're unlikely to have problems at a more fundamental level,' she says.

Despite her busy brief she is mindful of the importance of 'getting a grip on the children' and teaches every child PSHE. The door to her study (in the centre of the school and overlooking the playground), is (almost) always open. In the chaos of drop-off each morning, her small figure is to be found among a sea of parents and children as she greets them with a handshake ('I make sure each one looks me in the eye'). She regards the cramped hectic hall in the morning as being an important part of the school's relaxed and informal atmosphere and would hate to see children being dropped at the school gate.

Entrance: At nursery age – first come, first served, priority given to siblings. If your child is already in Robins (nursery to you and me) then an informal assessment before a seamless progression into kindergarten at four, otherwise a non threatening assessment in order of date of registration. 'We're not just looking for academic potential but want to see how well a child copes with being separated from his or her parents: Can they draw Mummy?'

At present no need to plan a C-section just before the closing date for registration. Always worth phoning for a place further up the school, especially if he's a boy under eight. Two mixed forms will reduce to one form of girls per year from 8–11. No second intake of girls to replace the boys who have left.

Exit: Almost all to their first choice. Broad range of (mostly) London day schools; girls go to St Paul's, Francis Holland, Godolphin & Latymer, Queen's Gate, St James, Putney High with a few choosing to board at e.g. Downe House, and Benenden. Boys leave at eight to go to Northcote Lodge, St Philip's, Fulham prep, and in previous years to Sussex House, Colet Court and Westminster Under. Occasionally boys go on to boarding schools.

Remarks: Redcliffe is not a small school. It's a tiny one. The open assembly we saw felt like an intimate gathering at home. A school with a big heart and a family feel. Even visiting staff know each child by name and it's not just the children who make good friends, 'at Redcliffe you make friends for life,' enthused a parent.

Everyone gets involved here (even the governors are mainly ex-parents). Each class participates at the weekly assemblies. Senior girls take it in turns to ring the hand bell between lessons. One of the girls was keen to show us photos of the school disco at which all the staff could be seen dancing with pupils (past and present) and parents (Mrs Bourne apparently refused to be photographed: her dancing was too embarrassing). One year a particularly diffident four year old was persuaded to sing a solo at the carol service.

Not a school for the highly competitive child. There are no scholarships. If your child needs nurturing then this is definitely worth a visit. Plenty of internal awards and these don't (necessarily) focus on the academic either. Displayed on a scholarship style board are the names of the one Wordsworth (Year 6) girl each year awarded the coveted prize for her 'services to the school'. Other lesser (but no less valued) awards given on a weekly basis for e.g. 'working quicker during lesson times', or 'being helpful and dependable'.

Parents are invited to lunch with Mrs Bourne and the children twice a term and sign up their availability. It's a popular event. Not surprising because the food is excellent and cooked fresh on the premises. A great full time chef who has children herself 'and so,' says Mrs Bourne 'knows not to sprinkle the spaghetti bolognese with parsley' but instead serves 'minced Transylvania bat on a bed of swamp weed' during Hallowe'en (turkey mince on green spaghetti!).

Classrooms are light, colourful and well equipped. High ceilings and large windows create the impression of there being more space. A small(ish) playground where children can be found with hula hoops and skipping ropes after their break time snack (normally fruit or vegetables, biscuits only once a week). Plenty of computers as well as interactive whiteboards throughout (there were only three of these when Mrs Bourne arrived). This is what she is about, she says firmly, preserving things that matter but moving with the times.

Redland High Junior School

Linked to Redland High School in the Senior section

1 Grove Park, Redland, Bristol, BS6 6PP

• Pupils: girls; all day • Ages: 3-11 • Non-denom • Fees: £5,760-£6780 pa • Independent

Tel: 0117 924 5796
Fax: 0117 924 1127
Email: admissions@redlandhigh.com
Website: www.redlandhigh.com

Head: Since 2006, Mr Jonathan Eyles BEd. Mr Eyles came from Millfield prep where he was assistant head of the junior and pre-prep schools and director of studies for six years. After graduation, he taught in schools in Devon, Weston Super Mare and Sri Lanka before joining Millfield. At the time of our visit, he was studying (part time) for a Masters degree in Cognitive Development at Bristol University, as well as finding time to be an ISI inspector.

Entrance: Non-selective into pre-prep then NFER tests used to monitor progress. Numbers practically double from Year 4 as state school parents wake up to advantages of getting daughters into senior school via this route. Early warning given if any girls unlikely to make grade.

Exit: Nearly all pupils proceed to senior school via entry examination at 11+.

Remarks: Safe, caring environment turns out friendly, polite girls; purposeful classroom atmosphere. Grove Park, two linked Victorian houses situated on one of leafier roads in this elegant Bristol suburb. Older junior school pupils have extensive access to senior school facilities for art, drama, PE. There is a separate music school equi-distant between junior and senior schools. Grove Park has been extended to accommodate higher demand for places, particularly in Years 5 and 6.

Outside play area recently revamped with new equipment. Inside, plenty of room for movement between activities; girls count well and displays include numerals, patterns and heights measured in handprints. We saw phonic work on letter X and some impressive writing in reception class plus displays from recent 'fairy week'. KS1 tests considered unnecessary. Good creative writing in prep – Year 4 pupils seen discussing own play scripts; library areas struck as cramped and uninviting; Year 6 teacher waxed lyrical whilst dissecting bluebells: girls generally do best at science at KS2 and when they get to senior school.

Own art room with colourful displays; lots of music – orchestra, choir and instrumental lessons. Often outplayed on sports field against tougher local opponents who probably get more practice. Annual stay at outdoor activity centre in Devon includes abseiling and caving. Two male teachers a welcome sight alongside female staff. SENCo works with individuals and follows through to seniors: mainly helping dyslexics. Girls from Year 3 upwards use senior school facilities for some specialist subjects and games; all but teenies have lunch there. Successful after school care (popcorn and video on Fridays makes it girls' favourite) and holiday schemes run by a classroom assistant.

Pleasant atmosphere and committed staff; provides good academic grounding and increasingly wide access to better facilities at senior school. Obvious enough way of getting your daughter into Redland High system early if you don't have to save your money for later.

Reigate St Mary's Preparatory and Choir School

Linked to Reigate Grammar School in the Senior section

Chart Lane, Reigate, Surrey, RH2 7RN

• Fees: £9,234-£10.869 pa • Independent

Tel: 0173 7244 880
Fax: 0173 722 1540
Email: office@reigatestmarys.org
Website: www.reigatestmarys.org

Rendcomb College Junior School

Linked to Rendcomb College in the Senior section

Rendcomb, Cirencester, Gloucestershire, GL7 7HA

• Pupils: girls and boys • Ages: 3-11 • Fees: £5,760-£9,270 pa
• Independent

Tel: 01285 832310
Fax: 01285 832 311
Email: info@rendcomb.gloucs.sch.uk
Website: www.rendcombcollege.co.uk

Head: Since 2002, Mr Martin Watson BEd MA (fifties), studied history at Exeter then London for MA. Joined Rendcomb after 19 years at The Downs, Wraxall (last fifteen as deputy head) to set up junior school. Passionate about co-education, the outdoor classroom and children 'needing to be happy to learn'. Played top class rugby while at St Luke's; qualified rugby referee but now umpires rounders to international level. Sport is still a great interest as is travel abroad. Married to Lynne who teaches Year 5 class as well as overseeing school's green flag eco programme. Daughter, Rachel, played rounders consistently for England from 13–18 and is due to study geography at Exeter after Rendcomb. Martin Watson has bags of experience – lovely rapport with children and at ease with parents. A tower of strength, he knows how to select and retain good staff (including four males). A safe pair of hands if ever we saw them.

Entrance: Majority from pre-school nurseries and own nursery (entrance from term after 3rd birthday). Shadow/taster day for youngest. Assessments in English, maths, VRQ and report from current school for all aged 7+.

Exit: Virtually all to senior school at 11 via entrance examination.

Remarks: Now in its tenth year, junior school occupies former senior day house accommodation to side of main school building. Large classrooms for younger ones on ground floor plus older children expanding on upper floors into main building. Not the most imposing of entrances (at least in contrast to senior school) but emphasis here is on industry rather than show. Bouncy, smiling pupils everywhere with sensible red and navy uniform (ties for high days). Outside areas are perfect for youngest – protective surfaces to save bruises – then skip round a corner or two into beautiful grounds via a variety of outside play equipment. Rendcomb tinies are used to the outdoor life and so are in their element here. Since nursery opened in 2005, nearly all recruitment is at 3–4 year old level with most staying on.

1:4 teacher:pupil ratio in nursery with two assistants and two teachers so never more than 16 children at one time. Lovely display and lots of fun. Jolly phonics scheme started here. Head plans to increase to two form entry from reception. Staff work closely with parents to develop each child's reading. Book corners in classrooms look well maintained. Oxford Reading Tree heavily used – 'boys like Fireflies' (the non fiction offshoot) we were told. Abacus for maths; plenty of numerical stimuli on display. Lots of topics – 'minibeasts' providing endless entertainment when we visited. Staff really on the ball: well kept learning journals record all significant milestones. Smartboards sit comfortably alongside book corners with teachers using old and new resources to full effect. Years 1 and 2 known as otters (not quite sure why) – could it be because they all have swimming on their timetable?

Specialist teaching for music, PE and French right from Reception with more specialism from Year 3 upwards; by Year 6 the class teacher is taking one or two subjects only. This leads nicely into transition to senior, reinforced by the physical location of the upper junior classrooms. Some juniors flexi board in seniors' lower school houses – makes another step towards senior school life effortless. ICT has a suite with 18 pcs and head says that some pupils have a 'phenomenal aptitude'. Large art area doubles up for D&T (pupils recently scored as young active designers of the year) plus some science (otherwise in classrooms) though senior labs can always be booked if required. Pupils screened for dyslexia and specialist help provided by discrete learning support department.

Year groups have one main trip per term plus a 3 day residential trip for Year 6 to Kilve activity centre. Authors visit to talk to pupils on World Book Day and main junior library is heavily used. Most pupils stay for prep club and/or activities after school. New big thing here is the forest school with trails through the wood, woodcraft and a proper log cabin for indoor activities. Heavily used (e.g. one afternoon per week from Reception to Year 2, thereafter 12 children at a time from upper years on a termly basis). Set-up good enough to be used by forest school association for training purposes. One of first independent schools to be awarded international eco-school green flag award following an intensive two year programme on site.

Games and PE very popular with inclusive policy to encourage all pupils to play at all levels. Usual range of main sports for boys and girls; separate sports days for juniors and otters. Keen cross country club teaches young muscles about hills; mixed pop-lacrosse team became recent national prep school champions. Own outside areas plus bonus of access to senior sports hall for PE and College pitches for games. Designated music room for juniors used by younger ones whilst older pupils use main music school. Juniors are offered a free taster instrumental lesson and can use school instruments in early stages. Music concert each term showcases junior school orchestra and choir. Juniors also enjoy using the food studies facilities for cookery club. Acting is popular – ambitious performances (recent ones include 'Fleeced' and 'Alice in Wonderland') in Dulverton Hall. Ballet pupils enter Cheltenham festival across full range. Full programme of LAMDA speech and drama with excellent plaudits. Riding and polo are popular and some pupils compete in the UK mega chess finals annually. Parents at Rendcomb Junior seem a pretty sociable lot – lots of events under aegis of 'Jest' for general letting down of hair.

Cornerstone of the 'new' Rendcomb and a life saver in a fiercely competitive part of Gloucestershire. Definitely a success and an end to worries if you're looking for a complete 3–18 package.

RGS Springfield

Linked to RGS The Grange in the Junior section
Linked to RGS Worcester in the Senior section

Britannia Square, Worcester, Worcestershire, WR1 3DL

• Pupils: 115 pupils • Ages: For boys and girls aged 2½-11 years • Non-denom • Fees: £3,798-£9,162 pa • Independent

Tel: 01905 24999
Fax: 01905 27957
Email: springfield@rgsw.org.uk
Website: www.rgsw.org.uk

Head: Mrs Marion Lloyd.

Entrance: Children will be admitted to RGS Springfield half-termly during the academic year. However, arrangements may be made for pupils moving into the area to be admitted at other times of the year.

Exit: Majority to the senior school, RGS Worcester.

RGS The Grange

Linked to RGS Springfield in the Junior section
Linked to RGS Worcester in the Senior section

Grange Lane, Claines, Worcester, Worcestershire, WR3 7RR

• Pupils: 380 girls and boys; all day • Ages: 2½-11 years • Non-denom • Fees: £5,688-£9,036 pa • Independent

Tel: 01905 451 205
Fax: 01905 757 917
Email: grange@rgsw.org.uk
Website: www.rgsw.org.uk

Head: Mr Gareth Hughes, previously head of lower school at RGS Worcester and director of sports. He is a top sportsman himself, having played fly-half for Saracens in the 1990s and subsequently for Worcester RFC. His wife Sophie is a local primary school music teacher. Two children.

Entrance: Children admitted to RGS The Grange half-termly during the academic year. Arrangements may be made for pupils moving into the area to be admitted at other times of the year. Interview and assessment as appropriate to the age of the child. For example, entry to Year 1 would involve a morning spent working in class with some reading and sums. Into Year 5 there would be a more formal entrance examination with standardised tests in maths and English plus both verbal and non-verbal reasoning questionnaires.

Exit: Vast majority go on to RGS Worcester unless advised this would not be appropriate. Head will help these parents/children select a less academic school.

Remarks: For further details see the senior school, RGS Worcester.

Rhodes Avenue Primary School

Rhodes Avenue, London, N22 7UT

• Pupils: 470, rising to 500 in 2011 • Ages: 3-11 • Non-denom • State

Tel: 020 8888 2859
Fax: 02088 817 090
Email: admin@rhodes.haringey.sch.uk
Website: www.rhodes.haringey.sch.uk

Head: Since 1996, Mrs Christine Witham (forties). Mrs Witham is definitely the driving force behind this remarkably successful primary school. In her fourteen years at the helm, she has taken the school from mediocre to marvellous and to the top of every league table, both academic and sporting. Positive and upbeat, she's widely liked by parents, pupils and teachers. 'She's very approachable,' said one. 'She loves children,' said another. 'She knows all their names, sees them all as individuals and is very visible about the school.' Optimistic and determined, even the recent threat to the school rebuild did not leave her deterred. Her skill to deal at dealing with the sometimes demanding clientele is also worthy of note. 'When one parent went into complain that their child was special and deserved special treatment, she just replied, "We feel all our children are special."' Married, with two children.

Entrance: The school is currently undergoing a significant expansion and, in 2011, will move from a two-form entry, with an intake of 60, to a three-form entry with 90. Admission to Rhodes Avenue is by means of the local authority criteria, which means that, on the whole, first come siblings and then those living as near as possible. With four applications for every place, this has meant within a quarter of a mile. The success of the school – and its neighbouring comprehensive – have undoubtedly had an impact on local property prices.

Exit: The school backs directly on to Alexandra Park, one of the borough's best secondaries, and the majority of pupils proceed here. Most of the rest to north London selective schools, both state and independent. 'There are an increasing number of parents who assume their children will be going private at 11,' said one parent. Those who are looking in that direction tend to coach.

Remarks: Rhodes Avenue has for some years consistently dominated the local authority league tables and Ofsted can barely think of a word of criticism. SATs results here are truly outstanding, in 2010, 78 per cent of pupils gained the highest level possible in maths; 80 per cent in English – results that would put a smile on the face of most prep-school heads. Mrs Witham has done the job by building up a very successful team of teachers. 'There's a good mix of the thoroughly experienced and the young and enthusiastic,' said one mother and the pupils agree: 'The teaching is really great,' said one boy. Though the pupils are of above average ability on entry, the school gives everyone that little bit more, particularly in the later years. An extensive enrichment programme in art, drama and creative writing (in which teachers receive regularly training) includes workshops and specials events, such as Book Week. Last year a string of well-known children's authors pitched up to entertain, but the highlight of the week was The Bedtime Story evening, when, accompanied by teddies, children were given hot chocolate and gripping fiction. Hardly surprising then, a recent nationwide writing competition saw nine Rhodes Avenue finalists. Academic progress is charted minutely and parents kept well informed, with three parents evenings and three reports a year. Strong support, too, for the struggling. 'My son has a special literacy person and she's fantastic,' said one parent. 'He gets taken out during the literacy hour and taught in a small group to ensure he'll cope at secondary school.' French taught from Year 3 and 'parlez-vous' is supplemented with fun activities like a French breakfast, croissants included.

Music and sport are as high up the agenda as the three Rs. All Year 4 learn cello, violin, trumpet or clarinet and specialist teachers, provided by the local authority, offer individual tuition during the school day. Sport is taken seriously and Rhodes Avenue tends to sweep the board in local competitions, whether it's athletics or tennis, football or netball. 'There's an exceptionally good PE teacher,' said one mother, adding that in-school provision is also often supplemented with private coaching. Loads of trips, clubs and workshops, with outings to the cinema, theatre and museums and a regular stream of visiting artists, actors and dancers. Plenty of activity on the pupils' parts, too, with impressive assemblies and regular performances and concerts. 'A lot is done around creativity,' said one parent. After-school clubs include cross-country, orchestra, cricket, recorder, choir, Bollywood dance, Spanish, French, pottery, drama, yoga, computer, netball and badminton. Lots of competitions entered and usually won – whether that for the school's abundant and much-loved vegetable garden or for pupils' Christmas card designs. After-school play centre on site 3.30-6pm.

This is a local primary school and most families live within feet of the gates, giving the school a strong community feel, though whether that is diluted when Reception numbers rise to 90 remains to be seen. Either way, from 2011, Rhodes Avenue will enjoy three smart new buildings to add to the current modern Year 6 space, which houses two classrooms and an IT suite Strong pupil involvement. School council, with two elections a year, debates hot topics like school uniform, sustainability and healthy eating. Peer mediators protect against playground perils. Plenty of praise is the recipe for good behaviour though pupils consider Mrs Witham 'very strict' and the naughty are given focused 'reflection' on wrong doing. Despite, the friendly upbeat mood, some feel the school places too great an emphasis on obvious winners, whether in the classroom or the sports fields. 'If you are slightly unusual and don't fit in,' said one parent, 'you can slip under the wire a bit.'

Parents, who are increasingly prosperous and professional, are heavily involved. Those with interesting jobs – like astronauts or newspaper editors – come into to share their expertise with the kids. Needless to say, the Parents Association – Rhodes Avenue Primary School Association – is buzzing, organising a hectic cycle of events including a summer and Christmas fair, school raffle, jumble sale, fireworks and Burns Supper. Class reps are required to stage two cake sales a year. Oodles of extra funds raised.

Richmond House School

170 Otley Road, Far Headingley, Leeds, West Yorkshire, LS16 5LG

• Pupils: 220 boys and girls; day • Ages: 3-11 • Non-denom though with a strong Christian base • Fees: £4,383-£6,843 pa • Independent

Tel: 0113 275 2670
Fax: 0113 230 4868
Email: enquiries@rhschool.org
Website: www.rhschool.org

Head: Mrs Jane Disley BA (Hons) PGCE.

Entrance: Maximum 30 children enter nursery each September. Nursery and Reception classes are housed together in the Foundation Stage. There are two classes of 18 per year group from Year 1 to Year 6. Most children remain in the school from the age of three, very few additional places available later. The entry to school is not academically selective at the earliest stages.

Exit: Pupils tend to remain within private sector from 11, many aiming for scholarships at local favoured schools:

Ashville, Harrogate Ladies', Bradford Grammar, The Grammar School at Leeds, Gateways, Woodhouse Grove.

Remarks: Opened on present site in 1935, housed in large stone Victorian villa, typical of area. Became charitable trust in 1979, further buildings and land added since. Main buildings house core classrooms, some a little small but all imaginatively decorated with children's work in evidence. Feels small, yet is tardis-like as additional accommodation materialises around site. In main building some areas appear rather under-sized (child-sized?). Note the diminutive doorways between reception and Year 1 classrooms – does nothing to help generate feeling of spaciousness but does create safe and comforting environment for pupils who all appear happy and focused.

Children busy with excellent range of extra-curricular activities, choir and orchestra flourishing; pupils form basis of school council and organise charity events. Reward schemes are part of a proactive approach to pastoral care; problems are dealt with promptly; 'friendship stops', like miniature bus stops, feature prominently in the playground as a safety zone/stop-off point for children short of a friend; it was very gratifying to see children hovering timidly near them at playtime being quickly picked up and drawn into other children's games.

Attractive sports pavilion, 10 acres of sports grounds, tennis, and this has to be one of the very few schools with its own crown bowling green (a Yorkshire marketing niche?); proximity of Carnegie College provides access to additional sporting facilities plus use of other local squash and badminton courts and swimming pools

Many restrictions on site as this is a residential area on busy main route into Leeds; some parents may find the lack of a car park problematic. However others (predominantly Leeds doctors, lawyers, financiers, business people, college/university staff) find both location and before and after school care convenient.

Parents demand (and get) high academic standards and, although head baulks at term 'hothouse', gets good results from good teaching; undoubtedly a highly competitive and industrious environment, with high expectations. No scholarships available but bursaries are available. Uncommon minimal differential between fee levels at various ages – a consequence of this is that it discourages parents from using the nursery without the intention of continuing through school.

Reputation of enabling children to get into good schools at 11 and in the face of stiff local competition within private sector; this reputation is of vital importance to whole school community. Many choose this school with the next stage very much in mind; it is a means to an end and it delivers.

Riddlesworth Hall Preparatory School

Diss, Norfolk, IP22 2TA

- Pupils: Co-ed nursery/pre-prep. Girls only prep, boarding and day
- Ages: main school 4-13; nursery 2-4 • C of E
- Fees: Boarding £15,720-£16,695; Day £3,300-£9,975 pa • Independent

Tel: 01953 681 246
Fax: 01953 688 124
Email: rhps@riddlesworthhall.com
Website: www.riddlesworthhall.com

Head: Since 2007, Mr Paul Cochrane Cert Ed (late forties). Previously head of prep and lower school at Tettenhall College, Wolverhampton. A lover of traditional boarding life, he's hugely popular with pupils and parents who recognise that if anyone is going to move the school forward it's this antithesis to a 'la-de-dah southerner'. Impressively determined and energetic he bowls about the place teaching geography and boys' PE in addition to tackling all those millions of jobs heads have to do. Married to Sally – she gives that extra something to make this place feel like home and is in the throes of creating a sensory garden for the pupils. They live on site with their four children – the younger three are at the school.

No board of governors – instead a sole owner, Colonel Boulter (owns and heads Barnardiston Hall as well), with whom Mr Cochrane has a good working relationship.

Entrance: 'No strings attached' day at school. Low key observation of performance in English and maths. Formal assessment of special educational needs to see if they can be accommodated.

Exit: To a range of schools at 11 and 13. They say all get to 'where they want to go'.

Remarks: Narrowly escaped closure in 2000 but with some timely help plus the introduction of boys – school due to become fully co-ed in 2011 – it continues to battle on. Recent partnership with an 'international' school in Thailand (apparently its owner loves the Diana connection – Princess Di was the school's most famous past pupil) may bring in between 12 to 25 competent English speaking pupils for a year at a time. First batch, into the top two forms won't, according to Paul Cochrane, 'be more than 12. We want to be sure it doesn't impact on the ethos of the place.' As one parent said 'we're used to having foreign students coming and going. Being in the sticks in Norfolk is great to a point so a tranche of foreign input can only be a good thing.' Time will tell.

Lovely setting deep in farming country where children safely roam. Tennis courts, adventure play area and hutches for small pets make the outdoors even more attractive. Main body of school in listed Georgian pile with welcoming hall, a good library and decent science lab. Adjacent outbuildings provide adequate classroom accommodation – small class sizes suit the timid or those who might just drift along in larger schools. Littlies (4–7) are in nearby self contained stable block with courtyard play area at its centre.

SEN provision with CreSTeD accreditation.

Games for all, every day. According to a parent 'they somehow manage to cobble something together' and play matches. Weekly swimming at pool in nearby Diss. For its size, good range of extra-curricular activities most of which are charged on top of basic fees – music tuition (including the harp), speech and drama, riding and martial arts. Flexible boarding provision with activities at the weekend. Scholarships for military and diplomatic offspring.

Happy, fresh-faced pupils endlessly skip and hug but aren't bothered by the charred wreck of a swimming pool and need for TLC in several areas. Tremendously supportive parents from all walks of life give up occasional Saturday mornings to join the 'task force' – that's gardening in return for a big breakfast get together.

Homely place filled with echoes from the past. Admirably positive head and his wife don't appear to be fazed by the challenges which lie ahead. We wait to see if proposed 'international' link can be happily absorbed and provide the financial boost needed for future developments.

Ripon Cathedral Choir School

Whitcliffe Lane, Ripon, North Yorkshire, HG4 2LA

• Pupils: 35 girls, 45 boys; 15 board 65 day • Ages: 3-13 • C of E • Fees: Day £6,075-£10,065; Boarding £13,401-£14,544 pa • Independent

Tel: 01765 602 134
Fax: 01765 608 760
Email: admin@cathedralchoirschool.co.uk
Website: www.cathedralchoirschool.co.uk

Head: Since 2009, Mr Chris McDade.

Entrance: By assessment and parental interview. Not a school just for choristers or musicians, those without a musical bent still enjoy their time here in part because of the strong emphasis on sport. Not a soft option for male choristers who are selected through voice trials and receive a 50 per cent fee remission. Girl choristers receive 20 per cent fee remission. Choristers can now be boarding or day pupils.

Exit: Roughly 40 per cent leave at 11+ – mostly to Ripon Grammar School (qv) – the rest at 13 plus. Have considerable musical success in scholarships to senior schools every year. Popular leaver destinations include Uppingham, Winchester, Ripon Grammar School, Sedbergh, Queen Margaret's and St Peters.

Remarks: Usual facilities: large hall for assembly, gym and musical productions (of which there are many), with separate dining hall doubling for exams and similar; classrooms, housed in a wooden block resembling stables, err on the small side with only a canopied walkway between, so expect to get wet on rainy days. School hope for a rebuild and outline planning permission has been obtained.

Subjects taught discretely from Year 4, with music school and specialist rooms for ICT, CDT, art, humanities, English and the ever popular science. Library plus dedicated reference book sections in subject rooms. Study all usual subjects plus French, Latin, music and dance. Smallish classes, average 12. All take SATs but school refused to let us see results so do ask when you visit, said their value-added was fine but again didn't produce any evidence to support that so we had to take their word for it (school add it's IAPS policy not to disclose SATs info to publications).

Staff run catch-up clinics for those needing extra support and there's one-to-one help available for mild dyslexia or dyspraxia. IEPs where appropriate. Trying to introduce individual education plans for all children to indicate strengths and weaknesses to be addressed, keen to ensure very able are stretched too. No Saturday school though pupils expected to turn up for any school-related events. Choristers have a busy weekend programme with limited free time. School recognise demands and responsibilities placed on choristers and the need to keep a careful eye on them. Say full boarding tends to suit those children who are happiest at home as those with problems at home tend to fret more in school too. Choristers spend a term or so on probation – carefully monitored but, as elsewhere, doesn't always work out.

Fantastic musical productions; 90 per cent of children play at least one instrument over 60 per cent two, with a handful playing three to grade 7 or 8 standard. Masses of orchestras, bands, and choirs. We saw impressive rehearsals with pupils not only singing and playing but accompanying too. Lots of successes in regional and national music competitions. Half of all pupils involved with LAMDA speech and drama as well as school productions. Well-endowed with sports fields plus adventure playground, aerial runway and separate play area for very youngest. Sport popular, plenty on offer all usual, plus tennis, golf, athletics, dance etc. Play competitively and with success against other preps and schools in locality. Extra-curricular clubs include chess, sewing, cookery, ICT, art, photography, judo etc ...

Dorms have now been upgraded. Boys are housed in big, light, airy rooms with great views, girls have attic rooms, bright with a sky light. Fortunately proposed rebuild includes boarding. Brand new common room on ground floor provides a pleasant area for boys and girls to relax, watch TV, play games and with facilities for tea and snackettes.

Undoubtedly children enjoy their time here and most get the opportunity to shine at something with some, such as the Ripon Young Musician of the Year, positively glowing. Pupils say they have great relationships with teachers and that everyone knows everybody, a real family feel. Not the place for those who don't like being with others and joining in.

You don't have to sing for your supper to come here but those who do, do so in fine voice and good spirit.

Robert Gordon's College Junior School

Linked to Robert Gordon's College in the Senior section

Schoolhill, Aberdeen, AB10 1FE

• Pupils: boys and girls, all day • Ages: 4-11 • Inter-denom
• Fees: £6,270-£9,090; Nursery £3,475-£7,300 pa • Independent

Tel: 01224 646758
Fax: 01224 630301
Email: p.skingley@rgc.aberdeen.sch.uk
Website: www.rgc.aberdeen.sch.uk

Head of Junior School: Mrs Mollie Mennie.

Remarks: For details, see senior school.

Roch House Preparatory School

Linked to Abbots Bromley School For Girls in the Senior section

Abbots Bromley, Rugeley, WS15 3BW

• Pupils: Girls and boys, some board • Ages: Boys in Kindergarten, to move through until aged 11, Girls throughout, boarding from aged 8
• Fees: £4,095-£8,700 pa • Independent

Tel: 01283 840 232
Fax: 01283 840 988
Email: enquiries@abbotsbromley.net
Website: www.rochhouse-ab.co.uk

Head: Since 2005, Mrs Ann Johnson. Bubbly extrovert engenders happy buzz and teaches all pupils at some point every week. Believes in approachability and communication. Has introduced parents' social evenings and gives space in her newsletter to parents' achievements as well as children's.

Entrance: Non selective with new kindergarten lowering age to three.

Exit: Most to senior school.

Remarks: Roch House is a huge rambling 1910 building with bags of space including an unused fourth flour (playground isn't as generous). Bright corridors and rooms offering bespoke dance studio and comfy commonrooms as well as science lab, library, art and technical rooms. Dressing up rail beside pre-prep library and happy girls who chuckle with teachers. Dance possible from day one, riding from sixth birthday. English and maths taught in divisions in Year 6. Each year votes two girls onto forum to present views to staff. Universal thumbs up for food with strong belief, 'Ours is better than over the road; if you don't like it here it's because you're picky.' Housepoints for helpfulness, good work, trying hard. Children say, 'They're quite strict – they don't like you leaving your stuff strewn about the changing room.' Sanctions in line with school's restorative justice policy so include, for example, having to apologise to the cleaner.

The Roche School

11 Frogmore, Wandsworth, London, SW18 1HW

• Pupils: 200 boys and girls, all day • Ages: 2½-11 • Fees: £9,690-£10,470 pa • Independent

Tel: 020 8877 0823
Fax: 020 8875 1156
Email: gcac@therocheschool.co.uk
Website: www.therocheschool.co.uk

Principal : Since 1988, Dr James Roche BSc PhD (sixties). Educated at St Paul's, read physics at Bristol and has a PhD in general relativity from Manchester. Taught for 2 years in a London state school then spent 19 years teaching A level physics at Collingham College, Kensington, where his wife Carmen taught languages. She founded the school in 1988. He teaches maths, history and RE. They have two daughters. We caught him recovering from flu and looking quite grey (think Jon Pertwee as Dr Who) but he was a joy to chat to. Very bright, has a quote for everything. Apparently Bernard Levin said, 'institutions are best if you don't have quite enough room to run them'. So it's a compact school but it isn't overcrowded. Dr Roche handwrites everything even the children's homework indeed (thanks spy) – when he was absent from a lesson a bright pupil (dyspraxic but a maths whiz kid) insisted on setting homework in the doc's style, handwritten and complete with hints and tips! Parents say, 'he can appear to be completely off the wall (think mad professor) but he's wonderful with the children and the children adore him though he's not so at ease with parents. Children not parents are his priority, which is great.'

Entrance: Majority join in the September of their nursery or reception year but handful of occasional places crops up so always worth checking. Visit on an open morning or request an individual tour. All new entrants spend a familiarisation afternoon in school. For some reason, parents get the idea this is a special needs school – it's not but, on the other hand, if your child has a difficulty they'll be helped. To set the record straight they have a mixed ability intake – lots of very bright children (couple of scholars – one boy was offered four scholarships last year) some with SEN, lots without. Can cater for dyslexia, dyspraxia, Asperger's, Down's syndrome, speech & language difficulties, ASD, ADD and those with EFL needs as long as they have the ability to catch up with their year group (also recognise that many children with SEN will be academically very able). Smallish site, so can only have odd one or two who require constant learning support assistance. Have flexibility, too so, if it's better for a child to be out of their chronological age group that's what they'll do. Lift (in pipeline) will improve wheelchair access. Will look at the child, their profile, strengths and difficulties but it's not the place for those needing a totally different programme. Wants children who'll fit in, be integrated and included.

Exit: Some to boarding schools, majority to London day schools. At 8+ to The Harrodian, Putney High and

Northcote. At 11+ to St Paul's, Lady Margaret's, Dulwich, The Hall, Ibstock Place, Wimbledon High, JAGS, Royal Russell, Kings, Bedales etc.

Remarks: Average class size of 16 ensures plenty of individual attention. Very recently praised by Ofsted, no weaknesses, couple of minor considerations. All take SATs – good results – above national norms. Most take 8+ or 11+ for next schools too so get lots of exam practice to lessen the stress. Specialist teachers for French, gym, art and music. Sets for maths and English from Year 1 or 2 to allow slower children to get a secure understanding and the high fliers to soar.

A parent of a child with dyslexia said she couldn't praise the school enough; they bend over backwards to help. If your child needs it they can have as much SEN help as necessary (though you'll be charged extra for one-to-one and there may come a time when a specialist school is suggested if no real progress). The gifted and talented needing extension work will also be given some one-to-one help. IEPs disseminated to all staff and reviewed regularly. Team to help with dyslexia, dyspraxia and speech and language problems (have therapist). Run social skills and friendships groups if need arises. Strong belief that children with SEN enrich the school, teaching others to be kind, considerate and thoughtful.

Lessons are lively affairs that hold the children's interests – then again work's much more fun when you understand it. Have a good sprinkling of investigative and practical work with trips and visits supplementing the diet. Say it's really important to ensure children do as well here as they would anywhere.

Lots happening outside the classroom, parents lyrical about the amazing productions, 'my nine year old was in 'As You Like It'. I was cynical but she learned her lines, understood it and it's given her a taste for Shakespeare – I felt so proud.' We caught the final throes of a West Side Story rehearsal not going quite as well as hoped. Productions are very inclusive – everyone gets to perform and share the limelight. Music's popular too – lots learn instruments or sing, all have a couple of music lessons a week and there's a choir and band. We had the privilege of being shown round by the head boy and head girl – took their duties very seriously, even showing us the paper store – and, fine though the facilities are, we were more impressed by the children. They've a keen awareness of others, a confidence to discuss strengths and weaknesses, they're lively, interested and, try as we might to find at least one child who couldn't explain their work, we failed.

Good sized (for inner London) playground – which children would like grassed (nice idea but with the British weather probably best left), dedicated art room (impressive art work everywhere), well-stocked library, ICT suite, science lab with apparently (according to kids) brilliant interactive whiteboard, good sized hall for PE, assemblies, productions, lunches. All do sport and, although school wouldn't suit aspirant athletes or potential polo players, for vast bulk of youngsters who're content with archetypal primary school sport it's just fine – usual on offer with fixtures against other schools, after-school clubs (most attend at least one extra-curricular club per week) etc.

Not posh or much patronised by the posh. Not the smartest place either (odd holey jumper and shirts hanging out brought back happy memories for this editor.) Children can be children here and they still get into all the top schools. What's more they're well-mannered and polite without a whiff of arrogance or priggishness. All children, from the non-academic through to the very brightest, are kept happy and there's a genuine belief that everyone has strengths. Older children look after younger. Mixed age tables at lunchtime (packed lunch only; no chocolate, nuts or fizzy drinks) and all of the 11+ class have a role or responsibility. Not a school where staff hide away – they're chatty and helpful just like the children.

Roedean Junior School

St Mary's Hall, Eastern Road, Brighton, East Sussex, BN2 5JF

• Pupils: 70; boys and girls • Ages: 3-11 • Fees: £6,300-£12,150 pa
• Independent

Tel: 01273 647763
Fax: 01273 620 782
Email: info@roedean.co.uk
Website: www.roedean.co.uk

Head: Since April 2007, Mr Huw May LRWCMD ADRWCMD PGCE MA Ed NPQH (fortyish, apparently, but we'd have guessed ten years younger). Those lengthy qualifications derive from The Royal Welsh College of Music and Drama where Mr May spent his student days studying singing. He began professional life as a counter tenor in Cardiff and fell into education – 'it was the last thing I wanted to do' – as a result of being asked to do a little singing teaching – 'then I really got into it'. Disarming, engaging, entertaining, Mr May is an enthusiast. 'It was making a difference that I really liked. I had that feeling of, my god, they didn't know that ten minutes ago and now they do!'

He was appointed to the headship of the pre-prep at St Aubyn's in Rottingdean in 2001 and went to St Mary's Hall as head of the junior school in all innocence six years on. Now, with smiling incredulity, he finds himself head of the new Roedean Junior School – a somewhat different prospect. It was a measure of his impact on St Mary's and his popularity therein that there was never any question over his coming to Roedean, as part of the package, so to speak. When the news of the 'merger' with Roedean came he knew that, unlike the St Mary's Senior School, he and his school had 'dodged a bullet'. He is clearly energised by the challenge and the opportunity the 'merger' presents. 'I'm building a community. The parents are a huge part of what goes on – making it more than just a school – much more a family in which we all contribute to the buzz of the place.' This approach makes Mr May the ideal man for the job – the job being to fashion a junior school to be reckoned with – a feeder for Roedean, of course, but a stunningly good little prep in its own right and one which this most attractive of Brighton 'suburbs' should take to its heart.

Entrance: Taster days for nursery and Reception and teacher observation and 'assessment' as much as you can assess at this age. From Year 1, non-verbal and verbal reasoning tests, taster day and assessments of their ability to socialise. Second taster day for those who impress on the first one. Reports from current school. Previously, first come first served at St Mary's Hall. Mr May changed that even before Roedean loomed. At the time of writing, there are still spaces at each level, though a recent Open Day was packed out. Get Max in now and he'll be well prepared for whatever feels right when he's 11. Get Lily in now and you can relax till she's 18.

Exit: The hope is that all girls will go up the road and along the cliff to the Big Sister – of which, of course, by then they will have no fear as much PE, drama etc will have been done there for years. Mr May is adamant that 'preferential treatment' has been agreed so that even if Lily performs poorly on the day of the entrance tests, he has leave to speak on her behalf to the senior branch. Those thought unlikely to thrive in an academic senior school will be warned well before and pointed at less demanding senior schools. Boys will leave at 11 for wherever best suits them. Brighton College is the nearest and arguably the best local co-ed. Others likely to travel to Eastbourne College, Lancing or St Bede's.

Remarks: St Mary's Hall Junior School was newly built in 2006 across the drive from its the long-established and now sadly missed senior school. Its inception was a sound move – build a feeder for the senior school – a bright, cleverly-designed modern pre-prep and prep – just what was needed. Sadly, whereas the junior school got off to a promising start, the senior school derived less benefit than had been hoped and numbers continued to slide. The crunching of credit, the resurgence of Brighton College, the current delusion that it is more 'natural' to educate senior boys and girls together – whatever the evidence – all contributed to its demise. Hence the approach to Roedean and the proposed 'merger' in early 2009.

What remains is a re-energised Roedean which has acquired not only several St Mary's girls throughout the senior school but also, for the first time in its history, its own, purpose-built brand new junior school in the heart of Kemp Town. If you could fly over the top of St Mary's Hall you could see Roedean proper perched on its cliff – it's that close – about four minutes by car. The junior school is one road up from the Brighton promenade, cool in the leafiest, quietest and most desirable bit of Brighton – an anchor's toss from the marina and fifteen minutes stroll to the pier. Roedean has also been left with, of course, the sorry husk that was the St Mary's Senior School and much discussion over how best – and when – to use it.

The Roedean Junior School is co-ed. It is an imaginative building on two floors. The nursery has its own separate entrance into a big light room – windows on three sides – and full of activities which made you want to be three years old. It has its own outside space with a soft surface next to the main school playground. There is an inviting infants' library exhibiting, when we visited, an intriguing collection of musical instruments – maracas, tambourines, slide whistles and bells. Reception similarly engaging with a 'word wall' showing new words in big blots – liked that. Also on the ground floor, Years 1 and 2 – all in good, spacious accommodation with – so important – really nice loos.

On the first floor, Years 3–6 enjoy much architectural ingenuity with a super slanting ceiling and porthole for Year 4s and an imaginative window onto the hall below – a good hall full of really good singing when we dropped in. Children here – well, their head was a professional – clearly really encouraged to sing out here – hooray! The choir was preparing for a tour of Bruges! An excellent music room. Everyone learns a series of instruments here – by Year 5 and 6 all are given free lessons – and instrument loan of violin or cello. DT is taught with an emphasis on learning skills – we loved the little slippers and were impressed by clever designs for chairs. Jolly nice art room though unnaturally tidy, we felt – and we liked the papier mache Roman bowls made by Year 3 and Year 6's Clarice Cliff-style teapots, inspired by a visit to Charleston, along with the comical 'junk' pictures made by Year 5.

Very good library in unusually shaped room – dealing with a leaky ceiling when we visited – with 13 PCs, books and tables – not over-supplied with books but each classroom has its own store too. Lively teaching here. Inspirational teaching evident, too, in Year 6's work on WW2 evacuation – children were writing evacuees' letters home and, even more imaginatively, letters from those who had taken in evacuees complaining about their charges! Excellent displays derived from teacher's own collection – gas masks, wartime radio, ration book, old money etc, making it all very real. High teacher:pupil ratio plus lots of classroom assistants.

Unlike the senior school the junior school is modern and can accommodate children with physical special needs – lift and so on. SENCo is in school 3 days weekly and runs diagnostic tests on anyone thought not to be thriving – close collaboration with parents. School has those with various dys's, mild sensory problems, wheelchairs. In class support and one-to-one – chargeable separately – but all children have their own IEPs, reviewed termly.

Outside is a good field; Mr May has upped the amount of sport done by all – at least an hour a day for Years 3–6. PE mostly done in the hall but, of course, Roedean's sports facilities and specialist coaches now used by juniors. That and the access to the Roedean theatre and so on adds enormously to what the junior school can offer to its pupils and parents.

It's a good little school and it opens door to a good notable one. It is a gift if you are of the impoverished clergy. Worth getting ordained for.

Rokeby School

George Road, Kingston-upon-Thames, Surrey, KT2 7PB

• Pupils: 265 boys, all day • Ages: 4-13 • Non-denom
• Fees: £8,475-£12,330 pa • Independent

Tel: 020 8942 2247
Fax: 020 8942 5707
Email: hmsec@rokeby.org.uk
Website: www.rokebyschool.co.uk

Head: Since 2007, Mr Jason Peck BEd Hons. Joined Rokeby as a science teacher in 1996, having previously worked in the state sector and before that he ran his own business. Originally intending to stay just a few years, he kept moving steadily up through the ranks to deputy head, acquiring NPQH along the way. He had resigned and was all set for a move to a headship elsewhere, when previous head Michael Seigel left. Mr Peck was persuaded to step up to the top job and he has been a very popular appointment with staff ('we're much happier,' confided one) and parents describe him variously as motivated, approachable, 'absolutely delightful,' and 'a very nice guy doing a first class job'. He has definite ambitions for the school and is already perceived as making a significant difference. Democratic style of leadership but in no doubt that buck stops with him and that, 'leaders should lead'. Describes himself as 'innovative and a good delegater' and works hard to make boys, staff and parents feel comfortable with the Rokeby offering. Proud of his strong senior leadership team, which has been further strengthened by the appointment of a new deputy from King's College, Wimbledon.

Entrance: To make entry less stressful and more child-friendly, Rokeby has dropped the previous system of assessments in favour of a ballot system. For entry at age four into pre-prep, register asap from birth for a non-refundable fee of £50. In the March prior to year of entry (i.e. 18 months before starting school), provided that the parents have visited the school, the first 44 boys chosen by ballot will be offered a place, with the rest (averagely 80) going on to a waiting list. All offers are subject to a 'positive' nursery report and siblings are given priority provided the older sibling is 'doing well'. At age seven there are 48 places available in the main school and transfer from pre-prep is 'automatic,' although parents of any boys thought unlikely to thrive will have been previously advised to look for an alternative. External candidates will sit an entry test for the additional places available – usually 6 to 8. Majority of boys come from Wimbledon, Putney and Kingston, with The Squirrels, Putney Park, Merlin, Park Hill and Hurlingham the main feeders.

Exit: At 13 to all the top-notch senior schools. Lots to King's College, Wimbledon, the others in ones and twos to a spread including Epsom College, Charterhouse, St Paul's, Hampton, Kingston Grammar and Eton. Occasionally to Tiffin (state grammar in Kingston) and head relaxed about such boys exiting at 11. 'It's only ever one or two and it's no help if we make a fuss,' says Mr Peck.

Remarks: Does the business and is right up there in the top ranks of the competitive world of Surrey independent boys' preps. Strong academic core but not a hothouse – school prefers the term 'powerhouse'. Certainly it is now offering a more nurturing environment than some similar set-ups and is very keen on the idea of 'extending childhood'.

Established in 1877, the present day school opened in Kingston Hill in 1966 in a very leafy part of town on the swanky private, residential Coombe Estate. Main building is a large Victorian house originally part of the Galsworthy Estate (John Galsworthy of Forsyte Saga fame). Extensively remodelled since then but main building still retains a homely feel. Pre-prep building is newer (1990s) with updated music facilities and an art wing added in 2000s. Most recent investment has concentrated on improving the library, dining hall and IT. It's well resourced, clean and bright. Some classrooms in the original house are a little cramped but the modern additions are airy and spacious. Site is largely built upon, there is little open space not occupied by tennis courts, Astroturf or car-parking.

A school for hardworking, academic boys, a broad-based curriculum includes Spanish, German, Greek and thinking skills. Latin from Year 5. 48-strong staff, split 50:50 male/female, average age 40ish – a hard-core of a dozen or so long servers balanced with some new blood. Teaching style is fairly traditional with the teacher standing and orchestrating the class rather than being a facilitator. 'But we want to embrace good quality innovation where it helps to focus learning,' says Mr Peck. Good focus and flow in the lessons we saw. 'Teaching is fantastic,' says one mother, 'very imaginative and broad-ranging.' Parents and boys agree homework is reasonable and manageable – one hour a night from Year 5 devoted to a single subject on a 14-day rota.

Together with the necessarily academic focus, Mr Peck believes it is an absolute necessity for the boys to relate well to others. 'Personalised learning may be a very good idea but cooperation and competition are just as vital to a boy's success,' he says. 'Their prospective senior schools are increasingly looking beyond the individual to see how he has worked with others or where he has 'taken part'; not just where he has excelled and left the crowd behind.' One father felt strongly that Mr Peck was to be applauded for gradually changing the ethos from 'success at any cost' to one where boys receive a more all-encompassing education. 'But it's not changing over-night, we are, after all, coming from a long way back.' This changing ethos seems to be the thinking behind the school's new Peck-inspired motto, 'Smart, Skilful and Kind' – 'though it might sound better in Latin,' mused one parent. And smart the boys generally are. Parents are largely the professional, prosperous types who proliferate in south west London suburbs and, despite lack of pre-entry testing, nature and nurture seem to ensure that the boys are all up to the high standards of learning here. No SATs but regular assessment. Most get their first choice senior school, with plenty of scholarships among them.

Any boy seeming to struggle will be assessed and individual learning support is provided by trained staff throughout the school. Currently some 26 boys receive extra help, such as one-to-one or withdrawal from lessons. Parents make a contribution towards the cost of any SEN support. Moderate, specific learning difficulties such as dyslexia and dyspraxia can be accommodated while extension work is offered to particularly gifted boys.

Classrooms are generally specialist subject rooms where all appears cheerful and purposeful. Interactive whiteboards and laptops abound. Outside the classrooms, like most schools of this type, sport consumes many hours of effort and discussion. Football, rugby and cricket are the big interests here and taken seriously, though some parents feel efforts could do with a boost. The Astroturf pitch on site is used mainly for pre-prep. For senior field sports, the boys are bussed 15 mins to 10-acre, super-duper sports grounds in Worcester Park – 'they must be the best in south-west London,' says one parent. All boys get a chance to play, though head acknowledged the F teams might struggle to find a fixture against other schools.

Art, music and drama are all valued and well catered for. Lovely art wing. Music has a nice area and is well supported with 128 boys learning a musical instrument of whom 90 take grades, with 15 reaching grade 5 and higher. There's an annual Rowe cup for instrumental and Allen cup for singing, which are strongly contested. An orchestra, two choirs, assorted ensembles and generally lots of opportunities to perform. At least one drama production a year – most recently a charming Toad of Toad Hall. Full range of lunchtime and after school clubs – from the usual sports and music to magic and Warhammer.

Former bugbear among parents was a dearth of trips and outings – all is much improved under Mr Peck, who believes it criminal to be so close to London without making the most of it. Further afield, boys have travelled to Rome, Greece, France, South Africa and Canada recently. Food has also been a gripe here. It's cooked on the premises, but was generally voted not up to scratch in the past. But again the consensus seems to be that things are on the up. Looked good when we visited.

Mr Peck is a good communicator – letters home have a lighter touch, the website has had a makeover, tearful mums have been kindly reassured and generally everyone seems to know where they are and what's expected of them. There's been a fresh focus on pastoral care (an area where parents have voiced concerns in the past). Together with the head of pastoral care, Mr Peck established a properly functioning school council and a buddy system, where older boys undertake to look after a younger schoolmate. There's zero tolerance of bullying and parents are impressed by improvements here. 'It's never been rife or anything but, in the past, I felt the school had a certain naivety in this area, which now seems to have been sharpened up,' one mother commented. 'And I'd now rate them 20 out of 10 in willingness to sort things out.' The emphasis is on managing behaviour with a simple system of rewards (such as house points) and sanctions (such as short detentions). Mr Peck believes boys respond best to something quick and immediate. 'I like to see them smiling,' he says.

Unashamedly academic, Rokeby had something of a tough guy image – we previously described it as not for weaklings and worriers. Still not for real tremblies but under this head a much warmer and positive place.

Rose Hill Westonbirt School

Linked to Westonbirt School in the Senior section

Tetbury, Gloucestershire, GL8 8QG

• Pupils: 130 boys and girls; all day • Ages: 3-11 • C of E
• Fees: £6,108-£9,195 pa • Independent

Tel: 01666 881 400
Fax: 01666 881 391
Email: rosehill@rhwestonbirt.co.uk
Website: www.rhwestonbirt.co.uk

Head: Since September 2009, Mr Neil Shaw BA MA PGCE (thirties), educated at Nottingham High School before reading geography at Exeter then PGCE at Nottingham and MA at Loughborough. Began career at St George's, Edgbaston where he was promoted to deputy headship thence to first headship at Kingswood School, Solihull. Married with one daughter. His high energy levels have already been put to the test: recent ambivalence over 11–13 provision and a fair amount of associated parental angst have necessitated levels of tact and diplomacy that he is unlikely to have anticipated. Parental consensus is that he is winning on most fronts though we feel that he still has an uphill task. Following the merger (see below) and his appointment to the 'new' post thus created, he won over quite a few by holding evening sessions (in the term before he took up his post) to listen to parental concerns from both camps. Pro-active and determined but not yet universally appreciated, we discovered, although school tells us that since our visit this has changed and he is very much appreciated!

Entrance: Visit then taster day when child is assessed in classroom situation.

Exit: 11+ entry to Westonbirt most likely route for girls; otherwise either sex to local grammars, comprehensives or other independents that admit at 11.

Remarks: Created by the merger of Rose Hill (long established and traditional co-ed prep formerly at Alderley, Gloucestershire) and Querns Westonbirt in August 2008. The good news is that the remodelling of the school has produced two much improved buildings (plus some useful temporary accommodation) where previously there was one. A converted girls' boarding house provides the multipurpose school hall, office accommodation and some pleasant classrooms for older pupils. Former Querns building works well for the younger ones and includes hard, bark and grass outside play areas. Nearby copse is being integrated as an 'outdoor classroom' space. Parents love the way that pupils play and share together across the age groups and praise the 'family feel'. Flourishing nursery and highly successful reception class feed the lower years. Parents we spoke to were very impressed with both the teaching and the level of care all the way through the school.

Learning support is well co-ordinated from designated area: 'the beehive' and moves straight in with appropriate (individual or small group) help as soon as a need is seen by teachers. One mother praised this positive intervention, telling us how her daughter now loved reading as a result and was 'zooming through her books.' At 5+ she was also playing the piano and loving her sport. Gosh.

Separate ICT suite for Year 3 upwards and pupils benefit from proximity of super sports, music and other facilities shared with the senior school. Vibrant art area (temporary accommodation proved versatile here) supports sculpture and fashion as well as regular art classes; French is introduced from nursery level. Music teacher cited as 'miraculous'. Forty children have individual music tuition. Singing, recorder and other instrumental groups; 'outstanding concerts and musical productions,' we were told. Choir performs locally and pupils are entered for Cheltenham Festival music and drama events as well as LAMDA examinations in which they excel. Visits out of school are many and varied: educational for all age groups and lots of sporting fixtures for 7+.

Lots of parental involvement and fun activities with and without the children: karting for all ages, parental rock band, 'Querns and Roses' lined up for summer ball gig. Children 'love it' and parents we spoke to describe it as 'a fabulous school'. After recent uncertainties associated with the merger, RHW can now settle down to its dedicated rôle of providing a happy educational environment for 3–11 year olds.

Rosemead Preparatory School

70 Thurlow Park Road, Dulwich, London, SE21 8HZ

• Pupils: 330; 180/150 girls/boys;- all day • Ages: 3-11 • Inter-denom
• Fees: £8,595-£9,120 pa • Independent

Tel: 020 8670 5865
Fax: 020 8761 9159
Email: admin@rosemeadprepschool.org.uk
Website: www.rosemeadprepschool.org.uk

Headteacher: Since 2003, Mrs Catherine Brown Cert Ed Dip Ed RSA Dip SpLD (fifties). Previously taught at Orley Farm and Dulwich College Prep School. Married with three grown-up children, one of whom attended Rosemead. She has a keen interest in the arts, the influence of this can be seen around the school. Since taking up headship she has overseen expansion of the school to two sites with a dedicated Early Years department. An energetic and imaginative head, say parents.

Entrance: Informal assessment morning at 3+ for nursery places, then by assessment at 4+, 7+ and casual vacancies in other year groups. Pupils are a broad cultural and socio-economic mix; catchment area is expanding.

Exit: At 11 to Dulwich College, Alleyn's, JAGS, St Dunstan's, Emanuel, Sydenham High, Trinity, Whitgift, City of London. Good proportion receive offers for academic, sport, art and music scholarships. Odd one to boarding and increasing numbers to state grammar schools.

Remarks: A very active, busy school with some excellent new facilities in the prep department including library, ICT suite and art room equipped with potter's wheel and photographic equipment. The pre-prep is housed in the new premises, Elm Court, which has its own head and has been completely refurbished. Well balanced fairly traditional academic curriculum, enhanced with an ample range of sport, art, dance and music. All pupils are taught French and there are Spanish, Mandarin and Russian clubs. Spanish has recently been introduced to the Year 6 curriculum. The school takes care to try and match the capacities and needs of each pupil. Full and part-time SEN staff provide support for specific learning difficulties as long as individuals can keep up to speed in class. Pupils progress is carefully monitored and there are opportunities for accelerated learning. Both premises have multi-purpose halls, colourful playgrounds and attractive classrooms though some are on the small side.

Inspiring art displays deck the classrooms and corridors and there is a dedicated art teacher. Two dedicated PE staff; head of sport is also captain of the England ice hockey team. Professional PE coaches add to PE staff in the junior school; pupils do well in many local matches and competitions, including ISA events. The school has a good reputation for spotting and developing individual sporting talents.

Music notably strong, individual tuition is available on a number of instruments, all pre-prep pupils learn the violin, all juniors the recorder. Impressive variety of music groups, an orchestra, jazz band and 3 choirs which sing in the Albert Hall Charity Christmas Concert. Drama is also popular, the school puts on regular plays and everyone has an opportunity to be in a production. Good choice of sport, music, dance and art after-school clubs.

Founded in 1942 the school is run by Thurlow Educational Trust, a parent co-operative and governed solely by parents. Active PTA runs a number of social and charity fund raising events, and an annual family skiing trip. Whilst much expanded, Rosemead remains a family school with a comfortable atmosphere, a place where children can discover and develop their strengths. Good all-round education preparing children for the more academic senior schools.

Rossall Junior School

Linked to Rossall School in the Senior section

Broadway, Fleetwood, Lancashire, FY7 8JW

• Pupils: girls and boys; 125 (4 boarders) • Ages: 7-11 in prep, 2-7 in pre-prep • C of E • Fees: Day £6,990-£7,260 pa; Boarding £11,880-£17,700 pa • Independent

Tel: 01253 774 222
Fax: 01253 772 052
Email: enquiries@rossall.org.uk
Website: www.rossallschool.org.uk

Head of Juniors: Since September 2010 Mrs Katie Lee MEd, former head of pastoral care and director of sport, joined Rossall in 1992 as head of girls' games and spent 10 years as a senior girls' housemistress. A career educationalist, with 30 years' teaching experience, her early years were in comprehensive education. Further experience in higher and adult education, so this appointment completes the circle from 'cradle to grave'. Has a pragmatic and decisive approach, is energetic and results driven. Changes are already visible in the creative use of public space and empty classrooms, strengthening the links and collaboration between the nursery and reception, re-invigorating school council and improving communications with parents. Introduced ties for school captains (infant and juniors) and house captains, as a mark of office and to raise the profile of these posts of responsibility. Believes the Primary Years Programme (PYP) gives children a real confidence and wants to develop this further by providing public platforms and presentation opportunities for them.

Mrs Lee is a director of Blackpool Grand Theatre Trust Board and the theatre's child protection officer. She is also a school governor of Millfield Science and Performing Arts College in Thornton. Breeds Weimaraner dogs and has two much loved pets.

Entrance: At two into the nursery in an informal play session. Into reception by assessment of social skills at a taster day. Infill in other years on assessment and report from previous school.

Exit: All to 'Dragon', transition to senior school for Years 7 and 8.

Remarks: Nursery and Infants in stand-alone building at edge of campus, accessible from nearby car park making drop-off and collection easy. Entrance area work in progress, early' years library and meeting room being created but on arrival no 'buzz' usually associated with this age group. Pre-lunch preparations?

Due to reduction in numbers in recent years, plenty of classroom space available. Has enabled alternative use as cloakrooms and storage areas, allowing uncluttered passage, a benefit in an infant school. Enclosed outside play area leads directly from Early Years' allowing free flowing outdoor play.

Junior School is housed in a separate building in front of the main school, a short walk away. Narrow circulation areas and some small classrooms cope with current numbers but any expansion and space will be at a premium. Contemporary class photos adorn the impressive room allocated to school council meetings. Both buildings in need of a facelift though good provision of IT with whiteboards evident.

However, the environment belies the work in the classroom. In 2006, the IB Primary Years Programme (PYP) was introduced. This enquiry-led learning programme promotes the development of the whole child, a holistic educational approach fostered at Rossall. It is particularly strong in developing communication skills, certainly evident in our conversation with pupils. Building on early success, the programme continues to be embedded and developed in the curriculum. Each classroom has key phrases on display so that pupils understand expected learning outcomes and can reflect on their learning style.

A SENCo covers both infants and juniors, providing continuity. Working one on one or in small groups, work is related to the class mainstream unit of enquiry work.

A full programme of 21 different weekly activities provides a full range of extra-curricular clubs and activities. Swimming, hockey and rugby are curriculum sports, with clubs for football, basketball, fives and badminton in addition. Junior choir for the singers and flute club for budding musicians.

A very clear rewards and sanctions system, with pupils' success being collected for their house. Three houses and healthy inter-house rivalry, culminating in House Challenge Day. The high spot in the social calendar for Year 6 is the Leavers' Ball, complete with a pink stretch limo for the girls and a black version for the boys!

A palpable feeling that learning is fun and a happy atmosphere of pupils engaged in learning exists in the classrooms of both buildings. A real leap of faith, the PYP programme is proving to lay good foundations for senior school, although in an environment without the extensive international element so evident with the older pupils.

Rowan Prep School

6 Fitzalan Road, Claygate, Claygate, Surrey, KT10 0LX

• Pupils: 255 girls; includes nursery and kindergarten (40), all day
• Ages: 2-11 • Non-denom • Fees: £8,799-£11,277 pa • Independent

Tel: 01372 462 627
Fax: 01372 470 782
Email: school.registrar@rowan.ucst.co.uk
Website: www.rowan.surrey.sch.uk

Head: Since 2004, Mrs Kathy Kershaw Cert Ed (fifties). Her fourth headship, previously head of nursery and pre-prep at Colfe's School (qv). A gushing enthusiast she quickly got her feet under the table and established herself as an instigator of change – academic, pastoral and cosmetic. She's a terrific advocate for the school with a warm manner and very keen to please, 'though perhaps too many people all the time,' comments a parent. She undoubtedly talks the talk and received an outstanding Independent Schools Inspectorate that was well received by the parents – some of whom can be more vocal than most. However, her more approachable style of management has so far generally won approval among parents as a 'breath of fresh air'. The girls also are on board – Mrs Kershaw says, 'my approach is more user friendly. However, the girls respect this and seem to relate to this more positively.' Lots of exciting plans for the school's future, not least to challenge its competitive ethos. She feels it's, 'important to do your best rather than just be a winner.' However, she has to tread a fine line – 'it is important that parents feel comfortable that the changes will not affect the high academic standards the school is renowned for.'

Entrance: Priority in kindergarten is given to those girls moving up from nursery (other places on first-come-first-served basis). Then automatic transfer to pre-prep at 4, followed by prep department at 7. There is usually also a small intake at 7, places permitting. Selection to prep takes form of informal 'activity day', its purpose seemingly to meet the girls and weed out any glaring unsuitables. However, Rowan retains its policy as a non-selective school and will take everyone from those who need learning support through to gifted and talented. Numbers are beginning to climb again. It is always worth trying for occasional places at odd times.

Exit: To top local independent schools – every year, large numbers to Lady Eleanor Holles, Tormead, Guildford High, St Catherine's Bramley. Regularly some to Surbiton High and a couple to board, usually Benenden. Consistently one or two to highly sought after state Tiffin Girls' in Kingston. 2010 saw 5 academic scholarships to a range of highly academic schools. Interestingly, only a few girls to co-ed senior schools – parents and girls are clearly pleased with the way Rowan continues to demonstrate virtues of single-sex education.

Remarks: In our last edition, we said, 'interesting times ahead' as the head continues to implement her vision for the school. The question was – how she would marry a softer, more gentle, approach, with the tip-top academic results parents have come to expect? Rowan parents are traditionally a competitive bunch, so the pressure is on the head to prove that the regime can be all things to all academic abilities. Now in her seventh year, Mrs Kershaw seems to be meeting the expectation of parents with the Schools' Inspectorate referring to the quality of education and affirming, 'girls at Rowan benefit from an extremely high-quality range of stimulating educational opportunities within a caring, supportive atmosphere in which all are encouraged to constantly strive to do their best'.

Academically, the impressive list of next schools at 11, from an unselected start, is a reflection of the rigorous academic structure – often the reason parents chose the school. But it does not suit all – in the past there were clashes with some parents who felt the need for a more nurturing atmosphere (and they often departed to pastures new). School is keen to emphasise that it 'remains consistent in preparing the girls for the senior school of their choice and will not compromise the academic rigour necessary to ensure success for every girl.' Mrs Kershaw adds, 'we also have a designated teacher who is actively involved in teaching the staff and providing reinforcement and help related to the talented and gifted girls in the school.' PHSE is now timetabled for more pastoral support and was noted as a particular area of improvement on the inspection report.

Class sizes run at around 18, with a maximum of 20. Head seems to have a team of excellent supportive staff – school lost several initially but this felt to be natural consequence of change rather than any mass walkout. There is now more of a Learning Support infrastructure and Learning Support markedly improved recently. New, though not glamorous, portable classrooms at Rowan Hill provides facility for one full-time learning support specialist with extra dyslexia and maths help as required from two other support teachers who are specialists in this area. Cost depending on need.

The school is split physically and administratively into Rowan Brae, the pre-prep, and Rowan Hill, the prep. They are a few minutes walk from each other, but both under the aegis of Mrs Kershaw from her office at Rowan Hill. Much effort is being made to achieve a closer relationship between the two departments on a curriculum level, and this has proved most successful. The inspection report, under ' The Quality of Education', states: 'besides being extremely well planned, the curriculum throughout the school shows continuity and clear progression from Nursery to Year 6' with girls being 'very well prepared for their move from Rowan Brae to Rowan Hill and from there to the next stage of their education.'

Rowan Brae, which houses the nursery to Year 2, is overseen by its own head, Mr James Tilly, in post since September 2007. However, he is by no means a stranger to the school having been part of the Senior Management team and having taught at the school for nine years. Both premises are converted Edwardian redbrick houses (that blend seamlessly with surrounding imposing properties) – hence a combination of slightly odd-shaped classrooms in the original buildings with more spacious later additions. The whole school has nearly completed a huge face-lift, with funding clearly not an issue. Immaculate inside and out, feels very well looked after.

In Rowan Brae, lovely, bright, airy classrooms. Lots of it is purpose-built, so layout really works and rooms have their own direct access to playground. Strong on presentation and handwriting, some outstanding Year 1 samples. Wonderful, imaginative topics and artwork – Year 2 'Healthy Living' project involves participation in Adopt-A-Chef scheme – they visit a commercial kitchen, at the House of Commons! Children and parents seem particularly thrilled with this part of the school.

As girls progress through Rowan Hill, they move around the school to be taught in excellently equipped, bright classrooms with evidence of much hard work and inspired teaching adorning walls and corridors. Fab new parent-funded IT suite, doubling as Year 6 classroom. New 'smartboards' everywhere. Mrs K has left no stone unturned in a bid to update and enhance the environment for all. It's not only the bits that show which make a glossy impression to parents, but staff also appreciate what she's doing i.e. centralising resources, improving access to facilities, etc – 'her standards are very high,' approves one. FoR (Friends of Rowan) continues to support the school with vigorous fundraising, a smart new mini-bus and caretaker's van having been presented in 2008.

The grounds at both sites have not escaped the head's beady eye. Extensive landscaping was well underway when we visited, bark chippings even laid in the spinney, an ever popular wooded play area previously inclined to mud! New outdoor games equipment available from specially designed sheds where girls help themselves – and very diligent in returning it all.

Sports facilities at Rowan Brae rather limited although there is a gym, a small field and lovely large playground with areas segregated by picket fencing for different age groups – loads of toys. At Rowan Hill there are two netball courts which become a playground and a hard tennis court. Girls are bussed out to Reed's School for swimming and to the local community recreation ground for athletics.

Excellent music, class and instrumental, backed up by lots of scholarships for leavers. At Rowan Brae all girls in Year 1 receive free tuition in either the violin or the cello which culminates in an impressive concert for parents at the end of the year. Three quarters of girls at Hill learn an instrument with their practice sessions timetabled into school day. All the usual ones played plus development of some more adventurous ideas, percussion club with samba drum workshops currently proving popular. Participation in orchestra and ensembles actively encouraged. Good choir, who have taken part in national competitions and won the Woking Music Festival in the last academic year.

Head has strong community conscience and has begun to involve the school in lots of schemes, sponsored events e.g. planting bulbs on traffic island. She feels the need for school to have 'less arrogance and more humility than before,' for girls to be 'better equipped for life beyond it'. To keep up this momentum after leavers' exams in Year 6 , new 'life skills programme' has been devised, ranging from community work and cycling proficiency.

Very polite, natural and open, happy-looking girls. Nice, relaxed atmosphere – gentle hum of activity ... not overly quiet or noisy. Distinctive, attractive uniform based on school tartan.

Rowan is a school very much reflecting its locality – the school of choice for socially mobile, mainly professional parents (lots of first-time buyers) living in the affluent environs of the gated private estates close by. Parental parking at each site is limited to the roadside, which has created its share of issues with local residents; however the school operates a 'drop and go' system which has addressed this and has a serious commitment to the 'Golden Boot challenge' encouraging girls and parents to walk to school.

Rowledge Church of England Primary School

School Road, Rowledge, Farnham, Surrey, GU10 4BW

• Pupils: 110 boys, 100 girls; all day • Ages: 4-11 • C of E • State

Tel: 01252 792 346
Fax: 01252 795 750
Email: admin@rowledge.hants.sch.uk
Website: www.rowledge.hants.sch.uk/

Head: Since 2006, Mr Richard Catchpole, previously the school's deputy head and class 6 teacher.

Entrance: Non-selective and always oversubscribed (although the numbers vary). In 2010 there were 60+ applications for 30 places. Proximity to the school is key, so consider moving into the village to get the best chance of a place and check the map on the school website. Attending local nurseries in the village does not guarantee a place, despite what you might be told. Usual state criteria apply with priority given to those living closest to the school and then siblings. The entire new intake has a visit at home from the Year R teacher before they start.

Exit: Almost all to two local state secondary schools – Eggars in Alton or Weydon in Farnham. A handful of leavers to local independents.

Remarks: A super village school where children enjoy learning – they put a lot into their school life and school ensures they get a lot out. Academically standards are good. All Year 5 take an English Speaking Board exam to assess their reading and public speaking ability. 'It does wonders for their confidence,' said one mother.

Average class size 30 with learning support assistants in every class. Very well staffed, mainly female, several student teachers, parish youth worker and parent volunteers. A new deputy head and Key Stage Two coordinator joined the school in 2007. A pat on the back for teaching skills – the school often provides teaching practice for Winchester College. School caters well for SEN: about 15 per cent of the school pupils receive extra help, taught mainly with the class or in groups by one part-time SEN teacher – school is fully accessible for the disabled. Equal emphasis on 'special needs' of those at the other end of the academic spectrum with assistance from an Able Child Coordinator who visits once a week.

On a quiet lane in an affluent village on the Surrey/Hampshire border, the original Victorian building has been extended and refurbished over the years with additional spacious classrooms and a fab multi-use hall. An extension to the hall completed in 2008. This provides four extra rooms for music lessons and focus groups. Well equipped ICT, all classrooms have interactive whiteboards and projectors. The whole place is immaculately maintained – a refreshing change; a well loved feel about the place. Lots of fantastic work displayed and the children are very proud of their school. Superb outside space – refurbished playground, extensive playing fields (complete with trim trail), the school has its own private access to the adjacent Alice Holt Forest used for lots of activities and assemblies in the summer.

Choir and orchestra, lots learn an instrument. Sport, particularly football, rounders and netball is good, with regular competitions against other local schools. A buzzing hive of activity throughout the day and this continues after school with the usual extra-curricular activities run by staff or privately organised. Residential and day trips. Very informative, award winning website, 'all the usual news and kept up to date,' said a parent. Also includes pages of jokes, quizzes and articles posted by pupil webmasters. 'It's really cool!' said one pupil.

Pupils are an extremely well behaved bunch and few problems arise – 'the children lead very busy lives,' said one parent 'but they love it.' Regular 'Friendship Weeks' ensure that all are aware of, and signed up to, the zero tolerance of bullying policy in the school. Young Governors' scheme involves pupils in the running of the school and teaches them about decision-making including whether to allow girls to wear trousers to school!

Royal Grammar School Junior School (Newcastle)

Linked to Royal Grammar School (Newcastle) in the Senior section

Lambton Road, Jesmond, Newcastle upon Tyne, Tyne and Wear, NE2 4RX

• Pupils: all day • Ages: 7-11 • Non-denom • Fees: £24,642 pa
• Independent

Tel: 0191 281 5711
Email: admissions@rgs.newcastle.sch.uk
Website: www.rgs.newcastle.sch.uk

Head: Mr Roland Craig.

Entrance: Assessment days held in mid January for prospective Year 3 and in November for Year 5 entrants.

Exit: All to the senior school (provided that internal assessments confirm suitability).

Remarks: Self-contained, purpose-built junior school. Years 3 and 4 self-contained in one building – pupils move across the road to new accommodation in Year 5 and 6. Shares facilities with the senior school.

Royal High School, Bath, Junior School GDST

Linked to Royal High School, Bath GDST in the Senior section

Hope House, Lansdown Road, Bath, BA1 5ES

• Pupils: 200 girls, plus nursery school; boarding from Year 5 • Ages: 3-11 • Non-denom • Fees: Nursery £5,760; Day £6,978; Boarding £14,508-£16,647 pa • Independent

Tel: 01225 422 931
Fax: 01225 484 378
Email: royalhigh@bat.gdst.net
Website: www.gdst.net/royalhighbath

Head: Since 2005, Mrs Helen M Fathers who knows every child in the school and is keen to develop the school as an academically strong school offering a stimulating curriculum. She is proud of all her girls and quick to make the most of parental input.

Entrance: By assessment and interview with head; children at the nursery school are assessed at entry to the Reception class and take up the first available places.

Remarks: On the site of the former high school a short walk or drive down the hill from the current senior school. There is regular overlap with the juniors using the sports and facilities weekly, and there is some shared staff. Big, sunny classrooms all fitted with interactive whiteboards in fine Georgian buildings with magnificent views. Grounds are on a steep hillside but somehow children are not seen careering out of sight at playtimes. Rolling is only allowed occasionally. Everywhere there is something thought-provoking to look at, inside and out. A huge mosaic and a fading mural enhance the concreted areas. Another nice touch is the provision of laminated games tables (chess, ludo, snakes and ladders) in part of the playground. Early birds may arrive at school from 8.00am and the after-school care provision is registered with Ofsted and is available till 6.00pm each day. At some stage, date to be determined, the junior school will be moving to a new home in Bath. Cranwell House is one of the city's finest properties, sitting in 11 acres of parkland. It will incorporate a purpose built new nursery school.

Definitely a more stimulating and buzzy atmosphere than up the hill. Girls look you in the eye and have things to say. Strong home school links are a feature of the school. The girls were able to make a huge copy of a Gainsborough painting, when it was donated by a parent from the school to a Bath Museum.

Fairly traditional timetable concentrating on English and maths and using as a base the core requirements of the National Curriculum. French and music are taught to all children from nursery up. Computers play an important part, and there is a fully equipped ICT room with 30 computers linked to the internet. Loads of clubs. The school is very good at providing basic skills (tables, handwriting etc) necessary for coping with secondary school, so much so that those that take the entrance exam for the senior school are pretty unphased by the process and almost all go on. This pleases parents. Those who are not going to make it through the tests are gently weeded out ('but in a nice way' comments one parent) in advance.

Small but well-equipped nursery school within the grounds, has separate facilities, but children participate in school assembly and eat lunch (if staying) with the big girls. Everyone has school dinner cooked on site, 'no packed lunches, for health reasons – we believe in providing a substantial midday meal'.

Cheerful, enclosed and safe, a perfect environment for the girls to do what the GDST does best, expand into themselves.

Royal Masonic School for Girls Prep & Pre-prep

Linked to Royal Masonic School For Girls in the Senior section

Rickmansworth Park, Chorleywood Road, Rickmansworth, Hertfordshire, WD3 4HF

• Pupils: 180. All girls • Ages: 4-11 • Fees: Boarding: £12,870-£22,020; Day £7,380-£13,770 pa • Independent

Tel: 01923 773 168
Fax: 01923 896 729
Email: admissions@royalmasonic.herts.sch.uk
Website: www.royalmasonic.herts.sch.uk

Head: Since 1996, Ms Linda Beckett BEd Hons (late forties). Educated at Christ Hospital Girls High School, Lincoln. Previously deputy head of Leaden Hall, Salisbury. Proud of her charges, gets a real buzz from seeing former pupils in sixth form, transformation complete.

Entrance: Mainly at four and seven, from a range of independent and mainstream nurseries and primary schools; there are also limited opportunities for entry throughout the prep department. Entry at each stage is competitive as most year groups are oversubscribed. Entrance assessments are classroom based and broad, focusing not merely on English, mathematics and reasoning, but also on approach, potential and the extra qualities that a girl may have.

Exit: All guaranteed a place at the senior school. Odd one leaves mainly because of relocation or for financial reasons, very few to other independent schools.

Remarks: On same campus but with own facilities, library, playground, ICT room etc though older girls begin transition by using some specialist facilities in senior school. Youngest taught in classes of 16, rising to 20 or 22 in older classes.

Corridors teeming with bright, frequently changed displays, allocated so all classes, and most pupils, get a chance to display their wares.

Lots of earnest, chatty children as keen to work as to play. We observed lessons with lots of hands on, differentiated, learning and happy children. Plenty of activities ensure something for everyone. Learning support for those who need a boost, whether for a specific learning difficulty or to enhance literacy or numeracy skills. Gifted looked after too; girls had chance to quiz author Michael Morpurgo about his literary prowess when he visited on

Prize Day and there are regular Enrichment Activities on offer.

Have annual play or production involving lots of eager participants. All encouraged to play an instrument, recently cello lessons offered on free trial basis to boost orchestra shortages. All Year 3 play the violin as part of the Music Curriculum, recorders not really the thing here. Plenty of sport, competitive matches from Year 4.

Sunny, homely boarding house with good facilities, including TV and extensive DVD collection but so much to do, few have time to sit in front of a screen. Numerous after school activities, plus games and in-house events, offer plenty of distractions, homesickness a rarity. Few full boarders, majority weekly or occasional nevertheless a bustling bargain even for full timers, with plenty offered at weekends too.

Rudolf Steiner Junior School (Kings Langley)

Linked to Rudolf Steiner School (Kings Langley) in the Senior section

Langley Hill, Kings Langley, WD4 8NB

• Pupils: 410 • Independent

Tel: 019232 262 505
Fax: 01923 270 958
Email: info@rsskl.org
Website: www.rsskl.org

Remarks: See senior school.

Rudolf Steiner School South Devon; Early Childhood Dept

Linked to South Devon Steiner School in the Senior section

Hood Manor, Dartington, Totnes, Devon, TQ9 6AB

• Pupils: boys and girls • Ages: 3-7 • Christian foundation - Non-denominational • Fees: £2,040-£4,350 pa • Independent

Tel: 01803 897 377
Fax: 01803 762 374
Email: admissions@steiner-south-devon.org
Website: www.steiner-south-devon.org

Mandate Co-ordination administrator: None. As for main school, monthly mandate circles (bringing teachers and parents together to review, discuss and plan) form the first level of organisation which then carries on through weekly collegiate and departmental meetings.

Entrance: Applications via admissions co-ordinator. Prospective parents for early years invited to attend a special monthly afternoon session hosted by current parents. Afternoon includes tour, peek-in at lessons and talks by parents and teachers. Nursery and kindergarten both oversubscribed so contact in good time.

Exit: Most proceed seamlessly to main school aged six.

Remarks: The department is passionate about fulfilling Steiner's mission for early childhood education – lovely hobbit-like learning environment where childhood can be enjoyed to the full away from gaze of older children. Teachers we met were very protective of children's dream-like experience and were disinclined to let us intrude. Understandable enough. Mothers appreciate how 'school gives children the space they need' and how children 'learn to be still'. Classrooms have been conceived from natural materials and are alive with light, fun and a sense of wonder. Welcome back to 'never never land'. Each day starts outside 'come rain or shine': 'children need to interact with nature,' we were told and they are much calmer by the time they go indoors around 9.30am.

Teachers follow through themes for four weeks with the emphasis on developing imagination. Simple crafts, making dens and a play house, gathering for ring time with songs and movement games, listening to a story and celebrating festivals are all part of what happens. Children also learn reverence for the divine in nature and respect for others. Helping with tasks such as breadmaking, tidying and arranging are important. Parent and toddler group for tinies, a nursery group for those aged 3–4 and a kindergarten for 4–6 year olds. Mental concepts are 'caught' through sensory experience rather than 'taught' through rote learning. Great emphasis is placed upon development of fine motor skills and manual dexterity. Steiner trained early years specialists (school is participating as a centre for Plymouth based students – many of whom spend time here), classroom assistants plus parents ensure children lack for nothing. Books and computers strictly taboo – 'parents don't cheat' we were assured 'but support Steiner philosophy'. Great for those who accept what Steiner advocated and intend their children to remain within this system.

The Russell Primary School

Petersham Road, Petersham, Richmond, Surrey, TW10 7AH

• Pupils: 240; 120 boys and 120 girls in main school plus 52 in nursery; all day • Ages: 3-11 • Non-denom • State

Tel: 02089 401 446
Fax: 02083 320 985
Email: info@russell.richmond.sch.uk
Website: www.russell.richmond.sch.uk

Head: Since 2005, Mr Darren Harrison BA PGCE NPQH (thirties). Comes from Cumbria but has worked in the Borough of Richmond for fifteen years, his previous position was deputy head of The Queen's School, Kew. Very informal and chatty, he has an approachable and energetic manner with a palpable love of his school. 'He's a great listener,' 'he always takes on board what you say,' 'he really seems to care about what parents think,' 'he's very go-ahead' – just some of the very positive views expressed by parents. He has a stable staff so he must be doing something right in that department as well – you get the impression he's the sort of chap who would let them get on with their job as much as possible. Lives locally with his wife and two young sons. Interests include travelling, sport and mathematics.

Entrance: Over-subscribed every year: 50 plus applicants for 34 places. Nursery place does not guarantee a place in reception class. Clear criteria for admission given on school website: children with a statement of SEN get first priority, followed by siblings, then those living closest to the school. With the current baby boom, there aren't many places left for non-siblings. You'll need to live on the doorstep even to stand a chance.

Exit: Very few leave after Year 2 to go to local prep schools. Local secondary Grey Court is the 'linked school' taking about two thirds of the leavers for senior school. A few go each year to the local grammar schools in Kingston – Tiffin Girls and Tiffin School, which are notoriously difficult to get into (you will need to get special coaching for the entrance exam). A handful move on to local independent day schools, for example, Kingston Grammar, Hampton or Surbiton High – an ex-Russell child is likely to be the only entrant from there in their year group. Mr Harrison is happy to give advice to parents about the independent schools as well as the state sector.

Remarks: A school that stands out for its SEN provision, wrap around care and wonderful grounds – you get the feeling that it is a place that really does belong to the children. One member of staff remarked that she feels privileged to be allowed care of such a wonderful group and the head has recently consulted all pupils about what they want to study – 'there is a lot of science to be learned from magic,' he says. The new child-centred topic approach to learning is now well underway. For those parents wanting a formal and authoritarian atmosphere this is not the place but for those parents in situ things couldn't be better – 'a strong focus on the development of the individual child,' remarked a mother, 'they aim to nurture every child,' says another.

A school that is proud of its history – it was originally founded in Richmond Park as the village school of Petersham by Lord John Russell in the 1850s. It retains something of the 'village school' feel – a true social mix where city bonuses rub shoulders with artists and with the council estate. The current school was built in the 1950s and some of the buildings look a bit tired but the beautiful outdoor space, which feels like a little corner of Richmond Park, more than compensates for this. There are two ponds teeming with wildlife, wooded areas, pathways to explore, wild areas, a vegetable garden cared for by the pupils and a popular outdoor classroom enclosed by bushes. This is in addition to the abundant playground areas with climbing equipment of all shapes and sizes. Shaded areas have been constructed and there is no outdoor area which cannot be put to good use. Some buildings are quite far apart, so no choice but to get wet when it rains!

Inside, the facilities are more than adequate for a small school: two halls, a science room, an art room (even has a kiln, though there was no sign of any pottery at the time of our visit), a small cookery room allowing for groups of six children, updated summer 2008. Libraries are cosy and welcoming and there are plenty of computers and interactive whiteboards in each classroom.

Education is far more than wanting a top place in the league table; SATs results are certainly not the be all and end all here – that said, the school is usually mid ranking in the borough. In Key Stage 1, classes are mixed between two year groups in order to remain within the maximum class size of 30. Parental concerns about this set-up have proved unfounded, especially since the birth month of the children is taken into account and Ofsted reports that standards are above average at this stage (the school has taken on board the comment that more able children could achieve more in reading and writing). Within the core curriculum, the school is always looking for ways to add breadth – hence the consultation about what children want to learn – and are ahead of the game when it comes to government requirements. Children learn French from reception and German from Year 5, with the help of students from the next door German School, and science is taught by specialist teachers. Children with English as an additional language are few, so can be helped within the classroom environment.

SEN is given high priority and there is much expertise within the school. Specialist SEN unit for children with statements which feels very much part of the school, although physically separate. (The multi-sensory room can be booked for use by anyone, not just the children in the unit). The SEN unit is recognised in the local area as very successful and is staffed by highly qualified personnel. The children join in as many mainstream activities as possible – 'a great benefit to both sides,' says the head. 'In an assembly the SEN child will take a role and be helped to do so by one of the children from the main school.' Parents also like this situation – 'my child is beginning to understand other children's needs.'

Music also enjoys specialist teaching; the choir is open to all age groups and performs annually in the Richmond Music Festival. One parent was delighted to find the music teacher in the nursery as well. Brentford Football Club teaches sport; swimming takes place at the German School for younger ones and in Richmond for older age groups. 'Sport is on the up,' remarked one parent, though another pointed out that there is not enough practice for the school teams thereby minimising their chances of winning. However, Mr Harrison is keen to add that relatively recently the school was 'the winner of the indoor athletics tournament and also the small schools' football tournament.'

The staff are 'adored' by the children according to one mother and, despite high house prices in the area, remain a remarkably stable bunch. One teaching assistant, who has been at the school for longer than anyone can remember, has applied to continue after retirement age. Apart from the head though, there is rather a lack of male presence though Mr Harrison reminds us that 'a classroom assistant, the Brentford sports coaches and a reading volunteer from the local community are also male.'

Pupils seem calm and motivated to learn, with 'exemplary discipline' according to Ofsted. Before and after school club (Fit for Sport) from 7.30am till 6pm catering for children from six months to 11 years at reasonable rates. For those who just want to enjoy an after-school club, there is plenty to choose from, ranging from indoor golf to maypole dancing (very popular). As with many Richmond primaries, part of what makes the Russell a good school is the parents – committed and ambitious enough to ensure that their children don't fail. If the topic is the Egyptians, you'll find a chunk of Richmond parents at the British Museum on Saturday. The Russell parents are no different and they are happy with the role they play – 'it's a lovely place for parents,' says one mother – and they find communication with the school more than adequate through newsletters, class assemblies, regular parents' evenings, a parents' forum and easy access at the end of the day to class teachers and, of course, the head who is regularly to be found in the playground. The website could do with an update – but this is 'in hand'.

This is not a substitute prep school with the kind of traditional methods and competition that implies, and the move to secondary school from such a close family set-up is not going to be easy. However, if you are looking for a good state school, a caring and friendly learning environment with plenty to inspire your child you need look no further. You just somehow need to find a way to get a place.

Ryde School with Upper Chine, Junior School

Linked to Ryde School With Upper Chine in the Senior section

Queen's Road, Ryde, Isle of Wight, PO33 3BE

• Pupils: boys and girls; day and boarding • Ages: 3-11 • C of E
• Fees: £4,860-£9,330 pa • Independent

Tel: 01983 612901
Fax: 01983 564714
Email: admissions@rydeschool.org.uk
Website: www.rydeschool.org.uk

Head: Mr Howard Edward BSc PGCE.

Remarks: In a converted house on the same campus as the senior school but operates almost completely separately, with few staff in common except those in learning support. Traditional feel, desks in rows, but bright and cheerful. 'We have a policy that all the children's work goes up on the walls.' Open until 4.45pm every day, after-school arts, crafts, sports and homework clubs. The Island is a fertile site for dinosaur bones and houses two dinosaur museums. Most pupils go on to the senior school.

The Ryleys School

Ryleys Lane, Alderley Edge, Cheshire, SK9 7UY

• Fees: £7,860-£8,985 pa • Independent

Tel: 01625 583 241
Fax: 01625 581 900
Email: headmaster@ryleys.cheshire.sch.uk
Website: www.theryleys.com

Head: Since 1997, Mr Patrick (Pat) Barrett (mid fifties). Has been here since 1975 'Ryleys man and boy'. Runs school with his wife Barbara from desks either side of the front room of the old building that's more like a comfy sitting room than a head's study. Their two sons were here and they still have a parental air for the pupils and gappies. Great belief of triangle of child, parents and school as core of each pupil's success, certainly the head's door is always open to parents although a quiet word with Barbara will often suffice. In term times at least Ryleys is a lifestyle, not just a job. In the hols they love Italy.

Entrance: Spaces available in some years but not all. Not selective as such although all families are interviewed but generally, unless a child has needs the school cannot meet, they're welcome. Some music scholarships. Reductions for second and third siblings and a fourth child goes free while you've four in the school.

Exit: A core aim is to ensure each child progresses to the best next school for them. All prepped for 11+ exams even if they plan to stay to 13. About half to Manchester Grammar. Kings Macclesfield, Cheadle Hulme and Stockport Grammar also popular. At 13 Shrewsbury, Sedburgh, Repton, Uppingham, Ampleforth are amongst the choices. A few bag music or sport scholarships.

Remarks: Delightful prep full of boys fair busting with enthusiasm and having the time of their lives. A few stay to 13 and, since 2009, girls have been included in nursery and infants in response to parental request to include female siblings (and, we suspect, to keep enrolment up). Admits all abilities, 'we are an academic school but we're not a hothouse in any way, we look for each child's special ability'. Impressive then that traditionally about half bag places at Manchester Grammar. Secrets include keeping classes to absolute maximum of 19, specialist teachers from 8 years old in bespoke rooms for science, music, ICT, DT and art, and lots of prizes most notably for endeavour. Prizes and merits presented in full school Friday assemblies, full and half colours for sport. Children describe school as 'challenging but the teachers are funny', and there's a can-do atmosphere, 'you can make anything you want in woodwork ... well, as long as it's not sharp'. Colour is everywhere in the nursery and infants from the playground to the murals in the loos and in class even four year olds stand to the instruction 'levez vous'.

Fabulous music, choirs swept the board winning all five choir category prizes in the 2009 Alderley Edge Music Festival. 'The whole world knows about our choirs' boys confidently tell us and in fact the whole world does know about former soloist Laurence Jeffcoate, one of the BBC's I'd Do Anything Olivers. Six coach loads travelled to see him in the West End. Music experience voluntary for litties but they can start instrument lessons as soon as they're capable and by 13 many pass grade VI, partly because school (hats off to this) teaches Grade V theory.

Boys describe sport here as 'hard core but fun; football, cricket, proper full-on contact rugby which most of us love, a tiny bit of tennis' and the 25m pool set in neat landscaped grounds brings a luxury holiday camp air to the heart of the attractive campus. Boys trundle to and from eight acres of pitches in two big yellow minibuses and younger pupils use a five aside astro at school. Their only complaint is that the changing rooms are a bit cramped. Annual trip to learn survival skills on a Rua Fiola, an island near Oban.

Clad in black and yellow, with caps and felt hats for girls, pupils are ultra polite but not stuffy. Good mornings, pleases and thankyous abound. They love earning house points, hate getting minuses or having to 'see the head'. The house with most points gets to miss a day of school for a treat, 'last year we went to Waterworld – how mint is that?' There's a discreet silence about just who comes here but, as befits the area, there's a fair share of celeb and footballer offspring. School has two TEFL trained teachers and has seen many a child become bi-lingual here after arriving with barely any English. Three favourite members of staff are the live-in 'gappies' from down under or South Africa, two boy and one girl gap year students who help with sport or the younger children. They appreciate chef Mark's ministrations to them just as much as the children who say, 'the food's great, very healthy ... and there's always cake'. Pupils and teachers share the dining hall and queue and pupils have no hesitation approaching teachers for a word during lunch. The only parental grumble is the congested road and nightmare parking. Ryleys still runs a minibus on into Wilmslow Girls' Prep for sisters.

S Anselm's School

Bakewell, Derbyshire, DE45 1DP

• Pupils: 230; 49 per cent girls. About one half board. 45 in pre-prep and 12 in nursery • Ages: Nursery to 13 • C of E
• Fees: Prep Day £12,360-£15,510; Boarding £18,210 pa • Independent

Tel: 01629 812 734
Fax: 01629 814 742
Email: headmaster@anselms.co.uk
Website: www.sanselms.co.uk

Head: Since 2007, Mr Simon Northcott, formerly history teacher and housemaster at Oakham. Educated at Marlborough and St Andrew's University and has a business background. Wife, Michelle, was an international netball player and head of girls' games at Oakham. Two young children.

Entrance: Automatic transfer from nursery and pre-prep at seven (no exam). One non-examined, means-tested bursary worth up to 100 per cent of fees for a child of seven or eight, which can be continued at six independent schools. Pupils from Derbyshire, Yorkshire, Lincolnshire, and from abroad; mainly professional middle class parents.

Exit: Impressive number of scholarships (in some years over 75 per cent of the year) to Winchester, Wycombe Abbey, Cheltenham Ladies, Ampleforth, Malvern, Oundle, Repton, Oakham, Rugby, Shrewsbury, Uppingham. Others go to wide variety of schools nationally.

Remarks: Idyllic setting with beautiful views of grounds and dales. Small, friendly, attractively furnished girls' boarding houses (14–17 per house, 10 in youngest). Boys in the main boarding house in small, homely, recently refurbished dorms. Almost all start as day pupils and by Year 5 almost all board; they start 'when they want to'.

Children present as happy, confident, articulate, polite, and enthusiastic about their school, especially sports and teaching. 'Bullying charter' displayed prominently all over school, signed by all pupils at start of each term. But bullying not a problem – in such a small school staff soon learn about unhappiness and deal with it effectively. All new children assigned a guide from their own year, as well as an older pupil as mentor. This has 'proved successful and is taken extremely seriously.' Top children also hear younger ones read.

Average class size is 12. Attractive, well equipped classrooms (interactive whiteboards etc), and there are two up-to-date IT suites and well stocked library, with reading area furnished with comfy chairs; children have daily reading period after lunch. National Curriculum covered (and beyond), with focus on CE and scholarship exams. Maths setted from 8+, core subjects and languages set in following year, when Latin starts (Greek available in final years). French starts in nursery. Strong learning support – two full time dyslexia specialists. About one third of pupils on support register, about half of them with dyslexic problems (individual lessons have to be paid for).

Described by a parent as 'academically outstanding; the children are eager to learn and enjoy it.' We saw two classes working in complete silence without a teacher; in a maths lesson a child waiting to see the teacher had her problem pleasantly resolved by another child. English clearly a strength, much excellent creative writing. Lots of science practicals and visits. Effort and attainment grades sent to parents every three weeks; pupils with best effort grades over year were taken out for a meal by the head. Interest in current affairs fostered – older boarders listen to news every morning. The staff is stable, with a touch of new, younger blood.

Lots of art on display, in a range of media. Strong drama – two school plays a year – and a lot of music goes on: two thirds of school learn an instrument, perform in concerts in and out of school, e.g. at Buxton opera house and on choir tours – last one to Austria in 2009. Terrific choice of extra-curricular activities includes astronomy, fly fishing, metal modelling and chess (over half the school play). Games played four or five times a week; lacrosse, fencing and rock climbing too. Sports tours in England and abroad. Brand new indoor swimming pool and common room complex is a fantastic resource for all pupils.

Pre-prep attractively decorated and well resourced. Subject specialists used for IT, DT, drama, music,sport, art and French, along with main school facilities. Lots of extra activities.

Refurbished nursery next to pre-prep also very well equipped, with very enthusiastic teacher. Mixed age activities make it more like family life, and contact with older siblings is encouraged.

Overall a delightful school, in many ways very traditional, where children's happiness is a priority. As one parent put it – 'A fabulous springboard for senior school.'

St Albans High School for Girls - Preparatory School

Linked to Saint Albans High School For Girls in the Senior section

Wheathampstead House, Codicote Road, Wheathampstead, Herts, AL4 8DJ

• Pupils: 310 girls, all day • Ages: 4-11 • Christian • Fees: £9,330-£9,840 pa • Independent

Tel: 01582 839 270
Fax: 01582 839 271
Email: admissions@stalbans-high.herts.sch.uk
Website: www.stahs.org.uk

Head: Since 2009, Ms Gillian Bradnam BEd MA NPQH. Previously deputy head of St Catherine's Preparatory School, Bramley for six years with over 24 years teaching experience. She aims to ensure a family atmosphere where everyone is encouraged, supported and valued. School says she is particularly keen on the use of new technologies, thinking skills, independent learning and helping the girls to acquire skills for life. Beyond school, she enjoys photography and world travel.

Entrance: Selective. Majority at 4 with handful of places at 5 and 7 (waiting list operates). At 4 and 5, informal assessment via play, looking at how girls problem solve, work with peers etc. 7+ entrants examined in maths, English and VR, looking for potential as well as actuals.

Exit: Virtually all to St Albans High, occasional one to local state school or boarding. Those unlikely to make demanding senior school standard are given ample warning and helped to find a suitable alternative.

Remarks: All NC subjects plus French taught from Year 3; extra- curricular clubs for Latin, Italian and Spanish. A busy school – many are encouraged to take LAMDA speech and drama exams; music strong, plenty of bands and choirs; fabulous art work evidenced. Lots happening: activity days; curriculum trips; clubs for everything from Funky Science, puzzles, dancing, sports, through to orienteering (regional winners). Runs enrichment groups for English, maths and thinking skills; talented join senior girls for music and sport.

A comfortable, focused and creative environment, worked hard to develop a 'can-do, have a go attitude'. Some limited support for dyslexia and dyspraxia, all screened in Year 3 and will discuss with parents if they feel additional assessment is needed.

Moved from co-located site at senior school to the former Polaroid Building in 2005. Hard to imagine, the modern well-planned interior, with specialist rooms for science, art, ICT and DT plus library and large sports hall, was ever anything other than a school. Stands in 18 glorious acres; a children's paradise of gardens, dens, adventure playgrounds and an outdoor learning classroom. Use of swimming pool at senior school.

A charming school – Sunday Times Independent Preparatory School of the Year 2008/2009. A lovely homely atmosphere with high standards achieved through nurture, endeavour and opportunity. Ideal for the scholarly. Weaker sisters will wilt.

St Aloysius' College Junior School

Linked to Saint Aloysius' College in the Senior section

45 Hill Street, Garnethill, Glasgow, G3 6RJ

• Pupils: 425 all day; 40 boys and girls in kindergarten • Ages: 5-11; kindergarten 3-5 • RC • Fees: £6,669-£8,379 pa • Independent

Tel: 0141 331 9200
Fax: 0141 353 0426
Email: hm.secretary@staloysius.org
Website: www.staloysius.org

Remarks: For details, see senior school entry.

St Anthony's Preparatory School

90 Fitzjohn's Ave, Hampstead, London, NW3 6NP

• Pupils: 295 boys; all day • Ages: 5-13 • RC • Fees: £12,945-£13,305 pa • Independent

Tel: 020 7431 1066
Fax: 020 7435 9223
Email: gill.hooper@stanthonysprep.co.uk
Website: www.stanthonysprep.org.uk

Headmaster: Since 2010, Paul Keyte (late forties) MA (first class honours in philosophy and theology, Oriel College, Oxford). Initially followed research interests in Oxford before his first teaching post at Dulwich College. Subsequently taught RS and philosophy at KCS, Wimbledon and Winchester College, progressing to deputy headships at Highgate and South Hampstead High School. He is keen on ensuring that, at prep school level, pupils experience the joy and freshness of learning that can be denied by the pressures at senior school level. Plans to integrate ICT and e-learning into the school curriculum as well as introducing philosophy throughout the school. Married to Emily, who teaches English at South Hampstead High School, with a two year old son Benedict. Enjoys a variety of interests: music (particularly Schubert Lieder, Bach and Sinatra), cinema, theatre, swimming, tennis and basketball. He writes comedy in his spare time!

Entrance: 'Register interest' (and pay £25.00) on or soon after 1 September after your child's birth. This is a change from the previous sign-up-straight-after-birth system under which autumn-born children filled up almost all the places. When your child is two, you will be invited for a visit and may register for an assessment and pay £75.00. Around 50-55 four-year-old boys are assessed for around 30 Year 1 places – this may increase to around 100 assessments in future. There are also a few places in Years 2 and 3, though Year 3 places are likely to diminish. On accepting a place, you pay a term's fees as deposit. NB 'The admissions process will reflect a 70 per cent Catholic acceptance.' Rarely takes in boys after Year 3.

Exit: One or two leave at 11 for state schools such as Cardinal Vaughan and The Oratory but most stay till 13. The most popular destinations are University College School (just up the road, with its similar liberal ethos), City, Highgate, Mill Hill, St Paul's, Westminster, including several scholarships, with the odd one or two heading for mostly Catholic boarding schools such as Ampleforth, Downside and Stonyhurst.

Remarks: The school was founded in Eastbourne by Richard Patton and run as a traditional prep school. It moved to Hampstead after World War Two under the leadership of Richard's son, Anthony and, in the late '60s, Richard's son, Tim, took over as head. A pony-tailed bohemian, he brought in the first-names, no-bell ethos which has endured to the present day. He ran a wine club and was responsible for the stained glass window in the senior house showing a glass of Guinness rather than the more traditional Virgin Mary. 'We've moved with the times but there's still the spirit of Tim here,' said previous head and Paul is keen to maintain the ethos of the school with its warmth between pupils and staff .The ownership of the school has recently passed from the Patton family to the Alpha Plus Group.

Inevitably, the selection process is becoming less gentle as larger numbers are assessed and the academic bar is rising. 'The more academic the children, the more you can retain the relaxed ethos. You can focus on education in the broader sense.' A parent commented, 'the academic education is fantastic here.' Mandarin now taught from Year 1. 'We do it because it's a different way of learning – it's tonal, and young children have better tonal awareness. It helps with listening and with singing.' French also from Year 1, Latin from Year 6, optional Spanish, German, Arabic and Ancient Greek. Re-jigged history syllabus to a chronological format, starting with dinosaurs (very popular) and skating rather rapidly through the millennia to reach the 17th century or so in Year 8.

Non-exclusive after-school scholarship classes now from Year 7. Those at both ends of the academic spectrum are well served by the in-house learning support team. The teaching assistants are all qualified teachers, many from Eastern Europe. The school can't take children with mobility problems because of its many-floored lay-out, but can accommodate learning difficulties and has included a boy with Asperger's, who comes with his own support staff. 'We will accept children with disabilities if we can but they've got to be given appropriate structure and help.' A physiotherapist runs seven motor-coordination classes for Year 2, which consist of gym circuits designed to improve balance and eye-hand coordination. These often identify conditions such as dyspraxia.

Sport is important here; the school has produced prep-school tennis and cross-country champions and wins plenty of matches. The junior house has a playground with areas for basketball, football and hopscotch, plus – to the delight of at least one non-football-fan – a giant chess set. There's also a vaulted hall for PE and table-tennis tables and a smallish covered swimming pool in the grounds of the senior house across Fitzjohn's Avenue. Boys from Year 2 upwards travel by coach to Brondesbury cricket club.

A large proportion of the boys plays a musical instrument – with rock groups at least as popular as classical ensembles. Ex-pupils are members of Razorlight, Bombay Bicycle Club and Cajun Dance Party (your children will know of these groups). Art was once a weaker link but 'we're moving in the right direction' – a new head of art has been appointed and the art room refurbished. Art and DT share a studio in the grounds of the senior house. There are reproductions of famous paintings on the junior school walls with questions to encourage boys to study them. 'I'm keen that teachers are aware that boys can learn visually and use visual stimulation in lessons.' In the last year, the school has undergone a full ICT refurbishment. Both school buildings have been networked and new computer suites added in both junior and senior house. Almost all teaching rooms will soon have electronic smart boards and the school is joining a 25 school wide learning portal from October 2010.

Plenty of drama, including eight productions a year in the junior house and several in the senior house. The Tempest was performed on the small outside wooden stage in stormy conditions. Other recent productions have included *Toad of Toad Hall* and *The Pirates of Penzance.* A National Theatre producer is in charge of drama and runs workshops 'to universal praise'. Twice-termly GAW ('groove awhile') celebration assemblies, a relic of Tim, see boys singing, playing the saxophone, reciting poetry.

After-school clubs for Year 3 upwards may include e.g. rounders, touch typing, clay modelling. Ski trip, activities weeks, outward bound courses, plenty of outings to e.g. Legoland, Hampton Court.

Catholicism is an integral part of the school ethos, with masses, hymns and prayers, though mass is optional for non-Catholics. 'The spiritual side is very important. But it is not an issue. We are not evangelical. We do our own thing.' The diocese criticised a lack of multi-faith education in the curriculum but new head feels that his academic training and teaching experience place him in an excellent position to tackle this. This is a school with a strong social conscience which raises large sums for schools overseas and hospices.

Parents praise the 'warm, caring' teachers and the 'sense of informality balanced by very clear boundaries.' Some feel they are being kept at a distance, with no class reps or parents' council. Instead, an active parents' charity committee runs social/fund-raising events. Alongside the informal, liberal ethos is a hard-line attitude to misdemeanours.

Families fairly typical of the area – 'north London parents are by reputation the most difficult in the country but mostly we get on very well' – though new head would like to broaden the racial mix. Combines a liberal, informal atmosphere with a strong Catholic ethos and high academic standards.

St Bede's College Prep School

Linked to Saint Bede's College in the Senior section

Alexandra Park, Manchester, Lancashire, M16 8HX

• Pupils: 210 girls and boys; boarding and day • Ages: 4-11 • RC
• Fees: £5,814 pa • Independent

Tel: 0161 226 7156
Fax: 0161 227 0487
Email: prep@stbedescollege.co.uk
Website: www.stbedesprep.co.uk

Head: Mr Peter Hales.

Entrance: By assessment.

Exit: No automatic right of transfer to the senior school though the vast majority do so.

Remarks: Housed in a new building on the same site as the senior school. Bright, colourful classrooms. Shares facilities with the main school.

St Bede's Preparatory School

Linked to Saint Bede's Senior School in the Senior section

Duke's Drive, Eastbourne, East Sussex, BN20 7XL

• Pupils: 400 boys and girls • Ages: 3 months - 13 • Inter-denominational
• Fees: £8,085-£13,275; Boarding +£6,210 pa • Independent

Tel: 01323 734 222
Fax: 01323 746 438
Email: prep.school@stbedesschool.org
Website: www.stbedesschool.org

Headmaster: Since 2007, Mr Nick Bevington (thirties) married with one child soon to start in the nursery. His wife is a consultant rheumatologist. The St Bede's Trust obviously favours youthful heads; he is boyishly young, enthusiastic and eager. He says the school is not a complete product of the changes he's made but that he and his 'marvellous SMT team have been ambitious with extensions and want every child is as happy and excited to be there as he is.' He believes that education begins with the individual and therefore should be child centred. His interests are walking, tennis is a passion and he coaches the U9 football and rugby team.

Entrance: Non-selective. Any child is welcome unless their behaviour distracts themselves and others from learning.

Exit: Ninety per cent go on to the senior school and this percentage is increasing. Some will choose a more traditional curriculum and move elsewhere.

Remarks: Situated at the end of Eastbourne seafront on the cliffs – wonderful sea views and a quick jaunt to the beach but still sporting enough greenery for two rugby/football/cricket pitches. Perched high on the cliff top is a large architecturally pleasing home where Mr Peter Pyemount, the founder of the now flourishing St Bede's Trust lives. Tells pupils that the house was strategically placed so that he could keep a vigilant eye on their antics – so, of course, the pupils revel in recounting his more mischievous behaviour. He is apparently a 'thrilling and inspirational history teacher' given to the spontaneous acting out of battle scenes.

The school has sympathetically been extended to include large, light classrooms ultra modern dining hall, renovated boarding houses, large sports hall, swimming pool, a new pre-prep and nursery school, all with high spec fire and safety systems. Due to the trust's culture of inclusion for parents, staff, and pupils – everyone has similar to a coded Oyster card and is given clearance to suit their timetable.

Rather like the senior school, they have identified a particular cohort in the middle range of ability that were not reaching their full potential and they are putting systems in place to address this. 'The ethos is about teaching children how to think and not concentrate on tests and league tables which often neglects their thinking development.' We are not concerned with 'spoon feeding' or being academically the top dog. Many children come here because they have floundered elsewhere but 'they really do cater to the individual, this is not mere lip service. I saw my child grow in confidence and it was uplifting seeing him succeed.' Around a third have a special need of some description; strong learning support specialist team run by 'an amazing head of department' with a reputation for unlocking the potential of pupils and many come through to study medicine, engineering, politics at prestigious universities. The head believes that if a child experiences success in one area that often transfers to success in other areas. A gifted and talented coordinator; extension classes and master classes are given to those pupils spotted as very able.

All the heads of department speak with gusto about their subject. This sense of fun comes through when visiting the science department – live reptiles on display, an replica solar system (and tales of when the self-confessed Peter Pan head of science lit up the science room which could be seen from the beach). The boarding houses are across the road from the seafront and children can board from Year 7 although special circumstances will be considered.

Every year group does a dramatic production where everyone takes part. Lots of sport, serious and recreational and the top teams can specialise five afternoons a week. Good to see girls' cricket at prep school level plus the staff coach netball to local schools. Huge range of clubs and activities. Art is a strength – school exhibits at festivals. Annual year group concert plus all the usual choirs, orchestras, drummers and guitarists that compete for 'St Bede's Got Talent' concerts.

An innovative school, not worried about ticking boxes. It is hard not to be impressed with the facilities and continuing success of the school obviously delivering on their promise of a good, all-round education for all abilities.

St Benedict's Junior School

Linked to Saint Benedict's School in the Senior section

5 Montpelier Avenue, Ealing, London, W5 2XP

• Pupils: 215 boys and 65 girls – plus co-ed nursery of 30. All day • Ages: 3-11 • RC (very) and Benedictine, but a good proportion of other denominations • Fees: £10,560 pa • Independent

Tel: 020 8862 2050
Fax: 020 8862 2058
Email: jssecretary@stbenedicts.org.uk
Website: www.stbenedicts.org.uk

Head: Since 2005, Mr R G Simmons, BA, the second secular head.

Entrance: Non-selective at 3 or 4.

Exit: Almost all to senior school on site.

Remarks: Junior school housed in very large, very attractive Victorian red-brick building across the playground from senior school (playground shared but times staggered so tinies not swamped by six foot rugger types). Playground also encloses new small area for tots. Building recently and carefully extended to provide lovely, light new hall and classrooms. New rooms include excellent new ICT suite with modern low tables and matching chairs and inviting, comfortable library overlooking the abbey and lawns. Interactive whiteboards in every classroom and well used. Leafy Ealing far more apparent here – super trees with space to grow and local family homes just across the way. Excellent displays everywhere – really interesting too on stone carving, perspective, shape and colour. A good orderly feel with happy, confident-looking pupils in a school recently commended in ISI report for excellent music and ADT. Pastoral care, too, clearly exceptional. A super start for your son or daughter and big school just across the playground! New nursery housed in super refurbished Victorian house just down the road. June 2008 Ofsted inspection rated the Early Years foundation stage provision as outstanding.

St Catherine's Preparatory School

Linked to Saint Catherine's School in the Senior section

Station Road, Bramley, Guildford, Surrey, GU5 0DF

• Pupils: 260 girls, all day • Ages: 4-11 • C of E • Fees: £7,050-£11,895 pa • Independent

Tel: 01483 899 665
Fax: 01483 899 669
Email: annie.daniell@stcatherines.info
Website: www.stcatherines.info

Head: Since 2001, Mrs Kathy Jefferies BSc, born and educated in the USA. Married with four children, she is very enthusiastic and driven and believes every child should be happy at the school. The children adore her.

Entrance: Selective entrance, at four and at seven, by test, interview and taster day. Girls come from a variety of local nurseries – both state and private.

Exit: To senior school across the road, not automatic, but only a small minority go elsewhere.

Remarks: A thriving, happy, academic school with strong competition for places and high expectations of its pupils. A recent building and refurb programme has provided very attractive and spacious accommodation. The prep school also benefits from being able to use extensive facilities and the chapel in the senior school across the road.

Academically very strong but not too pressured according to parents. Pupils are 'stretched' but there is a balance and the school's aim is to bring out qualities in all. Average class size 20 (smaller class sizes in pre-prep), and pupils are also grouped vertically through the school for tutoring – 12 to 14 girls in each group. The school feels these groupings are very influential – parents not so sure though school says 'the girls like them'. Super ICT suite in the new building and interactive whiteboards, internet etc in all classrooms.

Music and sport are encouraged. Instruments are introduced in Year 2 and almost 75 per cent continue to learn up to grade 5. Excellent brass and strings groups and several pupils have gained music scholarships to the senior school. Parents comment that the 'music tuition is wonderful'. Sport, which includes netball, swimming and gymnastics, is very important with many pupils representing the school in local competitions and at higher levels. All the usual extra-curricular activities – swimming, gym, chess (very popular) and some more unusual, including Mandarin and tap dancing. Main problem seems to be what to choose.

Staff are mainly female although there is one very popular male teacher. Any problems are dealt with efficiently and thoroughly by teachers and senior management team. Village location not far from Guildford equals the usual parking problems especially in the morning. Head has introduced a drop-off system for parents to ease the traffic flow and many use the school transport organised by parents, although this seems to be geared primarily to the needs of the senior girls.

St Christopher School Junior School

Linked to Saint Christopher School in the Senior section

Barrington Road, Letchworth Garden City, Hertfordshire, SG6 3JZ

• Pupils: 140 boys and girls plus Montessori nursery with 20 children • Ages: 4-11, Montessori: rising 3-4; boarding from 11+ • Non-denom • Fees: £3,375-£10,800 pa • Independent

Tel: 01462 650 947
Fax: 01462 481578
Email: admissions@stchris.co.uk
Website: www.stchris.co.uk

Head: Since 2010, Mr Paul Mason, previously head of Abercorn Junior School.

Entrance: Many children come up from the Montessori nursery, others join Reception and more join Year 3 or 4, though entry at any age is considered. Will take a broad range of ability, 'but our community exists on self-discipline and they must be able to cope.'

Exit: Almost all to the senior school.

Remarks: Lovely, light buildings adjacent to the senior school, full of paintings and projects. Much of the work is project-based (which can upset inspectors from traditional prep schools). 'The teachers know each child's strengths and weaknesses. It is most important to push their strengths and enrich those areas they find difficult. Being kind and having high expectations are not mutually exclusive.' Play areas include an orchard – children are encouraged to climb the trees and pick the apples. 'Childhood should be celebrated. We try to preserve it as long as possible.'

In 2008, the Montessori nursery ('The Monte') relocated to Arunwood, a Grade II listed building and former childhood home of Sir Laurence Olivier. Extensively refurbished, provides classroom space and outdoor facilities for learning and play. The Monte will take up to 50 children in due course.

For further details, see the senior school entry.

St Christopher's School

32 Belsize Lane, Hampstead, London, NW3 5AE

• Pupils: 235 girls, all day • Ages: 4-11 • Non-denom • Fees: £11,169 pa
• Independent

Tel: 02074 351 521
Fax: 02074 316 694
Email: admissions@st-christophers.hampstead.sch.uk
Website: www.st-christophers.hampstead.sch.uk

Head: Since 2003, Mrs Susan (Susie) West BA Hons PGCE MA Educational Management (fifties). Educated at Howell's, University of Newcastle, Oxford (PGCE) and OU. Began teaching career at Oakham School with 11–18 year olds and to say she has had a wide range of jobs since would be an understatement. Highlights include head of St Bede's Eastbourne pre-prep, head of English at a school in Kuala Lumpur, housemistress at Sherborne School for Girls, Year 4 teacher at Sussex House, plus a few spells in business. Most recently was deputy head at Kensington Prep. Divorced with grown son and daughter. A breath of fresh air in the intimidating world of London preps – down to earth, straight-talking, no hint of snobbery. Always puts the girls first, occasionally exasperating some mums. Cycles to school every day from Pimlico.

Entrance: Unique, we think, and hinges entirely on the fact that the school possesses 13 classrooms rather than 14. With two classes per year group, this leaves only one room (capacity 18 girls) for reception. Now read carefully: girls born in September to February enter reception at four-and-a-half and spend seven years at the school. Those with March to August birthdays stay at nursery an extra year and start in Year 1 at 5+, spending six years at the school. Name down at birth – 'we have had calls from the maternity ward'. The school closes the register at 200 names (for 38 slots) but tries to make allowances for people who have suddenly moved to the area. All places awarded on the results of assessments (of potential, not accomplishment) and play. Looking for bright berries, but also a mixture of personalities – 'some leaders, some quieter girls, the odd eccentric'. Sisters accepted automatically unless they are screamingly unsuited to the place. Vacancies arise from time to time, mainly at the end of Year 2. Over a third of pupils live within walking distance. Rest mainly from, Highgate, St John's Wood, Maida Vale and Islington. 100 per cent fees means-tested scholarships available.

Exit: Girls go in pretty even numbers to St Paul's, Haberdashers' Aske's, City of London, Channing, North London Collegiate, South Hampstead High. Some also go to Francis Holland, Queen's College and Highgate. Handful to boarding schools: Queenswood, Wycombe Abbey, Downe House, Badminton. Sometimes one to Henrietta Barnett.

Remarks: High-achieving, girls' prep in large, airy Victorian dwelling in leafy back road. Dates back, in a convoluted way, to 1883, but was established in its current form in 1950 by the writer Rosemary Manning. Strong family feel, sheltered, cosy, but not twee. Stairs central to proceedings, with throngs of confident little girls making their way up and down, oblivious to headmistress and teachers battling through the crowd. New uniform 100 per cent cotton – 'good for the skin but hell to launder,' said a mum. When we visited, girls were dressed in a mixture of summer and winter wear, shorts and tracksuit trousers, dresses and tunics, shoes and trainers – somehow all gelling into an attractive and comfy uniform. No specific school rules, just the word 'respect'. 'The school has a feeling of controlled but bubbling energy,' said a mother.

Completed building work 2008 with seven new classrooms. Every class has an interactive board. Lovely inside, with super rooms for DT, science, art etc. Library and computer building designed in Scandinavian style with light wood and big windows. Unusually broad range of subjects on offer. French and Spanish both taught, plus Mandarin club, and head dreams of 'putting Latin back' in the programme. Chess part of the curriculum Years 2–6. Reading taught mainly through Jolly Phonics, with other methods as back-up. No scholarship class and no setting, with exception of one investigative maths lesson per week in Years 4–6. Practice tests every Friday at the beginning of Year 6 help to insure that girls shine in senior school entrance exams. Homework burden can get a bit intense as girls progress up the school. Parents gush about special needs help (with no stigma attached) for the few girls – mostly younger siblings – who need support. 'They've done everything they can to help my daughter,' said one grateful parent. Another, whose daughter was attending a special programme for her disability out of school, was impressed that her form teacher had volunteered to attend a course to help her continue the programme in class. Similarly, school takes pains to integrate loners and to thwart cliquishness.

In keeping with the tradition started by Miss Manning, the school excels in music. Over 50 per cent of girls learn at least one instrument at school (plus loads outside). Four music competitions each year (wind, strings, piano and ensemble) plus senior, junior and chamber choirs, two orchestras, and – our favourite – junior and senior piano clubs to take the isolation out of learning that lonely instrument. Recently held joint concert with nearby boys' prep, The Hall, and keen to do more in this vein. High quality artwork displayed throughout school and art history taught as a separate subject in its own room. Less emphasis on PE. Cramped site allows netball, short tennis, rounders. Also some unihock, tag rugby, cricket, pop lacrosse etc. Gymnastics in school hall which doubles as canteen. Tarmacked playground heavily used, plus small play area out back – somehow sufficient. Huge range of school trips to theatre and museums, taking advantage of London on the doorstep.

Interesting parents – media, City, entertainment – with strong opinions. Extremely useful e.g. in helping to organise themed special studies days in the summer term with visiting speakers. Multi-cultural, though not particularly multi-ethnic. No beef, pork, ham, bacon, shellfish or nuts on menu – we suspect you're out of luck if you don't like chicken. Assembly every Monday, hymns sung, but tone is non-denominational – many children out of school on Jewish holidays.

Not traditional, not high-tech, not woolly. But a well-thought-out and jolly nice school.

St Columba's Junior School

Linked to Saint Columba's School in the Senior section

Knockbuckle Road, Kilmacolm., PA13 4EQ

• Pupils: 380 boys and girls • Ages: 3-11 • Non-denom
• Fees: Day £9,150; Nursery £2,380 pa • Independent

Tel: 01505 872768
Fax: 01505 874642
Email: secretary@st-columbas.org
Website: www.st-columbas.org

Head: Mrs D L Cook, DCE Jordanhill ITQ DipAdPrStudies DipEd Man Strathclyde.

Entrance: By assessment and test.

Exit: Automatic transfer to senior school.

Remarks: Positively buzzing, with fabulous new facilities. Two parallel classes throughout, 24 pupils in each.

St Dunstan's College Junior School

Linked to Saint Dunstan's College in the Senior section

Stanstead Road, Catford, London, SE6 4TY

• Pupils: boys and girls, all day • Ages: 3-11 boys and girls
• Anglican foundation • Fees: £7,467-£12,429 pa • Independent

Tel: 020 8516 7225
Fax: 020 8516 7244
Email: rscard@sdmail.org.uk
Website: www.stdunstans.org.uk

Remarks: For details see the senior school's entry.

St Edmund's Junior School

Linked to Saint Edmund's School in the Senior section

St Thomas Hill, Canterbury, Kent, CT2 8HU

• Pupils: 135 boys and 105 girls. 40+ full/weekly boarders; lots of flexi-boarding • Ages: 3-13 • Christian foundation but all faiths welcome
• Fees: Boarding £15,861-£17,406; Day £12,195; Pre-prep / nursery £3,420-£8,640 pa • Independent

Tel: 0122 7475 600
Fax: 01227 471 083
Email: juniorschool@stedmunds.org.uk
Website: www.stedmunds.org.uk

Head: Since 1996, Mr Robert Bacon BA (fiftyish). Educated at Bradfield and Durham where he read modern history and gained his PGCE. Previously at Stamford School where he taught history and was boarding housemaster in the Junior School. Reports to the head of the senior school and Janet Frampton Fell, Head of Early Years, reports to him. The three heads collaborate closely and in partnership and the Junior and Pre-prep Heads both have considerable autonomy to run their own schools. A great enthusiast who loves outdoor pursuits – he takes children on an annual adventure survival course to a Scottish island and leads sixth form of the Senior School on various adventure trips. Married to Dominique, an occupational therapist, they have two children, one at university and the other in the senior school at St Edmunds. Takes great trouble to maintain good relations with parents – always encourages them to come and talk about problems and happy for parents to ring him at home in the evening if they are worried about something.

Entrance: Up to age about 10, children spend a day at the school and sit tests. Both parents and children interviewed. School requires two years of reports and a report from the current head. Set great store by the attitude of the child and the family – enthusiasm essential. For entry to the top two years, children sit formal tests and attend an interview plus reports and reference from the current head. If a child offers a weak performance in the tests (they don't like to think in terms of failure), they are welcomed back to meet the curriculum support staff to see if their needs can be met. Can accommodate a wide ability range but those with severe learning difficulties would struggle. Quite a few join in Year 7 often from the primaries.

Exit: Most to the senior school. About half of the choristers move on to the senior school, the rest go on to other independent schools or into the state sector.

One or two pupils a year leave at 11+ for the grammars. The school prepares them for the Kent Test but does not coach them or change the curriculum for them. The school no longer routinely prepares children for Common Entrance – sounds as if it could be a problem but most senior schools can offer their own entrance exam so any St Ed's children wanting to move on at 13+ can take this. They will prepare a child for Common Entrance if absolutely necessary. Some to King's Canterbury, Tonbridge and Sevenoaks. Have also recently won music scholarships to Eton, Harrow and Oundle and an academic scholarship to King's Canterbury.

Remarks: When the Choir School of Canterbury Cathedral closed in 1972, the Cathedral choristers joined St Edmund's Junior School. The 26 choristers live in a separate recently refurbished house within the cathedral precincts. They lead extraordinarily busy lives with 20 hours a week singing and attending evensong every day except Wednesdays, plus recordings etc but they are also fully involved in school life and many are keen sportsmen as well. Here, as elsewhere, the presence of choristers makes a major contribution to the quality of school life.

Setting from Year 6 and for maths from Year 4. Some subjects taught by senior school teachers from Year 6 to ensure seamless transition at 13+. Start Latin in Year 5 and touch typing in Year 6. Good curriculum support department. Can cope with mild SEN only – dyslexia, dyscalculia, dyspraxia, Asperger's and mild autistic spectrum – about 45 children need some form of learning support. Can accommodate a wide ability range but those with severe learning difficulties would struggle. Two full time SEN teachers plus two members of staff who can teach EAL when required. Annual screening for general problems. Access to educational psychologists if necessary. School says they feel well ahead of the game and alert to problems. Class sizes 14–18. No scholarship stream but bright children offered scholarship tutorials for the last year. Academic scholarships available for senior school.

About two thirds of children learn a musical instrument – practice done at home. Plenty of after school clubs – squash, fencing, mountain biking etc. Academic clubs for the Gifted and Talented e.g. Seriously Hard Sums Club and Young Engineers Club. Maths masterclass for primary school children on Saturday mornings. Plenty of opportunities to stand up in public and build confidence – big musical every year plus drama club, lower school play and lots of small scale events. Poetry evening every year – some write their own poems. English Speaking Board exams and Junior School music festival. Informal recitals, concerts, etc all abilities welcome with great emphasis on having fun. 2008 BBC Radio 2 Chorister of the Year award. Woodland survival skills day, teambuilding and leadership day, water sports week, scarecrow building challenge – something for everyone. Children can compete in Senior School sports teams if they are good enough and also take part in Senior School orchestra. The East Kent Children's Orchestra is run by St Edmund's Junior School and incorporates the Junior School Orchestra.

St Edmund's has established itself as a 'through' school aimed at giving children a seamless education from 3–18. Established in Yorkshire in 1749 as the Clergy Orphan School, it moved to Canterbury via London and settled in its present location in 1855. It is clustered around an impressive ecclesiastical high Victorian building, with chapel attached, set in 50 acres with views of the Cathedral. The Prep School, pre-prep and nursery all have their own buildings, some purpose built, and all have use of the grounds and specialist facilities of the Senior School including the dining hall, swimming pool, sports hall, theatre and music school.

Has the same caring, nurturing ethos as the senior school. Children develop a strong sense of self worth and self confidence which means they are keen to do their best. The school is determined to find hidden talents and endeavour is rewarded in every field.

A cosy, happy school where great store is set by civilised behaviour and being nice to each other. Popular with parents who like the idea of their child being able to stay in one school from 3–18 without the trauma of the 11+ or Common Entrance.

St Edmund's Prep

Linked to Saint Edmund's College in the Senior section

Old Hall Green, Ware, Hertfordshire, SG11 1DS

• Pupils: 175, boys and girls • Ages: 3-11 • RC • Fees: £7,620-£11,145 pa • Independent

Tel: 01920 821 504
Fax: 01920 823 011
Email: admissions@stedmundscollege.org
Website: www.stedmundscollege.org

Head: Since April 2010, Mr Leonard Blom BED BA NPQH. Mr Blom joins the school from Edgeborough Prep School in Surrey, where he was head of geography. Prior to that, he held headships at St Dominic's Priory Junior School and Erica Girls' Primary School, both in Port Elizabeth, South Africa. Originally from Port Elizabeth in South Africa, Mr Blom is married with two teenage children and in his spare time he is a keen runner and cyclist – regularly taking part in triathlons and marathons. He has a BEd Honours degree specialising in Educational Management and a BA degree in History, Psychology and Philosophy, both gained from universities in South Africa, plus he recently obtained his National Professional Qualification for Headship in the UK (NPQH).

Entrance: Entrance to nursery from the term when children have their third birthday. Further admissions at four and at seven by interview and assessment. Entry to nursery and early years based on interview with the head of St Hugh's and assessment. References from any previous school also considered.

Exit: Majority into St Edmund's but some, inevitably, to wide range of good local state schools.

Remarks: Right next to the main school, parents couldn't hope to find a safer environment and with rather more space – inside and out – than most juniors can muster. A less imposing building than the college – built as a family home by Pugin – the school is well-resourced and appealing. It has a good hall and its own modern chapel. Lots of outdoors with a nice selection of play equipment. A large open plan art/DT/cookery area – bright, well-equipped, orderly – made us want to get our hands dirty. Relaxed, contented children.

The nursery runs both morning and afternoon sessions and there is a Tea Time Club available from 3.30pm–6pm each day for use by all pupils at the school.

Children in Years 3–6 can use the extensive College bus service to travel to and from school. Most children in Year 6 then transfer on to the College for their senior school education.

St Elizabeth's Catholic Primary School

Queen's Road, Richmond, Surrey, TW10 6HN

- Pupils: 215 boys and girls (plus 25 boys and girls in nursery), all day
- Ages: 4-11, nursery 3 • RC • State

Tel: 02089 403 015
Fax: 02083 320 986
Email: info@st-elizabeths.richmond.sch.uk
Website: www.st-elizabeths.richmond.sch.uk

Head: Since 1988, Ms Christine Brett MEd (in mathematics education) BEd (in English) DipMathsEd. Describes herself as 'over 21.' Previously deputy head at St Mary's Clapham. Comes across as sweetly old fashioned (though we are sure there is a steely resolve there as well), completely at home in this intimate, friendly, school. Still does some teaching – Year 6 maths and hymn practice. Parents say the school and the pupils are an important part of her life. 'Our children become her family,' says one mother 'but that's not to say she is a soft touch; she takes absolutely no nonsense.' Indeed she has great presence and we can understand why she is held in awe by parents (and pupils). 'She is quite scary but is a deeply religious person,' said one ex-mum. Dedicated to the school and the Catholic faith, Ms Brett is very keen on consistency, discipline and tradition – she's only the seventh head since school was founded in 1840. But she's also bang up to date with new ideas in education. Knows every child in the school, and she is very caring and involved. Also a good sport – has attended school summer fair dressed as a fairy to lead the fancy dress parade.

Entrance: No point applying unless you are on first name terms with your Catholic priest. Serving four parishes covering Richmond, Kew, Ham and East Sheen, with a few from St Margaret's, the school is single form entry and heavily oversubscribed. Typically 70 applications for the 30 places on offer and of these more than 50 per cent of the applicants fulfil the number one criteria of being a baptised, practising Catholic. After that priority goes to siblings (always lots) and then admission is based on proximity to the school. Nursery is separate unit on the same site in premises due for upgrading – same admissions criteria as school. Other feeder nurseries are Wyndham and The Barn.

Exit: To a wide range of schools including Catholic state secondaries, Gumley House Convent, Wimbledon College, The Ursuline Convent, The Sacred Heart Convent, The Cardinal Vaughan and the London Oratory. Some to Kingston schools, including two or three to Tiffin. Not many to Richmond secondaries. A few to independent sector including St Benedict's in Ealing, Hampton School and Lady Eleanor Holles in Hampton. 'Lots of doors open from here,' says Ms Brett, though one ex-mother queried how much independent schools' advice was on offer.

Remarks: Great SATs results, a clutch of glowing reports from Ofsted and the like, and a host of happy parents all pay tribute to this hugely popular school.

Academically it certainly does the business, producing well above average results at Key Stage two. Level 5s were achieved by 70+ per cent of the pupils in English and maths, 90 per cent in science. A fairly stable, female, teaching staff numbering just 12, so everybody knows everybody – no hiding place for the feckless. It's a very expensive area of the country and high living costs mean there is some movement of staff; however, nearby are the well-respected teacher training facilities of St Mary's and Roehampton, so a good supply of fresh student blood is on hand.

A traditional place but the ICT is all there – whiteboard and wireless laptop means the teacher is not stuck at the front of the class, but can be more flexible. Well-equipped ICT suite large enough for whole class teaching – just a few years old. More languages than many junior schools manage. Years 3, 4, and 5 learn Italian (courtesy of an arrangement with the Italian Embassy, which provides a teacher). Year 6 pupils learn French, visit France and study for the Lingua Bronze award – gives them a head start at their secondary school. There's also a Spanish club among the after school activities programme which takes children from age five.

Aesthetics not squeezed out by academia – music, art and drama all valued here. School views drama as a resource to be used whenever the opportunity arises. Every child in Years 2 and 3 learns recorder and all year groups study singing. Most learn an additional instrument, typically cello, brass, flute, violin or guitar. All culminated in a highly praised production of *Joseph and the Amazing Technicolour Dreamcoat* for KS2.

Pupils do extremely well at swimming – all four junior classes swim every year, six weeks on, six weeks off – head believes no point in teaching them for one term and ticking the 'they can swim' box. Mixed-age team champions in Richmond Schools Swimming Gala. Other sports include netball, football, athletics, basketball and mixed tag rugby (Small School Champions).

Almost the only gripe from parents does concern the lack of space and facilities for sport on site. There's no playing field, only hard surface provision – basically the junior playground. 'It's a lovely place but I wish the children, particularly the boys, had more room to run around,' says one mother. Pupils do use the outdoor facilities of a nearby secondary school.

In ritzy residential Richmond, built to an unusual semi-open plan arrangement which survives nearly 40 years on. Staff and parents like it, feeling that it helps to promote an open atmosphere which pervades the whole institution. Don't worry; there are classrooms, but also lots of shared work and quiet areas. 'It has the advantage of helping to achieve consistency of teaching, as well as promoting openness of spirit and mind,' says Ms Brett. Light floods in through partially glazed ceilings giving a nice airy aspect to the place. Super security; gates are locked during the school day, entryphone access both at the gates and the main building.

Largely upmarket intake; some of these families could undoubtedly afford the private sector, but head describes intake as 'much more mixed than you might imagine for this area.' About 9 per cent of the children qualify for a free school meal, which is more than twice as many as at other schools round about. Mainly white British or Irish, but 25 per cent of the school has EAL. Lots of immigrant families tend to be Catholic – so there are Italian, Spanish, Polish, Filipino, Eritrean, Chinese and Indian children on the roll. About 18 per cent of pupils have some special need, most commonly specific learning difficulties around language acquisition and some behavioural issues such as ADHD. No testing on entry, but school says it is happy to cater for all SEN and gifted and talented that fall within mainstream remit.

Children encouraged to take a real pride in their work; lovely displays and workbooks are the result. Perhaps it's the need to be considerate of others, necessitated by the open layout, which promotes the caring atmosphere in evidence. The older children take a fair degree of responsibility for helping their school mates in the lower years, lunch time monitoring, hearing them read and so on. Our Year 6 tour guides were almost mobbed in an act of pure hero worship as we visited the class they monitored.

Parents rave about the friendly atmosphere between the children, transcending year groups, and bill and coo over the pastoral care. The religious ethos is strong – whole school assembly most days; mass celebrated periodically and on special occasions, prayers at beginning and end of day and grace before lunch; all on top of what's included in the syllabus of course.

School is fairly demanding and standards are high, homework must be done on time, uniform absolutely on spec and so on – check that's you before signing up. Parents are a big part of the school: 'some parents get very involved in both daytime and after school activities and without them it would not be, for example, the great swimming school that it is,' said one former mum. 'However it is assumed that you want to give your time.' She felt that parental efforts were not always fully appreciated.

In a nutshell, the school ticks all the boxes for what parents would want from an ordered Catholic education – very strong spiritually, academically and pastorally. Not for the lackadaisical, nor for those hankering for informality and wide open spaces.

St Faith's

Linked to Leys School (The) in the Senior section

Trumpington Road, Cambridge, Cambridgeshire, CB2 8AG

• Pupils: 500 pupils; 310 boys and 190 girls, all day • Ages: 4-13
• Inter-denom • Fees: £9,360-£11,790 pa • Independent

Tel: 01223 352 073
Fax: 01223 314 757
Email: info@stfaiths.co.uk
Website: www.stfaiths.co.uk

Head: Since 2002, Stephen Drew MA Oxon. Previously head at The Chorister School, Durham, following twelve years at Eton and eight at Rugby as head of English then housemaster. Married to Julie. They have two grown-up daughters. Conventional exterior a bit of a red herring – turns out to be loquacious (a mine of information plus the odd off piste anecdote) with an ample helping of sparky enthusiasm. Is hugely proud of St Faith's, the staff and children – 'they have great respect for him but he isn't frightening,' said one mum. When not teaching English to Year 8s he likes to identify children who need a boost and give them an opportunity to shine. Interested in theatre, ballet and music, he plays in a local orchestra and sings in the school's adult choir made up of a 'random collection of people who are fond of St Faith's.'

Entrance: Name on the waiting list as soon as possible as demand for places is strong. Entry to pre-prep is offered by the head after a parental visit and a meeting with the child at their nursery. For all other years there are assessments in English and maths plus observation by learning support. Sibling policy gives priority on the waiting list.

Exit: Nearly 50 per cent to The Leys – otherwise to the Perse schools, Oundle, Oakham, Uppingham, Eton, Felsted, King's Ely, Friends', Stowe and Rugby. Past pupils include Maynard Keynes, Christopher Cockerell (inventor of the Hovercraft) and Sir John Tusa.

Money Matters: Scholarships are available covering Years 3–8 and Leys and St Faith's Foundation Scholarships are also offered specifically for older children who move on to the Leys. These are awarded at age 11 and cover two years at St Faith's and five years at the Leys School. Occasional bursaries are given to cover temporary financial need. The odd gripe about extras which are billed ('the moment the school day stops the meter starts ticking') countered by the head who says there are plenty of after school activities which are included in the fees e.g. Early Start – school breakfasts for all the family – and Late Stay – looks after children – playtime, homework time and sticky buns – until 5.30 or 6.00 and he feels it's a better deal than employing a child minder.

Remarks: Rounded, nurturing, not overly pressured. Lots of laughter and commitment – the head's approach puts zing into school life.

Pupils interact well with the enthusiastic, mainly young staff (two thirds are women), and when parents 'look to see who will be the form teacher next year no-one is disappointed with who they'll get.' Comments suggest science teaching is particularly good and that a great deal of effort is put into English. Extension scheme (with its own coordinator) for the gifted and talented. Stimulating end of year projects including one where children made a scale model of the universe and sited further flung planets in villages round Cambridge. The sun – in a free interpretation of its form – is in the school grounds. Sadly nothing quite as glamorous for those lower down the pile.

Judged from standardised tests taken by the pupils in Years 4–8, their achievement is well above the national average although a minority of children including learners with difficulties and/or disabilities (LDD) and any with special educational needs (SEN) are aided by the Learning Support Unit. Parents comment on the particularly caring approach of staff and the way in which problems are flagged up straight away. 'You don't have to wait for a report to find out that there's a problem' – 'the school picked up that our son was struggling with spelling and put on an extra class for him and about 10 others.'

Head has built up the arts to balance the long held perception that this is the sportier of the top three Cambridge preps – King's College and St John's being the other two. Increased provision for design technology. Also music (two thirds learn a musical instrument and every yr 2 pupil has violin lessons to identify those with aptitude) – all comers are valued but school not known to be the absolute tops if a child turns out to be another Mozart. Plentiful displays of interesting and expressive artwork.

Games two afternoons a week. Although the school isn't sport driven it is an important feature of school life and there's a definite competitive edge. A,B,C,D teams for the major sports so all get a chance to compete against other schools – much appreciated by the parents of those who aren't obvious stars. Touch rugby starts in yr 3 but tackling isn't introduced until yr 5. Playing fields on site but other facilities shared with The Leys which is just within walking distance.

Opened in 1884 as a boys' school (girls joined in 1995) St Faith's shares the same foundation as The Leys but in every other respect is a separate entity. Accommodation is mixed – some shoehorned into four slightly forbidding, late 19th century town houses which face the busy Trumpington Road like gappy teeth. Most of the rest (including a large library and generous hall where older pupils can arrange and operate the lighting for plays and performances) in bright, new buildings which help create a sizable courtyard. Library has 'Discovery Zone' to support learners with difficulties or disabilities and those who are gifted and talented. Look out for the low level 'climbing walls' – a popular challenge at play time – and wonderfully eccentric entrance gates commissioned in a scheme to promote the work of local craftspeople. To counter problems with traffic – 'delivery in the morning can be a nightmare' – the school runs free buses from a Park and Ride, but only in the morning. (Little ones are chaperoned across the school to their classrooms). They've also produced a useful section in the school handbook about travel options.

Children readily talk about their work and clearly enjoy being here. Parents have high expectations – a variety of backgrounds but professionals and ex pupils predominate. Unmistakable uniform – garish red, black and white striped blazers topped in the summer with red caps.

Saint Felix School Junior School

Linked to Saint Felix School in the Senior section

Halesworth Road, Reydon, Southwold, Suffolk, IP18 6SD

• Pupils: 125 girls and boys in the Junior School, 70 in nursery • Ages: 1-11 girls and boys • Non-denom • Fees: £6,000-£18,900 pa • Independent

Tel: 01502 722 175
Fax: 01502 722 641
Email: schooladmin@stfelix.suffolk.sch.uk
Website: www.stfelix.co.uk

Head: Since 2004, Mr David Ward – also head of the senior school. Head of junior school – Mrs Julia Campbell who took on the role in early 2009 when pre-prep and prep schools merged into new junior school.

Entrance: Not difficult but all entrants are screened and parents are forewarned if progression isn't likely. Junior School (reception to Year 3) – a day in school plus evidence of work and report from previous school. Transfer from the nursery to pre-prep is automatic. Junior (Years 4 to 6) – formal assessment.

Exit: Nearly all to the senior school although entrance isn't guaranteed.

Remarks: Hot on manners and consideration for others. Smiley, fresh faced children who appreciate the benign environment.

Preparatory department in stand alone 1906 Queen Anne style ex-boarding house adjacent to the senior school. Large, airy classrooms and wide corridors with squeaky wooden floor boards. Approximately 13 in a class and an unpressured teaching style which veers towards the traditional. French for all and a Latin club for Year 6. Assemblies, art, games and music (50 per cent have instrumental lessons) in the senior school. Specialist teachers for Years 5 and 6.

Library has been revamped and re-stocked and there are enough wireless laptops for an entire class. Two compulsory extra-curricular slots after school. Music, touch typing, board game construction, scrabble, climbing and clay are experienced by all with extra special awards for those who shine.

One or two full boarders. Flexi-boarding with the house parent and her family is a popular option. Junior school (nursery to Year 2) situated in Bronte House, a large building opposite the senior school with Years 3 to 6 situated in adjacent building. Attentive classes with questioning and co-operation. Long pavements (perfect for trikes and pedal cars), new wooden outdoor play equipment consisting of pirate boat, lighthouse and new adventure playground – all safely contained in a large grassy corral. Two new outdoor classrooms. Little ones in sweetly pretty dark green and white plaid dresses or polo shirts and shorts.

Recent shot in the arm for SEN provision with the appointment of Julia Campbell who did a sterling job at Riddlesworth – her remit is to get the school CReSTeD registered.

St George's Junior School

Linked to Saint George's School (Edinburgh) in the Senior section

Garscube Terrace, Edinburgh, EH12 6BG

• Pupils: girls, (boys in nursery) • Ages: 18 months - 11 years • Fees: £6,600-£8,625 pa • Independent

Tel: 0131 311 8000
Fax: 0131 311 8120
Email: admissions@st-georges.edin.sch.uk
Website: www.st-georges.edin.sch.uk

Remarks: See main school for details.

The School of St Helen and St Katharine Junior School

Linked to Saint Helen and Saint Katharine (The School of) in the Senior section

Faringdon Road, Abingdon, Oxfordshire, OX14 1BE

• Pupils: all girls, all day • Ages: 9-11 • Anglican foundation
• Fees: £11,235 pa • Independent

Tel: 01235 520173
Fax: 01235 532934
Email: info@shsk.org.uk
Website: www.shsk.org.uk

Remarks: For further details, see senior school entry.

St Hilary's School

Holloway Hill, Godalming, Surrey, GU7 1RZ

• Pupils: 75 boys, 180 girls • Ages: 2-11 (girls), 2-7 (boys) • Non-denom
• Fees: £7,950-£11,550 pa • Independent

Tel: 01483 416 551
Fax: 01483 418 325
Email: registrar@sthilarysschool.com
Website: www.sthilarysschool.com

Headmistress: Since 1999, Mrs Susan Bailes BA MA PGCE (early fifties). Married to long serving history teacher and archivist at St Paul's Girls' School and has two sons (one went to St Hilary's before she took up post). Has a solid gold pedigree in education – formerly deputy head and head of English at Bute House (where she was 'very, very popular and much lamented' according to one in the know), and prior to that, posts at Durston House, Falkner House and the secondary departments at Guildford High and St Catherine's Bramley. A clued-up, approachable, caring lady, with an extremely realistic approach to education and has a hands-on involvement with the school at all levels, 'I'm not in an ivory tower.' An experienced ISI inspector, she teaches English to Years 5 and 6 – she can get to know the girls individually and better advise on senior schools (she maintains very close links with all the local senior schools – 'it's a very important part of the job'). On a lighter note, she is in charge of the school play every summer – she writes it, directs it, and produces it – the whole shebang. 'Mrs Bailes is a major selling point for the school,' says one mother, who has the head summed up in a nutshell.

Entrance: A non-selective school and very popular locally. Best bet for entrance is through the nursery (en passant – nursery is 'fabulous' say all – a well-equipped space with a magical feel – entrance via Winnie the Pooh tree mural in the corridor!). Places do come up later on ('there's always some movement,' says head, due to parents' relocation) and there's another opportunity in Year 3 for girls (as the Year 2 boys move out). Pupils are invited to spend the day in the appropriate year group, staff assess how they will cope and look at the most recent school report. Scholarships available for girls going into Year 3.

Exit: Boys leave at 7 and move on to one of the local boys' day schools – Aldro is popular, then Lanesborough, Cranleigh, St Edmund's. Girls leave at 11 either for one of the Guildford academic powerhouses of Tormead, Guildford High or St Catherine's or more locally to Prior's Field in Godalming. Also a few to Cranleigh, Frensham Heights, St Swithun's, Downe House, Wycombe Abbey and The Royal, Haslemere. 'The girls really couldn't be better prepared for the next school,' says an enthusiastic parent. Academic, art, music drama and dance scholarships recently to Prior's Field, Frensham Heights, Tormead, St Catherine's, The Royal and Feltonfleet – on average ten scholarships a year.

Remarks: A thriving, buzzy, place with a warm and happy atmosphere and very impressive academic achievements for a non-selective school. Founded in 1927 by local worthy Miss Marjorie Hiorns, the school holds its traditions and family values dear, whilst embracing the new. Mrs Bailes aims to nurture a love of learning and for the school experience to be 'an appetiser for life.' Keen to stress the 'pressure off' approach and the school certainly does not come across as a hothouse. Small class sizes – you can see their little brains buzzing with all the stimulation. All classes seemed happy, involved, confident and enjoying their lessons. Pupils take SATs and are geared up slowly but surely for the myriad of entrance exams. A parent says, 'they are eased into school life gently in the lower school but, once they get to the upper school, the brakes are off.' The school follows the National Curriculum, and in the lower school (Years 1 and 2) most classes are taught by the class teacher. More specialist teaching from then on. 'Outstanding' Foundation Stage in all areas (see most recent Ofsted Inspection Report).

Excellent SEN provision – a lot of thought and care has gone into it. SEN department carries out an initial detailed assessment in consultation with parents. Mrs Bailes says, 'each year we have one or two pupils with severe problems but the majority of pupils needing SEN support have mild dyslexia or dyspraxia.' Those who need extra help spend time in one-to-one sessions with dedicated teachers in a well-equipped room. Sessions are during normal lesson time, but pupils are not taken out of core subject lessons. 'Children on our SEN register are regularly discussed so that pastoral care and discipline are seen to be fair and a child with poor organisational skills is not punished but encouraged.' SEN pupils are given (cost inclusive) support in the nursery and lower school, and (at additional cost) in the upper school.

Music, drama and dance are particular strengths of the school (scholarships abound to top-flight senior schools) – quite wonderful and inspirational music teacher was getting excellent performances out of the Year 5 class (every single pupil sang a solo – perhaps for our benefit – but impressive nevertheless). Also much praised speech and drama teacher. Ex-pupils in the drama genre include Jenny Seagrove and David Farr.

School buildings, a Victorian house with later additions, are atmospheric. 'It's a bit of a rabbit warren,' admits Mrs Bailes. Classrooms are bright and well equipped with interactive whiteboards. Superb ICT suite also enables pupils to carry out research and use the internet, enhancing all-round skills. Music room well equipped (grand piano and keyboards) and enhanced by recent addition of further practice room for drums and musical instrument walk-in store room for pupils. Brand new Hiorns' Centre next to all-weather pitch, allows for wet games, drama, music rehearsals, meetings as well as attractive venue for parents/players watching matches and post-match teas.

Design & Technology is housed in one of the less gorgeous portable style classrooms on site but there are some wonderful and imaginative activities going on in there. Super art studio that looks like Hansel and Gretel's cottage filled to the brim with examples of imaginative art. Art projects link to topics in other lessons – some beautiful knot garden collages made after a visit to Hampton Court. Science lab well laid out. Good sized library.

Small site – part of the reason why boys are off at age 7 to pastures new to let off steam and participate more in competitive sport. The lack of space doesn't detract too much and is the only giveaway that you are in a school almost in central Godalming. 'It would be fantastic if they had their own pool,' said one mum, but this seems to be the only downside for parents. New all-weather courts maximise the space – hockey, netball, tennis can now be played on site throughout the year. Sporting activities are wide ranging and 'very inclusive' so that all can enjoy, regardless of talent and 'there are fixtures for all the teams left right and centre,' says a mum. Head has been instrumental in introducing a wider range of extra-curricular clubs and activities including gardening, golf, judo, archery and chess.

Nurturing atmosphere. Mrs Bailes has a communication box in which anonymous messages can be left to alert her to any problems. Any bullying dealt with through class teachers or through 'our lovely matron' – children are encouraged to write down events and talk about them. Exemplary weekly newsletter from Mrs Bailes, well laid out and full of information in an easy to digest format.

St Hilary's has something of a reputation amongst parents at other local schools as being rather prissy and precious, particularly for boys (there are some boys from all-boy families in attendance – parents like the gentle start to formal school life – but boys in the main usually have sisters at the school). Doesn't feel like this to us – our 10-year-old guides were assertive, jolly, fun, and interesting. Even so, perhaps not the ideal place for a boisterous five-year-old.

Uniform is a slightly scary combination of brown and yellow ('I was horrified when I first saw it,' says head) but it's very distinctive to say the least. Summer dresses are pretty gingham, with new addition of attractive winter tartan skirts and bright yellow fleeces which add to the maximum bumble bee effect. Boys have the pleasure of wearing brown jumpers and shorts with yellow shirts, also with optional yellow fleece.

Wide catchment of much of south Surrey including Farnham, Haslemere and Cranleigh and villages in between. Introduction of morning transport service in collaboration with Aldro and Prior's Field is very popular with parents and pupils. Parents are generally professionals, many have moved out of London for better quality of life for their children. Old Hilarians (yes, really) are very loyal to the school – there are children and grandchildren of old boys and girls at the school and ex-pupils stay in touch.

St Hugh's School (Faringdon)

Carswell Manor, Faringdon, Oxfordshire, SN7 8PT

• Pupils: 165 boys, 135 girls. 50 weekly/flexi board, the rest day • Ages: 3-13 • C of E • Fees: Day £8,340-£14,160; Weekly boarding £16,950 pa • Independent

Tel: 01367 870700
Fax: 01367 870 707
Email: registrar@st-hughs.co.uk
Website: www.st-hughs.co.uk

Headmaster: Since 2006, Mr Andrew Nott BA (forties). Married to Sarah who copes with a multitude of tasks including managing the superb website. Family of five ranging from a delightfully lively three-year-old up to teenagers. Fascinating background – both are children of the vicarage and the head's father was the Bishop of Norwich. At the start of his career Mr Nott worked for the Church Commissioners. Since entering teaching at St Andrew's, Eastbourne he has advanced rapidly up the career ladder, St Hugh's being his second headship. He was previously head at Davenies School, appointed at the relatively young age of 34. School has had only six heads in just over 100 years.

Open, accessible and charming, the head also has a very clear understanding of the market and the place St Hugh's has in it. He values the school's remarkable stability and is building on the successes of his predecessor without altering this fundamentally very successful mix. Parents seem pleased that he has tidied up the admin and improved communication between home and school.

Mr Nott has a pleasantly relaxed approach to the pupils – clearly part of the St Hugh's tradition which remains alive and well. He wants to listen and his introduction of a School Council and regular boarder soirées in his house aid this objective. We were particularly impressed by the informal and friendly relationships we saw everywhere. It was lovely to see gaggles of happy children engaged in friendly banter with relaxed staff.

Entrance: Interview and where appropriate a simple assessment. Oversubscribed, and becoming yet more popular – don't wait to the last minute, you may be disappointed!

Exit: You will not find hoards of children on lists for Eton and Wycombe Abbey but plenty of respectable scholarships to places like Marlborough, Cheltenham, Radley, Rugby, Abingdon and St Edward's. The school has produced a few Winchester scholarships too. Able children are well catered for but in the context of a well rounded positive school experience. Leavers go to a wide range of schools as far away as Malvern, Rugby, and Uppingham but the majority move on to senior schools within a 25 mile radius. Virtually all the children, girls as well as boys, stay until they are 13. It gives the school a genuine co-ed feel and reflects the well-founded confidence of the parents.

Remarks: Not a hothouse and, in this respect, perhaps, an atypical example of the Thames Valley prep school type. Not selective, mainly by design rather than necessity. Academic performance very sound. Outstandingly good special needs support which is provided as part of the general fee (unusual). Wide catchment area for a predominantly day school, children come from as far away as Chipping Norton, Abingdon and Cirencester. Parents mainly local professionals and business people with a fair smattering of London refugees.

Sprawling 17th century mansion with lots of attractive outhouses, surrounded by over 40 acres of playing fields and woods. Children are allowed a great deal of freedom to explore the grounds. This is an ideal child-centred environment – Just William would have loved being here and, as Richmal Crompton's nephew was at St Hugh's, perhaps he was! Open, unsophisticated, naturally well-mannered children who are clearly blissfully happy. One parent remarks that in six years her child has never not wanted to go to school. Pastoral care is a strong feature, aided by the division into three sections: pre-prep, middle school and upper school. Each section has their own suite of classrooms surrounding a small central hall, giving the pupils a real sense of group cohesion. Bullying is rare and a huge focus is put upon the individual care of each child. No one gets lost here!

Some lovely facilities including a delightfully quirky art area located in the recently renovated orangery and a huge and well used sports hall as well as a barn recently converted into a modern theatre. The pre-prep area is especially charming, magnificent colourful displays of the children's work, all surrounded by beautiful gardens and extensive woods. The head has produced a realistic development plan, annually updated, which is circulated to all parents – ask for a copy. Recent improvements include a new all-weather pitch, two ICT suites, outdoor education area and brand new Nursery.

Young enthusiastic staff balanced by a core of older experienced teachers – a successful mix. This sense of staff continuity is perhaps one reason that the school has a slightly old-fashioned feel about it. The excellent staff/pupil ratio allows for an extensive range of activities and clubs after 4.30pm. A significant number of the children stay for these activities; some of the older day children also remain for supper and prep – NB all included in the fee. This arrangement offers great flexibility for working parents and is an important attraction. Saturday school remains for the final three years, the younger children benefit from a five day week.

Sport is taken very seriously with a philosophy of sport for all. It is quite difficult for a child to avoid being in a team and there is a team photograph for all. Extensive and well maintained sports fields; every child in the middle and upper schools plays some sport every day. This helps the school's aim of producing self-reliant children, further fostered by the school's imaginative personal development and leadership programme over the final four years culminating with a week long camp.

Music and drama are strong, especially music – three-quarters play at least one instrument. This small school boasts four choirs, a brass ensemble, string group, guitar group as well as a large orchestra. Most children take part in a play each year, this is seen as an integral part of the school experience. Unusually there is no annual magazine, the school produces instead lively half-termly newsletters called the 'St Hugh's News' – full of fascinating information.

The school gave up offering full boarding six years ago. It now has 55 places for weekly and more usually flexi-boarding. Most nights the boarding house is full. At £30 a night this is excellent value. Most of the final year boards most weeknights even if they are going on to a day school. The boarding experience is obviously great fun (NB the food here is rather special – all locally sourced ingredients). Since our visit we are told the dorms and washrooms have all recently been refurbished, providing attractive, comfortable accommodation.

St Hugh's offers a humane, smallish, cosy school option for Thames Valley parents who are uncomfortable with the often smart, pressurised alternatives. Produces unpretentious, relaxed, confident young people.

St Hugh's School (Woodhall Spa)

Cromwell Avenue, Woodhall Spa, Lincolnshire, LN10 6TQ

• Pupils: 105 boys and 100 girls, boarding and day • Ages: 2-13 • C of E
• Fees: Day £6,300-£11,670; Boarding £15,285-£15,570 pa • Independent

Tel: 01526 352 169
Fax: 01526 351 520
Email: office@st-hughs.lincs.sch.uk
Website: www.st-hughs.lincs.sch.uk

Head: Since 1997, Mr Stephen Greenish. Previously deputy head of Crosfields, Reading. Teaching is in his blood with both father and grandfather being headmasters of prep schools. Came to St Hugh's with dwindling numbers and has had a huge impact turning it, and its reputation, around. A good, solid chap. His wife is very involved and as a team, they sell St Hugh's as a family orientated school.

Entrance: Majority of the children rise through the ranks of the school's pre-prep. Prospective pupils spend a day at the school for assessment.

Exit: Independent senior schools in the A1 corridor, Uppingham, Oundle, Oakham, Repton, Queen Margaret's provide 75 per cent of the places. The remaining 25 per cent get places at local grammar schools at 13.

Remarks: Set in a leafy residential road in this sleepy Victorian town, with a good acreage of well-maintained grounds. Strong sense of family, excellent facilities – not surprising that it is popular, drawing children from a relatively local area. About 30 per cent of the children are from Services families, many from the RAF bases nearby.

The headmaster doesn't have to sell boarding as the children seem to make that decision for themselves and become weekly boarders in their last years. There are full-time boarders who are well looked after at weekends and kept busy. Everyone (children, teachers and parents) agrees that the food is 'fantastic', with plenty of choice. The place is absolutely spotless throughout the boarding and school side.

Classes are grouped according to ability from Year 5 with an average of 14 in a class. If a child has the ability, the school is prepared to push but generally, the teaching is taken at a gentle pace. Some of the children are statemented and the SEN department is well-staffed, with one-to-one lessons available. Staff are on average in their 40s and the headmaster is 'proactive in helping with career moves'.

Everyone is given the opportunity to contribute to the school either on the games field, musically or in drama but it's sport that rules the roost. Matches are played at all levels, involving as many as possible. The school is prepared to travel up to two hours for matches and the calendar is full of fixtures, taking the teams hither and thither. No-one is left out.

St Hugh's turns out well-rounded children who are polite and have discreet self-confidence. Happy children – and parents.

St James Junior School

Linked to Saint James Independent School For Senior Boys in the Senior section

Linked to Saint James Senior Girls School in the Senior section

Earsby Street, Kensington Olympia, London, W14 8SH

• Pupils: 255 boys and girls, all day • Ages: 4-11 • Non-denominational
• Fees: £10,650 pa • Independent

Tel: 020 7348 1777
Fax: 020 7348 1790
Email: admissions@stjamesjunior.org
Website: www.stjamesjuniors.co.uk

Head: Since 2009, Mrs Catherine Thomlinson (forties) BA in English and history from Roehampton. Head only since 2009 but through and through a St James' girl having been educated at sister school, St Vedast. Her own teaching career, likewise, spent at St James though with a pre-maternal spell at a pre-prep in South Africa whence she returned so that her own children could be schooled here. If her own education and career sound a bit narrow, the head in person is anything but that. She pays warm tribute to the traditions of the school and the work of her predecessor (Mr Paul Moss who, as principal, has an ambassadorial role) but Mrs Thomlinson is clearly her own woman with gentle innovation in mind. She is easy to chat to, astute and relaxed but she is also carefully and determinedly bringing the place up to date and more in tune with today's parental expectations. But it's not all done yet. The St James schools come from a unique tradition and carry the weight of a particular philosophy. Much of the old is treasured and celebrated but much still needs to change and old ways cannot be swept away overnight. Mrs Thomlinson, like the equally admirable head of the St James Girls' School, has the intelligence, diplomacy, dedication and enthusiasm needed to preserve all that is best in her school while shedding that which is now due for the history books. 'My aim is to open up our children's awareness and to give them the best that we can.'

Entrance: They see everyone who wants an assessment. Assessments take place informally with small groups of children whilst their parents enjoy coffee with the Head. 'We need to know they will be happy here.' Popular but not swamped, always worth calling for an occasional place.

Exit: Almost all to the respective senior schools, although the distance to the senior boys' school in Ashford, Middx, makes this unattractive for some. In recent years, these have found places at e.g. Fulham Prep, Latymer Prep, Colet Court, The Harrodian and Kings College, Wimbledon. Occasional girl to e.g. Bute House.

Remarks: Unique. The school has a relaxed and focused atmosphere unlike any we have encountered elsewhere. That this is so is testament to the school's 'philosophy' and this word, 'philosophy', is inescapable when one visits any of the St James schools. What is meant by it? In the words of the head, 'all human beings have the same divine essence and are full of consciousness, knowledge and happiness – equally everyone has their own particular nature and talents.' It is the schools' conscious and deliberate focusing on these ideas and on the 'virtues' – e.g. helpfulness, magnanimity, that gives them their special character. The junior school makes this palpable with practices like the silence observed by all classes at the start and finish of lessons, a greeting in unison at the start of a lesson and a chanted thank you to the teacher at the end, the grace said before lunch and the meditation which all are taught and which assumes more importance as the children grow older. 'It could become precious,' says Mrs Thomlinson but, in the main, it isn't now. 'It's not a pretentious school,' we were assured by very unpretentious parents.

We toured everywhere and saw only quietly concentrating, relaxed classrooms. Maths is partly based on National Curriculum maths and partly based on Vedic principles – we saw some pages in St James's own maths text books which draw attention to the beauty in geometric shapes. Top mathematicians would applaud. This intelligently explored on a trip to Chartres – maths in practice if ever it was. We applaud too. Hitherto there had been no computers in this school – or, at least, not used by the pupils. To this particular editor, this made enlightened and uplifting educational sense. However, modern life has intruded to the extent that Year 6 is now introduced to computing – but very firmly as a tool, not an end. Interactive whiteboards have begun to make a tentative appearance in Year 6 too – much relished, of course – but strictly for sound educational purposes. The most distinctive feature of the curriculum is Sanskrit which everyone learns from Year 1. Why? The answer, you guessed it, is 'philosophical' as well as linguistic and academic and ties in with the schools' belief that wisdom is to be derived from the great eastern traditions.

Boys and girls taught separately for all subjects. A Year 6 boy opined that 'girls always think they know everything – it would do them good to have lessons with us and see that they don't!' But the children eat, play, rehearse and go on trips together. Little difference in their curricula though girls still do needlework and dance while boys do woodwork or DT. We sense that this is one of the anachronisms Mrs Thomlinson will gently ease out and, surely, a good thing too! This particular female GSG writer, allergic to needles of all kinds, would have loved a try at woodwork! An exceptionally well-stocked library – busting for space – a big light art room, various music practice rooms and classrooms bigger than average for this number of children. A new pottery kiln much enjoyed and giving opportunity for lovely clayey hands and some clever modelling. The Art of Hospitality is a much-vaunted discrete subject – but the pupils we met said, rather sadly that they wished they could do more of it. 'One lesson in a whole term isn't much,' we were told.

Smallish classes – up to 22 – and the class teacher stays, whenever possible, with the class as it moves up the school. The intake is mixed ability as academic aptitude is not the main criterion for acceptance. What is? A genuine understanding of and sympathy with the school's 'philosophy'. 35 children with EAL needs at the time of our visit; these supported where necessary by a speech and language therapist – charged extra. 57 children on the learning support register ranging from School Action to School Action Plus – no statemented children when we went. Children have a range of learning difficulties, as you'd expect, and the school provides help either by giving individual or small group sessions. If the need is more extensive or the need for specialist help is identified then a number of therapists are brought in – also charged for. 'The school does not portray itself as highly academic and yet it subtly manages to tease out what skills/knowledge/experience a child has,' enthused an appreciative parent.

Masses of music – we heard exceptional singing and no-one is self-conscious about it here. Lots of drama too – again, a lack of self-consciousness is a notable feature. Frequent visits from outside speakers and companies – we coincided with a 'Victorian Day' and encountered tots wearing bustles or the helmets of various armies engaged in the Crimea. There is a good-sized gym, a large playground and a brightly painted climbing wall. There is some kind of physical activity each day; older children are bussed out for athletics at Barn Elms and everyone has weekly swimming at Fulham Pools. Girls and boys allowed to play football – this having been seen under previous regime as fostering aggression. There are lots of clubs and 'forest school' – ecological and good fun.

School moved into present buildings in 2000 – a Victorian school which has been many things in its time and now presents a rather daunting aspect to visitors. Within a ball's throw of Olympia, one is met by a sheer wall, built in 2005, CCTV, an electronic portcullis-like gate operated by entryphone. Once inside, it is very different. The three-sided old school has been cleverly added to, to provide a cloistered quadrangle enclosing a welcoming courtyard and bordered by glassed-over light and airy corridors. Refreshing to see something so architecturally imaginative. Junior school shares the building though few rooms with the senior girls. Desks are topped by adjustable mini-lecterns – hugely sensible for children who may well be the same age but cover a range of heights and builds – should be compulsory everywhere. Rooms are orderly and we were pleased to see more pupil work on display than hitherto. All rooms are in very good nick and the place feels cared for and inviting. Good new balcony in the hall will allow for bigger audiences and flexibility.

Food is eaten in a large dining room where good manners and courtesy are inculcated and expected. All looks extraordinarily civilised and civilising. Food is vegetarian and crunchy. Good system of 'buddies' – Year 5 children taking tots from reception under their wings – clearly really enjoyed and valued by all. Thriving 'Friends of St James' which organises a multitude of social events and, in fact, masses of parental involvement in all areas of school life. School has a bursary fund and a bursary committee to which current and prospective parents can apply. Bursaries are needs-based and not dependent on scholarship.

In 2010, the St James schools 'merged' with St David's Ashford – a girls' school forced to close, what with the recession and all – much missed by its aficionados. St James boys moved from the Twickenham site in Sept 2010 and now have a splendid, far bigger site in which to expand and deliver. This provides both opportunities and problems for the St James Junior boy leavers – if they want the St James brand of education for their senior school, then a trek to Ashford is the only option and a fleet of buses are now plying the routes. Hence, while the junior girls still leave for their senior schools at the end of Year 5 – and the vast majority go on to the girls' school onsite – the boys now stay on and do their Year 6 in situ. It must be strange for them to be suddenly girl-less and to see their 'sisters' suddenly elevated to seniorhood.

St James Junior school is part of the family of schools founded by The School of Economic Science and now administered by a charitable trust called The Independent Educational Association Ltd. The SES has its passionate adherents but has been controversial in the past. (For a fuller picture, see our entry on The St James Independent Boys' School.) SES members still make up around three quarters of the school's governing body so, although we are told that, 'the SES has no direct influence on the day schools', the family connection is alive and well. A certain rigidity and regimentation has characterised the school's approach in the past but there is far less sense of this now. 'If you are happy with the SES philosophy, it's a great school,' said one parent on our last visit and that remains the case. For many people looking for more than results and qualifications, the values embedded in the St James schools will feel wonderfully refreshing. Mrs Thomlinson talks of 'exploring' and of the children 'expressing themselves.' New, tangible sense now of the past being precisely that and the school feels healthy, forward-looking and sensible. Offers a rare combination of an unusual curriculum, an ethical approach, dedicated staff and a safe, unpressured environment. Unique in London.

St James's Catholic Primary School

260 Stanley Road, Twickenham, Middlesex, TW2 5NP

• Pupils: 315 boys and 320 girls (including 50 in the nursery); all day
• Ages: 3-11 • RC only • State

Tel: 02088 984 670
Fax: 02088 933 038
Email: info@st-james.richmond.sch.uk
Website: www.st-james.richmond.sch.uk

Head: Since 2000, Mrs Veronica Heffernan BD MA (mid-fifties). Previously head for seven years at St Mary's, Chiswick. Neat and petite, she comes across as calm and very capable – completely on top of her brief of running this expanding school, while still managing to fit in some regular teaching and weekly choir practice. 'She is fantastic – and very approachable,' says one mother. 'I think the children are in awe of her and eager to please, but in a positive way.' She knows most children by name and regularly paces corridors, classrooms and playground. 'Visionary,' says another parent. 'She has fantastic ideas and is very friendly and happy.' She is strict and takes no nonsense from the children. 'I have heard her say that she won't entertain playground gossip but if there is a genuine issue over anything you can get to see her quickly and she is very very fair,' said another mother. 'She goes by the book and I have nothing but praise for her.'

Entrance: At three to nursery, and four to the main school. Non-selective academically, St James's is a Roman

Catholic school serving the parishes of St James Twickenham, St Francis de Sales Hampton Hill, St Margaret East Twickenham and St Theodore Hampton. The school expanded to three-form entry to cope with over-subscription in 2002 and reached capacity in 2008. But it's still over-subscribed with almost two applicants for every place in both Nursery and Reception. Getting into the Nursery does not guarantee a Reception place but, in practice, most do go on to the main school. If you want a place 'your child must be baptised as Catholic and you must be a weekly attender at your parish.'

Exit: Popular choices are Hampton and The London Oratory for boys and Gumley House for girls. Recent scholarships to St George's, Weybridge for academic achievement, St Catherine's(for PE). Three boys into Tiffin Boys.

Remarks: Brand new, state of the art accommodation, a gift for local Catholic families. Its very strong Catholic ethos and excellent academic results make it a popular choice around these parts. The school's expansion into a new building on the same site has been welcomed by parents. 'The whole place seems to have been rejuvenated,' says one happy parent. The building is attractive and the school staff worked with the architect to get things right. A good example of being 'built for the purpose' is the ICT suite – where all the computer workstations face front for whole class teaching, rather than the more usual arrangement where they face the wall. Interactive whiteboards are in every classroom – including the nursery. The front of the school is one storey, rising to two storeys at the back (with a lift as well as stairs). Nursery children enjoy an additional outside classroom. Sunny yellow decoration gives a warm, almost Mediterranean, feel to the place (indeed Italian is taught from Year 3, and to any interested parents after school, as part of an initiative with the Italian embassy). Great use of space outside as well, with covered ways to provide some shelter, tables for lunch in good weather, and a huge climbing frame.

St James's has been up and running since the 1960s, gradually expanding from a single entry school to the current three-form entry, but retaining its good local reputation throughout. 'We heard fantastic reports of it and moved nearby to be sure of a place,' said one parent. 'We feel it has given our children a really good foundation and that they will get into a good secondary school after this.' Certainly there is a purposeful buzz about the place. Classrooms have a bright and industrious air and the children – all very smart and wearing proper ties – seem engaged in what they are doing.

Expect your child to work hard. There is a structured approach to teaching and a lot of homework (for a state school). 'I was shocked at the amount of homework – 1½ to 2 hours three nights a week when my daughter was in Year 4,' said one mother. Mainly literacy and numeracy, there are spellings to learn and reading 'without fail'. The head agrees with the parents we spoke to. She says, 'it's a big commitment which means a lot of parental involvement, especially with the younger children. We expect high standards of academic excellence and behaviour here.'

But it's not all work. 'They play hard too,' said another parent. 'My kids have lots of fun and are very happy.' And don't be discouraged if your child is not an academic high-flier. Parents of children whose talents lie elsewhere seem just as pleased. 'I feel my daughter, who is not so academic, has fared very well here,' says one mother. 'She is young in her year but got lots of extra help and has gained tremendous confidence. She is good at art and I feel this has been encouraged. The teachers seem to nourish talent, wherever it lies.'

There is an SEN co-ordinator and support teacher – and facilities have been enhanced by the move to the new building, which has more quiet rooms for group and individual work and assessment. St James's also houses The George Tancred Centre for autistic children. Ten places are available here and are open to non-Catholic children. Fantastic facilities include partitioned work areas so the children can control their immediate environment and a 'time-out' room filled with soft play equipment. The playground is separated from, but adjacent to, that of the main school and a regulated number of children from the main school are allowed to go in and play with the George Tancred children at break time – and compete to do so.

Plenty of praise for a delightful and stable staff – a mix of ages, but not gender, with just one male classroom assistant. School is very good at netball (Middlesex and Surrey champions) and chess, but does not really excel in other sporting pursuits. 'There is plenty of sport played and we take part in lots of things – but we don't actually win much,' one parent reports. Musical abilities are nicely encouraged – with a dedicated teacher and practice room and annual presentations of a music cup and another for 'Most Promising' musician.

Located in a cul de sac, opposite another school, access by car in the morning is not the best. Helping to overcome this, the school is heavily involved in a 'green transport policy', running several 'walking buses' and encouraging children to ride bikes and scooters to school, where 'parking' is provided. A very Catholic school – prayers are said three times a day in classrooms and whole school gathers for Mass on holy days.

St John's Beaumont School

Priest Hill, Old Windsor, Old Windsor, Berkshire, SL4 2JN

• Pupils: 300 boys; 60 board, 240 day • Ages: 3-13 • RC (owned by Jesuits) • Fees: Day £7,470-£9,645; Boarding £18,525-£21,465 pa • Independent

Tel: 01784 432428
Fax: 01784 494048
Email: admissions@stjohnsbeaumont.co.uk
Website: www.stjohnsbeaumont.org.uk

Headmaster: Since 2006, Mr Giles Delaney (thirties). Educated at Hereford Cathedral School and Cardiff University (music and theology), Cambridge PGCE. Joined school in 1996, deputy head 1999, acting head following sudden death of predecessor 2005. Has emerged from under shadow of remarkable Mr Dermot Gogarty: a superb leader, charismatic, autocratic, larger-than-life. It is a tribute to Mr Delaney (and his staff) that the school thrives under a very different leadership style; calmly confident, thoughtful, patient, 'management by conversation' – which doesn't mean he doesn't know his own mind or where he wants the school to go – though his suits and ties are a touch less stunning than Mr Gogarty's. He's around the site a lot; his spell as deputy means he knows boys and parents very well. Wife Katie a medieval history student at King's, London – as well as mother of four girls under nine.

Entrance: First come first served, rigorously adhered to – though some turned down after educational psychologist's report, 'if we can't help them'; long waiting list. Most enter at age four but places are kept open for another small intake at Year 3.

Exit: Eton, Ampleforth, Stonyhurst, Hampton, St Paul's, Westminster, Tonbridge, Harrow, Wellington, Winchester, The Oratory, Bradfield, Marlborough, i.e. the whole range, but skewed towards the more demanding senior schools.

Remarks: Fine 1888 buildings on a hilltop, by the architect of Westminster Cathedral. Lovely Gothic chapel, purpose-built music and drama block (there is a strong musical and artistic tradition), cheerful junior classrooms. A £2.5M sports complex with 8m climbing wall, fitness suite, drama studio and iMac design studio was opened by Her Majesty the Queen in October 2009. Everywhere inside is bright and wholesome (cleaners on constant duty and introduced to us by boys as 'This is Mr/Mrs X'), including dorms and loos. Extensive rolling grounds of over 70 acres, bordering Windsor Great Park, including 'one of the finest cricket squares to be found in an English prep school'. Significant recent leap forward in ICT provision, including Microsoft-sponsored intranet system: freer information flow means parents can find out what's going on, e.g. video link to 1st XV match, and can be aware of normal peaks and troughs of schoolboy life. Head claims beneficent effect on teaching styles – more efficient and creative. Usual broad curriculum, including Latin and Spanish options from Year 5 and Greek for some. Streaming operates from Year 5; boys and parents seem happy about this. There is a strong academic drive about the school, without the less gifted being neglected; high standards for all. Everyone 'hits the ground running', which shows up in remarkable record at senior school entrance – from a non-selective school. A very structured, hard-working place. Class size averages 14; Strong EAL provision and the Campion Unit has teachers in all fields of SEN requirements.

It has a reputation for being a pretty sporty place – games every day and typical RC emphasis on rugby (annual tours), but also has a wide extra-curricular programme, in which all staff are involved (including fly-fishing, French films and debating – SJB boys tend to be articulate); swimming also very good in 25 metre pool. Many trips at home and abroad. Pupils are kept busy right through the day; school ends for Years 4–5 at 5pm and for Years 6–8 at 6pm. The sixty boarders have full weekend programmes, including cultural visits and relaxation time. They sleep in long, old-fashioned dorms, divided into sacrosanct cubicles; plenty of resident staff (nine on duty every evening). Staff are a healthy mixture of young and long-serving and clearly relish the school's success and sense of purpose. When you sidle into a classroom they will march over and shake you by the hand, without apparently losing disciplinary hold or pedagogic flow.

Most pupils come from London and the south east; some from as far as Mexico, Korea, Japan. About 25 per cent are non-Catholic – all denominations 'positively welcomed'. Non-Christians are invited to share as far as they feel comfortable in the school's religious life; this seemingly difficult balancing trick is managed with some ease. Parents are issued with an amazingly detailed 'family handbook' which covers everything from a mission statement to what eight year olds are doing at 4.05pm on Thursday. Also useful booklets on helping with tinies' reading, and what to do if you're worried (about the school, that is). Means-tested bursaries available for deserving cases.

A famously prescriptive school, expects high standards of discipline. Successful, with a strong sense of community. 'Glammy Berkshire – turn up in the Rolls,' advises one parent; maybe, but boys seem untouched by the more idiotic Home Counties parental expectations. Head claims private tutoring 'on the way out'. Pupils are well-mannered and confident, at ease with themselves and with others – much respect both ways between boys and staff; ambitious and socially alert, keen joiners-in ('We believe in pushing all the buttons we can find'). Everyone seems to enjoy being there.

St John's College School

Grange Road, Cambridge, Cambridgeshire, CB3 9AB

• Pupils: 250 boys, 210 girls. 40 boy and girl boarders, 420 day
• Ages: 4-13 • C of E • Fees: Day £9,000-£11,874; Boarding £18,753; Choristers £6,252 pa • Independent

Tel: 01223 353 652
Fax: 01223 355 846
Email: admissions@sjcs.co.uk
Website: www.sjcs.co.uk

Head: Since 1990, Mr Kevin Jones (early fifties) MA. Educated Woolverstone Hall (state boarding) and Caius, Cambridge. Head of English and drama then deputy head at the Yehudi Menuhin School before deputy headship at St John's. A maverick: someone who takes nothing for granted and continues to search for even better ways to educate – interest in the acquisition of knowledge, combined with the development of creativity and self confidence, is deep seated. Parents speak of a well managed school (nothing is left to chance and his finger is firmly on every button) and his breezy, fun loving manner with the children – we watched some little ones closely examining and feeling his hairless pate – a novel twist to hands-on learning. Married with two sons – time with them is number one on his list of top ten pastimes closely followed by reading poetry and supporting Chelsea FC.

Entrance: Oversubscribed. 'Live waiting list with cap'. Sibling priority followed by boy/girl balance. Be under no illusions children are academically well above average and, as one mum commented, parents are 'fiercely competitive in the nicest of ways'. And there's a 'gentleman's agreement' on the parents side that the child will stay until they are 13 – so think twice before skipping off at 11. New children and parents made very welcome – links with existing parents are encouraged so new bods know someone before they start. Very civilized.

At four: no testing. School is cleverer than this – sequencing and other indicators are monitored instead.

Even at this early age a pretty reliable assessment can be made. At seven: assessments in English and maths plus observation of child over half a day of normal schooling.

Yearly scholarships for up to five choristers. At seven means-tested bursaries for those who would particularly benefit from being at the school.

Exit: One or two at seven and 11 – school says they 'don't evict' but occasionally, after discussion and mutual agreement, it's decided that a move would be in the child's best interests. Otherwise nearly all at 13. Masses of help from the head who is 'spot on' re the best school for his pupils. About 50 per cent gain awards/scholarships. Impressive number to The Perse (co-ed). Uppingham, Perse Girls, St Mary's and Oundle also popular.

Remarks: Pleasant environment with copious helpings of purposeful buzz, friendly fun and encouragement. Semi suburban setting, not far from St John's College, with ample space for play areas, pitches, indoor swimming pool and ongoing redevelopment. Three close but separate sites: intimate, purpose built Byron House (infants), a revamped boarding house (mainly boys and on the up since recent appointments) and the junior section – a well tended melange with a huge willow tree sturdily propped to create an organic climbing frame.

'Completely magic teaching' coupled with finely tuned management of learning/thinking processes help children 'go as far as they can go' without pressure or cramming – school has a full time psychologist and Ed Psych. 'The intellectual ability of my kids has really picked up and they're interested in finding out. They aren't behaving like baby birds sitting there accepting knowledge.' Parents also praise excellent lines of communication and staff who do anything to help. Pupils seem carefree and bubbly – school 'somehow empowers and gives them confidence.' All in Year 8 take on roles of responsibility from the 'mail run' to managing classroom recycling boxes. And there are competitions – during our visit we noted a short story competition with entries carefully pasted onto numerous windows (according to our guides winners 'get to choose a book and have a hot chocolate'), a wonderfully dotty extreme reading photo competition, a make a model out of rubbish competition, a science competition and the best decorated classroom door competition.

No exams until the penultimate year when out of lesson clinics are available for all. Extension work (from Year 7 'invitation only' Greek and debating) and scholarship standards in the top sets. IN (individual needs department) for those who need some extra help. Tucked into the web site blurb is the elliptical 'the school is therefore able to intervene in a child's best interest at a very low 'threshold' of difficulty.' Despite the odd exception this broadly translates to: school only wants to deal with minor difficulties (and it does so fantastically well). See 'exit' if issues turn out to be more than minor.

Parents are pleased that arts and sport aren't sacrificed at the altar of academia. Music is strong: 80 per cent of the older pupils learn one instrument and 60 per cent learn two or more – and a good number achieve grades 5 and 6. Head of drama 'totally charismatic and an absolute luvvie – some of the plays are a bit mad (pupils play a part in their development) but all have a fantastic time.' Enthusiastic librarian, productive DT department, airy art room decorated with interesting 2 and 3D work, extra-curricular activities ('every minute filled with something') and plenty of sporting fixtures for teams plus alternatives including real tennis and rowing. This is a fine school where children are highly motivated and magically happy.

St John's-on-the-Hill School

Castleford Hill, Tutshill, Chepstow, Monmouthshire, NP16 7LE

• Pupils: 305 boys (27 board) and girls (17 board); 350 boys and girls in three linked nurseries • Ages: 4-14 (3 months - 3+ in nurseries) • C of E • Fees: Day £6,450-£10,650; Boarding £15,000 pa • Independent

Tel: 01291 622 045
Fax: 01291 623 932
Email: registrar@stjohnsonthehill.co.uk
Website: www.stjohnsonthehill.co.uk

Head: Since 1993, Mr Ian Etchells BEd (mid-fifties). Educated at Marple Hall Grammar School in Stockport then St Luke's, Exeter where he studied history and played 1st XV rugby. Teaching career began at Kingswood House, Epsom then 5+ years at Exeter Cathedral School (head of history and games), further five years as deputy head at Haileybury Prep before spell as housemaster at Shapwick in Somerset. Appointed to try and 'save' St. John's during recession of early '90s. Married to Anne (daughter of legendary Somerset wicketkeeper, Harold Stephenson) whom he met at college. Described as 'much more than a meeter and greeter,' she doubles up as registrar and head of performing arts. They live on site (head's house not much of an inducement by the looks of it from outside) and have two grown-up daughters: Becky (who works in London) and Katy (who teaches at St John's).

Much admired, approachable head who eats, sleeps and drinks the school. 'If every head were like Ian we'd have a fantastic school system,' glowed one dad. 'One of the really super old school headmasters,' said another. Children love him and he has a knack for attracting tip top teachers who are 'committed to prep school life.' Has raised the school from near closure to outstanding academic, sporting and commercial success. Admits to being 'terribly driven' though he appears very relaxed. Not someone to take his eye off the ball towards end of career. Huge presence around the school, loads of experience and expert at advising parents on senior schools – 'horses for courses' he smiles modestly. Dads say that, 'He stands no malarkey but applies discipline wisely and consistently.' Thankful parents agree that 'he knows every child individually' and that he's 'always there at school events.' Phew! Enjoys playing golf, walking his dogs (Wilko and Carling) and getting away to the Greek islands.

Entrance: Mixed ability intake but school will say if it thinks applicants are unable to cope. Gives the benefit of the doubt where it can. Assessment is based on a 'taster day' in English and maths plus report from previous school. Procedure is 'painless' say parents and compared it favourably with other schools. Pupils may enter at any point provided spaces are available. Main catchment area is Newport/Cardiff through Monmouthshire to Forest of Dean and West Gloucestershire. Boarders come from all over.

Exit: Has gained reputation for gaining awards near and far. Recently, 30 children winning 40 awards at 11 different schools including Shrewsbury, Rugby and Cheltenham College as well as nearer placed Monmouth, Clifton etc.

Money Matters: Bursaries for services, police, clergy and staff children. 'School really helped to ensure we could afford to educate all our five children at St John's and had something left to live on,' said one grateful parent.

Remarks: St John's has risen phoenix like from ashes of early '90s' recession to become a thriving and successful school. Perched above river Wye, a short stone's throw into England, school overlooks Chepstow in Wales. Founded in 1923 in a rambling Georgian manor (rebuilt in 1805 after a fire). Succession of proprietorial heads until '60s but co-ed and charitable trust (incorporating former Brightlands School) since then. Has expanded successfully in recent years. New buildings fit well into overall scheme of things on a pleasant 8-acre site (plus 12 more acres of playing fields across the road).

Spectacular growth of nursery education (now provided on three sites including one in Newport) complete with state-of-the-art baby units (Tutshill site boasts a six-seater 'baby charabanc' paid for by the parents' association and appropriately pushed out from what was once the local garage). Seventy per cent of pre-prep intake come from the school's own nurseries. Our visit on a 'Foodie Friday' coincided with 'wormy pasta salad' on classroom menus. Highly professionalised early years teachers and assistants ensure tinies are happy and cared for. Impressive range of activities for these tots – stimulation in the nursery section includes sensory and soft play rooms plus safe outdoor play areas for all.

'Seamless' progression to reception level on Tutshill site where children 'learn to read without noticing' say committed staff. Phonic introduction alongside activities such as puppets and story telling. Loads of measuring and counting too. Each day begins with assembly in spacious hall; weekly link-up with nursery from below and to prep (in their hall) once a week. Communication between teachers and pre-prep parents includes 'wow cards' and home-school link books. Wide corridors in this modern, purpose-built building boast frequently changed displays including output of creative arts club and strong evidence of cross-curricular work: e.g. 'forces of movement' incorporating art, science and ICT work. Smart boards in each year group and laptops already in use at this level not to mention school intranet on plasma screen. Huge choice of readers ('fireflies' non fiction popular with boys). Tea after school for those involved in clubs, activities or post-lessons care.

Pupils leave the swish pre-prep for the cleverly converted coach house which accommodates Years 3 to 5 in what the head describes as 'a bit of a tardis.' Smallish but cheery classrooms (maximum class size is 16) for these years. Next project is to build a six classroom block to replace outside mobiles which have served older pupils well but whose shelf life is definitely nearing the end. We observed a mock Jewish wedding taking place during an upbeat RS lesson in one of these when we visited.

Much better than average prep school facilities for science: junior (in a quaint outpost) and senior (modern) laboratories with well qualified teachers to match. Lovely dining area combines best of cafeteria and sit down traditions whilst civilised entrance (with memorabilia on show) and meeting room (referred to as the Embassy) add gravitas. Prep is awash with subject specialists (some escapees from state sector others ex-independent) who can take pupils as far as they want to go. Art teachers (ex-Monmouth senior) explained how they are adapting OCR syllabus for St John's and thereby widening pupils' artistic horizons. We appreciated the on-going Picasso exhibition whilst annual Arts Week gives pupils a chance to let their creativity run wild. Athletic head of DT (he manages British universities' cross-country team) oversees a well resourced area which includes 3-D model making.

Somewhat dated school hall serves for assemblies as well as concerts and school productions (last one was a full blown 'Oliver'). Music has a large classroom base plus three individual practice rooms. Everyone in Year 3 gets a violin and learns to scrape – like it or not. Orchestra and wind band plus choirs (school subs for Newport cathedral choir and also sang at recent IAPS conference) are all well supported and three ex-pupils have graduated to national youth orchestra. Head is keen to see a new performing arts centre built but this may have to wait a while yet. Specialist ICT rooms are well used but school maintains a healthy balance between new technologies and more traditional approaches.

Sports facilities include (almost) half size Astroturf and hard tennis/netball courts, attractive 15 metre swimming pool and oodles of playing fields. School more than holds its own against larger preps with an impressive fixture list (includes Millfield and Cheltenham College). Wide choice of sports features rugby, soccer, cricket (boys and girls) as well as netball, rounders, swimming, tennis and golf. All pupils encouraged to participate as best they can. Fit looking sports staff include Haka savvy Kiwis. Pupils punch above their weight at national events – e.g. recent national runners-up in national JET cricket competition beating Cheam by one wicket in semi-final. Athletics and cross-country involve large numbers; lots of alternatives for non team players.

Refreshingly open, happy pupils – well turned out and polite nonetheless. We observed a school council meeting chaired effectively by a Year 8 boy. Plenty of evidence of pupils' ideas bearing fruit e.g. new homework diary and rewards system not to mention refurb of pupils' loos. Pupils also discussed making a new outdoor classroom interactive – cutting edge stuff for 12–13 year olds. Large number (33 last time) go for a whole month's exchange with host schools in Stirling and Cape Town, South Africa. Led (ten visits so far) by a staff member who hails from those parts. Does wonders for pupil personal development and bonding. Pupils wax eloquent about how they are all 'given a chance' by 'kind teachers' and how 'friendship' is the magical ingredient at St John's. We were shown a wide variety of pupils' work – impressive in its quality and diversity. Alumni include Olympic showjumper Richard Mead, Welsh rugby player Marc Batten and Rebecca Watts (in first group of ordained women priests).

Head of learning support 'took on' rôle initially because of dyslexic/dyspraxic needs in her own family. Four statemented children (each with a key worker), seven EAL pupils and forty-seven withdrawn for a variety of reasons. Thorough screening and intensive support from pre-prep upwards enable most children to proceed to senior schools of their choice. 'My bright, dyslexic son couldn't read when he started in the prep and now he's scored a high CE mark,' confided one very satisfied mum. Lots of input too for the most able (school is in membership of NACE) and organises trips (e.g. to theatres) and participates in events (e.g. maths challenges, languages show etc) to extend and inspire. Membership of Comenius project another way of widening horizons; some competed in Eurotalk competition (taking on tasks in previously unknown languages) at Olympia, London. School intranet, increasingly used to improve learning resources, provides cyber information for pupils, staff and parents. All years get to go on well chosen choice of trips not to mention year camps which get progressively more adventurous.

Fleet of minibuses ('drivers are really kind,' say parents) to ferry day pupils twixt home and school. Boarders get a good deal here with lovely, mixed (not the dorms) accommodation, dedicated and well qualified houseparents who 'go the extra mile' to develop a family, 'home from home' atmosphere. Houseparents even cook for boarders on Saturdays (take-aways are not unknown) but school roast on Sundays is 'to die for' they confess. Junior boarders write home (plus ICT and reading) on Saturday mornings whilst their seniors are in lessons. Dorm points add up so that winners get a reward outing. Regular 'Boarders' Bugle' adds to monthly school newsletters to keep boarding parents well informed. Flexi-boarding clearly popular with parents. Active Parents' Association have raised loads of dosh for worthwhile projects plus social and sporting events such as Bollywood Summer Ball and PA Golf Day. Parents help children's fund- raising through their four houses to benefit of a wide range of local, national and international good causes.

Great 'family' school for youngsters with 'gunpowder in the barrel' – 'we'll take them as far as they want to go,' insists head. Parents were at a loss to pick out a single outstanding feature – 'excellent teachers'; 'all pupils get involved'; 'a super school in all respects' was the consensus.

St Leonards - New Park

Linked to Saint Leonards School in the Senior section

The Pends, St Andrews, Fife, KY16 9QH

• Pupils: girls and boys; all day • Ages: 4½-12 • Fees: £7,653-£8,580 pa • Independent

Tel: 01334 472 126
Fax: 01334 476 152
Email: slnp@stleonards-fife.org
Website: www.stleonards-fife.org

Headmaster : Mr Andrew Donald.

Remarks: For further details, see senior school.

St Margaret's Nursery, Pre Prep and Junior (Prep) School (Exeter)

Linked to Saint Margaret's School (Exeter) in the Senior section

147 Magdalen Road, Exeter, Devon, EX2 4TS

• Pupils: 85 boys and girls; all day • Ages: nursery, pre-prep and prep: co-ed 3-11 • C of E • Fees: £5,010-£9,750 pa • Independent

Tel: 01392 273 197
Fax: 01392 251 402
Email: info@stmargarets-school.co.uk
Website: www.stmargarets-school.co.uk

Head: Since September 2010, Mr Richard Raistrick BA PGCE (early fifties), who succeeds long-serving and much valued predecessor, Ms Sarah Agg-Manning, who remains on staff. Educated at Bolton School before reading modern literature and linguistics at Cardiff then PGCE at Bristol. Taught at Saltus Grammar School, Bermuda for 12 years before return to UK and launching into a prep school teaching career beginning with St Aubyn's, Rottingdean where he was director of studies. Deputy head at St John's, Sidmouth for yonks then associate headships at Bramcote Lorne and Lincoln Minster. Clearly happy to be coming back to his old haunts and to have a project to get his teeth into. Has been round the block a few times so looks like he'll move the prep up a gear or three. Married to Beverley, a teacher, they have two sons moving towards and through university respectively. Still teaches English and is a keen sportsman. Enjoys theatre and walking the family dog.

Entrance: By application, entrance test and interview.

Exit: Girls' transfer to senior school unconditional although all sit entrance exam.

Remarks: All change here in recent times. Co-ed nursery opened in refurbished accommodation in 2009 alongside pre-prep in Westall House. Well qualified staff run early years section and it shows: children have a lovely, safe outdoor walled garden in which to play when they are not inside flitting twixt 'sunshine' and 'rainbow' rooms as the fancy takes them. Children feel happy and free but parents we spoke to recognise that the day is carefully structured and that the learning process is carefully monitored. Pre-reading phonic work starts here as does measuring, counting etc. When we visited it was café time for the tinies in their 'messy' room. Seamless progression from nursery (some go to state alternatives) to reception class where topics (e.g. 'Space' or 'The Seaside') generate lots of ideas for a range of work.

Years 1 and 2 expand the topic work but English and maths are taught discretely. French, drama and ICT begin at this level with smartboards and a suite of 15 PCs shared between pre-prep and prep in a recently converted suite. Parents get a termly curriculum focus which outlines areas for study. Linked access to senior school from Baring Lodge (prep school building) makes it easy for juniors to access specialist and dining facilities. 'Everyone knows everyone,' say parents who see great benefits from pupils being in smaller classes. 'St Margaret's teaches them values for life,' said one mum for whom the 'Christian underpinning' was also important.

'Learning success' department operates from the earliest years: identifying and helping those with specific learning difficulties. Some EAL teaching too though the girl we met in Year 4 who told us that the teaching was 'absolutely extraordinary' seemed already to have outgrown the need for it.

Blazers are worn throughout the day from reception except for practical work. Children get to be part of the wider community in a variety of ways – e.g. Tuesday assemblies involve Years 3 to 8. Our visit coincided with one by local radio as a result of a letter written to them by a Year 2 girl. Plenty of room to let off steam outside; sunken netball court provides an excellent hard play area for juniors. Book corner is inviting as is the art room which serves for reception class upwards. Former prep head now let loose in DT room which she loves almost as much as her other passion: performing arts. Performances sometimes involve nursery upwards – witness *The Littler Muncher* set in Lazy Daisy Village to the delight of parents or else, Years 2 to 6 as in the case of *Wind in The Willows*.

'Sport for all' motto is reflected in pupils' enjoyment of a range of sports. Without being over-competitive prep has built up a fixture list against local schools in netball, hockey, rounders and kwik cricket. Gymnastics, dance and swimming (at St Luke's pool nearby) all figure and Year 6 have a full games afternoon. Pupils enjoy inter-house competition through events such as annual swimming gala and athletics. Creative development is emphasised from the start – junior choir and junior orchestra perform regularly and a majority of junior children have group or individual instrumental lessons. Pupils are articulate at an early age we found; lots of visiting specialists for music as well as speech and drama (LAMDA exams). Horizons have been broadened through involvement with EU Comenius project which has recently involved reciprocal visits with pupils from Denmark and Belgium. Year 6 pupils make annual cultural pilgrimage to London for a few days and take in a range of activities (e.g. galleries, museums and a show). Visits lower down school are well thought out – lots involve natural settings (e.g. seashore centre at Goodrington) and inspire follow-up work in class.

Sensible arrangements for delivery and collection of pupils and for care before and after school (at a cost). Parents seem to be fully involved and help to organise social and fund-raising events through active PSA.

Distinctive, holistic start to schooling with an emphasis on the creative. 'If you fall over at St Margaret's someone will be there to help you back onto your feet,' explained one mum who suggested that elsewhere this was not necessarily the case. Boys will make a difference but so too will the new head of prep.

St Margaret's School for Girls Junior Department (Aberdeen)

Linked to Saint Margaret's School For Girls (Aberdeen) in the Senior section

17 Albyn Place,, Aberdeen, AB10 1RU

• Pupils: All girls, all day • Ages: 3-12 girls, all day • Non-denom
• Fees: £5,580-£8,844 pa • Independent

Tel: 01224 584 466
Fax: 01224 585 600
Email: info@st-margaret.aberdeen.sch.uk
Website: www.st-margaret.aberdeen.sch.uk

Head: Since 2010, Dr Julie Land (fifty) BSc (maths) PGCE EdD. Educated at Dame Allan's Girls' School, Newcastle and Manchester and Newcastle universities. Taught maths for nine years before taking 10 years out to look after a young family and did most of her doctoral research during this time. Returned to teaching in 2000 and joined St Margaret's in 2003, becoming deputy head in 2004.

Intends to lead and support staff through a period of educational change and oversee new buildings such as a new school hall and classrooms together with improvement of games facilities.

Married with two grown up children she enjoys walking and gardening as well as table tennis (an accomplished player in her youth).

Remarks: For details, see senior school entry.

St Margaret's Junior School (London)

Linked to Saint Margaret's School (London) in the Senior section

18 Kidderpore Gardens, London, NW3 7SR

• Fees: £9,042-£10,419 pa • Independent

Tel: 020 7435 2439
Fax: 020 7431 1308
Email: principal@st-margarets.co.uk
Website: www.st-margarets.co.uk

Head: Remarks: See senior school.

St Martin's Ampleforth

Linked to Ampleforth College in the Senior section

Gilling Castle, Gilling East, York, North Yorkshire, YO62 4HP

• Pupils: 115 boys, 85 girls; 80 boarders from age 7 • Ages: 3-13
• RC - accepts pupils of other denominations but they must be prepared to be a full participant in the religious life of the school
• Fees: Day £6,420-£11,910; Boarding £18,705 pa • Independent

Tel: 0143 9766600
Fax: 01439 788 538
Email: headmaster@stmartins.ampleforth.org.uk
Website: www.stmartins.ampleforth.org.uk

Head: Since 2004, Mr Nicholas Higham, educated at Mount St Mary's College, BA in PE and geography from Leeds Carnegie. Played rugby for Headingley and Saracens. Taught at Douai, housemaster at Pangbourne, head of Moreton Hall prep school, Suffolk, increased roll from 95 to 140. Charming, brisk, businesslike, loves his job (and children), has clearly got a grip on the place. He and wife Louise (ex-BBC, does school marketing) used to live on site with their three children and dog(s) but housemaster and housemistress now in situ instead, 'to give special pastoral care to all boarders'.

Entrance: By interview, assessment, and report from current school. All entrants encouraged to come for taster day.

Exit: Ninety per cent to Ampleforth College, rest to Oundle, St Peter's York, Eton, maintained schools. Many scholarship winners, especially in music. Though linked closely with Ampleforth, Mr Higham points out that it is 'a prep school in its own right'.

Remarks: Prep school of Ampleforth, founded in 1929, merged with St Martin's RC prep in 2001, which brought in girls, pre-prep and nursery. Main building is imposing Gilling Castle – Grade 1 listed, with unbelievable sixteenth century Great Chamber, probably the finest Tudor interior in England (don't miss the ceiling and stained glass); the children eat there. The castle has another life as the inspiration for Hogwarts in the Harry Potter films, according to JK Rowling's cousin, who went to the college – though site not used for filming. Southern pupils catch a Hogwarts Express at the beginning of term, and the school gardener bears an uncanny resemblance to Hagrid. Three miles from the senior school, with the freedom of its 3,000 acres; '10-year-olds can climb trees instead of hanging round the café'. Boarding is important, and growing; quite a few persuade parents to let them convert from day. School day ends at 5.30 for all.

Catholics make up 70 per cent; other denominations are clearly happy to be there, 'being educated in the life of the Christian faith', as the school puts it. Like its Benedictine big brother, it 'asks much from the children's strengths and supports their weaknesses'. Boarders come from all over UK, day pupils from Yorkshire. A good sprinkling from abroad.

Standard curriculum up to Common Entrance, pupils also tested at KS 1 and 2. Games predictably important: rugby and cricket for boys; hockey, netball, rounders for girls. Athletics, swimming, cross-country also on offer. School has a floodlit all-weather Astroturf pitch. Golf taking off (Mr Higham 'has taken a personal interest in its development'). Plenty of activities, including riding and shooting. Music superb, now based in fine new performing arts block. ISI noted 'high level of musicianship, inspirational teaching'. Schola (choir) in process of being elected to full membership of Choir Schools' Association, sings with senior school, has toured Malta and Hungary. Over 100 pupils learn instruments.

Pastoral care very good (there are three monks associated with the school); children are confident, courteous and seem to be happy in their extended school family. Catholic parents who want a safe but stimulating environment for their children should look no further. Good place for a weekend break, too.

St Mary's Hall

Linked to Stonyhurst College in the Senior section

Stonyhurst, Lancashire, BB7 9PU

• Pupils: 275; 55 Boarding and 220 day • Ages: 3-13 • Roman Catholic in the Jesuit tradition • Fees: Boarding £15,912-£18,087; Day £6,297-£12,552 pa • Independent

Tel: 01254 826 242
Fax: 01254 827 136
Email: saintmaryshall@stonyhurst.ac.uk
Website: www.saintmaryshall.com

Head: Since 2004, Mr Lawrence Crouch BA MA PGCE (forties), married with four children. After studying English at Nottingham, an action-packed gap year and a spell teaching English in a comprehensive school, returned to his alma mater in 1982 as head of drama, later appointed head of English. A keen sportsman, a rugby, cricket and golf fan, also the current Stonyhurst campus squash champion; plays piano and oboe and, as a singer, is renowned for a definitive performance of 'Great Balls of Fire'. Warm, thoughtful, caring, approachable and, despite his impressive achievements, extremely modest; clearly enjoying the role of prep school headmaster enormously, his enthusiasm is infectious.

Entrance: Pupils enter all years but most commonly at three, five, eight and 11. Admission to nursery and reception via interview with the head and head of pre-prep; older children admitted following an interview and on receipt of a school report. Ages 10–12 require additional tests in maths, English and verbal reasoning. Two academic scholarships and one for music awarded for entry at 11.

Exit: Straight on to Stonyhurst College. It is rare for a pupil to stray elsewhere, however school will advise appropriately if it feels Stonyhurst would be unsuitable.

Remarks: Set in glorious countryside amongst rolling fields, the inspiration is clear. However, you and your children may have to learn a whole new vocabulary to enter the world of Jesuit traditions and beliefs in this 400-year-old school. For starters 'lines' are school houses, 'playrooms' are common rooms, 'playroom masters' are housemasters and then there is the Latin ... And yet the school is forward-thinking enough to pick up on the whims of modern children, issuing a 'credit card' for consistent good work that allows you jump the lunch queue, MSN offering an active forum for after-school chat and the top year producing their own web page. Traditional in that scholarship classes exist to 'push' the brightest; German taught from four and French from seven; school performances are enjoyed in the theatre; sport is popular as is the usual carousel of after-school activities and the ARK with goats, ponies, sheep et al is a joy for those children who are animal lovers.

A long school day but children cope and parents are grateful. Strong boarding ethos with a mix of local children and others from Mexico, Hong Kong, Spain, Germany, Korea and beyond. Saturday school until lunchtime for day pupils. Charitable giving is important; the school has its own charity and a link with a school near Harare supporting the culture of 'men and women for others'.

Parents are a mixed bag of Old Boys and local professionals. 70 per cent Catholic, other denominations accepting the liturgy also welcome. The nursery and pre-prep are lovely, in attractive modern surroundings with delightful teaching areas and a multi-sensory approach to learning. By contrast, the prep school goes in for more formal teaching in higgledy-piggledy, but nevertheless much-loved, old buildings. Pupils appear confident and are hugely loyal, dreading the day when they must leave the security of these warm and supportive surroundings.

St Mary's Junior School (Cambridge)

Linked to Saint Mary's School, Cambridge in the Senior section

1 Brookside, Cambridge, CB2 1JE

• Pupils: 170 girls, all day • Ages: 4-11 • RC, but all faiths welcome
• Fees: £7,710 – £9,570 pa • Independent

Tel: 01223 311 666
Fax: 01223 472 168
Email: juniorschool@stmaryscambridge.co.uk
Website: www.stmaryscambridge.co.uk

Remarks: See senior school entry.

St Mary's Junior School (Shaftesbury)

Linked to Saint Mary's School Shaftesbury in the Senior section

Donhead St. Mary, Shaftesbury, Dorset, SP7 9LP

• Pupils: girls, boarding and day • Ages: 9-11 • RC
• Fees: Boarding £21,570; Day £14,820 pa • Independent

Tel: 01747 852 416
Fax: 01747 851 557
Email: admin@st-marys-shaftesbury.co.uk
Website: www.st-marys-shaftesbury.co.uk

Remarks: For further details, see the senior school entry.

St Mary's School (Gerrards Cross) Junior House

Linked to Saint Mary's School Gerrards Cross in the Senior section

Packhorse Road, Gerrards Cross, Buckinghamshire, SL9 8JQ

• Fees: £3,420-£10,065 pa • Independent

Tel: 01753 883 370
Fax: 01753 890 966
Email: registrar@st-marys.bucks.sch.uk
Website: www.stmarysschool.co.uk

St Mary's School, Hampstead

47 Fitzjohn's Avenue, Hampstead, London, NW3 6PG

• Pupils: 240 girls and 35 boys • Ages: 2-11 • Fees: £5,550-£10,380 pa
• Independent

Tel: 020 7435 1868
Fax: 020 7794 7922
Email: enquiries@stmh.co.uk
Website: www.stmh.co.uk

Head: Since 2003, Miss Angela Rawlinson BA MA (1st class honours) DipTchng NPQH (forties), previously head of Marlborough Primary School in Kensington and Chelsea. Started her teaching career in her native New Zealand and has also been acting head and deputy head of other London primaries. Enthusiastic, engaging, acclaimed by one and all. 'She's fantastically good,' said a parent. 'She's very approachable, very dynamic,' said another. 'She gave me lots of support when my older daughter was having problems at senior school. Everyone thinks she's great.'

Entrance: Non-selective in the nursery and lower school. Siblings get first priority, then Catholic girls up to two thirds of places, then Catholic boys. Any remaining places go to children of other faiths. Waiting lists close at 50, but it's always worth trying for a place higher up; boys leave at five, six or seven as they get places at boys' preps. Girls coming into the upper school are assessed, but only to ensure that they reach a basic level – 'we try to meet children's needs', school says.

Exit: Boys, as previously mentioned, leave between reception and Year 2 for boys' preps. Girls nearly all stay till 11, moving on to a range of mostly north London independent schools ranging from St Paul's to More House, with a good sprinkling of scholarships. A few to boarding school.

Remarks: Universal praise for its family feel and caring ethos. Excellent academic results, too, particularly for a non-selective school; in the top 20 prep schools in the country in recent years. Recent ISI and Diocesan inspection. By no means a hothouse, though the present head has upped the ante on the academic front. She has introduced very careful monitoring of progress so any dips in achievement are noted and rectified. 'But parents choose our school because they like the broad curriculum. The children are not sitting in rows, cramming. They leave with confidence and self-esteem as well as academic results.' Setting in English and maths from Year 3, but not for every lesson. 'Our groups are flexible. Some children might be good at fractions, for example, but find shapes difficult.' Staff set work for three different ability groups from reception onwards.

'They may not extend the more able end quite as much as they could,' said a parent, 'but the wealth of totally unpressured spiritual and physical experiences make up for it. They end up with a wide spectrum of physical skills and even the slower children get into perfectly good secondary schools.'

For a week at a time the school happily throws the curriculum aside to study science or maths or PSHE. 'It's hard for the teachers but lovely for the children.'

The site excludes children with mobility problems but the school can cope with most other needs including sight and hearing difficulties, dyspraxia and dyslexia. Some get one-to-one help (at extra charge), others are helped in small groups or in the classroom. A few pupils have emotional and behavioural problems. 'I've never yet had to say that we can't cope any longer, and I would try not to do so. It's very important for children to have consistency.'

Sport is a great strength, with football,netball and dance part of the wide range on the curriculum. There's also clubs and squad practices before, during and after school, plus inter-school and inter-house matches. Gymnasts compete nationally and internationally. 'The PE teacher is tireless,' commented a parent. Another added, 'even the ones who are hopeless at sport are all out there passionately doing things.'

Strong art and music too; the four choirs and two music ensembles perform in concerts. Choirs have won places at the North London Music Festival for the last three years. Plenty of clubs; each member of staff runs at least one, ranging from chess to Latin to Green Fingers gardening club. Year 5 has an adventure week at Ross-on-Wye, Year 6 visits France, and there is a ski trip every year. The grounds include a netball court, climbing frame and shady lawn; sports lessons also take place further afield higher up the school.

The school was founded in 1926 by the Congregation of Jesus, which decided in the early 1990s to close the school. A group of parents formed a company limited by guarantee to save it from closure and it now has a lay staff and headteacher. A fair ethnic mix; popular with American families. Around 80 per cent of pupils are Catholic. Other faiths are welcomed but everyone must take part in the religious life of the school. 'Our Catholic ethos underpins everything we do.' The chapel is an integral part of the school, used for mass, assemblies, choir practice and praying together. The school priest is available as a listening ear.

'We are not Catholics,' said a mother, 'but that hasn't mattered at all. My daughter has always felt included. But the faith side is very strong, very much part of their whole education, and that has certainly influenced her.'

'The children come first,' says the head. 'If all our decisions are made with the good of the children in mind then we're moving in the right direction.'

Parents agree – 'the ethos is a very special one. They really do make all the children feel they're important.'

St Mary's Music School Junior School

Linked to Saint Mary's Music School in the Senior section

Coates Hall, 25 Grosvenor Crescent, Edinburgh, EH12 5EL

• Pupils: girls and boys, some boarders • Ages: 9-13 • Non-denom
• Fees: individually assessed • Independent

Tel: 0131 538 7766
Fax: 0131 467 7289
Email: info@st-marys-music-school.co.uk
Website: www.st-marys-music-school.co.uk

Remarks: For details, see senior school entry.

St Mary's School (Melrose)

Abbey Park, High Street, Melrose, TD6 9LN

• Pupils: 120 boys and girls in main school; 25 in the Kindergarten
• Ages: main school 4-13; nursery 2.5-4 • Non-denom • Fees: Weekly boarding £15,750; Day £9,750-£12,600 pa • Independent

Tel: 01896 822 517
Fax: 01896 823 550
Email: office@stmarysmelrose.org.uk
Website: www.stmarysmelrose.org.uk

Head: Since 2010, Mr Liam Harvey BEd (forties). A former pupil of the school he went on to George Watson's College followed by a BEd in PE at Liverpool John Moores University. Taught PE to A level in the state secondary sector before moving to Belhaven Hill School where he became housemaster, head of history and PE. His wife, Marnia, originally from Canada, works alongside him. They have two young daughters at the school.

Entrance: All things to all men. The only independent school in the borders, children come from within a 20–30 mile radius, can come mid-term at any time if space available, otherwise automatically up from kindergarten. The odd state child has been known simply to come for an 'eighteen-month blast' before going back into the maintained sector again. And some come at 11 to do CE.

Exit: 'Most but not all' stay on until they go to their senior school which may be at 11, 12, or 13, depending whether they are going to continue in the independent vein in which case it is Glenalmond, Fettes, Merchiston, Loretto, St George's in Edinburgh as well as Longridge Towers in Berwick, Queen Margaret's York or dive back into the state sector and Earlston High School.

Remarks: Jolly useful little school, incredibly flexible, with flexi, weekly and day pupils; one or two toffs, but mostly farmers and local professionals who stay to the bitter end, plus 'masses of' first time buyers. Tiny classes, max 18 but usually much less, only one stream but scholars will be 'hived off' and setted at 10 if necessary. Latin from eight, languages from five, taster term of French, then specialise in French for Common Entrance. Science taught separately for the last four years, and pupils move round the staff. 'Excellent' dyslexia department, and good support for the very bright as well. Withdrawn help and staff will go into class as well – 'pretty flexible' (might be the school motto). Keen on handwriting.

Drama strong and timetabled, the school has links with local theatrical costumiers. Good music, rehearsals and lessons in functional school hall, whilst pre-prep have own gym, with Noah and his ark drawn by the young, main school has to use the hall. Somewhat surprising cloistered classroom corridor and incredible conversions and add-ons (or subtractions) on the classroom side, very rabbit warreny. Charming little Foyle library, with computers all over the place and dedicated resource centre for every age group. Brand new Hamilton building opened 2010, housing the top three year groups.

Day children can stay from 7.30 am (and breakfast in school) right through to 7.30 pm, by which time they will have done their prep and had supper. Kindergarten can stay till 4 pm, tinies wear delightful green and white check tabliers, and girls evolve from tartan gym slips to kilts. Jolly dorms upstairs, all brightly painted with splendid (unironed) stripy duvet covers. Dining room with proper menu (beware the 'sandwitch') and over-high benches for littlies to sit at the table. Brown bread only, and lots of sugar-free puds, and mainly organic as far as possible. Robert the chef comes complete with starched chef's hat and sparkling white uniform. Cor. He also makes scrumptious millionaire's shortbread for the head's guests – not sugar-free at all.

Squads and teams triumph all over the place. Swimming off-site in Gala(shiels) and main games pitches just across some National Trust land. Smashing little school.

St Michael's CofE Voluntary Aided Primary School

North Road, Highgate, London, N6 4BG

• Pupils: 465 boys and girls; all day • Ages: 3-11 • State

Tel: 02083 407 441
Fax: 02083 409 452
Email: admin@stmichaelsn6.haringey.sch.uk
Website: www.stmichaelsn6.com/

Head: Since 1997, Mrs Barbara Smith (late fifties). Formerly head of St John's, Angell Town, Brixton. Cert Ed, Christchurch, Canterbury. BA, Birkbeck, English, MA South Bank University, Education. Impressively focused and coolly efficient head who's taken a good primary school and turned it into an outstanding one. Enormously hard working and dedicated – she once spent her entire summer holiday reworking the curriculum to ensure her pupils didn't lose out from the government diktat for non-contact time – she's also a good sport, willing to join in the school panto. A keen drama enthusiast, she still manages to find time to produce and direct an annual Christmas play and a leavers' Shakespeare production. Married to an engineer.

Background and Atmosphere: One of north London's most sought-after primary schools, St Michael's has high academic standards and a high proportion of pupils who reach well beyond the government's expectations at seven and 11. This is partly due to intake – 'average children here would be above average in most other schools,' says the head – but also due to strong teaching throughout and well-organised classrooms where calm and well-behaved boys and girls sit quietly in their neat and practical navy uniform.

The curriculum is a particular strength of the school, with specialist subject teaching from Year 3, Italian (courtesy of the Italian government), and a notable maths programme with an early-morning maths club for the most able run with neighbouring Highgate prep and booster lessons in curriculum time for the struggling.

Afternoon teaching unique, with specialist subject teaching in extension maths, PE, art, science, geography, history and music from Year 3. 'I wanted to play to teachers' strengths,' says Mrs Smith. 'We had all these specialists in the school and only a proportion of the children were getting the benefit. It made absolute sense.'

A good range of sport – gymnastics, football, tennis, cricket, netball and basketball – taught in lesson time. Swimming too, taught in Years 5 and 6, a strength – the school has won the Haringey swimming shield so often it's now on permanent display.

Founded in the mid 19th century as a school to train up young locals to go into service, by 1852 it was on its current three-and-a-half acre site. The green fields and listed Victorian buildings have since been joined by a block built in the 1970s, two large, well-equipped playgrounds and a large, new all-weather court. The immaculately maintained grounds are still the pride of the school. 'The school manager, Troy, has to be one of the best in London,' enthused one parent – and, as well as play time and games, the grounds are made full use of for the popular summer fair and Bonfire night festivities.

Excellent drama, with two or three plays annually, plus a nativity play and annual summer concert. Dynamic extra-curricular programme, with after-school cricket, drama (led by the school's celebrated drama teacher, Bob Williams, CBE), orchestra, recorder groups, French, chess, etc. Higher than average special needs, with a good SENCo, plus a gifted and talented co-ordinator.

Unusually energetic Parents' Association, which raises impressive sums each year with an endless medley of social events. 'I have never come across such a strong body of parents' reps,' says Mrs Smith. Fund-raising drives have paid for a £35,000 computer suite, resurfacing and remodelling the infant playground, new cloakrooms, new stage lights and books galore.

Children mainly from comfortably off professional and media homes who are more than happy to use the state if it's as near to private as you can get. 'The parents here are wonderfully involved but you can feel excluded if you aren't in with the right set,' said one 'and parents can be quite demanding'. 'They sometimes don't seem to realise this isn't a prep school,' says the head.

Very much a community school, however, which children remain very attached to, often turning up to annual celebrations well into their secondary school years. 'It's one of unique things about the school.'

Entrance: Heavily oversubscribed at nursery and reception. Some 100 or so apply for 52 nursery places, 60 reception places, which are allocated on a points system. (five points for church attendance at St Michael's Church, three for living in N6. Thereafter, local Christians, siblings, other faiths.) Christianity very much part of the ethos but the school tries to be as wide ranging as possible in its intake. Open days every term and, if a vacancy is available, parents are welcome to look round. Places do arise, particularly in the higher years.

Exit: On the border of three boroughs – Haringey, Islington and Camden – St Michael's sends its leavers to as many as 30 secondary schools. About half to independent schools (many with scholarships) – particularly Highgate, with which the school has a close association – and City of London, but also Channing, UCS, Westminster, North London Collegiate, Haberdashers' Aske's, and South Hampstead, plus top grammars, Henrietta Barnett, Latymer, St Michael's Catholic Girls and Queen Elizabeth's Boys. Two boys, too, have recently been accepted by Eton. A considerable chunk each year to Fortismere School, the popular local comprehensive in Muswell Hill. The school doesn't prepare children for entry tests but parents tend to be very clued up (with a secondary school evening run by the Parents' Association) and coach accordingly.

Remarks: Oustanding local primary, with a strong head, wonderful grounds and a real sense of community, which endures long after the children have moved on to secondary school.

St Olave's School

Linked to St Peter's School (York) in the Senior section

Clifton, York, North Yorkshire, YO30 6AB

• Pupils: Co-ed; day and boarding from 8+ • Ages: 3-8 Clifton Pre-prep; 8-13 St Olave's • C of E but open to all • Fees: Day £9,483-£11,469; Boarding £17,382-£19,314 pa • Independent

Tel: 01904 527 416
Fax: 01904 527 303
Email: enquiries@st-olaves.york.sch.uk
Website: www.st-peters.york.sch.uk

The Master: Since September 2005, Mr Andy Falconer MBA BA (late thirties). An ISI inspector, current Chairman of IAPS and a Walter Hines Page Scholar. Previously deputy head at Chafyn Grove School and before that was head of geography at Craigclowan School. Married to Lesley, a nurse, with three young daughters. Enjoys skiing, grew up near a Scottish ski resort and is a qualified instructor, still gets commissions as a travel writer, otherwise free time is family time.

Kind, charming, with a soft Scottish lilt. Pupils say he's strict, 'he goes bonkers if you don't have your jumper on' but love the fact he gets involved with boarding: 'he's interested in what we do, not just the boys and their rugby but girls' matches too.' Popular with parents: 'last head was a hard act to follow but he's stepped comfortably into his shoes. He has a lovely manner, takes time to get to know the children and even sends personal letters for achievements.' Head hopes to dispel school's elitist image, keen to get the local community into the school, even if it's just for evening classes. Hopes to maintain academic rigour and wants pupils to work outside of their comfort zone. Says he wants to develop confident youngsters who'll give things a go.

Entrance: Automatic from Clifton Pre-prep, otherwise selective but not massively so, looking for NVR of 100+. All entrants are tested in maths, English, reading, spelling, and reasoning. Entrance examinations end of January. Means-tested bursaries for both boarding and day places available.

Exit: Odd one occasionally helped to find an alternative school, otherwise all to St Peter's.

Remarks: Good facilities, shares fencing salle and indoor pool with senior school, but have own sports hall with indoor nets, music block, science lab, language rooms, DT, cookery (not as a discrete subject but linked e.g. to maths, DT etc), art, pottery rooms, dining hall – (school holds Healthy Schools Award though children say food is 'not great' – what do they know?) and Shepherd Hall for assemblies and regular productions. Library bright, airy, well used, children encouraged to read and are rewarded with a series of certificates. Elegant Queen Anne Hall with galleried landing, and lovely art displays, but some incongruous additions including grey corrugated monstrosity and lurid yellow and green corridors (both of which have now been redecorated!).

DT popular. All do French, with Latin or classical studies and choice of Spanish or German for older ones. Have exchange programmes with two schools in South Africa as well as in Germany and France. Girls feel boys get better deal with sports and tours, boys feel girls get the better deal in the classroom. Pupils would like less prep, improved playground facilities (have a lovely quiet garden with benches designed by children) and more to do during wet breaks, otherwise no grumbles. Cosy, well-equipped junior boys' and girls' boarding house, complete with snack area, games room, computer room, model room, two TV rooms and a piano.

No issue with bright dyslexics (currently 23 on SEN register), have strategies to help, including links with Dyslexia Action (formerly DI), extra lessons and extra time for those who need them. Average class size 16 with maximum set at 20. Chapel held in senior school twice a week, traditional C of E service.

Pupils think those not into sport would struggle saying, 'we are competitive, we're not a Quaker school, competition is very important to us, we are more disciplined.' (A reference to a local rival!) Parents of non-sporty children disagree, saying their children enjoy all the school has to offer including drama (regular productions) and music; pupils regularly gain places on the IAPS national orchestra and strings groups. Sporting successes include four times winners of the National Rugby Sevens Tournament, current modern biathlon, indoor rowing and cross-country champions. Pupils enjoy charity days and fund-raising, pink day for breast cancer, organised by pupils, and green day in support of NSPCC, among recent events. Range of after school clubs and activities, including prep clubs for day children of working parents.

Parents say the teachers are conscientious, work hard for the children and create a lovely atmosphere, offering something for everyone and encouraging success. Ideal for those wanting guaranteed continuity.

St Paul's Catholic Primary School, Thames Ditton

Hampton Court Way, Thames Ditton, Surrey, KT7 0LP

• Pupils: 140 girls and 150 boys; all day • Ages: 4-11 • RC • State

Tel: 020 8398 6791
Fax: 0208 398 6080
Email: info@stpauls-thamesditton.surrey.sch.uk
Website: www.stpauls-thamesditton.surrey.sch.uk/

Head: Since 1990, Mrs Fionnuala Johnson, BEd (late forties), married with two children, the younger one is at the school. Garners huge respect from parents, who regard her as the architect of the school's (and their children's) success. Descriptions of her vary along the spectrum from 'strong impressive leader', through 'powerful personality' to 'formidable' (we'll vouch for that) – but most also mention her caring side. 'The children adore her – tempered by due reverence,' said one mother. 'I've seen children run across the playground to hug her,' said another.

Has plenty to say about the school – of which she is fiercely proud – and is full of plans and ideas for the future. She knows all the children by name – and promises to keep this up even when the school has doubled in size. As it is, parents wonder at her grasp of all the smallest details of their lives and the praise continues – 'she's fantastic – the school is as good as it is because of her. She talks to the children quietly and they all listen – she never needs to raise her voice. They want to please her and if ever they are in trouble and sent to see her they are not frightened but sorry they have incurred her disapproval'.

Entrance: Heavy over-subscription has allowed funding for expansion from single to two-form entry. From 2002, the school has accepted 60 children per year (instead of 30) and the pressure has eased up a little – but Catholic families whose children have been baptised (and you need the certificates to prove it) still take 99 per cent of the places. The school serves the parishes of Cobham, Esher and Thames Ditton, a mostly white middle-class lot. It is non-selective academically – regular church attendance will get you a long way.

Exit: Where to go next is the most vexing question for parents. 'I just wish this school had a secondary equivalent,' sighed one mother, echoing the view of many. St Paul's pupils are guaranteed entry to the RC Salesian School in Chertsey, but few choose it. Among the more popular choices of secondary school are Wimbledon College, Ursuline High, Tiffin School and Tiffin Girls School in Kingston.

Remarks: An academically strong school with a solid Catholic ethos. Set back from a busy dual carriageway, in functional rather than beautiful accommodation, purpose-built in the mid-1960s. There is plenty of space, including a large playground and a grass playing field. The smart new block built to provide the necessary seven extra classrooms does make the older classrooms look a little tired, but good art displays line the walls and lift the spirits. A well-resourced school, with a shiny IT suite and three well-stocked libraries. All classrooms are spacious and light; and each is named after a saint – reflecting the importance of Catholic teaching at the school.

The Catholic Church schools' 'Search for Excellence' theme is seen as key here – both in the spiritual and academic development of the children. Academic standards are high. At Key Stage 2, 93 per cent gained level 4 and above in English, and 100 per cent in maths and science – there were more level 5s than 4s in all three subject areas. Many parents tell us that this is a school for academic girls rather than non-academic boys. Even parents who are not quite so dogmatic believe the environment is more suited to the academically inclined. 'It is not a hothouse, but there is just a general expectation of achievement,' said one mother. Mrs Johnson disagrees strongly – so does Ofsted, who also single out the SEN teaching for praise. The number with SEN is below the national average but those with SEN do as well as their peers. There is an SEN teacher with two assistants on hand and the school also brings in outside specialists.

High praise from parents for an able and effective teaching staff. 'Every time we change classes we say we wish we could have that teacher again – and then the next one is just another delight,' said a mother who has had children at the school for many years. 'Discipline is strong, the children know their boundaries and understand them,' said another. There is plenty of praise and reward, with a system of highly-prized stickers and certificates, not just for academic work but also for helpfulness, cheerfulness and so on. Prayers are said at the end of each day, and children attend mass regularly. The religious teaching really kicks in at Year 3 as the children are preparing for Holy Communion.

All the parents we spoke to agree their children are happy at the school which they describe time and time again as 'very caring'. Pupils are respectful and polite – and also extremely smart – with even the reception children wearing neat ties. 'The fact they can get a four-year-old to tie a tie says a lot about this school,' enthused one mother. Mixed feelings abound over sports provision with some parents feeling it is not a particular strength, especially among the boys – though the school does well in the borough in netball and cross-country.

A real sense of community, which staff and parents are keen to maintain as the school expands. Some parents have expressed concerns that the strong sense of community they have enjoyed may be eroded as the school grows. However, the niggles are few and far between, and overall the positive comments far outweigh the negatives. It is still a first choice for parents seeking a good education for their child in a distinctively Catholic environment.

St Paul's Cathedral School

New Change, London, EC4M 9AD

• Pupils: 240 boys and girls, including 30 boy choristers; choristers board, the rest day. • Ages: 4-13 • C of E, but other faiths welcome, though choristers mostly Christian • Fees: Day £11,001-£11,844; Boarding + £6,852 pa • Independent

Tel: 02072 485 156
Fax: 020 7329 6568
Email: admissions@spcs.london.sch.uk
Website: www.spcs.london.sch.uk

Head: Since 2009, Mr Neil Chippington MA (Cantab) FRCO (forties). Music scholar at Cranleigh, organ scholar at Cambridge, Fellow of the Royal College of Organists, music is certainly in his blood. Came from Winchester College where he was a housemaster for eight years and, having himself been a quirister (chorister) at Winchester Cathedral, seems to be the ideal person to have taken the responsibility of thirty boarding choristers and a school bursting with music. Says he wants to make sure that all children reach their academic potential and are stretched to the limit of their abilities without the school becoming a hothouse. Feels it is crucial to get the balance right so that both choristers and day children get a wide breadth of educational experience and benefit from each other's talents.

Currently reviewing the curriculum, looking at different ways of approaching CE. Open minded and not afraid of change. Says 'the bottom line is to instil a love of learning'. Has introduced a more significant staff appraisal system. Communication apparently an issue when he arrived but believes he has opened up the lines. Responds quickly to emails and maintains an open door policy. Parents acknowledge this improvement. Married with two small sons, the elder of whom is at the school.

Entrance: 70 on list for 20 available places at 4+, so best to put children down early. Informal assessment in November before year of entry. More places at 7+ when boarding choristers also start. January assessment and short test for day children (also taken by those in pre-prep); informal audition with director of music for choristers, followed by formal audition and same academic test as day children. More places for choristers at 8+ and occasionally 9+. Choristers' fees paid by Dean and Chapter of St Paul's Cathedral with parents paying boarding fee. This will carry on even if a boy's voice breaks early. If in need, bursaries available for day children also. Head is keen to build up a fund and expand this.

Exit: At 11+ and 13+ to a mixture of London day schools and top boarding schools. Majority of girls at 11+ though head eager to keep girls and maintain balance. Choristers mostly to boarding schools at 13+. An impressive number of music and the occasional academic scholarships. Westminster appears high among day schools, with City of London (girls and boys) and JAGS also featuring. King's Canterbury popular amongst a wide selection of good boarding schools. Recently, Eton, Stowe, Uppingham and Oundle have all offered academic and music scholarships. Famous ex pupils include Alastair Cooke (England cricket captain) and Simon Russell Beale (actor).

Remarks: A small school, nestling in the precincts of St Paul's Cathedral, providing an excellent all round education in a traditional setting with a formal, spiritual context to everything it does. In amongst the hustle and bustle of the City of London, an oasis of orderliness and calm. Boy choristers have been around since 1123, originally linked to a grammar school which became St Paul's School, London, about 400 years later. Only tenuous links remain. In 1989, the Dean and Chapter decided to expand the tiny choristers' only school to include day boys as well. Girls arrived in 1998 and the school grew to the size it is today.

Two low concrete towers house the classrooms and are linked by the school hall, the gym, the library and various other communal activity areas. We seemed to wander up and down and across as enthusiastic pupils showed us their school but 'once you know the two towers it's easy,' they assured us. Three lovely bright classrooms for the pre-prep years, two each for Years 3 and 4, then subject-based doubling up as home rooms from Year 5 onwards.

Broad based curriculum with all subjects well taught. Parents praise 'inspirational teachers' who are 'passionate about everything they do'. Average age 39 seems about right. Our guides also spoke enthusiastically about their teachers, singling out science and Latin/Greek as exceptional. Certainly pupils did look happy and absorbed in the excellent science lab, however the French class we looked in on appeared chaotic. Mixed ability classes throughout with some discreet setting, particularly in Years 7 and 8. Previously some complaints about lack of preparation for 11+ entrance exams but new head is driving this forward and has already made important changes, revamping part of the curriculum and timetabling non-verbal reasoning, study skills etc into earlier years. Parents very happy about this. Creative writing, apparently, a great strength. Latin compulsory from Year 5. Modern languages not the strongest point, though French taught from the beginning and Spanish available as an extra. Head's wife a linguist, so change could be in the air. Interactive white boards in classrooms and good IT suite. All special needs problems dealt with by head of learning support. Teachers flag up concerns and he is immediately involved. Any necessary help is provided, mostly free of charge. Additional staff available for one-to-one and in-class support when necessary. Parents kept fully in the picture and involved from the beginning.

Reasonable art. Studio also contains a printing press (given by the Stationers' Company) and a kiln for firing imaginative clay models. Location excellent for visiting Tate Modern as part of extended art lesson. Drama strongish and everyone gets a chance to take part in a production. As one of our guides said, 'if you're not particularly musical, you can still do drama and have fun'. LAMDA exam course available.

Inevitably the greatest strength is music, huge both instrumentally and vocally. Virtually every child in the school learns an instrument of his or her choice (no bagpipes!). Choristers learn two, piano being compulsory. Over 300 music lessons given each week, beginners all the way to grade 8. At least six different choirs plus 15 orchestras and ensembles from classic to rock band. Something for everyone you might say. For musical, creative children it is a great place to be. Opportunities abound. Choristers are in the minority but it is their talent that is the backbone of the school. Head feels that one of the most crucial things he needs to do is clarify the way they are perceived. The day school exists because of them and they are getting a wider breadth of education because of the day school. Thus both sides are gaining a huge amount and it is important to maintain the balance. Choristers are acquiring an excellent academic education and day pupils are seeing, hearing and being involved in music of an exceptionally high standard. All of them are equally at home in the Cathedral, which they treat as an extension of the school. Assemblies and occasional special services held and the majority get the chance to sing there. A parent told us 'the Christmas service was something to behold ... about six or seven different choirs were fielded, including a combined one which seemed to involve most of the school'.

Choristers have a pretty heavy schedule with singing practice before school every morning, evensong on Tuesdays, Wednesdays, Fridays and Saturdays plus Saturday morning rehearsals and Sunday services. Alongside a multitude of other occasions when they have to perform. One of the first things the Head did for them was to negotiate Monday evenings off as well as Thursdays. Seems only fair after an action packed week end. He also stresses the importance of watching the development of their voices and becoming more aware of change – necessary with the earlier physical growth that now occurs. 13 year old trebles are rarer. Both the cathedral's director of music and organist are also committed to their personal development and nurture.

A father said, 'sport at the school is active, fun and inclusive.' Despite its inner city site, it is well catered for. Pupils are bussed to Coram's Fields and Regent's Park for seasonal activities. Matches fielded against other schools in hockey, football, cricket, rounders, fencing and netball. Have been runners up in u12 London Schools' Cricket Association Cup, winners of the Girls' Football South London Tournament and pupils have been selected for the U10 National Fencing Squad and the U11 Surrey County Cricket squad. Also swim at local baths recreationally and competitively. Rubber surfaced playground, marked up for ball games, for the prep where teachers also arrange impromptu games and sports practice. Brand new, larger, grass and woodchip playground with climbing equipment for the pre-prep. Older children allowed to play quiet games here but not allowed to climb.

A variety of after school clubs, mainly on Thursdays to enable choristers to join in, but on other days too. Range from cookery to dance to computer etc. Bound to be something for everyone. Also children may stay to do supervised prep at school, charged as an extra but useful for working parents. Plenty of outings and expeditions, academic, cultural and sporty. Home and occasionally abroad. A lot to see within walking distance as well.

Parents stress the happy atmosphere – 'it has been the making of our little boy' – (of a chorister) and 'our unsettled, troublemaker has been transformed' – (of a dayboy). 'Very good discipline, they don't tolerate bad behaviour'. General feeling that children are treated as individuals, academically stretched and made to work to their own levels; that the school is 'well managed and well ordered'. Much of this appears to lie in the vertical tutor system. Pupils are assigned to a tutor from day one and, in normal circumstances, remain with him/her until they leave the school. Thus tutor groups mixed in both ability and age and there is easy rapport between all children across the school. The older ones love helping the younger ones.

According to parents excellent pastoral care, particularly for the boarders. 'They get well cared for, individual treatment and feel they are part of a family'. Several raved about the deputy head (pastoral) who, they say, really carried the school through recent difficult times. Definitely feel there's a good team in place now.

Effective and active PTA. General feeling is that head is in tune with all pupils and ideal person to be running the boarding section as well. Watch this spot for further developments.

St Peter's Eaton Square CofE Primary School

Lower Belgrave Street, Belgravia, London, SW1W 0NL

• Pupils: 265 primary and 50 nursery (intake 30 per year to the nursery and 40 per year to the reception class). All day • Ages: 3-11 • C of E • State

Tel: 020 7641 4230
Fax: 020 7641 4235
Email: office@stpeaton.org.uk
Website: www.stpeaton.org.uk

Head: Since 2010, Ms Nicola Cottier BEd Cantab. Previously head of St Matthew's, Westminster since 1996. Extensive experience in church schools and internationally. Keen to promote the fantastic school ethos and supportive school community. Passionate about providing enriching learning experiences for all.

Entrance: Register in the academic year before the date of entry (part of the pan-London system). Two points of entry (September and January) for reception and nursery children. Visit school. Priority given to children whose parents attend St Peter's Church; those who attend church regularly; children with siblings in the school; children baptised as Anglicans etc etc. Always oversubscribed at early levels, and there is no automatic transfer from nursery to reception classes. Offers are made in the April preceding the year of entry.

Exit: To local state schools, particularly Greycoat Hospital, St Marylebone, Lady Margaret, Pimlico, London Nautical etc. Thirty per cent to private schools – Christ's Hospital, JAGS, City of London, Godolphin & Latymer, Clapham Hill and Streatham High etc.

Remarks: Super, central London, primary school which got a deservedly glowing Ofsted report. Good social mix – very broad spectrum of socio-economic backgrounds – 'everything from duchesses to dustmen and politicians,' in the words of one previous head. Loyal parents and PTA (good fund-raisers, these), exceptionally committed and dedicated professional staff. Terrific swimming school (all except nursery and reception use nearby Queen Mother's Sports Centre pool every week). Local district swimming competitions abandoned as other schools do not commit to similar regular swimming programmes through the year. Good music and getting better all the time. The IT suite has its complement of thirty computers, in addition to each classroom's own computers and interactive whiteboards. Teaching assistants allocated to classes in proportion to need and the number of pupils with Special Educational Needs. Special needs provision competent according to parents; school by turns forthcoming and clam-like about what's on offer.

Maximum class size 30 (several classes smaller than this). French, Italian and Mandarin are now an 'option' in after-school clubs. Spanish taught in Years 3–6. Maintenance of school supported by London Diocesan Board. Every inch of the school is used, with cunning timetabling and doubling up of rooms for various purposes. Jolly shouts from the playground (playtimes are staggered – a clever move), with a regular supply of 'mid-day supervisors' overseeing fair play. New playground soft surface and climbing wall. Library recently refurbished by active and enthusiastic parents.

School first mentioned in survey carried out by the National Society for Promoting Religious Education in 1864–7, sited in Eccleston Place. Moved to present building in 1872 on a site given by the Marquess of Westminster. Assumed its present form in 1949. Visited by HM Queen in 1972 (centenary year) and by HM Queen Mum in 1995. Strong links with St Peter's Church and the clergy pop in and out (church very high Anglican – so high, in fact, that a passing arsonist mistook it for Roman Catholic and burned it down not so long ago). Lots of parental involvement.

Super nursery. Morning or afternoon sessions. New nursery teacher who is well respected by the parents and has made an early, very positive mark, supported by two teaching assistants. Has an indoor/outdoor area for structured play and opportunities for development of gross motor skills. Drawback of the main school is that it is very cramped for space (though NB, many local private schools are even more cramped) and playground can be horrifically noisy and bursting at seams at breaktime. Children are not 'hothoused'- but, with more than two-thirds of pupils reaching level 5 in Year 6, they are well ahead of national expectations. English achievements of Year 6 pupils in 2010 showed that 70 per cent were two years ahead of national expectations (Level 5), mathematics 96 per cent (Level 5) and science 90 per cent (Level 5).

St Philip's School

6 Wetherby Place, London, SW7 4NE

• Pupils: 110 boys, all day • Ages: 7-13 • RC • Fees: £11,955 pa
• Independent

Tel: 02073 733 944
Fax: 02072 449 766
Email: info@stphilipschool.co.uk
Website: www.stphilipschool.co.uk

Head: Since 1990, Mr H Biggs-Davison MA (early fifties), educated St Philip's, Downside, Fitzwilliam College, Cambridge, where he read geography – and came straight back to St Philip's to teach in 1978. Aims to run an 'even more excellent little prep school and develop it, not in terms of expansion but as a place'. Seriously good looking – though wants us to delete this, can't think why! Good at recruiting and good with children. Open. Recently won the school's annual Conker Competition. Wife is the one with ideas – they want this deleted too!

Entrance: Standard not difficult but oversubscribed like everywhere else. Several tests, but priority is given to Catholics who make up over 80 per cent of the pupils.

Exit: A variety of schools including the London Oratory, St Benedict's Ealing, Westminster, St Paul's, Dulwich, and out-of-London boarding schools e.g. Eton, Winchester, Downside, Ampleforth, Harrow, Worth and The Oratory (Reading).

Remarks: Central London Catholic prep school – could be a solution. Housed in large red-brick Kensington building. Cramped classrooms but wonderful leafy and paved playground which runs the whole length of the block. Maximum class size 20; top form streamed. The school provides its own learning support team for boys with mild learning difficulties; learning support co-ordinator is the headmaster's wife. Several recent academic and music scholarships. Pupils a riot of different nationalities.

St Richard's School

Brendenbury Court, Bromyard, Herefordshire, HR7 4TD

• Pupils: 90 boys and girls, about 40 per cent boarding, 40 per cent day, the rest flexi. Plus pre-prep and nursery: 50 boys and girls
• Ages: 17-13, pre-prep 3-6 • RC, but all faiths welcome
• Fees: Boarding £15,300-£16,500; Day £4,155-£11,115 pa • Independent

Tel: 01885 482 491
Fax: 01885 488 982
Email: schooloffice@st-richards.org.uk
Website: www.st-richards.org.uk

Head: Since 2005, Mr Nathan Cheesman BEd (forties), only the fourth headmaster since school was founded in 1921. Educated in the state system in Henley-on-Thames (where he met his wife, Alexis – they have five children, two of whom are at the school). He then spent two years founding 'White Stuff', a ski clothing company, before studying for his teaching degree at Exeter. His first post, at Compton Primary School in Plymouth, was interrupted by a sabbatical in 2000 where he taught for a year at the Catholic St John Boscoe School in Melbourne, Australia, followed by two more terms at Compton and four years as deputy head at Moreton Hall in Suffolk.

Teaches across the board: Eng, geog, maths, sport and PSHE. A Catholic energetic all-rounder, he and his wife have moved St Richard's firmly into the 21st century. She comes from a theatrical background, and has plunged them both into pantomime productions. He has enthusiastically embraced the equestrian provision at the school resulting in cracked ribs! The ponies are still kept free of charge, although bad behaviour is always punished with the ultimate sanction – expulsion!

Entrance: Ninety per cent up from the nursery and pre-prep, or wherever: Hereford, Leominster Bromyard, Worcester and with enquiries from all continents. Pupils can and do come at any time (assuming space available) plus the odd overseas pupils, who may come for a term, or two, or a year. Boarders from all over the UK. Good mixture of trad parents and first time buyers, many with a 'rural' background.

Exit: To all the strong Catholic schools – Ampleforth, Downside, Prior Park, Shrewsbury, The Malverns – St James and College, St Mary's Shaftesbury, Moreton Hall, St Mary's Ascot, Eton, Harrow, Stowe, Tudor Hall. Otherwise to the local independents or the (very strong locally) state system. Horses for courses.

Remarks: School was founded (though elsewhere) in 1921. Richard Coghlan owned and ran it from the early 1980s. A happy, friendly, and deliciously old-fashioned school, in the nicest possible way, it became a charitable trust in 2006 and, while Mr Coghlan remains a benign eminence in the background, he is gradually fading from view. Mr Cheesman implemented an complete overhaul of the computers so that a whole class can learn on the computer at the same time and not just sit around producing natty (and sometimes very natty) graphics. Plans remain for a proper games/sports hall (the current one is terrific, and there was a glorious game of skool-rules rounders in progress during our tour – but it is a bit more like a hay shed than a sports hall with open spars at roof height. Astroturf is on the wish list.

The dorms have received a great dose of TLC, bright and jolly, with oodles of input from the boarders as well as Ikea, and there has been a re-vamp for the Delft-tiled bathrooms with new showers. Set in 37 acres of rolling Herefordshire (couple of point to pointers riding on an adjacent field during our visit), the school is based in an Edwardian shooting lodge, with various classroom extensions and, equally important, barn and farmyard additions: ducks, goats, dogs, plus ponies. Manège as well as games fields, tennis courts and outdoor heated swimming pool. The school plays a full part in the local community and as EVERYONE had to be the first to tell us it is deeply un-PC; the hunt meets here and the school hosts the hunt breakfast.

Terrific teaching too, tiny classes, 15/18, and a strong scholarship form, masses of awards. The list is impressive, art and music as well as sports and academic, averaging seven per year. Latin and French, and now some Greek. Inspired and ridiculously complicated circle-segmenting going on in maths class and outstanding remedial teaching. All pupils assessed annually for both verbal and non-verbal communication and any residual problems are hit on the head immediately. Two part-ish time remedial teachers, help particularly with English and maths, and quite considerable help if need be; one-to-one; straight slog and good use of computers. We saw a stunning and fun remedial snakes and ladders programme demonstrated with great pride. This is a fun school and children quite obviously enjoyed learning. Forget the fact that the place needs a bit of a face lift and the boys are time-warped in shorts in January (until their last year), the pupils are chatty, polite and allowed to climb trees and muck about like proper children. A smashing school, strong on games and music, with trips and tours in every discipline and a jolly good academic record.

Popular pre-prep which runs on same timetable as main school, plus nursery which operates till 5 pm during term time. Outstanding recent Ofsted nursery report.

St Ronan's School

Water Lane, Hawkhurst, Kent, TN18 5DJ

• Pupils: 320 boys and girls. Mainly day with flexi boarding. • Ages: Nursery 3 yrs to Reception age; pre-prep to rising 7; prep school from 7-13+ • C of E • Fees: Pre-prep £8,244; Prep £14,133 pa • Independent

Tel: 01580 752 271
Fax: 01580 754 882
Email: info@saintronans.co.uk
Website: www.saintronans.co.uk

Head: Since 2003, Mr William Trelawny-Vernon (early forties). Educated at Exeter University. Briefly a fund manger in the city before moving to Stowe School to teach biology. Seven years a housemaster of Chatham House, Stowe. Married to Emma who is the registrar and teaches divinity. They have three children in the prep school, first one dispatched to public school in 2009. Very enthusiastic and energetic – he has managed to bring the school into the 21st century without losing its old fashioned charm.

Head of the pre-prep since September 2007, Kathryn Bender, a worthy successor to the popular Jos Mawdsley.

Entrance: All children wanting a place in Reception upwards have an assessment. This is observation based for pre-prep entry and for the prep involves a taster day with testing in English and maths and a reasoning test. Children need to be of a fairly good standard but nonetheless cover a wide ability range. Most children join in the nursery or pre-prep but there are sometimes spaces further up the school.

Exit: About two thirds go on to public schools, of which Tonbridge, King's Canterbury, Benenden and Eastbourne are currently the most popular. Harrow, Eton, Sevenoaks and Stowe also favourites. Scholarships most years. 2009 scholarships to King's Canterbury (music), Tonbridge (academic), Eastbourne, Sutton Valence, Mayfield and King's Canterbury (art). 2010 Scholarships to King's Canterbury (art), Eastbourne (art), Kent College (academic and sport), Sutton Valence (academic), Cranbrook (academic). Also received a Prox Acc from Eton. One third go on to local grammar schools at 13+, principally Cranbrook. Occasionally children leave at 11 to go to the grammars but the school does not prepare them for the Kent Test or encourage them to leave at this age – keep them children for as long as possible! At 11+, it is up to the parents to organise extra tuition if they wish to take entry papers at this time. All Year 5 parents are invited for an individual meeting with the head to discuss secondary school options.

Remarks: Spiritually a home from home, a relaxed and informal school – a touch quirky and unusual with a happy and busy feel to it – where teachers are approachable and mud is unremarkable. A school which aims to develop each individual rather than impose a style and is committed to nurturing self confidence, academic as well as social, and independence. Academic achievement is valued and it is cool to be clever for boys as well as girls. A wide range of parents – lots of commuters, new money, old money and others who make notable sacrifices to send their children to the school. Maximum class size is 18 and average is 16. Fewer in Years 6, 7 and 8 where the classes are divided into three smaller groups. The children are setted from Year 4 in certain subjects and streamed from Year 7, with the scholarship children being taught separately for the last year. Latin is taught as a major subject from Year 6.

Although there is good learning support (mainly for dyslexia and dyspraxia) with one SENCo in the pre-prep and one full-time and three part-timers in the prep school, the school would not suit a child who really struggles academically. The school no longer offers full boarding but flexiboarding is a popular and oversubscribed option and most children ask to do this at some stage. As a result there is no longer a Sunday chapel service but visiting speakers are often invited to the Friday evensong. The chapel is used four mornings a week. Long school day as the older children (10+) do not finish until 6.30pm but all prep is done at school and it does mean that there is plenty of time for play, fun and extra activities during the day. Prep can be done at home if preferred – but school is favoured by most. Staff and children eat together in the dining room where an eye can be kept on table manners.

Games are played every afternoon. Major sports for the boys are football, rugby, hockey and cricket. Girls play netball, hockey, rounders and lacrosse plus lots of tennis for everyone on the newly refurbished courts. Strong tradition of cross country running – marvellous practice running round all those acres. Minor sports on offer include riding, golf (on the school's own small course), fencing, gymnastics and archery. The children also seem to find time for modelling, craft, fishing and trampolining, as well as tending their gardens. The children in the pre-prep can stay until 5.15pm and can take part in various clubs including den building, nature club, mad scientist club and cookery.

One week towards the end of the summer term is dedicated to expeditions for Years 6, 7 and 8. These can involve anything from camping in the woods to sailing, canoeing and raft building and rock climbing – all aimed at building self confidence and enhancing team-building and problem solving skills. The Year 8 leavers plan, organise and help with the fundraising for their own expedition which can be anywhere from the UK to Morocco to Iceland. 2010 found Year 8s kayaking up the River Wye and the Year 7s sailing catamarans off the coast of Brittany.

The school was founded in 1883 in Worthing and moved to its present site in 1946. It is housed in a rambling Victorian mansion built by an OXO magnate and set in 247 acres – it has its own 100 acre wood, lakes and a pinetum. There is a splendid one-time ballroom (with sprung floor and painted ceiling) known as The Great Space which is used as a centre for performing arts. It is certainly a school where children can be children for longer.

Saint Ronan's has undergone something of a renaissance and has doubled in size over the past five years but has no plans to grow further. In January 2007 it opened a new pre-prep, music and ICT building in addition to the nursery, art and science departments opened in 2006. 2006 also saw the opening of a refurbished swimming pool (heated – very un-Saint Ronan's!!) and further pitches and netball courts. Further capital investment is planned, with lots of new projects in the pipeline. New sports was opened in June 2010. An all-weather pitch is also in the plans.

Music now plays an important part in the life of the school with over two thirds of the children learning a musical instrument (anything from the more popular piano and violin to the double bass, bassoon and euphonium). There is an orchestra, various musical ensembles, a chapel choir and a number of lunchtime concerts throughout the term. The appointment of a new director of music in 2007 has further strengthened the department.

Drama is part of the curriculum and the school stages two major productions a year as well as more informal reviews and mini house plays. The children also have the opportunity to stand up in public through the LAMDA and the English Speaking Board exams, as well as the debating society and assemblies – all good confidence builders.

Parents very involved in raising fun and funds – there is a thriving Friends of Saint Ronan's parents' group who organise summer balls, parents' quizzes, Burns Night parties etc. (They raised well over £120,000 in five years.)

Old Boys include the WW2 fighter ace, Laddie Lucas, the politician Airey Neave, the artist Piers de Laszlo and cartoonist Sir Osbert Lancaster, whose Latin master used to tear up his sketches and demand prep instead. Also Charles Saumarez Smith, former director of The National Gallery.

St Swithun's Junior School

Linked to Saint Swithun's School in the Senior section

Alresford Road, Winchester, Hampshire, SO21 1HA

- Pupils: 180, 24 per year. Mostly girls; a few boys in the pre-prep.
- Ages: 3-11: girls to 11, boys to 7 • C of E • Fees: £7,485-£9,660 pa
- Independent

Tel: 01962 835 750
Fax: 01962 835 781
Email: office.juniorschool@stswithuns.com
Website: www.stswithuns.com

Headmistress: Since 2007, Mrs Pim Grimes (forties). Read English at Sussex University and had children before starting a career in teaching. Somehow maintains her poise and elegance, even when dealing with children's wet knickers and skinned knees. Everything you would want a prep school head to be. 'A breath of fresh air', said parent after parent we spoke to. 'I couldn't stop pinching myself when I realised how lucky we'd been!' enthused a mum whose daughter arrived at the school around the same time as Mrs Grimes. Married with two daughters in university.

Entrance: Non-selective but oversubscribed.

Exit: Boys go on at seven to local prep schools e.g. the Pilgrim's School, Twyford, Farleigh. The majority of girls go on to the senior school but also to other girls' boarding schools – Downe House, Godolphin, St Mary's Calne – or King Edward VI. No automatic entry to senior school.

Remarks: Here we have something really special: sparky, fun and innovative, while maintaining traditional values and academic standards. A cosy school that allows pupils to develop at their own pace but is never lax.

Physically in the shadow of the main school, but feels autonomous. Lovely classrooms, two colourful library areas and an interactive whiteboard in every classroom from reception up. Specialist music, PE and French teaching to begin with, and by Year 5 most subjects have specialist teachers. Copes well with full range of ability levels. No overt streaming, but classes of 24 girls are broken up into smaller groups of 12, or sometimes fewer, to scoot the more able along at a swifter pace or to give strugglers a chance to consolidate. 'Brilliant' learning support and the school advises parents regarding future school choice (will they make the senior school cut?) with delicacy. A new SENCo specifically to work with gifted and talented children. Currently one statemented child (deaf).

Much emphasis on getting along with one another, manners, self esteem. The standard of behaviour is exemplary, 'but without the girls being squashed', said a mum. Music (classical music softly wafts in the background throughout) and, especially, drama are outstanding. Cooking part of the curriculum and foundation stage pupils produce a healthy snack for morning break. 'The Apprentices' school council. Residential stays at Beaulieu (Year 5), Cornwall (Year 6) and now France. Inclusive sport using senior school fields; lacrosse taught to bigger girls. Upstairs gymnasium a bit hot and sticky. Only quibble we heard was over a shortage of competitive sport. 'They get plenty of exercise, but there aren't enough matches.'

Co-ed aspect of the pre-prep continually reviewed, particularly now that Pilgrim's (with which this school has links) has opened its co-ed pre-prep. Parents say it does fine by little chaps, at least until the end of the reception year. Now offers full day nursery from age three (and accepts government vouchers).

St Teresa's Nursery and Preparatory School

Linked to Saint Teresa's Senior School in the Senior section

Beech Avenue, Effingham Hill, Surrey, RH5 6ST

• Pupils: 120 girls, 5 board • Ages: 2-11 • RC but others welcome
• Fees: Boarding £17,475-£20,085; Day £6,945-£10,365 pa • Independent

Tel: 01372 453 456
Fax: 01372 451 562
Email: a.charles@stteresas.surrey.sch.uk
Website: www.stteresasschool.com

Head: Since 2010, Mrs Mary Arnal – very much liked and extremely approachable.

Entrance: Entry into the co-ed nursery is from two. Entry into the prep is by report and informal assessment during a Welcome Day as well as references from previous school.

Exit: The vast majority of girls move on to the senior school but have to sit entrance exam in competition with increased numbers of children from outside. Whilst there is no guarantee of a place at the Senior School, few girls have been turned away in the past.

Remarks: Girls achieve well academically, are settled and happy. 'A very friendly, happy environment,' says a parent.

St Vincent de Paul RC Primary School

Morpeth Terrace, London, SW1P 1EP

• Pupils: 250 boys and girls; all day • Ages: 3-11 • RC • State

Tel: 020 7641 5990
Fax: 020 7641 5901
Email: office.svp.westminster@lgfl.net
Website: www.st-vincents.westminster.lgfl.net

Head: Since 2002, Mr Jack O'Neill STB/MA (forties), single. Enthusiastic, effective and guitar-playing, came on a fast track to this post – a class teacher for four years in Hammersmith and Fulham, then deputy here before being promoted. He is resourceful and keen to squeeze a lot out of slim funding – they did without a deputy head for a year because of a budget cut. Keen on improvement and feedback: got an 81 per cent return on parents' questionnaire.

Entrance: Well over-subscribed and no guaranteed transfer from nursery to main school, so priority given to practising Roman Catholics. Within this category, first Catholic looked after children, then baptised, practising siblings, then baptised practising Catholics, then baptised siblings, with distance from school used as a tie-breaker.

Exit: Usually to first choice secondary schools; popular ones are St Thomas More, Greycoat Hospital, Sacred Heart, Salesian College and the London Oratory.

Remarks: Founded in 1859 by the Sisters of Charity of St Vincent de Paul. Sited in the shadow of Westminster Cathedral and a family Mass is held there every month, which many parents and pupils attend – some are altar servers there or at other neighbouring RC churches. Principles of the religious community pervade the school but not in an exclusive or heavy-handed way. Prayer corners in every classroom and the school chaplain regularly comes into the school. Also regular other faith weeks – we attended an astounding assembly on Hinduism with hip wiggling dancing, Hindu vocab cards and discussion of blue-skinned gods and goddesses.

On three levels with disabled access to ground floor at the rear; 20 CCTV cameras and new boundary railings mean security is effective. A new chapel has been built just inside the entrance; a double height sports hall also used for assemblies and meals – all of the class areas accessed from it. The formrooms are well decorated with quiet areas in between, beanbagged for reading and rainy day play. Outside, both a nursery playground and a bigger one with a child and parent maintained garden. Playground, dining hall and corridor rules are written by the elected school council, whose influence has extended to Mr Soapy Soap in all bathrooms and renewal of a water fountain.

Huge social mix with no one dominant racial or cultural grouping; EAL for 80 per cent and over 15 languages spoken. EAL teacher is in school for one day per week on an individual or group basis as needed. The teaching is of exceptional quality. Very low turnover since professional development is important here. Student teachers, parents and volunteers from BAA, DCSF and the Home Office help with the nursery, reading and walking pupils to swim at the nearby Queen Mother Sports Centre, freeing teachers for specialist SEN courses and the like. Record on SEN is deceptive since pupils seem to be making too much progress to get statements – staff pick up on SEN children early. Focuses on targeting social, emotional and behavioural issues; circle time and an anonymous comments box are well used. Buddy friendship scheme and charity initiatives such as a Childline skipathon encourage a caring outlook.

Children are known for their good behaviour and ongoing participation in events in the Royal Albert Hall, Westminster Archive Centre, Wallace Collection and throughout the West End; if 'there is something going on we'll get involved'. Head is very proud of zero unauthorised attendance record and only having to see two children a week for misdemeanours such as pushing. During his time has explained the ethos behind his rules and curriculum to parents and been rewarded by low pupil mobility and huge continuous support – half the cost of the interactive whiteboards in every class was covered by PTFA fundraising, the whole of the inside of the school was decorated by volunteers. The PTFA is dynamic and the weekly newsletter from the head helps the non-school gate parents feel in touch. Priority is 'children's individual success' – head aims to help them gain what they are expected to and more, while not being focused towards one area of the curriculum.

A fantastically happy, disciplined and effective school. Ofsted 2009: school 'makes a real difference to the community'; 'outstanding early years foundation stage' and 'above average' at the end of Year 6.

Salisbury Cathedral School

The Old Palace, 1 The Close, Salisbury, Wiltshire, SP1 2EQ

- Pupils: prep: 145 (90 boys, 60 girls), 35 board; pre-prep: 40
- Ages: 7-13, pre-prep 3-7 • C of E choir school
- Fees: Boarding £18,270; Day £6,450-£12,510 pa • Independent

Tel: 01722 555 300
Fax: 01722 410 910
Email: headsec@salisburycathedralschool.com
Website: www.salisburycathedralschool.com

Head Master: Since 2007, Mr Paul Greenfield BEd, formerly assistant housemaster at St John's College School, Cambridge, head of history at Malsis School, head of Scarborough College Junior School and head of the lower section of Norwich School. Read history at Westminster College, Oxford and teaches history and RE. Keen to promote what he sees as the school's 'two selling points' – its central location and its close ties with the Cathedral (the Chapter of Salisbury owns the school and the Dean of Salisbury is the chair of governors of both the school and the Cathedral) and the associated Christian ethos. While proud of the school's music, he emphasises that music is not the only string in the school's bow. 'Music is strong but we want the school to be seen as an all-round education.' A considered decision certainly, and no doubt true. But we can't help wonder whether, with so many prep schools in Salisbury, the musical excellence niche might not be a fair one to settle for. Wife, Jane, teaches in the prep school; they have three grown-up children.

Entrance: Many come up from the pre-prep, otherwise at all stages. Hugely oversubscribed chorister places (usually at eight) are offered as a result of a voice trial (January for boys, February for girls), academic assessment and interview. For others there is an informal test. Scholarships are available for music, sport and academic ability at seven and 11. Day children predominantly come from local primaries. Boarders come from a wide area: 'choristership knows few boundaries'. A few Services children; occasional Spanish, South African and Chinese boarders but none needing extra English. Like all the co-ed preps in the area, it could use a few more girls – Leaden Hall next door hoovers up plenty, as does Godolphin a few minutes down the road. Genuinely endeavouring to keep a lid on fee increases – last year's was under four per cent.

Exit: Most at 13 to a range of mainly local senior schools e.g. Bryanston, Dauntsey's, Sherborne, St Mary's Shaftesbury and Canford – many with music awards (13 last year). Some go further afield e.g. Eton, Marlborough, Wells, Lancing, Downside and Francis Holland. A quarter (a small number, says the school) leave at 11 to Salisbury's grammars.

Remarks: Founded in 1091 by St Osmund to educate the choristers of his cathedral at Old Sarum. Moved to its present home – centred in the 13th century buildings and grounds of the Bishop's Palace – in 1947. The children probably don't notice the magnificence of their surroundings but the parents certainly do. Trying to get there in rush hour traffic rather punctures the idyllic spell, however.

Sound teaching on all fronts in mainly 'old school' style classrooms (occasional feeling of being in a warren with rooms leading off rooms). Small class sizes – 12 on average – a big draw for many parents. Welcoming SEN room provides help for around 17 'mainly dyslexic' children. Swish new ICT room. Brilliantly well-stocked library. Imposing 'Big School Room', with pictures of every Bishop of Salisbury, used for assemblies and drama productions. Strong on science teaching; Latin from Year 6 for everyone. No scholarship set but able pupils given what they need. Nice to see DT includes the feminine arts of textiles and cookery. Lovely ancient chapel within the school and whole school worships once a week in the Cathedral. Unusual exchange programme with a South African school – two Year 7 pupils can spend a term at a boarding school deep in Cape Province.

About 85 per cent of pupils play at least one musical instrument; some learn three. There is a school orchestra, concert band, annual music festival, plus 17 different music ensembles including a jazz band. 'Everyone' sings and there are three school choirs apart from the two cathedral choirs. 48 choristers are treated much the same as the rest of the school although they clearly have an extra workload with choir practices etc. Monday concerts (concerts 'all the time' said a parent) and lots of music clubs take place over lunch breaks. Music practice sessions scheduled for boarders and some day pupils. You don't have to be interested in music to come here but it would be difficult not to develop one in such surroundings. Good Astroturf, three rugby pitches, and sports scholarships woo the sporty. Being a small school means almost anyone can walk into a school team, so lots of involvement. Usual list of prep school sports on offer – and an impressive and full fixture card – but perhaps not a school that hones the killer instinct when it comes to competitive games (results are on the up, says school). 'Eco' club uses the lake.

Switched on to the needs of busy parents: day pupils may arrive from 7.30am and stay until 6.30pm at no extra charge. No Saturday morning lessons. Boarding house charmingly tucked behind a cream tea shop five minutes' walk away, so boarders stride off to school at 7.20am and do not return until 7 or 8pm. Boarding house rather wholesome, with largish dorms for youngsters shrinking to doubles for some of the oldest children, lots of common areas downstairs and no internet access. Lovely boarders' handbook refers to teddies as 'important members of the boarding house, even in the Year 8 dorms!'. Boarding remains very English, with no overseas boarders at all when we visited – definite room for expansion on this front. Supervised shopping trips into Salisbury for boarders on Saturday afternoons (with a limited amount of pocket money tailored to the age group). As there are always two choirs in residence over the weekend for cathedral services, usually plenty of boarders around.

Former pupils include MPs Robert Key and Michael Mates, actress and singer Amy Carson (Kenneth Branagh's The Magic Flute), organist Bernard Rose, composer Peter Gritton and Sir Anthony Lewis, former president of the Royal College of Music. Judging by the strength of the alumni association and the lasting friendships between former pupils, a happy and very special place to spend your early school years.

Sandroyd School

Rushmore, Tollard Royal, Salisbury, Wiltshire, SP5 5QD

• Pupils: 200 (150 boys, 40 girls) in prep school; 35 in pre-prep. • Ages: 4-13. • C of E • Fees: Day £16,830; Boarding £20,130; Pre-prep £7,170 pa • Independent

Tel: 01725 516 264
Fax: 01725 516 441
Email: office@sandroyd.com
Website: www.sandroyd.org

Headmaster: Since 2003, Mr Martin Harris BSc (Hons) PGCE (fortyish). Educated at The Skinners School and read geography at Loughborough University. Began teaching at Sevenoaks Prep but has spent most of career at Ashdown House in East Sussex eventually rising to deputy head and then acting head. Keen sportsman, plays cricket, golf and tennis. Married to Catherine (a chartered physiotherapist) who plays a pastoral role in the school. Two young sons, the eldest now in the school. Has overseen big changes since arriving – the opening of The Walled Garden pre-prep, the introduction of girls in the main school, a new classroom block and arts centre.

Entrance: Not selective but all children are assessed and then interviewed by the head. Pupils can start at The Walled Garden from four, at the main school generally at seven or eight, but pupils start at all ages. Some enter at 10 or 11, specifically for the boarding. Flexi-boarding available but all pupils must properly board in the last two years. 70 per cent come from Wiltshire and Dorset, a few from London – a top drawer lot, with the school roll a festival of double-barrelled surnames. 16 boys from overseas, half British expats, half foreign, some of the latter receiving extra English tuition. Numbers of girls not growing as fast as hoped – good nearby girls' preps no doubt the reason. Minibuses from Gillingham, Blandford and Salisbury.

Exit: Virtually all leave at 13, very occasionally at 11 – girls now entering the school intend to stay all the way through. Quite a few to Radley, Sherborne and Eton and several to Bryanston and Marlborough. Otherwise all over, far and wide. Pupils have secured places at their first choice schools for the last eight years. Academic awards to top national schools (Eton, Radley, Sherborne, Bryanston) in the last three years. Strangely few to Canford and Dauntsey's.

Remarks: A happy school, bursting with all the extras. Ofsted 2007 full of praise. Founded in 1888 by the Revd L H Wellesley Wesley as a 'small coaching establishment' in his own home, for 'sons of friends who were due to go to Eton'. The school was evacuated here during the war and later bought the Pitt-Rivers' family house plus paddocks, playing fields and houses for many of the staff. Still a relatively formal and traditional prep, now co-ed. School currently owns 55 acres within the 400 acre Rushmore estate, next door to the Rushmore Golf Course (pupils and staff play for free). The park teems with wild life and the school was undergoing something of a pheasant infestation when we visited. Slightly isolated feel, a bit of a world unto itself. The main building has elegance in its bones and has been smartened sympathetically recently.

Grand wood-panelled hall, with classrooms off it. Has been much added to – recent inspirational new theatre, chapel, and girls' boarding wing which are cosy. Entire school – classrooms, dormitories, swimming pool, chapel etc under one roof, connected by a warren of corridors. Children terribly polite – say 'Sir', and stand up as soon as you appear. Dress code rather than uniform on school days: any check shirt, no tie, any brown shoes, green or blue cords – looks great. Girls wear a blue kilt or navy cords, blue blouse, Sandroyd sweatshirt and black shoes. Smarter wear for chapel and outings.

Still strong on traditional teaching: French from seven, Latin from nine, Greek for those who want it, plus a non-timetabled Spanish/German option. Head was keen on sharpening up the academic side when he arrived and he has been rewarded with a clutch of good awards to senior schools in recent years. Max class size 15 but average is 13 (and many are smaller). 30 children receive extra lessons – mainly for dyslexia and extra maths. Up to four sessions a week, if needed, with times varying so pupils miss different lessons or activities. Low tech IT – no interactive whiteboards, old computers – but sufficient. Four gap students, fill in here and there, read with the younger children every day. Parents given lots of feedback: termly reports, weekly assessments for effort, twice termly assessments for achievement. Exams every term in the top two years to iron out exam technique and quell any nerves.

Big on sport, especially rugger – the school reached the National Prep School 7s final at Rosslyn Park one year and won the Wiltshire U13 Rugby Cup and there is an annual rugby tour. Every boy represents the school in a rugby match and there are four [XVs] at the top of the school. Cricket also very strong. Girls play hockey and netball against other schools and some have played in boys' teams. Sport every day, though some peel off to attend special lessons – roughly half the pupils do tennis coaching as an extra; many learn squash with pro who visits three times a week. Still offers pistol shooting. A quarter of the school ride – on school's own horses, or you can bring your own. School contines to host an annual National Tetrathlon with 160 children competing. Glass-like cricket pitch, three quarter size Astroturf, rifle range, pets area (with few lodgers), indoor pool (18 and a half metres!), gym 'held together by Sellotape but well-loved'. Adventure playground for use by the youngest.

On Saturdays and Wednesday afternoons, less gamesy older children may seek refuge in the DT room, which is also open on winter evenings. Pupils make their own tuck boxes and decorate them in the holidays. The school still has general knowledge quizzes, with notable national success. Lots of activities on offer, and this is a key facet of the school. Something for everyone, from the nerdy (magic tricks, electronics, Russian) to the sporty (clay pigeon shooting, golf, fencing). God important. Lively music, especially the choir, and the orchestra is 'improving'. 108 pupils learn an instrument. 'We'll teach anything,' says the head. Violin tuition given by a houseparent who used to play in The Royal Philharmonic Orchestra (and in a backing band for Elton John!). Busy art in big, airy room, with outstanding ceramics. Drama offered through class lessons and a drama club. The school has drawn up plans for a theatre, which would be a super addition, and has purchased equipment for a film-making club. Cookery in a dedicated room, organised by the mums.

Brilliant boarding with good care throughout. Seven to nine boys in dorms in younger years – perfectly pleasant. Smaller dormitories of three to four boys in top year, and prep at this age is done in dorm – unusual for a prep school. Common room with telly, playstation, table football – a stepping stone to public school. No mobile phones, except for overseas boys who keep them in the office. Good food served family style in bright and airy dining room. Fruit available all day. Snacks galore. Top year can make toast and cocoa. Exeats every third weekend. Two Sundays a term pupils must stay in school but school enthusiastically woos them to stay more – and most do. Regular Sunday outings on horseback or cycling. Swallows and Amazons camping weekend for Year 4. School does all the childrens' laundry, even for the day children (it was at this point that we were sold on the place). OBs include the Lords Avon, Carrington, Snowdon, Wilberforce, Gladwyn, Sainsbury plus Archbishop Ramsay of Canterbury, Ian Gow, Max Aitken, Sir Terence Rattigan, Sir Anthony Eden, Sir Ranulph Fiennes.

The Walled Garden pre-prep opened in 2004. Still less than half full but numbers growing. Beautiful curving design, light, bright and cheery – all built to child size including mini whiteboards and beautiful loos. The children play and learn confidently in their bright purple sweatshirts – very focused. Spacious outdoor play area and these littlies use the main school's swimming pool and computers. One third of them have older siblings in the school. Their day finishes at 3.30pm but many stay for a late club until 5.15pm where they can take part in activities like football or pony club.

Sarum Hall School

15 Eton Avenue, London, NW3 3EL

- Pupils: 175 girls (including nursery); all day • Ages: 3-11 • C of E
- Fees: £7,050-£11,700 pa • Independent

Tel: 0207 794 2261
Fax: 0207 431 7501
Email: admissions@sarumhallschool.co.uk
Website: www.sarumhallschool.co.uk

Head: Since 2008, Mrs Christine Smith BA, Cert Ed RSA (SpLD), early 50s. Mrs Smith spent the previous 17 years at Lochinver Prep in Potter's Bar. Began her career teaching Home Economics and Textiles at Edmonton County School before having her two daughters. Lured back to teaching to work with deaf children, eventually becoming director of studies at Lochinver and setting up their learning support unit. When her children left home, she felt ready for a new challenge. 'I walked into Sarum Hall and knew immediately I could see myself here.' Describes herself as 'a calm person', and is widely seen as a sensible, soothing presence. Parents find her very approachable – 'Mrs Smith is so nice, she smiles all the time.' Married to an actuary. Interests include Tai Chi, cooking, the theatre and martial arts (she spent time in Beijing learning about swords).

Entrance: Main intake in September after third birthday. Register as soon after birth as possible with a non-refundable deposit of £100. Parents are invited two years before entry to visit the school on a working day and then write to confirm their continued interest in a place. The school is non-selective but priority is given to siblings and to the children and grandchildren of former pupils. The remainder of the 22–24 nursery places are based on the head's decision. 'I meet all the parents and discuss what kind of school they hope for for their daughter. This is very much a community school.' Most pupils are local, ideally within walking distance. Occasional vacancies arise after nursery. From Year 1, applicants are tested in English and maths.

Exit: Practically all to their first-choice school at 11. To Francis Holland, Clarence Gate (whose head is a governor at Sarum Hall), as well as strong numbers to all the leading London day schools, including St Paul's Girls, City of London School for Girls, South Hampstead, North London Collegiate, Highgate, Mill Hill and Queen's College. Also, unusually for a north London prep, a reasonable contingent to board (five in 2009, to Wycombe Abbey, Queenswood, Wells Cathedral School).

Remarks: If a school can have the 'wow factor', then Sarum Hall definitely does. Housed in a superb, RIBA-lauded contemporary building, which provides plenty of well-planned light and airy space to work, move about and play. 'Even on the most dismal day,' says the head, 'the school is flooded with natural light.' High design standards are complemented with attractive displays of fresh flowers. The school moved from just down the road in 1997 and the property-savvy governors have made further updates with a recent rooftop extension providing a quiet room for music exams and practice.

Though a relatively new appointee, the head has a clear vision of a continuing tradition. 'Sarum Hall is an academic school whose girls go onto further education and develop a lifelong love of learning. But the school places as strong an emphasis on the cultural and social as the academic. Music, art and drama have a central role.'

Good, solid, traditional teaching using the National Curriculum but not the dreaded SATS. 'The school really prepares pupils superbly for 11 plus,' says one mother with two daughters who've successfully surmounted that hurdle. Specialist subject teaching in PE, music, IT and French from nursery, science from Year 3, English, maths and humanities in Years 5 and 6. Inspired science teaching ('very practical and relevant', said one parent), taught in a well-furnished lab to the accompaniment of classical music. Some setting in maths, but 'we don't make too much of that'. There is, however, significant 'differentiation' to meet individual needs, with additional work, for example, for those sitting boarding school entrance exams and plenty of classroom assistance throughout. Imaginative cross-curricular teaching. One girl found a flattened toad in Africa and it was incorporated into the study of Macbeth,' says the head. Long serving ('people come to stay') highly-regarded staff. 'Some of the teachers have a real passion for their subject,' says one mother. Learning support unit (with one dedicated member of staff) copes with dyslexia, dyspraxia and the 'gifted and talented', at no additional cost. (Girls are taken out of lessons for individual or group support, though this 'not a huge part of the school'.) Homework introduced gently in Year 2, rising to a maximum of one hour a night in Year 6. All pupils expected to read daily. Bright and breezily decorated library open to all in lunch and break, plus library lessons as part of the curriculum.

Music, art and drama all lively and strong. Majority of girls study one or more instruments after Year 2 and get plenty of opportunity to 'show off' in class assemblies, frequent concerts and house drama. Also sit the English Speaking Board exams to build up communication skills. Stunning studio art room with north-facing light is made full use of and pupils study sculpture, print, textiles and woodwork. Also frequent exposure to the real thing, with outings to exhibitions as well as in-house visits from professional artists.

Though outdoor space is not extensive, the outside is as well planned as the interior and daily sport or PE takes place on three Astroturf courts (used for netball, hockey, rounders, soccer, cricket and tennis) or in the Assembly Hall which triples as a gym (for dance as well as gymnastics) and theatre. Swimming once more part of the curriculum, at nearby Swiss Cottage Baths. Annual athletics meet on Hampstead Heath.

Plenty of nourishing after-school clubs (yoga, sewing, knitting, Mandarin) and plenty of enriching outings to theatres etc 'we take full advantage of what's on our doorstep'. Year 6 summer programme to manage post 11-plus drag offering first aid, cookery, Mandarin and other handy skills. Residential trips to Flatford Mill and a chateau in France.

Very much a family-based school. 'We care about the whole family and want to nurture the natural talents of every girl,' says the head, and parents feel it lives up to its aims. I've had three daughters here and enjoyed it all the way; it's a wonderful school,' says one. Traditional good manners (from Year 2 girls leap to their feet when head enters and chorus, 'Good morning, Mrs Smith'.) We don't have any behavioural problems,' says Mrs Smith. Positive rewards for good behaviour, constant emphasis on Golden Rules – We are gentle, kind and helpful. We listen and are honest and work hard. We look after property. We don't hurt anybody's feelings etc. Three houses, with house points for good work and good behaviour, lots of praise and positive reinforcements. Food prepared daily on site with vegetarian option and faithful stalwarts like syrup sponge and custard. No packed lunch. Staff eat with girls. No mobile phones, no email, supervised internet use only. Affiliated to the Church of England and the large number of Jewish girls and other faiths join in daily assembly with the Lord's Prayer and hymns.

Enthusiastic charitable fundraising. 'These girls are very privileged and we try and get them to see that,' says the head. Parents and pupils are predominantly affluent, white, middle-class professionals – accountants, lawyers, city, etc, not too many media – with a strong international contingent, mainly European, Indian and Chinese. Many girls have brothers at The Hall and Arnold House (and head does her best to ensure coordinated term dates). No scholarships or bursaries, though will support parents if they fall on hard times.

A very well-run, small, intimate, traditional girls' prep in a wonderful modern setting that gets the very best out of a broad range of ability without too much pressure and provides a rich education in every sense. Possibly not the ideal school for the maverick child (or parent) or one who doesn't deal happily with authority.

The Schools at Somerhill

Linked to Yardley Court in the Junior section
Linked to Somerhill Pre-prep in the Junior section
Linked to Derwent Lodge School in the Junior section

Somerhill, Tonbridge, Kent, TN11 0NJ

- Pupils: 250 boys at Yardley Court; 130 girls at Derwent Lodge
- Ages: 3-13 • Non-denom • Fees: £7,920-£12,165 pa • Independent

Tel: 01732 352 124
Fax: 01732 363 381
Email: office@somerhill.org
Website: www.schoolsatsomerhill.com

Head: Headmaster of Yardley Court and Principal of The Schools At Somerhill: since 1998, Mr John Coakley MA PGCE (early fifties). Educated at Bishop Wordsworth Grammar School in Salisbury, went on to read English at York and did his PGCE at Oxford followed by an MA in English at New Brunswick University in Canada. Previously headmaster of Ryde Junior School on the Isle of Wight and of Saltus Grammar School in Bermuda. Delightful, charismatic. Softly spoken and welcoming, he has a knack of putting people immediately at their ease and is highly regarded by pupils and parents alike – though we are sure he'd stand no nonsense from any of them. Knows every child in the school and is able to greet them by name. Teaches PSHE to the boys at Yardley Court, and coaches some sport.

Head of Derwent Lodge: Since 2009, Mrs Sam Michau, previously director of studies at Ardingly College Prep School. BA and MA from Magdalen College, Oxford, did a PGCE at Roehampton Institute. Teaches science, maths and PE. Energetic, keen to foster a spirit of intellectual risk-taking and challenge throughout the school. Knows every girl personally and is keen to nurture strong relationships with their families.

Entrance: Not selective – astonishing when you see the leavers' lists. Most start in the nursery or pre-prep and priority is given to siblings – i.e. if this is the school for you, get your name down asap. Limited spaces after nursery other than in Year 3, when the boys and girls separate and move to either Yardley Court or Derwent Lodge. A number of children arrive from local primaries at this stage.

Exit: About 40 per cent of boys leave at 11 to go to the grammar schools. Otherwise Tonbridge, Sevenoaks, Sutton Valence and Cranbrook are popular options. The school prepares them for the Kent Test to the grammar schools and also the Sevenoaks test. All girls leave at 11 and about 80 per cent go to the grammar schools, otherwise Walthamstow Hall, Kent College and Sevenoaks are popular with regular major awards won. In 2010, Somerhill pupils gained 24 scholarship awards.

Remarks: With separate prep schools for boys and girls, and a co-educational school for young children, The Schools at Somerhill are unique in the area. They are for children aged between three and 13 (11 for girls) with the older boys and girls being taught apart but sharing the same specialist facilities and being members of one community.

Yardley Court School was founded in 1898 as a boys' prep school. In 1990, it, together with the pre-prep school moved to the Somerhill Estate – a Grade I listed Jacobean mansion set in 150 acres on a hill overlooking Tonbridge. In 1993 a girls' prep school, Derwent Lodge, joined Yardley Court from Tunbridge Wells, where it had been based for forty years, to form The Schools at Somerhill. The three schools value their individuality but are very much part of Somerhill.

In contrast to some other Kent prep schools where education is no laughing matter, the number one priority here is happiness, with an emphasis that learning should be fun whilst still enabling children to get very good results. A very nurturing school with lots of encouragement and praise; there is a strong emphasis on manners and general consideration for others – the children always stand up when an adult walks into the room and they are happy to look them in the eye. Not-overly-pushy parents who are comfortable with the ethos – very few are disappointed – they know the environment and understand that this is a mixed ability school. Lots of people buy into the prep school to get into the grammars. Lots of working mothers. Lots of first time buyers.

The maximum size of the classes is 20 and the average is 18 – a bit lower for the girls, as the Grade I listing of the Jacobean building governs the class sizes, and girls occupy the major part of it.

Yardley Court boys are setted in Year 4 for maths and in Year 5 for English, maths and science. The scholarship children join a special set for the last eighteen months where they also learn Spanish. The girls are setted for maths. All children start French in Year 2 and most boys start Latin in Year 5. All classrooms are networked and there are interactive whiteboards in all teaching classrooms.

Staff are a good mix of clever people – some NQTs straight out of college and some old hands – none have been there for more than 15 years – the head 'likes to have new blood'. Lots of musical events throughout the year and a concert most terms. About 75 per cent of girls and 60 per cent of boys play at least one musical instrument and Yardley Court provides choristers for Tonbridge School's chapel choir. Big drama productions every year and a play for almost every year group with the emphasis on all taking part. Plenty of opportunities for standing up in public – Yardley Court Years 4 and 7 do English Speaking Board work as do the girls in Years 3 and 4. Yardley Court are the local league champions at chess and had a boy who played chess for England.

The boys play soccer, rugby, cricket, athletics and tennis. Both the boys' and girls' schools enjoy a strong sporting reputation. All are given the opportunity to play regularly in school teams. The girls play netball, hockey, rounders, gymnastics and athletics. There is a strong and successful tradition of cross country running for both boys and girls – one of the major Kent schools' running events is held at the school, and the boys and girls combined team regularly wins the West Kent League. All the mod cons – fine sports hall, Astro pitch, four artificial wickets; new indoor swimming pool and newly constructed dining room.

The school day is normally 8.30-4.30 followed by afterschool clubs until 5.30pm. Saturday school for boys in Year 8 when the children focus on exam preparation but children are required to come in on Saturdays when there are matches.

Some children with special needs, mainly dyspraxia and dyslexia. In Yardley Court about 40 children need extra help, and this is given either one-to-one or in small groups, and is usually by withdrawal from lessons. The head of the pre-prep takes particular care to talk parents through the school's special needs provision. No statemented children. Standardised testing when everyone arrives in verbal reasoning, reading and maths, and if any problems are found the SENCo would talk to parents. Would not suit a child with profound difficulties.

Famous Old Boys include Frederick Forsyth, Peter West (the former BBC commentator) and the cricket coach Bob Woolmer.

Sedbergh Junior School

Linked to Sedbergh School in the Senior section

Danson House, Loftus Hill, Sedbergh, Cumbria, LA10 5RX

• Pupils: 90 girls and boys; boarding and day • Ages: 4-13 • Fees: Day £6,300-£9,390; Boarding £14,940-£16,125 pa • Independent

Tel: 01539 622 295
Email: jb@sedberghschool.org
Website: www.sedberghjuniorschool.org

Head: Since 2010, Mr Scott Carnochan.

Entrance: Ages four to nine by assessment, thereafter by written exam.

Exit: Almost exclusively to the senior school at 13 provided entrance examinations/scholarships met satisfactorily.

Remarks: Recently moved from its old site back to Sedbergh alongside its parent school.

Servite RC Primary School

252 Fulham Road, London, SW10 9NA

• Pupils: 235 girls and boys • Ages: 3-11 • Roman Catholic • State

Tel: 02073 522 588
Fax: 02073 514 024
Email: info@servite.rbkc.sch.uk
Website: www.serviteprimaryschool.co.uk

Head: Since 2002, Mrs Kathleen Williams BEd NPQH (thirties). Was previously deputy head of St Mary's Primary in Ladbroke Grove. Has been in teaching for 17 years and is married. Affable and approachable. Pupils look round eagerly as she enters the classroom trying to catch her eye. Shares a headship with another school and is passionate about developing leadership skills in schools. With the help of two able deputy heads she has raised the academic standard over the past few years. Achieved an outstanding Ofsted as well as an exceptional delivery of the national school sports strategy in 2007.

Entrance: At 3+ into the nursery but this does not guarantee a place in the primary. Very over-subscribed. Sibling priority only in the event of a tie breaker. 30 pupils per class. Parish boundaries denote the catchment area and only practising Catholics bearing a reference to prove it from their Parish Priests need apply. The Servite Priory (and trustees of the school) is next door and participates fully in school life; 'very keen to keep strong links.' Children celebrate Founders' Day on 17 February each year.

Exit: Mostly to the London state Catholic day schools: Cardinal Vaughan, London Oratory, Sacred Heart, Gunnersbury, St Thomas More and Chelsea Academy. Those who go down the private path tend to opt for Queensgate or Wimbledon High.

Remarks: This is a mixed, inclusive school on Fulham Road opposite the Chelsea and Westminster Hospital (NB in the Congestion Charging Zone). Many pupils come from the Worlds' End Estate on King's Road and the head promotes an atmosphere of 'community cohesion and racial harmony' within the school. The staff are young and energetic but a solid core in leadership positions gives 'strong and consistent leadership.' With an EAL level of 68 per cent, Servite offers 12 support staff, with one working full time in most classes. There is also a special needs teacher to give additional support to those who need extra help. Catch up programmes, an early intervention team plus part-time therapists help to bridge the gap between school and home. The school prides itself on having strong links with external agencies such as a social worker, a nurse, an educational psychologist and a play therapist. Specialist teachers are brought in for Spanish, French, Gymnastics, dance, music and art; 'A broad and balanced curriculum is essential for raising standards and preparing pupils for the future. Encouraging creativity of thought at a young age can lead to independence in learning and high achievement,' says the head. Although the building is modern and boxy its very practical design helps communication and the large classrooms facilitate shared teaching and other such initiatives. A recently started Parent Council offers a useful consultation platform while the PTA concentrates on fund raising. The large gym doubles as a theatre for drama productions and musical concerts. Each class holds an assembly each week giving all an opportunity for public speaking thus building their self confidence from a young age. The playground is concrete but spacious. Awnings and umbrellas are available in summer to afford some protection from the sun. Clubs and activities are offered as part of the wrap around school care between 8am and 6pm. As a voluntary aided school, all parents are asked to make a set contribution each year of £30-£45, in addition to paying for after school clubs.

This is a perfectly competent inner city primary school which aims to provide its pupils with a sound education whilst embracing the teachings of Christ. Religious assemblies and collective worship take place in the classroom with prayers at the beginning of the day, before lunch and at going home time. Religious education is taught for several hours a week and is one of the core subjects underlying the school's mission statement: 'Learning to love, loving to learn.'

Shapwick Prep School

Linked to Shapwick School in the Senior section

Mark Road, Burtle, Bridgwater, Somerset, TA7 8NJ

• Pupils: 43 boys and girls • Ages: 6-13 • Non-denominational
• Fees: £14,001-£19,272 pa • Independent

Tel: 01278 722 012
Fax: 01458 210 111
Email: prep@shapwickschool.com
Website: www.edingtonshapwick.co.uk

Joint heads: Mrs Margaret Kingham, experienced deputy head, in consultation with the joint heads Mr David Walker and Mr Jon Whittock, leads the teaching team here.

Entrance: Pupils can join at any stage. Open days include the opportunity for applicants to be assessed to ascertain level of need. Some via tribunal process but most enter privately or in mid-process depending on need or desperation.

Exit: Almost all to senior school though a few may re-enter mainstream education.

Money Matters: Parents pay extra for uniform and some trips: e.g. skiing.

Remarks: Recently re-branded as Shapwick Prep from former Edington and Shapwick Junior School. Provides small scale, specialist education way out on Somerset Levels. School has become centre of excellence for SpLD – is organising a diploma/Masters course for practising teachers, receives students from Exeter university and elsewhere. Site includes former farmhouse, vicarage and village school, a collection of 'temporary' classrooms and a purpose-built complex for youngest children plus therapy rooms known as the ARC (assessment and resource centre).

Pupils have English and maths classes all morning; therapy sessions arranged throughout day in ARC – withdrawal negotiated with staff. Remainder of day largely related to National Curriculum work, includes lots of sport, art and music. Lovely science lab with specialist teaching from senior school. Small classes throughout school and plenty of one-to-one.

School is welcoming and visually attractive with stimulating display work in classrooms. Super outside play and activity area as well as large playing fields. Loads of ICT including individual laptops for pupils in Year 8. Focus here on tackling SpLD within supportive, friendly environment. Children seem relaxed and confident. Super solution for those lucky enough to have the right funding at this earlier stage in schooling.

Sheen Mount Primary School

West Temple Sheen, East Sheen, London, SW14 7RT

• Pupils: 450 (roughly equal numbers of boys and girls), all day
• Ages: 4-11 • Non-denom • State

Tel: 020 8876 8394
Fax: 020 8878 6568
Email: info@sheenmount.richmond.sch.uk
Website: www.sheenmount.richmond.sch.uk

Head: Since 1999, Mrs Elaine England (mid-fifties), has thirty years teaching experience, and was previously head at Stanley Infant School in Teddington. Not an obviously touchy-feely 'my door is always open' type of head, but very much a strong leader. Parents describe her as 'efficient', 'well-respected', 'dynamic', 'a good motivator' and 'very involved'. She thinks long-term and is currently planning major building works for the next ten years.

Entrance: Over-subscribed every year. Priority to very special needs then siblings. After that, it's location, location, location – not just the road you live in but the house number in that road can determine whether your child gets a place. Around 90 per cent of the children have been to one of the many local nurseries – too numerous to list. Unlike other local state primaries, places only rarely become available higher up the school – hardly anyone leaves Sheen Mount at seven to go to the local prep schools, it's more likely to happen the other way round.

Exit: Mention any local independent school and someone from Sheen Mount has gone there and we're talking top academic schools – St Paul's, Lady Eleanor Holles, Putney High, Kingston Grammar, Latymer Upper, Godolphin, Hampton as well as St Catherine's, Surbiton or Halliford. Obviously lots of private tutoring goes on for the entrance exams but Mrs England feels it is unnecessary – 'we get them to the required level anyway,' but not all parents are quite that confident. Head does not try to advise parents on the choice of independent school – she admits that she doesn't know enough about them. She concentrates instead on the local state schools – Christ's, Waldegrave and Shene. Christ's is the most popular, with Waldegrave hard to get a place in from this side of the borough. With such a choice of exit schools, there is never more than a handful of pupils going on to each.

Remarks: The best primary school in the area according to parents in the know, and we are not going to argue. If you have the money, it is worth moving to be on its middle class doorstep – many see it as a real alternative to the local preps.

A sea of scooters greets you at the school gates – somehow symbolic of children who want to be at school – and as quickly as possible. Everywhere you see groups of eager, self-confident, happy children enjoying their learning and teachers enjoying their teaching. Reception is regarded as particularly strong – described by mothers as 'a really secure and happy start', 'gets children well-socialised'.

'A vibrant and lively education,' says one mum, who sums up the feeling of many; parents agree that the curriculum is well-taught with lots of visits to help bring subjects to life, but some mutter that SATs results ought to be higher given the intake. Class sizes are typical of state primary schools – average about 30. Despite the high cost of local housing, staff turnover is low and there are four male teachers including a male deputy head. Parents are very welcome in school, they take an interest in what their children are learning and buy appropriate books or visit museums. At least one child was taken to Egypt because she was studying the Egyptians.

The school prides itself on the help given to children with special needs – there is a small dedicated special needs room and the SENCo is highly experienced with children with specific learning difficulties. Some parental grumbles that more minor problems in children's learning are ignored.

Music, drama and the arts are strengths – two music rooms, with mountains of individual instruments piled up on the floor reflecting the range of individual music lessons and the myriad musical groups practising each lunchtime. In the summer term there's a musical drama production and an art show, and last year the choir sang at the Royal Albert Hall.

Children introduced to a wide range of sports, rather than concentrating on winning in a few. Sports facilities are nothing special. Loads of extra-curricular activities – produces mini chess champions, as well as budding Jamie Olivers through its cookery club (though school lunches themselves not invariably popular).

Buildings pretty standard for a primary school – fairly scruffy but with loads of artwork on display. A nice computer suite is well-used and all classrooms have interactive whiteboards. All sorts of use made of the spacious grounds – reading circles, weather stations, nature trails to name but a few. The hall has been rebuilt to double its size which must make a real difference to its usefulness for the school and the community. Parents raised £125,000 towards the hall! The summer fete alone raised a phenomenal £18,000. Leafy and suburban catchment, predominantly middle-class parents with a smattering of film stars and media types. Some of the school's success is due to these highly committed, well-off, parents – they undoubtedly know how to give generously, but some less affluent souls aren't so happy at being regularly asked for money – 'they say it will only cost me the same as a daily cappuccino – well I can only afford a cup of instant!'

Sheffield High School Junior Department

Linked to Sheffield High School in the Senior section

5 Melbourne Avenue, Sheffield, South Yorkshire, S10 2QH

• Pupils: girls; all day • Ages: 4-11 • Non-denom • Fees: £6,678 pa • Independent

Tel: 0114 266 1435
Fax: 0114 267 8520
Email: gatkins@she.gdst.net
Website: www.sheffieldhighschool.org.uk

Head: Since 2002, Mrs Jones. She first joined the school as a teacher in 1993. Earlier experience in the maintained sector.

Entrance: Entry to the junior school is through observation during a child-friendly session – they are looking for bright, lively girls who are ready for school. Admission to years above Reception is by assessment in maths and English.

Exit: The vast majority of junior pupils transfer to the senior school.

Remarks: Specialist teaching for almost all subjects in Years 5 and 6. French taught from reception to Year 3, Spanish in Years 4 & 5 and German in Year 6; specialist PE teaching and use of senior school sports facilities. Maximum of 18 in infant classes; 20–25 in Years 3–6. Support from specialist Dyslexia teacher available. Excellent ICT provision. The library has recently been upgraded. New outdoor play areas. Bright, light well resourced classrooms. The National Curriculum is followed selectively; good artwork on display. Infant department is housed in the adjoining building.

Sherborne Preparatory School

Acreman Street, Sherborne, Dorset, DT9 3NY

• Pupils: 260 total. 195 in the prep; 40 boarders. 65 in pre-prep
• Ages: 3-13 • C of E • Fees: Boarding £18,495–£19,350; Day £11,025–£13,515; Pre-prep £7,305+ pa • Independent

Tel: 01935 812 097
Fax: 01935 813 948
Email: registrar@sherborneprep.org
Website: www.sherborneprep.org

Head: Since 1998, Peter Tait MA, DipEd, DipTeaching, FRSA (fifties). Non-conformist, hands-on New Zealander whom we found crouched under his desk when we arrived (digging in a toolbox, preparing to hang a picture). Educated in New Zealand and spent much of his teaching career there (deputy head of a prep, then head of English, head of history and housemaster in senior schools). Two separate spells at Sherborne Prep in the eighties swayed him to settle there permanently when the headship came up. Brought school back from the brink (down to 101 pupils in 2000). Governor of Chafyn Grove prep and Chair of the IAPS education committee and involved in the management of the Independent Schools Examination Board (the folks who create CE papers). Campaigning gently, from within, to transform CE: 'the current exam tyrannises two years of the curriculum.' Not averse to putting pen to paper, Mr Tait publishes collections of his think pieces from school newsletters (on education, childhood, modern life, international relations, history) in compilations called 'Headmaster's Musings'. Wrote hard-hitting article in IAPS magazine (Winter 2007) bemoaning prep schools' submissiveness to senior schools and their willingness to straightjacket themselves to the CE syllabus rather than provide education for life. Hates spoon-feeding – 'it goes on all the way up to A level while universities are crying out for creative, independent learners!' Keen to keep prep down to a manageable level – '40 per cent of prep set in most schools is a waste of time. It's got to be really worthwhile to deprive a child of his or her childhood.'

Entrance: Non selective, non snooty. Interview with head and school report. Informal assessment when the pupil comes in for a trial day before joining the school. Mainly local families, plus London drift, plus 10 from overseas. Scholarships available for academics (papers in maths and English), music, sports and all-rounders. Bursaries awarded on a case by case basis for existing parents. New parents may apply if their child wins a scholarship. Forces discount. A few JET (Joint Educational Trust) children accepted.

Exit: Mainly to Sherborne School – some years more children move there than to all other destinations combined. Surprisingly few to Sherborne Girls' however. Others dot around in ones and twos to schools in the region (Leweston, Bryanston, King's Bruton, Clayesmore usually feature). Loads of scholarships – for everything – with more variety of destinations. Occasional pupil to a state school.

Remarks: Characterful prep marching to the beat of its own drum. Founded in 1885, the school is now a bustling community hidden behind a mild-mannered Sherborne street-front. Difficult to capture in words – Sherborne Prep looks traditional but thinks outside the box. Open to new ideas; indeed Mr Tait actively seeks them out. Has looked closely at IB early years programmes, among other options and we nod approvingly, noting that this was the first prep in the area to dump Key Stage exams. Ditched Saturday school in 2007 in favour of optional, non-academic Saturday morning programme. Pupils may choose from vast menu of activities and come along – in mufti – for only one hour, or up to three. So families used to their children being occupied on Saturday mornings are happy, teachers enjoy the variety, there is more flexibility for the child who has Saturday commitments outside school etc. Also takes pressure off weekdays – play rehearsals can take place on Saturdays rather than after school or during lunchtimes. Ambitious offerings include e.g. extra languages for pupils and/or parents, rock and music tech workshop, sports coaching, tae kwon-do. Sounds fab, and parents we spoke to were enthusiastic. Two years on, 90 per cent of the children take part and according to parents, 'it is an outstanding success' with activities supported by Sherborne School and Sherborne Girls. Saturday afternoon matches continue as before.

Keen on international links. Not only is the head from New Zealand but the head of art is Spanish, head of science is French, a senior French teacher is Zimbabwean, the German teacher is Swiss, the Mandarin teacher is Chinese, the EFL teacher is Swiss, gappies come from New Zealand and Australia – not to mention the 12 pupils from abroad (four each from Hong Kong, Russia and Spain). Breaking the mould when it comes to languages. In Years 1 to 4 pupils learn French, Spanish, German and Mandarin (one each year). Everyone hunkers down to French in Years 5 and 6 plus Latin/classical civilisation. In the final two years, when streaming kicks in, pupils can continue with French or shift to Spanish. Pupils in the CE stream may drop Latin and opt for Spanish alongside French, emerging with two living languages – an option not available to scholars (though the keen can do extra languages on Saturdays).

Thirty-three pupils currently receive help for SEN in big, airy learning support room. Beauteous new library (shoes off before entering) and art room – a wonderful open space, full of light and colour. Having glass walls, 'our art room is a place of discovery; pupils learn about themselves while looking at the world, literally!' DT, also well-housed, produces interesting projects, a notch above standard prep school fare. Main computer room adequate rather than cutting edge. Lots of sport, with girls' sport on a high, says school. Netball best season ever and reached final of Dorset Championships. Girls' hockey is becoming stronger each year as the coaching improves. 2010 saw their best performance at the County Tournament where they narrowly lost in the semi finals. The U13 girls' hockey team were undefeated last year. Swimming going from strength to strength with new swimming coach in place and pupils competing at the IAPS National Finals and winning medals. Boys' hockey is strong, they finished in the top 10 at the Nationals last year and boys' cricket had an excellent 2010, only losing one match. Makes use of some Sherborne School sports facilities e.g. its Astro (school has its own smaller version). Over 90 per cent of pupils play a musical instrument, from beginners up to grade 6; three concerts a term. School now fundraising to double the size of the music block. Head has recently appointed Sherborne Prep's first head of drama to indicate the subject's importance within the school.

Lovely children with nice manners. What do they like best? Their 'funny, nice teachers'. Gripes? Would like better match teas ('we get baked beans and sausages instead of cakes'). Retains some of the best prep school traditions like an intricate assortment of lapel badges to indicate accomplishment or responsibility, and teachers dolloping out lunch family-style. Many teachers double up their teaching in weird and wonderful ways e.g. DT and maths, science and maths, art and basketball and, in the music department, you will find one busy (talented) gentleman teaching cello and violin and all the brass. Cosy girls-only common room for Years 6–8, an unusual touch. Religion present but inconspicuous. Boarding appealing (especially girls'), flexible and low key. Boarders are mainly children of local working parents, plus pupils from overseas and small Services contingent. The majority pop home on weekends, including non-Brits who may enjoy the hospitality of their local friends. A trip is organised on Sundays for those who remain in school. Cheerful pre-prep and nursery, with small classes and much encouragement. Also mother-toddler group. OBs include poet Louis MacNeice and the literary Powys brothers.

Shrewsbury High Prep School

Linked to Shrewsbury High School in the Senior section

Old Roman Road, Kingsland Grange, Shrewsbury, Shropshire, SY3 9AH

• Pupils: junior dept 200; 175 girls, 25 boys, all day; Kingsland Grange Prep there are 75 boys • Ages: girls 4-11, boys 4-6; nursery 2-4 boys and girls. Kingsland Grange Prep boys 7-13 • Non-denom
• Fees: £6,978-£9,627 pa • Independent

Tel: 01743 494 000
Fax: 0174 349 4039
Email: enquiries@shr.gdst.net
Website: www.shrewsburyhigh.gdst.net

Exit: Girls to senior school following entrance examination, boys mostly to Shrewsbury School.

Remarks: Now fully co-ed pre-prep and prep. For further details, see senior school (girls only) entry.

Shrewsbury House School

107 Ditton Road, Surbiton, Surrey, KT6 6RL

• Pupils: 310 boys aged 7-13 in main school; all day; Shrewsbury Lodge pre-prep 210 children aged 3-7 years co-educational. • Ages: 3-13 • C of E • Fees: £13,275 pa • Independent

Tel: 02083 993 066
Fax: 02083 399 529
Email: office@shspost.co.uk
Website: www.shrewsburyhouse.net

Headmaster: Since 2010, Mr Kevin Doble (forties) BA (law and political sciences) PGCE. Educated at St John's College, Johannesburg and has a post grad degree in management. Previously second master at Edge Grove prep but has taught in a number of prep schools including Newlands school (head of English and housemaster) and Vinehall prep (head of English and scholars' tutor). Member of IAPS & IAPS major committee for sports. A keen sportsman he has coached and managed senior representative hockey squads and cricket teams. Other hobbies include children's literature (writing and analysis); opera; poetry; painting and drawing; amateur dramatics.

Entrance: Up to 50 places available annually for boys aged seven. A few occasional places may be offered at other ages. Two types of entry test: competitive test held in the autumn preceding anticipated entry and offer of places made to those attaining the highest marks. Alternatively, a guaranteed place test (in the autumn before anticipated entry) can be taken by some whose parents make the school their first choice. Head says, 'these parents will have the assurance of knowing that their son's joining the school is not dependent on performance in a competitive test.' Most do enter via this route and a hefty deposit of half a term's fees is required prior to a child sitting the test. School can afford to be picky – three applicants for every place. Head says that his aim is to pick only parents who believe in the school's philosophy. Boys come mainly from pre-prep schools but with about 30 per cent from state primaries. Head says that children have to be 'a good average at least' to get in.

Exit: Almost unknown for a boy not to attain a place at his first choice senior school and these include St John's Leatherhead, Hampton, Epsom College, Kingston Grammar School, St Paul's and King's College School, Wimbledon. Some to boarding schools including Charterhouse, Winchester, Eton and Wellington College. About a quarter of the boys win scholarships to their chosen schools. Head will not accept pupils who do not intend to stay until 13 and is supported in this stance by heads of local senior schools. If a boy takes an assessment to leave at an age other than 13+, it is understood that he will leave at the end of the academic year, regardless of the result.

Remarks: Popular, high-achieving school, which suits boys of wide ranging academic ability. Imposing Victorian house in classy residential area within reach of west London and Kingston area generally – easy from the A3. Founded in 1865, it went through a rocky period prior to previous head's appointment, nearly closing in 1979; however, a group of parents raised sufficient funds to keep it going. Only 190 on the roll when previous head took over, 310 now, so he was clearly successful. Staff numbers have increased from 13 to 34 and class sizes down from an average of over 20 to around 15, with maximum of 18.

Staff are 'friendly and accessible,' according to one parent. Head believes strongly that only someone with expertise in their chosen subject should teach pupils – all twelve of the sports staff, for example, have been outstanding in their particular sport even though they may lack formal teaching qualifications. All academic staff are fully qualified.

Boys setted according to ability from 8 for maths and English and from 10 for French. Scholarship stream from 11. Some parents expressed concern over the intensive internal exam timetable – up to three exams sat in one day – but others say that, as a result, their sons are now not in the least bit fazed by exams. All boys learn Latin and some Greek and Spanish taught 'for fun' after exams. There is no provision for SEN but the school identifies those in need of support and recommends appropriate action to parents, any specialist help being the responsibility of the parents and to be obtained out of school hours. A mother adds, 'the school realised after only one term that my son had a problem – we hadn't realised at all. He was subsequently diagnosed as mildly dyspraxic and the school has been wonderful, doing everything in its power to help.' All boys learn to touch type and some boys with SEN use laptops for their work. Longer than usual school day – boys can be dropped off at 8am for an 8.30am start and finish at 4.15pm, but they can stay to 6pm to do club activities and their prep. No packed lunches allowed – not easy for those who don't like school meals, but sandwiches and fruit may be brought in to be eaten at times other than lunch hour.

Generally smallish classrooms, all of which have specially designed desks with computers in. Also projectors linked to the teachers' laptop computers. The old prefabricated classrooms in the junior school department have been demolished and replaced by long awaited and outstanding £4 million block which houses the library (also incorporating a resources centre), the assembly hall/theatre, kitchens and canteen. It includes 9 new classrooms, a music room, art room and 10 practice rooms.

Heated swimming pool covered by a prefabricated rigid shell (bit on the basic side), an adventure playground and small putting green. School very fortunate (considering its location) to have playing fields within own grounds and owns another 7 acres, equally good, at nearby Chessington. School very sporty; head stresses, 'non-academic pursuits are very important,' and parents say that the sporting prowess played a large part in their choice of the school – 'the boys all play to win,' says one parent. Successful in numerous sporting tournaments both locally and nationally. Every boy can be in a school football team if he wishes (unlike in many other preps), and the vast majority are able to play in a cricket or rugby team, although head points out that it is not so easy to get matches with other schools for weaker teams in these sports. Regular sports tours and trips abroad including ski trips and a recent visit to Pompeii. Lots of extra activities on offer e.g. on-site shooting range for air rifles, scuba diving club and magic club and many more. Drama very strong and popular, with no fewer than six plays produced every year, so that every boy may participate. 'Even if a boy is not sporty, the school does its best to find him a niche in which he can shine,' says one mother.

Music strong – over 80 per cent of pupils learn a musical instrument, some with impressive grades (grade 7) for this age group. Pupils have to miss a regular lesson for their music session. A musical dinner is held every year for the heads of other local schools – a black tie occasion, with the guests being entertained by the numerous musical groups in the school. School magazine states that one head of music at a senior school described it as 'at least as good as, and probably better than, schools who specialise in music.' Regular concerts for parents, which one described as 'truly inspiring.'

Parents are largely prosperous, professional, south west London and Surrey types, British and a smattering of other nationalities, some who live in immediate locality with others ferried in from (much) further afield – fleet of minibuses transport the boys up and down the A3 and elsewhere, wherever there is the demand. As with all schools in a built-up area, parents' parking was seen as problematical by some locals – however, pick-up facilities supervised by staff has much improved this and has been appreciated.

In all, a traditional all-round school, not one for wild anarchists – those kicking against the system would not go down well here.

Sibford Junior School

Linked to Sibford School in the Senior section

Sibford Ferris, Banbury, Oxfordshire, OX15 5QL

• Pupils: 60 boys and girls; all day pupils • Ages: 4-11 • Quaker
• Fees: £7,050-£8,529 pa • Independent

Tel: 01295 781200
Fax: 01295 781204
Email: admissions@sibfordschool.co.uk
Website: www.sibford.oxon.sch.uk

Head: Mr Michael Goodwin.

Remarks: For details, see senior school: Sibford School, Banbury.

Sidcot Junior School

Linked to Sidcot School in the Senior section

Oakridge Lane, Winscombe, North Somerset, BS25 1PD

• Pupils: 65 girls; 65 boys in junior school (of whom 6 boys and 7 girls in nursery) • Ages: 3-11 • Quaker and welcomes all religions or none
• Fees: Day £5,550-£8,550 pa • Independent

Tel: 01934 845 200
Fax: 01934 844 964
Email: juniors@sidcot.org.uk
Website: www.sidcot.org.uk

Head: Since 2002, Ms Rosie Craig BEd DCE (forties), born in Glasgow and educated at Dundee High School then Dundee university. Family hails from Inner Hebridean island of Islay where they still have a home. Career began in Perthshire then moved to C of E primary in Glastonbury, Somerset where she became deputy head; seconded to county literacy initiative; has written children's books and spent a year in publishing before joining Sidcot as curriculum leader in 2000. Has doubled school roll since taking over and rationalised the place, bringing whole junior school together in exciting new building. Popular and involved head; enjoys exploring Hebridean roots with her dogs; cycling, theatre, ballet, films and reading. Has renovated own listed cottage and loves fast cars.

Entrance: Non-selective, entry based on school reports and interview. Admission tests for Years 5 and 6.

Exit: Nearly all pupils proceed to senior school. All take a baseline entrance assessment for the start of senior school life.

Remarks: Originated as The Hall School, Wedmore, and transferred to present site in 1990. Recently established as Sidcot Junior and now thriving in attractive, ecologically friendly new building joined to former school. Space limited in reception class but places not a problem once junior classes begin. Light, welcoming foyer and futuristic hall ideal for dance and music.

Quaker ethos but no teacher belongs to Society. Creative and nurturing atmosphere – children enjoying junk band workshop when we visited. More visits and experiential stuff than most junior schools. Innovative approaches include 'brain gym' to keep everyone mentally on their toes. Visually exciting environment. Links with seniors (e.g. helping with fund-raising) and use of some senior school facilities. Lots of activities at lunchtime. Emphasis on citizenship in PSHE. Specialist teaching e.g. in Spanish and French, own ICT suite, space for reading and research.

Shares SENCo with senior school; average of 2 IEPs per class; range of special needs: dyslexia, dyscalculia, dyspraxia and mild Asperger's currently accommodated but numbers kept within manageable limit. Overall academic standard is good. The majority of children remain in Sidcot environment once they have experienced Quaker approach.

Sir John Cass's Foundation Primary School

St James's Passage, 27 Duke's Place, Aldgate, London, EC3A 5DE

• Pupils: 270 (including Cass Child and Family Centre, up to 76) half girls, half boys • Ages: 3 months to 5 (Cass Child and Family Centre), primary school 5-11 • C of E but other faiths welcomed • State

Tel: 020 7283 1147
Fax: 020 7626 5071
Email: sirjohncassprimary@cityoflondon.gov.uk
Website: www.sirjohncass.org

Head: Since January 1993, Mr Gerry Loughran (early fifties), a bright eyed-Geordie who steadfastly refuses to be tempted away into inspecting or the like – 'I don't want to leave the chalk face!' He's taught and co-ordinated and led at four other primaries in central London before Sir John Cass and still works alongside teachers.

Efficient and enthusiastic, he moves easily between talking to pupils – 'why are you in the classroom at lunch? I'm listening, you listen to me' – parents, (about updating their work skills and what they need to look for in a secondary school) and bigwigs such as the Mayor. Very proud of success stories, e.g. a young mother just finished qualifying in Cambridge and keen to return to her old school to teach.

Entrance: At 3+, over-subscribed (75 applications for 30 places) and priority given to families/children in need in the City of London, then those who attend St Botolph's or neighbouring churches and live in the area, siblings. Worth ringing since places do open up when families move out of the area. If your child gets a place in the nursery, the school will do its utmost to keep them throughout the school.

Exit: To full range of secondary schools – church, community, independent and residential e.g. City of London Girls, City of London Boys, Christ's Hospital, City Academy in Southwark. Since performing arts and music are so strong here parents are advised to look for opportunities for their children to continue.

Remarks: Founded in 1710, the only voluntary aided school in the City of London (so not short of resources); this Georgian mass is open 50 weeks a year and is so much more than just a school. An oasis in the traffic that is Aldgate (the pollution monitor in the playground registers remarkably low readings), pedestrians can peer down at the little ones in the courtyard of the Cass Child and Family Centre – 90 reading and language partners from surrounding offices volunteer at lunchtime. The main entrance is opposite a café and visitors walk directly into the playground – the day we did, there was a line of helmeted children ready, with their trusty steeds, for their cycle safety test.

Between them pupils and parents speak 36 languages and backgrounds range from two families sharing a flat to one with a Barbican pad and a house in the country. Two teachers and a nursery officer work alongside class teacher to support those with English as a second language (50 per cent of the kids are Bangladeshi). A SENCo liaises with children, four LSAs and nine TAs to foreground reading development and is also in touch with CAMHs. Snoezelen room in the nursery section is fully equipped with sensory equipment to calm children (and staff!). The school is totally inclusive of those with relevant support – at present four with statements and one with Downs Syndrome.

A key worker is assigned to four or five families and they are visited before children's entrance. The centre also offers an extended school service to the community with health and social visitors, Job Centre Plus and lots of advice and support sessions for parents in a family learning room and Sp@ce: computer lessons, volunteering at your school, child development classes, first aid, ESL and getting back to work training. Many social functions for parent and community group (e.g. summer market, international food night) and art projects have led to work exhibited in the V&A and the Bethnal Green Museum of Childhood.

The teaching team is stable and ranges from the newly qualified to those with thirty years of experience. RE is popular, with two terms on Christianity, the other on another world faith and, as with sex education, parents can withdraw their children from these lessons but none do! The curriculum is made real in all manner of ways: artist and poet residencies, a roof garden with class planters and greenhouse overlooked by the Foster's Gherkin, maths linked to musical notation and vice versa, the home beat police officer in class to talk about peer pressure and avoidance of gangs, after school clubs (including knitting with senior citizens who provide tales of the war years to those kids with no extended family). Key Stage 2 get to go on two school journeys for a week to experience life with their friends outside London.

A musicianship teacher begins the Strings Project with the little ones (nursery to Year 3) and by Years 4, 5 and 6 all play a violin, cello etc. of their own – groups have performed for the Lord Mayor, Prince Phillip, Bill Clinton and Tony Blair. The choir has sung on the Queen's Christmas broadcast and at the Royal Albert Hall (three part harmony!).

The school coach runs relays to St George's Pool on the Highway or a crocodile of children snakes to the one in Golden Lane. The annual sports day takes place at Mile End stadium, the school competes as the City's team for the London Heathrow Games and occasionally plays rugby against other schools but, since it is the only one in the borough, there is not much competition. There's a traditionally equipped sports hall (huge windows and high ceilings throughout the school) on the second floor in addition to the lines of different courts painted in the playground.

The basement (a secure area in case of bomb threat) houses the computer suite with fifteen workstations networked to a couple in each class and an interactive whiteboard. This technology doesn't come without an awareness of the environment, the school received an award for work on recycling paper, printer cartridges, composting and installing timers on light switches.

Food is cooked on the premises and served in what is now called 'the restaurant' on the top floor; there are themed days with the menu scribed up on a whiteboard (tropical fruit, bread), 35 per cent free school meals and a comments book for the children. Manners are incredibly important here – one child says a prayer before everyone tucks in – everyone learns to behave politely according to their surroundings, whether it is lunch at Mansion House or breakfast club.

The Behaviour for Learning Policy is applied positively, however a series of sanction slips are given out for ignoring the school code of conduct (respect, cooperation, truth and honesty, trying your best etc) – four of these mean the child will be excluded and this hardly ever happens. Fire drills and bomb alerts are necessarily slick with the head's bleeper linked directly to the City of London police. Ofsted 2008 reads impressively.

Somerhill Pre-prep

Linked to Schools At Somerhill (The) in the Junior section
Linked to Derwent Lodge School in the Junior section
Linked to Yardley Court in the Junior section

Somerhill, Tonbridge, Kent, TN11 0NJ

• Pupils: 280 boys and girls • Ages: 0-5 • Non-denom
• Fees: £3,960-£9,165 pa • Independent

Tel: 01732 352 124
Fax: 01732 363 381
Email: office@schoolsatsomerhill.com
Website: www.schoolsatsomerhill.com

Head: Ms Ruth Sorensen – experienced, capable and well-liked by both parents and children.

Remarks: One of the largest pre-preps in the area, highly popular. Based round the courtyard of the Jacobean House. Warm encouraging atmosphere – want children to feel that learning is fun. Cute corduroy uniforms. After school clubs include such activities as ballet, short tennis and modern dance. There is also after-school provision for children from kindergarten upwards to help parents with children in the main schools. Computerised library. Primary emphasis is on literacy and numeracy. SEN help mainly with language and mathematical difficulties. Lessons well planned. Max class size 20. Close relationship with parents, regular reporting, meetings, workshops etc.

South Farnham Community Junior School

Menin Way, Farnham, Surrey, GU9 8DY

• Pupils: 535 boys and girls • Ages: 7-11 • Non denom • State

Tel: 01252 716 155
Fax: 01252 718 260
Email: info@south-farnham.surrey.sch.uk
Website: www.south-farnham.surrey.sch.uk

Head: Since 1988, Mr Andrew Carter BEd OBE (late fifties). Married (his wife Mary also teaches at the school) with three grown-up children. Avuncular and urbane, he is intensely proud of the school which one parent described as 'his invention'. Others describe him as 'visionary', 'dynamic' and 'dedicated'. Supportive yet demanding of his staff. 'He simply believes that however well the school is doing, there is a constant need to improve things,' said one parent. His conversation is peppered with literary quotes and commercial references, leaving parents in little doubt that he knows what he's about. In 2001, he featured in a BBC2 TV programme – he exchanged places with a head of a Birmingham school which was at the bottom end of the league tables.

Entrance: Non-selective and greatly oversubscribed. So many families are attracted to the area by the school that its website has a direct link to an estate agent! Four form entry and usual state criteria apply. In practice, most children come from neighbouring partner infant schools including The Bourne, St Andrews, St Mary's, Frensham St John's, Churt and All Saints, Tilford.

Exit: Most to the local Weydon Comprehensive School in Farnham. About 35 per cent to the private sector – to the impressive big name schools such as Royal Grammar, Guildford High, Tormead and St Catherine's Bramley.

Remarks: An absolute star in the state system and it stands head and shoulders above many private schools. Academically at the very top of the tables but not at the expense of a really rounded curriculum. 100 per cent of pupils at level 4 and above for KS2 SATs in maths, science, and English. More than 60 per cent level 5.

Class sizes average just over 30 and each one has a full time classroom assistant. All children are tested on entry to Year 3 and given targets accordingly. Teaching style is where possible 'to gather at the master's feet,' with children all sitting on the floor in front of the teacher, returning to their desks to complete the task. Pupils who look as though they might fall short of level 4 are taken out of class to work in 'focus' groups of eight, covering the same work as the rest of the class but at a different pace. 90 pupils on the special needs register and, at the other end of the spectrum, there is provision for the most able pupils.

Yet when parents describe what they like best about the school, this academic excellence appears to be almost taken for granted. Instead parents stress how happy their children are and talk about the 'fantastic' shows. Every child takes some part in the famed Christmas production – 'all the children get tremendous confidence from this,' says the head. A large number of pupils learn a musical instrument and sport is similarly encouraged with trophies lining the corridors. South Farnham has the Sportsmark Gold award. Two of the female teachers are trained football referees, which encourages an unusually keen interest in football among the girls. High praise also for a thriving and varied range of after-school clubs including sports, pottery, chess and even circus skills.

Facilities above average for a state school. Classrooms are large, bright and airy. Playground mapped into separate areas for football and other sports, leaving room for children who prefer to sit quietly. Children are very visibly valued – there are vases of flowers in their toilets and 150 spare coat pegs so they have room for all their extra bits and pieces. Such touches reinforce the school's belief that you don't improve maths teaching simply by teaching more maths – you have to get other things right so that the whole atmosphere is conducive to learning. Certainly pupils appear confident and happy and are all neatly turned out. 'There is such a warm friendly atmosphere at the school,' said one mother. 'Every child has the opportunity to do their very best – the ethos is that we want to achieve things.'

Staff largely female – five men at the last count – and includes 'leading practitioners'. All are closely monitored, with each teacher watched in action by a superior once a week. Staff training is a priority and the school rents out its training facilities to generate income. Lots of staff promotion both internally and to external posts, which does mean a fair turnover – just one member of staff has been at the school for more than 10 years. Mr Carter and staff are at the school gate morning and night and appear to know most of the parents by name. Easy to get to see a teacher, problems are dealt with promptly. 'The only child I could imagine not thriving here would be a bully,' said one mother.

Expect to be involved. The school asks as many parents as possible to come in and discuss their jobs and give children ideas about possible applications for their skills. Parents are also welcome to join their children for lunch in the canteen.

Said a parent who left the private system in favour of South Farnham, 'my daughter simply cannot get there fast enough in the mornings. You don't need to pay for a private school with this on your doorstep.'

South Hampstead High School Junior Department

Linked to South Hampstead High School in the Senior section

5 Netherhall Gardens, London, NW3 5RN

• Pupils: 250 girls, all day • Ages: 4-11 • Non-denom • Fees: £9,342 pa • Independent

Tel: 020 7794 7198
Fax: 020 7431 2750
Email: senior@shhs.gdst.net
Website: www.gdst.net/shhs/juniordepartment.html

Head: Since September 2006, Mrs Christine Lough (pronounced Lock) MA, a modern linguist (fiftyish) and highly experienced. She took up her position as her husband, Philip, took up his as head of The Hall, down the road. Clever stuff, this! Calm, professional, smart and warm, Mrs Lough was assistant head (to her husband's head) at Windlesham House, where they were immensely popular and successful, prior to which they taught at Marlborough. They have three grown-up children. This is clearly an excellent appointment and Mrs Lough's quiet and affectionate pride in her domain and its open-faced denizens was a pleasure to see.

Entrance: Register interest between birth and the September two years before your daughter is due to enter at four. On 1 October, the school sends out application forms to all the families who have registered – generally 400–600. The first 250 to reply get a place for assessment. This is for 24 places. Assessment takes place in groups of 12 and girls who are bright, sociable, collaborative are looked for – not those who know their tables. Half invited back and seen in groups of four. At seven, standardised tests are used – again, very competitive.

Exit: The majority to the senior school but some feel that the grass a further stage on the metropolitan line is greener and cart their girls off elsewhere – often with later regrets. Parents of girls who are thought likely to struggle in the senior school are warned by Year 5 and supported in the search for a less demanding school elsewhere.

Remarks: Five minutes from the main school and housed in two smaller versions of the same thing – solid, substantial Victorian redbrickery in quiet, tree-lined, south Hampstead, just above the busy Finchley Road – this is a sought-after junior school which offers, if you can get it, the opportunity of a place till 18 for your bright little girl. The two buildings are in what is now a cul de sac so no dangerous through traffic and parents operate a safe stop and drop system to avoid the potential twice-daily awfulness of 100 four wheel drives all attempting the same thing at once.

'Number 12' houses the 4–8 year-olds and the 9–11s are over the road in 'number 5'. Number 5 has a good new playground with safe surface and play apparatus; the rooms are lively, orderly and colourful but 22 nine-year-olds in rooms this size is ambitious. Music and art are well and enthusiastically taught and enjoyed; the food in the dining room was about the best we have seen in a London junior – mouth-watering fruit and seriously appetising main courses. Good displays throughout – we especially enjoyed 'Women in Science'. Specialist teachers for everything. Number 12 is similar – playground with safe surface though a lack of things to do. Bright, stimulating, structured classrooms. New science lab located on top floor of no 12. Bussing to sports facilities which offer good range of activities – used by Year 2 upwards. Swimming pool at University College School round the corner.

We were struck by the friendliness and openness of the girls we met and particularly by the warmth with which they greeted their head. Most children here seem bubbly and relaxed. Mrs Lough meets them all at the door each morning and, though obviously relishing the brightest and the best, says, 'my worry is that we miss the quiet, creative ones'. Large number of clubs – mostly arty/creative – in lunchtimes and after school.

A happy, secure, stimulating and privileged start for a girl. School now in expert hands and likely, one hopes, to set its pupils on a course they will feel lucky to stay for their entire scholastic lives.

Southbank International School (NW3)

Linked to Southbank International School (W1) in the Senior section
Linked to Southbank International School (W11) in the Junior section

16 Netherhall Gardens, Hampstead, London, NW3 5TH

• Pupils: 210 boys and girls • Ages: 3-11 • Fees: £12,00-£18,900 pa • Independent

Tel: 020 7243 3803
Fax: 020 7727 3290
Email: admissions@southbank.org
Website: www.southbank.org

Remarks: For information see senior school.

Southbank International School (W11)

Linked to Southbank International School (NW3) in the Junior section

Linked to Southbank International School (W1) in the Senior section

36-38 Kensington Park Road, London, W11 3BU

• Pupils: 215 boys and girls; all day • Ages: 3-11 • Fees: £4,000-£6,300 pa • Independent

Tel: 020 7243 3803
Fax: 020 7727 3290
Email: admissions@southbank.org
Website: www.southbank.org

Remarks: For further information, see senior school.

Spratton Hall

Smith Street, Stratton, Northampton, Northamptonshire, NN6 8HP

• Pupils: Pre-prep (Years 1-2) 110. Prep (Years 3-8) 300. Roughly 50-50 boys and girls throughout • Ages: Ages 4-13
• Christian ethos but all denominations accepted
• Fees: Pre-prep £7,950; Prep £10,200-£10,800 pa • Independent

Tel: 01604 847 292
Fax: 01604 820 844
Email: afj@sprattonhall.com
Website: www.sprattonhall.com

Head: Since 2004, Mr Stephen Player (fifties). Previously head of Brandeston Hall in Suffolk where he was fully involved in coaching games and teaching English before his translation. Read Sports Science and English at Loughborough before taking his MA in Educational Management. It shows.

Initially his talk is of graph-filled, objective assessments of his SMT ('outstanding'), the beauty and effectiveness of appraisals (parents are encouraged to contribute their ideas), attainment targets, and EYFs : jugfuls of jargon but always with an underlying sense of humour, a twinkle amidst the statistics. Ambitious for the school ('I certainly have no thoughts of moving on') some parents feel he has turned it into an academic hothouse. Mr Player's response is that he believes in setting realistically high standards now that he has an excellent teaching staff in place and he wants the best for the children. He certainly believes in 'celebrating the children's work': the walls are plastered with paintings, pictures, photographs and poems – NB the poeTREE – and to visit a classroom in the pre-prep with him is to risk a minor injury as budding scholars home in to show off their latest examples of joined up handwriting, coloured in drawings, arithmetical triumphs. The buzz is tangible. There's a faint whisper of 'cloning at Spratton' in the Shires: Mr Player certainly believes in structure. For instance, boys and girls in the pre-prep and prep are told where to sit and always with a boy next to a girl (or the other way round). But within the 'safety of structure' there is much fizz and bounce. The variety of activities for which pupils are awarded their colours makes the idea of 'cloning' difficult to accept. Mr Player is an enthusiastic Inspector of schools with an eye for detail but a manner which is quick to praise. The overall atmosphere is best summed up by the mum who told us, 'the children are happy because they feel secure and know Mr Player and his staff care about them.' No assessment of Mr Player is complete without Mrs Player who is Head of the Learning Support Department, rides with the children, clearly loves them and seems to have the enviable gift of eternal youth.

Entrance: 'We are selective but not overly,' says the headmaster. No obvious formal assessment; more importance attached to the taster days: how the children respond to the novelty and how others respond to them. Will they fit in? Boys and girls may enter at any age and stage, providing there is room. Children are screened on arrival for any learning difficulties and those who need it are given expert help. Scholarships are not available but bursaries are. In terms of finance, there is little difference. Don't be afraid to ask.

Exit: As might be imagined with a day school, most children exit to the usual local suspects: Oakham, Uppingham, Oundle, Rugby, Kimbolton etc though the head is characteristically active in getting around and widening the pool. Shrewsbury, Harrow, Winchester, Tudor Hall, Cheltenham Ladies get an occasional mention and a significant fact is that 60-70 per cent of children go on to board, so distance is not automatically perceived as a problem. The head is assiduous in trying to encourage parents to consider the right school for their child ('parents don't always understand that') and he knows a lot of registrars and heads. He is also prepared to recommend a child leaving early if in his opinion Spratton is not turning out to be the right school. This has been occasionally misunderstood but the overall message is that the head is 'approachable and empathetic.' There is an impressive annual harvest of scholarships, many of them serious ones.

Remarks: Set in 50 acres of attractive countryside, the main house around which the school has developed is a handsome 18th century building with Victorian additions, in particular a lot of brickwork. The gardens and grounds at Spratton are intelligently conceived and beautifully tended. To stand on the mound in the front of the house is to be astonished by the beautiful sweep of games pitches, tennis courts, Astroturf and grass athletics track. Nearer the teaching buildings a garden adjoins the science block and is stocked with suitable herbs and plants to aid academic research; another garden is for peace and quiet.

As far as facilities are concerned, everything looks bright and functional. The pre-prep is a delightful airy building with interesting levels and bags of space for running around; the science block is well equipped and encouraging, or so we thought. But it's undergoing a complete make over in a building programme which includes a sports dome (completed 2010) with an indoor tennis court and in 2011 a performing arts building. How does the school manage such expenditure in these hard times? 'We own everything and owe nothing,' says the head. Even so ...

There is bags of music with endless orchestras and jazz bands, choirs and smaller groups, computers to aid composition and opportunities for performing in assembly and wider audiences. Lively art and drama with much involvement all round. A breath-taking library with a full time librarian where, another example of the head's attention to detail, even the chairs have been carefully selected to give a feel of encompassment and warmth. Lots of guest speakers and suitable activities with which to catch young book worms. There are no lessons on Saturdays but bags of matches with much success. Some parents told us that the selection of teams was a little static and that if your child hadn't been selected early on in his or her career there wasn't much chance of playing for the top teams; others disagreed. All talked of the competitive way in which Spratton Hall pupils approach their sport and their sporting behaviour, something not always shared by the parents.

This is an extraordinary school which would seem to be surfing the wave under its experienced and confident headmaster. He has assembled some outstanding teachers, has the imagination and financial back up to build new facilities and improve on existing ones, understands the necessity for good food (the lunch we had was excellent) and has set up a clearly delineated framework within which children can feel safe and appreciated. Some may feel that the organization is too anodyne, too predictable, too carefully constructed without room for mystery and muddle, barked shins and the tears of disappointment. Others will feel this is the ideal arena within which to learn and grow; in the words of the prospectus, to 'blossom.' Registration numbers for the next three years apparently suggest that most parents feel the latter. Anyone living within commuting range should certainly check it out. Not a school to be overlooked.

Stamford Junior School

Linked to Stamford High School in the Senior section
Linked to Stamford School in the Senior section

Kettering Road, Stamford, Lincolnshire, PE9 2LR

• Pupils: 170 boys, 170 girls; 6 board • Ages: 2-11 • C of E
• Fees: Boarding £13,188-£16,548; Day £9,324 pa • Independent

Tel: 01780 484 400
Fax: 01780 484 401
Email: headjs@ses.lincs.sch.uk
Website: www.ses.lincs.sch.uk

Head: Since 1997, Miss Libby Craig MA (late fifties). Miss Craig has been teaching in the Stamford Endowed Schools (SES) for over thirty years and is a much-loved local institution. She began as a PE teacher in Stamford High School and was steadily promoted from then on. Her MA, taken well into her headship, was on higher performing children in the independent sector. Parents drool, 'the junior school is outstanding. The head is generally adored,' was one of the less enthusiastic comments we heard. She says, frankly, 'I love the school, I love my children and the staff. I'm onto my third generation. I taught six members of my staff.' She still teaches – as do all the SES heads – we approve most strongly. Miss Craig is central to the SES management and works closely with the other two heads and principal. She has a wider remit and bigger profile outside the, somewhat inward-looking, Stamford community being the vice chair of IAPS in 2008–9. But there can be few members of the local community who don't think of her affectionately and with gratitude.

Principal: The three schools in the Stamford Endowed Schools foundation are overseen by the Principal, Mr Stephen Roberts, who arrived in September 2008 from Felsted School of which he had been head for 15 years – a safe pair of hands then. This was a clever appointment and Mr Roberts sees eye to eye with the three heads of the individual schools over the aims – near and far – of the foundation. There is a substantial programme of renewal going on but the SES is not at pains to 'up the academics' (i.e. position in the league tables) which would mean doing itself out of much of its loyal traditional market. Nonetheless, the schools deserve to be far better known and appreciated. This writer can see little reason why some locals might choose the big three, relatively close-by, independents given all on offer here. Mr Roberts is affable, forward looking and a true educationalist. It is, in part, his job to up the school's confidence, to bruit abroad the excellence of his foundation and let Stamford's pride be more than just a local secret.

Entrance: First come, first served into nursery and Reception. 40 taken into nursery of which 20 move on to reception, with another 12 children arriving from elsewhere. This is a sizeable junior school overall. Occasional places thereafter in all years, testing from 7+. The brilliant thing here is, that if you get in at the beginning, you can stay till 18.

Exit: Around 50 per cent leave for the state sector or elsewhere after nursery. Automatic entry for Year 6 into the senior school and most do go on. Perhaps two or so a year warned early that they should look elsewhere as junior may not cope with the senior school curriculum. A few to the state sector or other independents.

Remarks: What you see is not quite what you will get – yet. Part of the vast programme of rebuilding, renewing and expanding in which the SES is engaged means that the nursery is in a super new building but still with the lovely, leafy outside space it currently enjoys. The whole junior school is privileged in terms of its site and green spaces. It is situated just outside the town close to the A1/A43 interchange – not that you'd know it in the pervasive rural peacefulness. The main junior school building is 1970s low-rise, pale brick and, though hardly a match for the architectural glories of the senior school, avoids the worst crimes of scholastic building of the period. It nestles between generous car parking space (lots of large people movers and 4x4s when we arrived) and fabulous, flood-lit courts, pitches and Astroturf, some shared with the senior branches. A little bridge over the railway charmingly leads to the nursery and we enjoyed the sight of crocodiles of smartly uniformed tots, two by two, chatting along their way – seemingly a sight from the 1950s – red berets, blue caps, blazers and sensible red backpacks – aah!

You don't need parents – or pupils – to tell you that this is a happy school – you can feel it as you walk through the orderly – but not neurotically so – classrooms with pockets of clutter here and there suggesting lively work in progress that doesn't need to be tidied away for visitors – so disconcerting elsewhere. It's colourful but not distractingly so with lots of nice touches – bird feeders on the trees, little windmills in the playspaces to encourage the breeze, super gardens and outside areas. We liked Thumbelina's Garden – a large basin full of pot pourri but were sad when an earnest pupil confided that Thumbelina had 'lost her wings'. We liked the door labeled Room 7½ and wondered what it concealed! Large, light hall, multi-purpose and used for celebrating – 'we're good at awarding things'. Everyone – staff and children – eats school lunch – prepared onsite and good manners are particularly encouraged during meals.

The school combines a safe environment with traditional values with up-to-the-minute provision. We saw trolleyfuls of laptops, plasma screens celebrating latest events (in this case the birth of nine ducklings to a resident duck) and saw evidence of sound, even inspirational teaching here and there. Stimulating work done by attentive and absorbed children – who might be even more absorbed in some classes if a few more windows were opened! Setting in some subjects. Those children who manifest learning problems are supported by the Additional Learning Opportunities Team which assesses and then monitors, withdrawing children from class where necessary or supporting them one-to-one or in small groups. Dys-problems seen as no bar to success here and all teachers on the look-out for probs and will replay them to the team. Nine pupils have EAL requirements. Two have individual EAL support. The other children's needs are catered for in the classroom. Arts and sports provision very strong. Music overseen by head of dept for all three schools which ensures continuity in planning and consistency of approach – the music in the senior school is outstanding but begins here. All Year 2 learns the violin. 200 timetabled individual lessons weekly – no-one misses classes – excellent. 60+ in the orchestra. Art and DT skillfully taught by specialists – lots of good stuff here. We met the head of chess! Giant sports hall used by whole school but on the junior school site, excellent 25m pool, immaculate athletics track and the prettiest games pitch we have seen anywhere.

Extra-curricular activities abound – many stay after school. Many come early and stay late – small boarding contingent makes school breakfast and late provision – until 8pm – a real boon for busy families and school has very flexible approach to flexi-boarding when needed. Ten full boarders – mostly from Services families – well provided for – lots of weekend trips, use of pool etc. Family atmosphere in boarding house.

The junior school sows the seed for what happens – increasingly impressively – higher up. Hard to see why anyone living locally would look elsewhere.

Stockport Grammar School Junior School

Linked to Stockport Grammar School in the Senior section

Buxton Road, Stockport, SK2 7AF

• Pupils: 370 boys and girls • Ages: 3-11 • Fees: £6,840 pa • Independent

Tel: 0161 419 2405
Fax: 0161 419 2435
Email: sgs@stockportgrammar.co.uk
Website: www.stockportgrammar.co.uk

Headmaster: Since 2000, Mr L Fairclough BA.

Entrance: From SGS Nursery or alternative preschools in the area.

Exit: Mainly to SGS Senior School.

Remarks: Junior school is on own site, adjoining senior school. Shares dining hall and some sports facilities with senior school. Curriculum is geared to senior school entrance examination, which vast majority pass. Lovely, light classrooms and happy, busy atmosphere. Evidence of projects and artwork bursting out to cover all available space. Staff dedicated. As with senior school, traditional values are centre stage, but lots of scope for exploration and fun.

Stonar Preparatory School

Linked to Stonar School in the Senior section

Cottles Park, Atworth, Melksham, SN12 8NT

• Pupils: 90 girls (15 board) in pre-prep and prep school; plus nursery; boys to age 7. • Ages: 2-11 • Non-denom • Fees: Boarding £15,090; Day £6,540-£10,530 pa • Independent

Tel: 01225 701 741
Fax: 01225 701 797
Email: admissions@stonarschool.com
Website: www.stonarschool.com

Head: Since January 2009, Mr Mark Brain, formerly deputy head of Kelly College Prep.

Entrance: Non-selective. Boarders from Year 3 upwards (usually overseas or military).

Exit: Nearly all girls to senior school.

Remarks: Excellent nursery accommodation with good outside play areas to include a newly opened forest school. Progressive teaching in reception class based on Jolly Phonics foundation and extended national numeracy strategy. Well managed development through prep with calm environment for getting basics right; basics in morning, then enrichment in afternoons: lots of self-expression and use of specialist facilities at senior school for games, riding, art, languages, PE etc.

Frequent reporting on academic progress. Not a money-grabbing approach: girls and boys can be dropped off from 8am and enjoy free pre-school care; tea is available after school for those who wish to stay . Free care for all until 6pm. Lots of after school clubs including riding, swimming etc; girls can go to supper with boarders and on to boarding house if not collected until late.

Shares SENCo with senior school plus help from LSAs (about 20 girls with IEPs); special needs specialist for early years; first screening for dyslexia in Year 1. Severe cases often go to Calder House in Colerne and sometimes return when able to cope in mainstream.

Much more dynamic than many girls' preps with bonus of amazing facilities for riding on doorstep. Previous head went down a storm but then zipped off like lightning to King's School, Ely.

Stover Preparatory School

Linked to Stover School in the Senior section

Stover, Newton Abbot, TQ12 6QG

• Pupils: Nursery : 30 girls and boys. Preparatory : 82 boys and 83 girls (some board). • Ages: 3-11 • Christian • Fees: Day £6,330-£7,755; Boarding £14,460-£16,575 pa • Independent

Tel: 01626 331 451
Fax: 01626 361 475
Email: fwhite@stover.co.uk
Website: www.stover.co.uk

Assistant Principal: Since 2006, Ms Caroline Coyle BEd MA (forties). Before that, deputy head. Wise, warm and approachable, 'lovely person' (said a mum), full of ideas of treating even the youngest as 'real people'. Loves them without patronising them and is very good fun to meet. Keen to select the best of modern teaching practice without being a slave to trendiness. Healthily sceptical about some ideas. 'Common and sense and love is what drives her,' said another parent. Enthusiastic about emotional intelligence.

Entrance: Seven and under are by interview and report. Those who are 7 + have assessments in reading, mathematics and non verbal reasoning. All prospective pupils are encouraged to spend a taster day at the school. 'Very rarely does anyone fail to get in'. Boys and girls are taught together in the Pre-Prep but divided for most lessons from Year 3. Otherwise they play happily together.

Exit: About 60 per cent of nursery pupils move up into the prep school; nowadays most prep school pupils move on to the senior school.

Remarks: Designed to be safe for horses and hounds, the school is built around the quadrangle of the original stables, complete with clock. Our guides were tremendously proud of the computer room, art room, the winding passages and staircases that followed the building round, the fresh bright paint, the colourful classrooms and the library. There we met a studious-looking boy reading with fierce concentration. 'I've read every Harry Potter book five times' he said airily. 'He's a reading legend' said one of our guides. Regular library sessions with young bibliophiles devouring books.

The Forest School in the woods below the house is very popular. Not long ago it was demolished by a freak wind. 'It offered a good lesson in facing up to adversity' said a teacher. ' The children sat around the ruins and discussed ways in which they must improve the next construction.' Our guides were thrilled about their participation in the school council which had already resulted in improvements in the playground. ' You don't get everything you asked for,' said one, 'but they listen.' A good lesson for life. An excellent, cheerful, well-run pre- and prep school – especially for those wanting to embark on the complete Stover experience, aged 11. Even those who are not going on to the senior school will benefit from a sound education in preparation for the next step.

The Study Preparatory School

Wilberforce House, Camp Road, Wimbledon Common, London, SW19 4UN

• Pupils: 315 girls, all day • Ages: 4-11 • Non denom • Fees: £9,885 pa • Independent

Tel: 020 8947 6969
Fax: 020 8944 5975
Email: wilberforce@thestudyprep.co.uk
Website: www.thestudyprep.co.uk

Headmistress: Since January 2011, succeeding Mrs Joyce Nicol, head since 2003, Mrs Susan Pepper MA, who comes from Francis Holland School SW1. Mrs Pepper (early fifties) joined Francis Holland in 1988 as head of history, thereafter becoming deputy head, so this is a considerable change after such long service in a different capacity. Mrs Pepper is lively and capable – an interesting appointment.

Entrance: Non-selective entry at 4+ by ballot; priority given to siblings. Thereafter girls have an informal assessment and interview for occasional places. Girls mainly local, Wimbledon and the surrounding areas of Roehampton, Kingston, Barnes and Putney.

Exit: Regularly get sports, music and academic scholarships at 11+. Record 12 scholarship offers in 2010. Majority go to day schools: Wimbledon, Putney and Surbiton High Schools, Lady Eleanor Holles, Kingston Grammar, Notre Dame. Some to boarding schools Woldingham, Benenden, Wycombe Abbey, Downe House etc, odd one to the state sector.

Remarks: Lively prep school founded in 1893 by a governess, now on two sites bordering Wimbledon Common. Preprep girls at Wilberforce House in large purpose-built ex-local authority premises, surrounded by well maintained gardens and play areas. Year 4 upwards on the original site, Spencer House, which was acquired in 1903 and has a small playground.

Both buildings have been redecorated and modernised recently. Classes are mixed ability with settings for maths and English from Year 2; a committed band of staff.

Girls are taught to enjoy learning; certainly not a hothouse say parents, but all the girls are 'encouraged to reach their potential,' Produces confident, friendly and well adjusted girls, without pressure. Science lab particularly well designed and the teaching is very high standard. A learning support team assists girls with specific difficulties and EFL. Gifted and Talented Co-ordinator has developed extension programme for the more able.

A good choice of clubs, with sports being very popular; girls have been selected for SW London athletic squads and swimming teams. No sports field: makes use of the many public sports facilities in the area. Drama and public speaking also thriving – many do New Era exams. The jewel in the crown is undoubtedly music; four choirs, an orchestra, a jazz group and smaller strings groups that provide music for assemblies. There is always a waiting list for individual instrumental tuition, so put your name down early. School awarded Artsmark Gold status by Arts Council England in 2010 for its excellence in the arts.

We will watch with interest as Mrs Pepper takes over this attractive school.

Summer Fields

Mayfield Road, Summer Fields, Oxford, Oxfordshire, OX2 7EN

• Pupils: 240 boys; 220 boarders, 20 day • Ages: 7-13 • C of E
• Fees: Boarding £21,768; Day £16,857 pa • Independent

Tel: 01865 454 433
Fax: 01865 459 200
Email: admissions@summerfields.com
Website: www.summerfields.com

Headmaster: Since 2010, Mr David Faber MA (modern languages). Was himself a boy at Summer Fields, continuing onto Eton and Balliol College, Oxford. Says he has 'enjoyed a long and happy association with the school over many years – as a boy, a parent, and most recently, as a governor.' This is the first time that a headmaster has been appointed whose background is not from within education. Previously a Member of Parliament, holding position as shadow foreign minister, Mr Faber stood down from Parliament in 2001 to pursue his career as an author and historian and has published two history books. He teaches RS to the youngest boys and history to the older pupils. Married to Sophie, with a son down the road at Balliol College, Oxford and two young daughters.

An unusual but interesting appointment.

Entrance: Names down early. Boys come for assessment two terms before they are due to start but the report from head of previous school is 'the key thing'. School has traditionally been viewed as an upper-class place but more of a mix than before and head says 'we attract a very great cross-section of people.' Around 40 per cent of boys are from London but others from Gloucestershire, Hampshire, East Anglia, Scotland, and up to 15 from abroad. No flexi or weekly-boarding but small number of day boys, mostly from Oxford, including a 7+ day entry class introduced in 2006. School very accommodating to busy working parents – one day boy arrives at 7.15 every morning to join boarders for breakfast. Range of academic and music scholarships on offer, including the Maclaren Foundation scholarship, offered to a boy of 'outstanding ability' starting in Year 6 or 7 whose parents could not otherwise afford the fees. About ten per cent of pupils are sons of Old Boys.

Exit: School 'very proud' of its links with Eton and is one of its main feeders, with up to 40 per cent heading there each year. Lots to Harrow, Radley and Winchester too, though, and a smattering to other schools – Marlborough, Shrewsbury, Stowe, etc. More than 40 scholarships and awards won in the last five years – details proudly framed along school corridor. The 2009 leavers secured some of the greatest scholarship results in recent years with eight awards in total: six to Eton, one to Shrewsbury and one to Winchester.

Remarks: Founded in 1864 and set in 72 acres in highly sought-after North Oxford. Grounds are stunning – elegantly manicured lawns and playing fields stretching towards the river as far as the eye can see. Setting is so delightfully rural that it's hard to believe that the dreaming spires are only a few minutes away. The large bow-fronted main building houses some classrooms and adjoins fantastic sports complex with three squash courts, fives courts, climbing wall, 22-metre indoor swimming pool (there's an outdoor one too), light and airy art department (complete with fabulous giant dinosaur made from computer packaging) and pottery and DT workshops. The boys say there's so much to do that they never get bored – no wonder.

Interactive whiteboards and computers everywhere. Boys are allowed to email during their free time. Internet access available subject to certain restrictions. Max class size 17, 'invisible' setting almost from the start (scholarship form and streaming for last two years) and one-to-one learning support available. All but very youngest boys taught by subject specialists. Latin for all and the scholarship group does Greek too. Pupils also get opportunity to practise their French during ten-day visit to chateau near Avranches in Normandy in their third year, followed by a two-week trip in their fourth. Two recently refurbished science labs and boys keen to get involved in scientific projects at weekends – everything from brewing lavender essential oil to building rockets when we visited. Well-stocked library and boys encouraged to read widely.

Drama and music strong. Plays and musicals performed in terrific theatre conversion – performances range from The Taming of the Shrew to Little Shop of Horrors. Around 85 per cent of boys learn a musical instrument. Orchestras, three choirs – senior choir performs all over, from Westminster Cathedral to Oxford's Keble College, and there have been recent trips to France, Germany, Italy, even New York. Sport is a vital feature of school and, in an age when many parents worry about their children's lack of exercise, Summer Fields' boys do games most days. Everything from rugby, football, hockey and cricket to cross-country, golf (the school has its own nine-hole golf course) and sailing. Lots of silverware on display for sporting feats. Masses of activities on offer – from chess to the Adventure Quest programme of camping, adventure activities and leadership training. 'You name it, it's there and the boys do it full throttle,' a parent told us last time round – and it's still the case.

Boarders assigned to one of seven lodges, arranged 'horizontally' according to age. Each lodge is run by lodge parents, a husband and wife team (many with young families of their own) with lots of experience of the particular age group they're looking after – whether they are eight-year-olds getting used to being away from home for the first time or older boys revising for exams. Lodges are wholesome, homely and welcoming. Boys don't take schoolwork or prep back to their lodges at night – 'it's their down-time,' says head. 'They play, wind down, drink hot chocolate and get into their pyjamas.' Cosy dorms, with brightly-coloured duvets, lots of teddies, Tintin and Asterix books, Jenga towers, marble runs, remote control cars etc and between three and 11 boys to a room. Each boy has his own bedside light and everyone reads for at least 15 minutes before lights out.

School prides itself on having 'three layers of care'. Each boy has lodge parents, a tutor (who usually stays with him throughout his time at Summer Fields) and a form teacher, all of whom work closely together. Contact with home not encouraged for first ten days while new boys find their feet (lodge parents thoughtfully make regular phone calls to update parents on how their sons are settling in though) but after that boys get phone cards, send emails, write weekly letters home and go out with their parents on a regular basis. Senior boys are allowed into nearby Summertown – but only in small groups. Boys are well behaved and discipline isn't an issue. 'We set very clear guidelines and make sure the parameters are in place,' says head. His words borne out by one of the oldest boys, who told us, 'there's a good atmosphere here and I really enjoy it. In the summer holidays I was looking forward to coming back to school!' Prefect system – six prefects on tenterhooks when we visited, waiting to hear who would be chosen to be head boy. Lovely chapel with impressive stained glass – services three times a week and on Sundays (when parents can attend too). Huge dining room – lined with portraits of the great and the good, including former Prime Minister Harold Macmillan, an Old Summerfieldian and the current headmaster's grandfather! Food committee (called Guzzlers – very appropriate!) means boys have their say on school meals and food gets the thumbs-up. There's also a school shop called Buzzer, which sells toys, stationery etc.

Boys are polite, jolly and purposeful as they scurry round the school in their smart Guernseys and polo-shirts. For parents looking for an all-boys' full-boarding prep (albeit with a handful of day pupils) Summer Fields is hard to beat. A happy place which fizzes with fun and activity while achieving fine academic results.

Summerhill School (Junior)

Linked to Summerhill School in the Senior section

Westward Ho, Leiston, Suffolk, IP16 4HY

• Fees: Boarding: £8,160-£14,181; Day £3,558-£8,505 pa • Independent

Tel: 01728 830 540
Fax: 01728 830 540
Email: office@summerhillschool.co.uk
Website: www.summerhillschool.co.uk

Remarks: See senior school.

Sunningdale School

Dry Arch Road, Sunningdale, Ascot, Berkshire, SL5 9PY

• Pupils: 100 boys, all board except a handful. • Ages: 8-13 • C of E
• Fees: Boarding: £17,640 pa • Independent

Tel: 01344 620 159
Fax: 01344 873 304
Email: headmaster@sunningdaleschool.co.uk
Website: www.sunningdaleschool.co.uk

Headmaster: Since 2005, Mr Tom Dawson, who took over the reins from his father and uncle. Mr Dawson was educated at Eton then Edinburgh and Bristol universities. He taught at Harrow before joining Sunningdale. Married to Elisabeth, one son, one daughter.

Entrance: At eight – 'they settle in better at this age' – from a wide variety of pre-preps all over the country including Scotland. Some from London but not as many as expected given the proximity to the London SW postcodes. Also happy to take boys at 10 or 11 from day schools.

Exit: Fifty per cent to Eton, 25 per cent to Harrow, five per cent to Stowe. One or two to Marlborough, Radley, Charterhouse, Wellington and Milton Abbey.

Remarks: Small, cosy, old-fashioned prep school. A large country house with lots of add-ons including new-fashioned classroom blocks, one furnished with old-fashioned wooden 'lift-up lid' desks. Refurbished ICT room and theatre, a new cinema and a newly built library complex in the planning. New house system encourages boys to earn points for their respective houses through good work and behaviour. Houses named after previous headmasters – Sheepshanks, Crabtree, Fox, Girdlestone. Attention given to individual academic needs. Much movement between classes. A brighter boy may end up doing two years in a top class which gives him a tremendous advantage at Common Entrance. Well-behaved boys juxtaposed with seemingly informal teaching staff. Very good results at Common Entrance and scholarships won on a regular basis.

Around 80 per cent learn a musical instrument. Active chess club with a part-time chess teacher and a wide-ranging extra-curricular programme that includes cooking, model-making, pottery, fencing, pirates and rifle shooting. Lots of sport including Eton fives. Full boarding although boys may weekly board in their first two years. Masses to do at weekends from paintballing to go-karting. Pastoral care has improved dramatically. Present matron is kind and cosy. Carpeted dorms for younger ones (piles of teddies on the beds), cubicles for the older boys, hot chocolate offered as a reward for tidiness. A large communal bathroom with eight miniature-sized cast iron baths with claw feet – new shower block too. House in Normandy used by the week. Boys allowed to walk the Dawsons' dogs in the grounds (wonderful at cheering up a homesick child). Excellent food. Boys have happy, cheery faces with sparkling eyes. Excellent manners and well disciplined. Lots of praise too.

Sunny Hill Preparatory School

Linked to Bruton School for Girls in the Senior section

Sunny Hill, Bruton, Somerset, BA10 0NT

- Pupils: girls; boys welcome in nursery and pre-prep until 7
- Ages: 3-11; day and boarding from 7 • Fees: Day £9,000-£9,300; Boarding £14,820-£16,635; Pre-prep £6,000 pa • Independent

Tel: 01749 814427
Fax: 01749 813202
Email: admissions@brutonschool.co.uk
Website: www.brutonschool.co.uk

Head: Since 2010, Mrs Helen Snow BEd, previously deputy head. Has had experience in primary and secondary education at state and independent schools. Lived in Berlin for eight years and worked in senior management at Berlin's leading British School. Married with one daughter. Aims to 'set the very highest expectations regarding behaviour and academic performance. To provide an environment which is safe, secure and stimulating, where each and every child is happy and nurtured.'

Entrance: Open entry into pre-prep.

Exit: Seamless entry to senior school at 11.

Remarks: Housed comfortably in rambling, two storey, former boarding house, overlooks shared swimming pool and rolling countryside beyond. Level site adjacent to senior school tennis courts which double as a hard surface play area for the prep. Plentiful car parking for drop-offs and collections a definite plus. Nursery (starts with 2+ children) and pre-prep in cedar clad annexe – plenty of space indoors and outside. Children feel safe and happy here. Well planned phonic and number work in pre-prep before girls move into adjacent prep classroom where we saw them writing scripts for a *Cinderella* performance. Work is differentiated sensibly for older and younger girls in a way designed to work well for both age groups.

Close contact between staff and parents encouraged at all levels. We noted this feedback from a prep 2 parent in her daughter's reading diary, 'I am pleased Charlotte is enjoying her reading so much. Fantastic.' Teachers monitor girls' choice of reading to ensure it fits emotional as well as reading ages.

Good interactive IT suite (accommodates 17 girls) plus specialist science and art/DT rooms. After-school clubs and prep continue to 5.35pm. Multi-purpose hall with staging for in-house performances; girls share senior school gym for PE (taught by specialists) and senior theatre for school productions. Prep has own SENCo with NFER materials used to screen for dyslexia at prep 3 level. Individual SpLD support followed through into senior school if necessary. Languages teacher uses *La Jolie Ronde* for French and also introduces Spanish. Peripatetic music lessons on site include Suzuki violin for all prep 3s; music showcased annually in prep prom. Yummy lunches at senior school supervised by prep staff ahead of main rush. Regular competition in netball, hockey and rounders. Swimming and tag rugby also on offer. Recent success for prep 6 girls in national indoor rowing championships. Inclusivity ensures all can have a go – severely asthmatic had managed to play in a hockey match a few days before our visit. Enticing library adds to reading ethos – popular annual book week with visitors. Excursions and on-going programme of activities for all ages. Lovely dorm in the nearby junior boarding house accommodates small number of prep boarders (currently seven). Idyllic learning environment – no wonder girls in the senior school look back nostalgically at their beginnings here.

Surbiton High Boys' Preparatory School

Linked to Surbiton High Junior Girls' School in the Junior section
Linked to Surbiton High School in the Senior section

3 Avenue Elmers, Surbiton, Surrey, KT6 4SP

- Pupils: 145 boys, all day • Ages: 4-11 • Christian ethos but all denominations accepted • Fees: £7,326-£9,801 pa • Independent

Tel: 02083 906 640
Fax: 020 8255 3049
Email: surbiton.prep@surbitonhigh.ucst.co.uk
Website: www.surbitonhigh.com

Head: Since 2006, Ms Cath Bufton BA PGCE (thirties). See Surbiton High Junior Girls' School.

Entrance: At four – informal assessment in November for 22 reception places. At other times subject to availability. No need to register at birth.

Exit: With no in-house repository at 11, school achieves a very creditable set of places/scholarships at local independent schools including Hampton, Kingston Grammar, Reed's and St George's College.

Remarks: Good academically but with limited space particularly outdoors. Surbiton Prep is the junior boys' school of Surbiton High School and shares many of its facilities including dining rooms and gym (100 metres down the road, so the boys get plenty of short walks each day) and sports fields (impressive, though a three mile bus journey away). The prep building has been a school since 1862 (it became part of Surbiton High in 1987) and, while this gives the place a certain homely charm, the downside is that physical surroundings are not great and space is at a premium. 'Reception classroom is small and hot,' said one parent. Several others voiced concerns about the playground – 'too small – no space for the boys to have a good run about,' said one, though school reminds us that they have extensive playing fields in Hinchley Wood. 'Not enough equipment,' said another parent.

Does not follow the National Curriculum to the letter (boys additionally take French from reception) but pupils sit SATs at Key Stages 1 and 2. In 2007, at Key Stage 1, 100 per cent reached level 2 (the national target) and more than half reached level 3 – 85 per cent in English, 80 per cent in maths. At Key Stage 2, 94 per cent of pupils reached the national target level 4 in English, 100 per cent in science, and 100 per cent in maths. Again many bettered this – level 5s by 57 per cent of the boys in English,

79 per cent in maths and 79 per cent in science. All classrooms have electronic whiteboards. Lots of opportunities for arty children – regular drama productions and a good range of music tuition available as an extra. Plenty of after-school clubs.

Pastoral care and discipline generally considered good. 'It's a very close community where the boys all know each other and the teachers all know them,' said a mother of two boys at the school. 'It's a safe and supportive environment where the children feel secure.' Any issues over behaviour problems are considered well handled – with the occasional miracle turnaround of a difficult child. Relaxed atmosphere, boys are polite and well turned out. Parents mostly English professional couples – both working, with a sprinkling from overseas. Strong parent association with plenty going on – more social than fund-raising. 'Friendly, not snooty,' said one.

Generally a feel that the prep is a bit of a poor relation of the main school but, 'there's a happy atmosphere and they turn out a good product,' said a father – 'makes you wonder what they could do if the facilities were slightly better.'

Surbiton High Junior Girls' School

Linked to Surbiton High Boys' Preparatory School in the Junior section
Linked to Surbiton High School in the Senior section

95-97 Surbiton Road, Kingston Upon Thames, Surrey, KT1 2HW

• Pupils: 230 girls, all day • Ages: 4-11 • Christian ethos but all denominations accepted • Fees: £7,467-£9,993 pa • Independent

Tel: 020 8439 1309
Fax: 020 8974 6293
Email: surbiton.juniorgirls@surbitonhigh.ucst.co.uk
Website: www.surbitonhigh.com

Head: Since September 2006, Ms Cath Bufton BA (thirties). She took a PGCE ('to get it under my belt for the future'), but actually intended to join the police force. While waiting to begin police training she did some supply teaching in Somerset, 'got bitten by the bug' and decided to begin teaching straight away. After five years teaching in junior and middle schools in Somerset, she moved to Bute House Prep in Hammersmith, where she spent five more years before arriving at Surbiton. In the past, there has been some parental feeling that the junior and boys' prep heads are mere puppets of senior school head (qv). However with a new head at the senior school all could change and Ms Bufton says they are already working work well as a team.

She is certainly full of enthusiasm, with just a whiff of head girl about her; describes herself as 'super-organised and approachable' and feels she has already tightened things up and strengthened the school's structure. Well-intentioned, proactive and good at PR, parents find her friendly and agree that she's approachable – if occasionally a little on the defensive side 'and hot under the collar when stressed'. 'I like her and feel she's brought a fresh perspective to the place,' says one mother. 'She's got a great attitude and I've got a good feeling about her,' says another. Outside school she is a keen musician (she plays trumpet) and is also very sporty (played rugby for Wales in her time) enjoying netball and triathlons. Married with a baby son.

Entrance: All girls are assessed prior to entry – an age appropriate and child-friendly exercise. At 4+ the tests are based on cognitive and social development, with the girls doing simple tasks observed by teachers. At 7+ girls are tested in line with the National Curriculum for English and maths and a school report is also requested. Most families come from immediate surrounding areas (11 school bus routes and 10 mins from BR station). Main feeders are Thames Ditton Infant School, Dicky Birds Nursery, Bushy Tails Nursery and Maple Road Infants School.

Exit: Most go to linked senior school as entry is now automatic (school prefers term 'natural progression'). Otherwise it's local grammars or other independents. Some parental moans that girls are not prepared for entry to other schools. The head counters that Surbiton is basically an all-through school, which parents know when they choose the junior section. Further, she maintains girls leave the juniors with good results and are therefore quite capable of gaining a place elsewhere.

Remarks: Vibrant happy place, modern yet homely, with a good local reputation and turning out confident, articulate girls, largely for its own senior department.

Attainment is high. Teaching is rigorous and lessons move along at a brisk pace. Even the youngest quickly prove capable of working alone or in small groups for short periods. Ms Bufton describes teaching styles as 'relaxed but productive – I don't mind a bit of noise as they process what they're learning and I want them to feel confident enough to take a risk, make a mistake, as they learn – it's the best way to learn.' Girls follow the National Curriculum closely, but not exclusively, and take SATs in Year 6, generally with great success – 100 per cent achieving the target of level 4, and many bettering it. Pupils work hard and go home tired – so homework is scaled back accordingly to three 30-minute sessions a week and absolutely none during the holidays (though some will be provided at parents' request). Nice teacher/pupil relationships. Some girls from Korea and Indian subcontinent supported with EAL lessons. Learning support for mild difficulties such as dyslexia and dyspraxia, along with support and access improvements to help the physically disabled. Parents can pay extra for one-to-one SEN support. School has an SEN teacher who works three days a week. Enrichment groups in English, maths and science are laid on for the gifted and talented, in addition to in-class support through planned differentiation.

Outside pure academia there is lots going on. Plenty of clubs and outings, including residential trips from Year 4. As with senior school, sport has been a concern here (small site militates against it) but generally seen as improving and the junior girls use the off site extensive sports grounds at Hinchley Wood. Regular music and drama productions.

Lovely modern building was purpose-built – so no complaints there. 10 minutes from central Surbiton it's a very urban space – local parking a nightmare so school has organised staggered start times to give all year groups a fair crack at the limited drop off area. Works well. Inside it's a bright and stimulating environment, a purposeful place with some outstanding specialist facilities – particularly art, music and science. Parents give special mention to the breadth of the curriculum and the child-centred approach – 'I like the ethos and the moral fabric of the school,' says one mother. The pupils are listened to and are happy that they have a voice – strong school council system.

Real sense of pride in the place – very small girls who didn't realise they were being watched were seen holding doors open for each other and another nonchalantly picked up an overturned waste paper bin as she passed without missing a beat. Lunchtimes have been much improved by a new system called 'family service' where, having previously chosen what to eat, the girls sit at the appropriate small table and are served by a member of staff or a Year 6 pupil – changes the mix and fosters sense of community. Even the necessary but unappealing table-clearing duties carried out cheerfully afterwards. 'The whole lunchtime set up is lovely now – and the food's improved,' says one pleased mum. A kindly atmosphere pervades. 'There's no such thing as a perfect school – but what makes the difference is the way the school deals with any issues – here I always feel listened to and where it's been warranted, something has been done,' a mother says. A few gripes about home/school communication – claims that school is flaky over notifications of after school clubs being cancelled and the like. However, with the linked boys' prep and seniors there's a real family feel to the place, with many families having children at all three schools.

Sussex House School

68 Cadogan Square, London, SW1X 0EA

• Pupils: 180 boys; all day • Ages: 8-13 • C of E • Fees: £14,040 pa • Independent

Tel: 02075 841 741
Fax: 02075 892 300
Email: registrar@sussexhouseschool.co.uk
Website: www.sussexhouseschool.co.uk

Head: Since 1994, Mr Nicholas Kaye MA ACP (mid fifties). Was deputy head here before. In his many years at the school, Mr Kaye has made his mark. His room is more reminiscent of a Victorian parlour, stuffed to the gunwhales with objets d'art, pieces of porcelain, figurines, potted plants, embroidered banners (made for the school jubilee in 2002 and used on special occasions), leather armchairs, lampshades, oriental carpets, rugs and comfy sofas. It even accommodates an ornately decorated pianoforte. The walls, needless to say, are covered with antique tomes, old school photos, house shields, clocks and portraits. At one end sits a fine stained glass window. During break the staff assemble amongst all this finery to partake of coffee and biscuits. It is hard not to like this room and this man. Indeed, parents as well as pupils become very attached to the school. The 'Olim Alumni' listed in the (very impressive) school magazine date back to the 1950s and reunions always see a good turnout from the Old Cadogans.

Entrance: At 8+ mostly from Wetherbys, Eaton House, Garden House and other local pre-preps. Not suited to any other than the high fliers as this is a school with an unashamedly academic agenda. Tends to attract families familiar with the English boarding system. Despite the pressures on his time (he still teaches English to the top three classes and is always demonstrating the delights of creative writing to the younger set) Mr Kaye resolutely meets all prospective parents and they are shown round the school on an individual basis – 'we are a personal school. The individual matters.'

Exit: Majority to Eton and Winchester. Harrow and Marlborough are also popular. Just under a third go to London day schools such as St Paul's, Westminster and Alleyn's. Generally achieves a smattering of scholarships.

Remarks: One could just describe this school as a centre of academic excellence and leave it at that but that would not give a true picture. Mr Kaye has created a remarkable place where he believes boys should have something to look forward to every day. One such is the sight of the School Marshal, Sergeant Khim Sherchan, formerly of the Gurkhas, looking very donnish in his black gown, welcoming the boys and their parents at the school entrance every morning; guaranteed to bring a smile to your face.

From Year 1, lessons are given by dedicated staff qualified to teach their subjects to A level. Each class has a pastoral teacher but the boys quickly become used to being taught by a variety of specialist teachers. This is an excellent preparation for their future public school education and beyond. Outside of academia, countless activities are offered before, after and during school and at weekends. For a small school in central London, the range available is astonishing and is the result of slick time organisation, 'rather like running a small railway company,' says the head. With limited space on the actual premises, musical and dramatic performances take place in Cadogan Hall, the Royal Court Theatre and St John's, Smith Square. All the junior boys now have an opportunity to develop in drama and music as they put on their own production. The school does not want the pupils to 'go into an academic tunnel. Boys who like music also want to play football.' Current activities on offer as classes or clubs include oil painting, fencing, cricket, football, creative writing, Greek, architecture, pottery and music, music everywhere. The school's annexe off Cadogan Square has a surprisingly large gym on the top floor. Art is particularly strong with the art room 'open for business all the time (including weekends)'. Examples of the boys' work are displayed throughout the school, starting with an awe-inspiring model of St Pancras station in the entrance hall. Everything here is done with skill, enthusiasm, enjoyment and hard work. Standards are high and it shows. Sussex House deserves its reputation as an excellent boys' prep.

Sutton High Junior School

Linked to Sutton High School in the Senior section

55 Cheam Road, Sutton, Surrey, SM1 2AX

• Ages: 4-11 girls, all day • Non-denom • Fees: £7,212-£2-£9,342 pa
• Independent

Tel: 020 8642 0594
Fax: 020 8642 2014
Email: office@sut.gdst.net
Website: www.gdst.net/suttonhigh

Head: Since 2010, Ms Manda Cooper.

Remarks: For details, see the senior school entry.

Sutton Valence Preparatory School

Linked to Sutton Valence School in the Senior section

Church Road, Chart Sutton, Maidstone, Maidstone, Kent, ME17 3RF

• Pupils: 175 girls and 195 boys; day • Ages: 3-11 • Fees: £10,680 pa
• Independent

Tel: 01622 842 117
Fax: 01622 844 201
Email: enquiries@svprep.svs.org.uk
Website: www.svs.org.uk

Head: Since 2010, Mr Richard Johnson LLB PGCE. Educated at Pocklington School and Gordounstoun before going on to Newcastle University to read Law. Worked in prep schools in the Lake District and Hertfordshire before becoming deputy head of St Francis School, Wiltshire in 2004.

Entrance: Entry in Kindergarten – Year 2 is non selective. For entry to Years 3–6, an assessment with the director of studies, involving reading, spelling, maths and non-verbal reasoning to ascertain the child's academic levels.

Exit: Mostly to Sutton Valence School, other independent schools and to local grammar schools.

Remarks: Set in 22 acres of grounds in the village of Chart Sutton, one mile from Sutton Valence School. Small classes, high standards and the same commitment to extra-curricular activities as the senior school.

Sydenham High Junior School GDST

Linked to Sydenham High School GDST in the Senior section

15 Westwood Hill, London, SE26 6BL

• Pupils: 255 girls; all day • Ages: 4-11 • Fees: £9,342 pa • Independent

Tel: 020 8557 7000
Email: d.hogarth@syd.gdst.net
Website: www.gdst.net/sydenhamhigh

Head: Mrs Barbara Risk Cert Ed MA. Friendly, chatty, open. Pupils really like the fact she always calls them 'my girls', makes them feel part of a big happy family. Enjoys a good working and personal relationship with head of senior school (who's in overall charge).

Entrance: Informal entry assessment at 3½ – 'gives us an edge over some of our competitors who do formal assessment – children skip out of here, find experience enjoyable, even fun.' 'Weed out the stroppy and difficult' so hope it doesn't fall on a day when your child's in a bad mood!

Exit: Between 60 and 70 per cent to senior school, rest to a range of schools: JAGS, Alleyn's, St Dunstan's College, Royal Russell, some boarding, some state, some to other GDSTs because they're nearer to where a girl is living. No automatic entry to senior school.

Remarks: Good facilities, new library and IT suite, classrooms brimming with lively displays. New playgrounds, additional classrooms and specialist science, art and ICT facilities have all been added in 2009/10. Close links with senior school – head spends an afternoon a week in the junior school, takes assembly which girls love and say is a very special time. Year 6 girls permitted to wear senior uniform and dine in senior school.

French for all from four, Latin is taught to the top two years; emphasis on music, sport and drama. Currently caters for range of mild SEN: dyspraxia, dyslexia, dyscalculia, Asperger's, autism, ADD, ADHD and EBD, but all must be able to manage the curriculum. Some specialist support available.

A very welcoming environment.

Talbot Heath Junior School

Linked to Talbot Heath School in the Senior section

Rothesay Road, Bournemouth, Dorset, BH4 9NJ

• Pupils: 120 girls in junior school and 95 pupils in pre-prep, including 10 boys • Ages: 3-11 • C of E • Fees: £3,315-£8,220 pa • Independent

Tel: 01202 763 360
Fax: 01202 768155
Email: jsoffice@talbotheath.org
Website: talbotheath.org.uk

Head: Since 1987, Mrs Karen Leahy BA PGCE MEd – a teaching head, having her own form and teaching 12 periods a week, but spends time with all of the children so that she knows every child in school and has a good understanding of each age group.

Entrance: Youngest children come along for a chat. Entrants to Years 1–6 spend a whole day in the school and pupils entering in Years 3–6 sit formal tests in VR, maths and English. Bar for entry not a high one: 'Most of our pupils are little Miss Average,' says the head. No longer taking boys from 2011.

Remarks: Junior school housed in what was once a school boarding house – so plenty of loos! Own dining rooms, computer suites and play areas as well as purpose built Jubilee Hall for assemblies, drama and music. Interactive whiteboards in all classrooms from Year 1 up. Traditional feel, small classes, tidy hair, smart uniform, emphasis on manners and handwriting. 'Not a place for eccentrics or slackers,' says school.

Music and PE taught by specialist staff at all ages, and senior school facilities are used when appropriate. Junior school has its own strings group and two choirs but able girls can join the senior orchestra. From Year 4 specialist teaching extends to English and maths, then French and art from Year 5. By Year 6 the girls are attending half their classes – and eating lunch – at the senior school. Four PE lessons per week, including fencing, volleyball and badminton in Year 6. Peripatetic special needs teacher gives one-to-one help to a half dozen pupils.

TASIS - The American School in England (Lower School)

Linked to TASIS - The American School In England in the Senior section

Coldharbour Lane, Thorpe, Surrey, TW20 8TE

• Pupils: 180 • Ages: 3-10 boys and girls; day • Non-denom
• Fees: £15,250-£17,100; Pre-K £8,950 pa • Independent

Tel: 01932 565 252
Fax: 01932 564 644
Email: ukadmissions@tasisengland.org
Website: www.tasisengland.org

Head of Lower School: Since 2003, Ms Susan Porter BA MEd. Previously taught in Exeter, New Hampshire, public school district before moving to England and joining TASIS in 1985 as a second grade teacher. In the ensuing years, she held several administrative posts before being appointed head.

Remarks: For details, see the senior school entry.

Taunton Pre Prep and Nursery

Linked to Taunton School in the Senior section

Taunton School, Taunton, Somerset, TA2 6AE

• Ages: 2-7 • Inter-denom • Independent

Tel: 01823 349209
Fax: 01823 349202
Email: enquiries@tauntonschool.co.uk
Website: www.tauntonschool.co.uk

Remarks: For details, see senior school entry.

Taunton Preparatory School

Linked to Taunton School in the Senior section

Staplegrove Road, Taunton, Somerset, TA2 6AE

• Pupils: Nursery 75 day; pre-prep 90 day; prep 300 day and boarding. Boys and girls throughout. • Ages: Nursery to pre-prep 2-7; prep 7-13 • Inter-denom • Fees: Day £5,580-£12,180; Boarding £10,635-£19,275 pa • Independent

Tel: 01823 703 307
Fax: 01823 703 308
Email: admissions@tauntonschool.co.uk
Website: www.tauntonschool.co.uk

Head: Since 2010, Mr Jimmy Beale (early forties) BSc (Geography) PGCE. Educated at Bryanston School, Dorset and was a police officer prior to a move into teaching. Taught at Stamford School, Lincolnshire before Taunton School, where he rose through the ranks becoming deputy headmaster. A keen cricketer and potter – planning to run the pottery club at TPS. Aims to 'provide a challenging environment for the young, where confidences will grow based on secure relationships with excellent teachers.' Key developments at TPS will be a major thrust towards independent learning and thinking skills.

Married to Tina who will be supporting the school, both as the head's wife and as a mother – two young children, both at the school.

Entrance: There are three rungs to the school's ladder. Entry into the nursery classes aged 2+; then the pre-prep and finally at 7+ the prep school itself. The first two rungs involve no formal assessment but rather familiarisation sessions to ensure all parties are happy. Entry into the prep school in Year 3 is when those moving up from the pre-prep are joined by some half dozen or so new pupils. Since the prep school year groups grow in size from 36 in Year 3 to 72 in Year 7, entry is usually possible at all ages. Potential pupils spend a day in the school individually or in pairs, joining their peers for lessons, before sitting papers in maths, English and non-verbal reasoning.

Strong special needs ('learning success') department. All pupils are assessed on entry and provision is put in place, if appropriate. The department consists of a full time head of department and five part time teachers and is housed in its own area which is bright and homely. There is also a 'gifted and talented' extension programme.

Scholarships available at 11+ for internal and external candidates, academic, music, sport or all rounder. The all rounder involves the academic papers plus two of sport, music, drama, art and technology.

Exit: Not surprisingly the majority go on to the senior school which is bang next door and offers a gentle and friendly way of moving on with little cultural and social shock. The prospect of spending so many years together doesn't seem to faze the pupils. 'They make friends for life,' said a parent with a child in both schools. No CE but children are set according to the prep school exams and detailed reports. The headmasters of the prep and senior schools have regular meetings, anyway. Entry to the senior school is almost, but not quite, automatic. Occasionally pupils are recognised as not being up to it and are 'diverted to somewhere else where they can succeed.' The school aims to help the parents select a suitable alternative and to avoid sudden hatchet jobs. 'Nothing should be a shock,' says the headmaster. Occasionally parents do choose to send their children elsewhere. In the last two years pupils have won scholarships to Winchester, Millfield and Sherborne School for Girls. 'Staff love the challenge and it's healthy to have some variety,' says the headmaster.

Remarks: An excellent indoor swimming pool, very good teaching facilities – new, brightly coloured and functional – with an atmosphere of busy purpose which some of the tattier buildings do nothing to disperse. Indeed one boy showed us with justifiable pride a hole in a prefab-looking building where he had driven a cricket ball ('It was an off drive, you see'). Games are taken very seriously. The dormitory arrangements (girls named after hills and boys after rivers) were very popular with our guides as were the (segregated) common rooms with televisions, presided over by a splendid matron who said she enjoyed being at 'the hub of things'. Members of the teaching staff preside overall. Tasters are available.

The most stunning aspect of the school is its music. Lessons are offered on an astonishing variety of instruments. There is an orchestra, a jazz band, a clarinet ensemble and a percussion group amongst other formal and informal groups. 60 per cent of pupils learn at least one instrument and there are over 100 in the (voluntary) choir. A smaller and selected singing group, coached and conducted by a flaming haired Celt who could charm sweet music out of a buffalo, has recently sung in Venice. Previous destinations have included Rome, Barcelona and Prague. This year, four pupils played in national orchestras and 11 sang with the national children's choir. A vast range of out of school activities. Weekend activities for the 40 or so boarders are well organised and popular.

The matter of bullying is tackled thoroughly. 'Buddy Groups' – vertical rather than horizontal – meet regularly, as do form captains. In groups and assemblies all are constantly reminded that 'different people have different sensibilities.' Leavers' questionnaires deal with the topic and regular self-assessment reports provide opportunities for airing anxieties. There is even, rather touchingly, a Friendship Bench overlooking the playground. The story is told of an exhausted member of staff plonking himself on the bench only to be approached by a young child asking if he had no friends.

This is a school for children with stamina. It's an action packed day and given that some of the children set off early on school buses from as far afield as Bristol and Exeter, Glastonbury and Sidmouth, it's a long one. Just as well the food – eaten separately from the main school but sharing the same kitchen – is as good as it is. It really is excellent.

Teesside Preparatory School

Linked to Teesside High School in the Senior section

The Avenue, Eaglescliffe, Stockton-on-Tees, TS16 9AT

• Pupils: 135 girls, all day • Ages: 3-11 • Non-denom
• Fees: £4,293-£8,334 pa • Independent

Tel: 01642 782 095
Fax: 01642 791 207
Email: abullen@teessidehigh.co.uk
Website: www.teessidehigh.co.uk

Head: Since 2005, Mrs Julie Richardson head of pre-prep and since 2010 Mr Graham Twist head of prep.

Remarks: Has its own separate building and play area next to the senior school. Bustling and cheerful atmosphere. French taught from eight and IT throughout. Children very proud of their school. Two ten-year-olds who took us round insisted on showing us everything from the staff room to the contents of every cupboard! Since 2007 boys have joined the school in Years 5 and 6. Exciting times.

Tetherdown Primary School

Grand Avenue, London, N10 3BP

• Pupils: 300 • Ages: 4-11 • Non-denom • State

Tel: 020 8883 3412
Fax: 02088 833 414
Email: admin@tetherdown.haringey.sch.uk

Head: Since 1999, Ms Evelyn Pittman BEd MA (late forties). Ms Pittman is a thoroughly experienced, clear-sighted and level-headed presence, who knows precisely what she wants for her school: a community school in which parents are closely involved and pupils have fun. 'She's a very competent, committed head,' said one mother. 'Very sorted.' 'Business brained,' was another's admiring description. 'She knows what the big issues are and doesn't get involved with the irrelevant.'

Entrance: The school has recently doubled in size to admit 60 pupils in reception, but there's still fierce competition to get in. In the past it was only siblings and those living feet from the gates who reasonably stood a chance, now at least an address in the same street might reasonably be expected to do the trick. (Needless to say property prices nearby have their own exotic micro-climate.) Parents can view the school in the autumn term prior to entry, kids visit in the summer term before they start.

Exit: Not only is Tetherdown one of the country's top-performing primary schools, if you're clever enough to have got your child in here you're also pretty much guaranteed a smooth transition to one of the capital's best comprehensives. Smug parents, who've sorted it all by the age of 4, tend to assume their children will proceed to Fortismere and the vast majority go on here. The rest to north London grammar schools or leading independents ('This is Muswell Hill,' said one mother, 'parents tutor without hesitation.')

Remarks: This is a school which regularly sits near the top of the local authority league tables and, even in an average year, over 50 per cent of pupils reach the highest score possible in English and maths. 'Pupils here make outstanding progress,' waxes Ofsted and do so, because of 'extremely effective teaching' and a 'dynamic and vibrant curriculum'. Add to the mix, meticulous monitoring, a dollop of regular homework ('there's not a lot of pressure') and dedicated parents willing to supervise nightly reading from reception to Year 6 and you get some idea how these results happen. The school follows the National Curriculum but adds its own flourishes.

Fun is very much part of the academic recipe, both in the classroom and outside, whether that's learning fractions in history by means of tricky Tudor recipes, studying maths with the help of a visiting Maths Clown or sharpening up those multiplication tables in Beat the Parents at Mental Maths. 'The children have a lovely education,' says one parent. Pupils are grouped, extended and supported according to ability. 'If they're struggling, it gets noticed. My son was given extra spelling and extra handwriting.' Special needs are caught early by a dedicated Special Needs Coordinator, who works with classroom teachers and outside specialists to set appropriate targets. The recent requirement for the inclusion of modern language teaching is provided (courtesy of the Italian consulate) in weekly Italian lessons and French is also offered as an after-school club.

Plenty of stretching and thinking in all directions, whether in an opera workshop or an after-school street-dance club. Plenty of creative parents, too, who come in to share their expertise. All children learn to play the recorder and read music in Year 3 and individual instrumental tuition, subsidised by the local authority, is provided during the working day. Sport is perhaps the school's weakest link, 'There isn't much and what there is isn't competitive,' said one mother of boys. In recent years, this has been partially due to a rebuild. Now the outdoor space is both more expansive and better equipped. In Year 6, all children learn swimming and travel outside the school for specialist coaching. Schools meals are nutritious – parents have their own tasting to ensure their experience matches their kids' – and naughty sweets, chocolates and fizzy drinks are banned from the premises. Plenty of after-school clubs – football, drama, etc – and while there's no after-school care on site, those who want it can be collected from the playground and taken to a nearby club. Regular school trips include an annual outing to the seaside for Years 2 and 5, where the deputy head sets a good example by leading the troops into the bracing waves.

Virtually all parents and pupils live within a few surrounding streets and the school has always offered an exceptionally tight-knit community. Expansion has marginally diluted the atmosphere, but has brought advantages. 'It used to be very much like a village school, where everyone knew each other and older pupils looked out for the younger ones,' says one mother with children at both ends of the spectrum. 'That was comforting, but sometimes your child didn't have a particularly wide choice of friends. Now there's plenty of scope.'

Until 2009, Tetherdown was a square and solid Victorian board school, but an exciting £6.5 million redesign had provided lots of lovely light interiors and well-planned playgrounds for infants and juniors. The make-over has also brought up-to-the-minute wireless IT, with interactive whiteboards in every classroom and two computer suites.

The school has no uniform and rules are kept to a minimum. 'We have just two rules,' says the head: 'Respect yourself, and respect others. If you respect yourself you are going to work hard to become the best you can.' Parents admire the way these principles are implemented. 'We had to go and see her about a case of bullying and she wasn't at all emotional, just reassuring,' said one. Those demonstrating behavioural difficulties are given the same support as those with academic problems, with intervention and targets. Children are encouraged to get involved: with the School Council; with each other's welfare (by becoming play leaders and buddies); and with the broader community (for example, running a soup kitchen at Harvest time). They are also lavished with praise. Regular 'Achievements Assemblies' recognise work, effort and attitude.

Tetherdown is located in north London's prosperous, professional Muswell Hill and the parent body is a mirror of the locality, with plenty of engaged, full-time mums who devote the same attention to reading rotas and library duty they once gave to successful careers. Parents, too, provide support in a very concrete fashion and the enthusiastic Parent School Association generously underwrites school trips and playground extras. Parents know each other well in and out of school, are ambitious for their kids and for the school.

Thomas's Battersea

Linked to Thomas's Clapham in the Junior section

Linked to Thomas's Kensington in the Junior section

28-40 Battersea High Street, London, SW11 3JB

- Pupils: 525 boys and girls. All day • Ages: 4-13 • Christian
- Fees: £13,560-£15,300 pa • Independent

Tel: 020 7978 0900
Fax: 020 7978 0901
Email: battersea@thomas-s.co.uk
Website: www.thomas-s.co.uk

Headmaster: Mr Ben Thomas MA (forties). Educated Eton, Durham and ultimately at the Institute of Education. First teaching job, aged 26, head of Thomas's Kensington, a bit of baptism by fire. After four years took over headship of Battersea and parents now say 'outstanding' and 'really has his finger on the pulse'. Says that this definitely affected his style of headship and believes that it makes him less didactic. Vice principal of the group, Jill Kelham, based at Battersea, has, apparently, been a huge help to him. Has built up excellent teaching team, including well respected heads of year, and now believes his main function, as far as parents are concerned, is advising on senior schools at 13+. Visits several of these each term and feels he really does know the heads. Parents praise his 'excellent advice'. Says that the school should be about 'enjoyment for the lower school, learning for the middle school and achievement for the upper school,' and is a big believer in the most important school rule, 'be kind'. One of the four principals of the whole group of Thomas's London Day Schools, originally founded by his parents, David and Joanna Thomas in 1971, describes himself as the headmaster, 'doing the fun stuff', and his brother Tobyn as the administrator controlling finance, buildings etc. It is a huge business and would appear to be extremely profitable, though some parents feel that the fees are increasing a little too fast. '4 to 5 per cent is a bit steep in the current financial climate.' Married to Katie, a full time mum, with three children all at the school and totally satisfied with his current existence. 'I love being head. It's great for family life.'

Entrance: Mainly at four. Competitive and oversubscribed. Register as soon as possible, preferably at birth. Assessments in November prior to entry in September the following year. Three applicants for each place offered. Up to six boys and girls per hour's session. Looking for children who 'have a measure of confidence, are responsive, sociable, with a light in their eyes.' Sibling priority but not absolutely guaranteed. Occasional places further up the school when candidates are assessed while spending half a day with their peer group. Written report from previous school also necessary. More places at 11+ but majority of these tend to be taken by children from Thomas's, Kensington.

Exit: At 11+ and 13+ but not normally at 7+ or 8+ as no preparation for these exams. Although, inevitably, the odd trickle whose parents are scared they may not make it later. Impressive range of destinations at both levels with St Paul's Boys, King's Wimbledon, Westminster, the Harrodian and the various girls' high schools featuring most as day schools and Wellington, Cheltenham Ladies', Oundle, Eton and Marlborough for boarders.

Remarks: A big, busy, slightly chaotic school for cosmopolitan parents who want their children to have the best English education money can buy. That is what they want and, to a large degree, that is what they get. Plenty of opportunities for pupils to excel but withdrawn types might find it all somewhat overwhelming.

Occupying an attractive listed ex-grammar school building, with many modern additions and plenty of playground space. This last is easily transformed into a car park at the beginning and end of each day as public transport not particularly convenient. Has own fleet of buses which convey children from Kensington and ferry the whole school to sports venues etc. All the facilities for a broad curriculum. Great science labs – 'we do chemistry, physics and biology here,' said our youthful guides, computer suites and all the modern aids to a tip top education. Plus loads of music, with 245 individual lessons taking place each week on instruments that range from piano to cornet; an orchestra, various bands and ensembles, choirs at all levels (recent concert had the school orchestra playing alongside the Southbank Sinfonia) and their own choral society where they are joined by parents from the other schools and members of the local community. Two great art studios and two pottery rooms with their own kiln. Imaginative creations displayed all over the school. We particularly liked the charcoal drawings lining one staircase alongside a written request to please not rub against them. And, of course, being a Thomas's school, the drama is outstanding with huge productions by each year group being put on over the year. 'Only drawback', said one parent, 'is that they are always musicals. Not much use if your child can't sing'. School assures us there's always something for everyone. Great Hall where they perform is pretty splendid.

Lots of sport, say it takes up about twenty per cent of the timetable from Year 3 onwards. All the usuals with sculling added in the summer term at the top of the school. Matches inter-house, inter-Thomas's and against other schools. Great gym and school playground excellent place for organised and unorganised games. Also use facilities at Battersea Park, Barns Elms and the Wandle Centre. Youngest children, Reception to Year 2, have fantastic and imaginative rooftop playground on high.

Academically, teaching deemed pretty good, though lots of coaching still occurring in the last years. 'Just as insurance,' say the parents. We did feel that this was definitely more about anxious and ambitious parents than inadequately taught children. As in all the schools, some specialist teaching from the beginning. Mixed ability classes, with setting in maths and English only, until they reach the upper school when they are divided into those doing 11+ and those staying on and academia becomes the be all and end all, with all classrooms subject based and a tutor system coming into operation. Not a wide choice of languages, although 11+ leavers have the option of German, Spanish or Italian after their exams. French from Reception, Latin compulsory from Year 5.

Enthusiastic, experienced head of learning support who also teaches maths in the lower and middle schools and study skills to Years 7 and 8. Determined to catch children early so that they can let go of support by Year 6 or 7. Works closely with class teachers, showing them how to help pupils. Mainly milder end of the spectrum but one-to-one teaching available for more serious problems and laptop training when absolutely necessary. Parents always involved and communication apparently good.

Probably most cosmopolitan of all the Thomas's schools, with a wide ranging mix of international parents and 19 different foreign languages spoken at home. About 25 per cent of children on the EAL register. A few of these need extra support which is well provided. School celebrates and appears to make the most of this range of different cultures.

Thomas's Clapham

Linked to Thomas's Kensington in the Junior section
Linked to Thomas's Battersea in the Junior section

Broomwood Road, Wandsworth, London, SW11 6JZ

• Pupils: 580 girls and boys; all day • Ages: 4-13 • Non-denominational • Fees: £12,660-£14,310 pa • Independent

Tel: 020 7326 9300
Fax: 020 7326 9301
Email: clapham@thomas-s.co.uk
Website: www.thomas-s.co.uk

Headmistress: Since 1993, Mrs Carol Evelegh DipCE DipSpLD (fifties). Joined Thomas's consortium in 1979, after two years teaching in the state system in Edinburgh, and has moved up and up. At one time, head of drama for all the schools, then deputy head of Kensington, then, after three years as head and director of the kindergartens, became head of the new Thomas's, Clapham at its inception. And here she plans to stay – well, probably, for the next five years anyhow. She doesn't visualise remaining into her dotage – after all, her children (who were both educated at Thomas's) are now at and almost at university. A strong, ambitious leader who knows what she wants and where she wants the school to go. Someone who 'makes decisions and gets things moving'. Old fashioned values, children all leap to their feet when she enters the room and say 'good afternoon Mrs Evelegh'. Says she just wants them all to be happy – 'we're here to enjoy everything with them. Let them have fun and do their best.' A good philosophy in a school where there appears to be quite a lot of pressure, where we are told children who are not clever enough, or are without interest in learning would not fit; a school where, some say, 'weaker children can get lost'.

Entrance: Competitive and oversubscribed. Need to be put on the list at birth. Interview and assessment take place a year before 4+ entry. Looking for an all rounder child who will 'get fun and joy out of a big school' and who will take advantage of the amount on offer. Sibling preference but not guaranteed. Individual assessments held when the occasional place occurs further up the school. Used to be several at 11+, when there is a small exodus; less likely in future as school is now the automatic follow on for Thomas's, Fulham which opened in 2005. No scholarships or bursaries but there is a fund to help in dire need.

Exit: At 11+ or 13+ but categorically not at 7+ or 8+ for which they will not be prepared. Head discusses destinations individually with all parents and is resolutely firm if she feels they are aiming too high. School says 100 per cent to first choice – but whose first choice? At 11, mainly girls, to local day schools, often with scholarships. Alleyn's, JAGS, Emanuel and Streatham Hill & Clapham High feature highest in the last few years. At 13, seventy per cent to boarding schools, again with quite a few scholarships. Head's favourites at the moment, apparently, King's Canterbury and Tonbridge. Recent results show Sherborne, Benenden, Wellington, King's Wimbledon and Alleyn's popular as well. Despite really top notch teaching standards we are told quite a lot of coaching still takes place. That's ambitious parents for you.

Remarks: A big, ambitious, busy school, with amazing facilities, continually moving forward, embracing every latest innovation, determined to give the children of local, successful and ambitious parents a kick start in their climb up the educational tree.

The tall, redbrick, grade 2 listed building, was originally built early in the twentieth century, to house Clapham County Girls' School. What would those girls think now if they could see the state-of-the-art facilities provided today? Bright classrooms, the majority of which are subject based, well equipped science labs, great IT suite, and a specialist art block where children can expand their creative skills in many different ways. Music is big, drama is huge. Choirs and orchestras galore, children can learn pretty well any instrument they want. Performances abound. Fantastic theatrical productions put on by each year group, masses of singing and dancing, this is an important part of the curriculum and all modern technology is there to help.

Elegant school hall with plenty of room for good sized audiences. Reception classes housed in their own recently built, specially designed single floor, block. Each classroom with its own outside area to enjoy and cultivate. Safety flooring everywhere. A garden where they can climb and play and have fun. This same building contains rooms where all children needing special assistance come to work one-to-one with their helpers. Art block alongside. All other classrooms up and down the stairs of the main school, divided into lower, middle and upper sections, one per floor. All meet and mix together at lunch time except for Years 7 and 8 who have canteen service in their own dining area. Very grown up. Head believes totally in the mixing up of the age groups. 'We are one big happy family.'

An academic school which starts gently and gets harder and harder as they move up through the years. 'For outgoing children it is terrific,' say parents. Mixed ability classes with setting in maths and English only until they reach the upper school when they are divided into those doing 11+ and those staying on and academia becomes the be-all and end-all. French from reception, Latin compulsory in Year 5, classics apparently one of the most popular subjects at CE. Tutor system for the top two years. Good SEN provision. Any learning problems are taken seriously, 'nothing can slip under the radar'. Children externally assessed and parents involved and kept fully in touch. 'It is not a taboo subject.' Support department has open door policy, children can drop in or parents can ring at any time. Or so they tell us. Parents said 'when things go wrong they don't always spot it that fast. Though, once it's pointed out, they do pick up the ball and get on with it.' Others said teachers, all of whom are handpicked by the head, 'go above and beyond to help the students'.

Sport also very important. Takes up about 20 per cent of the time table from middle school onwards. Lucky school, on large site, has huge playground adaptable to supply cricket nets, netball and tennis courts, football and other practice areas, plus plenty of space to line up all the 4 x 4s that arrive at collection time. (Though as the majority live very locally we wonder why there are quite so many.) Fantastic climbing wall for adventurous children. Also use nearby Trinity Fields, Clapham Common and Wandle Sports Centre. Matches played inter-house, inter-Thomas's and against other schools home and abroad. Gives sporty children a chance to show what they are made of. Apparently girls more successful than boys at the moment. Great gym catering for indoor sports as well. There are several more of these on the extensive 'clubs' list that guarantees another hour's worth of activity at the end of the school day. These children must tumble into bed exhausted each night; there's homework to be done as well.

Excellent system of class prefects and each class has separate representatives, whom they elect themselves, on the school council and the innovative ABC (Anti-Bullying Committee). However, we do still get occasional distressing reports of bullying which is less than well-handled by the school. A sense among some parents that you can sink or swim here. Green Unicorns elected to promote sustainable issues and further environmental friendliness. Older children are involved in helping the younger ones and love 'doing their reading with them'.

Lots of outings, using everything London and surrounds have on offer, and a wide variety of trips. Years 5 to 8 have a residential one included in the curriculum. Others optional, usually sports, music or subject based, and can be to faraway places. Some parents feel these can sometimes be a tad too expensive and exotic for such young children. Why not leave something for public school? But then one does get the feeling that this is a preparatory school with a public school ethos.

Thomas's Kensington

Linked to Thomas's Clapham in the Junior section
Linked to Thomas's Battersea in the Junior section

17-19 Cottesmore Gardens, London, W8 5PR

• Pupils: 360 girls and boys • Ages: 4-11 • Non-denominational
• Fees: £15,195-£16,545 pa • Independent

Tel: 020 7361 6500
Fax: 020 7361 6501
Email: kensington@thomas-s.co.uk
Website: www.thomas-s.co.uk

Headmistress: Since 2001, Mrs Diana Maine MA BEd NPQH (fifties). Formerly head of biology and director of sixth form at St Marylebone CE School, sixth form consortium co-ordinator for Greenwich, and deputy head at Blackheath High School (junior department). Also author and consultant on a number of science books for Dorling Kindersley and instrumental in developing the science curriculum for the school. Extremely professional, business-like and well organised. Inspires confidence in parents who find her 'straightforward and approachable' and say 'runs a tight, happy ship as far as staff concerned'. Thirty-four years of teaching experience certainly shows. Says she loves school ethos and very excited about introduction of intranet for all pupils to use. Married with two grown-up children.

Entrance: School full of large families, mainly from Kensington and Chelsea, with a few from further afield, Brook Green and Notting Hill Gate figuring highly. Mostly within walking, or at any rate, cycling distance. School keen to discourage motoring. Very over subscribed, so best to get on list as soon as possible after birth. Assessments in January before four-year-old entry in September. Sibling priority but not guaranteed. 'We must feel child will be able to cope.' Occasional places further up the school, so always worth asking.

Exit: About a third, mainly boys, to Thomas's Battersea but stress this is not the easy option. Need to pass internal exam. Parents say, despite sameness, children find it quite hard to break into and the move across is tough but also say good step up and preparation for bigger school. Otherwise a few leave at 7 and 8, but not prepared for these entrance exams, and the rest at 11+. Mainly to senior London day schools – Francis Holland, Godolphin and Latymer, Queen's Gate and Latymer Upper amongst others.

Remarks: A busy, happy, international school where children learn to love learning and have fun at the same time. A cosmopolitan place, reflecting the changing face of London, where the 'be kind' ethos seems to work and children and teachers alike are exceptionally supportive of each other. Not for the shy, withdrawn type, the pace is fast and the endless opportunities need to be grabbed with both hands. But there is a world of education to be had in the grabbing.

A school on three sites with very little outdoor play area, so much use is made of local tennis courts and the park. Tall Kensington buildings, with several staircases meandering in and out of bright, smallish classrooms and learning areas, give a comfortable old fashioned feel but teaching and facilities bang up to date. Parents say 'wonderful, local, cosy school'.

Lower school, housed in old Lady Eden premises, an entire unit of its own. Bright classrooms, own hall, dining facilities, library, IT, music and art rooms. Go round the corner to the preparatory school for pottery. Also have own outdoor play area; presumably, as has historically been a school for a long time, neighbours are used to it and don't mind a little noise. Space for planting and growing too. A teaching assistant in each class. A gentle, friendly place to start.

Pace speeds up on the move to the preparatory school and setting begins in maths, French and Latin. Specialist teachers, so classrooms become subject based and much more moving around. Teachers enthusiastic and relaxed, average age mid-thirties, a third have been at the school for more than ten years. Good male representation. Particularly high quality reading and writing. In recent national competition to write to the Prime Minister, a Year 4 boy was runner up. Small outdoor area, for quiet study only, so mid-morning break in classrooms with quick race around neighbouring tennis courts to expel surplus energy. Lunch takes place in converted Leith centre round the corner. Fantastic ultra modern kitchen and cafeteria style service. Dining area doubles up as gym with plenty of equipment. This building also contains exciting, purpose-built theatre for all those ambitious, glitzy productions. Seats eighty to ninety. Also used for concerts and as extra play space, probably much needed on wet winter days. Two music rooms as well. Around 42 per cent learn an individual instrument, currently up to grade 4.

Sport perhaps less successful although does take up 20 per cent of the timetable. Lack of playground and size of school not helpful and for boisterous boys it is not perfect, although parents say school is 'struggling hard to crack the problem'. School says 'when we play schools of similar size, we have been very successful' and 'in running and swimming we are right up there with the very best'. Some parents feel this does not help with integration when they move across to Battersea at 11+. Lots of bussing to various different grounds and sports centres, as at their sister schools, and several sport-based after school clubs. Having said that, the top classes can go for a 3k run in the park before school and sports scholarships to senior schools are not unknown.

Assistant head also head of learning support. Sympathetic, trained and highly experienced. Makes sure all staff are well informed and the youngest pupils are properly monitored so problems can be picked up early. 'Must know how to spot and observe.' Good relationships with local dyslexia centre and occupational therapists. One-to-one support and laptop training when necessary. Makes sure specialist sports staff also aware of problems. Feels that school culture helps: 'sympathetic and calm'. Approximately a third exposed to language other than English at home. Plenty of help with speech and writing.

Parents say communications excellent and 'teachers very approachable and seem to really care' 'children really supportive of each other'. As at all Thomas's schools, loads of expeditions and outings but here anything not involving overnight stay is included in the fees. Huge variety of after school clubs including athletics in the summer. Lots of charity projects too. These children are really encouraged to help others.

Thomas's Fulham

Hugon Road, London, SW6 3ES

• Pupils: 400 • Fees: £10,065-£14,625 pa • Independent

Tel: 020 7751 8200
Fax: 020 7751 8201
Email: fulham@thomas-s.co.uk
Website: www.thomas-s.co.uk/schools/fulham.html

Headmistress: Since it opened its doors in 2005, Miss Annette Dobson BEd from Homerton, Cambridge and Dyslexia Institute Certificate. Was head of Thomas's lower school in Clapham for 10 years and prior to that, class teacher at Northbridge House. Experienced, professional, approachable. Quick to put one at one's ease. Doesn't stand on ceremony. Gets down with the children in a comfy sitting area to hand out Golden Unicorns (for merit) several times a week.

Entrance: Selective so all are assessed at 3½ – 4 in January/February for September entry. Sibling policy where appropriate. Each child must be able to cope. 'Needs to relish' what school offers. At interview they are looking for children with confidence and an ability to socialise. Already oversubscribed with waiting lists. Screening tests take place in Year 1 to track progress. SENCo will alert parents to specific problems. Individual needs are catered for. Also have gifted and talented and EAL co-ordinators.

Exit: First set of Year 6 leavers in 2010. A quarter transferred into Year 7 at Thomas's Battersea. 11+ leavers went on to Wycombe Abbey, Oundle, St Catherine's Bramley, Emanuel and Wimbledon High.

Remarks: Very much part of the Thomas's stable which now consists of six schools around and about in south west and west London. Miss Dobson is keen to put her own stamp on the place while keeping to the underlying Thomas ethos and liaising on matters of syllabus. There is a good deal of coming and going between the schools and the pupils are never short of another school to play matches against. At the moment the oldest children team up with Clapham for sport. Twenty per cent of the timetable is devoted to sport – the head feels that as they are 'London kids they need sporting opportunities and space.' There are three unstructured outside playtimes a day; helps them socialise with their peers. Judo, football, ballet, art, hockey are offered as after-school activities.

Drama is always a hotspot at a Thomas's school. Collaborations with the fantastic music department which has raised orchestras, five choirs (only one where you have to be able to sing). The Green Team encourage sustainability and walking, cycling and scooting to school. Assemblies use a stimulus, with a moral theme, to encourage the children to just talk about their thoughts. Food is excellent. Ofsted declared it the best school food ever. Totally nut-free zone, even PTA meetings eschew peanuts with their drinks. Kitchen staff specifically allocated to check food for allergies and all pupils with allergies have their photographs displayed in the school office next to details of their doctor and any medication taken. The site in Hugon Road was formerly Chelsea Art College and the airy rooms with enormous windows allow light to pervade everywhere. This is particularly evident in the science labs and art room. Parents tend to be less traditional than their Clapham counterparts. Very relaxed, young, cosmopolitan – French, Spanish, Italian and American alongside the local Fulhamites. Active PTA. A good new addition to the Fulham educational scene.

Tormead School Junior School

Linked to Tormead School in the Senior section

Cranley Road, Guildford, Surrey, GU1 2JD

• Pupils: 205 girls, all day • Ages: 4-11 • Inter-denominational
• Fees: £5,685-£10,035 pa • Independent

Tel: 01483 575101
Fax: 01483 450592
Email: registrar@tormeadschool.org.uk
Website: www.tormeadschool.org.uk

Head: Since 2010, Mrs Christina Foord – also head of senior school – junior section is one of four sections in Tormead and communications between the four are obviously good. Day to day running of the junior school is by head of the department, Miss Karen Tuckwell NPQH MEd who joined the school in September 2006 having previously been deputy head of the British International School in Seoul, South Korea and, before that, director of studies at Cranleigh Prep.

Entrance: Selective entrance at four and at seven by a basic assessment test.

Exit: All the junior girls sit the entrance exam for the senior school and have priority on places over external candidates who fight it out for the remainder of places. Around 95 per cent of junior girls go on to the senior school – those who don't make the grade (although very few fail) are handled sensitively and are advised on 'a senior school better suited to their educational needs'.

Remarks: Traditional, high-achieving girls' school, situated opposite the senior school. Academically the pupils enjoy a wide curriculum very much reflecting the senior school – there is a gradual stepping up of subjects – more are added each year – and by Year 5, speech and drama plus Latin are taught as well as the usual subjects, including French and ICT. Girls are gradually prepped for the entrance exam to senior school, although everyone is keen to stress the lack of pressure – pupils included. SEN provision is on an individual need basis. School has three visiting specialists, one a dyslexia expert. Extra help given at lunchtimes, after school etc, room set aside for this purpose in junior school. Certainly not an issue for the school, and no stigma attached – pupils all very open about it.

Facilities impressive. Outside space a little lacking but no complaints from girls. Sport high on the agenda – athletics, dance, gymnastics (very big at Tormead), hockey, netball, rounders and tennis. Sports facilities are shared with the senior school (including impressive gymnasium) although space is tight at the senior school, hence no on-site pool. Lunch is also at the senior school so the girls get a taste of life over the road and feel less daunted about the transfer.

The aim is for an all-round education – 'we work hard and play hard' – and expectations are high. Everyone is encouraged to find their niche over and above the purely academic; whether it's music, sport, art or other activity, and extracurricular activities are particularly encouraged. A wide range available – some are selective e.g. chamber choir and gymnastics but all pupils are encouraged to have a go if keen, regardless of talent. The majority of girls play a musical instrument or are part of the choir.

Girls appointed prefect, librarian, games captain etc by staff and everyone gets a chance to prove themselves in these roles. Pupils don't feel intimidated by their teachers yet have a respectful attitude. Guided tour given to us by confident, articulate and bubbly pupils with obvious pride in their surroundings. All in all, an excellent academic preparation for the senior school.

Tower House Preparatory School

188 Sheen Lane, London, SW14 8LF

- Pupils: 180 boys, all day • Ages: 4-13 • Non-denom
- Fees: £9,750-£11,055 pa • Independent

Tel: 020 8876 3323
Fax: 020 8876 3321
Email: secretary@thsboys.org.uk
Website: www.thsboys.org.uk

Headmaster: Since 2009, Mr Gregory Evans MA BSc PGCE. Formerly a science teacher and thereafter a senior manager at Sussex House School in London. Is aiming to combine a traditional approach to teaching and challenging boys, with modern ideas on pedagogy. A passionate supporter of all extra-curricular activities; always makes time to be a visible presence on the touch line or helping out with the many charitable activities of the boys.

Entrance: From lots of different nursery schools mainly within couple of miles radius. Early (before first birthday) registration to guarantee place at 4+. Late applicants held on waiting list, many get in this way, 'people do move around here'. A few places can become available at 8+ and often taken by those from Falcons, Putney Park and Orchard House. Non-selective entry at 4. Short assessment in maths, English and non verbal reasoning for those joining later.

Exit: Academically wide-ranging, reflecting intake. St Paul's, King's College, Epsom College, Ibstock, Hampton, Kingston Grammar, Harrodian, Latymer Upper popular among day schools with a few to board further afield at Marlborough and Charterhouse, Abingdon, Cranleigh. Discussions about destination schools begin 'earlier and earlier out of necessity with more schools pre-testing at 11,' says head, 'we now start the process in Year 4'. Lots of support and advice given by the head.

Remarks: Small, gentle, essentially traditional (though more progressive than it used to be) all-round prep school which has always had a cosy environment and strong sense of purpose.

Split academically and physically into junior and senior schools linked by shared, rather bijou but recently updated, playground. Pressure on playground space is clearly an issue for nearly two hundred boys but they appear to make the most of it. Small area with climbing frames available for littlies and older boys encouraged to play 'gently', no bats/batons allowed. Junior school houses boys to Year 3 where every inch is maximised to give bright, quirkily-shaped classrooms each adorned with two state-of-the-art computers. Boys are taught in classes of about 18 by a class teacher and assistant. Great importance attached to 3Rs and school is noted particularly for innovative ideas to get them all reading, e.g. paired reading schemes with senior boys very popular. Senior school housed in similarly attractive, late-Victorian building. Again, space is at a premium but there is what the head describes as, 'a lovely science lab', an extensive and much-used library, amazingly large, well equipped new ICT suite, light airy loft-style art room and a large newly built hall which is used for drama and music as well as assemblies. Except for these sessions, boys remain in their own classrooms for lessons, specialist teachers coming to them.

Academically, school does well for broad spectrum of needs. Strong science and maths (setting from Year 3). End of year exams held every summer. In Years 4 and 5 CAT tests – a thorough assessment of where children are at and what can be expected of them. Incentive scheme for both work and behaviour by system of house plus and minus points, 'life's a mirror' type chat with head very productive for ironing out any concerns. Learning support for dyslexia, dyspraxia, Asperger's and ADHD from full time experienced SEN specialist. No extra cost.

Lack of on-site sports facilities, so boys bussed to fabulous Bank of England Sports Ground in Roehampton to play a range of sports that would impress many a bigger school – football, hockey, rugby, cricket, tennis, athletics and swimming (for ages 5–8 yrs). 70 per cent now learning an instrument up to grade 6, although no practice sessions are timetabled. Two active choirs, a swing band, a guitar ensemble and orchestra practise weekly after school. Tower House undertook its first ever music tour to Germany in summer 2008.

School day is longer for seniors and can include before/after school clubs – these vary according to current pupil and staff interests and can include fencing, squash, 5-a-side football, drama, chess and Greek. Child-care provision before and after school; the school is keen to be working-parent friendly. Lots of charity fundraisings, many driven by the boys – the previous head was particularly keen on responsibility coming with privilege and community awareness. Dan Phillips Award taken in Year 8 where work in the community, taking on new skills and environmental awareness are all part of the focus. Unusual with this age group.

Tregelles

Linked to Mount School (The) in the Senior section

Dalton Terrace, York, YO24 4DD

• Pupils: 130 girls and boys • Ages: 3-11 • Quaker • Fees: £5,565-£8,430 pa • Independent

Tel: 01904 667 513
Fax: 01904 667 538
Email: registrar@mountschoolyork.co.uk
Website: www.mountschoolyork.co.uk

Head: Ms Mary Anderson.

Entrance: Entrance by observation (looking for potential), supplemented at 6 by informal examination.

Exit: Most girls move up to The Mount School at the end of Year 6, boys to other independent schools in the local area.

Remarks: Has the benefit of the facilities and involvement of the senior school, from academic staff (three foreign languages are offered), music and food to mentoring by older girls. Before- and after-school care from 8.00am to 5.30pm, for an additional charge.

Trevor-Roberts School

55-57 Eton Avenue, London, NW3 3ET

• Pupils: 100 boys, 80 girls; all day • Ages: 5-13 • C of E
• Fees: £10,650-£12,600 pa • Independent

Tel: 020 7586 1444
Fax: 020 7722 0114
Email: trjunior@trevor-robertsschool.co.uk

Senior Head: Since 1999, Mr Simon Trevor-Roberts BA, son of founder Christopher Trevor-Roberts LVA, who died in 2005. Educated at Westminster School, and formerly head of the junior department. His son and daughter both attended the school, as does the daughter of his sister Amanda, who now heads the junior department. A mathematics teacher, he prepares Year 6 and Year 8 exam classes, and gives individual help both to strugglers and to those aiming at scholarships. Reticent and engaging, with the somewhat geeky air of a dedicated mathematician. 'He's brilliant at batting for the children over secondary transfers,' said a parent.

Entrance: No Reception class – 'I don't think four-year-olds should be sitting at desks. They should be playing in a sandpit.' Each intake, for reasons best known to the school, consists of children who were born in the same calendar year, so some will already be five-and-a half when they join whilst those with autumn birthdays will not yet be five. Parents generally tour the school soon after the baby's birth (not before), and the school registers the first 100 (refreshingly, no registration fee).

A year before entry, the first 50 on the list are invited for assessment. 'We show them the hens and the science lab and the fish tank,' says Amanda Trevor-Roberts, 'so they generally think it looks all right.' Each child has 10 minutes with the Year 2 teacher. 'We try to pitch the assessment at their level, whether it's using letters or looking at pictures. We're not testing or scoring – just getting to know them.' Nine boys and nine girls are offered places and generally about half of these are siblings. 'We're not trying to cream off the elite. We go for a spread of ages and a mix of personalities.'

The eccentric age range of junior classes, covering two school year age groups, is smoothed out by dividing Year 4 into two forms, joined by other children from outside. There is only one Year 5 class but the forms split again in Year 6, with those – mostly girls – who are going for the 11+ spending a term and a half concentrating on maths and English. Small intake at 11. Worth trying for places at odd moments.

Exit: Most, but not all, girls leave at 11, generally for London day schools such as Francis Holland, South Hampstead and Godolphin and Latymer. A few girls, and most boys, stay on to 13, aiming at a mix of London schools (e.g. City of London, Westminster, UCS, Mill Hill) and boarding schools (e.g. Eton, Haileybury, St Edwards, Wycombe Abbey). Most get their first choice.

Remarks: Christopher Trevor-Roberts set up the school in the early 1950s in his house in Hampstead's Vale of Health, frequently taking pupils for lunch at the local

Chinese restaurant, before relocating in 1981 to two Victorian houses in Belsize Park. He was an inspirational and much-loved teacher, and some of his former pupils' children now attend the school.

It is still determinedly individualistic and happily ready to disrupt the timetable when, for example, an Indian professor turned up at short notice with his family to take Vedic maths sessions with the top classes during our visit. 'We are fairly unencumbered by having to ask someone else's permission. Things can happen quickly.' This can also result in, for example, ad hoc backstage tours of the Royal Opera House and hockey coaching from England team members.

But the teaching methods are very traditional. 'I believe it is important to discipline children's thinking from an early stage. I want them to learn the correct methods for doing things – tools they can use later on. They need structure and guidelines. It's like learning a musical instrument – you need to know the basics before you can move on.'

Most parents feel their children are extremely well taught. 'They're very skilled at bringing out the best in the children – academically and in extra-curricular fields.' Some mention uneven teaching standards and the ISI commented on a lack of challenge for the brightest pupils, although the report also said: 'the school prepares pupils extremely well for the next stage of their education.' The school is taking advice on stretching its gifted and talented students. French throughout, Latin from Year 5 and some learn Greek in Year 8. Specialist teachers throughout, except for maths and English in the youngest classes.

The school is 'not geared up for special needs' but does take siblings in particular with a degree of dyslexia or dyspraxia. Those in need can have weekly sessions with the learning support coordinator (at no extra charge – everything is included in fees except the Mandarin club) and the school works with outside specialists. 'It's mostly about getting children to recognise their difficulties, and giving them the tools to deal with them.'

Strong anti-competitive ethos – children are not ranked in order and are rewarded for effort as much as achievement. 'They make them feel good about themselves rather than concerned about where they are in class.' This spills over into sport. The older forms have a 10 minute PE session in the playground after assembly each day, Year 3 upwards swims at Swiss Cottage baths, and there's a games lesson once a week on the small soft-surface pitch behind the senior school. But while pupils can play sport on Primrose Hill on Wednesday and Friday afternoons, equally they can join the choir, orchestra or art group. 'Football tends to be the default activity if you're not musical.' The head, with unpleasant memories of competitive sport from his own schooldays, wants his pupils to look on games as a pleasant release. The school does play occasional matches against other preps but teams are chosen with an endearing disregard for ability and they invariably lose.

Christopher Trevor-Roberts was passionate about music, as is his daughter Amanda, and it still plays a large part in the life of the school (though class music lessons are squeezed out of the timetable in the top two years by the demands of Common Entrance). The head of music is a professional singer and composer. As well as the orchestra and choir, there are jazz, brass and guitar groups. Talented young teachers come in to give instrumental lessons, and there are frequent concerts.

Performance is an integral part of school life. Pupils recite poems, play instruments and sing songs in assembly. Each class puts on two plays a year, and everyone has a speaking part. Main roles rotate so everyone gets a chance to star. 'It becomes normal for them to perform in public. The confidence they get stays with them for life.' Inspirational art displayed in bright top-floor art-room, with a kiln room next door; the head of art is always a practising artist. 'Much better than employing someone who is very good at teaching but has no love for the subject.'

Kind, caring, uncompetitive ethos. 'Because it's so small, they really do know everyone and take care of everyone,' said a parent. Another commented that the children like and respect their teachers, and look out for each other. 'But some of the older ones can begin to push the boundaries, and it can get rather wild after Common Entrance,' said a parent, though the school comments that play rehearsals and outings always fill the last few weeks of term. Rewards are more conspicuous than sanctions; awards in assembly, to much applause, for hard work, improvement, taking part.

'It's an extraordinary mixture of old-fashioned prep school with a trendy, media-friendly feel,' said a parent. Informal semi-uniform of polo shirt and sweatshirt. No great social or ethnic mix; a few glitterati families, plus a fairly homogenous lot of professional families from a wide area of North London.

Small, family-run school with an individualistic ethos that gives a firm academic grounding in a genuinely non-competitive and unpressurised atmosphere. Not the place for the rough-and-tumble rugby fanatic but most children will thrive in the friendly surroundings. 'They're given confidence and they're happy,' said a parent.

Tring Park School for the Performing Arts Preparatory School

Linked to Tring Park School For The Performing Arts in the Senior section

Tring Park, Tring, Hertfordshire, HP23 5LX

- Pupils: Boarding and day places for boys and girls. • Ages: 8-11
- Fees: Boarding £20,070; Day £12,600 pa • Independent

Tel: 01442 824 255
Fax: 01442 891 069
Email: info@tringpark.com
Website: www.tringpark.com

Remarks: See main school.

Truro High School Preparatory Department

Linked to Truro High School in the Senior section

Falmouth Road, Truro, Cornwall, TR1 2HU

• Pupils: 105 day girls; 6 boarders (from 7+); 6 boys in nursery • Ages: 3-11 • C of E • Fees: Boarding £18,390-£18,615; Day £6,075-£9,489 pa • Independent

Tel: 01872 272830
Fax: 01872 279393
Email: admin@trurohigh.co.uk
Website: www.trurohigh.co.uk

Head: Since 2002, Mrs Alison Miller BSc PGCE (forties) educated at North London Collegiate School before reading psychology at Manchester. Married with two sons. Early career in business then PGCE in primary education at Bristol Poly before teaching first at a Cornish primary and later Truro High. Rated as 'a great team leader,' she clearly loves what she does and is respected in all quarters: 'sets very high standard and shows respect for children's opinions,' say satisfied parents.

Entrance: By application, then stress free taster day for girls to get to know the place and for head to make an informal assessment as to suitability.

Exit: Girls transfer to senior school seamlessly although all sit entrance exam to determine setting etc. Ninety per cent move down a corridor they already know well by the time they leave Year 6.

Remarks: Lovely, safe setting for nursery and reception at Trevean: a separate complex with its own hard and grass outside areas. Plenty of apparatus for imaginative play, climbing and swinging. Room for up to twenty tots per session in current building but extension is planned to allow for an increase. Lovely feel to accommodation: safe and exciting all in one. Switched on, specialist staff to get young minds and limbs off to a happy start. Reception class make good headway with reading (incorporate various approaches including synthetic phonics) and lots of different number work. Changing topics throughout the year with classroom displays and activities to match. Close contact with parents through diaries etc to monitor progress with individual readers.

Years 1 and 2 enjoy large classrooms for the comparatively small numbers: amazing pupil:teacher ratio which enables pre-prep girls to make rapid headway. IT used in classrooms plus head teaches in specialist suite for Year 3 upwards. Topic based work combines humanities and other disciplines. Older girls also benefit from some teaching by senior specialists and use facilities in senior school for science, art, food and nutrition plus games (even joining senior teams where appropriate).

Reading culture obvious here with a separate and well used junior library. Academic atmosphere in older classes where girls can gain confidence in their abilities. One parent we spoke to transferred his daughter after a local primary had 'given up on her.' After some initial learning support, she is now making 'thrilling' progress and thriving on all the extra-curricular opportunities. Head hands over to Year 6 girls during part of annual prize-giving to give a Powerpoint presentation of the year's activities. No gawkiness – just happy girls who enjoy working as much as playing. 'Golden time' rewards on Friday afternoons when younger girls get to do their favourite things. Girls are allocated to one of four houses (all linked to Cornish benefactors) in prep and remain in the same house through the senior school. Good sized hall accommodates the 100+ children here for assemblies (they join seniors once a week). Tinies first into senior dining room for lunch. Healthy snacks at other times: e.g. before clubs meet after school. Wide range of activities at lunchtime. Tiered reward system with gongs for top achievers. School council meets twice termly. Amazing standard of music with high percentage having individual tuition. Junior choir particularly keen. Separate plays produced for older (currently *Snow White*) and younger ('tea towel' nativity) contingents at Christmas. Lots take LAMDA examinations. Parents fully involved in helping where appropriate – Friends of Truro High recently raised over £700 in three hours at a fun day. Pick up times are staggered to avoid congestion at end of school day. Boarding available from Year 3 upwards for the far flung.

Parents recognise that what they get here is a great deal more than academic results (which come more or less as a given). Nurturing atmosphere, caring and communicative staff who produce great results.

Truro School Prep

Linked to Truro School in the Senior section

Treliske, Highertown, Truro, Cornwall, TR1 3QN

• Pupils: 225; 130 boys and 95 girls; all day • Ages: prep 7-11, nursery and pre-prep 3-7 • Methodist • Fees: £7,395-£10,185 pa • Independent

Tel: 01872 243120
Fax: 01872 222 377
Email: jeg@truroschool.com
Website: www.truroprep.com

Head: Since 2004, Matthew Lovett (forties). Educated at Habedashers' Aske's and Exeter university (BA Ed). Discovered a wanderlust and journeyed under its influence to Spain (head of science and ICT at St Anne's), thence to Banda School, Kenya. Came home. Head of Forest Prep at the absurdly young age of 31, whence to Truro. Strong thespian tendencies – has strutted the boards, sometimes semi-professionally. Instantly recognisable by trademark braces (red when we visited). Has been a force for change since his arrival, arguably not too soon. A listener, they say, and his own man, he puts his foot down firmly and fairly. Possesses, they reckon, the authority and diplomacy required to bring about necessary change. Energetic, levels with you, quick to tune to your wavelength. Into choral singing, gardening, photography and playing cricket with like-minded and similarly hopeful but hopeless players. Married to Laura. Three young children.

Entrance: Entry to the nursery and pre-prep via application, thereafter automatically to the prep. To the prep at age 7 by written exam, report, interview and day spent in the school. Automatic admission from pre-prep.

Exit: All at age 11. Almost all to Truro school, some to senior schools up country. It's getting more difficult to pass the senior school entry exam, a source of some teeth-gnashing. For boys who fall short, Kelly College. For some girls the High School provides a safety net. Progression to Truro School is by head's recommendation.

Remarks: Delicious, semi-secret location at the end of a winding, rhododendron bordered drive. Small manor house built to last forever by a tin miner made good but he sank every last penny into it and was bankrupted. Tragic. Other school buildings good, mostly – the odd portakabin but children like those. Sports hall and swimming pool. Classrooms well presented, tidy and all with recent displays. Purpose-built nursery and pre-prep set slightly apart. Fine playing fields and swathes of woodland. A most attractive spot.

Academically, parents give it a clean bill of health. Until the arrival of Mr Lovett the tendency seems to have been to lionise the best and somewhat to overlook the rest. All change. Indeed, in all things this is now a much kinder, more inclusive school – 'if they're not brilliant academics we try and bring them out in other ways, find out what they're good at', says Mr Lovett. The departure of some old-school teachers has helped, as has their replacement by bright young things with here-and-now, professionalised glints in their eyes. For children who reveal special needs there is specialised help but you can see that what Mr Lovett thinks they need most to be egged on, urged to be daring, and rewarded frequently. It's both an effective and laudable remedial strategy. Some specialist teaching in Year 3 and all specialist teaching from Years 4 to 6. No testing till KS1 at age seven, and only then. Around a third of teachers are male, an unusually high percentage in what's becoming a feminised business. Mr Lovett is determined to maintain this.

Sport tremendously important as you might expect but parents say, 'it is more balanced these days'. Previously, the less good didn't get much of a look in but in the Lovett era we have B teams and we may not be brilliant but we get to play for our school and have people cheer us on. A quirk of the school is its excellence in sabre fencing – here you discover the litter from which most of the England under-12 squad is picked. Growing list of after-school activities.

The arts are thriving as a result of closer ties with the senior school. Drama good, art good, music on the way up. All children learn an instrument in Year 4 and can borrow one for a year to see if they're any good at it.

Stern criticism by some parents of the harshness of the ancien regime serves to highlight changes and mark progress towards kindness and proper focus on the individuality of each pupil. Parents say that Mr Lovett has not been a winnowing wind but has, rather, 'made changes subtly, sensibly, not disjointedly'. Others talk now of 'the same strong sense of community and mutual support you get at the senior school'. It's also much more fun, of course. Lunch here may well be the best in the UK. All food locally sourced, meat from a local organic farm, cooked with huge pride. And, they'll have you know – 'we've been doing this since before Jamie Oliver'.

Parents are not spoiled for choice down here when it comes to choosing a prep school. It is appropriate that Truro offers educational breadth. Emphasis on humanity has unquestionably brightened eyes and enhanced its effectiveness.

Twickenham Preparatory School

Beveree, 43 High Street, Hampton, Middlesex, TW12 2SA

• Pupils: 270; 50/50 boys and girls; all day • Ages: 4-13 • Families do not have to be practising Christians but the school has a strong Christian ethos • Fees: £8,490-£0-£9,180 pa • Independent

Tel: 020 8979 6216
Fax: 020 8979 1596
Email: office@twickenhamprep.co.uk
Website: www.twickenhamprep.co.uk

Head: Since 2005, Mr David Malam BA Hons, Southampton, (history), PGCE King Alfred's College, Winchester. Taught in junior and first schools in the Southampton area before working at Lagos International School, Cyprus, teaching ages 7–16. Married with five young children, four of whom are at the school. Enjoys all sports, especially football and squash, and has played chess at high level.

Entrance: Children on the Reception entry list are guaranteed a place. Other places in the school are on an occasional basis and subject to an assessment test in English, maths and reasoning.

Exit: Vast majority to a variety of local independent day schools and only occasionally to boarding schools (e.g. Sherborne). Boys mostly stay to 13 and many go to Hampton, Kingston Grammar, St James's, Ashford, Reeds, Halliford or St George's, Weybridge. Girls leave at 11, many for The Lady Eleanor Holles, Surbiton High, Kingston Grammar, Sir William Perkins's, Claremont Fan Court and Arts Educational. One music scholarship 2007, top academic scholarship to Hampton 2010, all-rounder to Reeds 2009 and scholarship to Lady Eleanor Holles 2010.

Remarks: Not a hothouse for the bright but a place where everyone is encouraged and helped to do their best. An all-round school, which aims to give every child a chance to take part in as many activities as possible, rather than dividing children according to ability (except where necessary).

Main school is housed (since 1992) in a handsome building which has been adapted well. The old building has recently been refurbished and interactive whiteboards have been introduced into all classrooms. Pre-prep is a lovely modern, purpose-built building with small but charming outdoor areas set apart for the young ones. What a pleasant change to see the youngest pupils housed in the smartest buildings, instead of in tacky temporary ones. Classrooms are just big enough and there is adequate space and facilities for art and science. Both rooms have been recently refurbished to a high standard. Outdoor space for the main school is limited but they have walking access to a large sports field for football etc.

Curriculum is as you'd expect in a prep school; specialist teaching for each subject after pre-prep. 'Standards are constantly improving,' said one parent, 'though they don't rest on their laurels.' RE is taught from the Bible alongside a programme about other faiths for older pupils. Classes are fairly small (18) and are mixed gender and ability, apart from setting for maths.

School has a website and ICT is very strongly used across the curriculum as evidenced by work on display. Computer suite has one terminal per child and they begin to learn computer skills in reception and continue to have timetabled lessons throughout the school. Music is strength – 'it has come on in leaps and bounds,' a longstanding parent said, with lots of individual tuition going on in separate buildings. In line with the ethos of the school, the annual concert is not just for these children – everyone takes part. Similarly, school or class plays have a role for all.

Sports teams play competitively but there will always be a C or D team so everyone can represent the school at some time (wish more prep schools followed this example). In such a small school, sport organised in this way is not going to lead to winning many competitions, 'but when I see them playing cricket I'm still very proud,' a mother remarked. Extra-curricular sport is offered in after school clubs as is a range of other activities – most successful is chess – school regularly appears in the local paper after winning chess tournaments. U11 IAPS National Chess Champions. One mother mentioned how disappointed her daughter was when she couldn't join the oversubscribed maths club run by a particularly strong teacher, 'but there are clubs every day,' she added.

Children are well-behaved and 'on task' in the classroom. Welcoming atmosphere almost tangible – from one's initial phone call to the school onwards. 'The community feeling is what attracted us,' one parent said. 'It's very family orientated,' said another, who added, 'I feel that I can go and discuss anything with my son's teacher.' At a recent governors' meeting, parents were invited to attend and voice any concerns but none turned up. When asked why, they reportedly said that they didn't have any.

There is a strong sense in the school that everyone is trying hard to do well and will be helped to achieve but if an Eton scholarship is what you have in mind this may not be the place for you – you'll be the only one heading in that direction. On the other hand, if you are looking for the small classes and the extras that no state primary school can give you, but still want the non-competitive atmosphere of an all round, local, mixed school – Twickenham Prep might suit very well.

Twyford School

High Street, Twyford, Winchester, Hampshire, SO21 1NW

• Pupils: 260 in prep school (a third girls); mostly day with some weekly- and flexi-boarding. 115 in pre-prep (over half girls) • Ages: pre-prep 3-7; prep 7-13 • C of E • Fees: Nursery - Y3 £4,227-£7,674; Prep: £11,550-£15,024; Boarding £18,924 pa • Independent

Tel: 01962 712 269
Fax: 01962 712 100
Email: registrar@twyfordschool.com
Website: www.twyfordschool.com

Head: From 2010, Dr Steve Bailey BEd PhD FRSA, formerly taught history at Winchester College and was housemaster for 11 years. He holds an international reputation as a historian of sport and the Olympic Games and is a Fellow of the Royal Society of Arts. Author of six books, and a Research Fellow of the International Olympic Committee. A keen sportsman – county and southern England hockey player – and enjoys tennis, water polo and surfing. His wife, Paula, has been involved in running Morsheads House and has an MSc in health psychology. She taught information and computer technology in Winchester since 1983 and is also a specialist teacher of boys and girls who have specific learning difficulties. They have three school age children, two boys and a girl.

Entrance: Children come for a half day informal assessment in the November before they are due to enter the school. Threshold for passing this not too high – 'academically average and above'. Will always try to accommodate siblings. Most pupils live within a 30 mile drive of the school.

Exit: Half to Winchester College, Canford and King Edward VI (Southampton). The rest all over but mainly to Bedales, Bradfield, Harrow, Marlborough, Radley, Sherborne, Sherborne Girls', St Swithun's, Wellington, Wycombe Abbey and Winchester state schools. Good news on the scholarship front, especially for academics and music. Over the past three years scholarships and awards have included academic, sport, music, design and art.

Remarks: Happy, high-achieving school – 'calm but whizzy,' says the head – but no longer offering full boarding. 'We were a seven-day-a-week boarding school with very few seven-day-a-week boarders,' says the head. In 2005 Twyford bit the bullet and moved to weekly and flexi-boarding only. The school retains its boarding ethos and continues, in the main, to behave like a boarding animal, with most pupils doing some boarding in the final two years. Best things about boarding according to the children – 'being with friends and Wednesday evening barbecues in the summer!' Worst – 'having to get up earlier than I did when I lived 20 minutes away!' No mobile phones. Taffies (tuck) twice a week. Boarding accommodation newly refurbished. Overseas pupils and children of expats will now be housed with guardians on Saturday and Sunday nights.

Interesting place – goes back to the middle of the 17th century and lays claim to being the oldest 'proper' prep school in the country. Converted to its current C of E foundation for the 'sons of Middle Class Persons' in 1809. Wonderful list of OBs, including composer Hubert Parry, Douglas Hurd and Thomas Hughes, author of Tom Brown's Schooldays. Alexander Pope (who wrote The Rape of the Lock) spent a year at Twyford, where he wrote 'a satire on some faults of his master,' which led to his being 'whipped and ill-used ... and taken from thence on that account.' Pupils from a relatively wide social mix. 'Not everyone is stinking rich,' said a mum.

Inscrutably complex setting/streaming system. Evening tutorials for serious scholarship hopefuls – discussing unfathomables like ethics and evolution. Class sizes average 14 to 17. Science taken seriously, Latin for all from Year 5. French from the start. The school is 'not set up for lower ability children'. Some 20 pupils receive extra tuition – for mild dyslexia, revision technique, maths struggles. Two or three with moderate SpLD requirements. Prep done at school; day pupils home at 6pm. Much investment in IT.

Top-class art department and evidence of pupils' work on walls all over the school. Small art display room – a lovely space and unusual for a prep. Drama provision increased over last few years. Year 8 have Shakespeare Week with a professional theatre company once exams have finished. Music exceptionally strong – two children have reached grade 8 on their instruments in each of the last few years and many more have reached grade 7. 83 per cent of pupils learn at least one instrument and there are three choirs, a jazz band, orchestra, many ensembles, 20 concerts a year, unusual instruments taught (harp!). Large, light music room with soundproof studio, overlooking playing fields, below which squats an open-air amphitheatre. Pleasant 20-acre country site close to Winchester, which includes the original old school hall (wood panelling and echoes of centuries of schoolboys). Religion informal, with a mix of visiting speakers in the charming chapel. Dining hall with long tables and benches – anyone can sit anywhere but pupils must ask to leave table.

Everyone plays on a team in Year 3. Six acres of extra sports fields, so all play major sports. The A teams are chosen by the sports coach based on merit, end of story – 'even I can't change the selection!' says the head. Very bad behaviour = being dropped from the team = 'leads to some interesting scenes in the car park.' Excellent swimming pool and sports hall. Brand new Astroturf pitch for hockey and football. Strong on boys' games, especially cricket. 'Court cricket', Twyford's very own invention, is a summer obsession. Girls' sport also humming with two age groups reaching the national netball finals in recent years. Dance (ballet, tap and modern) offered as an extra.

Pastoral care 'amazing' say parents and the matron 'deserves a knighthood'. Eternal vigilance on bullying. Revamped house system with lots of competitions (sport, music, public speaking, Easter egg decorating, boat building). Pupils cheerful, bouncy and informally attired. Parents emphasize the importance of staying to age 13 – 'you're not the finished product unless you finish the cycle.' Even the mighty St Swithun's – who used to scare parents into removing their daughters at 11 – has learned to accept this. A well-thought-out school from tip to toe.

Pre-prep with its own identity and not all children go on to Twyford. Children may start from the September following their third birthday. Two classes of 16 children per year group. Year 3 now in prep school which has three forms per year group. Pleasant classrooms and own hall for assemblies, dance etc. Large play area, very nice if you don't mind the traffic noise. Learning support teacher helps the 'most and least able'.

The Unicorn School (Abingdon)

20 Marcham Road, Abingdon, Oxfordshire, OX14 1AA

• Pupils: 48 (37 boys and 11 girls), all day pupils • Ages: 6-13
• Fees: £14,820 pa • Independent

Tel: 01235 530 222
Fax: 01235 536 889
Email: info@unicorndyslexia.co.uk
Website: www.unicorndyslexia.co.uk

Head: Since 2004, Mrs Jackie Vaux MA (Oxon), BSc psychology (fifties). Joined Unicorn in 1998 as special needs co-ordinator from state sector. Modern languages graduate St Catherine's, Oxford, husband an Oxford medical tutor, four grown-up children. Very open and enthusiastic with energy to spare and to share. Hugely supportive of highly dedicated staff and derives immense pleasure from pupils' progress. (During our visit, one boy read out a poem he'd written, prompting this response from the head – 'you have no idea what a great personal achievement that was. It's wonderful.') Big plans for the future, which have governors' full support, include some expansion as have now reached capacity on current site. But head quick to point out, 'we would not change the nature of the school. We're like a family.'

Entrance: All pupils must have report from educational psychologist identifying moderate to severe dyslexia as primary need or alternatively, dyspraxia, dyscalculia or speech and language difficulties. Some referred from primary or prep schools, most contact though initiated by anxious parents who see their children under-achieving and floundering in schools without the specialist skills or facilities. Entry on first come first served basis. Demand for places very high in Years 5 and 6 when learning difficulties normally identified.

Exit: Pupils expected to stay between one and three years. School's stated aim is 'to try to give all the appropriate help needed to address literacy and numeracy difficulties as quickly as possible so that he or she can return to mainstream education.' Places sought at known supportive schools and parents given plenty of help and advice in finding the right one for them. Popular choices include Pangbourne College (near Reading), Bartholomew's (Eynsham), Larkmead (Abingdon), Leckford Place in Oxford and Sibford School (Oxon.)

Remarks: A small but vital school which does wonders with its children. Founded in 1991 with just five pupils, demand has forced it to grow quickly and keep moving to larger premises. It now leases a large Edwardian house near the centre of the town with good playgrounds. The classrooms aren't huge, but there's no need as there are seldom more than 10 youngsters in them at any one time. Rooms are well fitted out with computers and interactive whiteboards in all, plus an IT suite with interactive whiteboard. Also small one-to-one tuition rooms. Lessons in numeracy and literacy held in mornings when children at their most receptive, also every child given at least 30 minutes individual teaching a day. Rest of timetable is along National Curriculum lines – including humanities, science, DT, drama, French and ICT – but tailored to specific needs. Touch-typing taught from day one. All classes very hands-on and children encouraged to develop their strengths as much as strengthen their weaknesses. SATs are taken but marked internally. Also extra exam time allowed where necessary. Teaching staff of 22, all specialists so appropriate help can be given. Children given free rein to express themselves but within disciplined and well-structured environment. Head recognises self-esteem likely to be very low and sense of failure high when new pupils arrive so much effort spent on rebuilding confidence first and foremost. 'Children are never put in a position where they could fail here,' says head.

Four sports periods a week – football, hockey, touch rugby, sailing and swimming. After-school clubs include art, shooting, cookery, sports. Lawns and hard play areas to use at break. PE hall and larger sports field thanks to Abingdon School. Unicorn's long term aim to be Centre of Excellence for dyslexia. Saturday morning school currently running for parents whose children need significant help with literacy or maths but can't afford private tuition. Staffed by qualified specialists and already proving great success. Also, established outreach programme in local state schools and independent schools.

Unicorn now building up capital to fund annual bursary. High teacher:pupil ratio ensures high standards of pastoral care. Children know where to turn for help and recently completed questionnaire as part of anti-bullying campaign. Vulnerable areas swiftly identified and corrected. Very supportive network of parents. Those questioned could not praise school highly enough. Said one, 'I don't know what we'd have done without it. It's been a life-saver.'

Unicorn School (Richmond)

238 Kew Road, Richmond, Surrey, TW9 3JX

• Pupils: 170, all day, roughly 50:50 boys and girls (including 22 part-time places in nursery) • Ages: 3-11 • Non-denom • Fees: £8,835-£9,870 pa • Independent

Tel: 020 8948 3926
Fax: 020 8332 6814
Email: registrar@unicornschool.org.uk
Website: www.unicornschool.org.uk

Head: Since 2004, Mrs Roberta Linehan BA PGCE (fifties). She came to the school (highly recommended both formally and informally according to one parent) from Danes Hill Prep in Oxshott where she was a deputy head and she has also worked in an international school in Hong Kong, Lady Eleanor Holles and Tiffin Girls. Very smiley and welcoming, she comes across as open and capable. No-one (parents, pupils, staff) has a bad word to say about Mrs Linehan, including the inspectors who've given her their seal of approval. Teaches Year 6 once a week, visits every class on Monday morning and greets parents and children at the front door of the school most days.

Entrance: Very popular school so names down at birth for entrance at age three, at other times from the long waiting list according to availability. Siblings take priority, often leaving just a relatively small number of places for new families, which will be allocated 'at the discretion of the headmistress'. One mother advised, 'my top tip would be to persist – keep ringing and asking – at the last minute we got a place.' Non-selective at nursery but for entry at six children will have an interview and/or informal tests.

Exit: To all the major London day schools including Emanuel, Godolphin & Latymer, Hampton, King's College Wimbledon, Lady Eleanor Holles, Latymer Upper School, Notting Hill & Ealing, St Benedict's, St Paul's Girls' and Colet Court. Also boarding schools such as Bedales and Downe House. In 2008 four academic, one drama and two music scholarships were awarded to children in a class of 16.

Remarks: A favourite with the chattering classes of south west London, the school comes up with the goods academically but with the trump card of a nurturing and creative atmosphere. Bang opposite Kew Gardens, Unicorn was founded in 1970 by a group of parents who couldn't find the type of education they were looking for elsewhere. Now run as a non-profit making company – one parent from each family becomes a member when their child joins the school. 'We could get a horrible shock if the roof fell in, as fees are adjusted according to spend,' said one father. But generally it is not an issue. Parents also loan the school £2,500 per family (regardless of how many children they have there) payable the term before admission. Realistically, you will not get much (if any) negative feedback from parents who own a school. 'It is a wonderful school where the children are well-motivated and made interested in what they are learning,' says one mother. Another equally positive soul adds, 'it is friendly, fun and creatively stimulating with a really caring ethos.'

Occupies a large three-storey Victorian house and a separate coach house, linked by a small, but well-equipped, playground. Newly acquired and landscaped 'quiet garden' has almost doubled the outdoor space, although overall the site remains small and more boisterous children might struggle to let off steam. Unicorn is homely rather than flashy and much of it has recently been refurbished, particularly the school hall and a new, well-equipped specialist music room. Visitors won't be bowled over by the facilities – 'but it is all there, they have everything they need – it is just not as pretty and impressive as some of the competition,' says one parent. Classrooms are small but visually stimulating with lovely displays all around. Less impressive is a new, rather narrow, design and technology room.

Academically impressive – children do well but are not pressured. Last SATs results: 96 per cent level 5s at Key Stage 2, with 100 per cent in English. Not sitting SATs in 2009. Yet, despite very creditable results, several parents said that they had chosen the school because it is not massively academic. 'I don't think it is for real high-fliers,' said one mother. The head disagrees (as you would expect). Another parent added, 'too many schools view results as the be-all and end-all – here you get a richer, more rounded education.' Staff are described as 'spot-on' with one mother commenting, 'you feel they have a good handle on your child from day one'. Pupils are attentive in class, working at different speeds and frequently assessed. Class size 22 and the school is very keen on equipping them with learning strategies and thinking skills. French from age five. Parents praise special needs provision.

Not the school for a seriously sporty child (the head does not agree – 'there are seriously sporty children at the school who thrive') – there are no playing fields and team performances in traditional sports are not top of the league table stuff. 'Newsletters contain reports of plucky rather than winning performances,' laughs one mother. However the children are bussed five minutes down the road to the Old Deer Park in Richmond for sports – mainly football, rugby and netball in the winter and the usual summer sports. And every Thursday afternoon the junior children go to clubs – badminton, cookery, carpentry, sailing and horse riding, among lots of other choices.

A rather arty cohort of parents is attracted by the strong focus on arts and music, which is described as 'fantastic.' There are regular and impressive assemblies, drama productions and music concerts. Many children start by learning the recorder and almost two thirds of the pupils learn at least one other instrument, some very successfully including music scholarships awarded by Putney High, Emanuel, Westminster Under School, Latymer and

Hampton in the last few years. Gorgeous artwork displays line the walls and on the day of our visit, some of the infant children were literally hurling paint to create a giant firework picture.

Older children have lots of involvement with the younger ones – partly because the school is small and everyone is rather thrust together, but also purposely, with Year 6 children coming into the infant classes to read stories and act as monitors. 'The children get to know each other very well, very quickly,' said a mother 'and they are all taught to be concerned about each other – it creates a really lovely caring atmosphere.' There are currently 12 second generation 'Unicorns' in the school as former pupils choose it for their own children. One mother summed up the appeal of the place – 'when I first toured the school my over-riding impression was of how nice the children were and I thought I would be really proud and happy for my children to be like them.' The school benefits from lots of parental involvement. 'Actors, directors, choreographers, writers and producers all share their experiences with the children, making everyday life so much more alive and interesting,' said one mother. On a more pedestrian level, there are also plenty of the usual opportunities to get involved in helping in class and at clubs. 'You could be there all day if you wanted to,' said one slightly weary-sounding mother. Rotas posted outside all the classrooms – 'you are always being asked for something and it can be hard on working mums.'

Happy, confident children with good social skills (as well as impressive academic results). Good impressions of the head. Not a place for the parent who wants to remain detached from their children's education or for the boisterous child who wants acres of space to let off steam.

University College School Junior School

Linked to Phoenix School in the Junior section

Linked to University College School in the Senior section

11 Holly Hill, London, NW3 6QN

• Pupils: 230 boys; all day • Ages: 7-11; pre-prep (The Phoenix School, a separate entity) 3-7 • Non-denom • Fees: £14,280 pa • Independent

Tel: 020 7435 3068
Fax: 020 7435 7332
Email: juniorbranch@ucs.org.uk
Website: www.ucs.org.uk

Head: Mr Kevin J Douglas BA Cert Ed; also works as a schools inspector – 'it keeps you on the ball'. Taught at QE Boys and then at Belmont for 19 years, the last 10 as deputy head. Married with three daughters. 'He's very involved, very approachable,' said a parent.

Entrance: Some 170 applicants for 48 places at seven and 12 at eight. At the initial assessment, in the autumn term, staff hear boys read – 'we're looking for two years above chronological age' – then read them a story and ask them questions in groups. Meanwhile, the head takes parents on a tour of the school, 'to make sure they want us'. Confident readers are asked back for English, maths and non-verbal reasoning tests in the spring term, with attention also paid to how they interact in groups.

The main feeder pre-preps tend to be The Phoenix, Mulberry House, Golders Hill School and Hampstead Hill School. Although The Phoenix is the UCS pre-prep, applicants take the same entrance test as everyone else. 'All things being equal they'll get a place. But they must be able to cope.'

Exit: Virtually all to the senior school, without taking the entrance exam. 'If a boy is really struggling we'll talk to his parents – but that has only happened once whilst I've been here.'

Remarks: Compact site tucked away at the top of Hampstead behind the Everyman cinema with views across London from every classroom. Nice boy-friendly science lab with tarantulas and poisonous frogs, which doubles as recording studios where boys can come in to write and record songs at lunchtime (an apprenticeship, no doubt, for the rock band culture of the senior school).

Art, woodwork and cookery rooms, all well-used: plenty of time here for creative activities. Some impressive photography displayed: came third in the Prep School Photographer of the Year competition. Smallish rubber surface playground/football pitch; boys play rugby, football, cricket and hockey at the senior school grounds in West Hampstead. Also use the senior school swimming pool and theatre and have concerts in the great hall. Giant chess set in the playground; the Under 11 team recently won the National Schools gold award.

Does not have to prepare boys for Common Entrance, so no huge academic pressure – can spend less time on maths and English and more on other activities. Relaxed pace. Undoubtedly some parents feel that their children are not stretched academically and some complain of lack of homework, though the latest Independent Schools Inspectorate report (following a bad inspection previously) praised standards. 'I think we've turned it round,' says the head.

Happy to accept able boys with physical disabilities. 'If they're bright and can cope I'll take anyone,' says the head. 'They've been amazing helping with all his needs,' said the parent of one disabled boy. Full-time school nurse who 'knows all the boys and is involved in their personal development'. Two part-time SEN teachers.

Warm, friendly atmosphere. 'It's a very happy school,' said a parent.

Vinehall School

Mountfield, Robertsbridge, East Sussex, TN32 5JL

• Pupils: 350 pupils of whom 100 in pre-prep and kindergarten and 250 in prep. Boy/girl ratio roughly 60/40 • Ages: 2-13 • C of E (with provision for Roman Catholics and other faiths) • Fees: Boarding £17,970; Day £13,770; Pre-prep £7,800 pa • Independent

Tel: 01580 880 413
Fax: 01580 882 119
Email: office@vinehallschool.com
Website: www.vinehallschool.com

Head: From 2011, Mr Richard Follett (late thirties) BA PGCE Dip Sp Psych. Previously housemaster at Pangbourne College. His wife Jo will teach in the school and their two daughters will join the school at the same time as their parents thus completing the family atmosphere.

Entrance: Most children either join the nursery in their third year or reception two years later – via an informal meeting and taster day. Partly selective as it is a fairly competitive environment and they want children who can cope with Common Entrance. Vinehall requires a fair bit of conformity. Small intake at age nine and occasionally some spaces higher up the school – have to sit a test and attend a visiting day.

Exit: To a wide range of local schools, the most popular being Tonbridge, Eastbourne, Benenden, King's Canterbury, St Leonard's Mayfield, Sevenoaks, Battle Abbey and increasingly to Cranbrook plus a few further afield to e.g. Eton and Winchester. A few girls leave at 11 but this is not encouraged. They do not actively prepare children for the 11 plus grammar school entrance exam but have incorporated verbal reasoning into the curriculum. Children are, however, prepared for the Cranbrook entrance exam at 13 plus.

Remarks: Founded in 1938, the school is centred round a large country house set in 47 acres of the East Sussex countryside It has a very light and airy and purposeful feel to it. The front hall and staircase are lined with shields which tell the story of every child who has attended the school. Much silverware and children's artwork also in evidence. A very glossy and shiny school with excellent facilities which takes itself seriously. Purpose built pre-prep and nursery schools.

Proud of its scholarship record – art and music as well as academic. 23 awards in 2008. Major academic scholarship to Sevenoaks in 2008. Setting in some subjects but the scholars are catered for within their own year group – they are streamed from Year 6. Staff a stable team – no trouble attracting good teachers. Top ICT: computers, smartboards, interactive whiteboards, intranet, and the library bristles with new computers. The school can cater for mild special needs, but would not suit someone who struggles academically unless they are very gifted at music, art or sport.

Day children start at 8.20am, after-school clubs end variably. Saturday morning school ends at 12.35pm – matches on two Saturdays per term but most of them are on Wednesdays. Sport a high profile activity. Girls play netball, hockey, lacrosse (as a club option) and rounders and the boys play rugby, cricket, hockey and soccer. All can do swimming, athletics, gymnastics, cross country running, judo, archery, riding, tennis and golf – virtually everyone who wants to can play in a team. Hooray!

Music strong – most play an instrument, two orchestras and several smaller ensemble groups. Lots of musical evenings. Very well equipped art department plus design technology, carpentry, textiles, pottery etc. Drama is also a major feature of school life: five or six productions each year. Plenty of opportunities for children to learn to speak in public by reading in assembly and chapel as well as music and poetry evenings. All regularly prepare English Speaking Board presentations.

Lots of extra-curricular activities – after school clubs, school trips, camping expeditions, cultural visits and visits abroad.

Although the academic standards are high, this not a hothouse. The school believes that its purpose is to discover the children's talents and nurture them as best it can. The school caters for the all-round child with a great emphasis on happiness and the development of a sense of self. A code of conduct known as 'The Vinehall Way' is used to promote thoughtful, caring behaviour. There are awards not just for merit but for kindness and consideration as well, as is borne out by the school motto 'to do our best for the benefit of others'. It does produce children who are extremely self confident but not precocious, and ready to face the challenges of their next schools. There is a strong sense of community and the children who showed us round were extremely proud of their school. It is a great school as long as you are good at something. The food is good with some of the finest chocolate brownies in East Sussex!

Predominantly a day school with 50-60 full time boarders with flexiboarding a very popular option. Mr and Mrs Caithness, the houseparents, provide a cosy family environment for the boarders and most of the top year ask to board. Plenty to do at weekends with special outings arranged.

A number of pupils on means-tested bursaries from the Vinehall Foundation.

Mostly happy parents – a broad mix, many from business, the media and medicine and a number of first time buyers. Mainly local, lots commute to London, some Services children and some high achieving foreign nationals. High priority given to communication with home. Parents are able to communicate with staff on a daily basis plus parents' information evenings. The emailed weekly newsletter 'Vinelines' provides constant links with the life of the school. Parental involvement very much encouraged, various social activities organised by the parents. Active Old Boys' and Girls' association with Vines Day each year when they can come back to the school. Old boys include Tim Smit of Eden Project fame, the members of the band 'Keane' and the explorer, Tom Avery.

Wakefield Girls' High School Junior School

Linked to Wakefield Girls' High School in the Senior section

2 St John's Square, Wakefield, WF1 2QX

• Pupils: 475 girls and (up to age 7) boys, all day • Ages: 9-11 • Inter-denom • Fees: £7,047-£7,692 pa • Independent

Tel: 01924 374 577
Fax: 01924 231 602
Email: admissions@wghsjs.org.uk
Website: www.wgsf.org.uk

Head: Mrs D St C Cawthorne BEd, Dip TEFLA; has been head of a school in the Middle East as well as teaching in England; pleasant, enterprising and very capable, relishes her independence from the senior school to the extent of having her own budget.

Entrance: No entrance requirement for the co-ed nursery – the first 50 children on the list get in; names are put down at or even before birth! Priority given to children with siblings in the Foundation. Almost all proceed to the pre-prep. Assessment for those wanting to join at this point from outside in English and maths, in late January or early February. Means-tested Foundation awards available, if parental annual income is below £35,000, at seven years, for 25/50 per cent of the fees; usually six a year.

Exit: Boys leave at the end of Year 2, creating space for more girls. Almost all Year 6 girls move up to the senior school but it's not automatic (parents are warned in advance if a child looks unlikely to be able to cope). They usually just do the verbal and non verbal part of the entrance test.

Remarks: Pre-prep Mulberry House (as in 'Here we go round the mulberry bush', the original mulberry tree is in the pre-prep garden).

For further details see senior school entry.

Warwick Junior School

Linked to Warwick School in the Senior section

Myton Road, Warwick, Warwickshire, CV34 6PP

• Pupils: 240 boys, currently all day (but boarders accepted) • Ages: 7-11 • C of E • Fees: £7,860-£9,996 pa • Independent

Tel: 01926 776 418
Fax: 01926 776 478
Email: jt@warwickschool.org
Website: www.warwickschool.org

Head: Mr Guy Canning BA.

Remarks: Housed in separate redbrick building on Warwick School site, junior school has same ethos and feel as its senior counterpart. Most boys enter the junior school at seven but entry is possible at eight, nine and, occasionally, for the final year. Lessons are initially taken mainly by the boys' form teachers and thereafter increasingly by specialists. Great opportunities for extracurricular activities – music, art, drama, sport etc – using senior school's facilities. Most boys progress to the senior school, sitting entrance exam in January of Year 6.

Wellesley House School

114 Ramsgate Road, Broadstairs, Kent, CT10 2DG

• Pupils: 135 boys and girls; 60/40 boys/girls; mainly boarding • Ages: 7-13 • C of E • Fees: Boarding £25,950; Day £15,600 pa • Independent

Tel: 01843 862 991
Fax: 01843 602 068
Email: hmsec@wellesleyhouse.net
Website: www.wellesleyhouse.org

Headmaster: Since 2006, Mr Simon O'Malley MA PGCE (forties). An ambitious, enthusiastic headmaster, universally seen as 'approachable', much liked and respected by parents, who has managed to pull this school up by its bootstraps and is justifiably proud of what he has done so far. With his own parents working overseas, he was sent to boarding school himself at a young age so really knows how important it is to feel secure and happy as well as being well educated. He was cut out to be a prep school headmaster. Previously a housemaster, and later deputy head, at Beaudesert Park in Gloucestershire, where he started at the same time as a new headmaster. This gave him, he believes, invaluable experience in avoiding some of the pitfalls of his present job.

A keen sportsman, he teaches English and cricket and seems to know every child in the school inside out. Met his wife, Katy, while they were both teaching in Kenya. She used to teach art at their previous schools but now confines herself to running the domestic side of the school, giving tlc to needy children and generally helping her husband in any way that she can. She does 'cooking activities' with the boarders and has completely turned round the nutritional aspect, introducing a new caterer, a brilliant new chef and providing not only good healthy meals but plenty of them as well. 'No longer does my son wake up every morning with a tummy aching from hunger!' said a parent. They have a son at the school.

Entrance: Non selective from 7. An interview with the headmaster and a letter and reports from any previous school is all that is required. Several means-tested bursaries, academic, sports or musical available. Discounts for army families. Any child with potential learning difficulties will be assessed by the headmaster and Mrs Wallace and will only be turned down if they feel that they could not give him/her the right sort of care, the priority being 'can we help?' A child will be taken at any age, at any time provided there is room.

Exit: All over. Boys to Eton and Harrow, girls to Benenden, quite a lot to King's Canterbury, others to Tonbridge and Stowe. Over a third with scholarships in recent years – academic, art, music and sports. A bursary appeal has recently been set up in order to be able to offer means-tested scholarships to senior schools.

Remarks: The school began life under a different name in 1866 and moved to its present, purpose-built site thirty years later. Since then it has grown, added several more buildings, amalgamated with another school and, in 1977, become co-educational. The headmaster's wife has made great inroads into brightening up the long corridors that inevitably wind round a school built at different stages, 'light and colour are really important'. Walls are now covered with artwork, photographs and sports ladders, and pipes have been painted in a variety of colours. She's very proud of her pipes! The only old-fashioned room left is the library and that will, one hopes, not be changed – large, leathery and very comfortable, just how a library should be. Their own built-in chapel off the main school hall where a full choral Sunday service is held with a visiting preacher.

The junior boys have their own house where they sleep, work and play while the senior boys are all in the main building. Wherever they are, the dormitories are large and homely with exceptionally neat looking beds. Lego and other toys lie around and each child has his own peg board on the wall. Common rooms sport televisions but there is so much else to do, they are rarely watched! Day pupils often opt to have supper at school so that they can take part in activities and merely go home to bed!

The girls live away from the boys in Orchard House on the other side of the playing fields, through an apple orchard, which is their private domain. This is where they can really have a girlie time out of school hours in the capable charge of the geography master Mr Nichol and his wonderful, petite, bubbly, caring, Spanish wife. Lots of pink in their dormitories and lots of cuddly toys. An older girl always sleeps in with the younger ones. Mrs Nichol oversees all health matters in Orchard House alongside the local doctor and the school nurses. The Nichols have been in charge of the house for 18 years and it really does feel like home from home.

Small classes with experienced teachers, many of whom have been at the school for over ten years, and good imaginative lessons going well beyond the National Curriculum seem to get good results. Several scholarships and awards to senior schools and the last few years have seen every pupil obtaining a place at his/her first choice of school.

Teachers aim to make all lessons fun and interesting and to 'open up a world of possibilities'; certainly the pupil/teacher relationships seem to hit the right spot, respect without awe and, according to parents, shy children are brought out of themselves and quickly learn to participate. All the children we saw and spoke to appeared happy and relaxed and interested in what they were doing. Some spoke enthusiastically about their science teacher and the experiments they had done with him, a parent told us of the popularity and exceptional teaching ability of the head of biology and the new head of the junior house is much liked and a great Latin teacher.

Large bright classrooms everywhere but, so far, not a huge amount of IT assisted teaching. Only two classrooms employ interactive white boards – 'I want to be sure that they are going to be used effectively before putting them everywhere.' A good IT room though with an enthusiastic teacher where children learn necessary computer skills and are taught to touch type but, as one parent said, 'is one lesson a week enough?' No doubt this will change as the head continues with his improvement programme.

Fantastic sports facilities and, for such a small school, their achievements are amazing. They have a long record of winning national and county events in hockey, rounders and cricket (the only school to have produced two England cricket captains, Mann and Cowdrey) including being five times winners of the JET National Cricket competition and Under 13 winners of the JET National Rounders Competition four times and again in 2007. Cricket is coached all year round. Soccer and rugby are also played in the winter terms against other local schools. Particularly strong in golf being winners of the Stowe Putter for the first time in 2007 and County Champions the same year (they do have their own putting green and are very close to The Royal St George's which must help). Squash, tennis, cross country ('the only thing I don't like about the school,' said one boy) – you name it they do it. A well equipped sports hall, a sunny, heated indoor swimming pool and, to cap it all, a 25 yard shooting range. Wow! Six of the 2007 Eton Shooting VIII were old Welleslians.

Lovely, imaginative, exciting art on display everywhere, sometimes even specially framed, and an art teacher who really can show even the most inept child how to draw, paint and create. Head has reintroduced 'six of the best' displaying six framed pictures in his study over the course of the year. Good design technology as well. Lots of drama with two musicals a year on a home built set. Great fun. A 20 child choir sings at school services three times a week; extra singing tuition is available. 70 per cent learn an instrument though parents do not feel this is the school's strongest point.

All sorts of other cultural happenings: they sang songs from Oliver during the Broadstairs Dickens Festival; there was a traditional haggis supper followed by Scottish dancing on Burns night; Red Nose Day, Jeans for Genes day, whatever, they participate; some went on a day trip to France, and there's an annual Outward Bound trip for the penultimate year group. A choir trip to Belgium at Christmas and French canal holidays too. After school activities range from chess to fencing to carpentry to sailing.

A truly dedicated head of Learning Support who has been at the school for seven years and has 30 years experience of special needs teaching. She understands the needs of each child and works very hard to help him/her. One parent said, 'she is wonderful but sadly does not always get proper support in the classroom,' although she went on to say that she reckons the new head has made a huge difference and the staff are definitely listening properly now.

Good communication set up, all the necessary links are there; Mrs Wallace has an open door policy and is always available to help with parental concerns. They have access to an educational psychologist and have set up an excellent relationship with East Court School in Ramsgate where they use the Occupational Therapy and Educational Psychology departments. Mrs Wallace is a great believer in the value of sport as an aid to children with learning problems. One full-time EFL teacher who teaches children either individually or in groups depending on their needs. Parents are charged for a maximum of three lessons a week but she is always available should a child need her.

Very good pastoral care as well. 'We don't have school rules, we expect the children to know what's right and what's wrong,' says Simon O'Malley. 'There are no behavioural problems in the school,' says Phyl Wallace.

'Wellesley is brilliant at getting on top of bullies and any other problems very fast,' says a parent. Tolerance, respect and good manners are expected of all. The occasional episodes of verbal bullying are quickly dealt with. The policy is to talk about problems and bring things out into the open. Excellent documentation about pastoral care and comprehensive child records are kept by the Director of Boarding. Sensible, caring matrons in each house, some stricter than others. No expat problems. This is a kind and thoughtful school. Overseas children quickly pick up English and the local children love taking their friends home for exeat weekends.

Pupils and parents are mainly from Kent and London but also Essex and East Sussex. Others come from further away and there is a steadily increasing trickle from overseas. Some parents easily able to afford the fees, some struggling to do so but all are certain they are giving their children the best start in life.

A unique school. Not a school for sophisticated, glitzy children, an old fashioned boarding school for the 21st century. Excellent teaching, sports and activities to suit everyone, 'except' said one girl 'I can't bring my pony!' What a wonderful way to spend up to five formative years. The seniors even get to dress up for the weekly dinner party with the O'Malleys. To quote some parents, 'the older children are so nice to the younger ones'; 'our sons made friends for life'; 'it's such a cosy environment'; 'it produces well rounded, nice children'. Certainly all the children we spoke to were open, straightforward and looked at our faces. Perhaps the only drawback is at the end of this gentle, nurturing interlude, when they have to face the real world and moving on is not always easy. One challenge to Simon O'Malley must be how to prepare them to swim in a big pond. It's a challenge we're sure he'll meet and, even if some do have to struggle to cope initially, the benefit they will have had from their time at Wellesley will always stand them in good stead. This was amply illustrated when the 30th anniversary of going co-ed was celebrated in 2007 and old girls poured into Orchard House laughing and talking, reliving happy days. A school on the up again with an excellent ISI inspection in 2007. A school with traditional values where, to give the last word to a satisfied parent, 'it's very special to be part of something where the child really matters.'

Wellington School Primary

Linked to Wellington School in the Senior section

Carleton Turrets, Craigweil Road, Ayr, KA7 2XH

• Pupils: boys and girls • Ages: 3-11 • Fees: £4,962-£9,000; Nursery £3,750 pa • Independent

Tel: 01292 269 321
Fax: 01292 272 161
Email: info@wellingtonschool.org
Website: www.wellingtonschool.org

Remarks: See senior school.

Wells Cathedral Junior School

Linked to Wells Cathedral School in the Senior section

8 New Street, Wells, Somerset, BA5 2LQ

• Pupils: 155 (80 boys and 75 girls) of whom 6 board; 12 in the nursery • Ages: 3-11 • C of E • Fees: Boarding £19,545; Day £11,265; R-Y2 £6,054 pa • Independent

Tel: 01749 834400
Fax: 01749 834401
Email: juniorschool@wells-cathedral-school.com
Website: www.wells-cathedral-school.com

Head: From January 2011, Mrs Katherine Schofield, previously deputy head of Combe Down School, Bath – a large state primary school. Has experience in teaching, leadership and management, from the Early Foundation Stage to Key Stage 2. Married to Paul, a design and technology teacher, and has two young daughters who will be joining the junior school in due course. The family live on site.

Entrance: No assessment tests for pre-prep but 'friendly' tests for all for the junior school. On the edge of full most of the time. Chorister auditions in January and June.

Exit: The vast majority of pupils go on to the Wells Cathedral School senior school.

Remarks: Sunny bright buildings with lovely gardens, well maintained and used frequently as outdoor classrooms. A lush conservatory is also used as teaching resource – hot though. Enthusiastic staff, many of whom have been with the school for a long time – some have never taught anywhere else. Pre-prep includes small, cheery nursery, reception class and Years 1 and 2 in very brightly coloured classrooms. There are four year groups and classes are small – 10–18.

In the arts, even the nursery children receive specialist music and drama teaching and the school has won the Artsmark Gold Award. Every second year a cast of 50 pupils performs to sell-out audiences at the Edinburgh Fringe. Community drama and music workshops on Saturday mornings. Highly thought of choir consists of 18 boys and 18 girl choristers (two separate choirs) plus adults. Plenty of sport also available, with matches against nearby schools.

Westbourne House School

Shopwyke, Chichester, West Sussex, PO20 2BH

• Pupils: 430 pupils; 230 boys, 200 girls; 40 board • Ages: 2.5-7 pre-prep; 7-13 prep • C of E • Fees: Boarding £16,395; Day: £7,620-£13,380 pa • Independent

Tel: 01243 782 739
Fax: 01243 770 759
Email: office@westbournehouse.org
Website: www.westbournehouse.org

Headmaster: Since 2003, Mr Brendan Law (early forties). Born and educated in South Africa where he taught at their first-ever multiracial school. Came by way of Sweden to Bedford School, where he was meteorically made senior housemaster. Sports mad – coaches the lot. Dyed in the wool boarder. The great Colin Sharman, head for 28 years and father of today's school, says feelingly and with understatement, 'we were very lucky to get him'. Brendan (he's a first name man) is clearly an effective force and affectingly anxious to head a kind, happy, achieving school. Early changes spooked some teachers but the force is with him. Parents like him exceedingly and say his door really is always open. His wife, Linda, is seen by parents as a 'huge asset'. She does a bundle of liaison and coordination things – she's the school mum. Two children, one of each, both at the school. Golden retriever, just as there ought to be.

Mr Law will be leaving in July 2011 to take up the position of first headmaster of Brighton College's new outpost in Abu Dhabi. A bit different.

Entrance: Most from a 15-mile radius. Unfiltered for nursery and pre-prep, assessment for entry to Year 3. Because this is a local school the mesh is not fine, but big SENs are urged to think again. Best get in early – roughly 36 go on from the pre-prep to be joined by 18 or so brand new Year 3s. Very few chinks higher up. Scholarship: 50 per cent for music and recent additions for academic excellence. Also Centenary Bursary from Year 6 with follow-on links to Radley and Cranleigh. Sundry bursaries for those who fall on hard times and five per cent off for brothers and sisters. Racial mix reflects the local community i.e. almost none – but there is a charming smattering of Germans from nearby Rolls Royce.

Exit: Almost all stay to Year 8, then fly to the full rainbow of independent seniors of which the most flavoursome are Marlborough, Canford, Sherborne, Charterhouse, Eton, Winchester, Radley, Harrow, Wellington, Cranleigh, Portsmouth Grammar, Bryanston, Bedales, Lancing, Benenden, St Swithun's, St Mary's Ascot, Downe House. Scholarship hit rate an arrestingly high 35 per cent of all leavers. Eminent outgoers include R4's Marcus Brigstocke (funny) and the late Nick Clarke (news); and Monarch of the Glen, Alastair McKenzie.

Remarks: Here's a school which has responded nimbly to a changing market with no sense of reactive incoherence. Until 1990 it was all boys, all boarding. Now it serves a prosperous local community which prefers day early on with some weekly boarding in the last two years as a rehearsal for a boarding senior. Saturday morning school survives impregnable. Parents say the school has done the transition from the old to the now brilliantly.

Blessed with a high acre:pupil ratio, this is a spacious place with a campus-y feel and all the playing fields you can count. In the midst is the early Victorian (1840) house and, liberally disposed, the usual school buildings, some characterful, some not. They've spent well over £2 million in the last five years – including good science labs, IT, dining, classrooms and theatre – and are inordinately and justly proud that the lion's share of that came from prudently husbanded fee income. Indoor swimming pool, sports hall, lake for canoeing, separate music and art. Latest additions include a new dance studio and all weather Astroturf pitch (hockey + 12 tennis courts).

Academically the range is wide. Those scholarships tell it all for top-notch teaching, but parents say strugglers are well supported too because all are lauded for what they're good at – 'the teachers really care'. The accent in all things is on making children feel good about themselves. There are extension lessons for the bright and reinforcement lessons for the not-so. Emergent special needs are swiftly spotted and fixed by the superb SEN department where the emphasis is on not creating dependence. Children come only if they choose and include a sprinkling of prospective scholars. All do SATS and results feed internal monitoring systems. Talking about the right senior school starts in Year 2.

Art and ceramics flourish luxuriantly and joyously in an inspirational environment where colour blazes and craft skills are taught to the accompaniment of the romping of the imagination. Music is eye-blinkingly good. An unusual number play at grades 6–8, and 80 per cent of the children learn an instrument. Every year, fantastic scholarships and super concerts, but the rigour can be chilling. We are promised that more fun is afoot, and a broader range. Vital.

Sport is played with full fervour and results to match. Observable at every level is a high level of coaching. Whatever they teach you here they teach you to do it well. Matches well supported by parents, with lots of bonding and dogs on the many touchlines. Picnics in the grounds after Saturday lessons all year round.

Boarding is the tradition and it lives on, most popularly in Years 7 and 8. No sloppy sleepover stuff, and 'although we are always open for business over weekends' almost all go home. Most sleep in the main house with some boys in outhouses, looked after by houseparents. Boarding facilities across the board are being upgraded. New girls' outhouse completed in 2008. It's not much to look at, not as fluffy as some – but the pastoral care is in place and misses little. A key feature, now copied elsewhere, is their system of Friends, trained Year 8 counsellors – impressively successful and testimony to strong seriousness. Lots to do after school, it's on the up, and the point is this – the children love it.

Here is a school which does more than it says on the tin. We have never met so many parents who never thought to look elsewhere. The boys and girls are chummy, charming and bright-eyed. In an environment of humanity and hard work parents get what they want – happy, confident children who do the best they can.

Westminster Abbey Choir School

Dean's Yard, Westminster Abbey, London, SW1P 3NY

- Pupils: 33 boys, all boarders, 1st year (probationers) weekly boarders
- Ages: 8-13 • C of E • Fees: £6,064 pa - after subsidy • Independent

Tel: 020 7222 6151
Fax: 020 7222 1548
Email: headmaster@westminster-abbey.org
Website: www.westminster-abbey.org

Headmaster: Since 2002, Mr Jonathan Milton BEd (fifty-ish), married, formerly head of The Abbey School in Tewkesbury. Bred, if not born, into the choir school tradition – he was a choral scholar at York. Music was his degree subject, though he now teaches geography. A gentle man, whose quiet, friendly manner betrays a profound love of his unique school, the tradition it enshrines and the community of boys and staff which gives it ever-fresh life. Clearly, an inspired appointment. Mr Milton is, at once, a traditionalist and a moderniser – exactly the right balance for the place. 'When I came, there were no carpets or curtains and it felt tense – that's now completely gone. It was dark too. We've tried to make it gentler.' He showed us the little IT room next to the dormitories, 'it's a marvellous way for boys to stay in touch – much simpler than writing a letter. And the staff communicate with parents every week electronically.' Gentler the school may well be but he has also tightened the academics, keeping step with the outside world in which senior school places are no longer assigned in little chats between heads of 'big' schools and trusted prep heads. Mr Milton's openness, thoughtfulness and warmth are mirrored in his boys. Those we talked to were similarly relaxed, candid and friendly. Head and boys share their view of life here, 'it's tough, you get very tired but ... it's fabulous.'

Entrance: No formal entrance test day or the like. Over the year, school will see around 25 boys for voice trials – usually in ones and twos – and usually in Year 3. The Master of the Choristers will hear them and the head will chat to the boy and parents and, if the lad looks promising he will be invited back to spend a day in the school. This will include a more formal voice trial, a chance to play their instruments and testing in maths and English. What is looked for is not grade 8 in six instruments but musical aptitude and the kind of attitude to music, community and learning that make for a happy and successful Westminster Abbey chorister. 'They have to enjoy being part of a close-knit team and they must have personality and character,' says Mr Milton. Academic brilliance is less important though, clearly, the boy must enjoy learning. Of the 25 they see, places may be offered to between 4–6, on average, though one or two may be invited to come back some months later.

These days, more than half come from state primaries and can be caught up and supported where necessary. 'With year groups of 6 or 7, we can tailor-make classes,' says head. School fees are subsidised by the Abbey and no-one, however impecunious, should be put off applying if their boy is a natural chorister. Funds will be found. 'Some pay nothing at all,' says Mr Milton. Boys now come from further afield – Yorkshire and even overseas. Quite tough for an eight-year old, you might think. 'And,' says Mr Milton, 'few of our parents would have chosen a boarding school – when they see it, they realise it's a way of life.' Yes. This represents the most amazing opportunity for the right child and a peerless preparation for life.

Exit: An astonishing list of leavers' destinations over the last three years. Everyone wins a music scholarship to a prestigious school and many win academic and/or art schols too. Most popular senior schools are King's Canterbury, Eton, Winchester with the rest hither and yon and doing very well wherever they end up.

Remarks: This is the only choir school in the country which is only a choir school – no day pupils, no girls, no non-choristers. Average class size six, maximum is nine – in a way that says it all. The place hums with quiet activity – mental, physical and musical. It all happens in a tall, unobtrusive building in Dean's Yard – right under Big Ben, the Houses of Parliament and Westminster Abbey. Dean's Yard is a grassy square lined by augustly solid houses. Opposite is the modest arch which leads to Westminster School – no connection with the choir school except that the large pupils and the little choristers see each other passing all day which makes the business of scholarship and growing up in this – the heart of the great centre of London – seem quite the normal thing.

Five floors accommodate all learning, admin and living space. All is freshly-painted and feels light, comfortable and well-cared for. There's a super ground floor 'music room' used for assemblies and the like – a splendid stained glass window commemorating Purcell and the other Masters of the Choristers who between them make up a history of English choral music – Gibbons, Blow, Simon Preston et al. Classrooms are small with conventional desks, whiteboards and it all looks a bit dolls house in scale – enhanced, when we visited – during exam week – by the very cuddly teddies (for good luck) sitting reassuringly on desks. More teddies in the dorms which – it is a boys' school – are, if not Spartan, certainly not prettified. Bunk beds with integral cupboards in airy rooms. Good shower rooms, good ICT provision and a very nice sitting room with sofas, piano, TV, books and games and feeling really snug.

Everyone does standard prep school curriculum but flexibility can be built into the system with such small classes and so small a school. Individual help is the norm. No boys with SENs, we are told, though the odd mild dyslexic may creep in. A boy with dyslexia would find chorister-life tough, says Mr Milton – what with having to read music and a foreign language at speed and so on. 'It wouldn't be fair.' Yes. Sports take place via buses to Battersea Park, The Queen Mother Sports centre in Victoria and water sports in Docklands – Mr Milton is a keen sailor. They kayak, rock climb and sail and Mr Milton sees this – and the opportunity to get away from the closed chorister world as essential for good relations.

Evidence of boy-life and wit abounds. 'WACS Lyrical' – the boys' own noticeboard, details competitions, initiatives, jokes and notices – full of fun and ideas. The art room – open in the evenings – similarly lively – we were terrified by the huge multi-tusked cardboard, paper and paint beast which 'would be tamed by listening to Palestrina'. Boys enjoy textile work, DT – they make fan-powered vehicles for racing, and knitting – 'very popular', we were told. Obviously, music is central to life. Singing practice in the song school happens each morning and each afternoon before evensong – except on Weds and alternate Mons. Instrumental practice is timetabled and very much a normal part of everyday life. Musical guests and ensembles visit, there is a composer in residence – a real privilege for such boys – and school takes full advantage of the concert halls and galleries roundabout. Likewise, the school goes into local primaries – boys take their instruments – to inspire others – 'just to give music a boost'.

What do the boys say – and their parents? 'You have to be very independent and organised,' a seasoned 12-year-old told us. 'You can't rely on your parents to pack your bag and find your pencil case – you have to do it all yourself. You have to manage your own revision and music practice.' (Sounds like a course in choristership might be handy all round!) 'It is very tiring – I'd like to have more of a rest after concerts.' On the other hand – 'singing all the special services we do is brilliant. We did a special service for the spies! (100 years of MI5.) They just looked normal. They don't wear T-shirts saying 'I'm a spy'. And 'We're on TV, we go on tours and make CDs.' 'It can be exhausting,' said a parent, 'but they bounce back. It's unbelievably rewarding.' And they clearly enjoy the Abbey community with whom they share Christmas and Easter meals and so on. A choristership here is a treasure. A huge commitment for boys and family while it lasts but a gift for life.

Westminster Cathedral Choir School

Ambrosden Avenue, London, SW1P 1QH

• Pupils: 126; 27 boarding choristers, 99 day boys • Ages: 7-13 • RC for choristers, rest ecumenical • Fees: £7,125-£14,055 pa • Independent

Tel: 020 7798 9081
Fax: 020 7630 7209
Email: mwilson@choirschool.com
Website: www.choirschool.com

Headmaster: Since September 2007, Mr Neil McLaughlan (late thirties). Joined from Downside School, near Bath, where he was head of English and director of development. Before that he taught English at Worth and Stonyhurst. He was educated at Durham University and spent a few years with Andersen Consulting in London before embarking on a teaching career in 1997. His interests include poetry, drama and cooking. He is married with two small children and is utterly charming.

Entrance: Boys come into the school in Year 3 or 4 (choristers must start in Year 4) and leave at the end of Year 8. Testing for would-be choristers, who must be Catholic and full-time boarders, is thorough. Information is sent out to every RC parish in the UK, inviting children along to the school's 'Chorister For A Day'. Those who are still interested after that can then apply for the six or so places. If candidates (a) survive the academic assessment and (b) sing their way past Martin Baker, the Cathedral's Master of Music, they spend two trial nights at the school. Only then, if they're judged suited to chorister life, are they offered a place. The head dismissed any 'misconception that chorister boys are whey-faced and insipid' – they need to be 'robust, fit, fun-loving and go-getting'. Around 80 to 100 boys also apply for 24 day places and are academically assessed like the choristers, in English, maths and verbal reasoning. Unlike choristers, these boys are mostly from local pre-preps (Eaton House etc), and can be of any faith. RC and C of E predominate but we spotted a Patel and a Rabinowitz on the roll as well. Sibling policy is strong – 'We like to keep families together.'

Exit: Exit record is outstanding, a significant factor in parents choosing WCCS for their sons. Choristers win music scholarships to the major Catholic boarding schools (Ampleforth, Downside, Stonyhurst etc), day boys go on to a raft of top London schools including Eton, Harrow, Westminster, St Paul's, KCS Wimbledon and Alleyn's.

Remarks: The sound of Moments Musicaux drifting down to us as we waited in reception, set the tone for our visit. Music is everywhere in this lovely little school – with just 126 pupils, it fields two orchestras, four chamber ensembles, any amount of singing and a huge breadth of instrumental tuition. Many pupils achieve grades 7 or 8 in their chosen instrument(s) by the time they leave and the choral singing is internationally renowned. The choristers are, in the headmaster's words, 'completely immersed' in music, and the day boys get a pretty thorough soaking too. The musical repertoire has been classical to date but new head of music, Mark Kennedy, is determined to introduce a contemporary note as well – African music has made its way into the classroom and musicals are planned for later in the year.

The school is tucked away behind the red and white brick splendour of Westminster Cathedral and consists of a labyrinth of smallish rooms surrounding a splendid playground, round which we saw posses of healthy little boys throwing themselves. Football, rugby and cricket are the main sports here and are played enthusiastically at local pitches, swimming and PE at the Queen Mother Sports Centre. The classrooms are nothing out of the ordinary – our tour guide proudly showed us the gas tap in the science lab – but the standard of work on the walls was excellent and bore testimony to imaginative teaching. Parents describe the teachers as 'motivated', 'easy to approach' and 'inspirational'. A recent critical ISI report commented unfavourably on boarding facilities and the over-use of practice exams over the final two years – neither was a cause for concern when we last visited and parents we have spoken to before and since (with one notable exception) do not agree with the ISI.

The boys seem happy, confident, articulate, proud of their school and very well-mannered. Superb food is cooked on the premises by 'three funky young chefs'; a wide range of clubs and societies (debating, chess, reading, fencing). For the boarders, film nights, toast parties and other treats are held in their own spacious commonroom, equipped with two pianos and a TV. A remarkably warm and caring head of boarding (a parent himself) supervises regular pillow-fights. One diminutive chorister admitted that he'd found the first couple of nights difficult but the matrons were 'big on cuddles' and he'd soon settled in. And indeed the junior dormitory, where teddy bears are compulsory, is delightful, resembling a children's bedroom in an IKEA showroom. The senior facilities are a little bleaker but due for a makeover this year, and our tour guide assured us that juniors only used the senior bathroom 'when the plumbing was bad' – which, judging from the state of the French classroom ceiling, must be pretty often.

Scored poorly on its pastoral care in its previous Ofsted report, but the new head has already turned this round and it is now rated as 'outstanding'. Boys are consistently rewarded for kind and caring behaviour and bullying is all but unknown. Parents report improvements in staff-parent communications. 'Concerns are now dealt with in a really professional and positive way,' wrote one parent. 'The children are very happy and the school is definitely on the up,' was another comment.

The headmaster is proud of the school's Catholic ethos, that 'prayer should be a natural and happy part of a child's life.' We were very struck by one recent innovation – the entire school (day boys and choristers) now sings together every Wednesday in Westminster Cathedral at their own special Mass. All the staff go and all the parents are invited. It is, says the headmaster, 'a unifying thing'. Certainly this seemed to us a cheerful, affectionate and successful community.

Westminster Under School

Adrian House, 27 Vincent Square, London, SW1P 2NN

• Pupils: 260 boys; all day • Ages: 7-13 • C of E • Fees: £14,181 pa
• Independent

Tel: 0207 821 5788
Fax: 0207 821 0458
Email: lyndsay@westminster.org.uk
Website: www.westminsterunder.org.uk

Master: Since September 2010, Mrs Elizabeth Hill MA CertEd DipEd. Previously deputy head of Dulwich Prep for 15 years. Educated at Leeds Girls High School, Homerton College, Cambridge followed by an MA in education at London University. Spent 13 years teaching science, physical education and PSHE in maintained sector comprehensive schools in London. Was head of department, housemistress then senior teacher at Camden Girls, deputy head of Raines Foundation and spent one year at Alleyn's Junior School. An Inspector for ISI since 2002. She is married to Humphrey with five children, three sons and two daughters (now university and beyond).

Entrance: Boys sit tests in maths, English and reasoning and all are interviewed by Mrs Hill. Entrance points are at 7+, 8+ and 11+. While other schools are experiencing a drop in the number of applicants, Westminster's is soaring. In recent years, there have been 6 for each place at the first two stages and 9 for each place at 11+. Applicants come from many pre-preps, among which figure Wetherby, Eaton House, Norland Place, Garden House, Eaton Square, Hampstead Hill, Mulberry House, St John's Wood, Basset House, Orchard House and Charterhouse Square. At 11+, they come from Ravenscourt Park, Kew College, Blackheath Prep and a large number of state primaries. Mrs Hill will not poach boys from other top preps which teach up to 13 so very few move across from these, despite the temptations of a perceived cruise into Westminster School – 'Great School'. However, it should be appreciated that this is a small school. Only 20 are taken into each of the first two years and a further 20 at 11.

This smallness of the Under School needs to be understood by parents. There are vastly more very able applicants than Mrs Hill has places for. Jack's brilliance in Whiteboard House and his pre-eminence there in music, sports, languages and art may well be matched by other boys from St Elsewhere's and his possible failure to gain a place at the Under School has to be seen in this context. However, the intake at 11+ gives truly able boys from state primaries a real chance and there are bursaries available for the genuinely needy which can provide for up to 100 per cent of fees and which continue into the senior school. More than 50 per cent of the intake at 11 is from the state primaries. Since 2001, no boy who has entered at 11 has failed to make the grade for Great School.

Exit: An average of 80 per cent of Under School pupils continue to Westminster School. Of the rest, most go to Eton and a few to Marlborough, Winchester, Highgate, St Paul's, Bradfield, Harrow and City of London. No flops then. They achieve between them an average of 16 awards per year – i.e. more than 25 per cent get awards. Most parents send their boys to the Under School in hopes of an eventual easy transition to Dean's Yard but the pre-test in Year 6 which results in conditional places for most, will be inconclusive for some – most frequently because the boy's maths is felt to be less than impressive. Certainly, more emphasis – here as elsewhere – is now placed on maths as a diagnostic and this, here as elsewhere, allows less leeway for the wayward genius whose talents lie in other intellectual areas – a development we regret but not one for which the fault can be lain at the door of the Under School. We can recall a number of Westminster School boys who were given places despite their maths and who had distinguished academic careers thereafter. Boys frequently make immense progress in Years 7 and 8 and further assessments take place in those years. As the Mrs Hill says, 'everyone is found the right school in the end.' The uncertainty, though, is not appreciated by parents and anxiety can be contagious.

Remarks: A top prep in the heart of London. You would walk past it if you didn't know – this unimposing, five-storey redbrick building at the south-west corner of Vincent Square. The square itself surprises – large, even for a London square – and, though only yards from the dusty din of Vauxhall Bridge Road, is tranquil and leafy. The square is fringed by a mix of architectural styles including some splendid Georgian stuff but the real surprise is its green centre – playing fields, grass and all-weather – topped off by a small but unmistakable pavilion. And for much of each day small, high-pitched boys rush around playing games or troop cheerfully across the narrow road up the steps into school. Very few London preps have such space on their doorstep and although it is shared with the pupils at the Great School, it is very much part of the Under School and its attractiveness. Inside, the old building blends seamlessly with the new-build and, apart from some rather narrow corridors and stairwells, feels less cramped and in far better nick than many London preps. The surprise is the huge hall/dining room. Inevitably, more space would be very nice and school is looking skywards to see if more can be added in that direction.

Everyone takes a standard curriculum, Latin being added in Year 6 and Greek in Year 8. Football and cricket are the main sports – don't look here if Jack is to be the next Jonny Wilkinson. High achievement is normal. In recent years the school won the IAPS General Knowledge quiz, the senior choir reached the finals of the BBC Radio 3 Choir of the year and the 1st XI cricket team were unbeaten. Remarkably, the school's chess team were south-east champs in the English schools' U18 tournament in the same year and the school produced major successes in drama and art alongside numerous other academic triumphs. Sport is now good and enthusiastic. Everyone enjoys drama. They also managed to raise £42,000 for charity in 2008.

Between 5 and 10 per cent of boys have special needs, the vast majority mild dyslexia or dyspraxia. The school has a lift and can accommodate wheelchairs in all but a few tight corners – and has done so. The Study Skills Coordinator spends two days a week at the school and has one-to-one sessions with those who need her support. The special needs help is praised by parents. As just about all boys could be described as Gifted and Talented. In Year 8, boys are divided into two scholarship classes and two CE classes, much to the chagrin of a few but 'usually parents accede in the end and it works out for the best.'

Classes are orderly, civilised and quivery with cerebral activity and fun. Excellent displays – of work and of interesting information – cover every wall. The library has a wonderful mix of fiction from CS Forester, Agatha Christie and Ian Fleming to Caroline Lawrence and Garry Kilworth with comforting dollops of Blyton to gladden the hearts of ancient visitors. It doubles as a bookshop on Mondays and a Latin classroom and is good source of print info of all kinds. Art is lovely, varied and imaginative. Splendid models, drawings, collages and paintings are wonderfully expressive of guidance and the opening of minds rather than instruction. Boys are taught in groups of only 7–10 and, from Year 5, all do history of art complete with gallery visits. How civilised is that? A top class computer room also accommodates 'our brilliant technician'. Boys enthuse, 'he always helps with problems – even at home.' Music is exceptional and standards attained exemplary. There is an impressive range of ensembles and events for so small a school – jazz band, brass group, string quartets, two orchestras, two choirs, House music competition, choir tours to Belgium, Brazil, USA etc every two years. Everyone is encouraged to be involved in the musical life of the school. Some reach grade 8 before they leave and grade 5 is usual. We enjoyed the crumhorns and shawms fixed to the wall in the director of music's office – a nice change from recorders and triangles!

The clientele is, inevitably, moneyed and brainy but the mix changes at 11 when those from the state schools and the preps which end at 11 join – most of whom import lots more brain but less money. School manages social matters expertly and the master is keen that if not, 'all shall have prizes' that honours are equitably distributed. There is a different head boy for each of the three Year 8 terms and virtually everyone will be a house captain or some such officer. Prizes, too, are awarded with care to reward as many as possible and not always the same Cleverclogs.

It was hard to find a critical parent. 'Our boys absolutely love it,' we were told – and told. 'The school knows how to deal with the most energetic and the brainiest – they always find new challenges for them.' 'They are wonderfully caring when pupils hit problems – academic or emotional.' 'The care is very individual.' 'Even though everyone is clever, they are always eager to support you if you have a blip.' 'The staff are wonderful – the teaching is great.' The sports are much better now – brilliant director of PE.' 'The food is great – it's far better now.' And so on.

To be happy here a boy must love learning and love the fun of exploring. This is as far from being a crammer as you can get. But, for the brightest and most intellectually curious, as one seasoned parent said, 'without question, the best.'

Westville House School

Carter's Lane, Middleton, Ilkley, West Yorkshire, LS29 0DQ

• Pupils: 80 boys, 55 girls; day only • Ages: 3-11 • C of E
• Fees: £4,260-£7,395 pa • Independent

Tel: 01943 608 053
Fax: 01943 817 410
Email: westville@epals.com
Website: www.westvilleschool.co.uk

Head: Since 1995, Mr Charles Holloway BA PGCE (mid forties), educated at King's Worcester, Leeds University and Westminster College, Oxford. Studied English, teaches English and some drama to the older pupils – 'vital in order to know the children.' Taught previously at Dulwich and Heath Mount. Married to Katharine, two children. Calm, warm, approachable yet determined demeanour, chats with the children with ease and bangs the drum for co-education. Proud of the children and their achievements as well as of the strides the school has made in an area rife with competition, where survival of the fittest is the watchword.

Entrance: Children from Ilkley, Skipton, West and North Yorkshire. Most enter at three (encouraged), occasional admissions at other ages. Introductory morning and then trial day before starting.

Exit: Feeding local maintained and independent senior schools, wide choice of good schools: Ashville, Bradford, Casterton, Ermysted's, Gateways, Giggleswick, Harrogate, Ilkley, Leeds, Sedbergh, St Peter's York and Woodhouse Grove, with a good scattering of art, academic and all-rounder scholarships.

Remarks: Good and traditional prep school with lots going on. Old-fashioned teaching though responding cautiously and expediently to changing times whilst ensuring a keen emphasis on the basics, right from the start. Handwriting and basic skills given prominence and even the nursery is 'no playground'. Everyone knows what is expected, however, so happy children, ditto staff and presumably parents too, who demonstrate their support through energetic and enthusiastic fund-raising – essential in a school that is far from cash rich and, in places, a little tired around the edges. Parents know what they want and understand and appreciate the school's mantra of traditional teaching. They recognise the school as a well-trodden and reliable path to the senior school of their choice. Not selective on intake but formal teaching and attention to detail leads to a good number of scholarships and high test scores in the final year. National Curriculum tests prove a useful benchmark (and results are excellent), but nothing stops for them and they aren't allowed to dominate thinking or teaching. Maximum 22 per class, some a little boy-heavy but the pattern does vary from year to year.

Rather surprising building on approach, somewhat out of kilter with the surrounding rolling hills and Yorkshire gritstone houses – would look perfectly placed on the seafront in Brighton. Towering, stark, white-rendered, with blue detail (it's everywhere – blue uniforms, blue windows, blue walls, blue blinds, blue website and the rest – a recurring theme throughout) and if you simply pulled up outside with your small offspring, you may be hesitant to venture inside. But those who do are met by bright-eyed, breezy children, purposeful and focused, happy to chat to visitors, very busy but also having enormous fun. Even the support staff are fiercely loyal and keen to tell us what a 'lovely and special school this is', very much a part of the Westville 'family'. Small turnover of teaching staff, decent overall blend of experience and newer younger staff. A warren of small(ish) yet bright, cheery classrooms, ICT, art, library, and narrow corridors with plenty of attractive work on display. Family service at lunch, remarkably civilised, no choice of menu though special diets are catered for.

A real boon is the relatively new multi-purpose hall, serving chiefly as a sports hall but also used for a range of other activities including assemblies, plays and speech day. A well-designed and attractive space and 'a bit like a microwave in that we wondered how we ever managed without it.' Small but attractive adventure playground area, tennis/netball courts. Short bus ride for major games as no playing fields, also swimming. Nevertheless, sport still manages to remain high profile and successful. Plus point is the annual sports tour, a rarity in a day school, competing against (mainly) boarding schools – an enjoyable romp for children and their parents who, post-matches, party the night away in hotels whilst their children slumber in dorms. Prospectus is slightly disappointing, it works for the school in that it is easily updated, but lacks the wow factor and the expected gloss; even the map lacks sufficient detail but it typifies this no-frills school. We await a newly developed website.

No major changes afoot, but then nobody would wish it. This is a school with only four heads in its forty year history – like Ilkley Moor on the hillside opposite, it has stood firm in all weathers. Small traditional school with a warm heart and a sense of purpose and there is a genuine feeling that, whilst not cocooned, children have a very secure education here.

Wetherby Preparatory School

Linked to Wetherby School (The) in the Junior section

Bryanston Square, London, W1H 2EA

• Pupils: 210 • Ages: 7-13 • Non denominational • Fees: £13,995 pa • Independent

Tel: 020 7535 3520
Fax: 020 7535 3523
Email: admin@wetherbyprep.co.uk
Website: www.wetherbyprep.co.uk

Head: Since 2008, Mr Nick Baker BA PGCE (late thirties). After reading geography at UCL aquired teaching qualifications at Newcastle. Taught in state secondary and middle schools and then Chesham Prep in rural Buckinghamshire. Joined Wetherby Prep at its inception in 2004. Initially senior master, then deputy head, before taking over the reins in January 2008. Quiet, does not have a huge ego and doesn't push himself forward but parents are full of praise for him, say he is honest and open and 'a very strong leader for boys'. 'Totally transparent, what you see is what you get'. 'An inspiration for boys and staff alike'. Feel he has definitely put his own mark on the school and they like it. Has a completely open door policy as wants to have a community, family school. Feels it is important to be a high profile head and stands outside to greet all the boys as they come off the buses in the morning. Teaches geography to Common Entrance classes and helps out elsewhere when he can. Watches, listens, thinks and really does seem to know each boy. Married to an ex-teacher with two small sons who he adores. Parents say 'when he is making decisions he thinks like a father.' Has high expectations of his pupils and runs 'a tight ship with no shady corners. If one appears he deals with it.' Boys like and respect him. A head who is constantly striving to improve his school and looking for ways to make it the best in London.

Entrance: At seven and eight, tests in English, maths and reasoning during an assessment day at the school, when will also take part in group activities. Places further up the school will be treated individually. Open evening in Autumn term but otherwise no open days. However parents are invited to visit the school and meet the head at any stage, doors are never closed. Unless circumstances are exceptional, automatic transfer from the pre-prep.

Exit: Early days yet but first set of results is impressive. A mix of London day schools and top boarding schools with scholarships to King's College Wimbledon, St Paul's and Winchester. The future looks rosy.

Remarks: A well structured, well balanced, caring school offering a slightly less pressurised alternative to the top London preparatory schools. One parent feels that, at the moment, it is her ' little secret'. We doubt it will stay that way much longer.

Opened in 2004 in Notting Hill Gate, has now moved to larger premises in tall, elegant listed Georgian house in central London. Parents and boys alike are delighted. 'Fabulous' said one 'and the bussing system is brilliant.' The additional space means that class rooms can now be subject based with each floor having its own identity. Two staircases, one, stylish and unadorned, for up in the old part of the house, one for down, winding round the lift shaft, in the newer, non-listed back addition. Rules say no running anywhere in the school. Huge hall right across the front on first floor, so far lacking in much wall decoration as conservation limits what can be done. Used for various activities and three times a week assemblies. Rooms aplenty, all bright and airy, staff can even escape to their own suite for R and R.

Broad curriculum and good teaching prepare the boys well for CE. Young staff (average age mid thirties), half male, half female and smallish classes, max 20, at the moment more like 14/15. Standard high and boys are expected to perform well. Setted from Year 4 in English, maths and French but classes are names not numbers – on English floor, Dickens, Conan Doyle and Woolf – so no superiority and boys do not know which set they are in. Interactive white boards and a computer in every classroom. IT embedded in curriculum with 60 laptops (in IT suite) available to be collected and used by the boys whenever and wherever necessary.

Good music. About a third learn individual instruments, some to grade 8. Choir (audition necessary) and string ensemble. Two concerts a year, all perform in the first one. Art and design room at top of the extension, so no problem putting stuff on the walls there. Humanities at the back on the ground floor and two decent sized science labs in basement, with more advanced equipment for the seniors. These boys have everything. Lots of outings and visits, within London, the UK and overseas.

No outdoor exercise area on site but much use is made of Seymour Leisure Centre just a few minutes walk away and parents say 'loads of sport'. All the usuals plus rowing to competitive levels. Awards for all. We met some older boys in the basement lining up to go in for a delicious looking lunch, wonderful quirky menus sent home for parents to see each week. We asked what the symbols on their ties meant: 'I've got my football half colours' and 'I've got my full ones'. This is a traditional prep school with modern innovations. A particularly effective one has been to cancel all Friday afternoon lessons and have compulsory clubs instead. Range from the cerebral, like European culture or maths, to the creative, like model making, to the sporty such as badminton and horse riding. Several others as well. So Friday afternoons are fun and both boys and parents think this is a brilliant idea.

Excellent pastoral care and help for SEN children. They are aware of how boys are learning and quick to pick up on any problems. Teachers plan weekly and make sure that those who need extra help are given it. Specialist teachers are available out of lesson time for more severe cases and if they feel all is still not going right they bring in other agencies. Their sister school, Abingdon House in South Kensington, is always there to help and the Dyslexia Centre round the corner provides occasional teachers. Policies for everything. PSHE for all every week. Head of PSHE and boys' fitness 'a real father figure who the boys find easy to talk to.' Parents very impressed with communications. Any email sent to a staff member is replied to within twenty four hours and feedback is equal for all children, academic or non academic. Parents say that learning difficulties are well dealt with and the individuality of each child is properly catered for. 'If a boy is picked on the head is on to it in milli-seconds and deals with it.'

Not a cosy, laid back school but one where every pupil is expected to perform and participate. Where parents are constantly kept up to date with their child's progress and tutors have been known to ring them even over half term. Not all expected to be A students but are expected to try and all boys are rewarded in some way or other. Parents say, 'very inclusive. Lots of leeway for each boy to be rewarded in front of the school.' 'You can trust the school to keep you in touch.' 'Very traditional, very strong values. Manners, decency and social responsibilities count. So does respect for peers.'

Wetherby School

Linked to Wetherby Preparatory School (The) in the Junior section

11 Pembridge Square, London, W2 4ED

• Pupils: 245 boys • Ages: 4-8 • Non-denom • Fees: £14,595 pa • Independent

Tel: 020 7727 9581
Fax: 020 7221 8827
Email: learn@wetherbyschool.co.uk
Website: www.wetherbyschool.co.uk

Head: Since 2008, Mr Mark Snell BA PGCE (forties). Busy, enthusiastic, hearty, noisy, ebullient, much loved by boys and parents alike. Passionate about education. Deputy for two years before taking over as head. Read business studies at University of Westminster before going to Brighton University to get his teaching qualification. Taught at Eaton House the Manor and Westminster Under before becoming head of maths at King's College School, Wimbledon, Junior where he stayed for five years. Teaching is definitely 'in the blood' – his wider family own Mowden School in Brighton and Ludgrove in Berkshire. Married with two young children, lives in Wimbledon where his wife teaches maths at King's College School.

Has, according to parents, made the school 'more touchy-feely' or 'a bit more chilled without affecting standards'. 'All the staff like him and the boys think he's their best friend'. But they still respect him and would not dream of doing something of which he did not approve. One child's father jokingly called him 'Mr Smell' which so horrified his son he told him off severely. Another parent told us 'he is a mixture of charm and strictness, he gives children boundaries with humour'. Teaches maths to the older boys and helps out with the younger ones. Believes you need to teach in order to know the boys properly and really does appear to know boys and parents inside out. Holds open staff meetings so that all can have their say. Believes teachers should be the core guidance in future planning although he will always make the final decisions. Determined that school should be a happy, fulfilling, jolly place – 'I am really here for the kids and I'm scared of silence'. A notice on his office door says, 'Stop. Smile before entering or do not enter!' That says it all.

Entrance: Non selective, first come first served, so get on the waiting list fast. Staggered throughout the year so ages properly mixed. The majority live locally although one parent said that the net seems to have spread further round London these days. Some spaces occur at other times for the lucky ones. Lots of multi-national families but speaking English is regarded as a necessity.

Exit: About a third to Colet Court and Westminster Under and a third to Wetherby Prep, with the remainder split between the other London day schools and boarding preps.

Remarks: No longer the glitzy glam place of yesteryear, now a busy, buzzing, caring, cosy school where all boys are exceptionally well prepared for the next stage. They are not only taught how to learn but also how to be kind and the importance of good manners. Yet they have an enormous amount of fun at the same time. 'Just the right balance,' say parents.

Young, (average age 32), teachers who parents say are 'superb' and 'relate to the boys, enthuse them and have a very good rapport'. The head has rejigged the timetable so that the serious lessons – maths and English – are in the first two periods of the morning. These are structured classes when the boys know that they have to work hard. All other lessons are holistic and cross-curricular, partly to make them more fun and relaxing but also to introduce different styles and ways of learning. Speaking and listening is an important part of the curriculum in Years 1, 2 and 3. A teaching assistant per class. Three mixed ability classes per year. Maximum number in each 21. Classrooms quite small but all bright and jolly containing happy, chatty children working informally at different levels. No 'silence in class' here. EYFS directive means that reception classes are now much more play based. 'No bad thing', says the head, 'but we do build in some structure because we feel it helps the children intellectually when they enter Year 1'.

Good music. Over 50 per cent learn an individual instrument. Several choirs and bands which regularly perform externally. Art and DT now perform a much larger part in the school as is indicated by the number of masterpieces decorating the walls, some showing exceptional talent for such young children. Unexciting library, with rather bare shelves, also contains computer area. ICT taught in half sized classes. Interactive whiteboards everywhere.

No outdoor play space but parents don't seem worried. All younger children have 15 minutes twice a day running around in the communal square and the upper school also have four activity sessions a week. A parent said, 'the sport is excellent and Mr Burgess, head of sport, is the hero of the school'. The previously rather formal annual sports day has, apparently, been transformed into a jolly, fun day for all, 'now a wonderful and relaxed time'.

Exceptional SEN support and pastoral care. Secure system in place for spotting boys with even minor learning difficulties. Parents are involved from the beginning and all necessary help is provided. Unless this is one-to-one or specific, it is regarded as part of the service. One parent with a boy who was desperately lacking in confidence, said it was 'awesome' how they helped him build it up. Another one, with a dyslexic child, was full of praise for the way they handled his difficulties. 'Golden Rules' encourage honesty and gentleness amongst the boys.

Parents say, 'a small, charming, smarty pants school which nurtures boys and sets them up with a baseline for life'. 'Our three boys are totally different yet all are doing well and love it.' 'At Wetherby they are not going to let anyone fall through the crack.' 'Really teaches children rules and gives them pride in their education.'

Wimbledon Chase Primary School

Merton Hall Road, London, SW19 3QB

- Pupils: 615 boys and girls (including 105 in the nursery); all day
- Ages: 3-11 • Non-denom • State

Tel: 020 8542 1413
Fax: 020 8542 1668
Email: wcps@wimbledonchase.merton.sch.uk
Website: www.wimbledonchase.merton.sch.uk

Head: Since 2001, Mrs Sue Tomes BEd (sixties), has been at the school for 35 years, moving up the ranks from head of French, senior mistress and then deputy head for 15 years. Married, a self-confessed workaholic and perfectionist, she freely admits that the school plays a major part in her life. Her lovely, large office is very homely but, when she can be prised away from work, she enjoys reading, music, travelling and collecting antiques.

Mrs Tomes also tries to maintain her links with France and is keen to support the teaching of primary modern foreign languages across the borough. A modest and unassuming woman, she is popular with pupils (knows all their names) and parents. 'She is pretty amazing,' sums up one mother. Generally seen as very approachable and open to suggestion and famed for her huge attention to detail. 'We have to sit on her a bit sometimes or she would be ordering the jammy dodgers for the school fair,' jokes one of her many fans.

Entrance: At 3+ to nursery, and 4+ to the main school. Non-selective academically. Applicants must list the school as their first preference, with special needs taking priority, followed by the usual sibling, then proximity criteria. Families need to move close to the school to be sure of a place.

Exit: A regular trickle to selective grammars: both of the Tiffin schools, Sutton Grammar and Nonsuch, while majority move locally to Ricards Lodge, Rutlish Secondary and Raynes Park Secondary School.

Remarks: A school with a heartbeat – lively and likeable; we didn't find anyone with a bad word to say about this happy place. In fact, quite the opposite. 'My children absolutely love going to school,' says one mother. 'It's an amazing place – the opportunities it offers and the way the kids are catered for are as near to a private school as I could get without opening a cheque book.'

At first sight it's a bit like visiting a senior school with very small pupils. Despite its location near the centre of Wimbledon, the school enjoys the size, site and facilities rarely found at primary level. Buildings date back to 1924 (when they were home to the local senior girls school) consequently there is lots of wood-panelling (slightly Harry Potterish feel to some of it) but, more importantly, lots of dedicated space. In 2001, and overseen by Mrs Tomes, the school began its conversion from middle to a primary school with its first intake of reception children and the addition of a big bright nursery. 'Its transition seemed daunting at the time but we're out the other side and it's great,' said one mother.

Academically all is more than sound – all well above national averages at the relevant Key Stages. What makes this school really stand above other primaries is the sheer range and variety of experiences over and above the National Curriculum. The philosophy is to give children a chance to try things and to make learning fun. So there are lots of themed days and weeks (everything from maths to black history) – the highlight of which is the well-planned 'Enrichment Week' where the afternoon timetable is suspended entirely in favour of workshops on all sorts from boxing to jewellery making. 'We want to find and foster talents wherever they may lie,' says Mrs Tomes. Talent is also nurtured through the inspiring extra-curricular activities after school and at lunchtimes – most of them free. Simple but easily lost skills like skipping, knitting and story telling are promoted via clubs, alongside the more usual sports, dancing (including tap), drama and French. (The children learn French from reception including a residential stay in France for Year 5). Lots of days out and trips. Pupils and parents are hugely appreciative of the range and quality of what's on offer.

A very inclusive place (lots of Koreans, Tamil speakers make up the second largest section) – 73 pupils speak 23 different languages. With the mix of languages comes a mix of abilities – but the school does well by them all. Every EAL pupil, except a few SEN children, attained at least a level 4 in their SATS. Similarly, provision for SEN is of high quality. There is a dedicated SENCo, early identification of special needs (including a gifted and talented register) and lots of additional support and catch up programmes. Additionally, the school has a unit for children with additional learning needs (ALN), previously aimed at moderate needs, but in 2006 this changed to cater for children with language and communication disorders. It now offers 14 places – with top priority for entrance to the school. There are also facilities for physically disabled children such as ramps and purpose-built toilets. Head feels this mix is good for all the children. Certainly the place is buzzing: from the front hall, packed with trophies, certificates and photographs extolling the achievements of pupils and staff, to the back door leading to beautiful grounds (well used – especially for sports and science); there's lots going on.

A happy school – it's not silent or regimented, but still has a slightly traditional feel and pupils quite smartly dressed. There is a 'positive behaviour management system' – largely stickers and crystals (full jar of gems equals golden time). All the teachers use – and encourage the children to use – 'language of choice', as in 'Is this (behaviour) a good choice? What are the consequences if I do this?' Parents encouraged to use the idea at home. The school also has a worry box, peer mediators, strong school council, buddy bus stop in the playground – all geared for children to sort out any problems. A boon for working parent is the wrap-around care on offer (breakfast and after-school) – another benefit of having the space. Even the half-day nursery children can be accommodated for the rest of the day. Hugely supportive parents are keen to help in the classroom and by raising impressive sums of money. The school returns the favour by providing a dedicated parents' room in school where helpers have somewhere to keep their things and (most importantly) get tea and biscuits!

Wimbledon High School Junior School

Linked to Wimbledon High School in the Senior section

Mansel Road,, London, SW19 4AB

• Pupils: 320 girls, all day • Ages: 4-10 • Non-denom • Fees: £9,387 pa • Independent

Tel: 020 8971 0902
Fax: 020 8971 0903
Email: info.juniors@wim.gdst.net
Website: www.wimbledonhigh.gdst.net

Head: Since 2003, Miss Catherine (Kate) Mitchell BEd MA (forties). Formerly deputy head at Alleyn's Junior School, Dulwich; before that deputy head of junior school at Ashville College, Harrogate, and Stamford School, Lincolnshire. Highly rated by parents as professional, approachable and dedicated, 'I'd say it's her vocation,' says one mother. 'She's lovely,' chorus others. Hasn't rocked any boats, preferring to 'refine things here and there'. Teaches verbal reasoning in preparation for 11+ and hears the infant readers. Has super rapport with the girls, knows them all and even recognises matching parent. Out of school, Miss Mitchell enjoys playing bridge and going to the theatre.

Entrance: Selective, mainly at 4+ with a handful of places available at 7+. Occasional vacancies as they arise. Popular and over subscribed – there's a one in three and a half chance of a place. 'It's hard to assess a child at four,' says head, 'but we're looking for potential, rather than how much a child has learnt so far.' A series of short assessments covering everything from maths and language to social skills and understanding of the world, are held in a relaxed nursery-style environment. At 7+, English, maths and non-verbal reasoning tests are more formal. 'We're aiming to get a cross-section of children, not just to pick up the more extrovert types.' No priority for siblings – little sisters sometimes disappointed, so entrance procedure evidently more than a formality. Attracts a predominantly local intake from Wimbledon and environs.

Exit: Most to the linked senior school (qv), where 98 per cent are offered places, some with academic and music scholarships. Parents are warned in good time (Year 5 at the latest) if their daughter unlikely to make the grade. Some academic and music scholarships elsewhere, including St Paul's and Kingston Grammar. A few to local grammars.

Remarks: Fantastic reputation means locals flock, attracted by the school's well rounded offering and a (virtually) guaranteed transition to the equally well regarded senior school. Does the business academically, following the National Curriculum and achieving sparkling SATs results – Key Stage 2 level 5 in English 100 per cent, maths and science both 91 per cent (nationally 32, 33 and 46 per cent respectively). Girls here are high-achieving but not pressured.

For a private school, class sizes are not small – 24 per class for Years 3 to 6. Mix of class-based and specialist teaching keeps things lively and the pace picks up as the girls move up the school. There's a co-ordinator to mentor the gifted and talented and parents of these bright girls are delighted how their daughters are motivated and extended in lots of subject areas. All pupils are screened for SEN in Year 2, with up to five per cent receiving extra help – parents make an additional payment. SEN is not a big issue here – few need SEN help probably because they are bright buttons to start with. Teachers work with a learning support co-ordinator to ensure SEN pupils are accommodated in lesson plans – typically for barriers to learning such as dyslexia and dyspraxia. Targets are drawn up with parents, with progress monitored.

Like many London schools, the site is relatively small and further space was lost recently when the new performance centre was built. Head's office looks out on to the junior playground – rather a hard grey site, but colour recently added and new trees planted. There are plenty of games and equipment to keep the girls busy and a new Wildlife Garden is proving popular with young gardeners. Junior school is housed in bright and cheery accommodation, purpose-built, set back behind the senior school (building comes as a pleasant surprise to visitors who can't see it from the road).

School is keen on the creative stuff, IT and sport which all have specialist rooms and facilities, share senior school facilities including fab pool and shiny new Rutherford Centre for the Performing Arts – named after (very) old girl, actress Margaret Rutherford. (More recent OGs include children's author Michelle Paver and journalist Rosie Millard). Playing fields, games pitches and courts are a few minutes walk away (at least no need for buses) on the site of the original All England Lawn Tennis Club. Though 'Sport for All' is one of the school's boasts, virtually the only parental disquiet about the place is that only the best players are chosen for the competition squads. More run of the mill players have to make do with what's on the time-table. 'It's frustrating if your daughter just falls short,' says one mother. Lots of extra-curricular clubs on offer – all sorts of music, languages, art and chess etc.

Happy and purposeful atmosphere. 'I like the way the girls are really supported but never mollycoddled,' said a mother. 'They are taught to be quite independent by the time they reach the top of the school, which is great for their move to the seniors. I'd say a real stand-out feature of this school is the way the girls develop confidence as they go through.' Although a real shrinking violet may initially be a little overwhelmed, the encouraging nature of the school means that even quieter types should thrive here. Since her arrival the head has beefed up the previously low-key house system. There's also a weekly 'celebration' assembly where the girls can show and tell about any out-of-school achievements. Parental praise for accessibility of (staff and) the head – she runs regular 'open mornings' when parents can drop in on her. Pupils too seem to have good relationships with the staff. 'Teachers make the lessons fun,' said our accomplished Year 6 guides, who also appear to believe the number one rule around the place is 'to smile'. An amused Miss Mitchell has issued no such edict – but was delighted to hear that was the only rule the girls could come up with. 'I'm very fortunate that the children behave beautifully and I can keep things fairly relaxed. It's certainly not a strict place,' she says. Discipline not really an issue with these keen and motivated young girls – worst sanction seems to be a missed playtime.

Run by The Girls' Day School Trust, the school celebrated its 125th anniversary in 2005. Knows exactly what it's about and parents perceive it as excellent value for money and appreciate that they are not preyed upon to write countless cheques for extras. Parents are a mixed bunch – not all from the multi-million pound houses on nearby swanky Wimbledon Hill – and they value the fact that the school has a community feel about it. Multicultural, with the emphasis on professional types from financial and legal world.

In a nutshell, it's not a hothouse but is academically pacey and does very well by its brightest girls. Highly recommended by parents who generally don't seem to have a bad word to say about the place.

Winchester House School

44 High Street, Brackley, Northamptonshire, NN13 7AZ

• Pupils: 385 boys and girls; 140 boarders (25 of whom are full boarders). • Ages: 7-13, plus pre-prep 3-7 • C of E • Fees: Boarding £15,645-£19,740; Day £8,610-£14,940 pa • Independent

Tel: 01280 702 483
Fax: 01280 706 400
Email: duncang@winchester-house.org
Website: www.winchester-house.org

Headmaster: Since 2004, Mr Mark Seymour BA CertEd (fifties), an historian and previously head of Cargilfield (qv) from 2000 and senior housemaster at Haileybury. Interests include playing the drums, power boating, cricket and golf. Three children, two at the school, eldest at Sibford. Married to Andrea who has been involved in school PR. Head charming, smiley, thought by some parents to be too marketing orientated – he's certainly got the numbers up. Feels settled, intends to stay for the long haul. Says he walked in and was immediately impressed by the diversity of opportunity and the way the staff pull together.

Entrance: Preferably in September. Day pupils move up via hugely popular pre-prep, others come for an informal test. Most boarders come from within 50 mile radius. Non-selective.

Exit: To a range of schools – Rugby, St Edwards, Oundle, Uppingham, Stowe, Radley, Eton etc. Girls to Tudor Hall, Downe House, Cheltenham Ladies', Wycombe Abbey etc. All accepted by (guided) first choice senior schools.

Remarks: Founded in 1876, moved to its present 18-acre site in Brackley in 1923. The school, a former Victorian hunting lodge, maintains traditional co-ed prep school values but offers occasional, weekly and full boarding. Very much a local school, and popular as such. Thriving well-run pre-prep and nursery over the road.

Good facilities including new Years 3 and 4 teaching block. All subjects have own dedicated areas including music block, specialist art and DT rooms, science labs and library; some in better nick than others. Children say it's a friendly school and everyone gets on really well, grumble is the lack of interesting displays in some classrooms. Maximum class size 16, sound teaching on all fronts, including Greek for the brightest, strong classics and maths for scholars.

Learning support located in the heart of the school, SEN not a problem, but children must be able to get involved and to access everything. 'Once we make a decision to accept a child then there is a real commitment that we do everything to teach them.' One-to-one, and small group help for dyslexia and similar – co-ordinator is director of studies (but also trained in special needs), employ occupational therapist for dyspraxics et al. Dys strata, MLD and mild sensory impairment OK but not behavioural difficulties or anything requiring specialised intervention.

Keen games, no need to be the next Flintoff but boys suggest those not into sport might struggle – girls disagree citing wealth of other activities – music, drama, chess, dance etc. Super activity centre for younger ones, with new adventure playground for older. Fantastic art and DT work displayed in the purpose built forum, including award-winning Wallace and Gromit style animation. Choirs, bands and orchestras offer something for all from the budding bassist to the fully-fledged flautist. Good sports facilities including extensive playing fields, modern sports hall, tennis courts and heated outdoor pool but alas no Astro (use that of nearby school). Continuing parental grumbles that the same 'top' children have all the fun, though annual school mag celebrates myriad of achievements by all.

Operates as a boarding school with day pupils, late finish and compulsory Saturday school. Boys' boarding recently improved, good facilities for all but girls overflowing – currently cramming 12 to a room. Recently regenerated house system a popular feature, not just for competitions but for socialising too, eat in house groups, lunch a formal sit-down occasion, no complaints re food. Children say head has introduced lots of new things and made life more exciting. They especially enthuse about 'Learn to Lead', say they love the varied opportunities, especially the challenge weekends – 10 such a year; helps build confident, responsible individuals.

Windermere Preparatory School

Linked to Windermere School in the Senior section

Windermere, Cumbria, LA23 1AP

- Pupils: 130 girls and boys • Ages: 3-11, boarding from 7+ • C of E
- Fees: Day £8,655-£12,069; Boarding £20,271-£21,414 pa • Independent

Tel: 01539 443 308
Fax: 01539 446 803
Email: wps@windermereschool.co.uk
Website: www.windermereschool.co.uk

Head: Since April 2007, Mr Ben Freeman (forties), previously deputy at Malsis. Brought up on the Wirral, educated at Rossall School, studied DT at University of West of England, later a postgraduate in education leadership at Leeds Metropolitan. Keen sportsman with bags of energy, coaches rugby and is a marathon runner. Charming and affable character enjoying the challenge of moving staff and school forward and still finding time to teach DT and kick a ball around with the boys – not an office man, far happier out of doors. Keen to convert Windermere Prep School 'from a primary to a prep' by increasing academic rigour, encouraging house competitions and adding further outdoor pursuits and challenges into the curriculum. Has one step-child and a large black labrador with him at Windermere Prep with two step-children at the senior school.

Entrance: Not overly selective: children 'assessed' in class for entry at KS1 and KS2.

Exit: Virtually all pupils carry on through into the senior school. Several scholarships a year to Casterton and Queen Margaret's. Six pupils have made it into Lancaster Grammar in the last three years.

Remarks: Housed in a former Lakeland private house – fabulous views, reminiscent of a country house hotel. Some lovely light classrooms in the main building and additional buildings in the grounds provide large spacious rooms for the younger ones; two information centres, one for prep, one for pre-prep, and three new pod-shaped classrooms in woods – very unusual, two for Year 6 and the other a science lab. New ICT infrastructure so now every room connected to server. Wooded landscape with great den building potential for pupils and gentler play areas for little ones.

Wasn't entirely happy with primary years IB programme (senior school does IB) so created their own curriculum along the same lines but with more depth. Has used science as backbone; also new homework policies. Lower down using Forest School initiative – one fully trained member of staff and others to follow, to re-inforce the outdoor curriculum for age three. New Elleray Adventure Award for Years 3–6: two hours/week, 10 areas, e.g. biking, camping, canoeing, kayaking (proper qualifications in these). Children record levels they reach in log book – the award eventually goes from bronze to silver and gold. Ultimate expedition for Year 6 – small groups map-reading themselves to remote camp in woods. Aim is for this to be continued into main school, resulting in industrial level trained 18 year olds.

Older pupils encouraged to take responsibility by carrying out duties – playground sweeping, table-laying etc – on a rota basis. Appealing lunches cooked on site using locally sourced food. French from reception; additional specialist teaching Year 3 upwards; plenty of extra-curricular activities and homework club after school; sports coaching on Saturdays. Children are bright and cheery, enjoying a busy life – indoors and outdoors; wellies are essential school kit. Round Square ethos aims to develop pupils beyond academic excellence into responsible all round individuals. Boarders sleep at senior school site a short distance away.

Windlesham House School

Washington, Pulborough, West Sussex, RH20 4AY

• Pupils: 285 pupils in main school (145 boys, 95 girls; 75 per cent board); 45 boys and girls in pre-prep (Little Windlesham). • Ages: 7-13, pre-prep 4-7 • C of E • Fees: Boarding £17,050-£20,280; Day £15,500-£17,280; Pre-Prep £7,350-£8,550 pa • Independent

Tel: 01903 874 700
Fax: 01903 874 702
Email: office@windlesham.com
Website: www.windlesham.com

Head: Since September 2007, Mr Richard Foster BEd (early fifties). Warm, friendly, approachable. Educated at Kenton College, Kenya and Clifton College. A very experienced headmaster. First headship was at Pembroke House School in Kenya, then, after 9 years to S. Anselm's in Derbyshire for 14 years. Takes 'great pleasure in seeing all the children flourish.' A stickler for manners. Good relationship with parents. Married to Rachel, a qualified junior teacher – very open and welcoming and a 'mother to all the children' according to one parent and who is immersed in all aspects of school life. We're getting a steady stream of delighted parental comment. Three grown-up children.

Entrance: Via registration and assessment day – mainly for setting purposes. Generally non-selective but the ultimate test is Common Entrance. Want those who will make the most of their time at Windlesham and enjoy themselves. About a third from London, a third local and a third from overseas – both foreign nationals and children whose parents are working abroad – 16 nationalities in the school. Quite a gang of Spanish and French children come for a term or a year – strong friendships are made and many ask to stay longer. EFL available for a fee of £815 per term. Most children pick up the language incredibly quickly. Since 2007, children from the pre-prep may remain as day children and there are a few day places further up the school – 75 per cent board. No flexi-boarding. Most children join the school in Years 3 or 4 or in Year 6 for the last two years.

Exit: To a huge range of schools (30 in 2010) – mostly to co-eds of which Marlborough the most popular but includes Harrow, Eton, Stowe, Winchester, Benenden, Bryanston, Hurstpierpoint, Sevenoaks, Wellington and King's Canterbury, to name a few. Very few leave at 11+.

Remarks: Windlesham is centred on a Queen Anne house set in 60 acres on the South Downs north of Worthing. Founded in 1837 on the Isle of Wight at the suggestion of Dr Arnold, headmaster of Rugby School, it moved to its present position in 1934 and became a charitable trust in 1963. A warm and welcoming school with a happy family atmosphere, excellent pastoral care much praised in the official reports. Inspection called it 'a happy school with happy children, with staff who are committed to providing very high standards of care.'

Great sense of freedom – children are allowed to play in the woods, climb trees and skateboard and ride the school's mountain bikes around the grounds. Although it's quite big for a prep school at 285 pupils, Windlesham's children get the kind of care and attention you would expect at a smaller establishment. Boarders are given responsibility at an early age – peer listeners group, food committee and school council. Strong house system with house parents and staff tutors within each house. Always someone to talk to if they need to. Boys and girls housed separately. Bright, jolly dorms, each girl has her own bedside light (wow!). Special 'chill out' common room, where they can have supervised quiet time. Top year has own common room which they see as a great privilege. No uniform but the headmaster is tightening up the dress code. Moral leadership is a strong theme and central to school life and is reinforced through chapel, school assemblies, House tutor group meetings etc. House colours are awarded for particularly considerate children and there is an annual citizenship prize. Cafeteria style dining system with child height servery and brightly coloured plates and cups – good range of food with lots of salads and fruit. Staff sit amongst the children.

The top two sets (out of five) would be considered for scholarship depending on where they want to go. Special scholars' evenings when outside speakers come to give talks. Spanish and Latin introduced at age 9 and 10. Average class sizes 14 with max of 18. IT an integral part of all academic subjects – four computer rooms within the school. Children do a course in touch typing. Interactive whiteboards everywhere. Marvellous art department with a huge range of opportunities – glass fusing, mosaics, pottery, graphics, product design etc. Top year children have each designed their own lamp and we saw a stunning array of pottery feathers. The school recently raised £2,500 from a silent auction of children's art work. 10–15 per cent of children need some level of SEN support mainly for dyslexia or dyspraxia. Three full time and two part time teachers – good links with subject departments ensure that children are supported at all levels and individual education plans and programmes are created where necessary.

Parents generally understated, broadminded and supportive, who, above all want their children to be happy. Children confident, friendly and well mannered without arrogance. Consistently urged to try new things – emphasis on instilling self belief. Much praise and encouragement with many prizes and certificates. Reports home to parents several times a term.

Everyone is encouraged to have a go, e.g. everyone painted a self portrait – all displayed around the school. Very dedicated team of staff – good mix of long-serving and newly appointed teachers – plenty of natural change. Every year some sort of adventure is planned: 2010 was in a school for disadvantaged children in the southern region of Andhra Pradesh, India. Year 5 survival weekend combined with DT where they have to design and make a shelter, bag, soap, torch and 'bush tucker' and camp out in the woods in the grounds.

The Malden Family Theatre (doubles as a sports hall) was opened in 1988 to mark the five generations of the Malden family who had been headmasters since 1837 (The last Malden Heads retired in 1994 and two daughters are still governors – one of which is now the Chairman of Governors). Opened by Old Boy Sir Michael Hordern who called it 'a small jewel in the crown of English Theatre'. All children have drama lessons; drama production once a term and a junior play so every child has the chance to be involved. Lots of other opportunities to perform in public.

Music at Windlesham is in a league of its own under inspirational directorship. The spectacular event staged in 2010 was Odyssey – 'The most advanced show ever staged by a UK school.' Almost 1000 children from Windlesham and the surrounding area gave performances in music, dance and readings themed on various forms of travel and journeys. It combined live performances with computer generated music, lasers, flypasts and parachutists from the Red Devils plus a link up with Russian astronauts aboard the International Space Station! – and raised money and awareness for the children's medical research charity, Sparks. About 80 per cent learn a huge variety of musical instruments, with 58 children learning the drums.

The usual range of sports on offer and all children take part in athletics and can have tennis coaching all year round on floodlit courts. Indoor heated swimming pool plus nine hole golf course. Huge range of activities and outings – cooking very popular – juniors have lessons and senior children not keen on games can cook, or do other activities, instead of playing matches. Also taught useful things like sewing on buttons and wiring plugs.

Pupils must stay in school for two fixed weekends per term, but with so many from abroad there is no general exodus on Sundays and there are plenty of outings and things to do. Regular bus from Putney on Sunday evenings. Parents' involvement and participation, but not interference, encouraged – always welcome to visit and stay in regular contact with house parents or other members of staff. Recent introduction of annual dinners for parents to get to know each other.

Limited bursary and scholarship fund – academic, all rounder, Services, sibling and financial need. The Windlesham House Association formed in 1910 keeps the Old Boys and Girls in touch and there is a leavers' reunion at the school every year. The Association marked its Centenary in 2010. Former pupils include Guy Ritchie, Tina Cook, Duncan Goodhew, Otis Ferry and Sir Michael Hordern.

In the capable hands of Shirley Mead, the pre-prep school is fondly known as Little Windlesham. Boys and girls from age 4 to 7+. Housed in bright airy buildings within the Windlesham complex. Same relaxed, happy atmosphere as the prep school. Runs from 8.30-3.30 with optional after school clubs until 6pm. The relaxation of boarding school rules has meant that nearly all children now move on to Windlesham House at the age of 7+.

Witham Hall Preparatory School

Witham-on-the-Hill, Bourne, Lincolnshire, PE10 0JJ

• Pupils: 240: 130 boys, 110 girls • Ages: Pre-prep 4-8; Prep 8-13 • C of E
• Fees: Boarding £15,630; Day £6,990-£11,460 pa • Independent

Tel: 01778 590 222
Fax: 01778 590 606
Email: headmaster@withamhall.com
Website: www.withamhall.com

Headmaster: Since 2009, Mr Charles Welch (forties) BEd, Educated at Oakham, and Exeter University. Previously director of sport, and then foundation director at Oakham School, where the Welch's also ran a junior girls' boarding house for 5 years. Head feels that 'a high level of pastoral care is at the heart of a Witham education. This, coupled with a highly inclusive approach across the total curriculum, brings happiness, nurtures confidence, widens opportunities and experiences and encourages a high level of individual achievement.' Married to Jo (who teachers part time in the school) with two young children, aged 4 and 2.

Entrance: No entry requirements for pre-prep and the majority pass automatically to prep. New entrants to the prep take standardised tests. Early application is strongly advised.

Exit: More than 30 scholarships have been gained in the last three years. Many go on to schools that are reasonably local e.g. Oundle, Oakham, Uppingham, Stamford and Worksop, but others go further afield, to Rugby, Stowe, Tudor Hall and Queen Margaret's. A few to Eton, Shrewsbury and Winchester.

Remarks: Considering its academic achievements, it is surprising that the school has a fairly low profile on the UK scene, attracting only local families in the main. It should really be broadcasting its successes in the classroom, the arts and sport more widely. For a small school, they are certainly at the top of their tree. With every year that passes, greater goals are being achieved.

Previous heads undertook a major building project every two years, all funded from within. Teaching blocks, sympathetically built, complement the comfortable Queen Anne manor that houses the boarding side. In 2006, the school opened the Stimson Hall, an excellent hall/theatre with fully electronic retractable seating and in January 2008 an Olympic size Astro plus four additional netball/tennis courts arrived. Everything has a ring of quality.

The school moves with the times, offering flexi-boarding. Children fit in to this side of the school very easily alongside the weekly boarders. The excellent food is prepared on site and they like to think they were years ahead of Jamie's Dinners; milk is on tap all day with bowls of fruit being refilled on demand. Class representatives from both the pre-prep and prep have weekly meetings with the head cook to discuss menus.

Academically, the school is hitting the right buttons. Staff are in their 30s and 40s, with four teaching special needs. Average class size in the prep is 14.8 and in pre-prep 10.1. The computerised Accelerated Reading Programme has made a big improvement in boys' reading. The school is in the enviable position of having to throw books away – from over use. Art deserves a special mention, not only the scholarships awarded in this medium. There is achievement at all levels. The pictures that cover the walls are eye-catching, well-conceived with a great use of colour and finished to a high standard. Some of the scholarship pupils work on large sculptures, giving them the opportunity to break free of size boundaries that can so often limit talent. Lots of music is being taught and at the last speech day, there were 153 children performing together on stage. LAMDA classes are very popular with a waiting list.

The prowess of the school also filters into sport, where they adopt a sport-for-all policy. Reaching national finals in rugby, hockey, netball, cricket and rounders and travelling to other matches all over, sees the school well-represented on both national and local scenes.

The school is solid and unflashy with a real warmth about it.

Withington Girls' Junior School

Linked to Withington Girls' School in the Senior section

Wellington Road, Fallowfield, Manchester, Greater Manchester, M14 6BL

• Pupils: 85 girls • Ages: 7-11 • Non-denom • Fees: £7,440 pa • Independent

Tel: 0161 224 1077
Fax: 0161 248 5377
Email: office@withington.manchester.sch.uk
Website: www.withington.manchester.sch.uk

Head: Since 2004, Mrs Kathryn Burrows (fifties). Was head girl here in 1977/8 before St Andrew's University and postgraduate studies at Bristol. Taught senior school geography and PE in Northern Ireland and Cyprus, then an army wife. Four children later, her husband is now a vicar, their daughter's still in the senior school here. Mrs Burrows returned to teaching at Lady Barn House School (qv), her own primary school, before moving to Withington as junior head and Year 6 teacher. 'I love it here,' she enthuses, 'the girls are a joy to teach.' She's warm and friendly and prides herself on being easy for parents to reach by email or phone.

Entrance: By an entrance exam half day in school in January, 'which is gentle, not scary, and which involves chocolate muffins'. Looking for an inbuilt love of learning, an inner spark, girls who're probably off the reading scale and from the top five per cent of the ability range. Would rather leave places empty than take girls who might not cope with the pace so while the top years are oversubscribed by those eager to eventually secure a senior school place, there may well be spaces in the lower years. Parents given detailed feedback after the day and often a girl who's been absolutely top of the class in another primary school will find she's just middle of the road here.

Exit: Almost all to Withington senior school.

Remarks: Just four classes, one per junior year, of up to 28 happy, busy, super-bright little girls from seven years up along a ground floor corridor with laminated thinking questions along its walls. Own junior hall and resources library but their extensive use of main school facilities, including the favourite 'little critters pets corner' in the science department, mean these mini-versions of the senior girls are everywhere bringing a serious 'aaah' factor, softening the place – not that it needs it but they're so sweet no big girls would want to risk trampling them on their routes between lessons. The adoration works both ways and sixth form prefects who take on peer support in the juniors speak happily of being 'bombarded' during their duties.

Head says this is 'academically the hardest school to get into locally'. Add to that a wide variety of specialist teaching from senior school staff with big school facilities, a wealth of trips, visits and visiting speakers and no wonder most girls carry on to further success in the seniors, 'and that's our hope, our aim'. Yet there's no shortage of fun. A magic carpet in the middle of Year 1's classroom takes them on imaginary journeys through time and space and fractions are being taught using Smarties which they're allowed to eat when they've finished their homework.

Lots of clubs at lunchtime and after school and there's a junior council and a 'chatterbox' outside the head's study where girls can post ideas; a tapestry club is the latest result from this. Head describes the school as multicultural and multi-faith, 'very healthy, we have cracking discussions'. Assemblies include a hymn or song and a thought or prayer which girls can use as 'thinking time' if they like. It's a small, protected place where girls are known through and through and where discipline is based on respect and responsibility.

Woodcote House School

Snows Ride, Windlesham, Surrey, GU20 6PF

• Pupils: 105 boys; 80 boarders, 25 day • Ages: 7-13 • C of E
• Fees: Day £13,275; Boarding £18,150 pa • Independent

Tel: 01276 472 115
Fax: 01276 472 890
Email: info@woodcotehouseschool.co.uk
Website: www.woodcotehouseschool.co.uk

Headmaster: Since 2009, Mr Henry Knight. Took over from Mr Nick Paterson who is still involved in running the school. Taught English here for seven years, after a career in the wine trade. Lives next to the main school building with his wife, Susannah, who oversees the pastoral care, and their three young children.

Entrance: Individual visits rather than Open Days, with an informal assessment and interview with head about a year before entry. Always prepared to talk to parents right up to the last moment. Takes new boys in at the beginning of all three terms.

Exit: Biggest numbers to Sherborne, Radley, Bradfield, Harrow, Charterhouse but boys go on to 27 different schools.

Remarks: Super little school, where each boy is carefully cocooned so that the shock of leaving nursery environment for prep school life is cushioned. Main problem might be the shock of leaving Woodcote for their public school! Family involvement and large staff (average class size 10) ensure very close monitoring of social and academic progress. Generous exeats every third week (Friday – Monday) and school will always make arrangements for 'abroad' boys with other families. Lots of other activities/outings on in-school weekends when parents are welcome to join in but not take out. Minuscule but extremely informative, yearly magazine which kicked off recently on the very first page, 'Food. Always the most interesting part of any small boy's day.' Prep done in the mornings and early afternoon to leave evenings clear for a wide variety of hobbies including nice old-fashioned boy things, such as making model aeroplanes, and less old-fashioned things such as 'Warhammer', boys have converted the school cellar into the 'Warhammer Dungeon'.

Set in its own 30 acres, which includes some attractive woods, the main building is Regency and elegant but delightfully worn at the edges, with additional modestly built classroom blocks round the back and charming little chapel across the lawn, made of corrugated iron (painted black) and wooden inside. 'Buildings like hen houses,' said one visiting parent disappointedly. New all-year round uniform is much smarter than before – school now runs its own clothes shop, both new and second-hand.

All main team and sports played to a high standard, particularly rugby; also golf, polo, squash, shooting amongst a dozen individual sports; five tennis courts, two Astroturf hockey pitches and indoor/outdoor telescopic swimming pool. Several parents join large ski party in early January and head concentrates on placing boys in the school of their parents' choice rather than on getting scholarships – though they got six in 2007. Small and very competent remedial unit – recommended by special needs organisations for dyslexia and dyspraxia. Fully qualified teacher who works in a small unit – some 15 per cent of the boys receive help – also excellent EFL teacher.

One or two gems among the staff including the super dynamic head of science, and the archetypal schoolmaster, Colin Holman, who has been here for yonks and lives in the lodge and, amongst other things, looks after the grounds lovingly. Recent development programme has transformed the school's academic and extra-curricular facilities; music particularly strong – 80 per cent learn at least one instrument. Choir tours to Holland. About one third are sons of soldiers or ex-pats, one-third London or local and a third from 'far afield'. One or two Thais (long-standing tie with Thailand), a few 'Europeans' (mainly Spanish). One of a dying breed – the family-owned school – and, unlike some, by and large it works. Continuing good reports.

Wycliffe Preparatory School

Linked to Wycliffe College in the Senior section

Ryeford Hall, Stonehouse, Gloucestershire, GL10 2LD

• Pupils: 380 boys and girls; 75 boarders. • Ages: 2-13
• Fees: Day £5,445-£11,265; Boarding £14,250-£18,135 pa • Independent

Tel: 01453 820470
Fax: 01453 825604
Email: prep@wycliffe.co.uk
Website: www.wycliffe.co.uk

Head: Since 2003, Mr Adrian Palmer BA (fifties). An ex maths and PE teacher with a range of bright and almost horrific ties, he has been a head for 16 years. After a spell as head at Warminster Preparatory School he moved to Rendcomb where he started the Junior School and built up numbers rapidly before moving to Wycliffe 'because I didn't want to get stale'. Works in close tandem with the senior school head and 'we get on very well.' The feeling is mutual. Married to the delightful Julie, who is deeply involved in the running of the place, and with a son and daughter in the school.

Experience has not brought pomposity to this head. Much of what he achieves is through lightness of touch, a sense of humour and a palpable love for the children. 'They must feel they're having fun. If they are happy, they'll work hard; if they work hard, they'll feel fulfilled.' A simple philosophy but one which seems to work. He is a hands-on leader (we saw him tidying away plates in the dining room after the first sitting for lunch) and is on easy terms with the boys and girls, joking his way around the place with a cheerful and individual remark for everyone. The children from the nursery and pre-prep, in particular, seem very excited to see him, swarming around shouting out his name and chattering about their recent experiences. A whale amongst minnows. He is clearly approachable, something confirmed by the parents we spoke to. 'He knows the children well and nothing is too much trouble,' said one very satisfied mum. No plans for leaving.

Entrance: Over 90 per cent from the nursery and pre-prep (Windmills) across the road, via a charming bridge built in the 1930s to make it safe from the volume of traffic; some, 'an increasing amount', join from other schools via relaxed interview and a good report. Fleets of buses from all over the place. Parents may apply at any time of the year and pupils may join whenever there is room. Scholarships available at 11 and there are awards in music, drama, dance, sport and art.

Exit: About 98 per cent move on to the senior school. Transition is very nearly automatic (examinations are for setting purposes) and the school aims to give plenty of warning to parents if it is felt that the senior school would not be appropriate.

Remarks: Initially the campus feels rather cramped and it is virtually impossible to find a parking space. Best to park on the senior school side where there is plenty of room. The main house bears the unmistakeable stamp of an institution but is essentially handsome and spacious within. A recently built conservatory through which parents enter is welcoming and functional, designed to show off children's art and make you feel happy to be there. A welcome board with your name on can work wonders.

As with the senior school, computers and interactive whiteboards are everywhere. ICT is taught as 'a discreet subject' and from the age of seven each pupil has two lessons a week. But these are not budding geeks: computers and their uses seem as natural as telephones. We saw some lively and imaginative teaching with interactive white boards: a history lesson involving The Peasant's Revolt, which culminated in the head being decapitated amidst yells of approval and Latin irregular verbs brought to life. Super computer room. Even the bright and airy library employs computer power and pupils were happy to demonstrate how you could remove and return books using thumb prints. Good fun and, presumably, effective.

Gifted and talented pupils benefit from the school's accreditation with NACE and shortly after our visit a party of pupils was due to go to the Sheldonian to talk and discuss. Good work with dyslexics. The school is CResTed. Debating is popular as are court room trials, conducted locally under the supervision of legal beavers. Excellent looking drama in the charming little theatre, complete with happy mum painting flats. 'Even mums can discover a talent here.' Good art in dedicated building.

Delightful head of pastoral care organising PHSE programme; regular tutorial meetings with tutees who retain the same tutor for their last two years. There is a zero tolerance of bullying and the head can 'be very frightening about that sort of thing,' said an older pupil, 'he takes it very seriously.' Trouble taken to recognise the difference between good natured banter and persistent bullying. 'That takes constant alertness,' says the head.

Most of the boarders are Service children and each house – one boy, one girl – is presided over by a house mistress who is not a teacher, which gives them a different perspective on their charges. Super bright accommodation where the décor is unashamedly girly for the girls and boyish for the boys. No problem if you were asked to close your eyes and guess which house you are in. Imaginatively designed common rooms, welcoming bedrooms – some with very daring colours – plenty of games available. Tea and toast making facilities. The boarding accommodation is across the road from the main buildings and up a gentle slope past the all weather pitches and next door to the nursery. 'I like it like this,' said an obviously happy girl. 'It's good to get away from the school. It's a bit like walking home. Weekends are fun with lots of activities arranged and sometimes we have special feasts.' The food in the main dining room is very good with the ladies serving behind the cafeteria counters noticeably kind and motherly. Staff sit with pupils. Healthy amount of noise. Optional Saturday morning school for Years 3 and 4; thereafter it is compulsory with a mixture of formal and informal.

No consideration of the prep school is complete without visiting the nursery and pre-prep. Behind carefully locked doors and gateways are the classrooms built in the style of log cabins. These are the pioneers of the Wycliffe experience and from their exalted position on the hill they can look down at the prep school, the goal for most of them. Masses of toys – 'learning toys' – everywhere with attentive and experienced staff. Good library – 'the nursery eats books,' said one teacher. Other meals are taken in the prep school dining room, down the hill and over the bridge. A very happy set up, well equipped and imaginatively run. Good after school care. Beds are even available for children exhausted by it all.

The Wycliffe empire, incorporating as it does children from 2–18, is a homogeneous package, closely knit both geographically and in ethos. For those embarking on the Wycliffe adventure the prep school is an ideal launching pad. Well equipped and well run, it is a happy school with sensible, worthwhile standards.

Yardley Court

Linked to Somerhill Pre-prep in the Junior section
Linked to Schools At Somerhill (The) in the Junior section
Linked to Derwent Lodge School in the Junior section

Schools at Somerhill, Five Oak Green Road, Tonbridge, Kent, TN11 0NJ

• Fees: £12,165 pa • Independent

Tel: 01732 352 124
Fax: 01732 363 381
Email: office@schoolsatsomerhill.com
Website: www.schoolsatsomerhill.com

Headmaster: Mr John Coakley BA MA PGCE.

Remarks: See The Schools at Somerhill for write-up.

Yarlet School

Yarlet, Near Stafford, Stafford, Staffordshire, ST18 9SU

• Pupils: 155; 95 boys, 60 girls; 70 in the pre-prep and nursery • Ages: 2-3 nursery, 3-7 pre-prep, 7-13 main school • C of E / inter-denom • Fees: Pre-prep £5,925-£ 7,425; Prep £9,285-£9,885 pa • Independent

Tel: 01785 286 568
Fax: 01785 286 569
Email: info@yarletschool.org
Website: www.yarletschool.co.uk

Head: Since 2009, Mr Ian Raybould BEd Hons ALCM NPQH (early forties), studied music and education (4–12 years) at University College, Winchester, and London College of Music, taught at King's College, Madrid, where he was head of music and boarding; head of first IAPS prep school in Spain; as ISI inspector visited prep, senior and international schools in Europe. Teaches music at school (and plays organ for chapel services) – keen to develop it and performing arts in general; also particularly interested in SEN provision and technology – has worked creatively on school's website and is introducing electronic management, tracking and registration systems (a lot of work to do here as school has lagged behind on the ICT front); also raising standards of teaching and learning.

Thoughtful, fair minded and unassuming, someone who listens rather than dominates – takes account of parental views and appreciates school's traditions whilst modernising. Well liked by children and parents – 'The children respect and are eager to please him. He is very focused on them, knows them very well and speaks to them in a gentle, kindly way'. Financially shrewd – solid plans to achieve security – but doesn't want to increase numbers to a point where the school's family atmosphere is lost. Wife, Zoe, enthusiastic, very involved (PR, domestic services); two boys, six and eight, one at school.

Entrance: Not selective – takes average/above average children; mild LDD/SEN accepted. Most move up from pre-prep. Takes children at any age after interview with head; taster day to assess ability.

Two bursaries (RS Plant awards) at 11+ for children who show at interview 'a real aptitude and enthusiasm for independent education' – up to 50 per cent fees. Sibling discounts in main school. General bursary fund for parents needing assistance.

Offers a combined scholarship for up to two local primary school children from 11, with a secured place at a senior school. At the time of visiting, two combined scholars were bound for Repton and Rugby respectively. Aimed at children with an 'aptitude for independent education and boarding whose progress is impeded by home or school circumstances'. Interview at 10 – need ability to pass CE into senior school and a particular strength in at least one arts, music, sports or academic subject; means-tested. School keen to extend range of primary and public schools involved.

Exit: Most at 13, though some girls at 11. All pass CE and a third to a half win academic, music and art scholarships. Most to independent schools – Denstone, Shrewsbury,

Stafford Grammar, Repton, Abbotsholme, the odd one to Rugby.

Remarks: Good recent ISI report on academics; homework from age seven; twice yearly exams till Year 7, then termly; no achievement gender divide; fine to be ambitious and work hard, according to our guide. Small classes – 14 average, but fewer from Year 7. Specialist teachers for all subjects by Year 5; children see teachers as 'helpful and understanding'. A parent said: 'The staff are amazing – they work very long hours, know the children very well and bring out the best in them.' She also liked the frequent use of the outdoors for lessons – 'They're not penned in the classroom'. New maths head to raise standards; very experienced, enthusiastic French and Latin teacher really stretches children and takes all of Years 7 and 8 to Normandy for five days to practise their oral skills plus visit historical sites – 'Languages tuition second to none,' praised a parent with experience of the Swedish school system. Moving to Latin for all in last three years.

Some classrooms darkish with small windows and in need of decoration (rolling programme for this, says head) but lovely large maths room (loft conversion) and light, purpose built art room. Only one computer per classroom and one interactive whiteboard, in a well resourced IT suite used for all subjects; library has four computers; more networking planned.

Very good SENCo – can cope with mild physical disabilities, dyslexia, dyspraxia, ADHD/autism/Asperger's: 'Would take each case on its merits'. IEPs; lots of discussion with all teachers about strategies. All Year 2s and late entries screened by Dyslexia Action for minimal fee; parents can pay for DA one-to-one support or opt for free individual/small group outside or inside classroom support. Also annual standardised testing of all, Years 1–6, and above if required, for English, spelling and maths. Detailed G and T policy – keeps a register.

EYFS – ISI report not glowing but praised relationships, personal development and care; well staffed, small classes, attractive, spacious, well equipped classrooms and pleasant outdoor play area. Five- and six-year-olds learn Spanish.

Daily traditional sports (including dance once a week for girls); very successful record – head wants to maintain this and introduce a more inclusive approach to teams; outside professional coaches; some children at county and national levels. Rugby, football (girls compete too) and cricket pitches, Astroturf, netball and tennis courts, sports hall, outdoor swimming pool.

Strong music and getting stronger ('fantastic head of music') – good choice of instruments; head is developing (popular) chapel choir, which performs outside school and is acquiring a reputation locally. Orchestra, string and woodwind groups, e.g. 'Champagne Flutes'; annual Young Musician of the Year competition. Ambitious drama productions (*Macbeth, Guys and Dolls, West Side Story*) in central hall with seating arranged on three sides of stage; theatre trips, e.g. Stratford on Avon, and visiting companies, e.g. a Spanish performing arts school; poetry reciting competition. Ballet/dance exams and performances. Yarlet Academy of Performing Arts run by Stagecoach available to three-year-olds upwards, taken up by a quarter of the school (can replace sport once a week).

Good range of art options – printing, ceramics, 3D, photography, textiles – and record for art scholarships, but we didn't see anything special on display. Other options include chess, model making, computer club (digital projects). Fund raising for various charities; several trips, local and national, for science, geography, history, ICT; outward bound week (plus community work) for Year 8.

Between Stafford and Stone, originally a late 18th century residence – turreted façade, ivy clad walls, welcoming entrance hall with sofas, open fire and, on one wall, framed black and white photographs of old heads and sports teams, whilst on another enlarged colour photos of current children engaged in various activities, suggesting the school's combination of the traditional with the modern. Of the two, the former rather prevails, through the lovely views of tranquil, open countryside (the grounds amount to 33 acres), the secure atmosphere of this small community and the very attractive, smart uniform – boys in open collar gingham shirts with sleeveless jumpers and dark trousers or shorts, girls in red and green tartan skirts and red jumpers; the very littlies wear blue or red gingham smocks over their home clothes. Founded in 1873 as a prep school for boys, it went fully co educational in 1994, though some classes have a preponderance of boys. Grand staircase and black and white chequered flagstones in main hall with another open fire, but some drab areas elsewhere.

A day school with flexi-boarding for main school children on Thursday and Friday nights; Saturday morning school – flexible for Years 3–4, following parental feedback. Comfortable, well decorated accommodation. The head has introduced more activities for children who board, e.g. camping evening, bowling, karaoke, which they appreciate. After school care available till 6pm in pre-prep (for a cost). Flexible finishing times between 4.30 and 7pm in main school (no additional cost). Prep periods so most can be done during school day – very popular with parents. Happy, family feeling – cross age friendships, lots of siblings, children help each other; ethos of mutual respect.

Pleasant dining room – staff eat with children, who have table clearing, floor sweeping and washing up duties. Healthy, filling food (spaghetti bolognese, garlic bread and trad pudding the day we visited, with salad, fruit/yoghurt options). Intriguing small chapel in the style of those built by Victorians for use in the then British Empire – green corrugated iron on the outside, with wooden pews, small organ and attractive green stained glass windows within. Traditional daily service with 'upbeat' content, says head, who has introduced more staff and child participation. Small garden outside for quiet reflection. Wildlife venture – pool with two islands and observation hide – open to other local schools, maintained under the auspices of Staffordshire Wildlife Trust.

Clear anti-bullying policy – head says not a problem (as do parents) but is realistic about possibility. Head boy and girl plus prefects from Year 8 chosen by staff (this year all are prefects) who keep tabs on younger children and enter issues in a book for head to handle. Children told us (approvingly) discipline better now with new head. ISI report praised effective handling of any problems and good behaviour. PSHE programme, including citizenship, from Year 3. Parents happy with support for emotional needs and preparation for transition to senior school. Three houses – points for excellence of any kind, including 'kind spirit', leading to certificates (pre-prep) or badges (prep) and end of year cups.

Parents from Stafford, Stone and surrounding rural communities. Wide variety of backgrounds – professional, farming, business – but very few ethnic minority (school aiming to develop multi cultural exposure). Confident, happy, polite children who enjoy energetic activities (running cross country even in snow!). Good links with parents, who are widely consulted and feel they can approach school at any time with concerns that are dealt with effectively – focus groups, regular information meetings (e.g. on e-safety), newsletters ('Y, Sir?' – say it aloud), detailed information booklets; questionnaire responses (warts and all) published on very good website, with a restricted area bearing delightful photos of children taken by parents at matches etc; grandparents' tea the day we visited.

An appealing, cosy school affording a very protected environment. On the up with energetic, talented, new head.

Yarm Preparatory School

Linked to Yarm School in the Senior section

Grammar School Lane, Yarm, TS15 9ES

• Pupils: 32 boys and girls in the nursery, 115 in Early School, 180 in the prep • Ages: 3-11 • Multi-faith with a Christian tradition • Fees: From £4,158 pa • Independent

Tel: 01642 781 447
Fax: 01642 787 425
Email: gt@yarmschool.org
Website: www.yarmschool.org

Head of Foundation Stage: Mr P H Hardy. Head of Prep School: Mrs Gillian R Taylor.

Head of Prep is to retire in July 2011 and they have advertised for a replacement.

Remarks: A perfect preparation for the senior school. Little 'Yarmers' have the phoenix badge on them from age three and progress with the same mix of expectation, opportunity and enjoyment as their senior school peers.

Well-equipped nursery (term times only) offers a blend of play and teaching on a one adult to eight children ratio. Boasts play rooms, maths room, literacy room, conservatory and nice outside play area. Play based curriculum moves swiftly into early literacy/numeracy. Youngsters begin French at age three. Children enjoy food cooked by senior school chef – lucky things!

Early School takes four- to seven-year-olds in seven classes (two reception, two Year 1, three Year 2). Play based learning phased out and pupils are down to work by end of reception, ready to tackle KS1 in Year 1 through a National Curriculum enriched with geography, history, music and PE. All classes, reception to Year 2, get weekly ICT lesson in the ICT site at the prep school.

School takes youngsters from age seven to eleven and pupils can join from other schools, following half day selection including NFER tests. Follows National Curriculum but cherry picks other subjects from art, design technology, sport, PE. For two lessons a week children can choose what they want to do, and they select anything from horse riding to Italian. Strong on sports, music, modern languages and ICT; small class sizes (around 20) help enormously. Two playgrounds – one noisy, one quieter. The prep and senior school are to have a £20m redevelopment scheme.

Great opportunity to try lots of different subjects and sports. Residential trips start at Year 3, typically with a visit to Grasmere, then York in Year 4, Robinwood Activity Centre and London in Year 5, France in Years 5/6, Milan and the Inner Hebrides in Year 6.

Happy, bright, confident little children.

Yateley Manor

51 Reading Road, Yateley, Hampshire, GU46 7UQ

• Pupils: 440 boys and girls, all day • Ages: Pre-prep (Wyndhams) 3-7; prep 7-13 • C of E roots • Fees: £4,125-£11,175 pa • Independent

Tel: 01252 405 500
Fax: 01252 405 504
Email: office@yateleymanor.com
Website: www.yateleymanor.com

Head: Since 2009, Mr Rob Williams MA (economics) PGCE, formerly head of St Peter's Prep School at Lympstone in Devon. Had a couple of spells in management in industry before moving back into teaching. He is a passionate believer in the importance of the broad educational experience and outside of school he enjoys sport, particularly the triathlon. On gaining the post he commented, 'I really am absolutely thrilled to have the chance to take on what is so obviously such a great school.'

Entrance: 'Moderately selective,' they say – informal interview and assessment. Generous scholarships: academic up to 50 per cent of fees, music 35 per cent, sport 25 per cent, chess 15 per cent, all-rounders 15 per cent. Discount for brothers and sisters. Galloping popularity means early registration a must.

Exit: Royal Grammar School Guildford, The Abbey Reading, Lord Wandsworth, Wellington, Bradfield, Leighton Park, then a smattering of other nearby top independents. Around 30 out of a typical year group of 76 leave aged 11 for local independents and grammars: Farnborough Hill, Guildford High, Reading Grammar, Kendricks.

Remarks: A tight ship – 450 children in eight acres. It ticks like a Swiss watch but efficiency banishes stress – cheeriness is general. The day starts at 8am if you want breakfast, and can finish as late as 6.30pm if you want supervised homework. Academically brisk, success is prized, scholarships are mopped up a-plenty, yet headmaster's commendations reward effort, and charmingly so – for 'being brave this week', for 'telling a lovely story'. Oh, yes, this is a humane place. Everyone learns Latin. And, in Years 3 and 4, cooking. Learning support established and growing – specialist fine tuning in class for problems as they arise, individual tuition charged for. Chess unusually big, taught by an international master, and more than twenty children play for Hants and Berks.

We were shown round by a boy and a girl, picked at random, licensed to take us anywhere. What confidence! We went everywhere. The IT is amazing. Message screens stand at junctions and bring the latest news. All pause and peer. Everyone does email – to each other, to their teachers. Interactive whiteboards abound. It's slick but it serves. We had to go see matron because she's so nice. Much new building, all of it excellent, and a painted rainbow along one wall to guide the weenies. Homework posted daily on the superb website, which keeps parents up to speed with everything. Reporting is meticulous and monthly – pupils are monitored not quizzically but with care. Their record book goes home daily, in which parents can have their say and, every week, their child makes a new resolution.

Music is a matter of pride. More than half the school learn an instrument. Art is good, ceramics especially. An alluring variety of after-school activities – and, in the holidays, arty and sporty activity weeks. Sport is hot and well done, cricket especially, though some parents say they'd like to see more coaching. All can play in a team if they want in many years. Socially, the climate is warm and sunny, the children notably natural and affectionate. Seniors take turns at being team leaders to supervise things, and patrol at break with snazzy walkie-talkies. There's a school council and a food committee with truly democratic elections. Communications are superb. Every week there's a bustling newsletter which comes home. Thriving PTA. For parents there is a strong sense of transparency and partnership, and much praise for the pastoral head, who solves problems thoroughly. However some feel that intimacy has lost out in the recent expansion and it can sometimes be hard to talk to your child's teacher in person.

A fast-moving, high-achieving school dedicated to best possible results. It keeps relentlessness at bay because it places such high value on courtesy, right conduct and happiness. There is something very rooted and very modern going on here.

Yehudi Menuhin Junior School

Linked to Yehudi Menuhin School in the Senior section

Stoke d'Abernon, Cobham, Surrey, KT11 3QQ

• Pupils: 70 boys and girls (entire school); mostly boarders • Ages: 8-13 • Non-denom • Fees: Boarding £41,106; Day £40,044 pa for those not on music and dance scheme. • Independent

Tel: 01932 864 739
Fax: 01932 864 633
Email: admin@yehudimenuhinschool.co.uk
Website: www.yehudimenuhinschool.co.uk

Remarks: See senior school for details.

Preparatory School: Nursery to age 11
Ages 11-18 HMC Day and Boarding
Preparatory School
01622 842117
Senior School
01622 845206
www.svs.org.uk
SUTTON VALENCE SCHOOL
'Early Years provision is excellent'
ISI Inspection Report 2009
'.... a broad ability school that attains very good results whilst providing a friendly, supportive atmosphere which my children are thriving in.'
Parent survey 2010
'A broad, challenging, well-balanced curriculum, flexibly delivered to suit pupils' needs is enriched by an outstandingly strong and varied co-curricular provision.'
ISI Inspection 2009
Sutton Valence School
A member of the United Westminster Schools' Foundation
Founded in 1576 by William Lambe

STEINER EDUCATION
Educating the whole child-
head, heart and hands
OPEN AFTERNOON
Saturday 12 February 2011 • 2-4pm
Rudolf Steiner School Kings Langley is set in 10 acres of attractive grounds in an historic site, and offers an education committed to the development of the whole child – Kindergarten to A Levels.
Rudolf Steiner School
Kings Langley
Introductory talks and tours throughout the afternoon – no need to book.
telephone: 01923 262505
email: info@rsskl.org
web: www.rsskl.org
Langley Hill, Kings Langley, Herts WD4 9HG

Discover the magic at Unicorn School
'An excellent programme of extra-curricular activities provides an educational experience of high quality ...
Personal development is outstanding ...
Good and often outstanding teaching enables pupils to learn effectively'
Independent Schools Report, March 2010
Unicorn School is a co-educational, parent-owned prep school. We provide a friendly, creative and stimulating learning environment in which a child's potential can be nurtured - with excellent results.
Places are occasionally available throughout the school. For enquiries, please contact the Registrar on 0208 8948 3926 or email registrar@unicornschool.org.uk
Unicorn School
238 Kew Road
Richmond
Surrey TW9 3JX
The school is registered as an Educational Charity, number 312578, and is a non-profit-making company.
UNICORN SCHOOL

The key to entrance exam success...
www.goodschoolsguide.galorepark.co.uk

SEAFORD COLLEGE

The Johnson Trust. Registered Charity No. 277439

Seaford College is a co-educational independent day and boarding school, situated in an unrivalled position, amid 400 acres of rolling parkland in the heart of West Sussex.

With just under 600 pupils aged from 7-18, Seaford is a caring community in which relationships are based on mutual respect and students are given a strong sense of belonging.

A centre of excellence for art, music and sport. Added value in all academic subjects.

Further details from the admissions secretary
Julie Mackay Smith

Telephone: 01798 867456
Fax: 01798 867606
email: JMackay@seaford.org - web: www.seaford.org

THE ROCHE SCHOOL

Independent Prep and Nursery School off Putney Bridge Road
11 Frogmore, London SW18 1HW
www.therocheschool.co.uk **Tel: 020 8877 0823**
Nursery schools in Wandsworth, Putney and Fulham

- Good, clear teaching and personal attention in small groups
- Places regularly gained at top academic secondary schools
- Plenty of sport, music and art and drama

"The Roche School provides an outstanding quality of education and meets its aims fully." (**OFSTED November 2008**)

2011 Open mornings:
26th January, 10th March, 6th May, 9th June, 13th October, 18th November and Saturday 24th September, or by appointment

ROWAN
PREPARATORY SCHOOL
AN OUTSTANDING SCHOOL FOR GIRLS AGED 2+ TO 11+

ROWAN BRAE
FOR GIRLS AGED 2 - 7 YEARS
41 GORDON ROAD, CLAYGATE, ESHER KT10 0PJ

ROWAN HILL
FOR GIRLS AGED 7 - 11 YEARS
6 FITZALAN ROAD, CLAYGATE, ESHER KT10 0LX

You are welcome to attend our Open Morning or arrange a visit to our school

Please visit the website for further details or contact Mrs Drake, School Registrar

United Church Schools Trust
The best in everyone™
Registered Charity Number: 1016538 Company Number: 2780748
23-25 Chapel Street, Titchmarsh, Northamptonshire NN14 3DA

FOR FURTHER INFORMATION PLEASE CONTACT US:
01372 462 627
school.office@rowan.ucst.co.uk
www.rowan.surrey.sch.uk

Elstree

Home Farm
(Elstree Pre-Prep) Boys and girls, 3 – 7

Elstree School
(Independent Boarding & Day) Boys, 7 – 13

OPEN MORNINGS

For details of our Open Mornings, please refer to our website

Please contact us if you are interested in attending an Open Morning
E registrar@elstreeschool.org.uk T 0118 971 3302 www.elstreeschool.org.uk
Elstree School Woolhampton Berkshire RG7 5TD

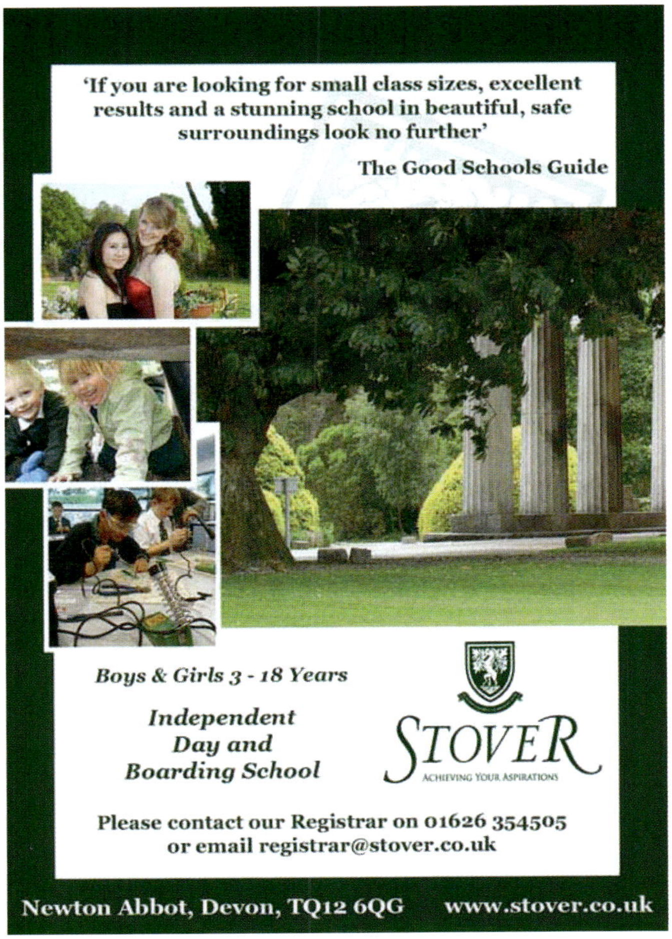
'If you are looking for small class sizes, excellent results and a stunning school in beautiful, safe surroundings look no further'
The Good Schools Guide
Boys & Girls 3 - 18 Years
Independent Day and Boarding School
STOVER
ACHIEVING YOUR ASPIRATIONS
Please contact our Registrar on 01626 354505 or email registrar@stover.co.uk
Newton Abbot, Devon, TQ12 6QG
www.stover.co.uk

MERCHISTON
EDINBURGH | Boys first
WE ONLY DO WHAT'S BEST FOR THE BOYS
Call 0131 312 2200
or visit www.merchiston.co.uk
A Boarding and Day School for Boys aged 8-18.
Merchiston Castle School, Colinton Road,
Edinburgh, EH13 0PU, Scotland.
Recognised by the Inland Revenue
as a Charity, number SC016580

Improving Performance
Building Confidence
Private Tuition in Your Own Home
Britain's leading tutoring service provider has 33 years experience. Qualified, experienced, enhanced-CRB checked tutors deliver personalised tuition programmes & excellent results. The Good Schools Guide recommended.
Primary, 7/8/11/13+/Common Entrance, GCSE, A1/A2 Level & beyond
Catering also for special needs, remedial, dyslexia & gifted
Excellent acceptance rate at leading selective schools and universities
Fleet Tutors
Helping students reach their potential
0845 644 5452
www.fleet-tutors.co.uk
Relieving Anxiety
Realising Success

Help your child gain entry to his or her school of choice...
www.goodschoolsguide.galorepark.co.uk

MAPS

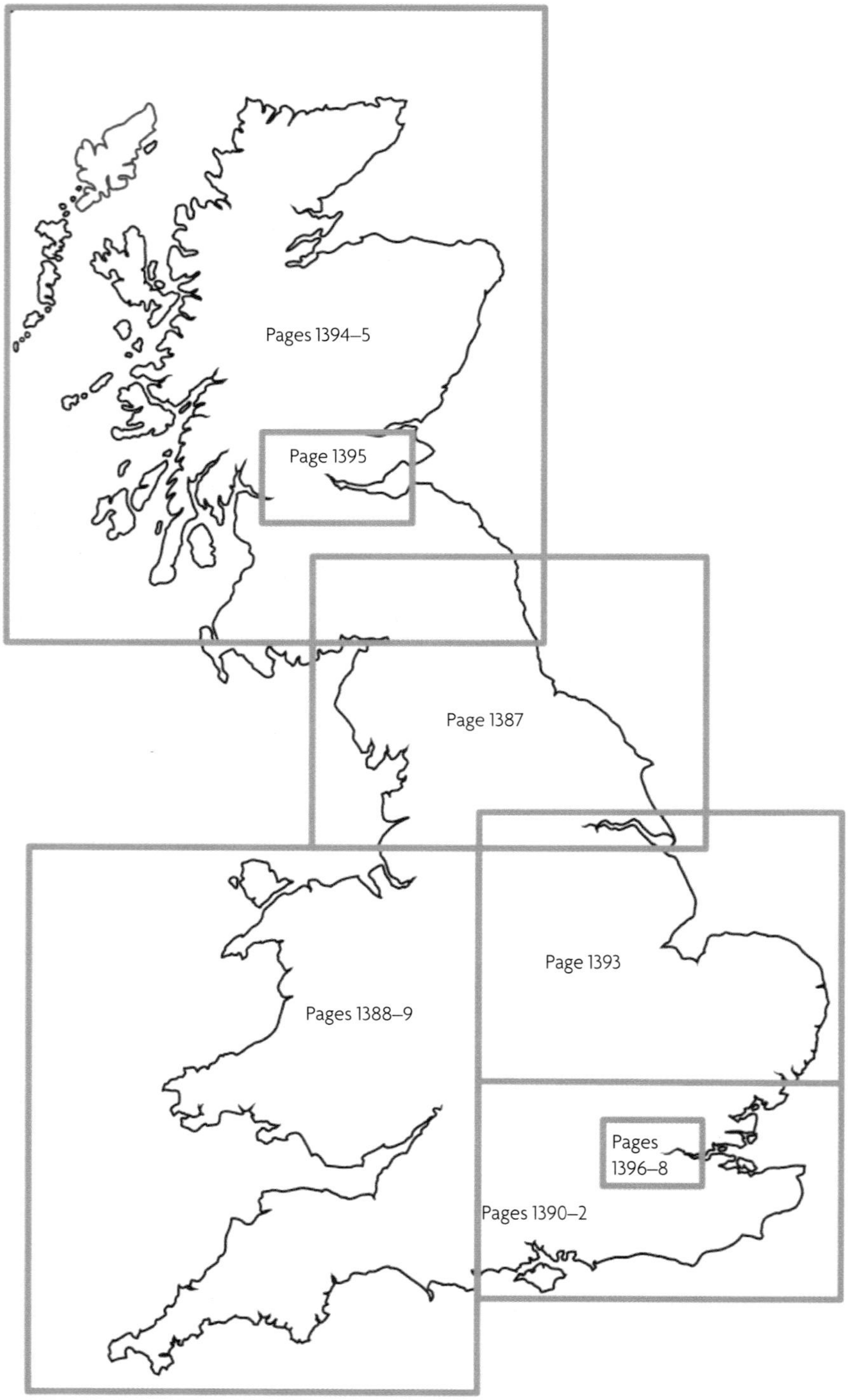
Pages 1394–5
Page 1395
Page 1387
Page 1393
Pages 1388–9
Pages 1396–8
Pages 1390–2

NORTH ENGLAND

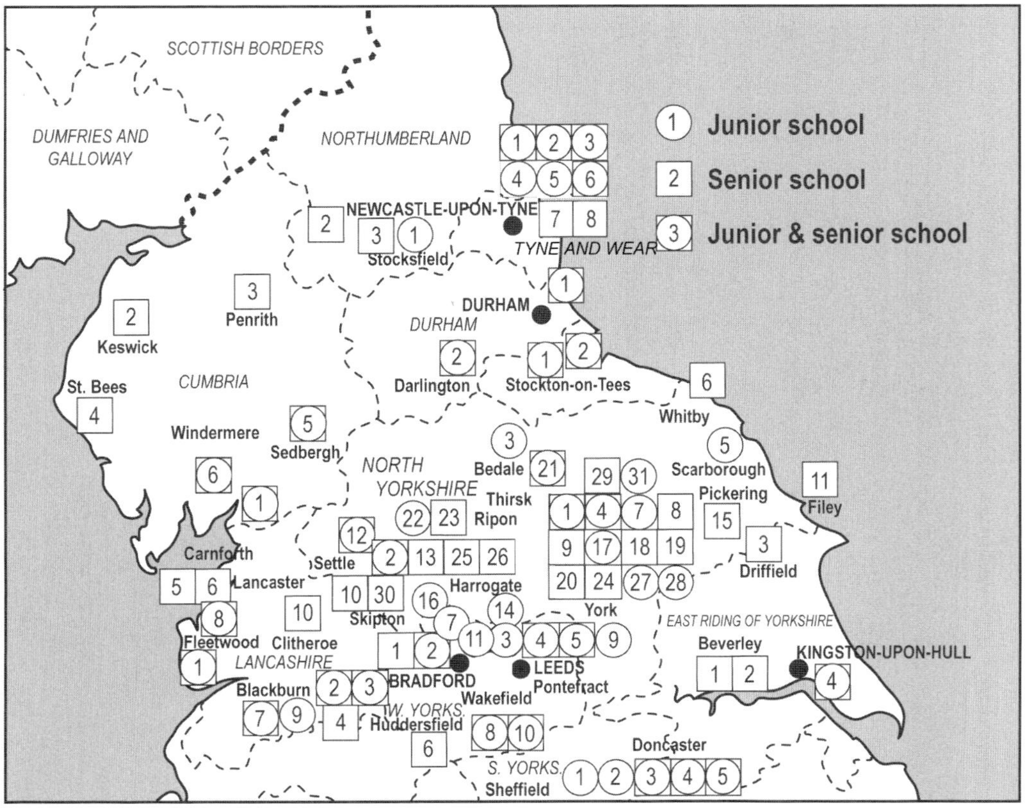

WEST OF ENGLAND & WALES

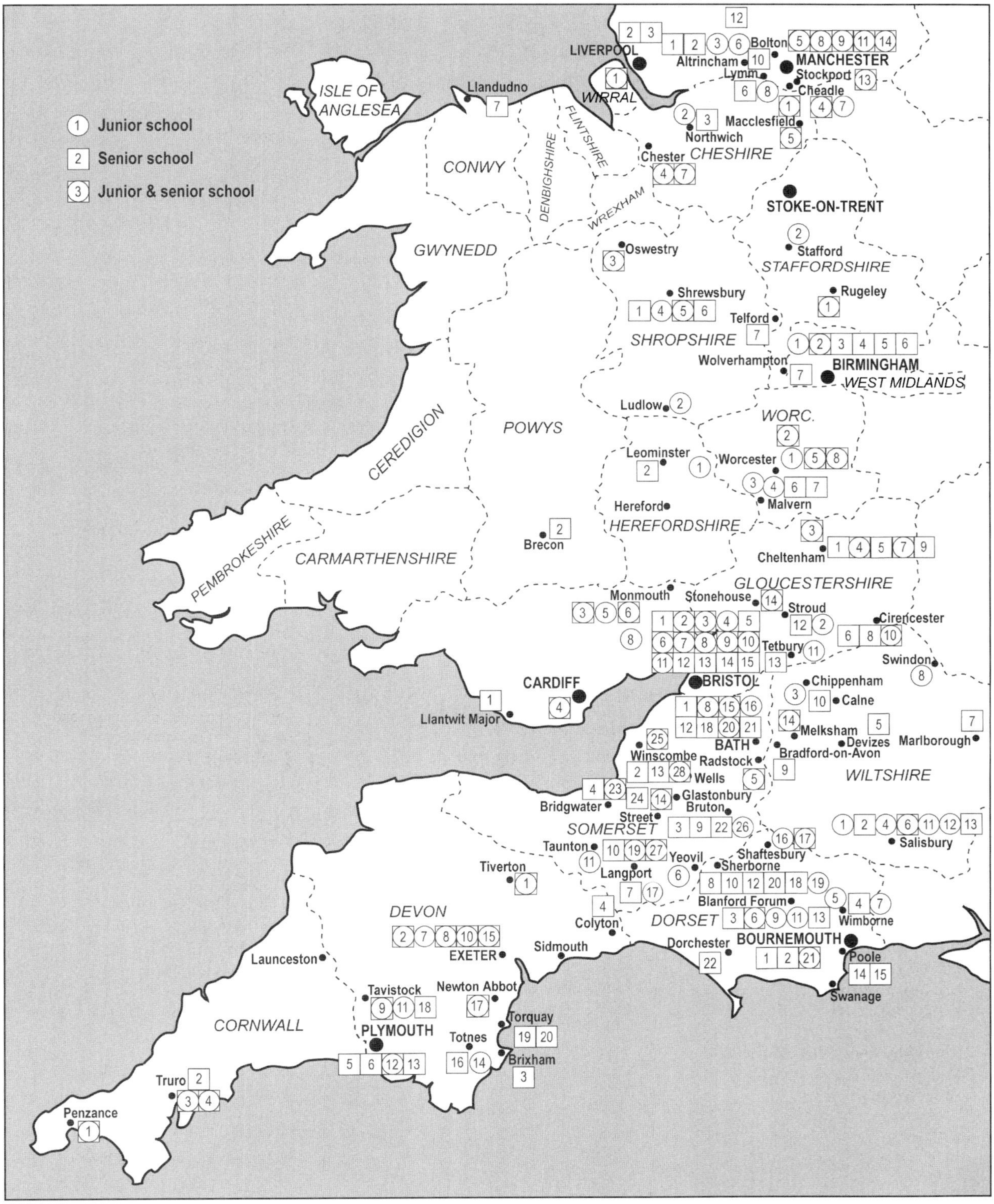

9 St Laurence School 763
10 St Mary's Calne 775
11 Salisbury Cathedral School 1299
12 Sandroyd School 1300
13 South Wilts Grammar School for Girls 833
14 Stonar School 846

WORCESTERSHIRE

1 Abberley Hall 965
2 Bromsgrove School 192
3 Downs (The), Malvern College Preparatory School 1069
4 Elms School (The) 1088
5 King's School (Worcester) 481
6 Malvern College 534
7 Malvern St James 536
8 RGS Worcester 683

SOUTH EAST ENGLAND

BERKSHIRE — Page

BRIGHTON & HOVE

BUCKINGHAMSHIRE

EAST SUSSEX

ESSEX

HAMPSHIRE & IoW

HERTFORDSHIRE

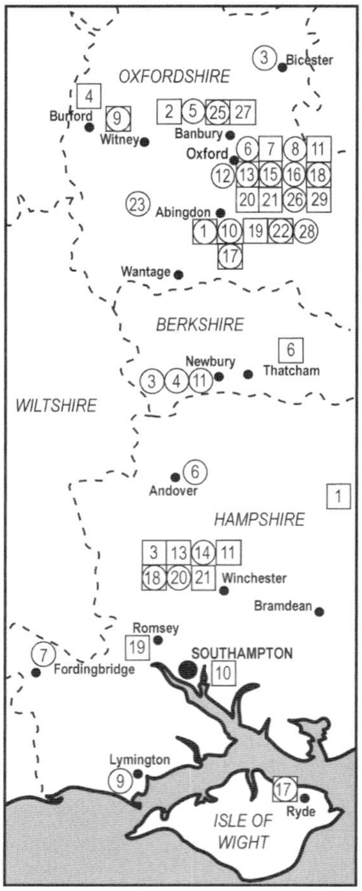

KENT

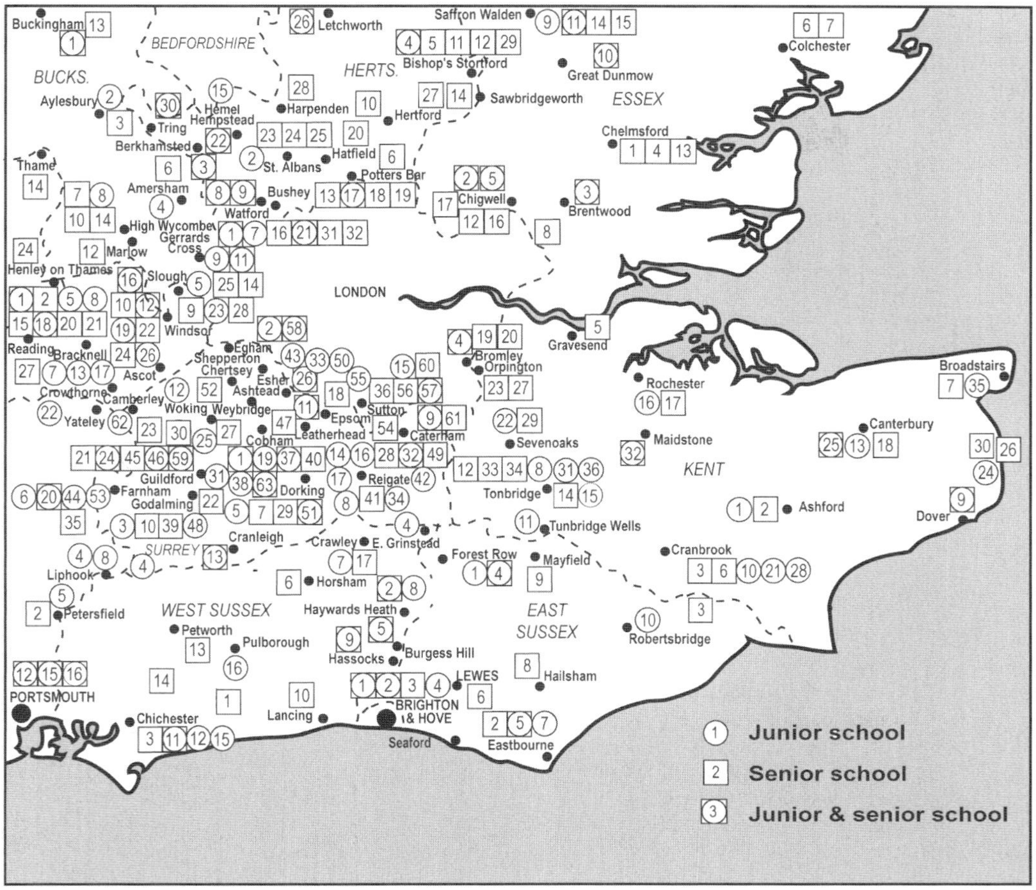

13 Junior King's School 1153
14 Kent College 458
15 Kent College Preparatory School, Pembury 1156
16 King's Preparatory School 1161
17 King's Rochester 478
18 King's School Canterbury (The) 483
19 Langley Park School for Boys 506
20 Langley Park School for Girls 507
21 Marlborough House School 1186
22 New Beacon School (The) 1200
23 Newstead Wood School for Girls 581
24 Northbourne Park School 1209
25 St Edmund's 741
26 St Lawrence College 764
27 St Olave's and St Saviour's Grammar School 787
28 St Ronan's School 1296
29 Sevenoaks School 802
30 Sir Roger Manwood's School 821
31 Somerhill (The Schools at) 1303
32 Sutton Valence School 862
33 Tonbridge Grammar School 880
34 Tonbridge School 882
35 Wellesley House School 1340
36 Yardley Court 1358

OXFORDSHIRE

1 Abingdon School 79
2 Bloxham School 161
3 Bruern Abbey School 1020
4 Burford School and Community College 199
5 Carrdus School 1028
6 Chandlings School 1032
7 Cherwell School (The) 228
8 Christ Church Cathedral School 1038
9 Cokethorpe School 255
10 Cothill House 1051
11 d'Overbroeck's College 292
12 Dragon School 1073
13 Headington School 406
14 Lord Williams's School 524
15 Magdalen College School 532
16 New College School 1201
17 Our Lady's Abingdon 613
18 Oxford High School GDST 614
19 Radley College 671
20 St Clare's, Oxford 732
21 St Edward's Oxford 743
22 St Helen and St Katharine (The School of) 752
23 St Hugh's School (Faringdon) 1277
24 Shiplake College 812
25 Sibford School 816
26 Summer Fields School 1317
27 Tudor Hall School 898
28 Unicorn School (Abingdon) (The) 1336
29 Wychwood School 951

SURREY

1 ACS Cobham International School 81
2 ACS Egham International School 83
3 Aldro School 973
4 Amesbury School 977
5 Belmont School (Dorking) 1000
6 Bentley Church of England Primary School 1001
7 Box Hill School 173
8 Burys Court 1022
9 Caterham School 214
10 Charterhouse 220
11 City of London Freemen's School 242
12 Coworth-Flexlands School 1054
13 Cranleigh School 273
14 Cranmore School 1058
15 Cumnor House School (Croydon) 1060
16 Danes Hill School 1064
17 Downsend School 1071
18 Epsom College 321
19 Feltonfleet School 1098
20 Frensham Heights School 341
21 George Abbot School 348
22 Godalming College 358
23 Gordon's School 363
24 Guildford High School 376
25 Halstead Prep School for Girls 1124
26 Hampton Court House 392
27 Heathside School (Weybridge) 409
28 Howard of Effingham School 424
29 Hurtwood House School 431
30 Knowl Hill School 491
31 Lanesborough School 1168
32 Manor House School 542
33 Milbourne Lodge School 1190

WEST SUSSEX

MIDLANDS & EAST ENGLAND

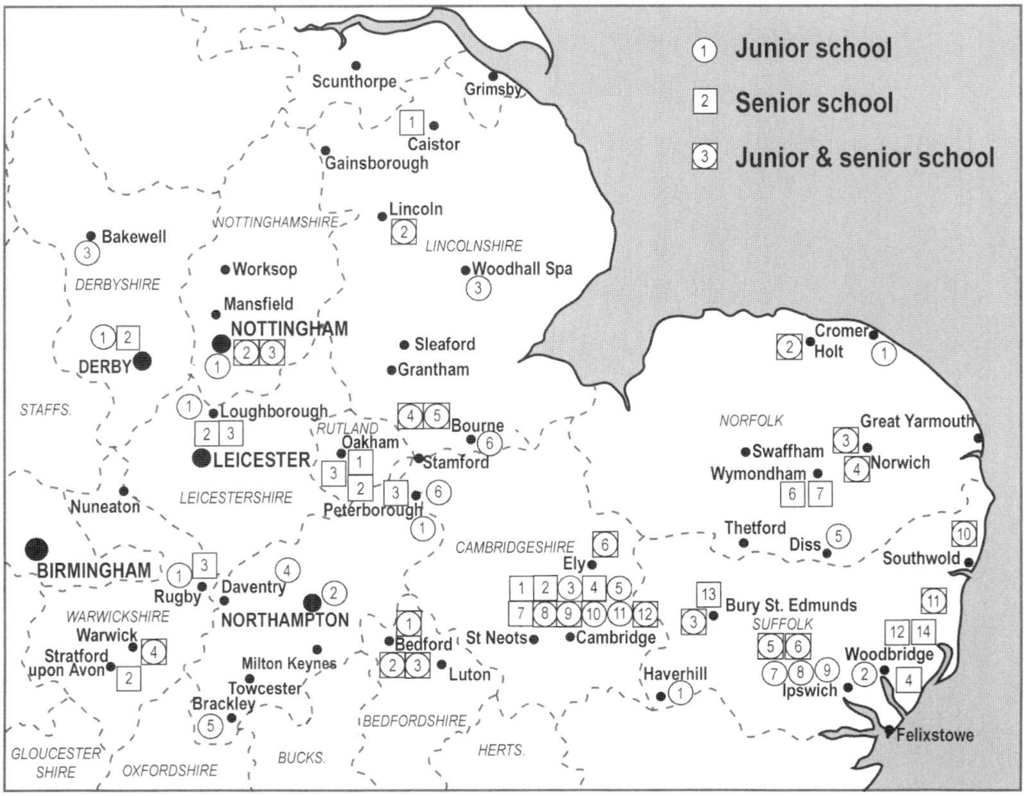

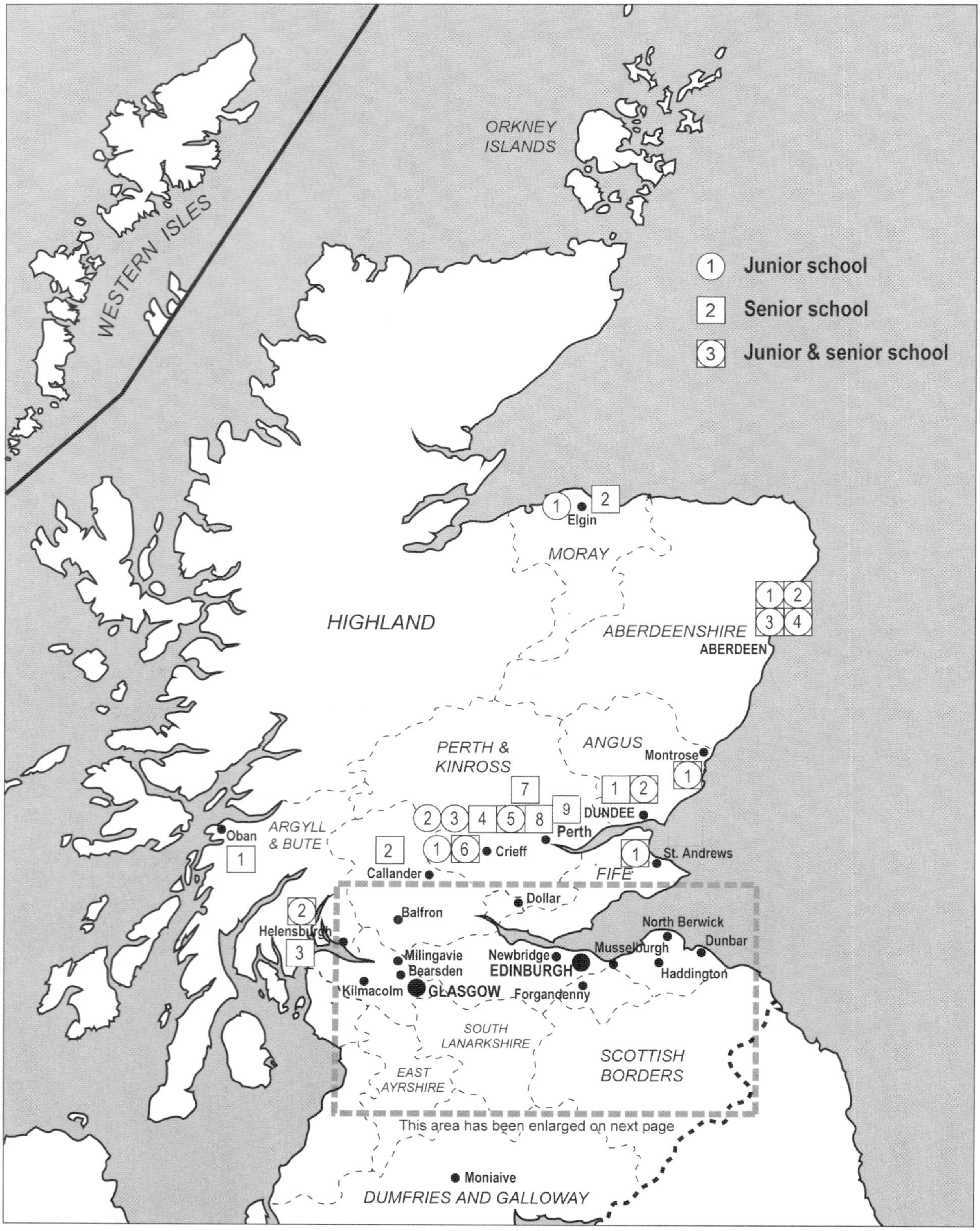

WESTERN ISLES
ORKNEY ISLANDS
Junior school
Senior school
Junior & senior school
HIGHLAND
MORAY
Elgin
ABERDEENSHIRE
ABERDEEN
PERTH & KINROSS
ANGUS
Montrose
DUNDEE
Perth
Crieff
ARGYLL & BUTE
Oban
Callander
St. Andrews
FIFE
Dollar
Balfron
Helensburgh
North Berwick
Dunbar
Milingavie
Bearsden
Newbridge
EDINBURGH
Musselburgh
Haddington
Kilmacolm
GLASGOW
Forgandenny
SOUTH LANARKSHIRE
EAST AYRSHIRE
SCOTTISH BORDERS
This area has been enlarged on next page
Moniaive
DUMFRIES AND GALLOWAY

SCOTLAND

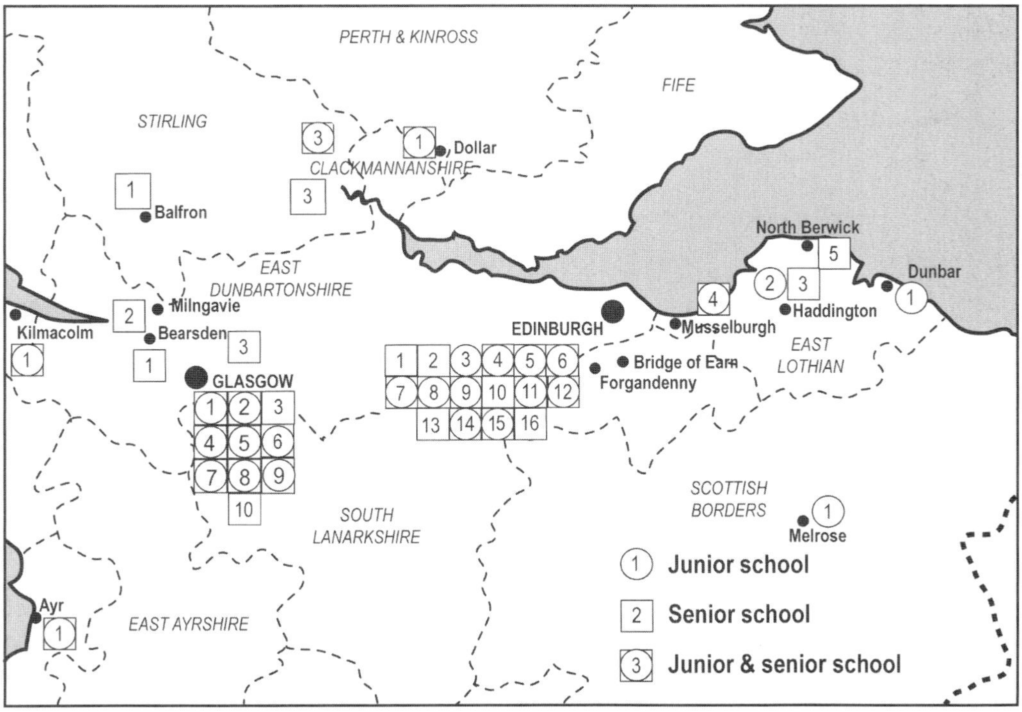

PERTH & KINROSS
FIFE
STIRLING
Dollar
CLACKMANNANSHIRE
Balfron
North Berwick
EAST DUNBARTONSHIRE
Dunbar
Milngavie
Haddington
Kilmacolm
Bearsden
EDINBURGH
Musselburgh
EAST LOTHIAN
Bridge of Earn
Forgandenny
GLASGOW
SCOTTISH BORDERS
SOUTH LANARKSHIRE
Melrose
Ayr
EAST AYRSHIRE
Junior school
Senior school
Junior & senior school

LONDON

1 Prep school

2 Senior school

3 Prep & senior school

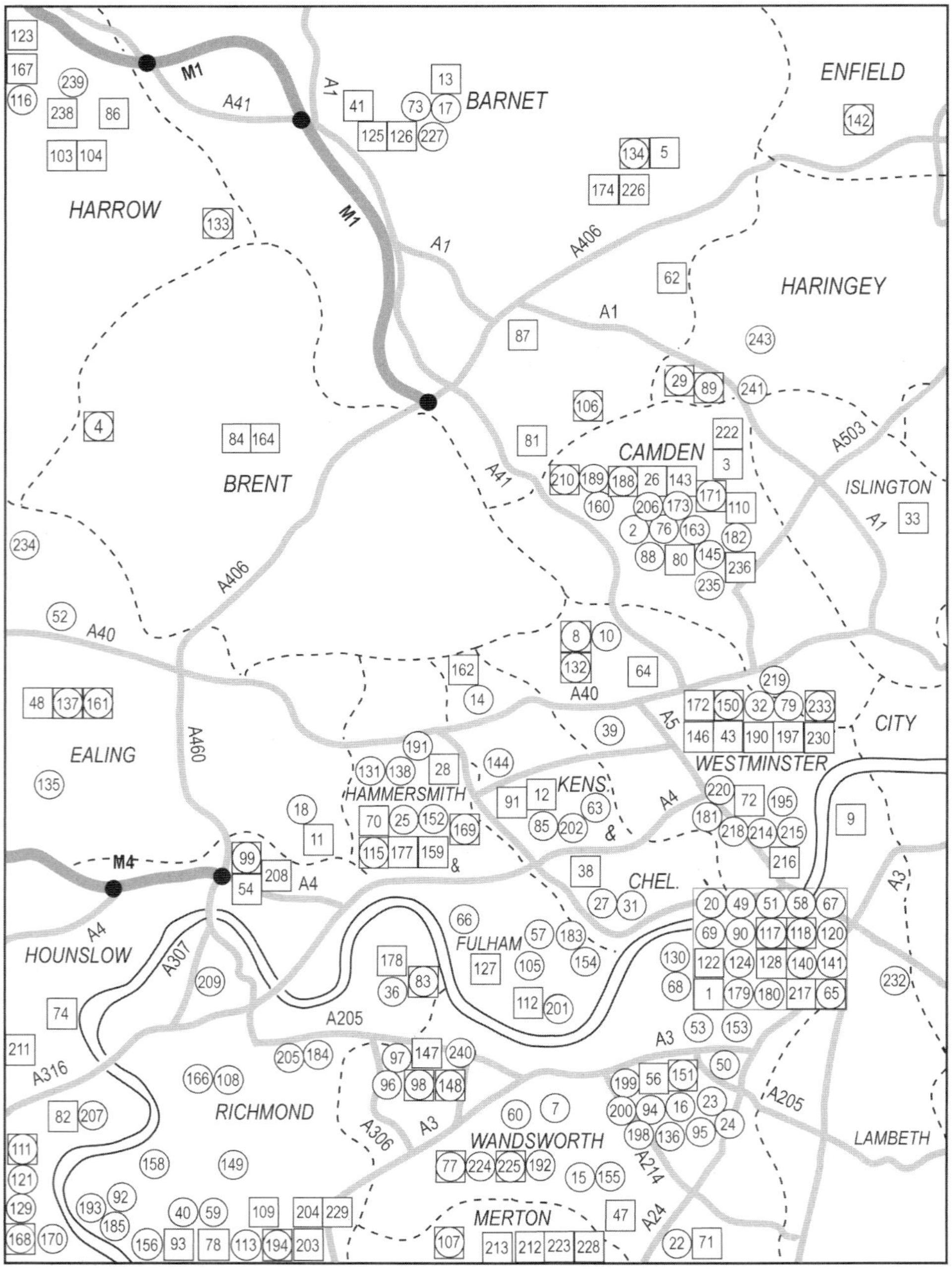

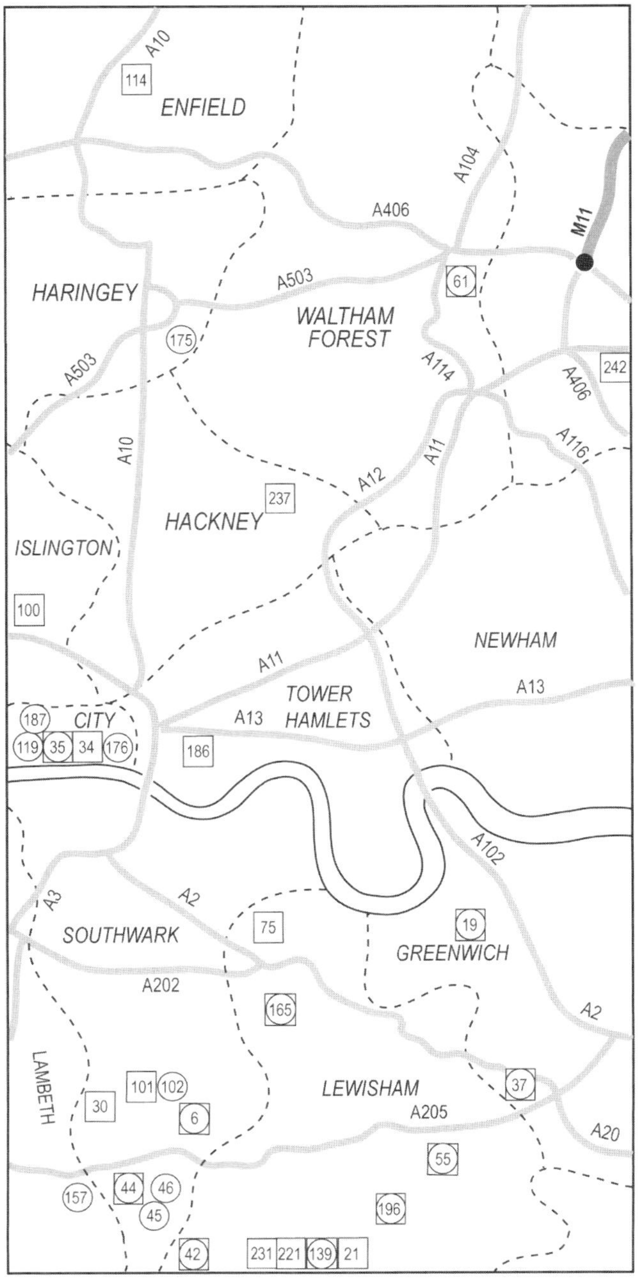

ENFIELD
114
A10
A104
A406
M11
HARINGEY
A503
61
WALTHAM FOREST
175
A114
A406
242
A503
A10
A116
A11
A12
237
HACKNEY
ISLINGTON
100
NEWHAM
A11
TOWER HAMLETS
A13
A13
187
CITY
119
35
34
176
186
A102
A3
A2
SOUTHWARK
75
19
GREENWICH
A202
165
A2
LAMBETH
101
102
30
6
LEWISHAM
A205
37
A20
55
157
44
46
45
196
42
231
221
139
21

Addendum